S0-AFF-592

Who's Who
Among American
High School Students®
Honoring Tomorrow's Leaders Today®

1985-86
Twentieth Annual Edition
Volume II

WHO'S WHO AMONG AMERICAN HIGH SCHOOL STUDENTS® is a publication of Educational Communications, Inc. of Lake Forest, Illinois and has no connection with "Who's Who In America" and its publisher, Marquis — Who's Who, Inc. Students featured in this volume attended school in the following states: Delaware, District of Columbia, Maryland, New Jersey and Pennsylvania.

Educational Communciations, Inc.
721 N. McKinley Road
Lake Forest, Illinois 60045
Printed in U.S.A.
ISBN 0-930315-14-6
ISBN 0-930315-12-X (10 Volume Set)
Library of Congress Catalog Card Number 68-43796

TABLE OF CONTENTS

* *Wherever students attend school out of state they will be listed in the state where they attend school.*

IN MEMORIUM:

Salvatore R. Salato
1925 - 1985

This book is dedicated to the memory of Salvatore R. Salato who served WHO'S WHO AMONG AMERICAN HIGH SCHOOL STUDENTS as a member of the Ethics, Standards and Practices Committee for six years. His untimely death in November, 1985, saddened all who came into contact with this warm, caring, compassionate human being. Sal had a long and distinguished career in public and private schools. At the time of his death, he was Principal of Thornridge High School, a school with 2,050 students, in Dolton, Illinois. He held that position since 1976. He joined the Thornridge faculty in 1961 as a physical education teacher and assistant varsity football coach. Recognizing his skills in working with adolescents, he was appointed Dean of Students in 1964 and then Assistant Principal at Thornridge in 1968.

Before coming to Thornridge High School, Sal taught and was head football coach at St. Mel High School in Chicago. A former Crane Technical High School and Drake University football player, he continued his interest in sports and young people by promoting and developing youth football. Starting in 1970 he served as the coach of the 7th and 8th grade football team at Holy Ghost Parish. Principal Salato received his bachelor's degree from Drake University and earned his master's degree from Purdue University.

Sal was the devoted husband of Mary Lou and father of four children and grandfather of five. As he dedicated his life to the development of youth, we respectfully dedicate the twentieth edition of WHO'S WHO AMONG AMERICAN HIGH SCHOOL STUDENTS to Sal Salato, professional educator, husband, father, coach, teacher and friend.

PUBLISHER'S CORNER:

After 20 years, some things are still the same.

Welcome to the 20th Annual Edition of WHO'S WHO AMONG AMERICAN HIGH SCHOOL STUDENTS. This is a very special, exciting anniversary edition.

In twenty years we have honored and recognized just under 5,000,000 students. We have helped over 700 students go to college by awarding over $800,000 in scholarships. We have made 2,000,000 referrals to colleges and universities through our College Referral Service and sponsored seventeen Annual Surveys of High Achievers.

Over the past twenty years we have witnessed and observed a multitude of changes and a few consistencies — through the end of the 60's, the entire 70's and now into the mid-80's. Much has changed including styles, music, politics, national leadership, morals, values, national interests, priorities, strengths and weaknesses. Big wars have ended, skirmishes and conflicts continue. Terrorism incidents startled us all when they first occurred and now they rarely make the front page of most of our newspapers. Our nation's morale reached an all-time low in the early 70's only to see a re-birth of patriotism and pride in the past few years, peaking perhaps as we celebrated Miss Liberty's 100th birthday this past summer.

Yet, through all this turbulence and change, one thing has remained conspicuously the same —the pursuit of academic excellence by a substantial percentage of American high school students. And, academic excellence is even more respected today than it was twenty years ago because educational reforms and higher standards have become a national priority resulting from several major reports issued in the past several years.

Historically we have been a nation which has honored, sometimes even worshiped, athletes, movie stars, politicians and celebrities of every ilk. From time-to-time we have gone overboard in this fanaticism. While we still reserve a special place in our collective hearts for those media marvels, we are finally coming to grips with the importance of recognizing and rewarding our best students, teachers and educational administrators.

At WHO'S WHO AMONG AMERICAN HIGH SCHOOL STUDENTS we are proud to be counted as one of the many organizations in the educational community which has always recognized the significance of spotlighting students who achieve excellence. For twenty years we have witnessed a constant and growing parade of outstanding young men and women who have been committed to achievement. Day in and day out they grind out their work, master their lessons, find time to contribute to their schools, communities and families. They may have stumbled and even fallen sometimes, but they persevered and never gave up their pursuit for excellence. To us, these students have always been heroes worthy of the applause usually reserved for individuals of lesser talent, but greater visibility.

To these students, their teachers, administrators and families we say congratulations for a job well done. The students we recognized twenty years ago, fifteen years ago and even ten years ago are already taking their rightful places of leadership in our nation's businesses, industries, professions, schools and the arts. We are confident that the students now being recognized on the following pages will similarly follow in their footsteps. We are proud of all of you.

Who's Who Review

A Summary of the Objectives, Programs, Policies for WHO'S WHO AMONG AMERICAN HIGH SCHOOL STUDENTS®

Since 1967, WHO'S WHO AMONG AMERICAN HIGH SCHOOL STUDENTS® has been committed to celebrating outstanding students for their positive achievements in academics, athletics, school and community service. Our first edition recognized 13,000 students from 4,000 high schools; the current, 20th edition, published in ten regional volumes, honors over 440,000 junior and senior class high school students representing 18,000 public, private, and parochial high schools nationwide.

As our publication has grown and matured over the years, we have expanded the scope and depth of the services and benefits provided for listed students and refined our policies and procedures in response to the needs of the schools and youth organizations who share our objectives.

Commencing with the 1986-87 academic year, we have expanded eligibility for recognition in WHO'S WHO to freshman and sophomore class students. This policy change was in direct response to educators who requested the opportunity to nominate younger students at a crucial point in their academic careers and reward those who excel through listing in the publication.

In our view, the growth, acceptance, and preeminence of WHO'S WHO AMONG AMERICAN HIGH SCHOOL STUDENTS as the leading student recognition publication in the nation, can be attributed to the involvement of educators in the policy-making areas of our programs.

During the past several years, we have hosted over 90 day-long reviews with key educational association executives to exchange ideas and perspectives regarding our standards, criteria, and services.

Most importantly, we must acknowledge the contributions of our Committee on Ethics, Standards and Practices, a group of distinguished educators representing relevant areas in secondary and post-secondary education. The committee was created in 1979 in order to formalize appropriate standards for our program which could be used as a guide for all student recognition programs. These standards are distributed to 80,000 high school principals, guidance counselors, and other faculty members each year.

It is a tribute to the committee that the standards they developed have been used as a model by several educational associations who have created their own guidelines for evaluating student recognition programs on a uniform basis. WHO'S WHO is proud of its well documented leadership role in promoting standards and ethics for all student recognition programs.

The committee meets each year and reviews literature, policies, programs, and services. They bring a perspective to the company which assures students and school administrators that WHO'S WHO policies and programs are in compliance and compatible with the standards and objectives of the educational community.

Major Policies and Procedures

Free Book Program—Guarantees extensive recognition through wide circulation

WHO'S WHO sponsors the largest Free Book Program of any publisher in any field. The book is automatically sent free to all participating high schools and youth organizations and offered free to all 7,500 libraries and 3,000 colleges and universities. Up to 15,000 complimentary copies are distributed each year.

The major purposes of this extensive free distribution system are to provide meaningful, national recognition for listed students among insitutions traditionally concerned with student achievement, and to make it convenient and easy for these students to view their published biography without purchasing the book.

For students who cannot locate an inspection copy of the book in their community, a listing of libraries within their state which received the most current edition is available upon request.

The recognition and reference purpose(s) of WHO'S WHO AMONG AMERICAN HIGH SCHOOL STUDENTS® have been acknowledged in the favorable review of the publication by the Reference and Subscription Books Reviews Committee of the American Library Association (*Booklist*, 3/1/82).

Financial Policies—Legitimate honors do not cost the recipient money

There are no financial requirements whatsoever contingent upon recognition in WHO'S WHO AMONG AMERICAN HIGH SCHOOL STUDENTS. The vast majority of students featured in all past editions have not purchased the book, but have received the recognition they have earned and deserve.

For those students who do purchase the publication or any related award insignia, satisfaction is guaranteed. Refunds are always issued on request.

Nominating Procedures—Representation from all areas of student achievement

Each year all 22,000 public, private, and parochial high schools are invited to nominate junior and senior class students who have achieved a "B" grade point average or better and demonstrated leadership in academics, athletics, or extracurricular activities. On rare occasions, students with slightly under a "B" average have been included when their achievements in non-academic areas were extraordinary. Nominators are requested to limit selections to 15% of their eligible students. Most nominate less.

Approximately 13,500 high schools participate in our program by nominating students. An additional 5,000-7,500 schools are represented by their outstanding students as a result of nominations received from bona fide youth organizations, churches with organized youth activities, scholarship agencies, civic and service groups. Most of our nation's major youth groups participate in our program by nominating their meritorious student leaders.

Editing—Maintains the integrity of the honor

Occasionally, nominators recommend students who are not qualified for recognition. When these students receive our literature and forms, there may be confusion concerning our standards and criteria. When biography forms are submitted for publication, they are all reviewed and edited to monitor compliance with our high standards. In the past ten years, approximately 167,300 students were disqualified by our editors because they did not meet our standards, including several thousand who ordered the publication. More than $1,106,500 in orders were returned to these students. Our standards are never compromised by the profit motive. (Auditor's verification available upon request.)

Verification of Data—A continuous safety check on the effectiveness of our procedures

To monitor the accuracy and integrity of data submitted by students, a nationally respected accounting firm conducts annual, independent audits of published biographical data. Previous audits reveal that up to 97.2% of the data published was substantially accurate. (Complete studies available upon request.)

Educational Communications Scholarship Foundation Committee members meet to select 50 scholarship winners for the 1983-84 academic year. Each winner receives a $1,000 award. Left: Dr. Norman Feingold, President, National Career & Counseling Services; Morton Temsky, Educator; Lester Benz, Executive Secretary Emeritus, Quill & Scroll Society; Wally Wikoff, Former Director, National Scholastic Press Association; Lily Rose, Scholarship Committee Chairperson and Director of Admissions, Roosevelt University; Fred Brooks, Asst. VP for Enrollment Services & Management, SUNY at Binghamton; Aline Rivers, 1979-80 Executive Board, National Association of College Admissions Counselors, Robert MacVicar, President Emeritus, Oregon State University; and Dr. James Schelhammer, Dean of Admissions, Austin Peay State University. Committee members not shown: Neill Sanders, Associate Director of Admissions, Washington State University and Dr. Hilda Minkoff, 1983-84 President, American School Counselor's Association.

Programs, Services and Benefits for Students

Scholarship Awards—From $4,000 in 1968 to $100,000 annually since 1982

The Educational Communications Scholarship Foundation®, a not-for-profit organization which is funded by the publishing company, now sponsors three separate scholarship award programs, which award over $100,000 in college scholarships each year. Over $800,000 has been funded to date.

Through the general high school program, 65 awards of $1,000 each are awarded to students by a committee of knowledgeable educators on the basis of grade point average, class rank, test scores, activities, an essay and financial need. An additional $15,000 in scholarships is funded through grants to youth organizations where we sponsor awards for their officers or contest winners. For students already in college, $25,000 in scholarships is awarded through THE NATIONAL DEAN'S LIST® Program.

Our research indicates that the Educational Communications Scholarship Foundation's programs represent one of the 10 largest scholarship programs in the nation funded by a single private sector organization. The Foundation is listed in numerous government and commercial directories on financial aid and scholarships.

Grants-In-Aid—Financial support for organizations who work with or for students

Since 1975, we have funded grants to youth and educational organizations to support their programs and/or services on behalf of high school students. The stipends fund scholarships or subsidize research, educational publications or competitive events, and programs. A brief summary of grants issued or committed to date, totaling approximately $346,000 appears in this review.

The College Referral Service (CRS)® — Links students with colleges

WHO'S WHO students receive a catalog listing all 3,000 colleges and universities. They complete a form indicating which institutions they wish us to notify of their honorary award. This service links interested students with colleges and universities and serves as a "third party" reference.

Certainly, listing in WHO'S WHO will not assure a student of admission into the college of his or her choice any more than any other award or honor society. Most selective colleges rely almost exclusively on grade point average, class rank, and test scores. Nevertheless, several hundred colleges have indicated that the CRS and/or the publication is a valuable reference source in their recruitment programs. (Letters from colleges available for inspection.)

17th Annual Survey of High Achievers™ —The views of student leaders are as important as their achievements

Since 1969, we have polled the attitudes and opinions of WHO'S WHO students on timely issues of interest. This study provides students with a collective voice otherwise not available to them. As young voters and future leaders, their views are important. Therefore, survey results are sent to the President, all members of Congress, state Governors, educational agencies, high school administrators, and the press.

Each year, survey results are widely reported in the press and have been utilized in academic studies and research indicating the educational value of this program.

WHO'S WHO Spokesteen Panel™— Another voice for student leaders and a service for media

Because WHO'S WHO has become an authoritative source on high school students, we receive frequent inquiries from reporters when they are preparing special features on teen views, lifestyles, etc. To assist reporters and to assure teens of appropriate representation of their views, we have created a network of articulate and well-informed students, nationwide, who are made available to the press for interviews of local and national coverage. WHO'S WHO Spokesteens have appeared on the "CBS Morning News," NBC "Today Show," "Merv Griffin Show," "Hour Magazine," and numerous other broadcasts, newspaper and magazine stories.

College-Bound Digest®—What students need to know

A compilation of articles written by prominent educators covering the various opportunities available to college-bound students, i.e., financial aid opportunities, the advantages of large schools, small schools, research universities, achievement test usage, and preparation and numerous other topics of similar relevancy. The Digest appears in the introductory section of this publication and is offered as a separate publication, free of charge, to 20,000 high school guidance offices, 20,000 principals, and 3,000 college admissions offices.

Local Newspaper Publicity—Additional recognition for honored students

Consistent with our primary purpose of providing recognition for meritorious students, we routinely provide over 2,000 newspapers nationwide with rosters of their local students featured in the publication with appropriate background information. (Students must authorize this release.)

Other Publications

Who's Who Among Black Americans®

This publication has been extremely well received by librarians, government agencies, educational institutions, and major corporations. All four major library trade journals reviewed and recommended earlier editions for their subscribers. The book was selected by the American Library Association as one of the "Outstanding Reference Books of the Year" and by *Black Scholar* as "A Notable Book," one of only 19 publications to receive this distinction.

WHO'S WHO AMONG BLACK AMERICANS was one of 380 titles chosen by the Library of Congress to be exhibited at The White House Conference on Library & Information Services held in November, 1979 and was selected for inclusion in the Presidential Library at Camp David.

William C. Matney, of WHO'S WHO AMONG BLACK AMERICANS, was introduced on the "Today Show" by book and theatre critic Gene Shalit. The publication has received numerous awards and honors.

The National Dean's List®

The ninth edition of THE NATIONAL DEAN'S LIST® recognizes 94,000 outstanding students representing 2,500 colleges and universities. All students were selected by their respective deans or registrars because of their academic achievements. This year, $25,000 in scholarships were distributed to twenty-five students. For 1986-87, a minimum of $25,000 in scholarships will again be awarded.

Memberships

Educational Communications, Inc. or its publisher is a member of the following organizations:

- American Association of Higher Education
- American Association of School Administrators
- Chicago Metropolitan Better Business Bureau
- Distributive Education Clubs of America, National Advisory Board
- Educational Press Association
- Future Farmers of America, Executive Sponsor
- National Association of Financial Aid Administrators
- National School Public Relations Association
- Office Education Association, National Business Advisory Council

Profile of Who's Who Student

(Statistics From 1986 Edition)

General Listing

Total Number of Students	440,000
WHO'S WHO Students as Percentage of 6,500,000 Juniors and Seniors Enrolled Nationwide	6½%
Females (%)	61%
Males (%)	39%

Academics

Grade Point Average (%)	
"A"	70%
"B"	29%
"C"	less than 1%
Local Honor Roll	203,025
National Honor Society	133,597
Valedictorian/Salutatorian	9,836

Leadership Activities/Clubs

Student Council	80,740
Boys State/Girls State	35,672
Senior Class Officers	35,159
Junior Class Officers	47,713
Key Club	27,876

Major Vocational Organizations

Future Homemakers of America	30,655
4-H	30,473
Junior Achievement	23,156
Future Farmers of America	15,577
Distributive Education Clubs of America	9,663
Office Education Association	6,447

Varsity Athletics

Basketball	79,238
Track	66,706
Cheerleading/Pom Pon	59,390
Football	52,476
Volleyball	39,969
Soccer	30,085
Baseball	28,307
Tennis	27,300
Cross Country	22,450
Wrestling	12,386

Music/Performing Arts

Orchestra/Band	91,555
Chorus	66,629
Drama	43,744

Miscellaneous

Church/Temple Activities	162,913
Yearbook	89,455
School Paper	68,727
Students Against Driving Drunk	43,776
Community Worker	32,161
Fellowship of Christian Athletes	28,930

Grants to Youth and Educational Organizations

American Association for Gifted Children
$2,000, 1 Grant
To sponsor a conference for educators concerning "The Gifted Child, the Family and the Community."

American Children's Television Festival
$2,000, 1 Grant
To promote excellence in television programming for our nation's youth. Founded by the Central Educational Network.

American Council on the Teaching of Foreign Language
$500, 1 Grant
To support the general goals and objectives in the field of foreign language.

American Legion Auxiliary Girls Nation
$20,000, 8 Grants
Scholarships for Vice President and Outstanding Senator of program where students participate in mock government structure.

American Legion Boys Nation
$21,000, 9 Grants
Scholarships for President and Vice President of program where students learn about government through participation.

Animal Welfare Institute
$1,582, 2 Grants
For biology textbook on experiments which do not involve cruelty towards animals. Second grant to fund convention booth equipment.

Black United Fund
$5,000, 1 Grant
Scholarships for Black students selected by BUF Committee.

Colorado Forum of Educational Leaders
$1,000, 1 Grant
To fund a series of quarterly activities regarding the educational successes of Colorado Schools.

Contemporary-Family Life Curriculum
$1,500, 1 Grant
Funded formal grant request, resulting in $100,000 grant from government to test this contemporary curriculum.

Distributive Education Clubs of America (DECA)
$42,800, 12 Grants
ECI serves on the National Advisory Board for this major vocational/educational organization and sponsors scholarships for national officers.

Earthwatch
$3,000, 3 Grants
Scholarships for students conducting scientific expeditions with scientists, researchers.

Education Roundtable
$5,000, 1 Grant
To fund the creation of a committee of representatives from government, education, private industry, and the general public to support and improve education in America.

Fellowship of Christian Athletes
$12,800, 5 Grants
Original stipend funded seminar of athletic directors. Subsequent grants for scholarships for coaches' conferences concerning spiritual, professional and family growth.

Joint Council on Economic Education
$11,000, 4 Grants
Funds ongoing economic education program for students and educators from elementary school to college level.

Junior Achievement
$14,000, 7 Grants
Scholarship for the winner of the WHO'S WHO Essay Contest.

Junior Classical League
$6,000, 6 Grants
Funds a scholarship to the outstanding member selected by an educational committee for this organization whose members study the civilizations of Greece and Rome to provide a better understanding of our culture, literature, language and arts.

Junior Engineering Technical Society
$6,000, 2 Grants
Stipends were used to help revise the National Engineering Aptitude Search Test.

Key Club International
$1,000, 1 Grant
For two scholarships of $500 each for two outstanding Key Clubbers.

Law & Economic Center, University of Miami Law School
$4,500, 1 Grant
Funded study on use of media to effectively communicate economic issues and policies to general public.

Miss Teenage America Scholarship Program
$33,000, 8 Grants
Currently funds a $5,000 scholarship for student selected as Miss Teenage America; previously funded four $1,000 awards for each of the semifinalists.

Modern Miss
$1,000, 2 Grants
Scholarship for the National Academic Winner.

Modern Music Masters
$4,500, 2 Grants
For chapter expansion program of this national music honor society, high school level.

Mr. U.S.A. Teen Program
$5,500, 4 Grants
Scholarships for outstanding student selected on basis of leadership, citizenship, academics, and community involvement.

National Cheerleaders Association
$8,100, 8 Grants
Scholarships for winners of state drill team contests.

National Federation for Catholic Youth Ministry
$3,000, 2 Grants
Funds a scholarship of $1,000 for the student elected President of the National Youth Council and a $500 scholarship for another Catholic Teen Leader selected by the National organization.

National Forensic League
$10,000, 5 Grants
For two scholarships of $1,000 each to the members of the first place National Debate Team.

National Foundation for Advancement in the Arts
$3,000, 3 Grants
For general support for the Arts, Recognition, and Talent Search Program of this Foundation.

National 4-H Council
$21,500, 8 Grants
Grants are used for scholarships for outstanding 4-H students.

National Future Farmers of America (FFA)
$29,000, 10 Grants
Grants are used for scholarships for outstanding FFA students.

Office Education Association (OEA)
$44,000, 11 Grants
ECI serves on the National Business Advisory Council and sponsors scholarship program for national officers.

Performing & Visual Arts Society (PAVAS)
$4,000, 2 Grants
To conduct expansion program for high school chapters.

The President's Committee on the Employment of the Handicapped
$5,000, 5 Grants
Scholarship for the winner of the President's Committee National Poster contest, high school division.

Quill & Scroll Society
$10,000, 5 Grants
For two scholarships of $1,000 each to students who apply as contestants in Quill & Scroll's Current Events Quiz and National Writing/Photography Contest.

Soroptimist International of the Americas, Inc.
$4,000, 4 Grants
Scholarship for organization's Youth Citizenship Award Winner.

Special Olympics, Inc.
$1,000, 1 Grant
Scholarship for outstanding student volunteer and direct mail promotion to high school athletic directors requesting volunteers to work with handicapped children.

Standards for Who's Who Among American High School Students and Other Recognition Programs and Societies

1. Nominations will be from established organizations that work with and for the benefit of high school aged youth. Under no circumstances will recommendations be accepted from students, their parents or solicited from standard commercial lists.

2. Criteria for students to be selected will be clearly defined and reflect high personal achievement.

3. Listing in "Who's Who" will not require purchase of any items or payments of any fees.

4. Additional programs and services which are available to those listed in "Who's Who" at cost to the students, will be clearly described in the literature provided.

5. A refund policy will be clearly stated in all literature.

6. Nominators will be able to recommend students without releasing confidential data or fear of having confidential data released by program sponsors.

7. Student information will be confidential and will not be released except where authorized by the student.

8. Home addresses will not be published in the book or made public in any way.

9. Under no circumstances will "Who's Who" sell student information or lists.

10. The publisher will describe, disseminate and verify the methods employed to assure national/regional recognition to students listed.

11. The publisher will respond to all inquiries, complaints and requests for relevant background information.

12. The basis for the scholarship program competition will be defined. Number and amount of awards will be stated, lists of previous winners will be available. Finalist selection process and funding method will be clearly defined. Employees or their relatives will not be eligible for scholarships.

13. There will be an advisory council (external to the organization) to review and make recommendations regarding the policies, procedures, and evaluation process of the "Who's Who" programs.

14. The publisher will set forth in writing and make publicly known the policies and procedures it follows in the implementation of these standards.

Our company's adherence to the above standards has been attested to by an independent public accounting firm. A copy of their report is available upon request.

Members of the Committee on Ethics, Standards and Practices:

Dr. Wesley Apker
Executive Director
Association of California School Administrators
Sacramento, CA

James T. Barry
Assoc. Vice President for College Relations
St. Ambrose College
Davenport, IA

Phyllis Blaunstein
Executive Director
National Association of State Boards of Education
Alexandria, VA

Dr. Harold Crosby
Regents Professor
University of West Florida
Pensacola, FL

Dr. S. Norman Feingold
President
National Career & Counseling Services
Washington, DC

Charles R. Hilston
Executive Director
Association of Wisconsin School Administrators
Madison, WI

Dr. Betty James
Assoc. Dean for Academic Affairs
Livingstone College
Salisbury, NC

Dr. John Lucy
Asst. Superintendent for Curriculum & Instruction
Downers Grove Public School District 58
Downers Grove, IL

Paul Masem
Superintendent
Ames Community School Dist.
Ames, IA

Dr. Edward J. Rachford
Superintendent
Homewood-Flossmoor Community High School
Flossmoor, IL

Dr. Vincent Reed
Vice President for Communications
The Washington Post
Washington, DC

On the NBC "Today Show," host Tom Brokow (center) interviews WHO'S WHO Spokesteens (left) Burnell Newsome, Hazelhurst, Mississippi, Amy Krentzman, Deerfield Beach, Florida, Tari Marshall, ECI Representative, and Mike McGriff, Chicago, Illinois.

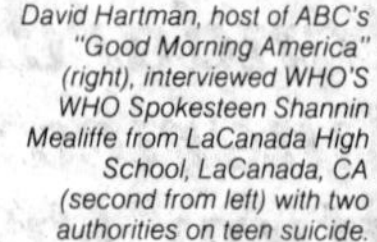

David Hartman, host of ABC's "Good Morning America" (right), interviewed WHO'S WHO Spokesteen Shannin Mealiffe from LaCanada High School, LaCanada, CA (second from left) with two authorities on teen suicide.

Merv Griffin interviews WHO'S WHO Spokesteen Steven Silver from South Shore High School, Brooklyn, New York on the nationally televised talk show.

WHO'S WHO Spokesteens are interviewed by Gary Collins, host of the popular, nationally syndicated TV talk show, "Hour Magazine."

President Reagan greets Miss Teenage America, Amy Sue Brenkacz in the Oval Office. WHO'S WHO sponsors a $5,000 scholarship for Miss Teenage America and listed Amy Sue in the publication.

Bill Kurtis, host of the "CBS Morning News," interviews WHO'S WHO Spokesteens Stephanie Woolwich, Long Beach, New Jersey and Alex Tachmes, Miami Beach, Florida.

A group of 12 WHO'S WHO Spokesteens appear with host Pat Robertson (center) on the popular TV magazine program, "700 Club" (CBN) to present teen leaders' views on America's future in a special 7 part, 8 hour debate.

WHO'S WHO sponsors $1,500 and $1,000 scholarships for the president and vice-president of the American Legion Boy's Nation program. (Left to right) Marcus R. Dilworth, Jr., 1985 Boy's Nation President; Mike Ayers, Director, Americanism and Children & Youth Division; and Daniel Bricken, 1985 Boy's Nation Vice-President.

Penni Ann McClean, right, Congress delegate advisor from North Carolina, presents a citation to Mrs. Jackie McGuinn, assistant to the publisher of WHO'S WHO, for five years support of the 4-H Citizenship-Washington Focus program.

Right to left: Debbie Moyer from Allentown, PA pointing to her prize winning poster in the high school category with Harold Russell, Chairman, President's Committee on Employment of the Handicapped. WHO'S WHO sponsors a $1,000 college scholarship for this annual contest.

College-Bound Digest®

As a public service to the 96% of WHO'S WHO students who will continue their education after graduation from high school, we have invited a group of distinguished educators to use our publication as a forum to inform and assist students through the articles in this section.

While we do not presume that these articles contain "everything you need to know" about preparing for college, we believe you will find they will be helpful in learning "some of the things you need to know."

We wish to acknowledge the special contribution of Robert McLendon, Executive Director, Brookstone College of Business, High Point, North Carolina, who was instrumental in selecting appropriate topics and authors for this section.

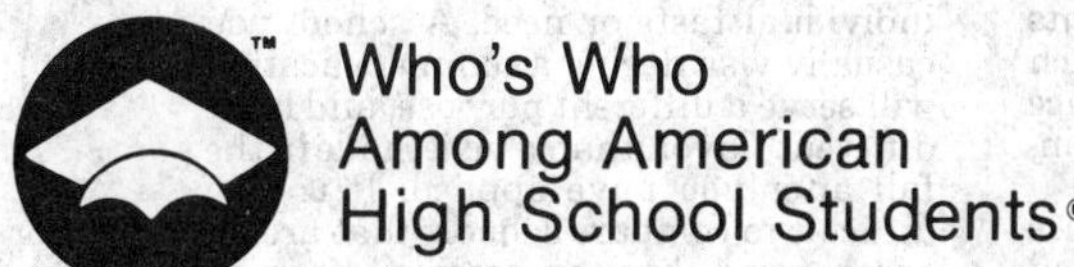

Getting the most from your high school counselor

By James Warfield

A high school counselor, helping you apply to college, is able to provide a wide variety of services tailored to your needs. The nature of this assistance will depend upon your abilities and achievement as well as the nature and quality of the colleges to which you apply. Effective use of the counselor's services will require you to have frequent discussions. Although your ideas about which colleges to apply to will change often, the more closely you work with your counselor the more valuable he/she will be to you.

Finding, selecting and applying to the colleges that are right for you is a long and studied process. It involves a lot of letter-writing, telephoning, research, weighing alternatives, and just plain old thinking. It's a decision-making process.

Your counselor makes recommendations as to which courses you should be taking in high school. These recommendations should be based upon your academic abilities and goals. This is a critical issue because the appropriateness of this advice is determined by the consistency between your aspirations and aptitudes. Verifying the accuracy of your self-perceptions is important in order to avoid sudden surprises caused by false hopes or unrealistic expectations. The reason why your counselor exists, is to help you become everything you are capable of within a realistic framework.

For many students, the college selection process begins with the PSAT, taken in the fall of the junior year. Your counselor should advise you which of the college entrace tests to take, SAT, ACT, ACH and AP, and when to take them. The type of college you apply to will determine which tests to take. The quality of the college, or the quality of your own academic program, and whether or not you plan to apply Early Decision, will determine when you should take such tests. Many students don't know in their junior year to which schools they'd like to apply, so advance planning is necessary in order to maintain open options.

Finding the right college will require you to know yourself, your likes and dislikes. In what kind of environment do you see yourself being most comfortable? Can you picture yourself at a small college or a mid-size or large university setting? Do you want a school to be in a rural community, a suburb or to be in an urban environment? Do you want to be in a different geographic part of the country or is being close to home important to you? What are some of your academic areas of interest? What kind of extra curricular offering do you want to participate in? As you answer these questions the attributes of your ideal college will become more clear. Through discussion with your counselor you'll be able to assess your needs, and more clearly focus your perceptions of yourself and of the schools you will be researching.

Your counselor should help generate a list of colleges that meet your requirements by drawing upon his/her own wealth of knowledge or utilizing the many reference materials available.

Many counselors have access to computers that will provide a list of colleges for you to investigate, once you have determined the characteristics you are looking for. If the guidance office does not have a computer, the same information can be obtained, with a little effort, from the commercially published reference books that are available through your counselor. After generating a list of perhaps twelve to twenty schools, your research really begins.

Resource books provide a wealth of statistical and narrative descriptions on virtually every college. The counseling office is likely to have college catalogs as well as files on each college containing brochures, view books and leaflets of the various academic and extracurricular offerings available at that particular school. Although college catalogs are boring reading material, information relating to admission procedures and requirements, course offerings and requirements for each of the academic majors are outlined. In addition, course prerequisites and methods of exempting yourself from some prerequisites are also indicated. As your research continues, you'll be able to eliminate schools and determine some colleges in which you are seriously interested.

Many high schools set up procedures whereby students may meet with representatives from colleges to obtain more information or answer individual questions. These representatives may be the Director of Admission, Admissions officers, or personnel hired to represent the college. Of course, the more you know about the college, before talking with the college representative, the more value they will be to you. Some colleges require an interview either by the representative, an alumni, or by an admissions officer. Your counselor should help you determine if an interview is necessary in your situation.

Campus visits are the most effective means to determine if the college is right for you. When to visit is a matter of individual taste or need. A school you casually visit during a summer vacation will serve a different purpose, and have different flavor, than a visit made in the fall after you have applied. It is also difficult to compare schools that are on break from those in session. Keep in mind that as you visit more schools your observational skills will become more sophisticated and your reflections of each will be altered. It may be more prudent to visit only those schools to which you have been accepted, after you have received all your admissions decisions.

As you narrow your choice of colleges, your counselor should review with you the possibilities of acceptance or rejection at each. At least one of your choices should be a safety choice, one in which you are almost guaranteed of being admitted.

After the list of colleges to which you are going to apply has been determined, it is your responsibility to obtain the application and meet deadline dates. Many colleges require a counselor's recommendation or a Secondary School Reference. Some require additional recommendations from specific teachers. Establish application procedures with your counselor so that he/she, the teacher, and school have adequate time to do their part in order to meet your deadline dates. If you are required to write an essay, or personal statement, discuss this with your counselor. These discussions serve several purposes: help you generate ideas and narrow topics that you wish to write about; provide you with suggestions that will enhance your applications; and provide the counselor with insights that will compliment your application.

It is your responsibility to file your applications on time, see that your test scores are sent to the admissions office, and file the financial aid applications. Your counselor will help you determine which scores to send, which financial aid form is required and how to fulfill these requirements.

Selecting and applying to a college is a decision-making process. The truly wise decision maker knows that he must clarify questions, obtain the most information possible, and probe until no new information becomes evident. Generally, the more information obtained, the better the decision, and the happier the college experience.

Jim Warfield is Director of Guidance at Lake Forest High School, Lake Forest, Illinois. Jim is currently involved and active in a number of professional organizations, and presently serving on the National Advisory Council for The Educational Records Bureau, Wellesley, Massachusetts.

The use of the SAT at selective colleges

By Dr. Judith Gatlin

For many students the numbers — from 200 to 800 on the verbal and on the quantitative sections of the College Board examination — seem to be the voice of doom; for others, they announce the possibility of admission into the nation's most selective colleges. But just how important, really, are those scores, and how will college admissions committees interpret them?

It is important to remember that the SAT (or ACT) is only one part of your total record. Your rank in your high school class, your grades, extracurricular activities which show leadership potential, and your recommendations are all extremely important. In addition, some colleges will consider your geographic location (it may be easier for the valedictorian of a South Dakota high school to enter Harvard than for the top student in a Connecticut prep school), your relationship with alumni, your religious preference at some denominational colleges, and the success of other graduates from your school at the institution.

Colleges treat scores, grades, rank, activities and recommendations in a variety of ways, but very few use arbitrary cut-off scores to determine acceptance. Every selective college or university attempts to select a class which will be successful (they don't want you to flunk out after your first year). Students who are admitted are those who they can predict will do well; and admissions staff experience with standardized tests suggests that certain levels of achievement, can be predicted with a fair degree of accuracy when used in conjunction with the high school record.

Often the total score on the SAT is less important than the individual score on either the verbal or the quantitative aptitude section. While colleges and universities may publish their average SAT as a combination, many liberal arts colleges believe that the verbal score is a particularly good indicator of ability, and many technically oriented engineering programs will be impressed with a very good quantitative score. A pre-engineering student with an 1150 SAT may be a very good candidate if his scores are 450 on the verbal section and 700 in the quantitative area; he might be substantially less impressive with 650/500.

One of the problems that many students confront when they first look at their scores is a sinking feeling that their numbers do not match their high school achievement level. The 'A' student who is third in her class and barely makes a 450/450 on the SAT is disappointed for days afterwards. It is important, however, to understand what your scores mean. The national average on the verbal section of the SAT is 427; on the mathematics section it is 467. Clearly, many college bound students will have a total score under 900. Many colleges and most state universities have average scores at this level or below it; more selective institutions will generally have average scores that are substantially higher, but even among these colleges there will be a number of students whose scores are at this level if their grades and rank indicate a strong chance of success.

But how can you explain or understand an average score when you have been an excellent student? It may be that you had a bad day (or a bad night before); a headache, too little sleep, a testing environment that is too hot or too cold may cause your scores to be less than your best. It may be that the scores are an accurate indicator of your aptitude and that you are a high achiever. Or it may mean that your grades have been inflated and that you have not been challenged by teachers or peers. One way that you can determine if it was just the specific test day is to compare your scores on the SAT with your PSAT. If you scored, for example, 48/50 on the PSAT and have a combined total on the SAT of from 970 to 1020 your test is probably valid. If, on the other hand, your PSAT was 55/58 and you scored 1020 on the SAT, you probably should plan to retake the examination to see if the second time might show real improvement.

In addition to the "bad day" low score there are other reasons that good students do not do well on standardized tests. It may be that they panic under time pressure, that they are unfamiliar with national tests and the testing environment, or that their skills and abilities cannot be shown on such tests. Really creative students, those with talents in the arts, and those who work very slowly through a problem, analyzing as they go, are sometimes at a disadvantage. If you fall in one of these categories, it is especially useful for a teacher whose recommendation you have requested be asked to discuss your other strengths in an admissions letter.

Some students retake the SAT two or three times to see if they can improve their overall scores, and it is important to realize that scores will vary slightly every time you take a Scholastic Aptitude Test. A variation of 30 points in either direction is normal; more than 50 points, unusual. How worthwhile is it to retake the SAT if your scores are under the average published by the college of your choice? Some schools, like Furman, accept your best scores from each test. Others may average your test results. It is probably true that you can improve your quantitative score with tutoring over several months; improving verbal scores is far more difficult. You should remember, however, that while selective colleges have many high-scoring students, their *average* SAT is just that: there have been many others whose scores are under the average but who have the proven achievement to be admitted.

Suppose, however, that you are very interested in an institution which indicates an average SAT of 1275; your score is 1050, but your parents are alumni, you graduated in the top 20% of your class, and you have been an outstanding high school leader. Academically you would be in the bottom quarter of your class, yet you may well be admitted because of your parents and your activities. Should you attend such a college? Will you be able to compete at a level comfortable for you with students whose high school backgrounds may be substantially superior? Are you ready to make a number of "C's" or to study harder and longer than your roommates?

You should consider, too, that very high scores do not necessarily mean admission to the college of your choice. Several years ago a young man with an SAT score of 1440 applied to a selective Southeastern liberal arts college. He had graduated in the lower half of his high school class and although he had been involved in some extracurricular activities, he also had been a discipline problem in high school. After substantial discussion, he was not admitted, but the college admissions office was interested enough to trace his career several years later. He had flunked out of two other colleges. SAT scores indicate aptitude — the ability to learn — not achievement. They do not show the desire to learn, the ambition to succeed or the perserverance necessary for academic excellence. College admissions officers are aware of these facts and they will read your entire application with an awareness that you are more than a score on a computer printout.

Dr. Judith Gatlin is the Director of Educational Services and Assistant Professor of English at Furman University, Greenville, South Carolina. She has authored various articles for the *Journal of College Placement* and is a former columnist for the *Charlotte Observer.*

Tips on taking the SAT

By Dr. Ernest W. Beals

If you are college-bound or plan to be, chances are that you will be required to take a college admissions test such as the Scholastic Aptitude Test (SAT) of The College Board or the American College Testing Program's assessment test (ACT).

The SAT's format and content have changed enormously over its 55 years of existence, and is now designed to measure the extent to which your reasoning abilities, that is skill with verbal expressions and mathematical concepts, have been developed up to the time you take the test.

It is important to realize that students are neither accepted nor denied admission to an institution solely on the basis of SAT or other test scores. When looking at prospective students, institutions of higher learning also stress to varying degrees such factors as your high school record (including courses taken, grade patterns, and class rank or high school average) and extracurricular activities. Other factors may be the outcome of personal interviews and teacher or counselor recommendations, as well as the student body needs of the college or university itself.

Students frequently ask: What can I do about raising my SAT scores or about making them better than they would be otherwise? The answer is: Quickly and immediately, probably not much. Over longer periods it depends on how much time, effort and concentration goes into the preparation. The abilities measured by the test are related to academic success in college. These abilities grow over a period of time through learning experiences such as those encountered in the family, in the classroom, with your friends and associates, and in reading and independent study.

The best preparation for the SAT is to have had varied opportunities of this kind and to have made the most of them. The contents of the tests cover such a broad area that trying to "cram" for it has never been found to yield validly measurable results. You may, however, find it useful to review some of the fundamental principles of algebra and geometry in order to refresh your memory for the mathematical section of the test.

In order to reduce anxiety and increase confidence when test time arrives, here are some valuable tips: First, become familiar with the format of the test. Obtain a copy of the informative booklet, *Taking the SAT*, from your guidance counselor. This free booklet describes the nature and components of the SAT and, provides a full sample SAT which you can administer and score yourself. By taking this sample test, you will familiarize yourself with the directions and the format of the questions. You will also gain valuable practice in allocating your time to each item.

You will also learn that, as a rule, the easier questions of each section come at the beginning of that section, with the questions growing progressively more difficult to the end of the section. Use your time wisely. If you find the individual items of a particular section are extremely difficult for you, read quickly through the remaining questions in the group, answering only those that you feel you know. You should then begin work on the next set of questions, returning to the omitted questions in that section if you have time. You receive as much credit for answering correctly the questions you find easy as you get for answering the hard ones. Above all, don't panic. You receive one point for each question correctly answered; you lose a fraction of a point for each item incorrectly answered. You neither gain nor lose points for omitted questions. Therefore, keep in mind that random guessing on questions will rarely increase your scores, and might even have the effect of reducing your raw score. However, some selective guessing can pay off for you: If you can confidently eliminate as incorrect at least two of the possible four or five answers to a question, then it would be to your advantage to take a stab at one of the remaining answers to that question.

Your raw score on the SAT is determined by adding up all correct answers and subtracting from that total the sum of the fractions for all incorrect answers. The raw score is then converted to the College Board scale ranging from a low of 200 to a high of 800 on the verbal and mathematics sections of the SAT.

The Test of Standard Written English (TSWE) is a 30-minute multiple-choice test administered with the SAT. The questions evaluate your ability to recognize standard written English, the language of most college textbooks and the English you will be expected to use in the papers you write for college courses. The scores may be used to place you in a freshman English course that is appropriate for you.

Contrary to the anxiety-ridden expectations of students taking the SAT and TSWE for the first time, these tests do not require specialized knowledge in science, social sciences, literature, or any other field.

In brief summary, the best strategies to follow in order to prepare yourself for taking the SAT include: enroll in college preparatory courses that your school offers, maintain good solid and consistent effort in your everyday classroom work and classroom tests, force yourself to read as many and varied outside readings as possible, brush up on your algebra and geometry lessons, become familiar with the SAT format, content, directions, etc. (obtain a copy of *Taking the SAT* booklet from your counselor and take the sample SAT test, score it yourself, and read the suggestions and explanations included with it), get a good night's sleep the night before the examination and take a positive attitude with you to the test center. If you do all of the above, you will be putting your best foot forward and enhancing your chances of obtaining good test scores. Good luck to you.

Dr. Ernest W. Beals is Association Director of the Southern Regional Office of The College Board. Dr. Beals has worked in the field of education for the past 26 years at the high school and college level including 13 years in college admissions.

Can you prepare for the SAT?

By Stanley H. Kaplan

The discussion of the issue of preparation for the SAT has come full circle since the 1950's. In the 1957 Bulletin, issued to the students, the College Board stated, "Coaching may be a sound and rewarding method. If coaching means an honest effort, under the guidance of a good teacher, over an extended period of time, to improve those skills in which you are weak, then it can be recommended as effective study." In the 1960's, the statement about the possible positive effects of coaching was withdrawn. The reason, I was told, was the proliferation of cram schools that preyed on students' (and parents') anxieties and offered little of educational value and little possibility of an improvement on the SAT. And now in the 1980's, the College Board and ETS which constructs the SAT, once again are distinguishing between cramming and long-term coaching which is now looked upon as "supplementary education."

Can one be prepared for the SAT? My answer is an emphatic yes. Some students can prepare by self-study. There are many materials, including tests released by the College Board and SAT review books available at bookstores.

My organization has been preparing students for the SAT for more than thirty years. Actually — and this is important — we are not preparing for the SAT per se. Rather, we are working to improve a student's basic math, verbal, and reasoning skills. The SAT does not measure a scholastic aptitude — if by aptitude we mean an innate, unchangeable indication of academic potential. The SAT measures the level of verbal and mathematical achievement, including the ability to handle innovative, non-routine approaches in these areas. The SAT evaluates the learning experiences of students in and out of school. The more the experience, the higher the level of achievement and therefore the higher the SAT score. Only an improved student can achieve an improved score. It seems that many students and parents still believe that all a test preparation program has to do is teach a few test techniques and strategies, wave a magic wand, and presto — a higher score. The goal of an SAT preparation program should go beyond that of improved SAT scores. It should provide improved skills to insure better performance at the college level. In fact, parents are beginning to realize the valuable long-range effects of SAT preparation. When reports of declining SAT scores made a big splash in the press, several years ago, the enrollments in our programs increased dramatically, despite the decreasing importance of SAT scores in the college admissions process. Declining SAT scores indicate a deficiency in basic skills which in turn could mean a poorer performance at the college level. Years of experience have convinced me that the "specter" of the SAT is an excellent device in motivating students toward working and improving these skills necessary for success at the college level.

Unfortunately, too many students memorize facts that teachers and textbooks provide, regurgitate this information on a test, and then promptly proceed to forget. A review can be of immense value in "bringing it all back," in making what one has learned more meaningful, and in giving the student an opportunity to think more creatively. This does not mean that every student should enroll in an SAT preparation program. Certainly, you should take at least one of the released exams to become familiar with the instructions, format, content, and time pressures of the test. If you feel, however, that you would like to enroll in a structured program of preparation, here are some tips you might follow in choosing a legitimate program that could give you the maximum benefit:

1) The program should be a long-range one — extending over a period of at least several months. Cram courses are of little value. The lessons should be held weekly with home-study assignments in between to reinforce what has been taught in class.

2) The classes should be small — not seminars of 100 or so. A class size should not exceed 25.

3) There should be an opportunity to make up missed lessons. Very frequently, you might miss a lesson because of illness or other commitments. Certainly,

you should not give up studying for an important school exam in order to attend a class session.

4) The program should offer you the option of continuing your study for the SAT if you choose to take the exam for a second time.

5) Most important, the school should have a *permanent* location where you might look at the materials and be able to talk in depth with a person in charge. Beware of fly-by-night programs that advertise by box numbers, have telephone answering services, hold classes in hotels or other meeting rooms, and silently steal away when the course is over.

6) The better programs offer scholarship assistance if you cannot afford to pay for the program.

7) You should check a program out with others who have taken it previously. Their experiences as to the quality of the teaching, the adequacy of the materials, and most important, the improvement they have achieved, can be most helpful in making your decision.

Be suspicious of high pressure tactics designed to corral you as a student — such as statements that the SAT is the most important exam you will ever take, claims of fantastic improvements, and guarantees of improved scores. Avoid correspondence courses. They are often expensive — almost as much as a course with live class programs. Usually the purchase of an SAT review book and use of materials supplied by the College Board itself is just as helpful.

Remember, the SAT is *not* the most important exam you'll ever be taking. It is only one of many criteria used by admissions officers to make a decision. Certainly your high school record is more important than the SAT score you will get.

Perhaps one of the best reasons for some kind of preparation is to make sure that the SAT score evaluates your achievement as reliably as possible. After all, you wouldn't enter a tennis tournament cold. I've seen hundreds of cases of underachievers or poor "test-takers" whose self-images have been enhanced by improved scores that more accurately evaluated this academic achievement.

Remember, there is much you can do on your own long before you take a preprartion course or even decide to do so. You can start reading — newspapers, magazines, best-sellers, — read something that interests you, but read! At the same time, you'll be improving your vocabulary and the ability to integrate ideas. In math, as well as in science, don't just memorize rules and standard ways of attacking problems. Try to reason things through and find out the why as well as the how as well as the what. Then, when the time comes to review for the SAT, you will have done most of your preparation already. Good luck!

Stanley H. Kaplan is Executive Director of the Stanley H. Kaplan Educational Center, Ltd., New York, New York with offices nationwide and abroad. Kaplan has been featured in numerous articles including *Time, Newsweek,* and the *New York Times.* He has also appeared on numerous public radio and television programs as an authority on test preparation.

Searching for student financial aids

By S. Norman Feingold and Marie Feingold

The purpose of this article is to suggest practical techniques and pathways for gathering accurate information about financial aids that are available and to indicate time frames within which it is advisable to initiate financial aid seeking efforts.

1. Start Early

The high school student should begin not later than the beginning of the junior year of high school. Many scholarships require that the student have taken the Scholastic Aptitude Test or the Preliminary SAT. The National Merit Scholarship competitions start the beginning of the junior year in high school. Many organizations use the results of this exam for the selection of their recipients; and this includes some companies which provide scholarships for the children of its employees. Some colleges select student aid recipients from National Merit competitors. Some competitions for research fellowships, overseas grants may close a year before recipients are announced.

2. Federal Publications

A. The U.S. Department of Education publishes two helpful pamphlets, that are revised annually. They are *Five Federal Financial Aid Programs: A Student Consumer's Guide* and *Federal Financial Aid for Men and Women Resuming Their Education or Training.* They are both available without cost from Federal Financial Aid, Box 84, Washington, DC 20044.

B. Veterans Administration each January publishes *Federal Benefits for Veterans and Dependents.* It contains details of educational assistance and is available from the Superintendent of Documents, U.S. Printing Office, Washington, DC 20402. Cost $1.50.

C. The Department of Defense. Each of the armed forces has ROTC programs and annually revises its pamphlets about programs.

Achievement through Education, Air Force ROTC is obtained from the Department of the Air Force, Air Force Reserve Officers Training Corps, Maxwell Air Force Base, AL 36112.

Navy-Marine Corps Scholarship Programs. U.S. Department of the Navy, Navy Recruiting Command, 4015 Wilson Boulevard, Arlington, VA 22203.

Information about Army ROTC scholarships can be obtained by writing to:
Army ROTC, P.O. Box 7000
Larchmont, NY 10538.

D. The U.S. Department of Health and Human Services, Washington, DC 20201 maintains up-to-date publications about social security benefits. Details should be obtained from the local Social Security office. Generally dependents of deceased or disabled contributors to Social Security are eligible for benefits while they are full-time elementary or high school students under the age of 19. Until April, 1985, there is a phasing out of the benefits as they existed until August, 1981.

Information about financial aid for students in the health and allied health professions is available from the U.S. Public Health Service, Bureau of Health Manpower, Student Assistance Branch, Center Building, Room G-23, 3700 East-West Highway, Hyattsville, MD 20782.

E. The U.S. Department of the Interior, Bureau of Indian Affairs, Washington, DC 20245 publishes pamphlets about educational assistance for native Americans.

If you are having difficulty locating information about Federal financial assistance for training and education, write to your Congressman or Senator at either his local office or at his Washington, DC office in the House of Representatives of the Senate.

3. State Publications

Most if not all states publish booklets or flyers about the student financial aid programs they administer. *Five Federal Financial Aid Programs: A Student Consumer's Guide* lists the names, addresses and telephone numbers of every state agency that provides information on the Guaranteed Student Loan Program and *Federal Financial Aid for Men and Women Resuming Their Education or Training* lists the names and addresses of each state scholarship agency. For details write to the state scholarship agency of the state in which you are a resident.

States also publish material on scholarships for special groups within the state such as veterans and their dependents, policemen, prison guards and firemen. It is likely that the state scholarship agency can give you the name and address you need.

Your state Senator can help you locate state aids.

4. Local Publications
(City and County)

Many communities have a printed or typed listing of student aids available to their residents. Your counselor may be helpful in directing you to these sources.

5. Know the ethnic, religious, and place origins of your family.

A fairly large amount of student financial aid is awarded by private organizations to persons of specific origin. Consult *Scholarships, Fellowships and Loans, Volumes VI and VII,* by S. Norman Feingold and Marie Feingold, and the *Scholarships, Fellowships, and Loans News Service and Counselors Information Services,* Bellman Publishing Company, P.O. Box 164, Arlington, MA 02174-0164.

6. Know for whom your parents or guardian work.

Some corporations and labor unions provide awards for their employees and members respectively. Have your parents speak to the personnel department of the company and the steward of the labor union for details. Company and union newspapers/magazines are good sources of keeping abreast of these financial aids.

7. As soon as practical for you, try to determine a **field of interest and hobby.** Some aids are given for majoring or studying certain subjects or having engaged in specific activities.

8. Enter Contests.

There are many different kinds of contests. The National Federation of Music Clubs, 310 South Michigan Ave., Suite 1936, Chicago, IL 60604 publishes scholarships and awards charts for two-year periods.

9. Get your own work experience.

Students who have been caddies or delivered newspapers or worked in other capacities are often eligible for scholarship competitions. Tuition refunds from the company for which you work cover a part or all of the fees for courses. Generally, the course must be related to your work and permission must be obtained.

10. Attend free post-secondary institutions of education and training.

The military academies and the Webb Institute of Naval Architecture are schools for which there are no tuition or room and board fees.

11. Consider scholarship loans.

In areas of work in which there are manpower shortages, it is possible to convert a loan to a scholarship by working in a given geographical area or in a specific subject matter field. Teaching the handicapped and working in rural poverty areas where there are shortages of specific personnel are two ways. Generally these programs are federally or state sponsored.

12. Loans to parents, to children of employees, to residents of service areas.

Such loans may be administered and awarded by business, foundations, banks, non-profit corporations. Two programs for which you should write for information are those of the United Student Aid Funds, Inc., 200 East 42nd St., New York, NY 10017 and Richard C. Knight Insurance Agency, Inc., 53 Beacon St., Boston, MA 02108.

13. Attend Cooperative or Work-Study Schools.

Your earnings will cover much if not all of your tuition and living expenses. More than 200,000 college students are enrolled in cooperative education pro grams. In the "typical" co-op program, students alternate semesters of study and supervised paid work. More than 1,000 colleges now offer co-op programs. Request *Undergraduate Programs of Cooperative Programs in the United States and Canada* which is available at no cost from the National Commission for Cooperative Education, 360 Huntington Ave., Boston, MA 02115.

14. Apprenticeship Training

In the skilled trades this is a way to learn and earn. Details are available from the following four sources: State Bureau of Apprenticeship and Training (one office is located in each state capital); a network of approximately 2,300 local and state employment offices; in a number of states there is a state apprenticeship council; U.S. Department of Labor, Bureau of Apprenticeship and Training, 601 D St., N.W., Washington, DC 20213.

15. Teachers, principals, ministers, lawyers, bankers, business people, counselors may know of individuals who anonymously assist deserving individuals to obtain the training and education they are seeking.

16. How do you locate the donors and administrators of financial aid programs?

There are a number of publications that should either be in the public library, school library, or college library. If not, request the library to order them. Some are:

Need a Lift, American Legion, P.O. Box 1055, Indianapolis, IN 46206. Revised every fall.

Scholarships, Fellowships and Loans, Volumes VI and VII, S. Norman Feingold and Marie Feingold. Bellman Publishing Company, P.O. Box 164, Arlington, MA 02174-0164, 1977 and 1982 respectively.

Scholarships, Fellowships and Loans News Service and Counselors Information Services, quarterly newsletter. Bellman Publishing Company, P.O. Box 164, Arlington, MA 02174-0164.

Don't Miss Out. The Ambitious Student's Guide to Scholarships and Loans, 5th ed., 1980/82, Robert Leider, Octameron Associates, Alexandria, VA. Published biennially.

Financial Aids for Higher Education 1980-81 Catalog, 9th ed., 1980, Wm. Brown Publisher, Dubuque, IA.

AFL-CIO Guide to Union Sponsored Scholarships, Awards, and Student Financial Aid, 1981. AFL-CIO Department of Education, 815 16th St., N.W., Washington, DC 20006.

Additionally, there are local newspapers, particularly suburban ones. They generally announce who won what and provide a name or address you can contact.

Local banks, community foundations, and social service agencies are aware of funds about which there is little or no publicity.

Usually there is less competition for local student aid funds in comparison with those available to candidates on a national level.

Many states publish directories of local aids. Your guidance counselor or public librarian will know how to obtain a copy or will have a copy for you to read.

17. The financial aid office of the institution you wish to attend or are attending.

Many funds are administered by the schools themselves, and you must let the financial aids officer know of your need for assistance. Many schools and colleges and universities publish a directory of their aids; they are usually free.

18. Answer all letters and application forms with great care.

Be certain that you have answered *every* question; for those not applicable, write N/A. If at all possible, type; be certain of accuracy and neatness. Meet all deadline dates. Deadline dates may change from those listed in directories. You need enough time to edit your answers several times. The quality of essays when they are required with the application blank is an important screening device. Be certain you remind your references and schools you've attended to submit requested material on time.

19. If you try each one of the methods described above and have ability and potential, you have a good chance of getting student aid. A study by the authors showed that with students of equal ability, the ones who applied to more resources were more successful in obtaining assistance. You may get a scholarship on your second try from the same fund.

Good luck. Don't let the lack of money deter you from seeking further education and training. Your post-secondary education can open up rewarding careers to which you otherwise would not have access.

Dr. S. Norman Feingold is President, National Career and Counseling Services, Washington, DC; Honorary National Director of B'nai B'rith Career and Conseling Services; Past-President of the American Personnel and Guidance Association and the author of several publications including seven volumes of *Scholarships, Fellowships and Loans.* Marie Feingold is a Rehabilitation Counselor, Washington, DC and co-author of volumes six and seven of *Scholarships, Fellowships and Loans.*

Tough questions to ask any admissions officer

By Robert G. McLendon

As a college admissions officer for the past fouteen years, it is clear to me that today's prospective students are carefully comparing colleges and striving to learn all they can about the colleges to which they apply. The age group of 18 to 24 year olds is declining in the United States, and this is creating a type of "buyer's market" in the market place of higher education.

In order to assure yourself that your expectations of a college are met, you, the student consumer, need not hesitate to ask admissions officers some "tough questions." This article will offer you a few suggestions of some tough questions that I hope will help you make the right choice when selecting a college.

Academic Questions

1. How many students in last year's

freshman class returned for their sophomore year?

2. What percent of the freshman class obtained a 2.00 (C) average or above last year?

3. If accepted, will you tell me my predicted freshman grade-point average?

Many colleges use a mathematical formula based on studies of currently enrolled students to predict an applicant's freshman grade average.

4. What is the college's procedure for class placement?

This is especially important in the areas of English and mathematics because freshmen often vary significantly in their ability to handle these important academic skills.

5. What procedure is used to assign a faculty advisor when the student is undecided as to the major area of study?

6. What type of additional academic services does your college offer at no additional cost to the student (e.g., tutoring, career or personal counseling, study-skills workshops, improving reading speed, etc.)?

7. How effective is your college's honor code? What is the penalty for cheating?

Social Questions

1. What is the average age of your student body and what percent resides on campus?

Many colleges today have a large and increasing population of commuting part-time adult students and a dwindling enrollment of 17 to 18 year old full-time, degree-seeking students residing on campus.

2. Is your college a "suitcase college" on the weekends? If not, what are some typical weekend activities for students on your campus?

3. What procedure is used to select roommates if no preference is listed?

4. What are some of the causes of students being suspended or dismissed from your college? Is there a system of appeal for those who have been dismissed?

5. How can a prospective student arrange a campus visit?

Clearly the best possible way to evaluate a college socially is to plan a visit to the campus. When you visit, try not to be shy. After your talk and tour with the admissions officer, walk around by yourself and informally ask students their opinions. A good place to chat with students is in the college's student center or at the dining hall.

6. What are some of the rules and regulations that govern residence hall life? Are there coeducational residence halls?

Financial Questions

1. What percent of your students received financial aid based on financial need?

2. What percent of your students received scholarships based on academic ability?

3. What percent of a typical financial aid offer is in the form of a loan?

4. How much did your college increase cost (room, board, tuition, and fees) from last year to current year?

5. If an accepted student must submit a room deposit, when is the deposit due, and when is it refundable?

The deposit should be refundable in full up to May 1, if the college or university is a member of the National Association of College Admissions Counselors.

6. If my family demonstrates a financial need on the FAF or FFS forms; what percent of the established need will typically be awarded? When can I expect to receive an official financial aid award letter?

The distinguishing quality of any person is the quality of the mind, and the college you select will have a long-lasting impact on your career and life. I realize that you are painfully aware of the need to make the right college choice because most high school students realize that the college years are often the most productive stage of life. Knowing what questions to ask an admissions officer is an important part of this decision-making process. Most admissions officers want you to ask "tough questions" because if you make the wrong choice we, too, have failed in our job.

Bob McLendon is Executive Director, Brookstone College of Business, High Point, North Carolina. He served on the Admissions Practices Committee of the National Association of College Admissions Counselors and has been Chairman of the Admissions Practices Committee of the Southern Association of College Admissions Counselors. He is a member of the Executive Board of SACAC and President-Elect of the Carolinas Association of Collegiate Registrars and Admissions Officers.

Common mistakes students make in selecting a college

By William B. Stephens, Jr.

The process of choosing a college can be a rewarding, worthwhile experience or it can be an endless, frustrating series of mistakes. Those mistakes are common and are usually the result of inadequate research and preparation— both characteristics you will need as a successful college student. The selection of a college is a good place to begin developing those virtues.

Begin the process with a series of questions. Am I most interested in a small, medium, or large college? Do I want to stay close to home or go away? What will be my major? Does the college have a broad curriculum if my major is undecided? How academically competitive do I want my college to be? What are the costs? Is financial aid available? Which extracurricular activities are the most important to me? When these questions are satisfactorily answered, it is time to begin the next stage.

Research is of primary importance in selecting a college. Do not make the mistake of choosing a college simply because your friends go there. List priorities. Be willing to invest time and effort in investigating colleges which share these priorities.

In writing to colleges for information, be neat, concise, and accurate in providing information about yourself. Many students forget to include the address to which the college should send material. Also include your high school graduation date, the high school you attend, your anticipated major (if that has been decided), and any pertinent information regarding grades and test scores. Decisions are made about students on the basis of their initial contact with the college. Do not be careless in this important decision.

There are numerous publications which are helpful in gathering information. These publications may be located in school and public libraries, bookstores, and guidance offices. Many are cross-referenced according to majors offered, geographic locations, costs, and sizes. Once familiar with college publications, the task of choosing a college becomes an easier one. Do not make the mistake of floundering with too many college options.

Your school guidance office can offer an abundance of information. Among the many contributions of guidance counselors is the provision of data concerning financial aid, college representatives scheduled to visit the school and/or vicinity, College Fairs, and testing for college entrance. In addition, most schools provide counseling to help students choose colleges compatible with their scholastic aptitudes, personality, financial means, and extracurricular interests. Often these guidance resources are not tapped, yet they can be among the most beneficial that you could explore.

Do not neglect the value of contacting alumni, college representatives, and currently enrolled students. Alumni can provide firsthand accounts of life at college while representatives will have the current facts about admissions requirements, new majors offered, scholarships, sports, and campus activities. Students who are currently enrolled in a particular college can provide additional insight into the actual experiences you can expect at the institution.

It is important that you visit the colleges which are your first preferences. Never will catalogs, counseling, or recommendations from alumni replace an actual visit to the campus. Much can be learned from sitting in on a few classes, walking through dormitories, and talking to faculty and staff. It is extremely risky to choose a college without personal observation.

Many colleges have orientation programs to acquaint students and their parents with the facilities and various aspects of student and faculty involvement. Investigate the colleges being considered to discover their plans for orientation programs. Do not fail to be present at the programs in which you are most interested.

Since the cost of attending college can be one of the greatest factors determining your choice, the possibility of obtaining financial aid is to be taken into careful consideration. Watch for the deadlines in applying for financial assistance, and have the appropriate forms completed well in advance. If financial aid is offered, be certain to compare the amount of aid offered and the total cost of attending that particular college. Remember that the matter of final importance is in determining the amount which has to be paid by you and your family.

College preparations should begin in the ninth grade. Solid academic courses (usually beyond the minimum required for high school graduation) should be completed each year. Four years of English is normally expected. Most colleges expect a student to complete at least three years of math, including two years of algebra and one of geometry. Although requirements vary from college to college, it is generally advantageous to have a sound background in biology, chemistry, physics, history, and a foreign language.

High schools administer PSAT, SAT, and ACT exams to juniors and seniors. It is wise to plan to take a College Board exam more than once. As these exams take four to six weeks to be graded, you should allow plenty of time so as not to delay the application process. Your score on a college board exam will further indicate the type of college to attend. Colleges vary considerably in their College Board score requirements.

By October of your senior year, choices should be narrowed to two or three prospective colleges. You should be aware of all admission requirements for each institution considered. Do not delay the application process until after Christmas. Many colleges begin waiting lists very soon after the beginning of each new year. Your application and all required documents should be on file by November 1 at each college considered. Do not expect high schools to send transcripts or teachers to send recommendations the day the request is made. Allow a couple of weeks for these items to be completed and mailed to the college.

Incomplete or illegible applications will greatly diminish the opportunity for rapid processing. These types of delays can mean the difference between being able to attend your first choice of colleges and having to wait another full academic year to enroll.

College-bound students should never hesitate to ask questions. Begin early and be organized. Parental involvement is essential in choosing a college that will meet the need of you and your family. Diligent research and careful planning are the keys to the prevention of the most common mistakes made by college applicants today.

Bill Stephens is Director of Admissions at Florida Southern College, Lakeland, Florida and has worked in the Admissions field for ten years. Stephens is a member of the National Association of Admissions Counselors, the Southern Association of Admissions Counselors, the American Association of Collegiate Admissions and Registrar Officers, and the Southern and Florida Associations of Collegiate Admissions and Registrars Officers.

The advantages and pitfalls of advanced placement and credit by examination for the freshman year of college

By Carl D. Lockman

I think we all agree that gifted young people need help in order to recognize their potential role in society. Through advanced placement and credit by examination programs, secondary school systems and universities alike are making a bona fide effort to encourage the development of academic talent, thus helping students to better understand their contributions to society and self.

Perhaps an explanation of the main difference between advanced placement and credit by examination is appropriate at this point. Both programs serve the purpose of awarding the student college course credit for acceptable scores on examinations. However, the Advanced Placement Program is a function of the College Entrance Examination Board. It is a formally structured program of instruction culminating with an examination. Institutions also may give departmental examinations which may be referred to as advanced placement. Credit by examination may or may not be a formally structured program. The College Level Examination Program (CLEP) is an example of the former, through which a student can receive credit for non-traditional (learning outside the classroom) educational experiences by presenting satisfactory scores on examinations.

All programs designed to award credit at the university level have advantages that are worth the student's consideration. Credit programs complement conventional instruction by allowing students to begin academic study at a level appropriate to their experience. They require students to demonstrate that they have achieved at a level equal to college experience. By being given this opportunity, the student can save both time and money.

A second advantage is that studies indicate that advanced placement continues throughout the undergraduate years. Quantitatively and qualitatively the student benefits. Course credit granted through advanced placement generally allows for increased hours to be completed in a four-year program, much of which may be completed at the junior level and above. This certainly allows for greater flexibility and versatility in designing one's curriculum. Somewhat the opposite has shown up in early studies of CLEP credit. Students with CLEP credit tend to graduate earlier. However, this still permits the student the advantages of having saved money and time and allows the opportunity to move into graduate studies at an earlier date. The challenge for the student is brought to the front when he/she is placed into courses recognizing achievement when his/her ability surpasses basic proficiency level courses.

Another advantage to the participation in and the receiving of credit through these programs is the quality of instruction associated with advanced placement. Generally speaking, it is safe to say that some of the best secondary instructors are asked to conduct the advanced courses. These instructors will stretch to stay ahead of these bright students who comprise the classes. Also, students in these programs not only benefit from the quality of instruction, but from the fact that most schools set up programs by drawing on the experiences of other school systems. In effect, students are being exposed to highly researched programs that have been trial tested for years by many systems.

A closer look at these programs reveals additional advantages. Many advanced placement programs borrow lectures, lab facilities, and equipment from local businesses and universities to accelerate their programs. Schools sometimes pool courses to give a wider curriculum offering. Credit programs allow secondary schools and colleges to articulate their programs, thus helping to bridge the curriculum gap that has been prevalent for years. In bridging this gap the student with an outstanding background can be recognized.

The advantages far outweigh the disadvantages when studying advanced placement and credit by examination programs. Two negative comments might be made at this point. There is always the possibility that students entering these programs do not have a thorough understanding of the extra demands that will be placed on them. Remember that the courses offered in the secondary schools are rigorous college-level courses. College credit granted may result in the student being placed in upper-level courses, which in turn will demand more effort on the student's part. It is not a bad idea either that parents be made aware of what is to be expected of students involved in advanced placement programs and of those having received credit by examination.

Secondly, uninformed secondary and college personnel cause very definite problems. After a student has participated in an advanced placement program or has the experience to achieve credit through examination, it is imperative that the secondary counselors advise students and their parents of colleges that have established policies that would meet the needs of the student. I can think of few things more disappointing than for a student to miss the opportunity to have more flexibility in his courses and to avoid repetition. The other fears are that the college officials may not have required faculty members in the subject areas covered by the tests to review the examinations and that the procedures and practices of the college regarding credit have not been carefully studied. As you can see, such omissions by the institution in establishing policies could lead to improper credit and, even worse, improper placement in courses "over the head" of the student.

In conclusion, whether a student goes through the CEEB Advanced Placement Program, participates in the institution's own advanced placement program by taking departmental examinations, or receives credit for life experiences, the importance of the programs is that they are attempts to equate classroom and/or non-classroom experience to college-level learning. The programs are models of learning closely conforming with college courses. Placement and credit programs are relatively new opportunities which each year seem to become more and more accepted by the academic communities. These are ways to recognize the individual differences in students, an attempt to confront the age-long problems of recognizing the variety of experiences students bring to college, and a breaking from the tradition that all students need to enroll in core curricula.

For students with exceptional learning experiences and/or intellectual talents, advanced placement and credit by examination programs are recommended. The rewards for such accomplishments are great.

Carl D. Lockman is Assistant Director of Admissions at Georgia Institute of Technology, Atlanta, Georgia. Lockman serves on the Admissions Practices Committee of the Southern Association for College Admissions Counselors and is a member of the American and Georgia Associations of Collegiate Registrars and Admissions Officers. He was appointed to the Governor's Committee to study recruitment techniques and is a board member of the Middle Georgia Drug Council.

The academic and social benefits of large American universities

By James C. Blackburn

There is no type of collegiate experience which is most appropriate for all students. The purpose(s) of this essay are to identify and discuss the academic and social benefits of large universities. In almost every state in the union, there is at least one large university whose enrollment exceeds 10,000 persons. More than a score of states have within their borders, universities enrolling more than 30,000 students. There are several community colleges whose enrollments meet the criterion of having 10,000+ enrollments. Those institutions are not included within the scope of this essay.

A substantial number of large universities are state-supported. However, more than a few large universities are private institutions of higher education. Such universities are more common in the more populous regions of the nation, e.g. the East Coast and upper Midwest. The tuition prices of large universities vary from nominal charges to $10,000 per year. It is, therefore, possible to select a large university from any price range. Some of America's most expensive and least costly institutions can be classified as large universities.

Large universities are located in large cities such as New York, Boston, and Los Angeles, as well as in small towns, e.g. Bloomington, Indiana and Tuscaloosa, Alabama. The selectivity of admission to large universities is also quite varied. Some universities admit as few as one in five of its applicants. Other moderately large institutions offer admission to more than 90% of their applicant pools.

In short, the diversity between and among large universities makes it possible for almost every student who desires to attend such an institution. Enrollment at a large university is not the private privilege of any socioeconomic or intellectual sub-segment of American society. That being the case, there must be some good reasons for matriculation at and graduation from a large university.

There are academic benefits which apply to each size and type of college or university. The academic benefits of enrolling at a large university are especially striking.

Few freshmen actually complete the academic major which they begin. At a large university, the available academic majors often number in the hundreds, not dozens. If a student changes his or her major or career choice, the large university is most likely to be able to accommodate that change.

As a result of the "knowledge explosion," many undergraduate *curricula* now require extensive equipment and large library resources. Because of their graduate and professional schools, large universities tend to offer more sophisticated laboratory equipment and libraries of considerable size. So called "economies of scale" seem likely to perpetuate this circumstance. At a large university, undergraduates often compete with others for these resources. The point is that the equipment and libraries are available.

For most students, post-graduate employment is a major reason for college enrollment. Large universities typically offer a multiplicity of services designed to help students in the identification and pursuit of career options. Selecting a career and finding a job are not often easy; it may be well to get as much help as possible.

There is an additional "job search" benefit to holding a degree from a large university. Most such institutions are well known on at least a regional basis. Assuming the reputation of a given institution is good, the employer or graduate school may be more impressed if they are familiar with an applicant's university.

Each type and size of college and university has academic benefits to offer. Ony a few of the academic benefits of the large university have been addressed here. There are other benefits related to the academic learning environment of each large university. Academic learning is clearly the primary reason for the existence of colleges and universities. It would be foolish to suggest that all of the benefits of college attendance happen inside the classroom, laboratory, and library. Many of the non-academic benefits of college attendance are social in nature. It is well that those benefits be discussed.

The typical ages of college attendance (18-22) constitute an important period of intellectual and social development. It is important that these changes take place in the most nearly appropriate environment possible. Intellectual development is obviously an academic enterprise. Social development, which means more than just dating, parties, and football games, happens throughout the campus environment. As with the academic areas, each type of college or university has social benefits to offer prospective students. The social benefits of large universities are significant; those benefits should be considered carefully by aspiring freshmen.

It is reasonable to state that larger universities offer more student activities and more varied opportunities to associate with other students. In fact, many freshmen who enroll at the largest university find themselves inundated with opportunities for social involvement, community service, etc. It may be difficult to select the activities, clubs, and personal associations which are most appropriate for individual students.

The variety of opportunities for student involvement at a large university are often more impressive than the sheer number of such involvements, activities, clubs, etc. Many larger universities offer organizations which cater to a plethora of interests ranging from handicrafts to hang gliding. There are often religious organizations for many faiths and denominations. The opportunities for political involvement are often wide ranging. From the most serious of religious or political convictions to the desire for big or small parties, large universities can frequently provide activities which meet the needs of all their students.

As universities grow, the size of the student services staffs also grow. With regard to academics, this growth in student services results in improved opportunities for career identification and job seeking. In the arena of social development, this growth means more opportunities for personal counseling and other activities which are designed to help a person to improve their social awareness and skills.

A final social benefit of large universities has to do with one's classmates.

Because of their size, large universities often enroll students whose backgrounds present a wide variety of experiences, values, and perspectives. Exceptions to this rule do exist, but is is generally true that one's classmates at a large university will be less homogeneous than might be the case at smaller colleges and universities.

There is an important social benefit in this lack of sameness among a student's classmates. Most students will study, work, and live out their lives in a world composed of a huge variety of persons. Our society has become more pluralistic in recent years. It seems, therefore, likely that there is a good in being able to live and work with a wide variety of persons. College is an excellent place to gain experience in dealing with people whose backgrounds and perspectives may be different from your own. Large universities offer many opportunities for such experiences.

By way of the above, it is hoped the nature(s) and benefits of large universities may be better understood by qualified prospective students. The more important points of this essay are that American higher education is quite varied and that no type of colleges or universities is inherently superior to any other type or types. Each student must make his or her own decisions about the appropriateness of small colleges, community colleges, church affiliated colleges, and large universities.

This writer's bias for large universities should be obvious. Huge varieties of academic and social opportunities are available at large universities. Those varieties serve to make such institutions an excellent choice for many aspiring freshmen. Large universities, although varied themselves, are not for everyone. They do present very appropriate choices for many prospective students.

Jim Blackburn is Director of Admissions at the University of Northern Colorado, Greeley, Colorado and has been involved in the college admissions process for over ten years. He has conducted a number of conference presentations for admissions personnel at various association meetings.

The academic and social advantages of a private church-related college or university

By A. Mitchell Faulkner

Many educators in recent days are concerned that moral and ethical matters have been so largely excluded from the educational experience. Under the influence of a technology expanding beyond all expectations, the demands placed upon most professions, including the social and natural sciences, have worked to exclude serious consideration of moral and ethical concerns inseparably bound up in that expanding technology.

But the assumption that our complex society can be safely led by technicians untrained in the making of serious ethical decisions affecting our corporate well being is totally unacceptable to any thinking person.

As Bruce Haywood has written in *The Chronicle of Higher Education,* "too many of our colleges and universities have become vocational schools... Whereas once they offered our children avenues to a larger sense of their humanity, they now direct them to the market place. Instead of seeing themselves enlarged under the influence of great minds and grand ideas, students find themselves shrunken to fit the narrowing door of the graduate school or tailored to a job description. It is time for our colleges and universities to talk again about the worth of a free life, time while we are still able to distinguish between the *training* of young people and their *education.*" (1/8/79)

Young people are not born with moral and ethical convictions. They are learned in the educational process, if learned at all, by precept and by example, by being in the presence of people with convictions. Healthy self identity, says Lloyd Averill, emerges out of an environment which has convictional distinctiveness, in which the maturing self has access to a range of clear and competing values where the competition serves to sharpen and enliven the options rather than to subjugate or obliterate them.

A subtle but pervasive element emerging in our day is what Archibald MacLeish has called the diminution of man, the "long diminishment of value put upon the idea of man" in our society. Why has this happened now at the moment of our greatest intellectual triumphs, our never equalled technological mastery, our electronic miracles? "Man was a wonder to Sophocles when he could only sail and ride horseback and plow; now that he knows the whole of modern science he is a wonder to no one," says MacLeish.

At least part of this loss of the humane is caused by the knowledge explosion, the sheer weight of information in the print and electronic media, so that man despairs of any cognitive wholeness and surrenders ever increasing areas of knowledge to a vast array of experts.

Earl McGrath, former Commissioner of Education, says on the other hand, that this vast array of facts and theories needs to be collated and evaluated within the framework of philosophic convictions and religious beliefs in order for the wisdom of the ages to again invest dehumanizing facts with meaning for man.

One further point of definition needs stating. Our sense of community has well nigh been lost, and every social philosopher recognizes the need to restore it. What is at stake here, says John Gardner, is the individual's sense of responsibility for something beyond the self. The "me" generation threatens the cohesiveness of our social fabric, and a spirit of concern and caring is virtually impossible to sustain in a vast, impersonal society.

All of the above points directly to the purpose of the church-related liberal arts college. The essence of the liberal arts is the passion for man, the development of the humane values in literature, philosophy, history, and religion; and the great ideas of the race, such as truth, justice, love, beauty, honor, and wisdom are precisely the vehicles through which the deepest purposes of religion are served. Religion is only secondarily a matter of creeds and rituals. At its heart it is a matter of meaning, and this meaning is conveyed most effectively through the wisdom of the ages, the liberal arts.

Education is more than a learned set of mental exercises, the ability to respond properly to fixed mental inquiries. A computer does this admirably. To be fully human is to add to this a capacity for imagination, the ability to feel reverence and awe in the presence of mystery, a capacity for caring and compassion, and appreciation for the mixed grandeur and misery of the human experience. These represent the uniquely human accomplishment and point the direction for the church-related liberal arts college.

Further, the church-related college, usually smaller, offers a community in which students have more opportunity to learn through experience the interpersonal skills so necessary to effective participation in today's society. The development of the whole person involves taking responsibility for the care of the community, its governance, its social life, its ethical and moral tone, its operative effectiveness. A broad participation in all aspects of the campus community should mark the church-related college.

Students are not uniformly at the same place in their development, and ought not to be coerced to march lock step through some standardized program. The undergraduate program, through flexibility made possible by forms of governance and individual care, ought to allow as much as possible for diversity of interest and differences in development as the student progresses. A college ought to find ways to encourage each student to develop to the fullest potential his individual gifts and educational aspirations. A student's goals ought to be headed by the desire not only to master the curriculum but to develop himself. The church-related college will seek to aid this through the total experience, intellectual, social, cultural and religious.

The church-related college, if dedicated to the fully human development of its students, will retain a healthy respect for the vocational skills. In order to fully *be*, a person must be able to *do.* Life cannot be divorced from work, and a healthy self identity depends in part upon the ability to make some significant contribution to society. Thus the great truths of the liberal arts must be brought to focus and a point of service through competency in a chosen area of the world's work, where one may serve and fully live.

After all, as Montaigne said a long time ago, the purpose of education is not to make a scholar but a man.

A. Mitchell Faulkner is the former Executive Director, Council for Higher Education, Western North Carolina Conference, The United Methodist Church. He is on the Board of Trustees for Pfeiffer, Greensboro, High Point and Brevard Colleges, and is a member of many educational associations including the North Carolina Association of Independent Colleges and Universities, Secretary, S.E. Jurisdictional Commission on Higher Education.

Advantage of attending a state university

By Stanley Z. Koplik

For most students and their families, the cost of a four-year college education is an important consideration, and for this reason alone, many choose state colleges and universities. These institutions are usually considerably less expensive than private institutions and in many cases provide students with the option of living at home while pursuing a degree.

State scholarship programs are frequently available providing monetary incentives even to those who attend state institutions. Some families appreciate the opportunity of utilizing a system they continue to support with their tax dollars. But state universities are a wise choice for the college bound for many reasons other than simply economics. For young people growing toward independence, the proximity of the state college or university to parents, friends and home communty can provide the firm base of support students need as they adjust to the academic, social and emotional pressures of a more demanding way of life.

High school graduates seeking to continue their education in an atmosphere of intellectual challenge and academic diversity should also look to the state universities and colleges. With a wide range of courses and curricula from which to choose, state institutions of higher education provide a solid grounding in most fields from vocational and technical training to liberal arts education. No longer stereotyped as teacher training schools, state colleges and universities now emphasize engineering, computer technology, business, and science as well as teacher education and the humanities.

As a first step for those seeking professional careers, state institutions offer programs in such fields as medicine, dentistry, law and architecture. Virtually, any area of academic interest can be satisfied through state college programs. At the University of Kansas, for example, there are 112 degree programs offered; the University of Missouri offers approximately 125. Other states offer an equally broad array of programs. With outstanding faculties in many disciplines, and national reputations in many areas, state institutions have developed into comprehensive universities where intellectual inquiry and academic excellence flourish.

A large number of state colleges and universities are equipped with fine research facilities and outstanding libraries providing unlimited opportunities for questioning and stimulating creative minds. In some areas the most complete and comprehensive library in the state thrives on the campus of the state university, while inter-library loan systems enhance access of all state residents to study and research materials.

For those who are concerned about "being lost in the crowd," state higher education systems usually provide a variety of campus sizes ranging from the very samll school with 1-2,000 students to the "mega-campus" with a student population of 25,000 or more. Attendance at a smaller campus does not imply inferior educational quality or diminished services. Excellent instruction, stimulating classroom discussion and challenging extracurricular activities can be found on all state college campuses regardless of size.

Providing an integrated educational program with a maximum of flexibility is the goal of many state systems. To facilitate student choice, states such as Kansas and Missouri have developed clear articulation or transfer agreements with junior college for a senior institution. Many junior college graduates enter four-year institutions as juniors with legitimate standing.

Continuous attendance at college or university is ideal for those pursuing a degree but it is not always possible. When attendance must be interrupted, many state universities provide cooperative extension programs and programs of continuing education for those who cannot attend classes full-time on campus. State higher education institutions also use sophisticated telecommunications systems to bring the university and its courses to the most outlying areas of the state.

The college years are, for many, a time to develop relationships which will provide a source of friendships and professional contacts for a lifetime. Attending college in one's home state increases opportunities to establish such long-lasting relationships and to be woven more fully into the fabric of state life.

Young people are increasingly aware of significant roles they will play in the social, political and economic life of this country. A college education in the state in which they are most likely to live can provide students with early involvement in the complexities of state activity. Increasingly, states are encouraging participation by student government groups in legislative activities. Some states, including Kansas, have authorized the appointment of a Student Advisory Committee to the Board of Regents, thus ensuring direct student participation in the decision making process.

State universities have long been known for athletic as well as academic excellence, and this continues to be true. On many campuses, intramural sports along with intercollegiate sports, enable large numbers of students to develop athletic prowess. As early responders to the growing need for quality in women's athletics, state universities provide equal opportunity in such sports as basketball, volleyball, swimming and tennis. Large multipurpose buildings springing up on many campuses indicate a dedication of state institutions to physical development and the cultural development of both campus and community. In some areas, the state college campus is the site of important cultural events, bringing lecturers, exhibits and the performing arts to an entire region. Attention must be given to the academic interest, the scholastic ability and the social and emotional maturity of the student as well as to the range of curricula, quality of instruction and extracurricular activities of the institution. A close examination of state university systems in the United States will indicate that there is virtually around every corner a quality institution of higher education solidly grounded in academics and attuned to the social and cultural needs of both students and community. State colleges and universities are a vital link in the network of public educational services and as such, merit serious consideration by the college bound.

Stanley Z. Koplik is Executive Officer of the Kansas Board of Regents, the governing body of public higher education in Kansas. Prior to assuming his current duties, Koplik served as Commissioner of Higher Education for the State of Missouri, where he directed activities of the Coordinating Board for Higher Education.

Advantages of a women's college

By Dr. Julia McNamara

Women's colleges are alive and well, even in 1982's all-too-realistic environment which predicts financial aid cuts, decreasing numbers of traditional college-age students, and a tight job market. Today, the mission and goals of 117 women's colleges in the United States matches neatly and clearly those of thousands of young women precisely because of these realities which they must face.

Women's colleges affirm and strengthen a woman's talent and ability; they exist specifically to develop the potential of their students; they demand and expect student participation and involvement. Women's colleges implant in women an attitude that is invaluable for success and achievement: "I can accomplish this task *and* I am a woman," not "even though" or "because" one is a woman. Rather the emphasis is on the fact that being a woman *and* accomplishing the task are quite compatible. Women's colleges instill in students the attitude that there is no sex-based limit to their potential for success. "I've lost that 'If-you're-a-woman-maybe-you-can't' attitude," said a 1982 women's college graduate who was also a student governor.

At a women's college, women learn that they can handle things because they have to handle them. They run the show; they exert influence; they wield power in student organizations which are exclusively their own. No one ever tells them that a particular leadership role is inappropriate for a woman. They can become properly aggressive and assertive without fear of seeming unattractive to men.

They learn to compete intellectually in an environment that consciously prepares them to realize that, if they seek it, the opportunity is there to excel. Their femininity will not be a deterrent at a women's college. Thus, women in leadership roles are not conspicuous at a women's college. Theirs is the only leadership that will occur, and they become comfortable with it. Women have to be in front of and behind all campus activities and events through which they learn to expect the best of themselves and of one another.

One woman, slightly overwhelmed by the extent of her responsibilities as student government treasurer, a task which involved budgets and planning, told me that she learned more from that experience than from some of her accounting classes, because she had final responsibility, and she had to make hard and unpopular decisions. She also said that her shyness and timidity would, in another setting, have prevented her from running for that office. "I would have thought some sharp guy could do it better."

When considering a women's college, it is important to understand several facts: First, women's colleges are not havens for people who could not survive elsewhere. Challenges and difficulties are just as much a part of this educational scene as any other, but there is emphasis on assisting women to meet the challenges which are special to them. Second, traditional views of women's colleges as protective shelters for innocent girls just do not pertain in 1982. Women's colleges are usually exciting places where learning and living mesh to create a viable educational and human experience. Third, women's colleges are not islands or ivory towers which exist by themselves, tiny spheres of influence which no other form of life can touch. Today, women's colleges often share facilities, faculty, and activities with neighboring schools so that students do participate in other educational environments. Thus, women's colleges can and do enjoy the benefits of co-education while maintaining their basic identity. This identity distinguishes her college and gives the young woman a chance to become a competitor, an achiever, a doer in an environment that is specifically concerned with her own development as a woman.

If women's colleges do not apologize for their *raison d'etre* of being for and about women's education, neither do they ignore men. Quite the contrary: women at a college for women, know well that this environment is only a temporary one, a step on the way to fuller participation in the human, common endeavor. If the college does its job well, the woman will realize that this environment prepares her for the next move and, indeed, sets the pace for it.

"You probably won't find your husband at a women's college," said one admissions counselor to a roomful of high school juniors, "but you will find out a lot about yourself, and about the kind of man you may want to marry." In considering a college, a woman needs to be clear about the reason for attendance at *any* college. Social life and experience are part of the rationale, but her intellectual development, the best and most comprehensive of which she is capable, is the key factor. To honor a woman's desire for quality education and self-development is the mission of a college which proclaims that it is *for* women.

Both academic and student services programs at women's colleges are consciously designed to achieve this mission. The opportunity to be leaders increases a student's self-awareness and inculcates a sense of feminine identity, preparing women for participation in every area of endeavor. No matter how secure or talented they are, young women do need affirmation and assistance in developing self-confidence. For example, two young women on my campus participated recently in the management of a political campaign. They were hired as business manager and associate to the candidate who was a woman. Because of specific communication skills that they had learned while working in a college office where the woman supervisor constantly exemplified a serious professional relationship with them, they succeeded admirably in a tough task. Of course, such training could occur on any college campus, but the point is that on a women's college campus specific efforts to develop a young woman's potential are a priority in all aspects of campus life from residence hall to classroom.

At women's colleges, career development offices train women for the competitive environment of the job market. Internship programs established in cooperation with local business and professional offices give students initial experience in administration or management or one of the professions, and provides a bridge between the world of academe and the business scene. When academic credit is linked with direct work experience a student's incentive increases; so does her personal satisfaction. And before she started out for the office, the student learned in a seminar room or through directed role-play what would be expected of her as a woman in the internship environment.

Faculties and administrative staffs at women's colleges are aware of their responsibility to develop young women's awareness of problems which she may face because she is a woman in a particular environment. The realities of discrimination and sexual harassment, can be a shock for the individual who needs to learn to deal with them effectively and, above all, to move beyond them.

When considering a women's college, these are questions which an applicant may want to ask during interviews:

1. Do the college's representatives seem to value their institution's specific identity as a women's college?
2. Does the college offer career guidance and advice for women?
3. Does the college have an internship program for its women?
4. What rapport has this institution established with neighboring universities and colleges?
5. What do students there say about their experience at a women's college?
6. Does the social life there give them a chance to meet men?

Responses to such questions give the prosepctive student a clear picture of the institution's commitment to the specific and unique character of a women's college. Certainly, a women's college is not for every woman. But equally as certain is the fact that these colleges continue to be extremely advantageous to the women who choose them.

Note: For more information on women's colleges, see: "A Profile of Women's Colleges" Women's College Coalition, Suite 1003, 1725 K St. N.W. Washington, DC 20006.

Dr. Julia McNamara is President of Albertus Magnus College in New Haven, Connecticut where she is also adjunct assistant professor of French literature. Dr. McNamara has also served as Dean of Students at this women's college. As an undergraduate she attended two women's colleges, Marymount Manhattan in New York City and St. Mary of the Springs, now Ohio Dominican, Columbus, Ohio and holds a Master's degree from Middlebury College and a Ph.D. from Yale University. She has been a Fulbright scholar and has studied for two years in Paris.

Opportunities at independent research universities

By F. Gregory Campbell

The diversity in American higher education is one of the greatest glories of our culture. No where else in the world does a prospective student enjoy such a wide range of choice. Public or private, large or small, urban or rural, secular or religiously oriented — American universities and colleges vary so greatly that any student should be able to find an institution seemingly tailor-made for that individual.

The major independent research universities constitute an important segment of American higher education. Frequently, they are considered primarily graduate or professional centers, and it is true that many students would be well advised to spend their undergraduate years elsewhere. But those universities typically possess vital undergraduate colleges offering a highly stimulating intellectual and extracurricular environment. For the right kind of student there is no better place.

In academic circles, the independent research universities enjoy an extraordinary reputation. That image depends on the quality of the faculty, and research is normally the means by which a scholar is evaluated. No one has yet devised a reliable method of measuring, comparing, and publicizing good teachers across the country. Good researchers are easy to spot, however, for they publish their discoveries for their colleagues around the world to evaluate. The research universities boast outstanding faculties containing highly innovative scholars with worldwide reputations.

But do they — or can they — teach? In ideal circumstances, the answer is yes. A standard view is that teachers are best when they continue to discover knowledge in their respective fields of scholarship. Conversely, the challenge of sharing their discoveries with critical young minds makes researchers better as a result of their also being teachers. Clearly, this ideal is not always realized. No university can guarantee that its most recent Nobel-prize winner will be teaching freshman chemistry, but such does happen.

The hope of learning from such scholars lures top-notch students to the research universities. Indeed, those institutions would have to do very little in order to produce outstanding graduates. Most college students quickly discover that they learn as much, or more, from their fellow students as from their professors. Inasmuch as the research universities serve as a meeting point for many bright young people, much of the intellectual stimulation on the campuses is provided by the students themselves. Compatibility with others who take their studies seriously is an essential prerequisite for prospective students.

But college life cannot be all work and pressure. There have been persistent efforts over the past fifteen years or so to reduce intellectual competition among students. Professorial complaints about "grade inflation" reflect the fact that it is much easier for a student to stay in the universities than to get into them to begin with. The drop-out rate is low, the failure rate even lower.

The learning experience extends beyond classrooms, libraries, and laboratories, and cannot be measured by grades alone. Extracurricular opportunities for learning and growth are central to a college experience. Most of the independent research universities seek to encourage informal association between professors and students. Professors may be encouraged to eat meals regularly with students in the dining halls. Leaders in public affairs or the arts and sciences may be invited to the campuses in order to engage in informal meetings with students. How does one measure the worth to a pre-law student of a breakfast conversation with a Supreme Court justice?

The independent research universities almost never appear on the list of major NCAA powers in football or basketball. Their teams normally compete at a lower level. But their programs do offer opportunities to participate in intercollegiate athletics to many young men and women who could not make the teams of the major powers. In addition, the intra-mural programs typically attract the vast majority of students on campus. The schools do not figure prominently in the sports pages, but the student communities are active and vigorous.

The undergraduate colleges within the independent research universities are normally quite small. Whereas they enroll more students than a typical liberal arts college, they have many fewer students than the state universities. That size both provides a critical mass for a wide variety of activities and allows for a sense of community and personal identity in a manageable environment.

The student bodies themselves are quite diverse. Admissions officers try hard to insure a nationally representative student body — including students from various regions of the country, diverse ethnic groups, and economic levels. There is also a significant number of foreign students. This intimate exposure to differences among people is a key element in the growth to adulthood.

The kind of education that is offered in the independent research universities is expensive, and tuition levels are high. Yet, since the 1960's, those institutions have tried to provide sufficient amounts of aid to enable students to matriculate regardless of financial need. It is an open question whether that policy can be maintained, even formally, in a more difficult economic environment.

The concept of a "University College" is the most apt way of thinking about undergraduate programs in an independent research university. Students find a relatively small college with a distinct identity of its own. Yet that college lives within a much larger institution possessing resources available for undergraduates to exploit. Those "University Colleges" are not appropriate for everyone, and there are many other excellent institutions from which to choose. But, when the match is right, a "University College" can offer gifted and serious young people opportunities seldom found elsewhere.

F. Gregory Campbell is Secretary of the Board of Trustees and Special Assistant to the President at The University of Chicago. He is a historian specializing in the history of international relations and Central and Eastern European history. In addition to administrative duties, he teaches in the college and the Graduate Divisions at Chicago.

Choosing the right college major

By James E. Moore

Implicit in this analysis is the assumption that there are some important decisions to make before choosing a major. A brief look at these is in order. First is the decision to enroll in a college or university. There is much rewarding and lucrative work in the world which does not require a college education. Furthermore, a wealth of adult programs have sprung up in the last decade, making the college education readily available later on to those who for a variety of reasons do not attend on a full-time basis immediately after high school. While there is immense peer and parental pressure in favor of college directly after grade twelve, there are many fascinating people who can attest to the value of travel or work after twelve years of formal schooling; these experiences shape and enrich the college experience when it is finally pursued.

Once the decision to go to college is made, one must choose the right college in order to be able to choose the right major. Not all schools teach everything, nor do they all teach as well as one another in a particular area. Obviously, the school should offer a program in what is the applicant's current major interest. Then, with some agressive questioning of students, faculty, and admissions personnel, the applicant can get a sense of how well the school does in that area and what, if any, particular perspective on the discipline is represented by that department.

The choosing of the major — in educational parlance, it is called "declaring the major" — is something which usually occurs toward the end of the sophomore year. While colleges and universities are interested in knowing what a prospective student intends to study and generally solicit that information on the application, that designation is neither binding nor necessary. Admissions officers and academic advisors are understanding of the many freshmen who simply do not know in what field they will concentrate, and it is not uncommon for a person to change directions a number of times during the first two years of college. It is, however, difficult to change majors as a junior or senior and still complete degree requirements in four years.

How does one determine what should be the major area of interest? A critical look at the high school record and aptitude and preference tests is a good way to start. What were the courses that proved exciting? In what did the student excel? Are the verbal or the quantitative skills more highly developed? The Kuder Preference Test asks the taker to respond to a variety of hypothetical situations and, by patterns that emerge from the responses, is a decent indicator of the general kind of work that will be congruent with the sense of self and others that is reflected in a person's answers.

Most colleges and universities require all students to complete course work in a variety of broad areas regardless of the intended major. This work commences during the freshman year and can be a useful way to further define the primary interest. Colleges offer courses in subjects that most high schools cannot or do not. In the process of meeting course requirements in the humanities, social sciences, and natural sciences or math, students expose themselves to new disciplines, one of which might well become the major.

In recent years, along with curricular development, there has been much interest and innovation in the issue of modes of learning. While the conventional classroom-lecture-textbook-test method of teaching and learning remains prevalent, the opportunity of "learning by doing" has become a widespread option. Some high schools offer their seniors the opportunity to do volunteer work for a variety of agencies, businesses, and charities. This work often evolves into summer employment for high school students. At the college level, the programs are more comprehensive, often involving both college credit and remuneration. Internships and cooperative education placements are an excellent way for students to discover exactly what a particular workplace is like and to determine just how suitable their preparation for that career is.

In addition to faculty, libraries, and laboratories, one of the most important resources for the undergraduate is the student who lives two doors down the hall. He or she probably studies in an area far removed from one's own or comes to the same interests for entirely different reasons. That person has parents who may well have had professional experiences and can share a sense of that professionalism from a perspective more personal than one that is offered in the classroom. The "bull session" is both misnamed and underestimated; these hours of informal exchange are often fundamental in shaping the direction and quality of life for many college students.

These are times when choosing the right major entails a gamble, regardless of how one sees it. The numbers of options are mind-boggling. The lack of certainty about the usefulness of a particular degree is a reality which should not be ignored, given rapid and constant change in the nature and needs of the workplace. Perhaps more than ever there is a case to be made for seeing the undergraduate years as ones for refining skills in reading, writing, and reasoning well, whichever department serves as the context for such endeavors. The risks are substantially reduced if the student is realistic about his or her capabilities and commitments, and thorough in exposure to the wealth of opportunity and resources colleges and universities offer. Above all, choosing the right major is cast in an appropriate light when seen as but one milestone of many in the process of learning, a venture which lasts a lifetime.

Jim Moore is an Admissions Officer at The American University in Washington, DC and previously worked in admissions at Aurora College, Aurora, Illinois; Goddard College, Plainfield, Vermont; and The New England Graduate Center of Antioch College, Keene, New Hampshire.

A yearn to earn

By Lawrence B. Durham

Throughout the 1970's much was made over the fact that the earnings differential between those with college degrees and those with only high school diplomas had shrunk. Many sought to interpret this statistical fact as evidence of the lessened worth of a college education. In the latter part of the decade, spiraling inflation and unemployment rates combined to produce a generation of college-bound young people more dedicated than ever to securing degrees which would assure them of employment upon graduation.

High school graduates of the early 1980's have thus been conditioned towards a very pragmatic view of the value of a college education. Yet, while post-college employment should be enhanced by this credentialing process, there is a real danger of overlooking the far more important and life-spanning aspects of the collegiate experience.

Indeed, many college faculties have contributed to this trend since the Russians launched their first Sputnik in 1957. Now, increasing numbers of these unwitting advocates of vocationalism are breathing fresh life into time-proven concepts such as core curricula and general education programs. Thus, the student entering college in the early 1980's faces the perplexing efforts of college faculties and our national economy as both seek to regain lost equilibrium through seemingly contradictory means.

In order to plot a realistic and rewarding course through the uncharted waters of higher education in this decade, students should be careful to expect neither too much nor too little from their collegiate experience. In an era where many college graduates may have to accept employment in jobs which had typically been filled by persons without degrees, certainly one would be unwise to expect a guaranteed position upon graduation. On the other hand, the rate of change in our society and in technological development is so rapid that a significant portion of the jobs in the next decade are non-existent at the present time. Consequently, one must seek to attain preparation for the unknown.

Education at its best results in the participant learning *how to learn* and *how to cope with change.* Given these two skills, the future can be faced with confidence. "Educational experiences" not producing these skills would better be labeled "training." And, it is crucial to note that such skills cannot be *taught,* they must be *learned.* As a result, the burden is on the student, not the teacher!

How then should one pursue such lofty goals? First, and foremost, there should be a commitment made to be an active participant in the educational process rather than to be satisfied as a passive subject. Then, a process of exploration should ensue during which the fear of the unknown is overcome by the excitement of discovery. In short, courage will lead to adventure!

Perhaps it would be useful at this point to emphasize the scope of these considerations. During the course of a life's work, a person may well change jobs eight to ten times. While several jobs may be in the same field, such as engineering, others may be in another field altogether, such as education. Generally, the different jobs are referred to as vocations, while the different fields are spoken of as careers. Thus an engineer might have several jobs within the field of engineering and then change careers to education where his vocation might be teaching in a particular college. In today's world and even more so in the future, students can ill afford to prepare for only a single career, let alone for a single vocation!

In this context, this author submits that the academic debate between specialized curricula and liberal arts programs is little more than a semantic exercise if the importance of developing both useful skills and broad perspectives is recognized. Just as an engineering program can include courses in the humanities, so can a liberal arts program include basic business courses. Studies continue to show that those who communicate effectively (orally as well as in writing), reason analytically, work well with others, and understand basic business principles find their respective pursuits far more rewarding.

A word of caution is in order, too, lest the reader fail to acknowledge consciously that the most important "rewards" are not financial. Over the years, studies of worker attitudes and values have increasingly revealed that pay ranks below other aspects of work such as the nature of the job environment the degree of individual autonomy, and the self-esteem derived from performing the work. Therefore, students should be careful not to choose a career path for purely financial reasons.

The process of choosing a course of study is no mean feat! Unless one has a burning desire to qualify for a particular profession, it is quite likely that several fields are of interest. Naturally, in the former case, the student would follow that academic track leading to certification in the chosen field. However, even in such cases, sampling courses in other fields and apprenticeships in the field of primary interest will often pay unexpected dividends. A person who is undecided should not develop an inferiority complex and go through senior high school and college apologizing! Rather, that individual should seek counsel and work experiences in areas of interest and engage in a sound, broadly-based course of study up to the point where declaration of a major field is required.

As of this writing, energy and computer science head the list of promising fields with other engineering and business areas and health services close behind. As we become more and more dependent on information exchange, related vocations in that field will increase in their attractiveness. And who knows where we are headed in the fields of microelectronics and genetic engineering. Yet, the reader who selected a course of collegiate study based solely on this or any similar listing would have missed the real point of this article. The true value of a college education cannot be quantified. To the contrary, its qualitative dimensions transcend the relatively narrow considerations of vocation and career to affect our entire lives.

Yearn to learn and you will learn to live. Live to learn and you will learn to earn.

Dr. Lawrence B. Durham is Dean of Admission Services, The University of Alabama. He holds memberships in many associations including the American, Southeastern and Alabama Associations of Collegiate Registrars and Admissions Officers. He has published numerous articles in the field of education.

The two-year experience

By Dr. Jacob C. Martinson, Jr.

It is a difficult adjustment for a student to go from a high school, sometimes a small high school at that, directly into a multi-complex university often with thousands and thousands of other students. Are the majority of high school graduates equipped for this kind of transition? The answer, of course, is that some are, and some are not. There is an alternative approach.

There is a wide range of academic programs available among two-year colleges today. There are many accredited institutions which offer outstanding two-year terminal programs in areas such as business arts, computer science, and medical arts. This article, however, will focus on the two-year colleges that are designed to prepare the students for continuation at a four-year college or university. It will address the belief that, in many cases, the pursuit of the baccalaureate degree is greatly enhanced by "The Two-Year Experience."

When it comes to the role of a college education in career performance, an academically recognized two-year college can provide the essential foundations of undergraduate training often better than the best universities. After all, it doesn't take an expert to see that faculty qualifications are not that different from one center of learning to another. For example, a survey of the educational credentials of faculty members at good two-year colleges reveals that they have received their graduate training at the finest colleges and universities in the country.

The advantages of getting a good start at a two-year college are numerous. I will cite some reasons why a two-year college program should be considered.

1. Access to the Faculty

A faculty member ordinarily does not choose to teach at a two-year college unless he/she is specifically dedicated to teaching. Those faculty members who are interested in publishing or research usually go to the multi-complex universities where much of their undergraduate teaching responsibilities are delegated to graduate assistants. Classes in two-year colleges are generally taught by first-line faculty members.

Students have a right to expect some time with their professors who have spent many hours embodying much of the knowledge in which the students are interested. In the smaller two-year colleges, the opportunity is provided to know professors on a one-to-one basis. It is not uncommon to observe ballgames between faculty and students, or for faculty to invite students to their homes for refreshments.

2. A Good Beginning

The first two years of college are probably the most important of a student's college career. With the exception of kindergarten and first grade, they are all-important to the pursuance of formal education. Statistics show that when a students does well in an academically sound two-year college, he/she seldom does poorly academically anywhere else. A good start can make the difference.

3. Budget Appropriations

Many multi-complex universities give the "lion's share" of the funds to the upper-level undergraduate courses and to the graduate programs. Two-year colleges, on the other hand, give their entire budget to those critical first two undergraduate years.

4. Less Expense to the Student

One can attend a fine two-year college with a superb academic reputation for less than one can attend most universities. The community colleges are less expensive to the student, but even the private residential two-year colleges are relatively inexpensive. Of course, if commuting is possible, the expense is even less. Since the private college also wants to serve the surrounding community, special scholarships to commuting area residents are offered by some colleges.

5. Opportunities for Leadership and Participation

The freshmen and sophomores at a two-year college will have no juniors and seniors to compete with in extra-curricular activites for campus leadership roles, team sport participation, and faculty time. The individual has an opportunity to become involved more quickly and more deeply in the total life of the college. Where else could a student be a representative to the college committees and the Board of Trustees at the age of 18? In short, there is no "sophomore slump" in the two-year college.

6. Vocational Future

The two-year college can enrich one's vocational future. The fact is that too many college graduates today are ignorant of the English language, history, science, and math. Many are deficient in their ability to get along with others and in that all-important skill of communication. One need only watch a nationally televised athletic event to observe the inability of some students from the so-called "prestigious" centers of learning to speak proper English. This is not to imply that the two-year college student will consistently perform any better; however, at good two-year colleges, there is a concerted effort to start wherever a student is academically and teach him/her to read and write effectively. For example, some of the better two-year colleges have 3 or 4 different levels of beginning English. The same is true of math. These schools place great emphasis on English and math with the conviction that if one can read and write and add and subtract, one has the educational foundation to function in the world. The hallmark of the best two-year colleges is that of toughness with caring. Such colleges encourage the formulation of long-range educational goals and positive views on how education can assist one in meeting vocational objectives. Obviously, there are some limitations to the depth to which one can pursue objectives in a two-year setting, but the seeds are planted and the incentives aroused.

7. The Best of Both Worlds

A student can have the best of the two-year and the four-year educational systems. During those critical first two years of college, a fine two-year school can provide an excellent academic program and curriculum, caring faculty members, and a concerned college community, all of which prepare the student to transfer to the larger college or university.

There are those in educational circles who would have one believe that transferring is dangerous to one's educational future. In most cases this belief is unfounded. On the contrary, it is sometimes easier to get into the best four-year schools after a two-year Associate of Arts/Science/Fine Arts degree than to apply right out of high school. Academic credits from a good, academically sound, two-year college are accepted by most of the finest universities. In fact, transfer students are not only accepted, they are actively recruited because of the natural attrition in the senior colleges and universities after the first and second years. Also, some students perform better in a two-year college than they did in high school; therefore, these students are more likely to have their application accepted when they leave the two-year college than when they graduated from high school. Further, there are certain rights and responsibilities which are uniquely applicable to the transferring student. A statement of these rights and responsibilities has been approved by the NACAC (National Association of College Admissions Counselors) in 1980 and revised in 1982.

In conclusion, today's two-year college generally offers a university-parallel curriculum. It is nearly always designed for the brilliant as well as the average student. The task is to successfully meet and challenge each student where he/she is academically despite varying aptitudes, dispositions, and outlooks.

The two-year college experience is not for everyone, but it certainly fills a need. It is a good place to start in higher educational pursuits — a good place to begin on the way toward the baccalaureate degree.

Jake Martinson is President of Brevard College, Brevard, North Carolina. Before going to Brevard in 1976, he was President of Andrew College in Cuthbert, Georgia. Dr. Martinson holds degrees from Huntingdon College, Duke University, and Vanderbilt University. Beyond serving Brevard College, he has been President of the Brevard Chamber of Commerce and Secretary of the Independent College Fund of North Carolina and is an elected Board member of the National Association of Schools and Colleges of the United Methodist Church. Born of Norwegian-American lineage, he is an honorary member of the American-Scandinavian Foundation.

The value of a liberal arts education

By Dr. David Maxwell

We are in the midst of a crisis that threatens the very fabric of higher education in America today, and that endangers the quality of education that we all desire for our children. The crisis centers on the relationship between undergraduate education and the so-called "real world": What are we preparing our students for? The resolution of this crisis has serious implications for the undergraduate curriculum, for the nature of the demands placed on our students by the institutions, by their parents and by themselves — and profound consequences for the continuing health and vitality of our nation.

A liberal education has always been measured in terms of its relevance to society's needs, and there is no reason that it should not continue to be; the notion of utility is firmly ingrained in our national character. The crisis to which I refer lies in the determination of precisely what those needs are, for it is in those "needs" that we express the relationship between education and the "real world."

I have witnessed a trend in American College students that I find particularly disturbing. An increasingly large number of students are demanding what they term "relevance" in their studies. Clearly, I feel that liberal education has profound relevance to the "real world," but these students have a definition of that term that is different from mine. By "relevance," they often mean professional training; training not for the future, but for jobs. With an entirely justifiable concern for their future economic well-being, they are making — I am afraid — a terrible and potentially devastating error of logic.

Although few of our students would accept the state of our "reality" as ideal, many are allowing the priorities of that reality — as expressed in economic terms — to dictate the priorities of their education. They are mistaking financial reward, prestige, and excitement for genuine intellectual interest. Many, I fear, view the undergraduate experience as a "credentialling" process, rather than as an education that will make them productive, fulfilled adults. I am not suggesting that our students do have neither genuine intellectual curiosity nor the thirst for pure knowledge, for they have ample supplies of both. But they are subjected to enormous pressures from the outside: the fear that the field in which they are truly interested will not provide them with a comfortable income; the fear that their parents (often professionals themselves) will not approve of their interests; the fear that their ambitions are not sufficiently "prestigious" in the eyes of their peers. These are all very real fears and pressures that must be recognized as valid, but they have two important — and destructive — consequences. It is my sense that many of our students go on to careers in the so-called "professions" with very little idea of what these professions entail and, what is worse, they have tailored their entire undergraduate education to fit what they feel is appropriate preparation for those professions.

We are engaging in the process of creating many unhappy adults as such students grow up to find that they have no real intellectual investment in the occupation toward which they have aspired since they were teenagers. Having focused their education at an early stage, with the mistaken impression that you have to major in economics to go into business, in political science to enter law school, or in biology to be a physician, they will be plagued with the gnawing feeling that they have missed something — but without knowing quite what it was that they have missed.

Furthermore, the misplaced emphasis on grades caused by the intense competition for professional schools discourages many students from their natural inclination to question, to challenge, to experiment, to take risks. Rather than risk the uncharted waters of their own ideas and their own imagination, many students choose the safe route of repeating what they've heard and read as they write their examinations and papers.

Clearly, it is our responsibility to find ways to encourage our students to follow their natural inclinations, to resist the pressures — we must make it clear to them that, as teachers, we will reward initiative, originality, and risk-taking. Perhaps most important is that we must convince them that it is precisely these skills that are the most "pre-professional," that no business ever grew without developing original ideas, that every physician must take calculated risks daily, and that the practice of law rests on the principle of challenge to ideas.

Most people with professional aspirations hope to advance beyond entry-level positions into managerial or executive roles; positions in which they can assume responsibility, control, and authority and positions in which they can implement their own visions. It is precisely these roles that demand breadth of education — not only in subject matter, but breadth in the range of personal and intellectual skills that the student acquires in his/her studies.

There is growing evidence that the "real world" is taking notice of the correlation between liberal arts skills at the professions. For the past twenty-nine years, AT&T has been conducting longitudinal studies of its managers, correlating field of undergraduate major to career advancement and managerial skills. The AT&T study showed clearly that those with non-technical majors (humanities and the social sciences) were "clearly superior in administrative and interpersonal skills." (Robert E. Beck, *The Liberal Arts Major in Bell System Management*, [Washington, D.C.: 1981], pp. 6, 8). Significantly, "Nearly half of the humanities and social science majors were considered to have potential for middle management, compared to only thirty-one percent of the business majors . . ." (p. 12) Within eight years of employment, the average management level of humanities and social science majors was significantly higher than that of other groups. As the author of the Bell report states: "One overall conclusion from these data is that there is no need for liberal arts majors to lack confidence in approaching business careers." (p. 13) It is interesting to note that this affirmation of the professional value of a liberal education comes from the experience of one of the world's largest high-tech corporations!

I am not presenting this evidence to argue that those who genuinely love engineering and the sciences should not pursue them, for their love is the best reason to enter those fields. Rather, the evidence presents a powerful argument for those whose interests lie elsewhere to *follow* their interests without fearing that their skills and knowledge will not be needed.

Not long ago, I had a meeting with several people who work in admissions at the Harvard Business School. We discussed the criteria for evaluating applicants, and they stressed that the single most important criterion was academic excellence at a respected, selective institution. Certainly, a few courses in economics and a familiarity with mathematics were an advantage, but the field of undergraduate major was not significant. As do the law and medical schools, they stress breadth of excellence and potential ability as reflected in the quality of the student's educational experience. It is significant that at Harvard, like many of the nation's best business schools, ninety-seven percent of their admitted applicants have had at least one year of full-time work experience before applying.

It should be clear from what I've said that liberal education *is* valued in certain segments of the "real world," and that there is often no correlation between choice of major and choice of career. Therefore we must encourage our students to spend their first year or more exploring, taking courses in a broad range of fields; courses in which they suspect they might be interested because of previous experience, courses in which they might be interested because they sound fascinating, courses in subjects that they know nothing about.

They should talk with their teachers, their advisors, their deans, their fellow students, with their parents, with other adults. In this process of exploration —if they are allowed to explore without pressure — they will find something in which they are genuinely fascinated. Pursuit of that fascination will lead them not only to sophisticated knowledge of a particular field, but to the development of intellectual and personal skills that will enable them to survive, happily and productively, as adults. The fascination will lead them to accept challenges, exercise their creativity, to take risks in the name of learning, to find out what they are good at and what to avoid, to be critical rather than accepting, and to be pathfinders rather than followers. It will also lead them, the evidence suggests, to a career that will allow them to use what they've learned in the broadest sense; one which they will find rewarding, interesting and challenging. To put it simply, they should decide *who* they want to be when they grow up, not just *what* they want to be.

David Maxwell has been the Dean of Undergraduate Studies at Tufts University since 1981. Formerly the Director of the Program in Russian at Tufts, he has been teaching Russian language and literature nearly fifteen years, and in 1979 was the recipient of the Lillian Leibner Award for Distinguished Teaching and Advising. A Fulbright Fellow in Moscow in 1970-71, Dean Maxwell is the author of numerous scholarly articles on Russian literature. He is active in a number of organizations concerned with liberal arts education, and is a charter member of the Council on Liberal Learning.

Preparing for a career in the arts

By Gene C. Wenner

Although the notion that there is no future in a career in the arts is still espoused by many, the number and quality of opportunities in the arts has dramatically increased in the past ten years. Not every vocational opportunity is with the Metropolitan Opera, Carnegie Hall or on Broadway but nationally the growth of the arts organization and career opportunities is much improved.

Many colleges and universities are responding to this trend, by greatly expanding their programs in the arts (music, dance, theater, visual arts and writing) that develop performers, creative artists, arts educators and arts administrators. In addition, there are many course offerings in the arts for those students less determined to pursue a career in the arts, but who also desire further training and experience in the arts.

Many young people are able to combine their artistic and academic skills in preparation for the demands of being an artist. Combination of skills are also necessary for careers in the management of artists or arts organizations.

If you are seriously considering further training and education in either music, dance, theater, visual arts or writing, you should be aware of a program designed to assist young artists. The Arts Recognition and Talent Search (ARTS) program of the National Foundation for Advancement in the Arts is a national program to recognize and support excellence in the arts. Over 5,000 high school seniors from every state participate in ARTS nationally every year.

The Educational Testing Service (ETS) of Princeton, N.J. administers the screening and adjudication activities of ARTS for the Foundation. Applications received from aspiring young artists include; a video tape of performance in dance and theater, an audio tape of solo music performance, a slide portfolio for visual artists and a portfolio of compositions by writers.

Each year, students with ability in the arts who will be high school seniors register for the ARTS program by these two dates: a regular registration deadline, May 15, (as a junior) and a late registration deadline, October 15 (as a senior).

The decisions made by panels of expert judges in each art field made solely on the basis of the artistic content of the student's performances as submitted. No other criteria, such as grades or academic standing have any bearing on their decisions.

As the result of these judgements four categories are selected: Finalists, awarded $3,000 in cash, Semifinalists, awarded $1,500, Merits, awarded $500 and Honorable Mention, a non-cash award. In addition, the registrants and award winners are recruited by leading colleges, universities and professional arts organizations who offer over 3 million dollars in scholarships and internships.

The Foundation recommends their top artistically talented students to the Presidential Commission on Scholars each year and twenty are selected as Presidential Scholars in the Arts. These young artists are presented in concert at the John F. Kennedy Center for the Performing Arts in Washington, D.C.

If you aspire to a creative career, you need to be realistic about your talent, for that is what is most important in getting a job in the arts or establishing a reputation. Practical experience outside of the school environment — with local theaters, music and dance groups, galleries and community newspapers — can give you an extra edge. Even the most talented artist must be willing to spend years of their lives mastering their skills so it is not too early to develop that necessary sense of dedication.

A life in the arts can be very rewarding because you give of yourself to others and what you get in return makes it more than worth the hard work and dedication.

Gene Wenner is the Vice President of Programs for the National Foundation for the Advancement in the Arts.

Guide to guides for high-school students

Reprinted with permission from the "Chronicle of Higher Education."

The Best Buys in College Education, by Edward B. Fiske (Times Books; 393 pages). Mr. Fiske, the education editor of the New York *Times,* has published his *Selective Guide to Colleges* since 1982. This fall he released *Best Buys*, which lists 200 colleges — both public and private — that are identified as particularly good values. The institutions range from Pratt Institute ($10,088 tuition) to Cooper Union ($300). Included are statistics (including admissions and financial-aid figures), and essays describing what Mr. Fiske calls "the academic and social climate" of the institutions.

The Insider's Guide to the Colleges, by the staff of the Yale *Daily News* (St. Martin's Press; 568 pages). "Obviously," the editors say in their preface, "it's impossible to capture the full scope and breadth of any institution in two or three pages of text." The editors of the Yale *Daily News* — and student correspondents on more than 150 campuses — offer readers, according to the book's cover, an account of "what . . . colleges are really like."

The brief descriptive sections tend to give colleges labels, provide a sweeping sense of the atmosphere, and describe campus social life. The book also provides an introduction to college "trends in the Eighties" and includes lists of colleges in categories such as "liberal arts colleges with an emphasis on preprofessionalism," and "colleges de-emphasizing varsity sports."

100 Top Colleges, by John McClintock (John Wiley & Sons, Inc.; 225 pages). In addition to its statistical descriptions of what it calls "America's best" institutions, *100 Top Colleges* suggests a systematic method for selecting a college. By answering a series of multiple-choice questions and plugging the answers into boxes, students may narrow their choice of institutions to conform to the qualities they value. "Choosing a college may never become a strictly scientific process," writes Mr. McClintock, "but it can be rational." The profiles of institutions rely heavily on statistics of all kinds, including ratings for "personal life," "mix of students," and "student motivation."

Rugg's Recommendations on the Colleges, by Frederick E. Rugg (Whitebrook Books; 65 pages). Mr. Rugg, a high-school guidance counselor, organizes his book by academic majors, from agriculture to zoology. In each section, the book recommends several colleges whose departments are felt to be among the best in the country. Within majors, the lists are divided into three categories: "most selective," "very selective," and "selective." Information about the colleges was obtained primarily through random interviews with students and others affiliated with institutions, according to the book.

"I even did weird things like interview the scorer and timer at the halftime of a basketball game at Williams College," Mr. Rugg writes. "We ended up discussing the classics department there (small, but good)." Mr. Rugg rates William's classics department among the best in the nation.

Lisa Birnbach's College Book, by Lisa Birnbach (Ballantine Books; 515 pages). Lake Forest College has the best salad bar of any College. The most promiscuous students are at Boston University. Connoisseurs of such information will find plenty of it in Ms. Birnbach's book, which describes student life at 186 colleges. "This is the inside scoop," writes Ms. Birnbach, "the juicy stuff you can only learn by visiting the campuses, by going to school there. This is the real thing." Entries place little emphasis on statistics and list such categories as "best professors," "gay situation," and "best thing about school."

The Public Ivys: A Guide to America's Best Public Undergraduate Colleges and Universities, by Richard Moll (Viking; 289 pages) "Even the parents with ready cash are wondering if Olde Ivy is worth two or three times the price of a thoroughly respectable public institution," Mr. Moll writes. His book contains lengthy narrative and statistical descriptions of 17 public institutions he says are comparable to Ivy League universities. Mr. Moll chose the 17 based on admissions selectivity, "quality" of "undergraduate experience," institutions' financial resources, and prestige.

America's Lowest Cost Colleges, by Nicholas A. Ross (Freundlich Books; 253 pages). North Carolina residents will be delighted to learn that, according to Mr. Ross's book, 13 institutions in their state charge $150 or less for one year's tuition. Californians have more reason to celebrate: 36 colleges are identified here as charging $100.

"This book was written," Mr. Ross writes, "because too many parents have been forced to sacrifice for their children's education. . . . Worst of all, too many young people have decided not to go to college, because they think they can't afford it." The book includes brief descriptions of more than 700 colleges with annual tuitions of less than $1,500.

The College Handbook, 1985-86 (College Entrance Examination Board; 1,900 pages). The College Board's guide is filled with facts and figures that answer any basic question a prospective student might have about more than 3,000 institutions: number of students, a description of the location ("city," "small town," etc.), major fields of study, and special programs. It also gives a brief "class profile" and statistics on the number of applicants admitted from the most recent pool. The introduction offers students advice on how to choose a college.

Selective Guide to Colleges, by Edward B. Fiske (Times Books; 482 pages). "If you are wondering whether to consider a particular college," Mr. Fiske writes, "it is logical to seek out friends or acquaintances who go there and ask what it's like. What we have done is exactly this. . . ." Mr. Fiske has written brief, general descriptions of what the book calls "the 275 colleges you are most likely to consider." The descriptions tend to emphasize various components of student life, as well as the academic reputations of institutions. In addition to the narrative descriptions, Mr. Fiske rates three qualities — "Academics," "Social Life," and "Quality of Life," on a subjective one-to-five scale.

GENERAL CATALOGUES

Barron's Guide to the Two-Year Colleges (Barron's Educational Series, Inc.; volume one: 319 pages; volume two: 282 pages). The first volume of this two-volume set lists facilities, costs, programs and admissions requirements of more than 1,500 two-year institutions. Using charts, the second volume identifies institutions offering programs in five general categories: business and commerce; communications, media, and public services; health services; agricultural and environmental management; engineering and technologies. It also provides a separate list of institutions offering liberal-arts programs.

Barron's Profiles of American Colleges (Barron's Educational Series, Inc.; 1,151 pages). In addition to providing statistical information — including median S.A.T. scores, student-faculty ratio, and tuition costs — *Barron's* ranks each college on a scale from "most competitive" to "non-competitive." The book's introduction says the rankings are determined by a combination of the institution's rate of acceptance and the average high-school grade-point average and median S.A.T. scores of students who are accepted.

Comparative Guide to American Colleges, by James Cass and Max Birnbaum (Harper & Row; 706 pages). While it includes many of the statistical laundry lists of other fact-filled guides, Cass and Birnbaum's book also throws in an introductory paragraph giving a general description of each institution. Each entry also includes sections on "academic environment," "religious orientation," and "campus life" and information on the proportion of degrees conferred in various departments. Like *Barron's,* the book uses what it calls a "selectivity index," rating institutions with competitive admissions from "selective" to "among the most selective in the country."

Lovejoy's College Guide, edited by Charles Straughn and Barbarasue Lovejoy Straughn (Monarch Press; 604 pages). Listing more than 2,500 colleges and universities, *Lovejoy's* is concise and informative but offers less statistical material than do some of the other catalogues. Its descriptions are much briefer than those in most of the other guides, such as *Barron's* and Cass and Birnbaum.

Peterson's Competitive Colleges, Karen C. Hegener, editor (Peterson's Guides; 358 pages). In its fourth edition, it includes one-page profiles of 301 "selective" institutions — those whose students do well on standarized tests and which consistently have more applicants who meet entrance standards than are admitted. The book contains lists of the colleges and universities by cost, size, religious affiliation, and other factors. It also includes one-paragraph profiles of selective arts colleges and conservatories.

Peterson's Four-Year Colleges 1986, Andrea E. Lehman, editor (Peterson's Guides; 2,237 pages). In a volume larger than the Manhattan telephone directory, *Peterson's,* which is updated annually, provides general information about more than 3,000 institutions. It also includes a section of two-page "messages from the colleges," profiles provided by institutions that each pay $895 for the space. In addition, the book provides a chart with a state-by-state breakdown of colleges, listings of institutions organized by majors offered, difficulty of admission, and costs.

Lovejoy's Concise College Guide, edited by Charles Straughn and Barbarasue Lovejoy Straughn (Monarch Press; 375 pages). "The criteria used for the selection of the 370 institutions are varied to include the most diverse selection of schools for you to choose from," says the introduction. The book never explains those criteria, but the editors seem to have included the most selective institutions. The descriptions of the colleges are slightly abbreviated selections from the larger *Lovejoy's,* including information on enrollment, cost, academic majors, and student life.

SPECIALIZED GUIDES

Who Offers Part-Time Degree Programs? edited by Karen C. Hegener (Peterson's Guides; 417 pages). The listings include more than 2,500 institutions offering part-time undergraduate and graduate degree programs. The guide also includes separate directories of colleges with evening, summer, and weekend programs.

The Black Student's Guide to Colleges, edited by Barry Beckham (Beckham House Publishers; 495 pages). Mr. Beckham, a professor of English at Brown University, writes in his introduction that he wishes to provide information "in both objective and subjective terms" to help black students choose among colleges. Each campus profile is based on information supplied by the institution and by five of its students, whose individual statements are often noted. In narrative form, the book provides details on topics including race relations, support services, cultural opportunities, and black organizations.

Everywoman's Guide to Colleges and Universities, edited by Florence Howe, Suzanne Howard, and Mary Jo Boehm Strauss (Feminist Press; 512 pages). For each of the 600 colleges it evaluates, *Everywoman's Guide* provides a ranking — on a three-star scale — for each of several categories: "students," "faculty," "administrators," "women and the curriculum," and "women and athletics." An introduction notes that those are areas of "special importance." In narrative form, each entry provides additional material under such headings as "policies to ensure fairness to women," "women in leadership positions," and "special services and programs for women."

A Guide to Colleges for Learning Disabled Students, edited by Mary Ann Liscio (Academic Press, Inc.; 490 pages). In addition to some basic information about admissions requirements and tuition, each entry lists services for learning disabled students, "modifications to the traditional learning environment" (including such details as tape recorders provided to tape lectures, and "longer time to complete exams"), and a person on campus for learning-disabled students to contact.

Learning a new role

By Paul and Ann Krouse

Most literature directed to parents of college-bound students focuses on financial matters, an area of great

(Continued next column)

interest and concern to most of us. Yet there are other roles besides bankrolls which require attention and involvement. Some are obvious and others more subtle. Having just completed the college admissions process with our eldest daughter, my wife and I would like to share our experiences and views.

Be involved.

Selecting a college is just one more experience in the parenting process with the usual mixture of risks, rewards, joys, and uncertainties. You will find yourself pouring over directories, college catalogs, counselor recommendations, applications, and financial aid forms. The more you do together, the less tedious the tasks and the more enlightening the process becomes. We found ourselves engaged in a very productive cycle which started with counselor/student meetings. From this counselor-to-parent shuttle which was repeated several times over a period of a few weeks, our daughter developed a list of six or seven college choices. We visited several of her college choices on a 4-day car trip and ultimately she selected a college which happily accepted her. Waiting for the acceptance letter was agonizing, receiving it was joyous. The family celebration which followed was memorable.

Our experiences were undoubtedly quite common. The subtleties merit equal awareness.

Listen to your child.

Most of us have our own preferences of where we would like our children to go to school, but we've had our chance(s) and now it's their turn. Certainly your guidance, opinions, and views are important. You may have some inflexible requirements which your child must be responsive to such as financial limitations. Nevertheless, it is imperative that you listen to your child's preferences and to the best of your ability and with your best judgement encourage your child to fulfill his or her dreams, not yours.

Be patient and "tune-in."

The separation between child and family is beginning and it impacts on everyone involved in different ways and at different times. So much of the college admissions process requires that the children initiate action which will cause separation that there is frequently a reluctance to complete a task which can easily be misinterpreted as laziness or irresponsibility. An application may remain untouched, an essay delayed, a conference postponed. You must "tune-in" to your child's emotions and try to determine when he or she is being lax and when normal anxieties are rising to the surface, slowing down progress. Try to be patient, guide instead of push and acknowledge your mutual feelings instead of hiding them. The closer the family is, the more pronounced these experiences may be.

Respect your child's privacy.

Social gatherings will undoubtedly bring you into contact with other parents of college-bound students and the plans and experiences of your children will become timely topics of conversation. Sharing experiences with other parents can be mutually beneficial. But, revealing your child's exact SAT scores, GPA, class rank and similar information is an invasion of privacy. If your child wants to announce this information to friends, relatives or other parents, that's his or her business and choice — not yours. Certainly you wouldn't want your child publicizing your income or other personal information to outsiders. Similarly, your child probably would prefer that some aspects of this process remain within the family. You will be amazed at what remarkably bad taste some parents exhibit in discussing their children's experiences.

Shop carefully.

As adults, you are undoubtedly a more experienced and sophisticated shopper than your child and your experience can be significant as your child shops for a college. Most colleges are very ethical and professional in their recruitment practices, but remember they are "selling." At college fairs, admissions officers can be persuasive which is not to their discredit. College catalogs can be slick and attractive which is also understandable and acceptable. But remember, most colleges are selling a package that can cost $5,000 to $15,000 per year or $20,000 to $60,000 over four years. They need from 100 to 10,000 new students each year to keep their doors open. That's not an indictment of their motives, but simply a representation of their realities. Read between the lines and beyond the pretty pictures. Don't hesitate to confer with your child's counselors about the choices and options available — counselors are generally objective and committed to serving the student, not a particular institution. When you visit campuses allow enough time to wander on your own *after* your formal tour, usually conducted by the admissions office. Walk into the library, dormitories, student union and even classrooms, if possible. Talk to students around the campus and observe as much as you can. Virtually all college admissions officials will encourage such "investigations" on your part since they don't want your child to make a mistake and stay for one year or less anymore than you do.

Naturally, each family's experiences will be a little different. The process is not very scientific yet, inspite of computerbanks, search services, video presentations, etc. Like looking for a house, there is more emotion in the process than some are ready to acknowledge. Nevertheless, as we look back, it was another enjoyable family experience where the rewards far outweigh the risks.

Paul and Ann Krouse are the publishers of WHO'S WHO AMONG AMERICAN HIGH SCHOOL STUDENTS and the parents of four delightful children. This article was written shortly after they completed the college selection/admissions process for the first time with their eldest daughter Amy who entered the freshman class at Tufts University, Medford, Massachusetts in the fall of 1983. WHEW!

THE EDUCATIONAL COMMUNICATIONS SCHOLARSHIP FOUNDATION®

During the 1985-86 academic year, approximately 20,000 students competed for scholarship awards sponsored by the Educational Communications Scholarship Foundation® which is funded by the publishing company. Students competed by completing an application which requested data regarding aptitude test scores, grade point average, extracurricular activities, work experience and general background information. Semifinalists were selected based on careful examination of all this information and were then requested to provide information regarding financial need. In addition, semifinalists were asked to write an essay from which the Scholarship Awards Committee attempted to evaluate the overall maturity of the students.

Fifty winners were selected and a total of $50,000 was awarded. Over $800,000 has been distributed through the Scholarship Foundation to date.

1985-86 SCHOLARSHIP WINNERS

Susan Lynn Abbott
Greens Farms Academy
Southport, CT
Williams College
Williamstown, MA

Katherine Chen
Lowell High School
San Francisco, CA
Stanford University
Stanford, CA

Amy Ferry
Gowanda Central School
Perrysburg, NY
SUNY University at Buffalo
Buffalo, NY

Preetinder Bharara
The Ranney School
Eatontown, NJ
Harvard University
Cambridge, MA

Kenneth C. Chern
W.T. Woodson High School
Annandale, VA
Northwestern University
Evanston, IL

Mei-Ling Fong
Putnam City High School
Oklahoma City, OK
Pepperdine University
Malibu, CA

Philip T. Blazek
St. John High School
Ennis, TX
Harvard University
Cambridge, MA

William Lance Conn
McComb High School
McComb, MS
Princeton University
Princeton, NJ

Richard Gay
Rich East High School
Park Forest, IL
University of Pennsylvania
Philadelphia, PA

David Yu Sam Chang
H.S. for the Performing and Visual Arts
Houston, TX
Standford University
Stanford, CA

Ross Dickerson
York High School
York, NE
University of Iowa
Iowa City, IA

Leon L. Gebhardt
Charter Oak-Ute Community High
Charter Oak, IA
The University of Iowa
Iowa City, IA

Nancy S. Chang
Niles North
Morton Grove, IL
Northwestern University
Evanston, IL

Patrick Spencer Egan
Neah-Kah-Nie High School
Nehalem, OR
Williamette University
Monmouth, OR

Sabrina J. Goodman
Marina High School
Huntington Beach, CA
Massachusetts Institute of Technology
Cambridge, MA

1985-86 SCHOLARSHIP WINNERS

Robert A. Grothe, Jr.
St. Louis University
High School
St. Louis, MO
California Institute
of Technology
Pasadena, CA

Molly Ann McMahon
Marian High School
Troy, MI
University of
Notre Dame
Notre Dame, IN

Margaret S. Oertling
Trinity Episcopal High
School
Natchez, MS
Trinity University
San Antonio, TX

Elizabeth Marie Gruca
Bishop McCort High
School
Johnstown, PA
Penn State University
University Park, PA

Frances Mikasa
Orosi High School
Orosi, CA
College of the Sequoias
Visalia, CA

Lisa Patnode
Banning High School
Banning, CA
Ithaca College
Ithaca, NY

Liane Adele Hancock
Mary Institute
St. Louis, MO
Massachusetts Institute
of Technology
Cambridge, MA

Michele Chiyomi
Mitsumori
Waiakea High School
Hilo, HI
Yale University
New Haven, CT

Charles F. Pazdernik
Breckenridge Senior
High
Ithaca, NY
Cornell University
Ithaca, NY

Joseph Scott Howlett
Forest High School
Ocala, FL
Massachusetts Institute
of Technology
Cambridge, MA

Charles Wallace Moniak
Garden Grove High
School
Garden Grove, CA
University of California
Berkeley, CA

Krystle Quynh Pham
Redlands Senior High
School
Redlands, CA
Stanford University
Stanford, CA

Andrew Thomas Hudak
Greenway High School
Grand Rapids, MN
Itasca Community
College
Grand Rapids, MN

John S. Monical
Pontiac Township High
Pontiac, IL
University of Illinois
Champaign, IL

Gregory Randal Ralph
Wheeler High School
Hobart, IN
California Institute of
Technology
Pasadena, CA

Darin Scott Katz
George Washington
High School
Philadelphia, PA
Pennsylvania State
University
University Park, PA

John S. Neville
Miami Beach Senior
High
Surfside, FL
Dartmouth College
Hanover, NH

Todd H. Rider
Ole Main High School
N. Little Rock, AR
Massachusetts Institute
of Technology
Cambridge, MA

1985-86 SCHOLARSHIP WINNERS

Kevin Paul Schutz
Andrean High School
Schererville, IN
University of Chicago
Chicago, IL

Roger Dale Shipplett
Tennessee High School
Bristol, TN
Princeton University
Princeton, NJ

Karla Elizabeth Usalis
Thayer Academy
Hanover, MA
Princeton University
Princeton, NJ

Jay Bertram Seliber
Stoughton High School
Stoughton, MA
University of Pennsylvania
Philadelphia, PA

David M. Stevens
Soldotna High School
Soldotna, AK
California Institute of Technology
Pasadena, CA

Timothy Ray Vollbrecht
LaFollette High School
Madison, WI
University of Wisconsin
Madison, WI

Juan Pablo Semidey
Colegio San Ignacio de Loyola
Guaynobo, PR
Massachusetts Institute of Technology
Cambridge, MA

Adam Franklin Strassberg
Ramapo Senior High School
Monsey, NY
Harvard University
Cambridge, MA

Michael Edwin Wall
Santa Monica High School
Malibu, CA
Harvard University
Cambridge, MA

James Eric Sims
Jersey Village
Houston, TX
Rice University
Houston, TX

Ali Tabatabai
Lower Merion High School
Narberth, PA
Stanford University
Stanford, CA

Tracey Rae Winters
Robertsdale High School
Silverhill, AL
Rockford College
Rockford, IL

Volney Leo Sheen
Henry Clay High School
Lexington, KY
The John Hopkins University
Baltimore, MD

Roxanne Tapia
Los Lunas High School
Los Lunas, NM
Adams State College
Alamosa, CO

Joseph T. Woods
Chicopee Comprehensive High School
Chicopee, MA
Rensellaer Polytechnic Institute
Troy, NJ

Irene Shih
Calabasas High School
Calabasas, CA
Harvard University
Cambridge, MA

Cynthia A. Tarkowski
Carmel High School for Girls
Wauconda, IL
Northwestern University
Evanston, IL

GLOSSARY OF ABBREVIATIONS

Acpl Chr .... Acappella Choir
AFS .... American Field Service
Am Leg Boys St .... American Legion Boys State
Am Leg Aux Girls St .... American Legion Auxiliary Girls State
Aud/Vis .... Audio-Visual
Awd .... Award

Badmtn .... Badminton
Bsbl .... Baseball
Basktbl .... Basketball
Btty Crckr Awd .... Betty Crocker Award
Bus .... Business
Bwlng .... Bowling

C of C Awd .... Chamber of Commerce Award
Camp Fr Inc .... Camp Fire, Inc.
CAP .... Civil Air Patrol
Capt .... Captain
Cit Awd .... Citizenship Award
Clb .... Club
Cmnty Wkr .... Community Worker
Coach Actv .... Coaching Activities
Crs Cntry .... Cross Country

DAR Awd .... Daughters of the American Revolution Award
DECA .... Distributive Education Clubs of America
Dnfth Awd .... Danforth (I Dare You) Award
Drm & Bgl .... Drum & Bugle Corps
Drm Mjr(t) .... Drum Major(ette)

Ed-Chief .... Editor-In-Chief

FBLA .... Future Business Leaders of America
FCA .... Fellowship of Christian Athletes
FFA .... Future Farmers of America
FHA .... Future Homemakers of America
Fld Hcky .... Field Hockey
FNA .... Future Nurses of America
FTA .... Future Teachers of America
Ftbl .... Football

GAA .... Girls Athletic Association
Gov Hon Prg Awd .... Governors Honor Program Award
Gym .... Gymnastics

Hist .... Historian
Hon .... Honor
Hosp Aide .... Hospital Aide

Ice Hcky .... Ice Hockey
Intnl Clb .... International Club

JA .... Junior Achievement
JC Awd .... Jaycees Award
JCL .... Junior Classical League
JETS Awd .... Junior Engineering Technical Society Award
JP Sousa Awd .... John Philip Sousa Award
Jr NHS .... Junior National Honor Society
JV .... Junior Varsity

L .... Letter
Lcrss .... Lacross
Lion Award .... Lions Club Award
Lit Mag .... Literary Magazine

Mgr(s) .... Manager(s)
MMM .... Modern Music Masters
Mrchg Band .... Marching Band

NCTE Awd .... National Council of Teachers of English Award
NEDT Awd .... National Educational Development Test Award
NFL .... National Forensic League
NHS .... National Honor Society
Ntl .... National
Nwsp .... Newspaper

OEA .... Office Education Association
Opt Clb Awd .... Optimist Club Award
Orch .... Orchestra

PAVAS .... Performing & Visual Arts Society
Phtg .... Photographer
Pres .... President
Prfct Atten Awd .... Perfect Attendance Award

Rep .... Representative
Rptr .... Reporter
ROTC .... Reserve Officer Training Corps

S.A.D.D. .... Students Against Driving Drunk
Sal .... Salutatorian
SAR Awd ... Sons of the American Revolution Award
Schol .... Scholarship
Sec .... Secretary
SF .... Semifinalist
Sftbl .... Softball
Socr .... Soccer
Sprt Ed .... Sports Editor
St Schlr .... State Scholar
Stf .... Staff
Stu Cncl .... Student Council
Swmmng .... Swimming
Symp Band .... Symphonic Band

Tm .... Team
Thesps .... Thespians

Trea .... Treasurer
Trk .... Track
Twrlr .... Twirler

V .... Varsity
Val .... Valedictorian
VICA .... Vocational Industrial Clubs of America
Vllybl .... Volleyball
Voice Dem Awd .... Voice of Democracy Award
VP .... Vice President

Wrstlng .... Wrestling
Wt Lftg .... Weight Lifting

Yrbk .... Yearbook

Sample Biography

This sample is presented to familiarize the reader with the format of the biographical listings. Students are identified by name, school, home, city and state. In order to protect the privacy and integrity of all students, home addresses are not published.

KEY

1 Name
2 High School
3 Home, City and State
4 Nomination Source*
5 Class Rank (when given)
6 Accomplishments
7 Future Plans

*(S) = School Nomination
(Y) = Youth Organization Nomination

1 Wolk, Sheffield L.; 2 Normandy Isle H.S.; 3 Miami, FL; 4 (S); 5 10-350; 6 Pres Stu Cncl; VP Sr Cls; Ftbl; 4-H; NHS; Cit Awd; Am Leg Awd; 7 Harvard University; Biochemist

STUDENT BIOGRAPHIES

DELAWARE

ABERNATHY, REBECCA; Ursuline Acad; Wilmington, DE; (Y); Church Yth Grp; Hosp Aide; JA; Model UN; Service Clb; Spanish Clb; Nwsp Ed-Chief; Lit Mag; Hon Roll; NEDT Awd; Duracell Battery Comptn Fnlst 83; U DE; Engl.

ABRENICA, NORLISA; Archmere Acad; Wilmington, DE; (S); Cmnty Wkr; French Clb; Speech Tm; Church Choir; Lit Mag; JV Cheerleading; Hon Roll; NHS; NEDT Awd; 3rd Pl French II Oral Spkng Cntst 85; Chem Engr.

ACORD, JERRY; Salesanum Schl; Newark, DE; (S); 2/301; Chess Clb; Mathletes; Spanish Clb; Concert Band; Nwsp Rptr; High Hon Roll; NHS; Salesianum Schlrshp 83-87; 2nd Hghst Cumltv Index 85; Astrnmy.

ADAMCZYK, PATRICIA; Newark HS; Newark, DE; (Y); Hosp Aide; VP SADD; Stage Crew; Variety Show; Trs Frsh Cls; JV Tennis; Co-Capt Twrlr; Hon Roll; Pres Jr NHS; Stphne Sltr Ctznshp, Schlrshp & Ldrshp Awd 80-81; Natl Education Ctr; Med Asst.

ADAMS, MONICA L; Epworth Christian Schl; Laurel, DE; (S); Chorus; Church Choir; Yrbk Stf; Var Cheerleading; High Hon Roll.

AGEE, MARY BETH; Seaford SR HS; Seaford, DE; (Y); 11/205; Rep Frsh Cls; Rep Jr Cls; Stu Cncl; Var Crs Cntry; Var Sftbl; High Hon Roll; NHS; Church Yth Grp; GAA; Scholastic Bowl; Stu Of WA Dist Bible Quiz Tm 83-86; Stu Of WA IMPACT Tm 86; Stu Nazarene Yth Intl Councl 83-86; Clemson Coll; Med Technlgy.

AIKEN, MARGARET; Archmere Acad; Wilmington, DE; (Y); Var Bsktbl; Var Crs Cntry; Var JV Sftbl; Var Trk; High Hon Roll; Hon Roll; Cmmnctns.

AITKEN, PAUL; Salesianum HS; Wilmington, DE; (S); 45/272; Var Socr; Hon Roll; 1st All Cath Sccr 85; 1st All State Sccr 85; Capt Of Soccer Team 85; Bus.

ALESSANDRINI, TERRE; St Mark HS; Wilmington, DE; (Y); 2/360; Church Yth Grp; Yrbk Rptr; Lit Mag; Rep Soph Cls; Sec Pres Stu Cncl; Var L Bsktbl; Var L Sftbl; Gov Hon Prg Awd; High Hon Roll; Pep Clb; Mid-Atlantic Sr Girl Sftbl Champs 83; Biochem.

ALEXANDER, KIM; Dover HS; Dover, DE; (Y); 25/317; OEA; PAVAS; Var Co-Capt Cheerleading; High Hon Roll; Hon Roll; Jr NHS; NHS; US Chrldr Achvt Awd 83; Dickinson Coll Carlisle; Engl.

ALFIERI, MARIA; Padua Acad; Wilmington, DE; (Y); Dance Clb; Hosp Aide; School Musical; Hon Roll; ST U NY; Dance.

ALFREE, BETTY; Middletown HS; Townsend, DE; (Y); 36/147; French Clb; Library Aide; OEA; Teachers Aide; Rep Jr Cls; Cheerleading; Fld Hcky; Sftbl; Hon Roll; Secretarial.

ALLEN, CINDY; Glasgow HS; Newark, DE; (Y); 6/250; Math Tm; Scholastic Bowl; Capt Flag Corp; Mrchg Band; Rep Frsh Cls; Rep Soph Cls; Rep Jr Cls; Rep Sr Cls; Var L Sftbl; Var L Swmmng; U DE; Physcl Thrpy.

ALLEN, ERIN; Holy Cross HS; Selbyville, DE; (Y); Church Yth Grp; Spanish Clb; SADD; Band; Color Guard; Drm Mjr(t); Mrchg Band; Hon Roll; Jr NHS; NHS; Acadmc Achvt Awd 83; Outstndng Span Stu 82-83; Outstndng Math Stu 82; Salisbury ST Coll; Elem Educ.

ALLEN, MARY; Dover HS; Dover, DE; (Y); 8/300; Office Aide; Band; Mrchg Band; Symp Band; Bowling; High Hon Roll; NHS; Kent County Hnr Bnd 84; Bus.

ALLEN, SUSANNE; Lake Forest HS; Felton, DE; (Y); 6/165; FFA; Math Tm; OEA; SADD; Trs Frsh Cls; Trs Soph Cls; Trs Jr Cls; Trs Sr Cls; Hon Roll; NHS; Kent Cnty Med Axlry Schlrshp 86; Gld Med Natl Pltry Jdgng Tm 85; Towson ST U; Nrsng.

ALLEN, TRACEY; Smyrna HS; Smyrna, DE; (Y); Art Clb; Church Yth Grp; OEA; Spanish Clb; Bsktbl; Cheerleading; Gov Hon Prg Awd; Hon Roll; NHS; Prfct Atten Awd; Prncpls Awd Acad Excel; JR Mrshl; Artst Of Mnth; Stu Art Dir; Acad Hl Of Fame; Sci.

ALLEN, WILLIAM; Brandywine HS; Wilmington, DE; (S); 30/225; DECA; JA; Ski Clb; School Play; Var Lcrss; High Hon Roll; Hon Roll; Ntl Merit Ltr; DE Rep Wrld Affairs Sem U WI 85; Incentive Scholar U DE 86; Chem.

ALOISE, SUZANNE D; Padua Acad; Wilmington, DE; (S); JA; Pep Clb; Spanish Clb; SADD; Hon Roll; NHS; Ntl Merit Schol; Spanish NHS; U DE.

ALVAREZ, DANNY WILLIAM; Laruel HS; Laurel, DE; (Y); 11/123; Pep Clb; Ski Clb; Varsity Clb; Off Frsh Cls; Off Soph Cls; Off Jr Cls; Var L Bsbl; Var L Ftbl; Var L Wrstlng; Hon Roll; 1st Team All Conf Placekicker; 1st Team All Mason Div Ma & De Placekicker; 2nd Team All St Placekicker; Med.

ALVAREZ, ROBERT; Glasgow HS; Newark, DE; (Y); 17/290; Exploring; Rep Frsh Cls; Rep Soph Cls; Rep Jr Cls; Off Sr Cls; Bsbl; Ftbl; Wt Lftg; Wrstlng; High Hon Roll; Henry King Stanford Schlrshp MI U 86-87; MI U; Pre-Law.

AMOS, ERNEST; St Marks HS; Wilmington, DE; (Y); Church Yth Grp; VP JA; Political Wkr; Spanish Clb; Varsity Clb; Chorus; Off Frsh Cls; Off Soph Cls; Off Jr Cls; Crs Cntry; Bus.

ANDERSON III, ANGUS E; Christiana HS; Newark, DE; (Y); 15/350; Am Leg Boys St; Exploring; French Clb; JA; Quiz Bowl; SADD; VP Stu Cncl; JV Bsbl; NHS; Mltry Ofcr.

ANDERSON, BRIGITTE; Mt Pleasant HS; Wilmington, DE; (Y); 20/212; Chrmn Church Yth Grp; Chorus; Church Choir; Var Stu Cncl; JV Var Sftbl; Var L Vllybl; Hon Roll; Drama Clb; Ski Clb; Teachers Aide; Outstndng Choir Stu 86; U DE; Techng.

ANDERSON, RACHEL; Tower Hill HS; Wilmington, DE; (Y); Band; Chorus; Var Fld Hcky; Im Gym; Var Trk; Ntl Merit Ltr; 3rd Pl Spnsh & ST Oral Cmpt 84.

ANDREOLI, PAUL; Glasgow HS; Newark, DE; (Y); Latin Clb; Wt Lftg; Chem.

ANDREWS, ERIC; New Castle Baptist Acad; Newark, DE; (Y); Band; Pres Jr Cls; Pres Sr Cls; Stu Cncl; Var Capt Socr; High Hon Roll; Pres Acad Ftna Awd 86; Liberty U; Scndry Educ.

ANDREWS, LYNN M; Milford SR HS; Milford, DE; (Y); 11/185; Church Yth Grp; SADD; Church Choir; Flag Corp; School Musical; Yrbk Stf; Cheerleading; NHS; Prfct Atten Awd; Spec Bnd Achvt Ltr 86; Smmr Coll U DE 86; Mth.

ANGEL, CHRISTINA; Sussex Central HS; Millsboro, DE; (Y); 48/188; SADD; School Musical; Nwsp Phtg; Yrbk Phtg; Lit Mag; Sec Stu Cncl; Var L Cheerleading; Art Clb; Drama Clb; Key Clb; DE Miss Teen 85-86; Pres Acad Fit Awd 86; Hnr Bar Thesp 86; Temple U Tyler Schl Art Of; Art.

ANGEL, LISA; Seaford HS; Seaford, DE; (Y); 19/170; JA; Key Clb; Yrbk Phtg; Yrbk Stf; Capt Cheerleading; Tennis; High Hon Roll; Hon Roll; GAA; Band.

ARGO, YVETTE; Milford SR HS; Milford, DE; (Y); Pres Church Yth Grp; Pres Sec 4-H; SADD; Chorus; Church Choir; Nwsp Stf; Yrbk Stf; 4-H Awd; High Hon Roll; NHS; Jrnlsm Awd Disability Cnts 86; Ed.

ARMISTEAD, GRANT; Dover HS; Dover, DE; (Y); Hosp Aide; Band; Drm Mjr(t); Mrchg Band; Symp Band; JV Bsbl; Var Crs Cntry; High Hon Roll; Hon Roll; All Am Yth Hnr Band 85.

ARMSTRONG, DAWN; Wilmington HS; Wilmington, DE; (Y); 2/134; Church Yth Grp; Concert Band; Var Fld Hcky; NHS; Sal; JA; Yrbk Ed-Chief; Stu Cncl; Elks Awd; JC Awd; Wilmigtn HS Almn Assn Awd 86; PA ST U; Psychlgy.

ARNONE, MARC; Salesianum HS; Wilmington, DE; (Y); 100/320; Nwsp Rptr; Off Jr Cls; Im Bsktbl; Im Socr; JV Wrstlng; Hon Roll.

ASBURY, SHELIA; William Penn HS; Bear, DE; (Y); JA; Ski Clb; Spanish Clb; Bsktbl; Mgr(s); Score Keeper; Timer; Hon Roll; Outstndng Stu In Indstrl Arts 84-85; U Of DE; Chem Tech.

ASH, PHILLIP; Indian River HS; Frankford, DE; (S); Band; Chorus; Concert Band; Jazz Band; Pep Band; JV Bsktbl; L Var Ftbl; Var Wt Lftg; Var L Wrstlng; Hon Roll; Engrng.

ASUNCION, JENNIFER; Dover HS; Dover, DE; (Y); 3/368; JA; Math Clb; Band; Lit Mag; Var L Crs Cntry; Var L Trk; Gov Hon Prg Awd; High Hon Roll; NHS.

ATTIX, JOYCE; Milford HS; Lincoln, DE; (Y); Church Yth Grp; SADD; Band; Chorus; Church Choir; Concert Band; Jazz Band; Mrchg Band; School Musical; Ave U M Chrch Schlrshp To Wesley Coll-Orgn 86-87; Orgnst & Asst Mnstr Of Music-Av U M Chrch DE 85-87; Sacred Music.

AUSTIN, VICKI; New Ark HS; Newark, DE; (Y); Latin Clb; Flag Corp; Sec Jr Cls; Off Sr Cls; JV Capt Cheerleading; Hon Roll; Jr NHS; Food Technlgy.

AYRES, LARRY; Milford HS; Houston, DE; (Y); French Clb; Band; Concert Band; Jazz Band; Rep Frsh Cls; Crs Cntry; Trk; Hon Roll; 1st Chair Tuba Plyr Regnl Band 84; Cuny; Arch.

BACINO, KIMBERLY; Dover HS; Dover, DE; (Y); Math Tm; Quiz Bowl; Science Clb; SADD; Var Cheerleading; Var Crs Cntry; Var Sftbl; Var Capt Swmmng; High Hon Roll; Hon Roll; Fin Anlyst.

BACKUS, KELLI; William Penn HS; New Castle, DE; (Y); 166/485; Cmnty Wkr; Girl Scts; JA; Teachers Aide; Hon Roll; Lynchburg Coll; Fshn Merch.

BAFFONE, MARC; Salesianum HS; Newark, DE; (S); 20/301; Var Bsbl; Wt Lftg; High Hon Roll; NHS; Acctng.

BAILEY, KATHY; Smyrna HS; Smyrna, DE; (S); Church Yth Grp; Dance Clb; French Clb; Sec Band; Nwsp Stf; Lit Mag; Mgr(s); High Hon Roll; NHS; Prncpls Awd Acadmc Excllnc 84-85; Mst Outstndg Bnd Stu 84; Kent Cnty Hnrs Bnd 84-86.

BAIR, COURTNEY; Indian River HS; Bethany Bch, DE; (S); Art Clb; Pep Clb; SADD; Varsity Clb; Y-Teens; Chorus; Stu Cncl; Tennis; Hon Roll; U Of DE; Elem Educ.

BAKER, CHERYL; Dover HS; Dover, DE; (Y); Band; Flag Corp; Mrchg Band; Symp Band; CPA.

BAKER, TINA; Woodbridge JR SR HS; Seaford, DE; (Y); 3/110; Am Leg Aux Girls St; OEA; Speech Tm; SADD; Nwsp Ed-Chief; Cit Awd; High Hon Roll; NHS; Pres Schlr; Voice Dem Awd; Close-Up Fndtn Ctzn Bee 86; Close-Up Fndtn Gvrnmntl Pgm 86; Amer Lgn Ntl Ortrcl Cntst 85; US Air Force; Admin Mgmt.

BALDO, STEVEN; Salesianum HS; Newark, DE; (S); 7/272; Bsktbl; Ftbl; Socr; JV Wrstlng; Hon Roll; NHS; Ntl Merit Ltr; Notre Dame; Elec Engrng.

BALLAS, JENNIFER; Concord HS; Wilmington, DE; (Y); 24/277; Cmnty Wkr; Concert Band; Mrchg Band; Symp Band; Mgr(s); High Hon Roll; Hon Roll; NHS; Band; VP Frsh Cls; DE ST Stu Drvr Yr, Teen Improvizational Theatre 86; Psych.

BALSAMA, JOSEPH; Salesianum HS; Media, PA; (Y); 29/262; Spanish Clb; Concert Band; Mrchg Band; School Musical; Nwsp Rptr; Nwsp Stf; Yrbk Stf; Boston U Schlrp 86; Boston U; Grphc Dsgn.

BANKS, MARSHA; Indian River HS; Frankford, DE; (S); Drama Clb; SADD; Jazz Band; School Musical; Pres Soph Cls; Rep Stu Cncl; Var Cheerleading; Var Tennis; High Hon Roll; NHS.

BANKS, MICHELE; Indian River HS; Frankford, DE; (S); 1/210; English Clb; Mrchg Band; Rep Soph Cls; Rep Jr Cls; Rep Sec Stu Cncl; Capt Var Cheerleading; Gov Hon Prg Awd; High Hon Roll; NHS; Ntl Merit Ltr.

BARASCH, TODD; Concord HS; Wilmington, DE; (Y); Pres Temple Yth Grp; School Musical; School Play; Stage Crew; Nwsp Ed-Chief; Nwsp Rptr; Nwsp Stf; Rep Stu Cncl; Hon Roll; Boy Scts; VP-TEEN Imprvtnl Theatr Grp STOP; Co-Chair Wkend Yth Cnvntn; Dsgnd Logos-Schl Drama Prodctns; Comm.

BARCHOCK, JOYCE; Concord Christian Acad; Wilmington, DE; (S); 1/6; Art Clb; Chess Clb; Church Yth Grp; Computer Clb; Debate Tm; Math Clb; Speech Tm; School Play; High Hon Roll; Hon Roll; Highest GPA-BIBLE 84; Homecmng Qn 84; Supvs Awd 83; Brandywine Coll; Comptr Applctn.

BARICH, DAWN; Dover HS; Dover, DE; (Y); Chorus; Hon Roll; Elem Ed.

BARNES, MARY; Padua Acad; Ridley Park, PA; (S); 35/213; French Clb; Chorus; Yrbk Stf; Hon Roll; Elem Educ.

BARR, PAMELA C; Caesar Rodney HS; Magnolia, DE; (Y); Church Yth Grp; Cmnty Wkr; OEA; Spanish Clb; SADD; Teachers Aide; Hon Roll; NHS; Miss Magnolia Fire Prevention 86; Academic All-Am 86; Special Edu Teacher.

BARRETTA, DENISE; Padua Acad; Philadelphia, PA; (Y); 66/212; Church Yth Grp; Hosp Aide; Church Choir; Rep Jr Cls; Hon Roll; Peer Cnslng Awd 86; Human Concerns Grp Awd 86; Nrs.

BARRON, KENNETH E; Brandywine HS; Wilmington, DE; (S); 10/253; Pres DECA; Pres JA; Mrchg Band; Stage Crew; Symp Band; Var L Gym; Var Capt Lcrss; Var Capt Socr; High Hon Roll; Pres NHS; Govt.

BARROSSE, DAVID; St Marks HS; Newark, DE; (Y); 53/600; Boy Scts; Varsity Clb; Stage Crew; Rep Frsh Cls; Rep Soph Cls; Rep Jr Cls; Rep Sr Cls; Rep Stu Cncl; JV Bsktbl; L Ftbl; SR Patrol Ldr Scout Troop 85-86; Med.

BARRY, KEVIN; William Penn HS; New Castle, DE; (Y); French Clb; VP Sec JA; Spanish Clb; Teachers Aide; Yrbk Stf; Outstndng Stdnt Forgn Lang 85; Outstndng Achvt Art II 85; Art.

BARTO, AMY LYNN; St Andrews Schl; Phoenixville, PA; (Y); 3/67; Hosp Aide; Model UN; SADD; Chorus; Church Choir; Nwsp Stf; JV Fld Hcky; High Hon Roll; Ntl Merit Ltr; JCL; Yale U; Math.

BARTON, LOREN; Newark HS; Newark, DE; (Y); Exploring; Varsity Clb; Band; Concert Band; Jazz Band; Mrchg Band; School Play; Symp Band; Rep Stu Cncl; Trk; MVP Trck 85 & 86; 2nd Pl JR Olympcs Ntl Chmpshps 85; Math.

BASCIANI, PAM; Ursuline Acad; Toughkenamon, PA; (Y); AFS; Am Leg Aux Girls St; French Clb; VP Model UN; Science Clb; VP SADD; Nwsp Sprt Ed; Yrbk Bus Mgr; Im Bsktbl; Fld Hcky; HOBY Ldrshp Delg; All Catholic Ten Tm 84-86; Wake Forest U; Bus.

BASLER, ROBERT; Brandywine HS; Wilmington, DE; (Y); Church Yth Grp; Drama Clb; School Play; Stage Crew; Var L Trk; JV Wrstlng; Hon Roll; Cmmnctns.

BAYNARD, PAUL; Milford SR HS; Houston, DE; (Y); SADD; Varsity Clb; Bsbl; Ftbl; Mgr(s); Wrstlng; U Of DE; Archl Engrng.

BEATY, KAREN; St Marks HS; Newark, DE; (Y); 7/343; Key Clb; Math Tm; Office Aide; Mrchg Band; School Musical; High Hon Roll; Hon Roll; NHS; Prfct Atten Awd; U DE; Bus Adm.

BECK, SHARON C; Middletown HS; Bear, DE; (Y); 10/130; Am Leg Aux Girls St; Sec Pres OEA; Science Clb; Sec Soph Cls; Sec Jr Cls; Sec Sr Cls; Stu Cncl; Var Fld Hcky; Sec NHS; John B Lynch Scholar 86; NHS Scholar 86; U DE; Bus Adm.

BECKER, ANDREW; Tower HS; Greenville, DE; (Y); Art Clb; JA; Nwsp Sprt Ed; Yrbk Ed-Chief; Yrbk Stf; Soph Cls; Jr Cls; Socr; Tennis; Hon Roll; Physcs Encnmcs.

BECKER, KAREN; Caesar Rodney HS; Dover, DE; (Y); 68/343; French Clb; Sec GAA; OEA; SADD; Band; Trs Soph Cls; Trs Jr Cls; Trs Sr Cls; Var Capt Cheerleading; Hon Roll; Girls Athletic Assic Schlrshp 86; All Sch Letter 86; DE U; Accntng.

BEEBE, JEFFREY; New Castle Baptist HS; New Castle, DE; (Y); Church Yth Grp; L Var Bsbl; L Var Bsktbl; Hon Roll; Wilmington Coll; Sprts Brdcstng.

BEHAN, MARGARET ANNE; Smyrna HS; Smyrna, DE; (S); 9/193; Am Leg Aux Girls St; Church Yth Grp; French Clb; OEA; Teachers Aide; Band; Concert Band; Mrchg Band; Stage Crew; Lit Mag; Prncpls Awd Exclnc 84-86; MVP Gymnstcs 85; Schlr Athlt 86; Phys Thrpy.

BELL, GREG; Seaford HS; Seaford, DE; (Y); 30/235; Teachers Aide; Yrbk Rptr; JV Bsktbl; L Golf; Bus Admin.

BELLAFANTE, MARK; Archmere HS; Wilmington, DE; (S); Computer Clb; Service Clb; Rptr Nwsp Rptr; Rep Soph Cls; Rep Stu Cncl; Var L Bsktbl; JV Ftbl; High Hon Roll; NHS; Spanish NHS; Med.

BELLEVILLE, BETH; Padua Acad; Wilmington, DE; (S); 8/213; French Clb; High Hon Roll; NHS; NEDT Awd; Hnr Soc 85-86; Soc Dstngshd Amer HS Stu 85.

BELLEW, KEVIN; Archmere Acad; Glenolden, PA; (Y); SADD; Band; Concert Band; School Musical; School Play; Im Bsktbl; Im Bowling; JV Ftbl; JV Trk; Hon Roll.

BENNETT, FRANKIE; Indian River HS; Dogsboro, DE; (Y); Mgr(s); Wrstlng; Hon Roll; Prfct Atten Awd; Bus.

BENO, TRACEY; The Christian Acad; Wilmington, DE; (Y); Church Yth Grp; Varsity Clb; Acpl Chr; Church Choir; Rep Frsh Cls; Trs Soph Cls; Sec Jr Cls; Pres Sr Cls; Stu Cncl; Cheerleading; Outstndg Typng Stu 85-86; Bus.

BERGERON, SUZANNE; Padua Acad; Middletown, DE; (S); Church Yth Grp; Cmnty Wkr; Library Aide; Math Clb; Yrbk Stf; Rep Stu Cncl; High Hon Roll; NHS; Elem Ed.

BERGSTROM, KIRSTEN; Seaford SR HS; Seaford, DE; (Y); 15/250; AFS; Band; Frsh Cls; Soph Cls; Jr Cls; Sftbl; Trk; Bsktbl; Mgr(s); Socr; Comp Sci.

BERNHARD, LISA; Delcastle Tech HS; New Castle, DE; (Y); Girl Scts; Yrbk Phtg; Yrbk Stf; Bsktbl; Mgr(s); Score Keeper; Hon Roll; Art Inst Of Seattle; Comm Art.

BERSTER, MICHELE MARIE; Padua Acad; Wilmington, DE; (S); Cmnty Wkr; Office Aide; Pep Clb; Bsktbl; Sftbl; Vllybl; Gov Hon Prg Awd; Govnrs Schl Excllnce Pgm 85; U Notre Dame; Bus.

BETHARD, CHRISTOPHER S; Caesar Rodney HS; Camden, DE; (Y); 104/388; Church Yth Grp; FFA; Latin Clb; Letterman Clb; Band; Bsbl; Bsktbl; Ftbl; JC Awd; Knt Gen Hosp Awd 86; CA U PA; Athltc Trng.

BETHEL, STEVE; Caesar Rodney HS; Wyoming, DE; (Y); JCL; Latin Clb; JV Var Bsbl; U Of DE.

BETTS, MICHELE; Cape Henlopen HS; Lewes, DE; (Y); SADD; Chorus; School Musical; Yrbk Stf; Var Bsktbl; Var Vllybl; Hon Roll; NHS; Pres Church Yth Grp; FCA; Schl Sprt Awd 84-85; Music Awd 84-85; U DE; Rdlgy.

BEYER, GREG; Newark HS; Newark, DE; (Y); 31/316; JA; Var Socr; Hon Roll; NHS; Mech Engrng.

BIBBINS, TRACY; Smyrna HS; Smyrna, DE; (Y); Teachers Aide; Chorus; Church Choir; Bsktbl; Hon Roll; Prfct Atten Awd; Acctng.

BIDEN, BEAU; Archmere Acad HS; Wilmington, DE; (Y); Am Leg Boys St; FBLA; Letterman Clb; Political Wkr; Ski Clb; School Play; Pres Frsh Cls; Pres Soph Cls; Pres Stu Cncl; Im Bsktbl; Pltcl Sci.

BIGGS, BAMBI; Lake Forest HS; Felton, DE; (Y); 16/170; Pres 4-H; Sec Girl Scts; Q&S; Band; School Musical; Nwsp Rptr; VP Soph Cls; Trk; NHS; Pres Schlr; 1st Pl ST JDG Spch; Wesley Coll; Spech Path.

BIRTWISTLE, MARK D; Christian Tabernacle Acad; Lincoln, DE; (S); 2/9; Church Yth Grp; Band; Chorus; Church Choir; Yrbk Sprt Ed; Capt Bsktbl; Coach Actv; Capt Socr; Var Sftbl; High Hon Roll; Christian Athl Awd 85 & 86; Messiah Coll; Comp Sci.

BITER, CAROL; Holy Cross HS; Dover, DE; (Y); Camp Fr Inc; Hosp Aide; Spanish Clb; SADD; Church Choir; Yrbk Stf; Hon Roll; NEDT Awd; Ntl Engl Merit Awd 86; Psych.

BLACK, MARVELLA; Newark HS; Wilmington, DE; (Y); JA; SADD; Teachers Aide; Lit Mag; Sftbl; Hon Roll; SAC Awd 86; Socio-Drama Awd 86; Bus Admin.

BLACKWOOD, RAYMOND; Salesianum Schl; Wilmington, DE; (S); 1/262; Chess Clb; Debate Tm; Math Tm; Scholastic Bowl; Concert Band; Mrchg Band; Nwsp Ed-Chief; NHS; Ntl Merit SF; Law.

BLAZES, WILLIAM J; St Marks HS; Newark, DE; (Y); Boy Scts; Egl Sct Awd 85; U Of DE; Mrn Bio.

BLESSING, RHONDA KAY; Milford SR HS; Milford, DE; (Y); Church Yth Grp; Drama Clb; Intnl Clb; PAVAS; Political Wkr; SADD; Teachers Aide; Varsity Clb; Sec Chorus; Concert Band; Drama Awd 86; Bst All Around SR 85-86; U Of DE; Law.

BOCK, PAMELA A; Dover HS; Dover, DE; (Y); 70/325; VP Church Yth Grp; Drama Clb; German Clb; OEA; PAVAS; Band; Mrchg Band; Stage Crew; Yrbk Phtg; Crs Cntry; Gvrnrs Schl For Exclnce Photo 85; Parsons Schl Of Dsgn Schlrshp 86; Parsons Schl Of Dsgn; Photo.

BOLKOVICH, LAURA; Glasgow HS; Newark, DE; (Y); FFA; Ski Clb; SADD; Mrchg Band; VP Frsh Cls; Var Fld Hcky; Var Mat Maids; Var Tennis; FFA Flwr Arrngng 1st ST, Indvdl 4th, 2nd Awd; U DE; Phy Thrpy.

BOOTS, MIKE; Dover HS; Dover, DE; (Y); Church Yth Grp; Teachers Aide; High Hon Roll; Hon Roll; Arch.

BOSCHER, SUSAN; Smyrna HS; Smyrna, DE; (Y); OEA; Teachers Aide; High Hon Roll; Prfct Atten Awd; Bus.

BOTHELL, TIM; Smyrna HS; Smyrna, DE; (S); Am Leg Boys St; Art Clb; Boy Scts; Chess Clb; Church Yth Grp; Teachers Aide; Varsity Clb; Band; Concert Band; Jazz Band; Cross Cty Captn Artist Mnth 8586; MVP Track; V Ltr Bsktbl 84-84; 2nd Pl Gold Key Awd 85-86; BYU; Physcl Ftns.

BOTLINGER, CHRISTOPHER; Caravel Acad; Middletown, DE; (S); 7/42; Drama Clb; Mathletes; School Play; Var L Bsbl; L Bsktbl; Var L Ftbl; Var L Socr; High Hon Roll; U Of DE; Aerntcl Engr.

BOUSH, MICHAEL A; Salesianum Schl; Wilmington, DE; (Y); Boys Clb Am; Computer Clb; Dance Clb; Pep Clb; Spanish Clb; Stage Crew; Im Bsktbl; Im Bowling; Im Socr; Hon Roll.

BOVANKOVICH, PAUL; St Marks HS; Newark, DE; (Y); 66/358; Ice Hcky; Lcrss; Flacon Fndtn Schlrshp 86; Vly Forge Fndtn Schlrshp 86; NROTC 3 Yr Schlrshp 87; Vly Forge Mltry JR Clg; Pilot.

BOWENS, MARLA; William Penn HS; New Castle, DE; (Y); French Clb; JA; Office Aide; Teachers Aide; Chorus; Comp Sci.

BOWERS, KATHLEEN; Archmere Acad; Wilmington, DE; (S); Spanish Clb; JV Var Bsktbl; Var Sftbl; JV Var Vllybl; Hon Roll; NHS; Spanish NHS.

BOWIE, BRIAN; Newark HS; Newark, DE; (Y); Rep Stu Cncl; Var Ice Hcky; Embry-Riddle; Aviation.

BOYD, EARL; Delcastle Technical HS; Newark, DE; (Y); Wldr.

BOYD, W DAVID; John Dickinson HS; Wilmington, DE; (Y); 32/237; Var Bsbl; Var Ftbl; Var Capt Wrstlng; Hon Roll; Jr NHS; Bio.

BOYLE, KATHLEEN; Padua Acad; Chadds Ford, PA; (Y); Art Clb; Fld Hcky; FIT; Illstrtn.

BOZZO, CARMELA; Padua Acad; Wilmington, DE; (Y); 31/212; VP Italian Clb 85-86; Hnr Rl 83-86; Goldey Beacon Coll; Acctng.

BOZZO, STEPHEN; Archmere Acad; Wilmington, DE; (S); German Clb; Concert Band; Jazz Band; Im Bsktbl; Im Bowling; Var Crs Cntry; Var Trk; Hon Roll; NHS; Pre-Med.

BRADLEY, DAVID; Mt Pleasant HS; Wilmington, DE; (Y); JA; Teachers Aide; Nwsp Stf; Graphic Arts.

BRADLEY, KAETI E; Cape Henlopen HS; Harbeson, DE; (Y); Drama Clb; Ski Clb; SADD; Thesps; Varsity Clb; School Musical; School Play; Nwsp Stf; Sec Jr Cls; Fld Hcky; JR Miss 86; 1st Rnnr Up DE JR Miss 86; U DE; Cmmnnctns.

BRADLEY, KEVIN; Archmere Acad; Claymont, DE; (S); Church Yth Grp; SADD; JV Bsbl; Im Bsktbl; Im Bowling; Var Ftbl; Im Wt Lftg; JV Wrstlng; High Hon Roll; NHS; Half Schlrshp Archmere Acad 84-87.

BRADLEY, MARK; Salesianum HS; West Chester, PA; (S); 20/319; Im Socr; NHS.

BRADY, JENNIFER; St Marks HS; Newark, DE; (Y); Key Clb; Pep Clb; Lit Mag; Rep Jr Cls; Hon Roll; Delaware ST Music Tchrs Assoc 86; PSYCH.

BRAKLY, ANTHONY; Indian River HS; Frankford, DE; (Y); 58/202; Boy Scts; Computer Clb; FHA; Office Aide; OEA; Spanish Clb; SADD; Var Capt Bsktbl; Var Ftbl; Prfct Atten Awd; U MD College Pk; Acctg.

BRANDRETH, LARA; Alexis I Dupont HS; Hockessin, DE; (Y); 1/240; Am Leg Aux Girls St; Cmnty Wkr; JA; Math Tm; Yrbk Stf; JV Vllybl; High Hon Roll; NHS; Awd Of Excllnc-Achvt In Engl I Hnrs 84 & Outstndng Achvt Bio 85; $100 Savings Bond High Grades 86; Bus.

BREAULT, NANCY ELIZABETH; Howard Career Center HS; Wilmington, DE; (Y); 5/202; Computer Clb; OEA; VICA; High Hon Roll; Hon Roll; NHS; Prfct Atten Awd; Acdmc Incntv Schlrshp 86; Prsdntl Acdmc Ftnss Awd 86; DE Tech CC; Data Prcssng.

BRESKE, SHARON; William Penn HS; New Castle, DE; (Y); 86/450; Office Aide; Service Clb; Ski Clb; Sec Spanish Clb; Var L Swmmng; Hon Roll; Mst Imprvd Swmr 85-86; U Of DE; Jrnlsm.

BRINKLEY, ANTHONY; Indian River HS; Frankford, DE; (Y); 38/154; Boy Scts; FHA; OEA; Spanish Clb; SADD; Rep Frsh Cls; Rep Stu Cncl; Var Capt Bsktbl; Var Capt Ftbl; Hon Roll; U Of DE; Accntng.

BRINKLEY, RENEE; Indian River HS; Frankford, DE; (Y); VICA; Mrchg Band; Stat Bsktbl; Cheerleading; Capt Fld Hcky; Mgr(s); Trk; High Hon Roll; Hon Roll; Jr NHS; Goldey Beacom Coll; Comp Info.

BROOKS, AMY; Indian River HS; Frankford, DE; (S); Spanish Clb; SADD; Chorus; Color Guard; Lit Mag; High Hon Roll; Hon Roll; Jr NHS; Tchr.

BROUGHTON, ALISHA L; Indian River HS; Dagsboro, DE; (Y); 50/202; Civic Clb; Drama Clb; JA; SADD; Chorus; Lit Mag; Stu Cncl; Cheerleading; Hon Roll; Prfct Atten Awd; Semi-Fin Scholar Outstndg Negro Stu 85-86; Nrsg.

BROWN, ALTHEA; Christiana HS; Newark, DE; (Y); SADD; Rep Frsh Cls; Stat Bsktbl; Hon Roll; Hghst Avg Govt 85; Mss Glttr Upwrd Bnd 85; Outstndng Achvmnt Eng 85; NC Central; Law.

BROWN, ANGELA M; William Penn HS; New Castle, DE; (Y); Camera Clb; Church Yth Grp; Library Aide; Church Choir; Hon Roll; Zoolgy.

BROWN, MICHELLE; Seaford SR HS; Seaford, DE; (Y); Band; Color Guard; Concert Band; Mrchg Band; JV Bsktbl; Var Trk; Hon Roll; Hampton U.

BROWN, MICHELLE A; Delcastle Tech HS; New Castle, DE; (Y); Dance Clb; Drama Clb; Girl Scts; Thesps; VICA; School Play; Stage Crew; Yrbk Stf; Hon Roll; Rep Stu Cncl; Actress.

BROWN, PATRICK; Salesianum Schl; Hockessin, DE; (Y); 1/301; Boy Scts; German Clb; Math Tm; Quiz Bowl; Yrbk Sprt Ed; High Hon Roll; NHS; Engnrg.

BROWNING, CRAIG; Delcastle Vocational HS; Wilmington, DE; (Y); Boys Clb Am; Church Yth Grp; Var Bsktbl; Var Ftbl; Var Tennis; Hon Roll; Bus.

BRUCK, JEFFREY; Salesianum Schl; Wilmington, DE; (Y); Computer Clb; Exploring; French Clb; Service Clb; High Hon Roll; Yrbk Caption Ed; Boston U; Med.

BRUCKER, MATT; Alexis I Du Pont HS; Hockessin, DE; (Y); JA; SADD; Nwsp Bus Mgr; Nwsp Phtg; Nwsp Rptr; Nwsp Stf; Rep Frsh Cls; Rep Soph Cls; Im Bsktbl; Im Ftbl; Top Scl Stdy Stu 83-84; Physcs Stu Awd Of Exc 85-86; Outstndng Physcs Stu 85-86; Bus.

BRUNOZZI, DIANA; Padua Acad; Wilmington, DE; (Y); 66/214; Cmnty Wkr; 4-H; Pep Clb; Red Cross Aide; Service Clb; Yrbk Stf; Tennis; 4-H Awd; Hon Roll; Aud/Vis; Ntl 4 H Awd Wnnr Breads 85-86; Bus Adm.

BRYNES, PAM; William Penn HS; New Castle, DE; (Y); Office Aide; Flag Corp; Mrchg Band; Twrlr; Hon Roll; U Of DE; Nrsg.

BRZOZOWSKI, MICHELLE; Delcastle Technical HS; Wilmington, DE; (Y); JA; Hon Roll; Gftd & Tlntd Prgm 85-86; Engrng.

BUCK, MARYANN; Dover HS; Dover, DE; (S); 124/400; Hst DECA; JA; OEA; Sec Pep Clb; Hon Roll; Interior Design.

BUNTING, KAREN; Indian River HS; Dagsboro, DE; (S); French Clb; Spanish Clb; Flag Corp; Nwsp Stf; Yrbk Stf; Rep Stu Cncl; High Hon Roll; Jr NHS; NHS; VFW Awd; Hugh O Brian Ldrshp Awd 85; Super Acdmc Achvt Awd 84; VFW Slvr Awd Ldrshp Citation 84.

BURCHFIELD, BETH; Delcastle Technical HS; Wilmington, DE; (Y); 8/387; Office Aide; VICA; Stage Crew; Rep Stu Cncl; Mgr(s); Bausch & Lomb Sci Awd; Cit Awd; Gov Hon Prg Awd; High Hon Roll; Trs NHS; Mltn & Httie Ktz Fndtn Schlrshp 86; Cncrd Prsbytrn Stu Educ Ln Fnd Schlrshp 86; Prsdntl Acdmc Ftnss 86; Beaver Coll; Chem.

BURGER III, DANIEL W; A I Du Pont HS; Newark, DE; (Y); 64/300; Key Clb; Latin Clb; JV Var Bsbl; JV Var Ftbl; U SC; Invstmnt Anlyst.

BURKE, MARY; Padua Acad; Wilmington, DE; (Y); Hosp Aide; Spanish Clb; Band; Concert Band; Mrchg Band; School Musical; Swmmng; Hon Roll; Vrsty Swmng Cptn 85-86; Histry.

BURKE JR, WILLIAM; Salesianum HS; Wilmington, DE; (S); 9/272; JCL; Rep Soph Cls; Rep Sr Cls; Var L Bsbl; Var Capt Ftbl; High Hon Roll; NHS; Bio.

BURKS, JEFF; Salesianum HS; Chadds Ford, PA; (Y); 70/305; JA; Band; Concert Band; Jazz Band; Symp Band; Var Cheerleading; Var Golf; High Hon Roll; Hon Roll; NC ST U; Acctg.

BURNS, LISA ANNE; William Penn HS; Newark, DE; (S); 41/487; Debate Tm; JA; Ski Clb; Spanish Clb; Teachers Aide; Nwsp Sprt Ed; Yrbk Ed-Chief; Yrbk Sprt Ed; Sec Jr Cls; Pres Stu Cncl; Spnsh Achvt Cert; Hmecmng Queen; Comm.

BURNS, MIA; Christiana HS; Newark, DE; (Y); 104/309; Church Yth Grp; Band; Chorus; Concert Band; Yrbk Stf; Cheerleading; Trk; Vllybl; Hon Roll; Jr NHS; Oustndng Ban Stu 83-84; Outstndng Achvt Soc Sci 85-86; Accntng.

BURNS, MICHAEL; Salesianum HS; Hockessin, DE; (Y); 6/301; Boy Scts; Church Yth Grp; French Clb; Mgr(s); JV Trk; High Hon Roll; Comm.

BURNS, ROBERT; William Penn HS; New Castle, DE; (Y); Computer Clb; Mgr JA; Ski Clb; VP Stage Crew; Rep Stu Cncl; Comp Mth I & II Cert Achvt 84-85; Drivers Ed Cert Achvt 85-86; Comp.

BURRIS, LEETRESS; Caesar Rodney HS; Magnolia, DE; (Y); Church Yth Grp; Exploring; Spanish Clb; Church Choir; Rep Frsh Cls; Rep Soph Cls; Rep Stu Cncl; Widener U Grnt 86-87; Alpha Kappa Alpha Schlrshp 86-87; Round Tbl Schlrshp; Widener U; Law.

BURRIS, WILLIE; Smyrna HS; Clayton, DE; (Y); Computer Clb; Concert Band; Jazz Band; Mrchg Band; High Hon Roll; Comp Sci.

BURTON, MIKE; Alexis I Du Pont HS; Hickessin, DE; (Y); Church Yth Grp; Drama Clb; Band; Concert Band; Mrchg Band; School Play; Stage Crew; JV Socr; Trk; Hon Roll; Bst Spprtng Actr-DE HS Theatr Fstvl 85.

BUSHWELLER, STEPHANY; Dover HS; Dover, DE; (Y); Debate Tm; Speech Tm; Trs Band; Concert Band; Drill Tm; Rep Frsh Cls; Rep Soph Cls; Pom Pon; High Hon Roll; Sci Olympiad Awds; All ST Hnrs Band; Kent Cnty Hnr Band.

BUTLER, RONNE E; John Dickinson HS; Newark, DE; (Y); Drama Clb; JA; Church Choir; Swing Chorus; Trk; Hon Roll; Bd Gov Schlrshp 86; Millersvlle U; Frng Lang.

BUTZ, NICOLE; St Marks HS; Newark, DE; (Y); 125/356; Church Yth Grp; Exploring; SADD; Drill Tm; School Musical; School Play; JV Var Cheerleading; Hon Roll; U Of DE; Bus Admin.

BYERS, DAVID J; John Dickinson HS; Wilmington, DE; (Y); 6/180; Rep Frsh Cls; Trs Soph Cls; Trs Jr Cls; Rep Sr Cls; Stu Cncl; Var Crs Cntry; Var Trk; Cit Awd; High Hon Roll; Jr NHS; Outstndng Male Stu,Athlete Awd 85-86; Kent Smith Meml Awd 85-86; Natl Hnr Soc Awd 85-86; PA U; Pre-Med.

CABAUD III, PHILIP; Caesar Rodney HS; Dover, DE; (Y); Camera Clb; Spanish Clb; Chorus; Var JV Ftbl; Var Trk; Hon Roll; Med.

CALES, PEGGY SUE; Dover HS; Cheswold, DE; (Y); Cmnty Wkr; Hosp Aide; OEA; Chorus; Hon Roll; Bkkpr.

CAMPANICKI, ROSEANNE; Dover HS; Dover, DE; (S); Church Yth Grp; JA; Library Aide; OEA; Hon Roll; DECA; FCA; FNA; Red Cross Aide; Var Sftbl; Bob Wheller Sprtsmnshp Awd Swmmng 83; Goldey Beacom; Accntg.

CAMPBELL, ANGELA; John Dickinson HS; Newark, DE; (Y); 10/218; Church Yth Grp; Exploring; SADD; School Play; Yrbk Stf; Pres Trs Stu Cncl; Mgr(s); Vllybl; Hon Roll; NHS; Bus.

CAMPBELL, CARMEN; Sussex Central SR HS; Millsboro, DE; (Y); 12/200; Am Leg Aux Girls St; Pres Drama Clb; SADD; School Musical; Sec Stu Cncl; DAR Awd; High Hon Roll; NHS; Prfct Atten Awd; U S Nvl Acad; Nvl Intlgnc Ofcr.

CANNON, ANTOINETTE; Howard Career Ctr; Wilmington, DE; (Y); 2/213; JA; Math Tm; VP Jr Cls; Trs Sr Cls; Sec Stu Cncl; Stat Bsktbl; Dnfth Awd; Hon Roll; Jr NHS; NHS; U DE; Engrng.

CARLSON, ANDREW M; Sanford Schl; Hockessin, DE; (Y); 1/40; Church Yth Grp; Scholastic Bowl; Band; Church Choir; School Musical; Pres Stu Cncl; Var L Bsbl; Cit Awd; High Hon Roll; Ntl Merit SF; Founders Schlrshp Sanford Schl 84-86; Delg Congrssnl Yth Ledrshp Conf 85.

CARLSON, KATHLEEN; Lake Forest HS; Camden-Wyoming, DE; (Y); 10/164; Church Yth Grp; VP Pres 4-H; Sec Pres Girl Scts; Concert Band; Ed Yrbk Stf; Capt Fld Hcky; Capt Swmmng; NHS; Drama Clb; French Clb; Hnr Awd-All Around Female Stu, Most Outstndng Sr Athl, Kent Co Med Aux Schlrshp 86; Washington Coll; Phys Ther.

CARNEY, CHRISTINE; Seaford HS; Seaford, DE; (Y); 38/200; GAA; Key Clb; School Play; Ed Nwsp Stf; Ed Yrbk Stf; Rep Frsh Cls; Rep Soph Cls; Rep Jr Cls; Co-Capt Cheerleading; Tennis; VA Tech; Vet.

CARROLL, MICHAEL; Salesianum HS; Wilmington, DE; (Y); 51/301; Spanish Clb; Im Bsktbl; Im Socr; Im Tennis; JV Wrstlng; High Hon Roll; Hon Roll.

CARTER, MICHAEL; Indian River HS; Selbyville, DE; (S); Pep Clb; SADD; Acpl Chr; Chorus; Lit Mag; JV Crs Cntry; French Hon Soc; High Hon Roll; Jr NHS.

CARTER, VONCEIA; Cape Henlopen HS; Milton, DE; (Y); DECA; Chorus; Nwsp Rptr; High Hon Roll; Hon Roll; Alpha Kappa Srty 86; Acdmc Incntv Schlrshp 86; Outstndng SR Awd 86; DE Tech; Bus Adm.

CARTOLANO, AMY; Padua Acad; Wilmington, DE; (S); 7/213; Hosp Aide; Pep Clb; Science Clb; Spanish Clb; Fld Hcky; Hon Roll; NHS; Span I & II Awds; Villanova; Bus Admin.

CARTWRIGHT, TINA; Smyrna HS; Townsend, DE; (Y); 18/192; FFA; OEA; Mrchg Band; Symp Band; Hon Roll; Prfct Atten Awd; Prncpls Awd Acad Excllnce 84-85; Cert Apprctn Stu Intern 86; Outstndg Acad Achvt H S U DE 86; Vet.

CARUSO, JEFFERY; Brandywine HS; Wilmington, DE; (Y); 12/228; Stu Cncl; Bsbl; Wrstlng; High Hon Roll; Pres Schlr; Dsitinquished Schlr; Fletcher Brown Found Schlrshp; John Lynch Found Schlsrhp; PA ST U; Pre-Med.

CASE, DEBBIE; Holy Cross HS; Dover, DE; (Y); 5/40; French Clb; Hosp Aide; Var JV Cheerleading; Mgr(s); French Hon Soc; Hon Roll; NHS; Nrsng.

CASKEY, PAT; Lake Forest HS; Felton, DE; (Y); 13/185; Am Leg Boys St; Letterman Clb; Quiz Bowl; Crs Cntry; Trk; Hon Roll; NHS; Army; Radio Rpr.

CASSEL, KEVIN; Salesianum HS; Newark, DE; (Y); 70/262; Boy Scts; Band; Jazz Band; Mrchg Band; School Musical; Symp Band; Hon Roll; Ntl Merit Ltr; Yrbk Rptr; Pickrd Schlrshp By Scts Amrca 86; U Of DE; Commnctns.

CASTAGNA, LISA; William Penn HS; New Castle, DE; (Y); 7/392; Trs Exploring; VP Key Clb; Math Clb; Ski Clb; Off Sr Cls; Stu Cncl; CC Awd; Lion Awd; NHS; Formosa Plstcs Math Awd 86; Acdmc Incntv Schlrshp 86; U DE; Chem Engrng.

CASTELLI, PATRICIA; Brandywine HS; Wilmington, DE; (S); Church Yth Grp; DECA; JA; Library Aide; Trs Frsh Cls; Rep Soph Cls; Rep Jr Cls; Sec Sr Cls; Rep Stu Cncl; Maryville Coll; Busnss Admin.

CATTS, STEVEN; Salesianum HS; Middletown, DE; (S); 49/301; Church Yth Grp; JV Bsbl; Im Bsktbl; JV Wrstlng; High Hon Roll; NHS.

CAVICCHIO, LISA; Padua Acad; Philadelphia, PA; (S); Pres French Clb; Library Aide; School Musical; High Hon Roll; NHS; Hgst Avg Frnch III 85; Ntl Sci Olympiad Awd Bio 84; Ntl Ed Dev Test Awd 84; PA ST U; Ed.

CELIBERTI, RACHEL; Dover HS; Dover, DE; (Y); 16/400; Church Yth Grp; Cmnty Wkr; OEA; Political Wkr; Yrbk Stf; High Hon Roll; NHS; Outstdng Acad Achvt From U Of DE 86.

CENTRELLA, LORI; Archmere Acad; Newark, DE; (S); Church Yth Grp; Cmnty Wkr; Exploring; Concert Band; Trs Frsh Cls; Trs Soph Cls; Trs Jr Cls; Fld Hcky; High Hon Roll; NHS; Hon Men All Cath Fld Hcky 85-86; Sci.

CERMINARO III, FRANK T; Delcastle Technical HS; Newark, DE; (Y); ROTC; VICA; JV Bsbl; JV Ftbl; Wt Lftg; Wrstlng; High Hon Roll; 155 Lb Blue Hen Conf Champn Wrstlng 85-86; Blue Hen Conf All Acadmc Confr Tm 85-86; Voc Dist Calndr 86; U Delaware; Law Enfrcmnt.

CHADWELL JR, ARTHUR; Woodbridge HS; Bridgeville, DE; (Y); Drama Clb; Quiz Bowl; Thesps; School Musical; School Play; Stage Crew; Variety Show; Hon Roll; Exploring; Library Aide; 1000 Hr Hon Trphy 86; Life Thespn Hon 86; U Delware; Thtr Arts.

CHAIT, ERIC; Dover HS; Dover, DE; (Y); 27/320; Science Clb; Band; Var L Socr; High Hon Roll; Ntl Merit Ltr.

CHALFANT, MARIBETH; St Marks HS; Wilmington, DE; (Y); Band; Concert Band; Mrchg Band; School Musical; Hon Roll; NHS; Bishop Mardaga Mem Merrit Schlrshp; Pres Acdmc Fit Awd; William H Melis Mem Awd; Goldey Beacom Coll; Admin Mgmt.

CHAMPANERIA, AARTI; Seaford SR HS; Seaford, DE; (S); 1/280; Hosp Aide; Key Clb; Scholastic Bowl; School Play; Hst Frsh Cls; Hst Soph Cls; Rep Jr Cls; JV Cheerleading; Gov Hon Prg Awd; NHS; Mst Outstndg Soph 84-85; Sci Olympd Mdl Wnr 83-85; Cmmnctns.

CHANDLER, LAURA; Indian River HS; Frankford, DE; (S); OEA; Spanish Clb; High Hon Roll; Grls ST Alt 86; Ctzn Bee 86; Crmnl Jstc.

CHANG, NINA J; Mount Pleasant HS; Wilmington, DE; (Y); 17/160; AFS; Mathletes; Science Clb; Yrbk Ed-Chief; Ed Lit Mag; JV Stat Bsktbl; JV Var Sftbl; Hon Roll; Ntl Merit Ltr; NEDT Awd; Diamond St Schlr 86; Mt Pleasant Schlrshp U Of DE 86; U Of DE; Bus Admin.

CHAPMAN, KELLY; Saint Marks HS; Elkton, MD; (Y); 34/362; Church Yth Grp; Sec Sr Cls; JV Bsktbl; Var Crs Cntry; Im Mgr(s); Var Trk; Church Yth Grp; Rep Soph Cls; Rep Jr Cls; Peer Counceling 85-86; Z Clb 85-86; Medicine.

CHARLES, MARIKA; Glasgow HS; Bear, DE; (Y); Cmnty Wkr; Office Aide; Chorus; Orch; Yrbk Rptr; Cit Awd; High Hon Roll; Hon Roll; NHS; Prfct Atten Awd; Arista Awd 84; Acctg.

CHARNEY, SHARON; Padua Acad; Wilmington, DE; (Y); Church Yth Grp; JA; Pep Clb; SADD; Teachers Aide; Church Choir; Nwsp Rptr; Nwsp Stf; Bowling; Tennis; Jrnlsm.

CHASSE, ERIC; Caesar Rodney HS; Hopewell Junction, NY; (Y); 5/300; VP JA; VP Letterman Clb; Capt Quiz Bowl; Nwsp Stf; Yrbk Sprt Ed; Rep Stu Cncl; Var L Bsbl; JV Var Socr; Gov Hon Prg Awd; NHS; Charles G Mortimer Schlrshp; U Of NC Chapl Hl; Bus.

CHEESEMAN, BRYAN; John Dickinson HS; Wilmington, DE; (Y); #1 In Class; Quiz Bowl; Scholastic Bowl; JV Bsbl; High Hon Roll; Hon Roll; Ntl Merit Ltr.

CHELTON, MELISSA; Seaford SR HS; Seaford, DE; (Y); AFS; Band; Concert Band; Drm & Bgl; Mrchg Band; Pep Band; Yrbk Stf; Hon Roll; Rep Frsh Cls; Rep Soph Cls; Prfct Attndnc Awds 84; Blue Jay & Spec Musc Awds 85; Bus.

CHEN, BETH; Archmere Acad; Wilmington, DE; (Y); SADD; School Musical; School Play; Yrbk Ed-Chief; Yrbk Phtg; Var Capt Cheerleading; Powder Puff Ftbl; Hon Roll; Comm.

CHEN, LIN-CHI A; St Andrews Schl; Milford, DE; (Y); Am Leg Aux Girls St; Hosp Aide; SADD; Varsity Clb; Band; Chorus; Church Choir; Concert Band; Jazz Band; Nwsp Stf; Govrnrs Schl For Excll 84; Amer Lgn Awd 83.

CHIN, KENNETH; Claymont HS; Wilmington, DE; (Y); OEA; Comp Pgmmng.

CHOU, HELEN; Alexis J Du Pont HS; Hockessin, DE; (Y); Variety Show; Yrbk Stf; High Hon Roll; Hon Roll; NHS; DE ST Music Tchrs Assn Solo Piano Fstvl-Excllnt Rtg 85; Govrs Schl For Excllnc 85.

CHUDZIK, TRINA; St Marks HS; Wilmington, DE; (Y); Intnl Clb; JA; Pep Clb; School Musical; High Hon Roll; Hon Roll; Silk Sqd Co-Capt 85-86; St Marks Blue/Gold All Star Comm 86; Bus.

CHUNG, DIANA; Alexis I Du Pont HS; Hockessin, DE; (Y); 27/254; Yrbk Ed-Chief; Ed Yrbk Phtg; Yrbk Stf; JV Bsktbl; JV Sftbl; Hon Roll; Math & Typg I Awd 83-84; Biomed Engrg.

CHURILLA, MONICA; Milford SR HS; Milford, DE; (Y); Art Clb; French Clb; Varsity Clb; Yrbk Phtg; Fld Hcky; Tennis; High Hon Roll; Hon Roll; Hnrb Mntn Holzmueller Art Gllry Cntst 84; Sea Wtch Intl Flg Dsgn Cntst 4th Pl 85; Cmmrcl Art.

CIERNIAK, KRYSIA; St Marks HS; Newark, DE; (Y); 77/310; JA; Pep Clb; SADD; Flag Corp; School Musical; Hon Roll; Bus.

CIMINELLO, TRICIA; St Marks HS; Wilmington, DE; (Y); Dance Clb; Drill Tm; Mrchg Band; School Musical; Capt Pom Pon; Dance.

CIRILLO, CHRISTINE; St Marks HS; Wilmington, DE; (Y); Dance Clb; Chorus; Mrchg Band; School Musical; Rep Stu Cncl; Hon Roll; NHS; Rep Soph Cls; Rep Jr Cls; Rep Sr Cls; U MD Coll Park 86; Towson ST U; Dance.

CIRITELLA, KATHRYN; St Elizabeth HS; Wilmington, DE; (Y); Church Yth Grp; Girl Scts; Service Clb; Rep Frsh Cls; Rep Soph Cls; Rep Jr Cls; Stu Cncl; Capt Bsktbl; Sftbl; Hon Roll; DE All St Bsktbl-1st Team 85-86; Convers All Amer 86; Gator Aid Bsktbl DE Wnnr 86; Towson ST U; Heatlh.

CLARK, JEFFREY; Smyrna HS; Kenton, DE; (S); 6/160; 4-H; French Clb; Math Tm; Band; Trs Band; Trs Mrchg Band; Trs Symp Band; Tennis; Gov Hon Prg Awd; High Hon Roll; Govnrs Schl Excllnce 84; DE Boys ST 85; West Point Appt 86; West Point.

CLAYTON, DARRELL A; Thomas Mc Kean HS; Wilmingtn, DE; (Y); 6/220; Art Clb; Church Yth Grp; Letterman Clb; Teachers Aide; Varsity Clb; School Musical; School Play; Stage Crew; Variety Show; Nwsp Rptr; U Of DE; Accntnt.

CLOYD, JENNIFER THERESA; Brandywine HS; Wilmington, DE; (Y); 50/250; JA; School Musical; Nwsp Phtg; Rep Stu Cncl; JV Fld Hcky; Mgr(s); Capt Twrlr; Hon Roll; Stu Of Statue Lbrty Drill Tm 86; Mc Guffy Schlrshp 86; $4000 Schlrshp Won Miss Teenager Pgnt 84; U Of DE; Lang.

COCHRAN, PATRICK; Salesianum HS; Newark, DE; (Y); 6/315; Boy Scts; Church Yth Grp; Drama Clb; Sec Trs Spanish Clb; Stage Crew; Yrbk Rptr; Im Bsktbl; JV Trk; High Hon Roll; NHS.

COCHRAN, WILLIAM; William Penn HS; New Castle, DE; (Y); Camera Clb; Computer Clb; Hon Roll; Law.

COGGINS, CLAIRE; Archmere Acad; West Chester, PA; (S); Girl Scts; Spanish Clb; School Musical; Var Fld Hcky; Stat Mgr(s); Im Powder Puff Ftbl; JV Sftbl; High Hon Roll; NHS; NEDT Awd; Schlrp To Archmere Acad 83; Hlf Schlrp To Villa Maria Acad H S 83; 2nd Tm All Cath Fld Hcky 85; U PA; Vet Med.

COLA, KIMBERLY; Dover HS; Dover, DE; (S); Church Yth Grp; Office Aide; OEA; SADD; Yrbk Stf; Stu Cncl; Powder Puff Ftbl; Var L Sftbl; Hon Roll; Elem Educ.

COLARIK JR, PAUL E; St Marks HS; Wilmington, DE; (Y); 31/358; Art Clb; French Clb; Intnl Clb; JA; Office Aide; Lit Mag; Off Frsh Cls; Off Soph Cls; Off Jr Cls; Off Sr Cls; Franklin/Marshll Clg; Invst Bus.

COLATRIANO, RENEE; Padua Acad; Wilmington, DE; (Y); 44/215; Church Yth Grp; Dance Clb; French Clb; Pep Clb; Flag Corp; School Musical; JV Trk; Hon Roll; Psych.

COLEMAN, NANCY; Delcastle Technical HS; Wilmington, DE; (Y); JA; Pres OEA; Church Choir; Hon Roll; Goldie Beacom Coll; Exec Sec.

COLEY, SHEENA; Christiana HS; Wilmington, DE; (S); JA; OEA; SADD; Varsity Clb; Var Capt Bsktbl; Var Trk; High Hon Roll; Hon Roll; Prfct Atten Awd; 1st Pl-Shrthnd I 84-85; 1st Pl-Shrthnd II 85-86; 4th Pl-Shrthnd-OEA ST Conf 84-85; Mngmt.

COLLENDER, STACIE; St Marks HS; Wilmington, DE; (Y); Ski Clb; Hon Roll; NHS; Pres Schlr; Boston U; Physcl Thrpy.

COLLINS, ANTHONY; Seaford SR HS; Seaford, DE; (Y); 7/184; Church Yth Grp; JA; Math Tm; Teachers Aide; Bsbl; Bsktbl; High Hon Roll; NHS; U DE Awd 86; JA Applied Econ Mgmt Awd 86; U DE; Elec Engrng.

COLLINS, DALE; Indian River HS; Frankford, DE; (Y); Computer Clb; JV Wt Lftg; Var Wrstlng; Hon Roll; JV Trk; Bst Stu Bldng Trades Shp Cls 83-84; Arch.

COLLINS, MICHAEL; Salesianum HS; W Chester, PA; (S); 13/320; Chess Clb; Spanish Clb; Im Bowling; High Hon Roll; NHS; U Of Notre Dame; CPA.

COLLISON, BETH; Lake Forest HS; Harrington, DE; (S); Church Yth Grp; French Clb; German Clb; OEA; Q&S; Varsity Clb; Nwsp Rptr; Var Cheerleading; Hon Roll; Princeton U; Engl.

COLLOM, KIMBERLY; Padua Acad; Wilmington, DE; (S); JA; JCL; Latin Clb; High Hon Roll; NHS; NEDT Awd; Hghst Avg In Latin-Padua Acad 84-85; Italian Clb Sec-Padua Acad 83-84; Italn Clb Pres-Padua Acad 84-85; U Of DE; Marine Bio.

COMEGYS, CARL RODNEY; William Penn HS; Delaware City, DE; (S); Aud/Vis; Cmnty Wkr; Math Tm; Political Wkr; Scholastic Bowl; Ski Clb; Cmnty Wkr; JV Bsbl; JV Socr; NHS; Close Up Clb Treas; Engrng.

COMEGYS, RODNEY; William Penn HS; Delaware City, DE; (Y); Am Leg Boys St; Library Aide; Math Tm; Scholastic Bowl; Science Clb; Stu Cncl; Bsbl; Socr; Hon Roll; NHS; Ctzn Bee ST Fin 86; U DE Summr Coll 86; Engrng.

COMPONOVO, CHRIS; Salesianum Schl; Wilmington, DE; (S); 8/262; JA; Symp Band; Nwsp Rptr; Stu Cncl; Im JV Bsktbl; Var Capt Trk; Hon Roll; NHS; ST Chmpn Pole Vault 85; Notre Dame; Pre Law.

COMPTON, HEATHER; Ursuline Acad; Wilmington, DE; (Y); 10/62; AFS; VP French Clb; Scholastic Bowl; Service Clb; Yrbk Stf; L Var Bsktbl; Var L Vllybl; VP NHS; New Cstle Cnty Chmbr Of Cmmrc Svc Awd 86; Schls Serviam Awd 85; Neilia Hunter Biden Awd For Svc 86; Ursinus Coll; Cnslng Psych.

CONARD, JEREMY; Wilmington HS; Wilmington, DE; (Y); 17/173; Camera Clb; Church Yth Grp; Band; Concert Band; Hon Roll; Prfct Atten Awd; Marine Sci.

CONCAVAGE, DONNA; Ursuline Acad; Newark, DE; (Y); Pres Aud/Vis; Pres Library Aide; Science Clb; Chorus; Flag Corp; Yrbk Phtg; Hon Roll; Ntl Merit Ltr; Dupont Explr; PA ST U.

CONNER, CHRISTOPER J; Seaford SR HS; Seaford, DE; (Y); Am Leg Boys St; Chrmn Church Yth Grp; Key Clb; Teachers Aide; Ed Yrbk Stf; Mgr Tennis; High Hon Roll; Hon Roll; Outstndng Art Stu 85-86; U VA; Hist Arch.

CONNER, SUSAN; Dover HS; Dover, DE; (Y); Dance Clb; SADD; Teachers Aide; Drill Tm; Mrchg Band; Symp Band; Rep Jr Cls; L Pom Pon; L Powder Puff Ftbl; Hon Roll; All Amer Yth Hnr Band Paris 85; Pom Pon Cmp 3 1sts, 2 2nds 85; All Amer Yth Hnr Band Germny & Austr 86; Elem Ed.

CONSIGLIO, AMY MARIE; Saint Marks HS; Newark, DE; (Y); 43/360; Am Leg Aux Girls St; Church Yth Grp; SADD; Acpl Chr; Chorus; School Musical; School Play; Swing Chorus; Variety Show; Lit Mag; Engl.

CONTE, MICHELE; Padva Acad; Philadelphia, PA; (S); 4/213; Pep Clb; Yrbk Stf; Hon Roll; NHS; NEDT Awd; Sci Olympiad Awd 85; Bio Awd 85; Acdmc All-Amer Schlr Awd 84; St Josephs U; Law.

COOK, BLAINE O; Brandywine HS; Wilmington, DE; (Y); 5/256; Am Leg Boys St; Boy Scts; Drm Mjr(t); School Musical; Var Capt Gym; Var Lcrss; Trs NHS; Ntl Merit Ltr; Pres Church Yth Grp; Drama Clb; Trustees Schlrshp BYU 86; Bys Ntn Sntr 85; DE ST Plc Trpr Yth Wk 86; BYU; Pltcl Sci.

COOK, CATHY; Seaford SR HS; Seaford, DE; (Y); AFS; Key Clb; Color Guard; Yrbk Stf; Hon Roll; Wntrgrd 84; Archtct.

COONEY, JANET; Archmere Acad; Wilmington, DE; (Y); French Clb; Concert Band; Im Bowling; Hon Roll; Italian Clb; Italian Hnr Soc; Comm.

CORDREY, TABATHA; Indian River HS; Dagsboro, DE; (S); 24/213; Drama Clb; French Clb; SADD; School Play; Hon Roll; NHS; Drama Prtcptn Awd 85; Qlty Prtnrs Educ Pgm Outstndng Stu Recog Awd 86; Acting.

CORPUS, RACHAEL; Caesar Rodney HS; Dover, DE; (Y); GAA; Hosp Aide; Math Tm; OEA; Spanish Clb; School Play; Stage Crew; Im Powder Puff Ftbl; Var L Trk; High Hon Roll; 16th Annual ST OEA Conf 85; U DE; Bio Sci.

CORSO, TERESA; Smyrna HS; Clayton, DE; (S); 19/140; Art Clb; French Clb; OEA; Teachers Aide; Yrbk Ed-Chief; Yrbk Stf; Trs Stu Cncl; Capt Cheerleading; Hon Roll; NHS; Var Ltr 83-86; MVP Chrldng 86; Acad Hall Fame Frnch 86; U DE.

COULBOURN, AMY; Seaford HS; Seaford, DE; (Y); 31/184; 4-H; Key Clb; Library Aide; School Play; Yrbk Stf; Trs Soph Cls; Trs Jr Cls; Trs Sr Cls; Rep Stu Cncl; 4-H Awd; Key Clb 86; Niriam Nebekah Ldg No 20 86; Outstndg Svc Class 86; Lynchburg Coll; Elem Ed.

COUNRTNEY JR, JAMES J; St Marks HS; New Castle, DE; (Y); 36/363; Am Leg Boys St; Drama Clb; Key Clb; Math Tm; Quiz Bowl; Chorus; School Play; Nwsp Rptr; Rep Stu Cncl; Hon Roll; Hstry.

COURTNEY, JENNIFER; Saint Marys HS; New Castle, DE; (Y); 49/358; Trs Church Yth Grp; Dance Clb; Hosp Aide; Office Aide; Trs Jr Cls; Trs Sr Cls; Rep Stu Cncl; Capt Cheerleading; Hon Roll; NHS; John B Lynch,Jim O Hanlon Schrlshp Awd 86; Blue Gold All Star Chrldr 86; U DE; Physcl Thrpy.

CRESCENZO, JAMES; Alexis I Du Pont HS; Wilmington, DE; (Y); Computer Clb; JA; Wrstlng; High Hon Roll; Hon Roll; Engrng.

CRISCUOLO, BARRY; St Marks HS; Townsend, DE; (Y); DECA; Band; Concert Band; Jazz Band; Mrchg Band; School Play; Stage Crew; Lcrss; Hon Roll; Cmptr Sci.

CRISTIANO, LISA; Smyrna HS; Dover, DE; (Y); Trs Church Yth Grp; Drama Clb; Spanish Clb; Drm Mjr(t); Rep Mrchg Band; School Musical; Rep Jr Cls; Stu Cncl; Mgr(s); Prfct Atten Awd; Embry Riddle; Aerospc.

CRITZER, LISA; Padua Acad; Brookhaven, PA; (S); 1/191; Library Aide; Service Clb; Color Guard; Yrbk Stf; NHS; NEDT Awd; Spanish NHS; Art Clb; Pep Clb; Spanish Clb; Svc Awd 84; Engl III Awd 85; PA Hghr Ed Assistnc Agncy; U PA; Finance.

CROCKETT, DON; Smyrna HS; Townsend, DE; (Y); 42/190; Band; Concert Band; Drm Mjr(t); Jazz Band; Mrchg Band; Var Socr; JV Var Trk; Hon Roll; Kent Cnty Hon Band 85-86; Goldey Beacom Coll; Ecnmcs.

CRONIS, CHRISTOPHER; Caesar Rodney SR HS; Dover, DE; (Y); 25/380; Letterman Clb; Nwsp Rptr; Rep Stu Cncl; JV Bsktbl; Var Capt Crs Cntry; JV Ftbl; Var Capt Trk; Hon Roll; NHS; All Conf Hrns Crss Cntry 2nd Tm 84-85, 1st Tm 85-86; Conf Champ Trk 85-86.

CROUSE, MICHELLE; Caravel Acad; Newark, DE; (S); 1/46; Am Leg Aux Girls St; Math Tm; Service Clb; Teachers Aide; Chorus; School Musical; School Play; Yrbk Stf; VP Frsh Cls; Sec Jr Cls; Treas, VP ST Stu Govt 85-87; Outstndng Achvt Awds 83-85; Hmcmng Prncss 83-85; Phys Thrpy.

CRUTCHER, JANET; Alexis I Du Pont HS; Newark, DE; (Y); 26/260; Church Yth Grp; Band; Chorus; Church Choir; Concert Band; Mrchg Band; Stu Cncl; Var L Bsktbl; Var L Fld Hcky; Var L Tennis; Fld Hcky 1st Tm All-Conf & 2nd Tm All-St 85; Jr Olymp Fld Hcky Tm 86; 2nd Tm All-Conf Bsktbl St Rnr-Up.

CULVER, DEAN; Laurel HS; Laurel, DE; (Y); SADD; Varsity Clb; L Bsbl; Var Ftbl.

CUMMINGS, KATHLEEN; Delcastle Technical HS; Wilmington, DE; (Y); VICA; Hon Roll; Church Yth Grp; Teachers Aide; Nwsp Stf; Yrbk Stf; Gov Hon Prg Awd; GATE 85-87; MI ST U; TV.

CUNDIFF III, BRUCE T; Brandywine HS; Wilmington, DE; (S); 49/249; DECA; Model UN; Scholastic Bowl; Var Bsbl; Var Socr; Ntl Merit Ltr; Georgetown U; Intl Rltns.

CUNHA, LISA; Caesar Rodney HS; Dover, DE; (Y); 22/343; GAA; Math Tm; Q&S; Thesps; Stage Crew; Yrbk Stf; NHS; Sec Computer Clb; German Clb; Teachers Aide; Caesar Rodney All Schl Actvts Ltr 86; Pres Acad Ftns Awd 86; German Awd 86; U DE; Civil Engr.

CURRAN, PETER; Salesianum HS; Wilmingon, DE; (Y); 127/301; Dance Clb; Rep Soph Cls; Rep Jr Cls; Socr; Swmmng; Mrktng.

CURTIS, GLEN; Caesar Rodney HS; Camden, DE; (Y); Trs Church Yth Grp; OEA; Spanish Clb; Color Guard; 5th Pl ST Ofc Ed Assn Cnfrnc In Vrbl I 86; Bus.

DALLAS, EDITH; Ursuline Academy HS; Wilmington, DE; (Y); AFS; Hosp Aide; Chorus; Variety Show; Rep Frsh Cls; Trs Jr Cls; Var Bsktbl; Im Fld Hcky; Mgr(s); Im Vllybl; Villanova U; Mrktng.

DANAHY, COLEEN; Dover HS; Dover, DE; (Y); Church Yth Grp; Cmnty Wkr; Hosp Aide; Office Aide; OEA; Pep Clb; SADD; Varsity Clb; Var Capt Cheerleading; Hon Roll; Sports Med.

DANBER, SHARON; Dover HS; Dover, DE; (Y); 15/380; AFS; Pres Boy Scts; NFL; Pres Speech Tm; Flag Corp; Symp Band; Var Cheerleading; NHS; Voice Dem Awd; Intl Affrs.

DARBY, RENEE; Seaford SR HS; Seaford, DE; (Y); 36/184; AFS; Cmnty Wkr; GAA; VP Key Clb; Office Aide; OEA; Yrbk Stf; Stu Cncl; L Mgr Fld Hcky; Mgr(s); Bll Rth Ldrshp Cnfrnc 85; U Of DE; Crmnl Jstc.

DAVID, MARK F; Salesianum Schl; Wilmington, DE; (Y); 67/262; Church Yth Grp; Exploring; Var Trk; Hon Roll; Ntl Merit Ltr; Valparaiso U; Elec Engr.

DAVIES, BRIAN; Christiana HS; Newark, DE; (Y); 2/357; Am Leg Boys St; Boy Scts; Math Tm; Political Wkr; Quiz Bowl; Scholastic Bowl; Science Clb; Service Clb; Spanish Clb; SADD; Distngshg Hnr Rll 4.o Avg; Govrnr Sch6 Acadmc Excllnc; Top Sci Awd; RPI; Engrng.

DAVIS, ANGELIQUE; Wilmington HS; Wilmington, DE; (Y); French Clb; Math Tm; Varsity Clb; Yrbk Stf; Var Cheerleading; Trk; JV Vllybl; Hon Roll; NHS; Upward Bound Pre Coll Prep Pgm 84-86; Pediatric.

DAVIS, KAREN; Padua Acad; Wilmington, DE; (S); 26/173; JA; School Musical; Variety Show; Hon Roll; Schlrshp-Anna Maries Dance Studio 84-86; Pres Of Dancers Unltd Prfrmng Ensmbl 85-86; SUNY-PURCHASE; Dance.

DAVIS, KELLEY; Christiana HS; Newark, DE; (Y); DECA; French Clb; Var Sftbl.

DAVIS, STACIE; William Penn HS; New Castle, DE; (Y); Sec Key Clb; Ski Clb; Teachers Aide; Chorus; Yrbk Rptr; Yrbk Stf; Rep Frsh Cls; Rep Soph Cls; Rep Jr Cls; Rep Sr Cls; Drvrs Ed Awd 85; U Of DE; Tchng.

DAVIS, TRINA; Laurel Senior HS; Laurel, DE; (Y); Pres JA; Pep Clb; SADD; School Play; Hon Roll; U Of DE; Jrnlsm.

DAVOLOS, STEPHANIE; Archmere Acad; Wilmington, DE; (S); Church Yth Grp; Cmnty Wkr; French Clb; SADD; Band; Lit Mag; JV Fld Hcky; Powder Puff Ftbl; JV Trk; Hon Roll.

DAY, NICK; Cape Henlopen HS; Rehoboth, DE; (Y); Am Leg Boys St; Cmnty Wkr; Jazz Band; Mrchg Band; Nwsp Ed-Chief; Trs Sr Cls; Pres Stu Cncl; Var Bsbl; NHS; Ntl Merit SF; Pol Sci.

DE PRISCO, JOSEPH R; Salesianum HS; Wilmington, DE; (S); 3/301; Band; Concert Band; Mrchg Band; Symp Band; Var Cheerleading; Wt Lftg; JV Wrstlng; High Hon Roll; Hon Roll; NHS; Duke U; Chemst.

DE VORE, LISA; Delmar HS; Delmar, MD; (Y); Keywanettes; Pep Clb; Ski Clb; SADD; Band; Chorus; Off Jr Cls; Bsktbl; Fld Hcky; Hon Roll; U Of MD Coll Pk; Chem Engrng.

DEAKYNE, DANIELLE; Smyrna HS; Smyrna, DE; (Y); French Clb; Teachers Aide; School Musical; Sec Frsh Cls; Sec Soph Cls; Pres Jr Cls; Var Cheerleading; Var Crs Cntry; Var Fld Hcky; Var Gym; Econ.

DEAN, FRANCES; Lake Forest HS; Harrington, DE; (Y); 47/164; 4-H; FHA; Girl Scts; OEA; Spanish Clb; SADD; VICA; 4-H Awd; High Hon Roll; Hon Roll; DE Tech & CC; Data Prcssng.

DEELY, DAVID; Salesianum School For Boys; Wilmington, DE; (Y); 93/292; SADD; JV Crs Cntry; Hon Roll; Comp.

DEHEER, CHRISTOPHER; St Marks HS; Bear, DE; (Y); 3/375; Math Tm; Science Clb; Rep Jr Cls; JV Crs Cntry; JV Trk; High Hon Roll; NHS; Ntl Merit Ltr; 3rd Pl DE ACS Chem Exam 86; DE Sci Olympd Tm 1st Pl 86; Envrnmntl Bio.

DELLEDONNE, MICHELLE; Padua Acad; Wilmington, DE; (Y); 22/216; Cmnty Wkr; Girl Scts; JA; Pep Clb; SADD; Band; JV Var Cheerleading; High Hon Roll; Hon Roll; NEDT Awd; Dale Carnegie Prsnl Prog Awd 85; West End Volunteer Tutor Awd 85; U DE; Comm.

DELLOSE, STEVE; Alexis I Du Pont HS; Hockessin, DE; (Y); SADD; Rep Jr Cls; Rep Stu Cncl; Bsbl; Ftbl; Wrstlng; Hon Roll.

DELTUFO, MICHAEL; Holy Cross HS; Dover, DE; (Y); #1 In Class; Math Clb; Math Tm; JV Bsbl; Var Bsktbl; High Hon Roll; Hon Roll; NHS; Spanish NHS; 1st Hnrs 84-86; Outstndng Acad Achvt 86; Achvt Awds 84-86; Engrng.

DEMNICKI, DAMIAN; Archmere Acad; Broomall, PA; (Y); Hosp Aide; NFL; SADD; Concert Band; Jazz Band; Ftbl; Hon Roll; Prfct Atten Awd; Pres Schlr; Cmnty Wkr; NROTC, AROTC & Air Force ROTC 86; CUA Gibbon Schlrshp 86; La Salle Acad Schlrshp 86; St Josephs U; Pre-Med.

DEMPSEY, AIMEE; Padua Acad; Wilmington, DE; (S); 18/240; Pep Clb; Spanish Clb; Crs Cntry; Trk; High Hon Roll; US Bus Educ Awds 84-85; Villanova U; Phy Thrpy.

DENNIS, MICHAEL; Indian River HS; Dagsboro, DE; (S); Trs Church Yth Grp; Cmnty Wkr; Band; Chorus; Concert Band; Jazz Band; Mrchg Band; Pep Band; School Musical; School Play; Intl Yth Yr 85; Am Leg Oratrcl Cntst Wnnr; Dir Awd Band 84; Law.

DESMOND, KELLY; Claymont HS; Claymont, DE; (Y); VP Church Yth Grp; Spanish Clb; SADD; Teachers Aide; Varsity Clb; Lib Band; Mrchg Band; Yrbk Stf; Hon Roll; NHS; Peer Helper Awd 86; Stu Of Mth-Math 86.

DETTRA, MARK; William Penn HS; New Castle, DE; (Y); Band; Concert Band; Jazz Band; Mrchg Band; Symp Band; Radio/TV Technlgy.

DEVENEY, MICHELLE D; Claymont HS; Claymont, DE; (Y); 12/150; VP Pres SADD; Nwsp Stf; Trs Jr Cls; Trs Sr Cls; Rep Stu Cncl; JV Var Cheerleading; NHS; Cmnty Wkr; Computer Clb; French Clb; Governors Schl For Exclnnc 84; John B Lynch Merit Schlrhsp 86; Elizabeth Coll.

DI CAMILLO, RAYMOND; Salesianum School For Boys; Wilmington, DE; (S); 2/260; Pres Church Yth Grp; Capt Scholastic Bowl; Nwsp Ed-Chief; Bowling; Bausch & Lomb Sci Awd; Pres NHS; Ntl Merit Ltr; Voice Dem Awd; Exploring; JCL; Schl Rep Cntry III Ldrs Pgm; Slvr Mdl-Ntl Latin Exm; Med.

DI DONATO, DORI; Archmere Acad; Folcroft, PA; (Y); Spanish Clb; Im Bowling; High Hon Roll; Spanish NHS; Itln Hnr Soc 86; Intl Law.

DICK, RONALD; Dover HS; Dover, DE; (Y); 17/320; Rep Frsh Cls; Rep Soph Cls; Rep Jr Cls; Bowling; VP Golf; Tennis; High Hon Roll; NHS; Playtex Schlrshp 86; U Of DE 86; U Of DE; Med.

DICKERSON, DIANA L; Dover HS; Dover, DE; (Y); 52/316; JA; OEA; Chorus; Nwsp Phtg; Yrbk Phtg; Rep Sr Cls; Capt Cheerleading; Powder Puff Ftbl; High Hon Roll; Pres Schlr; 1st Pl Comp Lit 83-84; U DE; Comm.

DICKERSON, SCOTT; Milford SR HS; Milford, DE; (Y); 3/220; Am Leg Boys St; Boy Scts; Quiz Bowl; School Musical; Nwsp Stf; Yrbk Ed-Chief; Lit Mag; High Hon Roll; Hon Roll; NHS; Nacel France Am Exc 85; Am Leg Ortrcl Cntst ST Champ 86; Eagle Scout 85; Brdcst Jrnlsm.

DICKSON, KIM; Dover HS; Hartly, DE; (S); Rptr DECA; Yrbk Stf; Var Bowling; U Of Delaware; Bus Admin.

DIEFFENBACH, LAURA; Brandywine HS; Wilmington, DE; (S); 13/249; Am Leg Aux Girls St; Trs DECA; Drama Clb; Hosp Aide; Sec Ski Clb; Band; Mrchg Band; School Play; Stage Crew; Var L Fld Hcky; Intl Yth Yr Awd 85; Penn U; Nrsng.

DIETZ, LORIE; Newark HS; Newark, DE; (Y); 4-H; Teachers Aide; 4-H Awd; Hon Roll; NHS.

DIHENIA, BHAVNA; Seaford HS; Seaford, DE; (Y); VP Intnl Clb; OEA; JV Var Badmtn; Hon Roll.

DILLON, MIKE; Salesianum HS; Wilmington, DE; (Y); Church Yth Grp; Cmnty Wkr; FCA; German Clb; Political Wkr; Varsity Clb; Var L Ftbl; Var L Lcrss; Im Socr; Wt Lftg.

DIMAURO JR, MICHAEL J; Mt Pleasant SR HS; Wilmington, DE; (Y); #26 In Class; Boy Scts; JA; Rep Jr Cls; Rep Stu Cncl; Var Ftbl; Score Keeper; Var Trk; Var Wrstlng; Hon Roll; U DE; Comp Pgmr.

DIXON, TRACY; Smyrna HS; Smyrna, DE; (Y); Drama Clb; Teachers Aide; Chorus; Color Guard; Mrchg Band; Yrbk Rptr; Pre-Med.

DODSON, MICHELLE; Laurel SR HS; Laurel, DE; (Y); 15/139; French Clb; FNA; Pep Clb; SADD; Hon Roll; Jr NHS; Prfct Atten Awd; Pres Schlr; 1st Pl Bones, Blncng Eqtns Sci Bwl 86; Bio.

DOMINO, ANTHONY; Archmere Acad; Middletown, DE; (Y); Cmnty Wkr; German Clb; Stu Cncl; JV Var Bsktbl; Var Capt Ftbl; Hon Roll; Jr NHS; NHS; Pre-Vet.

DORFF, HOLLY; Indian River HS; Selbyville, DE; (S); 6/178; French Clb; Spanish Clb; Rep Frsh Cls; Rep Soph Cls; Var Fld Hcky; Var Trk; High Hon Roll; Jr NHS; NHS; NEDT Awd; Awd Acadmc Excllnc & Math Excllnc & Frnch Excllnc 84-85; E Carolina U.

DORSEY III, DANIEL RICHARD; Howard Career Ctr; Wilmington, DE; (Y); 14/231; Church Yth Grp; Ski Clb; Trs VICA; Stu Cncl; High Hon Roll; Hon Roll; DE Bus Ed Assoc Partl Schlrshp 86-87; Auto Mech Cls 85-86; Goldey Beacon Coll; Mrktng Mgmt.

DOUGHERTY, DANIEL; Salesianum HS; Wilmington, DE; (S); Church Yth Grp; Yrbk Stf; Trs Jr Cls; Trs Sr Cls; Stu Cncl; High Hon Roll; NHS; Bus.

DOUGHERTY, ESTHER; Delcastle Tech HS; Newark, DE; (Y); Art Clb; Church Yth Grp; Drama Clb; FFA; JA; Chorus; Church Choir; School Musical; School Play; Hon Roll; Hnr Roll 85-86; Hnrd Pres Of Clss 85-86; Fshn Dsgn.

DOUGHERTY, JOHN; Salesianum Schl; Wilmington, DE; (Y); 16/262; Quiz Bowl; Scholastic Bowl; SADD; Im Bsktbl; Im Bowling; Im Socr; High Hon Roll; Hon Roll; Community Wrk 84-85; Brown Belt Karate 86; U DE; Mech Engr.

DOUGHERTY, SHARON; Alexis I Du Pont HS; Hockessin, DE; (Y); Art Clb; Drama Clb; Exploring; Hosp Aide; School Play; Stu Cncl; Var JV Fld Hcky; JV Trk; Hon Roll; Photo.

DOWRICK, ED; Salesianum HS; Aston, PA; (Y); Cmnty Wkr; Debate Tm; Drama Clb; Hosp Aide; Speech Tm; SADD; Im Bsbl; Diving; Im Ftbl; Im Golf; Partial Schlrp Archmere 84; Piano & Art Awds 84-86; Temple; Pre-Med.

DOYLE, GREGORY; St Andrews Schl; Wilmington, DE; (Y); JCL; SADD; School Musical; Stage Crew; Nwsp Stf; Lit Mag; Crs Cntry; Hon Roll; Princeton U.

DRUMMOND, MICHELLE; Indian River HS; Clarksville, DE; (S); 32/213; SADD; Band; Chorus; Concert Band; Jazz Band; Mrchg Band; School Musical; Var Sftbl; Hon Roll; Jr NHS; Music.

DU ROSS, SUZANNE; Middletown HS; Smyrna, DE; (Y); 1/139; Science Clb; Spanish Clb; Yrbk Bus Mgr; Yrbk Ed-Chief; Rep Stu Cncl; Mgr(s); High Hon Roll; NHS; HOBY Ldrshp Sem 85; Gov Schl Excllnce 85; Grls ST 86; U DE; Bus.

DUJARI, RAJEEV; Seaford HS; Seaford, DE; (Y); 3/300; Capt Math Tm; Scholastic Bowl; Jazz Band; Mrchg Band; Var L Tennis; Bausch & Lomb Sci Awd; NHS; Boy Scts; Library Aide; High Hon Roll; Ntl Sci Sympsm 85 & 86; Ntl Frnch Cont 84-86; Amer Rgns Math Leag; Engrng.

DUNLAP, JIM; A I Dupont HS; Wilmington, DE; (Y); JV Socr; Hon Roll; Awd For All A's In Alg I & II 83-86; U Of DE.

DUNSMORE, MICHELLE; Glasgow HS; Newark, DE; (Y); 40/257; JA; JCL; Latin Clb; OEA; SADD; Teachers Aide; Sec Stu Cncl; Var Mgr(s); Var Sftbl; Hon Roll; Acad Exc Bio; Stu Gov Assoc Ltr; Psychlgy.

DUPHILY, DIONNE; Holy Cross HS; Dover, DE; (Y); Drama Clb; French Clb; JA; SADD; Church Choir; Bsktbl; U DE; Psychol.

DUPRE, SHELLEY; Seaford SR HS; Seaford, DE; (Y); OEA; VP Frsh Cls; VP Soph Cls; VP Jr Cls; VP Sr Cls; Var Capt French Clb; High Hon Roll; Hon Roll; Cert Pres U Of DE Acdmc Achvt 86; Pre-Law.

DURHAM, KAREN MARELLA; Dover HS; Dover, DE; (Y); 8/298; Church Yth Grp; French Clb; SADD; Teachers Aide; Flag Corp; Mrchg Band; Symp Band; Rep Stu Cncl; High Hon Roll; NHS; Awd Otstndng Frnch Stu 86; Awd Otstndng Schlsc Achvmnt 86; Awd Otstndng Srv Sci Dpt 86; VA Wesleyan Coll; Frnch Educ.

DURHAM, KEN; Dover HS; Dover, DE; (Y); French Clb; Hon Roll.

DURKIN, KEVIN; Archmere Acad; Brookhaven, PA; (S); SADD; Stage Crew; Bsbl; Bsktbl; High Hon Roll; Hon Roll; NHS; Philadelphia Phillies Regnl Hm Rn Champ 84 & 85; Engrng.

DUZAN, GARY; Christiana HS; Newark, DE; (Y); 13/310; Computer Clb; JA; Library Aide; Math Tm; Science Clb; SADD; Acpl Chr; Chorus; School Musical; NHS; Compu Sci.

DZIELAK, JEFFREY; Salesianum HS; Wilmington, DE; (S); 61/262; NHS; Ntl Merit Ltr; Partl Schlrshp Salesianum 82; U Of DE; Bus Adm.

EANES, JULIE; Dover HS; Dover, DE; (Y); 44/320; Hosp Aide; SADD; Chorus; Madrigals; Rep Frsh Cls; Rep Soph Cls; Bowling; Powder Puff Ftbl; Tennis; High Hon Roll; Outstndng Stdnt Kent Cnty 86; Henlopen Conf Champ Sngls 86; All Henlopen Conf Tm 86.

ECKBOLD, JANICE; Delcaste Vo Tech; Wilmington, DE; (Y); 5/419; Church Yth Grp; JA; VICA; Trs Stu Cncl; Bsktbl; Hon Roll; Pres NHS; Pres Schlr; VICA 1st Pl Wnnr Natl Competition Med Asstng 86; 3 Time 1st Pl Wnnr In ST VICA Competition Med Ast; Sacred Heart Hosp; Surg Tech.

ECKERSON, BETH; Alexis I Dupont HS; Hockessin, DE; (Y); Cmnty Wkr; FHA; Hosp Aide; Stage Crew; Yrbk Stf; Cheerleading; Hon Roll; Outstndng Wrk Chld Dvlpmt, Engl 85 & 86; Elizabethtwn Coll; Psych.

ECKRICH, DANIEL; Salesianum HS; Wilmington, DE; (Y); 5/292; Stu Cncl; Trk; High Hon Roll; NHS; All Cnty-Trck 86; All ST-TRCK 86.

EDWARDS, CHERYL; Wilmington HS; Wilmington, DE; (Y); 14/190; French Clb; JA; Math Tm; Pep Clb; SADD; VP Frsh Cls; Var Vllybl; Hon Roll; NHS; Prfct Atten Awd; Med.

EDWARDS, JENNY; William Penn HS; New Castle, DE; (Y); Am Leg Aux Girls St; Drama Clb; Science Clb; Ski Clb; Drill Tm; Flag Corp; School Play; Rep Stu Cncl; Capt Band Frnt 85-87; Pres Ldr Corps 85-86; Lead SR Clss Ply 85-86.

ELLINGSWORTH, BONNIE; Seaford HS; Seaford, DE; (Y); AFS; Church Yth Grp; JA; Math Tm; OEA; SADD; Capt Band; Concert Band; Drill Tm; Mrchg Band; NLSA-NATL Ldrshp & Srvc Awds 86; Rcgnzd DE Hse Reps-Schl & Commnty Achvts 85; U Of DE; Educ.

ELLIOTT, CHRISTINE; Indian River HS; Dagsboro, DE; (Y); 30/200; Church Yth Grp; French Clb; SADD; Chorus; Concert Band; Jazz Band; Mrchg Band; Pep Band; Capt Cheerleading; Hon Roll; Math.

ELLIS, ANDREW; Delmar JR SR HS; Delmar, DE; (Y); 8/95; Key Clb; Bsbl; Bsktbl; High Hon Roll; Hon Roll; NHS; U DE.

ELLIS, DAWN; Dover HS; Dover, DE; (Y); SADD; Band; Concert Band; Flag Corp; Mrchg Band; Symp Band; Bowling; High Hon Roll; Hon Roll; NHS; Outstndng Acdmc Achvt U DE 86.

ELLIS, MARGARET; Newark HS; Newark, DE; (Y); Church Yth Grp; Girl Scts; Office Aide; OEA; SADD; Teachers Aide; School Play; JV Cheerleading; U Of DE; Psychlgy.

ELLZY, JANELLE; Wilmington HS; Wilmington, DE; (Y); Cmnty Wkr; GAA; Girl Scts; JA; Pep Clb; SADD; Teachers Aide; Chorus; Mgr(s); Var L Trk.

ELSWICK, ROBIN; Laurel SR HS; Laurel, DE; (Y); VICA; VP Stu Cncl; Dance Clb; Chorus; Church Choir; School Musical; Im Cheerleading; Cit Awd; Hon Roll; Voice Dem Awd; Prprd Spch Lcls 1st Plc 84-85; Prprd Spch Lcls 4th Plc 85-86; DE ST Prep Spch Hon Men 85-86; Comp.

EMERICK, KRISTEN; John Dickinson HS; Wilmington, DE; (Y); 10/217; Church Yth Grp; JCL; Latin Clb; Color Guard; Nwsp Stf; Stu Cncl; Mgr(s); Tennis; Hon Roll; NHS; Fshn Merch.

EMORY, H ANDREW; Milford HS; Milford, DE; (Y); Pres Church Yth Grp; SADD; Varsity Clb; Church Choir; Pres Jr Cls; Stu Cncl; Var L Bsktbl; Var L Tennis; Hon Roll; NHS; 1st Tm All Cnfrnc Vrsty Bsktbl 85-86.

EMORY, SCOTT; Milford SR HS; Milford, DE; (Y); Varsity Clb; Stage Crew; Nwsp Stf; Im Ftbl; VP Tennis; Im Vllybl; Im Wt Lftg; JV Var Wrstlng; Hon Roll; Aero.

ENERIO, DEVI; Indian River HS; Dagsboro, DE; (Y); Church Yth Grp; Band; Sec Soph Cls; Sec Jr Cls; VP Stu Cncl; Var Cheerleading; High Hon Roll; NHS; Acadmc Excllnc Awd 86; Med.

ENERIO, EDELYN; Indian River HS; Dagsboro, DE; (S); 13/180; Math Tm; SADD; Band; Mrchg Band; School Musical; VP Soph Cls; Rep Sec Stu Cncl; JV Capt Cheerleading; High Hon Roll; NHS.

ENNIS, PAT; Smyrna HS; Smyrna, DE; (S); Stage Crew; Rep Frsh Cls; Rep Soph Cls; Rep Jr Cls; Var L Ftbl; Var L Trk; Hon Roll; NHS; Prfct Atten Awd; Bus Adm.

EPPS, CHRISTINA; Mount Pleasant HS; Wilmington, DE; (Y); 29/174; Office Aide; Band; Concert Band; Mrchg Band; Pep Band; Yrbk Bus Mgr; Yrbk Sprt Ed; Yrbk Stf; Hon Roll; Ger Soc PA 84; Nrsg.

ERFLE, DAVID; Salesianum HS; West Chester, PA; (S); 23/301; SADD; Var Ftbl; Im Socr; Var Wt Lftg; JV Wrstlng; NHS; Notre Dame; Pre-Med.

ERLING, LISA; Saint Marks HS; West Grove, PA; (Y); 50/356; Pep Clb; Rep Jr Cls; Var Capt Cheerleading; Var Coach Actv; Var Mgr(s); Hon Roll.

ERSKINE, BRIAN M; Salesianum HS; Newark, DE; (Y); 61/292; Church Yth Grp; Cmnty Wkr; Hosp Aide; Band; Drm & Bgl; Jazz Band; Mrchg Band; Orch; Trk; All Am Mc Donalds Band 86-87; Mech Engr.

ERVIN, SHERONDA; Mt Pleasant SR HS; Wilmington, DE; (Y); 65/173; JA; Pep Clb; Radio Clb; JV Vllybl; Prfct Atten Awd; Bus.

EVERHART, CHRISTOPHER; Alexis I Du Pont HS; Hockessin, DE; (Y); 10/210; Computer Clb; JA; Math Clb; Variety Show; Socr; Hon Roll; NHS; Acdmc Awd Indvl Subj 82-86; Larry Dubin Sci Awd 86; Clemson U; Elec Engrng.

EVERSMANN, ERIC; Salesianum Schl For Boys; Newark, DE; (Y); 45/300; SADD; Concert Band; Jazz Band; Mrchg Band; Symp Band; Im Bsktbl; Im Bowling; JV Crs Cntry; JV Trk; Ntl Merit SF.

FABIAN, KATHERINE F; Padua Acad; Wilmington, DE; (S); Pep Clb; Spanish Clb; Var Sftbl; Hon Roll; NHS; Spanish NHS; Medcn.

FALKOWSKI, TRACY; Padua Acadh; Boothwyn, PA; (Y); 32/213; Hosp Aide; Pep Clb; Red Cross Aide; Service Clb; Sec Soph Cls; Rep Jr Cls; Trs Stu Cncl; JV Fld Hcky; JV Swmmng; High Hon Roll; Med.

FARISS, KIMBERLY J; John Dickinson HS; Wilmington, DE; (Y); 45/185; Hon Roll; Offc Occptns Pgm Awd-Bst Co-Op 85-86; DE Tech CC; Bus Adm.

FARKAS, ALEXANDER P; Kent North Vo-Tech; Camden, DE; (S); OEA; 1st Pl Comp Emphss 86; 2nd Pl Comp Ltrcy 86; Poly-Tech Prgm 86; Del Tech; Data Prcssng.

FARMER, KELLY L; Thomas Mckean HS; Wilmington, DE; (S); 30/210; Chorus; School Musical; School Play; Variety Show; Nwsp Bus Mgr; Stu Cncl; Mgr(s); High Hon Roll; Hon Roll; NHS; Am Assoc U Women Schlrshp 86-87; U De Summer Theatre Inst 85; Drama.

FARRELL, ELIZABETH; Padula Acad; Wilmington, DE; (S); 22/215; JCL; Latin Clb; Pep Clb; SADD; JV Fld Hcky; Hon Roll; NHS; NEDT Awd; Govnrs Schl Excllnce 85; Notre Dame.

FARRELLY, LAURA; Laurel SR HS; Laurel, DE; (Y); 3/123; AFS; Am Leg Aux Girls St; Band; Concert Band; Pres Soph Cls; Trs Stu Cncl; Capt Fld Hcky; Sftbl; NHS; Hmcmng Attendnt 84-85; Psnsh I Dectfl Awd 84; Miss Laurel 86-87; Frgn Lang.

FATORA, STEVE; Salesianum HS; Wilmington, DE; (Y); 25/292; Aud/Vis; Cmnty Wkr; French Clb; SADD; Var L Ftbl; Im Socr; High Hon Roll; NHS; Norte Dm; Prmed.

FAVAZZA, YVETTE; Glasgow HS; Glendale Newark, DE; (S); DECA; Hosp Aide; JA; OEA; SADD; Chorus; Nwsp Stf; Bowling; Vllybl; Cit Awd; Wrttn Manual Awd App/Accss; Cert Awd Job DE Grads; Hghst Avg Bowling Lg; Bus.

FEELEY, JIM; St Marks HS; Claymont, DE; (Y); Var Crs Cntry; Var Trk; Dentist.

FEENEY, BROOKE; Delmar HS; Delmar, MD; (Y); 1/80; Am Leg Aux Girls St; FHA; Keywanettes; Pres Jr Cls; Hon Roll; NHS; VFW Awd; Frnch II Awd 3rd Plc 84-85; Frnch III Awd 1st Plc 85-86; Ge Awd 2nd Plc 85-86; Engl III Awd 2dn Plc.

FEENEY, KAREN; Archmere Acad; Greenville, DE; (Y); Cmnty Wkr; SADD; School Musical; School Play; Var Trk; NHS; Ntl Merit Ltr; Spanish NHS; AFS; Church Yth Grp; Schlrshp Archmere Acad 83; 2nd Pl Oral French Cntst 86; Frgn Rltns.

FEHL, RONALD D; Christiana HS; Newark, DE; (Y); 28/310; VP French Clb; OEA; SADD; Socr; Trk; Hon Roll; NHS; Outstndng Perf Wrld Studies; Accntng.

FELICE, CHARLES; Salesianum Schl; Westchester, PA; (Y); 102/298; Church Yth Grp; Cmnty Wkr; Hosp Aide; Spanish Clb; Off Soph Cls; Off Jr Cls; Bowling; JV Ftbl; Wt Lftg; Hon Roll; Med.

FELTY, MICHELE; Dover HS; Dover, DE; (Y); 54/300; Cmnty Wkr; Office Aide; Teachers Aide; Flag Corp; Mrchg Band; Symp Band; High Hon Roll; Hon Roll; NHS; All Amer Yth Hnr Band 85; Longwood Coll; Psychlgy.

FIELDS, JODI; Delmar HS; Delmar, MD; (Y); Am Leg Aux Girls St; Sec Key Clb; VP Frsh Cls; Rep Soph Cls; Sec Jr Cls; Var Bsktbl; Var Cheerleading; Var Sftbl; Hon Roll; Prfct Atten Awd; Salisburg ST; Elem Ed.

FIGGS, KIMBERLY; Delmar HS; Delmar, DE; (Y); 2/100; Church Yth Grp; FHA; Keywanettes; Color Guard; VP Soph Cls; VP Jr Cls; Var Co-Capt Cheerleading; Sec NHS; Cmnty Wkr; Hon Roll; Hghst Avg Engl III 85-86; Ntl NES Guld Awd 84-86; Messiah Coll; Elem Educ.

FILANDRO, CHRIS; Dover HS; Dover, DE; (Y); 26/400; Pres Church Yth Grp; JV Var Ftbl; Var Tennis; High Hon Roll; Jr NHS; Wnnr DE JR Sci Olympiad-Comp Sci 86; Comp Prgmr.

FINK, FRANKLIN; John Dickinson HS; Stanton, DE; (Y); 34/218; Hon Roll; Mchnst.

FINK, JONATHAN; Concord Christian Acad; Downingtown, PA; (S); 1/4; Chess Clb; Church Yth Grp; Computer Clb; Debate Tm; Chorus; Church Choir; Capt Bsktbl; Capt Socr; Theolgy.

FISHER, CATHY; Milford SR HS; Milford, DE; (Y); 2/200; Pres Church Yth Grp; VP Pres Varsity Clb; School Musical; VP Frsh Cls; VP Soph Cls; VP Jr Cls; Co-Capt Cheerleading; Tennis; High Hon Roll; Trs NHS; Gvrnrs Schl For Excllnc 85; 1st & 2nd Pl ST Spnsh Spkng Cntst 85-86.

FISHER, TARA; Concord HS; Wilmington, DE; (Y); Church Yth Grp; Cmnty Wkr; Girl Scts; JA; Trk; MVP Trck Tm 85-86; Set Trck Rcrd William Penn HS 800 M 83-84; Mrktng.

FITZGERALD, BRENDA; Delmar JR SR HS; Laurel, DE; (Y); FHA; FTA; Keywanettes; SADD; Rep Soph Cls; Rep Jr Cls; Trs Stu Cncl; Cheerleading; Hon Roll; 1st Pl Awds Shrthnd I & II 84-86; Goldey Beacom; Exec Secy.

FITZPATRICK JR, THOMAS J; Newark HS; Newark, DE; (Y); 8/335; Am Leg Boys St; Exploring; Trs German Clb; VP Intnl Clb; Capt Quiz Bowl; Rep Jr Cls; Off Sr Cls; NHS; Cngrss Bndstg Schlrshp Alt; Ctzn Bee Semi Fnlst; Biochem.

FLEETWOOD III, THOMAS C; St Marks HS; Wilmington, DE; (Y); 12/360; Chess Clb; Quiz Bowl; Scholastic Bowl; Teachers Aide; Stage Crew; Rep Jr Cls; Rep Sr Cls; Rep Stu Cncl; Var Tennis; Hon Roll; Prsdntl Acdmc Ftns Awd Prgrm 85-86; U Of DE; Law.

FLEISCHAUER, KAREN; Christian Tabernacle Acad; Greenwood, DE; (S); 1/9; Church Yth Grp; Band; Chorus; Church Choir; Yrbk Ed-Chief; Sec Jr Cls; Stu Cncl; Var Capt Bsktbl; Var Cheerleading; Var Vllybl; Intl Frgn Lang Assoc 84-85; Liberty U; Bus.

FLEISCHMAN, HEATHER; Brandywine HS; Wilmington, DE; (Y); DECA; Nwsp Phtg; Yrbk Stf; Var L Fld Hcky; Var L Gym; Hon Roll; Blue Hen Cnfrnc Acdmc All-Cnfrnc Tm; Syracuse U; Cmmnctns.

FLENNER, KATHERINE; Brandywine HS; Wilmington, DE; (Y); 43/245; Church Yth Grp; Hosp Aide; Office Aide; Band; Mrchg Band; Yrbk Stf; Capt VP Crs Cntry; L Trk; Hon Roll; Rotary Awd; Rtry Clb Schlrshp 86; U Of Delaware; Educ.

FLETCHER, DONYILE; Indian River HS; Frankford, DE; (Y); 68/202; Trs FFA; Im JV Bsbl; Im Ftbl; Green Hand Of Indian Rvr Chptr Degree 84; Mech Engr.

FLORIANI JR, BERNARD P; Dover HS; Dover, DE; (Y); 8/350; Math Tm; Science Clb; SADD; VP Frsh Cls; Rep Soph Cls; Rep Jr Cls; Var Capt Bsbl; Var L Golf; High Hon Roll; NHS; DE ST JR Golf Champ 85-86; All Henlopen Conf Bsktbl 86; All Henlopen Conf Golf 84-86.

FLOYD, JENNIFER; William Penn HS; New Castle, DE; (Y); Q&S; Ski Clb; Band; School Play; Nwsp Ed-Chief; Nwsp Rptr; Stat Bsbl; Score Keeper; Hon Roll; Concert Band; Outstndng Prfrmnc Jrnlsm William Pen 86; DE Schlstc Press Assn Outstndng Achvt Shlstc Jrnlsm 86; U Of AZ; Jrnlsm.

FLYNN, TRISHA; Padua Acad; Philadelphia, PA; (Y); Cmnty Wkr; JCL; Nwsp Rptr; Lit Mag; Hon Roll; Gifted Young Wrtrs Pgm 86; Poetry Publctns 86; Villanova U; Engl.

FOESTER, CHARLENE; Concord HS; Wilmington, DE; (Y); 8/300; Church Yth Grp; Latin Clb; Band; Color Guard; Concert Band; Sftbl; Vllybl; High Hon Roll; NHS; Nrsng.

FOLEY, CHRISTIAN; St Marks HS; Landenberg, PA; (Y); JA; Ski Clb; Rep Stu Cncl; Im Ftbl; Var Trk; Drexel 1; Financ.

FOLTZ, BECKI; Mt Pleasant HS; Wilmington, DE; (Y); Acpl Chr; Chorus; Church Choir; Madrigals; School Musical; Yrbk Rptr; Yrbk Stf; Hon Roll; Ntl Merit Ltr; Govs Schl Excllnce 85; Photo Mgr Yrbk 85; Yth Rep Uster Proj 85-86; Mrktng.

FORD, PAUL; Salesianum Schl; Wilmington, DE; (Y); Art Clb; Pres VP Church Yth Grp; Cmnty Wkr; JCL; Office Aide; Political Wkr; Band; Concert Band; Symp Band; Nwsp Stf; Soc Sci.

FORD, YVETTE; Dover HS; Little Creek, DE; (Y); Office Aide; Sec OEA; Teachers Aide; Bowling; High Hon Roll; Hon Roll; Hugh Brian Yth Cnfrnc Awd 84; OEA Fll Ldrshp Cnfrnc 84; Sec.

FORESTER, VINCENT; Salesianum HS; Wilmington, DE; (S); 13/272; Boy Scts; VP French Clb; Mrchg Band; Orch; Symp Band; Ed Yrbk Rptr; NHS; Ntl Merit Ltr; Elec Engr.

FORTUNA, MARIA G; Padua Acad; Philadelphia, PA; (S); 1/213; Dance Clb; Hosp Aide; VP Science Clb; Rep Service Clb; Stu Cncl; Fld Hcky; High Hon Roll; NHS; Ntl Merit Ltr; Ellis Fdtn Tuition Schlrshp 82-85; Slvr Mdl Ntl Latin, Cert NEDT 84; Immaculata; Pre Med.

FOSKEY, KAREN; Seaford SR HS; Seaford, DE; (Y); Church Yth Grp; Cmnty Wkr; Office Aide; SADD; Color Guard; School Play; JV Var Cheerleading; Hon Roll; German Stu Mnth 86.

FOSS, DAVID; Alexis I Du Pont HS; Hockessin, DE; (Y); 16/216; Boy Scts; Church Yth Grp; VP Exploring; Teachers Aide; Stage Crew; Variety Show; Hon Roll; NHS; Ntl Merit Ltr; Pres Acadmc Fitns Awd 86; Oberlin Coll.

FOSS, LAUREN; A I Du Pont HS; Hockessin, DE; (Y); 7/260; Church Yth Grp; Dance Clb; Pres Trs Exploring; Church Choir; Flag Corp; Stage Crew; Hon Roll; NHS; Mst Outstndng Stu IPS Sci 84; Mst Outstndng Stu Albgra II Trig 85.

FOSTER, SEAN; Saint Marks HS; Newark, DE; (Y); Aud/Vis; Chess Clb; Computer Clb; Chorus; Stage Crew; U Of DE; Chem Engrng.

FOULK, BRIAN; Alexis I Du Pont HS; Hockessin, DE; (Y); 65/220; Church Yth Grp; CAP; German Clb; ROTC; Concert Band; Symp Band; Stu Cncl; Ftbl; Hon Roll; Prfct Atten Awd; CAR VP 85; Air Force ROTC Schlrshp 86; Delaware U; Physics.

FOUNTAIN, MICHAEL; Smyrna HS; Smyrna, DE; (Y); French Clb; Band; Concert Band; Jazz Band; Mrchg Band; Symp Band; Nwsp Rptr; Nwsp Stf; Rep Frsh Cls; Rep Stu Cncl.

FOX, ANDREA; Dover HS; Dover, DE; (Y); French Clb; Band; Concert Band; Mrchg Band; Symp Band; Comp Sci.

FOXX III, HENRY TIMOTHY; William Penn HS; New Castle, DE; (Y); Church Yth Grp; Key Clb; Library Aide; Scholastic Bowl; Spanish Clb; Yrbk Stf; Pres Stu Cncl; Ftbl; Wt Lftg; Prfct Atten Awd; Corp Law.

FRALLIC, DEBBIE; Seaford SR HS; Seaford, DE; (Y); AFS; VP Church Yth Grp; Hst Key Clb; OEA; Color Guard; Mrchg Band; School Play; Pediatrican.

FRANCIS, SIMONE; Claymont HS; Wilmington, DE; (Y); Drama Clb; Office Aide; Scholastic Bowl; Spanish Clb; Chorus; Church Choir; Flag Corp; Mrchg Band; FAME 82-85; BDEA 83-86; SADD Pstr Cntst-1st Pl 85-86; Howard U; Photo.

FRANCISCO, PAUL; Caravel Acad; Newark, DE; (S); 1/35; Cmnty Wkr; Math Tm; Teachers Aide; Temple Yth Grp; Yrbk Phtg; Yrbk Stf; Var Bsbl; Var Ftbl; High Hon Roll; Stage Crew; H S Schlrshp 84-86; ST Calculator Fair-1st Pl 85; U Of MI.

FRENCH, MISSY; New Castle Baptist Acad; Bear, DE; (Y); Church Yth Grp; Sec Frsh Cls; Trs Sec Jr Cls; Var Cheerleading; Hon Roll; Natl Englsh Mrt Awd 84; Englsh.

FRENCK, SCOTT; Newark HS; Newark, DE; (Y); 69/316; VP L Tennis; Aerospc Engr.

FRESE, PAUL; Dickinson HS; Wilmington, DE; (Y); Rep Frsh Cls; Rep Soph Cls; Rep Jr Cls; Var Capt Ftbl; Var Capt Swmmng; Var L Trk; Hon Roll; Jr NHS; Chrprctcs.

FREY, MATTHEW; Delmar HS; Delmar, MD; (Y); 3/112; AFS; Am Leg Boys St; Boy Scts; Key Clb; School Play; Yrbk Stf; Pres Frsh Cls; Pres Soph Cls; JV Var Ftbl; JV Wrstlng; Congrss Bundestag Yth Exchng Prg 85-86; Senator Bill Roths Yth Ldrshp Conf 85; Sci Olympiad 84-85; U Of MD; Pol Sci.

FRIEDRICH, CHERYL; Mount Pleasant HS; Wilmington, DE; (Y); #28 In Class; VP Capt JA; Teachers Aide; Trs Yrbk Stf; Hon Roll; Exec Scrtry.

FRIES, NICOLE; Tower Hill HS; Newark, DE; (Y); Sec Trs AFS; Drama Clb; French Clb; Chorus; School Musical; School Play; Yrbk Rptr; Lit Mag; Sec Trs Soph Cls; Var JV Fld Hcky; Olympcs Mind ST Champ Cptn 84-86; Med.

FROEHLICH, JENNIFER; Concord HS; Wilmington, DE; (Y); 30/300; Sec Church Yth Grp; Chorus; School Musical; High Hon Roll; Hon Roll; NHS.

FROGGATT, STACY; Claymont HS; Claymont, DE; (Y); 15/127; French Clb; JA; Teachers Aide; Varsity Clb; Band; Concert Band; Drm Mjr(t); Mrchg Band; Orch; NHS; Alld Chemcl Awd 86; Al-ST Band 82; Acadmc Al-Conf Tm 85; St Andrews Presbytrn; Chem Engr.

FUCHS, KIRA; Tower Hill Schl; Wilmington, DE; (Y); Teachers Aide; Var Tennis; High Hon Roll; Im Trk; JV Im Fld Hcky; Im Bsktbl; Lit Mag; SADD; JA; AFS; Natl Spnsh Cont 3rd Pl Lvl 3 & 4th Pl Lvl 4 85-86; 1st Pl Natl Frnch Cotn Rgnl Lvl-Lvl 2.

FUKUMURA, SANDY; Indian River HS; Selbyville, DE; (Y); Church Yth Grp; Math Tm; SADD; Stu Cncl; Mgr(s); Trk; High Hon Roll; Atlantic Rgnl Math Lge 85.

FULLER, JERRY; William Penn HS; New Castle, DE; (Y); French Clb; French Hon Soc; High Hon Roll; Hon Roll; Prfct Atten Awd; U Of Delaware; Comp Sci.

FULLER II, RICHARD; Salesianum HS; Brookhaven, PA; (Y); 12/292; Cmnty Wkr; Hosp Aide; Im Bowling; Hon Roll; NHS; Drexel U; Comp Eng.

FURBUSH, PAM; Smyrna HS; Smyrna, DE; (S); 15/200; Rep Jr Cls; Sec Stu Cncl; JV Fld Hcky; Capt Var Trk; High Hon Roll; NHS; Prncpls Awd Acad Achvmnt 84-86; U Of DFE Rcgntn Acad Achvmnt 85-86; Med.

GABLE, ANNE; St Marks HS; Newark, DE; (Y); 20/346; Office Aide; Yrbk Stf; Rep Jr Cls; Rep Sr Cls; Mgr(s); High Hon Roll; Hon Roll; NHS; Pres Acdmc Ftns Awd 86; Schlrshp Genrl Educ Fnd 86; Pst Scndry ST DE Schlrshp 86; U Of DE; Spec Educ.

GACKENBACH, MINDY; Concord HS; Wilmington, DE; (Y); 25/300; Pres Church Yth Grp; FCA; Office Aide; Church Choir; Mrchg Band; Rep Frsh Cls; Var Fld Hcky; Powder Puff Ftbl; Hon Roll; NHS; Elem Educ.

GALL, CHRISTINA; Dover HS; Dover, DE; (Y); French Clb; German Clb; Hosp Aide; JA; Tennis; High Hon Roll; NHS.

GALLO, MARIA ELIZABETH; Cape Henlopen HS; Lewes, DE; (Y); Drama Clb; Mathletes; Ski Clb; Pres Thesps; Band; Chorus; Mrchg Band; School Musical; School Play; Nwsp Rptr; U Of DE; Cmmnctns.

GANN, VICKI; William Penn HS; Del City, DE; (Y); JA; Office Aide; Teachers Aide; Schlrshp Dale Carneige Crs 83-85; Goldey Beacom; Comp Prog.

GARNIEWSKI, CHRISTINA; Padua Acad; New Castle, DE; (S); Dance Clb; Im Bsktbl; Im Sftbl; High Hon Roll; NHS; Ntl Merit Ltr; Lang Awd Tchrs Assn Amer 85; Italian Clb Treas 85-86; Phrmcy.

GARRISON IV, NORRIS B; Dover HS; Dover, DE; (Y); 13/301; Am Leg Boys St; Boy Scts; Trs French Clb; Office Aide; Political Wkr; SADD; Teachers Aide; Church Choir; Concert Band; Mrchg Band; Kent Cnty Acad Awd 85; Princeton U; Aerospc Engrg.

GARZA, GAYLE; Caravel Acad; Newark, DE; (S); 3/43; Dance Clb; Teachers Aide; School Musical; Yrbk Stf; Im Bsbl; Var Co-Capt Cheerleading; JV Vllybl; High Hon Roll; Hon Roll; Pres Schlr; Spnsh Outstndng Achvt Awd 85; Eng,Math Awd 83-85; West Chester; Elem Ed.

GAUCHER, MICHAEL R; Thomas Mc Kean HS; Wilmington, DE; (S); 34/217; Cmnty Wkr; Q&S; Nwsp Sprt Ed; Nws Edtr; Feature Edtr; Engl.

GAWINSKI, TERESA; St Elizabeth HS; Wilmington, DE; (Y); 7/100; Am Leg Aux Girls St; Sec Church Yth Grp; Pep Clb; Service Clb; SADD; Nwsp Ed-Chief; Lit Mag; Rep Sr Cls; Crs Cntry; Trk; John B Lynch Schlrshp 86; Pres Acad Ftns Awd 86; U DE; Eng.

GEANOPULOS, GEORGIEAN; Corcord HS; Wilmington, DE; (Y); 14/270; Drama Clb; Hosp Aide; JA; Library Aide; Office Aide; Teachers Aide; Chorus; School Musical; Yrbk Rptr; Yrbk Stf; Merit Schrlshp U DE 86; Hellenic U Clb Schlrshp 86; Fnlst Miss Teen DE 85; U DE; Pol Sci.

GEESE, JANET; Newark SR HS; Newark, DE; (Y); Church Yth Grp; French Clb; Yrbk Phtg; JV Var Socr; Hon Roll; U Of DE.

GEMPP, STEVEN; Salesignum HS; Hockessin, DE; (Y); Church Yth Grp; Pep Clb; Rep Jr Cls; Rep Sr Cls; VP Stu Cncl; Im Bsktbl; Im Socr; Hon Roll; Oblates St Francis De Sales Awd Ldrshp & Svc 86; Loyola Coll; Predntstry.

GERAN, DENISE; Padua Acad; Wilmington, DE; (S); 7/185; Hosp Aide; Library Aide; High Hon Roll; NHS; NEDT Awd; Spanish NHS; Natl Sci Olympiad Awd-Bio & Chem 83 & 84; Bus Adm.

GERKEN, MELISSA; Indian River HS; Dagsboro, DE; (S); Cmnty Wkr; Library Aide; Office Aide; Spanish Clb; Stat Bsbl; Var L Fld Hcky; High Hon Roll; Jr NHS; NHS; Early Chldhd Ed.

GERSHMAN, JEFFREY D; Newark HS; Newark, DE; (Y); 13/348; Pres Band; Jazz Band; Sec Mrchg Band; Symp Band; Variety Show; Gov Hon Prg Awd; High Hon Roll; NHS; All-ST Bnd Tuba 84-86; Music.

GESTY, DIANE; Archmere Acad; Claymont, DE; (Y); Church Yth Grp; VP JA; Math Tm; Concert Band; Lit Mag; Stu Cncl; Var Mgr Bsktbl; Var Mgr Ftbl; Var Mgr Socr; NHS; Oberlin Schlrshp 86; Boston U Schrlshp 86; Syracuse Schrlshp 86; Oberlin Coll; Biochem.

GIAMBRONE, BIAGIA; Padua Acad; Wilmington, DE; (Y); Cmnty Wkr; Dance Clb; Pep Clb; Tennis; Hon Roll; Dectfl Oral Lang Cont Italian II 2nd Pl 85, 3rd Pl III 86; Hghst GPA Italian III 86; Neumann Coll; Pol Sci.

GIBBS, PAULETTE; Dover HS; Dover, DE; (S); 133/400; Church Yth Grp; VP DECA; JA; Leo Clb; OEA; Pep Clb; Church Choir; Rep Sr Cls; High Hon Roll; Hon Roll; Delaware ST; Mktg.

GILBERT, ADONIS; Cape Henlopen HS; Milton, DE; (Y); Computer Clb; Letterman Clb; Spanish Clb; Varsity Clb; JV Bsbl; Var Bsktbl; Var Bowling; JV Ftbl; High Hon Roll; Hon Roll; De Vry Inst Of Tech; Elctrncs.

GIORDANO, CAROLYN; Padua Acad; Philadelphia, PA; (S); Science Clb; Hon Roll; Ntl Sci Merit, Bio & Typng Awds 85; Drexel U; Engrng.

GIRARDI, ANDREW; St Marks HS; Wilmington, DE; (Y); 84/360; Church Yth Grp; Cmnty Wkr; SADD; Rep Jr Cls; CC Awd; Hon Roll; U DE; Lawyer.

GIULIANI, JENNIFER; Padua Acad; Newark, DE; (Y); Church Yth Grp; JA; Pep Clb; Spanish Clb; Hon Roll; Spanish NHS; AATSP Spnsh Cntst 1st,3rd,2nd Pl 83-86; U DE; Bus Adm.

GIUNTA, KIMBERLY ANN; Archmere Acad; Westchester, PA; (Y); Cmnty Wkr; French Clb; JV Crs Cntry; JV Var Fld Hcky; Powder Puff Ftbl; Var Trk; Hon Roll; Boston Coll; Intnl Law.

GLAESER, BARBARA; A I Du Pont HS; Wilmington, DE; (Y); 69/275; Drama Clb; Hosp Aide; Var Fld Hcky; JV Swmmng; Hon Roll; U Of DE; Spcl Ed.

GLASS, LAURA A; Mount Pleasant HS; Wilmington, DE; (Y); Am Leg Aux Girls St; Pres Church Yth Grp; Cmnty Wkr; Ski Clb; Teachers Aide; Acpl Chr; Church Choir; School Musical; Stu Cncl; Prfct Atten Awd; Music Hon Awd 84 & 85; Erly Chldhd Educ.

GLAUM, MARK C; Salesianum HS; Thorndale, PA; (Y); 72/301; Church Yth Grp; Latin Clb; Ski Clb; Concert Band; Mrchg Band; Orch; Symp Band; Hon Roll; Notre Dame; Engrng.

GLOGOWSKI, CHRISTIE; Padua Acad; Wilmington, DE; (S); Cmnty Wkr; Drama Clb; JA; Latin Clb; Pep Clb; School Musical; Variety Show; Rep Jr Cls; Rep Stu Cncl; Var Cheerleading; USSCA 85-86; U Of VA; Arch.

GLOGOWSKI, KRISTI; Padua Acad; Wilmington, DE; (Y); Computer Clb; JCL; Pep Clb; School Musical; Rep Jr Cls; Cheerleading; Coach Actv; High Hon Roll; Ntl Merit Ltr; U S Stu Cncl Awd 85; Boston Coll; Pre-Law.

GLOYOWSKI, CHRISTIE; Padua Acad; Middletown, DE; (Y); Cmnty Wkr; Latin Clb; Pep Clb; School Play; Rep Jr Cls; Pres Sr Cls; Var Cheerleading; High Hon Roll; Ntl Merit Ltr; Lgl Prfsn.

GLYNN, MICHAEL; John Dickinson HS; Wilmington, DE; (Y); Bsbl; JV Socr; Archtrl Eng.

GOATE, DENISE; Dover HS; Dover, DE; (Y); 20/294; PAVAS; Band; Mrchg Band; Symp Band; Trs Frsh Cls; Trs Soph Cls; Gov Hon Prg Awd; High Hon Roll; NHS; Mary W Hearn Schlrshp 86; Teacher Of Year Schlrshp 86; Most Outstndng Instrmntl Music Stu 86; James Madison U; Erly Chldhd Ec.

GOLDBERG, DOUGLAS; Salesianum HS; Wilmington, DE; (S); 15/300; Aud/Vis; Spanish Clb; Band; Jazz Band; Jr NHS; NHS.

GOLDER, LYNN; Caesar Rodney HS; Magnolia, DE; (Y); 98/342; OEA; JV L Cheerleading; Hon Roll; 7th Pl Shrthnd I In ST 84-85; Kent Co Ed Sec Assn Schlrshp 86; Outstndg Bus Stu Of Yr Awd 86; Bradford Schl; Exec Sec.

GOODIER, SHAWN; Middletown HS; Middletown, DE; (Y); 3/135; Boy Scts; Computer Clb; Mathletes; ROTC; Science Clb; Spanish Clb; Varsity Clb; Var Capt Wrstlng; Bausch & Lomb Sci Awd; High Hon Roll; Wrstlng-6th ST, 2nd AAU Mid-Atlntc 85-86; Afrotc Schlrshp, Army Schlr-Athlt Awd 86; Prncpls Awd; Duke U; Elec Engrng.

GOPEZ, MELISSA; Archmere Acad; Greenville, DE; (S); Cmnty Wkr; French Clb; Hosp Aide; Concert Band; JV Capt Cheerleading; French Hon Soc; Hon Roll; NHS.

GORDON, EDWARD; Laurel SR HS; Laurel, DE; (Y); 7/114; Rep Jr Cls; JV Bsktbl; JV Ftbl; L Var Trk; Hon Roll; NHS; 49th Boys St Rep 86; Sci Olympcs 84.

GOSLEE, JOHN; Seaford SR HS; Seaford, DE; (Y); Drama Clb; Scholastic Bowl; School Play; Stage Crew; Rep Stu Cncl; Hon Roll.

GOTTSCHALCK, AL; Thomas Mc Kean HS; Hockessin, DE; (Y); 29/250; Nwsp Rptr; Nwsp Sprt Ed; Nwsp Stf; Bsktbl; Hon Roll; Jr NHS; U Of DE; Bus.

GOULD, LORRI; Indian River HS; Selbyville, DE; (S); 25/202; Library Aide; Spanish Clb; Sec Yrbk Stf; High Hon Roll; Hon Roll; Jr NHS; Outstndng Acad Achvt HS Awd 86; Psychlgy.

GRAHAM, RODNELL; William Penn HS; New Castle, DE; (Y); Art Clb; JA; Church Choir; Hon Roll; Signfcnt Imprvmt Engl 83-84; Comp Sci.

GRALEWSKI, ROBERT; Salesianum HS; Wilmington, DE; (S); 15/301; Church Yth Grp; SADD; Stu Cncl; Var Bsbl; JV Bsktbl; NHS; Law.

GRANEY, COLLEEN; St Marks HS; Newark, DE; (Y); Church Yth Grp; JA; Sftbl; Hon Roll; U DE; Child Psychlgy.

GRANITO, STEFAN; Saint Andrews Schl; Manasquan, NJ; (Y); Model UN; School Play; Nwsp Ed-Chief; Ed Lit Mag; High Hon Roll; Ntl Merit SF; Pres Schlr; Camera Clb; JCL; Math Tm; Sci, Drama, Crafts Awds 83 & 85.

GRANT, MATTHEW; Salesianum HS; New Castle, DE; (Y); 28/292; Spanish Clb; SADD; Bowling; High Hon Roll; NHS; Arch.

GRAY, MAURICE M; William Penn HS; New Castle, DE; (Y); 27/480; Spanish Clb; Acpl Chr; Chorus; Church Choir; Nwsp Stf; Hon Roll; Pres Schlr; Acadmc Schlrshp U Of De 86; U Of DE; Jrnlsm.

GREEN, JACKIE; Claymont HS; Claymont, DE; (Y); 5/100; Spanish Clb; SADD; Varsity Clb; Mrchg Band; Trs Soph Cls; Trs Jr Cls; Trs Sr Cls; Sec Rep Stu Cncl; High Hon Roll; Hon Roll; Govrnr Schl 85; Grls ST 86; Ctzn Bee 86; Phy Thrpy.

GREEN, JULIA; Paucua Acad; Middletown, DE; (Y); 44/213; Sec Church Yth Grp; Pres 4-H; Band; Mrchg Band; Symp Band; Nwsp Ed-Chief; Mgr(s); Sftbl; 4-H Awd; Hon Roll; Outstndng Yth In DE 86; Lbrl Arts Coll; Brdcst Jrnlsm.

GREEN, KELLY; Middletown HS; Smyrna, DE; (Y); 2/130; Mathletes; Science Clb; Spanish Clb; Nwsp Ed-Chief; Mgr(s); High Hon Roll; Jr NHS; NHS; Sci Olympcs 84-86; VFW Girls St 86; Distngshd Amer Stu 85; Pub Rltns.

GREEN, LESLIE; Brandywine HS; Wilmington, DE; (Y); 14/250; Cmnty Wkr; Dance Clb; VP Drama Clb; Ski Clb; Chorus; Church Choir; School Musical; School Play; Stage Crew; Variety Show; Dstngshd Schlr 86; All ST Chrs 84-86; James Madison U; Comm.

GREEN, WENDY; Padua Acad; Wilmington, DE; (Y); 51/180; JCL; Pep Clb; Church Choir; Nwsp Phtg; Nwsp Rptr; Rep Soph Cls; Rep Jr Cls; VP Stu Cncl; Alpha Kappa Alpha Debutante 86; Hampton U; Bus Mgmnt.

GREENLY, JEFF D; Milford SR HS; Milford, DE; (Y); Cmnty Wkr; Varsity Clb; Var Capt Bsbl; JV Bsktbl; High Hon Roll; Hon Roll; Bsbl Schlrshp DE ST Coll 86; All-ST Selctn All Henlpn Conf 86; DE All-Star Carpntr Cup Membr 86; DE ST Coll; Arts.

GREGORY, ALLISYN; Delcastle Technical HS; Wilmington, DE; (Y); Yrbk Stf; Phtgrphy.

GREGORY, MATTHEW; Wilmington Friends HS; Wilmington, DE; (Y); Am Leg Boys St; Library Aide; Chorus; Nwsp Ed-Chief; Nwsp Rptr; Lit Mag; Trs Frsh Cls; Pres Soph Cls; JV Bsktbl; Var L Ftbl; Cmmndtn Acad Excllnce Advncd U S Hstry 86; Hnrb Mntn Gavel Princeton Mod Cngrss 85; Prism Lit Cont 86; Law.

GRELAK, KURT; St Marks HS; Newark, DE; (Y); Hnr Rll 85-86; Del Tech; Music.

GRIECO, JUDY; Padua Acad; Claymont, DE; (Y); Church Yth Grp; Cmnty Wkr; JA; Trk; Hon Roll; Awd Tutrng Clymnt Cntr Excptnl Wrk 84-85.

GRIETEN, JOHN; Newark HS; Newark, DE; (Y); Boy Scts; Pres Church Yth Grp; Library Aide; VP SADD; Chorus; Church Choir; Drm Mjr(t); Nwsp Rptr; Wrk Human Rel Pgm Org 86; U DE; Aviation.

GRIFFIN, CRISTI; John Dickinson HS; Newark, DE; (Y); Am Leg Aux Girls St; Thesps; School Musical; Swing Chorus; Var Capt Cheerleading; NHS; Church Yth Grp; Chorus; School Play; VP Frsh Cls; All St-Chorus 86; Natl Choral Awd 86; Miss Teen Of DE 86-87; Miss DE US Teen 86; U Of DE; TV.

GRIFFITH, JULIE; Brandywine HS; Wilmington, DE; (Y); Art Clb; Dance Clb; Hosp Aide; JA; Pep Clb; Political Wkr; Spanish Clb; SADD; Flag Corp; School Musical; Princeton; Drama.

GRIFFITH, WENDY; Laurel SR HS; Laurel, DE; (Y); 5/129; Trs AFS; Am Leg Aux Girls St; Hst OEA; Band; Trs Sr Cls; VP Stu Cncl; Sftbl; Bausch & Lomb Sci Awd; Hon Roll; Sec NHS; Hugh O Brian Yth Fndtn Ldrshp Conf 84; U Of DE; Chem Engrng.

GRINE, TIFFANY; Christiana HS; New Caslte, DE; (Y); 1/350; Pres Am Leg Aux Girls St; French Clb; Math Tm; SADD; Chorus; School Musical; Off Jr Cls; Off Sr Cls; Var Tennis; High Hon Roll; U Of DE.

GROCE, DINETTA; Padua Acad; Chester, PA; (Y); 58/213; Hosp Aide; Pep Clb; SADD; Rep Frsh Cls; Rep Soph Cls; Bsktbl; Hon Roll; Spanish NHS; Pres Spanish Clb; Actvty-Xinos Sorority Phi Del Kappa; Pre Med.

GROSS, MARLENE; Brandywine HS; Wilmington, DE; (S); Cmnty Wkr; DECA; Exploring; JA; Hon Roll; Bus.

GROSS, PAULA; Ursuline Acad; Wilmington, DE; (Y); 6/62; Church Yth Grp; Model UN; Pres Frsh Cls; Rep Jr Cls; Pres Jr Cls; Bsktbl; Var Capt Tennis; Var Capt Vllybl; Hon Roll; NHS; Le High U.

GUTOWSKI, SLOAN; Salesianum HS; Newark, DE; (Y); 59/301; JV Trk; Hon Roll; Archit.

HACKETT, SHERRI; Ursuline Acad; Wilmington, DE; (Y); SADD; Bsktbl; Mgr(s); Hon Roll; Mt St Marys; Bus.

HAHN, ROBERT; Salesianum Schl; Wilminton, DE; (Y); 25/301; JCL; Band; Concert Band; Mrchg Band; Symp Band; High Hon Roll; Hon Roll; NHS; Cert Hnrb Merit Maxima Cum Laude Natl Latin Exam; Elec Engrng.

HALL, BRIAN L; Sussex Central SR HS; Millsboro, DE; (Y); 3/216; Am Leg Boys St; Church Yth Grp; Rep Soph Cls; JV Bsktbl; High Hon Roll; NHS; Amer Lgn Boys ST 86; GA Tech MITE Engrng Pgm 86; Bill Roth Yth Ldrshp Conf 86; DE ST Coll; Engrng.

HALL, KIRK; John Dickinson HS; Wilmington, DE; (Y); Art Clb; Im Vllybl; Hon Roll; Acad Recgtn Assn 85; Sci.

HALL, LAREESE; Concord HS; Claymont, DE; (Y); 32/274; Pres AFS; Teachers Aide; Drill Tm; Ed Yrbk Stf; JV Tennis; Hon Roll; Pres Schlr; Alpha Kappa Alpha Sorority Scholar 86; Oberlin Coll; Jrnlsm.

HALL, MARY ELIZABETH; Seaford SR HS; Seaford, DE; (Y); 12/186; Am Leg Aux Girls St; GAA; Sec Jr Cls; Sec Sr Cls; Var Fld Hcky; Capt Trk; Gov Hon Prg Awd; NHS; Pres Schlr; Yrbk Stf; Acorn Clb Schlrshp 86; Kutz Fndtn Schlrshp 86; Irene F Larrimore Schlrshp 86; James Madison U; Elem Educ.

HALL, TIM; Dover HS; Dover, DE; (Y); 1/306; Am Leg Boys St; Math Tm; Band; Pres Frsh Cls; Pres Soph Cls; Socr; Swmmng; Tennis; Bausch & Lomb Sci Awd; Gov Hon Prg Awd; Engr.

HALLEY, CHRISTY; Alexis I Du Pont HS; Newark, DE; (Y); 2/260; Drill Tm; Mrchg Band; Rep Soph Cls; Trs Jr Cls; Stu Cncl; Var L Mgr(s); Pom Pon; Var L Sftbl; High Hon Roll; Sec NHS; Physcl Thrpy.

HAMBRIGHT, STEPHEN; Concord HS; Wilmington, DE; (Y); 45/277; Boy Scts; FCA; Science Clb; Teachers Aide; Thesps; Band; Concert Band; Jazz Band; Mrchg Band; School Play; Blue Hen Conf All Acad Awd 85-86; Engrng.

HANCE, LAWRENCE; Salesianum HS; Wilmington, DE; (Y); 62/301; Aud/Vis; Chess Clb; JCL; Scholastic Bowl; Off Soph Cls; Off Jr Cls; Im Bsktbl; Im Bowling; Im Socr; Elks Awd; Natl Latin Exam Cum Laude 84; Delaware Latin Exam Cum Laude 84; Notre Dame; Bus.

HANDSBERRY, LISA; Smyrna HS; Smyrna, DE; (S); 1/218; Am Leg Aux Girls St; OEA; Var JV Bsktbl; Var JV Tennis; High Hon Roll; NHS; Voice Dem Awd; Lit Mag; Prfct Atten Awd; Top Mag Sls Jr; Phoenix Prog Gftd Stu; Amer Lgn Awd Civics; Tufts; Arch Engr.

HANNA, MICHAEL; Milford HS; Milford, DE; (Y); 24/143; Boy Scts; Cmnty Wkr; Pep Clb; Varsity Clb; Nwsp Stf; Yrbk Stf; VP Soph Cls; Var Capt Ftbl; Var Wrstlng; Hon Roll; MVP-VRSTY Ftbl 84; U Of FL; Sys Engrng.

HANSON, JAMES; Christiana HS; Newark, DE; (Y); 81/301; Ski Clb; Var Bsbl; Var Ftbl; Hon Roll; Acad All Conf Ftbl 84-86; 1st Team All Conf Ftbl 85-86; Wrld Studies Awd 85-86.

HANSON, JAMES; Salesianum Schl; Wilmington, DE; (S); 15/301; Boy Scts; Church Yth Grp; Cmnty Wkr; Office Aide; Spanish Clb; Off Soph Cls; Off Jr Cls; Mgr(s); High Hon Roll; Hon Roll; Lehigh U; Cvl Engr.

HARACH, MARY; Saint Marks HS; Newark, DE; (Y); Math Tm; Mrchg Band; Trk; Hon Roll; Prfct Atten Awd; U Of DE; Lab Tech.

HARISTON, KELLY; Brandywine HS; Wilmington, DE; (Y); 30/250; Am Leg Aux Girls St; Civic Clb; Cmnty Wkr; Exploring; Latin Clb; Pep Clb; Stat Bsktbl; Stat Fld Hcky; Hon Roll; NEDT Awd; Mech Engrng.

HARMON, BILLY; Delcastle Technical HS; Wilmington, DE; (Y); 129/508; Church Yth Grp; SADD; Church Choir; JV Bsbl; Var Ftbl; JV Wrstlng; Hon Roll; Boys Clb Am; Boy Scts; Sheet Mtl Fbrctn Cmndtns 84-86; Bsbl, Ftbl, Wrstlng Ltrs 84-86; Sheet Mtl Mchnc.

HARPER, KATHERINE; Claymont HS; Wilmington, DE; (Y); 17/118; DECA; French Clb; JA; Office Aide; OEA; Scholastic Bowl; Yrbk Stf; Hon Roll; Keeping Pace Wilmington Acad Awd 85; Richard A Wright Outstndng Enrollee Awd 85; Accntnt.

HARRELL, ERICA; William Penn HS; New Castle, DE; (Y); Sec JA; Teachers Aide; Mrchg Band; Symp Band; Rep Stu Cncl; Hon Roll; Nursing.

HARRIS, LISA; Dover HS; Dover, DE; (Y); Church Yth Grp; OEA; Trk; High Hon Roll; Hon Roll; NHS; Otstndng Stu DE 86; Accntng.

HARRIS, MAJOR; Wilmington HS; Wilmington, DE; (Y); Cmnty Wkr; Debate Tm; JA; Political Wkr; Temple Yth Grp; Drill Tm; Variety Show; Stu Cncl; Bsktbl; Coach Actv; Comp Sci.

HARRIS, SANDRA J; Christian Tabernacle Acad; Georgetown, DE; (S); Church Yth Grp; Cmnty Wkr; Political Wkr; Yrbk Stf; Sec Frsh Cls; Bsktbl; Capt Cheerleading; Capt Sftbl; Capt Vllybl; Hon Roll; Liberty U-Lynchburg; Bus Adm.

HARRISON, CHRISTINE; Indian River HS; Dagsboro, DE; (S); Spanish Clb; SADD; Chorus; Concert Band; Mrchg Band; Rep Stu Cncl; Var Fld Hcky; Var Tennis; High Hon Roll; NHS; Acad Excell Awd; Psych.

HARRISON JR, RODNEY; Dover HS; Dover, DE; (Y); Math Clb; ROTC; Varsity Clb; Bsbl; Bowling; Hon Roll.

HARTNAGEL, KATE; Archmere Acad; Wilmington, DE; (Y); Drama Clb; Chorus; School Musical; Rep Stu Cncl; Score Keeper; Stat Socr; Gov Hon Prg Awd; High Hon Roll; Hon Roll; All-ST Chorus 85; Delaware All-ST Chorus 86; Music.

HARTNETT, JENNIFER; Ursuline Acad; Hockessin, DE; (Y); 2/62; Trs Church Yth Grp; French Clb; Model UN; Science Clb; Var Capt Fld Hcky; Var Capt Sftbl; High Hon Roll; NHS; Ntl Merit Ltr; Sal; Pres Schlr SF, Century III St Fnlst, Echols Schlr 86; U VA; Pol Sci.

HARVEY, DIANE; Indian River HS; Dagsboro, DE; (S); 8/220; Band; Chorus; Concert Band; Stage Crew; Rep Soph Cls; Sftbl; High Hon Roll; Jr NHS; NHS.

HARWITZ, STEVEN R; Concord HS; Wilmington, DE; (Y); Am Leg Boys St; Political Wkr; Band; Drm Mjr(t); School Musical; Var Tennis; Hon Roll; NHS; Ntl Merit SF.

HASTINGS, GLENA; Laurel SR HS; Laurel, DE; (Y); 10/136; AFS; Church Yth Grp; Drama Clb; OEA; Drill Tm; Flag Corp; Mrchg Band; Stage Crew; Rep Sr Cls; Hon Roll; Chesepeake & Potomac Assc Private Schl 86; Woodridge Bus Schlrshp 86; Woodridge Bus Inst; Med Sec.

HAZLEBECK, THOMAS; Alexis I Du Pont HS; Wilmington, DE; (Y); 5/221; Pres Am Leg Boys St; Drama Clb; JA; Band; Var Socr; Cit Awd; High Hon Roll; NHS; Ntl Merit SF; Church Yth Grp; Air Force ROTC 4 Yr Schlrshp 86; Prsdnts Hnr Awd 86; Diamnd ST Schlrshp 86; Purdue U; Aerontcl Engnrng.

HEARN, SUSAN LEAH; Sussex Central SR HS; Georgetown, DE; (Y); Church Yth Grp; Cmnty Wkr; French Clb; Hosp Aide; Office Aide; Political Wkr; SADD; Teachers Aide; Band; Church Choir; William Roth Ldrshp Awd 85; US Army Rsrv Schlr Athlt Awd 86; SCHS Golden Knight Schlrshp 86; VA Wesleyan; Bus Admin.

HECK, DIANE; Padua Acad; Wilmington, DE; (S); 5/250; JA; Pep Clb; Science Clb; Nwsp Stf; Gov Hon Prg Awd; High Hon Roll; NHS; NEDT Awd; Italian Awd 83; Prnctn; Psychlgy.

HEESTERS, SUSAN; St Marks HS; Wilmington, DE; (Y); Pep Clb; SADD; Yrbk Stf; Stu Cncl; Gym; Hon Roll; Z-Clb; U Of DE; Sci.

HENDRICKS, DARYL; Archmere Acad; Newark, DE; (Y); Hosp Aide; Chorus; School Play; Var L Bsbl; Var L Ftbl; Wt Lftg; Hon Roll; U Richmond; Pre Med.

HERON, TERENCE; Dover HS; Dover, DE; (Y); Mgr Drama Clb; JA; Letterman Clb; Thesps; School Play; Stage Crew; Rep Sr Cls; E TN ST U; Engrng.

HEYDEN, CAROLYN; St Marks HS; Lincoln Universit, PA; (Y); 4-H; Ski Clb; Teachers Aide; Bsktbl; Lcrss; Sftbl; Vllybl; 4-H Awd; Hon Roll; Penn ST; Bio.

HIBBITTS, TAMMY; Delcastel Tech HS; Wilmington, DE; (Y); Dance Clb; 4-H; Office Aide; VICA; Nwsp Stf; Yrbk Stf; Off Jr Cls; Gym; Vllybl; Hon Roll; Med Lab Asstnt.

HIGGINS, PHILLIP; Dover HS; Dover, DE; (Y); 1/344; Capt Math Tm; Scholastic Bowl; Var Capt Ftbl; Gov Hon Prg Awd; NHS; St Schlr; Val; Elks Awd; High Hon Roll; NCTE Awd; All ST & All Conf Ftbll 84-85; Natl Schlr/Athlete Awd 86; Boys ST 85; Lafayette Coll; Elec Engrng.

HILL, DEESHA; Dover HS; Dover, DE; (Y); Am Leg Aux Girls St; Debate Tm; Hosp Aide; Flag Corp; Mrchg Band; Nwsp Bus Mgr; Bowling; High Hon Roll; NHS; Bkng.

HILLIS, CLIFTON; Cape Henlopen HS; Rehoboth, DE; (Y); Jazz Band; Nwsp Rptr; Crs Cntry; Music.

HILTNER, ERIK; Concord HS; Wilmington, DE; (Y); JA; Teachers Aide; Nwsp Stf; Hon Roll; DE Schlstc Press Assoc 86; PTA 2nd Pl Literature Cntst 86; Schlrshp MD Coll Art & Design 86; MD Coll; Grphc Cmmnctn.

HIMELREICH, KATY; Archmere Acad; Wilmington, DE; (Y); German Clb; Var Capt Crs Cntry; Var Capt Trk; Hon Roll; German Hnr Scty.

HISLER, KENNETH; Concord HS; Wilmington, DE; (Y); Boy Scts; Teachers Aide; Band; Concert Band; School Musical; JV Bsbl; Var L Ftbl; Var L Wrstlng; Hon Roll; NHS; U Of Delaware.

HITCH, STACY; Milford SR HS; Milford, DE; (Y); Hosp Aide; Intnl Clb; Quiz Bowl; SADD; Yrbk Stf; High Hon Roll; Lion Awd; NHS; U Of DE; Educ.

HITCHENS, DARREN L; Howard Career Ctr; New Castle, DE; (Y); 21/239; Am Leg Boys St; VICA; Pres Jr Cls; Pres Sr Cls; Rep Stu Cncl; Gov Hon Prg Awd; High Hon Roll; Howard H S Memrl Awd 86; U Of DE Full Acdmc Schlrshp; U Of DR; Corp Finc.

HITCHENS, PAMELA; Laurel SR HS; Laurel, DE; (Y); 14/113; VP Church Yth Grp; Drama Clb; Pres 4-H; SADD; Chorus; Church Choir; Drill Tm; School Musical; School Play; Stage Crew; Del Tech; Radlgy.

HITCHENS, STEPHANIE; Indian River HS; Ocean View, DE; (S); Band; Chorus; School Musical; Var Sftbl; Library Aide; Church Choir; Concert Band; Mrchg Band; School Play; Var Bsktbl.

HOAGESON, DANIELLE; Sussex Central SR HS; Georgetown, DE; (Y); 11/210; Sec SADD; Pres Jr Cls; VP Sr Cls; Rep Stu Cncl; Var Capt Cheerleading; High Hon Roll; Pres NHS; AFS; Am Leg Aux Girls St; French Clb; 1st Pl Indvul Cheer U Dela Chrldng Comptn 85; Hmcmng Queen 85-86; MVP Awd Chrldng 85; Salisbury ST Coll; Ed.

HOBACK, GLENN; Newark HS; Newark, DE; (Y); Boy Scts; Debate Tm; Sec Drama Clb; German Clb; Sec Intnl Clb; JCL; Pres Latin Clb; Chorus; Madrigals; AFS; Hstry Tchr.

HOBAN, JAMES; Salesianum HS; Newark, DE; (S); 31/320; Bsbl; Trk; NHS.

HODGES, ELLEN; Alexis I Dupont HS; Hockessin, DE; (Y); 18/277; Mrchg Band; Symp Band; Nwsp Stf; Trs Frsh Cls; Stu Cncl; Var Cheerleading; Var Swmmng; Var Tennis; Hon Roll; NHS; Schlrshp PA Free Entrprs Wk 85; Strs & Poems Pblshd 82-86; Bus.

HOFFMAN, DAVID; John Dickinson HS; Wilmington, DE; (Y); 35/220; VP L Bsbl; Hon Roll; Bsbl All Conf 2nd Tm 86.

HOGAN, DAVID; Archmere Acad; Wilmington, DE; (Y); Am Leg Boys St; Aud/Vis; SADD; School Musical; School Play; Stage Crew; Sec Jr Cls; Pres Sr Cls; High Hon Roll; Hon Roll; Law.

HOLCOMBE, JAMI; Smyrna HS; Smyrna, DE; (S); 6/192; Church Yth Grp; Hosp Aide; Church Choir; Fld Hcky; Mgr(s); Trk; Hon Roll; NHS; Med.

HOLDREN, MIKE; William Penn HS; Bear, DE; (Y); Am Leg Boys St; Church Yth Grp; German Clb; Math Clb; Math Tm; Ski Clb; JV Debate Tm; JV Var Socr; Hon Roll; Chsn Spec PSAT Crse 85; Chsn Cnslng Pgm 85-86; Won Schl Essy Cntst 85; Phrmcy.

HOLLADAY, ROBERT; Indian River HS; Dagsboro, DE; (S); 30/202; Church Yth Grp; Computer Clb; FCA; 4-H; Spanish Clb; SADD; Church Choir; Bsbl; High Hon Roll; Hon Roll; Outstndg Acad Achvt Awd 86.

HOLLAND, KATHY; Newark HS; Newark, DE; (Y); JV Var Cheerleading; Hon Roll; Jr NHS; NHS; Church Yth Grp; Spanish Clb; SADD; Yrbk Phtg; Yrbk Stf; Rep Frsh Cls.

HOLLEY, RACHEL; Mount Pleasant HS; Wilmington, DE; (Y); Girl Scts; Chorus; School Play; Rep Soph Cls; Rep Jr Cls; Rep Stu Cncl; JV Capt Cheerleading; JV Fld Hcky; Var Swmmng; Var Tennis; Bronze Russian Awd Year II 84-85, III 85-86; NY Schl Arts; Drama.

HOLLOWAY, MATTHEW; Salesianum HS; New Castle, DE; (S); 9/310; Office Aide; Yrbk Rptr; Var Crs Cntry; Im Socr; Var Wrstlng; High Hon Roll; NHS; Salesianum Minuteman 85-86; Engrng.

HOLMES, SUSAN E; Wilmington Friends Schl; Durham, NC; (Y); Hosp Aide; Math Tm; Concert Band; School Musical; Yrbk Stf; JV Fld Hcky; JV Lcrss; Ntl Merit Schol; Chorus; Rep Soph Cls; Bush Awd 85; A B Duke Schrlshp Duke U 86; Duke U; Sci.

HOLT, JEROMIE; Christiana HS; Newark, DE; (Y); JA; Ski Clb; U Of DE; Avtn.

HOOD, SABRINA; Cape Henlopen HS; Milton, DE; (Y); Church Yth Grp; Hosp Aide; Math Tm; Science Clb; Chorus; Nwsp Rptr; 1st Pl Trphy Antmy-Physlgy 86; Cert Mth Tm 86; Phys Thrpst.

HOOPES, PATRICIA-JO; Padua Acad; New Castle, DE; (S); 20/214; Church Yth Grp; Im Bowling; Hon Roll; U Of DE; Comp Sci.

HOPKINS, CONNIE; Cape Henlopen HS; Milton, DE; (Y); Dance Clb; Drm Mjr(t); Mrchg Band; Bsktbl; Cheerleading.

HORGAN, NEIL; Archmere Acad; Wilmington, DE; (S); Concert Band; Jazz Band; Var Crs Cntry; JV Trk; High Hon Roll; NHS; Spanish NHS; DE Cncl On Teachers Of Foreign Lang-1st Prize Oral Spnsh II Cont 85.

HORN, ANDREA M; Padua Acad; Philadelpia, PA; (Y); French Clb; Hon Roll; Jr NHS; Resp Thrpst.

HORTON, BLAIR A; Seaford HS; Seaford, DE; (Y); 10/200; Am Leg Boys St; Key Clb; Mrchg Band; Yrbk Stf; JV Bsbl; Var Bsktbl; Hon Roll; NHS; Engrng.

HOVINGTON, ANTHONY; Indian River HS; Frankford, DE; (S); 10/202; Am Leg Boys St; Church Yth Grp; French Clb; Math Tm; Pep Clb; SADD; Chorus; Church Choir; Socr; High Hon Roll; Ntl Ldrshp & Merit Awd 86; Math.

HOVIS, KEVIN; Laurel HS; Laurel, DE; (Y); 22/128; Church Yth Grp; Science Clb; SADD; Yrbk Phtg; Yrbk Stf; Var Crs Cntry; Var Trk; Goldley Beacom Coll; Accntng.

HOWARD, LEON; Indian River HS; Dagsboro, DE; (Y); VP FFA; Nwsp Stf; Hon Roll; Pres Acad Fit Achvt Awd 86; FFA Diamond ST Farmer Degree 85; Bus Mgmt.

HOWE JR, RICHARD O; Salesianum HS; Newark, DE; (Y); Chess Clb; Cmnty Wkr; SADD; Hon Roll; U Delaware; Physcs.

HSIAO, PHYLLIS; Concord HS; Wilmington, DE; (Y); 5/322; Cmnty Wkr; Spanish Clb; Acpl Chr; Band; Chorus; Church Choir; Madrigals; Mrchg Band; School Musical; Symp Band; Piano In DE St Music Tchrs Assoc 81-86; DE Miss TEEN Pgnt 3rd Rnnrup 85; Talent Wnnr; Sci.

HSU, ALISSA J; John Dickinson HS; Wilmington, DE; (Y); 3/180; Am Leg Aux Girls St; Pres Latin Clb; Nwsp Stf; Sec Jr Cls; Sec Stu Cncl; Pres NHS; Hugh O Brien Yth Ldrshp Smnr 84; Hnrbl Mntn Arts Recgntn & Tlnt Srch 85-86; Wilmington Ballet Co 82-86.

HUDSON, HEATHER; Smyrna HS; Smyrna, DE; (Y); 21/200; Sec Church Yth Grp; Hosp Aide; Pres Spanish Clb; Ed Yrbk Stf; Lit Mag; VP Soph Cls; Rep Stu Cncl; Var Gym; Var Mgr(s); Voice Dem Awd; Olympcs Mnd 1st Pl ST Wnnrs 86; Commnctns.

HUDSON, SUSAN; Indian River HS; Millsboro, DE; (S); 9/213; Church Yth Grp; Spanish Clb; Rptr Nwsp Rptr; Lit Mag; High Hon Roll; Jr NHS; NHS; Prfct Atten Awd.

HUEBNER, AMY; John Dickinson HS; Wilmington, DE; (Y); 24/224; JCL; Latin Clb; Band; Symp Band; Sftbl; Swmmng; Vllybl; Hon Roll; NHS; Concert Band; Cum Honore Mazimo Egregio; Engr.

HUFFMAN, ERIC A; Glasgow HS; Newark, DE; (Y); 21/310; Nwsp Ed-Chief; Nwsp Sprt Ed; VP Sr Cls; Am Leg Boys St; Drama Clb; Model UN; Political Wkr; SADD; Nwsp Rptr; Yrbk Rptr; Ntl HS Inst, Ed Chief Eye Mag 86; YMCA Yuth Govt 85-86; Jrnlsm.

HUGHES, KELLY; Padua Acad; Chadds Ford, PA; (S); 9/213; Var Fld Hcky; JV Tennis; JV Trk; Hon Roll; Natl Ldrshp Merit Awd 85; Spcl Educ.

HUNT, JANINE; William Penn HS; New Castle, DE; (Y); Am Leg Aux Girls St; Math Tm; Scholastic Bowl; Science Clb; Symp Band; Rep Trs Stu Cncl; Var Capt Tennis; Var Capt Vllybl; NHS; Girl Scts; DE Assoc Stdnt Cncls Treas 86-87; Forum Adv Minrties Engrng 82-87; AIM At GMI 86; Engrng.

HUNT, MARTIN KYLE; William Penn HS; Newcastle, DE; (Y); 14/490; VP Sr Cls; Pres Stu Cncl; L Capt Ftbl; L Capt Tennis; L Capt Wrstlng; High Hon Roll; NHS; Math Tm; Science Clb; Pres Frsh Cls; Acdmc All Amer; Mc Cabe Schlr Swarthmore Coll; Blue Gold All Str; Swarthmore Coll; Biomed Engr.

HURLEY, CHRISTINE; Dover HS; Dover, DE; (Y); DECA; FHA; Office Aide; OEA; Yrbk Stf; Capt Bowling; Hon Roll; Elem Ed.

IMLER, SHELBY; Dover HS; Dover, DE; (Y); Pres Church Yth Grp; Drama Clb; Exploring; Band; Concert Band; Mrchg Band; Symp Band; Hon Roll; Psych.

INDEN, BILL; Brandywine HS; Wilmington, DE; (S); DECA; JA; Model UN; Ski Clb; Gym; Lcrss; Socr; Hon Roll; NHS.

INMAN, MELINDA; Claymont HS; Claymont, DE; (Y); 10/94; Am Leg Aux Girls St; Drama Clb; Spanish Clb; Sec SADD; Varsity Clb; School Musical; Yrbk Ed-Chief; Capt Cheerleading; Hon Roll; NHS; Salisbury ST U.

IPLENSKI, GENEVIEVE; Dover HS; Hartly, DE; (Y); Drama Clb; SADD; Band; Concert Band; Mrchg Band; Symp Band; Bowling; Hon Roll; Arch.

IRONS, STACEY; Milford HS; Milford, DE; (Y); Intnl Clb; Varsity Clb; Var Capt Cheerleading; Hon Roll; Church Yth Grp; Spanish Clb; Rep Jr Cls.

IRVING, LEE; Alexis I Dupont HS; Hockessin, DE; (Y); 70/260; Boy Scts; Church Yth Grp; SADD; Band; Jazz Band; Mrchg Band; Orch; Pep Band; School Play; Stage Crew.

ISEMANN, MICHELLE; Dover HS; Dover, DE; (Y); Rep Stu Cncl; Var Capt Cheerleading; High Hon Roll; Hon Roll; 2nd Pl Best Indvl Chrldr Regnl Champ 86; Advrtsng.

JACKSON, CATHERINE; Newark HS; Newark, DE; (Y); Am Leg Aux Girls St; Spanish Clb; SADD; Chorus; Madrigals; Crs Cntry; Wt Lftg; Hon Roll; Jr NHS; NHS.

JACKSON, DOUGLAS; Seaford SR HS; Seaford, DE; (Y); 9/178; Am Leg Boys St; Boy Scts; Key Clb; Math Tm; Political Wkr; Mrchg Band; School Play; Yrbk Stf; Off Sr Cls; L Socr.

JACKSON, ELIZABETH; Seaford HS; Seaford, DE; (Y); 5/252; AFS; 4-H; Key Clb; Math Tm; Rep Frsh Cls; Rep Soph Cls; Rep Jr Cls; Var L Bsktbl; Var L Fld Hcky; NHS; Hugh O Brian Yth Ldrshp Cnfrnc 85; Bus Admin.

JACKSON, FELICIA; Dover HS; Dover, DE; (Y); 3/344; Am Leg Aux Girls St; Girl Scts; Hosp Aide; Capt Math Tm; Scholastic Bowl; Symp Band; Ed Lit Mag; Capt Pom Pon; NHS; Arch.

JACOBS, ANDREA; Brandywine HS; Wilmington, DE; (Y); AFS; Pres Church Yth Grp; Cmnty Wkr; Trs Drama Clb; Teachers Aide; Pres Temple Yth Grp; Chorus; Church Choir; School Musical; School Play; OK All ST Choir 84-86; DMEA Vocl Fest Supr Ratng 85; Distngshd Schlr 86; Brandeis U.

JARRELL JR, RALPH; Wilmington Christian Schl; Newark, DE; (Y); 2/52; Math Tm; VP Sr Cls; Rep Stu Cncl; L Bsktbl; Hon Roll; NHS; Sal; Acdmc Incntv 86-87; Edw C Davis Trst Schlrshp 86-89; U Delaware; Engrng.

JEFFERSON, KAREN; Seaford SR HS; Seaford, DE; (S); Key Clb; VP Frsh Cls; Hst Church Yth Grp; Hst Jr Cls; Hst Sr Cls; Hst Stu Cncl; Var Capt Bsktbl; Var Fld Hcky; Var Golf; Sec NHS; Girls ST 85; 1st Tm All Conf Fld Hockey 85-86; 1st Tm All ST Fld Hockey 85-86; James Madison U; Elem Educ.

JENNINGS, ANNMARIE; Claymont HS; Claymont, DE; (Y); 1/96; Am Leg Aux Girls St; Cmnty Wkr; Drama Clb; JA; Spanish Clb; Varsity Clb; Band; Chorus; Church Choir; Concert Band; All St Band 86; Gov Schl Music 85; Outstndng Jr Band Mbr 86; Oberlin Conservatory; Music.

JENNINGS, JACK; Archmere Acad; Winston Salem, NC; (Y); Church Yth Grp; German Clb; SADD; Stage Crew; Lit Mag; Bowling; Hon Roll; American Hollies Fndtn Drwg-Excllnc Awd 85-86; Cmmrcl Art.

JEROMINSKI, ANN; St Marks HS; Wilmington, DE; (Y); Exploring; Office Aide; Service Clb; Yrbk Ed-Chief; Yrbk Stf; Off Stu Cncl; Hon Roll; NHS; Pres Schlr; Hopwood Schlr 85; John B Lynch Schlrp Fndtn Grant 86; U DE; Biol.

JOCHEN, MICHAEL; Newark HS; Newark, DE; (Y); 40/325; Boy Scts; Exploring; Band; Concert Band; Drm Mjr(t); Mrchg Band; Symp Band; Lit Mag; Wrstlng; Hon Roll; U Of DE; Biochem Engrng.

JOHNSON, JEFF A; New Castle Baptist Acad; New Castle, DE; (Y); Chess Clb; Bsbl; Bsktbl; Hon Roll; Prfct Atten Awd; Sears Schlrshp 86; Silver Hnr Rll Awd 86; Goldey Beacom Coll; Cmptr.

JOHNSON, JEFFREY; Salesianum HS; Wilmington, DE; (S); 1/272; Mathletes; Spanish Clb; Yrbk Rptr; Bsbl; Socr; Hon Roll; NHS; Ntl Merit Ltr; Gold Medl Hghst Cumltv GPA; Rensselaer Medl Outstndng Achvt Mth & Sci; Engrng.

JOHNSON, LA SHAWN; Dover HS; Dover, DE; (Y); Church Yth Grp; Cmnty Wkr; Teachers Aide; VP Trs VICA; Var Capt Bsktbl; Var Socr; Var Sftbl; Var L Trk; Hon Roll; 1st-VICA Rep DE-NTL Conf 86; Spcl Rcgntn-Grad Of Knt Cnty Vo-Tech Schl 86; OH ST U; Fshn Dsgn.

JOHNSON, SHERRI; Seaford SR HS; Laurel, DE; (Y); Hst SADD; Teachers Aide; VICA; High Hon Roll; Hon Roll; Outstndng Stu Of Mnth 86; Dnstry.

JOHNSON, TOBY; Caesar Rodney HS; Wyoming, DE; (Y); French Clb; Band; Concert Band; Jazz Band; Mrchg Band; Pep Band; Nwsp Rptr; Nwsp Stf; Yrbk Rptr; Yrbk Stf; Outstndng Band Awd 84; Bst Trombone Plyr Yr 84; 2nd Chair All ST Band 84; Elec Desgnr.

JOHNSON, TONYA; Dover HS; Dover, DE; (Y); Church Yth Grp; FCA; German Clb; Office Aide; ROTC; Nwsp Stf; Var Capt Bsktbl; Mgr(s); Var Capt Trk; Hon Roll; Ntl Hnr Rll 84-85; MVP Vrsty Bsktbl 85-86; Outstndng Cdt ROTC & Mst Acad 85-86; OH ST U; Bus Admin.

JONES, KIM; Mc Kean HS; Wilmington, DE; (Y); 9/220; Computer Clb; Pep Clb; Spanish Clb; Jr Cls; Sr Cls; Var Fld Hcky; Var L Sftbl; Hon Roll; Engr.

JONES, LISA; Caravel Acad; Newark, DE; (S); 2/42; Pres AFS; Teachers Aide; Var Bsktbl; Var Capt Cheerleading; Pres Frsh Cls; Pres Soph Cls; Pres Jr Cls; Pres Sr Cls; Rep Stu Cncl; Mgr(s); Awd Certs Soc Sci, Chem 85; Sec DE Assn Stu Cncls 85-86; Ms DE Ntl Tn-Agr 85; Embry-Riddle Aero U; Aero Sci.

JORDAN, BRIAN; Indian River HS; Frankford, DE; (Y); Boy Scts; FFA; FHA; OEA; Pep Clb; SADD; Chorus.

JORDAN, KAREN; Caesar Rodney HS; Dover, DE; (Y); 7/350; Am Leg Aux Girls St; French Clb; Math Clb; Nwsp Rptr; Capt L Bsktbl; Powder Puff Ftbl; Capt L Sftbl; High Hon Roll; NHS; Ntl Merit Ltr; USAFA; Aero Engrng.

JOSEPH, DAWN; Delmar JR SR HS; Delmar, MD; (Y); 17/88; Church Yth Grp; FHA; Keywanettes; SADD; Teachers Aide; Chorus; Capt Color Guard; Stu Cncl; Hon Roll; Bus Achvt Awd 86; Wor-Wic Tech CC; Radlgc Tech.

JOYCE, ROBERT; Salesianum HS; Wilmington, DE; (Y); Church Yth Grp; Exploring; JA; Nwsp Rptr; Ftbl; Wrstlng; Beaver Coll; Phy Thrpy.

JUNE, CLAUDIA; Milford SR HS; Milford, DE; (Y); Am Leg Aux Girls St; Pres Intnl Clb; SADD; School Musical; Yrbk Phtg; Yrbk Stf; Tennis; Hon Roll; NHS; Church Yth Grp; Nacel Cultrl Exchng; Intl Bus.

KAHN, AMY; Brandywine HS; Wilmington, DE; (S); Am Leg Aux Girls St; Cmnty Wkr; Exploring; FBLA; Model UN; Scholastic Bowl; VP Soph Cls; Pres Jr Cls; Rep Stu Cncl; JV Sftbl; Publc Spkng Awds; Dale Carnegie Scholar; Johns Hopkins; Pre-Med.

KALONS, LESLY; Thomas Mc Kean HS; Wilmington, DE; (S); 14/210; AFS; Church Yth Grp; Drama Clb; GAA; Q&S; Varsity Clb; School Musical; School Play; Stage Crew; Variety Show; Hmecmng Cls Rep 83-85; Bus Mgmt.

KAMINSKI, DANA; John Dickinson HS; Wilmington, DE; (Y); 111/224; Teachers Aide; Nwsp Stf; Prfct Atten Awd; Goldy Beacon Coll; Mrktng Mgmt.

KANE, SUSAN; Padua Acad; Wilmington, DE; (Y); Church Yth Grp; JA; Pep Clb; SADD; Fld Hcky; Sftbl; Trk; Hon Roll; Prfct Atten Awd; MVP-FLD Hcky & Stbl 86; All ST Wntr Trck 86; All Cthlc-Fld Hcky 85-86; Immaculata Coll; Dietcs.

KASSING, EDWARD; Dover HS; Dover, DE; (Y); 83/383; Computer Clb; French Clb; Office Aide; OEA; Teachers Aide; Band; Mrchg Band; Symp Band; Outstndng Acdmc Achvt Hgh Schl Awd 86; Bus Adm.

KELLAM, JACKIE; Dover HS; Dover, DE; (Y); 92/306; JA; OEA; Teachers Aide; Hon Roll; Awd U DE Outstndng Acad Achvt HS 86; Wesley Coll; Inter Decor.

KELLEHER, ANN; Mt Pleasant HS; Wilmington, DE; (Y); 5/150; Math Tm; Band; Chorus; School Musical; Ed Nwsp Stf; Ed Yrbk Stf; Trk; Hon Roll; NHS; Prfct Atten Awd.

KELSEY, KIMBERLY D; Dover HS; Dover, DE; (Y); Office Aide; Band; Concert Band; Drill Tm; Jazz Band; Mrchg Band; Symp Band; Pom Pon; Powder Puff Ftbl; High Hon Roll; Perfect Attndnc 86; U Of De Jr Acad Awd 86; Millersville U; Elem Educ.

KESSINGER, CLYDE; Thomas Mc Kean HS; Wilmington, DE; (Y); 50/217; Boy Scts; Church Yth Grp; Trs OEA; Yrbk Stf; Stu Cncl; Crs Cntry; Trk; Hon Roll; NHS; Acdmc All-Cnfrnc Wntr Trck 86; U Of DE; Acctg.

KIMBLE, PAULA; Cape Henlopen HS; Lincoln, DE; (Y); 41/215; Math Tm; OEA; Political Wkr; Ski Clb; Chorus; Flag Corp; Nwsp Rptr; Yrbk Stf; Mgr(s); Hon Roll.

KING, DAWN; Seaford SR HS; Seaford, DE; (Y); AFS; Color Guard; Hon Roll; Wesley Col6; Prlgl.

KING, KEITH; Glasgow HS; Bear, DE; (Y); 88/359; Boys Clb Am; Drama Clb; Varsity Clb; Bsbl; Bsktbl; Ftbl; Wrstlng; Hon Roll; All ST Bsbll Tm 85-86; Bsbll Schlrshp Towson ST U 86-87; Towson ST U; Bio.

KING, KEVIN E; Glasgow HS; Ephrata, WA; (Y); 88/359; Boys Clb Am; Drama Clb; Varsity Clb; Bsbl; Bsktbl; Ftbl; Wrstlng; Hon Roll; All Sst Bsbll Tm 85-86; Bsbll Schlrshp Towson ST U 86-87; Towson ST U; Bio.

KINSLER, EDMUND; William Penn HS; New Castle, DE; (Y); Computer Clb; Math Tm; Science Clb; Ski Clb; Hon Roll; Natl Sci Olympiad 85; Engineering.

KIPP, SUZANNE; Padua Acad; Wilmington, DE; (Y); 63/200; Church Yth Grp; Pep Clb; Fld Hcky; Hon Roll; Ed.

KIRLAN, DEANNA; St Marks HS; Elkton, MD; (Y); Key Clb; Math Tm; Natl Beta Clb; Quiz Bowl; Science Clb; Service Clb; School Play; Mgr(s); High Hon Roll; Hon Roll; Prtl Acad Schlrshp St Marks HS 83-87; U Of DE.

KISER, SANDRA; Alexis I Du Pont HS; Hockessin, DE; (Y); 3/218; Trs Church Yth Grp; Trs FHA; Hosp Aide; JA; Math Tm; High Hon Roll; NHS; Keywanettes; Yrbk Stf; Yrbk Undrclssmn Edtr; Outstndng Calcls And Comptr Awds 86; U Of DE; Spec Educ.

KIT, KEVIN; Salesianum HS; Wilmington, DE; (S); 27/272; Boy Scts; Computer Clb; Spanish Clb; SADD; Concert Band; Mrchg Band; Symp Band; Bowling; NHS; VA Tech; Chem Engrng.

KLEIN, MARC; Salesianum HS; Sewell, NJ; (Y); 52/301; Boy Scts; Pres 4-H; French Clb; Boys Clb Am; Yrbk Ed-Chief; Hon Roll; Engrng.

KLINGE, BRIAN T; Salesianum Schl; Wilmington, DE; (Y); 41/262; Church Yth Grp; French Clb; Im Bsktbl; Im Var Socr; Elks Awd; Hon Roll; NHS; John B Lynch Found Schlrshp 86; Wilmington Rotry Clb Schlrshp Fnlst 86; VA Tech; Comp Sci.

KOOKER, KEITH; Dover HS; Dover, DE; (Y); 9/298; Am Leg Boys St; Math Clb; Band; Lit Mag; Bowling; Tennis; High Hon Roll; NHS; Pres Schlr; Concert Band; La Fayatte Coll; Cvl Engrng.

KOPECKI, ROBERT; St Marks HS; Wilmington, DE; (Y); Art Clb; Yrbk Stf; Var Ftbl; Var Swmmng; Pre-Med.

KORANT, DEBORAH; Mount Pleasant HS; Wilmington, DE; (Y); Girl Scts; Nwsp Stf; Yrbk Stf; JV Cheerleading; Hon Roll; Grl Sct Gld Awd 86; Brd Dir Chesapeake Boy Grl Sct Cncl 86-87; Bus.

KOSTIC, MARK; Salesianum Schl; Wilmington, DE; (S); 6/262; Pres Sr Cls; Rep Stu Cncl; JV Bsktbl; Var Ftbl; High Hon Roll; NHS; US Senate Yth Pgm Schlrshp; Hon Ment All ST Ftbl; Mike De Lucia Mem Ftbl Awd; Bio.

KOTOWSKI, MICHELLE R; St Marks HS; Wilmington, DE; (Y); 13/346; Cmnty Wkr; Office Aide; Trs Service Clb; Lit Mag; Var Co-Capt Cheerleading; Var Co-Capt Pom Pon; NHS; Pres Acad Ftns Awd 86; Hnrbl Ment Acad Awd Exc Bio 86; U DE; Genticst.

KOTZ, BRIAN C; St Andrews Schl; Charles Town, WV; (Y); Church Yth Grp; Math Tm; Church Choir; Lit Mag; Rep Sr Cls; Rep Stu Cncl; Ftbl; Cit Awd; Hon Roll; Ntl Merit Ltr; 1st Tm All St Ftbll 85; 1st Tm All Conf Ftbll 83-85; Harvard U; Math.

KOUTOUFARIS, MARCOS; Dover HS; Dover, DE; (Y); AFS; VP JA; OEA; VP Ski Clb; Pres Sr Cls; Stu Cncl; Var JV Bsbl; JV Bsktbl; Var JV Socr; Yth Govt Bst Legsltr Awd 85; ST Rep Natl Conf 85; Sci Olympd 3rd Pl 86; Johnson & Wales Scholar 86; PA ST; Htl/Rest Adm.

KOVAL, CATHERINE; John Dickinson HS; Wilmington, DE; (Y); 7/278; Am Leg Aux Girls St; Yrbk Ed-Chief; Yrbk Phtg; VP Jr Cls; VP Sr Cls; Stu Cncl; Mgr(s); Capt Swmmng; High Hon Roll; NHS; Outstndng News Jrnl Crrier Of Yr 86; Biomdcl Engrng.

KOZA, STEPHEN; Salesianum HS; Ridley Park, PA; (S); 25/315; French Clb; Im Bsktbl; Im Socr; High Hon Roll; Hon Roll; Villanova U; Pre Law.

KRAL, KIM; William Penn HS; New Castle, DE; (Y); Key Clb; Jazz Band; Mrchg Band; Symp Band; Hon Roll; Office Aide; Band; Swmmng; Comp.

KRAMEN, HOWARD; Claymont HS; Claymont, DE; (Y); Am Leg Boys St; Pres Computer Clb; Capt Scholastic Bowl; Pres Science Clb; Pres Spanish Clb; Pres SADD; School Musical; Var L Golf; Hon Roll; NHS; Student Of The Month Social Studies 82-83,Industrial Arts 85-86; Case Western Resrv U; Aerospace.

KRAUSS III, GRANVILLE C; Claymont HS; Claymont, DE; (Y); CAP; Latin Clb; Office Aide; SADD; Varsity Clb; JV Var Bsbl; JV Var Bsktbl; Var Bowling; Var Capt Crs Cntry; Var Capt Trk; Cross Cntry MVP, Track MVP, NSCTA Crss County, Coach MVP 84-86; U Of Delaware; Agriculture.

KRAWCZUK, LINDA; Padula Academy; Wilmington, DE; (Y); Church Yth Grp; Girl Scts; JA; Model UN; Science Clb; SADD; Mrchg Band; Rep Stu Cncl; Hon Roll; NEDT Awd; JR Achvmnt Awds Exec & Mgmt 85; Htl Mgmt.

KREBS, JEFFREY; Salesianum Schl; Wilmington, DE; (S); 2/350; Chess Clb; Cmnty Wkr; SADD; Rep Trs Stu Cncl; JV Crs Cntry; High Hon Roll; NHS; Boy Scts; JV Trk; Schlrshp To Salesinum; Hugh O Brian Yth Ldrshp Smnr; DE Gvnrs Schl Of Exc; Mngmnt.

KREWSON, STEPHANIE; Wilmington Friends HS; Wilmington, DE; (Y); Am Leg Aux Girls St; Cmnty Wkr; GAA; Chorus; Fld Hcky; Trk; Gov Hon Prg Awd; NHS; 4th In ST Div II Grls 800m Run 85/6th In 86; 1st In Conf For 1600m & 800m 86; Pre Med.

KROEBER III, MAL; A I Du Pont HS; Hockessin, DE; (Y); Boy Scts; Concert Band; Mrchg Band; Symp Band; Hon Roll; Pres Acad Fit Awds Prog 86; Certs Hon Outstndg Achvt Band, Sci & Alg 83-86; U DE; Engrg.

KROLL, CHRIS; Tower Hill Schl; Wilmington, DE; (Y); Teachers Aide; Yrbk Stf; Var Cheerleading; JV Lcrss; Hon Roll; Ntl Merit Ltr.

KRUEGER JR, RICHARD L; Dover HS; Dover, DE; (Y); 44/316; AFS; Church Yth Grp; English Clb; Library Aide; Office Aide; Band; Mrchg Band; Symp Band; Capt Bowling; High Hon Roll; Harrington H S Almn Assn Schlrshp 86; Millersville U; Libry Sci.

KUBICKI, BARBARA A; St Marks HS; West Grove, PA; (Y); Hnr Rl 83-86; Westchester U; Bus Adm.

KULIS, MIKE; Archmere Acad; Boothwyn, PA; (Y); Church Yth Grp; Bsktbl; Bowling; Ftbl; Trk; Hon Roll; Vrsty Ftbl 84; Top 90 Prcnt Ntl Ed Dvlpmnt T St 84.

LA BORDE, MARIBETH; Padua Acad; Bear, DE; (Y); French Clb; Pep Clb; Pep Band; Yrbk Stf; Rep Jr Cls; Var Crs Cntry; Var Trk; NEDT Awd; Prfct Atten Awd; All-ST X-Cntry & Trk 86.

LA POINTE, SUZANNE F; Padua Acad; Newark, DE; (Y); Church Yth Grp; Sec French Clb; Bowling; Tennis; Hon Roll; St Joseph U; Elem Educ.

LACAVA, VINCENT; Archmere Acad; Claymont, DE; (Y); Art Clb; Lit Mag; Bowling; Var Wrstlng; Gov Hon Prg Awd; Hon Roll; Am Hollies Fdtn 1st Pl 85-86; Schlrshp Hussian Schl Of Art 85-86; 1st Pl ST Schlstc Art Comp 85-86; Art.

LAGUNZAD, ROWENA; Caesar Rodney SR HS; Dover, DE; (Y); 83/301; French Clb; Band; Capt Mrchg Band; Orch; Symp Band; Bst Mellophone Marchng Season 83-84; Bst Librarn 85-86; Acad Scholar 86-87; DE ST Coll; Civil Engrng.

LAMB, K SCOTT; Concord HS; Wilmington, DE; (Y); Boy Scts; FCA; Ski Clb; Teachers Aide; Varsity Clb; Var L Socr; Hon Roll; Aerosp Engrng.

LAMBDIN, PATRICK M; Smyrna HS; Clayton, DE; (S); 5/183; French Clb; Lit Mag; JV Trk; High Hon Roll; Hon Roll; NHS; Ntl Merit Ltr; Prfct Atten Awd; Acdmc Hall Of Fame 85-86; Cvcs Awd Amer Lgn 83-84; U DE; Chmcl Engrng.

LAND, HAROLD; Newark HS; Newark, DE; (Y); Yrbk Phtg; Pres Soph Cls; Off Jr Cls; Off Sr Cls; Var L Golf; Var L Swmmng; Jr NHS; NHS; Natl Citizen Bee Cntst 86; St & Regl Wnnr Citizen Bee Cntst 86; Bus.

LANG, ANNETTE; Padua Acad; Wilmington, DE; (S); 5/213; Church Yth Grp; VP French Clb; Pep Clb; Science Clb; Pep Band; Ed Yrbk Stf; Mgr(s); Hon Roll; NHS; NEDT Awd; Frnch Awd 84 & 85; Hlth Awd 84; Bus.

LANGHAM, SUSIE; Dover HS; Dover, DE; (Y); German Clb; JA; Library Aide; Lit Mag; Cheerleading; High Hon Roll; Hon Roll; NHS; Sci Olympiad 86; U DE Acdmc Achvt 86.

LANTZY, BRIAN; Dover HS; Dover, DE; (Y); Rep Frsh Cls; Rep Soph Cls; VP Jr Cls; Pres Stu Cncl; Var Tennis; Var Wrstlng; High Hon Roll; Hon Roll; NHS; Law.

LARDEAR, SHARON; St Marks HS; Wilmington, DE; (Y); 10/360; Cmnty Wkr; Service Clb; SADD; Yrbk Stf; Rep Jr Cls; Rep Stu Cncl; Lcrss; High Hon Roll; DE Sci Sympsium 86; Alternate Gov Schl 85; Recpnt Exc Schlrshp 86; Pol Sci.

LARRIMORE, AMY; Seaford SR HS; Seaford, DE; (Y); Key Clb; Office Aide; Trs OEA; Capt Color Guard; Capt Drill Tm; School Play; Yrbk Ed-Chief; Capt Twrlr; Hon Roll; ST Sussex Cnty Regnl Dir OEA 84-85; Spec Music Awd 85-86; Acctng.

LAUDERBAUGH, DAVID; Dover HS; Dover, DE; (Y); 9/329; Debate Tm; Mrchg Band; Symp Band; Var L Bsktbl; Var Golf; High Hon Roll; NHS; Ntl Merit Ltr; German Clb; ST DE Sci Plympiad Mdlst; ; Engrng.

LAW, LORRIE; Indian River HS; Selbyville, DE; (S); 8/227; Church Yth Grp; Drama Clb; Library Aide; Office Aide; Church Choir; Stu Cncl; Capt Cheerleading; High Hon Roll; Pres Jr NHS; NHS; U DE; Bus Adm.

LAWRENCE, CHRIS; Dover HS; Dover, DE; (Y); 20/400; Var JV Bsbl; Capt Var Bsktbl; JV Ftbl; High Hon Roll; NHS; 1st Tm All Conf, 3rd Tm All ST Bsktbl 86; 1st Tm All Conf Bsbl 86; Bus Adm.

LAWRENCE, KIMBERLY; Dover HS; Dover, DE; (Y); OEA; Band; Chorus; Nwsp Rptr; High Hon Roll; Hon Roll; Prfct Atten Awd; Alpha Kappa Alpha Srorty Schlrshp 86; Dlta Sgma Thta Srorty Cthrn B Mddlton Schlrshp 86; Howard U; Engl.

LAWS, MIA; Delcastle HS; Wilmington, DE; (Y); 14/508; Letterman Clb; Library Aide; VICA; Rep Stu Cncl; Var Trk; Hon Roll; Piraview Texans; Chem Engrng.

LAWSON, CHRISTOPHER; Holy Cross HS; Dover, DE; (Y); 12/42; Cmnty Wkr; Letterman Clb; Math Tm; Political Wkr; Pres Frsh Cls; Pres Soph Cls; JV Var Bsktbl; JV Mgr(s); Score Keeper; Timer; Bus Admin.

LAYFIELD, CYNTHIA; Delmar JR SR HS; Delmar, MD; (Y); 6/93; Drama Clb; FHA; Keywanettes; SADD; School Play; Trs Frsh Cls; Trs Soph Cls; Trs Jr Cls; Co-Capt JV Cheerleading; Hon Roll; Hnr Homecomming Attndnt 84-85; Awd 3rd Hghst Engl Grade 84-85; Awd 2nd Hghst French III Grade 85-86; Elem Educ.

LE, LOAN; Seaford HS; Seaford, DE; (Y); 20/194; AFS; Church Yth Grp; DECA; Drama Clb; Math Tm; Office Aide; Science Clb; SADD; Stage Crew; Yrbk Sprt Ed; Reliance Grange No 58 86; Presdntl Acad Fitness Awd 86; U Of DE.

LECATES, MARILYN; Delmar HS; Delmar, MD; (Y); Pres Trs Church Yth Grp; Drama Clb; FHA; Keywanettes; Sec Band; Church Choir; Concert Band; Drm Mjr(t); Mrchg Band; School Play; Sclgy.

LEE, BARBARA; Brandywine HS; Wilmington, DE; (Y); Cmnty Wkr; Pres FHA; JA; Latin Clb; Library Aide; Stage Crew; Hon Roll; Math Commndtn 86; Biotech.

LEE, BRENDA; Seaford SR HS; Seaford, DE; (Y); Chorus; Church Choir; School Musical; School Play; Nwsp Rptr; Nwsp Stf; High Hon Roll; Hon Roll; County Chorus 83-84; Del Tech; Jrnlsm.

LEMANSKI, STAN; St Marks HS; Newark, DE; (Y); Boy Scts; Ski Clb; SADD; Band; Concert Band; Jazz Band; Mrchg Band; Pep Band; School Musical; Var Trk.

LEMON, BRADLEY TODD; Delmar JR SR HS; Delmar, MD; (Y); 1/95; Am Leg Boys St; Key Clb; VP SADD; Stu Cncl; Var L Bsbl; Var L Bsktbl; Var L Ftbl; Gov Hon Prg Awd; High Hon Roll; NHS; 1st Pl Span I, 2nd Pl World Hist, 4th Pl Chem 84-85; 1st Pl Trigonmtry & World Geog 85-86; Pre Med.

LEONARD, MALINDA; Christiana HS; Wilmington, DE; (Y); Church Yth Grp; Pep Clb; Chorus; Bsktbl; Cheerleading; Mgr(s); Timer; Hon Roll; Del Tech; Bus.

LEONARDO, EDWARD; Salesianum HS; Parkside, PA; (Y); 46/262; Boy Scts; Nwsp Rptr; Nwsp Stf; Im Bsktbl; Im Bowling; Elks Awd; Hon Roll; NHS; Acad Scholar Duquesne U 86; Eagle Scout 84; John B Lynch Scholar Fndtn 86; Duquesne U; Advrtsng Exec.

LESSARD, COLIN; Caesar Rodney HS; Kenton, DE; (Y); 117/348; FCA; French Clb; Teachers Aide; Band; Capt Var Crs Cntry; Capt Var Trk; MVP Cross Cty 86; All Conf Cross Cty 85-86; Chroprctr.

LEWIS, MICHELLE; Christiana HS; New Castle, DE; (Y); VP Church Yth Grp; JA; Latin Clb; Office Aide; Pep Clb; Spanish Clb; SADD; Church Choir; Variety Show; Stu Cncl; Pre-Med.

LEWIS, TAMMY; Smyrna HS; Smyrna, DE; (S); 20/160; Art Clb; FHA; Chorus; Hon Roll; NHS; Prfct Atten Awd; Wesley Coll; Cmmnctn Arts.

LIEBAL, SHARON; John Dickinson HS; Wilmington, DE; (Y); Band; Rep Frsh Cls; Var Cheerleading; Mgr(s); Hon Roll; U Of DE; Acctng.

LILLIS, BRAD; Salesianum HS; Wilmington, DE; (S); 16/272; JV Socr; Capt Var Swmmng; High Hon Roll; Blue Hen Cnfrnc Acdmc/Athlt Hnrs 82-84; Bucknell; Bus.

LIND, DAVID; Salesianum Schl; Wilmington, DE; (Y); 95/301; Computer Clb; Nwsp Stf; Hon Roll; Jrnlsm.

LINDE, JASON P; John Dickinson HS; Wilmington, DE; (Y); Am Leg Boys St; Boy Scts; Rep Stu Cncl; Var Bsktbl; Capt Tennis; Gov Hon Prg Awd; Brigham Young U; Pre-Med.

LINDSEY, STEVEN; St Elizabeth HS; Wilmington, DE; (Y); Boys Clb Am; Boy Scts; Church Yth Grp; Computer Clb; Nwsp Phtg; Nwsp Rptr; Nwsp Stf; Yrbk Phtg; Yrbk Stf; Lit Mag; Perf Atten Awd 82-86; Mt St Marys; Eng.

LINK, JEFF; Dover HS; Dover, DE; (Y); Church Yth Grp; Computer Clb; 4-H; German Clb; Math Clb; Math Tm; Science Clb; Teachers Aide; Chorus; Coach Actv; Wrld Krtng Assoc 84; WKA Ntl Pts Chmpn 85; 3rd Pl WKA Ntl Pts 84; Aerospc Engrng.

LIS, KATHLEEN; William Penn HS; New Castle, DE; (Y); Key Clb; Quiz Bowl; Color Guard; Jazz Band; Mrchg Band; Symp Band; JV Var Fld Hcky; Capt L Swmmng; Var Tennis; Hon Roll; U Of DE.

LISS, ERIC; Mc Kean HS; Wilmington, DE; (Y); DECA; Key Clb; Stage Crew; Off Sr Cls; Stu Cncl; VP Bsbl; JV Bsktbl.

LISSY, PETER; Archmere Acad; Glen Mills, PA; (Y); Ski Clb; Spanish Clb; Wt Lftg; High Hon Roll; Hon Roll; NHS; Spanish NHS; Econmcs.

LITTLE, AMY C; Dover HS; Dover, DE; (Y); 38/383; SADD; Band; Drill Tm; Symp Band; JV Var Cheerleading; Var Pom Pon; Im Powder Puff Ftbl; High Hon Roll; NHS; French Clb; Kent Cnty Hnr Band 85-86; All Amer Hnrs Rbnd 86; St Fnlst Miss DE Ntl Teen-Ager 86; Lawyer.

LITTLE, D RENEE; Dover HS; Dover, DE; (Y); Var L Crs Cntry; Timer; Var Trk; Hon Roll; Outstndng Acad Achvt Awd 85-86; Wilma Boyd Career Schl; Flight.

LITTLETON, ANGEL; Sussey Central SR HS; Georgetown, DE; (Y); Girl Scts; VICA; Band; Drill Tm; Mrchg Band; Twrlr; Hon Roll; Ntl Guard; Bus.

LIU, SUSAN; Christiana HS; Newark, DE; (Y); FBLA; JA; Ski Clb; SADD; Band; Mrchg Band; Var Tennis; Excllnc Typng II 86.

LOCKE, AMY; Smyrna HS; Clayton, DE; (S); 7/217; Church Yth Grp; Spanish Clb; Mrchg Band; Symp Band; Gym; High Hon Roll; NHS; Voice Dem Awd; Acad Hall Fame Spnsh 85; Schlr Athlete Gymnstcs 86.

LOCKERMAN, JACKIE; Dover HS; Dover, DE; (S); 42/344; Drama Clb; Office Aide; Trs OEA; Church Choir; Trs Bus Mgr; Yrbk Stf; High Hon Roll; Hon Roll; NHS; 1st Pl Bus Math 83-84; 4th Pl Prepared Vrbl I 84-85.

LOGULLO, CHRISTOPHER; Thomas Mc Kean HS; Hockessin, DE; (Y); 19/225; School Musical; School Play; Variety Show; Nwsp Sprt Ed; Nwsp Stf; Stu Cncl; Capt Swmmng; Hon Roll; Pres NHS; Best Actor 86; Amer Schlr Prss Assoc Mst Otstandng Story Awd 86; U Of DE; Attourney.

LORT, SARAH E; Indian River HS; Selbyville, DE; (S); 19/213; Pres Church Yth Grp; Girl Scts; Math Tm; Spanish Clb; Band; Chorus; Rep Stu Cncl; Hon Roll; NHS; Cataweba Coll NC; Elem Ed.

LOUDERBACK, DAN; Glasgow HS; Newark, DE; (Y); 16/280; Math Tm; Ski Clb; Teachers Aide; Var L Bsbl; Var L Ftbl; Var L Swmmng; Var L Trk; Wt Lftg; High Hon Roll; NHS; 1st Pl DE ST Comp Fair Pgmg Cntst 86; Outstndng Sci Stu 86; Pres Acad Ftns Awd 86; U Of DE; Elctrcl Engr.

LOUGHRAN, MAUREEN; Alexis I Du Pont HS; Greenville, DE; (Y); AFS; Drama Clb; School Play; Cheerleading; JV Swmmng; Hon Roll.

LOVENSHEIMER, KATHRYN; Thomas Mc Kean HS; Wilmington, DE; (Y); Church Yth Grp; Yrbk Stf; Off Stu Cncl; Mgr(s); Var Swmmng; High Hon Roll; Hon Roll.

LOWMAN, SUZANNE; Smyrna HS; Kenton, DE; (Y); OEA; Spanish Clb; Teachers Aide; Lit Mag; Var L Trk; Hon Roll; Prfct Atten Awd; U Of NC Chapel Hill; Bio.

LU, DENNIS; Archmere Acad; Wilmington, DE; (S); German Clb; Math Tm; Varsity Clb; VP L Crs Cntry; VP L Trk; High Hon Roll; NHS; NEDT Awd; Distngshd Prfrmnc Natl Ger II Test 85; Ger Hnr Soc 85; Elec Engr.

LUCAS, FRANCINE; Padua Acad; Wilmington, DE; (S); Hosp Aide; Science Clb; Spanish Clb; High Hon Roll; Pres NHS; JCL; Latin Clb; Band; Rep Frsh Cls; Bio.

LUCAS, TONIA; Padlia Acad; Wilmington, DE; (S); 6/213; Pres French Clb; Pep Clb; Science Clb; Spanish Clb; Ed Yrbk Ed-Chief; Gov Hon Prg Awd; Hon Roll; NHS; NEDT Awd; Frnch Awd 85; Hnrb Mntn In Englsh 84; Yrbk Awd 85; Intl Jrnlsm.

LUCK, KIM; New Castle Baptist Acad; Middletown, DE; (Y); Trs Frsh Cls; Var Cheerleading; Acadmc Excllnc Amer Histry Awd 85; Vet.

LUU, NGANHA; Claymont HS; Claymont, DE; (Y); 14/117; Library Aide; Chorus; Mrchg Band; Hon Roll; Outstndng Awd, Home Ec Awd, Libr Aide Awd-Bac Son HS Viet Nam 82-83; Anatomy.

LYNCH, DAVID; Alexis I Du Pont HS; Wilmington, DE; (Y); Aud/Vis; Trk; High Hon Roll; Hon Roll; Stock Mkt Game Awd 86; Swimmint Inst At YMCA 86; Mech Engr.

LYNCH, KATHY; Laurel SR HS; Laurel, DE; (Y); 6/113; VP AFS; FNA; Pep Clb; Ski Clb; SADD; Varsity Clb; Band; Concert Band; Mrchg Band; Rep Soph Cls; Educ.

LYNCH, MARY; Dover HS; Dover, DE; (Y); Cmnty Wkr; Office Aide; Teachers Aide; Band; Concert Band; Mrchg Band; Symp Band; Im Powder Puff Ftbl; High Hon Roll; NHS; Mrn Bio.

LYONS, DEBBIE; Delcastle Technical HS; Newark, DE; (Y); VICA; Hon Roll; 1st Pl Med Termnlgy St HOSA Conf 86; 1st Pl HOSA Bowl St Conf 86; U DE; Elem Ed.

MACMILLAN, RICHIE; Salesianum HS; Wilmington, DE; (Y); Boy Scts; Camera Clb; Yrbk Rptr; Yrbk Stf; Bowling; Hon Roll; Eagle Scout Awd 86; Bus Adm.

MACTURK, CHRIS; Mt Pleasant HS; Wilmington, DE; (Y); 21/200; Am Leg Boys St; Boy Scts; Rep Band; Concert Band; Jazz Band; Mrchg Band; Golf; JV Tennis; Hon Roll.

MAGUIRE, KAYLYN; Middletown HS; Middletown, DE; (Y); 15/136; Am Leg Aux Girls St; Hosp Aide; Teachers Aide; Mrchg Band; Rep Sr Cls; Stat Sftbl; Capt Twrlr; Hon Roll; NHS; Hnr Rank 86; U DE; Elem Ed.

MAGUIRE, PATRICK H; St Marks HS; Newark, DE; (Y); 95/400; Am Leg Boys St; Church Yth Grp; JA; Latin Clb; SADD; Varsity Clb; Rep Stu Cncl; Var Wrstlng; Hon Roll; Pre-Law.

MAKRAM, MAURICE; Salesianum HS; Parkesburg, PA; (S); Chess Clb; Computer Clb; JV Swmmng; NHS.

MALANEY, LISE; New Castle Baptist Acad; New Castle, DE; (Y); Pres Church Yth Grp; Cmnty Wkr; Hosp Aide; Library Aide; Chorus; Church Choir; VP Frsh Cls; JV Var Bsktbl; L Var Mgr(s); Var Capt Sftbl; Vrsty Vllybl & Sftbl Christian Char Ad 85-86; Miss DE Nat Tnagr Smfnlst 85.

MALESKY, STEVEN; St Marks HS; Wilmington, DE; (Y); 6/346; Exploring; JA; Key Clb; Mgr Band; Ed Yrbk Ed-Chief; Lit Mag; Stu Cncl; High Hon Roll; Hon Roll; NHS; Northwestern U; Jrnlsm.

MALZONE, KIM; Milford SR HS; Milford, DE; (Y); Church Yth Grp; Cmnty Wkr; Drama Clb; Intnl Clb; Political Wkr; SADD; Teachers Aide; Church Choir; School Musical; School Play; Outstndng Acdmc Achvt U DE 86; Soc Wrk.

MANCARI, ADRIANA; Christiana HS; New Castle, DE; (Y); SADD; Color Guard; Flag Corp; Prfct Atten Awd; U DE; Bus Adm.

MAND, GREGORY S; Wilmington Friends Schl; Wilmington, DE; (Y); Am Leg Boys St; Camera Clb; JA; Model UN; Teachers Aide; Temple Yth Grp; Chorus; School Musical; Nwsp Rptr; Yrbk Ed-Chief; Character, Schlrshp, Svc Bush Awd 85-86; Accntnt.

MANGALE, MICAHEL; Salesianum Schl For Boys; Wilmingotn, DE; (Y); Church Yth Grp; Yrbk Stf; Rep Stu Cncl; Var Bsktbl; Capt Crs Cntry; Var Tennis; DE All St Crss-Cntry Tm 84 & 85; Bsktbll Spirit Awd; Aerospc Engrng.

MANLOVE, EILEEN F; St Elizabeth HS; New Castle, DE; (Y); Sec Girl Scts; Hosp Aide; Pep Clb; Service Clb; SADD; Chorus; Church Choir; School Musical; Variety Show; Natl Fndtn For Advncmnt-Arts 86; Carnegie-Mellon U; Music Theatr.

MANNING, MARK; Delcastle Votech HS; Claymont, DE; (Y); Hon Roll; NHS; Ntl Merit Schol; Elect Trades.

MANUCCI, LYNN; Thomas Mc Kean HS; Wilmington, DE; (Y); AFS; Concert Band; Mrchg Band; School Play; Tennis; Hon Roll; Drama.

MARCUS, DESIREE; Dover HS; Dover, DE; (Y); German Clb; Hosp Aide; OEA; NHS; Gregg Shorthand Awd 86; DE Tech & CC; Crmnl Justice.

MARLAND, BELINDA D; Laurel JR SR HS; Marion, VA; (Y); AFS; Cmnty Wkr; French Clb; Office Aide; Pep Clb; Science Clb; Band; Chorus; Color Guard; Drill Tm; Majrtt, Chrldng Awd 82-83; Sci Awd 83; Aidine Stewardess Schl; Arln St.

MARQUEZ, PAUL; Smyrna HS; Smyrna, DE; (S); 5/160; Camera Clb; Church Yth Grp; OEA; Church Choir; Nwsp Phtg; Yrbk Phtg; Mgr(s); Var L Tennis; NHS; St Schlr; Texaco USA DE OEA Stdnt Yr & Rookie Yr DIKC 83; P Mc Gorman Awd 86; U Of DE; Bus Adm.

MARTENS, TAMMY; Seaford SR HS; Seaford, DE; (Y); AFS; Church Yth Grp; Concert Band; Mrchg Band; Yrbk Stf; Hon Roll; Prfct Atten Awd; Tournmnt Of Bnds Outstndg Achvmnt 85-86; Letter Band 83-84; U Of DE; Bus.

MARTIN, PATTI; Dover HS; Dover, DE; (Y); DECA; Library Aide; JV Sftbl; JV Vllybl; Hon Roll; Busnss.

MASCITTI, MICHELLE; Pajvd Acad; Philadelphia, PA; (S); JCL; SADD; Nwsp Ed-Chief; Rep Soph Cls; VP Jr Cls; VP Sr Cls; High Hon Roll; NHS; NEDT Awd; Phila Coll Of Pharm & Sci.

MASINO JR, THOMAS R; Caesar Rodney HS; Dover, DE; (Y); 4/343; Drama Clb; Latin Clb; Spanish Clb; Trs Chorus; School Musical; School Play; Pres Stu Cncl; DAR Awd; High Hon Roll; Trs NHS; Govrnr Schl Excllnc DE 84; 48th Boys ST DE 85; All ST Chorus DE 86; U Of DE; Bus Adm.

MASLANKA, FRANCIS C; Salesianum HS; Landenberg, PA; (S); 6/300; Exploring; German Clb; Yrbk Rptr; JV Bsbl; JV Socr; Var Capt Trk; High Hon Roll; NHS; 2nd Hgst Grade Pt Avg 83-84; Minuteman 85-86; Orthrpdcs.

MASSEY, HEATHER L; Seaford SR HS; Bridgeville, DE; (Y); GAA; Teachers Aide; Var Bsktbl; Var Capt Fld Hcky; Capt Sftbl; Hon Roll; Kiwanis Awd; All Cnfrnc In Fld Hcky 85; All Cnfrnc In Bsktbll/All Team All ST Grd 85; PA ST; Sprts Med.

MASTEN, JACKIE; Smyrna HS; Kenton, DE; (Y); 19/180; OEA; Teachers Aide; Hon Roll; 3rd Pl For Recrds Mgmt I In OEA ST Conf 86; Princpls Awd For Sci 85; Del Tech; Bus.

MATARESE, TRACEY; Delcastle Technical HS; Newark, DE; (Y); VICA; Yrbk Stf; VP Jr Cls; Sr Cls; Stu Cncl; JV Fld Hcky; JV Trk; Hon Roll; Prmdc.

MATHISON, MARY ANN; Padua Acad; Philadelphia, PA; (S); 16/213; Hosp Aide; JCL; Science Clb; Nwsp Rptr; Nwsp Stf; NEDT Awd; Drexel U; Engrng.

MATLUSKY, JOHN; Salesianum Schl; Greenville, DE; (S); 5/285; Pres French Clb; Political Wkr; Scholastic Bowl; Nwsp Stf; Im Bsktbl; Im Bowling; High Hon Roll; Ntl Merit Ltr; Jr Statesmen Soc 85; Pol Sci.

MATTHEWS, VICTORIA; Indian River HS; Ocean View, DE; (S); 2/180; Am Leg Aux Girls St; Spanish Clb; SADD; Nwsp Ed-Chief; Gov Hon Prg Awd; High Hon Roll; Jr NHS; NHS; Intl Frgn Lang Awd 85-86; Sci Awd Sci Olympics 84-85; Natl Math Awd 84-85 & 85-86; U DE; Acctg.

MAXIMO, VICTORIA; Dover HS; Dover, DE; (Y); Am Leg Aux Girls St; Capt Math Tm; Ed Nwsp Rptr; Sec Stu Cncl; Var Capt Cheerleading; High Hon Roll; NHS; HOBY Fndtn Intl Ldrshp Sem 85; DE Miss TEEN 84; Say No To Drugs Natl Pgm Vlntr 86; Emergncy Med.

MAXWELL, STACEY; Padua Acad; New Castle, DE; (Y); Pep Clb; Var L Bsktbl; Var L Sftbl; Hon Roll; NEDT Awd; Tchr.

MAYEW, CHRISTINA; St Marks HS; Wilmington, DE; (Y); Church Yth Grp; Ski Clb; Rep Soph Cls; Rep Jr Cls; Rep Sr Cls; Rep Stu Cncl; Var L Fld Hcky; Var Lcrss; Var L Swmmng; Var Hon Roll.

MC ALLISTER, CHERYL; St Marks HS; Newark, DE; (Y); 31/346; Chorus; Rep Stu Cncl; Hon Roll; NHS; Church Yth Grp; Cmnty Wkr; Intnl Clb; School Musical; Frnch Acdmc Awd 86; Pres Acdmc Ftns Awd 86; DE Hrtg Comm Cnstnl Schlrshp 86; U Delaware; Engl.

MC CABE, LORI; Indian River HS; Ocean View, DE; (S); 7/183; Trs Spanish Clb; Sec SADD; Concert Band; School Musical; Trs Jr Cls; Trs Stu Cncl; Bsktbl; Capt Fld Hcky; Capt Sftbl; NHS; John Hopkins Tlnt Srch 83.

MC CABE, TROY; Indian River HS; Selbyville, DE; (Y); Church Yth Grp; Computer Clb; FFA; Hosp Aide; Red Cross Aide; Spanish Clb; Socr; FFA Achvt Awd Outstndg Perf Sentinel 84; Persnl Apprectn Awd Gov M N Castle 85; Emergncy Mgmt Inst 86; Dentist.

MC CLOSKEY, MATTHEW J; Salesianum HS; Aston, PA; (Y); Boy Scts; Pres Church Yth Grp; German Clb; SADD; JV Crs Cntry; Im Socr; Var Swmmng; Hon Roll; Law.

MC CLURE, CHRISTA; Dover HS; Dover, DE; (Y); Library Aide; OEA; SADD; High Hon Roll; Hon Roll; NHS; Spanish NHS; Natl Sci Olympd 86; Bus.

MC CLURE, REBECCA; Mount Pleasant HS; Claymont, DE; (Y); 22/176; Office Aide; Capt Service Clb; Varsity Clb; Chorus; Ed Nwsp Stf; Var L Vllybl; Prfct Atten Awd; Econ.

MC CORMICK, BRIAN; Delcastle Technical HS; Newark, DE; (Y); VICA; Bsbl; Hon Roll; Prfct Atten Awd; Welder.

MC CORMICK, MARK; Brandywine HS; Wilmington, DE; (Y); 20/256; Varsity Clb; Mrchg Band; Pep Band; School Musical; Symp Band; Stu Cncl; Var L Bsbl; Var L Socr; High Hon Roll; NHS; Penn ST U; Pre-Law.

MC CORMICK, MICHAEL; Salesianum HS; Wilmington, DE; (S); 6/320; Church Yth Grp; JCL; SADD; Im Bsktbl; JV Crs Cntry; JV Ftbl; NHS; 1st Pl DE Math Lge 83; Jhns Hpkns Awd TSWE 83; U Of DE; Accntng.

MC CURDY, CHRIS; A L Du Pont HS; Newark, DE; (Y); 20/340; VP Sr Cls; Stu Cncl; Capt Socr; High Hon Roll; Hon Roll; Jr NHS; Trs NHS.

MC DEVITT, CHRISTINE; Concord HS; Wilmington, DE; (Y); Yrbk Stf; Rep Frsh Cls; JV Sftbl; JV Capt Vllybl; Hon Roll.

MC DONALD, TOM; A I Du Pont HS; Newark, DE; (Y); Boy Scts; High Hon Roll; Hon Roll; Jr NHS; Outstndng Achvt Spn I & II; Outstndng Achvt Alg II & Trig; Outstndng Achvt Engl II; U DE; Elec Engr.

MC ELRATH, JAMIE R; William Penn HS; Port Penn, DE; (Y); 13/487; Am Leg Aux Girls St; Girl Scts; Intnl Clb; Math Clb; Office Aide; Capt Quiz Bowl; Science Clb; Soroptimist; Pres Band; Concert Band; Adv Studies Pgm 85; Century Ldrs ST Rnnr Up 86; Soroptmst Yth Citznshp Awd 86; U DE; Bio.

MC GARRY, MARIE; Archmere Acad; Media, PA; (Y); Trs Church Yth Grp; Spanish Clb; Band; JV Fld Hcky; Trk; Hon Roll; Drama Clb; Latin Clb; School Musical; School Play; Business.

MC GINNIS, SANDY; Cape Henlopen HS; Lewes, DE; (Y); Camera Clb; Ski Clb; L Var Bsktbl; Var L Fld Hcky; Hon Roll; Jr NHS; Hosp Aide; Office Aide; Yrbk Stf; Stu Cncl; Hmn Svcs.

MC GRAW, DAWN; Glasgow HS; Newark, DE; (Y); 10/475; Chess Clb; Scholastic Bowl; Yrbk Phtg; Cheerleading; Gov Hon Prg Awd; High Hon Roll; NHS; Ntl Merit SF; Camera Clb; Girl Scts.

MC GUINNESS, MOIRA; Archmere Acad; Wilmington, DE; (Y); Cmnty Wkr; 4-H; French Clb; Yrbk Phtg; JV Bsktbl; Var Fld Hcky; Var Tennis; JV Vllybl; 4-H Awd; Hon Roll; Won Trip To Natl 4-H Congress In Chicago For Photo 85; Med.

MC ILVAINE, JOSH; John Dickinson HS; Wilmington, DE; (Y); 29/229; Church Yth Grp; JCL; Latin Clb; Symp Band; Yrbk Stf; Stu Cncl; Socr; Swmmng; Hon Roll; NHS; VA Tech; Lbrl Arts.

MC INTOSH, CAREY; Ursuline Acad; Newark, DE; (Y); GAA; Yrbk Stf; Var Swmmng; Var Vllybl; Swmmng All-Amercn Tm 86; 1st Tm All-Cthlc Swm Tn 85-86.

MC KENNA, SHANNON; Ursuline Acad; Middletown, DE; (Y); VP Church Yth Grp; Model UN; Science Clb; Spanish Clb; Im Bsktbl; Im Fld Hcky; High Hon Roll; NHS; Ntl Merit Ltr; Diamond ST Schlr 86; Womns Clb Odessa Schlrshp 86; U Of NC Chapel Hill; Med.

MC KINNEY, MITCHELL M; Wilmington HS; Wilmington, DE; (Y); 32/168; Boy Scts; VP Church Yth Grp; Pres SADD; Varsity Clb; Band; Stage Crew; Rep Stu Cncl; Hon Roll; JA; Spch & Drama Awd 86; Boston U; Htl Rstrnt Mgmt.

MC KOLVOY, ROBIN; A I Du Pont HS; Greenville, DE; (Y); Aud/Vis; VP JA; Scholastic Bowl; Crs Cntry; Capt Trk; Hon Roll; Ntl Merit SF; U DE.

MC MILLAN, MARK; John Dickinson HS; Newark, DE; (Y); Ski Clb; Mrchg Band; School Play; Stage Crew; Symp Band; JV L Ftbl; Var L Swmmng; Var L Tennis; Wt Lftg; Hon Roll; Bus Adm.

MC NELIS, MICHELLE E; Caesar Rodney HS; Dover, DE; (Y); Aud/Vis; Debate Tm; Drama Clb; VP German Clb; Natl Beta Clb; Scholastic Bowl; VP Science Clb; Teachers Aide; Nwsp Rptr; Nwsp Stf; Jrnlsm Awd 84; Gov Hnrs Regnl 84; U DE; Jrnlsm.

MEHAN, ANDREW; William Penn HS; New Castle, DE; (Y); Boy Scts; Church Yth Grp; Computer Clb; Drama Clb; JA; Speech Tm; Band; Concert Band; Mrchg Band; Symp Band; Fest Of Musc 86; Engrg.

MEIER, LISA M; Mt Pleasant HS; Wilmington, DE; (Y); 5/170; Sec AFS; Cmnty Wkr; Exploring; Math Clb; Band; Mrchg Band; Yrbk Ed-Chief; Ed Yrbk Phtg; Trs NHS; Ntl Merit SF; Psych.

MELSON, PATRICIA L; Cape Henlopen HS; Lewes, DE; (Y); Thesps; Band; Chorus; Concert Band; Mrchg Band; Yrbk Rptr; Yrbk Stf; Stat Fld Hcky; Sftbl; Hon Roll; Acad Awd Engl 86; Pres Acad Fit Awd 86; U FL; Phrmcy.

MELVIN, KELLIE; Dover HS; Dover, DE; (Y); Girl Scts; JA; Library Aide; Office Aide; OEA; Capt Bowling; High Hon Roll; Hon Roll; NHS; Outstndng Stu Kent Cnty 86; Cntst Mdrn Ms Pgnt 86; Bus.

MENZEL, ANNE-MARIE L; William Penn HS; New Castle, DE; (Y); 10/486; Church Yth Grp; JA; Key Clb; Math Tm; Spanish Clb; NHS; Pres Schlr; Acad Incntv 86; U Of DE; Comp Sci.

MERCANTE, VINCENT; Salesianum Schl; Wilmington, DE; (Y); 82/292; Boy Scts; Im Bowling; High Hon Roll; Hon Roll; Sfty Twn Teen Of Day Awd 85; U Of DE; Arch.

MERKLEY, MELINDA; Seaford SR HS; Seaford, DE; (S); Church Yth Grp; Math Tm; SADD; Band; Trs Frsh Cls; Rep Soph Cls; Sec Jr Cls; JV Fld Hcky; NHS; Johns Hopkins Prog For Gifted & Tlntd 82-85; Rnnr Up Govnrs Schl Excllnc; Pre Law.

MERRILL, ANTHONY J; Indian River HS; Ocean View, DE; (Y); 36/200; Drama Clb; Band; Concert Band; Mrchg Band; School Musical; School Play; Var Ftbl; Socr; Wt Lftg; High Hon Roll; U Of DE; Poli Sci.

MESHREKI, SAMER; Concord HS; Wilmington, DE; (Y); Boy Scts; Computer Clb; Concert Band; Jazz Band; Mrchg Band; Symp Band; High Hon Roll; Hon Roll; NHS; Church Yth Grp; DSYMPY Acclrtd Math Pgm 84-87; Comp Sci.

MESSICK, WENDY; Seaford SR HS; Seaford, DE; (Y); 12/190; Hst GAA; VP SADD; School Play; Ed Yrbk Stf; Hst Frsh Cls; Stu Cncl; L Fld Hcky; Capt Tennis; Cit Awd; NHS; Blue Gold Queen St Of DE 86; AU Conf Tm Fld Hockey & Tennis 84-85; U Of GA; Pblc Rltns.

MESSINA, JOSEPH A; Mt Pleasant HS; Wilmington, DE; (Y); JV Bsbl; Hon Roll; Elec Engrng.

METCALF, ANDREW O; The Tatnall Schl; Wilmington, DE; (Y); Chorus; Jazz Band; Yrbk Phtg; Var L Crs Cntry; Hon Roll; Ntl Merit SF.

METZLER, ERICH; Salesianum Schl; Wilmington, DE; (S); 10/272; Jazz Band; VP Mrchg Band; School Musical; Symp Band; Off Sr Cls; Rep Stu Cncl; NHS; Ntl Merit Ltr; Drexel U; Comp.

MEYER, DAVID M; Concord HS; Wilmington, DE; (Y); 6/250; Computer Clb; Library Aide; Math Tm; Scholastic Bowl; Teachers Aide; Nwsp Stf; Hon Roll; NHS; Ntl Merit SF; U VA; Elec Engrng.

MICALLEF, JANE; Archmere Acad HS; Wilmington, DE; (S); Sec French Clb; School Musical; Stage Crew; Nwsp Rptr; Rep Frsh Cls; Rep Soph Cls; Var Im Fld Hcky; Socr; High Hon Roll; NHS; Ursuline Acadmy Acad Schlrshp 83; Archmere Acadmy Acad Schlrshp 83.

MICHALCEWIZ, WILLIAM W; Archmere Acad; Wilmington, DE; (S); Trs Church Yth Grp; Dance Clb; JV Crs Cntry; JV Ftbl; JV Trk; Wt Lftg; High Hon Roll; Hon Roll; NHS; NEDT Awd; Mst Imprvd JV Ftbl Plyr 84; Johns Hopkins Tlnt Srch 82-86.

MIKEAL, KONOVIA; Padua Acad; Wilmington, DE; (Y); Hosp Aide; JA; Latin Clb; Pep Clb; Service Clb; Spanish Clb; SADD; Var Mgr(s); Hon Roll; Geo Washington U; Bus Admn.

MILHOAN, SUSAN; Caesar Rodney HS; Dover, DE; (Y); 80/365; Alderson Broaddus Coll; Nrsng.

MILLER, CHRIS; St Marks HS; Newark, DE; (Y); Rep Soph Cls; Rep Jr Cls; Var Crs Cntry; Var Gym; Var Trk; Hon Roll; Phy Thrpy.

MILLER JR, JAMES W; Salesianum Schl; Townsend, DE; (Y); 58/301; Church Yth Grp; Cmnty Wkr; French Clb; JCL; Latin Clb; School Play; Yrbk Stf; Crs Cntry; Ed.

MILLER, JON; Concord HS; Wilmington, DE; (Y); Boy Scts; Pres Band; Chorus; Concert Band; Drm Mjr(t); Jazz Band; Madrigals; Mrchg Band; School Musical; Symp Band; Naval ROTC Scholar 86; Outstndng Musician 86; VA Tech; Engrng.

MILLER, LESLI R; Sussex Central SR HS; Georgetown, DE; (Y); 36/187; Cmnty Wkr; Pres Key Clb; SADD; Varsity Clb; Rep Stu Cncl; Var Fld Hcky; Cit Awd; DAR Awd; Elks Awd; NHS; Gov Yth Vlntr Svc Awd 86; Elks Lodge Schlrshp; SICO Fndtn Schlrshp Alternate; Salisbury ST Coll; Phy Ed.

MILLER, LYNN; Seaford SR HS; Seaford, DE; (Y); GAA; Key Clb; OEA; SADD; Teachers Aide; Crs Cntry; Trk; Hon Roll; 2nd Tm All-Cnfrnc Soph Yr X-Cntry 84; Corp Law.

MILLER, MIKE; Smyrna HS; Kenton, DE; (Y); Computer Clb; Var Bsbl; Hon Roll; Archtctr.

MILLOY, KIMBERLY; Indian River HS; Bethany Bch, DE; (S); 2/187; Ski Clb; Band; Chorus; Var Cheerleading; Var Pom Pon; Var Tennis; High Hon Roll; NHS.

MILLS, DENNIS I; Milford HS; Milford, DE; (Y); 12/198; SADD; High Hon Roll; Hon Roll; NHS; Occupations Awd 86; Farming.

MILLS, DIANNE A; Mc Kean HS; Hockessin, DE; (Y); Drama Clb; French Clb; Q&S; School Musical; School Play; Variety Show; Nwsp Phtg; Nwsp Rptr; Pres Frsh Cls; Rep Soph Cls; Acad All Conf Fld Hcky , Tnns; Rosemont Coll; Bus Admn.

MIMS, RAE; Dover HS; Dover, DE; (Y); Library Aide; Math Tm; Band; Flag Corp; Mrchg Band; Lit Mag; Rep Soph Cls; Rep Jr Cls; Rep Stu Cncl; Outstndng Kent Cty Stu 86; Jrnlsm.

MITCHELL, BONNIE; Indian River HS; Frankford, DE; (S); 13/201; DECA; Drm Mjr(t); Capt Twrlr; Dnfth Awd; High Hon Roll; Hon Roll; Jr NHS; NHS; Prfct Atten Awd; 1st Pl ST Lvl Pepsi Lrn & Ern 84-85; Deca Stu Of Yr 84-85; Accntng.

MITCHELL, TONYA; Indian River HS; Frankford, DE; (S); Office Aide; SADD; Chorus; Nwsp Rptr; Var Cheerleading; Var Sftbl; Capt Twrlr; High Hon Roll; Hon Roll; Off Jr NHS.

MODI, JIGNESH; John Dickinson HS; Wilmington, DE; (Y); 5/186; JA; Socr; Hon Roll; IN U; Optomtry.

MOFFETT, RHONDA; Concord HS; Wilmington, DE; (Y); 20/253; Sec JA; JCL; Latin Clb; Science Clb; VP Jr Cls; VP Sr Cls; Cheerleading; Capt Twrlr; High Hon Roll; NHS; VA Tech; Bio.

MONACO, MEG; Archmere Acad; Wilmington, DE; (Y); Trs German Clb; SADD; Chorus; Coach Actv; Score Keeper; Wt Lftg; High Hon Roll; NHS; Ntl Merit SF; Grmn Ntl Hnr Soc 86; DE ST Music Tchrs Assoc Trphy 84; Semi-Fnlst Cngrs Bndstg Yth Exchng Pgm 86; Pre-Med.

MONAGHAN, MEGAN; Ursuline Acad; Wilmington, DE; (Y); Am Leg Aux Girls St; Church Yth Grp; Trs French Clb; Model UN; Political Wkr; Chorus; School Musical; School Play; Nwsp Phtg; Gov Hon Prg Awd; Amer Lgn Auxlry Girls Nation Senetors 86; Ballet Stu & Soloist Lcl Ballet Co 83-84; Musical Thtr.

MONEY, BRIAN; Smyrna HS; Clayton, DE; (Y); Chess Clb; CAP; Quiz Bowl; Band; Hon Roll; Delaware U; Physcs.

MONGELUZI, DONNA; Padua Acad; Philadelphia, PA; (S); Pep Clb; Pres Science Clb; Hon Roll; NHS; Drexel U; Med.

MONIGLE, MELODY; Padua Acad; Middletown, DE; (Y); 60/214; Sec Church Yth Grp; Dance Clb; Pep Clb; School Musical.

MOODY, THOMAS; Laurel SR HS; Georgetown, DE; (Y); Computer Clb; 4-H; Teachers Aide; VICA; 4-H Awd; Penn ST.

MOORE, BILL; Salesianum Schl; Aston, PA; (Y); Cmnty Wkr; Exploring; Hosp Aide; SADD; Var L Bsktbl; Hon Roll; Acctg Mgmt.

MOORE, CHARLES; Dover SR HS; Dover, DE; (Y); Var Socr; Bus Admin.

MOORE, DARRYL; Dover HS; Hartly, DE; (Y); Church Yth Grp; Debate Tm; 4-H; ROTC; Var L Ftbl; Powder Puff Ftbl; Trk; Vllybl; Wt Lftg; Hon Roll; TROA ROTC Mdl 86; DE ST Coll; Agri-Bus.

MOORE, DEENA; Milford SR HS; Milford, DE; (Y); 34/198; DECA; Office Aide; Nwsp Rptr; Nwsp Stf; JV Cheerleading; High Hon Roll; Hon Roll; 3rd Pl ST Wnr DECA Cndy Sales 84, 5th Pl 85; ST Achvt Awd Gen Mrchndsg DECA 86; U DE; Fshn Mrchndsg.

MORGAN, PATRICK; Salesianum HS; Wilmington, DE; (Y); 53/292; Cmnty Wkr; Spanish Clb; Band; Concert Band; Im Bsktbl; Im Bowling; JV Crs Cntry; Im Socr; Hon Roll; Comm.

MORGAN, RAYMOND; Delmar HS; Delmar, MD; (Y); 10/93; Computer Clb; Teachers Aide; VICA; Hon Roll; Prgmng.

MORRIS, H QUENTIN; Cape Henlopen HS; Lewes, DE; (Y); Am Leg Boys St; Church Yth Grp; Exploring; Math Tm; OEA; Church Choir; Bsktbl; High Hon Roll; Sec NHS; Sci Olympd Awd 83-85; Ldrshp Day Awd 84-86; Brd Of Govr Schlrshp Acadmc Achvmnt 85-86; Shippensburg U; Mech Engrng.

MORRIS, LORI; Delmar HS; Delmar, DE; (Y); 21/106; Pres Church Yth Grp; Trs FHA; Sec FTA; SADD; Teachers Aide; Chorus; Nwsp Rptr; St Schlr; Church Choir; Hon Roll; Geo E Gordy Schlrshp 86; DE Post Secndry Schlrshp 86; Salisbury ST Coll; Elem Ed.

MORRIS, MEMORY; Padua Acad; Wilmington, DE; (Y); Church Yth Grp; Cmnty Wkr; JA; Pep Clb; Service Clb; Stage Crew; Yrbk Stf; U Of DE.

MORRISSEY, TIMOTHY; Salesianun HS; New Castle, DE; (S); 29/300; Boys Clb Am; Capt Var Bsktbl; High Hon Roll; NHS; Comm.

MOSLEY, MICHAEL; Lake Forest HS; Felton, DE; (Y); 8/164; French Clb; OEA; Varsity Clb; Yrbk Stf; Capt Crs Cntry; Capt Tennis; Trk; High Hon Roll; NHS; U Acdmc Achvt Schrlshp 86; U Delaware; Elec Engrng.

MUELLER, BARBARA; Archmere Acad; Media, PA; (Y); NFL; Drill Tm; School Musical; Var Capt Crs Cntry; Var Capt Trk; Hon Roll; Hosp Aide; Ntl Catholic Forensic Leag Ourn Fnlst 83; Gettysburg Coll; Physcl Thrpy.

MUELLER, KRISTIN; Mt Pleasant HS; Claymont, DE; (Y); 14/150; Trs AFS; Church Yth Grp; Concert Band; Mrchg Band; School Musical; Stage Crew; Yrbk Stf; Co-Capt Sftbl; JP Sousa Awd; NHS; 2 Outstndng Achvts German 83&84; Orch-Musical, Best Orch Mbr Awd 8 4; Schlrshps Valpo; Valparaiso U; Pre-Med.

MULLARKEY, SUZANNE; Ursuline Acad; Wilmington, DE; (Y); Model UN; Soph Cls; Bsktbl; Fld Hcky; Tennis; Vllybl; High Hon Roll; NHS; Ntl Merit Ltr; Schrlshp Ursuline Acad 82; NEDT Awd 84; Schlrshp St Josephs U 86; Boston Coll; Elem Ed.

MUMFORD, DARLENE; Indian River HS; Frankford, DE; (S); 18/213; VP OEA; Spanish Clb; Teachers Aide; Concert Band; Mrchg Band; Stat Bsktbl; High Hon Roll; Jr NHS; Masonic Awd; NHS; Acadmc Achvt Awd 85-86; Presdntl Acadmc Achvt Awd 85-86; DE ST Coll; Acctng.

MUNIZ, MARCO A; A I Du Pont HS; Wilmington, DE; (Y).

MUNYON, ROBERT; Mount Pleasant HS; Wilmington, DE; (Y); Ski Clb; Bsbl; U Of DE; Electrical Engrng.

MURPHY, BETTY L; New Castle Baptist Acad; New Castle, DE; (Y); Church Yth Grp; Chorus; Church Choir; Nwsp Stf; Var Capt Cheerleading; Hon Roll; Prfct Atten Awd; Liberty U; Busnss Admin.

MYNUK, NICHOLAS M; Claymont HS; Claymont, DE; (Y); Ftbl; Wrstlng.

NACZI, MAUREEN; Concord HS; Wilmington, DE; (Y); 16/330; Am Leg Aux Girls St; VP JA; VP JCL; Pres Sec Latin Clb; Nwsp Rptr; Nwsp Stf; Bsktbl; Vllybl; Gov Hon Prg Awd; Hon Roll; Brown U Distngshd JR Englsh Awd 86; Englsh.

NAGY, KAREN; Delcastle Tech HS; Wilmington, DE; (Y); 13/384; Cmnty Wkr; Hosp Aide; VICA; High Hon Roll; Hon Roll; NHS; Pres Schlr; Ntl Merit Sci Awd; Medcl Asst.

NASH, AMY; Mc Kean HS; Wilmington, DE; (Y); Church Yth Grp; DECA; Color Guard; School Musical; School Play; Nwsp Stf; Yrbk Stf; Off Stu Cncl; Var Cheerleading; Hon Roll; Pltcl Sci.

NEAL, JAMES P; Newark HS; Newark, DE; (Y); 60/295; Boy Scts; JA; Ski Clb; Var Lcrss; Var Socr; Hon Roll; U Of IL; Statstcs.

NELSON, BOB; Smyrna HS; Smyrna, DE; (S); 10/190; Am Leg Boys St; Pres Church Yth Grp; Drama Clb; Hosp Aide; Pres Frsh Cls; Pres Soph Cls; Var L Bsktbl; Var L Ftbl; Var L Trk; High Hon Roll; West Pt; Med.

NELSON, GARY; Sussex Central HS; Millsboro, DE; (Y); SADD; Band; Chorus; Church Choir; Concert Band; Var L Crs Cntry; Var L Trk; Im Wt Lftg; Hon Roll; Achvmnt Music 86; 1st Chr Cnty Band Tuba 85&86; Music.

NETTA, BILL; Christiana HS; Newark, DE; (Y); Am Leg Boys St; Church Yth Grp; Ski Clb; Varsity Clb; Var Capt Crs Cntry; Var Capt Trk; Hon Roll; French Clb; SADD; All ST Crs Cntry 85; Alasa ST Champ 86; All Cnty Crs Cntry 85.

NEVDICK, HEATHER; Dover HS; Scotts Valley, CA; (Y); 49/328; French Clb; Office Aide; SADD; Teachers Aide; Band; Drill Tm; Mrchg Band; Symp Band; Rep Stu Cncl; JV Var Cheerleading; All Amer Hnr Bnd 86; Kent Cnty Bnd 85-86; ST Fnlst Miss DE Natl Tn-Agr 86; Pltcl Sci.

NEWSOME, STACEY; Milford SR HS; Houston, DE; (Y); GAA; Office Aide; Varsity Clb; Nwsp Rptr; Nwsp Sprt Ed; Bsktbl; Sftbl; High Hon Roll; Jr NHS; NHS.

NGUYEN, LINH; Delcastle Vocational Tech; Wilmington, DE; (Y); VICA; Hon Roll; Elec.

NGUYEN, TUAN H; Christiana HS; Newark, DE; (Y); 8/285; Chess Clb; Computer Clb; Exploring; French Clb; Hosp Aide; VP JA; Library Aide; Mathletes; Math Tm; Red Cross Aide; Math Dep Excllnt In Calculus 85-86; David Chambers Awd 85-86; Newark Jaycees Schlrshp 85-86; Uof DE; Pre-Med.

NICOLL, KATHLEEN; Padua Acad; Wilmington, DE; (S); 8/185; Girl Scts; Science Clb; Y-Teens; Nwsp Ed-Chief; Yrbk Phtg; Gov Hon Prg Awd; NHS; Yth In Govt.

NOREM, APRIL; Claymont HS; Claymont, DE; (Y); French Clb; Band; Chorus; Concert Band; Drm Mjr(t); Mrchg Band; School Musical; Hon Roll; All ST Band; U DE; Comm.

NORRIS, SHERRI J; Christiana HS; Newark, DE; (Y); Am Leg Aux Girls St; Chess Clb; Girl Scts; Science Clb; SADD; Band; Stu Cncl; Trk; NHS; Prfct Atten Awd; Pre Med.

NORRIS, TERRI L; Christiana HS; Newark, DE; (Y); Am Leg Aux Girls St; Girl Scts; Model UN; Science Clb; Band; Lit Mag; Rep Stu Cncl; Var Capt Fld Hcky; Trk; NHS; All ST Band 85; Yth In Govt 85; Grl Sct Gld Awd 84; Sci.

NORWOOD, GEMEZ; Sussex Central HS; Millsboro, DE; (Y); Hon Roll; Bus.

O BRIEN, ERIN P; Archmere Acad; Media, PA; (Y); Art Clb; Chorus; Stage Crew; Villanova U; Law.

O BRIEN, KATHLEEN A; Padua Acad; Wilmington, DE; (Y); 28/180; French Clb; Hosp Aide; Math Clb; Pep Clb; Service Clb; SADD; Im Trk; High Hon Roll; Goldey Beacom Coll Bacclrt Schlrshp 86; John B Lynch Schlrshp Fndtn Grnt 86; Goldey Beacom Coll; CPA.

O CONNELL, CIARA M; Archmere Acad; Wilmington, DE; (S); 5/110; Pres 4-H; JV Crs Cntry; Var Fld Hcky; Var Swmmng; Var Trk; French Hon Soc; Gov Hon Prg Awd; High Hon Roll; NHS; Var Powder Puff Ftbl; Oxford; Foreign Affrs.

O NEAL, ANNETTA LILLIAN; Newark HS; Newark, DE; (Y); 3/316; Library Aide; Office Aide; SADD; Teachers Aide; Church Choir; Rep Stu Cncl; L Mgr(s); Score Keeper; Trk; Hon Roll; FAME 81; Miss Feb 86, Miss Calndr Girl 86; Debtnt; Fnce.

O NEAL, SHARON; Ursuline Acad HS; Wilmington, DE; (Y); Am Leg Aux Girls St; French Clb; Nwsp Ed-Chief; Nwsp Stf; Lit Mag; Var Fld Hcky; Dnfth Awd; Hon Roll; NHS; NEDT Awd; 3rd Pl Essay Cntst 85; HOBY Ldrshp Sem 85; Boston U; Jrnlst.

O NEILL, MARY; Ursuline Acad; Wilmington, DE; (Y); Var L Swmmng; VA Common Wealth U; Phych.

O ROURKE, GERARD; Salesianum HS; Wilmington, DE; (S); 19/272; Pres Chess Clb; Math Tm; Jazz Band; Mrchg Band; School Musical; Symp Band; Variety Show; NHS; Natl Mrt Lttr 86; Achvt Acdmy; Dstngshd Amer HS Stu Soc; Chem Engrng.

OBORYSHKO, KATHLEEN; John Dickinson HS; Wilmington, DE; (Y); 20/280; Church Yth Grp; PAVAS; SADD; Band; Mrchg Band; School Musical; Symp Band; Hon Roll; NHS; Accntng.

OGRODNICK, STAN; Christiana HS; Newark, DE; (Y); French Clb; Var Socr; Var Tennis; Hon Roll; U Of DE; Mchnl Engnr.

OLSEN, ARTHUR; Newark HS; Newark, DE; (Y); Aud/Vis; Church Yth Grp; Exploring; Lit Mag; High Hon Roll; Hon Roll; U Of DE; Elec Engrng.

OLSEN, MELANIE; Smyrna HS; Smyrna, DE; (S); 5/192; Co-Capt Math Tm; Trs Mrchg Band; Trs Symp Band; Gov Hon Prg Awd; High Hon Roll; NHS; Cmnty Wkr; Drama Clb; Quiz Bowl; SR Delaware All-ST Band 85-86; DE All-Orch; 2nd Chair Kent Cnty Hnrs Bnad; Coll Of William & Mary; Biochem.

OLSON JR, JAMES; Lake Forest HS; Harrington, DE; (Y); 13/165; Church Yth Grp; Pres French Clb; Spanish Clb; Pres Band; Chorus; Church Choir; Concert Band; Jazz Band; Mrchg Band; Orch; 1st Pl ST Wide Spnsh Cntst 85-86; Am Music Found Awd 85-86; West Chester U; Music Ed.

ORLANDO, SUSAN; Smyrna HS; Smyrna, DE; (S); #11 In Class; French Clb; OEA; Mrchg Band; Trs Jr Cls; Cheerleading; Fld Hcky; Hon Roll; NHS; Phys Ther.

ORR, KEN; Archmere Acad; Newark, DE; (Y); Drama Clb; Chrmn SADD; Band; Concert Band; Mgr Jazz Band; School Play; Stage Crew; Capt Bowling; Golf; Wrstlng; Bus Mgmt.

ORTIZ, ROBIN; Wilmington HS; Wilmington, DE; (Y); 3/140; Am Leg Aux Girls St; Hosp Aide; Ski Clb; Pres Frsh Cls; Pres Soph Cls; Pres Jr Cls; Pres Sr Cls; Capt Fld Hcky; Capt Tennis; Pres Schlr; WHS Otstngdng Female Athlt 86; Dickinson Coll; Pre-Med.

OSBORNE, ANN C; Newark HS; Newark, DE; (Y); Am Leg Aux Girls St; Spanish Clb; SADD; Flag Corp; Mgr(s); Swmmng; Lion Awd; NHS; Church Yth Grp; Drama Clb; ALMNI Cls Of 85 Schlrshp 86; Var Ltr & Hgh Gpa Awd 82-86; Amrcn U; Intl Stds.

OSHAUGHNESSY, MARY; Seaford SR HS; Seaford, DE; (Y); AFS; GAA; Key Clb; Math Tm; Concert Band; Mrchg Band; Crs Cntry; Var L Trk; Hon Roll; Woodwind 1st Lt Mrchg Bnd 84; Woodwind Capt 85-86; Phys Ther.

OSHAUGHNESSY, STEPHANIE; St Marks HS; Newark, DE; (Y); Church Yth Grp; Ski Clb; SADD; Rep Soph Cls; Rep Jr Cls; Rep Stu Cncl; JV Var Cheerleading; Lcrss; U Of VA; Jrnlsm.

PALALAY, HEIDI; Dover HS; Dover, DE; (Y); VP French Clb; Math Tm; Pres Band; School Musical; Pres Symp Band; Var Capt Tennis; Gov Hon Prg Awd; Hon Roll; Outstndng Acad Achvt Awd 86; B & B Music Awd 84; YMCA Yth In Govt 86; Music.

PALLACE, CHRISTINE; Caesar Rodney HS; Dover, DE; (Y); 14/349; Am Leg Aux Girls St; Pres French Clb; Sec Frsh Cls; Sec Soph Cls; Sec Jr Cls; Sec Sr Cls; Var Capt Cheerleading; Elks Awd; High Hon Roll; Sec NHS; Wake Frst Acdmc Schlrshp; Wake Forest U; Math.

PALMER, MARK; Salesianum HS; Wilmington, DE; (S); 11/310; VP French Clb; Concert Band; Mrchg Band; Im Tennis; High Hon Roll; Jr NHS; NHS; Stanford U; Govt Law.

PAMPUCH, KIM; John Dickinson HS; Wilmington, DE; (Y); 18/250; Church Yth Grp; Drama Clb; Ski Clb; School Musical; School Play; Stage Crew; Mgr Ftbl; Mgr(s); Swmmng; Hon Roll; CPA.

PANTULIANO, NANCY; Padua Acad; New Castle, DE; (Y); Band; Concert Band; Mrchg Band; Symp Band; U Of DE; Acctng.

PAPA, TONI NICOLE; Padua Acad; Philadelpia, PA; (Y); Church Yth Grp; Cmnty Wkr; JCL; Latin Clb; Library Aide; Pep Clb; Science Clb; SADD; Teachers Aide; Hon Roll; Law.

PAPP, DEBBIE; Dover HS; Dover, DE; (Y); Church Yth Grp; Cmnty Wkr; OEA; Yrbk Stf; Bowling; Powder Puff Ftbl; High Hon Roll; NHS; Outstndng Acadmc Achvt Awd 86.

PARKINSON, LISA; Sussex Central HS; Millsboro, DE; (Y); 4/250; Aud/Vis; French Clb; SADD; Rep Frsh Cls; Rep Stu Cncl; Cheerleading; Tennis; Jr NHS; NHS; Law.

PARMAN, TRACI; Mt Pleasant HS; Wilmington, DE; (Y); 40/170; Art Clb; JA; U DE; Mrktg.

PARRAMORE JR, JAMES WM; Indian River HS; Selbyville, DE; (Y); Boy Scts; Church Yth Grp; Band; Chorus; Concert Band; Jazz Band; Mrchg Band; Bsbl; Ftbl; Trk; Cnty Bnd; Cert Of Exclnc In Mech 85; Auto Mech.

PARROTT, VICKI K; Seaford HS; Seaford, DE; (Y); Library Aide; Teachers Aide; School Play; Yrbk Stf; Lit Mag; Im Sftbl; Hon Roll; German Book Awd 86; Sunday Schl Nrsry Class Teacher & Aide 80-86; Elem Educ.

PARSONS, DAVID; Indian River HS; Selbyville, DE; (S); 20/200; French Clb; Math Clb; Concert Band; Mrchg Band; School Musical; JV Bsbl; High Hon Roll; Hon Roll; Jr NHS; Pres NHS; Outstndg Acdmc Achvmnt HS Awd 85-86; Acdmc All Amer 85-86; Natl Merit Awd 85-86.

PASQUARELLA, WILLIAM; Salesianum HS; Philadelphia, PA; (Y); 114/292; Chess Clb; Hosp Aide; SADD; Band; Rep Stu Cncl; Im Capt Bsktbl; Im Capt Bowling; Im Capt Ice Hcky; Im Capt Socr; Im Capt Sftbl; U Of FL; Comp Sci.

PASTERNAK, BRYAN; Salesianum HS; Hockessin, DE; (S); 14/301; Church Yth Grp; Math Tm; Service Clb; SADD; Trk; JV Capt Wrstlng; High Hon Roll; Ntl Merit SF.

PATCHEL, STEVEN J; Salesianum School For Boys; Kennett Square, PA; (Y); 57/262; Camera Clb; Drama Clb; Chorus; School Musical; Nwsp Stf; Stu Cncl; Hon Roll; Schlrshp Oberlin Consrvtry 86-87; Schlrshp Cathlc U Of Amer; Oberlin Conservatory.

PAVCO, LUANNE; Padua Acad; Wilmington, DE; (S); Pep Clb; Spanish Clb; Sftbl; Swmmng; Vllybl; Hon Roll; NHS; NEDT Awd; Library Aide; Math Awd; Phy Ed Awd.

PEARSON, JOY; Seaford SR HS; Seaford, DE; (Y); 19/270; GAA; Stage Crew; Rep Soph Cls; Rep Jr Cls; Rep Stu Cncl; JV Var Fld Hcky; Var L Trk; Hon Roll.

PEARSON, TAMIKA; Christiana HS; Newark, DE; (Y); VP FBLA; JA; Office Aide; OEA; Pep Clb; Spanish Clb; SADD; Teachers Aide; Cheerleading; Trk; Lttrs Vrsty Chrldg; OEA VP Awd; Hampton Inst U; Bus Adm.

PEEL, PAUL; Holy Cross HS; Dover, DE; (Y); 2/34; Boy Scts; Bsbl; Socr; Bausch & Lomb Sci Awd; High Hon Roll; NHS; Sal; Spanish NHS; Loyola Coll MD 86; Ofcrs Wives Clb Schlrshp 86; Natl Hnr Socty Schlrshp 86; Loyola Coll MD; Bus.

PELAIA, MARIA TERESA; Padua Acad; Wilmington, DE; (S); 8/181; JA; Stage Crew; Nwsp Rptr; Nwsp Stf; Off Jr Cls; Sec Trs Sr Cls; Cheerleading; High Hon Roll; NHS; NEDT Awd; Dectfl Italn Oral Lang Cont 1st Pl 83-85; USSCA Wnnr 85-86; Pre-Law.

PELEGRIN, KATHY; Padua Acad; Wilmington, DE; (Y); JCL; Latin Clb; Pep Clb; SADD; Rep Stu Cncl; Vllybl; Hon Roll.

PEPE, MATTHEW D; Salesianum HS; Wilmington, DE; (S); 22/272; Church Yth Grp; Spanish Clb; Concert Band; Im Bsktbl; Im Socr; Im Wt Lftg; High Hon Roll; NHS; NROTC Schlrshp Fnlst; Bus.

PEPETA, GERRY; Salesianum HS; Wilmington, DE; (Y); 115/299; Cmnty Wkr; Hosp Aide; SADD; Nwsp Rptr; Hon Roll; U DE; Nrsng.

PEPPER, TERESA; Cape Henlopen HS; Milton, DE; (Y); Math Tm; Band; Sftbl; Bausch & Lomb Sci Awd; High Hon Roll; Jr NHS; NHS; Prfct Atten Awd; SICO Schlrshp 86; U Of DE; Comp Sci.

PERNA, KEVIN; William Penn HS; New Castle, DE; (Y); Library Aide; Scholastic Bowl; Bsbl; Ftbl; Wt Lftg; Hon Roll; Capt Ftbl 86; Capt Bsbl 87; Outstndng JR Lnmn Ftl & MVP-MI JV Bsbl 85; Engrng.

PERRY, LETITIA; Delcastle Technical HS; Wilmington, DE; (Y); Church Yth Grp; Girl Scts; Library Aide; Office Aide; Pep Clb; Radio Clb; Band; Chorus; Concert Band; Jazz Band; Hon Mntn Sci Fair 83; 2nd Pl Mdl HOSA Bwl 86; Hampton U; Bus Admin.

PERRY, MELISSA R; Sussex Central SR HS; Georgetown, DE; (Y); AFS; Church Yth Grp; Library Aide; OEA; Teachers Aide; Thesps; School Musical; CC Awd; High Hon Roll; Jr NHS; Acctng Achvt Awd 86; U Of NC Chrltt; Acctng.

PESCE, LUCIA; Padua Acad; Wilmington, DE; (Y); 60/210; Church Yth Grp; Pep Clb; Hon Roll; U DE; Comm.

PETERS, KRIS; William Penn HS; New Castle, DE; (Y); Key Clb; Office Aide; Ski Clb; Spanish Clb; Teachers Aide; Yrbk Stf; Rep Stu Cncl; Var Capt Cheerleading; Hon Roll; Bus.

PETTIJOHN, TRACEE W; Claymont HS; Claymont, DE; (Y); 2/117; Computer Clb; Sec Pres Latin Clb; Scholastic Bowl; Ski Clb; SADD; School Musical; Pres Rep Stu Cncl; Stat Bsktbl; Var Cheerleading; NHS; Stu Mnth; Aerospace Engrng.

PEUGH, DEBBIE; Seaford SR HS; Seaford, DE; (S); 4/250; Key Clb; Science Clb; Band; Mrchg Band; Sec Frsh Cls; Sec Soph Cls; Var L Cheerleading; DAR Awd; High Hon Roll; NHS; Physcn.

PEYTON, KELLY; Newark HS; Landenberg, PA; (Y); Debate Tm; French Clb; Speech Tm; Thesps; School Play; Rep Stu Cncl; High Hon Roll; NHS; Ntl Merit SF; Voice Dem Awd; 5th UIL Lincoln Douglas Debate 85; Hnrbl Ment Actng 85; Recgntn Frnch 85.

PEZELY, DANIEL; Newark SR HS; Newark, DE; (Y); Art Clb; Boy Scts; Church Yth Grp; Computer Clb; Lit Mag; JV Socr; Comp Pgmmr Apprntce 85; 1st Pl AIASA Comp Aided Drftg Cont 86; Drexel U; Comp Pgmmr.

PFEIFER, CHRIS; Milford SR HS; Milford, DE; (Y); Am Leg Boys St; Boy Scts; Concert Band; Jazz Band; Mrchg Band; L Capt Socr; Var L Trk; High Hon Roll; NHS; ST Champion Track & Field 86; All Conf Socr 85; Aero-Space.

PHILHOWER, DAVE; Newark HS; Newark, DE; (Y); 15/332; Am Leg Boys St; Ski Clb; SADD; Teachers Aide; Variety Show; Pres Frsh Cls; Rep Soph Cls; VP Pres Stu Cncl; JV Socr; High Hon Roll; Biolgcl Sci.

PHILLIPS, CASANDRA LYNN; Sussex Central SR HS; Georgetown, DE; (Y); AFS; Church Yth Grp; Cmnty Wkr; Dance Clb; Key Clb; OEA; Capt Pep Clb; PAVAS; Spanish Clb; Pres SADD; Miss DE Natl Teenager 86; Miss DE Natl Teenager Miss Congenialty Awd 86; Ms DE Ms Hemisphere 86; OK City U; Fashion Merch.

PIERCE, D J; Archmere Acad; Wilmington, DE; (Y); Concert Band; School Musical; School Play; Stage Crew; Coach Actv; Ftbl; Mgr(s); Socr; Tennis; Hon Roll; Band Coordinator 86-87; Swmmr Of Wk & Mst Imprvd Swmmr Of Season 85; Arch.

PIERCE, LISA; Indian River HS; Dagsboro, DE; (S); 6/170; CAP; Computer Clb; Drama Clb; English Clb; Math Clb; Office Aide; Quiz Bowl; Pres Spanish Clb; SADD; Nwsp Rptr; Fclty Schlrshp 86; Pres Fit Awd 86; DE Tech CC; Humn Svcs.

PIETROBONO, LISA M; Archmere Acad; Wilmington, DE; (Y); Spanish Clb; Bowling; Cheerleading; Sftbl; Spanish NHS; Itln Clb 85-87; Itln Ntl Hnr Soc 86-87; Chrstn Svc Pgm 86-87; U Of DE; Bus Adm.

PIGEON, DANIEL W; Thomas Mc Kean HS; Wilmington, DE; (Y); Boy Scts; JA; JV Wrstlng; Mech Engrng.

PILEGGI, THERESA M J; Archmere Acad; Chadds Ford, PA; (Y); Cmnty Wkr; French Clb; Yrbk Stf; Pres Soph Cls; Trs Sr Cls; Stat Bsbl; Stat Socr; French Hon Soc; NHS; Ntl Merit Schol; Acad All Am 85-86; U VA; Pre-Med.

PITCHER, SANDRA L; Middletown HS; Townsend, DE; (Y); Science Clb; Yrbk Sprt Ed; Yrbk Stf; Rep Frsh Cls; VP Jr Cls; Rep Sr Cls; Rep Stu Cncl; Var Fld Hcky; JV Sftbl; Townsedn Wmns Clb Schlrshp 86; Stu Lison Cmmittee 86; Schagrin Gentile Specl Schlrshp 86; Wesley Coll; Nrsng.

PIZZO, STEPHANIE; Padua Acad; Philadelpia, PA; (Y); Dance Clb; Library Aide; Service Clb; Teachers Aide; Concert Band; Jazz Band; Variety Show; Yrbk Phtg; Rep Frsh Cls; Rep Jr Cls; Art Schlrshp 84; Stu Councl Awd 86; Library Adie Awd 85; Psych.

PLEASANTON, ANNETTE; Dover HS; Dover, DE; (S); Church Yth Grp; OEA; Nwsp Ed-Chief; Nwsp Stf; Yrbk Rptr; VP Soph Cls; CC Awd; High Hon Roll; Stu Mth 86; 5th Pl Rec OEA 86; Comp Prcsng.

PLEASANTON, MIKE; Smyrna HS; Smyrna, DE; (Y); 60/240; Library Aide; Spanish Clb; Varsity Clb; Nwsp Rptr; Nwsp Stf; Ftbl; Tennis; Prfct Atten Awd; Prfct Attndc 83-84.

PLYSTAK, CAROL; Padua Acad; Claymont, DE; (Y); Art Clb; Church Yth Grp; Cmnty Wkr; Capt Flag Corp; Mrchg Band; Rep Jr Cls; Rep Stu Cncl; JV Var Mgr(s); L Twrlr; Acad All-Amer 86; U Of DE; Art Edu.

POCIUS, MARY; Dover HS; Dover, DE; (Y); 36/306; Library Aide; JV Bsktbl; L Bowling; JV Mgr(s); High Hon Roll; Hon Roll; NHS; Ntl Merit SF; U Of DE; Mech Engrng.

POHLAND, OLIVER; Salesianum Schl; Wilmington, DE; (S); 8/272; VP Im Tennis; Hon Roll; NHS; Amer Assn Tchrs Ger Cert Merit 84-85; Cornell U; Physcs.

POPE, MICHAEL; Holy Cross HS; Milford, DE; (Y); Computer Clb; Varsity Clb; JV Var Bsbl; JV Var Bsktbl; U DE; Comp Sci.

PORTER, BRIAN; Dover HS; Hortley, DE; (Y); DECA; Var L Ftbl; Wt Lftg; Bus Adm.

PORTER, KEVIN J; John Dickinson HS; Wilmington, DE; (Y); 2/200; Am Leg Boys St; JCL; Latin Clb; Capt Math Tm; Scholastic Bowl; Trs Sr Cls; Stu Cncl; Var Crs Cntry; Var Capt Swmmng; Var Tennis; Govnrs Schl Of Excel 84; Prfct Scr Ntl Ltn Exam 84; 1st Pl ST Calcltr Cntst 86; Swarthmore Coll; Engrng.

POSDON, AMY; Dover HS; Dover, DE; (Y); JA; Band; Symp Band; Lit Mag; Bowling; Crs Cntry; Powder Puff Ftbl; Sftbl; Tennis; Hon Roll; Art Mgmt.

POSTLES, CHRISTINE; Dover HS; Cheswold, DE; (Y); FNA; German Clb; Hosp Aide; JA; OEA; SADD; Lit Mag; Rep Frsh Cls; Rep Soph Cls; High Hon Roll; Art.

POZSGAY, BRIAN; Seaford SR HS; Seaford, DE; (Y); 2/184; Speech Tm; Concert Band; Mrchg Band; Stage Crew; Yrbk Stf; High Hon Roll; NHS; Sal; St Schlr; 2nd Pl St For Amer Chem Soc Test 86; GA Inst Of Tech; Elec.

PRICE, JACQUELINE D; William Penn HS; Wilmington, DE; (Y); 4/487; Exploring; Math Tm; Scholastic Bowl; Trs Spanish Clb; Band; Rep Stu Cncl; Capt Cheerleading; DAR Awd; Gov Hon Prg Awd; Pres NHS; Hghst Acad Achvt Grl Inst Aim Engnrng Prog 85; Natl Achvt Schlrshp Outstndng Minrty Stu Semi Fin 85; GMI Eng & Mng Inst; Indust Eng.

PRICE, MICHELE; Indian River HS; Millville, DE; (S); 14/176; Spanish Clb; SADD; Nwsp Stf; Var Tennis; High Hon Roll; Jr NHS; NHS; Museum Stds.

PRILLAMAN, DEREK; Smyrna HS; Smyrna, DE; (Y); 16/150; Art Clb; Varsity Clb; Stu Cncl; Var JV Bsbl; Var JV Bsktbl; Var JV Ftbl; Hon Roll; French Clb; Prfct Atten Awd; 1st Tm All Conf Ftbl 85-86; 3rd Tm All ST Ftbl 85-86; VP Art Clv 85-86; Visual Comm.

PRITCHARD, LAURI; Cape Henlopen HS; Rehoboth, DE; (Y); Am Leg Aux Girls St; Ski Clb; School Play; Nwsp Stf; Var Cheerleading; High Hon Roll; Jr NHS.

PRITCHARD, ROBERT; Christiana HS; Newark, DE; (Y); FBLA; VP JA; Spanish Clb; Var L Bsbl; Hon Roll; NHS; U DE; Acctg.

PRITCHETT, SELENA; Dover HS; Dover, DE; (Y); FFA; German Clb; ROTC; Im Bsbl; Im Sftbl; Im Tennis; Im Vllybl; Im Wt Lftg; Embrlgy.

PROCINO, MICHELE; Laurel SR HS; Laurel, DE; (Y); AFS; Pep Clb; Varsity Clb; Band; Rep Frsh Cls; Rep Soph Cls; Rep Jr Cls; Trs Pres Stu Cncl; L Var Fld Hcky; High Hon Roll; Law.

PRUCKMAYR, BETTINA; Archmere Acad; Media, PA; (Y); German Clb; Spanish Clb; Stage Crew; Lit Mag; Trk; Hon Roll; NHS; Spanish NHS; Foriegn Lang.

PRUITT, JULIE REED; Delmar JR SR HS; Delmar, MD; (Y); 26/105; Drama Clb; FHA; Pres OEA; SADD; Chorus; Stu Cncl; Hon Roll; Acad Achvt Awd-2nd Pl Engl III 85 & 3rd Pl Shrthand II 85; Sussex Trust Bank Bus Awd 86; Salisbury ST Coll; Comm Arts.

PRUSAK, STEVEN; St Marks HS; Newark, DE; (Y); 1/350; L Var Golf; L Var Ice Hcky; High Hon Roll; NHS; Val; Channel 6 & Gms Bst Clss 86; St Marks HS U Of DE Schlrshp; St Marks HS Schlr Athlt Awd; U Of DE; Chemcl Engr.

PUDVAN, ROBERT; Thomas Mc Kean HS; Wilmington, DE; (Y); 17/256; High Hon Roll; Hon Roll; Prfct Atten Awd; Engl Phys Ed Wads 85; Math,Comp Sci 86; Annapolis; Engrng.

PURANDARE, SANJAY; Seaford SR HS; Seaford, DE; (S); 19/300; VP Key Clb; Library Aide; OEA; Pres Jr Cls; VP Stu Cncl; Var Socr; Var Tennis; Hon Roll; Prom Chrmn 86; Aerosp Engrng.

PURSE, VICKIE; Padua Acad; Wilmington, DE; (S); 18/180; Band; Sec Trs Mrchg Band; Symp Band; Rep Soph Cls; NHS; NEDT Awd; Spanish NHS; U Of Norte Dame; Math.

PUSEY, MARK; Laurel SR HS; Laurel, DE; (Y); Cmnty Wkr; Computer Clb; Office Aide; Aud/Vis; Teachers Aide; VICA; High Hon Roll; Hon Roll; Prfct Atten Awd; Outstndng Stdnt Awd Sussex Vo Tech 86.

QUIGLEY, MELISSA; Newark HS; Newark, DE; (Y); Nwsp Rptr; Nwsp Stf; Hon Roll; Bus Mgmt.

QUILLEN, DIA; Sussex Central HS; Georgetown, DE; (Y); 2/207; AFS; Am Leg Aux Girls St; Thesps; School Musical; Rep Stu Cncl; L Capt Cheerleading; High Hon Roll; Hon Roll; Jr NHS; NHS; Bill Roth Ldrshp Cnfrnc 86; Intl Rltns.

QUINLAN, JEFFREY; A I Du Pont HS; Wilmington, DE; (Y); Chess Clb; Drama Clb; Band; Concert Band; Jazz Band; Mrchg Band; School Play; Symp Band; Yrbk Phtg; Yrbk Stf; Wrtg.

RAFFEL, ALLISON; Newark HS; Newark, DE; (Y); 7/350; VP Drama Clb; Pres French Clb; School Play; Stage Crew; Nwsp Rptr; Yrbk Stf; Lit Mag; Jr NHS; NHS; ST DE Gov Schl Exclince 85; Natl Engl Essay Comptn Contstnt 86; U DE Summr Coll 86.

RANDALL, RUSSELL; Dover HS; Dover, DE; (Y); Office Aide; VP Chorus; Church Choir; Madrigals; Hon Roll.

RANISZEWSKI, PATRICIA; Padva Acad; Wilmington, DE; (S); 16/181; Art Clb; Library Aide; Science Clb; Yrbk Rptr; Lit Mag; Hon Roll; NHS; Ntl Merit Ltr; NEDT Awd; Plnt Sci.

RASERO III, LAWRENCE J; Tower Hill Schl; Hockessin, DE; (Y); JA; Socr; Tennis.

RASH, REBECCA; St Marks HS; Wilmington, DE; (Y); Church Yth Grp; Drama Clb; Hosp Aide; JA; Key Clb; Service Clb; School Musical; School Play; Yrbk Rptr; Lit Mag; U DE.

RAYNE, SUSAN; Indian River HS; Selbyville, DE; (S); 15/202; French Clb; Spanish Clb; Yrbk Stf; Co-Capt Cheerleading; Fld Hcky; High Hon Roll; Jr NHS; NHS; Cmmrcl Art.

REED, ANTOINETTE; Alexis I Du Pont HS; Wilmington, DE; (Y); 91/273; Pep Clb; SADD; Band; Concert Band; Mrchg Band; Pep Band; Symp Band; VP Frsh Cls; Rep Soph Cls; Pres Jr Cls; Frm To Advnc Mnrts In Engrng 82-85; Gynclgy.

REED, GREG; Smyrna HS; Clayton, DE; (Y); VP Chess Clb; Pres Church Yth Grp; OEA; Quiz Bowl; Spanish Clb; Lit Mag; Rep Frsh Cls; Rep Soph Cls; Rep Jr Cls; Rep Stu Cncl; ST Ctzn Bee Fnlst 86; Econ.

REED, STEPHANI; Concord HS; Wilmington, DE; (Y); 56/250; AFS; JA; Yrbk Stf; Cheerleading; Twrlr; Hon Roll.

REES, BRIAN; Salesianum HS; Wilmington, DE; (S); 44/272; Cmnty Wkr; Rep Stu Cncl; Var Ftbl; Im Socr; Wt Lftg; High Hon Roll; Hon Roll; Jr NHS; 1st Tm Al-Cathlc Conf Ftbl 85.

REGAN, LAUREN; Padua Acad; Wilmington, DE; (Y); French Clb; JCL; Latin Clb; Pep Clb; Rep Soph Cls; Rep Jr Cls; Rep Stu Cncl; JV Bsbl; Var Cheerleading; Var Capt Crs Cntry; Phys Educ Awd 84-85; Notre Dame; Med.

REISS JR, ROBERT J; Smyrna HS; Smyrna, DE; (Y); 33/192; CAP; Spanish Clb; Var Crs Cntry; JV Trk; Ntl Merit Ltr; Prfct Atten Awd; Prncpls Awd Acad Excel 85; Aerosp Sci.

REISTER, ELIZABETH; Indian River HS; Ocean View, DE; (S); 1/213; Am Leg Aux Girls St; Drama Clb; Political Wkr; Pres SADD; Chorus; School Musical; Swing Chorus; Stu Cncl; Fld Hcky; Gov Hon Prg Awd; Hstry.

RENDE, PAUL; Salesi Anum HS; Wilmington, DE; (S); 34/315; Cmnty Wkr; Office Aide; Im Bsktbl; High Hon Roll; Hon Roll; NHS; JV Bsbl; Im Tennis; Boston Coll; Law.

RENZETTE, ANTHONY J; Salesianum HS; Newark, DE; (Y); Camera Clb; French Clb; SADD; Stage Crew; Yrbk Phtg; Yrbk Stf; Hon Roll; Pre-Med.

REPPERT, JOCELYN; Caravel Acad; Elkton, MD; (S); Church Yth Grp; Math Tm; Chorus; School Musical; Yrbk Rptr; Stu Cncl; Var Fld Hcky; Var Sftbl; High Hon Roll; DE Comp Faire Calcltr Tm; Psych.

REYNOLDS, MARK; Milford SR HS; Milford, DE; (Y); FFA; SADD; Varsity Clb; Stage Crew; Var Capt Crs Cntry; Var L Wrstlng; High Hon Roll; Hon Roll; MVP Wrstlng 84-86; Bus Ed Awd 86; Messiah Coll; Acctg.

RIBLETT, GREG; Caesar Rodney HS; Dover, DE; (Y); Debate Tm; JA; Latin Clb; JV Var Socr; Hon Roll; NHS; JCL; Letterman Clb; Prfct Atten Awd; ST Fnlst VP Prod JR Achvt 86; Cum Laude Ntl Latin Exam Latin I 84; DE U; Bus.

RICE, CHRISTOPHER; Caravel Acad; Bear, DE; (S); Computer Clb; Drama Clb; Math Tm; School Musical; School Play; JV Var Socr; High Hon Roll; Hon Roll; Chess Clb; Church Yth Grp; 1st Pl ST Comp Prog Cntst 84-85; 1st Pl Tm ST Cncl Math Lgu 83-84; Comp Sci.

RICKARDS, TERRI; Indian River HS; Dagsboro, DE; (S); 16/160; Church Yth Grp; Spanish Clb; SADD; Yrbk Ed-Chief; Stu Cncl; Fld Hcky; Sftbl; Trk; High Hon Roll; Hon Roll; Supr Acad Achvt 84-86; Math And Ldrshp Awd 86; Soc Of Dstngsd Am H S Stu 86; U Of DE; Bus.

RIDER, JAY; Delmar JR SR HS; Laurel, DE; (Y); VP Key Clb; JV L Bsktbl; JV L Ftbl; Acdmc Awd 2nd Trig & Alg III 85-86; U Of DE; Ag.

RIES, KEVIN; St Marks HS; Newark, DE; (Y); Rep Frsh Cls; Rep Soph Cls; Rep Jr Cls; Rep Sr Cls; Rep Stu Cncl; JV Lcrss; Var Socr; Var Tennis; Hon Roll; U Of DE; Bio.

RIGGLEMAN, KAREN; Seaford SR HS; Seaford, DE; (Y); Church Yth Grp; Band; Chorus; Church Choir; School Play; Stu Cncl; Var Capt Cheerleading; High Hon Roll; Hon Roll; Concert Band; Aplchn Srv Prjct 84 & 85; U DE; Nrsng.

RILEY, PAUL; Salesianum HS; Wilmington, DE; (S); 1/300; French Clb; Speech Tm; Thesps; Chorus; School Musical; School Play; Rep Stu Cncl; Gov Hon Prg Awd; High Hon Roll; NHS; Hgst Rank Cls 84-85; Acad Schlrshp 84-87; Med.

RILEY, SUSAN; Padua Acad; Wilmington, DE; (Y); French Clb; Flag Corp; School Play; Stat Var Bsktbl; JV Var Score Keeper; Hon Roll; Prfct Atten Awd; U Of DE; Bus Adm.

RILEY, TINA; Concord HS; Wilmington, DE; (Y); VP AFS; Chorus; Yrbk Bus Mgr; Mgr(s); Var L Score Keeper; Mgr Sftbl; Hon Roll; U Of DE Schlrshp 86; U Schlrshp Grnt 86; U Of DE; Comp Sci.

RIMMER, CHRIS; Milford HS; Milford, DE; (Y); Am Leg Boys St; Church Yth Grp; Varsity Clb; Band; School Play; Var L Ftbl; Var L Trk; JV L Wrstlng; Hon Roll; NHS; Mst Dedctd Ftbl Plyr 85; Coachs Awd Wrstlg 84-85; Susquehanna U; Pharmclgy.

RITTENHOUSE, KATHY; Seaford SR HS; Seaford, DE; (Y); 16/174; Drama Clb; Math Tm; Office Aide; Concert Band; Mrchg Band; School Play; Rep Stu Cncl; Hon Roll; NHS; JA Appld Eco Mngmt Game-1st Pl-ST 86; Lttrd-Band 83-84; Clemson U; Accntng.

ROBBINS, SYLVIA D; Thomas Mc Kean HS; Wilmington, DE; (S); 25/217; Am Leg Aux Girls St; Church Yth Grp; Chorus; Variety Show; Nwsp Rptr; Rep Frsh Cls; Rep Soph Cls; Pres Jr Cls; Stu Cncl; Q&S; Close-Up Pgm WA D C 86; Comm.

ROBERTS, DEBRA; Dover HS; Dover, DE; (Y); 54/328; Sec Church Yth Grp; OEA; Sec Church Choir; Rep Soph Cls; Trk; High Hon Roll; NHS; German Clb; JA; Pep Clb; Outstndng Stdnt Achvt U Of DE 86; ST Sci Olympd 3rd Pl Medl 86; OEA Bus 3rd Pl Troph ST Conf 86; Law.

ROBINO, GREGORY; Salesianum HS; Westchester, PA; (Y); 33/292; Cmnty Wkr; Dance Clb; SADD; Yrbk Rptr; Yrbk Stf; Rep Stu Cncl; Hon Roll; NHS; Chem Engrng.

ROBINSON, ALYSSA BLAKE; Newark HS; Newark, DE; (Y); #7 In Class; VP JA; Teachers Aide; Nwsp Bus Mgr; Nwsp Ed-Chief; Lit Mag; Hon Roll; Jr NHS; NHS; JA 3rd Pl Offcr Yr Awd 83 & 84; Pres Acad Fit Awd 86; 2nd Pl Awd Page Layout DE Schltc Press 84; U DE.

ROBINSON, CAROL LYNN; Concord HS; Wilmington, DE; (Y); 30/250; Drama Clb; French Clb; German Clb; School Musical; Nwsp Ed-Chief; Yrbk Stf; Var Trk; Elks Awd; VP NHS; Scripps Howard Journlsm Schlrshp 86; John B Lynch Fndtn Schlrshp 86; 1st & 3rd Gov Comm 85-86; Boston U; Journlsm.

ROBINSON, JEFF; Salesianum HS; Newark, DE; (Y); 92/292; Church Yth Grp; Rep Frsh Cls; Rep Soph Cls; Var Ftbl; Golf; Hon Roll; Bus.

ROBINSON, KARLA; Seaford HS; Seaford, DE; (Y); 13/184; GAA; Band; Church Choir; School Play; Ed Yrbk Stf; Mgr Soph Cls; Var Trk; High Hon Roll; Hon Roll; Prfct Atten Awd; Hnr Key 86; George E Gordon Schlrshp 86; Div II Long Jump ST Champ 86; Syracuse U; Lawyer.

ROBINSON, KELLEY A; Padua Acad; Chester, PA; (S); 5/181; Hosp Aide; VP JA; SADD; School Musical; NHS; NEDT Awd; Spanish NHS; Church Yth Grp; Grl Sct Slvr Ldrshp & Slvr Awds 83; Natl Sci Olympd Co Medlst Chem 85; Excllnc Awd Bio, Spnsh 84-85; Neumann Coll; Bus Adm.

ROBINSON, KIM; Caesar Rodney SR HS; Dover, DE; (Y); GAA; Office Aide; Spanish Clb; Rep Soph Cls; JV Var Cheerleading; Hon Roll; U Of DE.

ROBINSON, MARK; Alexis I Du Pont HS; Hockessin, DE; (Y); Var Ftbl; JV Wrstlng; Hon Roll; Salisbury ST Coll; Sprts Med.

RODAN, JEANETTE; Caesar Rodney HS; Dover, DE; (Y); FFA; Spanish Clb; Color Guard; Mrchg Band; Hon Roll; NHS; Acadmc All Amercn 85-86; Vet.

RODDY, MICHAEL; Salesianum HS; Wilmington, DE; (S); 23/263; Am Leg Boys St; Aud/Vis; Chrmn Church Yth Grp; Cmnty Wkr; Mathletes; Service Clb; Sec Trs Stu Cncl; Capt Swmmng; High Hon Roll; NHS; ST Semi Fnlst Japan USA Sen Exchg 84; Engr.

RODGERS, CHARISSE L; St Marks HS; Wilmington, DE; (Y); Am Leg Aux Girls St; Office Aide; Rep Stu Cncl; Mgr Trk; High Hon Roll; NHS; Ntl Merit SF; Church Yth Grp; Civic Clb; Cmnty Wkr; Oustndng Stdnt FAME Prog 83; GMI Schlrshp 85; Calcls Awd GMI Smmr 85; Corp Acctg.

RODRIGUEZ, MARIA; Dover HS; Dover, DE; (Y); 118/306; Art Clb; Library Aide; Hon Roll; Cmrcl Art.

ROGERS, GRANT; Laurel HS; Laurel, DE; (Y); 16/123; Pres SADD; Band; Trs Stu Cncl; Trk; Hon Roll; Church Yth Grp; JA; Math Tm; Pep Clb; Bus.

ROSAS, ANN MARIE; Saint Andrews HS; Seaford, DE; (Y); Chorus; Concert Band; VP Frsh Cls; Trs Soph Cls; Var Fld Hcky; Var Tennis; High Hon Roll; Art Clb; Camera Clb; Cmnty Wkr; Gordon H Sunbury Awd 85; MIP Tnns Awd 85 & 86; Discipln Cmmtte Pres 84-86; Prefectshp 86.

ROSE, JEFF; Sale Sianum HS; Wilmington, DE; (Y); Exploring; SADD; Band; Im Bowling; Im Socr; Hon Roll; Music.

ROSE, LISA; Holy Cross HS; Dover, DE; (Y); Am Leg Aux Girls St; Church Yth Grp; Hosp Aide; Speech Tm; Nwsp Stf; Yrbk Ed-Chief; Rep Soph Cls; Sec Jr Cls; Sec Stu Cncl; Var JV Sftbl.

ROSSELL, DANA; St Marks HS; Wilmington, DE; (Y); Church Yth Grp; Drama Clb; FNA; SADD; Acpl Chr; Chorus; Church Choir; School Musical; School Play; Gov Hon Prg Awd; Elizabeth Quigley Music Schlrshp Vcl 86; U Of DE Newark; Nrsg.

ROSSER, BARBARA; Thomas Mc Kean HS; Wilmington, DE; (Y); 11/210; Am Leg Aux Girls St; Chorus; Drill Tm; School Musical; Swing Chorus; Hon Roll; NHS; Rep Stu Cncl; Mgr(s); Church Yth Grp; John B Lynch Schlrshp 86; Best Band Front Mbr 84&85; Mc Keon Choir Booster Schlrshp Awd 86; Westchester U; Psych.

ROWE, SHAWNEEN; Padua Acad; Wilmington, DE; (S); 2/213; Church Yth Grp; Pep Clb; School Musical; School Play; Variety Show; High Hon Roll; NHS; Govrnrs Schl For Excllnc 85; Hugh O Brien Yth Ldrshp Smnr 85; Comm.

RULLO, JOSEPH; Salesianum HS; West Chester, PA; (Y); 170/297; Aud/Vis; Church Yth Grp; SADD; Crs Cntry; Trk; Bus Admn.

RUMSEY, MELISSA; Smyrna HS; Clayton, DE; (Y); Pres 4-H; French Clb; Band; Capt Color Guard; Concert Band; Rep Frsh Cls; Var JV Trk; 4-H Awd; Hon Roll; Rcvd Trphy Bnd Frnt Lylty, Spirit & Attitd 85-86; U Of Deleware.

RUSDEN, CHRISTINE; Vrsvline Acad; Wilmington, DE; (Y); Trs AFS; French Clb; JA; Ski Clb; Flag Corp; Nwsp Stf; Yrbk Stf; 3rd Pl St Frnch Cntst 83; St Josephs U.

RUSSELL, GARRY; Saint Marks HS; Newark, DE; (Y); JA; DAR Awd; Hon Roll; Chem Engr.

RUSSO, CHARLES; Claymont HS; Claymont, DE; (Y); 10/150; Am Leg Boys St; Computer Clb; VP DECA; Pres JA; Scholastic Bowl; Spanish Clb; SADD; Teachers Aide; Stat Bsktbl; JV Trk; Sec Intl Yth Yr Awd 85; 3rd Natl Rest Mktg&mgt DECA, 1st St Pub Spkg DECA 86; U DE; Bus Admin.

RUST, LOWELL; Alexis I Dupont HS; Wimington, DE; (Y); 22/260; Am Leg Boys St; Church Yth Grp; JCL; Latin Clb; Var L Bsktbl; JV Ftbl; Var L Tennis; High Hon Roll; Dance Clb; Score Keeper; Excllnce Awd Alg, Trig & Amer Hist.

RUTKOWSKI, VICKI; Delcastle Technical HS; Wilmington, DE; (Y); Cmnty Wkr; Mgr VICA; High Hon Roll.

RYAN, CHRISTIAN; Archmere Acad; Wilmington, DE; (S); 1/110; Church Yth Grp; Math Tm; Scholastic Bowl; Chorus; School Musical; Var Socr; Spanish NHS; Jazz Band; Swing Chorus; VP Soph Cls; Rickover Sci Schlr, Attnd 6 Wk Inst & Wrote Math Rsrch Paper 85; Hugh O Brien At ST & Alt Natl; MIT; Engrng.

SACRE, ANTONIO; Archmere Acad; Newcastle, DE; (Y); JA; Acpl Chr; Chorus; School Musical; School Play; Var Bsbl; Var Socr; High Hon Roll; Hon Roll; Spanish NHS; All ST Chorus; Number 1 Mrktng VP-ST JR Achvt; Coaches Awd-Vrsty Soccer; Leigh; Librl Arts.

SADOWSKI, JOHN; Indian River HS; Millville, DE; (S); Cmnty Wkr; Teachers Aide; Band; Chorus; Concert Band; Jazz Band; Mrchg Band; DE All ST Band 82-86; Outstndng Band Stu Awd 81-83; DE All Cty Band 82-86; Music.

SADUSKY, STEFANIE; St Marks HS; Wilmington, DE; (Y); Am Leg Aux Girls St; Concert Band; Drm Mjr(t); Mrchg Band; Church Yth Grp; Girl Scts; Math Tm; Model UN; Political Wkr; SADD; Yth In Govt-Pres Of Senate 86; Grls ST Govrnr-YMCA Pgm 86; Yth Conf-Ntl Affrs 86; Law.

SALAMEDA, RICKY; St Marks HS; Wilmington, DE; (Y); JA; SADD; Yrbk Bus Mgr; Yrbk Stf; Rep Jr Cls; Rep Sr Cls; Var Tennis; Hon Roll; U Of DE; Bus Mrktg.

SAMPLE, KEVIN; Mc Kean HS; Wilmington, DE; (Y); School Play; Stage Crew; Variety Show; Nwsp Rptr; Nwsp Stf; JV Var Crs Cntry; JV Trk; Hon Roll; Archlgy.

SANCHEZ, ADELAIDA; Wilmington HS; Wilmington, DE; (Y); Church Yth Grp; Cmnty Wkr; JA; Office Aide; Teachers Aide; JV Var Vllybl; Hon Roll; Prfct Atten Awd; FHA; Im Badmtn; Otstndng Hispanic Yth Of Yr 85; Otstndng Concert Stu Chorus 83-84; Coldey Beacom Coll; Bus Admin.

SANTORE, CHRISTOPHER; Salesianum HS; New Castle, DE; (Y); Bowling; Ftbl.

SANTOS, MARICEL; Seaford SR HS; Seaford, DE; (S); Cmnty Wkr; Key Clb; Math Tm; Nwsp Stf; Pres Frsh Cls; Pres Soph Cls; Rep Jr Cls; Stu Cncl; Var L Crs Cntry; Var L Trk; Natl Wnr Essay Cont 500 Scholar 85; Outstndg Frsh Soph 83-85; Eng.

SARGENT, BRETT; Delmar HS; Delmar, DE; (Y); 12/115; Key Clb; Science Clb; Rep Frsh Cls; Var L Bsbl; Var L Ftbl; Hon Roll; Sci Olmpd Tm 86; Widener U; Elctrcl Engrng.

SARKISSIAN, BRIAN; Salesianum HS; Claymont, DE; (Y); 115/250; Art Clb; Boy Scts; Church Yth Grp; Exploring; Band; Concert Band; Mrchg Band; Orch; Symp Band; Hon Roll; MIP Music 82-83; U DE; Photo.

SATTERFIELD, KAREN; Christiana HS; Newark, DE; (Y); Cmnty Wkr; French Clb; Hosp Aide; Library Aide; Ski Clb; SADD; Teachers Aide; Color Guard; Drill Tm; School Play; Top 10 Pct Natl Score PSATS 85; Elizabethtown U; Boutique Ownr.

SCAFARIA, JEFFREY; Salesianum HS; West Chester, PA; (S); 17/262; Church Yth Grp; Exploring; JCL; Rep Stu Cncl; Var Capt Socr; High Hon Roll; Ntl Merit Ltr; Cert Merit SAT/ACT Cmmnwlth PA 85; All-Cath Tm Soccer 85; William & Mary; Acctg.

SCARBOROUGH, FAITH; Laurel SR HS; Laurel, DE; (Y); OEA; VP VICA; Hon Roll; Prfct Atten Awd; Data Entry-4th St Ofc Educ Assn 86, 4th Lcl Comp VICA 86, & 13th Natl OEA 85; DE Tech & CC; Bnkng Svcs.

SCARSONE, THERESA; St Marks HS; Wilmington, DE; (Y); 99/362; Var Gym; Var Vllybl; Hon Roll; NEDT Awd; Pre-Med.

SCHEIBE, DEBBIE; Saint Marks HS; Claymont, DE; (Y); Mrchg Band; Var Crs Cntry; Var Trk; Capt Twrlr; Hon Roll; U Of DE; Bus Admin.

SCHEING, BRIDGET; Padua Acad; Wilmington, DE; (S); 3/213; Hosp Aide; JCL; Latin Clb; Pep Clb; Science Clb; Yrbk Stf; NHS; NEDT Awd; Ntl Sci Olympd Bio Awd 85; Ntl Sci Olympd Gen Sci Awd 84; Ntl JR Clsscl Leag Magna Cum Laude Awd 84; Villanova U; Bus Adm.

SCHIAVI, HARRY; Salesianum HS; Wilmington, DE; (S); 20/270; Var Bsktbl; Var Capt Ftbl; Var Trk; Hon Roll; NHS; 2nd Tm All ST Ftbl 84-85; Chem.

SCHLERF, SUSAN; Brandywine HS; Wilmington, DE; (S); DECA; Hosp Aide; Sec Frsh Cls; Sec Stu Cncl; Var Fld Hcky; Var Lcrss; Var Swmmng; Var Trk; High Hon Roll; Hon Roll; Gen Mktng I 3rd Pl DECA 85; Engl Commendatn 86; Nrsng.

SCHMEELCKE, KRISTEN E; Alexis I Dupont HS; Hockessin, DE; (Y); 30/206; Pres Am Leg Aux Girls St; Political Wkr; Pres SADD; Off Band; Yrbk Stf; Off Sr Cls; Pres Schlr; Church Yth Grp; AFS; Mrchg Band; Grls Nation-Amer Legn SR Sen 85; Citznshp Awd 86; Psychlgy Excl Awd 86; American U; Govt.

SCHMIDT, KARLA; St Marks HS; Kennett Square, PA; (Y); 4-H; Rep Jr Cls; Rep Stu Cncl; Fld Hcky; Var Trk; 4-H Awd; Hon Roll; US Natl Champ 1/2 Arabian Hunter 84; Var Champs Horse Shows/Yth Achvt Awds 83-86; Rgnl Horseshow Bond; Rutgers; Vet.

SCHMIT, JOHN PAUL; St Marks HS; Elkton, MD; (Y); Boy Scts; Chess Clb; Scholastic Bowl; Science Clb; Im Bowling; Hon Roll; NHS; Grinnell Hnr Schlrshp, Pres Schlrshp Loyola, Exclnce Bio 86; Grinnell Coll; Bio.

SCHMITT, KAREN; Middletown HS; Townsend, DE; (Y); Computer Clb; English Clb; Office Aide; OEA; Teachers Aide; Cit Awd; Hon Roll; Tres Ofc Ed Assn 85; Goldey Beacom Coll; Exec Secy.

SCHNEIDER, CHRISIE; New Castle Baptist Acad; Newark, DE; (Y); Concert Band; Yrbk Stf; Var Cheerleading; Hon Roll; Rep Soph Cls; Ntl Ldrshp, Svc Awd 85-86; Ntl Band Awds 85-86; Acad All Amer Hist Awd 84-85; Civil Engr.

SCHOEN, GREGORY; Christiana HS; Newark, DE; (Y); 32/301; Radio Clb; SADD; JV Var Socr; Hon Roll; Bblcl Schlr Awd 85; Outstndng Achvt Wrld Hstry 85; Pre-Med.

SCHOOLS, GRANT; Smyrna HS; Clayton, DE; (Y); Varsity Clb; JV Var Golf; Coll Prk; Pharm.

SCHRECKENGOST, DAWN; William Penn HS; Middletown, DE; (Y); Key Clb; Office Aide; Ski Clb; Teachers Aide; Band; Mrchg Band; Off Sr Cls; Stu Cncl; Var Capt Cheerleading; U DE; Elem Ed.

SCHRECKENGOST, TRICIA; William Penn HS; Middletown, DE; (Y); Key Clb; Ski Clb; Teachers Aide; Band; Mrchg Band; Stu Cncl; JV Var Cheerleading; Hon Roll; Bus.

SCHUBERT, MARY; Thomas Mcrean HS; Wilmington, DE; (Y); 18/225; Church Yth Grp; 4-H; Keywanettes; School Musical; School Play; Pres Sr Cls; Rep Stu Cncl; Var L Fld Hcky; 4-H Awd; Hon Roll; Hugh O Brien Yth Fndtn Ambssdr 85; Drama.

SCHUMM, PAM; A I Du Pont HS; Wilmington, DE; (Y); Band; Concert Band; Drill Tm; Mrchg Band; Symp Band; Crs Cntry; Girl Scts; Socr; Mgr Wrstlng; Hon Roll.

SCHWARTZ, SHERRI; St Marks HS; Wilmington, DE; (Y); Dance Clb; Service Clb; Co-Capt Cheerleading; Trk; Hon Roll; Radlgc Tech.

SCHWER, JENNIFER; Padua Acad; Newark, DE; (Y); 32/216; Church Yth Grp; Girl Scts; Hosp Aide; Spanish Clb; SADD; Hon Roll; Soc Wrk.

SCIPLE, JUDI; Dover HS; Dover, DE; (Y); JA; Library Aide; Office Aide; Mrchg Band; Symp Band; Var Powder Puff Ftbl; High Hon Roll; Hon Roll; Chld Psych.

SEBOK, MELISSA A; Thomas Mckean HS; Wilmington, DE; (Y); 19/236; Sec AFS; Rep Church Yth Grp; DECA; Sec Keywanettes; SADD; Nwsp Rptr; Nwsp Sprt Ed; Nwsp Stf; Off Jr Cls; Trs Stu Cncl; Acdmc All Cnfrnc In Fld Hcky 85; 3rd Pl Fnc & Crt DECA 86; PA ST; Fnc.

SELLERS, KELLY; Caesar Rodney SE HS; Camden Wyoming, DE; (Y); 56/327; GAA; Office Aide; OEA; Spanish Clb; Teachers Aide; Band; Concert Band; Mrchg Band; VP Soph Cls; JV Var Cheerleading; Teenager Yr 86; Rnd Tble Clb Schlrshp 86; Laura M Jennings Schlrshp 86; U DE; Acctng.

SELVAGGI, TINA; Archmere Acad; Wilmington, DE; (Y); JA; Spanish Clb; Stu Cncl; Crs Cntry; Powder Puff Ftbl; Trk; Hon Roll; NHS; Spanish NHS; Schlrshp Loyola Coll MD 86; St Josephs U; Lbrl Arts.

SENSENIG, DIANA; Christiana HS; Newark, DE; (Y); DECA; Goldey Beacom; Bus.

SETTLES, ALEXANDER; Glasgow HS; Newark, DE; (Y); 9/258; Am Leg Boys St; Boy Scts; Concert Band; Mrchg Band; Symp Band; JV Var Wrstlng; Hon Roll; NHS; Eagle Sct Awd 85; Gvrnrs Schl For Excll 85.

SEVERSON, TAMMY ANNA; Dover HS; Dover, DE; (S); 77/344; Trs Drama Clb; Pres FFA; OEA; Pres SADD; Stu Cncl; Im Badmtn; Var L Socr; Hon Roll; Pres Church Yth Grp; Cmnty Wkr; Comm Svc Awd 83-84; 3rd Pl Office Ed Assoc 85; Millersville U; Ed.

SHARP III, WILLIAM H; Mt Pleasant HS; Wilmington, DE; (Y); 7/180; Boy Scts; Church Yth Grp; VP JA; Math Tm; Band; Mrchg Band; Var L Golf; Hon Roll; NHS; Tech Assoc Of Mt Cuba Astrnmcl Obsrvtry 84-86; Bucknell U; Elect Engrg.

SHARPE, MARY; Christiana HS; Newark, DE; (Y); 13/311; Soph Cls; SADD; Teachers Aide; Acpl Chr; Chorus; Church Choir; Mrchg Band; School Musical; Hon Roll; NHS; Advncd Hnrs Prgm 84-85; Prncpls Awd-Acad Exclnc 84-86.

SHAUBACH, JENNIFER L; Indian River HS; Dagsboro, DE; (Y); Computer Clb; French Clb; Red Cross Aide; Science Clb; SADD; Drm Mjr(t); Mrchg Band; Nwsp Rptr; JV Bsktbl.

SHEPEARD III, JESSE T; William Penn HS; Wilmington, DE; (Y); Boys Clb Am; Var L Bsktbl; Var L Ftbl; Wt Lftg; MVP Bsktbl 83-84; Bst Dfnsv Plyr Bsktbl 84-85; Lttrmn-Ftbl & Bsktbl 85-86; Comp.

SHEPHERD, MIA; Holy Cross HS; Dover, DE; (Y); Church Yth Grp; Cmnty Wkr; 4-H; French Clb; Hosp Aide; Service Clb; SADD; Var L Bsbl; Var L Bsktbl; Var JV Mgr(s); Alt Girls St 86; Catholic U; Forensic Pthlgy.

SHEPPARD, DAVID; William Penn HS; New Castle, DE; (Y); 5/390; Math Clb; Var L Bsktbl; Var Capt Crs Cntry; Var Capt Trk; CC Awd; Hon Roll; Lion Awd; NHS; Schlrshp US Mltry Acad Wst Pnt 86; West Pnt; Cmptr Sci.

SHERIDAN, MATTHEW; Caravel Acad; Bear, DE; (S); Computer Clb; Math Tm; Yrbk Stf; High Hon Roll; 1st Pl DE Comp Cont 84-85; 1st Pl Tm Mth Lg 82-83; Comp Sci.

SHERIDAN, SCOTT; Laurel SR HS; Laurel, DE; (Y); 9/113; AFS; Am Leg Boys St; VP Church Yth Grp; Trs Frsh Cls; Trs Soph Cls; Trs Jr Cls; Trs Sr Cls; VP Stu Cncl; Var Bsbl; Var Ftbl; High Point; Sports Med.

SHERMAN, GERRI; Glasgow HS; Newark, DE; (Y); Am Leg Aux Girls St; Church Yth Grp; Drama Clb; SADD; Yrbk Ed-Chief; VP Jr Cls; Cheerleading; High Hon Roll; NHS; Prin Awd Acdmc Excllnce 83-85; Excllnce Math 84 & 85; Excllnce Spanish I, II, III 83-85; U DE; Chldhd Stu.

SHIELS, KIM; Dover HS; Dover, DE; (Y); Pres Debate Tm; Hosp Aide; NFL; Pres Speech Tm; Var Bowling; Hon Roll; Voice Dem Awd; ASSE Stu Exchng Spain 86; 1st Pl Hmrs Intrprtn-3rd Pl Dramatc Intrprtn DE ST Spch Trnmnt 86; Law.

SHOCKLEY, LYNDA; Indian River HS; Dagsboro, DE; (S); 83/202; OEA; Band; Chorus; Concert Band; Jazz Band; Mrchg Band; Pep Band.

SHOEMAKER, DAVID T; Brandywine HS; Wilmington, DE; (Y); Am Leg Boys St; Boy Scts; CAP; Debate Tm; Drill Tm; Rep Stu Cncl; Bausch & Lomb Sci Awd; God Cntry Awd; Church Yth Grp; Drama Clb; Pltcl Sci.

SHORT, STEPHEN W; Sussex Central HS; Georgetown, DE; (Y); 11/207; Am Leg Boys St; VICA; NHS; NEDT Awd; Hghst Acad Data Proc 84-85 & 85-86; Acad Excllnce Awd 84-85; 2nd Pl DE VICA Skills Olympcs 85-86; Comp Sci.

SHUMAKER, TAMMY; Archmere Acad; Hockessin, DE; (Y); Church Yth Grp; Chorus; School Musical; Var Fld Hcky; Powder Puff Ftbl; Trk; Hon Roll.

SIEGELL, HEIDI; Concord HS; Wilmington, DE; (Y); AFS; Math Tm; Band; Chorus; Concert Band; Jazz Band; Madrigals; Mrchg Band; Orch; Pep Band; Hnbl Mntn Natl PTA Eflections Cntst, All Mus All St Band, Chorus, Jazz Band, Orch 86; Columbia U; Mus.

SIEJA, CHRISTINE; Alex I Du Pont HS; Wilmington, DE; (Y); Band; Concert Band; Mrchg Band; Symp Band; Var Crs Cntry; JV Sftbl; Hon Roll; Trig Awd Hghst Avg 85; Tiger Awd-X-Cntry 85; U Of DE; Psych.

SILEO, ANGELA; Archmere Acad; Wallingford, PA; (Y); JCL; Latin Clb; Spanish Clb; School Musical; School Play; Stage Crew; Sec Soph Cls; Im Bowling; JV Crs Cntry; JV Fld Hcky; Law.

SILFIES, MARK; Salesianum HS; Wilmington, DE; (S); 22/268; Hosp Aide; JA; Mathletes; Im JV Socr; Var L Swmmng; High Hon Roll; NHS; Natl Hon Rl 85; Notre Dame; Chem Engrng.

SIMMONS, DEBBIE; Holy Cross HS; Dover, DE; (Y); Pep Clb; Nwsp Stf; Yrbk Stf; Cheerleading.

SIMMONS, STEVE; Seaford SR HS; Seaford, DE; (Y); Church Yth Grp; Concert Band; Rep Soph Cls; Var Socr; Hon Roll; Bus Admin.

SIMONE, MICHELLE; Indian River HS; Fenwick Island, DE; (S); 4/213; Drama Clb; Chorus; School Musical; Stage Crew; Capt Cheerleading; Powder Puff Ftbl; Var Trk; NHS; VP Stu Cncl; NC ST; Math.

SIMPLER, EARLLAINE; Indian River HS; Selbyville, DE; (S); 11/187; Band; Chorus; Rep Stu Cncl; Capt Cheerleading; Sftbl; Tennis; High Hon Roll; Jr NHS.

SIMPSON, STEVEN A; William Penn HS; New Castle, DE; (Y); 22/487; FBLA; Quiz Bowl; Variety Show; Stu Cncl; Capt Ftbl; Capt Powder Puff Ftbl; Capt Wt Lftg; Capt Wrstlng; Gov Hon Prg Awd; UFCW; High Hnr Schlrshp 86; Ftbl Grant From Widener 86; Widener U; Bus Mgmt.

SIPE, KATHY; Brandywine HS; Wilmington, DE; (S); Computer Clb; DECA; Girl Scts; JA; SADD; Stu Cncl; Fld Hcky; Lcrss; Trk; Hon Roll; Gnrl Mktg Awd 2nd Pl ST 86; Med.

SKAGGS, NANCY; Smyrna HS; Clayton, DE; (Y); Pres Church Yth Grp; Pres VP 4-H; VP OEA; Teachers Aide; Church Choir; Concert Band; Mrchg Band; Symp Band; Rep Stu Cncl; Lcrss; 1st Pl ST Pblc Spkng Rcrd Bk 85; Mss Hsptlty At Mss TEEN Pgnt 85; Ganger Schl ST Run OEA 85-86; U Of Delaware; Cmmnctns.

SKOMORUCHA, LISA; Padua Acad; Glen Mills, PA; (Y); 30/230; Hosp Aide; JA; Library Aide; Chorus; JV Var Fld Hcky; Im Tennis; Hon Roll; NHS; Acdmc All-Amer Schlr 85-86; Hi-Avg Grmn Awd 83-86; Vet Med.

SLAUGHTER, MICHELE; Dover HS; Hartly, DE; (S); 16/287; Cmnty Wkr; DECA; Drama Clb; Girl Scts; Office Aide; OEA; Teachers Aide; Varsity Clb; Bowling; Stat Fld Hcky; Accntng.

SLAVENS, CHARIDTH K; Epworth Christian Schl; Millsboro, DE; (S); 2/12; Church Yth Grp; Drama Clb; Office Aide; Chorus; Church Choir; School Musical; Stage Crew; Yrbk Ed-Chief; Yrbk Stf; Cheerleading; 2nd Hghst Engl Avg; 3rd Hghst Soc Stud Avg; Hghst Sci Avg; Beebe School Of Nrsg; Nrsg.

SMILEY, DEAN; Laurel SR HS; Laurel, DE; (Y); 43/129; Church Yth Grp; Cmnty Wkr; Drama Clb; FCA; FHA; SADD; Varsity Clb; Band; Chorus; Church Choir; Mercer Cnty CC; Mortuary Sci.

SMILEY, ZYON; Dover HS; Dover, DE; (Y); 73/373; Am Leg Boys St; Boy Scts; Church Yth Grp; CAP; 4-H; Math Tm; ROTC; SADD; Capt Bowling; Var Trk; DE St News Carrier Of The Mnth 85; U Of DE Cert Of Acad Achvt 86; Cert Of Partcptn-Kent Cnty Govt 86; Brigham Young U; Law.

SMITH, GORDON; Caesar Rodney HS; Dover, DE; (Y); 60/348; Am Leg Boys St; Debate Tm; Science Clb; Ski Clb; Speech Tm; Teachers Aide; Yrbk Stf; Lcrss; Wrstlng; Hon Roll; Clarkstown Yth Ct 85; Sci.

SMITH, JEREMY; Willam Penn HS; New Castle, DE; (Y); French Clb; Acpl Chr; Chorus; Swmmng; Hon Roll; Exc Engl,Choir; Comm.

SMITH, KATHY; Laurel SR HS; Laurel, DE; (Y); 2/123; Am Leg Aux Girls St; Drama Clb; Band; Chorus; School Musical; Off Soph Cls; Off Jr Cls; High Hon Roll; NHS; SADD; Lt Gvnrs Awd For Exc In Engl Cmpstn 82-83; DECTFL Awd 2nd Pl In DE 83-84; Hstry.

SMITH, KRISTINA; St Marks HS; Hockessin, DE; (Y); Church Yth Grp; Nwsp Rptr; JV Cheerleading; Var Lcrss; Hon Roll; Cmmnctns.

SMITH, MARK JAMES; Dover HS; Dover, DE; (Y); Cmnty Wkr; Computer Clb; Mgr Drama Clb; German Clb; JA; School Musical; School Play; Mgr Stage Crew; High Hon Roll; NHS; U DE; Vet Med.

SMITH, MICHAEL; Brandywine HS; Wilmington, DE; (Y); DECA; Model UN; Political Wkr; Stu Cncl; Lcrss; Wrstlng; Boy Scts; JA; Hon Roll; St DECA Awd 85-86; Eagle Sct 85; Hugh Obrien Yth Fndtn Rep 85; Yth For Undrstndng Rep To Wst Grmny 86; Lafayette Coll; Intl Affrs.

SMITH, RANDY K; Mount Pleasant SR HS; Wilmington, DE; (Y); Political Wkr; Nwsp Stf; JV Bsbl; Prfct Atten Awd; U Of DE; Bus Mgmt.

SMOOT, EMILY; Newark HS; Newark, DE; (Y); Ski Clb; Var Fld Hcky; Church Yth Grp; Drama Clb; German Clb; Varsity Clb; Orch; School Musical; School Play; Var Cheerleading; Field Hockey 84-86; U Of PA; Engrng.

SMYSER, AMY L; Thomas Mc Kean HS; Wilmingtn, DE; (Y); School Musical; Rep Frsh Cls; Rep Frsh Cls; Rep Stu Cncl; JV Cheerleading; Var Fld Hcky; Capt Var Trk; Hon Roll; NHS; Outstndng Female Athlt 85-86; VA Cmmnwlth U; Physcl Thrpy.

SNARSKY, CHRISTINE; Cape Henlopen HS; Milton, DE; (Y); Girl Scts; Band; Flag Corp; Nwsp Rptr; Var L Crs Cntry; Var L Trk; Hon Roll; 1st Tm All St Crss Cntry 85-86; Bonnie Bell Hon Ment All Amer Crss Cntry 85-86; All St Indr Trck 85-86; George Mason; Chemist.

SNYDER, BRIAN; Caesar Rodney HS; Dover, DE; (Y); Boy Scts; JCL; Latin Clb; Hon Roll; NHS; U DE; Chem Engr.

SNYDER, JONATHAN; Newark HS; Newark, DE; (Y); 15/340; Var Golf; High Hon Roll; Hon Roll; Jr NHS; Real Est.

SOCTT, KEVIN; Dover HS; Dover, DE; (Y); Church Yth Grp; OEA; PAVAS; Y-Teens; School Play; Nwsp Sprt Ed; Rep Frsh Cls; Var L Bsktbl; Im Crs Cntry; Trk; USC; Jrnlsm.

SOEHLKE, JEANIE; St Marks HS; Newark, DE; (Y); Band; Rep Frsh Cls; Rep Sr Cls; Bsktbl; Crs Cntry; Trk; 2nd Hons; U Of DE; Accntng.

SOLOMON, MARGARET; Padua Acad; Philadelphia, PA; (S); 14/250; Church Yth Grp; Library Aide; Pep Clb; Science Clb; SADD; High Hon Roll; Med Tech.

SOLWAY, BARRY; Smyrna HS; Smyrna, DE; (Y); Trs Chess Clb; CAP; Dance Clb; Math Tm; Teachers Aide; Stage Crew; Yrbk Phtg; Var Trk; Hon Roll; U DE; Engr.

SOUTAR, JAMIE; Mount Pleasant HS; Wilmington, DE; (Y); #10 In Class; Band; Concert Band; Mrchg Band; Var Bsktbl; Var Capt Socr; Var Tennis; Hon Roll; US Marine Corp Distngshd Athl Awd 86; Kenneth Donovan Mem Awd Bsktbl 85; Engrg.

SOWERS, JAYSON WILLIAM; Caesar Rodney HS; Dover, DE; (Y); 12/343; Am Leg Boys St; JCL; Thesps; Band; Chorus; NHS; Boy Scts; Church Yth Grp; Debate Tm; Drama Clb; Acdmy Of Achvmnt Goldn Scroll Awd 86; Cntry III St Ldr Awd 86; Boy Scout Schlrshp 85; S Hall Mrt Awd; William & Mary; Gov Svc.

SPADAFINO, LISA; Holy Cross HS; Dover, DE; (Y); Am Leg Aux Girls St; Church Yth Grp; Spanish Clb; SADD; Varsity Clb; Rep Frsh Cls; Rep Soph Cls; Pres Jr Cls; Pres Sr Cls; Var Capt Bsktbl; Hnrbl Mntn All Cthlc Sftbll Bsktbll 84-85; Hnrbl Mntn All Catholic Bsktbll Vllybll 86.

SPECHT, TREVOR U; Brandywine HS; Wilmington, DE; (Y); Boy Scts; Church Yth Grp; Math Tm; Quiz Bowl; Scholastic Bowl; Ski Clb; Band; Chorus; Concert Band; Jazz Band; Eagle Scout Awd 85; Ordr Of Arrow Awd 84; All ST Cncrt Band, Jazz Band & Chrs 83-86; Towson ST U; Music Prfmnc.

SPENGLER, KEN; Caesar Rodney HS; Dover, DE; (Y); 10/343; Church Yth Grp; Debate Tm; JCL; VP Latin Clb; Letterman Clb; Teachers Aide; Nwsp Stf; Lit Mag; Im Bsktbl; Var JV Ftbl; J Miller Mem Prize 86; Latin Clb Awd 86; Pres Acadmc Ftnss Awd 86; Swarthmore Coll; Lib Arts.

SPIKER, TED; St Marks HS; Wilmington, DE; (Y); 10/345; Jazz Band; VP Mrchg Band; School Musical; Variety Show; Rep Stu Cncl; Hon Roll; NHS; Blue Gold All Star Band 85-86; DE All ST Jazz Ensmbl 86; Semper Fidelis Awd Outstndng SR Solist 86; U Of DE; Comm.

SPINK, MICHAEL; Salesianum HS; Newark, DE; (Y); 118/300; Church Yth Grp; SADD; Var Bsbl; Var Ftbl; Hon Roll.

SPRIGGS, STEPHANY; Dover HS; Dover, DE; (Y); Pres Church Yth Grp; FBLA; German Clb; Office Aide; OEA; Pep Clb; Teachers Aide; Band; Chorus; Church Choir; Hampton U VA; Bus Adm.

SPRINGER, KIMBERLY; Padua Acad; Newark, DE; (S); 30/213; Church Yth Grp; Spanish Clb; Rep Frsh Cls; Rep Stu Cncl; Bsktbl; Coach Actv; Mgr(s); Hon Roll; Swmmng; Acdmc All Amer Schlr; Ntl Ldrshp & Srv Awd; Villanova; Astrnmy.

SRINVASAN, RAM; Mt Pleasant HS; Wilmington, DE; (Y); #4 In Class; Computer Clb; Math Tm; Ski Clb; Stage Crew; Nwsp Sprt Ed; JV Socr; Var Tennis; High Hon Roll; Hon Roll; NHS; Engr.

STACHECKI, JOHN; Dover HS; Dover, DE; (Y); Hon Roll; Ntl HS Mth Exam 3rd Pl Dover Hgh 85-86; Comp Sci.

STACHECKI, JOY; Smyrna HS; Smyrna, DE; (Y); Art Clb; Church Yth Grp; OEA; Spanish Clb; Yrbk Sprt Ed; Var Cheerleading; JV Capt Fld Hcky; Lcrss; Hon Roll; Bio.

STARKEY, BRENDA; William Penn HS; New Castle, DE; (Y); #67 In Class; Library Aide; Ski Clb; SADD; Yrbk Stf; Sec Stu Cncl; Fld Hcky; Hon Roll; ST Offcr, Treas & VP HOSA; Outstndng Dntl Asstng Stu; Awd Outstndg Envlmnt Stu Actvts; Dntl Asst.

STASIUNAS, CAROLYN; Archmere Acad; West Chester, PA; (Y); Spanish Clb; Im Bowling; Fld Hcky; JV Score Keeper; Hon Roll; NHS; Spanish NHS; Bus.

STAYTON, KRISTIN; Caesar Rodney HS; Dover, DE; (Y); 8/306; GAA; Spanish Clb; Nwsp Stf; Lit Mag; Capt Cheerleading; Cit Awd; Hon Roll; NHS; Pres Schlr; DE U; Biolgcl Sci.

STEIN, CHRISTOPHER L; Archmere Acad; Wilmington, DE; (Y); Boy Scts; French Clb; Ski Clb; Stage Crew; Im Bowling; JV Ftbl; JV Socr; Var Trk; JV Wrstlng; Hon Roll; CAR ST Rgstr 84-86; Brthrhd Ordr Arrw Chptr Secty 85-86; Ad Altare Dei Mdl Scts 84; Virginia Tech; Arch.

STELLA, ROBERTO; Saint Marks HS; Wilmington, DE; (Y); Rep Jr Cls; Bsbl; Ftbl; Lcrss; U Of Pennsylvania.

STELLINI, STEPHANIE; St Marks HS; Newark, DE; (Y); 29/367; Church Yth Grp; JV Fld Hcky; Lcrss; Mgr(s); Hon Roll; Phy Thrpy.

STEVENS, JILL; Dover HS; Dover, DE; (Y); 33/300; Cmnty Wkr; Girl Scts; Capt Color Guard; Mrchg Band; Symp Band; JV Var Fld Hcky; Var Sftbl; Gov Hon Prg Awd; High Hon Roll; NHS; Grls ST Rep 86; Occptnl Thrpy.

STEVENSON, CONNIE; Indian River HS; Frankford, DE; (S); 20/213; Office Aide; OEA; Spanish Clb; SADD; Yrbk Stf; Rep Stu Cncl; Hon Roll; Prfct Atten Awd; U DE; Psych.

STEWART, SHARON; William Penn HS; Middletown, DE; (Y); French Clb; Ski Clb; Band; Mrchg Band; Var L Cheerleading; Hon Roll; NHS; Frgn Lang Stu Of Yr 86; DE Govr Schl For Excell 85; Chem.

STILL, DAVID; Salesianum Schl; Elsmere, DE; (Y); 100/300; Band; Concert Band; Hon Roll; Lion Awd; Prfct Atten Awd; U Of DE.

STILL, JOSEPH; Salesianum HS; Wilmington, DE; (S); 25/270; French Clb; Band; Mrchg Band; Orch; Variety Show; Im Bowling; High Hon Roll; NHS; U Of DE; Acctng.

STISO, MICHAEL; Alexis I Du Pont HS; Newark, DE; (Y); 49/230; VP JA; Trs Band; Concert Band; Jazz Band; Mrchg Band; Symp Band; Hon Roll; JP Sousa Awd; Ntl Merit Ltr; 1st Pl JA Co Ofc Regn 85; U Of DE; Chem Engnrng.

STJOHN, CHEREE; Dover HS; Dover, DE; (Y); Church Yth Grp; Band; Concert Band; Mrchg Band; Symp Band; Lit Mag; Bowling; Psych.

STONESIFER, CRAIG; Dover HS; Dover, DE; (Y); 42/350; Band; Jazz Band; Mrchg Band; JV Bsbl; Hon Roll; NHS; U Of Delaware; Bio.

STONESIFER, MARK; Dover HS; Dover, DE; (Y); 7/360; Math Tm; Science Clb; Mrchg Band; Symp Band; Var L Crs Cntry; High Hon Roll; NHS; SADD; Band; Outstndng Acad Achvt Awd 86; All Amer Yth Hnr Band 85 & 86; Arch.

STOOPS JR, RICHARD; Dover HS; Dover, DE; (Y); Var L Bsbl; Var L Bsktbl; Ftbl; High Hon Roll; Hon Roll; NHS; Wesley College; Acctg.

STORMER, JEFF; Smyrna HS; Clayton, DE; (Y); 85/147; Chorus; School Musical; Ftbl; Trk; Wrstlng; Most Outstndng Stu Music 86; Ltr Music; Ltr Wrstlng Ftbl 82-85; Gym Tchr.

STORNIOLO, LISA; Padua Acad; Claymont, DE; (S); Art Clb; Computer Clb; Math Clb; Pep Clb; JV Trk; Hon Roll; NEDT Cert; Penn ST; Arch.

STOUT, SUZANNE; Padua Acad; Landenberg, PA; (Y); Church Yth Grp; Cmnty Wkr; Office Aide; Hon Roll.

STRASSER, JOELLEN; Delcastle Technical HS; Wilmington, DE; (Y); High Hon Roll; Hon Roll; Coll; Comp.

STRAWSER, LYNNE; St Marks HS; Newark, DE; (Y); 19/379; Cmnty Wkr; Dance Clb; SADD; School Musical; Yrbk Rptr; Rep Frsh Cls; Rep Soph Cls; Rep Jr Cls; Rep Stu Cncl; Hon Roll; Chld Psych.

STRELECKIS, MICHAEL J; Salesianum HS; Exton, PA; (Y); 28/262; Chess Clb; Exploring; Concert Band; Bowling; Crs Cntry; Socr; Trk; Ntl Merit SF; Pre Med.

STRICKER, CHRISTINE; Sussex Central HS; Apo, NY; (Y); 19/195; Church Yth Grp; Math Clb; Math Tm; Spanish Clb; Teachers Aide; Aud/Vis; Concert Band; Mrchg Band; Sftbl; Acad Fit Awd; Phys Fit Awd; VA Wesleyan Coll; Phys Ther.

STRILKO, HILLARY A; Brandywine HS; Wilmington, DE; (Y); Pres Drama Clb; Temple Yth Grp; Chorus; School Musical; School Play; Variety Show; Nwsp Rptr; Yrbk Stf; NHS; Vassar Coll.

STRUPE, LISA; Dover HS; Dover, DE; (Y); OEA; Nwsp Rptr; Nwsp Stf; Bowling; Hon Roll; Outstndg Acadmc Achvt In HS Awd 85-86.

SUBRAMANIAN, ASHOK; Alexis I Du Pont HS; Hockessin, DE; (Y); Am Leg Boys St; Hosp Aide; SADD; Jazz Band; Mrchg Band; Pres Soph Cls; Pres Stu Cncl; NHS; Church Yth Grp; Math Tm; Outstndg Frshmn 84; All-ST Band 84&86; Gvrnrs Schl Excllnc 85; Pre-Med.

SULLIVAN, PATRICK; Indian River HS; Bethany Bch, DE; (S); 29/202; Boy Scts; Chorus; Concert Band; Mrchg Band; School Musical; Rep Stu Cncl; Socr; Tennis; Trk; Hon Roll; Gld Mdl, Math Comptn, Sci Olympd 85; 2nd Chr Frnch Horn, Sussex Cnty Band 84-86; West Point-Dartmouth; Mltry Sci.

SULLIVAN, ROBIN; Delmar JR SR HS; Delmar, MD; (Y); Church Yth Grp; Drama Clb; FHA; Keywanettes; Pep Clb; Spanish Clb; VP SADD; Nwsp Rptr; Nwsp Stf; Yrbk Rptr; Sentrl Schlrshp 86-87; Salisbury STS Coll; Psych.

SULLIVAN, TAWANA; Delcastle Technical HS; Wilmington, DE; (Y); Church Yth Grp; VICA; Church Choir; Flag Corp; Mrchg Band; Rep Frsh Cls; Trk; Vllybl; Hon Roll; Med Tech.

SWAFFORD, LISA; Sussex Central HS; Rehoboth Beach, DE; (Y); 20/214; Dance Clb; Var Capt Cheerleading; Hon Roll; NHS; DE Right To Ed Scholar 86-87; Pell Grant 86-87; U OF DE; Med Tech.

SYLVESTER, LEE; Christiana HS; New Castle, DE; (Y); FCA; Pres JA; Ski Clb; Teachers Aide; Band; Mrchg Band; Rep Jr Cls; Stu Cncl; Var Capt Ftbl; Capt Trk; Schlrshp US Naval Acad Track 86; US Naval Acad; Pre-Law.

TADALAN, TERESA; Padua Acad; Elkton, MD; (S); 13/213; Art Clb; Church Yth Grp; Pep Clb; Science Clb; Spanish Clb; NHS; Medcl.

TADDEI, DEBBIE; William Penn HS; New Castle, DE; (Y); Key Clb; Office Aide; Ski Clb; Teachers Aide; Color Guard; Flag Corp; Mrchg Band; Stu Cncl; Hon Roll; Leader Corps Pres & Recrdg Secy; Art Insts Of Philadelphia.

TALL, KAREN; Christiana HS; Newark, DE; (Y); Girl Scts; JA; Ski Clb; SADD; Teachers Aide; Var Cheerleading; Mgr(s); Score Keeper; Hon Roll; U Of DE; Law.

TAN, MICHELLE; Brandywine HS; Wilmington, DE; (Y); 1/239; Church Yth Grp; Trs Pres 4-H; Church Choir; School Musical; School Play; Yrbk Sprt Ed; NHS; Val; DECA; Drama Clb; James T Mc Kinstry Schlrshp 86; Diamond ST Schlrshp 86; Pres Schlrshp Frm VA Intl Coll 86; VA Intermont Coll; Bus.

TANNER, CELESTE; Indian River HS; Selbyville, DE; (S); #19 In Class; Church Yth Grp; French Clb; SADD; Teachers Aide; Band; Church Choir; Mrchg Band; Cheerleading; High Hon Roll; NHS; Natl Jr Hnr Soc 83-84; DVMPSY Pgm 83-84.

TARNEY, CORI; Alexis I Du Pont HS; Hockassin, DE; (Y); Church Yth Grp; Stage Crew; Stu Cncl; Bsktbl; DECA; Vllybl; HOBY Ldrshp Smnr 85; Pre-Med.

TATMAN, CINDY; Milford SR HS; Milford, DE; (Y); Intnl Clb; OEA; Varsity Clb; Cheerleading; Hon Roll; Pres All Amer Ftns Tm 84-85; Mst Vlbl Chrldr In Ftbll & Wrstlng 85 & 86; Lockhaven U; Spnsh.

TAYLOR, ANTHONY; Dover HS; Dover, DE; (Y); Church Yth Grp; VICA; Var Capt Ftbl; Var Trk; High Hon Roll; Hon Roll; Prfct Atten Awd; Art Inst Of Philadelphia; Art.

TAYLOR, BRIAN; William Penn HS; New Castle, DE; (Y); Office Aide; Ski Clb; Var L Bsbl; Var L Ftbl; Wt Lftg; Hon Roll; NHS; Arch.

TAYLOR, EARL; Claymont HS; Wilmington, DE; (Y); Boys Clb Am; Church Yth Grp; Computer Clb; Drama Clb; Quiz Bowl; Scholastic Bowl; Science Clb; Chorus; Church Choir; School Musical; Sunday Schl Man Yr 84; Howard U; Chem Engr.

TAYLOR, JANELLE; Seaford HS; Seaford, DE; (Y); #30 In Class; Trs Pres 4-H; Sec Cheerleading; High Hon Roll; Lion Awd; Pres Schlr; Hosp Aide; VP OEA; Teachers Aide; Nwsp Stf; 4-H Awd; Hugh Obrien Yth Conf 84; Natl 4-H Cngrss, Natl Schlrshp Wnr-Food Presvtn 84; PAFC Inst 84-86; Salisbury ST Coll; Librl Arts.

TAYLOR, KIMBERLY; Delmar JR-SR HS; Delmar, MD; (Y); 40/80; AFS; FHA; Hosp Aide; Trs Keywanettes; SADD; Church Choir; Sftbl; Vllybl; Hon Roll; Variety Show; Mst Outstndng Soph Keytt 85; JV Sftbl Ltr 84; Pin Recog Compltn Hrs Cndy Strpr 84; Bus.

TAYLOR, LAURA; Newark HS; Newark, DE; (Y); 21/321; Spanish Clb; Band; Chorus; Concert Band; Mrchg Band; School Musical; Trk; High Hon Roll; Hon Roll; VP NHS; DE Right To Ed Schlrshp 86; DE Postcndry Schlrshp Fund 86; DE U; Med Tech.

TAYLOR, PATRICIA; Dover HS; Dover, DE; (Y); OEA; Pep Clb; Chorus; Var JV Cheerleading; High Hon Roll; Hon Roll; NHS.

TESTERMAN, JENNIFER; St Marks HS; Wilmington, DE; (Y); Pres Pep Clb; Yrbk Rptr; Rep Jr Cls; Stu Cncl; Gov Hon Prg Awd; Pre Med.

TETI, EDWARD; Salesianum Schl; Claymont, DE; (Y); 31/301; Spanish Clb; Stage Crew; High Hon Roll; Hon Roll.

THOMPSON, JUDY; Dover HS; Hartly, DE; (S); Office Aide; OEA; Teachers Aide; Rep Stu Cncl; High Hon Roll; Hon Roll; 2nd Pl Extemporaneous Spch, 4th Pl Typing St OEA Comp 84; Exec Sec.

THOMPSON, NANCY; Concord HS; Wilmington, DE; (Y); 27/298; Church Yth Grp; Band; Concert Band; Mrchg Band; Var L Fld Hcky; Hon Roll; NHS; Jazz Band; Symp Band; Im Powder Puff Ftbl; 2nd Tm All-St In Fld Hcky 85; 1st Tm All-Conf In Fld Hocky 85; All-Acad Awd 84-85; Phy Thrpy.

THOMPSON, PAUL; Salesianum HS; Wilmington, DE; (Y); 82/292; Chess Clb; Chorus; Concert Band; Mrchg Band; Orch; School Musical; Trs Frsh Cls; High Hon Roll; Hon Roll; Ntl Merit SF; Super Mstng Awd Mrbrk Elem Schl 81; Bus Acctg.

THOMPSON, PHILLIP; Indian River HS; Selbyville, DE; (Y); Teachers Aide; Socr; Tennis; Engrng.

THROCKMORTON, BRIAN; Delmar JR SR HS; Delmar, DE; (Y); 4/80; Boy Scts; Library Aide; VICA; Variety Show; JV Var Ftbl; Hon Roll; NHS; ST Semi Finlst Congress Bunde Stag Schlrshp 86; Comp Prog.

TICE, LEROY; Milford HS; Milford, DE; (Y); Church Yth Grp; Drill Tm; Pep Band; School Musical; Variety Show; Nwsp Rptr; Nwsp Stf; Hampton U; Acctg.

TIMMENEY, BARBARA; Christiana HS; Newark, DE; (Y); 3/311; Am Leg Aux Girls St; Math Tm; Acpl Chr; Chorus; Lit Mag; Var Sftbl; Var Capt Vllybl; High Hon Roll; Pres NHS; All ST Chorus 85-86; Govs Schl Excllnc 85; Brown U Awd Outstgndg Achvmnt Engl 86; Liberal Arts Coll; Ecnmcs.

TIMMONS III, BAKE; Indian River HS; Dagsboro, DE; (Y); 5/213; Pres Computer Clb; Capt Math Tm; Var Tk; Gov Hon Prg Awd; NHS; Ntl Merit Ltr; St Schlr; Am Leg Boys St; Stu To Mensa 85; Lions Club Awd 86; Upward Bnd Cmmnty Serv Awd 85; Princeton U; Cgntv Sci.

TIMMONS III, BONARD; Indian River HS; Dagsboro, DE; (S); 3/213; Am Leg Boys St; Capt Math Tm; Lit Mag; Trk; Gov Hon Prg Awd; Jr NHS; NHS; Ntl Merit Ltr; Upward Bound Tutoring Cert 85; USAA Math & Ledrshp 84-85; Princeton U; Comp Engrng.

TINNEY IV, W SCOTT; Christiana HS; Newark, DE; (Y); 62/306; Am Leg Boys St; Boy Scts; SADD; Stu Cncl; Var Socr; Trk; Var Wrstlng; Hon Roll; Lion Awd; Teenager Of Yr & Boy Scout Of Yr 85-86; MD Boys ST 86.

TIRABASSI, TINA; Smyrna HS; Smyrna, DE; (Y); Drama Clb; School Musical; Yrbk Stf; Var Cheerleading; JV Co-Capt Fld Hcky; Lcrss; Hon Roll; Prfct Atten Awd; Cmmnctns.

TOBIN, PATRICIA; St Marks HS; Wilmington, DE; (Y); 67/379; Band; Concert Band; Mrchg Band; School Musical; School Play; Rep Jr Cls; High Hon Roll; Hon Roll; U DE; Lang.

TOLLEFSON, BRIAN; Salesianum HS; Wilmington, DE; (S); 20/309; Church Yth Grp; Stu Cncl; Bsktbl; Ftbl; Swmmng; High Hon Roll; NHS; Engrng.

TOLMAN, KENNETH J; Concord HS; Wilmington, DE; (Y); 26/255; Church Yth Grp; Cmnty Wkr; Latin Clb; Math Tm; Stage Crew; Nwsp Stf; NHS; Ntl Merit SF; High Score Chem Exam; Natl Math Awd.

TONOGBANUA, AROBERT; Salesianum Schl; New Castle, DE; (Y); 10/292; Spanish Clb; Stage Crew; Nwsp Ed-Chief; Yrbk Stf; Rep Stu Cncl; Im Bsktbl; JV Var Trk; High Hon Roll; Hon Roll; NHS; Annl Yth Ldrshp Conf; Pre Med.

TORRANCE, SUSAN; Dover HS; Dover, DE; (Y); Math Tm; Spanish Clb; Nwsp Bus Mgr; Nwsp Rptr; Rep Jr Cls; Var L Cheerleading; Coach Actv; Swmmng; High Hon Roll; NHS; Hmcmng Crt 84; Snwbl Crt 84; 1st Pl Edtrl Awd DE Schlstc Press Assn 86; Jrnlsm.

TOTINO, MEGAN L; Archmere Acad; Wallingford, PA; (Y); Spanish Clb; Chorus; School Musical; Sec Stu Cncl; Stat Bsktbl; JV Var Cheerleading; Im Fld Hcky; JV Mgr(s); Stat Socr; Hon Roll; Psd 3 Fgr Sktng Tsts In Dnc, Fgr, & Frstyl 84-85; Cert By Red Crs 85; ST Fnlst In Miss PA Pgnt 86; Pre-Med.

TOWERS, MICHELLE D; Seaford Christian Acad; Denton, MD; (S); 2/13; Church Yth Grp; Teachers Aide; Chorus; Church Choir; Yrbk Stf; Hon Roll.

TOWLE, KRISTIN; Mt Pleasant HS; Wilmington, DE; (Y); 14/230; Office Aide; Service Clb; Teachers Aide; Rep Frsh Cls; Rep Jr Cls; JV Var Fld Hcky; Bus.

TOWNSEND, MURIEL; Indian River HS; Frankford, DE; (Y); FFA; Library Aide; Office Aide; SADD; Teachers Aide; Chorus; Hon Roll; FFA 84-85; Accntng.

TOWNSEND, RONNIE; Indian River HS; Frankford, DE; (S); 21/202; Church Yth Grp; Var Ftbl; High Hon Roll; Hon Roll; Jr NHS; NHS; Math.

TRACY, MELODY; Dover HS; Dover, DE; (Y); Library Aide; Office Aide; OEA; Rep Soph Cls; Rep Jr Cls; Stu Cncl; Mgr Fld Hcky; High Hon Roll; Hon Roll; NHS; U Of DE; Acctg.

TRETTEL, JIM; Smyrna HS; Smyrna, DE; (S); 8/192; Math Tm; Quiz Bowl; Jazz Band; Mrchg Band; Stage Crew; Capt Crs Cntry; Capt Trk; Gov Hon Prg Awd; NHS; Prfct Atten Awd; U Of DE; Chmcl Engrng.

TRITELLI, KAREN; Padua Acad; Wilmington, DE; (Y); Art Clb; Ed Nwsp Phtg; Ed Nwsp Stf; Yrbk Phtg; Ed Lit Mag.

TROWER, SHAUNA; Alexis I Dupont HS; Shaker Hts, OH; (Y); Church Yth Grp; Drama Clb; French Clb; Hosp Aide; JA; Math Clb; Model UN; Office Aide; Varsity Clb; Concert Band; Euler Math Awd 86; Sports Med.

TRUMBORE, WILLIAM PAUL; Broadmeadow HS; Middletown, DE; (S); 1/5; Church Yth Grp; Intnl Clb; JA; Trs Jr Cls; Rep Stu Cncl; Var Lcrss; Var Socr; Hon Roll; Lib Arts.

TRYON, JUANITA M; Ursuline Acad; Chadds Ford, PA; (Y); Science Clb; Ski Clb; Nwsp Stf; Yrbk Stf; Var Sftbl; Stat Swmmng; Stat Vllybl; AFS; Cmnty Wkr; Dance Clb; 2nd Hons 86; PA ST U; Bus Admin.

TUCKER, ROBERT; St Marks HS; Newark, DE; (Y); Varsity Clb; Im Bowling; Im Wt Lftg; Var Wrstlng; High Hon Roll; Hon Roll; Drexel U; Elec Engrng.

TUMA, JULIO; St Andrews Schl; Dover, DE; (Y); Trs Am Leg Boys St; Pres Chess Clb; Cmnty Wkr; Debate Tm; Model UN; Pres Spanish Clb; Teachers Aide; Var Socr; Gov Hon Prg Awd; English Clb; 2nd-Boat Crew 85-86; 1st-Boat Crew 86-87; Teachers Aide 85-87; Harvard U; Bus.

TUSO, STEVEN; Salesianum HS; Philadelphia, PA; (Y); Pres Church Yth Grp; Ski Clb; VP Spanish Clb; NHS; Art.

TWADDELL, MICHAEL; Delcastle Technical HS; Wilmington, DE; (Y); VICA; DE JR Sci & Huamnities Sympsm 2nd Awd 86; DE Sci Bowl 3rd Pl 86; Chem.

TWILLEY, KIMBERLY; Dover HS; Dover, DE; (Y); 15/300; Office Aide; Chorus; Sftbl; Vllybl; High Hon Roll; NHS.

TWITCHELL, JENNIFER; St Marks HS; Newark, DE; (Y); Trs 4-H; French Clb; Nwsp Rptr; Nwsp Sprt Ed; Trs Frsh Cls; Rep Jr Cls; Stat Bsktbl; Mgr(s); 4-H Awd; Hon Roll; U Of DE; Law.

TYNDALL, KAREN; Laurel SR HS; Laurel, DE; (Y); AFS; Office Aide; Pep Clb; JV Fld Hcky; Hon Roll; Sen Roths Yth Ldrshp Conf 86; Govt Srvc.

ULDIN, LINDA; Christiana HS; Newark, DE; (Y); Church Yth Grp; Drama Clb; Library Aide; Office Aide; SADD; Teachers Aide; Chorus; Church Choir; Excllnce Bus Machines 86; Job Well Done Libr Aide 85; Intr Desgn.

UNRUH, THOMAS S; St Andrews Schl; Townsend, DE; (Y); 11/71; Church Yth Grp; Cmnty Wkr; Pres 4-H; Spanish Clb; SADD; School Play; Stage Crew; Yrbk Bus Mgr; Var Bsbl; Var Ftbl; Rcvd $1500 Womens Clb Schlrshp 86-87; Emory; Doctor.

UPADHYAY, ASHISH; Glasgow HS; Newark, DE; (Y); 5/283; Am Leg Boys St; Math Clb; VP Sr Cls; NHS; Acdmc Incntv Schlrshp For U DE 86-87; Prncpls Awd For Exc; U DE; Chmcl Engrng.

UPDIKE, ERIC; Alexis I Du Pont HS; Newark, DE; (Y); JV Wrstlng; High Hon Roll; Hon Roll; Pres Acad Fitness Awd 86; Awd Of Spec Hnrs 85-86; U Of DE; Engrng.

URICK, GREG; Dover HS; Dover, DE; (Y); Boy Scts; Church Yth Grp; ROTC; SADD; Rep Sr Cls; Off Stu Cncl; Var Ftbl; Hon Roll; U Of DE; Physcl Thrpst.

URION, REBECCA; Thomas Mc Keon HS; Wilmington, DE; (Y); 39/211; Pres Sec AFS; Teachers Aide; Band; Concert Band; Jazz Band; Mrchg Band; School Musical; School Play; Hon Roll; Jr NHS; Am Field Svc Awd 85-86; Band Awd 84-85; Chemical Engr.

VAGLE, KIRK; John Dickinson HS; Newark, DE; (Y); Pres Church Yth Grp; Trs 4-H; JA; Rep Frsh Cls; Var L Bsbl; JV Bsktbl; Var L Ftbl; L Tennis; 4-H Awd; Hon Roll; 4th Awd 2 ST Pblc Spkng 2 ST Dmnstrtns 81-83; 2 Trphs Bsbll & Bsktbl 85; All Cnfrnc Bsbll 86.

VALENTINE, LAUREEN; Christiana HS; Newark, DE; (Y); 23/301; FNA; Math Tm; Political Wkr; Spanish Clb; SADD; Band; Concert Band; Mrchg Band; Hon Roll; NHS; Pharm.

VALERIUS, KARYN; Padua Acad; Hockessin, DE; (S); 3/200; Pep Clb; Band; Rep Jr Cls; Hon Roll; NHS; Libry Arts.

VANCE, DAVID; Mount Pleasant HS; Wilmington, DE; (Y); Church Yth Grp; JA; Pres JCL; Pres Latin Clb; Math Tm; Nwsp Rptr; Socr; Hon Roll; Hon Mntn Ntl Ltn Exam; Comp Sci.

VANDERHOST, CHANTEL; Howard Career Ctr HS; Wilmington, DE; (Y); Cmnty Wkr; GAA; OEA; SADD; Yrbk Stf; Rep Stu Cncl; Cheerleading; Mgr(s); Hon Roll; Gftd-Talntd; Morgan ST U; Ecnmcs.

VASSILATOS, PETER; Concord HS; Wilmington, DE; (Y); 6/250; Pres Church Yth Grp; Capt Math Tm; Jazz Band; Madrigals; Mrchg Band; School Musical; Gov Hon Prg Awd; Pres NHS; Ntl Merit SF; St Schlr; ST 1st Pl Math League 83; Natl Sco Prfssnl Engr Schlrshp 86; All ST Chorus 86; U DE; Chem Engr.

VAUGHAN, CRAIG; Concord HS; Wilmington, DE; (Y); Am Leg Boys St; Church Yth Grp; Ski Clb; Acpl Chr; Church Choir; Madrigals; School Musical; Stage Crew; Nwsp Stf; Yrbk Stf; Bill Roth Yth Conf; New Castle Cnty Govt Day; Comp Faire; Cornell U; Arch.

VELASCO, TINA; Archmere Acad; Middletown, DE; (Y); 4-H; Mathletes; Math Clb; Spanish Clb; Speech Tm; Varsity Clb; Variety Show; Nwsp Phtg; Yrbk Phtg; Yrbk Stf; Capt 1st Vrsty Fld Hcky Tm 86; MIJV Awd Fld Hcky 85; 3.33 Fnl Rprt Crd 86; U Of DE.

VENABLES, CHIP; Laurel SR HS; Laurel, DE; (Y); 11/150; AFS; Letterman Clb; VP Varsity Clb; Ftbl; Trk; Wt Lftg; High Hon Roll; Hon Roll; NHS; Prfct Atten Awd; Athlt Of Wk 85; Sussx Cnty Outstndng Stu Awd 86; U Of D; Chem Engrng.

VENABLES, MATIA; Laurel SR HS; Laurel, DE; (Y); 9/123; AFS; Cmnty Wkr; SADD; Band; Chorus; Concert Band; Mrchg Band; School Musical; Off Frsh Cls; Off Soph Cls; Salisbury ST Coll; Elem Tchg.

VENSEL, HEIDI; Caravel Acad; Newark, DE; (S); 1/44; Sec AFS; 4-H; Math Tm; Yrbk Ed-Chief; Trs Sr Cls; Var L Cheerleading; Var L Fld Hcky; High Hon Roll; Prfct Atten Awd; DE Mus Tchrs Assn 85; Amer Reg Math Leag 84.

VERMA, SANDHYA; Dover HS; Dover, DE; (Y); Church Yth Grp; Cmnty Wkr; Drama Clb; Hosp Aide; Office Aide; PAVAS; Band; Chorus; Church Choir; Madrigals; Voice Prfrmnc.

VERONESI, CHRIS; Dover HS; Dover, DE; (Y); 29/316; Pres Church Yth Grp; Yrbk Stf; Socr; Dnfth Awd; High Hon Roll; Hon Roll; NHS; Wesley Coll; Bus Admin.

VIOLA, TODD CARLO; William Penn HS; New Castle, DE; (S); Church Yth Grp; Pres French Clb; Math Tm; Scholastic Bowl; Yrbk Phtg; L Swmmng; Gov Hon Prg Awd; High Hon Roll; NHS; Engrng.

VITCUSKY, TANIA; Christiana HS; Newark, DE; (S); 5/273; OEA; Sec Hst Stu Cncl; Var L Fld Hcky; Hon Roll; NHS; 1st Pl-Typng II-DE OEA 85; 1st Pl-Job Mnl-Emplyd-DE OEA 86; 2nd Pl-Typng III-DE OEA 86; U Of DE; Bus Adm.

VIVOLO, TINA; Padua Acad; Wilmington, DE; (Y); 33/217; Cmnty Wkr; Pep Clb; Rep Frsh Cls; Hon Roll; 4th DE ST Itln Cont 86.

VOIGT, MEGAN; Newark HS; Newark, DE; (Y); 6/316; Capt Drill Tm; Mrchg Band; Symp Band; VP Sr Cls; JV Bsktbl; JV Cheerleading; L Var Tennis; Capt Twrlr; High Hon Roll; NHS; Arch.

VOSHELL, KATHRINE MARIE; Tower Hill HS; Wilmington, DE; (Y); AFS; Teachers Aide; Var Bsktbl; Im Wt Lftg; Hon Roll; 5th Pl Delaware French Concours 84; Advncd Ballet Cls Acadmy Of Dance 86; Arch.

VU, BAO; Holy Cross HS; Dover, DE; (Y); 3/30; Computer Clb; Am Leg Boys St; Scholastic Bowl; L Socr; Computer Clb; High Hon Roll; Hon Roll; NHS; Natl Engl Merit Awd 86; Elctrcl Engrng.

WAGNER, GAYLIA; Alexis I Du Pont HS; Wilmington, DE; (Y); Drama Clb; JA; Mrchg Band; Symp Band; Nwsp Rptr; Cheerleading; Hon Roll; Eng.

WAIBEL, DIANE; Alexis I Du Pont HS; Newark, DE; (Y); 6/250; Church Choir; Mrchg Band; Symp Band; Gov Hon Prg Awd; High Hon Roll; NHS; Concert Band; Yrbk Stf; Hon Roll; Jr NHS; Handbell Chr 84-85; Awds Of Excllnt & Supr-Flute & Piano Fstvls 84-86; All ST Band 85-86; Music.

WALKE, JOHN; Brandywine HS; Wilmington, DE; (Y); Scholastic Bowl; Band; Jazz Band; Mrchg Band; School Musical; Var Lcrss; Pres French Hon Soc; Gov Hon Prg Awd; High Hon Roll; VP NHS; Duke U; Pre-Med.

WALLACE, DAVID; St Marks HS; Wilmington, DE; (Y); 50/320; VP Frsh Cls; Rep Soph Cls; Rep Stu Cncl; JV Ftbl; Stat Wt Lftg; Var Wrstlng; DE U; Chem Engrng.

WALLACE, ROSE; Dover HS; Hartly, DE; (Y); Library Aide; OEA; SADD; High Hon Roll; NHS; 1st Pl Acctng I OEA Conf 86; U DE; Acctng.

WALLS, KATHRYN E; Wm Penn HS; New Castle, DE; (Y); Key Clb; Library Aide; Ski Clb; Chorus; Yrbk Stf; Stu Cncl; Cheerleading; Hon Roll; US Stu Cncl Awds 86; Psychlgy.

WALLS, MARY ELIZABETH; St Marks HS; Wilmington, DE; (Y); Church Yth Grp; GAA; Bsktbl; Coach Actv; Hon Roll; Goldey Beacom; Accntng.

WALSH JR, GEORGE JAMES; Claymont HS; Claymont, DE; (Y); Dance Clb; Office Aide; Pep Clb; SADD; Jr Cls; Ftbl; Wt Lftg; Hon Roll; Prfct Atten Awd; Ftbl Haig Hupjan Mem Awd Most Athltc; Bowling Hi Series; U Of DE; Computer Analyst.

WALSH, MARIE; Archmere Acad; Milmont Park, PA; (S); Pres German Clb; Math Tm; Concert Band; Jazz Band; Mrchg Band; Symp Band; Bowling; High Hon Roll; NHS.

WALTON, SHARON; Delcastle Vo-Tech; Wilmington, DE; (Y); FFA; SADD; Hon Roll; FFA Awd 86; Hrtcltr.

WANG, SUSAN; Alexis I Dupont HS; Hockessin, DE; (Y); 19/257; Church Yth Grp; Math Tm; Science Clb; Drill Tm; School Play; Symp Band; Yrbk Phtg; Var Pom Pon; Var Trk; NHS; UCSD; Comp Sci.

WARD, DAVID A; Claymont HS; Claymont, DE; (Y); 20/109; Am Leg Boys St; Church Yth Grp; AFS; Spanish Clb; Varsity Clb; School Musical; JV Bsbl; Var L Crs Cntry; Var Trk; Hon Roll; Engrng.

WARD, PHILIP J; Concord HS; Wilmington, DE; (Y); Exploring; FCA; Math Tm; Socr; Trk; High Hon Roll; NHS; Outstndng Chem Achvt Awd 85; U DE; Chem Engrng.

WARD, TOM; Mount Pleasant HS; Wilmington, DE; (Y); 3/180; Math Tm; VP Soph Cls; VP Jr Cls; JV Bsbl; Var Ftbl; JV Trk; High Hon Roll; NHS; Rensselaer Math & Sci Awd 86; DE Amer Chem Soc Awd 86; Blue Hen Conf Acad Hnrs-All Conf Cert 85; U Of DE; Chem Engrng.

WARDEN, TAMMIE GAIL; Christiana HS; Newark, DE; (Y); French Clb; Ski Clb; Color Guard; Hon Roll; NHS; U DE; Sci.

WARNER, DEBORAH; New Castle Baptist Acad; New Castle, DE; (Y); 2/34; Church Yth Grp; Yrbk Ed-Chief; VP Sr Cls; High Hon Roll; Sal; Var Capt Vllybl; Var Capt Bsktbl; Sec Frsh Cls; Sec Soph Cls; VP Jr Cls; Timothy Awd 86; MVP Vrsty Bsktbl, Vllybl 86; Pensacola Christian Coll.

WARNER JR, GARY; New Castle Baptist Acad; New Castle, DE; (Y); 3/36; Quiz Bowl; Teachers Aide; Pres Frsh Cls; VP Soph Cls; Var Bsbl; Var Capt Bsktbl; Var L Socr; High Hon Roll; Pres Schlr; Pensacola Chrstn Coll; Comp Sci.

WARNER, TRACY; Smyrna HS; Hartly, DE; (S); 11/158; Art Clb; Drama Clb; Trs Spanish Clb; Teachers Aide; School Musical; School Play; Stage Crew; Stat Bsktbl; Fld Hcky; Mgr(s); Princpls Awd Acad Excllnce; U New Haven; Justice.

WASFI, YASMINE; Dover SR HS; Dover, DE; (Y); 2/325; Math Tm; Band; Gov Hon Prg Awd; High Hon Roll; NHS; Ntl Merit Ltr; Am Leg Aux Girls St; Office Aide; Mrchg Band; School Musical; Rensselaer Mth & Sci Awd 86; Mth Assn Amer Awd 86; Amer Lg Aux Awd Amer Hstry 86; Wellesley Bk Awd 86.

WASHINGTON, TAMMY; Christiana HS; Newark, DE; (Y); 30/300; French Clb; Ski Clb; Pres SADD; Mgr Band; Pres Stu Cncl; Capt Trk; Hon Roll; NHS; Schlr Athltc Awd 85; Won Delta Sigma Theta Annl Ortrcl Cntst 85; Engrng.

WATERS, ANGELA; Delcastle Technical HS; Wilmington, DE; (Y); 8/400; 4-H; Hosp Aide; VP JA; VICA; JV Vllybl; Gov Hon Prg Awd; Hon Roll; NHS; Pres Schlr; Voice Dem Awd; John H Tylr Chem Awd 86; Mt Joy Chrch Schlrshp 86; Hofstra U; Chem.

WATSON, SHELVIA; Glasgow HS; Newark, DE; (Y); Cmnty Wkr; English Clb; FFA; Girl Scts; Latin Clb; Library Aide; Office Aide; Spanish Clb; SADD; Teachers Aide; 1st Rnnr-Up-Mdrn Miss Pgnt 85; U Of DE; Engl.

WATSON, VANESSA; Indian River HS; Showell, MD; (Y); DECA; OEA; Hon Roll; FFA; FHA; Chorus; Prfct Atten Awd; Best Stu Soc Minrties 82-83; Woodridge Bus Inst; Recptnst.

WATTENBARGER, KELLY; Cape Henlopen HS; Lewes, DE; (Y); Thesps; Chorus; Mrchg Band; Stage Crew; L Cheerleading; L Tennis; Var Vllybl; High Hon Roll; Hon Roll; Schlstc Awd Mth, Sci 86; Cmptn Awd 83; U Delaware; Acctnt.

WEAVER, SCOTT; Mt Pleasant HS; Wilmington, DE; (Y); 4/168; Church Yth Grp; Ski Clb; Band; Concert Band; Jazz Band; Mrchg Band; Rep Stu Cncl; Var Socr; Hon Roll; NHS; Blue Hen All Acad Tm Soccr; Ski Tm; Comp Engrng.

WEBER, MARCIA; Smyrna HS; Smyrna, DE; (S); Church Yth Grp; Drama Clb; French Clb; Teachers Aide; School Musical; Rep Frsh Cls; Stat Bsbl; JV Cheerleading; Stat Ftbl; Var L Mgr(s).

WEBER, STACIE N; Seaford Christian Acad; Frankford, DE; (S); 1/13; Church Yth Grp; Band; Chorus; Concert Band; Var Capt Bsktbl; Hon Roll.

WEEKS, JOSEPH; Delcastle Technical HS; Wilmington, DE; (Y); Boys Clb Am; Boy Scts; Cmnty Wkr; JA; Ski Clb; VICA; Nwsp Rptr; Nwsp Stf; Bsbl; Ftbl; Crpntr.

WEINBERG, ILENE; Dover HS; Dover, DE; (Y); Yrbk Ed-Chief; Cmnty Wkr; Debate Tm; Drama Clb; Hosp Aide; Library Aide; Office Aide; SADD; School Play; Bowling; Outstndng Stu Edtr.

WEINKOWITZ, JOHN; Salesianum Schl; New Castle, DE; (Y); 86/292; Cmnty Wkr; Band; JV Var Bsktbl; Comp Sci.

WEIR, MIKE; Salesianum HS; Wilmington, DE; (Y); School Play; Ftbl; Trk; Hon Roll; NHS.

WEISS, JOHN A; Smyrna HS; Smyrna, DE; (Y); 20/180; Art Clb; French Clb; JA; Yrbk Phtg; Yrbk Stf; Stu Cncl; Capt Bsbl; Ftbl; Hon Roll; Prfct Atten Awd; 1st Pl Art Awd DE Museum Of Natl Hist 86; Archtctr.

WEISSGERBER, TERI; Christiana HS; Newark, DE; (S); 1/280; Dance Clb; OEA; Orch; Trs Stu Cncl; High Hon Roll; Hon Roll; NHS; NEDT Awd; Val; Prncpl Awd For Exc 83-85; Ntl Merit Cmndtn 85; Gvrnrs Schl For Exc 84; Hood Coll Frdrck MD; Bus Adm.

WELCH, SEAN; Salesianum Schl For Boys; Wilmington, DE; (Y); Chess Clb; Church Yth Grp; Cmnty Wkr; French Clb; Political Wkr; Chorus; School Musical; Stage Crew; Var Mgr(s); USAF Summer Sci Seminar; Comp Sci.

WELLMAN, TERRANCE; Delcastle Technical HS; Wilmington, DE; (Y); Var Ftbl; Var Capt Trk; Hon Roll; 1st Tm All ST Indr Trk 85-86; ST Rcrd Dstnc Mdly Rly Tm 85-86; 2nd Tm All ST Undftd 85-86; U Of GA; Athltc Dr.

WELSH, STEVE; Dover HS; Dover, DE; (Y); 2/344; Math Tm; Bsktbl; Var Capt Ftbl; Var Capt Golf; High Hon Roll; NHS; Sal; Rensselaer Inst Awd Excllnce Mth & Sci 85; Am Leg Schl Awd; Outstndng Achvt Mth & Sci 86; Duke U; Econ.

WELTER, KEITH; Salesianum HS; Newark, DE; (Y); Ski Clb; Band; Concert Band; Jazz Band; Orch; School Musical; Symp Band; Variety Show; Im Bowling; Var Capt Socr; Bus.

WENDLAND, SUSANNE; A I Du Pont HS; Hockessin, DE; (Y); 42/260; Church Yth Grp; Dance Clb; FFA; German Clb; PAVAS; Ski Clb; Mrchg Band; Yrbk Stf; Pom Pon; Tennis; U Of DE; Bio.

WESTCOTT, KRISTEN; Seaford SR HS; Seaford, DE; (Y); 12/150; Trs GAA; Key Clb; Band; Yrbk Stf; Rep Stu Cncl; Capt Cheerleading; Tennis; Hon Roll; NHS; U Of DE; Erly Chldhd Educ.

WHALEY, JOHN SCOTT; Laurel SR HS; Laurel, DE; (Y); VP Drama Clb; Band; Concert Band; Jazz Band; Mrchg Band; Pep Band; School Musical; School Play; Stage Crew; Bus.

WHEATLEY, LISA; Seaford HS; Seaford, DE; (Y); Trs Key Clb; Color Guard; Off Frsh Cls; Off Soph Cls; Off Jr Cls; Off Sr Cls; Stage Crew; Nwsp Rptr; Yrbk Stf; Prm Chrmn 86; Gftd Engl Stu Prog 82-87; U Of DE; Engl.

WHERRY, MATTHEW; Newark HS; Newark, DE; (Y); Am Leg Boys St; Latin Clb; Pres Jr Cls; JV Ftbl; Var Capt Tennis; Hon Roll; NHS; Pre Law.

WHETZEL, PATRICIA; Archmere Acad; Wilmington, DE; (S); Church Yth Grp; Exploring; 4-H; Concert Band; Jazz Band; High Hon Roll; NHS; Spanish NHS; Service Clb; Spanish Clb; 4-H Sec 83-85; Scholar Stu 85; Wndrlnd Farms Equine Studs 85; Vet.

WHITE, APRIL; Broadmeadow HS; Chestertown, MD; (Y); Girl Scts; Nwsp Stf; Yrbk Stf; Pres Sr Cls; Var L Fld Hcky; JV Var Mgr(s); Hon Roll; AFS; Drama Clb; Chorus; Richard Chichester Du Pont Memrl Awd 86; Athltc Awd 86; Fclty Awd 86; Western MD Coll; Lbrl Arts.

WHITE, JENNIFER; Laurel SR HS; Laurel, DE; (Y); AFS; FNA; Pep Clb; Spanish Clb; SADD; Band; Chorus; Concert Band; Mrchg Band; Hon Roll; Salisbury ST; RN.

WHITE, KASEY; Wilmington HS; Wilmington, DE; (Y); JA; Math Tm; Teachers Aide; Rep Stu Cncl; Mgr(s); Hon Roll; NHS; Prfct Atten Awd; Cmnctns.

WHITE, MONICA; William Penn HS; New Castle, DE; (Y); JA; Library Aide; Math Tm; Quiz Bowl; Spanish Clb; VP Teachers Aide; Sec Church Choir; Rep Stu Cncl; High Hon Roll; Hon Roll; Oustndng Stu Chem, Englsh, Hstry, Math AP Englsh 84-85; Hon Mntn Math Spnsh 85-86; Phrmcy.

WHITE, ROBIN; Alexis I Du Pont HS; Hockessin, DE; (Y); Flag Corp; Mrchg Band; Var Capt Cheerleading; Trk; Hon Roll; Jr NHS.

WHITE, TOMMI; Christiana HS; Newark, DE; (Y); Church Yth Grp; German Clb; Trs Ski Clb; SADD; VICA; Chorus; Church Choir; School Musical; Stage Crew; Cheerleading; DE U; Aerontcl Engnrng.

WHITEHEAD, DIANE; Middletown HS; Middletown, DE; (Y); Church Yth Grp; Library Aide; Teachers Aide; Stage Crew; Sftbl; Hon Roll; Sftbl Schlrshp To Mtchll Coll 86; Mtchll Coll; Acctng.

WHITTEN, KRISTIN; Padua Acad; Hockessin, DE; (Y); Drama Clb; French Clb; Hosp Aide; Pep Clb; Service Clb; SADD; School Musical; School Play; Hon Roll; NEDT Awd.

WICKS IV, GEORGE; Smyrna HS; Smyrna, DE; (Y); 3/143; Am Leg Boys St; Pres FCA; Pres French Clb; Math Tm; OEA; Mrchg Band; Pres Frsh Cls; Pres Soph Cls; Pres Jr Cls; Pres Sr Cls; DE ST Fedrtn Womns Clb 86; U Of DE Pres Awd 86; U S Army Rsrv Schlr Athl Awd 86; U Of DE; Physcs.

WIDGOWSKI, MAUREEN; Padua Acad; Wilmington, DE; (Y); Am Leg Aux Girls St; Model UN; Pep Clb; Science Clb; Yrbk Stf; Hon Roll; NHS; Club Yth Govrnmnt 86; Yrbk Awd 85-86.

WIDZGOWSKI, MAUREEN; Padua Acad; Wilmington, DE; (S); 7/213; Church Yth Grp; Model UN; Pep Clb; Sec Science Clb; Yrbk Stf; Hon Roll; NHS; Yrbk Awd 85.

WIESNER, DIANE; Padua Acad; Bear, DE; (Y); Church Yth Grp; Intnl Clb; Pep Clb; Ski Clb; SADD; Yrbk Stf; Hon Roll; Govrnrs Schl Of Excllnc 86; Won Mny Wtr-Ski Awds-Comptn 84-86; U Of DE.

WILDS, PAUL; Alexis I Du Pont HS; Newark, DE; (Y); Church Yth Grp; Debate Tm; Natl Beta Clb; Band; Concert Band; Jazz Band; Mrchg Band; Symp Band; Trs Soph Cls; Hon Roll; Hghst Schlstc Avrg Frosh Clss 83-84; U Of GA; Attrny.

WILLEY, VINCENT; Salesianum HS; Claymont, DE; (Y); 10/315; Office Aide; Im Bsktbl; NHS; Claymont SR Lg All Star Hnrs Bsbl; 1st Hnrs; Phrmcy.

WILLIAMS, BARBARA; Christiana HS; Newark, DE; (Y); Church Yth Grp; Ski Clb; SADD; Teachers Aide; Nwsp Sprt Ed; JV Bsktbl; L Sftbl; JV Vllybl; Elem Educ.

WILLIAMS, HEATHER; Woodbridge JR SR HS; Bridgeville, DE; (Y); 9/116; Am Leg Aux Girls St; Pres Church Yth Grp; OEA; Trs Thesps; Band; Chorus; Drm Mjr(t); School Play; Sec Frsh Cls; Hon Roll; Music.

WILLIS, JULIE; Dover HS; Dover, DE; (Y); Church Yth Grp; Debate Tm; Spanish Clb; Band; Mrchg Band; Nwsp Rptr; Swmmng; Tennis; Hon Roll; Jr NHS; Kent Cntys Outstndg Stu 86; Bus.

WILLS, JOHN S; Te Tatnall Schl; Wilmington, DE; (Y); Math Tm; Political Wkr; Band; Chorus; School Musical; Var Socr; Var Trk; Hon Roll; NHS; Ntl Merit SF.

WILSON, AMY; Seaford SR HS; Seaford, DE; (Y); AFS; Off GAA; Off Key Clb; Concert Band; School Play; Yrbk Stf; Sec Soph Cls; Stu Cncl; Cheerleading; Fld Hcky; Cnfrnce Wnr 2nd Dbls Tns 84; Staff Club Schlrshp 86; Cnfrnce Wnr 1st Dbls Tns 86; Clemson U; Elem Educ.

WILSON, DENNIS; Milford SR HS; Milford, DE; (Y); Intnl Clb; Concert Band; Jazz Band; Mrchg Band; School Musical; School Play; Off Jr Cls; Var L Bsbl; High Hon Roll; Hon Roll; Pre-Med.

WILSON, JAMIE; Brandywine HS; Wilmington, DE; (Y); Art Clb; Nwsp Stf; JV Bsbl; Hon Roll; NHS; Outstndng Achvt Awd Fine Art 86; ST Awd Wnnr Natl Holly Fine Art Cont 85; Golden Poet Awd 85-86; Phila Coll Art; Graphc Art.

WILT JR, CHARLES E; Caear Rodney HS; Dover, DE; (Y); 62/307; Letterman Clb; Trs Stu Cncl; JV Var Bsbl; Var Golf; JV Socr; JV Var Wrstlng; Lion Awd; Mrn Corp Dist Athlt Awd 85-86; Wrstlng Bsts Schlrshp 86; Drthy Brwn Schlrshp 86; U Of DE; Math.

WINDISH, RICHARD; Salesianum Schl; Chaddsford, PA; (S); 15/320; Church Yth Grp; VP French Clb; Drm & Bgl; Jazz Band; Mrchg Band; Symp Band; Tennis; High Hon Roll; NHS; Poli Sci.

WINDLE, WILLIAM; Dover HS; Hartly, DE; (Y); Debate Tm; Exploring; FBLA; Speech Tm; JV Bsbl; Im Crs Cntry; Im Wrstlng; Penn ST Coll; Crmnl Law.

WINDSOR, STACY; Smyrna HS; Smyrna, DE; (Y); OEA; School Play; Lcrss; Prfct Atten Awd.

WISHER, PAMELA; Dover HS; Dover, DE; (Y); Band; Symp Band; Chld Psych.

WOLFGANG, TAMARA; Laurel SR HS; Laurel, DE; (Y); 3/128; AFS; Sec Trs JCL; Sec Letterman Clb; Math Tm; Sec Trs Science Clb; Sec Varsity Clb; Drm Mjr(t); Var L Trk; High Hon Roll; JP Sousa Awd; U Of DE Pres Achvt Awd, Acad Achvt Awd & HS Awds 86-88; U Of DE; Psych.

WOLFGONG, BARRY; Dover HS; Dover, DE; (Y); DECA; Ftbl; Wt Lftg; U S Navy; Nclr.

WOMBLE, LESLIE; Ursuline Acad; Newark, DE; (Y); Model UN; Science Clb; Nwsp Phtg; Yrbk Ed-Chief; JV Bsktbl; Var Sftbl; High Hon Roll; Trs NHS; Rensselaer Awd 86.

WOMMACK, J BRIAN; Brandywine HS; Wilmington, DE; (Y); Am Leg Boys St; Drama Clb; JCL; Latin Clb; Model UN; Quiz Bowl; Nwsp Ed-Chief; Golf; Gov Hon Prg Awd; DECTFL Oral Lang Cont 1st Pl Germn III Statewide.

WOOD, TERESA; Lake Forest HS; Felton, DE; (Y); Am Leg Aux Girls St; French Clb; Math Tm; OEA; Teachers Aide; Varsity Clb; Capt Cheerleading; High Hon Roll; Hon Roll; Trs NHS; DE Gov Schl Excllnc 85; CPA.

WOODHALL, KIM; Dover HS; Dover, DE; (Y); Girl Scts; Math Tm; Office Aide; SADD; Band; Mrchg Band; Stage Crew; Symp Band; Hon Roll; DE Tech & CC; Bus.

WOODHEAD, MARY; Seaford SR HS; Seaford, DE; (Y); Church Yth Grp; School Play; Stage Crew; High Hon Roll; Hon Roll; Prfct Atten Awd; AAUW Schlrshp 86; Acad Ftnss Awd 86; 1st Pl Art Leauge Comp 83; Beaver COLL; Intr Dsgn.

WOODS, MICHAEL; Caravel Acad; Lincoln Univ, PA; (S); 10/42; Am Leg Boys St; Computer Clb; Mathletes; School Musical; Sec Jr Cls; Pres Stu Cncl; L Bsbl; L Socr; Hon Roll; Bus.

WOODWARD, BEVERLY; William Penn HS; New Castle, DE; (Y); 81/489; Key Clb; Spanish Clb; Hon Roll; Outstndng Stu Spanish 86; Wilmington Coll; Spanish.

WORTMAN, CHARLES; Salesianum De; Wilmington, DE; (Y); 75/300; Sec Am Leg Boys St; JA; Nwsp Rptr; Rep Stu Cncl; Rep Im Bsktbl; JV Crs Cntry; Hon Roll; Bill Roth Yth In Govt Ldrshp Pgm 86; Volunteer A I Du Pont Inst 85 & 86; Jstc & Peace Clb 85-87; Law.

WOTEN, LISA; Caesar Rodney HS; Camden Wyoming, DE; (Y); 43/350; French Clb; Teachers Aide; Band; Concert Band; Mrchg Band; NHS; Shippensburg U.

WRIGHT, DIANA; Caesar Rodney HS; Camden, DE; (Y); French Clb; FHA; FNA; GAA; Hosp Aide; Office Aide; ROTC; Chorus; Mgr Bsktbl; Hon Roll; Nrsg.

WRIGHT, MICHELLE; Dover HS; Dover, DE; (Y); Church Yth Grp; Band; Church Choir; Concert Band; Mrchg Band; Symp Band; Var JV Bsktbl; Hon Roll; U Of DE & Kent Cnty Outstndng Acadmc Awd 86; Bibleway Temple Chrch Of God-Outstndng Achvr 83; Chem.

WRIGHT, TROY; Smyrna HS; Clayton, DE; (Y); Art Clb; Boy Scts; Church Yth Grp; Spanish Clb; Band; Mrchg Band; Yrbk Phtg; Prfct Atten Awd; UCLA; Dentist.

WYATT, VIRGINIA; St Marks HS; New Castle, DE; (Y); Hon Roll; Med Sec.

YEN, JESSICA; Caesar Rodney SR High; Dover, DE; (Y); 7/334; French Clb; Math Tm; Chorus; Hon Roll; NHS; St Schlr; Fnlst YKAA Intl Piano Comptn 85; Soloist Newark Symp Orch Piano Solist 85.

YERGER, BRIAN; Salesianum HS; Newark, DE; (Y); 27/315; Var Ftbl; High Hon Roll; NHS.

YOUNG, CHRIS; Salesianum HS; Chaddsford, PA; (S); 20/270; Church Yth Grp; Jazz Band; Mrchg Band; Orch; School Musical; Bowling; High Hon Roll; Ntl Merit Ltr; U Of VA; Engrng.

YOUNG, JEFFREY; Dover HS; Dover, DE; (Y); 3/525; Am Leg Boys St; Math Tm; Var L Bsbl; JV L Bsktbl; Var L Socr; High Hon Roll; NHS; Amer Lgn Dstngshd Achvt Awd Hstry 85-86; Natl Sci Olympd 84-86; U DE Acadmc Achvt Awd 85-86; Engrng.

ZABIELSKI, LORRAINE; Padua Acad; Glen Mills, PA; (Y); JV Var Fld Hcky; Im Mgr Tennis; Natl Sci Olympd-Bio 85; Wioner U; Bus Adm.

ZARKOWSKI, ED; Dover HS; Dover, DE; (Y); 98/306; Band; Mrchg Band; Yrbk Stf; Rep Stu Cncl; High Hon Roll; Hon Roll; Med.

ZDROJEWSKI, ANTHONY; Del Castle HS; Wilmington, DE; (Y); Bsbl; High Hon Roll; Hon Roll.

ZEISLOFT, KARI; Christiana HS; Newark, DE; (Y); 50/400; AFS; Church Yth Grp; FHA; SADD; JA; Library Aide; Teachers Aide; Var Stat Fld Hcky; Outstndng Chld Care Stu; Outstndng Tchrs Aide-Lib Aide; Educ.

ZEVNIK, VERONCEE M; Mc Kean HS; Wilmington, DE; (Y); 43/215; AFS; French Clb; Keywanettes; PAVAS; Scholastic Bowl; Variety Show; Rep Stu Cncl; Cit Awd; Hon Roll; NHS; U Of DE; Music.

ZIEJEWSKI, CHRISTINE; Padva Acad; Wilmington, DE; (Y); Church Yth Grp; JA; Pep Clb; SADD; Rep Sr Cls; Stu Cncl; Tennis; U DE; Acctg.

ZIEMIANSKI, PATTI; A J Dupont HS; Newark, DE; (Y); Church Yth Grp; Debate Tm; Drama Clb; FBLA; JA; Office Aide; Pep Clb; Service Clb; Spanish Clb; SADD; Spanish Awd 85.

ZIMMERMAN, ANDREW C; Caesar Rodney HS; Dover, DE; (Y); 15/400; Am Leg Boys St; English Clb; JA; Latin Clb; Letterman Clb; Rep Political Wkr; Varsity Clb; Nwsp Sprt Ed; Yrbk Stf; Rep Soph Cls; Smmr Coll Pgm U Of DE 86; Poly Sci.

ZIMMERMAN, CHRIS; Salesianum Schl; Cladds Ford, PA; (S); 42/301; German Clb; Var Tennis; Im Wt Lftg; High Hon Roll; NHS; Lehigh U; Mech Engrng.

ZIPPE, ANNE; John Dickinson HS; Wilmington, DE; (Y); 17/218; SADD; Band; Drill Tm; Symp Band; Sec Trs Stu Cncl; Capt Var Swmmng; Hon Roll; Jr NHS; NHS.

D.C.

ADAIR, ALMAZ; Banneker SR HS; Washington, DC; (Y); Church Yth Grp; Cmnty Wkr; Debate Tm; Girl Scts; JA; Library Aide; Scholastic Bowl; Teachers Aide; Chorus; Sec Church Choir; Schlrshp Acadmc Excllnc 84; Most Outstndng Stu Eng 86; Outstndng Tutr Migrnt Wrkrs Of Am 86; Psychtry.

ADAMS, MARK; Dunbar SR HS; Washington, DC; (S); Pres DECA; French Clb; FHA; Red Cross Aide; Teachers Aide; Crs Cntry; Diving; Swmmng; Trk; Dstngshd Svc Awd DECA 86; Inter-Hgh Dvng Chmpn 86; Tenn ST U; Mrktng.

ADAMS, MICHELLE; Woodrow Wilson SR HS; Washington, DC; (Y); 23/380; Spanish Clb; Chorus; Rep Jr Cls; Rep Sr Cls; Rep Stu Cncl; Hon Roll; Jr NHS; NHS; Cty Spnsh Cnst Oratory 85; Carol Schwartz Commdntn Svc Awd 86; Stdnt Govt Awd 86; Crew Ltr & Trphy 86; U CO.

ADEBUSOYE, STELLA; Calvin Coolidge HS; Washington, DC; (Y); French Clb; Girl Scts; Vllybl; Cit Awd; Spelling Bee Awd 84; U DC; Med.

AGBRO, VICTORIA; Woodrow Wilson HS; Washington, DC; (Y); 4/387; Intnl Clb; Science Clb; Trk; French Hon Soc; High Hon Roll; Jr NHS; NHS; Rotary Awd; Drama Clb; French Clb; Sci & Engr Schlrshp 86; Mst Outstndg 86; Svc Clb Awd Excl Svc 86; U Of MD; Med.

AGER, LORA; Woodrow Wilson SR HS; Washington, DC; (Y); 75/431; Drama Clb; JA; Pep Clb; Spanish Clb; Band; Concert Band; Jazz Band; Mrchg Band; School Play; Symp Band; Hnry Svc Awd 84; Engl Achvt Awd 86; Spanish Achvt Awd 84; Math.

ALEXANDER, CRESCYNTHIA; Roosevelt SR HS; Washington, DC; (Y); Church Yth Grp; Computer Clb; Mrchg Band; Cit Awd; Prfct Atten Awd; Outstndng Imprvmt Engl 82-85; Awd Chrch Chr 86; Awd Mrchng Bnd 84; MD U; Data Proc.

ALI, MOHAMED; Woodrow Wilson HS; Suitland, MD; (Y); 40/431; Pres Science Clb; Var Ftbl; Var Socr; Var Trk; Hon Roll; Crossroads Africa Schrlshp 86; :Md U Engr Comp Sci 86; Comp Sci.

ALLEN, DARRYL; Frank W Ballou HS; Washington, DC; (S); Teachers Aide; Cit Awd; Hon Roll; Cert Recog Engl 85; Cert Excllnc Cvcs & Soc Stud 83; Elec Engr.

ALLEN, JACQUELINE; Ballou SR HS; Washington, DC; (S); Church Yth Grp; FBLA; ROTC; Teachers Aide; Sftbl; Cit Awd; Hon Roll; Jr NHS; NHS; Prfct Atten Awd; Bus Mgmt.

ALSTON, CASSANDRA; Mc Kinley Tech/Burdick Career Ctr; Washington, DC; (Y); Debate Tm; Spanish Clb; Variety Show; Cit Awd; Hon Roll; Jr NHS; Prfct Atten Awd; 3rd Pl-Essy Cntst-All Career Ctrs In DC Area 85; Comp Sci.

ANDERSON, BARBARA; Georgetown Visitation Prep Schl; Mclean, VA; (Y); 32/97; Off Church Yth Grp; English Clb; Hosp Aide; Math Clb; Service Clb; Var Mgr(s); Var Capt Socr; Var Capt Sftbl; Var L Tennis; Hon Roll; Excellence In Math 84; Excellence In Spanish 85; Mvp Softball 85; U Of VA; Arch.

ANDERSON, LAURA ELISABETH; Georgetown Visitation Prep Schl; Silver Spring, MD; (Y); Spanish Clb; SADD; Chorus; Yrbk Stf; VP Sr Cls; Hon Roll; Camera Clb; Church Yth Grp; Dance Clb; Math Clb; Excllnc Geom 84-85; Black Wmns Soc-Treas-Pres 84-87; Pol Oprtrs-Lfgrd Certs Based Tstng 85-86; Bus Adm.

ARGIRO, MEGAN; Georgetown Visitation Prep; Alexandria, VA; (Y); Model UN; Political Wkr; Service Clb; School Musical; Variety Show; Lit Mag; Pres Frsh Cls; Rep Stu Cncl; Capt Cheerleading; Hon Roll; Excellnce In Art & Music, Algebra II; Pep & Spirit Awd; Pol Sci.

ASFAW, MARY; Woodrow-Wilson HS; Burke, VA; (Y); Art Clb; Church Yth Grp; FHA; Intnl Clb; Library Aide; Spanish Clb; Chorus; Church Choir; Lit Mag; High Hon Roll; Intnl Rltns.

ASONGWE, ALICE; Woodrow Wilson SR HS; Washington, DC; (Y); FBLA; Intnl Clb; JA; Keywanettes; Teachers Aide; Yrbk Phtg; Yrbk Stf; Pres Jr Cls; JV Sftbl; JV Timer; Comm Svc Awd 84-86; Most Imprvd Awd 84; Cafeteria Aid Awd 86; Howard U; Fashion.

AVANS, MARGUERITE; Eastern HS; Washington, DC; (Y); Debate Tm; Hosp Aide; JA; Hon Roll; Ntl Merit Schol; Prfct Atten Awd; Thrpy.

BADRICH, MARINA; Immaculata Prep Schl; Washington, DC; (Y); French Clb; Tennis; French Hon Soc; Natl Hnr Rl 86; Music Awd Piano 86; Natl Frnch Cont 84; George WA U; Intl Affairs.

BAKER, MONICA; Duke Ellington School Of The Arts; Washington, DC; (Y); Spanish Clb; Speech Tm; Thesps; School Play; Rep Frsh Cls; Rep Soph Cls; Trs Jr Cls; Pres Sr Cls; Pres Stu Cncl; Swmmng; Mst Outstndng Schltc Thtre Stu 84-85; Mst Outstndng Stu Govt Ofcr 84-85; Jr Miss Pgnt Fnlst 86; Cornell U; Comm.

BANKS III, CHARLES; Dunbar SR HS; Washington, DC; (Y); Computer Clb; JA; Science Clb; Pres Jr Cls; Cit Awd; High Hon Roll; Jr NHS; NHS; Prfct Atten Awd; Sal; Ost Outstndng Boy No 2 Boys Clb 84; Mayers Cert Merit 84; Comp Prog.

BANKS, MICHELLE A; Model Secondary School For The Deaf; Washington, DC; (Y); Thesps; School Play; Variety Show; Ed Lit Mag; Rep Frsh Cls; JV Var Bsktbl; High Hon Roll; Kiwanis Awd; SF Drama Art Recgntn Talnt Srch 86; 2nd Prz Ntl Drama 86; Ntl Assoc Deaf 2nd Pl 84; Gallaudet Coll; Fash Desgn.

BARARIA, VINAY; Gonzaga Coll HS; Lanham, MD; (Y); Drama Clb; French Clb; Science Clb; Nwsp Stf; Yrbk Stf; Rep Stu Cncl; High Hon Roll; K Dulin Folger Smr Schlrshp 86; DC Sci Fair 1st Pl 86; US Army DC Sci Fair Hnrb Mntn 86; Johns Hopkins; Med.

BARNES, SHERRY; Theodore Roosevelt HS; Washington, DC; (Y); Computer Clb; Pep Clb; ROTC; Drm Mjr(t); Cheerleading; Cit Awd; Hon Roll; Prfct Atten Awd; Johnsn & Wales Culnry Coll; Chf.

BARNHILL, PHILLIP; Archbishop Carroll HS; Washington, DC; (S); 13/188; Pres Chorus; Church Choir; VP Madrigals; Capt L Ftbl; Hon Roll; NHS; JV Bsbl; JV Bsktbl; Score Keeper; Sci Fair Awd 84; All-Archdiocesan Chorus 84; All-Met Ftbl 85; Acctng.

BARNUM, DEVAUHN; Eastern HS; Washington, DC; (Y); Cit Awd; Hon Roll; NHS; Arch.

BARON, CRISTAL J; Georgetown Visitation HS; Washington, DC; (Y); 2/97; School Play; Variety Show; High Hon Roll; Hon Roll; NHS; Ntl Merit Ltr; Danc.

BASCOMB III, PAUL L; Theodore Roosevelt SR HS; Washington, DC; (Y); Math Clb; ROTC; Drill Tm; Yrbk Stf; Pres Stu Cncl; Hon Roll; Jr NHS; Prfct Atten Awd; Outstndng Achvt Awd Comp Mth 84; Atlntc Pcfc Mth Lg Cert 82; Outstndng Accmplshmnts In Hnrs Mth 81-82; Georgetown U; Bus Comp Pgmr.

BASILE, ALEXIS; Georgetown Visitation Prep; Lanham, MD; (Y); 3/100; Art Clb; Drama Clb; Science Clb; School Musical; Church Yth Grp; SADD; Stage Crew; Yrbk Stf; Badmtn; Vllybl; Amer Hrt Assoc Srch 86; Bio.

BECHTEL, KELLI; Georgetown Visitation Prep; Potomac, MD; (Y); Drama Clb; Math Clb; NFL; Speech Tm; Stage Crew; Nwsp Stf; VP Jr Cls; Sftbl; Hon Roll; Trs NHS; Margaret Mary Spirit Awd.

BECKWITH, RHONDA BERNADETTE; Frank W Ballou HS; Washington, DC; (Y); 18/435; Drama Clb; Chorus; Church Choir; School Play; NHS; Wilhelmina Rolark Awd 86; Ballou Dsapphire Modlg Tm 86; Dynmcs Reltnshp Achvt 86; Langston U; Intl Lwyr.

BELK, RALPH; Banneker Academic HS; Washington, DC; (Y); Pres Church Yth Grp; Cmnty Wkr; VP Exploring; Office Aide; Pres Church Choir; Yrbk Stf; Hon Roll; 10th St Baptist Church Pastor Awds 83-85; Cmmnty Svc Awd 84 & 86; Mayor Barry Yth Ldrshp Inst Cert 84; Duke; Med.

BELL, LISA; Frank W Ballou HS; Washington, DC; (S); Mrchg Band; Twrlr; Cit Awd; Hon Roll; NHS; Jrnlsm.

BENN, SAMUEL; Ballou SR HS; Washington, DC; (S); Quiz Bowl; ROTC; Science Clb; Teachers Aide; Drill Tm; Trk; Cit Awd; Hon Roll; JETS Awd; NHS; 1st Pl Earth Sci Sci Fair 85; Geol Soc WA Awd 85; Armd Frcs Cmmnctn & Elec Awd 84; Acad Achvt Awd 85; U Sthrn CA; Aerospc Engrng.

BENNETT, TARSHA; Paul Laurence Dunbar SR HS; Washington, DC; (Y); French Clb; FBLA; Mrchg Band; Capt Sftbl; Hon Roll; Jr NHS; Sal; Mst All Arnd Stu 84-85; Otstdng Sphmr 84-85; U VA; Accntng.

BENOVIL, JACQUES A; The Duke Ellington Schl Of The Arts; Washington, DC; (Y); CAP; Intnl Clb; Nwsp Phtg; Yrbk Ed-Chief; Yrbk Phtg; Yrbk Stf; Stu Cncl; Trk; Woodward Fndtn Fnd Fncl Aid Schlrshp 85-86; MD Art & Dsgn Coll Tlnt Srch Schlrshp 86.

BETHEA, MICHAEL; Mc Kinley Technical SR HS; Washington, DC; (Y); Aud/Vis; Rep Jr Cls; Var JV Ftbl; Var Trk; Hon Roll; Jr NHS; NHS; Ntl Merit Ltr; Sal; Perfct Attndnc Awd 86; Cert Of Accomplshmnt 86; Citznshp Awd 86; Clark Coll-Atlanta; Communctn.

BIGGER, SARAH; U S Senate Page Schl; Bossier City, LA; (S); 1/29; Key Clb; Math Clb; Natl Beta Clb; ROTC; SADD; Nwsp Stf; Yrbk Ed-Chief; Trs Frsh Cls; Rep Soph Cls; U S Senate Page 85-86; 1st Pl LA ST Schltc Rally Bio I 85; Acad Stu Sem 85; Polit Sci.

BISHOP, WILLIAM B; The Sidwell Friends Schl; Chevy Chase, MD; (Y); Var Lcrss; Var Socr; Var Ntl Merit SF; Magna Cum Lauda Ntl Ltn Exam 83.

BLACK, CRYSTAL; Dunbar SR HS; Washington, DC; (Y); Dance Clb; Model UN; Ctznshp Awd 84; Atten Awd 84; Howard U; Bio.

BLAINE, SHERRON; Dunbar SR HS; Washington, DC; (Y); Girl Scts; Math Clb; Band; Church Choir; Soph Cls; Bsktbl; Cheerleading; Sftbl; Swmmng; Hon Roll; MS Humnts 84-85; 2nd Rnr-Up Ms JR 85-86; Pediatrcn.

BLANKENSHIP, WARREN; Mackin Catholic HS; Washington, DC; (Y); 2/34; Cmnty Wkr; Debate Tm; French Clb; Science Clb; Sec Sr Cls; High Hon Roll; Hon Roll; NHS; Ntl Merit Ltr; Prfct Atten Awd; U Dist Columbia; Mass Cmmnctns.

BLASSENGALE JR, CLYDE; Takoma Acad; Washington, DC; (Y); Computer Clb; Yrbk Stf; Hon Roll; NHS; Best Stu Music Apprectn 85-86; William & Mary; Bus Adm.

BLOUNT, GALEN ANTHONY; Dunbar SR HS; Washington, DC; (Y); Aud/Vis; Computer Clb; ROTC; SADD; Drill Tm; Nwsp Stf; Yrbk Stf; VP Soph Cls; Diving; JV Ftbl; U Of Miami FL; Pre-Med.

BLYTHER, SHARRON; Eastern HS; Washington, DC; (Y); Cmnty Wkr; Dance Clb; French Clb; Hosp Aide; JA; Office Aide; Teachers Aide; Stage Crew; Tennis; Cit Awd; Outstndng Job Perfrmnce Awd 85; John Hopkins U; Pre-Med.

BONNER, PAUL; St Anselms Abbey Schl; Chevy Chase, MD; (S); Mgr Stage Crew; Nwsp Ed-Chief; Ntl Merit Ltr; German Clb; Yrbk Stf; Socr; Macalester Coll; Anthrplgy.

BRACKETT, LYNDA; Springarn HS; Washington, DC; (Y); 3/25; Art Clb; Church Yth Grp; Cmnty Wkr; Dance Clb; Debate Tm; Drama Clb; Girl Scts; JA; Library Aide; Red Cross Aide; Lawyer.

BRADLEY III, WILLIAM G; Mc Kinley Tech HS; Washington, DC; (Y); Boy Scts; Chess Clb; Cmnty Wkr; Computer Clb; Drama Clb; French Clb; Intnl Clb; Pres VP JA; School Musical; Socr; Georgetwon U Law Ctr Mock Trial Comptn 86; JA Awd Excllnce 86; Pres Phys Fit Awd 84; Intern 86; U DC; Arch.

BRANCH, DAWANA; Frank W Ballou SR HS; Washington, DC; (S); 2/500; Sec Computer Clb; FBLA; Office Aide; Yrbk Stf; Sec Stu Cncl; Cit Awd; Jr NHS; NHS; 1st Pl Clrk Typng Cntst 84; George Washington U; Comp Sci.

BRANCH, SARAH; Eastern HS; Washington, DC; (Y); Church Yth Grp; Cmnty Wkr; Church Choir; Cit Awd; DAR Awd; Hon Roll; Prfct Atten Awd; Amer Heart Assn 85; Close Up Fndtn 86; Health Careers Pgm; U DC; Mortury Sci.

BRAZAITIS, SARAH; Woodrow Wilson HS; Washington, DC; (Y); 1/380; Pres Drama Clb; Pres French Clb; Office Aide; Chorus; School Play; Stage Crew; Nwsp Rptr; Rep Stu Cncl; NHS; Val; U Of PA; Psych.

BREWER, DARRYL; Woodrow Wilson HS; Washington, DC; (Y); 152/431; Boy Scts; Chess Clb; Civic Clb; Cmnty Wkr; Computer Clb; Teachers Aide; Varsity Clb; Mrchg Band; Var Ftbl; Patrick Pope Comp Achvt Awd 84; VP Capp 84; 9th Grd Gftd Talntd Prog 84; NCA&T ST U; Finance & Law Sch.

BREWTON, SAMANTHA; Immaculata Prep; Washington, DC; (Y); Cmnty Wkr; Dance Clb; Pres Orch; VP Jr Cls; Var L Cheerleading; Var Gym; Cit Awd; Civic Clb; French Clb; FBLA; LEAD Prg Wharton U Of PA 85; Outstndg Music Awd 85-86; Tufts U; Fornsc Pthlgst.

BRONSTEIN, SARAH; Woodrow Wilson HS; Washington, DC; (Y); 42/431; Art Clb; VP French Clb; German Clb; Chorus; Nwsp Stf; Hon Roll; 3rd Pl Citywide Frnch Cntst Amer Assc Tchrs & 6th Pl Reg 86; Lang.

BROOKS, JAMES FRANKLIN; Calvin Coolidge SR HS; Washington, DC; (S); Church Yth Grp; JA; Office Aide; Teachers Aide; Varsity Clb; Church Choir; School Musical; Yrbk Phtg; Yrbk Stf; Cit Awd; Awd For Excllnc In Mktg Educ Pgm 86; Awd JR Achvt Position VP Pblc Rel 86; Awd Calvin Coolidge 86; Catholic U Of Am; Medicine.

BROOKS, KENNETH; Archbishop Carroll HS; Washington, DC; (Y); 10/188; Chess Clb; Computer Clb; Science Clb; Concert Band; Mrchg Band; Ed Nwsp Phtg; Bausch & Lomb Sci Awd; High Hon Roll; NHS; Spanish NHS; 1st Pl Sci Fair-Physcs 86; George Washington U; Chem Engrn.

BROOKS, MARSHA ANN; Calvin Coolidge HS; Washington, DC; (S); Church Yth Grp; Civic Clb; Pres DECA; Pep Clb; Teachers Aide; Church Choir; Stu Cncl; Cit Awd; Long Island U; Prsnl Mgmt.

BROOKS, MAURICE; Mc Kinley Technical HS; Washington, DC; (Y); VP Pres Aud/Vis; Pres Camera Clb; Pres Civic Clb; English Clb; JA; Math Clb; Radio Clb; Science Clb; Stage Crew; VP Frsh Cls; IBM Pgm At Mc Kinley Tech 85 & 86; Metcom Clb-Howard U 85; Johns Hopkins; Bio-Med.

BROWN, CAROLYN J; Duke Ellington Schl Of The Arts; Upper Marlboro, MD; (Y); 35/88; JA; Red Cross Aide; Band; Church Choir; Flag Corp; Variety Show; JV Var Trk; Hon Roll; MD Distngsshd Schlr 85; JA Ldrshp Awd 83; Peabody Consrv Music; Music Ed.

BROWN, JAMIE; Mc Kinley SR HS; Washington, DC; (Y); English Clb; Library Aide; Math Clb; Science Clb; Off Frsh Cls; Bsktbl; Vllybl; Cit Awd; Hon Roll; NHS; Grgetwn U Citatn Otstndng Schlstc Achvmnt 86; Jerry A Moore Awd 84; Rgn C Awd 84; Georgetown U; Pre-Med.

BROWN, LESLIE; All Saints HS; Washington, DC; (Y); Computer Clb; Pep Clb; Rep Stu Cncl; Hon Roll; Prfct Atten Awd; Cert Awd Schllstcly & Comm Svcs 86; DCARC Rggs Bnk Schlrshp Pgm 86; U Maryland; Comp Pgmng.

BROWN, ROCHELLE; Benjamin Banneker SR HS; Washington, DC; (Y); Off Jr Cls; Im Bsktbl; Hon Roll; Jr NHS; Pltcl Sci.

BROWN, TONYA; Dunbar SR HS; Washington, DC; (Y); Art Clb; Computer Clb; English Clb; French Clb; Teachers Aide; Chorus; Church Choir; Cit Awd; French Hon Soc; Hon Roll; Womens Bar Assoc Awd 84; Attndnc Gram 85; Prft Attnd 86; Howard U; Bus Admin.

BROWN, WILLIAM A; Washington Intl HS; Washington, DC; (Y); Dance Clb; Capt Debate Tm; PAVAS; Speech Tm; Chorus; School Play; Nwsp Rptr; Lit Mag; Rep Sr Cls; Trs Stu Cncl.

BROWNE, COLLEEN; Georgetown Visitation HS; Rockville, MD; (Y); Cmnty Wkr; Computer Clb; Drama Clb; Latin Clb; Math Clb; Model UN; Thesps; School Musical; Swmmng; U RI; Acctng.

BRYANT, SYLVETTA; Theodore Roosevelt SR HS; Districts Heights, MD; (Y); Church Yth Grp; GAA; Girl Scts; Math Clb; Science Clb; SADD; Teachers Aide; Pres Jr Cls; Pres Sr Cls; Bsbl; Best Dressed Award 83-86; Outstanding Business Student 85-86; Bus Admn.

BUCKLEY, PAUL; Gonzaga Coll HS; Rockville, MD; (Y); 17/170; Church Yth Grp; Drama Clb; French Clb; Latin Clb; Math Clb; Math Tm; Chorus; Church Choir; School Musical; School Play; Maxima Cum Laude-Ntl Latn Exm 83 & 84; Ntl Merit Schlr 85; Fnlst MD Math Cmptn 85 & 86; Coll Of The Holy Cross; Math.

BUMBREY, WAVERLY; Archbishop Carroll HS; Washington, DC; (S); 20/180; Church Yth Grp; Drama Clb; Pep Clb; PAVAS; Band; Church Choir; Jazz Band; Cit Awd; High Hon Roll; NHS; George Mason U; Acctng.

BURBRIDGE, LEILANI; Sidwell Friends Schl; Washington, DC; (Y); Dance Clb; GAA; Spanish Clb; Teachers Aide; Chorus; School Musical; Variety Show; Bsktbl; Cheerleading; Sftbl; U Of HI; Chines Lang.

BURNETTE, ANITA; Theodore Roosevelt S H S; Washington, DC; (Y); Church Yth Grp; Cmnty Wkr; JA; Office Aide; Science Clb; Teachers Aide; Church Choir; Cit Awd; Hon Roll; NHS; Pdtrcn.

BURROUGHS, ALENDA; Woodrow Wilson SR HS; Washington, DC; (Y); 28/431; Sec Church Yth Grp; Chorus; Pres Mrchg Band; Orch; Pres Jr Cls; Pom Pon; Hon Roll; Jr NHS; Sal; Ntl Sci Merit Awd 85; Acad All-Amer 86; Acad Awd 86; Law.

BURROWS, ALICIA; Eastern SR HS; Washington, DC; (Y); Chorus; Capt Color Guard; Stage Crew; Nwsp Ed-Chief; Yrbk Stf; Rep Jr Cls; Cit Awd; High Hon Roll; Jr NHS; Howard U; Jrnlsm.

BUTLER, DUANE; Springarn S HS; Washington, DC; (Y); Art Clb; Computer Clb; English Clb; JA; Math Clb; ROTC; Science Clb; Teachers Aide; Church Choir; Stage Crew.

BUTLER, SCOTT P; Gonzaga College HS; Washington, DC; (Y); Cmnty Wkr; Science Clb; Service Clb; Rep Stu Cncl; Hon Roll; Ntl Merit Ltr; Amer Heart Assn Fllwshp 85; Chem.

BYARS, DARLENE; Frank W Ballou HS; Washington, DC; (Y); Dance Clb; SADD; Teachers Aide; Bsktbl; Cit Awd; Prfct Atten Awd; 1st Pl In Martin Luther King Essy Cntst 86.

CALDWELL, PAUL C; Gonzaga College HS; Capital Heights, MD; (Y); 87/176; French Clb; Hon Roll; Ntl Achvt Cmm Schlr 85; Econ.

CARTER, DORLISA; Calvin Coolidge HS; Washington, DC; (S); Church Yth Grp; JA; Math Clb; Office Aide; Science Clb; Yrbk Stf; Hon Roll; NHS; Rensselaer Medal 85; Sci Awd 84; Spanish Awd 84; Howard U; Bus Mgt.

CARTER, RUTH; Anacostia SR HS; Washington, DC; (Y); Library Aide; Hon Roll; Bus Pgmng.

CASEY, KENNETH; Washington-Dix Street Acad; Washington, DC; (Y); Church Yth Grp; ROTC; Church Choir; Capt Drill Tm; Nwsp Rptr; VP Sr Cls; Stu Cncl; Prfct Atten Awd; Ldrshp Awd 85; Schltc Exclnce ROTC 86; UDC; Anim Sci.

CASTILLO, MARGARITA; Cardozo HS; Washington, DC; (S); FBLA; Cit Awd; Hon Roll; Prfct Atten Awd; Bus.

CAWOOD, ROBERT; Gonzaga College HS; W River, MD; (Y); 51/190; Art Clb; Aud/Vis; Drama Clb; German Clb; PAVAS; Hon Roll; Barnes Awd 83-84; Syracuse U.

CHAMBERS, ERIC; Archbishop HS; Washington, DC; (S); 16/188; Cmnty Wkr; Yrbk Phtg; VP Jr Cls; Stu Cncl; Crs Cntry; Ftbl; High Hon Roll; Pres NHS; VP Spanish NHS; 1st,3rd Pl Sci Fair Wnnr 84-85; Med.

CHANDLER, DIMETERICE; Cardozo SR HS; Washington, DC; (Y); FBLA; ROTC; Band; Color Guard; Drill Tm; VP Stu Cncl; Vllybl; Cit Awd; Hon Roll; Jr NHS; Citation From Georgetown U For Oustndng Schlstc Achvt 86; Acctg.

CHESEN, PAUL; Gonzaga College HS; Washington, DC; (Y); French Clb; Ski Clb; Nwsp Stf; Capt JV Bsbl; Im Bsktbl; Capt JV Ftbl; Im Tennis; Im Wt Lftg.

CHIN, MICHAEL; Ballou SR HS; Washington, DC; (S); 16/425; Boy Scts; Chorus; Drill Tm; School Musical; School Play; Variety Show; Cit Awd; Hon Roll; NHS; Prfct Atten Awd; Hnr Rl; Aerosp Engrng.

CHLOUPEK, SHARON; Georgetown Visitation Prep Schl; Potomac, MD; (Y); Varsity Clb; Trs Jr Cls; Var Capt Bsktbl; JV Socr; Hon Roll; Hstry Awd 84; Mst Imprvd Bstkbl Plyr Awd 85; Margaret Mary Sprt Awd 84; Lbrl Arts.

CLARK, CLETUS; Archbishop Carroll HS; Washington, DC; (S); 2/134; Library Aide; Pep Clb; Stage Crew; VP Sr Cls; Rep Stu Cncl; High Hon Roll; NHS; Citation Outstndng Schlstc Achvt Georgetown U 85; U MD College Park; Acctg.

CLARK, CONNIE; F W Ballou HS; Washington, DC; (Y); Teachers Aide; Hon Roll; Jr NHS; NHS; Prfct Atten Awd; Val; Georgetown; Bio.

CLAYTON, BRIAN; House Of Representatives Page Schl; Katy, TX; (Y); Drama Clb; Yrbk Stf; 4-H Awd; Hon Roll; Church Yth Grp; 4-H; Math Clb; Science Clb; UIL Persuasive Spkng 1st & 2nd Distg 84-85; Congressional Page Hse Of Rep 85-86.

COEHMIS-FRAZIER, KIM; Dunbar HS; Washington, DC; (Y); 4-H; FBLA; Pep Clb; SADD; Church Choir; Cit Awd; Hon Roll; Prfct Atten Awd; Bus Awd 85; Chem Awd 86; Bus.

COHEN, DAVID; Woodrow Wilson HS; Washington, DC; (Y); 22/431; Scholastic Bowl; Ski Clb; Chorus; Off Frsh Cls; Tennis; Hon Roll; JETS Awd; Ntl Merit Ltr; DOD Sci & Engrng Rsrch Appnrntcshp Pgm 85 &86; UDC Natl Tech Assn 1st Plmth Cont 85, 3rdp Pl Sci 85; Mth.

COLBERT, DELORES; Eastern SR HS; Washington, DC; (Y); Church Yth Grp; JA; Sec Ski Clb; Church Choir; School Musical; Sec Jr Cls; Hon Roll; Jr NHS; NHS; Sal; Howard U; Pre-Med.

COLEMAN, JOHNNIE L; Calvin Coolidge HS; Washington, DC; (S); Computer Clb; Math Clb; Scholastic Bowl; Church Choir; Off Sr Cls; Bsbl; Trk; High Hon Roll; Hon Roll; Jr NHS; Hnr Roll Awd & Gldys Tylr Schlrshp 85-86; Cmptr Sci Awd 84-85; U MD Coll Pk; Aerosp Engrng.

COLLUM, MICHELE; Washington International Schl; Washington, DC; (S); Hosp Aide; Orch; School Musical; Yrbk Stf; Lit Mag; Socr; Cit Awd; Exc Poetry Eng 84; Hnrbl Ment Spnsh 85; Exc Hist 85; Chem Engr.

CONEY, LESLIE; Dunbar HS; Washington, DC; (Y); FHA; Hosp Aide; VP Frsh Cls; Capt Crs Cntry; Capt Trk; Hon Roll; Jr NHS; NHS; Val; Prfct Attnd 85-86; 3rd Pl Ctywide Frgn Lang Cntst Spnsh 86; Systm Anlyst.

CONNOR, M COLLEEN; Georgetown Visitation HS; Ft Washington, MD; (Y); Drama Clb; Nwsp Rptr; Yrbk Rptr; Var Crs Cntry; JV Lcrss; Var Swmmng; Var Trk; Hon Roll; Jr NHS; Hnrs In Algbra I 84; Hnrs In Gmtry 85; Hnrs In Chem 86; Sprts Med.

COOLEY, RENEE; Cardozo HS; Washington, DC; (S); Camp Fr Inc; Drama Clb; Science Clb; High Hon Roll; Hon Roll; GWU Fellowshp Awd 85; Acad Excllnce Awd 85-86; Tuskegee Inst; Bio.

COOPER, FAITH E; Dunbar SR HS; Washington, DC; (Y); Girl Scts; Office Aide; Church Choir; Prfct Atten Awd; Psych.

COPELAND, KIMBERLY; Howard D Woodson SR HS; Washington, DC; (Y); Hosp Aide; ROTC; Yrbk Stf; Frsh Cls; Soph Cls; Jr Cls; Sr Cls; Cit Awd; Hon Roll; Prfct Atten Awd; U DC; Nrs.

COPEMANN, SHATIKA; William Mc Kinley SR HS; Washington, DC; (Y); Art Clb; Cmnty Wkr; JA; Science Clb; Ski Clb; Spanish Clb; SADD; Pres Jr Cls; Cit Awd; WA U; Med.

COPLAN, DAVID; Woodrow Wilson HS; Washington, DC; (Y); 48/431; Chess Clb; JA; Temple Yth Grp; Im Bsktbl; Hon Roll; Jr NHS; Sci Fair Wnnr & Prtcptn; Prtcptn Howard/Metcon Engrng Prg; Chvd Highest Score Schl Math Cntst; Bus.

CORMENY, SARA L; Banneker Academic HS; Washington, DC; (Y); 7/105; Cmnty Wkr; Debate Tm; Model UN; NFL; Stu Cncl; NHS; Ntl Merit SF; School Play; High Hon Roll; Rugby Tm 85-87; Folger Shakespeare Fllwshp 86-87; Hi-SCIP George Washington U 86-87; Wrtr.

CRAWLEY, WENDY; Calvin Coolidge HS; Washington, DC; (S); Church Yth Grp; Math Clb; Pep Clb; Ski Clb; Spanish Clb; Church Choir; Yrbk Ed-Chief; DECA; Var Mgr(s); Var Sftbl; Hmcmg Qn 85; Miss Jabberwock 84; Emry-Riddle Aeronaut U; Aviatn.

CREIGHTON, MARIA; Roosevelt SR HS; Washington, DC; (Y); Drama Clb; Math Clb; Teachers Aide; School Play; Sec Stu Cncl; Vllybl; Cit Awd; Hon Roll; NHS; Prfct Atten Awd; Armd Frcs Comm & Elctrncs Assn 83; Grgtwn U Ctatn Of Schltcs Achvt 86; Inclsn Of Poem-Amer Ptry Anthlg; Catholic U; Drmtc Arts.

CROWLEY, SUSAN; Georgetown Visitation Prep Schl; Washington, DC; (Y); Church Yth Grp; Computer Clb; French Clb; Library Aide; Math Clb; Science Clb; Yrbk Stf; Lit Mag; Hon Roll; Crtv Wrtng Awd 84; Natl Schlstc 84; Awd Eng & Frnch 85; Ad Ancient Hstry 83; Georgetown U; Gvrnmnt.

CUNNINGHAM, THOMAS T; St Anselms Abbey Schl; Silver Spring, MD; (Y); Boy Scts; Pres Debate Tm; Band; L Wrstlng; Ntl Merit SF; Gld Mdl Nlt JR Clsscl Leag Latin Tst 83-84; Slvr Med Ntl JR Clsscl Leag Latin Tst 85.

CURTIS, IRIS; Frank W Ballou HS; Washington, DC; (S); Church Yth Grp; VP FBLA; Band; Church Choir; Concert Band; Mrchg Band; Cit Awd; Hon Roll; Prfct Atten Awd; Excel Rtng Band Solo & Ensmble 84-85; Lane Coll; Acctng.

DANIEL, M KEITH; Archbishop Carroll HS; Hyattsville, MD; (S); #6 In Class; Var L Ftbl; Im Trk; Im High Hon Roll; Im Hon Roll; Im NHS; Im Spanish NHS; Hnbl Mntn Schl Scsi Fair 83; 1st Bapt Chrch Promo SR Dept 83; Elec Engrng.

DARGAN, KAREN; Calvin Coolidge HS; Washington, DC; (Y); JA; Crs Cntry; Trk; High Hon Roll; Hon Roll; NHS; Ntl Merit Ltr; George Washington U; Pltcl Sci.

DAVILA, KIMBERLY; Theodore Roosevelt HS; Washington, DC; (Y); JA; ROTC; Sec Spanish Clb; Trs Church Choir; Rep Jr Cls; Capt Cheerleading; Trk; Jr NHS; Prfct Atten Awd; Spanish NHS; Acad Excllnce Engl III 86; Supr Acad Achvt U S Hstry 86; A Avg Piano 86; Coll Prof.

DAVIS, EVETTE; Woodrow Wilson SR HS; Washington, DC; (Y); 17/431; Church Yth Grp; FBLA; JA; Office Aide; Sec Service Clb; Chorus; Cit Awd; NHS; Cmnty Wkr; Computer Clb; Smith Coll Book Awd 86; Mayors Yth Ldrshp Inst 86; CPA.

DAVY, FREDERICK; Calvin Coolidge SR HS; Washington, DC; (S); Church Choir; Cit Awd; NHS; Val; Church Yth Grp; Math Clb; Trk; Vllybl; High Hon Roll; Jr NHS; 1st Pl City Sci Fair 85.

DEADWYLER, ROSS; Model Secondary School For Deaf; Atlanta, GA; (Y); Drama Clb; School Play; Cheerleading; Wrstlng; Wnr Intl Crtv Arts Fstvl 86; Drama.

DEAN, GORDON; Edmund Burke HS; Washington, DC; (Y); JV Bsbl; Var Crs Cntry; Var Trk.

DEAN, JANICE; Coolidge HS; Washington, DC; (S); Church Yth Grp; FBLA; Math Clb; Science Clb; Church Choir; Mrchg Band; Rep Sr Cls; Rep Stu Cncl; Cit Awd; Hon Roll; Acad All Amer Stu Awd 84-85; Outstndng Schltc Achvt Citatn 85; Elec Engrng.

DEAN, TAURUS; Mc Kinley HS; Washington, DC; (Y); Computer Clb; FFA; Library Aide; Office Aide; Rep Jr Cls; Cit Awd; Hon Roll; Prfct Atten Awd; Teachers Aide; Stage Crew; Outstndng Stu 83-84; UDC Coll; Comp Pgm.

DEAUSEN, JOSEPH; Gonzaga College HS; Potomac, MD; (Y); 65/180; Camera Clb; Chess Clb; Latin Clb; Science Clb; Spanish Clb; JV Crs Cntry; JV Trk; Hon Roll; Latin Schlr 86; Engr.

DICKENS, TRYPHENIA; Theodore Roosevelt HS; Washington, DC; (Y); Teachers Aide; Drm Mjr(t); Nwsp Rptr; Yrbk Phtg; Cheerleading; Pom Pon; Cit Awd; Hon Roll; Jr NHS; Prfct Atten Awd; Outstndng Schlrshp & Crtv Wrtng Awd 84; Spnsh I, Gmtry Awds, & Engl Schlrshp 85; Spnsh II Awd 86; Hwrd U; Comp Sci.

DICKEY, LISA M; Calvin Coolidge SR HS; Washington, DC; (S); Cmnty Wkr; Computer Clb; Office Aide; Pep Clb; Teachers Aide; Rep Soph Cls; Cheerleading; Mgr(s); Hon Roll; Val; Amer Lgn Awd 83; George Mason Coll; Engrng.

DINAN, MARK; Gonzaga College HS; Alexandria, VA; (Y); 1/180.

DIXON, RYNELL; Frank W Ballou SR HS; Washington, DC; (S); Office Aide; NHS; Outstndng Stu Span I 85; Outstndng Stu US Hist 85.

DIXON, TANENA; Calvin Coolidge HS; Washington, DC; (S); Computer Clb; Im Bsktbl; Var Cheerleading; Im Vllybl; Cit Awd; High Hon Roll; JC Awd; Jr NHS; Prfct Atten Awd; JR Miss Schlrshp Prog 86; Phys Thrpy.

DOHERTY, BRIAN; Gonzaga Coll HS; Silver Spring, MD; (Y); 49/180; Aud/Vis; Drama Clb; Pep Clb; School Musical; Nwsp Rptr; Im Bsktbl; Hon Roll; Ntl Merit Ltr; Natl Latin Exam 86.

DOLLOSON, KEVIN; Gonzaga College HS; Suitland, MD; (Y); 70/177; Ed Aud/Vis; Office Aide; Var Bsktbl; Var Mgr(s); Var Timer; Var Wt Lftg; Hon Roll; Pres Schlr; Prtcptd Mnrty Schlrs Cmptr Sci 85; US Bus Educ Awd Wnnr 86; VA Wesley Coll; Bus Mrkng.

DOUGLASS, KAREN; Theodore Roosevelt HS; Washington, DC; (Y); Church Yth Grp; ROTC; Teachers Aide; Church Choir; Drill Tm; Yrbk Stf; VP Frsh Cls; Stat Score Keeper.

DUCKETT, EARL; Theodore Roosevelt HS; Washington, DC; (Y); 5/325; Cmnty Wkr; Drama Clb; ROTC; Science Clb; Varsity Clb; School Play; Rep Stu Cncl; Capt Var Tennis; Hon Roll; VP NHS; $2000 Schlrshp-4th Dist Plc Sta-Strng Spprt Cmnty Svcs 86; U Of Pittsburgh; Chem.

DUPREE, JENNIFER; Mckinley Tech; Washington, DC; (Y); Church Yth Grp; Band; Rep Jr Cls; Cheerleading; Hon Roll; Jr NHS; Acadmc All-Am 84; U MD; Comp Sci.

DUVALL, ROBERT; St Johns College HS; Gaithersburg, MD; (Y); 21/150; Cmnty Wkr; French Clb; Pep Clb; Off ROTC; Varsity Clb; Trs Soph Cls; Trs Jr Cls; JV Bsbl; Im Coach Actv; JV Var Ftbl; Promoted Rank Of Cadet Capt Of Regiment 86-87; Med.

ECHOLS, AL J; Dunbar HS; Washington, DC; (Y); Office Aide; Nwsp Rptr; Hon Roll; NCTE Awd; Prfct Atten Awd; Pres Acdmc Ftnss Awd 86; Schlrshp Frm Clss Of 86; Woodward Fndntn Aw 85-86; Essey Cnty Coll; Marines.

EDWARDS, BRENT H; St Albans Schl; Washington, DC; (Y); 4/70; Debate Tm; Madrigals; Yrbk Bus Mgr; Ed Lit Mag; Off Frsh Cls; Off Soph Cls; Off Jr Cls; Off Sr Cls; Stu Cncl; Socr; Wnr Ptry Cntst DC Metro Chptr Of Links Inc 84-85; Lawyer.

EKUBAN, EDNA; Cardozo HS; Washington, DC; (S); Dance Clb; Drama Clb; Science Clb; Tennis; Bausch & Lomb Sci Awd; Cit Awd; High Hon Roll; Hon Roll; Prfct Atten Awd.

ELLIS, KENNETH M; Archbishop Carroll HS; Landover Hills, MD; (S); 12/160; Church Yth Grp; Drama Clb; Library Aide; Chorus; School Musical; School Play; Stage Crew; Hon Roll; Law.

ELLIS, LORI R; Georgetown Visitation HS; Washington, DC; (Y); Cmnty Wkr; Hosp Aide; Library Aide; Office Aide; Teachers Aide; Var Capt Cheerleading; Mayor Barrys Yth Incentive Awd 83; Mayor Barrys Yth Ldrshp Inst 84; Achv Prog Cmmnd Stu 85; Chem Engrng.

EVELY, ROBERT A; Springarn HS; Washington, DC; (Y); Boy Scts; Church Yth Grp; Computer Clb; Church Choir; Cit Awd; Hon Roll; JETS Awd; NHS; Prfct Atten Awd; Comp Sci.

FARLEY, MELVINA; Calvin Coolidge SR HS; Washington, DC; (Y); Church Yth Grp; Drama Clb; Intnl Clb; Pep Clb; School Play; Nwsp Rptr; Var Sftbl; Cit Awd; Hon Roll; Ntl Merit Ltr; Excllnc-Engl 85; Archry Trphs & Rbbns 85-86; John Hopkins U; Med.

FAZZARI, GIOVANNA; Georgetown Visitation Prep; Falls Church, VA; (Y); 1/100; Sec Service Clb; Speech Tm; Teachers Aide; Chorus; Stage Crew; Ed Lit Mag; High Hon Roll; NHS; Computer Clb; Math Clb; Archdiocesan Hnr Choir; Hnrs Schlrshp Mdl; GWU Schl Of Engrng & Appld Sci Engrng Mdl; Appld Math.

FENSTER, GAYLE; National Cathedral Schl; Bethesda, MD; (Y); Cmnty Wkr; Math Tm; Model UN; Sec Temple Yth Grp; Lit Mag; Sec Jr Cls; Sec Stu Cncl; Ntl Latin Exam Cum Laude Awd 86.

FERREN, PETER; Woodrow Wilson SR HS; Washington, DC; (Y); 2/431; French Clb; Hosp Aide; Quiz Bowl; Chorus; Socr; Tennis; Bausch & Lomb Sci Awd; Jr NHS; NHS; Sal; U Dist Columbia Mth Cont 8th Pl 85, 3rd Pl 86; YMCA Intl Essay Cont 1st Pl 86; East Asian Studies.

FISHER, RONELL; Dunbar SR HS; Washington, DC; (Y); Math Clb; School Play; Cit Awd; Hon Roll; Prfct Atten Awd; Dntl Tech.

FITZGERALD, JUSTINE; Georgetown Vistation HS; Potomac, MD; (Y); Cmnty Wkr; Computer Clb; Hosp Aide; Math Clb; Nwsp Stf; Im Bsktbl; JV Var Cheerleading; Var High Hon Roll; Var NHS; Awd Otstndng Cntrbtn Chrstn Actn Scty; Archtctr Bus.

FITZGERALD, MARC; Archbishop Carroll HS; Capitol Hgts, MD; (S); 7/146; Church Yth Grp; Cmnty Wkr; Office Aide; Pep Clb; Spanish Clb; Pep Band; Variety Show; Pres Jr Cls; Rep Stu Cncl; JV Ftbl; Altar Server Awd 84; Howard U; Pre-Law.

FLEMING, DONNA; Woodrow Wilson HS; Washington, DC; (Y); 58/431; Church Yth Grp; GAA; Girl Scts; JA; Office Aide; Service Clb; Stage Crew; Rep Stu Cncl; Var Capt Bsktbl; Stat Ftbl; Cert Of Schlstc Achvt 86; Cngrsnl Cert Of Apprctn 82; Outstndng JR Stu 86; NC ST U; Comp Engrng.

FORD, REGAN; Woodrow Wilson SR HS; Washington, DC; (Y); 87/431; Aud/Vis; Church Yth Grp; Cmnty Wkr; Pres JA; Keywanettes; Speech Tm; Chorus; Cheerleading; Mgr(s); Cit Awd; Ntl Latn Exm-Cum Laude Awd-86; Brdcstg.

FOX, MARK; United States Senate Page Schl; Fairfax, VA; (Y); Letterman Clb; Political Wkr; Nwsp Stf; Yrbk Phtg; Yrbk Stf; Var L Ftbl; Hon Roll; Senate Pg Schl & Head Pg Senate Flr 85-86; U Of VA; Pltcs.

FRANCIES, VALERIE; Frank W Ballou HS; Washington, DC; (S); Church Yth Grp; Pep Clb; Church Choir; Mrchg Band; Hon Roll; NHS; Prfct Atten Awd.

FRANCIS, VICTORIA; F W Ballour HS; Washington, DC; (S); 3/425; Church Yth Grp; Key Clb; Math Clb; Yrbk Stf; Stu Cncl; Hon Roll; Jr NHS; NHS; Prfct Atten Awd; Woodwrd Fndtn Fllwshp Awd 84-85; Acad All Amer 85; Dstngshd Amer HS Stu Soc 85; MA Inst Of Tech; Elec Engr.

FREE, ANTHONY C; Dunbar SR HS; Washington, DC; (Y); 2/375; Church Yth Grp; Civic Clb; Church Choir; Mrchg Band; Nwsp Rptr; Trs Sr Cls; Trk; NHS; Rotary Awd; Drama Clb; Ntl Cncl Of Tchrs Of Englsh Wrtng Awd 85; Brown Book Awd 85; Elec Engrng.

FREEMAN, HARRINE ENID; Banneker SR HS; Washington, DC; (Y); 30/108; Camp Fr Inc; Trs Church Yth Grp; Cmnty Wkr; Dance Clb; Teachers Aide; Pres Church Choir; Trs Sr Cls; Im Socr; Im Vllybl; Hon Roll; Hnr Mayor Barry Youth Ldrsp Inst 86; Norte Dame MD; Comp Sci.

FREEMAN, TRACY; Georgetown Visitation HS; Washington, DC; (Y); Am Leg Aux Girls St; Camera Clb; Model UN; Chorus; Rep Soph Cls; VP Jr Cls; Pres Sr Cls; Black Stu Union Treas 83-84, VP 84-85; Mother Theresa Lalor Awd 86; UCLA; Econ.

FRYAR, YVETTE; Benjamin Banneker HS; Washington, DC; (Y); 18/108; Debate Tm; Exploring; Model UN; Sec Jr Cls; VP Stu Cncl; Cit Awd; Hon Roll; Jr NHS; Prfct Atten Awd; Pre-Med.

GAITAN, RICARDO I; Gonzaga College HS; Mc Lean, VA; (Y); 27/177; Cmnty Wkr; Spanish Clb; Nwsp Stf; Ed Lit Mag; Var Lcrss; Var Socr; JV Tennis; Hon Roll; Art Clb; Yrbk Phtg; Coll Holy Cross Bk Awd 84-85; Natl Art Hnr Scty; Boston Coll.

GALMORE, JAMES; Benjamin Banneker SR HS; Washington, DC; (Y); 12/108; Drill Tm; Pres Sr Cls; Stu Cncl; Swmmng; Wt Lftg; Hon Roll; Prfct Atten Awd; Wnnr Concrnd Black Men Imc Oratory Cntst 86; Poli Sci.

GANTT, LEON; Theodore Roosevelt SR HS; Washington, DC; (Y); Boy Scts; Chess Clb; Spanish Clb; Ftbl; Wt Lftg; Cit Awd; Prfct Atten Awd; Outstndng Bnkng 86; Outstndng French 86; Detroit U; Bus Mgnt.

GASTON, LESLIE; Woodrow Wilson HS; Washington, DC; (Y); 172/431; Church Yth Grp; Drama Clb; FCA; Girl Scts; JA; Teachers Aide; Church Choir; Capt Pom Pon; Sigma Gamma Rho Soror Blue Review 85; Howard U.

GAUL, CHRISTIAN; Gonzaga College HS; Chevy Chase, MD; (Y); Nwsp Rptr; Lit Mag; Ftbl; Var Lcrss; Hon Roll; U Notre Dame.

GENERAL, DEXTER; Theodore Roosevelt HS; Washington, DC; (Y); 4-H; JA; Im Bsktbl; Var Ftbl; Var Swmmng; 4-H Awd; Prfct Atten Awd; Brigham Young U; Comp Tchncn.

GESSNER, DAMIAN; Archbishop Carroll HS; Washington, DC; (Y); Boy Scts; Chess Clb; Church Yth Grp; Science Clb; Mgr(s); Socr; Hon Roll; NHS; Hugh Obrien Yth Fndtn Awd 84; G Washington U Hi Scip 85-86; Juanita Coll Huntngdn; Bio.

GIBSON, JULIA L; Woodrow Wilson HS; Washington, DC; (Y); Sec Art Clb; JA; Teachers Aide; Ntl Merit SF; Computer Clb; Variety Show; Rep Frsh Cls; Schlrshp Carnigie Melon U; Sci Fair Awds 83, 84 & 85; Art.

GINYARD, VON; Theodore Roosevelt HS; Washington, DC; (Y); Church Yth Grp; Computer Clb; Drama Clb; Band; Chorus; Church Choir; Concert Band; Bsktbl; Gym; Hon Roll; Comp Spec.

GLENN, RHONDA L; Benjamin Banneker HS; Washington, DC; (Y); 3/78; Chess Clb; Cmnty Wkr; Drama Clb; Model UN; Spanish Clb; NHS; Harvard Book Prize 85; U Dist Columbia Mth Cont 85; U Dist Columbia Mth/Comp Sci Scholar 83; Aerospc Engrng.

GNATEK, MARY; Georgetown Visitation HS; Washington, DC; (Y); 30/98; Computer Clb; Drama Clb; SADD; Varsity Clb; Stage Crew; Variety Show; Lit Mag; Var Socr; Art Clb; Dance Clb; Latin Awd 86; Frnch Awd 85; Athltc Awds 85; Loyola Coll.

GODFREY, SONYA L; All Saints HS; Suitland, MD; (Y); Debate Tm; Hosp Aide; Chorus; Pres Soph Cls; Rep Stu Cncl; Gospel Chr 82-86; Smphrmr Cls Awd 83-84; U Of Columbia; Bus Admin.

GONZALEZ, EILEEN; Woodrow Wilson HS; Washington, DC; (Y); Hon Roll; Intl Studies Pgm 85-86; Sci Fair Cert 85-86; Transltr.

GOODWELL, ELIZABETH; Cardozo SR HS; Washington, DC; (S); Dance Clb; Drama Clb; Science Clb; Hon Roll; NHS; Troph RIF Cntst 85; Acad Schlrshp Awd 85; Diffrnt Subjs Awds 84-85.

GORSUCL, STEPHANIE; Georgetown Visitation Prep Schl; Falls Church, VA; (Y); Cmnty Wkr; Drama Clb; Service Clb; Speech Tm; School Play; Stage Crew; JV Co-Capt Sftbl; Hnr Brd Rep, Sec; Awd Outstndng Svc Christian Actn Soc; Pre Med.

GRAHAM, BETTIE ANN; Benjamin Banneker HS; Washington, DC; (Y); 23/108; Church Yth Grp; Girl Scts; Library Aide; Office Aide; Teachers Aide; Trs Church Choir; Orch; Pres NCYC WA Dstr AME Zion Ch 86; 2nd Pl Essy Cont Am Constnlsm DC Br Assn 86; Econ.

GRAHAM, RICO; Dunbar SHS; Washington, DC; (Y); French Clb; Latin Clb; Varsity Clb; Bsbl; Ftbl; Swmmng; Trk; Wt Lftg; Cit Awd; Hon Roll; Coll NC ST; Bus Adm.

GRAY, ROBERTINA V; Howard Dilworth Woodson HS; Suitland, MD; (S); DECA; Drama Clb; Girl Scts; JA; ROTC; Teachers Aide; Boy Scts; Nwsp Ed-Chief; Nwsp Rptr; Frsh Cls; Princpls Awd 83; DECA Pres 86-87; U Southern CA; Jrnlsm.

GREEN, VALERIE; Edmund Burke HS; Washingtone, DC; (Y); VP Church Yth Grp; Debate Tm; Sec French Clb; Model UN; SADD; Yrbk Stf; Var JV Bsktbl; JV Socr; Var Vllybl; Hon Roll; Pre-Law.

GREENBERGER, SCOTT; Woodrow Wilson HS; Washington, DC; (Y); #11 In Class; JCL; Political Wkr; Chorus; Nwsp Sprt Ed; Yrbk Stf; Var Capt Bsktbl; Hon Roll; Jr NHS; Pres NHS; "how I Can Wrk For Peace" Cty-Wide Essay Cntst 1st Pl 85; Natl Latin Exam Cum Laude 85; Pltcs.

GREENE, KELLY A; Benjamin Banneker HS; Washington, DC; (Y); 19/81; Cmnty Wkr; Model UN; VP Drill Tm; Rep Sr Cls; Hon Roll; Art Clb; Sec French Clb; Girl Scts; Library Aide; Office Aide; Outstdng Svc Barrys Yth Ldrshp Inst 85; Outstndg Svd Lamond-Riggs Libr 84; Excllnce Wrk Prfrmnce 83; U Miami; Mar Biol.

GRIGG, RHEEMA; Immaculata Preparatory HS; Silver Spg, MD; (Y); Art Clb; French Clb; Intnl Clb; Political Wkr; Yrbk Stf; Powder Puff Ftbl; JV Vllybl; Ldrshp Schlrshp Of Manhattanville Clg 86; Natl De Frangous 85; Manhattanville Achvt Grant 86; Manhattanville Cgl; Intl Affrs.

GRIMALDI, FELICIA; Georgetown Vistation Prep Schl; Washington, DC; (Y); Am Leg Aux Girls St; Art Clb; Service Clb; Lit Mag; Var Fld Hcky; JV Capt Golf; Var Swmmng; Hon Roll; NHS; GAA; Prince Of Mardi Gras; Spcl Hon/Recog In Chem; Girls ST; Law.

GRISSETT, SIDNEY; Archbiship Carroll HS; Mitchelleville, MD; (S); #23 In Class; Aud/Vis; Boy Scts; Church Yth Grp; Teachers Aide; Yrbk Phtg; Pres Stu Cncl; JV Ftbl; Score Keeper; Hon Roll; NHS; In-Schl Wrk Pgm Awd 85; Mayor Barrys Yth Ldrshp Inst 83; Yth Incentive Awd 83; Elec Engr.

GUISHARD, TERRENCE; Archbishop Carroll HS; Washington, DC; (Y); 8/171; Pres Aud/Vis; Church Yth Grp; Nwsp Rptr; Yrbk Ed-Chief; Trk; High Hon Roll; Hon Roll; NHS; Spanish NHS; U Of MD; Bus Adm.

GUMBS, LESLIE JEROME; Mc Kinley Tech; Washington, DC; (Y); Camera Clb; Drama Clb; Gym; Socr; Cit Awd; Hon Roll; NHS; Coll Of The VI; Bio.

HAGINS, ERICA; Le Reine HS; Washington, DC; (Y); 27/148; Hosp Aide; French Hon Soc; High Hon Roll; Pres Schlr; Val; Outstndng Achvmnt Math 82-83; Mayors Schlstc Achvmnt Awd 83; Towson ST U Mnrty Schlrshp 86; Towson ST U; Comp Sci.

HALL, ERICA L; MSSD Galluadet Campus HS; Oxon Hill, MD; (Y); Church Yth Grp; Dance Clb; Drama Clb; Bsktbl; Cheerleading; Score Keeper; Swmmng; Trk; Cit Awd; NTID.

HAMILTON, MONIQUE; Woodrow Wilson HS; Washington, DC; (Y); Pres Church Yth Grp; Cmnty Wkr; Latin Clb; Science Clb; Pres Chorus; Pres Church Choir; Nwsp Rptr; Rep Stu Cncl; Bsktbl; Cit Awd; DC Cty Wd Sci Fair Wnnr 83-84; 2nd Pl Behvrl Sci 83-84; 2nd Pl SF DC Publc Schl Spch Cntst 84-85; Duke U; Bio.

HAMMOND, CRYSTAL; Dunbar SR HS; Washington, DC; (Y); 2/39; Church Yth Grp; Cmnty Wkr; 4-H; FHA; Sec Jr Cls; Cit Awd; Hon Roll; Prfct Atten Awd; 1st Pl Awd Dsgnng 86; Strghts As Awd 86; Eastern Shore Coll; Fashn Dsgn.

HARDY, KIKI; Eastern SR HS; Washington, DC; (Y); English Clb; Exploring; Math Clb; Science Clb; SADD; Nwsp Stf; Yrbk Rptr; Stu Cncl; NHS; Val; Hist & Engl Awds 86; Howard U; Pedtrcs.

HARPER, JANA; Senior HS; Arlington, VA; (Y); Art Clb; Camera Clb; Cmnty Wkr; Intnl Clb; Quiz Bowl; Rep Frsh Cls; Hon Roll; Teachers Aide; Rep Soph Cls; Early Coll Accptnc 86-87; Mock Trial Superior Ct Of DC 85-86; Translator For Hearing Impaired 85-86.

HARPER, JOYCE; Ballou SR HS; Washington, DC; (Y); Library Aide; Spanish Clb; Cit Awd; Hon Roll; Prfct Atten Awd; Pre-Med.

HARRIS, ELAINE; F W Ballou SR HS; Washington, DC; (S); 6/425; Cit Awd; Hon Roll; NHS; Accntng.

HARRIS, TERESA; Dunbar SR HS; Washington, DC; (Y); Computer Clb; French Clb; Red Cross Aide; Mrchg Band; Pom Pon; Cit Awd; Hon Roll; Jr NHS; Prfct Atten Awd; Sal; Mth.

HARRISON, ROBYN A; Georgetown Visitation Prep; Washington, DC; (Y); Drama Clb; Science Clb; Teachers Aide; Acpl Chr; Sec Chorus; Madrigals; Stage Crew; JV Mgr(s); Excllnc Awd-Frnch 82-84; Excllnc Awd Alg 84-85; Pre Med.

HARTWELL, JOE; Edmund Burke HS; Washington, DC; (Y); Model UN; Var Crs Cntry; Var Trk; Katherine Dulin Folger Smr Schlrshp 85; Cvl Engr.

HATTIS, ELEANNE; Maret Schl; Washington, DC; (Y); Teachers Aide; School Musical; Yrbk Ed-Chief; Yrbk Phtg.

HAWKINS, DONALD; Dunbar SR HS; Washington, DC; (Y); Church Yth Grp; Office Aide; Teachers Aide; Rep Jr Cls; Var Bsbl; Var L Bsktbl; JV Ftbl; Im Swmmng; Hon Roll; Kober Awd Encllnc Fds & Ntrtn 86; Physcl Thrpy.

HEDGEPETH, TONYA; Eastern HS; Washington, DC; (Y); DECA; Math Clb; Pres Stu Cncl; Capt Cheerleading; Wt Lftg; Cit Awd; High Hon Roll; NHS; Prfct Atten Awd; Val; Vldctrn 84; Hnr Roll 76-86; Ctznshp Awd 76-86; Bus Mgmt.

HENLEY, ALTON J; Banneker Academeis S HS; Washington, DC; (Y); 10/81; Cmnty Wkr; Stu Cncl; NHS; Ntl Merit Ltr; Pres Schlr; Chess Clb; Church Yth Grp; Library Aide; Math Clb; Science Clb; Natl Achvt Semi Fnlst 85; Natl Hist Day Cont 1st Pl City 84; UDC Annl Math Cont 6th Pl 85; Howard U; Pre-Dent.

HENRY, MAXINE; Roosevelt SR HS; Washington, DC; (Y); Dance Clb; FBLA; Model UN; OEA; ROTC; Nwsp Stf; Cit Awd; Hon Roll; Prfct Atten Awd; Harvard U; Med.

HERMAN, THOMAS; Archbishop Carroll HS; Washington, DC; (S); #14 In Class; High Hon Roll; NHS; Math & Vrbl Tlnt Srch Johns Hpkns U 82; Georgetwn U Amtr Sci Pgm 85; U Of VA; Arch.

HERNANDEZ, CLAUDIA; Francis L Cardozo HS; Washington, DC; (S); Debate Tm; Drama Clb; FBLA; Band; Chorus; School Musical; School Play; VP Soph Cls; Cit Awd; Hon Roll; Acctg.

HERRINGTON, RYAN; Gonzaga College HS; Alexandria, VA; (Y); 14/180; French Clb; Latin Clb; Nwsp Stf; Var Socr; High Hon Roll; Hon Roll; The Barnes Awd 84; Med.

HIGGINS, SUSAN; Georgetown Visitation Prep Schl; Washington, DC; (Y); Art Clb; Church Yth Grp; Cmnty Wkr; Math Clb; Model UN; Service Clb; Nwsp Rptr; Sec Sr Cls; Cheerleading; Crs Cntry; Cmmnded Schlr 85.

HIGHTOWER, MARK; De Matha Catholic HS; Washington, DC; (Y); Church Yth Grp; Cmnty Wkr; Ski Clb; Band; Concert Band; Outstndng Prgs Awd In Cncrt Bnd 85-86; Med.

HILL, EMILY; Woodrow Wilson HS; Washington, DC; (Y); 58/388; Cmnty Wkr; Chorus; Pres Soph Cls; Var Cheerleading; Var Mgr(s); Cit Awd; Dnfth Awd; Hon Roll; Prfct Atten Awd; Rep Frsh Cls; Mst Vlbl Coxswan Awd 86; JR Ldrshp Awd 85; Schlstc Achvt Awds 82-86; U Of PA; Nrsng.

HILL, JACQUELINE D; Academy Of Notre Dame; Washington, DC; (Y); 11/63; Church Choir; Drm Mjr(t); Yrbk Stf; Sec Jr Cls; Cheerleading; Trk; High Hon Roll; Frdrck Douglass Schlrshp Awd 86; Hi-Scip Stu 85-86; Miss Silhouette Mdl Of Yr 86; American U; Biolgy.

HILL, NANCY L; Paul Lawrence Dunbar HS; Washington, DC; (Y); 4/360; Church Yth Grp; Cmnty Wkr; Debate Tm; VP French Clb; Math Clb; Office Aide; Science Clb; Speech Tm; Nwsp Rptr; Yrbk Stf; D C Blk Rpblcn Cncl Schlrshp Awd 86; Gnrl Mtrs Engrng Schlrshp Awd 86; MD Brd Of Ed Schlrshp Awd 86; Crnl U; Neuro Srgn.

HOFFMAN, TONIA; Frank W Ballou SR HS; Washington, DC; (Y); Camp Fr Inc; Computer Clb; Girl Scts; Hosp Aide; Scholastic Bowl; Spanish Clb; Band; Church Choir; Drm Mjr(t); Mrchg Band; Hnr Roll 85; Sci Fair 86; Phys Thrpy.

HOGAN, MAURA; Georgetown Visitation Prep; Washington, DC; (Y); Cmnty Wkr; Pres English Clb; French Clb; Teachers Aide; Chorus; Madrigals; Yrbk Ed-Chief; Yrbk Stf; Rep Stu Cncl; Badmtn; U Of Notre Dame.

HOLLOMAN, KISHA; Woodrow Wilson HS; Washington, DC; (Y); 79/431; Science Clb; Band; Concert Band; Mrchg Band; Symp Band; Pom Pon; Hon Roll; NC ST; Accntnt.

HOLT, DENETRIOUS; Theodore Roosevelt HS; Washington, DC; (Y); Science Clb; Var Cheerleading; Var Pom Pon; Var Tennis; Var Trk; Hon Roll; NCTE Awd; Prfct Atten Awd; Sec Soph Cls; Rep Jr Cls; Convntn II Awd 86; Hampton U; Mktng.

HORNER, DAVID; Gonzaga College HS; Washington, DC; (Y); Nwsp Rptr; Lit Mag; JV Tennis; High Hon Roll.

HOWARD, KERMIT; Mackin Catholic HS; Wahsington, DC; (Y); #7 In Class; Church Yth Grp; Acpl Chr; Church Choir; Sftbl; High Hon Roll; Hon Roll; Chem Achvt Awd; Religion Awd; USAF Acad; Physics.

HOWARD, LOLITA RENEE; Dunbar SR HS; Washington, DC; (Y); Dance Clb; FBLA; FNA; Math Clb; OEA; Cheerleading; Gym; Cit Awd; Hon Roll; NEDT Awd; Outstndng Attndnce Awd 84; Norfolk ST U; RN.

HOWARD, WESLEY; Theodore Roosevelt HS; Washington, DC; (Y); Chess Clb; FBLA; Math Clb; Rep Jr Cls; Ntl Merit Schol; Its Academic 85-86; Engrng.

HUTCHENS, MICHAEL; Edmund Burke Schl; Bethesda, MD; (Y); Model UN; Political Wkr; Temple Yth Grp; Orch; School Play; Stage Crew; Yrbk Stf; Ntl Merit Ltr.

HYATER, JOHN E; Archbishop Carroll HS; Washington, DC; (Y); Aud/Vis; Computer Clb; Var Bsktbl; Ntl Merit SF; Natl Hnr Merit Schlrshp Cmmnd Stu 86; Howard U; Cmmnctns Engr.

JACKSON, CRYSTAL; Fracis L Cardozo SR HS; Washington, DC; (S); Library Aide; Trs Yrbk Stf; Lit Mag; Cit Awd; Hon Roll; Prfct Atten Awd; Sal; Pres Phy Fit Awd 83; WA JR Acad Sci Awd 85; Amer Ed Wk Essy Wnnr 85.

JACKSON, CYNTHIA; Woodrow Wilson HS; Washington, DC; (Y); Art Clb; Church Yth Grp; Cmnty Wkr; Girl Scts; Office Aide; Red Cross Aide; Science Clb; Spanish Clb; Teachers Aide; Band.

JACKSON, DERRICK; Cardozo HS; Washington, DC; (Y); Pres Art Clb; Cmnty Wkr; Drama Clb; FBLA; FHA; Intnl Clb; Science Clb; Stage Crew; Cit Awd; Hon Roll; WA JR Acad Sci 85; Dept Hlth/Phys Ed Safety 86.

JACKSON, JANET M; Central HS; Andrews Afb, DC; (Y); Intnl Clb; Pep Clb; Spanish Clb; Yrbk Bus Mgr; Rep Jr Cls; Stu Cncl; Bsktbl; Socr; Sftbl; High Hon Roll; Prince Georges CC; Accntnt.

JACKSON, KENNETH ALAN; Mc Kinley Tech; Washington, DC; (Y); 2/400; Aud/Vis; AFS; Computer Clb; Library Aide; Im Bsbl; Im Bsktbl; Im Vllybl; Hon Roll; Outstndng Achvt Prting 84-85; Howard U; Comp Svc.

JACKSON, MARSHALL; Frank W Ballou HS; Washington, DC; (Y); Church Yth Grp; Nwsp Stf; Var Trk; Cit Awd; Hon Roll; Stu Govt Assn Cls Rep 84-85; Wrtg & Readg Fun 83-84; Spn I Excllnce Plq 84-85; American U; Mech Engrng.

JACKSON, TONYA; Ballou SR HS; Washington, DC; (Y); FNA; Hosp Aide; Chorus; Pres Church Choir; Variety Show; Washington Schl Sec; Word Proc.

JACOBS, LINDA; Georgetown Visitation HS; Washington, DC; (Y); Cmnty Wkr; Dance Clb; English Clb; Chorus; Cheerleading; Hnr Rl 83-86; Am Heart Assn Resrch Pgm 86; Lawyer.

JERNBERG, HEATHER; Woodrow Wilson HS; Washington, DC; (Y); 60/382; AFS; Debate Tm; French Clb; Model UN; NFL; Political Wkr; Quiz Bowl; Science Clb; Ski Clb; Speech Tm; Macalester; Frnch.

JOBE, OMAR; Theodore Roosevelt HS; Washington, DC; (Y); Var Bsktbl; Var Socr; MD; Ag.

JOHNSON, DERRICK C; Archbishop Carroll HS; Washington, DC; (S); 18/146; Cmnty Wkr; Ftbl; Timer; Trk; Hon Roll; NHS; Engr.

JOHNSON, GILLIAN; Woodrow Wilson HS; Washington, DC; (Y); 52/431; Ski Clb; Chorus; Nwsp Stf; Stu Cncl; Socr; Hon Roll; Jr NHS; Arch.

JOHNSON, PETER; Gonzaga College HS; Oakton, VA; (Y); 22/180; Cmnty Wkr; French Clb; JCL; Latin Clb; Ski Clb; School Musical; Stage Crew; Nwsp Rptr; Lit Mag; JV Socr; Law.

JOHNSON, ROBERT D; Benjamin Banneker SR HS; Washington, DC; (Y); 5/83; Band; Concert Band; Yrbk Stf; Pres Jr Cls; Pres Sr Cls; Im Bsktbl; Hon Roll; VP NHS; Aerontc Engr.

JOHNSON, TERRANCE POWELL; Calvin Coolidge HS; Washington, DC; (S); Boys Clb Am; Camp Fr Inc; Off Trs DECA; 4-H; Rep Stu Cncl; Var Bsbl; Im Bsktbl; Var Ftbl; Var Trk; Church Yth Grp; Mayr Barrys Yth Ldrshp Inst 85-86; Calvin Coolidge Ftbl Tm 85-86; Rec Bsktbl Tm 86; Morgan ST U; Advertising.

JOLLY, ALLISON; Banneker HS; Washington, DC; (Y); 2/108; Church Yth Grp; Cmnty Wkr; Chorus; Pres Church Choir; Yrbk Stf; Rep Stu Cncl; High Hon Roll; Pres Jr NHS; NHS; Georgetown U Outstndt Schltc Achvt 86; Benjamin Banneker B Ltr 86; Natl Ldrshp & Svc Awd 86; Pthlgy.

JONES, ANDREA; Theodore Roosevelt SR HS; Washington, DC; (Y); #4 In Class; Radio Clb; Spanish Clb; Stage Crew; Crs Cntry; Capt Trk; Hon Roll; Sec NHS; Spanish NHS; Athletic & Acdmc Achvmnt 86; Achvmnt In Latin 86; Achvmnt Alge I 85; VA ST U; Compu Prg.

JONES, EVELYN; Frank W Ballou HS; Washington, DC; (Y); Pres Church Yth Grp; Cmnty Wkr; Acpl Chr; Stu Cncl; Cit Awd; Hon Roll; NHS; Maude Hughes Mem Schlrshp 86; Outstndg Soloist 86; De Pauw U; Chemstry.

JONES, LISA; All Saints HS; Capitol Hts, MD; (Y); 7/92; Camera Clb; Computer Clb; Sec FBLA; Girl Scts; Office Aide; Teachers Aide; School Play; Variety Show; Rep Stu Cncl; Hon Roll; Bus Awd 86; Typng I & II Awd 85-86; Eng Awd 85; Morgan ST U; Bus.

JONES, LISA; Woodrow Wilson HS; Washington, DC; (Y); 62/431; Drama Clb; Library Aide; Teachers Aide; Church Choir; School Play; Cit Awd; Hon Roll; Ntl Merit Schol; Prfct Atten Awd; Mass Media.

JONES, MIKKI; Mc Kinley SR HS; Washington, DC; (Y); FHA; Girl Scts; Hosp Aide; JA; Library Aide; Math Clb; Teachers Aide; Pres Frsh Cls; Pres Soph Cls; Pres Jr Cls; Hwrd U; Pre-Med.

JONES, PAMELA M; Anacostia SR HS; Washington, DC; (Y); 23/110; Girl Scts; Office Aide; Pep Clb; Spanish Clb; Teachers Aide; Nwsp Stf; Cheerleading; Cit Awd; Hon Roll; U Of DC; Psych.

JONES, SONJA; Benjamin Banneker HS; Washington, DC; (Y); 12/81; Dance Clb; Drama Clb; FHA; FNA; Hosp Aide; Chorus; School Play; Variety Show; Yrbk Stf; Stu Cncl; Benjamin Banneker Ntl Hnr Scty Schl 86; U Of Pittsburgh; Pre-Med.

JOYNES, ARDRA; Eastern HS; Washington, DC; (Y); Church Yth Grp; Cmnty Wkr; Dance Clb; Hosp Aide; Math Clb; Office Aide; Science Clb; Teachers Aide; Chorus; Church Choir; Lincoln U; CPA.

JUNG, CARMEN; Georgetown Visitation Schl; Falls Church, VA; (Y); Art Clb; Drama Clb; French Clb; Latin Clb; Model UN; Science Clb; Varsity Clb; School Play; Variety Show; Yrbk Stf; French Hnrs Awd 84-85.

KABEISEMAN, JIM; Gonzaga HS; Reston, VA; (Y); 42/187; Chess Clb; Latin Clb; Pep Clb; Ski Clb; Nwsp Rptr; Yrbk Rptr; Lit Mag; Im Bsktbl; Var Socr; Hon Roll; Capt Of Herdn, Chntlly Selct Sccr Clb 85; Natl Latn Exm Cum Laude 86; U Of VA; Engrng.

KAUPP, TATI; The Maret Schl; Washington, DC; (Y); Cmnty Wkr; Drama Clb; Band; School Musical; School Play; Lit Mag; Bowling; Socr; Trk; Wt Lftg; Outstndh Achvt Awd Art 84; Fine Arts.

KEARNEY, RENEE; Dunbar HS; Washington, DC; (Y); Cmnty Wkr; FTA; Hosp Aide; Science Clb; Teachers Aide; Var Pom Pon; Cit Awd; Hon Roll; Prfct Atten Awd; Pres Schlr; Sec Bits & Bytes Clb 85-86; Mst Outstndngpre Nrsng Stu 84-85; First Aide & Hm Nrsng Crd 84-85; Nrsng.

KECK, SAARIN; Georgetown Visitation HS; Washington, DC; (Y); Art Clb; Science Clb; Service Clb; Chorus; Madrigals; Nwsp Phtg; Lit Mag; Im Bsktbl; Im Lcrss; Im Tennis; Aesthetics Awd Relgn Awd 82-83; Math Awd 83-84; Frnch Awd 84-85; U Of MD; Engrng.

KELLEY, ANNE SCHOFIELD; Woodrow Wilson SR HS; Washington, DC; (Y); 55/500; Cmnty Wkr; French Clb; Teachers Aide; Acpl Chr; Chorus; Rep Stu Cncl; Var Socr; Hon Roll; Acdmc Achvmnt Awd 85-86; Hon Roll 84-85.

KHAN, AMINA; Georgetown Visitation Prep Schl; Mclean, VA; (Y); Computer Clb; Pres Debate Tm; Trs Model UN; Office Aide; Service Clb; Pres Speech Tm; Nwsp Stf; Drama Clb; English Clb; Math Clb; Debator Of Yr 83; Erpn Hstry Achvt Awd 84; Frnch III Achvt Awd 85; Grgtwn U; Corp Law.

KING, CONLEY B; Benjamin Banneker Academic HS; Washington, DC; (Y); 1/81; Cmnty Wkr; Math Tm; Cit Awd; High Hon Roll; NHS; Prfct Atten Awd; Natl Achvt Scholar Outstndg Negro Stu 85; Harvard Alumni Assn Bk Awd 85; Schl Ltr Acad Excllnce 85; MIT.

KLIMES, DONNA; Georgetown Visitation Prep Schl; Washington, DC; (Y); Computer Clb; Latin Clb; Library Aide; Chorus; Nwsp Rptr; Lit Mag; Cheerleading; Outstndng Spnsh Stu Awd 85-86; Comp Engrng.

KNIGHT, TELENA C; Benjamin Banneker SR HS; Washington, DC; (Y); Church Yth Grp; Cmnty Wkr; Girl Scts; Library Aide; Church Choir; Hon Roll; Natl Cncl Tchrs Math 64th Annl Meetg Stdnt Aide 86; Traing Prog Peer Cnslg 85; Acctg.

KRAMER, CHRIS; Edmund Burke College Prep; Washington, DC; (Y); Capt L Socr; Church Yth Grp; Ski Clb; Varsity Clb; Chorus; Church Choir; Yrbk Stf; Im Sftbl; Capt L Trk; Im Wt Lftg; Watr Skiing 4th Pl Awd-Intl Comp Japan 83; Snow Skiing 1st Pl Awd Cmptn Tyrol Austria 86; Middlebury VT; Sprts Med.

LADEN, JONATHAN; Maret HS; Washington, DC; (Y); Math Tm; Yrbk Stf; Lit Mag; Crs Cntry; Tennis; Trk; Jr NHS; NHS.

LAGOC, ROSABEL; Georgetown Vistiation Prep; Washington, DC; (Y); Church Yth Grp; Computer Clb; Service Clb; Teachers Aide; Chorus; Church Choir; Madrigals; Nwsp Stf; Excllnce For Achvt In Rlgn 84 & Spnsh 86; Catholic U Of Amer; Pre-Med.

LAMBERT, ALIX S; Edmund Burke Schl; Washington, DC; (Y); School Musical; MCPS Gftd & Tlntd Vsl Art Ctr 85-86; Schl Of Vsl Arts; Fine Arts.

LATCHIS, MARK; Edmund Burlee Schl; Chevy Chase, DC; (Y); Church Yth Grp; Cmnty Wkr; French Clb; Math Tm; Band; Mrchg Band; Ftbl; Var Socr; Tennis; Var Trk.

LAWRENCE, RHODA N; Duke Ellington Schl Of The Arts; Washington, DC; (Y); 12/88; Trs French Clb; Sec Math Clb; Pres Natl Beta Clb; VP Science Clb; Chorus; Church Choir; VP Mrchg Band; VP Soph Cls; Cheerleading; Hon Roll; WRC-TV Comm Schlrshp 86; DC Blk Wmn SAJ Awd 86; Mst Wndrfl Prince Schlrshp 86; U Of MD College Pk; Music.

LAWSON, LINDA; Calvin Coolidge HS; Washington, DC; (S); Computer Clb; Sec Science Clb; Pres Church Choir; Co-Capt Cheerleading; Capt Sftbl; Capt Twrlr; Cit Awd; NHS; Prfct Atten Awd; Val.

LEDBETTER, VERONICA; Cardozo HS; Forestville, MD; (S); Debate Tm; Science Clb; Varsity Clb; Chorus; Nwsp Phtg; Yrbk Stf; Stu Cncl; Swmmng; Hon Roll; Boston U; Psych.

LEE, FANMIE; Woodrow Wilson HS; Washington, DC; (Y); JA; Chorus; Pom Pon; Vllybl; Hon Roll; Jr NHS; Sal; Bus.

LEGALL, SHELLEY A; Benjamin Banneker SR HS; Washington, DC; (Y); Drama Clb; Thesps; Hon Roll; Sec NHS; Smith Coll Bk Awd 85; Yth Undrstndg Exch Stu Japan 85; Med.

LEITCH, STEPHANIE; Georgetown Vistiation Prep Schl; Aquasco, MD; (Y); Art Clb; Drama Clb; French Clb; Pep Clb; Teachers Aide; Acpl Chr; Chorus; School Musical; School Play; Yrbk Stf; Awds Hstry & Engl 86; Psychlgy.

LEONG, NG; Gonzaga College HS; Washington, DC; (Y); 7/200; French Clb; Latin Clb; Math Clb; Hon Roll.

LESLIE III, JOHN; Calvin Coolidge HS; Washington, DC; (S); Debate Tm; DECA; Drama Clb; Thesps; School Play; Nwsp Ed-Chief; Bsktbl; High Hon Roll; Cty-Wd Chmpnshp Mock Trial Tm 84-85; Cty-Wd Chmpnshp Drama Clb 84-85; Duquesne U; Prnt Jrnlsm.

LEVINE, DAN; Benjamin Banneker HS; Washington, DC; (Y); 1/128; Chess Clb; Debate Tm; Model UN; High Hon Roll; NHS; Ntl Merit SF; Im Bsbl; Im Bsktbl; Georgetown U Book Awd 86.

LIGGINS, WILLIAM; Archbishop Carroll HS; District Hts, MD; (S); 5/155; Boys Clb Am; Var Capt Bsktbl; Cit Awd; High Hon Roll; Hon Roll; NHS; Prfct Atten Awd; Archbishop Carroll Acad Schlrshp 83; Elec Engrng.

LINEHOUSE, BARRY; Congressional Page Schl; Green Pond, SC; (Y); Church Yth Grp; Political Wkr; Spanish Clb; SADD; Orch; School Play; Ftbl; Swmmng; Auburn; Vet Med.

LINSON, MICHELLE; Georgetown Visitation HS; Bethesda, MD; (Y); Cmnty Wkr; Drama Clb; School Musical; School Play; Sec Jr Cls; Rep Sr Cls; Var Cheerleading; Hon Roll; NHS; Ntl Merit SF; Bio.

LISA, DAVIS; Dunbar SR HS; Washington, DC; (Y); Art Clb; FHA; JA; Band; Chorus; Concert Band; Mrchg Band; Off Soph Cls; Cit Awd; Hon Roll; Apprctn Awd Dedctd Srv Dunbar 86; Mdl Perfect Attndnc 85; Awd Apprctn Prt Cptn Poster Cntst 86; American U; Psychlgst.

LITTLEJOHN, VALERIE; Eastern HS; Washington, DC; (Y); 1/500; VP Church Yth Grp; Church Choir; Rep Jr Cls; Hon Roll; VP Jr NHS; NHS; Prfct Atten Awd; Val; Georgetwn U Bk Awd 86; G Washington Math, Sci Awd 86; Howard U; Pediatrcn.

LIVINGSTON, BOBBY L; Woodrow Wilson HS; Washington, DC; (Y); 57/450; VP Stu Cncl; Var Capt Ftbl; Var Hon Roll; Ntl Merit Ltr; Aerosp Engr.

LIVINGSTON, DIONNE; T Roosevelt SR HS; Washington, DC; (Y); Church Yth Grp; Pres Natl Beta Clb; Church Choir; Pep Band; Pres Frsh Cls; Off Sr Cls; Var Trk; Hon Roll; Science Clb; Pres Stu Cncl; US Hist, Biol & Bus Stu Awds 85-86; Med.

LIVINUS, STELLA; Dunbar SR HS; Washington, DC; (Y); French Clb; FHA; FNA; Hosp Aide; Math Clb; Red Cross Aide; Stu Cncl; Bsktbl; Cit Awd; Hon Roll; Sci, Englsh, Gen Math, Bio, Chem, Geomtry, Adv Math, Algbra I & II, Trig 80-86; U District Columbia; Nrsng.

LONG, MIA; Coolidge HS; Takoma Park, MD; (S); Aud/Vis; Pres DECA; French Clb; Intnl Clb; Cit Awd; Jr NHS; 1st Pl ST Entrprnrl Wrttn Evnt 86; 1st Pl ST Gen Merch Comptn 86; 1st Pl ST Anti-Shoplftng Evnt 85; Johnson & Wales; Bus Mgmt.

LONG, TONYA; Eastern SR HS; Washington, DC; (Y); Dance Clb; Band; Flag Corp; Mrchg Band; Nwsp Rptr; Rep Frsh Cls; Trk; High Hon Roll; Hon Roll; Hgh Hnr Rl Band Awd 85-86; Acctng Awd 85-86; Bio Awd 84-85; Phys Ed Awd 83-84; Alg Excllnce Awd 83-84; Norfolk ST; Acctng.

LOTT, MARSHA; Eastern HS; Washington, DC; (Y); Library Aide; Pep Clb; Chorus; Church Choir; Cit Awd; Hon Roll; Jr NHS; Jr Medics; Gnl Svcs & Schlrshps; Fed Prtnrshp In Ed; Crmnl Lawyer.

LOUVIERE, PAUL; Gonzaga College HS; Forestvl, MD; (Y); 67/200; VP Church Yth Grp; VP French Clb; Latin Clb; Stage Crew; Hon Roll.

LYON, RENE; Eastern SR HS; Washington, DC; (Y); Church Yth Grp; Exploring; Hosp Aide; Drm Mjr(t); Mrchg Band; Rep Stu Cncl; Cit Awd; Womns Bar Assn 85; Proj Explr 85; Acdmcs 86; Howard U; Pathlgst.

MANUEL, MICHAEL; Gonzaga College HS; Mitchellvl, MD; (Y); 25/177; Computer Clb; French Clb; Latin Clb; Math Clb; Science Clb; Ski Clb; Rep Sr Cls; JV Ftbl; Var Trk; Var Wrstlng; 1st Gonzaga Sci Air 85; Loyola Coll Baltimore; Pre Med.

MARCELIN JR, JEAN A; Archbishop Carroll HS; Mount Rainier, MD; (S); Drama Clb; Band; Concert Band; Mrchg Band; Pep Band; School Play; Yrbk Stf; Hon Roll; Pedtrcn.

MARCIA, JORGE; Woodrow Wilson HS; Washington, DC; (Y); 158/433; Camera Clb; Church Yth Grp; Intnl Clb; Library Aide; Spanish Clb; Teachers Aide; Crs Cntry; Swmmng; Cit Awd; Prfct Atten Awd; Engl As 2nd Lg Awd 84; Montgomery Coll MD; Comp Engrg.

MARTIN, DAVID A; St Anselms Abbey Schl; Reston, VA; (Y); Chess Clb; Cmnty Wkr; Model UN; Scholastic Bowl; Yrbk Bus Mgr; Yrbk Stf; JV Golf; Ntl Merit SF; NEDT Awd; Summa Cum Laude Natl Ltn Exm 83-84; JR Sci & Hmnts Sympsm Georgetwn U 85; Engrng.

MARTIN, MONIQUE; Academy Of Notre Dame HS; Washington, DC; (Y); Computer Clb; Dance Clb; FBLA; FHA; JA; Cheerleading; Hon Roll; Yale U; Bus Mgt.

MATHEWS, PATRICE; All Saints HS; Washington, DC; (Y); 15/86; FBLA; FHA; Office Aide; Pep Clb; Service Clb; Masonic Awd; Hosp Aide; Stage Crew; Engl Awd 84-85; US Hstry 84-85; Bio 84-85; U Of DC; Fash Mdsg.

MATHIAS, WILLIAM T; Saint Anselms Abbey Schl; Hyattsville, MD; (S); Debate Tm; Stage Crew; Nwsp Phtg; Yrbk Phtg; Trs Soph Cls; Stu Cncl; Var Capt Bsbl; Var Capt Bsktbl; Hon Roll; Boy Scts; Century III Ldrshp Awds 86; Civitation Award.

MATTHEWS, LISA; Frank W Ballou HS; Washington, DC; (S); Pep Clb; Stu Cncl; Cit Awd; Hon Roll; Prfct Atten Awd; Ameri Lgn Awd 84; U Of MD; Lawyer.

MAXTED, ANN; Georgetown Visitation Prep Schl; Mclean, VA; (Y); Camera Clb; Red Cross Aide; Science Clb; Spanish Clb; Teachers Aide; Chorus; Yrbk Stf; NHS; Headmstrss Awd 86; Georgetown U; Bio.

MAYS, DAVID M; Woodrow HS; Washington, DC; (Y); 4/450; French Clb; Chorus; Nwsp Ed-Chief; Nwsp Rptr; Rep Stu Cncl; JV Capt Bsktbl; Var L Tennis; Hon Roll; Pres NHS; Ntl Merit SF; Rnsslr Mdl Outstndng Sci & Math Stu 84-85; 1st Pl Essay Cntst 84-85; Engr.

MC CABE, BRIAN; Gonzaga College HS; Ptomac, MD; (Y); 24/190; Cmnty Wkr; French Clb; Latin Clb; Pep Clb; Im Bsktbl; Lcrss; Hon Roll; Ntl Merit Ltr; Johns Hopkins Tlnt Search 82; Genl Excllnc 83; Herlihy Awd-Outstndng Male Grad 83; Pre-Med.

MC CASHIN, DAWN; Georgetown Visitation Prep; Vienna, VA; (Y); 4/100; Cmnty Wkr; Drama Clb; French Clb; Hosp Aide; Political Wkr; Nwsp Ed-Chief; JV Bsktbl; JV Sftbl; Var Tennis; Hon Roll; Intern Capitol Hill 86; Model 84; Fair Oaks Teen Fash Panel 85-86; Coll Wm & Mary; Pol Sci.

MC CLAFFERTY, LAWRENCE; St Johns College HS; Washington, DC; (Y); 26/189; Aud/Vis; Drama Clb; Q&S; Nwsp Stf; Rep Jr Cls; Stu Cncl; JV Tennis; VP NHS; Ntl Merit Ltr; Ntl Ed Dvlpmnt Tst Awd 83 & 84; Pres Acad Ftns Awd 86; Boston Coll; Pltcl Sci.

MC CREA, NICOLE; Cardozo SR HS; Washington, DC; (S); 15/279; Camera Clb; Computer Clb; 4-H; FHA; Church Choir; Concert Band; Nwsp Rptr; 4-H Awd; Hon Roll; NHS; Gftd & Tlntd Pgm 82-83; Humanities Pgm 83-84 & 84-85; Its Acdmc Tm 83-84; Duke U; Med Tech.

MC FADDEN, CRAIG; Frank Kl Ballou SR HS; Washington, DC; (S); Hon Roll; NHS; Sal; Pionr Of Jehovahs Wtnss.

MC GUIRK, SUSAN; Immaculata Prep; Cheverly, MD; (Y); Am Leg Aux Girls St; Church Yth Grp; Cmnty Wkr; Hosp Aide; Intnl Clb; Spanish Clb; Yrbk Phtg; Yrbk Rptr; Off Stu Cncl; Ntl Merit Ltr; Bnfcl Hdgsn Schlrshp Wshngtn Coll 86-87; Washington Coll; Intl Stds.

MC KENNA, JAMES D; Gonzaga College HS; Bethesda, MD; (Y); 4/174; Drama Clb; Latin Clb; VP Math Clb; Trs Spanish Clb; School Musical; Nwsp Ed-Chief; Ed Lit Mag; Rep Soph Cls; Im Bsktbl; Ntl Merit SF; 1st Prize-Jr Wrtng Cont 84-85; Fnlst-Jr Speech Comp 84-85; U Of VA; Engl.

MC KINZIE, ANTONIO; Cardozo HS; Washington, DC; (Y); Boys Clb Am; Computer Clb; 4-H; Math Clb; SADD; Variety Show; Nwsp Bus Mgr; Bsbl; Bsktbl; Ftbl; Atten Awd 85-86; VA Tech; Bus Admnstrtn.

MC LAUGHLIN, LORNE; Gonzaga College HS; Suitland, MD; (Y); Cmnty Wkr; Im Bsktbl; Capt Trk; Howard U; Arch Engr.

MC NAIR-SCOTT, ERIC; Maret HS; Washington, DC; (Y); Cmnty Wkr; Nwsp Rptr; Nwsp Stf; Stu Cncl; Var Socr; Var Tennis; Im Vllybl; Hon Roll; Ntl Merit Ltr; Stu Tutor Prog 85-86.

MC NEILL, JENNIFER; Frank W Ballou HS; Washington, DC; (Y); ROTC; Chorus; Church Choir; Var Vllybl; Cit Awd; Hon Roll; NHS; Prfct Atten Awd; Pre Med.

MIDDLETON, DAVID; Woodrow Wilson SR HS; Washington, DC; (Y); 11/431; Office Aide; Var Capt Ftbl; Hon Roll; Trs NHS; Vrsty Ftbl Rookie Of Yr 84-85; Comp Sci.

MIDDLETON, VERONICA; Ballous SR HS; Washington, DC; (Y); DECA; FHA; FNA; Library Aide; Math Clb; Pep Clb; Spanish Clb; Chorus; Church Choir; School Play; Acad All Amer Schlr 86; SUNY; Comp Engr.

MILBOURNE, KIMBERLY; H D Woodson SR HS; Washington, DC; (Y); Cmnty Wkr; Computer Clb; Dance Clb; Drama Clb; Pres JA; Pep Clb; Chorus; Rep Jr Cls; Hon Roll; Jr NHS; Georgetown U; Pol Sci.

MILLER, ANNE; Woodrow Wilson HS; Washington, DC; (Y); 16/431; Church Yth Grp; Cmnty Wkr; Pres French Clb; Office Aide; Teachers Aide; Chorus; Church Choir; Yrbk Stf; Var L Swmmng; High Hon Roll; Ed.

MILLER, ERWIN; Roosevelt SR HS; Washington, DC; (Y); Computer Clb; FBLA; Off Jr Cls; VP Stu Cncl; Cit Awd; Hon Roll; NHS; Math Clb; Nwsp Stf; Wmns Bar Assoc Awd 84; Pres Am Ftnss Awd 85; Sprntndnts Vol Svc Awd 86; Data Processor.

MILLER, FREDERICK; Gonzaga HS; Ft Washington, MD; (Y); 81/187; Church Yth Grp; Latin Clb; Letterman Clb; Varsity Clb; Bsbl; Ftbl; Wt Lftg; Hon Roll; Accntng.

MILLER, ROBERT; Gonzaga HS; Washington, DC; (Y); 60/175; Office Aide; Science Clb; Bsbl; Cit Awd; High Hon Roll; Hon Roll; Prfct Atten Awd; Barnes Awd 82-84; Amrcn Lgn Awd 81-82; Mrtn Lthr Kng Schlrshp 85-86; Coll Of Holy Cross; Microbio.

MINGO, LA SHAUN; Anacostia SR HS; Washington, DC; (Y); ROTC; Teachers Aide; Band; Drm Mjr(t); School Play; Twrlr; Hon Roll; Cortez Peter Typg Awd 85-86; Acad Exc Engl & US Hist 85-86; Outstndg Ldrshp 85-86; ROTC Promotn 85-86; Howard U; Pre-Law.

MITCHELL, ALEXANDER; Ballou SR HS; Washington, DC; (S); Teachers Aide; Cit Awd; High Hon Roll; Hon Roll; NHS; Prfct Atten Awd; Cert Of Excllnc Math & Chem 84-85.

MITCHELL, MELISSA; Benjamin Banneker HS; Washington, DC; (Y); Cmnty Wkr; Yrbk Stf; Teachers Aide; Hon Roll; Im Tennis; Lincoln U; Psych.

MOORE, JEFFERY; Mckinley SR HS; Washington, DC; (Y); 20/360; Boy Scts; ROTC; Drm Mjr(t); Nwsp Sprt Ed; Bsbl; Bsktbl; Bowling; Ftbl; Lcrss; Wrstlng.

MORGAN, VALERIE; Roosevelt SR HS; Washington, DC; (Y); JA; Prfct Atten Awd.

MORRIS, ALISON W; Duke Ellington School Of Arts; Springfield, VA; (Y); 10/75; Camera Clb; Drama Clb; English Clb; PAVAS; Red Cross Aide; Thesps; School Musical; School Play; Stage Crew; Nwsp Rptr; Ellington Exclnc Awds-Theatr & Engl 85; Johns Hopkins Tlnt Srch Wnnr 83; Schepp Fndtn Schlrshp 86; NY U; Dramatic Wrtg.

MORRIS, YOLANDA; Springarn SR HS; Washington, DC; (Y); Library Aide; Concert Band; Sec Jr Cls; Rep Stu Cncl; Var Sftbl; Hon Roll; NHS; Spec Cert Awd Comp Sci 86; Spec Cert Engl III 86; Cert Hon Acdmc Achvt 86; MIT; Comp Pgmr.

MORRISEY, VANESSA ANN; Paul Laurence Dunbar HS; Washington, DC; (Y); Drama Clb; FBLA; Chorus; Pres Soph Cls; Capt Bsktbl; Swmmng; Trk; Cit Awd; Hon Roll; Jr NHS; Woodward Fellwoship Fndtn 85-86; Outstdng Athlt In Fld Evnts 85-86; Typwrtng Awd 85-86; Lwyr.

MOSLEY, PAULA; Ballou SR HS; Washington, DC; (Y); Church Yth Grp; Teachers Aide; Rep Soph Cls; Hon Roll; Jr NHS; Prfct Atten Awd; Bus Adm.

MOTON, TERESA; Calvin Coolidge HS; Washington, DC; (Y); Cmnty Wkr; Service Clb; Sec Frsh Cls; Rep Stu Cncl; Capt Pom Pon; Cit Awd; Hon Roll; Jr NHS; Ntl Merit Schol; Jerry A More Schlrshp Awd, Math Hnr Soc 84fexcllnce Eng/Span 85; Howard; Pre-Med.

MULLINS, GEORGE; Howard D Woodson HS; Washington, DC; (Y); Library Aide; Office Aide; ROTC; Teachers Aide; Color Guard; Nwsp Ed-Chief; Nwsp Rptr; Nwsp Sprt Ed; Nwsp Stf; Yrbk Rptr; Trck Schlrshp Santa Fe Comm Coll 86; All Amer Hnrbl Mntn For Trck 86; Santa Fe Comm Coll; Cmmnctns.

MURRAY, MICHELLE; Woodrow Wilson HS; Washington, DC; (Y); Church Yth Grp; Girl Scts; Spanish Clb; Band; Church Choir; Stu Cncl; Crs Cntry; Swmmng; Trk; Hon Roll; Howard U; Arch.

MURRELL, RAPATRICK; Ballou SR HS; Washington, DC; (S); Church Yth Grp; Var Wrstlng; Hon Roll; Jr NHS; NHS; MD U; Comp Tech.

MUSE, KIMBERLY; Theodore Roosevelt SR HS; Washington, DC; (Y); Am Leg Aux Girls St; Co-Capt Cheerleading; Hon Roll; Bus.

MUTCHLER, MAMIE; Georgetown Visitation HS; Washington, DC; (Y); Drama Clb; Model UN; Speech Tm; Pres Jr Cls; Pres Stu Cncl; JV Lcrss; High Hon Roll; Hon Roll; NHS; Ntl Merit SF; Awd Acdmc Excllnce 84; Princeton U.

MUTH, MONICA; Georgetown Visitation Prep; Washington, DC; (Y); Drama Clb; Ski Clb; Spanish Clb; Yrbk Stf; Bsktbl; JV L Sftbl; High Hon Roll; Hon Roll.

NEAL, AYOKA Z; Georgetown Day HS; Washington, DC; (Y); Cmnty Wkr; Red Cross Aide; Yrbk Phtg; JV Var Mgr(s); Score Keeper; Vllybl; MD U Smmr Engrng Pgm 85; Engrng.

NEIL, AMAATE; Gonzaga College HS; Washington, DC; (Y); CAP; Drama Clb; Speech Tm; School Play; Variety Show; JV Tennis; High Hon Roll; Hon Roll; 2nd Pl Metro Cath Spch Cont Fnls 85; 2nd Pl Dr M L King Mem Spch Cont 85; Wnr Oratorical Cont 84 & 86; Chem.

NICHOLAS, STEFAN C; Georgetown Day HS; Silver Spring, MD; (Y); Model UN; Nwsp Stf; Yrbk Stf; Var Tennis; Bus Law.

NICHOLS, BRIAN; Woodrow Wilson HS; Washington, DC; (Y); 83/423; German Clb; Key Clb; Ski Clb; Chorus; Nwsp Stf; Crs Cntry; Swmmng; Hon Roll; Kiwanis Awd; Ntl Merit SF.

NICHOLS, COLLETTE; Mc Kinley Tech; Washington, DC; (Y); Church Yth Grp; Computer Clb; Drama Clb; JA; Math Clb; Stage Crew; Variety Show; Stu Cncl; Gym; Howard; Law.

NUTALL, DEXTER; Archbishop John Carroll HS; Washington, DC; (S); 12/147; Church Yth Grp; Varsity Clb; Church Choir; JV Bsktbl; Var L Ftbl; Var L Socr; Hon Roll; NHS; Radio-TV Cmnctns.

O ROURKE, RYAN P; St Anselms Abbey Schl; Washington, DC; (Y); Chess Clb; Computer Clb; School Musical; School Play; Stage Crew; Nwsp Ed-Chief; Im Coach Actv; Ntl Merit SF; Summa Cum Laude Natl Latin Exm 82-83; Georgetwn U JR Sci & Hum Sympsm 84-85; Writer.

ONLEY, JAMES; Archishop Carroll HS; Washington, DC; (Y); 9/170; Cmnty Wkr; Pep Clb; Nwsp Stf; JV Var Bsbl; JV Ftbl; Var Sftbl; High Hon Roll; Hon Roll; NHS; Yth Cnclmbr Myr Barrys Th Ldrschp Instl 85-86; Yth Bd Mem Nghbrhd Plnng Cncl 18 85-86; Howard U; Finnc.

OSTOJA-STARZEWSKI, NGA; Immaculata Preparatory Schl; Potomac, MD; (Y); Art Clb; German Clb; Yrbk Stf; U Scrntn Pres Schlrshp 86; U Scrntn; Pre-Med.

PACE, TARA; Theodore Roosevelt HS; Washington, DC; (Y); Sec Rptr FBLA; Library Aide; Math Clb; Cit Awd; Hon Roll; Jr NHS; NHS; Sal; Rptr Spanish NHS; Ftr Bus Ldrs AM Ldr Yr 86; Outstndng JR Achvt Awd 86; Myrs Schlstc Achvt Awd 84; Jrnlsm.

PADDACK, MICHELLE; Woodrow Wilson HS; Washington, DC; (Y); 32/431; Art Clb; PAVAS; Lit Mag; Trs Soph Cls; U Of CA; Mrn Bio.

PALTING, KAREN; Georgetown Visitation Prep Schl; Mitchellville, MD; (Y); Sec Church Yth Grp; NFL; Pres Speech Tm; Pres Chorus; Madrigals; Lit Mag; Var Cheerleading; Im Fld Hcky; Im Socr; JV Capt Sftbl; Hugh O Brian Yth Fndtn DC Ldrshp Smnr 85; Dist Of Columbia Grl Rep HOBY Intl Ldrshp Smnr.

PANG, JUANITA; Woodrow Wilson HS; Washington, DC; (Y); 8/431; Spanish Clb; Concert Band; Mrchg Band; Symp Band; Vllybl; Hon Roll; Pres Jr NHS; NHS; Prfct Atten Awd; Val; Sedarmocs Shlrshp Awd 84; Jerry A Moore Citation 85; Med.

PARKER, RAYMOND; Cardozo HS; Washington, DC; (Y); Computer Clb; English Clb; FBLA; Varsity Clb; Bsktbl; Ftbl; Swmmng; Cit Awd; Hon Roll; JETS Awd; Coll; Bus Mgmt.

PARKER, ROSALIND; Woodrow Wilson SR HS; Washington, DC; (Y); 26/431; Pres Keywanettes; Orch; Hon Roll; Jr NHS; Cty-Wide Sci Fair Wnr 85 & 86; Drtmth Col Book Awd 86; Outstndng JR In Top 10 Of Cls; Lawyer.

PATE, ALEXIS; Woodrow Wilson HS; Washington, DC; (Y); Church Yth Grp; 4-H; Pep Clb; Spanish Clb; SADD; Chorus; Church Choir; Off Soph Cls; Swmmng; Vllybl; Columbia U; Psych.

PEABODY, JENNIFER J; Woodrow Wilson HS; Washington, DC; (Y); 6/380; Chorus; Madrigals; School Musical; Variety Show; Yrbk Phtg; Sec Stu Cncl; Capt Swmmng; NHS; French Clb; Ski Clb; Time-Life Schlrshp Awd 86; Middleburg Coll; Intl Pol.

PERRY, NAOMI; Benjmain Banneker HS; Washington, DC; (Y); 9/108; Cmnty Wkr; Exploring; VP Ski Clb; Church Choir; Concert Band; Yrbk Rptr; Yrbk Stf; Hst Sr Cls; Hon Roll; Bowie ST COLL Careers Sci Prtcpnt 85; Hmn Envrnmnt Ctr Mnrty Envrmnntl Smmr Intern 86; Sci Fair Wnnr; Drexel U; Hydrology.

PERRY, VERNA; Benjamin Banneker HS; Temple Hills, MD; (Y); Church Yth Grp; Dance Clb; Teachers Aide; Chorus; Church Choir; Variety Show; Yrbk Stf; Rep Stu Cncl; Pre-Med.

PHILLIPS, LESLIE; All Saints HS; Washington, DC; (Y); 5/89; FBLA; Pep Clb; Red Cross Aide; Science Clb; Service Clb; Church Choir; VP Soph Cls; High Hon Roll; Hon Roll; Jr NHS; Catholic U Of America; Nrsng.

PILKERTON, JOSEPH A; St Johns College HS; Potomac, MD; (Y); Capt ROTC; Yrbk Stf; Pres Frsh Cls; Pres Soph Cls; Pres Jr Cls; JV Var Ftbl; Ntl Merit Ltr; Cathloic U Am; Bus.

PITTS, WALTER DAVID; Ballou SR HS; Washington, DC; (Y); Cmnty Wkr; Library Aide; ROTC; Service Clb; Color Guard; Rep Stu Cncl; Var Tennis; Cit Awd; Life Sci Awd 84; Outstndng Srv Awd 84; Cntnvl Cmnty Coll; Pre-Law Bus.

POOLE, MONIQUA; All Saints HS; Washington, DC; (Y); Church Yth Grp; FBLA; Girl Scts; Library Aide; Pep Clb; Variety Show; Trs Jr Cls; Rep Stu Cncl; Hon Roll; Jr NHS; Hghst Achvt Alg I 83; Hugh O Brian Yth Ldrshp Awd 84; U DC; Accntg.

PORTER, ERIN; Maret HS; Washington, DC; (Y); Cmnty Wkr; Drama Clb; Teachers Aide; School Musical; Stage Crew; Yrbk Phtg; Sec Trs Soph Cls; Pres Jr Cls; VP Sr Cls; Var Bsktbl; Alumni Spirit Awd 86; U Of VA; Chld Psychlgy.

POSEY, MICHELLE; Eastern HS; Washington, DC; (Y); 4/34; Cmnty Wkr; Debate Tm; Intnl Clb; Latin Clb; Library Aide; Thesps; Chorus; Church Choir; Nwsp Ed-Chief; Nwsp Rptr; Mayor Of Mayor Barry Yth Ldrshp Inst 84-85; Pres Atten Clb 85-86; Pres Career Awareess Prog 85-86; UDC; Psychology.

POWE, RALPH; Benjamin Banneker HS; Washington, DC; (Y); Debate Tm; Drama Clb; Model UN; Speech Tm; Orch; Nwsp Rptr; VP Soph Cls; Im Bsktbl; Im Sftbl; Im Vllybl; Corp Law.

PREVOST, ANDREW; Edmund Burke Schl; Washington, DC; (Y); Model UN; SADD; School Musical; Nwsp Rptr; Bsktbl; Im Golf; Var Socr; Var Tennis.

PRINCE, BETH; Woodrow Wilson SR HS; Washington, DC; (Y); 85/431; Church Yth Grp; FBLA; Office Aide; PAVAS; Political Wkr; Science Clb; Acpl Chr; Chorus; JV Bsktbl; Hon Roll; Art.

PROCTOR, RONALD; Woodrow HS; Washington, DC; (Y); Boy Scts; Camera Clb; Church Yth Grp; Varsity Clb; Church Choir; Stage Crew; Nwsp Rptr; Nwsp Sprt Ed; Nwsp Stf; Pres Soph Cls; Gld Mdl Trck Dlb 86; VP Yth Ushr Brd Chrch 84-86; Pro Athlt.

PURVIS, KIMBERLY; Theodore Roosevelt HS; Washington, DC; (Y); Teachers Aide; Hon Roll.

RASEVIC, MARK; Gonzaga College HS; Washington, DC; (Y); 5/180; Camera Clb; French Clb; Latin Clb; Math Clb; Math Tm; Nwsp Phtg; Nwsp Rptr; Nwsp Stf; Yrbk Phtg; Yrbk Rptr; Georgetown; Med.

RASPEN, RENEE; Georgetown Visitation HS; Herndon, VA; (Y); Girl Scts; Office Aide; Science Clb; Service Clb; Chorus; Nwsp Rptr; Lit Mag; Mgr(s); Hon Roll; Ntl Merit Ltr; Psych.

RAZZA III, JOSEPH C; Banneher HS; Washington, DC; (Y); 10/108; Capt Debate Tm; Model UN; NFL; Hon Roll; Asst Prgrm Drctr Pyramid Cmmnctns Intrl 85; Co-Lost All Wy Radio Prgrm NBC WUY 85-86; Co-Fndr Yth; Pltcl Sci.

REDMAN, IRENE; Theodore Roosevelt HS; Washington, DC; (Y); Church Yth Grp; Drama Clb; Exploring; GAA; Hosp Aide; Intnl Clb; SADD; Church Choir; Mrchg Band; Nwsp Stf; Lawyer.

REDMOND, SAYNORA D; Ancostia & Chamberlin HS; Washington, DC; (Y); Church Yth Grp; Drama Clb; Red Cross Aide; Chorus; Church Choir; School Play; Cit Awd; Hon Roll; Prfct Atten Awd; Eng Awds 86; Spansh Awd 83; Sci Awd 83.

REGALA, MARIA-ISABEL; Georgetown Visitation Prep Schl; Burke, VA; (Y); Church Yth Grp; Drama Clb; Chorus; Madrigals; School Musical; School Play; Lit Mag; Rep Frsh Cls; Rep Soph Cls; Rep Jr Cls.

RHODES, JONATHAN; Mckinley Tech; Washington, DC; (Y); Art Clb; Church Yth Grp; JA; ROTC; Off Soph Cls; U Dstrct Clmb; Comp Prgmr.

RICKS, FELICIA; Woodrow Wilson HS; Washibgton, DC; (Y); 37/485; Church Yth Grp; Cmnty Wkr; Debate Tm; Girl Scts; Key Clb; Service Clb; Spanish Clb; Teachers Aide; Church Choir; Mrchg Band; Georgetown; Psychiatrist.

ROBERSON, GERALDINE; Eastern HS; Washington, DC; (Y); 3/371; Teachers Aide; Chorus; Mrchg Band; Mgr(s); Capt Twrlr; Cit Awd; High Hon Roll; Hon Roll; JP Sousa Awd; Masonic Awd; Potomac Prsnl Awd 86; Eastrn Star Schlrshp 86; Schlrshp Frm Crnl U 84-85; DE ST Coll; Fshn Dsgn.

ROBINSON JR, CHARLES D; Archbishop Carroll HS; Hyattsville, MD; (Y); 1/177; Chess Clb; Church Yth Grp; Computer Clb; Stage Crew; Yrbk Ed-Chief; Cit Awd; High Hon Roll; NHS; Ntl Merit Ltr; Spanish NHS; Natl Achvt Scholar Outstndg Negro Stu 86; WJLA Tv Sta Bst Of Cls 86; Mdl Mod Lang Spn 86; MA Inst Tech; Elec Engrng.

ROBINSON, CHRISTOPHER; F W Ballou SR HS; Washington, DC; (S); 10/103; Drama Clb; Pep Clb; Science Clb; SADD; Thesps; Chorus; School Play; Variety Show; Nwsp Stf; Yrbk Rptr; USA Today Scope Hgh Hnrs 85-86; Kennedy Ctr X-Mas Chldrns Spcl; GW; Srgn.

ROBINSON, DIANA; Calvin Coolidge HS; Washington, DC; (S); French Clb; Office Aide; Pep Clb; Jr NHS; Outstndng Achvt Awds In Scl Studies 84-85; Accntng.

ROBINSON, LISA A; Frank Washinton Ballou HS; Washington, DC; (S); 20/400; Office Aide; Teachers Aide; Chorus; School Musical; Yrbk Stf; Rep Soph Cls; Rep Jr Cls; Rep Sr Cls; Pres Stu Cncl; Pres Lbry Clb 84-85; Sci Awd 84-85; Ntl Hnr Soc 85-86; George Wshngtn U.

ROBINSON, VERONICA; F W Ballou SR HS; Washington, DC; (S); 5/425; Church Yth Grp; Sec FNA; Key Clb; Nwsp Bus Mgr; Yrbk Stf; VP Frsh Cls; Rep Stu Cncl; Cit Awd; Hon Roll; Jr NHS; Myrs Schltc Achvt Awd 83; Frgn Exchng Pgm Yth Isrl Ambssdr 84; Med.

ROBINSON, VICTORIA; Woodrow Wilson SR HS; Washington, DC; (Y); 70/431; Church Yth Grp; Concert Band; Jazz Band; Mrchg Band; Symp Band; Mgr(s); Cit Awd; Hon Roll; Jr NHS; Prfct Atten Awd; Sedarmocs Awd 84; Oral Lang Cntst Spnsh Levels I & II 84-85.

ROBLES, TONY; Cardozo HS; Washington, DC; (Y); Dance Clb; Chorus; Swmmng; Off Jr Cls; Stu Cncl; Trk; Vllybl; Winston-Salem ST Coll; Soclgy.

RODGERS, MONEVE; All Saints HS; Washington, DC; (Y); 44/86; FBLA; JA; Latin Clb; Library Aide; Pep Clb; Church Choir; Nwsp Rptr; Yrbk Stf; Stu Cncl; George Washington U.

ROSS, THERESA; Dunbar SR HS; Washington, DC; (Y); FHA; Capt Cheerleading; Sec Pom Pon; Trk; Cit Awd; Hampton U; Crmnl Jstc.

RUSHING, ROSSLYN; Dunbar SR HS; Washington, DC; (Y); Band; Concert Band; Mrchg Band; Jr Cls; Sftbl.

RYAN, KATHLEEN; Georgetown Visitation Prep HS; Washington, DC; (Y); Art Clb; Hosp Aide; Office Aide; Teachers Aide; Nwsp Rptr; Hon Roll; NHS; Bus.

SALLAY, RAYMOND; Benjamin Banneker HS; Washington, DC; (Y); 38/108; Boy Scts; Church Yth Grp; Cmnty Wkr; Spanish Clb; Church Choir; Yrbk Stf; Coach Actv; Hon Roll; Wrd 5 Rep DC Yth Cty Cncl 86; NC A&t; Accntng.

SALVADOR, ALEXANDER; Gonzaga College HS; Burke, VA; (Y); 90/179; Church Yth Grp; French Clb; Im Bsktbl; Hon Roll; 1st Pl Sci Fair/Envrnmntl Sci 85; Cert For DC Sci Fair 85; Wlm & Mary; Elctrncs.

SAUNDERS, ANITA; Benjamin Banneker SR HS; Washington, DC; (Y); 51/108; Church Yth Grp; Cmnty Wkr; Girl Scts; JA; Political Wkr; Red Cross Aide; Band; Yrbk Stf; Wt Lftg; Mayor Barrys Yth Ldrshp Inst 84; Congrss Aide Awd 84-85; Hampton Inst; Soclgy.

SCHORR, JONATHAN L; Sidwell Friends Schl; Washington, DC; (Y); Radio Clb; SADD; Stage Crew; Nwsp Ed-Chief; Art Clb; JV Tennis; Ntl Merit SF; Thomas W Sidwell Meml Awd-Svc & Ldrshp Schl Cmmnty 85.

SCHULZ, MAX; Gonzaga College HS; Washington, DC; (Y); 25/195; Church Yth Grp; Political Wkr; Speech Tm; School Musical; Nwsp Stf; Yrbk Stf; Stu Cncl; Capt Bsktbl; Coach Actv; Cmnty Wkr; Mayor Marion Barrys DC Yth Ldrshp Congrss 84; Parish CYO Bsktbl Tm MVP 85-86.

SCOTT, CATHY; Mc William T Mc Kinley HS; Washington, DC; (Y); Church Yth Grp; Church Choir; Nwsp Stf; Cit Awd; Hon Roll; Prfct Atten Awd; Awd Cobol Prgrmmng I & II At UDC 86; William T Mckinley; Cmptr Tech.

SCOTT, PHILLIP; T Roosevelt HS; Washington, DC; (Y); Computer Clb; French Clb; FBLA; Science Clb; Hon Roll; Comp Tech.

SCURLOCK, TAMARA; Woodrow Wilson HS; Washington, DC; (Y); 30/429; Art Clb; Church Yth Grp; Girl Scts; Service Clb; Chorus; Yrbk Stf; Cit Awd; High Hon Roll; Scholastic Bowl; Jr NHS; Psychlgy.

SEAY, DOROTHY; Eastern HS; Washington, DC; (Y); 2/526; Chorus; Capt Drill Tm; School Musical; School Play; Pres Jr Cls; Rep Stu Cncl; Hon Roll; Pres Jr NHS; NHS; Holy Cross; Pre-Med.

SENG, WILLIAM F; St Anselms Abbey Schl; Vienna, VA; (Y); Computer Clb; Political Wkr; Capt Scholastic Bowl; Ski Clb; Acpl Chr; Yrbk Stf; Lit Mag; Ntl Merit SF; Pres Video Nws Pblctns 85; DAR 80; Maxima Cum Laude 83-84; Physcs.

SENKYIRE, PATRICIA B; Roosevelt HS; Washington, DC; (Y); Dance Clb; FBLA; Chorus; Trk; Hon Roll; Prfct Atten Awd; Outstndg Stu In Acctg 1 86; Howard U; Law.

SHAHEEN, KERRIE; Georgetown Visitation Prep Schl; Washington, DC; (Y); Art Clb; Cmnty Wkr; Nwsp Ed-Chief; Nwsp Rptr; Yrbk Stf; Im Badmtn; Mgr Sftbl; Mgr Tennis; High Hon Roll; Prfct Atten Awd; Comm.

SHARKEY, MICHAEL; Woodrow Wilson HS; Washington, DC; (Y); 21/431; Boy Scts; Latin Clb; Model UN; Office Aide; High Hon Roll; Hon Roll; Jr NHS; Hnrblment Physics 86; Wilson Acad T V Tm 86; 2nd Pl Math Cntst 86.

SHARPE, LORRAINE; Woodrow Wilson SR HS; Washington, DC; (Y); Drama Clb; Pep Clb; Science Clb; Varsity Clb; Bsktbl; Perf Attndnc 85; Nrsng.

SHAW, CARLOS; Archbishop Carroll HS; Suitland, MD; (S); #15 In Class; Aud/Vis; Computer Clb; Library Aide; School Musical; School Play; Yrbk Stf; Pres Sr Cls; Rep Stu Cncl; High Hon Roll; Hon Roll; U Of MD; Comp.

SHELTON, BYRON; Theodore Roosevelt SR HS; Washington, DC; (Y); 5/300; Teachers Aide; Nwsp Rptr; Nwsp Sprt Ed; Prfct Atten Awd; Frdrk Dgls Schlrshp 86; Bst Essy 86; 2nd Pl Wnr In Mrtn Lthr King Jr Essy Cntst 86; Amer U; Prnt Jrnlst.

SHELTON, WILLIAM; Mackin Catholic HS; Washington, DC; (S); 1/71; Boys Clb Am; Spanish Clb; Teachers Aide; Pres Frsh Cls; Pres Soph Cls; Soph Of Yr 84-85; Boys Of Mnth Boys Clb 83-84; Pre-Law.

SIMANIS, JOSEPH; Gonzaga College HS; Washington, DC; (Y); 67/177; Boy Scts; Church Yth Grp; Computer Clb; Science Clb; Ski Clb; Nwsp Stf; Im Socr; Magna Cum Laude Natl Lat Exam; Engrng.

SIMONS, AINSLEY; Cardozo SR HS; Washington, DC; (Y); Debate Tm; Rep Jr Cls; Rep Stu Cncl; Bsktbl; Tennis; Trk; Cit Awd; Hon Roll; Prfct Atten Awd; Grgtwn U Schlrshp Awd 86; U Of VA; Comp Tech.

SINGLETON, CATHY; Wilson HS; Washington, DC; (Y); Library Aide; Office Aide; Teachers Aide; JV Cheerleading; High Hon Roll; Hon Roll; Prfct Atten Awd; Mall Pgm 86; Drivers Ed Ad 85-86; Outstndng Church Helper 85; Howard U; Law.

SMITH, CAMILLE; Woodrow Wilson HS; Washington, DC; (Y); 52/431; Hosp Aide; Chorus; Hon Roll; Cert Of Achvt In D C Hstry 84; Cmnctns.

SMITH, DERRICK; Theodore Roosevelt HS; Washington, DC; (Y); CAP; FBLA; Letterman Clb; Radio Clb; Chorus; Church Choir; Nwsp Phtg; Nwsp Sprt Ed; Yrbk Phtg; Yrbk Sprt Ed; Outstndg Future Bus Ldrs Of Amer 85-86; Howard U; Broadcasting Comm.

SMITH, LA SHONDA L; Ballou SR HS; Washington, DC; (Y); Church Yth Grp; Library Aide; Teachers Aide; Church Choir; Off Frsh Cls; Off Soph Cls; Off Jr Cls; Rep Stu Cncl; Pom Pon; Cit Awd; A&T Tech Coll; Accounting.

SNEAD, ANTHONY D; Gonzaga College HS; Mt Rainier, MD; (Y); 62/177; Im Bsktbl; Var Crs Cntry; Var Trk; Hon Roll; Ntl Merit Black Semifnlst 84; Engr.

SOUTHERLAND, CYNTHIA R; Duke Ellington School Of The Arts; Washington, DC; (Y); 5/88; Church Yth Grp; Nwsp Rptr; Yrbk Stf; Trs Jr Cls; Trs Sr Cls; Im Bsktbl; Im Vllybl; NHS; Schlstc Art Awd Mdl 85; 4th Pl Anti-Drnkng & Drvng Poster Cont 85; Outstndg Visual Arts Stu 85; Indstrl Dsgn.

SPEAKS, MICHAEL; Mackin Catholic HS; Washington, DC; (Y); 4/65; Pep Clb; Teachers Aide; Church Choir; Drm & Bgl; Rep Stu Cncl; Var Sftbl; High Hon Roll; Hon Roll; NHS; Church Yth Grp; Citatn Outstndng Schlstc Achvt Awd Georgetown U 85-86; Spec Achvt Awd Chem 85; U S Air Force Acad; Pilot.

SPOHR, DAVID; The Maret Schl; Washington, DC; (Y); Boys Clb Am; Church Yth Grp; Nwsp Stf; Var Bsktbl; Im Vllybl; Var Wrstlng; Ntl Merit SF.

STARKS, MICHELLE; Paul Lawrence Dunbar HS; Washington, DC; (Y); Church Yth Grp; Drama Clb; Hosp Aide; VP JA; Band; Concert Band; Rep Soph Cls; Pom Pon; Jr NHS; NHS; Acad All Am 84-85; Elec Engr.

STEWART, SEAN JEROME; T Roosevelt HS; Washington, DC; (Y); Am Leg Boys St; Math Tm; VP Frsh Cls; Rep Soph Cls; Rep Jr Cls; Off Stu Cncl; Var Capt Bsbl; Var Ftbl; Mgr(s); Stat Sftbl; UPO Smmr Pgm 84; Amer Hrt Rsrch Pgm 85; Georgetown U Strt Law Pgm 86.

STOKES, LA RAHN; Spingarn HS; Washington, DC; (Y); Boys Clb Am; Band; Concert Band; Mrchg Band; Pep Band; Hon Roll; Solo Ensmble Awd 86; Outstndng Band Awd 86; Norfolk ST U; Elec Engr.

STOKESBERRY, ERIC J; Gonzaga College HS; Ijamsville, MD; (Y); 6/170; Am Leg Boys St; Math Tm; Var L Bsbl; Var L Bsktbl; Var Capt Socr; JETS Awd; Ntl Merit SF; Acdmc Team 85; Smmr Sci & Engr Apprntc 85; Gonzaga Sci Fair 1st Pl Engr 83; Elec Engr.

STROTHER, LISA; Roosevelt SR HS; Washington, DC; (Y); PAVAS; Teachers Aide; Chorus; Cit Awd; Hon Roll; Prfct Atten Awd; Alma Thomas Memorial Awd 84; Accomplishment Cert 86; DC U; Word Processing.

SWERCZEK, JEFFREY; Archbiship Carroll HS; Landover Hills, MD; (S); 14/160; Boy Scts; Computer Clb; Letterman Clb; Pep Clb; Ski Clb; Var L Socr; Var L Wrstlng; Hon Roll; Engrng.

SYDNOR, GAIL; Frank W Ballou HS; Washington, DC; (Y); FBLA; Var Bsktbl; Hon Roll; Prince Geo Acadmc Achvt Awd 84; Bus Admin.

TAYLOR, ARTHUR L; Duke Ellington Schl Of The Arts; Washington, DC; (Y); VP Church Yth Grp; Drama Clb; ROTC; Thesps; Church Choir; Drill Tm; School Musical; School Play; Stage Crew; Trk; Duke Ellington Awd Excllnc-Outstndg Artstc Achvt 84; Duke Ellington Awd Excllnc-Perfct Atten 85; Theatr.

TEARE, HALEY; Georgetown Visitation Prep Schl; Bethesda, MD; (Y); Cmnty Wkr; GAA; Library Aide; Service Clb; Var L Bsktbl; Var L Civic Clb; Hon Roll; Excellence Math 85-86; Mary Kay Mc Guire Schlrshp Awd 86; Bus.

TEED, REBECCA; Georgetown Visitation HS; Arlington, VA; (Y); 1/97; Math Clb; Political Wkr; Science Clb; Lit Mag; High Hon Roll; NHS; Ntl Merit SF; Val; George Washington U Engrng Medal; Sci Medal; Williams Coll; Phys.

THOMAS, DOROTHY C; Duke Ellington Schl Of The Arts; Washington, DC; (Y); Variety Show; Pres Jr Cls; Pres Sr Cls; Hon Roll; Ntl Merit SF; Schlrshp-Corcoran Schl Of Art-Painting 83; Hnr 2 Gold Keys For Schltc Art Awd 86; Cooper Union; Fine Arts.

THOMAS, VICKIE R; Benjamin Banneker SR HS; Washington, DC; (Y); 8/81; Cmnty Wkr; French Clb; Hosp Aide; Yrbk Stf; Sec Jr Cls; Sec Sr Cls; Hon Roll; NHS; Library Aide; Band; Poetry Awd The Links Inc 85; Psych.

THOMPSON, CHARLEAN; Ballou SR HS; Washington, DC; (Y); French Clb; Hosp Aide; Rep Frsh Cls; Cit Awd; French Hon Soc; High Hon Roll; Jr NHS; NHS; Computer Clb; Office Aide; Grgtwn U Citn Outstndng Schlstc Achvt 86; Outstndng JR Awd 86; Hosp Admn.

THOMPSON, KERRI; Woodrow Wilson HS; Washington, DC; (Y); 7/320; Church Yth Grp; FBLA; Acpl Chr; Chorus; Church Choir; Madrigals; School Musical; Nwsp Ed-Chief; Frsh Cls; Cit Awd; Oberlin Coll Book Awd 86; Communctns.

THOMPSON, WENDY; Georgetown Visitation Prep Schl; Potomac, MD; (Y); 4/95; Service Clb; Rep Frsh Cls; Stu Cncl; Tennis; Chorus; Pom Pon; Hon Roll.

TIANO, KIMBERLY ANNE; Georgetown Visitation Prep Schl; Mc Lean, VA; (Y); 10/97; Am Leg Aux Girls St; Cmnty Wkr; School Musical; School Play; Nwsp Ed-Chief; Lit Mag; Rep Stu Cncl; JV Lcrss; High Hon Roll; Sec NHS; Cntry III Ldrshp Schlrshp For D C Altrnt; Grls Ntn; Hugh O Brian Ldrshp Smnr; U VA.

TILLMAN, CHARMIN J; Benjamin Banneker Academic HS; Washington, DC; (Y); 4/81; Camp Fr Inc; Cmnty Wkr; Dance Clb; French Clb; Hosp Aide; Office Aide; Teachers Aide; Pres NHS; Corp Law.

TRAVER, JARED; St Anselms Abbey; Hyattsville, MD; (S); Cmnty Wkr; Debate Tm; German Clb; JCL; Band; School Play; Stage Crew; Variety Show; Nwsp Stf; Yrbk Stf; Emory U; Libl Arts.

TRUMAN, DAVID; The Maret Schl; Chevy Chase, MD; (Y); Drama Clb; Model UN; Acpl Chr; Church Choir; School Musical; School Play; Nwsp Ed-Chief; Nwsp Sprt Ed; Mgr(s); Score Keeper; Cum Laude Soc, Span Awd 86; Mus Awd; Amherst Coll; Frgn Govt Svc.

TUBBS, TONGELINA; Anacostia SR HS; Washington, DC; (Y); Computer Clb; FHA; Math Clb; ROTC; Science Clb; Band; Mrchg Band; Cit Awd; Hon Roll; Prfct Atten Awd.

TURNER, PATRICIA L; National Cathedral Schl; Washington, DC; (Y); Pres VP Church Yth Grp; Cmnty Wkr; Math Tm; Model UN; Pres Science Clb; SADD; Pres Jr Cls; Var Swmmng; Var Trk; Masonic Awd; Ntl Achvt Schlrshp 86; Bnjmn Frnkln Schlrshp 86; Red Crss Outstndng Vlntr Awd 86; U PA; Nrsrgry.

TURNER, SARAH P; US Senate Page Schl; Pittsburgh, PA; (Y); AFS; Camera Clb; Church Yth Grp; Pep Clb; Political Wkr; Teachers Aide; Varsity Clb; Yrbk Stf; VP Fld Hcky; VP Lcrss; U VA.

TURNER, YOLONDA; F W Ballou HS; Washington, DC; (S); 24/450; Pep Clb; Stu Cncl; Cit Awd; Hon Roll; Jr NHS; NHS; Yrbk Asst Edtr Layout 85-86; Math Engr Tech Scty 84-86; Its Acad Team 83-86; Peer Tutrng Coord 85-86; Penn ST U; Biomed Engr.

VESSELS, DEREK; Calvin Coolidge HS; Washington, DC; (Y); Art Clb; Church Yth Grp; Teachers Aide; Church Choir; Stage Crew; Ftbl; Wt Lftg; Cit Awd; Hon Roll.

VIEIRA, KAREN; Woodrow Wilson SR HS; Washington, DC; (Y); 62/380; FNA; Pep Clb; Teachers Aide; School Play; Variety Show; Pom Pon; Hon Roll; NHS; Prfct Atten Awd; Mdl Cty Wide Foreign Lang Pstr 85; Rober Awd Cltnry Arts 86; 4 Yr Tutor Schlrshp IN 86; Norfolk ST U; Nrsng.

WALKER, ALISON M; Benjamin Banneker HS; Washington, DC; (Y); Cmnty Wkr; Computer Clb; Debate Tm; Im Vllybl; Hon Roll; Jr NHS; Natl Achvt Scholar Pgm 85; Yth Cty Cncl Rep Mayr Barrys Yth Ldrshp Inst 84-85; Schlrs Pgm Comp Sci 85; Williams Coll; Comp Sci.

WALL, GINA; Woodrow Wilson HS; Washington, DC; (Y); Dance Clb; Pep Clb; Variety Show; Pres Frsh Cls; Pres Stu Cncl; Capt Cheerleading; Mgr(s); Cit Awd; Hon Roll; Spllng Bee; Schl Ltr W/Star; Carlow Coll; Soc.

WARD, CHRIS R; Gonzaga College HS; Alexandria, VA; (Y); Aud/Vis; Church Yth Grp; Math Tm; Concert Band; School Musical; Symp Band; JV Bsktbl; Var Golf; Hon Roll; Ntl Merit Ltr; MTH.

WASHINGTON, CAROLYN; Dumbar SR HS; Washington, DC; (Y); Church Yth Grp; Computer Clb; Debate Tm; FBLA; FHA; JA; Office Aide; Stu Cncl; Cheerleading; Hon Roll; U DC; Psych.

WATSON, DARYL; Dunbar SR HS; Washington, DC; (Y); Am Leg Boys St; Church Yth Grp; ROTC; Band; Church Choir; Var JV Ftbl; Cit Awd; Mechanic.

WATTS, CATHY; Woodrow Wilson HS; Washington, DC; (Y); 148/431; Church Yth Grp; Chorus; Church Choir; Outstndng Contrbtn To Chrl Music Dept; Htl Rest Mgmt.

WEAVER, ANTHONY; Frank W Ballou HS; Washington, DC; (S); VP Church Yth Grp; FBLA; Rep Stu Cncl; Var Swmmng; Cit Awd; Hon Roll; Jr NHS; NHS; Prfct Atten Awd; Amer Lgn Schl Awd 82; Myrs Schlstc Achvt Awd 82; Valdctrn Winston Ed Ctr 82; Bio.

WEBB, MELODY R; Banneker Academic HS; Washington, DC; (Y); 2/83; Chess Clb; Cmnty Wkr; Debate Tm; English Clb; Model UN; Spanish Clb; Teachers Aide; High Hon Roll; NHS; Ntl Merit SF; Schl Ltr Acad Achvt 83-84; Africare Essay Cont Wnnr 83-85; Century III Ldrs Scholar 85-86; Harvard; Law.

WELLS, TOMIKO; T Roosevelt HS; Washington, DC; (Y); Office Aide; School Musical; Rep Sr Cls; Hon Roll; 1st Pl Chem Sci Fair 85; Coll Internshp Pgm Geo WA U 85-86; Engr.

WEST, KIMBERLY; Ballou SR HS; Washington, DC; (Y); Dance Clb; Girl Scts; Pep Clb; Mrchg Band; Var Cheerleading; Var Pom Pon; Var Twrlr; Cit Awd; Hon Roll; Rep Frsh Cls; George Mason U; Law.

WEST, TIFFANY B; Sidwell Friends HS; Washington, DC; (Y); Cmnty Wkr; Latin Clb; Math Tm; Chorus; School Musical; Nwsp Rptr; Nwsp Stf; Frsh Cls; JV Fld Hcky; JV Socr.

WESTRAY, MAURICE; Mackin HS; Washington, DC; (Y); 2/62; French Clb; Rep Stu Cncl; High Hon Roll; Hon Roll; NHS; Stu Of Yr & Frshmn Of Yr 83-84; Spcl Achvt Algr I, Englsh, Physcl Sci & P E 83-84; Airforce Acad.

WHITE, MARY; Roosevelt SR HS; Washington, DC; (Y); Spanish Clb; Church Choir; Rep Jr Cls; Trk; Hon Roll; Jr NHS; Prfct Atten Awd; Spanish NHS; PA ST U; Bio.

WHITFORD, ANGELINA; Georgetown Visitation Prep Schl; Rockville, MD; (Y); Church Yth Grp; Hosp Aide; Service Clb; Speech Tm; Hon Roll; NHS; Ntl Merit Ltr; Cmnty Wkr; Debate Tm; Model UN; Am Heart Assoc Flsp 85; Pol Sci.

WICKS, JENIFER; Mavet HS; Chevy Chase, MD; (Y); Cmnty Wkr; Math Tm; Chorus; Nwsp Rptr; VP Jr Cls; Var JV Bsktbl; JV Socr; Var Capt Tennis; Cum Laude Soc 85-86.

WILEY, AMPERITA; Francis L Cardozo HS; Washington, DC; (S); JA; Pep Clb; Sec Frsh Cls; Rep Soph Cls; Var Bsktbl; Var Sftbl; Hon Roll; NHS; Prfct Atten Awd; Holy Cross Bk Awd 85; Elctrcl Engrng.

WILKERSON, TONI; Ballou SR HS; Washington, DC; (S); Key Clb; Yrbk Stf; Stu Cncl; Hon Roll; NHS; Smithsnian Carer Awrns Pgm 83-84; Woodward Fndtn Fellow 85-86; Arts Recgntn Talent Srch Competr 85-86; Graphc Dsgn.

WILLIAMS, ADRIENNE; All Saints HS; Washington, DC; (Y); Art Clb; Pep Clb; Prfct Atten Awd; Pres Frsh Cls; Off Jr Cls; VP Rep Stu Cncl; George Washington U; Psych.

WILLIAMS, ANITA; Theodore Roosevelt SR HS; Washington, DC; (Y); Cit Awd; Prfct Atten Awd; Bus Adm.

WILLIAMS, CYNTHIA V; Frank W Ballou HS; Washington, DC; (S); Ski Clb; Socr; Stat Tennis; Cit Awd; Hon Roll; Jr NHS; Undrstndng Yth Pgm; Engrng Yth Pgm; Howard U; Chem Engrng.

WILLIAMS, DARICE; Georgetown Visitation Prep Schl; Brookeville, MD; (Y); Dance Clb; Drama Clb; Model UN; Speech Tm; Variety Show; Lit Mag; Lcrss; Socr; Hon Roll; VP NHS; Rcptn Amer Cancer Soc Katherine Dulin Folger Smmr Rsrch Schlrshp 85; Amer Hrt Assoc Schlrshp 86; Intl Rltns.

WILLIAMS, DIANE; Dunbar SR HS; Washington, DC; (Y); French Clb; FHA; JA; Chorus; French Hon Soc; Hon Roll; Awd Partcptn Its Acdmc 86; Pres Futr Lingstcs Amer 86; Toursm Clb Metcn Engr Clb 84; Jrnlst.

WILLIAMS, LA VERNE C; Academy Of Notre Dame; Washington, DC; (Y); 4/62; Cmnty Wkr; Computer Clb; Intnl Clb; JA; Pep Clb; Yrbk Stf; Sec Frsh Cls; Rep Soph Cls; High Hon Roll; VP NHS; Myr Barrys Yth Ldrshp Inst Parents Assoc86; Georgina Thomas Grnd Chptr Ordr Eastrn Str Pha 86; Pennsylvania ST U; Bus Admnst.

WILLIAMS, MARC; Benjamin A Banneker HS; Washington, DC; (Y); 8/108; Boy Scts; Am Leg Boys St; Am Leg Aux Girls St; Art Clb; Aud/Vis; Rep Stu Cncl; JV Ftbl; Var Wrstlng; Jr NHS; NHS; Hghst Avg In Engl 85-86; Johns Hopkins U; Med.

WILLIAMS, MARITHA; Ballou SR HS; Washington, DC; (S); Church Yth Grp; Key Clb; SADD; Church Choir; Tennis; Cit Awd; Hon Roll; Jr NHS; NHS; Prfct Atten Awd; Wdwrd Fndtn Awd; Org Of Chinese Amer Wmn Awd; Amer Hrt Assn Rsrch Pgm; Chld Psych.

WILLIAMS, MARK; Roosevelt HS; Washington, DC; (Y); JA; Math Clb; Science Clb; Acpl Chr; VP Jr Cls; Sftbl; Swmmng; Hon Roll; Comp Sci.

WILLIAMS, REGINALD; Eastern SR HS; Washington, DC; (Y); Am Leg Boys St; Boys Clb Am; Camera Clb; Church Yth Grp; Drama Clb; ROTC; Science Clb; Band; Concert Band; Drm & Bgl; Acdmc Achvmnt Awd 83-84; Jrry A Moore Jr Awd 83-84; Rgn-D Spch & Drama Awd 85-86; Comp Techncn.

WILLIAMS, WANDA; Theodore Roosevelt HS; Washington, DC; (Y); Camp Fr Inc; ROTC; Band; Church Choir; Drill Tm; Orch; Cit Awd; Prfct Atten Awd; Howard U; Socl Welfr.

WILSON, CONAN; Banneker Academic HS; Washington, DC; (Y); Art Clb; Boy Scts; Church Yth Grp; Cmnty Wkr; Spanish Clb; Stage Crew; Hon Roll; Elec Engr.

WILSON, JULIETTE G; Benjamin Banneker SR HS; Washington, DC; (Y); 9/108; Trs Church Yth Grp; Science Clb; Chorus; Trs Soph Cls; Pres Jr Cls; Hon Roll; Mtrpltn Cnsrtm Mnrty Engrs Awd 85-86; Bnkr B Awd 85-86; Sci Career Opprtnties Awd 85-86; Engr.

WINTERS, TONYA; Dunbar HS; Washington, DC; (Y); JA; WSS; Sectry.

WISEMAN, ROSALIND; The Maret HS; Washington, DC; (Y); Political Wkr; Chorus; Stage Crew; Nwsp Stf; Pres Frsh Cls; Var Bsktbl; JV Socr; JV Sftbl; Var Tennis; JV Vllybl; Natl Hist Comptn 5th Pl 85; All Met/All Leauge Var Tnns 85-86; Poltcl Sci.

WITHERALL, SCOTT; Calvin Coolidge HS; Washington, DC; (S); Chess Clb; Math Clb; Science Clb; High Hon Roll; Prfct Atten Awd; Its Academic Tm Rep 86; Htl/Rest Mngmnt.

WOODS, WENDY MICHELLE; Benjamin Banneker Academic HS; Washington, DC; (Y); 16/108; Pres Church Yth Grp; Cmnty Wkr; Hosp Aide; Library Aide; Math Clb; Band; Chorus; Yrbk Stf; Hon Roll; Jr NHS; Duke U; Med.

WRIGHT, CHRISTIAN; Joel Spingarn HS; Washington, DC; (Y); VP Art Clb; Computer Clb; JA; SADD; Chorus; Mrchg Band; Nwsp Rptr; Yrbk Ed-Chief; Rep Jr Cls; High Hon Roll; Inst Of Archtctr; Archtct.

WRIGHT, LA TANYA D; Benjamin Banneke HS; Washington, DC; (Y); 20/108; Church Yth Grp; Hosp Aide; Spanish Clb; Band; Chorus; Variety Show; Sr Cls; Stu Cncl; Hon Roll; 1st Pl City Wide Group Perf Ntl Hist Day 86; 1st Pl Schl Wide Ntl Spnsh Exam 85; Spanish.

WYNNE, GARY; Gonzaga College HS; Washington, DC; (Y); 45/177; Camera Clb; VP Computer Clb; Jazz Band; Symp Band; Nwsp Rptr; Yrbk Phtg; Im Bsktbl; Church Yth Grp; Pep Band; Hghst Awd Achvt Comp Sci 86; US Nvl Acad Engrng & Sci Smnr 85; DC Myrs Annl Ldrshp Inst 85; Lehigh U; Comp Sci.

YOSHIMOTO, MIKI; The Washington Intl Schl; Arlington, VA; (S); Art Clb; Cmnty Wkr; Debate Tm; Ski Clb; Chorus; School Musical; Bowling; Awd For Excllnc In Math & Art 82-83; Awd For Excllnc In Math 83-84; Awd For Progrss In Chem 84-85; Oxford ; Fine Art.

YOUNG, DENISE M; Immaculata Preparatory Schl; Washington, DC; (Y); Girl Scts; Hosp Aide; Variety Show; Rep Jr Cls; Mgr(s); Mgr Trk; Natl Achvt Scholar Pgm Outstndg Negro Stu 85; Cert Recog Outstndg Achvt & Ded Trk 84; Stu Cncl Ldrshp; Ped Nrsg.

YOUNG, ROXANNA A; Duke Ellington Schl Of The Arts; Takoma Park, MD; (Y); AFS; Intnl Clb; VP Jr Cls; Rep Stu Cncl; Hon Roll; Trs VP NHS; Pres Dance Dept; Ellington Excllnc Awds Dance,Spanish & French 82-86; Georgetown U Citation Awd 85; Suny Purchase; Dancer.

YOUNG-BOWMAN, HOPE E; All Saints HS; Washington, DC; (Y); 16/86; Sec Trs Church Yth Grp; Drama Clb; Girl Scts; Hosp Aide; Library Aide; Pep Clb; Chorus; Trs Pres Church Choir; School Musical; Variety Show; Gospel Choir 82-86; Music 82-86; Algebra II 84-85; Natl Symphony Orchestra 84-85; Mckendrea Un Meth Chur; UDC; Bio.

YUN, JOON K; St Albans Schl; Rockville, MD; (Y); 5/73; Church Yth Grp; Intnl Clb; Math Tm; Science Clb; Stage Crew; Nwsp Rptr; Yrbk Stf; JV Bsbl; Var Capt Bsktbl; Var Socr.

MARYLAND

ABADIA, ANDY; Bowie HS; Bowie, MD; (Y); Church Yth Grp; French Clb; JA; Math Tm; Science Clb; SADD; Var L Crs Cntry; Var Trk; Hon Roll; U Of MD; Engrng.

ABALAHIN, ANDREW; Mt St Joseph HS; Glen Burnie, MD; (Y); 14/300; Chess Clb; Intnl Clb; Library Aide; Quiz Bowl; Off Frsh Cls; Off Soph Cls; Stu Cncl; High Hon Roll; Hon Roll; NHS; Summa Cum Laude Natl Latin Exm 82; Johns Hpkns Cty Math & Vrbl Tlnt Srch 82; Mrn Burk Knott Schlrshp; St Johns Coll; Frgn Lang.

ABBEY, JENNIFER MARIE; Connelly School Of The Holy Child; Bethesda, MD; (Y); Church Yth Grp; Math Tm; Service Clb; Nwsp Rptr; Lit Mag; Mgr(s); Swmmng; Hon Roll; NHS; Prfct Atten Awd; Highest Hnr Span, Latin & Western Civilization 85; U NC; Spec Educ Tchr.

ABBOTT, JENNIFER; Frederick HS; Fred, MD; (Y); 11/358; AFS; Church Yth Grp; French Clb; German Clb; Band; Church Choir; Concert Band; Mrchg Band; Off Jr Cls; Powder Puff Ftbl; Brigham Young U; Languages.

ABBOTT, REBECCA; Montrose Christian HS; Gaithersburg, MD; (Y); Church Yth Grp; Drama Clb; Spanish Clb; Chorus; Jr Cls; Stu Cncl; Score Keeper; Cit Awd; High Hon Roll; Scholar Awd 83-85; Acctg.

ABDINOOR, JULIE M; Walkersville HS; Walkersville, MD; (Y); 106/227; Office Aide; SADD; Teachers Aide; Ed Yrbk Stf; Lit Mag; VP Frsh Cls; Sec Sr Cls; Powder Puff Ftbl; Var Tennis; Hon Roll; U TX Austin; Clsscs.

ABEL, CATHY; La Plata HS; La Plata, MD; (S); 1/528; Math Tm; Science Clb; Spanish Clb; SADD; Chorus; Rep Jr Cls; Stat Socr; High Hon Roll; Jr NHS; NHS; Comp Sci.

ABELL, MARK; La Plata HS; La Plata, MD; (S); Ski Clb; Teachers Aide; Rep Frsh Cls; Rep Stu Cncl; Var L Socr; Var L Tennis; Jr NHS.

ABELL, VANESSA; St Vincent Pallotti HS; Laurel, MD; (S); 19/115; AFS; Ski Clb; Varsity Clb; Trs Jr Cls; Rep Stu Cncl; Stat Bsktbl; Var Socr; Var Trk; Hon Roll; NHS.

ABELLA, CHERRIE; Perry Hall HS; Baltimore, MD; (Y); SADD; Co-Capt Drill Tm; Mrchg Band; Stage Crew; Sec Soph Cls; Pres Jr Cls; Co-Capt Pom Pon; Im Powder Puff Ftbl; Stat Tennis; Ltr Awd Pom Pons,Drill Tm 83-84; Cert Band Awd 85-86; Four Blue Rbbns Sueprstar Drill Tm 85-86; Arch.

ABERNATHY, MARK; Arlington Baptist Schl; Baltimore, MD; (Y); Var Wrstlng; Comp Engnrng.

ABNER, PAMELA; Northern HS; Owings, MD; (Y); Cmnty Wkr; Score Keeper; Hon Roll; Sftbl; Frostburg; Acctnt.

ABOSCH, DEBBIE; Pikesville SR HS; Lutherville, MD; (Y); AFS; Temple Yth Grp; Powder Puff Ftbl; Var JV Sftbl; Var JV Vllybl; Hon Roll; NHS; Grt Bks Clb 84-86; Pyscl Thrpst.

ABRAHAM, SALLY; Takoma Acad; Clarksville, MD; (Y); Sec Church Yth Grp; Sec Science Clb; Ski Clb; Concert Band; Yrbk Stf; Off Sr Cls; Trk; Hon Roll; Prfct Atten Awd; Pres Schlr; Hgh Hnr Awd Earth Sci 82-83; Trck Awd 83; Columbia Union Coll; Med Fld.

ABRAHAMS, DAVID; Pikesville SR HS; Baltimore, MD; (Y); AFS; PAVAS; Acpl Chr; Chorus; School Musical; School Play; Stage Crew; Trk; Pre-Med.

ABRAMS, SUZY; Rockville HS; Rockville, MD; (S); 14/464; AFS; Cmnty Wkr; NFL; SADD; School Play; Nwsp Rptr; Nwsp Stf; Rep Stu Cncl; Wrstlng; High Hon Roll; Stu Of Yr Gourmt Food; Ldrshp Svc Sem Natl Svc Corps Exec; Brdcst Jrnlsm.

ABRECHT JR, DOUGLAS F; Gov Thomas Johnson HS; Frederick, MD; (Y); 13/323; Latin Clb; Science Clb; SADD; Chorus; Madrigals; School Musical; Gov Hon Prg Awd; High Hon Roll; Prfct Atten Awd; Merit Schlstc Awd 86; Excllnc & Achvt Advncd Plcmnt Bio 86; Thrghnss,Compstns,Assgnmnts Engl 86; Western MD Coll; Bio.

ABRUSCATO, GINA; Thomas S Wootton HS; Potomac, MD; (S); DECA; Teachers Aide; Stu Cncl; Hon Roll; Rotary Awd; DECA Chptr Pres 85-86; 3rd Pl ST Petrium Mrktng 85-86; AZ ST U; Intl Bus.

ABSHER, BILLY; La Plata HS; Waldorf, MD; (Y); Boy Scts; Church Yth Grp; Computer Clb; Science Clb; SADD; Var Tennis; 1st Pl Sci Fair Awd Laplata & Charles Co HS Botney 83; MD U; Comp Sci.

ACEBAL, MARIA L; The Holton-Arms Schl; Potomac, MD; (Y); Cmnty Wkr; Dance Clb; Varsity Clb; Diving; Swmmng; Var Tennis; JV Vllybl; Ntl Merit SF; Harvard Bk Prz 85; Cum Laude Pres 85-86; George WA U Engrng Mdl 85; Gntc Cnslr.

ACKER, AMY E; Academy Of The Holy Cross; Silver Spring, MD; (Y); 2/123; Art Clb; Math Clb; Red Cross Aide; SADD; Church Choir; JETS Awd; NHS; Ntl Merit Ltr; Sal; St Schlr; VA Tech Marshall Hahn Engrng Merit Schlrshp 86; AP Calculus Awd 85; Chem Awd 85; VA Tech; Engrng.

ACOSTA, DONALD J; Loyola HS; Dundalk, MD; (Y); 34/197; Camera Clb; Cmnty Wkr; Yrbk Rptr; Yrbk Stf; JV Var Ftbl; Ntl Merit SF; NEDT Awd; Opt Clb Awd; GA Inst Tech; Nuc Engr.

ADAM, ERDAL; Fiendly HS; Ft Washington, MD; (Y); Math Tm; Rep Frsh Cls; Var Socr; Var Tennis; French Hon Soc; High Hon Roll; Hon Roll; NHS; Pres Schlr; Prncpls Awd 82-83; MD U College Pk.

ADAM, LARRY; Fallston HS; Fallston, MD; (Y); Church Yth Grp; Teachers Aide; JV Capt Bsbl; JV Bsktbl; JV Var Socr; Cit Awd; High Hon Roll; Hon Roll; NHS; Prfct Atten Awd; Hon Men Sci Fr 85; Cnslr Harford Glen Tchng 5th Grdrs 85; Hd Dntns Fallstn Natl Hnr Scty 86; Bus.

ADAMS, ANTHONY; Carver Vo Tech HS; Baltimore, MD; (Y); 10/20; Aud/Vis; Cmnty Wkr; Drama Clb; FBLA; JA; SADD; Chorus; Church Choir; School Play; Sr Cls.

ADAMS, ARTHUR; Paul Laurence Dunbar HS; Baltimore, MD; (Y); Pres Art Clb; Boy Scts; Cmnty Wkr; Computer Clb; Library Aide; PAVAS; Spanish Clb; JV Ftbl; Cit Awd; God Cntry Awd; Flee Omega Psi Phi Tlnt Hunt & Flemington Fur Dsgn Cntst Hnr Mntn 85 & 86; Omega Psi Phi 1st Pl 86; Hlth Care Occup.

ADAMS JR, CHARLES A; Bladensburg HS; Hyattsville, MD; (Y); School Play; Trs Sr Cls; Hon Roll; Outstndg Stu Data Prcssng I 86; Cert Achvmnt Grmmr/Cmpstn II 86; Capitol Tech; Elctrnc Engnrng.

ADAMS, GREG; Northwestern HS; Hyattsville, MD; (Y); French Clb; Concert Band; Jazz Band; School Musical; High Hon Roll; NHS; Towson ST U; Music.

ADAMS, HEATHER; Great Mills HS; Lex Pk, MD; (Y); Office Aide; Pep Clb; Spanish Clb; Mrchg Band; Symp Band; Pres Frsh Cls; Rep Soph Cls; Rep Jr Cls; Sec Stu Cncl; Mgr(s); Jobs Dghtrs Schlrshp; Arch.

ADAMS, JAMES; Centennial HS; Ellicott City, MD; (Y); Art Clb; Camera Clb; Drama Clb; Acpl Chr; Chorus; School Musical; Yrbk Phtg; Yrbk Darkroom Ed; Lab Aide; Chem Engrng.

ADAMS, JOHN; Great Mills HS; Patuxent River, MD; (Y); 16/263; Church Yth Grp; FBLA; Intnl Clb; Math Clb; Model UN; Spanish Clb; SADD; Thesps; Church Choir; Pres Schlr; Data Proc Awd Sthrn CA Sectn FBLA 84; CSF 83-84; U FL Gainesville; Elec Engrng.

ADAMS, JULIE; Western HS; Balt, MD; (Y); 5/412; Church Yth Grp; Pres Debate Tm; Hosp Aide; Spanish Clb; School Musical; Nwsp Rptr; Lit Mag; NHS; Spanish NHS; Awd Naturlstc Poetry 84; Intl Corrspndnt.

ADAMS, MARIA T; Bethesda-Chevy Chase HS; Silver Spring, MD; (Y); 20/449; Political Wkr; Ed Yrbk Sprt Ed; Bsktbl; Commended Natl Negro Achvt Pgm; Kappa Alpha Psi Frat Awd; Harvard U; Hist Prof.

ADAMS, ROBERT D; Bishop Mcnamara HS; Suitland, MD; (Y); 1/149; Pep Band; Symp Band; Nwsp Rptr; Yrbk Stf; Rep Jr Cls; High Hon Roll; NHS; Ntl Merit SF; Genetic Rsrch Sci.

ADAMS, SHONDA; La Plata HS; La Plata, MD; (Y); Latin Clb; Science Clb; Band; Chorus; Concert Band; Mrchg Band; Variety Show; Prfct Atten Awd; Ntl Engl Mrt Awd 86; Pre-Med.

ADAMS, STEVE; Oakland Mills HS; Columbia, MD; (Y); Math Tm; Teachers Aide; Nwsp Ed-Chief; Nwsp Rptr; Nwsp Stf; Hon Roll; Tlnt Recog Awd Poetry 85-86; Its Acadmc Tm 86-87; Recog For Stories 84; U Chicago; Engl.

ADAMS, WANDA; Takoma Acad; Takoma Park, MD; (Y); Hon Roll; NHS; Nrs.

ADAMSKI, RONALD; Archbishop Curley HS; Baltimore, MD; (S); 19/138; Am Leg Boys St; Computer Clb; Quiz Bowl; Red Cross Aide; SADD; Nwsp Rptr; Yrbk Rptr; Hon Roll; NHS; Rep Frsh Cls; Blk & White Awd 84; Cent III Ldrshp Scholar 85; U MD College Park; Mech Engrng.

ADDISON, TRACEY; Westminster HS; Westminster, MD; (Y); Church Yth Grp; Cmnty Wkr; VP Jr Cls; High Hon Roll; NHS; Bio.

ADERHOLD, BRUCE; Thomas Stone HS; Waldorf, MD; (Y); 61/288; Jazz Band; Mrchg Band; Pep Band; School Musical; Hon Roll; All Cnty Hnrs Band 84-86; Tri Cnty Hnrs Band 84-86; Lions Clb Band 84-86; Charles Cnty CC; Comp Sci.

ADILSOLTANI, FARHAD; Friendly HS; Ft Washington, MD; (Y); Teachers Aide; NHS; PG CC; Dntstry.

ADKINS, JAMES; Parkside HS; Pittsville, MD; (Y); Cmnty Wkr; Exploring; Teachers Aide; High Hon Roll; Berlin Middle Schl.

ADKINS, SCOTT THOMAS; Eleanor Roosevelt HS; Laurel, MD; (Y); 4-H; Teachers Aide; 4-H Awd; High Hon Roll; NHS; Ntl Merit Ltr; Natl JR Hrtcltr Assn Judg Cntst Natl Champ 85; OH ST Ag Merit Schlrshp 86; Pres Acdmc Fit Awd 86; OH ST U; Plnt Prtctn.

ADKINS, TRACEY; Stephen Decatur HS; Ocean City, MD; (Y); Church Yth Grp; Am Leg Boys St; Library Aide; Yrbk Bus Mgr; Yrbk Stf; Stu Cncl; Hon Roll; Schltc Achvt Awd 85-86; Accntng Clrk 86; FBLA-BUS Math II-1ST Pl 86; Salisbury ST Coll; Accntng.

ADLER, JONATHAN; Palmudecal Acad; Baltimore, MD; (S); Varsity Clb; Nwsp Ed-Chief; Lit Mag; Pres Frsh Cls; Var Capt Bsktbl; Hon Roll; NEDT Awd; Youthline Writer-Local Newspaper; Johns Hopluns; Lawyer.

AFANASIEFF, LISA ELIZAVETA; Immaculata College HS; Potomac, MD; (Y); JA; Trs Spanish Clb; Church Choir; Variety Show; VP Jr Cls; Pres Stu Cncl; Mgr(s); Var Socr; JV Tennis; High Hon Roll; Bio.

AGNES, MATTHEW; Randallstown SR HS; Randallstown, MD; (Y); 10/500; Boy Scts; Church Yth Grp; Rep Stu Cncl; Capt Ftbl; Capt Lcrss; High Hon Roll; NHS; Ntl Merit Ltr; Opt Clb Awd; Air Force ROTC Schlrp 86; Cornell U; Aerospc Engrg.

AGRAFIOTIS, AMY; Parkdale HS; New Carrollton, MD; (Y); Sec AFS; Church Yth Grp; Pep Clb; Chorus; Drill Tm; School Musical; Ed Yrbk Stf; Trs Sr Cls; Stat Bsbl; Hon Roll; Schl Ltr 86; U MD; Psych.

AGUILERA, MARIA CARMEN; Paint Branch HS; Silver Spring, MD; (Y); 98/387; Church Yth Grp; 4-H; Sec Stu Cncl; 4-H Awd; Hon Roll; Acadmc Ftns Awd 86; Stephens Coll; Elem Ed.

AIREY, KATHLEEN; Northern HS; Huntingtown, MD; (Y); Dance Clb; Gov Hon Prg Awd; High Hon Roll; Hon Roll; NHS; Ntl Merit Schol; Pres Schlr; Treas Ntl Hnr Soc 86-87; MD Sci Symp 83-87; Olympics Mind 85-86; Vet.

AKERS, JEFF; North Harford HS; Jarrettsville, MD; (Y); Church Yth Grp; FTA; Spanish Clb; Teachers Aide; Varsity Clb; Bsktbl; Socr; High Hon Roll; Hon Roll; NHS; Engr For A Day Awd 86; VA Tech; Elec Engrng.

AKERS, MICHELLE R; Eleanor Roosevelt HS; Landover, MD; (Y); Sec Church Yth Grp; Dance Clb; Girl Scts; Variety Show; Yrbk Ed-Chief; Yrbk Stf; Hon Roll; Ntl Merit Ltr; Pep Clb; Teachers Aide; Ntl Achvt Schlrshp Comptn Semifnlst 86; P G Cnty Sci & Tech H S Pgm 82-86; Intl Stds.

AKINS, DEANNA; Surrattsville HS; Clinton, MD; (Y); Am Leg Aux Girls St; French Clb; Pep Clb; Lit Mag; Stu Cncl; Crs Cntry; Hon Roll; Med.

AKINS, MONICA; Forestville HS; Capitol Heights, MD; (Y); Office Aide; Teachers Aide; Rep Frsh Cls; Var Crs Cntry; Im Gym; Capt Trk; Cit Awd; Hon Roll; NHS; Pres Schlr; Acdmc Exclnc Awd 84-85; Stu Of Mnth 86; OH U; Pre-Law.

AKIYAMA, TARO; T S Wootton HS; Gaithersburg, MD; (Y); Mathletes; Math Tm; Orch; Tennis; Hon Roll; NHS; Grand Prze Mntgmry Cnty Sci Fair 85; Yth Schlrs Inst Lebanon Vly Coll 86; Mntgmry Cnty Yth Orch 85-86; Harvard U; Med.

ALBERDING, TERESA; Montgomery Blair/Northwood HS; Silver Spring, MD; (Y); 81/399; French Clb; Letterman Clb; Office Aide; Teachers Aide; Temple Yth Grp; Varsity Clb; VP Jr Cls; Capt Socr; Bausch & Lomb Sci Awd; Hon Roll; U Of MD College Park.

ALBERT, KIMBERLY S; Boonsboro HS; Boonsboro, MD; (Y); Teachers Aide; Varsity Clb; Band; Variety Show; Yrbk Ed-Chief; Yrbk Phtg; Yrbk Rptr; Yrbk Stf; Rep Frsh Cls; Rep Soph Cls; Radford U; Bus Adm.

ALBERTS, NOREEN M; Edgewood HS; Edgewood, MD; (Y); 9/199; Art Clb; Church Yth Grp; Girl Scts; Science Clb; Spanish Clb; Teachers Aide; Chorus; Cheerleading; High Hon Roll; NHS; Harford CC Hons Schlrshp 86-87; Presdntl Acadmc Fitness Awd 86; Acadmc Lttr 86; Harford CC; Engrng.

ALBERTSON, RHONDA; Great Mills HS; Lex Pk, MD; (Y); Church Yth Grp; Cmnty Wkr; Computer Clb; Library Aide; Spanish Clb; Teachers Aide; Church Choir; Var Capt Crs Cntry; Var Capt Trk; High Hon Roll; Coches Awd Trk; Shrthand I Awd 85; MVP Cross Cntry & All SMAC 85; Bonne Bell Crs Cntry 85; PA ST; Bus Admin.

ALDER, JOHN; Mount Saint Joseph HS; Baltimore, MD; (S); NHS; Prfct Atten Awd; Acdmc Schlrshp 83; Physcs.

ALDERSON JR, MICHAEL; Great Mills HS; Lexington Park, MD; (Y); Church Yth Grp; Cmnty Wkr; DECA; Var JV Wrstlng; Hon Roll; Tri County Resources Conservation Dept Of Envrnmntl Cmap Schlrshp 85; Business.

ALDERTON, LINDA; Bishop Walsh HS; Cumberland, MD; (Y); Cmnty Wkr; Hosp Aide; Office Aide; Hon Roll.

ALDRIDGE, MARK; Great Mills HS; Lexington Park, MD; (Y); English Clb; Office Aide; Pep Clb; Spanish Clb; Capt Bsktbl; Hon Roll; Bus.

ALEXANDER, ANGIE; La Plata HS; Bryantown, MD; (Y); Church Yth Grp; FHA; Science Clb; Teachers Aide; Church Choir; Color Guard; Flag Corp; Yrbk Rptr; Hon Roll; U Of MD; Astro Engr.

ALEXANDER, BETH; Gwynn Park HS; Brandywine, MD; (S); Cmnty Wkr; Band; Chorus; Concert Band; Mrchg Band; Hon Roll; Cnty & St Solo & Ensmbl Fest I & II Rtng 85; Music.

ALEXANDER, DONALD; Bishop Walsh HS; La Vale, MD; (Y); Rep Sr Cls; Var L Bsbl; Var L Bsktbl; Var L Socr; High Hon Roll; NHS; Acadmc All Amer 85; James Madison U; Ec.

ALEXANDER, JEFFREY KIRK; Loch Raven SR HS; Baltimore, MD; (Y); AFS; Boy Scts; Church Yth Grp; Exploring; Model UN; Yrbk Stf; Trs Soph Cls; Rep Stu Cncl; High Hon Roll; Hon Roll; 1782 Scty Schlrshp 86; Bnfcl Hodson Trst Schlrshp 86; Outstndng Art Achvmnt 86; Gettysburg Coll; Pltcl Sci.

ALEXANDER, JENNIFER; Queen Anne HS; Ft Washington, MD; (Y); Cmnty Wkr; Dance Clb; Hosp Aide; Model UN; Pep Clb; Political Wkr; Ski Clb; Temple Yth Grp; Acpl Chr; Chorus; Congrssnl Yth Ldrs Conf 86; Intrn Congrssmn Captl Hill Pg MD ST Senate 86; Brdcst Jrnlst.

ALEXANDER, KATHY ANN M; Eleanor Roosevelt SR HS; Upper Marlboro, MD; (Y); Dance Clb; Pep Clb; Stage Crew; Ed Yrbk Stf; Var JV Powder Puff Ftbl; French Hon Soc; Jr NHS; NHS; French Clb; Teachers Aide; Awd For Outstndng Acdmc Achvt 85; Doctor.

ALEXANDER, MICHAEL E; Governor Thomas Johnson HS; Frederick, MD; (Y); 11/349; Church Yth Grp; Letterman Clb; Science Clb; Off Jr Cls; Co-Capt Tennis; High Hon Roll; Hon Roll; NHS; MD Acad Sci Intro Arch U MD 86; Extraord Stu Amer 85-86; Arch.

ALEXANDER, MICHELE; Great Mills HS; Leonardtown, MD; (Y); Pres 4-H; Pep Clb; Spanish Clb; SADD; 4-H Awd; Nmrs Chmpnshp Awds Wstrn & Englsh Eqstrn Evnts 84; Mny Prsnl Awds Trng Hrses & Tchng Othrs Ride 85-86; Bus Adm.

ALFORD JR, MICHAEL J; Frederick HS; Frederick, MD; (Y); 20/360; Am Leg Boys St; Pres Computer Clb; JCL; VP Latin Clb; Math Tm; Scholastic Bowl; Science Clb; Teachers Aide; Hon Roll; NHS; Elec Engr.

ALFORD, STACY; Baltimore Polytechnic Inst; Baltimore, MD; (Y); Dance Clb; Girl Scts; Office Aide; Red Cross Aide; Rep Stu Cncl; Mgr(s); USAF; Computer Repair.

ALIFF JR, DAVID R; Maurice J Mc Donough HS; Pomfret, MD; (Y); Computer Clb; VICA; Band; Hon Roll; Prfct Atten Awd; Church Yth Grp; Concert Band; Jazz Band; Mrchg Band; Symp Band; Outstndng Post Carrier 81-84; All Am Yth Hnr Muscns 85; Edward Rorer Schlrshp 86; Skill Olympcs 86; Charles City CC; Electnc Tech.

ALIPIO, AMY; Immaculata College HS; Rockville, MD; (Y); Drama Clb; School Play; Stage Crew; Nwsp Ed-Chief; Nwsp Rptr; Lit Mag; Church Yth Grp; Cmnty Wkr; 4-H; French Clb; Cmmtns.

ALLEN, ALICIA; Hammond HS; Columbia, MD; (Y); Am Leg Aux Girls St; Art Clb; French Clb; Lcrss; Trk; NHS; Pres Schlr; Penn State; Engrng.

ALLEN, CHRISTOPHER; Northeast HS; North East, MD; (Y); 1/250; Church Yth Grp; Intnl Clb; Q&S; Pres Stu Cncl; Var L Tennis; Bausch & Lomb Sci Awd; VP NHS; Val; SADD; Teachers Aide; MD Distngshd Schlr Fnlst 86; SR Schlr/Athlt Awd 86; Franklin & Marshall Coll.

ALLEN, DALE EUGENE; Franklin HS; Owings Mls, MD; (Y); Boy Scts; Yrbk Sprt Ed; Off Jr Cls; Off Sr Cls; Var L Ftbl; Var L Lcrss; Var L Wrstlng; NHS; Am Leg Boys St; FBLA; Mryldn Bys ST Guidon 1st Pl Lgn Cty 85; NROTC Schlrshp 86; The Citadel; Cvl Engr.

ALLEN, DOUGLAS; Surrattsville HS; Clinton, MD; (Y); Office Aide; Teachers Aide; Yrbk Ed-Chief; Yrbk Stf; Hon Roll; NHS; Staff Achvt Awd Yrbk 85-86; Acad Exclnc Awd 84-87; Sci Fair Hnrb Mntn Awd 84-85; Pre-Med.

ALLEN, JEROME; Northern HS; Baltimore, MD; (Y); Dance Clb; Teachers Aide; Variety Show; Cit Awd; High Hon Roll; Hon Roll; Prfct Atten Awd; Chef.

ALLEN, RONALD W; Cambridge South-Dorchester HS; Cambridge, MD; (Y); Boy Scts; Church Yth Grp; Teachers Aide; Band; Mrchg Band; Symp Band; Var Capt Bsktbl; Var L Ftbl; Jr NHS; NHS; U Of MD; Accounting.

ALLGAIER, JONATHAN; Brunswick HS; Brunswick, MD; (Y); 150/300; Boy Scts; VP French Clb; Band; Concert Band; Jazz Band; Mrchg Band; Pep Band; Hon Roll; Dir Awd Mst Imprvd Band 85; Arch.

ALLISON, BRENDA; Thomas Wootton HS; Gaithersburg, MD; (Y); Church Yth Grp; Drama Clb; Ski Clb; SADD; Lit Mag; Tennis; Trk; Cit Awd; Hon Roll; Ntl Merit SF; Med Dr.

ALLISON, CRYSTAL; Parkville HS; Parkville, MD; (Y); Church Yth Grp; Jazz Band; Var Capt Bsktbl; Var Sftbl; Var Capt Vllybl; High Hon Roll; NHS; Key Clb; Band; Church Choir; 2nd Team All Cnty Vlybl 85-86; 1st Team All Cnty 1st Base Sftbl Team 84-85; Hnrb Mntn All Cnty Bsktbl.

ALOUPIS, SOPHIA; Thomas Stone HS; Waldorf, MD; (Y); Church Yth Grp; Office Aide; Yrbk Phtg; Yrbk Stf; Rep Sr Cls; Rep Stu Cncl; Hon Roll; Towson; Law.

ALSTON, ANGELA J; La Reine HS; Capital Heights, MD; (Y); 3/175; JA; SADD; Varsity Clb; Band; Yrbk Rptr; Var Capt Bsktbl; Var L Trk; Var Vllybl; High Hon Roll; NHS; Schlr Athl Awd 84-85; MD Dist Schlr 85; Comp Engr.

ALSTON, MARK E; Woodlawn HS; Baltimore, MD; (Y); Band; School Musical; Ftbl; Trk; Prfct Atten Awd; MVP JV Ftbl 84; U MD; Engr.

ALSTON, THOMAS; Crossland HS; Capital Hgts, MD; (Y); Teachers Aide; Hon Roll; U MD; Elctrnc Engr.

ALT, MELISSA; Westminster HS; Westminster, MD; (Y); Church Yth Grp; Varsity Clb; Band; Church Choir; Concert Band; Mrchg Band; Orch; Pep Band; Symp Band; JV Trk; ST Solo Ensmbl II Plyng Flute 86; Al-Cnty Band Flute 84; Fnlst Ms Tn MD Pgnt ST 86; Comps.

ALTON, JAQUETTA; Western SR HS; Baltimore, MD; (Y); Art Clb; PAVAS; Med.

ALTOZ, ELIZABETH; Archbishop Keough HS; Baltimore, MD; (Y); Cmnty Wkr; Hosp Aide; Chorus; Var Cheerleading; Hon Roll; Elem Educ.

ALVAREZ, PETER; Laurel HS; Laurel, MD; (Y); Im Sftbl; Im Vllybl; Capt Var Wrstlng; High Hon Roll; Hon Roll; NHS; Spanish NHS; Harvard Bk Awd 85; Margaret A Myerly Schrlshp Awd 86; Am Leg Schl Awd 86; Clemson U; Engrng.

ALVAREZ, VINCENT; Gaithersburg HS; Gaithersburg, MD; (Y); 119/528; Aud/Vis; Cmnty Wkr; Library Aide; Science Clb; Ski Clb; Swmmng; Jr NHS; NHS; GA Tech; Aero Engrng.

ALVEY, TROY; Chopticon HS; Clements, MD; (Y).

AMA, LYNNETTE; Bowie HS; Bowie, MD; (Y); Intnl Clb; Office Aide; Hon Roll; Masonic Awd; Bowie Sci Fair Hon Mntn 86; MD U; Crmnlgy.

AMAYA, MARITZA; Albert Einstein HS; Silver Spring, MD; (Y); Teachers Aide; Drill Tm; Yrbk Stf; Pom Pon; Svc Awd 85-86; Montgomery Coll Scholar 85-86; Mst Mentionabl Art Object 84-85; U MD; Phys Thrpy.

AMBEY, TERESA; Carver Vocational HS; Baltimore, MD; (Y); Camera Clb; FBLA; Chorus; NHS; Perfect Attendance Awd 87; Hnr Roll 83; Secretry.

AMBURGEY, ALISHA; Laplata HS; Bryantown, MD; (Y); Am Leg Aux Girls St; Church Yth Grp; Jr Cls; Sr Cls; Bsktbl; Crs Cntry; Pom Pon; Trk; Hon Roll; Audiology.

AMELI-TEHRANI, ROSHANAK; Gaithersburg HS; Gaithersburg, MD; (Y); 36/568; AFS; Yrbk Ed-Chief; Socr; Trk; Hon Roll; Mntgmry Awd Wrtng 84; Mntgmry Ldrshp Awd 86; Mntgmry Achvmnt Awd Jrnlsmn 86; U Of Maryland; Lawyer.

AMIRYZYAN, GEMMA; Laurel HS; Laurel, MD; (Y); Intnl Clb; Outstndg Achvt Frnch 85-86; Langs.

AMOROSI, MARK; Landon Schl; Potomac, MD; (S); Cmnty Wkr; Pres Band; Pres Jazz Band; Pres Frsh Cls; Pres Soph Cls; Pres Jr Cls; Pres Stu Cncl; JV Bsbl; JV Capt Ftbl; Hon Roll.

AMOS, MELISSA L; Linganore HS; Ijamsville, MD; (Y); 10/295; FCA; Hosp Aide; School Musical; Trs Frsh Cls; Trs Soph Cls; Capt Cheerleading; JC Awd; NHS; Frederick Cnty JR Miss 87; Intrnshp Mayor Yng Frederick Cty 85; Stu Rep Brd Of Ed 85-86; Envrnmntl Law.

AMYX, JENNIFER; Walkersville HS; Woodsboro, MD; (Y); 1/250; Computer Clb; FCA; Scholastic Bowl; Orch; Pres Soph Cls; Pres Jr Cls; VP Sr Cls; VP Stu Cncl; High Hon Roll; NHS; 9 St Chmpnshps Cross Cntry, Indoor Track, Outdoor Track 84-86; Acdmc All Amer 86; Japan Schlrshp 86; Math.

ANASTASSOPOULOS, ANDREAS N; Good Counsel HS; Olney, MD; (Y); 8/217; Chess Clb; Drama Clb; French Clb; Pres Math Clb; Math Tm; School Play; Im Mgr Bsktbl; Im Mgr Ftbl; Im Mgr Vllybl; NHS; Engrng.

ANDERSCH, LISA; Hammond HS; Columbia, MD; (Y); German Clb; Frsh Cls; Soph Cls; Jr Cls; JV Var Bsktbl; Var Socr; Var Sftbl; Var Trk; Female Athlt Of Yr 84-86; Business.

ANDERSON, AMANDA; Maurice J Mc Donough HS; Waldorf, MD; (Y); Cmnty Wkr; Q&S; Pres Thesps; School Musical; School Play; Stage Crew; Nwsp Ed-Chief; Rep Stu Cncl; Cit Awd; High Hon Roll.

ANDERSON, BETH; Parkdale HS; New Carrollton, MD; (Y); Latin Clb; Teachers Aide; Chorus; Off Frsh Cls; Off Soph Cls; Off Jr Cls; Pres Sr Cls; Var Sftbl; Var Swmmng; Hon Roll; Handbell Choir; Spcl Educ.

ANDERSON, BETH; Patapsco HS; Baltimore, MD; (Y); Art Clb; Camera Clb; Symp Band; JV Bsktbl; JV Lcrss; Hon Roll; MD Inst Art; Commercial.

ANDERSON, CATHRYN; Leonardtown HS; Leonardtown, MD; (Y); VP Church Yth Grp; Hosp Aide; Letterman Clb; Teachers Aide; Band; Madrigals; Mrchg Band; School Musical; School Play; Swing Chorus; Mst Imprvd Band 84-85; ID ST U; Music Ed.

ANDERSON II, DONALD T; Gwynn Park SR HS; Clinton, MD; (Y); Church Yth Grp; Cmnty Wkr; SADD; Varsity Clb; Church Choir; Rep Stu Cncl; Bsktbl; Ftbl; Wt Lftg; Cit Awd; Cert Awd Nu Zeta Omega Chptr Recgntn 85; MD ST Sentrl Schlrshp 86; Salisbury ST Coll; Elect Engr.

ANDERSON, HEIDI; Glenelg HS; Mt Airy, MD; (Y); Pres Church Yth Grp; 4-H; Key Clb; Teachers Aide; Church Choir; Variety Show; 4-H Awd; Prfct Atten Awd; Accntng.

ANDERSON, KAREN L; Notre Dame Prep; Monkton, MD; (Y); 20/119; Church Yth Grp; Hon Roll; NHS; Germn NHS 84-86; VA Tech; Vet Med.

ANDERSON, KARI; Highland View Acad; Frederick, MD; (Y); Band; Nwsp Sprt Ed; Yrbk Ed-Chief; Yrbk Stf; Sec Jr Cls; Var L Bsktbl; Var L Vllybl; High Hon Roll; Prfct Atten Awd; Acad All-Amer 85-86; Comm.

ANDERSON, KATHRYN; Mount De Sales Acad; Baltimore, MD; (Y); Church Yth Grp; Drama Clb; School Musical; School Play; Hon Roll; Archry Excllnc, Swmng Excllnc; Apprctn Art 86; Vet Sci.

ANDERSON, KATHY; Montgomery Blair HS; Silver Spring, MD; (Y); 98/357; Drama Clb; Office Aide; Thesps; Chorus; Church Choir; Madrigals; School Musical; School Play; Stage Crew; American U; Cmmnctns.

ANDERSON, KIRSTEN; Friendly SR HS; Ft Washington, MD; (Y); 60/367; Letterman Clb; PAVAS; Stage Crew; Variety Show; Sec Frsh Cls; Rep Jr Cls; Rep Stu Cncl; Var Capt Trk; High Hon Roll; Hon Roll; Hall Of Fme Grls Outdr Trck 86; 1st Rnnr Up Mss Debutnt 86; Eastern Kentucky U; Crpte Law.

ANDERSON, LAKESHIA; Oakland Mills HS; Columbia, MD; (Y); Church Yth Grp; Civic Clb; Cmnty Wkr; Dance Clb; ROTC; Teachers Aide; Church Choir; School Musical; Sftbl; Hon Roll; Peabody Inst Of John Hopkins 84; Hampton Inst; Music.

ANDERSON, LAURIE; Archbishop Keough HS; Baltimore, MD; (Y); 3/225; Church Yth Grp; Drama Clb; NFL; Speech Tm; Thesps; School Play; Lit Mag; Gov Hon Prg Awd; NHS; Ntl Merit Ltr; Aid Assn Lthrns All Coll Schlrshp 86-87; Vassar Coll Schlrshp 86-87; Smth Coll Grnt 86-87; Vassar Coll; Wrtr.

ANDERSON, MARK; Fairmont Heights HS; Landover Hills, MD; (Y); Intnl Clb; JA; Pep Clb; Quiz Bowl; Band; Concert Band; Symp Band; Stu Cncl; Im Bsktbl; Cit Awd; Awd Outstndng Achvt Arch 86; Prfct Attnd Awd 83; Prince Georges CC; Comp Pgmng.

ANDERSON, MAXWELL; Cardinal Gibbons HS; Baltimore, MD; (Y); 32/141; Chess Clb; Church Yth Grp; Computer Clb; Quiz Bowl; Church Choir; Rep Frsh Cls; Var L Bsktbl; JV Capt Socr; French Hon Soc; Svc Awd 86; C Markland Kelly Jr Athltc Svc Awd 86; Baltimore City Acad; Firefghtr.

ANDERSON, RICHARD; Takoma Acad; Takoma Park, MD; (S); Office Aide; VP Orch; Yrbk Stf; VP Jr Cls; JV Bsktbl; Var Trk; NHS; Most Outstndng Am Lit,Bio,World Hist Stu Yr 84-85; Sci.

ANDERSON, SCOTT; Thomas Stone HS; Waldorf, MD; (S); Chess Clb; Math Clb; Math Tm; Science Clb; Golf; Hon Roll; NHS; Prfct Atten Awd; Olmpcs Of Mnd Comptr Compttn 2nd Pl Wrlds Fnls & MD ST Champ 85; Engr.

ANDREW, GOULET; John Carroll HS; Aberdeen, MD; (Y); Debate Tm; NFL; Nwsp Ed-Chief; Yrbk Stf; French Hon Soc; High Hon Roll; NHS; Church Yth Grp; Quiz Bowl; Speech Tm; Full Scholar Jrnlsm U MD 85; Harford Law Day Wrtg Cont 86; MD Nrs Assn Teen Hlth Essay Cont Awd 85; Hstry.

ANDREW, JOHN; St Michaels Senior HS; Easton, MD; (Y); 6/66; Am Leg Boys St; Pres Chess Clb; Jazz Band; Nwsp Stf; Yrbk Phtg; Rep Stu Cncl; Var Socr; L Tennis; Capt Wrstlng; Model UN; Hugh O Brian Yth Fndtn 85; Engrng.

ANDREW, SHERRI; Catoctin HS; Emmitsburg, MD; (Y); Boy Scts; Red Cross Aide; Science Clb; VICA; Color Guard; Hon Roll; Cert Of Achvt Nrsng Assist Cert 86; HOSA ST Comptn 3rd Pl Wnnr First Aid/CPR 86; Nrs.

ANDREWS, ERIC; Fort Hill HS; Cumberland, MD; (Y); Wt Lftg; Hon Roll; Hnr Rl 84; Frostburg ST Coll; Bio.

ANDREWS, MICHELE; Ft Hill HS; Cumberland, MD; (S); 1/252; Trs 4-H; Thesps; Concert Band; Jazz Band; School Musical; Yrbk Bus Mgr; 4-H Awd; NHS; NEDT Awd; MD Distngshd Schlr 85; Cumberland Music & Arts Clb Schlrshp 84; Bst Sprtng Actress 84; WV U; Elec Engrng.

ANDREWS, RACHEL; Fort Hill HS; Cumberland, MD; (Y); Church Yth Grp; Cmnty Wkr; Sec Chorus; Church Choir; Concert Band; Mrchg Band; Orch; NHS; School Play; Rep Frsh Cls; Ctznshp Awd 85; Cert Ed Devlpmnt Natl 83; Flute Perfrmnce.

ANDREWS, RANETTA; Western HS; Baltimore, MD; (Y); 114/400; Cmnty Wkr; Dance Clb; Teachers Aide; Mrchg Band; Hon Roll; Accntng.

ANDREWS, RAYMOND; Potomac HS; Fort Washington, MD; (Y); Letterman Clb; Varsity Clb; L Var Bsbl; Capt L Ftbl; Im Wt Lftg; Hon Roll; All Cntyt LB 85-86; Tm Dvnsv MVP 85-86; Hon Men Bsbl 85-86.

ANDREWS, SEAN; Northern HS; Baltimore, MD; (Y); Outstndg Achvt Vo Tech 85-86; Vo Tech Stu Of Yr Awd 85-86; Cert Awd Wrk Stdy 85-86; USAF; Elec Syst.

ANDREWS, SUSAN; Oldfields Schl; Nashville, TN; (Y); 10/50; Varsity Clb; Pres Acpl Chr; Pres Frsh Cls; Pres Soph Cls; Pres Jr Cls; Pres Stu Cncl; Var Bsktbl; Lcrss; Pres Chorus; Church Choir; J T Brennan Prz 85; Polvogt Prz 86.

ANG, CHRISTINE MARIE; Academy Of The Holy Cross; Ashton, MD; (Y); 20/123; Art Clb; Hosp Aide; Spanish Clb; Nwsp Stf; Yrbk Stf; Sec Frsh Cls; Sec Soph Cls; Hon Roll; NHS; Spanish NHS; U Of DE; Acctng.

ANTHONY, CHRISTINE; Milford Mill SR HS; Balt, MD; (Y); Hon Roll; Acctng.

ANTHONY, STEWART; Sparrows Point SR HS; Baltimore, MD; (Y); Var Capt Bsbl; Var Socr; Wt Lftg; High Hon Roll; Hon Roll; All Cnty 1st, 2nd Tm Bsbl 85-86; Bus.

ANTLITZ, JOYCE; Chesapeake HS; Pasadena, MD; (Y); French Clb; FBLA; OEA; Teachers Aide; Yrbk Ed-Chief; Hon Roll; Dept Defense Awd 86; Ltr Apprctn Dept Defense 85; Anne Arundel CC; Bus.

ANTOINE, ROMY I; Stone Rdg Cntry Dy Schl Of The Scrd Hrt; Silver Spring, MD; (Y); Church Yth Grp; French Clb; Hosp Aide; Pres VP Leo Clb; Speech Tm; Chorus; Lit Mag; Med.

ANTONAKAS, ANTHONY; Mt St Joseph HS; Columbia, MD; (Y); Church Yth Grp; Computer Clb; Drama Clb; Quiz Bowl; School Play; Stage Crew; Hon Roll; UMBC; Engr.

ANTONOVICH, CARIN; La Reine HS; Clinton, MD; (Y); VP Church Yth Grp; Mgr Drama Clb; JA; Band; Concert Band; Mgr School Musical; Stage Crew; Nwsp Rptr; Lit Mag; Coach Actv; MD U; Pilot.

APOLITO, ADRIANA M; Regina HS; Adelphi, MD; (Y); 1/62; Yrbk Phtg; Yrbk Stf; Sec Frsh Cls; Trs Jr Cls; L Tennis; Bausch & Lomb Sci Awd; High Hon Roll; NHS; Ntl Merit SF; NEDT Awd; MD Distinguished Scholar Finalist 85; Geico Family Scholars Shclrshp 86; Tufts University Schlrshp 86; Tufts U; Engrng.

APPEL, ERIK; Dulaney SR HS; Glen Arm, MD; (Y); Church Yth Grp; JA; Natl Beta Clb; Concert Band; Jazz Band; Mrchg Band; Orch; High Hon Roll; U Of VA; Aerosp Engrng.

APPELT, GARTH; Loyola HS; Baltimore, MD; (Y); Chess Clb; Church Yth Grp; FCA; French Clb; JA; Model UN; SADD; Varsity Clb; Lit Mag; Off Frsh Cls.

APPERSON, CHERYL; Maurice J Mc Donough HS; La Plata, MD; (S); Chorus; Madrigals; School Musical; School Play; Swing Chorus; Symp Band; Variety Show; Rep Jr Cls; Jr NHS; NHS; Hghst Rtg ST & Dstrct Solo & Ensmbl 84-85.

ARAUJO, AUGUSTO; Walter Johnson HS; Bethesda, MD; (Y); Hosp Aide; Im Bsbl; Im Bsktbl; Var Capt Socr; Im Sftbl; High Hon Roll; Hon Roll; MD; Dentistry.

ARAUJO, LIZA MICHELLE; Juppatonwe HS; Edgewood, MD; (Y); Aud/Vis; Drama Clb; Chorus; Church Choir; Variety Show; Sftbl; High Hon Roll; Howard U; Psych.

ARBAUGH, MICHELE; Westminster SR HS; Westminster, MD; (Y); Hosp Aide; Office Aide; Ski Clb; Teachers Aide; Chorus; Swing Chorus; Stu Cncl; Var Capt Cheerleading; JV Trk; Hon Roll; Hmcmng Crt 85-86; Sec Of Chorus 85-86; Frostburg ST; Elem Ed.

ARCA, LORRAINE; Archbishop Keough HS; Baltimore, MD; (Y); 2/220; Church Yth Grp; Hosp Aide; Sec Thesps; Chorus; Yrbk Stf; Stu Cncl; Var Capt Cheerleading; Gym; Hon Roll; Church Choir; LIFE Grp; Cmnty Sftbl Trvlng Tm; Peer Facilitator Pgm; Soc Wkr.

ARCHER, ERIC; Grace Brethren HS; Temple Hills, MD; (S); Aud/Vis; Camera Clb; Church Yth Grp; Computer Clb; Science Clb; Teachers Aide; Yrbk Phtg; Lit Mag; Ntl Merit Ltr; Outstndng Negro Stu 85; Bio Awd 83; William & Mary; Marine Bio.

ARCHER, FREDERICK I; Grace Brethren Christian HS; Temple Hills, MD; (Y); Chess Clb; Church Yth Grp; Teachers Aide; Stat Bsbl; Hon Roll; Ntl Merit Ltr; Top Bio Stu In Class 82; Outstndng Negro Stu 85; Coll Of Atlantic; Mrn Bio.

ARCHER, THOMAS; Walter Johnson HS; Kensington, MD; (Y); Debate Tm; Pres Jr Cls; Socr; Trk; Dnfth Awd; High Hon Roll; Pres NHS; NFL; Hugh O Brian Yth Ldrshp Fndtn 85; Prncpls Wrtng Awd 86; Marin Bio.

ARCHIBALD, ISABEL MARIA; Washington HS; Westover, MD; (Y); 1/130; Am Leg Aux Girls St; Ski Clb; Thesps; School Play; Stu Cncl; Var Tennis; High Hon Roll; NHS; Rotary Awd; Cmmrcl Art.

ARCIAGA, CYNTHIA; Notre Dame Prep; Timonium, MD; (Y); Model UN; Rep Frsh Cls; Rep Soph Cls; Rep Jr Cls; Stu Cncl; Var JV Lcrss; Cmnty Wkr; Pep Clb; SADD; Chorus; Intl Rel.

ARFAA, BABAK E; John Carroll HS; Bel Air, MD; (Y); Orch; School Musical; School Play; Variety Show; Rep Jr Cls; Rep Sr Cls; Im Tennis; French Hon Soc; All ST Orch Violin I ST MD 84-86; Gift & Talent Smmr Ctr Goucher Coll 85-86; 1st Ratg ST MD Fstvl; Law.

ARGETAKIS, ANGELA; Patterson HS; Baltimore, MD; (Y); Math.

ARISTORENAS, AGNES; Seneca Valley HS; Germantown, MD; (Y); Yrbk Stf; Vllybl; U Of MD.

ARMEL, ROBERT; North Hartford HS; Forest Hill, MD; (Y); Hon Roll; Ntl Merit SF; Bus.

ARMSHAW, MICHELE; Hammond HS; Columbia, MD; (Y); 100/270; Church Yth Grp; Drama Clb; PAVAS; Speech Tm; School Musical; School Play; Stage Crew; Variety Show; Ed Yrbk Stf; Var Capt Cheerleading; Acad All Amer 84-86; Natl Chrldng Cmptn 84-86; U Of Steubenville; Comm.

ARMSTRONG, ERICA; Fort Hill HS; Cumberland, MD; (Y); Sec 4-H; Thesps; Band; Chorus; Drm Mjr(t); Swing Chorus; Sec Soph Cls; Var L Tennis; Jr NHS; NEDT Awd; Cumberland Music & Arts Schlrshp 85; Dstngshd Schlr Talent Arts Nom 86; U Of MD; Music Educ.

ARMSTRONG, KATIE; Fairmont Heights HS; Hyattsville, MD; (Y); Church Yth Grp; Computer Clb; Trs FBLA; Yrbk Stf; High Hon Roll; Hon Roll; Jr NHS; NHS; Comp Prgmr.

ARNOLD, GEORGE; Allegany HS; Lavale, MD; (Y); 13/220; Debate Tm; Band; Concert Band; Jazz Band; Mrchg Band; Yrbk Phtg; Yrbk Stf; Frsh Cls; Soph Cls; Jr Cls; Giftd Talntd Camps 84-85; WV U; Bus.

ARNOLD, GINA; Walter Johnson HS; Waldorf, MD; (Y); Var Bsktbl; Var Fld Hcky; Var Sftbl; Hon Roll; Charles County CC; Bus Mgt.

ARONSON, SAMUEL; Thomas Wooton HS; Gaithersburg, MD; (Y); Pres Debate Tm; NFL; Teachers Aide; Trs Temple Yth Grp; High Hon Roll; Hon Roll; NHS; Ntl Merit Ltr; Natl Fornsc Leag Ruby 85; Fnlst Natl Catholc Frnsc Lag 86; Yth Schlrs Prog Microb And Gentcs 86.

ARVIN, CHRISTIE; Williamsport HS; Hagerstown, MD; (Y); 33/227; Drama Clb; Ski Clb; Spanish Clb; Teachers Aide; Rep Jr Cls; Rep Sr Cls; JV Var Cheerleading; Capt Powder Puff Ftbl; Score Keeper; Hon Roll; Hagerstown JC; Flght Attndt.

ASCOSI JR, JOHN; De Matha HS; Silver Spring, MD; (Y); Political Wkr; Science Clb; Service Clb; Ski Clb; Teachers Aide; Y-Teens; High Hon Roll; Hon Roll; Prfct Atten Awd; Catholic U; Engrng.

ASH, DAVID; Pikesville HS; Owings, MD; (Y); FBLA; Science Clb; Ski Clb; Spanish Clb; Var Badmtn; JV Bsbl; Im Bsktbl; Var Mgr(s); Hon Roll; NHS; Bus.

ASHBROOK, KATHERINE; Gaithersburg HS; Gaithersburg, MD; (Y); Pres Boy Scts; Exploring; Library Aide; Ski Clb; Teachers Aide; Orch; Hon Roll; Gold Awd & Outstndng Achvt Trail Clb & Mr S Mordensky 84; Pricnpls Wrtng Awd Engl 86; Secndry Ed.

ASHFORD, ROSLYN; Springbrook HS; Silver Spring, MD; (Y); 139/488; Church Yth Grp; Library Aide; Teachers Aide; Rep Sr Cls; Var Cheerleading; L Pom Pon; Trk; Hon Roll; Natl Lat Exam 83; Magna Cum Laude 84; Cum Laude; Bus Comp.

ASHLEY, BRANT F; Washington HS; Allen, MD; (Y); Am Leg Boys St; Boys Clb Am; Chess Clb; Church Yth Grp; Computer Clb; 4-H; Ski Clb; Band; Chorus; Church Choir; Physcn.

ASHRUF, SAMIA; Archbishop Keogh Schl; Baltimore, MD; (Y); #2 In Class; French Clb; High Hon Roll; Hon Roll; NHS; MD Dstngshd Schlr Awd 86; Loyla Coll Presdntl Schlrshp 86; H S Relgn Awd 86; Loyola Coll; Bio.

ASHRUF, SUMERA; Archbishop Keough HS; Baltimore, MD; (Y); French Clb; Hon Roll; Prfct Atten Awd; George Washington U Schl Of Engrng & Appld Sci Engrng Mdl 86; Hist.

ASHWOOD, JENNIFER; Institute Of Notre Dame HS; Baltimore, MD; (Y); Service Clb; Rep Frsh Cls; Sec Soph Cls; Pres Sr Cls; Hon Roll; NHS; Part Schlrshp To IN 84-87.

ASKEW, LINDA; Rockville HS; Rockville, MD; (S); VP JA; Ed Nwsp Rptr; Ed Lit Mag; Co-Capt Var Socr; Var Capt Trk; JV Vllybl; Hon Roll; U AL Minority Jrnlsm Wrkshp Scholar 85; U MD College Pk; Jrnlsm.

ASLAM, SHEZANA; Archbishop Keough HS; Baltimore, MD; (Y); Cmnty Wkr; Spanish Clb; Hon Roll; Acdmc Achvt Awd Coll Notre Dame 86; Coll Of Notre Dame; Bus.

ASPLEN, NANCY; Cambridge-South Dorchester HS; Cambridge, MD; (Y); 2/300; AFS; School Musical; Variety Show; Nwsp Stf; Yrbk Stf; Pom Pon; Jr NHS; Stage Band Vocalist 84-85; Tlntd & Gftd Pgm; Bus.

ASUNCION, JOANNE; Queen Anne Schl; Cheverly, MD; (Y); 1/30; VP Symp Band; Ed Lit Mag; Rep Stu Cncl; Var Capt Bsktbl; Var Socr; Var Sftbl; High Hon Roll; Lion Awd; Cum Laude Soc 85-86.

ATKINSON, TOBI; Western SR High Schl No HS; Baltimore, MD; (Y); Church Yth Grp; Dance Clb; German Clb; Acpl Chr; School Musical; Mayors Rsltn 86; U MD Balto County; Acctnt.

ATLEE, CANDIS; Lackey HS; Bryans Rd, MD; (Y); Dance Clb; Intnl Clb; Spanish Clb; SADD; Chorus; Rep Stu Cncl; JV Var Cheerleading; Stat Trk; Prfct Atten Awd; VFW Awd.

ATTIAS, STEVEN; Boys School Latin; Lutherville, MD; (Y); 11/55; Church Yth Grp; Cmnty Wkr; Dance Clb; Letterman Clb; Pep Clb; Varsity Clb; Pres Jr Cls; Pres Sr Cls; Pres Stu Cncl; Capt Bsbl; DAR 84; Barton Cup Ctznshp 85; Almn Awd Ldrshp & Char 86; Washington Coll; Psych.

ATWELL, JOHN; Chopticon HS; Charolette Hall, MD; (Y); Var Socr; Allc Nty Hon Mntn Sccr; Comp Tech.

AUCOIN, LYNN; Seneca Valley HS; Germantown, MD; (Y); 115/490; Drama Clb; Office Aide; Pep Clb; School Musical; School Play; Rep Jr Cls; Capt L Pom Pon; Hon Roll; Asst Make-Up Dsgnr & Chrprsn Of Make-Up Crew 86; E Carolina; Commnctns.

AUDI, STEVE; Capitol Christian Acad; Cheverly, MD; (Y); 5/22; Church Yth Grp; Office Aide; Band; Yrbk Stf; Jr Cls; Sr Cls; Bsbl; Socr; U MD.

AUKERMAN, MIRIAM; Westminster HS; Union Bridge, MD; (Y); 1/500; VP Church Yth Grp; Pres Latin Clb; Pres Political Wkr; Thesps; Orch; JV Crs Cntry; High Hon Roll; Drama Clb; Math Tm; Band; Telluride Schlr 86; Silv Mdls Natl Latin Exam 84 & 86; HOBY Fndtn Ambssdr 85; Med.

AUMAN, MATT; Parkside HS; Salisbury, MD; (Y); 1/275; Rep Stu Cncl; Var L Golf; Var L Wrstlng; Cit Awd; Hon Roll; NHS; Outstndng Perfrmr Awd Golf 83 & 85; Unsung Hero Awd Golf 84; Acad Ltr 85-86; Bus Adm.

AUSTIN, CESSILY; Bladensburg HS; Seat Plsnt, MD; (Y); Aud/Vis; Church Yth Grp; Library Aide; Office Aide; Science Clb; Teachers Aide; Rep Stu Cncl; Var L Bsktbl; Var L Vllybl; Hon Roll; Engrng.

AUSTIN, JOHN; Cardinal Gibbons HS; Baltimore, MD; (Y); 1/124; Drama Clb; Q&S; School Play; Stage Crew; Nwsp Rptr; Yrbk Ed-Chief; Trs Stu Cncl; Hon Roll; NHS; Top Spnsh Stu Spnsh I, II, III; Hgh Obrn Ldrshp Smnr; Schl Plys.

AUSTIN, VICTORIA; Laplata HS; La Plata, MD; (Y); Pres Church Yth Grp; Cmnty Wkr; Pres Science Clb; Rep Sr Cls; Cit Awd; DAR Awd; High Hon Roll; Ntl Merit Schol; VFW Awd; Voice Dem Awd; Jycee Amrcnsm Essy Awd 84; MD Modn Miss ST Finlst 85; Prncpls Awd Spnsh 86; Brigham Young U; Socl Sci.

AVARA, SUSAN; Notre Dame Prep; Cockeysville, MD; (Y); Camera Clb; Cmnty Wkr; Nwsp Phtg; Yrbk Phtg; Im Badmtn; Var Bowling; Im Fld Hcky; JV Swmmng; Hon Roll.

AVEY, VICKI; Fort Hill HS; Cumberland, MD; (S); Church Yth Grp; Office Aide; Capt Bsktbl; Var Crs Cntry; Var Trk; Hon Roll; NHS; MD Distngushd Schlr Hnrbl Ment 85; Won MD ST Cls A 1600 M Run Trck 85; Acctng.

AVIN, JACQUELYN; Sherwood HS; Ashton, MD; (Y); 13/317; Chorus; Ed Nwsp Rptr; Hon Roll; NHS; Spanish NHS; Mst Outstndng Stdnt 85-86; Merit Schlstc Awd 86; Pres Acdmc Fit Awd 86; Syracuse U; Publ Cmmnctns.

AWKWARD, AARON; Great Mills HS; Lex Pk, MD; (Y); Church Yth Grp; Debate Tm; Church Choir; Nwsp Stf; Lit Mag; Im Bsbl; Im Bsktbl; JV Trk; Hon Roll; Mst Dvtd Univ & Coll Opprtnty Clb 84; Vetrnrn Med.

AXLINE, JEFF; Brunswick HS; Knoxville, MD; (Y); 8/146; Pres Computer Clb; Church Choir; Concert Band; Mrchg Band; School Musical; Rep Stu Cncl; Var Bsbl; Var Socr; Hon Roll; Schl Lttr Grds & 1st Str Grds For Actvts & Attndnc 84-86; Hstry.

AYERS, ANGELA; Western HS; Baltimore, MD; (Y); 95/391; CAP; JA; Variety Show; Rep Jr Cls; Rep Sr Cls; High Hon Roll; U Of MD-BALTO Cnty; Bus Adm.

BABA, DENNIS; Gaithersburg HS; Gaithersburg, MD; (S); 27/630; Boy Scts; Science Clb; Orch; Hon Roll; FL Inst Of Technlgy; Physcs.

BABYLON, JON; Sherwood HS; Silver Spring, MD; (Y); Boy Scts; Church Yth Grp; Latin Clb; Var JV Socr; Hon Roll; NHS; Eagle Scout 86; ST Champs Soccr Div A 85; Kenyon Coll; Humanities.

BACHMAN, LAURA; Bethesda-Chevy Chase HS; Bethesda, MD; (Y); Chorus; Church Choir; DAR Awd; Hon Roll; Trinity Pres Schlrshp 86; Vanderbilt U; Law.

BACK, JOHN; Franklin HS; Reisterstown, MD; (Y); Boy Scts; Church Yth Grp; Debate Tm; Science Clb; Chorus; Tennis; Hon Roll; MD JR Sci Smpsm 86; Gftd & Tlntd Sci Smnrs 84-85; Mltry Of Wrld Wars Ldrshp Cnfrnc 86; Aerospace Engnr.

BADEN III, AUBREY G; Queen Anne Schl; Riva, MD; (Y); 7/41; Church Yth Grp; Drama Clb; Chorus; Church Choir; School Play; Nwsp Stf; High Hon Roll; Hon Roll; Drw Tdlr Awd Chrctr 86; Mtths Dsowa Fllwshp 86; Awds Drama, Vcl Music & Spnsh 86; St Marys Coll Of MD; Engl.

BADGER, CATHERINE; Lackey HS; Indian Head, MD; (Y); Drama Clb; Ski Clb; Teachers Aide; Variety Show; Yrbk Stf; Rep Stu Cncl; Cheerleading; Pom Pon; Hon Roll; Score Keeper; Cert Wrkng Spcl Olympcs 85; Mrt Awd Amrcn Automobile Assoc Pstr Cntst 86; Art.

BAER, DARCY; Northern HS; Chesapeake, MD; (Y); 1/300; Stage Crew; VP Jr Cls; VP Sr Cls; Fld Hcky; High Hon Roll; VP NHS; Pres Schlr; Val; MD Distngshd Schlr 86; Suprntndt Awd 86; FL ST U; Htl Mgmt.

BAER, DAVID; Takoma Acad; Adelphi, MD; (Y); Church Yth Grp; Im DECA; Im Ftbl; Im Socr; Hon Roll; NHS; CPA.

BAGLEY, BRENDAN J; Archbishop Spalding HS; Severn, MD; (Y); Am Leg Boys St; Church Yth Grp; School Musical; Pres Jr Cls; Pres Sr Cls; Var Capt Bsbl; Var Capt Ftbl; Drama Clb; Aud/Vis; Denise Alvarez Schlrshp 85-87; Mccrmck Usung Hero Ftbll Awd 85-86; U S Mltry Acad; Engnrng.

BAGLEY, DAVID; Dundalk HS; Baltimore, MD; (Y); Cmnty Wkr; JA; Latin Clb; Spanish Clb; Varsity Clb; Capt Var Bsktbl; Im Coach Actv; Im Wt Lftg; High Hon Roll; Hon Roll; Acad All Amer Awd 84-85; UMBC; Bus Admin.

BAGWELL, ANN NICOLE; Institute Of Notre Dame; Baltimore, MD; (Y); 17/105; Church Yth Grp; French Clb; FBLA; Hosp Aide; Yrbk Stf; Lit Mag; Sec Trs Jr Cls; JV Var Badmtn; Partl Schlrshp 82-86; Loyola College Balto; Jrnlsm.

BAGWELL, KIMBERLY; Wicomico SR HS; Salisbury, MD; (Y); 2/243; Am Leg Aux Girls St; Pres French Clb; Pres Band; Stu Cncl; Tennis; Elks Awd; NHS; Sal; Randolph-Macon Coll Pres Schlrshp 86-90; Randolph-Macon Coll; Financ.

BAHLMAN, LAUREN; Notre Dame Prep; Baltimore, MD; (Y); Boy Scts; Church Yth Grp; Exploring; Nwsp Rptr; Nwsp Stf; Lit Mag; Var Badmtn; U MD Coll Pk; Jrnlsm.

BAHRAINI, RAMINE; Georgetown Prep Schl; Potomac, MD; (Y); Cmnty Wkr; Drama Clb; Science Clb; Ski Clb; Thesps; School Musical; School Play; Stage Crew; High Hon Roll; Hon Roll; Drama.

BAIK, JENNIFER; Dulaney SR HS; Timonium, MD; (Y); Dance Clb; VP Key Clb; Model UN; PAVAS; SADD; Chorus; JV Trk; Hon Roll; Towson Balto MD Hstry Fair 85; Fshn Merch.

BAILE, JULIE; Westminster SR HS; Westminster, MD; (Y); 3/500; Drama Clb; Band; School Musical; High Hon Roll; NHS; Ntl Merit Ltr; Scndry Educ.

BAILEY, ANDREA L; Springbrook HS; Silver Spring, MD; (Y); 60/488; Spanish Clb; Flag Corp; Stage Crew; High Hon Roll; NHS; MD Piano Tchrs Assoc Pino Solo Awd; Schltc Art Awd Gld Key; Conway Schlrshp Cntst Fnlst; U Of MI; Frgn Lang.

BAILEY, BRIAN; Thomas Stone HS; Hughesville, MD; (S); Boy Scts; Pres 4-H; Band; Concert Band; Mrchg Band; Var L Ftbl; 4-H Awd; Hon Roll; U MD.

BAILEY, CHERYL; Archbishop Keough HS; Columbia, MD; (Y); Church Yth Grp; Cmnty Wkr; Computer Clb; French Clb; Hosp Aide; Acpl Chr; Rep Soph Cls; Rep Stu Cncl; Bsktbl; Hon Roll; Pre-Med.

BAILEY, DENISE; St Frances-Charles Hall HS; Baltimore, MD; (Y); Art Clb; JA; School Play; Trs Soph Cls; VP Jr Cls; Pres Sr Cls; Stu Cncl; JV Bsktbl; Hon Roll; Val; Dghtrs Amer Art Awd; Sr Mary Paul Lee Schlrshp; Gen Excllnc Awd; Morgan ST U; Bio.

BAILEY, LYN; Laurel HS; Laurel, MD; (Y); Swmmng; Engl Achvmnt 86.

BAILEY, RAESHANNE; Arlington Baptist Schl; Baltimore, MD; (Y); Church Yth Grp; Varsity Clb; Church Choir; Var Bsktbl; Var Trk; VA U; Heart Srgn.

BAILEY, RONALD G; Largo HS; Capital Heights, MD; (Y); Teachers Aide; Hon Roll; Ntl Merit Ltr; Accntng.

BAILOR, CHRISTINE; Thomas S Woollton HS; Gaithersburg, MD; (Y); Art Clb; Church Yth Grp; Drama Clb; JA; Sftbl; Hon Roll; Rotary Interact Clb 85-86; Psych.

BAINBRIDGE, SHERYL; Holy Cross Acad; Rockville, MD; (Y); 30/126; Church Yth Grp; VP Spanish Clb; Chorus; Socr; Vllybl; High Hon Roll; Hon Roll; Spanish NHS; Vanderbilt U.

BAINE, KIM; Thomas Stone HS; Waldorf, MD; (Y); FHA; High Hon Roll; Hon Roll; NHS; Charles CC; CPA.

BAISEY, DEBBIE; Poolesville HS; Poolesville, MD; (Y); 14/108; Sec Frsh Cls; Sec Soph Cls; Sec Jr Cls; Sec Sr Cls; Pres Sec Stu Cncl; Cit Awd; Hon Roll; AFS; FHA; Office Aide; Presdntl Acadmc Ftns Awd 86; Spcl Rcgntn Stu Govt Pre, Sec 85 & 86; Acadmc Achvt Awds 84-86; U Of MD; Erly Chldhd Educ.

BAKER, BONNIE; Thomas S Wootton HS; Potomoc, MD; (Y); Church Yth Grp; JA; Teachers Aide; Rep Frsh Cls; Var JV Sftbl; Hon Roll; Govrnmnt.

BAKER, CAROLE; Western HS; Baltimore, MD; (Y); 100/400; Trs FBLA; Teachers Aide; Yrbk Stf; Hon Roll; Acctng II Awd 86; VITA Tax Awd 86; FBLA Bus Math Awd 1st Pl Citywd, 8th Pl ST 86; Temple Bus Coll; Acctg.

BAKER, DANIEL; Potomac SR HS; Temple Hills, MD; (Y); Boys Clb Am; Church Yth Grp; Church Choir; School Play; Lit Mag; Var Bsktbl; High Hon Roll; Hon Roll; NHS; HS Schlr Athlete 85-86; Bio Med Engr.

BAKER, DANITA; Thomas Stone HS; Lubbock, TX; (Y); 89/390; Church Yth Grp; Cmnty Wkr; Drama Clb; Latin Clb; Thesps; Acpl Chr; Church Choir; Stage Crew; Variety Show; JV Vllybl; Miss Mistletoe 84 & 85; TX Tech U; Mass Comm.

BAKER, DAVID; Potomac SR HS; Temple Hills, MD; (Y); Boys Clb Am; Church Yth Grp; Science Clb; Church Choir; JV Bsktbl; Gov Hon Prg Awd; High Hon Roll; Hon Roll; NHS; St Schlr; Prince Geo Cnty Acadmc Excell Awd 84-86; PHS Schlr Athlt 84-86; Biomdcl Engr.

BAKER, DEREK; La Plata HS; Charlotte Hall, MD; (Y); Church Yth Grp; 4-H; Library Aide; Office Aide; Church Choir; Nwsp Stf; Off Jr Cls; Coach Actv; Hon Roll; Maryland U; Law Enfrcmnt.

BAKER, MICHELE; James M Bennett SR HS; Salisbury, MD; (Y); Art Clb; Church Yth Grp; Cmnty Wkr; Intnl Clb; Drill Tm; Trk; Hon Roll; Prfct Atten Awd; 2nd Pl Art Prjct Awd 86; Sci Fair Prjct Awd 84.

BAKER, NATHAN; Allegany HS; Cumberland, MD; (Y); 13/240; Var JV Bsktbl; Var JV Crs Cntry; Var JV Socr; Var JV Trk; Hon Roll; NHS; USAFA; Engrng.

BALDANZA, J TODD; Dulaney SR HS; Cockeysville, MD; (Y); Boy Scts; Church Yth Grp; Cmnty Wkr; Ski Clb; Stage Crew; JV Capt Socr; Hon Roll; NHS.

BALDWIN, KRISTA; Maurice J Mc Donough HS; Waldoff, MD; (S); 29/310; Office Aide; Band; Concert Band; Mrchg Band; Cheerleading; Score Keeper; High Hon Roll; NHS; Charles County CC; Bus Adm.

BALDWIN, SUE; Southern HS; Baltimore, MD; (Y); 2/300; Nwsp Ed-Chief; Nwsp Rptr; Nwsp Stf; Hon Roll; Prfct Atten Awd; Mayors Stu Achvt Awd 86; Coppin ST Coll Schlrshp 86; 2nd Pl Schl Sci Fair Awd 86; Chld Dvlpmnt.

BALL, KIM; Everton R III HS; Everton, MO; (S); Office Aide; Teachers Aide; Nwsp Ed-Chief; Nwsp Rptr; Nwsp Stf; Yrbk Phtg; Yrbk Rptr; Yrbk Stf; Hon Roll; Mst Lkly Sccd; Prntg.

BALLARD, MICHELLE; North Carroll HS; Manchester, MD; (Y); #7 In Class; Pres VP Spanish Clb; Chorus; School Musical; Swing Chorus; Off Sr Cls; Hon Roll; NHS; Presdntl Ftns Awd 86; Centry III Ldrs Rnr-Up 85; St Marys Coll Of MD; Bio.

BALLESTEROS, MARIA; Notre Dame Prep; Towson, MD; (Y); Church Yth Grp; Hosp Aide; Chorus; Yrbk Stf; Prfct Atten Awd; Ntl Stu-Ntl Piano-Plyng Audtns 84; Dist Stu-Ntl Piano-Plyng Audtns 85 & 86; Bus Adm.

BALOG, LAURA; John Carroll HS; Jarrettsville, MD; (Y); 5/238; Drama Clb; Sec German Clb; Nwsp Stf; Yrbk Stf; Stat Bsbl; Var Swmmng; High Hon Roll; NHS; Natl Sci Olympd Awd 84; Germn Natl Hon Soc 86; Engrg.

BALOGH, ERIKA; Westminster SR HS; Westminster, MD; (Y); French Clb; GAA; Tennis; JV Trk; High Hon Roll; Hon Roll; Gannon Univ Acad 86-87; Gannon Univ; Phys Asst.

BANASHAK, MICHAEL; Archbishop Curley HS; Baltimore, MD; (S); Spanish Clb; Varsity Clb; Yrbk Ed-Chief; Yrbk Stf; Rep Soph Cls; Var JV Bsbl; Var JV Socr; Hon Roll; Jr NHS; Spanish NHS; K Of C Scholar 83-86; Elec Engr.

BANDELL, MICHAEL; Patterson SR HS; Baltimore, MD; (Y); Church Yth Grp; Cmnty Wkr; Office Aide; Teachers Aide; Var Lcrss; Wt Lftg; Hon Roll; NHS; John Hopkins; Comp Sci.

BANE, JAMES BENJAMIN; Frederick Christian Acad; Harpers Ferry, WV; (Y); 1/8; Q&S; Chorus; Nwsp Rptr; Nwsp Sprt Ed; Pres Frsh Cls; Bsbl; Bsktbl; Cit Awd; High Hon Roll; NHS; Loats Fndtn Inc Schlrshp 86; Chrstn Walk Awd 86; Sigm XI Scintfc Rsrch Soc Awd 86; VA Polytech Inst; Engr.

BANJANIN, RICHARD C; Frederick Douglass HS; Upper Marlboro, MD; (Y); Boy Scts; Church Yth Grp; Rep Frsh Cls; Rep Soph Cls; Rep Jr Cls; VP Sr Cls; French Hon Soc; High Hon Roll; Hon Roll; Eagle Scout 86; Civil Engrng.

BANKS, CHARLEITA; Porkside SR HS; Fruitland, MD; (Y); Spanish Clb; Chorus; Hon Roll; Salisbury ST Coll; Phys Ther.

BANKS, JULIANNE; Takoma Acad; Columbia, MD; (Y); Chorus; Church Choir; Rep Frsh Cls; Bsktbl; Mgr Cheerleading; Mgr(s); High Hon Roll; Hon Roll; NHS; Schl Lttr 86; MD U; Psych.

BANKS, PAULA; Parkside HS; Fruitland, MD; (Y); Church Yth Grp; Chorus; School Play; Stage Crew; Variety Show; Sftbl; Art Sclptr Awd 86.

BANNER, MARY A; Catonsville HS; Catonsville, MD; (Y); Church Yth Grp; Spanish Clb; SADD; Yrbk Phtg; Hon Roll; Jr NHS; Schlrshp-Outstndng Prfmnc 84-85; Prfrmnc In Spnsh 86; Duke U; Pre Med.

BARBEE, LORI; Maurice J Mc Donough HS; Waldorf, MD; (Y); Church Yth Grp; FBLA; Office Aide; Drill Tm; Trs Jr Cls; Trs Sr Cls; Rep Stu Cncl; Cheerleading; Pom Pon; Hon Roll; Comp.

BARBELY, ERIC; Sherwood HS; Olney, MD; (Y); 3/317; Math Tm; Band; Concert Band; Jazz Band; Mrchg Band; Pep Band; School Musical; School Play; Bsktbl; Var JV Socr; U Of MD.

BARBER, CYNTHIA; Great Mills HS; Lex Pk, MD; (Y); Office Aide; VP Chorus; Sec Church Choir; Sec Frsh Cls; Rep Stu Cncl; High Hon Roll; Hon Roll; Howard U; Bus Adm.

BARBER, DIANE; Smithsburg HS; Smithsburg, MD; (Y); 20/188; Latin Clb; VP Band; Mrchg Band; School Musical; Rep Jr Cls; Stu Cncl; Co-Capt Vllybl; Henry King Stanford Schlrshp U Of Miami 86; U Of Miami; Engl.

BARBER, TAWANDA; Woodlawn SR HS; Baltimore, MD; (Y); Pep Clb; Variety Show; Trk; Intr Dsgnr.

BARBOUR, AVON; Farimont Heights HS; Landover Hls, MD; (Y); Computer Clb; Ftbl; Trk; Wt Lftg; Grabmling ST; Cmptr Sci.

BARCHOWSKY, DAMIEN; John Carroll HS; Aberdeen, MD; (Y); 49/238; Trs Art Clb; French Clb; Var Lcrss; French Hon Soc; Hon Roll; Ntl Merit Ltr.

BARCLAY, ANNE BROOKS; Severn HS; Severna Park, MD; (Y); French Clb; Chorus; School Musical; Lit Mag; Cheerleading; Im Fld Hcky; Im Tennis; High Hon Roll; Hon Roll; Pres Schlr; Art Awd 86; Ntl Piano Playing Aud Dist Wnnr 85-86; U PA; Music.

BARFIELD, KIMBERLY; Crossland SR HS; Temple Hills, MD; (Y); Church Yth Grp; Pep Clb; Science Clb; Spanish Clb; Teachers Aide; Concert Band; Mrchg Band; Pep Band; Symp Band; Rep Soph Cls; Engrng.

BARGERON, JULIE; Oakland Mills HS; Columbia, MD; (Y); 19/275; Church Yth Grp; Hosp Aide; Teachers Aide; Acpl Chr; Chorus; Church Choir; Madrigals; Yrbk Stf; Lit Mag; Hon Roll; Pres Acdmc Fit Awd 86; Johns Hopkins U Physcs Lab Schlrshp 86; Brigham Yng U Dean Schlrshp 86; Bringham Young U; Accntng.

BARGERON, LISA; Oakland Mills HS; Columbia, MD; (Y); Church Yth Grp; Var Vllybl; NHS; BYU.

BARKER, GWENAE; Catoctin HS; Thurmont, MD; (Y); 1/196; FBLA; Band; Yrbk Stf; Rep Frsh Cls; Score Keeper; Hon Roll; Ntl Merit SF; Pres Schlr; Val; Am Leg Scholar 86; Grnt Messiah Coll 86; Deans Scholar Messiah Coll 86; Messiah Coll; Acctg.

BARLOW, JOANNA; Riverdale Baptist HS; Mitchellville, MD; (S); 1/66; Church Yth Grp; Band; Chorus; Sec Stu Cncl; High Hon Roll; Pres NHS; Val; Voice Dem Awd; Library Aide; Natl Awd Musc Comptn 84; Liberty U; Psych.

BARNCORD, MONICA; Mount Savage HS; Corriganville, MD; (Y); French Clb; Library Aide; Teachers Aide; Chorus; Concert Band; Jazz Band; Mrchg Band; Nwsp Phtg; Hon Roll; NHS; U Of MD.

BARNES, KIMBERLY R; Eleanor Roosevelt HS; Lanham, MD; (Y); VP Pep Clb; Red Cross Aide; Teachers Aide; Rep Jr Cls; Rep Sr Cls; Rep Stu Cncl; Powder Puff Ftbl; Hon Roll; Cmnty Wkr; Chorus; Natl Achvt Schlrshp Prgm 86; Eleanor Roosevelts Sci & Tech Ctr 82-86; JR SR Debutante For Links Inc; Bus.

BARNES, LARRY; Cambridge South Dorchester HS; Woolford, MD; (Y); Cmnty Wkr; Rep Stu Cncl; Var Bsbl; JV Var Ftbl; Wt Lftg; Cit Awd; Hon Roll; NHS; Variety Show; Outstndng Acad Achvt Lftme Sprts & Envrnmntl Sci 85-86; JR Scuba Diver; Salisbury ST.

BARNES, MELISSA ELAINE; Joppatowne HS; Edgewood, MD; (Y); 39/161; Cmnty Wkr; French Clb; SADD; Teachers Aide; Chorus; Stu Cncl; JV Lcrss; JV Var Powder Puff Ftbl; Hon Roll; Baltimore Wmns Clb 2nd Pl Schlrshp 86; Joppatowne Wnmns Clb 3rd Pl Schlrshp 86; Catherine I Riley Sch; U MD Baltimore; Cmmnctns.

BARNES, SHEILA; Du Val HS; Landover, MD; (Y); Hosp Aide; ROTC; Church Choir; Sec Stu Cncl; Hon Roll; Ntl Merit Ltr; St Schlr; Norfolk ST U; Accntng.

BARNES, TIMIKO; Walbrook HS; Baltimore, MD; (Y); Cmnty Wkr; FBLA; JA; Red Cross Aide; Teachers Aide; Church Choir; Gym; Trk; Cit Awd; Prfct Atten Awd; Math.

BARNHART, CHRISTOPHER; Hancock JR SR HS; Hancock, MD; (Y); 7/49; Office Aide; Var Bsbl; Var Bsktbl; Stat Score Keeper; Sftbl; Cit Awd; Elks Awd; High Hon Roll; Lion Awd; Moose Clb 86; HJC Hagerstown; Phy Ed.

BARNHART, STEPHANIE; Williamsport HS; Hagerstown, MD; (Y); 22/224; Capt Band; Drill Tm; Powder Puff Ftbl; Hon Roll; Hnr Clb 84-86; Hagerstown JC; Bus Admin.

BARNHOUSE, KIMBERLY; Patterson HS; Baltimore, MD; (Y); Library Aide; Prfct Atten Awd; Perfect Atten 81; Schl Store Attndnt 81; Engl.

BARR, BRIAN; Smithsburg HS; Smithsburg, MD; (Y); 3/177; Church Yth Grp; Latin Clb; Church Choir; School Musical; NHS; Ntl Merit Schol; Am Chemical Soc Awd 85; Biochemistry.

BARR, CHARLES D; Edgewood SR HS; Joppa, MD; (Y); Teachers Aide; Yrbk Rptr; Yrbk Stf; Var Trk; High Hon Roll; Hon Roll; NHS; Pres Schlr; Schlrshp Awd 86; U Of MD; Cmptr Sys Anylst.

BARR, GILLIAN R; Annapolis SR HS; Annapolis, MD; (Y); 13/520; Church Yth Grp; Spanish Clb; Ed Nwsp Stf; Ed Yrbk Stf; Rep Frsh Cls; Sec Stu Cncl; JV Sftbl; High Hon Roll; Jr NHS; NHS; MD Smmr Ctrs Gftd & Tlntd 82-85; Lib Arts.

BARRACK, KRISTEN; La Plata HS; Waldorf, MD; (Y); Church Yth Grp; Cmnty Wkr; Girl Scts; Science Clb; Acpl Chr; Chorus; Church Choir; All-ST Hnr Chorus 86; 1st Charles Cnty Chmbr Ensmbl 86; MD U; Music.

BARRANCO, DENISE; North Harford HS; Whiteford, MD; (Y); Church Yth Grp; French Clb; German Clb; Varsity Clb; Band; Mrchg Band; Pep Band; Yrbk Stf; Jr Cls; Cheerleading; Hnr Roll 83-86; Frostburg ST; Chem.

BARROW, JAMES; Glenelg HS; Glenwood, MD; (Y); Varsity Clb; Trs Jr Cls; Var L Bsktbl; Var L Socr; Var L Trk; Hon Roll; NHS; Im Wt Lftg.

BARROWS, AMY; John Carroll HS; Churchville, MD; (Y); 45/238; Am Leg Aux Girls St; Drama Clb; School Musical; Rep Jr Cls; Var Sr Cls; Var Mgr(s); Hon Roll; NHS; Spanish NHS; Church Yth Grp; Ltn Ntl Hnr Soc 84-85.

BARTELS, JOHN; Westminster SR HS; Westminster, MD; (Y); Camera Clb; Computer Clb; Hst 4-H; VP JA; Teachers Aide; Chorus; Lit Mag; JV Ftbl; JV Lcrss; High Hon Roll; Jr Firefighter Yr Gamber/Cmm Vol FD 82; Coll Virgin Islands; Mar Bio.

BARTHOLOMEW, SARA; Sherwood HS; Olney, MD; (Y); Pres Church Yth Grp; Cmnty Wkr; Hosp Aide; Red Cross Aide; Ski Clb; Hon Roll; NHS; Vctnl Awd $100 For Hlth Occupations 86; Svc Awd 86; Volunteer Awd Over 50 Hrs Hosp Svc 86; U Of DE; Phys Thrpy.

BARTLETT, CATHERINE; Surrattsville HS; Clinton, MD; (Y); French Clb; Teachers Aide; Nwsp Stf; VP Jr Cls; Pom Pon; Tennis; Hon Roll; Jr NHS; Busnss Admin.

BARTOLETTI, ANDREA; Regina HS; Adelphi, MD; (Y); Yrbk Stf; Sec Soph Cls; JV Sftbl; Var Vllybl; Bausch & Lomb Sci Awd; High Hon Roll; Sec NHS; NEDT Awd; Prfct Atten Awd; MD Distinguished Schlr 86; Engrng.

BARTOLOMUCCI, BETH ANN; Archbishop Martin Spalding HS; Arnold, MD; (Y); 9/128; Scholastic Bowl; Yrbk Stf; High Hon Roll; Latin Awd 85; Acad Merit Ltr 85-86; Acad Achvt Awd 86; Notre Dame MD; Med.

BARTON, FREDRICK; La Plata HS; Newburg, MD; (Y); Church Yth Grp; Computer Clb; Science Clb; Band; Concert Band; Rep Sr Cls; Crs Cntry; Wt Lftg; Teachers Aide; Church Choir; Brwn Blt Karate; Gld Adtn Ntl Frat Stu Mscns Amer Coll Mscns 86; Elec Engr.

BARTON, LISA; Northern HS; Owings, MD; (Y); Drama Clb; Chorus; School Play; Yrbk Stf; Rep Stu Cncl; Pom Pon; High Hon Roll; Varsity Clb; Color Guard; Acdmclly Intllctlly Able Adv; Spnsh III Awd; Intl Exchng Stu; Chld Psych.

BASHEIN, JILL; Charles E Smith Jewish Day Schl; Rockville, MD; (Y); Sec Church Yth Grp; Cmnty Wkr; SADD; Yrbk Rptr; Yrbk Stf; Var Jr Cls; Var Capt Bsktbl; Sftbl; Vllybl; Sftbl Mst Vlbl Offns Hnbl Mntn All-Lg 85-86; Hnr Roll & Jwsh Hstry 85-86; Stfbl & Bsktbl 83-84.

BASHORE, MELISSA E; Walt Whitman HS; Bethesda, MD; (Y); 138/445; Church Yth Grp; Swmmng; Tennis; Hnrbl Ment Awd Arts 86; Recgntn Talent Srch Dance; Ballet Dancer.

BASINGER, BETH; Calvert HS; Prince Frederick, MD; (Y); 2/256; Science Clb; Band; Concert Band; Mrchg Band; Var Tennis; High Hon Roll; NHS; Prfct Atten Awd; Sci Fair 2nd Pl 86; Spnsh 1st Pl 84; Millersville; Marine Bio.

BASKWILL, ANNE; Dulaney SR HS; Lutherville, MD; (Y); Church Yth Grp; Dance Clb; Ski Clb; Band; Church Choir; Concert Band; Mrchg Band; Variety Show; Stat Bsbl; Hon Roll; UMBC; Bus Admn.

BASS, KIRSTEN; Maryvale Preparatory Schl; Timonium, MD; (Y); Dance Clb; Drama Clb; Hosp Aide; Chorus; School Musical; High Hon Roll; NHS; NEDT Awd; Marquis Schlr La Fayette Coll 86; La Fayette Coll; Bio.

BASSANI, ALEXANDRA; Maurice S Mc Donough HS; White Plains, MD; (Y); Church Yth Grp; Ski Clb; Hon Roll; NHS; NAA Awds 86; Charles County CC; Bus.

BASSETT, LENEAR; Regina HS; Washington, DC; (Y); Church Yth Grp; Computer Clb; Model UN; Stat Bsktbl; Mgr(s); Score Keeper; Var L Tennis; Timer; High Hon Roll; VP Dubutnt Bll Acdmc Schlrshp 85; Awd Prtcptn Mck Trl Clb 86; Hnrs Govt Crs 86; Bus Admin.

BATCHELOR, DARRIN; Lackey HS; Bryans Rd, MD; (Y); Drama Clb; French Clb; Math Tm; School Musical; Yrbk Ed-Chief; Yrbk Phtg; Yrbk Stf; Sec Stu Cncl; High Hon Roll; NHS; Wrstlng; Pol Sci.

BATDORF, JOHN B; Walkersville HS; Frederick, MD; (Y); 1/187; Pres Frsh Cls; Pres Soph Cls; Stu Cncl; JV Socr; Var L Tennis; Elks Awd; High Hon Roll; JETS Awd; NHS; Val; Pres & VP Soc Sci Clb; Lwyr Mock Trl Team; Georgetown U; Bus.

BATEMAN, LISA; Southern HS; Mt Lake Park, MD; (Y); Church Yth Grp; Cmnty Wkr; Office Aide; Church Choir; High Hon Roll; Hon Roll; Ntl Merit Ltr; Prfct Atten Awd; Sec.

BATEMAN, WILLIAM; Calvert SR HS; Prince Frederick, MD; (Y); 47/272; Boy Scts; Varsity Clb; Band; Concert Band; Var L Bsktbl; Var L Socr; Var L Tennis; Hon Roll; MVP Tennis 84-86; All Cnfrnce Tennis 84-86; Ordr Of The Arrow 86; Aerospace.

BATES, HEATHER; Fort Hill HS; Cumberland, MD; (S); Church Yth Grp; Pep Clb; Pres Band; Pres Concert Band; Pres Mrchg Band; Yrbk Phtg; Cit Awd; Hon Roll; Trs NHS; Hosp Aide; Med.

BATTLE, ISAAC; Surrattsville HS; Clinton, MD; (Y); Aud/Vis; Computer Clb; Library Aide; Sec Frsh Cls; Rep Stu Cncl; JV Ftbl; Var Trk; Hon Roll; US Naval Acad; Math.

BAUCOM, ADRIENNE; Sherwood HS; Olney, MD; (S); Church Yth Grp; Dance Clb; Hosp Aide; Teachers Aide; School Play; Var Cheerleading; JV Lcrss; Var Socr; Var Swmmng; Hon Roll; 2nd Pl Trophy Geo Upward Bound Prg 85; Phy Thrpy.

BAUER, KATHY; South Carroll HS; Woodbine, MD; (Y); Pres 4-H; Ski Clb; Teachers Aide; Varsity Clb; Mrchg Band; Yrbk Stf; Trs Soph Cls; L Var Crs Cntry; L Var Trk; Hon Roll; Acadmc Ltr 83; UMBC; Nrsng.

BAUER, LAURIE; Chopticon HS; Mechanicsville, MD; (Y); Letterman Clb; Ski Clb; Chorus; Variety Show; L Trk; Yth Ftnss Achvt Awd 84; Bus Recdkpg Awd 86; Bus Mgmt.

BAUERNSCHUB, LISA; Westminster HS; Westminster, MD; (Y); Church Yth Grp; Hosp Aide; Spanish Clb; Teachers Aide; Church Choir; Capt Flag Corp; Mrchg Band; Symp Band; Var Trk; Bio.

BAUGHER, APRIL HEATHER; Allegany HS; La Vale, MD; (Y); 3/220; French Clb; Band; Concert Band; Jazz Band; High Hon Roll; VP NHS; Ntl Merit Commnd Schlr 86; MD ST Schlr Fnlst 86; Washington Coll; Math.

BAYLIS, MATTHEW; Potomac HS; Ft Washington, MD; (Y); Band; Concert Band; Jazz Band; Mrchg Band; Lit Mag; Math.

BAYNE, GLORIA; Eastern Vo Tech HS; Baltimore, MD; (Y); Art Clb; Church Yth Grp; Pres Chorus; Hon Roll; Pres-NTO; Mchnst.

BEACH, JENNIFER; Arch Bishop Spalding HS; Glen Burnie, MD; (Y); 18/140; Drama Clb; Pep Clb; Ski Clb; Thesps; School Musical; Stage Crew; Yrbk Stf; Sec Frsh Cls; Sec Soph Cls; Sec Jr Cls; Drama Awd 86; MD Ctr Arts Dance 83-84&85; Brandeis U; Jrnlsm.

BEAHN, THOMAS; Georgetown Prep; Rockville, MD; (Y); 11/106; Political Wkr; Ski Clb; Var Ftbl; Var Trk; Hon Roll; Law.

BEAL, DANA; Thomas Stone HS; Waldorf, MD; (S); High Hon Roll; Acadmc Ltr 85; Acadmc Pin 84; Dickinson Coll; Ecnmcs.

BEAL, TERRY; Northern HS; Grantsville, MD; (Y); 15/116; Church Yth Grp; Band; Chorus; Concert Band; Mrchg Band; Pep Band; Rep Stu Cncl; Var Bsbl; JV Ftbl; JV Capt Wrstlng; Garrett Ntl Bnk Schlrshp 86; Sprtsmnshp Awd For Wrstlng 85-86; Algny CC; Cmnctns.

BEALE, JANET; Forestville HS; Forestville, MD; (Y); Office Aide; Capt ROTC; Church Choir; Drill Tm; Nwsp Rptr; Sec Sr Cls; Var Pom Pon; Hon Roll; Brd Trst Schlrshp Prince Georges Comm Coll 86; Forestvilles Fclty Awd 86; Pr Georges Com Coll; Bus Admin.

BEALL, BARBARA; Seneca Valley HS; Gaithersburg, MD; (Y); French Clb; Spanish Clb; SADD; Teachers Aide; Nwsp Rptr; Mgr Trk; Hon Roll.

BEALL, SUSAN; Sherwood HS; Highland, MD; (Y); Model UN; SADD; Capt Var Pom Pon; Hon Roll; NHS; Spanish NHS; Aerntcl Engr.

BEAN, JOHN; Eastern Vocational Tech; Baltimore, MD; (Y); Math Clb; Var Bsbl; Hon Roll; Hnr Rll 3 Trms 84-86; Dsl Mchncs 83-87; Engr.

BEAN, PAUL A; Chopticon HS; Mechanicsville, MD; (Y); Church Yth Grp; FBLA; Library Aide; Teachers Aide; Crs Cntry; Socr; Hon Roll; Jr NHS; 3rd Pl FBLA Rgnl Compttn Data Pros 86; CPA.

BEARD, RENEE; Patterson HS; Baltimore, MD; (Y); Mrchg Band; NHS; Hnr Roll 84-85; John Hpkns U; Lawyer.

BEASLEY, TIANNE; Cambridge South Corchester HS; Cambridge, MD; (Y); DECA; FBLA; FHA; Chorus; Church Choir; Flag Corp; Mrchg Band; Stu Cncl; Sftbl; Vllybl; Secy.

BEATTY, MARCIA; Sherwood HS; Olney, MD; (Y); Church Yth Grp; Cmnty Wkr; Hosp Aide; JA; Teachers Aide; Concert Band; Mrchg Band; Pep Band; School Musical; Hon Roll; Pin Awd For Volntr Svc 84-85; Psychlgy.

BEAUBIEN, SAMANTHA L; Ft Hill HS; Cumberland, MD; (Y); 50/251; Art Clb; Camera Clb; Cmnty Wkr; Band; Color Guard; Chld Psych.

BECHTEL, JULIE; Westminster HS; Westminster, MD; (Y); Church Yth Grp; French Clb; Mrchg Band; Hon Roll; NHS; Pres Schlr; Slvr Run Union Mills Lions Clb Scholar 86; George Washington U; Bus.

BECHTOLD, DIANNA CAROL; Parkdale HS; New Carrollton, MD; (Y); Yrbk Rptr; Off Jr Cls; Var Co-Capt Bsktbl; Var Capt Sftbl; Hon Roll; Army Acad & Athltc Exclnc Awd 86; Ron Walker Mem Schlrshp 86; Acad Ftns Awd 86; U Of MD Coll Pk; Bus.

BECHTOLD, KATHLEEN; Laurel HS; Laurel, MD; (Y); Church Yth Grp; French Clb; Teachers Aide; Yrbk Phtg; Capt Var Vllybl; French Hon Soc; Hon Roll; NHS; Outstndg Perfrmnc Chem 86; Achvmnt Earth Sci 84; Vllybll Bst Offensive Plyr 85.

BECK, JENNIFER; Hereford HS; Freeland, MD; (Y); Cmnty Wkr; Jazz Band; Orch; Trs Jr Cls; Trs Sr Cls; Var Capt Crs Cntry; Var Capt Trk; High Hon Roll; JP Sousa Awd; NHS; Outstndng Athltc Awd 86; X-Cntry Hero 86; Hereford-Sparks Almni Assoc Schlrshp 86; Mrchnt Marine Acad.

BECK, PATRICK; Hereford HS; Freeland, MD; (Y); Church Yth Grp; Varsity Clb; Band; Jazz Band; Lcrss; Sftbl; Wt Lftg; JV Var Wrstlng; Hon Roll; Prfct Atten Awd; 3rd-Wrstlng Rgnls 85; 2nd Wrstlng Cnty, 4th Rgnls 86; Acad Excllnc Phys Educ 83-86; Towson ST U; Math.

BECKER, MAUREEN; Elizabeth Seton HS; Riverdale, MD; (Y); 2/188; Girl Scts; JCL; Latin Clb; Service Clb; Symp Band; Cit Awd; High Hon Roll; Pres NHS; Ntl Merit Ltr; Sal; Niagara U Acad Pres Schrlshp 86; Girl Scout Gold Awd 86; Pres Acad Ftns Awd 86; Niagara U.

BECMER, CAROLYN; La Plata HS; La Plata, MD; (Y); Dance Clb; Office Aide; Ski Clb; Variety Show; Off Frsh Cls; Off Jr Cls; Stat Ftbl; Hon Roll; Acctg.

BECTON, STANWYN; De Matha Catholic HS; Lanham Seabrook, MD; (Y); Church Yth Grp; Cmnty Wkr; Service Clb; Im Bsktbl; Hon Roll; Nw Crrltn Boys & Grls Clbs Bsktbl Ref 83-84; Outstndng Vc Plque Asstn Ftbl NCB&G 84-85; Cert Hon Roll; Bus.

BEDFORD, KELLIE; Andover HS; Linthicum Hts, MD; (Y); 1/294; Rep Stu Cncl; Mgr Bsktbl; L Socr; Mgr Tennis; High Hon Roll; VP NHS; Ntl Merit SF; Val; Zonta Schrlsh P86; Womans Clb Linthicum Schrlsh P86; Ntl Hnr Soc Bk Schlrshp 86; U Of MD; Aero Sp Engr.

BEEMAN, AMY; Valley HS; Barton, MD; (Y); 2/82; Q&S; Chorus; Nwsp Ed-Chief; Trs Jr Cls; Trs Sr Cls; Stu Cncl; Capt Var Bsktbl; Hon Roll; Pres NHS; Sal; Cert Of Merit Awd 86; CWP Awd-Mck Trl 86; Shld Jrnlsm Awd 86; Frostburg ST Coll; Accntng.

BEEMAN, LESLIE L; Mount Savage HS; Corriganville, MD; (Y); 15/60; French Clb; FBLA; Library Aide; Pep Clb; Teachers Aide; Flag Corp; Btty Crckr Awd; Hon Roll; 2nd Pl Reg I FBLA Cmpttn 86; 3rd Pl MD ST FBLA Cmpttn 86; Schl Bus Patrol 85-86; Frostburg ST Coll; Accntng.

BEEMAN, MISSY; Maurice J Mc Donough HS; Waldorf, MD; (Y); Teachers Aide; Hon Roll; Comp Oper.

BEEMAN, TINA; Valley HS; Barton, MD; (Y); Church Yth Grp; FHA; Nwsp Rptr; NHS; Allegany CC; Rsprtry Thrpy.

BEERS, GLEN; Wicomico SR HS; Salisbury, MD; (Y); Church Yth Grp; FCA; Spanish Clb; Chorus; Church Choir; Hon Roll; Salisbury ST Coll.

BEESON, STEVEN; Sherwood HS; Olney, MD; (Y); Church Yth Grp; Ski Clb; Crs Cntry; Swmmng; Trk; Hon Roll; NHS; Physcs.

BEHE, PAUL FRANCIS; Northern HS; Dunkirk, MD; (Y); Church Yth Grp; Trk; Wt Lftg; JV Wrstlng; Hon Roll; Outstndng Achvt Cnstr Trades 86; Crim Just.

BEITZEL, CHRISTY; Northern Garrett HS; Grantsville, MD; (Y); Teachers Aide; Varsity Clb; Chorus; Nwsp Stf; Garrett CC; Sec Sci.

BELEN, ELAINE; Archbishop Keough HS; Baltimore, MD; (Y); Church Yth Grp; Computer Clb; Dance Clb; Var Cheerleading; Hon Roll; Girl Scts; Spanish Clb; Teachers Aide; Variety Show; Nwsp Phtg; Fll Dnc Schlrshp 84.

BELL, CINDY; Grace Brethren Christian Schl; Temple Hills, MD; (S); 1/24; School Play; VP Frsh Cls; VP Jr Cls; Sec Stu Cncl; Var Bsktbl; Var Vllybl; High Hon Roll; Jr NHS; NHS; U Of MD; Drama.

BELL, DONNA; Oakland Mills HS; Columbia, MD; (Y); 1/280; Sec Math Tm; Chorus; School Musical; Chrmn Frsh Cls; Chrmn Soph Cls; Chrmn Jr Cls; Chrmn Sr Cls; Hon Roll; NHS; French Clb; 1st Pl ST Concours Natl De Francais 83-84.

BELL, MARSHALL C; Randallstown SR HS; Owings Mills, MD; (Y); Church Yth Grp; Cmnty Wkr; FBLA; Political Wkr; Stu Cncl; Var Capt Lcrss; Socr; Var Trk; Hon Roll; Ntl Merit SF; Outstndng Blck Stu-Ntl Merit Semi-Fnlst 85; Howard U; Mrktng Cnsltnt.

BELL, PATTI; Grisfield HS; Marion, MD; (Y); 2/95; FHA; Science Clb; Church Choir; Nwsp Stf; Yrbk Stf; High Hon Roll; NHS; Rotary Awd; Elm Ed.

BELLO, JOSEPH; Surrattsville HS; Clinton, MD; (Y); Science Clb; Hon Roll; Jr NHS; NHS; Ntl Merit SF; Excllnt Achvt-Earth Sci 84; Acad Excllnc Awd 84 & 86; Engrng.

BELTON, SHARISE; Forest Park HS; Baltimore, MD; (Y); OEA; Drill Tm; Mrchg Band; Cheerleading; Crs Cntry; Rep Soph Cls; Rep Jr Cls; Comp Tech.

BENBOW, ARLENE; Potomac SR HS; Temple Hills, MD; (Y); Church Yth Grp; Dance Clb; Mathletes; ROTC; Science Clb; VICA; Pom Pon; Powder Puff Ftbl; Cit Awd; Hon Roll; Yth Employability Pgm 86; Chrch Eldrs 85-86; Wrk Elderly People 80-83; USAF; Welder.

BENDER, KATIE; Dulaney HS; Timonium, MD; (Y); 85/500; Hosp Aide; Service Clb; Var Tennis; Hon Roll; NHS.

BENDT, TIMOTHY; Du Val HS; Lanham, MD; (Y); Boy Scts; Church Choir; Golf; Hon Roll; Church Yth Grp; U Of MD.

BENEDICT, CHRISTINA; La Plata HS; Newburg, MD; (S); Computer Clb; Latin Clb; Math Tm; Ski Clb; Rep Sr Cls; High Hon Roll; Jr NHS; NHS; Ntl Sci Merit Awd 85; Acad All-Amer 85; Engr.

BENFIELD, LESLIE; St Elizabeth Seton HS; Landover, MD; (Y); VP Art Clb; Cmnty Wkr; JCL; Latin Clb; Stage Crew; Variety Show; Nwsp Rptr; Nwsp Stf; Ed Yrbk Stf; Hon Roll; Prncpls Awd Art; Grgtwn U Intl Rltns Pgm; Offcl Spec Olympcs; Comp Sci.

BENJACK, JAMES; Thomas Stone HS; Waldorf, MD; (Y); Chess Clb; Debate Tm; Quiz Bowl; Science Clb; Hon Roll; U Of MD.

BENJAMIN JR, ERNEST L; Smithsburg HS; Cascade, MD; (Y); Comptrs.

BENJAMIN, MAYA; Wheaton HS; Rockville, MD; (Y); 66/386; Pres FBLA; SADD; Yrbk Bus Mgr; Co-Capt Cheerleading; Pom Pon; Hon Roll; Office Aide; Pep Clb; Teachers Aide; Temple Yth Grp; Peer Cnslng 84-86; Rcgntn Of Contribtn To Yng Am X & XI Int Dsgn 84-85; Towson ST U; Accounting.

BENNETT, BRADLEY; Saint Andrew's Episcopal HS; Clinton, MD; (S); 6/43; Cmnty Wkr; Latin Clb; Chorus; School Play; Nwsp Ed-Chief; Nwsp Phtg; Nwsp Rptr; Bsktbl; Trk; Hon Roll; Awd JR Cntrbtd Mst Schl Scty 85; Slvr Medl Natl Latn Exm 84; Natl Latn Exm Magna Cum Laude 85; Dartmouth Coll; Jrnlsm.

BENNETT, CORALIE; Middletown HS; Middletown, MD; (Y); Sec Pres Church Yth Grp; Dance Clb; Band; Chorus; Madrigals; Mrchg Band; School Musical; School Play; High Hon Roll; Hon Roll; Music Ltr 86; Dance Excllnc Awd 86; Grp Actg Excllnc Awd 86; Phys Ther.

BENNETT, COURTNEY LOZELLE; Academy Of The Holy Names HS; Silver Spring, MD; (Y); Cmnty Wkr; Office Aide; Sec Service Clb; Spanish Clb; Socr; Outstndg Achvt Eng Awd 84; Bus Mgmt.

BENNETT, D MITCHNER; Perryville HS; Perryville, MD; (Y); 5/120; Am Leg Boys St; Intnl Clb; Key Clb; VP Soph Cls; Pres Sr Cls; Rep Stu Cncl; JV Var Bsktbl; Var Trk; High Hon Roll; NHS; Mech Engr.

BENNETT, JULIE D; Brunswick HS; Knoxville, MD; (Y); Am Leg Aux Girls St; Latin Clb; Chorus; School Musical; Yrbk Bus Mgr; Trs Frsh Cls; Rep Stu Cncl; Capt Cheerleading; High Hon Roll; NHS; Coll Notre Dame MD Pres Fllwshp 86; Coll Notre Dame MD.

BENNETT, LA TONYER; Forest Park SR HS; Baltimore, MD; (Y); JA; Rep Soph Cls; Rep Jr Cls; Co-Capt Sftbl; Vllybl; Outstndng Athl Awd 85-86; Mst Hmbl Athl Awd Sftbl 86; Coppin ST Coll; Crmnl Law.

BENNETT, MATTHEW; Oxon Hill HS; Ft Washington, MD; (Y); 8/581; Computer Clb; Lit Mag; High Hon Roll; Hon Roll; JETS Awd; Pres Schlr; Sci & Tech Stu Of Yr 85; Top 10% Grad Cls 86; Marshall Hahn Engrng Schlrshp 86; VA Tech; Engrng.

BENNETT, SYLVIA; Hammond HS; Columbia, MD; (Y); Teachers Aide; Bus.

BENNETT, TERRY; Baltimore City Clg; Baltimore, MD; (Y); 21/238; Dance Clb; Drama Clb; Trs Girl Scts; Chorus; School Musical; Nwsp Stf; Rep Chrmn Sr Cls; High Hon Roll; Hon Roll; Hst NHS; Edward L Torsch Clss Schlrshp 86; Acctg.

BENSON, MICHELLE; Fort Hill HS; Cumberland, MD; (Y); Church Yth Grp; Teachers Aide; Drill Tm; Off Frsh Cls; Off Soph Cls; Off Jr Cls; Off Sr Cls; Hon Roll; Allegany Cmnty Coll; Lbrl Arts.

BENSON, WALTER; Fort Hill HS; Cumberland, MD; (Y); Church Yth Grp; Library Aide; Rep Stu Cncl; Var Mgr(s); Hon Roll; Body, Mind & Spirit Awd Fnlst 85; Sprtsmnshp Awd Rec Bsbl League 86; :Bus.

BERASALUCE, ANTONIA; Baltimore Schl For The Arts; Columbia, MD; (Y); Church Yth Grp; Dance Clb; Library Aide; Red Cross Aide; Stu Cncl; Hon Roll; NHS; Kathleen Crofton Mem Scholar 82; 3 Arts Homeland Dance Awd 86; Dncr.

BERGER, ANDREW; Oakland Mills HS; Columbia, MD; (Y); AFS; Boy Scts; Cmnty Wkr; Temple Yth Grp; Nwsp Stf; Stu Cncl; Hon Roll; MD Assn Stu Cncl; Tech For Cable TV Show Graffiti; Polit Actn Cmmttee.

BERGER, MICHAEL; Oakland Mills HS; Columbia, MD; (Y); 10/270; Boy Scts; Co-Capt Math Tm; Off Sr Cls; Trs NHS; SAR Awd; Cmnty Wkr; Yrbk Stf; Hon Roll; Merit Schltc Awd 86; Outstndng Achvt Spn 86, Math 86; U MI; Math.

BERKENKEMPER, CATHY; Chesapeake SR HS; Baltimore, MD; (Y); Drama Clb; Teachers Aide; Chorus; Church Choir; Gov Hon Prg Awd; High Hon Roll; NHS; Pres Schlr; Art Clb; Gradtn Spkr 86; Drama Awds 2 Pins, 1 Ltr, 2 Plqs & 5 Certs 83-86; 2nd Pl Wnnr Crtv Wrtg Cmptns 84-86; Essex CC; Cmmrcl Art.

BERMAN, BONNIE; Mcdonogh Schl; Baltimore, MD; (Y); 18/116; ROTC; Science Clb; Trs AFS; Drama Clb; Thesps; School Musical; School Play; Stage Crew; Mgr Ftbl; Var JV Sftbl; Astro/Physics.

BERNARDO, JOSE; Spring Brook HS; Silver Spring, MD; (Y); 16/488; Church Yth Grp; Math Tm; Trs Ski Clb; Rep Sr Cls; Hon Roll; Wnnr Yng Amercn Comp-Dsgn Mid-Szd Hse 85-86; Nmd Ntl Hspnc Schlr Smifnlst 85-86; U Of MD; Arch.

BERNSTEIN, MARK; The Boys Latin Schl; Baltimore, MD; (S); 5/60; Chess Clb; Yrbk Bus Mgr; Var Bsktbl; JV Var Tennis; High Hon Roll; Hon Roll; U Of NC-CHPL Hill; Accntng.

BERNSTEIN, RICHARD; Arlington Baptist HS; Sykesville, MD; (Y); 10/65; Computer Clb; Variety Show; JV Var Bsktbl; Var Capt Socr; High Hon Roll; Hon Roll; Pres NHS; Pres Scholar Messiah Coll 86; Deans Scholar Messiah Coll 86; Vrsty Socr Coaches Awd 86; Messiah Coll; Comp Info Sys.

BERRY, BILL; John Carroll HS; Joppa, MD; (Y); 23/238; Variety Show; Var JV Bsktbl; Var Tennis; French Hon Soc; Hon Roll.

BERRY, LARISSA; Arlington Baptist Schl; Baltimore, MD; (Y); 16/59; Church Yth Grp; Varsity Clb; Band; Chorus; Drill Tm; Mrchg Band; Pep Band; Yrbk Stf; Sec Jr Cls; JV Cheerleading; Cedarville; Educ.

BERRY, STEPHANIE RENEE; Western HS; Baltimore, MD; (Y); 125/412; Spanish Clb; Princpls Schlr 83-84; Natl Art Hnr Soc 85-86; Photogrphy Clb 85-86; Hampton Inst; Law.

BERTAK, JANET; Joppatowne HS; Joppatown, MD; (Y); Drama Clb; Hosp Aide; Mrchg Band; School Musical; Nwsp Phtg; JV Bsktbl; Var L Mgr(s); Var Powder Puff Ftbl; Var Sftbl; Var Vllybl; Dr.

BESHA, KATY; Immaculata College HS; Washington, DC; (Y); Math Clb; Spanish Clb; School Play; Stage Crew; JV Bsktbl; JV Var Vllybl.

BEST, FRANK; La Plata HS; Waldorf, MD; (Y); Art Clb; Chess Clb; Church Yth Grp; FCA; Letterman Clb; Var L Bsbl; Var L Ftbl; Var L Socr; JV Var Wt Lftg; Hon Roll; MD U; Forestry.

BEST, GARY; Chopticon HS; Mechanicsville, MD; (Y); Computer Clb; Hon Roll; Acad Stu Yr Mth 84; Acad Stu Mnth Sci & Engl 86; U MD; Comp Engrng.

BEST, JOANNE; Regina HS; Adelphi, MD; (Y); Yrbk Stf; Trs Soph Cls; Var Socr; JV Sftbl; Hon Roll; Trs NHS; MD Distngshd Schlr Prog 86; Nrsg.

BESTPITCH, CATHY; Takoma Acad; Silver Spring, MD; (S); Church Yth Grp; GAA; Office Aide; Teachers Aide; School Play; JV Score Keeper; Var Trk; Hon Roll; NHS; Andrews U; Child Psych.

BETLEY, MICHAEL; Archbishop Curley HS; Baltimore, MD; (S); 20/150; Am Leg Boys St; Pres SADD; Pres Frsh Cls; Pres Soph Cls; Pres Jr Cls; Pres Sr Cls; Var Ftbl; Var Capt Lcrss; Hon Roll; NHS; Cornell; Elec Engr.

BETTS, CRYSTAL; Northern SR HS; Baltimore, MD; (Y); FBLA; ROTC; Color Guard; Stu Cncl; Pom Pon; Hon Roll; Prfct Atten Awd; Bus.

BEULAH, NEDRA; Colonel Richadson SR HS; Federalsburg, MD; (Y); 14/112; Am Leg Aux Girls St; Church Yth Grp; Girl Scts; Pres Spanish Clb; Teachers Aide; Nwsp Phtg; Nwsp Rptr; Nwsp Sprt Ed; Nwsp Stf; Yrbk Phtg; Bowie ST Coll; Comp Sci.

BHAM, SHAMEEM; John Carroll HS; Aberdeen, MD; (Y); 63/270; Nwsp Rptr; Yrbk Stf; French Clb; GAA; Girl Scts; Pep Clb; Science Clb; Ski Clb; Stage Crew; Variety Show; Frnch Merit Awd 85-86; Med.

BIALOZEWSKI, DEBORAH; The Institute Of Notre Dame; Baltimore, MD; (Y); Church Yth Grp; Spanish Clb; School Musical; School Play; Stage Crew; Variety Show; Lit Mag; Hon Roll; Prfct Atten Awd; Towsan ST U; Elem Educ.

BICE III, STANLEY; Surrattsville SR HS; Clinton, MD; (Y); Pres Church Yth Grp; Church Choir; Mrchg Band; Symp Band; Var L Tennis; God Cntry Awd; Hon Roll; NHS; Jr NHS; Band; Acadmc Excell Awd 85-86; Jesse J Warr Jr Mem Awd 86; Bus Mgmt.

BICKFORD, SAM; Stephen Decator HS; Ocean City, MD; (Y); Dance Clb; Drama Clb; Office Aide; Rep Frsh Cls; Fshn Shw; Pres Worchester Cnty Alchl-Drg Task Frc; Wilma Boyd Trvl Schl; Trvl Agnt.

BIDINGER, JENNIE; Mercy HS; Reisterstown, MD; (Y); Church Yth Grp; Drama Clb; Library Aide; School Play; NHS; Prfct Atten Awd; Hnrbl Mntn Schlrshp 83; Acctnt.

BIEBER, MARK; Gaithersburg HS; Gaithersburg, MD; (Y); 1/650; Church Yth Grp; Trs Key Clb; Mathletes; Science Clb; Trs Frsh Cls; Trs Soph Cls; JC Awd; NHS; Pres Schlr; Val; Maryland Distngshd Schlr 85-86; George Wshington U Engrng Mdl 84-85; Carnegie-Mellon U; Elec Engrng.

BIEGELEISEN, SHERRI; Baltimore City College HS; Baltimore, MD; (S); School Play; Lit Mag; Hon Roll; Sec NHS; Prfct Atten Awd.

BIEHL, BARBARA; Eleanor Roosevelt HS; Bowie, MD; (Y); AFS; Church Yth Grp; Drama Clb; Thesps; Church Choir; Stu Cncl; Hon Roll; Ntl Merit SF; Pres Schlr; Spanish NHS; Outstndng Acdmc Achvt Awd 85-86; Elizabethtown Coll; Bus.

BIELAT, KAROLYN; Oakland Mills HS; Columbia, MD; (Y); 29/240; Cmnty Wkr; Office Aide; Teachers Aide; Var L Fld Hcky; Hon Roll; Towson ST U; Spch Path.

BIERSAY, LISAGAYE; Wilde Lake HS; Far Rockaway, NY; (Y); 20/225; Camera Clb; Debate Tm; Drama Clb; French Clb; Intnl Clb; JA; JCL; Latin Clb; NFL; Nwsp Stf; Top 10 SR 86; Columiba U NY; Jrnlsm.

BIGGS, DANIEL P; Beall HS; Frostburg, MD; (Y); CAP; Teachers Aide; Thesps; School Play; Stage Crew; Zia Schlrs Hip-Estrn NM U 86; Estrn NM U.

BIGLER, BETTY; Clear Spring HS; Clear Spg, MD; (Y); Chorus; Color Guard; Child Care Cert 86.

BILENKI, JENNIFER; Southern Garrett HS; Deer Pk, MD; (Y); Band; Concert Band; Mrchg Band; Rep Sr Cls; Hon Roll; Psych.

BILLINGS, KELLY; Calvert HS; Pr Frederick, MD; (Y); Cmnty Wkr; Drama Clb; School Musical; School Play; High Hon Roll; Hon Roll; Accntng.

BINCO, POLLY; Fallston HS; Fallston, MD; (Y); 97/250; SADD; Teachers Aide; Powder Puff Ftbl; Hon Roll; Stu Of SAC 83-84; UNC-CHAPEL Hill; Accntng.

BIRCKHEAD, JANEEN L; Snow Hill HS; Snow Hill, MD; (Y); AFS; VP Church Yth Grp; Civic Clb; Cmnty Wkr; Trs 4-H; Hosp Aide; Natl Beta Clb; Mrchg Band; VFW Awd; Political Wkr; Congrssnl Page 86; Govs Yth Advsry Cncl 85-86; AKA 86; Law.

BIRCKHEAD, SCOTT; Gwynn Park HS; Accokeek, MD; (Y); Church Yth Grp; Lit Mag; Var Bsbl; Im Bowling; Capt Socr; Cit Awd; Hon Roll; Prfrmnc Awd In Vrsty Soccer 85; U MD; Psychlgy.

BIRCKHOOD, JUDITH; James M Bennett SR HS; Wetipauin, MD; (Y); Church Yth Grp; FBLA; Girl Scts; Band; Concert Band; Pres Sr Cls; High Hon Roll; Church Choir; Pres Frsh Cls; Pres Soph Cls; Acdmc All Amer 85-86; Howard U Washington; Bus.

BISHOP, SHANNON; Oldtown HS; Oldtown, MD; (Y); Church Yth Grp; FBLA; Sec FHA; Pres Frsh Cls; Pres Soph Cls; Off Jr Cls; Co-Capt Cheerleading; Hon Roll; NHS; Prfct Atten Awd; Soph Attndnt For Hmcmng Queen 84-85; USBEA Outstndng Bus Ed Stdnts 85; Allegany Cmnty Coll; Sec Sci.

BISHOP, TAMMY; Snow Hill HS; Snow Hill, MD; (S); Church Yth Grp; French Clb; Spanish Clb; Hon Roll; Prfct Atten Awd; Schltc Recgntn Awd 85; Htl/Rest Mgr.

BISSET, DIANNA; Bishop Walsh HS; Romney, WV; (Y); 23/104; Art Clb; Band; Concert Band; Mrchg Band; French Hon Soc; High Hon Roll; Hon Roll.

BITTINGER, BRENDA; Southern HS; Swanton, MD; (Y); High Hon Roll; Hon Roll; Acctng.

BITTINGER, DALE E; Southern Garrett HS; Oakland, MD; (S); JV Bsbl; JV Var Bsktbl; Hon Roll; NHS; Div Bsbl All Star Tm 85; Best Tm Plyr Bsktbl 84; Bus.

BIVENS, DAWN; Hancock Middle SR HS; Hancock, MD; (S); VP Am Leg Aux Girls St; Pres DECA; FHA; Pres JA; Teachers Aide; Color Guard; Flag Corp; Ed Yrbk Ed-Chief; Pres Jr Cls; VP Stu Cncl; Jrnlsm.

BIVENS, MATTHEW J; Sherwood HS; Olney, MD; (Y); 45/317; Boy Scts; Cmnty Wkr; Debate Tm; Model UN; Office Aide; Ski Clb; Stu Cncl; Hon Roll; JETS Awd; NHS; 2nd Pl Rqtbl Trnmnt 85; UNC Chpl Hl; Jrnlsm.

BLACK, JILL; Glenelg HS; Glenwood, MD; (Y); Cmnty Wkr; Q&S; Varsity Clb; Variety Show; Yrbk Stf; JV Capt Cheerleading; Hon Roll; Villa Julie Coll; Bus Adm.

BLACK, KAREN; Thomas Stone HS; Waldorf, MD; (S); Key Clb; Rep Stu Cncl; Var L Bsktbl; Var Capt Cheerleading; Var Capt Socr; Cit Awd; High Hon Roll; Jr NHS; NHS; Church Yth Grp; Exploring; Acad Ltr Awd; Miss Teen NE Semi-Fin Scholar Recog Pagnt 85.

BLACKBURN, SUSAN; Suitland HS; Forestvl, MD; (Y); Church Yth Grp; Cmnty Wkr; French Clb; Office Aide; Teachers Aide; Church Choir; Madrigals; Sr Cls; French Hon Soc; Hon Roll.

BLACKLEDGE, TOMI; Northern HS; Huntingtown, MD; (Y); Drill Tm; Pom Pon; Hon Roll; Ntl Merit Ltr; Early Entrnce Clg 86; MD Distngshd Schlr Schlrshp 85; Alpha Lambda Delta Hnr Soc 86; Alpha Gamma Delta; U MD; Dietetics.

BLACKMAN, MICHAEL; Thomas Stone HS; Waldorf, MD; (S); VP Chess Clb; Trs Church Yth Grp; Latin Clb; Trs Science Clb; VP Band; Mrchg Band; Pep Band; School Musical; High Hon Roll; MD ST Champ Tm Olymps Of Mind Prbl Slvng 85; Comp.

BLACKSTONE, COURTNEY; Charles W Woodward HS; Rockville, MD; (Y); Cmnty Wkr; Model UN; Rep Frsh Cls; Rep Soph Cls; Sec Jr Cls; Sec Sr Cls; Rep Stu Cncl; JV Cheerleading; Socr; Hon Roll; Excellence & Superior Attainment In Eng 86.

BLACKSTONE, SHERYL; Gaithersburg HS; Gaithersburg, MD; (Y); Concert Band; Mrchg Band; Orch; Pep Band; Symp Band; Nwsp Rptr; Ed Lit Mag; French Hon Soc; Jr NHS; NHS; Intl Bus.

BLACKWELL, NANCY; Walbrook SR HS; Baltimore, MD; (Y); AFS; French Clb; FBLA; Nwsp Rptr; VP Frsh Cls; VP Soph Cls; VP Jr Cls; Pres Stu Cncl; Badmtn; Capt Cheerleading; U Of MD; Trnlstr.

BLAIR, DIANE; Towson Catholic HS; Reistertown, MD; (Y); 2/76; Church Yth Grp; Rep Frsh Cls; Rep Soph Cls; Rep Jr Cls; Pres Stu Cncl; Gov Hon Prg Awd; High Hon Roll; Kiwanis Awd; NHS; NEDT Awd; Pres Schlrp St Francis Coll 86; Faculty Outstndg Recog Awd 86; Hghst Gen Avg & Salutatrn 86; St Francis Coll Loretto; Nrsng.

BLAIR, IRENE; Takoma Acad; Beltsville, MD; (S); 3/95; Church Yth Grp; Sec Office Aide; Teachers Aide; Concert Band; Rep Jr Cls; JV Cheerleading; Gym; Hon Roll; VP Pres NHS; Bst Stu Biol II & Alg II 84-85; Bst Stu Amer Hstry 84-85; Loma Linda U; Psych.

BLAIR, SHAWN; Smithsburg HS; Hagerstown, MD; (Y); Church Yth Grp; Latin Clb; Stage Crew; Pres Frsh Cls; VP Soph Cls; Pres Jr Cls; Im JV Bsktbl; Var Crs Cntry; Var Trk; Hon Roll; Law.

BLAKE, ERIN; Bishop Walsh HS; Cumberland, MD; (Y); 17/100; Cmnty Wkr; Pep Clb; Yrbk Stf; Rep Jr Cls; Stu Cncl; JV Var Cheerleading; Hon Roll; NHS; Spanish NHS; Allegahy Cnty Spcl Olympcs Vlntr; Duke U; Bus.

BLAKESLEE, JULIE; Mc Donough HS; Pomfret, MD; (Y); Cmnty Wkr; Office Aide; Q&S; Nwsp Rptr; Nwsp Stf; Yrbk Stf; Stat Bsbl; Hon Roll; ST Fnlst Miss MD Teen USA Pgnt 85; Elon Coll NC.

BLANCH, MATTHEW; Arlington Baptist HS; Ijamsville, MD; (Y); Art Clb; Church Yth Grp; Natl Assoc Christian Schls 1st Art Drwng 86; MD Assoc Christian Schls 1st Art Drwng 85-86; Towson ST U; Graphics.

BLAND, STACEY; Western HS; Baltimore, MD; (Y); 173/412; Girl Scts; Radio Clb; Rep Frsh Cls; Rep Soph Cls; Rep Jr Cls; Hon Roll; Prfct Atten Awd; Band; Drill Tm; Rcgntn Achvt Piano 85; Howard U; Cmmnctns.

BLAND, WALTER; Milford Mill SR HS; Baltimore, MD; (Y); Var Bsbl; Var Bsktbl; JV Var Ftbl; Grphc Arts.

BLANEY, MICHELE MARIE; Liberty HS; Marriottsville, MD; (S); AFS; Pres Church Yth Grp; Latin Clb; Mathletes; Varsity Clb; Chorus; Swing Chorus; Var L Socr; High Hon Roll; Prfct Atten Awd; Concord; Trvl Tourism.

BLANK, NOELLE; Montrose Christian HS; Kensington, MD; (Y); Nwsp Ed-Chief; Yrbk Stf; Stu Cncl; Var Trk; Var Vllybl; Ski Clb; Spanish Clb; Pres Jr Cls; Cit Awd; Jrnlsm.

BLANKENSHIP, JODI; Riverdale Baptist Schl; Shadyside, MD; (Y); 11/65; Office Aide; Teachers Aide; Chorus; Yrbk Phtg; Yrbk Rptr; Yrbk Stf; Rep Soph Cls; Rep Stu Cncl; High Hon Roll; NHS; Natl Musc Comptn Chrs 83; Musc Comptn Chrs 83-86; Yrbk Staff Achvt Awd 86; Prince George CC; Elem Educ.

BLANKS, SYLVIA; Northern HS; Owings, MD; (Y); Church Yth Grp; Political Wkr; Science Clb; Chorus; Church Choir; School Play; Hon Roll; Stage Crew; Intrnshps Wth Tlcmnctns Wrtr & Prfssn 84-85; Tch Jrnlsm Cls, Asst Dir Prfsn Prod 85-86; Harford U; Philsphy.

BLASBERG, ROBIN V; Charles W Woodward HS; Rockville, MD; (Y); Cmnty Wkr; Math Tm; Science Clb; Jazz Band; Pep Band; School Musical; Symp Band; High Hon Roll; Hon Roll; JETS Awd.

BLASE, JULIE; Springbrook HS; Brookeville, MD; (Y); Cmnty Wkr; Math Clb; Office Aide; Service Clb; SADD; Rep Frsh Cls; Rep Soph Cls; Rep Jr Cls; Rep Sr Cls; Stu Cncl; Hnrbl Mntn Sci Fair 84; Pom Pon Sqd 86; Schlstc Lttrs 85; Psychlgy.

BLASH, STEVEN J; Governor Thomas Johnson HS; Frederick, MD; (Y); 2/320; Science Clb; Ski Clb; Rep Concert Band; Rep Mrchg Band; Off Jr Cls; Tennis; Bausch & Lomb Sci Awd; High Hon Roll; JETS Awd; Trs NHS; PSAT Natl Merit SF 86; MD Acad Sci Lectures Astrnmy 86; 10 Annual Schlrs Sem Dinner Pgm 86; Med.

BLASS, DAVID; Talmodical Acad; Baltimore, MD; (S); 1/12; Cmnty Wkr; Math Clb; Yrbk Ed-Chief; Var Capt Bsktbl; Hon Roll; NHS; Ntl Merit Ltr; NEDT Awd; St Schlr; MD St Hist Fair Wnnr 85.

BLATZHEIM, JEANNIE; Worcester Country Schl; S Bethany, DE; (Y); PAVAS; Spanish Clb; SADD; Thesps; School Musical; Yrbk Stf; VP Frsh Cls; Tennis; Hon Roll; Church Yth Grp; Roland; Bus.

BLAZOSKY, KAREN J; Eleanor Roosevelt HS; Upr Marlboro, MD; (Y); Scholastic Bowl; High Hon Roll; Hon Roll; Ntl Merit SF; Spanish NHS; Natl Acad Champnshp 85; Acctng.

BLOCK, JONATHAN; Gaithersburg HS; Gaithersburg, MD; (Y); AFS; Math Tm; Yrbk Sprt Ed; Var L Crs Cntry; Var L Trk; Dnfth Awd; High Hon Roll; NHS; Spanish NHS; Odyssey Of Mnd St Champs & 7th In Natn 86.

BLOCKER III, ANANIAS; Eleanor Roosevelt HS; Laurel, MD; (Y); Math Tm; Acpl Chr; Concert Band; Orch; School Musical; Trs Sr Cls; Rep Stu Cncl; Var Bsbl; High Hon Roll; NHS; Engrng.

BLODGETT, TAMMY; Highland View Acad; Hagerstown, MD; (Y); 1/45; Chorus; Nwsp Stf; Yrbk Stf; Sec Soph Cls; VP Jr Cls; Sec Stu Cncl; Var Vllybl; High Hon Roll; NHS; Prfct Atten Awd; Andrews U.

BLOMMERS, KRISTIN; Thomas Stone HS; Waldorf, MD; (Y); 4-H; Science Clb; Teachers Aide; Varsity Clb; Bsktbl; Sftbl; High Hon Roll; Spanish.

BLOOM, CARMEN; Smithsburg SR HS; Cascade, MD; (Y); Latin Clb; Office Aide; Chorus; Nwsp Stf; Stu Cncl; Lion Awd; MD ST Brd Schlrshp 86; Funkstown Amer Legion 86; Hagerstown JC; Prsnnl Mngmnt.

BLOT, JEANNE; Gaithersburg HS; Gaithersburg, MD; (Y); Intnl Clb; Hon Roll.

BLUBAUGH, JIM; Flintstone HS; Oldtown, MD; (S); FFA; Service Clb; VP Pres Jr Cls; Rep Stu Cncl; Var Bsktbl; Var Socr; High Hon Roll; VP Pres NHS; Hugh Obrien Awd 85; Natl Sci Mrt Awd 86; WV U; Aerospace Engnr.

BLUBAUGH, MELISSA; Westminster HS; Westminster, MD; (Y); Latin Clb; Teachers Aide; Chorus; Flag Corp; Mrchg Band; Variety Show; Jr Cls; Hon Roll; Psych.

BLUM, JEREMY; Walt Whitman HS; Germantown, MD; (Y); Chess Clb; Debate Tm; German Clb; JA; Political Wkr; Spanish Clb; Pres Of Amnesty Intl Chapter Whitman 84-85.

BLUNDELL, KARYN; Frederick HS; Frederick, MD; (Y); 43/320; Hosp Aide; Spanish Clb; Off Jr Cls; Var Cheerleading; Var Gym; Var Powder Puff Ftbl; Var Sftbl; Mary & Ruth Smith Schlrshp 86; Slippery Rock U; Spec Educ Tchr.

BLYMAN, DOROTHY; Kent County HS; Chestertown, MD; (Y); 12/168; Trs FBLA; Teachers Aide; Rep Sr Cls; Hon Roll; Elmer T Hawkins Schlrshp 86; Presdntl Schlrshp Excllnce 86-87; Most Outstndng Stu Data Proc 85-86; Goldey Beacom Coll; CPA.

BOARD, JOHN; Seneca Valley HS; Gaithersburg, MD; (Y); Chess Clb; Computer Clb; MCC; Bus Adm.

BOBOLTZ, RENEE; Seneca Valley HS; Darnestown, MD; (Y); Dance Clb; Drama Clb; Science Clb; Service Clb; School Play; Nwsp Rptr; 4-H Awd; High Hon Roll; Ntl Merit Ltr; Rptr 4-H; Principals Awd Outstndg Writing 84; Vet Med.

BOCZAR, KENNETH; Archbishop Curley HS; Baltimore, MD; (Y); Computer Clb; Var Golf; Hon Roll; Excllnce Hist Awd, Pres Acdmc Ftns Awd, Senatorial Schlrshp 86; UMBC; Elec Engrng.

BODIE, MATTHEW T; Loyola HS; Cockeysville, MD; (S); Boy Scts; Church Yth Grp; NFL; Speech Tm; Nwsp Rptr; Hon Roll; NHS; Opt Clb Awd; Marian Burkknott Full Schlrshp HS 83-87; Psychlgy.

BOEBEL, SHELLEY; Franklin SR HS; Reisterstown, MD; (S); FCA; FBLA; Var Capt Cheerleading; Bus.

BOESZE, ASTRID; Lauren SR HS; Laurel, MD; (Y); Church Yth Grp; Ski Clb; Teachers Aide; Chorus; School Musical; Yrbk Stf; Pres Frsh Cls; Pres Soph Cls; Var Bsktbl; Powder Puff Ftbl; Pblc Rltns.

BOGDAN, CHRISTINE; Seton HS; Kingsville, MD; (Y); 8/108; NFL; Nwsp Ed-Chief; Rep Stu Cncl; Var Socr; Var Sftbl; Hon Roll; Pres Schlr; Drama Clb; French Clb; Acad All-Amer INSMA 85; Hghst Avg Geomtry Anatmy & Physc 84-85; Top 10 Engl Awd 86; Towson ST U; Mass Comm.

BOGDAN, MATTHEW; Archbishop Curley HS; Baltimore, MD; (S); 27/143; Var Crs Cntry; Var Trk; Hon Roll; NHS; Comp Pgmr.

BOGGS, JAMES; Liberty HS; Westminster, MD; (S); 2/300; AFS; Computer Clb; Mathletes; Teachers Aide; High Hon Roll; NHS; Ntl Merit Ltr; NEDT Awd; Prfct Atten Awd; St Schlr; U MD; Engrng.

BOGGS, KATHIE; Fort Hill HS; Winchester, VA; (Y); 5/263; Cmnty Wkr; French Clb; Hosp Aide; Pep Clb; SADD; Thesps; Chorus; Rep Frsh Cls; Rep Soph Cls; Rep Jr Cls; Tutoring Awd 85; Stu Cncl Senate Awd & Svc Ltr Awd 86; Outstndng Stu Of Allgny Cnty Achvt Awd 86; Shenandoah Coll; Phrmcy.

BOHANNON JR, GILBERT; Highland View Acad; Hyattsville, MD; (Y); Church Yth Grp; Stage Crew; Variety Show; Lit Mag; Rep Jr Cls; Im Ftbl; Im Sftbl; Im Capt Vllybl; Hon Roll; MD U.

BOLAND, LYNN; Great Mills HS; St Inigoes, MD; (Y); Spanish Clb; SADD; JV Co-Capt Bsktbl; Im Powder Puff Ftbl; High Hon Roll; NHS; Eng,Spnsh Awd 85-86; Cert Apprctn St Marys Cty Cncl Child Yth 86; MI ST U; Vet-Med.

BOLD, SHARON; Duval HS; Davidsonville, MD; (S); Drama Clb; Pres Girl Scts; Natl Beta Clb; Spanish Clb; Teachers Aide; Mrchg Band; School Play; Symp Band; Hon Roll; NHS; WA Coll; Engl.

BOLDEN, MARY; West Nottingham Acad; Oakland, MD; (Y); Am Leg Aux Girls St; Political Wkr; Pres Sr Cls; Stat Bsktbl; L Fld Hcky; Im Tennis; High Hon Roll; Hon Roll; Jr NHS; NHS; J H-W W Bratton Mem Schlrshp 86; Bus Mgmnt.

BOLDEN, WENDY; Fort Hill HS; Cumberland, MD; (Y); Church Yth Grp; Church Choir; Flag Corp; Yrbk Stf; Stu Cncl; Hon Roll; NHS; Cedarville Coll.

BOLLER, DAWN M; Catoctin HS; Sabillasville, MD; (Y); 1/205; Computer Clb; Drama Clb; French Clb; Science Clb; Bausch & Lomb Sci Awd; Hon Roll; NHS; Office Aide; Thesps; MD Jr Sci & Humants Sympsm Rep 86; L Alliance De Francaise Awd 86; Engl Awd 86; Pre-Med.

BOLYARD, SUSAN; Fort Hill HS; Cumberland, MD; (Y); Computer Clb; Natl Beta Clb; Pep Clb; Off Soph Cls; Off Jr Cls; Stu Cncl; Mgr(s); Hon Roll.

BONENBERGER, WILLIAM; Baltimore Polytechnic Inst; Baltimore, MD; (Y); 33/417; Church Yth Grp; Math Tm; Concert Band; Variety Show; Rep Stu Cncl; JV Tennis; Vllybl; High Hon Roll; NHS; German Clb; Amer Soc Of Mech Engrs Awd 86; Pres Acad Ftns Awd 86; Acad Achvt Awd 86; U Of MD Bltmr Cnty; Mech Engr.

BONNEY, CAREY; Bel Air HS; Abington, MD; (Y); Church Yth Grp; Hosp Aide; Office Aide; Pep Clb; ROTC; Spanish Clb; Drill Tm; God Cntry Awd; Hon Roll; Crmnlgy.

BONOMO, DAVID; Chesapeake HS; Balt, MD; (Y); French Clb; Bsbl; Var Wrstlng; French Hon Soc; Hon Roll; NHS; Mathmtcs.

BONSELL, JENNIFER; Fort Hill HS; Cumberland, MD; (Y); Hosp Aide; Band; Concert Band; Mrchg Band; Yrbk Stf; Rep Soph Cls; Rep Jr Cls; Stu Cncl; Hon Roll; Svc Ltr 85; Frostburg ST Coll; Ed.

BOON, WENDY LOUISE; Eleanor Roosevelt HS; Seabrook, MD; (Y); #10 In Class; Library Aide; Math Tm; Chorus; Hon Roll; NHS; Ntl Merit SF; Acad Excllnc Awd 84; Gld Medl Natl Latn Exm 83; U Of VA; Psych.

BOONE, JULIE; Queen Annes Co HS; Church Hill, MD; (Y); Drama Clb; Library Aide; Office Aide; Spanish Clb; SADD; Chorus; Stage Crew; Averett Coll.

BOONE, PAMELA; North Hagerstown HS; Hagerstown, MD; (Y); 73/327; French Clb; Key Clb; Teachers Aide; Chorus; Hon Roll; Hood Coll; Pre Law.

BOOTH, SCOTT; Seneca Valley HS; Gaitherstown, MD; (Y); Science Clb; Spanish Clb; Hon Roll; Engineering.

BORGGREN, TODD; Thomas Johnson HS; Frederick, MD; (Y); Var L Crs Cntry; Var L Trk; Sentrl Schlrshp; Frederick CC; Chem.

BORI, DENISE; Connelly Schl Of The Holy Child; Silver Spg, MD; (Y); Camera Clb; Cmnty Wkr; French Clb; Spanish Clb; SADD; Yrbk Stf; Off Soph Cls; Bsktbl; Vllybl; Accntng.

BOROWSKI, MARGARET; St Johns Literary Inst Prospct Hall; Frederick, MD; (Y); 2/34; Drama Clb; Pres Soph Cls; Pres Jr Cls; Var Bsktbl; Var Capt Vllybl; High Hon Roll; Jr NHS; Pres NHS; Sal; Ntl Hnr Roll 84-86; MD ST Merit Schlstc & Hdmstrs Awd 86; Wstrn MD Coll; Scl Wrkr Comm.

BORSONI, ERIC; Wilde Lake HS; Clarksville, MD; (Y); Boy Scts; CAP; Computer Clb; Rep Stu Cncl; Ftbl; Lcrss; Socr; Trk; Wt Lftg; Sci Achvt Awd 83; Ftbl ST, Reg Chmpns 85; Avtn.

BORTNICK, MARC; The Bullis Schl; Potomac, MD; (Y); 10/90; Cmnty Wkr; Key Clb; Model UN; SADD; Nwsp Rptr; Nwsp Stf; Tennis; High Hon Roll; Jr NHS; NHS.

BOSELY, SEAN; John Carroll HS; Bel Air, MD; (Y); 14/238; Ski Clb; Var L Lcrss; Var L Socr; High Hon Roll; Hon Roll; NHS; Slavic Hon Soc 86; MVP JV Scr 84-85; Aerosp Engrng.

BOSLEY, PATRICIA; Calvary Christian Acad; Cumberland, MD; (Y); 1/15; Pres Pep Clb; Chorus; Yrbk Stf; Pres Jr Cls; Pres Sr Cls; Rep Stu Cncl; Capt Cheerleading; High Hon Roll; Val; Prncpls Awd 85; Tchrs Awd 84; Liberty U; Elem Educ.

BOSLEY, WENDY; Southern Garrett HS; Oakland, MD; (Y); 2/230; GAA; Office Aide; Ski Clb; Var Capt Cheerleading; Gym; Sftbl; Hon Roll; NCA All Amer Chrldr 84-86; Hmcmng Ct 84; Flght Attendnt.

BOSTON, SHEILA; Oxon Hill HS; Clinton, MD; (S); Cmnty Wkr; Teachers Aide; Rep Stu Cncl; Capt Var Cheerleading; High Hon Roll; NHS; Rotary Awd; VP Soph Cls; Jr NHS; Head Of Morning Announcrs 83-86; Pres Germ Hnr Soc 84-86; Mistress Cerem Miss Teen Pgnt 85; Princeton; TV Brdcstng.

BOTTO, NICHOLE; Western HS; Baltimore, MD; (Y); 33/400; Church Yth Grp; NHS.

BOTZUM, KEYS; Oakland Mills HS; Columbia, MD; (Y); 10/270; Computer Clb; German Clb; Math Tm; Hon Roll; Ntl Merit Ltr; St Schlr; ST Chmpns Comp Team 86; Carnegie-Mellon U; Physcs.

BOUNDS, ANNABETH; James M Bennett SR HS; Salisbury, MD; (Y); Church Yth Grp; Intnl Clb; Varsity Clb; Variety Show; Cheerleading; Hon Roll; Hmecmng Crt; Psychlgy.

BOUNDS, HOLLY; Parkside HS; Salisbury, MD; (Y); French Clb; Latin Clb; Library Aide; Ski Clb; Chorus; Yrbk Ed-Chief; Yrbk Phtg; Yrbk Stf; Hon Roll; Stu Svc Awd 85; Jrnlsm.

BOURNE, MERI A; Calvert Christian Schl; Owings, MD; (Y); 4-H; Math Clb; Teachers Aide; Chorus; Church Choir; Nwsp Rptr; Nwsp Stf; Yrbk Bus Mgr; Yrbk Phtg; Yrbk Sprt Ed; Poltcl Sci.

BOWE, KIMBERLY; W Nottingham Acad; Mitchellville, MD; (Y); Art Clb; Camp Fr Inc; Drama Clb; Letterman Clb; Office Aide; Ski Clb; Spanish Clb; Teachers Aide; School Play; Trs Soph Cls; Schlrshps Foxcroft & W Nottingham Boarding Schls 83-87; Spelman; Law.

BOWEN, KEVIN A; Old Mill SR HS; Crownsville, MD; (Y); 5/509; Math Clb; Math Tm; Varsity Clb; Var Capt Crs Cntry; Var Capt Trk; High Hon Roll; Hon Roll; NHS; Schlrs Athlt Awd 86; MD Dstngshd Schlr Hnrb Mntn 85; Wrcstr Poly Tech Inst; Comp Sci.

BOWEN, LAVONDE; Patterson HS; Baltimore, MD; (Y); ROTC; Thesps; School Musical; School Play; Stage Crew; Variety Show; Var L Crs Cntry; Var L Mgr(s); Var Capt Sftbl; Var Mgr Wrstlng; Commn Wlth Agrmnt Prog 86; Cert Recog Perfrmng Arts & Stage Crft 86; Spec Olympcs Vlntr Awd 86; Humnts.

BOWEN, PATRICK; Landon Schl; Potomac, MD; (S); 1/71; Debate Tm; French Clb; Math Tm; Band; Yrbk Ed-Chief; High Hon Roll; JP Sousa Awd; Drama Clb; SADD; AATF Ntl Frnch Cont-1st Pl Mid-Atlantc, 3rd Pl Ntl 85; Amer Hrt Assn-Hrt Lectrs Fllwshp Wnnr 85; Premed.

BOWEN, SHANNON; Notre Dame Preparatory HS; Baltimore, MD; (Y); 20/125; 1st Hnrs Each Smstr-H S; Fordham U; Pre-Dntstry.

BOWER, TERRI; Westminster HS; Finksburg, MD; (Y); JA; Math Tm; Chorus; Teachers Aide; Rep Soph Cls; Rep Jr Cls; Trs Sr Cls; High Hon Roll; Hon Roll; NHS; MD Acad Sci Bio Seminar Johns Hopkins U 86; Young Schlrs Wester MD Coll 86; Bio.

BOWERS, BROOKS E; Du Val HS; Seabrook, MD; (Y); 3/389; Church Yth Grp; Q&S; Teachers Aide; Nwsp Ed-Chief; Yrbk Stf; Var Wrstlng; High Hon Roll; Hon Roll; NHS; Spanish NHS; Its Acad WA Schltc Quiz Show 85-86; Usher, Teller, Liturgist Oaklands Presbytrn Church 85-86; Jrnlsm.

BOWERS, JILL; Catoctin HS; Thurmont, MD; (Y); Cmnty Wkr; Rep Stu Cncl; Score Keeper; Trk; Hon Roll; Lion Awd; @episcopal Wmns Orphan Fnd Schlrshp 86; Western MD Coll; Psych.

BOWLES, CAROL; Wheaton HS; Rockville, MD; (Y); 1/386; Church Yth Grp; Red Cross Aide; Madrigals; High Hon Roll; Jr NHS; NHS; St Schlr; Val; Teachers Aide; Lit Mag; Soroptmst Yth Citznshp Awd, Soroptmst Intl Montgomery Cnty 86; Pres Schlrshp-U Evansville 86; U Of Evansville; Physcl Therpy.

BOWLES, NANCY; Wheaton HS; Rockville, MD; (Y); 39/386; Church Yth Grp; Thesps; Madrigals; Lit Mag; Rep Stu Cncl; Hon Roll; Jr NHS; Sec NHS; Ntl Merit Ltr; Pres Schlr; Alumni Merit Schlrshp 85; Music Major Schlrshp 86; Occptnl Thrpy Schlrshp Natl Soc DAR 86; U Of Evansvill IN; Music Thrpy.

BOWLIN, LEANN; La Plata HS; Waldorf, MD; (Y); Am Leg Aux Girls St; Church Yth Grp; FBLA; Pep Clb; Ski Clb; Chorus; Yrbk Stf; Hon Roll; Academic.

BOWLING, DANIEL; La Plata HS; Newburg, MD; (Y); 4-H; SADD; Teachers Aide; Variety Show; Capt Golf; 4-H Awd; Hon Roll; Olympics Of Mind 85-86; Dept Of Defnse Sci & Engrng Apprentce Prog 85-86; Chem Engrng.

BOWLING, MIKE; La Plata HS; La Plata, MD; (S); Off Frsh Cls; VP Soph Cls; VP Jr Cls; Rep Stu Cncl; Hon Roll; Bus Admin.

BOWMAN, CONNIE; Northern Garrett HS; Mchenry, MD; (Y); Office Aide; Ski Clb; SADD; Drill Tm; Rep Jr Cls; Rep Stu Cncl; Tri-St Beauty Acad; Beautician.

BOWMAN, KRIS; La Plata HS; La Plata, MD; (Y); 4-H; Chorus; Church Choir; Yrbk Sprt Ed; Var L Tennis; Var L Vllybl; 4-H Awd; Hon Roll; Jr NHS; NHS; U Maryland; Knslgy.

BOWYER, MICHAEL W; Northern HS; Friendsville, MD; (Y); Teachers Aide; Varsity Clb; Stage Crew; Var Capt Bsbl; Capt JV Bsktbl; High Hon Roll.

BOYD, ARTHUR; St Andrews Episcopal HS; Chevy Chase, MD; (Y); Art Clb; Computer Clb; School Play; Stage Crew; Nwsp Stf; Rep Stu Cncl; Mgr Vllybl; Science Clb; Hon Roll; Math.

BOYD, MICHAEL; Bishop Walsh HS; Cumberland, MD; (Y); 15/107; Am Leg Boys St; Cmnty Wkr; Political Wkr; Var L Bsbl; Var L Bsktbl; Var L Ftbl; Wt Lftg; Hon Roll; Prfct Atten Awd; Allegany CC Math Comp 87-88; Allegany CC; Engr.

BOYD, SHELLEY; Sparrows Point Middle/SR HS; Baltimore, MD; (Y); Pres Church Yth Grp; Band; Off Church Choir; Concert Band; Mrchg Band; Mgr Bsktbl; Mgr Lcrss; Mgr(s); Hon Roll; NHS; Comp Engrng.

BOYD, TAMMY LYNN; Gaithersburg HS; Gaithersburg, MD; (Y); 235/589; Church Yth Grp; Girl Scts; Office Aide; OEA; Pep Clb; ROTC; SADD; Teachers Aide; Varsity Clb; Chorus; Sec.

BOYD, TERESA; Havre De Grace HS; Bear, DE; (Y); Am Leg Aux Girls St; SADD; Pres Chorus; Sec Stu Cncl; Capt Fld Hcky; Capt Lcrss; VP NHS; Pep Clb; Color Guard; Jazz Band; Al Cesky Schlrshp 86; Mary A Brunner Schlrshp 86; Amer Legion Cert Of Schl Awd 86; Foreign Lang Pin 86; Flagler Coll; Intl Bus.

BOYER, EUGENE; Brunswick HS; Knoxville, MD; (Y); Computer Clb; Scholastic Bowl; Spanish Clb; Chorus; School Musical; JV Trk; Hon Roll; Acad Ltr 84-86; Sports Ltr 84.

BOYLE, BRENDA; S S Peter & Paul HS; Queen Anne, MD; (Y); 4/28; Pres Stu Cncl; Var Bsktbl; Var Capt Fld Hcky; Var Sftbl; CC Awd; DAR Awd; NHS; VFW Awd; Voice Dem Awd; MD ST Hse Dlgt Schlrshp 86; Pres Acdmc Ftns Awds Pgm 86; US Army Rsrv Schlr Athlt Awd 86; Salisbury ST Coll; Bus Admn.

BOZMAN, CINDY; Washington HS; Frenchtown, MD; (Y); Ski Clb; Sftbl; Hon Roll.

BOZZI, KEVIN M; Thomas Stone HS; Bryantown, MD; (Y); Drama Clb; Latin Clb; Rep Stu Cncl; Hon Roll; U Of MD; Acctg.

BRACKINS, ANGELA F; Rising Sun HS; Rising Sun, MD; (Y); 7/140; Pep Clb; Concert Band; Yrbk Stf; Off Stu Cncl; Cheerleading; Cit Awd; High Hon Roll; Hon Roll; NHS; MD ST Mrt Schlstc Awd 86; Prsdntl Acdmc Ftns Awd 86; Dplma Pls Prgrm Hnrs Cert 86; Cecil CC; Accntng.

BRACY, LISA; Suitland HS; Suitland, MD; (Y); French Clb; Trs French Hon Soc; Hon Roll; Trs NHS; Comptr Sci.

BRADLEY, DOLLY; Valley HS; Lonaconing, MD; (Y); Church Yth Grp; Cmnty Wkr; French Clb; Girl Scts; Q&S; Teachers Aide; School Play; Nwsp Bus Mgr; Nwsp Rptr; Nwsp Stf; Shield Awd 85-86; Good Knght Awd 84-85; Allegany CC; Nrs.

BRADSHAW, KRISTEN; Franklin HS; Reisterstown, MD; (Y); Hosp Aide; Office Aide; Band; Color Guard; Concert Band; Mrchg Band; Crs Cntry; Sftbl; Trk; Hon Roll; Radford; Law Enfrcmnt.

BRADSHAW, MICHELE; Centennial HS; Ellicott City, MD; (Y); Art Clb; VP Church Yth Grp; Cmnty Wkr; Hosp Aide; Library Aide; Teachers Aide; Co-Capt Drill Tm; Hon Roll; U Of MD; Elmntry Educ.

BRADY, MARK P; Bishop Walsh HS; La Vale, MD; (Y); 26/104; Thesps; Jazz Band; Mrchg Band; School Musical; School Play; Stage Crew; NHS; Ntl Merit SF; Grmn Hnr Soc 85; Natl Art Hnr Soc 85; Catholic U; Chem Engrng.

BRADY, THERESA; Dundalk SR HS; Baltimore, MD; (Y); Church Yth Grp; Hosp Aide; SADD; High Hon Roll; Hon Roll; NHS; Awd Outstndg Piano 85-86; Schl Svc & High Acad Achievmnt 85-86; U Of Maryland; Nursing.

BRADY, TIM; Northern HS; Grantsville, MD; (Y); Boy Scts; Chess Clb; Cmnty Wkr; VICA; Var L Bsbl; Stat Bsktbl; Stat Ftbl; Var L Golf; Hon Roll.

BRAFFORD, DEBORAH L; North Carroll HS; Manchester, MD; (Y); 12/300; Drama Clb; VP VICA; Hon Roll; NHS; Prfct Atten Awd; Carroll Co Advsry Cncl Voctnl Tech Ed 84-85; Pres Acdmc Fit Awd 85-86; ST MD Merit Schlstc Awd; Clemson U; Cvl Engrng.

BRAHAM, BECKY; Chopticon HS; Mechanicsville, MD; (Y); Sec Latin Clb; Flag Corp; Opt Clb Awd; Med Fld.

BRAND, STEVEN RENARD; Eastern HS; Baltimore, MD; (Y); 8/257; Boys Clb Am; FBLA; JA; High Hon Roll; Hon Roll; Prfct Atten Awd; Peabody Med 2nd Grd 85-86; Pres Acdmc Ftnss Awd 85-86; 1st Pl FBLA Cmptr Prg Reg IIB Cmptv 85-86; Cmptr.

BRANDENBURG, KARIN; Bowie HS; Bowie, MD; (Y); AFS; Church Yth Grp; Intnl Clb; Office Aide; Trs Pres Science Clb; Spanish Clb; SADD; Var L Bsktbl; Var L Sftbl; Hon Roll; Acdmc Achvt Awd 83-84; Outstndng Olympn Awd 84; Notre Dame U.

BRANDES, ALISA; Allegany HS; Lavale, MD; (Y); 11/250; Computer Clb; Library Aide; SADD; High Hon Roll; Hon Roll; NHS; Law.

BRANDON, STARCINDA; Potomac HS; Suitland, MD; (Y); ROTC; Band; Church Choir; Var Bsktbl; JV Vllybl; Hon Roll; Schlrshp Baptist Chrch 86; Law.

BRANDT, CHRIS; Cardinal Gibbons HS; Baltimore, MD; (Y); Rep Soph Cls; Rep Jr Cls; Rep Sr Cls; Rep Stu Cncl; Var L Bsbl; Var L Bsktbl; JV Socr; High Hon Roll; Hon Roll; Jr NHS; WA Coll; Bus.

BRANHAM, ANTONIO; Forestville HS; Suitland, MD; (Y); Capt ROTC; Pres Soph Cls; VP Stu Cncl; Var Trk; High Hon Roll; VP NHS; Prfct Atten Awd; Ed Nwsp Stf; Debate Tm; JA; Outstndng Frshmn, Soph, JR 84-86; 2nd Pl Reg Sci Fair 86; Engrng.

BRANNAN, CYNDI; Calvert HS; Pr Frederick, MD; (Y); Dance Clb; Sec Spanish Clb; Capt Cheerleading; Coach Actv; Trk; High Hon Roll; Pres Schlr; St Schlr; Deans Schlrshp Bus, Econ 86; Towson ST U; Intl Bus.

BRANNAN, VALERIE; High Point HS; Beltsville, MD; (Y); Varsity Clb; Variety Show; Off Jr Cls; Bsktbl; Var Cheerleading; Var Gym; Mgr(s); Hon Roll; Prfct Atten Awd.

BRANSON, LESLIE; Holton-Arms Schl; Washington, DC; (Y); Cmnty Wkr; Hosp Aide; Library Aide; Model UN; Office Aide; Pep Clb; Spanish Clb; Varsity Clb; Fld Hcky; Sftbl; Cmmnd Stdnt Ntl Achvt Schlrshp 85; Engrng.

BRAUER, JEFF; Thomas S Wootton HS; Gaithersburg, MD; (Y); AFS; Debate Tm; FBLA; Pres JA; Nwsp Phtg; Nwsp Rptr; High Hon Roll; City Of Rockville Phtgrphr 86; Natl JR Achvmnt Conf Attnd 86; Chldrns Smmr Vlg Cnslr 85; Intl Bus.

BRAWLEY, CHARISSA A; Gaithersburg HS; Gaithersburg, MD; (S); 136/680; Ski Clb; Teachers Aide; Rep Jr Cls; Rep Stu Cncl; Hon Roll; Marriott Awd For Exclnc 86; Culinary Inst Of Amer; Chef.

BRAXTON, TUAWANA; Porkdale HS; New Carrollton, MD; (Y); Office Aide; Pres Spanish Clb; Nwsp Rptr; Nwsp Stf; VP Sr Cls; Capt Vllybl; Mgr Wrstlng; High Hon Roll; NHS; Pres Spanish NHS; House Of Dlgts Schlrshp 86-87; Pres Acadmc Ftnss Awd 86; Merit Schltc Awd 86; U Of MD; Bio.

BREACH, SCOTT E; Severn Schl; Edgewater, MD; (Y); 1/78; Computer Clb; Nwsp Stf; Var Golf; Var Wrstlng; Bausch & Lomb Sci Awd; Elks Awd; French Hon Soc; NHS; Ntl Merit Schol; Val; Mdl Math And Sci 85; Benjamin Louck Meml Awd 85-86; Math Awd 86; Carnegie Mellon U; Elect Engrg.

BREDENBURG, DAVID E; North Carroll HS; Finksburg, MD; (Y); 20/320; Am Leg Boys St; Varsity Clb; Yrbk Stf; Off Soph Cls; Off Jr Cls; JV Bsbl; JV Ftbl; Hon Roll; Ntl Merit Ltr; Spanish Clb; Amer Lgn Boys Ntn 86; US Nvl Acad; Aerontcl Engrng.

BREEN, DANIEL; Dulaney SR HS; Timonium, MD; (Y); 63/420; Church Yth Grp; VICA; Var Socr; Im Sftbl; High Hon Roll; U Of SC.

BREHM, DANIEL; Fort Hill HS; Cumberland, MD; (Y); Church Yth Grp; Computer Clb; Service Clb; Chorus; Church Choir; Navy.

BRENNAN, FRED; La Plata HS; Bel Alton, MD; (Y); Computer Clb; Mrchg Band; Wt Lftg; High Hon Roll; Hon Roll; NHS; Frnch Awd 86; VPI Elec Engr.

BRIDGES, KELLIE; Western SR HS; Baltimore, MD; (Y); Cmnty Wkr; Thesps; Church Choir; Stage Crew; Variety Show; Rep Soph Cls; Hst Jr Cls; Hst Sr Cls; Prfct Atten Awd; Acctg.

BRIDGES, MARK; Wolbrook HS; Baltimore, MD; (Y); FBLA; Concert Band; School Musical; School Play; Im Wrstlng; Hon Roll; Prfct Atten Awd; Bus.

BRIDGES, MICHELE; Allegany County Vocational Tech Ctr; Mt Savage, MD; (Y); Hosp Aide; NHS; Computer Clb; French Clb; Office Aide; High Hon Roll; Hon Roll; HOSA 84-86; 1st Pl ST Wd Lvl Prprd Spch Cntst 85-86; 1st Pl Lvl Essy Cntst Natl Lvl 86; Med.

BRIGGS, BRIAN E; Mc Donough HS; White Plains, MD; (Y); Church Yth Grp; Church Choir; Concert Band; Jazz Band; Mrchg Band; Orch; School Musical; Symp Band; Hon Roll; JP Sousa Awd; Mst Otstndg Bnd Stu; Supr ST Slo Fstvl Rtngs; All-Cnty Hnr Bnd; Moody Bible Inst; Chrch Music.

BRINKLEY, RENEE; Crisfield HS; Marion, MD; (Y); Cmnty Wkr; Dance Clb; FHA; JA; Science Clb; SADD; Mrchg Band; VP Stu Cncl; Crs Cntry; Sftbl; Peer Ldrshp Cert Compltn Week Pro A; Georgetown; Bus Admin.

BRISUENO, RAMSEY; Baltimore Polytechnic Inst; Baltimore, MD; (Y); Nwsp Stf; Lit Mag; Rep Frsh Cls; Rep Soph Cls; Rep Jr Cls; Rep Sr Cls; Drmtc Spkng Awd Smmr Wrtng Prog SWOP 82; Scientc Wrtng Awd SWOP 83; Comm.

BRITTINGHAM, KEVIN; Arlington Baptist HS; Baltimore, MD; (Y); 4/60; Church Yth Grp; Band; Church Choir; Mrchg Band; Var Bsbl; High Hon Roll; Prfct Atten Awd; Schl Hnr Soc 86; Schl Svc Awd 86; Sci Awd MACS 1st 82-85; Sci.

BROADWATER, SAMANTHA; Valley HS; Lonaconing, MD; (Y); Church Yth Grp; FHA; Office Aide; Teachers Aide; Nwsp Stf; Stu Cncl; VP Var Cheerleading; Score Keeper; Timer; Var Capt Vllybl; Vllbyl Regnl Champs 84-85; NCA Chrldng Fnlst 85-86; Allegany CC; Sec Sci.

BROBST, JOHN; Northern Garrett HS; Mchenry, MD; (Y); Church Yth Grp; Computer Clb; SADD; Rep Sr Cls; JV Var Bsktbl; High Hon Roll; Hon Roll; Stu Of The Month 85; Outstndng Stu Of The Yr 85-86; Frostbury ST Coll; Elec Engr.

BROCKI, RAY; Mt St Joseph HS; Baltimore, MD; (Y); Band; Concert Band; Wrstlng; Towson ST U; Pol Sci.

BRODER, JOANNA; Walter Johnson HS; Bethesda, MD; (Y); Speech Tm; Stage Crew; Tennis; Trk; Hon Roll.

BRODEUR, DAWN; Mount De Sales Acad; Baltimore, MD; (Y); Cmnty Wkr; Drama Clb; School Play; Var Sftbl; Hon Roll; Drama Awd 84; Excllnc JR Trm Paper Eng 86; Psychlgy.

BRODY, LISA; Wilde Lake HS; Columbia, MD; (Y); Debate Tm; Math Tm; NFL; Pres PAVAS; Chorus; Var L Tennis; NHS; Ntl Merit SF; Hosp Aide; Lit Mag; Volntr Archlgy Natl Pk Serv 85-86; 1st Pl Marjorie Holt Essay Cntst 85; Archaeology.

BROGDEN, SHIRLEY; Walbrook SR HS; Baltimore, MD; (Y); VP Church Yth Grp; JA; Speech Tm; Church Choir; Yrbk Stf; High Hon Roll; Hon Roll; Jr NHS; NHS; Howard U; Med.

BRONSON, TONYA; Crossland HS; Temple Hills, MD; (Y); Cmnty Wkr; Drama Clb; Hosp Aide; Pep Clb; Teachers Aide; Band; Church Choir; Var Cheerleading; Var Trk; Hon Roll; Spellman; Acctng.

BROOKS, EDWARD; Dematha HS; Laurel, MD; (Y); Church Yth Grp; High Hon Roll; Hon Roll; Law.

BROOKS, KATHRYN A; Sherwood HS; Olney, MD; (Y); Church Yth Grp; Library Aide; Band; Chorus; School Musical; Hon Roll; NHS; Spanish NHS; Ski Clb; Concert Band; Prncpls Awd-Outstndng Wrtng 85; Sprior & Exclint Rtngs-Cnty & ST Solo Fstvls 84; Engrng.

BROOKS, KEVIN; Parkdale HS; Berwyn Heights, MD; (Y); French Clb; Teachers Aide; Yrbk Bus Mgr; Var Socr; French Hon Soc; Hon Roll; Pres Acad Ftns Awd 85-86; U MD; Bus.

BROOKS, KURT; Parkdale HS; College Park, MD; (S); Church Yth Grp; French Clb; Teachers Aide; Yrbk Stf; Rep Stu Cncl; Var L Socr; Pres French Hon Soc; Hon Roll; NHS; U MD; Biolgcl Rsrch.

BROOKS, STEVE; Baltimore Polytechnic HS; Baltimore, MD; (Y); Var JV Bsbl; Var L Wrstlng.

BROOME, KEITH; Allegany HS; Cumberland, MD; (Y); #1 In Class; AFS; Church Yth Grp; Concert Band; Sec Mrchg Band; High Hon Roll; Jr NHS; NHS.

BROSSEAU, SUZANNE; The John Carroll School; Havre De Grace, MD; (Y); Girl Scts; Pres Service Clb; Chorus; Lit Mag; Poetry Awd From Schl Lit Mag 84-85; Hist.

BROTH, RICHARD; Talmudical Acad; Baltimore, MD; (S); Varsity Clb; Nwsp Rptr; Nwsp Stf; Lit Mag; Pres Jr Cls; Rep Stu Cncl; Var Bsktbl; Hon Roll; NHS; MD Ec Awd Greatr Baltimore Hstry Fair 85; U Of PA; Pre-Med.

BROTHERS, STACY; Potomac HS; Oxon Hill, MD; (Y); Church Yth Grp; Office Aide; Teachers Aide; Church Choir; Nwsp Rptr; Hon Roll.

BROWER, MARY ELLEN; Montgomery Blair HS; Silver Spring, MD; (Y); 38/353; Church Yth Grp; French Clb; Girl Scts; Spanish Clb; Church Choir; Yrbk Stf; Mgr Vllybl; Hon Roll; NHS; Lenoir Rhyne Coll; Physns Assit.

BROWN, ALLERONDA; John F Kennedy HS; Silver Springs, MD; (Y); 118/480; Drama Clb; Pep Clb; Teachers Aide; Thesps; Yrbk Stf; Cheerleading; Hon Roll; Commended Stu 85; Intl Affairs.

BROWN, ANDREA; Baltimore City College HS; Baltimore, MD; (S); Drama Clb; School Musical; School Play; Nwsp Rptr; Nwsp Sprt Ed; Hst Soph Cls; Rep Jr Cls; High Hon Roll; NHS; Ntl Merit SF; Jrnlsm.

BROWN, ANTHONY; De Matha Catholic HS; Hyattsville, MD; (Y); Band; JV Trk; Hon Roll; Engrng.

BROWN, BARBARA; Thomas Stone HS; Waldorf, MD; (S); Drama Clb; FHA; Ed Yrbk Phtg; Yrbk Rptr; Yrbk Stf; High Hon Roll; Hon Roll; Charles Cnty CC; Comp.

BROWN, BARRY; Cardinal Gibbons HS; Baltimore, MD; (Y); JA; Im Var Bsktbl; Im Bowling; Im Score Keeper; Im Tennis; Hon Roll; Gld Mdl In Bsktbl 86; Slvr Mdl Yth Games In Bsktbl 85; Bus.

BROWN, BURTON; Queen Annes County HS; Millington, MD; (Y); DECA; Band; Mrchg Band; Pep Band; Widner U; Bus.

BROWN, CAROLYN; Centennial HS; Ellicott City, MD; (Y); VP Church Yth Grp; Cmnty Wkr; Political Wkr; Q&S; School Musical; Nwsp Rptr; Ed Nwsp Sprt Ed; Rep Stu Cncl; Var JV Fld Hcky; Hon Roll; MD Sci Smnr Fnlst 83-84; Prdctn Mgr For Nwspr 85-86; Howard Cnty Stu Cncl Chrmn 85-86; Bus.

BROWN, CATHERINE; Forestville HS; Forestville, MD; (Y); NFL; Spanish Clb; Yrbk Stf; Sec Jr Cls; Rep Stu Cncl; Var Pom Pon; Hon Roll; NHS; Mst Outstndng Jr 85-86; Harvard Clb Awd 85-86; Stu Mnth Engl 83-84; NC ST; Engr.

BROWN, CHARITY; Harford Vocational-Technical HS; Forest Hills, MD; (Y); VICA; Var L Cheerleading; Var L Trk; Hon Roll; Csmtlgst.

BROWN, DONNA-MARIE; Thomas S Wootton HS; Rockville, MD; (Y); Church Yth Grp; VP Intnl Clb; Science Clb; Teachers Aide; Var Cheerleading; Hon Roll; Chem.

BROWN, ERICA; Paul Laurence Dunbar HS; Baltimore, MD; (Y); 5/35; Computer Clb; Dance Clb; Girl Scts; German Clb; School Play; Symp Band; JV Bsbl; Cheerleading; Trk; Hon Roll; Trphy Top Engl Stu 83; Nrsng.

BROWN, GREGORY; De Matha HS; Washington, DC; (Y); Art Clb; Church Yth Grp; CAP; Debate Tm; Letterman Clb; Speech Tm; Trs Soph Cls; Var Bsktbl; Var Tennis; Hon Roll; Liberal Arts Coll; Arch.

BROWN, GREGORY; Rockville HS; Rockville, MD; (Y); 42/464; Quiz Bowl; SADD; Teachers Aide; Nwsp Rptr; Im Bsktbl; Hon Roll; Jr NHS; NHS; Ntl Merit Ltr; Nwsp Mngng Editor; Pres Acadmc Ftns Awd; Naval ROTC Schlrshp; U Of PA; Pre Law.

BROWN, JENNIFER; Catoctin HS; Thurmont, MD; (Y); Boy Scts; Pres Drama Clb; Red Cross Aide; Sec VP Science Clb; School Musical; School Play; Stage Crew; Rep Soph Cls; Pres Jr Cls; Stu Cncl; Numers Dancg Awds.

BROWN, JENNIFER A; Broadneck SR HS; Arnold, MD; (Y); 20/315; Girl Scts; Mrchg Band; Symp Band; Rep Soph Cls; Rep Jr Cls; Rep Stu Cncl; JV Cheerleading; Pom Pon; Hon Roll; NHS; Cert Of Recgntn Comptv Schlrshp Pgm 86; Millersvl U; Commnctns.

BROWN, JORG; Thomas Stone HS; Waldorf, MD; (S); Teachers Aide; Yrbk Phtg; Yrbk Rptr; Yrbk Stf; Hon Roll; U Of MD; Bus Admin.

BROWN, KATHLEEN; Patterson HS; Baltimore, MD; (Y); VP Church Yth Grp; Cmnty Wkr; Dance Clb; GAA; Chorus; Church Choir; Badmtn; Bsktbl; Trk; JV Vllybl; Comm Coll Schlrshp 86; Comp Pgmr.

BROWN, KELLY; St Marys HS; Gambrills, MD; (Y); Dance Clb; Speech Tm; SADD; Chorus; Jazz Band; Yrbk Stf; Rep Frsh Cls; Rep Soph Cls; Var Cheerleading; Var Capt Sftbl; U Of MD; Vet Med.

BROWN, KEVIN; Elkton HS; Elkton, MD; (Y); Boy Scts; Church Yth Grp; Teachers Aide; Church Choir; Hon Roll; Comp Prgmr.

BROWN, LAURA; Liberty HS; Westminster, MD; (S); 16/320; Drama Clb; Mathletes; Pres Thesps; Chorus; Church Choir; School Musical; School Play; Yrbk Stf; Hon Roll; NHS; Gftd & Tlntd ST Econ & Gov Internshp Prog 85.

BROWN, LEESA; Takoma Acad; Takoma Park, MD; (S); Church Yth Grp; Cmnty Wkr; Office Aide; Ski Clb; Teachers Aide; Ed Yrbk Stf; Hon Roll; NHS; Southern Coll.

BROWN, LISA LA RONDA; Mercy High Exemplary Schl; Baltimore, MD; (Y); Church Yth Grp; GAA; Chorus; Church Choir; School Musical; School Play; Variety Show; Rep Stu Cncl; Art Dctn Awd 85-86; Dstngsh Schlr Tlnt Art 85-86; Art Thrpy.

BROWN, MARK; Archbishop Curley HS; Baltimore, MD; (S); Am Leg Boys St; Aud/Vis; Chess Clb; Computer Clb; Science Clb; Mgr(s); Score Keeper; Trk; Hon Roll; NHS; Loyola Coll; Acctg.

BROWN, MARY; Institute Of Notre Dame; Baltimore, MD; (Y); Church Yth Grp; Cmnty Wkr; Service Clb; Spanish Clb; Hon Roll; Spcl Ed Tchr.

BROWN, MELISSA; Fort Hill HS; Cumberland, MD; (Y); Mgr Office Aide; Pep Clb; Off Frsh Cls; Off Soph Cls; Rep Jr Cls; Rep Sr Cls; Hon Roll; NHS; Allegany Comm Coll; Mgmt.

BROWN, NICHELLE; St Marys Ryken HS; Loveville, MD; (Y); 6/139; Spanish Clb; Rep Stu Cncl; JV Var Bsktbl; DAR Awd; Gov Hon Prg Awd; High Hon Roll; VP NHS; NEDT Awd; Rep Frsh Cls; Natl Achvt Commended Stu 85; U MD Baltimore; Elec.

BROWN, NICOLE; Western HS; Baltimore, MD; (Y); Dance Clb; Sec French Clb; Hosp Aide; Drill Tm; Rep Stu Cncl; Cit Awd; 4-H Awd; Hon Roll; NHS; Prfct Atten Awd; Cmptn 100 Hrs Of Vlntr Srv At GSH 84; Chld Dvlpmnt Psych.

BROWN, NORCLIFFE E; Thomas S Wootten HS; Potomac, MD; (Y); 63/401; AFS; Quiz Bowl; Science Clb; Nwsp Rptr; NEDT Awd.

BROWN, ORLENA; St Marys Ryken HS; La Plata, MD; (Y); Church Yth Grp; Drama Clb; Spanish Clb; JV Var Bsktbl; Mgr(s); Hon Roll; Child Psych.

BROWN, RAVI; Northern HS; Baltimore, MD; (Y); 53/298; Church Yth Grp; FBLA; Model UN; School Musical; Variety Show; Rep Jr Cls; Rep Sr Cls; Mgr Lcrss; Hon Roll; Prfct Atten Awd; Martha A Coleman Schlrshp 86; Alpha Phi Omega Natl Svc Frat Schlrhsp 86; Excllnce Speech I & ST Ii 86; Morgan ST U; Comp Sci.

BROWN, RHONDA; St Vincent Pallotti HS; Laurel, MD; (Y); French Clb; Office Aide; Teachers Aide; Varsity Clb; Capt Cheerleading; Capt Sftbl; French Hon Soc; Hon Roll; MVP Sftbl 82-83 & 84-85; Homecmng Prncess 83-85; Acad All Amer 83-84; Intl Foreign Lang Awd 83-84; U Of MD.

BROWN, ROBIN M; John F Kennedy HS; Silver Spring, MD; (Y); 98/468; Drama Clb; Office Aide; Pep Clb; Red Cross Aide; Teachers Aide; Lit Mag; Hon Roll; Intl Rltns.

BROWN, RONDA; Easton HS; Trappe, MD; (Y); Church Yth Grp; DECA; FBLA; FHA; Spanish Clb; Church Choir; Yrbk Stf; Var Trk; Hon Roll; Upward Bound Chesapeake Coll 84; Ldrshp Awd 85-86; Goldey Beacom; Exec Sec.

BROWN, RYAN A; Oxon Hill HS; Ft Washington, MD; (Y); Church Yth Grp; Math Tm; Ski Clb; Rep Stu Cncl; JV Bsktbl; French Hon Soc; NHS; Natl Achvt Scholar Pgm Commended Stu 85; Acad Excllnce Prince Geo Co 84; Dept Def Apprntcshp Pgm 85; Bio.

BROWN, SEAN R; Carver Voc Tech HS; Baltimore, MD; (Y); Boy Scts; Band; Var Swmmng; Cit Awd; Hon Roll; Howard U; Arch.

BROWN, SHARON; Dulaney R HS; Phoenix, MD; (Y); Church Yth Grp; Drama Clb; Key Clb; Service Clb; Church Choir; Crs Cntry; Trk; Hon Roll; Jr NHS; NHS; Outstndng Span Stu Awd 83-84; Lang.

BROWN, SHARON S; Du Val HS; Louisburg, NC; (Y); French Clb; Pep Clb; Pres Sr Cls; Stu Cncl; Stat Bsktbl; Hon Roll; Acdmc All Amer 84; Wake Frst U; Med Engrng.

BROWN, SUSAN; St Michaels SR HS; Bozman, MD; (Y); Pres Drama Clb; Library Aide; Band; Concert Band; Mrchg Band; Pep Band; School Play; Stage Crew; Mrktng.

BROWN, TIMOTHY W; Damascus HS; Damascus, MD; (Y); Pres Drama Clb; Off Leo Clb; Pres NFL; Q&S; Pres Thesps; School Musical; School Play; Stage Crew; Church Yth Grp; Off Debate Tm; Yrbk SR Edtr 85-86; 1st Thespian To Earn Ovr 100 Thespian Pts At DHS 85-86; Apptd MD ST Thspn Bd; Yale; Prfssnl Actr.

BROWN, TRACEY; North Harford HS; Jarrettsville, MD; (Y); Church Yth Grp; Pres 4-H; 4-H Awd; Hon Roll; NHS; Rep MD As Hrs Jdg At Estrn Ntl 4-H Hrs Rnd-Up 85; Twsn ST U; Sclgy.

BROWN, TRINA; Maurice J Mc Donough HS; Waldorf, MD; (Y); Teachers Aide; Chorus; JV Bsktbl; Capt Var Cheerleading; Var L Trk; Hon Roll; All European Chldr B-Ball Var 84; Staff Career-Day 83-84; All Cnty Hon Chorus 86; Bus Admin.

BROWN, VALERIE A; Westminster SR HS; Westminster, MD; (Y); AFS; Church Yth Grp; German Clb; Ski Clb; Concert Band; Jazz Band; Mrchg Band; Orch; School Musical; Symp Band; MD ST Band 83-86; MD ST Orch 85; All Amer Music Abrd Tour Europe 85; American U; Trnsltn Educ.

BROWNING, PAUL; Southern HS; Deer Park, MD; (Y); Church Yth Grp; Computer Clb; 4-H; Band; 4-H Awd; Frostburg ST Coll; Comp.

BROWNLEE, JULIE; Thomas Stone HS; Waldorf, MD; (Y); Hosp Aide; Library Aide; Teachers Aide; Drm & Bgl; Rep Sr Cls; Stu Cncl; JV Var Cheerleading; WV U; Med.

BRUNE, CAITLIN; Notre Dame Prep; Baltimore, MD; (Y); Model UN; Service Clb; Rep Stu Cncl; JV Var Bsktbl; Stat Ftbl; Sftbl; French Hon Soc; High Hon Roll; VP NHS; Prfct Atten Awd; S Williams Cunningham Mem Schlrsph 84; Georgtown Univ; Inter Stds.

BRUNE, SEAN P; Loyola HS; Baltimore, MD; (S); 27/197; Church Yth Grp; Drama Clb; FCA; French Clb; SADD; Nwsp Rptr; Nwsp Sprt Ed; Lit Mag; Rep Frsh Cls; Sec Soph Cls; Headmstrs Schlrshp 82-86; ST Chmpn Ftbl Tm 83; Engl.

BRUNHART, SUSANNE; Connelly School Of The Holy Child; Gaithersburg, MD; (Y); Drama Clb; Service Clb; School Play; Stage Crew; Yrbk Stf; Ed Lit Mag; Rep Soph Cls; High Hon Roll; NHS; Prfct Atten Awd; Acdmc Awds Frnch I, Gmtry, Fn Arts, Rlgn, Bio, Hstry, Englsh, Chem, Pres Acdmc Ftns, AP Bio 83-86.

BRUNNER, PATTI; La Plata HS; La Plata, MD; (Y); 5/300; Cmnty Wkr; Latin Clb; Teachers Aide; High Hon Roll; Jr NHS; NHS; Ntl Merit SF; Pres Schlr; St Schlr; La Plata Vol Fire Dept-Fire Prvntn Queen 85-86; U MD Coll Pk; Engl.

BRYAN, ROBIN; Northern HS; Huntingtown, MD; (Y); Trs Church Yth Grp; School Play; Nwsp Ed-Chief; JV Var Cheerleading; Hon Roll; Opt Clb Awd; Prfct Atten Awd; Cmnty Wkr; Varsity Clb; Yrbk Stf; Mentrshp Prog Awd Cnty Nwsp 86.

BRYANT, CAMERON; Franklin HS; Glyndon, MD; (Y); Key Clb; OEA; Concert Band; Mrchg Band; Stat Socr; Tennis; High Hon Roll; NHS; Ntl Merit Ltr; MD Distinquished Schlr; Engrng.

BRYANT, KAREN; Sparrows Point Mid/SR HS; Baltimore, MD; (Y); Church Yth Grp; Chorus; Soph Cls; Jr Cls; Var Bsktbl; JV Var Sftbl; Stat Vllybl; Hon Roll; Voice Dem Awd; Scndry Ed.

BRZOSTEK, KATHY; Institute Of Notre Dame; Baltimore, MD; (Y); Art Clb; Dance Clb; Drama Clb; Girl Scts; Chorus; Color Guard; School Play; Sec Frsh Cls; Trs Soph Cls; High Hon Roll; Sci Awd 84.

BUAN, ERWIN JAMES; Northwestern SR HS; Lanham, MD; (Y); Chess Clb; Science Clb; Teachers Aide; Chorus; Golf; Hon Roll; John Hopkins; Chem Engnr.

BUCHANAN, DAVID; Archbishop Curley HS; Baltimore, MD; (S); Service Clb; SADD; Mgr Stage Crew; Stu Cncl; Ftbl; Mgr(s); Wrstlng; Hon Roll; NHS; US Cst Guard Acad; Pilot.

BUCHANAN, EMILY; North East HS; Elkton, MD; (Y); 4-H; Q&S; Ski Clb; Yrbk Ed-Chief; Hon Roll; Cecil CC; Math.

BUCHAR, LISA; Institute Of Notre Dame HS; Baltimore, MD; (Y); Church Yth Grp; English Clb; GAA; Red Cross Aide; Nwsp Rptr; Nwsp Sprt Ed; Nwsp Stf; Lit Mag; Var Socr; High Hon Roll; Villa Julie Clg; Para Legl.

BUCHNESS, ELEANOR A; Parkside HS; Salisbury, MD; (S); #1 In Class; Trs Drama Clb; Sec Thesps; Church Choir; Mrchg Band; School Play; Symp Band; Pres Frsh Cls; Stu Cncl; Hon Roll; VP NHS.

BUCK, BRYAN; Wilde Lake HS; Columbia, MD; (Y); Math Tm; Ntl Merit SF; Comp Sci.

BUCK, PAUL; Annapolis HS; Annapolis, MD; (Y); German Clb; Quiz Bowl; Concert Band; Mrchg Band; Stage Crew; JV Stat Bsktbl; Mgr(s); Score Keeper; Stat Socr; Stat Sftbl; Omega Psi Phi Awd 85; Lang.

BUCKALEW, ELIZABETH C; Valley HS; Lonaconing, MD; (Y); Drama Clb; Teachers Aide; Chorus; Swing Chorus; Trs Soph Cls; Cheerleading; Hon Roll; Trs NHS; NEDT Awd; Hugh O Brian Yth Fndtn Ldrshp Awd 84; Frostburg ST Coll; Bus Admin.

BUCKEL, JEFF; Kent County HS; Chestertown, MD; (Y); School Musical; Stage Crew; Var Lcrss; Physcl.

BUCKLEY, ELLEN; Notre Dame Prep Schl; Glen Arm, MD; (Y); Cmnty Wkr; Rep GAA; Stage Crew; Rep Jr Cls; Im Badmtn; Im Bsktbl; Im Fld Hcky; Im Socr; Im Swmmng; Im Vllybl; Sci.

BUCKLEY, KATHRYN; Kent County HS; Chestertown, MD; (Y); 1/180; Cmnty Wkr; French Clb; Quiz Bowl; Stage Crew; Nwsp Rptr; Sec Frsh Cls; Trs Soph Cls; Cheerleading; Fld Hcky; High Hon Roll.

BUCKLEY, MIKE; Fallston HS; Fallston, MD; (Y); 75/250; Nwsp Stf; Ed Lit Mag; Rep Frsh Cls; Rep Soph Cls; Rep Jr Cls; Rep Sr Cls; Rep Stu Cncl; Var L Socr; Var L Tennis; Hon Roll; Stu Govt Assoc Recog Awd Chrmn Mrch Of Dms Fundrsng Comm 86; Cmmnctns.

BUCKLEY, SUZANNE; Elizabeth Seton HS; Laurel, MD; (Y); Church Yth Grp; Spanish Clb; SADD; Chorus; Church Choir; School Musical; Yrbk Rptr; Yrbk Sprt Ed; Yrbk Stf; High Hon Roll; Bus Law.

BUENDIA, MARIA; Harford Christian HS; Bel Air, MD; (Y); Church Yth Grp; Hosp Aide; School Play; Sec Pres Stu Cncl; Cit Awd; French Hon Soc; Hon Roll; Opt Clb Awd; Natl Math Awd; Loyola; Med.

BUGGS, MIRANGELA; M J Mc Donough HS; Pomfret, MD; (Y); Chorus; School Musical; Rep Stu Cncl; Var L Cheerleading; Hon Roll; NHS; Stu Superstr Shw Troupe 83-86; Acadmc Tm 83-86; Mathmtcs.

BULEY, CHRIS; The Bullis Schl; Gaithersburg, MD; (Y); Chess Clb; Computer Clb; Debate Tm; Key Clb; Model UN; Political Wkr; Q&S; Ski Clb; SADD; Varsity Clb; Duke; Law.

BULL, SHANNAN; North Carroll HS; Westminster, MD; (Y); VICA; Band; Concert Band; Mrchg Band; Pep Band; Hon Roll; Prfct Atten Awd; Intr Decorator.

BULLOCK, BRENDA; Carroll Christian Acad; Westminster, MD; (Y); Church Yth Grp; Sec Trs Band; Chorus; Trs Frsh Cls; Sec Soph Cls; Trs Sr Cls; Sec Stu Cncl; Var Vllybl; Cit Awd; Natl Choral Awd 82-86; TN Temple U; Chrstn Mnstries.

BUNDY, DANIELLE; St Frances Charles HS; Baltimore, MD; (Y); English Clb; French Clb; JA; Math Clb; Science Clb; Chorus; Color Guard; Drm Mjr(t); Mrchg Band; Nwsp Stf; Str Mary Paul Of Good Cncl Schlrshp 85-86; Awds In Typng Rgln Algbra II 86; Frostburg ST Coll; Med.

BUNTE, SUZANNE; Academy Of The Holy Cross; Wheaton, MD; (Y); 8/122; Cmnty Wkr; Hosp Aide; Math Clb; Rptr Nwsp Stf; Sec Sr Cls; High Hon Roll; Hon Roll; VP NHS; Spanish NHS; Church Yth Grp; Encllnc In Algebra Ii Trig 84-85; U Of IL; Bio Chem.

BUOB, BRENDA K; Parkside HS; Salisbury, MD; (Y); 8/237; Pres Spanish Clb; Varsity Clb; Var L Fld Hcky; Var L Sftbl; High Hon Roll; NHS; Bus Adm.

BUONACCORSI, WILLIAM; Loyola Blakefield HS; Ellicott City, MD; (Y); Cmnty Wkr; Spanish Clb; Chorus; Var Socr; Var Swmmng; JV Trk; High Hon Roll; Hon Roll; Sptsmnshp Awd Socr 84-85; Engrng.

BURCH, JULIE; Bowie HS; Bowie, MD; (Y); Church Yth Grp; Drama Clb; U Of AZ; Phtgrphy.

BURCHARD, RACHEL A; Catonsville HS; Catonsville, MD; (Y); Debate Tm; Drama Clb; Hosp Aide; Pres Speech Tm; Orch; Stage Crew; Lit Mag; Ntl Merit SF; U Of VA; Psych.

BURDOCK, ELIZABETH J; Southern Garrett HS; Oakland, MD; (Y); 45/222; French Clb; GAA; Q&S; Teachers Aide; Yrbk Bus Mgr; Yrbk Stf; JV Capt Cheerleading; Tennis; Hon Roll; Hmcomg Qun 85; Soph Hmcmng Prncss 83; Law.

BURFORD, WILHELMINA; Baltimore Polytechnic Inst; Baltimore, MD; (Y); Nwsp Rptr; Hon Roll; Howard U; Math.

BURGAN, ELLEN; Pikesville HS; Baltimore, MD; (Y); AFS; Cmnty Wkr; JA; Trs SADD; VP Temple Yth Grp; Ntl Merit Ltr; Applied Physics Lab Schlrshp, Cert Rcgntn Math, Natl Conf Synagogue Yth Rgnl Standards Awd 86; Carnegie Mellon U; Applied Math.

BURGER, ERICH; Loyola HS; Baldwin, MD; (Y); 23/197; Boy Scts; German Clb; Yrbk Bus Mgr; Im Bsktbl; Im Socr; Hon Roll; Ntl Merit SF; NEDT 90 Pct Scorer 82-84; Comp Sci.

BURGER, SHANNON P; North East HS; Elkton, MD; (Y); Church Yth Grp; Exploring; Library Aide; Teachers Aide; Sec Jr Cls; Stu Cncl; Cheerleading; Mu Alp Tht; NHS; Pres Acad Phy Fit Awd 86; NC St U; Engrng.

BURGESS, SHERYL; Capitol Christian Acad; Lanham, MD; (S); Church Yth Grp; Cmnty Wkr; Computer Clb; French Clb; Varsity Clb; Church Choir; Capt Var Cheerleading; Hon Roll; VP NHS; Typng Awd 84; Hmcmng Ct 84-86; Modern Miss Teen Schlrshp Pagnt 4th Rnnr Up 84; P G CC; Para Legal.

BURKE, ADAM; Ryken HS; Lex Pk, MD; (Y); Var Crs Cntry; Var Socr; Var Trk; Hon Roll; Engrng.

BURKE, AVDRA; Bowie HS; Bowie, MD; (Y); Church Yth Grp; German Clb; Key Clb; U Of MD; Psych.

BURKE, BRIDGID; Institute Of Notre Dame HS; Baltimore, MD; (Y); Dance Clb; Hosp Aide; Intnl Clb; Library Aide; Political Wkr; Stage Crew; Lit Mag; Rep Frsh Cls; Vlntr Awds 82-85; Pre-Law.

BURKE, NATALIE; St Vincent Pallotti HS; Laurel, MD; (S); 20/120; Spanish Clb; Pres Frsh Cls; Mgr(s); Capt Pom Pon; Score Keeper; Sftbl; High Hon Roll; NHS; Art Awd 85; Law.

BURKE, ROBERT; Sherwood HS; Olney, MD; (Y); 25/331; Boys Clb Am; Boy Scts; Var L Crs Cntry; Var L Trk; JETS Awd; NHS; Ntl Merit Ltr; Im Ftbl; Im Sftbl; Supts Wrtng Awd 84; Sci Fair Hnrb Mntn 86; Arch.

BURKE, SONJA; Kenwood HS; Baltimore, MD; (Y); Spanish Clb; Varsity Clb; Pres Frsh Cls; Off Soph Cls; Off Jr Cls; VP Sr Cls; Rep Stu Cncl; Var Sftbl; Var Vllybl; NHS; Reg Nrs.

BURKETT, CATHY; Fort Hill HS; Cumberland, MD; (Y); Church Yth Grp; Hosp Aide; Pep Clb; Capt Flag Corp; Off Soph Cls; Off Jr Cls; Hon Roll; Cap & Medlln Candy Striping 85.

BURKHARDT, KEITH; Dundalk HS; Baltimore, MD; (Y); 3/354; Am Leg Boys St; Varsity Clb; Rep Stu Cncl; JV Var Socr; High Hon Roll; Pres NHS; Frsh Cls; Soph Cls; Jr Cls; Powder Puff Ftbl; Distinguished Hnrs Awd 83-84; Acad & Svc Awd 85-86; Aero Engr.

BURKHARDT, LAURA; Seton HS; Baltimore, MD; (Y); 11/108; Church Yth Grp; Drama Clb; School Play; Ed Lit Mag; Rep Stu Cncl; Cheerleading; Hon Roll; Pres Schlr; Comp Awd; Presdntl Acadmc Ftns Awd; Seton Sci Awd; U Of MD Coll Pk; Pre-Law.

BURKMAN, NATALIE; Archbishop Keough HS; Balt, MD; (Y); Art Clb; GAA; Band; Im Badmtn; Im Bsktbl; Var Cheerleading; Var Im Lcrss; Im Sftbl; Im Vllybl; Hon Roll; Pre-Law.

BURKOFF, CAROLYN; Milford Mill SR HS; Baltimore, MD; (Y); Hosp Aide; JCL; Q&S; Teachers Aide; Nwsp Rptr; Nwsp Stf; Mgr(s); Milford Mill Comm Schlrshp 86; Svc Awd 86; U Of MD Baltimore; Occ Thrpy.

BURLEW, TRACI; Glenelg HS; Mt Airy, MD; (Y); Pep Clb; Spanish Clb; Varsity Clb; Drill Tm; Variety Show; Yrbk Stf; Hon Roll; Chorus; JV Cheerleading; Pom Pon; U Of MD; Pre-Med.

BURLEY, DIONNE; Southwestern HS; Baltimore, MD; (Y); Camp Fr Inc; Computer Clb; Dance Clb; Library Aide; Math Clb; Office Aide; Teachers Aide; Color Guard; French Hon Soc; Hon Roll; VA ST; Bus Adm.

BURLINGAME, BETH; Liberty HS; Sykesville, MD; (S); Varsity Clb; Concert Band; Mrchg Band; Fld Hcky; Sftbl; Pep Clb; Band; Pep Band; Symp Band; Rep Jr Cls.

BURNETT, CAROL; Wheaton HS; Rockville, MD; (Y); Pep Clb; Ski Clb; Teachers Aide; Variety Show; Rep Frsh Cls; Rep Soph Cls; Stu Cncl; Capt Cheerleading; Vllybl; Hon Roll; Dance.

BURNETTE, VALERIE; Parkville HS; Baltimore, MD; (Y); Cmnty Wkr; Key Clb; Red Cross Aide; Service Clb; Nwsp Rptr; VP Trs Stu Cncl; JV Vllybl; High Hon Roll; Political Wkr; Hon Roll; Librns Rpt Cont 1st Pl 85; Intl Ordr Jobs Daughters Hnr Queen 86; Chrch Camp Bd 86; Engl.

BURNS, JAY; Towson Catholic HS; Baltimore, MD; (Y); 1/74; Bausch & Lomb Sci Awd; Hon Roll; NHS; St Schlr; Val; Towson ST U; Marine Bio.

BURRELL, CHERYL; Batlimore City Coll; Baltimore, MD; (S); Concert Band; Mrchg Band; Nwsp Stf; VP Soph Cls; Rep Jr Cls; VP Sr Cls; VP Stu Cncl; JV Mgr Bsktbl; High Hon Roll; Hon Roll; Bltmr City Pblc Schl Sys Wnr Of Wrtng Cntst 86; ASCBC Hnr Of Outstndng Schl Ldrshp 85; Howard U; Comm.

BURRIS, GAIL; St Marys Ryken HS; Morganza, MD; (S); 15/138; FBLA; Spanish Clb; Yrbk Stf; Sftbl; High Hon Roll; Bus.

BURRISS, FREDERICK W; Our Lady Of Pompei HS; Baltimore, MD; (Y); Chorus; Yrbk Stf; Rep Sr Cls; Stu Cncl; Im Vllybl; Dundack CC; Comp Pgmr.

BURROUGHS, CYNTHIA T; Largo HS; Brandywine, MD; (Y); Church Yth Grp; Dance Clb; Office Aide; School Musical; Stu Cncl; Cheerleading; Hon Roll; Penn ST; Comp Prgrmr.

BURROUGHS, EUGENE; St Marys Ryker HS; Waldorf, MD; (Y); Boy Scts; Dance Clb; Exploring; Yrbk Stf; Chrmn Stu Cncl; JV Crs Cntry; Hon Roll.

BURROUS, STEPHANIE; Walbrook SR HS; Baltimore, MD; (Y); Church Yth Grp; Band; Chorus; Church Choir; Concert Band; Jazz Band; Mrchg Band; School Musical; Variety Show; Hon Roll; Cert Awd Cncrt & Mrchg Bnd 84; Sci Fair Eng & Bnd 85; Baltimores Best Piano Bnd 86; Howard U; Music.

BURT, THOMAS B; Loyola Blakefield HS; Baltimore, MD; (S); 23/200; French Clb; Nwsp Rptr; Rep Sr Cls; Var Ftbl; Var Capt Lcrss; Hon Roll; NHS; U Of VA; Bus.

BURTON, MICHELLE M; Chesapeake HS; Pasadena, MD; (S); DECA; Stu Cncl; Cheerleading; Socr; Hon Roll; Dstrbtv Educ Word Srch & Essay Trphy 86; Bus.

BURTON, MIKE; Allegany HS; Cumberland, MD; (Y); 1/208; VP Stu Cncl; Tennis; High Hon Roll; Sec NHS; Pres Schlr; St Schlr; Val; AFS; Ski Clb; Maryland Distqshd Schlr Schlrshp 86; Chanclr Schlrsp U Of MD 86; U Of North Carolina; Pre Med.

BURTON, SANDY; Northern HS; Huntingtown, MD; (Y); L Mrchg Band; Sec Stu Cncl; Var Tennis; Hon Roll; NHS; French I Awd 86; Frostburg; Bus Adm.

BURTON, VIRGINIA L; Thomas Stine HS; Waldorf, MD; (S); 6/350; Church Yth Grp; English Clb; Math Clb; Math Tm; Sec Science Clb; Yrbk Phtg; High Hon Roll; NHS; Ntl Merit Ltr; Jones-Trstes Shclrshp Peace Coll 85; Peace Coll.

BURTON, WENDY; Northwestern SR HS; Brentwood, MD; (Y); Cmnty Wkr; Debate Tm; Exploring; French Clb; Girl Scts; JA; Latin Clb; Letterman Clb; Library Aide; Natl Beta Clb; Natl Merit Schlrshp 85-86; MD U; Accntng.

BUSH, BETTY JUNE; Bel Air HS; Bel Air, MD; (Y); 9/226; Cmnty Wkr; SADD; Acpl Chr; Gov Hon Prg Awd; NHS; Pres Schlr; St Schlr; Church Yth Grp; Letterman Clb; Office Aide; All-ST Chrs 85-86; Snds Of Amer All-Hnrs Erpn Tour 86; 1st Anl Prncpls Awd Rcpnt 85-86; Shndh Coll & Cnsrvtry; Vcl Prfc.

BUSSARD, DANA; Middletown HS; Middletown, MD; (Y); Church Yth Grp; Cmnty Wkr; Computer Clb; Hosp Aide; Spanish Clb; SADD; Chorus; Variety Show; Hon Roll; Cert Apprctn Svc Frederick Mem Hosp 84; Frederick CC; Comp Sci.

BUSSARD, MICHELLE; Smithsburg HS; Smithsburg, MD; (Y); Church Yth Grp; Latin Clb; Red Cross Aide; Chorus; School Musical; Swing Chorus; Gym; Var Socr; MD ST Militia 86-87; Biol.

BUSTER, JERROD; Northwestern SR HS; Baltimore, MD; (S); Exploring; Pres JA; Math Tm; Red Cross Aide; Science Clb; SADD; Band; Chorus; JV Ftbl; JV Swmmng; Ntl Gvt & Hstry Awd 85-86; Hstry Hnr Stu Awd; U Of Brdgprt; Biolgcl Rsrch.

BUSTIN, ARI M; CES Jewish Day HS; Rockville, MD; (Y); Aud/Vis; Concert Band; Orch; School Musical; Nwsp Stf; Lit Mag; Off Sr Cls; Crs Cntry; Socr; Ntl Merit SF; Hnrs Recital-Schl Of Music 83; Presdntl Fitness Awd 83; MD Summer Ctrs For Gftd & Tlntd Stu 85; Engrng.

BUTCHER, CASSANDRA ARTRILL; Northwestern HS; Hyattsville, MD; (Y); Cmnty Wkr; French Clb; Model UN; ROTC; Drm Mjr(t); Pep Band; Nwsp Rptr; Nwsp Stf; VP Sr Cls; Bsktbl; Acad All Amer 84; Cadet Of The Quarter 83; AL A&m; Bus Admn.

BUTLER, ALFIE G; Meade SR HS; Severn, MD; (Y); 38/414; Drama Clb; FBLA; Science Clb; Yrbk Rptr; Yrbk Stf; Off Frsh Cls; Off Soph Cls; Off Jr Cls; Var Lcrss; Hmcmng Ct 85; Johns Hopkins U; Biomed Engrng.

BUTLER, BRENDA D; Southern Garrett HS; Oakland, MD; (Y); 3/222; Key Clb; Latin Clb; Concert Band; Mrchg Band; Cheerleading; High Hon Roll; NHS; Rtry Stu Of Qrtr 86; Gvrnrs Awd 86; Pres Awd 86; Bnkng.

BUTLER, BRIAN; Fairmont Heights HS; Landover Hls, MD; (Y); Hon Roll; Prfct Atten Awd; NC A&T; Mech Engrng.

BUTLER, CYNTHIA; Chopticon HS; Bushwood, MD; (Y); Church Yth Grp; DECA; FBLA; FHA; ROTC; SADD; Varsity Clb; Rep Frsh Cls; Hon Roll; NHS; Stu Govt Awd 84-86; U MD; CPA.

BUTLER, KIMBERLY; Queen Annes County HS; Grasonville, MD; (Y); FHA; Band; Mrchg Band; Mrchg Band; Bsktbl; Trk; Hon Roll; Outstndng Achvt Intro Acctng 86; Goldey Beacom; Acctng.

BUTLER, LORI; Du Val SR HS; Seat Pleasant, MD; (S); Church Yth Grp; French Clb; Trs Band; Church Choir; Mrchg Band; Symp Band; Stu Cncl; Pom Pon; High Hon Roll; NHS; Howard U; Elec Engrng.

BUTLER, MARY; St Frances - Charles Hall HS; Baltimore, MD; (Y); Pres Church Yth Grp; Hosp Aide; Teachers Aide; Pres Church Choir; Variety Show; Hon Roll; Sr Paul Lee Schlrshp-Acadmc Excllnc 85-86; Holy Name Soc 85-86; Elem Eductn.

BUTLER, MELINDA; Crisfield HS; Marion, MD; (Y); 1/89; Cmnty Wkr; Exploring; Science Clb; High Hon Roll; NHS; Rotary Awd; Engr.

BUTLER, PAIGE; Walt Whitman HS; Bethesda, MD; (Y); Pres Church Yth Grp; Chorus; Church Choir; Var JV Vllybl; French Hon Soc; Ntl Merit SF; Brwn U Brown Bk Awd 86; NCTE Wrtng Cntst 86.

BUTLER, STACY; Smithsburg HS; Hagerstown, MD; (Y); 6/177; Pres French Clb; Rep Soph Cls; Rep Stu Cncl; JV Bsktbl; Var L Trk; Var L Vllybl; High Hon Roll; Sec NHS; Intl Rel.

BUTSCHER, JAMES; Southern Garrett HS; Oakland, MD; (Y); Boy Scts; Drama Clb; French Clb; PAVAS; Political Wkr; ROTC; Ski Clb; Band; Concert Band; Drm & Bgl; Otstndng Actr 86; Mask & Spur Soc Actng Clb 86; Norfolk Sst U; Nvy Plt.

BUTTS JR, D TIMOTHY; North Hagerstown HS; Hagestown, MD; (Y); Var L Bsktbl; Hon Roll; NHS; CPA.

BUTTS, SHARYL; Magruder HS; Rockville, MD; (Y); 51/320; AFS; Girl Scts; Ski Clb; Spanish Clb; Stu Cncl; Pom Pon; Sftbl; High Hon Roll; Hon Roll; Top 10 Prcnt Of JR Cls 85; E Crlna U; Law.

BUYSSE, SHARON; Colonel Zadok Magruder HS; Derwood, MD; (Y); Bsktbl; Fld Hcky; Sftbl; Hon Roll.

BYNUM, EDWARD; Friendly SR HS; Fort Washington, MD; (Y); Boys Clb Am; Boy Scts; Church Yth Grp; Band; Hon Roll; Elec Engrng.

BYRD, LISA S; Randallstown SR HS; Randallstown, MD; (Y); Church Yth Grp; Civic Clb; Drama Clb; Library Aide; Natl Beta Clb; Band; Church Choir; Off Stu Cncl; Tennis; Hon Roll; Natl Merit Cmmnded Stu 85; Psych.

BYRD, VONDA; Patterson HS; Baltimore, MD; (Y); Cmnty Wkr; Dance Clb; Girl Scts; VICA; Church Choir; VP Stu Cncl; Cheerleading; Vllybl; Hon Roll; Engl Awd 85; Consumer Educ Awd 85; Food Svc Awd 85; VA ST U; Comp Sci.

BYRON, GLENN; Great Mills HS; Califronia, MD; (Y); Church Yth Grp; Sec Varsity Clb; Im Bsktbl; Im Crs Cntry; Var Ftbl; Im Sftbl; Im Trk; Im Vllybl; Im Wt Lftg; Im Wrstlng; Presdntl Athltc Awd 85; Naval Acad; Engrng.

BYRUM, CHERIE; St Michaels HS; St Michaels, MD; (Y); Am Leg Aux Girls St; Cmnty Wkr; Drama Clb; GAA; SADD; Teachers Aide; Chorus; Stage Crew; Trs Sr Cls; Var Capt Bsktbl; Guy M Reeser Schlr Athlt Awd 86; Babe Ruth Sprtsmnshp Awd 86; Outstndg Athlt 86; Guilford Coll; Sprts Med.

CABRERA, ALICE; Northwestern HS; Hyattsville, MD; (Y); JA; Teachers Aide; Chorus; Gym; Hon Roll; Ntl Merit Ltr; Acad All Am Schlr Pgm 86; U MD; Med Assist.

CAINE, ALEXANDER; Potomae HS; Oxon Hill, MD; (Y); Church Choir; Hon Roll; Acdmc All Amer 86; Comp Sci.

CAINE, SEAN; Fallston HS; Forest Hill, MD; (Y); 59/250; Church Yth Grp; SADD; Teachers Aide; Acpl Chr; Pres Chorus; Church Choir; Madrigals; School Musical; Nwsp Rptr; Nwsp Stf; All ST Chrus 86-87; All Cnty Chorus 84-86; Grp Dscssn Pres Reagan 85; Music.

CALBI, WENDI; Takoma Acad; Adelphi, MD; (S); Aud/Vis; Drama Clb; Office Aide; Teachers Aide; Nwsp Ed-Chief; Pres Soph Cls; VP Jr Cls; Pres Sr Cls; NHS; NEDT Awd; U MD; Comm.

CALDEJON, MARIVI; Annapolis Area Christian Schl; Annapolis, MD; (S); 2/13; Yrbk Bus Mgr; VP Stu Cncl; Capt L Bsktbl; Capt L Cheerleading; Capt L Sftbl; Capt L Vllybl; High Hon Roll; NHS; Chorus; Church Choir; Chrldr Of Yr-Chesapeake Chrstn Athltc Conf 84-85; All Conf Vllybl Tm 84-85; Hnr Stu-Drvng Schl 85; Paralegal.

CALDWELL, BERNARD; De Matha Catholic HS; Upper Marlboro, MD; (Y); Im Bsktbl; Im Coach Actv; JV Var Ftbl; Im Score Keeper; Hon Roll; Towson ST U; Acctg.

CALDWELL, KENDALL A; Old Mill SR HS; Crownsville, MD; (Y); Church Yth Grp; Teachers Aide; Rep Frsh Cls; Trs Soph Cls; Pres Jr Cls; Pres Sr Cls; Var Lcrss; Chem Engr.

CALISIURI, ANTHONY; Broadneck SR HS; Annapolis, MD; (Y); 40/344; Camera Clb; VP FBLA; Pres Intnl Clb; Model UN; Science Clb; Spanish Clb; Nwsp Phtg; Yrbk Ed-Chief; Navl Acad Frgn Affrs Cnf, Cnty Schl Bd Comm, ST Leg Page 86; Washington Coll; Intl Affrs.

CALL, WENDY L; Great Mills HS; Lexington Park, MD; (Y); 2/270; Pres French Clb; Yrbk Ed-Chief; NHS; Ntl Merit Ltr; Pres Schlr; Rotary Awd; Sal; Red Cross Aide; Rep Frsh Cls; Rep Soph Cls; Outstndng Achvt Engl 86; Outstndng Achvt Sci 86; Charlotte Hall Schl Merit Scholar 86; Oberlin Coll; Bio.

CALLAHAN, MARK; Easton HS; Easton, MD; (Y); 26/184; Church Yth Grp; French Clb; VP Latin Clb; Trs Letterman Clb; Varsity Clb; Rep Frsh Cls; Rep Jr Cls; Rep Stu Cncl; Capt Lcrss; Socr; Army ROTC 4 Yr Schlrshp 86; Army Rsrv Natl Schlr Athl Awd 86; Almn Assn Awd 86; Syracuse U; Acctg.

CALLAHAN JR, TOM; Seneca Valley HS; Gaithersburg, MD; (Y); Aud/Vis; Ski Clb; SADD; Teachers Aide; JV Crs Cntry; Hon Roll; Cmmnctns.

CALLOWAY, LISA; Frederick HS; Frederick, MD; (Y); 34/306; Art Clb; Teachers Aide; Lit Mag; Var Capt Fld Hcky; Powder Puff Ftbl; Var Sftbl; Hon Roll; MIP Sftbl 83-84; Goldn Glv Awd 84-85; Fld Hcky Awds 83-86; Art.

CALONGNE, DONNA; Northwestern HS; Hyattsville, MD; (Y); Dance Clb; Hon Roll; 3rd Grnd Prz-NRTHWSTRN HS Sci Expo 84; Acadmc Exclinc Awd-P G Cnty 84-85; Acctng.

CALTABIANO, SAL; Mount Saint Josephs HS; Ellicott City, MD; (Y); 102/300; Ski Clb; Socr; Hon Roll; Acctng.

CALVERT, THERESA; Dulaney SR HS; Glen Arm, MD; (Y); 4-H; Key Clb; Hon Roll; Essex CC; Art.

CAMERON, ROBERT; Bullis Schl; Potomac, MD; (Y); Varsity Clb; Nwsp Rptr; Nwsp Sprt Ed; Var Capt Bsktbl; Var Capt Socr; Trk; NEDT Awd; Psychology.

CAMPAGNA, MARC; Mount St Joseph Clg; Ellicott City, MD; (Y); Nwsp Rptr; Hon Roll; Intnl Clb; Q&S; Spanish Clb; Nwsp Stf; Commnctns.

CAMPAGNOLI, PATRICIA; Immaculate College HS; Rockville, MD; (Y); Cmnty Wkr; Sec Trs Spanish Clb; Lit Mag; Trs Jr Cls; Tennis; High Hon Roll; Intl Law.

CAMPANELLI, TINA; Saint Marys Ryken HS; Laplata, MD; (Y); Drama Clb; Spanish Clb; Varsity Clb; Stage Crew; Yrbk Phtg; JV Var Cheerleading; JV Var Pom Pon; Bus.

CAMPBELL, MARK; Carroll Christian Acad; Westminster, MD; (S); Chorus; Pres Sr Cls; Off Stu Cncl; Var Bsbl; Capt Bsktbl; Capt Socr; Hon Roll; Church Yth Grp; Nwsp Stf; Natl Chrstn Hnr Soc 84; MACS Fine Arts Prchng 1st Pl 85; TN Temple U; Pstrl.

CAMPBELL, MICHELLE; Parkdale HS; Riverdale, MD; (S); Art Clb; Church Yth Grp; Pep Clb; Teachers Aide; Cit Awd; Hon Roll; NHS; Spanish NHS; U MD; Pre-Med.

CAMPBELL, TERALEEN; North Hagerstown HS; Hagerstown, MD; (Y); 40/327; Band; Flag Corp; Nwsp Bus Mgr; Nwsp Sprt Ed; Rep Sec Stu Cncl; Hon Roll; Church Yth Grp; Pep Clb; Spanish Clb; Teachers Aide; Hnr Clb; Prm Committee; U Of MD; Jrnlsm.

CAMPBELL, TINA; Catoctin HS; Thurmont, MD; (Y); Pres Computer Clb; VP French Clb; Spanish Clb; School Musical; Pres Soph Cls; VP Pres Stu Cncl; Capt Cheerleading; Sftbl; Hon Roll; Perfmng Arts Allinc Awds Dance Achvt 80-86; ST Trnmnt Little Lgu Sftbl Awds 84-85; 1st Cls C Sftbl 86; James Madison; Comm.

CAMPITELLI, PAULA; Westminster SR HS; Westminster, MD; (Y); Teachers Aide; Mrchg Band; High Hon Roll; NHS.

CANADAY, TERRI L; North East HS; North East, MD; (Y); 1/247; Intnl Clb; Q&S; Nwsp Sprt Ed; VP Frsh Cls; Pres Soph Cls; Trs Stu Cncl; Capt L Bsktbl; Capt L Cheerleading; Hon Roll; Pres NHS; Schltc Awds Amer Lit, Geom, Spn 84-86; Hopwood Summr Scholar Pgm 86; Delg MD Sci & Humants Sympsm 86.

CANAN, CAROLINA; Northern HS; Accident, MD; (Y); 4-H; Lit Mag; Hon Roll; Nrsng.

CANGELOSI, MICHAEL; Franklin HS; Reisterstown, MD; (Y); Hst Stu Cncl; High Hon Roll; NHS; Prfct Atten Awd; Music Comp.

CANNER, REBECCA E; Catonsville HS; Baltimore, MD; (Y); 1/300; AFS; French Clb; Orch; School Play; Lit Mag; Rep Trs Stu Cncl; Crs Cntry; Capt Trk; Hon Roll; NHS; U Of MN; Msc Educ.

CANNON, ANJANETTE; Wicomico SR HS; Salisbury, MD; (Y); DECA; Church Yth Grp; Drama Clb; Girl Scts; Acpl Chr; Chorus; Church Choir; School Musical; School Play; Stage Crew; Acctg.

CANNON, MICHELLE LYNN; Sherwood HS; Olney, MD; (Y); School Musical; VP Sr Cls; JV Co-Capt Cheerleading; Var Pom Pon; Var L Swmmng; Var Trk; Hon Roll; Jr NHS; NHS; Spanish NHS; Serv Awd Montgomery Cnty Rec Dept 83; Fine Arts.

CANNON, TINA; Queen Annes County HS; Sudlersville, MD; (Y); French Clb; Office Aide; Color Guard; Flag Corp; Hon Roll; Rotary Awd; Salisbury ST Coll; Elem Ed.

CANTER, ANDY; Northern HS; Owings, MD; (Y); 8/301; Computer Clb; Wt Lftg; High Hon Roll; Hon Roll; Pres Acad Ftns Awd 86; Outstndng Acad Pgm 86; Merit Schlrshp Awd 86; U MD; Comp Sci.

CANTOR, JANICE; Montgomery Blair HS; Silver Spg, MD; (Y); Chess Clb; Cmnty Wkr; Ski Clb; Teachers Aide; Jazz Band; School Musical; Stage Crew; Variety Show; Yrbk Phtg; Yrbk Stf; Black Belt 84; Kodak Awd Photo Sci Fair 84; U DE; Comm.

CAPLES, CHANDRA; Dulaney HS; Cockeysville, MD; (Y); 118/475; Cmnty Wkr; Dance Clb; Pres 4-H; Off FHA; Pres Key Clb; Pom Pon; Hon Roll; Pres Eminent Schrlshp Awd 86; Ntl Merit Stu 85; Vol Svc Awd 85; Hampton U; Mass Media.

CARBACHO-BURGOS, ANDRES; Walt Whitman HS; Bethesda, MD; (Y); 119/435; Chess Clb; Intnl Clb; Jazz Band; Rptr Lit Mag; Ntl Merit Schol; Ntl Hisp Schlr Awds Prog 86; Creative Wrtng.

CARDANY, KEVIN G; Gaithersburg HS; Gaithersburg, MD; (Y); 41/568; Key Clb; Ski Clb; Yrbk Phtg; JV Vllybl; Hon Roll; Jr NHS; NHS; Ntl Merit Ltr; VA Tech; Engr.

CARE, BRIDGETTE; Notre Dame Prep; Baltimore, MD; (Y); Camera Clb; Computer Clb; French Clb; SADD; School Musical; Hon Roll; Loyola Coll; Comm.

CAREY, DANA; Wicomico SR HS; Parsonsberg, MD; (Y); Chorus; Hon Roll; HS Fine Art Contst-Cert Of Awd 86.

CAREY, LANA R; Parkside HS; Salisbury, MD; (Y); 8/233; Am Leg Aux Girls St; French Clb; Math Tm; Ski Clb; Varsity Clb; Yrbk Stf; Stu Cncl; Capt Var Cheerleading; Elks Awd; Sec NHS; Moose Schlrp 86; Wicomico Wmns Clb Awd 86; US Chrldg Assoc 3rd Pl Awd 85; U MD College Park; Bus.

CAREY, MICHELLE; Snow Hill HS; Snow Hill, MD; (S); Church Yth Grp; Band; Pres Jr Cls; Rep Stu Cncl; Mgr Bsktbl; Var Sftbl; Capt Var Vllybl; Hon Roll; NHS; Prfct Atten Awd; Hugh O Brian Ldrshp Prog Rnnr Up 84; U Of MD; Med Sci.

CAREY, REBECCA; Mt Hebron HS; Ellicott City, MD; (Y); Hosp Aide; SADD; Chorus; Drill Tm; Madrigals; School Musical; Fld Hcky; Hon Roll; NHS; Prfct Atten Awd; Douglas Drake Travel Stipend Of $100 At Grad 86; Most Dedicated Drill Tm Mbr 84; U Of MD; Intl Bus.

CARGILL, ANNE M; Albert Einstein HS; Silver Spring, MD; (Y); 2/304; Thesps; Madrigals; School Musical; Stage Crew; Nwsp Rptr; Sec Sr Cls; JV Bsktbl; NHS; Ntl Merit SF; St Schlr; Princ Wrtng Awd 85; Acad Lttr 84-85; PA ST U; Chem Engrng.

CARHART, CHRISTINA; Gwyan Park HS; Cheltenham, MD; (S); Spanish Clb; Band; Jazz Band; Stu Cncl; Dnfth Awd; Pres VP NHS; Dance Clb; Hosp Aide; Mrchg Band; Hon Roll; Cnty Acad Awd; Ntl Ldrshp & Svc Awd.

CARL, TRACEY; Harforad Voc-Tech HS; Forest Hill, MD; (Y); Pep Clb; SADD; VICA; Nwsp Rptr; Yrbk Rptr; Yrbk Stf; VP Jr Cls; Var Cheerleading; Powder Puff Ftbl; Hon Roll.

CARLOW, KAREN; Calvert HS; Lusby, MD; (Y); Cmnty Wkr; Hosp Aide; Latin Clb; VICA; Pom Pon; High Hon Roll; Hon Roll; Christopher Chinauh Nrsg Schlrshp 86; 1st Med Termnlgy Cntst 86; Prince George CC; Nrsg.

CARMEAN, KRISTIN L; North East HS; North East, MD; (Y); 3/300; Am Leg Aux Girls St; Intnl Clb; Q&S; Pres SADD; Nwsp Rptr; VP Pres Stu Cncl; VP Capt Cheerleading; VP Capt Fld Hcky; VP Sftbl; VP NHS; Cnty Sftbl Plyr 84; Cnty Fld Hcky Plry 85; Mbr Soc Disting Amer HS Stu 86; Math.

CAROL, TANYA LISA; Walbrook SR High School No 411; Baltimore, MD; (Y); FBLA; Mrchg Band; Sec Jr Cls; JV Bsktbl; Hon Roll; Prfct Atten Awd; Twrlr; Media Awd Algbra II Awd 85-86; Typng Awd 84-85; Howard U; Achrwmn.

CARPENTER, CAMI; Mc Donough HS; La Plata, MD; (Y); #14 In Class; Teachers Aide; Pres Varsity Clb; JV Cheerleading; Stat L Ftbl; Var L Trk; High Hon Roll; Hon Roll; L NHS; U Alabama.

CARPENTER, FRANCES; St Marys Ryken HS; Leonardtown, MD; (Y); Cmnty Wkr; Spanish Clb; High Hon Roll; Hon Roll; Cert Awd Frgn Lang Clb 85; Vol Nrsng Hm 85-86; Schlrshp Cert Hnr Spnsh III 86; St Marys Coll; Lang.

CARR, JODY; Patterson HS; Baltimore, MD; (Y); Cmnty Wkr; Dance Clb; Sec Frsh Cls; CC Of Balto; Early Chldhd Educ.

CARR, KRISTINA; Chesapeake HS; Pasadena, MD; (S); 150/400; Church Yth Grp; DECA; Stage Crew; Trs Jr Cls; Pom Pon; Sftbl; Hon Roll; DECA Co Treas 85-86; Church Yth Grp Choir 83-84; UMBC; Busnss.

CARR, LASHAWN; Oxon Hill SR HS; Ft Washington, MD; (Y); Drama Clb; Band; Var L Pom Pon; Hon Roll; Accntnt.

CARR, NICOLE; John Carroll HS; Edgewood, MD; (Y); 6/240; Church Yth Grp; German Clb; Library Aide; School Musical; School Play; Yrbk Sprt Ed; Var Mgr(s); Var Powder Puff Ftbl; Var Trk; High Hon Roll; Marion Burke Knott Schlrshp 83-87; Med.

CARR, PAULA; Springbrook HS; Silver Spring, MD; (Y); 71/488; Church Yth Grp; Office Aide; Spanish Clb; Varsity Clb; VP Stu Cncl; Var JV Cheerleading; Var Pom Pon; Hon Roll; NHS; James Madison U; Comm.

CARRILLO, RICHARD LAURENCE; Wicomico SR HS; Salisbury, MD; (Y); 25/250; Boy Scts; Church Yth Grp; Civic Clb; CAP; Letterman Clb; Spanish Clb; Varsity Clb; Band; Concert Band; Mrchg Band; Clemson U; ROTC.

CARROLL, DEANNA; St Marys Ryken HS; Dameron, MD; (Y); VP FBLA; Hon Roll; Bus.

CARROLL, EDDIE; La Plata HS; Waldorf, MD; (Y); Art Clb; Boy Scts; Chess Clb; Wt Lftg; High Hon Roll; Hon Roll; Jr NHS; NHS; U MD; Arch.

CARROLL, JANNA K; Southern SR HS; Lothian, MD; (Y); 1/230; Am Leg Aux Girls St; Pres Church Yth Grp; Political Wkr; Ed Lit Mag; Trs Frsh Cls; Trs Soph Cls; Sec Jr Cls; Elks Awd; VP NHS; Chess Clb; Schlrshps For Schlrs Anne Anerdel Co Brd Ed 86; Cntry III Ldrs Awd 86; Deans Schlr Awd 86; Emory U; Pre-Med.

CARROLL, KIMBERLY; Surrattsville HS; Clinton, MD; (Y); Office Aide; Nwsp Stf; Pres Soph Cls; JV Tennis; High Hon Roll; Hon Roll; Ntl Merit Ltr; Hugh O Brien Ldrshp 84; Homecmng Prncss.

CARROLL, LESLI; Surrattsville SR HS; Clinton, MD; (Y); Church Yth Grp; Office Aide; Yrbk Stf; Var Pom Pon; Var Powder Puff Ftbl; Hon Roll; Jr NHS; Princ George Cty Acadmc Achvt Awd 85; Towson ST U.

CARROLL, PHYLLIS; Fairmont Heights HS; Cheverly, MD; (Y); Cmnty Wkr; French Clb; FBLA; DAR Awd; Pres Schlr; Val; Dance Clb; English Clb; FHA; Math Clb; Supr Perf IRS 86; Sprltv Awd Mst Frndlst 85; Gftd & Tlntd Prog 83; MD U; Comp Prog.

CARROLL, RICHARD; Great Mills HS; Lex Pk, MD; (Y); Comp Anlyst.

CARROLL, WANDA; Lackey HS; Bryans Rd, MD; (Y); Hosp Aide; Letterman Clb; Teachers Aide; Varsity Clb; Cheerleading; Trk; Vllybl; High Hon Roll; Hon Roll; Clnl Hstlr Trphy At George Washington Vllybl Cmp 84; CCCC Cmnty Coll; Nrs.

CARSON, CHRISTOPHER; Northwestern HS; Baltimore, MD; (Y); JA; Math Clb; Drill Tm; Variety Show; Frsh Cls; Stu Cncl; 4-H Awd; Prfct Atten Awd; Drmtc Rdng Awd 81-82; Bltmre Cty Myr Ldrshp Awd 81-82; Yale U; Comp Tech.

CARSON, GENE; Friendly SR HS; Ft Washington, MD; (Y); Math Clb; Office Aide; Pep Clb; Teachers Aide; Band; Concert Band; Mrchg Band; Bsktbl; Trk; CC Awd; Acadmc Achvt Awd 85-86; Bowie ST Coll; Engr.

CARTALLA, DAVID; Lackey HS; Bryans Rd, MD; (Y); FBLA; Teachers Aide; Sec Stu Cncl; Var Mgr(s); Var L Tennis; Mgr Vllybl; Cit Awd; High Hon Roll; Hon Roll; Prfct Atten Awd; FBLA Awds In Stngrphr I Rgnl & St 86; Jrnlsm.

CARTALLA, LILLIAN; Lackey HS; Bryans Road, MD; (Y); 27/186; Trs Spanish Clb; Teachers Aide; Rep Frsh Cls; VP Soph Cls; Trs Jr Cls; Rep Sr Cls; VP Stu Cncl; Var L Sftbl; Var L Vllybl; Voice Dem Awd; Centry III Ldrshp Awd Schl Wnnr 86; Outstndng Athltc Svc 86; 1st Tm Vbl All Southrn MD Athl Conf 85; U Of MD; Phy Ed.

CARTER, BRICCA; Calvert HS; Lusby, MD; (Y); 12/316; SADD; Teachers Aide; Varsity Clb; Var JV Mgr(s); Var L Vllybl; High Hon Roll; NHS; Prfct Atten Awd; 4-H; Latin Clb; Karate/Green Belt 82; Soccer Refre 85; Phrmcy.

CARTER, DEMETRIA; Western HS; Baltimore, MD; (Y); Strayer Bus Coll; Comp Pgmmg.

CARTER, GAIL; St Marys Ryken HS; Indian Head, MD; (Y); Hon Roll; U Of San Diego; Comm.

CARTER, MARIA; Gaithersburg HS; Gaithersburg, MD; (Y); 142/600; Intnl Clb; Office Aide; Teachers Aide; Chorus; School Musical; Hon Roll; Ntl Art Hnr Soc 85-86.

CARTER, SHERRILL; Suitland HS; Capitol Heights, MD; (Y); 4/360; French Clb; Pres Letterman Clb; Capt Var Trk; French Hon Soc; Hon Roll; Sec NHS; Ntl Merit Schol; Pres Schlr; Rotary Awd; Sr Athlte Of Yr For Schl 85-86; Morgan ST U; Elect Engrng.

CARTER, TRACYE; Western SR HS; Baltimore, MD; (Y); Chorus; Church Choir; Bsktbl; Gym; Sftbl; Tennis; Vllybl; Volunteer Awd 84; Spelman Coll; Econ.

CARUSO, JOSEPH; Takoma Acad; Hyattsville, MD; (Y); Drama Clb; Science Clb; Hon Roll; Outstndng Effrt Bio 84-86; WIT VA Yth Kng 83-86; WIT Grnd Natl Yth King 86-87; Sci.

CARUTHERS, PATRICIA H; Southern Garrett HS; Oakland, MD; (S); 12/225; Pres GAA; Model UN; Concert Band; Mrchg Band; Rep Frsh Cls; Hon Roll; NHS; Elec Engr.

CARUTHERS, SUSAN R; Southern Garrett HS; Oakland, MD; (S); VP SADD; Teachers Aide; Church Choir; High Hon Roll; Hon Roll; NHS; Rotary Awd; Northwood Inst; Acctg.

CARVER, DARRYL H; Senior HS; Baltimore, MD; (S); Yrbk Stf; Var Lcrss; NHS; Acctng.

CARY, LAURENCE; Crossland HS; Temple Hills, MD; (Y); Boy Scts; Variety Show; Crs Cntry; Trk; Hon Roll; Oakwood Coll; Med.

CASALI, HEATHER; Allegany HS; La Vale, MD; (Y); Sec AFS; Cmnty Wkr; Drama Clb; VP FBLA; Drill Tm; Yrbk Phtg; Yrbk Stf; Rep Frsh Cls; U Of FL; Ed.

CASE, BRYAN; Elkton HS; Elkton, MD; (Y); Cmnty Wkr; Key Clb; Hon Roll.

CASHOUR, JENNIFER; John Carroll Schl; Bel Air, MD; (Y); Cmnty Wkr; SADD; French Hon Soc; High Hon Roll; Hon Roll; NHS; Ntl Merit SF; Church Yth Grp; Yrbk Stf; Lit Mag.

CASPER, STEVEN; Bowie SR HS; Bowie, MD; (Y); Letterman Clb; Spanish Clb; Varsity Clb; Concert Band; Nwsp Sprt Ed; Crs Cntry; Tennis; Cit Awd; DAR Awd; Hon Roll; U Of MD; Brdcstng.

CASSEDAY, CATHLEEN; Allegany HS; Cumberland, MD; (Y); 2/240; Sec AFS; Church Yth Grp; Drama Clb; Hosp Aide; Drill Tm; Yrbk Stf; Jr NHS; Office Aide; Pep Clb; Peer Cnslr 85-86; Madart Shop Tm 85-86; Drill Tm 1st Div Awd 84-85; Bus Mgmt.

CASSORLA, SHIRA LEA; Gaithersburg HS; Gaithersburg, MD; (Y); SADD; Teachers Aide; Lit Mag; Hon Roll; Spanish NHS; Math.

CASTLE, ELAINE; Notre Dame Prep; Timonium, MD; (Y); Art Clb; Drama Clb; Service Clb; Teachers Aide; Im Badmtn; Cheerleading; Im Fld Hcky; Im Socr; Im Sftbl; Im Vllybl; Adtsg.

CASTOR, LINNETTE; Woodlawn SR HS; Baltimore, MD; (Y); Church Yth Grp; Drama Clb; Girl Scts; School Play; Nwsp Phtg; Nwsp Stf; Prfct Atten Awd; Coop Ed Cert Prfrmnc 86; Lbrl Arts Cert Achvt 86; Liberty U; Jrnlsm.

CATALDO, STEPHEN M; Randallstown HS; Randallstown, MD; (Y); Pres Debate Tm; High Hon Roll; Ntl Merit SF.

CATIGNANI, CARYN; Bowie HS; Bowie, MD; (Y); 44/645; AFS; Trs French Clb; GAA; JA; Office Aide; Var Cheerleading; Hon Roll; U Of MD-COLLEGE Pk; Busnss.

CATLIN, JACQUELINE; Lackey HS; Bryans Rd, MD; (Y); Teachers Aide; Rep Frsh Cls; Rep Soph Cls; Var Fld Hcky; Hon Roll; USNSDA 84; Natl Sci Merit Awd 85; Natl Ldrshp And Serv Awd 86; Law.

CAUSEY, JULIA; St Andrews Episopal Schl; Chevy Chase, MD; (Y); Church Yth Grp; Dance Clb; Office Aide; SADD; School Play; JV Bsktbl; Cheerleading; Var L Crs Cntry; Var L Lcrss; JV Trk; Ldrshp Awd Bsktbl, MVP Lacrosse, Outstndng Cntrbutn Dance 86; Dickinson.

CAVANAUGH, OVERTON; Potomac SR HS; Washington, DC; (Y); French Clb; Yrbk Stf; Tennis; High Hon Roll; Hon Roll; NHS; Yale; Med.

CAVANAUGH, SHELLEY; Surrattsville HS; Clinton, MD; (Y); Church Yth Grp; Dance Clb; Drill Tm; Variety Show; Pom Pon; Hon Roll; Prince Georgias CC; Bus Adm.

CAYELLI, STEPHEN D; Wooton HS; Potomac, MD; (Y); JA; Stage Crew; U Of MD; Law.

CECIL, DEANA; Allegany HS; Cumberland, MD; (Y); 17/220; Church Yth Grp; Dance Clb; VP FBLA; Library Aide; Office Aide; Red Cross Aide; Yrbk Stf; Hon Roll; NHS; Starmkr Danc Cmptn-2nd Pl 86; Frostburg ST Coll; Med.

CEPHAS, CHARLES; Takoma Acad; Silver Spring, MD; (Y); Rep Frsh Cls; Rep Soph Cls; Rep Jr Cls; VP Sr Cls; Rep Stu Cncl; Stat Bsktbl; Im Ftbl; Im Socr; Var Trk; Im Vllybl; Outstndg Effrt In Trig/Pre-Cal 86; Mont Co All Star Swmmr-3 Yrs 84-86; Bus.

CESSNA, BRUCE; Flintstone HS; Clearville, PA; (S); Aud/Vis; Pres Church Yth Grp; Sec FFA; Service Clb; Var Bsktbl; Var Socr; High Hon Roll; NHS.

CESSNA, KRISTA; Flintstone HS; Clearville, PA; (S); Sec VP Church Yth Grp; Sec VP 4-H; Scrkpr FHA; Chorus; Yrbk Ed-Chief; VP Jr Cls; Stat Bsktbl; Var Cheerleading; DAR Awd; 4-H Awd; Allegany CC; Forstry.

CESSNA, TINA; Flintstone HS; Clearville, PA; (S); VP Sec Church Yth Grp; VP Pres 4-H; Sec Pres FHA; Service Clb; Teachers Aide; Chorus; Yrbk Stf; VP Jr Cls; Pres Sr Cls; Stat Bsktbl; Allegany CC; Retl Mgmt.

CHAFFINCH, LORNA G; Towson SR HS; Towson, MD; (Y); Church Yth Grp; Chorus; School Musical; School Play; Var Capt Cheerleading; St Schlr; VP Frsh Cls; Towson ST U; Theatr Arts.

CHAFFMAN, DENISE; Archbishop Keough HS; Ellicott Cty, MD; (Y); Pep Clb; Rep Soph Cls; JV Bsktbl; JV Var Fld Hcky; NHS; Med.

CHAKRABARTY, PRABIR; Good Counsel HS; Brookeville, MD; (Y); 24/214; Chess Clb; Cmnty Wkr; Pres Debate Tm; NFL; Pres Speech Tm; NHS; Ntl Merit Ltr; NEDT Awd; U Of MD Ldrshp Smnr 86; Dept Defnse Intrnshp Prog 86; Med.

CHAKY, MICHELE; La Reine HS; Pomfret, MD; (Y); 1/170; Church Yth Grp; JV Bsktbl; Var Capt Sftbl; High Hon Roll; VP NHS; Spanish NHS; Spanish Clb; Schlr Of Qrtr; Athlt Of Mnth; La Reinian Of Mnth; Med.

CHAMBERLAIN, DEBBIE; North Harford HS; Forest Hill, MD; (Y); French Clb; Pres Varsity Clb; JV Var Bsktbl; Var L Fld Hcky; Var Capt Socr; JV Var Sftbl; Hon Roll; Trs NHS; All Cnty Bsktbl & Sftbl Tm 86.

CHAMBERLAIN JR, ROBERT L; Georetown Prep; Washington, DC; (Y); Drama Clb; Model UN; Thesps; School Musical; School Play; Lit Mag; Var L Wrstlng; Ntl Merit Ltr; Spanish NHS; Catholic U Of Amer; Psych.

CHAMBERS, JAMES P; Montgomery Blair HS; Silver Spring, MD; (Y); 3/357; Band; ROTC; Color Guard; NHS; Ntl Merit Ltr; Pres Schlr; St Schlr; Political Wkr; Quiz Bowl; High Hon Roll; Pres Schlr GA Inst Of Tech 86; Rrensselaer Mdl For Math & Sci 85; Gov Awd ST Of MD 86; GA Inst Of Tech; Nuclear Engr.

CHAMBERS JR, LEONARD B; Cardinal Gibbons HS; Baltimore, MD; (Y); 45/120; Church Yth Grp; Im Bsbl; JV Var Bsktbl; Bowling; Capt Ftbl; Im Sftbl; Catonsville Comm; Phys Therapy.

CHAMOS, KATHY; North Hagerstown HS; Hagerstown, MD; (Y); 52/277; Red Cross Aide; Teachers Aide; Trs Jr Cls; Sec Sr Cls; Var Sftbl; Hon Roll; Pres Church Yth Grp; GAA; Chorus; Church Choir; Fncl Consltnt.

CHAMP, TIMOTHY BERNARD; Lakcey SR HS; Nanjemoy, MD; (Y); 18/190; Church Yth Grp; Concert Band; Mrchg Band; Variety Show; Yrbk Stf; Lit Mag; Ntl Merit SF; Prfct Atten Awd; 1st Pl Charles Cnty Flm Fest; Instrmntl Music Ltr; Carnegie Mellon U Schlrhsp; MD U; Comp Sci.

CHAN, ANNA; Western HS; Baltimore, MD; (Y); 4-H; Hon Roll; Cert Of Rcgntn As Prtcpnt In Afrcn Amrcn Scntsts Cntst 85; Towson ST U; Nrsng.

CHANCE, LISA; Hammond HS; Jessup, MD; (Y); 49/274; Church Yth Grp; Cmnty Wkr; Hosp Aide; Jr Cls; Sr Cls; Stu Cncl; JV Sftbl; JV Var Vllybl; High Hon Roll; Hon Roll; Pre-Med.

CHANDLER, HAROLD; Takoma Acad; Washington, DC; (Y); Boy Scts; Church Yth Grp; Drama Clb; Chorus; Church Choir; Color Guard; Drill Tm; School Play; Stage Crew; Pres Frsh Cls; Spec Hnrs Prfrmnce Physiolgy Howard U 83; Bst Chrl Stu 86; Bus.

CHANDLER, MILTON; Suitland SR HS; Capitol Hts, MD; (Y); Dance Clb; Letterman Clb; SADD; Teachers Aide; VICA; Stage Crew; Yrbk Stf; JV L Bsktbl; Var L Swmmng; Var Capt Trk; Swim Capt; Regnl Champ Butterfly; Boise ST Coll; Comp Tech.

CHANEY, BRANDI; Lackey HS; Bryans Rd, MD; (Y); Drama Clb; FBLA; SADD; Teachers Aide; Varsity Clb; Rep Frsh Cls; Rep Soph Cls; Rep Jr Cls; Rep Stu Cncl; JV Var Cheerleading; U MD; Comp Proc.

CHANEY, CHRISTINE L; Southern Garrett HS; Deer Park, MD; (S); Band; Concert Band; Jazz Band; Mrchg Band; Off Soph Cls; Off Jr Cls; Rep Stu Cncl; High Hon Roll; Hon Roll; NHS; Math.

CHANEY, EDDIE; Carver Voc-Tech HS; Baltimore, MD; (Y); Hon Roll; NHS; Prfct Atten Awd; Delta Sigma Theta Srty Awd 86; Jehovahs Wtnss; Crpntr.

CHANG, PATRICIA P; Bethesda-Chevy Chase HS; Chevy Chase, MD; (Y); 1/449; Mgr(s); Sec Soph Cls; Pres Jr Cls; Pres Sr Cls; Rep Stu Cncl; St Schlr; Val; Dance Clb; French Clb; Trs German Clb; Outstndt Stu Awd 85; Dartmouth Coll Bk Awd 85; Stu Rsch Fllwshp Pgm-Smmr Intrnshp 85; Yale U; Med.

CHAPIN, LISA; Oldfields Schl; Delray Bch, FL; (Y); 13/48; Camera Clb; Ski Clb; Spanish Clb; Varsity Clb; School Play; Ed Nwsp Phtg; Nwsp Stf; Yrbk Phtg; Yrbk Stf; Var L Badmtn; Ohio Wesleyan U.

CHASKO, DALE; La Plata HS; Waldorf, MD; (Y); Chess Clb; Office Aide; SADD; VICA; Band; Chorus; School Musical; Wt Lftg; Principals Awd Auto Body Prg 86; Auto Body.

CHASSE, CRAIG; Oakland Mills HS; Columbia, MD; (Y); Church Yth Grp; Cmnty Wkr; Math Tm; Teachers Aide; Var Crs Cntry; Var Trk; Hon Roll; Comp Engrng.

CHASTAIN, NICOLE; Maurice J Mc Donough HS; Port Tobacco, MD; (S); FBLA; Sec Jr Cls; Var Co-Capt Pom Pon; High Hon Roll; Hon Roll; Jr NHS; NHS; Outstndng Svc Awd 85; Bus Mgmt.

CHATHAM, CYNTHIA; Mardela HS; Hebron, MD; (Y); Cmnty Wkr; Library Aide; Mrchg Band; Var Fld Hcky; Hon Roll; U MD Eastern Shore; Phys Thrpy.

CHATHAM, JOHN; Parkside HS; Fruitland, MD; (Y); 4-H; Latin Clb; Mrchg Band; Symp Band; Crs Cntry; Aircrft Engrng.

CHATMAN, MARY; Northwestern SR HS; Baltimore, MD; (Y); Prfct Attndnce May 84; Highest Acdmc Achvt US Hist & Soc Stud 86; Pharm.

CHAVIS, TANDRA; High Point HS; Beltsville, MD; (Y); Pres Model UN; Hon Roll; Prfct Atten Awd; Acad Enclln Natl Spnsh Tst Awd 84-85; Pharm.

CHEEK, SUSAN; Colonel Richardson HS; Federalsburg, MD; (Y); Church Yth Grp; Drama Clb; French Clb; Teachers Aide; Capt Color Guard; Capt Flag Corp; School Play; Nwsp Rptr; Yrbk Stf; Var Cheerleading; Jrnlst.

CHEN, EDUARDO R; Our Lady Of Good Counsel HS; Rockville, MD; (Y); 10/214; Church Yth Grp; Cmnty Wkr; French Clb; High Hon Roll; Hon Roll; NHS; Spn Clb Treas 85; U MI; Bio-Med.

CHEN, LYNN; Walter Johnson HS; Bethesda, MD; (Y); Church Yth Grp; Math Tm; Band; Jazz Band; School Musical; JV Fld Hcky; Var L Trk; Sec French Hon Soc; Hon Roll; NHS; Natl Piano Plyng Audtns Dist 85 & 86.

CHEN, PEI-PEI; Parkdale HS; New Carrollton, MD; (Y); AFS; JCL; Latin Clb; SADD; Acpl Chr; Chorus; Yrbk Stf; Off Frsh Cls; Sec Soph Cls; Off Sr Cls; U MD.

CHEN, PETER; Gaithersburg HS; Gaithersburg, MD; (Y); Chess Clb; Church Yth Grp; Computer Clb; Intnl Clb; Math Tm; Rep Stu Cncl; Hon Roll; Wnnr Asn Pdfc Amer Hrtg Cncl Pstr Cntst 85; Top 3 Mid Atlntc JR Plympc Rep MD; U Of MD; Arspc.

CHEN, SHANTE S; Walt Whitman HS; Potomac, MD; (Y); Arts Cntst SF & Awds, Torpedo Fact, Pratt Natl Tlnt Srch, Carnegie-Mellon, MD Eq Fndtn Schlrshps; Carnegie-Mellon U; Vis Art.

CHENG, LEIGH K; Winston Churchill HS; Potomac, MD; (Y); Hosp Aide; JA; Office Aide; Lit Mag; Hon Roll; NHS; Ntl Merit SF.

CHENG, LINDSEY L; Walt Whitman HS; Bethesda, MD; (Y); Chess Clb; JA; Science Clb; Mrchg Band; Pep Band; Symp Band; Rep Frsh Cls; Schltcs Schlrshp Rgnls Prtflio Fin 86; MD Coll Art/Dsgn Jrd Exhbtn 86; Mntgmry SR Hnrs Band 86; Med.

CHENNY, CHIT; Surrattsville HS; Camp Spring, MD; (Y); Chess Clb; Computer Clb; Hon Roll; Elec Engrng.

CHERVENAK, PATRICK; Maurice J Mc Donough HS; Waldorf, MD; (Y); Camera Clb; Church Yth Grp; Intnl Clb; Ski Clb; SADD; Teachers Aide; Varsity Clb; Variety Show; Rep Frsh Cls; Rep Sr Cls; Bus.

CHESHIRE, WENDY; Bruce HS; Westernport, MD; (Y); 22/90; Drama Clb; Office Aide; Chorus; Mrchg Band; School Musical; School Play; Capt Bsktbl; Twrlr; Hon Roll; Frostburg ST Coll; Dancer.

CHESSICK, NICOLE; Gaithersburg HS; Gaithersburg, MD; (Y); Art Clb; Intnl Clb; Yrbk Phtg; NHS; Pres Schlr; Band; Pep Band; Yrbk Rptr; Yrbk Stf; Sftbl; Ntl Art Hnr Soc 85-86; G Street Fbrcs Outsgndng Stu In Fash Merch 85-86; Parson Schl Of Dsgn; Fash Dsgn.

CHESTER, MICHAEL; John Carroll HS; Bradshaw, MD; (Y); 15/240; Science Clb; Spanish Clb; Trk; High Hon Roll; Hon Roll; Spanish NHS; Phldlpha Gas & Elec Co Pstr Cntst Wnr 83-84; Aviation.

CHEUNG, NANCY; Walter Johnson HS; Potomac, MD; (Y); Intnl Clb; Key Clb; Science Clb; SADD; Stage Crew; Variety Show; Mgr(s); JV Capt Vllybl; Hon Roll; NHS; Harvard; Surgeon.

CHICK, STEPHEN M; Valley HS; Hopewell, VA; (Y); Church Yth Grp; Computer Clb; Library Aide; Ski Clb; Chorus; Church Choir; Rep Stu Cncl; Var JV Ftbl; Atlantic Baptist Bible; Misnry.

CHIEN, MARK H; Springbrook HS; Silver Spring, MD; (Y); Church Yth Grp; Math Tm; Swmmng; Hon Roll; JETS Awd; NHS; Math Hnr Soc Mu Alpha Theta 85; Elec Engrng.

CHILDS, CHERYL; Bladensburg HS; Seat Plsnt, MD; (Y); Church Yth Grp; School Play; Stage Crew; Rep Soph Cls; Pom Pon; Trk; Hon Roll; David L Dean Awd 85-86; Span Awd Of Merit 85-86; Typng Awd 84-85; Bennett Coll; Bus Admin.

CHIRDON, NOELLE; Bishop Walsh HS; Lavale, MD; (Y); 60/110; 4-H; Mrchg Band; Capt Bowling; Var Mgr(s); Allegany CC; Med Sec.

CHLUMSKY, SHANNON; Parkville HS; Balt, MD; (Y); Church Yth Grp; Variety Show; Yrbk Rptr; Yrbk Sprt Ed; Yrbk Stf; JV Bsktbl; Var Fld Hcky; Var Lcrss; Hon Roll; Jr NHS; Hcky Tm ST Fnlsts 85.

CHODNICKI, JENNIFER; Patapsco HS; Baltimore, MD; (Y); Art Clb; Camera Clb; Dance Clb; Stage Crew; Yrbk Stf; Hon Roll; Wmns Clb Art Awds 86; Baltimore Cnty & MD ST Film Fest Awds 86; Local Annual Art Show Awd 86; MD Inst Coll; Graphic Art.

CHOE, STEVEN; Liberty HS; Sykesville, MD; (S); Rep Soph Cls; Wt Lftg; JV Capt Wrstlng; High Hon Roll; Hon Roll; Engrng.

CHOI, SUN; Hammond HS; Columbia, MD; (Y); 6/262; Church Yth Grp; French Clb; Science Clb; Band; Mrchg Band; Symp Band; Cit Awd; High Hon Roll; Lion Awd; NHS; TX All ST Band 84-85; U MD.

CHOJNACKI, JOEY LEE; Clear Spring HS; Clear Spg, MD; (Y); Ski Clb; Im JV Bsktbl; Hon Roll; Rookie Yr Clear Spg Vol Fire Dept 85; Ladies Aux Clear Spg Vol Fire Dept Awd Good Ctznshp & Effrt 86; James Romsey Vo Tech; Elctrcn.

CHOVAN, CYNTHIA; Mercy HS; Parkville, MD; (Y); 1/64; Church Yth Grp; Girl Scts; Pres Library Aide; Model UN; Nwsp Stf; NHS; Ntl Merit Ltr; Grl Sct Gld Awd 85; MD Distngshd Schlr Schlrshp 85; Loyola Coll Marion Burke Knott Schlrshp 86; Loyola Coll; Frnch.

CHRISMAN, CRAIG M; Thomas Stone HS; Hughesville, MD; (S); Art Clb; Bsbl; Ftbl; Hon Roll; Jr NHS.

CHRIST, JASON J; Mc Donough HS; Pomfret, MD; (Y); French Clb; Math Clb; Var L Bsbl; Var L Ftbl; Var L Socr; Var L Wrstlng; NHS; Astronautical Engrng.

CHRISTIAN, THOMAS D; Woodlawn HS; Baltimore, MD; (Y); Band; Nwsp Rptr; Nwsp Stf; High Hon Roll; Prfct Atten Awd; Computer Clb; Concert Band; Jazz Band; Mrchg Band; Pep Band; Dirctrs Band Awd 83; Cert Of Recngtn Adv Bsc & Frtrn 84; Cert Of Achvt Lbrl Arts 86; Catonsville CC; Lbrl Arts.

CHRISTMAS, COLLEEN; Connelly Schl Of The Holy Child; Chevy Chase, MD; (Y); Art Clb; Church Yth Grp; Cmnty Wkr; GAA; Pep Clb; Service Clb; Varsity Clb; School Play; Cheerleading; Fld Hcky; Business Mgmt.

CHRISTOPHER, SHERI; S S Peter & Paul HS; Federalsburg, MD; (Y); 1/28; Varsity Clb; School Play; Yrbk Stf; VP Jr Cls; Pres Sr Cls; Var L Sftbl; Hon Roll; NHS; Val; WA Coll; Math.

CHRISTY, MARGARET; St Vincent Pallotti HS; Laurel, MD; (S); AFS; French Clb; Concert Band; Var Swmmng; French Hon Soc; High Hon Roll; Hon Roll; NHS; Grl Scout Slvr Ldrshp Awd 82 & Slvr Awd ; Grl Scout Gld Ldrshp Awd 83; Comp Sci.

CHRONIGER, JULIE; Regina HS; Lewisdale, MD; (Y); School Musical; Stage Crew; JV Bsktbl; JV Cheerleading; JV Sftbl; 2 Acctg Awds 85-86; Benjamin Franklin Coll; CPA.

CHRZANOWSKI III, STANLEY R; Glen Burnie HS; Glen Burnie, MD; (Y); 10/428; JV Bsbl; Var Ftbl; JV Lcrss; JV Socr; High Hon Roll; NHS; USAF ROTC Schlrshp 86; Natl Hispanic Schlrshp Semi-Fnlst 85 & 86; B Banneker Schlrshp Semi Fnlst 86; U Of MD; Aerospace Engr.

CHUN, HYE YEON; James M Bennett SR HS; Salisbury, MD; (S); 4/193; Art Clb; Drama Clb; Intnl Clb; Latin Clb; Spanish Clb; Chorus; Tennis; Hon Roll; NHS; 1st Pl Art Shw 84-85; Plaque For Bst In Painting 84-85; Acad Lttr 84-85; Yale; Engrng.

CHUN, HYE-YEON; James M Bennett SR HS; Salisbury, MD; (Y); 1/180; Art Clb; Trs Church Yth Grp; Drama Clb; Intnl Clb; Latin Clb; Chorus; School Musical; Tennis; Sec NHS; Spanish NHS; Painting 1sts, Plaqua Best Painting 84-85; Plaque Acdmc Achvt Awd 85-86; Gld Mdl Perf Score Natl Latin; Elec Engrng.

CHUN, HYESIN; James M Bennett SR HS; Salisbury, MD; (Y); 24/192; Art Clb; Intnl Clb; Spanish Clb; Varsity Clb; Chorus; Church Choir; Cheerleading; Hon Roll; Med Tech.

CHUNG, DAVID; John Carroll HS; Joppa, MD; (Y); 3/238; Science Clb; Orch; French Hon Soc; High Hon Roll; Ntl Merit Ltr; Prfct Atten Awd.

CHUNG, JAE JUN PHILLIP; Loyola HS; Tumonium, MD; (Y); Church Yth Grp; Cmnty Wkr; French Clb; Band; Jazz Band; Yrbk Phtg; Yrbk Stf; French Hon Soc; NHS; Var Tennis; Bus Adm.

CHUNN, BRENDA S; Old Mill SR HS; Millersville, MD; (Y); 1/482; Trs German Clb; Concert Band; Mrchg Band; Sec VP Stu Cncl; Var Lcrss; High Hon Roll; Pres NHS; St Schlr; Val; Westinghouse Fmly Schlrshp Awd 86; Edward J Anderson Top Stu Schlr 86; MD Dstngshd Schlr Fnlst 86; Duke U; Bio Med Engrng.

CIAMACCA, MAGDALENA; Catonsville HS; Baltimore, MD; (Y); French Clb; SADD; Chorus; High Hon Roll; Hon Roll; VFW Awd; Voice Dem Awd; Hood Coll Awd Partcptn, Frgn Lang & Lit 86; Penn ST; Lawyer.

CIAMILLO JR, LOUIS; Frederick HS; Clarksburg, MD; (Y); Camera Clb; Computer Clb; FBLA; Latin Clb; Crs Cntry; Trk; Wt Lftg; High Hon Roll; Hon Roll; Prospect Hall Schlrshp 87; Wharton Schl; Bus Admin.

CIBAK, DANA; Potomac HS; Temple Hills, MD; (Y); Teachers Aide; Powder Puff Ftbl; Score Keeper; Vllybl; Hon Roll; MIP Vllybll 85; Schlr Athlt 86; Photogrphy.

CIEKOT, DAVID; Cambridge South Dorchester HS; Cambridge, MD; (Y); 5/258; Band; Concert Band; Jazz Band; Mrchg Band; Orch; Pep Band; School Musical; Symp Band; Church Yth Grp; DAR Awd; All Shore Band 86; Frostburg ST Coll; Mgmt.

CISSEL, SUSETTE; Rising Sun HS; Rising Sun, MD; (Y); 14/166; Office Aide; High Hon Roll; Hon Roll; Prfct Atten Awd; US Bus Educ Awds 86; Acad All-Amer At Large 86; Goldey Beacon Coll; Autmtd Acct.

CLAGGETT, CATHY; La Plata HS; Newburg, MD; (Y); 61/302; Cmnty Wkr; Spanish Clb; SADD; Teachers Aide; Nwsp Stf; Rep Frsh Cls; Rep Soph Cls; High Hon Roll; Hon Roll; Voice Dem Awd; Physcn Mem Hosp Axlry Schlrshp $500 86; Emrgncy Med Tchncn Cert 85; Charles Cnty CC; Nrsng.

CLAPIN, CHRISTINA; Eastern Vo-Tech; Baltimore, MD; (Y); VP Church Yth Grp; Band; VP Church Choir; Concert Band; Variety Show; Lit Mag; Var Capt Cheerleading; Var Mgr(s); Var Score Keeper; Stat Vllybl; Varsty Ltr Awd 85-86.

CLARK, AARON; Bishop Walsh HS; Lavale, MD; (Y); Ski Clb; Nwsp Phtg; Yrbk Phtg; Avaition.

CLARK, ALLEN; Queen Annes County HS; Crumpton, MD; (Y); Am Leg Boys St; Letterman Clb; Var L Lcrss; Var L Trk; Im Vllybl; Im Wt Lftg; Hon Roll; Im Sftbl; Tech.

CLARK, CELESTINE; Southern HS; Baltimore, MD; (Y); 10/200; ROTC; Teachers Aide; Chorus; Drill Tm; Flag Corp; Rep Frsh Cls; Rep Jr Cls; Pres Stu Cncl; Bsktbl; Trk; Genatrl Schlrshp 86; Frostburg ST Coll.

CLARK, D; Northwestern HS; Hyattsville, MD; (Y); AFS; Boy Scts; Church Yth Grp; Teachers Aide; Socr; Hon Roll; Jr NHS; NHS; U Of MD; Engnrng.

CLARK, DANIEL; Northwestern HS; Hyattsville, MD; (S); Boy Scts; Church Yth Grp; Science Clb; Teachers Aide; Socr; High Hon Roll; Hon Roll; VP Jr NHS; NHS; U MD; Engrng.

CLARK, MARGARET; Crossland HS; Temple Hills, MD; (Y); 8/330; Spanish Clb; Swmmng; High Hon Roll; NHS; Spanish NHS.

CLARK, ROBERT; Gaithersburg HS; Gaithersburg, MD; (Y); Chess Clb; Math Tm; High Hon Roll; Hon Roll; Kiwanis Awd; Physcs Achvmnt Awd 86; Hnry Kiwani 85; Elec Engr.

CLARK, ROBERT L; Bishop Walsh HS; Cumberland, MD; (Y); #6 In Class; Pres Debate Tm; Drama Clb; Pres Speech Tm; Thesps; Cit Awd; DAR Awd; French Hon Soc; Sec Trs NHS; Opt Clb Awd; Voice Dem Awd; Prsdntl Merit Schlrhsp Loyola Coll 86; Full Acadmc Merit Schlrshp Frostburg St Coll 86; ST Sent Page; Attorney.

CLARK, THERESE; Archbishop Keough HS; Baltimore, MD; (Y); Art Clb; Computer Clb; Spanish Clb; Nwsp Rptr; High Hon Roll; Hon Roll; NHS; Salisbury ST Col6; Optmtry.

CLARK, THOMAS; Dundalk HS; Baltimore, MD; (Y); Band; Off Frsh Cls; Off Soph Cls; Off Jr Cls; Stu Cncl; Bsbl; High Hon Roll; Hon Roll; NHS; Engl.

CLARK, THOMAS D; Mount Saint Joseph HS; Catonsville, MD; (Y); 2/253; Hosp Aide; Ed Yrbk Stf; Capt Im Bowling; High Hon Roll; VP NHS; Ntl Merit SF; Sal; St Schlr; Ski Clb; School Play; Fll Tuition Marion Burke Knott Schlrshp; Its Acadamic Tm Mbr; Pre-Med.

CLARKE, HEATHER; St Marys-Ryken HS; California, MD; (S); Art Clb; Church Yth Grp; FBLA; Church Choir; School Musical; JV Sftbl; JV Vllybl; High Hon Roll; Hon Roll; Jr NHS; Hmcmg Qn 85; Bio Awd 83; Spnsh Awd 84; Bryn Mawr Coll; Intrprtr.

CLARKE, LISA RENEE; Fort Hill HS; Cumberland, MD; (Y); 26/284; Church Yth Grp; Pep Clb; Band; Church Choir; Capt Flag Corp; Rep Stu Cncl; Hon Roll; Rotary Awd; Rotary Clb Schlrshp 86; Allgny Cnty Med Aux Schlrshp 86; MD Senatorial Schlrshp 86; Allegany CC; Nrsng.

CLARKE, SCOTT; Walter Johnson HS; Bethesda, MD; (Y); Aud/Vis; Pres Church Yth Grp; Drama Clb; Key Clb; Pres Ski Clb; SADD; School Musical; School Play; Stage Crew; Nwsp Rptr; Intern-Natl Inst Of Health 85-86; Marine Bio.

CLAS, AMY; South Carroll HS; Woodbine, MD; (Y); Church Yth Grp; Varsity Clb; VICA; Var Capt Trk; Hon Roll; Outstndng SR Awd Grls Trk & Field 86; Intr Design.

CLAUDE, TONYA; Montgomery Blair HS; Silver Spring, MD; (Y); 157/357; Church Yth Grp; Cmnty Wkr; Drama Clb; Hosp Aide; Office Aide; Pep Clb; Red Cross Aide; Teachers Aide; Y-Teens; School Musical; Mrtn Lthr Kng Schlrshp 86; Pre Med.

CLAVIN, LAURA; Franklin HS; Reisterstown, MD; (Y); Am Leg Aux Girls St; VP Key Clb; Trs Stu Cncl; Var Sftbl; Var Vllybl; High Hon Roll; Kiwanis Awd; NHS; Opt Clb Awd; Pres Schlr; Rymnd Hysn Mem Schlrshp 86; Schl Srv Mdl 86; Hsptl Vlntr 84 & 85; Loyola U Chgo; Pre-Med.

CLAY, REGGIE; Loyola HS; Columbia, MD; (Y).

CLEGERN, JAMES B; Sherwood HS; Olney, MD; (Y); Boy Scts; Chess Clb; Church Yth Grp; Computer Clb; Church Choir; Co-Capt Vllybl; Hon Roll; NHS; U MD College Park; Aerosp Engr.

CLEMENTS, CHRIS; Gaithersburg HS; Gaithersburg, MD; (Y); SADD; Tennis; Hon Roll; Comp Sci.

CLEMENTS, SUSAN; La Plata HS; Bryantown, MD; (Y); Red Cross Aide; Science Clb; Y-Teens; Color Guard; Flag Corp; Cit Awd; Hon Roll; Flag Corps Ltr & Pins 86; Towson; Child Psych.

CLEMENTS JR, THOMAS; La Plata HS; La Plata, MD; (Y); Computer Clb; 4-H; Key Clb; Capt Crs Cntry; Capt Trk; Cit Awd; 4-H Awd; High Hon Roll; Church Yth Grp.

CLEMSEN, KIMBERLY; Dulaney SR HS; Lutherville, MD; (Y); 4-H; Ski Clb; Spanish Clb; 4-H Awd; High Hon Roll; Hon Roll; U Of MD; Engineering.

CLEVELAND, JANE; La Reine HS; Upper Marlboro, MD; (Y); Church Yth Grp; Band; Var Cheerleading; JV Sftbl; Hon Roll; NHS; Prfct Atten Awd; U Of MD College Park.

CLINE, MISSY; Williamsport HS; Williamsport, MD; (Y); 49/224; Church Yth Grp; Latin Clb; Band; Church Choir; Concert Band; Drill Tm; Flag Corp; Mrchg Band; Symp Band; Prfct Atten Awd; Hagerstown JC; Secy.

CLISE, KRISTA; Fort Hill HS; Cumberland, MD; (Y); Drill Tm; Flag Corp; Nwsp Stf; Trs Jr Cls; Hon Roll; Allegany CC; Resp Thrpy.

CLIZBE, MARY; Brunswick HS; Brunswick, MD; (Y); Dance Clb; Drama Clb; Office Aide; School Musical; School Play; Stage Crew; Rep Jr Cls; Off Stu Cncl; Var Cheerleading; Hon Roll; Intr Dsgn.

CLOUGH, PATRICK D; Riverdale Baptist Schl; Laurel, MD; (Y); Church Yth Grp; Band; Orch; Var L Bsbl; Var JV Bsktbl; Score Keeper; Im Vllybl; Hon Roll; 1st Pl ST Fine Arts Pol Sci/Econ; Mth.

CLOUSE, KEVIN; Central HS; Andrews Afb, DC; (Y); Aud/Vis; Chorus; Concert Band; Jazz Band; Mrchg Band; Pep Band; School Musical; School Play; Stage Crew; Band Stu Of Mnth 85; Natl Hnr Rl 86; VA Tech; Aero.

CLOYD, DAYNA JOY; Woodlawn HS; Baltimore, MD; (Y); DECA; Var Trk; Comp Analys.

CO, MARK S; Loyola HS; Cockeysville, MD; (S); 7/197; JV Swmmng; Hon Roll; NHS; Ntl Merit Ltr; NEDT Awd; St Schlr; Acdmc Awds 82-86; Engrng.

COATES, MONICA A; Randallstown SR HS; Randallstown, MD; (Y); Church Yth Grp; Band; Concert Band; Orch; VP Sr Cls; Rep Stu Cncl; Sftbl; Var Capt Vllybl; High Hon Roll; Hon Roll; Natl Achvt Prgm Cmmnd Stu 85; All Cnty Vlybl Tm 85; Psych.

COBB, LYNNE; Mount De Sales Acad; Baltimore, MD; (S); 7/53; Hosp Aide; Band; Chorus; Church Choir; Yrbk Stf; JV Sftbl; Hon Roll; Opt Clb Awd; Mathias D Sousa Flwshp 85-86; St Marys Coll; Mrn Bio.

COBLE, ELIZABETH; Surrattsville SR HS; Clinton, MD; (Y); Cmnty Wkr; French Clb; Teachers Aide; Nwsp Stf; Hon Roll; Georgetown; Intl Law.

COBLE, LAWRENCE; The Bullis Schl; Potomac, MD; (S); 1/97; Am Leg Boys St; Key Clb; Nwsp Stf; Yrbk Stf; Var Crs Cntry; JV Socr; JV Sftbl; JV Tennis; High Hon Roll; NHS; Natl Wldlf Awd Montgmry Cty Sci Fair 84; Natl Sci Merit Awd 85; Headmstr Awd 85.

COCCAGNA, JULIE; John Carroll HS; White Hall, MD; (Y); Ski Clb; Band; Var Trk; Acad Achvt 85-86.

COCKERELL, DANIEL; Thomas S Wootten HS; Rockville, MD; (Y); Exploring; JA; Ski Clb; VP Jr Cls; VP Sr Cls; Ftbl; Var Trk; Hon Roll; Montgomery Cty All Cty Rnngbck 86; Ftbl MVP 86; Bus.

COCKERHAM, GENE P; Aberdeen HS; Aberdeen, MD; (Y); 7/195; Mrchg Band; Lit Mag; Var Trk; High Hon Roll; Hon Roll; NHS; Acad Awd 82-86; Engl Awd 86; Marshal Hahn Engrng Mrt Schlr VA Tech 86; Virginia Tech; Aerosp Engrng.

CODY, SCOTT W; Frederick HS; Frederick, MD; (Y); Boys Clb Am; Capt Wrstlng; Hon Roll; U Of NC Chapel Hll; Art.

COFFIN, BRITT; Takoma Acad; Brinklow, MD; (S); Drama Clb; Ski Clb; School Play; Sec Jr Cls; VP Sr Cls; Co-Capt Cheerleading; Pom Pon; Swmmng; Trk; Hon Roll; Valentn Qn 84-85; Soc & PR Cmmttee Chrprsn 84-86; James Madison; Cmmnctns.

COFFMAN, ANNETTE; Northern HS; Dunkirk, MD; (Y); Church Yth Grp; Var JV Bsktbl; Dnfth Awd; High Hon Roll; Hon Roll; NHS; Opt Clb Awd; Cmnty Wkr; Calvert Cnty Supts Schlstc Awd 86; Freedm Fndtn Ldrshp Awd 86; Bsktbl Mst Spirtd Awd 84; Tchr.

COFIELD, STACY; Oakland Mills HS; Ellicott City, MD; (Y); AFS; FCA; Science Clb; Nwsp Phtg; Nwsp Rptr; Nwsp Stf; Hon Roll; Camera Clb; Cmnty Wkr; Library Aide; Merit Concours Ntl De Francais , MD Acad Sci Smnrs 85; ST Pgnt MS Amer Coed 86; U Medical Schl; Pre Med.

COHEE, BRIDGET; Archbishop Spalding HS; Glen Burnie, MD; (Y); 8/128; Drama Clb; School Musical; Var Bsktbl; Capt Fld Hcky; Var Capt Lcrss; High Hon Roll; NHS; Church Yth Grp; Math Clb; Red Cross Aide; Sr Sci Awd 86; Mt St Marys Acad Schlrshp 86; Unsung Hero-Vrsty Bsktbl 86; Mt St Marys Coll; Bio.

COHEN, DAVID; The Bullis Schl; Potomac, MD; (Y); Cmnty Wkr; Temple Yth Grp; Nwsp Rptr; VP Soph Cls; Bsktbl; Socr; Tennis; High Hon Roll; Outstndng Frgn Lang 86.

COHEN, DENNIS; Riverdale Baptist Schl; Hyattsville, MD; (Y); Church Yth Grp; Office Aide; Band; Yrbk Sprt Ed; Bsbl; Capt Socr; Wrstlng; Hon Roll; MVP Sccr; ST Champs Sccr; 1st Brass Solo; St Police Offcr.

COHEN, ELYSE; Joppatowne HS; Edgewood, MD; (Y); Service Clb; Temple Yth Grp; Chorus; School Musical; Trs Frsh Cls; Rep Stu Cncl; JV Cheerleading; L Pom Pon; Powder Puff Ftbl; Hon Roll; Mass Comm.

COHEN, ERIC S; Pikesville SR HS; Baltimore, MD; (Y); Computer Clb; Spanish Clb; Band; Concert Band; Jazz Band; Mrchg Band; Orch; Off Frsh Cls; Stu Cncl; Var JV Lcrss; U MA-AMHERST; Finance.

COKER, KAREN; Seton HS; Baltimore, MD; (Y); Drama Clb; French Clb; Intnl Clb; Chrmn Pep Clb; School Musical; Nwsp Rptr; Lit Mag; Stu Cncl; Dnfth Awd; Pres Schlr; Pres Ftnss Awd 86; Towson ST U; Prdcr.

COLACIELLO, DEBBIE; Gwynn Park HS; Brandywine, MD; (Y); Aud/Vis; Yrbk Stf; Lit Mag; Rep Stu Cncl; Var Bowling; Hon Roll; Jr NHS; Pres VP NHS; Prnc Geo Cnty Acad Excllnc Awd 84 & 85.

COLBORN, MICHAEL; Bladensburg SR HS; Edmonston, MD; (Y); Boy Scts; Chess Clb; Natl Beta Clb; Off ROTC; Trs Jr Cls; Var L Bsbl; High Hon Roll; Jr NHS; Acdmc Achvmnt Awd 84; Outstndng Stu Mnth 85; Elec Engr.

COLE, BRENDA; Crisfield HS; Crisfield, MD; (Y); Church Yth Grp; FHA; Band; Church Choir; Concert Band; Mrchg Band; Symp Band; Var Bsktbl; Var Sftbl; Comp.

COLE, CHERYL; Sherwood HS; Silver Spring, MD; (S); 3/317; German Clb; Model UN; SADD; Teachers Aide; Off Stu Cncl; Capt Cheerleading; High Hon Roll; Hon Roll; NHS; Pres Schlr; MD Dstngshd Schlr; Duke U; Biolgcl Sci.

COLE, MARIO; Surrattsville HS; Clinton, MD; (Y); Boy Scts; Hon Roll; Jerry Horton Awd 84; Areospc Engrng.

COLEIANNE, LISA; Glenelg HS; Sykesville, MD; (Y); Cmnty Wkr; Intnl Clb; Ski Clb; Teachers Aide; Varsity Clb; Bsktbl; Score Keeper; Sftbl; Hon Roll; NHS; Villanova U; Sprts Med.

COLEMAN, CHRISTY; Beall HS; Frostburg, MD; (Y); Church Yth Grp; Dance Clb; 4-H; Chorus; Church Choir; Drill Tm; Yrbk Rptr; Yrbk Stf; Pres Sr Cls; Capt Pom Pon; Frostburg ST Coll; Pre-Law.

COLEMAN, GLENN; Parkville HS; Baltimore, MD; (Y); French Clb; Key Clb; Math Tm; Concert Band; Trnty U; Med.

COLEMAN, RHONDA; La Plata HS; La Plata, MD; (Y); Ski Clb; Spanish Clb; SADD; Chorus; Ed Yrbk Stf; Hon Roll; Towson.

COLEMAN, SANDRA; Great Mills HS; California, MD; (Y); FBLA; Latin Clb; Spanish Clb; Teachers Aide; Var Fld Hcky; Hon Roll; FBLA Rgnl Cmptn Typg I 84; Frstry.

COLEMAN, SHERI; Mercy HS; Baltimore, MD; (Y); Towson St; Spec Ed.

COLEMAN, THELMA; Southern HS; Baltimore, MD; (Y); Math Tm; Office Aide; ROTC; Drill Tm; Sec Stu Cncl; Trk; West Point; Comp Spec.

COLEMAN, VERONICA; Parkdale HS; Cheltenham, MD; (Y); Church Yth Grp; Cmnty Wkr; Pep Clb; Hon Roll; SR Prom Commtt 85-86; Prince Georgeous CC; Bus.

COLEMAN-BLACK, SHARON; La Reine HS; Washington, DC; (Y); 28/149; Pres Church Yth Grp; Civic Clb; Cmnty Wkr; JA; Chorus; Pres Church Choir; Drill Tm; Hon Roll; Acad Hnrs In Trig 86; Acad Hnrs In Cmptr Pgmng 86; Howard U; Cmptr Pgmng.

COLLETTE, SANDRA; Oldtown HS; Oldtown, MD; (S); FBLA; Sec FHA; Chorus; School Musical; Nwsp Stf; Sec Jr Cls; VP Sr Cls; Trs Stu Cncl; High Hon Roll; Sec NHS; Homnng Attndt 85; Ms Amity MD Teen Pgnt 85; Citznshp Awd 85; Allegany CC; Med Sec.

COLLEY, MARLO; Snow Hill HS; Stockton, MD; (S); AFS; Color Guard; Flag Corp; Yrbk Stf; Sec Jr Cls; Stat Socr; Hon Roll; NHS; Prfct Atten Awd; Miss Snow Hill Merchant 84-85; MD Miss Tn Cntstnt 85; Salisbury ST Coll.

COLLIER, CHARLES; James M Bennett HS; Salisbury, MD; (Y); 4/180; JCL; Latin Clb; Math Clb; Band; Concert Band; Jazz Band; Mrchg Band; Orch; School Musical; Symp Band; Oberlin College; Chem.

COLLILLA, JANE; Walter Johnson HS; Bethesda, MD; (Y); Thesps; School Play; Stage Crew; Hon Roll; Prdcrs Choice Awd 86; Intl Rltns.

COLLINGS, KELLEY WOOD; Elkton HS; Elkton, MD; (Y); 3/287; Debate Tm; German Clb; Intnl Clb; Varsity Clb; Band; Concert Band; Mrchg Band; Frsh Cls; Soph Cls; Jr Cls; 1782 Soc Schlrshp 86; Beneficial Hodson Trst Schlrshp 86; WA College; Intl Relat.

COLLINS, FELICIA L; Springbrook HS; Silver Spg, MD; (Y); 10/488; Pres Church Yth Grp; Sec Math Clb; Church Choir; Pres Concert Band; Drm Mjr(t); School Musical; Yrbk Ed-Chief; High Hon Roll; NHS; Ntl Merit Schol; Yale U; Biochem.

COLLINS, JOE; Mount Saint Joseph HS; Reisterstown, MD; (Y); 51/305; Ski Clb; Var L Ftbl; Var L Wrstlng; Capt JV & Fresh-Soph Ftbl 83-85; MD U; Comp Sci.

COLOMBO, LISA JANE; Joppatowne HS; Joppa, MD; (Y); 3/180; Varsity Clb; School Musical; Off Jr Cls; Pres Sr Cls; Sec Stu Cncl; Var Cheerleading; Var Lcrss; JV Tennis; Hon Roll; NHS; MD Distngshd Schlr Hnrbl Ment 85; U Of MD; Mrktng.

COLSON, DEBRA; Northwestern HS; Hyattsville, MD; (Y); Pep Clb; Teachers Aide; Chorus; Jr Cls; Stu Cncl; Hon Roll; NHS; MD U; Elect Engr.

COLT, JOHN; Fallston HS; Fallston, MD; (Y); 49/257; Spanish Clb; Nwsp Stf; Yrbk Stf; JV Bsktbl; Var L Lcrss; Var L Socr; Im Tennis; Im Wt Lftg; Im Wrstlng; High Hon Roll; U Of NC; Engr.

COLTON, DAVID; Thomas S Wootton HS; Potomav, MD; (Y); Camera Clb; Trs JA; Ski Clb; Temple Yth Grp; Nwsp Phtg; Var L Trk; Hon Roll; Maryland.

COMBS, MICHELLE; Ft Hill HS; Cumberland, MD; (Y); 35/265; Church Yth Grp; Office Aide; Temple Yth Grp; Yrbk Stf; Off Jr Cls; Hon Roll; Delg Scholar 86; Senatrl Scholar 86; Frostburg ST; Bus.

COMBS, SHARI; Fort Hill HS; Cumberland, MD; (Y); Church Yth Grp; Hosp Aide; Office Aide; Pep Clb; Chorus; Lit Mag; Trk; Hon Roll; NHS; Delg Yth Gov Leg 86; Acctng.

COMEGNA, MICHAEL J; Loyola HS; Marriottsville, MD; (S); Church Yth Grp; Jr Cls; Hon Roll; NHS; Comp Engrng.

CONAWAY, SHELLY; Wicomico SR HS; Parsonburg, MD; (Y); AFS; FCA; Varsity Clb; Yrbk Stf; Sr Cls; Bsktbl; Sftbl; Vllybl; Hon Roll; Med.

CONDON, ERIN; Fransis Scott Key HS; Westmnster, MD; (Y); Drama Clb; Science Clb; Spanish Clb; Chorus; Swing Chorus; Nwsp Stf; Office Aide; Teachers Aide; School Play; Stage Crew; Crmnlgy.

CONFER, KRISTIN; Williamsport HS; Hagerstown, MD; (Y); 23/206; Cmnty Wkr; Drama Clb; VP Sec Exploring; Hosp Aide; Sec Spanish Clb; SADD; School Musical; School Play; VP Swing Chorus; Hon Roll; Acad All Am 86; Physcl Thrpy.

CONGDON, MARK; Mt Saint Joseph HS; Baltimore, MD; (Y); Art Clb; Boys Clb Am; Boy Scts; Camera Clb; Church Yth Grp; Ski Clb; Stat Lcrss; Score Keeper; JV Wrstlng; Prfct Atten Awd; Best In Show Awd 86; Art.

CONJELKO, PHILIP; Leonardtown HS; Hollywood, MD; (Y); Jazz Band; Mrchg Band; Symp Band; Hon Roll; NHS; Tennis; Spanish Clb; Model Gen Assmbly 85; Embry Riddle Aeronatcl U; Engr.

CONNELL, LISA; Northeast HS; Elkton, MD; (Y); French Clb; FBLA; FHA; Intnl Clb; Science Clb; SADD; Teachers Aide; Band; Chorus; Concert Band; All Count Chorus 85-86; Tchrs Aid Awd; Widener U; Bus.

CONNELLEY, ANGIE; Calvert HS; Huntingtown, MD; (Y); Pres Latin Clb; Rep Frsh Cls; Capt Pom Pon; High Hon Roll; Hon Roll; Prfct Atten Awd; Med.

CONNER, JEFFERY; Allegany HS; Cumberland, MD; (Y); 12/250; FBLA; Hon Roll; Frostburg ST; Bus Admin.

CONNER, SUZANNE; Eastern Vo-Tech HS; Baltimore, MD; (Y); VP Pres FBLA; Office Aide; Chorus; Pres Hon Roll; Baltimore Cnty Spch Fest 84 & 86; Bus Adm.

CONNER, VALERIE; T S Wootton HS; Gaithersburg, MD; (Y); Drama Clb; JA; Chorus; Orch; School Musical; Stage Crew; Lit Mag; Hon Roll; Bus Admin.

CONNOLLY, PATRICK J; Loyola HS; Ellicott City, MD; (S); Debate Tm; French Clb; NFL; Jazz Band; Nwsp Rptr; Lit Mag; NHS; NEDT Awd; USN Acad; Physcs.

CONNORS, JENNIFER S; Bowie HS; Bowie, MD; (Y); 6/611; French Clb; Key Clb; Latin Clb; Letterman Clb; Teachers Aide; Varsity Clb; Drill Tm; Off Frsh Cls; Off Soph Cls; Off Jr Cls; Hmcmng Ct Princess 83-86; Natl Superstar Drill Tm 84; Potomac Vly All Star Swm 83; Clemson U; Engrng.

CONNORS, ROBERT WILLIAM; Seneca Valley HS; Gaithersburg, MD; (Y); 80/600; Am Leg Boys St; ROTC; SADD; Church Choir; School Play; Im Crs Cntry; Var L Trk; Hon Roll; Schl Quadrathln Record 86; 2nd Pl Mile Relay Regnl Trk 86; 4th Pl 2 Mi Relay Regnl Trk 86.

CONRAD, AMY; Notre Dame Preparatory Schl; Ellicott City, MD; (Y); Cmnty Wkr; GAA; Math Tm; Office Aide; Pep Clb; Political Wkr; Service Clb; Teachers Aide; Im Mgr Badmtn; Im Mgr Bsktbl; Cert Merit Frnch Lang 85-86; Treas Grls Athltc Assn 86-87; Cert Excllnc NEDT Tsts 83-84; Atty Law.

CONWAY, VALERIE; Walbrook SR HS; Baltimore, MD; (Y); Hosp Aide; JA; Teachers Aide; Band; Church Choir; School Musical; Hon Roll; Hearng-Spch Thrpy.

COOGEN, MICHAEL; Good Counsel HS; Rockville, MD; (Y); 50/214; 4-H; French Clb; Im Bsktbl; Im Ftbl; Im Vllybl; Hon Roll; Crtcl Anlys Clb 84-86; West Point; Law.

COOK, GRETCHEN; Oakland Mills HS; Columbia, MD; (Y); 65/280; Cmnty Wkr; Hosp Aide; Nwsp Phtg; Nwsp Rptr; Nwsp Sprt Ed; JV Cheerleading; High Hon Roll; 4-Yr Acadmc Schlrshp Spelman 86-90; Votd Ms Iota Kopelle 86; Exec Edtr Voice Tomorrw 86; Spelman Coll; Econmcs.

COOK, JEFF; Clear Spring HS; Clear Spg, MD; (Y); 11/125; Pres Church Yth Grp; SADD; Band; Church Choir; JV School Play; Var Bsktbl; JV Socr; Var Trk; Hon Roll; NHS; Hstry.

COOK, JULIE; Middletown HS; Middletown, MD; (Y); Hosp Aide; Office Aide; Spanish Clb; Teachers Aide; Chorus; Var L Crs Cntry; Var L Socr; Var L Trk; Hon Roll; 4-H; PTSA Scholar 86; Slippery Rock U; Spec Ed.

COOK, LAURIE J; Maranatha Baptist Church Acad; Elkton, MD; (Y); 1/10; Sec Church Yth Grp; Chorus; Church Choir; Yrbk Stf; L Var Bsktbl; Capt L Cheerleading; L Var Vllybl; High Hon Roll; Val; Hon Soc 3 Yrs; French Hon Soc; Pensacola Tuition Schlrshp 86; Bob Jones U; Elem Ed.

COOK, ROBIN; Allegany HS; Cumberland, MD; (Y); Yrbk Stf; Capt Cheerleading; Gym; Tennis; Trk; NHS; U Of MD; Bus.

COOKE, CHRISTIE; High Point HS; W Hyattsville, MD; (Y); 20/640; Latin Clb; Math Clb; Yrbk Phtg; Pom Pon; Cit Awd; High Hon Roll; NHS; Prfct Atten Awd; St Schlr; Phi Delta Kappa Scholar 86-89; Senatorl Scholar 86-89; Towson ST U; Chem.

COOKE II, COLIN; La Plata HS; La Plata, MD; (Y); Church Yth Grp; Band; Concert Band; Jazz Band; Mrchg Band; Symp Band; Hon Roll; Prfct Atten Awd.

COOKE, DERRICK; Loyola-Blakefield HS; Baltimore, MD; (Y); Art Clb; Varsity Clb; Frnch Awd 84-85; William & Mary; Bus.

COOKE, MONICA; Suitland SR HS; Hyattsville, MD; (Y); CAP; Exploring; French Clb; Service Clb; Speech Tm; Teachers Aide; Drill Tm; Vllybl; Spanish NHS; Elec Engr.

COOL JR, RONALD J; Catoctin HS; Emmitsburg, MD; (Y); VP Computer Clb; Science Clb; Ftbl; Hon Roll; USAF Acad; Pilot.

COOLEY, TRACIE; Maurice J Mc Donough HS; Waldorf, MD; (Y); Art Clb; Letterman Clb; Office Aide; Teachers Aide; Stu Cncl; Stat Trk; Wt Lftg; Stat Wrstlng; High Hon Roll; Hon Roll; Sci Fair-Hon Mntn 82-83; Merit Awd Wgtlftg 83-84; Art Wrk Excptd At Charles Co CC Exhb 85-86; Charles Co CC; Fshn Dsgnr.

COOMBS, ABBY; Mc Donough HS; Pomfret, MD; (Y); Church Yth Grp; Intnl Clb; Mrchg Band; Hst Soph Cls; Hst Sr Cls; Rep Stu Cncl; Pom Pon; High Hon Roll; Hon Roll; Animal Tech.

COOMBS, DONNA; Great Mills HS; Great Mills, MD; (Y); Pep Clb; Spanish Clb; Pom Pon; Hon Roll; Curriculum.

COOMBS, GREG; St Marys Ryleen HS; Great Mills, MD; (Y); Computer Clb; Prfct Atten Awd; Mgt.

COOMBS, PAMELA; Maurice J Mc Donough HS; Pomfret, MD; (S); Church Yth Grp; Intnl Clb; Var JV Sftbl; Var JV Vllybl; High Hon Roll; Hon Roll; Bus.

COON, JENNIFER; Du Val HS; Lanham, MD; (Y); Ed Natl Beta Clb; Pres Spanish Clb; Mrchg Band; Pres Symp Band; Hon Roll; Spanish NHS; MD U; Medcl Sci.

COONEY, ANDREW J; Bel Air HS; Bel Air, MD; (Y); 12/226; Church Yth Grp; Acpl Chr; Church Choir; JV Tennis; Var L Trk; Var Vllybl; Hon Roll; NHS; Prfct Atten Awd; Deans Schlrshp From Messiah 85; Presdntl Schlrshp From Messiah 86; Messiah Coll; Behavioral Sci.

COONTZ II, DAVID; La Plata HS; Waldorf, MD; (Y); Letterman Clb; Varsity Clb; Var L Ftbl; Wt Lftg; High Hon Roll; Hon Roll; Princpls Hnrs 85-86; Natl Cncl Tchrs Englsh Wrtng Contlaplata Rep 85; Psych.

COOPER, BENJAMIN; C E S Jewish Day Schl; Potomac, MD; (Y); Pres Temple Yth Grp; Bsbl; Crs Cntry; Schlrshp Awd Trp Israel; Won 1st Pl Schl Sci Fair; Med.

COOPER III, CLINTON; Snow Hill HS; Stockton, MD; (S); 11/114; French Clb; Rep Band; Church Choir; Concert Band; Jazz Band; Mrchg Band; Hon Roll; NHS; Prfct Atten Awd; Music.

COOPER, DARYL; Paul Laurence Dunbar HS; Baltimore, MD; (Y); Aud/Vis; FBLA; Teachers Aide; Bsktbl; Var JV Ftbl; Swmmng; Wt Lftg; Cit Awd; Prfct Atten Awd; Sprts.

COOPER, DORA; Frederick Douglas HS; Baltimore, MD; (Y); JA 83; Pres Of Stu Cncl Fresh 83; Stu Rep JR Cls 85-86; Army; Comp Anlyst.

COOPER, KATHERINE; Maurice J Mc Donough SR HS; Waldorf, MD; (S); FBLA; Intnl Clb; Library Aide; JV Trk; Hon Roll; NHS; Frnch Star Of The Qtr 86; U Of MD College Pk; Bus Adm.

COOPER, MELODY L; La Plata SR HS; La Plata, MD; (Y); Church Yth Grp; Dance Clb; Sec Science Clb; Thesps; Chorus; Church Choir; Concert Band; Madrigals; Mrchg Band; School Musical; Zoolgy.

COOPER, SHANNON; North Carroll HS; Mancheter, MD; (Y); Spanish Clb; Yrbk Stf; Rep Jr Cls; Var Capt Cheerleading; High Hon Roll; Hon Roll; NHS; Latin Awd 86; Bio.

COOPER, STACY; Great Mills HS; St Inigoes, MD; (Y); 60/250; Cmnty Wkr; French Clb; Office Aide; Political Wkr; Teachers Aide; Concert Band; Mrchg Band; Yrbk Phtg; Yrbk Stf; Rep Soph Cls; Charles Co CC; Bus.

COPAKEN, JENNIFER R; Winston Churchill HS; Potomac, MD; (Y); #69 In Class; Cmnty Wkr; Drama Clb; SADD; Thesps; School Musical; Variety Show; Nwsp Rptr; Ed Nwsp Stf; Pres Jr Cls; Pres Stu Cncl; Cabin John Prncpls Awd For Outstndng Ldrshp & Ctznshp Schlrshp 83; 1st Pl Wrtg Cntst 83; Jrnlsm.

COPELAND, ELIZABETH; Hammond HS; Columbia, MD; (Y); French Clb; JV Var Bsktbl; Im Lcrss; JV Var Socr; JV Sftbl; Hon Roll; NHS; Coaches Awd JV Sccr, JV Bsktbll & Var Sccr 83-84.

COPPAGE, CARLA; Thomas Stone HS; Waldorf, MD; (Y); Art.

COPPER, TOWANDA; St Michaels HS; Wittman, MD; (Y); 1/65; Mrchg Band; Stu Cncl; Stat Bsktbl; Var Cheerleading; Score Keeper; Hon Roll; Sec NHS; Ntl Merit SF; Prfct Atten Awd; Val; Bst Of Class 86; Grls ST 85; Gldy Bcn Coll; Bus Mgmt.

COPPOLA, VICTOR; Boys Latin HS; Baltimore, MD; (S); Debate Tm; Drama Clb; School Play; Stage Crew; Nwsp Ed-Chief; Yrbk Stf; Lit Mag; JV Socr; JV Tennis; French Hon Soc; 1st In Cls; Fr Awd.

CORBIN, ALICIA; Archbishop Keough HS; Balt, MD; (Y); Sec Church Yth Grp; Pres Spanish Clb; Yrbk Phtg; Rep Jr Cls; Stat Ftbl; High Hon Roll; Hon Roll; Jr NHS; NHS; Spn I & II Schl Awds 84-85; Marion Burk-Knott Scholar Full Tuition 83-87; Intl Stud.

CORBIN, SHERRY; Pocomoke HS; Pocomoke, MD; (S); AFS; Pom Pon; Hon Roll; Opt Clb Awd; Legal Intern Pgm 85-86.

CORD, DANIEL; Oakland Mills HS; Columbia, MD; (Y); 25/275; Political Wkr; Ski Clb; Speech Tm; Teachers Aide; Pres VP Temple Yth Grp; School Play; Stage Crew; Nwsp Sprt Ed; Rep Stu Cncl; Tennis; Franklin & Marshall; Intl Bus.

CORLEY, DAVID; Bowie HS; Bowie, MD; (Y); Chess Clb; Drama Clb; Off Speech Tm; Teachers Aide; Thesps; School Play; Stage Crew; Hon Roll; 1st Pl Rdrs Theater & 3rd Pl Duet Acting ST Cmptn 86; Comm.

CORNELL, SUZANNE; Springbrook HS; Silver Spring, MD; (Y); Sec VP AFS; Church Yth Grp; Church Choir; Variety Show; JV L Trk; Var L Vllybl; Jr NHS.

CORNISH, KIMERLY S; Cambridge South Dorchester HS; Cambridge, MD; (Y); AFS; Mrchg Band; Stage Crew; Symp Band; Sec Frsh Cls; VP Soph Cls; Jr NHS; NHS; Aud/Vis; Church Yth Grp; Negro Achvt Schlr Cmmnd Stu 85-86; Great Bks Pgm 85; Its Acad Alt 85-86; Law.

CORNISH, MONICA; Gaithersburg HS; Gaithersburg, MD; (Y); VP Sec FBLA; FHA; Library Aide; Hon Roll; NHS; MD FBLA Clrk-Typst I 3rd Pl 86; MD Rgn Iii FBLA Typng I 1st Pl 86; Bus.

CORNISH, VERONICA; Washington HS; Princess Anne, MD; (Y); Band; Concert Band; Mrchg Band; Symp Band; Hon Roll; NHS; Schlstic Achvt 1st Yr Awd 86; U MD Eastern Shore; Bus Admn.

CORREA, LOURDES; Winston Churchill HS; Potomac, MD; (Y); 324/612; Sec AFS; Cmnty Wkr; VP JA; Spanish Clb; Chorus; Rep Stu Cncl; Hon Roll; French Clb; German Clb; JCL; Natl Hispnc Schlr SF 85; Bst Perfrmnce Mechncs 85; 2nd Pl Physcs Middle TN Sci & Engrng Fair 82; George WA U; Engrng.

CORRIGAN, LESLIE; Archbishop Keough HS; Glen Burnie, MD; (Y); Pres Church Yth Grp; School Play; Rep Soph Cls; Rep Jr Cls; VP Stu Cncl; Capt Cheerleading; Sftbl; Vllybl; High Hon Roll; NHS; MD Govr Yth Advsry Cncl 85-86; Rnnr-Up Towson U Indiv Chrldg Cmptn 85; Miss MD Teen USA Pgnt 86; Chem.

CORTESE, MELISSA; Immaculata College HS; Kensington, MD; (Y); French Clb; Political Wkr; Varsity Clb; Var Capt Sftbl; Var L Tennis; High Hon Roll; Hstry Clb Pres; Poltcs.

COSBY, EMILE; The Barrie Schl; Washington, DC; (S); Boys Clb Am; Boy Scts; Chess Clb; Computer Clb; Science Clb; Ski Clb; Band; Nwsp Ed-Chief; Lit Mag; JV Golf; Stanford; Comptr Sci.

COSENTINO, BECKY; Mt Hebron HS; Ellicott City, MD; (Y); 32/279; Thesps; Madrigals; School Musical; Rep Frsh Cls; Rep Soph Cls; Rep Jr Cls; Rep Sr Cls; Var Capt Cheerleading; Stat Mgr Lcrss; NHS; MD Jr Miss 86; Cncrt Choir 82-86; Mt Hebron Hall Fm 86; Western MD Coll; Comp Sci.

COTTEN, SHELLY LYN; Western HS; Baltimore, MD; (Y); 238/412; Art Clb; Debate Tm; Sec French Clb; Hosp Aide; Science Clb; SADD; Nwsp Stf; Lit Mag; Sweet Briar; Neonatal.

COTTER, KATHLEEN; St Vincent Pallotti HS; Laurel, MD; (S); 3/96; Camera Clb; French Clb; Hosp Aide; Teachers Aide; L Swmmng; Im Trk; French Hon Soc; High Hon Roll; NHS; Cert Of Hnr US Hstry 84; Cert Of Hnr Life Plnng 85; 2nd Pl Sci Fair 85-86; Loyola Coll; Med.

COTTON, CYNTHIA L; Western HS; Baltimore, MD; (Y); Hosp Aide; Capt Trk; Outstndng Ath Achvt Trk 86; Howard U; Pre Med.

COTTON, HEATHER; North Harford HS; Jarrettsville, MD; (Y); German Clb; Library Aide; Varsity Clb; School Musical; Nwsp Rptr; Nwsp Stf; Var Trk; Hon Roll; Psychlgst.

COUCH, ERICA; Northern HS; Friendsville, MD; (Y); Cmnty Wkr; Ski Clb; Varsity Clb; Yrbk Stf; Trs Jr Cls; JV Capt Vllybl; High Hon Roll; Hon Roll; Prfct Atten Awd; Stu Of Yr 85-86; Bst JV Ofnsv Plyr 85-86; Garrett CC; Phys Educ.

COUCH, TONJA; Northern HS; Friendsville, MD; (Y); Cmnty Wkr; Ski Clb; Teachers Aide; Var Twrlr; High Hon Roll; Hon Roll; Jr NHS; Top 10 Pct SR Grad Clss 86; Oakland Rotry Schlrshp 86; Garrett CC; Soclgy.

COULEHAN, KEVIN EDWARD; Bishop Walsh HS; Cumberland, MD; (Y); 26/112; Rep Sr Cls; Var Stu Cncl; Bsktbl; Ftbl; Hon Roll; Bsbl; Tennis; Trk; Wt Lftg; Acctg.

COURTNEY, EVONNE; North Carroll HS; Reisterstown, MD; (Y); AFS; Drama Clb; GAA; Sec Trs Spanish Clb; School Musical; Swing Chorus; Rep Jr Cls; Rep Sr Cls; Rep Sec Stu Cncl; Var Cheerleading; ST Fnlst Japan US Sen Schlrshp 85; Peer Cnslng Awd 85-86; Fnctnl Wrtng Assist Awd 85-86; U Of MD Coll Pk; Jrnlsm.

COVER, THERESE; Oakland Mills HS; Columbia, MD; (Y); 22/275; AFS; Church Yth Grp; Pres French Clb; Math Tm; Spanish Clb; Crs Cntry; Mgr(s); Wrstlng; Hon Roll; NHS.

COVI, GINA; Archbishop Keough HS; Balt, MD; (Y); Art Clb; Camera Clb; Trs Science Clb; Ski Clb; Chorus; Sftbl.

COVI, TINA; Archbishop Keough HS; Balt, MD; (Y); Science Clb; Chorus; Art.

COVINGTON, DAMIAN; De Matha Catholic HS; Washington, DC; (Y); VP Church Yth Grp; Im Bsktbl; Var Tennis; Hon Roll.

COX, CHRIS; Crossland SR HS; Suitland, MD; (Y); 9/346; Band; Concert Band; Jazz Band; Mrchg Band; Pep Band; Symp Band; Capt JV Socr; High Hon Roll; Hon Roll; Trs NHS; MD U; Musician.

COX, KAREN; Allegany HS; Cumberland, MD; (Y); 46/240; AFS; Church Yth Grp; Drama Clb; Library Aide; Office Aide; SADD; Teachers Aide; Band; Flag Corp; Mrchg Band; Allegany CC; Rsprtry Thrpy.

COX, LISA; Du Val HS; Seabrook, MD; (Y); Natl Beta Clb; ROTC; Sec Band; Sec Sr Cls; Pom Pon; Gov Hon Prg Awd; NHS; Spanish NHS; Teachers Aide; Prince Georges Cnty Acadmc Fitnss Awd 85; Spnsh Excllnc Awd 86; Outstndng Achvt ROTC 84; U Of MD College Park; Psych.

COX, ROBBIE; St Marys Ryken HS; La Plata, MD; (S); 15/168; Art Clb; Church Yth Grp; Rep Stu Cncl; JV Bsktbl; Var Socr; Var Tennis; High Hon Roll; Hon Roll.

COX JR, WOODY E; La Plata HS; La Plata, MD; (Y); Office Aide; Teachers Aide; Varsity Clb; Ftbl; Capt Trk; Wt Lftg; Hon Roll; All Cnty Ftbl Tm 85; Mst Outstndng Lnmn Ftbl 85; Vrsty Ltr Awd 5th Regnl Trck Mt 86; Gallaude U; Bus Admin.

COYLE, MEG; Governor Thomas Johnson HS; Thurmont, MD; (Y); 53/303; Chess Clb; Church Yth Grp; Debate Tm; Drama Clb; Latin Clb; Teachers Aide; Thesps; Acpl Chr; Church Choir; Orch; Hnr Thespian 85; Best Sup Actrss Best Thespian 86; Pres Scho 86; UME Scho 86; Allentown Coll; Theatre.

CRAEMER, MARK; Milford Mill HS; Balt, MD; (Y); Letterman Clb; Varsity Clb; Im Bsktbl; Var Ftbl; Var Lcrss; Var Trk; Im Wt Lftg; Var Wrstlng; Hon Roll; 1st Tm All Cty Ftbl Hon Ment 85; Comm.

CRAIG, LORRIE; Regina HS; Hyattsville, MD; (Y); Church Yth Grp; Cmnty Wkr; Dance Clb; Girl Scts; Hosp Aide; Pep Clb; Yrbk Ed-Chief; Yrbk Phtg; Yrbk Rptr; NHS; Intl Exchng Pgm-Canada 84-85; Advrtsng.

CRALL, KIMBERLY; Chesapeake HS; Pasadena, MD; (S); DECA; Flag Corp; Pom Pon; Hon Roll; Prfct Atten Awd; U Of MD; Flght Attndnt.

CRAMPTON, KELLY S; Brunswick HS; Jefferson, MD; (Y); 4/138; FBLA; Sec Latin Clb; Trs Chorus; Trs Jr Cls; Trs Sr Cls; Trs Stu Cncl; JV Var Fld Hcky; Im Powder Puff Ftbl; High Hon Roll; Hon Roll; Deans Schlrshp Wstrn MD Coll 86; Jffrsn Prtn Schlrshp 86; Western MD Coll; Bus.

CRAVARITIS, GEORGE; Gaithersburg HS; Gaithersburg, MD; (Y); Boy Scts; Church Yth Grp; Cmnty Wkr; ROTC; L Bsktbl; Capt Socr; L Trk; Hon Roll; NHS; Mt St Marys; Acctg.

CRAVEN, JOY; Lackey HS; Indian Head, MD; (Y); Cmnty Wkr; French Clb; SADD; Yrbk Ed-Chief; Rep Stu Cncl; Var Pom Pon; Hon Roll; Church Yth Grp; Teachers Aide; Variety Show; Ltr Acad Achvt 85-86; U MD; Bus Adm.

CRAWFORD, DANA; Potomac HS; Temple Hill, MD; (Y); Dance Clb; Chorus; Drill Tm; Pom Pon; Sftbl; Hon Roll; Penn ST U; Crmnl Lwyr.

CRAWFORD, LARRY; Williamsport HS; Fairplay, MD; (Y); Church Yth Grp; FCA; Intnl Clb; Latin Clb; Letterman Clb; Office Aide; Spanish Clb; SADD; Varsity Clb; Chorus.

CREATURO, KELLY; La Plata HS; Waldorf, MD; (S); Church Yth Grp; Off Frsh Cls; Sec Soph Cls; Sec Jr Cls; Off Stu Cncl; JV Var Sftbl; JV Var Vllybl; St Fnlst Grls Sftbl 85; Swthrt Prin 84; Christmas Prin 85; Fshn Merch.

CREEK, JILL; Hancock HS; Hancock, MD; (Y); Church Yth Grp; FHA; Chorus; Concert Band; Mrchg Band; Nwsp Rptr; Yrbk Bus Mgr; Yrbk Stf; Trs Jr Cls; Stu Cncl; Outstndng SR Bus Stdnt 86; MVP Bsktbl & Sftbl; Hagerstown JC; Elem Ed.

CREEL, VICTOR; Mt St Joseph HS; Linthicum, MD; (Y); Sec Pres Boy Scts; Cmnty Wkr; Hon Roll; NHS; Comp Sci.

CREIGHTON, HEATHER; Frederick HS; Frederick, MD; (Y); 12/377; VP FBLA; Ski Clb; Sftbl; JR Ldrshp Awd/Ftr Scrtrys 86; Cert Of Awd/Typng II 85; Cert Of Awd For Outstndng Achvt Shrthnd I 85; K Gibbs Schl; Exec Scrtry.

CREMEDAS, ANDRA; Albert Einstein HS; Silver Spring, MD; (Y); VP Drama Clb; Trs Thesps; Band; Orch; School Musical; School Play; Stage Crew; Sec Stu Cncl; NHS; Ntl Merit Ltr; Prncpls Wrtng Awd 85; U Of MD; Prfrmng Arts.

CRESWELL, PAMELA; Perryville HS; Pt Deposit, MD; (Y); Intnl Clb; Band; Concert Band; Mrchg Band; Rptr Yrbk Stf; Prfct Atten Awd; Pres JR Grls Unt VFW; Ltr Band 86; Psych.

CRIDER, AMANDA ANN; North Hagerstown HS; Hagerstown, MD; (Y); 3/275; Pres Church Yth Grp; Rep Frsh Cls; Rep Jr Cls; Rep Sr Cls; Capt Stu Cncl; Elks Awd; Hon Roll; NHS; St Schlr; Cheerleading; Goucher Coll Schlrshp-Bus & Publc Pol 86; Goucher Coll; Bus.

CRIST, SHARON ANNE; Northwestern HS; Hyattsville, MD; (Y); Church Yth Grp; VP French Clb; Red Cross Aide; SADD; School Play; Rep Sr Cls; Rep Stu Cncl; High Hon Roll; Hon Roll; Var NHS; Red Crss Bld Serv Awd 84; Merit Schltc Awd 86; Natl Hnr Soc Awd 86; U Of MD; Microbio.

CRITTENDEN, ROBERT; Thomas Stone HS; Waldorf, MD; (Y); Art Clb; Drama Clb; Math Clb; Math Tm; Science Clb; Color Guard.

CRITZER, PAMELA; Baltimore City College; Baltimore, MD; (S); Art Clb; Nwsp Rptr; Lit Mag; High Hon Roll; Hon Roll; NHS; Prfct Atten Awd.

CROCK, TERESA; Connelly Schl Of The Holy Child; Rockville, MD; (Y); Pres Drama Clb; GAA; Hosp Aide; Pres SADD; Church Choir; Mgr Stage Crew; Im Badmtn; Var Tennis; Ntl Merit Ltr; MD U Hnrs Prog 86-87; Schlrshp Connelly Schl Of Holy Child 82-86; MD U; Bio Sci.

CROCKETT, JEFF; North Hagerstown HS; Hagerstown, MD; (Y); 22/277; Latin Clb; Band; Concert Band; Mrchg Band; Orch; Stage Crew; Symp Band; High Hon Roll; Hon Roll; Clemson U; Elec Engr.

CROCKETT, MARY; Pocomoke HS; Pocomoke, MD; (S); 7/92; AFS; Am Leg Aux Girls St; Sec SADD; Yrbk Stf; Sec Stu Cncl; Var L Fld Hcky; Var L Sftbl; Hon Roll; Optimist Awd-Outstndng Yth 86; Poultry Sci.

CROMWELL, JEWEL; Northwestern HS; Baltimore, MD; (S); Pep Clb; Political Wkr; Yrbk Stf; Trs Jr Cls; Sec Sr Cls; Var Badmtn; Mgr(s); Hon Roll; Prfct Atten Awd; Stu Page MD Gen Assmbly 86; Mock Trial Comp 86.

CROPP, TIFFANI; Fort Hill HS; Cumberland, MD; (S); Church Yth Grp; Sec Thesps; Swing Chorus; Stu Cncl; Twrlr; Cit Awd; Hon Roll; Off Masonic Awd; NHS; Voice Dem Awd; Hugh O Brien Ldrshp Fndtn 83-84; U Of MD; Pol Sci.

CROSBY, GREGORY; Severna Pk HS; Severna Park, MD; (Y); 2/421; Pres Church Yth Grp; Math Tm; VP Science Clb; Church Choir; Mrchg Band; Symp Band; Gov Hon Prg Awd; NHS; NEDT Awd; Sal; Marshall Hahn Engrng Schlrshp 86; Natl Hon Soc Torch Awd 84; Boys ST Selection 85; VA Tech; Elec Engrng.

CROSS, GINA; Mc Donogh Schl; Timonium, MD; (Y); 12/132; Dance Clb; French Clb; Key Clb; Teachers Aide; Nwsp Rptr; Yrbk Rptr; Lit Mag; Rep Frsh Cls; High Hon Roll; Hon Roll; John Mc Conogh Mem Bible Prize 2nd Pl 84-85 & 1st Pl 86; Cum Laude Soc 86; Loyola Coll; Bus Mgmt.

CROSS, JOHN H; North Caroline HS; Denton, MD; (Y); Church Yth Grp; Band; Concert Band; Jazz Band; Mrchg Band; Pep Band; Symp Band; Wt Lftg; Hon Roll; Louis Armstrong Jazz Awd 86; Semper Fi Music Awd 86; All Am Yth Hnr Musicns 85-86; Towson ST U; Music.

CROSS, JULEE; Crossland SR HS; Camp Springs, MD; (Y); Drama Clb; Office Aide; Teachers Aide; Thesps; School Play; Stage Crew; Nwsp Stf; Yrbk Stf; L Pom Pon; Hon Roll.

CROSS, JULIA; Chopticon HS; Avenue, MD; (Y); Am Leg Aux Girls St; Pres FBLA; Latin Clb; Varsity Clb; VP Frsh Cls; Sec Stu Cncl; Pom Pon; CC Awd; Dnfth Awd; Bus Stu Yr 86; Bus Law Stu Yr 86; Acctng.

CROSS, MICHAEL; La Plata HS; Hughesville, MD; (Y); Church Yth Grp; Ski Clb; Spanish Clb; Crs Cntry; Tennis; Trk; Cit Awd; Hon Roll; Duke U; Elec Engrng.

CROSS, TARONDA; Carver Voc Tech HS; Baltimore, MD; (Y); Mrchg Band; High Hon Roll; Hon Roll; Ftr Bus Ldrs Am FBLA 84-85; Hnr Scty 84-85; Hnrs Attndnc 84-85; Cmptr Prgrmmr.

CROSS, WESLEY; Elkton Christian Schl; Northeast, MD; (S); 3/30; Church Yth Grp; Bsktbl; Socr; Hon Roll; NHS; Electrncs.

CROSSAN, FELICIA; Catocitin HS; Thurmont, MD; (Y); Art Clb; Office Aide; Pres Chorus; Accntng.

CROSSER, LORI; Fort Hill HS; Cumberland, MD; (Y); Church Yth Grp; Pep Clb; Yrbk Ed-Chief; Yrbk Stf; JV Var Cheerleading; High Hon Roll; Hon Roll; NHS; Schl Ltr 85 & 86; Pre-Med.

CROSSLAND, EDWARD; Valley HS; Frostburg, MD; (Y); Church Yth Grp; Computer Clb; Pres 4-H; Ski Clb; Band; Yrbk Ed-Chief; Pres Sr Cls; 4-H Awd; Hon Roll; NHS; VA Tech Yth Forum 86; Coop Ed 85; VA Tech; Dairy Sci.

CROSWELL, BILLIE JO; Parkside SR HS; Pittsville, MD; (Y); Hon Roll; Salisbury ST Coll; Acctng.

CROUCH, MARY; Queen Annes Co HS; Chester, MD; (Y); Church Yth Grp; Cmnty Wkr; Church Choir; Nwsp Stf; Hon Roll; 1st Pl Typng Spd Fleet Bus Schl 86; 1st Yr Merit Awd 86; Chesapeake Coll; Acctng.

CROUSE, LYNNELL; Hereford HS; Millers, MD; (Y); French Clb; Teachers Aide; Fld Hcky; Hon Roll; Hlth Care.

CROWDER, CHRISTOPHER S; Albert Einstein HS; Wheaton, MD; (Y); 27/304; Church Yth Grp; Computer Clb; SADD; Church Choir; Orch; School Musical; High Hon Roll; Hon Roll; NHS; Montgomery Cnty Yth Orch 82-86; Acolyte Crucifer St Luke Lutheran Chrch 82-86; Frostburg ST Coll; Bus Adm.

CROWE, REBECCA; Middletown HS; Middletown, MD; (Y); FBLA; Teachers Aide; Chorus; Concert Band; Mrchg Band; Sec Frsh Cls; Sec Soph Cls; Sec Jr Cls; JV Bsktbl; Hon Roll; U Of MD; Accntng.

CROWELL, COURTNEY; Laurel HS; Laurel, MD; (Y); 15/320; Drama Clb; Ski Clb; Socr; Vllybl; High Hon Roll; Hon Roll; NHS; Clemson U.

CROWLEY, JIM; Dulaney SR HS; Cockeysville, MD; (Y); Var Bsbl; JV Var Bsktbl; Sr Cls; Hon Roll; Jr NHS; Chem.

CROWLEY, LAUREN; Wilde Lake HS; Columbia, MD; (Y); Cmnty Wkr; Debate Tm; Ski Clb; Chorus; Off Jr Cls; Off Sr Cls; Stu Cncl; Sftbl; Hon Roll; NHS.

CROWLEY, MICHAEL; Loyola HS; Baltimore, MD; (Y); German Clb; Hon Roll; Slvr Medal Ger 85; Gld Medal Ger 86; Arch.

CROWLEY, SHARON; Eastern Vo Tech; Baltimore, MD; (Y); Church Yth Grp; Rptr FBLA; Office Aide; Sec Chorus; School Musical; Yrbk Stf; Hon Roll; NHS; Cert Of Commendation In Conf & Activities Of Bus Ed 86; Music Varsity E Awd 85-86; Sec.

CROWNOVER IV, ARTHUR; Gwynn Park HS; Clinton, MD; (Y); Drama Clb; Band; Concert Band; Hon Roll; Ski Clb; Teachers Aide; Mrchg Band; Orch; Crs Cntry; JR All-Amer Hall Of Fame Band Hnrs 85-86; Amer Musical Fndtn Band Hnrs 85-86; Music.

CRUM, SCOTT; Broadneck SR HS; Arnold, MD; (Y); Drama Clb; Science Clb; Teachers Aide; Thesps; Var Bsbl; Var Bsktbl; Ftbl; U Of MD; Math.

CRUM, WILLIAM; Brunswick HS; Brunswick, MD; (S); Church Yth Grp; Pres FBLA; FTA; Q&S; Red Cross Aide; Sec Spanish Clb; Teachers Aide; Nwsp Ed-Chief; Nwsp Rptr; Sec Sr Cls; Outstndg Ldrshp Awd-Cnslng 85; Most Dedictd Plyr-Var Ten 85; Mr FLBA-1ST Pl 85; Shepherd Coll; Elem Educ.

CRUSE, JOSEPH; Archbishop Corley HS; Baltimore, MD; (S); Office Aide; Radio Clb; Yrbk Stf; Var Crs Cntry; Var Capt Trk; Hon Roll; NHS; Spanish NHS; Embry-Riddle Aero U; Aero Engr.

CRUTCHFIELD, PATRISE SHANNON; Southern SR HS; Harwood, MD; (Y); Capt Church Yth Grp; Cmnty Wkr; 4-H; Office Aide; Spanish Clb; SADD; Chorus; School Musical; Var Bsktbl; Powder Puff Ftbl; Prsdntl Physcl Ftnss Awd 82; Howard U; Fshn Dsgn.

CRUTCHLEY, JULIE; Gov Thomas Johnson HS; Frederick, MD; (Y); 30/323; Latin Clb; Science Clb; Thesps; Concert Band; Mrchg Band; Orch; Pep Band; School Musical; Off Sr Cls; Hon Roll; Eng Comp Awd Excllnc Writing 86; SR Band Awd Outstndg Svc 86; PTSA Acadmc Awd 86; Frederick CC; Business.

CSULAK, EMERY JONATHAN; Gov Thomas Johnson HS; Frederick, MD; (Y); Chess Clb; Computer Clb; Trs 4-H; Sec Science Clb; Spanish Clb; Teachers Aide; 4-H Awd; Hon Roll; Awd Ldrshp Outdr Schl Stu Cnslr 86; PTSA Hnr Awd 86; G Washington U; Elec Engr.

CULBREATH JR, WALTER L; Potomac SR HS; Oxon Hill, MD; (Y); Church Yth Grp; ROTC; Teachers Aide; JV Bsktbl; Var Capt Socr; Var Trk; Hon Roll; Prfct Atten Awd; Schrl Athlt Awd 86; Sci Acadmc Awd 83.

CULLATHER, MARY; Wootton HS; Rockville, MD; (Y); JA; Ski Clb; SADD; Teachers Aide; Nwsp Stf; Yrbk Stf; Cheerleading; Crs Cntry; Co-Capt Fld Hcky; Hon Roll; U MD.

CULLEN, WENDY R; Wilde Lake HS; Columbia, MD; (Y); 7/225; Church Yth Grp; JV L Socr; Var L Sftbl; Var Capt Vllybl; NHS; Camera Clb; Covenant Coll; Phys Ed.

CULVER, KRISTINA; St Vincent Pallotti HS; Laurel, MD; (S); 3/100; Spanish Clb; Var Stat Swmmng; VP Var Tennis; High Hon Roll; Spanish NHS; Geom Awd 84; Alg II, Trig Awd 83; U MD; Acctg.

CUMBERLAND, DAWN; Patterson HS; Baltimore, MD; (Y); Aud/Vis; Dance Clb; Girl Scts; Hosp Aide; Math Clb; Science Clb; Spanish Clb; Stage Crew; Off Jr Cls; Cheerleading; Radiologist.

CUMMINGS, KELLEY; Hereford HS; White Hall, MD; (Y); FTA; Teachers Aide; Sec Frsh Cls; Rep Soph Cls; Rep Jr Cls; Stu Cncl; Var Crs Cntry; JV Fld Hcky; JV Lcrss; Var Trk.

CUMMINGS, KERMIT; Sparrows Point HS; Baltimore, MD; (Y); Church Yth Grp; Library Aide; Teachers Aide; Nwsp Rptr; Nwsp Stf; Pres Soph Cls; Pres Stu Cncl; Hon Roll; Opt Clb Awd; Voice Dem Awd; Accntng.

CUMMINGS, MARIA; Notre Dame Preparatory Schl; Baltimore, MD; (Y); 50/130; Cmnty Wkr; Pres Rep Frsh Cls; Sec Trs Jr Cls; Sec Trs Sr Cls; Stu Cncl; Badmtn; Co-Capt Lcrss; Mgr(s); Score Keeper; Swmmng; 1st Hnrs 86; Prfct Atten 76-86; Deaf Educ.

CUMMINGS, MELANIE; Springbrook HS; Silver Spring, MD; (Y); Chorus; Madrigals; School Musical; Variety Show; Nwsp Rptr; Nwsp Stf; Yrbk Rptr; Yrbk Stf; Lit Mag; Off Frsh Cls; Sprgbrk HS Vrsty Lttr & Pin 85-86.

CUMMINGS, SHANDRA; Suitland HS; Forestville, MD; (Y); Drama Clb; Science Clb; Teachers Aide; Drill Tm; School Play; Stu Cncl; Var L Cheerleading; Var L Tennis; Trk; Hon Roll; Crimonology.

CUNNINGHAM, BECKY; Smithsburg HS; Hagerstown, MD; (Y); 22/198; Latin Clb; Office Aide; Ski Clb; Sec Band; Concert Band; Mrchg Band; School Play; Rep Stu Cncl; Vllybl; Hon Roll; Scholar Bnqt Top 15 Prcnt Of Cls 86; U MD College Park; Fshn Mrchnd.

CUNNINGHAM, CHERYL; Forestville HS; Capitol Heights, MD; (Y); Teachers Aide; Sec Chorus; Nwsp Bus Mgr; Lit Mag; VP Soph Cls; VP Jr Cls; Pres NHS; Hon Roll; Stu Cncl; Nwsp Rptr; Jesse J Warr Jr Mem Awd 86; St Marys; Pharmacy.

CUNNINGHAM, CHRISTINE; Notre Dame Prep; Baltimore, MD; (Y); 1/119; Trs Soph Cls; Trs Jr Cls; High Hon Roll; NHS; Pres Schlr; Spanish NHS; St Schlr; Church Yth Grp; Cmnty Wkr; Dance Clb; Edgr N Gnstr Awd Gnrl Excllnc 86; MD ST Schlstc Awd 86; Loyola Prsdntl Schlrshp 86; Loyola Coll; Acctg.

CUNNINGHAM, KELI; Dulaney SR HS; Cockeysville, MD; (Y); 35/480; VP Church Yth Grp; Dance Clb; Key Clb; Service Clb; School Play; Stage Crew; Var Cheerleading; High Hon Roll; NHS; Ntl Merit Ltr; Outstndng Drama Perf 84; Adv.

CUNNINGHAM, LA SYDNEY; Surrattsville HS; Clinton, MD; (Y); Art Clb; Camera Clb; Cmnty Wkr; FNA; Model UN; Red Cross Aide; Ski Clb; Teachers Aide; Drill Tm; Dance Clb.

CUNNINGHAM, MICHELLE; Thomas Stone HS; Waldorf, MD; (Y); Church Yth Grp; Nwsp Stf; Stu Cncl; JV Var Sftbl; Hon Roll; U MD.

CUPPY, LAWRENCE; Mc Donough HS; Waldorf, MD; (Y); Band; Mrchg Band; Symp Band; High Hon Roll; Hon Roll; Prfct Atten Awd; U Of MI; Acctg.

CURBELO, MARCELLA; Thomas Stone HS; Waldorf, MD; (S); Church Yth Grp; Cmnty Wkr; Pep Clb; SADD; Teachers Aide; Capt Flag Corp; Pom Pon; High Hon Roll; Hon Roll; NHS; Charles Cnty CC; Fshn Merch.

CURRAN, MEGAN; Archbishop Keough HS; Ellicott City, MD; (Y); Church Yth Grp; Drama Clb; Teachers Aide; Nwsp Rptr; Lit Mag; Rep Soph Cls; Rep Jr Cls; Hon Roll; NHS; Cum Laude Awd Natl Latin Exam 86; Georgetown U; Lawyr.

CURRAN, MICHAEL; Gaithersburg HS; Gaithersburg, MD; (Y); 180/600; Debate Tm; ROTC; Science Clb; SADD; Concert Band; Mrchg Band; Sftbl; Amrcn Legn Schlstc Exclnce Rotc Awd 85; ROTC Awd 86; Distngushd Cadet Awd 85-86; Navy; Flight Ofcr.

CURRAN, PATRICK; Centennial HS; Ellicott City, MD; (Y); Cmnty Wkr; Drama Clb; French Clb; Chorus; Madrigals; School Musical; School Play; Variety Show; Sr Cls; Trs Stu Cncl; Politics.

CURRAN, TRICIA; Wilde Lake HS; Columbia, MD; (Y); Debate Tm; Intnl Clb; Sec Jr Cls; Stu Cncl; Cert Of Hnr Natl Frnch Exam 86; Poltcl Sci.

CURRY, FREDRICK; Maurice J Mc Donough HS; La Plata, MD; (Y); Sec Am Leg Boys St; Church Yth Grp; Church Choir; Stat Var Bsktbl; Var Mgr(s); Stat Score Keeper; Accntnt.

CURRY, LISA; Catoctin HS; Thurmont, MD; (Y); Camera Clb; Computer Clb; Trs French Clb; FBLA; Letterman Clb; Pep Clb; Yrbk Phtg; Yrbk Stf; L Fld Hcky; Hon Roll; Towson ST U; Exprmntl Psych.

CURRY JR, THOMAS; Capcata HS; Newburg, MD; (Y); Office Aide; Var Crs Cntry; Hon Roll; Ntrl Resourses.

CURTIN, MICHELE; Liberty HS; Eldersburg, MD; (Y); 47/206; Church Yth Grp; Ski Clb; Varsity Clb; Variety Show; Lit Mag; Var Capt Gym; Socr; Hon Roll; Towson ST U; Mass Comm.

CURTIS, KELLEY; Northern HS; North Bch, MD; (Y); Office Aide; Socr; Sftbl; Vllybl.

CURTIS, MARIANNE; Regina HS; Silver Spring, MD; (Y); Drama Clb; Office Aide; Pep Clb; School Musical; School Play; Stage Crew; Hon Roll; Prfct Atten Awd; Art And Intr Dec.

CURTIS, MARY; St Johnsd At Prospect Hall HS; Gaithersburg, MD; (Y); Debate Tm; 4-H; Science Clb; Ski Clb; Teachers Aide; Stage Crew; JV Capt Cheerleading; JV Sftbl; Var Vllybl; 4-H Awd; Top Score Cntry NEDT 84; Bus.

CURTIS, TRACEY; Chopticon HS; Charlotte Hl, MD; (Y); French Clb; Intnl Clb; Library Aide; Spanish Clb; Varsity Clb; Yrbk Stf; Off Jr Cls; Rep Stu Cncl; Var Capt Cheerleading; Gov Hon Prg Awd; Charlotte Hall Schlrshp Fnd 86; Charles Cnty CC.

CUSTER, BRYAN G; Southern Garrett HS; Oakland, MD; (S); 8/222; Color Guard; Drm Mjr(t); Jazz Band; Pres Jr Cls; Pres Sr Cls; Rep Stu Cncl; NHS; Aviatn.

CUTSHAW JR, RICHARD; Westminster SR HS; Westminster, MD; (Y); High Hon Roll; Prfct Atten Awd; Pres Schlr; U MD College Park; Cvl Engrng.

CZERWINSKI, MICHAEL M; Bohemia Manor HS; Earleville, MD; (Y); 8/104; French Clb; Bsbl; Ftbl; Wrstlng; Hon Roll; NHS; Sntrl Schlrshp; Towson ST.

D ALONZO, JOSEPH; Centennial HS; Ellicott, MD; (Y); Am Leg Boys St; Cmnty Wkr; Letterman Clb; Teachers Aide; Varsity Clb; Nwsp Sprt Ed; Rep Jr Cls; Var Capt Bsbl; Var Bsktbl; Hon Roll; All-Cnty 2nd Tm Catcher CHS 86; All-Star Amer Lgn Post 156 Bsbl 86; Title Of Hmcmng Prince 86; U Of Miami; Bus Mgt.

D SOUZA, MICHELE; Gaithersburg HS; Gaithersburg, MD; (Y); 14/568; Church Yth Grp; ROTC; Science Clb; SADD; Church Choir; Nwsp Rptr; Fld Hcky; DAR Awd; Hon Roll; JC Awd; US Naval Inst Awd 86; ST MD Merit Schltc Awd 86; Presidential Acad Fitness Awd 86; NJROTC Merit Awd; WV Wesleyan; Med.

DABBS, MICHELLE; North Harford HS; Street, MD; (Y); Art Clb; Cmnty Wkr; 4-H; French Clb; Varsity Clb; Score Keeper; Var Trk; Hon Roll; Physcl Ftns Excllnc Awd 84-85; Athltc Awd Trck & Fld 84-85; Vrsty Ltr Trck & ; Ld 85-86; Frgn Lang.

DACQUEL, LORELEI; Northwestern HS; Hyattsville, MD; (Y); AFS; School Play; Rep Sr Cls; Var JV Cheerleading; High Hon Roll; Trs NHS.

DAGGETT, TINA; North Carroll HS; Hampstead, MD; (Y); Church Yth Grp; GAA; Chorus; Cheerleading; Sftbl; Vllybl; Hon Roll; Rep Frsh Cls; Rep Soph Cls; Rep Jr Cls; Bus.

DAHL, KRISTIN; Sherwood HS; Olney, MD; (Y); Spanish Clb; Teachers Aide; Varsity Clb; Yrbk Stf; Im Badmtn; Mgr(s); Socr; Capt Var Vllybl; Hon Roll; UNC Chapell Hill; Spec Educ.

DAILEY, JENNIFER; Northern Garrett HS; Mountville, PA; (Y); SADD; Varsity Clb; Var Sftbl; Var L Tennis; Var L Vllybl; Bausch & Lomb Sci Awd; Hon Roll; Stu Of Yr; Outstndg Stu; Math.

DALE, THERESA; Oxon HS; Ft Washington, MD; (Y); Teachers Aide; Rep Stu Cncl; Var Co-Capt Cheerleading; Hon Roll; Comm.

DALEY, RICHARD; Central HS; District Hgts, MD; (Y); 4/195; Teachers Aide; Yrbk Phtg; Yrbk Stf; Rep Frsh Cls; Rep Soph Cls; Rep Jr Cls; Rep Sr Cls; Rep Stu Cncl; Var Tennis; Var Trk; Grad Top 5 Pct Cls 86; Superintndnts Awd Outstndng Achvt 86; MD ST Schrlshp Bd Awd 86; U MD; Aeronutlc Engr.

DALY, DAVID; La Plata HS; Kingman, AZ; (Y); Letterman Clb; Ski Clb; JV Ftbl; Wt Lftg; JV Var Wrstlng; Hon Roll; Bus.

DALY, DENEE; Franklin SR HS; Reisterstown, MD; (Y); AFS; Church Yth Grp; Pep Clb; Varsity Clb; Band; Concert Band; Drill Tm; Mrchg Band; Symp Band; Yrbk Stf.

DALY, KEVIN W; Loyola HS; Timonium, MD; (S); 16/196; Church Yth Grp; French Clb; Ski Clb; Yrbk Ed-Chief; Yrbk Stf; Lit Mag; Im Socr; Hon Roll; NHS; NEDT Awd; 200 Hrs Volnteer St Josephs Hosp; Med.

DALY, PATRICK; Westminster HS; Westminster, MD; (Y); Ski Clb; Teachers Aide; Off Frsh Cls; Off Soph Cls; Rep Jr Cls; JV Crs Cntry; Prfct Atten Awd; Berkley Coll Of Music; Rcrdng.

DALY, SARAH; Rockville HS; Rockville, MD; (S); 14/464; Sec Drama Clb; 4-H; School Musical; School Play; Variety Show; Ed Nwsp Stf; Im Vllybl; NHS; Ntl Merit Ltr; Comm.

DAMDAR, ASHA; Academy Of The Holy Names; Silver Spring, MD; (Y); Library Aide; Nwsp Ed-Chief; Nwsp Rptr; Nwsp Stf; Hon Roll; Trs NHS; Highst Avg, Bst Stu Typing Awd 86; Acctng.

DAMERON, DAVID; Surrattsville HS; Clinton, MD; (Y); Chess Clb; Computer Clb; NHS; Comp Sci.

DAMERON, NICOLE; Walbrook SR HS; Baltimore, MD; (Y); Art Clb; French Clb; Band; Variety Show; Hon Roll; Trs Frsh Cls; Trs Soph Cls; Wstnghs Dfns & Elctrncs Ctr 85; Ntl Hnr Soc For Mth 84; Bus Admin.

DAMICO, CHRISTINE; Bethesda-Chevy Chase HS; Chevy Chase, MD; (Y); 81/419; JV Cheerleading; U CA Davis; Anml Sci.

DAMON, LORIE A; Southern HS; Oakland, MD; (S); 1/225; Pres Church Yth Grp; Debate Tm; German Clb; VP GAA; Model UN; Stu Cncl; High Hon Roll; NHS; Rotary Stu 85; Md Distngushd Schrlshp Fnlst 85; Math.

DANDRIDGE, STEVE; Fort Hill HS; Westernport, MD; (Y); Var L Ftbl; JV Var Trk; Wt Lftg; High Hon Roll; Hon Roll; MD Dstngshd Schlr 86; Gifted & Talent Pgm 84; Engrng.

DANDRIDGE, TOWANDA; Western HS; Baltimore, MD; (Y); FTA; Band; NHS; Med.

DANG, AN; Parkville HS; Balt, MD; (Y); Church Yth Grp; Church Choir; Hon Roll; Prfct Atten Awd; Hnr Roll 83-86; Prfct Atten 84-85; U MD College Pk; Elec Engrng.

DANIEL, BARBARA; Western SR HS; Glen Burnie, MD; (Y); 133/412; Church Yth Grp; French Clb; School Play; Jr NHS; Prfct Atten Awd; Elon Coll; Stck Brkr.

DANIEL, LESLIE; Regina HS; Washington, DC; (Y); Computer Clb; Drama Clb; Pep Clb; School Play; Stage Crew; VP Frsh Cls; Hon Roll; Canadian Exch Stu Prog Awd 84; Bus Adm.

DANIEL, STEPHANIE; Hammond HS; Columbia, MD; (Y); Yrbk Rptr; Yrbk Stf; Sec Frsh Cls; High Hon Roll; Hon Roll; Bus.

DANIELS, ASA; Surrattsville HS; Clinton, MD; (Y); Cmnty Wkr; Varsity Clb; Band; Concert Band; Mrchg Band; Orch; Pep Band; Symp Band; Bsktbl; Ftbl; Ltrmn Ftbl 74-85; Bus Law.

DANIELS, DARLENE R; Oxon Hill HS; Ft Washington, MD; (Y); Stu Cncl; L Pom Pon; Hon Roll; Eacadmc Excllnc Aw D85; Townson ST.

DANIELS, ELAINE; Western SR HS; Baltimore, MD; (Y); Art Clb; Cmnty Wkr; Chorus; Nwsp Stf; Yrbk Stf; Lit Mag; Im Badmtn; Im Sftbl; Opt Clb Awd; Natl Art Hon Soc 85-86; Rhoer Club Sigma Gamma Rho Sorority 85-86; U Of NC; Tele Cmmnctns.

DANIELS, FELICIA; Friendly SR HS; Oxon Hill, MD; (Y); Stu Cncl; Hon Roll; UDC; Pub Adm.

DANIELS, JONATHAN; Oakland Mills HS; Columbia, MD; (Y); Debate Tm; Speech Tm; Nwsp Rptr; Nwsp Stf; Off Sr Cls; Hon Roll; Ntl Merit Ltr; Northwestern U; Jrnlsm.

DANIELS, TAMMY K; Mardela HS; Mardela Springs, MD; (S); 1/60; Cmnty Wkr; Mathletes; Political Wkr; Nwsp Stf; High Hon Roll; NHS; Natl Hnr Rl 86; Yth Achvmnt Awd 86; Hgh Hnrs Cls 86; Bus Adm.

DANKLEFS, JACQUELINE M; Edgewood HS; Abingdon, MD; (Y); Teachers Aide; Rep Frsh Cls; Rep Soph Cls; Rep Jr Cls; Var L Socr; JV Trk; Hon Roll; Jr NHS; NHS; Salisbury ST Coll; Vet.

DANNENHOFFER, LAURIE; Parkside HS; Salisbury, MD; (Y); Dance Clb; Nwsp Rptr; Nwsp Stf; JV Fld Hcky; Hon Roll; Physcl Thrpy.

DANNEY, WANDA; Mercy HS; Baltimore, MD; (Y); Church Yth Grp; French Clb; GAA; Rep Soph Cls; VP Jr Cls; Rep Stu Cncl; Mgr Gym; Hon Roll.

DANNHEISSER, LISA; Centennial HS; Columbia, MD; (Y); 1/270; Aud/Vis; Cmnty Wkr; Drama Clb; Rep French Clb; Q&S; School Musical; Variety Show; Nwsp Stf; High Hon Roll; NHS; Pres & Genl U Schlrs Am U 86; Tlnt Rcgntn Pgm 86; MD Distngshd Schlr 86; American U; Tv Correspondent.

DANS, PAUL; Dulanoy SR HS; Cockeysville, MD; (Y); Church Yth Grp; Debate Tm; Model UN; NFL; Off Frsh Cls; Off Soph Cls; Off Jr Cls; Off Sr Cls; Var Crs Cntry; JV Var Lcrss.

DANS, THOMAS; Dulaney HS; Cockeysville, MD; (Y); Church Yth Grp; Debate Tm; Model UN; NFL; Off Frsh Cls; Off Soph Cls; Off Jr Cls; Off Sr Cls; Var JV Bsktbl; Var Crs Cntry.

DARE, MARLENA; Riverdale Baptist Schl; Upper Marlboro, MD; (S); Office Aide; JV Cheerleading; Var Vllybl; High Hon Roll; NHS; MD U; Psych.

DARLING, ROBYN; Queen Annes County HS; Chester, MD; (Y); 11/349; VP Church Yth Grp; Girl Scts; Spanish Clb; Sec Band; Mrchg Band; Rep Soph Cls; Stat Lcrss; Score Keeper; High Hon Roll; Hon Roll; Senatorial Schlrshp 86; U MD Baltimore Co; Nrsng.

DAUGHERTY, KRISTA; Harford Christian Schl; Brogue, PA; (S); 1/30; Church Yth Grp; Math Tm; Varsity Clb; Chorus; Church Choir; School Play; Sec Frsh Cls; Pres Soph Cls; Rep Jr Cls; Chrmn Sr Cls; Frnch Awd Hghst Avg 82-83; Bob Jones U; Nrs Prctnr.

DAUGHERTY, MICHAEL TODD; Arundel HS; Odenton, MD; (Y); 75/455; Pres Computer Clb; Office Aide; Teachers Aide; Rep Sr Cls; Var JV Ftbl; JV Var Lcrss; Var L Trk; Hon Roll; St Schlr; Twsn ST U; Comp Sci.

DAUGHTON, WANDA Y; Bel Air HS; Bel Air, MD; (Y); 2/200; Hon Roll; NHS; Ntl Merit SF; MD ST Distngshd Schlr Awd 85; MD Inst Coll Of Art; Illstrtn.

DAUM, LAURA; Notre Dame Prep; Timonium, MD; (Y); Church Yth Grp; Service Clb; Teachers Aide; Chorus; JV Var Cheerleading; Elem Educ.

DAVIDGE, ERICCIA; Archbishop Keough HS; Baltimore, MD; (Y); Hosp Aide; NFL; Pep Clb; Spanish Clb; Lit Mag; Hon Roll; 1st Pl ST Frnsc Cmptn 86; 2nd Pl Lit Cont 86; 1st & 3rd Pl Lit Cont 85; U Of MD; Physcn.

DAVIDSON, DAWN; Northern HS; Dunkirk, MD; (Y); Church Yth Grp; Varsity Clb; VICA; Hon Roll; Mst Imprvd Stu Comp Pgmng Lvl I 85-86; Hnrbl Rcgntn Job Intrvw Cntst VICA Skls Olympcs 85-86; Frostburg ST; Comp Systms Anly.

DAVIDSON, ELIZABETH; North Carroll HS; Millers, MD; (Y); Pres Church Yth Grp; Service Clb; Chorus; Church Choir; Swing Chorus; Hon Roll; Acadmc Ltr 86; Nrsg.

DAVIES, TANYA; Great Mills HS; Lex Pk, MD; (Y); Sec Church Yth Grp; Teachers Aide; Varsity Clb; Stat Crs Cntry; Mgr(s); Trk; Hon Roll; Ntl Merit Ltr; Schl Msct 83-85; Bus Adm.

DAVIES, THOMAS; Sherwood HS; Olney, MD; (Y); Boy Scts; Model UN; Jazz Band; Var Crs Cntry; Var Trk; NHS; VP Spanish NHS; Eagle Sct 84; George Wash U Awd Exclnc Math & Sci 86.

DAVIS IV, ALDEN Q; Calvary Baptist Church Acad; Severn, MD; (Y); 2/23; Var Capt Bsbl; Var L Bsktbl; Var L Socr; Cit Awd; Ntl Merit Ltr; Sal; Church Yth Grp; Chorus; Church Choir; Dstngshd Hon Roll 83-86; ST MD Schlstc Merit Awd 86; Chaplain For Fresh, Soph & JR Clss; Messiah Coll; Radio.

DAVIS, ANGELA; Calvert HS; Lusby, MD; (Y); 7/240; Rptr French Clb; Sec FBLA; Pres FHA; Natl Beta Clb; Nwsp Stf; Stu Cncl; High Hon Roll; Ntl Merit Ltr; Pres Schlr; Baltimore Sun Minority Jrnlst Schlrshp 86; U MD Banneker Schlrshp 86; U MD College Park; Jrnlsm.

DAVIS, ANGELA M; Western HS; Baltimore, MD; (Y); 12/420; Cmnty Wkr; JA; Pres Math Clb; Chorus; Church Choir; Rep Sr Cls; High Hon Roll; Hon Roll; NHS; Natl Achvt Schlrp Prog Commnded Stu 85; Cert Outstndg Achvt In Schlrp 85; Western MD Coll; Pre-Med.

DAVIS, BARBARA; Northern HS; Chesapeake Bch, MD; (Y); Band; Concert Band; Mrchg Band; Symp Band; Mgr(s); Stat Sftbl; Hon Roll; Educ.

DAVIS, CARRIE; Northwestern HS; College Pk, MD; (Y); AFS; VP German Clb; Lit Mag; Pom Pon; Capt Vllybl; Hon Roll.

DAVIS, DANIEL; Montgomery Blair HS; Silver Spg, MD; (Y); French Clb; Science Clb; Thesps; Acpl Chr; School Musical; School Play; Variety Show; Music.

DAVIS, DEANDRA; Parkdale HS; Silver Spring, MD; (Y); Debate Tm; French Clb; FHA; Model UN; Science Clb; Gym; Swmmng; Vllybl; French Hon Soc; Prfct Atten Awd; Hnry Mtn Sci Fari 84-85; Prtcpnt Natl Frnch Tst 85; FL ST; Cprt Lwyr.

DAVIS, DEBORAH J; Mt Hebron HS; Ellicott City, MD; (Y); Church Yth Grp; Ski Clb; SADD; Church Choir; Drill Tm; School Musical; School Play; JV Bsktbl; High Hon Roll; Spanish NHS; MD Fed Wmns Clbs Inc Yth Art Cntst 1st Pl Awds Cnty, Dist & St Lvls 86; Art.

DAVIS, DOROTHY; Thomas Stone HS; Waldorf, MD; (S); Latin Clb; Fld Hcky; Sftbl; Hon Roll; Hnr Rl.

DAVIS, DWAYNE M; Parkdale SR HS; Landover, MD; (Y); Latin Clb; Math Tm; Rep Jr Cls; Trs Sr Cls; Rep Stu Cncl; Var Wt Lftg; Var Wrstlng; High Hon Roll; Trs NHS; Ntl Merit SF; Acad Exclnce Awd 84; Naval Acad; Engrng.

DAVIS, ERICA; Laurel HS; Laurel, MD; (Y); Church Yth Grp; Cmnty Wkr; Capt 4-H; Latin Clb; Ski Clb; Varsity Clb; Nwsp Rptr; Stat Bsktbl; Var Crs Cntry; Mgr(s); Coaches Awd For Swim Tm; Capt Of Numerous US Tm 84-86; Bst Swmmr Awd.

DAVIS, HEATHER; Glenelg HS; Glenwood, MD; (Y); Var Vllybl; U Of MD; Bus.

DAVIS, JENNI; La Reine HS; San Antonio, TX; (Y); 7/148; FCA; Letterman Clb; Ski Clb; Rep Sr Cls; Stat Bsbl; JV Var Cheerleading; High Hon Roll; NHS; Ntl Merit Ltr; Pres Schlr; Bst Clss Awds Physcs Hnrs & Amer Hstry 85-86; AFOWC & AOWC Schlrshps 86; Baylor U.

DAVIS, JOHN T; Bishop Walsh HS; Cumberland, MD; (Y); 3/106; Boy Scts; Speech Tm; Thesps; School Musical; School Play; Stage Crew; Var JV Socr; Hon Roll; NHS; Ntl Merit SF; Pre-Med.

DAVIS, MELISSA; Williamsport HS; Wiliamsport, MD; (Y); 21/227; German Clb; Ski Clb; Drill Tm; Nwsp Stf; VP Frsh Cls; VP Soph Cls; Trs Sr Cls; Rep Stu Cncl; Powder Puff Ftbl; Co-Capt Vllybl; Page MD Gen Assmbly 86; Elizabethtown Coll; Comm.

DAVIS, MELISSA A; Valley HS; Barton, MD; (Y); French Clb; Ski Clb; Teachers Aide; Band; Concert Band; Mrchg Band; Var Cheerleading; Trk; Frostburg ST Coll; Crmnl Jsctc.

DAVIS II, MICHAEL D; James M Bennett SR HS; Salisbury, MD; (Y); 101/346; Aud/Vis; CAP; JCL; Teachers Aide; Thesps; School Musical; School Play; Nwsp Sprt Ed; JV Socr; Ntl Merit SF; Scty Dstngshd Amer HS Stu 85-86; Duke Tlnt Id Prgrm 84-86; Boston U; Linguist.

DAVIS, MICHELLE; Thomas S Wootton HS; Gaitherburg, MD; (Y); 68/401; VP Frsh Cls; VP Jr Cls; VP Sr Cls; Rep Stu Cncl; Var L Socr; Var Tennis; Hon Roll; Rotary Awd; Most Promising Sr NHS 86; Hmcmng Queen/Princess 86&82; U MD Ldrshp Conf 85; James Madison U; Bus.

DAVIS, NICOLE; Forest Park SR HS; Baltimore, MD; (Y); Art Clb; ROTC; SADD; Chorus; Off Sr Cls; Stu Cncl; Bsktbl; Hon Roll; Prfct Atten Awd; Stu Of Wk 85; Coppin ST Clg; Law.

DAVIS, RAYMOND D; Edgewood HS; Edgewood, MD; (Y); Computer Clb; Hon Roll; Acad Ltr Pins Hnr Rl; Acad Tm; Elect Engr.

DAVIS, SUZANNE L; Camp Spring Christian HS; Waldorf, MD; (Y); Church Yth Grp; Teachers Aide; Acpl Chr; Chorus; Church Choir; School Musical; School Play; Sftbl; Hon Roll; Fomi Chrch Yth Grp 85-86; Slvr Awd MA Coll Mus, Nrsng Hm Aid 85-86; Hmcmng Qn, Theatre Grp 85-86; Shenandoah Coll; Voice.

DAVIS, TODD M; Springbrook HS; Silver Spring, MD; (Y); 32/478; VP Debate Tm; German Clb; VP Capt Crs Cntry; Var Trk; Hon Roll; NHS; Ntl Merit SF; Germ Hon Soc; Montgomery Cnty Debate Champ; U VA; Econ.

DAVIS, WENDY; North Carroll HS; Hampstead, MD; (Y); #1 In Class; Am Leg Aux Girls St; GAA; VP Soph Cls; VP Jr Cls; Pres Stu Cncl; Gov Hon Prg Awd; High Hon Roll; NHS; Ntl Merit SF; Rotary Awd; Balfour Key, Soc Stds Awds 86; Mst Vlbl Frshmn Stdnt Cncl; Western MD Col6; Pub Rel.

DAWNING, KELLY; Edgewood HS; Edgewood, MD; (Y); Church Yth Grp; Dance Clb; Drama Clb; 4-H; JA; Pep Clb; SADD; Varsity Clb; Stu Cncl; High Hon Roll; Ruff-Ross Scholar 86; Wrk Exprnce Awd 86f4 Yr 16 Qtr Hnr Roll Stu 86; U MD College Pk; Appld Hlth.

DAWSON JR, DAVID R; Parkside HS; Salisbury, MD; (Y); Trs Spanish Clb; VP Frsh Cls; Pres Soph Cls; JV Bsbl; JV Socr; Hon Roll; Med.

DAWSON, JOAN; North East HS; North East, MD; (Y); FHA; Intnl Clb; Teachers Aide; Stu Cncl; Capt Cheerleading; Hon Roll; Algebra I Part B 84; Early Wstrn Civlztn 84; Sci 86; U MD; Life Sci.

DAWSON, MICHAEL; John Carroll HS; Perryville, MD; (Y); 81/238; Pres Camera Clb; Church Yth Grp; Debate Tm; Spanish Clb; Nwsp Phtg; Yrbk Phtg; Lit Mag; Swmmng; Cit Awd; Mt St Marys; Med Tech.

DAY, DAWN; Brunswick HS; Brunswick, MD; (Y); German Clb; Chorus; School Musical; School Play; Jr Cls; Sr Cls; Stu Cncl; Cheerleading; Powder Puff Ftbl; Trk; Darryl Huffer Mem Awd 86; PTSA Scholar 86; Catholic U Amer; Theatre.

DAYS, CHRISTIE; Fairmont Heights HS; Cheverly, MD; (Y); 9/241; Dance Clb; Teachers Aide; Sec Sr Cls; Stu Cncl; Stat Var Bsktbl; Var Capt Pom Pon; Score Keeper; Var Capt Tennis; Hon Roll; NHS; Outstndng Bus Stu 86; Chrprsn Hmcmng Float & Parade Comm 86; Editor SGA Nwslttr 86; Spelman Coll; Pre-Law.

DE ANGELIS, TABATHA; Pocomoke HS; Pocomoke, MD; (S); 9/95; AFS; Drama Clb; Sec 4-H; Sec Spanish Clb; SADD; Church Choir; Jazz Band; School Play; Hon Roll; Co-Hldr Of 2 Ntl Rfl Shtng Rcrds; E TN ST U; Frgn Lng.

DE ANGELIS, TAMMIE; Pocomoke HS; Pocomoke, MD; (S); 3/95; AFS; Science Clb; Spanish Clb; SADD; Off Sr Cls; Var L Cheerleading; Trs NHS; Opt Clb Awd; Pres Clssrm 86; Math.

DE BERRY, THOMAS H; Southern HS; Oakland, MD; (S); 4-H; Rep Stu Cncl; Ftbl; Tennis; 4-H Awd; Hon Roll; Debate Tm; US Coast Guard; Acctng.

DE BRUYN, DOTTIE; Calvert Christian HS; Owings, MD; (Y); 1/5; Church Yth Grp; Drama Clb; Sec 4-H; Chorus; Church Choir; School Play; Yrbk Stf; Rep Jr Cls; Trs Stu Cncl; Var Capt Bsktbl; Dist Amer HS Stu Awd 85-86; Hmcmng Prncss 85-86; Art Show 1st Pl Champ Awd 84-85.

DE GENNARO, LAURA; La Reine HS; Temple Hills, MD; (Y); Pres Church Yth Grp; Chorus; Prfct Atten Awd; Schltc Achvt Awd Cntmpry Sci 86; Schltc Achvt Awd Bio 85; Psych.

DE GEORGE, JAMES J; Loyola HS; Columbia, MD; (S); 25/169; Spanish Clb; Yrbk Stf; Var L Bsktbl; Var L Golf; Var Capt Socr; High Hon Roll; Hon Roll; NHS; NEDT Awd; Pres Schlr; Outstndng Art Stu Awd 83; Headmstr & Schlr Ath Scholar 83-86; Miami Of OH; Bus Adm.

DE LANEY, PHILIP; Fort Hill HS; Cumberland, MD; (Y); Pres Computer Clb; Pres 4-H; Band; Mrchg Band; Nwsp Phtg; 4-H Awd; NHS; NEDT Awd; All-St Hnr Band-MD 84-86; Math.

DE LEO, CHRISTINE; Paint Branch HS; Silver Spring, MD; (Y); Church Yth Grp; Hosp Aide; Ski Clb; Sec Soph Cls; Sec Jr Cls; JV Var Cheerleading; JV Sftbl; Var Swmmng; Hon Roll; Bio.

DE LEON, ELMER; Walt Whitman HS; Bethesda, MD; (Y); Church Yth Grp; Spanish Clb; Band; Stu Cncl; Var L Ftbl; Im Socr; JV Trk; Var Wt Lftg; Hon Roll; NHS; Engrng.

DE LOATCH, MARGARET C; Springbrook HS; Silver Spring, MD; (Y); 110/477; Church Yth Grp; Cmnty Wkr; Church Choir; School Play; Stage Crew; Variety Show; Nwsp Rptr; Rep Stu Cncl; Var Pom Pon; Hon Roll; Natl Achvl Cmmnd Stu 85; Law.

DE MARTINO, TY; Bishop Walsh HS; Cumberland, MD; (Y); 21/104; Art Clb; Camera Clb; Drama Clb; Library Aide; School Play; Yrbk Phtg; French Hon Soc; Hon Roll; NHS; Frostburg St Coll; Engl.

DE POLLAR, SHERRI L; Magruder HS; Gaithersburg, MD; (Y); Rep Frsh Cls; Rep Jr Cls; Cheerleading; Heritage Club Rep; Modeling.

DE ROSA, JEANNE M; Westminster HS; Finksburg, MD; (Y); Latin Clb; Band; Mrchg Band; Symp Band; Yrbk Phtg; High Hon Roll; NHS; Ntl Latin Ex Awd 85-86; George Mason U; Hist.

DE SIMONE, ELINKA; John Carroll HS; Aberdeen, MD; (Y); 35/250; Dance Clb; Service Clb; French Hon Soc; High Hon Roll; Hon Roll; NHS; Prfct Atten Awd; Concours Ntl De Francais Cert Of Hnr 86; Intl Bus.

DE VAUX, ROSCHELLE; Pocomoke HS; Pocomoke City, MD; (Y); 35/93; AFS; Church Yth Grp; Drama Clb; FBLA; Girl Scts; Spanish Clb; SADD; Pom Pon; Vllybl; Prfct Atten Awd; Ltr Vlybl; Jump Rope For Heart; Coaches Plyr Of Yr; DE ST Coll; Computer Engngrng.

DE VORE, CHRIS; Northern HS; Huntingtown, MD; (Y); Church Yth Grp; Computer Clb; Trs Sec 4-H; Spanish Clb; VICA; Color Guard; Yrbk Stf; Stat Ftbl; Mgr(s); 4-H Awd; Eqstrn Awds & Trphys 83-87; Rcd Bk & Anml Sci Pgm Awds 83-87; Eqstrn Mgmt.

DE WALD, TEENA; The Catholic HS Of Balto; Baltimore, MD; (Y); 4/186; French Clb; Pres FHA; Mathletes; Trs Math Clb; Lit Mag; Gov Hon Prg Awd; High Hon Roll; NHS; Prfct Atten Awd; St Schlr; Hon Mntn Baltimore Hist Fr 86; Coll Notre Dame MD; Mathmtcs.

DEAKINS, LISA; Notre Dame Prep; Baltimore, MD; (Y); SADD; Var Socr; Schl Rep Soho Teen Nght Clb 85; Art.

DEAN, LISA; Glenelg HS; Dayton, MD; (Y); Church Yth Grp; Teachers Aide; Church Choir; Yrbk Stf; Stat Bsktbl; JV Var Fld Hcky; Var Trk; Hon Roll; Towson; Bus Mgmt.

DEAN III, ROBERT LEE; Harford Vocational Tech HS; Aberdeen, MD; (Y); Cmnty Wkr; FNA; Hosp Aide; Teachers Aide; Hon Roll; Chorus; Q&S; Red Cross Aide; SADD; Prfct Atten Awd; Spec Educ Vol 1985-86; Red Cross Cert Life Guard,Wtr Safety; AIKIDO 1980-86; 1st Pl Cmty Tennis 83-85; Hartford CC; Phys Thrpy/X-Ray.

DEAN, VICTORIA; Northwestern HS; Hyattsville, MD; (Y); Cmnty Wkr; JA; Library Aide; NFL; Red Cross Aide; Spanish Clb; Church Choir; Cert Of Hnr-MD ST Bar Assn 86; Cmnty Svc Awd-Dist Of Colmbia 85; Cert Of Aprctn-Red Crss 84; Culinary Inst Of Amer; Exec Chf.

DEANGELIS, LISA J; Seneca Valley HS; Germantown, MD; (Y); 73/490; Dance Clb; Drama Clb; Teachers Aide; Chorus; School Musical; School Play; Rep Soph Cls; Cheerleading; Gym; Hon Roll; 6th Pl Gymnstcs Metal Cnty Mt/Flr Routn 85; Vrsty Ltr Gymnstcs 85; Danc Capt 86; MD U College Pk; Cmnctns.

DEAS, REBEKAH; Harford Christian Schl; Aberdeen, MD; (S); 1/36; Church Yth Grp; 4-H; Math Tm; Scholastic Bowl; Varsity Clb; Chorus; Church Choir; Pres Soph Cls; Var L Fld Hcky; High Hon Roll; Schltc Awd-Hghst Grd Avg 85; Med.

DEAVER, BETH; Elkton HS; Elkton, MD; (Y); Ski Clb; Varsity Clb; Rep Frsh Cls; Rep Soph Cls; Rep Jr Cls; Stu Cncl; Var JV Cheerleading; Var JV Fld Hcky; Trk; Hon Roll; Gldn Elk Awd 85; 3-Yr Vrsty Lttrmn Plq 86; Trpl Crwn Awd 85; Elizabethtown PA; Anml Sci.

DEAVER, CHRISTOPHER; Joppatowne HS; Joppa, MD; (Y); 16/180; Computer Clb; Math Tm; Chorus; School Musical; Vllybl; NHS; Ntl Merit Ltr; Pres Schlr; Math Awd 86; Gldn Anchor Awd; Towson ST U; Engrng.

DEBRO, ANGELA; Northern SR HS; Baltimore, MD; (Y); Library Aide; Office Aide; Hon Roll; Prfct Atten Awd; Dynmcs Stu Fcltr Trng Cert Compltn 85; U Of Miami; Law.

DECKER, DAVID; Wicomico SR HS; Salisbury, MD; (Y); Church Yth Grp; Letterman Clb; Varsity Clb; Nwsp Sprt Ed; Sec Jr Cls; Rep Stu Cncl; Var Capt Bsbl; Var Capt Ftbl; Var Capt Wrstlng; NHS; Med.

DEDERER, SUSAN; Dulaney HS; Cockeysville, MD; (Y); Church Yth Grp; Yrbk Stf; Im Socr; High Hon Roll; Hon Roll; Jr NHS; Math.

DEEGAN, KATHLEEN; Elizabeth Seton HS; Rockville, MD; (Y); Church Yth Grp; Latin Clb; Coach Actv; Socr; Tennis; Trk; Hon Roll.

DEEMS, ANGELA; Southern Garrett HS; Mt Lake Pk, MD; (Y); 15/221; German Clb; Var Trk; Hon Roll; NHS; Pres Schlr; Garrett CC.

DEFFINBAUGH, DENISE; North Harford HS; Street, MD; (Y); 3/278; Cmnty Wkr; German Clb; Varsity Clb; Yrbk Stf; Capt Fld Hcky; Capt Lcrss; Swmmng; NHS; Pres Schlr; Voice Dem Awd; Schlrshp Jrrtsvll Lns 86; Schlrshp Tchrs Assoc Of Balto Cnty 86; Dstngshd Schlr Hrfrd Cnty 86; Wake Forest U; Comp.

DEHNE, KRISTEN; St Vincent Pallotti HS; Olney, MD; (S); 5/115; Spanish Clb; Rep Frsh Cls; Var L Bsktbl; Var L Crs Cntry; Var L Sftbl; Var Trk; High Hon Roll; Jr NHS; NHS; Spanish NHS; Acad All-Amer; US Ldrshp Merit Awd; Math.

DEL CAMP, DANIELLE; James M Bennett SR HS; Salisbury, MD; (Y); 34/210; Office Aide; Varsity Clb; Band; Variety Show; Yrbk Stf; Trs Frsh Cls; Hon Roll; Salisbury ST Coll.

DEL GENIS, LORI; Walkersville HS; Gaithersburg, MD; (Y); JCL; Ed Lit Mag; High Hon Roll; JC Awd; NHS; Pres Schlr; St Schlr; Art Clb; Church Yth Grp; Drama Clb; Charles Broadrup Schlrshp 86; Senatorial Schlrshp; Loyola Coll MD; Frgn Rel.

DEL PINO, JOHN A; Montgomery Blair HS; Takoma Park, MD; (Y); 5/212; French Clb; School Play; VP Sr Cls; Crs Cntry; Trk; NHS; Ntl Merit SF; Intnl Clb; Math Tm; Scholastic Bowl; Schlrshp To Telluride Assn Smmr Pgm At U Of Chgo 86; WA Area Hispanic Wrtng Cnst 86; Ofc In De Molay; Stanford U; Engrng.

DELIBRO, TINA; Kenwood HS; Baltimore, MD; (Y); Church Yth Grp; Cmnty Wkr; FBLA; Hosp Aide; SADD; Drm & Bgl; Drm Mjr(t); Yrbk Stf; Trs Soph Cls; Trs Sr Cls; Chld Psychlgy.

DELOACH, TINA; Western HS; Baltimore, MD; (Y); 31/473; Church Yth Grp; Pres Drama Clb; French Clb; Math Clb; Radio Clb; Pres Thesps; School Musical; School Play; Hon Roll; NHS; Frnklin & Marshall U; Bio.

DELOATCH, MARQUITA; Forestville HS; Forestville, MD; (Y); Computer Clb; FBLA; Hon Roll; Howard U; Psychlgy.

DELUCA, DONNA; Cambridge South Dorchester HS; Cambridge, MD; (Y); 1/220; AFS; Church Yth Grp; Stu Cncl; L Pom Pon; L Tennis; NHS; Tlntd & Gftd Pgm; Prom Cmmtt Chrmmn; Hmcmng Float Cmmtt.

DEMBY, RONALD; Kent County HS; Millington, MD; (Y); #5 In Class; VP French Clb; Band; Chorus; Concert Band; Jazz Band; Mrchg Band; School Musical; Stu Cncl; High Hon Roll; Hon Roll; MS All ST Jazz Band 86; MD Eastern Shore All Shore Band 84-86; Saulisbury ST Coll; Music.

DEMENT, JOEY; St Marys Ryken HS; Newburg, MD; (S); 5/168; Debate Tm; Pres Science Clb; Speech Tm; School Musical; Lit Mag; JV Trk; High Hon Roll; NHS; Ntl Merit Ltr; NEDT Awd; Bio Awd; Math.

DENCKLA, DEREK A; Walt Whitman HS; Bethesda, MD; (Y); Art Clb; Debate Tm; Pres Drama Clb; Q&S; Band; School Play; Variety Show; Nwsp Stf; Ed Lit Mag; Stu Cncl; MD Prs Wmns Assn Desgn 1st Pl, Clmbia Prs Assn Design 3rd Pl, Hnrb Mntn Edtrl Wrtng All In 85; Columbia U.

DENEAU, JUDY; Magruder HS; Derwood, MD; (Y); Cmnty Wkr; French Clb; SADD; Rep Stu Cncl; Hon Roll; Ntl Merit Ltr; Outstndng Schltc Achvt 86.

DENEEN, CHRISTA; Fort Hill HS; Cumberland, MD; (Y); Church Yth Grp; Cmnty Wkr; Hosp Aide; Natl Beta Clb; Office Aide; Church Choir; Hon Roll; Optimist Club Schlrshp; Allegany CC; Bus Tech.

DENEEN, MATTHEW; Allegany HS; Cumberland, MD; (Y); 20/212; Rep Soph Cls; JV Var Bsktbl; Boy Scts; Band; Concert Band; Jazz Band; Mrchg Band; Orch; Pep Band; School Musical; Band Ofcr 85-86; U S Naval Acad; Cmmnctns.

DENNENBERG, BETH; Dulaney SR HS; Cockeysville, MD; (Y); Hosp Aide; Band; Variety Show; Yrbk Phtg; Yrbk Stf; Stu Cncl; Hon Roll; Jr NHS; Svc Awd Soc Studies Aide 83-84; Exc Stu Cncl Help 85-86; Physcl Thrpy.

DENNIS, LEONIE; Western SR HS; Baltimore, MD; (Y); FBLA; Acctng.

DENSMORE, DONNA; Patterson HS; Baltimore, MD; (Y); Dance Clb; Office Aide; Pep Clb; Chorus; Yrbk Stf; Bsktbl; Cheerleading; Diving; Sftbl; Swmmng.

DENTON, KRISTIN; Thomas Stone HS; Waldorf, MD; (S); Drama Clb; Science Clb; NHS; Engrng.

DENTON, VELMA; Southern HS; Baltimore, MD; (Y); FBLA; SADD; Sftbl; Typng, Acctng Awds 85; Engl Awd 86; Bus.

DEREMER, DONELL; Fort Hill HS; Cumberland, MD; (Y); Church Yth Grp; Pep Clb; Drill Tm; Hon Roll; Sntrl Schrlshp 86; Sntnl Rcgntn Soc 86; Allegany CC; Rsprtry Thrpy.

DERGE, GILLMER; Governor Thomas Johnson HS; Frederick, MD; (Y); 7/309; Boy Scts; Computer Clb; German Clb; Math Tm; Science Clb; Teachers Aide; JV Trk; Hon Roll; NHS; YMCA Brd Drctrs 85-86; Duke U; Elec Engr.

DERNOGA, CHRIS; Notre Dame Prep; Baltimore, MD; (Y); Cmnty Wkr; Hosp Aide; Chorus; Gym; High Hon Roll; Prfct Atten Awd; Spanish NHS; Psych.

DESAI, MEENA; Franklin HS; Owings Mills, MD; (Y); Cmnty Wkr; High Hon Roll; Hon Roll; Jr NHS; NHS; Prfct Atten Awd; Soc Work.

DESAI, SHASHANK; Sherwood HS; Brookeville, MD; (Y); 8/317; Model UN; Ski Clb; Teachers Aide; Bausch & Lomb Sci Awd; Gov Hon Prg Awd; Hon Roll; Trs NHS; Bst Photo In Schl 86; Montgomery Co Med Soc Mst Promising Awd 86; Bst Math Stu In Schl 86; George Washington U; Pre Med.

DESAI, SONAL; Franklin SR HS; Reisterstown, MD; (Y); Cmnty Wkr; Service Clb; Teachers Aide; Mrchg Band; JV Score Keeper; Hon Roll; JC Awd; NHS; Ntl Merit SF; Sntrl Schlrshp 86; Cmnty Srvc Schlrshp & Awd 86; Cert Achvmnt Sci & Tech 86; Coll Park; Hlth Sci.

DETER, DAVID; Fort Hill HS; Cumberland, MD; (Y); Var JV Bsbl; JV Im Bsktbl; Var JV Ftbl; Var JV Timer; Hon Roll; Schl Ltr 85-86.

DETERS, THERESA; Gaithersburg HS; Gaithersburg, MD; (Y); AFS; Church Yth Grp; Drama Clb; FHA; German Clb; JA; Thesps; Stage Crew; High Hon Roll; NHS; Engrng.

DETRICH, JACQUELINE; SS Peter & Paul HS; Easton, MD; (Y); 5/28; Am Leg Aux Girls St; Pres English Clb; SADD; Varsity Clb; Stage Crew; Variety Show; Nwsp Bus Mgr; Yrbk Stf; Lit Mag; Pres Frsh Cls; Excptnl Acdmc Prgrs 86; Prsdntl Acdmc Ftns Awd 86; Rpblcn Wmn Talbt Cnty Awd 86; Mt St Marys.

DETWILER, MARK; Pocomoke HS; Pocomoke, MD; (S); 8/97; Church Yth Grp; Science Clb; Spanish Clb; SADD; Church Choir; Var Bsbl; Bowling; Hon Roll; NHS; Aeronutcl Engr.

DEVILLASEE, TYNETTE; Walbrook SR HS; Baltimore, MD; (Y); Church Yth Grp; Girl Scts; Library Aide; Teachers Aide; VICA; Band; Twrlr; Hon Roll; Prfct Atten Awd; Ldrshp Awd 86; Schl Awds 86; Csmtlgy.

DEVLIN, CHRISTOPHER; Towson HS; Towson, MD; (Y); Drama Clb; Thesps; JV Var Ftbl; JV Var Lcrss; JV Trk; Var Wrstlng; High Hon Roll; Hon Roll; Jv Cnty La Crosse Champns 84; Vrsty Cnty Ftbll Cham 85; Vrsty Hero La Crosse Townson 86; Towson ST; Actor.

DEVONSHIRE, DORIS; Perryville HS; Perryville, MD; (Y); Church Yth Grp; Library Aide; Church Choir; Hon Roll; Spnsh II Achvt 84-85; Perryville Acad Star 85-86; Rn.

DEVROYE, RAYMOND; Hammond HS; Laurel, MD; (Y); Spanish Clb; Teachers Aide; Yrbk Rptr; Yrbk Stf; Swmmng; Hon Roll; NHS; Comp Sci.

DI COCCO, DENISE; Suitland SR HS; District Height, MD; (Y); GAA; Sftbl; Hon Roll; Sprts Actvts Bsktbll 78-82; Sftbl 78-86; Botny Schl Sci Fair 86.

DI COSTANZO, SHARON; Gaithersburg HS; Gaithersburg, MD; (Y); 111/590; Chorus; Madrigals; School Musical; Stage Crew; Hon Roll; NHS; Band; Mrchg Band; Pep Band; School Play; MD Dstngshd Schlr Schlrshp For Vocal 85-86; Pres Acdmc Ftns Awd 86; U MD Coll Pk; Mscl Theatre.

DI GIOVANNANTONIO, FRANK; Surrattsville SR HS; Clinton, MD; (Y); Boys Clb Am; Chorus; Var Capt Ftbl; Trk; Hon Roll; Jr NHS; Supt Awd; Towson ST U; Bus Adm.

DI MASSIMANTONIO, CORINNA; The Catholic HS; Baltimore, MD; (Y); 22/170; Hosp Aide; Radio Clb; SADD; Stage Crew; Rep Jr Cls; Sec Stu Cncl; Socr; Cit Awd; Hon Roll; Awd Unsung Hrn 86; Acad Achvt Awd Coll Of Ntr Dm 86; Srptmst Yth Ctzshp Awd 86; Towson ST U; Mass Comm.

DI PIETRO, ANGELA JOAN; Archbishop Spalding HS; Crownsville, MD; (Y); 20/132; Aud/Vis; Church Yth Grp; Drama Clb; Library Aide; School Play; Stage Crew; JV Sftbl; Hon Roll; Prfct Atten Awd; Rlgn Awd 86; Schl Merit Lttr & 3 Achvt Stars; U Of MD College Pk; Cnmtgrphy.

DIALLO, AMADOU W; Calvert Hall College HS; Baltimore, MD; (Y); 40/220; Rep Band; Rep Concert Band; Jazz Band; Rep Mrchg Band; Pep Band; Rep Symp Band; Nwsp Rptr; Ed Nwsp Stf; Im Bsktbl; Im Ftbl; Natl Achvt Scholar Pgm 85-86; U MD College Pk; Corp Law.

DIAMONTE, CHRISTINA; North East HS; N East, MD; (Y); 19/330; Sec Frsh Cls; Sec Soph Cls; Sec Jr Cls; Sec Sr Cls; Var Capt Cheerleading; Var Tennis; Hon Roll; St Schlr; Towson ST U; Pltcl Sci.

DIAZ, JULIE; Roland Park Country Schl; Baltimore, MD; (Y); Chorus; School Play; Nwsp Rptr; Nwsp Stf; Yrbk Stf; Hon Roll; Cert Hnrb Mntn Natl Latin Exam 84; Cert Merit Natl Frnch Cont 85 & 86.

DIBBLE, ILKA; Broadneck SR HS; Annapolis, MD; (S); DECA; JA; Cnty Cmp 3rd Pl Fshn Crdntn 86; 2nd Pl Appl & Assrs 86; 2nd Pl Fshn Crdntn ST Cmp 86; Bus.

DICKENS, MICHELLE; Crossland HS; Camp Spgs, MD; (Y); Church Yth Grp; Teachers Aide; VICA; Var Bsktbl; Hon Roll; Med Asst Cert 85-86; CPR Cert; 1st Aide Cert; Phys Ther.

DICKENS, VICKIE; Great Mills HS; St Inigoes, MD; (Y); 30/275; Church Yth Grp; Cmnty Wkr; Sec FBLA; Trs Spanish Clb; SADD; Teachers Aide; Stat Bsktbl; Score Keeper; Cit Awd; Hon Roll; Humntrn Awd 86; Morgan ST U.

DICKERSON, ALISA; Forestville HS; Suitland, MD; (Y); Teachers Aide; Nwsp Rptr; Mgr(s); Socr; Hon Roll; NC Central U; Communications.

DICKERSON, LARYSSA; Chopticon HS; Loveville, MD; (Y); Pres Sec Church Yth Grp; Pres DECA; Pep Clb; SADD; Chorus; Church Choir; Swing Chorus; Variety Show; Rep Frsh Cls; Trs Soph Cls; Miss NAACP 85-86; St Marys Cncl Yth 85; Show Choir 84-85; Mis Gospel Queen 84-85; Bus Law.

DICKSON, BOB; Highland View Acad; Frederick, MD; (Y); Church Yth Grp; Band; Nwsp Rptr; Nwsp Stf; Ed Lit Mag; Off Frsh Cls; Rep Jr Cls; Im Ftbl; Var Socr; Im Vllybl; Mech Engnrg.

DICKSON, CARL; La Plata HS; Waldorf, MD; (Y); Drm Mjr(t); Ntl Merit Ltr; Comp Sci.

DIEDRICH, KELLY; Lackey HS; Indian Head, MD; (Y); Sec Latin Clb; Ski Clb; SADD; Variety Show; Yrbk Stf; Stu Cncl; Capt Pom Pon; Powder Puff Ftbl; Hon Roll; Jr NHS; Adv.

DIETZ, PATRICIA; Institute Of Notre Dame HS; Baltimore, MD; (Y); Chorus; High Hon Roll; Hon Roll; Bus.

DIFFENBAUGH, DAWN; Patterson HS; Baltimore, MD; (Y); Jr NHS; NHS.

DILGARD, VICKIE; Southern HS; Oakland, MD; (Y); Var Cmnty Wkr; Dance Clb; GAA; Var Bsktbl; JV Cheerleading; Var Sftbl; Var Trk; Church Yth Grp; Bst Trk Athltc Awd 86; MVP JV Bsktbl 84-85; Acctg.

DILLON, ERIN; Parkside SR HS; Salisbury, MD; (Y); Church Yth Grp; Drama Clb; French Clb; Ski Clb; Stage Crew; Tennis; Art.

DILWORTH, NANCY; John Carroll HS; Kingsville, MD; (Y); 81/238; Cmnty Wkr; Service Clb; Yrbk Stf; Pres Stu Cncl; Var Cheerleading; NHS; Spanish NHS; VFW Awd; Am Leg Aux Girls St; VP Church Yth Grp; H S Ldrshp Inst 86; MD Smmr Ctrs Giftd & Talntd; Mst Invlvd Awd 84-85; Dickinson; Psych.

DINGESS, VALERIE; Gwynn Park HS; Accokeek, MD; (Y); Am Leg Aux Girls St; Church Yth Grp; Cmnty Wkr; Variety Show; Pres Soph Cls; VP Pres Stu Cncl; Hon Roll; Certf Hon MD ST Bar Asso 85-86; Certf Compltn Prnc Georges CC Ldrhsp Wrksp 84-86; Law.

DINGLE, LISA; Western HS; Baltimore, MD; (Y); Dance Clb; Band; Concert Band; Mrchg Band; School Musical; School Play; Spanish NHS; Ed.

DINGUS, LINDA; Patterson HS; Baltimore, MD; (Y); Child Care.

DINGUS, TERESA; Patterson HS; Baltimore, MD; (Y); Rep Sr Cls; Child Care.

DINH, KIMTHOA; Richard Montgomery HS; Rockville, MD; (Y); High Hon Roll; Hon Roll; Montgomery Coll; Elec Engrng.

DIPASQUALE, CHRISTY; Institute Of Notre Dame; Baltimore, MD; (Y); Church Yth Grp; GAA; Varsity Clb; Var JV Cheerleading; Gym; Swmmng 86; All Star Sftbl, Sccr, Dance, Chrldng; Parson Schl Dsgn; Intr Dsgn.

DIPIETRI, PATRICIA; Surrattsville HS; Clinton, MD; (Y); FBLA; Red Cross Aide; Teachers Aide; Capt Flag Corp; Yrbk Stf; Hon Roll; Jr NHS; Acadmc Exclince Awd 84-85; PGCC; Hotel Mgt.

DISHAROON, KERRY SUE; Loch Raven SR HS; Baltimore, MD; (Y); Sec Dance Clb; Hosp Aide; Teachers Aide; Sec Band; Chorus; Color Guard; Concert Band; Mrchg Band; School Musical; Prfct Atten Awd; SR Band Awd 85-86; Cedar Crest Coll Schlrshp 86-87; Pine Grove Ele Schl Schlrshp 86; U Of MD Balto County; Nrsng.

DITTO, LISA; Milford HS; Balt, MD; (Y); Church Yth Grp; Church Choir; Variety Show; Var Fld Hcky; Var Lcrss; Mgr(s); Hon Roll; NHS; Spec Educ.

DIUGUID, DUNCAN; Walt Whitman HS; Bethesda, MD; (Y); Pres Civic Clb; Cmnty Wkr; Red Cross Aide; Ski Clb; Spanish Clb; Teachers Aide; Rep Frsh Cls; Rep Soph Cls; Rep Jr Cls; Pres Sr Cls; Pre Law.

DIVELBLISS, DONNA; Hancock HS; Hancock, MD; (Y); 3/49; Am Leg Aux Girls St; SADD; Capt Color Guard; Sec Sr Cls; Sec Rep Stu Cncl; Var Stat Bsktbl; Var Sftbl; Var JV Vllybl; Dnfth Awd; Elks Awd; Hagerstown JC; Bus Admin.

DIX, STEPHANIE; Gaithersburg HS; Gaithersburg, MD; (Y); JA; SADD; School Play; Stage Crew; Var L Fld Hcky; Hon Roll; Jr NHS; Coast Guard Acad 86; Chem.

DIXON, DWAYNE B; Centennial HS; Ellicott City, MD; (Y); 72/267; Church Choir; Orch; Ed Pep Band; Pres Sr Cls; Var Capt Trk; Hon Roll; Boy Scts; Church Yth Grp; Latin Clb; Band; All ST Orchstra 86; Cnty Chmpn Dscs Evnt 85; Bus Adm.

DIXON, GERRI; Friendly SR HS; Ft Washington, MD; (Y); Stat Ftbl; Hon Roll; Bio.

DIXON, JILL; Patapsco HS; Baltimore, MD; (Y); Office Aide; Teachers Aide; Band; Yrbk Sprt Ed; Yrbk Stf; Hon Roll; Loyola Coll MD; Bus Admn.

DIXON, LA SHENNA; Potomac SR HS; Temple Hills, MD; (Y); Dance Clb; Teachers Aide; Gym; U MD; Bus Mgmt.

DIXON, MARE; Southern Garrett County HS; Oakland, MD; (Y); Hon Roll; Wilma Boyd; Arln Rsrvnts.

DIXON, MICHELLE; Beall HS; Frostburg, MD; (Y); Cmnty Wkr; Chorus; Yrbk Ed-Chief; Yrbk Stf; Score Keeper; Hon Roll; NHS; Prfct Atten Awd; St Schlr; Frostburg ST Coll; Ed.

DIXON, ROBERT; Liberty HS; Westminster, MD; (S); Boy Scts; Computer Clb; Exploring; Mathletes; Office Aide; Spanish Clb; Hon Roll; Western MD Coll; Physcs.

DIXON, WAVERLEY; La Plata HS; Waldorf, MD; (Y); Cmnty Wkr; Ski Clb; SADD; School Musical; School Play; Stage Crew; Off Jr Cls; Off Sr Cls; High Hon Roll; Hon Roll; Film Animation.

DOCHTER, DANIELLE; John Carroll HS; Bel Air, MD; (Y); Camera Clb; Computer Clb; Dance Clb; FBLA; Ski Clb; Nwsp Rptr; Bsktbl; Var Swmmng; JV Trk; Vllybl; Imprvmnt Awd 86; Outrch Awd 85.

DODGE, GARY; Southern HS; Deer Pk, MD; (Y); JV Bsktbl; Hon Roll; Hndwrtng Awd 78-80; Splling Awd 78-80; WV Weslyn; Elec Engr.

DODSON, DAVID; Francis Scott Key HS; Union Bridge, MD; (Y); VP Church Yth Grp; Pres 4-H; Teachers Aide; Pres Varsity Clb; Var L Ftbl; Wt Lftg; Var L Wrstlng; 4-H Awd; Hon Roll; Salisbury; Phy Ed.

DOFFLEMYER, BETTY; Muarice J Mc Donough HS; Waldorf, MD; (Y); Church Yth Grp; Cmnty Wkr; Hosp Aide; Flag Corp; Mrchg Band; High Hon Roll; Hon Roll; HOSA 85-86; Johns Hopkins U; Trama Nrsng.

DOGGETTE, DAVID; Oakland Mills HS; Columbia, MD; (Y); Jazz Band; Variety Show; VP Stu Cncl; Var L Trk; Hon Roll; NHS; VP Soph Cls; Im Bsktbl; Im Bowling; Im Diving; AOA Geoge Biddle Kelley Awd 85; PALMS 86; Ldrshp Develpmnt Inst Howard U AOA 86; Pre-Med.

DOLAN, COLLEEN; St Vincent Pallotti HS; Laurel, MD; (S); 8/86; AFS; Am Leg Aux Girls St; Drama Clb; Ski Clb; Stage Crew; Trs Jr Cls; Var Capt Socr; Var Capt Swmmng; Var Trk; High Hon Roll; Grls Sccr Outstndng Plyr 85; Swm Tm Coaches Awd 85-86; MVP Swm Tm 84-85; Comm.

DOLAN, KELLY; Fort Hill HS; Old Town, MD; (Y); Church Yth Grp; CAP; Pep Clb; Chorus; Church Choir; Swing Chorus; Rep Stu Cncl; Bowling; Crs Cntry; MD U; Pltcl Sci.

DOLBEY, CHRISTY; James M Bennett SR HS; Nanticoke, MD; (Y); 50/184; AFS; Church Yth Grp; Girl Scts; Spanish Clb; Varsity Clb; Band; Church Choir; Concert Band; Drill Tm; Mrchg Band; Salisbry ST Coll; Med Lab Tech.

DOLL, RICHARD; Centennial HS; Columbia, MD; (Y); 17/274; Math Tm; Jazz Band; Pep Band; Symp Band; JV Crs Cntry; JV Trk; NHS; Cmnty Wkr; Teachers Aide; Concert Band; Pres Acad Fit Awd 86; Band Ltr & Pins 84-86; Centennl PTSA Awd 86; Earlham Coll; Math.

DOMCHICK, DIANNE; Parkdale SR HS; New Carrollton, MD; (Y); SADD; Rep Jr Cls; Var JV Cheerleading; Hon Roll; MD U; Art.

DOMENICO, STEPHANIE; Northern HS; Huntingtown, MD; (Y); 6/296; Am Leg Aux Girls St; Cmnty Wkr; School Musical; Rep Stu Cncl; Capt Pom Pon; High Hon Roll; NHS; Pres Acadmc Ftnss Awd 86; Niagara U; Acctg.

DOMNEYS, YOLANDA; Northern HS; Baltimore, MD; (Y); Office Aide; Stage Crew; Rep Soph Cls; Off Jr Cls; JV Tennis; Hon Roll; Pre Law.

DONAHUE, SHARON; Sherwood HS; Silver Spg, MD; (Y); Drama Clb; Model UN; Chorus; High Hon Roll; Hon Roll; Ntl Merit Ltr; MD U; Law.

DONAHUE, TOMMY; Calvert HS; Pr Frederick, MD; (Y); Church Yth Grp; Cmnty Wkr; Letterman Clb; Var L Bsbl; JV Bsktbl; Var L Ftbl; Var Wt Lftg; Hon Roll; Senatrl Schlrshp 86; All SMAC Quarterback Outstndng Back 85-86; Schlstc Recgntn Awd 86; Towson ST U; Athlete Trang.

DONALDSON, DAVINA; Regina HS; W Hyattsville, MD; (Y); Cmnty Wkr; Model UN; Pep Clb; Hon Roll; NEDT Awd; Mod U N Activities Awd 85; Mock Trial Awd 86; Howard U; Psych.

DONALDSON, KIM; Suitland SR HS; District Height, MD; (Y); Church Yth Grp; Science Clb; Spanish Clb; High Hon Roll; Hon Roll; Spanish NHS; Acad Encllnc; Vet Med.

DONATO, MARIO; Northwestern HS; Mt Rainier, MD; (Y); Hosp Aide; High Hon Roll; Pres Schlr; Ntl Latin Hnr Soc 86; Real Est Agnt.

DONLEY, SANDRA; Heritage Acad; Clear Sp, MD; (Y); Chorus; School Play; JV Var Cheerleading; TN Temple U; Elem Ed.

DONNELLY, KATHLEEN; Sts Peter & Paul HS; Stevensville, MD; (Y); 10/28; Pres Pep Clb; Quiz Bowl; Ski Clb; SADD; Varsity Clb; Yrbk Ed-Chief; Lit Mag; Co-Capt Cheerleading; Var Fld Hcky; Score Keeper; Most Impvd Acad Perfm 84-85; Hcky Awd 85-86; Gwynedd-Mercey Coll; Spcl Educ.

DONOHUE, DEBBIE; Archbishop Keough HS; Balt, MD; (Y); Church Yth Grp; High Hon Roll; Hon Roll; NHS; Ntl Merit Ltr; NEDT Awd; Prfct Atten Awd; Bus.

DONOHUE, MARK; Georgetown Prep; Potomac, MD; (Y); Latin Clb; Pep Clb; School Musical; Stage Crew; Yrbk Stf; Im Bsktbl; Im Ftbl; Var L Socr; Pol Sci.

DOOLEY, DEANNA R; Sherwood HS; Brookeville, MD; (Y); Sec Jr Cls; Rep Stu Cncl; JV Bsktbl; Var Mgr(s); Var Tennis; Hon Roll; Teachers Aide; NHS; Spanish NHS; Outstndng Stu Awd 83-84; Spn NHS 84-85.

DORICS, BECKY; Great Mills HS; Lexington Park, MD; (Y); Spanish Clb; Teachers Aide; Rep Frsh Cls; Trs Soph Cls; Rep Jr Cls; Rep Stu Cncl; Hon Roll; U Of FL Gainsville; RN.

DORMAN, ADRIAN; Wicomico SR HS; Salisbury, MD; (Y); 35/244; Drama Clb; French Clb; JCL; Latin Clb; Office Aide; Pep Clb; Temple Yth Grp; Thesps; Church Choir; Symp Band; Hgh Hnr Rl 82-86; Acdmc Achvmnt Awd 83-86; Pres Schlrshp 85-86; Harcom JC; Trvl/Trsm.

DORSETT, SUSAN LYNN; North Harford HS; Fallston, MD; (Y); Church Yth Grp; Dance Clb; French Clb; Acpl Chr; Chorus; Church Choir; School Musical; School Play; Stage Crew; Yrbk Stf; Mary Washington Coll; Pre-Med.

DORSEY JR, DANIEL R; Mount Saint Joseph HS; Baltimore, MD; (Y); 100/250; Church Yth Grp; Computer Clb; FCA; Intnl Clb; Ski Clb; SADD; Church Choir; Var JV Ftbl; JV L Swmmng; Rep Stu Cncl; US Naval Acad; Aerospace.

DORSEY, HARRY; South Western HS; Baltimore, MD; (Y); Art Clb; Aud/Vis; Boys Clb Am; Church Yth Grp; Cmnty Wkr; JA; School Play; Bsktbl; Prfct Atten Awd.

DORSEY, JUDY; La Plata HS; Newburg, MD; (Y); Cmnty Wkr; FBLA; Hosp Aide; Library Aide; VP Pep Clb; Chorus; Cit Awd; Hon Roll; Prfct Atten Awd; Miss Teen Pgnt Cntstnt 85; Mrch Of Dms Wlk A Thn 85; Cmmnty Bse Lrng Srv 84-85; U Of MD Coll Prk; TV.

DORSEY, KEITH; Centennial HS; Ellicott City, MD; (Y); Ski Clb; Stage Crew; Hon Roll; Engr.

DORSEY, LISA M; South Carroll HS; Sykesville, MD; (Y); Chrmn Church Yth Grp; Drama Clb; Pres 4-H; VP Chrmn Keywanettes; Nwsp Stf; Cit Awd; Dnfth Awd; DAR Awd; 4-H Awd; Opt Clb Awd; Key Awd 85; Grand Champ Art Exhibit C C Fair 85; Red Cross Blood Dr Chrprsn 85.

DORSEY, MISSY; St Marys Ryken HS; Prince Frederick, MD; (Y); Dance Clb; DAR Awd; Hon Roll; Md Life Spprt 85; The Toy Box 85; Md Miss Teen Pgnt 85; Bus.

DORSEY, RONALD; Takoma Acad; Hyattsville, MD; (Y); Church Yth Grp; Varsity Clb; Church Choir; Drill Tm; VP Frsh Cls; Var Bsktbl; Im Ftbl; Im Socr; Im Vllybl; Mst Stu In Algebra II/Takoma Acad 85-86; Archtctr.

DORSEY, STEPHANIE; Washington SR HS; Westover, MD; (Y); Am Leg Aux Girls St; Church Yth Grp; Cmnty Wkr; Chorus; Church Choir; Jazz Band; Swing Chorus; Variety Show; Yrbk Stf; VP Stu Cncl; Kthryn Wshbrn Schlrshp 86-87; Sntrl Schlrshp 86-90; Slsbry ST Coll; Ed.

DORSEY, VERNELL; Carver Voc-Tech HS; Baltimore, MD; (Y); Church Yth Grp; Library Aide; Office Aide; Nwsp Stf; JV Badmtn; JV Bsktbl; JV Vllybl; High Hon Roll; NHS; Prfct Atten Awd; Awd Printg Clss Trd 85-86; Comp Tech.

DORSIE, EDWARD; De Matha Catholic HS; Adelphi, MD; (Y); Pep Band; Symp Band; Im Bsktbl; High Hon Roll; All ST Band 84 & 86; Comp Sci.

DORWARD, SEAN; Centennial HS; Ellicott City, MD; (Y); 4/260; Chess Clb; Teachers Aide; Concert Band; Jazz Band; Mrchg Band; Pep Band; School Musical; Symp Band; Hon Roll; NHS; Fisher Sci Co Schlrshp 86; Princton U; Med.

DOTY, ERIKA; Dulaney SR HS; Timonium, MD; (Y); Church Yth Grp; Drama Clb; French Clb; Model UN; Pep Clb; Band; Chorus; Color Guard; Concert Band; Flag Corp; Exch Stu France Rotary Intl 86-87; Teachng.

DOUGHERTY, KELLY; Allegany HS; La Vale, MD; (Y); 35/220; Drama Clb; Office Aide; Thesps; Concert Band; Mrchg Band; School Play; Hon Roll; Allegany Med Auxiliary Schlrshp; Mt Aloysius JC; Med Lab Tech.

DOUGHERTY, MARY PAT; Frederick HS; Frederick, MD; (Y); Art Clb; FBLA; Stu Cncl; Capt Cheerleading; Powder Puff Ftbl; Sftbl; Swmmng; Hon Roll; NHS; Chrldng Ldrshp Awd 85; Chrldng Best All Arnd Awd 86.

DOUGLAS, JAMES; Glenela HS; Sykesville, MD; (Y); AFS; Church Yth Grp; Exploring; Ski Clb; Varsity Clb; Ftbl; Trk; Wt Lftg; Math.

DOUGLAS, RONALD; Wicomico SR HS; Salisbury, MD; (Y); 8/243; Boy Scts; Var L Crs Cntry; Var L Trk; Cit Awd; Hon Roll; NHS; Temple Yth Grp; Band; Mrchg Band; Symp Band; Wrstlng; Gold Mdl Achvt 86; Salisbury ST Clg; Aero Engrg.

DOUGLAS, RUTH; Thomas Stone HS; Waldorf, MD; (Y); Church Yth Grp; FHA; Girl Scts; Latin Clb; Teachers Aide; Band; Concert Band; Mrchg Band; Symp Band; Trk; Myles-Andrsn Coll; Eng Teachr.

DOUGLAS, WENDY; Thomas Stone HS; Hughesville, MD; (S); FBLA; Teachers Aide; High Hon Roll; Hon Roll; Accntng.

DOVE, MARIAN L; Sherwood HS; Olney, MD; (Y); 3/317; Church Yth Grp; SADD; Bsktbl; Fld Hcky; Sftbl; Gov Hon Prg Awd; High Hon Roll; NHS; Pres Schlr; Bsktbl Scholar U Richmond 86; Faculty Awd 86; Katie Jenkins Mem Scholar 86; U Richmond; Bus.

DOVEL, MARY LU; St Vincent Pallotti HS; Glenn Dale, MD; (S); 2/136; Church Yth Grp; Ski Clb; VP Soph Cls; JV Bsktbl; Var L Socr; Var L Sftbl; French Hon Soc; High Hon Roll; NHS; Sci Fair Comm Chrmn; James Madison U; Soc Wrk.

DOWDY, MIKE; Patterson HS; Baltimore, MD; (Y); Hst Soph Cls; Hst Jr Cls; Bsbl; Ftbl; Wt Lftg; Hon Roll; Jr NHS; NHS; Electrncs.

DOWDY, RAQUEL; North East HS; Elkton, MD; (Y); 28/260; Drama Clb; Leo Clb; Pres Q&S; School Play; Nwsp Rptr; VP Stu Cncl; Hon Roll; Lion Awd; Prfct Atten Awd; Cecil Whig Schlrshp Cntys Nwsp 86; Natl Hon Soc Achvt Awd 86; Tyler Schl Art; Cmmrcl Art.

DOWER, ERIN; Mount De Sales Acad; Baltimore, MD; (Y); 1/50; Church Yth Grp; Cmnty Wkr; Dance Clb; Drama Clb; School Musical; School Play; Hon Roll; NHS; NEDT Awd; Art Clb; Lamb God Cmmnty Schl Awd Hnr 83-84; Acad Excllnce Awd; Mth.

DOWHAN, REBECCA; Gaithersburg HS; Gaithersburg, MD; (Y); Camera Clb; Key Clb; SADD; Nwsp Rptr; Yrbk Stf; Mgr(s); French Hon Soc; High Hon Roll; NHS; Yrbk Phtg; Natl Art Hnr Soc 86.

DOWNING, ANNE; Hammond HS; Columbia, MD; (Y); AFS; Church Yth Grp; German Clb; Service Clb; Teachers Aide; School Play; Stage Crew; Variety Show; Nwsp Rptr; Nwsp Stf; Intl Bus.

DOWNS, JAMES; Sherwood HS; Olney, MD; (Y); Jazz Band; Variety Show; Rep Stu Cncl; Crs Cntry; Trk; Hon Roll; NHS; Spanish NHS; Am Leg Boys St; Church Yth Grp; AFOTEC-MITE Engrng Dsgn Cont Wnnr 85; Cmmrcl Art.

DOXZEN, MARY; Western HS; Baltimore, MD; (Y); 7/412; German Clb; Yrbk Stf; Hon Roll; Jr NHS; NHS; Math.

DOYE, NICHOLE; Academy Of The Holy Names; Silver Spring, MD; (Y); Art Clb; Church Yth Grp; Chorus; Trk; Hon Roll; NHS; Natl Hnr Soc Chptr Sec 86-87; Sunday Schl & Yng Adult Usher Brd Jerusalem Bapt Chrch 86; Penn ST; Arch Dsgn.

DOYLE, JOHN; Eastern Vo Tech HS; Baltimore, MD; (Y); Sec Church Yth Grp; Ftbl; Cit Awd; Hon Roll; Comp Pgmg.

DOYLE, KEVIN F; Loyola HS; Cockeysville, MD; (S); Cmnty Wkr; FCA; Varsity Clb; JV Lcrss; JV Var Socr; Wt Lftg; Jr NHS; NHS; Opt Clb Awd.

DOYLE, MATTHEW; Washington HS; Princess Anne, MD; (Y); Church Yth Grp; Computer Clb; Ski Clb; Chorus; Church Choir; Swing Chorus; Var Score Keeper; JV Socr; Var Timer; Hon Roll; All ST Chrs 86; All Shore Chrs 85; Rotry Intl Ltr-For-Peace 86; WA Coll; Music.

DOYLE, SHANNON; Notre Dame Prep; Baltimore, MD; (Y); Cmnty Wkr; Hosp Aide; Service Clb; Im Bsktbl; Im Lcrss; Im Socr; Hon Roll; Prfct Atten Awd; File Clrk At Drs Doyle & Silber PA 84-85; Costume Comm 85; Invit Comm 85; Pre-Med.

DRADRACH, IWONA; Gaithersburg HS; Gaithersburg, MD; (Y); AFS; Church Yth Grp; Girl Scts; Intnl Clb; Key Clb; SADD; Teachers Aide; Diving; Hon Roll; Spanish NHS; MCPS Frgn Lang Awd Russian 84-86; Comp.

DRAHEIM, CHERYL; Northern HS; Huntingtown, MD; (Y); Church Yth Grp; Band; Concert Band; Mrchg Band; School Play; Symp Band; Nwsp Stf; Yrbk Ed-Chief; Capt Var Cheerleading; JV Sftbl; Liberty U Lynchburg; Jrnlsm.

DRAKE, D CRAIG; De Matha Catholic HS; Washington, DC; (Y); JA; Yrbk Sprt Ed; Yrbk Stf; Cit Awd; Hon Roll.

DRAYTON, DANTE; Forest Park HS; Baltimore, MD; (Y); Off Sr Cls; Bsbl; Swmmng; Wt Lftg; Hon Roll; Dr.

DREGIER, KATHERINE; Notre Dame Prep; Towson, MD; (Y); Church Yth Grp; Drama Clb; PAVAS; Thesps; School Musical; School Play; Pres Soph Cls; Rep Stu Cncl; Hon Roll; Theatre.

DRENNER JR, DENNIS A; Mc Donough HS; Catonsville, MD; (Y); 3/120; German Clb; Variety Show; Yrbk Phtg; Yrbk Rptr; Lit Mag; Var Golf; Hon Roll; Natnl Merit Schlrshp Commnd Stu 87; Bio.

DRESSMAN, KEVIN; Bishop Walsh HS; Frostburg, MD; (Y); 30/120; Am Leg Boys St; Church Yth Grp; Drama Clb; Band; Concert Band; Jazz Band; Mrchg Band; Orch; School Musical; Stage Crew; Music.

DRESSMAN, SHAWN; Alegany HS; Lavale, MD; (Y); Computer Clb; Drama Clb; School Play; Nwsp Rptr; Nwsp Stf; Bsbl; Bowling; Hon Roll; Jr NHS; NHS; MD Acad Of Sci Smnr 86; Engrng.

DRISCOLL, SHARON L; St Maria Goretti HS; Hagerstown, MD; (Y); 10/36; Pres Art Clb; Drama Clb; Nwsp Rptr; Yrbk Stf; Off Jr Cls; Sec Rep Stu Cncl; Tennis; High Hon Roll; Visual Arts.

DROTER, DANA; Gaithersburg HS; Gaithersburg, MD; (Y); Boys Clb Am; Church Yth Grp; Cmnty Wkr; DECA; Girl Scts; Pep Clb; PAVAS; Ski Clb; SADD; Band; Wash Pst Carrier Of Yr; Bus Admin.

DRYDEN, REBECCA; Mc Donough HS; Waldorf, MD; (Y); Church Yth Grp; Cmnty Wkr; French Clb; FBLA; Latin Clb; Office Aide; Varsity Clb; Frsh Cls; DAR Awd; NHS; PA ST; Med.

DU BRUL, JEFFREY; St Vincent Pallotti HS; Laurel, MD; (S); 18/95; AFS; Boy Scts; Library Aide; Stage Crew; Socr; Kiwanis Awd; NHS; Rotary Awd; Comp Sci Stu Mnth 84; Villanova U; Engrng.

DUBAS, KEVIN; The John Carroll Schl; Abingdon, MD; (Y); Boy Scts; Ski Clb; Band; Chorus; School Musical; Variety Show; Crs Cntry; Trk; Hon Roll; Prfct Atten Awd; Navy; Pilot.

DUCK, ELAINE T; Middletown HS; Myersville, MD; (Y); 1/200; Am Leg Aux Girls St; Church Yth Grp; Spanish Clb; Band; Var Capt Crs Cntry; Var Capt Trk; High Hon Roll; NHS; Ntl Merit SF; St Schlr; Nrsng.

DUCK JR, WILLIAM C; Prkside SR HS; Salisbury, MD; (Y); 23/231; Am Leg Boys St; Boy Scts; Computer Clb; VP French Clb; Math Tm; Varsity Clb; Crs Cntry; Mgr Wrstlng; Hon Roll; Royd A Mahafy Wicomico Cnty PTA Schlrshp 85-86; MO ST Schlrshp Awd 85-86; Exam For Bys ST 85; U MO Coll; Cmnctns.

DUCKWORTH, CARLA; Oldtown Schl; Oldtown, MD; (Y); FBLA; VP FHA; Library Aide; Office Aide; Stage Crew; Nwsp Rptr; Yrbk Rptr; Sec Stu Cncl; Var JV Cheerleading; Hon Roll; Sec Sci Schlrshp 86; Allegany CC; Leg Sec.

DUCKWORTH, LORI; Beall HS; Frostburg, MD; (Y); 4/120; Thesps; Off Drill Tm; VP Stu Cncl; St Schlr; Thesps; Chorus; Church Choir; Yrbk Bus Mgr; NHS.

DUCOTE, JOY; Perry Hall Christian HS; Baltimore, MD; (Y); Church Yth Grp; FCA; Teachers Aide; Sec Soph Cls; Sec Jr Cls; Sec Stu Cncl; Bsktbl; Vllybl; All Star Bsktbl 83-84; Most Athltc 84; Most Vlbl Plyr Bsktbl 84-86; Awd Bsktbl 86; Essex CC; Elem Ed.

DUFFY, BRUCE; Pocomoke HS; Pocomoke, MD; (S); 10/95; AFS; Aud/Vis; Church Yth Grp; Drama Clb; Mathletes; VP Science Clb; VP Band; Concert Band; Drm Mjr(t); Jazz Band; Schltc Ltr 84-85; Elec Engrng.

DULIN, PAMELA; Easton HS; Cordova, MD; (Y); Cmnty Wkr; VP 4-H; Spanish Clb; VP Vllybl; Elks Awd; Hon Roll; Md St Hrtclture Jdgng Champ 84; On Team Plcng 3rd At Ntl Hrtclture Jdgng Cntst 84; Horticulture.

DUNCAN, BRIAN; Baltimore Polytechnic Inst; Baltimore, MD; (Y); Chess Clb; Computer Clb; Intnl Clb; Letterman Clb; Library Aide; Varsity Clb; Nwsp Rptr; Bsktbl; Socr; Trk; John Hopkins U; Elec Engr.

DUNCAN, CHRISTOPHER; Mt St Joseph HS; Laurel, MD; (Y); SADD; School Musical; Stage Crew; Variety Show; Rep Soph Cls; Var L Bsktbl; Var L Trk; High Hon Roll; Hon Roll; Bus.

DUNCAN, DAVID; North Hagerstown HS; Hagerstown, MD; (Y); 32/325; Church Yth Grp; Band; Concert Band; Mrchg Band; Ftbl; Trk; Hon Roll; Ntl Merit SF; Prfct Atten Awd; Comp Sci.

DUNCAN, MELISSA L; North Harford HS; White Hall, MD; (Y); Pres French Clb; FTA; Var Capt Bsktbl; Var Capt Fld Hcky; Var Capt Sftbl; Hon Roll; NHS; 4-H; German Clb; SADD; Acad Lttr 3.5 Avg 84-85; Vrsty Athl Lttr 85-86; Tch Hstry.

DUNITHAN, VALERIE; Northern HS; Friendsville, MD; (Y); Pres Sec Church Yth Grp; Office Aide; SADD; High Hon Roll; Hon Roll; Wdmn Wrlf Lf Ins Soc Outstndng Schlstc Achvt Amer Hstry 86; Stu Mo Awd 84 & 86; Srstlng Stat 84-85; Allegany Community; Bus.

DUNN, JAMES; Baltimore Polytechnic Inst; Baltimore, MD; (Y); Library Aide; Hon Roll; Rep Soph Cls; Rep Stu Cncl; Bio.

DUNN, KATHY; Crisfield HS; Marion, MD; (Y); Sec Trs Church Yth Grp; Trs Exploring; VP VICA; Church Choir; Military Svc.

DUNN, MARY BRIGID; Immaculata College HS; Olney, MD; (Y); Dance Clb; Drama Clb; French Clb; Math Clb; Chorus; Orch; School Musical; Variety Show; Lit Mag; Opt Clb Awd; Stu Arch Discn Wshngtn Chrs 86.

DUNSEN, DANA; Western HS; Baltimore, MD; (Y); Sec Girl Scts; SADD; Church Choir; High Hon Roll; Hon Roll; Morgan ST U; Elect Engrg.

DURKAN, CIARA; Regina HS; Silver Spring, MD; (Y); Church Yth Grp; Cmnty Wkr; School Musical; Pres Soph Cls; VP Sr Cls; Var Socr; JV Sftbl; Hon Roll.

DURKIN, JENNFIER; Istitute Of Notre Dame; Baltimore, MD; (Y); Drama Clb; Political Wkr; Spanish Clb; Chorus; School Musical; School Play; Stage Crew; Yrbk Stf; Var Lcrss; Page At Md Gen Assmbly 86; Seton Hall U; Ed.

DUTTA, SUBRATA K; Eleanor Roosevelt HS; Lanham, MD; (Y); Boy Scts; Computer Clb; Exploring; German Clb; Math Tm; Radio Clb; Science Clb; Speech Tm; Hon Roll; NHS; Grmn Hnr Soc-Sec 85; Prnc Georges Cntyh Acadmc Excllnc Awd 84; Outstndng Achvt Grmn Awd 85; U Of MD; Elctrcl Engrng.

DUTY JR, CLARENCE E; Northern HS; Owings, MD; (Y); Am Leg Boys St; Boys Clb Am; Pres Church Yth Grp; ROTC; Science Clb; Stage Crew; Var L Bsbl; Opt Clb Awd; Teachers Aide; Hon Roll; Forest Mem Untd Methdst Chrch Puppet Minstry 82-86; Appalacian Srvc Proj 84-85; F Warring Snd&rec Wksh; Mittary Acad; Aerospace Engr.

DUVALL JR, DAVID L; Severna Park SR HS; Arnold, MD; (Y); Pres FBLA; Hon Roll; Computer Clb; Bsbl; Wt Lftg; U Of MD; Comp.

DUVALL, DENISE; Mercy HS; Baltimore, MD; (Y); Drama Clb; GAA; School Play; JV Bsktbl; JV Var Sftbl; JV Capt Vllybl; Hon Roll; NHS; Prfct Atten Awd; Geom Awd 85; Math Anlys Awd 86; Chem Awd 86; Chem.

DYER JR, THOMAS; Laurel HS; Laurel, MD; (Y); Ski Clb; Teachers Aide; JV Var Bsktbl; Var Capt Golf; Var L Socr; Wt Lftg; Hon Roll; U Of MD; Accntng.

DYKES, RALPH; Forestville SR HS; Forestville, MD; (Y); Math Tm; Office Aide; Varsity Clb; Capt Var Bsktbl; Ftbl; Wt Lftg; Bsktbl Varsty ST Chmpnshp 84-85; Engrng.

DYMOWSKI, KIMBERLY; Inst Of Notre Dame HS; Baltimore, MD; (Y); 3/140; Church Yth Grp; Chorus; School Musical; Rep Soph Cls; Rep Jr Cls; Hon Roll; NHS.

DYSART, MARC J; Elkton HS; Elkton, MD; (Y); Key Clb; Band; Concert Band; Jazz Band; Mrchg Band; Stu Cncl; JV Socr; Var Trk; Hon Roll; Trs NHS; Engrng.

EALY, STACEY L; Hammond HS; Columbia, MD; (Y); 11/259; French Clb; Band; Concert Band; Mrchg Band; Crs Cntry; Trk; High Hon Roll; Hon Roll; NHS; Ntl Merit SF; Natl Merit Commended Stu 85; Natl Achvt SF 85; Aerospc Engrng.

EARLE, TAMALA; Western HS; Baltimore, MD; (Y); 167/412; Hosp Aide; Varsity Clb; Rep Frsh Cls; Socr; Trk; Vllybl; MVP Awd JV Vllybl 84-85; MSYABA Champshp Tourn 3rd Pl Sngls 85; Little Flower Scr Team 81-82; Pre Law.

EARNEST, RUSSELL; Seneca Valley HS; Germantown, MD; (Y); Boy Scts; ROTC; Drill Tm; Crs Cntry; Swmmng; Trk; Wt Lftg; Hon Roll; Ldrshp Acad-ROTC 86; Mini Boot Cmp-ROTC 85-86; Exec Ofcr-NJROTC 86; U Of NM; Rstrnt Mgmt.

EASLEY, KEITH; Maurice J Mc Donough HS; Waldorf, MD; (Y); Boy Scts; Trs Church Yth Grp; Intnl Clb; Ski Clb; Teachers Aide; Var L Trk; Wt Lftg; JV Wrstlng; High Hon Roll; Hon Roll; Cert Merit By Scts 84; 2nd Pl Chrls Cnty Sci Fair 83; Spcl Prtcpnt Enrgy Sci Fair Wash DC 83; TX A&m U; Engnrng.

EASTERDAY, CARY; Smithsburg HS; Smithsburg, MD; (Y); 10/194; Pres Chess Clb; Latin Clb; Band; Concert Band; Mrchg Band; Pep Band; School Musical; Var Bsbl; Im Bsktbl; Sec NHS; OH Valley Coll; Comp.

EASTON, MICHELE; Frederick HS; Ijamsville, MD; (Y); 65/365; Pres Church Yth Grp; French Clb; JA; Office Aide; OEA; SADD; Teachers Aide; Trs Stu Cncl; French Hon Soc; Hon Roll; Ntl Leukemia Soc Awd-Bus 85; Bus Ed Awd 85; FCC VA U; Med Fld.

EATON, JAIME; Mercy HS; Baltimore, MD; (Y); Hon Roll; Spd & Accrcy Typg I 85-86; A Avg US Hstry 85-86; Mstrng Stengrphy I 85-86; Bus.

EATON, RONALD; Northern HS; Baltimore, MD; (Y); Church Yth Grp; Computer Clb; Political Wkr; Stu Cncl; Swmmng; Hon Roll; Hampton Inst; Comp Sci.

EBELEIN, DENISE; Mercy HS; Baltimore, MD; (Y); Church Yth Grp; Cmnty Wkr; GAA; VP Spanish Clb; Trs Soph Cls; Rep Jr Cls; Sec Sr Cls; Rep Stu Cncl; Var Bsktbl; JV Var Sftbl; JV MVP Sftbl 84.

EBELKE, PATRICIA; Arundel SR HS; Gambrills, MD; (Y); 56/455; Drama Clb; Key Clb; Letterman Clb; Natl Beta Clb; SADD; Chorus; Rep Stu Cncl; Var Capt Bsktbl; Var L Socr; Var L Sftbl; 4 Seasons Womns Clb Scholar 86; All Cnty Socr & SR All Star 85-86; Acad Achvt Awd 86; Towson ST U; Occ Ther.

ECCLES, LA JUAN; Suitland HS; District Height, MD; (Y); Library Aide; Teachers Aide; Gym; Hon Roll; Certfct Comptn Chld Develpmnt I II 85-86; Gen Attrctvnss Neatness 83; Accntnt.

ECHEVARRIA, VERONICA; La Plata HS; Waldorf, MD; (Y); Church Yth Grp; Dance Clb; Girl Scts; Office Aide; Teachers Aide; Band; Concert Band; Jazz Band; Hon Roll; Prfct Atten Awd; Teacher Aide Awd-Spnsh Cls 85-6; Travel Agnt.

ECKLER, RHONDA; Great Mills HS; Lexington Prk, MD; (Y); 4-H; Office Aide; Pep Clb; Teachers Aide; Color Guard; Yrbk Stf; Rep Sr Cls; 4-H Awd; Hon Roll; Southern Sem JC; Bus Mgt.

ECKLOFF, SUZANNE; Dundalk HS; Baltimore, MD; (Y); 2/354; Varsity Clb; Trs Jr Cls; Rep Stu Cncl; JV Badmtn; Var Fld Hcky; JV Socr; JV Var Sftbl; Var Trk; High Hon Roll; Trs NHS; Distngshd Hnrs Awd 83-84 & 84-85; Cert NHS 85; Svc Awd 85; Coll Notre Dame; Phys Thrpy.

ECKSTORM, LISA ANN; Elizabeth Secton HS; Greenbelt, MD; (Y); Church Yth Grp; Hosp Aide; Pep Clb; Ski Clb; Trk; Prince Georges CC; Nrsg.

EDA, SERLE; Oxon Hill Science & Tech Ctr; Oxon Hill, MD; (Y); Intnl Clb; Letterman Clb; Office Aide; Yrbk Stf; Hst Sr Cls; Stat Bsbl; JV Capt Cheerleading; Hon Roll; Jr NHS; VFW Awd; Miss Vlntns-Prgrssv Allnc-Flpino Amer 86; Comps Sci.

EDELMAN, TAMARA; Eastern Voc-Tech HS; Baltimore, MD; (Y); FBLA; Office Aide; VICA; Lit Mag; Law.

EDELMANN, PAUL; Liberty HS; Ellicott City, MD; (S); 15/350; Mathletes; Teachers Aide; Varsity Clb; Var L Ftbl; Hon Roll; Ntl Merit Ltr; U MD; Comp Sci.

EDGECOMBE, NICOLE; Oakland Mills HS; Columbia, MD; (Y); Spanish Clb; Sec Frsh Cls; Sec Soph Cls; VP Jr Cls; VP Sr Cls; Rep Stu Cncl; JV Var Bsktbl; JV Sftbl; Hon Roll; NHS; Black Awareness Clb 85-86; Brown U; Bus.

EDMISTON, DEBORAH; Overlea HS; Baltimore, MD; (Y); Varsity Clb; Band; Yrbk Stf; Off Sr Cls; Var Cheerleading; Capt Powder Puff Ftbl; Capt Var Sftbl; Var Vllybl; Hon Roll; Rosedale Vol Fire Dept 86; Overlea HS Class 86; U MD Balto Co; Inf Sys Mgt.

EDWARDS, BELINDA; Andover SR HS; Glen Burnie, MD; (Y); 50/291; VP Church Yth Grp; Teachers Aide; Church Choir; Yrbk Stf; Rep Stu Cncl; Capt Bowling; L Cheerleading; L Pom Pon; L Sftbl; Hon Roll; Cert Achvmnt Adv Cmptr Stdies 85; IN Inst Tchnlgy; Cmptr Sci.

EDWARDS, BRIAN; Mc Donough HS; White Plains, MD; (Y); Am Leg Boys St; Jazz Band; Symp Band; Var L Ftbl; Var Capt Tennis; Hon Roll; Prfct Atten Awd.

EDWARDS, HANS; Dematha Catholic HS; Hyattsville, MD; (Y); SADD; Concert Band; Pep Band; Hon Roll; Band Awd 84-85 & 85-86; Maryland U; Elec Engnr.

EDWARDS, RENEE; Bethesda-Chevy Chase HS; Silver Spring, MD; (Y); Aud/Vis; Church Yth Grp; Chorus; Coach Actv; Mgr(s); Timer; Co-Capt Trk; Wt Lftg; French Hon Soc; Hon Roll; Hme Eco-Chld Devlpmnt Lab Awd 86; Svnteen Mgzn Btywrks Mdlng Cert 84; Cert-Jnne Brks Prdctn Fshn Shw; Engrng.

EDWARDS, RICHARD I; High Point HS; Adelphi, MD; (Y); 43/655; Am Leg Boys St; Church Yth Grp; L ROTC; Drill Tm; Im Stat Bsbl; Im Mgr Ftbl; Hon Roll; Prfct Atten Awd; Band; Im Bsktbl; VA Tech Smmr Engr Inst 85; Natl Achvt Schlrshp Top 7%; Outstndg Negro Stus Pgm 85; US Naval Acad; Aerosp Engr.

EGAN, ERIN; Walt Whitman HS; Bethesda, MD; (Y); 4-H; JA; Keywanettes; Pep Clb; Yrbk Rptr; Yrbk Stf; Off Soph Cls; Stu Cncl; Mgr(s); Pom Pon; 4-H Tp Modl Awd 81.

EGAN, THOMAS; North Hagerstown HS; Hagerstown, MD; (Y); Latin Clb; Rep Frsh Cls; Rep Stu Cncl; Var JV Bsktbl; Hon Roll; Duquesne; Bus Adm.

EGAN III, THOMAS J; Loyola HS; Baltimore, MD; (S); Yrbk Bus Mgr; Ftbl; Wrstlng; Hon Roll; NHS; U Of VA; Bus.

EGELI, ANASTASIA H; Severn Schl; Edgewater, MD; (Y); Variety Show; Fld Hcky; Gym; Lcrss; Powder Puff Ftbl; High Hon Roll; Hon Roll; Chairprsn Entertnmnt Commtte 86; U MD; Art.

EHMIG, MARYANN; Mount De Sales Acad; Baltimore, MD; (Y); 9/45; Chorus; Pres Soph Cls; JV Cheerleading; JV L Lcrss; L Var Mgr(s); Hon Roll; Prfct Atten Awd; Church Yth Grp; Baltimroe Cty Page Ct; Art Awd; Svc Awd; Pilot.

EHRLICH, GARY J; Charles E Smith Jewish Day Schl; Rockville, MD; (Y); French Clb; Temple Yth Grp; Yrbk Stf; French Hon Soc; NHS; MD ST Schlrshp 86; Johns Hopkins U; Cvl Engrng.

EHRMANTRAUT, MARY; Connelly Schl Of The Holy Child; Rockville, MD; (Y); Cmnty Wkr; Drama Clb; Red Cross Aide; Service Clb; SADD; Church Choir; School Play; Fld Hcky; Mgr(s); NHS; Jan Norton Memrl Schlrshp 85; Pedtrcn.

EINHAUS, JOHN; John Carroll School; Fawn Grove, PA; (Y); German Clb; Library Aide; Chorus; School Musical; Hon Roll; Ntl Merit Ltr; Adv Stdnt Peabody Prep, 6 Yr Schlrshp, Awd Peabody; Aerontcl Engrng.

EISELE, JAMES M; Good Counsel HS; Brookeville, MD; (Y); 5/228; Latin Clb; Capt Math Tm; Office Aide; Nwsp Stf; JV Golf; Var L Tennis; High Hon Roll; NHS; Ntl Merit Ltr; St Schlr; Schlrshp Loyole Coll VA Tech U Of MD 86; Archbishops Ctznshp Awd 86; Presdntl Acad Ftns Awd 86; Loyole Coll; Bus.

EISENTROUT, LADA; Allegany HS; La Vale, MD; (Y); 30/220; Church Yth Grp; Office Aide; Ski Clb; JV Var Cheerleading; JV Socr; JV Sftbl; JV Var Trk; JV Vllybl; Hon Roll; NHS; Frostburg ST Coll; Phrmcy.

EL-SHAMMAA, EMILE; Magruder HS; Rockville, MD; (Y); Church Yth Grp; Ski Clb; JV Socr; Var Trk; JV Var Vllybl; Hon Roll; Sci.

ELBURN JR, WILTON; Franklin HS; Reisterstown, MD; (Y); Church Yth Grp; Debate Tm; Mrchg Band; Swing Chorus; Nwsp Rptr; VP Sr Cls; Stu Cncl; JV Var Bsktbl; JV Var Socr; Cit Awd; Franklnshp Awd 86; WA Coll Schlstc Schlrshp 86; Bradey Sounders Hnrs Schlrshp-Lynchburg Coll 86; WA Coll; Pre-Med.

ELDER, MELANIE; La Plata HS; La Plata, MD; (S); Am Leg Aux Girls St; Ski Clb; Off Soph Cls; Off Jr Cls; Off Stu Cncl; JV Var Cheerleading; Var Trk; Stat Wrstlng; Hon Roll; Jr NHS; Gftd & Tlntd Prog 83-86; Phy Thrpst.

ELDRETH, KIM; Elkton HS; Elkton, MD; (Y); 8/289; Office Aide; Pep Clb; Concert Band; Mrchg Band; School Musical; Nwsp Stf; Stu Cncl; High Hon Roll; Hon Roll; NHS; Kenmore Elem Schl Acad Schlrshp 86; United Meth Men Schlrshp 86; Pres & Govrn Awd 86; U DE; Mdsng.

ELGIN, DARBY; Gaithersburg HS; Gaithersburg, MD; (Y); Trs Art Clb; SADD; Stage Crew; Yrbk Stf; Chess Clb; Swmmng; Comm.

ELKINGTON, CHRIS; The Key Schl; Annapolis, MD; (Y); Drama Clb; School Play; Chrmn Stage Crew; Variety Show; Yrbk Phtg; Var Co-Capt Lcrss; Var Co-Capt Socr; Nwsp Phtg; Nwsp Rptr; Im Bsktbl; All Independnt Coaches Boys Soccr Tm 85.

ELLERBE, CARLOS; Oxon Hill HS; Oxon Hill, MD; (Y); Var Wrstlng; High Hon Roll; Hon Roll; Spanish NHS; Prince Georges Acad Excllnce Awd 84 & 85; Pres Acad Fit Awd 86; ST MD Merit Schltc Awd 86; U MD College Pk; CPA.

ELLIOTT, GWEN; Northern HS; Huntingtown, MD; (Y); Church Yth Grp; JV Var Bsktbl; Var Fld Hcky; Var Trk; Hon Roll; Prfct Atten Awd; Wnnr Science Fair 86; James Madison U; Acctg.

ELLIOTT, ROBYN; North Hagerstown HS; Hagestown, MD; (Y); 1/300; Drama Clb; Key Clb; Red Cross Aide; Teachers Aide; Yrbk Ed-Chief; Rep Jr Cls; Dnfth Awd; High Hon Roll; NHS.

ELLIOTT, TAMARA; Bishop Walsh HS; Cumberland, MD; (Y); 41/101; Pep Clb; Service Clb; Yrbk Rptr; Yrbk Stf; Cheerleading; Trk; Hon Roll; Advncd Plcmnt Amercn Hstry 86-87; Engl.

ELLIS, CAROLYN; Fort Hill HS; Miami, FL; (Y); Trs Computer Clb; Hosp Aide; Thesps; Flag Corp; Nwsp Stf; Soph Cls; Jr Cls; Sr Cls; Stu Cncl; Var Trk; Ltrd Vrsty Trck 82-86; FL Intl U.

ELLIS, DORETHA; Eastern HS; Baltimore, MD; (Y); 2/300; JA; High Hon Roll; Pres Schlr; Sal; St Schlr; 1st Grade Peabody Mdl 86; Awd From Govnr Of ST Of MD For Acad Achvt 86; CC Of Baltimore; Comp Sci.

ELLIS, ERIN; Liberty HS; Eldersburg, MD; (S); Spanish Clb; Hon Roll; NEDT Awd; Prfct Atten Awd; Acad Ltr & Pns 82-85; Millersville U; Spcl Educ.

ELLIS, LESLIE; Southern Garrett HS; Mt Lake Pk, MD; (Y); Q&S; Nwsp Phtg; Nwsp Rptr; Nwsp Stf; VP Bsktbl; Off Sftbl; Var Capt Vllybl; Hon Roll; Pres Acad Ftns Awd 86; U Of MD; Elem Educ.

ELLIS, STEVE B; Gaithersburg HS; Gaithersburg, MD; (Y); 100/568; FBLA; German Clb; VP Intnl Clb; Ski Clb; SADD; Varsity Clb; Off Jr Cls; Stu Cncl; Capt Ftbl; Capt Trk; Sam & Esther Eig Rotary Schlrshp Awd 86-87; John W Griffith Mem Schlrshp Intern 86-87; U Of Notre Dame; Aerosp Engrng.

ELLIS, VICTORIA; St Michaels HS; Bozman, MD; (Y); 5/60; Band; Church Choir; Concert Band; Drm Mjr(t); Jazz Band; Mrchg Band; Pep Band; Nwsp Ed-Chief; Tennis; NCTE Awd; Nellie Ward Nance Schlrshp 86; Talbot Cnty Educ Assn Awd 86; Talbot Cnty Prfrmng Arts Soc Awd 86; Longwood Coll; Secndry Eng Educ.

EMBODY, STACY; Laplata HS; Waldorf, MD; (Y); FHA; Hosp Aide; SADD; Swmmng; Trk; Wt Lftg; Prncpls Awd Hlth Occptns 86; Physcl Thrpy.

EMGE, CATHERINE; Arlington Baptist HS; Millersville, MD; (Y); Church Yth Grp; Church Choir; Yrbk Ed-Chief; Yrbk Stf; Yearbk Hnr For Outstndng Wrk 86; Educ.

EMLEY, MEG; Mcdonough HS; Pt Tobacco, MD; (Y); Church Yth Grp; Dance Clb; Drama Clb; 4-H; Intnl Clb; Teachers Aide; Thesps; Chorus; School Musical; School Play; Pass Cecchetti Grds I And II 83-84; Hnr Rll 84-86; Acctpnc Sch Of Ballt 86; Pro Dncr.

ENDERS, MICHELE MARIE; Arlington Baptist HS; Baltimore, MD; (Y); 2/100; Trs Soph Cls; Trs Jr Cls; Trs Sr Cls; Var Bsktbl; Score Keeper; Cit Awd; Hon Roll; NHS; Prfct Atten Awd; Sal; MD ST Schrlshp Awd 86; Eng Awd Exc Compstn Spch 86; U MD; Physcl Sci.

ENG, DENNIS; Laurel HS; Laurel, MD; (Y); Teachers Aide; Im Bsktbl; Hon Roll; Acad Excel Awd 84-85; Hstry Hnr 85-86; U Of MD; Bus Ec.

ENGEN, BRITT; Montrose Christian HS; Rockville, MD; (Y); Ski Clb; Yrbk Stf; Pres Jr Cls; Pres Stu Cncl; Var Capt Bsktbl; Var Capt Socr; Var Swmmng; Var Trk; Cit Awd; Hon Roll; Female Athlt Of The Yr 85-86; Coaches Sprtsmnshp Awd 85; MVP Bsktbl Trck 85-86; Cmrcl Art.

ENGLAND, HOLLY; Elkton Christian HS; Rising Sun, MD; (S); Church Yth Grp; Chorus; High Hon Roll; Hon Roll; NHS; Nrsng.

ENNIS, DEAN; Pocomoke HS; Pocomoke, MD; (Y); AFS; Am Leg Boys St; Drama Clb; 4-H; FBLA; SADD; Teachers Aide; Stu Cncl; Mgr(s); 4-H Awd.

ENO, JACKIE; Surrattsville HS; Clinton, MD; (Y); Cmnty Wkr; Teachers Aide; Capt Co-Capt Flag Corp; School Musical; School Play; Yrbk Stf; Hon Roll; Schltc Achvt Awd 84; PG Comm; Acctg.

ENOFF, MARSHA; South Carroll HS; Sykesville, MD; (Y); Church Yth Grp; Spanish Clb; Teachers Aide; Varsity Clb; Jazz Band; Socr; NHS; Concert Band; Mrchg Band; House Of Delg Schlrp 86; Deans Schlrp Western MD Coll 86; Merit Schlstc Awd 86; Western MD Coll; Psychol.

ENSMINGER, KAREN M; Mount Sauage Schl; Corriganville, MD; (Y); 1/61; French Clb; Pep Clb; Q&S; Teachers Aide; Chorus; Yrbk Ed-Chief; Hon Roll; NHS; Val; Dstngshd Schlr Schlrshp Awd 86-87; Sntrl Schlrshp 86-90; Grdtn Math Svgs Bnd 86; Frostburg ST Coll; Math Educ.

ENSOR, MARIE; North Harford HS; White Hall, MD; (Y); FTA; Spanish Clb; Teachers Aide; Nwsp Ed-Chief; Lit Mag; Rep Soph Cls; High Hon Roll; Sec NHS; Prfct Atten Awd; Hugh O Brian Schlrshp 84-85; Bus.

EPP, TERESA M; Liberty HS; Eldersburg, MD; (Y); Exploring; German Clb; Band; School Play; Var Crs Cntry; JV Socr; Gov Hon Prg Awd; High Hon Roll; NHS; Pres Schlr; Germn Hnr Soc 86; U MD Baltimore; Pre-Med.

EPSTEIN, JESSICA L; Winston Churchill HS; Potomac, MD; (Y); 56/602; Debate Tm; French Clb; Drm Mjr(t); Crs Cntry; Swmmng; Hon Roll; NHS; Indstrl Engrng.

EPSTEIN, PAMELA; C E S Jewish Day Schl; Silver Spring, MD; (Y); Cmnty Wkr; Temple Yth Grp; Chorus; School Musical; School Play; Yrbk Stf; Rep Soph Cls; Rep Stu Cncl; Stat Bsktbl; Var L Vllybl; Excllnc Engl 83-84; Excllnc Physcl Educ 84-85; Excllnc Hstry, Rlgs Stdy 85-86.

ERENBERG, ROBERT S; Hammond HS; Laurel, MD; (Y); CAP; Ski Clb; Var L Ftbl; Var L Lcrss; Wt Lftg; Var L Wrstlng; Jet Fghtr Pilot.

ERVIN, JENNIFER A; Notre Dame Prep; Glen Arm, MD; (Y); 11/119; Math Tm; Chorus; Yrbk Stf; Lit Mag; High Hon Roll; NHS; Prfct Atten Awd; Spanish NHS; Notr Dame Prep Schlrshp 82-86; NEDT Awd 82; Loyola Coll.

ESBORG, ERIK; The Key Schl; Bowie, MD; (Y); Boy Scts; Chorus; School Play; Eagle Scout 83; 2nd Pl Heidelberg Chmpnsps-European Forces Swm League 80; U Of CA Santa Cruz; Bus.

ESCALANTE, ANGELI A; Archbishop Keongh HS; Baltimore, MD; (Y); FBLA; Trs Spanish Clb; Ed Lit Mag; Rep Soph Cls; Rep Jr Cls; Rep Sr Cls; Rep Stu Cncl; Var Lcrss; Var Vllybl; Hon Roll; Coucher Coll Schlrshp 86; Coucher Coll; Bus Mgmt.

ESKUT, KATHLEEN; South Carroll HS; Woodbine, MD; (Y); Band; Concert Band; Mrchg Band; Orch; Rep Soph Cls; Powder Puff Ftbl; Gov Hon Prg Awd; Hon Roll; Teachers Aide; Deans Schlrshp Western MD College 86; Gvrnrs Mrtrs Schlrshp Awd 86; Advncd Acclrtd Acdmc Crtfct 86; Wstrn MD Coll; Blgy.

ESSIG, WENDY; Northern HS; Huntingtown, MD; (Y); Girl Scts; Hosp Aide; Teachers Aide; Flag Corp; Stu Cncl; MD ST Schlrshp 86; Washngtn Coll 86; Washington Coll; Pre-Med.

ESTEVEZ, MARY; La Plata HS; La Plata, MD; (Y); Art Clb; Teachers Aide; High Hon Roll; Hon Roll; Natl Hstry & Govt Awd 86.

ETTMAN, ALYSON; Thomas S Wootton HS; Potomac, MD; (Y); AFS; Service Clb; SADD; Hon Roll; Entrnmnt Ind.

ETZLER, JANICE M; Capital Lutheran HS; Sanderland, MD; (S); Church Yth Grp; Teachers Aide; Chorus; Church Choir; School Play; Variety Show; Rep Jr Cls; Rep Stu Cncl; L Sftbl; L Vllybl; Accntnt.

EUKER, KATIE; Dulaney SR HS; Phoenix, MD; (Y); Church Yth Grp; Band; Church Choir; Pep Band; Variety Show; Soph Cls; Fld Hcky; Lcrss; Hon Roll; Jr NHS; MD All Star Swmtm Eastern Zones 83 & 84; Commercial Art.

EUTSLER, KARL; Franklin HS; Reisterstown, MD; (Y); Band; Mrchg Band; School Musical; Symp Band; Rep Frsh Cls; Bsbl; Bsktbl; High Hon Roll; Hon Roll; NHS; U Of MD; Bus Mgmt.

EVANS, AARON S; Oxon HS; Andrews AFB, DC; (Y); 58/581; Boy Scts; Church Yth Grp; ROTC; Science Clb; High Hon Roll; Ntl Merit Ltr; Germ NHS 85; Outstndng Stu Awd Excllnce 85; Prince Georges Cnty Awd Acad Excllnce 85; Physics.

EVANS, ANDREA; Thomas S Wootton HS; Gaithersburg, MD; (Y); AFS; Hosp Aide; Variety Show; Yrbk Ed-Chief; Pom Pon; NHS; NEDT Awd; Rotary Awd; Intl Rltns.

EVANS, ANN MARIE; Gaithersburg HS; Gaithersburg, MD; (S); Art Clb; DECA; SADD; Band; Mrchg Band; Pep Band; Hon Roll; MD St DECA Parliamentarian 85-86; Cmmrcl Art.

EVANS, ANTHONY; Baltimore City College HS; Baltimore, MD; (S); Boy Scts; Church Yth Grp; Cmnty Wkr; Church Choir; Rep Frsh Cls; JV Capt Bsbl; High Hon Roll; Hon Roll; NHS; Prfct Atten Awd; Smnr Emplymnt Coll 85-89; MD; Bus Law.

EVANS, COLLEEN; Institute Of Notre Dame; Baltimore, MD; (Y); 46/145; Var Lcrss; High Hon Roll; Church Yth Grp; Cmnty Wkr; GAA; Varsity Clb; Rep Frsh Cls; Rep Stu Cncl; Im Bsktbl; Score Keeper; U Of Maryland Collage Park; Med.

EVANS JR, DALE ESTEL; Southern Garret Co HS; Mtn Lake Pk, MD; (Y); 18/225; Church Yth Grp; Cmnty Wkr; Hon Roll; Lion Awd; NHS; Pres Schlr; Garrett Cnty Voctnl Drftng Awd 86; Lions Clb Awd Drftng 86; Vctnl Stu Mnth Awd 86; WV U; Mech Engr.

EVANS, DAVID; Gaithersburg HS; Gaithersburg, MD; (S); 28/568; Boy Scts; Var L Trk; Var L Vllybl; Hon Roll; NHS; Bus.

EVANS, JEFFREY M; Winston Churchill HS; Potomac, MD; (Y); Church Yth Grp; Crs Cntry; Swmmng; GA Inst Of Tech; Engrng.

EVANS, JOHN D; Southern Garrett HS; Oakland, MD; (S); Church Yth Grp; Var Ftbl; Var Wrstlng; Hon Roll; NHS; Engrng.

EVANS, JULIE; Dulaney SR HS; Phoenix, MD; (Y); Chorus; Stat DECA; Var Golf; Stat Socr; Jr NHS.

EVANS, KELLEY; Southern Garrett HS; Oakland, MD; (Y); Pres Church Yth Grp; JV Vllybl; Hon Roll; NHS; Stu Of Mnth Sci Jan 86; Vet Sci.

EVANS, KELLY; Forest Park HS; Baltimore, MD; (Y); FHA; Church Choir; Score Keeper; Swmmng.

EVANS, LINDA; Maurice J Mc Donough HS; Waldorf, MD; (Y); Math Tm; SADD; Symp Band; High Hon Roll; Band; Concert Band; Mrchg Band; Pep Band; Hon Roll; Prfct Atten Awd.

EVANS, MYRTLE SYLEN; Forest Park HS; Baltimore, MD; (Y); JA; Library Aide; Office Aide; Hon Roll; Sec NHS; 1st Pl Wnnr Of Blck Hstry Cntst For Bltmr City Pblc Schl Systm 86; U Of MD; Law.

EVANS, SHERRELL E; Western HS; Baltimore, MD; (Y); 16/420; Debate Tm; French Clb; Political Wkr; Scholastic Bowl; Spanish Clb; Nwsp Rptr; Nwsp Sprt Ed; Lit Mag; Ntl Merit Ltr; Spanish NHS; Intl Schllr Inst Ptry Cntst Hnrbl Ment; Sndy Nrsry Drctr 85; MD U Acad Schlrshp 85; Intl Rltns.

EVERETT, GERTRUDE TRUDY; Easteau HS; Baltimore, MD; (Y); Church Yth Grp; Cmnty Wkr; Library Aide; Office Aide; Teachers Aide; Chorus; Church Choir; Variety Show; Rep Stu Cncl; Bowling.

EVERHART, JEANINE; St Vincent Pallotti HS; New Carrollton, MD; (S); 10/115; Ski Clb; Pom Pon; Hon Roll; U MD.

EVERITT, ANN E; Gaithersburg HS; Gaithersburg, MD; (S); 38/568; German Clb; Band; Symp Band; Hon Roll; Ntl Merit SF; PA ST U.

EVERLY, KELLY; North Kagerstown HS; Hagerstown, MD; (Y); 14/277; Church Yth Grp; Key Clb; Latin Clb; Band; Chorus; Church Choir; Drm Mjr(t); Hon Roll; Ntl Merit Ltr; Prfct Atten Awd; Hagerstown JC; Nrsng.

EYLER, SCOT; Catoctin HS; Thurmont, MD; (Y); 4/190; Computer Clb; Science Clb; Teachers Aide; VP VICA; NHS; All Am Acdmc Bus Awd 85; Math Hnr 85-86; St MD Merit Schlstc Awd 86; Shepherd Coll; Bus Admin.

FACCHINA, PAUL; Maurice J Mc Donough HS; La Plata, MD; (Y); Office Aide; Varsity Clb; Var Ftbl; Var Trk; Var Wt Lftg; JV Wrstlng; Hon Roll; NHS; Villanova.

FACELLO, MICHAEL; Eastrn Vocational Technical HS; Baltimore, MD; (Y); Sec Church Yth Grp; Computer Clb; Trs FBLA; Teachers Aide; Chorus; Church Choir; Tennis; Hon Roll; Trs NHS; Ntl Merit Ltr; Johns Hopkins U; Elec Engr.

FADDIS, TRACY; Glenelg HS; Sykesville, MD; (Y); Dance Clb; Drama Clb; Pep Clb; Teachers Aide; Varsity Clb; School Play; Variety Show; Sec Sr Cls; Cheerleading; Hon Roll; Towson ST U; Dance.

FADELY, JOHN R; Mcdonogh HS; Ellicott City, MD; (Y); 2/135; AFS; French Clb; Orch; Nwsp Stf; Off Frsh Cls; Off Jr Cls; Off Sr Cls; Stu Cncl; Trk; High Hon Roll; Awd German Govt AFS 85; Awd Bst Wrtr Jr Clss 85; Awd Gen Acadmc Exclinc 85; Princeton U; Psychtry.

FADER, JENNIFER LYN; Linganore HS; Mt Airy, MD; (Y); 26/263; Sec Church Yth Grp; Girl Scts; Intnl Clb; Sec Spanish Clb; Teachers Aide; JV Fld Hcky; Powder Puff Ftbl; Var L Socr; Var L Swmmng; Grl Sct Gold Awd 85; Frostburg ST Coll; Elem Ed.

FAHNBULLEH, JANII; Duval HS; Landover Hills, MD; (S); Aud/Vis; Boy Scts; Computer Clb; Mgr Band; Concert Band; Jazz Band; Yrbk Stf; Pom Pon; Mgr Socr; Towson ST Coll; Comptr Sci.

FAIR, BRIAN; Linganore HS; Ijamsville, MD; (Y); Am Leg Boys St; Church Yth Grp; Computer Clb; Intnl Clb; Ski Clb; Hon Roll; Elec Engnrng.

FAIRFAX, KATIE; St Marys Ryken HS; Lexington Park, MD; (S); 15/138; VP FBLA; CC Awd; High Hon Roll; NHS; NEDT Awd; Distgshd Schlr Semi Fnlst MD 85; Frnch I, II Awds 83-85; Alg II, Soc Stds Awds 85; St Marys Coll MD; Chldhd Ed.

FAITH, MICHAEL; Hancock HS; Hancock, MD; (Y); Teachers Aide; Im Bsktbl; Var L Ftbl; Cit Awd; Elks Awd; Hon Roll; Hrrcn Islnd Outwrd Bnd Schl Schlrshp 84; Hgrstwn JC; Elec Engrng.

FANFLIK, PATRICIA; Wheaton HS; Rockville, MD; (Y); Dance Clb; French Clb; Pep Clb; SADD; Chorus; Yrbk Stf; Rep Frsh Cls; Pom Pon; Hon Roll; Math Schlr Awd 84; Pom Pon Athl Awd 84 & 85; U Of MD; Chld Psych.

FANUCCI, DARA; Rising Sun HS; Cloraa, MD; (Y); Church Yth Grp; Computer Clb; Pep Clb; Frsh Cls; Soph Cls; Jr Cls; Sr Cls; Stu Cncl; Bsktbl; Fld Hcky; Cls Athl; All Cnty Fld Hcky; All Cnty Bsktbl; Frostburg ST; Psych.

FARKASH, KATHLEEN; Highland View Acad; Quakertown, PA; (Y); Art Clb; Drama Clb; Ski Clb; Jazz Band; Lit Mag; Trs Soph Cls; Vllybl; High Hon Roll; Hon Roll; Jr NHS; Columbia Union Coll; Elem Educt.

FARLEY, RONALD; Patterson HS; Baltimore, MD; (Y); 10/300; SADD; Bsbl; Ftbl; Golf; Wt Lftg; Hon Roll; Vrsty Bsbl Ltr 84-85; Ltrs Bsbl, Ftbl, Weightlftng Trphy Awd 85-86; Law.

FARMER, MARY REBECCA; Governor Thomas Johnson HS; Frederick, MD; (Y); 85/323; Church Yth Grp; Pres FNA; Hosp Aide; Latin Clb; Quiz Bowl; Hon Roll; Most Outstndng Vo Stu, Bedside Nrs 84-85; 1st Pl Med Spelling ST Competition 84-86; Natl Spch Finlst; York Coll PA; Nrs.

FARMER, STEVEN; Governor Thomas Johnson HS; Frederick, MD; (Y); Church Yth Grp; 4-H; Bsbl; Outstndng Stu Vo-Tech Cert Accomplshmnt 85-86; Pres Schlrshp TN Temple U 86; TN Temple U; Educ.

FARNSWORTH, SYLVIA; Thomas Stone HS; Waldorf, MD; (S); Church Yth Grp; Teachers Aide; Var JV Vllybl; Charles Cnty CC 85-86; Charles Cnty CC; Actg.

FARR, SALLY; Maurice J Mc Donough HS; Waldorf, MD; (Y); Art Clb; Dance Clb; Drama Clb; Hosp Aide; Office Aide; Speech Tm; Thesps; School Musical; School Play; Rep Frsh Cls; Nrsng.

FARRA, JULIE; Wicomico SR HS; Salisbury, MD; (Y); Art Clb; Cmnty Wkr; Office Aide; Band; Concert Band; Var L Crs Cntry; JV Trk; Hon Roll; MD Miss TEEN Cont 86; Wicomico Cnty Sci Fair 2nd Pl 85; Vet Med.

FARRELL, RONALD; La Plata HS; Cobb Island, MD; (Y); Chess Clb; Ski Clb; Spanish Clb; Teachers Aide; Hon Roll; Prfct Atten Awd.

FARRINGTON, ERIC; North Harford HS; Jarrettsville, MD; (Y); Sec Am Leg Boys St; Church Yth Grp; Varsity Clb; JV Var Bsbl; JV Var Bsktbl; Hon Roll; Church Sftbl Tm & Soundroom Crew 86; Embry-Ridl Aerntcl U; Aviatn.

FARRIS, JENIFER; Atholton HS; Ellicott City, MD; (Y); Letterman Clb; Hon Roll; Var L Cheerleading; Var JV Gym; L Mgr(s); Stat Trk.

FARVER, ROBERT; Mc Donough HS; La Plata, MD; (Y); Church Yth Grp; Computer Clb; Math Tm; Q&S; Yrbk Stf; Chess Clb; Office Aide; Navy; Comp Sci.

FAULCONER, M CONWAY; The Gunston Schl; Orange, VA; (Y); Science Clb; Chorus; Rep Stu Cncl; Var Fld Hcky; Var Ice Hcky; Im Socr; Var Sftbl; Hnr Cts Hona Awd 84; Sterling Soc 85; Paul M Long Awd 86; Math.

FAULKNER, JACK A; Southern Garrett HS; Deer Park, MD; (S); 31/222; Band; Concert Band; Mrchg Band; School Play; Phrmcst.

FAURE-DIAZ, MIRIAM; Mercy HS; Baltimore, MD; (Y); Drama Clb; Model UN; Spanish Clb; School Play; Trk; Hon Roll; Pblc Rel II 85-86; Our Lady Of Perpetual Help Parish; Howard U; Lwyr.

FAUST, BRYON; Clear Spring HS; Clear Spg, MD; (Y); 18/125; Church Yth Grp; Cmnty Wkr; Ski Clb; SADD; Church Choir; Yrbk Bus Mgr; Rep Jr Cls; Hon Roll; NHS; Prom Cmmtt 85-86; Engrng.

FAY, STEVEN; The Bullis Schl; Potomac, MD; (Y); Boy Scts; Church Yth Grp; Cmnty Wkr; Key Clb; Letterman Clb; Varsity Clb; Bsbl; Ftbl; Wt Lftg; Hon Roll; Villanova; Bus.

FAZENBAKER, KIMBERLY M; Valley HS; Barton, MD; (Y); Q&S; Ski Clb; Teachers Aide; Yrbk Ed-Chief; Sec Stu Cncl; Capt Cheerleading; Hon Roll; Frostburg ST Coll; Elem Educ.

FEAGAN, KEVIN; Gwynn Park HS; Clinton, MD; (Y); Church Yth Grp; Library Aide; ROTC; SADD; VICA; Chorus; Church Choir; Rep Jr Cls; Var Bsktbl; Hon Roll; Prince Georges Cnty Hnrs Chrs 83-84; MD All-ST Choir 84; Prnc Georges Cnty Hnrs Chrs 84-85; Econ.

FEASTER, CYNTHIA; Western SR HS; Baltimore, MD; (Y); 108/412; Church Yth Grp; Church Choir; Concert Band; Mrchg Band; Orch; School Musical; Mgr(s); Vllybl; Western Cert Hnr Outstndng Svc 86; Gold Music Awd 84-85; Cert Attainmnt Music 86; Bus Adm.

FEDD, DENISE; Northern SR HS; Baltimore, MD; (Y); Church Yth Grp; Cmnty Wkr; FBLA; Sec Frsh Cls; Sec Soph Cls; Sec Jr Cls; Hon Roll; Prfct Atten Awd; Bus Adm.

FEDERMAN, BRAD; Sherwood HS; Olney, MD; (Y); 90/317; Am Leg Boys St; Dance Clb; Drama Clb; Model UN; Ski Clb; SADD; Temple Yth Grp; Chorus; Madrigals; Pep Band; SR Serv Awd 86; Ntl Bk Schlrshp 86; Mst Outstndng Chrl Stu 86; U Of MD; Bus.

FEDIS, JAMES; Sherwood HS; Silver Spg, MD; (Y); Hon Roll; MD U; Medcl Dr.

FEILER, DONNA; Archbishop Keough HS; Balt, MD; (Y); Cmnty Wkr; Hosp Aide; Stu Cncl; Cheerleading; Mgr(s); Score Keeper; Sftbl; VFW Awd; Outstndg Yth Of Yr 86; U Of Balto; Pediatric Phys Ther.

FELDMAN, CHRISTINA V; Institute Of Notre Dame; Baltimore, MD; (Y); FBLA; Service Clb; Stage Crew; Hon Roll; Villa Julie Coll; Med Lab Tech.

FELDMAN, JENNIFER; Charles E Smith-Jewish Day Schl; Potomac, MD; (Y); French Clb; Service Clb; Teachers Aide; Temple Yth Grp; Outstndng Achvt Chem Algebra 2 85-86; Outstndng Achvt Hstry 83-84; Educ.

FELDMAN, KIM; Roland Park County Schl; Baltimore, MD; (Y); Cmnty Wkr; Office Aide; Science Clb; Service Clb; Teachers Aide; Temple Yth Grp; Im Cheerleading; French Hon Soc; Hon Roll; Schlrshp Hbrew Coll 84; Frnch Hnr Awd 86; Spcl Svc Hnr Awd 86; Math.

FELDMAN, MITCHELL; Walt Whitman HS; Potomac, MD; (Y); 1/500; Ski Clb; VP Spanish Clb; Teachers Aide; Stat Tennis; Var Trk; Hon Roll; Ntl Merit Ltr; Spanish NHS; Amrcn Hrt Assn Fllwshp Rcpnt 86; Pre-Med.

FELDMAN, SCOTT; Thomas S Wootton HS; Rockville, MD; (Y); Office Aide; Temple Yth Grp; Varsity Clb; Trs Frsh Cls; Trs Soph Cls; Var JV Socr; MD ST Socr Champshp Boys 85.

FELICIANO, MELISSA K; Friends School Of Baltimor; Baltimore, MD; (Y); Intnl Clb; Chorus; Orch; Nwsp Ed-Chief; Var Badmtn; Var Bsktbl; Var Fld Hcky; Var Lcrss; Hon Roll; Ntl Merit SF; Aais All Star Lacrosse 1st Tm 85; Gld Mdlst ACTR Spoken Russian Olym 84-85; Slvr Mdlst ACTR Wrtn Rus; Russian.

FELLNER, SARA; Charles E Smith Jewish Day HS; Alexandria, VA; (Y); Cmnty Wkr; Computer Clb; French Clb; Math Clb; SADD; Teachers Aide; Temple Yth Grp; Chorus; Nwsp Stf; Yrbk Bus Mgr; Erly Chldhd Ed.

FELSEN, MARTIN; Barrie HS; Seabrook, MD; (S); Model UN; School Play; Rep Stu Cncl; VP Bsktbl; VP Socr; VP Capt Tennis; Hon Roll; Yrbk Stf; Jr Cls; High Hon Roll; Intrnshp & Job Skidmore Owings & Merrill 84; Archit.

FENNELL, MICHAEL; St Vincent Pallotti HS; Laurel, MD; (S); 5/95; Am Leg Boys St; Ski Clb; Var Golf; Co-Capt Var Socr; Dnfth Awd; High Hon Roll; NHS; 4-H; Germn Ntl Hnr Soc 84-85; Engrng.

FENNER II, ROBERT L; Mc Donogh HS; Ellicott City, MD; (Y); Chess Clb; Cmnty Wkr; Pres Exploring; FCA; German Clb; Hosp Aide; Science Clb; Variety Show; VP Ftbl; VP Trk; Eagle Scout Awd 85; Schlr Ath Ftbl 85; Sci.

FENWICK, KAREN; La Plata HS; Charlotte Hall, MD; (Y); FHA; Pep Clb; Teachers Aide; Hm Ec; U MD; Comp.

FENWICK, STEVE; St Marys Ryken HS; Leonardtown, MD; (Y); Rep Frsh Cls; Rep Soph Cls; Rep Jr Cls; JV Bsktbl; Tennis; Engrng.

FEOLA, LAUREN; Damascus HS; Gaithersburg, MD; (Y); 10/235; Drama Clb; Q&S; Thesps; Mrchg Band; School Musical; Nwsp Ed-Chief; Yrbk Sprt Ed; NHS; Pres Schlr; Rep Jr Cls; MD Top 10 Pct Awd 86; SF Natl Ed Cmmnctns Schlrshp 86; Penn ST; Cmmnctns.

FEREBEE, TARA; Baltimore City Clg; Baltimore, MD; (S); Office Aide; Red Cross Aide; High Hon Roll; Hon Roll; Prfct Atten Awd; Temple U; Pre-Med.

FERGERSTROM, LESLIE; Acad Of The Holy Cross; Gaithersburg, MD; (Y); 9/123; Spanish Clb; Var Capt Vllybl; Hon Roll; NHS; Spanish NHS; Hnr Mntn Ntl Hspnc Schlr Awds Prog 86; 1st Pl MD Ntl Spnsh Exm 85; Serv Awd 86; Pickinson Coll.

FERGUSON, ALONDA TRINETTE; Fairmont Heights HS; Landover Hills, MD; (Y); Church Yth Grp; Dance Clb; FBLA; NFL; Church Choir; VP Frsh Cls; VP Soph Cls; VP Stu Cncl; Capt Cheerleading; Frgn Lang.

FERGUSON, COLLEEN; Notre Dame Preparatory Schl; Baltimore, MD; (Y); Church Yth Grp; Cmnty Wkr; Dance Clb; Hosp Aide; Teachers Aide; Yrbk Bus Mgr; Yrbk Ed-Chief; High Hon Roll; Hon Roll; NHS.

FERGUSON, LAURIE; Elizabeth Seton HS; Riverdale, MD; (Y); Ski Clb; Trs Spanish Clb; Var Cheerleading; Var Trk; Intl Bus.

FERGUSON, MARK; Perryville HS; Port Deposit, MD; (Y); Am Leg Boys St; Key Clb; Varsity Clb; L Ftbl; L Trk; L Wrstlng; High Hon Roll; Hon Roll; NHS; Ofcr Air Frc.

FERNANDES, DAVID; Walter Johnson HS; Bethesda, MD; (Y); AFS; Political Wkr; Pres Science Clb; Hon Roll; NHS; Intl Reltns.

FERO, MARCIE; Franklin HS; Reisterstown, MD; (Y); Intnl Clb; Temple Yth Grp; Nwsp Ed-Chief; Nwsp Rptr; Nwsp Stf; Lit Mag; Hon Roll; Prfct Atten Awd; Capt Jewish Comm Cntrs Chrldg Sqd 83-84; 2nd Prz-Baltimore Hebrew Hgh Essy Cont 86; Brdcst Jrnlsm.

FERRELL JR, RAYMOND NORRIS; Cardinal Gibbons HS; Baltimore, MD; (Y); Church Yth Grp; Q&S; Nwsp Stf; Yrbk Stf; Rep Frsh Cls; Rep Soph Cls; Rep Jr Cls; Chrmn Stu Cncl; Hon Roll; NHS; Matter & Energy Awd Outstndng Wrk 83-84; Layout & Art Edtr For Nwsp 85-86; Cartoonst Cardinal Nwsp; UMBC; Sci.

FERRIER, JENNIFER E; North Carroll HS; Manchester, MD; (Y); 21/270; Hosp Aide; Office Aide; Teachers Aide; Jazz Band; High Hon Roll; NHS; Sec Church Yth Grp; French Clb; Ski Clb; WMC Genetics Inst Westminster MD 84; Summr Schlrs WA & Lee U 85; Top Frnch Awd 86; Wstrn MD Coll; Bio.

FEW, TRENA; Oxon Hill HS; Forest Heights, MD; (Y); Church Yth Grp; Cmnty Wkr; Office Aide; ROTC; Teachers Aide; Off Stu Cncl; Bsktbl; Air Force; Air Trffc Cntrllr.

FIDELI, KRISTINA; Thomas Stone HS; Waldorf, MD; (S); Debate Tm; Math Clb; Pres Soph Cls; Rep Hst Stu Cncl; Var JV Cheerleading; Var Fld Hcky; High Hon Roll; NHS; St Schlr; Grls ST 85; Intl Bus.

FIELDS, AMY; Western HS; Baltimore, MD; (Y); JA; Yrbk Stf; Off Frsh Cls; Hon Roll; Bus Adm.

FIELDS, DAVID P; St Marys Ryken HS; Charlotte Hall, MD; (Y); 34/138; Boy Scts; Debate Tm; French Clb; Speech Tm; Coach Actv; Crs Cntry; Wrstlng; High Hon Roll; Hon Roll; NHS; Pres Sprts Awd; Aero Engrg.

FIELDS, RICHETTA; Southern SR HS; Baltimore, MD; (Y); Sec FBLA; Sec JA; Red Cross Aide; Sec SADD; Sec Rep Frsh Cls; Sec Rep Soph Cls; Sec Rep Jr Cls; Prfct Atten Awd; Blood Donar Cmmttee 83-85; Spcl Olympcs Hlpr 83-86; Ldrshp Conf-U Of MD 86; Spcl Ed Tchr.

FIGGS, BRENDA; Snow Hill HS; Snow Hill, MD; (S); 1/80; AFS; Church Yth Grp; Pres French Clb; Sec Sr Cls; Var Sftbl; High Hon Roll; NHS; Cmnty Wkr; Political Wkr; Band; Miss Delmarva Fire Prev 85-86; All-Shore Bnd 85; Jazz Musician Of Yr 85; Salisbury ST Coll; Math Tchr.

FIGUEROA, MIMI; Bishop Walsh HS; La Vale, MD; (Y); Library Aide; Math Clb; Office Aide; Ski Clb; Concert Band; Jazz Band; Yrbk Stf; French Hon Soc; Hon Roll; NHS; Loyola Coll; Comp Sci.

FIKES, CYNTHIA D; Oakland Mills HS; Columbia, MD; (Y); AFS; Church Yth Grp; Church Choir; Var Mgr(s); Var Trk; Var Capt Vllybl; Hon Roll; Natl Achvt Cmmnd Stdnt & Outstndng Fld Evnt 85; B Hnr Rll & Outstndng Athl 84; Phy Thrpy.

FILA, SANDRA; Archbishop Krough HS; Glen Burnie, MD; (Y); Drama Clb; GAA; Sec Science Clb; Teachers Aide; Rep Jr Cls; JV Stat Bsktbl; Im Coach Actv; Score Keeper; Timer; CCD Tchr 84-86; CCC Ldrshp Hnr 84; Piano 83-86; Comp Sci.

FILIPOWICZ, MIRIAM; Severn Schl; Severna Pk, MD; (Y); 5/77; French Clb; Ski Clb; Spanish Clb; Pres Stu Cncl; Var Diving; Var Capt Fld Hcky; Var Lcrss; French Hon Soc; Jr NHS; NHS; MD Distinguished Schlr 86; U VA Jefferson Awd 85; C Markland Kelly Jr Athl Svc Awd 86; Duke U.

FILLYAW, JAMES; Forest Park SR HS; Baltimore, MD; (Y); Art Clb; Boy Scts; Church Yth Grp; Drama Clb; 4-H; JA; Red Cross Aide; Chorus; Church Choir; School Play; Bus.

FINCK, JENNIFER; Dundalk HS; Baltimore, MD; (Y); 31/297; SADD; Varsity Clb; Variety Show; Trs Stu Cncl; Mgr(s); Powder Puff Ftbl; Tennis; High Hon Roll; Hon Roll; Jr NHS; Hnr Select Anncmnts SADD 86; Pres Fit Awd 84-86; Mar Biol.

FINEGOLD, MITCHELL S; Bethesda-Chevy Chase HS; Chevy Chase, MD; (Y); Jazz Band; Variety Show; Bsktbl; JV Golf; Tennis; Vllybl; MD Ctr Gftd & Tlntd Smmr Pgm 83; Intl Annl Msc Cmpstn Tst Cert Awd 82; Peabody Cnsrvtry Msc 84; Philosophy.

FINKBEINER, DAVID; Grace Brethren HS; Accokeek, MD; (S); 1/25; Church Yth Grp; Drama Clb; FCA; Pep Clb; Science Clb; Chorus; Church Choir; Yrbk Ed-Chief; Yrbk Phtg; Pres Stu Cncl; VA Polytechnic U; Engr.

FINLEY III, CHARLES; Oxon Hill HS; Fort Washington, MD; (Y); Math Tm; Ski Clb; Lit Mag; Trs Sr Cls; Co-Capt Crs Cntry; Trk; French Hon Soc; High Hon Roll; NHS; Ntl Merit SF; Apt USMA, UNA, USAFA 86; ROTC Scholar AF, Army & Navy 86; USAFA; Aerospc Engr.

FINNIFF, ERNEST; North Hagerstown HS; Hagerstown, MD; (Y); 33/247; Boy Scts; Church Yth Grp; Church Choir; Hon Roll; UMBC; Pre-Law.

FINZEL, ELLEN; Northern HS; Grantsville, MD; (Y); SADD; Teachers Aide; Chorus; Drill Tm; Flag Corp; Stat Bsktbl; Score Keeper; Hon Roll; Allegany CC; Media Tech.

FIRLIE, AMY; Bishop Walsh Middle HS; Cumberland, MD; (Y); 11/104; Drama Clb; Model UN; Speech Tm; Yrbk Stf; Capt Cheerleading; Trk; High Hon Roll; NHS; Spanish NHS; Ntl Art Hnr Soc 85; Mock Trial Team Stu 86; Phmcy.

FISCH, SUZANNE; Dulaney HS; Timonium, MD; (Y); 74/485; Cmnty Wkr; Concert Band; Yrbk Stf; Swmmng; JV Vllybl; Hon Roll; NHS; Natl YMCA Swmmng & Dvng Champshps 84-86; Bio.

FISCHER, KENNETH; Westminster SR HS; Finksburg, MD; (Y); CAP; Hst German Clb; Latin Clb; Math Tm; Political Wkr; Mrchg Band; High Hon Roll; NHS; Gold Mdl Natl Latin Exm 86; Mitchell Awd 3rd Hghst Civil Air Ptrl Cadet Prog 85; U VA; Math.

FISCHER, MATTHEW; St Marys HS; Arnold, MD; (Y); 2/119; Drama Clb; Math Tm; Ski Clb; Elks Awd; High Hon Roll; NHS; Pres Schlr; Sal; St Schlr; MD ST Dstngshd Schlr-Rnr Up 86; ST MD Schlstc Merit Awd 86; Amercn U 86; American U WA DC; Intl Svc.

FISCHL, AMY; Friendly SR HS; Fort Washington, MD; (Y); Science Clb; Spanish Clb; Teachers Aide; Temple Yth Grp; Stage Crew; Yrbk Stf; Hon Roll; NHS; Spanish NHS; Voice Dem Awd; Cnty Exec Yth Advisory Cncl 86; Pre-Med.

FISHBURNE, EDWARD; The Bullis Schl; Rockville, MD; (S); 9/89; Church Yth Grp; Drama Clb; Letterman Clb; Thesps; Varsity Clb; School Play; Nwsp Stf; Yrbk Stf; Var Socr; JV Tennis.

FISHEL, REBECCA; Arlington Baptist Schl; Randallstown, MD; (S); 2/45; Church Yth Grp; Cmnty Wkr; Nwsp Stf; Cit Awd; High Hon Roll; NHS; Ntl Merit Ltr; Covenant Coll.

FISHER, ALEXANDRA; Mc Donough HS; Pomfret, MD; (S); 14/350; Intnl Clb; Letterman Clb; Teachers Aide; Varsity Clb; Band; Concert Band; Stu Cncl; Var Capt Cheerleading; JV Sftbl; Var Capt Vllybl; Outstndng Athlt 84; Clg Waiver 85-86; MVP Vllybl 86; Charles Cnty CC.

FISHER, CHRISTINA; Eleanor Roosevelt HS; Lanham, MD; (Y); Boys Clb Am; Church Yth Grp; Pep Clb; Acpl Chr; School Musical; JV Cheerleading; Hon Roll; MD ST Music Tchrs Assoc Mrt Cert 85; Natl Piano Plyng Adtns 85; Brigham Yng U; Bio Sci.

FISHER, DEBRA; Elizabeth Seton HS; Hyattsville, MD; (Y); Church Yth Grp; Ski Clb; Varsity Clb; Im Bsktbl; Var L Sftbl; Hon Roll.

FISHER, TERRI LYNN; Lansdowne HS; Baltimore, MD; (Y); SADD; Nwsp Ed-Chief; VP Jr Cls; Trs Stu Cncl; High Hon Roll; NHS; Pres Schlr; Spanish NHS; St Schlr; Acad All Amer 85-86; Chatham Coll; Vet Med.

FISHTER, COLLEEN; Riverdale Baptist HS; Davidsonville, MD; (S); Teachers Aide; Rep Soph Cls; JV Cheerleading; Var Sftbl; High Hon Roll; Psych.

FISTER, LORENA; Northwestern HS; Mt Rainier, MD; (Y); Spanish Clb; Stu Cncl; Pom Pon; Hon Roll; U Of MD; Actg.

FITCH, BONNIE; Gaithersburg HS; Gaithersburg, MD; (Y); Stage Crew; Mgr(s); High Hon Roll; Hon Roll; Engr.

FITCH, MONICA; Damascus HS; Damascus, MD; (Y); 69/249; Teachers Aide; Drill Tm; Yrbk Stf; Cheerleading; Cit Awd; Off Frsh Cls; Off Sr Cls; Outstndng Elem Aide 85; Shephard Coll.

FITZGERALD, DANITA; Walbrook SR HS; Baltimore, MD; (Y); Church Yth Grp; 4-H; Spanish Clb; Band; Cit Awd; 4-H Awd; Lion Awd; Prfct Atten Awd; :Data Proc.

FITZGERALD, ERIN; Walter Johnson HS; Bethesda, MD; (Y); Teachers Aide; Rep Stu Cncl; U Of MD; Intl Bus.

FITZPATRICK, KAREN; Bishop Walsh HS; Lavale, MD; (Y); Art Clb; Trs Church Yth Grp; Office Aide; Orch; Mgr Bsktbl; Mgr(s); Vllybl; U MD; Phrmcy.

FITZSIMMONS, BRENDAN; Loyola HS; Baltimore, MD; (Y); School Play; Nwsp Phtg; Yrbk Phtg; Yrbk Stf; Rep Frsh Cls; Im Ftbl; JV Mgr(s); Im Socr; NEDT Awd; Bus Ecnmcs.

FITZWATER, ARDRA; Bishop Walsh HS; Frostburg, MD; (Y); Church Choir; Rep Sr Cls; Var Bsktbl; Sftbl; Var L Trk; Var L Vllybl; Hon Roll; Pep Clb; Chorus; Mgr(s); Chrprsn Allegny Cnty Stdnt Pg Selectn Comm; Schl Masct; Intrmrl Asst; Frostburg ST Coll; Comp Sci.

FLAHERTY, DAWN; Centennial HS; Columbia, MD; (Y); 10/270; Cmnty Wkr; VP French Clb; Political Wkr; Yrbk Rptr; Rep Stu Cncl; Var Capt Cheerleading; Sec NHS; Hon Roll; Natl Merit Cmmnded Schlr 86; Outstndg SR Awd 86; Westinghouse Educ Fndtn Schlrp 86; James Madison U; Intl Rltns.

FLAHERTY, SHEILA; Thomas S Wootton HS; Rockville, MD; (Y); Band; Drm Mjr(t); Mrchg Band; School Musical; Bsktbl; Mgr(s); Hon Roll; Vetrinarian.

FLANNERY, JOHN; North Hagerstown HS; Hagerstown, MD; (Y); Band; Concert Band; Jazz Band; Mrchg Band; Pep Band; School Play; Symp Band; Rep Frsh Cls; Rep Soph Cls; Stu Cncl; Computer Science.

FLANNERY, TERRANCE; Brunswick HS; Jefferson, MD; (Y); 17/150; Computer Clb; Red Cross Aide; School Play; Stage Crew; Hon Roll; Chess Clb; Spanish Clb; Chorus; Nwsp Rptr; Tennis; U MD; Engrng.

FLATHMAN, JENNIFER; Roland Park County Schl; Baltimore, MD; (Y); Drama Clb; Thesps; Chorus; School Musical; Stage Crew; Hon Roll; French Honor Society 86; Theater.

FLAX, MEREDITH; Walt Whitman HS; Bethesda, MD; (Y); Hosp Aide; Teachers Aide; Temple Yth Grp; Orch; Yrbk Phtg; Yrbk Rptr; Var Gym; Var Trk; Ntl Merit Ltr; Intl Bus.

FLEEGLE, KIM; Mount Savage HS; Corriganville, MD; (Y); Im Var French Clb; Teachers Aide; Band; Church Choir; Drm Mjr(t); Mrchg Band; Stu Cncl; Hon Roll; NHS; Allegany Cmnty Coll; Gnrl Stds.

FLEET, ANTHONY; Walbrook SR HS; Baltimore, MD; (Y); Drama Clb; English Clb; PAVAS; School Musical; School Play; Nwsp Rptr; Nwsp Stf; Cit Awd; Hon Roll; Perf Art Awds 86; Lawyer.

FLEISHELL, JENNIFER; Glenelg HS; Woodbine, MD; (Y); Sec 4-H; French Clb; Quiz Bowl; Teachers Aide; Band; Concert Band; Mrchg Band; Hon Roll; Lion Awd; Intnl Clb; ST 4 H Rabbit Awd Wnnr 86; Animal Sci.

FLEISHELL, KAREN; Glenelg HS; Woodbine, MD; (Y); 100/271; Pres 4-H; French Clb; Office Aide; Q&S; Teachers Aide; Color Guard; Variety Show; Nwsp Bus Mgr; Nwsp Rptr; Nwsp Stf; Ptpsco Grnge Ag Schlrshp 86; MD Lmb & Wool Queen 85; 1st Altrnt Ntl Sheep Schlrshp 86; U MD; Ag.

FLEMING, CYNTHIA; Allegany HS; Lavale, MD; (Y); 87/250; Church Yth Grp; Office Aide; Pep Clb; Drill Tm; Yrbk Rptr; Yrbk Stf; Var L Cheerleading; Soc Distngushd Am Stu 84-86; Salisbury ST Coll; Elem Ed.

FLEMING, KATHARINE LEE; Queen Anne Schl; Washington, DC; (Y); 5/41; Church Yth Grp; Model UN; Chorus; Church Choir; Nwsp Ed-Chief; Yrbk Stf; Trs Stu Cncl; High Hon Roll; SR Chorus Awd 84-86; U Of SC; Journlsm.

FLEMING, PAULA; Forest Park SR HS; Baltimore, MD; (Y); Rep Jr Cls; Var Score Keeper; Cit Awd; Hon Roll; Jr NHS; NHS; Bus.

FLEMING, TINA; Westminster HS; Finksburg, MD; (Y); Spanish Clb; Yrbk Stf; Rep Soph Cls; Rep Jr Cls; JV Var Cheerleading; High Hon Roll; Hon Roll; NHS; Prfct Atten Awd; Cmnctns.

FLEMING, VERNA JEAN; South Carroll HS; Mt Airy, MD; (S); Hosp Aide; Teachers Aide; Band; Chorus; Concert Band; Mrchg Band; Pep Band; Symp Band; TSU All SR ST Hnr Band 85; Miss Mt Airy Fire Prevntn Qn 85-86; U Of MD Fire Inst; Med.

FLERLAGE, LOVIE; Maurice J Mc Donough HS; Waldorf, MD; (Y); Art Clb; Teachers Aide; Mrchg Band; Pom Pon; Hon Roll; Psych.

FLESHER, JAMES R; La Plata HS; La Plata, MD; (S); FCA; Ski Clb; Jr Cls; Var L Bsbl; Var L Ftbl; Wt Lftg; Var L Wrstlng; Hon Roll; Jr NHS; NHS.

FLETCHER, APRILLE; Friendly SR HS; Ft Washington, MD; (Y); Drama Clb; Teachers Aide; School Play; Im Gym; Hon Roll; Bus Mgmt.

FLICK, DIANE; St Vincent Pallotti HS; Silver Spring, MD; (S); 3/115; Church Yth Grp; Pres Ski Clb; Spanish Clb; Frsh Cls; Jr Cls; JV Cheerleading; High Hon Roll; Acad Lttr.

FLINN, MICHAEL; St Marys Ryken HS; Lusby, MD; (S); Boy Scts; Trs Church Yth Grp; Cmnty Wkr; Science Clb; Yrbk Sprt Ed; Stat Trk; High Hon Roll; Prfct Atten Awd; Bio Sci.

FLINT, HEIDI; Eastern Vo Tech; Baltimore, MD; (Y); Varsity Clb; Pres Sec VICA; Band; Concert Band; Var Crs Cntry; Var Trk; Twrlr; JP Sousa Awd; Vica Ldrshp Awd 85; Top Fundraiser Awd Vica 86; Hnrs Bio,Engl; Elect Engr.

FLOWER, TODD; James M Bennett SR HS; Hebron, MD; (Y); Boy Scts; Camera Clb; Church Yth Grp; Varsity Clb; Stage Crew; Im Badmtn; Var JV Bsbl; Var JV Ftbl; Im Sftbl; Im Vllybl; Engrng.

FLOWERS, LARRY B; Hancock Middle SR HS; Hancock, MD; (Y); Church Yth Grp; Stage Crew; Nwsp Rptr; Yrbk Sprt Ed; Yrbk Stf; Pres Soph Cls; Rep Stu Cncl; Var L Bsbl; Var L Bsktbl; Var L Ftbl; Bsbll Offnsv Plyr 84-85; Bsbll Vlble Plyr 85-86; Arch.

FLY, JASON; Polytechnic Inst; Baltimore, MD; (Y); Var Bsbl; Im Bsktbl; Hon Roll; MIT; Mech Engr.

FLYNN, KAREN; Elkton Christian Schl; Elkton, MD; (S); 2/16; Teachers Aide; School Play; Yrbk Stf; Var Bsktbl; Var Cheerleading; Var Sftbl; Vllybl; High Hon Roll; NHS; Word Of Life Bible Inst; Busnss.

FOARD, GRETCHERN; Wicomico SR HS; Salisbury, MD; (Y); Pres AFS; Pres Church Yth Grp; French Clb; Pep Clb; Varsity Clb; Chorus; Symp Band; Rep Jr Cls; Trk; Hon Roll; Schl Svc Awd 83; Acad Excllnce Awd 86; Cert Distngshd Svc 86; Gold Music Awd 86; High Point Coll; Mgr Psych.

FOARD, KIM; Wicomico SR HS; Salisbury, MD; (Y); 22/243; French Clb; Band; Mrchg Band; School Musical; Symp Band; Rep Jr Cls; Rep Sr Cls; Socr; High Hon Roll; Hon Roll; Acadmc Ltr 85-86; High Point NC; Med Tech.

FOGG, BRIAN; Linganore HS; Mt Airy, MD; (Y); Letterman Clb; L Socr; L Trk; High Hon Roll; Hon Roll; NHS; St Schlr; Church Yth Grp; Debate Tm; Math Clb; MD Distngushd Schlr Awd; Outstndng Achvt Frnsh III,IV Phycics; MD Merit Schlstc Awd; VA Tech; Elect Engr.

FOGG, ERIKA; Friendly SR HS; Ft Washington, MD; (Y); Church Yth Grp; Dance Clb; 4-H; Girl Scts; Pep Clb; Teachers Aide; Chorus; Church Choir; Color Guard; Stage Crew; Pre-Med.

FOLKART, MICHAEL; Franklin HS; Owings Mls, MD; (Y); Boy Scts; Computer Clb; Scholastic Bowl; Im Bsktbl; Im Vllybl; Gov Hon Prg Awd; High Hon Roll; NHS; Natl Assoc Physcs Tchrs Outstndg Physcs Stu 86; Edward P Colwill Schlrp 86; Acad Ltr 86; U MD College Park; Elec Engrg.

FOLSTEIN, SCOTT; Zak Magruder HS; Olney, MD; (Y); 85/316; Band; Concert Band; Wrstlng; Hon Roll; Hnr Rll 83-86; FL Inst Of Tech; Bus Mgmt.

FONSECA, THOMAS; St Vincent Palotti HS; Laurel, MD; (S); 25/120; Cmnty Wkr; Ski Clb; Spanish Clb; Speech Tm; VP Jr Cls; Var L Socr; Var L Trk; Im Wt Lftg; NHS; MD ST Bar Assoc Mock Trial Comp 85-86; Med.

FOOR, PENNY; Maurice J Mc Donough HS; Waldorf, MD; (Y); Letterman Clb; Teachers Aide; Jr Cls; JV Var Cheerleading; JV Var Sftbl; Hon Roll; UMBC; Physcl Thrpy.

FOOS, SHERI; Central HS; Andrews AFB, DC; (Y); Band; JV Socr; Hon Roll; NHS; U Northern CO; Comp Engr.

FOOTE, PAMELA; Fort Hill HS; Cumberland, MD; (Y); 110/222; Church Yth Grp; Computer Clb; Dance Clb; SADD; Teachers Aide; Drill Tm; Rep Jr Cls; Rep Sr Cls; L Pom Pon; Allegany CC; Lab Tech.

FOOTLICK, RANDI; Pikesville HS; Balto, MD; (Y); 1/285; Spanish Clb; Teachers Aide; Temple Yth Grp; Chorus; Rep Stu Cncl; Var Mgr Lcrss; Var Vllybl; NHS; Math.

FORBES, TONYA; Takoma Acad; Columbia, MD; (S); Church Yth Grp; Pep Clb; Church Choir; Drill Tm; Var Cheerleading; Trk; Hon Roll; NHS; Natl Ed Devlpmnt Tests/Superior Perfrmnce 84; Howard U; Med.

FORBES, YVETTE; Takoma Acad; Columbia, MD; (Y); Office Aide; Pep Clb; Science Clb; Teachers Aide; Yrbk Stf; Off Sr Cls; Trk; Hon Roll; Pres Physcl Ftnss Awd 83-84; Howard U; Pharm.

FORD, DANYA; Western HS; Baltimore, MD; (Y); 49/412; Bus Adm.

FORD, JANEEN VIONA; Cambridge-South Dorchester HS; Cambridge, MD; (Y); 11/229; Am Leg Aux Girls St; Church Yth Grp; Teachers Aide; Sec Band; Church Choir; VP Sr Cls; Stu Cncl; Sftbl; NHS; Prfct Atten Awd; Lcl Rtry Srvice Abve Slf Awd 86; Ntl Merit Schlr Awd 86; Prsdntl Schlrshp Bowie ST Coll; Bowie ST Coll; Pltcl Sci.

FORD, RAJEE; Carver Vo-Tech HS; Baltimore, MD; (Y); Boy Scts; Computer Clb; Exploring; FBLA; Math Clb; Science Clb; Chorus; Nwsp Rptr; Off Soph Cls; VP Trk; Morgan ST; Med Tech.

FOREMAN, BRIAN; Thomas Stone HS; Waldorf, MD; (Y); 15/400; Am Leg Boys St; Math Clb; Science Clb; Var Crs Cntry; Var Tennis; High Hon Roll; NHS; Cmnty Wkr; French Clb; Band; 2nd Pl Olymp Of Mnd Wrld Comptr Comptn 85; Acad Ltr 84-86; 1st Pl Cnty Sci Fair 84.

FORESTER, YASUE; Immaculata College HS; Potomac, MD; (Y); Cmnty Wkr; French Clb; Nwsp Rptr; Yrbk Phtg; Yrbk Stf; Sec Trs Soph Cls; Pres Sr Cls; Mgr(s); Var Swmmng; Hon Roll; Franklin Coll; Poli Sci.

FORREST, JAMES; St Marys Ryken HS; Ridge, MD; (S); Debate Tm; NFL; Science Clb; Speech Tm; High Hon Roll; Ntl Merit SF; Excell In Englsh Awd 83-85; Excell In Math Awd 83-84; VA Polytechnic Inst; Comp Sci.

FORT, ROCHELLE; Friendly SR HS; White Plains, MD; (Y); Office Aide; Nwsp Bus Mgr; Nwsp Rptr; Bausch & Lomb Sci Awd; High Hon Roll; Hon Roll; NHS; Ntl Merit SF; Pres Schlr; Pres Spanish NHS; Purdue Bus Scholar 86; Full Tuition Salisbury ST Coll 86; Pannel Scholar Sweetbriar 86; Salisbury ST Coll; Acctg.

FORTUNA, JOSEPH; Good Counsel HS; Germantown, MD; (Y); Chess Clb; Pres Drama Clb; Pep Band; School Musical; School Play; Symp Band; Nwsp Phtg; Nwsp Stf; Ed Lit Mag; Hon Roll; PSAT Natl Merit Schlrshp; Georgetown U.

FOSCO, MARIA; Surrattsville SR HS; Clinton, MD; (Y); Church Yth Grp; Teachers Aide; Varsity Clb; Chorus; School Musical; School Play; Nwsp Stf; Yrbk Stf; Var Co-Capt Cheerleading; Hon Roll; MD U; Nrsng.

FOSTER IV, ALFRED W; Bishop Walsh HS; Romney, WV; (Y); 11/106; Science Clb; Ski Clb; Speech Tm; Teachers Aide; Concert Band; Jazz Band; Mrchg Band; Trs Stu Cncl; Var Bsbl; NHS; Awd Dedctn & Outstndg Svc To Schl 86; Acdmc Excllnc Awd Music 86; Christian Bros Coll; Chem Engnr.

FOSTER, MICHELLE; Hereford HS; Parkton, MD; (S); Church Yth Grp; Sec 4-H; FTA; JA; Letterman Clb; Political Wkr; Spanish Clb; Sec SADD; Teachers Aide; Varsity Clb; VA Tech; Vtrnrn.

FOTIA, KELLI L; Edgewood HS; Edgewood, MD; (Y); 4/200; Girl Scts; Orch; JV Fld Hcky; Powder Puff Ftbl; Var Swmmng; Var Capt Tennis; High Hon Roll; Hon Roll; Trs NHS; ST MD Schlstc Merit Awd 86; Pres Acad Ftns Ad 86; Hnr Grad 86; Essex CC; Math.

FOUNTAIN, MONIQUE; Elizabeth Seton HS; Lanham, MD; (Y); 4-H; Sec Frsh Cls; Sec Soph Cls; Sec Jr Cls; VP Sr Cls; Bsktbl; Sftbl; Vllybl; 4-H Awd; Hon Roll; Northeasterns U WIE Smmr Prog 86; Awds & Trophies Dance Clss 75-86; Hampton U; Phys.

FOUTS, LISA; North Carroll HS; Manchester, MD; (Y); Church Yth Grp; Rep Frsh Cls; Rep Jr Cls; Var JV Cheerleading; Hon Roll; Phys Thrpy.

FOWLER, CANDY; Thomas Stone HS; Waldorf, MD; (S); Teachers Aide; Yrbk Phtg; Yrbk Rptr; Yrbk Stf; Lit Mag; Tp 10 Erth-Sci Awd Plcd 4th 83-84; Crmnlgy.

FOWLER, CRAIG; Outhern Garrett HS; Swanton, MD; (Y); Q&S; Ski Clb; Yrbk Stf; Hon Roll.

FOWLER, JANICE; Brunswick HS; Brunswick, MD; (Y); Church Yth Grp; FBLA; Office Aide; Chorus; School Musical; School Play; Crs Cntry; Powder Puff Ftbl; Hon Roll; FBLA Svc Awd 85-86; FCC; Bus Adm.

FOWLER, TIFFANY; Northern HS; Dunkirk, MD; (Y); Sec Church Yth Grp; Symp Band; Sec Jr Cls; Stu Cncl; Capt Pom Pon; High Hon Roll; Sec NHS; Opt Clb Awd; Cmnty Wkr; Red Cross Aide; Outstdng Englsh Stu 85; Guard Spirit Awd 85-86; Frgn Comm.

FOX, PAUL; Westminster HS; Westminster, MD; (Y); Teachers Aide; Gov Hon Prg Awd; Hon Roll; Pres Acdmc Ftns Awd 86; Acdmc Ltr 86; Loyola Pres Schlrshp 86; Loyola Coll; Engr.

FOYLES, VICTOR; Carver Voc Tech HS; Baltimore, MD; (Y); Hon Roll; John Hopkin U; Med.

FRAILER, SUSAN; St Michaels HS; Neavitt, MD; (Y); 2/74; Pres Drama Clb; German Clb; Library Aide; Chorus; Church Choir; School Play; Stage Crew; Nwsp Rptr; Nwsp Stf; High Hon Roll; St Michaels Rotry Clb 86; St Michaels Womns Clb 86; Outstndng Svc Libry Aide 86; Randolph Macon Coll; Premed.

FRALEY, LISA; Catoctin HS; Thurmont, MD; (Y); Church Yth Grp; Drama Clb; Chorus; Church Choir; School Musical; Nwsp Bus Mgr; Sec Soph Cls; Sec Jr Cls; VP Sr Cls; Rep Stu Cncl; Outstndng Schlr In Arts 86; Music.

FRANCE, HELLENA; Arlington Baptist HS; Baltimore, MD; (Y); Church Yth Grp; Hosp Aide; Concert Band; Mrchg Band; Mgr(s); Sftbl; Vllybl; Hon Roll; Ntl Merit SF; Band; Band Trophies & Pins Performnc 84-86; Trnsprttn Awd 84; Pre Med.

FRANCE, ROBERT; N Hagerstown HS; Hagerstown, MD; (Y); Church Yth Grp; Teachers Aide; Band; Concert Band; Mrchg Band; Pep Band; Symp Band; Band Lttr 86; Arch.

FRANCIOSI, VICKI; Fort Hill HS; Cumberland, MD; (Y); Teachers Aide; Drill Tm; Off Soph Cls; Off Jr Cls; Hon Roll; NHS; Natl Hnr Soc Vp 86; WV U; Bus Admin.

FRANEK, ANTOINETTE; Northern HS; Owings, MD; (Y); Dance Clb; Teachers Aide; Stat Bsktbl; Crs Cntry; Stat Trk; Hon Roll; U Of MD; Bus Admin.

FRANK, ELLEN; St Vincent Pallotti HS; Silver Spring, MD; (S); 1/120; AFS; Teachers Aide; French Hon Soc; High Hon Roll.

FRANK, JENNIFER L; Damascus HS; Clarksburg, MD; (Y); 33/250; Drama Clb; VP Quiz Bowl; VP Thesps; School Musical; School Play; Variety Show; Rep Frsh Cls; Rep Soph Cls; Hon Roll; Natl Merit Special Schlrshp 86; Theatre.

FRANK, KIMBERLY; Northern HS; Accident, MD; (Y); Church Yth Grp; French Clb; SADD; Teachers Aide; Chorus; Church Choir; Yrbk Stf; Rep Stu Cncl; Cheerleading; Tennis; Garrett CC; Phys Ther.

FRANK, LAURIE; Springbrook HS; Silver Spring, MD; (Y); Pom Pon; Mgr Socr; Mgr Trk; High Hon Roll; NHS.

FRANKLIN, JOSETTE; Central SR HS; Forestville, MD; (Y); Thesps; Church Choir; School Musical; Yrbk Stf; Sec Sr Cls; Jr NHS; NHS; Ntl Merit Schol; Rotary Awd; Hood Coll Pres Ldrshp Awd 86; Alpha Kappa Alpha Sorority Schlrshp 86; MD ST Schlrshp Bd 86; Hood Coll; Music.

FRANTZ, LINDA; Northern Garrett HS; Friendsville, MD; (Y); SADD; Teachers Aide; Drill Tm; Flag Corp; Mrchg Band; Stu Cncl; Hon Roll; Sawyer Schl Bus; Med Sec.

FRANTZ, SHERRI; Northern HS; Friendsville, MD; (Y); 9/110; GAA; Nwsp Phtg; Rep Sr Cls; Rep Stu Cncl; Var Vllybl; High Hon Roll; Hon Roll; MD Dstngshd Schlr, Acdmc All Am; Frostburg ST Coll; Acctg.

FRANZ, BETH; Lansdowne HS; Baltimore, MD; (Y); Dance Clb; Drama Clb; FBLA; Hosp Aide; School Musical; Variety Show; Sec Jr Cls; Sec Sr Cls; Rep Stu Cncl; JV Bsktbl; 200 Hr Pin Vlntr St Agns Hosp 84-85; Loyola; Mrn Bio.

FRAZIER, CRYSTAL L; Gaithersburg HS; Gaithersburg, MD; (Y); 70/568; Church Yth Grp; Hosp Aide; Pep Clb; Church Choir; Variety Show; Pom Pon; Hon Roll; Jr NHS; Lion Awd; NHS; German Hnr Scty 844-86; Chrch JR Ushr Brd 83; UMBC Schlstc Achvmnt Awd 86; U Of MD; Physcl Thrpy.

FREBURGER, ERIC; Patterson HS; Baltimore, MD; (Y); Cmnty Wkr; Key Clb; Political Wkr; Band; Drm & Bgl; Bnqt Awd & Trphy Cochng Littl Lge 85; Awd ASVAB; Essex CC.

FREDERICK, JEFF; Laurel HS; Laurel, MD; (Y); Pres Stu Cncl; JV Var Ftbl; Drama Clb; Office Aide; Ski Clb; Rep Jr Cls; Powder Puff Ftbl; Hon Roll; Appntd To Prnc Grgs Cnty Yth Advsry Cncl 86-87; Bus.

FREE, CYNTHIA; Catoctin HS; Thurmont, MD; (Y); Art Clb; Computer Clb; Sec Drama Clb; Letterman Clb; Pep Clb; Sec Science Clb; Chorus; School Musical; Capt Cheerleading; Hon Roll; Achvts-Comp Sci 85; Chrldng Athltc Awd 82-85; Awd Of Apprectn 85; Comp.

FREELAND, ADAM; Hereford HS; Hampstead, MD; (Y); JCL; Latin Clb; Varsity Clb; School Play; Lit Mag; Rep Stu Cncl; Var Bsbl; Im Wt Lftg; Var JV Wrstlng; Hon Roll; Steve Clay Mem Awd 86; Bltmr Cnty Stu Page 86; Nclr Engrng Schl; Nclr Engrng.

FREEMAN, KARA; Crossland HS; Camp Spgs, MD; (Y); Church Yth Grp; FFA; Math Tm; Pep Clb; Teachers Aide; Jr Cls; Pom Pon; God Cntry Awd; Spanish NHS; U MD Baltimore Cnty; Comp Sci.

FREEMAN, PETER; De Matha Catholic HS; Bethesda, MD; (Y); Nwsp Bus Mgr; Nwsp Ed-Chief; Nwsp Rptr; Yrbk Stf; Im Bsktbl; Most Vlbl Stffr-Stagline Nwspr 84-85; U Of MD; Jrnlst.

FREEMAN, VICTORIA; Sherwood HS; Olney, MD; (Y); Church Yth Grp; FBLA; FTA; SADD; Co-Capt Drill Tm; Co-Capt Pom Pon; Hon Roll; JV Var Sftbl; Prfct Atten Awd; Spanish NHS; Outstndng Stdnt Awd 84; MVP JV Sftbl 84; MD ST Pom Sqd Champs 85; Olney Mill Swim Team Trphy 84; Corporate Law.

FRENCH, FARABE; Washington HS; Westover, MD; (Y); 4/116; Am Leg Aux Girls St; Church Yth Grp; Cmnty Wkr; Dance Clb; Spanish Clb; Church Choir; Mrchg Band; Yrbk Stf; Wt Lftg; High Hon Roll; U Of MD Easternshore Schlrshp 86; Top 5% Of Grad Clss 86; Mc Masters Old Home Prz Essay 86; U Of MD Eastern Shore; Phy Thr.

FRENCH, YVONNE; Frederick HS; Frederick, MD; (Y); 6/310; Debate Tm; 4-H; Pep Clb; Chorus; Sec Jr Cls; Stat Bsktbl; Cheerleading; High Hon Roll; NHS; Scl Stds/Govt Awd 85; Sci Awd 83-84; Acadmc All Amercn 86; Educ.

FRERE, KEVIN; Mc Donough HS; White Plains, MD; (Y); Chess Clb; Natl Beta Clb; Ski Clb; Timer; High Hon Roll; Hon Roll; Charles CC; Bio.

FRESCO, ANGELO; Suitland HS; Forestville, MD; (Y); Trs French Clb; Library Aide; Trs Science Clb; Teachers Aide; Band; Church Choir; Pep Band; Symp Band; French Hon Soc; Hon Roll; U MD; Aerosp Engr.

FRETZ, LORI; Thomas S Wootton HS; Potomac, MD; (Y); 56/401; Church Yth Grp; Chorus; Madrigals; School Musical; Var Capt Cheerleading; Hon Roll; Ntl Merit Ltr; Teachers Aide; Acpl Chr; Soc Tchncl Cmmnctn Wrtg Cntst 84&85; MD All-ST HS Chorus 84-86; U S Naval Acad Smmr Sci Smnr 85; MA Inst Of Technlgy; Ocean Eng.

FREY, TROY; Elkton Christian HS; Newark, DE; (S); School Play; Pres Frsh Cls; Pres Soph Cls; Pres Jr Cls; Pres Sr Cls; Var Bsktbl; Var Capt Socr; Hon Roll; NHS; DE U; Mech Engr.

FRIDINGER, LAURIE; Allegany HS; Cumberland, MD; (Y); Hosp Aide; Pres Pep Clb; VP Ski Clb; Yrbk Ed-Chief; Yrbk Stf; Pres Frsh Cls; Off Soph Cls; Sec Stu Cncl; Mgr(s); Score Keeper; Hood; Psych.

FRIDOVICH, LAURA A; The Holton-Arms Schl; Silver Spring, MD; (Y); Nwsp Phtg; Nwsp Rptr; Ed Yrbk Phtg; Mgr Trk; Ntl Merit SF; Cath U Schlrshp 85.

FRIEDENBERG, JEFFREY; Oakland Mills HS; Columbia, MD; (Y); 24/240; Math Tm; Ski Clb; JV Crs Cntry; High Hon Roll; NHS.

FRIEDMAN, ALEX; The Park Schl; Baltimore, MD; (Y); School Musical; VP Frsh Cls; JV Var Bsktbl; JV Var Socr; JV Var Tennis; Var Trk; Pres Physcl Fit Awd 81; Johns Hopkins U; Engrng.

FRIEDMAN, BRENDON; Bullis Schl; Rockville, MD; (S); Ski Clb; SADD; Nwsp Rptr; Nwsp Stf; Var Bsbl; JV Bsktbl; Var Ftbl; Var Wt Lftg; Hon Roll; NHS; Med.

FRIEDMANN, MITCHELL ADAM; Randallstown SR HS; Randallstown, MD; (Y); Quiz Bowl; Pres Radio Clb; Scholastic Bowl; Pres Temple Yth Grp; Band; School Play; Hon Roll; NHS; Tp 5 Prcnt Grad Cls 86; Merrill Levin Memrl Schlrshp 86; Syracuse U; Pre-Dntstry.

FRIEND, STEPHEN; Southern Garrett HS; Swanton, MD; (Y); Pres Trs Church Yth Grp; Rep Sr Cls; Stu Cncl; Hon Roll; Pres NHS; Arch.

FRIER, SIMONE; Notre Dame Prep; Baltimore, MD; (Y); Capt JV Cheerleading; French Hon Soc; Hon Roll; NHS; Lat Hnr Soc 84-85; H S Pgm Georgetown U 86; Pre-Law.

FRISCH, HAROLD; St Marys HS; Annapolis, MD; (Y); 4/119; Drama Clb; Rep Jr Cls; Rep Sr Cls; Capt Var Lcrss; Var Socr; Bausch & Lomb Sci Awd; High Hon Roll; NHS; Anne Arundel Cnty Sn All Cnty Acad Athltc Tm 86; US Army Rsrv Nat Schlr Athlt Awd 86.

FRITH, JONATHAN; Laurel HS; Laurel, MD; (Y); Quiz Bowl; Ski Clb; Mgr(s); Socr; Tennis; Vllybl; French Hon Soc; High Hon Roll; Prfct Atten Awd; Acad Achvt Awds 85-86; Aeronautcs.

FRITSCHI, JEAN; John Carroll HS; Bel Air, MD; (Y); Church Yth Grp; Cmnty Wkr; Service Clb; Chorus; Church Choir; School Musical; Yrbk Stf; Rep Jr Cls; Rep Sr Cls; Drama Clb; Knghts Clmbs 80; Med Tech.

FROBENIUS, HEIDI; Thomas Stone HS; Waldorf, MD; (S); Rep Stu Cncl; High Hon Roll; Hon Roll; NHS; Acad Lttr 85; SGA Lttr 85, Pin 86.

FROME, PAMELA; T S Wootton HS; Potomoc, MD; (Y); Service Clb; Teachers Aide; Temple Yth Grp; Hon Roll; NHS.

FRY, MICHELE; Thomas Sprigg Wootton HS; Potomac, MD; (Y); Dance Clb; Drama Clb; Teachers Aide; School Musical; Rep Soph Cls; Pom Pon; Hon Roll; Cert Peer Cnslng.

FUJII, KAREN; Oxon Hill HS; Ft Washington, MD; (Y); Lit Mag; Var L Tennis; French Hon Soc; High Hon Roll; NHS; Ntl Merit Ltr; Gvrnrs Top 5 Prcnt 86; Pres Schlrshp 86; Awd For Excllnc In Rsrch Prctcm 86; Loyola Coll Bltmr; Pre-Med.

FULGHUM, KIMBERLY E; Queen Anne Schl; Davidsonville, MD; (Y); Office Aide; Ski Clb; Chorus; Yrbk Bus Mgr; VP Stu Cncl; Stat Bsktbl; Var Socr; Var Sftbl; High Hon Roll; Stu Govt Awd 86; Natl Assn Sccr Coaches Army Awd 86; Radford U; Bus.

FULLER, JASON; Fort Hill HS; Cumberland, MD; (Y); Yrbk Stf; Hon Roll; U Of MD; Engrng.

FULLER, JONATHAN; Northern HS; Baltimore, MD; (Y); Drama Clb; Math Tm; Science Clb; Teachers Aide; Chorus; School Play; VP Stu Cncl; Ftbl; Hon Roll; FBLA; Citywide Mth Comptn 2nd Pl 85; Chemst.

FULLER, NICOLE; Northwestern HS; Hyattsville, MD; (Y); French Clb; Hosp Aide; JA; Pep Clb; SADD; Band; Pres Frsh Cls; Rep Soph Cls; Rep Jr Cls; Rep Sr Cls; Hampton U; Pol Sci.

FUNICELLI, LISA; Gwynn Park HS; Accokeek, MD; (Y); Teachers Aide; Varsity Clb; Chorus; Yrbk Stf; Var L Sftbl; Hon Roll; Top Sr Latin I Stu 86; Secy.

FUNICELLI, MARCIE; Gwynn Park HS; Accokeek, MD; (Y); Teachers Aide; Chorus; Var Sftbl; Hon Roll; Cert Prfcncy Typng II 64 Wpm 85-86; Secrtry.

FUNK, CHARLES; Dundaik HS; Baltimore, MD; (Y); Varsity Clb; Var Lcrss; Var Socr; Essex CC; Bus Mngmnt.

FUNK, CYNTHIA; Allegany HS; Cumberland, MD; (Y); Art Clb; FBLA; Hosp Aide; Pep Clb; SADD; Teachers Aide; Nwsp Rptr; Nwsp Stf; ACC.

FUNK, LAURI ANN; Fallston HS; Fallston, MD; (Y); Church Yth Grp; Dance Clb; SADD; Variety Show; JV Bsktbl; Coach Actv; JV Sftbl; Hon Roll; Bus Admin.

FUNK, MICHELLE; Western SR HS; Baltimore, MD; (Y); 19/412; Church Yth Grp; FBLA; Hon Roll; NHS; Bus.

FUNKHOUSER, CHARLES; Gwynn Park HS; Brandywine, MD; (Y); Cmnty Wkr; Computer Clb; JA; Letterman Clb; Varsity Clb; Rep Stu Cncl; Bowling; Cheerleading; Golf; Socr; U Of MD; FBI Agent.

FURLONG, BETH; Crossland HS; Temple Hills, MD; (Y); Drama Clb; Office Aide; Stage Crew; Pom Pon.

FURR, KEVIN; Wicomico SR HS; Delmar, MD; (Y); 35/220; Trs AFS; VP French Clb; SADD; Pres Mrchg Band; Stage Crew; Pres Symp Band; Hon Roll; Schl Svc Awd 86; Wake Forest U; Law.

FUSARO, AMELIA; James M Bennett SR HS; Salisbury, MD; (Y); 6/200; Am Leg Aux Girls St; JCL; Latin Clb; Spanish Clb; School Musical; Symp Band; Hon Roll; JP Sousa Awd; NHS; Spanish NHS; All-ST Bnd 86; MD Dstngshd Schlr Smi-Fnlst 85; Prsdntl Acdmc Ftns Awd 86; Furman U; Envrnmntl Sci.

FUSCO, CHRISTOPHER J; Seneca Valley HS; Germantown, MD; (Y); Library Aide; Ski Clb; Stage Crew; Hon Roll; Princpls Awd Outstndng Writing 86; Lib Art.

FUTRELL, ANNE; Grace Brethren HS; Temple Hills, MD; (S); Church Yth Grp; Church Choir; Nwsp Rptr; Yrbk Stf; Trs Sr Cls; Rep Stu Cncl; High Hon Roll; Jr NHS; NHS.

GAALAAS, DEAN; Northwestern HS; Hyattsville, MD; (Y); Boys Clb Am; German Clb; Office Aide; Teachers Aide; JV Var Bsbl; High Hon Roll; Hon Roll; NHS; Renssalaer Sci & Math Awd 85-86; Physc & Engrg.

GABBARD, SUSAN; Seneca Valley HS; Germantown, MD; (Y); 107/490; Hosp Aide; Ski Clb; Teachers Aide; L Pom Pon; L Tennis; Hon Roll; Mary Baldwin Coll; Bus Admin.

GABBERT, MARY LYNN; Dulaney HS; Timonium, MD; (Y); Church Yth Grp; SADD; Drill Tm; Capt Pom Pon; Wake Forest; Psych.

GADRA, LISA M; Governor Thomas Johnson HS; Frederick, MD; (Y); 28/360; AFS; Church Yth Grp; VP German Clb; Hosp Aide; Latin Clb; SADD; Teachers Aide; Rep Frsh Cls; Rep Soph Cls; Rep Jr Cls; Intl Bus.

GAGNON, DEBBIE; Thomas Stone HS; Waldorf, MD; (S); Office Aide; Color Guard; Pres Jr Cls; Rep Stu Cncl; JV Var Cheerleading; Var Tennis; Hon Roll; NHS; MVP All Cnty All S MD Athltc Conf Vrsty Ltr 85; U MD; Phys Ther.

GAILUNAS, LYNN; Seton HS; Baltimore, MD; (Y); Church Yth Grp; NFL; School Play; VP Sr Cls; Stu Cncl; JV Capt Bsktbl; Dnfth Awd; Ntl Merit Ltr; St Marys Coll; Educ.

GAITHER, JO ANNE; Archbishop Keough HS; Pasadena, MD; (Y); Pres Spanish Clb; Sec Trs Church Yth Grp; Cmnty Wkr; Computer Clb; GAA; NFL; School Play; Yrbk Rptr; Yrbk Stf; Rep Stu Cncl; Sr Mary Virginia Awd 86; Spn Awd 84-85; Mst Spirit JR Awd 85; Loyola Coll; Engrng.

GAITHER, TIFFANY; Atholton HS; Simpsonville, MD; (Y); Church Yth Grp; Cmnty Wkr; Debate Tm; Letterman Clb; Office Aide; Political Wkr; Speech Tm; SADD; Varsity Clb; Pres VICA; ST Schlr 84; Jaycees Awd 85; Danforth 85; Poltcl Sci.

GALBREATH, GREG; Kent County HS; Chestertown, MD; (Y); 25/180; Camera Clb; Chess Clb; Church Yth Grp; Computer Clb; 4-H; School Play; Socr; Tennis; Hon Roll; Boys ST.

GALLAGHER, ANN MARIE; Archbishop Keough HS; Balt, MD; (Y); VP Art Clb; Yrbk Stf; Rep Frsh Cls; Rep Soph Cls; High Hon Roll; Hon Roll; Trs NHS; Pres Ntl Hnr Soc 86-87; Pre-Med.

GALLAGHER, JENIFER; Thomas Stone HS; Waldorf, MD; (Y); Debate Tm; French Clb; Teachers Aide; Trs Soph Cls; Pres Jr Cls; Pres Sr Cls; Rep Stu Cncl; Mgr(s); Score Keeper; High Hon Roll.

GALLAGHER, LESLIE; St Marys Ryken HS; Leonardtown, MD; (Y); Cmnty Wkr; Drama Clb; School Play; Stage Crew; Lit Mag; Tennis; High Hon Roll; NHS; NEDT Awd; Engl Awd 85; Spnsh II Awd 85; Spnsh III Awd 86; Lang.

GALLAGHER, MIKELLA; Notre Dame Prep; Glen Arm, MD; (Y); Dance Clb; Frsh Cls; Soph Cls; Stu Cncl; Hon Roll; Frgn Svc Diplomt.

GALLAHER, AMELIA; Bohemia Manor HS; Chesapeake City, MD; (Y); 11/95; Drama Clb; Trs French Clb; SADD; Nwsp Rptr; Rep Stu Cncl; Hon Roll; Towson U; Chld Ed.

GALLEY, SUZILYN; Seneca Valley HS; Germantown, MD; (Y); Pep Clb; ROTC; Ski Clb; JV Capt Cheerleading; Pom Pon; Var Socr; Hon Roll; Physcl Thrpst.

GALLION, JENNA; Fort Hill HS; Cumberland, MD; (Y); Pres Drama Clb; Teachers Aide; Pres Thesps; Band; Concert Band; Mrchg Band; School Play; Stu Cncl; Cit Awd; Kiwanis Awd; Intl Thspn Sco Awd 86; Schl Srv Awd 86; Ftr Nwspr Edtr 86; Frostburg ST Coll; Spch Comm.

GALLO, CHRISTOPHER; Mount Saint Joseph HS; Baltimore, MD; (Y); 42/285; Debate Tm; Drama Clb; NFL; Var JV Crs Cntry; Var JV Trk; Hon Roll; NEDT Awd.

GALLOP, MARK; Patterson SR HS; Baltimore, MD; (Y); Pres Drama Clb; Pres Thesps; Chorus; School Musical; School Play; Stage Crew; Variety Show; VP Frsh Cls; VP Soph Cls; VP Jr Cls; Intl Thespn Socty Awd ST Crft & Perfrmnc 85-86; Hofstra U; Drmaa.

GALUSKY, ROBIN; Leonardtown HS; Hollywood, MD; (Y); French Clb; VP Sec FBLA; Yrbk Stf; Rep Frsh Cls; Rep Soph Cls; NHS; High Hons Awd; 3rd Plc Reg Clrk Typst Comptn FBLA 85; 1st Plc Regnl Acct I & 2nd Plc ST Acct I 86; Charles Co CC; Accntng.

GAN, GERALDINE M; Dulaney SR HS; Timonium, MD; (Y); Hosp Aide; Lit Mag; Hon Roll; NHS; Ntl Merit SF; MD Distngshd Schlr Awd 86.

GAN, RICHARD; Walter Johnson HS; Germantown, MD; (Y); Teachers Aide; Chorus; Im Bsktbl; JV Ftbl; Hon Roll; U Of MD; Med.

GANCAYCO, JAMES; Georgetown Prep Schl; Bethesda, MD; (Y); 28/106; Cmnty Wkr; Ski Clb; Trs Sr Cls; Var JV Ftbl; Var Capt Wrstlng; Hon Roll; Church Yth Grp; Science Clb; Im Bsktbl; Achvd Black Belt Martial Arts, Natl Wnnr Natl Piano Auditions, MD Rgnl Karate Champ 86.

GANLEY, DUSTIN K; Middletown HS; Middletown, MD; (Y); 86/235; Leo Clb; Ski Clb; Teachers Aide; Varsity Clb; JV Bsbl; JV Var Bsktbl; JV Var Ftbl; Var L Trk; High Hon Roll; Hon Roll; Engr.

GANNI, DINA; Thomas Stone HS; Waldorf, MD; (S); Acpl Chr; VP Sec Chorus; Madrigals; Swing Chorus; Variety Show; High Hon Roll; Hon Roll; NHS; Spanish NHS; Tri Cnty & All Cnty Hnrs Chorus 82-86; Top 5 SR Choir 86; Penn ST; Acctg.

GANNON, PATRICK; Lackey HS; Waldorf, MD; (Y); Trs Spanish Clb; JV Wrstlng; Engrng.

GANOE, KATRINA; Bishop Walsh HS; Romney, WV; (Y); Sec Church Yth Grp; VP 4-H; Band; Church Choir; Concert Band; Jazz Band; Mrchg Band; Var L Bsktbl; Hon Roll; Law.

GANOE, KELLY; Hancock HS; Hancock, MD; (Y); Exploring; SADD; Teachers Aide; Band; Pres Chorus; School Musical; Cit Awd; Elks Awd; JP Sousa Awd; Prfct Atten Awd; Hagerstown JC; Nrsng.

GANTT, LYNNETTE; Fairmont Heights HS; Seat Pleasant, MD; (Y); Camera Clb; Computer Clb; Dance Clb; ROTC; Variety Show; Var Cheerleading; Var Pom Pon; Hon Roll; Prfct Atten Awd; Pep Band; JROTC Achvt Awd 86; Morgan; Trvl Agnt.

GARDINER, CHRISTINE; Thomas Stone HS; Waldorf, MD; (Y); Office Aide; Concert Band; Mrchg Band; High Hon Roll; Spcl Recognition From Charles Cnty Brd Of Educ 84-86; Acad Let 84-86; Olympcs Of Mind St Champs 84-86; Psych.

GARDINER, HUGH; St Marys Ryken HS; La Plata, MD; (Y); Church Yth Grp; Nwsp Sprt Ed; Rep Frsh Cls; Rep Stu Cncl; Bsktbl; Var JV Socr; Var Tennis; Cit Awd; Hon Roll; NHS; Bus.

GARDINER III, JOSEPH L; St Marys Ryken HS; La Plata, MD; (Y); Am Leg Boys St; Concert Band; Trs Stu Cncl; L Mgr Bsbl; Var JV Wrstlng; High Hon Roll; NHS; Ntl Merit SF; St Schlr; MD Gftd & Tlntd Pgm 82-85; Dept Defns Smmr Sci & Eng Apprntcshp Pgm 85; Aero Eng.

GARDNER, LISA; Centennial HS; Ellicott City, MD; (Y); Art Clb; Yrbk Bus Mgr; Yrbk Phtg; Yrbk Rptr; Yrbk Stf; Hon Roll; Art.

GARG, AMIT; Gaithersburg HS; Gaithersburg, MD; (Y); German Clb; Ski Clb; Orch; Yrbk Stf; Im Bsbl; High Hon Roll; NHS; Hosp Aide; Hon Roll; Jr NHS; Olympcs Mnd 7th Wrld Comptn 85-86; Cellr Physlgy Semnr MD Acd Sci Johns Hopkins U 86; Le High U; Pre-Med.

GARGAR, MARIANNE; Whitman HS; Bethesda, MD; (Y); Art Clb; French Clb; Ski Clb; Honrbl Mention Art Maryland Coll Of Art & Design 86.

GARGES, KATHY; Thomas S Wootton HS; Rockville, MD; (Y); AFS; Cmnty Wkr; Service Clb; Teachers Aide; Socr; Trk; Hon Roll; Hnbl Mntn All County Soccer Sentinel 86; 3rd St 600-M Run-Indoor Trck 84; Spch Path.

GARGIULO, KELLY; Hammond HS; Columbia, MD; (Y); Camera Clb; Girl Scts; Spanish Clb; Yrbk Phtg; Yrbk Rptr; Yrbk Stf; Rep Frsh Cls; Stat Ftbl; Hon Roll; St Marys Coll; Bus.

GARLAND, RANDY; Liberty HS; Finksburg, MD; (S); Church Yth Grp; FCA; Timer; Wt Lftg; Hon Roll; Acad Awd 84; Military.

GARLITZ, MICHAEL F; Beall HS; Frostburg, MD; (Y); Thesps; Band; Concert Band; Mrchg Band; Nwsp Stf; Hon Roll; NHS; Allegany Cnty Hnr Band 84-86; Bst Supprtng Actr 1 Act Play Trnmnt 84; Tchng.

GARLOCK, BRIAN; Clear Spring HS; Clear Spg, MD; (Y); 39/125; Am Leg Boys St; Church Yth Grp; Computer Clb; Ski Clb; SADD; Teachers Aide; Stage Crew; Pres Stu Cncl; Socr; Hon Roll; Law Enfrcmnt.

GARNER, DENISE; Andover HS; Linthicum, MD; (Y); Varsity Clb; Yrbk Bus Mgr; Yrbk Stf; VP Soph Cls; Pres Stu Cncl; Mgr(s); Score Keeper; Sftbl; Hon Roll; Acctng.

GARNER, MARY; Liberty HS; Sykesville, MD; (S); Church Yth Grp; German Clb; High Hon Roll; Prfct Atten Awd; German Honor Scty 85; Principals Awd 83-85.

GARNER, PAMELA; La Reine HS; Temple Hills, MD; (Y); Church Yth Grp; Pep Clb; Church Choir; Stage Crew; Hon Roll; NHS; Spanish NHS; 3rd Pl Sci Fair 85-86; Natl Sci Olympd 86; Towson ST U; Child Psych.

GARNETT, CHERYL; Patterson HS; Baltimore, MD; (Y); Church Yth Grp; Cmnty Wkr; FTA; Teachers Aide; Hon Roll; Prfct Atten Awd; Math Awd 84; Delaware ST COLL; Comp Sci.

GARRETT, STEPHANIE; Fort Hill HS; Cumberland, MD; (Y); Teachers Aide; Chorus; Hon Roll; Spec Educ.

GARVER, DENNIS; Westminster HS; Westminster, MD; (Y); 18/530; Letterman Clb; Varsity Clb; Frsh Cls; Soph Cls; Jr Cls; Stu Cncl; Bsbl; Bsktbl; Ftbl; Ice Hcky; Carroll Countyson All Ath Acad Tm Hnrb Mntn 86; Acctng.

GAST, BARBARA; Eastern Vocational Tech; Baltimore, MD; (Y); Church Yth Grp; VICA; School Musical; Off Stu Cncl; Cit Awd; Hon Roll; Engr.

GAST, CAROL; Great Mills HS; Scotland, MD; (Y); 9/275; Spanish Clb; SADD; Var Capt Bsktbl; Var Sftbl; Var Capt Vllybl; Hon Roll; NHS; Wmns Sprt Fndtn HS All Star Awd 86; Achvmnt Awd Phys Ed 86; Sprts Med.

GASTILO, PHILIP ANTHONY; Oxon Hill HS; Fort Washington, MD; (Y); Am Leg Boys St; Dance Clb; ROTC; Drill Tm; School Play; Variety Show; Capt Bowling; Gym; Wt Lftg; Hon Roll; Jr Vp Sons Vfw 83-84; Pres Awd Cipaa 85-86; Us Mltry Acad; Engrng.

GATLIN, DOUGLAS; Laurel HS; Laurel, MD; (Y); 13/380; Pres Stu Cncl; Tennis; Dnfth Awd; Hon Roll; NHS; Ntl Merit Ltr; Sprntndnts Awd 86; Duke U; Law.

GATLING, KAREN; Northwestern SR HS; Baltimore, MD; (Y); ROTC; Drm Mjr(t); Mrchg Band; Bsktbl; Mgr(s); Pom Pon; Sftbl; Vllybl; Hon Roll; Acctng I Awd 86; CC Of Baltimore; Acctng.

GATLING, RYAN; Pocomoke HS; Pocomoke, MD; (S); Aud/Vis; Chess Clb; Church Yth Grp; Drama Clb; Math Tm; Band; Concert Band; Jazz Band; Pep Band; NHS; NC ST U; Comp Engr.

GATZKE, KRISTINE; Woodlawn HS; Baltimore, MD; (Y); Church Yth Grp; Ski Clb; Spanish Clb; Church Choir; Drill Tm; Mrchg Band; Rep Stu Cncl; Mgr Bsktbl; Mgr Ftbl; JV Lcrss; State Police Force.

GAUS, VAN; Ft Hill HS; Cumberland, MD; (Y); Church Yth Grp; Cmnty Wkr; Var Bsbl; Var Bsktbl; JV Ftbl; Babe Ruth Outstndng SR 86; Dapper Dan Bsbl Grnt 86; United Meth Schlrshp 86; Alleghany CC; Cmptr Sci.

GAUSS, VALERIE; Glenelg HS; Sykesville, MD; (Y); 26/268; Acpl Chr; Chorus; Church Choir; Madrigals; School Musical; Variety Show; Stu Cncl; Score Keeper; High Hon Roll; Hon Roll; Twsn ST U Brd Of Trst Merit Schlrshp 86-87; Vcl Msc Dept Awd 85-86; Twsn ST U; Elem Ed.

GAUTHIER, DANIELLE; St Marys Ryken HS; Prince Frederick, MD; (Y); Camera Clb; Dance Clb; Drama Clb; 4-H; SADD; Band; School Musical; School Play; Variety Show; Bowling; MD Ctr For Prfrmng Arts Gftd & Tlntd Pgm 85; Mrlnd Ctr For Gftd & Tlntd Pgm 86; Psych.

GAVER, VINCENT; North Hagerstown HS; Maugansville, MD; (Y); 9/272; VP Pres French Clb; FBLA; Band; Concert Band; Jazz Band; Mrchg Band; Orch; Pep Band; School Musical; Symp Band; Semper Fidelis Awd For Musical Excllnce 85-86; MD St Merit Schlstc Awd 85-86; Wake Forest U; Accntng.

GAVLAK, CHANTALE; St Marys Ryken HS; Waldorf, MD; (S); Pres Church Yth Grp; VP Science Clb; Im Bowling; Im Vllybl; Cit Awd; High Hon Roll; NHS; Fr Awd 84; Yng Cmmnty Ldrs Of Amer 85; Vlybl 85; U Of MD; Polit Sci.

GAWLER, BOB; Richard Montgomery HS; Rockville, MD; (Y); Boy Scts; Var Crs Cntry; Var Ftbl; Wt Lftg; Var Wrstlng; High Hon Roll; NHS; Boy Scts Of Amer Rnk Life 86; The Citadel; Pltcl Sci.

GAYLE, CAROLYN; Archbishop Keough HS; Columbia, MD; (Y); Church Yth Grp; Sec French Clb; Pres Church Choir; Off Soph Cls; Ntl Merit Ltr; Recgntn Ntl Ed Dev Tests 85; Ntl Piano Plyng Aud 84; Law.

GAYON, KIM; Mc Donough HS; Welcome, MD; (S); 26/310; GAA; Letterman Clb; Teachers Aide; Var Capt Bsktbl; Var Capt Sftbl; Var JV Vllybl; Hon Roll; Jr NHS; NHS.

GEARY, SHANNON; Woodlawn HS; Baltimore, MD; (Y); Church Yth Grp; Trs VICA; Hon Roll; CCC; Data Procng.

GEBAUER, CHRISTINE; Laurel HS; Laurel, MD; (Y); AFS; Cmnty Wkr; Office Aide; Bsktbl; Crs Cntry; Ftbl; VP JV Mgr(s); Trk; Hon Roll; Civic Clb; Athltc Trainer Ftbl Ltr 84-85.

GEDDINGS, KIMBERLY N; Queen Anne Schl; Ft Washington, MD; (Y); Church Yth Grp; Model UN; Science Clb; Rep Frsh Cls; Rep Soph Cls; Rep Trs Jr Cls; Trs Stu Cncl; Var Vllybl; Jr NHS; Opt Clb Awd.

GEELHOED, MIKE; Magruder HS; Derwood, MD; (Y); 17/315; Church Yth Grp; Latin Clb; Band; Hon Roll; Spanish NHS; Top 10% Of Cls; Slvr Mdl ACL Ntl Ltn Exm 85-86.

GEHR, THERESA; Joppatowne HS; Edgewood, MD; (Y); French Clb; German Clb; Concert Band; Jazz Band; Mrchg Band; Powder Puff Ftbl; Swmmng; Hon Roll; Stu Mnth 86; Saxaphone Pin; Mrchng Bar; Harford CC; Frgn Lang.

GEHRIG JR, JOHN F; Westminster HS; Westminster, MD; (Y); Cmnty Wkr; Varsity Clb; JV Var Bsbl; JV Var Bsktbl; Var L Ftbl; High Hon Roll; Prfct Atten Awd; Hon Mntn Carroll Cnty Schlr Athlt 85-86; Engrng.

GELLES, MICHAEL; Fort Hill HS; Cumberland, MD; (Y); Var Capt Var Capt Trk; Var Capt Wrstlng; West VA Wesleyan; Blgy.

GENYS, VICTORIA M; Bishop Walsh HS; Frostburg, MD; (Y); Hosp Aide; Ski Clb; Stage Crew; Pres Stu Cncl; High Hon Roll; Hon Roll; Homecomng Queen 86; Sweet Heart Queen 84; Best Persnlty 86; U Of MDSOCIAL Sci.

GEORG, SHANNON; Northern HS; Accident, MD; (Y); Trs Church Yth Grp; Sec FHA; Church Choir; Hon Roll; Stu Mnth Oct 85; Garrett CC.

GEORGE, ROBERT KEVIN; Queen Annes Co HS; Chester, MD; (Y); SADD; Stage Crew; Ed Nwsp Stf; Yrbk Phtg; Ed Yrbk Stf; Tennis; Trk; High Hon Roll; Most Creative Boy SR 86; Designer Of Yrbk Cover 86; E Carolina U; Illustration.

GERHARD, GREG; Bishop Walsh HS; Frostbury, MD; (Y); 23/110; Am Leg Boys St; Drama Clb; Speech Tm; Thesps; School Musical; School Play; Mgr Bsktbl; Hon Roll; NHS; Debate Tm; Clmbn Sqrs ST Ntry Of MD 84-87; Art.

GERMAN, CHRISSY; Hereford HS; Parkton, MD; (S); 1/209; Church Yth Grp; FTA; Varsity Clb; VP Sr Cls; Rep Stu Cncl; Cheerleading; Cit Awd; VP NHS; Opt Clb Awd; Optm Clb Yth Apprectn Citation 85; MD Distngushd Schlr SF 85; VA Poly Inst; Pre-Vet.

GERSHON, ARI A; Charles E Smith Jewish Day Schl; Silver Spring, MD; (Y); Computer Clb; Math Clb; Nwsp Stf; Ed Lit Mag; NHS; Ntl Merit SF; Spanish NHS; Rensselaer Awd Excllnc Math-Sci 85; Bio Sci.

GERSTENBERGER, LARA; Baltimore City College HS; Baltimore, MD; (S); Pres Sec Church Yth Grp; Church Choir; Yrbk Ed-Chief; Yrbk Stf; Rep Stu Cncl; Var Capt Diving; Var Swmmng; High Hon Roll; Jr NHS; NHS.

GERWIG, KATHLEEN; Notre Dame Prep; Baltimore, MD; (Y); Girl Scts; Hosp Aide; Office Aide; Teachers Aide; Rep Jr Cls; Hon Roll; NEDT Awd; Prfct Atten Awd; Spanish NHS; Aid For Physclly Handicapped Children MD Schl For Blind 85; U Of MD; Architecture.

GERWIN, DANIEL J; C E S Jewish Day Schl; Bethesda, MD; (Y); Temple Yth Grp; School Musical; School Play; Nwsp Rptr; Nwsp Stf; Ed Lit Mag; Rep Frsh Cls; NCTE Awd; Ntl Merit SF; St Schlr; U Synagoge Yths A J Heschel Hnr Scty 84; Ldrshp Awd 84; 1st Prize Schl Sci Fair 84.

GEYER, SHANNON; La Plata HS; Charlotte Hall, MD; (Y); Office Aide; Band; Concert Band; Flag Corp; Mrchg Band; School Musical; Symp Band; Off Soph Cls; Off Jr Cls; Rep Stu Cncl; Miss Democrt 4th Electn Dist 86; MD U; Psych.

GHEE, JOHN F; Crossland HS; Seat Pleasant, MD; (Y); 35/348; Teachers Aide; Band; Concert Band; Mrchg Band; Pep Band; Symp Band; Hon Roll; Lions Clb Band 86; SR Ythg Orch 86; DE ST Clg; Chem.

GHIORZI, ALFRED; Saint Johns Literary Inst; Lovettsville, VA; (Y); Computer Clb; 4-H; Rep Frsh Cls; Rep Soph Cls; Rep Jr Cls; JV Bsktbl; 2nd Pl Math Fair 85 & 86; NEDT Achvt Awd 85; Engrng.

GHIORZI, THOMAS J; Prospect Hall HS; Lovettsville, VA; (Y); 1/36; 4-H; Pres Frsh Cls; VP Jr Cls; Pres VP Stu Cncl; Stat Bsktbl; High Hon Roll; NHS; Ntl Merit SF; Hugh O Brien Leadrshp Semnr; Genetic Engrng.

GIBBONS, DEREK; Fallston HS; Fallston, MD; (Y); 40/242; Varsity Clb; Var Capt Bsktbl; Var Capt Lcrss; Var Capt Socr; Hon Roll; Sci Awd 85; Vrsty Let-Soccer & Bsktbl 84-86; St Champs 85; Comp Sci.

GIBBONS, JAMES; North Carroll HS; Hampstead, MD; (Y); JA; Var Ftbl; Hon Roll; Sytms Anlsyt.

GIBBONS, JAMES; Northeast HS; Elkton, MD; (Y); 16/250; SADD; Rep Soph Cls; Rep Sr Cls; Rep Stu Cncl; L Var Socr; L Var Tennis; DAR Awd; Hon Roll; NHS; Outstndng Achvt Awds-Math & Socl Studies 84-85; Grad With Diploma Plus 85-86; Norwich U; Mech Engr.

GIBBS, DAN; Walkersville HS; Walkersville, MD; (Y); Cmnty Wkr; Drama Clb; FBLA; Quiz Bowl; Science Clb; Teachers Aide; School Musical; School Play; Hon Roll; NHS; Sci Fair 1st Pl 85; Maryland FBLA Imprmpt Spkng Cont 4th Pl 84; Bio Sci.

GIBBS, KATIE; Saint Marys HS; Edgewater, MD; (Y); 18/118; Church Yth Grp; Drama Clb; Hosp Aide; Q&S; Service Clb; Band; School Musical; Nwsp Rptr; Yrbk Stf; Lit Mag; Pres Acad Ftns Awd 86; Trig Awd 85; Vassar Clg; Bio.

GIBSON, BRIAN; Patterson HS; Baltimore, MD; (Y); Boy Scts; Church Yth Grp; Crs Cntry; Wrstlng; Hon Roll; Jr NHS; NHS; Prfct Atten Awd; Ne Regnl Supdt Awd 84; Engrng.

GIBSON, CORELLA; Milford Mill SR HS; Balt, MD; (Y); Church Yth Grp; Cmnty Wkr; Drama Clb; English Clb; FBLA; GAA; Girl Scts; Letterman Clb; Library Aide; Office Aide; Wittenberg U; Atty.

GIBSON, DEREK; Thomas Stone HS; Waldorf, MD; (Y); Spanish Clb; SADD; JV Ftbl; Wt Lftg; Hon Roll; Elec Engrng.

GIBSON, DONNA; Parkdale HS; Riverdale, MD; (S); Teachers Aide; Chorus; Church Choir; Elks Awd; Sec French Hon Soc; High Hon Roll; NHS; SR Prom Comm; Brdcstg Club; U Of MD; Englsh.

GIBSON, MARY; Chopticon HS; Bushwood, MD; (Y); 9/249; Cmnty Wkr; FBLA; Sec Latin Clb; Band; Color Guard; Concert Band; Mrchg Band; Hon Roll; NHS; Opt Clb Awd; Senatorial Schlrshp 86-90; Salisbury ST Coll; Poli Sci.

GIELNER, DENISE; Easton Vo-Tech; Baltimore, MD; (Y); Computer Clb; Lit Mag; Rep Frsh Cls; Rep Soph Cls; Rep Jr Cls; Var L Cheerleading; Var Socr; Sftbl; Hon Roll; Jr NHS; Comp.

GIESKER, LEONARD; Queen Annes County HS; Stevensvle, MD; (Y); Boy Scts; Band; Mrchg Band; Pep Band; Hon Roll; Prfct Atten Awd; Aerospace Engrng.

GILBERT, ALLYSON; Crossland SR HS; Ft Washington, MD; (Y); Pep Clb; Band; Concert Band; Jazz Band; Mrchg Band; Symp Band; Trs Soph Cls; Trs Jr Cls; Trs Sr Cls; Wnnr PGMTA JR Concerto Cmptn 84; Natl Wnnr Of Natl Piano Auditions Of Amer Clg Of Music 85; U Of MD; Radio.

GILBERT, JENNIFER; Oakland Mills HS; Columbia, MD; (Y); Pres Band; Pres Concert Band; Drm & Bgl; Jazz Band; Pres Mrchg Band; Church Yth Grp; Jr Cls; Rep Stu Cncl; Hon Roll; NHS; Politics.

GILCHRIST, JUANA; Western HS; Baltimore, MD; (Y); Chorus; Orch; Off Stu Cncl; Hon Roll; Comp Prog.

GILES, TONJA; Northern HS; Owings, MD; (Y); Church Yth Grp; Office Aide; Hon Roll; Prnc George CC; Accntnt.

GILL, GINNY; Mc Donough HS; White Plains, MD; (Y); 49/295; Church Yth Grp; Letterman Clb; Teachers Aide; Varsity Clb; Crs Cntry; Trk; Hon Roll; Chns Cnty CC Inst Schlrshp 86; SR Athltc Awd 86; Bus.

GILL, LOUISE; St Vincent Palloitt HS; Fulton, MD; (S); 22/115; AFS; French Clb; Trs Pres Stu Cncl; Var Capt Sftbl; Var Capt Vllybl; French Hon Soc; Hon Roll; NHS; Ski Clb; Accntng.

GILL, RUTH; Parkside HS; Salisbury, MD; (Y); Drama Clb; Thesps; School Play; Stage Crew; Hon Roll; Best Actress Awd 85-86; TAG; U MD; Arch.

GILL, STEPHANIE; Northern HS; Huntingtown, MD; (Y); French Clb; Intnl Clb; Band; Concert Band; Jazz Band; Mrchg Band; Orch; Pep Band; Symp Band; Var Bsktbl; AIA & Hnrs Prog; Advncd Placement Engl; Superintndts Schlc Recognt Awd; Forgn Langs.

GILL, VALERIE; Liberty HS; Sykesville, MD; (S); Drama Clb; Office Aide; Band; Chorus; School Musical; Stage Crew; High Hon Roll; NHS; Carroll Al-Cnty Choir 85 & 86; MD Al-ST Choir 86; Towson ST U; Music Ed.

GILLAN, KAREN; Westminster HS; Westminster, MD; (Y); Trs German Clb; Pres JA; Teachers Aide; Yrbk Phtg; Hon Roll; Accelrtd Acad Cert 86; U MD.

GILLESPIE, ERICA; Beall HS; Frostburg, MD; (Y); Rptr 4-H; Speech Tm; Y-Teens; School Play; Yrbk Ed-Chief; Trs Frsh Cls; Off Stu Cncl; Var Trk; Hon Roll; NHS.

GILLIS, ANDREA; W Nottingham Acad; Columbia, MD; (Y); Drama Clb; SADD; Temple Yth Grp; Thesps; School Play; Stage Crew; Yrbk Rptr; Sec Stu Cncl; Mgr(s); Comm Svc Awd Schrlshp 86; Tour Guide Awd 84-86; Dorm Porctor Awd 85-86.

GILMAN, BOBBI-JO; Northern HS; Chesapeake Bch, MD; (Y); Hosp Aide; Teachers Aide; VICA; Hon Roll; HOSA 85-86; 1st Pl-Sklls Olympcs Med Spllng & Termnlgy In Voctnl Schl 85-86; Hgh ASVAB Tst Scr 85-86; CC; Med Asst.

GILPIN, KRISTINA; Fort Hill HS; Cumberland, MD; (Y); 1/254; Church Yth Grp; Band; Nwsp Stf; Var Tennis; Cit Awd; High Hon Roll; NHS; NEDT Awd; Computer Clb; Girl Scts; Music & Arts Clb Schlrshps 86; Wnnr MD Synod LCA Evnglsm Wrtg Cntst 85; Mcdnlds All-Amrcn Band 86.

GILPIN, TERESA; Northern HS; Sunderland, MD; (Y); 23/301; Stu Cncl; Hon Roll; Opt Clb Awd; Pres Acad Ftnss Awd 86.

GION, LISA; John Carroll Schl; Havre De Grace, MD; (Y); 5/238; Camera Clb; Yrbk Phtg; JV Fld Hcky; Powder Puff Ftbl; Var Sftbl; French Hon Soc; High Hon Roll; NHS; Prfct Atten Awd.

GIORIOSO, CHARLES; Mt St Joseph HS; Linthicum, MD; (Y); Hosp Aide; Ski Clb; High Hon Roll; Hon Roll; Salisbury ST; Bus.

GIPE, VIKI; Highland View Acad; Martinsburg, WV; (Y); Nwsp Ed-Chief; Yrbk Ed-Chief; Rep Frsh Cls; VP Sr Cls; VP Stu Cncl; Hon Roll; NHS; Girls Clb Treas 83-84; Schl Senator 82-83; Hagerstown Bus Coll; Paralgl.

GIVEN, DONNA; North East HS; Elkton, MD; (Y); Church Yth Grp; Leo Clb; Chorus; Color Guard; Mrchg Band; Hon Roll; Cedar Crest Grnt 86-87; Cedar Crest; Nclr Med.

GIZZI, CATHERINE; Allegany HS; Cumberland, MD; (Y); Ski Clb; U Of MD; Comp.

GLADMAN, TERRI; Westminster HS; Sykesville, MD; (Y); Church Yth Grp; 4-H; Hosp Aide; Latin Clb; Ski Clb; Spanish Clb; Capt Mrchg Band; Capt Twrlr; 4-H Awd; Chld Psychlgst.

GLASCOE III, WILLIAM O; Crossland HS; Fort Washington, MD; (Y); 27/370; Am Leg Boys St; Math Tm; Crs Cntry; Bausch & Lomb Sci Awd; Hon Roll; Jr NHS; Air Force Acad; Astro Engrng.

GLASER, BRIAN; St Marys-Ryken HS; Mechanicsville, MD; (S); 2/138; Am Leg Boys St; Drama Clb; Spanish Clb; Speech Tm; Swmmng; Trk; NHS; MD Dstngshd Schlr Fnlst 85; Waterpolo; Cnty Cncl On Yth 84-86; Bard Coll; Filmmaking.

GLASGOW, GREGORY; Friendly SR HS; Ft Washington, MD; (Y); Church Yth Grp; Computer Clb; Band; Hon Roll; Engrng.

GLASS, LISA; Francis Scott Key HS; Taneytown, MD; (Y); Yrbk Stf; Hon Roll; Pres Taneytown Jayteens 85-86; Schl Light-Sound Chrew 84-85; Mt St Marys Coll; Acctg.

GLASS, TRUDY F; Francis Scott Key HS; Taneytown, MD; (Y); Office Aide; Pres Spanish Clb; Teachers Aide; Nwsp Bus Mgr; Cit Awd; High Hon Roll; NHS; Ntl Merit Ltr; Hannah Shunk Mem Awd 86; Engl Achvt Awd 86; Spnsh Achvt Awd 86; Mt Ida Coll; Comm.

GLASSER, JASON; Pikesville SR HS; Balto, MD; (Y); Math Clb; Spanish Clb; SADD; Stat Bsktbl; Var Crs Cntry; JV Var Trk; Hon Roll; NHS; Jr Sci And Sympsm 86; Tufts U; Fnce.

GLENN, MICHAEL DARIN; Randallstown HS; Randallstown, MD; (Y); Political Wkr; Var Bsbl; JV Socr; Capt Var Trk; Church Yth Grp; Cmnty Wkr; Drama Clb; Band; Concert Band; Jazz Band; Six Flags Band Awd 83-84; MVP Trck 83-84; Ctznshp Awd Band 86; NC ST; Nvl Ofcr.

GLENNON, SUSAN; Pallotti HS; Laurel, MD; (S); AFS; Drama Clb; FBLA; Nwsp Rptr; Yrbk Stf; Var Crs Cntry; Stat Socr; Tennis; High Hon Roll; NHS; Soc Distngushd Am 86; U DE; Physcl Thrpy.

GLIME, BRYON; Colonel Richardson HS; Federalsburg, MD; (Y); French Clb; Rep Soph Cls; Var Capt Tennis; Hon Roll; Dist 6 Tnns Chmpn 84-86; MVP Vrsty Tnns 83-86; Achvt Awd 85-86; High Point Coll High Point; Bus.

GLINSKY, CYNTHIA; North Harford HS; White Hall, MD; (Y); Sec Dance Clb; French Clb; FBLA; Lit Mag; JV Fld Hcky; Hon Roll; Bus.

GLOVER, KATHERINE; The Bullis HS; Mclean, VA; (Y); Church Yth Grp; Cmnty Wkr; Drama Clb; Key Clb; Model UN; Band; Concert Band; Pep Band; School Musical; Rep Frsh Cls; Franklin & Marshall Coll Awd Hmnts 85-86.

GNIDZIEJKO, ROBIN; Mercy HS; Towson, MD; (Y); Cmnty Wkr; GAA; Rep Jr Cls; Cheerleading; Outstndng Rcgntn-Svc To Eldrly 85; Notre Dame MD; Scl Wrkr.

GODFREY, GEOFFREY R; Hereford HS; Millers, MD; (Y); Jazz Band; Var Crs Cntry; Var Trk; Hon Roll; Prfct Atten Awd; Acad All Amer 86.

GODSEY, ANNISA; Western HS; Baltimore, MD; (Y); German Clb; Hon Roll; Syracuse U; Psych.

GOEDEKE, MARY CLAIRE; Institute Of Notre Dame; Baltimore, MD; (Y); Church Yth Grp; French Clb; Math Clb; Flag Corp; Stage Crew; Yrbk Stf; Lit Mag; Rep Soph Cls; Hon Roll; Prfct Atten Awd; Towson ST U; Elem Educ.

GOHEEN, NANCY; Northwestern HS; Hyattsville, MD; (Y); 4-H; German Clb; Teachers Aide; Var Sftbl; Hon Roll; NHS; Acdmc Excel Awd 85; U MD.

GOLDBLATT, JEFF; The Bullis Schl; Potomac, MD; (S); 4/94; Am Leg Boys St; Letterman Clb; Office Aide; Varsity Clb; Nwsp Stf; Pres Frsh Cls; Pres Jr Cls; Var Socr; High Hon Roll; NHS; Dentstry.

GOLDBURN, SHARON; The Catholic HS Of Baltimor; Baltimore, MD; (Y); 10/189; Red Cross Aide; Spanish Clb; Stage Crew; Hon Roll; NHS; Spanish NHS; Delg Scholar Hibernian Soc 86-87; Senatorial Scholar 86-87; MD ST Scholar Fun 86-87; Loyola Coll.

GOLDEN, JUSTINE; Andover HS; Linthicum, MD; (Y); Drama Clb; 4-H; Science Clb; Spanish Clb; Lit Mag; Mgr(s); L Pom Pon; High Hon Roll; NHS.

GOLDGRABEN, FELICE; T S Wooton HS; Gaitherburg, MD; (Y); AFS; Science Clb; Temple Yth Grp; Hon Roll; Ntl Merit Ltr; Hnrb Mntn Montgomery Area Sci Fair 84.

GOLDMAN, ANTHONY; Patterson HS; Baltimore, MD; (Y); Hosp Aide; JA; Concert Band; Jazz Band; Pep Band; Ftbl; Gym; Lcrss; Wrstlng; FL ST; CIA.

GOLDMAN, SCOTT; Oakland Mills HS; Columbia, MD; (Y); 45/240; Office Aide; Teachers Aide; Ed Yrbk Stf; Hon Roll; Regnl Pres Bnai Brith Yth Orgnztn 85-86, Chptr Pres; Silvr Shield David Hghst Awd Yth Grp; Htl/Rest Mgmt.

GOLDMAN, WENDY; Rockville HS; Rockville, MD; (Y); 74/484; AFS; Drama Clb; Hosp Aide; PAVAS; Thesps; Stu Cncl; JV Cheerleading; Var Capt Crs Cntry; Var Co-Capt Trk; Ntl Merit SF; MD Ctr Arts 81-84; Montgomery Cnty Yth Orh 81-84; Peer Cnslr 85; Ocnogrphy.

GOLDSMITH, TINA; La Plata HS; Hughesville, MD; (Y); Art Clb; DECA; 4-H; Teachers Aide; Variety Show; 4-H Awd; Hon Roll; Comp.

GOLDSTEIN, MARC; Thomas S Wootton HS; Potomac, MD; (Y); Cmnty Wkr; JV Ftbl; Wt Lftg; High Hon Roll; NHS; Worked Giant Food Bagger 85; Worked PCFCU Bankteller 86; U Of VA; Architectur.

GOLIGHTLY, DOUGLAS; Fort Hill HS; Cumberland, MD; (Y); Boy Scts; Pres VP Church Yth Grp; Band; Concert Band; Mrchg Band; Hon Roll; NHS; Frostburg ST Coll; Bio.

GOMER, STEPHANIE; Beall HS; Frostburg, MD; (Y); AFS; Hst Service Clb; Chorus; Church Choir; Drill Tm; School Play; Rep Frsh Cls; Trs Soph Cls; Rep Jr Cls; VP Sr Cls; Frostburg ST; Elem Ed.

GOMEZ, ANGELA; Senca Valley HS; Gaithersburg, MD; (Y); 51/490; Teachers Aide; Hon Roll; Ball ST U Hnrs Dist Schlrshp 86-87; Ball ST U; Spec Ed Tchr.

GONZAGA, ROMMEL B; Bishop Walsh HS; Cumberland, MD; (Y); 50/113; Art Clb; Drama Clb; Ski Clb; Cheerleading; Gym; Socr; Tennis; Trk; Hon Roll; Towson ST U; Bus Admin.

GONZALEZ, ADALILA; Springbrook HS; Silver Spring, MD; (Y); 157/488; Pep Clb; Spanish Clb; Stage Crew; JV Pom Pon; Schlrshp Awd Brd Of Trustees Montgomery Coll 86; Modern Miss Schlrshp Pgnt 85; Spec Olympcs Awd 85; Montgomery Coll MD; Mrktng.

GONZALEZ, STEVEN; Seneca Valley HS; Gaithersburg, MD; (Y); 300/500; FFA; Variety Show; Wrstlng; Hon Roll; Semi-Fnlst Ntl Hispanic Awds Prog 86; U Of MD College Pk.

GOODEN, TISHA; Catoctin HS; Thurmont, MD; (Y); 3/198; Sec Church Yth Grp; Red Cross Aide; Science Clb; Teachers Aide; Chorus; Church Choir; School Musical; Stage Crew; Sec Stu Cncl; God Cntry Awd; 4th Pl FCSEF Medcl Hlth 84; ST Merit Schlstc Awd 86; Cert Prof Acctng 86; Messiah Coll; Hist.

GOODMAN, ELIZABETH J; Walt Whitman HS; Bethesda, MD; (Y); 39/445; VP Camera Clb; Drama Clb; PAVAS; Political Wkr; Thesps; Variety Show; Yrbk Phtg; Lit Mag; Off Jr Cls; Off Sr Cls; A GPA-HNR Role; Hnrb Mntn-Ntl Zoo Photo Cntst 85; Wesleyan U; Law.

GOODMAN, JILL; Snow Hill HS; Snow Hill, MD; (S); 4/84; Am Leg Aux Girls St; Drm Mjr(t); Pres Frsh Cls; Rep Soph Cls; Pres Jr Cls; Pres Sr Cls; Rep Stu Cncl; High Hon Roll; NHS; St Schlr; Yth Senate Schlrshp 85; Schl Spirt Awd 85; Capt Majrtt Sqd 85-86; Salisbury ST; Bio Tchr.

GOODWIN, BRUCE; St Andrews Episcopal Schl; Bethesda, MD; (Y); Computer Clb; Science Clb; Nwsp Stf; Bsbl; Bsktbl; Wt Lftg; Hon Roll; Prfct Atten Awd; Brn Blt In Karate 86; All Star Bsbl Team 86.

GOODWIN, LAURA E; Howard HS; Elkridge, MD; (Y); Church Yth Grp; Drama Clb; Hosp Aide; Thesps; Chorus; School Play; Variety Show; Sec Frsh Cls; Sec Soph Cls; Sec Jr Cls; Jr Miss Pagaent; Schl/AM Morning Annoucements; U Of MD; Fine Arts.

GOONERATNE, RAVI; Walter Johnson HS; Bethesda, MD; (Y); Church Yth Grp; Debate Tm; Math Tm; NFL; Speech Tm; High Hon Roll; Hon Roll; Math Clb; Im Bsktbl; Im Sftbl; Wltr Jhnsn Awds Stu Cngrss & Debate 86; Mntgmry Cnty Pblc Schls Stu Cngrss 2 Awds 86; Ntl Frnsc Lg 86; Comp Sci.

GORDON, CHRISTINE M; Western HS; Baltimore, MD; (Y); French Clb; Sftbl; Swmmng; Trk; Sci Achvt Awd 84; Towson ST U; Comp Prgmng.

GORDON, DAVID; Leonardtown HS; Hollywood, MD; (Y); #22 In Class; Computer Clb; French Clb; Letterman Clb; Office Aide; Pep Clb; Varsity Clb; Rep Jr Cls; Var Ftbl; Var Capt Wt Lftg; Var Capt Wrstlng; MVP Wrstlng 84-86; Mst Outstndng Lftr MD ST Pwrlftng Chmpnshps 85; U FL; Psychlgy.

GORDON, JOY; Andover HS; Linthicum Hts, MD; (Y); Church Yth Grp; Drama Clb; Science Clb; Lit Mag; Mgr(s); Pom Pon; Hon Roll.

GORDY, GRETTA A; Garrison Forest Schl; Baltimore, MD; (Y); Drama Clb; Spanish Clb; Thesps; Chorus; School Musical; Lit Mag; Hosp Aide; Latin Clb; Model UN; Service Clb; Vassar Coll; Psych.

GORRELL, BARBARA; John Carroll HS; Pylesville, MD; (Y); 113/238; Trs Church Yth Grp; Girl Scts; Hon Roll; Grmn Ntl Hnr Soc 86; Srvce Awd Hstng Grmn Exchnge Stud 85; U Of MD; Psych.

GOSLEE, JULIE; Wicomico SR HS; Salisbury, MD; (Y); 14/260; Am Leg Aux Girls St; French Clb; Soroptimist; Symp Band; Pres Jr Cls; Pres Sr Cls; Rep Stu Cncl; Trk; NHS; VFW Awd; Pharm.

GOSS, JUDITH M; Sherwood HS; Olney, MD; (Y); 83/317; VP Church Yth Grp; Model UN; Madrigals; School Musical; Swing Chorus; Stu Cncl; Var Cheerleading; NHS; Spanish NHS; SGA Svc Awd; Law.

GOSS, PATRICIA; Fort Hill HS; Cumberland, MD; (Y); 15/284; Sec Computer Clb; Pep Clb; Service Clb; Frsh Cls; Soph Cls; Jr Cls; Sr Cls; High Hon Roll; NHS; Sch Supply Store Stu Mgmr And Sec 84-86; Frstbrg Acadmc Merit Schlrshp 86; Acadmc And Serv Ltrs 86; Frostburg ST Clg; Acctg.

GOTO, DAVID M; Fairmont Heights HS; Tuxedo, MD; (Y); 3/270; Computer Clb; Math Clb; Var L Bsktbl; Var L Ftbl; High Hon Roll; NHS; NEDT Awd; Pres Schlr; Sprntndnts Cert 86; Nmrs Cmptr Awds 85-86; Maryland Coll Park; Cmptrs.

GOTTLIEB, ANDY; Magruder HS; Rockville, MD; (Y); Sec Am Leg Boys St; ROTC; Var Capt Crs Cntry; Hon Roll; Var Capt Trk; Amer Lgn Awd Acdmc Exclinc 84-85; Top 10 Pct Awd Soph, JR Clss 84-86; New Coll U South FL; Engl.

GOUDY, MILDRED; Patterson HS; Baltimore, MD; (Y); Var Cheerleading; Hon Roll; Jr NHS; Sec NHS; Loyola Coll; Comp Sci.

GOUKER, STEPHANNE M; Boonsboro HS; Boonsboro, MD; (Y); 17/203; Trs Church Yth Grp; Varsity Clb; Sec Yrbk Ed-Chief; VP Soph Cls; Rep Stu Cncl; Cheerleading; Cit Awd; High Hon Roll; Lion Awd; Opt Clb Awd; Gldn Egls Best All Arnd Chrldr 85-86; Clpr Mchl Pst 10 Schlrshp 86; Gldn Egls 1st Pl Jmp Cls Awd 85-86; Hagerstown JR Coll; Bus.

GOULD, ELIZABETH; Roland Park Country HS; Baltimore, MD; (Y); Drama Clb; Sec Model UN; Acpl Chr; School Musical; School Play; Yrbk Stf; Lit Mag; Ntl Merit Ltr; Haverford Coll.

GOULD, LAURA; North Hagerstown HS; Hagerstown, MD; (Y); 10/237; Am Leg Aux Girls St; Drama Clb; Pres Latin Clb; Orch; Ed Nwsp Rptr; Sec Soph Cls; VP Sr Cls; Rep Stu Cncl; Var L Tennis; Swmmng; SGA Cmmtte Chrprsn; Prom Cmmtte Chrprsn; Hugh O Brien Yth Ldrshp Semnr Ambssdr.

GOULD, SUZANNE M; Laurel HS; Laurel, MD; (Y); Ed Yrbk Stf; Var L Bsktbl; Var L Sftbl; Hon Roll; Aerospace.

GOUNDER, SUDHA; Potomac HS; Oxon Hill, MD; (Y); Lit Mag; High Hon Roll; Hon Roll; Acad Exclince Awd 84-85.

GOVE, TIMOTHY S; Linganore HS; Mount Airy, MD; (Y); Ski Clb; Socr; High Hon Roll; NHS; MD Dstngshd Schlr 85-86; MD JR Sci Sympsm, Ntl Engrng Apt Srch Outstndng Perf Cert 85; U DE; Elec Engrng.

GOVOTSOS, PANAGIOTIS DEMETRIUS; Linganore HS; Monrovia, MD; (Y); Boy Scts; Pres 4-H; Scholastic Bowl; Chorus; School Musical; 4-H Awd; Hon Roll; Ntl Merit Ltr; Chess Clb; Latin Clb; Ruth E & Mary E M Smith Scholar 86-87; Milton L Shifman Scholar Shepherd Coll 86-87; Shepherd Coll; Mth Tchr.

GOWL, LAURA; Brooklyn Park HS; Baltimore, MD; (S); 4/143; Pres Band; Church Yth Grp; Girl Scts; Teachers Aide; Concert Band; Mrchg Band; Yrbk Stf; Rep Stu Cncl; Mgr(s); Hon Roll; Cpa.

GRACE, DOUGLAS; Elkton HS; Elkton, MD; (Y); Am Leg Boys St; Aud/Vis; Intnl Clb; Key Clb; Library Aide; Mgr(s); Trk; Elks Awd; Hon Roll; Prfct Atten Awd; Prncpls Awd 83-86; Trpl Crwn Awd 83-84; Outstndg Stu In Alg II-TRIG 85-86; Acctg.

GRACE, MOYA; Western HS; Baltimore, MD; (Y); 42/460; Yrbk Stf; Rep Sr Cls; Hon Roll; Sal; Top Achvt Accntng I Hons 86; Schl Srvc Awd; Towson ST U; CPA.

GRAD, ALLISON; The Bullis Schl; Silverspg, MD; (Y); 17/87; Drama Clb; Hosp Aide; Thesps; School Musical; School Play; Nwsp Stf; Yrbk Stf; High Hon Roll; Hon Roll; Pres Schlr; Frgn Lang Excllnce Prize 86; American U; Psych.

GRADE, SHERYL R; Baltimore Polytechnic Inst; Baltimore, MD; (Y); 10/369; Church Yth Grp; Cmnty Wkr; Political Wkr; Hon Roll; U S Hse Reps Page 85; Cert Recog MD Dely Curtis Anderson 83; MD Dely Scholar 85; Towson ST U; CPA.

GRAF, RON; Laurel HS; Laurel, MD; (Y); Aud/Vis; Drama Clb; Science Clb; Band; Chorus; School Musical; Stage Crew; Yrbk Rptr; Rep Frsh Cls; Rep Sr Cls.

GRAFF, TAMARA; Wicomco SR HS; Delmar, MD; (Y); 6/260; Am Leg Aux Girls St; VP Spanish Clb; Drill Tm; VP Stu Cncl; Stat Sftbl; Stat Wrstlng; VP Pres NHS; Sec Pres Church Yth Grp; VP Intnl Clb; Math Tm; Rep Schl MD Hugh O Brian ST Ldrshp Smnr 84-85; USNA Smmr Sci Semnr 85-86; Yng Wrtrs Wrkshp U VA 85; Intl Rltns.

GRAHAM, AMY; Col Zadok Magruder HS; Derwood, MD; (Y); Am Leg Aux Girls St; Drama Clb; 4-H; Latin Clb; NFL; Thesps; School Musical; Yrbk Stf; Pom Pon; Hon Roll; Law.

GRAHAM, CHIPI; Annapolis Area Christian HS; Lothian, MD; (S); 1/26; Church Yth Grp; School Play; Nwsp Phtg; Yrbk Stf; Stu Cncl; Var L Bsktbl; Var Score Keeper; Var L Socr; High Hon Roll; NHS.

GRAHAM, JEFF; Fort Hill HS; Cumberland, MD; (Y); 4-H; Band; Concert Band; Mrchg Band; Pep Band; L Var Trk; Allegany CC; Elctrmchncl Tech.

GRAHAM, SUE; Gaithersburg HS; Gaithersburg, MD; (Y); 95/568; Church Yth Grp; Exploring; 4-H; Key Clb; Spanish Clb; Varsity Clb; Church Choir; Drill Tm; Im JV Sftbl; Var Capt Tennis; Distngshd Cadet Awd 85; Duke U; Engrg.

GRANDPRE, SUSAN M; Notre Dame Preparatory Schl; Cockeysville, MD; (Y); Office Aide; Teachers Aide; Nwsp Rptr; Var Socr; Cit Awd; High Hon Roll; Sec NHS; Ntl Merit Ltr; Grmn Hnr Soc 84; Senate Page MD Genl Assembly 86; St Bonaventure U.

GRANGER, TIM; North East HS; N East, MD; (Y); DE Tech; Civil Engrng.

GRANT, CHARSETTA M; Owings Mills JR SR HS; Owings Mills, MD; (Y); Church Yth Grp; Band; Rep Sr Cls; JV Var Sftbl; NHS; Drama Clb; Concert Band; Mrchg Band; Hon Roll; Ntl Merit Schlrshp Pgm Outstndng Negro Stu 85-86; Physcl Sci.

GRANT, DONALD; Potomac SR HS; Oxon Hill, MD; (Y); Cmnty Wkr; Letterman Clb; Varsity Clb; Var Capt Bsktbl; Var Crs Cntry; Hon Roll; Natl AAU All Trnmnt Tm 86; Var Bsktbl Capt 86; MIP Awd Bsktbl 86; 2nd Tm All Cnty Bsktbl 86; Schlr Ath; Acctng.

GRANT, STEVEN; Fort Hill HS; Rawlings, MD; (Y); Church Yth Grp; Exploring; Band; Church Choir; Concert Band; Mrchg Band; Pep Band; Hon Roll; Comp Sci.

GRANTHAM, STEVEN; Westminster HS; Westminster, MD; (Y); 21/500; Letterman Clb; Rep Frsh Cls; Stu Cncl; Ftbl; Hon Roll; Math.

GRAPES, TRACEY; Smithsburg HS; Hagerstown, MD; (Y); Pres Sec Church Yth Grp; Latin Clb; Pres Band; Concert Band; Drm Mjr(t); Jazz Band; Mrchg Band; School Musical; Stu Cncl; Var L Trk; Music.

GRAUZLIS, NANCY; Montgomery Blair HS; Silver Spring, MD; (Y); 24/356; French Clb; Rep Frsh Cls; VP Soph Cls; Rep Stu Cncl; Pom Pon; French Hon Soc; Hon Roll; NHS; Natl Sci Merit Awd 85; Pres Acadmc Ftnss Awd 86; U Of MD; Physcn.

GRAVELLE, AARON; Great Mills HS; Lexington Park, MD; (Y); #25 In Class; Church Yth Grp; Exploring; Pep Clb; Pres SADD; Mrchg Band; Var L Ftbl; High Hon Roll; Hon Roll; Jr NHS; NHS; Cntmpry Iss Achvmnt Awd; Engr.

GRAY, ANGIE; Northern HS; Huntingtown, MD; (Y); 133/300; Church Yth Grp; 4-H; FNA; Girl Scts; Hosp Aide; Library Aide; Office Aide; VICA; 4-H Awd; Hon Roll; Prince Georges CC; Resp Thrpst.

GRAY, COREY; Walt Whitman HS; Bethesda, MD; (Y); Pres Cmnty Wkr; Drama Clb; Office Aide; Pres Spanish Clb; Madrigals; Nwsp Bus Mgr; Rep Stu Cncl; High Hon Roll; Rotary Awd; Spanish NHS; Spcl Olympcs 85-87; Intrct Clb Pres 85-87; Lbrl Arts.

GRAY, FELICIA; Montgomery Blair HS; Takoma Pk, MD; (Y); SADD; Teachers Aide; Chorus; School Play; Ed Nwsp Stf; Var Cheerleading; Gym; Var Socr; Hon Roll; Jr NHS; Boston Clg; Pysch.

GRAY, GRETA; Oxon Hill SR Hill HS; Ft Washington, MD; (Y); Variety Show; Pom Pon; High Hon Roll; Hon Roll.

GRAY, SHEENEQUA; Forestville SR HS; Forestville, MD; (Y); Cmnty Wkr; Dance Clb; FBLA; Office Aide; Rep Frsh Cls; Rep Soph Cls; Hon Roll; Engl-Outstndg Achvt 83-84; Elizabeth City ST U; Bus Mgmt.

GRAY III, WALTER; Loyola Blakefield HS; Baltimore, MD; (Y); 30/197; Cmnty Wkr; Spanish Clb; Nwsp Bus Mgr; Yrbk Stf; Rep Sr Cls; Var Socr; Hon Roll; NHS; Natl Achvt SF 85; Brown U; Mech Engrng.

GREDLICS, JENNY; Hammond HS; Columbia, MD; (Y); 31/285; Camera Clb; Church Yth Grp; Teachers Aide; Varsity Clb; Drill Tm; Coach Actv; L Var Pom Pon; High Hon Roll; Hon Roll; U Of MD; Economics.

GREELEY, ROBERT S; Annapolis SR HS; Annapolis, MD; (Y); 20/520; Boys Clb Am; Math Clb; Math Tm; Spanish Clb; Band; Stage Crew; Ed Lit Mag; Var Capt Crs Cntry; High Hon Roll; Hon Roll; Sigma Math Leag Merit Awd 83; Annl Math Exam Awd 85; Eagle Scout 86; Engr.

GREEN, DEANNA; Notre Dame Prep; Towson, MD; (Y); Chorus; Yrbk Stf; NHS; NEDT Awd; Prfct Atten Awd; Aerospc Engrng.

GREEN, FRANCISCO; De Matha Catholic HS; Adelphi, MD; (Y); 9/254; Cmnty Wkr; Spanish Clb; SADD; High Hon Roll; NHS; Elect Engr.

GREEN, KATHERINE; Annapolis Area Christian Schl; Severna Park, MD; (S); 4/25; Nwsp Ed-Chief; Yrbk Stf; Var L Bsktbl; Var Cheerleading; Var Sftbl; Hon Roll; NHS; AACS Fine Arts Fest-1st Pl Cinquains & 1st Pl Charactr Sketch 85; Acadmc All Amer Awd-Bio 85; Eng.

GREEN, MELISSA; Bethesda-Chevy Chase HS; Silver Spg, MD; (Y); Variety Show; Bsktbl; Bowling; Mgr(s); Score Keeper; Sftbl; High Hon Roll; Hon Roll; Vrsty Lttr 86; Archery Awd 84; Swmmng Badge 84; Pre-Dent.

GREEN, MELISSA; North East HS; North East, MD; (Y); 2/238; VP French Clb; Leo Clb; Q&S; Sec SADD; Pres Sr Cls; NHS; Pres Schlr; Sal; Voice Dem Awd; Hnr Soc Schlrshp 86; Natl H S Choral Awd 86; Englsh Awd 86; Loyola Coll Baltimore; Spch Pat.

GREEN, RICKY; Brunswick HS; Point Of Rocks, MD; (Y); Chess Clb; Computer Clb; French Clb; Var Ftbl; Score Keeper; Timer; Var Trk; Wt Lftg; Hon Roll; Maryland U College Park.

GREEN, ROXANNE; Crossland HS; Clinton, MD; (Y); FNA; Stat Bsktbl; Capt Cheerleading; Hon Roll; Rn.

GREEN, SHELLY; Allegany HS; Cumberland, MD; (Y); Cmnty Wkr; FCA; Nwsp Stf; Rep Frsh Cls; Cheerleading; Gym; Trk.

GREEN, SUSAN G; Calvert HS; St Leonard, MD; (Y); 13/250; Church Yth Grp; Varsity Clb; Band; Mrchg Band; JV Var Bsktbl; Mgr(s); Score Keeper; Var L Sftbl; JV Var Vllybl; High Hon Roll; Eckerd Coll Hnrs, Acdmc Athl Schlrshp, Vllybl Assoc Schlrshp 86; Eckerd Coll; Comp Sci.

GREEN, TIA; Western HS; Baltimore, MD; (Y); Church Yth Grp; Girl Scts; Church Choir; Hon Roll; Prfct Atten Awd; Val; Wmns Conv Auxilary Cert Merit 84; Morgan ST U; X-Ray Tech.

GREEN, TINA M; Archbishop Keough HS; Balt, MD; (Y); Pres Art Clb; Rep Church Yth Grp; Rep Soph Cls; Rep Stu Cncl; High Hon Roll; Hon Roll; NHS; Opt Clb Awd; Actrss Yth Grp 1-Act Ply Cntst 86; Pre-Schl CCD Tchr 85-86; Cmptr Sci.

GREEN, WARREN; De Matha Catholic HS; Silver Spring, MD; (Y); Band; Concert Band; Jazz Band; Pep Band; Hon Roll; Arch.

GREENAWAY, TOM; Seneca Valley HS; Gaithersburg, MD; (Y); Boy Scts; JA; Science Clb; Ski Clb; Bsktbl; Vllybl.

GREENBACK, FRANCES; Northwestern HS; Riverdale, MD; (Y); AFS; Aud/Vis; Church Yth Grp; Drama Clb; Science Clb; Spanish Clb; Chrmn SADD; Jr NHS; NHS; Bradley U Grant 86; Bradley U.

GREENBERG, LARRY; Mc Donogh Schl; Owings Mills, MD; (Y); Key Clb; Office Aide; Nwsp Stf; Yrbk Stf; Swmmng; Trk; Law.

GREENBERG, MICHAEL LAWRENCE; Rockville HS; Rockville, MD; (Y); 60/501; AFS; Am Leg Boys St; Chess Clb; Capt Debate Tm; Nwsp Sprt Ed; High Hon Roll; NHS; VFW Awd; Voice Dem Awd; Md Gftd & Tlntd Smmr Schlrshp To Attnd Ctr For Math & Tech 83-85; Awd Smmr Intrnshp Naval Med Hosp 85; Uionon Coll; Pre-Med.

GREENE, TIMOTHY L; Southwestern No 412 HS; Baltimore, MD; (Y); Chess Clb; Church Yth Grp; Computer Clb; English Clb; Office Aide; Teachers Aide; School Play; Bsbl; Cit Awd; Prfct Atten Awd; Trphies Pins Bsbl Tm 84-86; Commendtn Hlth Dept 86; Bsbl.

GREENWALD, REBECCA; Walter Johnson HS; Bethesda, MD; (Y); Hosp Aide; School Play; Rep Jr Cls; Rep Stu Cncl; Fld Hcky; Gym; Sftbl; Swmmng; Hon Roll; Acad Sci Cell Physilgy Course; Cytogenetics Lab Stu Vol; Physician.

GREENWOOD, TIMOTHY; North Carroll HS; Hampstead, MD; (Y); Church Yth Grp; Ski Clb; Varsity Clb; Rep Stu Cncl; JV Bsbl; JV Var Bsktbl; Im Coach Actv; Capt Var Ftbl; Hon Roll; Prfct Atten Awd; Prfct Atten Awd 83-86; Acad Ltr Awd 84-86; Ath Ltr Awd 84-86; Ftbl Plyr Wk 84; PA ST; Phrmcy.

GREENWOOD-BRIGHT, PHYLLIS; Roland Park Country Schl; Baltimore, MD; (Y); Variety Show; Lit Mag; Hon Roll; Spanish NHS; Church Yth Grp; PAVAS; Spanish Clb; SADD; Schlrshp WA Schl Bllt 85-87; Smmr Schlrshp To The Clvlnd Bllt Schl 86; WA Bllts JR Co 86-87; Med.

GREER, KELLY; James M Bennett SR HS; Salisbury, MD; (Y); Church Yth Grp; Drama Clb; Thesps; Varsity Clb; School Musical; School Play; Yrbk Stf; JV Cheerleading; Cit Awd; Hon Roll; Dramatic Arts.

GREER, MONDI; Thomas S Wootton HS; Gaithersburg, MD; (Y); Church Yth Grp; Cmnty Wkr; Hosp Aide; Stu Cncl; Mgr Sftbl; Hon Roll; Med.

GREGORY, CHRISTINE; Southern Garrett HS; Oakland, MD; (Y); 54/220; Letterman Clb; Varsity Clb; Var L Bsktbl; Var L Sftbl; Var L Vllybl; Volleyball MVP 85 & 86; Garrett CC; Marine Bio.

GREGORY, CHRISTINE; Woodlawn SR HS; Baltimore, MD; (Y); Capt ROTC; Nwsp Rptr; Nwsp Stf; Rep Jr Cls; Var Pom Pon; Military Ordr Of Wrld Wars 85; Assn Of US Army Cert Of Commndtn 86; Superior Cadet Decrtnl Awd 86; Tuskeegee; Psych.

GREGORY, JONATHAN M; John F Kennedy HS; Rockville, MD; (Y); 66/468; Boys Clb Am; Teachers Aide; Nwsp Rptr; Yrbk Stf; Off Soph Cls; Stu Cncl; Var L Bsktbl; Var L Ftbl; Hon Roll; Ldrshp Trng Smnr-U Of MD 84; Natl Achvt Schlrshp 85; Prgm Outstndg Negro Stu; Bus.

GREGORY, KRISS; Thomas S Wootton HS; Gaithersburg, MD; (Y); 104/415; AFS; Church Yth Grp; VP JA; Teachers Aide; Stu Cncl; Gym; Pom Pon; Trk; Hon Roll; U Of MD; Finc.

GREGORY, NATALIE; Southern HS; Oakland, MD; (Y); 4-H; Rep Stu Cncl; Var Sftbl; High Hon Roll; Hon Roll; Hagerstown; Acctng.

GREISMAN, LISA; Howard HS; Elkridge, MD; (Y); Cmnty Wkr; 4-H; Teachers Aide; Band; Chorus; Concert Band; Jazz Band; Mrchg Band; Orch; School Musical; Pres Ldrshp Schlrshp 85-86; MD Distngshd Schlr In Arts Schlrshp 85-86; Sempre Fidells Music Awd 84-86; Hood Coll.

GRESSER, SHAWN E; Baltimore Actors Theatre Conserva; Lutherville, MD; (S); Acpl Chr; Band; Chorus; Concert Band; Madrigals; Mrchg Band; Orch; Pep Band; School Musical; School Play; Baltimore Actrs Theatre Consrvtry Scholar Piano 83-86; Music.

GREY, MATTHEW W; Loyola HS; Towson, MD; (Y); Boy Scts; French Clb; Nwsp Stf; Yrbk Stf; Im Ftbl; Hon Roll; Ntl Merit SF; NEDT Awd; Econ.

GRIER, MEG; Westminster HS; Westminster, MD; (Y); AFS; Pres Church Yth Grp; Ski Clb; Teachers Aide; Acpl Chr; Chorus; Madrigals; Swing Chorus; Off Sr Cls; Music Lttr & Pines 86-87; Psych.

GRIFFIN, BOBBI L; Suitland HS; Upper Marlboro, MD; (Y); Cmnty Wkr; French Clb; Science Clb; Cit Awd; French Hon Soc; NHS; Pres Schlr; Rotary Awd; Val; Franklin & Marshall; Phrmcst.

GRIFFIN, CLARICE Y; Gov Thomas Johnson HS; Frederick, MD; (Y); 44/330; Teachers Aide; Sec Chorus; School Musical; Var L Bsktbl; Var L Cheerleading; Hon Roll; Prfct Atten Awd; Girl Scts; Off Soph Cls; Off Jr Cls.

GRIFFIN, GREGORY; Thomas S Wootton HS; Potomac, MD; (Y); VP Camera Clb; Med Careers Clb; Med.

GRIFFIN, JANICE M; Centennial HS; Ellicott City, MD; (Y); 2/250; Church Yth Grp; Drama Clb; Hosp Aide; Teachers Aide; Chorus; Church Choir; Capt Drill Tm; Variety Show; Hon Roll; NHS; Capt Drll Tm 2 Yrs Rw 84-86; Pres Untd Meth Yth Fllwshp 85-86; Salisbury ST Coll MD; Socl Wk.

GRIFFIN, JOHN; Loyola HS Blakefld; Baltimore, MD; (Y); Boy Scts; Church Yth Grp; Nwsp Stf; Var L Crs Cntry; Var L Trk; Hnrs Pgm Loyola 83-87; Eagle Scout 86.

GRIFFIN, KAREN; Mt Hebron HS; Ellicott City, MD; (Y); Church Yth Grp; Cmnty Wkr; Sec Spanish Clb; Teachers Aide; Chorus; Stage Crew; Off Soph Cls; Hon Roll; Natl Span Soc 1st Plc Spkng 84; Natl Span Soc Merit Awd 85; Natl Span Soc 3rd Plc Wrttn 84; U MD Baltimore Cnty; Comp Sci.

GRIFFIN, RETHA CAROLE; Kenwood SR HS; Baltimore, MD; (Y); 97/250; GAA; Hosp Aide; Varsity Clb; Stage Crew; Yrbk Stf; Stu Cncl; Var Sftbl; Var Vllybl; NHS; Western Maryland U Summer Schlrshp 86; U Of Maryland Coll Pk; Law.

GRIFFIN, TAMMI; Paul L Dunbar SR HS; Baltimore, MD; (Y); Cmnty Wkr; Dance Clb; FBLA; Pep Clb; Frsh Cls; Schlrshp Mdcl Ofc Prcdrs I Bus Dept 86; Bauder Fashion Coll; Fashion.

GRIFFITH, AMY; Beall HS; Frostburg, MD; (Y); Sec Science Clb; Service Clb; Drill Tm; School Play; Nwsp Phtg; Trs Stu Cncl; Stat Socr; Hon Roll; JV Bsktbl; Suprstr Grl Drl Tm 86; Towson ST.

GRIGGSBY, LYDIA K; The Park Schl; Baltimore, MD; (Y); Sec Church Yth Grp; Acpl Chr; Chorus; Church Choir; Variety Show; Var Socr; Ntl Merit Ltr; Spnsh Exch Prog 84; Jack & Jill Of Amer; Pol Sci.

GRIM, ANGELLA; Fort Hill HS; Cumberland, MD; (S); Pep Clb; Thesps; VP Orch; Nwsp Ed-Chief; Lit Mag; Rep Jr Cls; Hon Roll; NHS; Fash Illust.

GRIMES, RYAN; Brunswick HS; Jefferson, MD; (Y); 6/130; Chess Clb; Computer Clb; Spanish Clb; Chorus; School Musical; Hon Roll; Aerospace Engrng.

GRIMM, BARBARA; La Plata HS; La Plata, MD; (Y); Math Tm; Science Clb; Concert Band; Mrchg Band; Bausch & Lomb Sci Awd; High Hon Roll; NHS; Cmnty Wkr; JA; Teachers Aide; MD JR Sci Symposm & Acad Of Sci 86; Olympcs Of The Mnd Tm Wnrs 85-86; U Of MD; Chem.

GRIMM, JENNIFER; Fort Hill HS; Cumberland, MD; (Y); Hosp Aide; Thesps; Band; Orch; Symp Band; Yrbk Stf; Stu Cncl; Trk; Hon Roll.

GRIMM, KIMBERLY; Southern Garrett HS; Mt Lake Park, MD; (Y); Drama Clb; GAA; Girl Scts; Teachers Aide; Bsktbl; Cheerleading; Sftbl; SR Atmn Glry Attndnt 86-87; Allegany CC; Comp Pgmg.

GRIMM, RICHARD; Lackey HS; Waldorf, MD; (Y); Boy Scts; Latin Clb; Math Tm; Quiz Bowl; Ski Clb; Trs Sr Cls; High Hon Roll; Mst Outstndng Hstry Achvt 85-86; Acad Ltr 84-86; Aerospc Engrng.

GRIMSHAW, MARK; Gov Thomas Johnson HS; Frederick, MD; (Y); 45/309; Chess Clb; Latin Clb; Jazz Band; Mrchg Band; Var L Swmmng; Var Capt Tennis; NHS; Max Kehne Awd 86; MVP In Tennis 83, 85 & 86; Nwspst Plyr Of Yr In Tennis 85 & 86; PA ST; Math.

GRINDLE, G TODD; Valley HS; Lonaconing, MD; (Y); 1/80; Cmnty Wkr; Debate Tm; Office Aide; Q&S; Teachers Aide; School Play; Nwsp Bus Mgr; Mgr(s); Score Keeper; Bausch & Lomb Sci Awd; Dstngshd Schlr Of MD 86; Vestvaco Schlrshp 86; Lonaconing Hall Fame Awd 86; Frostburg ST Coll; Pre-Law.

GRINEY, MICHELLE; Montgomery County Covenant Acad; Gaithersburg, MD; (S); 1/9; Church Yth Grp; Drama Clb; Yrbk Ed-Chief; VP Jr Cls; Rep Stu Cncl; Var Gym; High Hon Roll; Val; Bsktbl; Awd Of Superior Acadmc Excllnc 84; Elem Eductn.

GROAT, ROBERT; St Marys Ryken HS; Leonardtown, MD; (S); 19/140; Rep Stu Cncl; Var L Crs Cntry; JV Socr; Var L Trk; High Hon Roll; Hon Roll; NHS; NC ST; Engr.

GRODZINSKY, GIL; Pikesville SR HS; Balto, MD; (Y); Computer Clb; JA; Science Clb; Spanish Clb; Var JV Trk; NHS; Ntl Merit Ltr; MD Dstngshd Schlr Prgm 86; Bltmr Hebrew Coll Awd Of Exc In Hebrew & Hstry 86; U MD; Engrng.

GROENINGER, THOMAS M; Loyola HS; Towson, MD; (S); Rep Jr Cls; Var Lcrss; JV Capt Socr; High Hon Roll; NHS; NEDT Awd; 1st Tm All Metro Lcrs Goalie 85; Timothy E Wynn Mem Awd 85; Spn & Latin Mdls 85.

GROSS, JASON; Bethesda-Chevy Chase HS; Chevy Chase, MD; (Y); Cmnty Wkr; Variety Show; Nwsp Ed-Chief; Nwsp Rptr; Nwsp Sprt Ed; VP Frsh Cls; Pres Soph Cls; Pres Jr Cls; Pres Sr Cls; Pres Stu Cncl; Law.

GROSS, LAURA; Walter Johnson HS; Bethesda, MD; (Y); French Clb; German Clb; Chorus; Mrchg Band; Stage Crew; Diving; Swmmng; French Hon Soc; Hon Roll; NHS.

GROSS, MARY; Franklin HS; Owings Mills, MD; (Y); 1/296; FBLA; Teachers Aide; Hst Stu Cncl; High Hon Roll; Hon Roll; NHS; St Schlr; Val; 1st Pl ST FBLA Ecnmcs Comptn 86; 4th Pl Natl FBLA Ecnmcs Comptn 86; American U; Poltcl Sci.

GROSS, SHAWN MARIE; Joppatowne HS; Joppa, MD; (Y); 1/182; Hst FTA; Spanish Clb; Trs Yrbk Bus Mgr; Yrbk Stf; Var Capt Swmmng; Hon Roll; Pres NHS; Pres Schlr; St Schlr; Val; George Washington U-Outstndg Math/Sci Stu Awd 85; Miami U Almni Schlrshp 86; MD Dstngshd Schlr Prm 86; Miami U; Math.

GROSSMAN, JUDITH; Bethesda-Chevy Chase HS; Silver Spg, MD; (Y); French Clb; Intnl Clb; Math Clb; Math Tm; Office Aide; Science Clb; Hon Roll.

GROTZ, LAURA E; Roland Park County Schl; Timonium, MD; (Y); French Clb; PAVAS; Varsity Clb; Var Bsktbl; Var Fld Hcky; Var Lcrss; French Hon Soc; Hon Roll; Outstndg Athl Awd 83; Outstndg JV Plyr Awd 84; U Of DE; French.

GROVES, ANNETTE; Walkersville HS; Walkersville, MD; (Y); FBLA; GAA; SADD; Bsktbl; Fld Hcky; Powder Puff Ftbl; Hon Roll; Frederick CC.

GROVES, TIFFANY; Sherwood HS; Brookeville, MD; (Y); Pep Clb; Ski Clb; Spanish Clb; Var JV Cheerleading; Hon Roll; Prfct Atten Awd; Spanish NHS; Spirt Awds For Chrldng 84-86; Doctor.

GRUESSING JR, JOSEPH A; Mount Webron HS; Ellicott City, MD; (Y); 14/268; Band; Concert Band; Jazz Band; Mrchg Band; Symp Band; High Hon Roll; NHS; L Armstrong Jazz Awd 85; Pres Acad Ftnss Awd 86; U MD College Park; Elec Engrng.

GRUNIG, ANDREW; High Point HS; Adelphi, MD; (Y); Boy Scts; VP Church Yth Grp; JV Var Socr; Hon Roll; Prfct Atten Awd; Eagle Sct BSA 86; U Of MD; Comp Sci.

GRYMES, TAMMY; Great Mills HS; Lexington Prk, MD; (Y); 12/250; FBLA; Girl Scts; Spanish Clb; SADD; Teachers Aide; Powder Puff Ftbl; Bsktbl; Powder Puff Ftbl; JV Score Keeper; Sftbl; Dioces WA Schlrshp 86; Merit Schlrstc Awd 86; Morgan ST U; Bus Adm.

GRZELAKOWSKI, EDWARD; Gaithersburg HS; Gaithersburg, MD; (Y); 201/650; VP FBLA; Rep Frsh Cls; Rep Soph Cls; JV Bsktbl; Trk; Hon Roll; Elon Coll; Acctg.

GSCHEIDLE, MATT; Westminster HS; Westminster, MD; (Y); Comp Sci.

GUADALUPE, PHIL; Laurel HS; Laurel, MD; (Y); 50/430; Letterman Clb; Political Wkr; Varsity Clb; Im Coach Actv; Var Ftbl; Var Trk; Im Wt Lftg; Var Wrstlng; Hon Roll; Med.

GUARE, DOUGLAS; Queen Annes Co HS; Stevensvle, MD; (Y); Am Leg Boys St; Boy Scts; Chess Clb; Cmnty Wkr; Var Ftbl; NEDT Awd; Elect Engrng.

GUCKERT, JENNIFER; North Harford HS; Jarrettsville, MD; (Y); Drama Clb; French Clb; Pres FBLA; VP FTA; Hosp Aide; Teachers Aide; Varsity Clb; Im Powder Puff Ftbl; Var Socr; Var Sftbl; Perfrmnce Awd 86; Achvt Awd 86; Mc Donogh Schl Scholar 83; Cmmnctns.

GUEVARA, ABBY; Faith Christian Schl; Waldorf, MD; (S); 1/3; Church Yth Grp; Church Choir; School Play; Yrbk Stf; Trs Stu Cncl; Bsktbl; Capt Cheerleading; Hon Roll; Teachers Aide; Stat Sftbl; Chrstn Chrctr Awd 84; Hmcmng Queen 86; Hyles-Anderson Coll; Sec.

GUIDICE, CHRISTINE; C Milton Wright HS; Forest Hill, MD; (Y); 19/265; JV Var Cheerleading; Var Trk; Stat Vllybl; Hon Roll; NHS; Loyola Schlrshp 86; Srtrl Schlrshp 86; Prm Crt 86; Loyola Coll; Accntng.

GULATI, AVADESH; Thomas S Woolton HS; Rockville, MD; (Y); 141/401; Drama Clb; VP JA; Teachers Aide; School Play; Stage Crew; Ftbl; U MD; Arch.

GUNNARSON, ANDREA; Hereford HS; Whitehall, MD; (Y); Cmnty Wkr; 4-H; French Clb; FTA; JCL; Latin Clb; SADD; Yrbk Stf; Wt Lftg; Hon Roll; U KY; Psych.

GUPTA, SWAPANA K; Parkside HS; Salisbury, MD; (Y); 2/250; Math Clb; Math Tm; Spanish Clb; Tennis; Gov Hon Prg Awd; Hon Roll; NHS; St Schlr; Chncllrs Schlr U Of MD Coll Pk 86-87; Prkside HS Merit Schlrshp 86; Wicomico Cnty Med Assn Schlr 86; U Of MD; Elect Engr.

GUTHRIE, BRIAN; Bohemia Manor HS; Chesapeake City, MD; (Y); 2/95; Computer Clb; Pres French Clb; Band; Var L Bsbl; Var JV Wrstlng; DAR Awd; Hon Roll; NHS; Ntl Merit SF; Outstndg French Achvmnt 83-85.

GUTIERREZ, LOURDES; Acad Of The Holy Cross; Gaithersburg, MD; (Y); 21/125; Debate Tm; Math Tm; Model UN; Spanish Clb; Powder Puff Ftbl; Capt Swmmng; Capt Trk; High Hon Roll; NHS; Spanish NHS; 3rd Pl-Spnsh MD Plcmnt Exmntn 84; 15-18 Yr Hgh Pnt-Stdwck Swm Tm 85; VA Tech; Bio.

GUTTING, RANI; Queen Annes County HS; Church Hl, MD; (Y); Am Leg Aux Girls St; Church Yth Grp; SADD; Band; Mrchg Band; School Musical; School Play; Symp Band; Yrbk Stf; NHS; Med.

GUYTON, EMMETT; Dunbar HS; Baltimore, MD; (Y); Off Jr Cls; Ftbl; Wrstlng; VA ST; Med.

HABIG, BRENT; Gaithersburg HS; Gaithersburg, MD; (S); 1/750; Debate Tm; French Clb; NFL; Science Clb; Symp Band; Lit Mag; Rep Stu Cncl; Swmmng; Trk; French Hon Soc; Olympics Mind World Fnls 84; Music.

HACKETT, CRISTI; Western HS; Baltimore, MD; (Y); Church Yth Grp; Cmnty Wkr; Dance Clb; Girl Scts; Science Clb; Teachers Aide; Acpl Chr; Pres Church Choir; School Musical; School Play; Hon Mntn Awd Blk Hist Cntst 83-84; Harvard U; Law.

HADDEN, GRANT; Westminster HS; Finksburg, MD; (Y); Church Yth Grp; Letterman Clb; Off Frsh Cls; JV Bsbl; JV Var Bsktbl; JV Ftbl; High Hon Roll; Hon Roll; Prfct Atten Awd; Ltr Bsktbl 86; Bus.

HADDOCK, JENNIFER; Sherwood HS; Silver Spg, MD; (Y); Hon Roll; U MD.

HADEN, MICHELE; Leonardtown HS; Leonardtown, MD; (Y); Church Yth Grp; Hosp Aide; Office Aide; Pres Sec Spanish Clb; Stat Bsktbl; Mgr(s); Score Keeper; Mgr Stat Vllybl; Hon Roll; Hggr Spec Olympcs 85-86; Law.

HADSELL, KRISTA; Springbrook HS; Silver Spring, MD; (Y); Church Yth Grp; Drama Clb; French Clb; Hosp Aide; Church Choir; School Musical; Cheerleading; Gym; Hon Roll; Georgetown U; Nrsng.

HAEUSSLER, JILL; Eleanor Roosevelt SR HS; Lanham, MD; (S); Church Yth Grp; Var Pom Pon; High Hon Roll; NHS; Spanish NHS; Acadmc Ltr 85-86.

HAFER, WILLIAM; Allegany HS; La Vale, MD; (Y); Boy Scts; Ski Clb; Spanish Clb; Band; Hon Roll; U Of MD; Bus.

HAGE, KRISTIN; Academy Of The Holy Names; Washington, DC; (Y); SADD; School Play; Nwsp Stf; VP Frsh Cls; Pres Soph Cls; Sec Pres Stu Cncl; NHS; Done Mst For Schl 84-86; Mst Frndly 86; Bus.

HAGER, TINA; Pikesville HS; Pikesville, MD; (Y); AFS; Library Aide; Spanish Clb; Yrbk Stf; Mgr Var Bsbl; Mgr Var Bsktbl; Var Fld Hcky; NHS; Cmnty Wkr; FBLA; Baltimore Miss Teen Pgnt 86; 6 Yrs Spn 86; Spn.

HAGERMAN, SHERRY; North East HS; Elkton, MD; (Y); 20/254; FBLA; Ski Clb; SADD; VICA; Chesapeake & Potomac Assn Of Pvt Schls Schlrshp 86; Chldrns Hm Fndtn Schlrshp 86; Outstndg Achvt Art; Arundel Inst Of Tech; Drftg.

HAGGARD, LYNNE S; Newport Preparatory Schl; Silver Spring, MD; (Y); Chess Clb; Church Yth Grp; Office Aide; Church Choir; Orch; School Play; Yrbk Ed-Chief; VP Trk; High Hon Roll; Ntl Merit SF; MENC All Estrn Orch Violn 85; MD All ST Orch Cncrt Mstrss 83; Telluride Smmr Schlrshp SF 85; Humnties.

HAGY, MICHELLE DAWN; Boonsboro HS; Boonsboro, MD; (Y); Drama Clb; Chorus; School Musical; School Play; Yrbk Stf; Hon Roll; Opt Clb Awd; Shepherd Coll; Accntng.

HAHM, THOMAS; Centennial HS; Ellicott City, MD; (Y); Church Yth Grp; School Play; Off Frsh Cls; Off Soph Cls; Off Jr Cls; Off Sr Cls; VP Stu Cncl; Var Capt Ftbl; Var Gym; Trk; MVP Lineman Vrsty Ftbl Tm 85-86; Brnze Mdlst Flr Rtine Howard Cnty Champ 85-86; Engrng.

HAIGHT JR, WILLIAM; Sherwood HS; Rockvlle, MD; (Y); 2/317; Model UN; Office Aide; Gov Hon Prg Awd; Hon Roll; NHS; Pres Schlr; Sal; Olney Womens Repblcn Club Awd 86; LSU Pres Alumni Schlrshp 86; U Of NC; Pre Dntstry.

HAINES, DALE; Middletown HS; Middletown, MD; (Y); Church Choir; Orch; Church Yth Grp; Band; Voc Awd 86; Vol Fire Dpt 84-86; Wrk Stdy 85-86; Plmng.

HAINES, JANET; Fallston HS; Fallston, MD; (Y); 72/250; Cmnty Wkr; Hosp Aide; Service Clb; Rep Jr Cls; Stu Cncl; Stat Bsktbl; Var Mgr(s); Var Score Keeper; Tennis; Hon Roll; Yuth Apprctn Optmst Clb 85; Crmnl Psych.

HALL, BARBARA; Snow Hill HS; Snow Hill, MD; (S); Sec AFS; Sec French Clb; Spanish Clb; Var Capt Cheerleading; High Hon Roll; VP NHS; Opt Clb Awd; Church Yth Grp; Sec Frsh Cls; Sec Stu Cncl; Legl Intrn 85-86; Hugh O Brian Md Ldrshp Semnr 85; Amer Fld Svc Yr Prog Hst Fmly 85-86; Intl Law.

HALL, DOROTHY; Takoma Acad; Rockville, MD; (Y); Drama Clb; Teachers Aide; School Play; Nwsp Rptr; Nwsp Stf; Rep Sr Cls; Im Bsktbl; Im Sftbl; Hon Roll; Englsh.

HALL, KENNETH; Dunbar SR HS; Baltimore, MD; (Y); Mathletes; Ftbl.

HALL, KIM; La Reine HS; Ft Washington, MD; (Y); Pep Clb; ROTC; Drill Tm; Trk; Vllybl; Masonic Awd; Prfct Atten Awd; Johnson & Wales Coll; Fash Mer.

HALL, MARLON R; High Point HS; Beltsville, MD; (Y); 12/655; Am Leg Boys St; JA; Capt Ftbl; Wt Lftg; High Hon Roll; Hon Roll; Pres NHS; Prfct Atten Awd; Dartmouth Bk Clb Awd 85; Outstndng Acad Achvt Awd 85-86; PA ST U; Surgeon.

HALL, MARY; Elizabeth Seton HS; Hyattsville, MD; (Y); Cmnty Wkr.

HALL, PAMELA A; Largo SR HS; District Hts, MD; (Y); Cmnty Wkr; Drill Tm; Hon Roll; Metropltn Baptst Chch Schlrshp Awd 86; Hampton U; Bus Adm.

HALLOCK, DIANE; Queen Annes County HS; Chester, MD; (Y); 96/330; Trs FBLA; School Play; Yrbk Phtg; Var L Ftbl; Hon Roll; 2nd Plc Rgnl Cmptn Ms Ftr Bus Ldr Of Amer 85; 1st Plc Rgnl Cmptn FBLA Cmptr Applctn 86; U Of MD Baltimore; Physcl Thrp.

HAM, DAWN; North East HS; Elkton, MD; (Y); Drama Clb; Teachers Aide; School Play; Cheerleading; Hon Roll.

HAMELIN, DIANE; Liberty HS; Sykesville, MD; (S); 15/264; GAA; Spanish Clb; High Hon Roll; Prfct Atten Awd; Princpls Awd 83-84; Acctnt.

HAMILTON, CLARISSA; Elkton HS; Elkton, MD; (Y); 41/289; Church Yth Grp; Hosp Aide; Cit Awd; Stu Assctd Med Clb Schlrshp, Cert Prfct Attndnc Cecil Vo Tech Ctr 86; Hon Roll; Delaware U; Physcl Thrpy.

HAMILTON, JOHN; The John Carroll Schl; Bel Air, MD; (Y); Am Leg Boys St; Var L Band; Concert Band; Mrchg Band; Sec Stu Cncl; Computer Clb; Spanish Clb; Hon Roll; Ntl Merit SF; Villanova; Mech Engrng.

HAMILTON, KELLY; Bowie SR HS; Bowie, MD; (Y); Cmnty Wkr; Latin Clb; Pep Clb; Ski Clb; Band; Drill Tm; Pom Pon; Powder Puff Ftbl; Latin Maxima Cum Laude Awd 86; James Madison U; Human Dev.

HAMILTON, PATRICIA; Southern Garrett HS; Oakland, MD; (Y); 31/221; VP Sec 4-H; Pres VP FFA; Pres Soph Cls; VP Jr Cls; VP Sr Cls; Cit Awd; Voice Dem Awd; Dekalb Agric Accmplsmnt Awd 86; Prm Queen 86; Frostburg Sst Coll; Bus Admin.

HAMILTON, TRISHA; Thomas Stone HS; Waldorf, MD; (S); Pres Church Yth Grp; FCA; GAA; Latin Clb; SADD; Capt Fld Hcky; Hon Roll; Sec NHS; 2nd Pl Sci Fair Behavrl Sci 82; 2 Yrs 1st Tm Southrn MD Athltc Conf Fld Hcky 84-85; Frostburg ST Coll; Elem Ed.

HAMMAN, KRISTEN; Thomas Stone HS; Waldorf, MD; (S); SADD; Teachers Aide; Nwsp Bus Mgr; Symp Band; Yrbk Phtg; Yrbk Rptr; Rep Stu Cncl; JV Var Cheerleading; L Pom Pon; JV Sftbl; Law Enfrcmnt.

HAMMOND, KIMBERLY; Parkside HS; Pittsville, MD; (Y); 8/237; Office Aide; Yrbk Stf; Hon Roll; NHS; Prfct Atten Awd; Outstndng Stu Awd 85-86; Acadmc Achvt 85-86; Exec Sec.

HAMMOND, WILLIAM; Northern HS; Huntingtown, MD; (Y); Computer Clb; JV Var Ftbl; Var Capt Trk; Im Wt Lftg; JV Var Wrstlng; Hon Roll; Ntl Merit Ltr; Calvert Cnty Sci Fair-1st Pl Math 86; US Marine Corps Cert Achvt Sci 86; Army Cert Of Achvt Sci 86; UM College Park; Mech Engr.

HANCOCK, WILLIAM; Washington HS; Westover, MD; (Y); Computer Clb; JV Ftbl; Hon Roll; Nvy Career; Comp.

HANDY, MICHELLE; Crisfield HS; Crisfield, MD; (Y); Cmnty Wkr; Dance Clb; Concert Band; Capt Flag Corp; Symp Band; Pres Stu Cncl; Var Capt Cheerleading; Mgr(s); Sftbl; Wor-Wic Tech; Bus Admin.

HANDY, WYNNETTE; Stephen Decatur HS; Bishopville, MD; (Y); 3/200; Church Yth Grp; FBLA; Teachers Aide; Band; VP Jr Cls; VP Sr Cls; Capt Gym; Cit Awd; Gov Hon Prg Awd; NHS; MV Gymnst 84-86; Schlstc Achvmnt 84-86; Prfct Attndnc 86; Attnd WASHINGTON Coll.

HANES, JAMES; Capitol Christian Acad; College Park, MD; (Y); Drama Clb; Teachers Aide; Chorus; School Play; Yrbk Phtg; Pres Schlr; Score Keeper; Prince George CC; Bus Mgmt.

HANFORD, ELIZABETH; Great Mills HS; Lex Pk, MD; (Y); Church Yth Grp; Cmnty Wkr; French Clb; Pep Clb; Band; Mrchg Band; Symp Band; Rep Frsh Cls; Var Fld Hcky; Hon Roll; Aerspc Engrng.

HANKEY, SARAH; Gaithersburg HS; Gaithersburg, MD; (Y); Chorus; Var JV Cheerleading; Var Pom Pon; Var JV Sftbl; JV Swmmng; Hon Roll; George Washington U; Nutrtn.

HANKINS, KATHRYN; Hammond HS; Columbia, MD; (Y); Cmnty Wkr; German Clb; Hosp Aide; High Hon Roll; Hon Roll.

HANKINSON, ARETHA; Col Zadok Magruder HS; Rockville, MD; (Y); 55/310; Church Yth Grp; French Clb; Girl Scts; JCL; SADD; Church Choir; Yrbk Stf; Rep Stu Cncl; Pom Pon; Hon Roll; Cmnctns.

HANN, CAROLINE; Bishop Walsh HS; Frostburg, MD; (Y); 48/110; Church Yth Grp; Dance Clb; Drama Clb; Hosp Aide; Speech Tm; Thesps; Church Choir; School Musical; School Play; Variety Show; Hugh O Brian Awd 85; Acptd To John Csblnc Mdlng Schl & Agncy 85; Cmnctns.

HANN, KIMBERLY; Franklin HS; Reisterstown, MD; (Y); Church Yth Grp; Cmnty Wkr; FBLA; Powder Puff Ftbl; Hon Roll; Prfct Atten Awd; Prncpls Lst 83-87; Broadcasting Inst Of MD; TV.

HANNAN, BRYAN; Loyola-Blakefield HS; Baltimore, MD; (Y); Dance Clb; Spanish Clb; Nwsp Phtg; JV Trk; Hnrs Pgm 83-86; US Naval Acad; Pilot.

HANSEN, KIRSTEN; St Michaels HS; St Michaels, MD; (Y); Band; Jazz Band; Nwsp Rptr; Yrbk Bus Mgr; Pres Frsh Cls; Rep Jr Cls; Rep Stu Cncl; Score Keeper; Hon Roll; NHS; Chld Psych.

HARDEN, RICHARD; Franklin HS; Owings Mills, MD; (Y); AFS; Debate Tm; Band; Mrchg Band; Rep Soph Cls; Rep Stu Cncl; Stat Bsbl; Var Socr; Pres NHS; Prfct Atten Awd; Lagn.

HARDIE, ROBERT L; Crossland HS; Camp Springs, MD; (Y); Am Leg Boys St; Boys Clb Am; Rep Frsh Cls; Var Bsbl; Hon Roll; Wake Frst; Engrng.

HARDIN, ROBERT; Joppatowne HS; Joppa, MD; (Y); Yrbk Stf; Var Lcrss; Var Socr; Hon Roll; 2nd Pl Drawng Womns Club Cnty Contst 84; 1st & 2nd Pl Rnking Schl Art Show 86; Art.

HARDING, DAMON; Laplata HS; White Plains, MD; (Y); 4-H; Office Aide; Ski Clb; Spanish Clb; Teachers Aide; Varsity Clb; Socr; Tennis; Wt Lftg; Hon Roll; Rnr-Up Socr SMAC; All Cnty, All SMAC, Bst Off Plyr; MVP Socr; All Cnty Mix Dbls Ten; All SMAC.

HARDING, JIM; Gaithersburg HS; Gaithersburg, MD; (Y); Chess Clb; Computer Clb; Band; Jazz Band; Pep Band; High Hon Roll; Hon Roll; Word Proc Cert Awd 86; Comp Sci.

HARDING, JULIANA; Archbishop Spalding HS; Severna Park, MD; (Y); 2/129; Pres Sr Cls; Stu Cncl; JV Var Lcrss; Var Mgr(s); Var Socr; Pres NHS; Opt Clb Awd; Teachers Aide; Var Score Keeper; Sal; M Burke Knott Full Schlrshp 82-86; Hugh O Brien Yth Fdtn Ldrshp Amb 83-84; A Arundell Cnty Athl Tm; U Dayton; Bio.

HARDY, MICHAEL; Friendly SR HS; Tantallon, MD; (Y); Church Yth Grp; Drama Clb; Teachers Aide; School Play; Pres Frsh Cls; Rep Jr Cls; Pres Stu Cncl; Hon Roll; NHS; Pres Schlr; Benjamin Banneker Schlrshp 86; Sprtndnts Awd Otstndng Acad Achv 86; Pres Awd Acad Achvmnt 86; U Of Md; Pre-Med.

HARE, DANIEL JACK; Calvary Christian Acad; Cumberland, MD; (Y); Camera Clb; Pep Clb; Chorus; School Play; Variety Show; Yrbk Stf; Capt Var Bsktbl; Capt Var Socr; Tennis; Acad All-Amer 86; SR Bsktbl Sport Awd 86; 1st Tm All Cnfrnc Of Chrstn Schls Bsktbl 85 & 86; Allgny Cmnty Coll; Tchg.

HARE, KELLIE; Ft Hill HS; Cumberland, MD; (Y); Nwsp Stf; Hon Roll.

HARE, KIM; North Carroll HS; Hampstead, MD; (Y); Church Yth Grp; Drama Clb; JA; Church Choir; Trk; Hon Roll; Art.

HARFELD, MARC; Saints Peter & Paul HS; Greensboro, MD; (Y); Church Yth Grp; Band; School Play; Variety Show; Rep Frsh Cls; Var Wrstlng; Hon Roll; NEDT Awd; Hugh O Brian Yth Found Amb 85; Music Clb Pres 85-86.

HARGROVE, AARON; Crossland HS; Temple Hills, MD; (Y); 73/436; Chess Clb; French Clb; ROTC; VICA; Drill Tm; Var L Ftbl; Var Swmmng; Var Wrstlng; Ntl Merit SF; Pres Schlr; Cvl Engrng.

HARGROVE, DIANTHA LYNETTE; Carver Vo-Tech HS; Baltimore, MD; (Y); Computer Clb; Drama Clb; FBLA; SADD; VICA; Band; School Musical; School Play; Nwsp Phtg; Nwsp Rptr; Crtfct Achvmnt Data Prcssng I 86; Data Prcsng.

HARGROVE, SCOTT; High Point HS; Adelphi, MD; (Y); 120/425; Letterman Clb; Office Aide; JV Var Ftbl; Im Wt Lftg; High Hon Roll; Hon Roll; Prfct Atten Awd; Plcmnt Top 3 Hgh Pnt Sci Fr 84-86; Boys ST Slctn 86; Engr.

HARGROVE, VALENCIA; Leonardtown HS; Hollywood, MD; (Y); Office Aide; Teachers Aide; Chorus; School Musical; Variety Show; Capt Powder Puff Ftbl; Hon Roll; Outstndng Sv Bus Dptmt 85-86; Wrkd Spec Olympcs 84-85; Frstbrg ST Coll; Bus.

HARKINS, NOELLE LANDIS; Parkside HS; Salisbury, MD; (Y); Church Yth Grp; 4-H; GAA; Library Aide; Science Clb; Ski Clb; Spanish Clb; Varsity Clb; Off Jr Cls; Off Sr Cls; 3rd Pl Cnty Sci Fair 83; 2nd Pl Cnty Sci Fair 84; Lbrl Arts.

HARMAN, ANNE; Liberty HS; Sykesville, MD; (S); 20/264; Church Yth Grp; Drama Clb; Letterman Clb; Mathletes; Varsity Clb; Trs Chorus; Swing Chorus; JV Var Fld Hcky; Hon Roll; School Musical; All Cnty Choir 84.

HARMAN, ELAINE; North Carroll HS; Hampstead, MD; (Y); Rep Sec Drama Clb; Pres Service Clb; Pres Spanish Clb; Teachers Aide; Chorus; Church Choir; School Musical; Stage Crew; Rep Jr Cls; Stu Cncl; Spcl Olymcs Vlntr Awd 86; Messiah Coll.

HARMON, DEBRA; Thomas Stone HS; Waldorf, MD; (S); Math Clb; Science Clb; Hon Roll; NHS; St Schlr; Andrew Halstead Best Earth Sci Stu Awd 82-83; U Of MD; Elec Engrng.

HARMON, KELLY ANN; North Hartford SR HS; Jarrettsville, MD; (Y); 18/287; Drm Mjr(t); Mrchg Band; Stage Crew; Nwsp Bus Mgr; Crs Cntry; Trk; High Hon Roll; Voice Dem Awd; FBLA; German Clb; MD Masthead Awd 85-86; Band Drctrs Awd 84-86; U Of Smd; Cmmnctns.

HARNEY, MICHELLE; Crossland HS; Camp Springs, MD; (Y); Rptr FFA; ROTC; Hon Roll; Vctnl House Prjct/1st Pl Lndscp Dsgn 85 & 86; 1st Pl FFA Extmprans Spking Rgnl Cntst 85 & 86; Hortcltr.

HAROLD, TOM; Arlington Baptist Schl; Sparks, MD; (Y); Chess Clb; Church Yth Grp; Drama Clb; Concert Band; Pep Band; Ed Yrbk Phtg; Elec Engrn.

HARPER, KRISTINA A; Damascus HS; Gaithersburg, MD; (Y); 62/260; VP Church Yth Grp; Sec 4-H; Trs FFA; NFL; Teachers Aide; Church Choir; Hon Roll; Bus Mngmnt.

HARPER, MICHAEL; St Marys Ryken HS; Lexington Pk, MD; (Y); Church Yth Grp; Varsity Clb; Variety Show; Crs Cntry; Socr; Tennis; Trk; Hon Roll.

HARPER, WENDY; Gaithersburg HS; Gaithersburg, MD; (Y); Red Cross Aide; Ski Clb; SADD; Yrbk Sprt Ed; Var JV Cheerleading; Var Swmmng; NHS; Key Clb; Orch; Stage Crew; Yth For Understndng 86; Show Choir 84-86; Intl Bus.

HARPER, WILL; Charles W Woodard HS; Rockville, MD; (Y); 117/236; Pep Clb; Teachers Aide; Varsity Clb; Variety Show; Jr Cls; Sr Cls; Var Capt Bsktbl; JV Var Socr; Var Trk; Var Wt Lftg; Athlt Of Yr 85-86; Mst Vlbl Bsktbl Plyr 85; Mst Vlbl Trck Plyr 85-86; Miami Of OH; Bus.

HARPLE, KITTY; Surrattsville HS; Clinton, MD; (Y); Boys Clb Am; Cmnty Wkr; GAA; Library Aide; Office Aide; Political Wkr; Teachers Aide; Nwsp Stf; Bsktbl; JV Coach Actv; Crimnlgy.

HARRIGAN, NICHOLAS P; Damascus HS; Gaithersburg, MD; (Y); Drama Clb; VP Scholastic Bowl; VP Science Clb; VP Thesps; Hon Roll; JETS Awd; NHS; Ntl Merit Ltr; Church Yth Grp; Pres Computer Clb; Geo Wshngtn U Math & Sci Awd 86; Math Assoc Of Amrca Awd 85; Rtry Clb Lttr Peace Prz 86; Engnrng.

HARRINGTON, JANE; Laurel HS; Laurel, MD; (Y); Church Yth Grp; Dance Clb; Drama Clb; Office Aide; Teachers Aide; Band; Chorus; Church Choir; Concert Band; School Musical; Frostburg; Elem Tchr.

HARRINGTON, SCOTT; Montggmery Co Covenant Acad; Damascus, MD; (S); 1/21; Church Yth Grp; JA; Chorus; Pres Jr Cls; Rep Stu Cncl; Var Bsbl; Var Bsktbl; Var Capt Socr; JV Sftbl; High Hon Roll; Hstry Awd 84; Phys Fit Awd.

HARRIS, ANGELA; Eastern HS; Baltimore, MD; (Y); 3/244; Hosp Aide; Library Aide; Spanish Clb; Band; High Hon Roll; Hon Roll; NHS; Hnr Roll 85 Avg 2 Yrs 86; Hnr For Grad 3rd 86; Socl Studies Plaque 86; Coll Of Notre Dame-MD; Fashion.

HARRIS, CHAD; La Plata HS; La Plata, MD; (Y); SADD; Ftbl; Wt Lftg; Wrstlng; Hon Roll; 2 Acadmc Achvt Awds 85-86; Maryland U.

HARRIS, GENEVA; Potomac HS; Temple Hill, MD; (Y); Camp Fr Inc; Church Yth Grp; Pep Clb; Science Clb; Variety Show; Pom Pon; Tennis; Cit Awd; Hon Roll; Prfct Atten Awd; Vet.

HARRIS, GEORGE; Friendly SR HS; Suitland, MD; (Y); Camera Clb; Ski Clb; Varsity Clb; Band; Concert Band; Jazz Band; Mrchg Band; Stage Crew; Yrbk Phtg; Yrbk Rptr; Frostburg ST Coll; Bus Admn.

HARRIS, HENRY; Walter Johnson HS; Rockville, MD; (Y); Debate Tm; Nwsp Ed-Chief; Nwsp Rptr; Lit Mag; Crs Cntry; Sftbl; Var Trk; High Hon Roll; NHS; Ntl Merit Ltr; 2nd Pl Jrnlst Yr 85-86; Five Schlrshps Blair Smmr Schl Jrnlsm 85-86; Jrnlst.

HARRIS, KAREN; St Michael HS; Easton, MD; (Y); Teachers Aide; Key Clb; Off Frsh Cls; Score Keeper; Photo.

HARRIS, LEE; Milford Mill SR HS; Balt, MD; (Y); 6/225; Math Clb; Math Tm; Concert Band; Mrchg Band; Var Ftbl; Var Golf; High Hon Roll; NHS; Pres Schlr; St Schlr; Jnt Cmnty Schlrshp 86; 2nd Plc MD Math Cntst 86; David Sody Unsung Hero Awd 86; U Of MD; Engr.

HARRIS, LOIS; Archbishop Spalding HS; Glen Burnie, MD; (Y); 17/128; Red Cross Aide; Teachers Aide; Lit Mag; Rep Frsh Cls; Trs Soph Cls; VP Jr Cls; VP Sr Cls; Stat Bsbl; Var Capt Bsktbl; Var Sftbl; U Delaware; Elec Engrng.

HARRIS, MARIECA; Saint Michaels SR HS; Easton, MD; (Y); FHA; Office Aide; Teachers Aide; Chorus; Stu Cncl; Score Keeper; Hon Roll; Rotary Clb Of St Michaels Schlrshp 86; Childrens Home Fndtn Schlrshp 86; Goldey Beacom Coll; Exec Sec.

HARRIS, SUSAN; North Harford HS; Jarrettsville, MD; (Y); Art Clb; Spanish Clb; Nwsp Rptr; VP Soph Cls; Pres Jr Cls; Pres Sr Cls; Stu Cncl; Capt Cheerleading; JV Lcrss; FPA Sec; Newspaper Artist; Comm.

HARRIS, TARI; Bowie SR HS; Bowie, MD; (Y); 38/610; Library Aide; Teachers Aide; Chorus; Variety Show; Var L Cheerleading; Powder Puff Ftbl; High Hon Roll; Hon Roll; Prfct Atten Awd; Dance.

HARRISON, ELIZABETH; Roland Park Country Schl; Lutherville, MD; (Y); Acpl Chr; School Musical; Yrbk Stf; VP Rep Stu Cncl; Var Badmtn; Var Socr; JV Tennis; Hon Roll; Rep Frsh Cls; Rep Soph Cls; Mcick Schlrshp Wnr 86; Herbert E Witz Awd86; 5th Pl ST Spnsh Exam 86; Duke U.

HARRISON, ERICA; Southern HS; Baltimore, MD; (Y); Church Yth Grp; FHA; Girl Scts; Prfct Atten Awd; Comp.

HARRISON, JEANNE E; The Bullis Schl; Great Falls, VA; (Y); 32/89; Am Leg Aux Girls St; Drama Clb; SADD; School Musical; Var Cheerleading; Var Socr; Hon Roll; NHS; U S Chrldg Achvt Awd 85; Spts Med.

HARRISON, JON; Harford Christian HS; Delta, PA; (Y); 3/28; Sr Cls; Bsbl; Bsktbl; Hon Roll; NHS; Prfct Atten Awd; Clemson U; Engrng.

HART, E ANDREW; Bowie HS; Bowie, MD; (Y); Church Yth Grp; French Clb; German Clb; Im Bsbl; Bsktbl; French Hon Soc; High Hon Roll; NHS.

HART, MACEO; Lackey HS; Bryans Rd, MD; (Y); Art Clb; Boys Clb Am; Church Yth Grp; Rep Jr Cls; Wt Lftg; Hon Roll; Drwng-Dsgn 85-86; Oakwood Coll Of MD; Drftsmn.

HART, NOEL; Hammond HS; Columbia, MD; (Y); Spanish Clb; School Musical; Variety Show; Nwsp Rptr; Nwsp Stf; Mgr Frsh Cls; Rep Soph Cls; Rep Jr Cls; Var JV Cheerleading; Hon Roll; Pres Phy Ftnss Awd; Outstndng Spnsh & Physcs Stu 85-86; Psych.

HARTER, GERALD L; North East HS; North East, MD; (Y); Computer Clb; Intnl Clb; Pep Clb; Science Clb; Spanish Clb; Varsity Clb; Rep Jr Cls; Bsktbl; Hon Roll; Outstndng Englsh Stu, MVP Bsktbl Awd 85-86; ENGRNG.

HARTFORD, ALEXANDER N; Charles W Woodward HS; Rockville, MD; (Y); 55/234; Model UN; Spanish Clb; JV Bsbl; Hon Roll; Spanish NHS; Mst Imprvd Diving & Crs Cntry 86; Co-Capt Var Ltr Diving 86; Var Ltr Crs Cntry 86; ST Mt Qlfr Trk 86; Tulane U; Engrng.

HARTIGAN, KAREN; Queen Annes County HS; Chestertown, MD; (Y); 16/340; Drama Clb; Nwsp Rptr; Nwsp Stf; Hon Roll; NHS; Ntl Merit Ltr; Pres Acadmc Ftnss Awd 86; Chesapeake Fac And Staff Schlrshp 86; Herbert Goldste In Meml Schlrshp 86; Acctg.

HARTKA, JANET; Institute Of Notre Dame; Baltimore, MD; (Y); 3/140; Art Clb; Dance Clb; Girl Scts; JV Cheerleading; NHS; Folk Grp; Campus Ministry.

HARTMAN, LYNDA; Seneca Valley HS; Gaithersburg, MD; (Y); 121/500; Church Yth Grp; Dance Clb; Drama Clb; Band; Church Choir; Concert Band; Mrchg Band; Pep Band; Symp Band; Hon Roll; Penn ST; Psychlgy.

HARTMAN, MEGAN; Allegany HS; Lavale, MD; (Y); 31/240; AFS; Stat Bsktbl; Mgr(s); Score Keeper; Var Trk; JV Capt Vllybl; Hon Roll; U S Achvmnt Acdmy Grls Bsktbll 85-86; PA ST U; Chem.

HARTWICK, PETER; Wootton HS; Gaithersburg, MD; (Y); Boy Scts; Ski Clb; Concert Band; Tennis; Var Trk; Hon Roll; Jr NHS; Rotary Awd; Cmnty Wkr; Teachers Aide; Rnkd MD ST In 880 Yd 86; Mid Atlntc JR Tennis Circuit 84-86; Law.

HARVEY, CARROLL; Queen Annes County HS; Stevensvle, MD; (Y); Chorus; Tennis; Vllybl; Hon Roll; 1st Plc Awd Sci Fr Comp Prog 86; Comp Engr.

HARVEY, VIRGINIA; Chesapeake SR HS; Pasadena, MD; (S); Church Yth Grp; DECA; Church Choir; Yrbk Stf; Hon Roll; Acctnt.

HARWOOD, LAURA V; French International Schl; Bethesda, MD; (Y); 1/43; Art Clb; Aud/Vis; Yrbk Stf; Ntl Merit SF; Pres Schlr; St Schlr; Yr Abroad Lycee Pascal Abidjan Ivory Coast; Yale U.

HASAN, CHILER; Crossland HS; Camp Springs, MD; (Y); Pres Science Clb; Teachers Aide; Hon Roll; NHS; Pres Spanish NHS; Schlstc Merit Awd 86; Acadmc Excllnc Awd 84-86; U Of MD College Park; Pre-Med.

HASH, LORI; Elkton Christian Schl; Newark, DE; (S); 5/23; Pep Clb; School Play; Sec Trs Jr Cls; Var Bsktbl; Var Sftbl; Var Vllybl; High Hon Roll; Hon Roll; NHS; Phys Ed & Home Ec Awd 83-84; Sec/Treas 84-85; Liberty U; Acctng.

HASHIMOTO, SHARON; James M Bennett SR HS; Hebron, MD; (Y); 15/200; Symp Band; Yrbk Ed-Chief; VP Sr Cls; Var Fld Hcky; Var Tennis; Mu Alp Tht; Trs NHS; Ntl Merit Ltr; Pres Schlr; SAR Awd; Fld Hcky All-Star 1st Tm Bysd Cnfrnc 85; US Army Rsrv Schlr Athlt Awd 86; Med Soc Schlrshp 86; U Of MD Coll Pk; Indstrl Engr.

HASKELL, JAMES; Atholton HS; Fulton, MD; (Y); 112/270; Var Trk; Var Wrstlng; U MD; Engrng.

HASKER, DAVID ALLEN; Camp Springs Christian Schl; Temple Hills, MD; (Y); 7/42; Acpl Chr; Church Choir; School Musical; Stu Cncl; Jr NHS; NHS; Church Yth Grp; Teachers Aide; Orch; Natl Achvt Cmptn-Piano 3rd Pl & Vcl 2nd Pl 83; Natl Achvt Cmptn-Piano 2nd & Vcl 1st 84; Liberty U; Sacred Music.

HASKINS, STEPHANIE; St Michaels HS; Bozman, MD; (Y); 11/68; Church Yth Grp; Drama Clb; SADD; Band; Church Choir; Concert Band; Flag Corp; Mrchg Band; Pep Band; Stage Crew; BPOE Stu Of Mnth 86; U Of MA; Anthrplgy.

HATCHER, TARA; Walkersville HS; Loveland, OH; (Y); SADD; Band; Concert Band; Jazz Band; Mrchg Band; Rep Frsh Cls; Rep Soph Cls; Sftbl; Hon Roll; Mock Trial, Sci Sci & Sec 84-86; All Around Stu Awd 83-86; Bst Offns Sftbll 86; Miami; Journlsm.

HAUBE, SANDY; Atholton HS; Clarksville, MD; (Y); Dance Clb; Girl Scts; Teachers Aide; Chorus; Church Choir; School Musical; Variety Show; Hon Roll.

HAUF, FRANK; Eastern Voc-Tech HS; Baltimore, MD; (Y); JV Var Mgr(s); JV Var Score Keeper; Hon Roll; Engrg.

HAUGH, PAUL; Bullis HS; Arlington, VA; (Y); Church Yth Grp; Computer Clb; Key Clb; Office Aide; Nwsp Rptr; Var Bsbl; Var Golf; JV Tennis; Im Vllybl; High Hon Roll; Sci.

HAUPT, BYRON; Brunswick HS; Jefferson, MD; (Y); 21/140; Church Yth Grp; Computer Clb; French Clb; Stage Crew; JV Bsktbl; JV Socr; Var Trk; Hon Roll; Comp Sci.

HAWBAKER, BRENDA; Clear Spring HS; Clear Spg, MD; (Y); 16/125; Church Yth Grp; 4-H; Church Choir; Drill Tm; Mrchg Band; 4-H Awd; Hon Roll; NHS; Theology.

HAWBECKER, BRENDA; Clear Spring HS; Hagerstown, MD; (Y); 1/125; Sec Trs Church Yth Grp; School Play; Trs Jr Cls; Trs Stu Cncl; Stat Socr; High Hon Roll; NHS; Phrmcy.

HAWES, REBECCA; Gaithersburg HS; Gaithersburg, MD; (Y); Church Yth Grp; Teachers Aide; Church Choir; Var Fld Hcky; Var Mgr(s); Var Socr; Hon Roll; Rgnl Wnnr Spc Shttl Stu Invlvmnt Prjct 84; Vrsty Sccr MVP 86; Psychlgy.

HAWK, BARRY; Talmudical Acad; Baltimore, MD; (S); Chess Clb; Yrbk Stf; Rep Frsh Cls; Rep Soph Cls; Rep Jr Cls; Rep Sr Cls; Rep Stu Cncl; Var Bsbl; JV Bsktbl; Var Capt Ice Hcky; NEDT Cert 84; MD Dstngshd Schlr 85; Grtr Bltmr Hstry Fair 85; John Hopkins U; Law.

HAWK, JENNIFER; Fort Hill HS; Cumberland, MD; (Y); Church Yth Grp; Teachers Aide; Band; Symp Band; Capt L Bsktbl; Capt L Trk; L Var Vllybl; Grls Bsktbl Awd 86; Al-Cty Bsktbl Tm-Ldng Scorer 86; Al-WMIL Tm Hnrbl Mntn 86; Rcrd Hldr Shot Put 86; Frostburg ST Col; Geog.

HAWK, JERRY; Talmudical Acad; Baltimore, MD; (S); 2/12; Pres French Clb; Hosp Aide; Science Clb; SADD; Color Guard; School Play; Yrbk Stf; Lit Mag; Rep Frsh Cls; Trs Soph Cls; Cert Of Mrt For Outstdng Pblc Svc As VP; Johns Hopkins; Pre-Med.

HAWK, TINA; Catoctin HS; Taneytown, MD; (Y); Letterman Clb; Science Clb; Band; Concert Band; Flag Corp; Mrchg Band; Pep Band; Rep Frsh Cls; Rep Stu Cncl; Var Cheerleading; Stewardess.

HAWKINS, RITA; Great Mills HS; Scotland, MD; (Y); Hst FBLA; Library Aide; Office Aide; Pep Clb; Spanish Clb; SADD; Teachers Aide; Cit Awd; Hon Roll; Drug-Chem Free Grad Party 86; Aarons Beauty; Csmtlgy.

HAWLEY, PAMELA ANN; Gaithersburg HS; Gaithersburg, MD; (Y); 158/568; Church Yth Grp; Cmnty Wkr; 4-H; German Clb; JA; Pep Clb; Ski Clb; SADD; Teachers Aide; Coach Actv; Dept Of Air Frc Hnr For Sci Prjct 84; Dlta Epsln Phi Awd Excllnc In German 85; Old Dominion U; Mrn Sci.

HAWTHORNE, JILLIAN K; Mercy HS; Baltimore, MD; (Y); Aud/Vis; Drama Clb; GAA; Girl Scts; Library Aide; Model UN; Spanish Clb; Chorus; Stage Crew; Vllybl.

HAY, ANGELA; Francis Scott Key HS; Westminster, MD; (Y); French Clb; GAA; VICA; Chorus; School Musical; Swing Chorus; Stu Cncl; Socr; Sftbl; High Hon Roll; Army MVP Awd Grls Sccr 86; Data Prcssng Awd Crrll Cnty Voctnl Tech Ctr 86; Comp Oprtr.

HAY, REGINALD T; Oxon Hill HS; Ft Washington, MD; (Y); Boy Scts; Church Yth Grp; Cmnty Wkr; Computer Clb; Math Tm; Church Choir; Var L Crs Cntry; JV Var Trk; Hon Roll; JETS Awd; Crs Cntry Rnnr Yr 83; Acad All Amer 86; Engrng.

HAYDEN, JOANNE; Francis Scott Key HS; Union Bridge, MD; (Y); GAA; Spanish Clb; Chorus; Ed Nwsp Stf; Sec Frsh Cls; Var Trk; JV Var Vllybl; Hon Roll; NHS; Vocal Ensmbl 85-86; Union Bridge Fire Qn 85-86; Jrnlsm.

HAYDEN, MELONIQUE B; Takoma Acad; Silver Spring, MD; (Y); Computer Clb; Debate Tm; Drama Clb; Chorus; School Play; Nwsp Phtg; Yrbk Rptr; Stu Cncl; Cheerleading; Hon Roll; Advncd Diploma 85-86; Flag-Ftbl Trphy 85-86; Loma Linda U; Psych.

HAYDEN, MIKE; Wootton HS; Rockville, MD; (Y); Cmnty Wkr; Var Capt Bsbl; JV Var Bsktbl; Var Capt Golf; Hon Roll.

HAYDEN, VAUGHAN; Joppatowne HS; Edgewood, MD; (Y); Drama Clb; VP German Clb; Scholastic Bowl; Band; Orch; Rep Stu Cncl; High Hon Roll; Hon Roll; NHS; Cmnty Wkr; Stu Of Mnth 84; Elec Engr.

HAYES, DEREK; Potomac SR HS; Temple Hills, MD; (Y); Science Clb; Teachers Aide; High Hon Roll; NHS; Prfct Atten Awd; Its Acad Tm 86; Acad Excllnce Awd 85 & 86; Mech Engrng.

HAYES, JENNIFER; Sherwood HS; Silver Spring, MD; (Y); Chorus; Variety Show; Off Frsh Cls; Off Soph Cls; Off Jr Cls; Cheerleading; Gym; Hon Roll; All Amer Gymnstc Team 85; All Amer Chrldr 85-86; Vet.

HAYES, NICHELLE; Potomac HS; Temple Hills, MD; (Y); Church Yth Grp; Pep Clb; Hon Roll; Hampton U; Electrcl Engrng.

HAYMAN, CINDY; Colonel Richardson HS; Preston, MD; (Y); FBLA; FHA; Library Aide; Teachers Aide; Church Choir; High Hon Roll; Hon Roll; Prfct Atten Awd; Ntl Hnr Rl 85; Goldy Beacom Coll; Acctng.

HAYMAN, JANE; Wicomico SR HS; Salisbury, MD; (Y); 34/220; AFS; Church Yth Grp; French Clb; Varsity Clb; Stat Bsktbl; Var Fld Hcky; Mgr(s); Score Keeper; Hon Roll; Acdmc Cert 84-86; Fld Hcky Cert & Ltr 84-86; Bsktbl Mgr Cert & Pin 85 & 86; Intr Dsgn.

HAYWOOD, KAREN; Fort Hill HS; Cumberland, MD; (Y); Church Yth Grp; Cmnty Wkr; Hosp Aide; Library Aide; Office Aide; Teachers Aide; Off Frsh Cls; Off Soph Cls; Off Jr Cls; Swmmng; Allegany CC; Mgmt.

HEAD, LAURA E; Rockville HS; Rockville, MD; (S); 18/464; Church Yth Grp; VP Intnl Clb; School Musical; School Play; Variety Show; Nwsp Ed-Chief; Ed Nwsp Stf; Ed Lit Mag; High Hon Roll; NHS; Engl Awd 83; Princpls Wrtng Awd 83-84; Jrnlsm Awd 85; U Of MD; Brdcst Jrnlsm.

HEALANDER, JEFFREY; Good Counsel HS; Rockville, MD; (Y); 90/214; Church Yth Grp; Cmnty Wkr; Drama Clb; Service Clb; School Play; Lit Mag; Mgr(s); Educ.

HEALEY, SARAH; Walter Johnson HS; Bethesda, MD; (Y); Debate Tm; GAA; Red Cross Aide; SADD; Sec Stu Cncl; Var Bsktbl; Var Fld Hcky; Var Sftbl; French Hon Soc; Hon Roll; Spartan Awd Fld Hcky 83; MVP Sftbl 84-86; 2nd Tm All-Cnty Fld Hcky 84-86; 1st Tm All-Cnty Sftbl 85-86.

HEALY, JENNIFER ANN; Chesapeake HS; Pasadena, MD; (Y); French Clb; Math Tm; SADD; Teachers Aide; Yrbk Stf; Off Sr Cls; Tennis; Hon Roll; Maurice Mahr Mem Schlrshp Awd 86; Bd Educ Curriculum Comm 85; U MD Baltimore; Math Fld.

HEBB, RONNIE; Williamsport HS; Williamsport, MD; (Y); Var L Bsktbl; Law.

HEBRON, DANNY; The Bullis Schl; Fredericksburg, VA; (Y); Am Leg Boys St; Key Clb; SADD; Variety Show; Nwsp Rptr; Var Socr; Var Tennis; High Hon Roll; NHS; General Excllnc Studs 83 84 & 85; Med.

HECKL, JOSEPH C; Mt St Josephs HS; Ellicott, MD; (Y); German Clb; Scholastic Bowl; Speech Tm; High Hon Roll; Prfct Atten Awd; Chmstry.

HECKMAN, DIANNA; South Hagerstown HS; Hagerstown, MD; (Y); 65/275; Church Yth Grp; Computer Clb; Debate Tm; Trs Drama Clb; FBLA; Hosp Aide; Office Aide; SADD; Teachers Aide; Varsity Clb; Comp Opertr.

HECKMAN, JODIE; Bishop Walsh HS; Keyser, WV; (Y); Debate Tm; Drama Clb; Speech Tm; Thesps; Band; Chorus; Concert Band; Mrchg Band; School Musical; School Play; FL Rep WV Org 86; Law.

HEDAYATI, REZA; Mount Saint Joseph Coll; Baltimore, MD; (Y); CAP; Signfcnt Imprvmnt In Studies 85-86; 1st Hnrs 85-86; Math.

HEDGER, KAREN; Wicomico SR HS; Salisbury, MD; (Y); Varsity Clb; Nwsp Stf; Rep Soph Cls; Crs Cntry; Trk; High Hon Roll; NHS; Ntl Merit Ltr; Arch.

HEI, MARK; Duval SR HS; Seabrook, MD; (S); Chess Clb; Trs Jazz Band; Symp Band; Hon Roll; Engrng.

HEINBAUGH, SUSAN; Estern Vocational Tech HS; Baltimore, MD; (Y); Girl Scts; Hosp Aide; VICA; Band; Chorus; School Musical; Church Yth Grp; Girl Scouts-Slvr Awd 85; St Josephs Hospt 200 Hr Rcgntn Awd 85; Nrsng.

HEINERICHS JR, DON; Kenwood SR HS; Baltimore, MD; (Y); Boy Scts; SADD; Varsity Clb; Concert Band; Mrchg Band; Var L Ftbl; JV Trk; Var Wrstlng; Hon Roll; NHS; Eagle Scout 86; Towson ST; Bus Ed.

HEINLEIN, TINA M; Brooklyn Park JR SR HS; Baltimore, MD; (Y); Computer Clb; DECA; Latin Clb; Chorus; Nwsp Stf; Yrbk Stf; Stu Cncl; Cheerleading; High Hon Roll; Hon Roll; 2nd Rnr-Up Loylty Day Qun Cntst 85; Baltimore Bst JV, Vrsty Chrldrs 84 & 85; Awd Exclnc Chrldng Camp; Towson ST; Mdcl Secy.

HEINSELMAN, KURT; Westminster SR HS; Westminster, MD; (Y); 7/481; Teachers Aide; Orch; JV Crs Cntry; Dnfth Awd; High Hon Roll; Trs NHS; Ntl Merit Ltr; St Schlr; OH U Trstes Outstndng Schlr Awd 86; Hrm Roy Wlsn Chem Awd 86; Ohio U; Chem.

HEISS, PAUL J; Loyola HS; Ellicott City, MD; (S); 26/197; Camera Clb; Church Yth Grp; French Clb; VP Spanish Clb; SADD; Var Capt Bsktbl; Var Capt Trk; NHS; Hon Roll; Ntl Merit Ltr; Schlr Athlt Schlrshp To Atnd Loyola 82-86; Phtgrphy Awd 84; Corp Law.

HELBIG, THERESA MARIE; Southern Garrett County HS; Deer Park, MD; (Y); FBLA; Office Aide; Hon Roll; Garrett CC; Legl Sec.

HELFENBEIN, KIRK; Queen Anne Co HS; Stevensville, MD; (Y); Am Leg Boys St; Church Yth Grp; Civic Clb; Cmnty Wkr; Letterman Clb; SADD; Varsity Clb; Socr; Trk; Wt Lftg; Vrsty Lttrd Sccr; Best On Offense 86; 2nd String All Star Tm 86; Elon Coll.

HELLER, JAMES; Dulaney SR HS; Cockeysville, MD; (Y); Church Yth Grp; Cmnty Wkr; Trk; Hon Roll; NHS; Opt Clb Awd; Arch.

HELLER, JOHN; North Hagerstown HS; Hagerstown, MD; (Y); Boy Scts; CAP; Exploring; Crs Cntry; Trk; Hon Roll; Embry-Riddle; Aviatn Engrng.

HELLING, MICHAEL; Eleanor Roosevelt HS; Beltsville, MD; (Y); Am Leg Boys St; Church Yth Grp; Church Choir; Nwsp Rptr; Rep Stu Cncl; Var Capt Swmmng; Hon Roll; Powder Puff Ftbl; Teachers Aide; NSTA-NASA Spc Shttl Stu Invlmnt Proj Regnl Wnnr 84; US Sentr Am Leg Boys Natn 85; Natl JR Olymp 86; Cornell U; Politics.

HELMICK, RENEE; Southern Garrett HS; Deer Pk, MD; (Y); Band; Color Guard; Concert Band; Mrchg Band; High Hon Roll; Hon Roll; NHS; Captain Of Color Guard 86; U Of MD; Med.

HELMSEN, JOHN J; Good Coonsel HS; Kensington, MD; (Y); Boy Scts; Math Clb; Math Tm; Wrstlng; God Cntry Awd; High Hon Roll; Hon Roll; NHS; Ntl Merit SF; Amer Mensa 85; John Hopkins U Schlrshp 81-83; U Of MD Math Dept Schlrshp 82-86; Math.

HELSER, JULIE; Clear Spring HS; Hagerstown, MD; (Y); 27/125; Trs FBLA; Teachers Aide; Color Guard; Trs Jr Cls; Stat Socr; Bus.

HELTON, TRACY; Washington HS; Princess Anne, MD; (Y); Band; Color Guard; Concert Band; Mrchg Band; Symp Band; Miss Mt Vernon Vol Fires Dept 85-86; Worwich Tech; Acctg.

HEMMING, BERNIE; St Marys Ryken HS; Waldorf, MD; (S); Cmnty Wkr; Intnl Clb; Service Clb; Swmmng; High Hon Roll; Hon Roll; NHS; Math.

HEMPHILL, BRENDA; Williamsport HS; Hagerstown, MD; (Y); 10/234; Ski Clb; Teachers Aide; Drill Tm; Mrchg Band; Rep Frsh Cls; Rep Soph Cls; Rep Jr Cls; Rep Sr Cls; Im Powder Puff Ftbl; Tennis; HJC; Law.

HENDERSHOT, MICHAEL; Allegany HS; Cumberland, MD; (Y); AFS; Pres Drama Clb; Thesps; School Play; Nwsp Stf; U MD; Bio.

HENDERSON, DEBORAH J; Friends Schl; Baltimore, MD; (Y); Church Yth Grp; Dance Clb; Chorus; School Play; Lit Mag; Mgr(s); Hon Roll; Ntl Merit SF; Johns Hopkins U; Jrnlsm.

HENDERSON, RANI; Suitland HS; District Height, MD; (Y); Church Yth Grp; Cmnty Wkr; French Clb; Red Cross Aide; Science Clb; Teachers Aide; Pom Pon; Hon Roll; NHS; Prince Georges Cnty Acad Awd 84; Bio.

HENDRICKS, CARA; Takoma Acad; Silver Spring, MD; (Y); 1/96; Teachers Aide; Pres Stu Cncl; Hon Roll; NHS; Ntl Merit Schol; Val; Stu Obsrvr Schl Brd 85-86; Prncpls Advstr Cncl; Bryn Mawr Coll.

HENDRON, WILLIAM; Perryville HS; Perryville, MD; (Y); Am Leg Boys St; Church Yth Grp; FBLA; Intnl Clb; Capt L Trk; L Var Wrstlng; Cit Awd; DAR Awd; Hon Roll; NHS.

HENEGAR, AMY; Riverdale Baptist Schl; Laurel, MD; (Y); Church Yth Grp; VP Frsh Cls; Var Capt Cheerleading; Stat Socr; High Hon Roll; NHS; Wrstlng; Hon Roll; Ntl Hnr Rll, Acadmc All Amer, Ntl Sci Merit Awd, Ntl Physcl Ed Awd 84; US Chrldr Achvt Awd 85; Psychlgy.

HENKEL, JULIE; Bishop Walsh HS; Cumberland, MD; (Y); 9/110; Church Yth Grp; Pep Clb; Ski Clb; Yrbk Stf; Tennis; Trk; Vllybl; High Hon Roll; Hon Roll; NHS; Coll Of Notre Dame; Finc.

HENKIN, ANITA; Laurel HS; Laurel, MD; (Y); 10/315; Hosp Aide; Intnl Clb; Teachers Aide; Chorus; High Hon Roll; NHS; Pres Schlr; Its Acdmc Awd 85; Social Issues Awd 85; Engl Dept Awd 86; Carnegie Mellon U; Psychlgy.

HENNEBERRY, KARA; Archbishop Keough HS; Ellicott City, MD; (Y); Church Yth Grp; Drama Clb; VP Frsh Cls; VP Soph Cls; VP Jr Cls; VP Sr Cls; JV Fld Hcky; Var Sftbl; High Hon Roll; Hon Roll; NEDTS Top 10 Pct Co 84; U MD Baltimore; Nrsng.

HENNINGER JR, RICHARD L; Patterson HS; Baltimore, MD; (Y); Hon Roll; Ntl Merit Schol; Delta Lamboa Chap Meritrs Schlrshp Certf 86; Awd Drftng W Mobile Offcs 86; Grad Diploma Md 9th Hon 86; Archtct.

HENNINGER, TODD C; Eleanor Roosevelt HS; Upper Marlboro, MD; (Y); Boy Scts; Trs Church Yth Grp; Teachers Aide; Rep Jr Cls; Rep Sr Cls; NHS; Ntl Merit SF; High Hon Roll; Slavic Hnr Soc 84; Chem.

HENRICHSEN, SONYA R; La Plata HS; Waldorf, MD; (Y); Church Yth Grp; Science Clb; Chorus; Mrchg Band; Orch; Pep Band; High Hon Roll; Tri Cnty Hnrs Band & Hnrs Chorus 84-86; Brigham Young U; Music.

HENRY, DRISTA; Catoctin HS; Sabillasville, MD; (Y); 15/215; Sec Computer Clb; Science Clb; Spanish Clb; Teachers Aide; Church Choir; Hon Roll; Hist Awd; Fortran Awd; Basic Comptr Cls Awd; Comp Sci.

HENRY, LANA J; Kent County HS; Galena, MD; (Y); Am Leg Aux Girls St; 4-H; Spanish Clb; VICA; Mrchg Band; Hon Roll.

HENRY, MICHAEL; Westminster HS; Westminster, MD; (Y); JV Ftbl; Hon Roll; Towson ST U; Accntnt.

HENRY, SHANNON; Connelly School Of The Holy Child; Potomac, MD; (Y); Cmnty Wkr; Sec Debate Tm; Model UN; Service Clb; Nwsp Ed-Chief; Yrbk Stf; Lit Mag; JV Fld Hcky; Mgr(s); NHS; Engl.

HENSON, ALICIA; Clear Spring HS; Big Spg, MD; (Y); 7/111; FBLA; Office Aide; School Play; Stage Crew; High Hon Roll; Hon Roll; Hagerstown Bus Coll; Med Secy.

HENSON JR, DAVID W; Waldorf Christian Acad; Waldorf, MD; (Y); 2/23; Boy Scts; Church Yth Grp; Pres Exploring; Spanish Clb; Yrbk Phtg; Rep Soph Cls; JV Capt Ftbl; L Trk; Var Wrstlng; High Hon Roll; U Of MD; Law Enforcement.

HEPBURN, SHANNON; James M Bennett SR HS; Salisbury, MD; (Y); Art Clb; Hst Drama Clb; French Clb; Pres Thesps; School Musical; School Play; Stage Crew; Yrbk Stf; Hst Sr Cls; Hon Roll; MD Ctr Arts Goucher Coll 85; Theatre.

HERBERT JR, CHARLES E; Central HS; Capital Hts, MD; (Y); Pres Jr Cls; VP Sr Cls; Pres Stu Cncl; Var Crs Cntry; Var Tennis; Var Trk; Cit Awd; NHS; Rotary Awd; Jesse J Warr Jr Mem Awd 85; Supdt Cert Outstndng Achvt 82; Acadmc Excllnc Awd PG Cnty 83; Stanford U; Mech Engr.

HERMAN, ANDREW; Walt Whitman HS; Bethesda, MD; (Y); Nwsp Ed-Chief; Ntl Merit Ltr; 2nd Pl Temple U Schlstc Prss Assn Clmn Wrtg 86.

HERNANDEZ JR, CARLOS; Springbrook HS; Silver Spring, MD; (Y); French Clb; Office Aide; Teachers Aide; Var Socr; Hon Roll; Ntl Merit SF; Yng Am Trades Found Awd 85-86; Engrng.

HERNANDEZ, HERMAN I; Loyola Blakefield HS; Baltimore, MD; (S); Church Yth Grp; Spanish Clb; School Musical; JV Crs Cntry; Hon Roll; NHS; NEDT Awd; Msgr Roche Schlrp 83; Art Mdl 84; Elec Engrg.

HERNDON, GLENN; Mount Hebron HS; Ellicott City, MD; (Y); Trs Drama Clb; French Clb; Chorus; School Musical; School Play; Stage Crew; Hnr Roll 84; U Of MD; Crmnl Law.

HERRING, SCOTT; North Carroll HS; Manchester, MD; (Y); 10/250; Pep Clb; Ski Clb; Varsity Clb; Sec Frsh Cls; Trs Soph Cls; Off Jr Cls; Off Sr Cls; Stu Cncl; Bsktbl; Lcrss; Law.

HERRING, WHITNEY; Fort Hill HS; Cumberland, MD; (Y); Church Yth Grp; Pep Clb; Thesps; Church Choir; Flag Corp; School Play; Variety Show; Yrbk Stf; Rep Stu Cncl; Hon Roll; Chef.

HERSBERGER, DEE; Carroll Christian Acad; Westminster, MD; (S); 2/17; Church Yth Grp; Band; Chorus; High Hon Roll; NHS; Advncd Master Cls Piano 85; Baroque Fest 1st 85; Bob Jones U; Piano Perf.

HESSE, KIMBERLY L; Sherwood HS; Brookeville, MD; (Y); 48/317; Model UN; Thesps; Stage Crew; Yrbk Bus Mgr; Yrbk Ed-Chief; Var L Fld Hcky; NHS; Aud/Vis; PAVAS; Teachers Aide; Schlrshp Yrbk Dsgn & Grphcs 86; Mntgmry Gen Hosp Schlrshp 86; 1st Pl MSPAA For Cmnty Cvrg 85; Vanderbilt U TN; Biomed Engr.

HESSENAUER, MARTHA; Eastern Vocational Technical HS; Baltimore, MD; (Y); Sec Church Yth Grp; FBLA; Office Aide; Trs Band; Chorus; Hon Roll; Towson ST U; CPA.

HETTLEMAN, ROBERT; Baltimore City Coll; Baltimore, MD; (S); 4/390; Red Cross Aide; Nwsp Bus Mgr; Yrbk Stf; Lit Mag; Var L Socr; Var L Tennis; High Hon Roll; NHS; Computer Clb; Latin Clb; Natl Hnr Roll; Law.

HEUBECK, ANGELA; Paterson HS; Baltimore, MD; (Y); Church Yth Grp; Math Clb; Rep Soph Cls; Sec Jr Cls; Rep Stu Cncl; Hon Roll; NHS; Pg MD Gnrl Assmbly 86; Outstndg Stu Ldr 86; Fashion Inst Of Phil; Fshn Mrch.

HEURICH, BARBARA; Walkersville HS; Walkersville, MD; (Y); Computer Clb; Sec FBLA; Girl Scts; Office Aide; Science Clb; SADD; Band; Chorus; Concert Band; Stu Cncl; Katherine Gibbs Bus Schl; Bus.

HEWES, SUZANNE; North Carroll HS; Manchester, MD; (Y); AFS; Drama Clb; Hosp Aide; Spanish Clb; Chorus; School Musical; Stage Crew; Rep Jr Cls; Trs Sr Cls; Cheerleading; Acadmc Awd 85-86; Hosp Jnr Vlnteer Awd-Pin 84; Athltc Awd-Chrldng 84; Pre-Med.

HICKEY, DONNA; Springbrook HS; Silver Spring, MD; (Y); Church Yth Grp; Nwsp Rptr; Pom Pon; Twrlr; Hon Roll; Schl Let 86; Natl Latin Exam-Cum Laude 84; Busnss.

HICKMAN, LAURA; Pocomoke HS; Pocomoke, MD; (Y); Drama Clb; FBLA; Office Aide; SADD; Church Choir; School Play; Mgr(s); Score Keeper; Timer; Hon Roll; Worwic Tech Cmnty Coll; Med Sec.

HICKS, PAULETTE; Walbrook SR HS; Baltimore, MD; (Y); Girl Scts; JA; Math Tm; Band; Mrchg Band; Mgr(s); Hon Roll; Awd For Holding 95 Out Of 100 Grade Avg For 4 Quarters 84-85; U Of VA; Comp Sci.

HICKSON, DOROTHY J; Glenelg HS; Mt Airy, MD; (Y); Debate Tm; FCA; Letterman Clb; Q&S; Chorus; Yrbk Ed-Chief; Yrbk Stf; JV Var Diving; JV Swmmng; Ntl Merit SF.

HIGDON, TRACY; Maurice J Mc Donough HS; Pt Tobacco, MD; (Y); Church Yth Grp; Cmnty Wkr; 4-H; GAA; Hosp Aide; Intnl Clb; Letterman Clb; Varsity Clb; Var Fld Hcky; Var Trk; Sthrn MD Elctrc Coop Rep-Rurl Elctrc Yth Tour 86; Bus.

HIGGS, ANNE; Northern HS; Owings, MD; (Y); 12/301; Pom Pon; Hon Roll; Frnch V Awd 86; Merit Schltc Awd 86; Retired Tchrs Assn Calvertcnty Scholar 86; MD U; Elem Ed.

HIGGS, BRIDGETT; La Plata HS; Cobb Island, MD; (Y); Church Yth Grp; Intnl Clb; Ski Clb; SADD; Score Keeper; Tennis; Hon Roll; 5th Dist Vol Fire Dept & Rsc Sqd 85-87; Commnctns.

HIGHSMITH, RHONDA; Crossland HS; Camp Springs, MD; (Y); Church Yth Grp; Girl Scts; Math Clb; Church Choir; Concert Band; Symp Band; Hon Roll; U Of VA; Law.

HIGHTOWER, ANTHONY; Loyola Blakefield HS; Baltimore, MD; (Y); Church Yth Grp; Cmnty Wkr; Dance Clb; FCA; Political Wkr; SADD; Sec Stu Cncl; Var JV Bsktbl; Frsh-Sphmr Bsktbl Chmpns 83-84; Bus Mngmnt.

HIGSON, SONYA; Fort Hill HS; Cumberland, MD; (S); 9/252; Pres Church Yth Grp; Pep Clb; SADD; Teachers Aide; Drill Tm; Ed Yrbk Ed-Chief; Pres Sr Cls; Stu Cncl; Tennis; NHS; Mst Outstndg SR Girl 85; SR Homecmg Atten 85; Frostburg ST Coll; Phrmcy.

HILDENBRAND, SARAH; Williamsport HS; Williamsport, MD; (Y); 16/224; Band; Yrbk Stf; Sec Frsh Cls; Sec Soph Cls; Sec Jr Cls; Stu Cncl; High Hon Roll; Hon Roll; NHS; Dance Clb; WA Cnty Assn Of Stud Cncl Sec 86-87; Mbr Of MASC Exctive Cmmttee MASC MD Assn Stud Cncl 84-87; Corp Law.

HILGENBERG, JANET; La Reine HS; Suitland, MD; (Y); Church Yth Grp; JV Cheerleading; Var Capt Gym; Var Socr; Var Capt Trk; Ms Hustle Vrsty Trck 85-86; Phy Ed Awd 86; 3rd ST Gymnstcs 83-84; Salisbury ST; Phy Ed.

HILL, ALLISON; North Hergerstown HS; Hagerstown, MD; (Y); Church Yth Grp; Cmnty Wkr; French Clb; JV Bsktbl; Var Sftbl; Hon Roll; Boy Scts; Teachers Aide; Phys Fit Pres Awd 84; Var Sftbl Ltr 85; Aviatn.

HILL, JASON; La Plata HS; La Plata, MD; (S); Ski Clb; Chorus; School Musical; School Play; Variety Show; Off Jr Cls; Var Socr; Hon Roll.

HILL, RENEE MICHELE; Springbrook HS; Silver Spring, MD; (Y); 131/488; Pres Church Yth Grp; Dance Clb; Pres Exploring; Church Choir; Sec Rep Stu Cncl; Capt Pom Pon; Hon Roll; Jr NHS; Cmmnd Stu Natl Achvt Schlrshp Pgm Outstndng Negr Stu 85; Bus Adm.

HILL, SHERITA A; Eleanor Roosevelt HS; Upper Marlboro, MD; (Y); Church Yth Grp; Latin Clb; Sec Sr Cls; High Hon Roll; NHS; Spanish NHS; St Schlr; Key Clb; Pep Clb; Spanish Clb.

HILL, STACY; Oakland Mills HS; Columbia, MD; (Y); 1/275; Church Yth Grp; Pres VP 4-H; French Clb; Capt Math Tm; Ed Yrbk Stf; Trs Sr Cls; 4-H Awd; Hon Roll; NHS; Val; MD Distngshd Schlr 85; Howard Cnty Outstndng Stu 86; Chncllr Scholar U MD 86; VA Polytech Inst; Bus.

HILL, TINA; Seneca Valley HS; Germantown, MD; (Y); Nwsp Stf; Lit Mag; Rep Frsh Cls; Rep Soph Cls; Var Pom Pon; Var Socr; Trk; Twrlr; Hon Roll; Mst Val Twlr All Star Majrettes 85.

HILLIARD, ANDRE; National Christian Acad; Temple Hills, MD; (Y); Church Yth Grp; Computer Clb; French Clb; Spanish Clb; JV Bsktbl; High Hon Roll; Harvard.

HILLIARD, KATRINA; Surrahsville HS; Clinton, MD; (Y); Church Yth Grp; Girl Scts; ROTC; Teachers Aide; Church Choir; Drill Tm; Stat Bsktbl; Mgr(s); Hon Roll; U Of MD; Psych.

HILLMAN, JENNIFER; Archbishop Spalding HS; Pasadena, MD; (Y); 7/127; Ed Yrbk Stf; Hon Roll; NHS; Prfct Atten Awd; Ntl Sci Merit Awd, Merit Schlstc Awd 86; Frnch Awd 85; Salisbury ST Coll; Nrsg.

HILTON, BRENT; St Johns At Prospect Hall HS; Barnesville, MD; (Y); Science Clb; Varsity Clb; High Hon Roll; Hon Roll; VP NHS; Trs Frsh Cls; Rep Soph Cls; Rep Jr Cls; Rep Stu Cncl; JV Var Bsktbl; Mt St Marys; Bus Mgmt.

HILTON, KATHY; Allegany HS; Cumberland, MD; (Y); AFS; Church Yth Grp; Office Aide; Chorus; Capt Color Guard; Sec Stu Cncl; Frostburg ST Coll; Elem Educ.

HIMELRIGHT, LAURA; Glenelg HS; Mt Airy, MD; (Y); French Clb; Ski Clb; Teachers Aide; Varsity Clb; Var L Socr; Stat Trk; Hon Roll; NHS; Pre Med.

HIMMELHEBER, DIANE; St Marys Ryken HS; Leonardtown, MD; (S); 23/138; Sec Church Yth Grp; Cmnty Wkr; Dance Clb; French Clb; Library Aide; Service Clb; Teachers Aide; Variety Show; JV Var Fld Hcky; JV Trk; Jump Rope Heart Spec Awd 85; Schl & Chrch Retreats Grp Ldr 85-86; Engl.

HINDS, SELINDA; Fort Hill HS; Cumberland, MD; (Y); Church Yth Grp; Girl Scts; Flag Corp; Yrbk Stf; Off Jr Cls.

HINES, DEBORAH L; Elizabeth Seton HS; Upper Marlboro, MD; (Y); 21/197; Church Yth Grp; Quiz Bowl; Chorus; Church Choir; Jazz Band; Symp Band; Cheerleading; Hon Roll; U MD; Psych.

HINES-JENKINS, MICHELLE ANN; Old Mill HS; Glen Burnie, MD; (Y); VP Latin Clb; Teachers Aide; Rep Stu Cncl; Stat Crs Cntry; Stat Trk; Hon Roll; Cert Mrt Strghts A Spansh 84-85; Anne Arundel CC; Child Care.

HINKLE, MARK; Glenelg HS; Glenwood, MD; (Y); Church Yth Grp; Concert Band; VP Frsh Cls; VP Soph Cls; Rep Jr Cls; Rep Stu Cncl; Var L Bsktbl; Var L Tennis; Hon Roll; NHS; Muhlenberg; Lib Arts.

HINNANT JR, CHARLES H; Parkdale HS; New Carrollton, MD; (Y); 86/500; ROTC; Science Clb; Teachers Aide; Color Guard; Yrbk Phtg; Var L Ice Hcky; Var Lcrss; Var L Socr; High Hon Roll; JP Sousa Awd; Norwich U; Mltry.

HIRATA, ERNESTINE; Dulaney SR HS; Lutherville, MD; (Y); Sec VP Church Yth Grp; Key Clb; Band; Concert Band; Drm Mjr(t); Mrchg Band; Pep Band; School Musical; Symp Band; High Hon Roll; Mrchng Bnd Mst Outstndng Jr 85-86; Bus.

HIRRLINGER, LISA; Glenelg HS; Dayton, MD; (Y).

HIRSH, STEPHANIE; Winston Churchhill HS; Potomac, MD; (Y); Chorus; Rep Frsh Cls; Rep Soph Cls; Pom Pon; MD U; Med.

HIRSHMAN, LINDA; Crossland HS; Ft Washington, MD; (Y); 14/333; Dance Clb; Drama Clb; Teachers Aide; Rep Soph Cls; Rep Jr Cls; Var Pom Pon; Var Trk; Hon Roll; Sec NHS; Acadmc Excllnce Awd 84; U Of MD.

HO, SAMUEL; Parkdale HS; New Carrollton, MD; (Y); U Of MD; Elec Engrng.

HOBAN, CHRIS; Allegany HS; Cumberland, MD; (Y); Church Yth Grp; Church Choir; Stu Cncl; Bsktbl; Hon Roll.

HOBBS, AMY; Atholton SR HS; Dayton, MD; (Y); Church Yth Grp; Dance Clb; Flag Corp; Chorus; Church Choir; Drm Mjr(t); Variety Show; Var L Cheerleading; Twrlr; Hon Roll; MD ST U; Fshn Merch.

HOBBS, BARBARA; St Vincent Pallotti HS; Laurel, MD; (S); 14/86; Spanish Clb; Nwsp Stf; Yrbk Stf; Rep Jr Cls; JV Sftbl; High Hon Roll; Hon Roll; Trs NHS; Spanish NHS; PG CC; Bus Adm.

HOBBS, DEANNE; Catoctin HS; Thurmont, MD; (S); Dance Clb; DECA; 4-H; FBLA; FFA; FHA; Drm Mjr(t); Sftbl; Hon Roll; Prfct Atten Awd; 2nd Pl ST MD Food Mktng Manual 85; Frederick CC; Crimnl Justc.

HOBBS, DIANE; Liberty HS; Sykesville, MD; (S); Hosp Aide; Teachers Aide; VICA; Hon Roll; NEDT Awd; UMBC U; Nrs.

HOCH, BRYANT; Parkdale HS; Riverdale, MD; (Y); Church Yth Grp; Latin Clb; Chorus; Stage Crew; Wt Lftg; Wrstlng; Hon Roll; Acadmc Excllnc Awd 84-85; Bus.

HOCKMAN, LEE; Gaithersburg HS; Gaithersburg, MD; (Y); Art Clb; Cmnty Wkr; High Hon Roll; Hon Roll; Jr NHS; NHS; Ntl Merit SF; JV Sftbl; Prncpls Wrtng Awd; Coachd 6th Grd Bbll Tm.

HODGE, RALPH; Friendly SR HS; Ft Washington, MD; (Y); Church Yth Grp; Teachers Aide; Church Choir; NHS; Rep Frsh Cls; Var L Bsktbl; Var L Ftbl; Var L Trk; Prince Georges Acad Excllnc Awd 84-86; Prom Cmmtt 86; U NC; Dentistry.

HODGE, THERESA; Mt De Sales Acad; Baltimore, MD; (Y); JV Var Bsktbl; Var Socr; Hon Roll; NHS; NEDT Awd; Prfct Atten Awd; Schlr/Athl Awd.

HODGSON, MIKE; Hereford HS; White Hall, MD; (Y); Camera Clb; Yrbk Phtg; Ftbl; Hon Roll; Old Dominion U; Elec Engrng.

HOECK, BETH; Archbishop Keough HS; Ellicott City, MD; (Y); Church Yth Grp; Pres 4-H; French Clb; Var Swmmng; 4-H Awd; High Hon Roll; Hon Roll; Sec NHS; Ntl Merit Ltr; Prfct Atten Awd; Bus Adm.

HOF, DEAN; Hammond HS; Columbia, MD; (Y); Church Yth Grp; Political Wkr; Band; Yrbk Stf; Diving; Swmmng; Trk; Hon Roll; Frostburg ST; Engrng.

HOFF, MICHELLE; Northern HS; Huntingtown, MD; (Y); Sec Church Yth Grp; Band; Mrchg Band; Symp Band; Sec Sr Cls; JV Church Yth Grp7; Capt Var Cheerleading; High Hon Roll; Hon Roll; Sprntndnts Schlstc Awd 86; Mngmnt.

HOFFMAN, DAVID L; Glenelg HS; Ellicott City, MD; (Y); Varsity Clb; Rep Frsh Cls; Rep Soph Cls; Rep Jr Cls; Var L Lcrss; Var L Socr; Var Capt Wrstlng; Hon Roll; NHS; 1st Pl Cnty Wrstlng Trnmnt 86; 4th Pl ST Wrstlng Trnmnt 86; 2nd Tm All-Mtro Wrstlng Tm 86; Georgetown U; Engr.

HOFFMAN, DIANE; Frederick HS; Frederick, MD; (Y); Church Yth Grp; Computer Clb; Red Cross Aide; Spanish Clb; Teachers Aide; Cit Awd; High Hon Roll; Hon Roll; NHS; Outstndng Acctng I, Geo, Spnsh I, Alg II, Spnsh II, Typng I & Spnsh III Awds 83-86; Frederick CC; Sec Educ.

HOFFMAN, JULIE; Middletown HS; Middletown, MD; (Y); Church Yth Grp; FBLA; Spanish Clb; Sec Band; Chorus; Church Choir; Orch; Score Keeper; High Hon Roll; Hon Roll; Georgetown U.

HOFFMAN, LISA; Wicomico SR HS; Salisbury, MD; (Y); Church Yth Grp; JCL; Latin Clb; Math Tm; Pep Clb; Mrchg Band; Symp Band; Hon Roll; NHS; Acad All Am Schlr 86; Chem Engr.

HOFFMAN, MICHELLE L; Meade SR HS; Hanover, MD; (Y); 50/414; VP FBLA; SADD; Yrbk Ed-Chief; Lit Mag; Hon Roll; Engl Awd 86; Clnl Jrnlsm Awd For Outstndg Cpywrtg 85; Shphrd Coll; Engl.

HOFFMAN, ROBIN; Washington HS; Wenona, MD; (Y); 7/115; Church Yth Grp; Cmnty Wkr; Teachers Aide; Chorus; Nwsp Ed-Chief; Rep Stu Cncl; Var Tennis; High Hon Roll; NHS; Hood Coll-Frederick MD; Comm.

HOFFMAN, SUSAN; Wheaton HS; Rockville, MD; (Y); 32/386; Ski Clb; Spanish Clb; Teachers Aide; VP Concert Band; Trs Soph Cls; Trs Sr Cls; Crs Cntry; Socr; Hon Roll; NHS; SGA Treas; Pres Phy & Acad Awd; Hghst Rtng In Flute Solo; U Of MD; Bio.

HOFFMANN, STEPHANIE J; Severna Park SR HS; Severna Park, MD; (Y); Computer Clb; Drama Clb; Sec Trs Mrchg Band; Sec Trs Symp Band; Rep Stu Cncl; Hon Roll; NHS; Pres Schlr; Church Yth Grp; Sec Trs Band; Anne Arundel All Cnty H S Symphnc Bnd 85 & 86; Natl Lat Exm Magna Cum Laude 84 & 85; VA Polytech Inst; Elec Engr.

HOFFORD, STEVEN; Laurel HS; Laurel, MD; (Y); Hon Roll; Ltn Awd, Med Sci/Psych Awd, Tech Grphs Awd 85-86; Lang.

HOGAN, CINDY; Northern HS; Owings, MD; (Y); 31/301; Pres Church Yth Grp; Cmnty Wkr; Hosp Aide; Science Clb; Teachers Aide; Church Choir; Mgr Tennis; High Hon Roll; $500 Schlrshp From Calvert Mem Hosp 86; MD Modern Miss Pgnt 85; Prince George CC; Pre-Med.

HOGAN, JON P; Largo HS; Forestville, MD; (Y); Capt Chess Clb; Pres Sec Church Yth Grp; ROTC; Teachers Aide; Drill Tm; Nwsp Stf; Yrbk Stf; Lit Mag; Hon Roll; Military.

HOHL, LISA; Dulanes SR HS; Lutherville, MD; (Y); Church Yth Grp; Political Wkr; Nwsp Rptr; Nwsp Stf; Var Sftbl; Hon Roll; NHS; Scotland Yth Exchng 85; Intl Exchng Coordntr 86; Poltcl Sci.

HOHN, CHRISTINE MARIE; Potomac HS; Temple Hills, MD; (Y); 1/300; Church Yth Grp; Drama Clb; Office Aide; Teachers Aide; High Hon Roll; Trs NHS; Val; Senatrl Schlrshp 86; Its Acadmc Schlrshp 86; MD Merit Schlstc Awd 86; St Marys Coll Of MD; Humn Dvlp.

HOILER, DAVID; Loyola Blakefield HS; Towson, MD; (Y); French Clb; Band; Boston Coll; Intl Bnkng.

HOLDWAY JR, JOHN B; High Point HS; College Park, MD; (Y); Recgnzd MD Schlrshp Brd 86; MD Inst Of Art; Fine Arts.

HOLFELDER, KAIA; Western HS; Balt, MD; (Y); 20/412; Church Yth Grp; Acpl Chr; Church Choir; School Musical; Rep Soph Cls; Var Cheerleading; High Hon Roll; Hon Roll; NHS.

HOLLAND, ANTHONY; Thomas Stone HS; Waldorf, MD; (Y); Am Leg Boys St; SADD; Var L Bsktbl; Var Capt Trk; MVP Boys Trck, All Co Trck Team 86; Maryland; Comp Sci.

HOLLAND, JENNIFER; Hereford HS; Phoenix, MD; (Y); 1/215; Church Yth Grp; Cmnty Wkr; 4-H; FTA; JCL; FTA; Political Wkr; Teachers Aide; Varsity Clb; Band; Natl 4-H Prjct Schlrshp 85; FTA Schlrshp 86; Natl Hnr Sority Schlrshp 86; U Of Richmond; Pre-Med.

HOLLAND, MELANIE; Northern HS; Huntingtown, MD; (Y); VP VICA; Band; Var Fld Hcky; Hon Roll; Cert Elks Lodge Cmmnty Concern Needy 85-86; Locl & Regnl VICA Skills 2nd Pl 85-86; Cmmnctns Tech.

HOLLEY, NIKALL; Forest Park SR HS; Baltimore, MD; (Y); Church Yth Grp; Dance Clb; FBLA; Girl Scts; JA; Library Aide; Office Aide; Pep Clb; Science Clb; Teachers Aide; U Of MD; Sci.

HOLLINGER, JAMES; Northern HS; Owings, MD; (Y); 23/301; Scholastic Bowl; JV Bsbl; Var Wt Lftg; Var Wrstlng; Hon Roll; 1st Pl Cnty Sci Fair; VPI; Elec Engrg.

HOLLINGER, SHELLEY; Maurice J Mc Donough HS; Waldorf, MD; (Y); Dance Clb; Drama Clb; Thesps; Mrchg Band; School Musical; School Play; Stage Crew; Variety Show; Co-Capt Pom Pon; Stat Trk; Psd Grd I Cecchetti Exam Clasicl Ballet 84; Hmcmng Flt Cmmtte 85; Animal Studies.

HOLLINGSWORTH JR, CARL A; Landon Schl; Wheaton, MD; (Y); Church Yth Grp; Cmnty Wkr; Model UN; Pres Frsh Cls; Pres Soph Cls; Pres Jr Cls; VP Stu Cncl; JV Bsktbl; JV Ftbl; Mgr(s); G P Marshall Schlrshp 82-86; Amb Hugh O Brian Ldrshp Conf 84; U MD Stdnt Ldrs Conf 85; Psych.

HOLLINGSWORTH, DAWN; Francis Scott Key HS; Union Bridge, MD; (Y); Trs Drama Clb; VP GAA; Band; Chorus; Mrchg Band; JV Var Bsktbl; Var Fld Hcky; Var Trk; Hon Roll; NHS; Schlrshp From Bltmr Fld Hcky Assn Camp 85; Cert From MD Acad Of Sci In Psych 86.

HOLLINS, JAMES; Friendly SR HS; Ft Washington, MD; (Y); Pres Cmnty Wkr; Library Aide; Band; Nwsp Rptr; Nwsp Stf; Var Bsbl; JV Bsktbl; Var Crs Cntry; Hon Roll; OH U; Jrnslm.

HOLMAN, ANGELA; Francis Scott Key HS; Uniontown, MD; (Y); Drama Clb; Science Clb; Spanish Clb; Teachers Aide; School Play; Variety Show; Nwsp Stf; Hon Roll; Elem Ed.

HOLMES, SHERRI; Potomac HS; Temple Hills, MD; (Y); Pres Church Yth Grp; Office Aide; Band; Church Choir; Pom Pon; Hon Roll; NHS; Outstndg Ldrshp Yth Forum 84; Pm Pn Sprkl & Shn Awd 86; Hampton U; Law.

HOLMES III, THEODORE TED; Friendly SR HS; Ft Washington, MD; (Y); Boy Scts; Church Yth Grp; FCA; Yrbk Stf; Mgr Bsbl; Var Ftbl; Hon Roll; Cert Of Achvmnt GITEC & ONR 83-84; Engrng.

HOLT, JANET; Allegany HS; Cumberland, MD; (Y); 14/240; Hosp Aide; Band; Chorus; Concert Band; Drm Mjr(t); Jazz Band; Mrchg Band; Hon Roll; NHS; All St Band MD 85-86; WV Invtnl Hnrs Band 83-86; Music/Arts Schlrshp 86; Sci.

HOLT, LORA MARIE; Woodlawn HS; Baltimore, MD; (Y); JA; VP Madrigals; Rep Stu Cncl; Var Capt Cheerleading; Var Sftbl; NHS; Woodlaun Mddl Schl PTA Schlrshp 86; U Of MD; Engrng.

HOLT, MICHELLE; Parkville SR HS; Parkville, MD; (Y); Church Yth Grp; Hst FBLA; Hon Roll; Jr NHS; Camp Fr Inc; Hosp Aide; Villa Julie Coll; Dentl.

HOLTON, DANIEL; Chopticon HS; Charlotte Hall, MD; (Y); Chorus; Hon Roll; Art Awd 84; Sci Awd 84.

HOLTZ, JOHN ANDREW; Mc Donogh Schl; Mc Donogh, MD; (Y); Church Yth Grp; Computer Clb; Spanish Clb; Stu Cncl; Var Bsktbl; Var Coach Actv; JV Ftbl; Var Sftbl; Hon Roll; U Of Richmond; Bus.

HOLTZMAN, DEBORAH; Baltimore City College HS; Baltimore, MD; (S); School Musical; School Play; Nwsp Rptr; Ed Nwsp Stf; Var Swmmng; High Hon Roll; Jr NHS; NHS; Ntl Merit SF; Prfct Atten Awd; Magna Cum Laude Natl Latin Exam Level I & II 84-85; Hist.

HOM, HELLEN; Westminster HS; Westminster, MD; (Y); VP Trs Latin Clb; PAVAS; VP Political Wkr; Red Cross Aide; Capt Scholastic Bowl; Orch; Lit Mag; Rep Jr Cls; High Hon Roll; Trs NHS; Natl Latin Exam Magna Cum Laude Cert 86; Granite Hse Inc Bd Dir 85-87; Cover Art Stu Hnbk 86-87; Intl Rel.

HOMESLEY, DERRICK; Surrattsville SR HS; Clinton, MD; (Y); Boy Scts; Cmnty Wkr; Band; Concert Band; Mrchg Band; Symp Band; Var Bsktbl; Var Trk; Var Wt Lftg; Hon Roll; MVP Bsktbl 84-85; Coachs Awd Bsktbl 85-86; Outstndng Fld Prfrmr Trck 85-86; NC A&T ST U; Bus Mgmt.

HOOK, BRIAN; John Carroll HS; Joppa, MD; (Y); 52/238; Drama Clb; Pres German Clb; School Play; Nwsp Bus Mgr; Yrbk Stf; JV L Bsbl; Im Bsktbl; Var L Trk; Hon Roll; German Hon Scty 85; Accntng.

HOOKER, CARLA; Forest Park SR HS; Baltimore, MD; (Y); Chess Clb; Drama Clb; Stage Crew; Nwsp Phtg; Nwsp Rptr; Capt JV Gym; Capt Var Sftbl; Capt Var Vllybl; Hon Roll; JV Bsktbl; Cmnty Coll Bltmr Upward Bnd-Outstndng Achvt-Eng, Svc, Cmpltn Of 86 Pgm 86; Notre Dame MD; Psych.

HOOKER, IRIS TOWANDA; Eastern HS; Baltimore, MD; (Y); 17/248; FBLA; Hon Roll; NHS; Math, Engrng, Sci Achvt MESA 82-85; VIP Clb 85-86; Pres Acad Fit Awd 86; Villa Julie Coll; Paralegl.

HOOPER, KIMBERLY; Fallston HS; Fallston, MD; (Y); 76/225; FHA; PAVAS; SADD; Nwsp Rptr; Off Stu Cncl; JV Cheerleading; JV Powder Puff Ftbl; Hon Roll; Law.

HOOPER, STEPHEN; Cardinal Gibbons HS; Baltimore, MD; (Y); 24/124; Boy Scts; Church Yth Grp; Ftbl; Lcrss; Wt Lftg; Wrstlng; Hon Roll; MVP Lacrosse 84; Mech Engr.

HOOPES, MARY; Southern #70 HS; Baltimore, MD; (Y); Prfct Atten Awd; Engrng Plne 84-85; UMBC; Math & Sci.

HOOTS, DAVID; Laurel HS; Laurel, MD; (Y); Chess Clb; Computer Clb; School Play; Crs Cntry; Socr; God Cntry Awd; Hon Roll; MIT; Comp Asst.

HOOVER, SUSAN; Chopticon HS; Charlotte Hall, MD; (Y); DECA; Hon Roll; Charles Cnty Coll; Art.

HOPE, FRANCINE; Thomas S Wootton HS; Rockville, MD; (Y); AFS; Service Clb; Rotary Awd; Georgetown U; Chem.

HOPKINS, DEMITRY L; La Reine HS; Suitland, MD; (Y); 2/149; Church Yth Grp; Band; Yrbk Sprt Ed; Rep Stu Cncl; Var Capt Cheerleading; Var Socr; Var Capt Trk; Sal; Voice Dem Awd; Natl Achvt Semi Flnst 86; Acadmc All Am Natl Ldrshp & Serv Awd 86; MD ST Page 86; Princeton; Intl Econm.

HOPKINS, FAYE; Carver Voctional Technical HS; Baltimore, MD; (Y); FBLA; Mrchg Band; Hon Roll; Jr NHS; Ntl Merit Ltr; Comp Pgmng.

HOPKINS, MICHELE LEE; Westminster HS; Westminster, MD; (Y); Pres 4-H; Concert Band; Mrchg Band; School Musical; School Play; Symp Band; 4-H Awd; High Hon Roll; NHS; Hnrd Qn-Intl Ordr Of Jobs Dghtrs Bthl 86; Artist.

HOPKINS, MICHELLE L; Immaculata College HS; Washington, DC; (Y); 13/120; Cmnty Wkr; Drama Clb; Library Aide; Orch; Stage Crew; Yrbk Stf; Rptr Lit Mag; Rep Stu Cncl; Natl Merit Cmmnd Stu 85; Clsscl Hist.

HOPKINS, MONYETTE; Western SR HS; Baltimore, MD; (Y); Church Yth Grp; FBLA; Chorus; Church Choir; Bus Adm.

HOPP, MELANIE JEAN; Montgomery Blair HS; Silver Spring, MD; (Y); Exploring; Intnl Clb; VP Pres JA; Ski Clb; Teachers Aide; Stage Crew; Silv Spg Wmns Clb Scholar; Potomac Bus Studs Awd 86; Exec Awd JA 85; Blairs Bst 86; Hgh Advntr Explrers; U MD; Bus.

HOPWOOD, LISA; Annapolis Area Christian HS; Severna Park, MD; (S); 1/13; Hosp Aide; Stage Crew; Nwsp Rptr; Yrbk Ed-Chief; Yrbk Rptr; VP Soph Cls; Rep Jr Cls; Trs Sr Cls; NHS; St Schlr; MD ST Schlrshp Semi-Fnlst 85-86; Anne Arvndel Cnty Sci Fair Hon Ment 85; U Of MD; Comp Sci.

HORAN, LENNY; Glenelg HS; Woodbine, MD; (Y); 24/255; Church Yth Grp; Cmnty Wkr; Debate Tm; Letterman Clb; Rep Jr Cls; Var L Bsbl; Capt L Ftbl; Var L Trk; High Hon Roll; NHS; 1330 SAT Score 86; Intl Baccalaureate Cls 84-86; Leading Scorer Reciever Ftbl 84; Engrng.

HORKEY, LISA; Arch Bishop Keough HS; Glen Burnre, MD; (Y); Church Yth Grp; Hosp Aide; Spanish Clb; Off Frsh Cls; Off Soph Cls; Stu Cncl; Hon Roll; Prfct Atten Awd; Loyola Coll; Bus Mktg.

HORN, KEVIN; Thomas Stone HS; Waldorf, MD; (S); Chess Clb; Debate Tm; Latin Clb; Science Clb; High Hon Roll; Hon Roll; Its Acad Cnty Champs 85; Sci Fair 2nd Schl 1st Cnty Hon Men Area 85; Olympcs Of Mnd Great Art Lives 86; Med.

HORNATKO, ADRIENNE M; Mt De Sales Acad; Baltimore, MD; (S); 1/60; Cmnty Wkr; French Clb; Lit Mag; Hon Roll; NHS; Voice Dem Awd; MD Dstngshd Schlr Fnlst 85-86; Hugh O Brian Yth Fndtn Ldrshp Smnr Cls Rep 83-84; U Of MD-COLL Prk; Anml Sci.

HORNBECK, MARK; Baltimore City College; Baltimore, MD; (Y); 5/238; Church Yth Grp; Quiz Bowl; Yrbk Rptr; Yrbk Stf; Tennis; High Hon Roll; Hon Roll; VP NHS; Opt Clb Awd; Trsch Schlrshp 85-86; Pbdy Awd 85-86; Hvrfrd Coll; Lwyr.

HORNE, DAVID; James M Bennett SR HS; Salisbury, MD; (Y); 40/188; Towson ST; Engrng.

HORNE, KATIE; St Andrews Episcopal HS; Chevy Chase, MD; (S); Cmnty Wkr; French Clb; SADD; Nwsp Stf; Yrbk Stf; Var L Bsktbl; Lcrss; Var L Socr; Var L Sftbl; Hon Roll; Cert Apprctn Lgl Cnsl For Eldrly 84; Cert Grwth Drmtc Sklls; Suma Cum Laude Hnr Roll.

HORNER, BRENDA; Eastern Vocational Technical HS; Baltimore, MD; (Y); Church Yth Grp; FBLA; Library Aide; Band; Church Choir; Variety Show; Sftbl; Hon Roll; Teen Talent 86; YWEA 84; Lee Coll; Music.

HORNER, WENDY; Parkside HS; Salisbury, MD; (Y); Ski Clb; Spanish Clb; Varsity Clb; Var Bsktbl; Var Trk; Hon Roll; Acctng.

HORNUNG, JULIE; Andover HS; Linthicum, MD; (Y); 18/200; Thesps; Capt Pom Pon; Dance Clb; Drama Clb; French Clb; Radio Clb; Teachers Aide; School Musical; School Play; Cheerleading; Superstr Drill Tm 83-85; Towson ST; Dance.

HORSMON, SUSAN; Calvert HS; St Leonard, MD; (Y); Church Yth Grp; Teachers Aide; High Hon Roll; Hon Roll; St Marys Coll; Elem Tchr.

HORST, SCOTT K; North Hagerstown HS; Hagerstown, MD; (Y); Church Yth Grp; Office Aide; Ski Clb; Spanish Clb; Teachers Aide; Sr Cls; Wt Lftg; Cit Awd; Elks Awd; Hon Roll; Elks Teenagr Yr 86; U Of MD Coll Pk; Bus.

HORTON, MARY; Gaithersburg HS; Gaithersburg, MD; (Y); Cmnty Wkr; Ski Clb; School Play; Var Fld Hcky; NHS; AFS; Drama Clb; 4-H; FFA; Rep Frsh Cls; Stu Mnth 84; Acad Achvt 84; 2nd Pl Subdiv Sci Fair 85; Bio-Med Engrng.

HORVATH, DAWN L; Sherwood HS; Olney, MD; (Y); Church Yth Grp; Cmnty Wkr; Office Aide; Spanish Clb; Hon Roll; Fash Merch.

HOSE, STEPHANIE; Fort Hill HS; Cumberland, MD; (Y); Cmnty Wkr; Hosp Aide; Intnl Clb; Letterman Clb; Political Wkr; Thesps; Nwsp Phtg; Nwsp Rptr; Stu Cncl; Crs Cntry; Law.

HOSE, STEVE; Clear Sprin HS; Big Spg, MD; (Y); 23/156; Exploring; French Clb; Teachers Aide; Band; Concert Band; Mrchg Band; Bsktbl; Socr; Trk; Hon Roll; U MD; Engr.

HOSFELD, MICHELLE; Williamsport HS; Hagerstown, MD; (Y); Cmnty Wkr; Computer Clb; DECA; FNA; Hosp Aide; Red Cross Aide; Spanish Clb; Swmmng; Tennis; Trk; Sheephard Coll; Nrs.

HOTCHKISS, STEPHEN; Beall HS; Frostburg, MD; (Y); Boy Scts; Church Yth Grp; Chorus; Stage Crew; Yrbk Rptr; Johns Hopkins Tlnt Srch 82; Engrng.

HOUSE, ERWIN; Northwestern HS; Baltimore, MD; (S); Pres Church Yth Grp; Cmnty Wkr; Pres JA; Yrbk Sprt Ed; Var Crs Cntry; Trk; Hon Roll; Prfct Atten Awd; Val; Hist Gov Awd 86; Comp.

HOUSER, SCOTT; Westminster HS; Westminster, MD; (Y); 1/550; Church Yth Grp; Letterman Clb; Varsity Clb; Band; Concert Band; Bsktbl; Socr; Trk; High Hon Roll; NHS; Engrng.

HOUZOURIS, ADRIENNE; John Carroll HS; Havre De Grace, MD; (Y); 31/238; Church Yth Grp; Cmnty Wkr; Ski Clb; Varsity Clb; Ed Yrbk Bus Mgr; Var Socr; 4-H Awd; Hon Roll; Sec NHS; Spanish NHS; MD ST Horse Judgng Tm 84-85; 2nd Pl Dist Pony Clb 85; 2nd Pl MD ST Horse Judgng Cont 84-85; Engrng.

HOWARD, AUDREY; Carver Vo-Tech HS; Baltimore, MD; (Y); Drama Clb; FBLA; School Play; Rep Jr Cls; Prfct Atten Awd; Awd Distingshd Achvt In Acadmc Fair 86; Morgan ST U; Cpa.

HOWARD, CHERYL; Liberty HS; Eldersburg, MD; (Y); Drama Clb; Chorus; Church Choir; Orch; School Musical; School Play; Stage Crew.

HOWARD, DEANNA; Glenelg HS; Glenwood, MD; (Y); AFS; Debate Tm; NFL; Political Wkr; Thesps; School Musical; School Play; Off Sr Cls; Stu Cncl; Cheerleading; Ntl Hnr Rl 84-85; Lawson ST U; Psychlgy.

HOWARD, HOLLY; Magruder HS; Derwood, MD; (Y); Drama Clb; Chorus; School Musical; Stage Crew; Rep Stu Cncl; Trs Pom Pon; JV Sftbl; Var Tennis; JV Vllybl; Hon Roll; U VA Mdcl Coll; Physcl Thrpy.

HOWARD, LEE; St Andrews Episcopal HS; Gaithersburg, MD; (Y); Boy Scts; Church Yth Grp; Dance Clb; Drama Clb; Exploring; SADD; Thesps; School Musical; School Play; Stage Crew; Toastmstrs Awd Preprd Spch 84; Dirctrs Awd Schl Musical 85; Shrt Stry Cntst 2nd Pl 86.

HOWARD, LISA; Northwestern HS; Baltimore, MD; (Y); #25 In Class; Church Yth Grp; Pep Clb; Chorus; Yrbk Rptr; Rep Sr Cls; Var Badmtn; Mgr Trk; Mgr Wrstlng; Prfct Atten Awd; Prncpl Awd 86; Chmstry II Awd 86; Cls Awd 86; Howard U; Educ.

HOWARD, TAMARA ANNETTE; Oxon Hill HS; Durham, NC; (Y); Drama Clb; French Clb; Math Tm; Church Choir; JV Cheerleading; Gym; Hon Roll; Church Yth Grp; Dance Clb; Intnl Clb; Latn Hnr Soc 85; Natl Achvt Schlrshp Pgm Outstndng Negr Stu 85; Hnrs Schlrshp Providence Baptst Chrch; Duke U; Neursrgry.

HOWDYSHELL, DIANA; Lackey HS; Nanjemoy, MD; (Y); Am Leg Aux Girls St; Cmnty Wkr; Concert Band; Drm & Bgl; Pres Rep Frsh Cls; VP Rep Stu Cncl; Pom Pon; Hon Roll; Jr NHS; Tennis; Tri-Cnty Natural Rsrc Camp 85; Rockett Tech Wkshps-NOS Of Indn Head 85; Alt Dlgt-Chrls Cnty Assn/Stu; FL Inst Of Tech; Flght Tech.

HOWELL, BILL; Archbishop Spalding HS; Glen Burnie, MD; (Y); Var Bsbl; U MD; Comp Sci.

HOWELL, CHERIE; Acad Of The Holy Names; Silver Spring, MD; (Y); Church Yth Grp; Cmnty Wkr; Drama Clb; Red Cross Aide; Church Choir; Nwsp Rptr; Stu Cncl; Hon Roll; NHS; Nwsp News Editor 86; U Of PA; Bio-Med Engrng.

HOWELL JR, ROBERT J; Mt St Joseph HS; Elliot City, MD; (Y); Church Yth Grp; Stu Cncl; Var Bsbl; Var L Bsktbl; Hon Roll.

HOWER, CRAIG; La Plata HS; La Plata, MD; (Y); Capt Aud/Vis; Camera Clb; VP Drama Clb; Exploring; Thesps; Chorus; School Musical; School Play; Nwsp Ed-Chief; Nwsp Phtg; Bst Sprtng Actr Musical 84-85; 4yr Outstndng Svc Awd 82-86; 7 Str Hnr Thspn 85-86; Actor.

HOWLEY, ANGELA; Connelly School Of The Holy Child; Rockville, MD; (Y); Church Yth Grp; Service Clb; Rep Soph Cls; Pres Jr Cls; Pres Stu Cncl; Var JV Bsktbl; Var JV Fld Hcky; Var Capt Sftbl; Art Clb; Cmnty Wkr; Frshmn Outstndng Athlt 84; Frshmn Of Mnth 84; All Lg Sftbl Tm 86; Ed.

HOYT, WILLIAM; Barrie HS; Silver Spring, MD; (S); Computer Clb; Im Bowling; Crs Cntry; JV Socr; JV Trk; Im Wt Lftg; High Hon Roll; Hon Roll.

HOYTE, BETTINA S; Academy Of The Holy Name; Washington, DC; (Y); Art Clb; Church Yth Grp; Cmnty Wkr; Hosp Aide; Q&S; Chorus; Pres Sr Cls; Bst Frnch Stu Recogntn Awd 86; PA ST U; Radiolgy.

HRYSOVERGIS, ELIZABETH; Archbishop Keough HS; Baltimore, MD; (Y); Hosp Aide; Ed Yrbk Stf; Ed Lit Mag; Rep Frsh Cls; Capt Bowling; High Hon Roll; Hon Roll; NHS; Prfct Atten Awd; U Of MD; Psychlgy.

HU, PEGGY; Walter Johnson HS; Kensington, MD; (Y); Math Tm; Thesps; Chorus; School Play; Stage Crew; French Hon Soc; High Hon Roll; Sec NHS; AFS; Drama Clb; Yth For Undrstndng Corp Schlrshp ,6; Lang.

HUBBARD, ANTHONY D; Owings Mills HS; Owings Mills, MD; (Y); JA; Bsbl; Bsktbl; Ftbl; Wt Lftg; Awd Engl Achvt 85-86; Top 10 Pct Cls 85-86; Human Rel Commtte 85-86; Bus Adm.

HUBBLE, DANA; Arlington Baptist HS; Mt Airy, MD; (Y); Off Frsh Cls; Off Soph Cls; Off Jr Cls; Var Bsbl; Hon Roll; Stu Mont 86; Natl Hnr Roll; Hnr Scty; Fire Dept.

HUBER, CATHERINE; Arch Bishop Spalding HS; Pasadena, MD; (Y); 15/128; Church Yth Grp; Cmnty Wkr; Pres FBLA; Lit Mag; Hon Roll; NHS; Salisburg ST; Bio.

HUBER, DIANE; Laurel HS; Laurel, MD; (Y); Church Yth Grp; Drama Clb; School Musical; Variety Show; Nwsp Sprt Ed; Stu Cncl; Capt Crs Cntry; Capt Sftbl; Trk; High Hon Roll; Athltc-Acadmc Achvt Awd 86; Outstndng Athlt Awd 86; Drln Peters Memrl Awd 86; U Of DE; Physcl Thrpy.

HUBER, STACY; Kenwood HS; Baltimore, MD; (Y); Hon Roll.

HUBER, SUE; Cambridge South Dorchester HS; Fishing Creek, MD; (Y); 20/230; AFS; Cmnty Wkr; SADD; Teachers Aide; Band; Concert Band; Mrchg Band; Symp Band; Sec Jr Cls; Rep Stu Cncl; Bayside Sftbl 84-85; MVP Sftbl 85-86; Miss CSD 85-86; U Of MD; Comm.

HUBER, TIMOTHY; Thomas Stone HS; Waldorf, MD; (Y); Am Leg Boys St; Sec Chess Clb; Pres Debate Tm; Drama Clb; Capt Math Tm; Capt Quiz Bowl; Pres Chorus; School Musical; Swing Chorus; Var Crs Cntry; Physics.

HUDSON, JILL; Regina HS; Lanham Seabrook, MD; (Y); Camera Clb; English Clb; Intnl Clb; Model UN; Yrbk Phtg; VP Soph Cls; Hon Roll.

HUDSON, JOSIE; Bishop Walsh HS; Cumberland, MD; (Y); Church Yth Grp; Dance Clb; Debate Tm; Drama Clb; Pep Clb; Chorus; Drill Tm; Flag Corp; School Musical; School Play; Towson ST; Med.

HUFFER, KIMBERLY; Brunswick HS; Jefferson, MD; (Y); 9/140; French Clb; Concert Band; Jazz Band; Mrchg Band; Pep Band; School Musical; Powder Puff Ftbl; Tennis; Hon Roll; Art.

HUGEL, KEVIN; Chopticon HS; Mechanicsville, MD; (Y); Church Yth Grp; Spanish Clb; Varsity Clb; Band; Church Choir; Concert Band; Jazz Band; Mrchg Band; Orch; Pep Band; Journlsm.

HUGHES, AMY; John Carroll HS; Kingsville, MD; (Y); 29/248; GAA; Spanish Clb; Chorus; School Musical; Lcrss; Powder Puff Ftbl; Trk; High Hon Roll; Hon Roll; Spanish NHS; Notre Dame Coll; Pre-Vet Sci.

HUGHES, ANGELA; Northwestern HS; Avondale, MD; (Y); French Clb; Church Choir; Rep Stu Cncl; Var Pom Pon; Hon Roll; Hnr Of Attndg PG Coll As Concrrnt 86-87; Hampton U; Crmnlgy.

HUGHES, AUDRA; Thomas Stone HS; Waldorf, MD; (S); Art Clb; French Clb; Teachers Aide; Var Tennis; Cit Awd; Jr NHS; Natl Leadrshp Awd 85; Interior Desgn.

HUGHES, KEVIN L; Loyola HS; Catonsville, MD; (S); German Clb; Yrbk Stf; JV Crs Cntry; Var Golf; Hon Roll; NHS; Ntl Merit SF; Latn Merit Mdl 85; Med.

HUGHES, KRISTIN; Thomas S Wootton HS; Rockville, MD; (Y); AFS; VP Drama Clb; Ski Clb; Teachers Aide; Thesps; School Musical; School Play; Stage Crew; Hon Roll; NHS.

HUGHES, MICA; Oakland Mills HS; Columbia, MD; (Y); Drama Clb; Math Tm; Pep Clb; Chorus; Madrigals; School Play; JV Bsktbl; Var Bowling; JV Cheerleading; JV Gym; Grace And Talnt Awd 83; Bsktbl Athltc Awd 84; Thats Entrnmnt Awd 86; Micro Surgn.

HUGHES, RAYMOND; Beall HS; Frostburg, MD; (Y); 1/151; Drama Clb; Pep Clb; Thesps; Band; Concert Band; Jazz Band; Mrchg Band; Orch; Pep Band; School Musical; MD Dstngshd Schlr 86; Frstbrg ST Coll Fndtn Schlrshp 86; Pres Merit Schlrshp FSC 86; Eng Awd 86; Frostburg ST Coll; Engrng.

HUGHES, STEPHANIE; Maurice J Mc Donough HS; Waldorf, MD; (S); Teachers Aide; Acpl Chr; Drm Mjr(t); Mrchg Band; School Musical; Symp Band; Stat Bsktbl; JV Var Sftbl; High Hon Roll; NHS; Engrng.

HUGHEY, TRACEY; Perryville HS; Perryville, MD; (Y); Church Yth Grp; FBLA; SADD; Hon Roll; 1st Pl Intermediat Typng Cecil Cnty 85; 1st Pl Steno II Rgn 86; Royala; Chld Psych.

HUI, ERIC C; John F Kenndy HS; Silver Spring, MD; (Y); 1/468; Computer Clb; Mathletes; Math Tm; Nwsp Bus Mgr; Crs Cntry; High Hon Roll; Hon Roll; Ntl Merit Ltr; Pres Schlr; MD Distinguished Scholar 85; Cornell U; Elec Engr.

HULBURT, HEATHER; Allegany HS; La Vale, MD; (Y); 1/200; VP AFS; Church Yth Grp; Pep Clb; Capt Drill Tm; Rep Soph Cls; High Hon Roll; NHS; Psych.

HULL, LESLIE; James M Bennett SR HS; Quantico, MD; (Y); 30/188; VP Church Yth Grp; FBLA; Girl Scts; Hon Roll; Prfct Atten Awd; Film Fstvl Awd, Stdnt Mnth Physcs 86; Sci Fair Awd 84; U MD; Econ.

HUMBERSON, THERESA; Southern HS; Deer Park, MD; (Y); Tennis; Hon Roll; US Ntl Art Awd 85; US Ntl Ldrshp Merit Awd 86; Ft Lauderdale Inst; Fshn Ill.

HUMPHREY, TARA LEE; Surrattsville HS; Clinton, MD; (Y); VP Church Yth Grp; Trs FBLA; Sec Trs Flag Corp; Pep Band; Rep Stu Cncl; Hon Roll; Ntl Merit Schol; Amer Red Crss Svc 86; Acdmc Excllnc Awd 85; Towson ST U; Acctg.

HUMPHREYS, GIL; Calvert HS; Huntingtown, MD; (Y); Civic Clb; Varsity Clb; Var L Ftbl; Var L Wt Lftg; Var L Wrstlng; Hon Roll; NHS; Opt Clb Awd; Freedoms Fndtn Vly Forge 86; Capt Rugy Tm 84-86; Pres Octagn Clb Calvert Cnty 85-86; U MD; Elec Engr.

HUNSBERGER, NATALIE; Liberty HS; Sykesville, MD; (Y); VP AFS; Sec Drama Clb; Pres Girl Scts; Thesps; School Musical; School Play; High Hon Roll; Hon Roll; Jr NHS; NHS; Marion Burk Knott Schlrshp Ntre Dame 86; 1st Pl Duet Acting Spch Cnfrnce 85; Amer Lgn Ortrcl Cntst 86; Coll Of Notre Dame; Pre-Law.

HUNT, DANITA; Our Lady Of Pompei HS; Baltimore, MD; (Y); GAA; Pep Clb; Spanish Clb; Yrbk Stf; Sec Frsh Cls; Sec Soph Cls; Sec Jr Cls; Sec Sr Cls; Cheerleading; Sftbl; Spnsh Hnr Awd 85; Svc Awd Yrbk 86; Savings Bond 86.

HUNTER, BRYSON; St James HS; Wilmington, DE; (Y); 7/37; Church Yth Grp; DECA; Exploring; JA; Ski Clb; Pres Spanish Clb; Stu Cncl; Capt Golf; Lcrss; Hon Roll; European Hstry Prize Excellence 86; DECA ST U Cometition 2rd Pl Awd Finance Crdt 85.

HUNTER, MICHELE; Seneca Valley HS; Gaithersburg, MD; (Y); Church Yth Grp; French Clb; Latin Clb; Ski Clb; Speech Tm; Rep Frsh Cls; Sec Jr Cls; Pom Pon; Hon Roll; Miss Pom Pon; Acad Excllnc Awd.

HUNTER, TAMMY; Northwestern HS; Lewisdale, MD; (Y); 12/425; Am Leg Aux Girls St; Cmnty Wkr; Latin Clb; Red Cross Aide; Science Clb; Spanish Clb; SADD; Teachers Aide; Lit Mag; Sec Stu Cncl; Prncpl Awd No 1 Clb 86; Xavier U; Bio.

HUNTER, YOLANDA; Oakland Mills HS; Columbia, MD; (Y); Cmnty Wkr; Office Aide; ROTC; Teachers Aide; Yrbk Phtg; Yrbk Rptr; Yrbk Stf; Stat Bsktbl; Elks Awd; NHS; Clmb Clctn Schlrshp 86; Ntl Sjrnrs Awd, Rbn & Mdl 86; NC A&T; Law.

HUR, SUE INN; Old Mill SR HS; Glen Burnie, MD; (Y); Sec JCL; Sec Frsh Cls; VP Soph Cls; Pom Pon; Rep Jr Cls; Rep Sr Cls; Rep Stu Cncl; MD ST & Sntrl Schrlshp 86; Pres Acdmc Ftns Awd 86; Sci Dept Awd & Frnch Awd 86; Advncd Acdmc Dplm 86; St Marys Coll MD; Nclr Engrng.

HURLBURT, DAVID; Arlington Baptist HS; Randallstown, MD; (Y); Pres Soph Cls; VP Jr Cls; Var Capt Bsktbl; Var Capt Socr; Hon Roll; Physcs.

HURLEY, ALLEN; Smithsburg HS; Boonsboro, MD; (Y); Church Yth Grp; Band; Chorus; School Musical; Nwsp Stf; Yrbk Stf; Hon Roll; Disc Jcky WCRH; Le Tourneau Coll; Elec Engrng.

HURLEY, DARYL; Milford Mill HS; Pikesville, MD; (Y); Church Yth Grp; Nwsp Phtg; Nwsp Rptr; Nwsp Stf; Hon Roll; NHS; Stu Of Yr; Elec Engrng.

HURLEY, JEFF; Pacomoke HS; Pocomoke, MD; (S); 5/91; Church Yth Grp; Trs Jr Cls; Stat Bsktbl; Ftbl; High Hon Roll; Hon Roll; NHS; Math Chllng Awd 84-85; Acad Lttr & Pin 84-85; Chem Clb 85-86.

HURLEY, JOHN; Maurice J Mc Donough HS; La Plata, MD; (Y); Chess Clb; Church Yth Grp; FFA; Jazz Band; School Musical; Hon Roll; Apprectn Awd Faithlf & Meritrs Svc 83; Green Hand FFA 85; Charles County CC; Bus Progmng.

HURLEY, TAMMY J; Mardela HS; Hebron, MD; (S); 2/70; Capt Flag Corp; Mgr Stage Crew; Yrbk Phtg; VP Frsh Cls; VP Stu Cncl; High Hon Roll; Pres NHS; Opt Clb Awd; Prfct Atten Awd; Hugh O Brien Yth Fndtn MD ST Ldrshp Sem 84; Schlrs Semnr 85; Rep To Brd Of Ed 85-86; Salisbury ST Coll.

HURLY, IRENE; Atholton HS; Laurel, MD; (Y); Church Yth Grp; French Clb; GAA; Ski Clb; Varsity Clb; Rep Stu Cncl; Var Capt Fld Hcky; Var Lcrss; High Hon Roll; Hon Roll; Med.

HURWITZ, STACEY ILENE; Pikesville HS; Baltimore, MD; (Y); Debate Tm; Trs Latin Clb; Pres Science Clb; Band; Orch; School Play; Chrmn NHS; AFS; Cmnty Wkr; Mrchg Band; Cert Hnrbl Merit Cum Laude Natl Latin Exam 86; Stu Page Balt Cnty 86; Mock Trials Cert Awd 85; U MI; Law.

HUSEMAN, CHRISTOPHER S; La Plata HS; La Plata, MD; (Y); Cmnty Wkr; Ski Clb; Off Jr Cls; Tennis; Cit Awd; High Hon Roll; Hon Roll; Jr NHS; NHS; Acctg.

HUSINGA, DANNIELLE; Glenelg HS; Woodbine, MD; (Y); French Clb; Intnl Clb; Capt Drill Tm; Flag Corp; Variety Show; Rep Soph Cls; Stat Bsktbl; Hon Roll; NHS; U Of MD College Park; Engrng.

HUTCHINSON, BRENDA; Northern HS; Owings, MD; (Y); Church Yth Grp; Spanish Clb; Church Choir; Var L Cheerleading; Stat Score Keeper; JV Sftbl; Hon Roll; NHS.

HUTT, MICHELE C; James M Bennet SR HS; Salisbury, MD; (Y); 58/188; Church Yth Grp; Civic Clb; Girl Scts; JA; Church Choir; Color Guard; School Musical; Var Cheerleading; Masonic Awd; Prfct Atten Awd; Mst Outstndg Chrldr 86; 1st Rnr Talent Miss TEEN Pagnt 85; 2nd Pl Miss OES Cont 85; U MD College Park; Bus Ad.

HYDE, HANK; Our Lady Of Good Counsel HS; Olney, MD; (Y); 30/228; Latin Clb; Nwsp Rptr; JV Bsbl; JV Bsktbl; Tennis; Hon Roll; NHS; Retreat Ldrs 84 & 85; US Army Res Natl Schlr Ath Awd 86; U Richmond; Bus.

HYMAN, BETTY; Forest Park SR HS; Baltimore, MD; (Y); Sftbl; Hon Roll; NHS; Prfct Atten Awd; Gate Clb 84-86; Schlrshp Awd-Wstside Skl Ctr 85-86; 1st Pl Blck Hstry Cntst 86; Howard U; Pediatrc Nrs.

HYMAN, ELYSE; Glenelg HS; Ellicott City, MD; (Y); Political Wkr; Yrbk Rptr; Yrbk Stf; Rep Frsh Cls; Rep Soph Cls; Rep Jr Cls; Rep Sr Cls; Rep Stu Cncl; JV Fld Hcky; Stat Lcrss; Cptn Of Natl Chmpnshp U S Pony Clb Games Tm 85; Invtd To Ride In Windsor Cup In England 86; U NC; Bus Admin.

HYNSON, AMY; Roland Park Country Schl; Baltimore, MD; (Y); Chorus; JV Badmtn; JV Lcrss; Hon Roll; Natl Latin Exam Gold & Silver Mdls; Mst Imprvd Plyr Lacrosse; Spirit Awd Badmittan; U Of VA; Intl Fin.

IBE, JOHN; Maurice J Mc Donough HS; Waldorf, MD; (S); 3/350; Am Leg Boys St; Church Yth Grp; Capt Math Tm; L Chorus; Rep Frsh Cls; Var L Trk; L NHS; St Schlr; Chess Clb; Acad All Amer 85-86; Altar Srvr/ Yr 85; Chas Cnty Bd Educ Awd 84; Elec Engr.

IBRAHIM, RAMY; Walt Whitman HS; Bethesda, MD; (Y); Church Yth Grp; Symp Band; Im Bsktbl; Var L Ftbl; JV Trk; Im Wt Lftg; Rotary Awd; Spanish NHS; Hnrs & Awds Prvt Piano Stdy 84-86; Prncpls Dstngshd Hnr Awd 85-86; AIME 86; Med.

IFERT, DANETTE; Linganore HS; Mt Airy, MD; (Y); 6/270; Debate Tm; Sec Trs Girl Scts; Capt Quiz Bowl; Color Guard; Concert Band; Drm Mjr(t); Mrchg Band; Pep Band; JP Sousa Awd; NHS; Scl Stds Deptmntl Awd 86; PTSA Cmmnded Schlr 83-86; MD Lgsltv Pg 86; WV Wesleyan; Hstry.

IFKOVITS, JILL; Bowie SR HS; Bowie, MD; (Y); Office Aide; Spanish Clb; Yrbk Stf; Rep Frsh Cls; Rep Soph Cls; Rep Jr Cls; Rep Sr Cls; Hon Roll; U Of MD.

IGNACIO, CYNTHIA; Notre Dame Preparatory School; Lutherville, MD; (Y); Political Wkr; Nwsp Stf; Lit Mag; Im Bsktbl; Im Fld Hcky; Im Socr; French Hon Soc; Hon Roll; Prfct Atten Awd; Writing.

IJEOMAH, PRISCILLA; Fairmont HS; Seat Pleasant, MD; (Y); FBLA; P G CC; Bus Mgt.

IMES, LARRY; Bishop Walsh HS; Cumberland, MD; (Y); 20/112; Debate Tm; Ski Clb; Yrbk Stf; Pres Frsh Cls; Rep Sr Cls; Var L Bsbl; Var L Crs Cntry; Var L Socr; Var L Trk; Hon Roll; Sccr Al-Trnmt Tm Bishop Walsh Invtnl 84; Bsbl Hot Stove Leag Al-Star 83-85; B Walsh Mock Trl Dfnd Atty; Sci.

IMES, MARC; Lackey HS; Laplata, MD; (Y); French Clb; Ski Clb; SADD; Yrbk Phtg; Rep Frsh Cls; Rep Soph Cls; Rep Jr Cls; Socr; Tennis; Hon Roll; Embry-Riddle U.

INGA, JOHN; Takoma Acad; Silver Spring, MD; (Y); 2/92; Computer Clb; Math Clb; Science Clb; Ski Clb; Spanish Clb; Teachers Aide; Band; JV Sftbl; JV Vllybl; NHS; Bst Stu European Lit 86; Outstndng Effort Physcs 86; SVA Biolgst 83; U MD; Pre-Med.

INGERMAN, BRETT; Mc Donogh Schl; Baltimore, MD; (Y); Computer Clb; VP German Clb; Nwsp Rptr; Lit Mag; Var Ftbl; Var Trk; Wt Lftg; Hnrs German 85-86; Hnrs Math 83-86; Advncd Plcmnt Hstry 84-86.

INGERSOLL, EVAN; The Barrie Schl; Silver Spring, MD; (S); 1/28; Chess Clb; Church Yth Grp; Science Clb; Teachers Aide; Acpl Chr; Church Choir; High Hon Roll.

INSLEY, DEBRA; Woodlawn HS; Baltimore, MD; (Y); Nwsp Sprt Ed; Off Jr Cls; Rep Stu Cncl; Var Capt Fld Hcky; Var L Sftbl; Var L Trk; Hon Roll; NHS; Prfct Atten Awd; ST Of MD Schlstc Merit Awd 86; Cert Of Achvmnt Math & Sci 86; Mt St Marys Coll; Bio.

INSLEY, KIM; Cambridge South Dorchester HS; Cambridge, MD; (Y); 17/241; Exploring; Office Aide; Spanish Clb; Mrchg Band; Nwsp Stf; Yrbk Stf; Var Capt Fld Hcky; Stat Lcrss; Var Pom Pon; Hon Roll; Wesley Coll; Nrsng.

INSLEY, MISTY; Parkville HS; Baltimore, MD; (Y); Church Yth Grp; Sec Band; Stu Cncl; Capt Cheerleading; Hon Roll; Prfct Atten Awd; Loyola Coll.

INTROCASO, MARY C; Cambridge-South Dorchester HS; Church Crk, MD; (Y); 3/270; AFS; Am Leg Aux Girls St; Capt Debate Tm; Drama Clb; Latin Clb; Political Wkr; Quiz Bowl; Spanish Clb; Band; Nwsp Rptr; Hugh O Brien Altrnte Intl Amb 85; Sci Math Fair Yr 83; Ntl Bio Sem 85; U Notre Dame; Law.

IRELAND, MELISSA; Kent County HS; Chestertown, MD; (Y); Church Yth Grp; French Clb; Church Choir; Color Guard; High Hon Roll; Hon Roll; NHS; Med.

IRVIN, DARRON; Gaithersburg SR HS; Gaithersburg, MD; (Y); Letterman Clb; ROTC; Color Guard; Drill Tm; Cit Awd; Hon Roll; Prmtn Lt Cmmndr JROTC Cmmndng Ofcr 86; Amer Lgn Mdl & Rbbn Mltry Exclnc 86; Brnz Str Aptd & Cndct; Pilot.

IRVINE, ALLISON; Archbishop Keough HS; Baltimore, MD; (Y); Art Clb; Drama Clb; Towson ST U; Music.

IRVING, DEBRA; Southern Garrett HS; Oakland, MD; (Y); Church Yth Grp; Office Aide; Band; Church Choir; Color Guard; Concert Band; Drill Tm; Flag Corp; Jazz Band; Mrchg Band; Soc Dstngshd Amrcn HS Stu 85-86; Ntl Ldrshp Svc Awd; U S Achvmnt Acad; Intl Beauty Schl; Csmtlgy.

IRWIN, MICHAEL; Liberty HS; Sykesville, MD; (S); 7/302; VP German Clb; Mathletes; Ski Clb; Im Bsktbl; JV Socr; Var Swmmng; High Hon Roll; VP NHS; MD State Games 2 Slvr Mdls In Swmng 85.

ISLE, BRITNEY; Gaithersburg HS; Gaithersburg, MD; (Y); SADD; Teachers Aide; Stu Cncl; Tennis; Hon Roll; Fld Hcky; Pom Pon.

ISLES, ERICA; Takoma Acad; Silver Spring, MD; (S); Church Yth Grp; Teachers Aide; Church Choir; High Hon Roll; NHS; Howard U; Mdcn.

ISOM, TAWNEY; Allegany HS; Cumberland, MD; (Y); 10/240; Sec Band; Pres Jr Cls; Stu Cncl; Var L Bsktbl; Var L Cheerleading; Var L Coach Actv; Capt L Crs Cntry; Var L Trk; NHS; Prfct Atten Awd; Outstndng Feml Crss Cntry Awd 85-86; Med.

ISRAEL, HENRY; St Andrews Episcopol Schl; Rockville, MD; (Y); Cmnty Wkr; Service Clb; Chorus; Yrbk Stf; Trs Stu Cncl; Crs Cntry; Lcrss; High Hon Roll; Maxima Cum Laude Ntl Latin Exam; Oceanogrphy.

ISRAEL, JASMINE; Takoma Acad; Silver Spgs, MD; (Y); Cmnty Wkr; Computer Clb; Office Aide; Science Clb; Chorus; Sec Sr Cls; Hon Roll; NHS; Maryland U; Pre-Med.

IVISON, CHRISTIE; Northern HS; Dunkirk, MD; (Y); Cmnty Wkr; Var L Bsktbl; Var L Sftbl; Var L Vllybl; Hon Roll; NHS; Superintndnts Schlstc Recgntn Awd 86; Comp Sci.

IZAT, DONNA; Bishop Walsh Middle HS; Lavale, MD; (Y); Office Aide; Science Clb; Concert Band; Jazz Band; Mrchg Band; Pep Band; Yrbk Stf; Hon Roll; NHS; Spanish NHS; Jazz Fest Solo Awd 85.

JACKS, LAWRENCE; Northern HS; Owings, MD; (Y); ROTC; VICA; Bsktbl; Ftbl; Wt Lftg; Cit Awd; Hon Roll; Prfct Atten Awd; Army; Elctrncs.

JACKSON, ANGELINE; Frederick HS; Baltimore, MD; (Y); Cmnty Wkr; Hosp Aide; Science Clb; Service Clb; Yrbk Stf; Sec Soph Cls; Pres Jr Cls; Pres Sr Cls; Trk; Hon Roll; Mayors Citation For Outstndng Stu 86; Hnrd At All Sch Salute 85; Hnrd At Brkfst For Schlrs Coppin 86; Coppin ST Coll; Nrse.

JACKSON, CHRISTA; Franklin SR HS; Reisterstown, MD; (Y); AFS; Intnl Clb; Red Cross Aide; Ed Yrbk Ed-Chief; Lit Mag; Pres Stu Cncl; Var Civic Clb; JV Fld Hcky; JV Var Lcrss; NHS; Randolph-Macon.

JACKSON, DEIDRE; Western HS; Baltimore, MD; (Y); Church Yth Grp; FBLA; Church Choir; Stage Crew; Rep Stu Cncl; Acctg I Hnr 86; Villa Julia; Acctg.

JACKSON, DENA; Regina HS; Washington, DC; (Y); VP Sec Church Yth Grp; Drama Clb; Pep Clb; Church Choir; School Play; Hon Roll; Bus Admin.

JACKSON, ERIC; Colonel Richardson HS; Preston, MD; (Y); 11/107; VP French Clb; FBLA; Jazz Band; VP Sr Cls; Capt Bsbl; Capt Bsktbl; Dnfth Awd; Hon Roll; Lion Awd; NHS; Hampton U; Accounting.

JACKSON, JOHNATHAN; Great Mills HS; Ridge, MD; (Y); Spanish Clb; VP Chorus; Church Choir; Stage Crew; Variety Show; Hon Roll; Presidntl Phys Fitns Awd 83-84; Tuskegee Inst; Engnrng.

JACKSON, KATHLEEN; Western HS; Baltimore, MD; (Y); 95/412; Drama Clb; School Play; Stage Crew; Yrbk Stf.

JACKSON, KRISTY; Westminster HS; Sykesville, MD; (Y); Drama Clb; Office Aide; Spanish Clb; Yrbk Rptr; Rep Frsh Cls; Rep Soph Cls; Rep Stu Cncl; Hon Roll; NHS; Towson ST U; Mass Cmmnctns.

JACKSON, LAWRENCE P; Loyola-Blakefield HS; Baltimore, MD; (Y); 52/197; Church Yth Grp; Cmnty Wkr; French Clb; Nwsp Rptr; Yrbk Stf; Var Crs Cntry; Var Co-Capt Trk; Wrstlng; Hon Roll; NHS; Ntl Achvt For Blk Stdnts Semi-Fnlsh 85-86; Art Hstry Awd Gld Mdl 84-85; Hdmstr Schlrshp 82-86; Gvrmnt.

JACKSON, LYDIA; La Plata HS; Issue, MD; (Y); Trs Church Yth Grp; Cmnty Wkr; Hosp Aide; Latin Clb; Teachers Aide; Hon Roll; Trk; Modrn Miss Pagnt For Schlstc Achiev 85; Charlse County CC; Child Dev.

JACKSON, MARK F; Paint Branch HS; Silver Spring, MD; (Y); Church Yth Grp; Ski Clb; Thesps; Chorus; School Play; Stage Crew; Nwsp Ed-Chief; Lcrss; Socr; Hon Roll; Outstndng Tech Dir 85; Thespian Awd 86; Outstndng Stage Mgr 84; Mech Engrng.

JACKSON, PAMELA; Cambridge-South Dorchester HS; Cambridge, MD; (Y); Church Yth Grp; Varsity Clb; Band; Rep Frsh Cls; Fld Hcky; Mgr(s); Pedtrcn.

JACKSON, ROBERT; Gaithersburg HS; Gaithersburg, MD; (Y); SADD; Teachers Aide; Stage Crew; Variety Show; Var L Bsktbl; Var L Ftbl; JV Socr; Var L Trk; Trk & Fld Athl Week Hnrs 86; Regnl Wnr Long Jump Triple Jump 1st Pl & 2nd Pl High Jump 86; Bus Mgt.

JACKSON, TABBY; Frederick HS; Fairmont, WV; (Y); Church Yth Grp; Office Aide; Band; Church Choir; Color Guard; Concert Band; Flag Corp; School Musical; Yrbk Stf; Hon Roll; Fairmont ST Coll.

JACKSON, TERRI; Calvery Baptist Church Academy; Millersville, MD; (Y); 4/23; Chorus; Yrbk Ed-Chief; Pres Frsh Cls; VP Soph Cls; Rep Stu Cncl; Stat Bsktbl; JV Var Score Keeper; Cit Awd; High Hon Roll; Hlth Awd 84.

JACOB, DAVID; Pikesville HS; Balto, MD; (Y); Latin Clb; Mathletes; Red Cross Aide; Science Clb; Ski Clb; Spanish Clb; Stage Crew; Med.

JACOBS, LISA MARIE; Walkersville HS; Walkersville, MD; (Y); 11/160; Art Clb; Church Yth Grp; FBLA; GAA; SADD; Teachers Aide; Variety Show; Lit Mag; Rep Sr Cls; JV L Cheerleading; Wmns Cvc Clb Schlrshp 86; Ruth & Mary E Smith Schlrshp 86; Mardi Gras Prncss 86; Grove City Coll; Comm.

JACOBS, MELINDA; Highland View Acad; Hagerstown, MD; (Y); Office Aide; Chorus; Nwsp Ed-Chief; Yrbk Bus Mgr; VP Frsh Cls; Rep Soph Cls; Rep Stu Cncl; Var Vllybl; High Hon Roll; NHS; Frederic Chopin Piano Awd 86; Andrews U.

JACOBS, MICHAEL J; Charles E Smith Jewish Day Schl; Rockville, MD; (Y); Nwsp Ed-Chief; VP Soph Cls; Pres Jr Cls; Var L Bsbl; Var L Bsktbl; Var L Socr; JETS Awd; NHS; Ntl Merit Ltr; Spanish NHS; Schl Athlt Of Yr 84-85; Schl Sprt Awd 86; Awd Otstndng Cntrbtn Schl Nwsppr 86; Duke U.

JACOBS, MOLLY; Sherwood HS; Olney, MD; (Y); Dance Clb; Pres VP Temple Yth Grp; Chorus; School Musical; Var Pom Pon; Hon Roll; NHS; Spanish NHS; Art Clb; NFL; Natl Art Hnr Soc 85-86.

JACOBS, RAMONA; Western HS; Baltimore, MD; (Y); 35/420; French Clb; Red Cross Aide; Hon Roll; Prfct Atten Awd; Senatorial Schlrshp 86; UMBC.

JACOCKS, JUSTIN P; Good Counsel HS; Kensington, MD; (Y); 10/228; Cmnty Wkr; Office Aide; Jazz Band; Nwsp Rptr; Lit Mag; VP Frsh Cls; High Hon Roll; Trs NHS; Ntl Merit SF; Chess Clb; Acad Scholar 82-84; U DE; Chem.

JACQUELINE, THOMAS; Maurice J Mcdonough HS; Waldorf, MD; (Y); Chorus; Variety Show; Rep Jr Cls; Hon Roll; Prfct Atten Awd; All Amer Yth Hnrs Choir 85; Tri Cnty Hnrs Chorus 84 & 86; Bus Adm.

JAGO, WENDI; Great Mills HS; Great Mills, MD; (Y); Rep Soph Cls; VP Jr Cls; Pres Sr Cls; Var Cheerleading; Fld Hcky; Pom Pon; Trk; Hon Roll; Cmnty Wkr; Girl Scts; Hmcmg Prncss & Qn 84-86; Cum Laude Natl Latn Awd 85-86; U Of MD; Pltcl Sci.

JAHNKE, ANDREW; Brunswick HS; Jefferson, MD; (Y); 33/150; Computer Clb; French Clb; Teachers Aide; Yrbk Ed-Chief; Yrbk Rptr; Yrbk Sprt Ed; Yrbk Stf; Capt Var Socr; Hon Roll; Psychlgy.

JAKUBCZAK, ANNE; Gaithersburg HS; Gaithersburg, MD; (Y); 100/650; Cmnty Wkr; Mgr(s); Socr; Spanish NHS; Hood Presdntl Ldrshp Schlrshp 86; Presdntl Acad Ldrshp Awd 86; Physics Awd 86; Hood Coll; Bio.

JAMES, DEWSILL; Lake Clifton SR HS; Baltimore, MD; (Y); #2 In Class; Library Aide; Spanish Clb; Hon Roll; NHS; Cert Merit-Cls Wnr Baltimore Math Cntst 86; Mayor Baltimore Schlstc Wnr 86; ST MD Merit Schlrshp Awd; U Of MD; Law.

JAMES, DOUGLAS BRANT; Queen Annes County HS; Centreville, MD; (Y); Band; Concert Band; Mrchg Band; Orch; Pep Band; School Musical; School Play; Stage Crew; Swing Chorus; Symp Band; Chspk Coll Fine Arts Fnlst 82-86; WV U; Jrnlsm.

JAMES, LISA; Damascus HS; Dickerson, MD; (Y); #2 In Class; Am Leg Aux Girls St; 4-H; French Clb; Math Tm; Lit Mag; Var Capt Diving; AFS; Leo Clb; Sec NHS; St Schlr; Elect Engr.

JAMES, MARISANO; Loyola Blakefield HS; Baltimore, MD; (Y); Chess Clb; Church Yth Grp; School Musical; Lit Mag; Rep Jr Cls; JV Crs Cntry; JV Trk; JV Wrstlng; 2 Unsng Hero Awds Vrsty Indr & Outdr Trck 83-84; Fll Tuitn Schlrshp Phlps Extr Acad Smmr Schl 86; Princeton; Comp Pgmg.

JAMES, NICOLE; Northwestern HS; Baltimore, MD; (Y); Church Yth Grp; Church Choir; Var Cheerleading; Bus Mgt.

JAMES, RACHEL; Franklin SR HS; Reisterstown, MD; (Y); Church Yth Grp; Band; Chorus; Concert Band; Drm Mjr(t); Mrchg Band; Swing Chorus; Variety Show; Stat Bsktbl; High Hon Roll; Vrsty Ltr Band 86; U S Intl U; Music Theatr.

JAMES, STEPHANIE; Academy Of The Holy Names; Wheaton, MD; (Y); Church Yth Grp; Cmnty Wkr; Hosp Aide; Trs SADD; School Musical; Trs Soph Cls; Trs Sr Cls; Var Trk; NHS.

JAMISON, JOHN DAVID; Elkton SR HS; Elkton, MD; (Y); Key Clb; SADD; Yrbk Stf; Rep Frsh Cls; Rep Jr Cls; Rep Sr Cls; Stu Cncl; JV Ftbl; Hon Roll; East Caroline U; Bus Admin.

JANNEY, JOEL; Gaithersburg HS; Gaithersburg, MD; (Y); Math Clb; Im Bsktbl; Hon Roll; Mu Alp Tht; NHS; Ntl Merit Ltr; Slctd Spllr Rep Schl 83-86.

JANOSKE, JENNIFER; Immaculata Clg HS; Burtonsville, MD; (Y); 54/122; Hosp Aide; Trs Math Clb; Varsity Clb; Trs Orch; School Musical; School Play; Variety Show; Sftbl; Capt Vllybl; Service Clb; Orch Awd & Svc Awd & Mth Clb Awd; Catholic U Of Amer; Sclgy.

JANOSKI, LEE ANN; Eleanor Roosevelt HS; Bowie, MD; (S); Yrbk Stf; Pom Pon; Hon Roll; Jr NHS; S Bowie Girl Of Yr 86; Phys Ther.

JARBOE, TERRI; Thomas Stone HS; Waldorf, MD; (S); Yrbk Stf; VP Frsh Cls; Trs Jr Cls; Trs Sr Cls; Rep Stu Cncl; Capt Cheerleading; Pom Pon; Hon Roll; Comp Sci.

JARMAN, HOLLY; Northwestern HS; Hyattville, MD; (Y); Drama Clb; Pep Clb; Science Clb; Spanish Clb; Yrbk Stf; Lit Mag; Hst Jr Cls; Rep Stu Cncl; Var Capt Cheerleading; High Hon Roll; Prince Georges Cnty Acad Excllnc Awd 84-85; Awd Human Factors Soc 84-85; U Of MD; Physcl Thrpy.

JARRAH, AYMAN; Bullis HS; Rockville, MD; (Y); Var Vllybl; Wt Lftg; JV Wrstlng; Cit Awd; High Hon Roll; Hon Roll; NEDT Awd; Hghst Grd Chem & Bio Awd 83-84; Awd For Outstdng JR In Sci 85-86; MD U; Aeron Engrng.

JARRETT, KIMBERLY; Prospect Hall HS; Frederick, MD; (Y); Drama Clb; Science Clb; Ski Clb; School Play; Nwsp Rptr; Yrbk Phtg; Lit Mag; Rep Jr Cls; Off Stu Cncl; Var Cheerleading; Brdcstng.

JARVI, DAVID; Great Mills HS; Patuxent Rvr, MD; (Y); ROTC; Band; Drill Tm; Var L Socr; Trk; Hon Roll; Exmplry Cndct ROTC, Dstngshd Apprnce ROTC 84.

JAVELLANA, GRACHEL; Gaithersburg HS; Gaithersburg, MD; (Y); Bsktbl; Vllybl; Hon Roll; NHS; Frgn Affairs.

JAYNE, ROBYN; Kent County HS; Rock Hall, MD; (Y); 2/175; Am Leg Aux Girls St; Church Yth Grp; Girl Scts; Band; Rep Frsh Cls; Rep Soph Cls; Rep Jr Cls; Rep Sr Cls; JV Bsktbl; High Hon Roll; Bus.

JEFFERS, LORA; Archbishop Martin Spalding HS; Pasadena, MD; (Y); Church Yth Grp; Cmnty Wkr; Hosp Aide; Yrbk Stf; Capt Var Sftbl; Hon Roll; Ntl Merit Schol; Prfct Atten Awd; ST Schlrshp Awd 86; UMBC; Nrsg.

JEFFERSON, MARK; Dematha Catholic HS; Hyattsville, MD; (Y); Rep Soph Cls; Rep Jr Cls; Tennis.

JEFFERSON, MICHELLE A; Crossland HS; Ft Washington, MD; (Y); Drama Clb; French Clb; Office Aide; Thesps; Church Choir; School Play; Stage Crew; Nwsp Stf; Hon Roll.

JENEY, VICTORIA; North Hagerstown HS; Hagestown, MD; (Y); French Clb; Ski Clb; Teachers Aide; Varsity Clb; L Band; Mrchg Band; Trs Sr Cls; Stu Cncl; Hon Roll; Rfl Corp Cpt, Co Cpt 85-87.

JENIFER, TAWANDA; Chopticon HS; Clements, MD; (Y); FBLA; JA; Office Aide; Pep Clb; Varsity Clb; Var Cheerleading; Var Pom Pon; Cit Awd; High Hon Roll; Ntl Merit Ltr; Indianapolis Inst; Bus Admin.

JENKINS, AARON; Mount Saint Joseph HS; Baltimore, MD; (Y); Chess Clb; Church Yth Grp; Computer Clb; Ski Clb; Church Choir; High Hon Roll; Hon Roll; JETS Awd; Elec Engr.

JENKINS, DEBORAH; Elizabeth Seton HS; Washington, DC; (Y); 65/195; Library Aide; Office Aide; Teachers Aide; High Hon Roll; Hon Roll; Acadmc Ltr 86; Spelman Coll; Eco.

JENKINS, ERYNN; Bowie HS; Bowie, MD; (Y); Drama Clb; JCL; Latin Clb; Office Aide; Spanish Clb; SADD; Powder Puff Ftbl; High Hon Roll; Ntl Merit Ltr; Maxima Cum Laude In Natl Lat Exam 86; Merchandising.

JENKINS, JENNIFER; Maurice J Mc Donough HS; Waldorf, MD; (Y); Letterman Clb; Trk; Hon Roll.

JENKINS, JODY LYN; South River HS; Riva, MD; (Y); 39/312; FBLA; Office Aide; Ski Clb; Varsity Clb; Var Bsktbl; Var Lcrss; Im Sftbl; Im Tennis; Hon Roll; MD State Schlrshp 86; Lawson ST U; Accntng.

JENKINS, KIM; Thomas Stone HS; Bryantown, MD; (Y); Church Yth Grp; French Clb; Office Aide; Science Clb; Teachers Aide; Varsity Clb; Lit Mag; Var Sftbl; High Hon Roll; Jr NHS; Vet Sci.

JENKINS, LA RONDA; Capitol Christian Acad; Cheverly, MD; (Y); #4 In Class; Church Yth Grp; Debate Tm; Hosp Aide; Teachers Aide; Church Choir; Concert Band; VP Jr Cls; NHS; Englsh, Spnsh & Typng Ii Awd Encllnc 83-86.

JENKINS, MARY; St Marys Ryken HS; Laplata, MD; (Y); Aud/Vis; Church Yth Grp; 4-H; Spanish Clb; Teachers Aide; Church Choir; Var Bsktbl; L Tennis; Hon Roll; Lenoir-Rhyne; Law.

JENKINS, MICHELLE; Mc Donough HS; Pomfret, MD; (Y); Intnl Clb; Q&S; Teachers Aide; Yrbk Stf; Var Fld Hcky; High Hon Roll; Hon Roll; NHS; Aerospc Engnrng.

JENKINS, NICOLE; Forestville HS; Forestville, MD; (Y); Office Aide; Teachers Aide; Church Choir; Lit Mag; Hon Roll; Outstndng Sci, Art Dnc & Chrch Choir Achvt 83-85; Med.

JENKINS, ROBERT EBEN; Thomas S Wooton HS; Rockville, MD; (Y); 7/401; Church Yth Grp; Pres Science Clb; Teachers Aide; Jazz Band; Mrchg Band; Rep Stu Cncl; Hon Roll; NHS; Ntl Merit SF; Hnrbl Ment AF Awd, Outstndng Proj Sci Fair 83; Maxima Cum Laude Ntl Latin Exm 84; Elec Engrng.

JENKINS, ROBYN E; Walkersville HS; Walkersville, MD; (Y); 14/251; Pres Church Yth Grp; FBLA; GAA; Office Aide; SADD; Sec Soph Cls; Trs Jr Cls; Rep Stu Cncl; Fld Hcky; Hon Roll; ATM; Cvl Engrng.

JENKINS, TIMOTHY; Maurice J Mc Donough HS; La Plata, MD; (Y); Chess Clb; Church Yth Grp; Var L Tennis; Hon Roll; U Of MD; Bus.

JENNINGS, PAMELA; Lackey HS; Bryans Rd, MD; (Y); Red Cross Aide; SADD; Stage Crew; High Hon Roll; Hon Roll; Charles Cnty CC; Tchr.

JENNINGS, PATTI; Parkdale HS; College Park, MD; (Y); Math Clb; Office Aide; Ski Clb; SADD; Teachers Aide; Yrbk Stf; Var Cheerleading; Gym; High Hon Roll.

JENSEN, BRIAN; Kent County HS; Rock Hall, MD; (Y); Am Leg Boys St; Chess Clb; Church Yth Grp; Drama Clb; Spanish Clb; School Musical; Crs Cntry; Trk.

JESSEN, BRIAN; Westminster HS; Westminster, MD; (Y); Band; Concert Band; Mrchg Band; Pep Band; Symp Band; Rep Jr Cls; JV Var Wrstlng; High Hon Roll; Hon Roll; Baltimore Schl Law; Pre-Law.

JESSUP, RICHARD; Gaithersburg HS; Gaithersburg, MD; (Y); Church Yth Grp; Cmnty Wkr; Dance Clb; Political Wkr; Ski Clb; Red Cross Aide; JV Var Bsbl; JV Bsktbl; JV Tennis; Hon Roll; Bst All Arnd Stdnt Awd 83-84; Troph Cmmnty Comptv Sprts Bsktbl & Bsbl 83-86; Penn ST; Law.

JIANNINEY, LINDA; North East HS; Elkton, MD; (Y); 33/221; Office Aide; VICA; Hon Roll; Prfct Atten Awd; Cecil Voc Tech Ctr 83-85; Outstndng Achvt Awd Food Serv 85.

JOGLEKAR, JAIRAJ; Bowie HS; Bowie, MD; (Y); Boys Clb Am; JA; Nwsp Rptr; Bsbl; Bsktbl; Coach Actv; Score Keeper; Tennis; Hon Roll; MD U; Comp Sci.

JOHANNES, ANGELA; Sparrows Point HS; Baltimore, MD; (Y); Hosp Aide; Chorus; Yrbk Sprt Ed; Var Capt Cheerleading; JV Lcrss; Hon Roll; Cmnty Wkr; Yrbk Stf; Rep Stu Cncl; Dundalk CC; Sec.

JOHENGEN, CATHERINE; La Reine HS; Andrews A F B, DC; (Y); Teachers Aide; Yrbk Stf; Var L Tennis; Hon Roll; Gldn Poet Awd 85; Southern Sem JC; Eqstrn Mgt.

JOHNG, STEVEN; Loyola Blakefield HS; Baltimore, MD; (Y); Church Yth Grp; Cmnty Wkr; Pep Clb; Nwsp Stf; Ed Lit Mag; JV L Ftbl; Var L Wrstlng; High Hon Roll; Ntl Merit SF; NEDT Awd; Schl Calndr Art Cont Wnr 85; Art Pgm Awd 84; Jesuit Wrstlng Tourn 85.

JOHNSON, APRIL LENISE; Western HS; Baltimore, MD; (Y); Pres Church Choir; Co-Capt Drill Tm; Mrchg Band; Variety Show; Lit Mag; Trophy, Certs Mrchng Band 85-86; Cert-Chrch Actvts 86; UMBC; RN.

JOHNSON, BENGT E; Annapolis SR HS; Annapolis, MD; (Y); 6/500; German Clb; Political Wkr; Trs Frsh Cls; Rep Jr Cls; Pres Stu Cncl; Var Socr; Jr NHS; NHS; Ntl Merit SF; St Schlr; Gldn Paddle Awd 82; Jrnlsm.

JOHNSON, BRIAN; Franklin HS; Reisterstown, MD; (Y); Jazz Band; Mrchg Band; JV Bsbl; Var Bsktbl; Var Lcrss; Capt Var Socr; High Hon Roll; Hon Roll; NHS; Office Aide; Louie Armstrng Jazz Awd 86; Bltmr Gas & Elctrc Co Schlrshp 86; U MO Coll Pk; Engrng.

JOHNSON, BRIAN; Oakland Mills HS; Columbia, MD; (Y); German Clb; Math Tm; Ski Clb; Yrbk Stf; Ftbl; Lcrss; Trk; Wt Lftg; Hon Roll; NHS; Engrng.

JOHNSON, BRUCE; Mc Donough HS; Waldorf, MD; (Y); 7/310; Chess Clb; Math Clb; Math Tm; Stu Cncl; Gov Hon Prg Awd; High Hon Roll; Jr NHS; NHS; Ntl Merit Ltr; Pres Schlr; Rensselaer Poly-Tech; Elec Engr.

JOHNSON, CLEMON A; Friendly SR HS; Ft Washington, MD; (Y); JA; Church Choir; Mrchg Band; Nwsp Stf; Yrbk Stf; Lit Mag; Hon Roll; Boy Scts; Band; Orch; Gld Key, Hnrbl Ment Awds Art 85; NMBC, Sovran Bnk Schlrshps 86; Cert Merit 85; Philadelphia Coll Arts; Arch Ds.

JOHNSON III, D CHRISTOPHER; Northwestern HS; Baltimore, MD; (S); Aud/Vis; Boy Scts; Jazz Band; School Musical; Stage Crew; Tennis; Trk; Opt Clb Awd; Jessie Owens Trck Awd 80; Peabody Conservatory; Music.

JOHNSON, DANEENE; Regina HS; Silver Spring, MD; (Y); Camera Clb; Computer Clb; Drama Clb; Model UN; School Play; Nwsp Stf; Tennis; Hon Roll; Cmnty Wkr; Library Aide; Psychlgy.

JOHNSON, DANYELLA R; Old Mill SR HS; Baltimore, MD; (Y); 16/509; Church Yth Grp; Cmnty Wkr; Science Clb; Spanish Clb; Drill Tm; Capt Crs Cntry; Capt Var Trk; Hon Roll; NHS; Pres Schlr; Acadmc Athlt Yr Anne Arundel Sun Paper 86; Schrlshp Natl Vetrns Asso 86; Oberlin Coll; Bio.

JOHNSON, DEANNA; Southern HS; Oakland, MD; (Y); Church Yth Grp; FFA; Band; Color Guard; Mrchg Band; Coach Actv; Mgr(s); Wrstlng; FHA; Trk; Mss MD Teen Acdmc Awd 86; FFA Jdgng Awd 86; WVA; Int Dsgn.

JOHNSON, DOUGLAS; Mc Donogh HS; Baltimore, MD; (Y); 14/133; Nwsp Rptr; Pres Frsh Cls; Pres Soph Cls; Off Jr Cls; Off Sr Cls; JV Var Bsbl; JV Var Socr; Var Swmmng; Cit Awd; Ntl Merit Ltr; Sci Faculty Awd 84-85; Var Water Polo 85-86; Duke U; Engrng.

JOHNSON, GEORGE; La Plata HS; Waldorf, MD; (Y); Church Yth Grp; Teachers Aide; Bsbl; Bsktbl; Socr; High Hon Roll; Prfct Atten Awd; Fairmont ST; Frst Rngr.

JOHNSON, HEATHER; Queen Annes Co HS; Queenstwn, MD; (Y); Drama Clb; Spanish Clb; Band; Chorus; Concert Band; Mrchg Band; School Musical; Yrbk Stf; High Hon Roll; NHS.

JOHNSON, HELENE; Sherwood HS; Silver Spg, MD; (Y); Cmnty Wkr; Teachers Aide; Yrbk Phtg; JV Var Vllybl; Hon Roll; Prfct Atten Awd.

JOHNSON, INGRID; Academy Of The Holy Names; Beltsville, MD; (Y); Art Clb; Chess Clb; French Clb; Service Clb; Spanish Clb; Chorus; Variety Show; Cheerleading; Trk; DAR Awd; Lead Prog Ltr 85-86; Acadmc All Am Schlr Prgm 85-86; Ped.

JOHNSON, JAMES; Maurice J Mc Donough HS; Pomfret, MD; (S); 13/390; Church Yth Grp; Letterman Clb; Varsity Clb; Acpl Chr; Chorus; Variety Show; Var Ftbl; JV Wrstlng; High Hon Roll; Jr NHS; Elec Engrng.

JOHNSON, JAMES; Pocomoke HS; Westover, MD; (Y); Boy Scts; Church Yth Grp; 4-H; Chorus; Church Choir; Swing Chorus; JV Var Bsktbl; Var Ftbl; JV Var Socr; Hon Roll; Chem.

JOHNSON, JEFF; Highland View Acad; Hagerstown, MD; (Y); 1/41; Computer Clb; Math Clb; Band; School Play; Yrbk Stf; Lit Mag; Im Bsktbl; Im Ftbl; Im Socr; Im Sftbl; Outstndng Hist Achvt Awd 86; Bus Adm.

JOHNSON, JULIE; Du Val SR HS; Glenn Dale, MD; (Y); Church Yth Grp; VP Natl Beta Clb; Spanish Clb; Hon Roll; NHS; U MD.

JOHNSON, KAREN M; Middletown HS; Middletown, MD; (Y); Girl Scts; Trs Intnl Clb; Concert Band; Jazz Band; Mrchg Band; Nwsp Ed-Chief; Lit Mag; NHS; Pres Schlr; St Schlr; Dept Hnrs Eng & Jrnlsm 86; All Cnty Bnd 85 & 86; Hnrb Men John Phillip Sousa Bnd Awd 86; U MD; Music.

JOHNSON, KARIN; Pallotti HS; Derwood, MD; (S); 10/86; Sec Trs Church Yth Grp; Sec FBLA; Letterman Clb; Spanish Clb; Teachers Aide; Var Bsktbl; Var Score Keeper; High Hon Roll; Hon Roll; Ntl Merit Ltr; Stdnt Mnth 83-86; Elon Coll; Bus.

JOHNSON, KATHERINE; Thomas S Wootton HS; Rockville, MD; (Y); Ski Clb; Sr Cls; Hon Roll; Pres Acad Fit Awd 86; U Rochester.

JOHNSON, KATHY; Poolesville JR SR HS; Dickerson, MD; (Y); 10/108; Cmnty Wkr; Pres 4-H; Pres Sec FHA; Pres SADD; Sec Concert Band; Sec Mrchg Band; Sec Stu Cncl; Stat Bsktbl; 4-H Awd; Hon Roll; Clover Awd 85; Holy Cross Book Awd 85; Montgomery Cnty Fair Princess 85; VA Polytech Inst; Ag.

JOHNSON, KATRICE SELENA; Baltimore Polytechnic Inst; Baltimore, MD; (Y); Sec AFS; Sec Church Yth Grp; Church Choir; Nwsp Rptr; Rep Sr Cls; Stu Cncl; Var L Tennis; Outstndng Perf Minority Intro Engrng USCGA 85; Natl Achvt Cmmnd Stu 85-86; Petro Engrng.

JOHNSON, KEVIN; Forest Park SR HS; Baltimore, MD; (Y); Computer Clb; FBLA; JA; Mathletes; Red Cross Aide; Teachers Aide; Varsity Clb; Variety Show; Yrbk Bus Mgr; JV Bsktbl; Loyola; Accntng.

JOHNSON, KOBI; Takoma Acad; Burtonsville, MD; (Y); Pres Church Yth Grp; VP Trs 4-H; VP Science Clb; Church Choir; Jr Cls; Im Socr; Hon Roll; NHS; Prfct Atten Awd; Montgomery Co 4-H Vet Sci Rcrd Bk Recog 84-85; U Of MD; Pre Vet.

JOHNSON, KRISTEN L; Brunswick HS; Jefferson, MD; (Y); 8/130; Computer Clb; French Clb; Teachers Aide; Band; Jazz Band; Mrchg Band; School Musical; High Hon Roll; Hon Roll; Girl Scts; Schl Schlstc Actvty Awd 84-86; Hodson Trst Schlrshp 86; WA Coll Schlrshp 86; Washington Coll; Bus.

JOHNSON, LAURA MARIE; John Carroll HS; Bel Air, MD; (Y); 20/235; VP Civic Clb; School Musical; Yrbk Stf; Pres Stu Cncl; Cheerleading; Hon Roll; Sec Trs NHS; Library Aide; Teachers Aide; Variety Show; Mss Teen Hrfrd Cnty Queen & Tlnt Awd 86; Egl Of The Crss Awd Outstndg Chrstn Ldrshp 86; Schl Spirt Awd; Lehigh U; Pre-Law.

JOHNSON, LESLEY; Potomac HS; Hillcrest Hts, MD; (Y); Church Yth Grp; English Clb; JA; Library Aide; Spanish Clb; Church Choir; School Play; Rep Stu Cncl; God Cntry Awd; Hon Roll; Georgetown U; Psych.

JOHNSON, LISA; Baltimore City College HS; Baltimore, MD; (Y); 3/238; Quiz Bowl; Var Badmtn; Var Vllybl; High Hon Roll; Pres NHS; Opt Clb Awd; Natl Achvt Schlrshp 86; Natl Merit Schlcommnded Stu 86; Schlr Athlt Awd 86; U Of PA; Acctng.

JOHNSON, LISA; Snow Hill HS; Snow Hill, MD; (Y); 1/80; Am Leg Aux Girls St; Debate Tm; Drama Clb; 4-H; French Clb; Pres Soph Cls; Rep Stu Cncl; Cit Awd; 4-H Awd; Val; SR Sci, Hstry Awd 86; Pres Acdmc Ftns Awd 86; VA Tech; Vet Med.

JOHNSON, LORI; Surratsville HS; Clinton, MD; (Y); Art Clb; Church Yth Grp; Library Aide; Church Choir; Yrbk Stf; Lit Mag; Hon Roll; NHS; VFW Awd; Ntl Merit Schlstc Achvt Awd 86; MD Coll Of Art & Dsgn; Arts.

JOHNSON, LYNNELL S; Gwynn Park HS; Upper Marlboro, MD; (Y); Church Yth Grp; JA; Teachers Aide; VP Jr Cls; Sftbl; Jr NHS; Kiwanis Awd; NHS; Pres Schlr; Towson ST U; Math.

JOHNSON, MARIE; Maurice J Mc Donough HS; Pomfret, MD; (S); Letterman Clb; Varsity Clb; Rep Stu Cncl; Var Bsktbl; Stat Ftbl; Var Sftbl; Stat Vllybl; Hon Roll; NHS; Prfct Atten Awd.

JOHNSON, MARTIN; Leonardtown HS; California, MD; (Y); Letterman Clb; Varsity Clb; Variety Show; Capt Ftbl; Capt Trk; Var Wt Lftg; All SMAC Ftbl 85 & 86; MVP 85; Salisbury ST; Comp Oper.

JOHNSON, MELISSA; Valley HS; Frostburg, MD; (Y); Church Yth Grp; French Clb; Ski Clb; Band; Concert Band; Mrchg Band; School Play; Yrbk Stf; Stat Bsbl; Stat Bsktbl; Pediatrc Nurse.

JOHNSON, SUSAN; Seneca Valley HS; Gaitherstown, MD; (Y); Church Yth Grp; Latin Clb; VP Sr Cls; VP SR High Yth Group 85-86; Exec Brd Of Yth Group 84-85; Psychology.

JOHNSON, TIMOTHY D; Parkside HS; Salisbury, MD; (Y); Hosp Aide; Pep Clb; Spanish Clb; Rep Sr Cls; JV Bsbl; Hon Roll; NHS; Opt Clb Awd; NC ST; Arch.

JOHNSON, TINA; Archbishop Keough HS; Balt, MD; (Y); French Clb; Spanish Clb; Nwsp Rptr; Nwsp Stf; Rep Soph Cls; Rep Jr Cls; Hon Roll; Prfct Atten Awd; Foreign Reltns.

JOHNSON, TROY; Forest Park HS; Baltimore, MD; (Y); Computer Clb; Trs JA; Science Clb; VP VICA; Ed Nwsp Stf; Chrmn Sr Cls; Var Ftbl; Hon Roll; Pres NHS; Prfct Atten Awd; Pres Ntl Hnr Soc 85-86; Omega Psi Phi Schlrshp 86-87; Coppin ST Coll Hnr Stu Awd 85-86; Manhattan Coll; Engr.

JOHNSON, YOLANDRA; Western HS; Baltimore, MD; (Y); Church Yth Grp; Lib Chorus; Church Choir; Hon Roll; Hampton U; Bio.

JOHNSTON, CHAD; West Nottingham Acad; Pt Deposit, MD; (Y); Camera Clb; Library Aide; Political Wkr; Ski Clb; Pres Frsh Cls; Pres Soph Cls; Pres Jr Cls; L Bsbl; L Bsktbl; L Ftbl; Finley Schrlsh P84-85; Hugh O Brien Yth Ldrshp Found 84-85; U MD Ldrshp Sem 85-86; Bus Adm.

JOHNSTON, ERIC; Wicomico SR HS; Salisbury, MD; (Y); Boy Scts; Dance Clb; Drama Clb; Capt JCL; Latin Clb; Acpl Chr; School Play; JV Lcrss; Var Tennis; Hon Roll; U Maryland C P; Comp Sci.

JOHNSTON, MARY M; Immaculata College HS; Washington, DC; (Y); Cmnty Wkr; Drama Clb; Spanish Clb; Thesps; Chorus; Church Choir; Lit Mag; Hon Roll; Wrtg.

JOHNSTON, MILLIE; Southern Garrett HS; Oakland, MD; (Y); Church Yth Grp; FHA; Girl Scts; Teachers Aide; Sec Trs VICA; Band; Hon Roll; Frostburg ST College; Elem Ed.

JOHNSTON, STEPHEN; Friendly HS; Ft Washington, MD; (Y); 70/390; Aud/Vis; Chess Clb; Stage Crew; Nwsp Rptr; Nwsp Stf; Wt Lftg; Hon Roll; UCLA Film Schl; Film Prod.

JONES, ALLISON MICHELLE; Queen Annes Co HS; Chester, MD; (Y); 85/400; Am Leg Aux Girls St; Church Yth Grp; DECA; FBLA; Hon Roll; Csmtlgst.

JONES, ANDRE; De Matha Catholic HS; New Carrollton, MD; (Y); 75/250; Art Clb; Aud/Vis; Church Yth Grp; Exploring; FCA; Pep Clb; Political Wkr; ROTC; Ski Clb; Spanish Clb; Poli Sci.

JONES, ARNICE; Potomac HS; Temple Hills, MD; (Y); Church Yth Grp; Girl Scts; Pres Frsh Cls; Pres Soph Cls; Pres Jr Cls; VP Stu Cncl; Cheerleading; Powder Puff Ftbl; Trk; High Hon Roll; Natl Ldrshp Awd 85-86; Natl Chrldrs Awd 85-86; Prince Georges Cnty Acad Awd 84-86; Comm.

JONES, BRONTE; Cambridge-South Dorchester HS; Cambridge, MD; (Y); Pres Church Yth Grp; Pres 4-H; Spanish Clb; Band; Stage Crew; VP Soph Cls; Pres Jr Cls; Var L Bsktbl; Var L Trk; NHS; Goucher Coll; Intl Affrs.

JONES, CARY; Laplata HS; Mount Victoria, MD; (Y); Varsity Clb; Symp Band; Rep Frsh Cls; Bsktbl; Capt Fld Hcky; Sftbl; Tennis; Vllybl; Hon Roll; NHS; Grl Athltc Of Yr 84; MIP Fld Hcky & Bsktbl 85 & 86; Estrn Reg All Star 3rd Bse 86; Sprts Med.

JONES, CHARLES; Gwynn Park SR HS; Upper Marlboro, MD; (Y); ROTC; Drill Tm; Church Yth Grp; Trk; Hon Roll.

JONES, COURTNEY; Western HS; Baltimore, MD; (Y); 129/412; Church Yth Grp; Cmnty Wkr; Office Aide; Radio Clb; Chorus; Rep Frsh Cls; Hampton U; Telecomm.

JONES, DANIEL; Liberty HS; Finksburg, MD; (S); JA; Mathletes; Ski Clb; Teachers Aide; Varsity Clb; Var L Crs Cntry; Score Keeper; Var L Trk; Hon Roll; Stdnt Pg Selctn Cmmttee; U S Air Force Acad; Aerontcl En.

JONES, DEBBIE; Cambridge South Dorchester HS; Fishing Creek, MD; (Y); Concert Band; Drill Tm; Mrchg Band; Nwsp Stf; Yrbk Stf; Sec Frsh Cls; Rep Stu Cncl; Pom Pon; Sftbl; Stat Wrstlng; Bus.

JONES, DEBORAH; Crossland HS; Andrews AFB, WA; (Y); FHA; Natl Beta Clb; Spanish Clb; Teachers Aide; Cheerleading; Powder Puff Ftbl; Sftbl; Vllybl; Hon Roll; Jr NHS; Acctg.

JONES, ELISE; Dulaney SR HS; Timonium, MD; (Y); School Play; Stage Crew; Yrbk Rptr; Yrbk Stf; Im Badmtn; Stat Bsbl; Stat Bsktbl; Stat Socr; Hon Roll; Bus.

JONES, ERNEST; Smithsburg HS; Hagerstown, MD; (Y); Drama Clb; Latin Clb; Ski Clb; School Musical; School Play; Nwsp Rptr; Rep Stu Cncl; L Crs Cntry; L Trk; Hon Roll; Bus Ecnmcs.

JONES, HEATHER; Magruder/Gaithersburg HS; Gaithersburg, MD; (Y); AFS; Church Yth Grp; Cmnty Wkr; Drama Clb; ROTC; SADD; Concert Band; Mrchg Band; Orch; Pep Band; Cert Shwng Cmpltn NJROTC Crs 85-86; Pn Shwng Invlvmnt Schl Orch 85-86.

JONES, HERVOYNA; Walbrook SR HS; Baltimore, MD; (Y); Church Yth Grp; VICA; Hon Roll; Voc Ind Am 86; Skilly Olympic Child Care 86; Cert Assist Preschlrs 86; Towson ST U; Bus Mgmt.

JONES, JACQUELINE; Great Mills HS; Lex Pk, MD; (Y); Dance Clb; Band; Concert Band; Mrchg Band; Ballet Dncng Outstndng Stu; St Marys Coll; Psych.

JONES JR, JAMES M; Westminster HS; Eldersburg, MD; (Y); German Clb; Teachers Aide; Concert Band; Jazz Band; Mrchg Band; Gov Hon Prg Awd; High Hon Roll; NHS; Ntl Merit Ltr; Pres Schlr; U Of MD Coll Pk; Engrng.

JONES, JENNIFER; Wilde Lake HS; Columbia, MD; (Y); Civic Clb; Cmnty Wkr; French Clb; Office Aide; Political Wkr; Orch; Stage Crew; Variety Show; Var JV Bsktbl; Ntl Merit Ltr; Cmmnded Schlr Math PSAT 86; Early AdmssnUW Madison 86; Engrng.

JONES, JESSICA COX; Academy Of Holy Names; Hyattsville, MD; (Y); Pres French Clb; VP Library Aide; Model UN; Office Aide; Political Wkr; Q&S; Chorus; Nwsp Rptr; Lit Mag; Hon Roll; Lib Club Key 85-86; Chem And Typg Awds 86; St Marys College; Bus.

JONES, KATHERINE E; La Plata HS; Faulkner, MD; (Y); Cmnty Wkr; FNA; Teachers Aide; Sftbl; Swmmng; Vllybl; Cit Awd; Hon Roll; Ntl Merit Ltr; Prfct Atten Awd; Pedtrc Nrse.

JONES, KEVIN; Crossland HS; Seat Pleasant, MD; (Y); Church Yth Grp; Cmnty Wkr; Ftbl; Wt Lftg; Hon Roll; Ntl Merit Ltr; MD U; Accntng.

JONES, KEVIN; Northern HS; Baltimore, MD; (Y); Church Yth Grp; Chorus; Church Choir; JV Var Bsbl; Var Ftbl; Hon Roll; Comp Engnrng.

JONES, LATONIA; Baltimore City College; Baltimore, MD; (Y); 2/243; Art Clb; Cmnty Wkr; Chorus; Nwsp Stf; Rep Jr Cls; High Hon Roll; Hon Roll; NHS; Sal; Johns Hopkins U Peabody Prz 86; Matthias D Sousa Fllwshp 86; Modern Music Natl Music Hnr Soc 86; Saint Marys Coll; Bus.

JONES, MELISSA; Mount De Sales Acad; Pasadena, MD; (Y); 2/47; Church Yth Grp; Cmnty Wkr; Girl Scts; JA; Office Aide; PAVAS; Teachers Aide; Acpl Chr; Chorus; Concert Band; 1st Pl Tm Bwlng Awds 84 &85; Muscular Dystrphy Telthn Of Music 85; Law.

JONES, MONIQUE ELIZABETH; Western SR HS; Baltimore, MD; (Y); 167/412; Church Yth Grp; Chorus; Pres Church Choir; School Musical; Rep Soph Cls; Off Jr Cls; Sec Sr Cls; JV Trk; Prfct Atten Awd; U Of VA; Actng.

JONES, NANCY; Paul Laurence Dunbar HS; Baltimore, MD; (Y); FBLA; Pep Clb; Hon Roll; Prfct Atten Awd; Coppin ST Coll; Pre-Law.

JONES, NATALIE; Parkside HS; Salisbury, MD; (Y); 2/225; JCL; Latin Clb; Teachers Aide; Chorus; Church Choir; High Hon Roll; Hon Roll; NHS; VFW Awd; 2 Cum Laude Awds Natl Achvmnt Latin Exam 84&86; 2 Schlrs Outstndg Stu Awd 85-86; Schl Srv Awd & Mdl 86; Howard U; Biology.

JONES, R; Loyola HS; Owings Mills, MD; (Y); Stage Crew; Rep Soph Cls; Rep Jr Cls; Hon Roll; Ntl Merit SF; Prfct Atten Awd; Rep Frsh Cls; Engr.

JONES, SCOTT; Capitol Christian Acad; Edgewater, MD; (S); Church Yth Grp; Teachers Aide; Band; Mrchg Band; Socr; Trk; Hon Roll; NHS; Aerontcs.

JONES, SHARILYN; Gaithersburg HS; Gaithersburg, MD; (Y); VP Sec Church Yth Grp; Cmnty Wkr; Dance Clb; Drama Clb; SADD; Chorus; Church Choir; School Musical; School Play; Stage Crew; Psychlgy.

JONES, SHARON; Archbishop Keough HS; Severn, MD; (Y); Sec Church Yth Grp; Girl Scts; Spanish Clb; Trs Church Choir; DAR Awd; Acctng.

JONES, TERESA; Surrattsville HS; Clinton, MD; (Y); Band; Concert Band; Rep Frsh Cls; Bsbl; Bsktbl; Pom Pon; Powder Puff Ftbl; Hon Roll; Grls Bsktbl Awd 84; Pom Pon Awd 85; Bus Mgt.

JONES, TERRI A; Liberty HS; Marriottsville, MD; (Y); 4/278; Letterman Clb; Mathletes; Teachers Aide; Nwsp Sprt Ed; Yrbk Bus Mgr; Hst Stu Cncl; Capt Socr; Bausch & Lomb Sci Awd; Gov Hon Prg Awd; High Hon Roll; Freedom Jaycees Sci Stu Of Month 85; Brent Calvert Fllwshp 86; Izaak Walton Aquatic Bio Schlrshp 86; St Marys Coll; Bio.

JONES, TERRY; Du Val SR HS; Glenn Dale, MD; (Y); VP 4-H; Natl Beta Clb; Pres Spanish Clb; Teachers Aide; Drill Tm; Yrbk Stf; Off Frsh Cls; Off Soph Cls; Off Sr Cls; Pom Pon; Ntl Beta Clb Awd Mrt 85 & 86; AP Hstry Cert 86; AP Bio Cert 86; U Miami; Mrn Bio.

JONES, WILHELMINA; Southern SR HS; Lothian, MD; (Y); 3/196; FBLA; Tennis; Hon Roll; Baltimore Conf Schlrshp 86; Morgan ST U; Accntnt.

JORDAN, ELAINE S; S River SR HS; Davidsonville, MD; (Y); 13/265; Dance Clb; Spanish Clb; Rep Frsh Cls; Rep Soph Cls; Rep Jr Cls; Rep Sr Cls; Var Capt Cheerleading; Var L Pom Pon; High Hon Roll; Hon Roll; U Of MD; Math.

JORDAN, MONIQUE; Leonardtown HS; Valley Lee, MD; (Y); Drama Clb; Latin Clb; Teachers Aide; Varsity Clb; Powder Puff Ftbl; Trk; Vllybl; Hon Roll; Comp Sci.

JORDAN, SANDRA; Queen Ames Co HS; Chestertown, MD; (Y); French Clb; Hosp Aide; SADD; Nwsp Rptr; Var Bsktbl; Coach Actv; Crs Cntry; Hnr Rl 83 & 84; Louisburg Coll NC; Law.

JORDEN, JIMIE; Great Mills HS; Lex Prk, MD; (Y); Church Yth Grp; 4-H; Yrbk Stf; Hon Roll; Opt Clb Awd; Senatorl Schlrshp 86; St Marys Coll; Math.

JOYCE, DOREEN; Bishop Walsh HS; Frostburg, MD; (Y); Cmnty Wkr; Hosp Aide; Library Aide; Hon Roll; Golden West Coll; Jrnlst.

JOYCE, DOUG; Gaithersburg HS; Gaithersburg, MD; (Y); Teachers Aide; Capt L Ftbl; Wt Lftg; Hon Roll; Prfct Atten Awd; Indr Trck Chmpn Shtpt 86; Outdr Trck Chmpn 86; Stu Ldrshp Orgnztn 84-86; Bus Admin.

JOYNER, TONI; Potomac HS; Temple Hills, MD; (Y); Computer Clb; Intnl Clb; Mgr(s); Score Keeper; Timer; Trk; 4-H Awd; High Hon Roll; Hon Roll; Air Traffic Cntrllr.

JOZWICK, KIMBERLY; Patapsco HS; Baltimore, MD; (Y); Chorus; Lcrss; Mgr(s); Score Keeper; Timer; High Hon Roll; Hon Roll.

JUBB, THOMAS PATRICK; Williamsport HS; Willamsport, MD; (Y); Church Yth Grp; Latin Clb; ROTC; SADD; Nwsp Rptr; Bsktbl; Crs Cntry; Trk; Hon Roll; Shippensburg U; Cmmnctns.

JUDD, JENNIFER; Great Mills HS; Lex Pk, MD; (Y); Hosp Aide; Concert Band; Mrchg Band; VP Soph Cls; Off Jr Cls; Var Fld Hcky; Var Trk; Hon Roll; NHS.

JUDD, MATTHEW; Wilde Lake HS; Columbia, MD; (Y); Debate Tm; NFL; Var L Bsbl; Var L Ftbl; Wt Lftg; Hon Roll; NHS; Acdmc All Amrcn 85-86; Archtctr.

JUDGE, ELLA; Thomas Stone HS; Brandywine, MD; (Y); Office Aide; Yrbk Sprt Ed; Sec Jr Cls; Stat JV Bsbl; Var Capt Cheerleading; Hon Roll; Busnss Admin.

JUDGE, JOHN; Frederick HS; Frederick, MD; (Y); Church Yth Grp; Latin Clb; Tennis; Hartford; Mech Engrng.

JUDY, TINA; Fort Hill HS; Cumberland, MD; (Y); Sec 4-H; Pep Clb; Teachers Aide; Chorus; Flag Corp; Soph Cls; Jr Cls; Sr Cls; Hon Roll; Sec NHS.

JUN, VILLY; De Matha Catholic HS; Hyattsville, MD; (Y); Church Yth Grp; Hosp Aide; SADD; Teachers Aide; Band; Concert Band; Hon Roll; NHS; Villanova.

JUNG, JEFF; Maurice J Mc Donough HS; Waldorf, MD; (Y); VP Church Yth Grp; SADD; Nwsp Stf; Var Capt Bsbl; Bsktbl; High Hon Roll; NHS; Tv.

JUNG, PAUL; Laurel SR HS; Laurel, MD; (Y); Chess Clb; Church Yth Grp; German Clb; Science Clb; Teachers Aide; Acpl Chr; Band; Chorus; Church Choir; Concert Band; Geo Wshngtn U Engrng Mdl 86; Schl Sci Fair Hon Mntn 86; Seton Hill Coll Instrmtl Music Awd 85; Med.

JUSKELIS, CAROLYN; Lansdowne HS; Arbutus, MD; (Y); Dance Clb; Key Clb; SADD; Orch; Off Sr Cls; Off Stu Cncl; Cheerleading; Pom Pon; French Hon Soc; NHS; La Salle U; Advrtsng.

JUSTICE, KEVIN; Parkside HS; Salisbury, MD; (Y); Aud/Vis; Latin Clb; Office Aide; Stage Crew; Hon Roll; Medl Svc 84; FL Inst Tech; Comp Engrng.

JUSTICE, TRICIA; Wicomico SR HS; Salisbury, MD; (Y); Trs French Clb; Varsity Clb; Band; Concert Band; Mrchg Band; Symp Band; Rep Jr Cls; Var L Tennis; Hon Roll; Acad Pndnt 83-86; Phys Thrpy.

KACZMAREK JR, EDWARD A; Archbishop Curley HS; Baltimore, MD; (Y); 30/138; Cmnty Wkr; Computer Clb; Math Clb; Stu Cncl; High Hon Roll; Hon Roll; U MD College Park; Elec Engrng.

KAHN, BRENDA; Seneca Valley HS; Germantown, MD; (Y); 47/600; Dance Clb; Drama Clb; Spanish Clb; Teachers Aide; School Musical; School Play; Pom Pon; Hon Roll; Spotlight Awd 85-86; Best Prod Contribution 85-86; Pres Acad Fitness Awd 85-86; Shippensburg U.

KAISER, NANCY; Walter Johnson HS; Rockville, MD; (Y); Church Yth Grp; Pep Clb; Political Wkr; Nwsp Rptr; Ed Nwsp Stf; Yrbk Phtg; Yrbk Rptr; Ed Yrbk Stf; Chrmn Stu Cncl; Sec Capt Pom Pon; Outstndng Dedctn-Svc Soph Cls 85, Soc Comm 86; Jrnlsm.

KALBACH, HEIDI; Franklin SR HS; Reisterstown, MD; (Y); Pres Church Yth Grp; Jazz Band; Mrchg Band; Var Crs Cntry; Var Socr; Var Trk; Hon Roll; NHS; Martha Van Gutton Schlrshp 86; Band Boostrs Schlrshp 86; Towson ST U; Music.

KALCHTHALER, DENNIS; Pocomoke HS; Pocomoke City, MD; (Y); 10/115; Am Leg Boys St; Math Clb; Science Clb; Spanish Clb; SADD; Hon Roll; Ftbl; Hon Roll; Prfct Atten Awd; Acad All Amer 85; Hnrb Mntn Bayside Cnfrnc Ftbll 85-86; Arspc Engrng.

KALIVODA, KRISTEN; Broadneck SR HS; Arnold, MD; (S); DECA; Hosp Aide; JA; Ski Clb; Chorus; School Play; Tennis; Hon Roll; Silver Mrt Awd 86; Speakers Bureau Awd 86; Pres Of Broadneck Deca Chptr 85-86; Ann Arundle CC; Bus.

KALLAS, TERRY LEIGH; Eleanor Roosevelt HS; Laurel, MD; (Y); AFS; Latin Clb; Math Tm; Office Aide; Var Pom Pon; NHS; Hon Roll; 1st Typg I Cntst,2nd Clara L Bricker Cnty Comptn 84; Acadmc Excllnc Awd 84; Latn I Natl Exm 85; Lat II; U Of MD; Food/Nutrn.

KALLON, ABDUL; Bladensburg HS; Landover Hills, MD; (Y); 1/340; Trs Sr Cls; Var Capt Crs Cntry; Var Capt Trk; Bausch & Lomb Sci Awd; DAR Awd; VP NHS; Pres Schlr; St Schlr; Val; Stu Cncl; Alpha Phi Alpha Schlrshp 86; Cross Country Most Valuable Player 85; Dartmouth; Bio.

KAMINETZKY, SHIMON ALTER; Yeshu Of Greater Washington HS; Silver Spring, MD; (Y); Cmnty Wkr; Temple Yth Grp; Varsity Clb; Yrbk Stf; Pres Stu Cncl; Bsktbl; Bus Mngmnt.

KAMIRU, NJOKI; Northwestern HS; Hyattsville, MD; (Y); Cmnty Wkr; ROTC; Teachers Aide; Chorus; Drill Tm; Variety Show; Rep Frsh Cls; Rep Soph Cls; Rep Stu Cncl; Hon Roll; Principals Awd 86; Outstndg Literary Wrtr 86; Outstndg Literary Wrtr 86; Sojourner Prtrtsm Awd 84; Georgetown U; Law.

KANE, MARY; Archbishop Keough HS; Columbia, MD; (Y); Church Yth Grp; Cmnty Wkr; Hosp Aide; Office Aide; Pep Clb; Spanish Clb; Nwsp Phtg; Hon Roll; Ntl Merit Ltr; Mt St Marys Coll; Sclgy.

KANG, JACK; Gaithersburg HS; Gaithersburg, MD; (Y); 17/684; German Clb; Pres Intnl Clb; Science Clb; Nwsp Rptr; Hon Roll; NHS; Pres Schlr; St Schlr; Stage Crew; Space Shuttle Proj Tm Awd 86; Delta Ersilon Phi 86; U Of MD Rsrch & Expermntatn Awd 84; NW U; Mechanical Engrng.

KANG, MIN H; Dulaney SR HS; Cockeysville, MD; (Y); Key Clb; Model UN; Var Mgr Fld Hcky; Var Mgr(s); Hon Roll; Jr NHS; NHS; Phtjrnlst Mag.

KANG, PAUL; North Hagerstown HS; Hagerstown, MD; (Y); 1/276; Trs Latin Clb; Hon Roll; NHS; Ntl Merit Ltr; Pre Med.

KANG, SARAH; The Garrison Forest Schl; Reisterstown, MD; (Y); Church Yth Grp; French Clb; Hosp Aide; Model UN; Service Clb; Nwsp Stf; Tennis; Hon Roll; 4-H; PAVAS; Natl Piano Playing Auditions Dist, ST, & Natl Wnnr 84-86.

KANIS, REBECCA; St Johns At Prospect Hall HS; Overland Park, KS; (Y); Pres Science Clb; VP Soph Cls; Sec Jr Cls; VP Stu Cncl; Var Bsktbl; Var Socr; Var Sftbl; Var Tennis; NHS; Ntl Merit Ltr.

KANTOWSKI, KRISTIE; Glenelg HS; Ellicott City, MD; (Y); 1/265; Church Yth Grp; Intnl Clb; Varsity Clb; Yrbk Stf; Var Bsktbl; Var L Sftbl; Var L Vllybl; Hon Roll; NHS.

KAOURIS, DEMETRIOS; Wicomico SR HS; Salisbury, MD; (Y); JCL; Latin Clb; Rep Frsh Cls; Var Bsbl; Var Ftbl; NHS.

KAPFHAMMER, DAVID; Frederick HS; Clarksburg, MD; (Y); Church Yth Grp; Computer Clb; Pres Science Clb; Spanish Clb; Teachers Aide; Im Bsktbl; Im Powder Puff Ftbl; JV Socr; Im Tennis; Hon Roll; Sci.

KAPLAN, JONATHAN; Thomas S Wootton HS; Rockville, MD; (Y); Camera Clb; Debate Tm; NFL; Science Clb; Hon Roll; NHS; Ntl Merit SF; St Champs Mock Trial Comptn 85-86; Fnlst Supt Of Schls Writng Cntst 86; Frgn Svc.

KAREEM, QUANITA; Balto Polytechnic Inst HS; Baltimore, MD; (Y); JA; School Play; Rep Frsh Cls; Rep Soph Cls; Rep Jr Cls; Sec Sr Cls; Rep Stu Cncl; JV Trk; Prfct Atten Awd; Outstndng Stu Ldr Assn Stu Cngrs Blto City 86; Stu Govt Assn Awd 86; Prfct Attnd 86; U MD Baltimore Co; Info Systm.

KARLOWA, RUTH; Bishop Walsh Middle HS; Cumberland, MD; (Y); 1/101; Concert Band; Drm Mjr(t); Mrchg Band; School Musical; Yrbk Ed-Chief; High Hon Roll; NHS; Ntl Merit SF; Drama Clb; German Clb; $1000 Per Yr Schlrshp Notre Dame 85; German Hnr Soc 86; Tri St Hnrs Bnd 85; Bus Admin.

KARMASEK, DOUG; Eastern Voc-Tech HS; Baltimore, MD; (Y); JV Lcrss; Hon Roll; Carpntr.

KARPIAK, VERONICA; Old Mill SR HS; Glen Burnie, MD; (Y); 14/509; Church Yth Grp; Pres Girl Scts; Teachers Aide; VP Stu Cncl; Stat L Socr; Hon Roll; Sec NHS; Pres Schlr; Sen Schlrshp 86; UMBC; Engrg.

KARR, CATHERINE J; Baltimore Polytechnic Inst; Baltimore, MD; (Y); 2/475; Political Wkr; Yrbk Ed-Chief; Mgr(s); Sftbl; Swmmng; High Hon Roll; NHS; Ntl Merit SF; Cmnty Wkr; JA; Engr.

KARR, CHERYL; S Carroll HS; Sykesville, MD; (Y); Office Aide; Ski Clb; Teachers Aide; Varsity Clb; Nwsp Stf; Rep Frsh Cls; Rep Stu Cncl; JV Var Cheerleading; High Hon Roll; Hon Roll; Acdmc Ltr; Frostburg ST Coll; Bio.

KARR, MARTHA E; Baltimore Poloytechnic Inst; Baltimore, MD; (Y); 1/475; Political Wkr; Yrbk Ed-Chief; Yrbk Phtg; Var Sftbl; Var Swmmng; NHS; Ntl Merit SF; Val; Cmnty Wkr; Nwsp Stf; Civil Engr.

KARRAS, POTA; Maryvale Preparatory Schl; Ellicott City, MD; (Y); Computer Clb; Hosp Aide; VP JA; French Hon Soc; High Hon Roll; Hon Roll; Jr NHS; NHS; Pres Schlr; Its Acdmc 84-85; Frnch Awd 83-86; Geo Ganas Awd Acdmc Achvmnt 86; AHEPA Awd 86; American U; Pre-Med.

KARUKAS, MARIA; John Carroll HS; Bel Air, MD; (Y); 11/260; Church Yth Grp; Chorus; Yrbk Stf; Rep Stu Cncl; Lcrss; Var Socr; Trk; Hon Roll; NHS; Spanish NHS; Psychlgy.

KASCH, DANA; Gaithersburg HS; Gaithersburg, MD; (Y); SADD; Teachers Aide; Rep Frsh Cls; Rep Soph Cls; Rep Jr Cls; Var Capt Cheerleading; Hon Roll; Outstndng Achvts-Wrd Processing 86; Bus.

KATILAS, KELLY; Eastern Voc Tech; Baltimore, MD; (Y); Band; Rep Frsh Cls; Rep Stu Cncl; Var Bsktbl; Var Cheerleading; JV Var Socr; JV Var Sftbl; Hon Roll; NHS; Awd Hon Rl 4 Terms 84-85; Geriatrc Aide Cert 85-86; Towson ST; RN.

KATZIN, REBECCA; Laurel HS; Laurel, MD; (Y); Art Clb; Ski Clb; Temple Yth Grp; Yrbk Rptr; Yrbk Stf; Hon Roll; Hlth Fld.

KATZKE, ROBIN; Sherwood HS; Brookeville, MD; (Y); Hosp Aide; Trs Sec Temple Yth Grp; School Musical; Variety Show; Nwsp Ed-Chief; Rep Frsh Cls; Rep Soph Cls; Rep Jr Cls; Hon Roll; NHS; Spirit Of Jr Miss Mntgmry Cnty 86; Prof Dance.

KAUFFMAN, TAMMY; South Carroll HS; New Windsor, MD; (Y); 75/300; Church Yth Grp; Key Clb; Teachers Aide; Yrbk Stf; Mgr(s); Score Keeper; Vllybl; Hon Roll; Coll Schlrshp Frm Villa Julie Coll 86; Villa Julie Coll; Chld Dvlpmnt.

KAUFHOLD, JUSTUS; Maurice J Mc Donough HS; Waldorf, MD; (S); Chorus; School Musical; Stage Crew; Crs Cntry; High Hon Roll; Tri-Cnty Hnr Chr 86; Lead Schl Ply/Mscl-Cndrlla-The Prnc 86; Octet/Cncrt Chr 86; UCLA.

KAUFMAN, REBECCA; Springbrook HS; Silver Spring, MD; (Y); Church Yth Grp; Key Clb; PAVAS; Church Choir; Pres Frsh Cls; Hon Roll; Amer Hrt Assn 85-86; Stu Fllwshp Rsrch Pgm Wnnr; Awd Stipend-Intrnshp Natl Inst Hlth-Wrkng Rsrch Lab; Bio.

KAUP, SAUMYA; Parkside HS; Salisbury, MD; (Y); French Clb; Ski Clb; Varsity Clb; Rep Soph Cls; Rep Jr Cls; Var Fld Hcky; Hon Roll; NHS; Tennis; Acad Achvt Vrsty Lttr & Pint 85 & 86; Arch.

KAVANAUGH, MARGIE; Allegany HS; Cumberland, MD; (Y); 28/240; VP AFS; Dance Clb; Office Aide; Drill Tm; Yrbk Rptr; Yrbk Stf; Rep Stu Cncl; Hon Roll; MADART 85-86; Peer Counslr 85-86; Allegany CC; Radlgy.

KAYOUMY, ROYA; Walter Johnson HS; Bethesda, MD; (Y); French Clb; Hosp Aide; Key Clb; Sec Science Clb; Sec SADD; Rep Jr Cls; L Trk; French Hon Soc; High Hon Roll; NHS; Med.

KAZEMIAN, PARISA; Set Andrews Episcopal Schl; Washington, DC; (Y); French Clb; Pep Clb; Rep Jr Cls; Socr; Wt Lftg; Best Ldrshp Cptn Of Girls JV Soccor Tm 85-86; VP French Clb 85-86; Tufts Schl; Pre-Law.

KEARNEY, TOD; Mt St Josephs HS; Baltimore, MD; (Y); Hon Roll; Spanish NHS; UMBC; Bus Adm.

KEAST, LAURIE; La Plata HS; Waldorf, MD; (Y); Bsktbl; Socr; Swmmng; Hon Roll; Special Olymps Hugger 86; Charles Cnty Cmnty Clg Seahawks 84-86; Bus Or Comp Schl; Comp.

KEEFE, BRIAN; Laurel HS; Laurel, MD; (Y); Letterman Clb; Ski Clb; Varsity Clb; Stage Crew; Var Ftbl; Golf; Hon Roll; Accntng.

KEELEY, KELLYANNE; Connelly School Of The Holy Child; Bethesda, MD; (Y); Debate Tm; Service Clb; Pres SADD; Orch; School Musical; Stat Fld Hcky; JV Lcrss; JV Tennis; Hon Roll; 10th Pl Le Grnd Cncrs Exm; Engrng.

KEENEY, RAYMOND E; La Plata HS; La Plata, MD; (S); Boy Scts; Ski Clb; Varsity Clb; JV Var Ftbl; Var Swmmng; Var Trk; Var Wt Lftg; JV Wrstlng; NH; Bus Adm.

KEHOE, KRISTIE C; Atholton HS; Laurel, MD; (Y); 7/280; Pres Pep Clb; VP Thesps; School Musical; School Play; Nwsp Stf; Pom Pon; Pres NHS; Opt Clb Awd; Rotary Awd; Voice Dem Awd; U Of S FL; Cmmnctns.

KEHR, DIANE; Capitol Christian Acad; Upper Marlboro, MD; (S); 8/27; Office Aide; Teachers Aide; Varsity Clb; Variety Show; Nwsp Bus Mgr; Nwsp Rptr; Nwsp Stf; Yrbk Bus Mgr; Yrbk Phtg; Yrbk Rptr; Treas Ntl Hnr Soc 85-86; Hnrbl Mntn All Cty Vllybl Tm 85-86; Prince Georges CC; Paralgl.

KEIPER, DEBORAH; Sherwood HS; Brookeville, MD; (Y); Teachers Aide; Chorus; Drill Tm; School Musical; Pom Pon; Hon Roll; Jr NHS; U Of MD; Accntng.

KEISTER, PATRICIA ANNE; Charles W Woodward HS; Kensington, MD; (Y); Church Yth Grp; Teachers Aide; Varsity Clb; Yrbk Ed-Chief; Yrbk Rptr; Var L Bsktbl; Var L Socr; Var L Vllybl; Hon Roll; MVP Vllybl 85-86; Co Athlt Wk Mntgmry Jrnl Vllybl 85; Mst Imprvd Bsktbl All Cnty Tm 85-86; Tchng.

KEITH, JEFFREY A; Thomas Stone HS; Waldorf, MD; (Y); Aud/Vis; Camera Clb; Nwsp Ed-Chief; Nwsp Phtg; Hon Roll; Chas Cnty Cmnty Coll; Cnmtgrphy.

KELK, WENDY; La Plata HS; Charlotte Hall, MD; (Y); 4-H; JA; Concert Band; Mrchg Band; Orch; 4-H Awd; Hon Roll; Lincoln Tech; Auto Mech.

KELLER, ANDI; Fort Hill HS; Cumberland, MD; (Y); 34/260; Church Yth Grp; Teachers Aide; Drill Tm; Yrbk Bus Mgr; Pom Pon; Allegany CC; Nrsng.

KELLER, BRIAN; Valley HS; Lonaconing, MD; (Y); Drama Clb; Ski Clb; Stage Crew; JV Var Ftbl; NHS; Chem Stu ACS 86; USAFA; Aerospace Engr.

KELLER, KATHLEEN E; Great Mills HS; Lexington Park, MD; (Y); Art Clb; French Clb; Teachers Aide; Var Bsktbl; Var Crs Cntry; JV Ftbl; Var Sftbl; Var Wt Lftg; Hon Roll; Pres Schlr; Pres Athl Fit Awd 85-86; St Mary Coll; Mgmt.

KELLER, KEVEN; Walkersville HS; Walkersville, MD; (Y); 13/225; Church Yth Grp; Computer Clb; Science Clb; Spanish Clb; Hon Roll.

KELLER, STEFFANIE; Seton HS; Baltimore, MD; (Y); Church Yth Grp; Drama Clb; NFL; Lit Mag; Pres Stu Cncl; Hon Roll; MD Dssstngshd Schlr Hnrb Mntn 85; Altrnt Dlgt U S Senate Yth Prgm 85; Sprt Awd 84-85; Englsh.

KELLEY, LISA; Gaithersburg HS; Gaithersburg, MD; (Y); Cmnty Wkr; Pep Clb; SADD; Teachers Aide; Mgr(s); Pom Pon; Score Keeper; Hon Roll; Spanish NHS; Marketing.

KELLEY, TAMRA; Southern Garrett HS; Oakland, MD; (Y); Color Guard; Concert Band; Mrchg Band; Hon Roll; Wintergrd Trvld London, Englnd 86; Nrsng.

KELLMAN, WENDI; Pikesville HS; Owings Mills, MD; (Y); AFS; Spanish Clb; SADD; Gym; Powder Puff Ftbl; Var Capt Socr; JV Var Sftbl; Pres Awd 83-85; G Wash Univ; Bus.

KELLY, BART; Bishop Walsh HS; Cumberland, MD; (Y); 8/104; Am Leg Boys St; Rep Frsh Cls; Pres Soph Cls; VP Stu Cncl; Capt Crs Cntry; Capt Socr; Capt Tennis; Var L Trk; NHS; Ski Clb; MVP Tennis; Best Offensive Player Awd Soccer.

KELLY, CATHLEEN; Thomas S Wooton HS; Gaithersburg, MD; (Y); Concert Band; Yrbk Stf; Hon Roll.

KELLY, CHERIE; Western SR HS; Baltimore, MD; (Y); 89/412; Cmnty Wkr; Red Cross Aide; Lit Mag; Rep Jr Cls; Cit Awd; Hon Roll; Jr NHS; Prfct Atten Awd; Prfct Attndnc Awd 84; Hnr Roll Awd 85; Howard U; Psych.

KELLY, JENIFER; The Catholic HS Of Balto; Baltimore, MD; (Y); 30/189; Drama Clb; GAA; Red Cross Aide; Spanish Clb; Stage Crew; Var Badmtn; Prfct Atten Awd; Badmintn Bst Dbls, Bst Sngls Plyr 84-85 & 85-86; Towson ST U; Comp Sci.

KELLY, JILL SUZANNE; Dundalk SR HS; Baltimore, MD; (Y); 2/325; Church Yth Grp; Teachers Aide; Band; Mrchg Band; School Musical; Rep Stu Cncl; High Hon Roll; Jr NHS; NHS; Pres Schlr; Liberty U Chancellors Schlrshp, Dundalk Area Schlrshp Trust Fund 86; Outstndng Pianist 86; Liberty U; Music.

KELLY, KEITH; Georgetown Prep; Washington, DC; (Y); German Clb; Latin Clb; Hon Roll; Bus.

KELLY, KIMBERLY; Bishop Walsh HS; Cresaptown, MD; (Y); 13/104; Office Aide; Rep Soph Cls; Pres Sr Cls; Var Stat Bsbl; JV Stat Bsktbl; JV Cheerleading; Var Stat Ftbl; High Hon Roll; Hon Roll; Sec NHS; Cert Achvt Partcptn Bus Cmnctns, Typng Cntsts-Annegany CC 86; B Walsh Spr Rep-Mrch Dms Wlk Amer 84; Law.

KELLY, LYNDA ANNE; Gaithersburg HS; Gaithersburg, MD; (Y); 31/658; 4-H; Science Clb; 4-H Awd; High Hon Roll; Jr NHS; NHS; Spanish NHS; Schlrshp U MD Rerch Del Proj 84; 3rd Pl Jrnlsm Cntst Sci Fair Awd 85; Montgomery Cty Fair Princess 85; U MD; Aero Sp Engr.

KELLY, MONICA; Thomas Stone HS; Waldorf, MD; (Y); Church Yth Grp; Pres 4-H; Science Clb; Teachers Aide; Stage Crew; Variety Show; Var L Crs Cntry; Var L Trk; Hon Roll; U MD Baltimore Co; Phys Ther.

KELLY, SUSAN; North Harford HS; Jarrettsville, MD; (Y); Church Yth Grp; French Clb; Varsity Clb; Lit Mag; Capt Bsktbl; Powder Puff Ftbl; Sftbl; Hon Roll; Bus.

KEMPISTY JR, F MITCHELL; Dundalk SR HS; Baltimore, MD; (Y); Am Leg Boys St; Camera Clb; Im Socr; Im Vllybl; JV Wrstlng; High Hon Roll; Hon Roll; NHS; Engr.

KENNAN, SHANNON; James M Bennett SR HS; Salisbury, MD; (S); Church Yth Grp; Drama Clb; Office Aide; Teachers Aide; Thesps; Chorus; School Musical; School Play; Variety Show; Cheerleading; Educ.

KENNEDY, CHARLES; Northeast HS; Elkton, MD; (Y); Pep Clb; VICA; Bsktbl; Wrstlng; Hon Roll; Prfct Atten Awd; MD U; Indus Engr.

KENNEDY, GARY MICHAEL; Seneca Valley HS; Gaithersburg, MD; (Y); 2/490; Ski Clb; Spanish Clb; Stage Crew; L Sftbl; Var Capt Tennis; High Hon Roll; Hon Roll; VP NHS; Sal; St Schlr; U VA; Comp Sci.

KENNEDY, KATHY; Springbrook HS; Silver Spring, MD; (Y); Ski Clb; Chorus; Off Frsh Cls; Off Jr Cls; Stu Cncl; Var JV Cheerleading; Pom Pon; Hon Roll; Aerontcs.

KENNEDY, KERRI; Archbishop Keough HS; Baltimore, MD; (Y); Church Yth Grp; Computer Clb; Stage Crew; Yrbk Stf; Var Bsktbl; Var Lcrss; Hon Roll; Comp Sci.

KENNEDY, SHARON; High Point HS; Beltsville, MD; (Y); Cmnty Wkr; Spanish Clb; Teachers Aide; Var Trk; Hon Roll; Prfct Atten Awd; U Of NC; Nursing.

KENNEY, ANNA; Great Mills HS; Great Mills, MD; (Y); Church Yth Grp; Spanish Clb; Fld Hcky; Trk; Hon Roll; NHS; Hist.

KENNEY, PATRICK; Mc Donough HS; White Plains, MD; (Y); Art Clb; Latin Clb; JV Bsbl; JV Socr; Hon Roll; Magna Cum Laude Awd Ntl Latn Soc 83-85; Cert Rcktry Wrkshp 84-85; Art Coll; Cmmrcl Art.

KENNEY, SHAWNA; Great Mills HS; California, MD; (Y); Lib Band; Jazz Band; Pep Band; Symp Band; Nwsp Rptr; Nwsp Stf; Hon Roll; NEDT Awd; Syracuse U; TV Brdcstg.

KENT III, EDGAR ROBERT; Gilman Schl; Baltimore, MD; (Y); 1/93; Church Yth Grp; Model UN; Varsity Clb; Yrbk Ed-Chief; JV Lcrss; Var Socr; Im Wt Lftg; High Hon Roll; Ntl Merit SF; Val; Cum Laude Soc; Harvard U Bk Prize; Bus.

KERHIN, JENNIFER; Parkville HS; Baltimore, MD; (Y); Am Leg Aux Girls St; Church Yth Grp; Girl Scts; Science Clb; Band; Trs Jr Cls; Var Badmtn; Var Capt Socr; Var Tennis; Hon Roll; 1st Pl Archdcs Drama Comptn 86; Intl Finc.

KERNEY, DAVID; St Andrews Episcopal Schl; Bethesda, MD; (Y); Boy Scts; French Clb; Model UN; Ski Clb; Pres Frsh Cls; Rep Soph Cls; Pres Stu Cncl; Var Capt Lcrss; Var L Socr; Church Yth Grp; Hugh O Brien Ldrshp Awd 85; Natl Squash 84; Acolyte Capt 85-86.

KERR, CINDY; Roland Park Country Schl; Baltimore, MD; (Y); Art Clb; Church Yth Grp; Drama Clb; Model UN; Pep Clb; Teachers Aide; Chorus; Stage Crew; Nwsp Phtg; Lit Mag; Poem Pblshd Susquehanna U Mgzn 86.

KERR, DANIEL C; Howard HS; Elkridge, MD; (Y); 6/280; Band; Concert Band; Jazz Band; Mrchg Band; School Musical; Symp Band; High Hon Roll; NHS; Ntl Merit Ltr; MD All-ST Orchstra 86; U Of MD.

KERR JR, JAMES H; Howard HS; Columbia, MD; (Y); Church Yth Grp; Civic Clb; Teachers Aide; Band; Church Choir; Mrchg Band; Symp Band; Nwsp Ed-Chief; Yrbk Bus Mgr; Rep Stu Cncl; Natl Achvt Schlrshp 85; NASA Smmn Apprntcshp Resh Prgm; Nvl Acad Smmn Smnr; Intro To Engrng Smnr U MD; Engrng.

KERR, MELISSA; Bethesda-Chevy Chase HS; Somerset, MD; (Y); 23/449; Camp Fr Inc; Computer Clb; Dance Clb; French Clb; Hon Roll; Ntl Merit Ltr; Bryn Mawr.

KERSHNER, DAVID; Williamsport HS; Hagerstown, MD; (Y); 1/223; Rep Stu Cncl; High Hon Roll; NHS; Prfct Atten Awd; Olympcs Of The Mind 83-86; Utley Co Covr Art Cntst 2nd Pl 85; Knowledge Mstr 84-86; Arch.

KESSELL, WENDY MICHELLE; Linganore HS; Monrovia, MD; (Y); VP Drama Clb; FCA; French Clb; VP Pep Clb; Red Cross Aide; Rep Frsh Cls; Rep Soph Cls; Rep Jr Cls; Rep Sr Cls; Rep Stu Cncl; Soroptomist Schlrshp Of Young Achvt 86; Lions Clb Schlrshp 86; MD Teen Miss Chrmn 85; George Mason U; Law.

KETCHUM, SARAH; Immaculata College HS; Washington, DC; (Y); Cmnty Wkr; Drama Clb; French Clb; Math Clb; Orch; Sec Trs Frsh Cls; VP Soph Cls; Pres Jr Cls; Pres Sr Cls; High Hon Roll; Psych.

KETTERMAN, JAMES; Catoctin HS; Thurmont, MD; (Y); 11/198; 4-H; Ski Clb; Teachers Aide; Band; Concert Band; Mrchg Band; Tennis; Trk; Hon Roll; Amer Legn Awd 86; Ruritan Awd 86; U Of MD; Fin.

KEVAS, GEORGE; Patterson HS; Baltimore, MD; (Y); JV Var Socr; Aerontcl Engr.

KEYS, ELIZABETH; Stone Ridge Country Day Schl; Bethesda, MD; (Y); Chorus; Madrigals; School Musical; School Play; Rep Frsh Cls; Pres Soph Cls; High Hon Roll; Ntl Merit Ltr; Chorus Awd 84-85; Musicl Theatr.

KEYS-SMITH, LEANNE; St Johns At Prospect Hall HS; Baltimore, MD; (Y); French Clb; Science Clb; Ski Clb; Cheerleading; Sftbl; Vllybl; Hon Roll; NHS; Natl Hnr Rl 85-86; Duquesne U; Psych.

KHANNA, RITU; Colonel Zadou Magruder HS; Rockville, MD; (Y); Art Clb; German Clb; Latin Clb; Math Clb; Math Tm; Red Cross Aide; Teachers Aide; Nwsp Rptr; Bausch & Lomb Sci Awd; Cit Awd; Montgomery Cnty Sci Fair-Botany 86; Bst Story Yr-Jrnlsm Awd 83; Hnrs Schlrshp Rutgrs U NJ 86; Biomedcl Engr.

KHAROD, CHETAN; Queen Anne Schl; Andrews Afb, MD; (Y); Model UN; Pep Band; VP Symp Band; Frsh Cls; Jr Cls; Stu Cncl; Var Bsbl; Socr; High Hon Roll; NCTE Awd; Cum Laude Soc 86; Cngrsnl Schlr Ntl Yth Ldrshp Cncl 86.

KIBUNJA, VICKY; Springbrook HS; Silver Spring, MD; (Y); Church Yth Grp; Dance Clb; Pep Clb; Cheerleading; Harvard U; Bus.

KIEBLER, DIANA; North Harford HS; Whiteford, MD; (Y); Cmnty Wkr; 4-H; JA; Spanish Clb; SADD; Teachers Aide; Varsity Clb; Score Keeper; Var Socr; JV Sftbl; Prfrmnc Awd, Vrsty Lttrs 86; The Medix Schl; Mdcl Asst.

KIGGINS, JENNIFER; Notre Dame Preparatory Schl; Baltimore, MD; (Y); Church Yth Grp; Im Vllybl; Hon Roll; NEDT Awd; Educ.

KILLEEN, CHIMAINE; Laurel HS; Laurel, MD; (Y); Pres Soph Cls; Rep Stu Cncl; Var Swmmng; Var Trk; Var Vllybl; Hon Roll; Med & Hlth Sci Fair 2nd Pl 85; Outstndng Scholar Area Civics 84; Outstndng Geo WA U Vllybl Camp 84-85; U NC; Photogrphy.

KILMON, MICHAEL; St Michaels SR HS; St Michaels, MD; (Y); 5/60; Am Leg Boys St; Chess Clb; Cmnty Wkr; Teachers Aide; JV Bsktbl; Hon Roll; Electronic Engineering.

KILPE, PETER G; Centennial HS; Columbia, MD; (Y); Art Clb; Cmnty Wkr; Ski Clb; Band; 3rd Pl Graphic Dsgn Comp 85; Rl Schl Of Dsgn; Grphc Dsgn.

KIM, ALEXIS; Lansdowne HS; Baltimore, MD; (Y); Cmnty Wkr; Drama Clb; Hosp Aide; Pres Key Clb; Chorus; School Musical; Variety Show; Hon Roll; NHS; Opt Clb Awd; Cpt Its Acadmcs; MD Acad Sci Smnrs; Mst Outstndng F Soph 85.

KIM, DONG; Joppatowne HS; Edgewood, MD; (Y); Church Yth Grp; Cmnty Wkr; Teachers Aide; Var Socr; High Hon Roll; Hon Roll; NHS; Prfct Atten Awd; Vrsty Ltr, Pin, Athltc Awd 85-86; Engrng.

KIM, EUGENE; Georgetown Prep; Potomac, MD; (Y); 17/107; Math Clb; Nwsp Stf; Rep Frsh Cls; Im Bsktbl; JV Golf; Var Socr; JV Trk; Var Wrstlng; Hon Roll; NEDT Awd.

KIM, GRACE; Riverdale Baptist Schl; New Carrollton, MD; (Y); 7/64; Hosp Aide; Church Choir; Trs Frsh Cls; Sec Soph Cls; Rep Stu Cncl; JV Var Cheerleading; Amer Chrstn Hnr Soc 85; Hmcmg Ct 82 & 84; Math Coll Prof.

KIM, JENNIFER; Wheaton HS; Silver Spring, MD; (Y); Latin Clb; Office Aide; Sec SADD; Teachers Aide; Rep Stu Cncl; Var Capt Pom Pon; Hon Roll; Jr NHS; NHS; Stu Of Mnth HS For Acdmcs 86; Achvmnt Awd Excllnc Frnch 84&86; Cert Apprctn Companion Trng Crs 85; Psychlgy.

KIM, JOANN; Immaculata College HS; Rockville, MD; (Y); Cmnty Wkr; French Clb; Sec German Clb; Hosp Aide; Math Clb; VP Science Clb; Orch; High Hon Roll; German II Lang,Hist Awd 86; Ntl Piano Plyng Audtns 85.

KIM, KENNETH; Arlington Baptist Schl; Baltimore, MD; (S); 7/58; Orch; VP Frsh Cls; VP Soph Cls; Pres Jr Cls; Var Bsbl; Var Socr; High Hon Roll; VP NHS; Prfct Atten Awd; Military Acad; Engrng.

KIM, LISA; Hammond HS; Columbia, MD; (Y); Church Yth Grp; French Clb; Nwsp Rptr; Rep Soph Cls; Rep Jr Cls; Co-Capt Pom Pon; Hon Roll; NHS; Schlrshp Peabody Consrvtry Of Mus 83-84; Law.

KIM, MIKE; Laurel SR HS; Laurel, MD; (Y); U Of MD; Engnrng.

KIM, MIN; Eleanor Roosevelt HS; Seabrook, MD; (Y); AFS; VP Church Yth Grp; Exploring; Nwsp Stf; JV Cheerleading; High Hon Roll; Magna Cum Laude-Natl Latin Exam 85; MD Acad Of Sci 86; PG Cnty Outstndng Acadmc Achvt Awd 85 & 86.

KIM, MIN; Kenwood HS; Baltimore, MD; (Y); Church Yth Grp; SADD; Varsity Clb; Nwsp Ed-Chief; Off Sr Cls; Sec Stu Cncl; JV Capt Cheerleading; Var JV Fld Hcky; Hon Roll; NHS; Jrnlst.

KIM, MOONSU; Walt Whitman HS; Silver Spring, MD; (Y); 64/445; Art Clb; French Clb; FBLA; Intnl Clb; JA; Orch; Jr Cls; Sr Cls; Hon Roll; Church Yth Grp; Cert Of Awd For Prfrmnc In Wrtng & Cert Of Merit For Frnch 84; U MD Coll Park; Doctor.

KIM, PHIL; Seneca Valley HS; Gaithersburg, MD; (Y); 51/486; Computer Clb; FFA; Office Aide; Ski Clb; Spanish Clb; Jazz Band; JV Mgr(s); Im Trk; Hon Roll; Carnegie Mellon U; Elec Engrng.

KIM, TAEHI; Thomas S Woolton HS; Rockville, MD; (Y); 38/401; Church Yth Grp; JA; Ski Clb; Stu Cncl; Stat Bsktbl; French Hon Soc; Hon Roll; NHS; Presdntl Acadmc Ftns Awd 85-86; Thomas Wootton Cert Merit Frgn Lang 85-86; Natl Hnr Roll 84-85; U Of MD; Life Sci.

KIM, TERESA; Archbishop Keough HS; Baltimore, MD; (Y); 10/220; Art Clb; French Clb; Chorus; School Musical; Nwsp Rptr; Nwsp Stf; Yrbk Stf; Rep Stu Cncl; Var JV Cheerleading; Hon Roll; U Of MD Balto Co; Optometry.

KIM, TOM; Mt Hebron HS; Ellicott City, MD; (Y); Pres German Clb; Chorus; Church Choir; Madrigals; School Musical; Stu Cncl; Hon Roll; All Estrn Hnrs Chrs 85; Pre-Med.

KIM, YOU; Mount Saint Joseph HS; Baltimore, MD; (Y); Chrmn Church Yth Grp; FCA; Q&S; Church Choir; Flag Corp; Variety Show; Hon Roll; Merit Awd-Maitland Art Fest Stu Div 84; 1st Pl Taw Kwon Do Comp In Form 86; Encrgmnt Awd Art Fest 81; U Of MD; Dntstry.

KIMBALL, KRISTIN; Archbishop Keough HS; Balt, MD; (Y); Church Yth Grp; Drama Clb; GAA; Teachers Aide; JV Cheerleading; Gym; JV Sftbl; Typing Hnr Rl 86; Typing Profcncy Cert 59 Net Wrds 86; U S Naval Acad.

KIMBERLY, PRIETZ; Patterson HS; Baltimore, MD; (Y); Bus.

KIMBROUGH, MYLA; Bethesda Chevy Chase HS; Chevy Chase, MD; (S); DECA; Mgr(s); Capt Pom Pon; Hon Roll; DECA Hnrbl Mntn Ntl Cmptn 86; NAACP Yth Cncl 85-86; Blck Awrnss Clb 84-86; Comms.

KIMMEL, HOLLY; Frederick HS; Frederick, MD; (Y); 37/307; Chess Clb; Pres Church Yth Grp; German Clb; Teachers Aide; Chorus; Variety Show; Stu Cncl; Mgr(s); Score Keeper; Sftbl; Music Awds; Hood; Tchr.

KINES, STEPHANIE ANN; Linganore HS; Monrovia, MD; (Y); 15/270; Am Leg Aux Girls St; Spanish Clb; Sec Soph Cls; Pres Sr Cls; DAR Awd; NHS; Rotary Awd; Church Yth Grp; Intnl Clb; Teachers Aide; Ruth E & Mary E Smith Schlrshp 86; Brigham Young U Ldrshp Schlrshp 86; John Loats Fund 86; Brigham Young U; Hmn Resrc Devl.

KING, DAWN; Bohemia Manor HS; Cecilton, MD; (Y); 4/105; Church Yth Grp; Computer Clb; Debate Tm; Drama Clb; French Clb; Spanish Clb; Band; Yrbk Stf; Pres Jr Cls; Trs Stu Cncl; Lang Intrprtr.

KING, DONNA; La Plata HS; Waldorf, MD; (Y); German Clb; Hosp Aide; Math Tm; Pep Clb; Teachers Aide; Flag Corp; High Hon Roll; U Of MD Coll Pk ; Systms Anlys.

KING JR, JAMES; Prospect Hall HS; Frederick, MD; (Y); Chess Clb; Church Yth Grp; Ski Clb; Yrbk Sprt Ed; Var L Bsbl; Var L Bsktbl; Var L Crs Cntry; 1st Bptst Chrch Of Frdrck Schlrshp 86; MD ST Schlrshp 86; FCCA Bkstbl All Star 85-86; U MD Bltmr Cnty; Ecnmcs.

KING, KARL; Queen Annes HS; Church Hill, MD; (Y); Church Yth Grp; 4-H; Varsity Clb; School Play; VP Jr Cls; Pres Sr Cls; Rep Stu Cncl; Ftbl; Lcrss; Hon Roll.

KING, SHARON; Maurice J Mc Donough HS; Waldorf, MD; (Y); FBLA; JV Cheerleading; Hon Roll; Bus Adm.

KINGWELL, KEN; Dulaney SR HS; Timonium, MD; (Y); Cmnty Wkr; JA; Red Cross Aide; Ski Clb; Trk; Hon Roll; NHS; Natl Latn Exm Cert Hnrbl Merit Magna Cm Laud 86; Bio.

KINLOCH, JULIE; Laurel HS; Laurel, MD; (Y); 3/425; Dance Clb; Drama Clb; School Musical; Variety Show; VP Sr Cls; Cheerleading; High Hon Roll; NHS; Ntl Merit SF; Rotary Awd; Rotry Clb Stu Mth 86; Clemson U SC; Mathmtcl Sci.

KIRBY, DOUGLAS; John Carroll HS; Bel Air, MD; (Y); 81/238; Camera Clb; Church Yth Grp; School Play; Hon Roll; Prfct Atten Awd; U MD; Elec Engr.

KIRCHNER, DAVID BRIAN; Smithsburg HS; Hagerstown, MD; (Y); Church Yth Grp; Latin Clb; Pep Clb; Stage Crew; Nwsp Rptr; Nwsp Stf; Yrbk Stf; Stu Cncl; L Bsktbl; Ftbl; U Of MD; Comp Pgmmg.

KIRK, EMILY; Queen Annes County HS; Grasonville, MD; (Y); 5/340; Am Leg Aux Girls St; Girl Scts; Q&S; Band; Nwsp Ed-Chief; Gov Hon Prg Awd; High Hon Roll; NHS; Pres Schlr; Rotary Awd; Its Acadmc Schlrshp; U Of Richmond; Math.

KIRK, SUZANNE; St Marys Ryken HS; Prince Frederick, MD; (S); Drama Clb; Office Aide; Teachers Aide; Stage Crew; Lit Mag; Trk; High Hon Roll; NEDT Awd; Phy Sci Sci Dept Hnr Cert 85; Spnsh I Hnr Schlrshp Cert 85; Geo Hnr Schlrshp Cert 84.

KIRKLAND JR, CHARLES B; Largo HS; Upper Marlboro, MD; (Y); Band; Concert Band; Flag Corp; Mrchg Band; School Musical; School Play; Stage Crew; Hon Roll; Drama Clb; French Clb; Pre-Med.

KIRKNER, MARY; Notre Dame Prep; Reistertown, MD; (Y); Church Yth Grp; Cmnty Wkr; Hosp Aide; Church Choir; School Play; Hon Roll; NEDT Awd; Im Badmtn; Im Fld Hcky; Im Socr; 2nd Optimist Oratorical Cntst 84; Yth Ldrshp Wkend Freedoms Fndtn 85; Christian Cmmnty Awrns Pgm 84-85.

KIRKSEY, WARREN; Northwestern HS; Hyattsville, MD; (Y); Church Yth Grp; 4-H; JA; Band; Rep Sr Cls; Stu Cncl; JV Bsktbl; Var Ftbl; Trk; Hon Roll; Howard; Bus.

KIRSCHBAUM, SHERRY; Lansdowne HS; Baltimore, MD; (Y); Key Clb; Chorus; Var Socr; Hon Roll; NHS; Acad All Amer 85-86; Towson ST; Scl Wrkr.

KIRSCHNICK, STEVE; Liberty HS; Sykesville, MD; (Y); Varsity Clb; Trs Frsh Cls; Rep Soph Cls; Rep Jr Cls; Rep Sr Cls; Rep Stu Cncl; Var L Ftbl; Var L Lcrss; Trk; Hon Roll; Bio Medical Engineering.

KIRSTEIN, STACEY; Oakland Mills HS; Columbia, MD; (Y); 98/250; Ski Clb; Spanish Clb; JV Bsktbl; JV Sftbl; Hon Roll; Mt St Marys Coll; Lbrl Arts.

KIRTINITIS, JOLIE; Glenelg HS; Glenelg, MD; (Y); Church Yth Grp; Cmnty Wkr; 4-H; French Clb; Hosp Aide; Intnl Clb; Red Cross Aide; Crs Cntry; Hon Roll; NHS; GATE Hnr Course Stu 84-86; Hgh Pt Horseshow Riding Champ 84-85; UWV; Phys Thrpy.

KISIELEWSKI, CONSTANCE; John Carroll HS; Fallston, MD; (Y); Stage Crew; Yrbk Phtg; Ed Yrbk Stf; Var Sftbl; Prfct Atten Awd; Spcl Svc Awd-Erth Sci 84-85; Hnrbl Mntn-Wise Use Energy Cntst 83-84; Archrl Engrng.

KISS, TIMOTHY; Good Counsel HS; Rockville, MD; (Y); Church Yth Grp; French Clb; VP Spanish Clb; Lit Mag; Im Bsktbl; Im Ftbl; Var Mgr(s); Var Socr; Im Vllybl; Hon Roll; Villanova; Engr.

KITCHENMAN, JENNIFER; Annapolis Area Christian HS; Arnold, MD; (S); 5/25; Church Yth Grp; Chorus; School Musical; Nwsp Rptr; Yrbk Stf; Sec Soph Cls; VP Jr Cls; Stu Cncl; Bsktbl; Socr; Messiah Coll.

KITTEL, JIM; Smithsburg HS; Hagerstown, MD; (Y); 49/176; Church Yth Grp; Cmnty Wkr; FFA; Ftbl; Prfct Atten Awd.

KITTRELL, BERNITA; Eastern HS; Baltimore, MD; (Y); FBLA; Band; High Hon Roll; Hon Roll; Prfct Atten Awd; Stu Of VIP 85-86; Morgan ST U; Acctng.

KLAFF, CHERYL; Charles E Smith Jewish Day Schl; Rockville, MD; (Y); Chrmn Service Clb; School Play; Rep Frsh Cls; Rep Soph Cls; Rep Jr Cls; JV Bsktbl; Var L Gym; Im Tennis; Spanish NHS.

KLANDER, LARS; Mt Hebron HS; Baltimore, MD; (Y); 8/260; Drama Clb; Math Clb; Scholastic Bowl; Mrchg Band; School Play; Symp Band; Var L Trk; High Hon Roll; NEDT Awd; Ski Clb; Full U Schlrshp U MD 86-90; U MD; Engrng.

KLAPKA, D MONIQUE; Notre Dame Prep; Baltimore, MD; (Y); Camera Clb; Cmnty Wkr; Hosp Aide; Office Aide; Ski Clb; SADD; Hon Roll; Im Badmtn; Im Bsktbl; Im Fld Hcky; Sci.

KLAUTKY, RUTH; Oakland Mills HS; Columbia, MD; (Y); 1/275; AFS; French Clb; Chorus; Mgr(s); Hon Roll; Ntl Achvt Fnlst 86; MD Dstngshd Schlr 86; Alpha Kappa Alpha Srorty Schlrshp Awd 86; Johns Hopkins; Biomdcl Engrng.

KLEBE, RACHEL; Sherwood HS; Olney, MD; (Y); Red Cross Aide; Spanish Clb; Nwsp Rptr; Nwsp Stf; Var Swmmng; Hon Roll; NHS; Spanish NHS; Cmnty Wkr; Jr NHS; Solo Pianist 83-84; Hnrs Smnr-U Of MD 85; US Swimming 83-86; Bus Cmnctns.

KLEIN, AMY; Oakland Mills HS; Columbia, MD; (Y); Debate Tm; Ski Clb; Trs Frsh Cls; Trs Soph Cls; Sec Jr Cls; Trs Sr Cls; Rep Stu Cncl; JV Var Mgr(s); JV Socr; Hon Roll.

KLEIN, CATHY; Laurel HS; Laurel, MD; (Y); Dance Clb; Office Aide; Church Choir; Orch; School Musical; Hon Roll; Outstndng Achvt Awd-Psych 86; U Of MD; Socl Wkr.

KLEIN, KAREN LEE; Perry Hall HS; Baltimore, MD; (Y); Office Aide; Spanish Clb; Chorus; Sec Soph Cls; Sec Jr Cls; Pres Stu Cncl; Powder Puff Ftbl; Hon Roll; Pres Schlr; Janis Jffry Hrris Ldrshp Awd 86; Gaucher.

KLEIN, RANDI; Gaithersburg HS; Gaithersburg, MD; (Y); Drama Clb; Hosp Aide; SADD; Teachers Aide; VP Temple Yth Grp; School Musical; School Play; JV Var Cheerleading; High Hon Roll; Stage Crew; Engrng.

KLEINBAUER, MEGAN; Eastern Vo Tech; Baltimore, MD; (Y); VP VICA; Yrbk Rptr; Sec Stu Cncl; Var Capt Bsktbl; Var Tennis; Var Capt Vllybl; Hon Roll; NHS; Baltimore Sun Athlt Of Wk 86; All Cnty 1st Tm Bsktbl 83-85; Bltmr Cnty Tnns Grls Dbls Chmpn 85; Sprts Trnr.

KLEM, ADENA; Gaithersburg HS; Gaithersburg, MD; (Y); Drama Clb; Office Aide; Temple Yth Grp; Chorus; School Musical; Stage Crew; Swing Chorus; Pom Pon; High Hon Roll; NHS; Placed In Horseshows 85-86; Psych.

KLINE, IAN; Middletown HS; Middletown, MD; (Y); 5/205; Band; Drm Mjr(t); School Musical; Var Socr; Capt Var Trk; High Hon Roll; NHS; Ntl Merit Ltr; Pres Schlr; VFW Awd; Cornell U; Pre Law.

KLINE, JENNIFER; Middletown HS; Chadds Ford, PA; (Y); 14/206; Church Yth Grp; Intnl Clb; Spanish Clb; Teachers Aide; Diving; Swmmng; Trk; Hon Roll; NHS; $250 Schlrshp Excllnc Spnsh Dept 86; U Of DE; Ntrtn & Hlth Fied.

KLINE, KELLI; Fort Hill HS; Cumberland, MD; (Y); Sec Church Yth Grp; Drill Tm; Off Frsh Cls; Off Soph Cls; Off Jr Cls; Pom Pon; Stat Wrstlng; Hon Roll; Nrsng.

KLINE III, KENNETH D; Williamsport HS; Hagerstown, MD; (Y); 17/218; Drama Clb; Exploring; Ski Clb; Chorus; School Musical; School Play; Stage Crew; French Hon Soc; Hon Roll; Hagerstown JC Fclty/Fndtn Schlrshp-Acad Excllnc 86-87; SR Suprltv-Most Dramatic 86; Hagerstown JC; Engrng.

KLINE, KRISTIN ANN; Elkton HS; Elkton, MD; (Y); 5/289; Teachers Aide; Capt Color Guard; Sec Soph Cls; Var L Tennis; Gov Hon Prg Awd; High Hon Roll; NHS; SAR Awd; Cmnty Wkr; Drama Clb; Elkton Womens Civic Club Schlrshp 86-87; U Of DE Schlrshp 86-87; U Of DE; Bus Admin.

KLINE, MICHELLE; Lackey HS; Indian Head, MD; (Y); FBLA; Teachers Aide; Bowling; JV Sftbl; Hon Roll; U MD; Bus Adm.

KLINE, MONICA; Allegany HS; Cumberland, MD; (Y); AFS; FBLA; Pep Clb; Ski Clb; Drill Tm; Rep Frsh Cls; Rep Soph Cls; Var Cheerleading; Stat Vllybl; Hon Roll; Bio.

KLOETZEL, JENNIFER M; Catonsville HS; Catonsville, MD; (Y); Madrigals; Orch; School Musical; School Play; Sec Jr Cls; Sec Sr Cls; Hon Roll; Pres NHS; AFS; Church Yth Grp; Dist Schlr MD 85-86; Arts Recgntn & Tlnt 86; Cellist.

KLOPCIC, J THADDEUS; John Carroll HS; Bel Air, MD; (Y); 3/250; Latin Clb; Scholastic Bowl; Acpl Chr; Jazz Band; School Musical; JV Ftbl; Bausch & Lomb Sci Awd; High Hon Roll; NHS; Boy Scts; US Naval Acad Smmr Sem 86; Russian Hnr Sco 85; Engrng.

KLOSE, J MICHAEL; St Marys HS; Annapolis, MD; (Y); 41/118; Ski Clb; Stage Crew; Nwsp Stf; JV Var Lcrss; Capt Var Socr; Soccr All Cnty, Plyr Of Wk 85-86; Soccr MVP 86; UNSUNG Hero 86; Loyola College; Acctg.

KLOTZ, LORI; Northern Garrett HS; Friendsville, MD; (Y); Ski Clb; Teachers Aide; Band; Chorus; Concert Band; Mrchg Band; Pep Band; Hon Roll; Allegany Comm Hosp; Med Lab Tec.

KLUG, MELINDA; Shertwood HS; Brookeville, MD; (Y); Church Yth Grp; Dance Clb; German Clb; SADD; Variety Show; Var Vllybl; Hon Roll; Prncpls Awd Outstndng Wrtng 85; Cmnctns.

KLUG JR, RICHARD; Frederick HS; Frederick, MD; (Y); Boy Scts; Computer Clb; Concert Band; Jazz Band; Mrchg Band; Var L Golf; Hon Roll; FFA; Spanish Clb; SADD; Eagle Scout 83; Frederick Co Consrvtn Workshp 84; Frostburg ST Coll; Wildlife.

KNAPP, LORRAINE; The Catholic High School Of Balto; Baltimore, MD; (Y); 12/200; Drama Clb; English Clb; Mathletes; Trs Math Clb; School Musical; Stage Crew; High Hon Roll; Hon Roll; Pres Schlr; St Frncs Coll IN Hnr Schlrshp 86; Spcl Educ.

KNAPTON, MARY A; C Milton Wright HS; Churchville, MD; (Y); Art Clb; Band; Mrchg Band; Crs Cntry; Swmmng; Tennis; Trk; Hon Roll; NHS; St Schlr; Rochester Inst Alumni Schlrshp 86; MD Inst Art Schlrshp 86; Pratt Schlrshp 86; Rochester Inst; Medcl Illustrn.

KNEESSI, KATHRYN; Walter Johnson HS; Bethesda, MD; (Y); Ed Yrbk Stf; Var JV Cheerleading; Hon Roll; Spanish NHS; Teachers Aide.

KNEIPP, GREGG; Parkdale HS; College Park, MD; (S); Boy Scts; Camera Clb; Band; Jazz Band; Pep Band; School Musical; Symp Band; Nwsp Phtg; Yrbk Phtg; Hon Roll.

KNIGHT, KERRY; Lansdowne HS; Baltimore, MD; (Y); Church Yth Grp; Sec Key Clb; Teachers Aide; School Musical; Variety Show; Var Mgr Bsbl; Mgr(s); Var Mgr Socr; Var Mgr Wrstlng; Hon Roll; Bus Admin.

KNIGHT, KIM; Sherwood HS; Silver Spg, MD; (Y); Church Yth Grp; Dance Clb; Pep Clb; SADD; Flag Corp; Mrchg Band; School Musical; Rep Frsh Cls; Rep Soph Cls; Rep Jr Cls; Stu Vlntr Ntl Inst Hlth 85; Bio.

KNIGHT, RANDALL; Allegany HS; Cumberland, MD; (Y); Boy Scts; Office Aide; SADD; Thesps; School Play; Stage Crew; Off Jr Cls; Sec Stu Cncl; JV Ftbl; Var Trk; Hurrican Island Outward Bound Schl 85; Mount St Marys; Poli Sci.

KNIGHT, REBECCA C; Mount Hebron HS; Cockeysville, MD; (Y); 5/207; AFS; Cmnty Wkr; Library Aide; Frsh Cls; Bausch & Lomb Sci Awd; High Hon Roll; Hon Roll; NHS; Ntl Merit Ltr; Opt Clb Awd; Grad Cert Bllet Pbdy Inst 83; Jhns Hpkns Schlrshp 85; Johns Hopkins U; Med.

KNIPPENBERG, RANAE; Bishop Walsh HS; Cumberland, MD; (Y); Church Yth Grp; Cmnty Wkr; Political Wkr; Band; Chorus; Church Choir; Concert Band; Jazz Band; Mrchg Band; Pep Band; Prncpl Hnrs Tlnt Show 1st Pl 85-86; Bnd & Jazz Bnd Ltr 84-85; U Of MD; Optometry.

KNISLEY, SUSAN; Allegany HS; Cresaptown, MD; (Y); 24/233; AFS; Drama Clb; Church Choir; Orch; Nwsp Bus Mgr; Nwsp Stf; NHS; Church Yth Grp; Pep Clb; SADD; 1st Pl Trphy Tlnt For Jesus Comptn 85; Sntrl Schlrshp; Frostburg ST Coll; Music.

KNITTLE, MANDY; St Pauls Schl For Girls; Phoenix, MD; (Y); AFS; Art Clb; Camera Clb; Hosp Aide; Key Clb; Model UN; Ski Clb; SADD; Nwsp Sprt Ed; Trs Jr Cls.

KNOTT, VICKI; Queen Anne Schl; Bowie, MD; (Y); Drama Clb; Library Aide; Model UN; Varsity Clb; Chorus; School Musical; Stage Crew; Nwsp Stf; Yrbk Stf; Lit Mag; Queens Coll; Secndry Ed.

KNOTTS, KEVIN; Paul Laurence Dunbar HS; Baltimore, MD; (Y); English Clb; Band; Concert Band; Var Trk; Hon Roll; 2nd Ctywide Blck Hstry Cntst 86; Schlrshp Engl Awd 86; U Of MD.

KNOTTS, LEIGH S; Southern Garrett HS; Kitzmiller, MD; (S); Church Yth Grp; German Clb; Pep Clb; SADD; Sec Frsh Cls; Sec Soph Cls; Sec Jr Cls; Rep Stu Cncl; High Hon Roll; NHS; U MD; Phrmcy.

KNOWLES, CECILY; Liberty HS; Westminster, MD; (Y); 4-H; Mathletes; Teachers Aide; Varsity Clb; Rep Frsh Cls; JV Var Fld Hcky; Powder Puff Ftbl; Var L Trk; Hon Roll; U Of MD; Engr.

KNOWLES, KRISTINE; Kenwood SR HS; Baltimore, MD; (Y); Art Clb; SADD; Cit Awd; Hon Roll; Art Awd 82 & 83; MD Inst Art; Intr Dsgn.

KNOWLTON, ANDREA; St Marys Ryken HS; California, MD; (S); Church Yth Grp; Cmnty Wkr; Spanish Clb; Chorus; Church Choir; School Musical; Var Bsktbl; Var Sftbl; Rep Stu Cncl; Capt Crs Cntry; Spnsh Awd 83-85; U S Hstry Awd 85; Phy Sci Awd 85; Hlth.

KNOX, PEGGY; Southern Garrett HS; Deer Pk, MD; (Y); 13/221; Church Yth Grp; NHS; Hazelwd Schlrshp; Alderson Broaddus; Math.

KOCH, VIVIAN; Beall SR-JR HS; Frostburg, MD; (Y); 1/163; Church Yth Grp; VP Pres Thesps; Band; Chorus; Church Choir; Jazz Band; Nwsp Ed-Chief; JV Var Vllybl; NHS; Ntl Merit Ltr; GSA Slvr Awd 83; Jrnlsm.

KOCHANSKI, RICHARD; Liberty HS; Eldersburg, MD; (S); Mathletes; JV Socr; Hon Roll; Comp Sci.

KOENIG, TANYA; Great Mills HS; Great Mills, MD; (Y); Church Yth Grp; Dance Clb; Science Clb; Variety Show; High Hon Roll; Hon Roll; Prfct Atten Awd; Achvmnt In Geo, Alg II & Compu Math I 84-86; Liberal Arts Coll; Math.

KOERMER, KELLY; Maryvale Prep; Freeland, MD; (Y); 7/48; Pres Church Yth Grp; Church Choir; Yrbk Phtg; Coach Actv; JV Fld Hcky; JV Lcrss; Vllybl; High Hon Roll; NHS; Vangoard Schlrshp Villa Julie Coll 86; Villa Julie Coll; Law.

KOKOSKI, JENNIFER ROSEMARY; Archbishop Keough HS; Ellicott, MD; (Y); Cmnty Wkr; Drama Clb; Hosp Aide; Science Clb; Acpl Chr; Chorus; Stage Crew; Rep Frsh Cls; Rep Soph Cls; Hd Cmmtee Advs Schl Chngs Mk Handicapable; U Of MD; Chld Psych.

KOLANDER, RAYNA; Parkdale HS; Lanham, MD; (Y); French Clb; Yrbk Sprt Ed; Pom Pon; Cit Awd; DAR Awd; French Hon Soc; High Hon Roll; Outstndng Acadmc Achvt Presdntl Acadmc Ftns Awd 86; Alumni Cls 76 Schlrshp 86; Acadmc Ltr 86; U Of MD Coll Pk.

KOLBFLEISCH, SUSIE; Northern HS; Accident, MD; (Y); Sec Church Yth Grp; Yrbk Stf; Rep Frsh Cls; Rep Jr Cls; Church Yth Grp; Var Capt Cheerleading; Hon Roll; Prfct Atten Awd; Best All-Arnd Chrldr Awd 84; Psych.

KOLUCH, JANET; Institute Of Notre Dame; Baltimore, MD; (Y); FBLA; Office Aide; Service Clb; High Hon Roll; Marion Burke Knott Full Tuition Schlrshp 83-87.

KONG, JILLIAN; Oakland Mills HS; Columbia, MD; (Y); Dance Clb; French Clb; Speech Tm; Madrigals; School Musical; School Play; Off Frsh Cls; Off Soph Cls; Rep Jr Cls; Off Sr Cls; Delta Sigma Theta Sorority Deb 86; Intl Rel.

KOPIT, WENDY; Rockville HS; Rockville, MD; (S); 35/464; AFS; Key Clb; SADD; Nwsp Stf; NHS; Mth.

KOPPENHAFER, MAUREEN; Gaithersburg HS; Gaithersburg, MD; (Y); Cmnty Wkr; Pep Clb; Teachers Aide; Var L Crs Cntry; JV Var Trk; High Hon Roll; Hon Roll; Jr NHS; NHS; Spanish NHS; Bus.

KOPPI, JEFFREY A; John F Kennedy HS; Silver Spring, MD; (Y); 39/468; Church Yth Grp; Nwsp Bus Mgr; JV Ftbl; Var Swmmng; Hon Roll; Ntl Merit Ltr; U Of MD; Compu Sci.

KORNAK, EUGENE P; Archbishop Curley HS; Baltimore, MD; (S); 1/137; Camera Clb; Cmnty Wkr; Computer Clb; Hosp Aide; Mathletes; Math Clb; Math Tm; Quiz Bowl; Science Clb; Nwsp Stf; Archbshp Crly Awd 84 & 85; Lwrnce Crdnl Shehan Awd 83; Pre-Med.

KORNEGAY, STACIE; Forestville HS; Suitland, MD; (Y); Computer Clb; VICA; Gym; Hon Roll; Rep Soph Cls; Law.

KOROPECKYJ, ULANA; Archbishop Keough HS; Baltimore, MD; (Y); German Clb; Girl Scts; Pres Quiz Bowl; Yrbk Stf; Rep Stu Cncl; Var Capt Vllybl; Hon Roll; NHS.

KOURTESIS, LAURIE; Mercy HS; Baltimore, MD; (Y); Church Yth Grp; Cmnty Wkr; Library Aide; Yrbk Stf; Stu Cncl; Hon Roll; Prfct Atten Awd; Algbra II Awd 85; Med.

KOVACH, DARIN M; Washington HS; Princess Anne, MD; (Y); Am Leg Boys St; Boys Clb Am; Chorus; Var Bsbl; Var Bsktbl; JV Var Ftbl; NHS.

KOVACH, JOHN; St Marys Ryken HS; Aquasco, MD; (S); 9/138; Church Yth Grp; Political Wkr; VP Spanish Clb; Nwsp Bus Mgr; Stu Cncl; Crs Cntry; Trk; NHS; MD Dstngshd Schlr 85; Stu Page MD Hse Delgts 86; NC ST; Engr.

KOVALCHICK, CHARLES DAVID; Frederick HS; Frederick, MD; (Y); Computer Clb; German Clb; JCL; Latin Clb; Rep Frsh Cls; Rep Soph Cls; Rep Jr Cls; Socr; Tennis; Hon Roll; Bio.

KOVALSKY, ERIC; Rockville HS; Silver Spring, MD; (Y); 1/482; Co-Capt Quiz Bowl; Variety Show; Ed Nwsp Stf; Wt Lftg; Pres NHS; Ntl Merit SF; Val; Key Clb; Mathletes; SADD; George Washngtn U Math/Sci Awd 85; Natl Chmpshp Knwldge Mstr Opn Acad Tournmnt 86; Rampage Nwsper; Northwestern U; Med.

KOVANDA, ELIZABETH C; Arundel SR HS; Gambrills, MD; (Y); 18/455; Church Yth Grp; Chrmn Red Cross Aide; Teachers Aide; Chorus; Church Choir; VP Stu Cncl; Var JV Fld Hcky; Hon Roll; Masonic Awd; NHS; Mabel Parker Educ Schlrshp 86; Intl Sci & Engrng Fair 83; U MD College Park; Educ.

KOWALSKI, JOSEPH; Archbishop Curley HS; Baltimore, MD; (S); 5/132; Ftbl; Debate Tm; Quiz Bowl; Scholastic Bowl; Nwsp Phtg; Nwsp Rptr; High Hon Roll; Hon Roll; Ltr Merit 85; Loyola Coll; Lwyr.

KOWALSKI, MELISSA; Montgomery Blair HS; Silver Spg, MD; (Y); Drama Clb; Latin Clb; SADD; Teachers Aide; Thesps; Chorus; Stage Crew; Trk; Hon Roll; NHS; 2nd Pl Sci Fair 84, 3rd Pl 86; Creatv Wrtng.

KRACH, CONSTANCE A; Kenwood HS; Baltimore, MD; (Y); 1/270; Library Aide; Quiz Bowl; Red Cross Aide; Ed Lit Mag; Sec Jr Cls; Sec Sr Cls; Rep Stu Cncl; DAR Awd; High Hon Roll; Hon Roll; Frostburg ST Coll; Bus Adm.

KRAFT, DANIEL; Montgomery Blain HS; Silver Spring, MD; (Y); 5/360; Jazz Band; Mrchg Band; School Musical; Trs Sr Cls; Stu Cncl; Bausch & Lomb Sci Awd; Pres Schlr; Science Clb; Ski Clb; Temple Yth Grp; 1st Grnd Prz Microbiol 85; Intl Sci & Engrng Fair 85-86; 1st Pl Natl Navy Sci Comp 86; JR Sci & Human; Brown U; Med.

KRAFT, LAURI; Atholton HS; Fulton, MD; (Y); 1/280; Sec Pep Clb; Teachers Aide; Trs Chorus; High Hon Roll; NHS; Pres Schlr; St Schlr; Howard Cnty Hnrs Chrs 85-86; MD Distngshd Schlr 85-86; Frnch Awd 85-86; U Of MD; Aerosp Engrg.

KRAMER, EVELYN; St Vincent Pallotti HS; Lauret, MD; (S); Art Clb; Dance Clb; German Clb; Variety Show; Var Pom Pon; German Hnr Socy 85; MD U; Cmnctns.

KRAMER, PETER A; Gaithersburg HS; Gaithersburg, MD; (Y); 69/568; Computer Clb; JA; Ski Clb; SADD; Off Frsh Cls; Vllybl; French Hon Soc; Hon Roll; JETS Awd; Jr NHS; U MD; Arntcl Engrng.

KRANTZ, BRAD; St Michaels HS; St Michaels, MD; (Y); Pres 4-H; Spanish Clb; SADD; Nwsp Phtg; Nwsp Rptr; Rep Frsh Cls; Rep Soph Cls; Rep Jr Cls; Pres Sr Cls; JV Crs Cntry; High Point Coll; Psychol.

KRANZ, JOSHUA; Charles E Smith Jewish Day Schl; Brookeville, MD; (Y); Trs Temple Yth Grp; Thesps; School Play; Variety Show; Nwsp Sprt Ed; Lit Mag; Rep Frsh Cls; JV Var Bsktbl; JV Socr; Jets Engrng Tst Hgh Score Cmmndtn 86; Amer Hgh Schl Math Exam Hgh Scorer 86; MD Math Leag 86.

KRAUCH, KELLY S; Linganore HS; Monrovia, MD; (Y); Teachers Aide; Pres Soph Cls; Capt L Fld Hcky; Var L Gym; Var Capt Powder Puff Ftbl; Var L Trk; Hon Roll; VFW Awd; Rep Frsh Cls; Rep Jr Cls; Natl Schlr Ath Awd 86; MVP Fld Hockey 85; Mst Outstndng Trck Rnnr 84; Shippensburg U; Bus Admin.

KRAUCH, MICHAEL RENE; Easton HS; Easton, MD; (Y); Spanish Clb; Teachers Aide; Soph Cls; Jr Cls; Sr Cls; Stu Cncl; Hon Roll; Trs NHS; Scl Sci Fair 2nd Pl Essay Cmpttn 86.

KRCMA, KATHY; Linganore HS; Monrovia, MD; (Y); Trs 4-H; Pres German Clb; Teachers Aide; Flag Corp; Mrchg Band; Hon Roll; Acdmc Achvmnt 86; Mst Imprvd Slk Awd 83; Frederick CC; Elem Educ.

KREILING, DAVID; Dulaney SR HS; Lutherville, MD; (Y); Church Yth Grp; Cmnty Wkr; Hon Roll; Engrng.

KREMER, JILL A; Southern Garrett HS; Oakland, MD; (S); 5/221; School Play; Trs Frsh Cls; Stu Cncl; Cheerleading; High Hon Roll; Hon Roll; NHS; Ntl Merit Ltr; U Of MD College Park; Physcs.

KRIGBAUM, KIM; Brunswick HS; Brunswick, MD; (Y); 17/157; Church Yth Grp; Spanish Clb; Chorus; Concert Band; Capt Flag Corp; Mrchg Band; School Musical; Capt JV Cheerleading; Var JV Crs Cntry; Hon Roll; Fredricks All Co Choir,Band 81-85; Fredrick Giftd Talntd Pgm 86-87; Music.

KRISHER, RHONDA; Patterson HS; Baltimore, MD; (Y); Girl Scts; Pres SADD; Thesps; Stage Crew; Nwsp Rptr; Yrbk Ed-Chief; VP Pres Stu Cncl; Stat Lcrss; Var Tennis; Hon Roll; Theatr.

KRONSCHNABEL, PETER; Crossland HS; Ft Washington, MD; (Y); Church Yth Grp; Drama Clb; School Musical; School Play; Yrbk Phtg; Yrbk Rptr; Yrbk Stf; Accntng.

KRUPIN, STEPHANIE; Gaithersburg HS; Gaithersburg, MD; (Y); Art Clb; SADD; Temple Yth Grp; Pom Pon; Hon Roll; NHS; Natl Art Hnr Soc 86; U Of MD; Advtsg Dsgn.

KRUSH, PAUL; Chopticon HS; Mechanicsville, MD; (Y); 1/250; Model UN; Pres Sr Cls; Var Capt Socr; Var Capt Wrstlng; NHS; SAR Awd; Val; Church Yth Grp; Trs Latin Clb; Science Clb; US Army Rsrv Natl Schlr/ Athlete Awd; George Washington U Engrng Awd; US Naval Acad; Aerospc Engrng.

KUBALA, THOMAS M; Thomas Stone HS; Waldorf, MD; (Y); Computer Clb; Office Aide; Rep Jr Cls; Rep Sr Cls; Var Bsbl; Hon Roll; Merit Schlrshp Awd Elon Coll 86; Elon Coll; Finc.

KUBOTA, CHRISTINA M; St Marys HS; Annapolis, MD; (Y); 3/119; Drama Clb; Sec Math Tm; VP Pep Clb; Sec Ski Clb; Nwsp Rptr; VP Stu Cncl; JV Lcrss; NHS; Disbld Am Vet Schlrshp 86; Pres Acad Ftns Awd 86; Wellesley Coll; Pre-Med.

KUCHARSKI, EDWARD; Cardinal Gibbons HS; Baltimore, MD; (Y); Bsktbl; Ftbl; Golf; NHS; WA; Pre Med.

KUEHL, KRISTIN; Walt Whitman HS; Potomac, MD; (Y); Drama Clb; Pep Clb; Service Clb; Trs Spanish Clb; SADD; School Play; Rep Stu Cncl; Cheerleading; L Trk.

KUHAR, TOM; Sparrow Point HS; Baltimore, MD; (Y); 3/185; Math Tm; Political Wkr; Band; Concert Band; Drill Tm; Jazz Band; Mrchg Band; Orch; Pep Band; School Musical; VP Of Sr High Band 86-87; Stu Mnth Engl 85-86; Stu Mnth Geom 85-86; Vet Med.

KUHN, KELLIE; Western HS; Baltimore, MD; (Y); 54/412; Rep Church Yth Grp; Library Aide; Science Clb; Intr Desgng.

KUHRMANN, CHUCK; Sparrows Point HS; Baltimore, MD; (Y); Art Clb; Teachers Aide; High Hon Roll; Hon Roll; Voice Dem Awd; Gftd-Tlntd Art Pgm 85-86; Carpntry.

KUJALA, ERIC; North Harford HS; Jarrettsville, MD; (Y); Boy Scts; FCA; Var JV Bsbl; High Hon Roll; Hon Roll; MS Hstry Awd 84; Gemntry Awd 85; Chem Awd 86; Math.

KULP, WILLIAM; Wicomico SR HS; Salisbury, MD; (Y); 14/160; Am Leg Boys St; JCL; SADD; Mrchg Band; Sec Stu Cncl; Trk; NHS; German Clb; JA; Latin Clb; Intrnshp Nasa Goddard Spce Flght Ctr 85; Rep, MD Natl Magntc Fusn Supr Cmptr Hnr Sem 86; U S Navl Acd; Sysm Engrg.

KULWICKI, DAWN; Arlington Baptist HS; Reisterstown, MD; (S); Varsity Clb; VP Frsh Cls; VP Soph Cls; VP Jr Cls; VP Sr Cls; Var L Sftbl; High Hon Roll; NHS; Prfct Atten Awd; Towson ST; Bio.

KUNTZ, LAURA; St Marys HS; Annapolis, MD; (Y); 78/118; JR Civitan 85-86; CCD Tchr St Andrew By The Bay 85-86; Maria Regina Coll; Fshn Mrchnds.

KUPERSMITH, ANDREW; Gaithersburg HS; Darnestown, MD; (Y); Debate Tm; Mrchg Band; School Musical; Symp Band; Nwsp Stf; Sec Sr Cls; High Hon Roll; NHS; Spanish NHS; Aud/Vis; Space Shuttle Stu Invlvmnt Proj Regnl Wnnr 84; Pre-Med.

KURDT, KATHRYN A; Gov Thomas Johnson HS; Frederick, MD; (Y); 5/303; Church Yth Grp; Latin Clb; SADD; Band; Trk; Hon Roll; Sec NHS; Ntl Merit Ltr; NEDT Awd; Coll Of Wm & Mary; Lbrl Arts.

KURTZ, MICHAEL; Archbishop Curley HS; Baltimore, MD; (S); 5/145; Computer Clb; Hosp Aide; Radio Clb; Science Clb; Im Bowling; Var Mgr(s); Var Trk; High Hon Roll; NHS; St Schlr; 3rd Hghst Quality Paint Avg Awd 85; 1st Hnrs 82-86; UMBC; Phys Thrpy.

KURYLO, MICHELLE; Gaithersburg HS; Gaithersburg, MD; (Y); Var Pom Pon; Var Swmmng; Hon Roll.

KUSMENKO, NELLA; Catholic HS; Baltimore, MD; (Y); Dance Clb; SADD; Rep Soph Cls; Hon Roll; Spanish NHS; Senatorial Schlrshp Sen Bonvegna; UMBC; Pre-Med.

KUTNER, KARA; Mount De Sales Academy HS; Baltimore, MD; (Y); Camera Clb; Spanish Clb; Stage Crew; Lit Mag; Im Lcrss; Awd Acdmc Excllnc 85-86; Jrnlsm.

KUTZERA, MICHELLE; St Vincent Pallotti HS; Laurel, MD; (S); 32/93; French Clb; GAA; Hosp Aide; Red Cross Aide; Service Clb; VP Jr Cls; Pres Sr Cls; Var Capt Vllybl; French Hon Soc; Kiwanis Awd; U MD; Visual Arts.

KWAH, MARJORIE; John Carroll Schl; Havre De Grace, MD; (Y); 17/238; Camera Clb; Ed Lit Mag; Scholastic Bowl; Ski Clb; Stage Crew; Nwsp Rptr; Nwsp Stf; Yrbk Phtg; Powder Puff Ftbl; JV Trk; Latinhnr Soc 85.

KWUN, YOUNG; Takoma Acad; Silver Spring, MD; (S); Computer Clb; Science Clb; Yrbk Phtg; VP Soph Cls; Stu Cncl; Trk; Hon Roll; Church Yth Grp; NHS; Hugh O Brian Yth Found 84-85; Treas Ntl Hnr Soc 85-86; Treas Biota 85-86; Med.

KYLE, MICHELLE; Northern HS; Owings, MD; (Y); Church Yth Grp; Ski Clb; Chorus; Mrchg Band; Var Pom Pon; Var Trk; DAR Awd; 5th Pl High Jmpng Regnl Meet 85; 3rd Pl Cnty Sci Fair 85; Special Awd Air Force Sci Proj 85; UMBC; Psychlgy.

LA BARRE, DEIRDRE A; Rockville HS; Rockville, MD; (Y); Drama Clb; Political Wkr; SADD; Chorus; School Musical; School Play; Rep Stu Cncl; Pom Pon; MD St Schlrshp In Talent 85-86; US Achvt Acad-Speech & Drama 86; Goucher Coll; Dance.

LA MOTHE, TAMMY JO ANN; St Marys Nyken HS; Waldorf, MD; (S); Church Yth Grp; FBLA; Rptr Yrbk Stf; Stat Fld Hcky; Stat Trk; Hon Roll; NHS; Typg Awd 84; Natl Yng Ldrs Conf 86; Pol Sci.

LA PARLE, FRANCIS; Allegany HS; Cumberland, MD; (Y); 50/200; Ski Clb; Band; Concert Band; Jazz Band; Mrchg Band; Orch; Pep Band; Variety Show; Wt Lftg; Georgetown:Dent.

LA ROSA, ANGELA; Connelly School Of The Holy Child; Potomac, MD; (Y); VP Debate Tm; Hosp Aide; Pres Model UN; Political Wkr; Service Clb; Nwsp Sprt Ed; JV Bsktbl; JV Socr; Hon Roll; NHS; Rcgntn Mrt Wstrn Cvlztn; Rcgntn Mrt Blgy; Hnrbl Mntn Acad Exclnc; Pre-Med.

LA ROSE, TRACIE; Annapolis Area Christian Schl; Annapolis, MD; (S); 2/13; Church Yth Grp; Hosp Aide; Stage Crew; Yrbk Ed-Chief; Yrbk Phtg; Rep Frsh Cls; Pres Soph Cls; Sec Sr Cls; Capt Bsktbl; Capt Socr; Messiah Coll.

LA VILLA, DANIELLE E; Gaithersburg HS; Gaithersburg, MD; (Y); 21/568; AFS; Intnl Clb; Concert Band; Bsktbl; Var Socr; Hon Roll; NHS; Montgomery Cnty Sci Fair Awds 83-86; IN U; Bio.

LADD, SAM; Thomas S Wootton HS; Gaithersburg, MD; (Y); Boy Scts; Church Yth Grp; Letterman Clb; Im Bsktbl; Var Ftbl; Var Trk; JV Wrstlng; God Cntry Awd; Hon Roll; Wootton 300 Pound Clb 86; Brigham Young U; Intl Bus.

LADIN, EVIE; Baltimore City College HS; Baltimore, MD; (S); JA; Nwsp Ed-Chief; Sftbl; Swmmng; High Hon Roll; NHS; Bk Awd Williams Coll.

LAGANA, GREGORY; Fort Hill HS; Cumberland, MD; (Y); Church Yth Grp; Band; Concert Band; Jazz Band; Mrchg Band; Var Trk; Wt Lftg; Best Marcher 84-85; Svc Ltr 84-85; Athl Ltr 85-86; Pol Sci.

LAGNESE, MELINDA; Academy Of The Holy Cross; Silver Spring, MD; (Y); Church Yth Grp; Cmnty Wkr; French Clb; Math Clb; Math Tm; Pep Clb; Science Clb; SADD; Tennis; French Hon Soc; Georgetown U; Psych.

LAGONERA, MICHAEL J; St Vincent Pallotti HS; Beltsville, MD; (S); 4/120; Ski Clb; Spanish Clb; Church Choir; Crs Cntry; Tennis; High Hon Roll; Hon Roll; NHS; Spanish NHS; Engr.

LAGOS, ROSALINO PAT; Good Counsel HS; Silver Spring, MD; (Y); 7/238; Band; Concert Band; Jazz Band; Pep Band; Symp Band; Coach Actv; High Hon Roll; NHS; French Clb; Library Aide; Dstngshd Schlr 85-86; Natl Hispnc Schlr 85-86; Music Awd 86; Stanford; Engrng.

LAKATOS, MICHELE; Gaithersburg HS; Gaithersburg, MD; (Y); AFS; Camp Fr Inc; Church Yth Grp; Cmnty Wkr; NFL; SADD; Teachers Aide; School Musical; Swmmng; Hon Roll; Hon Men Awd Wrld Ptry 84; Comm.

LAKEIN, MEIR J; Charles E Smith Jewish Day Schl; Potomac, MD; (Y); VP Temple Yth Grp; School Play; Ed Nwsp Stf; Yrbk Stf; Lit Mag; Pres Jr Cls; French Hon Soc; NHS; Ntl Merit Ltr; Natl Yng Ldrs Conf Yth Ldrshp Awd 85-86; Montgmry Cnty Yth Corp 86.

LAKEL, KARA; South Carroll HS; Woodbine, MD; (Y); Teachers Aide; Varsity Clb; Orch; Nwsp Stf; Yrbk Stf; Stu Cncl; Cheerleading; Trk; Wt Lftg; Hon Roll; Elem Eductn.

LAKIN, JUDY; Brunswick HS; Jefferson, MD; (Y); Computer Clb; French Clb; FBLA; Teachers Aide; Chorus; School Musical; Stage Crew.

LAM, CHERYL; Western HS; Baltimore, MD; (Y); 185/412; Math Clb; U Of College Park; Rep.

LAM, CLARISSA LINH; Oxon Hill HS; Temple Hills, MD; (Y); VP Intnl Clb; Mrchg Band; Symp Band; Ed Lit Mag; Crs Cntry; High Hon Roll; NHS; Church Yth Grp; Computer Clb; Concert Band; Sntrl Schlrashp Awd, Merit Schlrshp Awd & Pres Acdmc Ftns Awd 86; U MD Clg Pk; Accntng.

LAMANA, NORMA; Pikesville HS; Baltimore, MD; (Y); AFS; Church Yth Grp; Cmnty Wkr; Spanish Clb; Yrbk Ed-Chief; Yrbk Stf; Lit Mag; Debate Tm; SADD; Ntl Merit Ltr; Vlnv U Pres Schlrshp 86; Crtv Wrtng & Yrbk Awd 86; Schlrshps Coll Ntr Dame & Lasle U 86; Villanova U; Engl.

LAMB, IRENE; Great Mills HS; Lexington Park, MD; (Y); SADD; Yrbk Stf; Trs Soph Cls; VP Jr Cls; Var Fld Hcky; Var Tennis; Hon Roll; Art Clb; Church Yth Grp; Pep Clb; Charlotte Hall Flwshp 86-87; Art Awds St Marys Co Fair 86; Art Awd St Marys Co Wmns Clb 86; Lbrl Arts; Bio Illstrn.

LAMB, JOHN; Highland View Acad; Darlington, MD; (Y); Aud/Vis; Nwsp Phtg; Nwsp Rptr; Yrbk Phtg; Off Jr Cls; Gym; Hon Roll; Outstndg Attndnc Awd 83; Andrews U; Photo.

LAMKIN, JEFF; Thomas Stone HS; Waldorf, MD; (Y); Church Yth Grp; Crs Cntry.

LAMONICA, LISA; Walkersville HS; Walkersville, MD; (Y); English Clb; JA; Pep Clb; SADD; Chorus; Variety Show; Stu Cncl; Pom Pon; Gregg Typng Awd 85-86; Lab Tech.

LAMUSGA, LORI; Dulaney SR HS; Timonium, MD; (Y); Church Yth Grp; Drama Clb; Thesps; Band; Concert Band; Mrchg Band; Pep Band; School Play; Hon Roll; Pres NHS; U Schlr U Of N FL 86; PTSA Schlrshps 86; U Of N FL; Comm.

LANCELOTTA, KEVIN C; Loyola HS; Ellicott City, MD; (S); Chess Clb; Church Yth Grp; French Clb; JA; Ski Clb; Chorus; School Musical; School Play; Im Bsbl; Im Bsktbl; Med.

LANDER, DAWN MELODY; Rising Sun HS; Conowingo, MD; (Y); School Play; Variety Show; JV Bsktbl; Var L Fld Hcky; Var L Sftbl; Hon Roll; Church Yth Grp; Drama Clb; FHA; U S Bus Ed Awd 86; Acadmc All Am 86; Western MD Clg; Bus Adm.

LANDERKIN, GREG; N Harford HS; Jarrettsville, MD; (Y); FBLA; Varsity Clb; Var L Socr; Var Trk; Hon Roll; Schlstc Prfrmc Eng 85-86; Cmptr Prgrmr.

LANDES, HEATHER; Franklin HS; Hampstead, MD; (Y); Var Crs Cntry; Var Mgr(s); Var Trk; High Hon Roll; NHS; Rbbns, Medls & Plq Vrsty Crss Cntry & Trck 83-86; Towson ST U; Secdry Tchg.

LANDIS, DAVID; St Vincent Pallotti HS; Laurel, MD; (S); Boy Scts; Church Yth Grp; Debate Tm; Ski Clb; Spanish Clb; Var L Socr; High Hon Roll; Hon Roll; Spanish NHS; Stu Of Mnth Nov 84; Engnrng.

LANE, BRENDAN; Gaithersburg HS; Gaithersburg, MD; (Y); Church Yth Grp; Cmnty Wkr; Band; Im Socr; Im Sftbl; Hon Roll; Fresh Class Superltv 83-84; 1st Chr Bartn In Band 83-84; Bus.

LANE, MATTHEW; Gaithersburg HS; Gaithersburg, MD; (Y); 1/650; Church Yth Grp; Ski Clb; Var Bsktbl; Im Golf; JV Socr; High Hon Roll; Hon Roll; NHS; Val; MD Distngsh Schlr; Thomas J Watson Mem Schlrshp; Duke U; Engr.

LANE, SANDRA I; Hammond HS; Jessup, MD; (Y); 49/255; Church Yth Grp; Teachers Aide; Church Choir; Concert Band; Mrchg Band; Orch; Sftbl; Vllybl; High Hon Roll; Hon Roll; Natl Merit Commended Blck Schlr 85; Engrng.

LANE, SUSAN; Friendly SR HS; Ft Washington, MD; (Y); Cmnty Wkr; Y-Teens; Hon Roll; Acad Achvt Awd 85; Pres Acad Ftns Awd 86; U MD; Pre-Law.

LANE, TOMMY; Perryville HS; Pt Deposit, MD; (Y); L Tennis; L Wrstlng.

LANGE, ROBERT; Walt Whitman HS; Bethesda, MD; (Y); Cmnty Wkr; Red Cross Aide; Ski Clb; Pres Frsh Cls; Pres Soph Cls; Rep Jr Cls; Pres Sr Cls; Trk; Rotary Awd; Ntl Latin Exam/Magna Cum Laude I 85.

LANGEL, JOY; Parkdale HS; College Park, MD; (S); Yrbk Stf; Hon Roll; Ntl Acadmc Achvt Awd; ME U Delaware; Chld Dvlpmnt.

LANGHORN, AMY; Forest Park HS; Baltimore, MD; (Y); FBLA; Office Aide; Rep Soph Cls; Rep Stu Cncl; Hon Roll; Pres NHS; Prfct Atten Awd; Outstndng Achvmnt Schlrshp 85-86; Strayer Bus Coll; Bus.

LANGSDORF, JOHN; Gaithersburg HS; Gaithersburg, MD; (Y); German Clb; Band; Concert Band; Mrchg Band; Trusties Awd 85; Mech Engr.

LANGSTON, KIMBERLY; Walbrook SR HS; Baltimore, MD; (Y); 4-H; 4-H Awd.

LANHAM, KRISTEN; Maurice J Mc Donough HS; Waldorf, MD; (Y); Letterman Clb; Thesps; Varsity Clb; Mrchg Band; School Play; Rep Stu Cncl; Var Capt Cheerleading; High Hon Roll; NHS; Dance Clb; Mrn Bio.

LANHAM, TERI; La Plata HS; Waldorf, MD; (Y); FBLA; Teachers Aide; Trk; Hon Roll.

LANOCHA, DEBORAH; Kenwood SR HS; Baltimore, MD; (Y); GAA; Varsity Clb; Off Frsh Cls; Pres Soph Cls; Off Jr Cls; Stu Cncl; Var Bsktbl; Var Vllybl; Law.

LAPIDARIO JR, RENATO; Bishop Walsh HS; Cumberland, MD; (Y); 32/106; Am Leg Boys St; Pres Jr Cls; Pres Stu Cncl; Var JV Stu Cncl; Var Crs Cntry; Var L Socr; Hon Roll; Bi ST Sccr All Star Selectn 85; All City Sccr Selectn 85.

LAPPIN, PATRICIA; South Carroll HS; Sykesville, MD; (Y); Spanish Clb; Varsity Clb; Var Score Keeper; Var Socr; Var Sftbl; Sec NHS; St Schlr; Val; Acad All Amer 86; Western MD Coll; Bus Admin.

LARDIZABAL, LISA; Smithsburg SR HS; Hagerstown, MD; (Y); 4/197; Dance Clb; Latin Clb; Teachers Aide; Rep Frsh Cls; Stat Sftbl; Var JV Vllybl; Hon Roll; MD Dstngshd Schlr-Hnrb Mntn 85; Semi-Fnlst Natl Hspnc Schlrshp 85-86; Top Schlr-Clbrtn Of Exclnc 85-6; Cmnctns.

LARRANAGA, VIRGINIA; The Bullis Schl; Gaithersburg, MD; (Y); 10/90; Pres AFS; Drama Clb; Model UN; Thesps; School Play; Stage Crew; Swmmng; Hon Roll; NHS; NEDT Awd; Natl Hispnc SF Awd 85.

LASLEY, FELICIA; Suitland HS; District Height, MD; (Y); French Clb; Pres Frsh Cls; Pres Soph Cls; Pres Jr Cls; Pres Sr Cls; Pres Stu Cncl; High Hon Roll; VP NHS; Girl Scts; Pep Clb; HOBY Recpnt 84-85 Bowie ST Coll 6 Wk Resdntl Pgm 84; Intrnshp Gov U Of MD For Tlentd & Gftd Stu 86; Pre Law.

LATKOVSKI, CHRISTOPHER; Saint Johns At Prospect Hall; Frederick, MD; (Y); Science Clb; Ski Clb; Yrbk Phtg; Yrbk Rptr; Lit Mag; Var L Bsktbl; Var L Socr; Var L Tennis; High Hon Roll; Allnc Frncs Awd 86; Geogrphy Trsm & Trvl.

LATNEY, TAWANA; Duval HS; Seat Pleasant, MD; (Y); Cmnty Wkr; Hosp Aide; Natl Beta Clb; Office Aide; Pep Clb; Political Wkr; Church Choir; Sec Soph Cls; VP Pres Stu Cncl; Hon Roll; Page To MD Hse Of Reps 86; Order Of Eastern Star Schlrshp 86; Hampton U; Law.

LAU, YUEN; Wheaton HS; Wheaton, MD; (Y); 2/386; SADD; Nwsp Stf; Yrbk Stf; Var Vllybl; Hon Roll; Jr NHS; NHS; MD ST Dstngshd Schlr 86; Merit Schltc Awd 86; Pres Acadmc Ftnss Awds 86; U Of MD; Sysm Anlyst.

LAURIE, MARK; Aberdeen HS; Aberdeen, MD; (Y); 20/200; Pres Spanish Clb; Rep Sec Varsity Clb; Acpl Chr; Rep Stu Cncl; Capt Vllybl; High Hon Roll; Hon Roll; NHS; Prfct Atten Awd; St Schlr; Alpha Kappa Alpha Sorority Scholar 86; Ruff-Ross Scholar 86; Am Leg Post No 128 86; U MD College Pk; Corp Comp Law.

LAVALLEE, MARK; Severna Park SR HS; Severna Park, MD; (Y); 11/421; Pres AFS; Boy Scts; Church Yth Grp; French Clb; Hosp Aide; Math Tm; Teachers Aide; High Hon Roll; Hon Roll; Jr NHS; Ad Altar Dei And Pope Pius XII 83; Gould Inc Schlrshp 86; PA ST; Pre Med.

LAVAPPA, MALINI; Thomas S Wootton HS; Gaithersburg, MD; (Y); AFS; Science Clb; Chorus; JV Trk; Hon Roll; Kaveri Cultural Talent Awd 86; Bio.

LAVELLE, MICHAEL T; Eleanor Roosevelt HS; Largo, MD; (Y); SADD; Band; JV Crs Cntry; JV Ftbl; JV Trk; Human Bio Cls Awd 85; Bio.

LAVETT, DEENA; Regina HS; Washington, DC; (Y); Camp Fr Inc; Church Yth Grp; Cmnty Wkr; Pep Clb; Teachers Aide; Cheerleading; Swmmng; Pre-Law.

LAVINA, LISA; Notre Dame Prep; Hunt Valley, MD; (Y); Pres GAA; Chorus; Var Fld Hcky; Intl Bus.

LAW, TIMOTHY D; Bethesda-Chevy Chase SR HS; Chevy Chase, MD; (Y); 69/449; VP Camera Clb; Trs French Clb; Intnl Clb; Pres Science Clb; Teachers Aide; Yrbk Ed-Chief; Yrbk Phtg; Capt Bowling; Hon Roll; Ntl Merit SF; Hon Men MD ST Mth Comp 85; U VT; Pre-Med Engrng.

LAWRENCE, TRACY; Forest Park HS; Baltimore, MD; (Y); Art Clb; ROTC; Church Choir; Nwsp Rptr; Nwsp Stf; Rep Jr Cls; Off Sr Cls; Prfct Atten Awd; Acad All Amer 86; Art Merit Awd 86; Savannah Coll; Arch.

LAWYER, NATALIE; Laurel HS; Laurel, MD; (Y); Church Yth Grp; Spanish Clb; Hon Roll; Var Co-Capt Cheerleading; Outstndng Achvt Math Awd 84-85; Brigham Young U.

LAY, STEPHEN E; Lackey SR HS; La Plata, MD; (Y); Latin Clb; Thesps; Chorus; Church Choir; Jazz Band; Variety Show; Hon Roll; St Schlr; Fnlst MD Dstngshd Schlrshp 86; Semifnlst Yng Keybd Artst Assn 84 & 86; U Of MD; Music.

LAYNE, DONNA; John Carroll HS; Monkton, MD; (Y); 151/238; Cmnty Wkr; JA; Library Aide; Pep Clb; Yrbk Stf; Mgr Trk; Villa Julie Coll; Accntng.

LAYTON, KATHERINE; James M Bennett HS; Salisbury, MD; (Y); 10/200; Math Clb; Varsity Clb; VP Soph Cls; VP Stu Cncl; Var Bsktbl; Var Sftbl; Var Vllybl; Hon Roll; Math.

LAZO, MARK; Northwestern SR HS; Mt Rainier, MD; (Y); French Clb; Science Clb; Var Crs Cntry; Var Tennis; Var Trk; Bausch & Lomb Sci Awd; High Hon Roll; Hon Roll; Jr NHS; Acad Encllnc Awd 84-86; Natl Chmstry Olympd 85-86; U Of Smd; Nclr Sci.

LE, BAO LOC; Albert Einstein HS; Silver Spring, MD; (Y); French Clb; Intnl Clb; Office Aide; Trs Soph Cls; Bsktbl; Trk; High Hon Roll; Jr NHS; Ranked 2nd Dist Alg I Comptn 84; Pre-Med.

LE, DIEM; High Point HS; Beltsville, MD; (Y); Drama Clb; Intnl Clb; Math Clb; Math Tm; Hon Roll; MD U; Elec Engr.

LE, TRANG; Gaithersburg HS; Gaithersburg, MD; (Y); Trs 4-H; Pres Intnl Clb; U MD College Pk; Advrtsng.

LE BLANC JR, DONALD J; Glenelg HS; Wodbine, MD; (Y); Boy Scts; Church Yth Grp; JA; Hon Roll; Loyola Coll; Engrng.

LE BRUN, LAURA; Mercy HS; Baltimore, MD; (Y); Aud/Vis; Church Yth Grp; Cmnty Wkr; French Clb; GAA; Chorus; Rep Church Yth Grp; Stu Cncl; Hon Roll; Head Choirstr 83; Secr Chrch Yth Grp 85-86; Essex Comm Coll.

LEACH, SHARON; St Andrews Episcopal Schl; Gaithersburg, MD; (S); Thesps; Chorus; School Musical; Rep Stu Cncl; Var Capt Bsktbl; Var L Socr; Var L Sftbl; Var L Tennis; High Hon Roll; Hon Roll; Smith Bk Awd 85; MD Acad Sci Semnr 85; Clncl Psychlgy.

LEAHY, KEVIN; Thomas Stone HS; Waldorf, MD; (Y); Am Leg Boys St; Concert Band; JV Var Ftbl; JV Wrstlng; Hon Roll; Pilot.

LEAMAN, LISA DIANE; Oakland Mills HS; Columbia, MD; (Y); 89/240; Cmnty Wkr; ROTC; Nwsp Rptr; Nwsp Stf; Rep Jr Cls; Stu Cncl; Im Bowling; Im Pom Pon; Towson ST; Bus Admn.

LEASE, NANCY; Fort Hill HS; Rawlings, MD; (Y); Church Yth Grp; Chorus; Church Choir; Hon Roll; Allegany Comm Coll; Rn.

LEBER, MICHAEL; De Matha Catholic HS; Potomac, MD; (Y); 19/254; Church Yth Grp; Cmnty Wkr; Pep Band; Symp Band; Im Bsktbl; JV Socr; High Hon Roll; NHS; Bus.

LEBLANC, BRADLEY; Mount St Joseph HS; Baltimore, MD; (Y); Intnl Clb; Spanish Clb; Socr.

LECHMAN, ROSEMARIE; Fort Hill HS; Cumberland, MD; (Y); Church Yth Grp; Thesps; Band; Church Choir; Jazz Band; Mrchg Band; Soph Cls; Jr Cls; Sr Cls; Trk; Chem.

LEDGER, DARLA DEE; Catoctin HS; Thurmont, MD; (Y); Drama Clb; School Musical; School Play; Nwsp Bus Mgr; Nwsp Rptr; Fld Hcky; Gym; Trk; Hon Roll; 1st Pl Frederick Co Sci Fair 83-84; VP Of SHOP; Delegate In Yth & Govnmt MD Model Leg; Anthropology.

LEE, ALICIA; Elizabeth Seton HS; Landover, MD; (Y); Debate Tm; FBLA; Model UN; Pep Clb; ROTC; Speech Tm; Drill Tm; School Play; Yrbk Rptr; Yrbk Stf; Mntrl Stf Pres 85-87; U Maryland; Law.

LEE, CAROL; John Carrol HS; Fallston, MD; (Y); 1/238; Cmnty Wkr; Scholastic Bowl; Ski Clb; Yrbk Stf; Var Fld Hcky; JV Lcrss; French Hon Soc; Hon Roll; NHS; Ntl Merit Ltr.

LEE, CRYSTAL; Sparrows Point Middue SR HS; Baltimore, MD; (Y); Teachers Aide; Chorus; Hon Roll; Catonsville CC; Comp Pgmr.

LEE, DANA C; Connelly Schl Of The Holy Child; Silver Spring, MD; (Y); Cmnty Wkr; SADD; Nwsp Phtg; Yrbk Phtg; Stu Cncl; JV Capt Fld Hcky; NHS; Prfct Atten Awd; Stu Yr 86; Donna Howk Mem Awd Sci 86; Figure Skatng Assn Amateur Skater 82-86; Colgate U; Bio Sci.

LEE, DEMRIS; Frederick Douglass HS; Upper Marlboro, MD; (Y); 2/326; Yrbk Ed-Chief; Rep Stu Cncl; L Mgr(s); Elks Awd; High Hon Roll; NHS; Rotary Awd; Sal; Spanish NHS; St Schlr; Jesse J Warr JR Mem Awd 85; Sprintdnts Awd 86; VA Cmnslth U; Bio.

LEE, DONNA W; Paint Branch HS; Silver Spring, MD; (Y); Key Clb; SADD; Chorus; Sec Jazz Band; VP Frsh Cls; Rep Jr Cls; VP Sr Cls; Hon Roll; Dance Clb; Distngshd Schlr Tlnts Arts Schlrshp 85; Creatv & Perfrmg Arts Schlrshp 86; Yng Kybrd Artst Assn SF 85; U Of MD; Piano Perfrm.

LEE, EUN Y; Dulaney SR HS; Lutherville, MD; (Y); Key Clb; PAVAS; Orch; Badmtn; Hon Roll; Schlrshp Tnglwd Music Fstvl BU 85; Peabody Cnsrvrtry Music; Piano.

LEE, JAMES; Takoma Acad; Greenbelt, MD; (S); Church Yth Grp; Cmnty Wkr; Exploring; French Clb; Hosp Aide; Science Clb; Service Clb; Ski Clb; Band; Orch.

LEE, JENNY; Thomas S Wootton HS; Rockville, MD; (Y); AFS; Art Clb; Drama Clb; Science Clb; Fld Hcky; Mgr(s); Trk; Hon Roll; Trk Awds 85-86; Bio.

LEE, JHEMON; Gaithersburg HS; Gaithersburg, MD; (S); Pres Chess Clb; Mathletes; Quiz Bowl; Hon Roll; Jr NHS; Spanish NHS; Outstndng Profcncy 85; Math Ex 85; Chem Tm 85; U MD; Med.

LEE, KAREN; Dulaney SR HS; Timonium, MD; (Y); Dance Clb; Varsity Clb; Chorus; Im Mgr Powder Puff Ftbl; Var Tennis; Cit Awd; High Hon Roll; Hon Roll; NHS; Crmnlgy.

LEE, KENNETH; Thomas Stone HS; Waldorf, MD; (Y); Church Yth Grp; Teachers Aide; Rep Jr Cls; Rep Sr Cls; JV Var Bsbl; Im Bsktbl; Var L Ftbl; Hon Roll; Towson ST U; Bus.

LEE, MARK S; Loyola HS; Hunt Valley, MD; (S); Art Clb; Pep Clb; Band; Concert Band; School Musical; School Play; Nwsp Rptr; Nwsp Stf; Hon Roll; NHS; Med.

LEE, MIN CHRISTY; T S Wootton HS; Gaithersburg, MD; (Y); Church Yth Grp; Dance Clb; Pep Clb; SADD; Teachers Aide; Varsity Clb; Off Frsh Cls; Off Soph Cls; Off Jr Cls; Off Sr Cls; UMBC; Dentl Lab Tech.

LEE, ROSLYN; Maurice J Mcdonough HS; La Plata, MD; (Y); FBLA; Girl Scts; Teachers Aide; Bsktbl; Trk; Vllybl; Charles Cnty CC; Bus Admin.

LEE, SANDRA; Walt Whitman HS; Bethesda, MD; (Y); Var Capt Cheerleading; Var Sftbl; Var Vllybl; Bus Finance.

LEE, SEUNG H; Einstein HS; Kensington, MD; (Y); 9/304; Latin Clb; Model UN; Political Wkr; Nwsp Bus Mgr; Nwsp Ed-Chief; Nwsp Stf; Yrbk Stf; Lit Mag; Trs Soph Cls; Rep Stu Cncl; Darmouth.

LEE, SHANA; Lackey HS; Welcome, MD; (Y); Church Yth Grp; FBLA; Intnl Clb; Trs Spanish Clb; Teachers Aide; Church Choir; Rep Stu Cncl; JV Sftbl; Var L Trk; JV Vllybl; Awd Of Merit FBLA 86; Var Athltc Awd 86; Cert Of Apprctn March Of Dimes 86.

LEE, SOO; Magruder HS; Derwood, MD; (Y); Church Yth Grp; Church Choir; JV Vllybl; Hon Roll; Hnr Awd Top 10 Pct Clss 84-86; U MD; Arch.

LEE, STACEY; Carver Vo-Tech HS; Baltimore, MD; (Y); Church Yth Grp; FBLA; Church Choir; Pres Sr Cls; Hon Roll; Jr NHS; NHS; Bltmr Almnae Chptr Delta Sigma Theta Srty 84-86; Outstndng Achvmnt Data Proc 1 85-86; Systm Anlyst.

LEE, SUNG; Bladensburg HS; Hyattsville, MD; (Y); School Musical; PTSA Schlrshp 86-87; Math, Frnch I & Data Prcssng II Awds 86; Hse Of Delg Schlrshp 86-87; U Of MD; Phlsphy.

LEE, TANYA; John Carroll HS; Kingsville, MD; (Y); Pres Church Yth Grp; Cmnty Wkr; GAA; School Musical; Yrbk Stf; Powder Puff Ftbl; Trk; Hon Roll.

LEE, TAWANNA; Northwestern SR HS; Baltimore, MD; (Y); Debate Tm; FBLA; Red Cross Aide; ROTC; Tennis; Hon Roll; Hnd In Outstndng Achvmnt In TPC 85; Awd FBLA Canned Goods Dr 85; Awd In Co-Op Prtcptn In Hist Clb 85; ROTC Coll; Philologist.

LEE, THERESA; Crossland HS; Temple Hills, MD; (Y); Church Yth Grp; Drama Clb; Hosp Aide; Office Aide; Teachers Aide; Mrchg Band; Symp Band; Socr; Hon Roll; Cmnty Wkr; Frdm Awd; K Briggs Bus Inst; Lgl Secy.

LEE, VIVIAN; Surrattsville SR HS; Clinton, MD; (Y); French Clb; Pom Pon; Hon Roll; UNC-CHAPEL Hill; Busnss Admin.

LEE, WARREN; Potomac HS; Temple Hills, MD; (Y); Science Clb; Hon Roll; Acad Encllnc Awd 85; Elec Engrng.

LEE, YONG M; Arlington Baptist HS; Baltimore, MD; (S); 3/61; Chorus; Church Choir; School Musical; High Hon Roll; Hon Roll; NHS; Prfct Atten Awd; 2nd Pl Piano Comptn ST 84; Eastman Schl Music; Music Prfrm.

LEE, YOUNG; Western HS; Baltimore, MD; (Y); 25/412; Art Clb; Hon Roll; NHS; Math Awds 85; Cert Of Awds 85; Natl Art Hon 86; U MD; Pharm.

LEE, YUEN HO; Potomac HS; Temple Hills, MD; (Y); Aud/Vis; Office Aide; Hon Roll; NHS; Sal; Acad Exclnc 84-85; George Washington U Awd For Sci & Math 84-85; U MD.

LEES, TANYA; Maurice J Mcdonough HS; La Plata, MD; (Y); VP Church Yth Grp; Letterman Clb; Hst Frsh Cls; VP Soph Cls; Off Jr Cls; VP Stu Cncl; JV Var Bsktbl; Mgr Ftbl; Var Trk; Hon Roll; Stu Govt Ltr 83; Track Ltr 85; Jrnlsm.

LEGATES, KEVIN; Wicomico SR HS; Salisbury, MD; (Y); Boy Scts; JA; Rep Frsh Cls; Rep Soph Cls; JV Ftbl; Var Tennis; High Hon Roll; NHS; MD Acad Sci Salisbury ST Coll Micro-Elec 86; Guidance Advsry Comm 85-86; Elec Engrng.

LEHMAN, CLINTON; Gov Thomas Johnson HS; Frederick, MD; (Y); Cmnty Wkr; Computer Clb; Latin Clb; SADD; Var Bsktbl; Hon Roll; Acctg.

LEHMAN, RICHARD A; Thomas Stone HS; Brandywine, MD; (Y); Latin Clb; Chorus; Church Choir; School Musical; School Play; St Schlr; Ntl Ldrshp, Svc, Speech, & Drama Awd; All St Hnrs Choir; 1st Tenor Tri-Cnty Hnrs Choir; Music Bus.

LEISHEAR, BILLY; St Vincent Pallotti HS; Highland, MD; (S); 6/120; ROTC; Ski Clb; Spanish Clb; Pres Soph Cls; Pres Jr Cls; JV Bsbl; JV Var Ftbl; Var Trk; High Hon Roll; Hon Roll; Amer Ltrtr Awd 85; Acdmc Ltr 85; Bus Ecnmcs.

LEISTER, JASON; Westminster HS; Westminster, MD; (Y); Camera Clb; Letterman Clb; Teachers Aide; Varsity Clb; Var L Ftbl; Capt L Trk; Hon Roll; Engrng.

LEISTER, JUDY; Westminster HS; Westminster, MD; (Y); 70/501; Hosp Aide; PAVAS; Science Clb; Service Clb; Acpl Chr; Chorus; Church Choir; Swing Chorus; NHS; Pres Schlr; Grace Lutheran Chrch Schlrshp 86; Schl Chorus Solst 86; Cmnty Solost 82-86; Lebanon Vly Coll; Biochem.

LEITAO, AMY; Pocomoke HS; Pocomoke, MD; (S); 6/95; Church Choir; Nwsp Bus Mgr; Trs Sr Cls; Var Cheerleading; Var Fld Hcky; Var Sftbl; Sec NHS; AFS; Am Leg Aux Girls St; Math Tm; All Shore Band 85-86; Pres Clssrm Yung Amercns 86; Century III Schl Wnnr 85-86; Juniata Coll.

LEITAO, JENNIFER; Pocomoke HS; Pocomoke, MD; (S); 6/91; AFS; SADD; VP Jr Cls; Trs Stu Cncl; Var Capt Bsktbl; Sftbl; Hon Roll; Score Keeper; Church Yth Grp; Math Tm; Drug & Alcohol Task Force Yth Advsry Comm 85 & 86; Chrch Parish Cncl 85-86; Math Challenge 1st Tm 85; Elem Educ.

LEMLEY, SHERRY; Wilcomico SR HS; Salisbury, MD; (Y); 1/243; Sec Mrchg Band; Symp Band; High Hon Roll; Lion Awd; NHS; Pres Schlr; St Schlr; Val; U MD Collage Park.

LEMMERT, KAREN; Beall HS; Frostburg, MD; (Y); Art Clb; Hosp Aide; Band; Jazz Band; Symp Band; Nwsp Stf; High Hon Roll; NHS; MD Sci Sympsm Awd 85-86; MD Distngshd Schlr Art,Music 86; Graphic Arts.

LEMON, MONICA; Sherwood HS; Olney, MD; (Y); Model UN; Stage Crew; Nwsp Stf; Stat Bsktbl; Stat Ftbl; Mgr(s); Stat Socr; Hon Roll; Church Yth Grp; German Clb; Schl Svc 83-84; U Of MD; Bus Admin.

LENHART, MARILYN; Gov Thomas Johnson HS; Thurmont, MD; (Y); VP 4-H; Office Aide; Band; Concert Band; Mrchg Band; Pep Band; Capt Powder Puff Ftbl; Var Capt Sftbl; Hon Roll; All League Sftbl Plyr, MVP & Unsung Hero Awd 83-86; Mt St Marys Coll; Accntng.

LENHOFF, LESLIE; Mercy HS; Cockeysville, MD; (Y); Church Yth Grp; Drama Clb; French Clb; GAA; Hosp Aide; Library Aide; Stage Crew; Im Badmtn; Im Bsktbl; Var Gym; Frnch Clb Pres 85-86; Loyola Coll Of MD; Bus.

LENNON, JAMES; Thomas Stone HS; Waldorf, MD; (Y); Teachers Aide; Charles Co CC.

LENT, LAUREL A; Southern Garrett HS; Mt Lake Park, MD; (S); German Clb; Band; Church Choir; Concert Band; Mrchg Band; Hon Roll; NHS.

LEONARD, GINA; John Carroll Schl; Baltimore, MD; (Y); 78/238; Yrbk Stf; Capt Crs Cntry; Trk; French Hon Soc; Chmstry.

LEONARD, LORI; Takoma Acad; Takoma Park, MD; (Y); 32/94; Church Yth Grp; Science Clb; Ski Clb; Chorus; Trs Stu Cncl; Im Vllybl; Hon Roll; NHS; Bst Stu-Wrld Lit 85-86; Columbia Union Coll; Scl Wrk.

LEONARDO, JOHN L; Loyola HS; Timonium, MD; (S); Intnl Clb; Im Ftbl; Hon Roll; Jr NHS; NHS; Art Awd 84; Georgetown U; Med.

LEPLEY, TAMBI; Allegany HS; Cumberland, MD; (Y); Church Yth Grp; Dance Clb; Girl Scts; Library Aide; Office Aide; Drill Tm; Orch; Sftbl; Allegany CC; Nrs.

LEPOLD, JAN; John Carroll HS; Bel Air, MD; (Y); 40/238; Fld Hcky; Lcrss; Mgr(s); Hon Roll; Prfct Atten Awd; Phy Thrpy.

LESE, CHRISTA; Bishop Walsh HS; Cumberland, MD; (Y); 4/99; Art Clb; Model UN; Band; Yrbk Stf; Rep Soph Cls; Var L Cheerleading; Var L Tennis; High Hon Roll; NHS; Spanish NHS; Hugh Obrian Yth Ldrshp Conf; Hlth Field.

LESKO, ALLEN; Friendly HS; Fort Washington, MD; (Y); 3/450; Church Yth Grp; Office Aide; Spanish Clb; Nwsp Stf; Rep Frsh Cls; Im Var Swmmng; Hon Roll; Spanish NHS; Acadmc Excllnc Awd 83-85; Hnry Mntn Prince Georges Scnty Sci Fair Physcs 83-84; Bus.

LESSMANN, JEANNINE; Wicomico SR HS; Salisbury, MD; (S); 3/288; JCL; Sec Latin Clb; Letterman Clb; Teachers Aide; Orch; Var Bsktbl; Var Sftbl; JV Vllybl; High Hon Roll; NHS; Silver Medlst Ntl Latin Ex 83-84; Intl Frgn Lang Awds 85-86; Maryland Acad Sci Sem 85-86; William & Mary; Sci.

LESSTER, ANNE; Queen Anne School; Crofton, MD; (Y); Art Clb; VP Church Yth Grp; Cmnty Wkr; Teachers Aide; Variety Show; Lit Mag; Hon Roll; US Figur Sktg Assn-5th In Tst Figurs 85, Novice Freestyl Tst 85, Pre-Slvr Danc 83.

LESTER, JOHN; La Plata HS; Waldorf, MD; (Y); Aud/Vis; Teachers Aide; Concert Band; Jazz Band; Mrchg Band; Pep Band; Symp Band; High Hon Roll; Hon Roll; Tri-Cnty Hnr Bnd 86; MD ST Solo & Ensmbl Fstvl Spr Rtng 85; U MD; Aero Spc Engrng.

LETT, LAURA E; Centennial HS; Ellicott City, MD; (Y); Key Clb; Pep Clb; Ski Clb; Yrbk Stf; VP Frsh Cls; Stu Cncl; Capt Cheerleading; Gym; Trk; Hon Roll; Intl Chrldg Fndtn Mst Outstndg Chrldr 83-84; Nbatl Chrldg Assn All Amer Fnlst 86-87; Blkhwk Ctznshp; Comm.

LEVANTIS, CHRIS; Sherwood HS; Olney, MD; (Y); Hon Roll; NHS; Maryland U; Bus Adm.

LEVERANCE, TOM; Parkdale SR HS; College Pk, MD; (Y); Sec AFS; Boy Scts; Pres Church Yth Grp; School Musical; Symp Band; Hon Roll; Opt Clb Awd; Spanish NHS; Cls 83 Schlrshp 86; VA Polytech; City-Urbn Plning.

LEVIN, DANIEL Z; Walt Whitman HS; Bethesda, MD; (Y); 1/450; Temple Yth Grp; Orch; Ntl Merit SF; MD Dstngshd Schlr 85; Socl Sci.

LEVIN, PAULA; Franklin SR HS; Reisterstown, MD; (Y); Pres Church Yth Grp; Cmnty Wkr; Teachers Aide; Y-Teens; Chorus; School Play; Mgr(s); Mgr Trk; Hon Roll; Jr NHS; Scl Wrk.

LEVINE, ADAM S; Baltimore City Coll HS; Baltimore, MD; (Y); 6/283; Chess Clb; Civic Clb; Computer Clb; Nwsp Stf; Swmmng; High Hon Roll; NHS; Ntl Merit SF; Mayoral Citation Acad Excell 85; Delta Sigma Theta Awd Schlrshp 85; Magna Cum Laude 83; Lib Arts.

LEVINE, KAREN; Walter Johnson HS; Bethesda, MD; (Y); Teachers Aide; Varsity Clb; Yrbk Stf; Rep Soph Cls; Rep VP Jr Cls; Rep VP Sr Cls; Im Bsktbl; Im Fld Hcky; Var L Mgr(s); Im Sftbl; Outstndng Ldrshp Qulties 86; Psych.

LEVY, LAURA S; John F Kennedy HS; Silver Spring, MD; (Y); Engr.

LEWIS, ALISA; Elkto HS; Elkton, MD; (Y); Debate Tm; Drama Clb; Band; Chorus; Concert Band; Mrchg Band; School Play; Symp Band; Nwsp Rptr; Stu Cncl; Cecil Cmnty Coll Bd Of Trustee Schlrshp 86; UFS-ACI-D Schlrshp 86; All-Cnty Hnrs Seminar Choir 86; Cecil CC; Theatre.

LEWIS, BEVERLY; Southern HS; Oakland, MD; (Y); Office Aide; Nwsp Rptr; Nwsp Stf; Hon Roll; Tri-St Bty Acad; Co.

LEWIS, CHRISTINE; Wicomico SR HS; Salisbury, MD; (Y); Hosp Aide; Math Tm; Spanish Clb; Chorus; Drill Tm; School Musical; Hon Roll; NHS; Prfct Atten Awd; Cnstutnl Lwyr.

LEWIS, DIANE; Hammond HS; Laurel, MD; (Y); 1/280; Off Jr Cls; Stu Cncl; Var L Bsktbl; Var L Sftbl; High Hon Roll; NHS; Acdmc Achvmnt Awd; Chem Hon Roll 85-86; Otology.

LEWIS, HEATHER; Walter Johnson HS; Bethesda, MD; (Y); French Clb; NFL; Orch; Rep Frsh Cls; Rep Soph Cls; Rep Jr Cls; Rep Stu Cncl; Var Fld Hcky; Var Socr.

LEWIS, KIM; Frederick HS; Frederick, MD; (Y); Library Aide; Office Aide; Trs Jr Cls; Trs Sr Cls; Rep Stu Cncl; Im Crs Cntry; Im Socr; Hon Roll; Jr NHS; NHS; Intl Relations.

LEWIS, KIMBERLY; Riverdale Baptist Schl; Capitol Heights, MD; (S); 2/66; Dance Clb; Hosp Aide; Pep Clb; Band; Church Choir; Pep Band; School Play; Yrbk Ed-Chief; Yrbk Rptr; Yrbk Stf; Top 10 Fin MD Modern Miss Pag 85; Mst Acad Trophy MD Modern Miss Pag 85; Acad All Amer 82; UNC Chapel Hill; Lawyer.

LEWIS, LISA; Bishop Walsh HS; Frostburg, MD; (Y); 5/104; Math Tm; Ski Clb; Church Choir; Trk; High Hon Roll; Merit Schltc Awd 86; Clemson U; Biochem.

LEWIS, MICHELLE E; Parkdale HS; Landover, MD; (Y); FBLA; Pep Clb; Spanish Clb; Teachers Aide; Stat Bsktbl; Hon Roll; Hampton U; Bio.

LEWIS, RACHEL; Wilde Lake HS; Columbia, MD; (Y); Debate Tm; Hosp Aide; Math Tm; VP PAVAS; Chorus; Fnlst Baltimroe Forensic Leag Debate Tour 86; Awd Eng Exc 86; Outstndng Confirmand Awd 85; Law.

LEWIS, RANA; James M Bennett SR HS; Salisbury, MD; (Y); Hosp Aide; Varsity Clb; Hst Soph Cls; Off Jr Cls; Pres Stu Cncl; Var L Bsktbl; Var L Fld Hcky; Var L Sftbl; Hon Roll.

LEWIS, RICKY; Carver Voc Tech HS; Baltimore, MD; (Y); 2/20; Rep Soph Cls; Trk; Prfct Atten Awd; Prtcptn Schl Wide Math Cntst Alg 84; Morgan ST U; Aerospace Engrng.

LEWIS, SHERI; Crossland HS; Capitol Hts, MD; (Y); 21/333; Church Yth Grp; CAP; Hosp Aide; Math Clb; Math Tm; Teachers Aide; Stu Cncl; Hon Roll; Acad Encllnc Awd; Howard U; Phrmcy.

LEWIS, SOBRENA; Crossland HS; Landover, MD; (Y); Church Yth Grp; Band; Trs Church Choir; Concert Band; Mrchg Band; Pep Band; Symp Band; Variety Show; Hon Roll; Prince Georges County Solo & Ensemble Festival 85-86; C P Jones Music Contest 86.

LEWIS, SONYA A; Eleanor Roosevelt Science/Tech Cntr; Capitol Heights, MD; (Y); French Clb; Math Tm; Pep Clb; French Hon Soc; Hon Roll; Jr NHS; NHS; Ntl Merit Ltr; Math Clb; Teachers Aide; Natl Achvt SF 85; Prince Geo Cnty Awad Acad Excllnce 84; Engr.

LIANG, WENCHI; Parkside HS; Fruitland, MD; (Y); 12/306; Am Leg Aux Girls St; French Clb; Varsity Clb; School Play; Variety Show; Off Stu Cncl; Var L Cheerleading; Var Sftbl; NHS; Yrbk Stf; Sectn Edtr Yrbk; Pre-Med.

LIBBY, GENE; Calvert HS; St Leonard, MD; (Y); Am Leg Boys St; ROTC; Rep Stu Cncl; Var Capt Crs Cntry; L Var Trk; Cit Awd; High Hon Roll; Hon Roll; Ntl Merit SF; Prfct Atten Awd; Ldrshp Acadmy Naval ROTC 86; Math.

LIBERTO, TIMOTHY; Woodlawn HS; Baltimore, MD; (Y); Nwsp Sprt Ed; Var Lcrss; JV Wrstlng; Law Enfrcmt.

LIBOWITZ, SIGMUND; Baltimore Polytechnic Inst; Baltimore, MD; (Y); 12/475; Pres Drama Clb; Pres Quiz Bowl; Pres Thesps; Ftbl; Thspn Gld Pn 85; Hnr Rl 85; Dns Lst 85; NY U; Drama.

LICHTENFELS, MIKE; Elkton HS; Elkton, MD; (Y); Key Clb; Math Clb; Math Tm; Office Aide; Teachers Aide; Rep Frsh Cls; JV Socr; Hon Roll; NHS; U Of DE; Engrng.

LIEBL, GRETCHEN; North Hagerstown HS; Hagerstown, MD; (Y); 10/360; Church Yth Grp; French Clb; FBLA; Key Clb; Orch; Yrbk Bus Mgr; Yrbk Stf; Hon Roll; NHS; James Madison U Spring String Thing Orch 84; Hagerstown JC; Bus.

LIED, CHERYL-ANN; North East HS; Elkton, MD; (Y); Leo Clb; Church Choir; Stage Crew; Yrbk Stf; Lit Mag; Rep Stu Cncl; High Hon Roll; Hon Roll; NHS; Ntl Merit Ltr; Outstndng Svc NHS 86; Outstndng Engl Stu 86; Discussion & Debate Hnrs 86; MFA; Tech Prod.

LIGHTNER, YARINA; Carver Vocational Tech HS; Baltimore, MD; (Y); FBLA; Hon Roll; NHS; Cert Of Hon Data Prcssng 86; Cert Of Awd Accntng 86; Cert Of Awd Acdmc & Ldrshp Skills 86; Howard U; Compu Sci.

LIJERON, ANTOINETTE JULIA; The Catholic HS Of Bltmore; Baltimore, MD; (Y); Dance Clb; Red Cross Aide; Service Clb; Spanish Clb; SADD; Teachers Aide; Acpl Chr; Chorus; Nwsp Rptr; Nwsp Stf; Ladies Aux Of Cath War Vets Outstndng Yth Awd 86; Essex CC; Mntl Hlth.

LILLER, DWAYNE; Southern Garrett HS; Oakland, MD; (Y); Computer Clb; Pres Soph Cls; Pres Jr Cls; Rep Stu Cncl; NC ST U; Air Frc Pilot.

LILLIS, TOMMY; Queen Anne Schl; Upr Marlboro, MD; (Y); Math Tm; Chorus; School Play; Stage Crew; Nwsp Stf; Var Bsbl; Var Bsktbl; Var JV Socr; Hon Roll; Catholic U Of Amenca; Elec Eng.

LILLY, PAMELA; Southern HS; Baltimore, MD; (Y); FBLA; Office Aide; Red Cross Aide; Teachers Aide; Nwsp Bus Mgr; Nwsp Rptr; Nwsp Stf; Yrbk Stf; Rep Frsh Cls; Hon Roll; Bus Mgmt.

LIM, JACKIE; Parkdale HS; Berwyn Hts, MD; (Y); French Clb; VP Soph Cls; VP Jr Cls; French Hon Soc; Hon Roll; Sentrl Schlrshp 86-90; Prince Georges CC; Bus Mgmnt.

LIMA, CARA; St Johns At Prospect Hall HS; Gaithersburg, MD; (Y); Science Clb; Ski Clb; L Co-Capt Cheerleading; Var Crs Cntry; Capt Trk; High Hon Roll; NHS; Nwsp Stf; Yrbk Stf; Var Bsktbl; Exclnc Biolgy 85; Prtcptn Natl Spnsh Exm 86; Sccsfl Cmpltn Jr Ldr Vlntr Prgrm 85; Pre-Med.

LIMERICK, KARLA A; Old Mill SR HS; Glen Burnie, MD; (Y); 55/509; Church Yth Grp; Pep Clb; Varsity Clb; JV Bsktbl; Capt Pom Pon; JV Vllybl; Hon Roll; Townson ST U; Math.

LIN, ANDY; Thomas Wootton HS; Rockville, MD; (Y); Computer Clb; JA; Concert Band; Yrbk Stf; Bsktbl; Mgr(s); Tennis; Cit Awd; High Hon Roll; Pres Acad Fit Awd 85-86; Natl Hnr Rl Awd 84-85; Natl Ldrshp & Svc Awd 84-85; U MD; Engrng.

LIN, CHUN YI; Parkdale HS; Hyattsville, MD; (S); AFS; Chorus; Church Choir; Hon Roll; Ntl Piano Plyng Aud, MD ST Music Tchrs Assn Awd 85; U MD; Acctng.

LIN, EPHRAIM PAUCHUNG; Winston Churchill HS; Potomac, MD; (Y); 16/612; Debate Tm; Math Tm; Rptr Lit Mag; Var L Tennis; NHS; Ntl Merit Ltr; Rnnr Up Montgomery Cnty B Doubles Ten Champnshp 86; 1st Pl Piano Solo MD ST Music Tchrs Assn 85; MIT; Engrng.

LINDEMANN JR, MICHAEL J; Thomas Stone HS; Waldorf, MD; (S); Chess Clb; Pres Debate Tm; Math Clb; Science Clb; JV Crs Cntry; Hon Roll; NHS; Parade Magz Young Columbus Wnnr 86; Acadmc Ltr 84-85; Frgn Svc Offcr.

LINDEMON III, RICHARD M; Baltimore City College; Baltimore, MD; (S); 38/383; Cmnty Wkr; Band; Concert Band; Jazz Band; Mrchg Band; Symp Band; Nwsp Rptr; Nwsp Stf; JV Bsbl; Var Socr; Air Force Acad; Aviatn.

LINDNER, ANTHONY; Archbishop Curley HS; Baltimore, MD; (S); 2/143; Am Leg Boys St; Aud/Vis; Boy Scts; School Play; Nwsp Rptr; Yrbk Stf; Coach Actv; JV Capt Ftbl; JV Lcrss; High Hon Roll; Marion Burke Knott Schlrshp 4 Yrs Full 84; U Of Notre Dame; Mngmnt.

LINDUNG, VALERIE A; Notre Dame Prep; Phoenix, MD; (Y); Band; Im Badmtn; Var Socr; Mgr Tennis; Im Vllybl; Hon Roll; Prfct Atten Awd; Loyola Coll; Elmntry Ed.

LINEBERGER, ANNE; Bowie Sr HS; Bowie, MD; (Y); Pres Church Yth Grp; Church Choir; Mrchg Band; Symp Band; Rep Frsh Cls; Rep Soph Cls; VP Jr Cls; Rep Sr Cls; Hon Roll; Latin Clb; Tri-M Hnr Soc Pres & Vp.

LINSENMEYER, MARY ELLEN; St Vincent Pallotti HS; Laurel, MD; (S); 15/116; Sec Trs AFS; NFL; Red Cross Aide; Sec Stu Cncl; Var L Socr; Var L Swmmng; Var L Tennis; NHS; 1st Pl Sci Fair Physcs 85; Stu Of Mnth 85; Mock Trial Tm 85 & 86.

LINTON, LATHAN; Cardinal Gibbons HS; Baltimore, MD; (Y); Boy Scts; Band; Jazz Band; School Musical; Wrstlng; Wrstlng Awd 84-86; Bsbl Awds 78-85; U Of MD; Bus.

LINZ, LAURA; John Carroll HS; Whitehall, MD; (Y); SADD; Band; Concert Band; Mrchg Band; School Musical; Ed Yrbk Stf; Mgr(s); Powder Puff Ftbl; Boy Scts; Var Mgr Trk; Sci.

LIPMAN, TAMMY; Mc Donogh Schl; Owings Mills, MD; (Y); 6/130; Cmnty Wkr; Hosp Aide; Service Clb; Teachers Aide; Nwsp Sprt Ed; Var Cheerleading; JV Fld Hcky; JV Lcrss; Gov Hon Prg Awd; High Hon Roll; Cum Laude Membrshp 86; The Compassion Cup 86; Duke.

LIPPERT, RICHARD; Chopticon HS; Charlotte Hall, MD; (Y); Science Clb; Spanish Clb; Varsity Clb; Var Capt Socr; Var Capt Tennis; High Hon Roll; Hon Roll; Acad Studnt Of Mnth 83 & 86; Acad Studnt Of Yr 85-86; Educ.

LISTER, TRACY; Great Mills HS; Nas Patuxent Riv, MD; (Y); 5/210; Church Yth Grp; VP SADD; Band; Concert Band; Mrchg Band; High Hon Roll; Hon Roll; NHS; Prfct Atten Awd; Engl Awd.

LISTOPAD, STEVEN; Patterson HS; Baltimore, MD; (Y); #1 In Class; Computer Clb; High Hon Roll; Hon Roll; Jr NHS; Pres NHS; Loyola; Comp Prmmrng.

LITTLE, RODNEY; Smithburg HS; Smithsburg, MD; (Y); Latin Clb; High Hon Roll; Printng.

LITTRELL, JOYCE; Governor Thomas Johnson HS; Frederick, MD; (Y); Church Yth Grp; Chrmn Cmnty Wkr; Hosp Aide; Latin Clb; Sec Thesps; VP Chorus; Church Choir; Stage Crew; Swmmng; Hon Roll; Mst Imprvd Swm Tm 84; Drama & Msc.

LITZKY, SARA RENEE; Annapolis SR HS; Annapolis, MD; (Y); 12/520; Girl Scts; Temple Yth Grp; Band; Mrchg Band; Orch; Hon Roll; Jr NHS; NHS; Pres Schlr; St Schlr; Penn ST U; Hotel-Rest Mngmt.

LIU, RICHARD; Thomas S Wootton HS; Gaithersburg, MD; (Y); Church Yth Grp; Teachers Aide; Varsity Clb; JV Var Ftbl; Im Sftbl; Im Trk; Im Wt Lftg; JV Var Wrstlng; Hon Roll; 4th Pl Montgomery JV Wrstlng Tour 85; Poli Sci.

LIU, SHERRIE; Perry Hall HS; Kingsville, MD; (Y); 1/454; Hosp Aide; VP Pres Spanish Clb; Yrbk Stf; Stu Cncl; L Pom Pon; L VP Tennis; NHS; Ntl Merit SF; Drill Tm; Jr NHS; 1st Pl Cmmrcl Art 83-84; Med.

LIVELSBERGER, MELISSA; Mc Donough HS; Waldorf, MD; (Y); FNA; Intnl Clb; Library Aide; Mrchg Band; High Hon Roll; NHS; Art Clb; Office Aide; Teachers Aide; Pres Acad Fit Awd 86; Silver Maxima Cum Laude Awd Natl Lat Exm 86; Principals Hnr Roll 86; Charles Cnty CC; RN.

LIVENGOOD, WARREN; Southern HS; Oakland, MD; (Y); Computer Clb; VICA; Ftbl; Trk; Wt Lftg; MVP Ftbl, Gold Medal VICA 85-86.

LIVERMAN, HEATH; Maurice J Mc Donough HS; White Plains, MD; (Y); Church Yth Grp; Band; Church Choir; Concert Band; Mrchg Band; Symp Band; Prfct Atten Awd; Prvt Piano Lssns; Ntl Adtns; Ntl Roll Amer Coll Mscns; Charles County CC.

LIVINGSTON, GRETCHEN M; Northwestern SR HS; Hyattsville, MD; (Y); 2/480; Drama Clb; Girl Scts; Math Tm; Capt Quiz Bowl; School Play; Ed Lit Mag; NHS; Ntl Merit Ltr; Sal; AFS; Rnnslr Polytchnc Math & Sci Awd 85; Duke U; Psychlgy.

LLOYD, JAMES; Northwestern HS; Takoma, MD; (Y); Hon Roll.

LLOYD, LEE; Pikesville HS; Balto, MD; (Y); Var L Ftbl; JV Lcrss; Var Wrstlng; NHS; Vet Med.

LO GIUDICE, RAMONA; Du Val SR HS; Lanham Seabrook, MD; (Y); 4-H; Sec Natl Beta Clb; Spanish Clb; Band; Mrchg Band; Symp Band; Capt Pom Pon; High Hon Roll; Hon Roll; NHS; Strght A In A P Hstry & Spnsh 85-86; 2nd Pl Microbio Fld Sci Fair 85-86.

LOAR, ANGIE; Bishop Walsh HS; Cumberland, MD; (Y); Drama Clb; Pep Clb; Ski Clb; School Musical; Rep Soph Cls; Stat Bsktbl; Stat Jr Cls; Stat Socr; Stat Trk; Hon Roll; Acctg.

LOC KLEAR, MARK; Patterson HS; Baltimore, MD; (Y); Var Lcrss; Var Socr; Var Wrstlng; Unsung Hero Awd Socr; Towson ST; Phys Educ.

LOCKARD, MARY ANNE; Northeast HS; North East, MD; (Y); FBLA; Teachers Aide; Hon Roll; Outstndg Achvt Acctg II 85; Schl Bk Store 85 & 86; FBLA Awd 84-86; Goldey Beacom Coll; Acctg.

LOCKETT, STACI LYNE; Forest Park HS; Baltimore, MD; (Y); Church Yth Grp; JA; Library Aide; VICA; Church Choir; Variety Show; Nwsp Stf; Pres Frsh Cls; Rep Soph Cls; Rep Jr Cls; Cert Of Rec Voca Bible Schl 86; Cert Of Awd Intern Wllms Baer Schl 85-86; Cert Otstndng Work In Sci 84; Messiah Coll; Excptnl Chldcre.

LOCKLEAR, ELI; Patterson #405 HS; Baltimore, MD; (Y); Cmnty Wkr; Letterman Clb; Varsity Clb; VICA; Var Bsbl; Prfct Atten Awd; Bst Pctr Yr Awd 86; Comp Oprtr Licns Awd 84; Athlt Wk Awd; Profsnl Bsbl Plyr.

LOCKLEY, DERRICK; Carver Vo-Tech HS; Baltimore, MD; (Y); Mchnst.

LODER, MARYBETH; Colonel Zadok Magruder HS; Rockville, MD; (Y); Var Cheerleading; High Hon Roll; Hon Roll; Loyola Coll.

LODWIG, CHRISSIE; St Johns Literary Inst Prospct Hall; Woodbine, MD; (Y); Cmnty Wkr; Science Clb; Ski Clb; Yrbk Stf; Rep Frsh Cls; Trs Soph Cls; Off Stu Cncl; JV Var Cheerleading; JV L Tennis; Hon Roll; Attnd Pres Inaugrtn 84; Chld Psychlgy.

LOFLAND, SAM; Colonel Richardson HS; Federalsburg, MD; (Y); 1/104; Chess Clb; Church Yth Grp; Pres Civic Clb; Computer Clb; Drama Clb; Pres French Clb; VP FBLA; Capt Math Tm; Spanish Clb; Rep Stu Cncl; 1st Pl Acctg 1 ST Cont FBLA 86; 2nd Pl Prlmntry Prodcr-ST Cont FBLA 85; U Of MD Coll Pk; Physcs.

LOGAN, CHERYL; Severna Park HS; Severna Park, MD; (Y); 4/461; Church Yth Grp; Cmnty Wkr; Teachers Aide; Church Choir; Orch; Stu Cncl; Sftbl; High Hon Roll; NHS; Pres Schlr; Anne Arundel Cnty Publc Schls Schlrshp 86; Oberlin Conservatory; Music Tch.

LOGGIA, ANDREW T; Seneca Valley HS; Germantown, MD; (Y); Pres Aud/Vis; Sec Science Clb; Ski Clb; Temple Yth Grp; Crs Cntry; L Trk; Hon Roll; NHS; Orch; Rep Frsh Cls; Elec Engr.

LOGSDON, DAVID; Laurel SR HS; Laurel, MD; (Y); Boys Clb Am; Ski Clb; Teachers Aide; School Play; Nwsp Rptr; Rep Stu Cncl; Var L Crs Cntry; Im Ice Hcky; Var L Trk; Kamikaze Striders 84-86; U Of DE; Psych.

LOHINSKI, MARY; Mt De Sales Acad; Baltimore, MD; (Y); Library Aide; Chorus; Hon Roll; Nic Prsn Awd 84-85; Prfct Attndnc Awd 83-85; Cert Apprctn Awd 85-86; Catonsville CC; Paralgl Sec.

LOHMAN, CHAD; Bowie HS; Bowie, MD; (Y); Math Tm; Office Aide; Pres Science Clb; Im Coach Actv; Var L Crs Cntry; L Mgr(s); Var L Trk; Im Vllybl; Hon Roll; Awd Cert Excel Physics 85-86; JR Olympics 3rd Natls 84-85; Sci.

LOHMEYER, LEANNE; Archbishop Keough HS; Ellicott, MD; (Y); Sec GAA; VP Spanish Clb; Concert Band; Var JV Bsktbl; Var Sftbl; Var Vllybl; Hon Roll; NHS; NEDT Awd; Hghst Geom Hnrs Avg 85; Ed.

LOKER, ANNIE; Saint Marys-Ryken HS; Leonardtown, MD; (Y); Drama Clb; English Clb; School Play; Lit Mag; NEDT Awd; Art Awd Drwng & Dsgn 84; 1st Pl Art Cntst $50 84; MS Inst Of Art; Fine Arts.

LOLLI, JENNIFER; Frederick HS; Frederick, MD; (Y); AFS; Spanish Clb; Band; Concert Band; Off Frsh Cls; Sec Soph Cls; Off Jr Cls; Capt Cheerleading; Ice Hcky; Swmmng; Chrldng Ldrshp Awd 85; Attnded MD Ldrshp Wrkshp 84; U Of MD; Merch.

LOMACKY, LARISA O; Holton-Arms Schl; Silver Spring, MD; (Y); Library Aide; Math Tm; Office Aide; Nwsp Stf; Yrbk Rptr; Lit Mag; Ntl Merit SF; 1st Pl Stu Cat WV Poetry Soc Cont 84; 5th Pl Natl Frnch Cont 85; Indctn Cum Laude Soc 85; Coll William & Mary; Engl.

LOMAX, CHRISTINE; Dunbar HS; Baltimore, MD; (Y); FBLA; Pep Clb; Yrbk Stf; Rep Frsh Cls; Rep Soph Cls; Sec Jr Cls; VP Sr Cls; Var Co-Capt Cheerleading; Pom Pon; Hon Roll; Mrt Schlstc Awd 86; Dunbar Alumnic Schlrshp 86; Natl Assoc Bus 86; Towson ST U.

LONABERGER, CHERIE LYN; Bladensburg SR HS; Riverdale, MD; (Y); Office Aide; Teachers Aide; Ed Nwsp Stf; Ed Yrbk Stf; Pom Pon; Cit Awd; Lion Awd; Masonic Awd; Frn Schl Sprt Awd 86; Mst Imprvd Pom Pon 86; PG CC; Psych.

LONDON, DAVID L; Winston Churchill HS; Potomac, MD; (Y); 15/612; Debate Tm; NFL; Quiz Bowl; Spanish Clb; Pres Temple Yth Grp; Hon Roll; NHS; Ntl Merit SF.

LONG, JOHN; La Plata HS; Waldorf, MD; (Y); Aud/Vis; Boy Scts; Computer Clb; French Clb; Math Clb; Cit Awd; High Hon Roll; Hon Roll; Ntl Merit Ltr; CCCC; Bus.

LONG, KEITH; Middletown HS; Frederick, MD; (Y); Pres Church Yth Grp; Intnl Clb; Band; Jazz Band; Mrchg Band; Variety Show; Ftbl; L Trk; Hon Roll; Dir Awd Jazz Band 86; Al Cnty Jazz Band 85-86; Tutrng Awd Intl Clb 86; Liberty U; Biochem.

LONG, KEVIN; Takoma Acad; Bowie, MD; (S); Ski Clb; Chorus; Off Frsh Cls; Trs Soph Cls; JV Mgr Bsktbl; Sftbl; Vllybl; Hon Roll; Off NHS; All Trnmnt Tm, Hnrbl Ment All Conf Tm 84-85; USC; Med.

LONG, MICHAEL; Heritage Acad; Hagerstown, MD; (S); 3/25; Chorus; School Play; Capt Bsbl; Capt Bsktbl; Capt Socr; Cit Awd; High Hon Roll; Hon Roll; Opt Clb Awd; Army Schlr/Ath Awd 84-85; All Cnty Leadng Scorer Bsktbl 85; 2nd All Cnty Small Schl Tm 85; U VA; Publc Reltns.

LONG, MIKE; Joppatowne HS; Joppa, MD; (Y); Drama Clb; German Clb; JA; SADD; Band; Chorus; Concert Band; Jazz Band; Mrchg Band; School Musical; Harford CC; Electrncs.

LONG, MONA D; Calvert HS; Huntingtown, MD; (Y); Church Yth Grp; Trs Drama Clb; Church Choir; School Play; Rep VP Stu Cncl; Var Wt Lftg; High Hon Roll; NHS; Opt Clb Awd.

LONG, TINA; Calvert HS; Huntingtown, MD; (Y); Church Yth Grp; Cmnty Wkr; Computer Clb; Office Aide; High Hon Roll; Hon Roll; Prfct Atten Awd.

LOOMIS, REBECCA; La Plata HS; Newburg, MD; (Y); Science Clb; Teachers Aide; Rep Frsh Cls; Rep Soph Cls; Rep Stu Cncl; Hon Roll; NHS; Ntl Merit Ltr.

LOOMIS, SUSAN L; Southern Garrett HS; Deer Park, MD; (S); Church Yth Grp; German Clb; GAA; Ski Clb; JV Cheerleading; Trk; Intl Bus.

LOPEZ, CARLOS; Gaithersburg HS; Gaithersburg, MD; (Y); Drama Clb; Jazz Band; School Musical; Variety Show; Trk; Musician.

LORD, DWAYNE; Pocomoke HS; Pocomoke, MD; (Y); 22/100; Church Yth Grp; Computer Clb; Band; Jazz Band; Mrchg Band; Yrbk Phtg; FL Inst Tech; Comp Engrng.

LORE, LYNN; Friendly HS; Ft Washington, MD; (Y); Teachers Aide; Chrmn Sr Cls; Var JV Cheerleading; Pom Pon; Sftbl; Hon Roll; Natl Hnr Rl 86; Pgcc; Hotel Mgt.

LOTRICH, HEATHER; Elkton Christian Schl; Newark, DE; (S); VP Pep Clb; School Play; Yrbk Ed-Chief; Sec Frsh Cls; Sec Jr Cls; Sec Sr Cls; Capt Cheerleading; Var Sftbl; Hon Roll; NHS; Hmcmng Ct 84-85; Sccr Qn 85; Extraordnry Christian Stus Of Amer 84; U DE.

LOTT JR, FRED; Dematha Catholic HS; Riverdale, MD; (Y); Church Yth Grp; Cmnty Wkr; Office Aide; Spanish Clb; Varsity Clb; Chorus; Sec Soph Cls; Var Bsktbl; Var Mgr(s); Swmmng; Vlntr Svc Awd From Md Prk & Plnng 84; Bus Fnce.

LOUDAN, DENISE F; Brunswick HS; Knoxville, MD; (Y); Drama Clb; FBLA; Spanish Clb; Teachers Aide; Chorus; Concert Band; Mrchg Band; Pep Band; School Musical; Nwsp Rptr; Nrsg.

LOUIE, LINDA FAYE; Hammond HS; Columbia, MD; (Y); 33/262; English Clb; Intnl Clb; Math Tm; Spanish Clb; Teachers Aide; Lit Mag; Hon Roll; Jr NHS; NHS; Spanish NHS; Pres Acad Fit Awd 86; Acad Schl Ltr 85; U MD College Pk; Engrng.

LOVE, KERRY; St Marys Ryken HS; Lusby, MD; (Y); 10/175; School Play; Yrbk Stf; Var Fld Hcky; Var Trk; High Hon Roll; Spnsh Awd 85; Loyola; Math.

LOVE, ROBIN; Randallstown HS; Randallstown, MD; (Y); Temple Yth Grp; School Musical; Var Capt Fld Hcky; Hon Roll; NHS; Grad Comm 84-86; VA Polytechnic Inst.

LOVELLETTE, LISA; Snow Hill HS; Snow Hill, MD; (S); AFS; Sec Soph Cls; Trs Sr Cls; Rep Stu Cncl; High Hon Roll; Pres NHS; Ntl Merit Ltr; St Schlr; Hosp Aide; Score Keeper; Centry III Ldrshp Awd; Legal Intern; Notre Dame Maryland; Bio.

LOVICK, JENNIFER DENISE; Suitland HS; District Hts, MD; (Y); Office Aide; Radio Clb; Science Clb; Spanish Clb; Teachers Aide; VP Sr Cls; Capt Cheerleading; Var Gym; NHS; Ntl Merit Schol; Disabled Amer Vets Awd 86; Var Awd 86; Hall Fame Awd Chrldng 86; U MD College Pk; Pre-Med.

LOWE, GLENDA; Mardela HS; Sharptown, MD; (S); 5/54; Letterman Clb; Pres Sr Cls; Capt Bsktbl; Capt Fld Hcky; Capt Sftbl; Sec NHS; All-Conf MVP Field Hockey 84-86; Yth Achvmnt Awd 85-86; Longwood Coll; Bio.

LOWE, HELEN; Westminster HS; Westminster, MD; (Y); Drama Clb; 4-H; Thesps; School Play; Stage Crew; Lit Mag; 4-H Awd; High Hon Roll; NHS; Ntl Merit SF; Rochester Inst Tech; Phtgrphy.

LOWE, L MICHAEL; North Harford HS; Whiteford, MD; (Y); Computer Clb; German Clb; Teachers Aide; Crs Cntry; Swmmng; Hon Roll; MD U; Airplane Pilot.

LOWE, LAURA; Smithsburg HS; Hagerstown, MD; (Y); Latin Clb; Stage Crew; Nwsp Sprt Ed; Nwsp Stf; Sec Frsh Cls; Stu Cncl; JV Var Bsktbl; L Sftbl; JV Var Vllybl; Hon Roll; Physcl Thrpy.

LOWERY, TRACY; Fort Hill HS; Cumberland, MD; (Y); Jr Cls; Sr Cls; Cheerleading; Trk; Frostburg ST Coll; Acctnt.

LU, THOMAS; Bowie HS; Bowie, MD; (Y); Latin Clb; Office Aide; Spanish Clb; Swmmng; Hon Roll; Duke U; Engrng.

LUBITZ, JESSICA L; Eleanor Roosevelt HS; Laurel, MD; (Y); Cmnty Wkr; Teachers Aide; Rep Sr Cls; Hon Roll; U Of MD College Pk; Psych.

LUCAS, TERESA; Institue Of Notre Dame; Baltimore, MD; (Y); Art Clb; Service Clb; NHS; MD Inst Coll Of Art; Grphc Art.

LUCHINSKY, HOWARD; Pikesville HS; Balto, MD; (Y); Boy Scts; Computer Clb; French Clb; Band; Concert Band; Mrchg Band; Im Bowling; NHS.

LUDDEN, KEVIN; Northwestern HS; Chillum, MD; (Y); Boys Clb Am; Pres Church Yth Grp; Cmnty Wkr; German Clb; Library Aide; Office Aide; Var L Socr; Boy Of Yr 83; P B Cnty Insrnc Awd 85; U Of MD; Bus.

LUDEWIG, HOLLY K; Winston Churchill HS; Bethesda, MD; (Y); Church Yth Grp; Civic Clb; School Musical; Rep Stu Cncl; Im Powder Puff Ftbl; Schltc Arts Comptn Fnlst 86; Ntl Fndtn Advncmnt Arts Fnlst; Fine Artist.

LUDWIG, ANDREA; Archbishop Keough HS; Baltimore, MD; (Y); High Hon Roll; NEDT Awd; Towson ST U; Secndry Ed.

LUDY, LINDA; Glenelg HS; Dayton, MD; (Y); AFS; Cmnty Wkr; French Clb; GAA; Intnl Clb; Teachers Aide; Varsity Clb; Var Fld Hcky; Var Capt Socr; High Hon Roll; Nrsng.

LUFT, LISA; Middletown HS; Middletown, MD; (Y); Red Cross Aide; Ski Clb; Teachers Aide; Band; Chorus; Concert Band; Mrchg Band; School Musical; Hon Roll; Mardi Gras Prncss 86; Shepherd Coll; Ed.

LUHN, MELISSA; Heritage Acad; Middletown, MD; (S); 3/30; Q&S; Chorus; School Play; Nwsp Rptr; Yrbk Stf; High Hon Roll; Ntl Assn Christian Schls Fine Arts Cmptn Wnnr 85.

LUKAS, LISA; Archbishop Keough HS; Balt, MD; (Y); Art Clb; Hon Roll; Cmmtmnt Reqrmnt For Crfts Clb 85-86; Crfts Cntst 86; Typng Prfncy Cert 86; Comm Art.

LUMPKIN, NICOLE; Oxon Hill SR HS; Ft Washington, MD; (Y); Varsity Clb; Var Pom Pon; Hon Roll; Bus.

LUMPKIN, STEPHANIE; Notre Dame Prep; Baltimore, MD; (Y); Cmnty Wkr; French Clb; Hosp Aide; Latin Clb; Rep Frsh Cls; JV Var Mgr(s); JV Var Score Keeper; Var JV Tennis; Hon Roll; Outstndng Achvt NEDT 84; Schlrshp Study Abroad France 86; Bio.

LUND, PETER; Friendly SR HS; Ft Washington, MD; (Y); 71/394; Sec Church Yth Grp; CAP; Computer Clb; Science Clb; School Musical; Nwsp Stf; Hon Roll; 2nd Pl MD Chap Amer Lung Assn Commercial Wrtng Cont 86; Search & Rescue Rbbn 86; Mitchel Awd 86; Concordia Coll; Elec Engrng.

LUNDELL III, PERN ANDREW; Baltimore Polytechnic Inst; Baltimore, MD; (Y); 89/486; Chess Clb; Drama Clb; Church Choir; School Musical; Im Bsktbl; JV Crs Cntry; Golf; Im Capt Vllybl; Hon Roll; Prfct Atten Awd; Natl Sec Agncy; Engrg.

LUNDQUIST, CAROL A; Notre Dame Preparatory Schl; Lutherville, MD; (Y); 17/119; Church Yth Grp; Drama Clb; Sec 4-H; Teachers Aide; Rep Stu Cncl; Cheerleading; Hon Roll; NHS; Anml Sci Schlrshp 86; VA Tech; Vet.

LUNSFORD, LISA; John F Kennedy HS; Silver Spring, MD; (Y); 7/468; Church Yth Grp; Math Tm; Teachers Aide; Church Choir; Var L Vllybl; Hon Roll; Ntl Hispnaic Schlr SF 85-86; Engr Apprentce Pgm; U MD; Elect Engr.

LUPPINO, CHRISTINE; Gaithersburg HS; Gaithersburg, MD; (Y); Scholastic Bowl; SADD; Lit Mag; French Hon Soc; NHS; Ntl Merit Ltr; Tutr Elem Stu 85-86; Frnch.

LUSBY, LISA; Gov Thomas Johnson HS; Frederick, MD; (Y); Church Yth Grp; Debate Tm; Hosp Aide; Latin Clb; SADD; Jazz Band; Madrigals; School Musical; Sr Cls; Off Hon Roll; PA ST U; Sci.

LUSCONBE, NINA; Stephen Decatur HS; Ocean City, MD; (Y); AFS; Computer Clb; Band; Concert Band; Nwsp Phtg; Nwsp Rptr; Nwsp Stf; High Hon Roll; Hon Roll; Photo.

LUSK, HOLLY S; Maurice J Mc Donough HS; Port Tobacco, MD; (Y); Band; Concert Band; Jazz Band; Mrchg Band; Orch; School Musical; Symp Band; High Hon Roll; Hon Roll; Dist Solo & Ens 83-86; Typwrtng Awd 83; Charles Cnty CC; Psych.

LUSKUS, ADRIENNE; St Marys Ryken HS; Charlotte Hall, MD; (Y); Church Yth Grp; FBLA; Spanish Clb; Band; Bsktbl; Trk; Hon Roll; Stock Broker.

LUTHE, JOEY; Mount Hebron HS; Ellicott City, MD; (Y); SADD; Teachers Aide; Chorus; Rep Jr Cls; Rep Sr Cls; Var Capt Bsktbl; Var Capt Ftbl; Var Capt Lcrss; Hon Roll; Mst Blvl Plyr JR Vrsty Bsktbl 84-85; Heros Smmr All Str Lcrss 86; Mst Imprvd Frnch Stu 83-84; Engr.

LUTHER, FRED; Joppatowne HS; Joppa, MD; (Y); French Clb; Var L Bsbl; Var L Bsktbl; Var L Ftbl; Prfct Atten Awd; Marine Bio.

LUU, LOC; Parkdale HS; Riverdale, MD; (Y); French Clb; French Hon Soc; Hon Roll; U Of MD; Pre Med.

LUZIUS, TIM; Oakland Mills HS; Columbia, MD; (Y); Hon Roll; UMBC; Bus.

LY, CUC THI HONG; South Hagersstown HS; Hagerstown, MD; (Y); 18/227; Bausch & Lomb Sci Awd; Elks Awd; Hon Roll; NHS; Hood Coll; Med.

LYERLY, WENDY; Walkersville HS; Walkersville, MD; (Y); 11/231; GAA; Rep SADD; Chorus; School Musical; Var L Bsktbl; Powder Puff Ftbl; Var Capt Vllybl; High Hon Roll; NHS; Socl Sci Clb 84-86; Elem Ed.

LYNCH, BETH; John Carroll Schl; Fallston, MD; (Y); 17/238; Pres 4-H; Spanish Clb; School Musical; Stage Crew; Nwsp Sprt Ed; Yrbk Stf; Stat Bsktbl; JV Fld Hcky; Var Trk; 4-H Awd; Hlth.

LYNCH, DARCY; Dulaney SR HS; Phoenix, MD; (Y); 74/480; Drama Clb; Service Clb; Band; Stage Crew; Hon Roll; Jr NHS; NHS; Bltmr Co Yth Cnfrnc 86; Dcrtng Cmmtee Dncs; Evng Dnc Pgms.

LYNCH, PAM; Williamsport HS; Hagerstown, MD; (Y); 3/227; French Clb; SADD; Band; Symp Band; French Hon Soc; Hon Roll; NHS; Rotary Awd; Mrchg Band; Pep Band; Senatorial Schlrshp 86; Natl Assn For Women In Constructn Awd 86; Frostburg ST Coll; Cvl Engrng.

LYNCH, SUSAN L; Stephan Decatur HS; Bishopville, MD; (Y); Pres FBLA; Sec Sr Cls; Rep Stu Cncl; Var Gym; Cit Awd; Gov Hon Prg Awd; Hon Roll; Sec NHS; Ctznshp Svc Awd Gov Top 5 Percent FBLA Awd 86; Bus Awd Gym Coaches Awd 86; Film Fstvl 1st Pl Cnty 86; Towson ST U; Elem Ed.

LYONS, KRISTIN NOELLE; North Harford SR HS; Jarrettsville, MD; (Y); Pres German Clb; Varsity Clb; Nwsp Bus Mgr; Nwsp Rptr; Yrbk Stf; Co-Capt Fld Hcky; Var Mgr(s); Var Powder Puff Ftbl; NHHS Hgh Prfmnce 85; Hist.

LYONS, VICKI LYNN; Sherwood HS; Silver Spring, MD; (Y); 35/317; Debate Tm; Intnl Clb; Model UN; Yrbk Stf; Hon Roll; NHS; Ntl Merit Ltr; 4 Yr Hlf Tuitn Schlrshp Johns Hopkins U 86; Johns Hopkins U; Intl Stds.

MAAS, KATHLEEN G; Northern HS; Huntingtown, MD; (Y); 29/301; 4-H; Teachers Aide; Yrbk Phtg; Dnfth Awd; 4-H Awd; Hon Roll; Opt Clb Awd; Nwsp Phtg; MD ST Wnnr 4-H Dog Care & Trng Prog 84; Sci Fair Awds US Army, Air Force, Marines 85-86; VA Polytechnic Inst; Wldlf Res.

MABE, TAMMY; North East HS; Elkton, MD; (Y); VP Sec FHA; Chorus; JV Vllybl; Hon Roll; Cecil CC; Exec Sec.

MAC DONALD, MALCOLM; Oakland Mills HS; Columbia, MD; (Y); Chess Clb; Math Tm; Ski Clb; School Play; Hon Roll.

MACCHETTO, CLAUDIO; Georgetown Prep Schl; Rockville, MD; (Y); Church Choir; Science Clb; JV Ftbl; Var Swmmng; JV Trk; NHS; 1st Hnrs 83-86; Bus Adm.

MACDONALD, CATHERINE; Bowie HS; Bowie, MD; (Y); Cmnty Wkr; Hosp Aide; Office Aide; Spanish Clb; Drill Tm; Flag Corp; Rep Sr Cls; Pom Pon; Prfct Atten Awd; Starmaker Dance Comptn 3rd Pl 83; 3rd Pl Excllnce ADTA Assn Pom Pons 86; Outstndng Spirit Awd 86; Towson; Psych.

MACDONALD, NIKKI; Gaithersburg HS; Gaithersburg, MD; (Y); AFS; Dance Clb; Girl Scts; Pep Clb; SADD; Swmmng; Hon Roll; Fshn Mrchndsng 86; Engl.

MACE, ROBYN; John Carroll HS; Joppatowne, MD; (Y); Computer Clb; GAA; Ski Clb; Varsity Clb; JV Bsktbl; Stat Score Keeper; JV Var Sftbl; Intr Dsgn.

MACEY, JENNY; Northern HS; Huntingtown, MD; (Y); Chess Clb; Teachers Aide; Chorus; Concert Band; Jazz Band; Mrchg Band; School Musical; Swmmng; Trk; 4-H Awd; Morehead ST U; Music Eductn.

MACK, EDMUND J; Carver Vocational Tech; Baltimore, MD; (Y); Science Clb; Rep Jr Cls.

MACK, MICHELE M; Franklin HS; Reisterstown, MD; (Y); Yrbk Stf; Sec Sr Cls; Rep Stu Cncl; JV Var Sftbl; High Hon Roll; NHS; Prfct Atten Awd; Office Aide; Church Choir; Mrchg Band; Franklin HS Schltc Medal 86; Principals List Awd 86; Distngshd Svc Medal Awd 86; Towson ST U.

MACK, ROSCHELLE; Chopticon HS; Mechanicsville, MD; (Y); Church Yth Grp; Spanish Clb; Varsity Clb; Church Choir; Nwsp Stf; Cheerleading; JV Vllybl; High Hon Roll; Hon Roll; NHS; Charlotte Hall Fellowship 86; Comm.

MACKALL, KEVIN R; Calvert HS; Lusby, MD; (Y); 1/250; Computer Clb; VP Sr Cls; Stu Cncl; High Hon Roll; NHS; Opt Clb Awd; Val; Natl Mert Cmndtn Schlrshp 86-87; Carnegie Mellon; Chemcl Engrng.

MACKOWIAK, DEBBIE; The Fallston HS; Fallston, MD; (Y); 17/250; Church Yth Grp; Service Clb; Teachers Aide; Nwsp Rptr; L Mgr Bsktbl; L Sftbl; L Vllybl; High Hon Roll; NHS; Acad Ltrs 85 & 86; Loyola Coll; Econ.

MACQUEEN, RUTH C; Towson HS; Towson, MD; (Y); Band; Ed Yrbk Stf; Rep Jr Cls; Mgr Lcrss; Mgr Socr; Mgr Vllybl; Moore Coll Of Art Schlrshp 86-87; Moore Coll Of Art; Intr Dsgn.

MACWHA, DAVID; La Plata HS; Waldorf, MD; (Y); Aud/Vis; Church Yth Grp; Exploring; Science Clb; Lib Arts.

MADABHUSHI, RAJIV; John F Kennedy HS; Silver Spring, MD; (Y); 4/468; Debate Tm; French Clb; Mathletes; Math Tm; Natl Beta Clb; Quiz Bowl; ROTC; Science Clb; Color Guard; French Hon Soc; Prsdntl Acad Ftnss Awd, Frnch Awd, Acad All Amer Awd 85-86; U PA; Engrng.

MADDEN, SHANNON; Glenelg HS; Mt Airy, MD; (Y); AFS; Model UN; Sec Jr Cls; Capt L Bsktbl; L Var Tennis; High Hon Roll; Ntl Merit Ltr; Stu Cncl; Intnl Clb; Band; Balt Fld Hcky Assn Schlrshp, 6th MT Grnd Concouis Ntl Frnch 84; Duke U; Pre Med.

MADEY, DANIEL; Brunswick HS; Burkittsville, MD; (Y); 15/160; Am Leg Boys St; Drama Clb; Letterman Clb; Quiz Bowl; Spanish Clb; School Musical; School Play; Pres Rep Stu Cncl; Var L Trk; Hon Roll; Frederick Cnty Assoc Stu Cncls VP 86-87; Its Acadmc Tm 84-87; Loyola Coll.

MADIGAN, KELLEY; John Carroll Schl; Forest Hill, MD; (Y); 33/238; Am Leg Aux Girls St; Hosp Aide; Latin Clb; Ski Clb; JV Var Fld Hcky; JV Var Lcrss; JV Mgr(s); JV Trk; French Hon Soc; High Hon Roll; Arch.

MADINE, SHANNON; Magruder HS; Olney, MD; (Y); Hosp Aide; Latin Clb; Ski Clb; Yrbk Stf; JV Bsktbl; JV Sftbl; Var Tennis; Hon Roll; NHS; Psych.

MADISON, DEBORAH; Suitland HS; District Height, MD; (Y); FBLA; Pep Clb.

MAGEE III, MARSHALL; Evening HS; Waldorf, MD; (Y); VICA; US Air Force.

MAGENAU, GAIL; South River HS; Davidsonville, MD; (Y); 2/360; Dance Clb; Math Tm; Trs Stu Cncl; Cheerleading; High Hon Roll; NHS; HOBY Ldrshp Sem 85; Aero Engrng.

MAGGIO, JOSEPH; Patterson High School HS; Baltimore, MD; (Y); Art Clb; Church Yth Grp; Drama Clb; Key Clb; Pres Science Clb; SADD; Thesps; Chorus; School Play; Off Sr Cls; Hnr Serv Schl 86; Art Fest Awd 86; Am Legn Cert Brnz Mdl 86; Juniata College; Microbio.

MAH, LANI; Gaithersburg HS; Gaithersburg, MD; (Y); Sec AFS; Swmmng; Var Tennis; Hon Roll; Jr NHS; 22nd MD Tennis 84-85; U MA; Sports Psychlgst.

MAHAFFEY, THERESA; North East HS; North East, MD; (Y); Dance Clb; Key Clb; Leo Clb; Office Aide; Teachers Aide; Drm Mjr(t); Hon Roll; Coll.

MAHAFFEY JR, WAYNE DAVID; De Matha Catholic HS; Bowie, MD; (Y); Church Yth Grp; Cmnty Wkr; Teachers Aide; Varsity Clb; JV Bsbl; JV Var Bsktbl; Coach Actv; Var Sftbl; Hon Roll; NHS; Outstndg Acad & Athl Achvt 85-86; Schltc Athl Awd; Mrshl For Grad Cls 85 & 86; Sprts Med.

MAHAN, TOMMY; Wilcomico SR HS; Salisbury, MD; (Y); 34/256; Boys Clb Am; Chess Clb; Church Yth Grp; Dance Clb; JCL; Latin Clb; Pep Clb; Varsity Clb; Band; Concert Band; Acad Ltr 86; U Of MD Coll Pk; Vet Med.

MAHER, PATRICK; Georgetown Prep; Ijamsville, MD; (Y); 19/93; School Musical; L Ftbl; Capt Wrstlng; Var Hon Roll; Ntl Merit SF; Spnsh Medal 83; 2nd Pl IAC Wrestling 86; Villanova U.

MAHER, TINA; Great Mills HS; Nas Pax River, MD; (Y); 1/273; Trs Soph Cls; Trs Stu Cncl; Var L Bsktbl; Var L Fld Hcky; Var L Tennis; High Hon Roll; NHS; Opt Clb Awd; Herald Awd 85; U MD; Engrng.

MAHMOOD, RUBY; Mercy HS; Baltimore, MD; (Y); Yrbk Stf; Rep Frsh Cls; Rep Stu Cncl; Tennis; Cit Awd; High Hon Roll; Hon Roll; NHS; Outstndng SR Sci Stu 86; Gnrl Excllnc 86; Outstndng Physics Stu 86; UMBC; Med.

MAHONEY, JOAN MARGARET; Elizabeth Seton HS; College Park, MD; (Y); 4/195; Church Yth Grp; Ski Clb; SADD; Pres Frsh Cls; Trs Soph Cls; Rep Stu Cncl; Var Capt Cheerleading; Hon Roll; NHS; U MD.

MAIER, MATT; St Marys Ryken HS; Lexington Park, MD; (S); 22/138; Boy Scts; Drama Clb; French Clb; Band; Concert Band; Jazz Band; Orch; Pep Band; School Musical; Stage Crew; Bst Slsmn For St Marys Ryken Bnd 83-84; Schl Mus Awd 83-84; VA Inst Of Tech; Elec Engr.

MAJEROWICZ, LYNDA; Mount De Sales Acad; Pasadena, MD; (Y); VP Soph Cls; Pres Jr Cls; Rep Stu Cncl; JV Stat Bsktbl; Var Fld Hcky; Var Lcrss; Var Score Keeper; Var Socr.

MAJEWSKI, LEIGH ANN; Westminster HS; Westminister, MD; (Y); Office Aide; Ski Clb; Var Capt Bsktbl; Var Mgr(s); Stat Socr; High Hon Roll; Hon Roll; Im Lcrss; Mid Atlantic PGA Schlrshp 86; Prsdntl Acad Ftns Awd 86; Vrsty Bsktbl Unsng Hero 86; Delaware U; Anml Sci.

MALACHI, LORI; Regina HS; Washington, DC; (Y); Church Yth Grp; Intnl Clb; JA; Pep Clb; Yrbk Phtg; Yrbk Stf; Vllybl; Hon Roll; Food Sci.

MALAFEEW, ERIC J; Governor Thomas Johnson HS; Frederick, MD; (Y); 1/350; Computer Clb; German Clb; Math Tm; Science Clb; Orch; Golf; Tennis; High Hon Roll; NHS; Ntl Merit Ltr; Accptnce Ltd Astrnmy Cls Johns Hopkins 86; Vrsty Ltr, Top Schl Scorer AHSME Mth Cont 85; Princeton; Chem Engrng.

MALAK, MILES; Bishop Walsh HS; Cumberland, MD; (Y); 21/138; Chess Clb; French Clb; Library Aide; Bsbl; Capt Bsktbl; Capt Co-Capt Socr; High Hon Roll; Hon Roll; NHS; Prfct Atten Awd; 1st Bi ST All Trnmnt Sccr Tm 84; Intrmrls Chmps; Frostburg ST Coll; Acctg.

MALAT, JONATHAN; Loyola HS; Baltimore, MD; (Y); Church Yth Grp; Cmnty Wkr; NFL; Acpl Chr; Band; Chorus; Concert Band; Jazz Band; Stage Crew; JV Trk; Hdmstrs Awd Music; Loyola Coll; Pre Med.

MALBY, HEATHER; Thomas Stone HS; Waldorf, MD; (S); Teachers Aide; Sec Stu Cncl; Capt Crs Cntry; Sec Ftbl; Tennis; Capt Trk; NHS; St Schlr; Sec Bsktbl; High Hon Roll; All SMAC All Cnty Trk 84; All SMAC All Cnty MVP Ten 85; All SMAC All Cnty All Regn MVP Crs Cntry; U VA; Bus Adm.

MALIK, JAWAD A; Meade SR HS; Laurel, MD; (Y); 26/440; Pres VP Math Clb; Capt Math Tm; Concert Band; Mrchg Band; Symp Band; Hon Roll; Ntl Merit SF; County Math Comptn Champ 84; All Cty Band 84; 4th Pl Ntl Math League 85; Theoretical Physics.

MALINOW, LOUIS; Randallstown SR HS; Randallstown, MD; (Y); Church Yth Grp; JV Socr; Var Trk; NHS.

MALLERY, SCOTT; Mt Savage HS; Mt Savage, MD; (Y); 5/60; FBLA; Band; Nwsp Rptr; Trs Sr Cls; Rep Stu Cncl; Var L Bsbl; Var L Bsktbl; Var L Socr; Hon Roll; VFW Awd; Army Res Awd Hghst Schltc Avg Ath 86; Frostburg ST Coll; Bus Adm.

MALLORY, NANCY; Rockville HS; Rockville, MD; (S); 1/464; Church Yth Grp; Pres L 4-H; Hosp Aide; Spanish Clb; Nwsp Stf; Yrbk Ed-Chief; Jr NHS; NHS; St Schlr; Val; Prin Awd All A Yr; Bus.

MALONE, CHAD; Beall HS; Frostburg, MD; (Y); 4-H; Teachers Aide; Church Choir; 4-H Awd; Hon Roll; 1st Pl Garrett Cnty 4-H Trctr Optrs 82 & 84; 2nd Pl Garrett Cnty 4-H Trctr Optrs; Allegany Cnty Cc; Elecmechl Tec.

MALONE, KATHLEEN; Baltimore City College HS; Baltimore, MD; (S); Cmnty Wkr; School Play; Stage Crew; Nwsp Stf; Mgr(s); High Hon Roll; NHS; Off Trs Stu Cncl; Outstndng Stu Ldrshp Awd; Nrthstrn Coll; Hstry.

MALVEAUX, COURTNEY; Centennial HS; Columbia, MD; (Y); Chess Clb; Hosp Aide; Political Wkr; Red Cross Aide; Band; School Musical; Trs Stu Cncl; Var L Crs Cntry; Var L Lcrss; High Hon Roll; 1st Pl Wnr Hmn Rght Commsn Dr Mrtn Lthr King Jr Essay Cont 86; 2nd Pl Dr Mrtn Lthr Kng Jr Oratorcl 85; Bio.

MANALANSAN, RACHAEL; Archbishop Keough HS; Balt, MD; (Y); Dance Clb; Drama Clb; JV Cheerleading; JV Sftbl; High Hon Roll; Hon Roll; Gymnstcs Clb 84-85; Schl Ltr 83-86; UMBC; Comp Sci.

MANALO, DAWN MICHELE; South Carroll HS; Sykesville, MD; (Y); 1/300; Am Leg Aux Girls St; Church Yth Grp; Intnl Clb; JA; Orch; Cheerleading; Trk; Elks Awd; NHS; Val; U VA; Bus.

MANALO, MICHELE; South Carroll HS; Sykesville, MD; (Y); Pres VP Church Yth Grp; VP JA; Orch; Off Stu Cncl; JV Var Cheerleading; Var L Trk; Elks Awd; VP NHS; NEDT Awd; Val; U Of VA; Bus.

MANATOS, NICHOLAS; Walt Whitman HS; Bethesda, MD; (Y); VP Church Yth Grp; Cmnty Wkr; Political Wkr; Pres Trs Stu Cncl; Var Capt Ftbl; Wt Lftg; High Hon Roll; Hon Roll; Letterman Clb; Pep Clb; 1st Info Spkng Engl 84; Perfrmnce Wrtng Awd 85; Hmcmng Prince 85; Pol Sci.

MANCHESTER, STACEY; Springbrook HS; Silver Spring, MD; (Y); Cmnty Wkr; Chorus; Nwsp Stf; Yrbk Stf; Rep Frsh Cls; Rep Soph Cls; Rep Jr Cls; Stu Cncl; Hon Roll; Law.

MANDURA, WENDY; Fort Hill HS; Cumberland, MD; (Y); Church Yth Grp; Pep Clb; Drill Tm; Flag Corp; Nwsp Ed-Chief; Nwsp Stf; Pres Frsh Cls; Pres Soph Cls; Off Jr Cls; Off Sr Cls; Frostburg ST Coll; Biol.

MANIMBO, MICHELE; Laurel HS; Laurel, MD; (Y); Drama Clb; Var Pom Pon; High Hon Roll; Hon Roll; Acad Excllnc Awd 84-85.

MANLEY, TRACY; Kent County HS; Still Pond, MD; (Y); French Clb; Red Cross Aide; Chorus; Concert Band; Jazz Band; Mrchg Band; Var Cheerleading; NHS; Flute Choir 84-86; Olympcs Of Mnd 86; Salisbury ST Coll; Acctg.

MANN, LAURA; Leonardtown HS; Leonardtown, MD; (Y); 1/200; Trs French Clb; Trs FBLA; Yrbk Stf; Rep Frsh Cls; Rep Soph Cls; Rep Jr Cls; Hst Sr Cls; Var L Cheerleading; Var L Fld Hcky; High Hon Roll; 1st Rgn, 4th ST FBLA Conf Bus Math II 86; Law.

MANNING, LINDA D; Gaithersburg HS; Gaithersburg, MD; (Y); 12/600; Church Yth Grp; Hosp Aide; Church Choir; Mrchg Band; Nwsp Phtg; JV Var Sftbl; French Hon Soc; Pres NHS; Spanish NHS; Teachers Aide; Amercn Lng Assoc Awd 85-86; Duke U; Rmnce Lang.

MANNING, PAMELA; Springbrook HS; Silver Spring, MD; (Y); 104/488; Dance Clb; Letterman Clb; Pep Clb; Teachers Aide; Varsity Clb; Drill Tm; Off Frsh Cls; JV Mgr(s); Var Pom Pon; Var Swmmng; Ntl Hnr Roll 85; Prncpls Awd Outstndt Wrtng 84; PA ST U; Librl Arts.

MANNING, SEAN; Lackey HS; Indian Head, MD; (Y); Boy Scts; VP Latin Clb; Variety Show; Nwsp Ed-Chief; Rep Frsh Cls; Rep Soph Cls; Capt Crs Cntry; Var Ftbl; L Socr; Co-Capt Trk; Nuclr.

MANUEL, RODNEY; Northeast HS; N East, MD; (Y); 9/275; Church Yth Grp; FBLA; JV Socr; VP Trk; High Hon Roll; Sec NHS; Ntl Merit Schol; Pres Schlr; Church Choir; St Schlr; Spanish Hon 83-84; Economic Hon 84-85; Amerifcan Lit Hon 83-84; WA Coll; Pre Law.

MARALIT, MARIE; La Reine HS; Camp Springs, MD; (Y); 5/170; Church Yth Grp; Cmnty Wkr; French Clb; Hosp Aide; Science Clb; Chorus; School Musical; Variety Show; High Hon Roll; NHS; Pre-Med.

MARCELLAS, DIANE; Dulaney HS; Phoenix, MD; (Y); Cmnty Wkr; Band; Concert Band; Mrchg Band; Sftbl; High Hon Roll; Hon Roll; Jr NHS; NHS; U Richmond; Bus.

MARCHETTI, CHRISTOPHER; Eleanor Roosevelt HS; Bowie, MD; (Y); Church Yth Grp; Letterman Clb; JV Var Ftbl; Wt Lftg; Hon Roll; All Cnty Ftbl 85; MD ST Schlrshp 86; Ftbl Tm 86; Salisbury ST Clg; Mgmt.

MARCONI, CONNIE; Mercy HS; Baltimore, MD; (Y); Drama Clb; GAA; Sec Frsh Cls; Sec Soph Cls; VP Stu Cncl; Im Badmtn; Var Bsktbl; Var Socr; Var Sftbl; Im Vllybl; Athltc Hnr Awd 83-86; HS Ldrshp Isnt Cert 86; Drama Clb Awd 84-85; James Madison U; Cmmnctns.

MARCONI, LISA; Northern HS; Carney, MD; (S); Church Yth Grp; Office Aide; Stage Crew; Variety Show; Rep Jr Cls; High Hon Roll; Hon Roll; NHS; Drama Clb; Library Aide; HOBY Almnus 83-84; Rebbeca E Carral Drmtc Readg Fest Fnlst 84-85; Amer Socty Distngshd Schlrs 85-86; Towson ST U; Secdry Ed.

MARCOS, ALEXIS; La Plata HS; Waldorf, MD; (S); Church Yth Grp; SADD; School Musical; VP Frsh Cls; Rep Soph Cls; Rep Jr Cls; Rep Stu Cncl; JV Capt Cheerleading; Hon Roll; Fine Art.

MARCROFT, JULIA A; The Fallston HS; Kingsville, MD; (Y); 10/250; Church Yth Grp; SADD; Varsity Clb; Chorus; Var L Fld Hcky; High Hon Roll; Hon Roll; NHS; Acdmc Let 85-86.

MARCUS, ROBIN; Walter Johnson HS; Rockville, MD; (Y); Hosp Aide; Mrchg Band; Rep Soph Cls; Rep Jr Cls; Rep Stu Cncl; Var L Pom Pon; Var Socr; French Hon Soc; High Hon Roll; Hon Roll; Outstndng Srv To Frshmn Cls 83-84; Outstndng Srv To Sphmr Cls 84-85.

MARGARONIS, DEMETRIOS P; West Nottingham Acad; Alfred, NY; (Y); Boy Scts; Chess Clb; Computer Clb; Drama Clb; French Clb; Intnl Clb; Letterman Clb; Math Clb; Political Wkr; SADD; Ldrshp & Citznshp Awd Schlrshp; Influence Awd Best Influence; Alfred U; Intl Bus.

MARINO, ANTONINA; Randallstown SR HS; Baltimore, MD; (Y); Church Yth Grp; Teachers Aide; Stage Crew; Yrbk Stf; High Hon Roll; Randallstown Cmnty Schlrshp Awd 86; Towson ST U; Spcl Educ.

MARIS, CATHERINE L; Walt Whitman HS; Bethesda, MD; (Y); 68/450; Drama Clb; Hosp Aide; Key Clb; NFL; Pep Clb; Teachers Aide; Var Capt Crs Cntry; Var Trk; Smithsonian Dscvr Grphcs Schlrshp 85; Schltc Gld Key Awd 86; Psych.

MARK, TANYA; John Carroll Schl; Pylesville, MD; (Y); 45/250; French Clb; Ski Clb; Yrbk Ed-Chief; JV Lcrss; Var Mgr(s); French Hon Soc; Hon Roll; U MD; Bus.

MARKER, ROBERT; Fort Hill HS; Cumberland, MD; (Y); Band; JV Socr; Var Tennis; Hon Roll; Ed.

MARKOWSKI, KAREN; Archbishop Keough HS; Baltimore, MD; (Y); 2/200; Am Leg Aux Girls St; Sec Pres Spanish Clb; Nwsp Sprt Ed; Rep Stu Cncl; Var Im Bsktbl; Var Vllybl; High Hon Roll; NHS; Church Yth Grp; Drama Clb; MD Sci Smnrs 83-84; Careers For Wmn In Math & Sci Sympsm 83; Excllnc Spnsh III Awd 86; USN Acad; Engrng.

MARONE, SUSAN A; Gaithersburg SR HS; Gaithersburg, MD; (Y); 124/568; JCL; Latin Clb; Teachers Aide; Flag Corp; Hon Roll; Lion Awd; MS Bar Assc Awd Law Tm 85; U Of DE; Bus.

MARPLE, JOHNNA; Southern Garrett HS; Oakland, MD; (Y); 27/225; GAA; Q&S; Ski Clb; Trs Band; Yrbk Stf; Rep Stu Cncl; Hon Roll; US Ntl Bnd Awd 85-86; Prsdntl Acad Physcl Ftnss Awd 86; Sntrl Schlrshp 86; U Of ; Md.

MARPLE, RICHARD; Southern Garrett HS; Oakland, MD; (Y); VP 4-H; German Clb; VICA; JV Ftbl; Var Wrstlng; 4-H Awd; Hon Roll.

MARQUIS, SANDRA; Maurice J Mc Donough HS; La Plata, MD; (Y); Intnl Clb; Mrchg Band; School Musical; Symp Band; Pom Pon; Hon Roll.

MARROW, STEPHANIE; Baltimore Polytechnic Inst; Baltimore, MD; (Y); Church Yth Grp; JA; Yrbk Stf; Rep Jr Cls; Stu Cncl; Mgr Bsktbl; Mgr(s); Score Keeper; Timer; Hon Roll; Major P For Exemplary Svc 85-86; Major Stu Govt Assn 85-86; NC A&T ST U; Elec Engrng.

MARSALA JR, KENNETH J; Thomas Stone HS; Waldorf, MD; (S); Drama Clb; Pres Latin Clb; Math Clb; Math Tm; Science Clb; Thesps; Co-Capt Drill Tm; Var Bsktbl; High Hon Roll; Pres NHS; U Of MD; Elec Engrng.

MARSALA, MICHAEL S; Thomas Stone HS; Waldorf, MD; (S); Church Yth Grp; Drama Clb; Latin Clb; Science Clb; SADD; Color Guard; Capt Drill Tm; Mrchg Band; Im Bsktbl; Mgr(s); Maryland U.

MARSHALL, ANITA M; Catoctin HS; Thurmont, MD; (Y); 38/202; Pres Computer Clb; Sec FBLA; Capt Drm Mjr(t); School Musical; Sec Frsh Cls; Sec Soph Cls; Sec Jr Cls; Stat Bsktbl; Capt Pom Pon; Capt Twrlr; MD Distingshd Schlr Finlst Dance 86; U MD; Acctng.

MARSHALL, LORI; Serverna Park HS; Millersville, MD; (Y); Church Yth Grp; FCA; Key Clb; Hon Roll; South Eastern Coll; Busnss.

MARSHALL, VICKI; Dundalk SR HS; Baltimore, MD; (Y); SADD; Varsity Clb; Var Bsktbl; Powder Puff Ftbl; Var Socr; Var Sftbl; Var Tennis; Var Vllybl; High Hon Roll; NHS; U Sydney Australia; Chem Engr.

MARSIGLIA, LISA; Kenwood HS; Baltimore, MD; (Y); Off Frsh Cls; Off Soph Cls; Off Jr Cls; Off Sr Cls; Off Stu Cncl; Var Bsktbl; Var Capt Fld Hcky; Var Lcrss; NHS; 1st Rnnrup Schlrshp La Cross 86.

MARSTELLER, BRENDA; Hereford HS; Freeland, MD; (S); Yrbk Stf; VP Frsh Cls; Pres Soph Cls; Pres Jr Cls; Pres Sr Cls; Var Capt Bsktbl; Var Capt Fld Hcky; Var Capt Lcrss; NHS; MD Distngshd Schlr 85-86; Outstndng Stu 86; Hofstra U; Allied Hlth.

MARTIN, DARREN; Hancock Middle SR HS; Hancock, MD; (Y); 1/53; Am Leg Boys St; Church Yth Grp; Band; Jazz Band; Mrchg Band; Trs Sr Cls; Bsbl; Hon Roll; Prfct Atten Awd; SAR Awd; Woodmen Of Wrld Awd Hist; Clbrtn Excllnc Awd; Hagerstown JR Coll Fac Fndtn Schlrshp; Hagertown JC; Comp Sci.

MARTIN, LAUR; Valley HS; Lonaconing, MD; (Y); Church Yth Grp; 4-H; French Clb; Girl Scts; Service Clb; Ski Clb; Teachers Aide; Band; Concert Band; Mrchg Band; ACC Math Schlrshp 85; Frstbrg ST Coll; Mntl Hlth.

MARTIN, PAMELA; Crossland HS; Camp Springs, MD; (Y); Hosp Aide; Red Cross Aide; Mrchg Band; Pep Band; Symp Band; Crs Cntry; Trk; Hon Roll; Spanish NHS; Concert Band; I & II In Solo & Ensmbl Fstvl 84-85; Coll Crdts At Prince Geos Cmnty Coll 86; Hwrd U; Pre-Med.

MARTIN, RHONDA; North Carroll HS; Hampstead, MD; (Y); Am Leg Aux Girls St; GAA; JA; Spanish Clb; SADD; Rep Jr Cls; Rep Sr Cls; Var L Bsktbl; High Hon Roll; NHS; Acdmc All-Amrcn 86; US Ntl Math Awd 86; JR Achvmnt Vp Finance 84; U Of MD Baltimore; Chem Engnrn.

MARTIN, TRACI; Southern Garrett HS; Oakland, MD; (Y); Drama Clb; GAA; Girl Scts; Pep Clb; Teachers Aide; School Play; Yrbk Phtg; Yrbk Rptr; Yrbk Stf; Cheerleading; Hcmngn Princess 83-84, 84-85 & 85-86; Wilma Boyd Schl; Trvl Agnt.

MARTIN, WENDY; North Carroll HS; Manchester, MD; (Y); GAA; Rep Frsh Cls; Rep Soph Cls; Rep Jr Cls; Rep Stu Cncl; JV Bsktbl; JV Var Fld Hcky; JV Var Sftbl; Hon Roll; Towson ST; Phys Educ.

MARTOF, TANYA E; Oxon Hill Science & Technology Ctr; Suitland, MD; (Y); Church Yth Grp; Cmnty Wkr; Intnl Clb; Latin Clb; Band; Drm Mjr(t); Nwsp Stf; Rep Stu Cncl; High Hon Roll; Prfct Atten Awd; Cont Prince Georges Cnty Miss TEEN Pgnt 86; VA Polytech Inst; Vet.

MARX, BRIAN; Magruder HS; Brookeville, MD; (Y); Cmnty Wkr; JV Bsbl; JV Var Socr; Var Trk.

MARZULLO, CHRISTOPHER; Calvert Hall College HS; Baltimore, MD; (Y); 30/285; Letterman Clb; Ski Clb; Rep Sr Cls; Var L Ftbl; Var L Lcrss; Hon Roll; Pres Schlr; Cornell U.

MASEMORE, MICHELLE D; Arlington Baptist HS; Baltimore, MD; (S); VP Church Yth Grp; Pres Band; Church Choir; Concert Band; Drm Mjr(t); Mrchg Band; Pep Band; High Hon Roll; NHS; Comp Systms.

MASLANIK, WENDY; Bowie HS; Bowie, MD; (Y); Hosp Aide; Key Clb; Band; Orch; Symp Band; Rep Stu Cncl; Cheerleading; Powder Puff Ftbl; Score Keeper; Hon Roll; Vrsty Cheerldng Sqd Capt 85-86; Busnss Mgmt.

MASON, DAWN; Seton HS; Baltimore, MD; (Y); 4/108; Church Yth Grp; Cmnty Wkr; Hosp Aide; Teachers Aide; Yrbk Stf; Hon Roll; Villa Julie Coll Trustes Schlrshp 86; Schlstc Achvt Awd 86; Villa Julie Coll; Para Legal.

MASON, DEBORAH; Gaithersburg HS; Gaithersburg, MD; (Y); Pres AFS; Church Yth Grp; Cmnty Wkr; FCA; 4-H; Office Aide; Pep Clb; ROTC; SADD; Teachers Aide; Chld Dvlpmnt Awd 85; ROTC Awd 84; 1st Pl Bwlng Awd 85-86; Alderson-Broaddus; Erly Chldhd.

MASON, MICHAEL; Fairmont Heights HS; Landover, MD; (Y); Dance Clb; Debate Tm; JA; Teachers Aide; Varsity Clb; JV Ftbl; JV Wrstlng; Hon Roll; Highst Scor Cnty Biolgst Tst Awd 85; MD ST Bar & Law Awd 86; JR Fitns Awd 85.

MASON, SANDRA J; Southern Garrett HS; Oakland, MD; (Y); Church Yth Grp; GAA; Church Choir; Yrbk Phtg; Yrbk Stf; JV Capt Cheerleading; Var Sftbl; Hon Roll; Prfct Atten Awd; All Amer Chrldr Awd 85; Bus & Mgmt.

MASSEY, AMANDA; Pocomoke HS; Pocomoke, MD; (Y); AFS; Church Yth Grp; Drama Clb; Trs FBLA; Girl Scts; SADD; Band; Church Choir; Var Capt Cheerleading; Var Mgr(s); Salisbury ST Coll; Bus Mgmt.

MASTROIANNI, ELIZABETH; Springbrook HS; Silver Spring, MD; (Y); Church Yth Grp; Drama Clb; JA; Ski Clb; Chorus; Stage Crew; Hon Roll; Catholic U Of America; Music.

MASTROIANNI, MARIA; St Elizabeth Ann Seton HS; Adelphi, MD; (Y); Church Yth Grp; Hosp Aide; Pres Intnl Clb; SADD; Teachers Aide; Nwsp Rptr; Nwsp Stf; Hon Roll; NHS; Acdmc Ltr 84-85; Pdtrcn.

MATESIC, MATIJA; Archbishop Keough HS; Baltimore, MD; (Y); Dance Clb; Drama Clb; French Clb; GAA; SADD; School Play; Yrbk Stf; Lit Mag; Rep Frsh Cls; Rep Soph Cls; U VA; Bio.

MATHES, YOLANDA; Forestville HS; Suitland, MD; (Y); FBLA; Crs Cntry; High Hon Roll; Hon Roll; Acad Excllnc-3rd Qtr, 19th & 20th Centry US Hist & The FBLA ST Cnvntn 85-86; U Of TN; Exec Secy.

MATHEW JR, GEORGE; Arlington Baptist Schl; Cockeysville, MD; (S); 9/50; VP Church Yth Grp; Church Choir; Variety Show; Cit Awd; Hon Roll; NHS; Prfct Atten Awd; Boy Scts; Acpl Chr; MD ST Acad Awd Acdmc Tstng 1st 85; ST Fine Arts Awd Chrl Music 83; 1st Spngh Rgnl 85; U MD; Med.

MATHEWS, CHRIS; Bishop Walsh HS; Cumberland, MD; (Y); Chess Clb; Church Yth Grp; Cmnty Wkr; Debate Tm; Math Clb; Ski Clb; Bacgammon & Checkers Champ 84-86; Vllybl Tm Champ 86; Bus.

MATHIAS, ANDREA; Snow Hill HS; Stockton, MD; (S); #1 In Class; AFS; Pres Church Yth Grp; French Clb; Rep Jr Cls; Trs Stu Cncl; Twrlr; High Hon Roll; NHS; Rotary Awd; Cmnty Wkr; GEO/LOGUE Glbl Educ Outreach Pgm 84; Highest GPA 84-85; Supr Sat Salisbury St Coll Micro-Bio 83-84.

MATLICK, BRIAN; Allegany HS; Cumberland, MD; (Y); Computer Clb; Ski Clb; Stage Crew; JV Bsktbl; Var Bowling; Var Socr; Var Wrstlng; Hon Roll; WV U; Comp Sci.

MATTEGUNTA, SUNEETHA; Liberty HS; Sykesville, MD; (S); 1/285; Church Yth Grp; Drama Clb; Office Aide; Stage Crew; Rep Soph Cls; Stat Bsktbl; Mgr Vllybl; Hon Roll; NHS; Prfct Atten Awd; Prncpls Awd.

MATTHEWS, JEFFREY F; Mt Savage Schl; Corriganville, MD; (Y); 6/60; Pres French Clb; FBLA; Pep Clb; Science Clb; Chorus; Nwsp Ed-Chief; Yrbk Phtg; Yrbk Stf; Merit Schlrshp Frstbrg ST Coll 86; Frostburg ST Coll.

MATTHEWS, MIKE; Snow Hill HS; Eden, MD; (S); French Clb; Church Choir; High Hon Roll; NHS; Distngshd Hnr Rll-4 Trms 85; Natl Hnr Soc 85; Salisbury ST Coll; Comp Pgmr.

MATTHEWS, ROBERT; Wicomico SR HS; Salisbury, MD; (Y); Camera Clb; Church Yth Grp; Computer Clb; Dance Clb; Yrbk Phtg; Crs Cntry; Score Keeper; Timer; Trk; Hon Roll; Acdmc Ltr 85-86; U MD Coll Prk; Aero Spc Engr.

MATTIA, LINDA; Middletown HS; Middletown, MD; (Y); 26/195; Office Aide; Yrbk Stf; Lit Mag; Sec Sr Cls; Var Capt Cheerleading; Hon Roll; Frostburg ST U; Wildlife Mgmt.

MATTINGLY, JOHN; St Marys Ryken HS; Leonardtown, MD; (Y); Nwsp Rptr; Var Wrstlng.

MATTINGLY, LORI; Walter Johnson HS; Bethesda, MD; (Y); Church Yth Grp; French Clb; FHA; Pep Clb; Nwsp Rptr; Nwsp Stf; Rep Cheerleading; JV Mgr(s); Pom Pon; Jr NHS; Buyr.

MATTIS, BECKY; Gaithersburg HS; Gaithersburg, MD; (Y); 40/680; Pres Art Clb; Drama Clb; SADD; Off Madrigals; School Musical; Swing Chorus; French Hon Soc; NHS; Church Yth Grp; Ntl Art Hnr Soc 86; Choir Accompianist 80-86; Meth Yth Fellowshp 80-86; U MD-BALTIMORE; Hlth.

MATTOCKS, SANDRA; Bishop Walsh HS; Cresaptown, MD; (Y); 40/98; Sec Trs Church Yth Grp; Concert Band; Mrchg Band; Var Mgr Socr; Hon Roll; Band Awd 82-83; Allegany CC; Math.

MATTOCKS, TANYA; Crossland SR HS; Capital Hts, MD; (Y); Dance Clb; Teachers Aide; Rep Frsh Cls; JV Crs Cntry; Var Trk; Hon Roll; Grgtwn U; Bus Cmnctns.

MATTURRO, CHRIS; Gaithersburg HS; Gaithersburg, MD; (Y); Pep Clb; SADD; Rep Frsh Cls; Rep Soph Cls; Rep Jr Cls; Var Capt Cheerleading; Var Fld Hcky; Timer; Hon Roll; PA ST U; Comm.

MATZDORF, LEIGH; Dulaney SR HS; Baldwin, MD; (Y); Church Yth Grp; Hosp Aide; Trs Key Clb; Service Clb; Chorus; Ed Yrbk Stf; Capt Vllybl; Hon Roll; NHS; Nrsng.

MAUSER, JENNIE; Glenelg HS; Glenwood, MD; (Y); Intnl Clb; Office Aide; Q&S; SADD; Chorus; Church Choir; Co-Capt Flag Corp; Mrchg Band; Nwsp Ed-Chief; Hon Roll; Cert Merit Frnch 85; Engl Ed.

MAUST, CONRAD; Northern Garrett HS; Accident, MD; (Y); Art Clb; Aud/Vis; Camera Clb; Church Yth Grp; Cmnty Wkr; Church Choir; Stage Crew; Ed Nwsp Phtg; Nwsp Rptr; Nwsp Stf; Bus Mngmnt.

MAXWELL, MICHELLE; Lackey HS; Bryans Rd, MD; (Y); French Clb; Variety Show; Yrbk Rptr; Yrbk Stf; Rep Stu Cncl; Var Pom Pon; High Hon Roll; U Of MD; Engrng.

MAY, GENA L; Oxon Hill SR HS; Ft Washington, MD; (Y); Girl Scts; Teachers Aide; Ntl Merit Ltr; Pblc Rltns.

MAY, KIM; Gaithersburg HS; Gaithersburg, MD; (Y); Key Clb; SADD; Yrbk Stf; French Hon Soc; Hon Roll; Jr NHS; NHS; VA Plytchnc Inst; Pre-Vet Med.

MAY, STEPHANIE; Allegany HS; Cumberland, MD; (Y); 9/243; AFS; Pres Church Yth Grp; Drama Clb; 4-H; Band; Mrchg Band; Nwsp Sprt Ed; JV Bsktbl; High Hon Roll; NHS; Allegany Cnty HS Hnr Band 1st Chr Trmbn 86; Bus Mgmt.

MAYER, KATHLEEN; St Marys Ryken HS; La Plata, MD; (S); Church Yth Grp; Ski Clb; Spanish Clb; Var Vllybl; High Hon Roll; Hon Roll; NHS; Hstry Achvt Awd 85; Outdrs Clb & Socl Comm 86; 110 Prcnt Awd JV Vllybl 84 & 85; Bus.

MAYES, ANNETTE; Highland View Acad; Canada; (Y); 3/39; Church Yth Grp; Chorus; School Musical; Sec Sr Cls; Trs Stu Cncl; Sftbl; Vllybl; Cit Awd; High Hon Roll; NHS; Andrews U; Bus Secy.

MAYES, DARRON RENARD; Friendly HS; Ft Washington, MD; (Y); Church Yth Grp; Debate Tm; Library Aide; Pep Clb; Nwsp Stf; Rep Stu Cncl; JV Var Mgr(s); Score Keeper; High Hon Roll; Hon Roll; U Of MD-COLLEGE Park; Bus.

MAYNARD, ALEJANDRO; John Carroll HS; Bel Air, MD; (Y); 63/183; Art Clb; Debate Tm; English Clb; Intnl Clb; JA; Office Aide; Political Wkr; Science Clb; Spanish Clb; Teachers Aide; Natl Spanish Exam 85-86; Med.

MAYO, MONICA L; Regina HS; Hyattsville, MD; (Y); 4/62; Computer Clb; Hosp Aide; Red Cross Aide; Yrbk Phtg; Yrbk Stf; High Hon Roll; NHS; Prfct Atten Awd; St Schlr; Schrlshp Smmr Inst 86; Exc Adv Plcmnt Bio 86; 2nd Pl Vermont Ave Schrlshp 86; Syracuse U; Engrng.

MAYSE, JOAN; High Point HS; Adelphi, MD; (Y); Sec Soph Cls; Rep Jr Cls; Trs Stu Cncl; Var Cheerleading; High Hon Roll; Prfct Atten Awd; WA Soc Of Engrs Awd 85; Marine Tech Soc 85; Natl Latin Exam Cum Laude Awd 85; Engrng.

MC AFEE, STEVE; Capitol Christian Acad; Forestville, MD; (S); Band; Mrchg Band; Pep Band; Socr; Wrstlng; Hon Roll; Phys Sci Awd 85; Mech Engrg.

MC ALLISTER, PAUL; Du Val SR HS; Lanham, MD; (Y); ROTC; Sec Rep Stu Cncl; Var L Socr; Wt Lftg; Var L Wrstlng; Hon Roll; Ntl Merit Ltr; AF JR ROTC Ldrshp, Achvt, Phys Fitness, Longevity, Outstndg Flight 86; Awd Squad Cmmndr Corps 86; U Of MD; Engineering.

MC ALPINE, DEBBIE; Magruder HS; Olney, MD; (Y); 106/310; Spanish Clb; Drill Tm; Yrbk Stf; Var Capt Pom Pon; JV Mgr Sftbl; Hon Roll; Natl Superstar Drill Tm Hnr 85-86; Art Work Awds 83-85; Big Sister Pgm 85 & 86; Towson U; Psych.

MC ALPINE, MARY; Valley HS; Lonaconing, MD; (Y); 15/95; French Clb; Q&S; School Play; Nwsp Bus Mgr; Nwsp Rptr; Nwsp Stf; Trs Sr Cls; High Hon Roll; NHS; Church Yth Grp; Schlstc Cert Pin Ltr 84-86; Frostburg ST Coll; Soc Wrk.

MC BETH, ELLEN; Frederick Douglass HS; Upper Marlboro, MD; (Y); 1/326; Hosp Aide; VP JA; Yrbk Stf; Rep Stu Cncl; Capt Sftbl; Bausch & Lomb Sci Awd; Trs NHS; Ntl Merit Ltr; Val; Math Tm; MD Dstngshd Schlr 85; Sprntndnts Awd 83; Prsdntl Acdmc Ftnss Awd 86; VA Polytech Inst; Elec Engnrng.

MC BRIDE, JIM; Frederick HS; Fred, MD; (Y); 70/330; Church Yth Grp; Cmnty Wkr; German Clb; Letterman Clb; Band; Concert Band; Mrchg Band; Var Bsbl; JV Bsktbl; JV Ftbl; Church Yth Cncl Offcr 84-85; Chrstn Devlpmnt Dip 86; Furman U; Ped.

MC BROOM, TRACEY; Forest Park SR HS; Baltimore, MD; (Y); Intnl Clb; ROTC; Teachers Aide; Drill Tm; School Play; Rep Frsh Cls; Rep Soph Cls; Cit Awd; Hon Roll; Ron Thomas Schl; Csmtlgst.

MC CABE, CAROL; Bowie HS; Bowie, MD; (Y); AFS; Art Clb; Church Yth Grp; Ski Clb; Yrbk Stf; Hon Roll; U Of MD.

MC CALLIN, TRINA; Dundalk HS; Baltimore, MD; (Y); SADD; Teachers Aide; Varsity Clb; Y-Teens; Stat Ftbl; JV Var Lcrss; Var Mgr(s); Var Socr; High Hon Roll; Hood; Comm Arts.

MC CAMMON JR, GARY R; Perry Hall HS; Kingsville, MD; (Y); 7/434; Teachers Aide; Lit Mag; Var L Crs Cntry; Var Capt Golf; NHS; Ntl Merit Ltr; Pres Schlr; Math Clb; Math Tm; Science Clb; Baltimore Cnty Gifted/Tlntd Pgm 82-86; Kingsvlle Elem Schl PTA Txt Bk Awd 86; Acad Schl Ltr/Pin 84-86; U DE; Elec Engrng.

MC CANN, DANIEL; Patapsco HS; Baltimore, MD; (Y); Boys Clb Am; Church Yth Grp; CAP; Teachers Aide; JV Var Bsbl; JV Ftbl; Var Socr; Wt Lftg; High Hon Roll; Hon Roll; Towson ST; Comp.

MC CARROLL, SAMANTHA; Walt Whitman HS; Bethesda, MD; (Y); Acpl Chr; Chorus; Madrigals; School Musical; U Of TX.

MC CARRON, MARY AGNES; Institute Of Notre Dame; Baltimore, MD; (Y); 5/103; Cmnty Wkr; Yrbk Stf; Rep Frsh Cls; Rep Soph Cls; Rep Jr Cls; Rep Sr Cls; Var L Bsktbl; High Hon Roll; NHS; Pres Schlr; Prtl Schlrshp Inst Ntre Dame 82; MVP Vrsty Bsktbl 85; Outstndng Math Stu Awd 84; Acdmc Achvt Awd 86; Coll Notre Dame MD; Math.

MC CARTER, TAMMIE; Cambridge South Dorchester HS; Cambridge, MD; (Y); 10/248; Spanish Clb; Teachers Aide; Stu Cncl; Var Bowling; Capt Pom Pon; High Hon Roll; NHS; Med.

MC CARTHY, ANTHONY; Patterson HS; Baltimore, MD; (Y); Boys Clb Am; Teachers Aide; Varsity Clb; Socr; Loyola Coll; Comp Pgmr.

MC CARTHY, DENNIS E; Loyola HS; Columbia, MD; (S); Chess Clb; Church Yth Grp; German Clb; Nwsp Stf; NHS.

MC CARTHY, JANE MARIE; Gwynn Park HS; Accokeek, MD; (Y); Am Leg Aux Girls St; Church Yth Grp; Var Capt Sftbl; Hon Roll; JV Bsktbl; JV Crs Cntry; Prince Geroges Comm Coll; Comp.

MC CARTHY, STEPHEN; Barrie HS; Rockville, MD; (Y); 1/13; Church Yth Grp; Computer Clb; Latin Clb; Library Aide; Model UN; Teachers Aide; Varsity Clb; Yrbk Stf; Rep Stu Cncl; Var L Bsktbl; Valedctrn 86; ST MD Merit Schltc Awd 86; NASA Spec Achvt Awd 84; U Notre Dame; Law.

MC CARTNEY, JOANN; Leonardtown HS; Leonardtown, MD; (Y); 1/286; Pres Sec Church Yth Grp; Q&S; Speech Tm; Nwsp Ed-Chief; VP Jr Cls; Rep Stu Cncl; Var L Crs Cntry; High Hon Roll; NHS; French Clb; Cmmnctns.

MC CASKILL, LYNN; Sparrows Point M/S HS; Baltimore, MD; (Y); Spanish Clb; Teachers Aide; Ed Yrbk Phtg; Pom Pon; Tennis; Hon Roll; Spanish NHS; Voice Dem Awd; DCC; Psych.

MC CLAIN, TONYA; Kent County HS; Chestertown, MD; (Y); French Clb; Pep Clb; Radio Clb; Rep Frsh Cls; Rep Soph Cls; Rep Jr Cls; Sec Stu Cncl; Wt Lftg; Hon Roll; Olympcs Of Mnd 86; Frnch.

MC CLAM, CHERIE RENEE; St Elizabeth Seton HS; Washington, DC; (Y); Am Leg Aux Girls St; Church Yth Grp; Drama Clb; NFL; Pep Clb; Spanish Clb; Speech Tm; Chorus; Madrigals; School Play; Southern MD Oratory Awd, Mayor Barry Youth Ldrshp Inst 86; MLK Oratory Awd 85; Catholic U; Law.

MC CLELLAND, MICHAEL; Key Schl; Edgewater, MD; (Y); Boy Scts; CAP; Drama Clb; Band; Mrchg Band; Nwsp Rptr; Var Lcrss; Hon Roll; Engrng.

MC CLINTOCK, ERIN; La Plata HS; Hughesville, MD; (S); Latin Clb; SADD; Teachers Aide; Rep Soph Cls; Rep Jr Cls; Var Fld Hcky; Sftbl; High Hon Roll; Hon Roll; U MD; Pub Reltns.

MC CONNELL, RACHEL E; Bethesda-Chevy Chase HS; Silver Spring, MD; (Y); 79/400; Chess Clb; Latin Clb; Library Aide; Mathletes; Math Clb; Math Tm; Teachers Aide; Orch; Hon Roll; Ntl Merit SF; Montgomery Cnty Yth Orch Cello 84-86; Hampshire Coll; Comp.

MC COOL, KELLY; Perry Hall SR HS; Baltimore, MD; (Y); 21/450; Yrbk Stf; Rep Jr Cls; Lcrss; Socr; Sftbl; High Hon Roll; Hon Roll; Pres Schlr; Dept Of Defns Engrs Aprntc 86; U Of MD; Aerospc Engrng.

MC CORMAC, LINDA; Oxon Hill HS; Brandywine, MD; (Y); 32/630; Cmnty Wkr; 4-H; Hosp Aide; Cit Awd; French Hon Soc; 4-H Awd; Gov Hon Prg Awd; High Hon Roll; NHS; VFW Awd; Prince Georges Cnty Miss TEEN 86; U Of MD; Eductn.

MC CORMICK, DUANE; Bishop Walsh HS; Cumberland, MD; (Y); 20/110; Var L Bsbl; Var L Bsktbl; Hon Roll; NHS; Engrng.

MC CORMICK, MARGARET; La Reine HS; Temple Hills, MD; (S); 15/167; Church Yth Grp; Red Cross Aide; Yrbk Stf; Lit Mag; High Hon Roll; Hon Roll; NHS; HOBY Ldrshp Cncl 85; Congrssnl Natl Yng Ldrs Conf 85; JR Sci & Humants Sympsm 85; Engl.

MC COY, JENNIFER; Allegany HS; La Vale, MD; (Y); Cmnty Wkr; Office Aide; Chorus; Drill Tm; Yrbk Stf; Stu Cncl; Teaching.

MC CULLY, CHRISTINE; Thomas Stone HS; Hughesville, MD; (S); Cmnty Wkr; French Clb; Science Clb; Ski Clb; Teachers Aide; Inst Food Tech Outstndng Sci Proj 84; 1st Pl Hnbl Mntn Charles Cnty Sci Fair 84-85; Pre-Med.

MC CUSKER, DEANA; Flintstone HS; Little Orleans, MD; (S); Church Yth Grp; FFA; FHA; Trs Service Clb; Trs Chorus; Church Choir; Nwsp Ed-Chief; Nwsp Rptr; Nwsp Stf; Yrbk Stf; MD Dist Schlrs 85-86; Hagerstown JC; Radlgc Tech.

MC CUSKER, MICHAEL; Hancock HS; Hancock, MD; (Y); 14/49; Drama Clb; VP SADD; Band; Chorus; Concert Band; Mrchg Band; Sec Soph Cls; Var L Bsktbl; L Ftbl; Var L Trk; WA Cnty All Star Game; MVP Trk; HJC; Ed.

MC CUSKER, TAMMY; Flintstone HS; Little Orleans, MD; (S); Church Yth Grp; FHA; Sec Service Clb; Teachers Aide; Sec Chorus; Nwsp Bus Mgr; Yrbk Stf; Sec Soph Cls; Sec Jr Cls; Pres Stu Cncl; MD Dist Schlr 85; Hmcmng Queen 85; Frostburg ST Coll; Bus Admin.

MC DANOLDS, WENDY; Kent County HS; Still Pond, MD; (Y); Am Leg Aux Girls St; French Clb; Yrbk Stf; Stu Cncl; JV Bsktbl; Var Fld Hcky; Var Lcrss; Var Swmmng; Ntl Merit SF; Maryland Asso Stu Cncl Convntn 86; Dentistry.

MC DERMOTT, JOE; Good Counsel HS; Gaithersburg, MD; (Y); Church Yth Grp; French Clb; FFA; JV Bsbl; JV Capt Bsktbl; JV Crs Cntry; All Star Tm Bsbll 83; Babne Ruth All ST Tm 2nd Plc 86; Accptd Good Cnsl HS 84-85; Marine Bio.

MC DERMOTT, VICTORIA A E; North Carroll HS; Hampstead, MD; (Y); 10/280; Church Yth Grp; Drama Clb; JA; Office Aide; Sec Political Wkr; Spanish Clb; Speech Tm; SADD; Variety Show; Off Sr Cls; Semi Fnlst Mock Trl Team 84-85 Acad Lttr Awd 83-84 Lmp Of Lrnng Pin Awd 85-86; Peer Cnslng Cert 85; George Mason U; Ed.

MC DONAGH, AMY; Notre Dame Prep; Towson, MD; (Y); Cmnty Wkr; Dance Clb; Model UN; Lit Mag; Jr Cls; Im Socr; Hon Roll; Ntl Merit Ltr; Dance Chairprsn 85; Bus Adm.

MC DONALD, GAIL A; Charles W Woodward HS; Rockville, MD; (Y); 58/234; Sec AFS; Art Clb; Dance Clb; Hosp Aide; Office Aide; Science Clb; Ski Clb; Spanish Clb; SADD; Teachers Aide; Black Awareness Clb Pres 85-86; Pre-Med.

MC DONALD, LISA; Maurice J Mc Donough HS; Waldorf, MD; (Y); Am Leg Aux Girls St; Intnl Clb; Math Tm; Teachers Aide; Hon Roll; Frnch Poem Rectl Comptn 86; Bst Shw Awd Cermc Piece 85; Math.

MC DONALD, LYNN; Thomas S Wootton HS; Gaithersburg, MD; (Y); JA; Service Clb; NHS; Comp Sci.

MC DONALD, SHANDRA L; Seneca Valley HS; Potomac, MD; (Y); Church Yth Grp; Civic Clb; Cmnty Wkr; Debate Tm; Girl Scts; Radio Clb; Church Choir; VP Jr Cls; Bsktbl; Pom Pon; Acadmc Debutnt Black Stu 85-86; Brown U; Med.

MC DOWELL, ARWEN; Rising Sun HS; Rising Sun, MD; (Y); 4/166; Sec Church Yth Grp; Cmnty Wkr; Sec VP 4-H; Concert Band; Jazz Band; Trs Sr Cls; JV Var Vllybl; High Hon Roll; VP NHS; Ntl Merit Ltr; Lgsltv Page-MD Genl Assmbly Annapolis 86; Grnd Awd Wnnr-1st Pl Tm-Ntl Hortcltr Judg Cont 86; Wheaton Coll.

MC DOWELL, CHRISTIE; North Hagerstown HS; Hagerstown, MD; (Y); 24/277; Church Yth Grp; French Clb; Latin Clb; Political Wkr; Ski Clb; Yrbk Ed-Chief; Yrbk Stf; Rep Stu Cncl; Exploring; FBLA; Bst Tnns Plyr Awd Frnch Cmp 85; Hon Clb; Pltcl Sci.

MC ELHONE, THOMAS; Parkside HS; Eden, MD; (Y); FFA; Hon Roll; Schlrshp Ag Sci 86; Schlrshp Awd FFA 86; ST Ag Awd FFA 86; U Of MD; Ag.

MC ELWEE, MARK; Mount Saint Joseph Prep; Catonsville, MD; (Y); 70/315; SADD; Pres Jr Cls; VP Stu Cncl; JV Wrstlng; Hon Roll; NHS; Rotary Awd; Bd Advsrs Schl Prncpl 86.

MC FALL, THOMAS; John Carroll HS; Bel Air, MD; (Y); 88/278; Band; Var Ftbl; JV Lcrss; JV Wrstlng; Cit Awd; Hon Roll; Oceangrphy.

MC FARLAND, TRICIA; Bishop Walsh HS; Flintstone, MD; (Y); CAP; Dance Clb; Drama Clb; Pep Clb; Science Clb; Speech Tm; Thesps; Church Choir; School Musical; Score Keeper.

MC FAUL, KELLY; Patapsco HS; Baltimore, MD; (Y); 10/290; Dance Clb; French Clb; High Hon Roll; Jr NHS; NHS; Merit Schltc Awd 86; Cert Of Achvt For Sci/Tech 86; $500 Schlrshp From Rotary Club Of Durdalk 86; UMBC; Engrng.

MC GEE, AUDREY; Dunbar HS; Baltimore, MD; (Y); Church Yth Grp; Girl Scts; Yrbk Phtg; Off Sr Cls; DECA; Cheerleading; Vllybl.

MC GLONE, VERONICA A; Crossland HS; Suitland, MD; (Y); Cmnty Wkr; Debate Tm; French Clb; Hosp Aide; Teachers Aide; Rep Frsh Cls; Rep Sr Cls; Var Tennis; Cit Awd; High Hon Roll; Cert For Scl Stdys Achvt 86; MD ST Schlrshp Grnt 86; Awd For Acdmc Exc 86; U MD Clg Pk; Pre-Med.

MC GLYNN, STEVEN T; High Point HS; Beltsville, MD; (Y); Am Leg Boys St; JV Bsbl; Var Capt Trk; Hon Roll; JETS Awd; NHS; U Of MD; Engr.

MC GONNIGAL, J BRUCE; Loyola HS; Towson, MD; (S); #26 In Class; Cmnty Wkr; Spanish Clb; Var Bsbl; Var Bsktbl; Capt Var Ftbl; Hon Roll; Plyr Of Yr-Ftbl 85; U Of VA.

MC GOOGAN, BRUCE; Pocomoke HS; Pocomoke, MD; (S); 2/100; AFS; Church Yth Grp; SADD; VP Stu Cncl; JV Bsktbl; Var Capt Socr; High Hon Roll; NHS; Rotary Awd; Hugh O Brien Ldrshp Awd 85.

MC GREGOR, LONNIE A; Maurice J Mc Donough HS; Waldorf, MD; (Y); Am Leg Boys St; Chess Clb; Var Bsktbl; Hon Roll; Navl Ordnc Stat Rockts Tech Wrkshp 85; Acctng.

MC GREGOR, PAT; Allegany HS; Lavale, MD; (Y); Bsbl; Bsktbl; Trk.

MC GREGOR, TRACEY; Fort Hill HS; Cumberland, MD; (Y); VP Frsh Cls; JV Var Cheerleading; JV Var Gym; JV Pom Pon; Hon Roll; NHS; Teen-Of-Yr Cntrl Assmbly Of God 85; Pres Of Flwshp Chrstn Stus 86.

MC GRUDER, SHAWN SHYRLENA; Centennial HS; Columbia, MD; (Y); 10/275; Pres Church Yth Grp; VP Civic Clb; Church Choir; Drill Tm; Jazz Band; Symp Band; Hon Roll; NHS; Prfct Atten Awd; Howard U; Laywer.

MC GUIGAN, JENNIE; St Marys Ryken HS; Indian Head, MD; (Y); Cmnty Wkr; 4-H; French Clb; Chorus; Hon Roll; Actvts Awd Comm Svc 85-86; Soc Commtte 86; Soc Sci.

MC GUIRE, TRACEY; Chapticon HS; Mechanicsville, MD; (S); DECA; Spanish Clb; Teachers Aide; Band; Concert Band; Mrchg Band; Sec Stu Cncl; Deca Conf 3rd Pl Food Mrktng Mgmt 86; Schl Gov SGA 82-84; San Diego; Zoolgy.

MC GUNIGAL, MARGARET; St Vincent Pallotti HS; Clarksville, MD; (S); 2/86; Spanish Clb; Trs Stu Cncl; Var Swmmng; Stat Trk; High Hon Roll; Pres NHS; Sal; Spanish NHS; St Schlr; Cmptr Sci.

MC GUTHRY, TIMA; Friendly SR HS; Ft Washington, MD; (Y); Church Yth Grp; Band; Concert Band; Mrchg Band; Symp Band; Sec Jr Cls; Sec Sr Cls; Stat Bsktbl; Hon Roll; Latin Hnr Soc 86; Hnr Mntn Sci Fair 86; Pre Med.

MC HALE, BETH; Institute Of Notre Dame; Baltimore, MD; (Y); Church Yth Grp; Cmnty Wkr; Hosp Aide; Hon Roll.

MC HOLD, HEATHER; The Key Schl; Annapolis, MD; (Y); Dance Clb; Ski Clb; Chorus; Stage Crew; Yrbk Ed-Chief; Var Lcrss; Drama Clb; Political Wkr; Yrbk Phtg; Yrbk Stf; Bio.

MC ILWEE, KEITH ALAN; Linganore HS; Ijamsville, MD; (Y); 22/300; Var Wt Lftg; Hon Roll; Ntl Merit Ltr; Montgomery Coll; Comm.

MC INTYRE, GLEN; Cardinal Gibbons HS; Baltimore, MD; (Y); 7/124; Var Ftbl; Var Lcrss; Var Wrstlng; Hon Roll; NHS; Ntl Merit Schol; Acad All Amer Awd; Phys Ther.

MC INTYRE, JENNIFER; John Carroll Schl; Havre De Grace, MD; (Y); 7/238; Library Aide; School Musical; Lit Mag; JV Var Lcrss; Var Capt Socr; High Hon Roll; Nmn Maryland Dstngshd Schlr; Slvc Hnr Scty; Baltimore Grls Cthlc Sccr Lge Str; Intrntl Rltns.

MC KAY, COLLEEN; Fort Hill HS; Cumberland, MD; (Y); 66/236; Pres Trs Church Yth Grp; Sec 4-H; Teachers Aide; Var L Bsktbl; Var L Trk; Var L Vllybl; Hon Roll; Del Proud Foot Awd 86; Frostburg ST Coll; Phys Educ.

MC KEE, DANETTE; Hancock HS; Hancock, MD; (Y); 4/67; Am Leg Aux Girls St; Church Yth Grp; FHA; Band; Yrbk Stf; Jr Cls; Dnfth Awd; Hon Roll; FFA.

MC KEEVER, DAWN; Sherwood HS; Olney, MD; (Y); SADD; Teachers Aide; Nwsp Rptr; Nwsp Stf; Rep Soph Cls; Rep Jr Cls; Trk; Wt Lftg; Hon Roll; Pre Law.

MC KENDREE, JACKIE; M J Mc Donough HS; La Plata, MD; (Y); Cmnty Wkr; Letterman Clb; Varsity Clb; Rep Frsh Cls; Rep Soph Cls; Var L Crs Cntry; Var L Trk; Hon Roll; Outstdng Athlete Awd 84-85; Outstdng Track 84-85; Comm.

MC KENNA, JOE; Laurel HS; Laurel, MD; (Y); Computer Clb; Var Crs Cntry; JV Trk; Hon Roll; Outstndng Achvt World Hist 84-85; US Hist.

MC KENNA, SCOTT; La Plata HS; Charlotte Hall, MD; (Y); Church Yth Grp; Ftbl; Trk; Hon Roll; PA ST Altoona; Comp Sci.

MC KENZIE, BRENT; Fort Hill HS; Cumberland, MD; (Y); Art Clb; Teachers Aide; Nwsp Sprt Ed; Socr; Hon Roll; Frostburg ST Coll.

MC KENZIE, PATTY; Mount Savage HS; Mt Savage, MD; (Y); Cmnty Wkr; DECA; VP French Clb; GAA; Library Aide; Office Aide; Pep Clb; Science Clb; Teachers Aide; Capt Drm Mjr(t); Allegany CC; Resprtry Therp.

MC KENZIE, RICH; Allegany HS; Cumberland, MD; (Y); JV Var Bsbl; JV Var Bsktbl; JV Var Socr; Allegany CC; Bus Admin.

MC KENZIE, STACEY LINN; Allegany HS; Cresaptown, MD; (Y); 8/220; Drill Tm; Off Jr Cls; Off Sr Cls; Cheerleading; Kiwanis Awd; NHS; Voice Dem Awd; Ski Clb; Off Frsh Cls; Off Soph Cls; Sci Dept Awd; Horace Mann Awd & Hrvrd Bk Awd; Frstbrg ST Coll.

MC KENZIE, TERRI; North Hagerstown HS; Hagestown, MD; (Y); 27/327; Latin Clb; Office Aide; Pep Clb; Yrbk Rptr; Yrbk Stf; Prfct Atten Awd; Hag JR Coll 1/2 Days 86-87; Pre Law.

MC KENZIE, WENDY; Chopticon HS; Waldorf, MD; (Y); Church Yth Grp; Latin Clb; Ski Clb; Teachers Aide; Varsity Clb; Trs Jr Cls; Capt Var Vllybl; Church Yth Grp; Latin Clb; Ski Clb.

MC KEON, MARIE E; Arch Bishop Keough HS; Elliott City, MD; (Y); VP Soph Cls; Pres Jr Cls; Pres Sr Cls; Var Capt Cheerleading; Var Fld Hcky; Var Lcrss; Var Tennis; Hon Roll; NHS; Natl Hnr Roll 86; SAC Sec 85-86; Comm.

MC KINNEY, TAMARA; Friendly HS; Ft Washington, MD; (Y); Dance Clb; German Clb; Chorus; Hon Roll; Sci Cert Of Compltn At Bowie ST Coll 85; MD U; Libry Sci.

MC KINNEY, VICTORIA; Institute Of Notre Dame; Baltimore, MD; (Y); Church Yth Grp; Church Choir; Bsbl; Bsktbl; Socr; Sftbl; Tennis; Trk; Vllybl; Hnr Roll 84-85; Bus Mgr.

MC KNIGHT, ANGELA; North East HS; North East, MD; (Y); Church Yth Grp; SADD; JV Var Fld Hcky; Lbrl Arts.

MC KOY, KAREN; Roland Park Country Schl; Baltimore, MD; (Y); Art Clb; Cmnty Wkr; Hosp Aide; Nwsp Stf; Yrbk Stf; Socr; Hon Roll; Bio.

MC KOY, VERSHON; Oakland Mills HS; Columbia, MD; (Y); 66/240; Pres German Clb; Hosp Aide; Pres Latin Clb; Off Soph Cls; Off Jr Cls; Off Sr Cls; Rep Stu Cncl; Hon Roll; Yrbk Bus Mgr; Yrbk Rptr; Delta Sigma Theta Debutante 86; Delta Sigma Theta Outstndng Cmmnty Svc Awd 86; Duke U; Pre-Med.

MC LAUGHLIN, BILLY; Laplata HS; Saint Charles, MD; (Y); Boy Scts; Off Computer Clb; Ski Clb; Var Socr; Bendey Awd 84; Bsktbl Announcng 86; 1st Prize Hist Fair 85; FL Inst Tech; Elec Engrng.

MC LAWHORN, KAREN ANN; Archbishop Keough HS; Baltimore, MD; (Y); Sec Civic Clb; Dance Clb; Drama Clb; Thesps; School Musical; Var L Cheerleading; Hon Roll; NHS; School Play; Variety Show; Ntl Achvt Schlrshp Pgm Commended Stu 85; Fnlst Miss Ntl Pagnt 84; Grad Barbizon Schl Modlng 85; U MD; Physcl Thrpy.

MC LEAN, ELENOR L; Albert Einstein HS; Kensington, MD; (Y); 8/304; Nwsp Stf; Yrbk Ed-Chief; Yrbk Stf; Trs Jr Cls; JV Bsktbl; Tennis; JETS Awd; NHS; Pres Schlr; Rensselaer Mdl Math&sci 85; U VA; Engrng.

MC LEOD, JOHN; Northern HS; Baltimore, MD; (Y); Off Jr Cls; Capt Socr; Var Trk; Cert-Phys Chem 85-86; Athltc Awd 86; U Of MD; Aerospc Engr.

MC MAHON, GAIL; Valley HS; Midland, MD; (Y); Cmnty Wkr; 4-H; Hosp Aide; Library Aide; Nwsp Stf; Cit Awd; 4-H Awd; High Hon Roll; NHS; Sec Sci Cont 86; Georgetown U; Med.

MC MAHON, KAREN; South Carroll HS; Westminster, MD; (Y); Ski Clb; Band; Concert Band; Jazz Band; Mrchg Band; Orch; Pep Band; School Musical; Symp Band; High Hon Roll; U Of MD Baltimore.

MC MANUS, CATHIE; Thomas Stone HS; Waldorf, MD; (Y); Church Yth Grp; Science Clb; Boys Clb Am; Color Guard; Drill Tm; Capt Flag Corp; Rep Frsh Cls; Rep Stu Cncl; Var Twrlr; Hon Roll; Cha Mes County CC; Comp.

MC MILLAN, CHARMEL; Crossland HS; Ft Washington, MD; (Y); 1/333; Church Yth Grp; Math Tm; Church Choir; Sec Jr Cls; Rep Stu Cncl; Var Vllybl; High Hon Roll; NHS; Pep Clb; Teachers Aide; George Washington U Awd For Engrng 86; Jesse Warr Mem Awd 86; Piano Guild Awd 81-86.

MC MILLAN, DAWN; Smithsburg HS; Ft Ritchie, MD; (Y); Church Yth Grp; Cmnty Wkr; Computer Clb; Dance Clb; Debate Tm; Drama Clb; French Clb; FBLA; Pep Clb; Sec Science Clb; Med.

MC NAMARA, MICHELLE; Walter Johnson HS; Bethesda, MD; (Y); Key Clb; Teachers Aide; Hon Roll; U MD; Bus.

MC NEILL, JOYCE; Fairmont Heights HS; Lanham, MD; (Y); Hosp Aide; Intnl Clb; Orch; Yrbk Stf; Hon Roll; Jr NHS; NHS; Outstndng Achvt Englsh, Sci 83; Sci Fair 2nd Pl 83; House Of Delg Schlrshp 86; U Of MD; Med.

MC NEW, SANDRA; Dundalk HS; Baltimore, MD; (Y); School Musical; Hon Roll; Strng Cmmtee Cls 1987 85-87; Exec Brd Stu Cncl 87; Soc Wrk.

MC PHERSON, JENNIFER; St Vincent Pallotti HS; Laurel, MD; (S); 13/86; Hosp Aide; Office Aide; Red Cross Aide; JV Sftbl; Mgr Swmmng; JV Var Vllybl; High Hon Roll; Hon Roll; NHS; Prfct Atten Awd.

MC PHILLIPS, KIMBERLY; Archbishop Keough HS; Baltimore, MD; (Y); 30/230; Yrbk Stf; Rep Jr Cls; Im Bsktbl; Im Socr; Im Sftbl; Im Swmmng; Hon Roll; Phys Thrpy.

MC RAE, SAMANTHA; Potomac HS; Temple Hills, MD; (Y); 4-H; Hosp Aide; Office Aide; Teachers Aide; Y-Teens; Band; School Play; Yrbk Stf; Rep Sr Cls; Crim Law.

MC SPARRAN III, R BOYD; Kent County HS; Chestertown, MD; (Y); Am Leg Boys St; Cmnty Wkr; Trs French Clb; Concert Band; Drm Mjr(t); Jazz Band; Capt Mrchg Band; School Musical; Var L Trk; Hon Roll; All Shore Band 85-86.

MC VEY, MELISSA; Oakland Mills HS; Columbia, MD; (Y); 40/275; Ski Clb; Capt Cheerleading; JV Var Fld Hcky; Lcrss; La Salle U; Acctng.

MC WILLIAMS, SHARON; Patterson HS; Baltimore, MD; (Y); Hon Roll; VP NHS; Prfct Atten Awd; Rep Jr Cls; Cert Of Achvt In Schlrshp Delta Sigma Theta Sorty 86.

MC WOOD, JASON; Chopticon HS; Mechanicsville, MD; (Y); Church Yth Grp; FFA; Office Aide; Teachers Aide; Bsbl; Ftbl; Mgr(s); Sftbl; Wrstlng; Cit Awd; FFA Jr Advsr 86; FFA Fruit Veg Profncy Awd 84-86; FFA Trctr Drvng 1st 85; Farming.

MEAGHER, DEENA; Allegany HS; Lavale, MD; (Y); Pres Computer Clb; Nwsp Bus Mgr; Nwsp Stf; Score Keeper; Socr; Trk; Hon Roll; W VA U; Comp Pgmng Sci.

MEALO, ANTHONY; Northwestern HS; U Park, MD; (Y); Teachers Aide; Wt Lftg; Hon Roll; NHS; U MD; MBA.

MEDAIRY, JENNIFER; Notre Dame Prep; Columbia, MD; (Y); Chorus; DAR Awd; Hon Roll; NEDT Awd; Latin Hnr Soc 86; Natl Hnr Soc 86; NEDT Test Awd 84; Med Dctr.

MEDFORD, DORRIS; Surrattsville HS; Camp Springs, MD; (Y); Church Yth Grp; FBLA; Math Tm; Office Aide; Church Choir; Yrbk Stf; L Trk; High Hon Roll; Hon Roll; Acad Excllnc Awd 84; Sci Fair Hon Mntn 84; Trck Cert; Accntng.

MEEKINS, CATHY; Franklin SR HS; Reisterstown, MD; (Y); FBLA; Powder Puff Ftbl; Vllybl; Hon Roll; NHS; Prncpls List 85-86; Edward P Colwell Schlrshp 86; Touson ST U; Comp Sci.

MEEKINS, STEVE; Highland View Acad; Chestertown, MD; (Y); Church Yth Grp; FCA; Ski Clb; Varsity Clb; Band; Variety Show; Yrbk Phtg; Yrbk Stf; Lit Mag; Pres Soph Cls; Columbia Union Coll; Bus Mgmt.

MEEKS, AMY; Rising Sun HS; Rising Sun, MD; (Y); 12/159; Church Yth Grp; Hosp Aide; Math Clb; Spanish Clb; SADD; Tennis; Vllybl; Hon Roll; NHS; Prfct Atten Awd; Wmn Cncl Of Cecil Cnty Achvt Awd 86; Sntrl Schlrshp 86; Pres Acdmc Ftns Awd 86; U MD Estrn Shr; Physcl Thrpy.

MEHRER, GARY; Laplata HS; Bel Alton, MD; (Y); Church Yth Grp; Ski Clb; Teachers Aide; JV Var Socr; Hon Roll; BYU; Pre Law.

MEHTA, MONALI; Gaithersburg HS; Gaithersburg, MD; (Y); AFS; FFA; Intnl Clb; Key Clb; Political Wkr; Chorus; NHS; Awd Russian 86; Russian.

MEILHAMMER, DEBORAH; James M Bennett SR HS; Salisbury, MD; (Y); Exploring; Letterman Clb; Office Aide; Varsity Clb; Stage Crew; Sftbl; Vllybl; High Hon Roll; Hon Roll; Comp Sci.

MEININGER, STEPHEN O; Centennial HS; Columbia, MD; (Y); 15/276; Church Yth Grp; German Clb; Ski Clb; Var L Lcrss; L Socr; Var L Trk; Wt Lftg; Hon Roll; JETS Awd; VA Tech; Engrng.

MEJIA, JODI; Liberty HS; Eldersburg, MD; (Y); Am Leg Aux Girls St; Latin Clb; Quiz Bowl; Rep Jr Cls; Rep Stu Cncl; JV Var Bsktbl; High Hon Roll; Hon Roll; Hugh O Brian Youth Ldrshp Sem 84; Acad Ltr-Bar 83-85; Kent ST Univ; Adv.

MELLOR, THERESA; Mt De Sales Acad; Finksburg, MD; (Y); Chorus.

MELLOS, ANDRIANA; Bladensburg HS; Hyattsville, MD; (Y); Office Aide; VICA; Chorus; Rep Frsh Cls; Rep Soph Cls; Rep Jr Cls; Mgr(s); Prince Georges Cnty Med Soc Scholar Awd 86; Cert Nrsg Asst 86; Prince Georges CC; RN.

MELTZER, STEPHANIE; Walt Whitman HS; Bethesda, MD; (Y); Temple Yth Grp; Nwsp Stf; Stu Cncl; Var Capt Cheerleading; Var Gym; Var Trk; Cmnctns.

MELVIN, RANDALL; Northwestern HS; Baltimore, MD; (S); Boy Scts; Church Yth Grp; ROTC; Church Choir; Rep Frsh Cls; Rep Stu Cncl; Var Swmmng; Ntl Histry & Govt Awd 86; Bowie ST Coll.

MENAKER, DAVID; Gaithersburg HS; Gaithersburg, MD; (Y); Pres Key Clb.

MENESES, REGINALD B; Loyola HS; Catonsville, MD; (S); 21/196; Church Yth Grp; Hosp Aide; NFL; Nwsp Ed-Chief; Lit Mag; Trk; NHS; Chess Clb; Debate Tm; French Clb; Loyola Coll MD; Jrnlsm.

MENG, JAMES; Pikesville SR HS; Baltimore, MD; (Y); Pres Church Yth Grp; Church Choir; Stage Crew; Trk; NHS; Chem Engrng.

MENGUE, FRANCINE; Richard Montgomery HS; Rockville, MD; (Y); Church Yth Grp; Intnl Clb; SADD; Yrbk Phtg; Var Bsktbl; JV Gym; Cit Awd; Dnfth Awd; French Hon Soc; Ntl Merit Schol; John Hopkins U; Med.

MENINGER, JILL; Fallston HS; Fallston, MD; (Y); 33/251; Letterman Clb; Varsity Clb; Band; Concert Band; Mrchg Band; Nwsp Rptr; Rep Jr Cls; Rep Sr Cls; Var Capt Bsktbl; Var Capt Fld Hcky; Cougar Booster Clb Schlrsh 86; All Cnty La Crosse Team 86; VA Tech; Comp Sci.

MENON, ANITHA; Springbrook HS; Silver Spring, MD; (Y); Debate Tm; Chorus; School Musical; Variety Show; Hon Roll; Engrng.

MENSH, STACY; Charles E Smith Jewish Day Schl; Silver Spring, MD; (Y); Cmnty Wkr; Red Cross Aide; SADD; Temple Yth Grp; Rep Sec Stu Cncl; Vllybl; Hosp Aide; Nwsp Stf; Yrbk Stf; Rep Soph Cls; Tmpl Youth Grp USY Chrprsn Of Best Intrchptr Of Yr 84; Sports Bus.

MENZER, JOAN; Northwestern HS; Hyattsville, MD; (Y); AFS; Church Yth Grp; German Clb; Stage Crew; Hon Roll.

MEREDITH, JESSICA; Dulaney SR HS; Phoenix, MD; (Y); Church Yth Grp; Sec Key Clb; Band; Mktg.

MERELLA, MAUREEN CLARE; Bowie HS; Bowie, MD; (Y); 15/630; Math Clb; Q&S; Spanish Clb; Ed Nwsp Rptr; Off Sr Cls; Stu Cncl; Socr; High Hon Roll; Sec NHS; Pres Schlr; Fordham U NY; Cmmnctns.

MERENA, THERESA MARIE; Glen Burnie HS; Glen Burnie, MD; (Y); 7/429; Pres Computer Clb; Teachers Aide; Cheerleading; Hon Roll; Prfct Atten Awd; Prsdntl Acad Ftns Awds Prog 86; Cert Achvt Vctnl Prog 86; Prncpls Awd 86; Outstndng Bus Comp Prgrmg 86; U Of MD; Comp Sci.

MERKEL, KATHLEEN; Elizabeth Seton HS; Bowie, MD; (Y); 10/188; Sec Trs French Clb; Yrbk Bus Mgr; Yrbk Phtg; Yrbk Stf; Var L Trk; High Hon Roll; NHS; Rotary Awd; Its Acadmc Tm; U Of DE; Acctng.

MERRBAUGH, JOHNNA; Valley HS; Lonaconing, MD; (Y); 2/90; Trs Church Yth Grp; Q&S; Nwsp Ed-Chief; Nwsp Phtg; Nwsp Rptr; High Hon Roll; NHS; Voice Dem Awd; Computer Clb; Drama Clb; Hugh O Brian Yth Ldrshp Awd & Ambassador Staff 86; Journlsm.

MERRILL, CHRISTIE; Washington HS; Princess Anne, MD; (Y); Am Leg Aux Girls St; Yrbk Rptr; Yrbk Stf; Tennis; High Hon Roll; NHS; Acctnt.

MERRYMAN, MICHELLE; Westminster HS; Taneytown, MD; (Y); Drama Clb; Pres Thesps; Band; School Musical; School Play; Stage Crew; High Hon Roll; NHS; Zoology.

MESSARIS, KAREN; Notre Dame Prep Schl; Baltimore, MD; (Y); Chorus; Stage Crew; Hon Roll; NEDT Awd; Medicine.

MESSENGER, MARY; Takoma Acad; Takoma Park, MD; (Y); Church Yth Grp; French Clb; Ski Clb; Orch; Hon Roll; NHS.

MESSINA, FELICIA; La Reine HS; Temple Hills, MD; (S); 10/168; Cmnty Wkr; Intnl Clb; Trs Science Clb; Teachers Aide; High Hon Roll; Hon Roll; NHS; La Reinian Of Mnth 84; Dr Of Med.

METERKO, MATTHEW; Crossland SR HS; Temple Hills, MD; (Y); Math Clb; Golf; Mgr(s); Mgr Sftbl; Hon Roll; Rcvd ST Sntrl Schlrshp 86; Resrch Apprntc Pgm U Of DC 85; Maryland U; Engrng.

MEYER, AMANDA L; Wicomico SR HS; Salisbury, MD; (Y); Church Yth Grp; Cmnty Wkr; French Clb; Girl Scts; Teachers Aide; Band; Concert Band; Mrchg Band; Symp Band; Var Crs Cntry; Natl Piano Plyng Auditions 85 & 86; G & T Pgm 81-84; Music.

MEYER, CHRISTINE; Dulaney SR HS; Timonium, MD; (Y); Debate Tm; Hosp Aide; School Musical; Mgr Bsktbl; Mgr Fld Hcky; Mgr Lcrss; High Hon Roll; NHS; 50 Hrs Cndy Strpng Cert 85; Sales Awd Tp Selr Mnth At Gap 86; Bus.

MEYER, GRETA; Montgomery Blair HS; Silver Spring, MD; (Y); 5/357; French Clb; Hosp Aide; VP Soph Cls; Stu Cncl; French Hon Soc; Hon Roll; NHS; Cmnty Wkr; Frsh Cls; Gov Hon Prg Awd; MD Dstngshed Schlr 85; Mntgmry Cnty Med Socs Rec Hlth Care 86; 1st Pl Piano Duet Comptn 85; U Of NC At Chpl Hll; Bio Scis.

MEYER, JONATHAN; Captiol Christian Acad; Edgewater, MD; (S); Church Yth Grp; French Clb; Band; Mrchg Band; Pep Band; Var L Bsbl; Hon Roll; JP Sousa Awd; Mst Studious 84-85.

MEYER, VANESSA; Gaithersburg HS; Gaithersburg, MD; (Y); Art Clb; SADD; JV Vllybl; Hon Roll; MD U; Bus.

MEYERS, EVAN; Wootton HS; Potomac, MD; (Y); Church Yth Grp; Letterman Clb; Red Cross Aide; Ski Clb; Var Capt Swmmng; Wt Lftg; High Hon Roll; Honrbl Mentn-MD ST Sci Fair 84; Engrng.

MEYERS, KARYN; Patapsco HS; Baltimore, MD; (Y); 13/310; Church Yth Grp; Rep Stu Cncl; Stat Lcrss; Mgr(s); Hon Roll; Jr NHS; NHS; Prfct Atten Awd; Awd Grad Top 5 Pct Of Clss 86; Schlrshp Bear Crk Elem PTA 86; Outstndng Achvt Eng 86; UMBC; Grphc Dsgn.

MICHAEL, DAWN; Patapsco HS; Baltimore, MD; (Y); Cmnty Wkr; Hosp Aide; Spanish Clb; Varsity Clb; Band; Concert Band; Jazz Band; Mrchg Band; Pep Band; Symp Band; Nurse.

MICHAELS, DAVID; Northern HS; Friendsville, MD; (Y); Art Clb; Mrchg Band; Yrbk Stf; Sr Cls; Wrstlng.

MICHAELS, SANDY; Mt Savage HS; Mt Savage, MD; (S); 3/60; FBLA; Band; Chorus; Nwsp Rptr; Rep Stu Cncl; Var Capt Cheerleading; Trk; Twrlr; Sci.

MICHALISKO, STEPHEN; John Carrol Schl; New Park, PA; (Y); Boy Scts; Church Yth Grp; Library Aide; Nwsp Stf; Hon Roll; German Ntl Hnr Soc 86.

MICKLES, CRAIG; Walbrook SR HS; Baltimore, MD; (Y); Computer Clb; FBLA; JA; Rep Frsh Cls; Rep Soph Cls; Rep Jr Cls; Pre Med.

MICKLOS, SOPHIA; Patterson HS; Baltimore, MD; (Y); Church Yth Grp; Cmnty Wkr; Service Clb; SADD; Yrbk Rptr; Pres Stu Cncl; Cit Awd; DAR Awd; Prfct Atten Awd; Art Clb; Dptrtm Rcrtn Prks Vlntr Crps Crtfct Hnr 81; Crtfcit Awd Pstr Cnts 79; Crtfct Apprctn Hnrbl Mntn 79; Intrntnl Mgmnt.

MIDLETON, NATALIE; Institute Of Notre Dane HS; Baltimore, MD; (Y); Church Yth Grp; Cmnty Wkr; Drama Clb; Pres FBLA; Sec Intnl Clb; Church Choir; Cheerleading; Trk; High Hon Roll; Amrcn Legn Sch Awd 83; Med.

MIERZWICKI II, LEO A; Loyola HS; Bel Air, MD; (S); Nwsp Stf; Yrbk Stf; JV Bsbl; Bsktbl; Golf; Socr; High Hon Roll; Hon Roll; NHS; Religion & Spanish Mdl Fresh & Soph Yr 83-84; NEDT Test Awd 83; Notre Dame; Gen Practnr.

MIGNINI, KATHY; Catholic HS; Baltimore, MD; (Y); Church Yth Grp; Cmnty Wkr; Dance Clb; Church Choir; School Musical; Variety Show; Hon Roll; NHS; Voice Dem Awd; Paralegal Schlrshp To Villa Jilie Coll 86; Villa Julie Coll; Law.

MIGROCK, JOANNA; Glenelg HS; Glenwood, MD; (Y); 3/280; Chess Clb; Hosp Aide; Spanish Clb; Varsity Clb; Var Capt Crs Cntry; Var Trk; High Hon Roll; Hon Roll; NHS; MD Dstngshd Schlr SF 85-86; Loyola Pres Scholar 85-86; Loyola Coll; Engl.

MILBURN, MICHELLE; Carver Vocational Technical HS; Baltimore, MD; (Y); Pom Pon; Hon Roll; Prfct Atten Awd; ULLA; Csmtlgst.

MILES, BRIAN; Northwestern SR HS; Baltimore, MD; (Y); Church Yth Grp; ROTC; Church Choir; Var Wrstlng; Hon Roll; Towson ST; Vet Med.

MILES, PATRICK; Glenelg HS; Ellicott City, MD; (Y); Church Yth Grp; Varsity Clb; Rep Frsh Cls; Var Bsbl; Hon Roll; Hon Roll Athlt 84-86.

MILLER, ANDRETTA; Paul Laurence Dunbar HS; Baltimore, MD; (Y); Girl Scts; Pep Clb; Capt Mrchg Band; Pep Band; Yrbk Stf; Mgr(s); Capt Pom Pon; Hon Roll; Prfct Atten Awd; Coppin ST U; Nrsng.

MILLER, CARLA; Allegany HS; Front Royal, VA; (Y); 43/223; Drama Clb; Hosp Aide; Library Aide; Pep Clb; Thesps; Varsity Clb; Rep Frsh Cls; Rep Soph Cls; Stat Bsbl; Cheerleading; Miss Campera Hmcmng Queen 85-86; Psych.

MILLER, CAROLYN; Broadneck SR HS; Annapolis, MD; (S); DECA; Pres JA; Rep Frsh Cls; Var Gym; Homecoming Queen 85-86; 1st Pl Free Enterprise Essay Contst 86; Natl DECA Conf In Atlanta; Mktng.

MILLER, CHRIS; Cambridge South Dorchester HS; E New Market, MD; (Y); Sec Pres Aud/Vis; Church Yth Grp; Girl Scts; Office Aide; Bsktbl; Chesapeake Coll Socl Sci 85; Chesapeake Coll Socl Sci 86; Chesapeake Coll; Bus Mngemnt.

MILLER, CHRISTINA; Patterson HS; Baltimore, MD; (Y); Church Yth Grp; FBLA; Band; Church Choir; Color Guard; Concert Band; Sec.

MILLER, CHRISTINE; North Harford HS; Jarrettsville, MD; (Y); Church Yth Grp; Spanish Clb; Varsity Clb; Chorus; School Musical; Yrbk Phtg; JV Var Bsktbl; Powder Puff Ftbl; JV Var Sftbl; JV Var Vllybl; Harford Comm; Bus.

MILLER, CHRISTOPHER J; Loyola HS Blakefld; Baltimore, MD; (S); 19/197; French Clb; Hosp Aide; Band; Concert Band; Jazz Band; Mrchg Band; Im Ftbl; Hon Roll; NHS; Loyola Outstndg Math Awd 84; Loyola Clg; Math Sci.

MILLER, CINDY MARIE; Governor Thomas Jefferson HS; Frederick, MD; (Y); 7/341; Church Yth Grp; Debate Tm; Chrmn Science Clb; Thesps; Madrigals; School Musical; Sec Soph Cls; Sec Sr Cls; High Hon Roll; NHS; Mock Trial Comptn 86; 1st Pl Solo Actng Frnscs Trnmnt 86; MD Ctr Arts 84-85; All ST Chorus 84-86; UNC; Psych.

MILLER, COURTNEY; Sherwood HS; Olney, MD; (Y); Pres Church Yth Grp; Drama Clb; Jazz Band; Madrigals; School Musical; Variety Show; Rep Stu Cncl; Capt Pom Pon; Hon Roll; Sec NHS; Ctznshp Awd & Excllnc Art Awd, Hnrb Mntn Schlstcs Art Comp 84; Excllnc Music Awd 85.

MILLER, DAWN; Bishop Walsh HS; Cumberland, MD; (Y); 17/101; Art Clb; Civic Clb; Girl Scts; Pep Clb; SADD; JV Stat Bsbl; Hon Roll; Actvts Awd 85-86; Pre-Med.

MILLER, DUSTY; Seneca Valley HS; Gaithersburg, MD; (Y); Church Yth Grp; Drm Mjr(t); Band; Church Choir; Mrchg Band; Orch; Pep Band; Symp Band; Hon Roll; Pblc Rltns.

MILLER, ELIZABETH; Col Zadok Magruder HS; Rockville, MD; (Y); Latin Clb; SADD; Hon Roll; Bus.

MILLER, FRED; Beall HS; Frostburg, MD; (Y); Church Yth Grp; Teachers Aide; Frostburg ST Coll; Chem Engrng.

MILLER, ISAAC; Damascus HS; Damascus, MD; (Y); 24/243; Drama Clb; Leo Clb; NFL; Speech Tm; Thesps; School Musical; School Play; Stage Crew; Variety Show; Trk; Bst Dramatic Actor Awd Schl Play 86; Excllnce Spkg Awd 85; Forn Fnlst Duet Act & Humrs Intrprtatn 86; U MD; Engrng.

MILLER, JACOB; Boys Latin HS; Upperco, MD; (S); 2/60; VP Soph Cls; Sec Jr Cls; Sec Sr Cls; Var Capt Ftbl; JV Lcrss; High Hon Roll; Hon Roll; NHS; Sci Awd 83; Art Awd 82; Schlr-Ath Awd 85.

MILLER, JOSEPH; Our Lady Of Good Counsel HS; Silver Spring, MD; (Y); 86/214; SADD; JV Bsbl; JV Ftbl; Hon Roll; Sprtsmn Clb 85-86; Cmmnty Rep 85-86; Cmp Good Cncl.

MILLER, LANCE; Cambridge South Dorchester HS; Cambridge, MD; (Y); 5/213; AFS; Chess Clb; Latin Clb; Scholastic Bowl; Spanish Clb; Rep Stu Cncl; NHS; Outstndng Stdnt Awd Tech Drftng I, 1st Master Quiz Soc Sci Wrld Civlztn 85; Med.

MILLER, MARK; Oxon Hill HS; Oxon Hill, MD; (Y); Chess Clb; Church Yth Grp; Math Tm; High Hon Roll; NHS; Pres Acad Fit Awd 85-86; 2nd Pl Area Sci Fair Comp Sci 86; Acad Excllnce Awd 84-86; VA Tech; Elec Engrng.

MILLER, MELISSA; Notre Dame Prep; Lutherville, MD; (Y); 3/28; Art Clb; Aud/Vis; Camera Clb; Cmnty Wkr; Computer Clb; Dance Clb; SADD; Teachers Aide; Swmmng; Villa Julie Coll; Comp Sci.

MILLER, MICHELLE; Riverdale Baptist HS; New Carrollton, MD; (Y); 10/66; Teachers Aide; Stu Cncl; Capt Cheerleading; Trk; High Hon Roll; Hon Roll; NHS; Katherine Gibbs; Bus.

MILLER, PENNY; Francis Scott Key HS; New Windsor, MD; (Y); Drama Clb; French Clb; Science Clb; Chorus; School Play; Hon Roll; NHS; Elem Educ.

MILLER, SHARON; North Carroll HS; Manchester, MD; (Y); French Clb; Off Frsh Cls; Hon Roll.

MILLER, STEPHEN; Perryville HS; Pt Deposit, MD; (Y); Am Leg Boys St; Varsity Clb; Pres Band; Pres Concert Band; Jazz Band; Var L Ftbl; Hon Roll; VFW Awd; MD ST Schlrshp 86; Towson ST All Sr Hnr Bnd 85; Sr Music Hnr Awd 86; Salisbury ST Coll; Music.

MILLER, SYLVIA; Seton HS; Baltimore, MD; (Y); JA; Hon Roll; Jr NHS; Pres Schlr; Latin Ii Awd 85; Maryland Math League Comp Awd 85; Essex CC; Bus Mgnt.

MILLER, TRACI; Laurel SR HS; Laurel, MD; (Y); Cmnty Wkr; Hosp Aide; Spanish Clb; Hon Roll; Prfct Atten Awd; MD Mth Achvt Awd 3rd 85-86; Acctng.

MILLS, BOBBY; John F Kennedy SR HS; Silver Spring, MD; (Y); Drama Clb; Teachers Aide; School Play; Rep Soph Cls; Var JV Bsktbl; Var Trk; Cit Awd; High Hon Roll; Hon Roll; NHS; NHS 84-85; Law.

MILLS, CHERYL; Clear Spring HS; Big Pool, MD; (Y); 12/119; Teachers Aide; School Play; Nwsp Rptr; Sec Sr Cls; Stu Cncl; Stat Socr; Elks Awd; Misses Lizzie & Ella Snyder Educ Awd 86; Clr Sprng Schlrshp 86; George A Sites Mrl Schlrshp; Hagerstown JC; Cmmnctns.

MILLS, DAVID; Maurice J Mc Donough HS; Waldorf, MD; (S); Art Clb; Computer Clb; Latin Clb; Rep Jr Cls; Bsbl; Ftbl; High Hon Roll; NHS; Prfct Atten Awd; VA Polytechncl Inst; Arch.

MILLS, JENNIFER LYNN; Fort Hill HS; Cumberland, MD; (Y); 37/284; Computer Clb; Pep Clb; Color Guard; Off Sr Cls; Rep Stu Cncl; Prfct Atten Awd; Carl Ritchie Bus Schlrshp 86; Svc Awd Ft Hill 86; Stu Cncl Svc Awd 86; WV U; Mrktng.

MILLS, KATE DORINDA; Gaithersburg HS; Gaithersburg, MD; (Y); Camera Clb; U MD; Law.

MILLS, PEGGY; Gaithersburg HS; Germantown, MD; (Y); Trs Key Clb; Office Aide; Chorus; Bowling; Hon Roll; Cosmetlgy.

MILLS, STACEY; Atholton HS; Highland, MD; (Y); 23/263; Hosp Aide; Band; Concert Band; Mrchg Band; Yrbk Stf; Trs Frsh Cls; Pres Jr Cls; Var Socr; Hon Roll; Law.

MILLS, TERRI; Maurice J Mc Donough HS; White Plains, MD; (S); Teachers Aide; High Hon Roll; NHS; Acad Achvt Cls Partcptn Rcrd Keepng 85; 2nd Pl Charles Cnty Sci Fair 84-85; Accntnt.

MILOS, AMANDA; Fort Hill HS; Cumberland, MD; (S); 13/250; Church Choir; Yrbk Stf; NHS; Bio.

MILSTEAD, KATHY; St Vincent Pallotti HS; College Park, MD; (S); 14/88; Drama Clb; NFL; School Play; Yrbk Stf; VP Soph Cls; Var Cheerleading; Mgr(s); High Hon Roll; Hon Roll; NHS; Hugh O Briean Yth Found Ldrshp Sem 84; Sheperd Clg; Grphc Inter Dsgn.

MILSTEAD, MONIQUE; Gwynn Park HS; Accokeek, MD; (Y); Teachers Aide; Hon Roll; Nrsng.

MILTENBERGER, CHRIS; Bishop Walsh HS; Ridgeley, WV; (Y); 1/100; Computer Clb; German Clb; Library Aide; Math Clb; Science Clb; Var Bsbl; High Hon Roll; NHS; Exploring; Cit Awd; Allegany CC Math Schlrshp; VA Tech; Chem Engrng.

MINER, MIKE; North Hagerstown HS; Hagerstown, MD; (Y); French Clb; Varsity Clb; School Musical; Off Jr Cls; Stu Cncl; Socr; Aerontcl Engrng.

MINGIONI, MONICA; Arlington Baptist HS; Ferndale, MD; (S); 1/75; Church Yth Grp; Drama Clb; Spanish Clb; Band; Trs Jr Cls; JV Var Cheerleading; High Hon Roll; NHS; Val; Comp Sci.

MINICK, TINA; Fort Hill HS; Cumberland, MD; (S); Capt Drill Tm; Mrchg Band; Ed Yrbk Stf; Off Jr Cls; Off Sr Cls; Rep Stu Cncl; Cit Awd; High Hon Roll; Hon Roll; NHS; Allegany CC; Bus Adm.

MINN, KYONG; Lansdowne HS; Baltimore, MD; (Y); Office Aide; Chorus; Madrigals; School Musical; School Play; Variety Show; JV Var Cheerleading; Hon Roll; Comp Sci.

MINNICK, ADORA; Allegany HS; Cumberland, MD; (Y); AFS; Church Yth Grp; SADD; Church Choir; Drill Tm; Rep Stu Cncl; JV Bsktbl; JV Fld Hcky; Sftbl; Hon Roll; Fash Merch.

MINNICK, BARBARA; Notre Dame Prep; Fallston, MD; (Y); Church Yth Grp; Cmnty Wkr; JA; SADD; Variety Show; JV Var Cheerleading; JV Lcrss; Hon Roll; Bus Admin.

MINNICK, MICHELLE; Allegany HS; Cumberland, MD; (Y); Computer Clb; Drama Clb; FBLA; Office Aide; SADD; Thesps; Drill Tm; Stage Crew; Stat Wrstlng; Allegany CC; Sociolgy.

MINOR, BONINETTE; Lackey HS; Nanjemoy, MD; (Y); Church Yth Grp; FBLA; Church Choir; Hon Roll.

MINTZ, DARRYN; Montgomery Blair HS; Silver Spring, MD; (Y); Teachers Aide; Yrbk Ed-Chief; Yrbk Stf; Off Soph Cls; Off Jr Cls; Off Sr Cls; High Hon Roll; Hon Roll; NHS; Ldrshp Conf U Of MD 86; Jrnlsm Wrkshp Goucher Coll 85; Spcl Recgntn Mntgmry Cnty Brd Of Ed.

MIRANTE, LYNN; Fairmont Heights HS; Landover Hls, MD; (Y); Church Yth Grp; JA; Spanish Clb; High Hon Roll; Lion Awd.

MIRSKY, JONATHAN B; Bethesda-Chevy Chase HS; Chevy Chase, MD; (Y); 136/449; Co-Capt Debate Tm; Sec Sr Cls; Off Stu Cncl; Ntl Merit SF.

MISENAR, DEBBIE A; Francis Scott Key HS; New Windsor, MD; (Y); Cmnty Wkr; Teachers Aide; VICA; Chorus; Church Choir; Socr; Tennis; Hon Roll; NHS; Unsung Hero Awd 85; Catonsville CC; Scl Sci.

MISHRA, ANITA; Thomas S Wootton HS; Potomoc, MD; (Y); Chess Clb; Orch; Trk; Hon Roll; Physic Tm 85-86; U Of MD; Engrng.

MISRA, TIMIR; Seneca Valley HS; Germantown, MD; (Y); Aud/Vis; Computer Clb; Band; Rep Soph Cls; JV Socr; Timer; Trk; Hon Roll; NHS; Bio.

MITCHELL, CAROL; Mardela HS; Sharptown, MD; (Y); 2/61; Office Aide; Trs Spanish Clb; Chorus; Color Guard; School Musical; Stage Crew; Pres Jr Cls; Rep Stu Cncl; NHS; Natl Schlrs Sem-Salibury ST Coll 84-5 & 85-6; U Of MD Coll Pk Ldrshp Sem 85-6; Flager; Psych.

MITCHELL, CHRISTOPHER; Loch Raven HS; Baltimore, MD; (Y); Drama Clb; SADD; Band; VP Pres Stu Cncl; Var Gym; High Hon Roll; NHS; Boy Scts; Intnl Clb; Concert Band; Japan US Sen Schlrshp Summer 86; All ST Orch, All County Orch, All County Concertmstr 84-86; Liberal Arts.

MITCHELL, CURTIS M; Gaithersburg HS; Gaithersburg, MD; (Y); 80/620; Church Yth Grp; Trs Soph Cls; Stu Cncl; Mgr(s); Var L Socr; Jr NHS; NHS; Ski Clb; Trk; Hon Roll; Emory U Smmr Schlr Pgm 85; Olympcs Mind 7th Pl Wrld Chmpnshps 86; VA Polytech Inst; Elec Engrng.

MITCHELL, KARLA; Western HS; Baltimore, MD; (Y); Art Clb; German Clb; Mgr(s); Score Keeper; Stat Sftbl; Pre-Med.

MITCHELL, MICHELLE K; Kenwood SR HS; Baltimore, MD; (Y); VP Computer Clb; Drama Clb; Office Aide; Varsity Clb; Chorus; Mgr Concert Band; School Musical; School Play; Variety Show; Tennis; Essex CC; Music.

MITCHELL, PATRICK J; Southern Garrett HS; Oakland, MD; (S); Ski Clb; Teachers Aide; Band; Concert Band; Jazz Band; Mrchg Band; Pep Band; School Play; Stage Crew; Yrbk Stf; Drm Capt 84-86; Towson ST; Comm.

MITCHELL, SALLY; Gaithersburg HS; Gaithersburg, MD; (Y); Ski Clb; SADD; Pres Soph Cls; Rep Jr Cls; VP Stu Cncl; Pom Pon; French Hon Soc; Hon Roll; Jr NHS; NHS; PA ST U; Intr Bus.

MITCHINER, ANGELA; Western SR HS; Baltimore, MD; (Y); 7/412; Church Yth Grp; Civic Clb; Cmnty Wkr; Dance Clb; German Clb; Math Clb; Church Choir; Rep Stu Cncl; Var Coach Actv; High Hon Roll; Dance Awd 85; Typng Awd 86; Stnly H Kpln Schlrshp 86; Bus Admin.

MITTAN, CHERYL; Thomas Stone HS; Waldorf, MD; (S); Church Yth Grp; Office Aide; Band; Nwsp Rptr; Nwsp Stf; Hon Roll; Bennington Coll VT; Tchng.

MITTAN, CLARK; Thomas Stone HS; Waldorf, MD; (Y); USAF; Security Police.

MOESLEIN, TIMOTHY; Cardinal Gibbons HS; Baltimore, MD; (Y); Cmnty Wkr; Drama Clb; Hosp Aide; PAVAS; Chorus; School Musical; School Play; Stage Crew; Lit Mag; Rep Frsh Cls; Awd Excllnc Engl; Shenandoah Coll/Cnsrvtry; Nrsng.

MOFFETT, CINDY; Kent County HS; Chestertown, MD; (Y); Art Clb; Church Yth Grp; Cmnty Wkr; Pres 4-H; Hosp Aide; Trs VICA; Church Choir; 4-H Awd; Stanley B Sutton Awd 85; Bst 4-H Pres 85; Anne Arundle CC; Nrsg.

MOHAN, VIVEK; Thomas S Wootton HS; Gaithersburg, MD; (Y); Mgr Aud/Vis; Science Clb; Hon Roll; Dept Defns Sci Apprntcshp Pgm 86; Natl Bureau Standrds Resrch Intrnshp 86; Biomed.

MOIST, NATALIE; Frederick HS; Frederick, MD; (Y); Church Yth Grp; Cmnty Wkr; French Clb; Hosp Aide; Band; Church Choir; Concert Band; Mrchg Band; Hon Roll; Sci.

MOLER, JAMES E; Brunswick HS; Knoxville, MD; (Y); 1/138; Capt Scholastic Bowl; Band; High Hon Roll; JP Sousa Awd; NHS; SAR Awd; Val; Computer Clb; Math Tm; Spanish Clb; Band Dirctrs Awd 83-84; Gold B Awd 82-86; Frederick Cnty Phi Beta Kappa Awd 86; Duke U; Math.

MOLICKI, ERIC; Towson SR HS; Towson, MD; (Y); Church Yth Grp; Computer Clb; Math Tm; Teachers Aide; Varsity Clb; Band; Concert Band; Mrchg Band; Orch; Variety Show; Bucknell U; Bus Adm.

MOLLER, CAROLYN; North Hagerstown HS; Hagerstown, MD; (Y); 11/356; Church Yth Grp; Dance Clb; French Clb; Key Clb; Teachers Aide; Yrbk Stf; Dnfth Awd; French Hon Soc; Hon Roll; NHS; Frnch.

MOLTZ, DANIEL; Parkdale HS; College Park, MD; (S); Boys Clb Am; Capt Letterman Clb; Service Clb; Capt Varsity Clb; Rep Stu Cncl; Var Capt Bsbl; Var Ftbl; Var Socr; High Hon Roll; NHS; Bostic Esilen Awd 83; Mayor Davis Awd 84; Most Athltc 85-86; Bus Admin.

MONAHAN, DEANNA L; Mount Savage HS; Mt Savage, MD; (Y); FBLA; Pep Clb; Q&S; Teachers Aide; Chorus; Drm Mjr(t); Nwsp Ed-Chief; Sec Jr Cls; L Cheerleading; Sec NHS; Frostburg ST Clg.

MONAHAN, DEE DEE; Mount Savage HS; Mt Savage, MD; (Y); FBLA; Chorus; Nwsp Ed-Chief; Sec Jr Cls; Im Bsktbl; JV Var Cheerleading; Im Twrlr; Im Vllybl; NHS.

MONDELL, CAROLYN; Sherwood HS; Olney, MD; (Y); Office Aide; Teachers Aide; Nwsp Rptr; Nwsp Stf; Var Bsktbl; Var Sftbl; Var Tennis; Hon Roll; NHS; Nrsng.

MONIODIS, DEBRA M; Archbishop Keough HS; Catonsville, MD; (Y); Church Yth Grp; GAA; Hosp Aide; Office Aide; Political Wkr; Rep Soph Cls; Rep Jr Cls; Swmmng; Hon Roll; Candy Strpr Awd 85; Summr Camp Cnslr 85; Hosp Radlgy Clrk 85; Loyola College; Med.

MONIODIS, MICHAEL; Patterson HS; Baltimore, MD; (Y); Computer Clb; Drama Clb; PAVAS; Chorus; Concert Band; School Musical; School Play; Bsbl; Ftbl; High Hon Roll; Acting.

MONNINGER, DEBRA K; North Harford HS; Street, MD; (Y); 19/286; Pres Girl Scts; Varsity Clb; Rep Sr Cls; Var Capt Fld Hcky; JV Var Lcrss; Hon Roll; Prfct Atten Awd; Pres Schlr; Spanish Clb; SADD; Fuller-Baity Awd 86; Senatrl Schlrshp 86; U Of MD Coll Pk; Elem Ed.

MONROE, CAITLIN; Oakland Mills HS; Columbia, MD; (Y); 31/275; Latin Clb; Church Choir; Nwsp Rptr; Nwsp Stf; Var Capt Bsktbl; Var Fld Hcky; Var Capt Sftbl; Hon Roll; NHS; Western MD Coll.

MONTAGNA, LISA; North Harford HS; Forest Hill, MD; (Y); French Clb; Math Tm; Varsity Clb; Yrbk Stf; Sec Frsh Cls; Rep Stu Cncl; JV Capt Fld Hcky; Var L Swmmng; Hon Roll; Math Perf Awd 85.

MONTAGUE, KEVIN; Central HS; Capitol Hgts, MD; (Y); JA; Band; Rep Frsh Cls; Rep Soph Cls; Rep Jr Cls; Rep Sr Cls; Var Bsktbl; Var Tennis; Hon Roll; Jr NHS; Gen ST Schlrshp 86; Bwlng 85-86; Stage Crw 83; U MD College Park; Acctg.

MONTAGUE, TONYA; Friendly HS; Ft Washington, MD; (Y); Hon Roll; Prfct Atten Awd; P G CC; Acctng.

MONTECLARO, CONSTANCE; Eastern Vocational Tech HS; Baltimore, MD; (Y); FBLA; VP Jr Cls; Trs Stu Cncl; Var Bsktbl; Var Capt Socr; Var Capt Sftbl; Pres NHS; Rep Soph Cls; Stu Cncl Svc Awd 86; 1st All Cnty Dfns Sccr Team 85-86; 2nd Pl ST Comptn FBLA Bus Math I 84-85; DP.

MONTESANO, CHRIS; Thomas S Wootton HS; Rockville, MD; (Y); Boy Scts; Church Yth Grp; Acpl Chr; Chorus; Madrigals; School Musical; Variety Show; Rep Stu Cncl; Var L Ftbl; Southern Methodist U; Hist.

MONTGOMERY, DANELL; Fort Hill HS; Cumberland, MD; (Y); 57/251; Church Yth Grp; Computer Clb; Office Aide; Pep Clb; Flag Corp; Yrbk Stf; Volunteer Svc Awd 85; WVU; Bus.

MONTGOMERY, JULIA; La Plata HS; La Plata, MD; (Y); 1/450; Cmnty Wkr; Concert Band; Mrchg Band; Yrbk Stf; L High Hon Roll; NHS; Ntl Engl Merit Awd 85-86; Ntl Hstry Merit Awd 85-86; CA Schlstc Fedrtn 84-85; Elec Engr.

MOONEY, ALISSA; Archbishop Keough HS; Baltimore, MD; (Y); Am Leg Aux Girls St; Nwsp Ed-Chief; Yrbk Phtg; Var Socr; High Hon Roll.

MOORE, AMY; Academy Of The Holy Names; Silver Spring, MD; (Y); Pep Clb; Stage Crew; Yrbk Phtg; Rep Frsh Cls; U Of MD; Bus Admin.

MOORE, BRENDA; Bishop Walsh HS; Lavale, MD; (Y); 6/120; Cmnty Wkr; Drama Clb; Hosp Aide; Service Clb; Concert Band; Mrchg Band; Yrbk Stf; High Hon Roll; NHS; Delta Epsilon Phi Ger Hnr Soc 86; Notre Dame MD; Biochem.

MOORE, ERIC; Williamsport HS; St James, MD; (Y); 2/206; Trs Church Yth Grp; Orch; Tennis; NHS; Knowldg Mstr Open 85-86; Olympcs Of The Mnd 85-86; Engrng.

MOORE, FAE; Garrison Forest Schl; Minter City, MS; (Y); 4-H; French Clb; Model UN; 4-H Awd; Hon Roll.

MOORE, JOHN; Cambridge South Dorchester HS; Cambridge, MD; (Y); Church Yth Grp; Debate Tm; French Clb; Jr Cls; Hon Roll; NHS; U Of MD; Marine Engineering.

MOORE, KATHLEEN H; Arlington Baptist Schl; Baltimore, MD; (S); Church Yth Grp; Service Clb; Spanish Clb; Church Choir; Arlington Bapt Hnr Soc 84-85; Schlrshp Awd 84-85; Church Organist 84-86.

MOORE, LATRICIA; Potomac HS; Temple Hills, MD; (Y); Church Yth Grp; Variety Show; Lit Mag; VP Frsh Cls; VP Soph Cls; VP Jr Cls; VP Sr Cls; Powder Puff Ftbl; JV Capt Vllybl; Hon Roll; Yth Of Yr 85.

MOORE, MARLENA; Hammond HS; Columbia, MD; (Y); Spanish Clb; School Musical; Off Stu Cncl; JV Var Cheerleading; Gym; Hon Roll; NHS; Achvtmnt Span 84-85; Ed.

MOORE, MEGAN; Fallston HS; Joppa, MD; (Y); 6/250; Church Yth Grp; Cmnty Wkr; German Clb; Church Choir; Yrbk Ed-Chief; High Hon Roll; Hon Roll; NHS; Ntl Merit SF.

MOORE, MELANIE; Franklin SR HS; Reisterstown, MD; (Y); Teachers Aide; Band; Concert Band; Mrchg Band; Yrbk Stf; JV Bsktbl; Var Fld Hcky; Var Lcrss; Var Sftbl; Hon Roll; Towson ST U; Early Chldhd Educ.

MOORE, MICHAEL; Bladensburg HS; Landover, MD; (Y); Boys Clb Am; Boy Scts; Band; Off Sr Cls; Bsktbl; Ftbl; Data Prcssng Stu Yr 85; Mnrty Schlrs Compu Sci 85; Sci Fair 4th Pl 86; U Of MD; Compu Sci.

MOORE, PATRICIA; Western HS; Baltimore, MD; (Y); 199/412; Art Clb; Leo Clb; Office Aide; Radio Clb; Band; Jazz Band; Mrchg Band; Orch; Pep Band; U Of MD College Park; Comp Sci.

MOORE, RAQUEL; Oxon Hill HS; Fort Washington, MD; (Y); Red Cross Aide; ROTC; Church Choir; High Hon Roll; NHS; Pres Schlr; Spanish NHS; Pres Fit Awd 86; P G Cnty GPA Awd 84 & 85; MD U; Med.

MOORE, TANYA; Western HS; Baltimore, MD; (Y); Computer Clb; FBLA; JA; SADD; Rep Jr Cls; Rep Stu Cncl; Cheerleading; High Hon Roll; Hon Roll; Media Comm Awd Radio Brdcstng 85-86; Peer Cnslng Srvc Awd 85-86; US Army Rsrvs; Military Srvc.

MOORE, TERESA; Forest Park SR HS; Baltimore, MD; (Y); Drama Clb; Library Aide; Pres Math Clb; Science Clb; Chorus; School Musical; AFS; Nwsp Rptr; Yrbk Rptr; Sec NHS; Rebecca E Carol Dramatic Rdng Cntst 84; Crss Age Sci Tchng Proj 86; Elec Engr.

MOORE, THERESA; Friendly SR HS; Ft Washington, MD; (Y); Rep Frsh Cls; Rep Soph Cls; Rep Jr Cls; VP Stu Cncl; Howard U; Acctg.

MOORE, TONYA; Northern HS; Baltimore, MD; (S); Church Yth Grp; Cmnty Wkr; Computer Clb; FBLA; Math Clb; Teachers Aide; Church Choir; Var Bsktbl; Hon Roll; NHS; Mth Awds 80-84; Prfct Atten Sunday Schl Awd; Outstndg Stu Awd; CCB Coll; Bus.

MOORE, VALERIE; Elkton Christian Schls; Newark, DE; (Y); 4/15; Teachers Aide; School Play; High Hon Roll; Hon Roll; NHS; DE Tech CC; Bio Sci.

MOPSICK, MARC; Sherwood HS; Silver Spg, MD; (Y); Band; Var Crs Cntry; Var Trk; Hon Roll; Intern Montgomery Cntry Circuit Ct Judge L Lenard Ruben 86; Bus.

MORALES, JOHN M; Annapolis SR HS; Annapolis, MD; (Y); 1/520; German Clb; Latin Clb; Math Clb; Math Tm; Sec Frsh Cls; Rep Soph Cls; Rep Jr Cls; Sec Stu Cncl; Var Crs Cntry; JV Socr; Med.

MORAN, GLENN; Cardinal Gibbons HS; Baltimore, MD; (Y); 14/140; Q&S; Nwsp Stf; Yrbk Stf; Hon Roll; NHS; Pres Schlr; Ski Clb; Var Bsbl; Mt St Marys; Bus.

MORAN, MONICA; Elkton HS; Elkton, MD; (Y); 31/289; Church Yth Grp; Sec Civic Clb; Ski Clb; Teachers Aide; Varsity Clb; Rep Stu Cncl; JV Var Fld Hcky; Im Sftbl; Hon Roll; NHS; MD ST Schlrp 86; Salisbury ST Coll; Bus.

MOREKAS, STACIE; Dulaney SR HS; Cockeysville, MD; (Y); Speech Tm; Chorus; Pres Frsh Cls; Var JV Fld Hcky; Hon Roll; NHS; Edtr Yth Group Papr 85-87; Anncr Mrng Anncmnts 86-87; Tres Grk Orthdx Yth Of Am Leag 86-87; Engrg.

MORELAND, DANNYL M; Allegany HS; La Vale, MD; (Y); 40/220; Boy Scts; Church Yth Grp; Nwsp Stf; Yrbk Stf; Rep Stu Cncl; Bsktbl; Var JV Ftbl; Var Wt Lftg; Hon Roll; Most Imprvd Weight Lifter Awd 86; Church Usher 85-86; WV U; Forestry.

MORELL, LIANE; Gaithersburg HS; Gaithersburg, MD; (Y); 202/625; Pep Clb; Ski Clb; SADD; Teachers Aide; Band; Concert Band; Mrchg Band; Variety Show; Rep Soph Cls; Coach Actv; Outstndng Chld Dvlpmnt Stu Awd 83-85; Homecmng Prncss 85-86; Frostburg ST Coll; Chldhd Ed.

MORETTI, PAUL JOSEPH; Gaithersburg HS; Gaithersburg, MD; (Y); 116/568; Boy Scts; Church Yth Grp; Key Clb; Ski Clb; Teachers Aide; Trs Sr Cls; Vllybl; Hon Roll; Jr NHS; NHS; Miami U; Bus.

MOREY, SHELAGH; Centennial HS; Columbia, MD; (Y); French Clb; Pres Intnl Clb; Stage Crew; JV Bsktbl; Var Socr; Var JV Sftbl; Hon Roll; NHS; Pres Schlr; Most Outstndng Spansh Studnt 86; Russian Clb; Fairfield U; Spansh.

MORGAN, DANIEL S; Sherwood HS; Olney, MD; (Y); 25/317; Ski Clb; Spanish Clb; Chorus; Nwsp Sprt Ed; Mgr(s); Hon Roll; NHS; Pres Schlr; Spanish NHS; JV Ftbl; PTSA, Vanderbilt Schlrshps, UMBC Chncllrs Awd 86; U MD; Jrnlsm.

MORGAN, JODI; Martin Spalding HS; Glen Burnie, MD; (Y); AFS; Church Yth Grp; Drama Clb; Lit Mag; Hon Roll; Ntl Merit Ltr; Radford U; Spch Pthlgy.

MORGAN, KARA; Charles W Woodward HS; Rockville, MD; (Y); SADD; Teachers Aide; Orch; Mgr L Diving; L Fld Hcky; L Mgr(s); Mgr L Socr; Mgr L Swmmng.

MORGAN, LINDA M; Springbrook HS; Silver Spring, MD; (Y); 196/498; Cmnty Wkr; Office Aide; Teachers Aide; Chorus; Yrbk Stf; Off Stu Cncl; Sec L Pom Pon; High Hon Roll; Honors Spanish 83-86; Econ.

MORGAN, MARTHA E; Baltimore Polytechnic Inst; Baltimore, MD; (Y); 13/515; Math Clb; Science Clb; Thesps; Orch; Yrbk Stf; Var JV Badmtn; High Hon Roll; NHS; Drama Clb; JA; Pres Tutorng Clb 84-86; Harvard; Chem Engrng.

MORIATIS, JENNIFER; Archbishop Keough HS; Balt, MD; (Y); Church Yth Grp; Hosp Aide; Yrbk Stf; Lit Mag; Stu Cncl; High Hon Roll; NHS; Ntl Merit Ltr; Prfct Atten Awd; Bst Grmn Stu; Exclnc Precalc; M Capt Its Acdmc Qz Shw; Englsh.

MORRIS, BETH; Calvert HS; Huntingtown, MD; (Y); Q&S; Nwsp Ed-Chief; Var Fld Hcky; JV Tennis; High Hon Roll; NHS; Outstndg Achvt Soc Stds & Engl 86; Exemplry Attndnc 86; Cmmnctns.

MORRIS III, CHARLES E; Loyola HS; Baltimore, MD; (S); Cmnty Wkr; NFL; Speech Tm; Yrbk Stf; Hon Roll; NHS; Opt Clb Awd; Loyola Hdmstr Schlrshp; Var Spch Awds 85; Grtc Psych.

MORRIS, DIANNA; Crossland HS; Temple Hills, MD; (Y); Church Yth Grp; VP Thesps; School Musical; School Play; Nwsp Ed-Chief; Yrbk Ed-Chief; Var Capt Sftbl; Var Capt Swmmng; Var Capt Vllybl; NHS; Towson ST; Cmmnctns.

MORRIS JR, JAMES G; Parkside HS; Parsonsburg, MD; (Y); 20/250; Boy Scts; Church Yth Grp; Ski Clb; Band; Concert Band; Mrchg Band; Var Ftbl; Eagle Scout 84; Clarkson U; Elec Engr.

MORRIS, JOHN; Thomas S Wootton HS; Potomac, MD; (Y); 190/420; FCA; FBLA; Letterman Clb; Science Clb; Varsity Clb; Trs Frsh Cls; Trs Soph Cls; Trs Jr Cls; Trs Sr Cls; JV Var Bsbl; Loyola Coll; Finance.

MORRIS, RICHARD; Thomas S Wooton HS; Potomac, MD; (Y); Chess Clb; Teachers Aide; Temple Yth Grp; Varsity Clb; Nwsp Bus Mgr; JV Var Socr; Im Wt Lftg; Hon Roll; NHS; Rotary Awd.

MORRIS, RON; Parkside HS; Pittsville, MD; (Y); Var JV Ftbl; Var L Wrstlng; Hon Roll.

MORRIS, SUZI; Frederick HS; Frederick, MD; (Y); 11/358; Pres German Clb; Pres Girl Scts; Trs Science Clb; Concert Band; Mrchg Band; Off Jr Cls; Off Sr Cls; Var Sftbl; Hon Roll; NHS; Bst Mrchr Band 86; Its Acdmc Tm Cnty Champs 86; Engrng.

MORRIS, TREVOR; St James Schl; Shepherdstown, WV; (Y); 1/38; Drama Clb; Chorus; Crs Cntry; Socr; Tennis; Ntl Merit Ltr; Val; Wt Lftg; Excllnc Frnch, Chem 84-86; Cum Laude Soc 86; Math.

MORRISON, ANN; Fort Hill HS; Cumberland, MD; (Y); GAA; Service Clb; Spanish Clb; Yrbk Bus Mgr; Bsktbl; Tennis; Vllybl.

MORRISON, DELLA; Liberty HS; Sykesville, MD; (S); Church Yth Grp; Varsity Clb; Chorus; Church Choir; Var Bsktbl; Var L Vllybl; High Hon Roll; Arch.

MORRISON, FABIAN; Northwestern HS; Baltimore, MD; (Y); ROTC; Church Choir; Var Trk; High Hon Roll; Schoolwde Blck Hstry Cntst 1st Pl 86; Chemstry I Schlrshp Awd 86; Algebra 2 Schlrshp Awd 86; Elec Engrng.

MORSETTE, BONNIE; Highland View Acad HS; Smithsburg, MD; (Y); Church Yth Grp; Office Aide; Teachers Aide; Yrbk Stf; Fld Hcky; High Hon Roll; Hon Roll; Prfct Atten Awd; 2nd Prz Mem Cntst Poetry 85-86; 1st Pl Art Awd 83; Mt Ellis Acad; Neuro Physcl Reh.

MORTIMER, ED; Wilde Lake HS; Columbia, MD; (Y); Church Yth Grp; Cmnty Wkr; Var Socr; Var Capt Swmmng; Y-Teens; USAF Acad 86; Appt USMAPS 86; K Of C Leut Awd 86; West Point; Army Ofcr.

MOSBY, CHANEL; Baltimore City Coll; Baltimore, MD; (S); High Hon Roll; NHS.

MOSCHONAS, KATHERINE; Middletown HS; Middletown, MD; (Y); Art Clb; Drama Clb; Chorus; Color Guard; Stage Crew; Lit Mag; Hon Roll; 2nd Pl Regional Womens Ctr Cncl Art Cntst 86; 2nd Pl SR Cmpttn Frederick Sci Fair 86; Montgomry Coll; Art Thrpy.

MOSSER, RANDALL K; Allegany HS; Cumberland, MD; (Y); 25/200; Drama Clb; JV Bsktbl; Ftbl; Trk; Wt Lftg; High Hon Roll; Hon Roll; Schl Spllng Bee 2nd Plc 83; Salisbury St; Radio & TV Brdcs.

MOULTON, VERNELL; Paul Laurence Dunbar HS; Baltimore, MD; (Y); 4/219; Church Yth Grp; Debate Tm; Hosp Aide; Pep Clb; Spanish Clb; Drill Tm; Mrchg Band; Rep Frsh Cls; Rep Soph Cls; Rep Jr Cls; Delta Sigma Theta H S Hnrs Chptr 84-86; Hlth Sci Acadmc Excllnc 86; U MD Schlrshp Outstndng Jrs 86; MA Coll Phrmcy; Phrmcst.

MOULTRIE, CHELSEA; Crossland HS; Ft Washington, MD; (Y); Art Clb; Drama Clb; Girl Scts; Pep Clb; Band; Hon Roll; U Of Dstrct Clmb; Scl Wrk.

MOWEN, REBECCA; Allegany HS; Cumberland, MD; (Y); Church Yth Grp; Sec Pres FBLA; Office Aide; Chorus; Hon Roll; NHS; Frostburg ST Coll; Bus Educ.

MOWERY, SHAWN; Allegany HS; Cumberland, MD; (Y); 38/200; Church Yth Grp; Pep Clb; Ski Clb; Nwsp Stf; Sec Soph Cls; VP Jr Cls; Hon Roll; NHS; Bus.

MOXLEY, STEPHANIE A; Damascus HS; Damascus, MD; (Y); 45/245; Church Yth Grp; Letterman Clb; Ski Clb; Spanish Clb; Varsity Clb; Off Frsh Cls; Im Badmtn; Im Bsbl; Im Sftbl; Var Capt Vllybl; Vllybl MVP 83-86; U MD; Comp.

MOY, GARY; Crossland HS; Camp Springs, MD; (Y); 3/388; Math Tm; Teachers Aide; Var Capt Golf; Var Socr; Cit Awd; High Hon Roll; Hon Roll; Kiwanis Awd; Pres NHS; Prfct Atten Awd; MD Merit Schlr Awd 86; U Of MD; Bus.

MOYER, BRIAN; Surrottsville HS; Clinton, MD; (Y); 1/297; Am Leg Boys St; Office Aide; Church Choir; Bausch & Lomb Sci Awd; High Hon Roll; Jr NHS; NHS; Val; Cnty Sci Fair 86; MD Distingshd Schlr 86; U MD; Physcs.

MOYLAN III, CHARLES E; Friends Schl; Baltimore, MD; (Y); Camera Clb; Debate Tm; Yrbk Ed-Chief; Var Ftbl; JV Lcrss; Wt Lftg; Hon Roll; Ntl Merit SF; Eugene H Denk Awd Math 84; Astrophys.

MOYLAN, SANDY; Archbishop Keough HS; Balto, MD; (Y); Art Clb; Yrbk Stf.

MUHLHAUSEN, ROSE; Centennial HS; Ellicott City, MD; (Y); 28/268; Sec Trs Church Yth Grp; Hosp Aide; Ski Clb; Drill Tm; Trs Soph Cls; Pres Jr Cls; JV Var Fld Hcky; Var Trk; Hon Roll; NHS; Sec Correspndce Howard Cnty Assn Stu Cncls 86-87; Homecmng Princess 85; SGA Rep Howard Cnty Stu Cncls; Bus.

MUHLY, THERESA; Gaithersburg HS; Gaithersburg, MD; (Y); 14/600; AFS; Dance Clb; Ski Clb; SADD; Lit Mag; Trk; French Hon Soc; NHS; Pres Schlr; Spanish NHS; MD U; Bus Adm.

MUHONEN, JENNIFER; Northern HS; Owings, MD; (Y); 1/325; Chorus; Jazz Band; School Musical; Sec Soph Cls; Pres Sec Stu Cncl; Pom Pon; NHS; Debate Tm; High Hon Roll; Ntl Merit Ltr; Geo Wshngtn U Outstndng Schlr In Math & Sci 86; Boolian Math Aws 85; Pythgrs Math Awd 86; Bus.

MULDROW, NACHELE TOVA; Regina HS; Washington, DC; (Y); Computer Clb; Intnl Clb; Cheerleading; Bus.

MULLENIX, CURTIS; Williamsport HS; Williamsport, MD; (Y); 7/229; Pres Church Yth Grp; Drama Clb; Latin Clb; SADD; Teachers Aide; School Musical; School Play; Rep Frsh Cls; Rep Soph Cls; Trk; Military.

MULLENS, LAURI; Heritage Acad; Hagerstown, MD; (S); 1/31; Chorus; School Play; Yrbk Stf; Stat Bsktbl; High Hon Roll; 2nd Pl Sci & 3rd Pl Engl All ST Chrstn Schl Awds 84; 2nd Pl All ST Chrstn Schl Hstry/ Geogrphy Awd.

MULLICAN, LYNN M; Fairmont Heights HS; New Carrollton, MD; (Y); Intnl Clb; Yrbk Phtg; Yrbk Stf; Hon Roll; Jr NHS; NHS; Pres Academic Fitness Awd 86; Maryland Gen ST Schlrshp 86; 3rd Pl Schl Sci Fair 86; Advertising.

MULVIHILL, GRACE; The Bullis Schl; Bethesda, MD; (S); Church Yth Grp; Nwsp Ed-Chief; Var Swmmng; JV Capt Tennis; High Hon Roll; Mst Vlbl Swmr Awd 84-85; Law.

MUNDEY, ALISA; Clear Spring HS; Clear Spring, MD; (Y); 3/111; 4-H; FFA; Office Aide; Flag Corp; Nwsp Rptr; Nwsp Stf; Stu Cncl; Stat Socr; Stat Sftbl; High Hon Roll; Pres Acad Ftns Awd 86; Merit Schlstc Awd 86; Hagerstown JC; Photo.

MUNDY, VICTORIA; Howard HS; Columbia, MD; (Y); Church Yth Grp; Drama Clb; Hosp Aide; Thesps; Chorus; Church Choir; Madrigals; School Musical; Hon Roll; NHS; Schls Dlgt MD Acad Of Sci Hmnts Sympsm 86; VA Polytech Inst; Vet Med.

MURDOCK, JONAH; Charles E Smith Jewish Day HS; Silver Spring, MD; (Y); Yrbk Stf; JV Var Bsktbl; Coach Actv; Socr; Var Tennis; NHS; Spanish NHS; Mbr Ntnl Yng Ldrs Cnfrnc WA 85; Fndng Mbr VP Schl Athltc Bstr Clb 84-87.

MURNANE, MATT; Parkville HS; Baltimore, MD; (Y); Var JV Socr; Hon Roll; Prfct Atten Awd; Accntng.

MURPHY, CRAWFORD; Saints Peter & Paul HS; Cambridge, MD; (Y); Am Leg Boys St; Chess Clb; Computer Clb; Band; Concert Band; Variety Show; Lit Mag; Bowling; NEDT High Scores 83-85; Comp Sci 4.00 Avg 85-86; GA Inst Tech; Elec Engr.

MURPHY, DAMIANA K; Stone Ridge Country Day Schl; Cheltenham, MD; (Y); Church Yth Grp; Political Wkr; Spanish Clb; Teachers Aide; Natl Achvt Schlrshp Pgm-Negro Stu Commended Stu 85; Stu Ldr Soc Actn Pgm 85-86; St Marys Jr Aux 82-85; Law.

MURPHY, JEFFREY SCOTT; Cambridge South Dorchester HS; Cambridge, MD; (Y); 6/228; VP Frsh Cls; Rep Soph Cls; Var L Bsbl; Var Capt Ftbl; VP NHS; Prfct Atten Awd; Pres Schlr; Monmouth Coll Trustees Scholar 86; Cynthia L Calabro Scholar 86; Top Scr Amer Mth Exam 86; Monmouth Coll; Elec Engrng.

MURPHY, JULIE; Gaithersburg HS; Gaithersburg, MD; (Y); Church Yth Grp; SADD; Hon Roll; Var L Swmmng; Acctng.

MURPHY, KIMBERLY; St Pauls Schl For Girls; Towson, MD; (Y); 3/40; Church Yth Grp; Cmnty Wkr; Key Clb; Lit Mag; Mgr(s); Score Keeper; Timer; High Hon Roll; Hon Roll; NHS; Trustee Awd 86.

MURPHY, PATRICIA; Oakland Mills HS; Columbia, MD; (Y); Math Tm; Political Wkr; Var Capt Bsktbl; Var Capt Fld Hcky; Hon Roll; Ntl Merit SF; Pres Schlr; St Schlr; Pres Schlrshp 86; JHU APL Comptv Schlrshp 86; Sharp Schlrshp 86; Loyola College; Mth Tchr.

MURPHY, YO LANDA L; Governor Thomas Johnson HS; Frederick, MD; (Y); Computer Clb; FBLA; Spanish Clb; Teachers Aide; Var L Bsktbl; Sftbl; Hon Roll; Bowie Alumni Awd 86; Sen Schlrshp 86; Loats Fndtn Inc 86; Bowie ST Clg; Elem Ed.

MURRAY, BRIDGET; Archbishop Keough HS; Severn, MD; (Y); Cmnty Wkr; Pres NFL; Red Cross Aide; Speech Tm; Ed Yrbk Stf; Pres Frsh Cls; Pres Soph Cls; Pres Jr Cls; Hon Roll; VP Church Yth Grp; Schl Spirit Awd 84; Frnsc Lge St Fnlst & Ntl Qlfr 86; Outstndng Svc Awd 5 Yrs Of Ctchtcl Tchng 85; Liberal Arts Coll; Pub Rltns.

MURRAY, CAROL; Queen Annes County HS; Wye Mills, MD; (Y); Sec Am Leg Aux Girls St; Chorus; Church Choir; Color Guard; Drm Mjr(t); Madrigals; Mrchg Band; Rep Stu Cncl; Spanish Clb; School Musical; Am Leg Oratorical Cntst Wnnr 86; Stu Advsry Comm 84-85; Rep Eastern Shore Assoc Tu Cncl 85-86.

MURRAY, CATHY; Eastern Voc-Tech HS; Baltimore, MD; (Y); Church Yth Grp; Ed Lit Mag; Sec Frsh Cls; Sec Soph Cls; Sec Jr Cls; Pres Sr Cls; Rep Stu Cncl; Var Capt Cheerleading; Hon Roll; Prfct Atten Awd; JR Litho Clb 85; Psych.

MURRAY, KELLY; Fallston HS; Baldwin, MD; (Y); Teachers Aide; Var Capt Swmmng; Hon Roll; Bus.

MURTAUGH, DAWN; Northwestern HS; Riverdale, MD; (S); Church Yth Grp; OEA; Teachers Aide; Rep Stu Cncl; Hon Roll; NHS; Outstndng COE Stu 86; Montgomery CC; Psych.

MUSCARA, MARIA; Gaithersburg HS; Gaithersburg, MD; (Y); 51/560; Ski Clb; Nwsp Stf; Stu Cncl; Cheerleading; Powder Puff Ftbl; Socr; Swmmng; Hon Roll; Jr NHS; NHS; Law Tm 85-86; Pres Acad Fit Awd 85-86; Supts Wrtng Awd 82-83; Colgate U.

MUSCELLA, DOMINIC; Joppatowne HS; Joppa, MD; (Y); 20/215; Concert Band; Jazz Band; Madrigals; School Musical; Sec Sr Cls; Diving; Lcrss; NHS; All Cnty LA Crss 86; MVP-LA Crss 86; Chmcl Engrng.

MUSE, PAMELA; La Reine HS; Clinton, MD; (Y); Computer Clb; Chorus; Trk; Hon Roll.

MUSOTTO, ANTHONY J; Loyola HS; Lutherville, MD; (Y); Spanish Clb; Comp.

MUSTERIC, SUSAN; Bishop Walsh HS; Cumberland, MD; (Y); Church Yth Grp; Drama Clb; Hosp Aide; Library Aide; Pep Clb; Ski Clb; SADD; School Musical; Rep Jr Cls; Sec Trs Sr Cls; Cert Hon MD ST Bar Assn 86; Awd Prtcptn Cmmnty Invlvmnt Cncl 83-84; Cert Trng MADART Shp Trng Pgm.

MUSTERMAN, LAURA; Bowie HS; Bowie, MD; (Y); Letterman Clb; Office Aide; Ski Clb; Band; Cheerleading; Mgr(s); Powder Puff Ftbl; Hon Roll; Salisbury ST.

MUTH, CHARLES; Archbischop Curley HS; Baltimore, MD; (S); 18/143; Yrbk Ed-Chief; Crs Cntry; Socr; Trk; Hon Roll; NHS; Spanish NHS; U Of MD Coll Park HS Ldrshp Confrnce 86; US Natl Jrnlsm Awds 86; Let Of Merit 85-86; Elec Engr.

MYERS, AMANDA; Walter Johnson HS; Bethesda, MD; (Y); JA; Key Clb; SADD; Yrbk Bus Mgr; Yrbk Phtg; Yrbk Rptr; Yrbk Stf; Sec Stu Cncl; Stat Mgr(s); Im Sftbl; Outstndng Schl Svc Stu Govt 85-86; Schlrshp MD Stu Ledrshp Wrkshp 86; Liberal Arts.

MYERS, ANGELA; Hancock Md SR HS; Hancock, MD; (Y); SADD; Nwsp Stf; Yrbk Bus Mgr; Rep Stu Cncl; JV Capt Cheerleading; Timer; Capt Trk; High Hon Roll; Hon Roll; Comp Sci.

MYERS, MATT; Centennial HS; Ellicott City, MD; (Y); JA; Ski Clb; Spanish Clb; Varsity Clb; Stage Crew; Rep Frsh Cls; Rep Sr Cls; Var Capt Bsbl; Var Capt Bsktbl; Hon Roll; All-Cnty Bsbl Tm 86; Amer Lgn All-Star Bsbl Tm 86.

MYERS, MICHELE; Notre Dame Prep Schl; Towson, MD; (Y); Service Clb; Im Bsktbl; Im Fld Hcky; Im Socr; Var Swmmng; Im Vllybl; Hon Roll; NHS; NEDT Cert 84; Chem.

MYERS, WAYNE; Catoctin HS; Thurmont, MD; (Y); Hon Roll; Computers.

NAGY, KATRINA; Thomas Stone HS; Waldorf, MD; (S); Cmnty Wkr; Math Clb; SADD; Teachers Aide; Stat Bsktbl; Score Keeper; Tennis; Vllybl; High Hon Roll; MVP Vrsty Ten 83-84.

NAGY, SANDRA LEE; Oxon Hill Science & Tech Ctr Ohhs; Fort Washington, MD; (Y); 28/560; ROTC; Pres Frsh Cls; Pres Jr Cls; Pres Sr Cls; Var L Cheerleading; Stat Socr; NHS; Rotary Awd; Am Leg Aux Girls St; Trs VP Church Yth Grp; Senate Page 85; AFROTC 4 Yr Schlrshp 86; US Naval Acad Appntmnt 86; US Naval Acad; Pol Sci.

NANZETTA, KATHY M; Col Zadok Magruder HS; Rockville, MD; (Y); Crs Cntry; Hon Roll; United Daughters Confed Scholar 86; Top 10 Prcnt Cls 85-86; U MD Baltimore; Elec Engrng.

NARULA, JASMINE; Thomas S Wootton HS; Gaithersburg, MD; (Y); 18/401; Church Yth Grp; SADD; Rep Frsh Cls; Var Fld Hcky; Hon Roll; NHS; NEDT Awd; Prsdntl Acdmc Ftns Awd 86; ST MD Schlstc Mrt Awd 86; Montgomery Area Sci Fr Cert Awd 84; U Of MD.

NARVA, SANDRA; Thomas S Wootton HS; Rockville, MD; (Y); AFS; Computer Clb; Drama Clb; Service Clb; SADD; Sec Temple Yth Grp; Hon Roll; NHS; Pltcl Sci.

NASON, TERESA C; Liberty HS; Sykesville, MD; (Y); 8/300; Trs Church Yth Grp; Thesps; Chorus; Church Choir; Color Guard; School Musical; JC Awd; NHS; Ntl Merit Schol; Knights Of Columbus No 7612 Robert H Clark Mem Schlrshp; Presdntl Acadmc Fitness Awd; Gettysburg Coll; Biological Sci.

NASRALLAH, LAURA; St Pauls School For Girls; Baltimore, MD; (S); 1/40; French Clb; Model UN; Acpl Chr; VP Sec Soph Cls; VP Sec Jr Cls; High Hon Roll; NHS; Ldrshp Awd; Pres Clsrm Young Am; SF Sen Schlrshp-Japan; Frnch Comp 3rd-7th MD; Solo Hnbl Mntn Piano; Govt.

NATALE, ANGELA; Regina HS; University Pk, MD; (Y); Cmnty Wkr; Hosp Aide; Model UN; Rep Frsh Cls; Rep Soph Cls; Sec Stu Cncl; Var Socr; Hon Roll; NHS; Ambssdr MD Hugh O Brian Yth Ldrshp 86; Eng.

NATHANSON, JESSICA; Eastern Vocational Technical HS; Baltimore, MD; (Y); Church Yth Grp; FNA; Hosp Aide; Socr; VFW Awd; Essex CC; Prctcl Nrsng.

NAUMAN, KAREN; Centennial HS; Ellicott City, MD; (Y); 16/278; Art Clb; Sec Church Yth Grp; Sec German Clb; Chorus; Church Choir; Drill Tm; School Musical; Stat Trk; Hon Roll; NHS; Math.

NAUS, EDWARD; Joppatowne HS; Joppa, MD; (Y); Church Yth Grp; French Clb; Church Choir; NHS; Engrng.

NAVE, LORI; Fort Hill HS; Cumberland, MD; (Y); Pres Sec Pep Clb; Off Frsh Cls; Off Soph Cls; Off Jr Cls; Off Sr Cls; Rep Stu Cncl; Stu Recgntn Awd 86; Salisbury ST Coll; Med Tech.

NEAL, CURTIS G; High Point HS; Beltsville, MD; (Y); French Clb; Var Trk; Var Wrstlng; Hon Roll; Natl Achvt Scholar Pgm Outstndng Negro Stu 86; Bus Adm.

NEAL, SABRINA; Mardela HS; Salisbury, MD; (Y); Aud/Vis; Spanish Clb; Chorus; Church Choir; School Musical; School Play; Stage Crew; Pres Frsh Cls; VP Jr Cls; Var Bsktbl; Chldrns Ped.

NEALE, SADARA; Maurice James Mcdonough HS; Pomfret, MD; (Y); Church Yth Grp; Cmnty Wkr; Girl Scts; Intnl Clb; Library Aide; Office Aide; Teachers Aide; Mgr Varsity Clb; Chorus; Swing Chorus; All-Cnty HS Hnrs Awd 84-86; Choral Adjdctn Prns 84-86; U Of Mrylnd Coll Prk; Nrsng Bus.

NEAVE, TRACY; Thomas Stone HS; Waldorf, MD; (S); Church Yth Grp; Trs Latin Clb; Var Crs Cntry; Co-Capt Mgr(s); Co-Capt Timer; Trk; High Hon Roll; NHS; Gftd & Tlntd Smmr Pgm 83-84; MD Ldrshp Pgm 85; Bus Admin.

NEEDLEMAN, ALYSSA; Parkside HS; Salisbury, MD; (Y); 4/275; Latin Clb; Pres Temple Yth Grp; Mrchg Band; Symp Band; Hon Roll; NCTE Awd; NHS; Cum Laude Ntl Latin Exam 84; 1st Pl Latin Day Comptn 85; 2nd Pl Sci Fair 85; Med.

NEELY, KELVIN; Queen Anne HS; Fort Washington, MD; (Y); Boy Scts; Teachers Aide; Nwsp Stf; Yrbk Stf; Lit Mag; Bsbl; Hon Roll; Wnnr Queen Anne Schl Sci Fair 85; Comm.

NEIRA, MARTHA; High Point SR HS; Hyattsville, MD; (Y); Dance Clb; Variety Show; Hon Roll; Prfct Atten Awd; Montgomery Coll; Mcrblgy.

NEJFELT, ABIGAIL; Mount De Sales Acad; Catonsville, MD; (Y); 4/50; Church Yth Grp; Cmnty Wkr; Var Cheerleading; Var Vllybl; High Hon Roll; NHS; Bio.

NELSON, BETH; Beall HS; Frostburg, MD; (Y); Hosp Aide; Band; Concert Band; Drm Mjr(t); Jazz Band; Mrchg Band; Pep Band; Nwsp Stf; Score Keeper; Hon Roll; Hnr Band 84-86; Typing I Wnnr 1st 85; Ldrshp Conf 86; Frostburg ST Coll.

NELSON, CLARA A; Oxon Hill HS; Accokeek, MD; (Y); Church Yth Grp; Computer Clb; Church Choir; Hon Roll; Ntl Merit Ltr; 2d Pl Sci Fair Chem 86; Prince Georges Cnty Sci-Technlgy 83-87; J Hopkins Yth Tlnt Srch Wnr 81; Elec Engr.

NELSON, DERRICK; Patterson HS; Baltimore, MD; (Y); Cmnty Wkr; Drama Clb; SADD; Thesps; School Play; Var Crs Cntry; JV Var Ftbl; Var Trk; Drexel U; Arch Engrng.

NELSON, JENNIFER; Wheaton HS; Silver Spring, MD; (Y); 38/386; Sec Trs Aud/Vis; Drama Clb; French Clb; Thesps; School Musical; School Play; Stage Crew; Hon Roll; Jr NHS; NHS; Pres Acdmc Ftns Awd 86; Asthtc Knght Mo 86; ROSE Awd 85; Goucher Coll; Cmnctns.

NELSON, JILL; Beall HS; Frostburg, MD; (Y); 1/151; Hosp Aide; Band; Concert Band; Mrchg Band; Nwsp Ed-Chief; Score Keeper; Bausch & Lomb Sci Awd; Pres NHS; Val; MD Dstngshd Schlr Semifnlst 86; MD Jr Sci & Hmnts Sympsm 85; Hugh O Brian Yth Ldrshp Smnr 84; Frostburg ST Coll; Bio.

NELSON, JULIA L; Wicomico SR HS; Salisbury, MD; (Y); 14/245; Soroptimist; Pres Spanish Clb; VP SADD; Varsity Clb; Drm Mjr(t); Mrchg Band; Trs Frsh Cls; Trs Soph Cls; Sec Sr Cls; Rep Stu Cncl; Hmcmng Queen 86; Miss 1986; Miss Wi Hi & Miss Congnlty 86; Salisbury ST Coll; Englsh Educ.

NELSON, JULIE; Bohemia Manor HS; Chesapeake City, MD; (Y); 2/100; Art Clb; Church Yth Grp; French Clb; Yrbk Ed-Chief; Frsh Cls; Fld Hcky; Tennis; NHS; Pres Schlr; Sal; M D Distinguished Schlr Finalist 85; Sr Schlr Athlete 86; Franklin & Marshall Coll.

NELSON, KELLY; Eastern Vocational Tech HS; Baltimore, MD; (Y); Church Yth Grp; Cmnty Wkr; Computer Clb; FBLA; Varsity Clb; Var Cheerleading; Var Socr; JV Sftbl; Hon Roll; NHS; Supt Yth Govt Day 85-86; Lwyr.

NELSON, LAURA; Bethesda Chevy Chase HS; Silver Spring, MD; (Y); 21/449; AFS; Hosp Aide; Mrchg Band; Symp Band; Stu Cncl; Var Swmmng; Var Vllybl; High Hon Roll; Church Yth Grp; Concert Band; Cnty Spntndnt Awd Otstndngn Wrtng 82; Harvard U; Bio.

NELSON, LAURA; Franklin SR HS; Upperco, MD; (Y); Am Leg Aux Girls St; Trs VP Drama Clb; VP Thesps; School Play; Stage Crew; Variety Show; Mount St Marys Coll; Bio.

NELSON, MARK; Brunswick HS; Brunswick, MD; (Y); High Hon Roll; Hon Roll; Vo-Tech Cost & Elec Booth 1st Pl For Bst Trade & Indstry Awd 86; Elec.

NELSON, SHERI; Cambridge-South Dorchester HS; Cambridge, MD; (Y); AFS; 4-H; Rep Stu Cncl; Var Fld Hcky; 4-H Awd; Bus.

NELSON, SUSAN; Great Mills HS; California, MD; (Y); French Clb; Yrbk Stf; Swmmng; Vllybl; High Hon Roll; Sec NHS.

NELSON, TINA M; Milford Mill HS; Randallstown, MD; (Y); 3/200; Church Yth Grp; Girl Scts; JCL; Math Clb; Office Aide; Teachers Aide; Nwsp Stf; Lit Mag; Pres Frsh Cls; Var JV Cheerleading; Engrng.

NEMATOLLAHI, KHATEREH; Walter Johnsn HS; Rockville, MD; (Y); Intnl Clb; SADD; Teachers Aide; Gym; Hon Roll; Med.

NESLER, RICHARD LEE; Central HS; Forestville, MD; (Y); 1/200; Debate Tm; Drama Clb; Science Clb; Band; Tennis; VP NHS; Rotary Awd; St Schlr; Val; Morgan ST U Engrng Scholar 86; Geo WA U Schl Engrng Mdl 85; Prince Geo Cnty Acad Exctlnce Awd 85-86; Morgan ST U; Elec Engr.

NEUBERGER, MARK; Westminster HS; Finksburg, MD; (Y); Boy Scts; Math Tm; JV Bsbl; JV Bsktbl; High Hon Roll.

NEUGENT, LUCY; Great Mills HS; Lexington Park, MD; (Y); Spanish Clb; Varsity Clb; Mgr(s); Mat Maids; Socr; Hon Roll; Psych.

NEUMAN, DOUG; The Bullis Schl; Potomac, MD; (Y); Math Tm; Yrbk Stf; Bsktbl; Socr; Cit Awd; Frnch, Cmptr & Math Awd; Jrnslm.

NEWBEGIN, TERRI; Surrattsville HS; Clinton, MD; (Y); Teachers Aide; Band; Chorus; Nwsp Stf; Ed Lit Mag; Rep Frsh Cls; Hon Roll; Jr NHS; NHS; Acdmc Achvt Awd 84-85; Bus Adm.

NEWBY, JEFF; Walter Johnson HS; Bethesda, MD; (Y); Trs Frsh Cls; L Var Bsktbl; Spec Svc Cls 83-84.

NEWMAN, STEPHEN; St Andrews Episcopal Schl; Potomac, MD; (Y); Boy Scts; Pres Church Yth Grp; SADD; School Play; Symp Band; Nwsp Rptr; JV Capt Bsktbl; Swmmng; High Hon Roll; Hon Roll; Physics Div-Sci Wnr 84; Coachs Awd Ldrshp & Skl In Bsktbl 86; MD ST Swmng Finals 83-84.

NEWSOME, TINA L; Eleanor Roosevelt HS; Lanham, MD; (Y); Key Clb; Pep Clb; Teachers Aide; Chorus; Off Sr Cls; Rep Stu Cncl; Powder Puff Ftbl; Hon Roll; NHS; P G Cty Acad Achvt Awd 84; Silver Metal Ntl Latin Ex 85; Commended Stu Ntl Achvt Schlrshp Pgm 85; Comp Sci.

NGUYEN, ANH TUAN; Senior HS; Baltimore, MD; (Y); Math Tm; High Hon Roll; Prfct Atten Awd; Blue Rbbn In Sci Prjct 83-84; 2nd Prz Wnnr Of Schl Wide Mth Cntst 85-86; Polytchnc Inst; Archtct.

NGUYEN, APOLLO T; Springbrook HS; Silver Spring, MD; (Y); Math Clb; Nwsp Rptr; Var Trk; Hon Roll; Aerospc Engrng.

NGUYEN, BINH; Chopticon HS; Charlotte Hall, MD; (Y); Socl Stdy & Phy Fit 85-86; Readng 84-85.

NGUYEN, HUAN; Richard Montgomery HS; Carmichael, CA; (Y); Teachers Aide; Socr; High Hon Roll; Hon Roll; American River Coll; Elec Engr.

NGUYEN, HY; Oakland Mills HS; Columbia, MD; (Y); 11/240; Band; Concert Band; Jazz Band; Mrchg Band; Orch; Variety Show; NHS; U Of MD College Park; Engrng.

NGUYEN, LAN; Oakland Mills HS; Columbia, MD; (Y); AFS; Trs French Clb; Chorus; Madrigals; Nwsp Bus Mgr; Nwsp Ed-Chief; Trs Jr Cls; Trs Stu Cncl; Mgr Trk; Stat Vllybl; 13th ST Le Grand Concours Lvl #b 84; Enonmcs.

NGUYEN, LE; Friendly SR HS; Ft Washington, MD; (Y); Cmnty Wkr; Math Tm; Teachers Aide; Temple Yth Grp; Hon Roll; NHS; Pres Schlr; St Schlr; Excllnt Achvmnt Awds 85&86; ST Merit Schlstc Awd 86; U Of MD College Pk; Engnrng.

NGUYEN, LOAN; High Point HS; Beltsville, MD; (Y); High Hon Roll; Hon Roll; Prfct Atten Awd; U Of MD; Optcn.

NGUYEN, TERESA; Seneca Valley HS; Germantown, MD; (Y); Art Clb; Church Yth Grp; German Clb; Office Aide; Teachers Aide; Varsity Clb; Variety Show; Nwsp Rptr; Yrbk Stf; Rep Frsh Cls; Chestnuthill Coll; Dnstry.

NGUYEN, THAO; Northwestern HS; Hyattsville, MD; (Y); Church Yth Grp; Spanish Clb; Teachers Aide; Hon Roll; NHS; Acad Excel Awd 85; Ntl Piano Plyng Audtns 86; Cert Of Achvt Recgntn Prvt Piano Study 85; U Of MD; Psych.

NIBALI, JENNIFER; Glenelg HS; West Friendship, MD; (Y); AFS; Hosp Aide; Intnl Clb; Q&S; Ski Clb; Yrbk Stf; Var JV Socr; Hon Roll; NHS.

NICHOLS, MARK; Walter Johnson HS; Bethesda, MD; (Y); Boy Scts; Ski Clb; SADD; Teachers Aide; Yrbk Phtg; Yrbk Rptr; Yrbk Stf; Swmmng; Hon Roll; Arch.

NICHOLSON, CATHY; Mercy HS; Baltimore, MD; (Y); Church Yth Grp; Library Aide; Teachers Aide; Church Choir; Hon Roll; Bus Awd For Excllnc 86; Towson ST; Bus.

NICHOLSON, DONNA; Queen Anns County HS; Millington, MD; (Y); Church Yth Grp; Cmnty Wkr; FFA; Office Aide; SADD; Teachers Aide; Hon Roll; Am Legion Schrlshp 87; Mac Queen Gibbs; RN.

NICHOLSON, ISAAC; Snow Hill HS; Snow Hill, MD; (S); 13/110; Church Yth Grp; Cmnty Wkr; French Clb; Spanish Clb; Speech Tm; Band; Chorus; Church Choir; Jazz Band; School Musical; Hugh Obrian Ldrshp Pgm-Rnnr Up 84-85; Acadmc Excllnc Awd-Wrcstr Cnty 84-85; Poltcl Sci.

NICKLOW, ROBERT; Gaithersburg HS; Derwood, MD; (Y); 100/680; Pres Art Clb; Boy Scts; Letterman Clb; Ski Clb; Varsity Clb; Concert Band; Var L Trk; High Hon Roll; NHS; Pres Schlr; Ntl Art Hnr Scty 85-86; U MD; Bio-Med Engrng.

NICOLAIDIS, ANTHONY; Archbishop Curley HS; Baltimore, MD; (S); 4/143; Aud/Vis; Boy Scts; Church Yth Grp; School Play; Rep Soph Cls; Im Socr; High Hon Roll; Hon Roll; NHS; Spanish NHS; Meritorious Awd; Engrng.

NIEBERDING, KATHERINE; Northern HS; Baltimore, MD; (S); Math Tm; SADD; Teachers Aide; Nwsp Bus Mgr; Nwsp Rptr; VP Stu Cncl; Pom Pon; Hon Roll; NHS; Pres Schlr; Bltmre Ctywide Prtcptn & Invlvmnt Awd 85; 1st Pl Math Bltimre Acad Fair 85; Coppin ST Coll Schlrshp; Towson ST U; Accntng.

NILAND, ERIC M; Bruce HS; Piedmont, WV; (Y); Yrbk Rptr; Yrbk Stf; Var L Bsbl; Var L Ftbl; Var L Wt Lftg; Hon Roll; David Nuzum Schlrshp 86; High Battg Avrg Bsbl 86; Most Home Runs Bsbl 86; Potomac ST Clg; Bus.

NIST, AMY; Stone Rdg Cntry Day Schl Of Scrd Hrt; Silver Spring, MD; (Y); Model UN; Nwsp Stf; Ed Yrbk Stf; Rep Stu Cncl; Lcrss; Var Capt Socr; High Hon Roll; NHS; St Schlr; Sacred Heart Goal I Goal Ii Awd; UC Berkeley; Law.

NIXON, CHRISTINE; Thomas S Wootton HS; Gaithersburg, MD; (Y); JA; ROTC; Var Socr; Hon Roll; MIT; Engr.

NIXON, MELINDA; Oldtown Schl; Oldtown, MD; (S); Trs FBLA; Pres FHA; School Musical; Yrbk Ed-Chief; Trs Soph Cls; Trs Jr Cls; Trs Sr Cls; Hon Roll; VP NHS; Church Yth Grp; Actvty Awd 85; Outstndng FHA/HERO Awd 85; Schl Tchr.

NIXON, STACIE N; Baltimore Schl For The Arts; Baltimore, MD; (Y); Church Yth Grp; 4-H; Political Wkr; School Play; Stage Crew; Variety Show; 4-H Awd; Hon Roll; Acting.

NIXON, STEVEN; Fort Hill HS; Cumberland, MD; (S); Pres Church Yth Grp; JV Bsbl; Hon Roll; Sec NHS; SR Sntr 85-86; Frstbrg ST Coll; Mech Engrng.

NIZIOLEK, MARY BETH; Our Lady Of Pompei HS; Baltimore, MD; (Y); Cmnty Wkr; Pep Clb; Nwsp Rptr; Nwsp Stf; VP Jr Cls; Rep Stu Cncl; Bsktbl; Im Socr; Sftbl; Im Vllybl.

NOBLE, JEANNE; Laurel SR HS; Laurel, MD; (Y); Church Yth Grp; French Clb; Pep Clb; Ski Clb; Teachers Aide; Stage Crew; Var Trk; French Hon Soc; Hon Roll; Frnch Hnr Soc Schlrshp 86; Salesprsn Mnth 84; Outstndng Achvt Bio 86; Appalachian ST U; Intr Design.

NOBLE, KASEY; Wicomico SR HS; Salisbury, MD; (Y); Camera Clb; Hon Roll; Phrmcst.

NOCK, CANDACE ELISE; Snow Hill HS; Pocomoke, MD; (S); Art Clb; Cmnty Wkr; Cheerleading; Mgr(s); Vllybl; Hon Roll; NHS; Pstv Yth Dvlpmnt Netwrk 84-85; Ldrshp Course Alclsm & Drug Abse 84-85; Outstndng Achvt In Art 85; Nrs.

NOCK, KIM; Wicomico SR HS; Salisbury, MD; (Y); Pep Clb; Spanish Clb; Varsity Clb; Chorus; VP Rep Frsh Cls; Rep Soph Cls; Rep Jr Cls; Var L Cheerleading; Gym; Var Sftbl; Acdmc Letter; Homecoming Court; Salisbury ST U; Alg Teacher.

NOEL, ANGELA; Elkton HS; Elkton, MD; (Y); 41/263; Church Yth Grp; Civic Clb; Drama Clb; Q&S; Teachers Aide; Chorus; Church Choir; School Musical; Nwsp Bus Mgr; Rep Frsh Cls; County Cncl Cecil Cnty 83-86 Pres County Cncl Cecil Cnty 85-86; All Eastern Seabord Choir 85; Journalism.

NOLAN, CHRISTOPHER; Georgetown Prep; Bethesda, MD; (Y); 11/110; Math Tm; NFL; Nwsp Rptr; Var Bsbl; Var Bsktbl.

NOLAN, DAWN; Mt Savage HS; Mt Savage, MD; (Y); FBLA; GAA; Office Aide; Pep Clb; Teachers Aide; Chorus; Drm Mjr(t); JV Var Bsktbl; JV Var Cheerleading; JV Var Vllybl; Allegany CC; Sec.

NOONAN, COLLEEN; Great Mills HS; Lexington Pk, MD; (Y); FBLA; Spanish Clb; JV Bsktbl; Var JV Crs Cntry; JV Vllybl; Hon Roll.

NOONKESTER, JACQUELINE; C Milton Wright HS; Bel Air, MD; (Y); 19/255; Church Yth Grp; JA; Sec Jr Cls; Rep Stu Cncl; Capt Pom Pon; NHS; Pres Schlr; German Clb; Math Clb; Chorus; Acdmc Achvmnt Awd 82-86; Sntrl Schlrshp 86; Outstndg Yng Prsn Of Mnth Hrfrd Cnty 86; Towson ST U; Lbrl Arts.

NORFOLK, JOHN; Northern HS; Huntingtown, MD; (Y); Boy Scts; Var L Crs Cntry; Var L Trk; Var L Wrstlng; Hon Roll; NHS; BSA Eagle, Sprntndnt Schlstc Awd, Natl Space Club Smmr Intern Pgm 86; Aerospace Engrng.

NORMAN, KIMBERLY S; Mc Donough HS; Waldorf, MD; (Y); 18/297; Sec Thesps; Chorus; School Play; Symp Band; Rep Jr Cls; Capt Co-Capt Pom Pon; High Hon Roll; NHS; Camera Clb; Cmnty Wkr; Frnch Awd 85; Pres Acad Ftns Awd 86; Frostburg ST Coll.

NORRIS, BRONNA; St Marys Ryken HS; Bryantown, MD; (Y); Church Yth Grp; FBLA; School Musical; Rep Frsh Cls; Rep Soph Cls; VP Stu Cncl; JV Cheerleading; NHS; Bus.

NORRIS, CHARLES; La Plata HS; La Plata, MD; (Y); 70/300; Aud/Vis; Drama Clb; Library Aide; Thesps; Band; Concert Band; Jazz Band; Mrchg Band; Pep Band; School Play; Charles Cnty Coll; Music.

NORRIS, KATHY; Allegany HS; Cumberland, MD; (Y); 48/250; Church Yth Grp; Cmnty Wkr; Band; Concert Band; Jazz Band; Mrchg Band; All Cnty Hnr Bands 83-86; WB U; Music Educ.

NORRIS, MARY; La Plata HS; La Plata, MD; (Y); Cmnty Wkr; Trs FHA; Flag Corp; Symp Band; Nwsp Rptr; 4-H Awd; Hon Roll; Jr NHS; NHS; U Of MD; Intr Dsgn.

NORRIS, WILLIAM; Bladensburg HS; Capitol Hts, MD; (Y); JV Bsktbl; Var Capt Ftbl; Hon Roll; Ntl Merit Ltr; Pres Schlr; U MD College Pk; Polc Offcr.

NORTH, MARTHA; Hereford HS; Monkton, MD; (Y); AFS; French Clb; Varsity Clb; Band; Lit Mag; Rep Stu Cncl; Fld Hcky; Lcrss; Trk; NHS; Fin.

NORTON, BRIAN; Frederick Douglass HS; Upper Marlboro, MD; (Y); JV Stu Cncl; Capt Var Bsktbl; JV Ftbl; Bausch & Lomb Sci Awd; NHS; Pres Schlr; Spanish NHS; St Schlr; Spanish Clb; Hon Roll; Army Res Schlr Ath Awd 86; Schl Sportsmnshp Awd 86; Civic Assn Cert Achvt Awd 85; U MD; Comp Sci.

NORWOOD, REGINALD A; Oxon Hill HS; Temple Hills, MD; (Y); AFS; CAP; 4-H; Math Tm; Off ROTC; Drill Tm; Rep Jr Cls; Hon Roll; Ntl Merit Ltr; Ntl Achvt Semi-Fnlst; VA Tech; Engrng.

NOVAK, KELLY; Old Mill SR HS; Millersville, MD; (Y); 110/509; Teachers Aide; Varsity Clb; VP L Cheerleading; Sec Lcrss; Frostburg ST Coll; Bus Adm.

NOVICK, MARSHA; Walt Whitman HS; Bethesda, MD; (Y); 75/465; JA; Band; L Mrchg Band; Pres Acad Ftnss Awd 86; U Of CA Santa Cruz; Bio.

NOVOTNAK, JOANNE; Fort Hill HS; Cumberland, MD; (Y); Concert Band; Mrchg Band; Yrbk Ed-Chief; Stu Cncl; Cit Awd; NHS; NEDT Awd; VA Polytech Inst; Vet Med.

NUGENT, JAMES; Friendly HS; Ft Washington, MD; (Y); 1/420; Boy Scts; Capt Debate Tm; Math Tm; ROTC; Nwsp Phtg; Hst Jr Cls; VP Sr Cls; Var L Socr; Pres Jr NHS; NHS; Eagle Scout-Boy Scouts Of Amer 84; Vigil Hnr-Order Of Arrow BSA 84; Superior Cadet Army JROTC Ld-1; U S Military Acad West Pt; Engr.

NULL, LARA; Westminster HS; Westminster, MD; (Y); Am Leg Aux Girls St; Math Tm; Red Cross Aide; Pres Spanish Clb; Teachers Aide; Rep Soph Cls; Rep Jr Cls; Pres Stu Cncl; JV Stat Bsktbl; High Hon Roll; St Marys Coll Of MD; Biology.

NUNN, MICHELLE; Mt De Sales Acad; Ellicott, MD; (Y); Intnl Clb; Lcrss; Swmmng; ACIS 86; Tchr.

NUSPL, TONY P; Walter Johnson HS; Bethesda, MD; (Y); 27/215; Drama Clb; PAVAS; School Play; Stage Crew; Swmmng; Chem.

NUSSBAUM, ELISE; Gaithersburg HS; Gaithersburg, MD; (Y); 6/600; Var Trs JA; Pres Var NFL; Ed Lit Mag; Var Tennis; Var High Hon Roll; Var NHS; Var Ntl Merit Ltr; Var Pres Schlr; Var Sal; Var St Schlr; Brandeis U.

O CONNOR, BRAD; North Hagerstown HS; Hagerstown, MD; (Y); Political Wkr; Pres Band; Concert Band; Jazz Band; Mrchg Band; Pep Band; School Musical; Symp Band; Sprts Admin.

O CONNOR, KEVIN; De Matha HS; Laurel, MD; (Y); 8/250; Band; Chorus; Socr; Tennis; Hon Roll; NHS; St Schlr; Natl Choral Awd; Presdntl Acamd Fitness; Villanova; Engrng.

O CONNOR, KEVIN; Our Lady Of Good Council HS; Germantown, MD; (Y); Boy Scts; Church Yth Grp; Trs Drama Clb; Pres Intnl Clb; Pres Model UN; Thesps; Mrchg Band; School Play; Nwsp Rptr; High Hon Roll; Best Actr On Rgnl Lvl 86; Best Dir In Theatrical Competition 85; Induction Into Order Of Arrow 82; Intl Affairs.

O DONNELL, KATE; Queen Anne Schl; Huntingtown, MD; (Y); Hosp Aide; Model UN; Red Cross Aide; Ski Clb; Band; Symp Band; Rep Soph Cls; Rep Jr Cls; Rep Sr Cls; Var Socr; Part In Ldrshp Dvlpmnt Conf To Red Cross 83; Psychology.

O DONNELL, ROBERTA; Great Mills HS; Lexington Pk, MD; (Y); Library Aide; Pep Clb; Spanish Clb; Teachers Aide; Band; Concert Band; Mrchg Band; Hon Roll; Span Clb Sec 85-86; Schl Span Awd 85-86; Schl Media Awd 85-86; Biology.

O DONOGHUE, JOHN; Elkton HS; Elkton, MD; (Y); Computer Clb; Key Clb; Ski Clb; Teachers Aide; Nwsp Rptr; Nwsp Stf; Yrbk Stf; Var Capt Bsbl; JV Bsktbl; Wt Lftg; LSU; Psych.

O HARA, SUZANNE M; Old Mill SR HS; Glen Burnie, MD; (Y); 18/510; Church Yth Grp; Pres Chorus; Church Choir; Madrigals; School Musical; Variety Show; Hon Roll; NHS; Voice Dem Awd; MD Distgshd Schlr Semi Fnlst 85; U Of MD; Music Educ.

O HARE, KEVIN; De Matha Catholic HS; Bowie, MD; (Y); Cmnty Wkr; Var Lcrss; JV Mgr(s); Var Socr; Hon Roll; Schlstc, Athltc Awd 85-86; Bus.

O KELLEY, KARMAN M; Maurice J Mc Donough HS; Waldorf, MD; (S); 40/314; Church Yth Grp; Intnl Clb; Church Choir; Swing Chorus; Variety Show; Ski Clb; Rep Stu Cncl; Hon Roll; Cmnty Wkr; Teachers Aide; Tri-Cnty Hnrs Chorus 86; Charles Cnty Gftd & Tlntd Choral Ensmbl 86; Sci Lab Asstnt 85-86; Carson Neman Coll; Pre-Med.

O NEAL, KIMBERLY; Allegany HS; Cumberland, MD; (Y); 2/230; AFS; Pres Sec Church Yth Grp; Drama Clb; Concert Band; Drm Mjr(t); Mrchg Band; Yrbk Stf; Rep Stu Cncl; High Hon Roll; NHS; Hlth.

O TOOLE JR, RICHARD JAMES; Patterson HS; Baltimore, MD; (Y); Art Clb; Computer Clb; Intnl Clb; Pres Key Clb; Math Clb; Science Clb; SADD; Varsity Clb; Concert Band; Yrbk Rptr; Pres Schlrshp 86; Studnt Of The Yr 85-86; Key Clb Intl Svc Awd 85-86; Cmnty Coll Baltimore; Comp Sci.

OATWAY, CHRIS; Walter Johnson HS; Bethesda, MD; (Y); Debate Tm; Var L Socr; Var L Vllybl; Church Yth Grp; JV L Bsktbl; Hon Roll; Scholastic/Kodak Photography Award 86; Intl Affairs.

OBENSTINE, CINDY LEE; Dundalk HS; Dundalk, MD; (Y); Teachers Aide; Yrbk Phtg; High Hon Roll; Jr NHS; NHS; Pres Schlr; St Schlr; Yrbk Stf; Hon Roll; Dist Schlr Hnrbl Mnt 85; Awd For Svc & Acad Excllnc In Soc Studies, Engl & Art 85; Book Prize 86; U Of MD Baltimore Cnty.

OBERAI, NAVJEET; Gaithersburg HS; Gaithersburg, MD; (Y); Boy Scts; VP Soph Cls; Capt Badmtn; Capt Socr; Capt Vllybl; Hon Roll; Cert Ovrll Merit 84; Comp Sci.

OCHOA, DAVID; Catoctin HS; Thurmont, MD; (Y); 11/203; Computer Clb; Debate Tm; Letterman Clb; Pres Science Clb; Spanish Clb; VP Band; Stage Crew; JV Bsktbl; L Trk; Hon Roll; Naval Acad Summr Sem 86; Naval Acad; Navl Archit.

OCONNOR, KATY; Beall HS; Frostburg, MD; (Y); Office Aide; Teachers Aide; Drill Tm; Mat Maids; Score Keeper; Shepherd Coll; Psychlgy.

ODEND HAL, ANDREA; Parkville HS; Baltimore, MD; (Y); Trk; Prfct Atten Awd; Psych.

ODENDHAL, ANDREA L; Parkville HS; Baltimore, MD; (Y); Trk; Hon Roll; Prfct Atten Awd; Psych.

OFFUTT, KERI; Westminster SR HS; Westminster, MD; (Y); Am Leg Aux Girls St; Hosp Aide; Quiz Bowl; Pres Frsh Cls; Rep Soph Cls; Rep Jr Cls; Rep Sr Cls; Trs Stu Cncl; Lcrss; Vllybl; Govnrs Cmmtte Of Emplymnt For Hndicpd Cntst Wnnr 86; CCSGA Publcty Rep Nwsltr Edtr In Chief 86; E Stroudsburg U; Telecomm.

OH, ESTHER; Bishop Waslh HS; Frostburg, MD; (Y); English Clb; Intnl Clb; Pep Clb; Science Clb; Ski Clb; Spanish Clb; Varsity Clb; Chorus; Yrbk Stf; Sec Stu Cncl; Acdmc 86; Principles Hon Roll 84; Pre Dntstry.

OH, HENRY; Laurel HS; Laurel, MD; (Y); Church Yth Grp; Ski Clb; Teachers Aide; Ice Hcky; Wt Lftg; Hon Roll; Bus.

OH, JU HYOUN; Loyola HS; Timonium, MD; (S); JV Trk; High Hon Roll; Hon Roll; Jr NHS; NHS; Pre-Med.

OH, SUKMIN; Mc Donogh Schl; Ellicott City, MD; (Y); 2/135; Chess Clb; Church Yth Grp; Cmnty Wkr; Library Aide; Office Aide; Spanish Clb; School Musical; Yrbk Sprt Ed; JV Bsbl; JV Crs Cntry; Jhn Mcdngh Memrl Schlrshp; Jack A Klschr Schlrshp; U Of PA.

OH, YOUNG K; Loch Raven SR HS; Baltimore, MD; (Y); 9/320; Church Yth Grp; School Musical; Lit Mag; Trs Soph Cls; Stu Cncl; Var L Fld Hcky; NHS; Ntl Merit SF; St Schlr; Baltimore Cnty Giftd-Tlntd Music Schlrshp 83-86; Peabody Hnrs Rectl Prtcpnt 85; Williams Coll; Medcn.

OHARA, SHANNON; Immaculata Coll HS; Cheverly, MD; (Y); German Clb; Math Clb; VP Frsh Cls; VP Sr Cls; Rep Off Stu Cncl; High Hon Roll; Hon Roll.

OKANE, DAVID; Jematta Catholic HS; Hyattsville, MD; (Y); Varsity Clb; JV Var Golf; JV Lcrss; JV Var Socr; Hon Roll; Engrng.

OLAYINKA, TIFFANY; Academy Of The Holy Names; Silver Spring, MD; (Y); Cmnty Wkr; Pep Clb; Chorus; Variety Show; Yrbk Stf; Jr NHS; Outstndng Acdmc Achvt Awd 86; Social Wrk.

OLES, MARIE; Glenelg HS; Woodbine, MD; (Y); 71/350; German Clb; Intnl Clb; Latin Clb; Band; Hon Roll; Intl Baccalrt Partcpnt 84-86; Latin IV Only Stu 85-86; U MD; Equine Bus Mgmt.

OLESKA, DIANE; Edgewood HS; Edgewood, MD; (Y); 4/222; Church Yth Grp; Teachers Aide; Concert Band; Mrchg Band; Powder Puff Ftbl; Var L Tennis; Hon Roll; NHS; Ntl Merit SF; Pres Schlr; Ntl Elks Fdtn, Widener 4 Yr Schlrshps 86; Widener U; Engrng.

OLEWNIK, RICHARD; De Matha Catholic HS; Washington, DC; (Y); High Hon Roll; Hon Roll; Bus.

OLINDE, JAY; Georgetown Prep; Baton Rouge, LA; (Y); Pep Clb; Rep Jr Cls; Rep Stu Cncl; Im Bsbl; Im Bsktbl; Im Ftbl; JV L Socr; Im Sftbl; Var L Swmmng; Var L Trk; Schlrshp To Sprnghl Coll; Sprnghl Coll Mbl AL; Pre-Med.

OLIVER, CHRISTOPHER; Paul Laurence Dunbar SR HS; Baltimore, MD; (Y); FBLA; JV Ftbl; Mgr(s); Hon Roll; Prfct Atten Awd; NC ST; Comptr Engrg.

OLIVER, JEAN; Northern HS; Catonsville, MD; (Y); Church Yth Grp; JA; Y-Teens; Band; Church Choir; Mrchg Band; Cheerleading; Mgr(s); Sftbl; Mgr Swmmng; Hampton Inst; Psych.

OLIVER, SCOTT D; Landsdowne HS; Baltimore, MD; (Y); Dance Clb; Band; Jazz Band; Mrchg Band; School Musical; School Play; Variety Show; Stu Cncl; Ftbl; Lcrss; PTSA Schrlshp 86; Ftbl Schlr Ath, Yuth In Govt Dpt Shrff 85; UMBC; Elec Engr.

OLIVER, TAMMY J; Eastern Vocational Techinal HS; Baltimore, MD; (Y); Church Yth Grp; FNA; Band; High Hon Roll; Pres NHS; MD Distngshd Schlr Hnbl Mntn 85; U Of MD; Nrsg.

OLIVER, VERTRELL; Western HS; Baltimore, MD; (Y); 143/412; Drill Tm; Yrbk Stf; Bsktbl; Vllybl; Howard U; CPA.

OLLERMAN, ANDREW; Maurice J Mc Donough HS; Pomfret, MD; (Y); Boy Scts; German Clb; Teachers Aide; Band; Mrchg Band; Stage Crew; Symp Band; Coach Actv; JV Socr; Var Trk; Best All Around Sci Stu 85; US Coast Guard; Ocean Engr.

OLLINGER, RACHEL; The Catholic HS Of Baltimre; Baltimore, MD; (Y); 20/196; Church Yth Grp; Girl Scts; Band; Church Choir; Hon Roll; St Schlr; Coll Of Notre Dame Of MD Grnt 86; Notre Dame Of MD; Elmntry Ed.

OLSEN, JENNIFER LYNN; Joppatowne HS; Joppa, MD; (Y); 5/161; VP FTA; Yrbk Sprt Ed; Rep Stu Cncl; Var Capt Bsktbl; Var L Fld Hcky; Var L Lcrss; Powder Puff Ftbl; High Hon Roll; Trs NHS; Pres Schlr; Marinr Awd 86; Hnrbl Mntn Fld Hcky 83; Fld Hcky Cls C ST Chmps 86; U Of MD College Park; Life Sci.

OLSEN, RANDY; Beall HS; Frostburg, MD; (Y); Boy Scts; Church Yth Grp; Teachers Aide; Varsity Clb; Chorus; Nwsp Phtg; Nwsp Rptr; Nwsp Stf; Bsktbl; Bowling; BYU.

ONESSIMO, GINA M; Meade SR HS; Ft Meade, MD; (Y); Drama Clb; FBLA; Library Aide; Office Aide; Chorus; Church Choir; Nwsp Stf; Bus Mgt.

ONYIRIMBA, KINGSLEY; Theodore Roosevelt HS; Washington, DC; (Y); 22/369; Boy Scts; Ftbl; Tennis; Hon Roll; Jean Curtis Natl Awd 86; Howard U; Phrmclgy.

ORAVECZ, LINDA; Great Mills HS; Lex Pk, MD; (Y); 6/315; Hosp Aide; Teachers Aide; Rep Frsh Cls; Rep Soph Cls; Rep Jr Cls; Rep Sr Cls; Rep Stu Cncl; Var L Fld Hcky; High Hon Roll; Hon Roll; Chem I Awd 85; Chem II Awd 86.

ORE, MONICA; Crossland HS; Suitland, MD; (Y); Church Yth Grp; Cmnty Wkr; Teachers Aide; Church Choir; Rep Frsh Cls; Rep Soph Cls; Pres Jr Cls; Pres Sr Cls; Rep Stu Cncl; Capt Var Cheerleading; Chld Psych.

ORNDOFF, KENNY; Westminster HS; Finksburg, MD; (Y); Varsity Clb; Var L Lcrss; Im Mgr(s); Var L Socr; Hon Roll; Arch.

ORNDOFF, MICHAEL; Fort Hill HS; Cumberland, MD; (Y); Pres Church Yth Grp; Hon Roll; Creatv Wrtng Awd, Gold Mdl 85, Slvr Mdl 86; Schlrshp Wrld Bible Quiz Indvl Chmp 85; Mt Vernon Nazarene Coll; Engl.

ORR, KAREN; John Carroll HS; Bel Air, MD; (Y); 39/240; Church Yth Grp; Cmnty Wkr; French Clb; GAA; Pep Clb; SADD; Varsity Clb; Band; JV Var Sftbl; French Hon Soc; Mst Invlvd In Outrch 84-86; Mst Vlbl Plyr In Sftbl 85; Scl Wrk.

ORRELL, ANNE E; Towson HS; Baltimore, MD; (Y); Sec Church Yth Grp; Drama Clb; Hosp Aide; Model UN; Spanish Clb; Chorus; Church Choir; School Musical; Variety Show; Hon Roll; Edyth Gorsuch Onion Awd Vocal Excel 85; Balti Cnty Gftd Tlntd Schlrshp 85; Peabody Prep Schlrshp 85; Gettysburg Coll; Music.

ORTH, KEVIN D; Gaithersburg HS; Gaithersburg, MD; (Y); VP JA; Ski Clb; SADD; Capt Vllybl; Hon Roll; Spanish NHS; Mck Trl Comptn Hon Law Team 86; Dist Sls Pro Wk 86; Williams Coll; Pltcl Sci.

ORTON, SHARON; Lackey HS; Indian Head, MD; (Y); French Clb; Yrbk Rptr; Ed Yrbk Stf; Rep Stu Cncl; High Hon Roll; Hon Roll; Comp Sci.

ORTT JR, RICHARD; Parkville HS; Baltimore, MD; (Y); Boy Scts; Nwsp Phtg; Trs Jr Cls; Pres Stu Cncl; Var Bsbl; Cit Awd; Hon Roll; Jr NHS; NHS; Prfct Atten Awd; Eagl Sct 84; Aerosp Engrng.

OSENBURG, KRISTIN; Notre Dame Preparatory HS; Baltimore, MD; (Y); Chorus; Nwsp Ed-Chief; VP Jr Cls.

OSHODIN, WILLIAM; Georgetown Preparatory Schl; Ft Washington, MD; (Y); Cmnty Wkr; Latin Clb; Hon Roll; Art Clb; Camera Clb; JV Bsktbl; JV Var Ftbl; JV Golf; JV Lcrss; JV Mgr(s); Engrng.

OTTERBEIN, JAMES; Mt Saint Joseph HS; Baltimore, MD; (Y); Boy Scts; Spanish Clb; U Of MD Balt County; Accntng.

OTTO, EMILY; Northern Garrett County HS; Accident, MD; (Y); Computer Clb; SADD; Teachers Aide; Color Guard; Hon Roll; Su Mth Awd 84 & 86; Cert Attndnc Awd 84; Typng Awd 86; Med.

OTTO, MARK; St Andrews Episcopal HS; Bethesda, MD; (S); Model UN; Spanish Clb; Stage Crew; Nwsp Rptr; Yrbk Phtg; Lit Mag; Var Bsbl; Ntl Merit SF; Music Achvt Awd 81-82; Drama Awd Achvt Tech Theatre 82-83; Rensselaer Polytech Inst; Engr.

OTTO, SALLY; Queen Annes County HS; Stevensville, MD; (Y); 40/343; Drama Clb; Nwsp Rptr; Nwsp Stf; Sec Stu Cncl; Hon Roll; NHS; Pres Schlr; French Clb; School Play; Stage Crew; Delgt Schlrshp 86-87; MD U; Ed.

OUTTEN, MICHAEL J; Delmar HS; Delmar, MD; (Y); 12/118; Camera Clb; Sec Key Clb; Ski Clb; SADD; Varsity Clb; Off Jr Cls; Var Capt Bsbl; Var Capt Ftbl; JV Wrstlng; Hon Roll; Hnrbl Mnt All Msn Dxn Ftbll Tm 85; Salisbury ST Coll.

OVERCASH, BETTY; Brooklyn Park JR SR HS; Baltimore, MD; (Y); 25/100; Church Yth Grp; Computer Clb; Latin Clb; Stu Cncl; Cheerleading; Score Keeper; Wt Lftg; Hon Roll; Jr NHS; NHS; Prfct Attdnce; Geo Prjct 2nd Pl; Art Apprctn; York Bus Schl; Pedtrcn.

OVERTON, MIKE; Wicomico SR HS; Salisbury, MD; (Y); Boys Clb Am; Varsity Clb; School Musical; Rep Jr Cls; Var Crs Cntry; JV Ftbl; JV Wrstlng; Hon Roll; Commnctns.

OWENS JR, FREDDIE JAMES; Baltimore Polytechnic Inst; Baltimore, MD; (Y); 15/273; JA; Im Bsktbl; Hon Roll; UMBC; Archtct.

OWENS, MARGUITA; Forest Park HS; Baltimore, MD; (Y); CAP; Dance Clb; Library Aide; Office Aide; Red Cross Aide; Mgr(s); Hon Roll; Mth Enrichmnt; Spelling Bee; Nrsng.

OWENS, SHERI; Arlington Baptist HS; Glen Burnie, MD; (Y); 6/64; Pres Church Yth Grp; Hosp Aide; Library Aide; Chorus; Church Choir; VP L Cheerleading; High Hon Roll; Hon Roll; Pres Schlr; Athletic Awd 85-86; Fnlst Miss Teen Pagnt 85; Soc Studies Awd 86; Lee Coll; Bio.

OWENS, VINCE; Mount Saint Joseph HS; Baltimore, MD; (Y); 25/300; Camera Clb; Debate Tm; Intnl Clb; Q&S; Speech Tm; Nwsp Rptr; JV Trk; NHS; Prfct Atten Awd; Law.

OWINGS, TERRI; Westminster HS; Westminster, MD; (Y); Var Socr; Var Trk; Athlt Of Wk Sccr 85; Sci.

PABIS, LEAH MELANEY; Havre De Grace HS; Darlington, MD; (Y); 5/141; Church Yth Grp; Cmnty Wkr; 4-H; Library Aide; Pom Pon; Cit Awd; High Hon Roll; Hon Roll; Jr NHS; Lion Awd; A Raymond Jackson Scholar 86; Schltc Merit Awd 86; Pres Acad Fit Awds 86; Joseph L Davis Post 47 86; Goldey Beacom Coll; Adm Off Mgm.

PACE, KIMBERLY A; Archbishop Keough HS; Baltimore, MD; (S); Computer Clb; Debate Tm; Drama Clb; Math Tm; NFL; Nwsp Rptr; Var Capt Gym; High Hon Roll; NEDT Awd; Rep Frsh Cls; Natl Math Awd 85; Natl Frnscs Leag Debate Octo Fnlst 84; MD ST Debate Fnlst 84-85; Elec Engr.

PACK, SHALISA; Dundalk SR HS; Baltimore, MD; (Y); Church Yth Grp; SADD; Chorus; Church Choir; Variety Show; Sftbl; High Hon Roll; Hon Roll; All ST Cncl Wash COLL 85-86; Black Heritage Clb 85-86; Peer Fclttrs 86-87; Bauder Fshn COLL; Fshn Dsgnr.

PACKARD, ANDREW; Hereford HS; Freeland, MD; (S); 9/209; Varsity Clb; Band; Concert Band; Jazz Band; Mrchg Band; Variety Show; Var Capt Golf; Var Capt Socr; Var Trk; Hon Roll; Alumni Assn Outstndng SR Boy 86; SR Speaker Graduatn 86; Schlr Athelete 86; Wake Forest U; Liberal Arts.

PACLAWSKYJ, THEODOSIA R; Charles W Woodward HS; Kensington, MD; (Y); 2/234; French Clb; Hosp Aide; Intnl Clb; Capt Math Tm; Capt Scholastic Bowl; Cit Awd; French Hon Soc; Hon Roll; Ntl Merit Ltr; Sal; Charles W Woodward Awd; Harvard Bk Clb Awd; MD Dist Schlr SF; Johns Hopkins U; Intl Health.

PADRE, LARRY; Crossland HS; Ft Washington, MD; (Y); Band; Concert Band; Jazz Band; Mrchg Band; Orch; Pep Band; Symp Band; JV Var Socr; Hon Roll; Lttr Symphnc Band 84; Cert GPA Typg 86; U S Naval Acad; Engnrng.

PALACIOS, STEPHEN; Good Counsel HS; Kensington, MD; (Y); 88/228; Sec Debate Tm; Latin Clb; Concert Band; Jazz Band; Mrchg Band; Symp Band; Nwsp Stf; Var Lcrss; Im Bsbl; Im Ftbl; Natl Latin Awd-Cum Laude 84; Reading List Schlr 85; Natl Hspnc Schlrs Pgm-Semi Fnlst 85-86; Hstry.

PALFI, CHRIS; Joppastowne HS; Joppa, MD; (Y); Var Lcrss; Var Capt Socr; Var Wrstlng; Var Hon Roll; Var NHS; Hnrbl Mntn V Sccr 85-86; Armd Frcs Offcr.

PALMER, ALAN JAY; Bethesda Chevy Chase HS; Chevy Chase, MD; (Y); Drama Clb; JA; Speech Tm; Band; Jazz Band; Mrchg Band; Orch; School Play; Stage Crew; Symp Band; Hon Ment ARTS 86; JA; Hart Schl Music; Afrcn Amer Msc.

PALMER, AYMALEE ALAYNE; Fallston HS; Fallston, MD; (Y); 18/256; Girl Scts; Hosp Aide; JV Sftbl; NHS; Hood Coll; Vet Med.

PALMER, CHRISTINE; S Carroll HS; New Windsor, MD; (Y); Teachers Aide; Varsity Clb; Var Cheerleading; Powder Puff Ftbl; Hon Roll; Villa Julie Coll; Bus.

PALMER, LEAH; Lackey HS; Indian Head, MD; (Y); French Clb; Intnl Clb; Spanish Clb; Teachers Aide; Sftbl; Hon Roll; Ltrd In Sftbl 86; Mrn Bio.

PALMER, RON; Fallston HS; Fallston, MD; (Y); JV Lcrss; Var Socr; Hon Roll; NHS; Loyola Coll; Bus.

PALMER, TIM A; Brunswick HS; Burkittsville, MD; (Y); Church Yth Grp; Computer Clb; Library Aide; Radio Clb; JV Ftbl; Wt Lftg; Hon Roll; Brktsvl Ruritan Lds Axlry 86; Prnts, Tchrs, & Stu Assoc 86; Lncln Tech Inst; Auto Tech.

PALMER, TROY; Baltimore Polytechnic Inst; Baltimore, MD; (Y); 13/210; Band; Concert Band; Mrchg Band; Pep Band; Hon Roll; Johns Hopkins U; Bio Physc.

PALMETER, CHRISTINA; Joppatowne HS; Joppatowne, MD; (Y); Yrbk Stf; Harford Cnty CC; Acctnt.

PALOMO, JOYCE; North Hagertown HS; Hagerstown, MD; (Y); Computer Clb; French Clb; FBLA; Key Clb; Spanish Clb; Y-Teens; Yrbk Stf; Hon Roll; Hnr Clb 83-86; ST & Dstrct Natl Piano Plyng Adtns 85-86.

PANCHOLI, SUSHIL; Park Dale HS; Lanham, MD; (S); Chess Clb; French Clb; French Hon Soc; High Hon Roll; Hon Roll; NHS; U Of MD; Engrng.

PANKEY, FONTELLA; Oxon Hill SR HS; Oxon Hill, MD; (Y); Church Yth Grp; FHA; Library Aide; Office Aide; Pep Clb; Teachers Aide; Church Choir; Pom Pon; High Hon Roll; Hon Roll; Mst Outstndng Stu Awd 82-83; Hampton U; Tv Brdcstg.

PAPAVASILIOU, JOHN A; Loyola HS; Timonium, MD; (S); Church Yth Grp; Var Swmmng; Timer; Hon Roll; NHS; USS All MD Swm Tm 84-85; MD All Star Eastern Zone Tm 84-85; Natl Age Grp Top 16 400 Med Relay 85; Mth.

PARCHMENT, GREG; Takoma Acad; Silver Spring, MD; (S); Ski Clb; Teachers Aide; Trs Frsh Cls; Off Soph Cls; Trs Jr Cls; JV Var Bsktbl; Trk; Hon Roll; NHS.

PARE, MARK; Rising Sun HS; Colora, MD; (Y); 9/167; Am Leg Boys St; VP Key Clb; Var Bsbl; Var Capt Bsktbl; Var Capt Ftbl; Hon Roll; NHS; Pres Schlr; SAR Awd; St Schlr; Schlr Athl Awd 86; Harvard.

PARETZKY, JESSICA C; Thomas S Wootton HS; Potomac, MD; (Y); AFS; DECA; Drama Clb; Temple Yth Grp; Stu Cncl; Var L Fld Hcky; JV L Tennis; Hon Roll; Ntl Achvt Schlrshp Outstndng Negro Stdnt.

PARK, KATHY; Allegany HS; Cumberland, MD; (Y); 10/233; Drama Clb; Pep Clb; Drill Tm; Orch; Hon Roll; NHS.

PARK, OGGI; Richard Montgomery HS; Rockville, MD; (Y); 1/250; Church Yth Grp; Drama Clb; Math Tm; Science Clb; Thesps; NCTE Awd; Trs NHS; Ntl Merit SF; Val; School Musical; Engrng Mdl 85.

PARK, SOOKY; Seneca Valley HS; Gaithersburg, MD; (Y); 13/490; Science Clb; Teachers Aide; Nwsp Ed-Chief; Nwsp Sprt Ed; Yrbk Rptr; Yrbk Stf; Rep Jr Cls; JV Var Cheerleading; L Pom Pon; Var Powder Puff Ftbl; Ntl Chrldng Assoc Excllnc Awd 84-85; Math Stu Of Mnth 85; MD U; Jrnlsm.

PARK, SUNG; Parkdale HS; Riverdale, MD; (S); Chorus; Var Bsbl; Hon Roll; NHS; Hnrs Pgm U MD 85-86; U Of MD; Elec Engrng.

PARK JR, WILLIAM R; Allegany HS; Cresaptown, MD; (Y); 71/350; Computer Clb; Office Aide; Ski Clb; Var Bsbl; Var Bsktbl; Var Ftbl; Var Wt Lftg; U MDFORTHODONTISTS.

PARKELL, NATALIE B; Kent County HS; Galena, MD; (Y); 1/168; Trs Spanish Clb; School Musical; Sec Frsh Cls; Sec Soph Cls; Sec Jr Cls; JV Cheerleading; Var JV Tennis; High Hon Roll; Pres NHS; Val; U VA.

PARKER, DONALD D; Colonel Zadok Magruder HS; Rockville, MD; (Y); 2/310; Boy Scts; Church Yth Grp; Pres Stu Cncl; Gov Hon Prg Awd; NHS; Pres Schlr; Val; Am Leg Boys St; Mathletes; SADD; Magruder Awd 86; Harvard Bk Awd 85; George WA Mdl 85; Vigil Hnr Order Arrow BSA 85; U IL; Comp Engrng.

PARKER, EMILY R; Friendly SR HS; Ft Washington, MD; (Y); Im Coach Actv; Var L Tennis; Var L Vllybl; French Hon Soc; Hon Roll; NHS; Acadmc Excllnc Awd 85; Art Recgntn Awd 85; Acadmc Recgntn Awd 85; Art.

PARKS, DAWN; Wshington HS; Westover, MD; (Y); Church Yth Grp; Dance Clb; 4-H; Teachers Aide; Chorus; 4-H Awd; 4-H Awd 83; Salisbury ST Coll; Tchg Mth.

PARKS, DONNA M; Parkside HS; Salisbury, MD; (S); 1/249; Trs VP Art Clb; Sec Girl Scts; Trs Math Tm; NHS; Val; Exploring; Spanish Clb; Hon Roll; George Washington U Schl Of Engrng & Appld Sci Engrng Medl 85; Distngshd Schlr Merit Schlrshp 85; U Of MD; Aerosp Engrng.

PARKS, GEORGE T; Cardinal Gibbons HS; Baltimore, MD; (Y); 9/125; Boy Scts; Church Yth Grp; 4-H; Church Choir; High Hon Roll; Hon Roll; NHS; Rep Frsh Cls; Rep Soph Cls; JV Bsbl; Citznshp Awd 81; Good Wrk & Depndbl Awd 82; High Acad Awd 84; Rets Electronics; Electncs.

PARKS, MELODIE; Highland View Acad; Delmar, DE; (Y); Chorus; Church Choir; Variety Show; Yrbk Stf; Lit Mag; Pres Frsh Cls; Im Var Bsktbl; Var Gym; Im Socr; Im Sftbl; Home Ec.

PARKS, VICKI; Snow Hill HS; Snow Hill, MD; (S); Hon Roll; NHS; Secry.

PARLETTE, HARRY L; Rockville HS; Rockville, MD; (Y); Key Clb; Ski Clb; Mrchg Band; Pep Band; Symp Band; Ftbl; Trk; Wt Lftg; Hon Roll; NHS; Engr.

PARRAN, JOSEPH; Calvert HS; Pr Frederick, MD; (Y); 41/249; 4-H; ROTC; Var L Wrstlng; High Hon Roll; Decaln Medal Pride Patrtsm 86; Most Imprvd Wrstlng 86; US Naval Acad; Engr.

PARRECO, RICH; Riverdale Baptist HS; Upper Marlboro, MD; (S); Church Yth Grp; Band; Pep Band; JV Bsbl; Var L Bsktbl; Var L Ftbl; High Hon Roll; NHS; U Of MD; Elec Engrng.

PARRY, KIMBERLY; Cambridge-South Dorchester HS; Crapo, MD; (Y); Church Yth Grp; Latin Clb; Library Aide; Office Aide; NHS; Pres Schlr; Natl Awd Merit Top 5 Prcnt Grad Cls 86; Gen Hnrs Awd 86.

PARSAPOUR, MITRA; Seneca Valley HS; Darnestown, MD; (Y); 10/653; Church Yth Grp; Pres Service Clb; Pres Spanish Clb; Church Choir; Rep Sr Cls; Var Socr; NHS; Spanish NHS; Cmnty Wkr; Math Clb; Charlotte Symphny Young Artst Piano Wnnr 86; NC Engl Tchrs Wrtng Cont Hnrb Mntn 86; Duke; Med.

PARSON, BRETT; Laurel HS; Laurel, MD; (Y); Cmnty Wkr; Pres Chorus; Rep Frsh Cls; Rep Soph Cls; Rep Jr Cls; Capt Bsbl; Capt Ice Hcky; Cit Awd; Hon Roll; U Of MD; Law.

PARSONS, JAMES; De Matha Catholic HS; Greenbelt, MD; (Y); Crs Cntry; Ftbl; Trk; Hon Roll; Physics.

PARSONS, JON; Walter Johnson HS; Bethesda, MD; (Y); Ski Clb; JV Trk; Var Wrstlng; Hon Roll; ; Bilgcl Sci.

PARSONS III, LANE W; Mc Donough HS; White Plains, MD; (Y); Am Leg Boys St; Chess Clb; Letterman Clb; Varsity Clb; Rep Frsh Cls; Off Soph Cls; Off Jr Cls; Ftbl; Wt Lftg; Var Capt Wrstlng.

PARSONS, LISA; Western HS; Baltimore, MD; (Y); Church Yth Grp; Spanish Clb; Chorus; Church Choir; Rep Soph Cls; Rep Jr Cls; Hon Roll; NHS; Archtctrl Engr.

PARSONS, MIA; Walkersville HS; Woodsboro, MD; (Y); 4-H; GAA; JV Bsktbl; Var Capt Fld Hcky; High Hon Roll; Hon Roll; Acad Excllnce 85; All Around Stu Awd 84; Bio.

PARSONS, STEVE; Allegany HS; Cumberland, MD; (Y); 41/240; Church Yth Grp; Cmnty Wkr; Chorus; Church Choir; Swing Chorus; High Hon Roll; All Cnty Chorus 85-86; Allegany CC.

PARTLOW, PAULA L; Paint Branch HS; Silver Spring, MD; (Y); Speech Tm; Rep Stu Cncl; Var Capt Cheerleading; U Of MD; Cvl Svc.

PARTRICH, ELLEN; Richard Montgomery HS; Derwood, MD; (Y); Church Yth Grp; Stu Cncl; Cheerleading; Sftbl; Swmmng; High Hon Roll; Hon Roll; NHS; Frsh Cls; Soph Cls; Lat I, Frnch I Profcncy 85; Germ IV Profcncy 84; Med.

PARTRIDGE, STEPHANIE; Surrattsville HS; Clinton, MD; (Y); 18/297; Am Leg Aux Girls St; Jazz Band; Mrchg Band; Symp Band; Yrbk Sprt Ed; Co-Capt Var Cheerleading; Powder Puff Ftbl; Tennis; Hon Roll; Trs Jr NHS; Prince Georges Cnty Acad Excllnc Awd 85; Prince Georges Cnty Area Sci Fair Natl Wld Soc Awd 85; Dance.

PASCOE, TODD; Takoma Acad; Spokane, WA; (Y); L Trk.

PATCHAK, JENNIFER; Notre Dame Preparatory Schl; Timonium, MD; (Y); Art Clb; GAA; Varsity Clb; Yrbk Stf; Lit Mag; Var JV Bsktbl; Var Fld Hcky; Capt JV Lcrss; Jr NHS; Asst Mgr & Mgr To Be Gym Meet Comptn NDP 85-87; Mst Athltc 84-86; Cmmrcl Art.

PATE, TERESA; Forestville HS; Suitland, MD; (Y); FBLA; Political Wkr; ROTC; Teachers Aide; Chorus; Rep Jr Cls; Var Cheerleading; Gym; Mgr(s); Score Keeper; Wayne Comm; Accntnt.

PATEL, HIREN R; Gaithersburg HS; Gaithersburg, MD; (Y); 51/568; Intnl Clb; Ski Clb; Yrbk Phtg; Yrbk Rptr; Var L Tennis; Hon Roll; Jr NHS; NHS; Olympcs Mnd Wrld Fnlsts 7th Pl 86; Pres Acad Ftns Awd 86; Accptnc MD Acad Sci Cllr 86; VA Tech; Pre-Med.

PATEL, PRAKASH; Laurel HS; Laurel, MD; (Y); Art Clb; Math Clb; Badmtn; Hnr Rll Twc 85-86; Prnc Georgs Cnty Coll; Cvl Engr.

PATRICK, ROBERT; Atholton HS; Highland, MD; (Y); 30/290; Chess Clb; Church Yth Grp; Computer Clb; Math Tm; Ski Clb; Teachers Aide; Var L Crs Cntry; Var Trk; Hon Roll; Ntl Merit Ltr; Pre-Med.

PATRULA, TONYA L; Jappatowne HS; Edgewood, MD; (Y); Teachers Aide; Chorus; Hon Roll; NHS; Schltc Mert Awd 86; Pres Acad Fit Awd 86; U MD.

PATTERSON, DAVID; Dulaney SR HS; Lutherville, MD; (Y); 39/500; Ski Clb; Rep Frsh Cls; Rep Soph Cls; Rep Jr Cls; Rep Sr Cls; JV Var Bsktbl; Var Capt Golf; JV Capt Socr; Hon Roll; NHS; Bobby Bwrs Mem Glf Schlrshp 86; Fthr Mthws Awd 85; Bus.

PATTERSON, DYLAN; The Bullis Schl; Bethesda, MD; (Y); 6/89; Pres Key Clb; Hosp Aide; High Hon Roll; NHS; JV Capt Bsktbl; Var Crs Cntry; Hon Roll; NEDT Awd; Boys Clb Am; Nwsp Rptr; Furman Clg Schlrshp 86; MD ST Schlrshp 86.

PATTERSON, JASON; Walbrook SR HS; Baltimore, MD; (Y); Library Aide; ROTC; Teachers Aide; Drill Tm; Flag Corp; Lcrss; Oceangrphy.

PATTERSON, LISA; Forestville HS; Suitland, MD; (Y); Dance Clb; Hosp Aide; Teachers Aide; Lit Mag; Pom Pon; Hon Roll; Sci Fr Hon Men 86; Pom Pon Comptn 3rd & 4th Plc 85-86; Obstrcn.

PATTEY, CHRIS; Snow Hill HS; Newark, MD; (S); 7/80; Art Clb; 4-H; 4-H Awd; Hon Roll; Outstndng Achvt Art 83-84 & 84-85; MD St Champs Rifle Mrksmnshp 4-H 80, 84 & 85; Rifle 4-H 3rd St 85; MD Inst Art; Cmmrcl Art.

PATTISON, SCOT; Du Val SR HS; Bowie, MD; (Y); 1/401; Sec Am Leg Boys St; CAP; Capt ROTC; Capt Scholastic Bowl; Color Guard; Rep Jr Cls; Var L Bsbl; Var L Socr; JV L Wrstlng; Off NHS; Amelia Earhart Awd Civil Air Patrl 85; Bst Acad Vrsty Socr Plyr 86; Jessie J Warr Mem Awd 86; USAFA; Engrng.

PATTON, ANGELA; Severna Park SR HS; Arnold, MD; (Y); 86/421; AFS; Church Yth Grp; Hosp Aide; Spanish Clb; Teachers Aide; Mrchg Band; Symp Band; Hon Roll; Prsdntl Acdmc Ftnss Awd 86; U Of MD Baltimore Cnty; Med.

PATTON, NANETTE; Seneca Valley HS; Germantown, MD; (Y); 4/490; Hosp Aide; Red Cross Aide; ROTC; Science Clb; Varsity Clb; Chorus; Var L Socr; Var Trk; Var L Vllybl; High Hon Roll; Air Force Acad Appntmnt 86; Army ROTC Schrlshp 86; Navy ROTC Schlrshp 86; Naval Acad; Pol Sci.

PATTON, TRACY; Westminster HS; Finksburg, MD; (Y); Cmnty Wkr; Girl Scts; JA; Library Aide; Hon Roll.

PATZER, KARIN; Howard HS; Ellicott City, MD; (Y); 5/301; Hosp Aide; Gov Hon Prg Awd; Hon Roll; NHS; Prfct Atten Awd; Pres Schlr; St Schlr; Church Yth Grp; English Clb; Teachers Aide; Cmmnty Serv Awd 4 Yrs; Awd Outstndg Peer Tutor In The Writer Pl 86; Dstngshd Schlr Cert Of Merit; Tawson ST U; Occptnl Thrpy.

PATZWALL, SUSAN; Notre Dame Prep; Lutherville, MD; (Y); Var JV Badmtn; JV Bsktbl; Im Fld Hcky; Im Socr; High Hon Roll; NHS; NEDT Awd; Spanish NHS; Bucknell U.

PAULIKAS, NICOLE; Linganore HS; Ijamsville, MD; (Y); 11/350; Letterman Clb; School Play; Yrbk Stf; Stu Cncl; Var JV Cheerleading; Hon Roll; NHS; Drama Clb; Ski Clb; Teachers Aide; PTSA Dstngshd Schlr 84 & 86; Yth Schlr Rcpnt Lebanon Vly Coll 86; Acad Ltr Rcpnt 84-86; Pre-Med.

PAULWELL, MONIQUE; Northwestern HS; Hyattsville, MD; (Y); Church Yth Grp; Cmnty Wkr; French Clb; Hosp Aide; Model UN; Pep Clb; Church Choir; Variety Show; Stu Cncl; Hon Roll; Good Sv Rndrd Martin Lthr Kng Soc 85; 1st Rnnr Tlnt Comp Miss MD Am Coed Pgnt 85; Hm Ec Gd Stu Awd 86; Howard U; Chld Psychlgy.

PAXTON, NANCY; Magruder HS; Rockville, MD; (Y); 59/310; Art Clb; Church Yth Grp; Cmnty Wkr; Office Aide; Hon Roll; Cert Montgomery Cnty Sci Fr 84; Fnlst Miss MD Ntl Tngr Pgnt 86; Drexel U; Mrktng Mngmnt.

PAYNE, KIMBERLY; Mc Donough HS; Waldorf, MD; (S); Am Leg Aux Girls St; Office Aide; Rep Jr Cls; Pres Stu Cncl; Stat Ftbl; High Hon Roll; Hon Roll; NHS; Media Cmmnctns.

PAZIENZA, MARC; Bullis Schl; Potomac, MD; (Y); 10/89; Key Clb; SADD; Thesps; Nwsp Ed-Chief; Pres Soph Cls; JV Wrstlng; Bausch & Lomb Sci Awd; Hon Roll; Mst Outstndng Jrnlst Of Yr 86; U Rchstr; Optics.

PEACOCK, DAWN; La Plata HS; Newburg, MD; (Y); Flag Corp; Mrchg Band; High Hon Roll; Hon Roll; Jr NHS; NHS; Orthdntc Asst.

PEAK, BONNIE; Westminster SR HS; Westminster, MD; (S); DECA; Chorus; High Hon Roll; Hon Roll; 1st Pl Gen Mrktg Supervisory Lvl MD DECA ST 85-86; 2nd Pl Mdse Dec Mkg Tm MD DECA ST 85-86; Marketing.

PEAKS, TIA D; Paul L Dunbar SR HS; Baltimore, MD; (Y); 4-H; FBLA; Pep Band; Rep Frsh Cls; Rep Soph Cls; 4-H Awd; Prfct Atten Awd; Acctng.

PEARCY, CYNTHIA; Riverdale Baptist HS; Forestville, MD; (Y); Church Yth Grp; French Clb; Girl Scts; Teachers Aide; Yrbk Ed-Chief; Yrbk Phtg; Yrbk Rptr; Yrbk Stf; Hon Roll; ST Fine Arts Fest Sci Awd 2nd & Regl 2nd 82-83; Starmkr Dance Comptn Tio Tap 3rd; PE CC; Prof Europn Hstry.

PEARRE, JEFF; Liberty HS; Sykesville, MD; (S); 23/300; VP Varsity Clb; JV Bsktbl; JV Var Ftbl; Wt Lftg; High Hon Roll; Pre Professnl.

PECK, KENDRA; Allegany HS; Cumberland, MD; (Y); 102/240; AFS; Drill Tm; Frostburg ST Coll; Law.

PECK, KENDRA A; Southern Garrett HS; Oakland, MD; (S); 4/225; Library Aide; Office Aide; Q&S; Teachers Aide; Yrbk Ed-Chief; High Hon Roll; NHS; Rotary Awd; Bus Admn.

PECUNES, DOREEN; Dulaney SR HS; Cockeysville, MD; (Y); Church Yth Grp; Letterman Clb; Varsity Clb; Yrbk Ed-Chief; Bsktbl; Var JV Sftbl; JV Vllybl; Cit Awd; Hon Roll; Jr NHS.

PEELER, HEATHER; Glenlg HS; Ellicott City, MD; (Y); Church Yth Grp; Exploring; Rep Jr Cls; Rep Sr Cls; Rep Stu Cncl; Capt Crs Cntry; Trk; NHS; Cmnty Wkr; Office Aide; Schlrshp US Coast Grd Acad Proj MITE 86; MVP Crss Cntry 85-86; Engrng.

PEELER, KIRSTEN; Glenelg HS; Ellicott City, MD; (Y); Cmnty Wkr; Teachers Aide; Rep Jr Cls; Rep Sr Cls; Rep Stu Cncl; Hon Roll; Church Yth Grp; Office Aide; Red Cross Aide; Ski Clb; Leah Thorpe Mem Schlrshp Ballet 86; Intrmdt Cert & Schlrshp Peabody Prep Ballet 86; Cert Achvmnt Dance; Mount Holyoke Coll; Dance.

PEER, MARSHA; Fort Hill HS; Cumberland, MD; (Y); Pep Clb; Yrbk Stf; Frostburg ST Coll; Accntng.

PEIFFER, H KIRK; Liberty HS; Sykesville, MD; (S); Church Yth Grp; Pres German Clb; Trs Stu Cncl; NHS; Ntl Merit Ltr; NEDT Awd; Prfct Atten Awd; Math Tm; Teachers Aide; Natl Frat Stu Musicians 83 & 85.

PEITSCH, CHRISTINE; Dundalk SR HS; Baltimore, MD; (Y); 13/300; Sec Church Yth Grp; Band; Jazz Band; Pep Band; Hst Jr Cls; Rep Stu Cncl; JV Var Fld Hcky; JV Lcrss; Powder Puff Ftbl; Var Tennis; Towson ST U; Sec Educ.

PEKAR, ANTHONY; Dematha HS; Hyattsville, MD; (Y); Am Leg Boys St; 4-H; Ski Clb; Varsity Clb; Bsbl; Bsktbl; Ftbl; Lcrss; Wt Lftg; Wrstlng; MD; Bus.

PELSTRING, MICHELLE ANNE; Easton HS; Easton, MD; (Y); 5/200; Am Leg Aux Girls St; Trs French Clb; Pres Frsh Cls; Pres Soph Cls; VP Jr Cls; Var L Crs Cntry; Var L Tennis; High Hon Roll; NHS; St Schlr; Congress-Bundestag Scholar 85-86; HOBY Ldrshp Sem 84; U MD Ldrshp Sem 85; Wake Forest U.

PENDER, KIMBERLY; Forest Park SR HS; Baltimore, MD; (Y); Church Yth Grp; Drama Clb; 4-H; Church Choir; School Play; Badmtn; Vllybl; 4-H Awd; High Hon Roll; Prfct Atten Awd; Pdtrcn.

PENNEPACKER, LENNY; Sparrows Point HS; Baltimore, MD; (Y); Varsity Clb; VP Sr Cls; Stu Cncl; Var Bsbl; JV Bsktbl; Var Ftbl; High Hon Roll; Hon Roll; Voice Dem Awd; Church Yth Grp; UNC Chapel Hill; Prof Sports.

PENNINGTON, JUDY; Calvary Christian Acad; Cresaptown, MD; (Y); 2/15; Hosp Aide; Pep Clb; Chorus; Yrbk Ed-Chief; Yrbk Phtg; Sec Jr Cls; Pres Stu Cncl; L Bsktbl; L Sftbl; L Vllybl; Alderson-Broaddus Coll; Nrsng.

PENROD, ANGELA; Allegany HS; Cresaptown, MD; (Y); 27/240; AFS; Church Yth Grp; Computer Clb; Drama Clb; GAA; Girl Scts; Office Aide; Pep Clb; Ski Clb; SADD; Air Force Acad; Aerontcl Engr.

PENSKY, JASON; Bullis HS; Potomac, MD; (S); 11/93; VP Varsity Clb; Ed Nwsp Sprt Ed; Bsktbl; High Hon Roll.

PEOU, VOUCHENG; Parkdale HS; Riverdale, MD; (Y); FBLA; Teachers Aide; CC Awd; Hon Roll; Ntl Merit Schol; Pres Schlr; 1st Pl Div II C L Bricker Typwrtng Cntst 85; 1st Pl Div III 86; Potomac Persnnl Bus Studies; Accntng.

PERDEW, MICHELLE; Allegany HS; Cumberland, MD; (Y); 27/250; FBLA; Girl Scts; Band; Concert Band; Mrchg Band; Bowling; Hon Roll; Jr NHS; Mu Alp Tht; 5th Pl Bus Englsh Cmptn In FBLA 86; Top 7th Stu In Trig Cls 86; Frstbrg ST Coll; Math.

PEREGOY, STACEY ANNE; Archbishop Spalding HS; Linthicum, MD; (Y); Drama Clb; Girl Scts; Thesps; Chorus; School Play; Variety Show; Nwsp Stf; Girl Scout Slvr Ldrshp Awd 84; Towson ST U; English.

PEREZ, APRIL D; Elizabeth Seton HS; Ft Washington, MD; (Y); 5/170; Drama Clb; Teachers Aide; High Hon Roll; Acad Ltr 85; 2nd Yr Acad Ltr Pin 86; Schlrshp To Mnrty Schlrs In Engrng U Of MD 86; Bus.

PEREZ, ARELYS; Gaithersburg HS; Gaithersburg, MD; (Y); Cmnty Wkr; ROTC; Chorus; Stu Cncl; Hon Roll; NC ST; Lwyr.

PEREZ, MARIA; Georgetown Vistiation Prep Schl; Silver Spring, MD; (Y); Pres Art Clb; Computer Clb; Drama Clb; Math Clb; School Play; Stage Crew; Capt Sftbl; Hon Roll; Co-Chrm Scl Comm Local CYO Teen Clb 85.

PERINA, RAQUEL; Connelly School Of The Holy Child; Washington, DC; (Y); French Clb; Hosp Aide; Intnl Clb; Pep Clb; Service Clb; Spanish Clb; Varsity Clb; School Play; Vllybl; Spanish NHS; Mdl-For A Well Christian Svc Done; Pediatrician.

PERKINS, CARRIE ALENE; Largo HS; Bowie, MD; (Y); Church Yth Grp; Cmnty Wkr; Trs Exploring; Teachers Aide; Church Choir; Var L Tennis; Hon Roll; U MD; Pre-Pharm.

PERKINS, DESIREE; Northern SR HS; Baltimore, MD; (Y); Church Yth Grp; Cmnty Wkr; Library Aide; Math Tm; Office Aide; Political Wkr; SADD; Stu Cncl; Stat Bsktbl; Hon Roll; Eastern U; Tchr.

PERKINS, JENNIFER; Regina HS; Takoma Pk, MD; (Y); Church Yth Grp; Drama Clb; Hosp Aide; Chorus; School Play; Stage Crew; Gov Hon Prg Awd; Hon Roll; NHS; Nrsng.

PERRIRAZ, ELISABETH ANN; Flintstone Schl; Little Orleans, MD; (S); VP 4-H; Library Aide; Science Clb; Service Clb; Chorus; Nwsp Stf; Yrbk Stf; Vllybl; High Hon Roll; NHS; PJAS 2nd Pl ST 84; JR Acad Of Sci 1st Pl Bar 84; Allegany Comm Coll; Child Dvlp.

PERROT, ROSEMARIE; Dundalk HS; Baltimore, MD; (Y); Service Clb; Im Powder Puff Ftbl; JV Sftbl; Var Tennis; Im Vllybl; High Hon Roll; Hon Roll; NHS; U Of MD; Acctg.

PERRY, DIERDRE; Crossland HS; Camp Springs, MD; (Y); 23/388; Pep Clb; Science Clb; Sec Spanish Clb; Chorus; Rep Stu Cncl; Stat Bsktbl; Mgr(s); Score Keeper; High Hon Roll; Hon Roll; Acadmc Excllnce Awd 84-85; Howard U; Pre-Med.

PERRY, SHA LONDA; Crossland HS; Ft Washington, MD; (Y); Church Yth Grp; Hosp Aide; Science Clb; Band; Mrchg Band; Pep Band; Symp Band; Hon Roll; JP Sousa Awd; NHS; Bio-Chem.

PERSIANI, JIMMY; Crossland HS; Camp Spgs, MD; (Y); Nwsp Stf; Wt Lftg; Hon Roll; MD U; Accntng.

PERSON, LESLIE; Frederick Douglass HS; Upper Marlboro, MD; (Y); 35/250; Cmnty Wkr; Teachers Aide; Lit Mag; Hon Roll; Acad Excll Awd Prince Georges Cnty 83-84; Bowie ST Coll; Cmnctns.

PESTRIDGE, DAWN; Western SR HS No 407; Baltimore, MD; (Y); 54/412; Cmnty Wkr; Drama Clb; Thesps; Stage Crew; Variety Show; Hon Roll; Cert Stage Crew 84-85; Schl Ltr 2nd Yr Stage Crew 85-86; U MD Baltimore Co; Theater.

PETERS, DORIS; Calvert Christian Schl; Lusby, MD; (S); 1/6; L Cheerleading; L Var Vllybl; Cit Awd; High Hon Roll; NHS; Prfct Atten Awd; Val; Excllnce Eng Awd; Optmsts Clb Yth Apprec Awd; Homecomg Qn; Intl Rel.

PETERS, ELIZABETH; Captiol Chrst Acad; Upper Marlboro, MD; (S); 6/29; Office Aide; Teachers Aide; Varsity Clb; Chorus; School Play; Stage Crew; Sec Jr Cls; Capt Cheerleading; Hon Roll; Vocal Achvt Awd 84-85; Fshn Merch.

PETERS, ELIZABETH ANN; The Catholic HS Of Balt; Perry Hall, MD; (Y); 1/188; English Clb; SADD; Rep Stu Cncl; JV Cheerleading; High Hon Roll; NHS; St Schlr; Val; Lyla Schlrshp 86; 3rd Rnnr Up-Miss TEEN Pgnt 86; Loyola Coll; Bio.

PETERS, KAREN; Geton HS; Baltimore, MD; (Y); 1/108; Church Yth Grp; Debate Tm; NFL; Pres Speech Tm; Var Capt Badmtn; Pres Schlr; Val; GAA; Nwsp Rptr; Setonite Of The Mnth 85; Towson ST U; Nrsng.

PETERS, TERESA; Wicomico SR HS; Delmar, MD; (Y); Trs SADD; Nwsp Rptr; Rep Frsh Cls; Rep Jr Cls; Rep Sr Cls; Rep Stu Cncl; High Hon Roll; Hon Roll; NHS; SAR Awd; Clss Hstrn 86; Merit Schlstc Awd 86; Tp Anatmy Stu 86; Salisbury ST Coll; Lbrl Arts.

PETERSON, REBECCA; La Reine HS; Dunkirk, MD; (Y); 17/148; VP Pres Church Yth Grp; Yrbk Ed-Chief; JV Cheerleading; Score Keeper; JV Sftbl; Hon Roll; NHS; PG Med Soc Schlrshp, Sntrl Schlrshp; U MD Baltimore County; Med.

PETONBRINK, MARK; Glenelg HS; Sykesville, MD; (Y); Var JV Bsbl; Var JV Ftbl; Im Wt Lftg; JV Wrstlng; Engineering.

PETTIGREW, LYNN; Middletown HS; Middletown, MD; (Y); Drama Clb; SADD; Teachers Aide; Thesps; VP Trs Chorus; School Musical; Trs Jr Cls; Trs Sr Cls; Sec Stu Cncl; Ruth & Mary E Smith Schlrshp 86; Frostburg STSCNDRY Ed.

PETTY, ELISABETH; Oldfields HS; Washington, DC; (Y); 6/60; Varsity Clb; Chorus; School Musical; School Play; Fld Hcky; Lcrss; Socr; Hon Roll; Aud/Vis; Acdmc All Am 86; Dewitt Rdrs Digest Schlrsh Awd 85&86; Intl Rel.

PEZZUTI, CHRISTINE M; Andover SR HS; Linthicum Hts, MD; (Y); Church Yth Grp; Red Cross Aide; Spanish Clb; Rep Soph Cls; Rep Jr Cls; Rep Stu Cncl; Var L Cheerleading; JV Vllybl; Hon Roll; NHS.

PFEFFERKORN, KRISANN; Liberty HS; Eldersburg, MD; (S); Ski Clb; Varsity Clb; Trs Soph Cls; VP Jr Cls; Var L Cheerleading; JV Fld Hcky; High Hon Roll; Hon Roll; Accntng.

PFEIFFER, MARY E; Bel Air SR HS; Bel Air, MD; (Y); Q&S; Chorus; Color Guard; Lit Mag; Hon Roll; Cornelia Archr Schlrshp 86; Harford CC Hnrs Schlrshp 86; Jurrs Awd HS Art Shw 86; Harford CC; Mass Comm.

PHEARS, VANESSA; Oakland Mills HS; Columbia, MD; (Y); Teachers Aide; Sec Church Choir; Rep Frsh Cls; Rep Sr Cls; High Hon Roll; 2nd Pl Howard Cnty Cltn Blck Hstry Pstr/Essy Cntst 85; Spnsh Excel 86; Alpha Phi Alpha Frng Lang Excel; Morgan ST U; Phlsphy.

PHEBUS, CONSTANCE; Catoctin HS; Thurmont, MD; (Y); Church Yth Grp; Drama Clb; Sec Letterman Clb; Varsity Clb; Band; Concert Band; Mrchg Band; Off Stu Cncl; Capt Var Cheerleading; Hon Roll; Schl Chrldr Awd 86; Frederick CC.

PHILLIPS, D SCOTT; Colonel Richardson HS; Federalsburg, MD; (Y); Boy Scts; Church Yth Grp; Drama Clb; Trs French Clb; Rep Stu Cncl; Tennis; Gov Hon Prg Awd; High Hon Roll; Hon Roll; NHS; Salisbury ST Coll; Bus Admin.

PHILLIPS, GINA; North Dorchester HS; Vienna, MD; (Y); 2/125; Am Leg Aux Girls St; Computer Clb; Keywanettes; Elks Awd; Gov Hon Prg Awd; High Hon Roll; NHS; Pres Schlr; Sal; St Schlr; E New Market/Secy Ruritan Schlrp 86; Monroe CC; Lib Arts.

PHILLIPS, KAMELIA; Friendly HS; Ft Washington, MD; (Y); Cmnty Wkr; Library Aide; Spanish Clb; Teachers Aide; Yrbk Stf; High Hon Roll; Hon Roll; NHS; Spanish NHS; 3rd Plc Awd Sci Fr 85; Acdmc Exclnc Awd 85; UCLA; Pdtrcn.

PHILLIPS, KRISTIN L; Perryville HS; Perryville, MD; (Y); FBLA; FHA; Intnl Clb; Math Tm; Varsity Clb; Concert Band; Mrchg Band; VP Soph Cls; Stu Cncl; Cheerleading; Presdntl Acad Fitness Board; U Of MD-COLLEGE Pk.

PHILLIPS, TODD M; North Dorchester HS; Vienna, MD; (Y); 1/133; Q&S; School Play; Nwsp Rptr; Yrbk Rptr; Yrbk Stf; VP Jr Cls; Elks Awd; VP NHS; Val; Computer Clb; MD Distngshd Schlr Fin 86; Amer Lg Awd; U MD; Aerospc Engrng.

PHILLIPS, TOM; Parkside HS; Eden, MD; (Y); Church Yth Grp; JA; Hon Roll; Parkside Acad Achvt Awd 85-86; Outdoor Fld.

PHILLIPS III, WILLIAM; Loyola HS; Timonium, MD; (Y); Church Yth Grp; Cmnty Wkr; FCA; Ski Clb; SADD; Chorus; JV Var Ftbl; Im Lcrss; Physcs Hnrs Clss 86-87; Aerontcl Engrng.

PHIPPS, HOLLY; Dulaney SR HS; Timonium, MD; (Y); Dance Clb; Variety Show; Yrbk Bus Mgr; Yrbk Stf; Rep Frsh Cls; Rep Soph Cls; Rep Sr Cls; Var Cheerleading; Hon Roll; NHS; Pres Ftns Awd 84-85; Bus Admn.

PIASKOWSKI, LISA; Woodlawn HS; Baltimore, MD; (Y); FBLA; Ski Clb; Spanish Clb; Mrchg Band; Stage Crew; Symp Band; Stu Cncl; Var Fld Hcky; Var Lcrss; Hon Roll; Young Life Woodlawn Chptr 84-87; Coll William & Mary; Psych.

PICKARD, CHERYL; Oxon Hill Science & Tech Center; Ft Washington, MD; (Y); Teachers Aide; Stu Cncl; Gov Hon Prg Awd; High Hon Roll; Ntl Merit Ltr; Spanish NHS; U Of TX; Accntnt.

PICKENS, CARMEN; Western HS; Baltimore, MD; (Y); 65/412; Church Yth Grp; Drama Clb; Thesps; Band; Chorus; Concert Band; Drill Tm; Mrchg Band; Howard U; Mgmt Info Systms.

PICKETT, JAY; Westminster HS; Westminster, MD; (Y); 45/500; Church Yth Grp; Rep Frsh Cls; L Socr; Hon Roll; Pres Schlr; Typng Awd 84; Liberty U; Comp Sci.

PIEKLO, HELENA; St Johns At Prospect Hall; Walkersville, MD; (Y); Church Yth Grp; Teachers Aide; JV Bsktbl; Var Tennis; Var Vllybl; High Hon Roll; NHS; Math.

PIEPER, FRANCINE; Fallston HS; Fallston, MD; (Y); Var Hosp Aide; Var SADD; Var Varsity Clb; Yrbk Stf; JV Bsktbl; Im Powder Puff Ftbl; Var Capt Sftbl; Var Capt Vllybl; Hon Roll; Prfct Atten Awd; U Of DE; Bus Admin.

PIERCE, SAMUEL; Highland View Acad; Rising Sun, MD; (Y); Church Yth Grp; Cmnty Wkr; Off Sr Cls; Im Bsktbl; Im Ftbl; Var Socr; Im Sftbl; Im Vllybl; Outstndng Sprtsmnshp Letter 83-84; Outstndng Sprtsmnshp Schlrshp 83-84; Coll Sccr Schlrshp 85-86; Columbia Union Coll; Bus.

PIERCE, SHAWN; Kenwood SR HS; Balto County, MD; (Y); Boy Scts; Drama Clb; SADD; Concert Band; Flag Corp; Jazz Band; School Musical; Stage Crew; Rep Stu Cncl; Cheerleading; Balto Cnty Stu Cncl Rgnl Exec Brd 85-87; ROTC; Data Proc.

PIERRE PHILIPPE, RICHARD N; Loyola Blakefield HS; Columbia, MD; (S); Church Yth Grp; French Clb; Orch; JV VP Wrstlng; NHS; Pre-Med.

PIKE, ARNE; Wootton HS; Rockville, MD; (Y); Ski Clb; JV Var Bsbl; Var Capt Ftbl; Hon Roll; NHS; Engrng.

PILARSKI, JERRI LYNN; Mercy HS; Baltimore, MD; (Y); French Clb; GAA; Variety Show; Var Capt Cheerleading; VP NHS; JR Miss Baltimore Cnty 86; 2nd Pl Ballet Solo Strmkr Comp 86; 1st Pl Ballet Duo Strmkr Comp 85; Dance-Theatre.

PIMENTO, WANDA; Western HS; Baltimore, MD; (Y); 161/467; Church Yth Grp; Chorus; 4R Deacnss Awd 85; Howard U; Acctg.

PIN, SAYNI; Havre De Grace HS; Havre De Grace, MD; (Y); 4/140; Hosp Aide; Hon Roll; NHS; Prfct Atten Awd; Pres Acad Fit Awd 86; Schl Ltr Cmmnty Svc 86; Svc Awd Cert 86; Harford CC; Phrmclgst.

PINDER III, WILLIAM D; Elkton HS; Elkton, MD; (Y); Am Leg Boys St; Church Yth Grp; Key Clb; Nwsp Stf; Stu Cncl; Bsbl; Ftbl; Hon Roll; NHS; Prfct Atten Awd; Greater Elktn Jycs Schlrshp 86; Senatorial Schlrshp 86; Ntl Yng Ldrs Cnfrnc 86; Towson ST U; Engl.

PINEDA, MARIA; Woodward HS; Rockville, MD; (Y); Intnl Clb; SADD; Hotel Bus.

PINKNEY, WANDA; Laplata HS; Faulkner, MD; (Y); FHA; Teachers Aide; Church Choir; Cit Awd; Hon Roll; Cert Of Recgntn From Fashion Show 85; Modeling.

PINTO, MONICA; Annapolis Senior HS; Annapolis, MD; (Y); 5/520; VP Frsh Cls; Rep Sr Cls; Rep Stu Cncl; JV Socr; High Hon Roll; Hon Roll; NHS; Pres Schlr; JV Var Socr; MD Distngshd Schlr 85-86; Mentorshp Prog US Naval Acad 85-86; Loyola Coll.

PIO RODA, CLARO; Mc Donogh Schl; Lutherville, MD; (Y); Church Yth Grp; German Clb; Band; Variety Show; Nwsp Rptr; Yrbk Sprt Ed; Bsktbl; Var Capt Golf; Var JV Socr; Im Tennis; Vrsty Golf Coachs Awd 85-86; Md Gold & Cntry Club Invtntl Boys 14-15 Wnnr 85; Engr.

PIOVESAN, RUSSELL; Calvert HS; Huntingtown, MD; (Y); Latin Clb; ROTC; JV Ftbl; Rifle Tm Capt Awd 85; Sharpshooter Awd 85; Sailsbury; Bio.

PISAPIA, JOSEPH; Kent County HS; Galena, MD; (Y); Church Yth Grp; Radio Clb; Spanish Clb; Pres Frsh Cls; Rep Soph Cls; Rep Stu Cncl; Var L Bsbl; Stat L Bsktbl; Var Capt Ftbl; Hon Roll; Electd Yth Rep St Dennis Prsh Cncl 86-87; Electd MVP Chrch Leag Bsktbl 85; Commnctns.

PISHIONERI, GINA; Walkersville HS; Walkersville, MD; (Y); 7/250; Church Yth Grp; Scholastic Bowl; Teachers Aide; Color Guard; Drill Tm; Sec Frsh Cls; High Hon Roll; Hon Roll; NHS; GAA; 2nd Pl Schl Sci Fr 85.

PITTMAN, ARNOLD; Southern HS; Baltimore, MD; (Y); Computer Clb; Office Aide; Spanish Clb; Teachers Aide; School Play; Stu Cncl; JV Bsbl; High Hon Roll; Hon Roll; MD Coll; Navy.

PLAUGER, JOELLE E; Southern Garrett HS; Mt Lake Park, MD; (S); German Clb; VP Pep Clb; SADD; Nwsp Stf; VP Pres Jr Cls; Rep Stu Cncl; High Hon Roll; Hon Roll; NHS; Awd Handbells For Grad 84-85; Chairprsn Stu Cncl 85-86; Med.

PLEASANTS, ANGELA MICHELE; John F Kennedy HS; Silver Spring, MD; (Y); 166/468; Church Yth Grp; Cmnty Wkr; Chorus; Stu Cncl; Var Capt Bsktbl; Var L Trk; Var L Vllybl; FCA; Teachers Aide; Varsity Clb; Athl Schlrshp U CT 86-90; Supr Writing Awd 85; Natl Achvt Schlrshp Pgm Negro Stud Cmmnd Schlr 85; U CT; Hist.

PLEINES, C LISA; Randallstown SR HS; Baltimore, MD; (Y); Latin Clb; JV Sftbl; JV Vllybl; Hon Roll; Brd Of Trsts Merit Grnt Towson St U 85-86; Erly Admtnc To Clg Skip SR Yr 85-86; Gifted & Tlntd 80-85; George Washington U; Intl Stds.

PLEINES, KRISTEN; South Carroll HS; Mt Airy, MD; (Y); Ski Clb; Band; Concert Band; Mrchg Band; Symp Band; Hon Roll; NHS; UMBC.

PLOTT, GRETCHEN; Hancock HS; Hancock, MD; (Y); 2/50; Boys Clb Am; Church Yth Grp; Rptr 4-H; FHA; SADD; Band; Chorus; Capt Color Guard; Concert Band; Mrchg Band; 1st Mid Atlantic Region Girls Club Am Poetry Cntst 85; U MD Baltimore Co; Psych.

PLOWDEN, SARAH; Patterson HS; Baltimore, MD; (Y); Pres Church Yth Grp; Computer Clb; Hosp Aide; Pres Church Choir; Im Bsbl; Bsktbl; Ftbl; Sftbl; Trk; Capt Vllybl; U Of MD; Comp Sci.

PLUMMER, JENNY; North Hagerstown HS; Hagerstown, MD; (Y); 4-H; French Clb; Latin Clb; Ski Clb; Varsity Clb; Hst Stu Cncl; Var Tennis; 4 H Teen Cncl 85-86; U MD-BALTIMORE; Engl.

PLUMMER, TAMMY; Fort Hill HS; Cumberland, MD; (Y); Church Yth Grp; Pep Clb; Teachers Aide; Hon Roll; NEDT Awd; Elem Ed.

POE, LYNN; Northwestern HS; Adelphi, MD; (Y); Debate Tm; Girl Scts; Office Aide; ROTC; Color Guard; Stu Cncl; Stat Coach Actv; Mgr(s); Pom Pon; Hon Roll; Maryland U; Law.

POE, NICHELLE A; Central HS; Suitland, MD; (Y); Intnl Clb; Trs Soph Cls; Trs Jr Cls; Trs Sr Cls; Trs Stu Cncl; Var Capt Cheerleading; High Hon Roll; Hon Roll; Trs Jr NHS; NHS; Omega Psi Phi Gamma Pi Chptr Schprshp 86; Sprntndnts Acdmc Awd 84-86; Law.

POINDEXTER, THOMAS; Thomas S Wootton HS; Rockville, MD; (Y); Church Yth Grp; Science Clb; Ski Clb; Stat Socr; Var JV Swmmng.

POIRIER, MARIE-CHRISTINE; Walter Johnson HS; Bethesda, MD; (Y); Art Clb; Office Aide; Teachers Aide; Varsity Clb; School Musical; Yrbk Phtg; Yrbk Stf; Fld Hcky; Smithsonian Intrnshp 86; Strathmore Art Cont 1st 86; Photo Journalism.

POKORNY, CHERYL LYN; Linganore HS; Monrovia, MD; (Y); 1/267; Church Yth Grp; Pres FFA; Spanish Clb; Church Choir; JV Fld Hcky; Var L Sftbl; Var L Tennis; Lion Awd; NHS; Val; Deans Schlrshp 86; Amer Lgn Gld Str Pst 191 Schlrshp 86; Sigma Xi Sci Awd 86; Wstrn MD Coll; Biolgy.

POLHAMUS, JOHN; Fallston HS; Fallston, MD; (Y); 20/251; Church Yth Grp; Pres German Clb; SADD; Yrbk Stf; Var L Crs Cntry; Im Ftbl; Var L Lcrss; JV Wrstlng; Hon Roll; NHS; Sigma Xi Sci Awd 86; NHS Germn Stu 86; Engrng.

POLK, LA CHANDA; La Reine HS; Suitland, MD; (Y); Math Clb; Trk; Pres Church Yth Grp; Pep Clb; Spanish Clb; Drill Tm; Var Cheerleading; Natl Chem Awd 85-86; Sci Fair 84-85; U NC; Engrng.

POMERANCE, ROBIN D; Annapolis SR HS; Annapolis, MD; (Y); 29/520; Drama Clb; Spanish Clb; Color Guard; Orch; School Musical; Var Capt Crs Cntry; Var L Trk; NHS; X-C 13th In Anne Arundel Cnty 83; X-C 7th In A A Cnty, 38th In St Of MD 84; X-C 17th In A A Cnty 85; U Of CA; Spanish Interpreting.

POMERANTZ, PHYLLIS M; Winston Churchill HS; Potomac, MD; (Y); 183/612; Temple Yth Grp; Yrbk Stf; Sec Frsh Cls; Rep Stu Cncl; Hon Roll; IN U Schl Music; Ballet.

POMS, KARI; Charles W Woodward HS; Rockville, MD; (Y); Red Cross Aide; SADD; Teachers Aide; Off Frsh Cls; Off Soph Cls; Sec Jr Cls; Off Sr Cls; Stu Cncl; Capt Pom Pon; Sftbl; U MD; Bio.

PONTIUS, KATIE; Heritage Acad; Clear Spring, MD; (S); 4/25; Sec Q&S; Chorus; School Play; Nwsp Sprt Ed; Yrbk Ed-Chief; Var Im Bsktbl; Var Sftbl; Capt Vllybl; Hon Roll; Ntl Merit Ltr; ST Chmpn Humorous Rdg MACS FAF 85; Teen Colmnst For Herald Mail Hagerstown 85-86; Cedarville Coll; Law.

POOLE, ALLEN; Calvert HS; Pr Frederick, MD; (Y); 15/265; Wt Lftg; Wrstlng; Prfct Atten Awd; U MD College Pk; Elec Engrng.

POOLE, JAMES; Chopticon HS; Charlotte Hall, MD; (Y); 1/200; Aud/Vis; Computer Clb; Model UN; Radio Clb; VP Soph Cls; VP Stu Cncl; High Hon Roll; NHS; Drama Clb; Intnl Clb; 4.0 Avg Awd 84-86; Semi-Fin Stu ST Brd Ed 86; Polit Sci.

POOLE, JULIE A; Parkside HS; Salisbury, MD; (Y); 2/253; Art Clb; Church Yth Grp; Trs French Clb; VP Girl Scts; Sec Math Tm; Lit Mag; God Cntry Awd; Hon Roll; NHS; Ntl Merit SF; Girl Sct Gold Awd 86; James Madison U; Chldhd Ed.

POOLE, LUCIA; Thomas Stone HS; Waldorf, MD; (S); FHA; Office Aide; Teachers Aide; Off Jr Cls; Hon Roll; MD U; Intr Dsgn.

POOLE, MICHELLE; Harford Vocational-Technical HS; Bel Air, MD; (Y); VICA; Hon Roll; Cosmetology.

POPE, LYDIA; Crossland HS; Temple Hills, MD; (Y); Teachers Aide; Hon Roll; Nght Clb Mgmt.

PORTCH, KEVIN T; Paint Branch HS; Silver Spring, MD; (Y); 99/337; Var Ftbl; Var Wrstlng; 4th Pl Montgomery Cnty & MD Regional Wrestling 85-86; Engrng.

PORTER, CHERISE; Paul Lawrence Dunbar SR HS; Baltimore, MD; (Y); FBLA; Pep Clb; VP Sr Cls; Cit Awd; High Hon Roll; Hon Roll; Prfct Atten Awd; U Of Baltimore; Acctg.

PORTER, DENISE; Patterson HS; Baltimore, MD; (Y); JA; Band; JV Var Bsktbl; Hon Roll; Hon-Cmmnwlth Prgm 86; Morgan ST U; Engrng.

PORTER, MELODY; Franklin SR HS; Reisterstown, MD; (Y); FBLA; Intnl Clb; Yrbk Stf; High Hon Roll; Jr NHS; NHS; Ntl Merit Ltr.

PORTER, NEIL ERIC; Brunswick HS; Brunswick, MD; (Y); 8/147; Church Yth Grp; Cmnty Wkr; Drama Clb; Library Aide; Office Aide; Chorus; School Musical; School Play; Stage Crew; Swing Chorus; Md St Schlr Athl 86; All Lge Ftbl 85-86; Schlrshp Awd 85; Bridgewater Coll; Hlth/Phys Ed.

PORTER, TINA; Allegany HS; Lavale, MD; (Y); 15/270; AFS; Drama Clb; Hosp Aide; Nwsp Ed-Chief; Nwsp Rptr; Yrbk Stf; Rep Frsh Cls; NHS; Med.

POSER, TOBY; Mc Donogh Schl; Baltimore, MD; (Y); AFS; Chorus; School Musical; School Play; Off Sr Cls; Var Tennis; NCTE Awd; Drama Clb; French Clb; Office Aide; Cls Of 40 Awd 84-85; Dedication Cup 85-86; Crtv Wrtng.

POSTEN, JENNIFER; Northern HS; Huntingtown, MD; (Y); Girl Scts; Teachers Aide; Mrchg Band; Orch; School Play; Nwsp Ed-Chief; Ed Yrbk Stf; Stat Sftbl; Stat Wrstlng; Hon Roll; U Of MD; Educ.

POSTEN, RAYMOND RYAN; Northern HS; Huntingtown, MD; (Y); 78/301; Boy Scts; CAP; Science Clb; Varsity Clb; Chorus; Nwsp Stf; Lcrss; Var Capt Wrstlng; Hon Roll; MD ST Sntrl Schlrshp 86; Mst Outstndng Wrstlr Coaches Awd 86; U Of MD; Aerosp Engrng.

POSTEN, TAMMY; Capitolchristian Acad; Upper Marlboro, MD; (S); 1/27; Church Yth Grp; Cmnty Wkr; French Clb; Letterman Clb; Office Aide; Teachers Aide; Varsity Clb; Church Choir; Yrbk Ed-Chief; VP Jr Cls; Hmecmng Queen 85; 2nd Pl Spch Cntst; 3rd Rnnr Up MD Mdrn Miss Teen Schlrshp Pgnt 84; Prince Georges CC; Nrsng.

POSTON, JANICE; Thomas S Wootton HS; Rockville, MD; (Y); Pres Trs Church Yth Grp; JA; Teachers Aide; Band; Concert Band; Pep Band; Var Bsktbl; Var Sftbl; Hon Roll; AIM Summer Pgm USCGA 86; Geog.

POTTER, GRAEME M; Northern HS; Dunkirk, MD; (Y); Church Yth Grp; Debate Tm; Acpl Chr; Band; Chorus; Concert Band; Jazz Band; Mrchg Band; Pep Band; Swing Chorus; Marine Corps Awd-Sci Excllnc 86; Math Awd 86; U Of DE; Anthrplgy.

POTTER, LYNN; Northern HS; Dunkirk, MD; (Y); 4-H; Library Aide; Band; Concert Band; Mrchg Band; Symp Band; Hon Roll; Ntl Merit SF; St Schlr; Awd 4th Hghst GPA Cls 84; U MD Coll Pk; Bus Mngmnt.

POTTS, DAVID; Takoma Acad; Silver Spring, MD; (S); Church Yth Grp; Office Aide; Band; Orch; Trs Stu Cncl; Hon Roll; NHS; Columbia Union Coll; Bio.

POUNCEY, KAREN; Calvert HS; Solomons, MD; (Y); Pres Church Yth Grp; Band; Nwsp Stf; Yrbk Stf; Sec Frsh Cls; Pres Sr Cls; Stu Cncl; Stat Fld Hcky; Lcrss; Concert Band; U MD.

POVEROMO, LORI; Academy Of The Holy Cross; Rockville, MD; (Y); 20/116; Church Yth Grp; French Clb; Latin Clb; Pep Clb; Nwsp Stf; Rep Frsh Cls; JV Cheerleading; Powder Puff Ftbl; Sec Trs French Hon Soc; High Hon Roll; Ntl Latin Exam Cum Lude 85; Ntl Music Gld Awd 84-85.

POWEL, NANCY; Mc Donogh Schl; Union Bridge, MD; (Y); 37/127; Art Clb; Cmnty Wkr; Pres 4-H; Key Clb; Office Aide; Variety Show; Rep Frsh Cls; Rep Soph Cls; Rep Jr Cls; Stu Cncl; 4-H Dairy Jdgng Tm Wn Natl Cont 85; Carroll Cnty Frm Qn 85; Carroll Cnty Dairy Towl Tm Cptn 85; Dairy Sci.

POWELL, DAMON A; De Matha Catholic HS; Upper Marlboro, MD; (Y); 139/255; Art Clb; Band; Jazz Band; Pep Band; Im Bsktbl; Ntl Merit SF; Im Crs Cntry; Im Trk; Pep Clb; Concert Band.

POWELL, MARY; Elizabeth Seton HS; Bladensburg, MD; (Y); Church Yth Grp; Ski Clb; Spanish Clb; SADD; Trk; Fshn Dsgn.

POWELL, NATHAN; Forest Park SR HS; Baltimore, MD; (Y); Computer Clb; Math Tm; Stu Cncl; Bsktbl; NHS; Prfct Atten Awd; Comp.

POWELL, ROBIN; Institute Of Notre Dame HS; Baltimore, MD; (Y); Chorus; Hon Roll; Prfct Atten Awd; Scl Wrk.

POWELL, SUSAN; Brunswick HS; Brunswick, MD; (Y); Church Yth Grp; Computer Clb; FBLA; Band; Concert Band; Mrchg Band; Pep Band; Nwsp Rptr; Nwsp Stf; Hon Roll; Band Dirctrs Awd 86; Hagerstown Beauty Schl; Csmtlgy.

POWERS, KAREN E; Smithsburg HS; Ft Ritchie, MD; (Y); 1/188; Trs Church Yth Grp; Spanish Clb; Church Choir; Stage Crew; Var Sftbl; JV Var Vllybl; NHS; Val; Ski Clb; Symp Band; Pres Acdmc Ftns Awd 86; MD Dist Schlr SF 86; Chas A Summers Awd Athl W/Highest GPA 86; Shippensburg U PA; Aerosp Engr.

PRANGE, STEPHANIE; Oakland Mills HS; Columbia, MD; (Y); Church Yth Grp; Hosp Aide; JCL; Band; Chorus; School Musical; Swing Chorus; JV L Vllybl; High Hon Roll; Pres NHS; Hstry.

PRANGLEY, MICHAEL; De Matha Catholic HS; Bowie, MD; (Y); Boys Clb Am; Cmnty Wkr; Political Wkr; Im Bsbl; Im Bsktbl; Hon Roll; Meterology.

PRATT, CHERYL E; Potomac HS; Oxon Hill, MD; (Y); Aud/Vis; FBLA; Girl Scts; Library Aide; ROTC; Im Vllybl; U Of MD; Bus Adm.

PRATT, DANDRA; The Institute Of Notre Dame; Baltimore, MD; (Y); Art Clb; Church Yth Grp; French Clb; Stage Crew; Rep Soph Cls; JV Badmtn; Hon Roll; Anasthslgy.

PRAUHS, PATRICIA H; Walt Whitman HS; Bethesda, MD; (Y); 169/445; 4-H; Hosp Aide; JA; Ski Clb; Honrbl Merit-Maxima Cum Laude-Natl Latin Exam 85; MD U; Busnss Mgmt.

PRENDERGAST, HOPE; Bishop Walsh HS; Cumbuerland, MD; (Y); 28/104; Cmnty Wkr; Drama Clb; Pep Clb; Science Clb; Speech Tm; School Musical; School Play; Stage Crew; Variety Show; Hon Roll; Schl Lttr For Drama; Psych.

PRESS, KEN; Oakland Mills HS; Columbia, MD; (Y); Chess Clb; Ski Clb; Teachers Aide; Hst Frsh Cls; Rep Stu Cncl; Bnai Brith Yth Org Pres, V-Pres & Sec; Bus.

PRESSLEY, ZIONNE; Elizabeth Seton HS; Washington, DC; (Y); Trs Pres Church Yth Grp; Pep Clb; Spanish Clb; Speech Tm; Nwsp Bus Mgr; Nwsp Rptr; Hon Roll; Cmnty Wkr; Debate Tm; Office Aide; Hugh O Brien Youth Ldrshp Awd 85; Amer Assn Blacks Energy 1st Pl 86; MD ST Bar Assoc Comp Awd 86; Law.

PRICE, DAWN; St Marys HS; Davidsonville, MD; (Y); Church Yth Grp; Hosp Aide; Ski Clb; Spanish Clb; Yrbk Stf; JV Fld Hcky; Hon Roll; St Benedict; Engrg.

PRICE III, JOHN H; Parkville HS; Baltimore, MD; (Y); Civic Clb; Cmnty Wkr; Varsity Clb; Stage Crew; Var L Wrstlng; Hllndale Elem Schlrshp Awd 86; Loch Raven Middle Schlrshp Awd 86; Towson T U; Sec Ed.

PRICE, JULIE; Northwester SR HS; Univ Pk, MD; (S); French Clb; Latin Clb; Chorus; Rep Stu Cncl; Capt Pom Pon; Hon Roll; Jr NHS; Kiwanis Awd; Pres NHS; Superintndnts Awd 83; MD Distngushd Schlr 85; U Park Womens Clb Schlrshp 86; Dickinson Coll; Frnch.

PRICE, LINNEA V; Middletown HS; Braddock Heights, MD; (Y); 29/189; German Clb; Latin Clb; Chorus; Concert Band; Jazz Band; Mrchg Band; School Musical; Lit Mag; Hon Roll; JP Sousa Awd; Natl Merit Commnd Schlr 86; U MD; Music Perf.

PRICE, MIMI; Archbishop Keough HS; Balt, MD; (Y); Art Clb; Church Yth Grp; German Clb; Latin Clb; Political Wkr; Stage Crew; Soph Cls; Jr Cls; Im Bsktbl; Hon Roll; Ntl Latin Exam Slvr Mdlst 86; Cert Excllnc Latin 86.

PRICE, SONIA; Forestville HS; Suitland, MD; (Y); Church Yth Grp; VP Soph Cls; VP Jr Cls; Stu Cncl; Pom Pon; High Hon Roll; Hon Roll; Kiwanis Awd; Ntl Merit Schol; Rotary Awd; St John GME Schlrshp $1000 86; Hampton U; Nrsng.

PRICE, WADE; Loyola HS; White Hall, MD; (Y); Church Yth Grp; Library Aide; Nwsp Bus Mgr; Var Crs Cntry; Var Trk; Hon Roll; Cmmnctns.

PRICKETT, ROSALYN; Westminster HS; Westminster, MD; (Y); AFS; Exploring; Sec Spanish Clb; Teachers Aide; Lit Mag; Gov Hon Prg Awd; High Hon Roll; NHS; Pres Schlr; St Schlr; Soc Studys Awd; American U; Cmmnctns.

PRILLMAN, CARLOS; Fairmont Heights HS; Lanham, MD; (Y); Church Yth Grp; JA; ROTC; Rptr Nwsp Rptr; Pres Jr Cls; Var Capt Ftbl; Cit Awd; High Hon Roll; Hon Roll; NHS; Awd Mltry Ordr Wrld Wrs Cert & ROTC Mdl 85; Awd Acdmc Exclince 84; Edtr Chf Schl Nwspaper 86; U Maryland; Jrnlsm.

PRIMACK, BRIAN; Montgomery Blair HS; Silver Spg, MD; (Y); Trs Drama Clb; Capt Math Tm; Quiz Bowl; Capt Scholastic Bowl; Pres Ski Clb; Thesps; School Musical; Stage Crew; Trs Frsh Cls; Bausch & Lomb Sci Awd; MD Dstngshd Schlr 86; U MD Math Cmptn Awd 86; U MD Hnr Schlrshp 82-86.

PRINGLE, LISA; St Michaels HS; St Michaels, MD; (Y); GAA; Band; Nwsp Stf; Fld Hcky; Sftbl; Hon Roll; Rep Frsh Cls; Pres Soph Cls; Pres Jr Cls; Rep Stu Cncl; Fshn Intr Dsgn.

PRITCHARD, JENNY; Friendly HS; Ft Washington, MD; (Y); 7/400; Band; Concert Band; Mrchg Band; Var L Bsktbl; Var L Sftbl; Var L Vllybl; Hon Roll; NHS; Acad Excllnc Awd 84-85; Latin Natl Hnr Soc 86; Physcl Thrpy.

PRITCHETT, CASSANDRA; Regina HS; Washington, DC; (Y); Aud/Vis; Church Yth Grp; Cmnty Wkr; Office Aide; Pep Clb; Chorus; School Musical; School Play; VP Jr Cls; Pres Sr Cls; Canadian Stu Exchng 84-85; Natl Hnr Soc 85-86; Towson U; Engrng.

PROCTOR, MICHELLE; Hammond HS; Jessup, MD; (Y); Church Yth Grp; French Clb; Math Tm; Church Choir; Cheerleading; Co-Capt Pom Pon; Trk; High Hon Roll; NHS; Variety Show; Ebony Schlrshp Soc Awd 85; Bus.

PROPHETER, KATHERINE; Dulaney HS; Glen Arm, MD; (Y); JV Var Fld Hcky; Powder Puff Ftbl; Var Sftbl; Hon Roll; JC Awd; Mst Vlbl Plyr JV Fld Hcky 84-85; Psych.

PROPST, SCOTT; Oldtown HS; Cumberland, MD; (S); Pres Computer Clb; Nwsp Ed-Chief; Rep Frsh Cls; Rep Soph Cls; Pres Jr Cls; VP Stu Cncl; JV Var Bsktbl; JV Var Socr; NHS; NEDT Awd.

PROVINCE, SUSAN; Montgomery Blair HS; Silver Spring, MD; (Y); Church Yth Grp; SADD; Church Choir; Pres Stage Crew; Nwsp Stf; Score Keeper; Var Mgr Vllybl; Hon Roll; Commctns.

PRYOR, SCOTT; Smithsburg HS; Smithsburg, MD; (Y); 44/193; Latin Clb; Office Aide; Bsktbl; Socr; All Monoccy Vly Athl Leag Hnbl Mntn Tm Sccr 86; All Cnty 2nd Tm Sccr 86; Hagerstown JC; Data Proc.

PTASHEK, AMY; T S Wootton HS; Potomac, MD; (Y); Dance Clb; Drama Clb; Intnl Clb; Teachers Aide; Temple Yth Grp; School Play; Mgr(s); Pom Pon; Sftbl; Hon Roll; Physcl Thrpy.

PUGH, JUNNETTE; Gwynn Park HS; Accokeek, MD; (Y); Pres Jr Cls; Pres Sr Cls; Rep Stu Cncl; Var L Cheerleading; Hon Roll; NHS; Acad Excllnce Awd 85; Soc Studs Awd 86; Jesse J Warr Jr Mem Awd 86; U PA; Acctng.

PUHALA, KIMBERLY; Walt Whitman HS; Bethesda, MD; (Y); Art Clb; Church Yth Grp; Cmnty Wkr; Yrbk Phtg; JV Sftbl; Hon Roll; U Of CA; Socl Sci.

PUKALSKI, CHRISTOPHER; Archbishop Curley HS; Baltimore, MD; (Y); 7/136; Aud/Vis; Hosp Aide; Library Aide; Science Clb; Lit Mag; Rep Frsh Cls; Rep Soph Cls; Rep Jr Cls; Rep Sr Cls; Hon Roll; Acad Lttr 86; Meritorious Awd 85; Loyola Coll; Bus.

PUMPHREY, DENISE; Institute Of Notre Dame; Baltimore, MD; (Y); French Clb; Service Clb; Stage Crew; Townson ST; Elem Ed.

PUNZALAN, CECILE M; The Bryn Mawr Schl; Towson, MD; (Y); Model UN; Quiz Bowl; Chorus; Ed Nwsp Stf; Ed Lit Mag; Hon Roll; Ntl Merit SF; Yale Bk Awd 85; Svc Awd 84.

PURBAUGH, JULIA; Beall HS; Frostburg, MD; (Y); Art Clb; CAP; Girl Scts; Library Aide; Pep Clb; Band; Color Guard; Flag Corp; Yrbk Stf; Capt Twrlr; Ushrs Clb Secy & VP 83-87; Allegany CC; Nrsg.

PURCELL, KYLELANE; The Bryn Mawr Schl; Baltimore, MD; (Y); Church Yth Grp; Model UN; Service Clb; SADD; Acpl Chr; Chorus; Madrigals; Nwsp Rptr; Var Capt Socr; Library Aide; Washington U St Louis; Intl Rel.

PURCELL, LISA; Suitland HS; Forestville, MD; (Y); Dance Clb; Hosp Aide; Pep Clb; Teachers Aide; Drm Mjr(t); Rep Stu Cncl; Var Cheerleading; High Hon Roll; Hon Roll; Sci Fair Wnnr 85; Cert Achvmnt Accmplshmnt Dnc 84; Achvmnt Outstndg Wrk Chld Grwth & Dvlpmnt 85; UMBC; Med Tech.

PURDUM, AMY; Westminster HS; New Windsor, MD; (Y); Debate Tm; GAA; Ski Clb; Speech Tm; Yrbk Stf; Stu Cncl; Cheerleading; Gym; Socr; Hon Roll; Al Cnty Sccr Select Tm 85-86; Reml Athlt Wk 85-86; Semi-Fnl Rgnl Trnmt-Sccr 85-86; Psych.

PURDY, TINA; Northern HS; Owings, MD; (Y); Varsity Clb; Flag Corp; Nwsp Bus Mgr; Nwsp Stf; Yrbk Bus Mgr; Yrbk Stf; Pom Pon; Hon Roll; Prfct Atten Awd.

PUSEY, JENNIFER; James M Bennett SR HS; Salisbury, MD; (Y); 18/182; JA; High Hon Roll; Hon Roll; Salisbury ST Coll; Bus.

PUTMAN, RONNI; Governor Thomas Johnson HS; Frederick, MD; (Y); 9/334; AFS; German Clb; Hosp Aide; Latin Clb; Science Clb; SADD; Mrchg Band; Var Twrlr; High Hon Roll; NHS; Excllnc Engl Awd 85&86; Jr Delgt For ST Of MD Sci Sympsm 86; Pre-Med.

PYATT, ELIZABETH J; Milford Mill HS; Baltimore, MD; (Y); 1/222; Sec Trs JCL; Math Clb; Capt Scholastic Bowl; Rptr Yrbk Rptr; Elks Awd; NCTE Awd; NHS; Ntl Merit Ltr; Val; Chrprson SR Prom Comm 85-86; Renslr Mdl Math & Sci 84-85; DE U; Physcl Sci.

QUANDER, LATRECE D; Regina HS; Chillum, MD; (Y); Cmnty Wkr; Model UN; Pres Stu Cncl; Capt Bsktbl; Capt Socr; Sftbl; Hon Roll; Prfct Atten Awd; Trk; Dept Defence Smmr Sci & Engrg Prog 85-86; Elect Engrg.

QUARTANO, MESIA; Leonardtown HS; Leonardtown, MD; (Y); 6/255; Trs Art Clb; Pres French Clb; NFL; Teachers Aide; Variety Show; Rep Jr Cls; JV Vllybl; High Hon Roll; NHS; Ntl Merit Ltr; Olga B Burgee Memrl Schlrshp 86-87; Jacksonville U Trstees Schlrshp 86-87; Awd For Frnch 85-86; Jacksonville U.

QUEEN, DARYL W; Old Mill SR HS; Severn, MD; (Y); 15/509; Sec Band; Concert Band; Jazz Band; School Musical; Lit Mag; Rep Stu Cncl; Var L Lcrss; Hon Roll; NHS; Ntl Merit Ltr; Engrng.

QUIDAS, KAREN; Col Richardson HS; Preston, MD; (Y); Am Leg Aux Girls St; Camera Clb; Church Yth Grp; Drama Clb; 4-H; Spanish Clb; SADD; Chorus; Church Choir; School Musical; Pblc Spkng Resrv Chmpn 84; 1st Pl Drmtc Scene Chesapeake Coll Comptn 85; Cnty Farm Queen 84-85; Western MD Coll; Corp Law.

QUINLAN, JOHN BERNARD; Severn Schl; Bowie, MD; (Y); VP Exploring; Im Bsktbl; Im Capt Ftbl; Var Ice Hcky; Var JV Lcrss; Im Powder Puff Ftbl; Hon Roll; Boy Scts; Ski Clb; SR Perf 85-86; Sentrl Schlrshp 86; Eagl Sct 82; Nav Acad Prep Schl.

QUINN, DEBBIE; Mount De Sales Acad; Baltimore, MD; (Y); Art Clb; Chess Clb; Church Yth Grp; Civic Clb; Pep Clb; Chorus; JV Bsktbl; Var Cheerleading; Var Fld Hcky; Var Golf; Vlntr Wrk; Sprts Ltrs; Aerontcl Engrg.

QUINTO, NORLITO; Friendly SR HS; Ft Washington, MD; (Y); Hon Roll; Annapolis Navl Acad; Engr.

QUISENBERRY, STACEY W; Northwestern HS; Hyattsville, MD; (Y); Church Yth Grp; French Clb; Teachers Aide; Church Choir; Var L Vllybl; Hon Roll; Genrl ST Schlrshp 86; Vlybl MVP 84-86; All-Cnty Vlybl Tm Hnrbl Mntn 84; U Of MD College Park; Pre-Bus.

QUITIGUIT, EUNICE; Notre Dame Preparatory HS; Pikesville, MD; (Y); Church Yth Grp; Cmnty Wkr; Dance Clb; Math Tm; Model UN; Pep Clb; Political Wkr; SADD; Chorus; Rep Frsh Cls.

RABINO, ELIZABETH; Surrattsville HS; Camp Springs, MD; (Y); Am Leg Aux Girls St; Pom Pon; Hon Roll; Accntng.

RABORG, RENEE; Pocomoke HS; Pocomoke, MD; (S); 1/91; AFS; Church Yth Grp; SADD; Capt Flag Corp; Sftbl; High Hon Roll; NHS; Hgst GPA Awd 85; Schlstic Ltr 85; Rotary Clb.

RACEK, PENNY; St Johns At Prospect Hall; Ijamsville, MD; (Y); Nwsp Rptr; Nwsp Stf; Yrbk Stf; JV Tennis; High Hon Roll; NHS; 3rd Pl Ntl Amer Essy Cntst 83; 1st Pl Math Fair 85; Bus.

RADCLIFFE, ALLYSON; St Andrews Episcopal Schl; Potomac, MD; (Y); Latin Clb; Nwsp Stf; Pres Soph Cls; Sec Stu Cncl; Cheerleading; Var Socr; Var Capt Sftbl; Hon Roll; Stu Govt Awd 85-86; Cum Laude-Natl Latin Exam 84-85; MVP-SFTBL 84-85; Bio.

RADCLIFFE, SHARON; Queen Annes County HS; Centreville, MD; (Y); Am Leg Aux Girls St; Church Yth Grp; French Clb; SADD; Hon Roll; NHS; NEDT Awd; MD JR Sci & Humanities Symposium 86.

RADMER, ANGELA; Archbishop Keough HS; Balt, MD; (Y); Hosp Aide; Orch; Ed Nwsp Stf; Ed Yrbk Stf; Bausch & Lomb Sci Awd; High Hon Roll; VP NHS; Ntl Merit Ltr; Prfct Atten Awd; Nwsp Rptr; Its Acad Tm; Cnslr.

RADO, ALEXANDRA; Walt Whitman HS; Bethesda, MD; (Y); Art Clb; School Musical; School Play; JV Vllybl; Econmcs.

RAFFERTY, MARY; Northern HS; Lonaconing, MD; (Y); FHA; Nwsp Rptr; Nwsp Stf; Hon Roll; Mgr.

RAFIK, HAROON; Gaithersburg HS; Gaithersburg, MD; (S); Intnl Clb; Tennis; Trk; Hon Roll; Med.

RAGSDALE, RHONDA; Eastern SR HS; Baltimore, MD; (Y); 10/280; Church Yth Grp; JA; Church Choir; Hon Roll; NHS; Ntl Merit SF; Prfct Atten Awd; Mrt Schlrshp Awd 85-86; Voctnl Intv Prog 85-86; Morgan ST U; Accntng.

RAIBLE, JENNIFER; Bishop Walsh HS; Cumberland, MD; (Y); 20/103; Church Yth Grp; 4-H; Band; Concert Band; Mrchg Band; Var Crs Cntry; Var Mgr(s); Var Trk; Hon Roll; Phys Thrpy.

RAID, MOHAMMED; Walter Johnson HS; Rockville, MD; (Y); Im JV Bsktbl; Var JV Ftbl; Im Sftbl; Var Capt Tennis; Im Wt Lftg; High Hon Roll; Hon Roll.

RAIDT, GINA; Williamsport HS; Hagerstown, MD; (Y); 104/206; Church Yth Grp; Teachers Aide; Flag Corp; Mrchg Band; Powder Puff Ftbl; Hon Roll; Cert Achvt Typng 85; Cert Achvt Accntntg 86; Law.

RAIN, MICHELE; Franklin SR HS; Owings Mills, MD; (S); Cmnty Wkr; FBLA; Rep Frsh Cls; Trs Soph Cls; Rep Jr Cls; Cheerleading; Hon Roll; Jr NHS; NHS; Prfct Atten Awd; Best Chrldr Awd 80; Most Sprtd Chrldr Awd 81; James Madison U; CPA.

RAINES, DAWN; Richard Montgomery HS; Rockville, MD; (Y); Ed Yrbk Stf; Rep Frsh Cls; Trs Soph Cls; VP Jr Cls; VP Sr Cls; Rep Stu Cncl; Var JV Bsktbl; Var Fld Hcky; Var JV Sftbl; Pres NHS; Prncpls Wrtng Awd 85; Outstndng Achvmnt Frnch 84-85; George Washington U Schl Of Engr & Appld Sci Mdl.

RAINS, SHANNON; Parkside HS; Parsonsburg, MD; (Y); High Hon Roll; Salisbury ST Coll; Law.

RALPH, LAURA; Western HS No 407; Baltimore, MD; (Y); 69/412; VP Church Yth Grp; Teachers Aide; Chorus; Church Choir; Hon Roll; Mount St Marys Coll; Comp Sci.

RAMI, DINAXI; Mercy HS; Owings Mills, MD; (Y); VP Camera Clb; VP French Clb; GAA; SADD; Concert Band; Rep Stu Cncl; High Hon Roll; Hon Roll; Jr NHS; NHS; U Baltimore; Phrmclgy.

RAMOS, MARCOS; Mc Donogh HS; Owings Mills, MD; (Y); Thesps; School Play; Nwsp Stf; Yrbk Stf; Pres Stu Cncl; Var Tennis; Boy Scts; Cmnty Wkr; Dance Clb; Drama Clb; Wnnr Ptry Rctn Cntst Frgn Lgn MD 86; Wnnr Chrctr & Inflnc Awd 86; Pre-Law.

RAMOS, SYLVIA A; Gaithersburg HS; Gaithersburg, MD; (Y); Church Yth Grp; Political Wkr; Bsktbl; Hon Roll; 2nd Pl Schl Sci Fr 83-84; St Marys Coll MD; Econ.

RAMSAY, DEANNA; La Reine HS; Camp Spgs, MD; (Y); Church Yth Grp; Drama Clb; FCA; Latin Clb; Spanish Clb; Concert Band; School Musical; School Play; Sftbl; Spanish NHS; AATSP Spnsh Level III 1st Pl 86; Broadcreek Piano Fstvl Wnnr 86; U Of DE; Fashn Merch.

RAMSEY, CAROL; Northwestern HS; Hyattsville, MD; (Y); AFS; Hosp Aide; Pres Latin Clb; Quiz Bowl; Nwsp Ed-Chief; Lit Mag; Hon Roll; NHS; Calvert Club MD Schlrshp 86; Cnsmr Cred Assoc 85; Grand Guardian Cncl Jobs Dau Schlrshp 86; U MD; Jrnlsm.

RAMSEY, LAURA; North Harford HS; Jarrettsville, MD; (Y); Cmnty Wkr; Dance Clb; Drama Clb; French Clb; Hosp Aide; Hon Roll; VFW Awd; Clncl Psychlgst.

RANDALL, LAURA; La Reine Catholic HS; Temple Hills, MD; (Y); Church Yth Grp; Civic Clb; Cmnty Wkr; Debate Tm; French Clb; Library Aide; Office Aide; Science Clb; Speech Tm; Church Choir; Howard U/U Of MD Cert Coll Of Engrng 84; MD ST Schlrshp Awd 86; Comp Exclnc 85; U Of MD; Math.

RANGANATHAN, RAJIV; John F Kennedy HS; Silver Spring, MD; (Y); 4/468; Mathletes; Natl Beta Clb; Quiz Bowl; Science Clb; Color Guard; French Hon Soc; High Hon Roll; JETS Awd; Ntl Merit Ltr; St Schlr; Frnch Awd 86; Acad All-Amer 86; Presdntl Acad Ftnss Awd 86; U Of PA; Elec Engrg.

RANKIN, ANTHONY; Bishop Mcnamara HS; Camp Springs, MD; (Y); 28/149; Spanish Clb; SADD; Rep Jr Cls; Var L Bsktbl; High Hon Roll; Hon Roll; Ntl Merit Ltr; White House Intern.

RAPISARDA, GINA; John Carroll HS; Bel Air, MD; (Y); 51/250; Church Yth Grp; Cmnty Wkr; Drama Clb; NFL; Chorus; School Musical; VP Sr Cls; Cheerleading; French Hon Soc; NHS; Pinnacle Prose Awd; Svc Awds; Engl.

RAPPAZZO, YVETTE; Eastern Voc-Tech HS; Baltimore, MD; (Y); Art Clb; FBLA; Spanish Clb; Yrbk Stf; Hon Roll; Prfct Atten Awd; Embry Riddle Aerontcl U; Aviatn.

RASCOE, KELLIE; Crossland SR HS; Upper Maryland, MD; (Y); Teachers Aide; Hon Roll; Chamberlayne JC; Fash Dsgn.

RASCON, JEFFREY LEE; Northern SR HS; Huntingtown, MD; (Y); 38/301; Church Yth Grp; Cmnty Wkr; Sec 4-H; Nwsp Rptr; Trs Stu Cncl; 4-H Awd; Hon Roll; Exploring; ST Scholar Yth Peer Ldrshp Trnng 85; Mntrshp Theolgy 85; Tchg.

RASMUSSEN, ETHEL; Hereford HS; Monkton, MD; (Y); Varsity Clb; Church Choir; Stu Cncl; Bsktbl; JV Var Fld Hcky; Capt Capt Tennis; NHS; Prfct Atten Awd; Unsung Hero Tennis 86; 3 Yrs Rgnl Games, 2 Yrs Ntl Games Capt 84-86; Capt Rgnl Cmbnd Trnng Rally 85; Educ.

RASTOGI, VINEETA; Seneca Valley HS; Gaithersburg, MD; (Y); 8/490; Cmnty Wkr; Drama Clb; Pres Latin Clb; Pep Clb; Red Cross Aide; Science Clb; Service Clb; Sec Spanish Clb; Speech Tm; SADD; Indn Clsscl Dncng; Med.

RATAJCZAK, THERESA; The Catholic High School Of Baltomor; Baltimore, MD; (Y); Dundalk CC; Acctng.

RATHJENS, JENNIFER; Arlington Baptist HS; Clarksville, MD; (Y); 2/60; High Hon Roll; Hon Roll; NHS; Art Awds 84-86; Extraord Chrstn Stu Amer 84-85; Edif & Conduct Awds 84-86; Chrstn Ed.

RATKE, KAREN; Fort Hill HS; Cumberland, MD; (Y); Cmnty Wkr; Dance Clb; Yrbk Phtg; Yrbk Sprt Ed; Sec Sr Cls; VP Rep Stu Cncl; Var Tennis; Hon Roll; NHS; NEDT Awd; Law.

RATLIFF, BRIDGETTE; Potomac HS; Temple Hills, MD; (Y); Art Clb; Camera Clb; Cmnty Wkr; OEA; Pep Clb; Hon Roll; Prfct Atten Awd; 1st Pl Awd Art Cntst; Hon Mntn Phtrphy Cntst; American U; Comp Anlys.

RATUE, KEVIN; Fort Hill HS; Cumberland, MD; (Y); Ski Clb; Bsktbl; Ftbl; Trk; Wt Lftg; Cit Awd; Hon Roll; Lttr Ftbll & Bsktbll 86; ST Plyoffs Ftbll 85&86.

RAUSCH, KAREN; Western HS; Baltimore, MD; (Y); 126/412; Cmnty Wkr; Drama Clb; FBLA; Library Aide; Red Cross Aide; Thesps; Chorus; Variety Show; Sftbl; 1st Rnnr Up Miss Lansdowne Pgnt 85; Finlst In Miss MD USA Pgnt 86; Music.

RAWLINGS, KIMBERLEIGH; St Pauls Schl For Girls; Baltimore, MD; (Y); Pres Church Yth Grp; Pres Dance Clb; Hosp Aide; Chorus; Church Choir; Yrbk Stf; Lit Mag; Hon Roll; Elizabeth Mackall Beetan Mem Awd Dnce & Music 86; Acctg.

RAY, STEPHANIE A; Largo SR HS; Mitchellville, MD; (Y); Sec Exploring; Vet Med.

RAY, TAMBRA; Hancock HS; Hancock, MD; (Y); 3/60; Sec Trs Church Yth Grp; Pres FHA; Lib Chorus; Church Choir; School Musical; School Play; Nwsp Rptr; Yrbk Stf; VP Jr Cls; High Hon Roll; Comp Bowl; Hagerstown JR Coll; Comp Sci.

RAY, WILLIAM; Northern HS; Baltimore, MD; (Y); FBLA; Hon Roll; Prfct Atten Awd; Bus Comp Dsng & Pgmng Cert 86; Frnch Cert 84; Comp Dsgn.

REA, LISA; Mc Donough HS; La Plata, MD; (Y); Hosp Aide; Library Aide; Scholastic Bowl; Cheerleading; Gym; Pom Pon; Cit Awd; Hon Roll; Art Awd Of Merit 83; 2nd Pl Art Show 84-85; Design.

READER, RACHELLE; Rising Sun HS; Rising Sun, MD; (Y); 26/165; Girl Scts; Pep Clb; SADD; Trs Sec Stu Cncl; Var Capt Cheerleading; Mgr Tennis; NHS; Rep Frsh Cls; Rep Soph Cls; Rep Jr Cls; Comptitn Chrldng Squad Won Tri ST Comptition 86; Hmcmng Crt 86; Hnrs Smnr 83-84; WV U; Intl Rltns.

READING, RICHARD A; Oxon Hill HS; Clinton, MD; (Y); Debate Tm; Intnl Clb; JV Crs Cntry; Var Trk; High Hon Roll; JETS Awd; NHS; Ntl Merit Ltr; Church Yth Grp; Jr NHS; Latin H Nr Soc; DOD Summer Sci Engrng Apprentice; Elec Engrng.

REALL, ANGIE; Southern Garrett HS; Mt Lake Pk, MD; (Y); 76/225; Sec Church Yth Grp; Pep Clb; VP Q&S; Teachers Aide; School Play; Nwsp Bus Mgr; Nwsp Ed-Chief; Nwsp Phtg; Nwsp Sprt Ed; Lion Awd; Frostburg ST; Educ.

REAMER, MICHAEL; Randallstown SR HS; Randallstown, MD; (Y); 16/462; SADD; Pres Sr Cls; Var Socr; Hon Roll; NHS; Schlrshp Rndllstwn Schlrshp Corp 86; Emory U.

REAVER, KELLY; St Vincetn Pallohi HS; Laurel, MD; (S); 7/115; AFS; Hosp Aide; NFL; Teachers Aide; School Musical; Pom Pon; French Hon Soc; Hon Roll; NHS; Stu Of Yr Frnch; Money Mgmt.

REAVER, LAURA; Catoctin HS; Emmitsburg, MD; (Y); 27/186; Sec Church Yth Grp; Letterman Clb; Math Tm; Teachers Aide; School Musical; Rep Soph Cls; Capt Trk; Capt Vllybl; Hon Roll; Lion Awd; J Coats Trst Fnd Schlrshp 86; E Moler Foundtn 86; Orphn House/Episcpl Free Schl Soc Schlrshp 86; MD U Baltimore; Physcl Thrpy.

REAVES, NICOLLA; Walbrook SR HS; Baltimore, MD; (Y); FBLA; Spanish Clb; Church Choir; JV Badmtn; JV Vllybl; Hon Roll; Jr NHS; Computer Analyst.

RECK, JEFF; Westminster HS; Westminster, MD; (Y); Church Yth Grp; Trs JA; Var L Golf; Var L Wrstlng; Hon Roll; Acctg.

RECKLEY, RODERIC N; Baltimore Polytechnic Inst; Baltimore, MD; (Y); Chess Clb; Rep Stu Cncl; Im Bsktbl; Im Vllybl; Ntl Merit Ltr; U MD College Pk; Aero Engrng.

RECKNER, KATIE; Andover Sr HS; Glen Burnie, MD; (Y); Radio Clb; Red Cross Aide; Thesps; School Musical; School Play; Stage Crew; Lit Mag; Sec Stu Cncl; Var Stat Mgr(s); Pom Pon; Tchncl Thtr.

REDD, DAVID; Milford Mill SR HS; Balt, MD; (Y); FBLA; Concert Band; School Musical; Stage Crew; Var Bsktbl; Var Sftbl; Var Trk; Cert Cmmndtn 86; Cert Achvmnt 86; Cert Mrt 86; High Point Coll; Comp Info Syst.

REDD, ROBERT; Magruder HS; Rockville, MD; (Y); AFS; Stat Boy Scts; French Clb; Pres Ski Clb; Varsity Clb; Rep Frsh Cls; Rep Soph Cls; Var L Trk; Hon Roll; Math.

REDMAN, ANDREW; Lackey HS; Indian Head, MD; (Y); Latin Clb; High Hon Roll; Hon Roll; Pre Med.

REDMOND, ERIC C; Eleanor Roosevelt HS; Forestville, MD; (Y); Concert Band; Symp Band; Rep Frsh Cls; Rep Stu Cncl; JV Crs Cntry; Var Capt Trk; Natl Achvt Cmmnd Schlr 85-86; VP Chrch Young Adlt Usher Brd 85-86; Biomed Engr.

REECE, CAROLE; Pocomoke HS; Pocomoke, MD; (S); 1/96; Debate Tm; Band; Jazz Band; Yrbk Ed-Chief; Sec Sr Cls; Rep Stu Cncl; Var Capt Fld Hcky; Tennis; Pres NHS; Val; Intl Yth Yr Awd Wnnr 85.

REED, BRAD; Fort Hill HS; Cumberland, MD; (Y); JV Bsktbl; Var L Ftbl; Var L Trk; Hon Roll; U Of MD; Pharm.

REED, LAURA; Laurel HS; Roanoke, VA; (Y); VP Church Yth Grp; Sec FCA; French Clb; Office Aide; SADD; Teachers Aide; Var Bsktbl; JV Var Trk; JV Var Vllybl; Hon Roll; Ath Yr 84-85; Rec Dirctr.

REED, SHAWN L; Southern HS; Accident, MD; (S); 2/226; Ski Clb; Drm Mjr(t); Mrchg Band; Trs Jr Cls; Trs Sr Cls; Pres Stu Cncl; Swmmng; High Hon Roll; NHS; Sal; Wake Forest U; Corp Law.

REED, VICKI; Snow Hill HS; Salisbury, MD; (S); 3/110; Pres 4-H; Spanish Clb; Nwsp Sprt Ed; Yrbk Stf; Var Bsktbl; Var Capt Vllybl; 4-H Awd; High Hon Roll; NHS; ST Altrnt 4-H Comptn Ag 85; Schlstc Ltr 85; Landscape Dsgn.

REEDER, TRINA F; Brunswick HS; Jefferson, MD; (Y); 13/143; Church Yth Grp; Chorus; Rep Sr Cls; Rep Stu Cncl; Fld Hcky; Powder Puff Ftbl; Trk; Hon Roll; NHS; PVYA Schlr Athlt 86; Lds Axlry To Jfrsn Vlntr Fire Co Schlrhp 86; Twsn ST U; Mth.

REEPING, ANN; Elizabeth Seton HS; Washington, DC; (Y); Drama Clb; Chorus; Bsktbl; Hon Roll; Catholic Univ Of America.

REES, CHRISTINE; Archbishop Keough HS; Ellicott City, MD; (Y); Church Yth Grp; Nwsp Rptr; Nwsp Sprt Ed; Nwsp Stf; Yrbk Sprt Ed; Yrbk Stf; JV Var Fld Hcky; Var Lcrss; High Hon Roll; Hon Roll; Western MD.

REES, MATT; Queen Annes County HS; Mrydel, MD; (Y); Band; Concert Band; Mrchg Band; Pep Band; Socr; High Hon Roll; Hon Roll; NHS; Ntl Merit Schol.

REESCH, RACHEL; La Reine HS; Ft Washington, MD; (Y); Church Yth Grp; Concert Band; Hon Roll; Spanish NHS; Sci Fair Prjct Hon Mntn 84; Mission Clb VP 85-86; U Of MD.

REESE, CHRIS; Gaithersburg HS; Gaithersburg, MD; (Y); Church Yth Grp; Cmnty Wkr; Dance Clb; FFA; Office Aide; Pep Clb; Political Wkr; Ski Clb; SADD; Sftbl; Gthrsbrg Area Drg Free Lvng You 85-86.

REESE, MIKE; Middletown HS; Middletown, MD; (Y); 25/190; Computer Clb; FBLA; Teachers Aide; Lit Mag; High Hon Roll; Pres Schlr; FBLA ST Accntng II 86; Frederick CC; Accntng.

REESER, CINDRA; Williamsport HS; Williamsport, MD; (Y); 3/215; Ski Clb; Sec Jr Cls; Sec Sr Cls; Rep Stu Cncl; Var Trk; French Hon Soc; NHS; Ntl Merit Ltr; Sec Frsh Cls; Comm Schl Intrnsp Prgm For Gftd Chld Psyc Phys Ther 86; MD Vllybl ST Champs Cls B 85; Shepherd Coll; Phys Ther.

REEVES, CRAIG; Northern HS; Huntingtown, MD; (Y); 110/301; Im Bsktbl; Im Coach Actv; JV Var Ftbl; Im Lcrss; Var Trk; Var Wt Lftg; Cmnty Wkr; Computer Clb; French Clb; Spanish Clb; Co Capt Vrsty Ftbl 85; UMBC; Athl Traing.

REEVES, JAMES L; Oxon Hill HS; Temple Hills, MD; (Y); Boys Clb Am; Teachers Aide; VP Frsh Cls; Trs Soph Cls; Trs Jr Cls; VP Sr Cls; Rep Stu Cncl; JV Bsbl; Var Wrstlng; Hon Roll; Schlr Athlt Awd In Bsbl 83; Cert Of Excllnc In Bsbl 84; Elec Engrng.

REGAN, LOUISE; Southern HS; Baltimore, MD; (Y); Church Yth Grp; Hosp Aide; Office Aide; Teachers Aide; Soph Cls; Prfct Atndnc 83-86; Schlstc Achvt Hnrb Mntn For 87 Avrg 83-84; Bus Adm.

REHDER, YVETTE; Kenwood HS; Baltimore, MD; (Y); Hosp Aide; Office Aide; Varsity Clb; Variety Show; Frsh Cls; Soph Cls; Jr Cls; JV Var Cheerleading; Hon Roll; Prfct Atten Awd; MD U; Dntl Hygn.

REICH, DAVID; Spring Brook HS; Silver Spring, MD; (Y); Boy Scts; Church Yth Grp; Im Bowling; Var JV Ftbl; Im Sftbl; Im Tennis; Im Vllybl; Im Wt Lftg; Im Wrstlng; Maryland; Psych.

REICHARD II, BOB; Liberty HS; Eldersburg, MD; (Y); Mathletes; Ski Clb; Spanish Clb; Band; Color Guard; Concert Band; Drm Mjr(t); Flag Corp; Jazz Band; Mrchg Band; James Madison; Comp Sci.

REID, DAVID; Centennial HS; Ellicott City, MD; (Y); 4/278; Boy Scts; Var L Ftbl; Var L Lcrss; Var L NHS; Im Wt Lftg; High Hon Roll; Pres NHS; German Clb; Math Tm; Science Clb; Eagle Sct Awd 84; Princeton Bk Awd 86; Publshd Mpls Star 86; Sci.

REID, LAURA; La Plata HS; Waldorf, MD; (Y); Church Yth Grp; Ski Clb; Thesps; Church Choir; Mrchg Band; School Musical; Off Frsh Cls; Rep Sr Cls; Cit Awd; Aud/Vis; 2nd Pl Tlnt Hnt Awd PSI PHI Frt Gmma Pi Chptr 86; Ctr Agng Wa Dc Vlntr Svs 85; Ntl Pn Ply Adtns 85; Dntstry.

REID, MICHAEL; Gaithersburg HS; Gaithersburg, MD; (Y); JV Socr; Tennis; High Hon Roll; Hon Roll; Jr NHS; NHS; Chem Engr.

REID, STEVEN G; St Pauls Schl; Baltimore, MD; (Y); Var Bsbl; Crs Cntry; JV Ftbl; Var Wrstlng; W Alton Jones Schlrshp To St Pauls 82; Hnr Rll; FIT; Spc Sci.

REINERT, MARY; Prospect Hall HS; Walkersville, MD; (Y); Yrbk Stf; High Hon Roll; NHS; Med.

REINHARDT, GREGORY; Arlington Baptist HS; Baltimore, MD; (Y); Church Yth Grp; Prfct Atten Awd; Natl Hist & Govt Awd 86.

REISLER, SHERRY; Rising Sun HS; North East, MD; (Y); 5/153; Am Leg Aux Girls St; Church Yth Grp; Debate Tm; 4-H; Spanish Clb; High Hon Roll; Lion Awd; NHS; Pres Schlr; U Of MD; Vet Med.

REITZ, BETH; Mercy HS; Monkton, MD; (Y); Dance Clb; GAA; Spanish Clb; Chorus; Yrbk Stf; Rep Stu Cncl; JV Fld Hcky; Hon Roll; Excllnc Algebra Awd 86; Loyola Coll; Elem Ed.

REITZ, KIMBERLY; Notre Dame Preparatory Schl; Towson, MD; (Y); Church Yth Grp; Cmnty Wkr; Drama Clb; German Clb; Pep Clb; SADD; Stage Crew; Nwsp Ed-Chief; Nwsp Rptr; Nwsp Stf; Rep For Christn Comm Awareness Pgm 83-84; Hollinsummer Expository Wrtng Pgm 86; Intl Affairs.

RELKIN, STACEY; Wheaton HS; Rockville, MD; (Y); 10/386; Cmnty Wkr; JA; Latin Clb; Temple Yth Grp; Nwsp Ed-Chief; Gov Hon Prg Awd; Hon Roll; Jr NHS; NHS; Pres Schlr; Claire Sodden Memrl Awd Outstndng Achvt 86; U Of MD; Soc Wrk.

REMEIKIS, GREGORY; Archbishop Curley HS; Baltimore, MD; (S); 10/143; Nwsp Stf; Yrbk Stf; Rep Frsh Cls; Rep Jr Cls; Var JV Bsktbl; Var Diving; Var Swmmng; Hon Roll; NHS; Spanish NHS.

REMMERS, CHRISTIE; Gaithersburg HS; Laytonsville, MD; (Y); Pep Clb; Yrbk Stf; Score Keeper; Vllybl; Hon Roll; NHS; Pharm.

RENARD, JOSEPH; Catoctin HS; Thurmont, MD; (Y); Boy Scts; Exploring; Letterman Clb; Radio Clb; Science Clb; Ski Clb; Band; Jazz Band; Pep Band; Var L Ftbl; Frederick CC; Aviatn Mech.

RENARD, MICHELLE J; Edgewood SR HS; Edgewood, MD; (Y); 2/222; Varsity Clb; Orch; Capt JV Cheerleading; Capt Powder Puff Ftbl; JV VP Sftbl; NHS; Pres Schlr; Sal; St Schlr; Stage Crew; Ntl Schl Orch Awd 86; Cngrssnl Schlr Ntl Yng Ldrs Cnfrnce 86; Virginia Tech; Chem Engr.

RENAULT, JOSETTE; Walt Whitman HS; Bethesda, MD; (Y); Pep Clb; Rep Stu Cncl; JV Fld Hcky; Psych.

RENDER, DAVID W; Richard Montgomery HS; Rockville, MD; (Y); Art Clb; Computer Clb; Drama Clb; German Clb; Red Cross Aide; Stage Crew; Var Hon Roll; NHS; Math.

RENESLACIS, JONATHAN V; Southern Garrett HS; Kitzmiller, MD; (S); 6/225; Church Yth Grp; Cmnty Wkr; Var Bsbl; Var Bsktbl; Coach Actv; Hon Roll; NHS; Ntl Merit SF; St Schlr; St Andrews Pres Coll; Math.

RENFROW, ANGELA; Surrattsville HS; Clinton, MD; (Y); French Clb; Teachers Aide; Church Choir; Hon Roll; NHS; Voice Dem Awd; Sprntndnts Awd 83-84; Amer Lgn Schlrshp 86; Rotary Clb Stu Of The Mnth 86; Utica Coll; Psych.

RENNER, STEVE; Thomas Stone HS; Waldorf, MD; (S); Science Clb; Teachers Aide; High Hon Roll; Hnrs Ltr 83-84; Engrng.

RENNER, TODD; Thomas Stone HS; Waldorf, MD; (S); Science Clb; Teachers Aide; Band; Concert Band; Drm Mjr(t); Jazz Band; Mrchg Band; Pep Band; School Musical; Symp Band; Tri Cnty Honors Band 86; All Cnty Hnrs Band 85-86; ST Solo/Ensmbl Fest-Grade VI Solo-Exclnt Rtng 85; Maryland U.

RENO, CHRISTINA LEA; Arundel SR HS; Odenton, MD; (Y); 7/455; Am Leg Aux Girls St; Var Rep Stu Cncl; Coach Actv; Var L Socr; Var Capt Sftbl; Hon Roll; JETS Awd; Sec NHS; Pres Schlr; St Schlr; 2nd Tm All Cnty Sccr Goalie 85-86; U Of MD; Elec Engrng.

RENOLL, DEBORAH LYNN; North Carroll HS; Millers, MD; (Y); 5/288; Pres Sec Church Yth Grp; Ski Clb; Spanish Clb; Sec Band; Mrchg Band; Rep Stu Cncl; Gov Hon Prg Awd; NHS; Prfct Atten Awd; St Schlr; Pual Garrett Schlrshp Am Leg 86; Soroptimist Intl Ctznshp Awd 86; Jack Markert Mus Awd 86; Western MD Coll; Math.

RESH, JOEY; Williamsport HS; Hagerstown, MD; (Y); 2/223; Rep Stu Cncl; Var Bsbl; Hon Roll; NHS; Lions Clb Essy Wnnr 85; Chem.

RETOMA, RACHELLE; Notre Dame Preparatory Schl; Baltimore, MD; (Y); Cmnty Wkr; Dance Clb; Hosp Aide; Math Tm; School Musical; Sec Soph Cls; Stu Cncl; Im Fld Hcky; Im Vllybl; High Hon Roll; 100 Vol Hrs Johns Hopkins Hosp 85; NEDT Awd 83-84; MD Math Lg Awd 4th 86; Bio.

REUSCHEL, JOE; Fort Hill HS; Cumberland, MD; (Y); Church Yth Grp; Dance Clb; Orch; Nwsp Stf.

REYES, ABIGAIL; Bladensburg HS; Capitol Hts, MD; (Y); Teachers Aide; Nwsp Bus Mgr; Nwsp Rptr; Nwsp Stf; Yrbk Bus Mgr; Yrbk Stf; Katherine Gibbs Bus Schl Ldrshp Awd 86; Jessie J Wait Jr Memrl Awd 86; Accntng.

REYES, LYNN CYNTHIA; Takoma Acad; Silver Spring, MD; (S); Church Yth Grp; Cmnty Wkr; Library Aide; Teachers Aide; Sec Acpl Chr; Sec Chorus; Yrbk Stf; Im Bsktbl; Im Ftbl; JV Score Keeper; Med.

REYNOLDS, JENNIFER; Mount De Sales Acad; Baltimore, MD; (Y); Chorus; Variety Show; Bsktbl; Cheerleading; Fld Hcky; Lcrss; Hon Roll; Opt Clb Awd; Towson ST; Pre-Law.

REYNOLDS, ROBIN; Parkside HS; Eden, MD; (Y); Ski Clb; Varsity Clb; Variety Show; Yrbk Stf; Var JV Cheerleading; Trk; French Hon Soc; Hon Roll; Old Dominion.

RHODES, CHRIS; Eastern Voc-Tech HS; Baltimore, MD; (Y); Boys Clb Am; Red Cross Aide; Im Bsbl; Capt Socr; Hon Roll; U Of MD; Data Prcssg.

RHODES, KATRINA; Allegany HS; Cumberland, MD; (Y); 32/220; Cmnty Wkr; Office Aide; Drill Tm; Trk; Allegany CC; Clinicl Psych.

RHODES, KIMBERLY; Allegany HS; Cumberland, MD; (Y); 11/220; Teachers Aide; Rep Stu Cncl; Var Co-Capt Vllybl; VP NHS; Alpha Phi Alpha Outstnndg Black SR Awd 85-86; Ralph Webster Awd 85-86; Ntl Hnr Soc Schlrhsp 85-86; Frostburg ST Coll; Bus.

RHODES, MEREDITH K; Gov Thomas Johnson HS; Frederick, MD; (S); Sec DECA; FBLA; VP FHA; Hosp Aide; Office Aide; Thesps; Drm Mjr(t); School Musical; Powder Puff Ftbl; Wt Lftg; ST Achvt Awd DECA-MGMT & Supv 84-85; DECA & FBLA-OUTSTNDG Ldrshp & Chrctr 84-85; DECA Sec 84-85; Fredrick CC; Bus.

RHODES, RACHEL; Fallston HS; Fallston, MD; (Y); Sec SADD; Church Choir; Nwsp Ed-Chief; Nwsp Rptr; Yrbk Stf; Rep Jr Cls; JV Var Cheerleading; JV Var Mgr(s); Hon Roll; NHS; Jrnlsm.

RHOE, MICHELLE; Williamsport HS; Hagerstown, MD; (Y); 20/206; French Clb; Hosp Aide; Band; Concert Band; Mrchg Band; Pep Band; Stu Cncl; Hon Roll; NHS; Soc Wrk.

RICCI, MARGARET; Catholic HS Of Balt; Baltimore, MD; (Y); JA; Mathletes; Concert Band; Jazz Band; School Musical; Variety Show; Hon Roll; NHS; Loyola Coll Scholar 86; Loyola Coll; Mth.

RICE, JEFFREY; Smithsburg HS; Smithsburg, MD; (Y); 38/188; Pres Church Yth Grp; Ski Clb; Spanish Clb; Chorus; Church Choir; Swing Chorus; Variety Show; JV Ftbl; Elin Bible Inst; Bible.

RICE, JODY; Charles W Woodward HS; Rockville, MD; (Y); 58/234; Pres Sec 4-H; SADD; Nwsp Stf; Soph Cls; VP Jr Cls; Sec Sr Cls; Stu Cncl; Var JV Crs Cntry; Trk; 4-H Awd; 1st Prncs At Mntgmry Cnty Fair 85; MD Mk It Yrslf Wool Wnr 84 & 85; 1st Altrnt To Rep MD 85; VA Poly-Tech Inst; Acctng.

RICE, MELISSA; Brunswick HS; Brunswick, MD; (Y); 1/150; DECA; FBLA; FFA; Frsh Cls; JV Var Bsktbl; Var Cheerleading; Powder Puff Ftbl; High Hon Roll; Hon Roll; Strght A 4 Trms 85-86; FCC; Bus.

RICE, NICOLE; Allegany HS; Cumberland, MD; (Y); 70/240; AFS; Art Clb; GAA; Ski Clb; SADD; Nwsp Stf; Trk; Vllybl; Wt Lftg; Biochem.

RICE, SHARON; Ft Hill HS; Cumberland, MD; (Y); Church Yth Grp; Office Aide; Church Choir; Sec L Flag Corp; Nwsp Stf; Allegany CC; Sec Stud.

RICE, ULYSSES; Potomac HS; Suitland, MD; (Y); Church Yth Grp; CAP; Cmnty Wkr; Prince George CC; Cmptr Sci.

RICHARD, LINDA; Fort Hill HS; Cumberland, MD; (S); 3/278; Drama Clb; Service Clb; Trs Thesps; Yrbk Ed-Chief; Yrbk Stf; Off Frsh Cls; Off Soph Cls; Off Jr Cls; Off Sr Cls; VP Stu Cncl; MD Dstngshd Schlr 85; U Of MD Baltimore; Phrmcy.

RICHARDS, JOHN; Seneca Valley HS; Gaithersburg, MD; (Y); Boy Scts; Drama Clb; Letterman Clb; School Play; Pres Soph Cls; Mgr Bsktbl; Mgr(s); Wt Lftg; God Cntry Awd; Hon Roll; Bradford Coll; Psych.

RICHARDS, ROBERT; Highland View Acad; Hagerstown, MD; (Y); Ski Clb; Socr; Columbia Un Coll Hi Grd 87; Hagerstwn; Elec Engrng.

RICHARDSON, ALEX J; Springbrook HS; Silver Spring, MD; (Y); 145/475; Boys Clb Am; Latin Clb; Office Aide; Rep Sr Cls; Rep Stu Cncl; JV Bsbl; JV DECA; Var Ftbl; Var Trk; Hon Roll; Natl Ltn Exam Awd 83; Natl Achvt Semi-Fin 85; Georgetown U; Lwyr.

RICHARDSON, DAWN; Mt De Sales Acad; Baltimore, MD; (Y); Church Yth Grp; Computer Clb; JA; Office Aide; Spanish Clb; Speech Tm; Church Choir; School Musical; Co-Capt Cheerleading; High Hon Roll; Hugh O Brien Yth Found Awd 84; Rita Larsen Mem Awd 83; Acad Exc 86; Catonsville CC; Med Sec.

RICHARDSON, KELLEY; Seneca Valley HS; Gaithersburg, MD; (Y); Church Yth Grp; Hosp Aide; Spanish Clb; Teachers Aide; Chorus; High Hon Roll; Hon Roll; Citzenshp Awd 85; U DE; Engrng.

RICHARDSON, KIM; Springbrook HS; Silver Spring, MD; (Y); 110/480; Dance Clb; Office Aide; Chorus; Yrbk Stf; Rep Frsh Cls; Rep Soph Cls; Rep Sr Cls; Cheerleading; Capt Gym; Hon Roll; Excllnc In Dance 84; U Of MD; Advrtsng Dsgn.

RICHARDSON, LISA; Walbrook HS; Baltimore, MD; (Y); FBLA; Library Aide; High Hon Roll; Hon Roll; Prfct Atten Awd; Cert For Stenography II 86; Dance.

RICHARDSON, REGINA; Westminster HS; Finksburg, MD; (Y); Sec Church Yth Grp; Spanish Clb; Teachers Aide; Variety Show; Yrbk Stf; Yrbk Rptr; High Hon Roll; NHS; Peer Cnslr; Stu Marshall; Vet.

RICHARDSON, STACEY; Laurel HS; Laurel, MD; (Y); Dance Clb; Drama Clb; PAVAS; Ski Clb; School Musical; School Play; Cheerleading; Powder Puff Ftbl; Hon Roll; U Of MD; Arch.

RICHARDSON, TRACIE; Surrattsville HS; Clinton, MD; (Y); Teachers Aide; Nwsp Ed-Chief; Rep Frsh Cls; Co-Capt Pom Pon; Hon Roll; VP Jr NHS; Princes Georges Cnty Acad Exclnc Awd 84-85; MD U; Psychlgy.

RICHARDSON-MARTIN, MARNI D; Western HS; Baltimore, MD; (Y); 2/420; Cmnty Wkr; English Clb; Latin Clb; Yrbk Ed-Chief; Yrbk Phtg; Yrbk Rptr; Yrbk Stf; Rep Frsh Cls; Rep Soph Cls; Rep Jr Cls; Latin Cumma Cum Laude Awd 83-85; Ntl PSAT Cmmnded Stu Awd 85; PA U; Jrnlsm.

RICHELS, ELISE; Baisyaakov Schl For Girls; Virginia Beach, VA; (S); Drama Clb; Pres Temple Yth Grp; School Play; Variety Show; Nwsp Ed-Chief; Yrbk Stf; Chrmn Stu Cncl; High Hon Roll; Jr NHS; Ntl Merit Ltr; VA Pilot Ledg Str Schlstc Tm 84; Natl Conf Synag Yth Nesyer Of Yr & Meritous Ldrshp 84; Pol Sci.

RICHMOND, PAULA ADELE; Gwynn Park HS; Accokeek, MD; (Y); Church Yth Grp; Cmnty Wkr; Teachers Aide; Nwsp Phtg; Nwsp Rptr; Nwsp Stf; Stu Cncl; Cheerleading; High Hon Roll; NHS; Dncr Berlin Ballet J F Kennedy Ctr Per Arts Wash DC 80; 1st Wnnr Voice Demcrcy Cntst 84-85; U Of MD; Comm.

RICKER, JEFFREY; Lackey HS; Bryans Rd, MD; (Y); French Clb; Latin Clb; Math Tm; Nwsp Stf; Yrbk Stf; Lit Mag; High Hon Roll; NHS; Cmnctns.

RICKETT, JAMES; Lackey HS; Waldorf, MD; (Y); Cmnty Wkr; Pres 4-H; French Clb; Math Tm; Teachers Aide; Yrbk Stf; 4-H Awd; High Hon Roll; NHS; Gentc Engrg.

RICKS, COREY; Joppastowne HS; Edgewood, MD; (Y); Church Yth Grp; German Clb; Ftbl; Lcrss; Wt Lftg; Hon Roll; Arch.

RIDDER, RICHARD L; Southern Garret HS; Oakland, MD; (S); 7/222; Teachers Aide; Concert Band; Jazz Band; Mrchg Band; High Hon Roll; Pres NHS; JR All Amer Band 84; All Amer Band 85; MD Coll.

RIDDICK, TIFFANY; Western SR HS; Baltimore, MD; (Y); 112/412; Church Yth Grp; French Clb; Chorus; School Musical; Ntl Merit Ltr; NC A&T ST U; Acctg.

RIDENOUR, MISTI L; Southern Garrett HS; Oakland, MD; (S); Pres Church Yth Grp; German Clb; Yrbk Phtg; Yrbk Rptr; Yrbk Stf; Sec Rep Stu Cncl; High Hon Roll; Hon Roll; NHS; Hugh O Brian Yth Ambssdr 85.

RIDER, TODD; Saint James Schl; Sharpsburg, MD; (Y); 10/40; Camera Clb; Drama Clb; Chrmn Library Aide; Nwsp Phtg; Yrbk Bus Mgr; Yrbk Phtg; Lit Mag; Var Bsbl; Var Capt Crs Cntry; JV Socr; Poetry Prz 85; M Onderdonk Prz For Ctznshp 86; Bates Coll; Englsh Ltrtr.

RIDGLEY, WILLIAM; Queen Annes HS; Queenstown, MD; (Y); Am Leg Boys St; Boy Scts; Chess Clb; Drama Clb; 4-H; Chorus; Church Choir; Madrigals; School Play; Stage Crew; Airline Pilot.

RIESETT, RANDAL; Archbishop Curley HS; Baltimore, MD; (S); 27/143; Quiz Bowl; School Musical; Nwsp Ed-Chief; Yrbk Stf; VP Jr Cls; Pres Sr Cls; JV Capt Lcrss; Hon Roll; NHS; Drama Clb; Marine Bio.

RIFE, STEFANIE; Walkersville HS; Woodsboro, MD; (Y); Pres 4-H; Girl Scts; Science Clb; Trs Soph Cls; VP Jr Cls; Pres Sr Cls; Rep Stu Cncl; Stat Fld Hcky; Cit Awd; 4-H Awd; JR Chrprsn March Dimes 84-87; Phrmctcls.

RIFFLE, PHYLLIS; La Plata HS; Charlotte Hall, MD; (Y); Library Aide; Science Clb; Hon Roll; Psychlgy.

RIGDON, JESSICA; Archbishop Keough HS; Columbia, MD; (Y); Computer Clb; Pres Drama Clb; French Clb; Thesps; Chorus; School Musical; School Play; Mgr Stage Crew; Yrbk Stf; Loyola; Comp Sci.

RIGGIN, KEVIN; Cambridge-S Dorchester HS; E New Market, MD; (Y); Church Yth Grp; Scholastic Bowl; Teachers Aide; Rep Frsh Cls; JV Ftbl; Var L Lcrss; Var Mgr(s); 1st Pl Shrt Stry Chesapeake Coll Lit Fair 86; Hist.

RIGGIN, TAMMY; North Carroll HS; Manchester, MD; (Y); GAA; Pres Service Clb; Teachers Aide; Socr; Trk; Hon Roll; Nrsng Home Volntr 83-85; Jr Olympics-Discus & Shotput 85; Bus.

RIGGINS, DON; Mt St Joseph College; Pasadena, MD; (Y); JV Bsktbl; High Hon Roll; NHS; Prfct Atten Awd; Fr Mc Giviney Prsnl Dvlpmnt Awd 83; A F Acad; Math.

RILEY, JEANIE; Regina HS; Washington, DC; (Y); Church Yth Grp; Pep Clb; Rep Stu Cncl; Var L Vllybl; Engl.

RILEY, JON; La Plata HS; Waldorf, MD; (S); Ski Clb; Varsity Clb; L Ftbl; Var Wt Lftg; Var Wrstlng; Hon Roll; Natl Merit Sci Awd 83; Natl Merit Sci Stds & Sci Awds 84; Psych.

RILEY, JULIE; North East HS; North East, MD; (Y); 24/230; Sec Church Yth Grp; Pep Clb; SADD; Band; Church Choir; Stat Bsbl; Capt L Bsktbl; L Var Vllybl; Cecil Cnty Art Awd 83-84; Houghton Coll; Ed.

RILEY, SEAN; Glenelg HS; Woodbine, MD; (Y); Boy Scts; Letterman Clb; Pep Clb; SADD; Varsity Clb; Acpl Chr; Chorus; School Musical; School Play; Variety Show; Schlrshp Shenandoah Coll Music Cmp 86.

RILEY, TIMOTHY; Mt St Josephs HS; Randallstonn, MD; (Y); JV Var Crs Cntry; Var Golf; Hon Roll; NHS; Pro Golf.

RING, KRISTEN; Parkdale HS; Lanham, MD; (S); Am Leg Aux Girls St; Church Yth Grp; Hosp Aide; Symp Band; Yrbk Stf; Pres Stu Cncl; Pom Pon; High Hon Roll; NHS; Pre-Med.

RINGLING, TINA; Maurice J Mc Donough HS; Waldorf, MD; (Y); Intnl Clb; Teachers Aide; Mrchg Band; Pom Pon; High Hon Roll; Hon Roll; NHS; Salisbury; Acctg.

RINGQUIST, DANIEL; Smithsburg HS; Smithsburg, MD; (Y); Boy Scts; Chess Clb; Church Yth Grp; ROTC; Teachers Aide; Stage Crew; Yrbk Rptr; Stu Cncl; Im Gym; Im Socr; ROTC Cadet Awd 85; FL U Jacksnvl; Miltry Intellgn.

RINI, DONNELL; Frederick HS; Frederick, MD; (Y); Church Yth Grp; Computer Clb; Science Clb; SADD; Yrbk Phtg; Off Sr Cls; Crs Cntry; Trk; Hon Roll; Ntl Merit SF; Semi-Fin In Natl Hspnc Schlr Awds Prog 85-86; Photo Awds-1st In Abstrct Schl & Cnty 83; Photo.

RINKER, BRIAN; Flintstone HS; Cumberland, MD; (S); FFA; Trs Jr Cls; Var L Bsktbl; JV L Socr; High Hon Roll; NHS.

RINKER, MELISSA; Fort Hill HS; Cumberland, MD; (Y); Trs FHA; Teachers Aide; Chorus; Bsktbl; Crs Cntry; Trk; Capt Vllybl; High Hon Roll; NHS; Semi Fin Distngshd Schlrs Of Amer 85.

RINKO, JOHN DAVID; Oxon Hill HS; Ft Washington, MD; (Y); Boy Scts; Chess Clb; Rep Soph Cls; Rep Jr Cls; Rep Sr Cls; Gov Hon Prg Awd; High Hon Roll; NHS; Ntl Merit Schol; Chancllrs Schlrshp U MD 86-90; Supt Awd 86; U Of MD Coll Pk; Chem Engr.

RIORDAN-LEE, JESSE; Centennial HS; Columbia, MD; (Y); Church Yth Grp; German Clb; Jazz Band; Mrchg Band; School Musical; Symp Band; High Hon Roll; NHS; Civic Clb; Band; Perfmng Arts Ltr 84-86; Johns Hopkins U; Astrphyscst.

RIPPEON, KARIN; Frederick HS; Frederick, MD; (Y); 44/286; Computer Clb; 4-H; SADD; Teachers Aide; Varsity Clb; Chorus; Church Choir; Bsktbl; Sftbl; Vllybl; Bsktbl Mst Improved Coaches Awd 84-86; Vllybl Outstndng Offenseive Ply MVP 85-86; Sftbl Coaches Awd; Nrsng.

RIPPLE, BRIAN; North Hagerstown HS; Hagerstown, MD; (Y); 5/277; French Clb; Key Clb; Latin Clb; Jr Cls; Stu Cncl; Hon Roll; NHS; Princpls Cert-Outstndng Achvt; Stu Ldr Awd; 1st Pl Impromptu Essay-Dist Key Clb Convntn; Coll Of William & Mary.

RISING, ANDREW; Joppatowne HS; Joppa, MD; (Y); Aud/Vis; Drama Clb; German Clb; Acpl Chr; Band; Church Choir; Jazz Band; School Musical; School Play; JV Ftbl; Music Ed.

RITCHEY, MELISSA; Rockville HS; Rockville, MD; (S); 18/464; Trs Drama Clb; 4-H; SADD; Madrigals; School Musical; School Play; Nwsp Rptr; Crs Cntry; NHS; Ntl Merit SF; US Spch-Drma Awd 85; Publc Rltns.

RITCHIE, JONATHAN; North Harford HS; Whiteford, MD; (Y); FTA; German Clb; Hon Roll; Harford Comm Coll; Comp Tech.

RITENOUR, JAMES; Governor Thomas Johnson HS; Frederick, MD; (Y); Church Yth Grp; Latin Clb; Science Clb; Acpl Chr; Chorus; Madrigals; School Musical; Hon Roll; U MD College Park; Engrng.

RITTENHOUSE, KELLY; Notre Dame Prep Schl; Eldersburg, MD; (Y); Church Yth Grp; Service Clb; Lit Mag; Variety Show; Hon Roll; Psych.

RITTER, JEFFREY C; Winston Churchill HS; Potomac, MD; (Y); 85/612; Cmnty Wkr; JA; Teachers Aide; Varsity Clb; Stat Bsktbl; Var L Socr; JV Vllybl; Hon Roll; JETS Awd; NHS; Coll Of William & Mary.

RITTER, MARIA; Regina HS; Silver Spring, MD; (Y); Cmnty Wkr; Drama Clb; School Play; Stage Crew; Yrbk Stf; Trs Stu Cncl; Var L Bsktbl; Var L Socr; JV Sftbl; Hon Roll; Navy; Aerospace Engineering.

RITTER, STAICIARANEE; Southern HS HS; Baltimore, MD; (Y); Girl Scts; Office Aide; SADD; Yrbk Rptr; Pres Jr Cls; Cheerleading; Hon Roll; Prfct Atten Awd; Phrmctcl.

RITZER, JEREMY; Sherwood HS; Silver Spr, MD; (Y); 35/317; Debate Tm; Model UN; SADD; Orch; Rep Stu Cncl; Var Capt Tennis; Hon Roll; Pres NHS; Pres Schlr; SAR Awd; Natl Hnr Socy Schlrshp 86; Natl Executive Svc Corps Ldrshp Ldrshp Seminar 85-86; Vassar Coll; Pol Sci.

RIVERA, GRACE; Gaithersburg HS; Gaithersburg, MD; (Y); Cmnty Wkr; FBLA; Intnl Clb; Political Wkr; Speech Tm; SADD; Chorus; Church Choir; Variety Show; Pres Frsh Cls; Bst Floor Dirctr TV Prodctn; Montgomery Coll; Psych.

RIVERA, LISA; Takoma Acad; Takoma Park, MD; (S); Church Yth Grp; Drama Clb; French Clb; Science Clb; Ski Clb; Teachers Aide; Cheerleading; Sftbl; Hon Roll; NHS.

RIVOIRE, MELANIE; Surrattsville SR HS; Clinton, MD; (Y); Dance Clb; Office Aide; Pom Pon; Powder Puff Ftbl; Hon Roll; Towson ST Clg; Pres Corp.

RIVOIRE, MELISSA J; Surrattsville HS; Clinton, MD; (Y); Office Aide; Pom Pon; Powder Puff Ftbl; Hon Roll; Twnsnd ST Coll; Accntnt.

RIZER, KEELY; Calvary Christian Acad; Cumberland, MD; (Y); Hosp Aide; Pep Clb; Church Choir; School Play; Yrbk Stf; Var Sftbl; Var Vllybl; Hon Roll; Dcns Awd 84; Allegany CC; Wrd Prcssng.

ROACH, JACKIE; Surrattsville HS; Clinton, MD; (Y); Am Leg Aux Girls St; Cmnty Wkr; Teachers Aide; Nwsp Stf; High Hon Roll; Hon Roll; Merit Awd From Prince Georges Cnty 85; Comp.

ROACHE, JOHN BRIAN; Ryken HS; Mechanicsville, MD; (Y).

ROANE, MARC W; Paint Branch HS; Silver Spring, MD; (Y); 83/337; Church Yth Grp; Ski Clb; Im Bsktbl; JV Mgr(s); JV Score Keeper; Hon Roll; Ntl Merit Ltr; Engr.

ROBB, KATHLEEN LOUISE; Lackey HS; Bryans Road, MD; (Y); Am Leg Aux Girls St; Teachers Aide; Capt Flag Corp; Hon Roll; Prfct Atten Awd; Frostburg ST Coll; Bus.

ROBB, TRACY; Fort Hill HS; Cumberland, MD; (Y); Dance Clb; Hosp Aide; Teachers Aide; Off Sr Cls; Co-Capt Cheerleading; Gym; Mgr(s); Twrlr; High Hon Roll; Tri Hi Y Alpah 86-87; Allegany CC; Nrsng.

ROBBINS, LISA; Cambridge-South Dorchester HS; Cambridge, MD; (Y); AFS; Hosp Aide; Teachers Aide; Nwsp Ed-Chief; Nwsp Rptr; Nwsp Stf; Yrbk Ed-Chief; Yrbk Stf; High Hon Roll; Jr NHS; Psych.

ROBERTS, DEREK JAY; St Michaels SR HS; St Michaels, MD; (Y); 8/56; Am Leg Boys St; Concert Band; Jazz Band; Mrchg Band; Yrbk Stf; VP Stu Cncl; Gov Hon Prg Awd; Hon Roll; JP Sousa Awd; Trs NHS; Amer Lgn Boys Ntn 85; Don Garner Awd 84; DE ST Coll; Accntng.

ROBERTS, LISA; Springbrook HS; Silver Spring, MD; (Y); Art Clb; Dance Clb; Spanish Clb; SADD; Teachers Aide; Chorus; Lit Mag; Rep Frsh Cls; VP Rep Soph Cls; Rep Jr Cls; Saks 5th Ave Teen Brd Charity Work 84-87; Excelled Hons Eng & Hist Clss; Creative Writing.

ROBERTS, THOMAS; Brunswick HS; Knoxville, MD; (Y); 22/150; Camera Clb; French Clb; Teachers Aide; Stage Crew; Yrbk Ed-Chief; Yrbk Phtg; Yrbk Rptr; Yrbk Sprt Ed; Yrbk Stf; VP Jr Cls; Photogrph Coll Art Shw 84; Frdrck Cnty Schl Of Vsl & Prfrmng Arts 86-87; Syracuse U; Photogrphy.

ROBERTS, TONY; Thomas Stone HS; Waldorf, MD; (Y); Church Yth Grp; Science Clb; Hon Roll; Comp Sci.

ROBERTSON, JOHN A; Central SR HS; Andrews AFB, DC; (Y); Drama Clb; Thesps; Nwsp Rptr; Var Crs Cntry; Var Capt Trk; Hon Roll; NHS.

ROBERTSON, MARTINA; Eastern HS; Baltimore, MD; (Y); Art Clb; Cmnty Wkr; Dance Clb; English Clb; Library Aide; SADD; Cit Awd; Prfct Atten Awd; JA; Hon Roll; Vlntr Awd Rognel Hts 84; Tauette Clb PI Chptr 84-85; Aerbcs Inst 84; MD U College Park; Accntng.

ROBERTSON, MONIQUE A; Eleanor Roosevelt HS; Laurel, MD; (Y); Church Yth Grp; Dance Clb; Drama Clb; Pep Clb; Yrbk Rptr; Mgr Crs Cntry; Mgr Trk; Hon Roll; Spanish NHS; Letterman Clb; Bio.

ROBERTSON, SCOTT; Catonsville HS; Baltimore, MD; (Y); Church Yth Grp; NFL; Pres Speech Tm; School Musical; School Play; Stage Crew; Nwsp Rptr; Capt Tennis; Lion Awd; Amer Lgn Ortrcl Cntst; East Stroudsburg U; Cmnctns.

ROBESON, MICHAEL; Northern HS; Frostburg, MD; (Y); Pres Letterman Clb; Var L Bsktbl.

ROBESON, TAMIRA; Carver Vocational Technical HS; Baltimore, MD; (Y); Cmnty Wkr; FBLA; Office Aide; Varsity Clb; Rep Frsh Cls; Rep Soph Cls; Rep Stu Cncl; Cheerleading; Crs Cntry; Prfct Atten Awd; Coppin ST Clg; Crmnl Jsut.

ROBEY, THOMAS; Frederick HS; Adamstown, MD; (Y); Computer Clb; French Clb; Science Clb; Hon Roll; Frederick CC; Fncl Plnr.

ROBINETTE, SHERRIE; Fort Hill HS; Cumberland, MD; (Y); Drama Clb; Teachers Aide; Thesps; Band; Sec Chorus; Concert Band; Mrchg Band; Pep Band; School Musical; School Play; Allegany CC; Nurse.

ROBINSON, AMY; Northern HS; Huntingtown, MD; (Y); Church Yth Grp; Hosp Aide; Spanish Clb; VICA; JV Bsktbl; VICA Spllng, Abbrev Cntst-1st Pl Nrsng 85-86; Obstetrcs Nrsng.

ROBINSON, ANITA; Rising Sun HS; Rising Sun, MD; (Y); 2/169; Debate Tm; Key Clb; Concert Band; Pep Band; Yrbk Ed-Chief; Yrbk Stf; Var L Fld Hcky; Pres NHS; Sal; Drama Clb; Daughtrs Amer Colonists 86; MD Distngshd Schlr Scholar 86; Jostens Golden Eagle Awd 85-86; Salisbury ST Coll.

ROBINSON, ANN; Connelly School Of The Holy Child; Washington, DC; (Y); Math Clb; Math Tm; Pep Clb; School Play; Stage Crew; Drama Clb; Capt Vllybl; Hon Roll; Comp Awd 85-86; COMP Sci.

ROBINSON, CHRISTINE; Wicomico SR HS; Salisbury, MD; (Y); 11/247; JCL; Latin Clb; Varsity Clb; Acpl Chr; VP Sr Cls; Var L Tennis; Var L Vllybl; Cit Awd; NHS; Pres Schlr; Salisbury ST Coll; Sclgy.

ROBINSON, CLAY; Baltimore Polytechnic Inst; Baltimore, MD; (Y); Church Yth Grp; Church Choir; Hon Roll; Howard U; Pre-Med.

ROBINSON, EDWARD L; Walt Whitman HS; Bethesda, MD; (Y); Art Clb; Church Yth Grp; French Clb; Intnl Clb; JA; Service Clb; SADD; Lit Mag; Youth Art Exhbt 86; VP Of PR JA Wash DC 84; U Of DE; Art Hist.

ROBINSON, GINA; Sherwood HS; Olney, MD; (Y); SADD; Swing Chorus; VP Soph Cls; Off Jr Cls; Off Sr Cls; Stu Cncl; Hon Roll; NHS; Spanish NHS; Drama Clb; Am Legn Awd 84; Serv Awd 85; Bio Sci.

ROBINSON, HEATHER; Gaithersburg HS; Gaithersburg, MD; (Y); Art Clb; Camera Clb; Band; Church Yth Grp; Exploring; Pep Clb; Concert Band; Mrchg Band; Pep Band; 1st & 2nd Plc Mntgmry Vllg Art Shw 86; Hon Men Schl Photo Shw 86; Art.

ROBINSON, JOANNA; Cambridge South Dorchester HS; Cambridge, MD; (Y); AFS; Cmnty Wkr; English Clb; Latin Clb; Science Clb; Spanish Clb; SADD; Teachers Aide; Nwsp Stf; Yrbk Stf; Outstndng Achvt Human Psylgy 85-86; Outstndng Achvt Adv Engl 84-86; Bst Spn Stu Awd 85-86; Bio Sci.

ROBINSON, LASEAN; Western HS; Baltimore, MD; (Y); 182/412; Cmnty Wkr; French Clb; FBLA; JA; Office Aide; Red Cross Aide; Teachers Aide; Chorus; Church Choir; Drill Tm; Perfct Attn; Towson ST Coll; Telecmnctn.

ROBINSON, LORI S; Springbrook HS; Silver Spring, MD; (Y); 142/487; Church Yth Grp; Cmnty Wkr; Teachers Aide; Band; Church Choir; Pom Pon; Twrlr; Hon Roll; Natl Achvt Schlrshp Prgm Outstndg Negro Stu 86; Spelman Coll; Fash Wrtr.

ROBINSON, MICHAEL; Broadneck SR HS; Annapolis, MD; (Y); 2/330; Drama Clb; Key Clb; Scholastic Bowl; School Play; Lit Mag; Mgr Bsktbl; JV Socr; High Hon Roll; NHS; Pres Schlr; Chncllrs Scholar 86; MD Dstngshd Schlr Fnlst 86; MD Merit Scholar 86; U MD Colle Pk; Physcs.

ROBINSON, RENEE; Franklin SR HS; Owings Mills, MD; (Y); Debate Tm; NFL; SADD; Var Cheerleading; JV Var Powder Puff Ftbl; Im Socr; Var Trk; Towson ST U; Engrng.

ROBINSON, SUSAN; Gaithersburg HS; Gaithersburg, MD; (Y); Orch; Hon Roll; Ntl Merit Ltr; U Of MD; Zoolgcl.

ROBINSON, TASHA; Montrose Christian HS; Kensington, MD; (Y); 1/16; Church Yth Grp; Drama Clb; School Play; Ed Lit Mag; High Hon Roll; Hon Roll; Ntl Merit Ltr; Val; Hgst Cls Avg Yr Awd 84-86; Drama.

ROBINSON, TAWANA; Gwynn Park HS; Cheltenham, MD; (Y); Church Yth Grp; FCA; Hosp Aide; JA; Red Cross Aide; School Musical; Sec Jr Cls; Stat Bsktbl; Pom Pon; Hon Roll; Showcase For St PG County Educators Assn 84; Am Drill Team Assn Most Outstdng Indiv 86; Howard U; Juvenile Psychologist.

ROBINSON, TERRI B; John Carroll HS; Joppa, MD; (Y); Debate Tm; Band; Chorus; Rep Soph Cls; Rep Jr Cls; Var Powder Puff Ftbl; L Stat Trk; Hon Roll; Spanish NHS; Ntl Achvt Schlrshp Outstndng Negro Stus 85; Peace Corp; Intl Rltns.

ROBLING, JASON; Gaithersburg HS; Gaithersburg, MD; (Y); Ski Clb; Band; Concert Band; Variety Show; Var Golf; Hon Roll; Engl Essy/Story Awd.

ROCA, BENJAMIN YNARES; Severn Schl; Glen Burnie, MD; (Y); 16/77; Rep Church Yth Grp; Yrbk Ed-Chief; Im Tennis; Cit Awd; Hon Roll; NHS; Opt Clb Awd; Spanish NHS; Archdiocesan Yth Advsry Cncl 85-86; MD ST Mus Tchrs Accoc 1st Piano Solo 83 & 86; U MD.

ROCA, KATHERINE; Centennial HS; Columbia, MD; (Y); 68/250; Spanish Clb; SADD; Nwsp Stf; Yrbk Stf; Rep Jr Cls; Rep Sr Cls; Var Capt Tennis; Var Vllybl; Hon Roll; NHS.

ROCHE, BRIAN; Westminster HS; Westminster, MD; (Y); Ski Clb; Jazz Band; Mrchg Band; Symp Band; Var Socr; Var Tennis; Hon Roll; Flght Aviatn.

ROCHE, WINIFRED J; Cambridge-South Drochester HS; Cambridge, MD; (Y); Drama Clb; Chorus; Mrchg Band; Nwsp Stf; Yrbk Stf; Rep Frsh Cls; Rep Soph Cls; Var Pom Pon; Var Tennis; Drill Tm; Acdmc Achvt Awd In Theatre & Related Arts 85-86; Fshn Merchandsing.

ROCHESTER, B J; Takoma Acad; Takoma Park, MD; (S); Church Yth Grp; Cmnty Wkr; Intnl Clb; JA; Ski Clb; Teachers Aide; Stage Crew; High Hon Roll; Hon Roll; NHS; Outstndng Effort Englsh Ltrtr & SR Rlgn; Pacific Union Coll; Bus Adm.

ROCK, DAWN; Western SR HS; Baltimore, MD; (Y); 167/412; Chorus; Rep Soph Cls; Hon Roll; Lock Haven U; Psych.

ROCK, LILDA; Bethesda Chevy Chase HS; Bethesda, MD; (S); 272/399; Pres DECA; Lit Mag; Rep Frsh Cls; Rep Soph Cls; Rep Jr Cls; Rep Sr Cls; Rep Stu Cncl; CC Awd; JP Sousa Awd; Hon Roll; MD Vctnl Assn Dstngshd In DECA Ldrshp Schlrsh& 86; Phllps Petro Co Ntl Achvmnt Awd 85; MD U; Engl.

RODAVITCH, ANN; Notre Dame Prep; Baltimore, MD; (Y); Church Yth Grp; Cmnty Wkr; Library Aide; SADD; Band; Chorus; School Musical; School Play; Stage Crew; Nwsp Rptr; Johns Hopkins U; Anthrplgy.

RODKEY, REBECCA; Francis Scott Key HS; Union Bridge, MD; (Y); 28/185; Chorus; Drm & Bgl; Stage Crew; Nwsp Phtg; Hon Roll; NHS; Accntng.

RODNEY, ROBIN; Kent County HS; Chestertown, MD; (Y); Am Leg Aux Girls St; VP Pres Church Yth Grp; 4-H; Hosp Aide; VICA; Off Frsh Cls; VP Stu Cncl; Capt Twrlr; Dnfth Awd; DAR Awd; 4-H Queen 85; Pres VICA Clb Bus Tm 84 & 85; U MD; Nrsng.

RODRIGUEZ, JULIE; Immaculata College HS; Bethesda, MD; (Y); Church Yth Grp; Drama Clb; VP Math Clb; Science Clb; Spanish Clb; Trk; High Hon Roll; 3rd Pl Math Comp 86; Rsrch Smmr Intrnshp Chldrns Hosp Nation Med Ctr 85 & 86; Pre-Med.

RODSKI, FRANK; Liberty HS; Eldersburg, MD; (S); Computer Clb; Mathletes; Band; Concert Band; Jazz Band; Mrchg Band; Pep Band; High Hon Roll; Hon Roll; U MD; Comp Sci.

ROGERS, DANNA; Mt Hebron HS; Ellicott City, MD; (Y); Civic Clb; Office Aide; Teachers Aide; Chorus; Drill Tm; Score Keeper; Hon Roll; Howard U; Bus.

ROGERS JR, JOHN F; Loyola HS; Towson, MD; (S); FFA; Nwsp Phtg; Yrbk Phtg; Hon Roll; NHS; Outward Bound 85; SR Lfsvng 85.

ROGERS, RHONDA; Franklin HS; Reisterstown, MD; (Y); Church Yth Grp; Yrbk Stf; Off Frsh Cls; Off Soph Cls; Off Jr Cls; Off Sr Cls; Stu Cncl; JV Bsktbl; Var Crs Cntry; Powder Puff Ftbl; Engrng.

ROGERS, SHELLY; Northwestern SR HS; Baltimore, MD; (S); Rep Soph Cls; Var Bsktbl; Var Vllybl; Lincoln U; Bus Adm.

ROH, JI; Crossland HS; Tmeple Hills, MD; (Y); 7/322; Church Yth Grp; Mrchg Band; Pep Band; Symp Band; Capt Var Swmmng; Hon Roll; NHS; Syracuse U; Psyclgy.

ROHE, ANNE RENEE; Queen Annes County HS; Stevensville, MD; (Y); 38/350; Capt Color Guard; Flag Corp; Capt Mrchg Band; School Play; Yrbk Ed-Chief; Yrbk Stf; Hon Roll; NHS; Pres Schlr; Lynchburg Coll; Archt Engr.

ROHME, DOUG; Bladensburg HS; Riverdale, MD; (Y); 5/300; Computer Clb; French Clb; Nwsp Sprt Ed; Nwsp Stf; Yrbk Sprt Ed; Yrbk Stf; Bsbl; Bsktbl; Socr; Trk; 1st Tm All Cnty Bsbll 85-86; Honrbl Mntn Bsktbll 85-86; FL ST; Engr.

ROLAND, JENNIE; Mc Donough HS; White Plains, MD; (Y); Cmnty Wkr; 4-H; School Play; Variety Show; Cit Awd; 4-H Awd; VFW Awd; $350 Schlrshp Chldrns Cncl 86; $100 Schlrshp Shenandoah Cnsrvtry 86; $100 Schlrsh P CCLA 85; Shenandoah Cnsrvtry; Music.

ROLAPP, JULIANE; Bullis Schl; Darnestown, MD; (S); Am Leg Aux Girls St; Church Yth Grp; SADD; Varsity Clb; Var Capt Bsktbl; Var Capt Socr; Var Capt Sftbl; High Hon Roll; Natl Sci Mrt Awd 85-86.

ROLFES, KIMBERLY; Mercy HS; Baltimore, MD; (Y); 5/63; GAA; Library Aide; Nwsp Rptr; Nwsp Stf; Rep Stu Cncl; High Hon Roll; Hon Roll; Sec Soph Cls; Sec Sr Cls; Im Badmtn; Acadmc Achvt Awd 86; Clg Of Notre Dame; Phys Thrpy.

ROLLINS, PAMELA M; High Point HS; Silver Spring, MD; (Y); 4/655; Teachers Aide; Rep Stu Cncl; Stat Bsktbl; Mgr(s); Hon Roll; VP NHS; Acadmc Excllnc 84-85; Natl Spnsh Exm Partcpnt 85; Natl Achvt Schlrshp Outstndng Negro Stdnts 85; Aerosp Engrng.

ROMANO, NINO; Frederick HS; Clarksburg, MD; (Y); Boy Scts; Church Yth Grp; Spanish Clb; Varsity Clb; Capt L Socr; Wt Lftg; Hon Roll; Engrng.

ROMER, STEPHEN; Sherwood HS; Brookeville, MD; (Y); Boys Clb Am; Crs Cntry; Wt Lftg.

ROMO, TRACY; Col Zadok Magruder HS; Rockville, MD; (Y); 107/300; GAA; Teachers Aide; Varsity Clb; Socr; Wt Lftg; Hon Roll; U MD; Psych.

ROOP, AMY; Towson HS; Lutherville, MD; (Y); AFS; Cmnty Wkr; Drama Clb; French Clb; Math Clb; School Musical; School Play; Stage Crew; Variety Show; Off Soph Cls; MD Distgshd Schlr 86; Pres Acad Fit Awd 86; Natl Merit Commnd Schlr 86; St Marys Coll Of MD; Bio.

ROPER, BELINDA; Elkton HS; Elkton, MD; (Y); 10/289; 4-H; Q&S; Concert Band; Mrchg Band; Yrbk Ed-Chief; Vllybl; High Hon Roll; NHS; Capt Natl Bwlg Tm 85-86; Full Tuitn Schlrshp ODU 86-90; Old Dominion U; Pre-Med.

ROSCHLI, DIANE; Bishop Walsh HS; Cumberland, MD; (Y); 12/103; Drama Clb; Pep Clb; School Musical; Yrbk Ed-Chief; Stat Bsbl; High Hon Roll; Hon Roll; NHS; Spanish NHS.

ROSE, DOUG; Oakland Mills HS; Columbia, MD; (Y); Boy Scts; Ski Clb; Var L Bsbl; Var L Ftbl; JV Trk; Im Wt Lftg; Hon Roll; Bus Admin.

ROSEMAN, JEFFREY; Thomas Stone HS; Waldorf, MD; (S); Science Clb; SADD; Band; Church Choir; Capt Drill Tm; Nwsp Ed-Chief; Nwsp Rptr; Crs Cntry; Trk; Hon Roll; Lttr & Pin-Trck 85; Aerosp Engrng.

ROSENBERG, STEVEN I; Eleanor Roosevelt HS; Bowie, MD; (Y); VP Church Yth Grp; Rptr Yrbk Phtg; Hon Roll; Trs NHS; Ntl Merit SF; Ntl Latin Ex Silver Medal 84-85; Arahan Joshua Herschel Hnr Soc 84-86.

ROSENSTEIN, JUDI; Thomas S Wootton HS; Rockville, MD; (Y); Cmnty Wkr; Red Cross Aide; Teachers Aide; Nwsp Stf; Capt Twrlr; Hon Roll; SC Schlstc Jrnlsm Wrkshp 2nd Plc Awd Sprtswrtng & 1st Plc Awd News Edtng 85-86.

ROSENTHAL, CHRISTINA; Governor Thomas Johnson HS; Frederick, MD; (S); Pres DECA; Office Aide; High Hon Roll; ST DECA Conf 1st Pl Gnrl Mrchndsng & Rtl Math & 3rd Pl Mrktng Cncpts 85-86; Data Prcssng.

ROSIER, LA TONYA; La Plata HS; La Plata, MD; (Y); Cmnty Wkr; FBLA; FHA; Pep Clb; Chorus; Hon Roll; Charles Co CC; Comp DP.

ROSIER, MICHELLE; Oakland Mills HS; Columbia, MD; (Y); 15/275; SADD; VP Jr Cls; Pres Sr Cls; Capt Fld Hcky; Sftbl; Hon Roll; NHS; Ntl Merit Ltr; Pres Schlr; F Lee Noel Schlrshp 86; Outstndng Howard Cnty Sr 86; Georgetown.

ROSS, DAVID; La Plata HS; Charlotte Hall, MD; (S); Am Leg Boys St; Church Yth Grp; Cmnty Wkr; FCA; Varsity Clb; Rep Sr Cls; Var L Ftbl; Wt Lftg; Var L Wrstlng; Hon Roll; Sports Med.

ROSS, JOE; Rising Sun JR SR HS; Rising Sun, MD; (Y); 20/185; Drama Clb; VICA; Yrbk Stf; Var Bsbl; Var Trk; Hon Roll; 1st And 2nd ST Comptn Mach Drftg 85-86; Outstndng Drft Stu 85; Engr.

ROSS, MICHELLE; Connelly Schl Of The Holy Child; Potomac, MD; (Y); Cmnty Wkr; Intnl Clb; Service Clb; SADD; Stage Crew; Yrbk Bus Mgr; Im Tennis; Hon Roll; The Cornelia Cannelly Awd 86; Fordham U.

ROSS, SUKI; Surratsville HS; Clinton, MD; (Y); Drama Clb; Teachers Aide; Thesps; Chorus; School Musical; School Play; Nwsp Stf; Sec Jr Cls; Sec Stu Cncl; Var Mgr(s); George Washington U; Pltcl Sci.

ROSS, TROY; Northwestern HS; Hyattsville, MD; (Y); Boys Clb Am; Wt Lftg; High Hon Roll; Hon Roll; ROTC Schlrshp 86; GA Tech; Elect Engr.

ROSWELL, MATTHEW V; Loyola HS; Baltimore, MD; (S); VP German Clb; NFL; JV Wrstlng; Hon Roll; NHS; Mil Hist.

ROTH, REBECCA; West Nottingham Acad; Livingston, NJ; (Y); Nwsp Rptr; Yrbk Rptr; VP Trs Jr Cls; Var L Bsktbl; Var L Fld Hcky; Var L Tennis; NHS; Fryer-De Courtenay Mem, Finley Schlrshps 86; Bus.

ROTH, TRESA; Southern HS; Deer Park, MD; (Y); Drm Mjr(t); Hon Roll; Church Yth Grp; Library Aide; Chorus; Church Choir; Fshn Cnstlnt.

ROTHAGE, DAVID; Broadneck SR HS; Annapolis, MD; (S); 153/340; Computer Clb; DECA; JA; Rep Sr Cls; Im Tennis; Hon Roll; 2nd Pl Trphy Career Exploration Manual 86; 1st Pl Trphy ST Career Exploration Manual 86; AACC; CPA.

ROTHENHOEFER, ROXANNE; Northern SR HS; Baltimore, MD; (S); JA; Office Aide; Teachers Aide; Off Sr Cls; Ed.

ROUILLER, DANIELLE; Westminster HS; Westmister, MD; (Y); Am Leg Aux Girls St; Q&S; Yrbk Sprt Ed; Rep Frsh Cls; Rep Soph Cls; Rep Jr Cls; Rep Stu Cncl; L Tennis; High Hon Roll; Hon Roll; Comm.

ROUNDTREE, KEITH; Paul Laurnec Dunbar SHS No 414; Baltimore, MD; (Y); Church Yth Grp; Computer Clb; FBLA; JA; Bsbl; Bsktbl; Ftbl; Cit Awd; Hon Roll; NHS; Bus Mgmt.

ROUNTREE, BRYAN; Crossland HS; Ft Washington, MD; (Y); 2/400; Pres Boy Scts; French Clb; Math Tm; Hon Roll; NHS; Acadmc Excllnc Awd 84-86; U Of MD; Computer Science.

ROVA, ROSELYN; Takoma Acad; Adelphi, MD; (S); Teachers Aide; Yrbk Stf; Stu Cncl; Hon Roll; NHS.

ROVINE, TIMOTHY J; John Carroll HS; Abingdon, MD; (Y); Church Yth Grp; JV Socr; U DE; Advrtsng.

ROWE II, G KENNETH; Mcdonough HS; Waldorf, MD; (Y); Science Clb; Mc Donough HS Sci Fr 85; Southern MD Elec Cooprtv Inc Spc Awd Engr 85; Charles Cnty Sci Fair 85; Engr.

ROWE, STEPHANIE; Delaney HS; Timonium, MD; (Y); Am Leg Aux Girls St; Pres Church Yth Grp; French Clb; FBLA; Rep Frsh Cls; Cheerleading; High Hon Roll; Hon Roll; ZCMI Fash Brd 86; Ms Teen Cntntl 85; Brghm Yng U; Corp Law.

ROWE, TAMARA; Friendly SR HS; Ft Washington, MD; (Y); AFS; Church Yth Grp; Cmnty Wkr; Library Aide; Office Aide; Nwsp Rptr; Im Bsktbl; Im Sftbl; Im Swmmng; High Hon Roll; Hampton U; Sys Analysist.

ROWLAND, ANNE; Oakland Mills HS; Columbia, MD; (Y); 10/275; French Clb; Scholastic Bowl; Chorus; Yrbk Ed-Chief; Rep Frsh Cls; Sec Sr Cls; Sec Stu Cncl; Im Swmmng; Sec NHS; UVA Echols Schlr; Cnty Ledrshp Awd; U Of VA; Econmcs.

ROWLAND, BRIAN D; Springbrook HS; Silver Spring, MD; (Y); 122/488; Church Yth Grp; Office Aide; JV Bsbl; Var Bowling; Hon Roll; Masonic Awd; NHS; Past Master Cnclr Meritorious Srv Awd 85; Rep De Molay Awd 84; VA Tech; Elec Engr.

ROWLAND, DWAYNE; North Hagerstown HS; Hagestown, MD; (Y); 65/333; Spanish Clb; Rep Frsh Cls; Rep Soph Cls; Stat Bsktbl; Stat Crs Cntry; JV Ftbl; Var Trk; JV Wrstlng; Widner U; Bus.

RUARK, STEVEN; Sts Peter & Paul HS; Cambridge, MD; (Y); Letterman Clb; Ski Clb; SADD; Varsity Clb; Yrbk Bus Mgr; Var L Lcrss; Var Socr; Outstndng Achvt-NEDT Tst 84; Duke Boston Coll; Fnanc.

RUBAK, EVELYN; Roland Country Schl; Baltimore, MD; (Y); Cmnty Wkr; Drama Clb; French Clb; Temple Yth Grp; Acpl Chr; Chorus; School Musical; School Play; Nwsp Rptr; Lit Mag; Thtr.

RUBEL, LAURIE; Thomas Sprigg Wootton HS; Potomoc, MD; (Y); Nwsp Rptr; Pres Frsh Cls; L Var Bsktbl; Stat Vllybl; Hon Roll; Spnsh Ntl Hon Soc; Chem Awd Excllnc, Math Awd Excllnc; SCI.

RUBIN, ALLAN; Parkside SR HS; Salisbury, MD; (Y); 6/239; Ski Clb; Trs Spanish Clb; Mrchg Band; Symp Band; Rep Stu Cncl; CC Awd; NHS; Pres Schlr; St Schlr; All Eastern Shore Band; Louis S Armstrong Jazz Awd 86; Pres Clsrm Yng Am Pgm 86; Franklin Marshall Coll.

RUDDY, LAURA; Maurice J Mc Donaugh HS; Waldorf, MD; (S); Office Aide; Stat Bsbl; JV Cheerleading; Capt Crs Cntry; Capt Trk; High Hon Roll; Hon Roll; Jr NHS; NHS; SMAC Cross Cty MVP 85; U MD; Physcl Thrpy.

RUDICK, BRIAN; The Boys Latin Schl; Baltimore, MD; (S); SADD; Teachers Aide; JV Ftbl; Var Tennis; High Hon Roll; Hon Roll; Hnrbl Ment Mst Imprvd Stdnt 84; Ntl Hnr Soc 85; Med.

RUDO, JAMIE; Randallstown HS; Randallstown, MD; (Y); FBLA; Ski Clb; Off Jr Cls; Stu Cncl; Var Lcrss; U MD; Bus.

RUDOLPH, KATHRYN; Oxon Hill HS; Ft Washington, MD; (Y); 4-H; Math Tm; Band; Mrchg Band; Hon Roll; NHS; Ntl Merit SF; Germ.

RUDOLPH, MARC D; Loyola HS; Baltimore, MD; (S); Var Bsktbl; Hon Roll; NHS; Schlr Athl Schlrshp 83-87.

RUFFIN, KELVIN T; De Matha Catholic HS; Mitchellville, MD; (Y); #63 In Class; Boy Scts; Church Yth Grp; Ski Clb; Band; Concert Band; Symp Band; Co-Capt Ftbl; Wt Lftg; Hon Roll; Ntl Merit Ltr; Aero Sp Engr.

RUHL, JOHNA; Allegany HS; Cumberland, MD; (Y); 18/240; Hosp Aide; Yrbk Ed-Chief; Yrbk Phtg; Trs Jr Cls; Rep Stu Cncl; Stat Bsktbl; Hon Roll; NHS; JV Vllybl; AFS; Nwpr New Editor; Gate; U MD College Pk.

RUMBARGER, RICHARD CHARLES; Winston Churchill HS; Potomac, MD; (S); Boy Scts; Church Yth Grp; DECA; Ski Clb; Teachers Aide; JV Ftbl; JV Wrstlng; Hon Roll; DECA 1st Pl St & Top 10 USA & Canada-Petro Mrktng Mgmt Level 86; Ldrshp Corp & Order Arrow 82-86; Ithaca; Mgmt.

RUMBLE, STACEY; Patapsco HS; Baltimore, MD; (Y); 20/400; Political Wkr; Nwsp Bus Mgr; Rep Stu Cncl; Capt L Fld Hcky; High Hon Roll; NHS; Opt Clb Awd; St Schlr; Church Yth Grp; Cmnty Wkr; Pres Hnrs Flwshp Schlshp 86-87; Amer Awd 86; Lcl Rec Cncl Schlrshp 86-87; Coll Of Notre Dame MD; Lwyr.

RUMMEL, JULIE; North Hagerstown HS; Hagestown, MD; (Y); 25/300; Church Yth Grp; French Clb; Pres Band; Capt Flag Corp; Mrchg Band; Rep Jr Cls; Rep Stu Cncl; Hon Roll; Prfct Atten Awd; Rep Soph Cls; Prom Commtte Chirprsn 85-86; Med.

RUMMEL, KELLI LYNN; Bowie HS; Bowie, MD; (Y); German Clb; Spanish Clb; SADD; Variety Show; High Hon Roll; Hon Roll; Prfct Atten Awd; Spch Pathlgy.

RUMRILL, MARTIN; Oakland Mills HS; Columbia, MD; (Y); 44/236; French Clb; JA; ROTC; Rep Frsh Cls; Rep Stu Cncl; JV Wrstlng; Engrng.

RUPINSKI, MELVIN; Mt St Joseph HS; Baltimore, MD; (Y); 29/295; Camera Clb; Nwsp Rptr; Ftbl; High Hon Roll; Hon Roll; Law.

RUPP, JENNIFER; La Reine HS; White Plains, MD; (Y); Cmnty Wkr; Office Aide; SADD; Nwsp Stf; Yrbk Stf; High Hon Roll; Hon Roll; 2nd Pl & Hnrb Mntn Sci Fair; Hnr Awds; Comm Acad Excllnce; U MD.

RUPPERT, KIM; Allegany HS; Lavale, MD; (Y); Art Clb; Lit Mag; Sci.

RUSEVLYAN, RONALD; Lackey HS; Bryans Rd, MD; (Y); Ski Clb; Band; Concert Band; Mrchg Band; Symp Band; Variety Show; Off Stu Cncl; Bsktbl; JV Socr; Var L Tennis.

RUSH, JODI; Northern HS; Friendsville, MD; (Y); 2/114; Sec Church Yth Grp; Pres 4-H; Chorus; Church Choir; Bausch & Lomb Sci Awd; High Hon Roll; Hon Roll; Ntl Merit SF; Sal; MD St Sch Brd Schlrshp 86; Outstndng Stu 85; Frstbrg ST Coll; Vcl Msc.

RUSH, KIM; Gaithersburg HS; Gaithersburg, MD; (Y); Church Yth Grp; Drama Clb; Ski Clb; SADD; Rep Stu Cncl; JV Cheerleading; Var Fld Hcky; JV Pom Pon; JV Socr; Hon Roll; Engrng.

RUSSELL, JAMES; Leonardtown HS; Valley Lee, MD; (Y); JV Var Crs Cntry; JV Trk; High Hon Roll; Hon Roll; US Armd Svcs; Comm Wiring.

RUSSELL, JEANNE; Hereford SR HS; Parkton, MD; (Y); Church Yth Grp; Teachers Aide; VP Jr Cls; Var Cheerleading; Var Mgr(s); JV Sftbl; JV Var Vllybl; Hon Roll; Natl Sci And Eng Merit Awds 84-85; Acadmc All Am 84-85; Towson ST U.

RUSSELL, MARK; Walter Johnson HS; Bethesda, MD; (Y); Debate Tm; Nwsp Stf; Trs Sr Cls; Rep Stu Cncl; Im JV Bsktbl; JV Ftbl; Var L Socr; Im Sftbl; JV Var Vllybl; Hon Roll.

RUSSIN, DAVID; Thomas Stone HS; Waldorf, MD; (S); Band; Jazz Band; Mrchg Band; Pep Band; Rep Jr Cls; VP Sr Cls; Rep Stu Cncl; High Hon Roll; Lion Awd; NHS; Acad Ltr; U MD; Comp.

RUSSO, DEENA; Magruder HS; Derwood, MD; (Y); 23/330; Hosp Aide; Teachers Aide; Var L Sftbl; Hon Roll; Acdmc Awd 85-86; Hlth Pro.

RUTH, DANA; Queens Annes County HS; Chester, MD; (Y); Cmnty Wkr; Girl Scts; Hosp Aide; SADD; Drill Tm; Mrchg Band; Trk; Hon Roll; NHS; Ntl Merit Ltr; Zoogrphy.

RUTH, DAVID; Smithsburg HS; Smithsburg, MD; (Y); Church Yth Grp; Spanish Clb; Church Choir; School Musical; Elks Awd; Hon Roll; St Senatorial Schlrshp 87-90; Awd Tchng Spnsh To Elem Schl Stu 86; Hagerstown JC; Scndry Educ.

RYAN, BETH; Notre Dame Prep; Cockeysville, MD; (Y); Hosp Aide; Variety Show; Yrbk Phtg; Im Badmtn; Im Bsktbl; Im Fld Hcky; Im Socr; Hon Roll; Vllybl; Gym Meet Capt 84-86; Stu Faculty Bd Rep 85-86; Bus Adm.

RYAN, CHRISTOPHER; Georgetown Prep Schl; Potomac, MD; (Y); Math Tm; NFL; Radio Clb; Nwsp Stf; Golf; Hon Roll; Amrcn Rep Of A Junior Golf Tm In England 86.

RYAN, MARY KATHERINE; Acad Of The Holy Cross; Brookeville, MD; (Y); 5/123; Church Yth Grp; Math Clb; Church Choir; Lit Mag; High Hon Roll; NHS; Ntl Merit Ltr; Pres Scholar Loyola Coll 86; Chncllrs Scholar U MD Baltimore 86; MD Dstngshd Schlr Semi-Fin 85; Loyola Coll Baltimore; Elec Eng.

RYAN, VALERIE; Potomac HS; Hillcrest Hts, MD; (Y); Dance Clb; Pep Clb; Church Choir; Hon Roll; Psyclgy.

RYBAK, SHEREE; Woodlawn HS; Baltimore, MD; (Y); Sec AFS; Spanish Clb; Chorus; School Play; Hon Roll; Prfct Atten Awd; VFW Awd; Voice Dem Awd; Ski Clb; MD Acad Of Sci Awd 84; Cert Of Achvt 86; Lebanon Valley Clg; Bio.

RYKIEL, MARIA THERESA; Northeast SR HS; Pasadena, MD; (Y); 6/210; Pres Thesps; Varsity Clb; Powder Puff Ftbl; Capt Sftbl; Vllybl; Hon Roll; NHS; Church Yth Grp; Drama Clb; Office Aide; Unsung Hero Awd Vlybl 86; ST Sftbl Champs 86; Sentrl, Cls 86, Ki Wives Schlrshps 86; Schlstc Merit 86; Towson ST U; Early Chldhd Ed.

SAADI, CINDI; Bowie HS; Bowie, MD; (Y); Hosp Aide; VP Office Aide; Spanish Clb; Chorus; Off Frsh Cls; Off Soph Cls; Off Jr Cls; L Pom Pon; Sec NHS; Spanish NHS; Jobs Dghtrs Hon Queen, 2nd Rnnr Up In Miss Jobs Of MD Pgnt; Outstndng Achvmnt Awd; Mock Trial Club; Law.

SAATHOFF, TINA L; Mt Savage HS; Mt Savage, MD; (Y); 5/61; Pep Clb; Q&S; Band; Chorus; Concert Band; Mrchg Band; Pep Band; Yrbk Stf; Twrlr; NHS; All Cnty Chrs; All Cnty Band And Orch; Bd Of Trustees Schlrshp; Alleghany CC; Nrsg.

SABOL, SHARON; Joppatowne HS; Edgewood, MD; (Y); 13/186; Church Yth Grp; Trs French Clb; Teachers Aide; Orch; School Musical; Rep Sr Cls; Cit Awd; Hon Roll; NHS; Prse Acad Fita Awd 86; George Washington U Scholar Grant 86; George Washington U; Intl Bus.

SABOURY, DAWN; Queen Annes County HS; Centreville, MD; (Y); 22/342; Trs Spanish Clb; Chorus; Yrbk Phtg; Var L Bsktbl; Hon Roll; NHS; Ntl Merit Ltr; Sprtsmn Yr Grls Bsktbl 85-86; Salisbury ST Coll; Physcl Educ.

SACHS, DARRIN; Bohemia Manor HS; Cecilton, MD; (Y); 11/95; Camera Clb; Church Yth Grp; VP French Clb; Political Wkr; SADD; Acpl Chr; Jazz Band; Pep Band; Hon Roll; Prfct Atten Awd; Mst Accmplshd Brass Sectnst 83-86; MD Film Festvl 2nd Pl 86; Oral Roberts U; Theology.

SACKETT, JEANINE; Dulaney SR HS; Timonium, MD; (Y); Church Yth Grp; Dance Clb; Chorus; Variety Show; Trk; Hon Roll; Towson ST; Music.

SACKS, MARY; Harford Vo-Tech HS; Forest Hill, MD; (Y); Cmnty Wkr; Hosp Aide; SADD; VICA; Yrbk Bus Mgr; Yrbk Ed-Chief; Yrbk Sprt Ed; Yrbk Stf; Off Jr Cls; Hon Roll; Harford CC; Nrsg.

SACKS, TAMMY; La Reine HS; Camp Springs, MD; (Y); 13/149; Dance Clb; Teachers Aide; Nwsp Stf; Rep Frsh Cls; Rep Soph Cls; Sec Jr Cls; Trs NHS; Tres Of Natl Hnr Soc 85-86; U Of MD; Comm.

SADANALA, RAJAKUMAR; Takoma Acad; Takoma Park, MD; (S); Church Yth Grp; Ski Clb; Yrbk Phtg; Rep Frsh Cls; VP Soph Cls; Pres Jr Cls; Stu Cncl; JV Bsktbl; Hon Roll; NHS; Columbia Union Coll; Med.

SADTLER, MICHELLE; St Timothys Schl; Cockeysville, MD; (Y); Church Yth Grp; Spanish Clb; Horseback Riding 80-84&85-86; Hrsbck Rdng Tm Spring 86; Bus.

SAHIN, AYSE; Northwestern HS; College Pk, MD; (Y); AFS; Art Clb; Drama Clb; French Clb; German Clb; JA; Stage Crew; Nwsp Stf; Lit Mag; Gym; Cross Crrnts Awd, Art Publctn Schl 85; Gymnstcs Champ 84; AFS; Ecnmcs.

SAKADUSKI, JOSEPH; Loyola Blakefield HS; Towson, MD; (Y); Boy Scts; Church Yth Grp; Cmnty Wkr; Science Clb; Ski Clb; Varsity Clb; Chorus; Church Choir; VP Frsh Cls; Rep Soph Cls; Med.

SALAMONE, CATHERINE; Maurice J Mc Donough HS; Waldorf, MD; (Y); Drama Clb; Pres Thesps; Chorus; School Play; Stage Crew; VP Sr Cls; High Hon Roll; Hon Roll; Voted By SR Clss Best Actress,Mostoptimistic 86; U MD; Commnctns.

SALAS, LISA; Notre Dame Preparatory Schl; Baltimore, MD; (Y); Cmnty Wkr; Hosp Aide; Variety Show; Bowling; Var Capt Cheerleading; Var Gym; Im Socr; Swmmng; Hon Roll; NHS.

SALAZAR, JERE; St Vincetn Pallotti HS; Lanham, MD; (S); 2/115; Ski Clb; Spanish Clb; Var Bsktbl; Var Sftbl; Var Swmmng; High Hon Roll; Hon Roll; NHS; Spanish NHS.

SALAZAR, MICHELLE; Potomac SR HS; Temple Hills, MD; (Y); Am Leg Aux Girls St; Church Yth Grp; FBLA; Science Clb; Gym; Var Pom Pon; Var Sftbl; Cit Awd; High Hon Roll; NHS; Schlr Athlt Sftbll Lttr & Bar; U Of TX; Psychlgy.

SALB, DAWN; New Covenant Christian Acad; Chester, MD; (S); Church Yth Grp; Quiz Bowl; Band; School Play; Pres Sr Cls; High Hon Roll; Ntl Merit Schol; Church Choir; Chess Clb; Tennis; Amer Chrstn Hnr Scty Awd 82-84; Qlfd As Fin For The U S Sen Yth Prog 85; Sec MD Govrnrs Yth Adv Cncl.

SALERNO, CHRISTY; Archbishop Keough HS; Baltimore, MD; (Y); NFL; Rep Red Cross Aide; Thesps; School Musical; School Play; Rep Soph Cls; Trs VP Stu Cncl; JV Cheerleading; Swmmng; Ntl Cthlc Frnsc Lg Qrt Fnlst Ortrcl 85; Ntl Cthlc Frnsc Fnlst 5th Pl Drmtc 86; Bltmr Ctlc Fnsc Lg ST; Cmnctns.

SALES, ROBERT; Dulaney SR HS; Phoenix, MD; (Y); Church Yth Grp; JV Bsbl; Var Bsktbl; Coach Actv; Var Capt Socr; High Hon Roll; Teachers Aide; Hon Roll; 1st Tm MD All ST Sccr Slctn 85; Mech Engrng.

SALIBURY, CINDY; James M Bennett HS; Salisbury, MD; (Y); Cmnty Wkr; FBLA; Hosp Aide; Nwsp Bus Mgr; Nwsp Rptr; Nwsp Stf; Hon Roll; Stu Of Mnth 86; Salisbury ST Coll; Scl Wrk.

SALLESE, KELLI A; The Institute Of Notre Dame; Baltimore, MD; (Y); Church Yth Grp; Hosp Aide; School Musical; Variety Show; St Gbrls Soc Schlrshp 86; Villa Julie Coll; Tvl.

SAMPSON, VICTORIA; La Plata HS; White Plains, MD; (Y); Off Church Yth Grp; FBLA; Office Aide; Teachers Aide; Concert Band; Mrchg Band; Symp Band; Rep Stu Cncl; Hon Roll; Cmnty Wkr; Volunteer Rescue Sqd 86; Nrsg.

SAMUEL, LEVERN; Carver Vo Tech; Baltimore, MD; (Y); Computer Clb; English Clb; Math Clb; SADD; VICA; Nwsp Sprt Ed; Yrbk Sprt Ed; Var Ftbl; Var Swmmng; Var Trk; Engr.

SAMUELS, TRACEY LYNNE; Lareine HS; Ft Washington, MD; (Y); 19/149; Drama Clb; French Clb; Pep Clb; Sec Science Clb; Teachers Aide; Ed Lit Mag; Rep Frsh Cls; Var Cheerleading; French Hon Soc; High Hon Roll; Outstndng Awd Of Merit In Frnch 83-86; Acdmc Schlrshp From Tulane 86-90; Tulane U; Intl Corp Lawyer.

SAN JOSE, MARIA; Immaculata Coll HS; Bethesda, MD; (Y); Cmnty Wkr; Drama Clb; Math Clb; Science Clb; Spanish Clb; Chorus; School Musical; Variety Show; Hon Roll; Schl Schlrshp Pin 83-84 & 84-85; Slvr Mdl Schl Math Comp 85-86; Intl Mbr Natl Piano Plyng Auditions 86; Bus Admin.

SANABRIA, SUZANNE; Oxon Hill HS; Ft Washington, MD; (Y); German Clb; Intnl Clb; Stage Crew; Yrbk Phtg; Ed Lit Mag; Hon Roll; NHS; Grmn Hnr Scty 83-86; 1st Pl In Rgnl Sci Fair 84; Natl Schlrshp Ccommended Stu 85; U Of MD College Pk; Jrnlsm.

SANDBERG, MARNEE; Oakland Mills HS; Columbia, MD; (Y); Pres Temple Yth Grp; Varsity Clb; Var Cheerleading; Var Gym; Stat Lcrss; Var Socr; Hon Roll; NHS; Latin Clb; Phys Ed Awd; Scndry Acad Awd; Phys Thrpst.

SANDERS, DOROTHY; Baltimore Polytechnic Inst; Baltimore, MD; (Y); Library Aide; Church Choir; Messiah Coll; Elem Ed.

SANDERS, JEFF; Heritage Acad; Hagerstown, MD; (S); Boy Scts; Chorus; Church Choir; Orch; School Play; VP Soph Cls; Rep Stu Cncl; Cit Awd; Hon Roll; Fine Art Fsvtl Amer Assn Chrstn Schls Piano Div 1st Pl 84; Natl Fed Music Clbs JR Fstvl Gold Cup 84; Piano Prfrmnce.

SANDERS, KIM; Colonel Richardson HS; Preston, MD; (Y); Spanish Clb; Sec Soph Cls; VP Jr Cls; Var Capt Cheerleading; Tennis; NHS; Hstry Clb Sec/Treas; U Of MD; Dietcn.

SANDERS, LAURIE; Elizabeth Ann Seton HS; Bowie, MD; (Y); 6/179; Pres Frsh Cls; Var Bsktbl; Var Socr; Var Sftbl; High Hon Roll; NHS; Basketball 2nd Team All-Met 86; Softball & Basketball Nationals 86.

SANDLER, DAVID; Walter Johnson HS; Bethesda, MD; (Y); AFS; Debate Tm; Key Clb; Office Aide; Political Wkr; Temple Yth Grp; Stu Cncl; JV Bsktbl; Var Capt Ftbl; Wt Lftg.

SANDLER, RISA; Thomas S Wootton HS; Gaithersburg, MD; (Y); Cmnty Wkr; Temple Yth Grp; Nwsp Bus Mgr; Nwsp Stf; Hon Roll; NEDT Awd; Bst Wrtng Awd-U Of SC-JRNLSM Wrkshp 85; Confrmtn Cls 85; HS In Isrl Pgm 85-86; Peer Cnslr 86-87.

SANETRIK, MARK; Mount Saint Joseph HS; Ellicott City, MD; (Y); 75/300; Im Ftbl; Hon Roll.

SANTANGELO, LISA; Elizabeth Seton HS; Landover, MD; (Y); Ski Clb; Rep Stu Cncl; Swmmng; Trk.

SANZ, FATIMA; Archbishop Keough HS; Baltimore, MD; (Y); Rep Stu Cncl; Tennis; Hon Roll.

SAPP, ANNA; Gaithersburg HS; Gaithersburg, MD; (Y); Office Aide; SADD; Teachers Aide; Band; Orch; JV Bsktbl; JV Sftbl; Swmmng; Hon Roll; Advrtsg.

SARALEGUI, GISELE; Winston Churchill HS; Potomac, MD; (Y); Drama Clb; French Clb; Trk; Vllybl; Hon Roll; Jr NHS; NHS; Page House Of Reps 85; Cngrssnl Intern 85 & 86; Yng Republicns 86; Georgetown U; Pol Sci.

SARGENT, VALERIE; Maurice J Mc Donough HS; Waldorf, MD; (S); Church Yth Grp; Intnl Clb; Office Aide; Teachers Aide; Nwsp Rptr; Nwsp Stf; Rep Frsh Cls; Rep Soph Cls; Hon Roll; NHS; Lttrd In Stu Govt 83-84; Lttrd In Natl Hnr Scty 84-85; U Of MD; Accntng.

SASTRO, RESA BARNADIWA; Wheaton HS; Wheaton, MD; (Y); 50/386; JCL; Latin Clb; Letterman Clb; SADD; Varsity Clb; Capt Socr; Var Tennis; Hon Roll; NHS; 3 Yr Vrsty Socr Plyr Cap; Vrsty Ten Tm 86NHS 85-86; Natl Hnr Roll 83-85; Lat Clb 84-85; MD; Bus Mgmt.

SATCHELL, STEVE; Easton HS; Easton, MD; (Y); Spanish Clb; Nwsp Rptr; Nwsp Stf; Trs Frsh Cls; Trs Soph Cls; Rep Stu Cncl; Var Capt Ftbl; L Golf; L Lcrss; Hon Roll; Brdcstng.

SATISKY, STEVEN; Pikesville HS; Balto, MD; (Y); Cmnty Wkr; Mathletes; Quiz Bowl; Scholastic Bowl; Nwsp Rptr; Nwsp Sprt Ed; Sec Sr Cls; Var Bsktbl; Var Lcrss; NHS; Mem US Yth Maccabi Tm Bsktbl 84; Mechncl Engr.

SATTERFIELD, SEAN; St John/Prospect Hall HS; Jefferson, MD; (Y); 6/35; Drama Clb; Capt JA; Hon Roll; NHS; Loyola Coll; Phlsphy.

SAUER, CARRIE C; Thomas Wootton HS; Gaithersburg, MD; (Y); Service Clb; Thesps; Orch; School Musical; Variety Show; Pom Pon; Hon Roll; NHS; Ntl Merit Ltr; MD ST Music Tchrs Assn Piano Comptn 1st Pl 85; Critics Cir Ntl Piano Playg Audtns 86.

SAUERS, GREG; Mt Hebron HS; Marriottsville, MD; (Y); Rep AFS; Office Aide; Chorus; Rep Frsh Cls; Rep Soph Cls; Rep Jr Cls; Rep Sr Cls; Rep Stu Cncl; Mgr Bsktbl; Mgr Tennis; UMBC.

SAUM, ANDREA; Liberty HS; Sykesville, MD; (S); Church Yth Grp; Ski Clb; Teachers Aide; Varsity Clb; Rep Jr Cls; JV Var Socr; Hon Roll; Peer Cnslr; MD ST Gifted & Tlntd; Psych.

SAUNDERS, ANTHONY W; Thomas Stone HS; Waldorf, MD; (Y); Drama Clb; Thesps; Band; Chorus; Church Choir; Jazz Band; Mrchg Band; Pep Band; School Musical; School Play; All Amer Yth Hnr Mscns 83-85; Embry-Rddl Aeron U; Aeroncl Sci.

SAUNDERS, GAIL; Northwestern SR HS; Baltimore, MD; (Y); FBLA; Hosp Aide; Library Aide; Office Aide; Band; Concert Band; Orch; Symp Band; Rep Frsh Cls; Rep Soph Cls; Real Estate Broker.

SAVAGE, DAINA A; Southern Garrett HS; Swanton, MD; (S); 24/225; 4-H; Ski Clb; Band; Rep Stu Cncl; Stat Score Keeper; Im Swmmng; Tennis; High Hon Roll; Masonic Awd; NHS; Vrsty Ltr Ski Rcng 84; SR Chmp Dist Swm Tm 85; Garrett Cty Farm Qn & Autumn Glory Prncss 85; Dentstry.

SAVAGE, DAVID C; Southern Garrett HS; Mountain Lake Pk, MD; (S); 53/222; Boy Scts; Church Yth Grp; Band; Color Guard; Concert Band; Jazz Band; Mrchg Band; Pep Band; Var Trk; Hon Roll; WSU; Bus.

SAVAGE, JOE; Clear Spring HS; Clear Spg, MD; (Y); 20/128; Band; Concert Band; Mrchg Band; Yrbk Stf; JV Bsktbl; JV Var Socr; Graphic Arts.

SAVELESKI, KAREN; Broadneck SR HS; Annapolis, MD; (S); DECA; SADD; Teachers Aide; Mrchg Band; Yrbk Stf; Rep Jr Cls; Var L Sftbl; Hon Roll; Church Yth Grp; VP Band; DECA Cnty Conf 3 Trphs Won 86; Towson ST U; Teaching.

SAVERINO, BETH; Mt De Sales Acad; Baltimore, MD; (Y); Chorus; Church Choir; Var JV Cheerleading; Var JV Lcrss; Hon Roll; Prfct Atten Awd; Cert Eductnl Dvlpmt 85; Cert Apprctn 85 & 86.

SAVIA, JOLYNN; La Plata HS; La Plata, MD; (Y); Debate Tm; Drama Clb; Pres Thesps; Chorus; School Musical; School Play; Stage Crew; Hon Roll; Jr NHS; Trvl Agnt.

SAVOY, DWAYNE; La Plata HS; Waldorf, MD; (Y); Computer Clb; Ski Clb; Teachers Aide; Hon Roll; RE Broker.

SAVOY, THOMAS; Lackey HS; Bryans Road, MD; (Y); JA; Rep Soph Cls; Pres Jr Cls; Rep Stu Cncl; Var Bsbl; JV Ftbl; VP Capt Wrstlng; Soutern Md Athl Conf Wrestling Champ 85; OK ST.

SAWERS, MARK ANDREW; Hammond HS; Columbia, MD; (Y); 26/252; Co-Capt Chess Clb; Cmnty Wkr; Computer Clb; Debate Tm; Math Tm; Ski Clb; Hon Roll; Pres Acadmc Fit Awd 86; U Of MD Coll Park; Aerosp Engr.

SAYERS, MITCHELL; Boys Latin Schl; Glen Arm, MD; (S); Computer Clb; Debate Tm; Ski Clb; Varsity Clb; Nwsp Rptr; Yrbk Stf; Lit Mag; L Crs Cntry; Im Lcrss; JV Tennis; Sci.

SAYLOR, SANDRA; St Vincent Pallotti HS; Laurel, MD; (S); 10/120; Var JV Bsktbl; Capt L Pom Pon; Score Keeper; Timer; High Hon Roll; Hon Roll; NHS; Prfct Atten Awd; Stu Mnth Am Lit 84-85; Stu Mnth Spnsh II 84-85; Coachs Awd Pom Pon Sq 84-85; Elem Ed.

SAYLOR, SHARON; Northwestern SR HS; W Hyattsville, MD; (Y); Pep Clb; Spanish Clb; Stage Crew; Hon Roll; P G CC; Comp Oprtr.

SCHADE, TERRI; Fort Hill HS; Cumberland, MD; (Y); Church Yth Grp; Office Aide; Yrbk Stf; Hon Roll; Towson ST Coll; Bus Admin.

SCHAEFER, BARBARA; Elkton HS; Elkton, MD; (Y); 1/289; Pres SADD; Nwsp Ed-Chief; VP Sr Cls; Var Capt Bsktbl; Var L Sftbl; Var Capt Vllybl; Pres NHS; Pres Schlr; Val; Math Tm; Swarthmore Coll Grant 86; Princpls Awd 86; Swarthmore Coll; Bio.

SCHAP, DEBBIE; Notre Dame Prep; Timonium, MD; (Y); Cmnty Wkr; JA; Chorus; Im Badmtn; Im Bsktbl; Law.

SCHARPER JR, PHILIP H; Loyola HS; Lutherville, MD; (S); 13/197; Art Clb; French Clb; Quiz Bowl; Service Clb; Teachers Aide; Y-Teens; Yrbk Phtg; Im Ftbl; Im Socr; Hon Roll; NEDT Awd; Naval Acad; Engrng.

SCHAUM, CHARLES; Eastern Voc Tech HS; Baltimore, MD; (Y); Aud/Vis; Church Yth Grp; Cmnty Wkr; Drama Clb; Red Cross Aide; Teachers Aide; Chorus; Dsl Mchnc.

SCHEINBERG, JASON; Thomas S Wootton HS; Rockville, MD; (Y); Political Wkr; Nwsp Rptr; Nwsp Stf; JV Bsktbl; Var Socr; JA; Teachers Aide; Rep Stu Cncl; Outstndng Jnrs MD Ldrshp Confrnc-U Of MD 86; Fngn Affrs/Anti-Aprthd Confrnc 86; Pre-Law.

SCHEINER, DAVID; Elkton HS; Elkton, MD; (Y); JV Bsktbl; Hon Roll; Prfct Atten Awd; Bio.

SCHEINER, MIKE; Elkton HS; Elkton, MD; (Y); JV Bsktbl; Hon Roll; NHS; Prfct Atten Awd; U Of DE; Bio.

SCHENENDORF, JOHN NOAH; Gaithersburgh HS; Gaithersburg, MD; (Y); AFS; French Hon Soc; High Hon Roll; NHS; Ntl Merit SF; Geog Wash U Medal Achvmnt In Math & Sci 86; Cert Of Merit In French Ntl Cntst 84-86.

SCHER, LESLIE; La Plata HS; La Plata, MD; (Y); Computer Clb; Drama Clb; Office Aide; Thesps; Chorus; School Musical; School Play; Stage Crew; Hon Roll; Young Lawyers Clb Treas 86; Anthplgst.

SCHIMKE, JON B; Calvert HS; St Leonards, MD; (Y); 5/242; Am Leg Boys St; Key Clb; Spanish Clb; Yrbk Stf; JV Bsbl; JV Bsktbl; JV Crs Cntry; JV Mgr(s); High Hon Roll; Lion Awd; U Of CA San Diego; Bio.

SCHLEICHER, TIM; Patterson SR HS; Baltimore, MD; (Y); Am Leg Boys St; Pres Church Yth Grp; VP Debate Tm; Church Choir; Pres Stu Cncl; Var Bsktbl; JV Ftbl; Cit Awd; Jr NHS; Prfct Atten Awd; Paul Smiths Coll; Htl Mgmt.

SCHLIMM, GREGORY; Archbishop Curley HS; Baltimore, MD; (S); Science Clb; Nwsp Ed-Chief; Lit Mag; NHS; Chess Clb; Nwsp Rptr; Nwsp Stf; Yrbk Stf; High Hon Roll; MD Distngshd Schlr SF; Gen Excllnce Ltr Schl Svc; Its Acad Tm; Loyola Coll; Jrnlsm.

SCHLITZER, MICHAEL; Arlington Baptist HS; W Friendship, MD; (Y); VP Church Yth Grp; Band; Chorus; Church Choir; Orch; School Play; Bsbl; Hon Roll; Cello, Bio Awds 85-86; U MD Baltimore Co; Bio Chem.

SCHMERSAL, JEFFREY; Dulaney SR HS; Phoenix, MD; (Y); Church Yth Grp; Band; Concert Band; Jazz Band; Mrchg Band; Pep Band; Symp Band; Hon Roll; NHS; Im Sftbl; Clemson; Engrng.

SCHMIDT, FRED; Mcdonough HS; La Plata, MD; (S); 34/315; Am Leg Boys St; Bsbl; Golf; Socr; Tennis; High Hon Roll; Jr NHS; NHS; Wake Forest; Intl Affrs.

SCHMIDT, KAREN; Mc Donough HS; Bryantown, MD; (Y); Letterman Clb; Teachers Aide; School Musical; Variety Show; Pres Soph Cls; Stu Cncl; Stat Ftbl; L Pom Pon; Hon Roll; Jr NHS; 1st & 2nd Pl Rgnl & Ntl Lvls 83-86; Ltn Awd 86.

SCHMIDT, SHARON; Lansdowne HS; Baltimore, MD; (Y); Dance Clb; Drama Clb; Service Clb; Ski Clb; SADD; Teachers Aide; Drm Mjr(t); Flag Corp; Mrchg Band; School Musical; Outstndg Athletes Amer; Med.

SCHMIGEL, GREGORY; Northwestern HS; Hyattsville, MD; (Y); AFS; Aud/Vis; Drama Clb; German Clb; Spanish Clb; SADD; School Play; Stage Crew; Rep Frsh Cls; Rep Soph Cls; Hugh O Brien Yth Fndtn Awd 85; U Of MD; Frng Lang.

SCHMITZ, MIKE; Magruder HS; Derwood, MD; (Y); Ski Clb; JV Ftbl; JV Golf; Var Trk; Wt Lftg; Hon Roll; E Carolina U; Bus.

SCHNEEWIND, HANNAH; Western HS; Baltimore, MD; (Y); 20/420; Drama Clb; English Clb; Quiz Bowl; Scholastic Bowl; Thesps; School Play; Stage Crew; Nwsp Rptr; Nwsp Stf; NHS; Schlrshp From Its Acadmc Tv Quiz Show; Vassar Coll; Drama.

SCHNEIDER, CHRISTINE; La Plata SR HS; La Plata, MD; (Y); 5/388; Math Tm; Science Clb; Swmmng; Var Capt Tennis; Cit Awd; High Hon Roll; NHS; Ntl Merit Ltr; All Co Tennis Tm Mixed Doubles 85; 3rd Tennis Rgnls Mxd Dbls, Prin Awd Achvt Math Lg 86; Comp Sci.

SCHOEN, KIM; Gaithersburg HS; Gaithersburg, MD; (Y); SADD; School Play; Nwsp Rptr; Yrbk Stf; Pres Stu Cncl; Var Tennis; JV Vllybl; French Hon Soc; NHS; Ntl Merit SF; W MD Coll Writing Awd 86; Superintdnts Writing Awd 85; Advtrsng.

SCHOLLENBERGER, LAURA; Thomas Stone HS; Waldorf, MD; (S); Am Leg Aux Girls St; Pres Drama Clb; Teachers Aide; Thesps; Chorus; School Musical; School Play; High Hon Roll; NHS; Salisbury ST Coll; Bus Adm.

SCHOLTZ, KRISTIN; Institute Of Notre Dame; Baltimore, MD; (Y); Pres Church Yth Grp; Cmnty Wkr; Drama Clb; Hosp Aide; Thesps; School Musical; School Play; Hon Roll.

SCHOLZ, JAMES ALLEN; Elkton HS; Elkton, MD; (Y); Band; Chorus; Concert Band; Jazz Band; Mrchg Band; School Musical; Symp Band; JV L Trk; Hon Roll; Trple Crwn 86; Ind Arts Outstndng Achvt 8j; Cmptr Tech.

SCHREDER, BRANDON; Cardinal Gibbons HS; Baltimore, MD; (Y); Gov Hon Prg Awd; NHS; Ntl Merit Ltr; Pres Schlr; Debate Tm; Red Cross Aide; School Play; JV Crs Cntry; Hon Roll; Pres Schlrshp 86; Sci Awd 86; U Of MD.

SCHROEDER, DIANE; Laurel HS; Laurel, MD; (Y); Church Yth Grp; Teachers Aide; Church Choir; Yrbk Sprt Ed; Yrbk Stf; Tennis; Hon Roll; Tennis Troph MIP 86; Tennis Pin & Ltr 86.

SCHUBERT, SHERRI; Allegany HS; Cumberland, MD; (Y); 32/230; AFS; Ski Clb; Drill Tm; Yrbk Stf; Tennis; Hon Roll; Salisbury ST Clg.

SCHUERHOLZ, TERRY; Parkville HS; Baltimore, MD; (Y); Church Yth Grp; JV Var Socr; Var JV Sftbl; JV Trk; High Hon Roll; NHS; Towson ST U; Acctg.

SCHULDEN, JEFFREY D; Queen Anne Schl; Bowie, MD; (Y); 1/41; Camera Clb; Chess Clb; Model UN; Ski Clb; School Play; Stage Crew; Nwsp Ed-Chief; Yrbk Phtg; Trs Frsh Cls; Trs Soph Cls; Cum Laude Scty 85; Math Awd 84 & 85; Hmnts Awd 85; Frnch & Chmstr Awds 83-85; Physcn.

SCHULTZ, BONNIE; Westminister HS; Westminster, MD; (Y); Church Yth Grp; French Clb; Office Aide; Concert Band; Hon Roll; Prfct Atten Awd; Comm.

SCHULTZ, MELODY; Roland Park Country Schl; Baltimore, MD; (Y); AFS; Church Yth Grp; Chorus; Sec Frsh Cls; Sec Sr Cls; Var Badmtn; Im Fld Hcky; Im Lcrss; JV Tennis; Hon Roll; Page For MD Gen Assem 86; Franklin/Marshll Coll; Poly Sci.

SCHUMANN, ERIK; St Andrews Episcopal Schl; Rockville, MD; (Y); Exploring; Latin Clb; Ski Clb; SADD; Varsity Clb; Trs Stu Cncl; JV Bsktbl; Var JV Socr; Trk; Wt Lftg; Soccer Vrsty Trphy 85; Mst Outstndng Forward 85; 2nd Team All League 85; 1st Pl Jr Whitewater Slalom 84.

SCHWAB, MICHELLE; Arlington Baptist Schl; Baltimore, MD; (Y); Teachers Aide; Trs Band; Concert Band; Flag Corp; Mrchg Band; Orch; Pep Band; Hon Roll; Goucher Coll.

SCHWARTZ, DEBRA E; Springbrook HS; Silver Spring, MD; (Y); 16/488; GAA; Ski Clb; SADD; Temple Yth Grp; Yrbk Sprt Ed; Im Mgr Fld Hcky; L Socr; Hon Roll; NHS; Math Clb; Ntl Hnr Roll; U DE; Vtrnrn.

SCHWARTZ, DORIS; C E S Jewish Day Schl; Potomac, MD; (Y); Cmnty Wkr; Dance Clb; SADD; Chorus; School Play; Yrbk Sprt Ed; Rep Frsh Cls; Rep Soph Cls; Rep Stu Cncl; Var L Cheerleading; Excellence In Eng 83-86; Excellence In Judaic & Chem 85-86.

SCHWARTZ, JACKIE; Notre Dame Prep School For Girls; Towson, MD; (Y); Cmnty Wkr; GAA; Pep Clb; Varsity Clb; Chorus; Stu Cncl; JV Var Fld Hcky; JV Var Lcrss; Timer; Hon Roll; Forestry.

SCHWARTZ, JEFFREY I; Mc Donogh Schl; Owings Mills, MD; (Y); Debate Tm; German Clb; Intnl Clb; Lit Mag; Socr; JV Var Tennis; Hon Roll; Ntl Merit SF; Gld Mask Awd 83; Bus Adm.

SCHWEDES, RONALD G; South Carroll HS; Mt Airy, MD; (Y); Church Yth Grp; JA; Jazz Band; Stu Cncl; Bsktbl; Trk; Vllybl; Hon Roll; Senatorial Schlrshp Charles Smelser Awd 86; Red Crss JR Lfsvng Cert 84; E Cst Trpl Jmp Awd 1st 86; Ambassador COLL; Info Sys Mgnt.

SCHWINGER, LAURI; Centennial HS; Ellicott City, MD; (Y); Art Clb; Key Clb; Office Aide; Ski Clb; School Musical; Yrbk Stf; Stu Cncl; Var L Fld Hcky; Mgr(s); Hon Roll.

SCOTT III, LEON F; Bishop Mc Namara HS; Temple Hills, MD; (Y); Model UN; Spanish Clb; SADD; Rep Jr Cls; VP Sr Cls; Rep Stu Cncl; JV Im Bsktbl; JV Ftbl; High Hon Roll; Hon Roll; US Senate Internshp 86; Ct Internshp Judge Femia 85; U MD; Acctng.

SCOTT, MELISSA; Harford Vo-Tech HS; Fallston, MD; (Y); VP SADD; U Of MD; Law.

SCOTT, RONALD; Suitland HS; Suitland, MD; (Y); Boys Clb Am; Church Yth Grp; Latin Clb; Spanish Clb; SADD; Teachers Aide; Nwsp Phtg; Yrbk Phtg; Yrbk Rptr; Yrbk Stf; Latin Hon Soc 84; Hampton U; Pre Law.

SCOTT, WILTON W; Springbrook HS; Silver Spring, MD; (Y); 294/488; Boy Scts; Church Yth Grp; Chorus; JV Bsbl; Var L Socr; Wt Lftg; Wrstlng; Montgomery Cnty Young Amer Arch Awd 84-85; Natl Achvt Commended Stu 84-85; Arch.

SCUNGIO, JOANNA; The John Carroll Schl; Abingdon, MD; (Y); 84/238; French Clb; JA; Yrbk Rptr; Mgr(s); French Hon Soc; Hon Roll; FBLA; Chorus; Variety Show; Yrbk Stf; Corporate Law.

SEAQUIST, CARL; Severn Schl; Annapolis, MD; (Y); 1/77; Chess Clb; Pres VP Key Clb; Latin Clb; Ed Lit Mag; NHS; Ntl Merit Ltr; Val; Tennis; High Hon Roll; Pres Schlr; Schl Ltn Awd 85 & 86; Bnjmn Frnkln Schlr U PA; 86-87; U PA; Physics.

SEARLES, AIMEE; Gaithersburg HS; Gaithersburg, MD; (Y); Church Yth Grp; Cmnty Wkr; Drama Clb; FBLA; JA; ROTC; SADD; Teachers Aide; Color Guard; Drill Tm; Reserve Ofcrs Assn Medal For Ctznshp 86; NC ST Clg; Educ.

SEARS, ROB; Pattersonn HS; Baltimore, MD; (Y); Computer Clb; Wrstlng; Auto Mchnc.

SEAY, MARIAN; Fallston HS; Joppa, MD; (Y); 68/250; DECA; Math Clb; SADD; Cit Awd; Hon Roll; Vlntrs In Ed Cert 85; Aero Space Engrng.

SEBURN, PATRICK W; North Hagerstown HS; Hagerstown, MD; (Y); 14/272; VP Latin Clb; Teachers Aide; VP Orch; Wt Lftg; Hon Roll; U MD C P; Bus.

SEEBER, ALYSON; St Marys Ryken HS; Colonial Bch, VA; (Y); Sec Church Yth Grp; FBLA; VP Frsh Cls; VP Soph Cls; Stat Bsbl; Var Stat Bsktbl; Mgr Ftbl; JV Sftbl; Hon Roll; Acctng.

SEESS, JULIA; Frederick HS; Frederick, MD; (Y); AFS; Church Yth Grp; German Clb; Spanish Clb; SADD; Teachers Aide; Ed Lit Mag; JV Socr; Hon Roll; Jrnlsm.

SEILBACK, JOHN; Fallston HS; Baldwin, MD; (Y); 36/250; Church Yth Grp; German Clb; Stage Crew; Hon Roll; USAF.

SEILER, PHIL; Dulaney SR HS; Timonium, MD; (Y); Teachers Aide; Church Choir; School Musical; School Play; Lit Mag; JV Crs Cntry; Rep Church Yth Grp; Band; Im Sftbl; JV Trk; Bronze Mdl In Russian Written Olypiada 85; 2nd Pl At Dulaney Natl Math Cntst 85; Bus Mgmt.

SEITER, JANE I; Rising Sun JR SR HS; Rising Sun, MD; (Y); 3/165; Pres Key Clb; Concert Band; Jazz Band; Pres Frsh Cls; Pres Soph Cls; Var L Fld Hcky; Var L Trk; Ntl Merit SF; St Schlr; Math Tm; Towson ST U All SR Hnr Band; All Cnty Band; Towson ST U Massed Clarnt Choir.

SEITZ, NIKKI; Thomas Stone HS; Waldorf, MD; (S); Cmnty Wkr; Drama Clb; Off Thesps; School Play; Yrbk Stf; Rptr Lit Mag; Hon Roll; PTP Plyrs 84-85; U S All Amercn Schlr 85-86; Psyclgy.

SELBY, TODD; North Carroll HS; Manchester, MD; (Y); Art Clb; JA; Stage Crew; Hon Roll; Art.

SELL, STEPHEN; Allegany HS; Cumberland, MD; (Y); Computer Clb; Drama Clb; Band; Concert Band; Jazz Band; Mrchg Band; Pep Band; School Play; High Hon Roll; Hon Roll; Music.

SELLARS, KISTION; Sparrows Point HS; Baltimore, MD; (Y); Computer Clb; GAA; Off Soph Cls; Var Fld Hcky; Var Lcrss; JV Var Socr; Var Trk; Hon Roll; Took 1st Rnnr Up Miss HS Cntst 84; Dundalk CC; Compu Prg.

SELSER JR, ALAN; Parkside HS; Salisbury, MD; (Y); Church Yth Grp; Cmnty Wkr; French Clb; JA; Band; Mrchg Band; Stu Cncl; Tennis; Hon Roll; NHS; Yng Democrts Wicomico Cnty Brd Mbr 84-87; Natl Frnch Exm Hghst Scr Schl 85-86; NC; Elec Engrg.

SEMIN, LORRAINE; Archbishop Keough HS; Balt, MD; (Y); Church Yth Grp; Library Aide; Nwsp Rptr; Off Frsh Cls; Off Soph Cls; Off Jr Cls; Rep Stu Cncl; Var Socr; Hon Roll; NHS; High Li Ldrshp Prog 86; 1st Plc 3rd Yr German Ptry Rectatn Cont 86; 1st Rnnr Up Bst Actrss 1 Act Ply86.

SENFT, DAVID; Laplata HS; Waldorf, MD; (Y); Chess Clb; Computer Clb; Intnl Clb; Ski Clb; Teachers Aide; Var Capt Socr; High Hon Roll; Hon Roll; NHS; First Team Confnc Sccr 86; MD U; Bus Finance.

SEO, HUI; Crossland HS; Temple Hills, MD; (Y); French Clb; Wrstlng; Hon Roll.

SERENYI, NICK; Gaithersburg HS; Gaithersburg, MD; (S); AFS; Church Yth Grp; Var Crs Cntry; Var Tennis; Var Trk; Cit Awd; French Hon Soc; Hon Roll; Lion Awd; Spc Shttl Stu Invlvmnt Prjct Reg Wnnr 84 & 85.

SERIO, CHRISTINE E; Centennial HS; Ellicott City, MD; (Y); 150/400; Drama Clb; Pep Clb; Ski Clb; Spanish Clb; Thesps; School Play; Rep Stu Cncl; Cheerleading; Gym; Opt Clb Awd; Hnds Across America 86; Newberry Coll; Communications.

SERIO, MICHAEL J; Archbishop Curley HS; Baltimore, MD; (S); 1/136; SADD; Var Capt Ftbl; Var L Lcrss; Var Capt Wrstlng; Pres NHS; Dstngshd Schlr Semi Fnlst 86; Schlr Athl Rgnl Wnnr 86; MD Schltc Assoc All Star Tm 86.

SETO, PAUL; Suitland HS; District Height, MD; (Y); Varsity Clb; Var JV Bsbl; Var JV Bsktbl; High Hon Roll; Hon Roll; Boys Clb Am; Letterman Clb; Office Aide; Spanish Clb; Teachers Aide; MD; Engrng.

SEWELL, TARA; Fallston HS; Fallston, MD; (Y); Church Yth Grp; Computer Clb; German Clb; Yrbk Stf; Hon Roll; German Natl Hnr Scty 86; Bio Sci.

SEWELL, VIVIAN; Glenelg HS; Ellicott City, MD; (Y); 12/255; Sec Ed Church Yth Grp; Cmnty Wkr; Church Choir; Nwsp Ed-Chief; Rep Jr Cls; Rep Sr Cls; High Hon Roll; Hon Roll; NHS; Trphy 3rd Pl Rsrch Paper 85; Occp Therapy.

SEXTON, GEOFF; Gwynn Park HS; Cheltenham, MD; (Y); Boys Clb Am; Camera Clb; Yrbk Phtg; Yrbk Rptr; Yrbk Stf; Lit Mag; Bsbl; Bowling; Hon Roll; Salisburg ST Coll; Bus.

SEYMOUR, PAULA; Ma Gruder HS; Olney, MD; (Y); AFS; SADD; Yrbk Stf; Rep Soph Cls; Rep Jr Cls; Pre-Law.

SEYMOUR, SANDRA; Archbishop Keough HS; Balt, MD; (Y); Pres Art Clb; Cmnty Wkr; Trs Spanish Clb; Yrbk Bus Mgr; Sec Soph Cls; Sec Jr Cls; Sec Sr Cls; Hon Roll; NHS; NEDT Awd; Comp Sci.

SHACOCHIS, CHARLES; Fallston HS; Fallston, MD; (Y); Drama Clb; Ski Clb; Thesps.

SHAFFER, BRUCE; Allegany HS; Cresaptown, MD; (Y); Art Clb; CAP; Cmnty Wkr; Library Aide; Office Aide; Science Clb; Teachers Aide; Stage Crew; Yrbk Ed-Chief; Yrbk Stf; Bowling Qesd Coca Cola Natl Schlrshp Tourney 84-85; Derry Inst Of Elec; Electrncs.

SHAFFER, ERIK; Mc Donough HS; Waldorf, MD; (Y); Computer Clb; SADD; Band; Concert Band; Mrchg Band; Pep Band; Outstndng Srv From Amer Scndnvn Stu Exch 78-86; CPR Cert From Ntl Red Cross; San Jose ST U; Bus Mngmnt.

SHAFFER, LORI A; Southern Garrett HS; Deer Park, MD; (S); 19/223; Band; Concert Band; Mrchg Band; Hon Roll; Gardner-Webb Coll; Frnch Ed.

SHAH, MONICA; Gaithersburg HS; Gaithersburg, MD; (Y); AFS; JA; Chorus; Nwsp Stf; Yrbk Stf; Lit Mag; Ntl Merit SF; Intnl Clb; NFL; Ski Clb; Fairchild Sp Co Jr Bd Dir 85-86; Am Nuc Soc Spcl Achvt Awd, Mus Awd 84; Georgetown; Intl Bus.

SHAHAN, LYNN; Bishop Walsh HS; Ridgeley, WV; (Y); Pep Clb; Rep Stu Cncl; Cheerleading; Bus Mgmt.

SHAHID, MOHAMMAD; Bennett SR HS; Salisbury, MD; (Y); 29/180; Chess Clb; FBLA; JA; Nwsp Rptr; Nwsp Stf; JV Socr; Hon Roll; 1st In Rgnl Comp Prgmmg Cont FBLA 85-86; 4th MD-COMP Prgmmg; Syracuse U; Comp Sci.

SHAIBU, JOHN; Northwestern HS; Hyattsville, MD; (Y); Church Yth Grp; Chorus; Church Choir; High Hon Roll; Hon Roll; Acdmc Awd 85; U MD; Chem.

SHAMBLEN, VICKI; La Plata HS; La Plata, MD; (Y); 12/500; 4-H; Thesps; Off Sr Cls; JV Cheerleading; 4-H Awd; High Hon Roll; VP Jr NHS; Trs NHS; Drama Clb; Schl Show Troupe; Med.

SHANE, LAURA E; Williamsport HS; Williamsport, MD; (Y); 2/227; Drama Clb; French Clb; Science Clb; Teachers Aide; Band; Frsh Cls; Soph Cls; Jr Cls; Stu Cncl; High Hon Roll; Mst Ideal Stu; George WA U; Intl Affairs.

SHANHOLTZER, ANDREA; Bishop Walsh HS; Romney, WV; (Y); Pres 4-H; VP Library Aide; Band; Flag Corp; L Pom Pon; 4-H Awd; Hon Roll; JR Ldrshp Awd 85; Blue And Gold 4-H Awd 86; Outstndng Flag Corp 86; Marywood College; Chld Psych.

SHANHOLTZER, LISA; Walt Whitmon HS; Bethesda, MD; (Y); Exploring; Mgr Socr; Ntl Latin Exam Gold Mdlst 86; Lang.

SHANK, DENNIS; Williamsport HS; Williamsoport, MD; (Y); Exploring; Var JV Socr; Var Tennis; Hon Roll; NHS; Prfct Atten Awd; Engrng.

SHANK, MIKE; Smithsburg HS; Hagerstown, MD; (Y); 18/188; Hagerstwon JC; Comm.

SHANNON, KATHY; High Point SR HS; Beltsville, MD; (Y); Church Yth Grp; Church Choir; Nwsp Stf; Yrbk Stf; Hon Roll; Prfct Atten Awd; Bryan Coll; Englsh.

SHANNON, MICHAEL; Goergetown Prep; Olney, MD; (Y); 1/100; Math Clb; Im Bsbl; Im Bsktbl; JV Crs Cntry; JV Golf; Var Trk; Hon Roll; First Hnrs 84-86; GA Inst Tech; Elect Engr.

SHANNON, TORRI; Eastern HS; Baltimore, MD; (Y); Library Aide; Spanish Clb; Band; Chorus; Hon Roll; Common Wealth Agreemnt 86; Villa Julie Coll; Comp Info Sys.

SHARAR, SHAHID; Gaithersburg HS; Gaithersburg, MD; (Y); Chess Clb; Intnl Clb; Science Clb; Crs Cntry; Trk; Bausch & Lomb Sci Awd; Hon Roll; HS Sci Fair Awd 85-86; U Of MD; Med.

SHARMA, RUCHI; James M Bennett SR HS; Salisbury, MD; (S); 2/225; French Clb; JCL; Trs Latin Clb; Math Clb; Var Tennis; Hon Roll; NHS; Acadmc Ltr Awd 84-85; Princeton; Bus Adm.

SHAW, CHARLES; Cardinal Gibbons HS; Baltimore, MD; (Y); 37/130; Varsity Clb; Rep Frsh Cls; Rep Soph Cls; Rep Jr Cls; Stu Cncl; JV Ftbl; JV Var Trk; U Of MD; Law.

SHAW, DAVID; St Andrews Epsicopa Schl; Bethesda, MD; (Y); Art Clb; Ski Clb; Spanish Clb; Teachers Aide; Stage Crew; Lit Mag; Bsbl; Crs Cntry; Hon Roll.

SHAW, JEANNE; Governor Thomas Johnson HS; Frederick, MD; (Y); Chess Clb; Debate Tm; Pres French Clb; VP Thesps; Mgr Stage Crew; High Hon Roll; NHS; ST Of MD Merit Schltc Awd; U Of NC-CHAPEL Hill; Frgn Lang.

SHAW, KELLY; Arundel SR HS; Gambrills, MD; (Y); Hosp Aide; Natl Beta Clb; Red Cross Aide; Teachers Aide; Drill Tm; JV Cheerleading; Var Capt Pom Pon; High Hon Roll; Prfct Atten Awd; Church Yth Grp; Ldrshp Cmp Spr Str Grl 85; Outstndng Schl Ldr 85; Hmecmng Queen 85-86; Loyola Coll; Bio.

SHAW, SUZANNE; Glenelg HS; Glenwood, MD; (Y); AFS; Intnl Clb; Letterman Clb; Ski Clb; Varsity Clb; Yrbk Stf; Rep Jr Cls; Rep Sr Cls; Var Tennis; Hon Roll; U Toronto Canada; Psych.

SHAWHAN, PETER S; Springbrook HS; Silver Spring, MD; (Y); 1/48; Pres Debate Tm; Capt Math Tm; Orch; School Musical; NHS; Ntl Merit SF; Val; Gold Key Schlstc Art Awds 83; Harvard Bk Awd 85; IA ST Debate 83; Physics.

SHEARER, DEBBIE; Surrattsville HS; Clinton, MD; (Y); Am Leg Aux Girls St; Sec Church Yth Grp; FBLA; Ski Clb; Thesps; Band; Church Choir; Concert Band; Drm Mjr(t); Jazz Band; De Moday Chptr Swthrt 84; 1st Pl Sci Fair Awd 84; Acdmc Exc Awd 85; U MD; Advrtsng Dssgn.

SHEARER, LINDA; Rockville HS; Rockville, MD; (Y); Aud/Vis; Drama Clb; Concert Band; Jazz Band; Mrchg Band; Orch; School Musical; Mgr Stage Crew; High Hon Roll; NHS; NIH Apprtcshp Pro 86; Fine Arts.

SHEETS, HAROLD; North Carroll HS; Westminster, MD; (Y); Boys Clb Am; Church Yth Grp; Cmnty Wkr; Letterman Clb; Library Aide; Math Clb; Teachers Aide; Var Bsbl; Var Bsktbl; Bowling.

SHEFFE, CHRISTINE; Lackey HS; Bryans Rd, MD; (Y); Am Leg Aux Girls St; Church Yth Grp; FCA; SADD; Band; Var L Bsktbl; Var L Sftbl; Var L Vllybl; High Hon Roll; Hon Roll; Math.

SHEFFIELD, KIMBERLY B; Gov Thomas Johnson HS; Frederick, MD; (Y); Pres Art Clb; Science Clb; Thesps; Chorus; Off Soph Cls; Off Jr Cls; Off Sr Cls; Stu Cncl; Var L Tennis; Hon Roll; Excllnc Engl 85-86; PTSA Acdmc Achvt Awd 85-86; Hood Coll; Cmmnctns.

SHEIFER, STUART E; Winston Churchill HS; Potomac, MD; (Y); 41/620; Boy Scts; Library Aide; Teachers Aide; Nwsp Rptr; Var Capt Crs Cntry; Mgr(s); Var L Trk; High Hon Roll; NHS; Ntl Merit SF; Co Art Sci Fairs Awds 84 & 85; Smmr Internshp David W Taylor Nvl Shp Rsrch Dvlpmnt Ctr 84-85; Duke U; Bio.

SHELL, BRENDA K; Eleanor Roosevelt HS; Laurel, MD; (Y); Hon Roll; NHS; Ntl Merit Ltr; German Hnr Soc 85; Prince Georges Acad Exc Awd 84-85; Pres Acad Ftns Awd 86; U FL.

SHELP, TAMARA; La Plata HS; Waldorf, MD; (Y); Aud/Vis; Debate Tm; Drama Clb; Spanish Clb; Thesps; Chorus; School Musical; School Play; High Hon Roll; Hon Roll; Pt Tbbco Plyrs Awd Bst Actrss 85-86; Prncpls Awd Outstndng Achvt 85-86; MD Ctr Arts Chrs 82-86; Drama.

SHEN, CYNTHIA; Thomas S Wootton HS; Gaithersburg, MD; (Y); 7/420; Cmnty Wkr; Drama Clb; Hosp Aide; Red Cross Aide; Teachers Aide; Thesps; Chorus; Madrigals; School Musical; Yrbk Stf; Natl Merit Cmmnded Stu 85; MA Inst Of Tech; Matrl Sci.

SHEN, ELLEN; Thomas Sprigg Wootton HS; Gaithersburg, MD; (Y); 1/450; Debate Tm; Sec Drama Clb; NFL; Service Clb; Sec Thesps; School Musical; School Play; High Hon Roll; NHS; Opt Clb Awd; Natl Mrt Cmmndd Stu 85; Engr.

SHEN, FRANCIS; Thomas S Wootton HS; Gaithersburg, MD; (Y); Off Church Yth Grp; Science Clb; Church Choir; Hon Roll; NHS; Ntl Merit Ltr; Computer Clb; Teachers Aide; Natl Piano Plyg Audtns Dist Mem Awd 86; Elect Engr.

SHENG, CHAIN; Charles Woodward HS; Rockville, MD; (Y); Dance Clb; Teachers Aide; Pom Pon; Vllybl; Hon Roll; Hnr & Awds Music Piano MSMTA Fest & Guild; Hnrs & Awds Chinese 80-86; Cmmnctns.

SHENTON, DAVID; Cambridge-South Dorchester HS; Cambridge, MD; (Y); AFS; English Clb.

SHEPARDSON, KEITH; Northern HS; Owings, MD; (Y); Drama Clb; Thesps; School Musical; School Play; Im Bsktbl; Var L Ftbl; Var Trk; JV Var Wt Lftg; Hon Roll; Penn ST; Pre-Med.

SHEPPARD, JILL; Wilde Lake HS; Columbia, MD; (Y); Cmnty Wkr; JA; Office Aide; Political Wkr; Teachers Aide; Chorus; Drill Tm; Stat Bsbl; Bus Admin.

SHEPPARD, WILLIEMAE; Parkside HS; Salisbury, MD; (Y); Church Yth Grp; French Clb; Chorus; Variety Show; French Hon Soc; Hon Roll; Crtfct Tkng Natl Frnch Exm 84-86; Morgan ST U; Ecnmcs.

SHERIDAN, JAMES D; Loyola-Blakefield HS; Timonium, MD; (S); Var Swmmng; Timer; Hon Roll; NHS; Mock Trial 83-84; USS MD All Star Swmmng Tm 85; MD Zone Swim Tm 85; Bus.

SHERR, SUSAN; Pikesville HS; Balto, MD; (Y); Pres Temple Yth Grp; Nwsp Rptr; NHS; AFS; French Clb; Science Clb; Ski Clb; Mgr(s); Hon Roll; Grad Hnrs Baltimore Hebrew Coll Hgh Schl Div 86; Jrnlsm.

SHERRILL, DAVID; Randallstown SR HS; Randallstown, MD; (Y); Aud/Vis; Church Yth Grp; Color Guard; JV Lcrss; GA Inst Of Tech; Aerospace Eng.

SHERWOOD, TRACY; Ft Hill HS; Cumberland, MD; (Y); Sec Church Yth Grp; Teachers Aide; Thesps; VP Chorus; Flag Corp; Swing Chorus; Hon Roll; NHS; Pep Clb; Church Choir; Delg To MD Yth & Gov Mod Leg 86; Selected As An Alt To All ST Chorus 87; Multi Lingual Interpreter.

SHESKIN, LISA; Rockville HS; Rockville, MD; (Y); SADD; Chorus; School Musical; Nwsp Rptr; Nwsp Stf; Stu Cncl; Im Fld Hcky; JV Mgr(s); Var Swmmng; Im Vllybl.

SHIBER, JOSEPH R; Loyola HS; Baltimore, MD; (S); 10/197; Cmnty Wkr; French Clb; Rep Stu Cncl; Var Bsktbl; Hon Roll; NHS; Acad All Amer 86; NMSA 86; NEDT 83-84.

SHIFLETT, BARBARA; Sparrows Point HS; Baltimore, MD; (Y); Teachers Aide; Chorus; Hon Roll; Towson ST U; Comp Prgmr.

SHIH, ANNIE Y; Seneca Valley HS; Gaithersburg, MD; (Y); 32/492; Keywanettes; Latin Clb; Math Clb; Teachers Aide; Chorus; Hon Roll; Natl Latin Exm 85; Outstndng Prfrmnc ESOL 83; Muscl Achvt Piano Prfrmnc 85; U Of MD College Pk; Psychtrst.

SHILLING, SYNDY; Glenelg HS; Ellicott City, MD; (Y); Varsity Clb; Band; Concert Band; Mrchg Band; Rep Frsh Cls; Rep Soph Cls; Rep Jr Cls; Rep Sr Cls; VP Stu Cncl; Capt Cheerleading; Pre-Law.

SHILLINGBURG, TONYA L; Brunswick HS; Brunswick, MD; (Y); 23/135; FFA; FHA; SADD; Teachers Aide; JV Cheerleading; Stat Timer; Hon Roll; Frdrck Comm Coll; Secy Sci.

SHILLMAN, ROBIN; Pikesville HS; Baltimore, MD; (Y); Model UN; Spanish Clb; Variety Show; Nwsp Rptr; Frsh Cls; Jr Cls; Var VP English Clb; Sec NHS; Mntn Frgn Lang Pblctn 86; Tufts U.

SHIN, CHRIS; Parkdale HS; Lanham, MD; (Y); Church Yth Grp; French Clb; Yrbk Stf; Var Tennis; French Hon Soc; Hon Roll; Pres Of Church Youth Club 86-87; Med.

SHINDLE, JODI; Laurel HS; Laurel, MD; (Y); Yrbk Sprt Ed; Yrbk Stf; Var Bsktbl; Var Crs Cntry; Im Powder Puff Ftbl; Var Capt Trk; Hon Roll; Outstndng HS Athtcs 86; Bonne Belle Cir Of Excllnc In Running 85-86; U Of MD; Chld Psych.

SHIPLEY, JULIE; Flintstone Schl; Flintstone, MD; (S); Library Aide; Teachers Aide; Chorus; Nwsp Stf; Yrbk Stf; Stat Bsktbl; Mgr(s); Var L Vllybl; Hon Roll; NHS; ACC Brd Of Trustees Schlrshp 86; Allegany CC; Libry Sci.

SHIPS, LISA; La Plata HS; Bryantown, MD; (Y); Trs Church Yth Grp; Computer Clb; Yrbk Stf; Rep Frsh Cls; Rep Soph Cls; Rep Jr Cls; Stu Cncl; Var L Tennis; High Hon Roll; NHS; Fnlst Miss MD Natl Teen Pgnt 85; Grad Barbzon Mdlng Schl 84; U Of MD; Cpa.

SHIRGAOKAR, SANDY; La Plata HS; Waldorf, MD; (S); Ski Clb; Spanish Clb; SADD; Rep Soph Cls; Rep Jr Cls; Sec Stu Cncl; Stat Bsbl; Stat Ftbl; Stat Sftbl; Hon Roll; Fash Inst Of Tech; Fash Merch.

SHIRODKAR, SHEELA; Archbishop Keough HS; Baltimore, MD; (Y); Art Clb; Computer Clb; Nwsp Bus Mgr; Nwsp Rptr; High Hon Roll; Hon Roll; NHS; Prfct Atten Awd.

SHIRVINSKI, LISA; Academy Of The Holy Cross; Silver Spring, MD; (Y); 24/123; Art Clb; Pres Camera Clb; JCL; Latin Clb; Rep Sr Cls; Rep Stu Cncl; Var Powder Puff Ftbl; JV Sftbl; Hon Roll; Ntl Hnr Scty 86; Ntl Ltn Hnr Scty 85-86; Phtgrpht Clb Srv Awd 85-86; U Hrtfrd; Bus.

SHIVES, TESSA; Heritage Acad; Funkstown, MD; (Y); Trs Q&S; Chorus; Nwsp Bus Mgr; Yrbk Ed-Chief; Sec Jr Cls; Sec Sr Cls; Stat Bsktbl; Stat Bsktbl; Stat Socr; Hon Roll; Messiah Coll; Elem Educ.

SHOMALI, MANUSR E; Loyola HS; Towson, MD; (S); 3/197; Church Yth Grp; Debate Tm; French Clb; NFL; Scholastic Bowl; Church Choir; Nwsp Rptr; Trk; High Hon Roll; NHS; Med.

SHOPE, SHANAN; Patapsco HS; Baltimore, MD; (Y); Church Yth Grp; Vllybl; Hon Roll; Sntrl Schlrshp 86; PTA Schlrshp 86; St Lukes Lthrn Chrch Schlrshp 86; U MD Bltmr; Nrsng.

SHORT, HEATHER; Parkville HS; Baltimore, MD; (Y); 4/275; Trs Sr Cls; JV Bsktbl; Var Fld Hcky; Var Lcrss; High Hon Roll; Hon Roll; NHS; Pres Schlr; Val; Am Lg Distinguished Scholar Awd 86; Parkville High Hall Of Fame 86; Eng Dept Awd 86; Loyola; Math.

SHORT, SEAN; Du Val HS; Lanham, MD; (Y); 29/382; Am Leg Boys St; ROTC; SADD; Soph Cls; Jr Cls; Stu Cncl; Var Tennis; JV Wrstlng; Hon Roll; VFW Awd; Air Force Seargeants Assc Awd 86; US Naval Sea Cadet Corps 85; US Naval Acad; Poli Sci.

SHORTALL, MARY; SS Peter & Paul HS; Trappe, MD; (Y); 3/28; Am Leg Aux Girls St; Yrbk Ed-Chief; Trs Rep Soph Cls; Rep Stu Cncl; L Stat Bsktbl; Stat Cheerleading; Stat Socr; NHS; Bcclrn 86; Immaculata Coll; Math.

SHRADER, SCOTT; De Matha Catholic HS; Hyattsville, MD; (Y); Spanish Clb; Hon Roll; U Of MD.

SHREEVE, NEAL; Friends Schl; Baltimore, MD; (Y); 8/21; French Clb; Natl Beta Clb; Ski Clb; Spanish Clb; Yrbk Phtg; Yrbk Stf; Lit Mag; Var Bsbl; Im Lcrss; Var Mgr(s); Intl Rel.

SHRESTHA, SUSHMA; Fairmont Height HS; Hyattsville, MD; (Y); Computer Clb; 4-H; FBLA; Girl Scts; Yrbk Stf; Off Jr Cls; Cit Awd; High Hon Roll; Hon Roll; Jr NHS; Geogetown U; CPA.

SHRIVER, RODDY; Frederich Christian Acad; Keymar, MD; (Y); Church Yth Grp; Quiz Bowl; Chorus; School Musical; School Play; Stage Crew; Stat Mgr(s); VP Soph Cls; VP Jr Cls; Var L Bsbl; MVP Sccr All Conf Sccr Tm 86; Mst Def Bsktbl 85-86; Frederick CC; Bus.

SHROPSHIRE, SONYA; Wilde Lake HS; Columbia, MD; (Y); 48/225; Pres Debate Tm; Drama Clb; Office Aide; Pres Speech Tm; Thesps; Chorus; Nwsp Rptr; JV Var Cheerleading; Hon Roll; Prfct Atten Awd; Howard U; Psychlgy.

SHRYOCK, SUSAN; Smithsburg HS; Hagerstown, MD; (Y); 24/188; Ski Clb; Band; Concert Band; Jazz Band; Mrchg Band; School Musical; Sec Jr Cls; Sec Sr Cls; Sec Stu Cncl; Var Trk; U MD; Inf Sys.

SHUMAKER, KIMBERLY L; Catonsville HS; Baltimore, MD; (Y); Church Yth Grp; Computer Clb; Political Wkr; Spanish Clb; VICA; JV Sftbl; High Hon Roll; Hon Roll; Jr NHS; Cert Merit Data Proc Vo-Tech 86; Catsonville CC; Data Proc.

SHUMAKER, SCOTT; Fort Hill HS; Cumberland, MD; (Y); Boy Scts; Pres Church Yth Grp; Computer Clb; Thesps; Chorus; Church Choir; School Musical; School Play; Mgr Stage Crew; Swing Chorus; Frostburg ST Coll; Music.

SHUMAN, YAFFA; Bais Yaakor School For Girls; Baltimore, MD; (S); Pres Cmnty Wkr; Chorus; Trs Frsh Cls; Trs Soph Cls; Trs Jr Cls; Trs Sr Cls; Ntl Merit SF; Ntl Dstngshd Schlr 86; Towson ST U; Tchr.

SIBIGA, JENNIFER JOAN; North Carroll HS; Hampstead, MD; (Y); 4/282; Mgr JA; Teachers Aide; Chorus; High Hon Roll; Hon Roll; Am Leg Ortrcl Cntst 83; Towson ST U; Elem Ed.

SIEGEL, DIANA; Eleanor Roosevelt HS; Upper Marlboro, MD; (Y); Teachers Aide; VP Sec Temple Yth Grp; Yrbk Phtg; Rep Stu Cncl; JV Cheerleading; High Hon Roll; Hon Roll; Acadmc Exlnc Awd 84-85.

SIEHLER, ANGELA; Fort Hill SR HS; Cumberland, MD; (Y); Chorus; Church Choir; Orch; School Musical; Swing Chorus; Nwsp Stf; Ed Lit Mag; Cit Awd; High Hon Roll; NHS; 1st Pl Exhibit Art Show 86; Mbr Sentinel Recogntn Soc 86; Frostburg ST Coll; Educ.

SIEMASKO, KARYN; Great Mills HS; Lexington Park, MD; (Y); Band; Concert Band; Mrchg Band; School Play; High Hon Roll; Hon Roll; Lion Awd; Pres VP NHS; Tri-Cnty Hnrs Band 85 & 86; St Marys Coll Wnd Ensmbl 86.

SIENKOWSKI, TAMMY; Gaithersburg HS; Gaithersburg, MD; (Y); AFS; Camera Clb; Church Yth Grp; Computer Clb; Key Clb; Teachers Aide; Stat Gym; Stat Vllybl; Hon Roll; Bus.

SIEVERS, LINDA M; Oxon Hill HS; Oxon Hill, MD; (Y); Church Yth Grp; Cmnty Wkr; Computer Clb; Girl Scts; Letterman Clb; Ski Clb; Teachers Aide; Band; Church Choir; Mrchg Band; Engineering.

SILBERSACK, TRACY L; C Milton Wright HS; Bel Air, MD; (Y); 48/243; German Clb; Teachers Aide; Yrbk Stf; Rep Jr Cls; Rep Stu Cncl; Fld Hcky; Powder Puff Ftbl; Swmmng; Trk; Pres Schlr; Sentrl Schlrshp 86; St Marys Coll Of MD; Bus Adm.

SILVER, DANIEL GLENN; Gaithersburg HS; Gaithersburg, MD; (Y); 60/580; Intnl Clb; Political Wkr; Ski Clb; Nwsp Stf; Rep Jr Cls; Rep Sr Cls; Hon Roll; NHS; Ntl Merit Ltr; Im Socr; Amer Assn Of Mid MD Smr Hlth Career Pgm 85; Pres Awd For Acdmc Ftns 86; Edsn-Mc Graw Cmptn Awd 86; Brandeis U; Bus.

SIMMONS, LISA; Liberty HS; Sykesville, MD; (S); Mathletes; Spanish Clb; Teachers Aide; High Hon Roll; Hon Roll; NHS; Ntl Merit Ltr; Opt Clb Awd; Prfct Atten Awd; Acad Pin 83-84; Comptr Prog.

SIMMONS, MARGARET; Calvert HS; Dowell, MD; (Y); Pres Art Clb; Off ROTC; Hon Roll; NHS; Latin Clb; JV Vllybl; Superintnts Schltc Awd 86; Freedoms Foundtn Conf 86; Acadmy Introdctn Mission Coast Guard Acad 86.

SIMMONS, RUSSELL; Cambridge-South Dorchester HS; Church Crk, MD; (Y); 1/350; Computer Clb; Office Aide; Scholastic Bowl; Spanish Clb; High Hon Roll; Hon Roll; NHS; Ntl Merit Ltr; Outstndng Stdnt Trigeo, Adv Engl Cert 86; Outstndng Stdnt Data Procssng 85; Watchtower Bible; Cmptr Tech.

SIMMONS, SHARONE; Lackey HS; Marbury, MD; (Y); Office Aide; SADD; Band; Concert Band; Mrchg Band; Pom Pon; Stat Trk; Hon Roll; Prfct Atten Awd; U Of MD; Pdtrcn.

SIMMS, ROBERT; James M Bennett SR HS; Salisbury, MD; (Y); 3/196; Boy Scts; Chess Clb; French Clb; Pres Math Clb; Math Tm; Var L Crs Cntry; Var L Trk; NHS; St Schlr; Eagle Scout 86; Pres Acad Fit Awd 86; Wicomico Cnty Mth Lg Hghst Scorer 86; Salisbury ST Coll; Aerospc Eng.

SIMON, DENISE; Dunbar SR HS; Baltimore, MD; (Y); Am Leg Aux Girls St; Library Aide; Varsity Clb; Church Choir; Yrbk Phtg; Var Bsktbl; Hon Roll; Prfct Atten Awd; Schlrshp Engl & Geo 86; 2nd Hghst Grd 84; Exclinc Engl & Hm Ecnmcs 84; Howard U; Med.

SIMONS, MICHELLE; Frederick HS; Fred, MD; (Y); AFS; Computer Clb; German Clb; Hosp Aide; Science Clb; Nwsp Stf; Var Bsktbl; Hon Roll; Exec Committee; Chem.

SIMPKINS, LAURA; Western SR HS; Baltimore, MD; (Y); 92/416; Pres Church Yth Grp; Dance Clb; Drama Clb; Latin Clb; Thesps; School Musical; School Play; Frsh Cls; Jr Cls; Cheerleading; Syracuse; Telecmnctns.

SIMPSON, BECKY; Gaithersburg HS; Gaithersburg, MD; (Y); Church Yth Grp; Trk; Vllybl; Hon Roll; St Marys; Lawyer.

SIMPSON, DIANE; Ft Hill HS; Cumberland, MD; (S); Pres 4-H; Trs Political Wkr; Concert Band; Drill Tm; Mrchg Band; Nwsp Rptr; Var Bowling; NHS; NEDT Awd; Towson ST Coll; Comm.

SIMPSON, JILL; Washington HS; Princess Anne, MD; (Y); Church Yth Grp; Science Clb; Chorus; Church Choir; Swing Chorus; High Hon Roll; Hon Roll; All St Chorus 86; St Teen Talent Wnr 86; Music.

SIMPSON, KATHLEEN ELLEN; Elizabeth Seton HS; Lanham-Seabrook, MD; (Y); 13/189; Am Leg Aux Girls St; VP French Clb; Girl Scts; Political Wkr; Ed Yrbk Stf; Im Tennis; Cit Awd; Kiwanis Awd; VP NHS; Pres Schlr; Citznshp Awd 86; Sci Clb Sec Ann Sci Day 82-84; Hgh Hnr Roll 86; U Of MD; Bio Med.

SIMPSON, KIMBERLY A; Southern Garrett HS; Deer Park, MD; (S); 10/222; Debate Tm; Pres VP GAA; Office Aide; Ski Clb; Rep Trs Stu Cncl; Score Keeper; Hon Roll; NHS; Math.

SIMPSON, MARTHA; Lapiata HS; Cobb Island, MD; (Y); Cmnty Wkr; Library Aide; Science Clb; Charles County CC; Educ.

SIMPSON, PATRICIA; Regina HS; Greenbelt, MD; (Y); Pres Church Yth Grp; Pep Clb; Service Clb; Sec Jr Cls; Rep Stu Cncl; Var L Bsktbl; JV Sftbl; Var Vllybl; U S Army Rsrv Schlr Athl Awd 85-86; MVP Bsktb JV 83-84.

SIMPSON, REBECCA; Gaithersburg HS; Gaithersburg, MD; (Y); Church Yth Grp; Key Clb; Teachers Aide; Trk; Vllybl; Hon Roll; St Marys Notre Dame; Sec Educ.

SIMPSON, RODERICK; Mount Saint Joseph HS; Baltimore, MD; (Y); Boy Scts; Ski Clb; Speech Tm; Bsktbl; Hon Roll; BUSINES Administration.

SIMS, AMY; Crossland SR HS; Forestville, MD; (Y); Camp Fr Inc; Church Yth Grp; Drama Clb; Girl Scts; Library Aide; Pep Clb; PAVAS; Teachers Aide; Band; Chorus; Supr Mdls Music Ablty 84; Scrtry Chrch Teen Grp 85; U Maryland; Med.

SIMS, NATALIE; Suitland HS; Capitol Heights, MD; (Y); VP FBLA; SADD; Nwsp Stf; DAR Awd; Hon Roll; JP Sousa Awd; NHS; Ntl Merit Schol; Prince Georges Cnty Acad Awd 84-85; Bus Admin.

SINANIAN, LAURA; Maurice J Mc Donough HS; Waldorf, MD; (Y); Intnl Clb; Q&S; Teachers Aide; Concert Band; Mrchg Band; Nwsp Stf; High Hon Roll; Hon Roll; Prncpls Hnr Rll 85.

SINCLAIR, NICOLE; Takoma Acad; Adelphi, MD; (S); 3/95; Teachers Aide; Yrbk Stf; Im Ftbl; NHS; John Hopkins U; Med.

SINCLAIR, PAMELA; Laurel HS; Laurel, MD; (Y); Yrbk Stf; Capt L Bsktbl; Powder Puff Ftbl; Capt L Sftbl; Capt L Vllybl; Hon Roll; All Str Womens Sprts Fndtn Vllybl, All Co 1st Tm Vllybl, Jr Cls Princess 85-86.

SINDLER, AMY; Pikesville SR HS; Baltimore, MD; (Y); Sec AFS; Sec Art Clb; Drama Clb; French Clb; Stage Crew; Lit Mag; JV Capt Cheerleading; Diving; Englsh.

SINES, KEVIN; Northern HS; Friendsville, MD; (Y); 23/111; Drama Clb; Pres Letterman Clb; Church Choir; Stage Crew; Var L Bsbl; Var L Bsktbl; Var Capt Ftbl; Schlr Athlete Awd; Frostburg ST Coll; Accntng.

SINGER, DANIEL; Baltimore City Coll; Baltimore, MD; (S); Trs JA; School Musical; Trs Soph Cls; Stu Cncl; Var Socr; Var Swmmng; High Hon Roll; Jr NHS; NHS; Ntl Merit Ltr; ST Stu Cncl Treas 85-86; Rgnl Sci Fair Awd; Bio.

SINGER, MARC; Mc Donogh Schl; Baltimore, MD; (Y); Political Wkr; Ski Clb; SADD; Nwsp Ed-Chief; Yrbk Stf; Im Bsktbl; Im Socr; Im Wrstlng; Hon Roll; Journlsm Schlrfshp 86; Law.

SINGER, RACHEL; Gaithersburg HS; Gaithersburg, MD; (Y); AFS; Cmnty Wkr; Intnl Clb; Red Cross Aide; Teachers Aide; Orch; Gym; Hon Roll; Edsn Elec Inst Sci Fctn Wrtng Cntst 2nd Pl Awd 86; Psych.

SINGFIELD, DANA; Baltimore City College; Baltimore, MD; (S); School Musical; Nwsp Rptr; Ed Lit Mag; Trs Stu Cncl; High Hon Roll; NHS; Prfct Atten Awd; Cum Laude Cert Prfrmnc Ntl Ltn Exm 86; Assoc Stu Cngrss Baltimore Cty Outstndg Stu Ldrshp Awd 86; Jrnlsm.

SINGH, MICHAEL; Takoma Acad; Takoma Park, MD; (Y); Art Clb; French Clb; Cit Awd; High Hon Roll; Hon Roll; NHS; Prfct Atten Awd; Physcn.

SINGH, RAM C; Winston Churchill HS; Potomac, MD; (Y); Chess Clb; Computer Clb; Debate Tm; Sec Trs German Clb; Math Tm; NFL; Science Clb; Orch; Lit Mag; Hon Roll; Benjamin Banneker Scholar 86-91; Hnrb Mntn Physics Catgy Montgomery Sci Fair 85; Cert Merit Forn 84-85; U MD College Park; Elec Engr.

SION, ROGER; Georgetown Prep; Rockville, MD; (Y); 6/106; Math Clb; NFL; Q&S; Radio Clb; Science Clb; Nwsp Stf; Lit Mag; Var Capt Ftbl; Var Tennis; Hon Roll; 2nd Pl Frshmn Elctn Cntst 83; Co-Chr Alchl & Drgs Awrns Comm 85; Pltcl Sci.

SIRILLA, MICHAEL; Georgetown Preparatory Schl; Rockville, MD; (Y); Thesps; School Musical; School Play; Cmnty Wkr; Drama Clb; Band; Off Soph Cls; JV Ftbl; Var Wrstlng; Musicn.

SIX, BOBBI JO; Francis Scott Key HS; Taneytown, MD; (Y); French Clb; SADD; Chorus; Hon Roll; Spec Educ.

SKALITZKY, KAREN; Notre Dame Preparatory Schl; Lutherville, MD; (Y); German Clb; Girl Scts; Hosp Aide; Latin Clb; Sec VP Service Clb; Band; Im Swmmng; High Hon Roll; Hon Roll; Pres NHS.

SKELTON, KIMBERLY; Patapsco HS; Baltimore, MD; (Y); Church Yth Grp; Trs SADD; Mrchg Band; Trs Soph Cls; Trs Jr Cls; Trs Sr Cls; JV Bsktbl; Var Mgr(s); Hon Roll; Girl Scts; Schltc Achvt Awd 84-86; Mathmtcn.

SKIDMORE, NANCY C; Wheaton HS; Wheaton, MD; (Y); Church Yth Grp; Letterman Clb; Ski Clb; Var Pom Pon; Powder Puff Ftbl; Var Socr; Hon Roll; Vet.

SKIDMORE, WENDY; Gaithersburg HS; Gaithersburg, MD; (Y); Church Yth Grp; Dance Clb; Key Clb; Rep Stu Cncl; JV Cheerleading; Var Pom Pon; Var Swmmng; High Hon Roll; NHS; Ntl Merit SF; Vvet-Med.

SKILES, EMILY STEPHENS; Annapolis HS; Annapolis, MD; (Y); Hosp Aide; Key Clb; Library Aide; Red Cross Aide; Flag Corp; Mrchg Band; Stat Bsktbl; Hon Roll; Church Yth Grp; SADD; Jr Nrsng Awd AAGH; Certified CPR; Candy-Striping Pin AAGH; UMBC; Nrsng.

SKORA, ROBERT; Laurel HS; Laurel, MD; (Y); Var L Ftbl; Var L Trk; Hon Roll; Elect Engr.

SKOUFALOS, CATHERINE ANN; Centennial HS; Columbia, MD; (Y); Church Yth Grp; Drama Clb; Capt Drill Tm; School Musical; Variety Show; Off Frsh Cls; Off Soph Cls; Off Jr Cls; Intr Dsgn.

SKRYPZAK, KAREN; St Vincent Pallotti HS; Silver Spring, MD; (S); 18/101; AFS; French Clb; Teachers Aide; Var L Vllybl; Hon Roll; Stu Of Mnth 85; Hnrb Mntn 85 & 86; Acadmc Lttr 85; Physcl Thrpy.

SLAGLE, MARY; Brunswick HS; Knoxville, MD; (Y); 17/140; Church Yth Grp; 4-H; Radio Clb; Spanish Clb; Chorus; School Musical; Yrbk Stf; Stu Cncl; Stat Bsbl; Bsktbl; Marine Bio.

SLANEY, MARK F; Lackey HS; Waldorf, MD; (Y); 3/315; Am Leg Boys St; Church Yth Grp; Capt Math Tm; Spanish Clb; SADD; Im Socr; High Hon Roll; NHS; Outstndg Mth Stu 84-86; Outstndg Biol Stu 85; Mech Engr.

SLANGER, MARC; Beall HS; Frostburg, MD; (Y); Art Clb; Church Yth Grp; DECA; Drama Clb; School Play; High Hon Roll; Karate Clb; 1st, 3rd & 2nd Rbns ST Fair Art 85; ST Fair Art Show 84; Sktbrd Clb 86; Frostburg ST Coll; Art.

SLATER, ANDREW P; New Cavenant Chrstn Acad Estrn Shore; Preston, MD; (S); 2/4; Church Yth Grp; Scholastic Bowl; School Musical; Yrbk Ed-Chief; Pres Stu Cncl; Cit Awd; High Hon Roll; SAR Awd; Amer Chrstn Hnr Soc Awd 84-85; U Of MD-BLTMRE Cnty; Comm Arts.

SLAVIN, TRACY L; Rockville HS; Rockville, MD; (Y); Key Clb; SADD; Rep Stu Cncl; Var Capt Cheerleading; Gym; High Hon Roll; High Hon Roll; NHS; Acctng.

SLIDER, SHELLY; Oldtown HS; Oldtown, MD; (S); Var Church Yth Grp; FBLA; FHA; Stage Crew; Nwsp Phtg; Cheerleading; Vllybl; Hon Roll; NHS; NEDT Awd; Dstngshd Schlr & Hugh O Brian Schlrshp Awd 85; Nrs.

SLIGER, KIMBERLY; Soouthern Garrett HS; Oakland, MD; (Y); 34/226; Sec FBLA; Office Aide; High Hon Roll; Hon Roll; Lion Awd; Joy Clb 83; Garrett CC; Sec.

SLIWA, JAMES A; Eleanor Roosevelt HS; Bowie, MD; (Y); Thesps; Acpl Chr; Chorus; Madrigals; School Musical; School Play; Rep Stu Cncl; Hon Roll; NHS; MD Dstngshd Schlr Semi-Fnlst 85; U Of MD; Music.

SLOTWINSKI, JOHN; Good Counsel HS; Gaithersburg, MD; (Y); 18/214; Boy Scts; Latin Clb; Teachers Aide; Orch; Pep Band; School Play; Symp Band; Nwsp Stf; High Hon Roll; NHS; Distngshd Sct 85; Meritorious Ldr 86; Phscs.

SLUDER, JEFF; Sherwood HS; Olney, MD; (Y); 141/317; JV Var Ftbl; West VA Wesleyan; Psychlgy.

SMALL, FRANK; Colonel Zadok Magruder HS; Derwood, MD; (Y); Boy Scts; Teachers Aide; Concert Band; Mrchg Band; Symp Band; Trs Rep Stu Cncl; L Var Ftbl; JV Socr; Hon Roll; NHS; Colgate U; E Asian Stud.

SMALL, JOHN COTA; Col Zador Magruder HS; Rockville, MD; (Y); 10/310; Stu Cncl; Bsbl; Ftbl; Gov Hon Prg Awd; High Hon Roll; NHS; Pres Schlr; St Schlr; IBM Thomas J Watson Schlrshp 86; US Army Resrv Natl Schlr/Ath Awd 86; Cornell U; Econ.

SMALL, PATRICIA; Academey Of The Holy Cross; Silver Springs, MD; (Y); Cmnty Wkr; Drama Clb; SADD; Chorus; School Musical; Diving; Swmmng; Pep Clb; Variety Show; Powder Puff Ftbl; 2nd Pl MD ST Modrn Miss Pagnt 85; Mntgmry Cnty Miss TEEN Pagnt 4th Pl Forml Presntatn Awd 85; Towson ST U; Bus.

SMARIGA, ROBERT; Governor Thomas Johnson HS; Frederick, MD; (Y); 16/303; Chess Clb; Church Yth Grp; Debate Tm; Math Tm; Quiz Bowl; Scholastic Bowl; Teachers Aide; Hon Roll; Ntl Merit Ltr; MD ST Schlrshp 86-87; MD Mck Trl Cmptn Prtcpnt 85-86; Awd Creatvty 85-86; Johns Hopkins U; Engr.

SMARR, MARYBETH; Cambridge South-Dorchester HS; Andrews, MD; (Y); AFS; Am Leg Aux Girls St; Church Yth Grp; Cmnty Wkr; Drama Clb; French Clb; Pep Clb; Political Wkr; Spanish Clb; SADD; Amer Lgtn Grls St 86; Brdcstng Awd Voice Of Dmcrcy 86; DAR Essay Wnr 86; Elon Coll; Brdcst Jrnlsm.

SMITH, ALICE; Williamsport HS; Williamsport, MD; (Y); 6/206; Orch; Rep Frsh Cls; Rep Soph Cls; Rep Jr Cls; Rep Sr Cls; Var Capt Bsktbl; Var Sftbl; Var Capt Vllybl; Hon Roll; NHS; Math.

SMITH, AMIE; Roland Park Country Schl; Baltimore, MD; (Y); Hosp Aide; Model UN; Chorus; Lit Mag; Lcrss; Mgr(s).

SMITH, ANDY; Thomas S Wootton HS; Potomac, MD; (Y); Am Leg Boys St; Church Yth Grp; Var JA; Rep Stu Cncl; Im Socr; Var L Tennis; Var L Trk; Hon Roll.

SMITH, BRAD; La Plata HS; Charlotte Hall, MD; (S); Chess Clb; Computer Clb; Capt Math Tm; Capt Scholastic Bowl; Rep Frsh Cls; Pres Stu Cncl; Var L Cheerleading; Var Capt Socr; Var Capt Trk; High Hon Roll; Astrnmy.

SMITH, CASSANDRA; Kent County HS; Millington, MD; (Y); Am Leg Aux Girls St; Church Yth Grp; Pres Girl Scts; Pep Clb; Spanish Clb; Speech Tm; Rep Frsh Cls; Elks Awd; Hon Roll; Speech Tm; Grl Sct 10 Yr Awd 86; 3rd Pl Prsusv Spkng Cmptn 85; 2nd Pl In Amrcn Lgn Ortrcl Cntst 85; Lwyr.

SMITH, DANIEL; John Carroll Schl; Forest Hill, MD; (Y); 57/238; Cmnty Wkr; Band; Concert Band; Mrchg Band; Pres Frsh Cls; Var JV Bsktbl; Var Capt Ftbl; Var JV Lcrss; High Hon Roll; Hon Roll; Brnz Medl Rssn Olympd 84-85; Slava Rssn Hnr Socty 85-86; Coll Prof.

SMITH, DEBRA L; Eleanor Roosevelt HS; Laurel, MD; (Y); Computer Clb; Math Tm; Teachers Aide; High Hon Roll; VP NHS; Ntl Merit SF; Spanish NHS; St Schlr; Sci Fair Awds In HS & Cnty Fairs 83-84; Awd For Acad Excllnc 84; U Of MD; Med.

SMITH, DECARLO; Northern HS; Huntingtown, MD; (Y); 71/301; Office Aide; VICA; Var L Bsbl; JV Var Bsktbl; JV Var Ftbl; L Trk; Wt Lftg; High Hon Roll; Prfct Atten Awd; Vctnl Prgm In Elctrncs 84-86; Cert Of Acptnc In U S Marines 85-86; 3rd Pl Elctrncs Skls Tst 85-86; Marines; Elec Tele Cmnctns.

SMITH, DEIDRE N; Springbrook HS; Silver Spring, MD; (Y); JV Var Bsktbl; Var L Sftbl; Hon Roll; Engrg.

SMITH, DELISA; Friendly HS; Fort Washington, MD; (Y); Church Yth Grp; Cmnty Wkr; Co-Capt Pep Clb; Ski Clb; VP Sr Cls; Hon Roll; Prfct Atten Awd; Spanish NHS; Stu Cncl; Prince Georges County Acad Excllnc Awd 85; Spanish Natl Hnr Soc Awd 85; Spelman; Comp Sci.

SMITH, DENISE; Western SR HS; Baltimore, MD; (Y); Art Clb; Aud/Vis; Girl Scts; Band; Concert Band; Mrchg Band; Hon Roll; U Of MD; Engrng.

SMITH, DONNA D D; Potomac HS; Suitland, MD; (Y); Church Yth Grp; Dance Clb; Red Cross Aide; Scholastic Bowl; Spanish Clb; Chorus; Flag Corp; School Musical; Bowling; Powder Puff Ftbl.

SMITH, EMILY; Beall HS; Frostburg, MD; (Y); 5/162; Pres 4-H; Thesps; Band; Nwsp Stf; Sec Frsh Cls; Sec Soph Cls; Sec Stu Cncl; High Hon Roll; NHS; Hugh O Brien Ldrshp Smnar MD 85; Intl Affairs.

SMITH, ERIC; Potomac HS; Temple Hills, MD; (Y); Library Aide; Socr; Trk; Hon Roll; Schlr Athlete Sccr 85-86; MVP Sccr 85-86; George Mason U; Child Pysch.

SMITH, GEOFFREY; Sandy Spring Friends Schl; Sandy Spring, MD; (S); Pres Math Clb; Scholastic Bowl; Concert Band; Mgr(s); Var JV Socr; Mgr Trk; Hon Roll; Ntl Merit SF; Chess Clb; Teachers Aide; Earlham Coll; Bio.

SMITH, HEATHER; Fort Hill HS; Cumberland, MD; (Y); 4-H; Political Wkr; Drill Tm; Rep Stu Cncl; 4-H Awd; Hon Roll; Opt Clb Awd; Lwyr.

SMITH, IVAN; La Plata HS; Bel Alton, MD; (Y); Church Yth Grp; Varsity Clb; Mgr(s); Prfct Atten Awd.

SMITH, JACK; Smithsburg HS; Smithsburg, MD; (Y); Hon Roll; Distngshd Hnr Roll 86; Columbus Schl Of Art; Comrcl.

SMITH, JENNIFER; Stephen Decatur HS; Berlin, MD; (Y); 2/200; FBLA; SADD; Pep Band; Trs Soph Cls; Rep Stu Cncl; Gym; Gov Hon Prg Awd; High Hon Roll; NHS; Sal; Bnfcl Hodson Acad Merit Schlrshp 86-90; Pres Acad Ftns Awd 86; Sci Awd 86; WA Clg; Chem.

SMITH, JESSE; Glenelg HS; Mt Airy, MD; (Y); Church Yth Grp; Library Aide; Hon Roll; Explrng Chldhd Awd 84-86; Elem Ed.

SMITH JR, JOHN R; Gaithersburg HS; Gaithersburg, MD; (Y); Church Yth Grp; Church Choir; Jazz Band; School Musical; School Play; Pres Sr Cls; Hon Roll; Jr NHS; NHS; Boy Scts; Annual Regnl Confrnc WA DC Yth Rep 86; Yth Bd Mem WA DC Diocese 86; UVA; Lw.

SMITH, JONATHAN; MT ST Joseph HS; Baltimore, MD; (Y); Church Yth Grp; Political Wkr; ROTC; Spanish Clb; Acpl Chr; Band; Church Choir; Concert Band; Orch; Pep Band; VA Tech; Pre-Law.

SMITH, JULIA HELENE; Dulaney SR HS; Towson, MD; (Y); Concert Band; Mrchg Band; Variety Show; Yrbk Stf; Var Crs Cntry; Var Swmmng; Var Trk; Hon Roll; NHS; Band; Rsn Olympd Slvr & Brnz Mdls 84, 85 & 86.

SMITH, JULIE; La Plata HS; La Plata, MD; (S); 4-H; Hosp Aide; Yrbk Ed-Chief; Pres Frsh Cls; Pres Soph Cls; Pres Jr Cls; Var Fld Hcky; Cit Awd; High Hon Roll; VP NHS; Hugh O Brian Yth Smnr 85; Wrld Afrs Smnr 85; Law.

SMITH, KATHRYN; Eastern Vo Tech; Baltimore, MD; (Y); JA; Off Frsh Cls; Bsktbl; Sftbl; Hon Roll; Towson ST; CPA.

SMITH, KEITH; John Carroll HS; Havre De Grace, MD; (Y); 109/237; Boy Scts; Church Yth Grp; Science Clb; Ski Clb; Var L Ftbl; Var L Lcrss; Im Wt Lftg; God Cntry Awd; Prfct Atten Awd; Acadmc Achvt Awds; Pre-Law.

SMITH, KIRA M; Stone Ridge HS; Washington, DC; (Y); Chorus; School Musical; Rep Soph Cls; Rep Jr Cls; Rep Sr Cls; Capt Cheerleading; Capt JV Socr; Capt JV Vllybl; Church Yth Grp; Cmnty Wkr; Cmmnded Blck Stu PSAT 85; Vlnteer Cmnty Svc Awd Miss DC Natl Teen Pgnt 85; Outstyndg Cmnty Svc 85; Prof Tm Physcn.

SMITH, LEE ANN; Fort Hill HS; Cumberland, MD; (Y); Pres Church Yth Grp; Drill Tm; Mrchg Band; Off Frsh Cls; Off Soph Cls; Off Jr Cls; L Pom Pon; Hon Roll; U Of MD; Bio.

SMITH, LEVELLE G; Notre Dame Prep; Baltimore, MD; (Y); 12/119; Church Yth Grp; Dance Clb; Pep Clb; SADD; Variety Show; Rep Yrbk Stf; Rep Sec Stu Cncl; Im Badmtn; Im Fld Hcky; Im Lcrss; MD St Senatorial Schlrshp 86; Loyola Coll; Intl Bus.

SMITH, LISA; Western HS; Baltimore, MD; (Y); 54/412; Sec Church Yth Grp; Church Choir; Hon Roll; Hampton U; Comp Analys.

SMITH, MATTHEW; St Marys Ryken HS; Great Mills, MD; (Y); Var JV Socr; Var Trk; Im Wt Lftg; JV Wrstlng; Hon Roll; Ntl Merit Ltr; Rtrt Ldr 86.

SMITH, MAXINE; Owings Mills JR-SR HS; Owings Mills, MD; (Y); Am Leg Aux Girls St; Art Clb; Church Yth Grp; Library Aide; Chorus; Church Choir; Var Vllybl; High Hon Roll; NHS; Prfct Atten Awd; Coll Parks Ldrshp Prog 86; Yng Miss Pgnt 85; 3rd Pl In Patriotic Art Cntst 85; Comp Sci.

SMITH, MELINDA; Cambridge South Dorchester HS; Cambridge, MD; (Y); 22/241; AFS; School Play; Nwsp Stf; Yrbk Stf; Trs Soph Cls; Pres Jr Cls; Pres Sr Cls; Jr NHS; NHS; Nathan Fndtn Schlrshp 86; Salisbury ST.

SMITH, MICHAEL; Beall HS; Frostburg, MD; (Y); Nwsp Phtg; Nwsp Rptr; Bsbl; Bsktbl; Ftbl; Socr; Var L Tennis; NHS; Ntl Merit Schol; Sal; Frstbrg ST Coll; Jrnlsm.

SMITH, MONIQUE; Friendly HS; Fort Washington, MD; (Y); Math Tm; Red Cross Aide; Rep Stu Cncl; L Trk; High Hon Roll; Hon Roll; Pres NHS; Edtr Prnc George Cnty Chptr Tots & Teens 85; Mock Trl Tm 84-86.

SMITH, PAULA; Catoctin HS; Taneytown, MD; (Y); Hon Roll; Bus.

SMITH, RICHARD; Westminster HS; Taneytown, MD; (Y); Church Yth Grp; Pres Political Wkr; Concert Band; High Hon Roll; Hon Roll; Muhlenburg; Psychlgy.

SMITH, ROBIN; Potomac HS; Suitland, MD; (Y); Drama Clb; Variety Show; Off Sr Cls; Var JV Cheerleading; High Hon Roll; Hon Roll; NHS; 1st Pl Carriage Hill Swmng Awd 84; Outstndng Elctrnc Stu 86; Ntl Chrng Assoc Camp 86; Stu Govt Assoc 86; U Of MD Coll Pk; Elctrncs.

SMITH, SAIMANTHA; Dundalle HS; Baltimore, MD; (Y); Rep Soph Cls; Rep Jr Cls; Var Mgr(s); Mdl MD St Legiltre 83-84; Accntng.

SMITH, SHANA; Riverdale Baptist Schl; Upper Marlboro, MD; (S); #1 In Class; Yrbk Rptr; Rep Stu Cncl; Var Socr; Var Trk; High Hon Roll; Ntl Merit Ltr; Prfct Atten Awd; US Army Resrv Schlr-Athl Awd 85; Natl Chrstn Hnr Soc 84; Mst Acad Sccr Plyr 85; Actng.

SMITH, SHANNON; St Marys Ryken HS; Maddox, MD; (Y); Church Yth Grp; Cmnty Wkr; Drama Clb; Teachers Aide; School Play; Crs Cntry; Trk; High Hon Roll; NHS; Cls Religion Awd 84; Office Child Yth Awd 86; Mary Washington.

SMITH, SHANON; Centennial HS; Columbia, MD; (Y); 16/265; Cmnty Wkr; French Clb; Math Tm; Teachers Aide; Rep Jr Cls; Rep Sr Cls; Rep Stu Cncl; Hon Roll; NHS; Natl Achvt Semfnlst; Treas Cultrl Awrns; U Of MD; Medcn.

SMITH, STEPHANIE; Clear Spring HS; Hagerstown, MD; (Y); 14/119; 4-H; Girl Scts; Pep Clb; Band; Concert Band; Mrchg Band; Trs Jr Cls; Var L Bsktbl; L Sftbl; NAWIC Schlrshp 86; Semper Fidelis Marine Awd 86; U MD; Mech Engrng.

SMITH, TAMMY; Forestville HS; Suitland, MD; (Y); Debate Tm; Model UN; Pep Clb; ROTC; Varsity Clb; Chorus; Church Choir; Mrchg Band; Variety Show; VP Sr Cls; U Of MD; Pre-Med.

SMITH, TANYA A; Central HS; Andrews AFB, DC; (Y); ROTC; Band; Chorus; Variety Show; Jr NHS; Church Yth Grp; Teachers Aide; Lit Mag; Gym; Hon Roll; Ntl Achvt Cmmdtn 85; Music.

SMITH, TODD; Allegany HS; Freeport, IL; (Y); 49/240; FCA; Ski Clb; Yrbk Stf; Ftbl; Tennis; Trk; Wt Lftg; Wrstlng; Wstrn IL U; Bus Admin.

SMITH, TONY; Frederick HS; Frederick, MD; (Y); 54/307; Art Clb; Church Yth Grp; FCA; Office Aide; Varsity Clb; Rep Stu Cncl; Var L Ftbl; Var L Trk; Wt Lftg; Opt Clb Awd; Schlr Athl 86; Coachs Awd Trck 86; ST Chmpnshp Boys Trck 86; Slippery Rock Coll.

SMITH, TRACEY; Sherwood HS; Olney, MD; (Y); Library Aide; Office Aide; Teachers Aide; Hon Roll; NHS; Prfct Atten Awd; Spanish NHS; Eng Cmndble Perf Composition 84; Sci.

SMITH, TRACY; Kent County HS; Millington, MD; (Y); Church Yth Grp; 4-H; Mrchg Band; Nwsp Phtg; Yrbk Phtg; Var Bsktbl; JV Trk; 4-H Awd; Hon Roll; Psych.

SMITH, VALERIE; Mercy HS; Baltimore, MD; (Y); 10/28; Cmnty Wkr; French Clb; GAA; Red Cross Aide; Stu Cncl; JV Var Cheerleading; Var Sftbl; Hon Roll; Opt Clb Awd; Prfct Atten Awd; MADD Srvc Wrk 85-86; MADD Tang Mrch 85; Miss Teen Pageant Stu 85; Towson ST U; Accntng.

SMITH, VANESSA; Frederick HS; Frederick, MD; (Y); 32/307; Cmnty Wkr; Computer Clb; Hosp Aide; JCL; Latin Clb; Concert Band; Mrchg Band; Vllybl; Hon Roll; Mrch Of Dms Hlth Careers Awd 86; Frederick CC; Occptnl Thpry.

SMITH, WENDY; Severna Park SR HS; Arnold, MD; (Y); 1/700; Church Yth Grp; Concert Band; Pres Mrchg Band; Pres Symp Band; Lit Mag; High Hon Roll; NCTE Awd; NHS; Ntl Merit SF; Natl Latin I Exm Gld Mdl Summa Cum Laude 84; Natl Latin II Exm Magna Cum Laude 85; Mtrls Instr Cmmtee; Englsh.

SMITHSON, LANSING; Montrose Christian Schl; Kensington, MD; (Y); Church Yth Grp; Drama Clb; Spanish Clb; School Play; JV Var Bsktbl; JV Score Keeper; Im Socr; JV Im Sftbl; Im Vllybl; Cit Awd.

SMITHSON, MARY E; Liberty HS; Eldersburg, MD; (Y); Art Clb; Church Yth Grp; Yrbk Stf; Sm-Fnlst Dstngshd Schlr Arts Comptn 85; 1st Pl Sykesvl Wmns Clb Art 85; Schlrp Columbus Coll Art/Dsgn; Columbus Coll; Commrcl Art.

SMITZ, SHERRY; Stephen Decatur HS; Ocean City, MD; (Y); Spanish Clb; Teachers Aide; Off Frsh Cls; Off Soph Cls; Hon Roll; Schlstc Achvmnt Awd 86; Accntng Clerk Bus Cert 86; Wor-Wic Tech CC; Compu Prg.

SMOOT, JANET; La Plata HS; Bel Alton, MD; (Y); FHA; Office Aide; Off Frsh Cls; Hon Roll.

SMYTHE, TERRI DAWN; North East HS; N East, MD; (Y); 50/250; Debate Tm; Political Wkr; Teachers Aide; Acpl Chr; Ed Lit Mag; Stu Cncl; Capt Pom Pon; Prfct Atten Awd; Mst Outstndng Bnd Frnt Stu 85-86; All Cnty Chrs 84-85; Westchester U; Music.

SNEAD, CARLA E; Montgomery Blair HS; Silver Spg, MD; (Y); Church Yth Grp; Red Cross Aide; Sec Frsh Cls; VP Soph Cls; Pres Sr Cls; Rep Stu Cncl; Pom Pon; Hon Roll; Jr NHS; Montgomery Cnty Miss TEEN Pg 85; Soc Sci.

SNELL, LEE; Gaithersburg HS; Laytonsville, MD; (Y); Art Clb; Teachers Aide; Band; Concert Band; Mrchg Band; Pep Band; School Musical; Symp Band; Lit Mag; Hon Roll; Art Adm.

SNIEZEK, JOHN; Our Lady Of Good Counsel HS; Silver Spring, MD; (Y); 4/216; Cmnty Wkr; Drama Clb; French Clb; Math Clb; Math Tm; SADD; Band; Jazz Band; Pep Band; School Musical; Religious Achvt Awd 85; All-Archdiocesan Band 86; Bus Mngt.

SNIVELY, MARSHALL W; North Hagerstown HS; Hagerstown, MD; (Y); Mrchg Band; Rep Frsh Cls; Rep Soph Cls; Rep Jr Cls; Rep Sr Cls; Sec Stu Cncl; Hon Roll; Var Trk; French Clb; Key Clb; Natl Achvt Commended Stu 86; Historian French Clb; Sr Rep Band; Arch.

SNODDERLY, KIM; Patapsco HS; Baltimore, MD; (Y); Church Yth Grp; Drama Clb; Varsity Clb; Chorus; School Play; Nwsp Stf; JV Bowling; JV Crs Cntry; Fld Hcky; Var Lcrss.

SNOW, WENDY; Fort Hill HS; Cumberland, MD; (S); Drama Clb; Pep Clb; Thesps; School Musical; School Play; Nwsp Ed-Chief; Hon Roll; Ms Outstndng MD Tn 84; Art Shw Grnd Prz 84 & 85; WA Coll; Pre-Vet.

SNOWDEN, LOUIS J; Edgewood SR HS; Edgewood, MD; (Y); Church Yth Grp; Computer Clb; Math Tm; Scholastic Bowl; Trs Science Clb; Var Crs Cntry; Var Trk; Hon Roll; Jr NHS; Pres NHS; Army & Navy ROTC Scholars 86; U S Naval Acad, U S Air Force Acad, U S Militry Acad Apptmnts 85-86; US Military Acad; Aero Engrng.

SNYDER, CHARLES L; Clear Spring HS; Big Pool, MD; (Y); 4/125; Am Leg Boys St; Church Yth Grp; Ski Clb; Band; School Play; Var Socr; Hon Roll; NHS.

SNYDER, CORI; Pikesville HS; Balto, MD; (Y); AFS; French Clb; Spanish Clb; School Play; Stage Crew; Nwsp Rptr; Nwsp Stf; Cheerleading; NHS; Hon Men M L King JR Essay Comp 84; 1st Prz Essay Cont 86; Natl Hnr Roll 86; Intl Rel.

SNYDER, JOHN; Fort Hill HS; Cumberland, MD; (Y); L Badmtn; JV Var Bsbl; JV Var Bsktbl; L Fld Hcky; JV Var Ftbl; Hon Roll; James Turner Awd Outstndng Jr Athlt 86; Commrcl Jet Plt.

SNYDER, KAREN L; Loch Raven SR HS; Baldwin, MD; (Y); Church Yth Grp; Drama Clb; Office Aide; Chorus; Church Choir; School Musical; School Play; Swing Chorus; Variety Show; Hon Roll; Chldrns Chorus MD 78-84; MD Gftd & Tlntd Music Prog 85-86; MD Acad Sci 86; Stdnt Sci Semnrs 86; Western MD Coll.

SNYDER, MARK G; Gaithersburg HS; Gaithersburg, MD; (Y); 83/568; Boy Scts; FCA; Ski Clb; Stu Cncl; Ftbl; Swmmng; Hon Roll; NHS; Pres Schlr; Spanish NHS; Natl Captial Area Cncl Sct Yth Rep 84; Natl UN Day Coord 84; Tm Contrib Awd Vrsty Ftbl 85-86; U Richmond; Spts Med.

SNYDER, TAMMY; Fort Hill HS; Cumberland, MD; (Y); 47/284; Church Yth Grp; Drama Clb; Thesps; Drill Tm; Yrbk Rptr; Yrbk Stf; Pom Pon; Hon Roll; S Cumberland Bus & Civic Assn Scholar 86; Allegany CC; Bus Tech.

SOBCHAK, EDWARD TED; Liberty HS; Eldersburg, MD; (S); Church Yth Grp; Cmnty Wkr; Mathletes; JV Socr; Hon Roll; Comp Sci.

SOBCHAK, TED; Liberty HS; Eldersburg, MD; (Y); Church Yth Grp; Cmnty Wkr; Socr; Comp Sci.

SOCKUM, JOAN; Carver Vocational-Tech HS; Baltimore, MD; (Y); FBLA; Hon Roll; Prfct Atten Awd; U Of MD; Physcl Thrpst.

SOEKEN, JEFF; Laurel HS; Laurel, MD; (Y); Boy Scts; Church Yth Grp; Political Wkr; Quiz Bowl; Stage Crew; Var L Socr; Hon Roll; Boy Sct Jmbree 85; Arch.

SOKOLOSKI, CAROLE T; Poolesville JR SR HS; Poolesville, MD; (Y); 3/113; Cmnty Wkr; School Play; Co-Capt Var Tennis; Hon Roll; VP NHS; Ntl Merit Ltr; Pres Schlr; St Schlr; Towson U Schlrshp 86; Acad Team Schlrshp 86; Towson St U.

SOLANKI, SUSHMA J; Franklin SR HS; Reisterstown, MD; (Y); Cmnty Wkr; Math Clb; Cit Awd; High Hon Roll; Hon Roll; JC Awd; NHS; Prfct Atten Awd; Cert Of Achvt Sl Of Merit 86; Sntrl Schlrshp 86; Cntry Clb Ests Schlrshp 86; U Of MD Baltimore; Bio.

SOLE, KIMBERLY; Oxon Hill HS Sci & Tech Program; Temple Hills, MD; (Y); Church Yth Grp; Yrbk Stf; Stu Cncl; Var Pom Pon; Hon Roll; Acadmc Excllnc Awd 84.

SOLOMAN, PRISCILLA; Joppatowne HS; Joppa, MD; (Y); French Clb; Band; Mrchg Band; Yrbk Ed-Chief; Ed Lit Mag; VP Jr Cls; Var Fld Hcky; Var Lcrss; High Hon Roll; NHS; 3rd Sci Fair 85; 25 Hr Svc Pin Cmnty Svc 86; Acctg.

SOLOMON, CHARLES; Fort Hill HS; Cumberland, MD; (Y); Church Yth Grp; Im JV Lcrss; JV Trk; JV Wrstlng; Mdrn Schl Spplies 86; Allegany CC; Arch.

SOLOMON, DAYNA; Walter Johnson HS; Bethesda, MD; (Y); GAA; Nwsp Rptr; Nwsp Stf; Yrbk Ed-Chief; Yrbk Rptr; Yrbk Stf; Var Capt Bsktbl; Var L Sftbl; Hon Roll; Sprtn Awd Sftbll 84; MVP JV Bsktbll 84-85; Jrnlsm.

SOLOMON, ROBERT; Walt Whitman HS; Bethesda, MD; (Y).

SONG, YOUNG O; Arlington Baptist HS; Baltimore, MD; (S); 5/63; Pres Church Yth Grp; L Vllybl; High Hon Roll; Hon Roll; NHS; Prfct Atten Awd; Drexel U; Intrior Dsgn.

SONGY, STEVE; Lackey HS; Bryans Road, MD; (Y); 18/186; Drama Clb; Math Tm; SADD; Band; Jazz Band; Pep Band; School Musical; School Play; Variety Show; Mst Outstndng Band Stu; MD U.

SOOD, KAVITA; Mercy HS; Baltimore, MD; (Y); Aud/Vis; Drama Clb; French Clb; GAA; Hosp Aide; School Play; Stage Crew; High Hon Roll; Hon Roll; Loyola Coll; Blgy.

SORDILLO, MAUREEN; North Carroll HS; Hampstead, MD; (Y); Pres VP Church Yth Grp; JA; VP Service Clb; Band; Stu Cncl; Var L Socr; Var L Trk; NHS; Pres Ftnss Awd 86; Gov Cert Merit 86; Towson ST U; Sprts Med.

SORIANO, CAMILLE; Seneca Valley HS; Germantown, MD; (Y); Church Yth Grp; ROTC; Yrbk Stf; Pom Pon; Var Socr; Var Swmmng; JV Vllybl; Amer Lgn Acadmc Excllnc Awd 86.

SOTIR, KRISONTHIE; Roland Park Country Schl; Baltimore, MD; (Y); Cmnty Wkr; French Clb; Ski Clb; Pres Soph Cls; Pres Rep Sr Cls; JV Bsktbl; Var Fld Hcky; JV Tennis; French Hon Soc; Hon Roll.

SOUDERS, DAVID; Gov Thomas Johnson HS; Frederick, MD; (Y); 3/345; Boy Scts; Church Yth Grp; FBLA; Latin Clb; Science Clb; JV Capt Bsktbl; High Hon Roll; Hon Roll; Prfct Atten Awd; Awds GPA 84-86; Engl Hnrs 86; Acctng II Hnrs 86; Penn ST; Acctng.

SOUTHARD, LAURA; Liberty HS; Sykesville, MD; (Y); Cmnty Wkr; Mathletes; Towson ST U; Bus Adm.

SOWARDS, SUSAN; Kenwood SR HS; Baltimore, MD; (Y); FBLA; Trs Pep Clb; Lit Mag; High Hon Roll; Prfct Atten Awd; Pres Schlr; Alex E Bmgrtnr Hstry Awd 86; MD Dstngshd Schlr Smi-Fnlst 85; Gld K Ltr-H S 86; Essex CC; Mrktng Mngmt.

SPALDING, DALE; St Marys Ryken HS; Leonardtown, MD; (Y); Camera Clb; Drama Clb; School Play; Variety Show; Nwsp Ed-Chief; Nwsp Phtg; Nwsp Rptr; Nwsp Sprt Ed; Nwsp Stf; Tennis; Engrng.

SPANN, JULIE; Laurel HS; Laurel, MD; (Y); Pres Church Yth Grp; Intnl Clb; Chorus; Church Choir; School Play; Variety Show; Rep Stu Cncl; Pom Pon; French Hon Soc; Hon Roll; Sorptmst Intl Prince Georgs Co Schlrshp 86; Laurel Oratorio Soc Awd/Schlrshp 86; U Of MD; Lbrl Art.

SPATES, ERIC; Landon Schl; Poolesville, MD; (S); Chess Clb; Church Yth Grp; Math Tm; Band; JV Bsbl; Var Crs Cntry; Im Socr; Var Wrstlng; Ntl Merit Ltr; Engr.

SPEAK, JUNE; Francis Scott Key HS; Taneytown, MD; (Y); 6/200; GAA; Latin Clb; Spanish Clb; Nwsp Phtg; Trs Sr Cls; Rep Stu Cncl; Var Fld Hcky; L Trk; High Hon Roll; NHS; U S Achvmnt Acad Awd 86; Ntl Engl Merit Awd 86; Acdmc Lttr 85; Elec Engnr.

SPEAR, KEVIN; Cambridge-South Dorchester HS; Cambridge, MD; (Y); Church Yth Grp; Band; Church Choir; Concert Band; Drm & Bgl; Jazz Band; Mrchg Band; Orch; School Play; Symp Band; Mrchng & Symphnc Band Ltr & Plq 85-86; MD All Shr Band Ptch & Mdl 85-86; Engrng.

SPECTOR, ELLEN; Thomas S Wootton HS; Potomac, MD; (Y); Aud/Vis; Hosp Aide; Band; Hon Roll; Rgnl & Chptr Pres Of Bnai Brith Yth Orgnzatn 83-86; 2nd Pl Psych Fair At Thms S Wttn Hgh 86; Comm.

SPENCE, DONIQUE; Northwestern HS; Baltimore, MD; (Y); Art Clb; Dance Clb; Drama Clb; Girl Scts; Church Choir; School Play; Hon Roll; Comp Pgmr.

SPENCER, KAREN; St Marys Ryken HS; Mechanicsville, MD; (Y); Math Tm; Sftbl; Hon Roll; Schlrsp Gftd Tlntd Prgrm 81; Bus.

SPENCER, SHANAN; Fort Hill HS; Cumberland, MD; (Y); Pres Church Yth Grp; Band; Church Choir; Concert Band; Drm Mjr(t); Jazz Band; Mrchg Band; Pep Band; Hon Roll; NHS; Brigham Young U; Music.

SPERRY, LAURA; Gaithersburg HS; Gaithersburg, MD; (Y); MD ST Chmpn Gymnstcs 85.

SPESSARD, PAMELA; Laurel HS; Laurel, MD; (Y); Physcl Thrpy.

SPIELMAN, DEBORAH; Williamsport HS; Hagerstown, MD; (Y); 10/206; Latin Clb; Teachers Aide; Yrbk Stf; Rep Jr Cls; Var Bsktbl; Mgr(s); Var L Trk; Hon Roll; NHS.

SPINDLER, KIMBERLY; Institute Of Notre Dame; Baltimore, MD; (Y); 21/139; Art Clb; Girl Scts; Spanish Clb; Sec Acpl Chr; Chorus; Drm & Bgl; School Play; Vllybl; Hon Roll; Marion Basketbll Schlrshp IND 83; HS Acadmc Team 85-86; Bio.

SPOSATO, TINA; Elkton HS; Elkton, MD; (Y); Church Yth Grp; French Clb; FHA; Office Aide; Pep Clb; Dntl Tech.

SPOTSWOOD, ROBERT; Balto Polytechnic HS; Baltimore, MD; (Y); 8/425; Chess Clb; JA; Library Aide; Off Jr Cls; Off Sr Cls; High Hon Roll; Hon Roll; U Of MD Coll; Chmcl Engrng.

SPRAGUE, JOAN; St Marys Ryken HS; Port Taboacco, MD; (Y); 4-H; Rep Frsh Cls; Rep Soph Cls; Rep Jr Cls; Trs Stu Cncl; Var Fld Hcky; Var Tennis; Hon Roll; High Hon Roll; Cert Hnr Excllnce Religious Studies 86; 1st Sqd Sthrn MD All Conf Ten 85, 2nd Sqd 86; Bus.

SPRIGGS, JOCELYN; Institute Of Notre Dame; Baltimore, MD; (Y); Art Clb; Library Aide; Spanish Clb; Yrbk Stf; Hon Roll; 2nd Hnrs 84; Salisbury ST; Cmmnctns.

SPRINGER, SCOTT; Bowie HS; Bowie, MD; (Y); Church Yth Grp.

SPURLOCK, LISA; Maurice Mc Donough HS; Pomfret, MD; (Y); Church Yth Grp; Hosp Aide; Intnl Clb; Concert Band; Mrchg Band; Hon Roll; Engl.

ST CLAIR, MICHELLE; St Marys Ryken HS; Compton, MD; (S); Cmnty Wkr; FBLA; Girl Scts; Hosp Aide; Yrbk Stf; Stat Trk; High Hon Roll; NHS; NEDT Awd; Latn, Hist & Typng Awds 82-84; Boston U; Nrs.

STACHURA, MICHAEL; Lackey HS; Nanjemoy, MD; (Y); Church Yth Grp; 4-H; Math Tm; SADD; Teachers Aide; Church Choir; 4-H Awd; Volntr Fire Wrk 86; Elec.

STADTER, PATRICK; Mt St Joseph HS; Glenwood, MD; (Y); Ski Clb; Speech Tm; Bsktbl; Tennis; High Hon Roll; NHS; Ntl Merit Ltr; Gftd And Talntd Summr Semnr 84; Navl Acad Summr Semnr 86; Natl Hnr Rl 86; Engrg.

STAFFORD, MISTY; Fort Hill HS; Cumberland, MD; (Y); Computer Clb; Rep Stu Cncl; Var Bsktbl; Var Vllybl; Hon Roll; U MD; Vet.

STALEY, STEVE; Clear Spring HS; Hagerstown, MD; (Y); 33/111; FFA; Ski Clb; VICA; Y-Teens; Concert Band; Mrchg Band; School Musical; School Play; Stage Crew; Rep Jr Cls; Pres FFA 85-86; Outstndng Frm Stu Awd 86; De Klb Ag Accmplshmnt Awd 86; Liberty Stmftng Schl; Steamftr.

STALEY, TARA; Forestville HS; Temple Hills, MD; (Y); ROTC; Teachers Aide; Yrbk Stf; JV Cheerleading; Gym; Var Sftbl; Swmmng; Hon Roll; U Of MD; Comp Sci.

STALLINGS, BRIAN; Suitland HS; Capitol Heights, MD; (Y); CAP; French Clb; ROTC; Color Guard; Drill Tm; Trk; NHS; Military; Sci.

STAMMINGER, MARK; Thomas S Wootton HS; Gaithersburg, MD; (Y); 1/401; Debate Tm; JA; Math Tm; NFL; Symp Band; Lit Mag; NHS; Ntl Merit SF; NEDT Awd; MD Distngshd Schlr; Elec Engrng.

STANCILL, STACEY G; John Carroll HS; Bel Air, MD; (Y); Camp Fr Inc; Cmnty Wkr; Girl Scts; Political Wkr; Chorus; Hon Roll; Trs Church Yth Grp; Debate Tm; Drama Clb; Trs 4-H; Campfire Horizn Ldrshp Conf CSU 85; Intrnshps In Govt W MD GT & Delg Behrman 84; Carnegie-Mellon U; Pre-Law.

STANFORD, CELENDA; Northwestern HS; Mt Rainier, MD; (Y); Flag Corp; Jazz Band; Symp Band; Pom Pon; High Hon Roll; Lion Awd; NHS; 1st Prz Schl Sci Fair 84; Wstrn MD Coll; Engl.

STANIEWICZ, CHRISTINE; John Carroll HS; Joppa, MD; (Y); 57/238; Church Yth Grp; Teachers Aide; Yrbk Stf; Stat Bsktbl; Mgr(s); Powder Puff Ftbl; Var L Sftbl; Vllybl; Hon Roll; Russian Hnr Soc 86; Vet.

STANISLAV, PATRICIA; Academy Of The Holy Cross; Rockville, MD; (Y); 25/120; Model UN; Pep Clb; Ski Clb; Spanish Clb; Nwsp Stf; Jr Cls; Pres Sr Cls; Var Trk; Hon Roll; Spanish NHS; Merit Awd Spnsh 84-85; Apprctn Awd Trtmnt Cntrs Of Amer 85; Apprctn Awd Amer Red Cross 86; Frstbrg ST Coll.

STANKIEWICZ, JOSEPH; De Matha Catholic HS; New Carrollton, MD; (Y); Band; Var L Lcrss; JV Socr; Hnr List 85-86.

STANLEY, MICHELLE; St Vincent Pallotti HS; Laurel, MD; (S); 20/116; Pres AFS; Cmnty Wkr; French Clb; Ski Clb; Nwsp Stf; Yrbk Stf; Trs Stu Cncl; JV Var Cheerleading; Var Pom Pon; Var Tennis; Acad Ltr 85; V Ltr 85; U VA; Comm.

STANSBERRY, SHELLEY; Oldtown HS; Oldtown, MD; (S); 1/35; Church Yth Grp; Sec FBLA; Trs FHA; Yrbk Phtg; Pres Stu Cncl; Bsktbl; Hon Roll; Pres NHS; VP Jr Cls; Rep Sr Cls; Chatham Coll.

STANTON, CHRIS; Walt Whitman HS; Potomac, MD; (Y); Latin Clb; Teachers Aide; JV Var Bsbl; JV Var Socr; Var Capt Swmmng; Lbrl Arts.

STANTON, JAMES; North Carroll HS; Hampstead, MD; (Y); 1/370; Church Yth Grp; Red Cross Aide; Rep Frsh Cls; Off Soph Cls; Off Jr Cls; Stu Cncl; Co-Capt Ftbl; Var L Lcrss; High Hon Roll; Hon Roll; CCSGA Smoking & Steering Del, SGA Parl 85; CCSGA Constitution & Previson Del 86; Johns Hopkin; Physics.

STAPLES, JULIA; Queen Anne HS; Upper Marlboro, MD; (Y); Church Yth Grp; Chorus; Lit Mag; Hon Roll; Martha B Beall Awd In Ltn 86; Coll Or U; Bus Admnstrtn.

STARBIRD, MELINDA; Mc Donough HS; White Plains, MD; (S); 12/320; Am Leg Aux Girls St; Intnl Clb; Latin Clb; Letterman Clb; Var Capt Bsktbl; Var L Socr; Var L Sftbl; Var L Vllybl; High Hon Roll; NHS; West Point; Med.

STARBUCK, MICHELLE; Lareine HS; Upper Marlboro, MD; (S); Girl Scts; Pres Science Clb; Yrbk Stf; French Hon Soc; High Hon Roll; NHS; Elec Engrng.

STARGHILL, SKYLAR; St Frances-Charles Hall HS; Baltimore, MD; (Y); 1/30; Art Clb; French Clb; Nwsp Stf; High Hon Roll; Hon Roll; Opt Clb Awd; Val; Pell Grant 86; Cncl Manc 86; MD ST Schlrshp 86; MD Inst Clg; Grphc Dsgn.

STARK, ERIC; Allegany HS; Lavale, MD; (Y); Church Yth Grp; Pres Computer Clb; Var Socr; Var Tennis; Var Trk; Hon Roll; Carnegie Mellon; Comp.

STARKE, BRIAN; Dunbar SR HS; Baltimore, MD; (Y); 20/203; FBLA; Stage Crew; Var Capt Ftbl; Var Trk; Hon Roll; Natl Ftrbl Fndtn Hl Fm Schlr Athl Awd, Dun-Mor Acdmc Schlrshp, Chi Psi Sigma Frat Gld Key Acctg 86; Morgan ST U; Bus Admin.

STARKE, KELLY; Mc Donough HS; Waldorf, MD; (Y); SADD; Teachers Aide; Stu Cncl; Var Stat Bsktbl; Var Cheerleading; JV Sftbl; Wt Lftg; High Hon Roll; Hon Roll; Fash Merch.

STARKEY, CHRIS; Highland View Acad; Hagerstown, MD; (Y); Spanish Clb; Nwsp Rptr; Nwsp Stf; Im JV Ftbl; Timer; High Hon Roll; Hon Roll; Atlantic Union Coll; Athletics.

STARR, DAVID; Fort Hill HS; Cumberland, MD; (Y); Bsbl; Bsktbl; Ftbl; Frgn Lang.

STARR, TODD; Middletown HS; Middletown, MD; (Y); 11/205; AFS; Cmnty Wkr; Debate Tm; Drama Clb; Latin Clb; NFL; Pep Clb; Ski Clb; Teachers Aide; Thesps; JR Wmns Cvc Clb; MD Senatrl Schlrp; Drama Schlrp; U MD; Engrg.

STASIOWSKI, KAREN; Archbishop Keough HS; Ellicott, MD; (Y); Drama Clb; Spanish Clb; School Musical; School Play; Rep Stu Cncl; JV Vllybl; Hon Roll; NHS; Ntl Merit Schol; New Coll USF; Intl Rltns.

STASKOWIAK, DONNA; Patapsco HS; Baltimore, MD; (Y); Chorus; Yrbk Stf; JV Var Socr; JV Var Sftbl; Essex CC; Gnrl Stdy.

STATESMAN, KIRSTIN; Leonardtown HS; Valley Lee, MD; (Y); Church Yth Grp; Band; Drm Mjr(t); Mrchg Band; Symp Band; Powder Puff Ftbl; High Hon Roll; Opt Clb Awd; Voice Dem Awd; Diocese Of WA Schlrp 85-86; Baltimore Sun Schlrp For Minrty Jrnlsts Fnlst 85-86; U MD College Pk; Jrnlsm.

STATON, JAMES; Potomac SR HS; Temple Hills, MD; (Y); Church Yth Grp; Church Choir; Ftbl; Hon Roll; E Carolina U; Accntng.

STATTEL, THERESA; Eleanor Roosevelt HS; Lanham, MD; (Y); AFS; Var Cheerleading; Letterman Clb; Hon Roll; Engrng.

STAUBS, RACHEL; Clear Spring HS; Clear Spg, MD; (Y); 7/125; Stage Crew; Yrbk Ed-Chief; Yrbk Stf; Trs Jr Cls; Var Tennis; High Hon Roll; Hon Roll; NHS; Sec Of Jnthn Nsbt Hstry Club 86-87; Chrprsn Prom Cmmttee 85-86; Shepherd Coll; Graphic Desgn.

STAUFFER, ANDREW M; Linganore HS; Monrovia, MD; (Y); Church Yth Grp; Debate Tm; Ski Clb; School Play; Nwsp Ed-Chief; VP Jr Cls; Rep Stu Cncl; Powder Puff Ftbl; L Tennis; NHS.

STEARNS, STEPHANIE; St Marys Ryken HS; Piney Point, MD; (Y); Church Yth Grp; Dance Clb; Chorus; Church Choir; School Musical; JV Var Cheerleading; JV Trk; Hon Roll; Only Feml-Pax-Hi Pgm 85-86; Relgs Retrt Cnslr Awd 83-84; Salisbury ST; Math.

STECKEL, CHRISTINE; Laurel SR HS; Laurel, MD; (Y); Ski Clb; Orch; Stu Cncl; Trk; Hon Roll; Pres Schlr; Presdntl Acadmc Ftns Awd 85 & 86; MD ST Schlrshp 86; Acadmc Schlrshp 86; Mt St Marys Coll; Psych.

STEELE, CAROLYN; Frederick Douglass HS; Upper Marlboro, MD; (Y); Drama Clb; Latin Clb; Office Aide; Var Pom Pon; High Hon Roll; Sec NHS; Acad Excllnce Awd 83-84; Pres Acad Excllnce Cert 85-86; Prince George Brd Trustee Scholar 85-86; P G CC; Legl Sec.

STEELE, DOUGLASS EDWARD; Southern HS; Baltimore, MD; (Y); Art Clb; FHA; Band; Drm Mjr(t); Mrchg Band; Bsktbl; Ftbl; Swmmng; Trk; Hon Roll; Lawyer.

STEELE, KAMERON HOLT; Mt Hebron HS; Ellicott City, MD; (Y); Aud/Vis; Ski Clb; Thesps; Band; Chorus; Church Choir; Jazz Band; Madrigals; Off Mrchg Band; School Musical; Louis Armstrong Awd 86; Jzz Bnd 86; Wnr ST Flm Fstvl 85; Drma.

STEELE, KAREN; Elkton HS; Elkton, MD; (Y); Pep Clb; Teachers Aide; Score Keeper; Hon Roll; Psych.

STEELE, PATRICK; Northern HS; Huntingtown, MD; (Y); Ftbl; Golf; Socr; Wt Lftg; Hon Roll; U Of MD; Bus Managmnt.

STEELE, TAMMY L; Mount Savage HS; Mt Savage, MD; (Y); French Clb; FBLA; Pep Clb; Chorus; Nwsp Ed-Chief; Hon Roll; Quill & Scroll 86; US Bus Ed Awd 85; FBLA Rgn I Comp 3rd Pl Bus Math 85; Hagerstown Bus COLL; Bus Mgnt.

STEER, WENDY; Dulaney SR HS; Cockeysville, MD; (Y); Sec Church Yth Grp; Church Choir; Var L Bsktbl; Var L Socr; JV Sftbl; Hon Roll; Jr NHS; NHS; Arch.

STEFANCIC, ANDREA; Linganore HS; Monrovia, MD; (Y); Ski Clb; Spanish Clb; Concert Band; Mrchg Band; Nwsp Stf; Frsh Cls; Soph Cls; Jr Cls; Sr Cls; Trk; Hewlett Packard Acad Scholar 86; Loyola Coll; Acctng.

STEFANSIC, KRISTINE; Notre Dame Prep; Towson, MD; (Y); Church Yth Grp; Cmnty Wkr; German Clb; Girl Scts; Library Aide; Ski Clb; Band; Church Choir; Concert Band; Orch; Greater Baltimore Yth Orch 85-87; Music.

STEFKO, KARIN; St Marys-Ryken HS; Indian Head, MD; (Y); Art Clb; Church Yth Grp; Lit Mag; Trk; High Hon Roll; Hon Roll; NHS; Art Awds 84-86; Charles County CC.

STEIDEL, RICKY; Northern HS; Huntingtown, MD; (Y); Church Yth Grp; Bsbl; Ftbl; Wrstlng; Penn ST; Accntng.

STEIGERWALD, PATRICIA M; Archbishop Keough HS; Columbia, MD; (Y); 1/225; Cmnty Wkr; Lit Mag; High Hon Roll; Hon Roll; NHS; Ntl Merit Ltr; Val; SR Joann Brosnan Awd Mth 86; Gerard A Heidrick Jr Mem Awd 86; Edgar N Ganster Awd 86; Johns Hopkins; Moleclr Bio.

STEIN, HOLLY ANN; Wicomico SR HS; Parsonsburg, MD; (Y); 2/243; Latin Clb; Math Tm; Office Aide; Spanish Clb; Capt Sftbl; Capt Vllybl; Pres NHS; Sal; Sci Awd, T H Williams Prz, D H Graham Awd Acad Excel 86; US Military Acad West Point.

STEINER, DAVID; Francis Scott Key HS; Union Bridge, MD; (Y); 2/202; Pres Church Yth Grp; Pres Drama Clb; Trs Pres French Clb; Chorus; School Play; VP Soph Cls; NHS; Sal; SAR Awd; St Schlr; Acad All Amer 86; Stu Govt Awd 86; Balfour Ldrshp Awd 86; Ashland Coll; Pol Sci.

STEMMLER, MARTIN B; German Schl; Potomac, MD; (Y); 1/32; Orch; Variety Show; Ntl Merit SF.

STEMPEL, ANDREW B; Pikesville HS; Baltimore, MD; (Y); AFS; Math Tm; Political Wkr; Pres Band; Concert Band; Mrchg Band; Orch; School Musical; Symp Band; Ntl Merit SF; Mc Donalds All-Amer Band 85-86; All-Eastern Coast Band 85; Astronomy.

STEMPLE, KENDRA D; Southern HS; Oakland, MD; (S); Church Yth Grp; Yrbk Stf; Var Bsktbl; JV Vllybl; Hon Roll; NHS; Ntl Merit Ltr; Jrnlsm.

STEPANSKE, NANCY; Takoma Acad; Silver Spgs, MD; (Y); Church Yth Grp; Cmnty Wkr; Hosp Aide; Office Aide; Yrbk Stf; Hon Roll; Bus Mgmt.

STEPHENS, DOUGLAS; Lackey HS; Bryans Rd, MD; (Y); Var L Bsbl; Im Bsktbl; Capt Var Socr; Charles Cnty CC; Physcl Educ.

STEPHENS, LESLIE B; Large HS; Upper Marlboro, MD; (Y); Church Yth Grp; Debate Tm; French Clb; Model UN; Pep Clb; Band; Rep Frsh Cls; Cit Awd; Hon Roll; Ntl Merit SF; Natl Achvt Schlrshp Pgm-Outstndng Stu 85; Cntry III Ldr Pgm Wnnr 85; Pltcl Sci.

STEPHENS, SAM; Brunswick HS; Jefferson, MD; (Y); 22/150; Computer Clb; Drama Clb; Teachers Aide; Chorus; School Musical; School Play; Stage Crew; Socr; Hon Roll; Schl Arts 86-87; Gftd Tlntd Pgm; Frdercktwn Plyrs Comm Thtre; MD ST Dstngshed Schlr Pgm 85-86; Engrng.

STEPHENS, WANDA; Bladensburg SR HS; Brentwood, MD; (Y); Teachers Aide; Rep Soph Cls; Hon Roll; Lion Awd; NHS; Pres Schlr; Willis R Cone Sci Awd Excllnce Dedctn Prsnl Achvt 86; U MD College Park; Comp Sci.

STERLING, OLGA J; Crisfield HS; Crisfield, MD; (Y); Church Yth Grp; Cmnty Wkr; Dance Clb; Drama Clb; FHA; Hosp Aide; Pep Clb; Science Clb; Teachers Aide; Band; Crmnl Jstc.

STERN, ANDRA; Charles W Woodward HS; Rockville, MD; (Y); Church Yth Grp; Ski Clb; Spanish Clb; SADD; Teachers Aide; Temple Yth Grp; Lit Mag; Sec Soph Cls; Score Keeper; Hon Roll; Princpls Awd Outstndng Cretv Wrtng 86; U MD.

STERN, JEFFREY; Thomas S Wootton HS; Potomac, MD; (Y); Yrbk Bus Mgr; Yrbk Stf; VP Soph Cls; JV Socr; High Hon Roll; Hon Roll; Aud/Vis; Cmnty Wkr; Library Aide; Office Aide; Spcl Hnr Stu Rep 84-86; Peer Cnslr; Bus.

STETAK, WENDY; Williamsport HS; Hagerstown, MD; (Y); French Clb; Ski Clb; Band; Concert Band; Drm Mjr(t); Mrchg Band; Pep Band; Symp Band; Rep Jr Cls; Var L Tennis; All Cnty Band 85-86; No 1 Rtng-Fredrick Cnty Solo Comptn 86; Municpl Band 86; Music.

STETS, ROBERT J; Magruder HS; Rockville, MD; (Y); Am Leg Boys St; Service Clb; Ski Clb; Bsbl; Bsktbl; Score Keeper; Hon Roll; NHS; Harvard Bk Awd 86; Comp Sci.

STETSON, CATHERINE; T S Wootton HS; Rockville, MD; (Y); Church Yth Grp; Drama Clb; Thesps; Band; Chorus; Church Choir; Flag Corp; Mrchg Band; Pep Band; School Play; Wnnr Montgomery Cty Music Comptn 86; Music Achvt Awd 85; Lib Arts.

STEVENS, JENNIFER LYNN; Middletown HS; Smithsburg, MD; (Y); 37/201; Chorus; Yrbk Stf; VP Frsh Cls; Pres Soph Cls; Pres Jr Cls; Pres Sr Cls; Capt Cheerleading; Hon Roll; Drama Clb; French Clb; Mst Outstndng Chrldr Intl Chrldng Fndtn 85; Hmcmng Queen 85; Ruritan & Loats Fndtn Inc Scholars 86; WVU; Graphic Desgn.

STEVENS, JULIE; Northern Garrett HS; Grantsville, MD; (Y); Teachers Aide; Chorus; Color Guard; Yrbk Stf; Off Jr Cls; Rep Stu Cncl; Var Sftbl; Stat Vllybl; Hon Roll; Medcl Technlgy.

STEVENS, KATHY; Hammond HS; Columbia, MD; (Y); AFS; Cmnty Wkr; Letterman Clb; Ski Clb; Nwsp Stf; Stu Cncl; Pom Pon; Hon Roll; Salisbury ST Coll; Intl Busnss.

STEVENS, NICHOLE; Thomas Stone SR HS; Waldorf, MD; (Y); Art Clb; Dance Clb; French Clb; FHA; Office Aide; Teachers Aide; Chorus; Fld Hcky; Hon Roll; Towson U; Psych.

STEVENSON, KELLY M; Williamsport HS; Hagerstown, MD; (Y); French Clb; Ski Clb; Rep Soph Cls; Rep Jr Cls; Rep Sr Cls; Stu Cncl; Capt Var Cheerleading; Powder Puff Ftbl; Stat Trk; Hon Roll; Hagerstown JC; Radiolgc Tech.

STEWARD, TONY; Eleanor Roosevelt HS; Upper Marlboro, MD; (Y); Boy Scts; Chess Clb; Computer Clb; Ntl Merit Ltr; Achvt Awd 85; Bridge Clb 84; Gaming Clb 84-86; SUNY; Engrng.

STEWART, DONNA; Arlington Baptist Chl; Baltimore, MD; (Y); Church Yth Grp; School Play; Cit Awd; High Hon Roll; Hon Roll; Prfct Atten Awd; Geneva Coll; Bus Adm.

STEWART, EDWARD W; Arlington Baptist HS; Baltimore, MD; (S); 1/63; Boy Scts; Church Yth Grp; Concert Band; Pres Frsh Cls; Pres Soph Cls; Pres Jr Cls; Pres Sr Cls; Crs Cntry; Trk; God Cntry Awd; Eagle Scout-Two Palms 82; Geneva; Mech Engrng.

STEWART, GEOFF; Seneca Valley HS; Gaithersburg, MD; (Y); Church Choir; Computer Clb; Latin Clb; Math Clb; Science Clb; Ski Clb; JV Socr; Var L Tennis; High Hon Roll; NHS; U Of MD; Engrng.

STEWART, KELLY; Brooklyn Park HS; Baltimore, MD; (S); 4/150; Am Leg Aux Girls St; Church Yth Grp; Cmnty Wkr; GAA; Teachers Aide; Trs Chorus; Yrbk Stf; Sec Sr Cls; Stu Cncl; Capt Cheerleading; NCA All Amer Chrldr 86; JR Class Sec 85; UMBC; Law.

STEWART, MARK; High Point HS; Silver Spg, MD; (Y); Art Clb; Church Yth Grp; Cmnty Wkr; Church Choir; Var Ftbl; Wt Lftg; High Hon Roll; Hon Roll; Round Missionary Bapt Chrch Schlrshp 86; Maryland Inst/Art; Arch Dsgn.

STEWART, SHANNON; Bowie HS; Bowie, MD; (Y); Church Yth Grp; Teachers Aide; Church Choir; Hon Roll; Jr NHS; Prfct Atten Awd; Potomac Acad Hair Dsgn; Csmtlgy.

STEWART, TONYA; Gaithersburg HS; Gaithersburg, MD; (Y); Church Yth Grp; Pep Clb; Band; Variety Show; JV Cheerleading; Swmmng; Trk; Hon Roll; MD U; Law.

STIDHAM, SUSAN; Notre Dame Prep; Towson, MD; (Y); Art Clb; JA; Math Clb; Pep Clb; PAVAS; Red Cross Aide; Varsity Clb; Pep Band; JV Capt Cheerleading; Swmmng; Merit Schlrshp Notre Dame Prep 83-84; Hgh Hnr Pgm 83-84.

STIGALL, MICHELLE; Archbishop Keough HS; Cartonsville, MD; (Y); Cmnty Wkr; German Clb; SADD; Nwsp Stf; Yrbk Stf; JV Var Fld Hcky; Hon Roll; NHS; MD Ldrshp Wrkshp 84; HS Ldrshp Inst 86; Frgn Exchng Stu-Grmny 85.

STILES, ANDREW A; Damascus HS; Clarksburg, MD; (Y); Am Leg Boys St; Boy Scts; Leo Clb; Quiz Bowl; Ski Clb; Band; Color Guard; Concert Band; Drm Mjr(t); Jazz Band; Eagle Scout 84; Engrng.

STILL, AMY; Cambridge-South Dorchester HS; Cambridge, MD; (Y); Drama Clb; 4-H; SADD; School Play; Stage Crew; Nwsp Rptr; Yrbk Stf; Tennis; 4-H Awd; Voice Dem Awd; Jrnlsm.

STIMMEL II, GEORGE RICHARD; Fort Hill HS; Old Town, MD; (Y); Office Aide; Ftbl; Hon Roll; Algny Cnty Pblc Schls Achvt Accolade 86; Algny CC; Auto Tech.

STINE, MELISSA; La Plata HS; Newburg, MD; (Y); Church Yth Grp; Cmnty Wkr; Teachers Aide; Chorus; Cit Awd; High Hon Roll; Hon Roll; Principals Awd Of Schlstc Achvt 86; Natl Engl Merit Awd 86; Comp Engr.

STINNETT, CINDY; Liberty HS; Sykesville, MD; (S); Teachers Aide; Stat Bsktbl; JV Var Mgr(s); Score Keeper; High Hon Roll; Hon Roll; Prfct Atten Awd; Acadmc Ltr & Pin; Hiwassee Coll; Nrsg.

STINNETTE, STEPHEN; Dundalk SR HS; Baltimore, MD; (Y); 4/306; Band; JV Socr; NHS; Dstngshd Schlr Awd 86; Phrmclgy Prgm/John Hpkns Hosp 86; U MD; CPA.

STIRN, MICHELLE; Randallstown HS; Randallstown, MD; (Y); Cmnty Wkr; FBLA; Hon Roll; Towson ST U; Bus Adm.

STIVERSON, SHARON; Crisfield HS; Marion, MD; (Y); Computer Clb; Sec Girl Scts; Library Aide; Nwsp Rptr; Rep Stu Cncl; Var Bsktbl; Hon Roll; Kiwanis Awd; Adult Educ Introduction Micro Computers 85-86; Cor Journalism.

STOGOSKI, JOHN P; John Carroll Schl; Bel Air, MD; (Y); 25/238; Boy Scts; Math Tm; Spanish Clb; Im Bsktbl; High Hon Roll; Hon Roll; Prfct Atten Awd; Spanish NHS; Archtct.

STOKES, KIMBERLY ANN; Eleanor Roosevelt HS; Mitchellville, MD; (Y); AFS; Yrbk Rptr; Frsh Cls; Soph Cls; Pom Pon; Hon Roll; Jr NHS; Spanish NHS; Stu In Sci & Technlgy Div 83-87; Mechncl Engrng.

STOLAR, ELIZABETH; T S Wootton HS; Potomac, MD; (Y); SADD; Hon Roll; Art Shw 2nd Pl Awd 84; Rotary Interact Attndnc Awd 86; Law.

STONE, JENNIFER; Holy Names Acad; Takoma Park, MD; (Y); Pres Art Clb; Trs Camera Clb; Cmnty Wkr; Nwsp Stf; Hon Roll; NHS; Band; Lab Sci Hghst Cls Avrg 84; MD St Music Tchr Assoc-Piano Rcgntn 85; MD St Music Tchr Accos 3rd Pl 86.

STONE, MICHELE; Bowie HS; Bowie, MD; (Y); Church Yth Grp; French Clb; SADD; Church Choir; Rep Sr Cls; French Hon Soc; Hon Roll; Prfct Atten Awd; Broadcreek Music Comp 1st Pl 85; MTAB Sprins Eval 3rd Pl 85; Natl Guild Auditions St Wnnr 86; Music Therapy.

STONE, ROBERT; Eastern Voc Tech; Baltimore, MD; (Y); Boy Scts; Church Yth Grp; JV Lcrss; Hon Roll; Var Trk; Hnr Rll 84-85; Air Force Acad; Elctrncs.

STONEBRAKER, ALAN T; Sherwood HS; Silver Spr, MD; (Y); 26/317; PAVAS; Band; Drm & Bgl; Variety Show; Trs Jr Cls; Trs Sr Cls; Var L Trk; St Schlr; Aud/Vis; Boy Scts; Mst Outstndng Sr 85-86; Schlstc Achvmnt Awd To UMBC 85-86; Prsdntl Acdmc Ftns Awd 85-86; U Of MD; Pre-Med.

STONEY III, CLEMENT PATRICK; Fallston HS; Fallston, MD; (Y); 27/250; Church Yth Grp; German Clb; Rep Frsh Cls; Rep Soph Cls; JV Var Bsbl; JV Var Ftbl; Wt Lftg; JV Wrstlng; High Hon Roll; NHS; Acadmc Ltr 86; Sigma X Sci Awd 86; Engrg.

STOPFORD, MICHAEL; Archbishop Curley HS; Baltimore, MD; (S); Red Cross Aide; Rep Soph Cls; Im Bsktbl; JV Crs Cntry; Var Ftbl; Hon Roll; NHS; Northland Coll; Envrnmntl Sci.

STOTT, AMY M; Bishop Walsh HS; Cumberland, MD; (Y); Cmnty Wkr; Drama Clb; 4-H; Hosp Aide; Pep Clb; Spanish Clb; Yrbk Stf; Hon Roll; Spanish NHS; Rep Frsh Cls; Frostburg ST Coll; Bus.

STOTTLEMYER, SHEILA E; Francis Scott Key HS; Middleburg, MD; (Y); Church Yth Grp; French Clb; Var Socr; JV Sftbl; Hon Roll; Prfct Atten Awd; Shephard Coll; Socl Wrk.

STOTTLEMYER, STEPHANIE; Glenelg HS; Mt Airy, MD; (Y); Acpl Chr; Chorus; Vet.

STOWE, DEBBIE; Crossland HS; Temple Hills, MD; (Y); Teachers Aide; Nwsp Phtg; Nwsp Rptr; Nwsp Stf; Yrbk Phtg; Yrbk Rptr; Yrbk Stf; Lit Mag; Var Pom Pon; Hon Roll; Crss & 1st Pl Div II Typng Cont 86; PG Co Prtcpt Typng Cont 86; Excel Acadmc Awd 86; Bus.

STRAUGHN, BRYAN; Cardnial Gibbons HS; Baltimore, MD; (Y); 1/141; Cmnty Wkr; Q&S; Ski Clb; Nwsp Ed-Chief; Nwsp Phtg; Nwsp Rptr; Yrbk Phtg; Yrbk Sprt Ed; Columbia U; Mech Engrng.

STRAUGHN, LONNIE; Cardinal Gibbons HS; Baltimore, MD; (Y); 38/128; Computer Clb; JA; Bsktbl; Ftbl; Wt Lftg; Jacksonville U; Computer Sci.

STRAUSSER, KRISTIN; Maurice J Mc Donough HS; Waldorf, MD; (Y); Church Yth Grp; VP Cmnty Wkr; Teachers Aide; Varsity Clb; Band; Concert Band; JV Var Cheerleading; JV Var Sftbl; JV Vllybl; High Hon Roll; All Cnty Hnrs Band 84; Brdcst Jrnlsm.

STREAKER, BEATRICE; Liberty HS; Westminster, MD; (S); 25/302; Drama Clb; Mathletes; Band; Chorus; Church Choir; Stat Bsktbl; Hon Roll; MD Dist Schlr Comp Fnlst 85; MD All ST Chorus 85-86; Amer Yth Incncrt Choir 85; U Of MD-COLLEGE Pk; Music Ed.

STRICKLER, TRACEY LYNN; Paint Branch HS; Laurel, MD; (Y); 13/373; SADD; High Hon Roll; Hon Roll; Tourmobile Sghtsng Schlrshp 86; Hlth Occptns Awd 86; Ftnss Awd 86; York Coll Of PA; Nrs.

STRITEHOFF, SHARON; Broadneck SR HS; Arnold, MD; (S); DECA; JA; Var L Gym; Hon Roll; MVP All Cnty Gymnstcs 85; Mktg Cncpts 3rd Pl Cntys 85; Trvl Indstry.

STRIZAK, MARY; Magruder HS; Rockville, MD; (Y); Church Yth Grp; Trs 4-H; SADD; Teachers Aide; Var Capt Bsktbl; Var L Fld Hcky; Var L Mgr(s); Var Capt Sftbl; 4-H Awd; Hon Roll.

STROH, ERIC J; South Hagerstown HS; Hagerstown, MD; (Y); 48/227; Trs Bowling; Exploring; Pres German Clb; Tennis; Hon Roll; Voice Dem Awd; Brooklane Ed Schlrshp 86; Rbl Actn Cncl Awd 86; U Of MD Coll Pk; Comp Sci.

STROSS, BEVERLY; Thomas S Wootton HS; Potomac, MD; (Y); Church Yth Grp; Teachers Aide; Var L Bsktbl; Var Capt Vllybl; High Hon Roll; NHS; Selctd All Cnty All Metro Vlybl Tms 86; Yth Schlrs Prog Chem 86; Sci.

STROTHER, FELICIA; Potomac SR HS; Temple Hills, MD; (Y); Concert Band; Mrchg Band; Bsktbl; Pom Pon; Powder Puff Ftbl; NHS; Acdmc Ltr Ptmc 86; Extrcrrclr Ltr Pom Poms 86; Extrcrrclr Ltr Mrchng Bnd Mt Vrnon 83-84; Vet.

STROTHER, JACQUELINE; Regina HS; Washington, DC; (Y); Computer Clb; French Clb; Hampton U; Comp Sci.

STROUP, GYNENE; Snow Hill HS; Salisbury, MD; (S); 10/80; Library Aide; Band; Church Choir; Concert Band; Mrchg Band; School Musical; School Play; Stage Crew; Hon Roll; Prfct Atten Awd; Schlstc Achvt Awd 85; Wor-Wic Tech CC; Htl Mngmnt.

STROUSE, DAVID; Oakland Mills HS; Columbia, MD; (Y); Chess Clb; Debate Tm; Chrmn Drama Clb; Pres Speech Tm; School Play; Rep Stu Cncl; JV Crs Cntry; Var L Tennis; Var Trk; Hon Roll.

STROVEL, CHRIS; Joppatowne HS; Baltimore, MD; (Y); Pres German Clb; Math Tm; Capt Quiz Bowl; Teachers Aide; Nwsp Ed-Chief; JV Var Bsktbl; Var L Vllybl; Hon Roll; Stu Of Mo 84; MD Schl Coll Math Assn Cert Achvt 86; U Of Maryland; Jrnlsm.

STRUNTZ, JULIE; Bishop Walsh HS; Cumberland, MD; (Y); 7/103; Art Clb; Math Tm; Pep Clb; Political Wkr; Band; Stat Socr; French Hon Soc; High Hon Roll; Hon Roll; Pres NHS; Dstngshd Catholic Action Cmnty 86; Auburn U; Pol Sci.

STUART, JEFFREY; Bowie HS; Bowie, MD; (Y); Spanish Clb; Teachers Aide; Aeronutcl Engr.

STUCKEY, ERIKA; Queen Annes County HS; Centreville, MD; (Y); 1/350; Mrchg Band; Rep Stu Cncl; Bausch & Lomb Sci Awd; High Hon Roll; Hon Roll; NHS; Ntl Merit Ltr; NEDT Awd; Pres Schlr; Val; MD ST Schlrshp 86; Rutgers U; Ind Engrng.

STUFFT, LESLIE; Thomas Stone HS; Hughesville, MD; (S); Sec Math Clb; Science Clb; Pom Pon; Trk; High Hon Roll; Mu Alp Tht; NHS; Ntl Merit SF; St Marys Coll Smmr Bio Inst Schlrshp 83; Wstrn MD Coll Smmr Bio Schlrshp 84; St Marys Coll Of MD; Engrng.

STUMP, DOUGLAS; Westminster HS; Finksburg, MD; (Y); 1/505; Boy Scts; Capt L Ftbl; L Var Lcrss; Var L Wrstlng; NHS; Pres Schlr; Val; Sec Trs Letterman Clb; Sec Trs Varsity Clb; Elks Awd; Greater Baltimore Metroditn Area Schlr Athlete 86; Carroll Cty Athlete Of Yr 86; MD ST Wrstlng Champ; U MD; Aero Sp Engr.

SU, CATHERINE KAI LIN; Walt Whitman HS; Bethesda, MD; (Y); 1/445; Cmnty Wkr; Intnl Clb; Mathletes; Im Pres Tennis; French Hon Soc; Hon Roll; Amer Hrt Assoc Stu Rsrch Fllwshp 85; YWCA Tn Schlrshp 86; Amer HS Math Exam Fnlst 86; Sci Awd 14 86; MA Inst Of Tech; Bio.

SU, WILBUR; Dulaney SR HS; Lutherville, MD; (Y); Political Wkr; Teachers Aide; Lit Mag; Var Badmtn; Hon Roll; NHS; Brnz Mdl In Rsn Wrtn Olympd 86; Slvr Mdl In Rsn Oral Olympd 86; Plstc Srgn.

SUBARAN, NADIA; Wheaton HS; Rockville, MD; (Y); 36/386; Art Clb; Church Yth Grp; Sec French Clb; Pres Intnl Clb; Church Choir; Variety Show; Yrbk Stf; Pres Soph Cls; Mgr Vllybl; French Hon Soc; Robert E Peary Schlrshp Awd 86; Peer Cnslng Awd 84; French Awd 84; Cooper Union Adv Sci/Art; Arch.

SUFFECOOL, KERRI; Clear Spring HS; Clear Spg, MD; (Y); 28/111; Hst FBLA; Pep Clb; Flag Corp; Ed Yrbk Stf; Hst Sr Cls; Cheerleading; Hon Roll; Hmcmng Queen 86; Hstry Clb; Art.

SUGGS, ROBIN; Mount Hebron HS; Ellicott City, MD; (Y); Office Aide; Rep Sr Cls; Var Swmmng; Hon Roll; NHS; Pres Acad Ftns Awd 86; Stu Sec Awd Guidance 86; Brandywine Coll; Fash Merch.

SUKACHEVIN, CHULACHAK; Takoma Acad; Silver Spring, MD; (S); Church Yth Grp; Pres Computer Clb; Pres Science Clb; Orch; Nwsp Phtg; Rep Frsh Cls; Rep Soph Cls; Stu Cncl; High Hon Roll; NHS; Columbia Union COLL; Pre-Med.

SULLIVAN, COLLEEN; Carroll Christian Acad; Westminster, MD; (S); 2/13; Church Yth Grp; Chorus; Sec Frsh Cls; Sec Jr Cls; Sec Sr Cls; Trs Stu Cncl; Cit Awd; High Hon Roll; Prfct Atten Awd; Natl Chrl Awd 82-83; Natl Chrstn Hnr Soc 83-86; TN Temple U; Scrd Music.

SULLIVAN, JENNIFER; Fort Hill HS; Cumberland, MD; (Y); Sr Cls; Stu Cncl; Hon Roll; Allegany CC; Bus Tech.

SULLIVAN, JOHN; Thomas S Wootton HS; Rockville, MD; (Y); 1/450; Church Yth Grp; Dance Clb; NFL; Speech Tm; Thesps; Madrigals; School Musical; Sr Cls; Ntl Merit Schol; Val; Optmst Outstndng Stu Rckvl MD 86; Pro Actr SAG & AFRTA 82-86; 1st Pl WA DC Metro Area Duet Intrp; Stanford U; Math.

SULLIVAN, KATHLEEN; Bowie SR HS; Bowie, MD; (Y); Church Yth Grp; Key Clb; SADD; Band; Concert Band; Mrchg Band; Var Pom Pon; Var Powder Puff Ftbl; Socr; Trk; Rgnl Champ 100 M High Hurdles 86; Dntstry.

SULLIVAN, KEVIN; Franklin HS; Reisterstown, MD; (Y); Church Yth Grp; Cmnty Wkr; Nwsp Sprt Ed; Nwsp Stf; Yrbk Ed-Chief; JV Tennis; Hon Roll; Jr NHS; Ntl Merit Schol; NEDT Awd; Jrnlsm.

SULLIVAN, PAULA; Great Mills HS; Ridge, MD; (Y); 12/242; Pres Sec Am Leg Aux Girls St; FBLA; Model UN; Office Aide; Color Guard; Stage Crew; Powder Puff Ftbl; Sftbl; High Hon Roll; NHS; Bus Law Awd 86; Pres Acad Fitness Awd 86; MD Merit Schlrshp Awd 86; Frostburg ST; Paralegal.

SUMMER, MICHELLE; Patterson HS; Baltimore, MD; (Y); Sec Church Yth Grp; Dance Clb; FBLA; Library Aide; Math Clb; Acpl Chr; Chorus; Church Choir; Pep Band; Scrkpr Bsktbl; Spec Olympcs Awd 86; Fshn Dsgn.

SUMMERS, LINDA; Brunswick HS; Jefferson, MD; (Y); FFA; Concert Band; Drm Mjr(t); Mrchg Band; Pep Band; Yrbk Stf; Var JV Bsktbl; Powder Puff Ftbl; Hon Roll; Rep Stu Cncl; Toured Europe-Amer Music Abroad 86; Florist.

SUMMERS, ROBERT; Cardinal Gibbons HS; Halethorpe, MD; (Y); 2/124; Drama Clb; School Play; Stage Crew; Rep Soph Cls; Trs Pres Stu Cncl; High Hon Roll; NHS; Rotary Awd; Excllnce Mth & Sci George Washington U 86; Engrng.

SUMMEY, MICHAEL D; Oxon Hill HS; Fort Washington, MD; (Y); Math Tm; L Crs Cntry; Var L Trk; Hon Roll; Natl Achvt Outstndng Negro Stu Pgm Fnlst 85-86; Stanford U.

SUMPTER, KIMBERLY; Western HS; Baltimore, MD; (Y); 83/412; Church Yth Grp; Dance Clb; English Clb; FBLA; Spanish Clb; Chorus; Lit Mag; Tennis; Hon Roll; Prfct Atten Awd; Acctg.

SUPERIOR, SCOTT; Great Mills HS; Lexington Pk, MD; (Y); Drama Clb; Library Aide; Office Aide; Teachers Aide; Var L Bsbl; Var Ftbl; Var L Golf; Im Wt Lftg; Var L Wrstlng; High Hon Roll; Comp.

SUTTON, PATRICIA A; Loch Raven HS; Baltimore, MD; (Y); 34/374; Church Yth Grp; Intnl Clb; Nwsp Ed-Chief; JV Sftbl; DAR Awd; Hon Roll; NHS; Prfct Atten Awd; Nwsp Rptr; Nwsp Stf; Gen ST Schlrshp 86; St Marys Coll; Sci.

SUTTON, SHANA; Sherwood HS; Ashton, MD; (S); 1/317; Model UN; Cheerleading; Trk; High Hon Roll; NHS; Pres Schlr; Val; Ltn Hnr Awd 85; Loyola Coll; Pre-Med.

SUTTON III, WILLIAM; Gaithersburg HS; Gaithersburg, MD; (Y); Teachers Aide; Variety Show; Pres Frsh Cls; VP Jr Cls; Rep Stu Cncl; JV L Bsktbl; JV L Ftbl; Var Trk; Hon Roll; Minorty Clb Treas 85-86; Cmnctns.

SVEJDA, ANDREA; Sherwood HS; Silver Spg, MD; (Y); Spanish Clb; Hon Roll; Spanish NHS; Cathlc U; Math.

SVOBODA, YASMINE; Elkton HS; Elkton, MD; (Y); Exploring; Math Tm; Varsity Clb; Band; Rep Jr Cls; Rep Stu Cncl; Var L Fld Hcky; Hon Roll; Jr NHS; NHS; Bicycle Club Sec; Triple Crown Attendance-Schlrshp, Behavior; Bio-Chem.

SWAIN, SHELLY; Hancock Mid/Sen HS; Hancock, MD; (Y); Church Yth Grp; FHA; SADD; Band; Chorus; School Musical; High Hon Roll; Concert Band; Mrchg Band; Nwsp Rptr; Most Imprvd Chorus Mbr Awd 86; All Cnty Corus & Band 84-86; Music.

SWANSON, WENDY; Oxon Hill SR HS; Accokeek, MD; (Y); Computer Clb; French Clb; Math Tm; Ski Clb; Variety Show; Crs Cntry; Var Trk; French Hon Soc; High Hon Roll; NHS; U Of MI; Aerospace Engrng.

SWARTZBAUGH, JAMES; Westminster SR HS; Westminster, MD; (Y); Hon Roll; Gen ST Schlrshp 86; Frstbrg ST; Acctng.

SWAUGER, TAMMY; Northern HS; Frostburg, MD; (Y); Pres Church Yth Grp; GAA; Yrbk Sprt Ed; Yrbk Stf; Pres Jr Cls; Trs Rep Stu Cncl; Var Vllybl.

SWEENEY, CHUCK; Parkville HS; Baltimore, MD; (Y); Rep Soph Cls; Rep Jr Cls; Mgr(s); Score Keeper; Hon Roll; Acctng.

SWEENEY, KELLY; James B Bennett SR HS; Salisbury, MD; (S); Hosp Aide; JA; JCL; Latin Clb; Pres Spanish Clb; School Musical; School Play; High Hon Roll; Mu Alp Tht; Spanish NHS.

SWEENEY, SHERESE; Institute Of Notre Dame HS; Baltimore, MD; (Y); Church Yth Grp; Spanish Clb; Church Choir; Color Guard; Mrchg Band; Trk; Hon Roll; Archdcsn Yth Advsry Cmmtt 85-87; Exec Brd Mbr Archdcsn Yth Cmmtt 85-86; Cmps Mnstry Tm 84-86; Loyola Coll; Med.

SWEITZER, CINDY; Clear Spring HS; Daleville, VA; (Y); 8/127; Pep Clb; Band; School Play; JV Var Cheerleading; Var Tennis; Var Trk; Mst Imprvd-Trk 85; 1st Chr-Frnch Horn-Band 84-86; Jr Cls Prom Comm 86; U Of MD Balt Co; Bio.

SWIFT, JAMIE; Gov Thomas Johnson HS; Frederick, MD; (Y); 27/250; AFS; Latin Clb; SADD; Teachers Aide; Rep Frsh Cls; Rep Soph Cls; Rep Stu Cncl; Var Capt Cheerleading; Stat Mgr(s); Powder Puff Ftbl; Purdu; Aviation.

SWITZER, PAUL; Montgomery Co Covenant Acad; Gaithersburg, MD; (S); Church Yth Grp; Drama Clb; Pres Jr Cls; Pres Sr Cls; Stu Cncl; Co-Capt Bsktbl; Co-Capt Socr; Sftbl; High Hon Roll; Hon Roll; Joshua Awd-Ldrshp 85; U Of MD; Bus Mgmt.

SYMES, MARIA; Gunston Schl; Virginia Bch, VA; (Y); AFS; Church Yth Grp; Cmnty Wkr; French Clb; VP Hosp Aide; Speech Tm; Chorus; School Musical; Nwsp Stf; Yrbk Stf; Gerontology.

SYNAN, GEORGE; Saint James Schl; Lonaconing, MD; (Y); 7/40; Ski Clb; Spanish Clb; Band; Nwsp Stf; Yrbk Ed-Chief; Pres Frsh Cls; Bsktbl; Crs Cntry; Ftbl; Lcrss; Excllnce Modern European Hstry 85; Bates Coll; Econ.

SYNODINOS, ANITA M; Eastern Voc-Tech HS; White Marsh, MD; (Y); Aud/Vis; Camera Clb; Mgr Church Yth Grp; Mgr Drama Clb; Office Aide; Mgr VICA; Chorus; School Play; Stage Crew; Hon Roll; Essex; Mgmt.

SZILAGYI, SHERRY ANN; Eleanor Roosevelt HS; Laurel, MD; (Y); AFS; Church Yth Grp; Cmnty Wkr; Math Tm; Im Swmmng; High Hon Roll; Spanish NHS; Computer Clb; Ski Clb; Teachers Aide; NM Tech Acadmc Tuitn Schlrshp 86; Presdntl Acadmc Fitns Awd 86; Sci & Tech Prgrm Cert 86; NM Inst Mng & Tech; Comp Sci.

SZOCH, JENNI; Archbishop Keough HS; Catonsville, MD; (Y); Trs Drama Clb; Trs Thesps; School Play; Stage Crew; Rep Frsh Cls; Rep Soph Cls; Rep Jr Cls; Rep Stu Cncl; JV Var Mgr(s); God Cntry Awd; Comp Sci.

SZWED, ROSE; St Marys Ryken HS; White Plains, MD; (Y); Drama Clb; Sec Intnl Clb; Library Aide; Speech Tm; School Play; Variety Show; Rep Frsh Cls; L Cheerleading; Sprstrs Shw Troupe 85-86; MD Gftd & Tlntd Smmr Pgm 85; Thtrcl Dance.

SZYMANOWSKI, MICHAEL; Archbishop Curley HS; Baltimore, MD; (S); 19/143; Church Yth Grp; Cmnty Wkr; Im Bsktbl; JV Capt Socr; Hon Roll; NHS; Spanish NHS; Black & White Awd; Towson ST U; Comp Engrng.

SZYMKOWICZ, JOHN; Surrattsville HS; Clinton, MD; (Y); 20/150; Am Leg Boys St; Drama Clb; Sec FBLA; Ski Clb; SADD; Thesps; School Musical; School Play; Nwsp Rptr; Yrbk Stf; Acdmc Awd MD Boys ST 86; Optmst Spch Clb Wnr 85; ST Dlgt MD Boys ST 86; Bus Law.

TABRON, MARCHETA Y; Archbishop Keough HS; Baltimore, MD; (Y); VP Church Yth Grp; Drama Clb; NFL; Stage Crew; Yrbk Stf; Cheerleading; Hon Roll; NHS; Prfct Atten Awd; Natl Achvt Schlrshp Pgm-Outstndng Negro Stdnt Commendtn 86.

TADJBAKHSH, SHAHRZAD; Walter Johnson HS; Bethesda, MD; (Y); Intnl Clb; Key Clb; Ski Clb; Spanish Clb; SADD; Teachers Aide; Lit Mag; Trs Jr Cls; Trs Sr Cls; Swmmng; Med.

TAGG, ROBERT; North Hagerstown HS; Hagerstown, MD; (Y); Boy Scts; French Clb; Teachers Aide; Lcrss; Hon Roll.

TAGLIABUE, ANDREW PHILIP; Walt Whitman SR HS; Bethesda, MD; (Y); Sec Church Yth Grp; Cmnty Wkr; Intnl Clb; Spanish Clb; SADD; Rep Stu Cncl; Hon Roll; Spanish NHS; Pres Envrnmntl Yth Awd 84 & 85; Sprntndnt Wrtng Awd 85.

TAI, YUEA; Walt Whitman HS; Bethesda, MD; (Y); Art Clb; Computer Clb; St Schlr; Schltc Art Cmptn Gld Key 85; Arch.

TAIT, PAULA; Oxon Hill HS; Ft Washington, MD; (Y); Math Tm; Lit Mag; L Mgr(s); Im Socr; L Trk; NHS; Ntl Merit SF; Chess Clb; VP Drama Clb; Intnl Clb; Itln Hon Soc 84-86; Its Acdmc TV Team 83-86; Shkspr Clb 84-85; St Johns Annapolis; Lbrl Arts.

TAKAGI, SARAH; Winston Churchill HS; Potomac, MD; (Y); 1/623; Dance Clb; French Clb; German Clb; Chorus; Swing Chorus; Hon Roll; Estrn Div Wnr Baldwin Jr Kybrd Achvts Cmptn 84; 1st Beethoven So Cmptn 84; Pbs TVMUSICL Encounter 84; U Of MD; Piano Prfrmnc.

TAKEDA, YOSHI; Oakland Mills HS; Columbia, MD; (Y); Computer Clb; French Clb; Rep Frsh Cls; Pres Sec Stu Cncl; JV Crs Cntry; JV Trk; Hon Roll; NHS; Sci & Humntrn Sympsm Rep 86; Howrd Cnty Assn Stdnt Cncls Rep 84-86; Georgetown U; Intl Bus.

TALBERT, CHERYL; Thomas Stone HS; Bryantown, MD; (S); Math Clb; Science Clb; Church Choir; Drm Mjr(t); School Musical; Pres Symp Band; High Hon Roll; NHS; Outstndg Pit Orch Stu 85; George Mason U; Comp Engrng.

TALBOT, KAMILLA K; Walter Johnson HS; Bethesda, MD; (Y); 23/215; Art Clb; VP Intnl Clb; Science Clb; Nwsp Stf; Rep Stu Cncl; Hon Roll; NHS; Hnrbl Mntn-Artwrk Schltc Art Cmpnt 86; Grphc Arts.

TALBOTT, DAVID; Lackey HS; Marbury, MD; (Y); 5/253; Am Leg Boys St; Math Tm; Ski Clb; JV Ftbl; Mgr(s); JV Trk; High Hon Roll; Hon Roll; NHS; Air Force Acad; Arntcl Engr.

TALBOTT, JAMES; Thomas Stone HS; Waldorf, MD; (S); Am Leg Boys St; Teachers Aide; Rep Stu Cncl; Var L Bsbl; JV L Ftbl; Socr; High Hon Roll; Hon Roll; Frostburg ST Coll; Bus Adm.

TALCOTT, APRIL; Gaithersburg HS; Gaithersburg, MD; (Y); 26/568; Church Yth Grp; Letterman Clb; VP Spanish Clb; Lit Mag; Var Capt Crs Cntry; Capt Lcrss; NHS; AFS; Intnl Clb; Comsat Spcl Schlrshp 86; Ntl Merit Cmmnded Stu 85; U Of Mrylnd Coll Pk; Pre-Med.

TAMASI, MICHELE L; Wicomico SR HS; Salisbury, MD; (Y); Pep Clb; Spanish Clb; Teachers Aide; Varsity Clb; Band; Color Guard; Yrbk Stf; Var Trs Cheerleading; Var Capt Sftbl; Hon Roll; Catawba Clg; Psych.

TAMBURELLO, JULIE; Notre Dame Prep; Baltimore, MD; (Y); Church Yth Grp; Drama Clb; Girl Scts; Hon Roll; Hnrb Mntn Art Comptn 86; Loyola Coll MD; Bus.

TAMBURELLO, PETER D; Thomas S Wootton HS; Potomac, MD; (Y); 33/401; Boy Scts; Pres Debate Tm; NFL; Speech Tm; Church Choir; Concert Band; Mrchg Band; Hon Roll; NHS; Ntl Merit SF.

TAMRES, SUZANNE E; Northwestern HS; Baltimore, MD; (Y); Art Clb; Science Clb; Spanish Clb; High Hon Roll; Hon Roll; Myrs Stu Achvmnt Awd 86; Schlstc Achvt In Phys Sci 85; Schlrshp In Hlth Risk Fctrs 85; Goucher Coll; Mec Stds.

TAN, KIMBERLY; Notre Dame Preparatory Schl; Fallston, MD; (Y); Chorus; Variety Show; Var Socr; Var Tennis; High Hon Roll; NHS; Ntl Merit SF; Spanish NHS; Church Yth Grp; Computer Clb; Hugh O Brien Ldrshp Semnr Notre Dame Prep Rep 84; Jefferson Schlrshp 86; Echols Schlr U Of VA 86; U Of VA; Intl Politics.

TANSILL, GEORGE J; Hammond HS; Jessup, MD; (Y); Chess Clb; Latin Clb; Math Clb; Math Tm; Im Crs Cntry; Im Ftbl; Im Socr; Im Sftbl; Im Swmmng; Hon Roll; Cert Magna Cum Laude 2nd Pl Annl Latn Bwl Coll Notre Dame 85; Cert Of Appectn MD ST Assn 85; U Of MD; Engr.

TAPPAN, TAMI; Laurel HS; Laurel, MD; (Y); Dance Clb; Drama Clb; School Musical; School Play; Variety Show; JV Cheerleading; Hon Roll; Helen Awd Outstndng Actrss 85; Inn Star Srch Cntst Grnd Prz Vclst 85; Advnture Awd Tnage Actrss 85; Prof Actrss.

TARBURTON, TODD; Laplata HS; Hughesville, MD; (Y); FCA; Ski Clb; Teachers Aide; JV Var Bsbl; JV Var Ftbl; Var Wt Lftg; JV Wrstlng; Hon Roll; Ctznshp Ship Awd 83; VA Polytech Inst; Arch Engr.

TARPLEY, DAMION; Thomas Stone HS; Waldorf, MD; (Y); Church Yth Grp; Rep Frsh Cls; Rep Soph Cls; Rep Jr Cls; Off Sr Cls; JV Var Bsktbl; JV Var Ftbl; Hon Roll; Var Trk; Cmnty Co-Bsktbl Coach Yr 85-86; Outstndng Rep Stu Govt Assn 85-86; Engrng.

TATE, MARGARET; Kent County HS; Millington, MD; (Y); Am Leg Aux Girls St; Church Yth Grp; Trs Girl Scts; Spanish Clb; Rep Stu Cncl; Hon Roll; NHS; Gftd & Tlntd Pgm 83-86; Pre-Med.

TAUSSIG, VAIL; Garrison Forest Schl; Towson, MD; (Y); Hosp Aide; SADD; Thesps; Acpl Chr; School Musical; School Play; Stage Crew; Mgr Bsktbl; JV Fld Hcky; Hon Roll; All Star Cast MD 86; Natl Piano Guild Cmptn Cert 80-86; Musical Thtr.

TAVENNER, KAREN; High Point HS; Beltsville, MD; (Y); Church Yth Grp; Hosp Aide; Teachers Aide; School Play; Stage Crew; Lit Mag; JV Capt Cheerleading; Var Gym; Var Pom Pon; Hon Roll; U Of MD College Park; Nrsng.

TAVIK, GREGORY; Archbishop Curley HS; Baltimore, MD; (S); 6/143; Am Leg Boys St; School Musical; Nwsp Ed-Chief; Nwsp Stf; Sec Frsh Cls; Pres Soph Cls; Var JV Trk; High Hon Roll; Hon Roll; NHS; Gen Excellence Awd 85-86; Elec Engr.

TAYLOR, ANDREW; St Vincent Pallotti HS; Laurel, MD; (S); 7/120; Ski Clb; Spanish Clb; Im Bsktbl; Var Crs Cntry; Var Tennis; Hon Roll; NHS; Spanish NHS; VA Tech; Engrng.

TAYLOR, ARETHA; Southern HS; Baltimore, MD; (Y); JA; Teachers Aide; JV Bsktbl; Hon Roll; Prfct Atten Awd; Math Awd 85; Bowie ST Coll; Bus.

TAYLOR, CINDY; Franklin HS; Reisterstown, MD; (Y); Pres Church Yth Grp; Girl Scts; Key Clb; Chorus; Church Choir; Yrbk Stf; High Hon Roll; Hon Roll; Prfct Atten Awd; Comp.

TAYLOR, DIANE; Snow Hill HS; Snow Hill, MD; (S); AFS; Trs 4-H; Library Aide; Pep Clb; Teachers Aide; Nwsp Stf; Twrlr; 4-H Awd; Hon Roll; NHS; Wor-Wic CC; Acctg.

TAYLOR III, JOHN C; Milford Mill HS; Balt, MD; (Y); Boy Scts; Church Yth Grp; Cmnty Wkr; Service Clb; Acpl Chr; Chorus; Church Choir; Madrigals; Variety Show; Hon Roll; Sing In Pres Inauguration 85; Prtcptd In The MD All St Chorus 86; Prtcpt In 2 European Tours 86; U Of MD; Elec Engr.

TAYLOR, JOSEPH; Lackey HS; Indian Head, MD; (Y); Church Yth Grp; Cmnty Wkr; FBLA; Pep Clb; Spanish Clb; SADD; Variety Show; Rep Frsh Cls; Rep Soph Cls; Rep Stu Cncl; Sci Fair, Schl Fair & Charles Cnty Fair Awds; Pharmacy.

TAYLOR, KARL; Northern HS; Baltimore, MD; (S); Hon Roll; Math Stu Of Mnth 85-86; Carpentry.

TAYLOR, KARYN; Maurice J Mc Donough HS; Waldorf, MD; (S); Church Yth Grp; Intnl Clb; Band; Mrchg Band; Orch; School Musical; Symp Band; Var L Pom Pon; Hon Roll; NHS; MD All St Hnrs Band 86; Law.

TAYLOR, KEILA A; Gaithersburg HS; Gaithersburg, MD; (Y); Teachers Aide; Band; Concert Band; Jazz Band; Mrchg Band; Symp Band; High Hon Roll; Hon Roll; CAPAPS Schlrshp 86; Stratford Schls; Bus.

TAYLOR, KIMBERLY; Western HS; Baltimore, MD; (Y); Hon Roll; Spanish NHS; Med Tech.

TAYLOR, LATESHA; Mercy HS; Baltimore, MD; (Y); Church Yth Grp; Drama Clb; GAA; Hosp Aide; Drill Tm; Rep Soph Cls; Hon Roll; NHS; Red Cross Aide; School Play; Eagle Of Cross Awd 86; Compu Sci I Awd 86; Towson ST U; Bus Admin.

TAYLOR, LESLEY; Washington SR HS; Eden, MD; (Y); 8/120; Church Yth Grp; Hosp Aide; Science Clb; Ski Clb; Spanish Clb; Chorus; Rep Stu Cncl; L Var Sftbl; DAR Awd; High Hon Roll; Med Tech.

TAYLOR, LISA; Frederick Douglass HS; Baltimore, MD; (Y); 2/295; Chess Clb; Office Aide; Science Clb; Mrchg Band; Orch; School Musical; High Hon Roll; NHS; Sal; NASA Schlrshp 86; Intl Mdrn Music Mstrs Soc 86; Mdrn Music Awd 86; Morgan ST U; Chld Psych.

TAYLOR, MARIA L; Southern Garrett HS; Oakland, MD; (Y); 17/221; Church Yth Grp; 4-H; French Clb; GAA; Office Aide; Q&S; Yrbk Stf; Sec Soph Cls; Stat Bsktbl; Cheerleading; Frostburg St Coll; Psychtry.

TAYLOR, MATTHEW; Arlington Baptist HS; Baltimore, MD; (Y); Church Yth Grp; Chorus; Stat Bsbl; Cit Awd; CPA.

TAYLOR, MELVIN; Patterson HS; Baltimore, MD; (Y); 40/480; Var Bsbl; Ftbl; Hon Roll; NHS; Ntl Ftbl Hall Fame Schlr Athlete 85; Sons Highlndtwm Yth Yr 86; Morning Sun 86; Salisbury; Med.

TAYLOR, PURSHELLE A; Eleanor Roosevelt SR HS; Lanham, MD; (Y); 4-H; Girl Scts; Pres Pep Clb; Teachers Aide; Chorus; Rep Frsh Cls; Rep Soph Cls; Rep Jr Cls; Rep Sr Cls; Powder Puff Ftbl; Bus Psychlgy.

TAYLOR, SHANNON; Snow Hill HS; Snow Hill, MD; (S); 8/110; AFS; Sec French Clb; Flag Corp; Mrchg Band; High Hon Roll; NHS; 1st Pl Sci Fair 85; Schltc Recgntn Ltr 85; MD Ldrshp Wrkshp St Marys Coll 84.

TAYLOR, SHARON; Snow Hill HS; Snow Hill, MD; (S); 3/100; 4-H; Band; Concert Band; Jazz Band; Mrchg Band; Pep Band; Nwsp Ed-Chief; Nwsp Rptr; Nwsp Stf; VP Jr Cls; Worcester Co Sci Fair 1st 85; Schlstc Recgntn Awd 85; Jrnlsm Awd 85; Bio.

TAYLOR, STEPHEN; Montgomery Blair HS; Silver Spg, MD; (Y); L SADD; Thesps; Chorus; Stage Crew; VP Jr Cls; Pres Stu Cncl; Var L Bsktbl; Im Sftbl; Im Vllybl; Prfct Atten Awd; Sci Fair Grnd Prz Crrnt Evnts Genetic Engrng 84; Outstndng Ldrshp Crtsy Crw 84; Solost Rock & Soul; Cmmnctns.

TAYLOR, TIMBERLY P; Walbrook SR HS; Baltimore, MD; (Y); Dance Clb; Cheerleading; Hosp Aide; Church Choir; Capt Mrchg Band; Hon Roll; Prfct Atten Awd; Schlrshp Awd Nrsng Asst 85; Reg Nrs.

TAYLOR, YULANDA; Oakland Mills HS; Columbia, MD; (Y); JA; ROTC; Speech Tm; Drill Tm; Nwsp Ed-Chief; Sec Jr Cls; Cheerleading; Score Keeper; DAR Awd; Opt Clb Awd; Cadet Yr 83-84; Air Force Assn Awd 85-86; Alpha Kappa Alpha & Delta Srty Schlrshp 85-86; NC A&T ST U; Engrng.

TEAGUE JR, REGINALD BAILEY; St Marys Ryken HS; Patuxent River, MD; (S); Church Yth Grp; Capt Scholastic Bowl; Science Clb; Nwsp Rptr; Lit Mag; VP Stu Cncl; Var Tennis; High Hon Roll; VP Jr NHS; NHS; VA Beach PTA Lit Cont-3rd Pl City; Med.

TEATHER, ERIC; Loyola Blakefield HS; Glen Arm, MD; (Y); Computer Clb; Jazz Band; Socr; Hon Roll; Acadmc Hnrs 85-86; Johns Hopkins; Engrg.

TEDESCO, JOEY; Cambridge South Dorchester HS; Cambridge, MD; (Y); 25/215; AFS; French Clb; Pres Soph Cls; Rep Jr Cls; L Lcrss; L Socr; Hon Roll; NHS; Peer Ldrshp Awd 84-85; UMBC; Psych.

TEMMERMEYER II, WILLIAM F; Lackey HS; Bryans Road, MD; (Y); 7/180; Am Leg Boys St; Boy Scts; VP Exploring; Office Aide; Teachers Aide; Crs Cntry; Capt Trk; Elks Awd; High Hon Roll; NHS; Ntural Resources Exc Awd 85; Pres Hnr Guard 84; Schlrshp Rotry Clb Elks 86; WV U; Mgmt.

TEMPLON, BEVERLY; Clear Spring HS; Hagerstown, MD; (Y); 3/125; Church Yth Grp; Concert Band; Mrchg Band; School Play; Yrbk Stf; Stu Cncl; Cheerleading; Trk; Vllybl; NHS; MD Art Ed Assn Awd 86; Art.

TENNANT, CHRISTOPHER; Oakland Mills HS; Columbia, MD; (Y); Ski Clb; Teachers Aide; Var JV Ftbl; Wt Lftg; God Cntry Awd; Hon Roll; Miami ST; Med.

TENNYSON, CAROL; Chopticon HS; Avenue, MD; (Y); Computer Clb; Rptr FBLA; FHA; Library Aide; Office Aide; Spanish Clb; CC Awd; Hon Roll; Acdmc Stu Of Mnth 84-86; Awds Rgnl & ST Lvls W FBLA 84-86; Mst Actv Frshmn FHA 83; Charles County CC; Data Prcssg.

TENNYSON, TROY; Crossland HS; Camp Spgs, MD; (Y); Math Tm; Teachers Aide; JV Ftbl; Hon Roll; NHS; Comp Sci.

TEPPER, KENNETH; Pikesville SR HS; Balto, MD; (Y); Mathletes; Math Clb; Ski Clb; Capt Var Crs Cntry; Var Lcrss; Capt Var Trk; Hon Roll; NHS; Ntl Merit Ltr; Indr Trck Champshp 85; U S Naval Acad; Elctrcl Engrng.

TERNENT, JOHN; Valley HS; Lonaconing, MD; (Y); Boy Scts; Sec Civic Clb; Ski Clb; Teachers Aide; Stage Crew; Yrbk Phtg; Arrow Awd-Boy Scouts 85; Bd Educ Dlgt Wtr Env Rsch Grnt 85-86.

TERNENT, MARK; Valley HS; Lonaconing, MD; (Y); Boy Scts; Band; NHS; MD Jr Sci Sympsm 86; Bio.

TERRELL, LISA M; Oxon Hill SR HS; Ft Washington, MD; (Y); Pep Clb; Teachers Aide; Chorus; Church Choir; Pep Band; Symp Band; Cheerleading; Co-Capt Pom Pon; High Hon Roll; NHS; U Of MD College Pk; Psych.

TERRILL, CHRISTINE; Eastern Vocational Technical HS; Baltimore, MD; (Y); FBLA; Pres Band; Rep Jr Cls; Rep Stu Cncl; Var Stat Bsktbl; Var L Cheerleading; Mgr(s); Hon Roll; Educ.

TERRY, GARRETT; Northern HS; Owings, MD; (Y); Spanish Clb; Crs Cntry; Trk; Hon Roll; Comp Oper.

TESORIERO, ROSEANNE; Pallotti HS; Laurel, MD; (S); 1/86; Drama Clb; Office Aide; Spanish Clb; Var L Swmmng; High Hon Roll; Sec NHS; Ntl Merit Ltr; Spanish NHS; MD Dstngshd Schlr Semi-Fnlst 85; U Of MD College Park.

TESTA, CHRISTOPHER; Joppatowne HS; Joppa, MD; (Y); French Clb; Rep Jr Cls; Var Tennis; Var Vllybl; Im Wt Lftg; Hon Roll; NHS; VA; Arch.

TESTER, SCOTT; Elkton SR HS; Wilmington, DE; (Y); 10/289; Church Yth Grp; Civic Clb; Cmnty Wkr; Key Clb; Math Tm; Office Aide; Political Wkr; Teachers Aide; Yrbk Rptr; Rep Stu Cncl; Gov Awd Top 5 Pct Cls 86; Pres Acad Fit Awd 86; Congressnl Yth Ldrshp Schlr 86; Wake Forest U; Pol Sci.

THACKER, MONICA; Notre Dame Prep; Baltimore, MD; (Y); Church Yth Grp; Cmnty Wkr; Nwsp Sprt Ed; Hon Roll; NHS; MD Yth Govt-Sen 85-86; German Hnr Soc 85; Latin Hnr Soc 85; Engrng.

THEIS, KIMBERLY; Roland Park Country Schl; Baltimore, MD; (Y); 4/42; AFS; Model UN; SADD; Yrbk Stf; L Fld Hcky; Lcrss; High Hon Roll; Spanish NHS; Cum Laude Soc 86; Sndy Schl Tchr 84-86; Mdl OAS 84-85; Duke U; Med.

THEK, KARENA M; Saints Peter And Paul HS; Seaford, DE; (Y); Sec Soph Cls; Pres Jr Cls; Sec Stu Cncl; Var Fld Hcky; NHS; Pres Schlrshp 86; Columbia Coll SC; Dance.

THEODORE, PIERRE R; St Pauls Schl; Randallstown, MD; (Y); Cmnty Wkr; Computer Clb; Ftbl; Lcrss; Socr; Tennis; Wrstlng; High Hon Roll; Hon Roll; Ntl Merit SF; Natl Achvt Awd SF 85; Rennes France Schl Yr Abrd 85; Princeton; Trnsplt Surgn.

THOMA, MICHAEL; Brunswick HS; Brunswick, MD; (Y); Aud/Vis; Church Yth Grp; Variety Show; Var Ftbl; Mgr(s); Stat Socr; Hon Roll; Balt Schl Culnry Arts; Caterer.

THOMAN, ERIC; Dulaney SR HS; Cockeysville, MD; (Y); Variety Show; Rep Soph Cls; Trs Jr Cls; Trs Sr Cls; Stu Cncl; JV Var Ftbl; JV Var Lcrss; JV Var Wrstlng; Hon Roll; Hmcmg Ct JR Clss 85; Ldrshp Awd 85; Pharm.

THOMAS, AMY; Kent County HS; Worton, MD; (Y); Am Leg Aux Girls St; Church Yth Grp; 4-H; French Clb; Church Choir; Stu Cncl; Var Fld Hcky; Stat Lcrss; 4-H Awd; Hon Roll.

THOMAS, ANN; Southwestern SR No 412 HS; Baltimore, MD; (Y); JA; Office Aide; Teachers Aide; Gym; Cit Awd; Hon Roll; Prfct Atten Awd; Schl Nwsppr; John Hopkins U; Gynclgst.

THOMAS, CAROL; Thomas Stone HS; Bryantown, MD; (S); Math Tm; Pres Science Clb; Hst Band; Mrchg Band; High Hon Roll; VP NHS; St Schlr; Church Yth Grp; Math Clb; Intl Sci Fair 84 & 85; Ntl Sci Sympsm 85; Aerospc Engrng.

THOMAS, DAVID; Gov Thomas Johnson HS; Frederick, MD; (Y); 4/303; Debate Tm; Latin Clb; Science Clb; SADD; Band; Chorus; Church Choir; Concert Band; Madrigals; Mrchg Band; Optmst Schlrshp Outstndng Yng Man Yr 85; Med.

THOMAS, DEBBIE; Dundalk HS; Baltimore, MD; (Y); SADD; Varsity Clb; Trs Concert Band; Mrchg Band; Yrbk Stf; Hst Frsh Cls; Hst Soph Cls; Rep Jr Cls; Rep Sr Cls; Rep Stu Cncl; 2nd Tm All Cnty Fld Hcky 85-86; Med Fld.

THOMAS, DIANE R; Williamsport HS; Hagerstown, MD; (Y); Art Clb; Drama Clb; Latin Clb; Ski Clb; Spanish Clb; Teachers Aide; Rep Jr Cls; Rep Sr Cls; Capt Cheerleading; Powder Puff Ftbl; Honor Club 82-83; Bauder Fashn Coll; Fashn Mrchdn.

THOMAS, DONNA; Fairmont Heights HS; New Carrollton, MD; (Y); FBLA; Teachers Aide; Orch; Var Cheerleading; High Hon Roll; Hon Roll; Ltr Apprectn Dept Commerce 85; Cert Partcitpn Womans Engl 85; Hampton Coll; Bus Mgt.

THOMAS, ERIN M; Sherwood HS; Ashton, MD; (Y); 79/317; Ski Clb; Spanish Clb; Teachers Aide; Hon Roll; Spanish NHS; Advsry Cncl Rep 84-85; Outstndg Schl Svc 83-86; Baldwin-Wallace Coll; Bus Admin.

THOMAS, HELEN; Cambridge-South Dorchester HS; Cambridge, MD; (Y); 6/229; AFS; Pep Clb; Spanish Clb; Teachers Aide; JV Var Cheerleading; NHS; Pres Schlr; St Schlr; Outstndg Spanish Stu 86; Dorchester Cnty Acdmc Hon 86; Dir Admssn To U Of MD Schl Of Bus 86; U Of MD; Bus.

THOMAS, JACKIE; Mc Donough HS; Waidorf, MD; (S); Chorus; Variety Show; Rep Jr Cls; Hon Roll; All Amer Yth Hnrs Choir 85; Tri Cnty Hnrs Chorus 84-86; Music.

THOMAS, JOHN; St Amrys Ryken HS; Waldorf, MD; (Y); Band; Pep Band; Golf; Ntl Merit Ltr; Amer HS Athlt 85-86; 1st Team All SMAC-GOLF 85-86; Retreat Ldr Hnr 85-86; Geo Mason U; Golf Pro.

THOMAS, LESLIE; Academy Of The Holy Cross; Chevy Chase, MD; (Y); 12/125; JCL; Latin Clb; Math Clb; Math Tm; Ski Clb; Stage Crew; Nwsp Phtg; Yrbk Phtg; Yrbk Stf; Coach Actv; Pascal Awd 86; Outstndng Svc Awd-Schl Athltc Dept 86; VI Polytech; Aerospc Engrng.

THOMAS, LIZZIE; Northwestern HS; Hyattsville, MD; (S); Church Yth Grp; Hosp Aide; Spanish Clb; Teachers Aide; Hon Roll; NHS.

THOMAS, MELODY; Maurice J Mc Donough HS; Pomfret, MD; (Y); Teachers Aide; Varsity Clb; Flag Corp; Mrchg Band; Bsktbl; Trk; Vllybl; Hon Roll; Prfct Atten Awd; Indoor Trck Awd 85-86; Physcl Thrpy.

THOMAS, MICHELLE; Western HS; Baltimore, MD; (Y); 173/412; Bus Admin.

THOMAS, NANETTE M; Calvert HS; Stleonard, MD; (Y); 27/229; Church Yth Grp; Drama Clb; French Clb; Intnl Clb; Science Clb; Var L Cheerleading; Mgr(s); Stat Tennis; Schlstc Awd 86; Distngshd Hnr Roll 86; Millersville U; Dentst.

THOMAS, PAGE FREDRICK; Severn Schl; Bowie, MD; (Y); VP French Clb; VP Service Clb; Ski Clb; Lit Mag; Var L Ftbl; Var Lcrss; Wt Lftg; Natl Achvt Schlrshp Prog Semi Fin 85; Arch.

THOMAS, RICHARD; Friendly SR HS; Ft Washington, MD; (Y); Church Yth Grp; Math Clb; Teachers Aide; Stage Crew; Pres Frsh Cls; Pres Soph Cls; Capt Bsktbl; Var Trk; Cit Awd; High Hon Roll; Tution Schlrshp 83-84; Citizenship 83-84; Law.

THOMAS, STEPHANIE; Laurel HS; Laurel, MD; (Y); Church Yth Grp; SADD; Nwsp Rptr; Rep Stu Cncl; Var Capt Cheerleading; Powder Puff Ftbl; High Hon Roll; U Of MD; Bus.

THOMAS, SUZIE; Northwestern HS; Hyattsville, MD; (Y); Church Yth Grp; Hosp Aide; Spanish Clb; Chorus; Rep Sr Cls; High Hon Roll; NHS; Ntl Merit SF; Pres Schlr; Prince Georges Cty Med Soc Schlrshp 86; Howard U; Med Tech.

THOMAS, TANYA; Walter Johnson HS; Bethesda, MD; (Y); 47/238; Church Yth Grp; Cmnty Wkr; Hosp Aide; JA; Key Clb; Pep Clb; SADD; Church Choir; Drill Tm; Var Co-Capt Pom Pon; Outstndng Stu Awd 85; MD ST Fin Miss Natl Teen Pag 85; Vlntr Cmmnty Svc Awd Miss Natl Teen 85; IN U; Psych.

THOMAS, TERI; Oakland Mills HS; Columbia, MD; (Y); VP French Clb; School Musical; School Play; American U; Intl Rltns.

THOMAS, TRACY; Allgany HS; Cresaptown, MD; (Y); 33/233; Dance Clb; Office Aide; Ski Clb; Teachers Aide; Hon Roll; Dancing Cumberland Dixettes; Frostburg ST Clg.

THOMPSON, ANDREA; Elizabeth Seton HS; Washington, DC; (Y); Church Yth Grp; French Clb; Hosp Aide; Pep Clb; SADD; Teachers Aide; Church Choir; Variety Show; Hon Roll; Bus.

THOMPSON, BECKY L; Arlington Baptist HS; Sykesville, MD; (S); #2 In Class; Church Yth Grp; Spanish Clb; Varsity Clb; Pres Chorus; Church Choir; Trs Frsh Cls; Cheerleading; High Hon Roll; NHS; Music, Engl & Spnsh Awds; Bob Jones U; Scndry Educ.

THOMPSON, CHRISTINE; Northwestern HS; Baltimore, MD; (Y); Drama Clb; German Clb; Pres Latin Clb; Ed Yrbk Ed-Chief; Var Capt Cheerleading; High Hon Roll; NHS; AFS; JA; Teachers Aide; P G Cnty Acad Excellence Awd 84-86; Number 1 Clb 85-86; Pres Acad Fitness Awd 85-86; Smith Coll; Gov.

THOMPSON, DEBRA; Thomas Stone HS; Waldorf, MD; (S); Church Yth Grp; Science Clb; Teachers Aide; Chorus; Church Choir; Mrchg Band; School Play; Symp Band; High Hon Roll; Hon Roll.

THOMPSON, DONNA; Chopticon HS; Mechanicsvl, MD; (Y); Art Clb; FBLA; FHA; Teachers Aide; Stu Cncl; High Hon Roll; NHS; Opt Clb Awd; Pres Schlr; St Schlr; Outstndng Bus Stu CHS 86; ST MS FBLA 86; ST Parlimntry Procdr Team Mem 85; Sec.

THOMPSON, ERIC; North Hartford HS; Monkton, MD; (Y); 16/286; Math Tm; Spanish Clb; JV Bsktbl; Hon Roll; NHS; Ntl Merit Ltr; Pres Acad Ftnss Awd, C Carlos Sprt Amer Mem Schlrshp 86; U MD College Park; Cmptr Sci.

THOMPSON, HILARY; St Pauls Schl For Girls; Baltimore, MD; (Y); Service Clb; Yrbk Phtg; Rep Frsh Cls; Rep Soph Cls; Rep Jr Cls; Sr Cls; Stu Cncl; Var Bsktbl; Var Capt Fld Hcky; Var Capt Lcrss; Sprts Sash For 3 Vrsty Sprts In A Yr 85.

THOMPSON, KEVANN; Bladensburg HS; Hyattsville, MD; (Y); Church Yth Grp; Pep Clb; SADD; Teachers Aide; Rep Soph Cls; Rep Jr Cls; Rep Sr Cls; Pres Stu Cncl; Stat Bsktbl; JV Var Cheerleading; Achvt Cert Grammer Comp 85-86; Diploma Merit Spanish 85-86; Nero-Surgeon.

THOMPSON, KIMBERLY; St Johns At Prospect Hall; Point Of Rocks, MD; (Y); Cmnty Wkr; Yrbk Stf; Sec Stu Cncl; Capt JV Bsktbl; Var L Socr; Var Sftbl; JV Var Tennis; JV Var Vllybl; High Hon Roll; NHS; Merit Schlrshp Prospct Hll 83; Certfct Merti Natl Spansh Exam 85.

THOMPSON, LORIE; Perryville HS; Perry Point, MD; (Y); 5/125; Intnl Clb; Varsity Clb; JV Var Bsktbl; JV Var Fld Hcky; Var L Sftbl; NHS; Pres Schlr; FBLA; FHA; Math Tm; Schrl Athlete Awd 86; Optmst Clb Awd 85-86; Marquis Regnl Schlr 85-86; Lafayette Coll; Engr.

THOMPSON, MARY ANNE; La Plata HS; La Plata, MD; (Y); Church Yth Grp; Cmnty Wkr; 4-H; Office Aide; Teachers Aide; Concert Band; Mrchg Band; Symp Band; Hon Roll; Certfd Tutr For Illiterate Adlts 86; Lwyr.

THOMPSON, MELISSA; Immaculata College HS; Germantown, MD; (Y); Cmnty Wkr; German Clb; Math Clb; Science Clb; JV Var Fld Hcky; Var Lcrss; Pres Schlr; Alg Awd; Scholar Awd; Pre-Calculus Awd; U FL; Chem Engrng.

THOMPSON, PAMELA; Hammond HS; Columbia, MD; (Y).

THOMPSON, RENEE; Potomac SR HS; Temple Hill, MD; (Y); Office Aide; JV Powder Puff Ftbl; High Hon Roll; Hon Roll; Towson ST U; Nrsng.

THOMPSON, SEJUAN; Laurel HS; Laurel, MD; (Y); Church Yth Grp; Cmnty Wkr; Dance Clb; Office Aide; Spanish Clb; Teachers Aide; Chorus; Church Choir; Hon Roll; Spnsh Tchr.

THOMPSON, TAMARA; Crossland HS; Temple Hills, MD; (Y); Drama Clb; French Clb; FBLA; Teachers Aide; School Play; Cheerleading; Pom Pon; Hon Roll; Comp Analyst.

THOMPSON, WILLIAM A; Good Counsel HS; Washington, DC; (Y); Church Yth Grp; Cmnty Wkr; Computer Clb; ROTC; Spanish Clb; SADD; Stu Cncl; Bsktbl; Mgr(s); Hon Roll; Springfield Coll; Math.

THOMS, HEATHER; Great Mills HS; Lexington Pk, MD; (Y); FBLA; FHA; Library Aide; Office Aide; Teachers Aide; Cheerleading; Gym; Sftbl; Timer; Hon Roll; Lgl Secy.

THORNE, CHARLES A; Maurice J Mc Donough HS; Waldorf, MD; (S); Intnl Clb; Teachers Aide; Thesps; Chorus; Drm Mjr(t); Mrchg Band; School Musical; School Play; Symp Band; Hon Roll; MD All ST Hnrs Chorus 86; Tri County Hnrs Band & Chorus 83-86; Charles Cnty Chamber Ensmbl 86.

THORNE, PHILLIP; Glenelg HS; Mt Airy, MD; (Y); AFS; Pres 4-H; German Clb; Var Ftbl; JV Lcrss; Var Trk; 4-H Awd; Engrng.

THORNTON, LISA M; Capital Lutheran HS; New Carrollton, MD; (S); 1/18; Teachers Aide; Yrbk Ed-Chief; Yrbk Phtg; Yrbk Rptr; Yrbk Stf; Var L Bsktbl; Var L Sftbl; Var L Vllybl; Hon Roll; Christs Carillon Hndbl Choir; Valparaiso U IN; Cmmnctns.

THORNTON, MIKE; Surrattsville SR HS; Clinton, MD; (Y); Office Aide; School Play; Var Golf; Hon Roll; Yth Ldrshp Cmp 85; Hnrbl Mntn Sci Fair 85; Us Air Force.

THRASHER, JOY; Southern Garrett HS; Deer Pk, MD; (Y); Pres Sec Church Yth Grp; Girl Scts; Q&S; Teachers Aide; Yrbk Stf; JV Var Bsktbl; Stat Tennis; Var L Vllybl; Comp Sci.

THRESS, THOMAS E; Parkside HS; Fruitland, MD; (S); 4/249; Boy Scts; Church Yth Grp; JCL; Pres Latin Clb; Pres Math Tm; Pres Band; Symp Band; Hon Roll; Pres VP NHS; Opt Clb Awd; Pre-Law.

THUNE, DIANA; Snow Hill HS; Snow Hill, MD; (S); 9/84; AFS; Church Yth Grp; Cmnty Wkr; Spanish Clb; Church Choir; Concert Band; Mrchg Band; VP Bsktbl; Vllybl; VP Vllybl; Govnrs Yth Cncl Hnr 85; Salisbury ST Coll.

THURBER, SAMUEL; North Hagerstown HS; Hagerstown, MD; (Y); Hagerstown JC; Comptr Pgmmg.

TICE, LORIE; Magruder HS; Derwood, MD; (Y); Church Yth Grp; Letterman Clb; Teachers Aide; Church Choir; Flag Corp; Rep Jr Cls; Trk; Perfrmng Art Schl Of Philadelp.

TICE, NIEDA; Bishop Walsh HS; La Vale, MD; (Y); 7/104; Cmnty Wkr; Math Clb; Jazz Band; School Play; Var Trk; French Hon Soc; High Hon Roll; Ntl Merit Ltr; Art Clb; Church Yth Grp; Prsdntl Hnrs Fllwshp Awd 86; Mbr Ntl Art Hnr Soc 85-86; Coll Notre Dame Fo MD.

TIHERMARY, REBECCA; Pocomoke HS; Pocomoke, MD; (Y); AFS; Am Leg Aux Girls St; Church Yth Grp; Drama Clb; SADD; Band; School Play; L Fld Hcky; High Hon Roll; NHS.

TILGHMAN, WILLIAM; Parkside HS; Willards, MD; (Y); Church Yth Grp; Cmnty Wkr; French Clb; Hon Roll; NHS.

TILLER, NATHAN; Montgomery Blair HS; Silver Spg, MD; (Y); Ski Clb; Thesps; Stage Crew; Nwsp Stf; Var JV Bsbl; Swmmng; NHS; Boy Scts; Church Yth Grp; Nwsp Rptr; 1st In Schls Annl HS Math Exam 86; Math.

TILLMANN, AMY; Liberty HS; Sykesville, MD; (S); Sec Church Yth Grp; Teachers Aide; Rptr VICA; Mgr(s); High Hon Roll; Hon Roll; Cosmtlgy.

TIMKO, GEORGE; Patterson High School No 405; Baltimore, MD; (Y); 3/342; Band; Rep Jr Cls; Var Lcrss; Var Wrstlng; Bausch & Lomb Sci Awd; Hon Roll; Hon Roll; Jr NHS; Pres NHS; St Schlr; Susan Marie Leto Mem Schlrshp Awd 86; David E Weglein Schlrshp 86; ST MD Merit Schlrshp Awd 86; Frostburg ST Coll; Mgmt.

TIMPE, BRYAN; Smithsburg HS; Cincinnati, OH; (Y); 4/197; Spanish Clb; Rep Frsh Cls; Rep Soph Cls; Rep Stu Cncl; Var Capt Crs Cntry; Var L Trk; Trs NHS; 4 Yr Army ROTC Schlrshp 86; MD Dstngshd Schlr Hnrbl Mntn 85; Chrls Smmrs Mem Awd 86; W MD Coll; Ecnmcs.

TINE, GREGORY; Westminster HS; Westminster, MD; (Y); Mrchg Band; School Play; Symp Band; Lcrss; High Hon Roll; NHS; All Cty Band 84-85; U DE; Elect Engr.

TINLEY, BROOKE; Roland Park Country Schl; Lutherville, MD; (Y); AFS; Art Clb; Camera Clb; GAA; Varsity Clb; Stage Crew; Var L Bsktbl; Var L Fld Hcky; Var L Lcrss; Hon Roll; All Star Lcrsse Team Cty Prvt Schls 86; Law.

TIPPETT, BRIAN; La Plata HS; La Plata, MD; (Y); Spanish Clb; Teachers Aide; Variety Show; Hon Roll; Jr NHS; NHS; Slvr Scrn Awd Plcng 3rd Natn 83; Film Festvl Awds Cnty ST & Nat 83; Span Stu Hons Awd 86.

TIPPETT, KELLY; Lackey HS; White Plains, MD; (Y); Office Aide; Ski Clb; Spanish Clb; SADD; Flag Corp; Yrbk Stf; Sec Frsh Cls; Pres Stu Cncl; Hon Roll; Church Yth Grp; Spnsh III Awd 85-86; U Of S FL; Marine Bio.

TISSUE, LEA; North Hagerstown HS; Hagerstown, MD; (Y); French Clb; Rep Frsh Cls; Trs Soph Cls; Pres Jr Cls; L Bsktbl; Capt L Crs Cntry; L Trk; Hon Roll; Lang.

TITTERMARY, REBECCA; Pocomoke HS; Pocomoke, MD; (S); AFS; Church Yth Grp; Drama Clb; SADD; Band; School Play; Fld Hcky; High Hon Roll; NHS; Lgl Intrn 85-86.

TITTLE, KARA; Oxon Hill HS; Ft Washington, MD; (Y); Trs Church Yth Grp; Ed Yrbk Stf; Capt Swmmng; Stat Trk; French Hon Soc; High Hon Roll; NHS; Intnl Clb; Math Tm; Ski Clb; Acad Fit Awd 86; 2nd Envrnmntl Sci Cnty Fair 85 & 86; U Of MD; Educ.

TJADEN, BRETT; Georgetown Prep; Rockville, MD; (Y); 19/106; Church Yth Grp; Computer Clb; Dance Clb; Debate Tm; Math Tm; Science Clb; Varsity Clb; Var Bsbl; Var Swmmng; Hon Roll; Mth Medal 85.

TOADVINE, THEODORE; James M Bennett SR HS; Hebron, MD; (S); 16/192; Pres Church Yth Grp; Pres 4-H; Pres French Clb; JCL; Thesps; Jazz Band; School Musical; 4-H Awd; Drama Clb; Latin Clb; Ruritan Awd 85; Natl Latin Exam 83; All-Cnty & All-Shore Chorus 84-85; Salisbury ST Coll.

TOBIAS, PAUL; Catoctin HS; Cascade, MD; (Y); 10/210; Pres Church Yth Grp; Computer Clb; Science Clb; Chorus; School Musical; Hon Roll; Ntl Merit Ltr.

TODD, DEBBIE; Northwestern HS; Hyattsville, MD; (S); Trs Spanish Clb; Teachers Aide; Var Vllybl; Hon Roll; NHS.

TODER, CAROL; Lackey HS; Indian Head, MD; (Y); Teachers Aide; Nwsp Stf; High Hon Roll.

TOENSMEYER, DEBRA; Elkton Christian Schl; Bear, DE; (S); 1/25; Church Yth Grp; 4-H; Chorus; Church Choir; School Play; 4-H Awd; High Hon Roll; NHS; U Of DE; Educ.

TOM, MICHAEL; Northern HS; Baltimore, MD; (Y); U Of MD; Mech Engrng.

TOM, STEPHEN; Linganore HS; Mt Airy, MD; (Y); Boy Scts; Computer Clb; FCA; Yrbk Stf; Bsktbl; Ftbl; Socr; Wt Lftg; Hon Roll; Brwn Blt Karate; Elon Coll; Comp Sci.

TOMECEK, DAVID; Thekenwood HS; Baltimore, MD; (Y); Church Yth Grp; SADD; High Hon Roll; Hon Roll; U Of MD; Fire Prvntn Engr.

TOMINOVICH, SCOTT; Archbishop Carroll HS; Bowie, MD; (S); 12/180; Computer Clb; Letterman Clb; Pep Clb; Varsity Clb; Nwsp Stf; Socr; High Hon Roll; Hon Roll; NHS; Sci Fair Grnd Prz-1st Pl 83; Sci Fair 1st Pl-Bio 84; US Naval Acad; Arch.

TOMS, MICHAEL; Catoctin HS; Thurmont, MD; (Y); Cmnty Wkr; Computer Clb; Science Clb; Band; Orch; Hon Roll; JC Awd; Rcvd Hg Achvr Mth Awd 86; U Of Maryland; Cmptr.

TONEY, DEREK; Carver Vocational-Technical HS; Baltimore, MD; (Y); Trs FBLA; Rep Jr Cls; Var Stat Bsktbl; 1st & 8th Pl Bus Math I, FBLA Regn II B 85; 3rd Pl Accntng I FBLA Regn IIB 86; Accntng.

TOWNSEND, ANNE; Oxon Hill HS; Accokeek, MD; (Y); Computer Clb; Ski Clb; Church Choir; Crs Cntry; Hon Roll; NHS; Pres Schlr; PTSA Schlrshp 86; Fndry Alida Smith Schlrshp 86; Hmn Fctrs Potomac Chptr Awd 86; PA ST; Indstrl Engr.

TOWNSEND, DEBBIE; Snow Hill HS; Snow Hill, MD; (S); #10 In Class; AFS; Church Yth Grp; FBLA; Spanish Clb; Church Choir; Nwsp Stf; Wt Lftg; Hon Roll; Woodridge Bus Inst; Lgl Secy.

TRACEY, PHILIP; Westminster SR HS; Finksburg, MD; (Y); JA; Coach Actv; Var L Gym; Mgr(s); Score Keeper; Timer; Wrstlng; High Hon Roll; Hon Roll; Stdnt Tchr Gymnstcs 85-86; NC ST Engr.

TRADER, LORI; Pocomoke HS; Pocomoke, MD; (Y); 30/95; AFS; Church Yth Grp; Pres 4-H; Office Aide; Drill Tm; Mrchg Band; Capt Pom Pon; Hon Roll; Salisbury ST Coll; Nrsg.

TRANCHITELLA, LYNDA; Archbishop Keough HS; Clarskvile, MD; (Y); Sec VP 4-H; Hosp Aide; Yrbk Stf; Trs Jr Cls; Trs Sr Cls; JV Var Fld Hcky; Var Tennis; 4-H Awd; Hon Roll; Rep Stu Cncl; Mrktg.

TRASK, DANIEL; Bishop Walsh HS; Frostburg, MD; (Y); #24 In Class; Am Leg Boys St; Letterman Clb; Bsbl; Bsktbl; Ftbl; Trk; Hon Roll; NHS.

TRAUB, HEIKE; Archbishop Keough HS; Balt, MD; (Y); German Clb; Spanish Clb; Vllybl.

TREACY, KATHLEENE; St Marys HS; Arnold, MD; (Y); 17/119; Civic Clb; Trs Pep Clb; Ski Clb; Yrbk Phtg; Yrbk Stf; Var L Bsktbl; JV Fld Hcky; Var L Lcrss; Var Capt Socr; NHS; C Markland Kelly JR Athltc Svc Awd 86; Math Stu Of Mnth 85; US Army Mst Vlbl Plyr Awd 86; Roanoke Coll; Athltc Trn.

TREER, PAM; Gaithersburg HS; Gaithersburg, MD; (Y); 190/568; Church Yth Grp; French Clb; Library Aide; Office Aide; Teachers Aide; Stu Cncl; Cheerleading; Pom Pon; Hon Roll; Jr NHS; ST SC Chrlstn; Chld Psychlgst.

TREGO, NANCY KAY; North East HS; Elkton, MD; (Y); 35/240; Hosp Aide; Teachers Aide; VICA; Band; Concert Band; Off Jr Cls; Off Sr Cls; Hon Roll; Masonic Awd; Cecil Cncl For Women Awd 86; Civics Awd For All A's 83; Goldey Beacom Bus Clg; Accntng.

TRENT, SHANICQUA; Walbrook SR HS; Baltimore, MD; (Y); Drama Clb; Sec French Clb; GAA; Girl Scts; Capt Varsity Clb; School Play; Var Capt Trk; Excllnt Rdng & Math Awd 78; Excllnt Achvt Trck 86; Above Avg Grds Englsh 84; NY Inst Of Tech; Math Engr.

TRENUM, GARY JOE; Valley HS; Barton, MD; (Y); VP Church Yth Grp; Teachers Aide; Stu Cncl; Var L Bsbl; Var L Bsktbl; Var L Socr; Hon Roll; Frstbrg ST Coll; Comp Pgmg.

TRIBBE, MICHAEL E; Loyola HS; Baltimore, MD; (S); Var Capt Bsbl; JV Bsktbl; Var Ftbl; NHS; NEDT Awd; Opt Clb Awd; Schlr/Athl Schlrshp 83.

TRIBBLE, MICHELLE; Perryville HS; Perryville, MD; (Y); Hosp Aide; Intnl Clb; Lit Mag; Hon Roll; Church Yth Grp; Teachers Aide; Postv Yth Devlpmnt Netwrk 86; Cecil CC; Nrsg.

TRIBECK, MELISSA K; Wicomico SR HS; Mardela Springs, MD; (Y); French Clb; Sci Fair 3rd Prz 84; Sci Smnr Slsbry ST Coll 85; U S Air Force; Acctg.

TRIEBEL, TOBIN; Great Mills HS; Lexington Park, MD; (Y); Ski Clb; Varsity Clb; Band; Concert Band; Jazz Band; Mrchg Band; Yrbk Phtg; Yrbk Sprt Ed; Capt L Socr; L Var Tennis; Soutehrn MD Athlete Confrnc Soccer 85-86; Math.

TRINCHITELLA, LYNN A; Riverdale Baptist HS; Upper Marlboro, MD; (Y); Yrbk Stf; Trs Stu Cncl; Cheerleading; Hon Roll; VP NHS; Natl Sci Mrt Awd 85.

TRIPLETT, MONICA R; Gwynn Park HS; Clinton, MD; (Y); Pres Drama Clb; Science Clb; School Play; Stage Crew; Yrbk Rptr; Yrbk Stf; Lit Mag; Hon Roll; Ntl Merit Schlrshp Comm 85; Actng.

TRIPP, DAVID; North Hagerstown HS; Hagerstown, MD; (Y); Boy Scts; Church Yth Grp; French Clb; Church Choir; Hon Roll; Aerospace Engr.

TROUSDALE, WILLIAM F; Boys Latin Schl; Catonsville, MD; (Y); 2/55; L Letterman Clb; Scholastic Bowl; School Play; Yrbk Bus Mgr; Var L Lcrss; Var L Wrstlng; High Hon Roll; Sec NHS; Ntl Merit SF; Sal; Naval ROTC Schlrhp 86; Freund Awd Chem, Phys, Bio 86; Winkleblech Math Awd 86; MA Inst Of Tech; Aerospace Eng.

TRUELOVE, MEEGHAN; St Pauls School For Girls; Baltimore, MD; (Y); 2/40; Debate Tm; Political Wkr; SADD; School Play; Ed Nwsp Stf; Pres Soph Cls; Pres Jr Cls; Pres Stu Cncl; NHS; AFS; Wgly Schlrshp-Acadmc 83-87.

TRUESDELL, JORDAN; Glenelg HS; Woodbine, MD; (Y); VP 4-H; Concert Band; Orch; School Musical; Variety Show; Trs Sr Cls; Hon Roll; NHS; Band; Mrchg Band; US Music Ambssdrs European Tour 85; 1st Pl Divng Awd West Howard Swim Clb 85; Grand Champ Goat Shwmn; Aerospc Engrng.

TRUITT, JILL; James M Bennett SR HS; Salisbury, MD; (S); 4/184; JCL; Latin Clb; Stage Crew; Yrbk Stf; Hon Roll; Prfct Atten Awd; Stu Of Mnth Engl Awd 84; JR Ed Yrbk 85-86; U Of MD Baltimore; Grphc Arts.

TRUITT, MARSHELLA; Eastern Voc-Tech; Baltimore, MD; (Y); Chess Clb; FBLA; Chorus; School Musical; Lit Mag; Jr Cls; High Hon Roll; Essex CC; Elec.

TRUMAN, NATALIE; Thomas S Wootton HS; Rockville, MD; (Y); Hosp Aide; JA; SADD; Teachers Aide; Rep Stu Cncl; Hon Roll; Hon Roll 84-86.

TRUMAN, PATRICK; Garthersburg HS; Gaithersburg, MD; (Y); 11/600; Math Tm; NFL; Science Clb; School Play; Lit Mag; Hon Roll; Jr NHS; NHS; Teachers Aide; French Hon Soc; Wlsn Schlrshp U Of Rchstr 86; U Of Rochester.

TRUMPOWER, BETH; Francis Scott Key HS; Union Bridge, MD; (Y); GAA; Spanish Clb; Teachers Aide; Rep Jr Cls; Var Trk; Var Vllybl; Hon Roll; NHS; Hstry.

TRUMPOWER, DAVID; Clear Spring HS; Clear Spg, MD; (Y); 4/125; FFA; Var L Bsbl; Var L Bsktbl; Var L Socr; Hon Roll; 1st Pl Indvl Frm Mgmt Cntst ST 84; 1st Pl FFA Cnvt Tlnt Cntst ST 85; Prom Cmmtte 86; Physcs.

TSANG, CYNTHIA; Baltimore Polytechnic Inst; Baltimore, MD; (Y); 2/400; Math Tm; Pres Science Clb; Capt Varsity Clb; Nwsp Stf; Yrbk Stf; Var Capt Badmtn; Var Capt Tennis; High Hon Roll; Hon Roll; NHS; Mayors Stu Achvt Awds 86; Pres Acad Ftns Awd 86; ST Of MD Merit Schltc Awd 86; MA Inst Of Tech; Cvl Engrng.

TSE, AILEEN; Gaithersburg HS; Gaithersburg, MD; (Y); 36/626; Camera Clb; Intnl Clb; Science Clb; Yrbk Phtg; Yrbk Rptr; High Hon Roll; Hon Roll; NHS; Art Clb; Variety Show; Natl Art Hnr Soc 85-86; Sci Engrng Apprenticeship Prog 86; Internatl Natl Piano Aud 86; Oddessy Mind 86; Brown U; Elec Engrng.

TSE, CAROLINE; Gaithersburg HS; Gaithersburg, MD; (Y); VP Intnl Clb; Model UN; Variety Show; Yrbk Phtg; Yrbk Rptr; Gym; Hon Roll; Ntl Wnnr Of Ntl Guild Of Piano Tchrs Aud 84-86; Odyssey Of Mind Comp 2nd Pl 86; Rcvd A MSMTA Exam 86.

TUCKER, BETH; Archibishop Keough HS; Baltimore, MD; (Y); JV Bsktbl; Socr; NHS; Comptrs.

TUCKER, DAWNA; Friendly HS; Fort Washington, MD; (Y); Church Yth Grp; Chorus; Church Choir; School Musical; Hon Roll; NHS; Prince Georges Cnty Acadmc Excllnc Awd 85-86; Prince Georges Cnty Hns Chorus 83-86; Elec Engr.

TUCKER, GARRETT; Capitol Christian Acad; Lothian, MD; (S); 1/40; Pres VP Church Yth Grp; Concert Band; Mrchg Band; Var L Socr; High Hon Roll; NHS; Prfct Atten Awd; VFW Awd; Voice Dem Awd; Hghst Acad Avg 83-85; Most Likely To Succeed 84-85; Sci Awd 84; Sci.

TUCKER, LAURA; Eleanor Roosevelt HS; Glenn Dale, MD; (Y); Church Yth Grp; Church Choir; Orch; Symp Band; Yrbk Rptr; Yrbk Stf; French Hon Soc; Hon Roll; All ST Orch & Bnd 83-86; MD Hnrs Bnd 84-86; Prince George SR Yth Orch 84-86; Music.

TUCKER, TERRI; Francis Scott Key HS; Union Bridge, MD; (Y); Sec Church Yth Grp; Sec Drama Clb; GAA; Teachers Aide; Variety Show; Capt Bsktbl; Capt Fld Hcky; Powder Puff Ftbl; Sftbl; Stat Trk; Robert Moton Schlrshp Awd 86; Hagerstown Bus Coll; Bus Adm.

TULL, GREGORY; Maurice Mc Donough HS; White Plains, MD; (Y); Art Clb; Church Yth Grp; SADD; Rep Soph Cls; Off Jr Cls; Var Capt Bsktbl; Var Capt Tennis; Hon Roll; Prfct Atten Awd; Tennis 1st Tm All Cnty 86; Tennis 3rd Pl St Of MD 86; Drexel U; Bus.

TULLY, KAREN; Linganore HS; Mt Airy, MD; (Y); Church Yth Grp; Drama Clb; Pep Clb; Spanish Clb; SADD; Sec Frsh Cls; Rep Soph Cls; Rep Jr Cls; Co-Capt Cheerleading; Var Gym; Acad Ltr 84-86; Gov Physcl Ftns Exc Awd 85.

TUN, MIMI AYE AYE; Pain Branch HS; Silver Spring, MD; (Y); 19/347; AFS; Key Clb; Hosp Aide; Yrbk Stf; Capt Tennis; NHS; Pres Acad Ftns Awd 86; Frnch Dprtmnt Awd 85-86; Haverford Coll.

TUNSTALL, PATRICIA D; Capital Lutheran HS; Washington, DC; (S); Church Yth Grp; Civic Clb; FCA; Church Choir; School Musical; Off Jr Cls; Bsktbl; Sftbl; Hon Roll; Howard U; Bus Mgmt.

TURANO, KATHRYN VANESSA; Bishop Walsh HS; Cumberland, MD; (Y); Chess Clb; Cmnty Wkr; Hosp Aide; Red Cross Aide; Ski Clb; Yrbk Stf; Mgr Ftbl; Stat Trk; James Madison U; Math.

TURNER, BENJAMIN; De Matha Catholic HS; Lanham, MD; (Y); 62/250; Band; Pres Sr Cls; Var Socr; Hon Roll; NHS; PAVAS; Varsity Clb; Chorus; Pep Band; Symp Band; Physics.

TURNER, BRENDA; Frederick Christian Acad; Jefferson, MD; (Y); 1/6; Church Yth Grp; Chorus; Church Choir; Cit Awd; High Hon Roll; Ntl Christian Hnr Soc 85-86; Missions.

TURNER, DARYL; Laurel HS; Laurel, MD; (Y); Hon Roll; Prfct Atten Awd; Outstdng Stu Auto Mech 86; William Ropka Mem Awd 86; James B Boss Mem Awd 86; U Of MD; Mech Engr.

TURNER, KATHERINE E; Gov Thomas Johnson HS; Thurmont, MD; (Y); 26/343; Debate Tm; Hosp Aide; Pres SADD; VP Stu Cncl; JV Var Cheerleading; Hon Roll; AFS; Latin Clb; Teachers Aide; Sec Frsh Cls; MD Gftd & Tlntd Cert Of Achvt 85; Frederick Cnty Assn Of Stu Cncls 84-86; Stu Advsry 85; Bus.

TURNER, LAURA; Baltimore Lutheran HS; Towson, MD; (Y); French Clb; Chorus; School Play; Nwsp Rptr; Yrbk Stf; High Hon Roll; Jr NHS; NHS; Prfct Atten Awd; Essex CC; Mass Cmmnctns.

TURNER, MICHAEL PAUL; Beall HS; Frostburg, MD; (Y); Band; Chorus; Concert Band; Jazz Band; Mrchg Band; Orch; Nwsp Stf; Badmtn; Bsbl; Bsktbl; Hnr Band 83-85; All-Area & All-WMT Lg Goalie Sccr Tm 85-86; Lttrs Band 83-84, Bsbll 84-86 Sccr 85-86; Math.

TURNER, SANDRA LEE; Williamsport HS; Sharpsburg, MD; (Y).

TURNER, SHANNAN; Wheaton HS; Wheaton, MD; (Y); 52/386; Ski Clb; Teachers Aide; Nwsp Stf; Yrbk Stf; Rep Stu Cncl; JV Var Cheerleading; Mgr Trk; Mgr Wrstlng; Hon Roll; Publc Reltns.

TURNER, STEVEN; La Plata HS; Mechanicsville, MD; (Y); Boy Scts; Church Yth Grp; Science Clb; Band; Mrchg Band; Symp Band; Off Soph Cls; Off Jr Cls; Wt Lftg; Wrstlng; Acad Amer Awd 85; Sci Merit Awd 84-86; Stu Engrng Apprntc Prog 86; Engrng.

TURPIN, KAREN; Wicomico SR HS; Salisbury, MD; (Y); Church Choir; Lit Mag; High Hon Roll; Eng.

TWIGG, ALLEN; Allegany HS; Cumberland, MD; (Y); Church Yth Grp; Computer Clb; Drama Clb; Teachers Aide; Band; Concert Band; Jazz Band; Mrchg Band; Orch; School Play; MD ST Schlrshp 4 Yrs; Hghst Merit SR Band Awd; Rbd Braun Memrl Awd; Frostburg ST Coll; Comp Tch.

TWIGG, YVONNE; Fort Hill HS; Cumberland, MD; (Y); Library Aide; Office Aide; Svc Ltr Awd & My Ltr F 85; Stu Lbry Aid Svc Awd 85; Psych.

TYLER, JASIRI; Mt St Joseph College HS; Silver Spring, MD; (Y); Computer Clb; Drama Clb; French Clb; Ski Clb; School Musical; Rep Stu Cncl; Stu Cncl Awd 85; Dartmouth; Bus.

TYMIUK, MARIA; The Catholic HS Of Balto; Baltimore, MD; (Y); 6/189; Pres Spanish Clb; High Hon Roll; Hon Roll; NHS; Prfct Atten Awd; Spanish NHS; Office Aide; Red Cross Aide; MD Gnrl ST Schlrshp 86; Schlstc Merit Awd 86; Amer Bus Wmns Assoc Schlrshp 86; U Of MD; Pre Phrmcy.

TYNDALL, ALTHEA; Walt Whitman HS; Bethesda, MD; (Y); French Clb; Intnl Clb; Science Clb; Spanish Clb; Teachers Aide; Orch; School Musical; MSMTA Judgd Rectl 1st Pl 85; D C Fed Of Music Clbs Judgd Rectl 1st Pl 86; Med.

TYSON, RODNEY; Woodlawn HS; Woodlawn, MD; (Y); Boy Scts; Thesps; Madrigals; Pres Frsh Cls; Pres Soph Cls; Pres Sr Cls; NHS; Bnjmn Bnnhr Schlrshp 86-90; Excllnc Awd For Ldrshp & Srv 85-86; U Of MD Coll Pk; Financl Exec.

ULEN, EISA N; Western HS; Baltimore, MD; (Y); Girl Scts; JA; Yrbk Phtg; Yrbk Stf; Rep Frsh Cls; Rep Soph Cls; Rep Jr Cls; Rep Stu Cncl; Natl Achvt Pgm Cmmnded Stu/Outstndg Negro Stu 85; Pre-Coll Pgm Syracuse U 85; Staff City Yth Nwspr; Frgn News.

ULLRICH, JENNIFER; Inst Of Notre Dame; Baltimore, MD; (Y); Church Yth Grp; Sec Math Clb; Pres Girl Scts; Service Clb; Flag Corp; Stage Crew; Variety Show; Yrbk Sprt Ed; Sec Stu Cncl; Hon Roll; Stu Volntr Mst 84; St Marys; Cmnctns.

ULMER, BROOKE; Sherwood HS; Brookeville, MD; (Y); Sec Art Clb; Cmnty Wkr; Ski Clb; Stage Crew; Yrbk Stf; Hon Roll; NHS; Spanish NHS; Outstdng Stu Awd Female 85; Early Chldhd Educ.

ULRICH, LINDA C; C W Woodward HS; Rockville, MD; (Y); 4/234; Cmnty Wkr; Debate Tm; Math Tm; Red Cross Aide; Pres Science Clb; Speech Tm; Orch; Ntl Merit SF; St Schlr; Mntgmry Cnty Heart Assoc Stu Resrch Fllwshp 85; Med.

UNDERWOOD, ELIZABETH S; Riverdale Baptist HS; Riverdale, MD; (Y); Church Yth Grp; Pep Clb; Speech Tm; Teachers Aide; Cheerleading; Hon Roll; U MD; Bus Adm.

UNGER, DANIEL; Rockville HS; Rockville, MD; (S); Sec Chess Clb; Quiz Bowl; SADD; Band; Concert Band; Mrchg Band; Nwsp Rptr; Hon Roll; Partcpnt Johns Hopkins U Ctr Adv Acadmclly Tlntd Yth; Hstry.

UNGER, PATRICIA; North Carroll HS; Hampstead, MD; (Y); JA; Sec Service Clb; Spanish Clb; VICA; Chorus; Flag Corp; Pep Band; Hon Roll; Chem, Bio &II, Geom, Alg I&II Tutor 84-86; RN.

UPHOLD, TERI; Fort Hill HS; Rawlings, MD; (Y); Computer Clb; Hosp Aide; Band; Church Choir; Concert Band; Drill Tm; Yrbk Stf; Trk; Cit Awd; Hon Roll; Phrmcst.

UPOLE, REBECCA; Southern Garrett HS; Mt Lake Park, MD; (Y); Sec FHA; Library Aide; Office Aide; Hon Roll; ICM Bus Coll; Lgl Sec.

URIAN, MICHAEL; Oakland Mills HS; Columbia, MD; (Y); Ski Clb; Var Bsbl; Var Crs Cntry; Var Diving; JV Ftbl; Var Swmmng; Var Wt Lftg; Bus.

USHER, BETSEY; St Pauls Shool For Girls; Baltimore, MD; (Y); Trs AFS; Art Clb; Church Yth Grp; Library Aide; Model UN; Chorus; Ed Yrbk Phtg; Lit Mag; Var Capt Socr; Hon Roll; Art Hons 84-86.

UTERMAHLEN JR, WILLIAM; Francis Scott Key HS; Taneytown, MD; (Y); 16/200; Letterman Clb; VICA; Var L Bsbl; Var L Ftbl; Var L Wrstlng; Hon Roll; NHS; JA; Key Clb; Off Sr Cls; Taneytown Bank & Trust Schlr-Ath Scholar 86; U S Marine Corp Dstngshd Ath 86; Salisbury ST Coll; Chem.

UTZ, ELIZABETH; St Marys-Ryken HS; Mechanicsville, MD; (Y); Cmnty Wkr; Drama Clb; Spanish Clb; Speech Tm; School Musical; School Play; Nwsp Rptr; Lit Mag; JV Fld Hcky; JV Trk; Outdoors Club 86; Ntl Mbr Piano Playing Audttns; Retreat Ldr 85; Theater.

VACHE, SUZANNE C; John Carroll HS; Havre De Grace, MD; (Y); Art Clb; Camera Clb; Church Yth Grp; Cmnty Wkr; Debate Tm; Drama Clb; 4-H; FHA; Letterman Clb; NFL; 1st Pl Cnty & ST Frnsc Mts; Pblc Rltns.

VADER, STEPHANIE; Magruder HS; Derwood, MD; (Y); 153/310; Pres VP Church Yth Grp; Pres 4-H; German Clb; SADD; Chorus; Church Choir; Swing Chorus; Rep Soph Cls; Rep Jr Cls; Rep Sr Cls; Natl 4-H Congrss 84; Seminar NY At The UN 84-85; St Dairy Bowl Tm 83-84; Music.

VAID, UPASANA; Allegany HS; La Vale, MD; (Y); AFS; Hosp Aide; Pep Clb; Mrchg Band; Yrbk Stf; Hon Roll; NHS; Med.

VAISHNAV, RAJAL; North Carroll HS; Hampstead, MD; (Y); Sec Drama Clb; French Clb; VP JA; Teachers Aide; Nwsp Ed-Chief; Lit Mag; Rep Jr Cls; Church Yth Grp; Library Aide; Office Aide; Mck Trial Tri-Cnty Chmps-ST Semi-Fnlsts 84-85; Peer Cnslng Achvt Cert 85-86; Advnc Acadmc Cert 86; Goucher Coll; Psychlgy.

VALENTINE, AMY; Catoctin HS; Thurmont, MD; (Y); Church Yth Grp; Dance Clb; FBLA; Letterman Clb; Teachers Aide; Varsity Clb; Chorus; Church Choir; School Musical; School Play; NE US Altrnt Mdlng 84; All Amer Tlnt Awd Ust Pl Dncng 85; Frrestyle Tm Rcrd Swmmng 83; Bus Mngmnt.

VAN BUREN, STEPHANIE; Magruder HS; Gaithersburg, MD; (Y); Hon Roll; Exe Secty.

VAN DE VEERDONK, NICOLE; Thomas Stone SR HS; Waldorf, MD; (Y); Drama Clb; Office Aide; Science Clb; Teachers Aide; Mrchg Band; Symp Band; Variety Show; Mgr(s); Pom Pon; Sftbl; Towson; Psychology.

VAN DER LINDEN, JEANETTE MARIA; M J Mc Donough HS; Waldorf, MD; (Y); 22/320; Drama Clb; Ski Clb; Chorus; Church Choir; Flag Corp; School Musical; School Play; Swing Chorus; Variety Show; Rep Frsh Cls; MD Acad Sci 85-86; Physcs Olympcs 85-86; US Navl Acad; Aviatn.

VAN DIEN, JACQUELYN; St Marys Piyken HS; Waldorf, MD; (Y); Band; Nwsp Ed-Chief; Rep Frsh Cls; Rep Soph Cls; Rep Jr Cls; Var Capt Cheerleading; Trk; Hon Roll; NHS; NEDT Awd; Law.

VAN LENTEN, DEBBY; Thomas S Wootton HS; Rockville, MD; (Y); 7/401; Trs Drama Clb; Teachers Aide; Trs Thesps; Mgr School Play; Stage Crew; Hon Roll; NHS; Pres Schlr; Frgn Lang Hnr Awd 86; Swarthmore Coll.

VAN METER, KELLY; Fort Hill HS; Cumberland, MD; (S); 20/251; Church Yth Grp; Pep Clb; SADD; Thesps; Church Choir; Drill Tm; School Play; Rep Frsh Cls; Rep Soph Cls; Rep Jr Cls; Demolay Sweetheart-Cumberland Chapter 84; Rainbow Girls-Grand Officer 85-86; Tutoring Awd 85; U Of MD; Phys Thrpy.

VAN NORMAN, BRIAN; Thomas Stone HS; Waldorf, MD; (S); Science Clb; JV Var Ftbl; JV Var Wrstlng; Acctg.

VAN OCKER, ALLISON; La Plata HS; Waldorf, MD; (Y); 9/400; Teachers Aide; Chorus; Rep Sr Cls; Stu Cncl; L Cheerleading; L Sftbl; Hon Roll; Pres Jr NHS; NHS; Prfct Atten Awd; Prncpls Awd 83; Rgnl & ST Semi-Fnl Sftbl Chmpnshp 85; Mrt Schlstc Awd 86; U Of MD.

VAN SPLINTER, DARLENE; St Vincent Pallotti HS; Laurel, MD; (S); Church Yth Grp; Office Aide; Spanish Clb; Rep Stu Cncl; Var L Cheerleading; Hon Roll; Ntl Art Hnr Soc; UMBC; Bus Fash Merch.

VAN TASSEL, DEANNA; St Marys Ryken HS; Lusby, MD; (Y); JV Var Cheerleading; Hon Roll; NEDT Awd; Engr.

VANCE, MARTINA; Southern Garrett HS; Mt Lake Pk, MD; (Y); Trs Church Yth Grp; Trs Q&S; Ed Nwsp Phtg; Var Vllybl; Vllybl Var Ltr 85; CPA.

VANCE, SERENA; Andover HS; Glen Burnie, MD; (Y); Dance Clb; Drama Clb; Drill Tm; Nwsp Rptr; Gym; Pom Pon; Suprstr Nomn 85; Dncr.

VANDERLINDEN, JEANETTE; Maurice J Mc Donough HS; White Plains, MD; (S); 20/320; Drama Clb; Pres Ski Clb; School Musical; Swing Chorus; Trs Sr Cls; Vllybl; Pres NHS; Camp Fr Inc; Science Clb; MD Sci Acad 86; Jr Sci & Hmnts Sympsm 86; US Nvl Acad; Marine Sci.

VANDROSS, CATRICE RENEE; Potomac HS; Temple Hills, MD; (Y); Church Yth Grp; Drama Clb; Hst FBLA; Intnl Clb; Office Aide; Red Cross Aide; School Play; Yrbk Stf; Pres Hst Stu Cncl; Stat Ftbl; FBLA Pblc Spkng Region III 2nd Pl, ST 7th Pl 86; Citatn Ldrshp; Cnty Council Ldrshp 86; U Of Eastern Shore.

VANLOON, CRAIG; Eastern Voc-Tech HS; Baltimore, MD; (Y); SADD; Band; Concert Band; Orch; School Musical; Hon Roll; U Of MD; Elctrncs Engrng.

VANMETER, BONNIE; Fort Hill HS; Rawlings, MD; (Y); Trs Church Yth Grp; Natl Beta Clb; Pep Clb; Chorus; Church Choir; Off Frsh Cls; Off Soph Cls; Off Jr Cls; Sftbl; Allegany CC; Secdry Tchrs Ed.

VANMETER, LISA; Fort Hill HS; Cumberland, MD; (Y); Dance Clb; French Clb; Natl Beta Clb; Varsity Clb; Drill Tm; Mrchg Band; Soph Cls; Jr Cls; Cit Awd; Hon Roll; Frostburg ST U; Lang.

VANN, DORIAN; Maurice J Mc Donough HS; Waldorf, MD; (S); 4-H; Sec Letterman Clb; Symp Band; VP Jr Cls; Sec Stu Cncl; Var Stat Bsktbl; JV Var Cheerleading; Var Stat Trk; High Hon Roll; NHS.

VANSKIVER, THOMAS; Southrew HS; Baltimore, MD; (Y); Red Cross Aide; Yrbk Stf; Swmmng; Wt Lftg; Hon Roll; Prfct Atten Awd; Hnr Rl 84-85; RTOC.

VARGAS, CONSTANZA EDITH; St Johns At Prospect Hall; Frederick, MD; (Y); Intnl Clb; Science Clb; Yrbk Ed-Chief; Lit Mag; Rep Frsh Cls; Trs Jr Cls; Var Tennis; Hon Roll; Trs NHS; NEDT Awd; Jrnlsm Yrbk Awd 87; Intl Stds.

VARGAS, LOURDES; High Point HS; Adelphi, MD; (Y); Church Yth Grp; Office Aide; Teachers Aide; Church Choir; Hon Roll; Private Indstry Cncl Merit 85; Med.

VARGEA, MELISSA; Gaithersburg HS; Gaithersburg, MD; (Y); AFS; Drama Clb; Pep Clb; School Play; Nwsp Rptr; Nwsp Stf; Hon Roll; Jrnlst Of The Yr 84; U Of MD; Jrnlsm.

VARMA, PAYAL R; Gaithersburg HS; Rockville, MD; (Y); 58/620; AFS; Cmnty Wkr; Intnl Clb; Science Clb; SADD; Rep Frsh Cls; Rep Sr Cls; Stu Cncl; French Hon Soc; Hon Roll; Prsdntl Ftnss Awd 86; U Of MD; Engnrng.

VARRON, JOHN; Good Counsel HS; Silver Spring, MD; (Y); 28/214; Aud/Vis; Exploring; Hosp Aide; ROTC; SADD; Ftbl; Trk; Wt Lftg; Hon Roll; NHS; U Of MD; Elec Engrng.

VAUGHAN, CHERIE; Maurice J Mc Donough HS; Pomfret, MD; (S); 12/316; Camera Clb; Computer Clb; English Clb; Intnl Clb; JV Cheerleading; High Hon Roll; Univ Wmn Amer Assoc 83; Comp Sci.

VAUGHAN, MONICA YVETTE; Crossland HS; Forestville, MD; (Y); FHA; Office Aide; Science Clb; Band; Pres Soph Cls; Bsktbl; Cheerleading; Sftbl; Tennis; High Hon Roll; Prfct Atten Awd 85; Pres Phys Fit Awd 83-84; U MD; Paralegal.

VAUGHN, AMY; North East HS; Rising Sun, MD; (Y); FBLA; Leo Clb; Spanish Clb; SADD; Teachers Aide; JV Bsktbl; Mgr(s); Hon Roll; Engl Hnrs Awd 84-85; Acctg.

VAUGHN, JULIE; Western HS; Balt, MD; (Y); VP Church Yth Grp; Trs Church Choir; Hon Roll; NHS; Prfct Atten Awd; 2nd Pl Awd Oratorical Cntst Rchmnd VA 83 Clevelnd Oh 84; Med.

VAUGHN, KATHERINE; Great Mills HS; Lex Prk, MD; (Y); 10/230; French Clb; SADD; Yrbk Stf; Lit Mag; Trs Sr Cls; Hon Roll; NHS; MD Merit Schlstc Awd 86; Presdntl Acadmc Ftns Awd 86; Engl Awd 86; U Of MD; Bio.

VAUGHN, VICKI; Parkdale HS; Lamham, MD; (Y); Church Yth Grp; Teachers Aide; School Play; Yrbk Stf; Var Cheerleading; Var Trk; Jr NHS; U Of FL; Tchng.

VAUSE, HEIDI; Great Mills HS; California, MD; (Y); Drama Clb; Trs French Clb; SADD; Teachers Aide; School Musical; School Play; Lit Mag; Sec Sr Cls; Hon Roll; NHS; MD ST Schlrshp 85-86; Typg 2 Awd 84-85; Prsdntl Acdmc Ftnss Awd 85-86; U Of MD Baltimore Cnty; Engl.

VEASEY, MARY R; Wootton HS; Gaithersburg, MD; (Y); Computer Clb; Drama Clb; JA; PAVAS; Speech Tm; School Musical; Nwsp Rptr; Lit Mag; High Hon Roll; Church Yth Grp; JEA USC Write Off Cntst 2nd Advrtsng 86; City Wide Stu Exchng Prog 84; George Washington U; Engrng.

VELARDE, DAVID JOSEPH; Walkersville HS; Walkersville, MD; (Y); Drama Clb; Thesps; Chorus; Orch; School Musical; School Play; Nwsp Bus Mgr; Nwsp Rptr; Nwsp Stf; Var L Socr; Octorian Theatr Co 86; All-ST Choir 86&87; MD Cntrs Thrtrs Smmr Pgms 82-86; Prfrmng Arts.

VENGINICKAL, PAUL; Archbishop Corley HS; Baltimore, MD; (S); 6/143; Church Yth Grp; Math Clb; Science Clb; Nwsp Rptr; Nwsp Stf; JV Trk; High Hon Roll; Hon Roll; NHS; Engrng.

VERGA, GREG; Maurice J Mc Donough HS; Port Tobacco, MD; (S); FBLA; JV Capt Socr; Hon Roll; NHS; U MD; Engrng.

VERRICO, BRADLEY J; Elkton HS; Elkton, MD; (Y); Debate Tm; Intnl Clb; Key Clb; Math Tm; SADD; Rep Jr Cls; Rep Stu Cncl; JV Socr; Var Tennis; JV Trk; Schl Rep PA Yth Debts Enrgy 85-86; Maryland Math Leag Awd 86; Maryland ST Tnns Fnlst 86.

VEST, ROBERT; Frederick HS; Clarksburg, MD; (Y); 4/377; Church Yth Grp; Computer Clb; JCL; Latin Clb; Math Tm; Teachers Aide; Off Soph Cls; Off Jr Cls; High Hon Roll; NHS; Physcs.

VICENDESE, JAMES; Loyola HS; Ellicott City, MD; (Y); Chess Clb; Rep Frsh Cls; Var L Bsbl; JV Trk; JV Wrstlng; NHS; U KY Bsbl Wildcat Awd 86; Pre-Med.

VICKERIE, STEWART; Potomac HS; Temple Hills, MD; (Y); Spanish Clb; SADD; Hon Roll; Comp Sci.

VICKERS, W JUDD; Cambridge South Dorchester HS; Cambridge, MD; (Y); AFS; Aud/Vis; Camera Clb; Cmnty Wkr; French Clb; Political Wkr; SADD; Band; Pltcl Sci.

VICTOR, CECELIA; Archbishop Keough HS; Catonsville, MD; (Y); NFL; Rep Frsh Cls; Trs Soph Cls; Rep Jr Cls; Rep Sr Cls; VP Stu Cncl; NHS; GAA; Hon Roll; H S Ldrshp Inst 85; Pltcl Sci.

VICTOR, SUJATHA; Takoma Acad; Takoma Park, MD; (Y); Library Aide; Ski Clb; Yrbk Stf; Socr; Hon Roll; NHS.

VIERS, SANDRA; Centennial HS; Ellicott City, MD; (Y); Pres Art Clb; Church Yth Grp; Dance Clb; Teachers Aide; Drill Tm; Mgr Cheerleading; Hon Roll; Salisbury ST; Math Ed.

VILLAMIN, MIRABELLE; Morthwestern HS; Hyattsville, MD; (Y); Hosp Aide; Math Tm; VICA; Chorus; School Musical; Tennis; High Hon Roll; Hon Roll; NHS; U Of MD; Accntng.

VILLELA, KHARI; Baltimore City College; Baltimore, MD; (S); Boy Scts; Concert Band; School Musical; School Play; Yrbk Bus Mgr; Pres Frsh Cls; Pres Soph Cls; Pres Jr Cls; Pres Sr Cls; Lcrss; Hugh O Brien Yth Ambssdr 85; Yale U; Bus Adm.

VINCENT, WM; Northwestern HS; Hyattsville, MD; (Y); JA; Latin Clb; Var Trk; Hon Roll; Bus.

VINES, LETETIA; Surrettsville SR HS; Clinton, MD; (Y); Chorus; Yrbk Stf; Cheerleading; Hon Roll; Acad All Amer 85; DR.

VINICK, CAROLE; Magruder HS; Olney, MD; (Y); Cmnty Wkr; VP 4-H; Letterman Clb; Speech Tm; SADD; Temple Yth Grp; Trs Jr Cls; Var L Fld Hcky; Pres NHS; NFL; Cert Hnrb Merit Cum Laude Natl Latin Exam 86; Stu Ldrshp Cls 85-86; U MD College Pk; Hlth Sci.

VISSERS, SUSAN E; Mount Hebron HS; Ellicott City, MD; (Y); 1/266; Chorus; Madrigals; Pres Stu Cncl; Var Capt Bsktbl; Var L Tennis; Var L Trk; Var Capt Vllybl; High Hon Roll; NHS; St Schlr; ROTC Schlrshp; Cnty Outstndng SR 86; GWU Awd Excel Math, Sci 85; Duke U; Atty.

VOCKE, NEIL; Parkville HS; Baltimore, MD; (Y); JA; Key Clb; Stat Var Vllybl; Hon Roll; Trs Stu Cncl; U MD; Info Systms Mgt.

VOGDES, JENNIFER; Gaithersburg HS; Gaithersburg, MD; (Y); AFS; Church Yth Grp; Concert Band; Mrchg Band; Fld Hcky; Swmmng; Jr NHS; NHS; Spanish NHS; Rep-Epscpl Diocs Of Washngtn-Peace Tour Of Svt Union 85.

VOITEK, PAUL; James M Bennett SR HS; Salibury, MD; (Y); Bsktbl; Ftbl; Trk; Hon Roll; Engnrng.

VOLK, JODY; Fort Hill HS; Cumberland, MD; (S); Church Yth Grp; Thesps; Ed Nwsp Stf; Off Frsh Cls; Off Soph Cls; Off Jr Cls; Rep Sr Cls; Off Stu Cncl; Stat Wrstlng; NHS; Frostburg ST Coll; Chem.

VOLTMER, AILEEN; Franklin SR HS; Reisterstown, MD; (Y); Cmnty Wkr; Service Clb; Drill Tm; Mrchg Band; Ed Yrbk Stf; NHS; Schlstc Medal 86; Community Schlrshp 86; Drexel U Philadelphia; Engr.

VON VACANO, MARCELA; Walter Johnson HS; Bethesda, MD; (Y); Debate Tm; French Clb; NFL; Science Clb; Service Clb; Spanish Clb; Chorus; School Musical; School Play; Nwsp Rptr; 2nd Pl Cnty Debate Leag Tourmnt 86; Ntl Ldrshp & Serv Awd 86; Law.

VOSS, DOUGLAS; Pocomoke HS; Pocomoke, MD; (S); 8/95; Am Leg Boys St; Boy Scts; Cmnty Wkr; Political Wkr; Science Clb; School Play; VP Sr Cls; High Hon Roll; NHS; Pres Clssrm Yng Amer 86; Legl Intrn ST Mck Trl Tm 85-86; U S Naval Acad; Aerosp Engrng.

VU, QUOCANH; Gaithersburg HS; Gaithersburg, MD; (Y); VP Chess Clb; Intnl Clb; Math Tm; ROTC; Spanish Clb; Drill Tm; Rep Stu Cncl; JV Capt Vllybl; Hon Roll; NHS; U Of MD; Pre Med.

VUITEL, JENNIFER; Dulaney SR HS; Timonium, MD; (Y); Nwsp Rptr; Hon Roll; Wildlife Presrvtn.

WADDY, TINA; Western SR HS; Baltimore, MD; (Y); 112/412; Mrchg Band; Variety Show; Yrbk Stf; Cheerleading; Trk; K Brich Sls Achvt Awd, Cert Attnmnt Music 86; Howard U; Bus Admn.

WADE, ANITA W; Arlington Baptist HS; Baltimore, MD; (S); 16/52; Red Cross Aide; Var Bsktbl; Cit Awd; Bio Awd 84-85; Econ-Govt Awd 84-85; Anstslgst.

WADE, BRENDA; Thomas Stone HS; Bryantown, MD; (S); Rep Am Leg Aux Girls St; Pres Church Yth Grp; Pres 4-H; Rep Stu Cncl; Trk; Vllybl; 4-H Awd; High Hon Roll; Hon Roll; NHS; Miss Congnlty Awd 85; Accntnt.

WADE, GENA; Northwestern HS; Brentwood, MD; (Y); Church Yth Grp; VICA; Trk; Hon Roll; Comp Repr.

WAGNER, EDWARD; Milford Mill HS; Balt, MD; (Y); 6/250; JCL; Concert Band; Trs Jr Cls; Capt Bsbl; Capt Socr; Var Wrstlng; Elks Awd; NHS; Ntl Merit Ltr; St Schlr; Best All Around SR 86; Schlr Athlete Awd 86; Acdmc Schlrshp 86; Stanford U; Sci.

WAGNER, KAREN; Laurel HS; Laurel, MD; (Y); Am Leg Aux Girls St; Church Yth Grp; Drama Clb; Letterman Clb; Office Aide; Church Choir; School Play; Variety Show; Capt Vllybl; Hon Roll; Tent Troupe Am Theater 84; Salibury ST.

WAGNER, KEITH; Walter Johnson HS; Silver Spring, MD; (Y); Art Clb; Cmnty Wkr; Intnl Clb; Science Clb; Ski Clb; SADD; Rep Stu Cncl; Bsktbl; Socr; Hon Roll; Hstry.

WAGNER, SANDRA; Queen Annes County HS; Queenstown, MD; (Y); 14/329; VP Spanish Clb; Chorus; Yrbk Phtg; Yrbk Stf; Gov Hon Prg Awd; Hon Roll; NHS; Pres Schlr; Senatorial Schlrshp 85-86; 1st Pl-Environmental Sci Fair 84-85; Queen Annes Cnty HS Merit Awd 85-86; Salisbury ST Coll; Engrng.

WAGNER, VALERIE; Harford Christian Schl; Bel Air, MD; (S); Church Yth Grp; Teachers Aide; Var Fld Hcky; Hon Roll; NHS.

WAGONER, AMY; Allegany County Vo-Tech Center; Cumberland, MD; (Y); Church Yth Grp; Computer Clb; Library Aide; SADD; Chorus; Church Choir; Orch; Variety Show; Yrbk Stf; Hon Roll; Frstbrg ST Coll; Comp Sci.

WAHL, STEPHANIE; Dulaney SR HS; Cockeysville, MD; (Y); Thesps; Chorus; Madrigals; School Musical; School Play; Stage Crew; Variety Show; Outstndng Wrk In Dance For Schl 86; Perf Arts.

WAINWRIGHT, CHERYL; Western SR HS; Baltimore, MD; (Y); English Clb; Hosp Aide; JA; Nwsp Bus Mgr; Lit Mag; JV Capt Bsktbl; Hon Roll; Cert Of Achvt Accomplshmnts Math 83; Plaq Recog Excptnl Lectr Chrch 84; 1st Fire Safty Slogan Cntst 85; Adelphi U; Pre Law.

WALCHER, SUSAN; St Pauls School For Girls; Towson, MD; (Y); VP Church Yth Grp; Cmnty Wkr; Church Choir; Lit Mag; Stat Bsktbl; Var Cheerleading; Mgr(s); Hon Roll; Alumni Sclrshp 85-86.

WALDEN, ELIZABETH; Sherwood HS; Brookeville, MD; (Y); AFS; Church Yth Grp; Ski Clb; Spanish Clb; SADD; Yrbk Ed-Chief; Yrbk Phtg; Yrbk Rptr; Yrbk Stf; Lit Mag; Agns Sailr Awd-Ptry 84; 1st-2nd Pl Mdls-Synchrnzd Swmmng 85; U Of MI; Arch.

WALESBY, AME H; Notre Dame Preparatory Schl; Ruxton, MD; (Y); Art Clb; Cmnty Wkr; Debate Tm; 4-H; German Clb; Math Tm; Rep Soph Cls; Im Badmtn; Im Bsktbl; Im Socr; German Natl Hnr Soc 85; Animal Sci Schlrshp VA Tech 86; VA Polytech; Vet Srgn.

WALKER, GREG; Thomas Stone HS; Waldorf, MD; (S); Chrmn Chess Clb; Debate Tm; Latin Clb; Concert Band; Mrchg Band; School Musical; Var L Golf; High Hon Roll; Hon Roll; NHS; Top 10 Earth Sci Stu 84; Solo/Ens Bnd Fstvl Excllnt Ratg 84 & 85; All Cnty H S Bnd 84 & 85; GA Inst Tech; Archit.

WALKER, JENIFER; Brunswick HS; Jefferson, MD; (Y); 4-H; Trs FFA; Girl Scts; Spanish Clb; Teachers Aide; Chorus; School Musical; School Play; Nwsp Stf; Yrbk Stf.

WALKER, JOHN; Oakland Mills HS; Columbia, MD; (Y); 60/240; Boy Scts; Latin Clb; Im Mgr Bsbl; Hon Roll; Ntl Merit SF; Engrng.

WALKER, NANCY; Colonel Richardson HS; Federalsburg, MD; (Y); Am Leg Aux Girls St; Church Yth Grp; Drama Clb; Teachers Aide; School Play; Nwsp Ed-Chief; Yrbk Ed-Chief; Dnfth Awd; NHS; Wesley Coll DE; Comm.

WALKER, ROBIN; Northern HS; Chesapeake Bch, MD; (Y); Hosp Aide; Trs VICA; Hon Roll; Health Occup Stu Amer; Resp Ther.

WALL, MARIA N; C Milton Wright HS; Bel Air, MD; (Y); 20/262; Cmnty Wkr; JA; Math Clb; Rep Frsh Cls; Powder Puff Ftbl; JV Sftbl; Var Trk; Hon Roll; NHS; Minorities Engr Prog VA Tech 85; Civil Engr.

WALL, WILLIAM; Governor Thomas Johnson HS; Frederick, MD; (Y); 27/309; Boy Scts; Church Yth Grp; VP Science Clb; Teachers Aide; L Wrstlng; God Cntry Awd; Hon Roll; NHS; PTSA Hnr Awd 83; Sci Dept Awd 83, 85, & 86; Army ROTC 4 Yr Schlrshp 86; WV U; Chem.

WALLACE, ALICIA; Forest Park SR HS; Baltimore, MD; (Y); Church Yth Grp; FBLA; Library Aide; ROTC; Church Choir; Drill Tm; Sec Soph Cls; Hst Jr Cls; Hon Roll; CAST 85-86; Med.

WALLACE, KEVIN; Fort Hill HS; Cumberland, MD; (Y); 1/254; Pres Church Yth Grp; Nwsp Ed-Chief; Nwsp Phtg; Pres Jr Cls; VP Sr Cls; Rep Stu Cncl; Var JV Bsbl; Cit Awd; High Hon Roll; NHS; Stu Cncl Hse Awd 86; Mind, Bdy, Spirt Awd YMCA 86; U Of MD; Phrmcy.

WALLACE, MANDY; North Harford HS; Whitehall, MD; (Y); Art Clb; 4-H; French Clb; Lit Mag; Mgr(s); Swmmng; 4-H Awd; Hon Roll; Hnr Rl 85-86; Intl Bus.

WALLACE, SCARLET; Fairmont Heights HS; Hyattsville, MD; (Y); 2/250; Dance Clb; Chorus; Church Choir; Rep Jr Cls; Var Cheerleading; Cit Awd; Hon Roll; NHS; Prfct Atten Awd; Math Awd; Spnsh And Mock Trial Awds; Pre Med.

WALLER, PAULA; Colonel Richardson HS; Federalsburg, MD; (Y); 14/107; Am Leg Aux Girls St; Church Yth Grp; French Clb; SADD; Teachers Aide; Band; Chorus; Sec Frsh Cls; Rep Soph Cls; Trs Jr Cls; Natl Bus Womn & A Locl Sorty & Solo Cup Co Schlrshps 86; Salisbury ST Coll; Socl Wrk.

WALLINGTON, CHARLYCE; Takoma Acad; Columbia, MD; (S); 1/90; Church Yth Grp; Pep Clb; Teachers Aide; Sec Jr Cls; Var JV Cheerleading; High Hon Roll; Hon Roll; NHS; Chrldng 81-86; Hgh Hnr Rll 83-86; Ntl Hnr Soc 84-86; Oakwood Coll; Pre Med.

WALLIS, DENISE D; Connelly Schl Of The Holy Child; Chevy Chase, MD; (Y); Art Clb; Dance Clb; Model UN; Red Cross Aide; Service Clb; Stage Crew; Variety Show; High Hon Roll; NHS; Frnch IV & Algbra II Awds 84-85; Comp, Algbra III/Trig & Frnch V Awds 85-86; Accntnt.

WALLMARK, JERI LYNN; ST Marys Ryken HS; Mechanicsville, MD; (S); FBLA; Rep Jr Cls; Fld Hcky; Capt Sftbl; High Hon Roll; Hon Roll; NHS; Church Yth Grp; Yrbk Stf; Cls Princss 84-85; Phys Sci Awd; Typng Awd; Loyola Coll; Elem Ed.

WALLS, TODD; Crossland HS; Temple Hills, MD; (Y); 5/380; Math Tm; Ski Clb; Capt Socr; Tennis; Capt Wrstlng; Hon Roll; NHS; Outstndng Yng Amer, Rotary Clb, P G Cnty 86; Hnr Acadmc & Athl Exclince, US Army Rsrv 86; MVP Soccer; MD U; Engr.

WALSH, CHRIS; North Carroll HS; Hampstead, MD; (Y); Teachers Aide; Varsity Clb; Rep Jr Cls; Rep Stu Cncl; JV Var Bsktbl; JV Var Socr; High Hon Roll; Hon Roll; Carroll Cnty Schlr Athlt Tm 86; WTTR AM Athlt Of Wk Bsktbl 85; All Conf MVAL Tms, Hnbl Mntn Bsktbl; Bus.

WALSH, COLLEEN; St Vincent Pallotti HS; Largo, MD; (S); Spanish Clb; Nwsp Rptr; Nwsp Phtg; Yrbk Rptr; Yrbk Stf; Pom Pon; High Hon Roll; Hon Roll; Spanish NHS; U Of MD; Jrnlsm.

WALSH, COLLEEN; Westminster HS; Westminster, MD; (Y); GAA; Rep Stu Cncl; Fld Hcky; Tennis; Hon Roll; Aud/Vis; Girl Scts; Math Tm; Ski Clb; Yrbk Phtg.

WALSH, DENNIS; Loyola HS At Blakefld; Baltimore, MD; (Y); Letterman Clb; Pep Clb; SADD; Varsity Clb; JV Var Bsbl; Im JV Bsktbl; JV Diving; High Hon Roll; Bus.

WALSH, MARYANN; St Marys HS; Annapolis, MD; (Y); Art Clb; Church Yth Grp; Civic Clb; Cmnty Wkr; Drama Clb; Pep Clb; Service Clb; Spanish Clb; SADD; School Play; Cthlc Dghtrs Amer Ptry Awd 83; Jrnlst.

WALSH, PAMELA; St Johns At Prospect Hall; Frederick, MD; (Y); 6/40; Science Clb; Nwsp Phtg; Nwsp Rptr; Nwsp Sprt Ed; Nwsp Stf; Lit Mag; Bsktbl; Crs Cntry; Tennis; High Hon Roll; 3rd Pl ST-WD Essay Cntst 85.

WALSTON, MARK; Pocomoke HS; Pocomoke City, MD; (Y); 15/90; AFS; Drama Clb; Math Tm; Spanish Clb; School Play; Ftbl; Coll Crdt 2 Cls Engl 101 & Math 111 Schlrshp U Of MD Coll 86; Worcester Cnty Vlntrsm Appr Awd 85-86; NC A & T; Comp Engrng.

WALTERHOEFER, KIMBERLY; St Marys HS; Annapolis, MD; (Y); 21/120; Drama Clb; Hosp Aide; Pep Clb; Ski Clb; Lcrss; Sftbl; NHS; NEDT Awd; Intnl Clb; Bowling; Military Order World War Essay Cont 86; Towson ST U; Psychology.

WALTERS, MICHELLE S; Towson HS; Towson, MD; (Y); French Clb; JA; Trs VP Key Clb; Political Wkr; School Play; Stage Crew; Hst VP Stu Cncl; Hon Roll; Pres Sec NHS; Voice Dem Awd; Pres MD Gvrnr Yth Advsry Cncl 86-87; TV Rprtr Hst Of Yng Crtcs & Crme File 85-87; Bst Slsprsn JA 83; Ivy League U; Pltcl Sci.

WALTON, AVERY; Patterson SR HS; Baltimore, MD; (Y); 4-H; Varsity Clb; Stage Crew; Bsktbl; Wrstlng; Kentucky ST U; Cmptr Sci.

WALZAK, JAMIE; Institute Of Notre Dame; Baltimore, MD; (Y); 5/144; Church Yth Grp; Math Clb; Scholastic Bowl; Pres Stu Cncl; High Hon Roll; NHS; Schl Scholar 84-87; Engr.

WANG, ANTHONY F; Gaithersburg HS; Gaithersburg, MD; (Y); 132/568; Band; Concert Band; Mrchg Band; Var L Swmmng; Ntl Merit Ltr; Pres Schlr; U Of IL; Engrng.

WANG, KAREN; Thomas S Wootton HS; Irvine, CA; (Y); Pres JA; Yrbk Phtg; Yrbk Rptr; Yrbk Sprt Ed; Rep Stu Cncl; Var Pom Pon; Var L Tennis; Hon Roll; Art Clb; Cmnty Wkr; Appeared On Natl Pres Acadmc Ftnss Awd Pposter 85-86; Stu Life Sectnn 85; Awd-Natl Schltc Prss All Ame; Bus.

WANG, LAWRENCE P; Thomas S Wootton HS; Rockville, MD; (Y); Chess Clb; Computer Clb; Debate Tm; SADD; Yrbk Stf; JV Trk; Hon Roll; NHS; Lebanon Vly Yth Schlrs Pgm 86; W MD Coll Summr Scholar Pgm 86; Duke U; Pre-Med.

WANG, SUE; Thomas S Wootton HS; Gaithersburg, MD; (Y); AFS; VP JA; Ski Clb; SADD; Lit Mag; JV Swmmng; Hon Roll; U Of MI-ANN Arbor; Busnss Mgmt.

WANNER, JEANNE; Mercy HS; Baltimore, MD; (Y); Model UN; Nwsp Rptr; Nwsp Sprt Ed; Nwsp Stf; Yrbk Rptr; Rep Soph Cls; Sec Jr Cls; Rep Stu Cncl; NHS; Fllws Schlrshp-High Point Coll 86-87; Flame Awd 85; High Point Coll; Bus Law.

WARD, CHRIS; Landon HS; Bethesda, MD; (S); Drama Clb; SADD; VP Band; VP Concert Band; VP Jazz Band; Variety Show; Var Socr; Hon Roll; Louis Armstrong Jazz Awd 85; Hnrs Recitals Schl Of Music WA Consvrtry; Arts.

WARD, CRYSTAL; Ft Hill HS; Cumberland, MD; (Y); Church Yth Grp; Office Aide; Teachers Aide; Drill Tm; Orch; Off Sr Cls; Pom Pon; Ltr Drl Tm 87; Allegory CC; Secr.

WARD, JEFF; North Hagerstown HS; Hagerstown, MD; (Y); 15/325; Varsity Clb; Jazz Band; Pres Soph Cls; Pres Sr Cls; Var L Socr; Var Capt Wrstlng; Ntl Merit SF; U S Naval Acad; Physcs.

WARD, JOHN; Fort Hill HS; Cumberland, MD; (Y); Off Soph Cls; Off Jr Cls; Off Sr Cls; Rep Stu Cncl; Var Capt Crs Cntry; Var Tennis; JV Var Trk; Hon Roll; Outstndng Crs Cntry Rnr 85-86; Al-Cnty Crs Cntry Tm-Allegany Cnty 85-86.

WARD, JOSEPH; La Plata HS; Charlotte Hall, MD; (Y); Debate Tm; Office Aide; Mrchg Band; Symp Band; Off Frsh Cls; Off Soph Cls; Off Jr Cls; Off Sr Cls; Tennis; La Plata Svc Awd 85-86; Cls Delg Awd 85-86; Band Awd 85-86; Boston U; Pub Rel.

WARD, KATHLEEN T; Mount Hebron HS; Ellicott City, MD; (Y); 31/271; Hosp Aide; Q&S; Yrbk Bus Mgr; Sec Stu Cncl; Hon Roll; NHS; Chrmn AFS; Art Clb; Chrmn Church Yth Grp; Milton L Shifman Schlrshp 86; Mt Hebron HS Journalism Awd Bus Mgr 86; JROTC Indiv Drill Awd 84; Shepherd Coll; Bus Admin.

WARD, KRISTEN; Liberty HS; Finksburg, MD; (S); Gym; JV Capt Vllybl; High Hon Roll; Hon Roll; Bus.

WARD, LAMONT; Washington HS; Manokin, MD; (Y); 7/121; Art Clb; Church Yth Grp; Computer Clb; Tennis; High Hon Roll; Tnns Schlrshp 86; SR Athltc Awd 86; Sntrl Schlrshp 86; UMES; Arch.

WARD, MELISSA; La Plata HS; La Plata, MD; (S); Church Yth Grp; Debate Tm; Ed Yrbk Rptr; Rep Jr Cls; Hon Roll; Jr NHS; NHS; Assn Amer U Women Sci Fair 85; Hnrb Mntn Sci Fair 84; Interior Desgn.

WARD JR, NATHANIEL; Snow Hill HS; Snow Hill, MD; (S); AFS; Am Leg Boys St; Trs Church Yth Grp; FBLA; VP Soph Cls; VP Jr Cls; Pres Stu Cncl; Hon Roll; VP NHS.

WARD, NICOLE; Poromac HS; Suitland, MD; (Y); ROTC; Color Guard; Drill Tm; Rep Jr Cls; Sftbl; High Hon Roll; Hon Roll; Natl Sojourners Awd Air Force 86; Cade Of Qrtr & Year 86; Howard U; Law.

WARE, DEBORAH; Northwestern HS; Mt Rainier, MD; (Y); Pep Clb; VICA; VP Jr Cls; VP Sr Cls; Trk; Cit Awd; Hon Roll; Jr NHS; Ntl HS Trck Hnrable Mtn Trck All-Amer 84; Med Assistnt Cmpltn Cert 86; Nrsng Adm.

WARE, RITA; Wicomico SR HS; Salisbury, MD; (Y); 13/244; Church Yth Grp; Cmnty Wkr; JCL; Latin Clb; Chorus; High Hon Roll; Hon Roll; NHS; Pres Schlr; Merit Schlrshp 86; Pres Acad Ftns Awd 86; Slsbry ST Coll; Phrmclgy.

WARFIELD, HEATHER; Connelly School Of The Holy Child; Rockville, MD; (Y); Pres Church Yth Grp; Speech Tm; SADD; Rep Jr Cls; Stat Fld Hcky; Stat Lcrss; Pce Comm Trip To Soviet Union, & Fine Arts Wk Speech Cntst Wnr 85; Exchng Studnt 86; Speech Pathology.

WARFIELD JR, HOWARD; Southern HS; Baltimore, MD; (Y); Draftng.

WARING, DAVID; Lackey Md; Marbury, MD; (Y); Var Bsbl; Var Bsktbl; Var Ftbl; Var Trk; Hon Roll; Maryland U; Constructn Wrk.

WARNER, CHERYL N; Francis Scott Key HS; Westminster, MD; (Y); Science Clb; VP Spanish Clb; Teachers Aide; Pres Trs Band; Concert Band; Jazz Band; Mrchg Band; Pep Band; School Play; Rep Jr Cls; WV U Hnr Bnd 85; Towson ST U Hnr Bnd 85; All Cnty Bnd & Orchstr 86; Shprd Coll; Msc Thrpy.

WARNER, TRACY; Wicomico SR HS; Salisbury, MD; (Y); Aud/Vis; Sec Drama Clb; Pep Clb; SADD; Teachers Aide; Thesps; School Play; Stage Crew; Lit Mag; High Hon Roll; Schl Acdmc Ltr 85-86; Chrch Asstnt Tchr Ltl Thtr Dir 85; AMRCN Muscl & Drmtc Acad; Drma.

WARNICK, RENEE; Northern Garrett HS; Frostburg, MD; (Y); English Clb; GAA; Varsity Clb; Nwsp Phtg; Nwsp Rptr; Var Bsktbl; Hon Roll; MD Cntrs Gftd & Tlntd 83-85; Stu Cncl Stu Actvties Cmmtee 84-85; Cngrssnl HS Art Comptn 86; Fine Arts.

WARO, DARRIN; Great Mills HS; Patuxent River, MD; (Y); Var L Bsbl; Var L Mgr(s); Hon Roll; Ntl Merit Ltr; Prfct Atten Awd; Algbra I Awd 83-84; Spnsh I Awd 83-84; Engr.

WARREN, AMOS; Leonardtown HS; Great Mills, MD; (Y); Church Yth Grp; 4-H; Band; Mrchg Band; Symp Band; Pres Sr Cls; Var L Crs Cntry; Var L Tennis; High Hon Roll; NHS; Engl.

WARREN, DANIELLE; Mc Donough HS; La Plata, MD; (Y); Church Yth Grp; Cmnty Wkr; Hosp Aide; Intnl Clb; SADD; Teachers Aide; Chorus; Stage Crew; Variety Show; Yrbk Stf; Miss Teen Pgnt Certfct Achvt 86; Nrsng.

WARREN, LAKEESHA; Dunbar SR HS; Baltimore, MD; (Y); Church Yth Grp; Dance Clb; Debate Tm; 4-H; Hosp Aide; Office Aide; Pep Clb; Red Cross Aide; Hon Roll; VP Frsh Cls; Towson ST U; Rn.

WARREN, LESLIE; Parkside HS; Sal, MD; (Y); Flag Corp; Yrbk Stf; Rep Frsh Cls; Rep Jr Cls; Trs Sr Cls; Hon Roll; Campbell U; Phrmcy.

WARREN, ROB; Thomas Stone HS; Hughesville, MD; (S); VP Debate Tm; Trs Math Clb; Science Clb; Ski Clb; High Hon Roll; Hon Roll; Jr NHS; NHS; Prfct Atten Awd.

WARREN, SIMON; Rockville HS; Rockville, MD; (Y); Pres Chess Clb; Debate Tm; Political Wkr; Lit Mag; Stu Cncl; Hon Roll; Natl Hspnc Schlr Awd Schlrshp Fnlst 86; Natl Yng Ldrs Conf Hnrs 85; MD U; Engl.

WARRINGTON, CAROL; Parkside HS; Pittsville, MD; (Y); Spanish Clb; Varsity Clb; Band; Chorus; Church Choir; Concert Band; Mrchg Band; Symp Band; JV Fld Hcky; Gym; Music.

WARTHEN, MARY C; Mount Desales Acad; Baltimore, MD; (Y); Drama Clb; Hosp Aide; Lit Mag; JV Cheerleading; Var Fld Hcky; Var Lcrss; Hon Roll; NEDT Awd; Cmnty Wkr; Chorus; Baltimore Cnty Page Pgm Towson MD 85; 250 Hr Awd-Vlntr St Agnes Hosp 85; Employee Mth 86; Scndry Ed.

WASH, RONALD LOREN; Thomas Stone SR HS; Waldorf, MD; (Y); JV Bsbl; High Hon Roll; Hon Roll; Bus.

WASHINGTON, BONNIE; Notre Dame Preparatory School; Towson, MD; (Y); Math Tm; Service Clb; Nwsp Rptr; Fld Hcky; Socr; French Hon Soc; Hon Roll; NHS; Opt Clb Awd; Intl Rel.

WASHINGTON, JENNIFER; Bladensburg HS; Capitol Hts, MD; (Y); Church Yth Grp; Library Aide; Teachers Aide; Band; Sec Frsh Cls; VP Stu Cncl; Cit Awd; Hon Roll; Jr NHS; NHS; USAF Acad; Med.

WASHINGTON, TIMOTHY; Crossland HS; Camp Springs, MD; (Y); 33/388; Boys Clb Am; Trs Church Yth Grp; Varsity Clb; Church Choir; Stu Cncl; Var Capt Ftbl; Var Capt Trk; Hon Roll; Masonic Awd; Rotary Awd; U Of Pttsbrgh Financial Awd 86; Acdmc Excllnc Awd Prnc Geo Cnty 84-85; Prsdntl Acdmc Ftnss Awd 86; U Of Pittsburgh; Elec Engnrng.

WATANABE, LESLIE MICHELE; Charles W Woodward HS; Rockville, MD; (Y); AFS; Spanish Clb; SADD; Spanish NHS; Arts Recog & Tlnt Srch Fnlst 86; Schltc Arts Awds 85 & 86; MD Dstngshd Schlr In Visual Arts 85; Pntg/Sclptr.

WATERFIELD, AMY; Sparrows Point HS; Baltimore, MD; (Y); Am Leg Aux Girls St; Church Yth Grp; Scholastic Bowl; Yrbk Stf; Rep Stu Cncl; Cheerleading; Tennis; Hon Roll; NHS; Hugh O Brien Ambssdr 85; Intl Bus.

WATERS, NICOL; Snow Hill HS; Snow Hill, MD; (Y); AFS; Church Yth Grp; Girl Scts; Pep Clb; Church Choir; Stage Crew; Var Cheerleading; Var Sftbl; Merchndsg.

WATKINS, ANGELA; Western SR HS; Baltimore, MD; (Y); FBLA; Teachers Aide; Band; Delta Sigma Theta Inc 86; Morgan U; Bus Admin.

WATKINS, CHRISTINE; Our Lady Of Mt Carmel HS; Baltimore, MD; (Y); 1/43; School Play; Yrbk Stf; Off Soph Cls; Off Jr Cls; Pres Stu Cncl; Cheerleading; Capt Sftbl; High Hon Roll; VP NHS; St Schlr; Edgar M Ganster Awd K Of C 86; Pres Phys Ftns Awd 85-86; MVP Sftbl; UMBC; Vet.

WATKINS, TONYA; Eastern HS; Baltimore, MD; (Y); 20/206; Church Yth Grp; Computer Clb; Dance Clb; Drama Clb; Girl Scts; Library Aide; Math Clb; Ski Clb; Spanish Clb; Church Choir; MD ST Schrlshp 86; Lenora E Crpntr Mem Schlrshp 86; Bltmr Cty Pblc Schl Bus Mgt Div Sch 86; Morgan ST U; Acctg.

WATKINS, TRACIE A; Western HS; Baltimore, MD; (Y); Cmnty Wkr; French Clb; JA; Political Wkr; Red Cross Aide; Pom Pon; Ntl Merit SF; Lawyr.

WATKINSON, ERIC; Parkville HS; Baltimore, MD; (Y); Cmnty Wkr; Teachers Aide; Band; Rep Soph Cls; Rep Jr Cls; JV Var Bsbl; JV Var Bsktbl; JV Var Ftbl; High Hon Roll; Hon Roll; MVP ST SF Bsktbl Tm, 3rd Tm All Balt Cnty 85-86; Hnrbl Ment All Balt Cnty Bsbl 86; Sprts Comm.

WATSON, CHERYL; Thomas Stone HS; Waldorf, MD; (S); Church Yth Grp; 4-H; VP FBLA; Science Clb; SADD; Church Choir; Mrchg Band; Symp Band; High Hon Roll; Lion Awd; Amercn Yth Hnrs Musicns 83-85; U Of MD; Bus.

WATSON, DEBORAH; Western HS; Baltimore, MD; (Y); Church Choir; Yrbk Stf; Crs Cntry; Trk; Hon Roll; Morgan St Upward Bound Prgrm 84-86; Towson ST U; Mrktng.

WATSON, KAREN; Mardela HS; Hebron, MD; (Y); Church Yth Grp; Letterman Clb; Chorus; Church Choir; Concert Band; Drm Mjr(t); Mrchg Band; School Musical; Sftbl; Hon Roll; UMBC; Nrsng.

WATSON, KELLY; James M Bennett SR HS; Quantico, MD; (Y); French Clb; FBLA; Girl Scts; Color Guard; Drill Tm; Flag Corp; Stage Crew; Hon Roll; Srvce Awd 85; Elem Ed.

WATSON, LYNN; Sherwood HS; Olney, MD; (Y); 42/312; Model UN; Ski Clb; School Musical; Nwsp Rptr; Stu Cncl; Cheerleading; Score Keeper; Ntl Hnr Soc; NAIMUN; Co Captn Chrldng Sq; NC ST U; Bus.

WATSON, MICHELLE GENEEN; Eleanor Roosevelt SR HS; Lanham, MD; (S); Church Yth Grp; Cmnty Wkr; Girl Scts; Red Cross Aide; Hst Pom Pon; Powder Puff Ftbl; God Cntry Awd; Hon Roll; Med Asst Cert 85; MD U Coll Prk Outstndng Mnrty Stu 85; U Of MD; Bio Sci.

WATSON, TERRI; Kenwood SR HS; Baltimore, MD; (Y); Cmnty Wkr; SADD; Hst Frsh Cls; Off Soph Cls; Off Jr Cls; Off Sr Cls; VP Stu Cncl; Var Fld Hcky; Var Lcrss; VP NHS; Med.

WATSON, WILLIAM BRIAN; Calvert HS; Prince Frederick, MD; (Y); 22/256; VICA; Chorus; Yrbk Stf; Hon Roll; Ntl Art Hon Soc-Hnry Stu 86; Calvert Career Ctr-Prncpls Awd, Outstndg Svc Awds 86; U Of MD Baltimore; Grphc Dsgn.

WATTERS, MARIE; La Plata HS; Waldorf, MD; (Y); Cmnty Wkr; Teachers Aide; Concert Band; Mrchg Band; Pep Band; School Musical; Symp Band; Rep Soph Cls; Hon Roll; Bd Of Ed Awd Superior Rtg ST Solo & Ensmbl Fstvl 86.

WATTS, MICHELLE; Westminster SR HS; Westminster, MD; (Y); Church Yth Grp; JA; Spanish Clb; Band; Church Choir; Color Guard; Flag Corp; Hon Roll; Comp Sci.

WAUGH, WILLIAM E; Maurice J Mc Donough HS; White Plains, MD; (Y); English Clb; Intnl Clb; Rep Stu Cncl; Hon Roll; MD Ntl Bnk Emplye 86; Finc.

WAY, ROBIN; Maurice J Mc Donough HS; White Plains, MD; (Y); Drama Clb; FBLA; Intnl Clb; Varsity Clb; Rep Frsh Cls; Rep Soph Cls; L Var Cheerleading; Gym; High Hon Roll; Hon Roll; Psych.

WAY, RUTH; Rising Sun HS; Conowingo, MD; (Y); 11/169; Am Leg Aux Girls St; Church Yth Grp; Spanish Clb; SADD; Church Choir; Nwsp Rptr; Yrbk Rptr; VP Sr Cls; Fld Hcky; Hon Roll; Sci & Engrng Apprntcshp Prog 85-86; U MD Baltimore Cnty; Lawyer.

WEAKLAND, SHEILA; Smithsburg HS; Cascade, MD; (Y); Computer Clb; Yrbk Stf; Bowling; Var Co-Capt Cheerleading; Stat Ftbl; High Hon Roll; Hon Roll; U Of MD; Med.

WEAVER, CHRIS; Mt St Joseph HS; Baltimore, MD; (Y); High Hon Roll; Hon Roll; U Of MD; Pre Med.

WEAVER, JOSEPH L; Allegany HS; Cumberland, MD; (Y); Sec Ski Clb; Jazz Band; Yrbk Stf; Rep Soph Cls; JV Capt Socr; Trk.

WEAVER, KRISTI; Walkersville HS; Walkersville, MD; (Y); GAA; SADD; Sec Trs Band; Sec Jr Cls; Stu Cncl; Bsktbl; Fld Hcky; Sftbl; Trk; Hon Roll; Outstndng French Stu Awd 85-86; All Around Stu Awd 83-86; Lttrs Earned In Sports Six 83-86.

WEAVER, LANCE; Valley HS; Barton, MD; (Y); Ski Clb; Var Bsbl; Var Ftbl; Hon Roll; Forestry.

WEAVER, ROSITA; Acad Of The Holy Names; Silver Spring, MD; (Y); Art Clb; Dance Clb; Hosp Aide; Chorus; School Musical; VP Sr Cls; Var Trk; Coll Prep Georgetown U 85; Supr Perf Coll Prep Alg Awd; Med.

WEBB, DEBORAH; Lackey HS; White Plains, MD; (Y); Am Leg Aux Girls St; FBLA; Ski Clb; SADD; Variety Show; Trs Frsh Cls; Rep Stu Cncl; Var L Pom Pon; Stat Sftbl; High Hon Roll; Pol Sci.

WEBB, STEVEN; Perryville HS; Colora, MD; (Y); 2/120; Am Leg Boys St; VP Intnl Clb; Varsity Clb; Band; Pres Stu Cncl; Var Capt Ftbl; Var Trk; Var Capt Wrstlng; Hon Roll; NHS; Engnrng.

WEBBER, PAULA L; Surrattsville HS; Clinton, MD; (Y); 30/310; Church Yth Grp; Cmnty Wkr; Debate Tm; FBLA; GAA; JA; Pep Clb; Radio Clb; Red Cross Aide; Spanish Clb; Emory & Henry Coll; Mass Cmmnct.

WEBER, CINDY; Kenwood HS; Baltimore, MD; (Y); Rep SADD; Rep Frsh Cls; Rep Soph Cls; Rep Jr Cls; Rep Stu Cncl; JV Socr; Var Tennis; Hon Roll; NHS; Nrsng.

WEBER, ROBERT L; Bethesda-Chevy Chase HS; Washington, DC; (Y); 36/469; Boy Scts; Computer Clb; French Clb; Concert Band; Jazz Band; Mrchg Band; Pep Band; School Musical; American U; Dentstry.

WEBSTER, JEFF; Westminster SR HS; Westminster, MD; (Y); Letterman Clb; Varsity Clb; Rep Frsh Cls; Var Capt Crs Cntry; Var L Trk; Hon Roll; Twsn ST; Anthrplgy.

WEBSTER, JENNIFER; Fallston HS; Baldwin, MD; (Y); Church Yth Grp; FBLA; Variety Show; Tennis; High Hon Roll; Hon Roll; Acadmc Ltr 86; Clercl Awd 86; Vanguard Schlrshp-Villa Julie Coll 86; Villa Julie Coll; Medcl Secy.

WEBSTER, KAREN; Du Val HS; Seabrook, MD; (Y); Office Aide; Drm Mjr(t); Trs Symp Band; Pom Pon; Hon Roll; U MD Coll Park.

WEBSTER, SUSAN; South Carroll HS; Sykesville, MD; (Y); Church Yth Grp; Spanish Clb; High Hon Roll; Hon Roll; NHS; St Jsphs Unsng Hr 85; Mrt Schlstc Awd 86; Mount ST Marys Coll.

WEDLOCK, TYRONE; Northwestern HS; Baltimore, MD; (Y); ROTC; Hon Roll; Outstndng Geom Achvts 85-86; Outstndng Alg Achvts 84-85; Engrng.

WEEKS, JARSIE; Eastern HS; Baltimore, MD; (Y); Church Yth Grp; Dance Clb; Office Aide; Im Bowling; Var Trk; Hon Roll; NHS; Goucher Coll MD; Engrng.

WEEKS, SHANNON NOEL; Bethesda-Chevy Chase HS; Chevy Chase, MD; (Y); 133/449; Concert Band; Jazz Band; Mrchg Band; School Musical; Symp Band; Variety Show; Capt Var Bsktbl; Ftbl; Var Socr; Var Sftbl; St Marys Coll-MD; Music.

WEEKS, WENDY L; Mt Lake Independent Baptist HS; Loch Lynn, MD; (Y); 1/4; Church Yth Grp; Cmnty Wkr; Church Choir; Acad Hons Awd-Pensacola Christian Coll 86; Pensacola Christian Coll; RN.

WEEMS, KRISTAL T; Oxon Hill HS; Ft Washington, MD; (Y); VP Pres Church Yth Grp; Dance Clb; Office Aide; Pep Clb; Teachers Aide; Band; Church Choir; Jazz Band; Symp Band; Cheerleading; 1st Pl Danc Grp Metro Tlnt Srch 85; 1st Pl Danc Grp In Tony Grant Tlnt Unltd 85; Towson ST Coll; Psych.

WEEMS JR, WILLIAM E; Calvert HS; Port Republic, MD; (Y); Church Yth Grp; Carpenter.

WEESE, BRIAN; Calvert Christian HS; Dunkirk, MD; (Y); Computer Clb; 4-H; Key Clb; School Play; JV Var Bsktbl; Var Crs Cntry; Var Socr; Var Trk; 4-H Awd; NHS; MD ST 4-H Key Clb & Clvr For Ctznshp, Achvt & Ldrshp 85; Comp.

WEIBLE, KERRI LYNN; Bohemia Manor HS; Earleville, MD; (Y); 33/92; Cmnty Wkr; FBLA; Girl Scts; Teachers Aide; Band; Chorus; Bsktbl; Hon Roll; Acad All Amer Large Div 84; Natl Ldrshp/Svc Awd 85; Bus Admin.

WEILACHER, GEORGE; Landon Schl; Potomac, MD; (S); Church Yth Grp; Math Tm; Band; Concert Band; Jazz Band; Nwsp Phtg; Ed Yrbk Phtg; Var L Ftbl; Hon Roll; Cmnty Wkr; Louis Armstrong Jazz Awd 86; Physcl Sci.

WEINER, MARCI A; Largo HS; Bowie, MD; (Y); 3/440; VP JA; Model UN; Office Aide; Temple Yth Grp; Ed Lit Mag; Capt Var Cheerleading; Hon Roll; NHS; MD Dstnghsd Scholar Hon Men 85-86; U MD; Comm.

WEINER, NEAL; Thomas S Wootton HS; Rockville, MD; (Y); Model UN; Radio Clb; Nwsp Stf; Stu Cncl; Hon Roll; Ntl Merit Ltr; NEDT Awd; Aud/Vis; Nwsp Rptr; Psych Fair Awd; Co Fndr, Pres, VP Frisbee Clb; Exec Intrshp TV; Comm.

WEINGARTEN, NICOLE; Gaithersburg HS; Gaithersburg, MD; (Y); Cmnty Wkr; SADD; Trs Temple Yth Grp; Sec Stu Cncl; Var Fld Hcky; French Hon Soc; High Hon Roll; Hon Roll; NHS; Intl Reltns.

WEINHOLT, SHEILA H; Arlington Baptist HS; Baltimore, MD; (S); FCA; Orch; Yrbk Stf; Trs Jr Cls; Trs Sr Cls; Var Bsktbl; Var Mgr(s); Var Score Keeper; Stat Sftbl; Stat Vllybl; 2nd Pl Rifle Shooting-Optimist Clb Of MD 85; Bus Mgt.

WEINHOUSE, BRETT A; Baltimore Actors Theatre Conserve; Baltimore, MD; (S); AFS; Art Clb; Dance Clb; Drama Clb; Chorus; School Musical; School Play; Stage Crew; Variety Show; NHS; Muscl Theatr.

WEINREICH, SANDRA; Queen Annes County HS; Kennedyville, MD; (Y); Drama Clb; French Clb; School Play; High Hon Roll; Hon Roll; NHS; Ntl Merit Schol; Presidental Accad Fitness Awd 86; Frank Owen Memorial Bk Schlrshp 86; MD Genl ST Schlrshp 86; WA Coll.

WEIRICK, SHARON M; Wicomico SR HS; Parsonsburg, MD; (Y); 23/244; VP Spanish Clb; Pres SADD; Drm Mjr(t); Mrchg Band; Symp Band; Rep Frsh Cls; Rep Soph Cls; Rep Jr Cls; Rep Sr Cls; Hon Roll; CC Baltimore; Dntl Hygn.

WEISS, CYNTHIA H; Gaithersburg HS; Gaithersburg, MD; (Y); 71/568; Mrchg Band; Orch; School Musical; Symp Band; NFL; Temple Yth Grp; Hon Roll; NHS; Montgomery Co Yth Symphny; Hye Hay Mem Awd; Montgomery Co SR Hnr Band; St Marys Invtnl Hnr Band; Miami U Ohio; Scl Stds.

WEISS, SARA; Hebrew Acad Of Greater Wshngtn; Silver Spring, MD; (Y); Debate Tm; Hosp Aide; FHA; Science Clb; Temple Yth Grp; Nwsp Phtg; Nwsp Stf; Yrbk Phtg; Yrbk Stf; Pres Frsh Cls; Bio.

WEITZEL, JENNIFER; Potomac HS; Temple Hills, MD; (Y); Church Yth Grp; Science Clb; Band; Concert Band; Lit Mag; Stat Bsbl; Co-Capt Pom Pon; Hon Roll; NHS; I Dare You Awd Ledrshp 86; SR Princess Intl Order Of Jobs Daughters 84; Towson ST U; Soc Wrkr.

WEKER JR, WILLIAM R; Dundalk SR HS; Baltimore, MD; (Y); 37/297; Band; Off Soph Cls; Off Jr Cls; Stu Cncl; High Hon Roll; Hon Roll; NHS; Opt Clb Awd; Engl Gftd & Tlntd Pgm 83-87; Mrch Of Dms Wlk-A-Thn 83-86; Jhns Hpkns Cncr Fndtn Bwl-A-Thn 83-86; Pre-Med.

WELBORN, RACHEL; Walbrook SR HS; Baltimore, MD; (Y); Cmnty Wkr; French Clb; FBLA; Pres Frsh Cls; Pres Soph Cls; Rep Jr Cls; Stu Cncl; Crs Cntry; Trk; Hon Roll; Outstndg Stu Ldr Awd ASCBC Assocd STU Cncl Of Balto City 86; Computer Programmer.

WELCH, KRISTEN; Calvert SR HS; Pr Frederick, MD; (Y); Sec Church Yth Grp; SADD; Mrchg Band; Pom Pon; Sftbl; Hon Roll; St Marys Coll; Psych.

WELLER, SUSAN; Hammond HS; Laurel, MD; (Y); 39/264; Church Yth Grp; Q&S; Jazz Band; Nwsp Rptr; Nwsp Stf; Var L Fld Hcky; Im Lcrss; Trk; High Hon Roll; NHS; U Of VA; Wrtg.

WELLINGTON, ANGELA; Potomac HS; Temple Hills, MD; (Y); Cmnty Wkr; Dance Clb; Girl Scts; Pep Clb; Chorus; Church Choir; School Musical; School Play; Cit Awd; Hon Roll; Athltc Prtcptn Awd 81; Crtfct Accmplshmnt Awd 83; Crtfct Apprctn Awd 82; Nova; Bus.

WELLS, ANDREA; Walt Whitman HS; Bethesda, MD; (Y); Political Wkr; Teachers Aide; Yrbk Rptr; Yrbk Stf; Stu Cncl; Var JV Sftbl; Var Swmmng.

WELLS, CHRISTINE; Bowie HS; Bowie, MD; (Y); Church Yth Grp; Key Clb; Yrbk Stf; Rep Frsh Cls; Rep Soph Cls; Rep Jr Cls; Rep Sr Cls; Powder Puff Ftbl; Hon Roll; NHS; ACL NJCL Natl Latin Exam Maxima Cum Laude 86; Acad Excllnce Awd 84 & 85; Cmmnctns.

WELLS, SHARESE; La Reine HS; Washington, DC; (Y); Camera Clb; Political Wkr; Red Cross Aide; School Musical; Rep Sr Cls; Hon Roll; Cmnty Wkr; Teachers Aide; Chorus; Stage Crew; Comp Skills Awd 86; Yth City Cncl Mbr Awd 84-85; Western Civilization Hnrs 85; George Mason U; Info Resource.

WELSH, KATE; Wicomico SR HS; Salisbury, MD; (Y); French Clb; Chorus; School Musical; School Play; High Hon Roll; NHS; Tchr Svc Awd, Sccmpnst Schl Mscl 82-83; Guld Ntl Audtns, Guld Ntl Hon Roll 86; MD Music Tchr Pian Exm; Bio.

WELSH, KRISTEN E; Loch Raven HS; Glen Arm, MD; (Y); 4-H; Scholastic Bowl; Concert Band; Sec Stu Cncl; High Hon Roll; NHS; Ntl Merit SF; MD Dstngshd Schlr 85; Engl.

WELTER, ANGELA; Gaithersburg HS; Gaithersburg, MD; (Y); FFA; Key Clb; OEA; SADD; Hon Roll; Clrcl Bus.

WELTY, TONY; West Nottingham Acad; Palestine, TX; (Y); Church Yth Grp; Spanish Clb; Varsity Clb; Concert Band; Var Ftbl; Var Lcrss; Var Socr; Var Tennis; Wt Lftg; Outstndng Spnsh Stdnt 85-86; Ftbl MVP 85-86; Ldrshp Conf U Of MD 85-86.

WENDEL, COLLEEN; St Johns At Prospect Hall; Walkersville, MD; (Y); Church Yth Grp; Pres Science Clb; Rep Soph Cls; JV Bsktbl; Hon Roll; NHS; Bio.

WENGEL, MARNI; Wilde Lake HS; Columbia, MD; (Y); Drama Clb; Temple Yth Grp; Chorus; Rep Frsh Cls; Rep Stu Cncl; Var Fld Hcky.

WENGER, LANCE COLE; The Bullis Schl; Bethesda, MD; (Y); Am Leg Boys St; Boy Scts; CAP; Exploring; Model UN; JV Socr; Var Swmmng; Ntl Merit SF; NEDT Awd; Eagle Scout 85; Civil Air Patrol 85; Hist.

WENNER, VIC; C Milton Wright HS; Bel Air, MD; (Y); Jazz Band; Orch; School Musical; Stage Crew; Variety Show; Off Jr Cls; Off Sr Cls; Stu Cncl; Hon Roll; Ntl Merit Ltr; U Of MD-COLLEGE Pk; Yth Mnstry.

WENZEL, TANYA; Westminster HS; Finksburg, MD; (Y); 13/525; AFS; Model UN; School Musical; Swing Chorus; Rep Soph Cls; Var Vllybl; Gov Hon Prg Awd; NHS; Ntl Merit SF; Pres Schlr; Smmr Schl Ctr Asthtc Dvlpmnt Englnd 83; Schlstc Lttr 86; MI ST U; Chinese.

WERDEBAUGH, CATHLINA; Southern Garrett HS; Oakland, MD; (Y); Pep Clb; Varsity Clb; Concert Band; Jazz Band; Mrchg Band; Pep Band; Rep Jr Cls; Rep Sr Cls; Trs Stu Cncl; Var Sftbl; Lttrd Sftbll 85; Lttrd Bnd 86; Ptmc Prk 86.

WERNER, WENDI; Towson SR HS; Towson, MD; (Y); Cmnty Wkr; JA; Concert Band; Stage Crew; Hon Roll; Pres Schlr; UMBC; Cnmtgrphr.

WERNSDORFER, MATTHEW; Baltimore City College HS; Baltimore, MD; (S); Drama Clb; School Musical; School Play; Stage Crew; Nwsp Stf; VP Lcrss; Hon Roll; NHS; Stu Of Chmpns Of Latin III Div Of Latin Bwl 85; Spcl Effcts.

WESSEL, DONNA; Kent County HS; Worton, MD; (Y); VP Chess Clb; Trs Church Yth Grp; Hon Roll; Odyssey Mind Awd Creativity 85-86; Psych Club 83-84; U MD; French.

WESSELS, SCOT; Snow Hill HS; Snow Hill, MD; (S); Computer Clb; French Clb; Math Tm; SADD; JV Ftbl; Score Keeper; High Hon Roll; JC Awd; NHS; Rotary Awd; Engrng.

WEST, MONA; Potomac HS; Temple Hill, MD; (Y); Lit Mag; JV Crs Cntry; JV Powder Puff Ftbl; JV Var Trk; Psych.

WEST, ROBERT; Glenelg HS; Glenelg, MD; (Y); Band; Jazz Band; Mrchg Band; Symp Band; Bsktbl; Trk; Hon Roll; MD Acad Of Sci Semnr 85; Bio.

WESTBROOK, JOYCE HARPER; Perryville HS; Perryville, MD; (Y); 3/120; Rep Intnl Clb; Nwsp Ed-Chief; VP Soph Cls; Off Stu Cncl; Var L Sftbl; Hon Roll; NHS; Cmnty Wkr; Teachers Aide; Nwsp Phtg; Its Acad 84-86; G & T Smmr Cntr For Comp At Wstrn MO Coll 84; G & T Smmr Cntr For Ecnmcs 85; Wstrn MO Coll; Chld Psych.

WESTERMAN, JOANNE; Joppatowne SR HS; Joppatowne, MD; (Y); Drama Clb; Spanish Clb; Teachers Aide; Chorus; Vllybl; Hon Roll; Voice Dem Awd; SR Athlt Awd 85-86; Towson ST U; Bio.

WESTGATE, KATHERINE; Western HS; Baltimore, MD; (Y); German Clb; JV Vllybl; Med.

WESTMORE, MICHELLE; Regina HS; Camp Springs, MD; (Y); 3/79; Cmnty Wkr; Intnl Clb; Spanish Clb; Pres Jr Cls; Rep Stu Cncl; High Hon Roll; NHS; MD Distngshd Schlr Pgm 86; Natl Ldrshp & Svc Awd Wnnr 86; Pre-Med.

WESTPHAL, CHRISTOPH H; German Schl; Bethesda, MD; (Y); Dance Clb; German Clb; Ski Clb; Orch; School Play; Nwsp Rptr; Nwsp Sprt Ed; Nwsp Stf; Pres Stu Cncl; Ntl Merit SF; Hnbl Mntn David Burhop Strng Comptn 84; 1st Pl MD Strng Comptn Cello 84; 1st Stnd MD All ST Orch 85; Harvard; Biochem.

WETZEL, BLAKE; North Hagerstown HS; Hagerstown, MD; (Y); 11/277; Am Leg Boys St; French Clb; JV Bsktbl; Var L Socr; Hon Roll; NHS; Prncpls Awd For Math 85-86; Washington Coll; Econ.

WETZIG, AMBER; North East HS; North East, MD; (Y); VP 4-H; French Clb; Intnl Clb; Pep Clb; Hon Roll; VP Stu Cncl; Var L Fld Hcky; Score Keeper; L Trk; MD U; Economics.

WETZOLD, JULIE; Annapolis Area Christian Schl; Severna Park, MD; (S); Band; Chorus; Orch; Yrbk Stf; Sec Jr Cls; Var Bsktbl; Var Cheerleading; Var JV Socr; JV Var Sftbl; Hon Roll; Lang.

WHARTON, MICHAEL A; Wicomico SR HS; Salisbury, MD; (Y); 15/250; AFS; Boy Scts; Dance Clb; Latin Clb; Spanish Clb; Orch; JV Crs Cntry; Var L Tennis; High Hon Roll; NHS; Arch.

WHEADEN, TONYA; Forest Park SR HS; Baltimore, MD; (Y); Pep Clb; Band; Mrchg Band; Rep Soph Cls; Off Jr Cls; Mgr(s); Hon Roll; Natl Engl Merit Clb 84; Coll Of Notre Dame; Child Psych.

WHEATLEY, ANTHONY; Laurel HS; Laurel, MD; (Y); Cmnty Wkr; Hon Roll; Prfct Atten Awd; Maryland U; Engrng.

WHEATLEY, PAUL; Milford Mill SR HS; Balt, MD; (Y); FBLA; Nwsp Ed-Chief; Nwsp Rptr; Nwsp Stf; Bsbl; Ftbl; Future Bus Ldrs Of Amer 86; U Of MD; Bus.

WHEATLEY, WENDY; Liberty HS; Sykesville, MD; (S); Cheerleading; Diving; Trk; High Hon Roll; Hon Roll; Citznshp & Acad Awds 81-84; Sec.

WHEELER, DAVID; Francis Scott Key HS; Union Bridge, MD; (Y); 51/185; Spanish Clb; Teachers Aide; Varsity Clb; Rep Stu Cncl; JV Var Ftbl; JV Trk; JV Wrstlng; Hon Roll; AAU JR Olympics Wrstlng Trnmnt 85; U S Navy; Arntcs.

WHEELER, DAVID; Highland View Acad; Laurel, MD; (Y); School Play; Nwsp Rptr; Nwsp Stf; Off Frsh Cls; Sec Soph Cls; Sec Jr Cls; Bsktbl; Ftbl; Gym; Vllybl; Ldrshp Schlrshp 86; Columbia Union Coll; Bus Adm.

WHEELER, ROBYN; Highland View Acad; Hagerstown, MD; (Y); Library Aide; Band; Yrbk Ed-Chief; Ed Yrbk Stf; Ed Lit Mag; Sec Frsh Cls; High Hon Roll; NHS; Prfct Atten Awd; Church Yth Grp; Bell Choir 83-86; Andrews U; Cmmnctn.

WHITACRE, RONDA; Allegany HS; Cumberland, MD; (Y); AFS; Chorus; Drill Tm; Swing Chorus; Chld Psychlgy.

WHITAKER, ANGELA M; Eleanor Roosevelt HS; Adelphi, MD; (Y); Pres Church Yth Grp; Red Cross Aide; Chorus; Church Choir; Sec Drill Tm; Yrbk Stf; JV Vllybl; Hon Roll; Girl Scts; Pep Clb; MD Acad Sci Sem-In-Dpth 86; Harry Diamond Labs Intrnshp 85-86; Untd Chrch Of Chrst Yth Rep 84; Cornell U; Cardiac Surgn.

WHITAKER, CINDY; La Reine HS; Suitland, MD; (Y); Dance Clb; Drama Clb; Office Aide; Drill Tm; Cheerleading; Howard U; Dntstry.

WHITAKER, JENEL; Northwestern HS; Baltimore, MD; (S); 1/250; Church Yth Grp; Cmnty Wkr; FBLA; Pres Jr Cls; Pres Sr Cls; Badmtn; Mgr(s); High Hon Roll; Hon Roll; NHS; Hghst Avg Soc Stud 85; NEH Summer Inst 85; Notre Dame; Comm.

WHITBRED, REBECCA; Frederick HS; Frederick, MD; (Y); AFS; German Clb; Science Clb; SADD; Teachers Aide; Rep Jr Cls; Hon Roll; Frederick CC; Lbrl Arts.

WHITE, CAROL; Takoma Acad; Takoma Park, MD; (Y); Camp Fr Inc; NHS; Columbia Union Coll; Oc Thrpy.

WHITE, CHRISTA; Fort Hill HS; Cumberland, MD; (S); VP Church Yth Grp; Pep Clb; Red Cross Aide; Teachers Aide; Thesps; Chorus; Church Choir; Frsh Cls; Soph Cls; Jr Cls; Amer Chmcl Scty Awd 85; Wrthy Advs Intl Ordr Of The Rnbw For Grls 83; Frstbrg ST Coll; Math.

WHITE, DINA; Wicomico SR HS; Salisbury, MD; (Y); 65/244; School Play; Hon Roll; Dorothy H Graham Awd Excllnc In Bus 85-86; Acad Achvt Awd 85-86; Century-21 Accntng Awd 84-85; Ministry.

WHITE, ELIZABETH; Westminster HS; Westminster, MD; (Y); GAA; Sec JA; Q&S; Speech Tm; Yrbk Rptr; Rep Jr Cls; Sec Sr Cls; Rep Stu Cncl; Var Socr; $50 Svngs Bond In Voice Of Dmcrcy Speech Cntst 85; St Andrews Presbyterian Clg.

WHITE, JENNIFER C; Lareine HS; Accokeek, MD; (Y); Church Yth Grp; Drama Clb; Ski Clb; Spanish Clb; Thesps; Band; Chorus; Church Choir; School Musical; School Play; Achvt Acad Ntl Awd 85; Ntl Ldrshp Svc Awds 86; Theater Arts.

WHITE, LISA; Oxon Hill SR HS; Fort Washington, MD; (Y); Intnl Clb; Teachers Aide; Church Choir; Variety Show; VP Stu Cncl; Mgr Bsktbl; High Hon Roll; Hon Roll; NHS; Pres Schlr; MD U; Nursing.

WHITE, MARTHA; Thomas Stone HS; Waldorf, MD; (S); Band; Symp Band; JV Bsktbl; Var L Crs Cntry; High Hon Roll; Trs NHS; Ntl Merit Ltr; Science Clb; Mrchg Band; JV Sftbl; JV Athlt Of Yr 82-83; Tri-Cnty Honors Band 84 & 85; Bio.

WHITE, RACHELLE; Walbrook SR HS; Baltimore, MD; (Y); Spanish Clb; Rep Jr Cls; Crs Cntry; Trk; NEDT Awd; Prfct Atten Awd; Spanish NHS; FBLA 84-86; Towson ST U; Med.

WHITENER, SHERRY; Patterson HS No 405; Baltimore, MD; (Y); JV Var Bsktbl; Morgan ST Coll; Cmptr Sci.

WHITFIELD JR, GUILFORD ARTHUR; Takoma Acad; Silver Spring, MD; (S); 23/96; Computer Clb; Off Frsh Cls; Off Soph Cls; Stu Cncl; Im Bsktbl; Im Ftbl; JV Mgr(s); Im Socr; Im Sftbl; Im Vllybl; UMBC; Medcn.

WHITFIELD, SEAN; Clearspring HS; Hagerstown, MD; (Y); 34/125; Chess Clb; Church Yth Grp; Computer Clb; ROTC; Science Clb; Ski Clb; Trk; Hon Roll; Prfct Atten Awd; H S Drftg Display 3rd Pl 84, 2nd Pl 85 & 86; MD; Arch.

WHITFORD, WENDY; La Plata HS; Charlotte Hall, MD; (S); Art Clb; Trs Science Clb; Jazz Band; Mrchg Band; Symp Band; Stu Cncl; Hon Roll; NHS; Math Tm; Spanish Clb; MD All ST H S Hnr Bnd 86; All-Amer Yth Hnr Bnd 85; Olympcs Of Mind 1st Pl Tm In Cnty 85; Music Ed.

WHITMER JR, GILBERT F; Glen Burnie SR HS; Glen Burnie, MD; (Y); Math Tm; Teachers Aide; Elks Awd; High Hon Roll; Hon Roll; NHS; Rotary Awd; St Schlr; U S Nvl Acad Mntrshp Pgm 85-86; JR Engnrng & Tchnlgcl Soc Sec 84-86; U Of MD College Pk; Elec Engnr.

WHITMER, LYNN; Riverdale Baptist Schl; Greenbelt, MD; (S); 2/65; Church Yth Grp; Cmnty Wkr; Drama Clb; Library Aide; Band; Pep Band; Nwsp Stf; Yrbk Stf; Rep Frsh Cls; Rep Soph Cls.

WHITNEY, AMY C; Brunswick HS; Jefferson, MD; (Y); 3/138; Am Leg Aux Girls St; Art Clb; Sec Trs Church Yth Grp; Scholastic Bowl; School Musical; Var L Crs Cntry; NHS; Ntl Merit Ltr; Sal; St Schlr; Henry Wells Schlr Schlrshp 86; Frederick Co Art Tchrs Awd & Art Assoc Schlrshps 86; Wells Coll; Studio Art.

WHITT, LILLIAN DANIELLE; Crossland HS; Camp Springs, MD; (Y); Church Yth Grp; Cmnty Wkr; Hon Roll; Outstndng Achvt In Acctng I 85-86; Excllnt Frnch Stu 84-85; U Of Ptsbrgh; Finance.

WHITTIER, TIMOTHY; Hammond HS; Columbia, MD; (Y); Church Yth Grp; German Clb; Yrbk Stf; Rep Stu Cncl; Var Tennis; Hon Roll; Ntl Merit Ltr; Bus Adm.

WHITTINGTON, MONIQUE; Bowie SR HS; Bowie, MD; (Y); Church Yth Grp; Latin Clb; Band; Nwsp Stf; Var Capt Cheerleading; Var Trk; Hon Roll; Prfct Atten Awd; Hampton Inst; Cmnctns.

WHORLEY, ANTHONY; Southern SR HS; Baltimore, MD; (Y); Boy Scts; AFS; ROTC; Music Hnr Awd Bay Brook Elem 80; High Achvt Soc Studies 82; Salisbury ST Coll; Brdcstng.

WIECHERT, RALPH; Good Counsel HS; Gaithersburg, MD; (Y); 12/212; Boy Scts; Chess Clb; Science Clb; High Hon Roll; Hon Roll; NHS; Crtcal Anlys Clb 85-86.

WIELAND, KARLA; James M Bennet SR HS; Salisbury, MD; (Y); Church Yth Grp; Cmnty Wkr; Sec Girl Scts; Latin Clb; Thesps; Varsity Clb; Band; Concert Band; Jazz Band; Mrchg Band; Al-Shore Band 1st Chr Bassoonst 85 & 86; Natl Ltn Exm Gld Mdl 86; Poli Sci.

WIEST, TERRENCE; Oxon Hill SR HS; Ft Washington, MD; (Y); Math Tm; Church Choir; Var Crs Cntry; Var L Ftbl; L Capt Wrstlng; French Hon Soc; Gov Hon Prg Awd; Hon Roll; NHS; Pres Schlr; AFROTC Shclrshp 86; PA ST U; Elec Engrng.

WIGGINS, ANNCHANETTE; Northwestern SR HS; Baltimore, MD; (S); Camera Clb; High Hon Roll; Hon Roll; Hghst Acadmc Avg In Cls 84-85; Amer Citznshp For High Standrd Of Excllnc 84-85; Frnch I Profcncy 84-85; U Of MD; Law.

WIGHTMAN, MICHELLE ETHELYN; Northeast HS; Pasadena, MD; (Y); Art Clb; Computer Clb; French Clb; Powder Puff Ftbl; Socr; JV Var Tennis; Hon Roll; Prncpls Hnr Roll & Hall Of Fame Awd For Art 86; Rvr Bch Elem Schl Schlrshp 86; MD Gnrl Schlrshp 86; U MD Bltmr.

WILBUR, RICHARD; Takoma Acad; Gaithersburg, MD; (Y); Church Yth Grp; Band; Im Socr; High Hon Roll; NHS; Pres Schlr; Computer Clb; Math Tm; Chorus; Grand Prz Takoma Acad Sci Fair 86; George Washington U Engrng Hnr Schlrshp 86; George Wasington U; Elec Engrng.

WILDE, CHRISTINE; Albert Einstein SR HS; Silver Spring, MD; (Y); Capt Cmnty Wkr; Sec Girl Scts; Capt Red Cross Aide; Ski Clb; Band; Concert Band; Jazz Band; Mrchg Band; Pep Band; Hon Roll; Rd Crss Srvc Awds 84-86; MD Ldrshp Sminar Ambssdr 85; Rd Crss Yth Ldrshp Confrnc Dlgt 85-86; Psych.

WILDER, CLAUDE H; Eleanor Roosevelt HS; Silver Spring, MD; (Y); Church Yth Grp; Computer Clb; Quiz Bowl; Teachers Aide; VP Ftbl; Im Wt Lftg; Hon Roll; Comp Engrng.

WILDER, SHARON B; Eleanor Roosevelt HS; Laurel, MD; (Y); Spanish Clb; Teachers Aide; VP Temple Yth Grp; Powder Puff Ftbl; Im Socr; Hon Roll; NHS; Ntl Merit SF; Spanish NHS; St Schlr; Bus.

WILES, DALE; Catoctin HS; Emmitsburg, MD; (Y); 17/198; Church Yth Grp; JV Bsktbl; JV Var Socr; Trk; ITS Acad Team 85-86; Elizabethtown Coll; Commnctns.

WILES, EVAN; Williamsport HS; Hagerstown, MD; (Y); Boy Scts; Church Yth Grp; FFA; Cit Awd; God Cntry Awd; Gov Hon Prg Awd; Prfct Atten Awd; Ftbl; Sftbl; Ranger Of Yr-Sectnl Level, Jr Ldrshp Trng Camp, Chrch & Chrstn Srvc Awds 86; Elec Engr.

WILEY, BETTY; Smithsburg HS; Smithsburg, MD; (Y); Church Yth Grp; Hst FBLA; Hosp Aide; Latin Clb; Band; Concert Band; Mrchg Band; Hagerstown JC; Bus Adm.

WILHELM, ANGELA; Thomas Stone HS; Waldorf, MD; (S); Sec Pres Church Yth Grp; Sec Church Choir; Flag Corp; Mrchg Band; Symp Band; Yrbk Rptr; Yrbk Stf; Lit Mag; Hon Roll; Latin Clb; Chrls Cnty Hnrs Band 84; Chrls Cnty Sci Fair Wnnr/Prnc Geo Area Sci Fair 84; Mrktng.

WILHELM, KIRSTEN; Cambridge-South Dorchester HS; Cambridge, MD; (Y); #6 In Class; Am Leg Aux Girls St; French Clb; Latin Clb; Spanish Clb; Nwsp Stf; Trs Soph Cls; Sec Jr Cls; VP Sr Cls; Tennis; NHS; Intl Rltns.

WILHELM, MICHAEL; Parkville HS; Baltimore, MD; (Y); JA; Key Clb; Rep Stu Cncl; L JV Trk; Hon Roll; NHS; U Of MD Baltimore; Phrmcy.

WILHIDE, STEPHANIE; Francis Scott Key HS; Keymar, MD; (Y); Church Yth Grp; GAA; Science Clb; Spanish Clb; Rep Stu Cncl; JV Bsktbl; Var Socr; JV Sftbl; Stat Trk; Hon Roll; Psych.

WILKERSON, LAURA; Gaithersburg HS; Gaithersburg, MD; (Y); Art Clb; Girl Scts; Lit Mag; JV Bsktbl; Trk; Hon Roll; Jr NHS; NHS; Prfct Atten Awd; Natl Art Hnr Soc 85-86; Achvt In Geo Awd 83-84; Art Awds 83-86; U Of NC; Pharmacy.

WILKINS, SHARON; James M Bennett SR HS; Salisbury, MD; (S); 18/192; Drama Clb; Sec Key Clb; Thesps; Chorus; Mrchg Band; Orch; School Musical; Symp Band; Var Trk; Hon Roll; Allshore Band 84 & 85; All Shore Chorus 85; Mus Educ.

WILKINSON, JAMES; Northwestern HS; Hyattsville, MD; (Y); AFS; French Clb; German Clb; Nwsp Sprt Ed; Ed Lit Mag; JV Bsbl; Capt Socr; Hon Roll; Pres NHS; Woodsmn Of Wrld Awd Excllnce US Hstry 85-86; U MO; Hstry.

WILKINSON, ROBIN; Parkdale HS; Lanham, MD; (Y); FBLA; OEA; Ski Clb; Teachers Aide; Chorus; WA Schl Sec 86; Hnr Roll 83-86; WA Schl Sec; Mgmt.

WILL, LISA A; New Covenant Christian Acad; Denton, MD; (S); 2/4; Church Yth Grp; Dance Clb; Office Aide; Political Wkr; Scholastic Bowl; Church Choir; School Musical; VP Stu Cncl; High Hon Roll; Teachers Aide; Amer Christian Hnr Soc 82-84; Src Awd 84-85.

WILLETTE, MARK; Cardinal Gibbons HS; Baltimore, MD; (Y); 20/124; Chess Clb; Church Yth Grp; Library Aide; Q&S; Teachers Aide; Nwsp Rptr; Nwsp Stf; Yrbk Rptr; JV Capt Crs Cntry; Towson ST U; Psychlgy.

WILLEY, ANNMARIE; Easton SR HS; Easton, MD; (Y); GAA; Spanish Clb; Nwsp Rptr; Nwsp Stf; Sec Jr Cls; Var Sftbl; Hon Roll; NHS; Jrnlsm Awd 85-86; Sftbl Awd MIP 83-84; Ldrshp Awd 84-85; Lib Arts.

WILLIAM, KIRSTEN; Parkside HS; Salisbury, MD; (Y); 10/270; Church Yth Grp; Spanish Clb; Varsity Clb; Band; Concert Band; Mrchg Band; Symp Band; Sftbl; Var Vllybl; Hon Roll; Bus Law.

WILLIAMS, ANDREA NICOLE; Western SR HS; Baltimore, MD; (Y); Hosp Aide; Office Aide; Band; Church Choir; Concert Band; Orch; School Musical; School Play; Cert Of Hnr Outstndng Srv 86; Med.

WILLIAMS, ARTHANAIS F; Randallstown SR HS; Randallstown, MD; (Y); FBLA; Library Aide; Office Aide; Hon Roll; Outstndg Negro Stu 86; Howard U; Acctg.

WILLIAMS, CARLA; Maurice J Mcdonough HS; La Plata, MD; (S); 36/318; Sec SADD; Thesps; Concert Band; Mrchg Band; School Play; NHS; Intnl Clb; Teachers Aide; Band; Symp Band; Charles Co CC; Early Chldhd Ed.

WILLIAMS II, CHARLES E; High Point HS; Beltsville, MD; (Y); JA; Ftbl; Trk; Wt Lftg; High Hon Roll; Hon Roll; NHS; Prfct Atten Awd; Athl Achvt Awd; Acdmc Excllnc Awd; MI ST U; Accntng.

WILLIAMS II, DANIEL; Northwestern HS; Mt Rainier, MD; (S); Boy Scts; Drama Clb; JA; Science Clb; Band; Stage Crew; Bsbl; High Hon Roll; NHS.

WILLIAMS, DONNA; Northern HS; Sunderland, MD; (Y); 3/301; Am Leg Aux Girls St; Varsity Clb; Color Guard; Yrbk Stf; Pom Pon; High Hon Roll; Pres NHS; Pres Schlr; Govrs Yth Advsry Cncl-Dlgt 84-86; Manhattanville Coll Acadmc & Hnrs Schlrshp 86; Rtry Clb Schlrshp 86; Manhattanville Coll; Frgn Svc.

WILLIAMS, EDWARD S; Mount Savage HS; Ellerslie, MD; (Y); 15/60; Aud/Vis; Cmnty Wkr; French Clb; Library Aide; Stage Crew; VP Sr Cls; Off Stu Cncl; Var Bsbl; Var JV Bsktbl; Var JV Socr; Dapper Dan Schlrshp 86; Allegany CC; Rsptry Thrpy.

WILLIAMS, JANE; Connelly Schl Of The Holy Child; Potomac, MD; (Y); Church Yth Grp; Model UN; Service Clb; Yrbk Stf; Rep Stu Cncl; Coach Actv; NHS; JV Bsktbl; JV Fld Hcky; Frgn Exch Pgm Ireland 85, Belgium 84; Chem-A-Thon 86.

WILLIAMS, JENNIFER; Surrattsville SR HS; Clinton, MD; (Y); Church Yth Grp; Hosp Aide; Political Wkr; Teachers Aide; Varsity Clb; Nwsp Stf; Yrbk Stf; Cheerleading; 4-H Awd; Hon Roll; Chrldr Athltc Cert 85; Comm.

WILLIAMS, JOHN S; Elkton HS; Elkton, MD; (Y); Exploring; VP Key Clb; Sec SADD; Band; Mrchg Band; Sec Stu Cncl; JV Socr; High Hon Roll; VP NHS; Elec Engrng.

WILLIAMS, KAREN; Crossland HS; Seat Pleasant, MD; (Y); Church Yth Grp; Dance Clb; FBLA; Pep Clb; Spanish Clb; Teachers Aide; Band; Rep Stu Cncl; Cit Awd; Hon Roll; Morgan; Psychlgy.

WILLIAMS, KATRINA; Mc Donough HS; Pomfret, MD; (Y); Church Yth Grp; Sec Computer Clb; Sec FBLA; Var Cheerleading; Var Pom Pon; High Hon Roll; Opt Clb Awd; Hon Roll; Digtl Elec Smnr Loyola Coll 86; Mst Outstndng Stu Chem 86; Rcvd Schlrshp NRL Smr Job Elec 86; Engr.

WILLIAMS, KEVIN; Washington SR HS; Princess Anne, MD; (Y); 19/136; Trs Church Yth Grp; Computer Clb; Drama Clb; Ski Clb; Thesps; Chorus; Trs Church Choir; Concert Band; Mrchg Band; School Play; Md St Stu Cncl Comm Awd 86; Mst Outspkn For Upward Bound 85; Great Excllnce In Chrch Actvts 85-86; Georgetown U; Crmnl Law.

WILLIAMS, KIMBERLY; Regina HS; Silver Spring, MD; (Y); Pres Frsh Cls; JV Cheerleading; High Hon Roll; Hon Roll; NHS; NASA Sharp Awd 85-86; Acadmc All Am 86; Math Awd 86; Med.

WILLIAMS, KRISTINE; Thomas Stone HS; Waldorf, MD; (S); Cmnty Wkr; Science Clb; SADD; Teachers Aide; Capt Flag Corp; Yrbk Phtg; Lit Mag; Capt Sftbl; Hon Roll; Chrmn NHS; Sci Fair 2nd Pl Awd; MD U; Engrng.

WILLIAMS, LA DONNA; Western HS; Baltimore, MD; (Y); 75/412; German Clb; Math Clb; Sftbl; Bsktbl; Trk; Prfct Atten Awd; Hon Roll; Acctg.

WILLIAMS, LISA; Mount Hebron HS; Marriottsville, MD; (Y); 25/253; Church Yth Grp; OEA; Service Clb; Teachers Aide; Merit U Of D 86; RISE Rm & Brd 86; Alpha Phi Alpha Awd-Excllnc Natl Sci 86; U Of DE; Chem Engrng.

WILLIAMS, LYNN; Delmar HS; Delmar, MD; (Y); Dance Clb; Girl Scts; Math Clb; Pep Clb; School Play; Sussex Co Vo-Tech; Hair Stylist.

WILLIAMS, MAURICE; Washington SR HS; Princess Anne, MD; (Y); 8/120; SADD; Chorus; Church Choir; Jazz Band; Swing Chorus; Rep Stu Cncl; Cit Awd; NHS; Pres Schlr; Cmpbls Soup Schlrshp 85-86; Hrry S Peacock Awd 86; All ST Chrs 86; Morgan ST U; Elec Engrng.

WILLIAMS, NOELLE; Academy Of The Holy Cross; Silver Spring, MD; (Y); Math Clb; Pep Clb; Pres Ski Clb; Church Choir; JV Coach Actv; Mgr(s); Var JV Socr; Var Swmmng; High Hon Roll; NHS; Outstndng Svc To Schl86; MD ST Schlrshp 86; Mt St Marys Coll Schlrshp 86; Mt St Marys Coll; Bio.

WILLIAMS, PAIGE; La Plata HS; Waldorf, MD; (Y); Church Yth Grp; Office Aide; Teachers Aide; Chorus; Church Choir; Rep Sr Cls; Cheerleading; Wt Lftg; Hon Roll; Sntrl Schlrshp 86; Charles County CC; Educ.

WILLIAMS, PAULA; Fort Hill SR HS; Cumberland, MD; (Y); Teachers Aide; Drill Tm; Mrchg Band; Rep Soph Cls; Rep Jr Cls; Rep Sr Cls; Cit Awd; Hon Roll; Sec NHS; Nrsg.

WILLIAMS, QUENTIN; Potomac HS; Temple Hills, MD; (Y); Church Yth Grp; Trs Jr Cls; Trs Sr Cls; Hon Roll; USA ABF Novice Div Champ 132 Lbs 86; Div Outstndng Boxer ABF 86; Golden Gloves Champ Jr Div 86; Elec Engr.

WILLIAMS, SCOTT; Friendly HS; Ft Washington, MD; (Y); Teachers Aide; Stage Crew; Wt Lftg; Hon Roll; Prince George CC; Law Enfrcmt.

WILLIAMS, SHAWNETTE; Western HS; Baltimore, MD; (Y); VP JA; Off Teachers Aide; Yrbk Stf; Hon Roll; Prfct Atten Awd; Good Scv Awd 83-84; MD Training Ctr; Data Entry.

WILLIAMS, TERESA; Great Mills HS; Pax River, MD; (Y); 20/251; Cmnty Wkr; Model UN; Pep Clb; SADD; Rep Frsh Cls; Rep Soph Cls; Rep Jr Cls; Rep Sr Cls; JV Trk; JV Vllybl; JV Vllybll MVP 85-86; Tchr.

WILLIAMS, TERESA; Regina HS; Greenbelt, MD; (Y); Drama Clb; Stage Crew; Var Socr.

WILLIAMS, VALERIE; Du Val SR HS; Landover, MD; (S); Debate Tm; French Clb; Pep Clb; Pres Chorus; VP Church Choir; Stu Cncl; Var Crs Cntry; Var L Trk; Natl Cncr Soc 82-86; U Of CA-BRKLY; Bus Admin.

WILLIAMS, VALERIE; Rising Sun HS; Colora, MD; (Y); 6/167; Pres Drama Clb; VP Key Clb; Math Clb; Chorus; Bsktbl; Sftbl; Tennis; Capt Vllybl; NHS; MD Dstngshd Schlr SF 85; WA Coll; Pre-Med.

WILLIAMS, VERMELLA; Southern SR HS; Baltimore, MD; (Y); Dance Clb; JCL; Office Aide; Pep Clb; ROTC; Teachers Aide; Band; Color Guard; Concert Band; Drill Tm; Outstndng ROTC Cadt 84; Most Vlbl Plyr Vllybl 85; Best Mgr 86; Loyola College; Comp Prgmr.

WILLOUGHBY, THOMAS; North East HS; Elkton, MD; (Y); Cmnty Wkr; Letterman Clb; Spanish Clb; Bsktbl; Hon Roll; NHS; Industrl Arts Awd 84-85; Am Lit Awds 84-85; Bus.

WILLS, BETHANY; St Marys HS; Annapolis, MD; (Y); 20/121; Church Yth Grp; Pres Pep Clb; Ski Clb; Ed Yrbk Rptr; Socr; Mgr Tennis; Hon Roll; Sec NHS; ST Senatorial Schlrshp 86; Pres Schlrshp 86; Salisbury ST Coll; Bus Adm.

WILLS, JENNIFER M; Thomas S Wootton HS; Gaithersburg, MD; (Y); Dance Clb; Drama Clb; Thesps; Band; School Musical; School Play; Stage Crew; Var L Tennis; High Hon Roll; Hon Roll; Hnrbl Mntn Algebra 83; Mst Dedicated Tennis 83; Citation Typng Speed 84; U Of WA; Engrng.

WILLS, JILL; Dundalk HS; Baltimore, MD; (Y); Model UN; Variety Show; Lit Mag; NHS; Ntl Merit Ltr; Pres Schlr; St Schlr; FBLA; Office Aide; Off Soph Cls; Rufus W Bailey Mem Schlrshp 86-87; Cert Achvt Seal Merit 86; Dundalk Cls 82 Schrlshp 86; Mary Baldwin Coll; Comm.

WILLS, LISA; Oxonhill High SR HS; Ft Washington, MD; (Y); Church Yth Grp; Varsity Clb; Band; Rep Frsh Cls; Rep Soph Cls; Rep Jr Cls; Rep Sr Cls; Capt Tennis; Cmmnd Stu Thru Partcptn In Natl Achvt Schlrshp Prog 85-86; Loyola; Biomed Engrng.

WILLSEY, ANGIE; Takoma Acad; Silver Spgs, MD; (Y); Church Yth Grp; Hosp Aide; Science Clb; Yrbk Stf; Hon Roll; NHS; Columbia Union Coll; Cardlgst.

WILMER, LENIS; Snow Hill HS; Snow Hill, MD; (S); Church Yth Grp; Color Guard; Mrchg Band; Vllybl; Wt Lftg; Hon Roll; NHS; Paralegal.

WILSON, CATHY; Southern Garrett HS; Deer Park, MD; (Y); Church Yth Grp; FBLA; Girl Scts; VICA; Var Vllybl; Hon Roll; Tri-ST Beauty Acad; Cosmtlgst.

WILSON, CHOATE; Walkersville HS; Frederick, MD; (Y); Cmnty Wkr; SADD; Teachers Aide; Varsity Clb; Orch; Rep Frsh Cls; Rep Soph Cls; Var Capt Bsktbl; Wt Lftg; Hon Roll; Bus Mgt.

WILSON, DAWN; Winston Churchill HS; Potomac, MD; (S); Rep DECA; PAVAS; Teachers Aide; Band; Jazz Band; School Play; Variety Show; Capt Powder Puff Ftbl; Hon Roll; JA; 2nd Pl Apprl & Accsrs Mrktng ST Wd Comp 86; Tri M Music Hnr Soc 85-86; Fshn Inst; Fshn Mrchndsng.

WILSON, DOUG; Potomac HS; Temple Hills, MD; (Y); Boy Scts; Church Yth Grp; Lit Mag; Var Bsbl; JV Ftbl; Var L Trk; Chem Engr.

WILSON, JOE; Carroll Christian Acad; Westminster, MD; (S); 1/18; Chorus; Pres Frsh Cls; Pres Soph Cls; Rep Jr Cls; VP Stu Cncl; Var Bsbl; Stat Score Keeper; High Hon Roll; NHS; Ntl Merit Schol; Liberty U; Hstry.

WILSON, KEVIN CLAIR; Hammond HS; Columbia, MD; (Y); 18/262; AFS; Q&S; VP Spanish Clb; Ed Nwsp Ed-Chief; Rep Stu Cncl; L Var Bsbl; L Var Bsktbl; L Var Crs Cntry; High Hon Roll; NHS; Howard Cnty Schlr Athl Awd 86; Air Force ROTC 4 Yr Schlrshp 86; VA Tech; Elec Engrng.

WILSON, SAMANTHA; Notre Dame Prep; Timonium, MD; (Y); Church Yth Grp; Dance Clb; Drama Clb; Chorus; School Musical; School Play; Gym; York; Vet Med.

WILSON, SHARI; Westminster SR HS; Finksburg, MD; (Y); Trs Pres AFS; Church Yth Grp; Spanish Clb; Chorus; Mrchg Band; Hon Roll; Hood Coll; Early Chld Devlpmnt.

WILSON, SHAUNN; Potomac HS; Temple Hills, MD; (Y); Church Yth Grp; Lit Mag; Pres Frsh Cls; Pom Pon; Cit Awd; Hon Roll; Pres Jr NHS; NHS; Ball ST U; Acctng.

WILSON, STACEY; Crisfield HS; Crisfield, MD; (Y); Church Yth Grp; Science Clb; VP Band; Jazz Band; Mrchg Band; Pep Band; School Play; Symp Band; Variety Show; Rep Frsh Cls; Ultra Sound Techn.

WILSON, STEPHEN THOMAS; John Carroll HS; Delta, PA; (Y); 35/224; Boy Scts; Service Clb; Ski Clb; Pres Band; Concert Band; Jazz Band; Mrchg Band; School Play; Stage Crew; Variety Show; Natl Sci Olympd-Chem 84-85; Outstndng John Carrol Stu Medl 86; J Carroll Svc Awd, Certs Acmplshmt 86; U Of ND; Airway Sci.

WILSON, WHITNEY; Walt Whitman HS; Bethesda, MD; (Y); 61/475; Ski Clb; Temple Yth Grp; Bsbl; Var Ice Hcky; Socr; Var Trk; High Hon Roll; Pres Schlr; Intl Rltns.

WILT, BARBARA; Fort Hill HS; Cumberland, MD; (Y); Sec Church Yth Grp; Drill Tm; Nwsp Stf; Frsh Cls; Soph Cls; Jr Cls; Pom Pon; Hon Roll; Trs NHS; NEDT Awd.

WILT, BRENDA; Allegany HS; Cumberland, MD; (Y); 18/220; Church Yth Grp; Office Aide; Chorus; Church Choir; Co-Capt Drill Tm; Co-Capt Pom Pon; Timer; Trk; Hon Roll; NHS; Miss Drill Tm 83-85; Superstar Girl 85-86; Allegany CC; Elem Ed.

WILT, JODI; Southern Garrett HS; Oakland, MD; (Y); Capt Color Guard; Concert Band; Mrchg Band; European Winterguard Intls 3rd Pl 86; Waynesburg Coll; Nrsg.

WILT, KRISTIANN H; Southern Garrett HS; Oakland, MD; (S); German Clb; Model UN; Trk; Rotary Awd; Pres Handbell Choir 85; Secy Untd Meth Yth Fndtn 85-86; U Of MD; Psych.

WILT, SHERRI; Southern Garrett HS; Oakland, MD; (Y); Church Yth Grp; Cmnty Wkr; Sec Trs 4-H; FBLA; Sec FFA; Girl Scts; Office Aide; 4-H Awd; Rotry Awd Outstndn Yht Garret Cnty Fair 84; 1t Runn Cnty Farm Qn 85; Dairy Prncss 86; Garrett CC; Med Sec.

WILTON, TIMIA; Dunbbar Community HS; Baltimore, MD; (Y); Church Yth Grp; Computer Clb; JA; Pep Clb; Church Choir; Rep Frsh Cls; Rep Soph Cls; Rep Jr Cls; Prfct Atten Awd; Alg II Schlrshp Awd 86; Montebello Elem Vol Awd 86; Schlrhsp 86; Towson ST U; Physcl Thrpy.

WIMMER, SUSAN E; South Carroll HS; Westminster, MD; (Y); 5/300; Am Leg Aux Girls St; Church Yth Grp; Spanish Clb; Teachers Aide; High Hon Roll; NHS; Ntl Merit SF; NEDT Awd; Acad Ltr 83-84; MD Dstngshd Schlr 85-86; Lingustcs.

WIMMS, HARRIETTE E; St Marys Ryken HS; Lexington Park, MD; (Y); Sec Church Yth Grp; Rep Trs Concert Band; Symp Band; Prncpls List; Emerson Coll; Comm.

WINDLAN, KAREN; Sherwood HS; Brookeville, MD; (Y); 70/300; Cmnty Wkr; SADD; Yrbk Rptr; Yrbk Stf; Stat Bsktbl; Mgr(s); Hon Roll; NHS; Spanish NHS; Computer Clb; Spcl Hnry Awd Sci Fair Proj 86; Outstndng Stu Awd 84-85; Marktng.

WINDSOR JR, LARRY V; Cambridge-South Dorchestger HS; Toddville, MD; (Y); Am Leg Boys St; Quiz Bowl; Teachers Aide; Concert Band; Jazz Band; Mrchg Band; Var Bsbl; Var JV Bsktbl; Var NHS; Bst U S Hstry Awd 85-86.

WINE, JEFFREY; Williamsport HS; Williamsport, MD; (Y); Art Clb; Drama Clb; SADD; Chorus; Concert Band; Jazz Band; Mrchg Band; School Musical; School Play; Hon Roll.

WINER, VALERIE; Thomas S Wootton HS; Rockville, MD; (Y); Hosp Aide; Pres JA; Temple Yth Grp; Bus.

WINESTOCK, MARK; Archbishop Carroll HS; Forestville, MD; (S); 20/188; Church Yth Grp; Office Aide; Nwsp Rptr; Im Bsktbl; Var Trk; Hon Roll; Engrng.

WINKERT, DANIEL R; Dleanor Rossevelt HS; Bowie, MD; (Y); Variety Show; Yrbk Sprt Ed; Var L Crs Cntry; Var L Trk; Hon Roll; NHS; Ntl Merit Ltr; U Of FL; Arch.

WINKLER, LISA; Mc Donough HS; White Plains, MD; (Y); Am Leg Aux Girls St; Church Yth Grp; Dance Clb; GAA; Office Aide; Teachers Aide; Varsity Clb; Sec Frsh Cls; JV Var Bsktbl; JV Var Sftbl; Cmmnctns.

WINNER, DARRIN; Beall JR SR HS; Frostburg, MD; (Y); Band; Pres Chorus; Rep Frsh Cls; Rep Soph Cls; Rep Jr Cls; Rep Sr Cls; Hon Roll; NHS; Boy Scts; PAVAS; All ST Chorus 86; Best Vocal Beall High 86; Frostburg ST Coll; Bus Admin.

WINSLOW, MICHELE; Perryville HS; Colora, MD; (Y); 1/120; Church Yth Grp; Intnl Clb; Quiz Bowl; Nwsp Ed-Chief; Yrbk Stf; Rep Stu Cncl; DAR Awd; Hon Roll; NHS; Hgh Plcmnt HS Math Lge Awd 85-86; Dlgt MD ST Sci Sympsm 85-86; Bus Adm.

WINSTON, LORI; Western HS; Baltimore, MD; (Y); 16/412; Church Yth Grp; FBLA; JA; Pep Band; Yrbk Stf; Rep Stu Cncl; Var Mgr(s); Var Trk; Hon Roll; NHS; Hampton U; Accntng.

WINSTON, TRACY; Southwestern HS; Baltimore, MD; (Y); Drama Clb; French Clb; Chorus; Stu Cncl; Bsktbl; Cheerleading; Pom Pon; Trk; Hon Roll; Prfct Atten Awd; Forecast Future Awd 83-84; Mth Cont Awd 85; Engrng Pipeline Awd 84; Bus.

WINTERBOTTOM, AUTUMN; James M Bennett HS; Salisbury, MD; (Y); Church Yth Grp; Hosp Aide; Varsity Clb; Var Bsktbl; Sftbl; Var Tennis; Var JV Vllybl; Hon Roll.

WIRTLEY, LARRY; Fort Hill HS; Cumberland, MD; (S); Band; Concert Band; Jazz Band; Mrchg Band; Pep Band; Rep Sr Cls; NHS; Frostburg ST Coll; Phrmcy.

WISE, GARY; Lackey HS; White Plains, MD; (Y); Intnl Clb; Letterman Clb; Ski Clb; Spanish Clb; Varsity Clb; JV Var Wrstlng; Hon Roll; Aerontcl Engr.

WISEMAN, ELIZABETH; Bishop Walsh HS; La Vale, MD; (Y); 4/103; Drama Clb; Science Clb; Thesps; Concert Band; Mrchg Band; School Musical; School Play; French Hon Soc; NHS; Cmbrland Music & Arts Schlrshp 84; Johns Hopkins U; Humanities.

WISEMAN, LISA; Parkville SR HS; Baltimore, MD; (Y); Am Leg Aux Girls St; Church Yth Grp; Trs Drama Clb; JA; Office Aide; School Musical; Nwsp Rptr; Hon Roll; Prfct Atten Awd; Jrnlsm.

WISK, THERESA; Liberty HS; Eldersburg, MD; (S); AFS; 4-H; Mathletes; High Hon Roll; Ntl Merit SF; Vet Med.

WISNER, DAVID; North Carroll HS; Millers, MD; (Y); Varsity Clb; Chorus; JV Bsbl; JV Var Bsktbl; JV Lcrss; JV Capt Socr; Hon Roll; Hnrbl Mntn Athltc Leag Soccr 85; 1st Tm Soccr 85; Brdcstg.

WITT JR, RAY; Fort Hill HS; Cumberland, MD; (Y); Drama Clb; English Clb; Exploring; FCA; FBLA; Radio Clb; Red Cross Aide; Scholastic Bowl; Service Clb; Ski Clb; Frostburg ST Coll; Bus Adm.

WITZGALL, LISBON; Gaithersburg HS; Gaithersburg, MD; (Y); CAP; Exploring; Girl Scts; Political Wkr; ROTC; Concert Band; Mrchg Band; Pep Band; Symp Band; JV Bsktbl.

WIZDA, SHARYN; Western HS; Baltimore, MD; (Y); 6/450; Drama Clb; Thesps; School Play; Stage Crew; Nwsp Ed-Chief; Rep Stu Cncl; Hon Roll; NHS; Barnard Coll Bk Awd 86; Outstndng Studnt Ldershp Awd 86; Coll Of NY; Journalism.

WOHLFORT, KATHY; Col Zadok Magruder HS; Derwood, MD; (Y); Sec Pres AFS; Nwsp Rptr; Var Diving; Var Vllybl; High Hon Roll; Hon Roll; NHS; Macalester; Anml Sci.

WOJTYSIAK, DIANE; Institute Of Notre Dame; Baltimore, MD; (Y); Church Yth Grp; Hosp Aide; Acpl Chr; Chorus; Variety Show; Rep Frsh Cls; Rep Jr Cls; Hon Roll; Frostburg ST; Early Childhd Ed.

WOLF, BARBRA; St Vincent Pallotti HS; Bowie, MD; (S); 5/100; Drama Clb; Nwsp Ed-Chief; Yrbk Bus Mgr; Yrbk Ed-Chief; Rep Jr Cls; Rep Sr Cls; Stat Bsbl; High Hon Roll; VP NHS; Eng Awd 83-85; German Hnr Soc 83-86; Brdcst Jrnlsm.

WOLF, DAVID; Middletown HS; Smithsburg, MD; (Y); Trs Church Yth Grp; Chorus; Church Choir; School Musical; VP NHS; Ntl Merit SF; Extraordnry Chrstn Stdnts Amer Awd 86.

WOLF, DEBRA; Southern Garrett HS; Oakland, MD; (Y); 38/225; Church Yth Grp; Q&S; Teachers Aide; Band; Church Choir; Color Guard; Yrbk Bus Mgr; Yrbk Phtg; Yrbk Stf; Yth For Chrst 85-86; Hagerstown Bus Coll; Law.

WOLF, DOUGLAS; T S Wootan HS; Rockville, MD; (Y); JA; Teachers Aide; JV Var Wrstlng; Hon Roll; Pres Trs Rotary Awd; Ntl Merit Cmmnded Schlr 85-86; Finance.

WOLF, KRISTIN M; Academy Of The Holy Cross; Rockville, MD; (Y); 22/122; Church Yth Grp; Hosp Aide; Church Choir; Yrbk Bus Mgr; Yrbk Stf; Lit Mag; Var L Vllybl; NHS; Ntl Merit SF; Spanish NHS; 5th Pl ST Wide Natl Spnsh Exmntn 85; Georgetwn U; Hlth Sci.

WOLFE, DENISE; Clear Spring HS; Big Spg, MD; (Y); 6/111; Q&S; School Play; Nwsp Ed-Chief; Pres Jr Cls; VP Sr Cls; Trs Stu Cncl; Stat Socr; High Hon Roll; Masonic Awd; NHS; 1st Stdnt Bd Ed 85-86; Hood Coll; Frgn Lang.

WOLFE, JENNIFER; Beall HS; Frostburg, MD; (Y); Church Yth Grp; Chorus; Church Choir; Co-Capt Cheerleading; Hon Roll; NHS; Towson; Math Tchr.

WOLFF, JEANNETTE; Archbishop Spalding HS; Glen Burnie, MD; (Y); Drama Clb; Red Cross Aide; Band; Off Jr Cls; Sec Sr Cls; Stu Cncl; JV Var Cheerleading; Var Sftbl; Jr NHS; SAR Awd; John And Mary Foley Schlrshp 86; U Of MD; Phys Thrpy.

WOLFF, JOHN; Parkville HS; Baltimore, MD; (Y); French Clb; Quiz Bowl; Yrbk Stf; Sec Stu Cncl; Ftbl; French Hon Soc; Hon Roll; Jr NHS; Prfct Atten Awd; Towson ST U; Tchr.

WOLFF, RONNIE; Fort Hill HS; Cumberland, MD; (Y); Camera Clb; Church Yth Grp; Library Aide; Wrstlng.

WOLFORD, HEATHER; Allegany HS; Cresaptown, MD; (Y); Church Yth Grp; Pep Clb; Capt JV Cheerleading; Gym; Child Psych.

WOLFORD, KEVIN; Takoma Acad; Laurel, MD; (Y); Church Yth Grp; Ski Clb; Chorus; Trk; Hon Roll; Sci.

WOLFORD, TAMMY; Southern HS; Mt Lake Park, MD; (Y); Sec Church Yth Grp; Civic Clb; Girl Scts; Rep Sr Cls; Grl Sct Slvr Awd 2nd Hghst Awd 86; Astrnmy.

WOLINSKI, LAURA; Fallston HS; Kingsville, MD; (Y); 27/256; Library Aide; Office Aide; Chorus; Nwsp Rptr; Cheerleading; Hon Roll; Pres Schlr; Twsn ST U; Elem Ed.

WOLLEY, DENNIS; Fairmont Heights HS; Hyattsville, MD; (Y); Boys Clb Am; Im Badmtn; Im Bsbl; Im Bsktbl; Var Ftbl; Im Socr; Im Sftbl; Im Vllybl; Im Wt Lftg; Hon Roll; Acadmc Excllnc Awd 84; U MD; Comp Sci.

WOMACK, MONICA; Suitland HS; District Height, MD; (Y); Church Yth Grp; VP French Clb; Girl Scts; Letterman Clb; ROTC; Sec Soph Cls; Sec Jr Cls; Var Im Bsktbl; Var Sftbl; Hon Roll; NJROTC Awd From Military Order Of Wrld Wars 86; NJROTC Awd From Navy Lg 85; Providence Coll; Comp Sci.

WOMACK, RODNEY; Fairmont Hgts HS; Cheverly, MD; (Y); French Clb; Math Clb; Science Clb; Jazz Band; Ftbl; Hon Roll; Howard U; Elec Engr.

WONG, DICK; Walter Johnson HS; Bethesda, MD; (Y); Hosp Aide; SADD; Off Stu Cncl; JV Capt Socr; Hon Roll; Computers.

WONG, REBECCA; Northwestern HS; Hyattsville, MD; (Y); 1/480; Church Yth Grp; Drama Clb; Chorus; Church Choir; Lit Mag; Off Sr Cls; Chrmn NHS; Pres Schlr; Rotary Awd; Val; 4 Yr Full Schlrshp U Of MD 86; Woodmen Wrld Awd 85; MD ST Dist Schlr Semi Final Awd 85; U Of MD; Music-Piano.

WONG, SUSAN; Oxon Hill Science & Technology Ctr; Ft Washington, MD; (Y); Chess Clb; Math Tm; Teachers Aide; VP French Hon Soc; High Hon Roll; NHS; Pres Schlr; Eclgy Clb Pres 85-86; Reg Schl Sci Fair Awd 83-86; U Maryland Coll Park; Microbio.

WOO, HO; Dulaney SR HS; Timonium, MD; (Y); Pres Church Yth Grp; Chrmn Key Clb; Church Choir; Hon Roll; NHS; Key Clb Hnry Awd For Svc 85-86; Commercial Art.

WOO, SHEILA; Oxon HS; Ft Washington, MD; (Y); Church Yth Grp; Church Choir; Crs Cntry; Trk; High Hon Roll; NHS; St Schlr; 1st Pl Cnty Sci Fair 86; Gov Top 5 Pct 86; Princpl Trophy Outstndng Female Schlr/Ath 86; U MD; Chem Engr.

WOOD, MARY M; Linganore HS; Monrovia, MD; (Y); 20/368; Camera Clb; Church Yth Grp; Pres 4-H; Concert Band; Mrchg Band; Pep Band; Stage Crew; 4-H Awd; Hon Roll; NHS; Math.

WOOD, PRESTON; Chopticon HS; Mechanicsville, MD; (Y); Science Clb; Varsity Clb; Concert Band; Jazz Band; Mrchg Band; School Musical; Nwsp Rptr; Nwsp Stf; Off Stu Cncl; Var Socr; Outstndng Band Stu Awd 85 & 86; Outstndng Sci Stu Awd 86; 4.0 Grd Pt Aver Awd 85 & 86; U Of MD; Aerontcl Engrng.

WOOD, ROBERT A; La Plata HS; Bel Alton, MD; (Y); 7/317; Am Leg Boys St; Wt Lftg; High Hon Roll; Jr NHS; NHS; Ntl Merit SF; Cit Awd; DAR Awd; Hon Roll; Acadmc All-Amer; Natl Engl Merit Awd 86; Embry-Riddle U; Aerontcl Engrng.

WOOD, SHELLY; Centennial HS; Columbia, MD; (Y); AFS; Ski Clb; Yrbk Bus Mgr; U Of MD; Soc Sci.

WOOD, WILLIAM A; Good Counsel HS; Rockville, MD; (Y); 1/228; Hosp Aide; Latin Clb; Math Tm; Nwsp Ed-Chief; L Crs Cntry; L Trk; Pres NHS; Ntl Merit Schol; Pres Schlr; English Clb; Acadmc Accmplshmt; VA Tech; Mech Engrng.

WOODALL, JENNIE; St Michaels HS; St Michaels, MD; (Y); 4/59; Hosp Aide; SADD; Band; Yrbk Stf; VP NHS; Church Yth Grp; Drama Clb; Chorus; Church Choir; Concert Band; Psych.

WOODARD, JOYCE; Paul Laurence Dunbar HS; Baltimore, MD; (Y); Var Bsktbl; Bsktbll & Vllybl 84-86; U Of Kansas; Nrsng.

WOODBREY, CAROLE S; Surrattsville HS; Clinton, MD; (Y); Church Yth Grp; Cmnty Wkr; Drama Clb; Chorus; Church Choir; Mrchg Band; Nwsp Stf; Yrbk Stf; L Var Pom Pon; Hon Roll; PGCC; Bus.

WOODS, KEITH; St Marys Ryken HS; California, MD; (S); Library Aide; Chorus; DAR Awd; Hon Roll; NHS; NEDT Awd; St Pius X Seminary; Priest.

WOODWARD, ERIC; Maurice J Mc Donough HS; Waldorf, MD; (Y); VICA; Nwsp Stf; Auto Body.

WOOLEY, KRISTINA R; Central HS; Andrews A F B, DC; (Y); VP Church Yth Grp; Spanish Clb; Nwsp Ed-Chief; Rep Soph Cls; Rep Jr Cls; Rep Stu Cncl; Var Fld Hcky; Var Mgr(s); High Hon Roll; Hon Roll; U Of MD; Journalism.

WOOTEN, JENNIFER; Arundel HS; Crofton, MD; (Y); 50/534; Dance Clb; Drama Clb; Teachers Aide; School Musical; Yrbk Stf; Co-Capt Pom Pon; Hon Roll; Cmnty Wkr; Debate Tm; DECA; Ctznshp Scholar 84 & 86; Outstndg Bus Stu Scholar 86; MD ST DECA Ofcr/Sec 85-86; U MD; Bus Adm.

WOOTTEN, MARIAN; Wicomico SR HS; Salisbury, MD; (Y); 13/300; French Clb; JCL; Latin Clb; Pep Clb; Teachers Aide; Hon Roll; NHS; Acad Lttr/Lamp Of Knowledge Patch 85-86; Art Inst Of Ft Lauderdale FL.

WRAY, TERRY; Great Mills HS; Monterey, CA; (Y); Church Yth Grp; JV Capt Bsktbl; Var Capt Golf; Var Capt Tennis; Hon Roll; Jr NHS; NHS; Won Schl Essy Cntst On Frdm 85-86; Comp Sci.

WRIGHT, JASON; Seneca Valley HS; Gaithersburg, MD; (Y); Ski Clb; JV Ftbl; Hon Roll; CO Coll; Shock Trauma Med.

WRIGHT, SEAN; Parkdale HS; Lanham, MD; (Y); Church Yth Grp; Varsity Clb; Church Choir; Yrbk Stf; Var Bsbl; Var Ftbl; Var Trk; Hon Roll; Cmptr Sci.

WRIGHT, TAMMERA; High Point HS; Beltsville, MD; (Y); 150/600; Church Yth Grp; Cmnty Wkr; Library Aide; Spanish Clb; Teachers Aide; Church Choir; Hon Roll; Prfct Atten Awd; UNCC Charlotte; Acctg.

WRIGHT, TAMMY; South Carroll HS; Westminster, MD; (Y); Church Yth Grp; Cmnty Wkr; Hosp Aide; Keywanettes; Teachers Aide; Hon Roll; Math Awd 78; Merit Schlstc Awd 86; Cert Pgm Achvt-Bus 86; Villa Julie Coll; Lgl Secy.

WRIGHT, TRACEY; Forest Park Ssr HS; Baltimore, MD; (Y); Church Yth Grp; Debate Tm; Girl Scts; Library Aide; Math Clb; Math Tm; ROTC; Band; Chorus; Church Choir; 95 Avrg Geography 84-85; Success Roll 83-84; Life Of Animals.

WU, BRYANT C; Springbrook HS; Silver Springs, MD; (Y); 134/488; Chess Clb; ROTC; Drill Tm; Yrbk Stf; Lit Mag; Tennis; Ntl Merit SF; Arch.

WU, LOUISA P; Catonsville SR HS; Catonsville, MD; (Y); 1/250; Trs Debate Tm; Nwsp Phtg; Yrbk Phtg; NCTE Awd; Sec NHS; Ntl Merit SF; St Schlr; French Clb; Hon Roll; MD ST Grnt; Johns Hopkins U Erly Admssn; John Hopkins U; Bhvrl Sci.

WUDARSKI, JULIE; Catoctin HS; Thurmont, MD; (Y); Pres Church Yth Grp; DECA; Drama Clb; Chorus; Church Choir; Hon Roll; Prfct Atten Awd; Frederick Cnty Vo-Tech Ctr-Outstndng Mrktng 86; 1st Pl Adward Finance & Crdt Written Stu 86; Mrktng.

WYATT, KELLY; Harford Vocational Technical HS; Jarrettsville, MD; (Y); Cmnty Wkr; SADD; VICA; Cheerleading; Gym; Tennis; Vllybl; High Hon Roll.

WYCLIFFE, JOY JOHN; Northwestern HS; Hyattsville, MD; (Y); Church Yth Grp; Cmnty Wkr; JA; Bsktbl; JV Capt Ftbl; Var Trk; U MD College Pk; Elec.

WYNKOOP, PATTI; Wheaton HS; Wheaton, MD; (Y); GAA; JA; Letterman Clb; Spanish Clb; Rep Frsh Cls; Pom Pon; Powder Puff Ftbl; Socr; Hon Roll; Jr NHS; MD U; Arch.

WYRICK, PHELAN; Walter Johnson HS; Bethesda, MD; (Y); Teachers Aide; National Juried Ceramics Awd 86; MD U.

YAAG, LORI; Takoma Acad; Takoma Park, MD; (S); Drama Clb; Teachers Aide; Chorus; Sec Soph Cls; Var Capt Cheerleading; Trk; Hon Roll; NHS; Sec Frsh Cls; Hnrs In Geometry; Cert Of Ed Dvlpmnt; Baruch Coll; Bus.

YAMAQUCHI, LINA; Walter Johnson HS; Bethesda, MD; (Y); Hosp Aide; Aud/Vis; Yrbk Ed-Chief; Yrbk Stf; Pom Pon; Vllybl; Hon Roll; Journlsm.

YANG, ANGELA; Paint Branch HS; Silver Spring, MD; (Y); 2/337; Key Clb; Math Tm; Capt Tennis; Hon Roll; NHS; Pres Schlr; MD Dstngshd Schlr Pgm; Natl Merit Cmmnd Stu; Duke A J Fletcher Music Schlrshp; Duke U; Sports Med.

YANG, BARBARA; Fallston HS; Fallston, MD; (Y); Trs Church Yth Grp; German Clb; Math Clb; Pep Clb; Band; Concert Band; Jazz Band; Orch; Pep Band; Symp Band; CA Music Ed Assn Cmmnd Prfrmnce & Supr Ratg 84; All Star Tm Fld Hcky 85; Pres Fit Awd 86; Johns Hopkins U; Polit Econ.

YATES, SIDNEY; Snow Hill HS; Snow Hill, MD; (S); Spanish Clb; Band; Concert Band; Mrchg Band; Capt Socr; Legal Intern; Boys ST; Navy.

YEAGER, SHARON; Kent County HS; Millington, MD; (Y); 11/163; Church Yth Grp; 4-H; FNA; Hosp Aide; Library Aide; Office Aide; Pep Clb; Spanish Clb; VICA; Band; Outstndng Hlth Occ Stu Awd, Hnbl Merit Awd 85-86; LPN; Nrsng.

YEH, KENNETH; Laurel HS; Laurel, MD; (Y); Boy Scts; Band; Var L Crs Cntry; Swmmng; Var L Trk; Hon Roll; Kiwanis Awd; UMBC Schltc Achvt Scholar 86; Laurel H S Schlr-Ath Awd 86; Laurel Crs Cntry MIP 84; Coaches Awd 84-85; U MD Baltimroe Cnty; Mech Engr.

YESKEY, DEBRA JOLENE; Old Mill SR HS; Crownsville, MD; (Y); 90/509; VP Trs Church Yth Grp; German Clb; Teachers Aide; Var Capt Fld Hcky; Tennis; Hon Roll; Anne Arundel Cnty Publc Schls Advncd Acadmc Cert 86; Towson ST U; Bus.

YESUDIAN, DAYANTHI; Takoma Acad; Beltsville, MD; (Y); Orch; High Hon Roll; Hon Roll; NHS; Church Yth Grp; Ski Clb; Acpl Chr; Chorus; Yrbk Stf; NC ST; Pre-Med.

YHIM, SUNG; Good Counsel HS; Wheaton, MD; (Y); 13/214; Church Yth Grp; Pres Spanish Clb; Capt Nwsp Stf; Hon Roll; NHS; Pre Med.

YI, SEUNG; Albert Einsteiin HS; Silver Spring, MD; (Y); 4/450; Ski Clb; Nwsp Stf; High Hon Roll; Hon Roll; Jr NHS; NHS; Cert Prfcncy Wrd Proc 86; Minister.

YIENGER, JUDITH M; Oakland Mills HS; Columbia, MD; (Y); 18/240; Church Yth Grp; JV Var Socr; JV Trk; Hon Roll; NHS.

YINGER, TAMMY; Frederick HS; Frederick, MD; (Y); 41/377; Sec Spanish Clb; Teachers Aide; Rep Frsh Cls; JV Bsktbl; Im Bowling; Powder Puff Ftbl; Var Sftbl; Hon Roll; Prfct Atten Awd; Excllnc Spnsh Achvt Awds 84-86; Typg Awd 84; Salisbury ST; Spnsh.

YOCKUS, SCOTT; Bishop Walsh HS; Cumberland, MD; (Y); Var Pres Sr Cls; Var L Bsktbl; Var L Crs Cntry; Var L Trk; MVP Track,Cross Cty 85-86.

YODER, DEBBY; Northern Garrett HS; Grantsville, MD; (Y); Trs Church Yth Grp; Chorus; Church Choir; Stat Var Bsbl; Var Score Keeper; Var Socr; High Hon Roll; Hon Roll; God Sqd Clb VP 84-85; God Sqd Clb Pres 85-86; Garrett CC; Soc Wrk.

YOKOYAMA, REIKO; Walt Whitman HS; Bethesda, MD; (Y); Art Clb; Camera Clb; Intnl Clb; Key Clb; School Play; Stage Crew; Lit Mag; Rep Frsh Cls; Var Trk; MD Coll Or Arts & Dsgn Exhbtn 86; Prnt Slctd For Dscvr Grphcs Stu Exhbtn 86; Intl Rltns.

YOMMER, KAREN; Northern HS; Accident, MD; (Y); Church Yth Grp; FHA; Teachers Aide; Chorus; Variety Show; Hon Roll; Music.

YOO, TOM; Loyola HS; Baltimore, MD; (Y); Church Yth Grp; Cmnty Wkr; Drama Clb; French Clb; SADD; School Musical; School Play; Im Socr; Var Tennis; Hon Roll.

YORK, CATHY; Joppatowne HS; Joppa, MD; (Y); Teachers Aide; Concert Band; Mrchg Band; School Musical; Trs Jr Cls; Trs Sr Cls; Powder Puff Ftbl; Swmmng; NHS; Girl Scts; Vrsty Lttrs Swmmng, Band 83-86; Vllnv U; Tchng.

YORK, MARIA; Gaithersburg HS; Gaithersburg, MD; (Y); Cmnty Wkr; Trs Exploring; Var L Swmmng; Var L Trk; High Hon Roll; Hon Roll; Jr NHS; NHS; 1st Sch Sci Fair 84; Metros Swm Meet 85-86.

YORKER, RHONDA; South Western HS; Baltimore, MD; (Y); Church Yth Grp; Chorus; Church Choir; Bus.

YOUNG, CYNTHIA; Valley HS; Midland, MD; (S); 2/82; Drama Clb; Trs 4-H; French Clb; Band; Chorus; Church Choir; Sftbl; NHS; NEDT Awd; FHA; Accolade Dinner 86; Frostburg ST Coll; Engl Techr.

YOUNG, HORACE MOO; Northwestern HS; Takoma Park, MD; (Y); Office Aide; JV Bsktbl; High Hon Roll; Hon Roll; NHS; Cvl Engrng.

YOUNG, JAMES; Fort Hill HS; Cumberland, MD; (Y); 23/253; Computer Clb; Thesps; Jr Cls; Sr Cls; Rep Stu Cncl; Stat Bsktbl; Ftbl; Trk; Cit Awd; Hon Roll; Mst Dpndbl Male SR Cls, RR YMCA Mnd, Bdy, Sprt Awd, Bst Actr Schl Ply 85-86; Western Maryland Coll; Intrpr.

YOUNG, JILL; Bishop Walsh HS; Cumberland, MD; (Y); Cmnty Wkr; Dance Clb; Hosp Aide; Pep Clb; Ski Clb; Yrbk Stf; Hon Roll.

YOUNG, JON; Walt Whitman HS; Bethesda, MD; (Y); Church Yth Grp; Intnl Clb; Model UN; Varsity Clb; Concert Band; Jazz Band; Mrchg Band; Symp Band; Socr; Wrstlng; Pre-Med.

YOUNG, KAREN; Seneca Valley HS; Germantown, MD; (Y); Church Yth Grp; Cmnty Wkr; Drama Clb; Church Choir; School Play; Prncpls Awd Otstndng Wrtng 83-84; Sprntn Dnts Awd Otstndng Wrtng 83-84.

YOUNG, KRISTIN TAYLOR; Takoma Acad; Silver Spring, MD; (S); Church Yth Grp; Drama Clb; Stage Crew; Variety Show; Cheerleading; Crs Cntry; Trk; Hon Roll; NHS; St Johns Coll; Eng.

YOUNG, LUCIA; Eleanor Roosevelt HS; Bowie, MD; (Y); AFS; VP Exploring; Sec Pres Spanish Clb; Hon Roll; Ntl Merit Ltr; Sec Pres Spanish NHS; Church Yth Grp; Stat Socr; Jr NHS; 1st Pl & 2nd Pl Natl Spnsh Exm 84-85; Natl Mrt Hspnc Outstndng Prfrmnc Hnr Cert 84-86; U Of MD.

YOUNG, MELISSA; Dulaney SR HS; Lutherville, MD; (Y); Church Yth Grp; Dance Clb; Hosp Aide; Teachers Aide; Variety Show; Yrbk Sprt Ed; Rep Soph Cls; Rep Jr Cls; Sec Stu Cncl; Powder Puff Ftbl; Med.

YOUNG, NANCY LYNN; La Reine HS; Largo, MD; (Y); 8/149; Church Yth Grp; SADD; Yrbk Stf; Mgr(s); L Mgr Trk; French Hon Soc; High Hon Roll; NHS; Cmnty Wkr; Dance Clb; Physics Olympiad Awd 85-86; Frnch V Awd 85-86; St Andrews Acad Schlrshp 86-87; St Andrews Coll; Soc Sci.

YOUNG, PAMELA; Calvert HS; Pr Frederick, MD; (Y); Office Aide; Teachers Aide; Chorus; Drm Mjr(t); Bsktbl; Score Keeper; Trk; Hon Roll; Pfct Attndnce 83-86; Katharine Gibbs; Data Proc.

YOUNG, WILLIAM; Frederick HS; Frederick, MD; (Y); Computer Clb; Red Cross Aide; Spanish Clb; Teachers Aide; Varsity Clb; Off Sr Cls; Rep Stu Cncl; Var Diving; Var Capt Swmmng; Hon Roll; Mst Imprvd Swmng Awd 84-85; Comp Sci.

YOUNGBLOOD, CARLA; Oldtown HS; Oldtown, MD; (S); Trs Church Yth Grp; FBLA; VP FHA; Office Aide; Sec Jr Cls; Bsktbl; Capt Cheerleading; Vllybl; High Hon Roll; NHS; Allegany CC; Med Sec.

YOUNGER, CHRISTOPHER; Cardinal Gibber HS; Baltimore, MD; (Y); 27/127; School Play; Trs Jr Cls; Off Sr Cls; Hon Roll; Prfct Atten Awd; Mt St Marys.

YOUNGER, CYNTHIA; Institute Of Notre Dame; Baltimore, MD; (Y); 35/140; Hosp Aide; Rep Frsh Cls; Rep Jr Cls; JV Capt Lcrss; Var Socr; Art.

YOUNGER, SAMUEL; Northwestern HS; Hyattsville, MD; (Y); Am Leg Boys St; Aud/Vis; Boy Scts; ROTC; Chorus; School Musical; Variety Show; Stu Cncl; Var Ftbl; Wt Lftg; Resrv Offcs Assm Mertrious Cntrbtn Awd 86; Lght Hvy Wght Pwr Lftng Chmpn 86; Bst All Arnd Awd-Tlnt Shw; Hampton U; Arntcs.

YOUSE, HOLLY; Elkton HS; Elkton, MD; (Y); 63/250; Civic Clb; Pep Clb; Teachers Aide; Band; Concert Band; Mrchg Band; Rep Frsh Cls; Rep Soph Cls; Rep Jr Cls; Rep Sr Cls; Senatorial Schlrshp 86; Salisbury ST Coll; Bus Admin.

YUFFEE, MICHAEL; Walt Whitman HS; Bethesda, MD; (Y); Civic Clb; Red Cross Aide; Rep Service Clb; Rep Temple Yth Grp; Band; Mrchg Band; Symp Band; Im Bsktbl; Schrlshp Pgm Adv Training Cell Molecular 86; Bio Aid Walter Reed Army Inst 86; Pre-Med.

YURCIK, LORRAINE; Franklin SR HS; Reisterstown, MD; (Y); 6/300; Concert Band; Drm Mjr(t); Mrchg Band; Symp Band; High Hon Roll; Hon Roll; Lion Awd; Pres NHS; Yuth Govt Day 85; Spec Schlr Awd, Won Essay 86; U MD Baltimore; Sec Ed.

YUTZY, JULIE; Allegany HS; Cumberland, MD; (Y); 1/240; Sec AFS; Am Leg Aux Girls St; Band; Concert Band; Mrchg Band; Trs Sr Cls; Cit Awd; High Hon Roll; NHS; Ocnogrphy.

ZADNAVEC, STEFANIE C; Bethseda Chevy Chase HS; Chevy Chase, MD; (Y); 92/450; Cmnty Wkr; Pres Drama Clb; French Clb; German Clb; Pres Thesps; Acpl Chr; Madrigals; School Musical; School Play; Lit Mag; Catherine Filene Shouse Theatr Awd 86; Ntl Spch & Drama Awd 86; Connecticut Coll; Theatr.

ZAHN JR, RICHARD S; Catonsville HS; Catonsville, MD; (Y); Debate Tm; Drama Clb; School Musical; School Play; Nwsp Rptr; Lit Mag; High Hon Roll; Hon Roll; Hnrb Mntn Natl Fndtn For Advancement In The Arts 85; Natl Merit Corp-Commended Stu 85; Carnegie-Mellon U; Fine Arts.

ZAHNER, WAYNE J; Archbishop Curley HS; Baltimore, MD; (S); 9/143; Chess Clb; Church Yth Grp; Concert Band; Nwsp Stf; High Hon Roll; Hon Roll; NHS; Mrn Brk Knott Schlrshp 83; Gnrl Exclnc 84-85; Accntnt.

ZAJIC, DAVID M; Randallstown SR HS; Randallstown, MD; (Y); Drama Clb; PAVAS; Acpl Chr; Chorus; Orch; School Musical; Hon Roll; NHS; Ntl Merit SF; Principal Violist Of Grtr Baltimore Yth Orch 84-86; Music Comp.

ZAMPINI, TRACEY; Dundalk HS; Baltimore, MD; (Y); Church Yth Grp; Band; Concert Band; Jazz Band; Mrchg Band; Orch; Pep Band; JV Var Mgr(s); Var Vllybl; Hon Roll; Prfrmng Arts.

ZANELOTTI, TONI; Mc Donough HS; White Plains, MD; (Y); Cmnty Wkr; Drama Clb; 4-H; Teachers Aide; Thesps; Chorus; School Musical; School Play; Stage Crew; Swing Chorus; Prt Tbbco Plyr Awds Bst Spprtng Actrs Mscl 86; Thspn Clb Trsr 86-87; Pres Mxd Choir 84-85; Prfrmng Arts.

ZANGL, LESLIE; Southern SR No 70 HS; Baltimore, MD; (Y); Nwsp Rptr; Nwsp Sprt Ed; Nwsp Stf; Var Cheerleading; Prfct Atten Awd; Intnl Clb; Teachers Aide; Var Badmtn; Var Gym; Engrng Pipeln 84-87; Penn ST; Comp Proc.

ZANNINO, SALVATORE V; Our Lady Of Pompei HS; Baltimore, MD; (S); Pep Clb; Varsity Clb; Church Choir; Nwsp Stf; Yrbk Bus Mgr; Pres Sr Cls; VP Stu Cncl; Var L Socr; Prfct Atten Awd; Church Choir Partcptn Awd 86; Outstndng Svc Awd 86; Mass Cmmnctn.

ZAWODNY, NICOLE; Harford Christian Schl; Nottingham, PA; (S); 4/31; Church Yth Grp; Chorus; Stu Cncl; Cit Awd; Hon Roll; Prfct Atten Awd; Hghst Av French Awd 85; Typing Awd 85; Bob Jones U; Nrsng.

ZAY, JENNIFER; Gov Thomas Johnson HS; Frederick, MD; (Y); Church Yth Grp; Cmnty Wkr; Latin Clb; Yrbk Stf; Stu Cncl; Bsktbl; Co-Capt Fld Hcky; Swmmng; Hon Roll; Voluntr Yr Awd ARC 86; All Cnty Fld Hcky Team 85; Slippery Rock U; Spec Educ.

ZEALAND, ELISE; Allegany HS; Cumberland, MD; (Y); 13/250; Pres Church Yth Grp; Pep Clb; Yrbk Stf; Off Frsh Cls; Stu Cncl; Cheerleading; Hon Roll; NHS; Commnctns.

ZEBARTH, LAURA; Mc Donough HS; White Plains, MD; (Y); Cmnty Wkr; Intnl Clb; Chorus; Fld Hcky; Trk; 4-H Awd; High Hon Roll; Hon Roll; Prfct Atten Awd; MD Miss Teen Pgnt Cntstnt 85; Bus Econ.

ZEGAL, CHRIS; Fallston HS; Kingsville, MD; (Y); 11/250; Boy Scts; Math Clb; Scholastic Bowl; Yrbk Bus Mgr; High Hon Roll; Hon Roll; Trs NHS; Ntl Merit Ltr; Acad Ltr 85-86.

ZEGLIN, MARY PATRICIA; Academy Of Holy Names; Silver Spring, MD; (Y); Pep Clb; School Musical; School Play; Yrbk Bus Mgr; Yrbk Rptr; Yrbk Stf; Lit Mag; Cheerleading; Socr; Trk; Chld Psych.

ZEIGLER, BRYAN; James M Bennett SR HS; Salisbury, MD; (Y); 11/200; Church Yth Grp; French Clb; Key Clb; Math Tm; Thesps; Church Choir; School Musical; Var Trk; Mu Alp Tht; Hon Roll; Prfct Score-MD St Math Comptn 85; Tied For Hgh Score-Rgnl Math Comptn 85; Comp Sci.

ZEILER, KAREN; Institute Of Notre Dame; Baltimore, MD; (Y); Art Clb; Spanish Clb; Nwsp Rptr; High Hon Roll; Crtfct Mrt 86; Ntl Spnsh Exm 86; Scnd Hnrs & Frst Hnrs 83-86; Washington Coll; Intrntl Rltns.

ZENDT, ABBY; Bishop Walsh HS; Cumberland, MD; (Y); NHS; U Of NC; Pharm.

ZEPP, AARON; Westminster SR HS; Westminster, MD; (Y); Teachers Aide; JV Crs Cntry; Hon Roll; Comp Sci.

ZERRLANT, WALTER; Patapsco HS; Baltimore, MD; (Y); Church Yth Grp; Chorus; Church Choir; Stage Crew; Rep Frsh Cls; Hon Roll; Relgn.

ZIEBA, JOHN; Parkdale HS; College Park, MD; (Y); 4/500; Pres Soph Cls; Pres Jr Cls; French Hon Soc; High Hon Roll; NHS; Pres Schlr; Prince Georges Cnty Bd Educ Stu Mbr 86; Its Acadmc Clb 85; U Of MD; Acctg.

ZIEGLER, ROBERT; Crossland SR HS; Upper Marlboro, MD; (Y); Lit Mag; Pres Frsh Cls; Rep Soph Cls; Rep Jr Cls; Pres Stu Cncl; Var L Ftbl; Wt Lftg; High Hon Roll; Hon Roll; Pres Jr NHS; West Point Military Acad.

ZIELINSKI, MAURITA; Seneca Valley HS; Gaitherstown, MD; (Y); 100/490; Dance Clb; VP Drama Clb; German Clb; Teachers Aide; Acpl Chr; Chorus; School Musical; School Play; Vllybl; Hon Roll; Prinicpls Wrtng Awd 86; SR Spotlight Chamber Singer 86; SR Of Mo For Aesthetics 85-86; Webster U; Theatre Arts.

ZILER, PAULA; Allegany HS; Cumberland, MD; (Y); 11/249; AFS; Pres Church Yth Grp; Hosp Aide; Pep Clb; Rep Frsh Cls; Rep Stu Cncl; Im Fld Hcky; Var Trk; Im Vllybl; Hon Roll; UMBC; Pre-Med.

ZIMMERMAN, DEBORAH; Suitland HS; District Hts, MD; (Y); Aud/Vis; Church Yth Grp; French Clb; Letterman Clb; Science Clb; Teachers Aide; Band; Mrchg Band; Mgr(s); Socr; Suitlands Spc Shuttl Tm 82-86; Sci Fair 83; Prnc Georges Bd Of Trustees 86; Prince George CC.

ZIMMERMAN, JENNIFER; Broadneck HS; Arnold, MD; (S); DECA; JA; Orch; Tennis; Wt Lftg; 3rd Pl Cnty Fshn Shw 85; 2nd Pl ST Fshn Shw 86; 3rd Pl Cnty Gnrl Mrchndse 85; Loyola U; Bus.

ZIMMERMAN, PAM; Mt Savage HS; Corriganville, MD; (S); Hosp Aide; Band; Chorus; Jazz Band; Nwsp Stf; Sec Stu Cncl; Cheerleading; High Hon Roll.

ZIMMERMAN, PAMELA; Mt Savage HS; Corriganville, MD; (Y); Trs French Clb; Band; Chorus; Concert Band; Jazz Band; Mrchg Band; Nwsp Stf; Sec Stu Cncl; Cheerleading; High Hon Roll; Allegany CC; Psychtrst.

ZINKHAN, VICKIE; Joppatowne HS; Edgewood, MD; (Y); Powder Puff Ftbl; Hon Roll; Stu Mnth 86; U MD; Acctng.

ZINN, KEVEN; Calvert HS; Lusby, MD; (Y); Church Yth Grp; Varsity Clb; JV Bsbl; Var JV Ftbl; Var Wt Lftg; Hon Roll; Bnkng.

ZINN, SUSAN; Northern HS; Sunderland, MD; (Y); 7/301; Am Leg Aux Girls St; Pres Church Yth Grp; Intnl Clb; Church Choir; Stu Cncl; Capt Cheerleading; Trk; High Hon Roll; Capt NHS; Opt Clb Awd; Campbell U.

ZIRKLE, CHRISTINE; Frederick HS; Frederick, MD; (Y); 100/380; Art Clb; Church Yth Grp; French Clb; Letterman Clb; SADD; Teachers Aide; Drm Mjr(t); Yrbk Phtg; Yrbk Rptr; Yrbk Sprt Ed; Mst Imprvd Vlybl Plyr 83-84; Mst Vlbl Dfnsv Plyr Vlybl 84-85; Sprklng Sprt Awd Chrldng 85-86; Commnctns.

ZISELBERGER, PATRICK N; Seneca Valley HS; Gaithersburg, MD; (Y); 157/550; Drama Clb; Capt Quiz Bowl; Science Clb; School Play; Stage Crew; Ntl Merit Ltr; Arts Schlrshp Search 85-86; Liberal Arts Ed; Engl Mjr.

ZULLO, STEPHEN; Fallston HS; Fallston, MD; (Y); 1/250; Boy Scts; Debate Tm; Math Clb; Scholastic Bowl; Yrbk Ed-Chief; NHS; Ntl Merit SF; German Clb; Science Clb; Yrbk Stf; Achvd Rnk Egl Sct 85.

ZUMBRUM, ANDREW; Crossland HS; Suitland, MD; (Y); 5/300; Math Clb; Math Tm; High Hon Roll; Hon Roll; NHS; GATE; MD U; Phrmcy.

ZURETTI, CHERYL; South Carroll HS; Mt Airy, MD; (Y); 7/350; Am Leg Aux Girls St; Varsity Clb; Band; Mrchg Band; Pres Frsh Cls; Pres Soph Cls; Pres Jr Cls; Pres Sr Cls; JV Var Bsktbl; Var L Tennis; Med Career.

NEW JERSEY

AANONSEN, ERIC; Morristown Beard HS; Whippany, NJ; (Y); AFS; Church Yth Grp; Model UN; Church Choir; Pres Sr Cls; JV Bsbl; Var L Socr; JV Swmmng; Architecture.

ABALOS, VERONICA; Columbia HS; S Orange, NJ; (Y); Aud/Vis; Cmnty Wkr; Political Wkr; Nwsp Rptr; Stu Cncl; Cheerleading; Communications.

ABASOLO, GARY; St Aloysius HS; Springfield, NJ; (Y); 11/111; Chess Clb; Spanish Clb; Nwsp Sprt Ed; Var Capt Bsbl; Capt Bowling; Var L Socr; Var L Tennis; High Hon Roll; NHS; All Around Spts Awd 86; NY U Schlrshp 86; Fordham U Lincoln Ctr; Pre Law.

ABBATTISTA, MICHAEL; Queen Of Peace HS; North Arlington, NJ; (S); 2/235; SADD; Band; Ed Nwsp Stf; Capt Yrbk Stf; Rep Stu Cncl; High Hon Roll; NHS; Dance Clb; Science Clb; Concert Band; Dstngshd Schlr Awd JR Cls; Mktg.

ABBE, DAVID J; Cinnaminson HS; Cinnaminson, NJ; (Y); Am Leg Boys St; Math Tm; Quiz Bowl; Scholastic Bowl; Science Clb; Var Bsbl; Var Bsktbl; NHS; Brlngtn Cnty Schlstc Lge All-Str Lbrty Div Bsbl 86; All-Grp 3 Bsbl S Jrsy 86; All Sth Jrsy Bsbl Hon Mn; Engr.

ABBOTT, CHRIS B; Pleasantville HS; Absecon, NJ; (S); 1/132; Rensselaer Medal 86.

ABBOTT, JENNY; North Hunterdon HS; Glen Gardner, NJ; (Y); Drama Clb; Chorus; Church Choir; School Play; Yrbk Stf; Empire Schl Of Beauty; Csmtlgst.

ABBOTT, MICHELE MARIE; St James HS; Penns Grove, NJ; (Y); 21/77; Am Leg Aux Girls St; Sec Church Yth Grp; Drama Clb; School Musical; Pres Frsh Cls; Rep Jr Cls; Off Sr Cls; Var Bsktbl; Var Fld Hcky; Var Sftbl; Girls Ctznshp Inst 85; St Josephs U; Poltcn.

ABBOTT, WAYNE; Hightstown HS; E Windsor, NJ; (Y); 70/343; Computer Clb; French Clb; Im Ftbl; Var L Socr; Hon Roll; NHS; Rutgers Engrng Awd 86; National Hnr Soc 85-86; Rutgers Engrng; Engrng Elec.

ABBRUZZESE, ALISA; Washington Township HS; Turnersville, NJ; (Y); Church Yth Grp; German Clb; Ski Clb; Spanish Clb; Rutgers; Psych.

ABDALLA, CHRISTINE; Mount St Mary Acad; Somerset, NJ; (Y); GAA; Spanish Clb; Yrbk Stf; JV Fld Hcky; Var Hon Roll; Outstndng Exc Soc Studies 85-86; Dentst.

ABDELAZIZ, AISHE; Dickinson HS; Jersey City, NJ; (Y); Computer Clb; French Clb; Hosp Aide; Prfct Atten Awd; Hrn Rl 83; Merit Rl 85; Comp.

ABELE JR, DONALD B; Gloucester City JR SR HS; Gloucester, NJ; (Y); Computer Clb; Hosp Aide; Library Aide; Science Clb; Ski Clb; Spanish Clb; Chorus; School Play; Nwsp Phtg; Nwsp Stf; Attnd Rotary Yth Ldrshp Awds Conf 86; Bio Resrch.

ABELLO, ROSALINA M; Hunterdon Central HS; Lebanon, NJ; (Y); 129/550; Church Yth Grp; Dance Clb; Band; JV Bsktbl; Var Sftbl; JV Trk; Hon Roll; Cert Merit Libr Aid 83-84; Natl Phys Fit Awd 83-84; S S Merit Cert 83-84.

ABITABILO, DONNA; B R HS West; Bridgewater, NJ; (Y); Church Yth Grp; Hosp Aide; Office Aide; Yrbk Stf; Off Soph Cls; Off Jr Cls; Stat Crs Cntry; Stat Socr; Stat Trk; Hon Roll; 2nd Rnr-Up Prom Queen 86; Stu Aid VP Schl 86; Psych.

ABOTSI, LEONE; St John Vianney HS; Aberdeen, NJ; (Y); Computer Clb; FBLA; Intnl Clb; Library Aide; Service Clb; Drill Tm; Trk; Hon Roll; Penn ST U; Accntng.

ABRAHAM, ERIC; Matawan Aberdeen Regional HS; Aberdeen, NJ; (S); #11 In Class; Ski Clb; Temple Yth Grp; Thesps; Band; Concert Band; Jazz Band; Mrchg Band; School Musical; Variety Show; Bus.

ABRAHAM, SHIBU; Union HS; Union, NJ; (Y); Computer Clb; Varsity Clb; Church Choir; Awds Rifle Team & NRA 85-86; Rutgers; Pre Med.

ABRAHAMSEN, LUCILLE; Riverdell Regional HS; Oradell, NJ; (Y); 40/222; DECA; Teachers Aide; Chorus; School Musical; Im Vllybl; Stat Wrstlng; Hon Roll; Prncpls List 85-86; Pace U; Mktng.

ABRAMO, TEDDY; Hudson Catholic HS; Hoboken, NJ; (Y); 25/182; Am Leg Boys St; Var L Bsbl; Var L Bsktbl; Coach Actv; Im Vllybl; High Hon Roll; Hon Roll; Pres Schlr; Pres Citatn Acad Achvt 86; Acad All Am 86; Am Leg Bsbl All Star 85-86.

ABRAMS, KAREN; Wood-Ridge HS; Wood-Ridge, NJ; (S); Service Clb; Spanish Clb; Nwsp Rptr; Yrbk Stf; Lit Mag; Var Cheerleading; Sftbl; Hon Roll; NHS; Elon Coll.

ABRAMS, MARTIN; Garden State Acad; Willingboro, NJ; (Y); Church Yth Grp; Chorus; Church Choir; School Play; Score Keeper; Capt Sftbl; Hon Roll; Columbia Unn Coll; Hsptl Adm.

ABRAMSON, DANIEL; River Dell SR HS; River Edge, NJ; (Y); 79/210; VP Chess Clb; Computer Clb; Var Golf; JV Tennis; 3rd Pl NBICL Chess 85-86; Bryant Coll; Comp Sci.

ABRAMSON, RICHARD; Lakewood Prep; Toms River, NJ; (Y); Chess Clb; School Play; Nwsp Phtg; Rep Soph Cls; Pres Sr Cls; Pres Stu Cncl; Var Tennis; Hofstra U-Distngshd Acadmc Schlrshp 86; Hnrbl Mntn-NJ Inst Tech Alum Assn Poetry Cntst 86; Syracuse U.

ABRELL, MATTHIAS; St Pius X Regional HS; Somerset, NJ; (Y); Off ROTC; Ski Clb; Drill Tm; Var Ftbl; Var Wrstlng; Hon Roll; Rider Coll German Comp 1st 86; Engl.

ACCATATTA, ANNETTE; Hillsborough HS; Neshanic Station, NJ; (Y); CAP; Drama Clb; Pep Clb; Ski Clb; Band; Chorus; School Play; Stage Crew; Lit Mag; Powder Puff Ftbl; Miss Coed Teen Amer Pgnt 86; Pen Wmn Amer Awd 82; Crmnl Jstc.

ACERRA, TONY; Hudson Catholic HS; Hoboken, NJ; (Y); SADD; Ftbl; Sftbl; Vllybl; Wt Lftg; High Hon Roll; Hon Roll; Acdmc All Amrcn 85-86; Rutgers; Acctnt.

ACEVEDO, ZULMA; Essex County Vo Tech HS; Orlando, FL; (Y); Var JV Sftbl; Prfct Atten Awd; Bus Adm.

ACHENBACH, DEBBIE; St Mary HS; E Brunswick, NJ; (Y); 21/118; Church Yth Grp; Library Aide; Ski Clb; SADD; Teachers Aide; School Play; Nwsp Stf; Yrbk Bus Mgr; Yrbk Stf; Ed Lit Mag; E Brunswick Regnl Chmbr Cmmrc Schlrshp Wnnr; Hgh Hnrs Ech Qrtr Evry Yr; Natl Multi Sclros Gld Medls; Lebanon Valley Coll; Elem Ed.

ACIERNO, MARK; Hopatcong HS; Hopatcong, NJ; (Y); 26/173; Boy Scts; Church Yth Grp; Exploring; Ski Clb; Ftbl; Wt Lftg; High Hon Roll; Hon Roll; Aiasa Tech Wrtng Awd 2nd 83; Stockton ST Coll; Envrnmtl Sci.

ACKERMAN, MARC; Indian Hills HS; Oakland, NJ; (Y); Drama Clb; Jazz Band; Ed Nwsp Phtg; Trs Frsh Cls; Trs Soph Cls; Trs Jr Cls; Trs Sr Cls; JV Socr; JV Hon Roll; Temple Yth Grp; IBM Ldrshp Seminar.

ACKERMAN, MICHAEL; Indian Hills HS; Franklin Lks, NJ; (Y); AFS; Temple Yth Grp; Nwsp Stf; Yrbk Stf; Rep Stu Cncl; JV Var Bsbl; Wt Lftg; Hon Roll; NHS; Ntl Merit Ltr; IBM Ldrshp Sem 85; Foster Parents Clb 85-86; Politcs.

ACKERMAN, THOMAS; Boonton HS; Boonton, NJ; (Y); 10/243; Church Yth Grp; Math Tm; Band; Jazz Band; Nwsp Stf; Rep Soph Cls; Rep Jr Cls; Capt Crs Cntry; Var Trk; High Hon Roll; Accntng.

ACKROYD, ELIZABETH; West Milford Township HS; West Milford, NJ; (S); 10/350; Church Yth Grp; French Clb; Nwsp Stf; Yrbk Stf; JV Var Fld Hcky; High Hon Roll; Hon Roll; NHS; Jrnlsm.

ACOSTA, ANNYA; Memorial HS; W New York, NJ; (Y); Church Choir; Color Guard; Orch; School Play; Lit Mag; Rep Frsh Cls; Rep Soph Cls; Rep Jr Cls; Stu Cncl; JV Sftbl; Lbrl Arts.

ACOSTA, GRISEL; North Bergen HS; North Bergen, NJ; (Y); Variety Show; Hon Roll; Seton Hall U; Spec Ed.

ACOSTA, JUAN; St Peters Prep; Manalapan, NJ; (Y); Dance Clb; Intnl Clb; Stage Crew; Tennis; Trk.

ACOSTA, RICHARD; North Bergen HS; N Bergen, NJ; (Y); 11/500; High Hon Roll; Hon Roll; Jr NHS; NHS; Ntl Merit SF; Italina Hnr Soc 84-86; Italian Clb 84-86.

ACTON, THOMAS; Clifton HS; Clifton, NJ; (Y); Boys Clb Am; Church Yth Grp; SADD; Nwsp Rptr; JV L Bsktbl; Var Capt Socr; Hon Roll; Jr NHS; Yth Wk-Schl Admstrtr 1 Day; Career Day Prudential Ins; Mst Imprvd Sccr Plyr; Acctng.

ADAMCHAK, SUE; Wayne Hills HS; Wayne, NJ; (Y); Church Yth Grp; GAA; Science Clb; Yrbk Stf; JV Socr; JV Sftbl; Var Vllybl; Hon Roll; Penn ST U; Nrsng.

ADAMS, ALLISON; Villa Victoria Acad; Trenton, NJ; (Y); Art Clb; Cmnty Wkr; Dance Clb; Chorus; School Musical; Yrbk Stf; Hon Roll; Philadelphia Coll Text; Fshn.

ADAMS, BRIAN; Rancocas Valley Regional HS; Mount Holly, NJ; (Y); 47/271; Computer Clb; Quiz Bowl; Orch; Arch.

ADAMS, JIM; Hamilton H S East; Hamilton Sq, NJ; (Y); 34/326; Band; Concert Band; Mrchg Band; Rep Stu Cncl; JV Bsktbl; NHS; Rutger U; Bio Chem.

ADAMS, KELLY; Absegami HS; Egg Hbr, NJ; (Y); 5/235; Pres 4-H; GAA; Key Clb; Rep Stu Cncl; L Crs Cntry; 4-H Awd; High Hon Roll; Trs NHS; Studies Piano 11 Yrs; Phrmcy.

ADAMS, KIM; Williamstown HS; Williamstown, NJ; (Y); Library Aide; Yrbk Stf; Sec Soph Cls; Rep Jr Cls; Rep Stu Cncl; Stat Bsktbl; JV Var Mgr(s); JV Var Score Keeper; VFW Awd; Voice Dem Awd; Secndry Educ.

ADAMS, KIMBERLY; West Orange HS; W Orange, NJ; (Y); 20/168; Am Leg Aux Girls St; Church Yth Grp; French Clb; School Play; Yrbk Stf; Off Sr Cls; Swmmng; French Hon Soc; Hon Roll; NHS; Southern Methodist U.

ADAMS, LISA; Howell HS; Howell, NJ; (Y); 43/400; FBLA; Stat Bsbl; JV Bsktbl; Var Capt Socr; Im Sftbl; Im Vllybl; Hon Roll; HS All-Time Grls Sccr Tm 86; Bst Offsnv Plyr Of Yr Sccr 86.

ADAMS, MARK; Steinert HS; Hamilton Sq, NJ; (Y); 87/315; AFS; Church Yth Grp; Exploring; School Musical; School Play; Stage Crew; High Hon Roll; Hon Roll.

ADAMS, SCOTT; Burlington City HS; Edgewater Park, NJ; (Y); 23/160; Drexel; Physics.

ADAMSON, LINDA; Wildwood HS; Wildwood, NJ; (Y); 17/121; Yrbk Ed-Chief; Rep Jr Cls; Rep Sr Cls; Rep Stu Cncl; Am Leg Scholar 86; Elon Coll; Mass Cmmnctns.

ADANAS, VAHRAM; Memorial HS; West New York, NJ; (Y); 40/480; Computer Clb; Key Clb; Spanish Clb; Var L Tennis; High Hon Roll; Hon Roll; Prfct Atten Awd; Hlth Clb 85-86; MVP For Mem Boys Tennis Team 86; Dstrct Tns Trnmnt 84; Pre-Med.

ADDIEGO, MATTHEW; Holy Cross HS; Burlington, NJ; (Y); Chess Clb; Computer Clb; Science Clb; Stage Crew; Hon Roll; Bus.

ADDIS, KIRK S; BCVT Medford Campus; Medford, NJ; (S); 9/153; VICA; Stu Cncl; Im Wt Lftg; Wrstlng; Hon Roll; 1st Pl VICA Wnnr Mchne Shp 84-85; Intramrl Wghtlftng Wnnr 82-85; Glouster Cnty Coll; Mktg.

ADDISON, ANN CAROL; Dickinson HS; Jersey City, NJ; (Y); GAA; Var Bsktbl; Var Sftbl; Comp.

ADELSBERG, RISA; Solomon Schechter Day Schl; Livingston, NJ; (Y); Hosp Aide; Service Clb; Nwsp Stf; Yrbk Ed-Chief; Yrbk Stf; Svc Awd Harlem Vly Mentl Hosp 84-85; Citatn Am Cancer Soc 85; Bus Adm.

ADELSOHN, DEBORAH; Livingston HS; Livingston, NJ; (Y); 51/496; Teachers Aide; Pres Band; Concert Band; School Musical; Stage Crew; Ed Yrbk Stf; JP Sousa Awd; Hosp Aide; Mrchg Band; School Play; Home, Schl Assn Music Awd 86; Cook Coll; Pre-Vet.

ADJOGA-OTU, NAA-MOMO A; Weequahic HS; Newark, NJ; (S); #8 In Class; Exploring; Library Aide; Speech Tm; Color Guard; VP Jr Cls; Rep Stu Cncl; Opt Clb Awd; Thomas Alva Edison-Max Mc Graw 84; Rutgers; Pre-Med.

ADLAKHA, MONA; Randolph HS; Randolph, NJ; (Y); 3/316; Hosp Aide; Sec Key Clb; Math Tm; Science Clb; Drill Tm; Stat Trk; Bausch & Lomb Sci Awd; High Hon Roll; NHS; Spanish NHS; Frgn Lang Forenc Trnmnt Spnsh 85; Rndlph HS Chem Awd 86; Distgshd Sec Awd At Key Clb Convtn 86; U Of VA; Engrng.

ADLASSNIG, SHARON; South Plainfield HS; S Plainfield, NJ; (Y); 44/206; Bus Admin.

ADLER, AMY; Buena Regional HS; Newfield, NJ; (S); Sec Church Yth Grp; Math Clb; Ski Clb; Varsity Clb; Drill Tm; Tennis; Hon Roll; Jr NHS; Mrktng.

ADLER, LORRIE J; Buena Regional HS; Newfield, NJ; (Y); 27/187; Art Clb; Spanish Clb; Varsity Clb; Rep Sr Cls; Sftbl; Tennis; Trk; Hon Roll; NHS; Seton Hill Coll; Grphc Dsgn.

ADLER, STEPHANIE; Jackson Memorial HS; Jackson, NJ; (Y); 31/343; DECA; FHA; German Clb; Hosp Aide; Drill Tm; Flag Corp; Nwsp Stf; Mgr(s); High Hon Roll; PTSO Lottery Schlrp Hgh Hon Rl 85-86; U DE; Dietetics.

ADOLPH, ROBERT; Wall HS; Manasquan Park, NJ; (Y); AFS; FCA; ROTC; Drill Tm; Bsbl; Bsktbl; Socr; Wt Lftg; High Hon Roll; Hon Roll; Chsn For All Cty Sccr Tm To Lndn 85; 2nd Tm All Conf Sccr 86; Fnc.

ADRIAN, CELESTE; Highstown HS; Robbinsville, NJ; (Y); Cmnty Wkr; Debate Tm; Drama Clb; French Clb; Chorus; Rep Jr Cls; Englsh.

ADSETT, ROGER J; Midland Park HS; Midland Park, NJ; (Y); Am Leg Boys St; Computer Clb; Debate Tm; Off Soph Cls; Off Jr Cls; Off Sr Cls; Var Socr; Gov Hon Prg Awd; High Hon Roll; NHS; Scl Stds Stu Of Yr HS 85-86; Hgh O Brn Yth Fndtn Rep 84-85; Outstndg Stu U S Hstry HS 85-86; Intl Rltns.

ADZEMA, DAVID; Morristown HS; Morris Plains, NJ; (Y); Exploring; Ski Clb; Var Lcrss; Hon Roll.

AFFINITO, JAMES; Manchestere Regional HS; Haledon, NJ; (Y); Am Leg Boys St; Aud/Vis; Band; Concert Band; Mrchg Band; Nwsp Ed-Chief; Nwsp Phtg; Rep Sr Cls; Rep Stu Cncl; Var Golf; Draftsman.

AFFLITTO, CHARLENE; Verona HS; Verona, NJ; (Y); Girl Scts; Hosp Aide; Chorus; School Play; Rep Frsh Cls; Cheerleading; Spanish NHS; Psych.

AGLIATA, NARDINA; Bishop George Ahr HS; Carteret, NJ; (Y); French Clb; Intnl Clb; Ski Clb; SADD; Drill Tm; Yrbk Stf; Pom Pon; Score Keeper; Vllybl; Hon Roll; Med.

AGLIOZZO, CHRISTINA; Oak Knoll Schl; Short Hills, NJ; (Y); Hosp Aide; Key Clb; Pep Clb; Service Clb; Spanish Clb; Chorus; Nwsp Rptr; Yrbk Stf; Hon Roll; Nrsng.

AGNESS, GARY; Audubon HS; Audubon, NJ; (Y); DECA; Office Aide; JV Bsktbl; Var Golf; Hon Roll; DECA 3rd Pl Gld Disply Diadrama 86; Camden Cnty Coll; Acctng.

AGNOLET, JEANINE; Queen Of Peace HS; Lyndhurst, NJ; (S); 7/231; Church Yth Grp; Model UN; NFL; Service Clb; SADD; Church Choir; Nwsp Ed-Chief; NHS; Opt Clb Awd; VFW Awd; Comm.

AGOSTINI, FRANCESCA; Parsippany Hills HS; Parsippany, NJ; (Y); 32/302; Church Yth Grp; School Musical; Variety Show; Lit Mag; Stu Cncl; Hon Roll; NHS; Service Clb; Chorus; Var Fld Hcky; U S Sec Of Educ Intl Yth Yr Awd 85; Jaycs Outstndng Yng Prsn Awd 86; Prnt Tchr Stu Assn Schlrshp 86; Loyola Coll Of MD; Psychlgy.

AGOSTINO, JOSEPH; Secaucus HS; Secaucus, NJ; (S); 14/169; Am Leg Boys St; Computer Clb; Math Clb; Math Tm; Varsity Clb; JV Bsbl; Var Trk; Hon Roll; Mu Alp Tht; NHS; Rutgers Coll; Arontcl Engr.

AGOSTON, DAVID; Oratory Catholic Prep; Montville, NJ; (Y); Chess Clb; Computer Clb; Ski Clb; Nwsp Rptr; JV Capt Socr; Im Vllybl; High Hon Roll; NHS; NEDT Awd.

AGRANOFF, PHIL; Wayne Valley HS; Wayne, NJ; (Y); Boy Scts; Cmnty Wkr; FBLA; JA; Ski Clb; Temple Yth Grp; Y-Teens; Hon Roll; Rotary Awd; Bus Adm.

AGRAWAL, NEELU; Marlboro HS; Marlboro, NJ; (Y); 1/500; Library Aide; Math Tm; Science Clb; Sec SADD; Teachers Aide; Band; Ed Lit Mag; Sec Stu Cncl; High Hon Roll; Jr NHS; Rutgers Dean Smmr Schlrshp 85; Yth Of Yr-Lcl Exch Clb 86; U Of PA; Comp Sci.

AGRAWAL, NEIL; Parsippany HS; Parsippany, NJ; (Y); German Clb; Math Tm; Spanish Clb; Hon Roll; NHS; Ntl Merit Ltr; Prfct Atten Awd.

AGRIFOLIO, MARY LYNN; West Essex HS; Fairfield, NJ; (Y); DECA; FTA; Girl Scts; Science Clb; Spanish Clb; Cheerleading; Sftbl; Cit Awd; Hon Roll; DECA Cls Hist 85-86; Hon Roll 85-86; Italian Club 82; Artistic Acad.

AGUILERA, ALICIA; St Mary Of The Assumption HS; Hillside, NJ; (S); 8/59; Dance Clb; Hosp Aide; Office Aide; Variety Show; Yrbk Stf; Rep Soph Cls; Sec Trs Sr Cls; Bowling; Hon Roll; Frnch II Awd 83-84; 2nd Pl Hstry Fair Awd 84; Hstry Fair Hnrbl Ment 85.

AHEARN, SHARON; Bernards HS; Bernardsville, NJ; (Y); AFS; Spanish Clb; Varsity Clb; Chorus; Orch; Stage Crew; Nwsp Stf; Yrbk Phtg; Var Capt Crs Cntry; Fld Hcky; Book Schlrshp To U Of FL 86-87; Cross Cntry Colonal Hills Ind Champ 85; U Of FL; Bus.

AHKAMI, SHERRY; Montclair Kimberley Acad; Clifton, NJ; (Y); Pres AFS; Hosp Aide; Ed Yrbk Phtg; Sec Frsh Cls; Sec Sr Cls; Var Fld Hcky; Var Lcrss; Hon Roll; Red & Blk Soc Pres; U Of VA; Govt.

AHLMAN, STACY; Hunterdon Central HS; Ringoes, NJ; (Y); 86/549; Sec Church Yth Grp; FCA; Pep Clb; Capt Drill Tm; School Musical; Variety Show; Timer; Hon Roll; Jr NHS; NHS; Bio.

AHN, LUCIA; Northern Valleγ Regional HS; Old Tappan, NJ; (Y); AFS; Intnl Clb; VP Chorus; Hon Roll; Julliard Awd; Uillard Coll; Piano.

AIBEL, MATTHEW B; Northern Valley Regional HS; Demarest, NJ; (Y); 2/246; Pres Drama Clb; Capt Quiz Bowl; Pres Temple Yth Grp; School Musical; School Play; Sec Stu Cncl; NCTE Awd; Ntl Merit SF; Math Tm; Office Aide; All Estrn & All ST Chrs 83-85; Dartmth Coll Alumni Awd 85; Hugh O Brian NJ Yth Ldrshp Smnr 84; Actor.

AIELLO, JULIA; Chatham Twp HS; Denville, NJ; (Y); 11/128; Church Yth Grp; Computer Clb; Model UN; Band; Yrbk Sprt Ed; Var Fld Hcky; Stat Ice Hcky; Var Sftbl; Hon Roll; Sec NHS; PTO SR Achvt Awd 86; NJ Dstngshd Schlr 86; Pres Acadmc Fit Awd 86; Smith Coll; Lib Arts.

AIELLO JR, PHILIP J; South Plainfield HS; S Plainfield, NJ; (Y); Cmnty Wkr; Varsity Clb; JV Var Bsbl; JV Var Bsktbl; Hon Roll; 1st Tm Grp 2 Pitcher All-St 86; US Army Rerserves Schlr Athlete Awd 86; Seton Hall; Bus.

AILARA, EDMUND; Parsippany HS; Parsippany, NJ; (Y); Boy Scts; Latin Clb; JV Socr; JV Trk; JV Wrstlng; Hon Roll; Ntl Hnr Rl 86; AF Acad; Aerosp Engr.

AIRES, CECILIA; St Marys Of The Assumptn; Linden, NJ; (S); Pres Jr Cls; Vllybl; High Hon Roll; Hon Roll; Lang.

AJJA, MICHAEL G; Waldwick HS; Waldwick, NJ; (Y); 4/135; Am Leg Boys St; Math Tm; Varsity Clb; Nwsp Sprt Ed; Capt Bsktbl; Capt Crs Cntry; Trk; Hon Roll; NHS; Ntl Merit Ltr; Villanova; Elec Engrng.

AKER, GREGORY; Linden HS; Linden, NJ; (Y); High Hon Roll; Hon Roll; NHS; Prfct Atten Awd; Germ Hnr Scty Delta Epsilon Phi 84; Amer H S Math Exam Achvt Pin 86.

AKER, SAMANTHA; Southern Regional HS; Manahawkin, NJ; (Y); Cmnty Wkr; Model UN; Drill Tm; Nwsp Bus Mgr; Stat Bsbl; Stat Bsktbl; Ftbl; JV Var Socr; High Hon Roll; Hon Roll; Qll & Scrll Awd JR; U Of DE; Phy Thrpy.

AKGUN, ALTAY; Pope John XXIII Reg HS; Hopatcong, NJ; (Y); Hosp Aide; Quiz Bowl; Scholastic Bowl; Var Swmmng; JV Var Wrstlng; Hon Roll; NHS; Ntl Merit SF; Math Clb; Lit Mag; Bwmn Ashe Schrlshp U Miami 86; Achvt Awd US Hstry I 85; Mst Imprvd Swmr 85; U Miami; Med.

AKIAN, BERJ; Belleville SR HS; Belleville, NJ; (S); Boy Scts; Key Clb; Acpl Chr; Band; Church Choir; Madrigals; Mrchg Band; Orch; School Play; Stage Crew; Acctg.

AKKAWAY, ALAN; Clifton HS; Clifton, NJ; (Y); Computer Clb; Drama Clb; Ski Clb; Spanish Clb; Hon Roll; Jr NHS.

ALAIMO, CHRISTOPHER; Holmdel HS; Holmdel, NJ; (Y); 8/207; Boy Scts; VP Band; Jazz Band; Mrchg Band; School Musical; Yrbk Phtg; High Hon Roll; NHS; Grmn Hnr Soc Pres 84-85; U Of MI; Engrng.

ALARCON, CLAUDIA; Hillside HS; Hillside, NJ; (Y); Med.

ALBANESI, LUCIA; Life Center Acad; Wrightstown, NJ; (S); 2/14; Aud/Vis; Church Yth Grp; Chorus; Mrchg Band; Orch; Yrbk Stf; Bsktbl; French Hon Soc; Hon Roll; NHS.

ALBANO, PETER; Verona HS; Verona, NJ; (Y); Church Yth Grp; French Clb; Nwsp Stf; Yrbk Stf; French Hon Soc; High Hon Roll; 3rd Pl Music Ed Cncl 83; 1st Pl Music Ed Cncl 84; 2nd Pl Music Ed Cncl 85; Orthodonture.

ALBANO, VICTORIA; Holy Spirit HS; Atlantic City, NJ; (Y); Stage Crew; Sftbl; Tennis; Hon Roll; NHS.

ALBERT, JANICE LYNN; Kingsway Regional HS; Swedesboro, NJ; (Y); Ski Clb; JV Cheerleading; Crs Cntry; Powder Puff Ftbl; Gloucester County Coll; Elem Ed.

ALBERT, NATALIE; Watchung Hills HS; Warren, NJ; (Y); 14/350; SADD; VP Temple Yth Grp; Rep Soph Cls; Pres Jr Cls; Pres Sr Cls; JV Fld Hcky; Trk; NHS; Ntl Merit Ltr.

ALBERT, PAUL; Seton Hall Preparatory School; Irvington, NJ; (Y); 40/200; French Clb; Var L Bsktbl; Hon Roll; NEDT Awd; Bus.

ALBERT, RANDI M; Livingston HS; Livingston, NJ; (Y); 8/498; Hosp Aide; School Musical; Stage Crew; Nwsp Bus Mgr; Nwsp Rptr; Lit Mag; Pres French Hon Soc; High Hon Roll; Jr NHS; NHS; Wellesley Coll Bk Awd Outstndg JR 85; Cmmndtn Merit Le Grand Concours Fr Comp 85.

ALBERT, WARREN; Neptune SR HS; Neptune, NJ; (Y); 21/343; Computer Clb; Spanish Clb; Varsity Clb; Band; Concert Band; Mrchg Band; Var Bsbl; Im Bsktbl; High Hon Roll; Hon Roll; Omega Psi Phi Scroll Of Hnr 85; Alpha Phi Alpha Acad Awd & Schlrshp 86; Presdntl Acad Fitness Awd 86; U Of MD; Elec Engrng.

ALBERTSON, APRIL; Arthur P Schalick HS; Elmer, NJ; (Y); 19/128; Dance Clb; DECA; OEA; Ski Clb; Band; Chorus; Color Guard; Concert Band; Mrchg Band; Variety Show; Sears Rbck Fndtn Schlrshp 86; Bst Sctn Clrnt Awd 85; Pom Pon Cptn Awd 85; Goldey Beacom Bus Coll; Accntng.

ALBERTSON, CHRIS E; Millville SR HS; Mauricetown, NJ; (Y); Am Leg Boys St; Latin Clb; Var Bsktbl; Var Tennis; High Hon Roll; NHS.

ALBERTY, ANGELA; Monsignor Donovan HS; Toms River, NJ; (Y); Church Yth Grp; Drama Clb; SADD; Stage Crew; Yrbk Stf; 2nd Hnrs For Semstr 85; TEAM 85-86; Bus.

ALBINO, MYRIAM; Pinelands Regional HS; Tuckerton, NJ; (S); 22/147; French Clb; Sec Soph Cls; Rep Jr Cls; Rep Sr Cls; JV Bsktbl; Var Capt Fld Hcky; Mgr(s); Var Trk; Hon Roll; All Ocean Cnty Tm Fld Hcky WOBM Star Ldgr 85; All Star Tm Fld Hcky Gdn ST 85; All Star Rider Cmp 84; Rutgers U; Intl Comm.

ALBRECHT, ANNE; Middletown H S South; Middletown, NJ; (Y); Church Yth Grp; VP Pres Girl Scts; Hosp Aide; Flag Corp; Yrbk Stf; Trk; Hon Roll; Bronze Congressnl Awd 85; Grl Scout Silv Awd 84; Sci.

ALBRECHT, GARY; Fair Lawn HS; Fair Lawn, NJ; (Y); Bsbl; Ice Hcky; Bus Mrktng.

ALCANTARA, MICHAEL T; Indian Hills HS; Franklin Lakes, NJ; (Y); 6/274; Chorus; Ed Nwsp Stf; NHS; Ntl Merit SF; Chem.

ALDANA, ALLYSON; Pope John XXIII Regional HS; Newton, NJ; (Y); 10/145; Hosp Aide; Ski Clb; Yrbk Stf; Lit Mag; JV Cheerleading; JV Stat Swmmng; High Hon Roll; NHS; Sussex Cnty Med Soc Aux Scholar Awd 86; Adv Engl Awd; Achvt Awd; Fairfield U; Bio.

ALDEN, CARIN; West Essex SR HS; Fairfield, NJ; (Y); 28/350; Art Clb; Key Clb; Yrbk Stf; Lit Mag; Stu Cncl; Var Sftbl; Hon Roll; NHS; Hnrbl Mntn NJ Dstngshd Schlr 86; Mst Artstc Grdtng Cls 86; VA Polytechnic; Bus.

ALDER, KEITH; West Essex HS; Upper Montclair, NJ; (Y); 200/352; Aud/Vis; PAVAS; Chorus; School Play; Stage Crew; Swing Chorus; Variety Show; Frsh Cls; Outstndg Achvmnt Awd 86; Brd Dir Masauers HS 85-86; Embry Riddle U; Pilot.

ALDERTON, JENNIFER; Mount Olive HS; Flanders, NJ; (Y); Dance Clb; Science Clb; Ski Clb; SADD; Capt Cheerleading; AFS; Art Clb; Variety Show; Yrbk Stf.

ALDERTON, TODD; Saint Joseph Regional HS; Rivervale, NJ; (Y); Ski Clb; Teachers Aide; Coach Actv; Ftbl; Trk; Hon Roll; Schl Hon Roll 86; Ftbl Prtcptn Awd 84-86; JV Ftbl Ltrs 85; Bus Law.

ALDINGER, KRISTINE; Ocean Township HS; Ocean, NJ; (Y); 110/333; French Clb; Ski Clb; SADD; Nwsp Rptr; Adv.

ALDRICH, TIFFANY; Freehold Twp HS; Freehold, NJ; (Y); Church Yth Grp; Drama Clb; German Clb; School Play; Stage Crew; Yrbk Phtg; Yrbk Rptr; Yrbk Stf; Lit Mag; Score Keeper; Art.

ALEJANDRO, DORIS; Hoboken HS; Hoboken, NJ; (Y); Latin Clb; Nwsp Stf; Rep Jr Cls; Acclrtd Stu 83-85; Accntng.

ALEMAN, DENISE L; Neptune SR HS; Neptune, NJ; (Y); 7/400; Debate Tm; GAA; Model UN; Drm & Bgl; Yrbk Rptr; Yrbk Stf; Stu Cncl; High Hon Roll; Hon Roll; NHS; Phy Therpy.

ALESSI, KELLY; Hamilton High West; Trenton, NJ; (S); Chrmn Concert Band; Drm Mjr(t); Mrchg Band; School Musical; School Play; Symp Band; Stu Cncl; Hon Roll; Intract Club Secy 86; Exec Secy.

ALESSIO, MARYANN; Nutley HS; Nutley, NJ; (Y); 14/338; Office Aide; Ski Clb; Spanish Clb; Teachers Aide; Stu Cncl; JV Vllybl; Hon Roll; NHS; Jose Lopez Memrl Schlrshp NYU 86; Vrsty Ltr Crew 85; NY U; Bio.

ALEXANDER, DANIELLE; Essex Catholic Girls HS; Irvington, NJ; (Y); 14/63; Drama Clb; GAA; Yrbk Stf; Rep Sr Cls; Capt Cheerleading; High Hon Roll; Hon Roll; NHS; Elem Educ.

ALEXANDER, ELLEN; Academy Of St Elizabet; Florham Pk, NJ; (Y); 2/58; Spanish Clb; School Musical; Nwsp Stf; Yrbk Stf; Lit Mag; Var Capt Cheerleading; High Hon Roll; Pres Schlr; Sal; St Schlr; Fairfied Schlr; Hnrs Evry Acdmc Sbjct; Fairfield U; Bus.

ALEXANDER, JOAN; Williamstown HS; Williamstown, NJ; (Y); Intnl Clb; Key Clb; Pres Band; Concert Band; Drm Mjr(t); Mrchg Band; Orch; School Musical; Rep Frsh Cls; Rep Soph Cls; Elem Ed.

ALEXANDER, KAKIVA; Lincoln HS; Jersey City, NJ; (Y); 10/260; Drama Clb; FBLA; Girl Scts; Nwsp Sprt Ed; Lit Mag; Crs Cntry; Sftbl; Prfct Atten Awd; Crmnl Lwyr.

ALEXANDER, KATRINA; Trenton Central HS; Trenton, NJ; (Y); Hosp Aide; Spanish Clb; Teachers Aide; Sftbl; Wt Lftg; Helen Fld Schl; Reg Nrs.

ALEXANDER, MARY JO; Red Bank Catholic HS; Rumson, NJ; (Y); French Clb; Pep Clb; Ski Clb; Color Guard; Drill Tm; Variety Show; Nwsp Stf; Yrbk Stf; VP Frsh Cls; VP Soph Cls; Bucknell U; Pre-Law.

ALEXANDER, SUSAN; Montville HS; Montville, NJ; (Y); Church Yth Grp; Cmnty Wkr; Spanish Clb; Trs SADD; Coach Actv; Var Fld Hcky; Var Gym; Var Sftbl; Hon Roll; Tchng.

ALEXANDER, WESLEY; Red Bank Catholic HS; Long Branch, NJ; (Y); Church Yth Grp; Pres Frsh Cls; Trk; Mary Carmody Fndtn Imprvd Acadmc Perfrmnc 86; Ltr For Trck; Bus.

ALEXANDRE, RAEANNE; Paul VI HS; Glendora, NJ; (Y); 80/510; Mrchg Band; Hon Roll; Perfect Attendance Awd 84-85; Hotel Mgmt.

ALEXANDROU, ANGELIKE; Verona HS; Verona, NJ; (Y); Church Yth Grp; Q&S; Symp Band; Nwsp Stf; Yrbk Stf; Cheerleading; Vllybl; French Hon Soc; High Hon Roll; NHS; Musicl Scholar Summr Cmp 84; Ophthalmgly.

ALFE, KAREN; Highland Regional HS; Blackwood, NJ; (Y); 10/318; Civic Clb; French Clb; Nwsp Rptr; Yrbk Stf; NHS; Ntl Merit Ltr; Med.

ALGEIER, SUSAN JANET; Hackensack HS; Maywood, NJ; (Y); 34/480; Am Leg Aux Girls St; Ed FBLA; Spanish Clb; Var Fld Hcky; CC Awd; Hon Roll; NHS; Spanish NHS; FBLA Awd 86; Montclair ST; Actg.

ALI, JIMMY; Piscataway HS; Piscataway, NJ; (Y); Drama Clb; Key Clb; Nwsp Rptr; JV Socr; JV Trk; High Hon Roll; Hon Roll; NHS; Ntl Merit Ltr; Prfct Atten Awd; Vrsty Scr 87; Pre-Med.

ALI, MARIA; St Rose HS; Belmar, NJ; (Y); 3/207; Art Clb; Dance Clb; Key Clb; Ski Clb; Spanish Clb; School Play; Nwsp Stf; Lit Mag; Rep Soph Cls; Pres Jr Cls; Rutgers Dean Schlr; Georgetown U; Frnch.

ALIA, CRAIG J; Saddle Brook HS; Saddle Brook, NJ; (Y); 6/120; Am Leg Boys St; Political Wkr; Yrbk Sprt Ed; Pres Soph Cls; Pres Stu Cncl; Var Bsbl; Var Ftbl; Capt Wrstlng; Hon Roll; VP NHS; W Point; Engrng.

ALICEA, IRMA; Trenton Central HS; Trenton, NJ; (Y); Camera Clb; Hon Roll; Bst Bhvr Awd 86; Accntng.

ALICEA, SAMUEL; Vineland SR HS; Vineland, NJ; (Y); Am Leg Boys St; Exploring; Political Wkr; Spanish Clb; Rep Jr Cls; VP Sr Cls; Rep Stu Cncl; Rutgers U; Poli Sci.

ALIMENTI, CAROL; Sacred Heart HS; Vineland, NJ; (S); 10/68; Pres Art Clb; French Clb; FNA; School Musical; Stage Crew; High Hon Roll; Hon Roll; Trenton ST; Nrs.

ALIMI, LISA; Colonia HS; Colonia, NJ; (Y); SADD; Varsity Clb; Chorus; School Play; Var L Bsktbl; Stat Crs Cntry; Mgr(s); Score Keeper; Hon Roll; Cnfrnc All Acad Hnrs Grls Bsktbl 86.

ALLEGRETTA, MASSIMILIANO; North Bergen HS; N Bergen, NJ; (Y); 15/404; Computer Clb; Intnl Clb; High Hon Roll; NHS; Soc For Acad Achvt 86; Prncpls 1000 Clb 86; Pres Acad Ftnss Awd 86; Stevens Inst Of Tech; Mech Engr.

ALLEN, ALTHEA; Academic HS; Jersey City, NJ; (Y); Pres Jr Cls; Var Bsktbl; Capt Trk; Capt Vllybl; Acadmc Athlt Yr 85 & 86; Howard U; Phy Thrpy.

ALLEN, ANDREA; Plainfield HS; Plainfield, NJ; (Y); Church Yth Grp; Hosp Aide; Chorus; Rep Frsh Cls; Rep Soph Cls; Rep Stu Cncl; Jr NHS; Upwrd Bnd-Rutgers U 84-86; Rutgers U Livingston; Fash Mdsg.

ALLEN, ARLENE; Clayton HS; Clayton, NJ; (Y); FHA; Sec Stu Cncl; Cheerleading; COSMETOLOGIST.

ALLEN, CHRIS; Hamilton High West; Trenton, NJ; (Y); Am Leg Aux Girls St; SADD; Drill Tm; Sec Sr Cls; Sec Hst Stu Cncl; Var Pom Pon; Im Vllybl; Hon Roll; Systms Analyst.

ALLEN, CLIFTON; Essex County Voc Tech HS; Irvington, NJ; (Y); Computer Clb; Drama Clb; FBLA; Pres Stu Cncl; Var Capt Bsbl; Var Capt Bsktbl; Im Ftbl; Wt Lftg; Hon Roll; Prfct Atten Awd; Stck Mrkt Game Spring Semstr Cmpttn 86; U Of Southern CA; Law.

ALLEN, CRYSTAL; East Orange HS; Newark, NJ; (S); 66/410; Sec Church Yth Grp; Church Choir; Capt Drill Tm; Yrbk Stf; Sec Frsh Cls; Sec Soph Cls; Pres Jr Cls; Pres Sr Cls; JV Cheerleading; Hon Roll; Soph Cls Queen 83-84; Hmcmng Queen 85-86; Essex Cnty JR Miss 85-86; Rutgers U; Coroner.

ALLEN, DAVID; Belvidere HS; Belvidere, NJ; (S); 11/120; Varsity Clb; VICA; Ed Yrbk Ed-Chief; Yrbk Rptr; Yrbk Sprt Ed; Yrbk Stf; JV Bsbl; Var L Bsktbl; Bowling; Hon Roll; Advncd Plcmnt Stdng In Englsh 85-86; Syracuse; Sprts Comm.

ALLEN, ELAINE THERESA; Manchester Township HS; Toms River, NJ; (S); Am Leg Aux Girls St; Church Yth Grp; Pep Clb; Color Guard; Drm Mjr(t); Nwsp Ed-Chief; Nwsp Rptr; Yrbk Ed-Chief; Score Keeper; Cit Awd; Grad From The Stirway To Stars Missionettes Prg 86; Ctznshp Awd Miss United Teenager Pgnt 84; Mass Cmmnctns.

ALLEN, ELIJAH; East Orange HS; East Orange, NJ; (S); 4/410; Debate Tm; French Clb; Math Tm; Scholastic Bowl; Lit Mag; Rep Stu Cncl; Stat Bsbl; Hon Roll; NHS; Prfct Atten Awd; Rutgers U; Polit Sci.

ALLEN, JON; Hopewell Valley Central HS; Pennington, NJ; (Y); Church Yth Grp; Nwsp Rptr; Hon Roll; Ntl Merit SF; Macalester Coll; Jrnlst.

ALLEN, KIA; Wilwood Catholic HS; Cape May, NJ; (Y); French Clb; SADD; Variety Show; JV Var Bsktbl; JV Tennis; Hon Roll; Cert Of Merit; Accntng.

ALLEN, NICOLE; Holy Cross HS; Willingboro, NJ; (Y); 17/375; Pres French Clb; Ed Nwsp Rptr; Coach Actv; Var L Crs Cntry; Var L Trk; Hon Roll; NHS; Ntl Merit Ltr; Pres Schlr; St Schlr; Charles G Berwind Fndtn Schlrshp 86; American U; Jrnlsm.

ALLEN, PAUL; John F Kennedy HS; Metuchen, NJ; (Y); 52/279; SADD; Teachers Aide; Trk; Hon Roll; Wt Lftg; Senator Bill Bradley NJ Young Citizens Awd 86; Capt Iselin 1st Aid Squad 86; William Patterson; Athltc Trnng.

ALLEN, SHARON M; Ewing HS; Trenton, NJ; (Y); 18/306; Am Leg Aux Girls St; Cmnty Wkr; Key Clb; Political Wkr; Ski Clb; Orch; School Musical; Stage Crew; Yrbk Stf; Off Soph Cls; Italn Amercn Natl Hl Fame Schlrshp 86; U Of DE; Poli Sci.

ALLISON, TINA; Toms River East; Toms River, NJ; (Y); 42/585; French Clb; FBLA; Drill Tm; High Hon Roll; Hon Roll; Elem Educ.

ALMANZOR, ARNOLD J; Hamilton East Steinert HS; Trenton, NJ; (Y); Am Leg Boys St; VP Exploring; Key Clb; NFL; Band; Concert Band; Mrchg Band; School Play; VP Stu Cncl; Tennis; Comp Engrng.

ALMEIDA, JANICE; Union Catholic Reg HS; Union, NJ; (Y); 81/319; Church Yth Grp; Office Aide; PAVAS; Service Clb; Ski Clb; School Play; Yrbk Phtg; Yrbk Stf; Var Cheerleading; Var Pom Pon; Vrsty Ltr Sccr Chrldg 85; Vrsty Ltr Bsktbl Wrstlg Chrldr 85-86; Med.

ALOI, PETER; Marist HS; Bayonne, NJ; (Y); 4/104; Am Leg Boys St; Church Yth Grp; Key Clb; Scholastic Bowl; Nwsp Stf; Capt Var Bsbl; High Hon Roll; NHS; Spanish NHS; Natl Ldrshp, Svc Awd 85; Brother Leo Sylvius Awd Schlrshp 83-86; Villanova.

ALPER, CURT; Matawan Regional HS; Holmdel, NJ; (Y); 106/353; Radio Clb; Ski Clb; Temple Yth Grp; Socr; Tele Comm.

ALSTON, DERRIC; Frank H Morrell HS; Irvington, NJ; (Y); Hon Roll; Accntng.

ALTENBURG, CARL; Toms River H S East; Toms River, NJ; (Y); 7/585; Computer Clb; FBLA; Key Clb; Math Tm; Science Clb; High Hon Roll; NHS; 3rd Pl FBLA ST Comptn Acctng 2 86; 3rd Pl Sci Lg Chem 86; Acctng.

ALTERA, ROSE MARIE; West Essex Regional HS; Fairfield, NJ; (Y); 37/350; Church Yth Grp; Computer Clb; Exploring; JV Fld Hcky; NHS; Stage Crew; Womens Clubs Schlrshp 86; Italian Natl Hnr Soc 84; Montclair ST Coll; Bio.

ALTMAN, MEREDITH; Manalapan HS; Manalapan, NJ; (Y); Thesps; Chorus; Madrigals; School Play; Stage Crew; Yrbk Stf; All Shrchrs 86; Bus.

ALTMAN, RICHARD; Highistown HS; E Windsor, NJ; (Y); 42/449; Boy Scts; Drama Clb; SADD; Thesps; Chorus; School Musical; School Play; Stage Crew; High Hon Roll; NHS; Econmcs.

ALTOM, JOHN; The Wardlaw-Hartridge Schl; Plainfield, NJ; (Y); 5/53; SADD; School Musical; Sec Frsh Cls; Sec Jr Cls; Sec Sr Cls; Var L Bsktbl; Var L Ftbl; Var L Trk; High Hon Roll; NHS.

ALVAREZ, CARLOS; North Bergen HS; North Bergen, NJ; (Y); 57/450; Im Coach Actv; High Hon Roll; Hon Roll; NHS; Ntl Merit Ltr.

ALVES, MARIA; East Side HS; Newark, NJ; (Y); Civic Clb; Hosp Aide; Chorus; Yrbk Stf; Rep Jr Cls; Hon Roll; NHS; Opt Clb Awd; Engrng.

ALVEZ, DEBBIE; Dwight Morrow HS; Englewood, NJ; (Y); Cmnty Wkr; Drama Clb; Hosp Aide; Spanish Clb; School Musical; School Play; Sec Stu Cncl; High Hon Roll; Hon Roll; Bergen Cnty Plned Prnthd Tn Pnl Stu 85-86; Stu Tn Lfe Prgm 85-86; Postve Imge Clb 85-86; Chld Psych.

AMABILE, MICHAEL; Toms River H S South; Toms River, NJ; (Y); 1/348; Boy Scts; Capt Math Tm; Sec Mrchg Band; VP Soph Cls; Bausch & Lomb Sci Awd; NHS; Ntl Merit SF; Val; Cmnty Wkr; Science Clb; WA Wrkshps Congrssnl Sem 86; Amer Chem Soc Awd Wnnr 85; Black Belt Karate 84; Physcs.

AMADIO, THOMAS J; Montville HS; Towaco, NJ; (Y); Church Yth Grp; Varsity Clb; Nwsp Phtg; Nwsp Stf; Ftbl; Lcrss; Powder Puff Ftbl; Wt Lftg; Wrstlng; MVP 1st Team All Cnfrnc Wrstlng 84 & 86; Trenton ST Coll; Bus.

AMADO, DAISY L; Our Lady Of Good Counsel HS; Newark, NJ; (Y); Church Yth Grp; Cmnty Wkr; Office Aide; Political Wkr; Chorus; School Musical; Yrbk Stf; Rep Frsh Cls; Rep Soph Cls; Rep Jr Cls; Perfect Attendence & Tardiness Award 83-84; Most School Spirit Award 84-85; Law.

AMAKER, HARRIS; Rahway HS; Rahway, NJ; (Y); Aud/Vis; Chess Clb; Computer Clb; Var Bsktbl; JETS Awd; Comp Repair.

AMARAL, JORGE; Harrison HS; Harrison, NJ; (Y); 3/158; Sec Church Yth Grp; Pres Computer Clb; Pres French Clb; VP Socr; Cit Awd; DAR Awd; Pres NHS; Opt Clb Awd; Al-ST Sccr 86; US Army Rsrv Natl Schlr/Athlt Awd 86; Blue Tide Bstr Clb Schlrshp 86; PTA Schlrshp 86; Montclair.

AMATO, HOLLY; Middlesex HS; Middlesex, NJ; (Y); 60/170; Church Yth Grp; Hosp Aide; Ski Clb; Spanish Clb; Varsity Clb; Band; Color Guard; Concert Band; Mrchg Band; Yrbk Ed-Chief.

AMATO, MICHAEL C; Hackensack HS; Rochelle Park, NJ; (Y); 86/386; Am Leg Boys St; Teachers Aide; Var L Ftbl; Hon Roll; Prfct Atten Awd; Rutgers.

AMBARDAR, MEENAKSHI; Westfield SR HS; Westfield, NJ; (Y); 4/450; 4-H; Capt Thesps; Trk; Vllybl; French Hon Soc; Gov Hon Prg Awd; High Hon Roll; NHS; Ntl Merit Schol; St Schlr; NJ Wrtrs Awd 86; Coll Womens Clb Schlrshp 86; Northwestern U; Med.

AMBARDAR, PARA; Westfield HS; Westfield, NJ; (Y); French Clb; Hosp Aide; Model UN; Science Clb; Ed Nwsp Stf; Yrbk Bus Mgr; Var Trk; French Hon Soc; Gov Hon Prg Awd; Sec NHS; 2 1st Pls Rider Foreign Lang Forensic Tournmnt 85-86.

AMBERG, JOHN; Middletown South HS; Leonardo, NJ; (Y); Camera Clb; Pres Church Yth Grp; Civic Clb; Drama Clb; FCA; Church Choir; School Play; JV Wrstlng; Yngst Stu Bd Dir 84-86; St Peters Coll; Photo Jrnlst.

AMBROSE, KATHLEEN M; Haddon Heights HS; Barrington, NJ; (S); Church Yth Grp; SADD; Concert Band; Capt Mrchg Band; L Bsktbl; JV L Sftbl; High Hon Roll; Hon Roll; Garnet & Gold Soc 85 & 86; Tchr.

AMBROSE, MARGARET K; St Rose HS; Brick, NJ; (Y); French Clb; JCL; VP Key Clb; SADD; JV Trk; French Hon Soc; High Hon Roll; NHS; NEDT Awd; Gen Excllnc Awd; Alg II & Trig Awd; Hnrs Engl II Awd; Intl Bus.

AMENDOLARO, SCOTT; Parsippany HS; Parsippany, NJ; (Y); Ftbl; Hon Roll; Rutfens; Aero Space.

AMIN, SAMEH; Lakewood HS; Lakewood, NJ; (Y); 103/294; Boy Scts; Chess Clb; JCL; Latin Clb; Mgr(s); Score Keeper; JV Var Socr; Hon Roll; Drew U.

AMKRAUT, BRIAN; E Brunswick HS; E Brunswick, NJ; (Y); 8/600; Key Clb; Math Clb; SADD; Variety Show; Bsktbl; JV Tennis; JV Wrstlng; French Hon Soc; Pres NHS; NJ St Sci Day-4th Pl Cumulative 86; NJ Sci League-1st Pl Chem Ii 86; Columbia Coll; Physician.

AMMERMAN, SHARI; Wayne Hills HS; Wayne, NJ; (Y); 26/300; Church Yth Grp; Spanish Clb; Varsity Clb; Variety Show; Nwsp Phtg; Nwsp Stf; Var Swmmng; Var Tennis; Var Trk; High Hon Roll; Librl Arts.

AMMONS, DAVID; Freehold Township HS; Freehold, NJ; (Y); 56/382; Boy Scts; Church Yth Grp; Drama Clb; School Musical; School Play; Stage Crew; Var Ftbl; Var Trk; Hon Roll; Econ.

AMON, ELIZABETH; Hopewell Valley Central HS; Hopewell, NJ; (Y); 54/203; Political Wkr; Nwsp Ed-Chief; Nwsp Rptr; NHS; AFS; French Clb; Red Cross Aide; Band; Chorus; School Musical; Four Short Stories Pblshd Aspirations 85-86; Oberlin; Engl Creative Wrtng.

AMON, EMILY; Hopewell Valley Central HS; Hopewell, NJ; (Y); 41/202; AFS; French Clb; School Musical; Nwsp Stf; Yrbk Stf; Rep Stu Cncl; Fld Hcky; Swmmng; High Hon Roll; NHS; 3rd Pl Arch Craft Fair Comptn 85.

ANASTASIOU, MARTHA; Mother Seton Regional HS; Irvington, NJ; (Y); Drama Clb; Math Tm; Stage Crew; Nwsp Stf; Yrbk Stf; Lit Mag; Rep Frsh Cls; Rep Jr Cls; Hon Roll; NHS; Drill Team 85-86; Frnch Awd 84-85; Sci League 85-86; Phrmcy.

ANDERSON, ADRIENNE; Mount Saint Mary Acad; S River, NJ; (Y); Art Clb; German Clb; PAVAS; Nwsp Phtg; Nwsp Rptr; Yrbk Ed-Chief; Yrbk Rptr; Hon Roll; Pres Ntl Art Hnr Soc; Work With Mentally Handcpd; Art.

ANDERSON, CYNTHIA; Millville SR HS; Heislerville, NJ; (Y); 25/317; Pres VP Church Yth Grp; Drama Clb; Pres Trs 4-H; SADD; Ed Nwsp Stf; Capt Bowling; Cit Awd; NHS; Key Clb; ST Rep 4-H Ntl Clb Cngrss 86; Cmmnctns.

ANDERSON, DARCIENA; Linden HS; Linden, NJ; (S); 53/353; Sec German Clb; Girl Scts; Concert Band; Mrchg Band; Orch; School Play; VP Stu Cncl; L Swmmng; Linden Debutante 86; Douglass Coll; Acctng.

ANDERSON, DARCY; Randolph HS; Randolph, NJ; (Y); 18/363; Drama Clb; Hosp Aide; Ski Clb; Spanish Clb; Stat Bsktbl; Sftbl; Var Trk; High Hon Roll; NHS; Spanish NHS; Ntl Hrsbck Rdng Chmpn 80-83; NJ & Grdn ST Hrsmns Accn Title 80-83; U WA; Frgn Lng.

ANDERSON, DAVID; Overbrook Regional HS; Clementon, NJ; (Y); Var Capt Bsktbl; Var Capt Socr; Var Trk; Hon Roll; Olympc Conf Ntl Div 2nd Tm For Sccr 85-86; Accntng.

ANDERSON, DEREK; North Brunswick Township HS; N Brunswick, NJ; (Y); Church Yth Grp; Cmnty Wkr; Key Clb; Letterman Clb; Mathletes; Spanish Clb; Concert Band; Mrchg Band; Rep Stu Cncl; Var Bsbl; All Conf Acad Bsktbl Tm 85 & 86; Pre-Med.

ANDERSON, EDWARD; Kingsway Regional HS; Mickleton, NJ; (Y); 31/181; Ski Clb; Crs Cntry; Swmmng; Drevel U; Vet.

ANDERSON, JAMES; Toms River High School East; Toms River, NJ; (Y); 34/585; Am Leg Boys St; Church Yth Grp; Chorus; Church Choir; Orch; Var Capt Swmmng; NHS; Ntl Merit Ltr; All ST Orchstra 85.

ANDERSON, LATISHA; Essex Co Vo-Tech HS; Newark, NJ; (Y); Chorus; Drill Tm.

ANDERSON, MEGAN; Chatham Borough HS; Chatham, NJ; (Y); Pres Church Yth Grp; Key Clb; Pep Clb; Acpl Chr; Chorus; Yrbk Stf; Var Bsktbl; Var Tennis; Var Trk; Hon Roll; Bell Awd Englsh; All ST Chr; ST Fnls Trk; Art.

ANDERSON, MELODY; Park Bible Acad; Carneys Pt, NJ; (Y); 4/5; JA; Spanish Clb; School Play; Nwsp Rptr; Yrbk Ed-Chief; Bsktbl; Cheerleading; Sftbl; Vllybl; Hon Roll; Plcd 3rd Chrstn Schl Fine Arts Comptn 85-86; Title Salem Cntys Jr Miss 85-86; Camden CC; Dental Hygnst.

ANDERSON, PAUL; Florence Memorial HS; Florence, NJ; (Y); 17/95; Math Clb; Jazz Band; Rutgers Schl/Engrng; Elec Engr.

ANDERSON, PAUL; Hillsborough HS; Bellemead, NJ; (Y); 25/285; Var L Bsbl; L Capt Bsktbl; Var Hon Roll; Coll; Comp Sci.

ANDIA, SANDRA; Mater Dei HS; Middletown, NJ; (Y); 21/150; Church Yth Grp; Pep Clb; SADD; VP Stu Cncl; Bsktbl; Cheerleading; Tennis; Hon Roll; Jr NHS; NHS; Catholic U; Bus Adm.

ANDOLPHO, DENENE; Mater Dei HS; Middletown, NJ; (Y); 53/155; Church Yth Grp; Exploring; JCL; Latin Clb; Sec Frsh Cls; Sec Soph Cls; Pres Jr Cls; Pres Sr Cls; Var L Crs Cntry; Hon Roll; Cthlc U Wash DC; Bus Mgmt.

ANDRASZ, LISA; Woodbridge SR HS; Hopelawn, NJ; (Y); 4/400; Dance Clb; French Clb; Hosp Aide; SADD; Concert Band; Mrchg Band; Hon Roll; NHS; Biol Rsrch.

ANDREA, OTTER; Hamilton High West; Trenton, NJ; (Y); Church Yth Grp; Exploring; Science Clb; SADD; Chorus; Madrigals; School Musical; Ed Lit Mag; Mgr Stat Bsktbl; Mgr(s); Outstndng Soph Choral Awd 85; Stockton ST Coll; Crmnl Justce.

ANDREASSEN, STEVEN; Scotch Plains Fanwood HS; Scotch Plains, NJ; (S); Computer Clb; English Clb; Quiz Bowl; Lit Mag; High Hon Roll; Hon Roll; NJ ST Sci Day Comp 85; Princeton U.

ANDREEKO, ANDREW A; Warren Hills Reg HS; Hackettstown, NJ; (Y); Am Leg Boys St; Boy Scts; Var L Chess Clb; Band; Concert Band; Mrchg Band; Var L Bsbl; Var Crs Cntry; Hon Roll; All County Bnd 85-86; Natl Boy Scout Jamboree Band 85; Jersey Boys ST Band 86; Arch.

ANDREJEWSKI, KEITH; St Marys HS; Spotswood, NJ; (Y); Am Leg Boys St; School Play; Im Bowling; JV Socr; High Hon Roll; Hon Roll; Olympics Mind Tm 86.

ANDREOPOULOS, NICK; Northern Valley Regional H S Old Tapp; Northvale, NJ; (Y); 33/281; AFS; Church Yth Grp; Math Tm; Ski Clb; Concert Band; Mrchg Band; Var Bowling; Hon Roll; NHS.

ANDREW, NYCIA; Orange HS; Orange, NJ; (S); Debate Tm; DECA; English Clb; Exploring; JA; Math Tm; Science Clb; SADD; Acpl Chr; High Hon Roll; Bst Discpline & Hard Wrkng Schlrshp 82; Sprts Awds 82-83; Sci.

ANDREWS, LAURA; Marylawn Of The Oranges HS; Nutley, NJ; (Y); 10/54; School Musical; VP Jr Cls; Rep Stu Cncl; French Hon Soc; High Hon Roll; Ldrshp Awd 85; Rtgrs; Elem Ed.

ANDRIAN, THERESA; Brick Memorial HS; Brick Town, NJ; (Y); 30/400; Am Leg Aux Girls St; Church Yth Grp; Pres Key Clb; Pep Clb; Sec Spanish Clb; Nwsp Stf; Yrbk Stf; Stu Cncl; Var Tennis; High Hon Roll; Most Outstndng Key Clubber Yr 85-86; Miss Rising Star 84; Miss Am Co Ed Most Photo Fnlst 84; Monmouth; Tchr.

ANDROLEWICZ, SHERIE; Paul VI HS; Turnersville, NJ; (Y); 9/463; Math Clb; Var Capt Bsktbl; JV Fld Hcky; French Hon Soc; NHS; Hugh O Brien Yth Ldrshp Awd; Lehigh U; Bus.

ANDRUS, HEATHER; Lower Cape May Regional HS; Cape May, NJ; (Y); Cmnty Wkr; Office Aide; Pep Clb; Yrbk Stf; JV Tennis; Hon Roll; Prfct Atten Awd; Rtry Yth Ldrshp Cnfrnc 86; ARCH.

ANDRUSIN, MICHAEL; Pompton Lakes HS; Pompton Lakes, NJ; (Y); Q&S; Hst Varsity Clb; School Play; Stage Crew; Yrbk Sprt Ed; Capt Socr; Capt Trk; Capt Wrstlng; Elks Awd; Hon Roll; US Marine Crps Dstngshd Athlt Awd 86; US Army MV Sccr Plyr Awd 86; East Stroudsburg U.

ANDZESKI, MARILYN; Central Regional HS; Bayville, NJ; (Y); Art Clb; French Clb; Hosp Aide; Library Aide; Ski Clb; SADD; Nwsp Rptr; Stu Cncl; Bsktbl; Mgr(s); Bus.

ANELLO, TIZIANA; Mary Help Of Christians Acad; W Paterson, NJ; (S); 4/68; Cmnty Wkr; Computer Clb; Letterman Clb; Stage Crew; Nwsp Stf; Trs Soph Cls; Trs Jr Cls; VP Stu Cncl; NHS; Computer, Algebra, & Italian Awds; Med Field.

ANGAROLA, CARLA; Hunterdon Central HS; Flemington, NJ; (Y); 144/550; Church Yth Grp; Ski Clb; Off Frsh Cls; Off Jr Cls; VP JV Fld Hcky; Im Lcrss; JV Trk; Im Vllybl; Hon Roll; Im Wt Lftg; Nrsg.

ANGELAKOS, PETER; Dwight Morrow HS; Englewood Cliffs, NJ; (Y); 48/250; Nwsp Stf; Var Bsbl; Var Socr; Hon Roll.

ANGELBECK, JOHN; Roselle Catholic HS; Maplewood, NJ; (S); 16/153; Boy Scts; Lit Mag; JV Var Crs Cntry; JV Var Trk; High Hon Roll; Hon Roll; NHS; Spanish NHS; Eagle Scout 85; Ad Altare Del Religious Medal 86; Patrol Ledr Of Year 83; Air Force Acad; Aeronautcl Engr.

ANGELES, MICHAEL; St Aloysius HS; Jersey City, NJ; (Y); NHS; Exploring; Rep Stu Cncl; Im Capt Bowling; Pres Citation Acad Achvt 86.

ANGELICA, JOHN; Don Bosco Prep HS; N Haledon, NJ; (Y); 25/192; Pep Clb; Rep Jr Cls; Stu Cncl; JV Var Bsbl; Var L Bsktbl; Var L Ftbl; High Hon Roll; Hon Roll; NHS; Local Govt Youth Week 86.

ANGELINI, LISA; Paulsboro HS; Gibbstown, NJ; (Y); 54/150; Art Clb; Sec VICA; JV Bsktbl; JV Fld Hcky; Var Sftbl; Hon Roll; Yth Ftnss Achvt Awd 86; Sec Of VICA 86; Burlington Cnty; Polc Offcr.

ANGELL, DAVID; Bayonne HS; Bayonne, NJ; (Y); Frsh Cls; Soph Cls; Jr Cls; Stu Cncl; Crs Cntry; Trk; Environ Mental Sci.

ANGEROLE, BETH; Wall Twp HS; Sea Girt, NJ; (S); 27/270; Church Yth Grp; Cmnty Wkr; Chorus; Church Choir; JV Bsktbl; Im Socr; Var L Sftbl; High Hon Roll; Im Powder Puff Ftbl; Intl Chrstn Yth Conf 83; Vrsty Lttr Sftbl 84-85; Natl Engl Merit Awd 85-86; Juniata Coll; Erly Chldhd.

ANGONA, KRISTINE L; Monsignor Donovan HS; Lanoka Harbor, NJ; (Y); 48/218; Am Leg Aux Girls St; Pres Drama Clb; Service Clb; Pres Thesps; Chorus; Church Choir; School Musical; School Play; Variety Show; Nwsp Rptr; Rutgers U; Lib Art.

ANGULO, E MICHAEL; Moorestown HS; Mt Laurel, NJ; (Y); 59/210; Am Leg Boys St; Church Yth Grp; FBLA; JA; Latin Clb; Letterman Clb; Pep Clb; Spanish Clb; SADD; Varsity Clb; Catholic U; Mrktng.

ANILO, RALPH; Scotch Plains Fanwood HS; Fanwood, NJ; (Y); 113/359; Church Yth Grp; Drama Clb; VP Leo Clb; Model UN; Stage Crew; Aud/Vis; Cmnty Wkr; Intnl Clb; Hon Roll; Key Clb Scholar 86; Joyce Bergman Mem Scholar 86; Natl Yth & Govt Pgm 86; VA Wesleyan Coll; Lib Art.

ANILONIS, RITA; Point Pleasant Boro HS; Pt Pleasant, NJ; (S); 11/240; Varsity Clb; Band; Mrchg Band; JV Var Fld Hcky; Hon Roll; NHS; Arch.

ANINIPOT, RODERICK L; Hudson Catholic HS; Jersey City, NJ; (Y); 20/200; Nwsp Sprt Ed; Var Crs Cntry; Var L Trk; Hon Roll; NHS; Seton Hall U; Crprt Law.

ANNUNZIATA, KELLY ANN; Kinnelon HS; Kinnelon, NJ; (Y); 34/160; Drama Clb; Hosp Aide; Pres Spanish Clb; Trs Varsity Clb; Chorus; Rep Stu Cncl; Capt Var Socr; Capt Var Swmmng; Spanish NHS; Spnsh Hnr Soc Awd & Schlrshp 86; Stu Cncl Awd 86; 4 Yr Vrsty Awd Sccr & Swmmg 86; Rutgers Coll; Psychlgy.

ANOTA, CATHERINE; Secaucus HS; Secaucus, NJ; (S); 2/166; Pres Computer Clb; Pres Math Clb; VP Spanish Clb; Varsity Clb; Chorus; School Play; VP Tennis; Mu Alp Tht; NHS; Spanish NHS; Bus Adm.

ANOTA, OSCAR; Secavcus HS; Secaucus, NJ; (Y); Math Clb; JV Bsktbl; JV Ftbl; Hotel Mgmt.

ANSBRO, KEVIN; Toms River South HS; Toms River, NJ; (Y); 28/360; Letterman Clb; Ski Clb; Varsity Clb; Variety Show; Crs Cntry; Var Capt Swmmng; Trk; Hon Roll; NHS; Ftbl Tm Mskt 86-87; 5th St Swmmng 85-86; Swm Rly HS All AM 85-86; Lehigh U; Engnrng.

ANSTETH, JOHN; St Peters Prep; Elizabeth, NJ; (Y); 100/215; Tennis; Hon Roll; Law.

ANTE, RODERICK F; Academic HS; Jersey City, NJ; (Y); French Clb; Orch; Variety Show; NEDT Awd; Prfct Atten Awd; Comp Sci.

ANTHONY, CATHY; Warren County Vo-Tech; Stewartsville, NJ; (S); Ski Clb; VICA; Yrbk Stf; Rep Stu Cncl; High Hon Roll; Hon Roll; NHS; Cosmtlgy.

ANTHONY, DWAYNE; Asbury Park HS; Asbury Pk, NJ; (Y); 45/133; Boys Clb Am; Church Yth Grp; Bsbl; Trk; Rutgers U; Bus.

ANTHONY, JOSEPH; Paul VI HS; Glendora, NJ; (S); 31/550; Drama Clb; Math Clb; School Musical; School Play; Variety Show; Pres Soph Cls; VP Jr Cls; Off Stu Cncl; Bowling; Hon Roll.

ANTON, DOUG; Ramsey HS; Saddle River, NJ; (Y); 27/241; Boys Clb Am; Church Yth Grp; Nwsp Ed-Chief; Stu Cncl; Wt Lftg; Wrstlng; Hon Roll; NJS JR Olympc Box Champ 85; Dist IV Wrstlg Champ 86; Villanova U; Polit Sci.

ANTON, JENNIFER; Highland Regional HS; Clementon, NJ; (Y); #14 In Class; Trs Drama Clb; School Musical; Trs Soph Cls; Trs Jr Cls; Rep Stu Cncl; Hon Roll; Kiwanis Awd; NHS; Voice Dem Awd; Natl Latn Exm Cum Laude 84-85; Rutgers Coll; Ecolgy.

ANTONAZ, ISABEL; Highland HS; Clementon, NJ; (S); 25/400; GAA; Latin Clb; Stu Cncl; Sftbl; Tennis; Med.

ANTONELLI, VINCENT; James Caldwell HS; Caldwell, NJ; (Y); French Clb; Nwsp Rptr; Ed Yrbk Stf; Trs Jr Cls; Sr Cls; Stu Cncl; High Hon Roll; NHS; Church Yth Grp; Key Clb; Gov Schl 86; Lawyr.

ANTOSHAK, ANN C; Northern Valley Regional H S Demarest; Closter, NJ; (Y); 48/250; Orch; School Musical; Rep Stu Cncl; Hon Roll; NHS; Tom Connor Art Schlrshp 85; Wrote For Suburbanite Sprts Rptr 82-83; Art Recgntn & Tlnt Srch 85; The Cooper Union; Art.

ANTUNES, LISA MARIE; Mother Seton Regional HS; Hillside, NJ; (Y); 22/102; GAA; Science Clb; Service Clb; School Play; Ed Yrbk Stf; Rep Jr Cls; VP Stu Cncl; Var Sftbl; Dnfth Awd; Hon Roll; Spec Educ.

ANUSZKIEWICZ, NICHOLAS S; Brick Township HS; Bricktown, NJ; (Y); Boy Scts; Church Yth Grp; Cmnty Wkr; Band; Concert Band; Mrchg Band; Variety Show; Rep Frsh Cls; Var Tennis; Hon Roll; U Notre Dame; Bus Mngmnt.

APGAR, SUZANNE; South Hunterdon Regional HS; Ringoes, NJ; (Y); 5/72; FBLA; Key Clb; Stu Cncl; Hon Roll; Psych.

APISA, DANIELLE; Red Bank Catholic HS; Colts Neck, NJ; (Y); Pres Jr Cls; Stat L Socr; Bus.

APONTE, JOANA; East Side HS; Paterson, NJ; (Y); Church Yth Grp; Dance Clb; Drama Clb; Hosp Aide; Library Aide; Teachers Aide; Band; Church Choir; Concert Band; Drm & Bgl; Best Martial Arts Girl Of Yr 85; EFA Schlrshp 85; Bst Musical Group In Band For Drums 86; Lawyer.

APONTE, MICHAEL W; Ornage HS; Orange, NJ; (Y); 46/180; Drama Clb; Band; Concert Band; School Play; Stage Crew; Var Tennis; Vrsty Ltr & Awd Boys Tnns 84-86; 3rd Pl Awd Orng Chmbr Cmmrc Art Cntst 85-86; Rutgers U Newark; Med.

APPEL, SHARI; Woodstown HS; Woodstown, NJ; (Y); 10/250; Pres Church Yth Grp; Drama Clb; Pres Sec 4-H; German Clb; Band; Chorus; Church Choir; School Musical; Hon Roll; NHS; Bus.

APPIO, MARYEILEEN; Passaic Valley HS; W Paterson, NJ; (Y); Trs Church Yth Grp; GAA; Var L Crs Cntry; Var L Mgr(s); Capt Var Trk; 2nd Tm Conf X-Cntry 84&85; Hnbl Mntn NNJIL X-Cntry 83; HS Hnr Soc 85; California U PA; Pre-Med.

APPLEBY V, J RANDOLPH; Central Regional HS; Seaside Park, NJ; (Y); 1/260; Golf; Eastern Surfing Assn 2nd Rank JR Mens Div 82-86; UC SLO; Arch.

APPLEGATE, BARBARA; Toms River H S East; Toms River, NJ; (Y); 25/586; Church Yth Grp; Intnl Clb; Church Choir; Orch; Sec Sr Cls; Var Bsktbl; Var Socr; High Hon Roll; Hon Roll; NHS; Church Scholar Natl Select Westminster Choir 85; Hnrb Mntn All Ocean Cnty Soccr 85; 2nd Tm Soccr 86; Engl.

APPLETON, SCOTT; Kinnelon HS; Kinnelon, NJ; (Y); Var Socr; JV Tennis; Chem Engrng.

APREA, ANDREA; East Brunswick HS; E Brunswick, NJ; (Y); Yrbk Phtg; Gym; Hon Roll; Middlesex Cnty Coll; Photo.

APRUZZESE, LISA; Belleville HS; Belleville, NJ; (Y); Church Yth Grp; Key Clb; Chorus; Church Choir; Color Guard; Nwsp Stf; Yrbk Stf; Rep Soph Cls; JV Sftbl; Var Tennis; Fashion Mgmt.

APY, MELISSA; Red Bank Regional HS; Red Bank, NJ; (Y); 18/285; VP Stu Cncl; Var Capt Swmmng; Var Capt Tennis; French Hon Soc; High Hon Roll; Hon Roll; Ski Clb; Rep Frsh Cls; Rep Soph Cls; Rep Jr Cls; Bus Admin.

AQUILA, FRANK; Hackensadk HS; Hackensack, NJ; (Y); 11/39; 4-H Awd; Engrng.

AQUINO, JOANNA M; Sussex County Vo-Tech HS; Lake Stockholm, NJ; (S); #9 In Class; Math Clb; Spanish Clb; Varsity Clb; Yrbk Stf; Sec Soph Cls; Trs Jr Cls; Rep Sr Cls; L Powder Puff Ftbl; Var JV Swmmng; High Hon Roll; Bus.

ARACENA, GIANILDA; Dickinson HS; Jersey City, NJ; (Y); English Clb; High Hon Roll; Prfct Atten Awd; Montclair ST Coll; Med.

ARANOWITZ, LAUREN; West Essex SR HS; Roseland, NJ; (Y); 47/356; Church Yth Grp; Key Clb; Color Guard; Yrbk Stf; Hon Roll; Spanish NHS; Roseland Yth Wk Actng Cnclprsn 84-86; U Of MA; Intl Bus.

ARASIN, JO ANNE; Saint James HS; Carneys Point, NJ; (S); 7/78; Trs Hosp Aide; School Musical; Yrbk Stf; Hon Roll; Soc Dstngshd Amer H S Stu 85.

ARATEN, MICHAEL; Cherry Hill HS West; Cherry Hill, NJ; (Y); 7/356; French Clb; Political Wkr; Trs Frsh Cls; Trs Soph Cls; Trs Jr Cls; JV Var Tennis; CC Awd; High Hon Roll; Hon Roll; NHS; Stanford U; Pol Sci.

ARAUJO, JOHN; Arthur L Johnson Regional HS; Clark, NJ; (S); 14/217; Key Clb; Spanish Clb; Stu Cncl; Socr; Hon Roll; Spanish NHS; Charles Johnson Jr Mem Scholar 86; U Chicago Scholar 86; U Chicago; Bio.

ARAUJO, JURANDIR; Roselle Catholic HS; Union, NJ; (S); 46/195; Lit Mag; Socr; French Hon Soc; Literary Art Editor Plaque Awd 85; Varsity Let 85; Arch.

ARBESFELD, GLENN; Manalapan HS; Englishtown, NJ; (Y); 34/430; Stage Crew; Variety Show; NHS; Engrng.

ARCABOS, LYNNETTE; Memorial HS; West New York, NJ; (Y); 18/436; Key Clb; Office Aide; Rep Stu Cncl; Hon Roll; NHS; Prfct Atten Awd; Rep Frsh Cls; Rep Soph Cls; Acctnt.

ARCHELUS, WESLINE; Vailsburg HS; Newark, NJ; (Y); 23/275; Church Yth Grp; Library Aide; Temple Yth Grp; Church Choir; Yrbk Stf.

ARCHER, DANA LEIGH; Toms River South HS; Toms River, NJ; (Y); Am Leg Aux Girls St; Church Yth Grp; Hosp Aide; Model UN; Science Clb; Band; Church Choir; Mrchg Band; Symp Band; TEAM Schlrshp 86; Ann May Sch; Nrsg.

ARCHER, STEVEN T; Ridge HS; Basking Ridge, NJ; (Y); Boy Scts; Ski Clb; Variety Show; JV Bsktbl; Var Capt Golf; Var Capt Socr; Hon Roll; All Smrst Cntry Sccr All Mntn Vlly Conf 85-86; All ST Sccr 85-86; All Mntn Vlly Conf Golf 85-86; Bus Adm.

ARCHIBALD, BARBARA; Middlesex HS; Middlesex, NJ; (Y); 19/200; Church Yth Grp; Computer Clb; Girl Scts; Ski Clb; Spanish Clb; Im Mgr Gym; JV Sftbl; Im Mgr Vllybl; High Hon Roll; Hon Roll; Rutgers; Bus.

ARCHIE, DESIREE DENISE; Immaculate Conception HS; Irvington, NJ; (Y); Chorus; Hon Roll; Exec Sec.

ARCISZEWSKI, CHRISTINE; South River HS; South River, NJ; (Y); 12/140; French Clb; Spanish Clb; Color Guard; Mrchg Band; Symp Band; Yrbk Stf; Hon Roll; NHS; Douglass; Bus.

ARENDT, EILEEN; Toms River High School North; Toms River, NJ; (Y); 2/412; High Hon Roll; Cert Rcgntn Amer Assn U Wmn 85; Acdmc Ltr 84; Acdmc Pin 85 & 86; 1st Pl Ocn Cnty Soil Cnsvrtn Dist; Math.

ARETZ, STEPHANIE; Buena Regional HS; Landisville, NJ; (S); Pep Clb; Ski Clb; Varsity Clb; Nwsp Phtg; Nwsp Rptr; Rep Frsh Cls; Rep Soph Cls; VP Jr Cls; Rep Stu Cncl; Crs Cntry.

ARETZ, TRACIE; Vineland SR HS; Vineland, NJ; (Y); 43/680; Sec Key Clb; Ed Lit Mag; Art Clb; Spanish Clb; Rep Frsh Cls; Rep Soph Cls; Rep Jr Cls; Rep Sr Cls; Rep Stu Cncl; Stat Wrstlng; JFK Awd Outstndng Comm Ser 86; Bnai Brthawd, Unsng Hero Awd 86; U Of Maryland; Zoology.

ARGITIS, VOULA; Wallington HS; Wallington, NJ; (Y); Band; Chorus; Mrchg Band; Pres Jr Cls; Sec Stu Cncl; Vllybl; Hon Roll; Nova Awd 85; Sys Anylst.

ARGUE, ROBIN; Central Regional HS; Bayville, NJ; (Y); Church Choir; Color Guard; Concert Band; Jazz Band; Mrchg Band; School Musical; Nwsp Rptr; Lit Mag; Fld Hcky; NHS; Hnrb Mntn NJ Poet Cont 86; Jazz Band ST Teen Arts Fstvl 86; ST Teen Arts Fstvl Poet 86; Elem Ed.

ARIAS, JERMAN A; James J Ferris HS; Jersey City, NJ; (Y); #3 In Class; Am Leg Boys St; Church Yth Grp; Debate Tm; French Clb; Math Clb; Scholastic Bowl; Rep Jr Cls; Off Sr Cls; Trs Stu Cncl; Var Socr; Hnbl Mntn STEP 85; Cert Partcptn Spc Shttl Stdnt Invlvmt Prog 85; Spring Garden Coll; Arch.

ARICO, FRANK; Morris Catholic HS; Rockaway, NJ; (Y); 46/155; Church Yth Grp; Math Clb; Varsity Clb; Sec Frsh Cls; Sec Sr Cls; Var Capt Crs Cntry; Var Trk; Hon Roll; Masonic Awd; Im Wt Lftg; 200 Club Schlrshp 86; X-Cntry MVP 85-86; James Madonna Trck & Schlrshp Awd 86; St Bonaventure; Advrtsng.

ARIE, RONIT; Hightstown HS; E Windsor, NJ; (Y); 28/343; VP Cmnty Wkr; Drama Clb; Intnl Clb; Model UN; Service Clb; Spanish Clb; SADD; Temple Yth Grp; Stage Crew; Rep Stu Cncl; Brandeis U; Math.

ARKLISS, NADINE; Lincoln HS; Jersey Cty, NJ; (Y); 4/250; JA; Mgr Cheerleading; Var Crs Cntry; Var Trk; Dnfth Awd; Hon Roll; VP Jr NHS; VP NHS; Ntl Merit Ltr; Rutgers Coll; Obstrcn.

ARKY, LAUREN; East Brunswick HS; E Brunswick, NJ; (Y); Dance Clb; Hosp Aide; Key Clb; Pep Clb; Ski Clb; Temple Yth Grp; Chorus; Nwsp Stf.

ARLAUS, RICHARD; Clifton HS; Clifton, NJ; (Y); 12/564; Boy Scts; German Clb; Science Clb; Rep Frsh Cls; High Hon Roll; NHS; Rotary Awd; NROTC Scholar 86; NJ Frgn Lang Tchrs Awd 86; Pres Acad Fit Awd 86; PA ST U; Engrng.

ARLES, CORINNE; Mount Olive HS; Flanders, NJ; (Y); AFS; Dance Clb; Science Clb; Ski Clb; Rep Frsh Cls; Rep Soph Cls; JV Swmmng; Var Trk; Hon Roll; Arch Dsgn.

ARLINE, DANIELLE; Pleasantville HS; Pleasantville, NJ; (Y); Art Clb; Dance Clb; Chorus; Church Choir; Flag Corp; Mrchg Band; Off Stu Cncl; Swmmng; Ntl Merit Schol; Acdmc Achvmnt Merit Rll 86; Comp.

ARMENIO, PETER J; De Paul Diocesan HS; Wayne, NJ; (Y); Chess Clb; Hosp Aide; Math Tm; Quiz Bowl; Science Clb; Nwsp Rptr; Yrbk Phtg; Off Frsh Cls; Off Sr Cls; Stu Cncl; Rutgers Schlr 84; Schlrshp Rutgers Deans Smmn Schlrs Pgm 85; Spnsh Awd; Physcn.

ARMOUR, KRISTIN; Hackettstown HS; Hackettstown, NJ; (Y); Trs Church Yth Grp; PAVAS; Red Cross Aide; Chorus; Drm & Bgl; Stu Cncl; Var Socr; JV Trk; Hon Roll; NHS; Phys Thrpy.

ARMSTRONG, JAMES M; Delbarton Schl; Madison, NJ; (Y); 1/101; French Clb; Math Clb; Model UN; Science Clb; Nwsp Rptr; Yrbk Rptr; JV Var Golf; JV Var Socr; High Hon Roll; Ntl Merit SF; 4V Lacrosse MVP Awd 84frutgers Pres Schl Awd 85.

ARMSTRONG, KIM; Ocean Township HS; Elberson, NJ; (Y); Church Yth Grp; Hosp Aide; Key Clb; Ski Clb; Spanish Clb; SADD; Varsity Clb; Variety Show; Stu Cncl; Var Cheerleading; SOCL Wrkr.

ARMSTRONG, LISA; Mainland Regional HS; Northfield, NJ; (Y); Stu Cncl; Mgr(s); Vllybl; Svrl Awds For Surfing 84-86; San Diego ST; Marine Bio.

ARMSTRONG, PETER; Morris Catholic HS; Denville, NJ; (Y); 4/147; Am Leg Boys St; Cmnty Wkr; Math Clb; Natl Beta Clb; Trs Soph Cls; Pres Stu Cncl; JV L Socr; Var L Trk; High Hon Roll; NHS; Acdmc All-Amrcn 86; Prncpls Hnr Rll; Ntl Beta Clb Pres; Ntl Hnr Soc; Acdmc Math & Langs; Stu Cncl Pres 86; Duke U; Comp Sci.

ARMSTRONG, SANDRA; Piscataway HS; Piscataway, NJ; (Y); 29/519; Church Yth Grp; French Clb; Mathletes; Radio Clb; Church Choir; Nwsp Rptr; Stat Tennis; High Hon Roll; NHS; Pres Schlr; Trntn ST Coll Almni Assn-$1000 Schlrshp 86; Trenton ST Coll; Elem Educ.

ARNELLA JR, BENEDICT; Christian Brothers Acad; Colts Neck, NJ; (Y); Stage Crew; Yrbk Stf; Mgr(s); Powder Puff Ftbl; Sftbl; JV Wrstlng; Hon Roll.

ARNOLD, ARNESIA; Notre Dame HS; Trenton, NJ; (Y); Church Yth Grp; Cmnty Wkr; Drama Clb; FNA; SADD; Church Choir; Lit Mag; L Var Bsktbl; L Trk; High Hon Roll; Shot Put Gold, Silvr & Brnz Mtl; Most Vlbl Plyr 85-86; Boston U; Psych.

ARNOLD, CHRIS; Notre Dame HS; Trenton, NJ; (Y); Trs Church Yth Grp; Dance Clb; Hosp Aide; Drill Tm; Mrchg Band; Stage Crew; Pom Pon; High Hon Roll; Hon Roll; NHS; Natl Bus Hnr Scty Trsr 86-87; Trenton ST Coll; Bus Admn.

ARNOLD, DONNA; Toms River North HS; Toms River, NJ; (Y); 250/412; DECA; Drama Clb; PAVAS; Ski Clb; School Musical; School Play; Prfct Atten Awd; Camp Fr Inc; FBLA; Office Aide; DECA Awds-Regnl Comptn 1st & 3rd 84-85; Tchr.

ARNOLD, RICHARD; Union HS; Union, NJ; (Y); Am Leg Boys St; Boy Scts; VP Church Yth Grp; Jr Cls; L Swmmng; Wrstlng; Hon Roll; NHS; Highest Acdmc Achvt Awd.

ARNOLD, SONIA; Colonia HS; Colonia, NJ; (Y); Drill Tm; Hon Roll; Fshn Inst Tech; Fshn Merch.

ARNONE, ELIZABETH; Paulvi Reg HS; Paterson, NJ; (Y); Church Yth Grp; Hosp Aide; Pep Clb; Ski Clb; SADD; Nwsp Stf; Yrbk Stf; Stu Cncl; Mgr(s); Hon Roll; Rutgers Coll Arts & Sci Newark.

AROCHO, TAMMY LEE; Emerson HS; Union City, NJ; (Y); Cmnty Wkr; Hosp Aide; Library Aide; Spanish Clb; Color Guard; Flag Corp; School Play; Nwsp Rptr; Nwsp Stf; Yrbk Rptr; DECA Mrktng Gld Mdl 85; Psych.

AROMANDO, JO ANN; Bayley Ellard HS; Florham Pk, NJ; (Y); Church Yth Grp; Service Clb; Yrbk Stf; Powder Puff Ftbl; Hon Roll.

ARON, JULIE; West Milford HS; Newfoundland, NJ; (S); 20/350; Civic Clb; Cmnty Wkr; Intnl Clb; Political Wkr; Nwsp Stf; Yrbk Ed-Chief; Yrbk Stf; Stat Bsktbl; JV Trk; Hon Roll; Vrsty Ltr; Cmnctns.

ARONOWITZ, DEBBIE; Hightstown HS; E Windsor, NJ; (Y); 75/439; Cmnty Wkr; Spanish Clb; VP Temple Yth Grp; Yrbk Stf; Off Jr Cls; JV Trk; High Hon Roll; Hon Roll; MD U; Psychlgy.

ARONSOHN, WILLIAM JOHN; Ramapo HS; Wyckoff, NJ; (S); 12/309; French Clb; Temple Yth Grp; School Musical; Variety Show; Nwsp Ed-Chief; Yrbk Stf; Lit Mag; High Hon Roll; Hon Roll; NHS; Dartmouth Coll; Comms.

ARRINGTON, DORIA MONIQUE; West Side HS; Newark, NJ; (Y); GAA; Trk; Hon Roll; Hnrbl Mntn Ntl HS Trck All-Amrcn 84; DE ST U; Phy Ed.

ARRINGTON, YVONNE D; Oak Knoll School Of The Holy Child; E Orange, NJ; (Y); Rutgers Schlr 85; Natl Achvt Lttr 85; Rutgers Coll Of Pharmacy; Pharm.

ARROGANTE, CHRIS; Union HS; Union, NJ; (Y); Art Clb; Chorus; Stage Crew; Var Tennis; Wt Lftg; CC Awd; Andrew Gorfman Art Awd 86; Achvmnt Awd In Sculpture 86; Kean Coll; Commercial Art.

ARTEAGA, MARIA; Wayne Hills HS; Wayne, NJ; (Y); 3/133; French Clb; Hosp Aide; Library Aide; Spanish Clb; School Musical; Yrbk Stf; Fld Hcky; Hon Roll; 100 Hrs Awd Cndystrprs 86; Med.

ARTEAGE, MADELYNE; St Patrick HS; Elizabeth, NJ; (S); #5 In Class; Church Yth Grp; Science Clb; Chorus; Church Choir; NHS; Wrld Hstry Awd; Sys Analisis.

ARTHUR, CHRIS; West Milford Twsp HS; W Milford, NJ; (S); Am Leg Boys St; Science Clb; Nwsp Phtg; Yrbk Phtg; Lit Mag; Bsbl; Mgr Ftbl; Mgr(s); Peer Cnslng 84-86; 4 X 4 Trckng Clb 85-86; IGWC 85; Astrnt.

ARTHUR, KEVIN; Maple Shade HS; Maple Shade, NJ; (Y); Am Leg Boys St; Boy Scts; Computer Clb; Key Clb; Scholastic Bowl; Yrbk Stf; Rep Stu Cncl; Var Capt Crs Cntry; Var Capt Trk; High Hon Roll; Eagle Scout; USAF Acad; Engrng.

ARTHUR, PATRICIA; Perth Amboy HS; Perth Amboy, NJ; (Y); Church Yth Grp; Girl Scts; Key Clb; Ski Clb; Church Choir; School Play; Stage Crew; Variety Show; Bsktbl; Skppd Grd-1st To 3rd; Bus.

ARTHUR, SHANNON; Middletown HS South; Middletown, NJ; (Y); Church Yth Grp; Drama Clb; French Clb; Hosp Aide; Natl Beta Clb; Varsity Clb; Chorus; Church Choir; Variety Show; Lit Mag; Chrldng Ltr 84-86; FL ST U; Bus Mngmnt.

ARYA, VIVEKANAND; Cliffside Park HS; Fairview, NJ; (Y); 6/250; Am Leg Boys St; Scholastic Bowl; School Play; Pres Jr Cls; Var Bsktbl; Var Trk; NHS; Boy Scts; Cmnty Wkr; Math Tm; Pres Acdmc Ftns Awd Pgm, Prin Awd Acdmc Exclnce&achvt, Am HS Math Exam 2nd 86; Stevens Inst Tech; Engrng.

ASARNOW, DAVID S; Mount Olive HS; Flanders, NJ; (Y); Trs PAVAS; Ski Clb; SADD; Varsity Clb; Yrbk Phtg; Var Swmmng; Var Capt Trk; Hon Roll; Voice Dem Awd; Gold Medl-Schltc Arts Awds 86; 8 Blue Rbbn Fnlst From Schltc Arts Awds 86; Rochester Inst Of Tech; Phtgrph.

ASARO, MARGARET H; Hopewell Valley Central HS; Hopewell, NJ; (Y); Church Yth Grp; Drama Clb; Latin Clb; Spanish Clb; SADD; Varsity Clb; Chorus; School Musical; School Play; Variety Show; FL ST U; Bus.

ASBRAND, JAMES; Hamilton HS East Steinert; Hamilton Sq, NJ; (Y); 69/311; Am Leg Boys St; Key Clb; Quiz Bowl; VP Speech Tm; Concert Band; Madrigals; Mrchg Band; School Musical; Lit Mag; Pres Stu Cncl; Hnry Mntn Rider Coll Litry Cntst 83-84; Advncd SR Hist Cours 85-86; Advncnd Compstn Coll Lvl Engl; Carneigie-Melbon U.

ASCENZO, MARYLOU; Lakeland Regional HS; Wanaque, NJ; (Y); 38/303; FNA; Math Clb; School Play; Capt L Fld Hcky; Var L Sftbl; High Hon Roll; NHS; Wanaque Brgh Wmns Clb Schlrshp 86; Wanaque Plc Assn Schlrshp 86; E Strdsbrg U; Pdtrcn.

ASCHOFF, JON; Northern Valley Regional HS; Old Tappan, NJ; (Y); Computer Clb; Exploring; Math Clb; Math Tm; Science Clb; Ski Clb; Im Bowling; Im Vllybl; High Hon Roll; Hon Roll; MIT; Med.

ASHE, PORTIA; Trenton Central HS; Trenton, NJ; (Y); Church Yth Grp; Cmnty Wkr; Church Choir; Cit Awd; Hon Roll; Engrg.

ASHFORD, ORLANDO; Franklin HS; Somerset, NJ; (Y); 27/313; Computer Clb; Model UN; Radio Clb; SADD; Pres Frsh Cls; Pres Soph Cls; Pres Jr Cls; Pres Sr Cls; JV Bsktbl; Cit Awd; Purdue U Merit Schlrshp, Ethicon Incs Minority Engrng Trng Pgm 86; Purdue U Minority Intro Engnrng 85; Purdue U; Mech Engrng.

ASHLEY, BONNIE; Audubon HS; Audubon, NJ; (Y); 24/119; Nwsp Stf; Yrbk Phtg; Stu Cncl; Capt Var Bsktbl; Stat Ftbl; Im Powder Puff Ftbl; Var Capt Sftbl; Capt Var Tennis; Voice Dem Awd; Off Frsh Cls; S Jersey Sftbl Plyr Of Yr 86; Furman U; Pre-Dent.

ASHTON, PATRICIA LYNNE; Pemberton Township HS II; Browns Mills, NJ; (Y); 27/410; Drama Clb; Library Aide; Teachers Aide; Acpl Chr; Chorus; Hon Roll; NHS; Tn & ST Arts Fstvl 82; Brlngtn Cnty Coll Alumi Schlrshp 86; Brlngtn Cnty Coll.

ASKIN, DAVINA; Lakewood Prep; Brick, NJ; (S); Scholastic Bowl; VP Sec Temple Yth Grp; Nwsp Ed-Chief; Yrbk Bus Mgr; Pres Rep Soph Cls; Sec Rep Stu Cncl; Var L Crs Cntry; Gov Hon Prg Awd; Exclsr Pgm Georgian Coll 83 & 84; Ex Sec United Synagogue Yth 84-85; Lakewood Prep Frgn Lang Hnr Soc; Cmmnctns.

ASSELTA, THOMAS; Delsea Regional HS; Newfield, NJ; (Y); Science Clb; JV Bsbl; JV Var Socr; JV L Trk; Wt Lftg; Annapolis; Sci.

ASTOR, TRACY; Burlington Twp HS; Burlington, NJ; (Y); Drama Clb; Chorus; School Play; Var Bsktbl; Schl Ldrshp Awd 84-85; LAW.

ASTUNI, ANN M; E Brunswick HS; East Brunswick, NJ; (Y); Girl Scts; Key Clb; Red Cross Aide; Var JV Fld Hcky; Var JV Score Keeper; JV Socr; All ST, All Cnty & MVP In Field Hockey 85; All Cnfrnce & All Cnty In Field Hockey 86; Monmouth Coll; Bus.

ATEHORTUA, MAGNOLIA; East-Side HS; Paterson, NJ; (Y); Boys Clb Am; Med.

ATEHORTUO, ELIZABETH; Hoboken HS; Hoboken, NJ; (Y); Church Yth Grp; Sec Key Clb; Chorus; Church Choir; Co-Capt Color Guard; Off Jr Cls; Twrlr; Nrsng.

ATKINS, PAT; Jackson Memorial HS; Jackson, NJ; (S); 14/428; Art Clb; Girl Scts; PAVAS; Q&S; Red Cross Aide; Band; Lit Mag; High Hon Roll; NHS; NEDT Awd; Hlth Occup Stud Of Amer-Rgnl Cmptn-1st Pl Medcl Termnlgy 86; ST Cmptn-Medcl Termnlgy 5th Pl 85; Pre-Med.

ATKINS, RACHEL S; Teaneck HS; Teaneck, NJ; (Y); 22/420; Pres Trs Drama Clb; Chorus; School Play; Lit Mag; Rep Sec Stu Cncl; Hon Roll; NHS; Ntl Merit Ltr; Thesps; Variety Show; Dartmouth Coll.

ATKINSON, LENWORTH; Dwight Marrow HS; Englewood, NJ; (Y); 31/268; Varsity Clb; Band; Socr; High Hon Roll; Hon Roll; Rutgers New Brunswick; Accntg.

ATKINSON, MICHELLE; Salem HS; Salem, NJ; (Y); Intnl Clb; Office Aide; Ski Clb; Spanish Clb; Hon Roll; NHS; RN.

ATLEE, EDWARD; Highland Regional HS; Clementon, NJ; (Y); Ntl Merit Ltr; Mus.

ATTANASIO, SCOTT; Queen Of Peace HS; Nutley, NJ; (Y); 18/229; Cmnty Wkr; SADD; Hon Roll; Church Yth Grp; Service Clb; High Hon Roll; Sphmr Hnr Soc; Jr Hstry Awd; Peace Clb; Games Clb; Peer Mnstry; Svc Gods Nm; Seton Hall U; Priesthd.

AUDIO, REGINA; Washington Township HS; Turnersville, NJ; (Y); 9/470; Church Yth Grp; Q&S; Teachers Aide; Nwsp Rptr; Lit Mag; Rep Stu Cncl; High Hon Roll; NHS; Voice Dem Awd; Awd For Continuing Ed Careers 86; Grdn ST Schlr 86; Hon Grad 86; Glasboro ST Coll; Elem Ed.

AUER, DAVID; Middletown HS South; Middletown, NJ; (Y); Capt Chess Clb; Math Tm; Temple Yth Grp; Bausch & Lomb Sci Awd; Gov Hon Prg Awd; Hon Roll; NHS; Ntl Merit Ltr; Math.

AUGER, MICHELLE; Bridgeton SR HS; Bridgeton, NJ; (Y); Art Clb; Drama Clb; Ski Clb; Sftbl; Tennis; Cit Awd; NHS; HOSA 1st Pl Reg, 2nd Pl ST Comptn Frst Aid 85-86; SCHLRSHP Glsbro Art Pgm 87; Art Awds 1st Pl; Camden County Coll; Dntl Hygnst.

AUGOSTINI, FRANK; Paulsboro HS; Paulsboro, NJ; (Y); 4/143; Wt Lftg; High Hon Roll; Hon Roll; Acad Achvt Awd 83-86; Mech Engrng.

AUGUSTIN, NATHALIE; Union Catholic Regional HS; Scotch Plains, NJ; (S); 6/318; Math Tm; Science Clb; Service Clb; Nwsp Rptr; Chrmn Jr Cls; Var Cheerleading; Var Tennis; High Hon Roll; NHS; Spanish NHS; Natl Spnsh Exam 3rd Pl 84; Natl Spnsh Exam 4th Pl 85; Intl Law.

AUGUSTINE, MARY SUE; Livingston HS; Livingston, NJ; (Y); 138/498; French Clb; Leo Clb; Teachers Aide; Yrbk Stf; JV Mgr Wrstlng; High Hon Roll; Hon Roll; Cert Achvt 83; Cert Svc 83; Towson ST U; Mktng.

AUGUSTYNIAK, MICHAEL; Marist HS; Bayonne, NJ; (Y); 3/134; Computer Clb; Key Clb; Science Clb; Ski Clb; Socr; Hon Roll; Jr NHS; NHS; St Schlr; Garden ST Distngshd Schlr Schlrshp 86; Hudson Cnty Schlstc Achvt Awd 86; Rutgers; Engr.

AULD, WILLIAM; Bound Brook HS; Bound Brook, NJ; (Y); 15/135; Art Clb; Debate Tm; Key Clb; Math Clb; Quiz Bowl; Science Clb; Ski Clb; Pep Band; Nwsp Rptr; Nwsp Sprt Ed; Gold Dble B High Hnrs Club 86; St Teen Art Awds; Rensselaer Polytech Inst; Arch.

AULETTO, LISA; Secaucus HS; Secaucus, NJ; (Y); Key Clb; Math Clb; Varsity Clb; School Play; Yrbk Stf; Rep Sr Cls; Var Capt Cheerleading.

AUMUELLER, CHERYL; Central Jersey Christian HS; Manasquan, NJ; (S); 7/18; Church Yth Grp; Drama Clb; Office Aide; Pep Band; Cheerleading; High Hon Roll; NHS; Sal; Stu Of Mth 83.

AURCA, CATHERINE; Emerson HS; Union City, NJ; (Y); Church Yth Grp; French Clb; Model UN; Flag Corp; Yrbk Stf; Elks Awd; Hon Roll; Prfct Atten Awd; Val; Acctg.

AURIGEMMA, SEAN J; River Dell SR HS; Oradell, NJ; (Y); 2/213; Am Leg Boys St; Spanish Clb; Speech Tm; Nwsp Rptr; Nwsp Sprt Ed; Sec Jr Cls; VP Sr Cls; Ftbl; Trk; Wrstlng; Book E Needle Clb Hghst Acad Avg 83-84; Alfred U Barkman Phys Educ Awd 83-84; U Of PA; Corp Law.

AURIN, KRISTINE; Long Branch HS; Long Branch, NJ; (Y); Science Clb; Drm Mjr(t); Stat JV Bsbl; Var Crs Cntry; Score Keeper; JV Var Swmmng; Var Trk; Twrlr; Phy Ed.

AUSTIN, ALISA; Spotswood HS; Milltown, NJ; (S); VP Intnl Clb; Trs Temple Yth Grp; Sec Soph Cls; Trs Jr Cls; Mgr(s); Var Socr; High Hon Roll; Hon Roll; Amer Cancer Soc Cert Of Merit 82-84; BAR Mitzvah 82; Tutor Hebrew Gold Seal 82-85; Psych.

AUSTIN, EDWARD; Emerson JR-SR HS; Emerson, NJ; (Y); 5/90; Computer Clb; Ski Clb; Spanish Clb; Band; Concert Band; Mrchg Band; Crs Cntry; Tennis; Trk; High Hon Roll; Amer Math Assoc Awd 85; Rensselaer Mdl Excllnc Math & Sci 86; Engrng.

AUSTIN, SHELTON L; St Marys Hall Doane Acad; Willingboro, NJ; (Y); Am Leg Boys St; Yrbk Stf; Trs Soph Cls; Bsbl; Capt Bsktbl; Coach Actv; Score Keeper; Socr; Cit Awd; Crmnlgy.

AVANT, ILA LITTLE; Frank H Morrell HS; Irvington, NJ; (Y); 35/400; Exploring; Key Clb; Library Aide; Pep Clb; Spanish Clb; SADD; Concert Band; Stage Crew; Nwsp Stf; Yrbk Stf; US Teen Miss Rep 85-86; Howard U; English.

AVEDISSIAN, LENA; Paramus HS; Paramus, NJ; (Y); 13/320; Church Yth Grp; Debate Tm; French Clb; Intnl Clb; Math Clb; NFL; Science Clb; Lit Mag; French Hon Soc; NHS; Cncl Schlrshp 86; Rutgers U; Bio.

AVELLA, CARRIE; Morris Knolls HS; Denville, NJ; (Y); 20/367; Concert Band; Mrchg Band; Yrbk Stf; Rep Stu Cncl; High Hon Roll; NHS; Summa Awd 84-86; Fencg; Frshmn Awrnss Ldr; Rutgers U; Bus.

AVERILL, LAURIE; Palmyra HS; Riverton, NJ; (Y); 13/130; French Clb; Varsity Clb; Var Bsktbl; Im Fld Hcky; Var Capt Socr; Var Trk; Hon Roll; Prfct Atten Awd; Rotary Awd; Soph Hmcmg Rep 84-85; 2nd & 3rd Tm Freedm Div All Str Sccr & Trck 84-86; Rutgers Coll; Bio.

AVILA, DENNY; Ferris HS; Jersey City, NJ; (Y); Rep Am Leg Boys St; Church Yth Grp; Computer Clb; Math Clb; Science Clb; Yrbk Phtg; Rep Frsh Cls; Rep Soph Cls; Off Jr Cls; Stu Cncl; Stevens Inst Tech; Elec Engr.

AYALA JR, CARMELO; Woodrow Wilson HS; Camden, NJ; (Y); Chess Clb; Cmnty Wkr; Red Cross Aide; Teachers Aide; Socr; Vllybl; Hon Roll; NHS; Med.

AYAYO, CHRIS; Emerson JR SR HS; Emerson, NJ; (Y); 2/96; Camera Clb; French Clb; Scholastic Bowl; Chorus; School Play; Stage Crew; Yrbk Phtg; Off Frsh Cls; Off Soph Cls; Off Jr Cls; Harvard; Economics.

AYERVAIS, DENA; Glen Rock JR-SR HS; Glen Rock, NJ; (Y); AFS; Ed Lit Mag; Im Socr; JV Vllybl; Hon Roll; Prncpls Stu Recmmndtn Brd 84-85; Attnd Smmr Arts Inst Creative Wrtng 84; Pol Sci.

AYMER, VALERIE; Columbia HS; S Orange, NJ; (Y); VP Church Yth Grp; Drama Clb; Library Aide; Chorus; School Play; Wellesley Bk Awd 86; French Music Studio Rctl Awd 86.

AYNEJIAN, JOHN; Park Ridge HS; Park Ridge, NJ; (Y); 23/120; AFS; Church Yth Grp; Varsity Clb; Band; Chorus; Var Bsktbl; Score Keeper; Var Socr; Quackenbush Schlrshp 86; Rutgers U; Acctng.

AYVAZ, AHMET; Hawthorne HS; Hawthorne, NJ; (Y); Radio Clb; Science Clb; Crs Cntry; Tennis; Vllybl; Hon Roll; PATH 81-85; NJ Inst Of Tech; Elec Engr.

AZHAR, ADNAN; Emerson HS; Union City, NJ; (Y); Science Clb; Hon Roll; Med.

AZZARITI, JENNIFER; Dwight Morrow HS; Englewood, NJ; (Y); 13/247; School Musical; Stage Crew; Yrbk Stf; Sec Frsh Cls; Rep Stu Cncl; JV Vllybl; High Hon Roll; NHS; 1st L Davinci Soc Art 84-85.

AZZARTO, MARY; Westfield HS; Westfield, NJ; (Y); Key Clb; SADD; Chorus; Pres Stu Cncl; Hon Roll; Bus.

AZZOLINA, ANDREA; North Hunterdon HS; Clinton, NJ; (Y); 131/340; Church Yth Grp; VICA; Stu Cncl; Trk; Dnce.

BAATZ, DENISE; Egg Harbor Twp HS; Pleasantville, NJ; (S); 31/317; German Clb; Yrbk Stf; High Hon Roll; Hon Roll; Ntl Merit Ltr; Comm Art.

BABARY, NAOMI; Ocean Township HS; Wanamassa, NJ; (Y); JCL; Latin Clb; Spanish Clb; SADD; Temple Yth Grp; Hon Roll; Pub Reltns.

BABB, ELLEN; Holy Cross HS; Medford Lakes, NJ; (Y); Drama Clb; School Musical; Stage Crew; Nwsp Phtg; Yrbk Phtg; Yrbk Stf; Hon Roll; Yrbk Photo Edtr Awd 85-86; NJ St Tnarts Fest-Phtgrphy 86; Burlington Cnty Tnarts Fest Gld Seal Wnr 86; Temple U; Photorgraphy.

BABB, KAREN; West Morris Central HS; Califon, NJ; (Y); 75/270; Cmnty Wkr; 4-H; Quiz Bowl; Drill Tm; Cit Awd; 4-H Awd; Hon Roll; NJ Eqstrn Yr 4-H 85-86; Rotary Clb Chester/Long Vly Scholar 86; Top 10 Hnrs NJ ST 4-H Horse 80-86; PA ST U; Agri-Bus.

BABICS, CATHERINE; East Brunswick HS; East Brunswick, NJ; (Y); Cmnty Wkr; Debate Tm; Key Clb; Letterman Clb; Political Wkr; Ski Clb; Varsity Clb; Band; Concert Band; Variety Show; Rutgers Coll; Law.

BABILINO, GINA; Our Lady Of Mercy Acad; Turnersvile, NJ; (Y); 1/41; Rep Frsh Cls; Pres Soph Cls; Pres Jr Cls; Pres Stu Cncl; Hon Roll; NHS; Ntl Merit Schol; Nwsp Rptr; Nwsp Stf; Im Badmtn; Ntl Sci Merit Awd Wnnr 85-86; Spnsh Awd 84-85; U Of PA; Bio.

BABLER, MICHAEL; Middletown HS South; Red Bank, NJ; (S); 36/240; Boy Scts; Pres Church Yth Grp; German Clb; Teachers Aide; Band; Church Choir; Mrchg Band; Pep Band; Nwsp Ed-Chief; Rep Stu Cncl; Most Likely To Succeed 83; NJ Pres Schlr 86; Bus Mgt.

BACCALA, MICHAEL; Ocean City HS; Marmora, NJ; (Y); 38/298; Church Yth Grp; Computer Clb; Science Clb; Spanish Clb; Band; JV Bsbl; Drexel; Comp Engr.

BACCARELLA, MICHELE; Holy Family Acad; Bayonne, NJ; (Y); 6/129; French Clb; NFL; Speech Tm; Chorus; Lit Mag; Bowling; High Hon Roll; Sec NHS; Frnch.

BACH, ERIKA; Lakewood HS; Lakewood, NJ; (Y); 13/258; Am Leg Aux Girls St; Pres English Clb; German Clb; Yrbk Ed-Chief; CC Awd; Hon Roll; NHS; Steuben Awd For Germn 86; Jostens Ldrshp Awd 86; Govrs Tchg Schlrs Prgm 86; Georgian Court Coll; Engl.

BACH, TAMI L; Paul VI HS; Blackwood, NJ; (S); 1/550; Drama Clb; Math Clb; Spanish Clb; Band; Jazz Band; Rep Stu Cncl; Capt Cheerleading; Hon Roll; Sec Trs Spanish NHS; Typng, Drvng & Sewng Cert; Villanova; Med.

BACINO, ROBERT; Sumit HS; Summit, NJ; (Y); 50/285; Boy Scts; Church Yth Grp; Computer Clb; Math Clb; Math Tm; Nwsp Stf.

BACKENSON, BRYON; Pope Paul VI HS; Stratford, NJ; (S); 20/475; Am Leg Boys St; Capt Quiz Bowl; School Musical; Hon Roll; NHS; Spanish NHS; Garden ST Distngshd Schlr 86; Drew U; Bio.

BACKLE, FRANK; Lakewood HS; Lakewood, NJ; (Y); 82/350; Church Yth Grp; Spanish Clb; Frsh Cls; Jr Cls; Sr Cls; Bsbl; Bowling; Ftbl; CO ST U; Pre-Med.

BACKMAN, DAVID; West Morris Central HS; Long Valley, NJ; (Y); 77/294; Socr; Coll; Comp Sci.

BACKOUS, SHERMAN; Dwight Morrow HS; Englewood, NJ; (Y); 23/247; Church Yth Grp; Math Tm; Church Choir; Jazz Band; Variety Show; Ftbl; Hon Roll; NHS; U MD; Acctng.

BACON, ANNETTE; Hopewell Valley Central HS; Pennington, NJ; (Y); 33/202; AFS; Girl Scts; Service Clb; Orch; Var Bsktbl; Var Sftbl; NHS; AFS Exec Brd 86-87; Engrg.

BACUNGAN, TEOFILO; Lower Cape May Regional HS; N Cape May, NJ; (Y); 15/243; Chess Clb; Varsity Clb; Crs Cntry; Trk; High Hon Roll; Hon Roll; NHS; 1st Pl Retail Sllng Acc Bus Sympsm 84-85; 4th Pl Tm NJ Stck Mrkt Game 85-86; 3rd Pl 800 M Trck Mt 86; Drexel; Elec Engr.

BADARACCA, WILLIAM; Cinnaminson HS; Cinna, NJ; (Y); Off Boy Scts; Church Yth Grp; Pres VP Exploring; Engnrng.

BADER, ERIC; James Caldwell HS; W Caldwell, NJ; (Y); Concert Band; Mrchg Band; Stage Crew; JV Socr; Engrng.

BADKE, SUE; Parsippany Hills HS; Morris Plains, NJ; (Y); Church Yth Grp; Band; Mrchg Band; School Musical; Symp Band; Var Crs Cntry; JV Socr; Var Trk; FBLA; Hon Roll; Girl ST; Accntnt.

BAER, LAUREN; Paramus HS; Paramus, NJ; (Y); Art Clb; FBLA; Ski Clb; Var Mgr Mgr(s); Var Socr; Var Trk.

BAEZ, LUZ; Barringer HS; Newark, NJ; (Y); Boys Clb Am; English Clb; Spanish Clb; Chorus; School Play; Rep Frsh Cls; Hon Roll; Montclair ST Coll; Bus Adm.

BAEZ, MARITZA M; Emerson HS; Union City, NJ; (Y); 20/277; Camera Clb; Cmnty Wkr; French Clb; Library Aide; Varsity Clb; Flag Corp; Nwsp Ed-Chief; Yrbk Stf; Hon Roll; NHS; Thms A Edsn Schl PTA Schlrshp 86; Rutgers U; Pre-Med.

BAGBY, ELSA; Cumberland Regional HS; Bridgeton, NJ; (Y); Church Yth Grp; Band; Color Guard; Concert Band; Drm Mjr(t); Jazz Band; Mrchg Band; School Musical; Hon Roll; Prfct Atten Awd; Colr Gd Outstndng Perfrmr; Outstndng JR Band Awd; Band Concrt Merit Awd; Cumberland Cnty Clg; Socl Serv.

BAGDADI, LINNETTE; Cliffside Park HS; Cliffside Pk, NJ; (Y); 36/236; Chorus; Swing Chorus; Yrbk Stf; VP Frsh Cls; VP Soph Cls; VP Jr Cls; VP Sr Cls; Rep Stu Cncl; Cheerleading; Hon Roll; Psych.

BAGGETTE, MICHELE; High Point Regional HS; Branchville, NJ; (Y); 22/215; Drama Clb; Q&S; SADD; Varsity Clb; Chorus; Drill Tm; School Musical; Nwsp Stf; Pres Frsh Cls; Rep Soph Cls; Sprntnds Rnd Tbl Awd 86; Stu Cncl Ctznshp Awd 86; Sprntnds Cup Trphy 86; Clemson U; Acctg.

BAGIN, CATHY; Washington Twp HS; Turnersville, NJ; (Y); 66/470; Church Yth Grp; Spanish Clb; Rep Stu Cncl; Var Bsktbl; Var Fld Hcky; Im Swmmng; Hon Roll; St Schlr; Tchg Schlrshp Awd 86; U Of DE; Phys Thrpy.

BAGLEY, MICHELLE; Teaneck HS; Teaneck, NJ; (Y); Dance Clb; Drama Clb; Hosp Aide; Spanish Clb; School Play; Nwsp Rptr; Yrbk Stf; Twrlr; Bronze Pin Awd Acad Achvt 84; Piano Achvt Awd 85; Law.

BAGLEY, STEVE; Hamilton East HS; Hamilton Sq, NJ; (Y); 11/311; Library Aide; Varsity Clb; Bsbl; Bsktbl; Hon Roll; NHS; Ntl Merit Ltr; Pres Acadmc Ftns Awd; Lehigh U; Comp Sci.

BAGLIERI, CHRISTOPHER; Arthur L Johnson Regional HS; Clark, NJ; (Y); 20/214; Boy Scts; Chess Clb; Exploring; JA; Math Clb; Math Tm; Chorus; School Musical; School Play; Hon Roll; Engrng.

BAGLINO JR, PATRICK J; Matawan Reg HS; Aberdeen, NJ; (Y); Pres Debate Tm; NFL; Pres Speech Tm; School Musical; School Play; Yrbk Stf; Rep Stu Cncl; Hon Roll; NHS; Pres Schlr; Trstee Schlrshp NYU 86-87; NY U; Bus.

BAGWELL, ROBIN T; Neptune SR HS; Neptune, NJ; (Y); VP Church Yth Grp; FHA; Library Aide; Teachers Aide; Chorus; Rep Sr Cls; JV Trk; Outstndng SR Awd-Music/Chorus 85 & 86; LORD Cmnty Choir Pres 83 & 86; Outstndng Pgm Ms Amer Co-Ed 86; DE ST Coll; Elem Ed.

BAHAM II, PAUL M; Hudson Catholic HS; Union City, NJ; (Y); #3 In Class; Chess Clb; Church Yth Grp; Cmnty Wkr; Computer Clb; Math Clb; Political Wkr; Science Clb; SADD; Rep Stu Cncl; Bowling; Natl Engrng Soc Scholar 86; Cooper Union Schl Engrng Scholar 86; NJ Inst Tech Scholar 86; NJS Schlrs; Cooper Union; Mech Engr.

BAHAMON, MARTHA; East Side HS; Newark, NJ; (Y); Civic Clb; Drama Clb; VP French Clb; Orch; Yrbk Stf; Rep Sr Cls; Rcgntn 3rd Annl HS Schlrs Day 84-85; IECC Outstnding Comm Svcs 85-86; Rutgers U; Pltcl Sci.

BAI, MARIO; St Peters Preparatory Schl; Lodi, NJ; (Y); 21/209; Pres Camera Clb; Sec Computer Clb; JCL; Nwsp Phtg; Ed Yrbk Phtg; Ed Lit Mag; Hon Roll; NHS; Ntl Merit SF; French Clb; US Naval Acad Smmr Session 86; Greek I Acad Gld Mdl 84-85; Rutgers U Deans Smmr Schlr 86; Carnegie-Mellon U; Comp Engr.

BAIER, STEPHEN; Toms River H S South; Toms River, NJ; (Y); 2/350; Church Yth Grp; FBLA; Math Tm; Science Clb; Stage Crew; Nwsp Stf; Var Crs Cntry; JV Trk; High Hon Roll; Hon Roll; 2nd FBLA ST Cnvt 86; 3 1st Art 84-85; Engrng.

BAIJNATH, WINSTON; Plainfield HS; Plainfield, NJ; (Y); ROTC; Drill Tm; Hon Roll; Natl Sojourners Awd ROTC 85-86; Outstndng Achvt Awd 85-86; Elec Engr.

BAILEY, CHRISTINE; Verona HS; Verona, NJ; (Y); 80/184; Sec DECA; Hosp Aide; 2nd Rnnr-Up Miss Teen NJ 85; DE JR Acadmc Stu Of Yr 86; Miss Photognc Miss Garden ST Pagnt 86; Rutgers; Bio.

BAILEY, DANIEL K; Haddon Township HS; Haddon Township, NJ; (Y); 5/177; Am Leg Boys St; Aud/Vis; Varsity Clb; Variety Show; Nwsp Rptr; Var Socr; Tennis; High Hon Roll; NHS; St Schlr; Rutgers Engrng; Chem Engr.

BAILEY, DONNETTE M; University HS; Newark, NJ; (Y); 9/59; Debate Tm; Drama Clb; JA; School Play; Nwsp Rptr; NHS.

BAILEY, GERRI; Camden HS; Camden, NJ; (S); 4/408; FHA; Sec JA; Drill Tm; School Play; Rep Sr Cls; Tennis; Hon Roll; Jr NHS; NHS; Prfct Atten Awd; Hampton U; Pre Med.

BAILEY, INDIRA; Plainfield HS; Plainfield, NJ; (Y); 33/439; Art Clb; English Clb; Y-Teens; Nwsp Stf; Yrbk Stf; JV Bsktbl; Var Mgr(s); Var Score Keeper; Hon Roll; Amer Assn U Women 86-87; Alpha Kappa Alpha Sorority 86-87; Outstndng Svc Cls 86; Pratt Inst; Illstrtn.

BAILEY, JOSEPH; Lower Cape May Regional HS; Cape May, NJ; (Y); Church Yth Grp; French Clb; PAVAS; SADD; School Musical; Yrbk Stf; Socr; Tennis; Prfct Atten Awd; Globe Trotters Trvl Club 85&86; Fshn Merch.

BAILEY, PAUL; Middletown HS South; Lincroft, NJ; (Y); School Musical; School Play; Yrbk Phtg; Hon Roll; Glasboro ST Coll.

BAILEY, SCOTT; East Brunswick HS; East Brunswick, NJ; (Y); Key Clb; Science Clb; Ski Clb; Temple Yth Grp; Rep Frsh Cls; Socr; Hon Roll; Biolgy Tm 84-85; Bus.

BAILEY, SHAWNELLE; Snyder HS; Jersey City, NJ; (Y); Var Bsktbl; Var Sftbl; NHS; Prnts Cncl Achvt Awd 85; Acad Tm 86; Bus Mgmt.

BAILEY, STEPHANIE; Roselle Catholic HS; Linden, NJ; (S); Art Clb; Civic Clb; French Clb; Hosp Aide; Stage Crew; Lit Mag; JV Crs Cntry; JV Trk; Hon Roll; Rotary Awd; Rotary Intl Exch Stu Belgium 86-87; RI Schl Design; Film/Animtn.

BAILEY, T JASON; East Brunswick HS; East Brunswick, NJ; (Y); Church Yth Grp; Church Choir; School Play; Nwsp Rptr; Yrbk Stf; Ftbl; Var Trk; Var Wt Lftg; Prfct Atten Awd; Rutgers; Engrng.

BAILEY, TYRONE; Camden HS; Camden, NJ; (S); Aud/Vis; Chess Clb; Church Yth Grp; Cmnty Wkr; Key Clb; Model UN; Stage Crew; Yrbk Stf; JV Ftbl; Im Vllybl; Prfct Attndnc Awd 82-85; Good Citznshp Awd 84-85; Civil Engr.

BAIME, ABIGAIL; West Essex SR HS; Essex Fells, NJ; (Y); 36/350; Debate Tm; French Clb; Key Clb; Chorus; Yrbk Stf; Var Fld Hcky; Tennis; Var Trk; High Hon Roll; Pres NHS; Alt NJ Grls Ctznshp 85; All Cnty & All Nrthrn NJ Field Hockey 85; WA U; Lawyer.

BAIRD, AIMEE; Northern Valley Old Tappan HS; Norwood, NJ; (Y); 48/281; AFS; Hosp Aide; Latin Clb; Ski Clb; Concert Band; Mrchg Band; Orch; School Musical; Symp Band; Hon Roll; Math.

BAIRD, JOHN; Mater Dei HS; Union Beach, NJ; (Y); 36/152; Variety Show; Yrbk Phtg; Yrbk Stf; Var Bowling; JV Socr; Acctng.

BAJADA, RICHARD; Central Regional HS; Bayville, NJ; (Y); Office Aide; Ski Clb; Pres Jr Cls; Rep Stu Cncl; Stat Crs Cntry.

BAJCIC, NANCY A; Monsignor Donovan HS; Toms River, NJ; (Y); Art Clb; Drama Clb; Library Aide; Thesps; School Musical; School Play; Stage Crew; Variety Show; Yrbk Stf; Var Stat Score Keeper; Setan Hall Schlrshp 86-89; Setan Hall U; Psych.

BAKER, AUDRA; Hillsborough HS; Somerville, NJ; (Y); #21 In Class; Dance Clb; Ski Clb; SADD; Varsity Clb; Rep Sr Cls; JV Bsktbl; Var Tennis; High Hon Roll; NHS; Perfrmng Arts Dance 84-85; Wake Forest U.

BAKER, CECILIA; Red Bank Catholic HS; Long Branch, NJ; (Y); Church Yth Grp; Latin Clb; Spanish Clb; SADD; Band; Concert Band; Drm Mjr(t); Mrchg Band; Rep Stu Cncl; Var Trk; Pre-Med.

BAKER, DONYALE; Cherry Hill HS West; Cherry Hill, NJ; (Y); Church Yth Grp; ROTC; Teachers Aide; JV Var Mgr(s); JV Swmmng; Var Trk; Im Vllybl; Hampton; Chld Day Cr.

BAKER, JODI; Spotswood HS; Milltown, NJ; (S); 14/189; Intnl Clb; Color Guard; Yrbk Phtg; Off Stu Cncl; Sec Crs Cntry; Mgr(s); Sec Trk; High Hon Roll; Hon Roll; NHS; Arch.

BAKER, KIM YVETTE; Dwight Morrow HS; Englewood, NJ; (Y); 45/270; Sec AFS; Pres Church Yth Grp; Girl Scts; Hosp Aide; Church Choir; Orch; Trk; Hon Roll; Sec Jr NHS; Civic Clb; Corp Law.

BAKER, MICHELLE; Fair Lawn HS; Fair Lawn, NJ; (Y); Drama Clb; Girl Scts; Chorus; School Musical; Hon Roll; Elem Educ.

BAKER, PAUL; Pascack Hills HS; Woodcliff Lk, NJ; (Y); 4/231; Am Leg Boys St; Math Tm; Science Clb; Nwsp Sprt Ed; JV Bsktbl; Var Trk; Hon Roll; VP NHS; Ntl Merit Ltr; Spn Awds 83-85; Burton Agency Scholar 86; Gdn ST Distngshd Schlr 85; U PA; Bio.

BAKER, THOMAS; Steinert HS; Trenton, NJ; (Y); Trs Church Yth Grp; DECA; VP Key Clb; SADD; Chorus; Madrigals; School Musical; All ST Chorus NJ 86; Princeton Opera Assn 85-86; Business.

BAKER, WILLIAM J; North Plainfield HS; North Plainfield, NJ; (Y); 2/153; Am Leg Boys St; Key Clb; Stu Cncl; NHS; Prfct Atten Awd; GA Inst Of Tech; Aerospace Eng.

BALAS, CATHY; Phillipsburg Catholic HS; Alpha, NJ; (Y); 14/78; Cmnty Wkr; Stage Crew; Capt Bsktbl; Sftbl; Hon Roll; The Boyd Schl; Trvl Agnt.

BALDANZA, SAL; Christian Brothers Acad; Manasquan, NJ; (Y); 5/220; Wrstlng; 1st Hnrs Awd Rec; Stanford; Law.

BALDERSTONE, THOMAS C; Cherry Hill East HS; Cherry Hill, NJ; (Y); Am Leg Boys St; Church Yth Grp; FCA; SADD; Chorus; School Play; Variety Show; VP Frsh Cls; Pres Soph Cls; Rep Sr Cls; Math.

BALDINO, REBECCA; Nutley HS; Nutley, NJ; (Y); 17/337; Spanish Clb; Variety Show; Yrbk Phtg; Rep Stu Cncl; Cheerleading; Hon Roll; NHS; Rutgers Coll.

BALDOSARO, THOS; Washington Township HS; Turnersville, NJ; (Y); JV Golf; Hon Roll; Accntng.

BALDWIN, BRIAN; Wall HS; Sea Girt, NJ; (Y); VP Church Yth Grp; Trs FCA; Rep 4-H; French Clb; Ski Clb; Band; Jazz Band; Mrchg Band; Pep Band; Rep Frsh Cls; Accptd Boston Coll Smmr Ses 86; Attnd U CO 19th Anl HS Hnrs Inst Prgm 86; Engrng.

BALDWIN, JANIS; Middletown HS South; Lincroft, NJ; (Y); 65/450; Church Yth Grp; Pep Clb; Ski Clb; Spanish Clb; Band; Church Choir; Mrchg Band; Pep Band; Symp Band; Socr; Bus.

BALESTRIERE, LISA; Wildwood Catholic HS; N Wildwood, NJ; (Y); Spanish Clb; Stage Crew; Fld Hcky; Mgr(s); Spanish NHS.

BALF, DEBORAH A; Toms River HS South; Beachwood, NJ; (Y); 16/360; Math Tm; Band; Mrchg Band; Symp Band; Var L Sftbl; JV Swmmng; Hon Roll; Top 4 Pct Of Clss; Acadmc Ltr 83-84; Spch Pathlgy.

BALICA, ANA; Kearny HS; Kearny, NJ; (Y); Church Yth Grp; VP German Clb; Science Clb; Ski Clb; Chorus; JV Crs Cntry; JV Trk; High Hon Roll; Hon Roll; NHS; Dela Epsilon Phi Germn Hnr Soc 85; JV Awd 85; Natl Sci Olympd 86; Phys Thrpy.

BALIK, AMY; Hunterdon Central HS; Ringoes, NJ; (Y); 182/548; Church Yth Grp; Pres 4-H; Spanish Clb; SADD; Stu Cncl; Cheerleading; 4-H Awd; Hon Roll; Spanish NHS; Prfct Atten Awd; Hnrd Mem JR Prom Ct 8l; Comp Sci.

BALKEMA, BRENDA L; Ramapo Regional HS; Wyckoff, NJ; (Y); AFS; Sec Church Yth Grp; Office Aide; Spanish Clb; Teachers Aide; Church Choir; Mgr(s); Var Socr; Sftbl; Hon Roll; Spcl Svcs Aide 86; APTS Schlrshp 86; TX A&M; Elem Ed.

BALKEY, MIKE; Cherokee HS; Marlton, NJ; (Y); 24/374; Am Leg Boys St; FCA; Rep Soph Cls; Rep Jr Cls; Rep Sr Cls; Var Capt Socr; Var Capt Wrstlng; High Hon Roll; NHS; St Schlr; 2nd Tm All S Jersey Wrstlng 85; Wrstlng Awd MVP 85 & 86; U Of VA; Engrng.

BALL, CHRISTOPHER L; Uncon Catholic Regional HS; North Plainfield, NJ; (Y); Am Leg Boys St; Science Clb; Concert Band; Nwsp Ed-Chief; JV Swmmng; High Hon Roll; NHS; Spanish NHS; Law Day Cnty Essay Wnnr 86; Natl Latin Exam-Cum Laude 84.

BALL, CURTIS C; Overbrook Regional SR HS; Lindenwold, NJ; (Y); 6/260; Office Aide; Pres Sr Cls; JV Var Trk; High Hon Roll; Hon Roll; NHS; Schlrshp Carnegie Mellon U 85; Chem Engrng.

BALL JR, EARLE WILLIAM; Toms River H S East; Toms River, NJ; (Y); Ski Clb; Var Ftbl; Var Swmmng; Var Trk; Hon Roll.

BALL, GARY; Kearny HS; Kearny, NJ; (Y); Am Leg Boys St; Cmnty Wkr; German Clb; Letterman Clb; Ski Clb; Varsity Clb; Var L Swmmng; High Hon Roll; Hon Roll; NHS; Grmn Hnr Soc 86.

BALL, LISA ANNE; Manasquan HS; Spring Lk, NJ; (Y); 15/250; Church Yth Grp; Drama Clb; Key Clb; Math Tm; Spanish Clb; Band; Chorus; Flag Corp; High Hon Roll; NHS; Bd Of Ed Awd 85-86; Bio.

BALLARD, LORI ANN; Piscataway HS; Piscataway, NJ; (Y); 82/600; French Clb; Acpl Chr; Chorus; Flag Corp; School Musical; Stage Crew; Hon Roll; NHS; Super Marchr Awd 86; Montclair ST Coll; Librl Arts.

BALLAS, CLEMENT P; Piscataway HS; Piscataway, NJ; (Y); 8/513; Am Leg Boys St; Science Clb; High Hon Roll; Hon Roll; NHS; Ntl Merit SF; Awd For Excellence In Chem From Union Carbide; Rutgers Coll; Econ.

BALLINA, MICHAEL; Toms River H S South; Toms River, NJ; (Y); Cmnty Wkr; Band; Chorus; Jazz Band; Mrchg Band; Orch; Symp Band; High Hon Roll; Hon Roll; NHS; Rgnl Awd AMSA Piano Comp 85; Supr Hnrs Natl Mbr Natl Piano Guild 85; Bronze Metal Intl Piano Comp 84; Paramedic.

BALLON, ANDREA; North Brunswick Township HS; N Brunswick, NJ; (Y); FBLA; Intnl Clb; Rep Jr Cls; Hon Roll; Miss Itly Awd 86; Bus.

BALLON, WENDI; Henry Snyder HS; Jersey City, NJ; (Y); Teacher Deaf.

BALSAMO, MARIA; Wall HS; Wall Township, NJ; (Y); German Clb; Key Clb; Ski Clb; Color Guard; Yrbk Stf; JV Var Trk; High Hon Roll; Hon Roll; March Of Dimes Volunteer 84; Psych.

BALSANO, ROSANA; Bound Brook HS; Bound Brook, NJ; (Y); VP French Clb; Office Aide; Stu Cncl; Cit Awd; Hon Roll; Somerset County Coll.

BALSLEY, ELIZABETH; North Hunterdon Regional HS; Lebanon, NJ; (Y); 88/348; Church Yth Grp; JCL; Latin Clb; Ski Clb; Lib Jazz Band; Stu Cncl; JV Ftbl; Golf; Im Lcrss; Hon Roll; Law.

BALTOZER, ROSE; Sacred Heart HS; Glassboro, NJ; (S); 5/65; Church Yth Grp; French Clb; Math Clb; Chorus; Church Choir; School Play; Yrbk Stf; Bsktbl; Hon Roll; NHS; US Math Achvmnt Awd 86; Var Let Bsktbll 86; Coaching Awd Sccr 86; Med.

BALZER, CLAUDIA; Chatham Twp HS; Chatham Twp, NJ; (Y); 35/150; Church Yth Grp; Key Clb; Pep Clb; Nwsp Stf; Yrbk Ed-Chief; Cheerleading; Sftbl; Hon Roll; Mst Imprvd Sftbl Plyr 85; Intl Rltns.

BANAAG, REUBEN; Passaic HS; Passaic, NJ; (Y); Am Leg Boys St; FBLA; Var Capt Tennis; Hon Roll; Prfct Atten Awd; Acctg.

BANASIAK III, STEPHEN J; Rahway HS; Rahway, NJ; (Y); 62/256; Am Leg Boys St; Boy Scts; Computer Clb; Exploring; Band; Concert Band; Jazz Band; Rep Stu Cncl; Cit Awd; Hon Roll; Lf Sct 86; Penn ST U; Bus.

BANDELLI, LISA; East Brunswick HS; East Brunswick, NJ; (Y); Rep Key Clb; Pep Clb; Ski Clb; SADD; Chorus; Drill Tm; Cheerleading; Hon Roll; NHS; Rutgers U; Bus.

BANE, MICHELLE R; Middletown HS South; Leonard, NJ; (Y); Ski Clb; Variety Show; Yrbk Phtg; Yrbk Rptr; Yrbk Stf; Trs Stu Cncl; Cheerleading; Mgr(s); JV Socr; Hon Roll; Cert Of Awd Yrbk Staff And Stu Cncl 84; Cert Of Awd JV Soccr 85-86; Spec Ed.

BANFE, EDWARD; Bishop Eustace Preparatory Schl; Medford, NJ; (Y); Boy Scts; Spanish Clb; JV Trk; Hon Roll; NHS; Achvt Awd Dale Carnegie Courses.

BANGASH, SHIREEN; Saddle River Day Schl; Ridgewood, NJ; (S); 30/69; School Play; Var Cheerleading; Var Capt Socr; Hon Roll; Key Clb; Math Tm; Natl Ldrshp & Serv Awd Wnnr 86; Psychlgy.

BANICK, TRACY; Woodstown HS; Woodstown, NJ; (Y); Dance Clb; Office Aide; Spanish Clb; Rep Frsh Cls; Sec Jr Cls; Sec Sr Cls; Var Capt Cheerleading; Cit Awd; Speech Pthlgy.

BANKER, DANNY; Lakeland Regional HS; Haskell, NJ; (Y); 35/303; Church Yth Grp; Math Clb; Teachers Aide; JV Var Bsbl; Im Capt Bowling; Im Coach Actv; Im Mgr(s); Hon Roll; NHS; Bergen CC; Bus Admin.

BANKOWSKI, JENNIFER; Kearny HS; Kearny, NJ; (Y); VP Church Yth Grp; German Clb; Science Clb; Concert Band; Mrchg Band; L Var Swmmng; Hon Roll; NHS; Chorus; Ltr Band 84; Vet-Med.

BANKS, ANDREW D; Seton Hall Prep; Cedar Grove, NJ; (Y); 20/199; Sec Art Clb; Boy Scts; Pep Clb; Ski Clb; School Play; Nwsp Rptr; Yrbk Ed-Chief; Var L Crs Cntry; Var L Tennis; High Hon Roll; Fairfield U; Bus.

BANKS, LORI; John F Kennedy HS; Willingboro, NJ; (Y); 13/294; Intnl Clb; Service Clb; Mgr Cheerleading; Mgr Trk; High Hon Roll; Hon Roll; Trs NHS; Bus Adm.

BANKS, MARK C; Highland Regional HS; Sicklerville, NJ; (Y); Service Clb; Spanish Clb; School Play; Var Swmmng; Trk; Hon Roll; Ntl Merit Ltr; Summr Actrl Prgm 86; Actrl Sci.

BANNISTER, ROBERT P; Cherodii HS; Atco, NJ; (Y); 8/408; Am Leg Boys St; Art Clb; Church Yth Grp; Frsh Cls; Soph Cls; Jr Cls; Stu Cncl; Bowling; NHS; Ntl Merit Ltr.

BANSEMIR, ANNE; Nutley HS; Nutley, NJ; (Y); 2/330; Sec German Clb; Math Tm; Capt Scholastic Bowl; Rep Stu Cncl; Var Capt Crs Cntry; Var Capt Trk; Pres NHS; Rotary Awd; Sal; Orch; Natl Mrt Fnlst; Cook Coll; Bio-Chem.

BAPTISTE, RUTH; Weequahie HS; Newark, NJ; (S); 13/353; Boys Clb Am; Church Yth Grp; Spanish Clb; Yrbk Stf; Pres Jr Cls; Rep Sr Cls; NHS; Engrng.

BARA, RACHEL; S River HS; S River, NJ; (Y); 18/132; Math Tm; Spanish Clb; Yrbk Stf; Var L Bsktbl; Coach Actv; Var L Fld Hcky; JV Sftbl; Var L Trk; NHS; Specl Ed Tchr.

BARABAS, KIMBERLY; Shore Regional HS; W Long Branch, NJ; (Y); Temple Yth Grp; Band; Concert Band; Mrchg Band; School Musical; Stage Crew; High Hon Roll; Hon Roll; Sci Fair 3rd Pl Awd Scl Sci Div; Sci Fair Hnrbl Mntn Bio Div; Hnrs Alg II, Geom/Trig, Hstry I; Med.

BARALL, ALLAN; Parsippany HS; Parsippany, NJ; (Y); Am Leg Boys St; Pres Computer Clb; Trs FBLA; Temple Yth Grp; Yrbk Stf; Hon Roll; NHS; Cntrl Hebrew H S Grad W Hnrs 86; Teen Ldrshp Mssn Wash DC 86; Understndg Amer Bus Rutgers U 86; Invstmt Bnkg.

BARANCO, LORRIE; Toms River H S North; Toms River, NJ; (Y); 37/412; Dance Clb; Ski Clb; School Play; Stu Cncl; JV Fld Hcky; JV Socr; High Hon Roll; Hon Roll; NHS; Church Yth Grp; Bio.

BARANOFF, JOSHUA; Cherry Hill West HS; Cherry Hill, NJ; (Y); 41/330; Aud/Vis; Cmnty Wkr; Computer Clb; Library Aide; PAVAS; VP Temple Yth Grp; School Play; Hon Roll; La Salle U Adio Vsul Spec Pgm 85-86; Slctn Poland/Isrl Smnr Pgrmg 85-86; Ithaca Coll; Cmnctns.

BARANOWSKI, FAITH; Hackettstown HS; Hackettstown, NJ; (Y); Am Leg Aux Girls St; Pep Clb; Q&S; Teachers Aide; Yrbk Ed-Chief; Stu Cncl; Var JV Cheerleading; Stat Wrstlng; Hon Roll; Pol Sci.

BARASCH, JON; Matawan Regional HS; Matawan, NJ; (S); 37/280; Math Clb; Math Tm; Ski Clb; Yrbk Stf; Stu Cncl; Var Ftbl; Var Wt Lftg; JV Wrstlng; Hon Roll; NHS; Fnce.

BARASH, JEFF; Montville HS; Montville, NJ; (Y); Computer Clb; FBLA; Temple Yth Grp; Mrchg Band; Symp Band; Socr; Tennis; High Hon Roll; Hon Roll; NHS; USY-OUTSTNDNG Mem-Temple Yth Grp 83-84; Comp Sci.

BARASH, SARA; Scotch Plains Fanwood HS; Westfield, NJ; (Y); Jazz Band; Orch; Symp Band; Co-Principal Flutist NJ Yth Symphny 85-86; NJ Gov Schl Of Arts 1st Flute 86; Ntl Flute Assoc 86; Music.

BARATY, DAMIAN; Paramus HS; Paramus, NJ; (Y); 5/364; Intnl Clb; JCL; Chorus; Ed Lit Mag; Capt Socr; NHS; Spanish NHS; Cornell U; Bio.

BARBAGIANNIS, OLGA; Immaculate Conception HS; Rochelle Park, NJ; (S); Dance Clb; English Clb; SADD; School Play; Bsktbl; Mgr(s); Score Keeper; Swmmng; Hon Roll; Ntl Merit Ltr; Natl Art Hnr Soc; Intl Bus.

BARBARA, DAN; Washington Township HS; Turnersville, NJ; (Y); 100/500; Am Leg Boys St; Church Yth Grp; Var L Bsbl; Var L Bsktbl; Var L Socr; Hon Roll; Rep S Jersey Gdn ST Bsbl Trnmnt Rutgers U 85 & 86; Bus Adm.

BARBARISI, LOUIS; West Essex HS; Roseland, NJ; (Y); Computer Clb; Stu Cncl; Capt L Bsbl; Coach Actv; Var Capt Ftbl; Ice Hcky; Swmmng; Wt Lftg; Kids Bsktbl Coach Awd 86; Tulane U FL; Bio Chem.

BARBEE, JENNIFER; Ridge HS; Far Hills, NJ; (Y); 16/220; VP Pres Church Yth Grp; VP Acpl Chr; VP Chorus; Madrigals; School Musical; School Play; Sec Sr Cls; Capt Cheerleading; NHS; NJ All ST Chorus 85-86; NJ Rgn II Chorus 85; Music.

BARBER, KELLIE; Gateway Regional HS; Westville, NJ; (Y); 50/184; JCL; Latin Clb; SADD; Swmmng; Hon Roll; NHS; Grls Ctnznshp Inst 86; Cmmrcl Art.

BARBER, LARRY; Paulsboro HS; Paulsboro, NJ; (Y); Var Bsbl; Var Ftbl; Wt Lftg; JV Var Wrstlng; High Hon Roll; Hon Roll; NHS; Acadmc Exllnc 84 & 85; Wrstlng Awds 84 & 85; Cert Of Appreciation 85; Colonial Conf HS Bsbl Champ 86.

BARBER, TRACY; Cumberland Regional HS; Bridgeton, NJ; (Y); 82/401; Camera Clb; Hosp Aide; Intnl Clb; JCL; Science Clb; Ski Clb; Chorus; Stat Crs Cntry; Var JV Mgr(s); Var JV Trk; Chorus & Choir High Achvt 84 & 85; Vet Sci.

BARBOSSA, DAVID; Hudson Catholic HS; Jersey Cty, NJ; (Y); 83/201; Stu Cncl; Bsbl; Ice Hcky; Hon Roll; MVP Hudson Cath Ice Hockey 84-86; ST NJ Ath Mnth 85-86; Amer Conf A Div Ice Hcky MVP 85-86; Bus.

BARBOUNIS, SOTIRI; Morristown HS; Morris Plains, NJ; (Y); Computer Clb; Radio Clb; Prnctn U; Arch Engrng.

BARCH, KIMBERLY; Parsippany Christian HS; Morris Plains, NJ; (Y); 2/18; Church Yth Grp; GAA; Chorus; Church Choir; School Play; Rep Frsh Cls; Sec Soph Cls; Var Capt Bsktbl; Var Socr; Cit Awd; Piano & Spelling 1st Pl ST 85 & 86; Piano 2nd Natls 85; Cedarville Coll; Nursing.

BARCKLEY, ANNETTA LYNN; Buena Regional HS; Landisville, NJ; (S); 20/191; Church Yth Grp; 4-H; Math Clb; School Musical; School Play; Stage Crew; Nwsp Rptr; Nwsp Stf; Hon Roll; Jr NHS.

BARCLAY, SUZANNE; Toms River H S North; Toms River, NJ; (Y); Church Yth Grp; Band; Chorus; Church Choir; Concert Band; Drm Mjr(t); Mrchg Band; School Musical; School Play; Var L Swmmng; Acadmc Ltr 85-86; Music.

BARD, DEBORAH; Fairlawn HS; Fair Lawn, NJ; (Y); 12/335; Rep Soph Cls; Rep Jr Cls; Rep Sr Cls; Var Capt Trk; High Hon Roll; Hon Roll; NHS; NJ ST Intrschlstc Athl Assn Schlr Athl Awd 86; JR Clss Marshall Grad 85; Le High U.

BARDSLEY, ROBERT; Clearview Regional HS; Mantua, NJ; (Y); 16/170; Boy Scts; Debate Tm; Nwsp Stf; Yrbk Stf; Crs Cntry; Trk; Pres NHS; Opt Clb Awd; Eagle Scout 83; Order Arrow Vice Chief 85-86; Rutgers; Ed.

BARGE, ANGELIQUE; Camden HS; Camden, NJ; (Y); 48/408; Dance Clb; Hosp Aide; Model UN; Jazz Band; Prfct Atten Awd; Church Yth Grp; Cmnty Wkr; Debate Tm; Band; Church Choir; Rcgntn Intrdnmntnl Mnstrs Wvs Cmdn & Vcnty 86; Douglass Coll; Spch Pthlgy.

BARGE, JAMES; South River HS; South River, NJ; (Y); 17/140; Am Leg Boys St; Church Yth Grp; German Clb; Math Tm; Church Choir; Im JV Bsktbl; L Var Crs Cntry; Var Stat Fld Hcky; L Var Trk; NHS; Cross Cty MVP Awd 85; Track MVP Awd 86; U VA; Comm.

BARHAM, CHRISTY; Absegami HS; Absecon, NJ; (Y); 26/250; French Clb; GAA; Drill Tm; Cheerleading; Librl Arts.

BARILLA, DENISE; Roselle Catholic HS; Union, NJ; (Y); Church Yth Grp; Ski Clb; Var Score Keeper; Var Tennis; French Hon Soc; Hon Roll; Jr NHS; NHS; Bio.

BARISH, RICHARD; Oakcrest HS; Mays Landing, NJ; (Y); 5/172; Math Clb; Var Bsktbl; Im Lcrss; Var Socr; Im Sftbl; Var Capt Tennis; High Hon Roll; Hon Roll; NHS; Pres Schlr; PTA Schlrshp 86; Am U.

BARK, JENNIFER; Paul VI HS; Haddonfield, NJ; (S); 6/551; Math Clb; Spanish Clb; High Hon Roll; Hon Roll; Spanish NHS; SUNY Coll; Bus.

BARKAUSKAS, RICHARD T; Mountain Lakes HS; Mtn Lakes, NJ; (Y); Sec Model UN; Nwsp Stf; Ed Yrbk Stf; Pres Frsh Cls; Var JV Bsbl; Bsktbl; Coach Actv; Var Capt Socr; Hon Roll; Athl Hnr Awd 83-86; MIP Soccr 84-85; Georgetown U; Ecnmcs.

BARKER, LISA; Cumberland Regional HS; Bridgeton, NJ; (Y); Art Clb; Church Yth Grp; Cmnty Wkr; Dance Clb; Hosp Aide; Intnl Clb; Band; Church Choir; Color Guard; Ski Clb; Miss Grtr Bridgetn 86; Art Inst Philadelphia; Vsl Comm.

BARKLEY, MONE; Washington Township HS; Sewell, NJ; (Y); Drama Clb; Math Tm; Model UN; Spanish Clb; School Musical; School Play; Nwsp Rptr; Hon Roll; Prism Excllnc Awd 84; Urban League Task Force 84; Intl Bus.

BARLOW, DEIDRA; Lakewood HS; Lakewood, NJ; (Y); FBLA; Pres Chorus; Church Choir; Hon Roll; Danckng Cls Awd 84; 1st Pl Rbbn Sewing Proj Fair 84; Math.

BARLOW, ERIC; Hightstown HS; Cranbury, NJ; (Y); Church Yth Grp; Spanish Clb; Im Bsbl; Im Bsktbl; Var Crs Cntry; Im Socr; Var Trk; Im Vllybl; Law.

BARLOW, THOMAS; Spotswood HS; Spotswood, NJ; (S); 17/174; Am Leg Boys St; Model UN; Scholastic Bowl; Nwsp Stf; Yrbk Stf; Off Stu Cncl; Capt Socr; St Schlr; Sr Rep Spotswood Bd Of Educ 85-86; Bus Admin.

BARLOW III, THOMAS B; Toms River HS East; Toms River, NJ; (Y); 75/585; Concert Band; Jazz Band; Mrchg Band; Symp Band; Schls 1st Recipient Of Louis Armstrong Jazz Awd 85-86; Medical Doctor.

BARNES, EDWINA; Franklin HS; Somerset, NJ; (Y); German Clb; Stu Cncl; Cheerleading; Pom Pon; Trk; Wt Lftg; VA ST U; Acctg.

BARNES, JEFFREY; Wildwood Catholic HS; Wildwood Crest, NJ; (Y); Cmnty Wkr; Varsity Clb; Nwsp Rptr; Nwsp Sprt Ed; Yrbk Stf; Var Bsktbl; Var Tennis; Hnrbl Mntn All Cape Atltc League Bsktbl 85-86; 2nd Tm All Cape May Cnty Bsktbl 85-86; Dfndr Yr 85-86; Brdcstng.

BARNES, LORRAINE; West Morris Mendham HS; Mendham, NJ; (Y); 15/300; Church Yth Grp; Band; Capt Flag Corp; Mrchg Band; High Hon Roll; Hon Roll; NHS; Rutgers U.

BARNES, MICHELE S; Vernon Township HS; Glenwood, NJ; (Y); VP DECA; VP FBLA; Chorus; Nwsp Stf; JV Capt Cheerleading; Stat Wrstlng; Hon Roll; Centenary Coll Fash Merch Scholar 86; DECA NJ Delg Natl Career Dev Conf 85 & 86; DECA NJ Fin Conf; Centenary Coll; Fash Merch.

BARNETT, BRIAN; Columbia HS; Maplewood, NJ; (Y); Boy Scts; Chess Clb; Cmnty Wkr; Exploring; FBLA; Ski Clb; Temple Yth Grp; Stage Crew; Golf; Natl Law Enfrcmnt Explorer Pistol Champ 86; Natl Law Enfrcmnt Explorer Conf Part 86; Stockton ST; Law Enforcement.

BARNETT, PENELOPE; Clifford T Scott HS; East Orange, NJ; (Y); 33/250; Cmnty Wkr; Office Aide; Hon Roll; FL A&m U.

BARNETT, PHILIP; Burlington Co Vo Tech; Willingboro, NJ; (Y); Computer Clb; VICA; Yrbk Stf.

BARNETT, ROBERT; Overbrook Regional HS; Lindenwold, NJ; (Y); 30/270; Spanish Clb; Varsity Clb; Bsktbl; Var Ftbl; Var Golf; Var Wrstlng; Hon Roll; Babe Ruth Sprtsmnshp Awd 86; Overbrook Vrsty Club Schlrshp Awd 86; Gettysuburg Coll; Bus Adm.

BARON, LINDA; Fair Lawn SR HS; Fair Lawn, NJ; (Y); Temple Yth Grp; Rep Jr Cls; Rep Sr Cls; Hon Roll; Compu.

BARON, SHERRY; Fairlawn HS; Fair Lawn, NJ; (Y); 40/336; Girl Scts; Temple Yth Grp; Band; Mrchg Band; Capt Bowling; Hon Roll; NHS; Rutgers Coll.

BARONE, ANDREW T; Seton Hall Prep; Newark, NJ; (Y); Church Yth Grp; Computer Clb; French Clb; Chorus; Lit Mag; Hon Roll; Caldwell Coll; Math Tchr.

BARONE, ANGELA; Bishop Eustace Prep Schl; Haddonfield, NJ; (Y); 10/182; Math Clb; Pep Clb; VP Spanish Clb; Var L Trk; High Hon Roll; NHS; Spanish NHS; St Wnnr Ntl Piano Audtns NGPT 86.

BARONE, LISA; Queen Of Peace HS; N Arlington, NJ; (Y); 66/234; Yrbk Stf; Jr Cls; Stat Bsktbl; Powder Puff Ftbl; Var Sftbl; JV Var Vllybl; Hon Roll; Secdry Ed.

BARONE, THOMAS C; Midland Park HS; Ho-Ho-Kus, NJ; (Y); Am Leg Boys St; Church Yth Grp; Ski Clb; School Musical; Nwsp Phtg; Nwsp Stf; Yrbk Phtg; Yrbk Stf; Off Frsh Cls; Off Soph Cls; Bio.

BARR, MAUREEN; Paul VI HS; Somerdale, NJ; (S); 10/474; French Clb; Math Clb; Var Crs Cntry; Var Trk; French Hon Soc; Hon Roll; NHS; Johns Hopkins U; Bio.

BARR, PETER; Haddon Heights HS; Haddon Heights, NJ; (S); Scholastic Bowl; Service Clb; Teachers Aide; VP Jr Cls; Var L Bsbl; JV Bsktbl; Var JV Ftbl; Hon Roll; Marine Physcl Ftns Awd 84-86.

BARR JR, ROBERT L; University HS; Newark, NJ; (Y); Leo Clb; Im Bsktbl; Var Capt Crs Cntry; Var Capt Trk; Cit Awd; Hon Roll; NHS; Aerspc Engr.

BARR, STEPHANIE; Wayne Hills HS; Wayne, NJ; (Y); 49/353; French Clb; FBLA; Nwsp Rptr; Stat Bsktbl; Var Capt Crs Cntry; Var Capt Trk; Hon Roll; Jrnlsm.

BARRE, AMY; N Bergen HS; Guttenberg, NJ; (S); 100/475; Exploring; SADD; Nwsp Stf; Yrbk Stf; Sec Jr Cls; Stu Cncl; Hon Roll; Stu Membr Midl ST Evltn Comm 85-86; Erly Chldhd Educ.

BARRESSE, GLENN; James Caldwell HS; W Caldwell, NJ; (Y); Church Yth Grp; Bsbl; Bowling; Hon Roll; Aerontcl Engr.

BARRETT, CHRISTINE; Scotch Plains Fanwood HS; Scotch Plains, NJ; (Y); AFS; FBLA; GAA; Key Clb; Nwsp Rptr; Var JV Cheerleading; Gym; Trk.

BARRETT, JO A; Ocean Township HS; W Allenhurst, NJ; (Y); Bus Admin.

BARRETT, MICHELLE; Highland Regional HS; Erial, NJ; (Y); Yrbk Bus Mgr; Score Keeper; Stat Sftbl; Glassboro ST; Elem Ed.

BARRETT, NELTON; Eastside HS; Paterson, NJ; (Y); #59 In Class; Capt Boy Scts; Trs Camera Clb; Church Yth Grp; Cmnty Wkr; VP Dance Clb; Drama Clb; Stu Cncl; Capt Socr; Tennis; Trk; NJ 1st Pl Awd In Crftmn Fair & Ptrsn Fair 84-86; Cert Of Merit In Chem,Hstry & Civics 84-85; Banking.

BARRETT, TRACY; Scotch Plains Fanwood HS; Fanwood, NJ; (Y); AFS; Drama Clb; French Clb; Chorus; School Play; High Hon Roll; Hon Roll; Ntl Merit Ltr; Prfct Atten Awd; Spanish NHS; Spnsh Awd 84-86; Erth Sci Awd 84; Hstry & Engl Recog Achvt Ltr 85; Boston U; Atty.

BARRIOS, JANIEN; Clifton HS; Clifton, NJ; (Y); Boys Clb Am; Office Aide; Chorus; Law.

BARRON, LISA; Weequahic HS; Newark, NJ; (S); 3/353; Pres Stu Cncl; NHS; Yale; Comp Prgrmr.

BARRY, CHRISTINE; Pompton Lakes HS; Pompton Lakes, NJ; (Y); 30/150; Spanish Clb; Varsity Clb; Yrbk Stf; Pres Frsh Cls; Pres Soph Cls; Pres Jr Cls; Cheerleading; Capt Sftbl; Hon Roll; Trenton ST Coll; Commnctns.

BARRY, HOPE; Hackettstown HS; Hackettstown, NJ; (Y); Girl Scts; Hon Roll; NHS; 1st Art Cntst Kiwanas Drnkng & Drvng 83-84.

BARRY, ROBIN; Montgomery HS; Skillman, NJ; (Y); 8/131; Cheerleading; Co-Capt Gym; Powder Puff Ftbl; Score Keeper; High Hon Roll; Hon Roll; NHS; Church Yth Grp; Rep Frsh Cls; Rep Soph Cls; Most Vlbl Plyr Awd Gymstcs 84-85; Ursinus Clg; Psych.

BARSCZEWSKI, BRIAN; Penns Grove HS; Penns Grove, NJ; (Y); 12/185; Church Yth Grp; JCL; Latin Clb; Var Socr; JV Var Wrstlng; Hon Roll; Sci.

BARSIK, SUSAN; Mary Help Of Christians Acad; Haledon, NJ; (S); 8/88; Computer Clb; Latin Clb; Math Clb; Service Clb; Teachers Aide; Nwsp Stf; High Hon Roll; Hon Roll; Prfct Atten Awd; Algebra, Bio & Histry Awds 85; Busnss.

BARSKY, DENNIS; Cliffside Park HS; Fairview, NJ; (Y); Am Leg Boys St; Pres Chess Clb; Nwsp Rptr; Nwsp Stf; Lit Mag; Ftbl; Golf; Wrstlng; NJ Acad Decath 86; STAIRS Frgn Rel Sem 86; Intl Affrs.

BARSKY, NOREEN; Chatham Twp HS; Chatham, NJ; (Y); Key Clb; Pep Clb; Yrbk Rptr; Yrbk Sprt Ed; Yrbk Stf; Rep Jr Cls; Stu Cncl; Var Cheerleading; Gym; High Hon Roll; Physcl Thrpy.

BARTEL, BRIAN; Middletown HS South; Middletown, NJ; (Y); Cmnty Wkr; Im Bsktbl; Im Wt Lftg; Hon Roll; Chiropractor.

BARTHA, MIRIAM; East Brunswick HS; E Brunswick, NJ; (Y); Dance Clb; 4-H; Latin Clb; Chorus; Orch; Trk; French Hon Soc; 4-H Awd; NJ All ST Orch 83-85; SR Regl Orch 83-86; Rutgrs Schlr Hnrs Merit Awd 86; Rutgers Coll; Theatr Arts.

BARTHOLOMEW, JUDY; Phillipsburg HS; Phillipsburg, NJ; (Y); 22/292; Key Clb; Nwsp Stf; NHS; Nwsp Rptr; High Hon Roll; Hon Roll; Warren Hosp Nrsg & Hlth Careers Schlrshp 85-86; Phillipsburg Rotary Schlrshp, Cls Of 48 Schlrshp 85-6; Trenton ST Coll; Psych.

BARTILUCCI, JENNIFER; Marlboro Reg HS; Morganville, NJ; (Y); Hon Roll; Var Cheerleading; Child Psychlgy.

BARTIROMO, LOUIS C; Lenape Valley Regional HS; Stanhope, NJ; (Y); CAP; Thesps; School Musical; School Play; Stage Crew; Spelling Be Champ; Eligible Took Sat John Hopkins U 81; Seek Pgm 81-82; E Stroudsburg U; Comp Sci.

BARTKUS, DAWN; Toms River HS East; Toms River, NJ; (Y); JV Cheerleading; High Hon Roll; Hon Roll; Cittone Inst TCI Awd; High GPA Awd-Accntng I; Coop Offc Eductn Studnt; Cittone Inst; Court Reprtr.

BARTLETT, LYNN ANN; Rutherford HS; Rutherford, NJ; (S); Church Yth Grp; Pep Clb; Varsity Clb; Rep Jr Cls; Stat Bsktbl; Stat Ftbl; Sftbl; Vllybl; High Hon Roll.

BARTLEY, CAROLYN; Hightstown HS; Cranbury, NJ; (Y); Am Leg Aux Girls St; Stu Cncl; JV Var Bsktbl; Var Capt Fld Hcky; Var Sftbl; All St Group IV Fld Hockey All-Star 85-86; Centrl Jersey All Star 1st Tm Fld Hockey 85-86; Phy Ed.

BARTOLINO, JODI; Notre Dame HS; Lawrenceville, NJ; (Y); Key Clb; VP Latin Clb; VP Ski Clb; JV Capt Fld Hcky; Hon Roll.

BARTOLO, MARCA LEIGH; Montclair School Of Performing Arts; Montclair, NJ; (Y); PAVAS; Chorus; Madrigals; School Musical; School Play; Stage Crew; Variety Show; Tlnt Srch 1st Pl Feml Voclst 86; Bst Supptg Actrss Drama 83; Bst Actrss Drama 84; Schl Svc Awd 83 & 86; Amer Musical & Dramatic Acad.

BARTON, ELAINE; Bridgewater-Raritan West HS; Bridgewater, NJ; (Y); Art Clb; Church Yth Grp; Debate Tm; French Clb; NFL; High Hon Roll; Hon Roll; Cnty Teen Arts 86; Ramapo Coll; Psych.

BASAVIAH, PREETHA; Montville Township HS; Montville, NJ; (Y); 3/270; Dance Clb; FBLA; Pres Intnl Clb; Key Clb; Science Clb; Lit Mag; Var Tennis; High Hon Roll; NHS; Ntl Merit Ltr; NJ Sci Day-Chem-1st Cnty 86; Rnr Up-HOBY Ldrshp Conf 85; FBLA Rgnl Comptn-1st Bus Eng 86; Pre Med.

BASELICE, MICHAEL J; Lyndurst HS; Lyndhurst, NJ; (Y); 18/180; Am Leg Boys St; Boy Scts; Math Clb; Science Clb; Ski Clb; Stu NJ Acdmc Decthln Tm 86; Compu Sci.

BASEM, LAURA; Parsippany HS; Parsippany, NJ; (Y); FBLA; Sec Spanish Clb; VP Temple Yth Grp; Band; Mrchg Band; School Musical; Var L Tennis; High Hon Roll; Hon Roll; NHS.

BASICH, MICHELE; Delsea Regional HS; Vineland, NJ; (Y); Science Clb; Im Mgr Sftbl; Im Mgr Vllybl; Jr NHS; NHS; Outstndng French II 85; Hnr Rl 84-86; Acctg.

BASILE, DAWN; Brick HS; Brick Town, NJ; (Y); 235/400; Color Guard; Drill Tm; Mrchg Band; Var Sftbl; Var Trk; Twrlr; Early Educ.

BASILE, JEFFREY; Cumberland Regional HS; Bridgeton, NJ; (Y); Church Yth Grp; Cmnty Wkr; Hosp Aide; Band; Jazz Band; Mrchg Band; Orch; Ftbl; Wt Lftg; Elec Engrng.

BASILE, LAURA; Parsippany HS; Lk Hiawatha, NJ; (Y); 26/318; FBLA; GAA; Ski Clb; Varsity Clb; Var Capt Socr; Stat Sftbl; NHS; Dora B Stolfi Memrl Schlrshp 86; Polc Athl Leag Schlrshp 86; Unico Schlrshp 86; E Stroudsburg U; Erly Chldhd Ed.

BASILE, NINA ANN; Fort Lee HS; Fort Lee, NJ; (Y); Trs Art Clb; Service Clb; Speech Tm; Rep Stu Cncl; Capt Var Cheerleading; Capt Var Sftbl; High Hon Roll; Hon Roll; NHS; Pep Clb; Italian Hnr Soc Pres 85-86; Textile Design.

BASILEO, MARYANNE; Washington Township HS; Turnersville, NJ; (Y); 63/480; Dance Clb; Office Aide; Stu Cncl; Hon Roll; Bond From Hrtge Bk For Cnstnt High Avg In Bus Courses 86; Won ONS Typing Cntst 86; Hon Grad 86; Rutgers U; Bus Mgmt.

BASKERVILLE, APRIL; Lincoln HS; Jersey City, NJ; (Y); 28/264; Cmnty Wkr; FHA; VP JA; Spanish Clb; Rep Jr Cls; Rep Sr Cls; Stu Cncl; Prfct Atten Awd; Merit Roll 4 Semstrs 85-86; Merit Achvt Roll & Perfect Attd 84-85; William Patterson Coll; Pre Med.

BASKERVILLE, BRIAN; West Side HS; Newark, NJ; (Y); Hon Roll; Outstndng Frshmn 83-84; Art Awd From The St Art 84-85; Trade Schl; Comp Pgmmng.

BASKERVILLE, JUNE; Lincoln HS; Jersey City, NJ; (S); 8/10; Art Clb; JA; Key Clb; Teachers Aide; Yrbk Ed-Chief; Stu Cncl; Yth & Elderly Svc Awd 85; Frgn Lang Pstr Cntnst Awd 85; Nrsng.

BASKIN, DAVID SETH; Morris Knolls HS; P O Dover, NJ; (Y); 8/392; Boy Scts; Science Clb; Temple Yth Grp; Varsity Clb; Chorus; Elks Awd; High Hon Roll; NHS; Pres Schlr; Eagle Scout 85; Gifted & Tlntd Prog 84; Fencing Vrsty Capt 86; Rutgers U; Engrng.

BASKIND, JENNIFER; Highland Regional HS; Erial, NJ; (Y); AFS; Art Clb; French Clb; FTA; Trs VP Library Aide; Hon Roll; Ed.

BASSETT, RICHARD; Holy Cross HS; Florence, NJ; (Y); JV Tennis; Hon Roll; Hnr Roll 84-86; Trenton ST Coll; Chemst.

BASSI, ANN MARIE; Keansburg HS; Keansburg, NJ; (Y); German Clb; Key Clb; Yrbk Stf; Lit Mag; Sec Sr Cls; Stu Cncl; Tennis; Hon Roll; NHS; US Hstry II Achvt Awd 84-85; Grmn Achvt Awd 85-86; Acadmc Awd Stu Govt Day 85-86; Mgmt.

BASSMAN, LORI C; Cherry Hill HS East; Cherry Hill, NJ; (Y); 2/690; French Clb; Color Guard; Yrbk Ed-Chief; Rep Stu Cncl; High Hon Roll; Ntl Merit SF; Temple Yth Grp; Cornell Ingenuity Awd Math & Sci 85; Rutgers Schlr 85; Cum Laude Soc Ntl Hnr Soc 84-85; Engr.

BASTOS, CRISTINA; Riverside HS; Riverside, NJ; (Y); Key Clb; Stu Mnth Art 83-84; Acctng.

BATALHA, MARIA; Benedictine Acad; Elizabeth, NJ; (Y); French Clb; JCL; Latin Clb; Library Aide; NFL; Church Choir; Nwsp Rptr; Pres Frsh Cls; Sec Jr Cls; Hon Roll; French II, Engl, Latin II, Jrnlsm, French I & Latin I 84-85; French III, Chem, Hist 86; Interpreter.

BATE, LINDA; Fair Lawn HS; Fair Lawn, NJ; (Y); 1/320; Sec Church Yth Grp; Sec Band; Sec Frsh Cls; Rep Soph Cls; Rep Jr Cls; Stu Cncl; Var L Crs Cntry; Var L Swmmng; High Hon Roll; NHS.

BATEN, MARK D; Indian Hills HS; Oakland, NJ; (Y); 27/270; Math Tm; Science Clb; Yrbk Phtg; Yrbk Stf; Rep Soph Cls; Rep Jr Cls; Rep Sr Cls; Var Socr; Hon Roll; Jr NHS; Lehigh U; Engrg.

BATES, BARBARA; Central Jersey Christian Schl; Neptune, NJ; (Y); FBLA; Hosp Aide; Yrbk Ed-Chief; Stu Cncl; French Hon Soc; High Hon Roll; NHS; Sal; Val; Sec Church Yth Grp; Christian Charctr, Ldrshp & Testmny Princep Awd 85-86.

BATES, CYNTHIA; Williamstown HS; Franklinville, NJ; (Y); Intnl Clb; Nwsp Bus Mgr; Im Bowling; Var L Fld Hcky; Girl Scts; Hosp Aide; Chorus; Flag Corp; Im Trk; Perf Attndnc 84; Pres Phy Ftnss Awd 86.

BATES, DEBBIE; North Warren Reg HS; Columbia, NJ; (Y); Library Aide; Color Guard; Nwsp Rptr; Yrbk Stf; 2nd Vc Of Dmcrcy 85; 2 Tn Arts Dstvl 83 & 84; E Straudsburg U; Hstry Tchr.

BATES, MICHELLE; East Brunswick HS; East Brunswick, NJ; (Y); Drama Clb; Hosp Aide; Key Clb; Pep Clb; Ski Clb; SADD; Pres Temple Yth Grp; Chorus; School Musical; School Play.

BATES, PAM; Pascack Valley HS; Hillsdale, NJ; (Y); VP Soph Cls; VP Jr Cls; VP Sr Cls; Htl Mgmt.

BATES, PHILLIP; Frank H Morrell HS; Irvington, NJ; (Y); Aud/Vis; Drama Clb; School Play; Yrbk Stf; Lit Mag; Bsbl; Trk; Wrstlng; Hon Roll; Prfct Atten Awd; Rutgers U; Bus Adm.

BATES, SHELLEY; Hillside HS; Hillside, NJ; (Y); 14/198; Church Yth Grp; Cmnty Wkr; Drama Clb; Hosp Aide; Thesps; Color Guard; School Play; Nwsp Rptr; Yrbk Stf; Bus Admin.

BATES, VIRGINIA LOGAN; Brick Township Mem HS; Brick, NJ; (Y); 8/307; Church Yth Grp; Hosp Aide; Math Tm; Church Choir; High Hon Roll; NHS; St Schlr; Ciba-Geigy Svngs Bond 86; AFL-CIO Of NJ Chck 86; Wmns Clb Of Brenton Woods Chck 86; Cook Coll At Rutgers; Pre Med.

BATRA, MONTY S; Pennsville HS; Pennsville, NJ; (Y); 18/210; Am Leg Boys St; Nwsp Ed-Chief; Nwsp Sprt Ed; Lit Mag; Capt Tennis; Hon Roll; NHS; Prfct Atten Awd; Tdys Sunbeam Plyr Of The Yr In Bys Tnns 86; U S Japan Schlrshp Rcpnt At Pennsville 85; Georgetown U; Intl Bus.

BATTIPAGLIA, DANIELE; Paul VI HS; Voorhees, NJ; (Y); 180/519; JV Cheerleading; Nrsng-Anesthesia.

BATTLE, TREON; Vailsburg HS; Newark, NJ; (Y); Debate Tm; Crs Cntry; Trk; Stu Of Teen Hlth Club 85; Essex Cnty Coll; Wrd Prcssr.

BATTS, JOSEPH K; Science HS; Newark, NJ; (Y); Am Leg Boys St; Boy Scts; Band; NRLGY.

BATWINAS, KIMBERLY; Kittatinny Regional HS; Newton, NJ; (Y); 32/222; Science Clb; Teachers Aide; Stage Crew; Nwsp Phtg; Yrbk Ed-Chief; Yrbk Sprt Ed; JV Var Sftbl; High Hon Roll; Hon Roll; NHS; Rutgers U; Genetics.

BATZLE, DAVID; Toms River North HS; Toms River, NJ; (Y); Boy Scts; 4-H; Trk; Hon Roll; Stevens Inst Tech; Electrnc Eng.

BAUAH, ANA; Essex Catholic Girls HS; E Orange, NJ; (Y); Debate Tm; FHA; Pep Clb; Church Choir; Drill Tm; Pre Med.

BAUER, KRISTINA; Lakeland Regional HS; Ringwood, NJ; (Y); 41/303; Chorus; Nwsp Rptr; Hon Roll; NHS; Chmbr Sngrs Gld Mdl Mntrl Music Fstvl 85; Gld Mdl Chmbr Sngrs WA DC Music Fstvl 86; Douglass Coll; Wrtr.

BAUER, MARGARET E; Sayreville War Memorial HS; Sayreville, NJ; (Y); 38/374; Science Clb; Spanish Clb; Concert Band; Mrchg Band; School Musical; School Play; Nwsp Ed-Chief; Nwsp Rptr; Nwsp Stf; Grls Ctznshp Inst 84-85; Hofstra U; Mrktng.

BAUER, MICHAEL; Manazquan HS; Mansquan, NJ; (Y); Church Yth Grp; Math Clb; Band; Concert Band; Jazz Band; Mrchg Band; Capt Crs Cntry; Trk; Hon Roll; Livingston Coll; Lawyer.

BAUER, RENEE; Manchester Regional HS; North Haledon, NJ; (S); Intnl Clb; Nwsp Rptr; Nwsp Stf; Yrbk Ed-Chief; Yrbk Stf; High Hon Roll; Hon Roll; NHS; Ntl Merit Schol; Spanish NHS; Gifted & Talented 84-85; NY U; Mag Edtr.

BAUM, ERIK; Clearview Regional HS; Sewell, NJ; (Y); Art Clb; Boy Scts; Church Yth Grp; Bsktbl; Crs Cntry; Swmmng; Tennis; High Hon Roll; Hon Roll; Psych.

BAUMAN, DAVID ALAN; Parsippany HS; Parsippany, NJ; (Y); Cmnty Wkr; Temple Yth Grp; Rep Frsh Cls; Rep Soph Cls; Var Socr; High Hon Roll; NHS; Intnl Clb; Ski Clb; Varsity Clb; ATS 83-84; Amer Stu Israel Pgm 86; Peer Cnslr Grp 85-86; Cornell U; Pol Sci.

BAUMAN, NANCY; Sacred Heart HS; Vineland, NJ; (Y); Art Clb; SADD; School Play; Yrbk Stf; Rep Frsh Cls; Im Bsktbl; Var Mgr(s); Im Vllybl; Hon Roll; NHS; Bus Adm.

BAUMANN JR, DANIEL; Roselle Catholic HS; Roselle Pk, NJ; (Y); Lit Mag; JV Swmmng; Im Vllybl; French Hon Soc; High Hon Roll; Hon Roll; Ntl Merit Ltr; Computer Clb; Drama Clb; Speech Tm; Proficiency Fren 84-85; Comp Sci.

BAUTZ, JENNIFER; Bloomfield SR HS; Bloomfield, NJ; (Y); 80/427; Church Yth Grp; Key Clb; Spanish Clb; Rep Soph Cls; Rep Jr Cls; Stu Cncl; Var Crs Cntry; Gym; Var Trk; Anl Audtns Music Edctrs Assn NJ-PIANO 84-85; Trinity Coll Music, London Thry 83-85; Physcl Thrpy.

BAUZA, JODEE; Paramus Catholic Girls HS; Englewood, NJ; (Y); Hosp Aide; Library Aide; Office Aide; Pep Clb; Frsh Cls; Stu Cncl; Cheerleading; Diving; Wt Lftg; Hon Roll; Rutgers U; Psychlgy.

BAXT, REBECCA; Dwight-Englewood Schl; Allendale, NJ; (Y); Hosp Aide; Orch; Ed Yrbk Stf; Co-Capt Var Tennis; Hon Roll; Ntl Merit Ltr.

BAYARD, BRAD; Cinnaminson HS; Cinnaminson, NJ; (Y); Political Wkr; Ski Clb; Off Jr Cls; Off Sr Cls; Trs Stu Cncl; JV Var Bsbl; Var Bsktbl; Capt L Socr; Hon Roll; Socr MVP 85; Accntng.

BAYERS, JEANNE; Saint Mary HS; W Keansburg, NJ; (Y); Church Yth Grp; French Clb; JV Var Cheerleading; Var Crs Cntry; High Hon Roll; Hon Roll; NHS; Cmnctns.

BAYLES, TANYA; Bishop Eustace Preparatory Schl; Haddon Heights, NJ; (Y); Nwsp Stf; Var L Cheerleading; Var L Crs Cntry; Fld Hcky; Var L Trk; High Hon Roll; Hon Roll; NHS; U Of VA; Chem.

BAZALO, SHARON; Kittatinny Regional HS; Newton, NJ; (Y); German Clb; Math Tm; Stage Crew; Trk; High Hon Roll; Hon Roll; NHS; 3rd Pl Pen Ink Drawing 86.

BEABER, TRACY; Washington Township HS; Turnersville, NJ; (Y); Am Leg Aux Girls St; Church Yth Grp; Sec Trs Latin Clb; Trs Ski Clb; Stage Crew; Ed Yrbk Stf; Rep Stu Cncl; Stat Bsktbl; Fld Hcky; Hon Roll; Bus Adm.

BEADLE, LA RAE; Scotchplains Fanwood HS; Scotchplains, NJ; (Y); Library Aide; Office Aide; Radio Clb; Spanish Clb; Teachers Aide; Yrbk Stf; Stu Cncl; Var Mgr(s); Cit Awd; Hon Roll; Psych.

BEAGON, DEBORAH; Red Bank Catholic HS; Lincroft, NJ; (Y); #3 In Class; Church Yth Grp; Cmnty Wkr; Ski Clb; Sftbl; Queen Hrts Amer Hrt Assn 85; Imprvd Acdmc Prfrmnc Mary Crmdy Fndtn 86.

BEAHAN, KELLEY; Wall HS; Wall, NJ; (Y); JCL; Latin Clb; Ski Clb; Stat Var Bsbl; JV Socr; High Hon Roll; Hon Roll; NHS.

BEAHM, JOHN; Kearny HS; Kearny, NJ; (Y); Boys Clb Am; Var L Ftbl; Wt Lftg.

BEAL, CHRISTOPHER J; St Rose HS; Spring Lake Hts, NJ; (Y); Am Leg Boys St; Chess Clb; Church Yth Grp; Cmnty Wkr; Latin Clb; Math Clb; Spanish Clb; SADD; Im Bsktbl; Var L Bowling; Towson St U; Pltcl Sci.

BEAL, JIMMY; Eastern HS; Voorhees, NJ; (Y); Church Yth Grp; Math Tm; Rep Frsh Cls; Rep Soph Cls; JV Bsbl; High Hon Roll; NHS; PA ST; Bus Adm.

BEALE, LISA; St Rose HS; Brick, NJ; (Y); Hosp Aide; Mgr(s); Var Sftbl; Hon Roll; VP NHS; NEDT Awd; Ntl Latin Exam Magna Cum Laude; Relgs Educ Tchr; Comm.

BEAM, LAURA; Warren County Technical Schl; Stewartsville, NJ; (S); Sec Key Clb; Ski Clb; Sec VICA; Yrbk Phtg; Yrbk Stf; Rep Frsh Cls; Pres Soph Cls; Trs Jr Cls; Rep Stu Cncl; Bsbl; Top Data Cls NJ ST Vica Comptor 86; Comp Sci.

BEAN, ADRIAN; Atlantic Friends Schl; Port Republic, NJ; (S); 3/9; Aud/Vis; Cmnty Wkr; Drama Clb; Teachers Aide; Pres Thesps; School Play; Stage Crew; Stu Cncl; Var Capt Bsktbl; Var Capt Socr; Vrsty Lttrs-Soccer & Bsktbl 83-86; Cmmnty Svc Cmmttee Chrprsn 85 & 86; Mech Engrng.

BEAN, KARIN; Ramapo HS; Wyckoff, NJ; (Y); 35/329; Cmnty Wkr; French Clb; Hosp Aide; Band; Symp Band; Yrbk Stf; Lit Mag; High Hon Roll; Hon Roll; NHS; Merit Achvt Geo, Engl, Frnch, Spnsh.

BEARD, JACQUELINE; St James HS; Mullica Hill, NJ; (Y); 21/78; Art Clb; Yrbk Stf; Stu Cncl; Bsktbl; Cheerleading; Tennis; Fshn Inst Of Tech NY; Fshn Mrc.

BEARD IV, TIMOTHY D; Ridge HS; Basking Ridge, NJ; (Y); 30/217; Var JV Crs Cntry; JV Trk; NHS; Spanish NHS; US Naval Sea Cadet Corps Scholar 86; Chief Petty Offcr USNSCC 86; 1st Degree Brown Belt 86; GA Tech; Nuclr Engrng.

BEASLEY, KIP L; Hackensack HS; Hackensack, NJ; (Y); Am Leg Boys St; Aud/Vis; Church Yth Grp; Computer Clb; FBLA; Church Choir; Orch; Bsbl; Cert Of Prtcptn-Yth Mnth-Stu Prsnnl Drctor 86; Mrtl Arts-Tae-Kwon-Do; Comp Sci.

BEATO, LOUIS R; Nottingham HS; Trenton, NJ; (Y); Am Leg Boys St; Exploring; Key Clb; Math Clb; Pep Clb; Var Crs Cntry; Var Tennis; Var Trk; JV Wrstlng; Hon Roll; Rtgrs Schlr Awd 86; Acclrtd Sci Pgm Lwrncvll Prep Schl; Chem.

BEATTIE, PHIL; Paslack Hills HS; Montvale, NJ; (Y); SADD; Nwsp Rptr; Var Bsbl; JV Bsktbl; Var Capt Crs Cntry; Hon Roll; All Leag, Sub, Cnty Crss Cnty 85; Leag Chmps Str Hcky 85-86; Villanova U; Bus.

BEATTY, BRIAN; Overbrook SR HS; Lindenwold, NJ; (Y); Church Yth Grp; FBLA; Jazz Band; Rep Soph Cls; JV Ftbl; Var Tennis; Hon Roll; Glassboro ST Coll; Comm.

BEATTY, TAWHESHIA; Neptune SR HS; Neptune, NJ; (Y); #23 In Class; Boy Scts; GAA; Science Clb; Teachers Aide; Yrbk Stf; Off Soph Cls; Off Jr Cls; Sec Sr Cls; Stat Bsktbl; Mgr Pom Pon; Omega Psi Frat Hnr Schlrshp 83; Nept JR HS Otstndng Stu 84; Nept JR HS Sci Fai 84; Elec Engnrng.

BEAVERS, HEDY; Our Lady Of Good Counsel; Newark, NJ; (Y); 23/106; Dance Clb; Teachers Aide; Yrbk Stf; Gym; 4-H Awd; Ultrsnd Tech.

BECK, DAVID E; John Fitzgerald Kennedy HS; Willingboro, NJ; (Y); 60/292; Radio Clb; Spanish Clb; Nwsp Rptr; Nwsp Sprt Ed; Nwsp Stf; Var Mgr(s); Mgr Wrstlng; Hon Roll; Spllng Chmp 82-83; Navy; Mngmt Spclst.

BECK, JACKIE; Morris Catholic HS; Succasunna, NJ; (Y); Math Clb; Yrbk Ed-Chief; Yrbk Stf; JV Cheerleading; Stat L Socr; Var L Tennis; Schl Scholar 83-84.

BECK, LAWRENCE; Parsippany Hills HS; Boonton, NJ; (Y); 6/325; Computer Clb; Key Clb; Math Tm; Political Wkr; Science Clb; Stu Cncl; Hon Roll; NHS; 2nd Pl Poetry Cont 84; Physcs.

BECKER, BARRIE LYNN; Hillsborough HS; Somerville, NJ; (Y); 27/293; Library Aide; Pep Clb; Band; Mrchg Band; Pep Band; High Hon Roll; Hon Roll; NHS; Art Stu 86; Musc Awd 86; Merit Awd 86; U Of NC Greensboro; Bio.

BECKER, PAMELA; B R East HS; Martinsville, NJ; (Y); Ski Clb; Chorus; Gym; JV Trk; Hon Roll; Psych.

BECKER, TIFFANY; Cherokee HS; Marlton, NJ; (Y); 1/372; Nwsp Rptr; Yrbk Stf; Var L Socr; Var Trk; Elks Awd; Gov Hon Prg Awd; NHS; Sec Spanish NHS; Val; Prsdntl Acad Ftnss Awd 86; PA ST U.

BECKER, TRACEY; Shawnee HS; Medford, NJ; (Y); 22/535; Exploring; Variety Show; Var JV Cheerleading; Hon Roll; NHS; Bridgewater Pres Scholar 86; Medford Home & Schl Assn 86; Bridgewater Coll.

BECKERMAN, NATALIE; Rancocas Valley Regional HS; Mt Holly, NJ; (Y); 9/242; Nwsp Ed-Chief; Sec Stu Cncl; Var Bsktbl; Var Capt Fld Hcky; Hon Roll; NHS; VFW Awd; Boston U Schlr Athlete Schlrshp86-90; Ntl Schlr Athlete Awd 86; Boston U; Sports Med.

BECKETT, DOROTHEA; Holy Cross HS; Medford, NJ; (Y); 99/385; Church Yth Grp; Mrchg Band; Var Cheerleading; Capt Pom Pon; Im Vllybl; Hon Roll; NHS; Advncd Lfsvng Cert 84; Cabrini COLL.

BECKFORD, CARLENE; John F Kennedy HS; Paterson, NJ; (S); Church Yth Grp; Sec Debate Tm; French Clb; Chorus; Church Choir; Orch; Rptr Nwsp Rptr; Ed Nwsp Stf; Rep Soph Cls; Sec Stu Cncl; Upward Bound 85; Rutgers; Accntng.

BECKWITH, ANDY; Bridgewater-Raritan West HS; Bridgewater, NJ; (Y); Var Socr; Var Wrstlng; High Hon Roll; Hon Roll; NHS.

BEDE, MARY; Lenape Valley Regional HS; Andover, NJ; (Y); 4-H; Girl Scts; Spanish Clb; Nwsp Stf; Capt Var Bsktbl; Var Fld Hcky; Var Powder Puff Ftbl; Sftbl; Var Wrstlng; Comp.

BEDESTANI, AHMET; Hamilton HS; Mercerville, NJ; (Y); Am Leg Boys St; VP FBLA; Rptr Nwsp Rptr; Rep Frsh Cls; Rep Soph Cls; Capt Swmmng; Capt Tennis; High Hon Roll; Hon Roll; Key Clb; Johns Hopkins; Pre-Med.

BEDNAROVSKY, JESSICA; Lakeland Regional HS; Wanaque, NJ; (Y); 67/339; JV Bsktbl; JV Vllybl; Hon Roll; Bus Adm.

BEDNARZ, THERESA; Wallington HS; Wallington, NJ; (Y); Art Clb; Dance Clb; Varsity Clb; School Play; Yrbk Stf; Var L Cheerleading; Hon Roll; Camera Clb; Drama Clb; Ftbl Queen Attndnt; Phys Therapist.

BEDOYA, CAROLYN; Academy Of The Holy Angels; Ft Lee, NJ; (Y); 38/169; Church Yth Grp; Civic Clb; Hosp Aide; Socr; Var Vllybl; Cmnty Wkr; GAA; Library Aide; Rep Frsh Cls; Rep Soph Cls; Miss Northern NJ Natl Tnagr Pgnt 85:Miss NJ Coed Pgnt 85-86; Engrng.

BEDOYA, NORHA; Abraham Clark HS; Roselle, NJ; (Y); 7/280; Debate Tm; Pres French Clb; Sec Latin Clb; Trs Spanish Clb; Capt Vllybl; French Hon Soc; High Hon Roll; Hon Roll; NHS; Spanish NHS; 10% Cls Awd 86; Chorus Msc Awd 86; Mst Outstndng In Spnsh, Frnch & Latin Awds 86; Rutgers U; Lngstcs.

BEDSER, JEFFREY R; Lonape Valley Reg HS; Stanhope, NJ; (Y); Aud/Vis; Intnl Clb; Key Clb; Model UN; SADD; Band; Concert Band; Jazz Band; School Play; Lit Mag; Amer Msc Fndtn Awd 83-84; USNBA Bnd Awd 83-84; Rtgrs U; Cmnctns.

BEER, CAROLYN; Toms River HS North; Toms River, NJ; (Y); 25/412; Church Choir; Orch; Mgr(s); Swmmng; Tennis; Trk; High Hon Roll; NHS; Pres Awd Phys Fit 85-86; Acad Ltr 85-86; Elec Engrng.

BEER, REBECCA; Central Regional HS; Bayville, NJ; (Y); Church Yth Grp; Band; Concert Band; Jazz Band; Mrchg Band; School Musical; Var Crs Cntry; JV Fld Hcky; JV Trk; God Cntry Awd; Advrtsng.

BEERS, SUZANNE; Sayreville War Memorial HS; Parlin, NJ; (S); 44/450; School Musical; Nwsp Rptr; Rep Frsh Cls; Rep Soph Cls; Rep Jr Cls; Rep Sr Cls; Pres Stu Cncl; Var Cheerleading; Hon Roll; NHS; Giftd And Talntd 85-86; Douglass Clg; Mktg.

BEESE, KERRY; Immaculate Conception HS; Carlstadt, NJ; (Y); Church Yth Grp; Cmnty Wkr; Sec Drama Clb; Math Tm; Office Aide; Political Wkr; Mat Maids; Hon Roll; Ntl Awds Yrbk Math; Stockton ST Coll; Poly Sci.

BEETEL, KEVIN; Northern Burlington County Reg HS; Bordentown, NJ; (Y); VP Church Yth Grp; VP 4-H; Band; Jazz Band; Symp Band; Var L Bsbl; Var L Bsktbl; Var L Ftbl; Burlington Cnty Ftbl Schlrp 86; Widener U.

BEGLEY, ANDREA; Villa Victoria Acad; Washington Xing, PA; (S); Cmnty Wkr; NFL; Teachers Aide; Lit Mag; Pres Frsh Cls; Bsktbl; Hon Roll; NEDT Awd; Mock Trl Cnty Champ; Prsdntl Clsrm; Advertsng.

BEHM, HEATHER; Clearview Regional HS; Glassboro, NJ; (Y); 10/150; Am Leg Aux Girls St; Teachers Aide; Concert Band; Drm Mjr(t); Nwsp Ed-Chief; VP Frsh Cls; High Hon Roll; NHS; Church Yth Grp; Debate Tm; Hugh O Brian Awd Otstndng Sphmr.

BEHREN, SCOTT M; Hightstown HS; E Windsor, NJ; (Y); Aud/Vis; Drama Clb; Model UN; Ski Clb; Temple Yth Grp; Yrbk Bus Mgr; Yrbk Stf; Var Swmmng; Muhlenberg Coll; Poltcl Econ.

BEHRENS, JOHN; Howell HS; Howell, NJ; (Y); Nwsp Rptr; Var L Crs Cntry; Var L Trk; High Hon Roll; Hon Roll; NHS; MVP Vrsty Outdr Trk Tm 85-86; MVP Vrsty Crss Cntry Tm 84-85; Pilot.

BEHRMANN, WALTER E; Lacey Township HS; Forked River, NJ; (Y); 14/256; Boy Scts; Math Clb; Science Clb; Rep Stu Cncl; Var L Bsbl; Var L Bsktbl; JV Ftbl; High Hon Roll; Hon Roll; NHS; Alumni Schlrshp From UPSALA Coll 86-87; Member Of Hnrs Prgm At UPSALA Coll 86-87; UPSALA Coll; Sci.

BEHSON, NOELLE; Wall Twp HS; Manasquan, NJ; (S); 14/315; German Clb; Ski Clb; Stage Crew; Var L Gym; Var L Trk; Stat Wrstlng; Hon Roll; NHS.

BEIER, JILLENE; North Brunswick HS; N Brunswick, NJ; (Y); 8/265; French Clb; Var Cheerleading; Var Golf; Var Gym; NHS; Ntl Merit Ltr; Schlrshp Nrthestrn U 86; Schlrshp PA ST U 86; Grdn ST Dstngshd Schlr 86; PA ST.

BEISEL, KELLEY; Pinelands Regional HS; Tuckerton, NJ; (S); 4/145; Chorus; Trs Jr Cls; Trs Stu Cncl; Stat Bsbl; Cheerleading; Stat Ftbl; Stat Wrstlng; High Hon Roll; Hon Roll; Acctg.

BEITZ, EILEEN; Bishop Ahr/St Thomas HS; Perth Amboy, NJ; (Y); Church Yth Grp; Spanish Clb; Nwsp Stf; Yrbk Stf; Bsktbl; Sftbl; High Hon Roll; Hon Roll; Cert Of Achvt Piano 82-83; Syracuse U; Bio.

BELAFSKY, PETER; Cherry Hill East HS; Cherry Hill, NJ; (Y); Camera Clb; Varsity Clb; Nwsp Stf; Bsktbl; Hon Roll; Cum Laude; Vassar Coll.

BELCASTRO, DEBBIE; Lenape Valley Regional HS; Andover, NJ; (Y); 60/241; Radio Clb; Yrbk Phtg; Yrbk Stf; Hon Roll; Prfct Atten Awd; Rutgers; Law.

BELCEA, AURORA; Shore Regional HS; Eatontown, NJ; (Y); Yrbk Stf; Tennis; High Hon Roll; NHS; U Of CA Sn Diego; Comp Sci.

BELCHER, SUE; Hunterdon Central HS; White House Stati, NJ; (Y); Church Yth Grp; Cmnty Wkr; Band; Concert Band; Mrchg Band; Somerset County Coll; Vet.

BELCHER, TODD; Vernon HS; Vernon, NJ; (Y); 77/300; Letterman Clb; Varsity Clb; Var Ftbl; Wt Lftg; Hon Roll; Vrty Ltr-Jr Yr; USC; Bio.

BELEM, PAULA; Mother Seton Regional HS; Hopelawn, NJ; (Y); Math Tm; Science Clb; Lit Mag; Sec Jr Cls; VP Sr Cls; Var Tennis; Hon Roll; NHS; Church Yth Grp; Stage Crew; Ltry Edtr Yrbk 86-87; Stg Mgr Schl Ply 86-87; Perfct Attndnc 83-86; Med.

BELINFANTI, FRANK A; Salem HS; Woodstown, NJ; (Y); Am Leg Boys St; Computer Clb; Office Aide; Spanish Clb; Varsity Clb; VP Stu Cncl; Var Ftbl; Im Sftbl; Im Vllybl; Im Wt Lftg; Salem Exchnge Clb Schlr Athlt Of The Mnth 85; Cntctn Tech.

BELING, GARY; Neptune SR HS; Ocean Grove, NJ; (Y); 1/415; Debate Tm; Exploring; VP JA; Model UN; Yrbk Bus Mgr; Yrbk Ed-Chief; Ed Yrbk Rptr; Var Tennis; NHS; Val; Congrssnl Awd 86; Natl Hist Day St Wnr 86; Princeton; Intl Rltns.

BELL, CAPRICIA; East Orange HS; E Orange, NJ; (Y); Aud/Vis; Drama Clb; Pep Clb; School Play; Stage Crew; Pres Frsh Cls; Stu Wk Bio 83; SR Athltc Awd Prtcptn Pep Sqd 85-86; Stphn S Thms Cvc Assn Schlrshp 86; Johncon C Smith U; Cmnctns.

BELL, DEBRA; Mainland Regional HS; Northfield, NJ; (Y); 21/300; Intnl Clb; Hon Roll.

BELL, JENNIFER; Bloomfield SR HS; Bloomfield, NJ; (Y); 30/450; Trs Drama Clb; VP Temple Yth Grp; Chorus; Flag Corp; School Play; Yrbk Stf; VP Jr Cls; Rep Stu Cncl; NHS; Opt Clb Awd; Nmntd Gvrnrs Schl Prfrmng Arts 86; Prfmng Arts.

BELL, KAREN; Holy Cross HS; Burlington, NJ; (Y); 97/370; Church Choir; Yrbk Stf; Rep Frsh Cls; JV Bsktbl; Var Trk; Im Vllybl; Hon Roll; Bus.

BELL, MICHAEL; Salem HS; Salem, NJ; (Y); 3/140; Am Leg Boys St; Church Yth Grp; Computer Clb; Math Clb; Band; Concert Band; Var Golf; JP Sousa Awd; NHS; Outstndg Stu Awd 86; Mamngtn Mlls Inc Schlrshp 86; Minstm Schlrshp 86; Susqhma U; Acctg.

BELL, NANCY; River Dell HS; River Edge, NJ; (Y); 28/210; Am Leg Aux Girls St; Band; Chorus; Color Guard; Concert Band; Jazz Band; Mrchg Band; Orch; Yrbk Stf; Cit Awd; Albright Coll; Psych.

BELL, STEPHANIE; Washington Twp HS; Turnersville, NJ; (Y); Office Aide; VP Spanish Clb; Rep Jr Cls; Rep Stu Cncl; Stat Crs Cntry; Stat Golf; Hon Roll; NHS; Coin Clb 85-86.

BELL, TOM; Paul VI HS; Turnersville, NJ; (Y); Im Bsbl; Im Bsktbl; Im Ftbl; JV Trk; JV Wrstlng; Temple; Bio.

BELLENGER, CINDY; Hunterdon Central HS; Somerville, NJ; (Y); 300/500; Civic Clb; Var Capt Cheerleading; Var Capt Pom Pon; NJ Nets All ST Cheerldr 85; Parker Awd-Best All Arnd Cheerldr 85; NCA All Amer Cheerldr 85; FL ST U; Fashn Retail.

BELLIN, LISA; Matawan Regional HS; Aberdeen, NJ; (S); 6/273; Math Clb; Concert Band; Jazz Band; Mrchg Band; Nwsp Stf; Stu Cncl; NHS; Spanish NHS; Eng.

BELLIUCAMPI, LISA; Raritan HS; Hazlet, NJ; (Y); 36/324; French Clb; Chorus; Hon Roll; NHS; Technlgy.

BELLO, NATALIE; St Dominic Acad; Jersey City, NJ; (Y); 55/138; Computer Clb; French Clb; GAA; Ski Clb; Church Choir; Sr Cls; Stu Cncl; Cheerleading; Sftbl; Hon Roll; 1st Hnrs 86; AFL-CIO Scholar Awd 86; Jersey City ST Coll.

BELLOFATTO, MARIELAINE; Manchester Regional HS; Haledon, NJ; (Y); 25/156; Cmnty Wkr; GAA; Hosp Aide; Rep Frsh Cls; Sec Soph Cls; Sec Jr Cls; Sec Sr Cls; Rep Stu Cncl; Cheerleading; Hon Roll; Unico Schlrshp 86; Acadmc Achvt 83; Montclair ST Coll; Acctng.

BELLUCE, TARRIN; Gateway Regional HS; Wenonah, NJ; (Y); 52/209; Latin Clb; Varsity Clb; Yrbk Stf; Rep Soph Cls; Rep Jr Cls; Stu Cncl; JV Bsktbl; Var Swmmng; Var Tennis; Hon Roll; Rutgers; Arch.

BELNAVIS, SCOTT; New Brunswick HS; New Brunswick, NJ; (Y); Chess Clb; Computer Clb; Capt Bsbl; Var Bsktbl; Var Ftbl; Var Hon Roll; Bsbl Cty ST All Conf 85; MVP Bsbl 86; Bus Adm.

BELORO, GINA; Lower Cape May Regional HS; N Cape May, NJ; (Y); 39/216; Yrbk Stf.

BELUM, SUZAN; Cherry Hill East HS; Cherry Hill, NJ; (Y); Color Guard; Stat Bsktbl; Ftbl; Powder Puff Ftbl; JV Var Sftbl; Hon Roll; NEDT Awd; Office Aide; SR Hl Of Fame 85-86; Dstngshd Serv 82-86; Crmnsn Shld For Dstnghsd Serv 83-84; Lebanon Vly; Occptnl Thrpy.

BEMBRY, LISA; Pleasantville HS; Pleasantville, NJ; (S); 2/136; Band; Concert Band; Mrchg Band; Yrbk Stf; Sec Frsh Cls; Trs Stu Cncl; Stat Var Bsktbl; Var L Sftbl; Cit Awd; Pres NHS; Pres Schlrshp-Fairleigh Dickinson U 85-86; Chem Awd-Amer Chem Soc 85-86; Gdn ST Dstngshd Schlr 85-86; Fairleigh Dickinson U; Psych.

BENDELE, SHERRIE; Sparta HS; Sparta, NJ; (Y); Chorus; Concert Band; Mrchg Band; School Musical; Yrbk Stf; High Hon Roll; Hon Roll; NHS; Pres Acad Ftns Awd; U Of DE; BS.

BENDER, DANNY; Plainfield HS; Plainfield, NJ; (Y); Computer Clb; Band; Var Socr; Var Tennis; NHS; Model Congress 86; Crtv Wrtng.

BENDER, JONATHAN; Woodstown HS; Woodstown, NJ; (Y); Drama Clb; Key Clb; Band; Pres Stu Cncl; Var L Socr; Var L Tennis; NHS; Rotary Awd; Trs Church Yth Grp; German Clb; Hugh O Brien Yth Ldrshp Foundtn 84-85; Phy Thrpy.

BENDER, MICHAEL S; Marlboro HS; Marlboro, NJ; (Y); 30/500; Key Clb; Red Cross Aide; Science Clb; VP Ski Clb; Spanish Clb; SADD; Ed Nwsp Ed-Chief; Ed Yrbk Rptr; JV Socr; NHS; WA U St Louis; Bus.

BENDINGER, JEAN MARIE; Bishop Eustace Prep; Haddonfield, NJ; (Y); Drama Clb; French Clb; Pep Clb; School Play; Rep Frsh Cls; Rep Stu Cncl; Var Trk; French Hon Soc; Hon Roll; NHS.

BENEDICT, LIANE; Toms River High School South; Pine Bch, NJ; (Y); Am Leg Aux Girls St; Flag Corp; Mrchg Band; Yrbk Sprt Ed; Frsh Cls; Soph Cls; Jr Cls; Sr Cls; Powder Puff Ftbl; Socr; U Of VT.

BENESH, SANDRA; Washington Township HS; Sewell, NJ; (Y); French Clb; Pres Girl Scts; Hosp Aide; Band; Concert Band; Mrchg Band; Yrbk Stf; Stu Cncl; JV Var Mgr(s); JV Var Score Keeper; Nrsng.

BENEVENTO, GINA TERESE; Scotch Plains-Fanwood HS; Fanwood, NJ; (Y); 116/347; AFS; Drill Tm; JV Cheerleading; Itln Natl Hon Soc 83-86; Itln Clb Awd 86; Outstndng Itln Schlrp 86-87; Syracuse U; Dsgn.

BENNER, DIANA LYN; Bridgewater Raritan HS East; Martinsville, NJ; (Y); Am Leg Aux Girls St; PAVAS; SADD; Orch; School Musical; Sec Soph Cls; Sec Jr Cls; Sec Stu Cncl; Var Cheerleading; High Hon Roll; Lehigh U.

BENNETT, ANTHONY; Burlington City HS; Burlington, NJ; (Y); Boy Scts; Church Yth Grp; Cmnty Wkr; Dance Clb; Band; Var Ftbl; Var Trk; Aerontcs.

BENNETT, CHRISTINE; Manalapan HS; Englishtown, NJ; (Y); 91/400; Cmnty Wkr; Pres Girl Scts; Hosp Aide; Church Choir; Lib Orch; School Musical; Govs Schl Arts Fnlst 85-86; Rgnl Orchstra 84-86; NJ Al-ST Orchstra Altrnt 86.

BENNETT, DAVID; Middletown South HS; Leonard, NJ; (Y); Church Yth Grp; Cmnty Wkr; Band; Concert Band; Jazz Band; Variety Show; Bowling; Golf; Socr; Hon Roll; Cngrssl Awd Silver 86; Dntstry.

BENNETT, DENISE; E Orange HS; E Orange, NJ; (S); 8/400; French Clb; JA; Nwsp Rptr; Nwsp Stf; Lit Mag; Var Tennis; High Hon Roll; Hon Roll; Prfct Atten Awd; Montclair ST Coll; Bus Admin.

BENNETT, LORNE; Frank H Morrell HS; Irvington, NJ; (Y); Bsktbl; Ftbl; Hon Roll; Comp Prog.

BENNETT, LUCIA; Dover HS; Dover, NJ; (Y); 10/160; AFS; Y-Teens; Orch; School Musical; Symp Band; Swmmng; DAR Awd; Gov Hon Prg Awd; High Hon Roll; NHS; AFS Schlrshp & Foreign Exchng Stu Malaysia & Srv Awd 85-86; Art.

BENNETT, LYNNE; Ysparta HS; Sparta, NJ; (Y); 8/235; Math Tm; Nwsp Rptr; Sec Frsh Cls; Sec Soph Cls; Rep Stu Cncl; Stat Bsbl; Capt Cheerleading; JV Sftbl; Var Swmmng; High Hon Roll; Math.

BENOR, REBECCA; Mount Olive HS; Flanders, NJ; (Y); Drama Clb; French Clb; Math Clb; Temple Yth Grp; School Musical; Yrbk Stf; French Hon Soc; High Hon Roll; Hon Roll; NHS; Linguist.

BENOWITZ, DAVID B; Leonia HS; Leonia, NJ; (Y); 5/150; Am Leg Boys St; Quiz Bowl; Yrbk Sprt Ed; Pres Stu Cncl; JV Bsktbl; Var Tennis; High Hon Roll; NHS; Ntl Merit Ltr; Trs Jr Cls; Amer Lgn Boy ST NJ Delegt 86; Pres-Stu Senate 86; Poli Sci.

BENSEL, ERIC; Pitman HS; Pitman, NJ; (S); 19/142; Church Yth Grp; Teachers Aide; VP Crs Cntry; Hon Roll; NHS.

BENSHOFF, KIM; Spotswood HS; Spotswood, NJ; (S); 21/189; JV Bsktbl; JV Sftbl; High Hon Roll; Hon Roll; Rutgers; Acctg.

BENSON, ERIC; Raritan HS; Hazlet, NJ; (S); 20/314; Science Clb; Trs Temple Yth Grp; Var Tennis; High Hon Roll; Hon Roll; Pres NHS; Ntl Hon Soc Schlrshp; Lehigh U; Bus.

BENSON, GARY; North Warren Regional HS; Blairstown, NJ; (Y); 40/120; VP 4-H; Quiz Bowl; Ski Clb; JV Wrstlng; 4-H Awd; Embry-Riddle Aerntucl U; Plt.

BENSON, KIRSTEN; Woodbridge SR HS; Woodbridge, NJ; (Y); 3/369; French Clb; Trs SADD; Acpl Chr; Chorus; Mrchg Band; School Musical; Stage Crew; Swing Chorus; Hon Roll; NHS; Phrmcy.

BENSON, LYN; Middletown HS South; Middletown, NJ; (Y); Drama Clb; Pep Clb; Teachers Aide; Sec Trs Thesps; School Musical; School Play; Stage Crew; Variety Show; Var L Cheerleading; Im Vllybl; Chrldng Awds 84-86; Theater.

BENSON, ROBERT E; Palmyra HS; Beverly, NJ; (Y); Am Leg Boys St; Church Yth Grp; Library Aide; Church Choir; Bsktbl; Ftbl; Wt Lftg; Cit Awd; Lion Awd; Comp Sci.

BENTHAM, SHERRIE; Lakewood HS; Lakewood, NJ; (Y); Church Yth Grp; Drama Clb; 4-H; VICA; Band; Chorus; Church Choir; Drill Tm; Mrchg Band.

BENTHIN, GUY; North Hunterdon HS; Hampton, NJ; (Y); Key Clb; Latin Clb; Ski Clb; School Musical; School Play; Stage Crew; Hon Roll.

BENTON, JENNIFER; Manalapan HS; Englishtown, NJ; (Y); 97/389; Chorus; JV L Socr; Monmouth Hts Swmmng & Diving Tm Coaches Trphy & Mst Vlbl Stu 83-84; Zoology.

BENTZ, DAVE; Mc Corristin Catholic HS; Trenton, NJ; (Y); Am Leg Boys St; Boy Scts; Varsity Clb; JV Bsbl; Var JV Bsktbl; Var Ftbl; Wt Lftg; High Hon Roll; Hon Roll; Comp Engrng.

BENTZ, ELLEN; Notre Dame HS; Morris, PA; (Y); 33/400; Cmnty Wkr; Drama Clb; French Clb; Varsity Clb; Off Frsh Cls; Off Soph Cls; Crs Cntry; Trk; French Hon Soc; Hon Roll; Fshn Dsgn.

BENZ, MARJORIE; Middlesex HS; Middlesex, NJ; (S); 1/161; Trs Red Cross Aide; Band; Trs Pres Chorus; Concert Band; Capt Mrchg Band; High Hon Roll; NCTE Awd; VP NHS; St Schlr; Rutgers Schlr; NJ Schlrs Pgm; Hugh O Brian Ldrshp Amb; Physcl Thrpy.

BENZELL, KIMBERLY BETH; Red Bank Catholic HS; Holmdel, NJ; (Y); Ed Q&S; Mrchg Band; School Musical; School Play; Nwsp Rptr; Nwsp Stf; Pres Frsh Cls; Pres Soph Cls; Sec Sr Cls; Stu Cncl; Dorothy Ann Carroll Trzepacz Schlrshp Awd 86; Jrnlsm.

BENZENHAFER, PATTI; Central Jersey Christian Schl; Jackson, NJ; (S); 8/16; Drama Clb; Chorus; Mrchg Band; School Play; Yrbk Stf; Pres Jr Cls; Var Bsktbl; Var Socr; VP NHS; Philadelphia Coill Bible; Bible.

BENZLER, FREDRIC; Mahwah HS; Mahwah, NJ; (Y); High Hon Roll; Hon Roll; Bus Mgmt.

BERARD, CLEMENT M; Hopewell Valley Central HS; Pennington, NJ; (Y); 51/207; AFS; Am Leg Boys St; Pres Church Yth Grp; French Clb; Math Tm; Service Clb; Chorus; School Musical; School Play; Stage Crew.

BERARDI, PAULA; Kittatinny Regional HS; Newton, NJ; (Y); 36/228; Dance Clb; Chorus; School Musical; Nwsp Rptr; Ed Yrbk Stf; Hon Roll; NHS; Dance Mstrs Amer JR Ms Dance 83; Hgh Score Awd NY Danc Olympcs 85; Bst Ballet, Technq Awds-Rochster; SUNY Binghamton; Bus Mgmt.

BERBERICH, CHRISTINE; Southern Regional HS; Barnegat, NJ; (Y); 9/391; Dance Clb; Girl Scts; Sec Spanish Clb; Yrbk Stf; Var Capt Cheerleading; Pom Pon; Var Trk; High Hon Roll; Hon Roll; NHS; Acad Hrns Awd 86; Phrmcy.

BERENYI, NORBERT; Northern Valley Regional HS; Northvale, NJ; (Y); 25/281; Exploring; Science Clb; SADD; Capt Crs Cntry; Var Trk; Hon Roll; NHS; 1st Tm All Cnty Crs Cntry 85; 1st Tm All Lg Sprng Trk 86; Comp Sci.

BERESIN, CRAIG W; Cherry Hill HS East; Cherry Hill, NJ; (Y); Cmnty Wkr; Math Tm; Model UN; Pres Ski Clb; JV Socr; JV Tennis; High Hon Roll; Ntl Merit SF; Cum Laude Soc 85; Ety Awd Bible Hist 85; Garden ST Distngushd Schlr 85; U PA; Bus.

BERG, DEBRA; Hightstown HS; East Windsor, NJ; (Y); 48/449; Drama Clb; French Clb; Service Clb; SADD; Stage Crew; Yrbk Sprt Ed; High Hon Roll; Hon Roll; NHS; Pro Marksman Riflery 84; Bus.

BERG, KELLY; West Morris Central HS; Long Valley, NJ; (Y); Capt Cheerleading; Fld Hcky; High Hon Roll; Hon Roll; NHS; Cert Amer Inst Frgn Stdy 85; Byr.

BERGE, JENNIFER; Immaculate Conception HS; Garfield, NJ; (S); 8/96; Off Church Yth Grp; Q&S; SADD; Nwsp Ed-Chief; Sec Frsh Cls; VP Soph Cls; Hon Roll; NEDT Awd; Spanish NHS; Volntr Wrk For TV 85; March Of Dimes Ofcr 85; St John Fisher; Jrnlsm.

BERGE, LAURA; Dover HS; Dover, NJ; (Y); 18/183; Trs AFS; Church Yth Grp; Latin Clb; Color Guard; Yrbk Stf; JV Socr; Stat Swmmng; Stat Trk; Hon Roll; NHS; Phys Ther.

BERGELSON, ILENE; North Brunswick Township HS; North Brunswick, NJ; (Y); 22/267; Cmnty Wkr; Dance Clb; Drama Clb; Key Clb; Thesps; Acpl Chr; VP Chorus; School Musical; School Play; Variety Show; NJ Dist Schlr Hon Mntn 86; Pres Awd For Acdmc Ftnss 86; George Mason U; Perf Arts.

BERGEN, CYNTHIA; North Warren Regional HS; Blairstown, NJ; (Y); 7/130; Church Yth Grp; Spanish Clb; Chorus; Var Gym; Hon Roll; NHS; Elem Ed.

BERGEN, PAUL; Bridgewater-Raridan H S East; Martinsville, NJ; (Y); 70/260; Off Church Yth Grp; French Clb; Hosp Aide; Math Tm; Quiz Bowl; Scholastic Bowl; School Musical; JV Crs Cntry; JV Trk; Ntl Merit Ltr; Quiz Bowl Awd 86; Lehigh U.

BERGER JR, CONNEY W; Dover HS; Dover, NJ; (Y); 7/187; Am Leg Boys St; Computer Clb; Math Tm; Band; Pres Stu Cncl; Var Capt Ftbl; Wt Lftg; Var Capt Wrstlng; High Hon Roll; NHS; Frshmn Coaches Awd Wrstlng 83-84; Physcs Awd 85-86; 2nd Pl East Trnmnt Wrstlng 85-86; Rutgers U; Chem.

BERGER, NICOLETTE; James Caldwell HS; W Caldwell, NJ; (Y); 5/265; Church Yth Grp; French Clb; Key Clb; Concert Band; Mrchg Band; Orch; School Musical; Yrbk Stf; High Hon Roll; NHS; Awd For Musical Exclinc 86; Acdmc Exclinc From Womans Clb 86; Awd Being 1st Girl In Clss 86; Lehigh U; Bus.

BERGER, PETER G; Sayreville War Memorial HS; Parlin, NJ; (Y); Drama Clb; PAVAS; Scholastic Bowl; Chorus; School Musical; School Play; Nwsp Ed-Chief; Yrbk Stf; Ed Lit Mag; Golf; NJ ST Wnnr Olympcs Of Mnd 83 & 86, 5th In Wrld 83, 8th Pl 86; Bd Ed Awd Exclinc Engl 86; Carnegie-Mellon U; Engrng.

BERGERON, LIESL; Randolph HS; Randolph, NJ; (Y); Am Leg Aux Girls St; French Clb; Rep Political Wkr; Ski Clb; Chorus; School Musical; Swing Chorus; Sec Soph Cls; Powder Puff Ftbl; Hon Roll; Nrthestrn U; Phrmcy.

BERGHEIMER, WILLIAM WARREN; Frank H Morrell HS; Irvington, NJ; (Y); 1/500; Am Leg Boys St; German Clb; Key Clb; SADD; Lit Mag; Bowling; High Hon Roll; Masonic Awd; NHS; Val; Suburbn Cablvsn Merit Schlrshp 86; Essex Cnty Socty Prof Engrs Schlrshp 86; Rutgers Schlr 85; Cook Coll; Gentc Sci.

BERGMAN, ANDREW; Chatham Township HS; Chatham, NJ; (Y); 20/140; Am Leg Boys St; Pres Stu Cncl; Var Bsbl; Var Capt Ftbl; Hon Roll; NHS.

BERGMAN, AURELIA; North Bergen HS; North Bergen, NJ; (Y); 33/404; Key Clb; Q&S; Yrbk Bus Mgr; Yrbk Sprt Ed; VP Sr Cls; Trk; Montclair ST Coll; Hlth Profss.

BERGMAN, KRISTINE; Howell HS; Howell, NJ; (Y); 4-H; Girl Scts; Capt Quiz Bowl; SADD; Var Color Guard; Flag Corp; Cit Awd; 4-H Awd; Hon Roll; 4-H Cnty Pomona Grng Mrt Awd 84; Cnty Vlntr Actn Cntr Cmmnty Svc Awd 86; NJ ST 4-H Rbbt Prjct Wnr 86; Rutgers; Vet Med.

BERGMAN, PETER; Princeton HS; Princeton, NJ; (Y); Chess Clb; French Clb; Letterman Clb; Var Ftbl; Im Socr; Var Tennis; Im Wt Lftg; High Hon Roll; Jr NHS; Ntl Merit Ltr; Suffolk Cnty Math Awd; Invstmnt Bnkr.

BERGMANN, TIMOTHY; Belvidere HS; Belvidere, NJ; (S); 8/125; Library Aide; VICA; Chorus; Madrigals; Pres Frsh Cls; VP Soph Cls; Pres Jr Cls; Var Wrstlng; High Hon Roll; NHS; Hugh O Brien Awd 84; 1st Dist, Regl, 4th NJ Wrstlng Finals 85; JR Yuth Grp 83; USAF Acad; Aviation.

BERGMUELLER, KAREN; Queen Of Peace HS; North Arlington, NJ; (S); 22/231; Model UN; Service Clb; Cheerleading; High Hon Roll; Hon Roll; Jr NHS; NHS; Villanova; Bus.

BERISH II, WILLIAM S; Hamilton High North; Trenton, NJ; (Y); 97/307; Am Leg Boys St; Pep Clb; Chorus; School Play; Variety Show; VP Bsbl; VP Ftbl; Chiroprctr.

BERK, NATHAN A; Holy Spirit HS; Linwood, NJ; (Y); Elctrcl Engr.

BERK, NOAM; East Brunswick HS; East Brunswick, NJ; (Y); Debate Tm; Model UN; VP Temple Yth Grp; Band; Mrchg Band; Symp Band; VP Bowling; Im Socr; JV Wrstlng; Gov Hon Prg Awd; Pre-Law.

BERKES, CHERYL; Cherry Hill East HS; Cherry Hill, NJ; (Y); Aud/Vis; Cmnty Wkr; Computer Clb; DECA; Drama Clb; FBLA; Girl Scts; JA; Latin Clb; Chorus; Hnrb Mntn DECA Cnfrnc In Gnrl Merch 86; Bst Make Up Artst For Stg Crw 84; Bus Mngmnt.

BERKO, MICHELE-LEE; Mt St Dominic Acad; Kearny, NJ; (Y); 1/57; JCL; NFL; Quiz Bowl; Speech Tm; School Musical; Lit Mag; High Hon Roll; NHS; Val; NJ JR Miss 86; NJ Outstndng Young Amer 84; Garden ST Distngshd Schlr 86; Drew U; Pol Sci.

BERKOWITZ, PAUL; Union HS; Union, NJ; (Y); Aud/Vis; Computer Clb; Science Clb; Temple Yth Grp; Cit Awd; Hon Roll; Svc Awd 83; PHA Awd 82; Comp Sci.

BERLIN, STEVE; Toms River HS East; Toms River, NJ; (S); 108/585; Q&S; Temple Yth Grp; Nwsp Rptr; Ed Nwsp Stf; JV Ftbl; Cmmnctns.

BERLINER, ROBERTA; W Morris Mendham HS; Brookside, NJ; (Y); FTA; Hosp Aide; Intnl Clb; Chorus; Drill Tm; Yrbk Stf; Stu Cncl; Hon Roll; NHS; Olympics Of Mind NJ ST Champ 86; Spec Ed.

BERLOCO, ANDREA; Clifton HS; Clifton, NJ; (Y); 54/637; French Clb; Yrbk Stf; Var Socr; Hon Roll; Accntng.

BERMAN, JESSICA; Cherry Hill HS West; Cherry Hill, NJ; (Y); Sec JCL; VP Trs Temple Yth Grp; L Color Guard; Mrchg Band; Mgr Stage Crew; Off Sr Cls; High Hon Roll; NHS; Yrbk Stf; Latin Clb; BIS Achvmnt Awd Ldrshp 86; Vldctrn Mdrasha Cls 86; USY Mst Vlbl 84; Pre-Med.

BERMEO, MARCELLA; Middletown High School South; Middletown, NJ; (Y); Var JV Bsktbl; Powder Puff Ftbl; Capt JV Socr; Var Sftbl; Hon Roll; MVP Girsl Sccr 85; Chiro Med.

BERMUDEZ, BETSY; Memorial HS; West New York, NJ; (Y); Spanish Clb; Teachers Aide; Hon Roll; Math Tchr.

BERMUDEZ, MICHELLE; St Joseph Of The Palisades HS; North Bergen, NJ; (S); 3/126; Math Clb; Spanish Clb; Variety Show; VP Sr Cls; Var Cheerleading; Hon Roll; NHS; Spanish NHS; Acad All Amer 84; Brown & Brown Tutors Scholar 85; Arch.

BERNARDINO, JAN; Somerville HS; Somerville, NJ; (Y); 32/226; Sec Trs Art Clb; Church Yth Grp; Teachers Aide; Rep Frsh Cls; Rep Jr Cls; Var L Bowling; Mgr(s); JV Sftbl; JV Tennis; Rutgers U; Bus.

BERNARDO, LUISITO; Academic HS; Jersey City, NJ; (Y); Art Clb; Chorus; Scholastic Bowl; School Play; VP Stu Cncl; Hon Roll; Brd Of Ed Art Awd 85; Citation From Myr Of Jrsy Cty 86; NYU; Comp Tech.

BERNATAVICIUS, ALBERT; Holy Cross HS; Cinnaminson, NJ; (Y); Church Yth Grp; Debate Tm; Ski Clb; Spanish Clb; Lit Mag; Rep Soph Cls; Rep Jr Cls; JV Socr; JV Wrstlng; Hon Roll; Amer Lgn Axlry Boys ST 86; Bus.

BERNSTEIN, DREW; Middletown HS South; Leonard, NJ; (Y); Am Leg Boys St; Band; School Musical; Trs Soph Cls; Jr Cls; Stu Cncl; Hon Roll; Cnvntn II Comm Chrmn 86; Hgh Obrn Yth Smnr 85.

BERNSTEIN, HOWARD; Burl Co Vo-Tech; Willingboro, NJ; (Y); Boy Scts; Exploring; Temple Yth Grp; VICA; Bsbl; Crs Cntry; Socr; Wrstlng; Acad Of Culinar Art-Atlantc Ci.

BERNSTEIN, LAURA; East Brunswick HS; E Brunswick, NJ; (Y); Ski Clb; Varsity Clb; Bsbl; Bsktbl; Ftbl; Var Mgr(s); Var Socr; Sftbl; Trk; Wrstlng; Athl Trng.

BERNSTEIN, SCOTT; Hightstown HS; E Windsor, NJ; (Y); Computer Clb; Ski Clb; Spanish Clb; Variety Show; Lcrss; Swmmng; High Hon Roll; NHS; Pres Schlr; Advisor To Prncpl 85-86; Featured Cable TV Report About HS 85-86; ST U Of NY; Law.

BERONIO, GEORGE F; Bridgewater-Raritan High Schl East; Martinsville, NJ; (Y); 99/278; Boy Scts; Church Yth Grp; Jazz Band; School Musical; Var L Swmmng; NHS; Ntl Merit SF; Val; Mathletes; Quiz Bowl; Grdn ST Dstngshd Schlr 85; Gldn Nggt Schlrshp 86; Presdntl Acadmc Ftns Awd 86; Princeton U; Elec Engrng.

BEROWITZ, JOSEPH L; Highland Park HS; Highland Park, NJ; (Y); 11/130; Am Leg Boys St; Political Wkr; Radio Clb; Stage Crew; Yrbk Rptr; Trs Frsh Cls; VP Soph Cls; Pres Jr Cls; VP Stu Cncl; Ftbl; Foriegn Lang Awd Spanish; Tower Soc; Cornell U.

BERRIEN, PAIGE; Henry Hudson Regional Schl; Atlantic Hghlds, NJ; (Y); 1/90; French Clb; Library Aide; Band; Concert Band; School Musical; Im Badmtn; Var Fld Hcky; Bausch & Lomb Sci Awd; High Hon Roll; NHS; RI Schl Of Dsgn; Arch.

BERRUTI, JOHN; Brick Township HS; Brick, NJ; (Y); 47/350; Intnl Clb; Ski Clb; Speech Tm; Varsity Clb; Nwsp Stf; Coach Actv; Ftbl; Trk; Wt Lftg; Hon Roll; Hofstra U; Acctg.

BERRY, ERIC; Pascack Hills Regional HS; Montvale, NJ; (Y); Computer Clb; Debate Tm; FBLA; NFL; Spanish Clb; SADD; Nwsp Bus Mgr; Nwsp Rptr; Rep Frsh Cls; VP Stu Cncl; Natl Frnsc Leag Degre Merit 84; Outstndng Achvt-Tnns 85; Middlebury Coll; Invstmt Bankng.

BERRY, ETHEL; Buena Regional HS; Collings Lakes, NJ; (S); Pep Clb; Nwsp Phtg; Nwsp Rptr; Trs Jr Cls; Stat Wrstlng; Hon Roll; Jr NHS; Soc Of Disngshd H S Amer Stus 85; Jrnlsm.

BERRY, GWEN; Lakeland Regional HS; Ringwood, NJ; (Y); Girl Scts; JV Bsktbl; JV Capt Sftbl; High Hon Roll; Hon Roll; Spirit Awd-Jv Sftbl 86; Bio.

BERRY, STEPHANIE; Holy Cross HS; Mount Laurel, NJ; (Y); 24/365; Church Yth Grp; Exploring; Girl Scts; JA; Service Clb; Spanish Clb; Church Choir; Stage Crew; Yrbk Phtg; Yrbk Stf; JA Awd; Cookie Cert Merit Grl Scouts; Adam Scholar; United Way Campgn Awd; WDAS FM Essay Cont Hnrb Mt; Temple U; Banking.

BERRYANN, MELISSA S; Millville SR HS; Millville, NJ; (Y); 90/468; SADD; Nwsp Stf; Yrbk Stf; Lit Mag; Hon Roll; NHS; Prfct Atten Awd; Art Scholar 86; Hnr Soc Scholar Svc 86; Scholar Saturday Art Cls Moore Coll Art 86; Hussian Schl Art; Advrt Illust.

BERTEKAP, ROBERT L; Woodbridge HS; Fords, NJ; (Y); 1/357; Chess Clb; Math Clb; Quiz Bowl; Jazz Band; Hon Roll; NHS; Ntl Merit SF; Spanish NHS; Computer Clb; Church Choir; Renslr Mdl Awd Exclinc Math & Sci 85; NJ Distngshd Schlr Awd; Cook Coll; Major Bio.

BERTHIAUME, CHRISTINE T; Pitman HS; Pitman, NJ; (Y); Dance Clb; Girl Scts; JA; Key Clb; Nwsp Rptr; Nwsp Stf; Stu Cncl; Var Capt Cheerleading; Stat Socr; Hon Roll; JR Achvmnt NAJAC Schlrshp Awd IN U 86; JR Achvmnt Bst VP Of Mrktng 86; Western MD Coll; Pre Law.

BERTOLOTTI, PAUL; North Bergen HS; North Bergen, NJ; (Y); 24/460; Computer Clb; Key Clb; Band; Concert Band; Jazz Band; Mrchg Band; Orch; School Musical; Bowling; High Hon Roll; Russian Hnr Soc 86.

BERTONE, LISA; Rutherford HS; Rutherford, NJ; (Y); 46/185; Drama Clb; French Clb; Ski Clb; Varsity Clb; School Play; Nwsp Rptr; Nwsp Stf; Lit Mag; Tennis; Var Tennis; 1st Tm All Lg Var Ten 85-86; Fordham Coll.

BERTONI, MICHAEL; Mc Corristin HS; Trenton, NJ; (Y); Key Clb; Hon Roll; Rutgers; Engrng.

BERY, NANDITA; Parsippany HS; Parsippany, NJ; (Y); Debate Tm; NFL; Speech Tm; Socr; Hon Roll; NHS; Prfct Atten Awd; Impromptu Spch At U PA Awd 86; Spnsh Spch Awd 85; Atnd Drew U For Spnsh Spch; Engrng.

BESHADA, ROBYN; Pompton Lakes HS; Pompton Lks, NJ; (Y); 20/151; Am Leg Aux Girls St; Office Aide; OEA; Q&S; Spanish Clb; Band; Concert Band; Mrchg Band; Nwsp Rptr; Nwsp Stf; Natl Hist Comptn 85; Loc Merchnt Schlrshp 86; Advncd Typg Comptn 2nd 86; U Of Scranton; Ecnmcs.

BESLER, SCOTT; Notre Dame HS; Trenton, NJ; (Y); Varsity Clb; Ftbl; Wt Lftg; La Salle; Accntg.

BESSLER, SANDRA A; Northern Burlington Regional HS; Burlington, NJ; (Y); NFL; Stu Cncl; JV Socr; Acctg.

BEST, ERIC; Delsea Regional HS; Clayton, NJ; (Y); Art Clb; Church Yth Grp; Band; Mrchg Band; Pres Frsh Cls; Rep Stu Cncl; JV Var Bsktbl; JV Ftbl; Im Wt Lftg; Foulshooting 82; Wrstlng 80; Track 79; Rutgers; Accounting.

BEST, STACEY R; Frank H Morrell HS; Irvington, NJ; (Y); Camera Clb; FBLA; Model UN; Chorus; Church Choir; Yrbk Stf; Pom Pon; Hon Roll; NHS; Prfct Atten Awd; FL A & M; Comp Engr.

BET, GINA; Northern Highlands Regional HS; Upper Saddle Rvr, NJ; (Y); 11/249; AFS; Rep GAA; Hosp Aide; Rep Spanish Clb; Var Socr; Var Sftbl; NHS; Math Hnr Soc; Natl Latn Exm-Magn Cm Laud; Hstry Soc.

BETHEA, JOHN; E Orange HS; E Orange, NJ; (S); Boys Clb Am; Church Yth Grp; Debate Tm; Math Tm; Spanish Clb; Church Choir; JV Bsktbl; Im Ftbl; Cit Awd; High Hon Roll; Dir Awd Ldrshp Stevnes Inst Of Tech 85; Schl Rep Sntr Bill Bradleys Ldrshp Smmnr 86; Pres Clsrm Prog; Bus.

BETHEA, LORRAINE; Lincoln HS; Jersey Cty, NJ; (Y); Drama Clb; Spanish Clb; Bowling; Sftbl; Twrlr; Ntl Merit Ltr; Prfct Atten Awd; KS ST U; Psychlgy.

BETHEA, YOLANDA; Weequahic HS; Newark, NJ; (Y); Flag Corp; High Hon Roll; NHS; Ntl Merit Schol; Exploring; Band; Mrchg Band; Nwsp Phtg; Hon Roll; Lyons Inst; Nrs.

BETKOWSKI, FRANCIS; St Peters Prep; Bayonne, NJ; (Y); 20/201; Pep Clb; Yrbk Ed-Chief; Var Diving; Capt Var Gym; Elks Awd; Ntl Merit SF; St Schlr; Art Clb; Church Yth Grp; Cmnty Wkr; Natl Jesuit Secdry Ed Assoc Awd; Rutgers Deans Smmr Schlr; Schl Spirit Awd; Georgetown U; Corp Law.

BETTENCOURT, MARK; Keensburg HS; Keansburg, NJ; (Y); 3/140; Computer Clb; Pres Jr Cls; Hon Roll; NHS; TEEN Arts & Hghst Math Awds 86; Brookdale Cmnty; Comp Sci.

BETTS, NICOLE; Eastside HS; Paterson, NJ; (Y); Church Yth Grp; Cmnty Wkr; Teachers Aide; Church Choir; MA Sch Phrmcy; Phrmcst.

BETZ, JAMES P; Northern Valley Regional HS; Harrington Park, NJ; (Y); Am Leg Boys St; Aud/Vis; 4-H; Stage Crew; Nwsp Phtg; Trk; Hon Roll; Photo Journlsm.

BEUKEMA, MICHELLE; West Windsor-Plainsboro HS; Princeton Jct, NJ; (Y); 40/232; AFS; FBLA; Band; Cheerleading; Hon Roll; Presddntl Acadmc Ftns Awd 86; 2nd Rnr-Up Ms NJ Natl Tn-Agr Pgnt 85; Area Rep USA Tn Ms NJ 85; Rutgers Coll; Bus Mgmt.

BEUTELL, BRIAN; Seton Hall Prep Schl; Springfield, NJ; (Y); Sec French Clb; JV Bsbl; Hon Roll.

BEVACQUA, CHRISTIAN J; Fair Lawn HS; Fair Lawn, NJ; (Y); 1/333; Am Leg Boys St; Computer Clb; Letterman Clb; Science Clb; Varsity Clb; Yrbk Phtg; Crs Cntry; Swmmng; Trk; High Hon Roll.

BEVAN, SHARON MARIE; Palmyra HS; Riverton, NJ; (Y); 18/119; Pres Cmnty Wkr; Trs FNA; Intnl Clb; Latin Clb; Red Cross Aide; Service Clb; Spanish Clb; NHS; Rutgers ST U; Pre-Vet Med.

BEVANS, LORI; Kittatinny Regional HS; Layton, NJ; (Y); Church Yth Grp; 4-H; Spanish Clb; Chorus; Church Choir; Stage Crew; JV Bsktbl; Hon Roll; Aero.

BEVERIDGE, STACIE; Pennsville Memorial HS; Salem, NJ; (Y); 6/210; FBLA; FHA; Ski Clb; School Play; Trs Frsh Cls; Bsktbl; Var Cheerleading; Mgr(s); Hon Roll; NHS; Fashn Merch.

BEVERIDGE, TEDDY; Bishop George A H R HS; Plainfield, NJ; (Y); Church Yth Grp; Varsity Clb; JV Ftbl; Var Capt Tennis; Im Vllybl; Hon Roll; All-Conf Tnns 1st Dlbs.

BEVIS, BLAINE R; The Pennington Schl; Princeton Junctn, NJ; (Y); 12/75; Am Leg Boys St; German Clb; Latin Clb; Ski Clb; Nwsp Rptr; Sec Frsh Cls; Rep Soph Cls; Rep Stu Cncl; JV L Bsbl; Var L Ftbl; Yr Abrd-Grmny 84-85; Peer Ldrshp 85-86.

BEYER, BONNIE; Washington Twp HS; Turnersville, NJ; (Y); Art Clb; Church Yth Grp; Q&S; Band; Stage Crew; Variety Show; Yrbk Stf; Lit Mag; Glassboro ST Clg; Acctg.

BEYERS, JOANN; Matawan Regional HS; Cliffwood Bch, NJ; (Y); 71/350; Var L Bsktbl; Var L Sftbl.

BEYROUTEY, NATALIE; Passai County Vo-Tech; Paterson, NJ; (S); Church Yth Grp; Girl Scts; Cheerleading; Pom Pon; Score Keeper; Hon Roll; Acad All Amer 85-86; Comp Pgrmng.

BHARARA, PREETINDER; Ranney HS; Eatontown, NJ; (Y); 1/38; VP Drama Clb; NFL; Trs Spanish Clb; Pres Speech Tm; School Play; Nwsp Ed-Chief; Yrbk Stf; Lit Mag; High Hon Roll; Ntl Merit Schol; Harvard U; Govt.

BHATIA, AARTI; Northern Valley HS; Northvale, NJ; (Y); AFS; Cmnty Wkr; Intnl Clb; Library Aide; Stage Crew; Lit Mag; High Hon Roll; Hon Roll; Mbr Quality Cir Ldrs 85-86; Child Psych.

BHATIA, RITU; Highland Reg HS; Somerdale, NJ; (S); #10 In Class; Sec German Clb; Hosp Aide; Science Clb; Trs Service Clb; VP Soph Cls; VP Jr Cls; VP Stu Cncl; Var Capt Tennis; NHS; Rotry Yth Ldrshp Awd 84; Boston U; Med.

BHATT, DIVYANG; Rutherford HS; Rutherford, NJ; (Y); Camera Clb; Debate Tm; VP Key Clb; Pres NFL; Speech Tm; Hon Roll; Math.

BHATT, RACHNA; North Bergen HS; North Bergen, NJ; (Y); 21/470; Office Aide; Spanish Clb; Band; Rep Frsh Cls; Hon Roll; NHS; Ntl Merit Ltr; VP Spanish NHS; Guidnc Hlpr 86; Rutgers Coll; Phrmcy.

BIAGI, SUSAN; Our Lade Of Mercy Acad; Vineland, NJ; (Y); Teachers Aide; Trs Frsh Cls; VP Soph Cls; Capt JV Cheerleading; Swmmng; Hon Roll; Seton Hall 1; Statistician.

BIALECKI, JANINE; Washington Towhship HS; Sewell, NJ; (Y); Cmnty Wkr; Hosp Aide; Teachers Aide; Hon Roll; NHS; Type A Thon Cert Of Merit 86; Cert Lyl & Vlbl Srvc JFK Hosp 84; Glouster Cnty Coll; Nrsng.

BIANCHETTA, TONY; Freehold Twp HS; Freehold, NJ; (Y); 2/292; Exploring; Capt Math Tm; Trs Frsh Cls; Trs Soph Cls; Trs Jr Cls; Var L Tennis; Cit Awd; NHS; Ntl Merit Ltr; Pres Schlr; Garden ST Dist Schlr 85; Rutgers Schlr 85; Patrt Schlr Awd Sci 86; Bucknell U; Pre-Med.

BIANCHI, DAVID; South Brunswick HS; North Brunswick, NJ; (Y); 2/250; Am Leg Boys St; Aud/Vis; Computer Clb; French Clb; Math Tm; Political Wkr; Ski Clb; Varsity Clb; Var Bsbl; Im Mgr Stu Cncl; Hnr Grad Sltrn; Ambssdr To Hugh O Brien Yth Fndtn; Dlgt To Amer Lgn Boys ST; Ntl Hnr Soc; Frnch Hnr Soc; U Of Notre Dame; Lbrl Arts.

BIANCHI, TERRY; Woodstown HS; Woodstown, NJ; (Y); Church Yth Grp; Spanish Clb; Rep Frsh Cls; Rep Soph Cls; Rep Jr Cls; Var Bsktbl; Stat Crs Cntry; Var Sftbl; Elem Ed Tchr.

BIANCIELLA, ANTHONY; De Paul Diocesan HS; Wayne, NJ; (Y); 24/171; Aud/Vis; Boy Scts; Church Yth Grp; JCL; Church Choir; School Musical; Variety Show; Bsbl; Var Socr; Cit Awd; 110 Pct Awd 82-86; 4 Yr Thlgy Awd 82-86; Rutgers U; Elec Engrng.

BIASE, DENISE; West Essex Regional HS; Roseland, NJ; (Y); 41/356; Color Guard; Flag Corp; Sftbl; Hon Roll; NHS; Darlene Pekalski Mem Schlrshp 86; Montclair ST Coll; Bus Admin.

BIBERICA, JOYCE; Cliffside Park HS; Cliffside Pk, NJ; (Y); 20/236; French Clb; Latin Clb; Nwsp Stf; Rep Frsh Cls; Rep Soph Cls; Rep Jr Cls; Stu Cncl; Score Keeper; Stat Tennis; Trk; Pre Med.

BICKEL, CHRIS; Atlantic City HS; Margate, NJ; (Y); Boy Scts; Teachers Aide; Rep Stu Cncl; Swmmng; Hon Roll; NHS; Vrsty Ltr For Crew Rowng 84-85; Vrsty Ltr & Swtr For Crew & Particptd In Fall Crew 85-86; Sci.

BIDDISON, DAWN; Wardlaw-Hartridge HS; Edison, NJ; (Y); 5/53; AFS; Key Clb; Leo Clb; Spanish Clb; SADD; Var L Bsktbl; Mgr(s); Var L Sftbl; JV Trk; High Hon Roll; Bsktbl MIP 86.

BIDWELL, SANDRA; Voorhees HS; White House Stati, NJ; (Y); 59/274; Ski Clb; Varsity Clb; Orch; Yrbk Stf; Stu Cncl; Var Fld Hcky; Var Trk; French Hon Soc; NHS; Girls Ctznshp Inst Alt 86; Vet Med.

BIELAVITZ, THOMAS C; Parsippany HS; Parsippany, NJ; (Y); Band; Ftbl; Wrstlng; Psych.

BIEN, ELAINE; Bridgewater-Raritan HS West; Bridgewater, NJ; (Y); Am Leg Aux Girls St; Science Clb; Acpl Chr; Nwsp Stf; Pres Jr Cls; Pres Sr Cls; Var Socr; Elks Awd; NHS; Church Yth Grp; 2nd Pl MEC Piano Comptn 85; Somerset Cnty Soccr Tm Hnrb Mntn 85; Biochem.

BIENIASZEWSKI, IRENE; Mother Seton Regional HS; Union, NJ; (Y); Church Yth Grp; Debate Tm; Drama Clb; GAA; Girl Scts; Nwsp Rptr; Nwsp Stf; Rep Frsh Cls; Rep Soph Cls; Rep Jr Cls; Ntl Hnr Soc Outstndg Achvmnt Awd 82; Acad Of Bus Careers; Ct Rprtng.

BIERALS, DANIEL P; Randolph HS; Randolph, NJ; (Y); Am Leg Boys St; Hon Roll; Var L Bsbl; Var Capt Bsktbl; Var Capt Ftbl; All Co Ftbl, 2nd Tm All St Ftbl 85; All Co Bsbl 86.

BIGLEY, KRISTINE; Paul VI HS; Haddon Heights, NJ; (Y); 55/514; Drama Clb; Hosp Aide; Math Clb; Spanish Clb; Lit Mag; Hon Roll; Phys Therapy.

BIGLOW, MICHAEL; Watchung Hills Regional HS; Warren, NJ; (Y); 17/323; Church Yth Grp; Cmnty Wkr; Key Clb; Ski Clb; Var L Bsbl; Var L Ftbl; Hon Roll; Voice Dem Awd; Ftbl Awd-Mst Hustle, Desire & Determination 85.

BILAL, BRIAN; Plainfield HS; Plainfield, NJ; (Y); Exploring; Capt JV Bsbl; Stat Bsktbl; L Ftbl; L Wrstlng; Hon Roll; Prfct Atten Awd; MIT; Engrng.

BILICSKA, DIANE; Union HS; Union, NJ; (Y); 6/455; Church Yth Grp; Sec Ftbl; Trs VP Spanish Clb; Yrbk Stf; Var L Bsktbl; High Hon Roll; NHS; Pres Schlr; Dance Clb; Math Clb; Rutgers Schlr 85; Girls Ctznshp Inst 85; Seton Hall U; Bus.

BILINSKI, SUSAN; Glen Ridge HS; Glen Ridge, NJ; (Y); AFS; Intnl Clb; Model UN; Spanish Clb; Band; Concert Band; Mrchg Band; Mgr Bsktbl; Cheerleading; Mgr(s); Erly Chldhd Educ.

BILL, JENNIFER; Woodstown HS; Monroeville, NJ; (Y); Cmnty Wkr; Hosp Aide; Spanish Clb; Flag Corp; Nwsp Stf; Yrbk Stf; Hon Roll; Elem Ed.

BILLEK, CARL; Bayonne HS; Bayonne, NJ; (Y); Intnl Clb; Office Aide; Hon Roll; Acctng.

BILLIES, KEVIN A; St Joseph Regional HS; Oradell, NJ; (Y); Boy Scts; Church Yth Grp; Franklin Pierce Coll; Arts.

BILLMANN, JOHN; Washington Twp HS; Turnersville, NJ; (Y); Latin Clb; Variety Show; Var Ftbl; Var Trk; Wt Lftg; Var Wrstlng; Hon Roll; Chicago Schl Of Perf Arts; Dram.

BILLY, KEITH; Pt Pleasant HS; Pt Plesant, NJ; (Y); 12/249; JV Var Socr; Hon Roll; Pres Schlr; Rotary Awd; U Of Hartford; Engrng.

BILNEY, ELIZABETH; Pope John XXIII HS; Newton, NJ; (Y); 29/131; Chorus; Yrbk Phtg; Lit Mag; Capt Crs Cntry; Trk; High Hon Roll; Outstndng Achvt Hnr 84-86; Hnr For Exclnc Schlrshp Englsh II 85; Outstndng Achvt Ldrshp Sklls 84; Pre-Vet.

BILOTTI, ROBT; Verona HS; Verona, NJ; (Y); Boy Scts; Letterman Clb; Stage Crew; Yrbk Stf; Im Sftbl; Var L Tennis; Hon Roll.

BILUCK, BARBARA; Holy Cross HS; Riverside, NJ; (Y); Chorus; School Musical; School Play; Rep Stu Cncl; JV Var Bsktbl; Fld Hcky; JV Sftbl; Hon Roll; NHS; Unsung Hero Bsktbl 84-85&85-86; US Army Rsrve Natl Schlr/Athl Awd 85-86; Fairleigh Dickinson U; Mar Bio.

BINACO, DEBBIE; Middletown HS South; Middletown, NJ; (Y); Cmnty Wkr; Drama Clb; Exploring; Thesps; Chorus; School Musical; Stage Crew; Yrbk Stf; Bowling; Ntl Merit Ltr; Engl Teacher.

BINDAS, PAMELA; Manalapan HS; Manalapan, NJ; (Y); 49/431; Yrbk Stf; Rep Soph Cls; Pres Jr Cls; Pres Sr Cls; Mgr Tennis; NHS; JR Prm Ct 86.

BINDER, CHARLES; Cumberland Regional HS; Bridgeton, NJ; (Y); Science Clb; Ski Clb; Ftbl; Trk; Wrstlng; Prfct Atten Awd; Schltc Art Awd Cert Of Merit 84; Schltc Art Awd Natl Achvt 84; Certfd Life Svr 85; High Achvt Physcs 86; Engrg.

BINNS JR, RUSSELL WM; Brick Township HS; Mantoloking, NJ; (Y); 18/415; Debate Tm; Key Clb; JV Var Crs Cntry; JV Trk; JV Wrstlng; High Hon Roll; Elctrncs Engnrng.

BIONDI, GLENN; Middlesex HS; Middlesex, NJ; (Y); Art Clb; Church Yth Grp; Exploring; 4-H; French Clb; Key Clb; Ski Clb; 4-H Awd.

BIONDI, JANETTE M; Scotch Plains Fanwood HS; Scotch Plains, NJ; (Y); FBLA; SADD; Concert Band; Mrchg Band; VP Frsh Cls; Rep Soph Cls; Pres Stu Cncl; JV Var Cheerleading; Hmcmng Queen 86; Bus.

BIONDO, KIM; Pope John XXIII HS; Matamoras, PA; (Y); German Clb; Trs Frsh Cls; Rep Stu Cncl; JV Bsktbl; Var Fld Hcky; JV Sftbl; High Hon Roll; NHS; Philips Exeter Acad.

BIRAMONTES, JOYCE; Frank H Morrell HS; Irvington, NJ; (Y); Church Yth Grp; Chorus; Church Choir; High Hon Roll; Hon Roll; Cert Apprctn 83; Chld Psychtrst.

BIRD, GEOFFREY; Clifton HS; Clifton, NJ; (Y); 134/637; Am Leg Boys St; French Clb; Teachers Aide; Pres Temple Yth Grp; JV Trk; Jr NHS; Cnty Chmpns Mck Trl Team 86; Bstn Coll Smmr Session 86; Wllsly Coll Smmr Session 85; Amer Hstry.

BIRD, JONATHAN; Clifton HS; Clifton, NJ; (Y); 118/637; Am Leg Boys St; French Clb; Temple Yth Grp; Crs Cntry; Trk; Jr NHS; Spanish NHS; Mst Imprvd Var Levl 85.

BIRD, LORETTA; Sayreville Ware Memorial HS; Parlin, NJ; (Y); 45/380; Church Yth Grp; French Clb; Sec Science Clb; Band; Mrchg Band; Orch; Yrbk Stf; JP Sousa Awd; NHS; Band Awd 86; Bio/Eclgy Clb Awd 86; Band Schlrshp 86; Douglass Coll; Bio.

BIRDSONG, MARY E; Southern Regional HS; Beach Haven Gdn, NJ; (Y); 34/350; Drama Clb; School Musical; School Play; Swing Chorus; Variety Show; Yrbk Stf; Sr Cls; Stu Cncl; High Hon Roll; NHS; Vtd Mst Tlntd SR Yrbk Poll 86; Partcptd Vocl Solost & Orig Ply Wrttn By Me NJ ST Teen Arts Fest 86; Prof Music.

BIRDSONG, VICKI; Hillside HS; Hillside, NJ; (Y); Church Yth Grp; Civic Clb; Cmnty Wkr; Dance Clb; Debate Tm; DECA; Hosp Aide; Service Clb; Temple Yth Grp; Band; Accntng.

BIRGL, K JOHN; Holy Cross HS; Delran, NJ; (Y); Am Leg Boys St; Bsktbl; JV Var Ftbl; JV Trk; High Hon Roll; Hon Roll; Ntl Merit Ltr; Ski Clb; Spanish Clb; Stage Crew; Schlrshp Smmr Stdy Lebanon Vly Coll VEA Exch Stdnt Prog; Ed.

BIRKHIMER, MARCO ALLEN; Mc Corristin HS; Bordentown, NJ; (Y); 37/280; Camera Clb; Math Tm; Chorus; Concert Band; Swing Chorus; Rep Jr Cls; Var Capt Socr; JV Wrstlng; Hon Roll.

BIRMINGHAM, EILEEN; Manalapan HS; Englishtown, NJ; (Y); 71/435; Church Yth Grp; Cmnty Wkr; Ed.

BIRNIE, REBECCA; Toms River South HS; Beachwood, NJ; (Y); 41/313; Church Yth Grp; Band; Concert Band; Mrchg Band; Orch; School Musical; School Play; Symp Band; Var JV Bsktbl; JV Fld Hcky; Seaside Italian Am Clb Schrlshp 86; Alpha Delta Kappa Lamba Schlrshp 86; Music Schlrshp 86; Carson Newman Coll; Music.

BISCHOF, WALTER; West Essex Regional HS; Fairfield, NJ; (Y); 53/355; Church Yth Grp; Cmnty Wkr; German Clb; Varsity Clb; Var Bsktbl; Coach Actv; Var Socr; Hon Roll; Soccer, All Cnty, All ST, MVP W Essex 85; U Of Scranton; Bus Adm.

BISCHOFF, AMIEE; Mater Dei HS; Middletown, NJ; (Y); 51/151; Church Yth Grp; Cmnty Wkr; Pep Clb; Red Cross Aide; Variety Show; Trs Sr Cls; Stu Cncl; Var Crs Cntry; Var Trk; Hon Roll; Cert Of Awd Stu Govt & Volntry Actn Cntr Tchr 86; Bsktbl, X-Cntry & Sccr Vrsty Awds 83-85.

BISCHOFF, THOMAS; Parsippany HS; Parsippany, NJ; (Y); 69/318; German Clb; Letterman Clb; L Bsbl; JV Bsktbl; JV Ftbl; Hon Roll; NHS; NJIT; Mech Engr.

BISCONTE, EUGENE; St Augustine Prep; Vineland, NJ; (Y); 2/50; Nwsp Sprt Ed; Yrbk Stf; Lit Mag; Pres Jr Cls; Var L Bsbl; NHS; Prfct Atten Awd; Sal; Aud/Vis; Church Yth Grp; Garden ST Distngshd Schlr 85-86; Exchng Clb Stu Of Mnth 85-86; DE U; Bus Law.

BISHOP, MEREDITH LOUISE; West Milford Township HS; West Milford, NJ; (Y); 39/350; Church Yth Grp; Pres Computer Clb; Teachers Aide; Rep Stu Cncl; High Hon Roll; Hon Roll; Lion Awd; NHS; Pres Schlr; Grmn Hnr Socty 85-86; Montclair ST Coll; Geo Sci.

BISOGNO, JOSEPH; Toms River H S North; Toms River, NJ; (Y); Letterman Clb; SADD; Varsity Clb; Nwsp Rptr; Nwsp Sprt Ed; Yrbk Sprt Ed; Var Capt Bsbl; Var Capt Bsktbl; Wt Lftg; Pres Physcl Ftnss Awd 83-85; Jrnlsm.

BITTAY, CARRIE; Manchester Twp HS; Toms River, NJ; (Y); 21/198; Intnl Clb; Letterman Clb; Science Clb; Spanish Clb; SADD; Chorus; Yrbk Stf; Var L Crs Cntry; Var L Trk; Hon Roll; Papp Scholar 86; Sci Lg Awd 83-84; Ann May Schl Nrsng; Nrsng.

BITTEN, KIM; Fairlawn HS; Fair Lawn, NJ; (Y); 26/330; Church Yth Grp; Chorus; School Musical; High Hon Roll; NHS; Natl Hnr Soc 85-86; Chorus 82-86; Hgh Hnr Rll 86; Douglass Coll; Bus Psych.

BITTENBINDER, SUSAN; Point Pleasant Borough HS; Pt Pleasant, NJ; (Y); 51/224; Aud/Vis; Sec Pep Clb; Chorus; School Musical; School Play; Stage Crew; Variety Show; Yrbk Ed-Chief; Yrbk Phtg; Stu Cncl; Bst SR Tech Stg Mngr 86; Syracuse U; Cmmnctns.

BITTLE, MARCY; Hillsborough HS; Somerville, NJ; (Y); 68/285; Band; Concert Band; Jazz Band; Mrchg Band; Pep Band; School Musical; Powder Puff Ftbl; Hon Roll; Score Keeper; Sftbl; Band Vrsty Ltr 85-86; Julliard Schl Music NY; Symph.

BITZ, JENNIFER; Ramapo Regional HS; Wyckoff, NJ; (S); 4/316; AFS; French Clb; Nwsp Ed-Chief; Yrbk Stf; Rptr Lit Mag; Rep Stu Cncl; Cit Awd; High Hon Roll; NHS; Rep Girls Citznshp Inst 85; Rep Natl Yng Ldrs Conf 86; Bill Bradley Yth Ctznshp Awd 86; Cornell U; Eng.

BIVONA, LAUREN; Red Bank Catholic HS; Red Bank, NJ; (Y); Dance Clb; French Clb; Ski Clb; Varsity Clb; Var Crs Cntry; Var Trk; Hon Roll; NEDT Awd.

BIXBY, DIANE A; Ocean City HS; Woodbine, NJ; (Y); 17/300; Drama Clb; VP 4-H; Science Clb; Chorus; Drill Tm; School Musical; Pom Pon; 4-H Awd; Hon Roll; Mech Engrng.

BIZZOCO, MICHAEL N; Shore Regional HS; Oceanport, NJ; (Y); 61/225; Am Leg Boys St; Thesps; School Musical; School Play; Nwsp Rptr; Var L Bsbl; L Var Ftbl; Var L Trk; High Hon Roll; Drama Clb; US Army ROTC Scholar 86; Drexel U; Engrng.

BJORSTAD, SUE; Point Pleasant Beach HS; Pt Pleasant Bch, NJ; (Y); 6/94; Church Yth Grp; Ski Clb; Band; Jazz Band; Mrchg Band; Mgr(s); Powder Puff Ftbl; Socr; Ithaca College; Phys Thrpy.

BLACK, LEEANNA; Newton HS; Andover, NJ; (Y); 11/193; Math Tm; Spanish Clb; Yrbk Bus Mgr; Sr Cls; Stu Cncl; Bsktbl; Sftbl; NHS; High Hon Roll; Rotary Awd; Grls Ctznshp Inst Delg 85; Presdntl Clsrm 85; Sorptimist Intl Yth Ctznshp Awd 86; Clemson U; Pre-Law.

BLACK, REGINA; Franklin HS; Somerset, NJ; (Y); 9/300; Hon Roll; NHS; Italian Clb Treas; Pres Acad Fit Awd 86; Rutgers Coll; Acctng.

BLACKISTON, MICHAEL; Deptford HS; Mantua, NJ; (Y); Varsity Clb; Var Bsbl; Var Bsktbl; Capt Ftbl; Wt Lftg; Soph Yr Awd 84; 2nd Team All Cnfrnce Ftbl 85; Capt Team 86; Sprts Med.

BLACKMAN, DEBRA; Essex Catholic Girls HS; Newark, NJ; (Y); Art Clb; FHA; Hosp Aide; Nwsp Stf; Nrsng.

BLACKMAN, GERALD; Overbrook SR HS; Lindenwold, NJ; (Y); School Play; High Hon Roll; Hon Roll; NHS; Future Pblm Slvng Tm NJ ST Fnls 83-84; Arch.

BLACKMON, SARAH; Wall HS; Manasquan, NJ; (S); 17/289; JV Var Fld Hcky; JV Var Powder Puff Ftbl; Var Socr; High Hon Roll; Hon Roll; Jr NHS; NHS; Kiwanis Ntl Hnr Scty; Accntng.

BLACKSTONE, JENNIFER; The Kings Christian HS; Medford, NJ; (S); 4/33; Church Yth Grp; Red Cross Aide; Teachers Aide; Chorus; Nwsp Stf; Yrbk Stf; Sec Soph Cls; Sec Jr Cls; Sec Sr Cls; Capt Cheerleading; ACSI Dstngshd Stu 85-86.

BLACKWOOD, DAVID; Hunterdon Central HS; Whitehouse Sta, NJ; (Y); 24/539; Pres Church Yth Grp; VP FCA; Hon Roll; NCTE Awd; NHS; Im Capt Bsktbl; Var Capt Socr; VA Tech; Mech Engrng.

BLAESE, NICCOLE; Northern Burlington Co Reg HS; Columbus, NJ; (Y); 54/198; FFA; Ski Clb; Teachers Aide; Rep Jr Cls; Rep Sr Cls; Rep Stu Cncl; Bsktbl; Capt Fld Hcky; Capt Sftbl; Hon Roll; Scholar Miss Columbia Pagnt 86; Athltc Awd 85-86; Wvu.

BLAIR, TAMMY; Cinnaminson HS; Cinnaminson, NJ; (Y); 57/257; Church Yth Grp; VP JA; SADD; Off Stu Cncl; JV Lcrss; JV Var Tennis; Hon Roll; Pres Schlr; Bought Own Horse; Cook Coll; Anml Sci.

BLAIR, TERRENCE; Cumberland Regional HS; Bridgeton, NJ; (Y); Intnl Clb; JCL; Lit Mag; JV Tennis; Prfct Atten Awd; 2nd Omnium Mag 85-86; Crmnl Just.

BLAIR, VALERIE; Cumberland Regional HS; Bridgeton, NJ; (Y); Pres Drama Clb; 4-H; Chorus; Madrigals; High Hon Roll; Jr NHS; NHS; Cmnty Wkr; Office Aide; School Musical; Hgh Obrn Yth Fndtn Ambsdr 84; NJ All ST Chrs 84-86; Ntl 4-H Clb Cngrs Dlgt 86.

BLAJDA, MARY BETH; Morris Catholic HS; Parsippany, NJ; (Y); 16/155; Debate Tm; JCL; Pres Latin Clb; Math Clb; Natl Beta Clb; NFL; Scholastic Bowl; Service Clb; Ski Clb; Speech Tm; Fnlst Natl Forensic Lg 85; Schl Rep Christian Svc Awd 86; St Marys Notre Dame; Cmmnctns.

BLAKE, ASTOR; Kearny HS; Kearny, NJ; (Y); Computer Clb; High Hon Roll; Hon Roll; Acadmc Achvt 83-84; NWK Coll Of Arts&sci; Comp Sci.

BLAKE, ELIZABETH; Haddonfield Memorial HS; Haddonfield, NJ; (Y); Hosp Aide; Intnl Clb; Office Aide; Rep Frsh Cls; Rep Soph Cls; Rep Jr Cls; Rep Stu Cncl; Var Capt Cheerleading; JV Sftbl; Elem Educ.

BLAKE, JANINE; Mainland Regional HS; Linwood, NJ; (Y); AFS; Church Yth Grp; French Clb; Intnl Clb; Ski Clb; George Washington U; Fash Merch.

BLAKE, JENNIFER; Mahwah HS; Mahwah, NJ; (Y); 52/189; Yrbk Stf; Var Capt Bsktbl; Var Capt Socr; Var Trk; Hon Roll; Latin Clb; JV Sftbl; MVP Bsktbll 85-86; 1st Team All Lge Bsktbll 85-86; 1st Team All Suburban Bsktbll 85-86; Phys Therapy.

BLAKE, SCOTT J; Wallkill Valley Reg HS; Franklin, NJ; (Y); 2/170; Math Clb; Science Clb; Trs Stu Cncl; Capt Ftbl; Capt Trk; Pres NHS; Sal; Dghtrs Amer Rvltn Good Dtzn Awd 86; Mel Sobel Mcrscps Bio Awd 86; Cornell U; Med.

BLAKELY, DAWN; John F Kenndey HS; Paterson, NJ; (S); Church Yth Grp; Civic Clb; VP Chorus; Church Choir; Co-Capt Color Guard; Nwsp Rptr; Bnkng & Fnanc.

BLAKESLEE, EVELYN; John F Kennedy HS; Willingboro, NJ; (Y); Hosp Aide; Intnl Clb; Chorus; Yrbk Stf; Swmmng; High Hon Roll; Hon Roll; NHS; Wllngbro Rtry Schlrshp 86; Pres Acdmc Ftns Awd 86; Trenton ST Coll; Acctg.

BLAKOVICH, PATRICIA L; Bayonne HS; Bayonne, NJ; (Y); 35/365; Church Yth Grp; Sec Key Clb; Nwsp Rptr; Yrbk Stf; Lit Mag; Stu Cncl; Hon Roll; NHS; Pres Schlr; St Schlr; Rose Mem Frshmn Schlrshp 86; Drew U; Pol Sci.

BLANCHARD, LAUREN; Hunterdon Central HS; Flemington, NJ; (Y); 219/548; VP Church Yth Grp; Dance Clb; SADD; Capt Flag Corp; Mrchg Band; School Musical; Variety Show; Rep Frsh Cls; Rep Soph Cls; Rep Jr Cls; Child Psychlgy.

BLANCHE, GREGORY; East Side HS; Newark, NJ; (Y); Boys Clb Am; Boy Scts; Radio Clb; Band; Concert Band; Jazz Band; Capt Mrchg Band; Bsbl; Cit Awd; Hon Roll; Blck Achvrs Awd 86; Seton Hall U; Pre Med.

BLANEY, ANNEMARIE; Neptune SR HS; Neptune, NJ; (Y); 25/390; Am Leg Aux Girls St; Church Yth Grp; GAA; Girl Scts; ROTC; Chorus; VP Frsh Cls; Trs Soph Cls; Trs Jr Cls; VP Sr Cls; All Shore Field Hockey 85; Outstndng Vocal Musician 84; Physcl Thrpy.

BLANK, MARCI; Parsippany Hills HS; Boonton, NJ; (Y); 20/342; Am Leg Aux Girls St; Cmnty Wkr; VP Temple Yth Grp; Varsity Clb; Nwsp Rptr; Stu Cncl; Var Cheerleading; Var Gym; Hon Roll; NHS; Jfrsn Cup Top 25 Stu 86; SUNY Bnghmtn.

BLANKS, DONALD R; Rahway HS; Rahway, NJ; (Y); Am Leg Boys St; School Musical; Rep Frsh Cls; Var Ftbl; Gym; Cit Awd; Hon Roll; NHS; Prfct Atten Awd; Philospher.

BLARR, RICK; Middletown HS S HS; Middletown, NJ; (Y); Cmnty Wkr; Library Aide; JV Socr; Trk; Im Wt Lftg; Hon Roll; NHS; Comp.

BLASBERG, TINA; Pope Paul VI HS; Bellmawr, NJ; (Y); 74/474; Bowling; Hon Roll; 2nd Hnrs Frshmn & Soph; Accptd Rtgrs Coll & Glssboro Coll; Glassboro ST Coll; Jrnlsm.

BLASS, PAUL; Washington Township HS; Sewell, NJ; (Y); Church Yth Grp; German Clb; Yrbk Stf; Sec Stu Cncl; Hon Roll; Rotary Awd; Rotary Yth Ldrshp Awd 86; History.

BLATT, KYRABETH; Mahawak HS; Mahwah, NJ; (Y); 5/181; Lit Mag; Gym; French Hon Soc; NHS; Ntl Merit Ltr; HSO Outstndng Accmplshmnt & Prfrmnce Physcs 86; Gym Yr Awd Elite Hawthorne 85.

BLEACHER II, EDWARD; Notre Dame HS; Kingston, NJ; (Y); Political Wkr; Red Cross Aide; Ski Clb; JV Ftbl; Hon Roll; Rutgers U; Accntng.

BLECKMAN, DAVID; Cresskill HS; Cresskill, NJ; (Y); Office Aide; Ski Clb; Rep Frsh Cls; Rep Soph Cls; Rep Jr Cls; Rep Stu Cncl; Var Crs Cntry; JV Ftbl; Var Trk; Im Vllybl.

BLEJWAS, AMY; Bridgewater-Raritan East HS; Bridgewater, NJ; (Y); Church Yth Grp; Intnl Clb; Ski Clb; Concert Band; Mgr Jazz Band; Mrchg Band; Var Capt Cheerleading; Powder Puff Ftbl; Hon Roll.

BLEJWAS, MARK; Bridgewater Raritan East HS; Bridgewater, NJ; (Y); Church Yth Grp; Ski Clb; Concert Band; Jazz Band; Mrchg Band; Im Bowling; High Hon Roll; NHS; Pres Schlr; Acadmc Tm Merit Awd 85-86; Awd-Outstndng Achvt-Scl Stds 85-86; Lafayette Coll; Elec Engrng.

BLEKICKI, JOHN; H G Hoffman HS; South Amboy, NJ; (S); 5/54; Chess Clb; Quiz Bowl; Teachers Aide; Trs Jr Cls; Stu Cncl; Math Clb; JV Bsbl; Var Bowling; Var Crs Cntry; Hon Roll; Stetson U; CPA.

BLEMINGS, DANIEL; Vorhees HS; Califon, NJ; (Y); 80/274; Church Yth Grp; 4-H; Rep Jr Cls; Stu Cncl; Capt Vllybl; NHS; 1st Deg Brwn Blt Isshin Ryu Karate 86; Lrng Cmnty Awd 84; Outstndg Ceramics Stu 84-86.

BLICH, JACQUELINE; Morris Catholic HS; Mine Hill Dover, NJ; (Y); Church Yth Grp; Dance Clb; French Clb; Hosp Aide; Teachers Aide; Chorus; Church Choir; Capt Flag Corp; School Play; Variety Show; Educ.

BLIGH, MARY; Holy Spirit HS; Ocean City, NJ; (Y); 42/435; Church Yth Grp; Political Wkr; Service Clb; Trk; Hon Roll; Spnsh Merit Cert 84; Fnlst Rtry Yth Ldrshp Awd 85; Mt St Mrys Coll Schlrshp 86; Mt St Marys.

BLITZSTEIN, BRETT; Clearview Regional HS; Mantua, NJ; (Y); Camera Clb; Cmnty Wkr; Drama Clb; Chorus; School Musical; Stage Crew; Rep Stu Cncl; Var Tennis; NHS; Tlntd & Gftd Prog 83-86; Pre-Med.

BLOCH, COLLEEN; Scotch Plains-Fanwood HS; Scotch Pl, NJ; (Y); AFS; VP French Clb; Band; Concert Band; Mrchg Band; Lit Mag; French Hon Soc; Hon Roll; Frnch Cls Achvt Awd 84; Ltr Commendtn Engl Tchr 84, Engl Dept 85; Engl.

BLOCH, ROBERT I; Ridgefield Memorial HS; Ridgefield, NJ; (Y); 1/100; Am Leg Boys St; Boy Scts; Mrchg Band; Orch; VP Stu Cncl; Cit Awd; High Hon Roll; Eagle Scout 85; NJ Young Citizens Awd 86; Acad Decathlon 86; Cornell U; Arch.

BLOM, JAMIE; Middlesex HS; Middlesex, NJ; (Y); Church Yth Grp; French Clb; SADD; Chorus; Elks Awd; Gov Hon Prg Awd; Hon Roll; NHS; Girl Scts; Nwsp Stf; Witness HS Mock Trial Tm 85-86; Slctd HS Stu Of Month 85-86.

BLOODGOOD, DAVID; Manasquan HS; Spring Lake Hts, NJ; (Y); 28/227; Drama Clb; Key Clb; Latin Clb; Spanish Clb; Chorus; School Musical; School Play; Stage Crew; Yrbk Stf; Bsktbl; Hugh O Brien Yth Fndtn Awd Fnlst 84; Pres Clsrm Grad Cls 3 86; Polt Sci.

BLOODGOOD, DONNA; Wall HS; Wall, NJ; (S); 6/296; Drama Clb; Latin Clb; Mrchg Band; Stage Crew; Stu Cncl; Socr; Var Tennis; High Hon Roll; Kiwanis Awd; Pres NHS; Natl Engl Merit Awd 84-86; Natl Art Hnr Soc 85-86; Phila Coll/Txtl & Sci; Txtl Dsg.

BLOOM, DAVID; Parsippany HS; Parsippany, NJ; (Y); 1/320; Cmnty Wkr; Trs French Clb; Nwsp Stf; JV Bsktbl; Capt Tennis; Gov Hon Prg Awd; High Hon Roll; NHS; Rtgrs Schlr 86.

BLOOM, DEBORAH F; East Brunswick HS; E Brunswick, NJ; (Y); Drama Clb; Mathletes; Nwsp Ed-Chief; High Hon Roll; Lion Awd; Ntl Merit SF; Pres Schlr; Sec Computer Clb; Latin Clb; Library Aide; MENSA 83-86; Comptr Clubs Leag 85-86; Golnd Nuggt Schlrshp 86; Yale U; Comptr Sci.

BLOUNT JR, DENNIS LEE; Memorial HS; West New York, NJ; (Y); Church Yth Grp; Cmnty Wkr; Political Wkr; Rep Frsh Cls; Rep Soph Cls; Pres Jr Cls; Rep Stu Cncl; Hon Roll; Stu Cncl Homeroom Awd 86; Advnc 1st Aid & CPR Awd 86; A&T Coll; 6aw.

BLOUNT, TOI KIMBERLY; Montclair HS; Montclair, NJ; (Y); 134/438; Church Yth Grp; FBLA; Chrmn Pep Clb; VP Frsh Cls; Off Stu Cncl; Cheerleading; Mgr Sftbl; High Hon Roll; Hon Roll; Lion Awd; Bus Adm.

BLUE, GEOFFREY N; Rumson-Fair Haven Regional; Fair Haven, NJ; (Y); 13/243; Nwsp Stf; Var Stu Cncl; Bsktbl; Ftbl; Var Socr; High Hon Roll; Hon Roll; NHS; Engl Brwn Bk Awd 86; Geo Wshngtn U Mdl 86; NJ Gvrnrs Schl Pblc Issues 86.

BLUM, JASON; Neptune SR HS; Neptune, NJ; (Y); 9/455; Cmnty Wkr; VP Debate Tm; Letterman Clb; Library Aide; Model UN; Office Aide; ROTC; Varsity Clb; Nwsp Rptr; Ed Nwsp Stf; Brnz Cngrssnl Mdl 86; Distgshd Cadet Grd For ROTC 85; Boston U; Diplmtc Corp.

BLUM, KENNY; Colonia HS; Colonia, NJ; (Y); Key Clb; Ski Clb; Varsity Clb; Band; Rep Soph Cls; Rep Jr Cls; Var Ftbl; Var Tennis; Hon Roll; Prfct Atten Awd.

BLUM, LISA; Rancocas Valley Regional HS; Mount Holly, NJ; (Y); French Clb; Nwsp Ed-Chief; Nwsp Rptr; Ed Nwsp Stf; Yrbk Rptr; Yrbk Stf; Sec Stu Cncl; Var Cheerleading; JV Lcrss; Mat Maids; NYU; New Correspondent/France.

BLUMBERG, JEANNE; Bishop Eustace Preparatory Schl; Cherry Hill, NJ; (Y); 48/183; Hosp Aide; Pep Clb; Spanish Clb; Cheerleading; Hon Roll; Spanish NHS; Villanova U; Nrsng.

BLUMENFELD, KARYN; Manalapan HS; Manalapan, NJ; (Y); Sec Debate Tm; Chrmn Frsh Cls; Rep Soph Cls; Trs Jr Cls; Stu Cncl; Hugh O Brien Yth Ldrshp Fndtn Ambssdr 84; Bus Clb Pres 85; Prom Crt 86; Bus Admin.

BLUTH, JAMIE; Cherry Hill East HS; Cherry Hill, NJ; (Y); French Clb; Trk; High Hon Roll; Hon Roll; Ntl Merit Ltr; Rep Frsh Cls; Rep Soph Cls; Rep Jr Cls; Rep Sr Cls; Rep Stu Cncl; Tufts U.

BLYSAK, JENNIFER; West Morris Central HS; Long Valley, NJ; (Y); Church Yth Grp; French Clb; Science Clb; Jr Cls; Bsktbl; Stat Crs Cntry; Stat Sftbl; Stat Trk; Wrstlng; Texas A&M; Bus.

BOATWRIGHT, KEISHA; West Side HS; Newark, NJ; (Y); Girl Scts; JV Crs Cntry; JV Trk; Hon Roll; NJ ST Mss Teen Glxy Pgnt 85; USA Tn Mss Schlrshp Pgnt Cntstnt 86; Goal Crd; Rutgers Schl Engnrng; Elec Engn.

BOBERG, KENNETH; Jackson Memorial HS; Jackson, NJ; (Y); 21/406; Debate Tm; Ski Clb; Var L Ftbl; Var L Golf; JV Socr; Var Trk; JV Wrstlng; High Hon Roll; NHS; Ntl Merit Ltr; Mst Vlbl Wrstlr Awd 84; Law.

BOBINIS, MIKE A; Phillipsburg HS; Phillipsburg, NJ; (Y); 70/315; Am Leg Boys St; Pres Boy Scts; Pres Exploring; L Ftbl; Trk; L Wrstlng; Prfct Atten Awd; Mst Outstndng Frshmn Wrstlr 84; Grp 4 ST Chmp Wrstlng Tm 86; Dist Runnrup Wrstlng 86; Elec Engrng.

BOCCIA, JEFF; Northern Valley Rgnl HS Old Tappan; Old Tappan, NJ; (Y); AFS; Bsktbl.

BOCCO, PATRICK; St Peters Prep; Hoboken, NJ; (Y); 30/200; Church Yth Grp; Im Bsbl; Im Bsktbl; Im Ftbl; Im Vllybl; High Hon Roll; Hon Roll; Slvr Mdl Acad Exclinc 85; Rutgers; Med.

BOCHI, NICOLAS; Palisades Park HS; Palisades Pk, NJ; (Y); Tennis; MVP Plyr 86; Mech Engr.

BOCHIS, GEORGE; Toms River HS East; Toms River, NJ; (Y); Am Leg Boys St; Debate Tm; FBLA; Key Clb; Political Wkr; Quiz Bowl; Scholastic Bowl; SADD; Nwsp Phtg; Yrbk Phtg; WA Workshops Congressional Sem 85; Chrmn NJ ST Modle Congres 85 & 86; Drew U; Economics.

BOCKER, SCOTT JOSEPH; Clifton HS; Clifton, NJ; (Y); 172/546; Am Leg Boys St; Cmnty Wkr; French Clb; Band; Jazz Band; Mrchg Band; Nwsp Ed-Chief; VP Stu Cncl; Duquesne; Pre-Law.

BOCKHOLT, TRACY; Bernards HS; Dallas, TX; (Y); 8/181; Jazz Band; Madrigals; School Musical; VP Swing Chorus; Rep Stu Cncl; Capt Cheerleading; Co-Capt Pom Pon; High Hon Roll; NHS; Pres Schlr; 2 Super Rtngs & Gld Cup Natl Fed Festvls Piano Comptn 84; Ltrs Chrldng, Bnd, Chorus & Pompon Sqd 85; Vanderbilt U.

BODDEN, SANDY LEE; Burlington City HS; Burlington, NJ; (Y); 36/180; Am Leg Aux Girls St; Church Yth Grp; Hosp Aide; Band; Concert Band; Jazz Band; Mrchg Band; Sftbl; Hon Roll; Masonic Awd; Ftur Physcns Clb 84-85; Lock Haven U; Phys Thrpst.

BODINE, MICHELE; Delsea Regional HS; Franklinville, NJ; (Y); 4-H; Capt Bsktbl; Crs Cntry; Diving; Score Keeper; Sftbl; Swmmng; High Hon Roll; Hon Roll; NHS; Zoolgy.

BODNAR JR, ROBERT J; Roselle Catholic HS; Roselle Park, NJ; (Y); School Play; Var L Bsbl; JV Im Bsktbl; JV Var Socr; High Hon Roll; Hon Roll; Glassboro U; Comm.

BODNER, ERIC; East Brunswick HS; E Brunswick, NJ; (Y); 1/600; Computer Clb; Hosp Aide; Math Clb; Band; Bausch & Lomb Sci Awd; High Hon Roll; NHS; St Schlr; ST Sci Day Cmptn Chem & Bio 84-86; Gradtd With Hghst Hnrs 86; U Of PA; Elec Engrng.

BODON, RENATA; Metuchen HS; Metuchen, NJ; (Y); 11/158; Math Tm; Band; Pres Frsh Cls; Rep Soph Cls; Sec Jr Cls; VP Sr Cls; Capt Var Socr; Var Sftbl; NHS; Spanish NHS; NJ Distngshd Schlr; Olympcs Of Mind; Rutgers U; Math.

BOEHM, KELLY; Buena Regional HS; Milmay, NJ; (S); Church Yth Grp; Band; Concert Band; Jazz Band; Mrchg Band; Jr NHS; Bst 1st Yr Musicn 83; Music.

BOEHMER, DARCIE; Toms River HS South; Beachwood, NJ; (Y); 28/360; Church Yth Grp; FBLA; Math Tm; Tennis; Trk; High Hon Roll; Hon Roll; NHS; Ocean County Coll; Paralegal.

BOEHMLER, JOEL A; Moorestown HS; Delran, NJ; (Y); Pres Church Yth Grp; ROTC; Trs Service Clb; Ski Clb; Church Choir; Yrbk Rptr; Rep Soph Cls; Rep Jr Cls; Var Bowling; Hon Roll.

BOELHOWER, SUSAN; Nottingham HS; Mercerville, NJ; (Y); FBLA; Girl Scts; Chorus; Lit Mag; Stu Cncl; Mgr(s); Score Keeper; Awd Mgmt Field Hocky 83-84; Daisy Chain For Grads 85-86; Fshn Designer.

BOEPPLE, LEANNE J; Westwood HS; Westwood, NJ; (Y); 6/235; Cmnty Wkr; Sec Hst Drama Clb; Library Aide; Office Aide; Quiz Bowl; Spanish Clb; Thesps; Chorus; School Musical; School Play; Schltc Writng Awd 83; Intl Thespian Scty 84; NJ Govs Awd 84; NY U; Comm.

BOER, PHAEDRA; Toms River East; Toms River, NJ; (Y); Church Yth Grp; FBLA; Key Clb; Ski Clb; Spanish Clb; SADD; Var Bowling; Powder Puff Ftbl; Mrktng.

BOETTICHER, ROBERT P; Passaic Valley HS; Totowa, NJ; (Y); Am Leg Boys St; Pres Aud/Vis; German Clb; Ski Clb; Concert Band; Mrchg Band; Stu Cncl; JV Wrstlng; Hon Roll; NHS; Comp.

BOFF, JOEL; Nutley HS; Nutley, NJ; (Y); 18/339; Am Leg Boys St; Pres Camera Clb; Latin Clb; Yrbk Phtg; Rep Stu Cncl; JV Var Wrstlng; High Hon Roll; Hon Roll; NHS; Nutley Acad Booster Clb Awd 85; Rosa Diploma 86; Hgh Hnrs Hstry, Hnrs Mth & Engl 86; Dickinson Coll; Econ.

BOGARDUS, CHRISTINE; Washington Twp HS; Blackwood, NJ; (Y); Church Yth Grp; Debate Tm; Girl Scts; JCL; Latin Clb; Library Aide; Spanish Clb; Lit Mag; Stat Socr; Stat Trk; Rutgers; Law.

BOGDA, MICHELE; Notre Dame HS; Trenton, NJ; (Y); 9/370; Drama Clb; School Musical; School Play; Off Frsh Cls; Off Soph Cls; Off Jr Cls; Off Sr Cls; High Hon Roll; Hon Roll; Trs NHS; German Hnr Soc 84-85; Rutgers Coll; Educ.

BOHOSSIAN, OCXEN; Memorial HS; W New York, NJ; (Y); 22/500; Key Clb; Band; Concert Band; Jazz Band; Mrchg Band; High Hon Roll; Music Awd 86; Band Schlrshp Awd For Lesson At Metropolitan Opera House Lincoln Cntr 85-86; PA ST U; Architecture.

BOHRMAN, CARYN; Bishop George AHR HS; Iselin, NJ; (Y); 11/250; Church Yth Grp; Cmnty Wkr; Dance Clb; Drama Clb; German Clb; Science Clb; School Musical; School Play; Bsktbl; High Hon Roll; Richard Stockton Scholar 86; Stockton ST Coll; Pre-Med.

BOKER, CAROLYN; Gloucester City HS; Brooklawn, NJ; (Y); 26/180; Church Yth Grp; Library Aide; Pep Clb; Chorus; School Musical; Trs Jr Cls; Cheerleading; Fld Hcky; FBLA; School Play; Scrtrl Sci.

BOLAND, KATE; Morris Catholic HS; Montville, NJ; (Y); 3/147; Church Yth Grp; Pres French Clb; Sec FBLA; Key Clb; Math Clb; Natl Beta Clb; Stu Cncl; JV Sftbl; High Hon Roll; NHS; Bus Admin.

BOLAND, KATHLEEN; Immaculate Conception HS; West Orange, NJ; (Y); Art Clb; Yrbk Stf; Rep Soph Cls; Rep Jr Cls; Rep Stu Cncl; JV Capt Cheerleading; Var Score Keeper; JV Capt Sftbl; High Hon Roll; Hon Roll; Hghst Avg Engl JR Cls Awd 86.

BOLANOWSKI, RICHARD; Oratory Prep; Cranford, NJ; (S); 1/46; Math Clb; Ed Nwsp Stf; Trs Frsh Cls; Pres Jr Cls; Rep Stu Cncl; Im Bsktbl; High Hon Roll; NHS; NEDT Awd; Pre-Med.

BOLDEN, DARWIN; Secaucus HS; Secaucus, NJ; (Y); Am Leg Boys St; L Capt Ftbl; Hon Roll; Varsity Clb; Variety Show; Lit Mag; L Trk; Manhattan Borough Pres Acad Achvt Awd 83; Liberal Arts.

BOLDEZAR, MICHAEL; Hawthorne HS; Hawthorne, NJ; (Y); Ski Clb; Stage Crew; Variety Show; Rep Stu Cncl; Ftbl; Wt Lftg; Wrstlng; Hon Roll; Archit.

BOLEN, ROBIN; Red Bank Catholic HS; Highlands, NJ; (Y); 64/327; Capt Gym; JV Sftbl; Mt Saint Marys Coll.

BOLES, MICHELE; Camden Catholic HS; Camden, NJ; (Y); Debate Tm; French Clb; Science Clb; Law.

BOLIN, SCOTT; Matawan Regional HS; Matawan, NJ; (S); 30/315; French Clb; Math Tm; Ski Clb; Band; Var L Bsbl; Var Bsktbl; Var Ftbl; Hon Roll; Psych.

BOLLENBACHER, ELIZABETH; St Joseph Of The Palisades HS; Weehawken, NJ; (Y); 30/129; Spanish Clb; Capt Varsity Clb; Variety Show; Nwsp Rptr; Cheerleading; Capt Sftbl; High Hon Roll; Spanish NHS; Cert Of Achvt Amer Chem Soc 85; St Peters Coll; Drmtlgst.

BOLLER, BRIAN R; Cinnaminson HS; Cinnaminson, NJ; (Y); 81/259; Church Yth Grp; Computer Clb; Key Clb; Band; Church Choir; Concert Band; Jazz Band; JV Crs Cntry; Rutgers; Elect Engr.

BOLLINGER, ERIC; River Dell Regional HS; River Edge, NJ; (Y); 70/213; Church Yth Grp; Pep Clb; SADD; Varsity Clb; Var L Bsbl; Var L Bsktbl; Im Vllybl; 1st Tm All-Lge Bsktbl & Bsbl 86; 2nd Tm All Bergen Cnty Bsktbl 86; 3rd Tm All Bergen Cnty Bsbl 86.

BOLOGNESE, LORI; Mary Help Of Christians Acad; Paterson, NJ; (S); 13/88; Computer Clb; Drama Clb; School Play; Stage Crew; Gym; Mgr(s); JV Var Score Keeper; Vllybl; Hon Roll; Sci Awd 83-84; Eng II, World Hist II, Spnsh II 84-85; Lttrmn 84-85; Rutgers U; Bio.

BOLTON, SCOTT; Mount Olive HS; Flanders, NJ; (Y); 17/324; Drama Clb; SADD; Temple Yth Grp; Varsity Clb; Church Choir; School Musical; School Play; Variety Show; Nwsp Rptr; Lit Mag; 1st Pl Mrs Cnty Chmpns; MVP Sccr; Rep To Bus Ldrshp Cnfrnc Rtgrs U; Crmnl Jstc.

BOMBEKE, KIKA; Our Lady Of Mercy Acad; Millville, NJ; (Y); 13/45; French Clb; Trs Jr Cls; Hon Roll; Spanish Awd.

BONACORDA, BILL; Mightstown HS; East Windsor, NJ; (Y); 200/449; Concert Band; Hon Roll; Cook Coll; Bio Sci.

BONADIE, JACQUELINE A; East Orange HS; East Orange, NJ; (S); 7/410; Church Yth Grp; JA; Math Tm; Nwsp Stf; Yrbk Stf; Lit Mag; Tennis; High Hon Roll; Hon Roll; Sec NHS; Rutgers Schlr 85; Minority H S Achvt Awd 86; Comptr Sci.

BONADO, LORENZO; Shore Regional HS; W Long Branch, NJ; (Y); 23/225; Cmnty Wkr; Office Aide; Science Clb; Teachers Aide; Band; Concert Band; Mrchg Band; High Hon Roll; Hon Roll; NHS; Stevens Inst Of Tech; Engrg.

BONAFEDE, ANTHONY; Clifton HS; Clifton, NJ; (Y); 149/550; JA; Letterman Clb; Office Aide; Varsity Clb; Var Wrstlng; Hon Roll; Jr NHS; Rutgers Coll; Biol.

BONAGUARO, DAWN; Glen Rock JR SR HS; Glen Rock, NJ; (Y); 10/153; Cmnty Wkr; Hosp Aide; Latin Clb; Library Aide; Spanish Clb; Varsity Clb; Tennis; High Hon Roll; Jr NHS; NHS; Reggie Weir Awd 85; Vet Med.

BONANATO, EVELYN; Washington Township HS; Turnersville, NJ; (Y); 141/470; Miss Mahaney Schlrshp Awd 86; Camden Cnty Coll; Nrsng.

BONAVITA, WENDY; Woodbridge HS; Fords, NJ; (Y); 36/336; Capt Dance Clb; Sec Spanish Clb; Capt School Play; Yrbk Stf; Lit Mag; Rep Stu Cncl; Stat Score Keeper; Hon Roll; NHS; Acdmc Exc Awd 86; Rutgers Coll; Ind Psych.

BOND, CHERYL; Hunterdon Central HS; Flemington, NJ; (Y); Church Yth Grp; 4-H; Girl Scts; Ski Clb; Chorus; Stage Crew; Stu Cncl; JV Crs Cntry; Hon Roll.

BOND, SHARON; Hunterdon Central HS; Flemington, NJ; (Y); 3/548; Church Yth Grp; Hosp Aide; Spanish Clb; Orch; Nwsp Rptr; High Hon Roll; Hon Roll; NHS; Ntl Merit SF; Germn I Achvt Awd 85-86; Pre-Med.

BONE, CHRISTOPHER CLARK; Cherry Hill HS East; Norfolk, VA; (Y); Model UN; PAVAS; Band; Concert Band; Mrchg Band; Pep Band; Symp Band; Im Lcrss; Hon Roll; NC ST U; Navy Pilot.

BONELLI, LISA; Hamilton High West; Trenton, NJ; (Y); Trs Key Clb; Political Wkr; SADD; Concert Band; Mrchg Band; Rep Stu Cncl; Hon Roll; GALRE; Jrnlsm.

BONESSI, BARBARA; James Caldwell HS; Caldwell, NJ; (Y); 47/280; Cmnty Wkr; Debate Tm; Key Clb; Soroptimist; Varsity Clb; Nwsp Rptr; VP Soph Cls; VP Sr Cls; Stu Cncl; Tennis; Le High U; Physics.

BONFIGLI, RICHARD M; Washington Twp HS; Turnersville, NJ; (Y); Var Tennis; Hon Roll; Drexel; Elec Engrng.

BONGIONE, JOHN; Toms River South HS; Beachwood, NJ; (Y); Camera Clb; Chess Clb; Drama Clb; Spanish Clb; Chorus; High Hon Roll; Hon Roll; Hon Roll Certf 1st - 3rd Quart 86; Acad Lltd & Pin 86; Acad Brkfst 86; Accntng.

BONHARD, KIRK; Hudson Catholic HS; Jersey City, NJ; (Y); Boy Scts; Cmnty Wkr; Varsity Clb; Band; Church Choir; Var Bowling; JV Crs Cntry; JV Swmmng; Cit Awd; Boy Scouts; Brookdale.

BONK, ROBERT M; High Point Regional HS; Newton, NJ; (Y); 9/210; Boy Scts; Computer Clb; Wt Lftg; God Cntry Awd; Hon Roll; Pres Schlr; Frankford Twnshp PTA 86; Hrld Pellow & Assoc Engrs 86; Wilkes Grant 86; Wilkes U; Materials Engr.

BONKER, WILLIAM; Lenape Valley Regional HS; Sparta, NJ; (Y); 51/207; Drama Clb; Varsity Clb; Chorus; Madrigals; Stage Crew; Pres Frsh Cls; Rep Jr Cls; Pres Sr Cls; Tennis; Hon Roll; Cnty Coll Of Morris; Soc Sci.

BONMAN, PATRICIA LYNNE; Ocean City HS; Ocean City, NJ; (Y); Cmnty Wkr; Drama Clb; Pres Spanish Clb; Chorus; School Musical; Variety Show; Stu Cncl; Cheerleading; Powder Puff Ftbl; Hon Roll; ST Wnnr Acting Teens Art Festvl 86; Firemans Mutual Benev Assoc 86; Gardens Civic Assoc 86; Trenton ST Coll; Comm.

BONNELL, LISA; Highland HS; Laurel Springs, NJ; (S); #28 In Class; Swmmng; Advrtsng.

BONNER, CHRISTINA; Belvidere HS; Hope, NJ; (S); 2/140; Ski Clb; SADD; Varsity Clb; Nwsp Stf; JV Bsktbl; JV Fld Hcky; Stat Ftbl; Var Golf; Hon Roll; NHS; Spnsh I Awd 84; MIP Golf Awd 85.

BONNER, CHRISTY; Montgomery HS; Belle Mead, NJ; (Y); Church Yth Grp; Model UN; Radio Clb; Ski Clb; Spanish Clb; Band; Church Choir; Mrchg Band; School Musical; Stage Crew; Pre Law.

BONNER, JEFFREY B; Freehold HS; Freehold, NJ; (Y); 21/237; Am Leg Boys St; Pres Computer Clb; Exploring; Stage Crew; Var Tennis; High Hon Roll; Hon Roll; Shld-N-Key 86; Rtgrs U; Elctrcl Engrng.

BONNER, KRISTINE; Toms River HS East; Toms River, NJ; (Y); 27/635; Varsity Clb; Chorus; Var L Bsktbl; Im Powder Puff Ftbl; Var L Socr; Im Sftbl; Hon Roll; NHS; Acctng.

BONNER, MICHAEL; Roselle Catholic HS; Roselle, NJ; (S); 35/205; Boy Scts; Drama Clb; School Musical; Stage Crew; Lit Mag; Var Crs Cntry; Var Wrstlng; High Hon Roll; Hon Roll; Spansh Proficncy 85.

BONNET, DEBORAH C; Morris Knolls HS; Denville, NJ; (Y); 30/420; Am Leg Aux Girls St; Church Yth Grp; Cmnty Wkr; Dance Clb; French Clb; Intnl Clb; Yrbk Stf; High Hon Roll; NHS; Suma Awd For Acadmc Excllnc 84-86; HOBY Awd For Outstndg Ldrshp 85; Morris Knolls Rep At Morris Co; Biology.

BONZEK, ANNE; Hamilton HS West; Trenton, NJ; (Y); Letterman Clb; SADD; Varsity Clb; Concert Band; Mrchg Band; Off Jr Cls; Off Sr Cls; Var Swmmng; Var Tennis; Var JV Trk; 2nd Tm All Cnty Swmmng 84; Physical Therapy.

BOODY, PATRICIA; Paul VI HS; Magnolia, NJ; (Y); School Play; Glassbora ST Coll; Bus Admin.

BOOKHOLDT III, DEWEY P; Hamilton H S North; Trenton, NJ; (Y); 80/265; Am Leg Boys St; Key Clb; Jazz Band; Madrigals; School Musical; Yrbk Sprt Ed; Capt Ftbl; Wt Lftg; Pep Clb; Political Wkr; ROTC 3 Yr Schlrshp To U Dayton 86; Cmpsd Lyrics & Msc For Schl Alma Mater 84; U Dayton; Chrprctr.

BOORSTEIN, STEVEN; Cinnaminson HS; Cinnaminson, NJ; (Y); 49/254; Exploring; Acpl Chr; Chorus; Var Trk; Rutgers U; Phrmcy.

BOORUJY, SUSIE; Mt St Mary Acad; Watchung, NJ; (Y); Church Yth Grp; Debate Tm; Rep Stu Cncl; Var Fld Hcky; Hon Roll; Art Clb; Off Frsh Cls; Off Soph Cls; Var Fld Hcky; Prfct Atten Awd; Bus.

BOOS, DEBORAH; Midland Prk HS; Newfoundland, NJ; (Y); 23/137; Am Leg Aux Girls St; Debate Tm; Library Aide; Varsity Clb; Nwsp Ed-Chief; Yrbk Stf; Lit Mag; Tennis; Hon Roll; NHS; Vrsty Vllybl Wrstlng & Sftbl Statstcn 85-86; Co Hst Live On 35 M P Cbl Tv Wrkshp 85-86; Geo Wshngtn U; Englsh.

BOOS, KAREN; Scotch Plains-Fanwood HS; Fanwood, NJ; (S); German Clb; Rep Frsh Cls; Var Diving; High Hon Roll; Prfct Atten Awd; Westfld YMCA Coachs Awd-Dvng 83-85; Nmrs Dvng Awds 81-86; Physcl Thrpy.

BOOTH, CHRISTINE LYNN; Butler HS; Bloomingdale, NJ; (Y); 12/197; Am Leg Aux Girls St; Radio Clb; Thesps; School Musical; Nwsp Stf; Yrbk Stf; Lit Mag; Pres Sec Stu Cncl; NHS; Drama Clb; HS Stu Cncl Schlrshp 86; Charles K Payne Schlrshp 86; PBA Schlrshp 86; Douglass Coll; Bus.

BOOZ, BRETT; Cumberland Regional HS; Brideton, NJ; (S); 10/425; Pres Church Yth Grp; Sec Drama Clb; 4-H; Church Choir; Jazz Band; Mrchg Band; School Musical; Stage Crew; High Hon Roll; NHS; S Jersey Chorus 85; 4 H Young Man Yr 85; Cumberlnd Co Hnrs Band 84-85; Audio Engrng.

BOPF, LYNN; Cranford HS; Cranford, NJ; (Y); AFS; JCL; Latin Clb; Spanish Clb; Chorus; Nwsp Rptr; Yrbk Stf; Swmmng; Hon Roll; Cum Laude Phila Latn Exm 86; Maxima Cum Laude Natl Latn Exm 86.

BOPP, JAMES; Paramus HS; Paramus, NJ; (Y); 4-H; Ski Clb; JV Var Bsktbl; Ntl Merit Ltr; Ntl Scl Stds Olympd US Hstry Awd 86; Aerontcl Engrng.

BORAD, ANIRUDH; Hoboken HS; Hoboken, NJ; (Y); Spanish Clb; Band; Concert Band; Mrchg Band; Variety Show; Elks Awd; High Hon Roll; VP NHS; Dctr.

BORDAMONTE, MAE HOPE; Paul VI Regional HS; Passaic, NJ; (Y); Boys Clb Am; Cmnty Wkr; Hosp Aide; Chorus; Church Choir; School Play; Yrbk Stf; Capt Cheerleading; Tennis; Hon Roll; Med.

BORDEN, STEPHANIE; St Cecilia HS; Englewood, NJ; (Y); Church Yth Grp; Cmnty Wkr; Girl Scts; Hosp Aide; Pep Clb; Church Choir; Pep Band; Variety Show; Yrbk Bus Mgr; Yrbk Stf; Boston U; Corp Law.

BORDNER, TERESA; Wall HS; Manasquan, NJ; (S); 2/260; AFS; Am Leg Aux Girls St; Church Yth Grp; French Clb; Powder Puff Ftbl; High Hon Roll; Hon Roll; Kiwanis Awd; Garden ST Dstngshd Schlr 86-87; Quinnipiac Coll; Phys Thrpy.

BOREN, SCOTT; East Brunswick HS; Newtown, PA; (Y); Key Clb; Orch; Gov Hon Prg Awd; 3rd Pl-$7500 Schlrshp-Pratt Inst Natl Merit Schlrshp Tlnt Srch 86; WOR-TV Apprnce-E Brnswck Yth Cmn; Roger Williams Coll; Arch.

BORG, KRISTINA; Bishop George Ahr HS; Fords, NJ; (Y).

BORGES, NICOLE; Notre Dame HS; Trenton, NJ; (Y); Hosp Aide; Yrbk Stf; Var Bowling; JV Trk; Hon Roll; NHS; Excllnc Antmy & Physlgy 85-86; Outstndng Achvmnt Hist 83-84; Excllnc Spnsh I & II 84-85; Chem.

BORINO, MARK; St Peters Preparatory Schl; Bayonne, NJ; (Y); 69/206; Band; Snd Rcrdng Tech.

BORKOWSKI, JODI; Audubon HS; Mt Ephraim, NJ; (Y); Office Aide; Acpl Chr; Yrbk Ed-Chief; Yrbk Stf; Sec Jr Cls; JV Var Bsktbl; Stat Cheerleading; Powder Puff Ftbl; Stat Trk; Psych.

BORKOWSKI, THERESA; Burlington Township HS; Burlington Twnshp, NJ; (Y); 5/120; Am Leg Aux Girls St; Sec VP French Clb; Ski Clb; Sec VP Spanish Clb; Cit Awd; High Hon Roll; Hon Roll; NHS; Prfct Atten Awd; Pres Schlr; Wilma Boyd Career Schl; Trvl.

BORNSTAD, CHRISTEN M; Roselle Catholic HS; Elizabeth, NJ; (Y); 34/153; Math Tm; Rep Soph Cls; Bsbl; Var Bsktbl; JV Socr; JV Trk; High Hon Roll; Hon Roll; Hnbl Mntn In Poetry 85; Lebanon Vly Coll; Physcl Thrpy.

BORNSTEIN, DAVID M; Westwood HS; Washington Twp, NJ; (Y); 9/217; Concert Band; Mrchg Band; Ftbl; Capt Wrstlng; High Hon Roll; Hon Roll; Jr NHS; NHS; St Schlr; NJ ST Schlr Athl 86; Penn ST; Pre-Med.

BORNSTEIN, IRA; Columbia HS; Maplewood, NJ; (Y); Band; Concert Band; Mrchg Band; Orch; Symp Band; Nwsp Bus Mgr; Stu Cncl; Bentley Coll; Finance.

BORNSTEIN, JUDY; John P Stevens HS; Edison, NJ; (Y); 2/479; Debate Tm; Exploring; Pres Key Clb; Yrbk Stf; Mgr(s); Var L Tennis; High Hon Roll; Hon Roll; Kiwanis Awd; NHS; Congrssnl Awd 86; Outstndg Stu 86; Duke U; Psychol.

BOROFF, GREGORY; Marine Acad Of Science & Tech; Rumson, NJ; (S); 2/26; ROTC; Spanish Clb; Nwsp Ed-Chief; Yrbk Ed-Chief; High Hon Roll; Hon Roll; Pres NHS; Fshn Inst Of Tech; Csmtc Mktng.

BOROTA, NICK A; Florence Township Memorial HS; Roebling, NJ; (Y); Am Leg Boys St; Latin Clb; Mathletes; Math Clb; Math Tm; Science Clb; NEDT Awd; Im Bsktbl; Im Golf; Im Gym; Crt Of Prtcpntn NJ Sci Leag For Bio & Chem 84-86; Cert Awd Chem 85-86; Aerospace.

BOROWSKY, DAVID J; John P Stevens HS; Edison, NJ; (Y); 16/471; VP Chess Clb; Debate Tm; Pres Exploring; Key Clb; Model UN; Ski Clb; Stage Crew; Yrbk Stf; Im Ftbl; Hon Roll; Century III Ldrs Pgm Schl Rep 85; Garden ST Distngushd Schlr 85; Rutgers U Schlr 85; Mechncl.

BOROWSKY, JOSEPH; St John Vianney HS; Morganville, NJ; (S); 6/283; Computer Clb; Math Clb; Stage Crew; High Hon Roll; NHS; HOBY Fndtn Sem 85; Engrng.

BORR, RICHARD; Matawan Regional HS; Matawan, NJ; (S); 25/350; Church Yth Grp; Band; Jazz Band; Nwsp Stf; Jr Cls; Stu Cncl; VP Crs Cntry; Engrg.

BORSA, LILAS; Manchester Reg HS; N Haledon, NJ; (Y); French Clb; Intnl Clb; Nwsp Rptr; Yrbk Rptr; Yrbk Stf; Crs Cntry; Psychlgy.

BORSTELMANN, CARRIE; Kinnelon HS; Kinnelon, NJ; (Y); 26/190; Sec German Clb; Yrbk Stf; Rep Frsh Cls; Rep Soph Cls; Rep Jr Cls; Rep Sr Cls; Rep Stu Cncl; Trk; NHS; Rotary Awd; Hugh Obrien Yth Ldrshp Awd 85; German Natl Hnr Soc 86-87; Fash Merch.

BORSUK, GLENN E; Monroe Twp HS; Hightstown, NJ; (Y); 5/180; Am Leg Boys St; Aud/Vis; Boy Scts; Pres Church Yth Grp; Mathletes; Science Clb; Church Choir; Cit Awd; Elks Awd; High Hon Roll; Garden ST Dist Schlr Schlrshp; Stevens Alumni Schlrshp; Stevens Inst Tech; Comp Mgnt.

BORUCKI, CHRISTINE; Hunterdon Central HS; Flemington, NJ; (Y); 31/539; Am Leg Aux Girls St; Key Clb; Band; Yrbk Stf; Var L Cheerleading; Var L Pom Pon; Hon Roll; Kiwanis Awd; NHS; Spanish NHS; Villanova U; Intl Bus.

BORYS, ROBERT A; Christian Brothers Acad; Monmouth Beach, NJ; (S); 15/214; Boy Scts; Band; Mrchg Band; Crs Cntry; Trk; High Hon Roll; NHS; Eagle Scout; Bio.

BOSCH, JOE; Fairlawn HS; Fair Lawn, NJ; (Y); 9/325; Am Leg Boys St; Bsbl; High Hon Roll; Hon Roll; Rutgers; Bus.

BOSCIA, ANNE MARIE; Mother Seton Regional HS; Westfield, NJ; (Y); 9/103; Art Clb; Drama Clb; Math Tm; School Musical; School Play; Nwsp Stf; Lit Mag; Chrmn Soph Cls; Cheerleading; NHS.

BOSCIA, JENNIFER; Clifton HS; Clifton, NJ; (Y); 286/637; Dance Clb; Office Aide; Spanish Clb; Hon Roll; Spanish NHS; William Paterson Coll; Elem Ed.

BOSCO, MARTIN; Gloucester County Christian Sch; Newfield, NJ; (S); 3/16; Church Yth Grp; Drama Clb; Chorus; School Musical; Rep Jr Cls; Trs Stu Cncl; Hon Roll.

BOSCO, STEPHANIE; Vineland SR HS; Vineland, NJ; (Y); Church Yth Grp; German Clb; Red Cross Aide; Stage Crew; Yrbk Stf; Rep Frsh Cls; Rep Stu Cncl; JV Cheerleading; Hon Roll; Bus Mgmt.

BOSIES, LOREN; Oakcrest HS; Egg Harbor, NJ; (Y); 4/240; Sec Keywanettes; Color Guard; Drm Mjr(t); Mrchg Band; Yrbk Ed-Chief; Sec Jr Cls; JV Sftbl; Hon Roll; Jr NHS; Pres NHS; Girls Ctznshp Inst, Douglass Coll, New Brunswick NJ 86; Amer Mgmt Assn, Oper Enterprise 86; Htl Mgmt.

BOSLER, SCOTT; Gloucester Coutny Christian Schl; Mantua, NJ; (S); Church Yth Grp; Quiz Bowl; Chorus; Var Bsbl; Var Bsktbl; Hon Roll; NHS; Pennsecola Chrstn Coll; Phy Ed.

BOSLEY, MARK; Monsienor Donovon HS; Long Beach Twp, NJ; (Y); Boy Scts; Pres Church Yth Grp; Off Ski Clb; U Of IN.

BOSLEY, RACHAEL; Monsignor Donovan HS; Long Beach Twp, NJ; (Y); 32/230; Sec Church Yth Grp; Drama Clb; Thesps; Band; Mrchg Band; School Musical; School Play; Nwsp Ed-Chief; Nwsp Rptr; Nwsp Stf; Highst 2nd Yr Latin Stu & Typng Awd 84-85; Rnnr Up Voice Democrcy 85-86; U Indianapolis; Librl Arts.

BOSOTINA, KAETHE; Hopatcong HS; Hopatcong, NJ; (Y); 49/199; Drama Clb; FBLA; School Play; JV Crs Cntry; JV Trk; Hon Roll; Nrs.

BOSQUE, ADA; Out Lady Of Good Counsel HS; E Orange, NJ; (Y); 9/111; Dance Clb; Debate Tm; Drama Clb; Capt Pep Clb; Science Clb; School Musical; School Play; Yrbk Bus Mgr; Capt Cheerleading; Hon Roll; Hstry Awd & 1st Hnrs; Law.

BOSS, CHRISTINE; Secaucus HS; Secaucus, NJ; (Y); 30/170; Dance Clb; Varsity Clb; Chorus; Color Guard; Mrchg Band; School Play; Lit Mag; JV Var Cheerleading; Hon Roll; Rutgers Coll; Cmmnctns.

BOSTIC, EBONY L; Delran HS; Delran, NJ; (Y); 14/179; Am Leg Aux Girls St; FBLA; Model UN; SADD; Concert Band; Var Bowling; Var Tennis; Hon Roll; Pres NHS; Church Yth Grp; LEAD Prog Bus 85; Bus.

BOSTON, LAURA JESSICA; Arthur P Schalick HS; Elmer, NJ; (Y); 9/128; Concert Band; Mrchg Band; Hon Roll; NHS; Salem Cnty Brass Soc Awd 86; Band Mgr Awd 86; Top Ten Awd 86; Bus Admin.

BOSTON, STACEY M; Henry Snyder HS; Jersey City, NJ; (S); Am Leg Aux Girls St; Pres FBLA; Office Aide; Yrbk Stf; Pres Jr Cls; Pres Stu Cncl; Pom Pon; Hon Roll; NHS; NEDT Awd; NJ Schlr 86; Acad Awds 82-84; Engl Awd 82; Accnt.

BOSTON, VALERIE; Vailsburg HS; Newark, NJ; (Y); Church Yth Grp; Church Choir; Color Guard; Drill Tm; Hon Roll; Prfct Atten Awd; Comp.

BOSWELL, SCOTT D; St Josephs HS; Piscataway, NJ; (Y); 2/224; Boy Scts; Pres French Clb; Model UN; School Musical; School Play; Nwsp Rptr; Lit Mag; Elks Awd; High Hon Roll; NHS; Wash Crossing Schlrshp 86; Golden Nugget Schlrshp 86; Exch Club NJ Yth Yr 86; Appalachia Svc Proj 86; Georgetown U; Intl Rel.

BOSZAK, DAWN; Hamilton High West; Yardville, NJ; (Y); FBLA; GAA; JV Socr; Var Swmmng; Var Trk; Im Vllybl; Hon Roll; Kthrn Gibbs Ldrshp Awd Future Sectys Hon Mntn 86; Comp.

BOSZE, JOAN A; Carteret HS; Carteret, NJ; (Y); 2/182; Drama Clb; FBLA; German Clb; JA; JCL; Latin Clb; Science Clb; Ski Clb; Capt Color Guard; Mrchg Band; Fnlst Gov Schl NJ Drew U 85; Tourmnt Of Excel 84-86; Sci Sympsm 84; Clncl Chld Psychgst.

BOSZE, JUDEE; Carteret HS; Carteret, NJ; (Y); 20/198; Ski Clb; Spanish Clb; Band; Mrchg Band; Pres Soph Cls; VP Jr Cls; Sec Sr Cls; Var Bsktbl; JV Var Sftbl; NHS; Nrsng.

BOTKIN, BRIAN; Manalapan HS; Englishtown, NJ; (Y); Aud/Vis; Off Jr Cls; JV L Wrstlng; Elec Engrng.

BOTSCHKA, ROBERT; Don Bosco Prep; Franklin Lks, NJ; (Y); Pep Clb; JV Var Socr; Hon Roll; Bus Adm.

BOTT, CHERRYL; Rutherford HS; Rutherford, NJ; (S); Church Yth Grp; Pep Clb; Varsity Clb; Rep Jr Cls; Var Bsktbl; JV Crs Cntry; Var Sftbl; High Hon Roll; Boston Coll.

BOTTINI, DOMENICK; Pascack Hills HS; Woodcliff Lake, NJ; (Y); Ski Clb; Im Bsbl; Im Trk; Im Wrstlng; Acctng.

BOTTITTO, LISA; Essey Catholic Girls HS; Union, NJ; (Y); 2/72; FHA; Science Clb; School Play; Yrbk Stf; Pres Jr Cls; Trs Stu Cncl; Bowling; High Hon Roll; Hon Roll; NHS; Kean Coll Of NJ; Acctg.

BOTTOMLEY, AMANDA; Lakewood Prep; Island Heights, NJ; (S); Sec Jr Cls; Var Cheerleading; Var Socr.

BOUDOUGHIAN, ALICE; Pascack Hills HS; Woodcliff Lk, NJ; (Y); Sec Church Yth Grp; Teachers Aide; Chorus; Church Choir; JV Var Bsktbl; Var Crs Cntry; Sftbl; Hon Roll; MVP Bsktbl Tm 86; MVP Arch Bishps Trnmnt 86; Montclair ST; Real Est.

BOULAZERIS, JOANNA; Atlantic City HS; Ventnor City, NJ; (Y); Church Yth Grp; Cmnty Wkr; English Clb; Office Aide; Spanish Clb; Variety Show; Bsktbl; Fld Hcky; Score Keeper; Sftbl; Glassboro ST Coll; Tchr.

BOULDIN, SHERI; Long Branch SR HS; Long Branch, NJ; (S); 33/213; Church Yth Grp; Cmnty Wkr; Dance Clb; French Clb; GAA; Hosp Aide; Q&S; Band; Color Guard; Concert Band; All Cnty Bsktbl 83; All ST Bsktbl 84; All Amer Bsktbl 85-86; UCLA; Pre-Med.

BOULWARE, SHEILA RENEE; Stuart Country Day HS; Piscataway, NJ; (Y); French Clb; Hosp Aide; Science Clb; VP Spanish Clb; Rep Frsh Cls; Rep Soph Cls; Rep Jr Cls; Rep Sr Cls; Capt Bsktbl; Swmmng; Goucher Coll; Med.

BOURNAZIAN, DAVID; Westfield SR HS; Westfield, NJ; (Y); Computer Clb; Sec Latin Clb; Spanish Clb; Im Ftbl; Hon Roll; Bus Admin.

BOURNE, AMY; Woodstown HS; Salem, NJ; (Y); 10/225; Church Yth Grp; FFA; German Clb; Office Aide; Church Choir; Yrbk Stf; High Hon Roll; Hon Roll; Ntl Merit SF; FFA Schlrshp Awd 86; Accntng.

BOUVIER, STEVEN; Penns Grove HS; Pedricktown, NJ; (Y); 1/144; Church Yth Grp; Trs German Clb; Chorus; Church Choir; Var Tennis; High Hon Roll; NHS; St Schlr; Val; Wheaton Coll; Math.

BOWER, STEPHANIE; Hopewell Valley Central HS; Pennington, NJ; (Y); 101/202; AFS; Pres Church Yth Grp; Service Clb; SADD; Chorus; Var Socr; JV Sftbl; Var Swmmng; Hon Roll; Hmcmng Prncss; Springfield Coll; Recrtnl Stds.

BOWER, TINA; West Morris Central HS; Long Valley, NJ; (Y); 8/285; Flag Corp; Off Jr Cls; Trs Sr Cls; Stu Cncl; Powder Puff Ftbl; NHS; Hosp Aide; Latin Clb; Science Clb; Ski Clb; Magna Cum Laude Ntl Latin Cntst; Mgmt.

BOWERS, CATHERINE; Point Pleasant Boro HS; Pt Pleasant, NJ; (Y); 5/225; Keywanettes; Socr; Tennis; Gov Hon Prg Awd; High Hon Roll; Hon Roll; Jr NHS; NHS; Itln Amer Cltrl Soc Ocn Cnty 86; JCP & 6 CAP Schlrshp WA Wrkshps Cngrssnl Smnr 86; Rutgers Coll; Pltcl Sci.

BOWERS, MICHELE; West Morris Central HS; Long Vly, NJ; (Y); Church Yth Grp; Chorus; Church Choir; Flag Corp; Hon Roll; JR Hon Grd Grad 84-85; Waynesburg Coll PA; Elem Ed.

BOWERS, STEVEN; Bound Brook HS; S Bound Brook, NJ; (Y); 21/143; Am Leg Boys St; French Clb; Key Clb; Sec Soph Cls; Trs Jr Cls; Rep Stu Cncl; Var L Bsbl; Var L Ftbl; NHS; Church Yth Grp; Knights Of The Altar Pres Chrch 85-86; Math.

BOWERS, SUSAN; Holy Spirit HS; Absecon, NJ; (Y); 56/366; Church Yth Grp; School Play; Yrbk Stf; Fld Hcky; NHS; Elem Ed.

BOWES, JIM; Christian Brothers Acad; Sayreville, NJ; (Y); 25/230; Yrbk Stf; Im Fld Hcky; Im Ftbl; Im Socr; High Hon Roll; Hon Roll; Engrng.

BOWLING, MARIA; Notre Dame HS; East Windsor, NJ; (Y); 33/353; Church Yth Grp; Pres Latin Clb; Nwsp Phtg; NHS; NJ Distngshd Schlr 86; Seton Hall U.

BOWMAN, DEBORAH; Saint Anthony HS; Jersey City, NJ; (Y); #6 In Class; Computer Clb; Dance Clb; Variety Show; Yrbk Stf; Pres Stu Cncl; JV Var Cheerleading; Sftbl; Trk; Twrlr; Vllybl.

BOWMAN, HEATHER; Gloucester City HS; Gloucester, NJ; (Y); 30/160; Girl Scts; Library Aide; Pep Clb; Varsity Clb; Stu Cncl; Capt Var Bsktbl; Var Fld Hcky; Hon Roll; Govt Yth Wk Elect; Homecmng Capt; Capts And Coaches Awd Bsktbl; Phys Thrpst.

BOWMAN, MARK CHRISTOPHER; Union Catholic Regional HS; Cranford, NJ; (Y); Am Leg Boys St; Boy Scts; SADD; Thesps; School Musical; Nwsp Sprt Ed; Stu Cncl; Capt Crs Cntry; Capt Trk; Hon Roll; Fnce.

BOWMAN, MELINDA M; Mainland Regional HS; Linwood, NJ; (Y); 5/300; Church Yth Grp; Intnl Clb; JCL; JV Fld Hcky; High Hon Roll; VP NHS; Pres Schlr; Rotary Awd; Gordon ST Distngushd Schlr 85-86; Bryn Mawr Coll.

BOX, VIVIAN JOAN; Red Bank Catholic HS; Shrewsbury, NJ; (Y); NFL; Ski Clb; Speech Tm; Teachers Aide; School Play; Nwsp Stf; JV Gym; JV Swmmng; Hon Roll; NHS; Mst Dedctd Gymnst 83-84; U MA; Ed.

BOYADJIAN, MARK; Brick Township HS; Brick, NJ; (Y); Am Leg Boys St; Pres Debate Tm; Math Tm; High Hon Roll; Hon Roll; Sports Med.

BOYCE JR, HENRY C; Raritan HS; W Keansburg, NJ; (Y); 14/342; Boy Scts; Church Yth Grp; French Clb; Teachers Aide; Yrbk Ed-Chief; Yrbk Stf; Cit Awd; God Cntry Awd; Hon Roll; NHS; Eagle Scout 85; Mock Trial Part-Cnty Crt House Freehold 86; Stevens Inst Of Tech; Sys Engrg.

BOYD, CHRISTINA; Kingsway Regional HS; Swedesboro, NJ; (Y); Church Yth Grp; Cmnty Wkr; Exploring; GAA; Office Aide; JV Powder Puff Ftbl; JV Swmmng; JV Tennis; Ski Clb; Variety Show; Acctng.

BOYD, KECIA; Essex Catholic Girls; Irvington, NJ; (Y); Pep Clb; Drill Tm; Im Bsktbl; Var Cheerleading; Chrldr Awd; Bus Merch.

BOYD, MACIO; Pemberton TWSH II HS; Pemberton, NJ; (Y); Science Clb; Im Ftbl; Im Wt Lftg; Indstrl Dsgn.

BOYD, PATTY; Harrison HS; Harrison, NJ; (Y); 23/170; Pep Clb; School Play; Var Capt Cheerleading; Gym; Var Capt Swmmng; Var Powder Puff Ftbl; High Hon Roll; NHS; Bergen CC; Lgl Asstnt.

BOYLE, BRIAN; Wayne Hills HS; Wayne, NJ; (Y); 42/330; FBLA; Latin Clb; Ski Clb; Yrbk Stf; Rep Frsh Cls; Rep Soph Cls; Rep Jr Cls; Pres Stu Cncl; Capt Var Swmmng; JV Trk; Fture Bus Ldrs Of Amer Outstndng Prfrmnce 85-86.

BOYLE, GEORGEANNE; Lakewood HS; Lakewood, NJ; (Y); Sec Girl Scts; Chorus; Church Choir; Mrchg Band; Stage Crew; Yrbk Stf; Mgr(s); Church Yth Grp; Cmnty Wkr; English Clb; Brnz Cngrssnl Awd Mdl 85; Grl Sct Gld Awd 86; Wider Opprtnty 85; Law.

BOYLE, SUZANNE; Vernon Township HS; Sussex, NJ; (Y); 22/219; JCL; Rep Sr Cls; Rep Stu Cncl; Capt Cheerleading; Stat Crs Cntry; Stat Swmmng; JV Trk; Hon Roll; NHS; Prfct Atten Awd; Sussex Kiwanis Schlrshp 86; Medlln Frm NJ Tchrs Of Yr 86; Pres Acad Ftns Awd 86; William Paterson Coll; Elem Ed.

BOYLE, TERESA; Rutherford HS; Rutherford, NJ; (S); French Clb; Varsity Clb; Variety Show; Yrbk Stf; Off Frsh Cls; VP Soph Cls; Trs Stu Cncl; Var JV Cheerleading; High Hon Roll; Hon Roll; Prfct Attndnc Dance 10 83-85; Ballet Schlrshp Dance 10 83; Awd For Maintaining Avg 84-85.

BOYLES, ERIKE; Hudson Catholic HS; Irvington, NJ; (Y); 51/143; Art Clb; Boys Clb Am; 4-H; Ski Clb; Swmmng; Trk; Hon Roll; Fisk U; Photogrphr.

BOZARTH, BRETT; Pinelands Regional HS; Tuckerton, NJ; (S); 6/150; Am Leg Boys St; French Clb; Band; Concert Band; Jazz Band; Mrchg Band; Yrbk Stf; Socr; High Hon Roll; Hon Roll.

BOZEWSKI, ANDRE; St Anthony HS; Jersey City, NJ; (Y); 6/64; Aud/Vis; Debate Tm; Library Aide; Spanish Clb; Stage Crew; Rep Soph Cls; Bowling; Hon Roll; NEDT Awd; Wrtng Profncy Test Awd 86; Stu Of Mnth/Max Awd 85; Englsh III Hnrs Cls 85-86; Jersey City ST Coll; Elem Ed.

BOZOLUS, CHERYL; Roselle Catholic HS; Union, NJ; (Y); Church Yth Grp; FCA; GAA; Service Clb; Lit Mag; Im Vllybl; High Hon Roll; NHS; Spanish NHS; Computer Clb; Medals Music Organ Piano 84; Princeton U; Physcl Thrpy.

BOZZA, MICHELLE; Shore Regional HS; Oceanport, NJ; (Y); 18/220; Pres French Clb; Thesps; Chorus; Mgr Stage Crew; Ed Yrbk Stf; Capt Gym; High Hon Roll; NHS; Frnch Achvt Awd 86; Pres Scholar FDU 86; Fairleigh Dickinson U.

BOZZELLI, CAROLE J; Livingston HS; Livingston, NJ; (Y); Church Yth Grp; Sec FBLA; Leo Clb; Band; Chorus; Score Keeper; Var JV Socr; Hon Roll; Jr NHS; Pre-Law.

BRABSON, KEVIN; Eastside HS; Paterson, NJ; (Y); Art Clb; Acpl Chr; Chorus; Concert Band; JV Mgr(s); Score Keeper; JV Wrstlng; RETS; Elec Tech.

BRACCO, JENNIFER; Howell HS; Howell, NJ; (Y); 103/435; French Clb; JCL; Latin Clb; Office Aide; Lit Mag; Rep Stu Cncl; Var Capt Cheerleading; JV L Socr.

BRACERAS, ROBBIE; James Caldwell HS; Caldwell, NJ; (Y); 1/265; Math Tm; Political Wkr; Ski Clb; VP Sr Cls; Stu Cncl; L Ftbl; L Tennis; Wt Lftg; High Hon Roll; NHS; Rutgers Schlr 86; Med.

BRACERO, NILDA; Hoboken HS; Hoboken, NJ; (Y); Cmnty Wkr; Spanish Clb; Teachers Aide; Mrchg Band; Yrbk Stf; Off Sr Cls; Var Pom Pon; Var Sftbl; Hon Roll; Perf Atten 83; Trophies 84-86; Bus Mgmt.

BRACKEN, AMY; Midland Park HS; Midland Park, NJ; (S); 54/137; Art Clb; DECA; Pep Clb; Ski Clb; Teachers Aide; Varsity Clb; Var Cheerleading; JV Sftbl; Var Tennis; Hon Roll; Bus Admin.

BRACKEN, DAVE; West Morris Central HS; Long Valley, NJ; (Y); FBLA; JA; Math Tm; Ski Clb; School Play; Stage Crew; Var Capt Swmmng; Hon Roll; Undrstndng Amrcn Bus Appnte; ST Fnlst Bus Mth FBLA; Rnnr Up ST VP FBLA; Bus Adm.

BRACKEN, JOHN; Delaware Valley Regional HS; Pittstown, NJ; (Y); 3/167; Am Leg Boys St; VP Church Yth Grp; Key Clb; Scholastic Bowl; Science Clb; Stage Crew; Var Socr; High Hon Roll; VP NHS; Pres Schlr; U VA; Elect Engr.

BRADBURY, THERESA A; Highland Regional HS; Erial, NJ; (Y); Church Yth Grp; Drama Clb; Spanish Clb; Band; Chorus; Mrchg Band; School Musical; School Play; Var Twrlr; Hon Roll; Choir Awd 86; Actvts Awd 86; Mrchng Band Awd 86; Glassboro ST Coll; Comp Math.

BRADEN, THOMAS; Colonia HS; Avenel, NJ; (Y); Am Leg Boys St; Trs Jr Cls; VP Sr Cls; JV Crs Cntry; JV Var Trk; JV Wrstlng; NHS; Debate Tm; German Clb; SADD; Debt Wnnr Schlrshp Close Up Pgm 86; NJ Yth St Gov 86; U S Naval Acad; Marine Eng.

BRADFORD, LAUREN; Spotswood HS; Milltown, NJ; (S); 8/174; Ski Clb; Concert Band; Orch; Nwsp Stf; Stu Cncl; VP Bsktbl; Capt Socr; VP Sftbl; Trs NHS; All Cnty & Conf Sftbl 85, Socr 85; Region II Hon Orch 85; Engrng.

BRADFORD, MARCIA; Westside HS; Newark, NJ; (Y); PAVAS; ROTC; Band; Church Choir; Concert Band; Drm Mjr(t); Mrchg Band; Nwsp Rptr; Nwsp Stf; Yrbk Stf; Psych.

BRADHAM, STEPHANIE; Henry Snyder HS; Jersey City, NJ; (S); Office Aide; Hon Roll; Pres NHS; Val; Achvt Awd 84; Valdctrn 83; Math Awd 83; Pedtrcn.

BRADLEY, DAVID ANDREW; Clifton HS; Clifton, NJ; (Y); 81/564; Ski Clb; Jazz Band; Orch; School Musical; Im Vllybl; JV Wrstlng; Hon Roll; Jr NHS; NHS; Ithaca Coll; Music Ed.

BRADLEY, JOHN; Queen Of Peace HS; N Arlington, NJ; (Y); 16/230; Church Yth Grp; Model UN; Ski Clb; SADD; Thesps; School Musical; School Play; Nwsp Rptr; High Hon Roll; NHS; Vrsty Ltrmn For Schl Nwspr; Rutgeis Clg; Pharm.

BRADLEY, MATT; Wildwood Catholic HS; Wildwood Crest, NJ; (Y); Bsktbl; Airlines.

BRADLEY, ROBIN; Voorhees HS; White House Stati, NJ; (Y); 55/274; Pres Trs Church Yth Grp; Stu Cncl; JV Fld Hcky; Hon Roll; NHS; Coll; Bus.

BRADLEY, THOMAS; Sacred Heart HS; Vineland, NJ; (Y); Cmnty Wkr; FBLA; Varsity Clb; JV Var Bsktbl; JV Tennis; JV Trk; JC Awd; Jycees Bus Awd 86; Frnk Luisi Awd 86; William Paterson; Bus.

BRADLEY, TIMIA; Holy Spirit HS; Atlantic City, NJ; (Y); Library Aide; Political Wkr; Pres Stu Cncl; Mrktng.

BRADLEY, WILLIAM; Jackson Memorial HS; Jackson, NJ; (Y); 50/310; Nwsp Rptr; Nwsp Sprt Ed; Trs Sr Cls; Stu Cncl; Wt Lftg; Wrstlng; French Hon Soc; Hon Roll; Ntl Merit Ltr; NEDT Awd; Natl Jrnlsm Achvt Awd 85, Engl 86; Rutgers U; Jrnlsm.

BRADSHAW, SEAN; Riverside HS; Riverside, NJ; (Y); 19/86; VP Pres Drama Clb; Jazz Band; School Musical; Nwsp Rptr; Ed Yrbk Stf; Pres Jr Cls; Pres Sr Cls; Rep Stu Cncl; Concert Band; Mrchg Band; Thomas Chorosiewski Mrl Bnd Schlrshp 86; Kiwanis Clb Awd Srv Schl 86; Yrbk Unsng Hero Awd 86; Roanoke Coll; Blgy.

BRADU, CATALIN T; S River HS; S River, NJ; (Y); French Clb; Math Clb; Math Tm; Quiz Bowl; Nwsp Stf; High Hon Roll; NHS; Ntl Merit SF; St Schlr; Gov Schl Sci Drew U 85; Calculus Lg 85-86; MIT; Nuc Physics.

BRADY, JACQUELINE A; Delaware Valley Reg HS; Frenchtown, NJ; (Y); 12/122; Church Yth Grp; Girl Scts; Varsity Clb; Chorus; Color Guard; Drill Tm; Nwsp Rptr; Var Crs Cntry; JV Trk; High Hon Roll; Hnr Grad 86; Polc Benevolent Assn Awd 86; Acad Scholar 86-87; Gannon U; Crimnl Justc.

BRADY, JAMES; Middletown South HS; Red Bank, NJ; (Y); Ftbl; High Hon Roll; Hon Roll; Bus.

BRADY, KATHRYN; Rutherford HS; Rutherford, NJ; (S); 1/186; Key Clb; Spanish Clb; Nwsp Stf; Yrbk Stf; Var Bsktbl; Sftbl; Var Capt Vllybl; High Hon Roll; Sec NHS; St Schlr; Board Of Ed Awds; Hnrbl Mntn All-League Vllybl; 1st Tm All-League Vllybl; Comm.

BRADY, PATRICIA; Bogota HS; Bogota, NJ; (Y); 10/100; Church Yth Grp; Drama Clb; Math Tm; Spanish Clb; Chorus; School Musical; Lit Mag; Hon Roll; NHS; Grls Ctznshp Inst Delg 86; Chsn Attnd Ramapos Enrchmnt Prog 86.

BRADY, TARA; Oak Knoll HS; Brookside, NJ; (Y); Art Clb; French Clb; Pep Clb; Ski Clb; School Play; Stage Crew; Nwsp Stf; Yrbk Stf; Lit Mag; Swmmng; Hnrb Mntn Consortium Of Art 84 & 85; Summer Art Study At Parsons 86; Stanford; Graphic Art.

BRAGG, KARLA D; John F Kennedy HS; Willingboro, NJ; (Y); Am Leg Aux Girls St; Church Yth Grp; Computer Clb; Intnl Clb; Band; School Play; High Hon Roll; Prfct Atten Awd; Pep Clb; Chorus; Gftd Prg From 1st Grd Thru 10th; US Air Force Acad; Nvgtr.

BRAHMANN, KIMBERLY; Madison Central HS; Old Bridge, NJ; (S); 71/360; Church Yth Grp; SADD; Chorus; School Musical; Stat Bsbl; JV Score Keeper; Hon Roll; Mus Awd 85; Co Arts-Dance 85.

BRAIN, TRACEY; Spotswood HS; Spotswood, NJ; (S); 8/174; Church Yth Grp; Intnl Clb; Band; Concert Band; Jazz Band; Mrchg Band; Nwsp Stf; Yrbk Stf; Stu Cncl; French Hon Soc; Bus Mgmt.

BRAININ, GREGORY; Vail-Deane HS; Elizabeth, NJ; (Y); 5/14; Art Clb; French Clb; School Play; Stage Crew; Nwsp Phtg; Nwsp Stf; Yrbk Phtg; Yrbk Stf; Pres Jr Cls; Pres Sr Cls; Lawyer.

BRAITHWAITE, DARREN; Burlington City HS; Edgewater Pk, NJ; (Y); Am Leg Boys St; Exploring; Jazz Band; Variety Show; Kiwanis Awd.

BRAMANTE, PRISCILLA; Washington Twp HS; Sewell, NJ; (Y); Hon Roll; Glassboro ST Coll; Elem Ed.

BRANCA, LEA; Delran HS; Delran, NJ; (Y); Hosp Aide; Psych.

BRANCH, SHEILA; Frank H Marrell HS; Irriston, NJ; (Y); Camp Fr Inc; Church Yth Grp; Library Aide; Spanish Clb; Church Choir; Variety Show; Twrlr; Gov Hon Prg Awd; Hon Roll; Prfct Atten Awd; Afro Amer Club 87; FBLA 87; Color Guard 87; Hampton Inst; Bus.

BRANCO, CHRISTINE; Washington Township HS; Turnersville, NJ; (Y); Church Yth Grp; Red Cross Aide; Science Clb; Yrbk Stf; Stu Cncl; Child Care.

BRAND, CLAUDIA L; Emerson HS; Houston, TX; (Y); 5/300; Stu Cncl; Var Cheerleading; Bausch & Lomb Sci Awd; CC Awd; Hon Roll; NHS; Ricky Del Valle Mem Awd 86; U Of Houston.

BRAND, DIANA; Brick Township HS; Brick Town, NJ; (Y); Radio Clb; Yrbk Stf; Hon Roll.

BRANDES, LISA; Hightstown HS; East Windsor, NJ; (Y); French Clb; Intnl Clb; Drill Tm; Mrchg Band; Chrmn Jr Cls; Stu Cncl; Mgr Socr; Trk; Twrlr; Wrstlng; Mercer Cnty Arts Fstvl 84-85; Awd For Outstndg Achvt-Sci 83-84; Txtl Dsgnr.

BRANDLEY, KIMBERLY; Overbrook Regional HS; Clementon, NJ; (Y); 10/270; FBLA; Trs Stu Cncl; Bsktbl; Fld Hcky; Sftbl; DAR Awd; JC Awd; NHS; Rotary Awd; Jr NHS; Vrsty Clb Schlrshp 86; Albert J Carino Bsktbl Clb Schlrshp 86; Trenton ST Coll; Accntng.

BRANDT, JENNIFER; Woodbridge HS; Woodbridge, NJ; (Y); 10/300; Quiz Bowl; VP Soph Cls; Rep Jr Cls; Rep Stu Cncl; Var Stat Bsbl; Var Capt Cheerleading; Hon Roll; NCTE Awd; NHS; Ntl Merit SF; Union Carbide WA Wrkshp Schlr 86.

BRANNON, WANDA D; Orange HS; Orange, NJ; (Y); 28/182; Dance Clb; 4-H; Varsity Clb; Y-Teens; Sec Soph Cls; Sec Jr Cls; Rep Stu Cncl; Var Capt Cheerleading; Sftbl; Trk; Mrs Orange HS 85-86; Ms JR 84-85; Mt Ida Coll; Comm.

BRANTLEY, BRYANT H; Pennsville Memorial HS; Pennsville, NJ; (Y); Am Leg Boys St; Church Yth Grp; Cmnty Wkr; Ski Clb; Church Choir; Rep Frsh Cls; Rep Soph Cls; Rep Jr Cls; Rep Sr Cls; Rep Stu Cncl.

BRASEK, CARL; Holy Cross HS; Medford, NJ; (Y); Am Leg Boys St; Church Yth Grp; Cmnty Wkr; Political Wkr; Var Crs Cntry; Var Trk; Hon Roll; Burlington Cnty Bar Asso Mock Trls; Yng Rep Clb TARS.

BRASWELL, CALANDRA; Hackensack HS; Hackenack, NJ; (Y); 153/368; Church Yth Grp; 4-H; FNA; Hosp Aide; Teachers Aide; Chorus; Church Choir; Yrbk Stf; Off Soph Cls; Bowling; Bergen CC; Dntl Hyg.

BRAUN, SUZANNE; Bruriah H S For Girls; Edison, NJ; (Y); 8/55; Temple Yth Grp; Pres Jr Cls; VP Stu Cncl; Hon Roll; NHS; Ntl Eductnl Dvlpmnt Tst Awd 83.

BRAUNWELL, PAMELA; High Point Regional HS; Sussex, NJ; (Y); #1 In Class; Debate Tm; German Clb; Science Clb; Ski Clb; Mrchg Band; High Hon Roll; NHS; Teachers Aide; Band; Concert Band; Peer Cnclng; Advncd Stdys Prgm; Tutor Elem Schl Math; Doctor.

BRAVACO, GUY; Bloomfield SR HS; Bloomfld, NJ; (Y); 38/442; Computer Clb; Key Clb; Rep Frsh Cls; Rep Soph Cls; Rep Jr Cls; High Hon Roll; Hon Roll; NHS; Bus.

BRAWER, ANDREW J; Glen Rock HS; Glen Rock, NJ; (Y); 6/150; Am Leg Boys St; Latin Clb; Math Tm; Quiz Bowl; Science Clb; Var Trk; Bausch & Lomb Sci Awd; High Hon Roll; NHS; JV Socr; Cum Laude Lat III Magna Cum Laude Lat I; Aeronautical.

BREAULT, SHARON; Brick Township HS; Brick Town, NJ; (Y); Key Clb; Political Wkr; Yrbk Stf; Powder Puff Ftbl; Hon Roll; Stockton ST; Socl Wrk.

BREAZEALE, LEE; Hamilton High West; Trenton, NJ; (Y); Key Clb; Math Clb; Math Tm; School Musical; School Play; Stage Crew; Key Clb Svc Awd 84-85 & 85-86; Bus Adm.

BRECHER, TODD; Westfield SR HS; Westfield, NJ; (Y); French Clb; Temple Yth Grp; Nwsp Ed-Chief; Nwsp Rptr; Nwsp Stf; Var Score Keeper; French Hon Soc; High Hon Roll; Hon Roll; VP NHS; Jrnlsm Awd-2nd Pl ST Cont-Sprts Wrtg 86; Hnrbl Mntn ST Sprts Wrtg 86; Hnrbl Mntn ST Cont Sprts 85; Jrnlsm.

BREDEHOFT, ANASTASIA ANN; Toms River HS; Toms River, NJ; (Y); Church Yth Grp; 4-H; FBLA; Chorus; VP Cheerleading; Cit Awd; 4-H Awd; Arnold Lehman Cmmnty Svc Awd 84; Hugh O Brien Ldrshp Awd 85; ST Awd Natr & Consrvtn John Deere 85.

BREDEHOFT, MARY ALICE; Toms River North HS; Toms River, NJ; (Y); Church Yth Grp; 4-H; FBLA; Chorus; Mrchg Band; Var Crs Cntry; Var Trk; Var Twrlr; Cit Awd; 4-H Awd; Howard Mann Publ Spkg Awd 84; Natl JR Hortcltr Cntst KY 85; ST Awd Plnt & Soil Sci Quakr Oats Co 85; Elem Ed.

BREEDEN, TAMMY; John F Kennedy HS; Paterson, NJ; (S); 72/438; Chorus; Church Choir; Bowling; Hon Roll; Cmmnctns.

BREEN, CHRISTA; Clifton SR HS; Clifton, NJ; (Y); 132/637; French Clb; SADD; Nwsp Rptr; Var Capt Bsktbl; Var L Sftbl; Var Capt Vllybl; Jr NHS; 1st Tm All Cnty, All Lg Vlybl 85; 2nd Tm All Lg, All County Hm Bsktbl 85-86; 2nd Tm All Lg Sftbl 86; Physical Therapy.

BREEN, NORA; Franklin HS; Somerset, NJ; (Y); 40/313; High Hon Roll; Hon Roll; ST Champs Guitar Ensmbl 82-86; Rider College; Bus Mgmt.

BREHENY, ANN MARIE; Manville HS; Manville, NJ; (Y); 2/99; Chorus; Church Choir; Yrbk Sprt Ed; Stu Cncl; Var JV Bsktbl; JV Sftbl; High Hon Roll; Hon Roll; NHS; Law.

BREITENBACH, WARREN M; Plainfield HS; Plainfield, NJ; (Y); Church Yth Grp; Science Clb; Var L Golf; Hon Roll; NHS; Ntl Achvmt Commnd Stu 85; Elec Engrng.

BREITHAUPT, KENNETH; Montville Township HS; Towaco, NJ; (Y); 52/272; FBLA; Key Clb; Ski Clb; SADD; Var Crs Cntry; Im Var Socr; Var Capt Trk; Var Capt Wrstlng; High Hon Roll; NHS; Exc Stu Japan 84; Mayors Awd Outstndng Civic 85; Schlott Reltrs Schrlshp Awds 86; Syracuse U; Mrktng Mgmt.

BRENNAN, HELEN; Ridge HS; Basking Ridge, NJ; (Y); Church Yth Grp; Latin Clb; Stat Socr; JV Sftbl; Hon Roll; Ntl Merit SF; Roselle Svgs Bus Educ Awd 86; Business.

BRENNAN, MICHAEL; Highland Regional HS; Blackwood, NJ; (Y); Var Capt Bsbl; Var Capt Bsktbl; Var Capt Ftbl; Lion Awd; Outstndng Athl 82-86; Schlr Athl USAR 86; All Grp 4 Bsbl & 2nd Tm All S Jersey Bsbl 86; U Of VA; Acctg.

BRENNAN, TARA; Queen Of Peace HS; Lyndhurst, NJ; (S); 18/231; Cmnty Wkr; Pres Speech Tm; SADD; Var Crs Cntry; Var Gym; Sftbl; Var Trk; Hon Roll; NHS; Kean Coll; Phy Thrpy.

BRESCH, KRISTEN; Riverside HS; Riverside, NJ; (S); Am Leg Aux Girls St; FTA; Yrbk Sprt Ed; Sec Soph Cls; Sec Jr Cls; Var Fld Hcky; Score Keeper; Var Sftbl; Comm.

BRESCIA, MICHAEL M; Saint Josephs HS; Fords, NJ; (Y); Pres Church Yth Grp; Cmnty Wkr; Model UN; Political Wkr; Service Clb; Ski Clb; Yrbk Bus Mgr; High Hon Roll; Outstndng Delg 84; Outstndng Yth Grp Memb 84-85; Hnrb Mntn Litry Cntst 85; Hist.

BRESCIA, MICHELLE; Toms River High School East; Toms River, NJ; (Y); 13/586; Am Leg Aux Girls St; Intnl Clb; Key Clb; Yrbk Stf; JV Socr; JV Trk; High Hon Roll; Drama Clb; NHS; Math Tm; TEAM 84-86; Pre-Law.

BRESLIN, DIANE; Kearny HS; Kearny, NJ; (Y); Gym; Swmmng; Trk; Hon Roll; Nrs.

BRESSAN, KAREN; Hackensack HS; Maywood, NJ; (Y); 17/375; Church Yth Grp; Yrbk Phtg; High Hon Roll; Prfct Atten Awd; Rotary Awd; Spanish NHS; Mywd Wmns Clb Exc In Frgn Lng Awd 86; N E Cnfrnc/Frgn Lng & Spnsh Awd 86; Ahcvt Awd In Acdmcs 86; Montclair ST Col6; Bus Adm.

BRETONES, ANTHONY; Roselle Catholic HS; Roselle, NJ; (Y); Drama Clb; Stage Crew; Var Wrstlng; Hon Roll; Forestry.

BRETT, JESSICA; Vineland HS; Vineland, NJ; (Y); 156/803; Art Clb; Drama Clb; Stage Crew; Frsh Cls; Soph Cls; Jr Cls; Var Mgr(s); Var Socr; NJ ST Teenarts Pgm 85-86; Exhbtn 2 3rd Plcs 85; Merit Roll 86; Art.

BRETT, SUSIE L; Abraham Clark HS; Roselle, NJ; (S); 11/180; French Clb; Latin Clb; Office Aide; VP Science Clb; Chorus; Concert Band; Mrchg Band; Symp Band; Var L Sftbl; Hon Roll; Awd Frnch; 3rd Frgn Lang Fair; Acctng.

BREUER, ROBIN; Cresskill HS; Cresskill, NJ; (Y); 4/111; French Clb; Spanish Clb; Temple Yth Grp; Yrbk Stf; Var Tennis; High Hon Roll; NHS.

BREWER, ANDREW M; De Paul HS; Pompton Lakes, NJ; (Y); 3/175; Math Tm; Science Clb; Ski Clb; Bsktbl; Var L Socr; Var L Trk; High Hon Roll; NHS; Ntl Merit SF; NJ Dinstingushed Schl Awd 85; USMA HS Workshop 85.

BREWER, ELIZABETH; Middletown H S South; Middletown, NJ; (Y); Girl Scts; Hosp Aide; Intnl Clb; Flag Corp; Stage Crew; Nwsp Stf; Yrbk Ed-Chief; Trk; Twrlr; Hon Roll; PA ST; Psychology.

BREWER, JULIE; Weequahic HS; Newark, NJ; (Y); Band; Drm Mjr(t); Mrchg Band; Lit Mag; Bowling; Sftbl; Twrlr; Baton Twrlng Cptn Awd 85; Bwlng Awds & Trphy 86; Pre-Med.

BREWER, KRISTIN; Hillsborough HS; Belle Mead, NJ; (Y); 33/274; Cmnty Wkr; SADD; Rep Sr Cls; Rep Stu Cncl; JV Var Sftbl; JV Var Tennis; Church Yth Grp; Pres Latin Clb; Library Aide; Im Crs Cntry; Northeastern U Boston; Intl Bus.

BREWINGTON, JOHN D; Montclair HS; Montclair, NJ; (Y); 15/438; Am Leg Boys St; Pres Jr Cls; Stu Cncl; Var Bsktbl; Var Tennis; High Hon Roll; Lion Awd; NHS; Yale Bk Clb Awd 85; WA Wrkshp Congsnl Sem 85; Law.

BRIAMONTE, FRANCIS; St Peters Prep; N Arlington, NJ; (Y); 6/201; Cmnty Wkr; Pep Clb; SADD; Stat Bsbl; Var L Ice Hcky; Mgr(s); High Hon Roll; NHS; St Schlr; Church Yth Grp; Retreat Tm Ldr; Euchriotc Ministr; Holy Cross.

BRIANTE, SUSAN C; Scotch Plains Fanwood HS; Fanwood, NJ; (Y); 12/311; Dance Clb; French Clb; Ed Nwsp Rptr; Lit Mag; Stu Cncl; Var Capt Cheerleading; Mgr(s); Im Vllybl; French Hon Soc; High Hon Roll; Poem-Rainsong-Pblshd In Susquehanna Univ Apprntc Wrtr 85; 3rd Pl NJ Prss Assn-Prss Dy Wrtng Cmptn 85; Englsh.

BRICENO, MARGARET; Roselle Catholic HS; Roselle, NJ; (Y); 16/207; School Play; Var Cheerleading; Im Gym; Var Socr; Var Sftbl; Im Vllybl; Hon Roll; Cert Merit Profcncy Frnch 85; Pine Forest Chrldng Camp All Amer Fin 85; Psych.

BRICENO, MAXIMO; Roselle Catholic HS; Roselle, NJ; (S); Science Clb; School Play; Stage Crew; Yrbk Stf; Im Bsktbl; JV Var Socr; Var Trk; Im Wt Lftg; Hon Roll.

BRICKER, SUSAN; Piscataway HS; Piscataway, NJ; (Y); 22/521; Key Clb; Sec Varsity Clb; Band; Var Fld Hcky; Var Sftbl; Var Swmmng; Hon Roll; NHS; Emory U; Engl.

BRICKETT, KAREN; West Essex SR HS; N Caldwell, NJ; (Y); Band; Chorus; Concert Band; Jazz Band; Mrchg Band; Pep Band; Symp Band; Ithaca; Music.

BRICKLEY, TARA; Bishop George Ahr/St Thomas; Edison, NJ; (Y); Cmnty Wkr; Dance Clb; Pres Intnl Clb; Pres Model UN; Ski Clb; Spanish Clb; School Play; Mgr(s); High Hon Roll; NHS; Vol Svc Awd 85-86; Ballet Dancing Awd 78-79; Dance.

BRIDENBAUGH, JOHN ERIC; Kittatinny Regional HS; Newton, NJ; (Y); 42/228; Boy Scts; Church Yth Grp; Math Tm; Band; Mrchg Band; Var Bsktbl; Var Capt Socr; Var Tennis; High Hon Roll; Hon Roll; Med.

BRIDGER, ELIZABETH; Hopewell Valley Central HS; Hopewell, NJ; (Y); 26/204; AFS; Service Clb; Var L Swmmng; High Hon Roll; Hon Roll; NHS; Spanish Clb; JV Fld Hcky; Var L Trk; Im Wt Lftg; Pres Acad Fit Awd 86; Dickinson Coll; Bio.

BRIEF, DAVID R; Livingston HS; Livingston, NJ; (Y); 50/498; Key Clb; Model UN; Temple Yth Grp; VP Frsh Cls; Crs Cntry; Trk; High Hon Roll; Hon Roll; Jr NHS; Ntl Merit SF; Cornell U; Elec Engrng.

BRIEN, DARRAUGH; Westfield SR HS; Westfield, NJ; (Y); 104/509; Church Yth Grp; Latin Clb; Var Swmmng; Hon Roll; Psych.

BRIEN, JAMES O; Hopatcong HS; Hopatcong, NJ; (Y); Varsity Clb; Var Ftbl; Var Trk; L Var Wrstlng; Rugers Coll; Engrng.

BRIERLEY, SUZANNE; Toms River HS South; Toms River, NJ; (Y); 18/354; Art Clb; Nwsp Rptr; Nwsp Stf; Off Jr Cls; JV Capt Bsktbl; JV Capt Fld Hcky; Powder Puff Ftbl; High Hon Roll; NHS; Math Tm; 2nd Pl Hallwn Wndw Pntg 83; 3rd Pl Hallwn Wndw Pntg 84; Artst.

BRIETENSTINE, LYNN L; Burlington County Vo Tech; New Lisbon, NJ; (S); 14/149; VICA; Trs Frsh Cls; Trs Soph Cls; Trs Jr Cls; Var Bowling; JV Mgr(s); Sftbl; Hon Roll; NHS; Prfct Atten Awd; FL Inst Tech; Aeronautics.

BRIGGS, NANCY; Paulsboro HS; Swedesboro, NJ; (Y); 25/135; Office Aide; Varsity Clb; Color Guard; Drill Tm; VP Soph Cls; Rep Jr Cls; Trs Sr Cls; Rep Stu Cncl; Im Badmtn; JV Bsktbl; Librarians Awd 86; Logan Twp Hm & Schl League Awd 86; Fairleigh Dickinson U; Radiolgy.

BRIGGS, SCOTT A; Montgomery HS; Belle Mead, NJ; (Y); Am Leg Boys St; Science Clb; Ski Clb; Stage Crew; Nwsp Rptr; Lit Mag; Rep Stu Cncl; JV Bsktbl; JV Tennis; Hon Roll; Bus.

BRIGHT, MICHAEL; Barringer HS; Newark, NJ; (Y); Computer Clb; Exploring; Math Clb; ROTC; Hon Roll; Ntl Merit Schol; Pre-Med.

BRIGNOLA, CHRIS; Shore Regional HS; Oceanport, NJ; (Y); Stage Crew; Var Capt Bsktbl; JV Socr; High Hon Roll; Hon Roll; Grphc Dsgn.

BRILL, VANESSA M; Cinnaminson HS; Cinna, NJ; (Y); Church Yth Grp; SADD; Rep Jr Cls; Var JV Socr; Var Swmmng; Hon Roll; NHS; Cmnty Wkr; Lcrss; Ntl Merit Schol; Cls Cabinet Schl Govt; Interact Club; Bus.

BRILLANTES, ROSANNA; Oak Knoll HS; Short Hills, NJ; (Y); Pres Aud/Vis; Boy Scts; Church Yth Grp; Sec Exploring; French Clb; Ski Clb; Teachers Aide; Im Vllybl; Hon Roll; Outstndgn Achvt Awd 86; Wnr Oak Knoll Schl Ptry Awd 84; Lbrl Arts.

BRILLES, HEATHER; Overbrook Regional HS; Berlin, NJ; (Y); 7/362; Drama Clb; German Clb; Girl Scts; Science Clb; Concert Band; Mrchg Band; Yrbk Bus Mgr; Yrbk Ed-Chief; High Hon Roll; Hon Roll; U Of PA; Chem.

BRILLHART, STEVEN; Middletown HS South; Lincroft, NJ; (Y); Boy Scts; Church Yth Grp; Jazz Band; Mrchg Band; High Hon Roll; NHS; Ntl Merit SF; Ski Clb; Church Choir; Pep Band; Brd Educ Cmndtns 86; Engrng.

BRIMLEY, GEORGE; East Side HS; Paterson, NJ; (Y); Boys Clb Am; Church Yth Grp; Y-Teens; Wrstlng; NEDT Awd; Howard U; Pre-Med.

BRINAMEN, MARIBETH; Mount Olive HS; Flanders, NJ; (Y); 26/296; AFS; Dance Clb; Ski Clb; Concert Band; Jazz Band; Mrchg Band; School Musical; Yrbk Stf; Lit Mag; NHS; Hugh O Brien Mst Outstndng Awd 85; Yng Comm Ldr Distngshd Yth Ldrshp & Svc 86; Librl Arts.

BRINGHURST, RICHARD; Victory Christian HS; Berlin, NJ; (S); 1/17; Church Yth Grp; Chorus; Pres Jr Cls; Pres Sr Cls; Timer; High Hon Roll; Ntl Merit Ltr; Prfct Atten Awd; Chrstn Charactr Awd; 4.0 Avg; Le Tourneau Coll TX; Comp Sci.

BRINKERHOFF, STEPHEN G; Midland Park HS; Midland Park, NJ; (Y); Am Leg Boys St; Chess Clb; Church Yth Grp; Math Tm; Science Clb; Ftbl; Trk; Wrstlng; High Hon Roll; Hon Roll.

BRINKLEY, DENARD; Hillside HS; Hillside, NJ; (Y); Church Yth Grp; Computer Clb; JA; Math Clb; ROTC; Science Clb; Church Choir; Nwsp Stf; Yrbk Stf; JV Trk; Achvt Acad 83; Elect Engrg.

BRINKLEY, RENE; Lacordaire Acad; Newark, NJ; (Y); School Play; Stage Crew; Nwsp Rptr; Yrbk Stf; Lit Mag; High Hon Roll; Hon Roll; Pres Schlr; Chorus; Syracuse U; Cmmnctns.

BRINTZINGHOFFER, TAMMY; Holy Cross HS; Burlington, NJ; (Y); 200/396; Art Clb; Church Yth Grp; Ski Clb; Spanish Clb; Concert Band; Mrchg Band; School Musical; Yrbk Phtg; Rep Jr Cls; Stat Ftbl; Sftbll ST Chmpnshp 85; Montclair ST; Bus Mngmnt.

BRION, PAUL; Freehold Township HS; Howell, NJ; (Y); 17/319; Boy Scts; Church Yth Grp; Sec Dance Clb; Exploring; Math Tm; Radio Clb; JV Wrstlng; Hon Roll; NHS; St Schlr; Prsdntl Acdmc Ftns Awd; Rutgers U; Biolgy.

BRISCOE, MONICA; Haddonfield Memorial HS; Haddonfield, NJ; (Y); Church Yth Grp; Church Choir; Var Capt Cheerleading; JV Stat Trk; Hon Roll; NHS; 2nd Rnnrup Mr Miss Blck Teen Wrld Pgnt Camdn Cnty 86; Awd Achvt Mt Pisgah A M E Chrch 86; Photo Jrnlsm.

BRISMAN, JONATHAN L; The Frisch Schl; Tenafly, NJ; (Y); Capt Math Tm; Nwsp Ed-Chief; Nwsp Rptr; Yrbk Sprt Ed; Rep Sr Cls; Bsktbl; Capt Mgr Tennis; High Hon Roll; NHS; Ntl Merit SF; Bio.

BRISTER JR, WILLIAM C; Plainfield HS; Plainfield, NJ; (Y); FBLA; Chorus; Church Choir; Mrchg Band; VP Jr Cls; Pres Stu Cncl; Model Congress 85-86; Prom King 85-86; Mont Clair ST; Bus Admn.

BRITO, MILADY; Emerson HS; Union City, NJ; (Y); Latin Clb; Spanish Clb; Variety Show; Hon Roll; Spanish NHS; FL Intl U; Med.

BRITSCH, KAREN; Pascack Hills HS; Montvale, NJ; (Y); Band; Capt Color Guard; Concert Band; Jazz Band; Mrchg Band; Lwyr.

BRITT, PHAEDRA; Northern Valley Regional HS; Norwood, NJ; (Y); 4/313; Drama Clb; Math Tm; Church Choir; School Musical; Stage Crew; Ed Lit Mag; Vllybl; NHS; Pres Acdmc Ftns Awd 86; U Rchstr; Med.

BRITTEN, KIM; Frank H Morrell HS; Irvington, NJ; (Y); Drama Clb; Exploring; Model UN; PAVAS; Radio Clb; Science Clb; Off Jr Cls; Hon Roll; Prfct Atten Awd; ABI; Exectv Secy.

BRITTON, ALLISON; Scotch Plains Fanwood HS; Fanwood, NJ; (Y); 15/330; Dance Clb; FBLA; Model UN; Quiz Bowl; Band; Mrchg Band; Yrbk Stf; Var Capt Tennis; High Hon Roll; Spanish NHS; Girls Citizenship Delegate 85; NJ Society Of CPAS Schlrshp 86; Coll Club Of Fanwood Schlrshp 86; PA ST U; Accntng.

BRIXIE, JOHN; Oratory Prep; Cranford, NJ; (Y); Church Yth Grp; Computer Clb; Math Clb; Math Tm; Science Clb; School Musical; Nwsp Stf; Yrbk Stf; Bsktbl; Vllybl; Pres Westfield JR Musical Clb 85-86; Biological Sciences.

BROADHURST, MARK; Hackettstown HS; Hackettstown, NJ; (S); 25/250; Am Leg Boys St; Band; Chorus; Church Choir; Nwsp Stf; Pres Frsh Cls; Pres Soph Cls; Pres Jr Cls; VP Stu Cncl; NHS; Law.

BROADNAX, CHRISTINE; Westside HS; Newark, NJ; (Y); Church Yth Grp; Dance Clb; GAA; JCL; Church Choir; Yrbk Stf; Stu Cncl; Tennis; Trk; Hon Roll; Howard U; Dancer.

BROADWATER, MICHAEL; Millville SR HS; Millville, NJ; (Y); 7/440; Am Leg Boys St; Church Yth Grp; Cmnty Wkr; Science Clb; SADD; Computer Clb; NHS; JV Bsbl; Im Bowling; JV Diving; Bys Ldrs Clb 85-86; Engnrng.

BROADWELL, LISA; Westfield SR HS; Westfield, NJ; (Y); 3/514; French Clb; Model UN; Orch; Var Capt Crs Cntry; Var L Trk; French Hon Soc; NHS; Ntl Merit Ltr; Cmnty Wkr; Latin Clb; YMCA Yth Yr Awd 86; 1st Pl Rider Coll Frgn Lang Cmptn 85 & 86; Frnch.

BROADWELL, NANCY E; Hunterdon Central HS; Whitehouse Sta, NJ; (Y); 1/550; Chess Clb; Sec German Clb; Library Aide; Sec Thesps; Orch; School Musical; School Play; Stage Crew; Gov Hon Prg Awd; High Hon Roll; Rutgers U; Englsh.

BROBERG, ERICA; Holmdel HS; Holmdel, NJ; (Y); 70/225; Intnl Clb; SADD; Yrbk Stf; Var Trk; Intr Dsgn.

BROCKMAN, MELISSA; Lakewood HS; Lakewood, NJ; (Y); English Clb; FBLA; SADD; Chorus; Stu Cncl; Cheerleading; Gym; Socr; Trk; Hon Roll; Pres Ftns Awd 82; Lawyer.

BROCKSON, MARGARET; Holy Cross HS; Mount Laurel, NJ; (Y); Church Yth Grp; Nwsp Stf; Yrbk Stf; Lit Mag; High Hon Roll; Hon Roll; Rider Coll; Accntng.

BRODER, HELEN A; Morristown Beard Schl; Short Hills, NJ; (Y); AFS; French Clb; Intnl Clb; Model UN; Science Clb; Hon Roll; Political Wkr; Chorus; Lit Mag; Rep Jr Cls; Yth For Understanding Awd 86; Intern For NJ Assemblywoman 85-86; Peace Corp 84-86; Bicentennial Const; Government.

BRODERICK, COLLEEN; Manchester Township HS; Lakehurst, NJ; (Y); 9/176; Am Leg Aux Girls St; Pres Church Yth Grp; Capt Mrchg Band; Nwsp Stf; Var Capt Pom Pon; L Var Socr; Var Stat Wrstlng; NHS; Cmnty Wkr; High Hon Roll; Pres Acad Ftnss Awd; Ambssdr HOBY Ldrshp Smnr; Trenton ST COLL; Psych.

BRODIE, REGINA; Egg Harbor Township HS; Cardiff, NJ; (Y); 20/266; Drama Clb; Key Clb; Pres Sec Band; Concert Band; Jazz Band; Mrchg Band; Rep Stu Cncl; Stat Bsktbl; Ntl Merit Ltr; Pres Schlr; Natl Engl Merit Awd; Soc Of Dstngshd Amer HS Stu 85-86; Natl Achvt Schlrshp Prgm Outstndng Stu 85-86; Trenton ST Clg; Comp Sci.

BRODKA, ROBERT; Paramus Catholic Boys HS; Garfield, NJ; (Y); 82/178; Computer Clb; Stage Crew; Capt Var Socr; Hon Roll; Prfct Atten Awd; 2nd Tm All-Lg Hnrbl Mntn All-Area 85; Mnlta Slct Tm Div I & II 84-85; Comp Sci.

BRODY, CARL E; New Milford HS; New Milford, NJ; (Y); 7/143; Am Leg Boys St; Ski Clb; Mrchg Band; Orch; Sec Stu Cncl; Var L Socr; Var L Tennis; Var L Trk; French Hon Soc; Jr NHS; Coachs Awd Trck 86; HM All Cnty Socr 85; Bio.

BRODZIAK, MICHAEL; St Marys HS; Sayreville, NJ; (Y); 13/145; Church Yth Grp; Library Aide; Quiz Bowl; Spanish Clb; JV Var Bsbl; Var Bsktbl; Var Crs Cntry; High Hon Roll; Hon Roll; Spanish NHS; Rutgers Coll; Engr.

BROGDEN, CAROLYN; Edgewood SR HS; Atco, NJ; (Y); 14/371; Rep Am Leg Aux Girls St; 4-H; German Clb; Pres Latin Clb; Yrbk Bus Mgr; Yrbk Phtg; Yrbk Stf; Rep Frsh Cls; Rep Soph Cls; Rep Jr Cls; Prom Qn 86; Trenton ST Coll; Psych.

BROGLE, STACYANN; Hamilton High West; Trenton, NJ; (Y); Cmnty Wkr; Key Clb; Chorus; School Musical; School Play; Variety Show; High Hon Roll; Hon Roll; NHS; Danc Comptns 83-86; Congrad All A Reprt Crd 83-85; Math Ed.

BROKAW, BRADFORD; Red Bank Regional HS; Little Silver, NJ; (Y); Boy Scts; Pres Church Yth Grp; Cmnty Wkr; Political Wkr; SADD; School Play; Variety Show; Nwsp Phtg; Nwsp Rptr; Yrbk Stf; Mock Trl Comptn-Cnty Chmpns 86; Stu Coordntr-Hnds Acrss Amer 86; Washngtn Wrkshps-April 85; Jrnlsm.

BROMBERG, JEFFREY; East Brunswick HS; E Brunswick, NJ; (Y); High Hon Roll; Ntl Merit Ltr.

BRONCANO, CARLOS; Memorial HS; West New York, NJ; (Y); Boy Scts; Cmnty Wkr; Library Aide; Spanish Clb; Teachers Aide; Nwsp Rptr; Off Jr Cls; Bsbl; Bsktbl; Coach Actv; Aerontcs.

BRONKEMA, ROBERT; Atlantic City HS; Ventnor, NJ; (Y); 22/446; Church Yth Grp; Cmnty Wkr; Soroptimist; JV Bsktbl; Var Capt Socr; Var Capt Tennis; Pres Schlr; MVP Rec Leag Bsktbl 85; All S Jersey Grp IV Sngls Tennis 86; Columbus Day Band 86; Swarthmore Coll; Mssnry.

BRONSTEIN, JAMIE L; The Pingry Schl; Succasunna, NJ; (Y); Debate Tm; Drama Clb; Temple Yth Grp; Concert Band; Mrchg Band; Nwsp Stf; Yrbk Stf; Lit Mag; NHS; Ntl Merit SF; Pblc Issues & Future NJ Gvrnrs Schl; Comm.

BROOKS, CHRISTOPHER; Lower Cape May Regional HS; Cape May, NJ; (Y); 27/225; Key Clb; Political Wkr; SADD; Nwsp Rptr; Nwsp Stf; Lit Mag; JV Swmmng; JV Trk; Hon Roll; George Washington U; Archlgy.

BROOKS, KIMBERLY; Saint Anthony HS; Jersey City, NJ; (Y); Church Yth Grp; Girl Scts; Band; Church Choir; Trs Sr Cls; Rep Stu Cncl; Bsktbl; Cheerleading; Coach Actv; Mgr(s); Dentistry.

BROOKS, LISA; Shore Regional HS; Oceanport, NJ; (Y); Church Yth Grp; French Clb; Girl Scts; Math Tm; Ski Clb; Nwsp Rptr; High Hon Roll; Engr.

BROOKS, TONYA; Penns Grove HS; Penns Grove, NJ; (Y); 22/177; Am Leg Aux Girls St; Pres Church Yth Grp; JCL; Pres Church Choir; Var Bsktbl; Hon Roll; Merit Typng Awd 85; Altrnate For Rtry Ldrshp Conf 86; Gftd And Tlntd Pgm 86; Psych.

BROPHY, KATHLEEN M; Roxbury HS; Succasunna, NJ; (Y); 25/389; Drama Clb; Quiz Bowl; Chorus; Concert Band; Mrchg Band; School Musical; Swing Chorus; Rep Chrmn Stu Cncl; Ntl Merit SF; St Schlr; Awd Acad Excell; William & Mary Coll.

BROPHY, MICHAEL; Pope John XXIII HS; Newton, NJ; (Y); 23/133; Boy Scts; Drama Clb; Quiz Bowl; Concert Band; Mrchg Band; School Musical; School Play; Lit Mag; Var Tennis; NHS; Military Acad; Hstry.

BROSEN, ANITA; Middlesex HS; Middlesex, NJ; (Y); French Clb; Sec Band; Hon Roll; Vrsty Lttrs Mrchng Cncrt Bnd 85-86; Stu Dance Ballt 12 Yrs 74-86; Psychology.

BROSSE, MIKE; South Brunswick HS; Monmouth Jct, NJ; (Y); 4/250; Math Tm; Bsktbl; Var Tennis; High Hon Roll; Mu Alp Tht; NHS; Ntl Merit Ltr; Spanish NHS; Law.

BROSSOIE, MICHELLE; Red Bank Regional HS; Little Silver, NJ; (Y); Cmnty Wkr; French Clb; Stage Crew; French Hon Soc; High Hon Roll; Hon Roll; NHS; Acad Ftns Awd 86; Rutger Douglas; Spch Pathlgy.

BROUGHAM JR, THOMAS J; Rahway HS; Rahway, NJ; (Y); Church Choir; Church Yth Grp; Tennis; Hon Roll; Rutgers; Fnancl Plnnr.

BROUGHMAN, JO ANN; Clayton HS; Clayton, NJ; (Y); Girl Scts; Mrchg Band; Yrbk Stf; Var Bsktbl; Var Cheerleading; JV Var Sftbl; Hon Roll; Camp Fr Inc; Pep Clb; Im Powder Puff Ftbl; Girls High Game 83; 1st Pl Girls Double 83; 1st Pl Lions Clb 83; Glassboro ST Coll; Mgt.

BROWER, DONNA; Mc Corristin HS; Trenton, NJ; (Y); Church Yth Grp; Hosp Aide; Church Choir; Off Stu Cncl; Hon Roll; Trenton ST; Parlgl.

BROWER, PAM; Midland Park HS; Midland Park, NJ; (S); Church Yth Grp; DECA; Pep Clb; Varsity Clb; Band; Chorus; Church Choir; Mrchg Band; JV Var Cheerleading; Hon Roll; Typeathon 85; Note Taker Deaf Stu Awds 83-85; Chld Psych.

BROWN, ANDREW; Hopewell Valley Central HS; Hopewell, NJ; (Y); Church Yth Grp; Cmnty Wkr; Debate Tm; German Clb; Chorus; JV Var Golf; Hon Roll; Corp Lwyr.

BROWN, AURELIA; John F Kennedy HS; Willingboro, NJ; (Y); Cmnty Wkr; Intnl Clb; Pep Clb; Spanish Clb; SADD; Yrbk Rptr; JV Capt Fld Hcky; JV Capt Lcrss; Trk; Hon Roll; Statue Of Liberty Essay Cntst SF 86; JV La Crosse MVP 85; Sadd Fndr 85-86; Westchester U; Sprts Med.

BROWN, CARMELITA; Clifton HS; Clifton, NJ; (Y); Office Aide; Spanish Clb; Church Choir; Drm Mjr(t); Yrbk Stf; Sec Soph Cls; Rep Jr Cls; Mgr(s); Twrlr; Spanish NHS; NJ USA Teen MISS SF 85; Miss Teen Passaic Cnty 85-86; Nwsp Hnr Rl 84; Dancing & Bowlng Awds; Lawyer.

BROWN, CHERI LYNN; Arthur P Schalick HS; Elmer, NJ; (Y); 7/128; Math Tm; Pres Jr Cls; Pres Sr Cls; Rep Stu Cncl; Fld Hcky; Sftbl; Hon Roll; NHS; Pres Schlr; Campbell U Pres Scholar 86; Elon Coll Trustees Scholar 86; Elon Coll; Bus Adm.

BROWN, CHERYL A; Mc Corristin Catholic HS; Trenton, NJ; (Y); 55/213; Hon Roll; Fash Illstrtn.

BROWN, CHRISTOPHER; Hudson Catholic HS; Jersey City, NJ; (Y); 90/201; Dance Clb; Bsbl; Bsktbl; Acctg.

BROWN, CORBIN; Williamstown HS; Williamstown, NJ; (Y); Church Yth Grp; Library Aide; Office Aide; Band; Mrchg Band; Variety Show; Wt Lftg; Hon Roll; 2nd Pl NJ Voc Arts; Glassboro ST Coll; Music.

BROWN, CYNTHIA L; Millville SR HS; Millville, NJ; (Y); 10/468; Debate Tm; French Clb; Intnl Clb; Political Wkr; SADD; Ed Lit Mag; JV Golf; Var Capt Socr; High Hon Roll; NHS; Dstngshd Achvt Awd; Fresh Schlrshp US FL; PTSA Schlrshp; U FL; Intl Relations.

BROWN, DAWN E; Spotswood HS; Spotswood, NJ; (Y); 69/160; Church Yth Grp; German Clb; Hosp Aide; Intnl Clb; Ski Clb; Varsity Clb; Band; Mrchg Band; Socr; Hon Roll; Brigham Young U; Zoolgy.

BROWN, DONNA; Cinnaminson HS; Cinna, NJ; (Y); 43/257; German Clb; Orch; JV Socr; High Hon Roll; Hon Roll; Prsdntl Acdmc Ftns Awd 85-86; Bermuda Karate Chmpnshp 83; Vrs Karate Awds; Rutgers U; Nrsng.

BROWN, GREG; Ocean Twp HS; Neptune, NJ; (Y); Aud/Vis; Boy Scts; Computer Clb; Exploring; Nwsp Rptr; Score Keeper; Timer; Hon Roll; Comp Sci.

BROWN, HEIDI; Lakewood HS; Lakewood, NJ; (Y); 19/300; Church Yth Grp; English Clb; Ed Lit Mag; Stat Ftbl; Var Socr; Hon Roll; NHS; Engl.

BROWN, HILARY; Bishop George Ahr HS; E Brunswick, NJ; (Y); 18/300; Church Yth Grp; Cmnty Wkr; French Clb; Model UN; Concert Band; Mrchg Band; School Musical; Hon Roll; NHS; NEDT Awd.

BROWN, JEFFREY; Maple Shade HS; Maple Shade, NJ; (Y); French Clb; Var JV Bsbl; Bsktbl; Var JV Socr; Im Vllybl; High Hon Roll; Hon Roll; Prfct Atten Awd; Arch.

BROWN, JEN; Lakeland Regional HS; Ringwood, NJ; (Y); 30/332; Acpl Chr; Chorus; Madrigals; School Play; High Hon Roll; Hon Roll; NHS; Var Ltr Fencng Tm 85-86; JV Ltr Fencing Tm 83-84; 3 Gld Medls At Intl Music Festvls 84-86.

BROWN, LARS; Belvidere HS; Belvidere, NJ; (Y); 5/118; Am Leg Boys St; Boy Scts; Varsity Clb; Bsbl; Ftbl; High Hon Roll; NHS; VFW Awd; Debate Tm; Drama Clb; 3 Yr NROTC Schlrshp 86; Eagle Scout Awd; Teal Scout Awd; ME Maritime Acad; Marine Engr.

BROWN, LISA; Woodrow Wilson HS; Camden, NJ; (Y); 4-H; Latin Clb; Acpl Chr; Chorus; Church Choir; Socr; Trk; Hon Roll; Med.

BROWN, LORETTA; Roselle Catholic HS; Roselle, NJ; (Y); 70/200; Church Yth Grp; Cmnty Wkr; GAA; Political Wkr; Teachers Aide; JV Bowling; JV Var Socr; Im Vllybl; Hon Roll; NHS; Spch Pthlgst.

BROWN, MICHELE; Hackettstown HS; Belvidere, NJ; (Y); Girl Scts; Band; Concert Band; Jazz Band; Mrchg Band; Orch; Fld Hcky; Trk; Hon Roll; Eng Tchr.

BROWN, PATRICIA; Union Catholic Regional HS; Elizabeth, NJ; (Y); Office Aide; Service Clb; Nwsp Stf; Hon Roll; Jhnsn & Wls Acdmc Schlrshp 86-87; Fairleigh Dickinson U; Htl Mgmt.

BROWN, RICHARD; Monsignor Donovan HS; Jackson, NJ; (Y); 118/254; Ski Clb; Jazz Band; Hon Roll; Science.

BROWN, ROBIN; Kingsway Regional HS; Harrisonville, NJ; (Y); 5/163; Office Aide; Concert Band; Mrchg Band; Var Capt Bsktbl; Var Capt Fld Hcky; Var Sftbl; Var Capt Trk; DAR Awd; High Hon Roll; Sec NHS; Hcky-Hnrb Mntn Tri-Cnty Glster Cnty Sth Jrsy/Bsktbl-1st Tm Tri-Cnty Glcter Cnty 84-85; Mt Union Coll; Sprts Med.

BROWN, ROBINETTE; Eastside HS; Paterson, NJ; (S); 2/440; Library Aide; Office Aide; Concert Band; Jazz Band; Nwsp Stf; Yrbk Stf; Hon Roll; NHS; Garden St Dist Schlr 86; Trenton ST Coll; Acctg.

BROWN, ROSEMARIE; Egg Harbor Township HS; Linwood, NJ; (S); 11/266; SADD; Yrbk Stf; Rep Stu Cncl; Hon Roll; NHS; 2nd Pl ACCS Bus Sympsm; Rider; Acctng.

BROWN, SCOTT M; Cherry Hill HS West; Cherry Hill, NJ; (Y); Chess Clb; Church Yth Grp; French Clb; ROTC; Bowling; Cherry Vly Civic Assn Schlrshp 86; Karate Blck Blt 84; Drexel U; Comp Sci.

BROWN, SHANYNE LASHON; Mother Seton Regional HS; Elizabeth, NJ; (Y); GAA; JA; Pep Clb; Church Choir; Drill Tm; Yrbk Stf; Off Sr Cls; Pom Pon; Elks Awd; Hon Roll; Womens Schlrshp Clb Elizabeth 86; Roselle Catholic Schlrshp Olympcs 82; City U Of NY; Crmnl Jstc.

BROWN, SHAWNETTE; Irvington Tech HS; Newark, NJ; (Y); 11/75; Girl Scts; Church Choir; Yrbk Stf; Var Bsktbl; Var Trk; Hon Roll; Montclair Coll.

BROWN, STEFANIE; Paul VI HS; Magnolia, NJ; (S); 6/544; Math Clb; Spanish Clb; Pom Pon; High Hon Roll; Hon Roll; John Hopkins U; Med.

BROWN, STEPHEN; Plainfield HS; Plainfield, NJ; (Y); Aud/Vis; Boys Clb Am; Boy Scts; Cmnty Wkr; Debate Tm; Political Wkr; Science Clb; Rep Soph Cls; Var Bsbl; Var Bsktbl; Model Congress Awd 86; Political Sci.

BROWN, TAWANA; Deptford Twnshp HS; Wenonah, NJ; (Y); 19/283; Chorus; Concert Band; JV Bsktbl; Var Cheerleading; Var Fld Hcky; JV Sftbl; Hon Roll; Jr NHS; NHS; Prfct Atten Awd; Tenor I Sctn Ldr All Sth Jrsy Chrs 86; Music.

BROWN, TELEEA; Lakewood HS; Lakewood, NJ; (Y); 142/275; Computer Clb; FBLA; Letterman Clb; Pep Clb; Coach Actv; Crs Cntry; Trk; Hon Roll; Ntl Merit Ltr; Prfct Atten Awd; GA Crt Coll Upward Bnd Prject Cmpltn Awd 86; Cert Of Aprctn As Spnsr Of Spcl Olympcs 85; Brkdl CC; Physcl Thrpy.

BROWN JR, THEODORE; Trenton Central HS; Trenton, NJ; (Y); Boy Scts; Chess Clb; Church Yth Grp; DECA; Bsktbl; Coach Actv; Ftbl; Trk; MD Estrn Shore Clg; Comp.

BROWN, THERESA; Memorial HS; North Bergen, NJ; (Y); Art Clb; French Clb; Hosp Aide; Yrbk Stf; Rep Frsh Cls; Rep Soph Cls; Bowling; Hon Roll; W New York Teen Art Awd 85; Med.

BROWN, TRACEY; Millville SR HS; Port Norris, NJ; (Y); Office Aide; Ski Clb; Spanish Clb; Nwsp Rptr; Yrbk Sprt Ed; Rep Stu Cncl; Var Crs Cntry; Var Trk; Im Vllybl; Hon Roll; Bus Adm.

BROWN, WENDY; Salem HS; Salem, NJ; (Y); VP Art Clb; Computer Clb; FBLA; JA; Spanish Clb; Rep Stu Cncl; Hon Roll; NHS; Var Cheerleading; Data Prcssng.

BROWN III, WILLIAM E; Somerville HS; Somerville, NJ; (Y); 10/226; German Clb; Letterman Clb; Ski Clb; Rep Stu Cncl; Var L Bsbl; Var L Socr; DAR Awd; High Hon Roll; NHS; NEDT Awd; 3 Yr Army ROTC Schlrshp 86; Amer Legion Awd 86; DAR Ldrshp & Patrtsm Awd 86; Lafayette Coll.

BROWNE, LORRIE; Union Catholic Regional HS; Scotch Plains, NJ; (Y); 21/300; Ski Clb; SADD; Nwsp Rptr; Nwsp Stf; Trs Sr Cls; JV Bsktbl; Var Golf; JV Sftbl; Var Tennis; High Hon Roll.

BROWNE, NINA M; Ridgewood HS; Paterson, NJ; (Y); 22/495; Science Clb; Nwsp Phtg; High Hon Roll; NHS; Pres Schlr; Natl Endwmnt Humanties Yng Schlr Awd 86; Barnard College.

BROWNING, PAUL; Morristown-Beard HS; Madison, NJ; (Y); 2/80; Quiz Bowl; Lit Mag; JV Crs Cntry; JV Trk; French Hon Soc; High Hon Roll; Jr NHS; NHS; Ntl Merit SF; Rensslr Mdl Math & Sci 86; Brown U; Engrng.

BROWNLEE, MICHELLE; The Hun Schl; Cranbury, NJ; (Y); 2/107; Drama Clb; Pres French Clb; Math Tm; Ski Clb; Var Fld Hcky; Var Lcrss; Var Sftbl; Var Swmmng; Ntl Merit SF; Sal; Paul R Cheseboro Sltry Awd 86; Rnsslr Math & Sci Mdl 85; Wllsly Bk Awd 85; Dartmouth Coll; Intl Rltns.

BROZEK, JEFF; Bridgewater-Raritan HS East; Bridgewater, NJ; (Y); Computer Clb; JV Bsbl; Var L Bsktbl; Var L Ftbl; Im Wt Lftg; Hon Roll; NHS; Hnrs Courses; Engrng.

BROZNAK, PETER; Spotswood HS; Spotswood, NJ; (S); 10/189; Math Tm; Model UN; VP Science Clb; JV Ftbl; Var Trk; Hon Roll; NHS; Astrophyscst.

BROZYNA, COREY; Seton Hall Prep; W Orange, NJ; (Y); 41/187; Computer Clb; Key Clb; Spanish Clb; Band; JV Var Wrstlng; Hon Roll; Accounting.

BROZYNA, ELIZABETH; Toms River High School South; Toms River, NJ; (Y); 5/360; Mrchg Band; Symp Band; Ed Yrbk Stf; High Hon Roll; NHS; Prfct Atten Awd; Wmns Clb Awds Hghst Fml Grd Pnt Avrg 84-85; 1st Pl Awds In Ltry Div Cltrl Olympcs 84-85; Anthropolgy.

BRUCA, GLENN; Cinnaminson HS; Cinna, NJ; (Y); Am Leg Boys St; Church Yth Grp; Math Clb; Science Clb; Var Socr; Var Tennis; NHS; Prfct Atten Awd; Rotary Awd; Govrs Schl Schlr 86; Engrng.

BRUCE, ERIC BRENDAN; Mater Dei HS; Middletown, NJ; (Y); 7/165; Pres Exploring; Trs Latin Clb; Math Clb; Model UN; School Musical; Nwsp Stf; Trs Stu Cncl; Trk; NHS; St Schlr; Brnz Cngrssnl Awd 85; Mater Dei Stu Of Qtr 84; Slvr Mdl Amrcn Clsscl Ltn Awd 83; Lafayette Coll; Engnrng.

BRUCE, MARLA; Middletown High Sch South; Middletown, NJ; (S); 11/436; Model UN; Yrbk Stf; Off Soph Cls; Off Jr Cls; Off Sr Cls; VP Fld Hcky; VP Lcrss; Capt L Tennis; Jr NHS; NHS; Congoleum Srve Stroke & Volley 2nd Pl 83; Middletwn Pks Mixed JR 1st Pl 83; 2nd Pl Racqt Clb 84.

BRUDON, DANIEL; Overbrook HS; Pine Hill, NJ; (Y); VP DECA; Office Aide; Spanish Clb; Teachers Aide; Yrbk Phtg; Yrbk Rptr; Yrbk Stf; Golf; Hon Roll; Yrbk JR Edtr; Widener Coll; Bus Cnsltnt.

BRUGAL, MAGGIN; Emerson HS; Union City, NJ; (Y); French Clb; Chorus; Yrbk Stf; Rep Stu Cncl; Bsktbl; Crs Cntry; Trk; Wt Lftg; Hon Roll; Seton Hall U; Lawyer.

BRUH, RONALD W; The Peddle Schl; E Windsor, NJ; (Y); Am Leg Boys St; Cmnty Wkr; Spanish Clb; Temple Yth Grp; Yrbk Stf; Var JV Bsbl; Var JV Bsktbl; Mathematics.

BRUMANT, ROLSTON JOSEPH; Frank H HS; Irvington, NJ; (Y); Am Leg Boys St; JV Var Socr; High Hon Roll; Hon Roll; Stephens Inst Tech; Mech Engr.

BRUMANT, RONNIE; Frank H Morrell HS; Irvington, NJ; (Y); Am Leg Boys St; JV L Bsbl; Var Capt Socr; Hon Roll; Civil Engr.

BRUNHOUSE, MELISSA; Westfield HS; Westfield, NJ; (Y); 121/525; GAA; Spanish Clb; Varsity Clb; Chorus; Var L Fld Hcky; Socr; Hon Roll; Lit Mag; Awd Tchrs Bst Stdnt Hstry 84; Poem Wrttn Spnsh Publ Schl Lang Mgzn 86; 3 Yrs Vrsty Fld Hcky 86-87.

BRUNO, ANGELA M; Cinnaminson HS; Cinnaminson, NJ; (Y); 26/256; Drama Clb; Math Tm; Thesps; Chorus; School Play; Stage Crew; Var Capt Bowling; NHS; Ntl Merit Ltr; Prfct Atten Awd; Tmstrs Lcl 107 Schlrshp 86; Edward Nangle Schlrshp 86; U Of VA; Engrng.

BRUNO, CHRIS; Holy Spirit HS; Mays Landing, NJ; (Y); 5/348; Hosp Aide; Yrbk Stf; High Hon Roll; NHS; Silver Mdl Ntl Ltn Exam, Histry Awd & Englsh Awds 85; PA U; Med.

BRUNO, CRISTIE; West Orange HS; W Orange, NJ; (Y); Spanish Clb; Band; Chorus; Concert Band; Lit Mag; Stat Wrstlng; Hon Roll; Jr NHS; Jr Hnr Guard 86; Sci Expo 84-86; Med Tech.

BRUNO, DANIELE E; Haddon Township HS; Westmont, NJ; (Y); 3/172; Am Leg Aux Girls St; Varsity Clb; Stage Crew; Var Capt Fld Hcky; High Hon Roll; NHS; Sal; Mgr(s); Score Keeper; Stat Sftbl; Pres Schrp 86-90; Outstndg Stu Awd 86; Alfred Litwak Awd All Arnd Stu 86; American U; Intl Bus.

BRUNO, DEBORAH ANN; Watching Hills Regional HS; Warren, NJ; (Y); 27/258; SADD; Rep Frsh Cls; Rep Soph Cls; Rep Jr Cls; Stu Cncl; Bsktbl; Cheerleading; Coach Actv; Sftbl; Hon Roll; Chrldg Capt 84; Coach-Chrldg & Judg For Sqds 83-86; Electn Bd Stu 85-86; Bus.

BRUNO, MARIANNE; Wall HS; Wall Township, NJ; (Y); Nwsp Rptr; Nwsp Stf; VP Frsh Cls; Sec Soph Cls; Trs Jr Cls; Off Sr Cls; Capt Cheerleading; Church Yth Grp; Yrbk Rptr; Yrbk Stf; Law.

BRUNO, MARISSA; Sacred Heart HS; Vineland, NJ; (S); 18/67; Church Yth Grp; FNA; Spanish Clb; School Play; Yrbk Stf; Elem Ed.

BRUNO, RICHIE; Morris Catholic HS; Boonton, NJ; (Y); 85/142; Drama Clb; Chorus; School Musical; School Play; Variety Show; Trk; Wrstlng; Prfrmng Arts.

BRUNSKILL, LYNN A; Morris Knolls HS; Denville, NJ; (Y); Art Clb; Drama Clb; 4-H; Library Aide; Teachers Aide; 4-H Awd; Gov Hon Prg Awd; High Hon Roll; Hon Roll; VFW Awd; Summr Arts Inst 84; Sch Of Arts 85; Rutgers U; Tchg.

BRUNSWON, TAMMY; Highland Park HS; Highland Park, NJ; (Y); 43/131; Trs German Clb; Pres SADD; Band; Mrchg Band; Sec Jr Cls; Pres Sr Cls; Sec Stu Cncl; JV Bsktbl; Var Tennis; Hon Roll; Rutgers Schlrs Prgm 85-86; Girls State 85; Howard U; Intl Bus.

BRUSCO, ROSANNA E; Palisades Park JR-SR HS; Palisades Pk, NJ; (Y); 20/122; Drama Clb; Chorus; School Musical; Variety Show; Nwsp Stf; Yrbk Stf; Var JV Tennis; Hon Roll; NHS; Italian Day Fordham U 85; $250 Schlrshp Mem Of T Gaiazzo Gvn By Babe Ruth Lge 86; Rutgers U; Accntng.

BRUZAITIS, ERIC MASON; Manchester Township HS; Toms River, NJ; (Y); Am Leg Boys St; Drama Clb; French Clb; Science Clb; School Play; Stage Crew; Variety Show; Nwsp Stf; Yrbk Phtg; Pres Stu Cncl; Mason Gross; Arts.

BRYAN, PAUL; Lakeland Regional HS; Wanaque, NJ; (Y); 13/303; Art Clb; Math Tm; Nwsp Ed-Chief; Lit Mag; High Hon Roll; Hon Roll; NHS; NEDT Awd; Rotary Awd; NJ Grdn ST Schlr 86; Ramapo Coll NJ.

BRYANT, BONNIE; Delsea Regional HS; Franklinville, NJ; (Y); L Church Yth Grp; FHA; JV Sftbl; Var Hon Roll; Bus Mgr.

BRYANT, DEBBIE; Manalapan HS; Englishtown, NJ; (Y); Church Yth Grp; Cmnty Wkr; Hosp Aide; Kiwanis Awd; Bus Adm.

BRYCE, JOSEPH; Lakewood HS; Lakewood, NJ; (Y); 2/275; Pres Stu Cncl; Var Capt Bsbl; Var Capt Socr; NHS; Ntl Merit Ltr; Sal; St Schlr; Am Leg Boys St; English Clb; Band; Golden Nugget Schlrshp, Athlete/Schlr Awd & All-ST/Soccer & Bsbl 86; U Of MD; Politics.

BRYNGIL, DAVID; St Peters Prep; Weehawken, NJ; (Y); 24/209; Sec Intnl Clb; Nwsp Stf; Lit Mag; Stu Cncl; Var L Trk; Hon Roll; Hugh O Brian Yth Ambsdr 85; Prep Schl Spirit Awd 86; All Cnty Track Team 86; Englsh.

BRZOZOWSKI, JAMES; Manasquan HS; Spring Lake Hts, NJ; (Y); Drama Clb; Stage Crew; Yrbk Stf; JV Ftbl; High Hon Roll; Board Of Edu Awd 86; Engnrng.

BRZOZOWSKI, KEN; South River HS; S River, NJ; (Y); 13/160; Am Leg Boys St; Computer Clb; VP French Clb; Variety Show; JV Var Bsbl; JV Im Bsktbl; Im Var Ftbl; Var Trk; High Hon Roll; Hon Roll; All Acad Tm-Sprts & Schlstc Awds 85-86; Arch.

BUCCI, CHRISTOPHER; Morris Catholic HS; Oakridge, NJ; (Y); Aud/Vis; Boy Scts; Cmnty Wkr; French Clb; FBLA; Library Aide; School Musical; School Play; JV Bsktbl; JV Ftbl; Acctng.

BUCCI, JANINE; Riverside HS; Delanco, NJ; (S); Drama Clb; Ski Clb; School Play; Yrbk Stf; Fld Hcky; Mgr(s); Score Keeper; Psych.

BUCCI, LISA; Bridgewater-Raritan H S West; Raritan, NJ; (Y); French Clb; Office Aide; Band; Color Guard; Mrchg Band; Yrbk Stf; High Hon Roll; Hon Roll; Jr NHS; NHS; Presdntl Acad Ftnss Awd 86; Outstndng Ovrll Intrst Dedctn Bus Ed 86; Berkeley Awd 86; Rutgers; Bus.

BUCCI, MARIA; Mount Saint Dominic Acad; Orange, NJ; (Y); Yrbk Phtg; Hon Roll; NHS; Arch.

BUCCINE, KATHLEEN; Hunterdon Central HS; Whitehouse Sta, NJ; (Y); 47/539; Church Yth Grp; Service Clb; Ski Clb; Band; Stage Crew; Off Jr Cls; Off Sr Cls; Hon Roll; NHS; Boston Coll; Nrsng.

BUCHANAN, ELIZABETH; Wildwood Catholic HS; Wildwood Crest, NJ; (Y); 12/110; French Clb; Hosp Aide; Yrbk Phtg; Yrbk Rptr; Yrbk Stf; Stu Cncl; Var Capt Tennis; High Hon Roll; Hon Roll; NHS; MVP Awd Tnns 84-85; Math Awd 85-86; Sci Fair 2nd Pl Chem 85-86; Rutgers; Clin Psychol.

BUCHICHIO, CHRISANN B; Wetwood Regional HS; Washington Twp, NJ; (Y); 26/226; French Clb; Ski Clb; Variety Show; Capt Fld Hcky; VP French Hon Soc; High Hon Roll; Hon Roll; NHS; Fordham 1; Fin.

BUCHOLTZ, MONIQUE; St Mary HS; S Amboy, NJ; (Y); 13/125; Spanish Clb; Hon Roll; Spanish NHS; Dermatlgst.

BUCHOLTZ, SARA; Solomon Schechter Day Schl; Maplewood, NJ; (Y); AFS; Temple Yth Grp; Varsity Clb; Cmnty Wkr; Drama Clb; School Play; Yrbk Ed-Chief; Ed Yrbk Stf; Stu Cncl; Var L Tennis; Natl Ed Dev Outstndng,JEA Israel Fnlst, Press Assn Cnvtn; NHS; UJA Fed Teen Lrshp,Intl Quis Jewish.

BUCK, JOHN; South Branswick HS; Dayton, NJ; (Y); 47/250; Boy Scts; Church Yth Grp; Ski Clb; Spanish Clb; Ski Clb; Pres Stu Cncl; Var L Ftbl; Var L Trk; Im Vllybl; Im Wt Lftg; Aerospc Engrng.

BUCKLEY, CATHY; Chatham HS; Chatham, NJ; (Y); 53/126; Church Yth Grp; German Clb; VP Latin Clb; School Play; Ed Nwsp Stf; Pres Soph Cls; Pres Jr Cls; Rep Sr Cls; Capt Cheerleading; Trk; Political Sci.

BUCKLEY, ELLEN; St Rose HS; Sea Girt, NJ; (Y); Church Yth Grp; Exploring; Key Clb; SADD; Lit Mag; Vllybl; High Hon Roll; Hon Roll; NHS; Ntl Merit SF; Bio.

BUCKLEY, KEVIN; Roselle Catholic HS; Elizabeth, NJ; (Y); Ski Clb; JV Bsbl; Im Bsktbl; JV Wrstlng; Bst Def Plyr Bsbl 85 & 86; Oceanogrphy.

BUCKLEY, PATRICK; Monsignor Donovan HS; Lanoka Harbor, NJ; (Y); 11/214; Am Leg Boys St; Math Clb; VP Sr Cls; Var L Bsbl; Pres NHS; Nw Jrsy Dstngshd Schlr Awd 85-86; 4 Yr Rotc Schlrshp Us Air Frc 85-86; Apntmt Us Cst Grd Acad 90; Us Air Frc Acad; Engrng.

BUCKLEY, SCOTT; Westwood HS; Westwood, NJ; (Y); Boy Scts; Church Yth Grp; Band; Concert Band; Mrchg Band; Var Bsbl; Var Socr; JV Wrstlng.

BUCKMAN, GAIL; Lower Cape May Regional HS; Cape May, NJ; (Y); Office Aide; Teachers Aide; CC Awd; Hon Roll; NHS; Prfct Atten Awd; Bus Stdnt Qrtr 85-86; Floyd Oliver Memrl Awd 86; Lwr Twnshp Moose Lodg 86; Fshn Merch.

BUCKMAN, LISA; Manasquan HS; Belmar, NJ; (Y); 1/234; Key Clb; Band; Drm Mjr(t); Jazz Band; Symp Band; Cheerleading; Hon Roll; Kiwanis Awd; NHS; Garden ST Schlrshp; Brd Of Educ Awd; Var Schlrshp; Rutgers U; Engrng.

BUCKWALTER, MARK; Moorestown Friends Schl; Medford, NJ; (Y); Am Leg Boys St; Model UN; Ed Yrbk Sprt Ed; Rep Sr Cls; Rep Stu Cncl; JV Var Socr; Hon Roll; Ntl Merit Ltr; Spanish NHS; JR Rotarian 84-85; Lafayette; Bus.

BUDA, CHUCK; St John Vianney HS; Manalapan, NJ; (Y); Boy Scts; Computer Clb; Ski Clb; SADD; School Musical; School Play; Ed Yrbk Stf; Lit Mag; Rep Soph Cls; Ftbl; Gold & White Awd; Outstndng Merit Spch & Drama Awd; Elec Engrng.

BUDAVARI, ADRIANE; Watchung Hills Regional HS; Watchung, NJ; (Y); AFS; Key Clb; Scholastic Bowl; SADD; Capt Var Bsktbl; Var Fld Hcky; Var Sftbl; High Hon Roll; Hon Roll; NHS; Cptn Of Bsktbll Team 83; Neuro Sci.

BUDDEN, RAY; Burlington City HS; Burlington, NJ; (Y); Am Leg Boys St; VP Church Yth Grp; FBLA; Nwsp Ed-Chief; Var Socr; Var Tennis; Hon Roll; NHS; Trenton ST Coll; Crmnl Just.

BUDGIN, JEANNE; Morris Catholic HS; Boonton, NJ; (Y); 18/142; Church Yth Grp; Cmnty Wkr; German Clb; Hosp Aide; Office Aide; School Play; Yrbk Stf; Powder Puff Ftbl; 4-H Awd; High Hon Roll; Ntl Lang Arts Olympd 83-84; 1st Hnrs-10 Qrtrs, 2nd Hnrs-2 Qrtrs 83-86.

BUDOWSKY, DAVID A; Secaucus HS; Secaucus, NJ; (Y); Am Leg Boys St; Computer Clb; Key Clb; Math Clb; NY U; Cmdts Flr Trd.

BUDZISKI, PATRICIA; Dover HS; Mine Hill, NJ; (Y); Church Yth Grp; French Clb; Math Tm; Ski Clb; Yrbk Stf; UCLA; Music Recrdng.

BUECHEL, FREDERICK; Seton Hall Prep; W Orange, NJ; (Y); Key Clb; Varsity Clb; Rep Jr Cls; JV Bsbl; L Ftbl; Var L Wrstlng; High Hon Roll; NEDT Awd; Pre-Med.

BUFFALINO, CARL; South River HS; So River, NJ; (Y); 17/150; Spanish Clb; Chorus; School Musical; Bsbl; Var L Bsktbl; Ftbl; Var Capt Golf; Var Capt Socr; Im Vllybl; Hon Roll; Hrtcltr Clb 85-87; Engrng.

BUFFINGTON, MELISSA; New Milford HS; New Milford, NJ; (Y); Art Clb; Cmnty Wkr; Mrchg Band; Sec Jr Cls; Pres Stu Cncl; Var Crs Cntry; Var Trk; Band; Concert Band; Pep Band; Rutgers St Champ Mt Track 86; NY U; Advertising.

BUFFO, TIM; Overbrook HS; Albion, NJ; (Y); Stage Crew; Bsktbl; Ftbl; Trk; Hon Roll; Most Outstndg Field Man Trck 86; Bryant Coll; Accntng.

BUFFOLINO, ROCCO; Bishop George Ahr HS; Hopelawn, NJ; (Y); 88/300; Bowling; Im Socr; Elect Engr.

BUFFONGE, SAMUEL A; The Lawrenceville Schl; Hyde Park, MA; (Y); Debate Tm; Church Choir; JV Var Wrstlng; NHS; Church Yth Grp; Intnl Clb; Stage Crew; Rep Soph Cls; Rep Stu Cncl; JV Diving; MA Yth Ldrshp Smnr 83.

BUGG, RONALD; Marist HS; Jersey City, NJ; (Y); Var Bsktbl; Capt Ftbl; Wt Lftg; All Cnfrnc, All Cnty & All ST In Ftbl 85 & 86; Dream Team 85 & 86; Bus.

BUKOWSKI, WILLIAM; Roselle Catholic HS; Linden, NJ; (Y); Service Clb; Vllybl; NHS; Spanish NHS; Elec Engrng.

BULER, KELLEY J; Delran HS; Delran, NJ; (Y); 18/180; Am Leg Aux Girls St; Science Clb; Yrbk Ed-Chief; Capt Tennis; Hon Roll; NHS; Pres Schlr; Yrbk Phtg; Yrbk Rptr; Yrbk Sprt Ed; Delran Schl Admin Awd 86; Hugh O Brian Yth Ldrshp Awd 84; Prncpls Awd-Outstndng Svc To The Schl 86; PA St U; Arch.

BULGAR, MICHELLE; Bruriah HS; Hillside, NJ; (Y); Computer Clb; English Clb; Temple Yth Grp; Yrbk Ed-Chief; NHS; Acpl Chr; Advrtsng.

BULGER, JOSEPH B; Pequannock Twp HS; Pequannock, NJ; (Y); 4/203; Am Leg Boys St; Varsity Clb; Stu Cncl; Var Capt Bsktbl; Var Ftbl; Var Capt Trk; High Hon Roll; Jr NHS; NHS; Ntl Merit SF; 12-Pack 85-87.

BULLARD, KISHA; Trenton HS; Trenton, NJ; (Y); Church Yth Grp; Chorus; Sec Church Choir; Socr; JV Trk; Hon Roll.

BULLOCK, CALANDRA; Holy Spirit HS; Pleasantville, NJ; (Y); Church Yth Grp; Cmnty Wkr; Dance Clb; Drama Clb; FNA; Library Aide; Chorus; Church Choir; School Play; Temple U; Phys Thrpy.

BULLOCK, KIRK; Hamilton High School East; Trenton, NJ; (Y); 83/327; Church Yth Grp; Var Capt Ice Hcky; Var JV Socr; Hon Roll; U Of DE; Landscpe.

BULLOCK, RYAN; Pemberton Twp HS No 2; Pemberton, NJ; (Y); Am Leg Boys St; Concert Band; Drm & Bgl; Jazz Band; Mrchg Band; Stage Crew; Rep Stu Cncl; Capt L Crs Cntry; Hon Roll; Prfct Atten Awd; MVP Awd Crss Cntry 85; Perf Atten Awd 84; Hornet Awd 83, 86; Trk Awd Wntr Trk Awds; Grambling ST U; Arch.

BULVANOSKI, CHRISTINA; Matawan HS; Matawan, NJ; (S); 14/315; Math Clb; Concert Band; Drm Mjr(t); Jazz Band; Mrchg Band; School Musical; Sec Soph Cls; Sec Jr Cls; Stu Cncl; Hon Roll; Outstndng Mus 84; Arch.

BUMBER, KIMBERLY; Southern Regional HS; Manahawkin, NJ; (Y); Dance Clb; GAA; VP Math Clb; VP Math Tm; VP Spanish Clb; Rptr Lit Mag; Im JV Sftbl; High Hon Roll; Hon Roll; NHS; Athlt Acdmc Awd 84-85; Elem Ed.

BUNCH, MICHELE; Marylawn Of The Oranges HS; Newark, NJ; (Y); Church Yth Grp; Spanish Clb; Chorus; Church Choir; School Musical; School Play; Nwsp Phtg; Nwsp Stf; Hon Roll; Spanish NHS; Schlrshp 83; Piano Tchrs Scty America 83 & 86; Music Eductrs Assoc NJ 85; Pre Med.

BUNDY, ERICA S; Elizabeth HS; Elizabeth, NJ; (Y); 8/800; Key Clb; Latin Clb; Spanish Clb; Yrbk Stf; Trk; High Hon Roll; NHS; Spanish NHS; Drama Clb; NFL; Malson Rice Memrl Awd 86; Hspnc Hnr Soc 86; Prncpls, Sprtndts Schlr 84-86; Rutgers; Comms.

BUNDY, RACHEL; Toms River High Schl North; Toms River, NJ; (Y); Church Yth Grp; Teachers Aide; Acpl Chr; Band; Chorus; Church Choir; Jazz Band; Mrchg Band; Swing Chorus; Symp Band; Elem Educ.

BUNKER, BRETT; Chatham Twp HS; Chatham Twp, NJ; (Y); 5/126; Key Clb; VP Sr Cls; Bsbl; Socr; High Hon Roll; NHS.

BUONCRISTIANO, PATRICIA; St Pius X HS; Metuchen, NJ; (Y); Church Yth Grp; Yrbk Stf; Lit Mag; Coach Actv; Hon Roll; Ntl Sci Merit Awd 84-85; Fshn Inst Of Tech; Fshn Merch.

BUONO, DEAN; Holy Cross HS; Medford, NJ; (Y); Am Leg Boys St; Spanish Clb; SADD; Rep Frsh Cls; VP Soph Cls; VP Jr Cls; Var Socr; Var Wrstlng; Med.

BUONO, ROBERT; St Marys HS; Passaic, NJ; (Y); 17/53; Boy Scts; Church Yth Grp; Cmnty Wkr; Letterman Clb; Library Aide; Ski Clb; Spanish Clb; Lit Mag; Rep Frsh Cls; Var Bsktbl; Eagle Scout 86; Mst Imprvd Athlt 86; Oceanogrphy.

BUONOCORE, DAWN M; Brick Memorial HS; Bricktown, NJ; (S); FNA; Hosp Aide; Red Cross Aide; VICA; Stage Crew; Powder Puff Ftbl; Sftbl.

BURANICH, RAYNA; Piscataway HS; Piscataway, NJ; (Y); Computer Clb; FBLA; OEA; Yrbk Stf.

BURCH, ANTOINETTE; Garden State Acad; Lauderhill, FL; (Y); Church Yth Grp; Nwsp Rptr; Yrbk Stf; Rep Jr Cls; Ed.

BURCHELL, ROBERT; Hamilton HS East; Hamilton Sq, NJ; (Y); 10/360; Church Yth Grp; FBLA; SADD; Im Bowling; NHS; Ftr Prblm Slvrs 84; Trntn ST Coll; Comp Sci.

BURCHETT, LAURA; Delaware Valley Regional HS; Milford, NJ; (Y); 7/183; Sec Pres Art Clb; Chorus; Church Choir; School Play; Stage Crew; Nwsp Rptr; Ed Nwsp Stf; JV Crs Cntry; JV Trk; Gov Hon Prg Awd; Visual Artist.

BURDICK, IAN; Egg Harbor Township HS; Mckee City, NJ; (S); 1/316; Trs Chess Clb; Nwsp Ed-Chief; High Hon Roll; Jr NHS; Ntl Ldrshp Merit Awe 85; Ntl Sci Merit Awd 84-85; Comp Prog.

BUREN, MARCY; Raritan HS; Hazlet, NJ; (S); 10/342; Ski Clb; Spanish Clb; VP Temple Yth Grp; Band; Hon Roll; Trs NHS; Grdn ST Dstngshd Schlrs Awd 86; U Of Michigan.

BURGER, TRACY; Hunterdon Central HS; Whitehouse Sta, NJ; (Y); 102/548; Church Yth Grp; SADD; Drm Mjr(t); Mrchg Band; Symp Band; Off Jr Cls; Off Sr Cls; Stu Cncl; Hon Roll; NHS; Mrchng Band Ltr 86; Educ.

BURGESS, CAROL A; Haddonfield Memorial HS; Haddonfield, NJ; (S); 22/138; Sec Drama Clb; Pres Orch; School Musical; School Play; Nwsp Rptr; French Hon Soc; Hon Roll; NHS; Ntl Merit Ltr; Emory U; Intl Bus.

BURGESS, JEFFREY; Buena Regional HS; Newtonville, NJ; (Y); 59/161; Acpl Chr; Chorus; Madrigals; Swing Chorus; JV Bsbl; JV Ftbl; JV Wrstlng; NJ ST Brbrshop Qrtet Champs 85; All S Jersey Chorus 86; Pennco Tech; Elctrnc Engrng.

BURGIEL, HEIDI L; Voorhees HS; Lebanon, NJ; (Y); 10/243; Exploring; Trs French Clb; Trs Key Clb; Math Tm; Sec SADD; Band; Mrchg Band; French Hon Soc; Gov Hon Prg Awd; Hon Roll; JV Fncg 85; MVP Bnd 85; Grdn ST Dstngshd Schlr 85; Mth.

BURGOS, ISABEL; Dwight Morrow HS; Englewood, NJ; (Y); Camera Clb; High Hon Roll; Hon Roll; Mdlng.

BURKART, DANIEL; Lenape Valley HS; Stanhope, NJ; (Y); Ski Clb; Varsity Clb; Bsbl; Ftbl; Vllybl; Wt Lftg; Hon Roll; Prfct Atten Awd; Bus.

BURKE, BRIAN; Burlington City HS; Beverly, NJ; (Y); Am Leg Boys St; JV Var Socr; JV Trk; Ntl Merit Ltr; Comp Engr.

BURKE, CYNTHIA; Washington Township HS; Turnersville, NJ; (Y); Chrmn Girl Scts; Spanish Clb; Im Fld Hcky; JV Sftbl; Var Capt Swmmng; Outstndng Swmr 84-86; Rep The US Swmng In Wst Grmny 85; Arch.

BURKE, JEANNE MARIE; St Rose HS; Neptune, NJ; (Y); 30/206; Pres Church Yth Grp; Key Clb; SADD; Chorus; Church Choir; School Musical; Rep Jr Cls; Hon Roll; NHS; NEDT Awd; Outstndng Dirctr Awd Catholic Yth Orgnztn; La Salle U; Spec Ed.

BURKE, JONAS; Freehold Township HS; Freehold Twp, NJ; (Y); 14/380; Drama Clb; Math Tm; VP Temple Yth Grp; Acpl Chr; Band; Chorus; Madrigals; L Bowling; Gov Hon Prg Awd; NHS; NJ All-Shore Choir 85&86; NJ All-ST Choir 86; Hgh Hnr Awd HS 84; Elec Engnrng.

BURKE, KEVIN; Matawan Regional HS; Matawan, NJ; (Y); 100/320; Ski Clb; Varsity Clb; JV Var Bsbl; JV Var Bsktbl; Stockton; Accntg.

BURKE, KEVIN P; Waldwick HS; Waldwick, NJ; (Y); Am Leg Boys St; Letterman Clb; Varsity Clb; Var Bsbl; Capt Bsktbl; Capt Socr; Hon Roll.

BURKE, MARIA; Morris Catholic HS; Randolph, NJ; (Y); 31/142; French Clb; Natl Beta Clb; Varsity Clb; Powder Puff Ftbl; Var Socr; JV Sftbl; Var Trk; Hon Roll; Trnsfr Stu Hon Roll Awd; Schl Athlt Mo Sccr; 1st Team All Cnfrnc Sccr; Physcl Thrpy.

BURKE, MARK J; Wildwood Catholic HS; Wildwood Crest, NJ; (Y); Am Leg Boys St; Boy Scts; Pres Jr Cls; Pres Sr Cls; Off Stu Cncl; JV Bsbl; Poli Sci.

BURKE, MAUREEN; Saint Rose HS; Neptune, NJ; (Y); 30/250; Church Yth Grp; Key Clb; Church Choir; School Musical; Yrbk Stf; Im Vllybl; Hon Roll; NHS; NEDT Awd; 2nd Pl Cake Dcrtng Cntst 85; Sci.

BURKE, PAM; John P Stevens HS; Edison, NJ; (Y); 71/469; SADD; Rep Jr Cls; Rep Sr Cls; Var Capt Bsktbl; Powder Puff Ftbl; Var Capt Trk; Hon Roll; NHS; Rep Stu Cncl; NJ Blck Achvr 84-85; Dstngshd Mrt Soc 85; Rtgrs Coll Engrng; Engr.

BURKETT, SANDRA L; Mountain Lakes HS; Mountain Lakes, NJ; (Y); 1/106; Var Capt Fld Hcky; Powder Puff Ftbl; JV Var Sftbl; Var Swmmng; Pres French Hon Soc; High Hon Roll; Trs NHS; Ntl Merit SF; Val; JCL; NJ Govrnr Schl Sci 85; Brown U Engl Awd 85; George Washington U Math & Sci Awd 85.

BURKLOW, TIMOTHY M; Pequannock Township HS; Pompton Plains, NJ; (Y); Am Leg Boys St; Boys Clb Am; Church Yth Grp; Latin Clb; Varsity Clb; Pres Band; Pres Sr Cls; Rep Stu Cncl; Ftbl; Capt Wrstlng; NJ Area Band 84; Princeton; Econ.

BURKMAN, SARAH; Hopewell Valley Central HS; Pennington, NJ; (Y); 48/200; AFS; Church Yth Grp; FBLA; GAA; Intnl Clb; Service Clb; Spanish Clb; Yrbk Stf; Stu Cncl; Fld Hcky; Penn ST; Bus.

BURLEW, DAN; Dover HS; Dover, NJ; (Y); Church Yth Grp; Math Tm; Yrbk Ed-Chief; Yrbk Rptr; Yrbk Stf; JV Bsbl; Bowling; Hon Roll; Jr Prom King 86; Accntng.

BURLEW, DONNA; Ocean Township HS; Ocean, NJ; (Y); 76/314; Pres French Clb; Ski Clb; Var Bowling; 1st Pl Frnch Frnscs Trnmnt 84; Keynt Spkr NJ Assn Schl Prncpls 84; Trp Frnc 84; U Of Rhode Island; Bus.

BURLEW, HEIDI; A P Schalick HS; Elmer, NJ; (Y); Church Yth Grp; Ski Clb; Church Choir; Sec Jr Cls; Stu Cncl; Stat Mgr(s); JV Sftbl; Var Trk; Law.

BURMEISTER, MARTA; Cherry Hill HS West; Cherry Hill, NJ; (Y); 50/335; Office Aide; Mrchg Band; Var L Bowling; Fash Merch.

BURNETTE, DAVID; Shore Regional HS; W Long Branch, NJ; (Y); Chess Clb; Math Clb; Math Tm; Science Clb; Elks Awd; High Hon Roll; 3rd Pl Sci Fair 85, 2nd Pl 86; Aerospc Engr.

BURNETTE, STACY L; Lakeland Regional HS; Ringwood, NJ; (Y); 49/298; Off Exploring; French Clb; Intnl Clb; SADD; Thesps; School Musical; Rep Stu Cncl; Cit Awd; High Hon Roll; Hon Roll; Outstndng Ldrshp In Exploring Awd 83-85; 2nd Pl St Lvl Hist Day Comp 83; E Stroudsburg U; Hosptlty Mgmt.

BURNEY, YOSHIA; Hamilton HS West; Trenton, NJ; (Y); 137/337; Band; Concert Band; Mrchg Band; School Musical; School Play; Symp Band; Rep Frsh Cls; Rep Soph Cls; Rep Jr Cls; Rep Stu Cncl; La Debu Debutante Parlimntrn 84-85; La Debu Debutante Treas 85-86; Most Sincere Debutante Awd 85-86; Trenton ST Coll; Bus Admin.

BURNHAM, JOHN; Ocean Township HS; Ocean, NJ; (Y); Church Yth Grp; Computer Clb; Latin Clb; Nwsp Rptr; Nwsp Stf; Lit Mag; Ntl Merit Ltr; Ocean Twnshp Spartan Schlr; Kings Coll Pres Schlrshp; Outstndng Achvt Sociology; Kings Coll; Law.

BURNHAM, LORRAINE; Manalapan HS; Englishtown, NJ; (Y); 83/386; Exploring; Teachers Aide; JV Var Bsktbl; JV Var Crs Cntry; JV Var Sftbl; Cert Of Hnr Grmn Awd 85-86; Pre-Law.

BURNHAM, YVETTE; Manalapan HS; Englishtown, NJ; (Y); 63/383; Cmnty Wkr; Drama Clb; Thesps; School Musical; School Play; Stage Crew; Lit Mag; Gvrnrs Awd Arts Fndtn 86; Wnr NJ Yng Plywrghts Fstvl 86; Bttlgrnd Arts Cntr Awd Cntng Career 86; NY U; Drmtc Wrtng.

BURNS, ADRIENNE; Middletown High Schl South; Middletown, NJ; (Y); French Clb; Ski Clb; Pres Band; Concert Band; Jazz Band; Mrchg Band; Pep Band; Yrbk Stf; VP French Hon Soc; NHS.

BURNS, CHRISTINE; Wallington HS; Wallington, NJ; (Y); 12/73; Church Yth Grp; Library Aide; Varsity Clb; Chorus; Rep Soph Cls; JV Var Bsktbl; Var Trk; Cit Awd; Hon Roll; NHS; Pres Acdmc Fit Awd 86; Homet Schl Orgnztn Schlrshp 86; Rutgers; Acctg.

BURNS, EDWARD; Seton Hall Prep; Madison, NJ; (Y); Math Clb; Math Tm; Rep Jr Cls; JV Var Bsbl; JV Var Socr; JV Trk; High Hon Roll; NHS; Cathlc Math Leag Outstndng Achvt 86.

BURNS, GREGORY E; Westwood HS; Westwood, NJ; (Y); 18/226; Science Clb; Ski Clb; Var L Ftbl; Im Wt Lftg; High Hon Roll; Hon Roll; $1000 Sci Awd & $2000 Merit Schlrshp 86; Seton Hall; Chemistry.

BURNS, JENNIFER; Abraham Clark HS; Roselle, NJ; (Y); 11/160; Chorus; Yrbk Sprt Ed; Lit Mag; Sftbl; Tennis; NHS; Ntl Merit Schol; Chess Clb; English Clb; Teachers Aide; Govrnrs Schl Arts Schlr 85; Alice G Robbins Schlrshp 86; Engl Awd 86; Douglass COLL; Engl.

BURNS, JOHN; Cherry Hill West HS; Cherry Hill, NJ; (Y); Church Yth Grp; Hosp Aide; Latin Clb; Science Clb; Spanish Clb; Teachers Aide; Im Bsktbl; JV Trk; Im Vllybl; Hon Roll; Bio.

BURNS, MICHAEL; Hamilton High West; Trenton, NJ; (Y); Am Leg Boys St; Boy Scts; Church Yth Grp; SADD; Orch; Crs Cntry; Hon Roll; Eagle Sct 86; Freelance Wrtr.

BURNS, MONET; St Mary HS; E Brunswick, NJ; (Y); French Clb; Girl Scts; Library Aide; School Play; Yrbk Stf; Ed Lit Mag; Rep Frsh Cls; Tennis; High Hon Roll; Olympcs Mind 85-86; Law.

BURNSTEIN, LIBA; Bruriah HS For Girls; Elizabeth, NJ; (Y); High Hon Roll; NHS; NEDT Awd.

BURO, JASON; Parsippany Hills HS; Boonton, NJ; (Y); 11/360; Am Leg Boys St; Church Yth Grp; Debate Tm; SADD; Chorus; School Musical; School Play; Off Sr Cls; Hon Roll; NHS; Engrng.

BURRIS, MARY MARGARET; Central Regional HS; Bayville, NJ; (Y); Hon Roll; Teen Talnt Wnnr 81; Saving Bond 85; Ocean City Coll; Med.

BURROUGHS, MARK; Wall HS; Manasquan, NJ; (S); 14/256; Am Leg Boys St; Scrkpr Pres Soph Cls; Pres Jr Cls; Pres Sr Cls; Off Stu Cncl; Var L Bsktbl; Var L Socr; DAR Awd; High Hon Roll; NHS; Senators Leadrshp Pgm 86; Most Likely To Succd 86; Most Popular 86; Wake Forest U; Law.

BURROW, THOMAS; Nutley SR HS; Nutley, NJ; (Y); 132/349; Chess Clb; JV Socr; William Paterson Coll; Bus Admn.

BURROWS, WENDY; Gloucester City HS; Gloucester, NJ; (Y); FBLA; Pep Clb; Teachers Aide; Chorus; School Musical; Rep Stu Cncl; Cheerleading; Cit Awd; Hon Roll; NHS; Elem Educ.

BURSHNICK, CHRISTINE; Piscataway HS; Piscataway, NJ; (Y); Hon Roll; Mock Trial Comp; Stu Drug Asst Pgm; Psych.

BURT, MARY; Paulsboro HS; Gibbstown, NJ; (Y); 49/133; Red Cross Aide; Varsity Clb; Rep Frsh Cls; Rep Soph Cls; VP Jr Cls; JV Bsktbl; JV Fld Hcky; Var Sftbl; Wt Lftg; Stu Cncl; Dr Chester I Ulmer Awd Persnl Svc 83; Kean Coll; Child Dev.

BURT, ROCHELLE; Vineland HS; Vineland, NJ; (Y); 115/803; DECA; Political Wkr; Pres Frsh Cls; Rep Soph Cls; Pres Jr Cls; Pres Sr Cls; Rep Stu Cncl; Var Mgr(s); Acctg.

BURT, SHERRI; St James HS; Gibbstown, NJ; (Y); 23/86; JA; Bsktbl; Sftbl; Hon Roll; Nrsng.

BURT, SUSAN; Pualsboro HS; Gibbstown, NJ; (Y); 14/128; Art Clb; Camera Clb; Computer Clb; Teachers Aide; Ed Yrbk Ed-Chief; High Hon Roll; Hon Roll; Jr NHS; Off NHS; Pres Schlr; Summer & Fall Schlrshps At Moore Coll Of Art 85; Paulsboro Faclty Mem Schlrshp 86; Music & Art Awd 86; Comm Art.

BURTON, LAUREN; John F Kennedy HS; Paterson, NJ; (S); 100/348; Church Yth Grp; Cmnty Wkr; Girl Scts; Hosp Aide; Library Aide; Office Aide; Teachers Aide; Chorus; Church Choir; Flag Corp; William Paterson Coll; Nrsng.

BURTON, MATTHEW THOMAS; Chatham HS; Chatham, NJ; (Y); Art Clb; Cmnty Wkr; German Clb; Nwsp Stf; Yrbk Stf; Im Bowling; Var Capt Crs Cntry; Im Vil Ftbl; Trk; Hnr Outstndng Vlntr Svc SLEEP 85-86; Subrbn Cltrl Ed Enrchmt Prog 84-86; Peer Awareness Cnclng 85-86; Stdo Art.

BURTON, TRACI; Mt Olive HS; Flanders, NJ; (Y); SADD; Hon Roll; Lang.

BURZYNSKI, TAMARA; Toms River HS East; Toms River, NJ; (Y); 8/586; NHS; High Hon Roll; Hon Roll; JV Trk; Intnl Clb; Mrchg Band; Key Clb; Spanish Clb; Powder Puff Ftbl; Math Tm; Chem Engr.

BUSH, JACQUELINE R J; Bridgewater-Raritan High Schl West; Bridgewater, NJ; (Y); Drama Clb; Speech Tm; SADD; Acpl Chr; Chorus; Madrigals; School Musical; Variety Show; JV Gym; Ms Irenand Irish Dy Parade Fund Raiser 86; Somerset County Coll; Chld Psyc.

BUSHELL JR, JOHN T; Central Regional HS; Seaside Park, NJ; (Y); 21/244; Aud/Vis; Var Ftbl; Trk; Jr NHS; Athletic Acad Awd Ftbl 85-86; Bus Adm.

BUSSE, G DIRK; Colonia HS; Colonia, NJ; (Y); 78/350; Art Clb; PAVAS; Rutgers U; Indstrl Dsgn.

BUSSIE, ALVIN; John F Kennedy HS; Paterson, NJ; (Y); Am Leg Boys St; Band; Nwsp Phtg; Nwsp Rptr; Nwsp Stf; Bsbl; Ftbl; Score Keeper; Rutgers U; Computer Tech.

BUSTARD, JOHN W; Cherry Hill HS West; Cherry Hill, NJ; (Y); 6/386; Variety Show; Nwsp Rptr; VP Stu Cncl; Var Golf; Var Socr; Var Capt Swmmng; High Hon Roll; NHS; Ntl Merit Ltr; St Schlr; Hll Of Fm Indctee 86; Schl Schlr 86; U Of VA; Comp Engnrng.

BUSTOS, NADINE; The Hun Schl; Belle Mead, NJ; (Y); 16/107; Library Aide; Teachers Aide; VP Frsh Cls; VP Soph Cls; Rep Stu Cncl; Var Fld Hcky; Var Capt Lcrss; High Hon Roll; Cum Laude Soc 85-86; Spnsh Awd 85-86; Red Rbbn Cert 82-84; Bryn Mawr Coll.

BUTKIEWICZ, ELISE; Bishop Geroge Ahr HS; Plainfield, NJ; (S); 31/240; French Clb; Nwsp Rptr; Crs Cntry; Gym; Socr; Trk; NHS; Ntl Merit Ltr; NEDT Awd; Eng.

BUTKOWSKI, LISA; Union Catholic HS; New Providence, NJ; (Y); 36/319; Drama Clb; Chorus; School Musical; School Play; Stage Crew; Nwsp Phtg; Yrbk Phtg; Yrbk Stf; Bio.

BUTKOWSKY, ROCHELLE; Manasquan HS; Brielle, NJ; (Y); Church Yth Grp; Drama Clb; Spanish Clb; Thesps; Band; School Musical; School Play; Ed Lit Mag; Hon Roll; Hugh O Brian Yth Ldrshp Fndtn Rep 84; Eng III Ptry Cntst 1st Pl 86; Eng.

BUTLER, CHRISTINA; Oak Knoll Schl; Jersey City, NJ; (Y); Camera Clb; Cmnty Wkr; GAA; Pep Clb; Service Clb; Ski Clb; Stage Crew; Yrbk Stf; Var Lcrss; Var Capt Tennis; Lacrosse MVP & Mst Outstndng All Star Lacrosse Tm 85-86; Tennis MVP Most Outstndng 85-86; Bus.

BUTLER, DONALD; Christian Brothers Acad; Middletown, NJ; (Y); 65/230; Nwsp Rptr; Nwsp Stf; Lit Mag; Im Capt Bowling; Ftbl; Im Capt Sftbl; Essy Pres Reagan Locl Nwsppr 83; Spnsh Postr Cntst 86; Rutgers; Metrlgy.

BUTLER, GWENDOLYN; Kittatinny Regional HS; Middleville, NJ; (S); 14/164; Band; Concert Band; Mrchg Band; Nwsp Rptr; Nwsp Stf; Hon Roll; NHS; 1st Pl Paramus Crftsman Fair Detl, Assmbly Drwg 84, Arch Renderng, Plns 85; Arch.

BUTLER, KAREN; Cumberland Christian Schl; Salem, NJ; (S); 2/14; Church Yth Grp; VP Soph Cls; Sec Sr Cls; Var Capt Bsktbl; Var Capt Fld Hcky; Var Sftbl; High Hon Roll; All Tornmnt Tm V Bsktbl, V Fld Hockey 84-85; Messiah Coll; Physical Educ.

BUTLER, KYLE L; Snyder HS; Jersey City, NJ; (S); Church Yth Grp; Pres DECA; Pres Jr Cls; Sr Cls; JV Ftbl; Var Wrstlng; High Hon Roll; Hon Roll; Jr NHS; NHS; U S Air Force Coll; Elctrncs.

BUTLER, LISA; St John Vianney HS; Hazlet, NJ; (Y); 43/282; Church Yth Grp; Intnl Clb; Library Aide; Yrbk Stf; Mgr(s); Powder Puff Ftbl; Stat Score Keeper; Trk; Hon Roll; Bus.

BUTLER, MARY; Marylawn Of The Oranges HS; Orange, NJ; (Y); 3/55; Math Clb; Science Clb; Service Clb; School Play; Nwsp Ed-Chief; VP Sr Cls; Sec Stu Cncl; Capt Sftbl; Capt Tennis; Sec French Hon Soc; Lwyr.

BUTLER, NICOLE; Red Bank Catholic HS; Farmingdale, NJ; (Y); 4-H; SADD; Band; Mrchg Band; Bsktbl; 4-H Awd; Hon Roll; Psychol.

BUTLER, PETER; Absegami HS; Egg Harbor City, NJ; (Y); #13 In Class; Computer Clb; Crs Cntry; Trk; Elec Engnrng.

BUTLER, STEPHANIE; Cherry Hill HS West; Cherry Hill, NJ; (Y); Drama Clb; Trs JCL; Library Aide; PAVAS; Thesps; Chorus; School Play; Bowling; NHS; Am Leg Aux Girls St; NCTE Schl Rep 85-86; Natl Home & Schl Assoc Awd 83-84 & 85-86; Gov Schl Of The Arts 85-86; Psychlgy.

BUTLER, SUE; Toms River East HS; Toms River, NJ; (Y); Ski Clb; Mgr Sftbl; Mgr Wrstlng; Math.

BUTLER, SYLVIA; Vineland HS; Vineland, NJ; (Y); 78/803; Girl Scts; Political Wkr; Orch; Rep Frsh Cls; Rep Soph Cls; Rep Jr Cls; ; Sociology.

BUTTE, ATUL JANARDHAN; Cherry Hill HS East; Cherry Hill, NJ; (Y); Am Leg Boys St; Boy Scts; Computer Clb; Debate Tm; Hosp Aide; Pres Latin Clb; Science Clb; High Hon Roll; Voice Dem Awd; Cum Laude Hnr Soc 86; Govs Sch Of Scis 86; Physcn.

BUYARSKI, JOHN; Pennsville Memorial HS; Pennsville, NJ; (Y); 4/210; Cmnty Wkr; Ski Clb; Speech Tm; Frsh Cls; Soph Cls; Trs Stu Cncl; JV Bsktbl; Tennis; High Hon Roll; Pres NHS; All S Jersey Grp 2 Dbls Plyr Ten 86; 4.0 Awd 83-85; Recgtn Day 84-86; VA Tech; Engrng.

BUZZELLI, PASQUALE; St Peters Prep; Jersey City, NJ; (Y); 18/205; Aud/Vis; Camera Clb; Varsity Clb; Yrbk Phtg; Yrbk Sprt Ed; Wrstlng; High Hon Roll; Gld Mdl Geo Hnrs 85; Brnz Mdl 84; Slvr Mdl 85; Stevens Inst Of Tech; Engr.

BYERS JR, JESSE EDWARD; Edgewood SR HS; Sicklerville, NJ; (Y); Camera Clb; Cmnty Wkr; Computer Clb; ROTC; Color Guard; Drill Tm; Var Ftbl; JV Trk; Im Wt Lftg; Hon Roll; RETS; Elec Engr.

BYK, KIMBERLEY; Mt Saint Mary Acad; Watchung, NJ; (Y); Church Yth Grp; French Clb; GAA; Office Aide; Lit Mag; Var L Tennis; French Hon Soc; Hon Roll; Bio.

BYLONE, MICHAEL; St Augustine Prep; Vineland, NJ; (Y); 15/50; Cmnty Wkr; Pep Clb; Capt Var Bsbl; Im Bsktbl; Coach Actv; Im Ftbl; Im Socr; Im Sftbl; Wt Lftg; Hon Roll; Stu Actvts Awd 86; Hons 82-86; Var Bsbll 82-86; St Josephs U; Bus.

BYRD, KANDY; Hillside HS; Hillside, NJ; (Y); Dance Clb; Drama Clb; Hosp Aide; Pep Clb; Chorus; Church Choir; Drill Tm; Variety Show; Nwsp Stf; Var Cheerleading; Bus Mgmt.

BYRD, KIMBERLY DENISE; Abraham Clark HS; Roselle, NJ; (S); Office Aide; Science Clb; Service Clb; Chorus; Madrigals; Rep Stu Cncl; NHS; Spanish NHS; Bus Adm.

BYRD, LIZETTE; River Dell HS; Oradell, NJ; (Y); 22/214; Camp Fr Inc; Chorus; School Musical; Crs Cntry; French Hon Soc; High Hon Roll; Hon Roll; NHS; French Clb; NJ Dstngshd Schlr Schlrshp 86; River Dell Ed Assc Schlrshp 86; Natl Schl Choral Awd 86; Rutgers Coll; Bus.

BYRD, LORI; Frank H Morrell HS; Irvington, NJ; (Y); Camera Clb; Color Guard; Flag Corp; Variety Show; Off Frsh Cls; Off Soph Cls; Off Jr Cls; Rep Stu Cncl; Twrlr; Hon Roll; Nrsng.

BYRD, TANYA; Franklin HS; Somerset, NJ; (Y); Church Yth Grp; SADD; Church Choir; Rep Frsh Cls; Rep Soph Cls; Rep Jr Cls; JV Capt Cheerleading; Fld Hcky; JV Sftbl; Hon Roll; Comm.

BYRNE, DAVID J; Ewing HS; Trenton, NJ; (Y); Am Leg Boys St; Cmnty Wkr; Debate Tm; Key Clb; Political Wkr; Ski Clb; Nwsp Sprt Ed; Yrbk Sprt Ed; Stu Cncl; Hon Roll; History.

BYRNE, ERIN; Mary Help Of Christian Acad; Lincoln Pk, NJ; (Y); Am Leg Aux Girls St; Computer Clb; Drama Clb; Letterman Clb; School Play; Im Cheerleading; Gym; Hon Roll; NEDT Awd.

BYRNE, ERIN; Roselle Catholic HS; Union, NJ; (Y); Church Yth Grp; SADD; Stat Bsbl; JV Bsktbl; Stat Socr; JV Swmmng; Hon Roll; Fashion Inst Tech; Int Dsgn.

BYRNE, KATHLEEN; West Orange HS; W Orange, NJ; (Y); Church Yth Grp; Cmnty Wkr; French Clb; Hosp Aide; Ski Clb; Rep Stu Cncl; JV Bsktbl; JV Cheerleading; JV Sftbl; Hon Roll; Sci Expo 85-86; Bus.

BYRNE, KELLY ANNE; Mt St Mary Acad; Cranford, NJ; (Y); 11/83; Dance Clb; Drama Clb; Service Clb; Spanish Clb; Pres Chorus; School Musical; High Hon Roll; Hon Roll; NHS; Spanish NHS; St Josephs U; Fd Mktg.

BYRNE, KELLY M; Academy Of The Sacred Heart HS; Hoboken, NJ; (Y); 3/48; Hosp Aide; Rep Sr Cls; Stu Cncl; JV Cheerleading; Co-Capt Pom Pon; NHS; Pres Schlr; Peer Cnslng 85-86; Seton Hall U; Accntng.

BYRNE, KEVIN; St Josephs HS; South Amboy, NJ; (Y); Am Leg Boys St; Church Yth Grp; Drama Clb; Model UN; SADD; School Musical; School Play; Yrbk Stf; Lit Mag; Stu Cncl; Robert Frost Ltrry Awd 85; Engl.

BYRNE, KRISTIN; South Plainfield HS; So Plainfield, NJ; (Y); 25/260; Chorus; Concert Band; Madrigals; Symp Band; French Hon Soc; Hon Roll; Church Yth Grp; Drama Clb; French Clb; Ski Clb; Order Rainbow 84-86; Central Jersey Region Chorus 85-86; Am Hist.

BYRNE, LISA; Southern Regional HS; Cedar Run, NJ; (Y); 22/380; Model UN; Service Clb; Trs Spanish Clb; Rep Jr Cls; Var L Ice Hcky; JV L Socr; High Hon Roll; NHS; Trs Church Yth Grp; Hosp Aide; Schlr Athl Awd Sccr 85; Acdmc Achvt Awds 85 & 86; Acctg.

BYRNE, STEPHANIE; Chatham Township HS; Chatham Twp, NJ; (Y); 18/130; Church Yth Grp; Key Clb; VP Service Clb; Stu Cncl; Capt Cheerleading; NHS; Rotary Awd; AFS; Math Tm; Model UN; Presdntl Acadmc Ftns Awd 86; Bus Educ Awd 86; Acadmc All Amercn 85; Jms Mdsn U Hnrs Schlr 86; James Madison U; Intl Bus.

BYRNE, STEPHEN J; Bridgewater-Raritan H S West; Bridgewater, NJ; (Y); Computer Clb; VP 4-H; Ski Clb; Varsity Clb; JV Bsbl; JV Ftbl; Var Lcrss; Im Vllybl; Elks Awd; Hon Roll; Comp Sci.

BYRNE, SUE ANN; St John Vianney HS; Manalapan, NJ; (Y); 39/283; SADD; Yrbk Stf; High Hon Roll; Hon Roll; Art Thrpy.

BYSTERBUSCH, RYAN; Eastern Christian HS; Hawthorne, NJ; (Y); Am Leg Boys St; Boy Scts; Camera Clb; Chess Clb; Church Yth Grp; Cmnty Wkr; Badmtn; Hon Roll; Elec Engr.

BZDEWKA, LAURA; St John Vianney HS; Hazlet, NJ; (Y); 16/283; Intnl Clb; Math Tm; Office Aide; Service Clb; Teachers Aide; Drill Tm; Mrchg Band; L Twrlr; Hon Roll; NHS; Pre-Med.

CABALAR, MARIA; Manchester HS; Toms River, NJ; (Y); Chorus; Bsktbl; Cheerleading; Score Keeper; Sftbl; Hon Roll; Var Lttrs Chrldng & Sftbl 85-86; UCLA; RN.

CABALU, RAY; West Essex SR HS; N Caldwell, NJ; (Y); 48/350; Sec Debate Tm; Exploring; Trs Key Clb; Latin Clb; Sec Model UN; Quiz Bowl; Science Clb; Hon Roll; Fncng Vrsty Cap 84-86; Boston Coll; Mgmt.

CABATIC, JEANNETTE; Mount Saint Dominic Acad; Bloomfield, NJ; (Y); 7/53; French Clb; Hosp Aide; JCL; Library Aide; Ski Clb; Chorus; Stu Cncl; Var L Sftbl; NHS; Prfct Atten Awd; Rutgers U; Med.

CABERA, BLANCA; Memorial HS; W New York, NJ; (Y); FBLA; Sr Cls; Katherine Gibbs Schl; Lgl Secy.

CABO, JENNIFER; Mainland Regional HS; Ocean City, NJ; (Y); 45/400; Church Yth Grp; Spanish Clb; SADD; Variety Show; Yrbk Stf; Off Soph Cls; Off Soph Cls; Off Jr Cls; Off Sr Cls; Stu Cncl; Prom Chairperson 86; Bus Seminar 84; Ldrshp Prgm 86; Rutgers U; Med.

CABRERA, MARIBEL; Newark Science HS; Newark, NJ; (Y); 13/131; Debate Tm; NFL; Ed Nwsp Rptr; Yrbk Stf; Mgr Tennis; Im Vllybl; Gov Hon Prg Awd; High Hon Roll; NHS; Ntl Merit SF; SF Pace U Lincoln-Douglas Debate 86; Quatrfin Mnchster L-D Dbte 86; Rutgers Schlr 85; Princeton U; Mech Engrng.

CACCATORE, CHARLES J; Hasbrouck Hgts HS; Hasbrouck Heights, NJ; (Y); 5/125; Am Leg Boys St; Drama Clb; French Clb; German Clb; Rep Key Clb; Letterman Clb; Nwsp Rptr; VP Jr Cls; Capt Bsbl; NHS; Itln Hon Awd; Hartwick Coll; Bus.

CACTABELLATTA, JIM; Don Basco Prep; River Vale, NJ; (Y); Hon Roll; ST Chmpn Rfl Shtr 85; JR Olympcs 86; Ntl Mtchs Rfl Trgt Shtng 82-86; Bus.

CADWELL, LAURA C; Triton Regional HS; Somerdale, NJ; (Y); 43/297; Sec AFS; Church Yth Grp; Pep Clb; Sec Trs Spanish Clb; Church Choir; Yrbk Stf; Stu Cncl; Hon Roll; Voice Dem Awd; Glasboro ST Coll; Spec Ed.

CAFASSO, ERMINIA; Mt St Dominic Acad; Newark, NJ; (Y); Cmnty Wkr; Trs Intnl Clb; JCL; Latin Clb; Library Aide; Political Wkr; Teachers Aide; Chorus; Nwsp Ed-Chief; Nwsp Rptr; Masonic Awd 86; Med.

CAFFIE, JANIQUE; St Dominic Acad; Jersey City, NJ; (Y); 59/131; Art Clb; Pres Church Yth Grp; French Clb; Girl Scts; Science Clb; Chorus; Church Choir; Yrbk Stf; Lit Mag; Trs Sr Cls; Corine Frazier Schlrshp 86; OH ST U; Pre-Med.

CAFONE, BOB; Bloomfield SR HS; Bloomfld, NJ; (Y); 57/442; Computer Clb; Crs Cntry; Golf; Socr; Trk; Hon Roll; Rutgers U; Ind Engrng.

CAGANDE, CONSUELO; Pope John XXII HS; Sparta, NJ; (Y); Teachers Aide; Lit Mag; Var Bsktbl; Stat Var Fld Hcky; Var Co-Capt Sftbl; High Hon Roll; NHS; Chorus; JV Golf; Sprta Twp Dstngshd H S Stu Awd 86; Santo Ptrnstro Awd-Athltcs & Acadmcs 86; Rutgers ST U; Bio.

CAGANDE, ERWIN; Pope John XXIII HS; Sparta, NJ; (Y); Hosp Aide; Office Aide; Spanish Clb; JV Bsktbl; Score Keeper; Timer; High Hon Roll; Hon Roll; Achvt Awd; Boys St; Dnstry.

CAGGIANO, JULIE; Pitman HS; Pitman, NJ; (S); 15/150; Teachers Aide; Flag Corp; Nwsp Rptr; Nwsp Stf; Rep Soph Cls; Pom Pon; Hon Roll; NHS; Olympcs Of Mnd Comptn Wrld Champ 85; Newsppr Featrs Edtr 85-86; Brdcstg Cmmnctns; Radio.

CAGNETTA, ROBERT; Verona HS; Verona, NJ; (Y); Camera Clb; Pres Frsh Cls; Rep Soph Cls; VP Jr Cls; Pres Stu Cncl; JV Bsbl; L Ftbl; L Trk; 3rd Pl Paramus Art Ahw Batik 86; Rep Hands Acrs Amer 86; Verona Yth Cmmtt 86; Syracuse; Arch.

CAHANAP, CONNIE; Wm L Dickinson HS; Jersey City, NJ; (Y); Computer Clb; Q&S; Scholastic Bowl; Science Clb; Nwsp Rptr; Yrbk Stf; Lit Mag; Rep Frsh Cls; Stu Cncl; Hon Roll; William M Dougherty Awd 86.

CAHILL, ARLA; Randolph HS; Randolph, NJ; (Y); 92/357; Hosp Aide; Trs Key Clb; Ski Clb; Concert Band; Mrchg Band; Symp Band; Nwsp Stf; Smmr Inst Gftd Blair Acad 85; Wrtr/Edtr Mrrs Cnty Fd Bnk Nwslttr 86; Nwcmrs Clb 85-86; Montclair ST Coll; Biochem.

CAIN, CAROLYN; Absegami HS; Absecon, NJ; (Y); Flag Corp; Hon Roll; B Hnr Rl 85-86; Accntng.

CAIN, JENNI; Williamstown HS; Williamstown, NJ; (Y); Var Stat Bsbl; JV Cheerleading; Var Stat Wrstlng; Hon Roll; Math.

CAIN, MARLO L; Hamilton HS West; Trenton, NJ; (Y); 129/345; Church Yth Grp; Bsktbl; Fld Hcky; Vllybl; Fairleigh Dickinson U; Acctng.

CAINE, PAMELA; Red Bank Catholic HS; Leonardo, NJ; (Y); French Clb; Lit Mag; Brookdale Coll; Jrnlsm.

CALABRESE, MARK; Memorial HS; Cedar Grove, NJ; (S); #3 In Class; Math Tm; Nwsp Rptr; Var Tennis; High Hon Roll; Hon Roll; NHS; Ntl Merit Ltr; Garden ST Distngshd Schlr 85; Senatr Bill Bradleys H S Ldrshp Semnr 86; Intl Rel.

CALAMITA, JACLYN; Wayne Hills HS; Wayne, NJ; (Y); Church Yth Grp; Cmnty Wkr; GAA; Hosp Aide; Red Cross Aide; Var Fld Hcky; Psych.

CALANTONI, MARIA L; Brick HS; Bricktown, NJ; (Y); SADD; Drm Mjr(t); Mrchg Band; Band; Rep Sr Cls; Stat Bsbl; JV Var Sftbl; High Hon Roll; NHS; Stockton ST Coll; Fash Mktng.

CALCAGNI, MELISSA; Washington Twp HS; Sewell, NJ; (Y); Spanish Clb; Yrbk Stf; Rep Stu Cncl; Stat Bsktbl; JV Socr; Hon Roll.

CALDERA, LAUREN; Matawan Regional HS; Matawan, NJ; (S); 38/315; Off Frsh Cls; Off Soph Cls; Off Jr Cls; Stu Cncl; VP L Bsktbl; VP Sftbl; Hon Roll; Mst Dedctd Sftbl Plyr 83-84.

CALDWELL, CHERYL; Rancocas Valley Regional HS; Mt Holly, NJ; (Y); 15/307; Am Leg Aux Girls St; Church Yth Grp; Trs Key Clb; Church Choir; Rep Stu Cncl; High Hon Roll; Hon Roll.

CALDWELL, HOPE; Clifford J Scott HS; E Orange, NJ; (Y); 26/254; Pres Dance Clb; VP Drama Clb; Camera Clb; Church Yth Grp; French Clb; FHA; JA; PAVAS; Service Clb; Nwsp Stf; Trntn ST Coll; Cmnctns.

CALDWELL, SHARON; Overbrook SR HS; Lindenwold, NJ; (Y); DECA; 4-H; Office Aide; Fld Hcky; 4-H Awd; High Hon Roll; Hon Roll; NY 4-H ST Hrs Shw Chmpn 85; Intr Dsgn.

CALDWELL, VINCENT RAYDELL; Clifford J Scott HS; South Orange, NJ; (Y); 8/250; Am Leg Boys St; Mgr Dance Clb; Library Aide; VP Math Clb; Math Tm; Varsity Clb; Acpl Chr; Chorus; Lit Mag; VP Jr Cls; Mancel Warwick Awd 86; Clifford J Scott Hall Fame 86; Trenton ST Coll; Acctg.

CALHOUN, BETH; Rutherford HS; Rutherford, NJ; (S); Spanish Clb; Rep Frsh Cls; Rep Soph Cls; Stat Bsktbl; Stat Sftbl; High Hon Roll; Hon Roll; Rutherford Bd Ed Schlstc Awd 84-85; Bus Adm.

CALHOUN, JACQUIE; Bishop Eustace Prepatory Schl; Audubon, NJ; (Y); 14/196; Cmnty Wkr; Pep Clb; Spanish Clb; Varsity Clb; Soph Cls; Stu Cncl; Var L Cheerleading; High Hon Roll; NHS; Spanish NHS; Natl Chmpnshps Chrldng 85-86; Cnty Govt Day Schl Rep 84-85; Red Crs Sr Lfesvng Bdge 83-85.

CALIENDO, BRENDA; Toms River HS North; Toms River, NJ; (Y); Church Yth Grp; Key Clb; Ski Clb; Varsity Clb; Variety Show; Yrbk Stf; Rep Frsh Cls; Rep Soph Cls; Rep Sr Cls; Var Socr; Presdntl Ftns Awd; Chiroprctr.

CALIFANO, ANDY; Middlesex HS; Middlesex, NJ; (Y); 14/158; VP German Clb; Math Clb; Rep Jr Cls; Var L Bsbl; JV L Ftbl; Bausch & Lomb Sci Awd; Elks Awd; Hon Roll; VP NHS; Stu Of Mnth Mrch 86; Babe Ruth Lge Batting Crown 84; Bus.

CALISTA, KATHY; Cherry Hill East HS; Cherry Hill, NJ; (Y); Church Yth Grp; Rep Stu Cncl; Mgr Bsktbl; Fld Hcky; Lcrss; Powder Puff Ftbl; Hon Roll; Ntl Merit Ltr; CBS Schlrshp 86; Class Achvt Awd 86; Rutgers Coll; Mth.

CALIVA, JOSEPH; Camden Catholic Schl; Cherry Hill, NJ; (Y); 80/300; Acpl Chr; Band; Church Choir; Concert Band; Jazz Band; Madrigals; Mrchg Band; Pep Band; School Musical; Symp Band; Temple U; Music Ed.

CALKIN, NANCY; Arthur P Schalick HS; Elmer, NJ; (Y); 1/130; JA; Math Tm; Ski Clb; Nwsp Ed-Chief; High Hon Roll; NHS; St Schlr; Val; OM Awd Mousemobile 83-4; OM Awd Ecology Dozer 84-5; OM Awd Treasure Hunters 85-6; Cornell U; Bio.

CALLAGHAN, MARK; Morris Catholic HS; Parsippany, NJ; (Y); Cmnty Wkr; Latin Clb; Rep Soph Cls; JV Crs Cntry; Score Keeper; JV Var Trk; Hon Roll; Engl Olympcs Awd 84; Mdls Cthlc Cnfrnc Frsh Chmpnshp Cnty 84; Pre-Med.

CALLAGHAN, MICHAEL; Edison HS; Edison, NJ; (Y); Boy Scts; Spanish Clb; Chorus; School Play; Nwsp Rptr; Yrbk Stf; Lit Mag; Crs Cntry; Engl.

CALLAHAN, DAWN; West Morris Central HS; Long Valley, NJ; (Y); Church Yth Grp; Dance Clb; Library Aide; Office Aide; Color Guard; Capt Flag Corp; High Hon Roll; Hon Roll; Dnc Acad Awd 83-85; Sec Awd 86; Bus Admin.

CALLAHAN, JONATHAN MATTHEW; Dwight Englewood HS; Leonia, NJ; (Y); 20/150; Boy Scts; Camera Clb; Cmnty Wkr; Letterman Clb; Varsity Clb; Band; Concert Band; Orch; Nwsp Phtg; Yrbk Phtg; Ctznshp Prz 83; Miclns Trsk Full Schlrshp Awd 85; Prep Schl All Amer Natl Wrstlg Tourn Lehigh U 86; UCS B; Aqua Cltr.

CALLAHAN, SHAWN P; Jefferson Township HS; Lake Hopatcong, NJ; (Y); 21/211; Am Leg Boys St; Church Yth Grp; Math Tm; SADD; Pres Chorus; School Musical; Rep Sr Cls; Var Socr; NHS; Rutgers Coll Of Engrng; Engrng.

CALLAMARO, JOHN; North Warren Regional HS; Blairstown, NJ; (Y); 8/150; Am Leg Boys St; Church Yth Grp; Ski Clb; VP Stu Cncl; JV Bsbl; Var Socr; High Hon Roll; NHS; Pilot.

CALVANESE, DINA; St James HS; Gibbstown, NJ; (S); 3/80; Ski Clb; School Musical; School Play; Yrbk Stf; Pres Frsh Cls; Pres Soph Cls; JV Sftbl; High Hon Roll; Hon Roll; Ntl Merit Ltr; Communications.

CALVERT, CHRISTOPHER; Cresskill HS; Cresskill, NJ; (Y); 17/126; Church Yth Grp; Band; Drm Mjr(t); Jazz Band; Mrchg Band; School Musical; Var Socr; Gov Hon Prg Awd; VP NHS; Pres Schlr; Crnll U; Hlth Svs.

CALVERT, EDWARD; Cresskill HS; Cresskill, NJ; (Y); 12/111; Drama Clb; Ski Clb; Spanish Clb; Chorus; School Musical; Crs Cntry; Trk; NHS; NJ All ST Choir 84-86; Bergen Cnty Choir 83-86; Music.

CALVIELLO, DAVID; St Marys HS; Rutherford, NJ; (S); 9/45; Debate Tm; Drama Clb; FBLA; Math Clb; Pres Soph Cls; Pres Jr Cls; Var Bsktbl; Var Ftbl; French Hon Soc; NHS; Polit Sci.

CALVO, CARRIE ANNE; Hunterdan Central HS; Whitehouse Sta, NJ; (Y); Am Leg Aux Girls St; Model UN; Stu Cncl; Trk; NHS; Spanish NHS; Voice Dem Awd; Hosp Aide; Political Wkr; Y-Teens; Hugh O Brian Ambssdr; Pres Clsrm Delg 85; Yth & Govt-Spkr Of House 86; Douglass Coll; Pol Sci.

CALVO, JOHN; St Mary HS; Passaic, NJ; (S); 1/44; Drama Clb; Pres Math Clb; NFL; School Musical; School Play; Nwsp Rptr; Crs Cntry; Hon Roll; VP NHS; Mock Trial-Cnty Champs; Law.

CAMACHO, EGDA; Linden HS; Linden, NJ; (Y); VP Sec FBLA; Office Aide; Hon Roll; NHS; Prfct Atten Awd.

CAMACHO, PETER; Frank H Morrell HS; Irvington, NJ; (Y); Var Swmmng; JV Timer; NY Inst Of Tech; Archctr.

CAMALIGAN III, COSME RUEL G; James J Ferris HS; Jersey City, NJ; (Y); 1/312; PAVAS; Yrbk Stf; JV Trk; Gov Hon Prg Awd; High Hon Roll; Hon Roll; Kiwanis Awd; NHS; ST Teen Arts Hnr 83-85; JC Msm Perm Art Collctn Hnr 83-85; Frnds Msc & Arts Hnr 83-85; Schl Of Vsl Arts; Comm Arts.

CAMBA, ROMEO G; Cherry Hill West HS; Cherry Hill, NJ; (Y); 22/380; Concert Band; Jazz Band; Mrchg Band; Orch; Stu Cncl; Wrstlng; Hon Roll; NHS; Computer Clb; Model UN; PAVAS; Mck Trl Tm; Rutgers Nw Brunswick; Bio.

CAMEJO, MARIA; Glen Rock HS; Glen Rock, NJ; (Y); 35/153; Art Clb; Cmnty Wkr; Hosp Aide; Spanish Clb; Teachers Aide; Varsity Clb; Yrbk Stf; Mgr(s); Trk; Capt Vllybl; Gvnrs Schl Vis Art 86; All ST Vllybl Tm 85-86.

CAMELI, JENIFER; Red Bank Catholic HS; Spring Lake, NJ; (Y); NFL; Ski Clb; SADD; Nwsp Rptr; Off Sr Cls; Hon Roll; NEDT Awd; NEDTS Cert Ed Dvlpmnt 84; Cum Laude Ntl Ltn Exm 86; Bus Admin.

CAMERON, HEATHER; Marris Knolls HS; Butler, NJ; (Y); 41/389; Yrbk Stf; JV Fld Hcky; JV Trk; High Hon Roll; Hon Roll.

CAMERON, LARRY; Delsea Regional HS; Franklinville, NJ; (Y); Am Leg Boys St; Church Yth Grp; Var L Bsbl; Var Capt Bsktbl; Var L Ftbl; Gov Hon Prg Awd; High Hon Roll; Hon Roll; NHS; Computer Clb; All Star Ltl Leag Bsbl 83-85; Olympcs Of Mnd Tm 83; Chmcl Engrng.

CAMERON, ROBERT; Ramapo Regional HS; Wyckoff, NJ; (Y); 4/329; Camera Clb; Cmnty Wkr; French Clb; Radio Clb; Mgr School Play; Lit Mag; Rep Stu Cncl; High Hon Roll; NHS; Ntl Merit Ltr; Geom & Engl Merit Awd 84; Engl & Frnch Merit Awd 85; Engl Merit Awd 86.

CAMERON, ROBERT W; Mountain Lakes HS; Mountain Lakes, NJ; (Y); 3/106; JCL; Latin Clb; Mathletes; Math Clb; Math Tm; Spanish Clb; SADD; Variety Show; Nwsp Sprt Ed; Nwsp Stf; NJ Amer Lgn Bsbl Schlrshp 85-86; Rtry Clb Outstndng Sr Awd 86; Schlr/Athlt Awd 86; Princeton U; Pre-Med.

CAMINITI, MELISSA; Paramus HS; Paramus, NJ; (Y); FBLA; Var L Cheerleading; Var Powder Puff Ftbl; Var L Sftbl; Ntl Merit Ltr; Italn Hnr Soc; Prelaw.

CAMLIN, ROBERT; Wayne Hills HS; Wayne, NJ; (Y); Aud/Vis; Computer Clb; PAVAS; School Musical; School Play; Stage Crew; JV Bsbl; Var Bowling; Var Wrstlng; Hon Roll; Communications.

CAMMALLERI, ROSA; Mary Help Of Christians HS; Paterson, NJ; (Y); Berkeley Schl; Lgl Sec.

CAMMILLERI, ROXANNE; Mary Help Of Christians Acad; Clifton, NJ; (Y); Art Clb; Dance Clb; Drama Clb; Drill Tm; School Musical; School Play; Variety Show; Hon Roll; Wrld Hstry I Cert Awd 84; Wrld Hstry II, Itln II & Engl II Cert Awd 85; Amercn Hstry Cert Awd 86; Drew U; Psychlgy.

CAMMILLERI, SANDRA; Mary Help Of Christians Acad; Clifton, NJ; (Y); Dance Clb; Drama Clb; Drill Tm; School Play; Variety Show; Nwsp Stf; Hon Roll; Theolgy Awd 84; Italian I, II, III Awd 84-86; Engl II & III Awd 85 & 86; Hghst Avg Soclgy Awd 86; Engl.

CAMPANELLA, BARBARA JEANNE; Sterling HS; Stratford, NJ; (Y); Civic Clb; Cmnty Wkr; DECA; GAA; Girl Scts; Pep Clb; PAVAS; SADD; Teachers Aide; Varsity Clb; Deca 1st Pl Mdlng NJ 85; Modelng 1st Reg ST 85-86; Wrttn Entrprnshp 1st 86; Mayors Trophy Com Inv 84; Fashion Inst.

CAMPANELLA, CHRISTOPHER J; Christian Brothers Acad; Matawa, NJ; (Y); 120/250; Var Bsktbl; Im Ice Hcky; Mgr(s); Im Tennis; JV Trk; Bus.

CAMPANELLA, JACKLYN; Hammonton HS; Hammonton, NJ; (Y); 5/185; Chrmn Key Clb; High Hon Roll; Hon Roll; Kiwanis Awd; NHS; John, Irene Papines Schlrshp 86; Maynard S Love Frnch Awd 86; Acadmc Achvt Awds 84-86; Seton Hall U; Mdrn Lang.

CAMPANELLA, LAURA; Secaucus HS; Secaucus, NJ; (S); 6/165; Chorus; High Hon Roll; NHS.

CAMPBELL, CYNTHIA; North Brunswick Twsp HS; N Brunswick, NJ; (Y); 43/300; Church Yth Grp; Key Clb; Varsity Clb; Flag Corp; Yrbk Stf; Rep Stu Cncl; Var L Swmmng; JV Trk; Hon Roll; Latin Clb; All Cnty Swm Tm 84-86; Fash Merch.

CAMPBELL, DEBBI; St Jammes HS; Salem, NJ; (Y); 4-H; JV Capt Cheerleading; Sftbl; 4-H Awd; Comp Sci.

CAMPBELL, DILLARD T; Holy Spirit HS; Atlantic City, NJ; (Y); 126/400; Church Yth Grp; Cmnty Wkr; Library Aide; Office Aide; Political Wkr; Scholastic Bowl; Coach Actv; Score Keeper; Rep Frsh Cls; Rep Soph Cls; Comp Engr.

CAMPBELL, IRENE; Middletown HS South; Atlantic Highland, NJ; (S); 30/450; Church Yth Grp; Capt Math Tm; Co-Capt Science Clb; Chorus; Capt Color Guard; Var Swmmng; Hon Roll; Monmouth JR Sci Symposm 86; Physics.

CAMPBELL, JEFF; Delron HS; Delran, NJ; (Y); 80/215; French Clb; Ski Clb; Varsity Clb; Stage Crew; Bsbl; Bsktbl; Capt Var Ftbl; Ice Hcky; 6th Man Club; Civl Engr.

CAMPBELL, JIM; Holy Cross HS; Cinnaminson, NJ; (Y); Church Yth Grp; Political Wkr; Ski Clb; Im Golf; Im Sftbl; Im Tennis; Im Vllybl; High Hon Roll; Hon Roll; Pre-Med.

CAMPBELL, JOSEPH M; Cinnaminson HS; Cinnaminson, NJ; (Y); Am Leg Boys St; Church Yth Grp; Math Clb; Pres Frsh Cls; Rep Soph Cls; Rep Jr Cls; Crs Cntry; Trk; Hon Roll; NHS.

CAMPBELL, KAREN; Middletown HS South; Middletown, NJ; (Y).

CAMPBELL, MICHAEL; James Caldwell HS; W Caldwell, NJ; (Y); Church Yth Grp; Yrbk Bus Mgr; Stat Bsbl; NHS; High Hon Roll; Hon Roll; Math.

CAMPBELL, NANCY; Chatham HS; Chatham, NJ; (Y); 11/128; Varsity Clb; Var Capt Bsktbl; Var L Socr; Var Capt Sftbl; High Hon Roll; NHS; OHO-HAAS Schlr Athlt Awd 85-86; Bell Achvt Awd In Bus 85 & 86; MVP In Sftbl & Bsktbl 85-86; Gtysbrg Coll; Bus Mngmnt.

CAMPISANO, GINA MARIE; Wayne Valley SR HS; Wayne, NJ; (Y); 29/340; French Clb; GAA; JA; Yrbk Stf; Lit Mag; JV Cheerleading; High Hon Roll; Hon Roll; NHS; Dance Clb; One To One 84; 4-H Camp Cnslr 86; Educ.

CAMPITELLI, NANCY; Jackson Memorial HS; Jackson, NJ; (S); 30/334; Stat Bsbl; High Hon Roll; Hon Roll; NHS.

CAMPO, ALBA; Asbury Park HS; Bradley Bch, NJ; (Y); Nwsp Rptr; Hon Roll; Frgn Lang Fornsc Trnmnt 85-86; Diploma Merit Excllnc Span NS 86; Chld Psychlgy.

CAMPOLO, CHRISTIAN; Egg Harbor Township HS; Pleasantville, NJ; (S); 6/266; Pres Ski Clb; Band; Drm Mjr(t); Mrchg Band; High Hon Roll; NHS; Ntl Merit SF.

CAMPOLO, LUCIEN; Egg Harbor Twp HS; Pleasantville, NJ; (S); Office Aide; Ski Clb; Varsity Clb; Band; Church Choir; Color Guard; Concert Band; Jazz Band; Mrchg Band; Pep Band; Princeton; Real Est Invstmnt.

CAMPOLUCCI, CHRIS ANNE; Highland Regional HS; Laurel Springs, NJ; (S); 17/326; Church Yth Grp; Library Aide; Political Wkr; Science Clb; Spanish Clb; Drill Tm; Rep Bowling; Pom Pon; Hon Roll; NHS; Law.

CAMPOREALE, CARL; St Peters Prep; Clifton, NJ; (Y); 56/209; Am Leg Boys St; Church Yth Grp; Cmnty Wkr; SADD; Yrbk Ed-Chief; Lit Mag; Pres Soph Cls; VP Jr Cls; JV Bsbl; Hon Roll; Diocesean Youth Rep To St Youth Council 86 & 87; Law.

CANADA, CHRISTOPHER M; Johnson Regional HS; Clark, NJ; (Y); 20/225; Am Leg Boys St; Pres Frsh Cls; Pres Soph Cls; Pres Jr Cls; Pres Sr Cls; JV Bsktbl; Var Ftbl; Var Lcrss; Hon Roll; Outstndg Prfrmnce JR Cls 85-86; Pol Sci.

CANADA, DERRICK; Clifford J Scott HS; E Orange, NJ; (S); Math Clb; Math Tm; Varsity Clb; Var Bsktbl; Var Trk; Hon Roll; NHS; Amer Ed Wk Essy Wnnr 85; Elctrcl Engrng.

CANADY, STEVE; Roselle Catholic HS; Roselle, NJ; (Y); Aud/Vis; Hosp Aide; School Play; JV Bsbl; Var Bsktbl; Ftbl; Olympcs Of Mind Tm; Gftd & Tlntd Pgm; Intrmrl Hcky, Bsktbl & Ping-Pong; Penn ST U; Phrmcy.

CANAHUATE, YOLIMAR; Bishop Eustace Prep Sch; Marlton, NJ; (Y); 10/183; French Clb; Nwsp Ed-Chief; Yrbk Rptr; Yrbk Stf; JV Bowling; French Hon Soc; High Hon Roll; NHS; Ntl Merit SF; Pre-Med.

CANCEL, DAMARIS; Buena Regional HS; Minotola, NJ; (Y); 6/161; Math Clb; Concert Band; Jazz Band; Mrchg Band; NHS; 2nd Hghst Math Avg; Pres Acdmc Fit Awd; Schlr Ltr; Rutger U; Engrng.

CANCELLIERI, TRACEY; Freehold Boro HS; Freehold, NJ; (Y); 28/230; High Hon Roll; Hon Roll; Spanish NHS; Shield & Key Awd; US Hstry Awd; Brookdale; Intl Bus.

CANCGLIN, JAMES; Pitman HS; Pitman, NJ; (Y); 44/136; Dance Clb; VICA; Nwsp Phtg; Nwsp Sprt Ed; Stu Cncl; Prfct Atten Awd; Stu Cncl Hrdwrkr Schlrshp; Chrisetman Semi Frml Dance Chrprsn; Stu Cncl Hon Soc; Prfrmng Arts.

CANCIELLO, STEPHANIE; Hightstown HS; E Windsor, NJ; (Y); 6/342; Am Leg Aux Girls St; Spanish Clb; Yrbk Stf; JV Var Sftbl; High Hon Roll; NHS; Pres Schlr; Rutgers U; Mktg.

CANCILA, GREGORY; St James HS; Gibbstown, NJ; (S); 5/80; Ski Clb; School Play; Stage Crew; Var JV Bsbl; JV Bsktbl; Var JV Ftbl; High Hon Roll; Hon Roll; Prfct Atten Awd; Rotary Awd; Acad All Amer; Elec Engrng.

CANDELINO, CHERYL; Roselle Cath; Roselle, NJ; (Y); Church Yth Grp; Cmnty Wkr; JA; Stage Crew; Lit Mag; Stat Bsbl; L Cheerleading; Pom Pon; Hon Roll.

CANDELORI, NEEVA-GAYLE; Gherry Hill Us West HS; Cherry Hill, NJ; (Y); Pres Church Yth Grp; Dance Clb; French Clb; JA; Acpl Chr; Chorus; Church Choir; Orch; Var Fld Hcky; Var Lcrss; Fld Hcky Mst Imprvd Plyr Awd 84-85; Bnkng.

CANDON, CHRISTA; Union Catholic HS; Clark, NJ; (Y); Drama Clb; Hosp Aide; PAVAS; VP Thesps; School Musical; School Play; Variety Show; Nwsp Stf; Hon Roll; 100 Hr Dvtd Sv Rahwy Hsp Vol 85; Hnr Thspn 85-86.

CANE, JOANNE; Parsippany HS; Parsippany, NJ; (Y); Church Yth Grp; FBLA; Hosp Aide; Letterman Clb; Pep Clb; Varsity Clb; Variety Show; Cheerleading; Fld Hcky; Sftbl; MVP Chrldng 85-86; Bus Adm.

CANGELOSI, SCOTT; River Dell Regional HS; Oradell, NJ; (Y); 23/213; Am Leg Boys St; Pres Ski Clb; JV Ftbl; JV Trk; Hon Roll; NHS; Spanish NHS; U Ntre Dm; Acctnt.

CANIZARES, LOURDES; Memorial HS; West New York, NJ; (Y); Art Clb; French Clb; Color Guard; Rep Frsh Cls; Rep Stu Cncl; Mgr(s); Timer; Hon Roll; Cert Offc Mgr 86; Inter Desgn.

CANNATA, MICHELE; Lenape Valley Reg HS; Stanhope, NJ; (Y); Church Yth Grp; 4-H; Girl Scts; Hosp Aide; SADD; Band; Color Guard; Concert Band; Mrchg Band; Lit Mag; NC ST-RALEIGH; Lwyr.

CANNICI, STEVE; Fair Lawn HS; Fair Lawn, NJ; (Y); Rep Frsh Cls; Rep Soph Cls; Rep Jr Cls; Im JV Bsbl; Capt Ice Hcky; VP Lcrss; Wt Lftg; Arch.

CANNING, KIMBERLY; Manchester Regional HS; Haledon, NJ; (Y); French Clb; GAA; Intnl Clb; High Hon Roll; Hon Roll; Acadmc Achvt Awd 86; Intl Bus.

CANNON, KIMBLE; Neptune SR HS; Ocean Grove, NJ; (Y); 3/375; Am Leg Boys St; Boy Scts; Pres Debate Tm; Drama Clb; Math Clb; Math Tm; Model UN; Science Clb; Ski Clb; School Play; Most Work Done Stu Cncl 86; Best Sci,Hist Stu 84; 1st Pl ST Sci Fair 86; Annapolis; Engrng.

CANNON, KOLLEEN; Mater Dei HS; Middletown, NJ; (Y); 2/169; Am Leg Aux Girls St; Nwsp Sprt Ed; Var L Bsktbl; Var L Trk; High Hon Roll; NHS; Sal; St Schlr; JCL; Pres Latin Clb; Rutgers Schlr 85; Acad All Amer 85; Schlr Ath 86; Emory U.

CANNON, LYNN; Holy Cross HS; Medford, NJ; (Y); 125/390; Yrbk Stf; Trk; Hon Roll; Lncrs For Life 84-85; Nrsng.

CANNON, MELISSA; Edgewood Regional SR HS; Sicklerville, NJ; (Y); 7/380; Pres Latin Clb; Pres Varsity Clb; Rep Frsh Cls; Rep Soph Cls; Sec Jr Cls; Rep Sr Cls; Var Bsktbl; Var Stat Ftbl; Var Sftbl; Var Tennis; Bus Adm.

CANO, MIRIAM; Dickinson HS; Jersey City, NJ; (Y); Intnl Clb; Prfct Atten Awd; Arista Awd 84; Gen Sci Awd 84; Comp.

CANSECO, EDUARDO; St Peters Prep; Bloomfield, NJ; (Y); 48/207; Stage Crew; Var Trk; High Hon Roll; Hon Roll.

CAO, HUY; Metuchen HS; Metuchen, NJ; (Y); Var Socr; Hon Roll; NHS; Numerous Concert & Musicl Perfs; Borough Rep; Sr Cls Secy; Yng Adlts Cncl; Rutgers U; Elec Engrs.

CAPALBO, KIM; Highland Regional HS; Erial, NJ; (Y); Dance Clb; Drama Clb; French Clb; Pep Clb; VP Frsh Cls; VP Soph Cls; Hon Roll; La Salle U; Acctg.

CAPERS, CORETTA; Eastside HS; Paterson, NJ; (Y); 1/600; Church Yth Grp; Church Choir; Stu Cncl; Mgr(s); Sftbl; Hon Roll; NHS; Prfct Atten Awd; Rtgrs Schlr 86; Gvrnr Schl Schlr 86; Rutgers; Law.

CAPESTRO, LISA; Matawan Regional HS; Matawan, NJ; (S); 9/350; French Clb; JCL; Math Clb; Math Tm; NFL; Color Guard; Rep Frsh Cls; Rep Soph Cls; Rep Jr Cls; Rep Stu Cncl; Teen Arts Fstvl Hnrbl Ment 84; Art.

CAPITAN, COLLEEN; Brick HS; Brick Town, NJ; (Y); 189/403; Ski Clb; Rep Frsh Cls; Rep Soph Cls; Rep Jr Cls; Var Gym; Var Powder Puff Ftbl; JV Trk; Dntl Hygnst.

CAPITANO, ROSANNE; Roselle Catholic HS; Roselle, NJ; (Y); 42/195; Stage Crew; Stat Bsbl; Stat Bsktbl; Hon Roll; Spanish NHS; 1st Yr Spnsh Awd 85; Rutgers U.

CAPIZZI, PETER; St Peters Prep; Union City, NJ; (Y); 9/205; Cmnty Wkr; Computer Clb; German Clb; Model UN; Co-Capt NFL; Stu Cncl; Cit Awd; High Hon Roll; Pres Schlr; Prep Spirit Awd 86; Bus.

CAPOBIANCO, JAMES M; Saddle Brook HS; Saddle Brook, NJ; (Y); 11/108; Am Leg Boys St; Quiz Bowl; Nwsp Ed-Chief; Lit Mag; Tennis; Hon Roll.

CAPONE, MICHELE; Washington Township HS; Blackwood, NJ; (Y); Yrbk Stf; Hon Roll; Prfct Atten Awd; Camden Cnty Coll; Electrncs.

CAPOZZI, JOSEPH J; Ridgefield Memorial HS; Ridgefield, NJ; (Y); Am Leg Boys St; Letterman Clb; Science Clb; Varsity Clb; Rep Frsh Cls; Rep Soph Cls; Rep Jr Cls; Rep Stu Cncl; Var L Bsktbl; Ftbl; Pre-Law.

CAPOZZI, LAINA; Nutley HS; Nutley, NJ; (Y); 70/350; Civic Clb; Latin Clb; Stu Cncl; Var Capt Cheerleading; Hon Roll; Silver N Awd 85; Vrsty Sprts Ltr 84-86; Lib Art.

CAPOZZI, MICHELE; James Caldwell HS; W Caldwell, NJ; (Y); 67/265; Key Clb; Rep Frsh Cls; Rep Soph Cls; Rep Jr Cls; Rep Sr Cls; Rep Stu Cncl; Var Bsktbl; Stat Ftbl; Var Sftbl; High Hon Roll; 2nd Tm All Cnty & 1st Tm All-Conf Sftbl 85; 1st Tm All-Cnty & 1st Tm All-Conf Sftbl 86; Rutgers U; Bus.

CAPPADONA, ROBERT; Christan Brothers Acad; Oakhurst, NJ; (Y); 65/225; Church Yth Grp; Stage Crew; Yrbk Stf; Hon Roll; Managmnt.

CAPPELLO III, FRANK; Rutherford HS; Rutherford, NJ; (Y); Bus.

CAPPOLA, THOMAS; Dwight-Englewood Schl; Middletown, NJ; (Y); AFS; Math Tm; Science Clb; Chorus; Concert Band; Jazz Band; Orch; School Musical; School Play; Gov Hon Prg Awd; Dwight Englewood Schl Comm Schlrshp Hdmstrs Awd 86-87; Bergen Yth Orchstr Co-Prin Trmbnst 85-86; Engr.

CAPPUCCIO, DONNA; Wayne Hills HS; Wayne, NJ; (Y); Library Aide; Math Clb; Rep Stu Cncl; Coach Actv; JV Swmmng; Hon Roll; Hnrs Engl 84-86; Hnrs Hstry 85-86; Ecolgy Clb 85-86; Stu John Casablancas Mdlng & Career Ctr 85-86; Sci.

CAPRARI, ELENA; Bishop George Ahr HS; E Brunswick, NJ; (Y); Church Yth Grp; Cmnty Wkr; Pres Sec 4-H; SADD; Teachers Aide; Church Choir; Concert Band; Mrchg Band; School Musical; Symp Band; Accntng.

CAPRARO, SUZANNE; Woodbridge HS; Woodbridge, NJ; (Y); 8/400; Chorus; Concert Band; Mrchg Band; Hon Roll; NHS; Ntl Merit Ltr; Prfct Atten Awd; Spanish NHS.

CAPRIO, BETH; Jackson Memorial HS; Jackson, NJ; (Y); 71/411; Katherine Gibbs Schl; Bus.

CAPUANO, KRISTIN; Bloomfield HS; Bloomfield, NJ; (Y); 90/432; Girl Scts; Band; Concert Band; Flag Corp; Mrchg Band; School Musical; Trs Soph Cls; Fld Hcky; Hon Roll; JP Sousa Awd; Slvr Awd Grl Scts 85; Lawyer.

CAPUANO, LOUIS; Clifton HS; Clifton, NJ; (Y); 150/637; Aud/Vis; Boy Scts; Key Clb; SADD; Band; Concert Band; Mrchg Band; School Musical; Mgr Stage Crew; Hon Roll; Rutgers; Chem.

CAPUTO, BOB; Toms River HS East; Toms River, NJ; (Y); 95/585; Computer Clb; Math Clb; Science Clb; L Var Ice Hcky; Var Trk; Hon Roll; Ice Hockey Unsung Hero 85-86; Engrg.

CAPUZZI, ALBERT; Morris Catholic HS; Morris Plains, NJ; (Y); 22/142; Church Yth Grp; Latin Clb; Trs Variety Show; Nwsp Stf; Rep Frsh Cls; Trs Soph Cls; JV Var Bsbl; JV Var Ftbl; High Hon Roll; Prfct Atten Awd; Natl Lang Arts Olympiad 84; Parsipany All-Star Bsbl Tm 84-85.

CARABALLO, KIMBERLY; Montville Twp HS; Boonton, NJ; (Y); Hosp Aide; Key Clb; High Hon Roll; Hon Roll; Rutgers; Psych.

CARALLUZZO, KAREN; Vine HS HS; Vineland, NJ; (Y); Church Yth Grp; Cmnty Wkr; Office Aide; Teachers Aide; Itln Clb 85-86; Music.

CARANO, KRISTIN; Lakeland Regional HS; Ringwood, NJ; (Y); 1/303; Capt Quiz Bowl; Nwsp Stf; Var Bsktbl; Cit Awd; Gov Hon Prg Awd; High Hon Roll; Pres NHS; Val; Govnrs Schlr Publc Issues 85; Gardn ST Distngshd Schlr 86; Pres Acadmc Ftnss Awd 86; Cornell U; Med.

CARANO, STEVEN M; Neumann Prep; Ringwood, NJ; (Y); 13/87; Am Leg Boys St; Red Cross Aide; Stage Crew; Lit Mag; Capt Swmmng; High Hon Roll; NHS; Spanish NHS; Semi Fnlst NJ Schlrs Prog 86; MIT; Elec Engrng.

CARAVELA, JOSEPH; James Caldwell HS; W Caldwell, NJ; (Y); 41/265; Church Yth Grp; Key Clb; Pres Soph Cls; Rep Jr Cls; Rep Sr Cls; Rep Stu Cncl; Var Bsbl; Var Capt Ftbl; Var Wrstlng; High Hon Roll; Ntl Ftbl Hall Fame Schlr Athlete 86; James Caldwell Schrlshp Fund 86; Essex Cty Athletic Dir Schlr; Fairfield U; Lib Arts.

CARAVELA, THOMAS; James Caldwell HS; West Caldwell, NJ; (Y); 80/267; Key Clb; Bsbl; Ftbl; Wt Lftg; Wrstlng; Hon Roll; Male Athl Of Yr 86; Gridiron Schlrshp 86; All ST Ftbl 86; All Conf Wrstlng 86; Plcd Top 8 In Wrstng 86; Rutgers Coll.

CARAVELLA, PETER; West Essex Regional HS; Fairfield, NJ; (Y); 39/360; Trs Sr Cls; Rep Stu Cncl; Var Capt Bsbl; Var Capt Ftbl; Hon Roll; Essx Cnty Schlr Athlt Awd 86; 1st Tm All-ST Grp III Bsbl 86; Mbr E Rgn Bsbl Tm US Olympc Tstvl 86; Yale U; Ec.

CARBERRY, KENDRA; Watchung Hills Regional HS; Millington, NJ; (Y); 10/320; Church Yth Grp; Trs Key Clb; Ski Clb; Spanish Clb; SADD; Varsity Clb; Nwsp Rptr; Rep Stu Cncl; Score Keeper; Var Score Keeper; Safe Rides.

CARBONARA, MICHAEL; De Paul HS; Fairfield, NJ; (S); Church Yth Grp; Library Aide; Varsity Clb; Bsktbl; JV Ftbl; Var Trk; Im Vllybl; High Hon Roll; NHS; Physcs Tm 84-85; Notre Dame; Lwyr.

CARBONE, CARL MICHAEL; Lyndhurst HS; Lyndhurst, NJ; (Y); 13/184; Am Leg Boys St; Chess Clb; Math Clb; Political Wkr; Science Clb; Teachers Aide; Nwsp Rptr; Ftbl; Trk; NHS; Engrg.

CARBONE, SAMUEL; Don Bosco Prep; Rutherford, NJ; (S); 16/179; German Clb; JV Bsbl; High Hon Roll; Arch.

CARD, DOUGLAS; Middletown HS South; Highlands, NJ; (Y); Drama Clb; Band; Chorus; Concert Band; Stage Crew; Variety Show; Yrbk Phtg; Trs Pres Stu Cncl; Gym; Capt Wrstlng.

CARDINALE, DONNA; Voorhees HS; Califon, NJ; (Y); 14/240; Stu Cncl; JV Crs Cntry; JV Trk; Hon Roll; NHS; Trs Spanish NHS; Church Yth Grp; Color Guard; Acdmc Achvt Socty 83-86; Peer Tutrng 83-86; Glassboro ST Coll; Elem Ed.

CARDINALE, DREW; Hillsborough HS; Belle Mead, NJ; (Y); 22/320; Church Yth Grp; Drama Clb; Latin Clb; Math Clb; NFL; Spanish Clb; School Musical; Tennis; Hon Roll; NHS; Romance Lang.

CARDINALE, MICHAEL; Lenape HS; Stanhope, NJ; (Y); Ftbl; Var JV Socr; Math Hons.

CARDINEZ, NATALIE; Norht Bergen HS; N Bergen, NJ; (Y); #140 In Class; Art Clb; Chess Clb; Chorus; Tennis; Wt Lftg; Prfct Atten Awd; Zoology.

CARDONE, ANTHONY; Dover HS; Mine Hill, NJ; (Y); Boy Scts; Church Yth Grp; Computer Clb; FCA; Latin Clb; Chorus; Ftbl; Trk; Wt Lftg; Wrstlng; Auto Mech.

CARDOSA, HEATHER A; West Morris Central HS; Hackettstown, NJ; (Y); Church Yth Grp; Chorus; Color Guard; Crs Cntry; Hon Roll; NHS; Messiah Coll; Bio.

CAREY, DAVID; Roselle Catholic HS; Roselle, NJ; (Y); 54/195; Ski Clb; Yrbk Stf; Var Bsbl; Var Socr; French Hon Soc; Hon Roll; Accntng.

CAREY, ERIN; West Morris Central HS; Long Valley, NJ; (Y); Am Leg Aux Girls St; Varsity Clb; Rep Jr Cls; Var Crs Cntry; Var Capt Trk; Cit Awd; High Hon Roll; Hon Roll; Jr NHS; NHS; Bus Mgmt.

CAREY, LAURA; West Morris Central HS; Long Valley, NJ; (Y); Ski Clb; Concert Band; Drm Mjr(t); Jazz Band; School Musical; Cit Awd; Jr NHS; NHS; Ltn Ntl Hnrs Soc 86; Ltn Cum Laude Awd 86; N Jrsy Area Band 85&86; N Jrsy Rgn Band 85; Music.

CAREY, LISE; Middletown HS South; Lincroft, NJ; (Y); Hosp Aide; Red Cross Aide; SADD; Swmmng; Hon Roll; Engrng.

CAREY, MICHAEL; Neptune SR HS; Neptune, NJ; (Y); 22/430; Boy Scts; Math Tm; Science Clb; School Play; Nwsp Rptr; Lit Mag; Var Capt Bowling; NHS; Drama Clb; Library Aide; Placed In Stockton DE Vly Sci Fairs 84; Eagle Scout 86; Cornell U; Aerospace Enrng.

CAREY, PATRICIA; St Rose HS; Spring Lake, NJ; (Y); Drama Clb; School Musical; Nwsp Stf; Yrbk Stf; Lit Mag; Rep Jr Cls; JV Cheerleading; Var Trk; Hon Roll; NEDT Awd; Maga Cum Laude Achvt Nat Tln Exm 86.

CARFAGNO, GLEN; Montville HS; Montville, NJ; (Y); Art Clb; Ski Clb; Hon Roll; Prfct Atten Awd; Comp Engr.

CARFIELLO, ANGELA; Pennsville Memorial HS; Pennsville, NJ; (Y); 21/210; Church Yth Grp; Girl Scts; Mrchg Band; School Musical; School Play; L Capt Pom Pon; Mgr Trk; Hon Roll; SPNSH.

CARITA, MICHAEL J; Bishop Eustace Prep Schl; Magnolia, NJ; (Y); 29/181; Am Leg Boys St; Drama Clb; Thesps; School Play; Var L Trk; NHS; School Musical; Stage Crew; Yrbk Stf; Lit Mag; Gloucester Twnshp Day Schlrshp 86; Coll Of William & Mary; Bus Mgm.

CARLIN, TODD; Roselle Catholic HS; Roselle, NJ; (Y); 35/160; Am Leg Boys St; Letterman Clb; Varsity Clb; School Play; Im Bsktbl; Var Crs Cntry; Var Trk; High Hon Roll; Hon Roll; Peer Grp Cnsllng 86; Villanova U; Law.

CARLL, DANA; Cumberland Christian HS; Bridgeton, NJ; (S); Church Yth Grp; Band; Chorus; Yrbk Phtg; Trs Soph Cls; Pres Jr Cls; Pres Sr Cls; Pres Stu Cncl; Var Fld Hcky; Trk; Scripture Mastery Awd; Eastern Coll; Intl Mrktng.

CARLO, THOMAS; Nutley HS; Nutley, NJ; (Y); Aud/Vis; Key Clb; Political Wkr; Nwsp Stf; JV Bsktbl; Var Socr; 2nd Tm All-Cnty Sccr 85-86; Nutley Untd Sccr Clb 83-86.

CARLSON, KRISTIN; Manalapan HS; Tennent, NJ; (Y); 10/450; Rep Church Yth Grp; Rep Sr Cls; Var Capt Cheerleading; High Hon Roll; NHS; Prfct Atten Awd; NJ Music Teachers Assn Hnrs Awd 85-86; Natl Piano Guild Hnrs 84-86; Intl Bus.

CARLSON, MICHAEL; Morsignor Donovan HS; Brick, NJ; (Y); 7/230; Political Wkr; High Hon Roll; Hon Roll; NHS; Boston U; Pre-Law.

CARLTON, KAREN; Morris Catholic HS; Parsippany, NJ; (Y); 73/142; Church Yth Grp; Hosp Aide; JV Bsktbl; Var Powder Puff Ftbl; Var Capt Socr; Nrsng.

CARMAGNOLA, TERESA; Morris Knolls HS; Denville, NJ; (Y); Var Socr; JV Sftbl; Hon Roll.

CARMAN, DESIREE; Woodstown HS; Elmer, NJ; (Y); Church Yth Grp; French Clb; Yrbk Stf; Var JV Sftbl; French Hon Soc; Acctg.

CARMELI, AUDREY; Parsippany HS; Parsippany, NJ; (Y); Church Yth Grp; Drama Clb; Trs Chorus; School Musical; School Play; Variety Show; High Hon Roll; Hon Roll; NHS; Prfct Atten Awd; N Jrsy Rgnl Choir 84-86.

CARMICHAEL, GREGORY; West Morris Central HS; Long Valley, NJ; (Y); 15/250; Church Yth Grp; Debate Tm; Drama Clb; FBLA; Acpl Chr; Swing Chorus; Nwsp Stf; Yrbk Stf; High Hon Roll; Jr NHS; 2nd Pl ST Wnnr Rssl E Lnning Piano Cmptn; WA ST U; Arch.

CARMODY, DAVID E; Hillsborough HS; Hillsborough, NJ; (Y); 3/292; Math Tm; Band; Pres Chorus; School Musical; Nwsp Rptr; NHS; Ntl Merit SF; St Schlr; Madrigals; Mrchg Band; Acad Tm; Yale U.

CARMODY, EILEEN; Rancocas Valley Regional HS; Mt Holly, NJ; (Y); Sec Church Yth Grp; Sec 4-H; Model UN; Band; Concert Band; Mrchg Band; JV Fld Hcky; Sftbl; Grls Ctznshp Inst Delg 86; Secndry Ed.

CARMOLINGO, CHRISTOPHER; Glassboro HS; Glassboro, NJ; (Y); Am Leg Boys St; Off Frsh Cls; Off Soph Cls; Off Jr Cls; Stu Cncl; Bsbl; Bsktbl; Ftbl; High Hon Roll; Hon Roll; Law.

CARMON, PAIGE; Villa Victoria Acad; Holland, PA; (Y); Math Clb; Chorus; Variety Show; Yrbk Ed-Chief; Lit Mag; VP Church Yth Grp; Capt Cheerleading; Var Sftbl; Hon Roll; Art Hnrs 84 & 85; La Salle U.

CARNATHAN, MARY THERESE; Mt Olive HS; Flanders, NJ; (Y); Church Yth Grp; Computer Clb; Exploring; FBLA; Service Clb; Coach Actv; High Hon Roll; Hon Roll; NHS; Pres Schlrshp Caldwell Coll 86; Caldwell Coll; Math.

CARNEY, MELISSA; Burlington Twp HS; Burlington, NJ; (Y); 20/116; French Clb; Ski Clb; Varsity Clb; Yrbk Stf; Var L Socr; Var L Sftbl; Hon Roll; Bus Adm.

CAROLA, LISA; Belleville HS; Belleville, NJ; (Y); OEA; Sec Frsh Cls; High Hon Roll; Hon Roll; Gregg Typng Awd 84 & 85; Booster Clb 85; Secy.

CAROLA, TERRY; Red Bank Catholic HS; Colts Neck, NJ; (Y); Latin Clb; Ski Clb; SADD; Off Frsh Cls; Soph Cls; Rep Jr Cls; JV Crs Cntry; Var Sftbl; JV Trk; Hon Roll.

CAROZZA, JOHN; South Hunterdon Regional HS; Lambertville, NJ; (S); 1/85; Am Leg Boys St; Trs Key Clb; Nwsp Ed-Chief; VP Jr Cls; VP Sr Cls; Pres Stu Cncl; Bsbl; Capt Crs Cntry; Golf; Pres NHS; Engrng & Appld Sci Medal Geo Wash U 86; Rutgers Schlr 86; Govs Schl 86.

CARPENTER, JOHN; Montville HS; Towaco, NJ; (Y); Letterman Clb; Varsity Clb; Rep Frsh Cls; Trs Jr Cls; Trs Sr Cls; JV Bsktbl; Var Ftbl; Var Lcrss; Cit Awd; High Hon Roll; 2nd Tm All Cnfrnc 85-86.

CARPENTIER, ROBERT JOHN; West Essex SR HS; Roseland, NJ; (Y); 124/351; Sec Church Yth Grp; Sec Model UN; Quiz Bowl; Band; Concert Band; Mrchg Band; Orch; School Play; Golf; Clara Luenther Schlrshp 86; Val Paraiso U; Pltcl Sci.

CARR, GREG; Kingsway Regional HS; Mickleton, NJ; (Y); 16/245; Mrchg Band; Variety Show; JV Var Bsktbl; Var Powder Puff Ftbl; Hon Roll; SICO Fndtn Schlrshp 86; Stockton ST Coll; Marine Sci.

CARR, JOHN; Roselle Catholic HS; Union, NJ; (Y); Boys Clb Am; Church Yth Grp; Computer Clb; Spanish Clb; Bsbl; Gym; Swmmng; Trk; Wrstlng; High Hon Roll; SONJ; Arch.

CARR, VICTORIA; Egg Harbor Twp HS; Cardiff, NJ; (S); 17/266; Art Clb; Cmnty Wkr; Key Clb; Stat Bsktbl; Stat Crs Cntry; Stat Trk; High Hon Roll; Jr NHS; NHS; Vrsty Letter In Acad 84-86; Hugh O Brian Ldrshp Sem 84-85; Riper Coll; Educ.

CARR, WARREN; East Orange HS; East Orange, NJ; (S); 80/438; Pres Church Yth Grp; Dance Clb; VP Exploring; Chorus; Church Choir; School Musical; Variety Show; Yrbk Bus Mgr; Capt Tennis; Gov Hon Prg Awd; Solo NJ All ST Opera Fstvl Comp 85 & 86; NJ Govnrs Awd Music Ed 85; Westminster Chrs Coll; Vocl.

CARRARA, DOUGLAS; James Caldwell HS; W Caldwell, NJ; (Y); Church Yth Grp; Debate Tm; Key Clb; Letterman Clb; Rep Stu Cncl; Var Bsbl; Capt Var Socr; Hon Roll; Drew U; Pol Sci.

CARRERA, MIRIAM; Hoboken HS; Hoboken, NJ; (Y); Church Yth Grp; Spanish Clb; Yrbk Stf; Hon Roll; Lion Awd; Bus.

CARRERAS, ANA; Linden HS; Linden, NJ; (Y); Orch; School Play; Off Frsh Cls; Off Soph Cls; Stu Cncl; Hon Roll; NHS; Fash Design.

CARRI, SUZANNE; Egg Harbor Township HS; Linwood, NJ; (S); Dance Clb; Bsktbl; Gym; Mgr(s); Sftbl; Trk; Hon Roll; Jr NHS; Prfct Atten Awd.

CARRINGTON, BIAFRA; Cumberland Regional HS; Bridgeton, NJ; (Y); 179/357; Cmnty Wkr; FBLA; Office Aide; Lit Mag; Hon Roll; Rutgers; Bus Adm.

CARRINGTON, DERRICK L; Pleasantville HS; Pleasantville, NJ; (Y); 12/136; Church Yth Grp; Church Choir; Capt Ftbl; L Trk; Capt Wt Lftg; Mst Lkly Succd, Mst Intllgnt 86; Trenton ST Coll; Acctg.

CARRINGTON, JOSEPH D; Camden Catholic HS; Camden, NJ; (Y); Am Leg Boys St; FBLA; ROTC; Scholastic Bowl; VP Spanish Clb; Concert Band; VP Frsh Cls; Var L Bsbl; JV L Bsktbl; Var VP Golf; Rutgers Coll; Crprtn Law.

CARRIZO, LUISA; Paterson Catholic R HS; Paterson, NJ; (Y); Rep Soph Cls; Rep Jr Cls; Rep Sr Cls; Rep Stu Cncl; Var Cheerleading; Score Keeper; Hon Roll; Acdmc All Amer Awd 86; Innr Cty Ensmbl Wrkshp Achvt Awd 86; Soc Stds Schlr Awd 85; Hofstra U; Soclgy.

CARROLL, DENYCE L; Trenton Central HS; Trenton, NJ; (Y); Dance Clb; Pep Clb; PAVAS; Teachers Aide; Drill Tm; VP Frsh Cls; Rep Stu Cncl; Hon Roll; Span Awd 84-85; Acctg.

CARROLL, TIM; Morristown HS; Morris Plains, NJ; (Y); Church Yth Grp; Cmnty Wkr; Political Wkr; Radio Clb; Stage Crew; Hon Roll; Electrical Engineering.

CARROW, THERESA; Pualsboro HS; Paulsboro, NJ; (Y); 33/152; Exploring; Coach Actv; Fld Hcky; Mat Maids; Wrstlng.

CARROZZA, PAUL; St Joseph Regional HS; Pearl River, NY; (Y); 4/167; Church Yth Grp; Civic Clb; Spanish Clb; JV Var Bowling; High Hon Roll; Hon Roll; Jr NHS; NHS; Spanish NHS; Marine Bio.

CARRUTH, KEVIN; Haddon Heights HS; Lawnside, NJ; (S); Aud/Vis; Church Yth Grp; JA; Church Choir; JV Bsbl; Ftbl; Var Trk; JV Wt Lftg; Var Wrstlng; Hon Roll; Bus Adm.

CARSON III, COLE; Linden HS; Linden, NJ; (Y); Church Yth Grp; Computer Clb; FCA; FBLA; Nwsp Sprt Ed; Rep Frsh Cls; JV Bsbl; JV Var Bsktbl; JV Var Crs Cntry; Hon Roll.

CARSON, LAVONNE; Barringer HS; Newark, NJ; (Y); Church Yth Grp; Exploring; Math Clb; Radio Clb; Teachers Aide; Chorus; Hon Roll; NHS; Opt Clb Awd; Jr NHS; Dr Pfeffer Awd 83-84; Wrld Impct Cmnty Teen Clb Ctznshp Awd 82; Fairleigh Dickerson U; Bio Engr.

CARSON, MATTHEW T; Delsea Regional HS; Newfield, NJ; (Y); Science Clb; High Hon Roll; Hon Roll; Prfct Atten Awd; Tchr.

CARSWELL III, JASPER LEE; St Pius X Reginol HS; Plainfield, NJ; (Y); Boy Scts; Church Yth Grp; Cmnty Wkr; Office Aide; ROTC; Varsity Clb; Band; Nwsp Stf; Bsktbl; Ftbl; Comp.

CARSWELL, JOHN E; Allentown HS; Clarksburg, NJ; (Y); Am Leg Boys St; Drama Clb; Chorus; Madrigals; School Musical; School Play; Stage Crew; VP Soph Cls; VP Jr Cls; Rep Stu Cncl; Law.

CARSWELL, KAREN L; Warren Hills Regional SR HS; Washington, NJ; (Y); 34/225; School Play; Lit Mag; Bsktbl; Crs Cntry; Powder Puff Ftbl; Hans P Meischner Art Schlrshp 86; Summer Arts Inst Vis Art STU 86; Beaver Coll; Vsul Art.

CARTAGENA, TRINI; North Bergen HS; North Bergen, NJ; (Y); 29/398; French Clb; Chorus; Color Guard; Yrbk Stf; Rep Frsh Cls; French Hon Soc; Hon Roll; NHS; Svc Awd-Stg Mngng NB Mdlng Clb 85-86; Cert Rcgntn-Teen Arts Fstvl-Chr 86; Columbia U; Bio.

CARTER, ALLEN; Carteret HS; Carteret, NJ; (Y); 17/198; Boy Scts; Science Clb; Nwsp Sprt Ed; Yrbk Sprt Ed; Var Crs Cntry; Var Trk; Carteret Sprtsmen Assoc Vrsty Wntr Trck 86; Vrsty Ltr Wntr Trck 86; Military Acad; Aero Engr.

CARTER, CARNEL; Highland HS; Blackwood, NJ; (Y); Church Yth Grp; Am Leg Aux Girls St; Latin Clb; Variety Show; Bsktbl; Tennis; Hon Roll; Hnr Rll 84-85; Georgetown U; Musc.

CARTER, COLLEEN; St Joseph HS; Franklinvilley, NJ; (Y); Chorus; Concert Band; Var Cheerleading; Hon Roll; Dance Awds US Trnmnt Dance 84 & 85; Hnr Awd Typng I 84; Hnr Awd Typng II 85; Nrsng.

CARTER JR, DONALD P; Seton Hall Prep; Newark, NJ; (Y); Boy Scts; Church Yth Grp; Key Clb; Science Clb; Varsity Clb; Church Choir; Nwsp Rptr; Yrbk Rptr; Im Bsktbl; Var Capt Trk; Biolgy Awd 84-85; Med.

CARTER, JAMES; Deran HS; Delran, NJ; (Y); VP Jr Cls; VP Sr Cls; Rep Stu Cncl; Var L Bsbl; Ftbl; Im Vllybl; Im Wt Lftg; NHS; Purdue U; Comp Dsgn Engr.

CARTER, SAUNDRA; Frank H Morrel-Irvington HS; Newark, NJ; (Y); 11/400; Pres Church Yth Grp; FBLA; Spanish Clb; Sec Church Choir; Ed Yrbk Stf; Rep Stu Cncl; Var Bowling; Var Trk; Hon Roll; Drama Clb; Spec Achvmnt Sci 82; Chorrus Prtcptn 82; De Vry Inst Of Tech; Compu Prg.

CARTER, SHANNON; A P Schalick HS; Bridgeton, NJ; (Y); Chorus; Variety Show; Stat Trk.

CARTER, STACEY; Wildwood Catholic HS; Cape May, NJ; (Y); Spanish Clb; Varsity Clb; Nwsp Ed-Chief; Nwsp Phtg; Nwsp Rptr; Nwsp Stf; Co-Capt Cheerleading; Diving; Swmmng; Tennis; 2nd Pl Cape May Cnty Art Lg 85-86.

CARTER, TAMIKO; Plainfield HS; Plainfield, NJ; (Y); 34/456; Model UN; Office Aide; Pep Clb; Teachers Aide; Flag Corp; Mrchg Band; Yrbk Stf; Lit Mag; Rep Jr Cls; Capt Pom Pon; Law.

CARTY, PATRICK; Wall HS; Sea Girt, NJ; (Y); Chess Clb; Band; Concert Band; Jazz Band; Mrchg Band; Symp Band; Var Bowling; High Hon Roll; Hon Roll; Mst Imprvd Bnd Mbr 85-86; Hstry Prfssr.

CARTY, TAMMI; Paulsboro HS; Bridgeport, NJ; (Y); Boy Scts; Office Aide; Brdgprt Vlntr Fire Co Ladies JR Axlry Pres 2 Yrs, Treas 2 Yrs; Berkley Schl Bus; Accntng.

CARUSO, ANDREA; St John Vianney HS; Middletown, NJ; (Y); 2/298; Math Tm; SADD; Yrbk Stf; Rep Stu Cncl; JV Var Socr; Cit Awd; Gov Hon Prg Awd; High Hon Roll; Hon Roll; NHS; Congrssnl Schlr 86; Engl Awd 86.

CARUSO, CARL; North Plainfield HS; N Plainfield, NJ; (Y); 21/180; Church Yth Grp; Math Tm; Scholastic Bowl; JV Bsbl; JV Var Ftbl; Wt Lftg; Hon Roll; NHS; Engrng.

CARUSO, DAVID; West Morris Central HS; Hackettstown, NJ; (Y); Am Leg Boys St; Radio Clb; Varsity Clb; Nwsp Rptr; Nwsp Sprt Ed; Sec Frsh Cls; Rep Jr Cls; Rep Stu Cncl; Var Socr; Var Capt Trk; Pol Sci.

CARUSO, KATIE; Wildwood Catholic HS; Cape May Ch, NJ; (Y); 1/120; Rep Frsh Cls; Var Capt Bsktbl; Var Sftbl; DAR Awd; High Hon Roll; Hon Roll; NHS; Spanish NHS; St Schlr; Rutgers Schlr 86; Chrstphr Clmbs Essay Cntst 86; Law.

CARUSO, VINCENT; Rancocas Valley Regional HS; Mount Holly, NJ; (Y); DECA; Varsity Clb; Var L Trk; Hon Roll; Prfct Atten Awd; Physical Ftns; Acctng Awd; Business Admin.

CARUSO, WILLIAM; Verona HS; Verona, NJ; (Y); Civic Clb; Ski Clb; Spanish Clb; Nwsp Rptr; Nwsp Sprt Ed; Nwsp Stf; Yrbk Rptr; Yrbk Sprt Ed; Yrbk Stf; Lit Mag; 2nd Tm Nrthrn Hls Cnfrnc Bsbl Ctchr 86; Cmmnctns.

CARVAJAL, LUZ ELENA; Memorial HS; West New York, NJ; (Y); Key Clb; Crs Cntry; Sftbl; Trk; NY U; Dentist.

CARVALHO, JOAQUIM; Toms River High Schl East; Toms River, NJ; (Y); Var Bowling; Hon Roll; Bwlng Vrsty Awd 83-86; Bus.

CARVER, JANET MARIE; Brick Twp HS; Brick Town, NJ; (Y); 16/318; Debate Tm; Drama Clb; French Clb; SADD; Thesps; School Musical; School Play; Stage Crew; Lit Mag; High Hon Roll; HOSA 85; Alpha Delta Kappa Schlrshp 86; Brick Rtry Schlrshp 86; E Stroudsburg U; Engl Lit.

CASAGRANDE, MARY; Monsignor Donovan HS; Toms River, NJ; (Y); German Clb; Science Clb; Hon Roll; NHS; High Yr Grd Avrg Germ II 85; Equine Sci.

CASALE, MICHAEL; James Caldwell HS; Caldwell, NJ; (Y); 6/265; Debate Tm; Drama Clb; Thesps; Band; Concert Band; School Play; High Hon Roll; NHS; Ntl Merit SF; Aud/Vis; NJ Distngshd Schlr 86; U Of PA; Bio Chem.

CASAMENTO, DAWN; Notre Dame HS; Belle Meade, NJ; (Y); 36/486; Ski Clb; Church Choir; Var Crs Cntry; Stat Fld Hcky; Mgr(s); JV Score Keeper; High Hon Roll; Hon Roll; NHS; Business.

CASAROW, ANDREA; Cumberland Regional HS; Bridgeton, NJ; (S); 1/400; Intnl Clb; JCL; Ski Clb; Stage Crew; Nwsp Rptr; Yrbk Stf; Lit Mag; High Hon Roll; Hon Roll; NHS; Maxima Cum Laude Silver Mdl Natl Latin Exam 83-84; Summa Cum Laude Gold Mdl Natl Latin Exam 84-85; Criminology.

CASASUS, ALBERTO; Memorial HS; W New York, NJ; (Y); 49/376; Computer Clb; Band; Concert Band; Drm & Bgl; Jazz Band; Mrchg Band; Rep Frsh Cls; Rep Soph Cls; Rep Sr Cls; Hon Roll; Rutgers U; Biochem.

CASAVINA, LOUIS R; River Dell SR HS; River Edge, NJ; (Y); 18/213; Am Leg Boys St; Band; JV Bsbl; Var Ftbl; Bsktbl; Wt Lftg; Wrstlng; Cit Awd; Hon Roll; NHS; NJ ST Intrschlstc Athltc Assoc Awd 85; Athltc Awd In Wrstlng 85-86; Ltl Lg ST Chmpns 81; Crmnl Lwyr.

CASAZZA, NANCY; Montville HS; Pine Brook, NJ; (Y); 135/250; FBLA; Ski Clb; Varsity Clb; Fld Hcky; Var Ftbl; Mgr Var Lcrss; JV Var Mgr(s); Powder Puff Ftbl; High Hon Roll; Hon Roll; Marist Coll; Comm.

CASCIANO, JENNIFER; Newton HS; Newton, NJ; (S); 19/210; Madrigals; School Musical; Variety Show; Yrbk Stf; Trs Frsh Cls; Trs Soph Cls; Trs Jr Cls; Stat Ftbl; Hon Roll; NHS; Bus Admin.

CASCIATO, CELESTE; Haddon Township HS; Westmont, NJ; (Y); Cmnty Wkr; Hosp Aide; Yrbk Stf; Sftbl; Hon Roll; Spec Awd For Outstndng JR Vlntr 85; Med.

CASEY, GINA MARIE; Holy Spirit HS; Margate, NJ; (Y); 2/336; Church Yth Grp; Cmnty Wkr; Exploring; French Clb; Speech Tm; Rep Frsh Cls; Pres Jr Cls; Rptr Sr Cls; Bsktbl; Var Capt Sftbl; Ordr Sns Itly Amer 86; Unico Schlrshp 86; Natl Army Rsrv Schlr/Athlt 86; Villanova; Lbrl Arts.

CASEY, KATHLEEN; Metawan Regional HS; Matawan, NJ; (S); 19/365; Girl Scts; Math Tm; Speech Tm; Band; Concert Band; Jazz Band; Mrchg Band; Yrbk Stf; Hon Roll.

CASEY, SEAN; Paramus Catholic Boys HS; Rochelle Pk, NJ; (Y); 42/178; Boy Scts; Interior Decorator.

CASHMAN, JANET; Chatham Twp HS; Chatham Twp, NJ; (Y); 24/138; Sec Church Yth Grp; Pres Frsh Cls; Pres Jr Cls; Rep Stu Cncl; Var Bsktbl; Var Capt Fld Hcky; Var Capt Lcrss; High Hon Roll; NHS; Key Clb; Peer Spprt Grp 84-87.

CASPER, BRIAN; High Point Regional HS; Augusta, NJ; (Y); 12/260; Aud/Vis; CAP; Debate Tm; German Clb; Quiz Bowl; JV Socr; JV Trk; High Hon Roll; Hon Roll; NC ST U; Comp Engrng.

CASPER, DEVIN; Cumberland Regional HS; Bridgeton, NJ; (Y); #82 In Class; Office Aide; Var Bsbl; Var Socr; Hon Roll; Bus.

CASSADAY, BRYAN J; St Augustine Prep; Clayton, NJ; (Y); 5/50; Drama Clb; Key Clb; Band; Chorus; Nwsp Ed-Chief; Yrbk Ed-Chief; Rep Stu Cncl; High Hon Roll; Art Clb; Church Yth Grp; Drxl U Prsdnts Frshmn Schlrshp 86; NJ Grdn ST Dstngshd Schlr; Drexel U; Finance.

CASSADAY, KATHLEEN; Woodstown HS; Woodstown, NJ; (Y); VP Trs Church Yth Grp; Spanish Clb; Co-Capt Flag Corp; Nwsp Rptr; Hon Roll; Exploring; Office Aide; Rep Stu Cncl; Stat Trk; Prs Volunteens 85-86, Historian 84-85; Pharm.

CASSEUS, SANDRA; Essec Catholic Girls HS; Irvington, NJ; (Y); 30/80; Pep Clb; Nwsp Phtg; Vllybl; :Doctor.

CASSIDY, DEBBIE; Newton HS; Newton, NJ; (Y); Ski Clb; Spanish Clb; Nwsp Stf; Gym; Var Sftbl; Prfct Atten Awd; Tchr Assoc Bk Schlrshp 86; Montclair ST.

CASSIDY, HEATHER; Glassboro HS; Glassboro, NJ; (Y); Drama Clb; Varsity Clb; School Play; Trs Soph Cls; Trs Jr Cls; Trs Sr Cls; Cheerleading; Trk; Hon Roll; Trs NHS; Chem Caravn Rtgrs 86; U Of IL; Chem Engnrng.

CASSIDY, JOSEPH; Long Branch HS; Long Branch, NJ; (Y); 3/299; ROTC; Bsbl; Coach Actv; Socr; Hon Roll; NHS; Elec Engr.

CASSIDY, LINDA; Kittatinny Regional HS; Newton, NJ; (S); 3/164; Hosp Aide; Band; Mrchg Band; Symp Band; Nwsp Stf; High Hon Roll; NHS; Rotary Awd; Wind Ensmble Area Band 86, Regn Band 86; Sussex Cnty Music Fndtn Scholar 83; Sci.

CASTAGNA, DINA; Holy Spirit HS; Northfield, NJ; (Y); 27/384; French Clb; NHS; Rotary Awd; Rotary Yth Exchng Pgm Brazil 85-86; Aviatn.

CASTAGNETTO, MARTIN; Perth Amboy HS; Perth Amboy, NJ; (Y); Camera Clb; Computer Clb; Math Clb; Radio Clb; Nwsp Phtg; Off Sr Cls; Socr; Tennis; SAR Awd; Dedry; Elec.

CASTAGNO, LOUIS; Hudson Catholic HS; Jersey Cty, NJ; (Y); 2/190; Computer Clb; Socr; Hon Roll; NHS; Ntl Merit Ltr.

CASTANEDA, LIANA; Vailsburg HS; Newark, NJ; (Y); Cit Awd; Hon Roll.

CASTELLANO, MIGUEL; Memorial HS; W New York, NJ; (Y); Art Clb; Boy Scts; Church Yth Grp; Science Clb; Band; Concert Band; Jazz Band; Mrchg Band; Pep Band; Symp Band; Ad Altare Dei-Boy Sct Rlgs Awd 84; Stevens; Elec Engr.

CASTELLANO, NEIL; Manalapan HS; Manalapan, NJ; (Y); Varsity Clb; Var L Bowling; Var L Trk; Comp Engr.

CASTELLO, MARIA T; Bishop George Ahr HS; So Plainfield, NJ; (Y); 40/240; Church Yth Grp; Dance Clb; Intnl Clb; Ski Clb; Rep Frsh Cls; Rep Soph Cls; Rep Sr Cls; Capt Cheerleading; Coach Actv; Var Gym; Nrsng Schrlshp 86; Coachng Awd; Hmcmng Princess 82-85; U DE; Nrsng.

CASTERLIN, DAWN; Newton HS; Andover, NJ; (Y); 27/190; German Clb; Varsity Clb; Chorus; Church Choir; Fld Hcky; Hon Roll; Jr NHS; Coaches Awd-Fld Hcky 85; U Of New Haven; Scl Wrkr.

CASTIGLIA, JEFF; Paramus Catholic Boys Schl; Lodi, NJ; (Y); 30/180; Church Yth Grp; Civic Clb; Cmnty Wkr; 4-H; Stage Crew; Nwsp Stf; Yrbk Stf; Stu Cncl; Fld Hcky; Ftbl; Unico Schlrshp Awd 86; Devry Inst Of Tech; Engrng.

CASTIGLIONE, PATRICIA; Glen Rock JR SR HS; Glen Rock, NJ; (Y); 28/153; Art Clb; Drama Clb; Hosp Aide; JCL; Latin Clb; School Play; JV Var Socr; High Hon Roll; Jr NHS; NHS; Law.

CASTILLO, VLADIMIR; John F Kennedy HS; Paterson, NJ; (Y); Latin Clb; Math Clb; Science Clb; Nwsp Rptr; Yrbk Rptr; JV Socr; NHS; Mech Engr.

CASTNER, DARLENE; Monsignor Donovan HS; Toms River, NJ; (Y); Church Yth Grp; Letterman Clb; Ski Clb; Sftbl; Trk; Wt Lftg; Psych.

CASTNER, KAREN; Kittatinny Regional HS; Middleville, NJ; (Y); 70/230; Sec Spanish Clb; Concert Band; Mrchg Band; Powder Puff Ftbl; JV Trk; Pysch.

CASTNER, SUE; Belvidere HS; Belvidere, NJ; (S); #7 In Class; Am Leg Aux Girls St; Letterman Clb; Varsity Clb; Nwsp Rptr; Var JV Bsktbl; Var JV Fld Hcky; Lcrss; Var JV Sftbl; Hon Roll; Trs NHS; Crmnl Justc.

CASTORO, ANTONIA; Emerson HS; Union City, NJ; (Y); Computer Clb; FNA; Hosp Aide; SADD; Varsity Clb; Rep Stu Cncl; Ftbl; Pom Pon; Socr; Sal; Montclair ST Coll; Acctng.

CASTRILLON, DANIEL M; Don Bosco Prep; Montvale, NJ; (Y); Boy Scts; Church Yth Grp; Cmnty Wkr; Pep Clb; Political Wkr; Red Cross Aide; Ski Clb; SADD; Stage Crew; Nwsp Phtg; Bob Fllr All-Str Bsbll 84-85; All-Sbrbrn Trck 85-86; Sndy Koufx All-Str Bsbll 82-83; Pre-Law.

CASTRO JR, EL; Piscataway HS; Piscataway, NJ; (Y); Drama Clb; Math Tm; Science Clb; Chorus; Church Choir; Madrigals; Orch; School Musical; School Play; Swing Chorus; Govs Hnr Prog Sci; Natl Mrt Ltr; Natl Hnr Soc; Columbia U Sci Hnrs Prog; Rutgers U Sci Apprntceshp Prog.

CASTRO, JAN A; Hunterdon Central HS; Flemington, NJ; (Y); 9/560; Nwsp Ed-Chief; Hon Roll; NHS; Ntl Merit SF; Russian Studies.

CASTRO, JHACCO; William L Dickinson HS; Jersey City, NJ; (Y); Pres Spanish Clb; School Play; Stu Cncl; Lion Awd; Sal; Glassboro ST Coll; Pltcl Sci.

CASTRO, MARIA C; Mary Help Of Christians Acad; Paterson, NJ; (Y); 40/68; Computer Clb; Chorus; School Play; Stage Crew; Tobe-Coburn NY; Fshn Buying.

CASTRO, NANCY; Montclair Kimberley Acad; Newark, NJ; (Y); Pres Sec Church Yth Grp; Intnl Clb; Service Clb; Church Choir; Lit Mag; Hon Roll; Ntl Merit Ltr; Funk Awd-Hghst Grd Pt Avg 83; Frank Poncho Brogn Memrl Schlrshp 85; Dartmouth Clb Bk Awd 85.

CASULLI, KRISTEN; Mount Olive HS; Flanders, NJ; (Y); AFS; Ski Clb; Varsity Clb; Rep Jr Cls; Rep Stu Cncl; Var Bsktbl; Var Fld Hcky; JV Sftbl; High Hon Roll; NHS; Vet.

CASWELL, JAMELL AHMAD; John F Kennedy HS; Willingboro, NJ; (Y); 18/270; Am Leg Boys St; Church Yth Grp; Church Choir; Crs Cntry; Trk; Hon Roll; NHS; ROTC; Aero Engrng.

CATALANELLO, ARTHUR L; Northern Valley Regional HS; Closter, NJ; (Y); 62/250; Church Yth Grp; Ski Clb; School Musical; Nwsp Phtg; Nwsp Rptr; JV Var Socr; JV Trk; Hon Roll; NHS; Pres Acadmc Ftns Awd; CSPA Outstndng Contrbn Jrnlsm; Ithaca Clg; Rado.

CATANZARO, JILL; Westfield SR HS; Westfield, NJ; (Y); 87/529; Nwsp Ed-Chief; Nwsp Rptr; Bsktbl; High Hon Roll; Hon Roll; NHS; Bnkg.

CATANZARO, TARA; St Aloysius HS; Jersey City, NJ; (Y); Civic Clb; Exploring; Spanish Clb; High Hon Roll; NHS; Pres Citn Acdmc Achvt Brnz Mdl 86; Awd Excllnce Stnogrphy I, Typng II 86.

CATERINA, SAM; Jackson Memorial HS; Jackson, NJ; (Y); 50/420; French Clb; Math Clb; Math Tm; Science Clb; Spanish Clb; Varsity Clb; Nwsp Sprt Ed; Nwsp Stf; Bsbl; Crs Cntry; J P Stevens Inst; Physics.

CATERINI, CORINNE; Wildwood HS; Wildwood, NJ; (Y); 32/113; Spanish Clb; Spanish NHS; School Play; Yrbk Stf; Rep Jr Cls; Mgr(s); Acad Achvt Spnsh 86; Spnsh.

CATLETT, CAROLYN; Paul VI HS; Lindenwold, NJ; (S); 24/474; Church Yth Grp; English Clb; Math Clb; Church Choir; JV Var Cheerleading; Hon Roll; NHS; Long Island U; Jrnlsm.

CATO, BRIAN; Abraham Clark HS; Roselle, NJ; (Y); Chess Clb; Service Clb; Church Choir; Tennis; Acctnt.

CATTELL, MEGAN; Clayton HS; Clayton, NJ; (Y); Drama Clb; VP Key Clb; Chorus; Mrchg Band; School Musical; Nwsp Rptr; Yrbk Stf; Bsbl; Sftbl; Thtre Arts.

CAUDA, LISA; Montville Twp HS; Pine Brook, NJ; (Y); 36/262; Art Clb; Hosp Aide; VP Intnl Clb; Spanish Clb; Lit Mag; Rep Jr Cls; High Hon Roll; Hon Roll; NHS; Grphc Arts.

CAUGHRON, KIMBERLY; Cumberland Regional HS; Bridgeton, NJ; (S); 12/369; Church Yth Grp; Drama Clb; Intnl Clb; JCL; Ski Clb; Varsity Clb; Yrbk Stf; Stu Cncl; JV Bsktbl; Var Fld Hcky; Cum Laude Latin Awd 84.

CAULTON, SUSAN; South Hunterdon Regional HS; Stockton, NJ; (Y); 6/65; Art Clb; Key Clb; Yrbk Stf; Hon Roll; Grad Hnr Guard 86; Art.

CAUTILLO, EUGENE J; Union Catholic Regional HS; Linden, NJ; (Y); Political Wkr; Service Clb; Spanish Clb; Teachers Aide; Rep Frsh Cls; Rep Soph Cls; Rep Jr Cls; Rep Sr Cls; Rep Stu Cncl; Tennis; Susquechanna U.

CAVACIER, BUCK; Atl City HS; Margate, NJ; (Y); Computer Clb; Office Aide; Trs Jr Cls; JV Bsbl; Bsktbl; Capt Golf; Hon Roll; NHS; Key Clb 84-86; Princeton; Invstmnt Banking.

CAVAGE, BILL; Highland Reg HS; Laurel Springs, NJ; (Y); Service Clb; JV Crs Cntry; JV Swmmng; Var Trk; RYLA 85; Arthur Calabrese Mem Schlrhsp 86; Ralph Citro Unsung Athlete Awd; WVU; Aerospace Engrng.

CAVALERI, GREG P; West Milford Twp HS; West Milford, NJ; (Y); Am Leg Boys St; Boys Clb Am; Varsity Clb; JV Ftbl; JV Wrstlng; ROTC.

CAVALERO, CATHERINE; Kittatinny Regional HS; Newton, NJ; (Y); 33/230; Boys Clb Am; Ski Clb; Spanish Clb; Pres Frsh Cls; Im Swmmng; Im Trk; Im Wt Lftg; High Hon Roll; Hon Roll; NHS.

CAVANAGH, ANNAMARIE; Red Bank Catholic HS; Red Bank, NJ; (Y); Cmnty Wkr; French Clb; Hosp Aide; Library Aide; Ski Clb; SADD; Flag Corp; Ed Nwsp Phtg; Yrbk Phtg; Var JV Sftbl; Vlntry Actn Awd 86; Sftbl All Star 84; Pltcl Sci.

CAVANAUGH, MAUREEN; Sacred Heart HS; Newfield, NJ; (S); 13/67; Church Yth Grp; Yrbk Ed-Chief; Sec Sr Cls; Stat Socr; High Hon Roll; Hon Roll; NHS; French Clb; Natl Hnr Rll Yrbk & Ldrshp Organztn 85; SR Clss Sec & Treas 85-86; Pre-Law.

CAVE, MEGIN; Manasquan HS; Manasquan, NJ; (Y); Political Wkr; VP Spanish Clb; Mgr(s); JV Socr; High Hon Roll.

CAVENDER, MELISSA; Cinnaminson HS; Cinnaminson, NJ; (Y); 18/254; German Clb; Frsh Cls; Rep Soph Cls; Rep Jr Cls; Rep Sr Cls; NHS; Natl Merit Recommended Schlr 85; Gladys Parker Mem Awd 86; Rutgers Coll.

CAVLOV, ANNEMARIE; N Bergen HS; North Bergen, NJ; (Y); Art Clb; Church Yth Grp; Coach Actv.

CECCOMANCINI, ANTHONY J; North Plainfield HS; N Plainfield, NJ; (Y); 28/195; Drama Clb; Key Clb; Model UN; Pep Clb; SADD; Chorus; School Musical; School Play; Yrbk Phtg; Trs Stu Cncl; Glf Vrsty Ltr 85; Cinematgrphy.

CECE, JENNIFER; Union HS; Union, NJ; (Y); Dance Clb; Girl Scts; Library Aide; Spanish Clb; Chorus; Jr Cls; Hon Roll; Bio Medcl Engrng.

CEHELSKY, ANNE; Roselle Catholic HS; Roselle, NJ; (S); Nwsp Rptr; Yrbk Stf; Rep Jr Cls; Trs Stu Cncl; Capt Bsktbl; Capt Socr; Hon Roll; NHS; French Clb; Grls Ctznshp Inst Delgt 85; Acctng.

CEKIC, LINDA; Franklin HS; Somerset, NJ; (Y); 9/313; Church Yth Grp; Trs French Clb; Library Aide; VP Model UN; Political Wkr; French Hon Soc; High Hon Roll; Hon Roll; Jr NHS; NHS; Outstndng Frgn Lang Stu Awd 86; Frgn Lang Ed NJ Awd 86; WA Wrkshp Congrssnl Sem Awd 85; Intl Rltns.

CELENTANO, VINCENT F; Lakewood HS; Lakewood, NJ; (Y); 60/300; English Clb; VP French Clb; FBLA; Band; Concert Band; Drm & Bgl; Jazz Band; Pres Mrchg Band; Pep Band; Symp Band; PA ST; Bus Adm.

CELENTANO, WILLIAM; St Peters Prep; Cliffside Pk, NJ; (Y); Cmnty Wkr; Computer Clb; ROTC; School Play; Lit Mag; Tennis; Rutgers; Corp Mgmt.

CELENZA, CLAIRE; St Mary HS; Rutherford, NJ; (S); 6/47; Drama Clb; Nwsp Stf; VP Frsh Cls; Sec Soph Cls; VP Jr Cls; Stu Cncl; Bsktbl; Sftbl; French Hon Soc; NHS.

CELESTE, CATHERINE; Wayne Valley HS; Wayne, NJ; (Y); 98/311; Ski Clb; Chorus; Lit Mag; Socr; Hon Roll; Fencing Tm 85-86; Math.

CELESTE, JOHN; North Bergen HS; Guttenberg, NJ; (Y); 56/470; Nwsp Bus Mgr; Nwsp Ed-Chief; Nwsp Stf; Lit Mag; Trs Soph Cls; Pres Jr Cls; Boy Scts; Chess Clb; Computer Clb; Rep Frsh Cls; Merit Soc 86-87; Ordr Of Arrow Ntl Brthrhd Of Sct Hnr Cmprs; US Sccr Fdrtn Lcnsd Ref; Comp Sys Anlys.

CELESTINE, NANCY; Middletown HS South; Middletown, NJ; (S); 17/434; Dance Clb; Math Clb; Math Tm; Pep Clb; Band; Jazz Band; Mrchg Band; Pep Band; Symp Band; Hon Roll; Outstndg Achvt Dance 83-86, Alg 83; Stevens Inst Tech; Chem Engr.

CELI, THOMAS; Burlington City HS; Burlington, NJ; (Y); 29/168; Am Leg Boys St; Cmnty Wkr; Letterman Clb; Bsbl; Bsktbl; Var L Ftbl; Var L Trk; Wt Lftg; Hon Roll; Springfield Coll; Bus.

CELIA, MARC; Clearview Regional HS; Mantua, NJ; (Y); 6/161; Boy Scts; Concert Band; Jazz Band; Mrchg Band; Yrbk Ed-Chief; Hon Roll; NHS; Bstn U; Med.

CENERI, SUZANNE; Wayne Valley HS; Wayne, NJ; (Y); 36/312; Church Yth Grp; FBLA; GAA; Red Cross Aide; Ski Clb; Spanish Clb; Var Socr; Hon Roll; NHS; One To One Schlrshp & Awd 86; Var Awd; U Of DE; Accntng.

CENSULLO, CHRIS; Northern Valley Regional HS; Harrington Pk, NJ; (Y); 87/400; ROTC; Crs Cntry; Var Trk.

CENSULLO, PATRICIA; North Bergen HS; North Bergen, NJ; (Y); French Clb; Key Clb; Office Aide; Rep Soph Cls; Rep Sr Cls; Var Stat Mat Maids; Var Stat Score Keeper; Var Tennis; Var Trk; Hon Roll; Georgetown U; Pol Sci.

CENTENO, JOSE; St Peters Prep; Jersey City, NJ; (Y); French Clb; Spanish Clb; Wrstlng; Hon Roll; Bus.

CENTOFANTE, FRANCES; Red Bank Catholic HS; Matawan, NJ; (Y); Hosp Aide; Math Clb; Pres NFL; School Musical; Nwsp Stf; NHS; NJ ST Teen Arts Qualfctn 86; Pre-Med.

CERASI JR, JOSEPH; Maple Shade HS; Maple Shade, NJ; (Y); Am Leg Boys St; Church Yth Grp; Bsbl; Ftbl; Jr NHS; Tm MVP Burlington Cnty Ftbl Clb 85; 1st Tm All Burlington Cnty Bsbl 86; 1st Tm All Grp I S Jersey Bsb; Business Mgmt.

CERASI, VICTORIA; Highland Regional HS; Blackwood, NJ; (S); #7 In Class; Computer Clb; Drama Clb; Concert Band; Capt Drill Tm; Trs Soph Cls; Sec Stu Cncl; JV Capt Socr; High Hon Roll; NHS.

CERBOLLES, ROD; Don Bosco Prep HS; Blauvelt, NY; (Y); Hon Roll; Natl Hon Roll 86; Architecture.

CERCHIO, PAM; Red Bank Catholic HS; Rumson, NJ; (Y); Ski Clb; SADD; Flag Corp; Lit Mag; VP Soph Cls; VP Jr Cls; Var Trk; Twrlr; Therapy.

CERESI, C ELISABETH; Morris Knolls HS; Denville, NJ; (Y); 35/367; Varsity Clb; Yrbk Stf; Rep Frsh Cls; Rep Soph Cls; Rep Jr Cls; Trs Sr Cls; Rep Stu Cncl; Var Capt Fld Hcky; Hon Roll; Pres Schlr; Schl Svc Schlrshp 86; Villanova U; Acctng.

CERESI, DEBORAH; Morris Knolls HS; Denville, NJ; (Y); 42/383; Sec Sr Cls; Cheerleading; Var Fld Hcky; JV Trk; Frshmn Awrns Ldr 85; Frshmn Awrns Strng Committee 86; Bus Mgmt.

CERNIGLIA, LISA; Kinnelon HS; Kinnelon, NJ; (Y); 30/176; Church Yth Grp; Exploring; German Clb; Hosp Aide; Spanish Clb; Var JV Bsktbl; JV Sftbl; Hon Roll; NHS; Spanish NHS; Psychlgy.

CERONE, ROSE; Haddon Township HS; W Collingswood Ht, NJ; (Y); Office Aide; Varsity Clb; Capt Drill Tm; Drm & Bgl; Stat Bsbl; Var Capt Cheerleading; Capt Pom Pon; Phys Thrpy.

CERPA, JULIO; Clifton HS; Clifton, NJ; (Y); 140/715; Boys Clb Am; Boy Scts; Church Yth Grp; Office Aide; Spanish Clb; Yrbk Stf; Frsh Cls; Pres Stu Cncl; JV Var Socr; Jr NHS; Yth Wk 84; Cnstrctn.

CERRA, MICHAEL; Roselle Catholic HS; Roselle, NJ; (S); Debate Tm; Math Clb; NFL; Speech Tm; Rep Frsh Cls; Stu Cncl; Hon Roll.

CERRATO, CHRIS A; Vernon Township HS; Sussex, NJ; (Y); 3/225; Am Leg Boys St; Trs JCL; Latin Clb; Scholastic Bowl; Wrstlng; High Hon Roll; Hon Roll; Kiwanis Awd; NHS; Prfct Atten Awd; SR Advisor 85-86; Elks Awd 86; Hnrb Mntn Natl French Test 85 & 86; Rutgers U; Bio.

CERTISIMO, ARTHUR; North Bergen HS; Gladstone, NJ; (Y); 47/470; Key Clb; Rep Jr Cls; Rep Sr Cls; JV Bsktbl; Hon Roll; NHS.

CERVINO, SCOTT; Brick Town HS; Bricktown, NJ; (Y); 92/364; Band; Concert Band; Jazz Band; Var Socr; Hon Roll; Coaches Awd-Sccr; Belmont Abbey Coll; Crmnlgy.

CERWINSKI, CHRISTINE; St Aloysius HS; Jersey City, NJ; (Y); Church Yth Grp; Office Aide; Political Wkr; SADD; Yrbk Stf; Rep Stu Cncl; Bsktbl; Bowling; Sftbl; Vllybl; Bus Mgmt.

CESAREO, SONIA; Hoboken HS; Hoboken, NJ; (Y); Sec Church Yth Grp; Spanish Clb; Church Choir; Yrbk Stf; JV Trk; Elks Awd; Kiwanis Awd; Nrsng.

CESTONE, CHRISTINA; Toms River North HS; Toms River, NJ; (Y); 38/412; Sec French Clb; Rep FBLA; Intnl Clb; Band; Color Guard; Mrchg Band; Rep Frsh Cls; Pom Pon; Trk; Hon Roll; Soph Yr Acadmc Ltr 85; U Of CT Bridgeport; Fash Merc.

CHA, KYUNG; Parsippany HS; Lake Hiawatha, NJ; (Y); Mgr Art Clb; Cmnty Wkr; Mgr Dance Clb; Mgr FBLA; Mgr Intnl Clb; Mgr JA; Mgr Math Clb; Mgr Pep Clb; Mgr PAVAS; Mgr Spanish Clb; Drew U.

CHACHKES, MICHELLE; Fort Lee HS; Ft Lee, NJ; (Y); Cmnty Wkr; French Clb; FBLA; Library Aide; Teachers Aide; Stu Cncl; Hon Roll; Rutgers U; Psychlgy.

CHADWICK, KATHLEEN; Holy Cross HS; Willingboro, NJ; (Y); 187/369; Church Choir; Stage Crew; Rep Frsh Cls; Rep Soph Cls; Rep Jr Cls; Rep Stu Cncl; Swmmng; Dance.

CHAFAR, GIOMARA; Our Lady Of Good Counsel HS; Belleville, NJ; (Y); 22/108; Chorus; School Musical; Nrsng.

CHAIT, DAVID; East Brunswick HS; E Brunswick, NJ; (Y); 3/600; Cmnty Wkr; Key Clb; Math Tm; Science Clb; Spanish Clb; Gov Hon Prg Awd; Hon Roll; NHS; Engrng.

CHALIAN, MARAL; Toms River HS North; Glendale, CA; (Y); 12/412; Am Leg Aux Girls St; Hosp Aide; School Musical; Yrbk Stf; Off Jr Cls; Rep Stu Cncl; High Hon Roll; NHS; Voice Dem Awd; Exploring; WA Wrkshps Cngrssnl Smnr 86; UCLA.

CHALSON, ERICA; North Brunswick Township HS; N Brunswick, NJ; (Y); 3/300; Drama Clb; French Clb; Key Clb; School Play; Sec Soph Cls; Pres Jr Cls; Pres Sr Cls; Rep Stu Cncl; High Hon Roll; NHS; Ambssdr Hugh O Brien Ldrshp Conf 85; Awd 6 Yrs Partcptn YWCA Synchrnzd Swm Tm 80-86.

CHAMBERLAIN, C SUZANNE; Middletown High School South; Red Bank, NJ; (Y); VP Sec Church Yth Grp; Girl Scts; Math Clb; Stage Crew; Yrbk Stf; High Hon Roll; Hon Roll; NHS; Accntng.

CHAMBERS, KEITH; Audubon HS; Audubon, NJ; (Y); Church Yth Grp; School Play; Stage Crew; Var Bsbl; Hon Roll; Insurance.

CHAN, CANYON; Bishop Eustace Prep; West Berlin, NJ; (Y); 1/187; French Clb; Math Clb; Pres Science Clb; Ed Nwsp Phtg; Yrbk Phtg; Yrbk Stf; Lit Mag; Bausch & Lomb Sci Awd; French Hon Soc; NHS; George Washington U Awd 86; Hghst Scr Schl Natl Frnch Cntst Lvl 3 86; Biomed Rsrch.

CHAN, CHERYL; Elizabeth HS; Roselle Park, NJ; (Y); 46/839; Boys Clb Am; Church Yth Grp; Cmnty Wkr; Exploring; Intnl Clb; Library Aide; Red Cross Aide; Teachers Aide; Var L Swmmng; High Hon Roll; Army; Med.

CHAN, SANDRA; Pascack Valley Regional HS; River Vale, NJ; (Y); Church Yth Grp; Spanish Clb; Varsity Clb; Chorus; Stage Crew; Nwsp Stf; JV Bsktbl; Score Keeper; Var L Trk; Hon Roll; Med.

CHANCE, ANGELITA; Pemberton HS II; Pemberton, NJ; (Y); Art Clb; Church Yth Grp; FNA; GAA; Quiz Bowl; Science Clb; SADD; Band; Church Choir; Bsktbl; MVP Awd Trk 86; MVP Winter Trk Awd 85-86; Vrsty 86; Dctr.

CHANDLER, CHRISTINE; Cresskill HS; Cresskill, NJ; (Y); 15/112; Debate Tm; Ski Clb; Spanish Clb; Chorus; Capt Color Guard; Concert Band; Yrbk Stf; JV Var Trk; Hon Roll; NHS; Biol.

CHANDLER, GARRETT; Gloucester County Christian HS; Deptford, NJ; (S); Church Yth Grp; Quiz Bowl; Yrbk Stf; Pres Frsh Cls; Pres Jr Cls; Var JV Socr; High Hon Roll; Hon Roll; NHS; Debate Tm; 1st Bibl Qz Tm ST Comp 85; Embry Riddle Aero U; Aero Engr.

CHANDLER, MARTIN R; Plainfield HS; Plainfield, NJ; (Y); Church Yth Grp; Church Choir; JV Ftbl; JV Trk; Var Wt Lftg; Boy Scts; Rep Soph Cls; Rep Stu Cncl; JV Gym; JV Var Wrstlng; Vldctrn; Smr Tech Ed Prgm 83; Ldrshp Inst 86; Elec Engrng.

CHANDRAKANTAN, ARUN; Manalapan HS; Manalapan, NJ; (Y); 1/431; VP Chess Clb; Debate Tm; Science Clb; Rep Frsh Cls; Rep Soph Cls; Sec Jr Cls; VP Sr Cls; Im Socr; Var Socr; NHS; Rutgers Schlr; Rutgers Smmr Schlrshp; Depart Awd Social Studies.

CHANEY, KENDIS; Monsignor Donovan HS; Seaside Heights, NJ; (Y); Church Yth Grp; Cmnty Wkr; Intnl Clb; Ski Clb; Chrmn Spanish Clb; Band; Color Guard; Concert Band; Jazz Band; Mrchg Band; GA Court Coll; Bus Adm.

CHANG, CAROLYN; John P Stevens HS; Edison, NJ; (Y); Church Yth Grp; Drama Clb; French Clb; Hosp Aide; Thesps; School Musical; School Play; Stage Crew; Yrbk Stf; Sec Frsh Cls.

CHANG, GRACE; Palisades Park JR SR HS; Palisades Pk, NJ; (Y); Library Aide; Math Clb; Speech Tm; Yrbk Stf; Ed Lit Mag; Var Crs Cntry; High Hon Roll; NHS; Ntl Hstry Day NJ Fnlst 84; NJ Govrnrs Schlr 86.

CHANG, JOANNIE CHIUNG-YUEH; Ranney HS; Hazlet, NJ; (S); 4/38; Hosp Aide; Yrbk Ed-Chief; Lit Mag; Rep Soph Cls; Rep Jr Cls; Rep Sr Cls; JV Fld Hcky; Var Socr; Var Swmmng; High Hon Roll; Rutgers Schlr 85; Pediatrcs.

CHANG, LYNDA; Memorial HS; West New York, NJ; (Y); Hosp Aide; Library Aide; Hon Roll; NHS; Rutgers; Phrmcst.

CHANG, PATRICK S; Seton Hall Prep; West Orange, NJ; (Y); Chess Clb; Hosp Aide; Math Tm; Science Clb; Ski Clb; Church Choir; Im Badmtn; Im Socr; Hon Roll; NHS; Kean Coll.

CHANG, SOFIA; Maple Shade HS; Maple Shade, NJ; (Y); 1/150; Computer Clb; Key Clb; Yrbk Stf; JV Badmtn; Var Fld Hcky; Cit Awd; Gov Hon Prg Awd; High Hon Roll; NHS; Rotary Awd; Acadmc All Amer Math 86; Acadmc All Amer Spnsh 85; Rutgers Schlr 86.

CHANG, STEVEN; Parsippany HS; Parsippany, NJ; (Y); Chess Clb; Computer Clb; Math Clb; Math Tm; Iron-Hill Math Leag 85; NJ Math Leag 85; NJ Math Leag 86; Comp Engr.

CHANG, SUE-LYNN; Governor Livingston Regional HS; Warren, NJ; (Y); 9/195; Chorus; Orch; School Musical; Variety Show; French Hon Soc; High Hon Roll; NHS; Summa Cum Laude NJ Msc Ed Cncl Piano Comptn 82-85; PTA Schlstic Achvt Awd 85-86; Piano/1st Pl Comptn; Physics.

CHANG, TINA; Newton HS; Newton, NJ; (S); Computer Clb; Latin Clb; Math Tm; Hon Roll; NHS; 2nd Comptr Leag Cntst 84-85; Comp Sci.

CHANN, DONNA LYNN; Bridgeton HS; Bridgeton, NJ; (Y); French Clb; Office Aide; Pep Clb; Yrbk Stf; Stat Ftbl; French Hon Soc; High Hon Roll; Hon Roll; 1st Art Awd Spring Art Show 86; Nurses Aide; Cumberland Co; Phys Ther.

CHANTI, CRAIG; Holy Cross HS; Roebling, NJ; (Y); Pres Church Yth Grp; School Musical; Yrbk Ed-Chief; Yrbk Stf; JV Trk; Hon Roll; Drew U.

CHAO, ANGELA; Parsippany Hills HS; Morris Plains, NJ; (Y); Sec Church Yth Grp; Sec Intnl Clb; Key Clb; Math Tm; NFL; Spanish Clb; Var Trk; High Hon Roll; Hon Roll; NHS; Arch.

CHAO, KAREN K; Montville Township HS; Montville, NJ; (Y); 6/276; Sec Church Yth Grp; FBLA; Sec Intnl Clb; Key Clb; High Hon Roll; NHS; Ntl Merit SF; St Schlr; Library Aide; Math Clb; FBLA Natl Convntn ST Comptn Fnlst 84; Sci Leag 27th ST Bio I & Chem I 84 & 85.

CHAO, KATHIE; Memorial HS; W New York, NJ; (Y); French Clb; Chorus; Color Guard; Lit Mag; Rep Jr Cls; Tchr.

CHAO, LINDA; Cinnaminson HS; Cinnaminson, NJ; (Y); Art Clb; SADD; Fld Hcky; Im Sftbl; Swmmng; Vllybl; Hon Roll; Accntg.

CHAO, MICHAEL; Montville HS; Montville, NJ; (Y); 5/250; Church Yth Grp; VP Computer Clb; Sec Jr Cls; Sec Sr Cls; JV Trk; High Hon Roll; NHS; Ntl Merit Ltr; Exploring; FBLA; Clmba U Sci Hons Pgm 85-87; Gvrnrs Schl Sci Drw U 86; 3rd Pl NJ Sci Day Chem I Div 86; Elec Engrng.

CHAPELL, MARYANNE; Toms River East HS; Toms River, NJ; (Y); Church Yth Grp; Chorus; Var Powder Puff Ftbl; Drama Clb; Key Clb; Church Choir; School Musical; School Play; Mgr Bsktbl; Phil Coll Of Bible; Soc Worker.

CHARACHE, DARRYL H; Lawrence HS; Lawrenceville, NJ; (Y); 11/230; Am Leg Boys St; Pres Spanish Clb; Jazz Band; Mrchg Band; Var Bsbl; Var Capt Crs Cntry; Var Capt Trk; NHS; Pres Schlr; Semper Fidelis Marn Band Awd 86; All Amer Band Awd 83; U Of DE; Physcs.

CHARETTE, GABRIELLE; Mount Saint Mary Acad; Fanwood, NJ; (S); 10/82; French Clb; Service Clb; Teachers Aide; Lit Mag; Im Swmmng; High Hon Roll; NHS; Natl Latin Exam Magna Cum Laude 85; Drew U Rose Memorial Scholar 86; Hstry Clb; Drew U; Econ.

CHARLES, ARLENE; Plainfield HS; Plainfield, NJ; (Y); FHA; Church Choir; Hon Roll; Industrl Engr.

CHARLES, GENEVIEVE; Emerson HS; Union City, NJ; (Y); French Clb; Capt Drill Tm; Yrbk Stf; Var Bsktbl; Capt Pom Pon; Var Trk; High Hon Roll; Hon Roll; Accntng.

CHARNITSKY, DANIEL; Sacred Heart HS; Glassboro, NJ; (Y); 10/70; Church Yth Grp; Hon Roll; Glassboro ST; Chem Engr.

CHASAR, BERNADETTE; Hopatcong HS; Hopatcong, NJ; (Y); Ski Clb; Varsity Clb; Lit Mag; Im Powder Puff Ftbl; Var Socr; Var Trk; Hon Roll; German Clb; Office Aide; Pres Jr Cls; Booster Clb Schlrshp 86; Most Imprvd Plyr Soccer 84; Sprtsmnshp Awd-Track 86; E Stroudsburg U; Elem Ed.

CHASE, VICTORIA; Southern Regional HS; Harvey Cedars, NJ; (Y); 2/400; School Musical; School Play; Trs Soph Cls; Trs Jr Cls; Trs Sr Cls; Trs Stu Cncl; Powder Puff Ftbl; Var Socr; High Hon Roll; NHS; Soccr Schlr Athl 84-86; Intl Bus.

CHASIN, LARRY; Manalapan HS; Manalapan, NJ; (Y); Computer Clb; Ski Clb; SADD; Temple Yth Grp; Yrbk Rptr; Yrbk Stf; Stat L Mgr(s); Var Socr; Hotel Mgmnt.

CHASKES, MICHAEL; Washington Township HS; Turnersville, NJ; (Y); 9/480; Am Leg Boys St; French Clb; Model UN; Temple Yth Grp; Jazz Band; Nwsp Stf; Gov Hon Prg Awd; Hon Roll; NHS; Rutgers U Deans Smmr Scholar 86; Eng.

CHAU, DOANH; Dover HS; Dover, NJ; (Y); Gmtry, Englsh & Frnch Awds 85-86; Morris Coll; Engrng Sci.

CHAUBAL, CHARU; Christian Brothers Acad; Tinton Falls, NJ; (Y); 8/230; Camera Clb; Hosp Aide; Math Tm; School Musical; Stage Crew; Ed Nwsp Sprt Ed; Yrbk Stf; Lit Mag; NHS; Engrng.

CHAUDHARI, SUSHIL N; Hamilton High East; Hamilton Sq, NJ; (Y); Spanish NHS; Engr.

CHEATHAM, JAMES; Camden HS; Camden, NJ; (S); Cmnty Wkr; Computer Clb; Quiz Bowl; Scholastic Bowl; Teachers Aide; Variety Show; Rep Frsh Cls; Rep Soph Cls; Rep Jr Cls; Rep Sr Cls; Math Awd 84; Slgn Cntst Wnnr 85; US Navy Comp Anlyst.

CHEATHAM, RAYMONETTE; Overbrook SR HS; Lindenwold, NJ; (Y); Dance Clb; Drama Clb; Pep Clb; Spanish Clb; Chorus; Church Choir; Drill Tm; Variety Show; Lit Mag; Church Yth Grp; Upward Bnd Awd Advncd Alg, Crrnt Evnts 85; Music Awd-Chorus 85-86; Stockton ST Coll; FBI Agnt.

CHECKO, TIMOTHY; Bridgewater East HS; Bridgewater, NJ; (Y); 81/278; Math Tm; Stage Crew; Variety Show; Var L Bowling; Var L Ftbl; Var L Golf; Wt Lftg; Hon Roll; Ntl Merit Ltr; Duke; Engr.

CHEDDAR, CHRISTINA; Woodbridge HS; Port Reading, NJ; (S); 18/396; Am Leg Aux Girls St; NFL; SADD; Mrchg Band; School Musical; Nwsp Ed-Chief; Lit Mag; Hon Roll; NHS; Cmnty Wkr; Acad All-Amer 87; Jrnlsm.

CHELPATY, HEATHER; Lenape Valley Regional HS; Sparta, NJ; (Y); 17/241; Var JV Bsktbl; Im Socr; Var JV Sftbl; Var Tennis; Hon Roll; Lenape Schlr 86; Acctg.

CHEN, ANDREW; Middletown HS South; Lincroft, NJ; (Y); Boy Scts; Var L Tennis; Hon Roll; NHS; Lehigh; Mech Engr.

CHEN, BELLONA; James Caldwell HS; W Caldwell, NJ; (Y); 22/256; Church Yth Grp; Crs Cntry; Var Trk; High Hon Roll; Kiwanis Awd; NHS; Prfct Atten Awd; Bio Awd 86; Med Career Clb VP 86; Muhlenberg Coll; Bio.

CHEN, BETTY; Morris Catholic HS; Denville, NJ; (Y); 5/142; Church Yth Grp; Debate Tm; Pres FBLA; Hosp Aide; Math Clb; NFL; Speech Tm; School Play; High Hon Roll; Sec NHS; Debate ST Chmpnshps 3rd Pl 85; 98 In Music Edctrs Assoc Piano Audtns 86; Rensselaer Polytech Inst; Dntst.

CHEN, CHIN CHIN; Scotch Plains-Fanwood HS; Scotch Plains, NJ; (S); Dance Clb; Drama Clb; French Clb; Model UN; Quiz Bowl; Chorus; Mrchg Band; Orch; School Musical; Lit Mag.

CHEN, CHRISTINE; South Brunswick HS; Kendall Park, NJ; (Y); 11/254; Am Leg Aux Girls St; Dance Clb; Math Clb; Nwsp Sprt Ed; Lit Mag; Cheerleading; Trs French Hon Soc; Hon Roll; NHS; Amanda Knowles Scholar 86; Wrld Poetry Hnrb Mntn 84; Hnr Grad 86; Rutgers Coll Phrmcy; Phrmcy.

CHEN, CHRISTOPHER S B; Princeton HS; Princeton, NJ; (Y); Am Leg Boys St; Key Clb; Science Clb; Jazz Band; Pep Band; School Musical; Symp Band; Rep Sr Cls; Var Socr; JV Trk; 1st Pl NJ Sci Lg Chem II 84-85; 4th Pl NJ Sci Nday Physcs II 85-86; Harvard.

CHEN, DAVID; Freehold Twp HS; Freehold, NJ; (Y); 2/341; Computer Clb; Math Clb; Math Tm; Drill Tm; Gov Hon Prg Awd; NHS; Rensselaer Math Sci Awd 86; Am Math Ex 86.

CHEN, DAVID; W Windsor-Plainsboro HS; Princeton Jct, NJ; (Y); 1/242; Co-Capt Math Tm; Off Model UN; Political Wkr; Scholastic Bowl; Service Clb; Orch; Ed Nwsp Stf; Chrmn Stu Cncl; Gov Hon Prg Awd; High Hon Roll; Duke; Law.

CHEN, PATTY; River Dell HS; Oradell, NJ; (Y); 23/218; FBLA; Orch; Yrbk Ed-Chief; Trs Frsh Cls; Sec Soph Cls; Rep Stu Cncl; JV Vllybl; VP French Hon Soc; NHS; Frnch Advncd Forensc Meet Wnnr; Presdntl Acad Ftns Awd; Boston Coll; Bus.

CHEN, PETER; Lyndhurst HS; Lyndhurst, NJ; (Y); 6/200; Pres Math Clb; Math Tm; Science Clb; Ski Clb; Varsity Clb; Drm & Bgl; Mrchg Band; Trk; High Hon Roll; NHS; Band Awd 85; Trck Vrsty Lttrs 85 & 86; Stanford U; Elec Engrng.

CHEN, PHILIP; Arthur L Johnson Regional HS; Clark, NJ; (Y); Am Leg Boys St; Boy Scts; Debate Tm; Spanish Clb; Orch; VP Frsh Cls; VP Soph Cls; VP Jr Cls; VP Sr Cls; Rep Stu Cncl; NY All St Orchstra 83-86; 2 Mdls Cntrl NJ Msc Ed Orchstra 84 & 86; Hlth Sci.

CHEN, RAYMOND R; The Lawrenceville Schl; Mercerville, NJ; (Y); Drama Clb; Model UN; Stage Crew; Lit Mag; JV Crs Cntry; Im Golf; Var Trk; JV Wrstlng; Hon Roll; Ntl Merit SF; Art.

CHENEY, JULIE; Haddon Township HS; Haddonfield, NJ; (Y); Am Leg Aux Girls St; Church Yth Grp; Girl Scts; Varsity Clb; Chorus; Church Choir; Rep Stu Cncl; JV Var Bsktbl; JV Var Fld Hcky; JV Var Sftbl; Sci.

CHENG, HO-KAN; Roselle Park HS; Roselle Park, NJ; (Y); Am Leg Boys St; Math Tm; JV Capt Socr; Var Trk; NHS; Awd For Achvt 84-85; Math Cntst Math Leag 85; Fnlst Govnrs Sch Sic 86; Schlrshp Close Up Fndtn 86.

CHENG, KAM; Clearview Regional HS; Sewell, NJ; (Y); 23/160; Drama Clb; Acpl Chr; Chorus; Madrigals; School Musical; School Play; Cheerleading; Hon Roll; DECA; Yrbk Stf; Hrnd Bd Of Educ ST Teen Arts Fstvl Wth Clrvw Vocal Ensmbl 84&86; Bus.

CHENG, LOUISA; Manville HS; Manville, NJ; (Y); 4/130; PAVAS; VP Pres Stu Cncl; DAR Awd; High Hon Roll; NHS; St Schlr; Model UN; Band; Concert Band; Mrchg Band; NJASC Exec Mem In Chrg Of Pub 84-86; Gov Schl Prfrmng Arts Schlr 85; Gov Awd In Arts Ed 86; U Of CA Los Angeles; Bus.

CHENG, TERAVAT; Dickinson HS; Jersey City, NJ; (Y); Yrbk Phtg; Yrbk Stf; Tennis; Schl Of Engrng; Engr.

CHEPENIK, LARA G; Cherry Hill HS East; Cherry Hill, NJ; (Y); Ed Art Clb; Church Yth Grp; Dance Clb; Drama Clb; Office Aide; PAVAS; Thesps; School Musical; Stage Crew; Swing Chorus; Douglass Coll.

CHERICHELLA, ANTHONY; Wood-Ridge HS; Wood-Ridge, NJ; (S); 4/92; Aud/Vis; Spanish Clb; Yrbk Ed-Chief; Bsbl; Bsktbl; Bausch & Lomb Sci Awd; High Hon Roll; NHS; Upsoln Coll; Accntng.

CHERICHELLA, ROBERT; Wood-Ridge HS; Wood-Ridge, NJ; (S); 2/90; Art Clb; Spanish Clb; Sec Frsh Cls; Sec Soph Cls; Sec Jr Cls; Sec Sr Cls; JV Bsbl; JV Bsktbl; High Hon Roll; NHS; Pharmcy.

CHERRY, BRAD; Phillipsburg HS; Phillipsburg, NJ; (Y); 80/334; Ski Clb; Varsity Clb; Pres Frsh Cls; Pres Soph Cls; Rep Stu Cncl; JV Var Ftbl; JV Var Wrstlng; Cit Awd; Lion Awd; Prfct Atten Awd; Cmnty Svc Awd; Bus Admn.

CHERVIL, BALAGUER; Memorial HS; West New York, NJ; (S); Computer Clb; French Clb; JA; Math Clb; Teachers Aide; Socr; Hon Roll; Lehman Coll; Elec.

CHESSA, JOHN; Don Bosco Technical HS; N Haledon, NJ; (Y); 8/95; Ski Clb; Mrchg Band; Yrbk Stf; Rep Soph Cls; Rep Jr Cls; Pres Stu Cncl; Var Capt Socr; Hon Roll; NHS; Sci Fair Bio 1st 83-84; Alumni Achvt Awd, Don Bosco Tech Outstndng Stu 86; Drexel U; Arch.

CHESSERE, JIM; Bishop George Ahr HS; Old Bridge, NJ; (Y); 127/300; ROTC; JV Bsbl; Var L Ftbl.

CHESTER, CHARLOTTE ANN; Arthur P Schalick HS; Elmer, NJ; (Y); 12/131; Spanish Clb; Pres Chorus; Rep Frsh Cls; Rep Soph Cls; Sec Jr Cls; Pres Sr Cls; Rep Stu Cncl; Wrstlng; Cit Awd; Hon Roll; Slm Co Acdmc Schlrshp 86; Arthr P Schlck Schlrshp 86; Stu Cncl Svc Awd 86; Gloucester County Coll; Nrsng.

CHEW, GEORGE; Cumberland Regional HS; Bridgeton, NJ; (Y); 32/369; Debate Tm; JCL; Office Aide; Varsity Clb; Pres Sr Cls; Capt Var Vllybl; Hon Roll; 3rd ST Wrstlng Chmpshps 85-86; Pol Sci.

CHEW, KIM; Hoboken HS; Hoboken, NJ; (Y); Computer Clb; French Clb; Chorus; Off Jr Cls; Swmmng; Hon Roll; Valedictorian 83; Innr Cir Awd 83; Hstry Awd 83; Acctng.

CHIACCHO, MARC; Penns Grove HS; Penns Grove, NJ; (Y); Exploring; JCL; Latin Clb; JV Ftbl; Wt Lftg; Bausch & Lomb Sci Awd; Hon Roll; Astrnmy.

CHIANG, EDMUNO P; The Lawrenceville Schl; Manhasset, NY; (Y); Exploring; Math Tm; Model UN; Service Clb; Orch; Nwsp Stf; Im Tennis; High Hon Roll; Ntl Merit SF; Computer Clb; Deans Lst 84-85; Econ.

CHIAPPETTA, DENNIS; Christian Brothers Acad; Manalapan, NJ; (S); 44/216; Boy Scts; Math Tm; Nwsp Stf; Yrbk Stf; Crs Cntry; Im Ftbl; Trk; High Hon Roll; NHS; Asbury Park Press Schrlshp 84; Eagle Scout Hnrs 83.

CHIARAVALLOTI, PINA; Lakewood HS; Lakewood, NJ; (Y); 73/325; Am Leg Aux Girls St; Dance Clb; French Clb; FBLA; JCL; Key Clb; Latin Clb; Rep Frsh Cls; Rep Soph Cls; Rep Jr Cls.

CHIARELLO, CHRISTINE; Millville SR HS; Millville, NJ; (Y); 27/468; Sec French Clb; GAA; SADD; Variety Show; Rep Sr Cls; Stu Cncl; High Hon Roll; NHS; Prfct Atten Awd; Stu Cncl Svc Awd Schlrshp 86; Glassboro ST Clg; Elem Educ.

CHIAROLANZA, MARK; Parsippany Hills HS; Parsippany, NJ; (Y); Stage Crew; Wrstlng; Engrng.

CHIEFFO, DIANNE; Scotch Plains-Fanwood HS; Fanwood, NJ; (S); Computer Clb; Pres 4-H; Teachers Aide; Chorus; Mrchg Band; Symp Band; Lit Mag; Sftbl; Cit Awd; L 4-H Awd; Citizenshp WA Focus 4-H 85; Spirit Of Amer Mrchng Bnd 86; Vet Med.

CHILDERS, LYNETTE; Bridgeton HS; Bridgeton, NJ; (Y); Office Aide; Teachers Aide; Yrbk Stf; Sec Frsh Cls; Sec Soph Cls; Sec Jr Cls; Sec Sr Cls; Mgr(s); CEP Asst Secy Law Office; Morgan St Univ; Bus Adm.

CHILSON, LYNETT; Red Bank Catholic HS; Eatontown, NJ; (Y); SADD; Nwsp Ed-Chief; High Hon Roll; Hon Roll; NHS.

CHIMES, MICHAEL J; Hightstown HS; E Windsor, NJ; (Y); 39/350; Yrbk Sprt Ed; Capt Var Swmmng; Hon Roll; Ntl Merit SF; French Clb; JV Ftbl; All Mercer Cnty & All Colonl Vly Conf Swim Tms 83-85; Sci.

CHIN, DEBBIE; Paramus HS; Paramus, NJ; (Y); Church Yth Grp; French Clb; Hosp Aide; JV Bsktbl; JV Crs Cntry; JV Socr; JV Trk; French Hon Soc; Nrsng.

CHIN, EDWIN; Parsippany HS; Parsippany, NJ; (Y); Trs Computer Clb; VP Debate Tm; Hosp Aide; Math Clb; Math Tm; NFL; Var L Tennis; High Hon Roll; NHS; Ntl Merit Ltr; 3rd Pl Trophy L-D Debate Hanover Pk Tournmnt 85; 4th Pl L-D Debate Trophy Montville Tournmnt 85; Bus Admin.

CHIN, ROSE; South Plainfield HS; S Plainfield, NJ; (Y); 7/287; Teachers Aide; French Hon Soc; High Hon Roll; Hon Roll; NHS; Pres Schlr; VFW Awd; Jrsymn; Cook Coll; Comp Sci.

CHIN, SABRINA; Ramapo HS; Wyckoff, NJ; (Y); 11/329; Rep Soph Cls; Chrmn Jr Cls; Mgr(s); JV Var Trk; High Hon Roll; Hon Roll; VP NHS; Ntl Merit Ltr.

CHIN, WENDY; Spotswood HS; Milltown, NJ; (S); 2/174; Am Leg Aux Girls St; Pres Church Yth Grp; Science Clb; Church Choir; Nwsp Stf; Yrbk Ed-Chief; VP Stu Cncl; Stat Crs Cntry; NHS; Garden ST Dist Schlr 85; Arch.

CHINCHAR, NANCY; Woodbridge HS; Woodbridge, NJ; (Y); 39/390; Sec Soph Cls; Sec Jr Cls; Sec Sr Cls; Stat Bsbl; Var Capt Cheerleading; Hon Roll; NHS; Cmmnctns.

CHING, LORNA; Morris Knolls HS; Denville, NJ; (Y); Math Clb; Math Tm; NFL; Sec Trs Science Clb; Chorus; Yrbk Stf; High Hon Roll; Hon Roll; Jr NHS; NHS; Summa Awd 84; Summa Medln Awd 86; Vldctrn At Chinese Schl 83; Yth Undrstndng Exchng Stu Schlrshp 83-84; Rutgers U; Finance.

CHIPMAN, KATHLEEN B; Delsea Regional HS; Newfield, NJ; (Y); Art Clb; Dance Clb; French Clb; Key Clb; Spanish Clb; Chorus; Church Choir; Flag Corp; School Musical; Im Fld Hcky; Phscl Thrpst.

CHIRIBOGA, RUGEL; Dover HS; Dover, NJ; (Y); 20/220; Am Leg Boys St; Church Yth Grp; German Clb; Band; Church Choir; Concert Band; Drm Mjr(t); Mrchg Band; Orch; Bowling; Mollie & Gertrude Turetsky Scholar 86; Holy Cross Awd 86; Supplmnlt Opprtnty Grant 86; U Notre Dame; Arch Engrng.

CHISHOLM, DANIEL J; Pascack Valley Regional HS; Hillsdale, NJ; (Y); 15/251; VP Crs Cntry; VP Trk; Hon Roll; NHS; Ntl Merit SF; Mech Engrng.

CHISHOLM, STEVE; Jackson Memorial HS; Jackson, NJ; (Y); 48/405; JV Var Trk; High Hon Roll; Hon Roll; 3rd Pl Shore Shp Stu Crftsmns Fr 85 & 86; Frstry.

CHITKARA, AJAY; Oratory Prep; Elizabeth, NJ; (Y); 5/40; Math Tm; Service Clb; Ski Clb; Ed Yrbk Stf; VP Sr Cls; Bsbl; Bsktbl; Wrstlng; High Hon Roll; Sec NHS; Latin Ltrary Awd 83; Litrary Latin Cmmdtn 83; Sci Awd-Bio 83; RPI; Bio-Mdcl Engrng.

CHIU, JOHN; Parsippany HS; Parsippany, NJ; (Y); Computer Clb; Debate Tm; Concert Band; Mrchg Band; Stage Crew; Symp Band; Swmmng; Hon Roll; Lib Arts.

CHLUDZINSKI, SUZANNE; East Brunswick HS; East Brunswick, NJ; (Y); Trs Chorus; Color Guard; Mrchg Band; Band Boosters Schrlshp Awd 86; E Stroudsburg U; Mgmt.

CHMIEL, ROBYN; Clifton HS; Clifton, NJ; (Y); 94/637; Drama Clb; Girl Scts; Pep Clb; Spanish Clb; Cheerleading; Pom Pon; Sftbl; Vllybl; Hon Roll; Jr NHS; Girl Sct Silvr Awd 83; Mayors Awd 83.

CHMIELENSKI, THOMAS; Burlington City HS; Edgewater Park, NJ; (Y); 11/168; Am Leg Boys St; Aud/Vis; Cmnty Wkr; JA; Mgr Stage Crew; Var Capt Crs Cntry; Var Trk; Hon Roll; NHS; Carnegie-Mellon U; Arch.

CHO, CHARLES; Westfield SR HS; Westfield, NJ; (Y); Chess Clb; Church Yth Grp; French Clb; Hosp Aide; Math Clb; Church Choir; Hon Roll; Outstndng Achvt Awds In Geomtry & Bio 84; 14th Annl ST Math Meet Awd 85; Pres Acad Fit Awd 86; Rutgers Coll; Pre Med.

CHODROFF, BRENDA; East Brunswick HS; East Brunswick, NJ; (Y); Am Leg Aux Girls St; Key Clb; Variety Show; VP Stu Cncl; Stat Bsktbl; Socr; Var Tennis; Stat Wrstlng; Prom Commtte Chrprsn 86; Hmcmng Commtte; Rep Stu Cncl; U MD; Bus.

CHOE, JENNIFER; Newark Acad; Randolph, NJ; (Y); Cmnty Wkr; Chorus; Church Choir; Nwsp Ed-Chief; Nwsp Rptr; Ed Lit Mag; JV Fld Hcky; JV Tennis; Gov Hon Prg Awd; Jullilard Pre Coll Music Shl 84-87; Smmr Intern At Morris County Ct House 85 & 86; English.

CHOE, YUN-HUI; Northern Valley Regional HS O T; Norwood, NJ; (Y); 19/289; AFS; Off Church Yth Grp; Hosp Aide; Ski Clb; Yrbk Stf; Hon Roll; Chrch Yth Grp Cbnt Offcr 86-87; Hosp Ad Physcl Thrpy 86; Hnr Rll.

CHOFF, JEFFREY; Christian Brothers Acad; Little Silver, NJ; (Y); Church Yth Grp; JV Bsbl; Im Bsktbl; Im Fld Hcky; Im Ftbl; Im Socr; High Hon Roll; Hon Roll; Econ.

CHOI, HAN WOOK; The Lawrenceville Schl; Pompton Lakes, NJ; (Y); Camera Clb; Church Yth Grp; Hosp Aide; Pres Library Aide; Ski Clb; Chorus; Nwsp Phtg; Ed Yrbk Phtg; Ed Lit Mag; Hon Roll; Rensselaer Polytechnic Inst.

CHOI, MAGGIE; Mount St Mary Acad; Plainfield, NJ; (S); 12/83; Red Cross Aide; French Hon Soc; Hon Roll; NHS; Engrng.

CHOI, SANDRA; Northern Valley Regional HS; Norwood, NJ; (Y); 10/281; AFS; VP Church Yth Grp; Library Aide; Teachers Aide; Band; Church Choir; Concert Band; Stage Crew; Nwsp Stf; Lit Mag; Accntng.

CHOKSHI, MANISH; Bayonne HS; Bayonne, NJ; (Y); 28/362; Computer Clb; Exploring; Math Tm; Science Clb; Mrchg Band; Var Tennis; High Hon Roll; NHS; Prfct Atten Awd; St Schlr; Silvr Medl Chem Hudson Cnty Sci Fair 86; U S Army Rsrv Schlr Athl Awd 86; Case Western Resrv U; Biochem.

CHOMINSKY, JOHN P; Wayne Hills HS; Wayne, NJ; (Y); 41/311; Art Clb; Letterman Clb; Math Tm; Spanish Clb; Jazz Band; JV Golf; Ice Hcky; High Hon Roll; Hon Roll; 2 Yrs Vrsty Rfl Tm; PA ST U; Music.

CHOMO, MATTHEW; St James HS; Carneys Point, NJ; (S); 3/76; Am Leg Boys St; Boy Scts; Drama Clb; School Musical; High Hon Roll; NHS; Ntl Merit Ltr; Hon Roll; NJ Garden St Distinguished Schlr 85; Johns Hopkins U; Physician.

CHONG, DAVID; Hunterdon Central HS; Flemington, NJ; (Y); 291/548; Chess Clb; Varsity Clb; School Musical; School Play; JV Var Ftbl; Var L Trk; Im Mgr Wt Lftg; Var Wrstlng; Hon Roll; Ntl Merit Ltr; Jacksonville; Flght Technlgy.

CHONG, STEPHEN; Kittatinny Reg HS; Stillwater, NJ; (Y); 1/228; Trs Church Yth Grp; Math Tm; Science Clb; Church Choir; Concert Band; Mrchg Band; School Musical; JV Trk; High Hon Roll; NHS; 1st Cnty Music Fdtn Schlrshp 85; Hnrbl Ment Inter Piano Div 84; Rutgars Scholar 86; Princeton U; Genetic Engrng.

CHOONG, LINDA; Marlboro HS; Marlboro, NJ; (Y); 69/500; French Clb; Ski Clb; Stu Cncl; Cornell U; Intr Dsgn.

CHOP, TRACY L; Morris Hills Regional HS; Rockaway, NJ; (Y); 2/289; Computer Clb; French Clb; French Hon Soc; High Hon Roll; NHS; Excelsior Awd 84 & 85.

CHORAZAK, TERESA; Roselle Catholic HS; Roselle, NJ; (S); 5/152; Church Yth Grp; Orch; Rep Frsh Cls; Off Stu Cncl; Var Bsktbl; Var Co-Capt Swmmng; High Hon Roll; NHS; Spanish NHS; Hstry, Engl & Spnsh Awds.

CHORDAS, DARRYL; South River HS; S River, NJ; (Y); 44/130; FNA; German Clb; Spanish Clb; Sec Jr Cls; Rep Stu Cncl; Im Bsbl; Var Capt Ftbl; Var L Trk; De Vry; Instrmntn.

CHORUN, ALAN FRANCIS; Lenape Valley Regional HS; Stanhope, NJ; (Y); 6/212; Am Leg Boys St; SADD; Chorus; Jazz Band; Nwsp Sprt Ed; Socr; NHS; Prfct Atten Awd; Spanish NHS; Church Yth Grp; Hofstra U; Psychology.

CHOU, ELLEN; Montville Twp HS; Pine Brook, NJ; (Y); 15/270; Key Clb; Ski Clb; Concert Band; Nwsp Bus Mgr; Yrbk Bus Mgr; Rep Stu Cncl; JV Var Lcrss; JV Var Socr; High Hon Roll; Jr NHS; Most Imprvd Plyr Gils Var Sccr 85; Rotary Schlrshp 86; 2nd Pl Voice Of Democracy Cont 85; Barnard Coll; Econ.

CHOU, JOSEPH; Hudson Catholic HS; Jersey City, NJ; (Y); 59/188; Chess Clb; Computer Clb; Dance Clb; English Clb; Math Clb; Spanish Clb; SADD; Varsity Clb; Yrbk Rptr; Yrbk Stf; NYIT; Cmptr Sci.

CHOU, JOSEPH H; Lawrenceville Schl; Cranbury, NJ; (Y); Pres Computer Clb; Pres Math Tm; Nwsp Stf; High Hon Roll; Hon Roll; Ntl Merit SF; St Schlr; Amer Invtnl Math Exmntn Hnr Roll 84-85; Sidney W Davidson Schlrshp 83-86; Bruce Mc Clellan Schlrshp Cp; Math.

CHOUDHURY, SAMBHU N; The Pingry Schl; Parsippany, NJ; (Y); Chess Clb; Math Clb; Quiz Bowl; Orch; Sr Cls; JV Crs Cntry; Var Swmmng; JV Trk; High Hon Roll; Debate Tm; Math Sci Prize Hnrb Mntn 86; Highest Schltc Avrg 81-82; Cum Laude 85-86; Med.

CHOWANEC, SANDY; Cedar Ridge HS; Old Bridge, NJ; (Y); 90/375; DECA; SADD; Yrbk Stf; Gym; Hon Roll; Cedar Ridge Booster Clb-Schlr/Athlt 86; Cedar Ridge-MV Sr-Gymnstcs 86; Trenton ST Coll.

CHRANOWSKI, STEVE; Maple Shade HS; Maple Shade, NJ; (Y); 1/150; Am Leg Boys St; Pres Computer Clb; Key Clb; Yrbk Stf; VP Jr Cls; Pres Sr Cls; JV Bsbl; JV Bsktbl; JV Socr; Pres NHS; Rutgers U; Elec Engrng.

CHRASTINA, RONALD; Parsippany Hills HS; Parsippany, NJ; (Y); 20/324; Key Clb; Concert Band; Jazz Band; Mrchg Band; School Musical; Bsktbl; Hon Roll; NHS; Annapolis; Comp Engr.

CHRISCO, HILLARY; E Orange HS; East Orange, NJ; (S); 18/410; Library Aide; Color Guard; Nwsp Stf; Yrbk Stf; Lit Mag.

CHRISTENSEN, GARY; Notre Dame HS; Princeton Jct, NJ; (Y); Var Swmmng; Hon Roll; NHS; Biochem.

CHRISTENSEN, TARA; Woodbridge HS; Wodbridge, NJ; (Y); 2/356; Hosp Aide; Quiz Bowl; Rep Soph Cls; Elks Awd; NHS; Sal; NJ Dist Schlr Awd; NJ Govrns Tchng Schlrs Awd; Montclair ST Coll Merit Schlr; Montclair ST Coll; Teacher.

CHRISTER, TRACY; Howell HS; Howell, NJ; (Y); 50/306; Crs Cntry; Trk; Drama.

CHRISTIAN, TAYNIA; Lincoln HS; Jersey City, NJ; (Y); Mt Clair ST Coll; Comp Engr.

CHRISTIANO, DIANA; Livingston HS; Livingston, NJ; (Y); Church Yth Grp; Ski Clb; Yrbk Stf; Off Stu Cncl; Swmmng; Jr NHS; Rutgers Coll-Engrng; Cvl Engrng.

CHRISTIANS, JILL; Rutherford HS; Rutherford, NJ; (Y); Church Yth Grp; Stat Var Bsbl; JV Var Bsktbl; Hon Roll; Rutgers; Bus.

CHRISTIANSEN, JUSTINE; Toms River East HS; Toms River, NJ; (Y); 87/586; Hosp Aide; Chorus; Mrchg Band; JV Cheerleading; JV Diving; Im Powder Puff Ftbl; Var L Swmmng; Bio.

CHRISTIANSEN, LYNN; Timothy Christian Schl; Aberdeen, NJ; (S); Church Yth Grp; Drama Clb; Chorus; School Play; JV Cheerleading; Var Sftbl; High Hon Roll; Hon Roll; NHS; Val.

CHRISTIE, DAVID ANDREW MICHAEL; Bayley-Ellard Catholic Regionl HS; Basking Ridge, NJ; (Y); 2/90; Am Leg Boys St; Model UN; NFL; Ski Clb; Chorus; School Musical; Yrbk Bus Mgr; Var L Crs Cntry; High Hon Roll; NHS; Hugh O Brien Ldrshp Fdtn 84-85; Boston Coll; Law.

CHRISTIE, DONNA-MARIE; Summit HS; Summit, NJ; (Y); AFS; FBLA; Varsity Clb; Orch; Yrbk Stf; Lit Mag; Crs Cntry; Capt Trk; Hon Roll; Prfct Atten Awd; Mst Imprvd Plyr For Trck & Fld 86; Mst Vlble Plyr For Union Cnty Coches Cnfrence 86.

CHRISTOPHER, FRANK L; John F Kennedy HS; Willingboro, NJ; (Y); 8/302; Am Leg Boys St; Trs Cmnty Wkr; Key Clb; Nwsp Stf; Yrbk Rptr; Var JV Ftbl; Hon Roll; Jr NHS; Computer Clb; Squire Of Mnth NJ ST Columbian Squires 85; Columbian Squires Sntry 83-84, Marshal 85-86, ST Purser; West Point; Med.

CHRISTY, TODD; Millville SR HS; Millville, NJ; (Y); 1/450; Am Leg Boys St; Ski Clb; Pres SADD; Im Bowling; JV Socr; High Hon Roll; Hon Roll; Pres NHS; Ntl Merit Ltr.

CHRZANOWSKI JR, FRANK A; Cherokee HS; Marlton, NJ; (Y); 5/408; Am Leg Boys St; Church Yth Grp; Math Tm; Scholastic Bowl; Var Swmmng; High Hon Roll; Pres NHS; Computer Clb; German Clb; Math Clb; NJ Govrns Schl Sci 86; Church Lector 83-86; Chem Lab Asst; Med.

CHU, ALICE; Westfield HS; Westfield, NJ; (Y); 49/514; Science Clb; Chorus; NHS; Bus Mngmnt.

CHU, BRIAN; Matawan Regional HS; Matawan, NJ; (S); 1/355; Band; School Musical; Nwsp Rptr; Yrbk Phtg; Trs Jr Cls; Capt Crs Cntry; Val; Computer Clb; Math Tm; Spanish Clb; Math Leag Awd 1st Pl 84; Pres Physcl Ftnss Awd 84; Ntl Lang Arts Olympd Awd 1st Pl 84; MIT; Bus Adm.

CHU, KEITH C; Hillsborough HS; Belle Mead, NJ; (Y); 103/292; Art Clb; Science Clb; Ski Clb; Cook Coll; Bio.

CHU, MARGARET; Dwight-Englewood HS; Englewood Cliffs, NJ; (Y); Camera Clb; Church Yth Grp; Cmnty Wkr; Church Choir; Fld Hcky; Trk; High Hon Roll; Bio.

CHUANG, JOHN; Dwight Englewood Schl; Orangeburg, NY; (Y); Pres Debate Tm; Hosp Aide; Math Clb; Ed Lit Mag; Var Crs Cntry; JV Tennis; High Hon Roll; Hon Roll; Ntl Merit Ltr; Atlantc Pacifc Math Leag Hgh Score Awd & NJ Math Leag 85-86; N Jersey Debt Leag Tourn 1st Tm 85; Bio.

CHUDKOWSKI, JOANN; Sayreville War Memorial HS; S Amboy, NJ; (Y); 26/380; French Clb; Girl Scts; Spanish Clb; Varsity Clb; Ed Lit Mag; Var Capt Tennis; Var Trk; High Hon Roll; NHS; Spanish NHS; Best Female Tennis Plyr 83-86; Cook Clg; Bio Sci.

CHULIVER, ANTHONY; Holy Cross HS; Delran, NJ; (Y); 10/391; Spanish Clb; Band; Concert Band; Mrchg Band; Orch; School Musical; Var Swmmng; High Hon Roll; NHS; Physcs.

CHUN, ESTHER; Parsippany HS; Parsippany, NJ; (Y); 2/315; Trs Pres Church Yth Grp; Pres VP French Clb; Hosp Aide; Pres Intnl Clb; Trs Key Clb; Concert Band; Pres Sr Cls; NHS; Sal; All Am Schlr, Natl Ldrshp Svc Awd 85; Intl Frgn Lang Awd 86; U PA; Pre-Med.

CHUN, MOO YOUN; Northern Valley Regional HS; Northvale, NJ; (Y); AFS; Math Tm; Chorus; Im Tennis; Hon Roll; Engrng.

CHUN, SAM H; Moorestown HS; Moorestown, NJ; (Y); Am Leg Boys St; Latin Clb; Band; Orch; School Play; Nwsp Stf; Lit Mag; Off Soph Cls; Off Sr Cls; Var Socr; Yth Of Amer 84.

CHUNG, DAVID; Riverside HS; Riverside, NJ; (S); 7/87; Am Leg Boys St; Sec Jr Cls; Sec Sr Cls; Stu Cncl; Socr; JV Var Trk; NHS; Rotary Awd; St Joes; Bio.

CHUNG, JAE E; New Milford HS; New Milford, NJ; (Y); 5/140; Pres Sec Church Yth Grp; Hosp Aide; Math Tm; Spanish Clb; Church Choir; Orch; Yrbk Stf; Cit Awd; NHS; Sec Spanish NHS; Supr Rtg Ntl Fed JR Fstvls Piano Solo 86; Top Ten 84-86; Rutgers Coll; Comp Sci.

CHUNG, JEE; St Aloysius HS; Jersey City, NJ; (Y); 39/118; Yrbk Phtg; Bowling; Tennis; Bus.

CHUNG, JOON; Northern Valley Regional HS; Harrington Pk, NJ; (Y); AFS; Math Clb; Acpl Chr; Chorus; Church Choir; Hon Roll; Medical.

CHUNG, JOYCE; Toms River H S East; Toms River, NJ; (Y); 76/579; Camera Clb; Intnl Clb; Lit Mag; JV Diving; JV Gym; Powder Puff Ftbl; Hon Roll; Church Yth Grp; Dance Clb; DECA; DECA Modlng, Billbrd Adv Hnrbl Mntn 85; Chrldng-Chrstn Yth Org 83-86.

CHUNG, SCOTT; Cresshill HS; Cresskill, NJ; (Y); 31/111; VP Church Yth Grp; Ski Clb; Yrbk Stf; Rep Soph Cls; JV Var Bsbl; Ftbl; High Hon Roll; Hon Roll; Econ.

CIALINI, MIKE; Atlantic City HS; Margate, NJ; (Y); Key Clb; Red Cross Aide; SADD; Yrbk Stf; JV Bsbl; Hon Roll; H S Rep Freedms Fndtn Yth Conf 86; GA Tech U; Aerospc Engrg.

CIAMPA, MATTHEW; Summit HS; Summit, NJ; (Y); Boy Scts; Cmnty Wkr; Varsity Clb; Coach Actv; Powder Puff Ftbl; Var Wrstlng; Hon Roll.

CIANCAGLINI, KELLI; Washington Township HS; Turnersville, NJ; (Y); Hosp Aide; Q&S; School Musical; Sec Stu Cncl; Mgr(s); Hon Roll; Rotary Awd; Med.

CIAVARRA, LEA; Ramapo HS; Wyckoff, NJ; (Y); 15/329; Sec French Clb; Lit Mag; Trs Jr Cls; Rep Stu Cncl; JV Capt Socr; High Hon Roll; Jr NHS; NHS; Ntl Merit Ltr; Grad Hnr Grd 86; Art Shw Awds & Photo Awd 84-86; Med.

CIAVATTA, CHRIS; Neptune HS; Ocean Grove, NJ; (Y); Pres Frsh Cls; Hon Roll; NHS; Ski Clb; Chorus; Bsbl; Villanova; Pol Sci.

CIBENKO, MICHAEL T; High Point Regional HS; Branchville, NJ; (Y); Chess Clb; Church Yth Grp; Debate Tm; German Clb; Quiz Bowl; Scholastic Bowl; Lit Mag; Crs Cntry; Trk; High Hon Roll; Boston U; Biochem.

CICALA, LAURA L; Phillipsburg HS; Phillipsburg, NJ; (Y); 6/284; Am Leg Aux Girls St; Model UN; Rep Stu Cncl; Mgr(s); Score Keeper; High Hon Roll; NHS; Voice Dem Awd; FFA; Key Clb; GFWC Easton Womens Clb Schlshp 86; Easton Unico Schlrshp 86; Seton Hall Acad Schlrshp 86; Seton Hall U; Finance.

CICARELLI, JILL; Holy Spirit HS; Brigantine, NJ; (Y); Cmnty Wkr; Nwsp Rptr; Yrbk Rptr; Yrbk Stf; Cit Awd; Hon Roll; Hnrs Writing 86; Pub Rel.

CICCARELLI, STEVEN T; Hopatcong HS; Hopatcong, NJ; (Y); 9/173; Church Yth Grp; Quiz Bowl; Scholastic Bowl; VICA; Yrbk Stf; Socr; Trk; Hon Roll; NHS; Pres Acad Fitness Awd 86; James Dickson Carr Schlrshp 86; Yth Ctznshp Awd Soroptmst Intl Amer 86; Rutgers U; Engrng.

CICCARINO, CHRISTOPHER; Oratory Catholic Prep; Scotch Plains, NJ; (S); 7/46; Chess Clb; Math Clb; Math Tm; Nwsp Stf; Im Vllybl; High Hon Roll; NHS; Prfct Atten Awd; Church Yth Grp; Dungeons & Dragons Clb VP 85-86; Hist.

CICCARRELLA, MELISSA; Bridgewater-Raritan HS East; Bound Brook, NJ; (Y); Intnl Clb; Latin Clb; Concert Band; Capt Drill Tm; Rep Jr Cls; Rep Sr Cls; Var Stat Swmmng; High Hon Roll; Hon Roll; NHS; Pace U Acadmc Schlrshp 86; Pace U; Acctng.

CICCHINI, MICHELLE; Union Catholic Regional HS; Hillside, NJ; (Y); 30/300; Latin Clb; Yrbk Stf; French Hon Soc; Rutgers; Engrng.

CICHON, AMY; Manville HS; Manville, NJ; (Y); 3/99; Church Yth Grp; Chorus; Drill Tm; Variety Show; Yrbk Rptr; Yrbk Stf; Pres Frsh Cls; Pres Soph Cls; Pres Jr Cls; Pres Sr Cls; Peer Pressr Cnclg Grp 86; Teen Arts Poetry 86; LTC 86; Bus Mgmt.

CICHON, SUZIE; Newton HS; Newton, NJ; (Y); Art Clb; Church Yth Grp; 4-H; French Clb; Ski Clb; SADD; Concert Band; Drill Tm; Rep Frsh Cls; Rep Jr Cls; Spch Ther.

CICHOWSKI, JOSEPH; Rahway HS; Rahway, NJ; (Y); Aud/Vis; Church Yth Grp; Exploring; Wrstlng; Hon Roll; Kiwanis Awd; NHS; Pre-Law.

CIECHON, CHRIS; Audubon HS; Mt Ephraim, NJ; (Y); 3/109; Computer Clb; French Clb; Scholastic Bowl; Varsity Clb; Var Ice Hcky; Tennis; High Hon Roll; Hon Roll; NHS; Rotary Awd; Acdmc Awd 85-86; Cvl Engr.

CIECIUCH, VERONICA; St Dominic Acad; Secaucus, NJ; (Y); Computer Clb; FNA; Ski Clb; Spanish Clb; VP SADD; Yrbk Stf; Gym; Sftbl; Swmmng; Vllybl; Fairleigh Dickinson U; Optmtrst.

CIEMNOLONSKI, LAURA; Burlington City HS; Burlington, NJ; (Y); FBLA; Office Aide; Chorus; Mgr(s); Score Keeper; Legl Sec.

CIFFO, RUSSELL; Lyndhurst HS; Lyndhurst, NJ; (Y); 68/180; Am Leg Boys St; Boys Clb Am; Boy Scts; French Clb; Key Clb; Variety Show; Pres Sr Cls; Var Bsbl; Var Capt Bowling; Prfct Atten Awd; Natl PTA Cltrl Arts 1st Plc Wnr; Stu Rep Lyndhrst Brd Educ; Bus.

CIGANEK, TODD; Monsignor Donovan HS; Lavallette, NJ; (Y); Am Leg Boys St; Church Yth Grp; Ski Clb; Spanish Clb; Varsity Clb; JV Ftbl; JV Ftbl; Var Wrstlng; Pepperdine; Med.

CIGNARELLA JR, ROBERT C; Watchung Hills Regional HS; Warren, NJ; (Y); 24/324; Key Clb; Ski Clb; Spanish Clb; Varsity Clb; JV Socr; Var Tennis; Hon Roll; Sec NHS; Voice Dem Awd.

CILIENTO, DAVID; Pinelands Regional HS; Tuckerton, NJ; (Y); JV Bsbl; JV Bsktbl; Var Ftbl; Var Trk; Var Wt Lftg; Hon Roll; Penn ST; Sci.

CILONA, JOSEPH; Pope John XXIII HS; Hackettstown, NJ; (Y); Church Yth Grp; Civic Clb; Cmnty Wkr; Hosp Aide; Ski Clb; Yrbk Phtg; JV Ftbl; High Hon Roll; Rotary Awd; Vrsty Lttrs Ski Tm; Pre-Med.

CINCOTTA, JANE; Pinelands Regional HS; Tuckerton, NJ; (Y); Church Yth Grp; Ed Nwsp Stf; Pres Stu Cncl; JV Bsktbl; JV Fld Hcky; Var Sftbl; Hon Roll; NHS.

CINCOTTA, KEITH; Cinnaminson HS; Cinna, NJ; (Y); Am Leg Boys St; Boy Scts; Church Yth Grp; German Clb; Library Aide; SADD; Stu Cncl; Var Socr.

CINEGE, CHRISTINE; Mount Saint Mary Acad; Linden, NJ; (Y); 12/110; French Clb; Ski Clb; VP Concert Band; Var Gym; Pom Pon; Swmmng; Tennis; Hon Roll; Gftd & Tlntd 85-86; Duke; Chem.

CINTRON, CELIA; Hoboken HS; Hoboken, NJ; (Y); Cheerleading.

CIPERSKI, JILL; Wayne Hills HS; Wayne, NJ; (Y); 81/300; Church Yth Grp; Cmnty Wkr; FBLA; Spanish Clb; Variety Show; Yrbk Stf; JV Bsktbl; Sftbl; Hon Roll; FBLA Hghst Grd Pt Avg Acctg 85; Cntstnt Miss Teen NJ 84; Peer Cnslg Grp 86; Fshn Merch.

CIPOLLETTI, CINDY; Manchester Regional HS; North Haledon, NJ; (S); Hosp Aide; Office Aide; Band; Chorus; Concert Band; Madrigals; Mrchg Band; Yrbk Stf.

CIPRIANI, DIANE; Hackettstown HS; Hackettstown, NJ; (Y); Chorus; Stu Cncl; Hon Roll; NHS; Fncg Vrsty Ltr; Fncg Capt; Fncg Rookie Of Yr; Intl Rel.

CIPRIANI, LYDIA; Park Ridge HS; Park Ridge, NJ; (Y); 7/106; Letterman Clb; Math Clb; Quiz Bowl; Teachers Aide; Varsity Clb; Stage Crew; Nwsp Stf; Yrbk Sprt Ed; VP Soph Cls; VP Jr Cls; Trck MVP Awd 85; Bsktbl Most Impvd Plyr 85; Hon Mntn Spnsh Cmptn 85; Econ.

CIRCONCISO, ALFONSO; Secaucus HS; Secaucus, NJ; (S); 10/200; Computer Clb; School Play; Nwsp Rptr; Ftbl; High Hon Roll; Hon Roll; NHS; Itln Natl Hnr Soc 85; Princeton; Med.

CIRELLI, JENINE; West Morris Central HS; Hackettstown, NJ; (Y); Church Yth Grp; Dance Clb; 4-H; Ski Clb; Capt Color Guard; Yrbk Stf; Stu Cncl; Stat Bsktbl; Powder Puff Ftbl; JV Score Keeper; Csmtlgy.

CIRELLO, VINCENT ANTHONY; Fair Lawn HS; Fair Lawn, NJ; (Y); Cmnty Wkr; Var Capt Ftbl; Var Capt Lcrss; 1st Tm All Lg Ftbl 85-86; Ref & Coach JR Ftbl 82-83; JR Elks 82; Psych.

CIRINCION, DAYNA; Rutherford HS; Rutherford, NJ; (Y); 66/185; Cmnty Wkr; Pep Clb; Ski Clb; Varsity Clb; Chorus; Variety Show; Yrbk Bus Mgr; Yrbk Stf; Cheerleading; Swmmng; Outstndng Voc 86; Rutgers Coll; Spcl Ed.

CIRRITO, KRISTEN; Scotch Plains-Fanwood HS; Scotch Pl, NJ; (Y); AFS; Key Clb; Sec SADD; Band; Capt Color Guard; Concert Band; Flag Corp; Mrchg Band; Var Socr; Hon Roll; Psych.

CITRON, MIKE; Lakewoood HS; Lakewood, NJ; (Y); 16/297; English Clb; Band; Rep Frsh Cls; Rep Jr Cls; Bsbl; Mgr Mgr(s); Var L Socr; Var Trk; High Hon Roll; Hon Roll; Bys ST NJ Gvrnmntl Pgm; Bys Grp III NJ; ST Indr Trck Chmpnshp; Bus Fnance.

CIUBINSKI, GEORGE; Lakewood HS; Lakewood, NJ; (Y); Boy Scts; English Clb; Key Clb; Spanish Clb; Mgr Color Guard; Nwsp Rptr; Var L Socr; Boy Scouts Of Amer Eagle Scout Awd; Bio Med.

CIUFO, LISA M; Watchung Hills Regional HS; Warren, NJ; (Y); 39/320; Key Clb; Var L Cheerleading; Powder Puff Ftbl; Hon Roll; Ldrshp Awd Fut Sec Katharine Gibbs 85; Birkeley Schl Awd Outstndng Achvt Bus Educ 86; Bus Mktg.

CIULLA JR, PETER; Nutley HS; Nutley, NJ; (Y); Boy Scts; Exploring; Math Clb; JV L Wrstlng; Hon Roll; Prfct Atten Awd; AF Acad; Engrng.

CIVA, DENISE ANN; Camden Catholic HS; Camden, NJ; (Y); 18/262; Am Leg Aux Girls St; Pres French Clb; Camera Clb; Drill Tm; Nwsp Rptr; French Hon Soc; NHS; Voice Dem Awd; Soc Sci Hnr Soc-VP 84-86; Pres Acadmc Ftns Awd 86; Close Up 85; Cabrini Coll; Cmnctns.

CIVIL, RICHARD; Wayne Hills HS; Wayne, NJ; (Y); Aud/Vis; Boy Scts; Library Aide; Radio Clb; Stage Crew; Comm.

CIVLLA, KAREN; Sacred Heart HS; Vineland, NJ; (Y); 18/67; Art Clb; Pep Clb; Spanish Clb; Chorus; School Musical; Stage Crew; Off Frsh Cls; Rep Soph Cls; Rep Jr Cls; Off Stu Cncl; Cert Apprctn Awd 86; PA Acad Fine Arts; Art.

CLAIR, SUSAN; St John Vianney HS; Colts Neck, NJ; (Y); 6/270; Church Yth Grp; Drama Clb; Intnl Clb; SADD; Chorus; School Musical; School Play; Yrbk Stf; Var Mgr(s); NHS; High Hons & Hons Cert 84-86; Shield & Key Gold & White Awd 84-86; Piano Guild Awd 85-86; Carnegie Mellon U; Communicatn.

CLANCY, JOHN M; New Milford HS; New Milford, NJ; (Y); Am Leg Boys St; Church Yth Grp; Var Bsbl; Var Bsktbl; JV Coach Actv; Var Ftbl; Im Trk; Cit Awd; Bsbl-BCSL Natl Ust Tm All Lge 86.

CLAPP, KRISTIN; Kittatinny Regional HS; Branchville, NJ; (Y); Dance Clb; Drama Clb; PAVAS; Spanish Clb; Rep SADD; Thesps; Acpl Chr; Chorus; School Musical; School Play; Sympsm Arts Thtr Wrkshps 85-87; Drama.

CLAPPI, KATHERINE M; Ramsey HS; Ramsey, NJ; (Y); 69/243; Art Clb; Church Yth Grp; Debate Tm; Drama Clb; Office Aide; Chorus; School Play; Nwsp Rptr; Nwsp Stf; Lit Mag; Fshn Inst Of Tech Advtsg & Intro To Bus In Fshn 85; Syracuse.

CLARK, AUDREY; Hackettstown HS; Hackettstown, NJ; (Y); Church Yth Grp; Cmnty Wkr; Hosp Aide; Key Clb; Teachers Aide; Church Choir; Sftbl; Wt Lftg; Hon Roll; Candystrpg 82; Wrkg N Vlg Yr 86; WV U; Phys Thrpy.

CLARK, EILEEN; Sparta HS; Sparta, NJ; (Y); Trs Concert Band; Drm Mjr(t); Jazz Band; Mrchg Band; Yrbk Stf; Gov Hon Prg Awd; High Hon Roll; JP Sousa Awd; Ntl Ski Ptrl 84-86; Rutgers U; Comp Sci.

CLARK, GEORGE; Timothy Christian Schl; Donellen, NJ; (S); Church Yth Grp; Drama Clb; Service Clb; Chorus; School Play; Var Bsbl; Var Bsktbl; Var Socr; High Hon Roll; Hon Roll; Pol Sci.

CLARK, GEORGE B; Hackensack HS; Hackensack, NJ; (Y); Pres Computer Clb; Yrbk Stf; JV Bowling; Hon Roll; Jr NHS; Prfct Atten Awd; Jerome Bentley JR Annual ST Sci Day 86; Lat Hnr Soc 86; Comp Sci.

CLARK, JANE; Arthur P Schalick HS; Bridgeton, NJ; (Y); 22/133; Teachers Aide; Hon Roll; Comm.

CLARK, JOANNE L; Oakcrest HS; Mays Landing, NJ; (Y); 26/220; French Clb; GAA; Hosp Aide; Key Clb; Yrbk Stf; Off Soph Cls; Off Sr Cls; Var Cheerleading; Jr NHS; Vrsty Schlr 83-85; Gftd & Tlntd 82-86; Pre-Med.

CLARK, JONATHAN A; Governor Livingston Reg HS; Berkeley Heights, NJ; (Y); Am Leg Boys St; Church Yth Grp; FBLA; School Musical; Yrbk Ed-Chief; Sec Stu Cncl; Powder Puff Ftbl; Var JV Socr; Hon Roll; Yrbk Phtg; Chrmn Welcoming Committee 86-87; Township Committee 85-87; The Underground; Lehigh; Economics.

CLARK, PAMELA; Kittatinny Regional HS; Blairstown, NJ; (Y); 29/222; Church Yth Grp; Chorus; School Musical; Cheerleading; Crs Cntry; Swmmng; Trk; Hon Roll; NHS; Natl Ldrshp Conf 86; 1st Pl NJ ST HS Crft Fair 84; Achvt Awds In Hist, Math, Eng, Clothing Construc; Liberal Arts.

CLARK, PATTY; Parsippany HS; Lk Hiawatha, NJ; (Y); Church Yth Grp; GAA; Bsktbl; Fld Hcky; Sftbl; Bus.

CLARK, SHANNON; Essex Catholic Girls HS; East Orange, NJ; (Y); Pep Clb; SADD; Rep Soph Cls; Sec Jr Cls; Yng Cmnty Ldrs Of Am 86; Intl Dir Of Distingquished Ldrshp 86; Natl Ldrshp And Svc Awd 86; ST Johns U; Med.

CLARK, SHARON; Bridgewater-Raritan East HS; Bridgewater, NJ; (Y); Sec Church Yth Grp; SADD; Off Frsh Cls; Sec Soph Cls; Off Jr Cls; Off Sr Cls; VP Stu Cncl; Var Capt Fld Hcky; Var Trk; NHS; Pres Acad Ftnss Awd 86; Bridgewater Wmns Clb Schlrshp 86; Hmcmng Queen 4th 86; Douglass Coll.

CLARK, TAMMY; Camden HS; Camden, NJ; (S); 25/408; Pres JA; Capt Color Guard; Yrbk Stf; Trs Soph Cls; Trs Jr Cls; Trs Stu Cncl; Hon Roll; VFW Awd; Voice Dem Awd; NJ Govrnr Schl 85; Seton Hall U; Law.

CLARKE, CHRISTIE ERIN; Northern Valley Regional HS; Haworth, NJ; (Y); 18/250; Cmnty Wkr; Pres French Clb; Pres Intnl Clb; NFL; VP Pres Ski Clb; Varsity Clb; High Hon Roll; Hon Roll; NHS; Pres Schlr; U Of VT; Psych.

CLARKE, DEBRA; Arthur P Schalick HS; Elmer, NJ; (Y); Color Guard; Flag Corp; Mrchg Band; Church Choir; GATE 83-85; Olympics Mind 83; Jrnlsm.

CLARKE, HEATHER; North Warren Regional HS; Blairstown, NJ; (Y); 50/158; Church Yth Grp; Pep Clb; Ski Clb; SADD; Chorus; Church Choir; School Musical; Stage Crew; Sec Frsh Cls; Sec Soph Cls; Women Soc Schlrshp $300 86; Hmcmng Queen 85-86; Prom Queen 84-85; County Coll Of Morris; Pblc Adm.

CLARKE, NOELLE; Washington Township HS; Sewell, NJ; (S); Chess Clb; Drama Clb; German Clb; Model UN; Soroptimist; Mrchg Band; School Musical; Nwsp Rptr; Lit Mag; Jr NHS; Stdnt Press Conf With NJ Cngrssmn Wm Hughs 85; Hofstra U; Med.

CLARKE, SHARON; Rahway HS; Rahway, NJ; (Y); Hon Roll; Prfct Atten Awd.

CLARKE, SHAUNE; Highland HS; Sicklerville, NJ; (Y); Dance Clb; Chorus; Concert Band; Sftbl; White Williams Schlrshp 85; Tylers Chrl-Voice & Piano Schlrshp 86; Outstndg Trphy-Miss Amer Coed Pgnt; Nrs.

CLASSEN, MAGDALENA; Eastside HS; Paterson, NJ; (S); 19/550; Pres Sec Church Yth Grp; Office Aide; OEA; Teachers Aide; Hon Roll; Ntl Merit Ltr; J Dvnprt Awd Excllnce Engl 86; Cert Of Awd Acdmc Excllnce 86; Schlrshp Cert For 3 Yrs SHABE 86; Passaic Cnty CC; Lgl Sec.

CLAUSS, CRAIG; Westwood Regional HS; Westwood, NJ; (Y); 30/220; Rep Stu Cncl; Var L Golf; French Hon Soc; High Hon Roll; Hon Roll; NHS; Rep Soph Cls; Rep Jr Cls; Rep Sr Cls; JV Bsktbl; Arspc Engrng.

CLAUSS, LAURIE; Salem HS; Salem, NJ; (Y); 4/140; Math Tm; Jazz Band; Mrchg Band; Orch; Stu Cncl; Gov Hon Prg Awd; NHS; Pres Schlr; Rotary Awd; Acadmc All Amer Lrg Div 86; Natl Math Awd 86; Ruth Kieth Schlrshp 86; CO ST U; Pre Vet Med.

CLAWSON, SCOTT; Voorhees HS; Califon, NJ; (Y); 1/300; Am Leg Boys St; Boy Scts; Varsity Clb; French Hon Soc; Gov Hon Prg Awd; High Hon Roll; NHS; Ntl Merit Ltr; French Clb; Key Clb; Fncng 3rd Tm All ST 86; Rensselaer Math & Sci Mdl 86; Elec Engrng.

CLAXTON, KELLIE; Central Reginal HS; Island Heights, NJ; (Y); 2/230; Nwsp Rptr; Fld Hcky; Mgr(s); Trk; High Hon Roll; Jr NHS; NHS; Spanish NHS; Georgian Court Coll; Scndry Ed.

CLAY, HUBERT O; Neptune HS; Neptune, NJ; (Y); 12/309; Drama Clb; Capt Math Tm; Science Clb; Pres Ski Clb; VP Stu Cncl; Crs Cntry; Golf; High Hon Roll; NHS; Ntl Merit Ltr; U S Army Sci & Humnties Symp 3rd Pl 85; ST Sci Fair 1st Pl 83-84; Outstndng Dramtc Perfmnc 85; Mech Engrng.

CLAYTON, DAVID; Wood-Ridge HS; Wood-Ridge, NJ; (S); 1/80; Pres Math Clb; Model UN; Science Clb; Pres Y-Teens; Ed Lit Mag; Capt Crs Cntry; Capt Trk; NHS; Voice Dem Awd; Natl Latin Exam Maxima Cum Laude Slvr Mdl 84-85.

CLAYTON, DIANNE; Clifford J Scott HS; E Orange, NJ; (Y); 2/253; Church Yth Grp; Cmnty Wkr; Computer Clb; 4-H; Intnl Clb; Key Clb; Spanish Clb; Yrbk Stf; Stu Cncl; Sftbl; Rutgers U HS Achvt Awd 86; Rutgers Schl Of Nrsg; Nrsg.

CLAYTON, KENNETH; Paterson Catholic Regional HS; Paterson, NJ; (Y); Pres Church Yth Grp; DECA; Chorus; Church Choir; Nwsp Rptr; Yrbk Bus Mgr; Stu Cncl; Hon Roll; Amercn Ldg 333 Tmpl 258 Ptry Awd-2nd Pl 86; Howard U; Comm.

CLEAR, DYLAN; Metuchen HS; Metuchen, NJ; (Y); Ski Clb; Var Bsktbl; Var Ftbl; NHS; Mst Imprvd Bsktbl Vrsty 86; Marine Bio.

CLEARY, COLLEEN; Red Bank Catholic HS; Brielle, NJ; (Y); Church Yth Grp; Math Clb; SADD; JV Co-Capt Cheerleading; Intl Finance.

CLEMENT, CHRISTINE; Middle Township HS; Cape May Ct Hse, NJ; (Y); VICA; Color Guard; Mrchg Band; Pres Jr Cls; Hon Roll; NHS; Vica Partcptn Awd 85-86; Vica Outstndng Achvtmt Awd 84-86; MTHS Band Actvty Awd 83-86; Cosmetology.

CLEMENT, JOHN; Arthur L Johnson HS; Clark, NJ; (Y); 14/195; Drama Clb; German Clb; Thesps; School Musical; School Play; Stage Crew; Rep Soph Cls; Rep Stu Cncl; Hon Roll; Ntl Merit SF; Germn Hnr Socty; Engrng.

CLEMENT, STEPHANIE; Steinert HS; Trenton, NJ; (Y); 43/315; Church Yth Grp; Color Guard; Drill Tm; Flag Corp; High Hon Roll; NHS; Mrchng Unt Schlrshp 86; Erly Chldhd.

CLEMENTE, JOSEPH P; De Paul HS; Lincoln Pk, NJ; (Y); 21/200; Am Leg Boys St; Spanish Clb; Nwsp Rptr; Var Tennis; High Hon Roll; Hon Roll; Pres Schlr; Rotary Awd; Rutges Coll; Bus.

CLEMENTE, PATRICIA; Paul VI HS; Clifton, NJ; (Y); Girl Scts; Key Clb; Pep Clb; Ski Clb; SADD; Chorus; Nwsp Stf; Yrbk Stf; Stu Cncl; Hon Roll; Jrnlsm.

CLEMENTS, TIMMY; Westside HS; Bronx, NY; (Y); Church Choir; Arts 79; Mth 85; Rdng 85; Plc Ofcr.

CLEVELAND, DAVE; Washington Township HS; Sewell, NJ; (Y); Church Yth Grp; Math Clb; Math Tm; Model UN; Sthrn Methadist U; Engrng.

CLIENTO, SUSAN; Lodi HS; Lodi, NJ; (Y); Cmnty Wkr; FTA; JA; Pep Clb; Spanish Clb; Teachers Aide; Varsity Clb; School Play; Sec Frsh Cls; Rep Soph Cls; Elmntry Tchr.

CLIFF, CAROLYN; Mary Help Of Christians Acad; Mahwah, NJ; (Y); Math Tm; Quiz Bowl; Chorus; Variety Show; Nwsp Rptr; VP Frsh Cls; JV Cheerleading; Hon Roll; Teachers Aide; Nwsp Stf; Irish Dncng Champ 74-86; North Amercn Regnl Irish Dncng Champ 80-86; Natl Irish Dncng Champ 83; Oxford U; Law.

CLIFFORD, MICHAEL; Bishop George Ahr HS; Iselin, NJ; (Y); Boy Scts; Socr; High Hon Roll; Hon Roll; St Johns U; Engr.

CLIFTON, ANASTASIA; West Central HS; Long Valley, NJ; (Y); 6/256; Var Debate Tm; Ed Nwsp Ed-Chief; Hon Roll; NHS; Air Frce ROTC 86; Lehigh U; Mech Engrng.

CLIFTON, ROBERT; St John Vianney HS; Matawan, NJ; (Y); Art Clb; JV Var Crs Cntry; JV Var Trk; Hon Roll.

CLOAK, KELLY; Delsea Regional HS; Monroeville, NJ; (Y); 10/195; Pres Science Clb; Mgr Bsktbl; Var JV Crs Cntry; Mgr(s); Score Keeper; JV Trk; High Hon Roll; NHS; Schlrshp Cstdl Stff Delsea 86; Frnklnvll VFW Pst 2071 Axlry Amrcnsm 86; 2nd Tm Vnlnd Times X-Cntry 86; Cabrini Coll; Acctg.

CLOUGHLEY, BARBARA; Dover HS; Dover, NJ; (Y); 21/220; Hosp Aide; Band; Mrchg Band; Var Capt Bsktbl; Var Crs Cntry; Var Capt Socr; Var Capt Trk; High Hon Roll; Hon Roll; NHS; Bnd Bstr Awd/Outstndng Instrmntlst 86; Sprngfld Col6; Physcl Ed.

CLOUR, RANDY; Salem HS; Salem, NJ; (Y); 9/131; Am Leg Boys St; Computer Clb; Math Tm; Ski Clb; Rep Sr Cls; Hon Roll; NHS; Rider; Bus Adm.

CLOUSER, DIANNA; Camden County Voc Tech Schl; Atco, NJ; (Y); 5/350; Trs VP DECA; Church Choir; Yrbk Stf; Stu Cncl; Hon Roll; NHS; Hnbl Mntn Radio Cmmrcl 84; 2nd Pl Indiv Tst & Hnbl Mntn Ovrll Gen Mtg 85; Camden Cnty Coll; Acctg.

COAKLEY, JEFFREY; Roselle Catholic HS; Elizabeth, NJ; (Y); Var JV Bsbl; Bsktbl; Wt Lftg; Hon Roll; Spanish NHS; Seton Hall; Bus.

COAN, GARRETT B; Dwight Englewood Schl; Cresskill, NJ; (Y); Var Bsktbl; U PA; Intl Rltns.

COATES, RICK; Holy Cross HS; Willingboro, NJ; (Y); Church Yth Grp; Red Cross Aide; Ski Clb; Rep Jr Cls; Rep Sr Cls; Rep Stu Cncl; JV Bsktbl; JV Var Ftbl; Var Wrstlng; Hon Roll; Yth & The Amer Pol Systm 86; Pilot.

COATES, STEVE; Delsea Regional HS; Franklinville, NJ; (Y); Key Clb; Spanish Clb; Varsity Clb; Var Bsbl; Var Ftbl; Var Wrstlng; Hon Roll; Prfct Atten Awd; Rutgers U.

COBB, JACLYN; Bridgeton HS; Bridgeton, NJ; (Y); Ski Clb; SADD; JV Sftbl; JV Tennis; NHS; Rensselaer Polytech Inst Math & Sci Awd.

COBB, LAVERN; Burlington County Vo-Tech HS; Willingboro, NJ; (Y); 12/260; Pres Church Yth Grp; VP Pres Computer Clb; VICA; Chorus; Capt Bsktbl; Capt Sftbl; High Hon Roll; Voice Dem Awd.

COBERT, MARIANNE; Edgewood SR HS; Blue Anchor, NJ; (Y); 10/300; Church Yth Grp; Cmnty Wkr; Exploring; Girl Scts; VP Frsh Cls; High Hon Roll; Hon Roll; Jr NHS; Gftd & Tlntd 82-86; NY U; Fashn.

COBLE, KENNETH; St Anthony HS; Jersey City, NJ; (Y); Spanish Clb; Variety Show; JV Bsbl; Var Bowling; Hon Roll; Prfct Atten Awd; Rtgrs Coll Of Engrng; Elec Engr.

COCCA, MICHAEL; St Peters Preparatory HS; Jersey City, NJ; (Y); 40/206; Church Yth Grp; Civic Clb; Cmnty Wkr; FBLA; FTA; Math Clb; Office Aide; Political Wkr; Teachers Aide; Nwsp Rptr; Seton Hall U; Math.

COCEANO, THOMAS; Saint Marys Hall Doane Acad; Willingboro, NJ; (Y); 2/18; Am Leg Boys St; Drama Clb; Nwsp Rptr; Lit Mag; VP Soph Cls; VP Stu Cncl; High Hon Roll; NEDT Awd; Engrng.

COCHRAN, BONNIE; South Hunterdon Regional HS; Stockton, NJ; (S); 10/72; Art Clb; Church Yth Grp; SADD; Chorus; Church Choir; Madrigals; School Musical; School Play; Yrbk Ed-Chief; Score Keeper; Marine Corps Rsrvs; Diesal Mech.

COCKERHAM, EVELYN; Eastside HS; Paterson, NJ; (Y); 10/500; Computer Clb; Yrbk Phtg; Yrbk Stf; Soph Cls; Hon Roll; Yrbk Awd; Frgn Lang Educ NJ Awd; Acdmc Excllnce Awd; Rutgers; Comp Sci.

COCOZZIELLO, MARISA; West Orange HS; W Orange, NJ; (Y); Ski Clb; Spanish Clb; Trs Frsh Cls; VP Soph Cls; Cheerleading; Hon Roll; Spanish NHS; Kean Coll; Lib Arts.

COCUZZA, DONNA; Toms River HS East; Toms River, NJ; (Y); Art Clb; Church Yth Grp; FBLA; Key Clb; SADD; JV Trk; High Hon Roll; Hon Roll; FBLA-RGNL Comptn-Accntng I 85; Awd-Outstndng Wrk-JV Trck Fld Evnts 85; Ocean County Coll; Accntnt.

CODERRE, ROBERT; Pope John XXIII Regional HS; Sparta, NJ; (Y); 5/133; Boy Scts; Drama Clb; Thesps; School Musical; School Play; Lit Mag; Var Bowling; High Hon Roll; NHS; US Naval Acad; Aerontcl Engr.

CODY, JAMES; St Mary HS; W Keansburg, NJ; (Y); 63/130; Church Yth Grp; Hon Roll; Schlrshp St Mary; Sec Ed.

COFFARO, STEPHANI; North Warren Regional HS; Blairstown, NJ; (Y); 22/131; Church Yth Grp; Cmnty Wkr; FBLA; Pep Clb; Stat Bsbl; JV Fld Hcky; Var L Trk; JV Vllybl; High Hon Roll; NHS; Bus Acctg.

COFFEY, MAUREEN; Toms River H S East; Toms River, NJ; (Y); 38/680; Aud/Vis; Computer Clb; Drama Clb; German Clb; Math Tm; Band; Concert Band; Drm & Bgl; Mrchg Band; School Musical; Bus Educ Assoc; Comp Prgmmng.

COGAN, WILLIAM E; Paul Vi Regional HS; Clifton, NJ; (Y); Camera Clb; SADD; School Play; Nwsp Phtg; Yrbk Ed-Chief; Yrbk Phtg; Yrbk Sprt Ed; Rep Sr Cls; Pres Trs Stu Cncl; Var Golf; Acctng.

COGEN, STEPHANIE; Teaneck HS; Teaneck, NJ; (Y); French Clb; SADD; School Play; Nwsp Ed-Chief; Rep Jr Cls; Var Capt Swmmng; French Hon Soc; High Hon Roll; NHS; Ntl Merit SF.

COHAN, ERIC; Montville Twp HS; Montville, NJ; (Y); 13/262; Pres FBLA; Math Clb; Science Clb; Ski Clb; JV Bsbl; Var L Ftbl; High Hon Roll; Trs NHS; FBLA 1st Pl Bus Law & Math Cmptn 85-86; Engr.

COHAN, SUSAN; Ocean Township HS; Ocean, NJ; (Y); French Clb; Temple Yth Grp; Band; JV Fld Hcky; JV Sftbl; Spartan Schlr 83-84; MVP Fld Hockey 82-83; Bentley Inst; Music.

COHEN III, ARTHUR L W; Lower Cape May Regional HS; Cape May, NJ; (Y); #12 In Class; Boy Scts; Spanish Clb; SADD; Band; Chorus; Church Choir; Concert Band; Mrchg Band; Orch; Pep Band; Arion Awd Music 86; Mus Compstn.

COHEN, BARBARA; Howell HS; Howell, NJ; (Y); #32 In Class; JCL; Latin Clb; Math Tm; Off Jr Cls; Rep Stu Cncl; Stat Bsktbl; L Socr; NHS; Bus.

COHEN, DAWN; Freehold HS; Freehold, NJ; (Y); Sec Sr Cls; Sec French Hon Soc; High Hon Roll; Hon Roll; NHS; Sec French Clb; Nwsp Stf; Yrbk Stf; Sec Jr Cls; Rutgers Coll.

COHEN, ERIC; Fair Lawn HS; Fair Lawn, NJ; (Y); Boy Scts; Cmnty Wkr; Varsity Clb; Y-Teens; Var JV Bsbl; Var Capt Bsktbl; Im Coach Actv; Var Ftbl; Acctg.

COHEN, JEFF; East Brunswick HS; East Brunswick, NJ; (Y); Cmnty Wkr; Hosp Aide; Lit Mag; Wrstlng; NHS; Nwsp Stf; Jr NHS; Distngshd Schlr 86; Acadmc Schlrshp 86; U Of MI Ann Arbor; Med.

COHEN, JENNIFER; James Caldwell HS; West Caldwell, NJ; (Y); 40/265; Am Leg Aux Girls St; Temple Yth Grp; Band; Capt Flag Corp; Stu Cncl; Tennis; Emory U; Bus.

COHEN, JEREMY; James Caldwell HS; W Caldwell, NJ; (Y); Key Clb; Temple Yth Grp; Nwsp Rptr; Stu Cncl; JV Var Socr; JV Trk; High Hon Roll; NHS; Computer Clb; Math Tm; Rtgrs Deans Smr Schlr 86; 1st Prz Israel Tst Schlrshp 86; Hrvrd; Bus.

COHEN, JILL A; Manalapan HS; Morganville, NJ; (Y); 19/385; Hosp Aide; Temple Yth Grp; Band; Concert Band; Mrchg Band; Stu Cncl; NHS; Cornell Schl Engrng; Engrng.

COHEN, JONATHAN; Bridgwater Raritan East HS; Bridgewater, NJ; (Y); French Clb; Ski Clb; SADD; Temple Yth Grp; Rep Frsh Cls; VP Stu Cncl; Ice Hcky; Lcrss; Var Socr; Var Tennis; Attndng Natl Assoc Of Stu Cncls Cnvntn 86; Fnlst For NJ Boys St 86; Bus.

COHEN, JULIAN M; Cherry Hill High School East; Cherry Hill, NJ; (Y); Am Leg Boys St; Model UN; Political Wkr; Ed Nwsp Stf; Rep Sr Cls; Rep Stu Cncl; JV Tennis; High Hon Roll; NHS; Ntl Merit Ltr; Delg 41st Amer Lgn Jersey Boys St 86; Pres Bet Kama AZA Chptr BBYO 85-87; NJ St Sci Day 20th 86.

COHEN, LINDA; Pompton Lakes HS; Pompton Lakes, NJ; (Y); 35/151; FNA; Q&S; Temple Yth Grp; Band; Flag Corp; School Play; Nwsp Stf; Lit Mag; Cheerleading; High Hon Roll; Hlth Career Clb Scholar 86; Bradley U; Nrsg.

COHEN, MIRIAM; Morris Knolls HS; Denville, NJ; (Y); 2/390; Trs German Clb; Hosp Aide; Math Clb; Pres Temple Yth Grp; Chorus; NHS; Pres Schlr; Sal; Math Tm; VP Science Clb; Hugh Obrien Ldrshp Fndnt Outstndng Sphmr 83; NJ Jr Acad Of Sci Grnt-In-Aid 84; NJ Rgnl Sci Fair 1st; Cornell U; Bio Chem.

COHEN, NEIL; Shore Regional HS; W Long Branch, NJ; (Y); Am Leg Boys St; French Clb; Varsity Clb; Concert Band; Mrchg Band; JV Bsbl; Var Bowling; Var Golf; High Hon Roll; NHS; Olympcs Mind-Ldrshp Awd 86; Rgnl Sci Fair-3rd Pl 85; Stock Mkt-3rd Pl 85; Pre-Med.

COHEN, ROBIN LORI; Lawrence HS; Lawrenceville, NJ; (Y); 28/227; AFS; Drama Clb; French Clb; Hosp Aide; JV Var Socr; Var Swmmng; Var Trk; High Hon Roll; Hon Roll; Grammarian Awd; Rutgers Coll.

COHEN, SCOTT; Cherry Hill West HS; Cherry Hill, NJ; (Y); Am Leg Boys St; Off Stu Cncl; Var Bsbl; JV Bsktbl; Var Ftbl; High Hon Roll; Pres Schlr; Im Sftbl; Im Vllybl; Pres Ftnss Awd; Pre Law.

COHEN, SHARYN; John F Kennedy HS; Willingsboro, NJ; (Y); 7/300; Am Leg Aux Girls St; Intnl Clb; VP Sec Service Clb; Pres VP Temple Yth Grp; Yrbk Stf; JV Fld Hcky; Var Mgr Lcrss; NHS; Rep Hugh O Brien Yth Ldrshp Semnr 85; Hebrew Hon Soc 82&84-85.

COHEN, STUART; Fair Lawn HS; Fair Lawn, NJ; (Y); Ski Clb; Spanish Clb; Stu Cncl; Var Socr; Hon Roll; Dvd Bernikes Srv Awd 86.

COHEN, SUSAN; Wayne Hills HS; Wayne, NJ; (Y); 47/350; Spanish Clb; Sec Temple Yth Grp; Chorus; Concert Band; Mrchg Band; School Musical; Nwsp Stf; Yrbk Stf; Lit Mag; Hon Roll; Journlsm.

COHEN, WENDY; Saddle River Day Schl; Orangeburg, NY; (Y); Art Clb; Camera Clb; Dance Clb; Math Clb; Pep Clb; Teachers Aide; Yrbk Stf; VP Pom Pon; VP Tennis; Hon Roll; Spanish Achvt Awd 84-85; U Of Rochester.

COHN, SHARRON; Franklin HS; Somerset, NJ; (Y); 84/313; French Clb; Teachers Aide; Temple Yth Grp; Varsity Clb; Concert Band; Mrchg Band; Nwsp Stf; Stat Bsktbl; Var Mgr(s); St Johns Cmptv Schlrshp; Hebrew U; Athltc Adm.

COILPARAMPIL, BAIJU; Orange HS; Orange, NJ; (S); Exploring; Band; Concert Band; Mrchg Band; Yrbk Ed-Chief; Yrbk Stf; Lit Mag; Pres Frsh Cls; VP Soph Cls; Rep Jr Cls; Med.

COKE, DONNA; Vailsburg HS; Newark, NJ; (Y); Church Yth Grp; FNA; Church Choir; High Hon Roll; Hon Roll; NHS; Ntl Physcin Clb 83; VP Chrch Yth Grp 86; Sec Chrch Choir 80; RN.

COLACINO, LISA; Holy Family Acad; Bayonne, NJ; (Y); 58/130; Computer Clb; French Clb; Bowling; Hon Roll; Math.

COLAIACOVO, DAREN; Montville HS; Pine Brk, NJ; (Y); Church Yth Grp; Key Clb; Varsity Clb; Rep Jr Cls; JV Bsktbl; Var Ftbl; Var Lcrss; High Hon Roll; Hon Roll; Art Clb; Bus.

COLANGELO, ANTHONY; Belvidere HS; Belvidere, NJ; (S); Scholastic Bowl; Varsity Clb; VP Jr Cls; Stu Cncl; Var L Bsktbl; Var L Ftbl; Var L Golf; 4-H Awd; Hon Roll; NHS; Engrng.

COLANGELO, VITA G; Belvidere HS; Belvidere, NJ; (S); 5/117; 4-H; French Clb; Varsity Clb; Rep Stu Cncl; Var Bsktbl; Var Capt Fld Hcky; Stat Ftbl; JV Sftbl; Cit Awd; Hon Roll; Occptnl Thrpy.

COLASURDO, JOSEPH; Hudson Catholic HS; Jersey Cty, NJ; (Y); Yrbk Stf; Hon Roll; NHS; US Bus Ed Awd 86; St Peters Coll; Bus Admin.

COLAVECCHI, LISA; Washington Township HS; Turnersville, NJ; (Y); Tennis; Athl Wk Tnns 84; Bus Admin.

COLAVITO, EDWARD; Secaucus HS; Secaucus, NJ; (S); Ski Clb; Spanish NHS; Bus Mgmt.

COLBERT, JOHN A; Maple Shade HS; Maple Shade, NJ; (Y); 9/158; Am Leg Boys St; Rep Sr Cls; Rep Stu Cncl; Ftbl; Trk; Wt Lftg; High Hon Roll; Jr NHS; NHS; Prfct Atten Awd; HS Sprts Clb Schlr & Grad Clss Schlr 86; Knights Of Columbus OLPH Schlr 86; Rutgers-Camden; Mech Engrng.

COLCLOUGH, REZENA; Henry Snyder HS; Jersey City, NJ; (Y); Church Yth Grp; Cmnty Wkr; FBLA; Office Aide; Church Choir; School Play; Sftbl; Spanish NHS; St Schlr; Acctng.

COLDEBELLA, GUS P; Nutley HS; Nutley, NJ; (Y); 34/327; Am Leg Boys St; Boy Scts; Key Clb; Capt Concert Band; Mrchg Band; Variety Show; VP Sr Cls; Im Socr; Hon Roll; Librl Arts.

COLDENHOFF, TIMITY; Matawan Regional HS; Cliffwood Bch, NJ; (S); 16/311; Radio Clb; Comp Sci.

COLE, DANIEL; Dover HS; Dover, NJ; (Y); Computer Clb; Stage Crew; Score Keeper; Elctrncs Engr.

COLE, JEFFREY; Eastside HS; Paterson, NJ; (Y); Church Yth Grp; JA; Prfct Atten Awd; Trenton ST Coll; Electrncs.

COLE, KELLY; Manasquan HS; Spring Lk Hts, NJ; (Y); Church Yth Grp; DECA; FBLA; GAA; Ski Clb; Varsity Clb; Socr; Sftbl; Soccer Vrsty Letter; Marymont Coll VA; Accntng.

COLE, LESLIE; John F Kennedy HS; Willingboro, NJ; (Y); Intnl Clb; SADD; JV Fld Hcky; Var Swmmng; Hon Roll; Chld Psychlgy.

COLE, LISA; Central Regional HS; S Toms River, NJ; (Y); 10/300; Church Yth Grp; Math Clb; Math Tm; Office Aide; Chorus; Church Choir; Nwsp Sprt Ed; Yrbk Sprt Ed; JV Bsktbl; JV Fld Hcky; 3 Wk Schlrshp Actrl Sci-Howard U 86; Howard U.

COLE, LISA ANN; Hackettstown HS; Hackettstown, NJ; (Y); 12/199; Exploring; Hosp Aide; Key Clb; Q&S; Nwsp Rptr; Ed Lit Mag; Rep Stu Cncl; Stat Bsktbl; Co-Capt Powder Puff Ftbl; JV Stat Sftbl; U Of Delaware; Biolgy.

COLE, RICHARD; Dover HS; Dover, NJ; (Y); 22/240; Stage Crew; Score Keeper; High Hon Roll; Hon Roll; NHS; NJ Inst Of Tech; Chem Engrng.

COLE, WILLIAM C; Moorestown HS; Moorestown, NJ; (Y); 1/200; German Clb; Concert Band; Jazz Band; School Musical; Ed Yrbk Stf; Lit Mag; Var Capt Crs Cntry; Var Capt Trk; Ntl Merit SF; Nwsp Rptr; Ehrenurkunde Excptnl German Stu 84; Schlrshp Telluride Assoc Smmr Pgm 85; Eng.

COLELLA, STEPHEN J; Cherokee HS; Marlton, NJ; (Y); Am Leg Boys St; Stage Crew; Stu Cncl; Ftbl; Wrstlng; Hon Roll; Won Automotive Schlrshp 86; Mech Engrng.

COLELLO, STEPHANIE; Northern Burlington R HS; Wrightstown, NJ; (Y); 37/200; Am Leg Aux Girls St; 4-H; Yrbk Stf; Trs Jr Cls; Trs Sr Cls; Var L Fld Hcky; Var L Mgr(s); Var L Trk; Cit Awd; Hon Roll; Jeff Hudson Memrl Schlrshp 86; 4-H Ctznshp Focus Wk WA DC 85; Grt Advntr Pres Awd 86; La Salle U; Bus.

COLEMAN, DEBBIE; Cresskill HS; Cresskill, NJ; (Y); Church Yth Grp; Band; Concert Band; Mrchg Band; Pep Band; School Musical; Stat Trk.

COLEMAN, DWAYNE; Lincoln HS; Jersey City, NJ; (S); JA; Varsity Clb; Yrbk Phtg; Pres Frsh Cls; Pres Soph Cls; Pres Jr Cls; Stu Cncl; JV Var Bsktbl; Swmmng; High Hon Roll; Hugh O Brien Yth Fndtn Ldrshp Awd 85; Polt Sci.

COLEMAN, KELLY; Holy Cross HS; Medford, NJ; (Y); 114/397; Cmnty Wkr; French Clb; FNA; Hosp Aide; PAVAS; Rep Frsh Cls; Stu Cncl; JV Crs Cntry; JV Trk; JV Wt Lftg; Lncrs Life Pro Abrtn Clb 84-85; Nrsng.

COLEMAN, KEVIN B; Lenape Valley Regional HS; Stanhope, NJ; (Y); Am Leg Boys St; Acpl Chr; Chorus; Church Choir; Madrigals; Swing Chorus; Nwsp Rptr; Lit Mag; Hon Roll; Pres Schlr; Fairleigh Dickinson Presdntl Schlr Awd 86-90; Fairleigh Dickinson U; Psych.

COLEMAN, PATRICE; Trenton Central HS; Trenton, NJ; (Y); 177/544; Computer Clb; FHA; Scholastic Bowl; VICA; Variety Show; Hon Roll; Csmtlgy.

COLEMAN, ROXANE; Malcolm X Shabazz HS; Newark, NJ; (S); 1/263; Computer Clb; Office Aide; Cit Awd; High Hon Roll; NHS; St Schlr; Val; Rensselaer Poly Inst Math,Sci Medal 85; Sci Essay Awd 83; PTA Awd 83; Rutgers Coll; Phrmcy.

COLERIDGE, JENNIFER; Hunterdon Central HS; Flemington, NJ; (Y); 150/550; VP Cheerleading; Stat Lcrss; Trvled Comp Squad; Natl Chrldg Chmpnshps FL 85; FL ST; Bus Adm.

COLESS, PATRICIA M; Memorial HS; Cedar Grove, NJ; (S); 6/120; Church Yth Grp; Pres Spanish Clb; Drm Mjr(t); Yrbk Ed-Chief; Stat Bsktbl; Capt Var Fld Hcky; Var Swmmng; Var Trk; NHS; Douglass Coll; Bio.

COLGAN, TIMOTHY; Don Bosco Prep HS; Wyckoff, NJ; (Y); 13/170; Pep Clb; Nwsp Rptr; Rep Frsh Cls; Bsktbl; Hon Roll; NHS; Atl Trnr Ftbl 3 Ltrs 83-86; Anncr Vrsty Bsktbl Gms 86; Exec Bd NHS Tres 86-87; Bus.

COLL, MELISSA; Woodstown HS; Woodstown, NJ; (Y); FBLA; Im Sftbl; High Hon Roll; Hon Roll.

COLLETTI, ROBERT; St Joseph Regional HS; Valley Cottage, NY; (Y); 21/170; Yrbk Stf; JV Crs Cntry; High Hon Roll; Hon Roll; Spanish NHS; JV Mst Vlbl Rnnr 85-86; JV Mst Impvd Rnnr 84-85; Manhattan Coll; Engnrng.

COLLETTI, ROYLENE; N Warren Regional HS; Blairstown, NJ; (Y); 37/129; Church Yth Grp; Pep Clb; Ski Clb; SADD; Yrbk Stf; Stat Bsbl; JV Socr; Rotary Awd; Athltc Trnng.

COLLIGAN, JEANNE; De Paul HS; Wayne, NJ; (S); 22/178; School Play; Nwsp Sprt Ed; Cheerleading; Stat Fld Hcky; Var Trk; High Hon Roll; Hon Roll; Mktg.

COLLINI, AMY; Pope John XXIII HS; Sparta, NJ; (Y); 16/137; French Clb; Hosp Aide; SADD; School Play; Lit Mag; Swmmng; Cit Awd; Sec NHS; Drama Clb; Altrnt Grls Ctznshp Inst 86; Srch Tm 86; Prm Chrmn 86.

COLLINS, DAWN; A T Schalick HS; Elmer, NJ; (Y); Pres Band; JV Stat Bsktbl; JV Var Fld Hcky; JV Sftbl; NHS.

COLLINS, EDWARD HARRIS; Red Bank Regional HS; Little Silver, NJ; (Y); Ski Clb; Variety Show; Ftbl; Golf; Hon Roll; Monmouth Teen Ctr 86; Advtsng.

COLLINS, JENNIFER; Roselle Catholic HS; Elizabeth, NJ; (Y); Rep Sr Cls; Var Capt Cheerleading; Var Socr; Var Sftbl; Var Capt Trk; Hon Roll.

COLLINS, MICHAEL; Holy Spirit HS; Ventnor, NJ; (Y); 3/375; Computer Clb; Exploring; Rep Soph Cls; Hon Roll; Jr NHS; NHS; Vrsty Crew 84-86; Engrng.

COLLINS, MICHELLE; Triton Regional HS; Laurel Springs, NJ; (Y); 63/320; Im Socr; Var Capt Trk; JV Vllybl; Hon Roll; Interact Clb 85-86; 3rd Pl Javelin Olympc Conf; Camden Cnty CC; Phys Ed.

COLLINS, PAUL; St John Vianney HS; Colts Neck, NJ; (Y); 55/260; Cmnty Wkr; SADD; Var L Golf; Hon Roll; Bus.

COLLINS, SUSAN; Middletown South HS; Middletown, NJ; (Y); Cmnty Wkr; Spanish Clb; Concert Band; Jazz Band; Mrchg Band; Var L Crs Cntry; Var L Trk; Hon Roll; Jr NHS; Sci.

COLLINS, TIMOTHY; Verona HS; Verona, NJ; (Y); Boy Scts; Nwsp Rptr; Yrbk Sprt Ed; Stat Bsktbl; Var L Crs Cntry; Var L Trk; SAR Awd; Spanish NHS.

COLOMY, HEIDI; Sacred Heart HS; Newfield, NJ; (S); 10/75; German Clb; Office Aide; Teachers Aide; Variety Show; Nwsp Sprt Ed; Yrbk Stf; Var Cheerleading; Score Keeper; Tennis; Hon Roll; Physcl Thrpy.

COLON, CAROLYN; J J Ferris HS; Jersey City, NJ; (Y); Color Guard; Nwsp Stf; Yrbk Stf; Rep Jr Cls; VP Stu Cncl; JV Bsbl; JV Sftbl; NHS; Comp.

COLON, DENISE; Immaculate Conception HS; Rockaway Boro, NJ; (Y); Drama Clb; Spanish Clb; Yrbk Stf; Var Cheerleading; Sftbl; Vllybl; 2nd Degree Chrldng Awd 86; Rutgers U; Acctng.

COLON, JOHNNY; St Marys HS; Jersey City, NJ; (Y); Acpl Chr; Chorus; Church Choir; School Play; Stage Crew; Hon Roll; Hnr Roll-Hudson Cnty Area Voc Tech Schl 86; St Marys Musical Prfrmr 85; Pftct Attnd 85; Fshn Dsgnr.

COLONNA, SUSAN; Holy Cross HS; Mount Holly, NJ; (Y); Church Yth Grp; Hosp Aide; SADD; Drill Tm; Pep Band; Yrbk Stf; Im Vllybl; Cit Awd; Hon Roll; Marine Bio.

COLUCCI, JAMES A; Wayne Valley HS; Wayne, NJ; (Y); 8/320; Am Leg Boys St; Church Yth Grp; Computer Clb; French Clb; Model UN; Nwsp Stf; Yrbk Stf; Lit Mag; High Hon Roll; NHS; Hnrb Mntn Bst Dely Mod U N 86; Hnrb Mntn Bst Dely Libya 86; Co-Chrmn 1 To 1 Help Mntlly Retard 85-86; Comp Sci.

COLUMBO, SHERRI; Pinelands Regional HS; Tuckerton, NJ; (Y); Stu Cncl; Bsktbl; Fld Hcky; Sftbl; Trk; Hon Roll; Opt Clb Awd; MVP Fld Hkcy 85; Al-Cnty Sftbl Tms 85; Tuckerton Optmst Clb-Yth Mth-Athltcs 85; Trvl, Toursm.

COLVIN, PATRICIA; Mount Olive HS; Budd Lake, NJ; (Y); Ski Clb; Varsity Clb; Stu Cncl; Cheerleading; Fld Hcky; Sftbl; Wt Lftg; Hon Roll; Most Imprvd Sftbnl 85; MVP Field Hockey 85; All Area Coaches Team; Boston Coll; Bus Adm.

COMBA, DENISE; Toms River North HS; Lakehurst, NJ; (Y); 39/410; Cheerleading; High Hon Roll; Hon Roll; Cook Coll; Bio.

COMEGYS, SUSAN; Holy Cross HS; Edgewater Park, NJ; (Y); Am Leg Aux Girls St; Church Yth Grp; French Clb; Ed Yrbk Stf; High Hon Roll; Hon Roll; Bus.

COMMENT, BONNIE; Clifton HS; Clifton, NJ; (Y); Office Aide; Acpl Chr; Chorus; High Hon Roll; Hon Roll; Jr NHS; Spanish NHS; Bus.

COMPTON, JEAN; South Hunterdon Reg HS; Lambertville, NJ; (Y); 10/72; Church Yth Grp; Band; Chorus; Capt Color Guard; Concert Band; Jazz Band; Mrchg Band; Pep Band; School Musical; School Play; Choral Dirctr Asst 86-87; Trenton ST Coll; Music Tchr.

COMPTON, WENDY; Eastern Regional HS; Gibbsboro, NJ; (Y); Var Crs Cntry; JV Fld Hcky; JV Lcrss; Im Vllybl; Im Wt Lftg.

CONCEPCION, JOSE; Hoboken HS; Hoboken, NJ; (Y); CAP; FCA; FBLA; Hosp Aide; Red Cross Aide; Spanish Clb; Bsbl; Gym; Phys Achvt 856; Cardiologist.

CONCIALDI, AMY; Toms River HS East; Toms River, NJ; (Y); Key Clb; Spanish Clb; Stat Bsktbl; JV Powder Puff Ftbl; Gftd-Tlntd 81-83; Rutgers; Psychlgst.

CONCINA, RONALDO; Abraham Clark HS; Roselle, NJ; (S); 4/187; Quiz Bowl; Science Clb; Teachers Aide; Chorus; Var Tennis; Best Sprtsmnshp-Tennis 84; PA ST; Pre-Med.

CONCORDIA, STEPHANIE; Triton Regional HS; Blackwood, NJ; (Y); 34/294; Teachers Aide; Rep Stu Cncl; Cheerleading; Trk; Hon Roll; Voice Dem Awd; Mrn Physcl Ftns Awd 83-85; Rutgers; Dntstry.

CONDINA, LINDA; Red Bank Catholic HS; Red Bank, NJ; (Y); SADD; Teachers Aide; Hon Roll; Elem Ed.

CONDON, JOY; Randolph HS; Randolph, NJ; (Y); Church Yth Grp; French Clb; Ski Clb; Orch; School Musical; JV Swmmng; NJ Regn I Orch 1st Chr 84; Lakeland Yth Symph 84-86; Bus.

CONDON, PETER; Christian Brothers Acad; Marlboro, NJ; (Y); 9/240; Cmnty Wkr; Math Tm; Service Clb; Nwsp Ed-Chief; Lit Mag; JV Crs Cntry; Im Ftbl; Im Socr; Im Sftbl; High Hon Roll.

CONFORTI, CAROLYN; Wall HS; Sea Girt, NJ; (Y); Ed Nwsp Bus Mgr; Nwsp Rptr; Nwsp Stf; Hon Roll; Gifted Yng Wrtrs Prgm 85-86; Jrnlsm.

CONFORTI JR, MICHAEL J; Toms River HS East; Toms River, NJ; (Y); Aud/Vis; Camera Clb; Political Wkr; Q&S; Nwsp Phtg; Nwsp Rptr; Nwsp Stf; Yrbk Phtg; Yrbk Stf; Wrstlng; Elon Coll; Jrnlsm.

CONGEDO, MICHAEL; Pascack Hills HS; Montvale, NJ; (Y); Cmnty Wkr; Math Tm; SADD; JV Capt Socr; JV Tennis; Hon Roll; Ntl Merit Schol; Boy Scts; Church Yth Grp; Band; Engrng.

CONGO, MICHELLE; Middletown HS South; Middletown, NJ; (Y); Powder Puff Ftbl; Var Swmmng; Var Trk; Hon Roll; Bottecappers Alcohol Awareness Club 86; Villanova PA; Psych.

CONIDI, FRANK; Hudson Catholic HS; Jersey City, NJ; (Y); Dance Clb; SADD; Ftbl; William Paterson Coll; Bus Admn.

CONIGLIO, NATALIE M; Notre Dame HS; Trenton, NJ; (Y); Cmnty Wkr; Dance Clb; Pep Clb; Yrbk Rptr; Yrbk Stf; Cit Awd; Hon Roll; Mrcy Pc & Jstc Clb 85-86; Pblcty Clb 85-86; Srv Awd 84; Scndry Ed.

CONKLIN, CHRISTIE; Toms River HS; Toms River, NJ; (Y); Dance Clb; Chorus; Wrstlng; High Hon Roll; Pres Schlr; Pep Clb; Color Guard; Jazz Band; Variety Show; Var Mgr(s); Prsdntl Athltc Awd 85; Ramapo Coll; Advrtsng.

CONKLIN, THERESA L; Sussex Vo-Tech HS; Hamburg, NJ; (S); #8 In Class; Church Yth Grp; Math Clb; Spanish Clb; Varsity Clb; Rep Jr Cls; Rep Sr Cls; Rep Stu Cncl; Var Cheerleading.

CONLEY, CRAIG; Manalapan HS; Englishtown, NJ; (Y); Church Yth Grp; Cmnty Wkr; SADD; Rep Jr Cls; Rep Sr Cls; Var Capt Socr; Accntng.

CONLEY, KATHY; St Peters HS; N Brunswick, NJ; (Y); 16/82; Art Clb; Chorus; School Musical; Yrbk Stf; Lit Mag; Stat Trk; Stat Wrstlng; NEDT Awd; PA ST U; Comm.

CONLON, STEPHANIE; Sayreville War Memorial HS; Parlin, NJ; (Y); 140/379; Sec DECA; Spanish Clb; Concert Band; Mrchg Band; Pom Pon; JV Var Mgr(s); Hon Roll; NJ Htl Mtl Assn Schlrshp 86; Awd Hghst Avg Mktg & Dstrbtv Educ Pgm 86; Awd Rstrnt Mktg DECA Reg Cnfr; Fairleigh Dickinson U; Htl Mgt.

CONN, VICKI; Notre Dame HS; Yardley, PA; (Y); 44/367; Jazz Band; Stage Crew; Nwsp Rptr; Yrbk Rptr; French Hon Soc; High Hon Roll; Hon Roll; Key Clb; Ski Clb; Band; Hnrs Englsh I 84; Advncd Art Encllnc 86; Bst Ovrll Art Dsply 86; Arspc Engr.

CONNELLY, DANIEL; Oratory Prep HS; Scotch Plains, NJ; (Y); Church Yth Grp; Political Wkr; Ski Clb; Nwsp Rptr; Golf; Trk; High Hon Roll; NHS; Ntl Merit Ltr; Latin Medal; Georgetown U; Pol Sci.

CONNELLY, DIANE; Scotch Plains-Fanwood HS; Scotch Pl, NJ; (Y); Model UN; Spanish Clb; SADD; Concert Band; Mrchg Band; Symp Band; Lit Mag; Cit Awd; Hon Roll.

CONNELLY, TARA; Red Bank Catholic HS; Monmouth Bch, NJ; (Y); Church Yth Grp; Cmnty Wkr; Elem Educ.

CONNELLY, TOM; Lower Cape May Regional HS; Cape May, NJ; (Y); Boy Scts; Camera Clb; Letterman Clb; Varsity Clb; Stu Cncl; JV Stat Bsktbl; Var L Ftbl; Stat Score Keeper; Im Wt Lftg; Hon Roll; Envrnmntl Stds.

CONNER, DANIEL; Southern Regional HS; Waretown, NJ; (Y); Trs Church Yth Grp; Cmnty Wkr; Ski Clb; Church Choir; JV Wrstlng; Hon Roll; NHS; Kiwanis Ldrshp Camp 83; Hist.

CONNER, MICHAEL; Plainfield HS; Plainfield, NJ; (Y); 16/464; Computer Clb; Library Aide; Concert Band; Mrchg Band; Hon Roll; NHS; Syracuse U; Comp Sci.

CONNOLLY, CHRIS; Kittatinny Regional HS; Newton, NJ; (Y); Pres VP 4-H; Girl Scts; Spanish Clb; School Musical; Rep Jr Cls; Capt Var Cheerleading; JV Swmmng; JV Trk; 4-H Awd; High Hon Roll; Psych.

CONNOLLY, CRAIG; St Joseph Regional HS; Stony Point, NY; (Y); 18/232; Capt Bsbl; Capt Ice Hcky; Hon Roll; Jr NHS; NHS; Ntl Merit Ltr; Spanish NHS; NJ All ST 1st Tm Ice Hcky Dfnsmn 86; Alkl Cnty NJ Bsbll Tm 86; U Of PA.

CONNOLLY, MARTIN; Seton Hall Prep; S Orange, NJ; (Y); French Clb; Math Clb; Math Tm; School Musical; Im Bsktbl; Hon Roll.

CONNOR, JAMES; Florence Twp Memorial HS; Roebling, NJ; (Y); Math Clb; Varsity Clb; Bsktbl; Ftbl; Mgr(s); Arch.

CONNOR, MARGARET; Indian Hills HS; Oakland, NJ; (Y); 8/279; Yrbk Stf; Socr; Sftbl; High Hon Roll; Hon Roll; NHS; Foster Parent 85-86.

CONNOR, MARK; Washington Township HS; Sewell, NJ; (Y); Boy Scts; Law.

CONNOR, MAUREEN; Villa Victoria Acad; Yardley, PA; (Y); Computer Clb; Drama Clb; Hosp Aide; Pep Clb; Lit Mag; Hon Roll; Pres Jr Cls; Rep Stu Cncl; Var Bsktbl; Im Coach Actv; Erly Chldhd Educ.

CONNOR, TIMOTHY; Saint Augustine Prep Schl; Linwood, NJ; (Y); 9/50; Chess Clb; Computer Clb; Lit Mag; Hon Roll; NEDT Awd; U Of DE; Bus Admin.

CONOVER, NANCY; Egg Harbor Township HS; Linwood, NJ; (S); 8/390; Dance Clb; Trs Key Clb; School Musical; Nwsp Ed-Chief; Sec Stu Cncl; Stat Bsbl; Capt Var Cheerleading; Office Aide; High Hon Roll; Var Schlr Awd; Chldhd Ed.

CONOVER, THERESA; Pemberton Twp H S II; Pemberton, NJ; (Y); 16/350; Church Yth Grp; Drama Clb; Yrbk Stf; Hon Roll; NHS; Cook Coll; Vet-Med.

CONRAD, CHERYL; Pinelands Regional HS; Tuckerton, NJ; (Y); Lit Mag; JV Fld Hcky; Hon Roll; Ed.

CONROY, THOMAS; Paramus HS; Paramus, NJ; (Y); 8/350; Trs French Clb; Pres Orch; Yrbk Stf; Elks Awd; French Hon Soc; NHS; Pres Schlr; Drama Clb; Intnl Clb; Math Clb; ITT Schlrshp 86; Ntl Orchestra Awd 86; Excllnc In Frnch Awd 86; Rutgers Univ; Bio.

CONRY, CAROLYN; Our Lady Of Good Counsel; Newark, NJ; (Y); 3/110; Cmnty Wkr; Dance Clb; Science Clb; Teachers Aide; Chorus; School Musical; Yrbk Stf; NHS; Prfct Atten Awd; Stu Of Mnth 86.

CONSER, SCOTT; Mount Olive HS; Flanders, NJ; (Y); Computer Clb; Math Tm; Ski Clb; JV Crs Cntry; Var Swmmng; JV Trk; High Hon Roll; Hon Roll; 1st Pl In Schl Fair-Arch Drafting I; 3rd Pl In Schl Fair-Mech Drawing I; Advance Plcmt Class; Comp Sci.

CONSTANTIN, BETH; Kittatinny Regional HS; Newton, NJ; (Y); 30/228; Rep Jr Cls; Rep Stu Cncl; JV Var Cheerleading; Gym; Powder Puff Ftbl; JV Var Sftbl; JV Var Swmmng; High Hon Roll; Hon Roll; NHS.

CONSTANTINE, LORAN; Shore Regional HS; Oceanport, NJ; (Y); Art Clb; Church Yth Grp; Drama Clb; Ski Clb; SADD; School Musical; Stage Crew; Cheerleading; Crs Cntry; Powder Puff Ftbl.

CONTE, JEFF; Red Bank Catholic HS; Lincroft, NJ; (Y); Church Yth Grp; Hon Roll; NEDT Awd; Rep Jr Cls; Merit Stu Emplymnt Awd Teledyne Brown Engrg; Rutgers Coll Of Engrg; Engrg.

CONTENTE, BILL; St Patrick HS; Linden, NJ; (S); 1/63; Science Clb; Ski Clb; School Musical; Rep Frsh Cls; Rep Jr Cls; Sec Stu Cncl; High Hon Roll; NHS; Frshmn Top Schlstc Av 84; Soph Top Schlstc Av 85.

CONTESTABLE, BARBARA; Middlesex HS; Middlesex, NJ; (Y); Drama Clb; Varsity Clb; Variety Show; Pres Frsh Cls; Fld Hcky; Score Keeper; Trk; Elks Awd; Hon Roll; Comp Progrmmr.

CONTI, FRED; West Morris Central HS; Long Valley, NJ; (Y); 53/283; JV Wrstlng; High Hon Roll; Ranked 1st Clss Awd 83; Mbr Italian Hon Scty; Rutger Coll Of Engr; Engr.

CONTI, RAY; Central Regional HS; Bayville, NJ; (Y); Var Golf; Hon Roll; Bus Mgmt.

CONTILIANO, JIM; Hightstown HS; E Windsor, NJ; (Y); 7/350; Cmnty Wkr; Var Bsbl; JV Bsktbl; Var JV Socr; High Hon Roll; NHS; Prfct Atten Awd.

CONTILIANO, RICK; Hightstown HS; East Windsor, NJ; (Y); 13/350; Cmnty Wkr; Var Bsbl; JV Bsktbl; JV Var Socr; High Hon Roll; NHS; Prfct Atten Awd.

CONTRACATOR, SHEETAL; Egg Harbor Township HS; Pleasantville, NJ; (S); 2/266; Pres GAA; Model UN; Pres Spanish Clb; VP Fld Hcky; High Hon Roll; Jr NHS; NHS; Sal; Grdn ST Dstngshd Schlr Awd 85; Natl Sci Merit Awd 84-85; Bus.

CONTRADY, JEFF; Holy Cross HS; Delran, NJ; (Y); 100/385; Church Yth Grp; Spanish Clb; Stage Crew; Ftbl; Hon Roll; Wilkes Coll PA; Engrng.

CONTZIUS, ERIK; Parsippany HS; Parsippany, NJ; (Y); Math Tm; VP Temple Yth Grp; Band; Mrchg Band; School Musical; School Play; Lit Mag; NHS; Ntl Art Hon Soc 86; Cmptr Sci.

CONWAY, COLLEEN; Cherry Hill HS West; Cherry Hill, NJ; (Y).

CONYERS, STEPHANIE; Dwight Morrow HS; Englewood, NJ; (Y); 49/225; Sec Church Yth Grp; Office Aide; Political Wkr; Teachers Aide; Varsity Clb; Band; Rep Stu Cncl; JV Var Bsktbl; High Hon Roll; Hon Roll; Natl Achvmnt Schlrshp Prog For Outstndg Negro Stus 85; FL A & M; Bus Mgmt.

CONZA, JOHN P; Burlington Co Voc Tech; Pemberton, NJ; (S); Computer Clb; Letterman Clb; Varsity Clb; VICA; Off Frsh Cls; Stu Cncl; Ftbl; Wt Lftg; Wrstlng; Prfct Atten Awd; 1st Pl-Voctnl Ind Club Of Amer 86; Camden CC; Automtv Engr.

CONZALEZ, RUTH; Hoboken HS; Hoboken, NJ; (Y); Model UN; Teachers Aide; Band; Chorus; Concert Band; Jazz Band; Mrchg Band; Orch; Pep Band; Variety Show; Berkeley School NYC; Fshn Mktg.

COOGAN, JOHN; St Peters Prep Schl; Upr Montclair, NJ; (Y); 21/206; Pep Clb; Nwsp Rptr; Im Bsktbl; Crs Cntry; Im Ftbl; Var Golf; Var Im Ice Hcky; Wt Lftg; High Hon Roll; West Point Annapolis; Arch.

COOK, ALANE; Abraham Clark HS; Roselle, NJ; (S); 17/187; Debate Tm; Teachers Aide; NHS; Media Stdys.

COOK, DAWN; Kittatinny Regional HS; Newton, NJ; (Y); 52/222; Spanish Clb; SADD; Lit Mag; Swmmng; Hon Roll; Spcl Olympics 2 Yrs 85-86.

COOK, GORDEN T; Hopewell Valley Central HS; Pennington, NJ; (Y); 30/200; Am Leg Boys St; Concert Band; Mrchg Band; School Musical; Var Trk; Var Capt Wrstlng; High Hon Roll; Hon Roll; NHS; 3rd Pl Dist Wrstlng Trnmnt 86; Wind Ensmbl 86; Amer Lgn Boys ST Elctd City Cnclmn & Cnty Exec; Rensalear Polytech Inst; Engrng.

COOK, HEATHER; Toms River HS East; Toms River, NJ; (Y); 5/478; Pres Intnl Clb; Political Wkr; Spanish Clb; Mrchg Band; High Hon Roll; NHS; Pres Schlr; Indpndnt Ordr Of Frstrs Schlrshp 86; Mst Outstndng Pol & Lgl Educ Stu 86; Trenton ST Coll Schlrshp 86; Trenton ST Coll; Bio.

COOK, LESLIE; Dover HS; Mine Hill, NJ; (Y); AFS; Band; Church Choir; Concert Band; Jazz Band; Mrchg Band; Orch; Symp Band; JV Cheerleading; Spanish Clb; N Jersey Area Band 86; County Coll-Morris; Comp Pgmmg.

COOK, MARIBETH; St Marys HS; Hazlet, NJ; (Y); Church Yth Grp; Cmnty Wkr; Stage Crew; JV Sftbl; Hon Roll.

COOK, MARK; North Warren Regional HS; Blairstown, NJ; (Y); Band; Chorus; Concert Band; Mrchg Band; Symp Band; Hon Roll; Boy Scts; Church Yth Grp; Drm & Bgl; School Musical; Fnlst NJ Gov Schl Arts 85-86; Berklee Coll Music; Music.

COOK, SHERI; Mount St Mary Acad; Milltown, NJ; (Y); Art Clb; 4-H; Yrbk Phtg; Hon Roll; Art Thrpy.

COOK, VICTORIA; Brunah HS; Beverly, NJ; (Y); Art Clb; Debate Tm; Drama Clb; Ed Yrbk Stf; VP Frsh Cls; Sec Soph Cls; Hon Roll; NHS; NEDT Awd; Johns Hopkins Schlr 84.

COOK, YOLANDA; Eastside HS; Paterson, NJ; (S); 17/558; Church Choir; Concert Band; Mrchg Band; Yrbk Stf; NHS; Soc Dstngshd Amer HS St U Awd 84; Acad Exclln Awd 86; Acad All Amer Awd 86; DE ST Coll; Nursing.

COOKE, ANDREW P; Pemberton Township HS; Browns Mills, NJ; (Y); 3/410; Trs Am Leg Boys St; FBLA; Math Tm; Scholastic Bowl; Yrbk Stf; High Hon Roll; NHS; NEDT Awd; Mc Guive Wvs Clb & Acdmc Schlrshp 86; Fclty Schlrshp; S Jrsy Vndng Co Hghst Schlstc Avg Math Schlrhp; U Of PA; Engr.

COOKE, ANTHONY; East Orange HS; E Orange, NJ; (Y); High Hon Roll; Hon Roll; 2nd Hnr Seton Hall Prep 83-84; Comp Tech.

COOKE, DENNIS; Lyndhurst HS; Lyndhurst, NJ; (Y); 25/180; Camera Clb; Chess Clb; Math Clb; Science Clb; Var JV Ftbl; Var JV Wrstlng; Hon Roll; NJ Inst Of Tech; Elect Engrg.

COOKE, JENNICE; Mother Seton Regional HS; Newark, NJ; (Y); Church Yth Grp; Cmnty Wkr; Church Choir; Madrigals; Rptr Nwsp Stf; Lit Mag; Pres Sr Cls; Rep Stu Cncl; Hon Roll.

COOKE, PAUL; De Paul Diocesan HS; Wayne, NJ; (S); 1/165; JCL; Trs Latin Clb; Math Tm; Nwsp Rptr; Trs Jr Cls; Var Bsbl; JV Bsktbl; Ftbl; High Hon Roll; NHS; Natl Sci Awd; Natl Latn Exm Magna Cum Laude; Cert Achvt Acadmc Excllnc Hnrs Ame Lit & Latn II; Bio.

COOLEY, BRAD; Voorhees HS; Califon, NJ; (Y); 2/274; JCL; Pres Latin Clb; Ski Clb; JV Bsktbl; Var Capt Tennis; High Hon Roll; NHS; Sal; Latin I, Latin Ii & Latin Iiii Achvt Awds 84 & 85 & 86; Natl JR Clsscl Lge 86; Var Tnnns Athl Awd 86.

COOLEY, SHEILA; Scotch Plains Fanwood HS; Scotch Plains, NJ; (Y); FBLA; Leo Clb; Political Wkr; Yrbk Bus Mgr; Yrbk Ed-Chief; Yrbk Stf; Off Frsh Cls; Off Soph Cls; Off Jr Cls; Vllybl; WIDENER U; Pol Sci.

COON, JANE; Jackson Memorial HS; Jackson, NJ; (Y); FBLA; Ski Clb; Band; Color Guard; Drm & Bgl; Mrchg Band; Nwsp Rptr; Twrlr; NEDT Awd; Georgian Court Coll; Childcare.

COONEY, CHRISTOPHER; Morris Knolls HS; Denville, NJ; (Y); 48/383; Am Leg Boys St; Church Yth Grp; Yrbk Phtg; JV Bsbl; Socr; Comp Sys Anlyst.

COONEY, KEVIN; Hoboken HS; Hoboken, NJ; (Y); Camera Clb; Yrbk Phtg; Yrbk Stf; Monmouth Coll; Retailr.

COONEY, WILLIAM; St Peters Prep HS; Jersey City, NJ; (Y); 50/250; Dance Clb; Pep Clb; Nwsp Stf; Yrbk Stf; Rep Frsh Cls; Var Bsbl; Var Bsktbl; Hon Roll; Jrnlsm.

COOPER, DANNY; Overbrook Regional HS; W Berlin, NJ; (Y); 27/402; Church Yth Grp; Computer Clb; Drama Clb; Pep Clb; Spanish Clb; Varsity Clb; Sec Soph Cls; JV Var Bsbl; Socr; Spanish NHS; Geo Wshngton U; Ele C Engrng.

COOPER, DAVE; Steinert HS; Hamilton Sq, NJ; (Y); 34/315; FBLA; SADD; Im Mgr Socr; Im Mgr Trk; JV Wrstlng; High Hon Roll; NHS; FBLA Rgnl Ldrshp Conf 1st Pl Accntng II 85; FBLA Ntl Entrprshp II Tm 86; Elizabethtown Coll; Bus.

COOPER, JEFFREY P; Pemberton Township HS; Pemberton, NJ; (Y); Am Leg Boys St; Exploring; Band; Concert Band; Jazz Band; Mrchg Band; Bsbl; Bowling; Hon Roll; NHS.

COOPER, LENNY; Washington Twp HS; Sewell, NJ; (Y); Ftbl; Ice Hcky; Trk; Vllybl; Wt Lftg; Wrstlng.

COOPER, PAUL; No Burlington County Regional HS; Columbus, NJ; (Y); 37/198; Nwsp Rptr; Var L Trk; French Hon Soc; Hon Roll; Stage Crew; Off Jr Cls; Off Sr Cls; Pres Schlr; St Joseph U; Systms Anlyst.

COOPER, RACHEL; Palmyra HS; Riverton, NJ; (Y); 16/109; Drama Clb; Office Aide; Ski Clb; Yrbk Stf; Rep Frsh Cls; Var Capt Fld Hcky; JV Trk; Hon Roll; NHS; Sci Awd Shermann Industries 86; Pres Fit Awd 86; Burlington Cnty Coll; Biol.

COOPER JR, THOMAS E; Brick HS; Brick Town, NJ; (Y); Var Bsbl; Var Ice Hcky; High Hon Roll; NHS; Hghst Acadmc Excllnc/Hocky Plyr & Bsbl Plyr 86; Hrn Roll; North Caroline ST U; Bus.

COPPOLA, DIANE; Gloucester City JR SR HS; Gloucester, NJ; (Y); 10/140; FBLA; Concert Band; Mrchg Band; Yrbk Stf; Cit Awd; Hon Roll; NHS; Prfct Atten Awd; Bus Schl.

CORACE, TRACY; Lenape Regional HS; Mt Laurel, NJ; (Y); Church Yth Grp; Varsity Clb; Trs Sr Cls; Lcrss; Var L Trk; Hon Roll; NHS; Pl 1st Gmtry Fnl All Stu Crs 83-84; Bus.

CORAL, CEIR; Dover HS; Dover, NJ; (Y); 11/249; Am Leg Boys St; French Clb; Ski Clb; Var Socr; Var Tennis; High Hon Roll; Hon Roll; Jr NHS; NHS; Allied Chem Sci Awd 86; USAF; Aeronutcl Engr.

CORAL, JULIE; Manchester Regional HS; Haledon, NJ; (Y); Camera Clb; William Paterson Coll; Elem Art.

CORALLO, DAVID; Passaic Valley HS; Little Falls, NJ; (Y); 1/359; Cmnty Wkr; Science Clb; High Hon Roll; NHS; Altrnt Amer Legn Boys ST 86; Pre-Med.

CORBETT, MELISSA; Monsignor Donovan HS; Toms River, NJ; (Y); 46/243; Drama Clb; Ski Clb; SADD; School Play; Yrbk Stf; Jrnlsm.

CORBETT, THOMAS; Monsignor Donovan HS; Bayville, NJ; (Y); 65/248; Ski Clb; Nwsp Stf; Debate Tm; Var Bsbl; JV Crs Cntry; Capt L Ftbl; Im Wt Lftg; Hon Roll; NHS; Mst Imprvd Rlgn & Math Awd 82; All Cnty Lnbckr Ftbl 85-86; Trphys Bsbe, Ftbl, Trck, Rqtbl 79-86; Holy Cross; Pltcl Sci.

CORBLIES, JOHN; Harrison HS; East Newark, NJ; (Y); Cmnty Wkr; Library Aide; VICA; Socr; Wrstlng; JETS Awd; Prfct Atten Awd; NJ ST Crftsmns Fair 1st Pl 86; Air Condtn Mech.

CORBO, FRANCO P; Fair Lawn HS; Fair Lawn, NJ; (Y); 29/330; Am Leg Boys St; Band; Mrchg Band; Rep Soph Cls; Rep Jr Cls; JV Var Lcrss; JV Var Socr; JV Var Wrstlng; Ntl Merit Ltr; Rutgers; Law.

CORBO, TERRI LYNN; Highstown HS; E Windsor, NJ; (Y); Drama Clb; Hosp Aide; Service Clb; Spanish Clb; SADD; School Musical; School Play; Hon Roll; Mgr Fld Hcky; Mgr(s); Sec Music Clb; Elem Ed.

CORBY, SUSAN; Mater Dei HS; Union Beach, NJ; (Y); 25/151; Church Yth Grp; Drama Clb; English Clb; Pep Clb; Spanish Clb; Lit Mag; Powder Puff Ftbl; Hon Roll; NHS; Spanish Awd 85-86.

CORCORAN, NANCY; Lakeland Regional HS; Ringwood, NJ; (Y); Church Yth Grp; Ski Clb; Off Frsh Cls; Rep Jr Cls; Rep Stu Cncl; Bsktbl; Powder Puff Ftbl; JV Socr; JV Sftbl; Hon Roll; Phys Therapy.

CORDEIRO JR, ROBERT; St Mary HS; Spotswood, NJ; (Y); 35/146; Church Yth Grp; Off ROTC; Capt Color Guard; JV Bsbl; Var Tennis; Var Wrstlng; Hon Roll; Petty Ofc Awd 86; Maritime Coll; Naval Ofcr.

CORDOVA, EMILIO; Belleville HS; Belleville, NJ; (Y); 11/387; Pres Church Yth Grp; Hosp Aide; Chorus; VP Soph Cls; Sec Jr Cls; Sec Sr Cls; NHS; Opt Clb Awd; Rotary Awd; Drew U; Bio-Chmstry.

CORDTS, ERIKA; Collegiate Schl; Nutley, NJ; (S); 2/10; Church Yth Grp; Office Aide; Stat Score Keeper; JV Var Vllybl; Hon Roll; NHS.

COREY, CATHERINE; Spotswood HS; Milltown, NJ; (S); 18/174; Sec Church Yth Grp; Dance Clb; Stu Cncl; Cheerleading; Co-Capt Trk; Gov Hon Prg Awd; Hon Roll; Sec NHS; Finance.

COREY, ROSEMARIE; Colonia HS; Avenel, NJ; (Y); 26/287; Hon Roll; NHS; Seton Hl U Acad Schlrshp 86; Acad Excel Awd 86; 5th Qrtr Clb SR Athltc Awd Archry 84-86; Seton Hall U; Acctng.

CORKE, KATHLEEN; Mt St Dominic HS; Livingston, NJ; (Y); 9/53; Church Yth Grp; Debate Tm; Girl Scts; Acpl Chr; Chorus; Church Choir; Madrigals; Yrbk Ed-Chief; Twrlr; High Hon Roll; Attnd H S On Schlrshp 83; Wrkshp Schlrshp 86; Bus Mgmt.

CORMAN, LILI; Roselle Catholic HS; Elizabeth, NJ; (Y); Drama Clb; PAVAS; Teachers Aide; School Musical; School Play; Stage Crew; Lit Mag; Spanish NHS; Aud/Vis; Computer Clb; Awd For Prfcncy In Spnsh 85; Asst Dir For Schl Musical Prod 86; Comm.

CORN, RONALD; Rancolas Valley Regional HS; Hainesport, NJ; (Y); 49/269; Church Yth Grp; Varsity Clb; Rep Jr Cls; Var L Bsbl; Var L Ftbl; Hon Roll; Farleigh Dickinson U Scholar; Garden ST Merit Scholar; NJ Tuition Grant; Farleigh Dickinson U; Hstry.

CORNEJO, DEBBIE; Paterson Catholic Regional HS; Paterson, NJ; (Y); 14/123; Sec French Clb; Pep Clb; Science Clb; Nwsp Rptr; Nwsp Stf; Yrbk Stf; French Hon Soc; High Hon Roll; Hon Roll; Amer Lodg 333 Poetry Cntst 2nd Pl 86; NYU; Cmnctn Arts.

CORNELIOUS, JUDITH A; Neptune SR HS; Neptune, NJ; (Y); Art Clb; Sec Church Yth Grp; Hosp Aide; Sec Latin Clb; Rep Soph Cls; Sec Jr Cls; Pres Sr Cls; Var Cheerleading; Mgr(s); Ntl Merit SF; Earontcs.

CORNELIUS, CHRISTINE; Middletown H S South; Leonardo, NJ; (S); 19/437; Dance Clb; School Musical; Variety Show; Cheerleading; High Hon Roll; Hon Roll.

CORNELIUS, SCOTT; Voorhees HS; Oldwick, NJ; (Y); Boy Scts; Church Yth Grp; JCL; Latin Clb; Radio Clb; Ski Clb; Stu Cncl; Hon Roll; Natl Sci Olympd Physcs 86.

CORONATO, THOMAS; Lenape Valley Regional HS; Sparta, NJ; (Y); 24/217; Color Guard; Concert Band; Jazz Band; Mrchg Band; Var Bowling; NHS; Prfct Atten Awd; Espirit De Corps Awd For Band 85-86; Brwn Belt Awd; Rtgrs Coll; Engrng.

CORRADO, ANNA M; Spotswood HS; Spotswood, NJ; (S); Capt Hosp Aide; Intnl Clb; Band; Symp Band; Pres Soph Cls; Pres Jr Cls; High Hon Roll; Hon Roll; NHS; Vlntr Yr St Peters Med Ctr 84-85; First Aid Squad Vlntr; German.

CORREA, STEPHANIE; Dover HS; Dover, NJ; (Y); Office Aide; Spanish Clb; Chorus; Church Choir; Lit Mag; Voice Dem Awd; Katharine Gibbs; Bus Mgmt.

CORREIA, SHARON; Howell HS; Howell, NJ; (Y); Church Yth Grp; 4-H; Math Clb; Mrchg Band; Crs Cntry; Trk; Twrlr; Cit Awd; NHS; Rutgers U; Phrmcy.

CORRELL, GREGORY; Brick Township HS; Brick, NJ; (Y); 21/400; Capt Debate Tm; Drama Clb; Math Tm; Temple Yth Grp; Thesps; School Play; Stage Crew; Leo Clb; High Hon Roll; NHS; Rutgers U Summr Schlrs Pgm 86; Drama Clb Awd 86; Tech Desgn.

CORRIS, STACEY; Belleville HS; Belleville, NJ; (Y); Church Yth Grp; Spanish Clb; Hon Roll; Advrtsng.

CORSON, ROSINA; Millville SR HS; Millville, NJ; (Y); Church Yth Grp; Cmnty Wkr; Office Aide; Hon Roll; Prfct Atten Awd; Won Merit Awd; Writng Contst Sfty; Salesprsn Schl Activties.

CORT, BRYAN; Roselle Catholic HS; Westfield, NJ; (Y); Boy Scts; Church Yth Grp; Red Cross Aide; JV Bsktbl; JV Ftbl; Var Trk; Cit Awd; Hon Roll; Ntl Merit Schol; Prfct Atten Awd; Schlrshp; Amteur Athltc Union Of The US Elem Athltc Leag; Princton U; Engrng.

CORTES, RAUL; Woodrow Wilson HS; Camden, NJ; (Y); 1/256; Scholastic Bowl; Science Clb; Concert Band; Mrchg Band; Yrbk Stf; Ed Lit Mag; Rep Sr Cls; Bausch & Lomb Sci Awd; NHS; Val; U PA; Bioengrng.

CORTESE, LINDA J; Mahwah HS; Mahwah, NJ; (Y); 16/149; Debate Tm; Drama Clb; Model UN; Chorus; School Musical; Nwsp Ed-Chief; Sec Frsh Cls; Trs Sr Cls; VP Cheerleading; Capt Sftbl; Ntl Hnr Soc 85-86; Hgh Hnr Roll 82-86; Pres Acad Fitnss Awd 86; Franklin & Marshall Coll; Lwyr.

CORTESINI, GEORGE; Notre Dame HS; Hamilton Square, NJ; (Y); 32/364; Nwsp Rptr; Nwsp Stf; Hon Roll; NHS; Yng Repblcns Clb 85-86; Peace-Justc Clb 85-86; St Josephs U; Ecnmcs.

CORTEZZO, LISA M; Phillisburg HS; Phillipsburg, NJ; (Y); 17/296; Cmnty Wkr; Teachers Aide; Flag Corp; Stu Cncl; Var Capt Bsktbl; Crs Cntry; Var Capt Sftbl; High Hon Roll; NHS; Eugene Quinn Mem Awd 86; Pohatcong Stf Schlrshp 86; Phillipsburg HS Mens Fclty Awd 86; Fairleigh Dickinson U; Bio.

CORTINAS, LINDA ANN; Queen Of Peace HS; Newark, NJ; (Y); French Clb; Girl Scts; NFL; Ski Clb; School Play; Yrbk Phtg; Im Bowling; JV Cheerleading; Var Crs Cntry; Hon Roll; Arch.

CORVINO, WILLIAM; Audubon HS; Audubon, NJ; (Y); #1 In Class; Am Leg Boys St; Scholastic Bowl; Spanish Clb; Pres Band; Church Choir; School Play; Yrbk Stf; Golf; High Hon Roll; Hon Roll; Rutgers Schlrs Prog 86; Fnlst Govnrs Sch 86; Ritz Theatre Schlrshp Actrs 86; Berklee Clg Of Musc; Musc Comp.

CORVO, LISA; Neumann Prep HS; N Haledon, NJ; (Y); Variety Show; Nwsp Sprt Ed; Yrbk Stf; Lit Mag; Rep Frsh Cls; Pres Soph Cls; Pres Jr Cls; Pres Stu Cncl; Cit Awd; NHS; H S Prep Awd 86; 1st Pl Dnc Schlrshp Wnnr 86; Catholic U Of America; Bus Adm.

CORY, CHRIS; Manasquan HS; Belmar, NJ; (Y); 8/227; Math Tm; Band; Mrchg Band; JV Var Bsktbl; Var Crs Cntry; High Hon Roll; Kiwanis Awd; NHS; Voice Dem Awd; Pres Of H S Band 86; Clemson U; Math.

COSENZA, SHARON; Matawan Regional HS; Matawan, NJ; (Y); Cmnty Wkr; Drama Clb; Library Aide; Science Clb; Chorus; School Musical; School Play; Variety Show; Cheerleading; Hon Roll; SUNY Stonybrook; Pre-Med.

COSENZO, ROBERT; Don Bosco Prep; Suffern, NY; (Y); Cmnty Wkr; Exploring; Radio Clb; Pres Soph Cls; Hon Roll; Pennsylvania ST U; Med.

COSGROVE, BILL; Audubon HS; Audubon, NJ; (Y); Am Leg Boys St; Boy Scts; Quiz Bowl; Spanish Clb; Nwsp Rptr; Sec Frsh Cls; VP Soph Cls; Sec Sr Cls; Crs Cntry; Trk; MVP Cross Cntry; Cptn Of Cross Cntry.

COSPER, PAUL; Maple Shade HS; Maple Shade, NJ; (Y); Computer Clb; JV Bsbl; JV Var Socr; JV Var Trk; Im Vllybl; High Hon Roll; Hon Roll; Jr NHS; Prfct Atten Awd; Engrng.

COSTA, CHARLENE; Maple Shade HS; Maple Shade, NJ; (Y); 12/160; Computer Clb; Key Clb; Spanish Clb; Yrbk Stf; Var Capt Cheerleading; Mgr(s); Var JV Sftbl; High Hon Roll; Hon Roll; Jr NHS; Drexel U; Int Desgn.

COSTA, TRACY; Eastern Regional HS; Voorhees, NJ; (Y); Church Yth Grp; Office Aide; Band; Color Guard; Flag Corp; Mrchg Band; School Musical; School Play; Variety Show; Yrbk Stf; Flight Attndnt.

COSTANGO, DEBORAH; Garfield HS; Garfield, NJ; (Y); 10/180; Math Tm; Varsity Clb; Concert Band; Mrchg Band; Sec Sr Cls; Var L Sftbl; Var Capt Tennis; Cit Awd; High Hon Roll; NHS; Montclair ST Coll.

COSTANZO, ANTHONY; Bricktown HS; Brick Town, NJ; (Y); 793/1000; Boy Scts; Chess Clb; Drama Clb; Exploring; 4-H; Key Clb; Radio Clb; Thesps; VICA; School Musical; Brick Voc/Tech.

COSTANZO, HOLLY; Steinert HS; Hamilton Sq, NJ; (Y); 35/328; AFS; Dance Clb; French Clb; Yrbk Stf; Off Jr Cls; Stu Cncl; Var L Cheerleading; Hon Roll; NHS; Rider Coll; Sports Med.

COSTANZO, MICHAEL V; Watchung Hills Regional HS; Warren, NJ; (Y); 41/325; Am Leg Boys St; Aud/Vis; Boy Scts; Church Yth Grp; Computer Clb; JA; Ski Clb; SADD; Band; Concert Band; U Chgo; Bus Law.

COSTELLO, FRANCIS V; Scotch Plains-Fanwood HS; Scotch Plains, NJ; (Y); 1/311; Science Clb; Capt Var Crs Cntry; Var L Trk; Bausch & Lomb Sci Awd; High Hon Roll; Ntl Merit Schol; Val; Am Leg Boys St; Church Yth Grp; Model UN; Ben Frnlkn Schlr U Of PA 86; Attnd NJ Gvnrs Schl Of Sci 85; U Of PA; Math.

COSTELLO, JIMMY; Roselle Catholic HS; Elizabeth, NJ; (Y); Church Yth Grp; Golf; Acctg.

COSTELLO, LISA C; Paul Vi HS; Haddonfield, NJ; (Y); 1/475; Math Tm; Trk; French Hon Soc; High Hon Roll; NHS; Ntl Merit SF; Pres Spanish NHS; Val; French Clb; Math Clb; Spnsh Ntl Hnr Soc Trvl Awd 85; George Washington U Engr Medal 85; Rutgers Schlr 85.

COSTELLO, MELISSA; Matawan Regional HS; Matawan, NJ; (S); 38/291; Math Clb; Math Tm; Band; Concert Band; Mrchg Band; Yrbk Stf; Sftbl; Hon Roll; Math Hnr Soc 85; Tele-Cmmnctns.

COSTELLO, ROBERT F; De Paul Diocesian HS; Pompton Plains, NJ; (Y); 28/164; Am Leg Boys St; School Play; Nwsp Rptr; Yrbk Rptr; Pres Stu Cncl; Var Capt Bsktbl; Var L Crs Cntry; Var L Trk; Hon Roll; Acad Awd Hstry 84-85; Acad & Ldrshp Awd Phys Ed 84-85; Socl Wrk.

COSTIGAN, MARY; Red Bank Catholic HS; Middletown, NJ; (Y); Science Clb; Yrbk Bus Mgr; Yrbk Stf; Jr Cls; Twrlr; Hon Roll; NHS; NEDT Awd; Pres Schlr; Intnl Clb; Mst Outstnndng Achvt US Hstry II Awd 84-85.

COTLER, TIM; Cumberland Christian HS; Bridgeton, NJ; (Y); 1/14; Var Capt Bsktbl; Trk; High Hon Roll; Hon Roll; Val; Pres Church Yth Grp; Pres Jr Cls; VP Sr Cls; All Star Tm Bsktbl, Lawrence Kimball Awd-Schlstc Achvt 86; Merit Awd Athl 84-86; Bob Jones U; Bus Ldrshp.

COTTELL, JENNIFER ANNE; Immaculate Conception HS; Woodridge, NJ; (Y); Math Tm; School Musical; Nwsp Rptr; Var Capt Bsktbl; Capt Var Sftbl; High Hon Roll; Hon Roll; NHS; Spanish NHS; All Star Slctn NJCGSL Hst Bttng Aver 85-86; MVP Plyr Vrsty Sftbl 84-85; All Star Slctn Vrsty Bsktbl; Pol Sci.

COTTER, SANDRA; Belleville HS; Belleville, NJ; (Y); 41/383; Key Clb; Ski Clb; Band; Chorus; Concert Band; Jazz Band; Mrchg Band; Stu Cncl; Capt Trk; 2nd Team All-League Essex Cnty Trck 86; U WI-MADISON; Pharmacy.

COTTINGHAM, BETH G; Wayne Valley HS; Wayne, NJ; (Y); 20/311; French Clb; GAA; Model UN; Trs Temple Yth Grp; Yrbk Ed-Chief; Lit Mag; Capt Socr; Trk; High Hon Roll; NHS; Bus.

COTTINGHAM, KATHRYN L; Shawnee HS; Medford Lakes, NJ; (Y); 1/537; Church Yth Grp; Stu Cncl; Fld Hcky; Lcrss; Gov Hon Prg Awd; High Hon Roll; NHS; Ntl Merit SF; Val; Cmnty Wkr; Pres Clsrm 85; Mst Likely Succeed 85; Bio.

COTTLE, MICHAEL L; Pemberton Township HS; Browns Mills, NJ; (Y); 26/450; Computer Clb; German Clb; Library Aide; Teachers Aide; High Hon Roll; Hon Roll; NHS; De Vry Tech Inst; Comp Info.

COTTMAN, DAWN; Delaware Valley Regional HS; Milford, NJ; (Y); 56/165; Radio Clb; Acpl Chr; Band; Chorus; Concert Band; Mrchg Band; School Musical; Hon Roll; Somerset Cnty Clg; Mrktng.

COTTONE, BELLA; Lodi HS; Lodi, NJ; (Y); Art Clb; Leo Clb; Varsity Clb; Cheerleading; Trk; Wt Lftg; High Hon Roll; NHS; Dermtlgy.

COTTRELL, KELLY; Norte Dame HS; Hamilton, NJ; (Y); 14/320; Varsity Clb; Chorus; Var L Bsktbl; Var L Socr; Var L Sftbl; Im Mgr Vllybl; High Hon Roll; Hon Roll; Pre-Med.

COUDEN III, MALCOLM V; Clifton HS; Clifton, NJ; (Y); 205/620; Church Yth Grp; Dance Clb; Library Aide; Chorus; Church Choir; Madrigals; School Musical; School Play; Variety Show; Yrbk Stf; N Jersey Rgn I Chrs 85-86; All ST Chrs 85-86; Voice Prfmnc.

COUGHLAN, CHRISTINE; Morris Knolls HS; Rockaway, NJ; (Y); 4/367; Pres 4-H; FBLA; Math Clb; Math Tm; High Hon Roll; NHS; Summa Awd 82-86; Garden ST Distngshd Schlr 86; Pres Acad Fit Awd 86; Boston U; Acctng.

COUGHLIN, CRAIG; Holy Cross HS; Burlington, NJ; (Y); JV Bsbl; Im Vllybl; Hon Roll; Rutgers; Mktg.

COUGHLIN, DOUGLAS; Don Bosco Preparatory HS; Hawthorne, NJ; (Y); 27/187; Pep Clb; Rep Jr Cls; Stu Cncl; Var L Bsktbl; Crs Cntry; Ftbl; High Hon Roll; Hon Roll; NHS; Top Area Scorer In Bsktbl 86; Hnrb Mntn In Bsktbl Team 86.

COUNIHAN, KATHIE; Middlesex HS; Middlesex, NJ; (Y); 29/169; Art Clb; Church Yth Grp; Computer Clb; Hosp Aide; Key Clb; Ski Clb; Spanish Clb; Nwsp Stf; Cheerleading; Hon Roll; Mst Dsrvng Stu Acad Achvt 86; Montclair ST Coll; Psych.

COURARD, FREDERIQUE M; Academy Of The Holy Angels; River Edge, NJ; (Y); 3/169; Girl Scts; Pres Spanish Clb; Yrbk Stf; Lit Mag; Hon Roll; NHS; Ntl Merit SF; VFW Awd; French Clb; Model UN; 1st Cls Awd Grl Scts, Amer Leg Ldrshp Awd 82.

COURTER, CAROL; Memoria HS; Cedar Grove, NJ; (S); 6/118; Camera Clb; Church Yth Grp; French Clb; Key Clb; Capt Color Guard; Nwsp Rptr; Yrbk Ed-Chief; Cit Awd; High Hon Roll; NHS; Acadmc Excllnc Awd-Adv Art I 84; Soc Of Distngshd Amer H S Studnts 86; Girls Citznshp Inst Pgm 85.

COURTNEY, DANIEL J; De Paul Diocesan HS; Wanaque, NJ; (Y); 13/171; Drama Clb; School Play; Var Crs Cntry; Var Trk; Hon Roll; NHS; Ntl Merit Ltr; William Lightfoot Schultz Schlrshp 86; Acadmc Achvt Awd Pres Acadmc Ftnss Awds Prg 86; Cert Of Achvt; U Of VA; Engrg.

COURTRIGHT, RALPH; Sussex City Vocational-Tech HS; Franklin, NJ; (Y); 7/175; Spanish Clb; Varsity Clb; Rep Soph Cls; Rep Jr Cls; Var Bsbl; Im Bsktbl; JV Ftbl; High Hon Roll; Hon Roll.

COURTRIGHT, ROBIN L; Sussex County Vo Tech; Mc Afee, NJ; (S); Am Leg Aux Girls St; Spanish Clb; Drm & Bgl; Trs Sr Cls; Stu Cncl; JV Bsktbl; Powder Puff Ftbl; High Hon Roll; Hon Roll; NHS; Comp Sci.

COUSINS, KRISTEN; Lakewood HS; Lakewood, NJ; (Y); Am Leg Aux Girls St; English Clb; Spanish Clb; Pres Soph Cls; Pres Jr Cls; Var Capt Cheerleading; Socr; Sftbl; Gov Hon Prg Awd; NHS; Pre-Med.

COUTINHO, ALBERT; Seton Hall Prep; Newark, NJ; (Y); 17/198; Boys Clb Am; Cmnty Wkr; Pres French Clb; Math Tm; Nwsp Stf; Var Socr; High Hon Roll; NHS; Prfct Atten Awd; Mathletes; Holy Name Soc Achvt Awd 83; Cty Math League 85; Math League 86; Econ.

COVELLO, JOSEPH; East Brunswick Vo-Tech; Laurence, NJ; (Y); Hon Roll; Bst In Shop-Cmmrcl Foods; Chef.

COVERDALE, MINDY; Buena Regional HS; Williamstown, NJ; (S); 21/191; Church Yth Grp; Debate Tm; Spanish Clb; Nwsp Rptr; Rep Frsh Cls; Rep Jr Cls; Stu Cncl; Tennis; Hon Roll; Ntl Merit SF; Engl.

COVERT, KATHLEEN; Cinnaminson HS; Cinna, NJ; (Y); Church Yth Grp; Service Clb; SADD; Rep Frsh Cls; Rep Soph Cls; Rep Jr Cls; Rep Stu Cncl; JV Lcrss; Hon Roll; NHS; Rutgers U; Bus.

COVIELLO, GINA; Lenape Regional HS; Medford, NJ; (Y); Cmnty Wkr; Varsity Clb; Var Cheerleading; Coach Actv; Mgr(s); Hon Roll; Med.

COVINGTON, MARC C; University HS; Newark, NJ; (Y); Boy Scts; 4-H; JA; Chorus; School Musical; Trk; Hon Roll; Culnry Arts.

COVINO, JOHN; John F Kennedy Memorial HS; Iselin, NJ; (Y); 131/279; Art Clb; Computer Clb; ROTC; Ski Clb; Varsity Clb; Rep Frsh Cls; Rep Stu Cncl; Var Golf; JV Capt Socr; Golf Awd 86; Rtgrs; Aerodynmcs.

COWDIN, PAMELA; Eastern HS; Berlin, NJ; (Y); Color Guard; Drill Tm; Flag Corp; Mrchg Band; Yrbk Stf; Hon Roll; Srgnt At Arms For Clrgrd 85; Coll.

COWDRIGHT, MICHELLE; Hammonton HS; Hammonton, NJ; (Y); JV Var Fld Hcky; Mgr(s); Score Keeper; JV Trk; Cit Awd; Hon Roll; Acadmc Achvt Awd 84; Amer Bus Womns Assn Schlrshp 86; Womns Cvc Clb Art Awd 86; Temple U Ambler; Phy Thrpy.

COWELL, MATT ALAN; Westfield SR HS; Westfield, NJ; (Y); 73/500; Church Yth Grp; Cmnty Wkr; Chorus; Var L Bsbl; Var L Bsktbl; Hon Roll; Bus.

COWEN IV, BILL; Delsea Regional HS; Newfield, NJ; (Y); Drama Clb; FTA; Concert Band; Mrchg Band; School Musical; Trs Jr Cls; Sec Stu Cncl; Tennis; High Hon Roll; NHS; Olympcs Of Mind Tm 1st & 3rd Plcs 84; Ranatra Fusca Crtvy Awd 84; Rad Brdcstg.

COWGILL, KATHRYN; Kittatinny Regional HS; Newton, NJ; (Y); 62/228; Hosp Aide; Ski Clb; Band; Concert Band; Mrchg Band; School Play; JV L Bsktbl; JV L Cheerleading; JV Crs Cntry; Var L Sftbl; Occupational.

COWGILL, KEVIN R; Kittatinny Regional HS; Newton, NJ; (S); 6/164; Church Yth Grp; Science Clb; Ski Clb; Concert Band; Mrchg Band; JV Var Bowling; JV Var Socr; High Hon Roll; NHS; St Schlr; Navy ROTC Schlrshp; NJ Dstgnshd Schlr Schlrshp; Ltr Comndtn Hgh PSAT NMSQT Scrs; Boston U; Pre Dntstry.

COWHERD, JAMES; Oakcrest HS; Mays Landing, NJ; (Y); Art Clb; Church Choir; Lit Mag; JV Var Ftbl; Var Trk; Hon Roll; Cmmrcl Art.

COWIE, ANTHONY; Don Bosco Prep; Hillsdale, NJ; (Y); Math Tm; Model UN; Pep Clb; Service Clb; Ski Clb; Yrbk Stf; Rep Frsh Cls; Rep Sr Cls; Var Ftbl; High Hon Roll; U Richmond; Bus.

COWIE, ELIZABETH; Freehold Township HS; Freehold, NJ; (Y); 64/335; Church Yth Grp; French Clb; Lit Mag; Rep Frsh Cls; Rep Soph Cls; Rep Jr Cls; Rep Sr Cls; Rep Stu Cncl; JV Cheerleading; Stat Socr; Metal Lathers Local 46 Scholar 86-90; IN U PA; Crimnl Just.

COX, HOLLY MARI; Florence Twp Mem HS; Roebling, NJ; (Y); Cmnty Wkr; French Clb; GAA; Stage Crew; Nwsp Stf; Hon Roll; Amer Lgn Twnshp & Cnty Essy Awd 83; Engl Awd Hgh Avg 85-86; Prncpls Lst Acdmc Imprvmnt 85-86; Bus.

COX, MELISSA; Toms River H S East; Toms River, NJ; (Y); Art Clb; Camera Clb; FBLA; Mgr Capt Variety Show; Lit Mag; Off Jr Cls; Rep Sr Cls; Rep Stu Cncl; JV Crs Cntry; JV Trk; 1st Pl FBLA Grphc Arts Cmptn 85; ; Mdrn Muses Awd For Art 86; Phldlpha Coll Of Art.

COX, PATRICIA ELIZABETH; Piscataway HS; Piscataway, NJ; (Y); Drill Tm; Flag Corp; Mrchg Band; Orch; Swmmng; Hon Roll; Outstndng Fres Orch 83-84; Rifl Capt Marchg Band 85-86; Drill Tm Capt Mrchg Band 86; Equin Sci.

COX, ROOSEVELT; The Visual & Performing Arts HS; Newark, NJ; (Y); Aud/Vis; Church Yth Grp; Cmnty Wkr; Debate Tm; Drama Clb; Leo Clb; Pep Clb; Political Wkr; Speech Tm; Teachers Aide; Union CC; Prsnl Mngmnt.

COX, TRACEY A; Sparta HS; Sparta, NJ; (Y); 32/250; Church Yth Grp; Hosp Aide; Church Choir; Nwsp Stf; Yrbk Stf; Rep Soph Cls; Capt Var Cheerleading; High Hon Roll; Hon Roll; 35th Annl ST Sci Day 85; Grove City Coll; Acctg.

COXSON, LA VERNE; Weequahic HS; Newark, NJ; (S); 5/355; Debate Tm; Exploring; Math Clb; Color Guard; Mrchg Band; Yrbk Phtg; Crs Cntry; Trk; Twrlr; Hon Roll; Stu Mnth 85; Penn ST U; Acctg.

COXSON, LAVERNE; Weequahic HS; Newark, NJ; (Y); 5/353; Debate Tm; Exploring; Color Guard; Mrchg Band; Nwsp Phtg; Yrbk Phtg; Crs Cntry; Trk; Hon Roll; NHS; Stu Of Mnth 85; Clark U; Econ.

COYNE, COLLEEN; Neptune SR HS; Neptune, NJ; (Y); 9/350; GAA; Hosp Aide; Office Aide; Ski Clb; School Musical; Rep Soph Cls; Rep Jr Cls; Var Diving; Jr NHS; NHS; Nrsng.

COYNE, THOMAS; James Caldwell HS; W Caldwell, NJ; (Y); VP Frsh Cls; Pres Soph Cls; Var Bsbl; Im Bsktbl; Var Capt Ftbl; Wt Lftg; 2-Tm Al-Conf Ftbl 85; Al-Conf Bsbl 86; Law.

COZINE IV, CHAUNCEY G; Oratory Prep; Basking Ridge, NJ; (Y); 30/60; Church Yth Grp; Cmnty Wkr; JA; Ski Clb; Im Bsbl; Var L Bsktbl; Im Ftbl; JV Var Score Keeper; Im Sftbl; Im Vllybl.

CRAMER, GLENN; Teaneck HS; Teaneck, NJ; (Y); VP Pres Debate Tm; Drama Clb; NFL; Political Wkr; Speech Tm; Nwsp Ed-Chief; Nwsp Rptr; Nwsp Stf; Lit Mag; Tennis; NJ Schlrs Prog 86.

CRAMMER, SCOTT B; Northern Burlington Regional HS; Columbus, NJ; (Y); Am Leg Boys St; Church Yth Grp; Var L Bsbl; Var L Bsktbl; Hon Roll; NHS; Spanish NHS; Engrng.

CRAMPTON, RITA; Paul VI Regional HS; Paterson, NJ; (S); SADD; Rep Frsh Cls; Rep Soph Cls; Sec Jr Cls; VP Sr Cls; Var Cheerleading; Var Crs Cntry; French Hon Soc; VP Pres NHS; JV Bsktbl; Rutgers; Law.

CRANDALL, JOANNA; Hunterdon Central HS; Flemington, NJ; (Y); 54/560; Girl Scts; Intnl Clb; Model UN; Political Wkr; Ski Clb; Spanish Clb; Varsity Clb; Band; Nwsp Stf; Rep Jr Cls; Recgntn Pgm Awd Achvt Wnnr 84; Recgntn Pgm Awd Svc Fellow Stu 84; Intl Rltns.

CRANE, BRIAN E; Admiral Farragut Acad; Colts Neck, NJ; (Y); 2/50; Am Leg Boys St; ROTC; Nwsp Ed-Chief; Sec Stu Cncl; DAR Awd; Ntl Merit Ltr; Voice Dem Awd; Vrsty Rfle Tm Capt; George Washington U Schl Engrng & Sci Awd; Cum Laude Soc 4R Instrctr; U S Nvl Acad; U S Marine Corps.

CRANE, TRACI; Clayton HS; Clayton, NJ; (Y); Am Leg Aux Girls St; Key Clb; Band; Chorus; Concert Band; School Musical; Stage Crew; Yrbk Stf; Sftbl; NHS; Bio.

CRANE IV, WILMER; St Josephs Catholic Schl; Hammonton, NJ; (Y); Chess Clb; Cmnty Wkr; Key Clb; Math Clb; Math Tm; Pep Clb; Red Cross Aide; Service Clb; Ski Clb; Ftbl; Exclnce Math Awd 86; U PA.

CRANSTON, MICHAEL; Paul VI HS; Westmont, NJ; (Y); 92/544; Am Leg Boys St; Church Yth Grp; Nwsp Stf; Lit Mag; Crs Cntry; Trk; Hon Roll; NHS; Bus Admn.

CRAWFORD, LISA TAHOE; Dwight Morrow HS; Englewood, NJ; (Y); 73/247; AFS; Church Yth Grp; Cmnty Wkr; Drama Clb; FBLA; Hosp Aide; Hampton Inst; TV Prod.

CRAWFORD, RICH; Washington Township HS; Sewell, NJ; (Y); Ski Clb; JV Tennis; High Hon Roll; Hon Roll; Bus.

CRAWFORD, SUSANNE; Egg Harbor Twsp HS; Cardiff, NJ; (S); 9/287; Drama Clb; French Clb; Rep Frsh Cls; High Hon Roll; NHS.

CRAY, ANN MARIE; Rutherford HS; Rutherford, NJ; (S); 2/188; Key Clb; Nwsp Stf; Rep Stu Cncl; Var Capt Cheerleading; High Hon Roll; NHS; Ntl Merit Ltr; Sal; Math Tm; Pep Clb; Divona Awd Outstndng Chrldng 86; Bd Ed Schlstc Awds 83-85; League County,ST Champ Track Tm 85; Math.

CREAM, CARLOS; Camden HS; Camden, NJ; (S); 21/408; Am Leg Boys St; Varsity Clb; Variety Show; Rep Sr Cls; Var L Ftbl; Var L Trk; Var Wt Lftg; Var Capt Wrstlng; Hon Roll; NHS; Bus Mgmt.

CREAMER, CLAYTON; Central Regional HS; Bayville, NJ; (Y); Cvl Engr.

CREED, PAMELA; Toms River H S South; Beachwood, NJ; (Y); 57/360; German Clb; Intnl Clb; Flag Corp; Lit Mag; Cheerleading; Powder Puff Ftbl; Hon Roll; Douglass Coll; Govt/Intl Rltns.

CREEGAN, MICHAEL; Don Bosco Prep; N Haledon, NJ; (Y); 75/190; Church Yth Grp; Pep Clb; Im Bsktbl; Var L Socr; Bus.

CREELMAN, LYNN; Vineland HS; Vineland, NJ; (Y); Cmnty Wkr; Key Clb; Pep Clb; Political Wkr; Rep Frsh Cls; Italian Clb 85-86; Law Enfrcmt.

CREO, JACQUALINE; Central Regional HS; Island Heights, NJ; (Y); 63/232; Art Clb; Church Yth Grp; Cmnty Wkr; Drama Clb; SADD; VICA; Chorus; Color Guard; Stage Crew; Capt Pom Pon; William Sprinkle Mem Schlrshp 86; Outstndg Stu Awd OCVTS 86; 1st Pl Essay Cont OCVTS 86; Hood Coll; Interior Design.

CRESSE, SUSANNE; Holy Spirit HS; Absecon, NJ; (Y); 36/380; Church Yth Grp; Stage Crew; Var L Crs Cntry; Hon Roll; Ec Awd 86; Lynchbrg Coll.

CRESSEN, LYNN; Toms River East HS; Toms River, NJ; (Y); Chorus; Church Choir; Hon Roll; JC Awd; NBA Firearms Safety Crs Awd 85-86; U PA; Bio-Chem.

CRESTI, ANTHONY; North Brunswick Township HS; N Brunswick, NJ; (Y); 10/269; Cmnty Wkr; Computer Clb; Dance Clb; Key Clb; Red Cross Aide; L Bsktbl; Hon Roll; NHS; Itln Ntl Hnr Soc 86; Mr Italy 86; Engnrng.

CREVELING, ERIC; Belvidere HS; Washington, NJ; (S); 9/130; Varsity Clb; Var L Ftbl; Var Capt Wrstlng; Hon Roll; NHS; Sci.

CRICHTON, LILLIAN A; St John Vianney HS; Freehold, NJ; (Y); 42/237; Church Yth Grp; Office Aide; Church Choir; JV Crs Cntry; JV Trk; Hon Roll; Gold & White Awd 84; Rutgers Coll; Math.

CRIMMINS, JULIE; Roselle Catholic HS; Roselle, NJ; (Y); Drama Clb; GAA; Ski Clb; School Play; JV Swmmng; High Hon Roll; Hon Roll; NHS; Frnch Gold Mdl Awd 1st Pl 86; Forn 3rd Pl 83; Wrld Poet Cont Hnrb Mntn 85; Douglass Coll; Psych.

CRINCOLI, AMERICO; Roselle Catholic HS; Elizabeth, NJ; (Y); Im Fld Hcky; JV Var Socr; Im Vllybl; Im Wt Lftg; Hon Roll; Spanish NHS; Pre-Med.

CRISAFI, LAURA; North Bergen HS; N Bergen, NJ; (Y); 14/400; Q&S; Speech Tm; School Musical; Nwsp Bus Mgr; Nwsp Rptr; Rep Soph Cls; Hon Roll; Jr NHS; NHS; Val; Pres Acad Fit Awd 86; Italian Natl Hnr Soc 86; JLA Schlrshp 86; Rutgers U; Pre Med.

CRISAFULLI, AL; Don Bosco Prep HS; Suffern, NY; (Y); Church Yth Grp; Cmnty Wkr; Yrbk Ed-Chief; Yrbk Rptr; Pres Jr Cls; Pres Stu Cncl; Hon Roll; Dance Clb; Key Clb; SADD; Local Rock Band 84-87; Childrens Bkstbl Coach; Comm.

CRISCI, DANA; Ocean Township HS; Ocean, NJ; (Y); 156/314; Church Yth Grp; Civic Clb; Drama Clb; French Clb; Hosp Aide; Key Clb; Office Aide; Ski Clb; Band; Chorus; Roger Williams Coll; Paralegal.

CRITIDES, BARRY; North Bergen HS; North Bergen, NJ; (Y); 6/404; VP German Clb; Math Tm; Science Clb; Service Clb; Ski Clb; Band; Variety Show; Yrbk Rptr; Rep Soph Cls; CC Awd; N Brgn Fire Dept Schlrshp 86; Rbrt Fltn PTA Schlrshp 86; NBHS Sci Awd 83-86; Air Force Awd 84&85; Columbia Schl Of Engnrng; Bus.

CRNARICH, JENNY; Dover HS; Mine Hill, NJ; (Y); 47/182; Am Leg Aux Girls St; Political Wkr; Bsktbl; JV Sftbl.

CROCE, BENJAMIN; Union HS; Madison, NJ; (Y); Trs German Clb; Math Tm; VP Service Clb; Ski Clb; Rep Frsh Cls; Rep Soph Cls; Ftbl; Socr; Trk; Hon Roll; Outstndng Chrctr & Schlrshp 84; Med.

CROCE, STEPHEN L; Ewing HS; Trenton, NJ; (Y); Am Leg Boys St; Cmnty Wkr; Key Clb; Varsity Clb; Stu Cncl; Var Bsktbl; Var Capt Crs Cntry; Var Trk; Hon Roll; NHS; Spnsh & Sci Awd Acad Excllnc 84; Outstndng X-Cntry Athlt Awd 85-86; Ewng Twp Grdn Clb Bio Awd 85; Princeton U Of VA.

CROKE, SANDY; Matawan Regional HS; Cliffwood, NJ; (Y); VICA; Cosmtlgy.

CROMER, TOWANDA; Central HS; Newark, NJ; (Y); Exploring; School Play; Human Rights Awd 84; Cert Attendance 86; Rutgers U; Legal Sec.

CROMMELIN, KIM; Hunterdon Central HS; Stanton, NJ; (Y); 82/539; Church Yth Grp; Trs 4-H; Ski Clb; Church Choir; Yrbk Phtg; Stat Crs Cntry; Capt L Trk; 4-H Awd; Hon Roll; NHS; Vrsty Clb Awd Trck 86; Natl 4-H Cngrss 85; Ctznshp WA Focus 85; E Stroudsburg U; Phy Ed.

CROMONIC, DEBRA D; Phillipsburg HS; Phillipsburg, NJ; (Y); 72/294; Drill Tm; Off Frsh Cls; Rep Soph Cls; Im Bowling; Southeastern Acad; Trvl.

CRONCE, JOYCE; Hightstown HS; Hightstown, NJ; (Y); Intr Dcrtng.

CRONENWETT, DONNA; Hightstown HS; E Windsor, NJ; (Y); Cmnty Wkr; Teachers Aide; Concert Band; Co-Capt Flag Corp; Mrchg Band; Symp Band; Yrbk Phtg; Stu Cncl; High Hon Roll; NHS; Penn ST; Advrtsg.

CRONIN, JENNIFER; Montville Township HS; Montville, NJ; (Y); 41/262; FBLA; Key Clb; Office Aide; Ski Clb; Concert Band; Var Cheerleading; Hon Roll; NHS; MIP Awd Chrldg 86; Miss Natl Teen Johnson & Wales Schlrshp 86; Rest Mgmt.

CROOM, LISA; Frank M Morrell HS; Irvington, NJ; (Y); Cmnty Wkr; Drama Clb; Hosp Aide; Key Clb; Nwsp Rptr; Hon Roll; ASSE Exc Stu Pgm 85-86; Columbia U; Print.

CROSIER, CHARLES; St James HS; Salem, NJ; (S); 2/80; Stage Crew; Rep Soph Cls; JV Ftbl; Im Wt Lftg; High Hon Roll; Hon Roll; NCTE Awd; Ntl Merit Schol; Val; Outstndg Achvt Math, Sci & Soc Stud Awds 85; Engrng.

CROSS, ANNEMARIE; Queen Of Peace HS; Kearny, NJ; (S); 4/265; Church Yth Grp; Model UN; VP Service Clb; Trs Spanish Clb; Church Choir; School Musical; Nwsp Bus Mgr; NHS; Ntl Merit Ltr; Spanish NHS; Garden ST Distngshd Schlr 86; Qn Of Peace Eng Awd 84; Rutgers Coll Of Rutgers U; Med.

CROSSLAND, BONNIE; Atlantic City HS; Ventnor, NJ; (Y); Model UN; Red Cross Aide; Sec Stu Cncl; Hon Roll; Jr NHS; NHS; Crew, Arista 83-86; Eng.

CROTTY, JOHN; Christian Brothers Acad; Spring Lake, NJ; (Y); 38/221; Stu Cncl; Var JV Bsbl; Var JV Bsktbl; Socr; Hon Roll; 1st Tm All Cnty Soph And JR Bsktbl 85-86; 1st Tm All ST JR Bsktbl 86; Euchrstc Mnstr 86; Bus.

CROTTY, PAUL; Kittatinny Regional HS; Stillwater, NJ; (S); 1/164; Math Clb; Quiz Bowl; Science Clb; Ski Clb; Var Capt Socr; JV Trk; High Hon Roll; VP NHS; St Schlr; Yth Mrt Awd Frm Rtry 86; Rnsslr Plytcnhc Inst; Mchn Engr.

CROUCH, KATHLEEN; Jackson Memorial HS; Jackson, NJ; (Y); 32/342; Spanish Clb; VP Jr Cls; VP Sr Cls; Stu Cncl; Var L Cheerleading; Ftbl; High Hon Roll; Hon Roll; NHS; Spanish NHS; Crowned Hmcmng Queen 85-86; Miss Teen USA Fnlst; Pres Acad Ftnss Awd 85-86; NJ Awd Foreign Lang; Rider Coll; Bus Adm.

CROWE III, THOMAS A; Millvilel SR HS; Leesburg, NJ; (Y); Varsity Clb; Im Bowling; Capt Crs Cntry; Var L Trk; Prfct Atten Awd; Ldrs Clb 85-87; Natl Sci Lge 85-86; Physcs.

CROWELL, JUNE; Brick Township HS; Brick Town, NJ; (Y); Yrbk Stf; Pres Frsh Cls; Pres Soph Cls; Rep Jr Cls; Pres Sr Cls; Rep Stu Cncl; Powder Puff Ftbl; Var Tennis; Stat Wrstlng; Hon Roll; Ed.

CROWLEY, CHRISTINA; Waldwick HS; Waldwick, NJ; (Y); Hosp Aide; Math Tm; Ski Clb; School Play; Stage Crew; Powder Puff Ftbl; Var Tennis; Var Trk; Hon Roll; Prfct Atten Awd.

CROWLEY, LAUREN; Ramapo HS; Wyckoff, NJ; (Y); 36/329; Church Yth Grp; Trs French Clb; Teachers Aide; Stage Crew; Nwsp Rptr; Yrbk Stf; Rep Stu Cncl; JV Cheerleading; JV Trk; High Hon Roll; Frnch Acdmc Awd 83-84 & 85-86.

CRUICKSHANK, DENISE; Hopewell Valley Central HS; Pennington, NJ; (Y); Church Yth Grp; Ski Clb; Church Choir; Yrbk Stf; Bus Stu Month 86.

CRUM, LAURIE; Pompton Lakes HS; Pompton Lakes, NJ; (Y); Mathletes; Spanish Clb; Sec Frsh Cls; Stu Cncl; Var L Cheerleading; Hon Roll; Montclair ST NJ.

CRUMB, WALTER; Salem HS; Salem, NJ; (Y); Am Leg Boys St; Art Clb; Boy Scts; Chess Clb; Computer Clb; Math Clb; Spanish Clb; Bsbl; Hon Roll; Rutgers; Elect Engr.

CRUMMEY, PATRICIA; Livingston HS; Livingston, NJ; (Y); 42/498; Concert Band; Mrchg Band; School Musical; Yrbk Sprt Ed; Var Capt Fld Hcky; JV Swmmng; Var Trk; NHS; Ntl Merit Ltr; Spanish NHS; Livingston Wms Clb Schlshp 86; Home & Schl Assn Band Schlshp 86; Njsiaa Schlr Athl Awd 86; Clg Of William & Mary; Bio.

CRUMP, CECIL LAWRENCE; The Vail-Deane School HS; Newark, NJ; (Y); Church Yth Grp; Dance Clb; Drama Clb; French Clb; Math Tm; Political Wkr; Ski Clb; Acpl Chr; Chorus; School Musical; Yng Achvrs Awd 85; Intl Bus.

CRUZ, ALLAN DELA; St Peters Prep; Jersey City, NJ; (Y); Chess Clb; Computer Clb; Crs Cntry; Trk; Comp Engrng.

CRUZ, LISA; Red Bank Catholic HS; Holmdel, NJ; (Y); Art Clb; French Clb; Ski Clb; SADD; Church Choir; Yrbk Stf; Lit Mag; Hon Roll; Gen Art Awd 86; Arch.

CRUZ, MAGDALA C; St Joseph Of The Palisades HS; West New York, NJ; (S); 1/135; Pres French Clb; Spanish Clb; Stage Crew; Nwsp Rptr; Yrbk Stf; Lit Mag; Rep Jr Cls; French Hon Soc; Hon Roll; Acdmc All Am Awd 84; Bkng.

CRUZ, MONSERATE; Academic HS; Jersey City, NJ; (S); Am Leg Aux Girls St; Variety Show; VP Jr Cls; Rep Stu Cncl; Var Powder Puff Ftbl; Var Sftbl; Trs NHS; NYU; Vet Med.

CRUZ, RALPH; Dover HS; Mine Hill, NJ; (Y); Church Yth Grp; Science Clb; Band; Concert Band; Mrchg Band; JV Wt Lftg; JV Wrstlng; Bnd Awd; Tyng Awd; Law.

CRUZ, SONIA; Oakcrest HS; Elwood, NJ; (Y); 20/209; Drama Clb; GAA; Girl Scts; Key Clb; Office Aide; Off Sr Cls; Stu Cncl; Hon Roll; Jr NHS; Georgian Ct Coll; Bio.

CRUZ, SUZY; Memorial HS; W New York, NJ; (Y); 29/408; Cmnty Wkr; Computer Clb; Math Clb; Variety Show; Sec Soph Cls; JV Cheerleading; JV Vllybl; Hon Roll; NHS; 1st Pl HS Math Exam 84; Comp Sci Hnr Mntn 85; Stevvens Inst Of Tech; Elec Eng.

CSASTELLITTO, CAROLINE; Immaculate Conception HS; N Bergen, NJ; (Y); Art Clb; Chorus; School Play; Var Tennis; Spanish NHS; Art Hnr Soc Natl 86; Pres Natl Spn Hnr Soc 86; Hgh Hnr Roll 83-84; Psych.

CSEH, KAREN ANN; Depaul HS; Lincoln Park, NJ; (Y); 55/169; Bsktbl; Montclair ST Coll; Acctg.

CUBILLA, PATRICIA; East Side HS; Newark, NJ; (Y); Exploring; High Hon Roll; Hon Roll; Prfct Atten Awd; Psych.

CUDNIK, DENISE; Hamilton High West; Yardville, NJ; (Y); 37/307; Debate Tm; Key Clb; Speech Tm; Color Guard; Variety Show; Nwsp Rptr; Nwsp Stf; Off Frsh Cls; Off Soph Cls; Off Jr Cls; Clr Grd Co-Cap 85-86; Hornet Of Wk 86; Temple U; Pharm.

CUELLAR, RAFAEL; Paul VI Regional HS; Paterson, NJ; (Y); 20/96; Chess Clb; Church Choir; JV Bsktbl; JV Ftbl; US Naval Acad; Aerospace Engr.

CUGLIARI, ROSEMARY; Bridgewater-Raritan West HS; Raritan, NJ; (Y); Ski Clb; Spanish Clb; Rep Jr Cls; Crs Cntry; Powder Puff Ftbl; Trk; High Hon Roll; Hon Roll; NHS; Hon Mntn Rider Coll Poetry Cntst 84; Math.

CULLEN, CHRISTOPHER W; Passaic Valley Regional HS; Little Falls, NJ; (Y); 137/349; Camera Clb; Cmnty Wkr; Key Clb; Varsity Clb; JV Var Bsktbl; JV Var Ftbl; U VA; Bus Mgt.

CULLEN, FRANCES; Mother Seton Regional HS; Clark, NJ; (Y); 10/124; Church Yth Grp; Hosp Aide; Math Tm; Science Clb; School Play; Stage Crew; Lit Mag; Soph Cls; Timer; NHS; Acctg.

CULLEN, GENE; North Warren Regional HS; Blairstown, NJ; (Y); 1/130; Am Leg Boys St; Church Yth Grp; Capt Quiz Bowl; Capt Scholastic Bowl; Var L Ftbl; Var Wrstlng; Bausch & Lomb Sci Awd; Gov Hon Prg Awd; NHS; Rutgers Schlr 86; Rutgers U; Bio.

CULLEN, MICHAEL J; Paterson Catholic Regional HS; Paterson, NJ; (Y); 11/120; Aud/Vis; DECA; Band; Mrchg Band; Pep Band; Nwsp Ed-Chief; Pres Jr Cls; Var Crs Cntry; Var Trk; Hon Roll; DECA NJ ST Ldrshp Conf 3rd Rest/Mktg 86; 2nd Cougar Run-Church, Hnbl Achvt Earth Sci/French 84; Rutgers New Brunswick; Ent Tchr.

CULLEN, TAMMY; Hackettstown HS; Hackettstown, NJ; (Y); 25/250; Hon Roll; Kiwanis Awd; NHS; Hackettstown Area Poster Child Muscular Dystrphy 85; Psychlgy.

CUMMINGS, APRIL ANITA; Garden State Acad; Massapequa, NY; (Y); Church Yth Grp; Cmnty Wkr; Office Aide; Teachers Aide; Mgr Band; Sec Chorus; Church Choir; Concert Band; School Play; Bsktbl; $4000 Schlrshp Columbia Union Coll 86; Columbia Union Coll; Nrsng.

CUMMINGS, CHRISTINE; Pinelands Regional HS; West Creek, NJ; (Y); 8/192; FHA; Science Clb; High Hon Roll; Hon Roll; NHS; Prfct Atten Awd; Elem Ed.

CUMMINGS, MEG; Haddonfield Memorial HS; Haddonfield, NJ; (Y); Intnl Clb; Concert Band; Mrchg Band; Orch; Nwsp Bus Mgr; Nwsp Rptr; Yrbk Rptr; Sec Frsh Cls; Hon Roll; NHS; Coll Frshmn Acdmc Schlrshp 86; Hibshmn Memrl Schlrshp 86; Wlf Memorl Schlrshp 86; Eastern Mennonite Coll; Engr.

CUMMINGS, PAMELA; Holy Family Acad; Bayonne, NJ; (Y); 4/130; Cmnty Wkr; French Clb; Orch; Var Tennis; High Hon Roll; Hon Roll; VP NHS; Prfct Atten Awd; Mst Imprvd Plyr Tnns 86; Supr Prfrmnc Certs Natl Educ Devlpmt Tsts 84 & 85; Dusquene U; Biochem Rsrch.

CUMMINGS, SCOTT; Bayonne HS; Bayonne, NJ; (Y); 57/402; Cmnty Wkr; Teachers Aide; Nwsp Stf; Rep Stu Cncl; Var Bsbl; Capt Var Bowling; Stat Ice Hcky; Im Vllybl; Cit Awd; Hon Roll; N Hudson Leag Bwlg All Str 1st Tm 86; Athltc Schlrshp Bsbl & Acdmc Schlrshp Union Coll 86-87; Union Coll KY; Jrnlsm.

CUMMINS, MAUREEN; Bishop George HS; Plainfield, NJ; (Y); Church Yth Grp; Girl Scts; Varsity Clb; Yrbk Stf; VP Stu Cncl; Var Bsktbl; Var Sftbl; Hon Roll; Physical Therapy.

CUMMISKEY, PEGGY; Mother Seton Regional HS; Clark, NJ; (Y); Cmnty Wkr; Hosp Aide; Math Tm; Office Aide; Political Wkr; Teachers Aide; Chorus; Church Choir; School Play; Stage Crew; Cert Awd Attendnce Regnl Tri Beta Conv 85; Cert Recgntn Sci Humanities Symp 86; Chem.

CUNIFF, KEITH; Nutley HS; Nutley, NJ; (Y); 23/325; Am Leg Boys St; Hosp Aide; Key Clb; Pres Frsh Cls; Pres Soph Cls; Pres Jr Cls; Pres Sr Cls; Hon Roll; NHS; Bus.

CUNNIGNHAM, LINDA; Paul VI HS; Berlin, NJ; (Y); 15/475; Math Clb; Concert Band; Jazz Band; Mrchg Band; Orch; School Musical; Variety Show; Lit Mag; NHS; Mdws Schl Arts Tlnts Schlr 86; Shsp Sttlmnt Music Schl 85-86; S Methodist U; Music.

CUNNINGHAM, ALLISON; Paul VI HS; Pine Hill, NJ; (Y); 78/468; Cmnty Wkr; Math Clb; Spanish Clb; Pres SADD; Yrbk Bus Mgr; Lit Mag; Rep Frsh Cls; Var L Cheerleading; Hon Roll; NHS; NIAATSP 83; Rutgers U Camden; Acctg.

CUNNINGHAM, BRUCE; Summit HS; Summit, NJ; (Y); Cmnty Wkr; Math Tm; Model UN; Political Wkr; Jazz Band; Rep Frsh Cls; Rep Soph Cls; JV Socr; JV Tennis; AFS; Contntl Math Lague Bronze; Best Delgtn Gen Assmbly; Bus.

CUNNINGHAM, CHENYCE; West Side HS; Newark, NJ; (Y); 15/235; Church Yth Grp; Computer Clb; Science Clb; Church Choir; Hon Roll; Math Achvt Awd 85-86; Bausch & Lomb Sci Awd 85-86; Acad Achvt Awd 85-86; NJ Inst Tech; Comp Sci.

CUNNINGHAM, KIERAN; Haddon Township HS; W Collingswood, NJ; (Y); Civic Clb; German Clb; Ftbl; Trk; Wt Lftg; Wrstlng; Hon Roll; All Grp II 2nd Tm Cntr Ftbl 85; All Colonial Conf 2nd Tm Off & Def 85; 5th Pl Javlin Thrw S Jersey 86; Spts Med.

CUNNINGHAM, LINDA; Paul VI HS; Berlin, NJ; (S); 16/475; Math Clb; Band; Church Choir; Concert Band; Jazz Band; Mrchg Band; Orch; Pep Band; School Musical; Variety Show; Cigna Schl At Settlemnt Music Schl 84-86; All S Jersey Orch & Wind Ensmbl 85-86; Music.

CUNNINGHAM, MARK; Clearview Regional HS; Mullica Hill, NJ; (Y); 23/175; Church Yth Grp; Varsity Clb; Var Bsktbl; Var Socr; U Of DE; Phys Thrpy.

CUNNINGHAM, MATTHEW E; Red Bank Catholic HS; W Allenhurst, NJ; (Y); 10/344; Natl Hnr Soc; Hgh Hnr Roll; Hnr Roll; Natl Merit Ltr; Pres Schlr ST Schlr & Prfct Atten Awd; Gen Acad Ex; Pre-Med.

CUNNINGHAM, SHERRI YVONNE; Salem HS; Quinton, NJ; (Y); Church Yth Grp; Computer Clb; FBLA; JA; Spanish Clb; Band; Concert Band; JV Var Bsktbl; Algbr, Hstry & Crs 85-86; Faccntng.

CUNNIUS, COLLEEN; South Hunterdon R HS; Lambertville, NJ; (Y); 20/73; Art Clb; French Clb; Key Clb; Spanish Clb; Varsity Clb; Rep Stu Cncl; Var JV Bsktbl; Var Capt Fld Hcky; Var JV Sftbl; Hon Roll; NJ All ST Honrbl Mention Fld Hcky 85; DE Vly Conf 1st Tm Fld Hcky 85; ; De Vly Conf Sftbl 86; Wilford Beauty Acad; Cosmotolgy.

CUOZZO, GREGORY; Kinnelon HS; Kinnelon, NJ; (Y); 22/184; Trk; Wrstlng.

CUPON, LEANNE N; Phillipsburg HS; Alpha, NJ; (Y); 43/334; Pres VP Exploring; Hosp Aide; Ski Clb; SADD; Church Choir; Variety Show; Nwsp Phtg; Nwsp Rptr; Sftbl; Trk; WA Wrkshps Cngrsnl Smnr Schlrshp 86.

CUPPARI, PASQUALE; Red Bank Catholic HS; Long Branch, NJ; (Y); Dance Clb; Acpl Chr; Church Choir; School Play; Stage Crew; Ftbl; Score Keeper; Vllybl; Pres Wt Lftg; JV Hon Roll; Monmouth Coll; Bus.

CURCIE, DAVID JOHN; Toms River High School North; Toms River, NJ; (Y); Church Yth Grp; Orch; High Hon Roll; Hon Roll; Acad Lttr 86; Phy Ftnss Awd 86; 4 Yr Lttr & Pin Orch; Rutgers Coll; Biomed Engrng.

CURCURA, BRIAN; Wayne Hills HS; Wayne, NJ; (Y); 91/340; Cmnty Wkr; FBLA; Ski Clb; Trs Frsh Cls; Trs Soph Cls; Trs Jr Cls; Rep Stu Cncl; Lib Arts.

CURE, JOAN ANN; Oak Knoll HS; Westfield, NJ; (Y); Church Yth Grp; Cmnty Wkr; Pep Clb; Ski Clb; Teachers Aide; Varsity Clb; Var Fld Hcky; Var Sftbl; Hon Roll; Math Awd 85; NJ Ski Tm 85 & 86; Mathematics.

CURIO, NICOLE; Haddon Twp HS; Wesgmont, NJ; (Y); Church Yth Grp; Red Cross Aide; Orch; JV Bsktbl; Var Trk; Im Vllybl; Hon Roll; MVP Trk 86; Mercer Cnty Coll; Draftng.

CUROTTO, JAMES; Sayreville War Memorial HS; Sayreville, NJ; (Y); 10/379; Pres Varsity Clb; Rep Stu Cncl; Var Capt Socr; Var L Tennis; Hon Roll; NHS; Ntl Merit SF; Spanish NHS; St Schlr; Spanish Clb; Tlntd & Gftd Pgm 82-86; Olympcs Of Mind 83-84; Acadmc Comptns Tm 84-85; Penn ST; Pre-Med.

CURRAN, PATRICK; Chatham HS; Chatham, NJ; (Y); Cmnty Wkr; Latin Clb; Model UN; Spanish Clb; Varsity Clb; Yrbk Stf; Var Bsktbl; JV Socr; Hon Roll; Ntl Merit Ltr.

CURRERI, MARK; Cumberland Regional HS; Bridgeton, NJ; (Y); Ski Clb; Chorus; Crs Cntry; Swmmng; Army; Wrrnt Offcr Flght Trng.

CURRIE, WALTER; Toms River H S East; Toms River, NJ; (Y); 22/585; Church Yth Grp; Var L Bsbl; Bsktbl; Ftbl; Trk; High Hon Roll; Hon Roll; NHS; Engrng.

CURRY, CLAUDINE; Essex Catholic Girls HS; East Orange, NJ; (Y); Spanish Clb; Church Choir; Nwsp Rptr; Yrbk Ed-Chief; High Hon Roll; NHS; Jrnlsm.

CURRY, DAWN; West Essex Regional HS; N Caldwell, NJ; (Y); Dance Clb; Pres FBLA; Key Clb; Pep Clb; Mgr Nwsp Ed-Chief; Ed Nwsp Stf; Ed Lit Mag; JV Var Cheerleading; Powder Puff Ftbl; Natl Mdlng Comptn 3rd Rnr Up 83; Model Extrvgnza Miss Tn 2nd Rnr Up 83; Miss Tn All Amer Pgnt Fnlst 84; Montclair ST Coll; Bus Adm.

CURRY, LISA M; Toms River HS South; Beachwood, NJ; (Y); 31/296; Drama Clb; French Clb; Library Aide; Thesps; Chorus; School Musical; Yrbk Stf; Rep Jr Cls; Rep Sr Cls; Rep Stu Cncl; Am Leg Dept NJ Awd; Acdmc Ltr Hi Hnr Rl; Georgian Court Coll; Frgn Lang.

CURTIS, ADRIENNE L; Bayonne HS; Bayonne, NJ; (Y); Key Clb; Yrbk Stf; Twrlr; Vllybl; Hon Roll; St Peters Coll; Accntng.

CURTIS, CANDACE; Camden HS; Camden, NJ; (S); 38/408; Dance Clb; FHA; Color Guard; School Play; Yrbk Stf; High Hon Roll; Hon Roll; Jr NHS; NHS; Cert Of Achvt-Spanish 84-85; Helen Fuld Schl Of Nursing; Med.

CURTIS, DARNICE Y; Paterson Catholic Regional HS; Paterson, NJ; (Y); 3/99; Concert Band; Mrchg Band; Rep Stu Cncl; Stat Bsktbl; JV Cheerleading; High Hon Roll; NHS; Ntl Merit Ltr.

CURTIS, GLENN; Deptfort Township HS; Deptford, NJ; (Y); 10/287; JA; Concert Band; Jazz Band; Var Capt Bsbl; Crs Cntry; Diving; Trk; Hon Roll; Jr NHS; NHS; Comp Sys Mgnt.

CURTSINGER, EVA; Rancocas Valley Reg HS; Mt Holly, NJ; (Y); Church Yth Grp; PAVAS; Thesps; School Play; Stu Cncl; Intl Thespian Soc; W VA U; Theatre.

CUSANO, DENISE; Pompton Lakes HS; Pompton Lks, NJ; (Y); 16/152; Latin Clb; Math Tm; Q&S; Varsity Clb; Ed Yrbk Stf; Ed Lit Mag; JV Sftbl; High Hon Roll; NHS; Art Clb; Pres Schlrshp For FDU 86; Rotary Intl Schlrshp 86; Julias Grass Awd Fencing 86; Fairleigh Dickinson U; Psychlgy.

CUSUMANO, LEANNE; Manalapan HS; Manalapan, NJ; (Y); 6/423; CAP; NFL; SADD; Ed Lit Mag; Pres NHS; Ntl Merit Ltr; NJ Drl Tm Cmndr, Cvl Air Patrl ,4; E Walsh Schl; Intl Rltns.

CUTINELLO, JOSEPH E; Roselle Park HS; Roselle Park, NJ; (Y); 42/170; Am Leg Boys St; Band; Concert Band; Jazz Band; Mrchg Band; School Musical; Crs Cntry; Trk; Instmntlst Mag Merit Awd 86; 3 Lttr Vrsty Awd Crs Cntry Wntr/Sprng Trck 84-86; Embry-Rddle Aero U; Air Frce.

CUTNEY JR, RICHARD S; Lakeland Regional HS; Ringwood, NJ; (Y); 46/305; Church Yth Grp; Cmnty Wkr; SADD; School Musical; Var L Socr; Var Capt Wrstlng; NHS; Aud/Vis; Boy Scts; Chess Clb; Eagle Sct 84; Army ROTC Schlrshp 4yr 86; Senator Bill Bradley Yng Ctzn Awd 86; Eastern KY U; Fire Protctn Adm.

CUTRO, MARY ANN; Bayonne HS; Bayonne, NJ; (Y); 47/362; Computer Clb; French Clb; Office Aide; Spanish Clb; Nwsp Rptr; Rep Stu Cncl; Hon Roll; NHS; Italian Clb Pres 822-6; Poliglotta Schls Lang Mag Editor-In-Chf 82-6; Natl Foreign Lang Tchrs Assn Awd; Seton Hall U; Polit Sci.

CUY, KENNETH; Teaneck HS; Teaneck, NJ; (Y); Aud/Vis; SADD; Ed Nwsp Phtg; Ed Yrbk Phtg; Rep Stu Cncl; High Hon Roll; NHS; Amrcn Lgn Outstndg Stu 84; Mry Fnmore Good Ctznshp Awd 84; JR Advsry Cncl 85; MIT; Elec Engnrng.

CUYLER, MARC; Marist HS; Jersey City, NJ; (Y); Computer Clb; Church Choir; Comp Prgmr.

CYGAN, LANCE; East Brunswick HS; E Brunswick, NJ; (Y); Art Clb; Boy Scts; Church Yth Grp; Key Clb; Chorus; Church Choir; Variety Show; JV Bsktbl; Hon Roll; Im Badmtn; Comm Desgn.

CYPHERS, KAREN E; Delaware Valley Regional HS; Milford, NJ; (Y); 37/190; Chrmn Key Clb; Sec Varsity Clb; Nwsp Rptr; Rep Stu Cncl; Var Cheerleading; Var Sftbl; Hon Roll; Montclair ST Coll; Psych.

CYRLIN, LANCE; Somerville HS; Somerville, NJ; (Y); 14/220; Cmnty Wkr; Drama Clb; Service Clb; Spanish Clb; School Play; Lit Mag; JV Var Ftbl; Var Trk; NHS; Band; Eagles Schlrshp 86; 1st Annual Don Elliott Mem Schlrshp 86; Civic League Schlrshp 86; Syracuse U; Communications.

CZAKO, CHRISTOPHER J; Bordentown Regional HS; Yardville, NJ; (Y); Am Leg Boys St; Pres Computer Clb; French Clb; VP Math Clb; Var Crs Cntry; Var Trk; Var Wrstlng; Mu Alp Tht; NHS; Rotary Awd; Amercn Hngrn Cvc Assn & H S Trcntnial Schlrshps 86; FBLA ST Ldrshp Conf 86; Rtgrs Schl-Engrng; Mchncl Engrn.

CZAPKOWSKI, JOE; South River HS; South River, NJ; (Y); 14/140; German Clb; Stu Cncl; Var L Bsbl; Var Capt Ftbl; Hon Roll; NHS; Montclair ST Coll; Bus.

CZAPLICKI, CARL S; Saint Mary HS; Jersey City, NJ; (Y); Am Leg Boys St; Chorus; School Musical; School Play; Yrbk Ed-Chief; Im Bsktbl; Timer; High Hon Roll; Jr NHS; NHS; Bio Awd 84-85; Hstry Awds 83-86; Bus.

CZARNECKI, ALLISON; Highstown HS; E Windsor, NJ; (Y); 150/344; Cmnty Wkr; Service Clb; Ski Clb; Rep Frsh Cls; Rep Soph Cls; Rep Jr Cls; Rep Sr Cls; Var Diving; Var Fld Hcky; Var Swmmng; CVC Fld Hcky Tm Hnrblmnt 84; Syracuse U; Mngmnt.

CZARNECKI, MICHAEL; Red Bank Regional HS; Shrewsbuy, NJ; (Y); Am Leg Boys St; Service Clb; Pres Ski Clb; Stage Crew; Rep Frsh Cls; Rep Soph Cls; Off Jr Cls; VP Stu Cncl; Var Golf; Var Socr; US Coast Grd Acad AIM Pgm; YMCA Yth In Govt Pgm; Outstndng-HOBY Ldrshp Schlrshp Pgm; Engr.

CZARNIAK, LISA; Roselle Catholic HS; Linden, NJ; (Y); 11/290; Hosp Aide; Math Clb; Ski Clb; JV Tennis; Gov Hon Prg Awd; High Hon Roll; NHS; Spanish NHS.

CZEBIENIAK, DANIEL J; Spotswood HS; Millton, NJ; (Y); Am Leg Boys St; Church Yth Grp; Church Choir; Crs Cntry; Trk; Most Impvd Rnnr Crs Cntry 84; Most Impvd Rnnr Winter Trck 85-86; Most Imprvd Rnnr Spg Trck 86.

CZEREPAK JR, JAN F; St Joseph Regional HS; Elmwood Park, NJ; (Y); 16/242; Jr NHS; NHS; Spanish NHS; Rtgrs Coll; Sprts Med.

CZERNIAWSKI, YOLANDA; Immaculate Conception HS; Wallington, NJ; (S); 3/98; Math Clb; Math Tm; Science Clb; Spanish Clb; Chorus; School Musical; School Play; Yrbk Stf; Lit Mag; Rep Jr Cls; Lit Awd Schl Mag 85; 3rd Pl Dune Cntst 83; Garden ST Arts Ctr Essay Cntst Wnnr 83; Rutgers; Phrmcy.

CZERNY, ANDREW; Chatham Twp HS; Chatham Twp, NJ; (Y); AFS; Yrbk Phtg; Var Ftbl; JV Trk; Marine Bio.

CZERWINSKI, THOMAS; Hillside HS; Hillside, NJ; (Y); 16/195; Trs Computer Clb; Science Clb; Trk; Ntl Merit Ltr; Prtcptd NJ Sci Leag Chem I, Bio II 85-86; Rutgers; Med.

D ADDOZIO, MICHELE; Memorial HS; Cedar Grove, NJ; (S); 17/120; VP Key Clb; Spanish Clb; Chorus; School Musical; Pres Jr Cls; Pres Sr Cls; Capt Cheerleading; JV Sftbl; High Hon Roll; NHS; Acad Achvt Phy Ed 83.

D AGOSTO, ANTHONY; Marist HS; Jersey City, NJ; (Y); Art Clb; Sec Key Clb; Ed Nwsp Stf; NHS; Marist Schlrshps 85 & 86; Rutgers; Bio.

D ALESSANDRO, GENE; Eastern HS; Gibbsboro, NJ; (Y); Pres Computer Clb; Mgr(s); Hon Roll; Pres Ecolgy Clb 85; Outstndng Comp Achvt 85; Comp Olympcs Camden Co Coll 7th & 9th Pl 85-87; Comp Engr.

D ALLESSIO, MARIA; Bishop George Ahr HS; Fords, NJ; (Y); Capt Drill Tm; Frsh Cls; Capt Bsktbl; Mgr(s); Score Keeper; Hon Roll; Chairperson Acad Cncl 86-87; Bus.

D ALOIA, TRICIA; Red Bank Regional HS; Shrewsbury, NJ; (Y); 54/232; Ski Clb; Spanish Clb; Band; Concert Band; Mrchg Band; Yrbk Sprt Ed; Yrbk Stf; JV Var Sftbl; Hon Roll; Tmstrs Lcl 11 Union Fnd Schlrshp 86; Bnd Prnts Schlrshp 86; Frnk & Louise Grff Fndtn Schlrshp 86; Catholic U Of America; Nrsng.

D ALUSIO, JIM; Brick Township HS; Brick, NJ; (Y); Hon Roll; Acctng.

D AMATO, JOELLE; Southern Regional HS; Barnegat, NJ; (Y); JA; Ski Clb; Varsity Clb; Capt Cheerleading; Var Mgr(s); Var Capt Powder Puff Ftbl; Var Score Keeper; Var Capt Sftbl; Var Trk; Vllybl; Fash Merch.

D AMATO, MICHAEL; Orange HS; Orange, NJ; (Y); Music.

D AMICO, JOHN F; Montgomery HS; Belle Mead, NJ; (Y); Am Leg Boys St; Spanish Clb; Nwsp Stf; JV Bsbl; JV Bsktbl; Hon Roll; NHS; Church Yth Grp; Science Clb; Nwsp Rptr; Engl Awd Colby Coll 86; Dfnsv Awd Bsktbl 86; Ntl Merit Prgrm 86.

D ANTON, NICOLE; Essex Catholic Girls; Newark, NJ; (Y); FHA; Stu Cncl; Btty Crckr Awd; High Hon Roll; Montclair ST Coll.

D APOLITO, PAUL; Christian Brothers Acad; Little Silver, NJ; (Y); Boy Scts; Church Yth Grp; Im Ftbl; Im Ice Hcky; Boy Scts Life Awd 84; Boy Scts Jr Asst Sct Mstr JASM 85; Boy Scts Wrkng Twrds Eagle.

D ARMIENTO, DEANNE; North Plainfield HS; N Plainfield, NJ; (Y); 9/177; Church Yth Grp; Girl Scts; Teachers Aide; Concert Band; Rep Stu Cncl; JV Var Bsktbl; Var Tennis; Var Trk; Capt Twrlr; Hon Roll; Math.

D ARRIGO, ARTHUR; Bridgeton HS; Bridgeton, NJ; (Y); Aud/Vis; French Clb; Varsity Clb; Nwsp Sprt Ed; Nwsp Stf; Rep Frsh Cls; Rep Soph Cls; Crs Cntry; Trk; Wrstlng; Law.

D AUGOSTINE, STEPHANIE; Clayton HS; Clayton, NJ; (S); 3/60; Sec Nwsp Stf; Yrbk Stf; Pres Sr Cls; VP Rep Stu Cncl; JV Var Bsktbl; Var Fld Hcky; JV Var Sftbl; Key Clb; Nwsp Bus Mgr; Grls St 85; Acdmc All-Amer 84-85; Pre-Med.

D AURIZIO, JOANNE; Paul VI Regional HS; Totowa, NJ; (Y); Pep Clb; Service Clb; Spanish Clb; School Musical; School Play; Hon Roll; Spanish NHS; Law.

D ORAZIO, FRANK; Bishop Ahr HS; East Brunswick, NJ; (Y); 36/240; Am Leg Boys St; Math Tm; Ski Clb; Nwsp Stf; Ftbl; Hon Roll; NHS; NEDT Awd 84; Fairfield U; Pltcl Sci.

D UVA, GENNARO; North Arlington HS; N Arlington, NJ; (Y); French Clb; Nwsp Stf; Yrbk Stf; Office Aide; Spanish Clb; Hon Roll; N Arlingtn Schlrshp Awd 86; Middlesex County Coll; Clnry.

DA SILVA, CARLOS; James Caldwell HS; Caldwell, NJ; (Y); 101/263; Trs Sr Cls; Trs Stu Cncl; Hofstra U; Mgmt.

DA SILVA, JACQUELINE; East Brunswick HS; E Brunswick, NJ; (Y); SADD; Drill Tm; School Play; Variety Show; Yrbk Stf; Rep Soph Cls; Rep Stu Cncl; Var Cheerleading; High Hon Roll; NHS; Rutgers Coll; Intl Bus.

DA SILVA, JENNIFER; Hunterdon Central HS; Flemington, NJ; (Y); Art Clb; Church Yth Grp; Key Clb; Band; Mrchg Band; Orch; School Musical; Stage Crew; Symp Band; Jenny Haver Revue 83-84; Pharmctcl.

DABNEY, CAROLYN; Teaneck HS; Teaneck, NJ; (Y); AFS; Art Clb; Church Yth Grp; Drama Clb; French Clb; German Clb; School Musical; Rep Frsh Cls; Var Swmmng; Hon Roll.

DABNEY, LISA; Leonia HS; Leonia, NJ; (Y); 1/132; Drama Clb; Math Tm; Yrbk Stf; Rep Frsh Cls; Rep Soph Cls; Pres Jr Cls; Pres Sr Cls; Var Bsktbl; Var Crs Cntry; Var Capt Trk; Columbia U; Doctor.

DABRAMO, MICHAEL; Cliffside Park HS; Cliffside Pk, NJ; (Y); 37/245; Math Tm; Pres Band; Concert Band; Jazz Band; Mrchg Band; Nwsp Stf; Lion Awd; ACTNV Union Schlrshp Awd 86; Pace U; Acctg.

DABROWSKI, DIANA; Highland Regional HS; Laurel Spgs, NJ; (Y); FTA; Spanish Clb; Varsity Clb; Stage Crew; Yrbk Stf; Var Bsktbl; Tennis; JV Trk; JR Yr Vrsty Ltr Bsktbll 84; Presdntl Phys Fitness Of Marines Corp 84; Buiness.

DACOSTA, NELSON; Queen Of Peace HS; Newark, NJ; (Y); 6/250; Ski Clb; Band; Concert Band; Variety Show; Nwsp Ed-Chief; Yrbk Ed-Chief; Rep Soph Cls; Rep Jr Cls; Bsktbl; NHS; Awd $500 Bond Mst Outstndg Thinker Of Yr 84; U Of Southern CA.

DADDIO, DONNA MARIE; Pemberton Twp HS; Hamilton Sq, NJ; (Y); 208/396; VP Church Yth Grp; Office Aide; SADD; Chorus; JV Capt Cheerleading; Mercer County Coll; Lgl Asst.

DAGBUSAN, HONEY DARLENE C; Piscataway HS; Piscataway, NJ; (Y); 19/519; Church Yth Grp; Office Aide; Science Clb; Church Choir; Yrbk Phtg; Yrbk Stf; Stat Tennis; High Hon Roll; Hon Roll; NHS; Govrnr Schl Sci 84; Pres Acdmc Fit 86; Cert Excllnc Forgn Lang Spnsh & Hlth 86; Med.

DAGGETT, AARON MARC; Middletown HS South; Red Bank, NJ; (Y); 48/436; Pres Church Yth Grp; Science Clb; Mrchg Band; School Musical; Symp Band; Crs Cntry; Var L Trk; Hon Roll; NHS; Howard Osborne Schrlshp 86; Pres Acad Ftns Awd 86; Le Tourneau Coll; Aviatn.

DAGOGLIANO, CAROLYN; Palisades Park JR SR HS; Palisades Pk, NJ; (Y); 1/120; Church Yth Grp; Nwsp Stf; Yrbk Stf; Stu Cncl; Var Capt Bsktbl; Vllybl; NHS; Val; Lit Mag; Crs Cntry; Rtgrs Schlr 86; Acad Decthlte 86; Engl.

DAGOSTINO, LEONARDO; Holy Spirit HS; Atlantic City, NJ; (Y); School Play; High Hon Roll; Hon Roll; Jr NHS; NHS; Prfct Atten Awd; Real Estat.

DAHL, ELISABET; De Paul Diocesan HS; Ringwood, NJ; (S); Yrbk Stf; Hon Roll; Ski Tm V Capt Ltr 84-86; Health Sci.

DAHLEN, PAMELA; Indian Hills HS; Oakland, NJ; (Y); 24/279; AFS; Nwsp Rptr; Lit Mag; Sec Frsh Cls; Sec Soph Cls; Hon Roll; Jr NHS; NHS; Debate Tm; Science Clb; Cert Merit Bio,Alg,Hist,Eng,Writers Wrkshp 83-85; U NC; Frgn Lang.

DAHLGREN, CRAIG; Ramapo HS; Franklin Lakes, NJ; (Y); 32/329; German Clb; Nwsp Rptr; Var L Socr; Var L Trk; Hon Roll; NHS; Ntl Merit SF; Yrbk Stf; Bsktbl; Nvl Acad Smr Smnr 86; ST Sci Dy 86; Physcs Tm 86.

DAHMEN, ROBIN; St Mary HS; Carlstadt, NJ; (Y); Dance Clb; Drama Clb; School Play; Capt Cheerleading; Mat Maids; Hon Roll; Art Awd 86; Barbizon Mdl 85; Felician Coll; Psych.

DAILEY, JENNIFER PAGE; Dover HS; Dover, NJ; (Y); 16/224; Am Leg Aux Girls St; Color Guard; Yrbk Ed-Chief; Cheerleading; Score Keeper; High Hon Roll; NHS; Latin Clb; Spanish Clb; Nwsp Stf; Acad St Schl PTA Schlrshp ; JR Olympc Archry Dvlpmnt; Lock Haven U; Med Tech.

DAILEY, SEAN; Roselle Catholic HS; Roselle, NJ; (S); 4/195; Boys Clb Am; Math Clb; Pres Frsh Cls; Pres Soph Cls; JV Bsbl; Var Crs Cntry; Mgr(s); Trk; Hon Roll; Hugh O Brien Ldrshp Schlr 85; St Peters Schlr 85.

DALESANDRO, STEPHANIE; Pitman HS; Pitman, NJ; (S); 14/147; Church Yth Grp; Cmnty Wkr; Keywanettes; Teachers Aide; Crs Cntry; Trk; Hon Roll; Jr NHS.

DALESSANDRO, MICHAEL; Elmwood Park Memorial HS; Elmwood Pk, NJ; (Y); 27/163; Boy Scts; Off Frsh Cls; Off Soph Cls; Stu Cncl; Var Capt Bsbl; Var JV Ftbl; Sftbl; Bio.

DALESSIO, ARTHUR; Bloomfield SR HS; Bloomfield, NJ; (Y); 13/450; Computer Clb; Debate Tm; Key Clb; Math Clb; Math Tm; PAVAS; Science Clb; Varsity Clb; Yrbk Rptr; Yrbk Stf; Ltr Tennis 86; ST Sci Day Comptn 86; Gov Schl 86; Med.

DALESSIO, FRANCES; Mary Help Of Christians Acad; Paterson, NJ; (Y); Computer Clb; Math Clb; Quiz Bowl; Chorus; Drill Tm; Variety Show; Gym; Vllybl; Montclr ST Coll; Mrktng.

DALEY, JANELL; Paul VI HS; Bellmawr, NJ; (S); 11/546; Math Clb; Spanish Clb; Hon Roll; Spanish NHS.

DALLAHAN, TRACEY; Pope John XXIII HS; Sussex, NJ; (Y); 16/131; Church Yth Grp; Cmnty Wkr; Spanish Clb; Teachers Aide; Thesps; School Musical; Yrbk Stf; Var L Swmmng; High Hon Roll; Biology.

DALLAIRE, DEVIN; Trenton Central HS; Trenton, NJ; (Y); Computer Clb; Debate Tm; Pep Clb; Varsity Clb; Var Ftbl; Var Golf; Var Tennis; Var Wt Lftg; Var Wrstlng; Hon Roll; U Of MI; Econ.

DALLAL, NANCY L; Dwight Englewood HS; Wyckoff, NJ; (Y); Church Yth Grp; Debate Tm; Orch; Lit Mag; Var L Socr; Var L Sftbl; High Hon Roll; Mu Alp Tht; Ntl Merit SF; Columbia Coll; Ecnmcs.

DALLAPORTAS, PATTY; Manasquan HS; Belmar, NJ; (Y); 9/240; Band; Mrchg Band; Var Bsktbl; Socr; Var Sftbl; High Hon Roll; NHS; Bus.

DALLING, DOUGLAS SCOTT; Newton HS; Newton, NJ; (Y); 92/192; FFA; Band; JV Ftbl; Wt Lftg; JV Var Wrstlng; Nclr Pwr.

DALOIA, PATRICIA; Red Bank Regional HS; Shrewsbury, NJ; (Y); 54/250; Hosp Aide; Ski Clb; Concert Band; Jazz Band; Mrchg Band; School Play; Yrbk Ed-Chief; Var JV Sftbl; Hon Roll; Spanish NHS; Teamsters Local 11 Union Ed Fund 86; Band Parents Scholar 86; Rosa Weiss Scholar 86; Catholic U Amer; Nrsng.

DALRYMPLE, ANDREW; Belvidere HS; Washington, NJ; (Y); Am Leg Boys St; Debate Tm; ROTC; Ski Clb; Varsity Clb; Yrbk Stf; JV Var Bsbl; JV Im Bsktbl; Im Bowling; JV Var Ftbl; Embry-Riddle Aerntcl U; Avtn.

DALTON, ANN MARIE; Point Pleasant Borough HS; Pt Pleasant, NJ; (S); 3/180; Pep Clb; Band; Concert Band; Jazz Band; Mrchg Band; Stu Cncl; High Hon Roll; NHS; Girls ST 86; Girls Citizenshp Alt 86; Psych.

DALY, CHRISTOPHER D; West Milford Township HS; West Milford, NJ; (Y); 4/350; Ntl Merit SF.

DALY, LYNDA A; Monsignor Donovan HS; Toms River, NJ; (Y); Art Clb; Drama Clb; FBLA; Service Clb; SADD; Thesps; Stage Crew; Yrbk Stf; Hon Roll; Teen Arts Fest 85-86; FBLA Convntn Cherry Hill NJ 85; Arts Recog & Tlnt Srch Pro Sprg 86; Georgian Court Coll; Psych.

DAMIANO, ANTHONY; Manalapan HS; Englishtown, NJ; (Y); Church Yth Grp; Trs SADD; Band; L Trk; 2nd Hnrs At Chrstn Brthrs Acad 84; 3rd Pl At 8th Annl Untd Crbrl Plsy Intl Krte Trnmnt 85; Physcl Thrpy.

DAMICO, JAMES S; Passaic Valley Regional HS; West Paterson, NJ; (Y); 28/349; Am Leg Boys St; Art Clb; Chess Clb; Key Clb; Yrbk Sprt Ed; Var Bsbl; Var Ftbl; High Hon Roll; Jr NHS.

DAMICO, JOHN; Passaic Valley Regional HS; West Paterson, NJ; (Y); Art Clb; Key Clb; Bsbl; Hon Roll.

DANCKWERTH, KIM; Wayne Valley HS; Wayne, NJ; (Y); Church Yth Grp; Dance Clb; FBLA; GAA; Ski Clb; Var Capt Cheerleading; Gym; Powder Puff Ftbl; Hon Roll; Mktg.

DANDRIDGE, MARSHA; Weequachie HS; Irvington, NJ; (S); 19/353; Service Clb; Band; Concert Band; Mrchg Band; Rep Stu Cncl; Trk; Vllybl; Hon Roll; Jr NHS; NHS; Rutgers-New Brunsbwick; Accntng.

DANESE, JOHN E; Bidgefield Memorail HS; Ridgefield, NJ; (Y); Am Leg Boys St; Rep Jr Cls; Var L Bsbl; High Hon Roll; Hon Roll; Elec Engr.

DANETZ, JEFFREY; Manalapan HS; Manalapan, NJ; (Y); Aud/Vis; Dance Clb; Temple Yth Grp; Ftbl; Wt Lftg; Wrstlng; High Hon Roll; Hon Roll; NHS; Pre Vet.

DANIEL, GREGORY; Wardlaw-Hartridge HS; Cranford, NJ; (Y); 7/53; Computer Clb; Hosp Aide; SADD; Concert Band; Jazz Band; Stage Crew; Rep Stu Cncl; JV Tennis; High Hon Roll; NHS; Bus.

DANIELS, JENNIFER; Weequahic HS; Newark, NJ; (S); #11 In Class; Church Yth Grp; Dance Clb; FNA; Hosp Aide; Spanish Clb; Band; Church Choir; Color Guard; Concert Band; Mrchg Band; Superior Achvt & Excllnt Perfrmnc Engl 84; Pursuit Excllnce Secndry Ed 84; Nrsng.

DANIELS, KAREN; Weequahic HS; Newark, NJ; (Y); Boys Clb Am; Church Yth Grp; French Clb; Office Aide; Church Choir; Bsktbl; Vllybl; NHS; Prfct Atten Awd; Prfct Attndnc Awd 85-86; Hon Roll 86; Elec Engrng.

DANIELS, KIM; Atlantic City HS; Ventnor, NJ; (Y); Key Clb; Var Bsktbl; Var Sftbl; Mst Vlbl Sftbl 85-86; Mst Outstndng Bsktbl 86.

DANIELS, KIMBERLY; Passaic Valley HS; Little Falls, NJ; (S); 40/358; Church Yth Grp; Dance Clb; Drama Clb; French Clb; Concert Band; Flag Corp; Mrchg Band; School Musical; Var Vllybl; High Hon Roll; Am Legn Awd 83; N Jersey Band 83; Pub Rel.

DANIELS, LEON THOMAS; St Joseph Regional HS; Spring Valley, NY; (Y); 23/201; Camera Clb; Computer Clb; Off Frsh Cls; Off Soph Cls; Off Jr Cls; Off Sr Cls; Stu Cncl; Wrstlng; High Hon Roll; Hon Roll; Rcktbl 83 & 84; Du Quesne U; Bus.

DANIELS, MICHAEL G; Pope John HS; Newton, NJ; (Y); 3/150; Church Yth Grp; Cmnty Wkr; Computer Clb; Math Clb; Scholastic Bowl; Teachers Aide; Nwsp Bus Mgr; Nwsp Rptr; Nwsp Stf; Yrbk Sprt Ed; Pres Schltc Ftns Awd 86; Math Awd; Garden St Distinguished Schlr; Johns Hopkins; Engnrng.

DANIELS, SUZETTE; Weequahic HS; Newark, NJ; (Y); #27 In Class; Church Yth Grp; Exploring; Church Choir; Mrchg Band; Cit Awd; Prfct Atten Awd; Rutgers New Brunswick; Bus Admn.

DANIESL, MICHAEL; Pope John HS; Newton, NJ; (Y); Boy Scts; Church Yth Grp; Cmnty Wkr; Math Clb; Math Tm; Quiz Bowl; Scholastic Bowl; Science Clb; Nwsp Bus Mgr; Nwsp Stf; Pres Schlrshp 86; Pres Schltc & Ftnss Awd 86; John Hopkins; Engrg.

DANKO, ROBERT; Freehold Township; Freehold, NJ; (Y); FCA; U SC; Pre Med.

DANN, KELLY; Delran HS; Delran, NJ; (Y); Drama Clb; Chorus; School Musical; School Play; Stage Crew; Nwsp Rptr; Yrbk Rptr; Rep Frsh Cls; Trs Soph Cls; Rep Jr Cls; Sprt Wk Awds 83-86; Chrs Vcl 83-86; Bus Tchr.

DANNER, HILLARY BLYTHE; Dwight Morrow HS; Englewood, NJ; (Y); 11/235; Drama Clb; School Musical; Stage Crew; Nwsp Phtg; Nwsp Stf; Yrbk Phtg; Yrbk Stf; JV Var Vllybl; High Hon Roll; NHS; Theater.

DANNER, MATTHEW; Woodstown HS; Woodstown, NJ; (Y); Exploring; FFA; Bus Adm.

DANZ, CHRISTI; Glen Rock JR SR HS; Glen Rock, NJ; (Y); Art Clb; Studio Art.

DARATA, MILISSA; Ridgefield Park HS; Little Ferry, NJ; (Y); Church Yth Grp; JV Cheerleading; Var Capt Sftbl; Var Vllybl; Unsung Hero Awd-Softball 86; Nrsng.

DARBY, CHRISTOPHER; Teaneck HS; Teaneck, NJ; (Y); Boy Scts; Drama Clb; Exploring; Office Aide; OEA; Service Clb; SADD; School Play; Yrbk Stf; Rep Stu Cncl; Eagl Sct; Rutgers College; Bus Adm.

DARCHI, DEBBI; Central Regional HS; Bayville, NJ; (Y); 1/240; Math Clb; Chorus; Nwsp Stf; Yrbk Bus Mgr; Yrbk Ed-Chief; Tennis; French Hon Soc; High Hon Roll; NHS; St Schlr; Rutgers Schlr Pgm Rep 86; Outstndng Schltc Achvt 86; Actuarl Sci.

DARCY, ANGELA; St Pius X HS; Piscataway, NJ; (Y); #27 In Class; Art Clb; Computer Clb; Quiz Bowl; Teachers Aide; Church Choir; Variety Show; Rep Frsh Cls; JV Sftbl; Hon Roll; Vet Med.

DARCY, FRANK; Brick Town HS; Brick Town, NJ; (Y); 55/455; Boy Scts; Key Clb; Political Wkr; Varsity Clb; VP Frsh Cls; Trs Stu Cncl; Var Bsktbl; Var Ftbl; Var Wt Lftg; Dnfth Awd; Engrng.

DARDIA, MIKE; Bridgewater Raritan HS East; Bridgewater, NJ; (Y); Var Ftbl; Capt Var Lcrss; Hon Roll; NHS; Pres Schlr; J T Pocaro Mem Awd 86; Bridgewater-Raritan Rgnl PTO Schlrshp 86; Ithaca Coll; Cinema/Photo.

DAREN, HEATHER; Hamilton HS; Trenton, NJ; (Y); Am Leg Aux Girls St; Hosp Aide; VP Intnl Clb; Pres Key Clb; Radio Clb; Pres SADD; Madrigals; Lit Mag; Rep Stu Cncl; Hon Roll; Outstndng Achvt Frgn Lang Trnmnt 86; Spch Pathlgy.

DARLING, RONALD; Montville Township HS; Montville, NJ; (Y); Church Yth Grp; Computer Clb; FBLA; Key Clb; Spanish Clb; Im Trk; High Hon Roll; Hon Roll; Arch.

DARNOI, DENNIS; Christian Brothers Acad; Ocean Twp, NJ; (Y); 100/237; Var L Socr; Region Soccer Tm 85; Pre-Law.

DAROCHE, MARILENE; Queen Of Peace HS; Newark, NJ; (Y); 31/224; Berkeley Schl; Sec.

DASARO, ANDREA; Bloomfield SR HS; Bloomfield, NJ; (Y); 195/442; Drama Clb; Key Clb; Chorus; Color Guard; School Musical; School Play; Yrbk Stf; Mgr(s); JV Capt Socr; Capt Var Wrstlng; U Of FL; Communications.

DASHEFSKY, CRAIG; Monalapan HS; Englishtown, NJ; (Y); 8/410; VP Latin Clb; Bsbl; JV Bsktbl; NHS; Cum Laude Ntl Latin Exam 86; Lehigh U; Accntng.

DASSATTI, MICHELE; North Bergen HS; North Bergen, NJ; (Y); Chairperson For HOSA; 85-86; Fairleigh Dickason; Dntl Hygnst.

DASTI, SOFIA; Piscataway HS; Piscataway, NJ; (Y); French Clb; JV Trk; Hon Roll; NHS; Middlesex Cnty Arts H S Visual Arts 85-86; Bus Admn.

DATTA, S DEBLINA; Memorial HS; Cedar Grove, NJ; (S); 8/120; School Musical; Nwsp Ed-Chief; Nwsp Sprt Ed; Ed Yrbk Stf; Var Fld Hcky; JV Trk; High Hon Roll; VP NHS; Ntl Merit Ltr; NJ Dstngshd Schlr 85-86; Grmn Achvmnt Awd 83-84; Vlntr Wrk Cty Hrvst 82-86.

DATUS, RUTH; Orange HS; Orange, NJ; (Y); Art Clb; Computer Clb; Exploring; Teachers Aide; Rep Frsh Cls; Rep Soph Cls; Rep Jr Cls; Var Tennis; Hon Roll; Prfct Atten Awd; Crtfct Achvmnt Excllnc 86; Hlth Occptns Stu Am Crtfct 86; Rutgers U; Med Dctr.

DATZ, JAMES; Holy Spirit HS; Port Republic, NJ; (Y); 10/330; Am Leg Boys St; Computer Clb; Lit Mag; Var L Socr; NHS; St Schlr; Voice Dem Awd; Crw Tm 82-86; Art Shw 1st Pl Mxd Mdia Pen & Ink 84-86; U Of PA; Med Law.

DAUBERSPECK, RICHARD; Delsea Reg HS; Newfield, NJ; (Y); Am Leg Boys St; Church Yth Grp; JV Socr; NHS; Engrng.

DAUDELIN, DONNALEE; Belleville HS; Belleville, NJ; (Y); Cmnty Wkr; GAA; Girl Scts; Ski Clb; Varsity Clb; Acpl Chr; Chorus; Orch; Rep Frsh Cls; Rep Soph Cls; Sprts Hnr Rll Crss Cntry 85; JR Olympcs Mdl 84; Orchstra 83-86; Hist.

DAUKSHUS, MICHELLE; Ocean Township HS; Wanamassa, NJ; (Y); 154/356; Church Yth Grp; CAP; Ski Clb; Spanish Clb; Varsity Clb; Chorus; Church Choir; Mrchg Band; Twrlr; Mst Hon Merit Ptry Cntst 86; Spec Mntn Ptry Cntst 84; Glassboro Coll; Elem Tchr.

DAURA, DAMON; Pope John XXIII HS; Lk Hopatcong, NJ; (Y); Church Yth Grp; Pres Spanish Clb; Pres Stu Cncl; Var L Bsbl; Var L Ftbl; Cit Awd; DAR Awd; NHS; Lakeland St Bk Schlrshp 86; Gettysburg Coll.

DAVALA, AMY; Hamilton High School West; Trenton, NJ; (Y); 1/330; Church Yth Grp; Chorus; Church Choir; Madrigals; School Musical; Variety Show; Sec Sr Cls; Cit Awd; Kiwanis Awd; NHS; Trenton ST Coll; Psych.

DAVENPORT, JENNIFER; Hunterdon Central HS; Flemington, NJ; (Y); 152/560; Cmnty Wkr; Hosp Aide; Stat Lcrss; Stat Socr; Stat Wrstlng; Hon Roll; Acctg.

DAVENPORT, TED; Mount Olive HS; Flanders, NJ; (Y); JA; Ski Clb; Varsity Clb; Pres Sr Cls; Var Ice Hcky; Var Socr; Var Tennis; Wt Lftg; Mhlnbrg Coll.

DAVID, CHARMAIN; Mother Seton Regional HS; Rahway, NJ; (Y); 3/124; Hosp Aide; Math Tm; Quiz Bowl; Science Clb; Nwsp Stf; Sec Lit Mag; Pres Soph Cls; Pres Stu Cncl; Vllybl; NHS; Rutgers U Deans Smmr Schlr Prgrm 86; Prtcptd W/ Dstnctn Natl Sci Olympd Chmstry 86; Hghst Avg Frnch; Rutgers Schl Of Phrmcy; Phrmcy.

DAVIDS, PAUL; Riverdell HS; River Edge, NJ; (Y); 30/213; Am Leg Boys St; Exploring; Ski Clb; JV Ftbl; Var Trk; Im Vllybl; French Hon Soc; Hon Roll; NHS; Engrng.

DAVIDSON, CAROL ANN; Cinnaminson HS; Cinnaminson, NJ; (Y); 4/257; Am Leg Aux Girls St; Church Yth Grp; Cmnty Wkr; Hosp Aide; Spanish Clb; Teachers Aide; Off Soph Cls; Off Jr Cls; Stu Cncl; Fld Hcky; Ithaca Coll; Physcl.

DAVIDSON, GUY A; Pitman HS; Pitman, NJ; (Y); 48/141; Am Leg Boys St; Cmnty Wkr; Spanish Clb; Var L Bsbl; Var L Ftbl; Wt Lftg; Var L Wrstlng; Hon Roll; All Tri Cnty Awd Ftbl 84-86; Pitman Wrstlg Acad Awd Hghst GPA 85-86; All Tri-Cnty Clssc Awd Wrstlg 86; Phys Ther.

DAVIDSON, LISA; North Brunswick Twp HS; N Brunswick, NJ; (Y); 11/265; Cmnty Wkr; Hosp Aide; Key Clb; Model UN; SADD; Teachers Aide; Yrbk Ed-Chief; Yrbk Stf; Lit Mag; Rep Sr Cls; Eunice Davidson Awd High Achvt Humntjes Classics 86; Vassar Coll.

DAVIDSON, SHANNON; Toms River HS North; Toms River, NJ; (Y); 250/410; Hosp Aide; Ski Clb; Yrbk Stf; Var Swmmng; JV Trk; Hon Roll; Communications.

DAVIE, DOUGLAS; Howell HS; Howell, NJ; (Y); 50/385; JV Var Socr; Tennis; Hon Roll; NHS; Opt Clb Awd; Stu Adv Bd.

DAVIES, GUY; Shore Regional HS; Monmouth Bch, NJ; (Y); Computer Clb; French Clb; Science Clb; JV Socr; Var Wrstlng; High Hon Roll; U New South Wales; Elec Engrng.

DAVIES, JUDY; Bayley-Ellard HS; New Providence, NJ; (Y); Varsity Clb; Band; Chorus; JV Var Bsktbl; Im Powder Puff Ftbl; JV Var Socr; Var Sftbl; Ldrshp Comm 84; Med.

DAVINA, LAURA; Fair Lawn HS; Fair Lawn, NJ; (Y); 115/346; Varsity Clb; Yrbk Stf; Rep Frsh Cls; Rep Soph Cls; Pres Jr Cls; Pres Sr Cls; Rep Stu Cncl; Capt Bsktbl; Coach Actv; Capt Sftbl; Athltc Schlrshp/Setn Hall U 86; 1st Tm All-Lge NBIL Sftbl 86; 2nd Tm All-Lge NBIL Vllybll 85; Seton Hall U; Physcl Educ.

DAVIS, BAYLEY; Christian Brothers Acad; Shrewsbury, NJ; (Y); 75/212; Chorus; VP Stu Cncl; Im Ftbl; Im Wt Lftg; Law.

DAVIS, CAROL; West Morris Central HS; Long Valley, NJ; (Y); Church Yth Grp; Dance Clb; Band; Concert Band; Jazz Band; Mrchg Band; Music.

DAVIS, CHERYL; Cumberland Regional HS; Bridgeton, NJ; (Y); 18/315; Church Yth Grp; Chorus; High Hon Roll; Hon Roll; NHS; Mozart Piano Awd 86; Choral Music Dept Soloists Awd 86; Choral Music Dept Awd 86; U Of DE; Nrsng.

DAVIS, CHERYL L; Burl County Vo-Tech; Browns Mills, NJ; (S); 15/180; Church Yth Grp; VICA; Church Choir; Variety Show; JV Capt Bowling; Hon Roll; NHS.

DAVIS, COLLEEN; Toms River HS; Toms River, NJ; (Y); 34/585; Drama Clb; Math Tm; Concert Band; Mrchg Band; School Musical; School Play; Stage Crew; NHS; Aud/Vis; Math Clb; Acdmc All Amer 86; Compu Sci.

DAVIS, DAVID; Hamilton West HS; Yardville, NJ; (Y); 41/334; Church Yth Grp; Cmnty Wkr; SADD; Varsity Clb; Band; Concert Band; Mrchg Band; Orch; Symp Band; Bsktbl; Natl Urban Leag Acadmc Achvt Awd 86; Excllnc Thru Eductn Schlrshp 86; Twigs Foundtn Schlrshp 86; Rutgers U; Biochem.

DAVIS, DEBORAH; Manalapan HS; Manalapan, NJ; (Y); SADD; Temple Yth Grp; Stage Crew; Nwsp Rptr; Nwsp Stf; Lit Mag; Pblc Rltns.

DAVIS, ERIC; Highland Park HS; Highland Park, NJ; (Y); Latin Clb; Radio Clb; Capt Crs Cntry; Var Trk; Church Yth Grp; German Clb; SADD; Band; Concert Band; Mrchg Band; Natl Achvt Scholar Pgm Outstndgn Negro Stu 85; MVP Crs Cntry 84-85; Hampton U; Acctng.

DAVIS, ETHEL; Woodrow Wilson HS; Camden, NJ; (Y); Sec Church Yth Grp; Office Aide; Church Choir; Yrbk Stf; VP Jr Cls; Hon Roll; Trs NHS; Church Conformation 84; Elite Club 84-85; Elem Educ.

DAVIS, GLEN D; Pennsville Memorial HS; Pennsville, NJ; (Y); 20/222; VP JA; Jazz Band; Mrchg Band; Orch; School Musical; School Play; Stu Cncl; Tennis; Band; Concert Band; Outstndng Band Awd 86; Salem Cty All Star Tennis Tm 86; Louis Armstrong Jazz Awd 86; Rutgers U.

DAVIS, GREGG S; Sayreville War Memorial HS; Parlin, NJ; (Y); Am Leg Boys St; Varsity Clb; Acpl Chr; Chorus; Swing Chorus; Var Diving; Var Capt Socr; Var Trk; High Hon Roll; NHS; All ST Chorus 85 & 86; Middlesex Co All Acadmc Tm 86; Middlesex Co Arts HS 85; Navy; Pilot.

DAVIS, JEFF; Manalapan HS; Manalapan, NJ; (Y); VP Trs Church Yth Grp; Cmnty Wkr; JCL; Latin Clb; Stage Crew; Woodworking Awd 85; Hon Engl 83-84; Rcvd Slvr Crss 6 Yrs Acolyte 84; Bus Admin.

DAVIS, JENNIFER; Manasquan HS; Brielle, NJ; (Y); Church Yth Grp; Math Tm; Spanish Clb; Church Choir; Nwsp Rptr; Nwsp Stf; Yrbk Stf; Lit Mag; Rep Soph Cls; Rep Jr Cls; Brielle Wmns Slb Schlrshp; Brielle Chna & Sllrs Schlrshp; Dickinson Coll; Law.

DAVIS, JOSEPH; Millville SR HS; Millville, NJ; (Y); 153/650; Office Aide; SADD; Teachers Aide; Band; Concert Band; Drill Tm; Mrchg Band; Orch; Pep Band; School Musical; Atlantic CC; Cul Art.

DAVIS, LESLEY; Bridgewater Raritan H S East; Bridgewater, NJ; (Y); Ski Clb; Spanish Clb; Teachers Aide; Varsity Clb; School Musical; JV Var Fld Hcky; Mgr Lcrss; Mgr Wrstlng; Hon Roll; Princpls Cncl 84-86; PA ST; Elem Ed.

DAVIS, LOUISE; Hamilton H S West; Trenton, NJ; (Y); FBLA; Spanish Clb; Badmtn; Gym; Mgr(s); Score Keeper; Vllybl; Hon Roll; Comp Sci.

DAVIS, MARIANNA; Salem HS; Salem, NJ; (Y); Latin Clb; Library Aide; Chorus; Yrbk Stf; NHS; Frnds Of Anmls 84-87; Tchr.

DAVIS, MARK; Kingsway Regional HS; Swedesboro, NJ; (Y); Art Clb; Aud/Vis; Computer Clb; Lit Mag; JV Crs Cntry; Trk; Wrstlng; San Diego U; Cinmtgrphy.

DAVIS, MARK; Northern Highlands Regional HS; Upper Saddle Rvr, NJ; (Y); 38/250; AFS; Church Yth Grp; Capt Quiz Bowl; Jazz Band; Symp Band; Var Trk; High Hon Roll; NHS; Ntl Merit SF; USMA Invitatnl Acad Wrkshp 85; Polit Sci.

DAVIS, MICHAEL; West Windsor-Plainsboro HS; Plainsboro, NJ; (Y); 14/238; Church Yth Grp; Key Clb; Spanish Clb; JV Bsbl; Var Capt Ftbl; DAR Awd; High Hon Roll; Hon Roll; NHS; NEDT Awd; Garden St Distngshd Schlr; Kerr Schlrshp; Princeton U; Engrng.

DAVIS, MICHAEL SCOTT; Washington Township HS; Sewell, NJ; (Y); Church Yth Grp; German Clb; JV Var Socr; Messiah Coll; Bus.

DAVIS, MICHELLE; Deptford HS; Deptford, NJ; (Y); Church Yth Grp; Hon Roll; Nrsg.

DAVIS, NANCY; Malcolm X Shabazz HS; Newark, NJ; (Y); Computer Clb; Dance Clb; Pep Clb; Science Clb; Chorus; Color Guard; Variety Show; Nwsp Rptr; Yrbk Stf; Capt Cheerleading; Spelman; Dntstry.

DAVIS, PAUL; Spotswood HS; Milltown, NJ; (S); Boy Scts; Computer Clb; Debate Tm; Math Tm; Science Clb; Wrstlng; Hon Roll; Middlesex Coll Comp & Elctrncs Wrkshp 84; U S Airforce Smmr Sci Semnr 85; Rutgers U Schl Of Engrng; Elctr.

DAVIS, PETER; La Salle Military Acad; Randolph, NJ; (Y); 4/89; Capt ROTC; NHS; Pres Schlr; Gld Hnrs 82-86; New Schl For Socl Rsrch; Music.

DAVIS, SAAH; Woodrow Wilson HS; Camden, NJ; (Y); Capt Chess Clb; Exploring; Capt Socr; Trk; High Hon Roll; NHS; Rotary Awd; Archtctr.

DAVIS, SHANNON; Essex Catholic Girls HS; Irvington, NJ; (Y); Art Clb; Drama Clb; Girl Scts; Pep Clb; Political Wkr; Spanish Clb; Hon Roll; Im Badmtn; Im Cheerleading; Im Sftbl; Flght Attndnt.

DAVIS, TAMMY; Lower Cape May Regional HS; N Cape May, NJ; (Y); Pep Clb; Varsity Clb; Var Sftbl; Var Vllybl; Hist.

DAVIS, TERRI; Bishop George Ahr HS; E Brunswick, NJ; (S); 7/250; Church Yth Grp; Spanish Clb; Trk; High Hon Roll; NHS; Rutgers Schlr Awd 85; 6th Pl Ntl Essay Cntst 84; Rsrch Gentcs.

DAVIS, VALERIE; Colonia HS; Colonia, NJ; (Y); 56/287; Varsity Clb; Yrbk Bus Mgr; Yrbk Stf; JV Var Mgr(s); JV Var Socr; Hon Roll; St George Pharmacy 86; PA Coll Pharm & Sci; Pharmacy.

DAVISON, SUZEN; Hightstown HS; East Windsor, NJ; (Y); Drama Clb; Spanish Clb; Band; Concert Band; Mrchg Band; Stage Crew; Symp Band; Mgr(s); Mngmnt.

DAWKINS, RICHARD; Toms River North HS; Toms River, NJ; (Y); Church Yth Grp; Ski Clb; Var Bsbl; Bsktbl; Var Capt Ftbl; Var Wt Lftg; U S Lifesaving Assn 85-86; CYO ST Chmpnshp Bsktbl Awd 86; SR Little Lg Dist Champ Awd 84; Spts Med.

DAWSON, FRANCINE; Eastside HS; Paterson, NJ; (Y); #10 In Class; Church Yth Grp; Church Choir; Pres Concert Band; Yrbk Stf; VP NHS; Prfct Atten Awd; Al-ST Chorus 85; JR Regnls 83.

DAWSON, KELLY; Spotswood HS; Spotswood, NJ; (Y); 38/189; Am Leg Aux Girls St; Church Yth Grp; Dance Clb; Drama Clb; GAA; PAVAS; Ski Clb; Spanish Clb; School Musical; School Play; Rider Coll; Bus.

DAY JR, JAMES; Christian Bros Acad; Colts Neck, NJ; (Y); Yrbk Rptr; Yrbk Stf; Lit Mag; Im Ice Hcky; Im Tennis; Bus.

DAY, LAURA; Pt Pleasatn Boro HS; Pt Pleasant, NJ; (Y); Church Yth Grp; Varsity Clb; Trs Frsh Cls; L Var Fld Hcky; Var L Sftbl; Hon Roll; NHS; Prfct Atten Awd; Tght Comp Sci Pt Pleas Adlt Nght Schl 85-86; Rep Schl Brd Mtngs 82-83; Radford U; Comp Sci.

DAY, LAURA LYNNE; Bernards HS; Gladstone, NJ; (Y); 55/170; Church Yth Grp; Varsity Clb; Lit Mag; Var Capt Crs Cntry; Var Capt Trk; Bernardsvl Tchrs Mem Schlrshp 86-87; St Lukes Episcopal Chrch Schrlshp 86-87; U MD; Elmntry Ed.

DAY, SHARLENE; De Paul Diocesan HS; Wayne, NJ; (S); 1/178; Debate Tm; Math Tm; Science Clb; Speech Tm; School Play; Crs Cntry; Trk; High Hon Roll; NHS; Biochem.

DAZ, ORLANDO; Toms River HS South; S Toms River, NJ; (Y); 42/360; Comp Pgmmr.

DE ALESSANDRO, SUSAN; Wood-Ridge HS; Moonachie, NJ; (S); 1/91; Art Clb; Church Yth Grp; Trs Math Clb; Spanish Clb; Yrbk Stf; Var Capt Bsktbl; Var Capt Sftbl; Var Capt Vllybl; High Hon Roll; Hst NHS; Grdn ST Dstngshd Schlr 85-86; Rutgers Schlr 85.

DE ANGELIS, MICHAEL; Parsippany Hills HS; Parsippany, NJ; (Y); Im Ice Hcky; Cmmnctns.

DE ANGELO, DANA; Hunterdon Central HS; Whitehouse Stat, NJ; (Y); 41/548; Hosp Aide; Stat Ftbl; Hon Roll; NHS; Spanish NHS; Rep Jr Cls; Rep Sr Cls; Rep Stu Cncl; Rcgntn Pgm For Excllnc In Engl, Ftbll Stats & Chld Dvlpmnt 84-85; Med.

DE BISSCHOP, MICHAEL; Ocean Township HS; Loch Arbour, NJ; (Y); 5/333; Boy Scts; Chess Clb; Computer Clb; Nwsp Stf; Sprtn Schlr 2 Awds 84-85; Ryder Coll Lng Trnmnt Grp Rssn Skt 85-86; Russian.

DE BRUNO, ROSA; Mary Help Of Christians Acad; Mahwah, NJ; (S); 9/87; Computer Clb; JCL; Service Clb; Hon Roll; Italian, Thelgy & W Hstry Awds 84-85; Rutgers U; Phrmcy.

DE CAGNA, JEFFREY S; West Orange HS; West Orange, NJ; (Y); 16/168; Am Leg Boys St; Quiz Bowl; Yrbk Bus Mgr; Stu Cncl; Gov Hon Prg Awd; Hon Roll; Jr NHS; NHS; Spkr Of Hse NJ Mod Congress; Cls Soc Sci Prze Wnnr 86; Itln NHS Pres; Johns Hopkins U; Intl Rel.

DE CANDIA, ROBERT; William L Dickinson HS; Jersey City, NJ; (Y); Debate Tm; Q&S; Nwsp Rptr; Nwsp Stf; Lit Mag; Stu Cncl.

DE CARLO, TAMMY; Paramus HS; Paramus, NJ; (Y); Off Church Yth Grp; Drama Clb; German Clb; Ski Clb; Yrbk Sprt Ed; Yrbk Stf; Rep Frsh Cls; Stu Cncl; Socr; Rutgers U; Phrmcy.

DE CAROLIS, EMILIA; David Brearley HS; Kenilworth, NJ; (Y); 18/186; Key Clb; Sec Latin Clb; Hon Roll; Montclair ST Coll NJ; Chem.

DE CESARE, R; Blair Acad HS; Portland, PA; (Y); 5/240; Ski Clb; Pres Concert Band; Mrchg Band; Rep Jr Cls; JV Trk; High Hon Roll; Jr NHS; Lions Clb Ldrshp Seminar 86; Medicine.

DE CHIARA, MICHAEL; Belleville HS; Belleville, NJ; (Y); 2/393; Key Clb; Spanish Clb; Rep Jr Cls; Rep Sr Cls; Bsktbl; Sftbl; Wt Lftg; Bausch & Lomb Sci Awd; High Hon Roll; Hon Roll; Mth Awd; Van Dyke Sci Awd; Daniel O Callaghan Scholar; Stevens Inst Tech; Engr.

DE CHRISTOPHER, MARY; Egg Harbor Township HS; Mays Landing, NJ; (S); 7/266; Hosp Aide; Pres SADD; Pres VP Stu Cncl; Var Tennis; High Hon Roll; Jr NHS; NHS; Ntl Merit Ltr; Mst Outstndng Chem Stdnt 85; Chem Ed.

DE CICCO, AMELIA A; Holy Rosary Acad; Jersey City, NJ; (Y); 4/57; Church Yth Grp; French Clb; Math Tm; Chorus; Nwsp Rptr; Trs Stu Cncl; Capt Co-Capt Bsktbl; Hon Roll; VP NHS; Rotary Awd; Pres Acdmc Ftns Awd 86; Us Army Natl Schlr/Athl Awd 86; History Achvt Awd 86; Montclair ST Coll.

DE CICCO, CYNTHIA; Egg Harbor Township HS; Linwood, NJ; (S); 8/325; Drama Clb; Pres French Clb; Sec Key Clb; Model UN; School Musical; School Play; Nwsp Stf; VP Stu Cncl; Var Cheerleading; High Hon Roll; Fash Inst Tech; Fash Merch.

DE COSTANZA, NEIL; Hackettstown HS; Hackettstown, NJ; (Y); 20/200; Boy Scts; Church Yth Grp; Socr; Trk; Hon Roll; NHS; Pres Acad Ftns Awd 85-86; Hon Mntn Grdn ST Schlr Prgm 85-86; Albright Coll; Ortho Surgn.

DE COSTE, TINA; Middlesex HS; Middlesex, NJ; (Y); 9/170; Sec French Clb; VP Girl Scts; Pres Key Clb; Chorus; School Musical; Var L Crs Cntry; High Hon Roll; Sec NHS; Ski Clb; Delegate To Oper Enterprise 86.

DE COSTER, DAPHNE; Belvidere HS; Belvidere, NJ; (S); 5/120; Cmnty Wkr; Drama Clb; Thesps; Band; Church Choir; Concert Band; Drm Mjr(t); Madrigals; Mrchg Band; School Musical; Engl/Hstry Awds 83-85; Pdtrc Phy Thrpy.

DE DOLCE, DAWN MARIE; St Mary HS; Kearny, NJ; (Y); 2/44; FBLA; Yrbk Bus Mgr; Rep Frsh Cls; Rep Soph Cls; Var Cheerleading; Var Crs Cntry; Var Trk; High Hon Roll; NHS; Spanish NHS; Cchs Awf For Trck; Columbia U.

DE FILIPPIS, CHRIS; Columbia HS; Maplewood, NJ; (Y); Boy Scts; Church Yth Grp; Spanish Clb; Yrbk Stf; Var L Lcrss; Var L Socr; Var Capt Wrstlng; Hon Roll; 4 Yr 3 Sprt Cgr Bstrs Athltc Awd 86; U Of DE; Engrng.

DE FILIPPIS, EILEEN; Manchester Regional HS; Haledon, NJ; (S); GAA; Hosp Aide; Chorus; Flag Corp; Madrigals; Yrbk Stf; Powder Puff Ftbl; Score Keeper; Var Trk; French Hon Soc; Intl Foreign Lang Awd 86; Acad All Amer 86; Foreign Lang Hnr Soc 86; Intl Bus.

DE FILIPPIS, MARIA; Wood-Ridge HS; Wood-Ridge, NJ; (S); 14/91; Science Clb; Spanish Clb; Nwsp Stf; Yrbk Stf; Sec Stu Cncl; Var Chess Clb; JV Sftbl; Var Trk; High Hon Roll; NHS; Wm Ptrsn Coll; Nrs.

DE FRANCESCO, ANTHONY; De Paul Diocesan HS; Ringwood, NJ; (Y); 57/178; Bsbl; Socr; Hon Roll; Livingstgon Coll; Math.

DE FREESE, DAVID A; Rahway HS; Rahway, NJ; (Y); Am Leg Boys St; Jazz Band; Mrchg Band; Tennis; High Hon Roll; Hon Roll; Jr NHS; VP NHS; Ntl Merit SF; Spanish NHS; Acad Awds Scis, Soc Scis & Math 85; Cornell; Engrg.

DE GIGLIO, RITA; Carteret HS; Carteret, NJ; (Y); FBLA; Ski Clb; Band; Chorus; Color Guard; Drill Tm; Mrchg Band; Pep Band; Variety Show; Rep Frsh Cls.

DE GRAAF, AMY; Clifton HS; Clifton, NJ; (Y); Church Yth Grp; Yrbk Stf; Mgr Bsktbl; Mgr Lcrss; Mgr(s); Gov Hon Prg Awd; Spanish NHS; Art.

DE GROOT, ALLISON; Kittatinny Regional HS; Newton, NJ; (Y); Hosp Aide; Band; JV Var Crs Cntry; JV Trk; Hon Roll; Intl Rltns.

DE GUARDIOLA, SUSAN; Ridgewood HS; Ridgewood, NJ; (Y); 9/491; Capt Quiz Bowl; Color Guard; School Musical; School Play; High Hon Roll; Hon Roll; Ntl Merit Schol; Pres Schlr; Phlsphy.

DE GUTIS, MICHELE; Central Regional HS; Seaside Park, NJ; (Y); 13/230; Library Aide; Ski Clb; Varsity Clb; Nwsp Rptr; Var L Trk; Prfct Atten Awd; St Schlr; Pres Acad Fitness Awd 86; Acad Schlrshp Catawba Coll 86; Catawba Coll NC; Physical Edu.

DE HART, HEATHER; Toms River High School East; Toms River, NJ; (Y); Church Yth Grp; Dance Clb; Mrchg Band; Var Pom Pon; Weber ST Coll; Bus.

DE HART, MICHAEL; Salem HS; Salem, NJ; (Y); Am Leg Boys St; Boy Scts; Chess Clb; Ski Clb; Var JV Wrstlng; Hon Roll; NHS.

DE HART, RENEE; Mother Seton Regional HS; Irvington, NJ; (Y); 2/103; GAA; Hosp Aide; Math Tm; Science Clb; SADD; Yrbk Stf; Hon Roll.

DE JESUS, IRAIDA; Visual & Performing Arts HS; Jersey City, NJ; (Y); 7/312; Debate Tm; Sec Latin Clb; Scholastic Bowl; VP Science Clb; Rep Sr Cls; High Hon Roll; Hon Roll; Trs NHS; Prfct Atten Awd; Hnrbl Mntn/Frnds Of Music & Art Hudson Cnty 85; Graphic Art.

DE JONG, CHRISTINA; Morris Knolls HS; Denville, NJ; (Y); 69/367; Math Tm; Band; Jazz Band; Sec Mrchg Band; School Musical; High Hon Roll; Hon Roll; JP Sousa Awd; Richard Cooke Mem Scholar 86; U TX Acad Scholar 86; Pres Acad Fit Awd 86; U TX; Astrnmy.

DE LA CRUZ, ANNE; Bishop George Ahr HS; Edison, NJ; (Y); French Clb; Ski Clb; Spanish Clb; Rep Frsh Cls; Sec Stu Cncl; Vllybl; High Hon Roll; Hon Roll; Bus.

DE LA CRUZ, MICHAEL S; Perth Amboy HS; Perth Amboy, NJ; (Y); 75/460; French Clb; Key Clb; Rep Stu Cncl; Var Tennis; JV Trk; Hon Roll; Rutgers U.

DE LOACH, LEE; Pennsauken HS; Pennsauken, NJ; (Y); Church Yth Grp; Band; Chorus; Church Choir; Concert Band; Drm Mjr(t); Jazz Band; Mrchg Band; School Musical; School Play; All-S Jrsy All-Grp IV All-Cnfrnce Bsbl 85; Olympc Cnfrnce Bnd 85 & 86; All-S Jrsy Bnd & Chrs 86; Rutgers U.

DE LONG, LARA; Kittatinny Regional HS; Newton, NJ; (Y); 2/228; Math Tm; Science Clb; Concert Band; Mrchg Band; School Musical; Symp Band; Bausch & Lomb Sci Awd; High Hon Roll; NHS; St Schlr; Cornell; Bio.

DE LUCA, MICHAEL S; Wayne Hills HS; Wanye, NJ; (Y); 33/310; Am Leg Boys St; Boy Scts; Church Yth Grp; Hosp Aide; Concert Band; Mrchg Band; Bsbl; Capt Var Wrstlng; Hon Roll; NHS; West Point; Med.

DE LUCA, SCOTT C; Nutley HS; Nutley, NJ; (Y); 62/335; Am Leg Boys St; Key Clb; Spanish Clb; Stu Cncl; Var Bsktbl; Capt Var Ftbl; Im Wt Lftg; Hon Roll; Ftbl-1st Tm All Cnty 85-86; Ftbl-1st Tm All Lge-NNJIL 85-86; Ftbl-EEE-ESTRN Ftbl Mag 86; Pre Med.

DE MAIO, DOUGLAS; West Morris Mendham HS; Mendham, NJ; (Y); 8/311; Church Yth Grp; Service Clb; Ski Clb; Rep Jr Cls; Var Capt Lcrss; JV Socr; High Hon Roll; Hon Roll; NHS; Hnrbl Mntn All Conf 85 & 86; Gftd & Tlntd 84-86; AP Chem Tm 86; Service Acad; Aerontcl Engrng.

DE MAIO, STEPHEN J; West Essex Regional HS; Fairfield, NJ; (Y); 50/350; Am Leg Boys St; Ski Clb; Pres Sr Cls; Var Capt Ftbl; Trk; Wt Lftg; Hon Roll; All-Cnty 1st Tm Ftbl, 2nd Tm All-ST 86; Essex Co Ftbl Hall Of Fame 86; Dartmouth.

DE MAIRA, ELAINE; Red Bank Catholic HS; Colts Neck, NJ; (Y); Intnl Clb; SADD; Teachers Aide; Stage Crew; Nwsp Stf; Yrbk Stf; Hon Roll; Spanish NHS; Bus.

DE MARCO, CINDY; Sussex County Vo-Tech HS; Hopatcong, NJ; (S); 10/150; Variety Show; Sec Frsh Cls; JV Cheerleading; Gym; High Hon Roll; Sec NHS; Teen Arts Fest Guide 85; Govt Day Supr Homestead 83; Spectrum Danc Shw 85; County Coll Of Morris; Secy Sci.

DE MARCO, EDWARD; Monroe Twp HS; Jamesburg, NJ; (Y); Am Leg Boys St; Mathletes; Science Clb; Var L Bsktbl; Var L Golf; Var L Socr; Im Vllybl; Wt Lftg; High Hon Roll; Hon Roll; Dist Judge Am Leg Bys ST 86; Stockton ST Coll Physics Olympics 86; Grtr Mddlsx Stdnt Athl 85-86; Pre Med.

DE MARCO, MARC D; Hamilton High Schl North; Trenton, NJ; (Y); Am Leg Boys St; Exploring; Latin Clb; Madrigals; School Musical; School Play; Rep Frsh Cls; Rep Stu Cncl; JV Var Ftbl; Trk; Phila Coll Pharmacy; Chem.

DE MARRAIS, JENNIFER; Teaneck HS; Teaneck, NJ; (Y); Dance Clb; Drama Clb; Hosp Aide; SADD; School Musical; School Play; Yrbk Stf; Sftbl; Hon Roll; NHS.

DE MARTIN, DAVID; The Pennington Schl; Ewing, NJ; (Y); 2/85; Am Leg Boys St; Quiz Bowl; Spanish Clb; School Play; Sec Sr Cls; JV Bsktbl; Var Socr; JV Stu Cncl; High Hon Roll; Pres NHS; Headmstrs Awd-Bst Al-Arnd Stu; Boston Coll.

DE MATTEO, NICHOLAS; Highland Regional HS; Clementon, NJ; (S); 1/332; Chess Clb; Computer Clb; Trs Key Clb; Spanish Clb; Thesps; School Play; Stage Crew; VP Jr Cls; Off Stu Cncl; Cit Awd; 2nd Dgre Blck Blt Tang Soo Do Korean Karat 83; Music.

DE NARDO, HOLLIE; Middlesex HS; Middlesex, NJ; (Y); Ski Clb; Varsity Clb; Var Capt Cheerleading; Var Trk; Rep Frsh Cls; Prfct Atten Awd; Rep Soph Cls; Rep Jr Cls; Fshn Mrchndsng.

DE NETTIS, LISA; River Dell HS; River Edge, NJ; (Y); 77/214; Church Yth Grp; 4-H; Girl Scts; ROTC; Ski Clb; SADD; Chorus; Variety Show; Im Cheerleading; Var L Sftbl; Emerson Coll MA; Mass Cmnctns.

DE NOIA, DARIA; Toms River High School North; Toms River, NJ; (Y); Church Yth Grp; Cmnty Wkr; French Clb; German Clb; Teachers Aide; Orch; School Musical; Variety Show; Nwsp Bus Mgr; Nwsp Stf; Acdmc Lttr & Pin 4.0 GPA 84-86; Brd Ed Awd South Jersey Rgnl Orchstr 84-86; All ST Orchstr 86; Music.

DE NOIA, LAUREN; Bishop George Ahr HS; Colonia, NJ; (Y); French Clb; Pres SADD; Pres Off Stu Cncl; Var Sftbl; Bus.

DE NUNZIO, CHRIS; St Peters Preparatory Schl; Secaucus, NJ; (Y); Am Leg Boys St; Cmnty Wkr; Band; Concert Band; Jazz Band; Pep Band; School Musical; School Play; Variety Show; Bsbl; Villanova.

DE PAUL, THOMAS; Pont Pleasant Boro HS; Point Pleasant, NJ; (Y); 17/250; Math Clb; Math Tm; Nwsp Rptr; Hon Roll; Dept Awd Comp Sci; Math League Awd; Stevens Inst Tech; Comp Engr.

DE PERRO, BARBARA; Lenape Valley Regional HS; Stanhope, NJ; (Y); 11/255; Am Leg Aux Girls St; Key Clb; Sec Chorus; Madrigals; Rep Stu Cncl; JV Capt Fld Hcky; JV Trk; High Hon Roll; NHS; Spanish NHS; 1st Frgn Lang Fornsc Trnmnt, IFLA Awd Spnch, Frnch 86; Spnsh Tchr.

DE POALO, TRACEY; Woodbridge HS; Pt Reading, NJ; (Y); 17/400; Hosp Aide; Varsity Clb; Mgr(s); Capt Trk; Hon Roll; NHS; Math.

DE PROSPO, TINA; Eastern Regional HS; Gibbsboro, NJ; (Y); 53/341; Hon Roll; Gordon Phillips Beatuy Schl.

DE RITIS JR, JOHN M; Holy Spirit HS; Absecon, NJ; (Y); Church Yth Grp; Political Wkr; Var L Tennis; Hon Roll; Hon Ment 86; All Head Liner Boys Tnns Tm 86; Mrktng.

DE RYDER, EDWARD; Ridgefield Park HS; Little Ferry, NJ; (Y); 4/183; Am Leg Boys St; Debate Tm; Math Tm; Nwsp Stf; High Hon Roll; VP NHS; Ntl Merit Ltr; Rensselaer Medl-Math & Sci 86; Comp Sci.

DE SANE, DAVID; Christian Brothers Acad; Ocean, NJ; (Y); 72/230; Church Yth Grp; Dance Clb; Pep Clb; Ski Clb; Nwsp Stf; Im Socr; Im Sftbl; JV Trk; Hon Roll; Law.

DE SHONG, BRIAN; Christian Brothers Acad; Middletown, NJ; (Y); 67/222; Church Yth Grp; Band; Yrbk Stf; Im Bowling; Im Sftbl; Hon Roll; Trnty Coll Msc Pianoforte Merit 84; Trnty Coll Msc Thry Msc Hnrs 83; Med.

DE SIMONE, ELIZABETH; Northern Valley Regional HS; Closter, NJ; (Y); 30/250; Church Yth Grp; Hosp Aide; Spanish Clb; Capt Color Guard; Stage Crew; Yrbk Stf; High Hon Roll; Computer Clb; NHS; Unico Natl Tuitn Asstnc Grnt 86; Marjorie Dotson Awd 86; Rutgers Coll.

DE SIMONE, SIMONE; Lacey Township HS; Forked River, NJ; (Y); 23/270; Cmnty Wkr; Rep Soph Cls; Pres Jr Cls; Pres Sr Cls; Rep Stu Cncl; Capt Powder Puff Ftbl; Var Tennis; Hon Roll; NHS; 3rd Pl Miss Am Co-Ed Pagent Miss NJ 86; Accntng.

DE SOPO, JAMES A; Passaic Valley Regional HS; W Paterson, NJ; (Y); 28/310; Church Yth Grp; Key Clb; Concert Band; JV Var Bsbl; JV Var Ftbl; JV Var Wrstlng; High Hon Roll; Hon Roll; NHS; Passaic Vly Hnr Soc 85; Marion Spinler Mem Schlrshp 86; Intl Fed Of Lbr Unions Schlrshp 4 Yrs 86; Montclair ST Coll; Bio.

DE SPIRITO, STEVEN; Sayreville Ware Memorial HS; Parlin, NJ; (Y); 44/380; Trs Church Yth Grp; Spanish Clb; Varsity Clb; Band; Concert Band; School Musical; Var Tennis; Hon Roll; Prfct Atten Awd; Spanish NHS; Pres Acad Ftns Awd 85-86; Rutgers U; Elec Engrng.

DE STEFANO, CHRIS; Spotswood HS; Spotswood, NJ; (S); Yrbk Stf; Var L Socr; JV Sftbl; High Hon Roll; Hon Roll; NHS; MD.

DE VENEZIA, BRENDA E; Mountain Lakes HS; Mountain Lakes, NJ; (Y); Ski Clb; SADD; Band; Nwsp Sprt Ed; Yrbk Ed-Chief; Var L Fld Hcky; JV Capt Sftbl; JV Var Swmmng; NHS; Ntl Merit SF; Smith Bk Awd 85; 5 Yr Band Awd 86; 3 Sprt Awd 84-86; Humnties.

DE VINCENTIS, RICHARD; Toms River North HS; Toms River, NJ; (Y); 24/412; Stu Cncl; Crs Cntry; Trk; Hon Roll; NHS; Ntl Merit Ltr; US Air Force Acad Summr Sci Sem Cert 86; Rutgers Career & Engrng Day 86; Acad Awd Ltr 84, Pin 86; Bio.

DE VIRGILIO, MICHAEL; Henry P Becton Regional HS; Carlstadt, NJ; (Y); 40/150; JV Bsbl; JV Var Ftbl; Seton Hall U; Mrktng.

DE VITO, KATHLEEN; Westfield SR HS; Westfield, NJ; (Y); Art Clb; Church Yth Grp; Frsh Cls; Socr; Swmmng; Trk.

DE VORE, RODNEY L A; Eastside HS; Paterson, NJ; (Y); 57/600; Cmnty Wkr; Dance Clb; Library Aide; Drm Mjr(t); Mrchg Band; Nwsp Bus Mgr; Yrbk Rptr; Trs Jr Cls; Stu Cncl; Hon Roll; Trenton ST Coll; Crmnlgy.

DE VOSE, SHANNON; East Orange HS; E Orange, NJ; (Y); John Jay; Law.

DE WALD, EDWARD T; Piscataway HS; Piscataway, NJ; (Y); 47/519; Chrmn Am Leg Boys St; Varsity Clb; Stu Cncl; Capt Var Ftbl; Capt Var Trk; Capt Var Wrstlng; Hon Roll; NHS; Pres Schlr; All Cnty Wrstlng 85-86; ST Wrstlng Champs 85-86; Schlr Ath Mid ST Conf & Cnty 86; US Naval Acad; Officer.

DE WITT, AMY; Clifton HS; Clifton, NJ; (Y); Camera Clb; Cmnty Wkr; Ski Clb; Spanish Clb; Chorus; Yrbk Phtg; Yrbk Stf; Hon Roll; Library Aide; Twrlr; Comm.

DE WITTE, PAMELA; Clifton HS; Midland Pk, NJ; (Y); 93/600; Am Leg Aux Girls St; Sec German Clb; Chorus; Mrchg Band; Sec Soph Cls; Sec Jr Cls; Var Trk; Hon Roll; Girl Scts; Ski Clb; 1st Clss Awd Girl Scouts 83; Mustang Band Schlrshp 86; Rutgers U; Accntng.

DEANE, JENNIFER; Wildwood Catholic HS; Wildwood Crest, NJ; (Y); 10/83; Nwsp Rptr; Yrbk Stf; Pres Soph Cls; Tennis; Hon Roll; Rotary Awd; Spanish Clb; Nwsp Stf; Yrbk Rptr; Sftbl; NJ Schl Arts Pgm Glassboro ST Coll, Sci Fair 2nd Med/Hlth Cat 85; Temple U; Mus.

DEANE, KAREN; Highstown HS; E Windsor, NJ; (Y); 36/449; French Clb; Ski Clb; Drill Tm; Off Frsh Cls; Off Soph Cls; Off Jr Cls; Stu Cncl; Trk; High Hon Roll; NHS; Bus.

DEANE, LARISSA; Queen Of Peace HS; N Arlington, NJ; (Y); 109/257; SADD; Var Cheerleading; Var Pom Pon; Hon Roll; Varsty Ltr Chrldng 85; Fashion Merch.

DEANGELIS, LAUREN; Manalapan HS; Englishtown, NJ; (Y); 160/400; Aud/Vis; Church Yth Grp; FCA; Spanish Clb; School Play; Stage Crew; Yrbk Stf; Johnson & Whales RI; Fshn Mrch.

DEANGELO, DONNA; Paul VI Regional HS; Cedar Grove, NJ; (Y); 11/124; French Clb; NFL; Pep Clb; Nwsp Ed-Chief; JV Cheerleading; Pres French Hon Soc; High Hon Roll; Pres Z-Clb 85-86; Seton Hall U; Acctng.

DEBIAK, LISA; Mary Help Of Christians Acad; W Paterson, NJ; (S); 8/69; Church Yth Grp; Computer Clb; Drama Clb; Quiz Bowl; Church Choir; School Play; Yrbk Stf; VP Soph Cls; VP Jr Cls; Im Co-Capt Cheerleading; Miss Congeniality 85 Miss N J Teen Pgnt 85; Art.

DECANDIA, MARC; Rutherford HS; Rutherford, NJ; (Y); Ski Clb; School Play; High Hon Roll; Hon Roll; Cert Coast Guard Aux Course 84; Pre-Law.

DECICCO, FRANK; Toms River H S East; Toms River, NJ; (Y); 34/585; Cmnty Wkr; Intnl Clb; Math Tm; Spanish Clb; Var L Bsbl; Var L Bsktbl; High Hon Roll; Hon Roll; NHS; Acctg.

DECINQUE, JIM; St James HS; Salem, NJ; (Y); School Play; Yrbk Stf; VP Frsh Cls; Pres Stu Cncl; Ftbl; Tennis; Cit Awd; Bus.

DECKER, DEBRA; Highland Regional HS; Sicklerville, NJ; (S); 8/332; Computer Clb; Dance Clb; French Clb; Service Clb; Off Stu Cncl; Var Capt Cheerleading; Hon Roll; NHS; Rutgers; Bus Mgmnt.

DECKER, JOHN; Toms River HS South; Beachwood, NJ; (Y); 7/352; Chess Clb; Church Yth Grp; CAP; Math Tm; JV Trk; High Hon Roll; Hon Roll; Ntl Merit Ltr; Engrng.

DECKER, MICHELLE MARIE; Toms River High School South; Beachwood, NJ; (Y); 18/300; Sec Church Yth Grp; Drama Clb; Pres FBLA; Model UN; Orch; Fld Hcky; Sftbl; NHS; Pres Schlr; St Schlr; Glassboro ST Coll Alumni Scholarship 86-87; Glassboro ST Coll; Commnctns.

DECREE, YOLANDA; Weequahic HS; Newark, NJ; (Y); Sec Art Clb; Pres Church Yth Grp; Cmnty Wkr; Debate Tm; Girl Scts; Hosp Aide; Office Aide; Political Wkr; VP Church Choir; Sec Stu Cncl; Rutgers.

DECTER, BENJAMIN C; Montclair HS; Montclair, NJ; (Y); Am Leg Boys St; Teachers Aide; Yrbk Stf; Rep Frsh Cls; Pres Soph Cls; Rep Jr Cls; Stu Cncl; Var L Tennis; High Hon Roll; NCTE Awd; Msc Edctrs Assoc NJ Gld Cert 83; Citatn Generl Assmbly ST NJ Acdmcs 86; Essex Cnty Dblr Trnmnt Wnr.

DEEGAN, DANIELLE; Holy Cross HS; Pennsauken, NJ; (Y); 15/378; Aud/Vis; Ski Clb; Spanish Clb; High Hon Roll; Hon Roll; High Hnr Rll 82-85; Rider Coll; Poltcl Sci.

DEEGAN, MARY; Benedictine Acad; Hillside, NJ; (Y); French Clb; Latin Clb; Nwsp Rptr; Yrbk Ed-Chief; Bausch & Lomb Sci Awd; Hon Roll; NHS; Ntl Merit SF; Sal; Spanish NHS; Eng Coll Eng 86; Psychology 86; CSMC Outstndg Ldrshp 86; Pharm.

DEEGAN, PETER; Parsippany Hills HS; Parsippany, NJ; (Y); Church Yth Grp; Trs FBLA; Nwsp Stf; Yrbk Stf; 4th Acctng I, 7th Acctng II Cmptn/Nrthrn Rgn FBLA 85 & 86; Bus.

DEEMER, MICHELLE; Delaware Valley Reg HS; Milford, NJ; (Y); Church Yth Grp; Varsity Clb; Yrbk Stf; Rep Stu Cncl; Bsktbl; Cheerleading; Var Fld Hcky; Im Gym; Var Trk; Hon Roll.

DEENEY, MAUREEN; Overbrook Regional SR HS; Clementon, NJ; (Y); 9/276; Spanish Clb; Acpl Chr; Chorus; Crs Cntry; Trk; High Hon Roll; Hon Roll; NHS; Prfct Atten Awd; Rider Coll Alumni Schlrshp 86; Rider Coll Trustees Schlrshp 86; Garden ST Schlrshp 86; Rider Coll; Comm.

DEFALCO, PAUL; Keyport HS; Union Bch, NJ; (Y); Am Leg Boys St; Church Yth Grp; FCA; Yrbk Stf; Var L Civic Clb; Var L Trk; Var Vllybl; Var L Wt Lftg; Hon Roll; Dean JR Coll; Bus.

DEFRANCESCO, LISA; Phillipsburg Catholic HS; Phillipsburg, NJ; (Y); 23/78; Cmnty Wkr; Stage Crew; Yrbk Stf; Fld Hcky; Hon Roll; Andvr-Mrrs Schlrshp; Coll Of St Elizabeth.

DEGAETANO, ARTHUR; Don Bosco Prep; Ramsey, NJ; (Y); 10/285; Cmnty Wkr; Ski Clb; Varsity Clb; Rep Frsh Cls; Rep Soph Cls; Stu Cncl; Var Ftbl; Var L Tennis; High Hon Roll; Hon Roll; Tennis All League,Suburban All Cty 86; Bergen Cty Ldrshp Forum Comm 85-86.

DEGAN, MISSY; Phillipsburg HS; Phillipsburg, NJ; (Y); 88/302; GAA; Key Clb; Varsity Clb; Mrchg Band; Yrbk Stf; Stu Cncl; Var L Bsktbl; Var L Sftbl; Hon Roll; Le High Vly All Star Sftbl 86; Moravian Coll; Pre-Law.

DEGROFF, CYNTHIA; Voorhees HS; Oldwick, NJ; (Y); Drama Clb; Intnl Clb; Latin Clb; Varsity Clb; School Musical; Yrbk Bus Mgr; Lit Mag; Var Fld Hcky; Hon Roll; NHS; Dir Mscl Ply 85-86.

DEGUZMAN, MICHAEL; Bishop Eustace Prep Schl; Kirkwood, NJ; (Y); 10/180; Church Yth Grp; Drama Clb; Spanish Clb; Church Choir; School Play; Nwsp Stf; High Hon Roll; Spanish NHS; Dean Summer Schlrs Pgm Rtgrs U 86.

DEIGNAN, JOHANNA; St Rose HS; Farmingdale, NJ; (Y); 21/225; Art Clb; German Clb; Chorus; Nwsp Rptr; Nwsp Stf; Yrbk Stf; Lit Mag; Bsktbl; High Hon Roll; NHS; Fnlst WNET Chanell 13 Annual Stu Art Festvl 86; Merit Visual Arts 85; German Awd 82-84; GA Court Coll; Art.

DEJESUS, JOHN; Don Bosco Prep; Fairfield, NJ; (Y); Chrprctr.

DEJESUS, LISSETTE; Memorial HS; West New York, NJ; (Y); Church Yth Grp; French Clb.

DEJNEKA, MATTHEW; Hunterdon Central HS; Stockton, NJ; (Y); 9/550; Boy Scts; Concert Band; Jazz Band; Orch; JV L Socr; Var L Trk; Hon Roll; NHS; Ntl Merit Ltr; Vrsty Blc Awd Spng Trck 86.

DEL DUCA, GARY V; Governor Livingston Regional HS; Berkeley Hts, NJ; (Y); 82/194; Church Yth Grp; Cmnty Wkr; Ed Yrbk Stf; Rep Sr Cls; L Bsbl; L Ftbl; Hon Roll; Govern Livingston Schlr Athlt Awd 86; Burgdorff Realtors Awd Intgrty Srvc 86; Susquehanna U PA; Comp Sci.

DEL FAVERO, MADALYN; Clifton HS; Clifton, NJ; (Y); 1/687; Am Leg Aux Girls St; Key Clb; Spanish Clb; Band; Concert Band; Mrchg Band; School Musical; Symp Band; Bsktbl; Jr NHS; Bio.

DEL ROSSO, DONNA MARIA; Wood-Ridge HS; Wood-Ridge, NJ; (S); 6/91; Math Clb; Model UN; Nwsp Rptr; Yrbk Stf; Trs Sr Cls; Var Bsktbl; Var Sftbl; Var Capt Vllybl; Cit Awd; Pres NHS; Rutgers U; Lawyer.

DEL VALLE, NANCY; Eastside HS; Paterson, NJ; (Y); High Hon Roll; Hon Roll; Flight Destntn Svc Persnnl.

DEL VESCOVO, PATRICIA; Secaucus HS; Secaucus, NJ; (S); 2/160; Sec Math Clb; Band; Concert Band; Drm Mjr(t); Sec Jr Cls; Mgr(s); High Hon Roll; NHS; Mrchg Band; Sec Frsh Cls; Italian Hnr Soc 84-86; Outstndng Stu Italina 83-85; 1st & 2nd Pl Italian Poetry 83-85.

DELAINE, PATRICIA; Overbrook SR HS; Lindenwold, NJ; (Y); Capt Pep Clb; Spanish Clb; Chorus; Church Choir; Trk; Hon Roll; NHS; Prfct Atten Awd; Trenton ST Coll; Journlsm.

DELANEY, COLLEEN; South River HS; South Rive, NJ; (Y); 12/130; Cmnty Wkr; Debate Tm; Mrchg Band; Symp Band; L Crs Cntry; Var Mgr(s); Var Trk; Hon Roll; Jr NHS; NHS; Rutgers; Accntng.

DELARGEY, RENEE; Triton Regional HS; Somerdale, NJ; (Y); Rep Soph Cls; Rep Jr Cls; Rep Stu Cncl; Var Capt Socr; JV L Sftbl; High Hon Roll; Exec Comm 84-86; Socr Captn 84-85; Cert Socr Var Sftbl; Educ.

DELAROSA, MARIA; Hoboken HS; Hoboken, NJ; (Y); Spanish Clb; Yrbk Stf; Off Jr Cls; Hon Roll; Hon Mntn Sci Fair 86; Nrsng.

DELAURO, DARRYL; Middletown South HS; Leonardo, NJ; (Y); L Bsbl; High Hon Roll; Hon Roll; Hghst Achvt Acctng 86; Seton Hall U; Acctng.

DELCAMP, ROBERT; Overbrook SR HS; Clementon, NJ; (Y); ROTC; Socr; Rutgers; Printing Ind.

DELCORE, ANGELO; North Brunswick Township HS; N Brunswick, NJ; (Y); 3/250; Dance Clb; Intnl Clb; Key Clb; Mathletes; Var Socr; High Hon Roll; Hon Roll; NHS; Mth.

DELEON, MARY; St Marys HS; Sayreville, NJ; (Y); Library Aide; Spanish Clb; High Hon Roll; Hon Roll; Mommouth Coll; Med.

DELFINO, MARIE; Scotch Plains-Fanwood HS; Scotch Plains, NJ; (Y); Acpl Chr; Chorus; School Musical; Lit Mag; Hon Roll; Trs Drama Clb; Quiz Bowl; Spanish Clb; SADD; Spanish NHS; NJ All ST Choir 84 & 86; NJ Regn Choir; Music.

DELGADO, MISAEL; Memorial HS; Guttenberg, NJ; (Y); FBLA; Off Jr Cls; Bowling; Spanish NHS; Rl Estate.

DELLA BADIA, RENEE; Piscataway HS; Piscataway, NJ; (Y); Varsity Clb; Rep Jr Cls; Var Fld Hcky; Var Capt Swmmng; JV Trk; All Cnty Swd Tm 85-86; Govt Alive Stdnts 86; Law.

DELLA RATTA, ANTHONY D; Manalapan HS; Englishtown, NJ; (Y); Science Clb; Band; Variety Show; High Hon Roll; NHS; Ntl Merit Ltr; Soc Studs Cert Hnr 86; Adv Alg & Trig Cert Hnr 86; NJ Sci Lg Physcs Cert 86; Engrng.

DELLANNO, ANTHONY; North Warren Reg HS; Blairstown, NJ; (Y); 15/145; Var Capt Bsbl; JV L Bsktbl; JV L Socr; Hon Roll; Math.

DELLAPI, DONNA; West Essex Regional HS; Fairfield, NJ; (Y); 23/350; Key Clb; Nwsp Ed-Chief; Yrbk Rptr; Lit Mag; JV Cheerleading; Var Trk; High Hon Roll; Hon Roll; NHS; Amercn Assn U Wmn Schlrshp 86; Stu Voic Schlrshp 86; Rutgers Coll; Bus.

DELLARATTA, KAREN; St James HS; Gibbstown, NJ; (Y); 17/78; Yrbk Stf; Trs Soph Cls; VP Stu Cncl; Var Capt Cheerleading; Hon Roll; Med Sci.

DELLE, ANDREJS M; Arthur L Johnson Regional HS; Clark, NJ; (Y); Am Leg Boys St; Chorus; Church Choir; Var L Ftbl; Var L Lcrss; Var L Trk; Gov Hon Prg Awd; Hon Roll; Pres Phys Fit Awd 84 & 85; GATE 85 & 86; Engrng.

DELORENZO, CHRISTINA; West Essex Regional HS; Fairfield, NJ; (Y); 17/385; Cmnty Wkr; Library Aide; Math Clb; Math Tm; Office Aide; Chorus; Rep Frsh Cls; Soph Cls; Stu Cncl; Var Gym; Scholar George Washington U Gym; George Washington U; Comm.

DELORENZO, JOSEPH; Oratory Prep; Morris Plns, NJ; (Y); 12/70; Church Yth Grp; JV Bsktbl; Var Capt Socr; Vllybl; Wrstlng.

DELOUISE, ELIZABETH; Monalapan HS; Englishtown, NJ; (Y); 51/431; Drama Clb; PAVAS; VP Thesps; Chorus; Madrigals; School Musical; Swing Chorus; Variety Show; Lit Mag; NHS; Thtr.

DELTUVIA, ELLEN; Monsignor Donovan HS; Jackson, NJ; (Y); Church Yth Grp; Drama Clb; Math Tm; SADD; Thesps; Chorus; Church Choir; Stage Crew; High Hon Roll; NHS.

DELUCA, HELENE; East Brunswick HS; Somerset, NJ; (Y); VP Art Clb; SADD; Trs Frsh Cls; Trs Soph Cls; Off Jr Cls; Stu Cncl; JV Fld Hcky; Var Swmmng; High Hon Roll; Hon Roll; Stu Liasn Cftra Cncrns 84-85.

DELUCA, JOHN; Morris Catholic HS; Denville, NJ; (Y); 25/150; Trs French Clb; Ski Clb; Varsity Clb; Var Socr; High Hon Roll; JV Trk; JV Wrstlng; Engl III Hnrs 85-86; Natl Lang Arts Olympd 83-84.

DELUCA, PAUL; Marist HS; Bayonne, NJ; (Y); 55/104; Key Clb; Spanish Clb; Stage Crew; Rep Soph Cls; Rep Jr Cls; VP Sr Cls; VP Stu Cncl; Var Tennis.

DEMARCO, LISA; Chatham Township HS; Chatham, NJ; (Y); Cmnty Wkr; GAA; Girl Scts; Key Clb; Pep Clb; Teachers Aide; Concert Band; Yrbk Stf; Im Stat Socr; Var JV Sftbl; Early Chldhd Ed.

DEMAREST, JACQUELINE; Scotch Plains-Fanwood HS; Scotch Plains, NJ; (Y); Pres Dance Clb; Drama Clb; Political Wkr; Pres Art Clb; Chess Clb; French Clb; Girl Scts; Key Clb; Model UN; PAVAS; T Rhytme Gym Champ 85; Schlrshp Rutgers 86; Dance,Ballet,Jazz,Awd 84-86; Psyclgst.

DEMARIA, LAURA; Holy Family Acad; Bayonne, NJ; (Y); 14/140; Church Yth Grp; Dance Clb; Girl Scts; Hosp Aide; Pep Clb; Spanish Clb; Varsity Clb; School Musical; School Play; Variety Show; Nrsng.

DEMAURO, KRISTINE; Vineland HS; Vineland, NJ; (Y); 60/675; Office Aide; L Drill Tm; Stage Crew; Lit Mag; VP Stu Cncl; Var Trk; Hon Roll; NHS; Italian Hnr Soc 86; Phys Thrpy.

DEMBOWSKI, GREGORY; St Peters HS; Milltown, NJ; (Y); Am Leg Boys St; School Play; Stage Crew; Yrbk Stf; Trs Jr Cls; JV Bsktbl; Var Ftbl; Var Trk; Hon Roll; NHS; Rutgers Coll.

DEMCHAK, DANIELLE LEE; St Marys Hall-Doane Acad; Florence, NJ; (Y); Cmnty Wkr; Girl Scts; Yrbk Stf; Sec Jr Cls.

DEMEDICI, LOUIS; Southern Regional HS; Manahawkin, NJ; (Y); 74/400; Aud/Vis; Lit Mag; JV Socr; High Hon Roll; Hon Roll; NHS; MVP Soccer 85-86; RIT; Graphic Comm.

DEMETRIADES, ELENI; Northern Valley Regional HS; Old Tappan, NJ; (Y); 90/311; AFS; Church Yth Grp; Band; Mrchg Band; Yrbk Sprt Ed; Var Capt Crs Cntry; JV Fld Hcky; Var Capt Trk; Hon Roll; NHS; All-Lg All-Cnty Hnrs Trck, Wntr Trck & X-Cntry 84-86; SUNY Stonybrook; Sprts Med.

DEMING, SUSAN; Manalapan HS; Manalapan, NJ; (Y); 46/431; VP Church Choir; Pres Madrigals; Swing Chorus; Rep Frsh Cls; Var Cheerleading; Gov Hon Prg Awd; High Hon Roll; All Shore & All ST Chorus 84-86; SF Miss NJ Teen Pag 85; USFSA Comptv Figure Sktr 79-87; Mth.

DEMM, CAROLYN; Morris Catholic HS; Morris Plains, NJ; (Y); 23/155; Varsity Clb; Rep Jr Cls; Stat Bsbl; Var Capt Bsktbl; Powder Puff Ftbl; Score Keeper; Var L Sftbl; Tennis; Var L Vllybl; Hon Roll; Amer Athlete Awd 85; Handy & Harman Schlrshp 86; U Of NC; Psychlgy.

DEMMA, ANDREW; Chatham Township HS; Chatham, NJ; (Y); 34/138; Church Yth Grp; Model UN; Concert Band; Jazz Band; Pep Band; Var Crs Cntry; Var Trk; Hon Roll; Flght Naval Offcr.

DEMPSEY, JAMES; Rutgers Preparatory Schl; Milltown, NJ; (Y); 6/66; Boy Scts; Drama Clb; Math Tm; Q&S; Chorus; Ed Lit Mag; Rep Stu Cncl; JV Socr; High Hon Roll; Aud/Vis; Army ROTC Schrlshp; Cum Laude Soc; WFCW Ntl & Lcl Union Schlrshp; Acdmc Team; U Of Pennsylvania.

DENCH, WENDY; Indian Hills HS; Oakland, NJ; (Y); 77/273; Dance Clb; Ntl Merit Ltr; Drew U.

DENITTO, JIM; Toms River North HS; Toms River, NJ; (Y); Church Yth Grp; Computer Clb; Ski Clb; Band; School Musical; JV Bsbl; Var JV Ftbl; Im Golf; Im Vllybl; Hon Roll; York Coll; Computers.

DENNIS, THOMAS; Oakcrest HS; Hammonton, NJ; (Y); 30/260; Dance Clb; Drama Clb; SADD; VP VICA; Pres Band; Pres Concert Band; Pres Mrchg Band; School Play; JV Crs Cntry; JV Wrstlng; NJ AIASA Publc Spkng 84; Vars Schlr 84-85; Rutgers U; Chld Psychol.

DENNIS, TRACY; Washington Township HS; Turnersville, NJ; (Y); Church Yth Grp; Office Aide; Spanish Clb; Yrbk Stf; Widener U; Accntng.

DENNO, LORI; Point Pleasant Boro HS; Pt Pleasant, NJ; (Y); 2/265; Rep Keywanettes; Pep Clb; Varsity Clb; Band; Stu Cncl; Cheerleading; Mgr(s); Capt Powder Puff Ftbl; Cit Awd; DAR Awd; Spnsh/Math Awds 85-86; Grls Ctznshp Inst 85; Rtgrs Coll; Bio.

DENNY, ADRIENNE; East Brunswick HS; E Brunswick, NJ; (Y); 85/676; Church Yth Grp; Dance Clb; Drama Clb; Girl Scts; Key Clb; Pep Clb; Chorus; Church Choir; Color Guard; NHS; PTSA Scholar 86; Alph Adelta Kappa Scholar Fut Tchrs 86; Boston U; Biol.

DENNY, KATHLEEN A; Lakeland Regional HS; Ringwood, NJ; (Y); 21/303; Art Clb; High Hon Roll; Hon Roll; NHS; WNET-CHNNL 13 Art Wrk Going To France 86; 3rd N Jersey Crftsmns Fair 85; 3rd Rngwd Mnr Assn Arts 85; Rutgers Coll; Art.

DENT, JACQUELINE; Trenton Central HS; Trenton, NJ; (Y); Church Yth Grp; Chorus; Church Choir; Rep Jr Cls; Pres Sr Cls; Var Bsktbl; Cit Awd; Hon Roll; Prfct Atten Awd; Val.

DENTE, ROBERT; Paramus Catholic Boys; Oakland, NJ; (Y); Boy Scts; Church Yth Grp; School Play; Nwsp Rptr; Eagl Sct 86; Tutrng Pgm 86; Ad Altare Dei Relgs Awd 84; Manhattan Coll; Engrng.

DENTLEY, DEBORAH; St Patrick HS; Elizabeth, NJ; (S); Dance Clb; Drama Clb; Science Clb; Ski Clb; Spanish Clb; Chorus; Stage Crew; Nwsp Rptr; Nwsp Stf; Off Frsh Cls; Fresh Svc Awd 84; Bio.

DENYSE, DAWN; Lakeland Regional HS; Ringwood, NJ; (Y); AFS; Church Yth Grp; Ski Clb; JV Socr.

DENZEL, STACEY; Middletown High Sch South; Leonardo, NJ; (S); 25/246; Chorus; Drm Mjr(t); Mrchg Band; School Musical; Symp Band; Cheerleading; High Hon Roll; Hon Roll; NHS; PA ST U; Ind Psych.

DEO, GREGORY; Seton Hall Prep; Hillside, NJ; (Y); Boy Scts; Church Yth Grp; FBLA; Key Clb; JV Wrstlng; Hon Roll; Camp Fatima Vlntr For Retarded Chldrn; Montclair ST Coll; Bus.

DEPALMA, JANET; Paul VI HS; Waterford, NJ; (Y); 226/544; Drexel; Bus Adm.

DEPALMA, JOHN C; Mt Olive HS; Budd Lake, NJ; (Y); Pres Church Yth Grp; Dance Clb; Math Clb; Ski Clb; Yrbk Stf; Capt Var Crs Cntry; Var Trk; High Hon Roll; Hon Roll; NHS; U Of CO-BOULDER; Comp Sci.

DEPPENSCHMIDT, ERIKA; Glassboro HS; Glassboro, NJ; (Y); Sec Pres Church Yth Grp; Church Choir; Orch; High Hon Roll; Hon Roll; NHS; Pre-Med.

DERAC, FLORINE; Lincoln HS; Jersey City, NJ; (S); JA; Key Clb; Yrbk Stf; Gov Hon Prg Awd; Hon Roll; Jr NHS; NHS; Acctg.

DERESH, JENNIFER; Manalapan HS; Manalapan, NJ; (Y); 65/431; SADD; VP Band; Capt Color Guard; Mrchg Band; Mgr Trk.

DEROSE, PETER; Vineland HS; Vineland, NJ; (Y); Drama Clb; English Clb; Key Clb; Library Aide; PAVAS; Ski Clb; Chorus; School Musical; Nwsp Stf; 4-H Awd; Jaycee Prfrmng Arts Awd Drama 85; Princeton U; Drama.

DERR, CHRISTOPHER M; Highland Regional HS; Blackwood, NJ; (Y); 14/300; Am Leg Boys St; Aud/Vis; Chess Clb; Computer Clb; Latin Clb; Science Clb; Im Bowling; Var Mgr(s); JV Socr; Hon Roll; Drexel U; Electrnc Engrng.

DERRICK, ROSS; Mendham HS; Chester, NJ; (Y); Church Yth Grp; Cmnty Wkr; Ski Clb; JV Wrstlng; Hon Roll; Im Bsbl; Im Bsktbl.

DESAI, NIRAJ S; Glen Ridge HS; Glen Ridge, NJ; (Y); 1/113; Trs AFS; Cmnty Wkr; Pres Model UN; Political Wkr; Nwsp Ed-Chief; VP Soph Cls; Ntl Merit SF; French Clb; Lit Mag; High Hon Roll; Rutgers Schlr 85; Yale Bk Awd 85.

DESANTIS, GINA; Emerson HS; Union City, NJ; (Y); Latin Clb; Drill Tm; Rep Frsh Cls; Rep Soph Cls; Rep Stu Cncl; Hon Roll; JC Awd; Wnr Hudson Cnty Teen Tlnt Comptn 85; Natl Assoc Dnc & Affltd Artst Inc Awd 83-85; Amer Hrt Assoc Awd; Rutgers U.

DESANTIS, JOLYN; Rancocas Valley Rgnl HS; Mt Holly, NJ; (Y); 22/307; Scholastic Bowl; Spanish Clb; Yrbk Stf; JV Fld Hcky; Var Trk; High Hon Roll; Hon Roll; Bus.

DESHEFY, LISA; Lakewood HS; Lakewood, NJ; (Y); 120/300; Church Yth Grp; English Clb; French Clb; Key Clb; Spanish Clb; Tennis; Bus.

DESHEPLO, CARMEN; Christian Brothers Acad; Longbranch, NJ; (Y); Cmnty Wkr; Hosp Aide; Letterman Clb; Radio Clb; Science Clb; Service Clb; Varsity Clb; Yrbk Stf; Rep Jr Cls; Var L Bsbl; Engrng.

DESHPANDE, BHALENDU; Columbia HS; S Orange, NJ; (Y); Chess Clb; Science Clb; Spanish NHS; Engrng.

DESILVIO, MICHELLE; Paul VI HS; Atco, NJ; (Y); 132/470; Am Leg Aux Girls St; Drama Clb; 4-H; Math Clb; SADD; Chorus; Church Choir; Mrchg Band; School Musical; School Play; Glassboro ST Coll; Pre-Law.

DESMND, KELLEY; St John Vianney HS; Old Bridge, NJ; (Y); 79/253; Hon Roll.

DESMOND, JULIE; Sparta HS; Sparta, NJ; (Y); 38/210; Am Leg Aux Girls St; Church Yth Grp; Key Clb; Stu Cncl; Capt Bsktbl; Capt Crs Cntry; Capt Trk; High Hon Roll; Hon Roll; Pres Schlr; Coaches Awd Bsktbll 84-85; Bst Defensive Plyr 86; Schlrshp Athlete 86; Army Reserve Schlrshp 86; West Point Military; Frgn Rltns.

DESMOND, MARY ELLEN; St John Vianney HS; Manalapan, NJ; (Y); 35/283; Cmnty Wkr; Dance Clb; Exploring; Hosp Aide; Service Clb; Variety Show; Nwsp Rptr; Hon Roll; Gym; Swmmng; US Cngrssnl Slvr Mdl 85; Sen Bill Bradleys Yng Ctznshp Awd 86; Gold & White Awd 84-85; Sci.

DESOPO, CARMINE; Willingboro HS; Willingboro, NJ; (Y); #17 In Class; Am Leg Boys St; Key Clb; Capt Bsbl; Capt Socr; Hon Roll; Lion Awd; Rutgers Coll; Hstry.

DESORT, JULIE; North Bergen HS; Guttenberg, NJ; (Y); 101/400; Am Leg Aux Girls St; Cmnty Wkr; Rep Frsh Cls; Rep Soph Cls; Rep Jr Cls; Var Sftbl; Var Trk; Merit Soc 85-86; 1st All Tm All-Cnty 55 Mtr Dash & High Hurdles 85-86; Busnss.

DESSICINO, ANDREA; The Pilgrim Acad; Mays Landing, NJ; (Y); Church Yth Grp; Pep Clb; Capt Cheerleading; High Hon Roll.

DESTEFANO, GEORGIANNA; Clifton HS; Clifton, NJ; (Y); 232/637; Key Clb; Office Aide; Sftbl; Jr NHS; Prfct Atten Awd; Montclair ST Coll; Psych.

DESTITO, ROSALINA; Holy Family Acad; Bayonne, NJ; (Y); 9/130; Bowling; Vllybl; High Hon Roll; Hon Roll; Acad All Amer 84; Biochem.

DETIZIO, CHRISTINE; Chatham Township HS; Chatham Twp, NJ; (Y); 50/136; Church Yth Grp; Key Clb; Pep Clb; Varsity Clb; Stu Cncl; JV Cheerleading; JV Fld Hcky; JV Lcrss; Hon Roll; Prfct Atten Awd; Finance.

DETRICK, LAURA; Oakcrest HS; Mays Landing, NJ; (Y); 5/255; Math Clb; Yrbk Ed-Chief; Yrbk Sprt Ed; Hst Soph Cls; Var Capt Tennis; Hon Roll; NHS; Computer Clb; SADD; Rep Frsh Cls; Vrsty Schlr 84-86; Presdntl Physcl Ftns Awd 85-86; Rtry Yth Ldrshp Awds Cnfrnc 86; Math.

DEUBEL, DONNA LYNN; St Pius X Regional HS; Spotswood, NJ; (Y); 15/123; 4-H; Spanish Clb; Varsity Clb; Color Guard; Lit Mag; Trk; High Hon Roll; Hon Roll; Ntl Merit Ltr; U Of TN; Hmn Frnscics Pthlgy.

DEUSCHLE, KEVIN P; Columbia HS; South Orange, NJ; (Y); 5/541; Am Leg Boys St; Church Yth Grp; German Clb; Science Clb; VP Stu Cncl; JV Socr; JV Trk; Ntl Merit Ltr; Prfct Atten Awd; Citizenship Awd 84; Stevben German Lang Awd 86.

DEUTSCH, EDWARD; Paramos HS; Paramus, NJ; (Y); Capt Debate Tm; Hosp Aide; NFL; Lit Mag; Pres Stu Cncl; Var L Bsbl; French Hon Soc; NHS; Cmnty Wkr; French Clb; World Affairs Sem 86; Ntl Conf Christians Jews Yth Conf 85; Hist.

DEUTSCH, JILL; Delran HS; Delran, NJ; (Y); 20/182; JV L Bsktbl; Var L Socr; Var L Sftbl; Hon Roll; NHS.

DEUTSCH, JONATHAN; Hunterdon Central HS; Ringoes, NJ; (Y); Chess Clb; Computer Clb; Radio Clb; Teachers Aide; Mrchg Band; Orch; School Musical; Variety Show; Im Vllybl; Comptrs.

DEVARIA, LAURIE; Washington Twp HS; Turnersville, NJ; (Y); Exploring; Spanish Clb; Bsktbl; JV Var Fld Hcky; JV Sftbl; Im Wt Lftg; Hon Roll; Ntl Merit SF; Bucknell U; Bus Admin.

DEVINCENS, DOUG; Toms River H S East; Toms River, NJ; (Y); Intnl Clb; SADD; Rep Frsh Cls; Rep Soph Cls; Rep Jr Cls; Rep Sr Cls; Pres Trs Stu Cncl; Var Capt Swmmng; High Hon Roll; NHS.

DEVINE, KERRY; Delran HS; Delran, NJ; (Y); Pres French Clb; Spanish Clb; Yrbk Stf; Var Stat Bsbl; Var Stat Bsktbl; JV Bowling; Var Fld Hcky; Bsktbl; Intl Stds.

DEVINE, MARGARET ANNE; West Milford HS; W Milford, NJ; (S); French Clb; Varsity Clb; Concert Band; Mrchg Band; Nwsp Rptr; Nwsp Stf; Rep Stu Cncl; Fld Hcky; Band; Ftrs Edtr Nwspapr; Fencng; Prom Cmmtte; Jrnlsm.

DEVINE, MARJORIE; Holy Cross HS; Mount Laurel, NJ; (Y); Hosp Aide; Sec Soph Cls; Rep Jr Cls; Sec Stu Cncl; Var Capt Crs Cntry; Var Capt Trk; High Hon Roll; Hon Roll; NHS; U Of DE; Phy Thrpy.

DEVINE, MELODY; Hackettstown HS; Hackettstown, NJ; (Y); 47/211; 4-H; Hosp Aide; Band; Concert Band; Jazz Band; Mrchg Band; School Play; JV Bsktbl; 4-H Awd; Hon Roll; Alt Girls ST Citznshp At Rutgers 85; $500 Home Ec Schlrshp Warren Cnty 4-H 86; $200 Band Schlrshp 86; U Of MN; Clthng/Txtls.

DEVINE, NORA R; St Joseph Of The Palisades HS; Hoboken, NJ; (S); 2/130; Spanish Clb; Stage Crew; Variety Show; Lit Mag; High Hon Roll; Spanish NHS; Acdmc All Amer 84; Tchr.

DEVIRGILIO, PATTI; Parsippany Hills HS; Morris Plains, NJ; (Y); Dance Clb; FBLA; Chorus; Rep Frsh Cls; Rep Soph Cls; Rep Jr Cls; Rep Sr Cls; Powder Puff Ftbl; Hon Roll; FBLA Awd For Cmptn 8th Pl 86.

DEVITT, KRISTINE; Brick Twp HS; Brick, NJ; (Y); Band; Mrchg Band; JV Bsktbl; Var Capt Powder Puff Ftbl; Var Capt Trk; High Hon Roll; Knights Of Columbus 86; Ocean Cnty Coll; Arch.

DEVLIN JR, JAMES F; Rancocas Valley Regional HS; Mt Holly, NJ; (Y); Latin Clb; VP Letterman Clb; Model UN; Red Cross Aide; VP Varsity Clb; Var JV Bsbl; Capt Var Socr; All Div All Cnty All Group Soccer 84-85; All St All Div All Cnty All Group Soccer 85-86; Rider Coll; Bus Mgmt.

DEVLIN, KATHLEEN; Paul VI Regional HS; Clifton, NJ; (S); 1/130; French Clb; VP Key Clb; Pres Office Aide; Cit Awd; French Hon Soc; High Hon Roll; NHS; Rutgers Schlr 85; Rutgers Mrt Schlrshp 85; NJ Dstngshd Schlr 86; Fairfield U; Sociology.

DEVLIN, LAURENCE; St James HS; Hancocks Bridge, NJ; (S); 1/81; School Musical; School Play; High Hon Roll; Ntl Merit Ltr; 1st Chair Trumpet All St Orchestra 85; 4th Chair Trumpet All St Wind Ensmbl 85; Solo Trumpet 84; U Of MI; Trumpet Perfrmr.

DEVORE, STEVEN; Cumberland Regional HS; Bridgeton, NJ; (Y); French Clb; Intnl Clb; Ski Clb; Lit Mag; VP Jr Cls; Var Ftbl; JV Tennis; Var Wrstlng; Hon Roll; Jr NHS; Engrg.

DEY, MATTHEW P; West Morris Central HS; Long Valley, NJ; (Y); Am Leg Boys St; Cmnty Wkr; Science Clb; SADD; Varsity Clb; Rep Stu Cncl; JV Var Bsbl; Coach Actv; Var Socr; JV Wrstlng.

DEZUTTI, KELLY; Cherry Hill West HS; Cherry Hill, NJ; (Y); Var Fld Hcky; Var Swmmng; High Hon Roll; Hon Roll; NHS; Marine Sci.

DI AMICO, MAUREEN; Passaic County Technical HS; Paterson, NJ; (S); Office Aide; Spanish Clb; Cheerleading; Sftbl; Hon Roll; Eng Prof.

DI BELLA, JOSEPH M; Sayreville War Memorial HS; Parlin, NJ; (Y); Am Leg Boys St; Drama Clb; Band; Chorus; Church Choir; Concert Band; Jazz Band; Mrchg Band; School Musical; Nwsp Sprt Ed; Musical Tlnt Shw Wnnr; Arrw Lght Sct Hldr; Seton Hall U; Cmnctns.

DI BENEDETTO, CHERYL; Franklin HS; Somerset, NJ; (Y); Trs Drama Clb; Chorus; School Musical; School Play; Stage Crew; Swing Chorus; High Hon Roll; NHS; NJ All ST Chorus 85-86; Franklin Pride Music Awd 85-86.

DI BERARDINO, DEBORAH; St James HS; Swedesboro, NJ; (S); 9/76; Church Yth Grp; Chorus; School Musical; School Play; Ed Nwsp Ed-Chief; Yrbk Stf; VP Frsh Cls; Pres Stu Cncl; NHS.

DI BIANCA, SUZANNE; Holy Spirit HS; Margate, NJ; (Y); Cmnty Wkr; French Clb; Key Clb; Pep Clb; Ski Clb; SADD; Stage Crew; Nwsp Stf; Yrbk Stf; Lit Mag.

DI BRUNO, JOSEPH; Highland Regional HS; Laurel Springs, NJ; (S); 20/332; Pres Chess Clb; Computer Clb; Latin Clb; Science Clb; Hon Roll; NHS; Rotary Awd; Engrng.

DI BUONO, AMY; Bridgeton SR HS; Bridgeton, NJ; (Y); 17/207; Office Aide; Teachers Aide; Yrbk Stf; Rep Jr Cls; Rep Sr Cls; High Hon Roll; Hon Roll; NHS; Edith Hepner RN Nrsng Schlrshp 86; Pres Acad Ftns Awd Prgrm 86; Cumberland Cnty Coll; Nrsng.

DI CARLO, FRANCINE; Morris Catholic HS; Boonton, NJ; (Y); Chorus; School Musical; School Play; Yrbk Stf; Var Capt Cheerleading; Powder Puff Ftbl; Score Keeper; Mst Imprvd Awd Chrldg 85-86; Nrsng.

DI COSIMO, FRANK; Bishop AHR St Thomas HS; Carteret, NJ; (Y); Vllybl; Hon Roll; Pres Schlr; Dntstry.

DI DONATO, KIM M; Mainland Regional HS; Linwood, NJ; (Y); 27/300; Nwsp Phtg; Nwsp Rptr; Nwsp Stf; Lit Mag; High Hon Roll; Pres Schlr; Hon Roll; Gregg Shrthnd Awd 83; Eva Andrsn Schlrshp 86; Rider Coll; Pblc Rltns.

DI ELLO, MICHELE; Roxbury HS; Succasunna, NJ; (Y); 7/378; Pres AFS; Am Leg Aux Girls St; Debate Tm; Chorus; Sec Stu Cncl; Trs NHS; Rotary Awd; VFW Awd; Acad All-Amer Schlr 85; Pres Acad Ftnss Awd 86; Villanova U; Librl Arts.

DI ENNA, MICHELE L; Haddonfield Memorial HS; Haddonfield, NJ; (Y); Intnl Clb; Spanish Clb; Var Cheerleading; Hon Roll; NHS; Spanish NHS; Accountant.

DI FRANCIA, VINCENT B; Pinelands Reg HS; Tuckerton, NJ; (S); 15/200; Church Yth Grp; Off Frsh Cls; Off Jr Cls; Stu Cncl; Bsbl; Ftbl; Trk; Wrstlng; High Hon Roll; Hon Roll; Ldrshp Hnr 85; Natl Ath Awd 85; Stevens Inst Tech; Engrng.

DI GIACOMO, MISSY; Mainland Regional HS; Northfield, NJ; (Y); Exploring; Ski Clb; SADD; Rep Frsh Cls; Rep Soph Cls; Rep Jr Cls; Sec Stu Cncl; Var L Fld Hcky; Im Vllybl; Srgcl Nrs.

DI GIACOMO, THOMAS A; Rancocas Valley Regional HS; Mt Holly, NJ; (Y); 3/250; Am Leg Boys St; Capt Math Tm; Capt Scholastic Bowl; Concert Band; Jazz Band; Mrchg Band; Orch; School Play; VP Frsh Cls; Pres Jr Cls; Outstndng Sci Stu 86; Grdn ST Dstngshd Schlrs Prog 86; MA Inst Of Tech; Elec Engr.

DI GIOVANNA, SEAN M; West Windsor/Plainsboro HS; Princeton Junctn, NJ; (Y); Am Leg Boys St; Boy Scts; Model UN; Chrmn Mrchg Band; VP NHS; Cmnty Wkr; Math Tm; Band; Concert Band; Jazz Band; Oprtn Entrprs Schlrshp 86.

DI GRAVINA, LAURA; North Arlington HS; N Arlington, NJ; (Y); 23/128; Spanish Clb; Hst Sr Cls; Hon Roll; Ntl Merit Ltr; Spanish NHS; Rutgers U.

DI JOSEPH, ROBERT; Cumberland Regional HS; Bridgeton, NJ; (Y); Computer Clb; Acpl Chr; JV Var Ftbl; Im JV Socr; High Hon Roll; Intnl Clb; Ski Clb; Chorus; Madrigals; School Musical; NJ All-ST Chrs 85-86; NJ All-Sth Jrsy Chrs 84-86; Cmbrlnd Rgnl Slct Chrs Mdrigal Grp 83-86; Med.

DI LEGGE, THERESA; East Brunswick HS; E Brunswick, NJ; (Y); Dance Clb; Trk; High Hon Roll; Hon Roll; Bio.

DI LORENZO, CONNIE; Holy Spirit HS; Smithville, NJ; (Y); #86 In Class; Var Capt Cheerleading; Mgr(s); Score Keeper; Hon Roll; Bus.

DI MATTEO, ROBERT; Delsea Regional HS; Malaga, NJ; (Y); Chess Clb; Science Clb; Hon Roll; Aero Engrng.

DI MAURO, LISA; Sacred Heart HS; Vineland, NJ; (S); 4/67; French Clb; School Musical; Yrbk Stf; Off Sr Cls; VP Cheerleading; VP Crs Cntry; High Hon Roll; Sec NHS; Prfct Atten Awd; 2nd Pl Trhy Vinelands Run Charity 83; 3rd Pl Schl Sci Extrvgnz 82-83; Prncpls Lst 84-85; Med.

DI MUZIO, DEBORAH; Manasquan HS; Brielle, NJ; (Y); Drama Clb; French Clb; Sec Thesps; Chorus; Stage Crew; Im Bsktbl; Hon Roll; U MD; Physcl Thrpy.

DI PADOVA, CHRISTINE; Point Pleasant Boro HS; Point Pleasant, NJ; (S); 4-H; Keywanettes; Math Tm; Pep Clb; Band; Hon Roll; NHS.

DI PAOLO JR, JOE; Sussex County Vo-Tech; Sparta, NJ; (Y); Nwsp Stf; Var JV Bowling; Hon Roll; Rotary Awd; OH Diesel Schlrshp 86; SEO Grnt 86; SCVT SR Shop Awd 86; OH Dsl Tech Inst; Dsl Mech.

DI PASQUALE, FRANK; Manalapan HS; Englishtown, NJ; (Y); Im Ftbl; Dntl.

DI PASQUALE, JEFF P; Dover HS; Dover, NJ; (Y); Am Leg Boys St; Computer Clb; Spanish Clb; JV Ftbl; JV Wt Lftg; JV Wrstlng; Hon Roll; U Of Bridgeprt; Comp Sci.

DI PERSIO, KIMBERLY A; Auduban HS; Philadelphia, PA; (Y); 12/119; Library Aide; Yrbk Stf; Rep Soph Cls; Rep Sr Cls; Var Cheerleading; JV Tennis; JV Trk; Hon Roll; VP NHS; Ntl Merit SF; US Ldrshp Mrt Awd 85; Richard J Hardenburgh Schlrshp 86; Trenton ST Coll; Crmnl Justice.

DI PIETRO, DONETTE; Holy Spirit HS; Pleasantville, NJ; (Y); Church Yth Grp; Cmnty Wkr; French Clb; Stage Crew; Hon Roll; Bus.

DI ROMA, MINA; Raritan HS; Hazlet, NJ; (Y); 7/314; Teachers Aide; Yrbk Ed-Chief; Yrbk Stf; Trs Soph Cls; Rep Jr Cls; VP Stu Cncl; Stat Crs Cntry; JV Tennis; NHS; Var Acdmc Let Schlstc Ldrs; VFW Ladies Auxlry Awd; Champ Jackets & Cert; Brookdale CC; Compu.

DI ROSA, MAUREEN; Highland Regional HS; Blackwood, NJ; (Y); German Clb; Stu Cncl; Stat Diving; Mgr(s); Var Socr; Var JV Trk; Gloucester Twnshp Grls Athl Assn 86; Glassboro; Bus Adm.

DI VUOLO, FERDINAND; Toms River High Schl South; Toms River, NJ; (Y); 28/360; Camera Clb; FBLA; Quiz Bowl; Frsh Cls; JV Bsbl; High Hon Roll; Hon Roll; 4th St FBLA Bus Math 84; Hofstra U; Bus Mgr.

DIAMOND, ALYSSA; Livingston HS; Livingston, NJ; (Y); Leo Clb; Temple Yth Grp; Chorus; School Musical; Stage Crew; Musicl Theatr.

DIAMOND, KENT; St John Vianney HS; Marlboro, NJ; (Y); 43/283; Stage Crew; L Var Socr; High Hon Roll; Hon Roll; NHS; Prfct Atten Awd.

DIANGELO, EDWARD; St Peters Prep; Jersey City, NJ; (Y); 125/207; Cmnty Wkr; French Clb; Library Aide; Pres SADD; School Play; Hon Roll; Lion Awd; Bus.

DIAS, DAVID; Livingston HS; Livingston, NJ; (Y); Am Leg Boys St; Var Bsbl; Var Ftbl; High Hon Roll; Hon Roll; Jr NHS; Law.

DIAS, MICHELE; Orange HS; Orange, NJ; (S); 6/182; Drama Clb; Math Tm; Science Clb; Teachers Aide; High Hon Roll; Hon Roll; Jr NHS; NHS; Ntl Merit Ltr; Comp Sci.

DIASPARRA, DIANA J; Pascack Valley HS; River Vale, NJ; (Y); 9/252; Computer Clb; Math Tm; Pep Clb; Spanish Clb; Chorus; Socr; Hon Roll; NHS; Ntl Merit SF; 1st Pl Montclair ST Coll Annl Prgmg Cntst & Rutgers Schlr 85; 22nd For Biol ST Sci Day 84.

DIAZ, ALEIDA; Roselle Catholic HS; Elizabeth, NJ; (Y); Dance Clb; French Clb; School Play; French Hon Soc; Hon Roll; Socl Actn 84; Frnch.

DIAZ, ANGIE; Passaic County Vo Tech; Paterson, NJ; (S); Hosp Aide; SADD; Variety Show; Var Cheerleading; Var Pom Pon; Hon Roll; Rutgers; Med.

DIAZ, EVELYS; Memorial HS; W New York, NJ; (Y); Var Trk; Outdoor Trck MVP 86; All-Cnty 2nd Tm, Long Jmp, 100 Mtrs & 400 Mtrs 86; Athlt Of Wk 86; Engrng.

DIAZ, PILAR; Manville HS; Manville, NJ; (Y); Scholastic Bowl; Hon Roll; NHS; Bus.

DIAZ, VICTOR; Central HS; Newark, NJ; (Y); 2/200; Science Clb; Var Ftbl; Cit Awd; High Hon Roll; Hon Roll; NHS; Prfct Atten Awd; Sal; Proj Pride Scholar 86; Stu Yr Scholar 85-86; Kean Coll; Acctng.

DIAZ, WILLIAM A; Roselle Catholic HS; Union, NJ; (S); 21/153; Am Leg Boys St; Church Yth Grp; Var Bsbl; Var Capt Bsktbl; JV Crs Cntry; High Hon Roll; Hon Roll; Spanish NHS; Ntl Engl Merit Awd 84-85; Ntl Ldrshp Awd 85-86; Acad All Amer 85-86; Stevens Inst Of Tech; Comp Engr.

DICKERSON, BRUCE LAWRENCE; New Brunswick HS; New Brunswick, NJ; (Y); Aud/Vis; Church Yth Grp; Civic Clb; Letterman Clb; Pep Clb; Varsity Clb; Band; Church Choir; School Play; Rep Frsh Cls; All Conf & Div All Star Ftbl Tm 85; Coachs Trck & Ftbl Awd 85-86; Mr Cngnlty 86; Chmcl Engrng.

DICKERSON, VALLEY M; Orange HS; Orange, NJ; (Y); 13/180; Church Yth Grp; Computer Clb; Chorus; Yrbk Stf; Trs Stu Cncl; Var Stat Bsktbl; Hon Roll; Elem Grad Commcmnt Add 84; Miss Blck Teen 85; All Am Schlrs 86; Rutgers U; Psych.

DICKEY, DAVID; Matawan Regional HS; Aberdeen, NJ; (S); 22/320; Debate Tm; French Clb; NFL; Speech Tm; School Musical; Stage Crew; JV Var Ftbl; Var Wt Lftg; High Hon Roll; Rutgers Engr Coll; Elect Engr.

DICKINSON, ALVIN; St Marys Hall/Doane Acad; Willingboro, NJ; (Y); Am Leg Boys St; VP Drama Clb; School Musical; School Play; Stage Crew; Trs Sr Cls; Rep Stu Cncl; L Var Bsbl; L Var Bsktbl; L Var Socr; Math.

DICKINSON, DAWN; Lower Cape May Regional HS; Cape May, NJ; (Y); 20/300; Am Leg Aux Girls St; 4-H; Key Clb; Spanish Clb; Varsity Clb; Chorus; Church Choir; School Musical; Yrbk Stf; Trs Soph Cls; Hugh O Brien Yth Fndtn Awd 84; Outstndng Ung New Jerseyan Awd 86; St Sen B Bradley Ctznshp Awd 84; Trenton St Coll; Elem Ed.

DICKINSON, JAMES; Camden HS; Camden, NJ; (S); 27/408; Rep Soph Cls; Var Capt Ftbl; Capt Trk; Var Wt Lftg; Hon Roll; NHS; Prfct Atten Awd; Pre-Med.

DICKSON, JOHN A; Rancocas Valley Reg HS; Mt Holly, NJ; (Y); 2/250; Am Leg Boys St; Scholastic Bowl; VP Stu Cncl; Var Ftbl; Var Capt Swmmng; Gov Hon Prg Awd; Ntl Merit SF; Pres Schlr; Sal; St Schlr; Duke U.

DICKSON, KEVIN; Eastside HS; Paterson, NJ; (Y); 40/650; Boy Scts; Computer Clb; Spanish Clb; Drill Tm; US Army; Engr.

DICTON, CAROLE; Warren Hills Regional SR HS; Hackettstown, NJ; (Y); Church Yth Grp; Chorus; Flag Corp; Mrchg Band; Yrbk Phtg; Lit Mag; Powder Puff Ftbl; Hon Roll; Aud/Vis; Camera Clb; York Of Penn; Commnctns.

DIDGEON, NADINE; Benedictine Acad; Clark, NJ; (Y); Sec GAA; Office Aide; Service Clb; Acpl Chr; Bsktbl; Trk; Var L Vllybl; French Clb; Ski Clb; Chorus; Aprrec Cert City Of Elizabeth 84; Outstndg Cert AAU 85; Green Bee Of Yr Awd 84.

DIEDRICHS, JOAKIN; Cresskill HS; Cresskill, NJ; (Y); 7/114; Am Leg Boys St; Math Tm; Ski Clb; Var Socr; Var Tennis; High Hon Roll; NHS; 1st Team All League Tennis Group I 85-86; 3rd Team Al Lcnty Tennis Group I 85-86; Brown; Invst Bankng.

DIEFFENBACH, KRISTA; Morris Catholic HS; Morris Plains, NJ; (Y); Cmnty Wkr; French Clb; Hosp Aide; Math Tm; Service Clb; Ski Clb; School Musical; School Play; Trk; Hosp Volntr Awd 100 Hrs Of Serv 83; Advrtsng.

DIEHL, ROBERT; Cumberland Regional HS; Seabrook, NJ; (Y); 50/300; Var Ftbl; Trk; Hon Roll; Bus Admin.

DIEKHAUS, RICHARD; Secaucus HS; Secaucus, NJ; (Y); Hon Roll; Kean Coll; Chem.

DIENER, SCOTT; Fair Lawn HS; Fair Lawn, NJ; (Y); 23/335; Computer Clb; Political Wkr; Spanish Clb; Nwsp Rptr; Rep Jr Cls; Hon Roll; NHS; St Schlr; Brandesi U; Pltcl Sci.

DIERTL, ROBERT; Montville HS; Towaco, NJ; (Y); Mrchg Band; JV Lcrss; Hon Roll.

DIETEL JR, KENNETH W; North Hunterdon HS; Lebanon, NJ; (Y); 15/298; Pres VP Church Yth Grp; German Clb; Chorus; Church Choir; Madrigals; School Musical; Socr; JV Tennis; JV Trk; Ntl Merit SF; Intl Yth Music Festival 83; Acadmc Achvmnt Society 83-85; Elec Engr.

DIETER, BRIAN; Victory Christian HS; Williamstown, NJ; (S); Church Yth Grp; Yrbk Stf; Off Soph Cls; Off Jr Cls; Mgr Bsktbl; Mgr Socr; High Hon Roll; Prfct Atten Awd; Awana Yr 84; Pensacola U; Aviation.

DIETRICH, PAUL E; Ocean City HS; Petersburg, NJ; (Y); 44/346; Am Leg Boys St; Church Yth Grp; Computer Clb; Quiz Bowl; Science Clb; Jr Cls; Var Crs Cntry; Cvl Engrng.

DIETZ, DAVE; Jonathan Dayton Regional HS; Mountainside, NJ; (Y); 24/231; Church Yth Grp; Drama Clb; French Clb; Thesps; Band; Concert Band; Jazz Band; Mrchg Band; Pep Band; School Musical; Angelo Martino Band Schlrshp 86; Best Thespn 86; Pres Acadmc Ftnss Awd 86; Northwestern U; Mech Engrg.

DIFIORE, MICHAEL; St Josephs Regional HS; Montvale, NJ; (Y); 23/170; Am Leg Boys St; Var Ftbl; JV Trk; Capt JV Wrstlng; NHS; Chrprctr.

DIFRANCEISCO, PAUL; Washington Twp HS; Turnersville, NJ; (Y); Spanish Clb; Var Bsbl; Im Bsktbl; Im Ftbl; Im Wt Lftg; NHS; Vrsty Ltr Bsbl; Med.

DIGEROLANO, RITA; Edgewood Regional SR HS; Blue Anchor, NJ; (Y); Hon Roll; Psych.

DIGIOVANNI, LAURA; Wildwood Catholic HS; Wildwood Crest, NJ; (Y); French Clb; JA; Mgr(s); Tennis; French Hon Soc; Hon Roll; NHS; Rotary Awd; Natl Ldrshp & Svc Awd 85; Engr.

DIGNEO, COSMO; Cherry Hill HS West; Cherry Hill, NJ; (Y); 90/360; Var Bsbl; Capt JV Bsktbl; Var Ftbl; Hon Roll; Bus.

DIKUN, CATHLEEN M; Jefferson Twp HS; Newfoundland, NJ; (Y); 54/216; Am Leg Aux Girls St; Varsity Clb; School Musical; Rep Stu Cncl; Capt Cheerleading; High Hon Roll; Hon Roll; NHS; Hmcmng Queen 85-86; Mntclr ST Coll; Art.

DILEO, LISA; Roselle Catholic HS; Linden, NJ; (Y); French Clb; Bowling; Hon Roll; Natl Bus Hnr Soc 85-86; Linden Amer-Italian Ladies Assn Awd 86; Union Coll Hnrs Pgm Schlrshp 86; Union Coll; Bus Admin.

DILEO, RUSSELL; Palmyra HS; Palmyra, NJ; (Y); 19/121; Church Yth Grp; Office Aide; Var Bsbl; Bsktbl; Var Socr; High Hon Roll; Hon Roll; Comp Sci.

DILEONARDO, JOSEPH; Palmyra HS; Palmyra, NJ; (Y); 5/131; Varsity Clb; Rep Frsh Cls; Var Bsbl; Var Socr; Var Capt Wrstlng; High Hon Roll; NHS; Rotary Awd; 1st Tm Frdm Div-Wrstlng 84-86; Amercn H S Athlt 84-85.

DILGER, DOROTHEA; Triton Regional HS; Bellmawr, NJ; (Y); Debate Tm; Chorus; Mrchg Band; School Musical; School Play; VP Stu Cncl; Powder Puff Ftbl; Hon Roll; Computer Clb; Drama Clb; Peer Fcltatr In The SJ Yth Cmmmssn 85-87; Dlgate To Grls Ctznshp Inst 86; Cmmnctns.

DILKS, LISA; Sacred Heart HS; Bridgeton, NJ; (Y); 17/65; Dance Clb; French Clb; Hosp Aide; Band; Variety Show; Nwsp Bus Mgr; Nwsp Ed-Chief; Nwsp Rptr; Lit Mag; Yrbk Rptr; 2nd Prize Schl Talent Show 86; Marymount Manhattan Coll; Dance.

DILL, ANGEL; Pemberton Twp High School No 2; Pemberton, NJ; (Y); 10/412; Church Yth Grp; Scholastic Bowl; Science Clb; Church Choir; Flag Corp; Variety Show; Hon Roll; NHS; Sec Rotary Awd; Math Clb; Duke U; Pre Med.

DILL, CHRIS; Ocean Township HS; Ocean, NJ; (Y); 69/337; Speech Tm; Band; Concert Band; Mrchg Band; School Play; Spartan Schlr Awd 83-84; Emerson; Pro Writing.

DILLER, REBEKAH R; Monmouth Regional HS; Tinton Falls, NJ; (Y); 3/225; Drama Clb; German Clb; Math Clb; Pres Temple Yth Grp; School Play; Sec Sr Cls; Hon Roll; Ntl Merit SF; Latin Clb; Ski Clb; Rutgers Schlr 85; Fin.

DILLON, ANNIE; Union HS; Union, NJ; (Y); Key Clb; Variety Show; Yrbk Stf; Off Soph Cls; Rep Jr Cls; Sec Sr Cls; Rep Stu Cncl; Var Crs Cntry; Cit Awd; NHS; Grls Ctznshp Inst 86; Theatr Arts.

DILLON, JOE; Butler HS; Butler, NJ; (Y); 20/197; Am Leg Boys St; Church Yth Grp; Math Tm; Political Wkr; Radio Clb; SADD; Yrbk Phtg; JV Socr; Hon Roll; NHS; Wnr Bst In ST Hstry Fair 84; Rep Sntr Bill Brdly Ldr-Smnr 85; Drexel U; Elctrcl Engrng.

DILLON, LISA A; Manalapan HS; Freehold, NJ; (Y); 4-H; Mgr Bsktbl; Cit Awd; 4-H Awd; Comm Dvlpmnt Awd Bill Bradley Awd 83; Katharine Gibbs Schl; Ex Sec St.

DILLON, TIMOTHY; Burlington Twp HS; Burlington Twp, NJ; (Y); 1/115; Pres Key Clb; Pres Varsity Clb; Var Capt Bsbl; Var Capt Bsktbl; Bausch & Lomb Sci Awd; Pres NHS; Val; VFW Awd; Am Leg Boys St; VP Church Yth Grp; S Jersey Athl Schlr Awd, Pres Acdmc Ftns Awd, Occidental Chem Corp Sci Schlrshp 86; Rensselaer Poly-Tech Inst; Engr.

DIMEO, TRACI; Cumberland Regional HS; Bridgeton, NJ; (Y); 49/357; VP Church Yth Grp; Intnl Clb; JCL; Latin Clb; Ski Clb; Var Bsktbl; Bowling; Var Fld Hcky; Stat Ftbl; Var Sftbl.

DIMMLER, GERARD; St Joseph Regional HS; Garnerville, NY; (Y); 3/163; Drama Clb; Math Tm; Model UN; Church Choir; School Play; Yrbk Stf; JV Crs Cntry; Var Trk; High Hon Roll; Hon Roll; Havard Bk Awd 86; Engr.

DIMUZIO, KENNETH; St James HS; Gibbstown, NJ; (Y); Bsbl; Bsktbl; Pre Law.

DINCER, SEMA; Manchester Twp HS; Whiting, NJ; (Y); 1/185; VP French Clb; Math Tm; Science Clb; Jazz Band; School Musical; Variety Show; Bausch & Lomb Sci Awd; Jr NHS; Pres NHS; Val; Grdn St Distngshd Schlr 86-87; NJ Smmr Arts Inst 85; Rutgers Coll; Pharmacy.

DINCUFF, BETH ELLEN; South River HS; South River, NJ; (Y); Sec German Clb; Math Tm; Quiz Bowl; Nwsp Stf; Yrbk Stf; Trs Frsh Cls; VP Jr Cls; JV Cheerleading; JV Sftbl; Gov Hon Prg Awd; The American U; Film Maker.

DINN, DEBORAH; St John Vianney HS; Holmdel, NJ; (Y); Church Yth Grp; Mrchg Band; Orch; Lit Mag; High Hon Roll; NHS; Govs Schl Semi Fnlst 86; Rtgrs Schlr 86; Deans Smmr Schlr Rtgrs U 86; Engnrng.

DINN, MICHELE; St John Vianney HS; Holmdel, NJ; (Y); #12 In Class; Boy Scts; Cmnty Wkr; Sec Trs Exploring; Hosp Aide; Math Tm; Political Wkr; SADD; Band; Concert Band; Drm Mjr(t); Bill Bradley Yng Ctzns Awd 86; Excptnl Explorer Awd 86; Rel Awd 83; Acdmc Ltr 83, 84, 85&86; Muhlenberg Coll; Med.

DINOLA, RALPH; Kittanny Reg HS; Newton, NJ; (Y); German Clb; Swmmng; Corp Awd Exxon Rsrch & Engrng 86; Arctctr.

DINSHAH, ANNE; Delsea Regional HS; Malaga, NJ; (Y); Concert Band; Jazz Band; Mrchg Band; Rep Stu Cncl; Var Diving; Var Swmmng; Var Trk; Im Wt Lftg; Var Hon Roll; NHS.

DIONISIO, ROMMEL; Morristown-Beard Schl; Parsippany, NJ; (Y); 1/81; Trs Model UN; Nwsp Ed-Chief; Var L Bsbl; DAR Awd; Gov Hon Prg Awd; High Hon Roll; Jr NHS; Ntl Merit Ltr; Opt Clb Awd; St Schlr; Morristown Beare Schl Merit Schlr 81-87; Cum Laude Hon Socty 86; Med.

DIRIL, HALIME; John F Kennedy HS; Paterson, NJ; (Y); Trs German Clb; Nwsp Stf; Yrbk Stf; Rep Frsh Cls; Rep Soph Cls; Rep Jr Cls; Var Score Keeper; Trk; Hon Roll; Soc Stds Fair 84-86; Saint Leo Coll; Comp Prgmmr.

DISCIENZA, JOSEPH; Pope Paul VI HS; Williamstown, NJ; (S); 5/514; Math Clb; School Play; Rep Soph Cls; JV Crs Cntry; JV Trk; High Hon Roll; Hon Roll; Spanish NHS; Dentistry.

DISISTO, ANELLE; Bound Book HS; Bound Brook, NJ; (Y); 20/147; Sec Drama Clb; Key Clb; Trs Thesps; Concert Band; Flag Corp; Rep Stu Cncl; Var Tennis; Var Trk; Hon Roll; NHS; Arch.

DISISTO, EILEEN; St John Vianney HS; Colts Neck, NJ; (Y); 31/298; Nwsp Rptr; Rep Frsh Cls; Pres Soph Cls; Pres Jr Cls; Pres Stu Cncl; JV Var Bsktbl; JV Var Crs Cntry; Capt Var Sftbl; NHS; Cert Of Merit Outstndg Achvt Frnch 85-86.

DISMUKES, REUBEN; Linden HS; Linden, NJ; (Y); French Clb; Concert Band; Jazz Band; Orch; School Play; Bsbl; Bsktbl; High Hon Roll; Hon Roll; NHS; Marchg Sprts Rpt And Trivia 86.

DISMUS, DIANA; Dwight Morrow HS; Englewood, NJ; (Y); 39/225; Drill Tm; Yrbk Phtg; Capt Cheerleading; High Hon Roll; Hon Roll; Natl Hnr Soc 85; Chprn Club Schlrshp Awd 86; Boston U; Engrg.

DISPOTO, MICHAEL; Bricktown HS; Brick Town, NJ; (Y); 15/345; Boy Scts; Ski Clb; Bsbl; Socr; High Hon Roll; Ocean Cnty Artst Guild Schlrshp 86; Govnrs Schl Of Arts Prog 85; Trenton ST Coll; Cmmrcl Art.

DISTEFANO, DAVID; Belleville HS; Belleville, NJ; (Y); Orch; Bsktbl; Hon Roll; Mthmtcs.

DITTMANN, CHRISTINE; Wood-Ridge HS; Wood-Ridge, NJ; (S); 14/91; Math Clb; Spanish Clb; Nwsp Stf; Yrbk Stf; Stat Bsktbl; Stat Ftbl; VP Trk; High Hon Roll; Hon Roll; NHS; William Patterson Coll; Nrsg.

DITTMEIER, KRISTI; Toms River HS East; Toms River, NJ; (Y); Cmnty Wkr; Spanish Clb; Variety Show; Var L Bsktbl; Powder Puff Ftbl; Var L Tennis; Trk; Observr All-Cnty Awd Tns 85-86; Ocean Cnty Tns All Star 85-86; All Shr Hnrbl Mentn Tns 84-85; Coll Of Boca Raton; Bus.

DIVERIO, KEVIN J; Don Bosco Prep; Hasbrouck Hts, NJ; (Y); 44/171; Church Yth Grp; Letterman Clb; Pep Clb; Service Clb; Varsity Clb; Yrbk Stf; Var Bsbl; Var Capt Bsktbl; NHS; Drew U Mem Schlrshp 86; Don Bosco Alumni Schlrshp 86; Don Bosco Ironman Awd Schl Ath Awd 86; Drew U.

DIVITO, TRACY; Immaculate Conception HS; Elmwood Park, NJ; (Y); 21/89; Cmnty Wkr; Drama Clb; Pres Chorus; School Musical; School Play; Hon Roll; Trs Spanish NHS; Amer Legion Awd 83; Wm Paterson Coll; Comm.

DIX, LAURA L; Northern Valley Regional HS; Haworth, NJ; (Y); 25/250; French Clb; Hosp Aide; Ski Clb; School Play; Score Keeper; Hon Roll; NHS; Rutgers Coll; Pre-Med.

DIXON, CHARMANE; John F Kennedy HS; Willingboro, NJ; (Y); 27/298; Church Yth Grp; Color Guard; Concert Band; Mrchg Band; Nwsp Stf; Yrbk Stf; Capt Bsktbl; Cheerleading; Hon Roll; Prfct Atten Awd; AKA Clndr Cntstnt Schlrshp 86; Temple U; Bus Adm.

DIXON, SHERI; Mary Lawn Of The Oranges HS; E Orange, NJ; (Y); #8 In Class; Hosp Aide; Service Clb; Chorus; Yrbk Stf; Rep Sr Cls; Capt Cheerleading; NHS; Spanish NHS; St Schlr; James Dickson Carr Schlrshp 86; Intl Union Opertng Eng 86; Union Baptist Church Schlrshp 86; Drew U Madison Nj; Communicatns.

DIXON, STEVEN; Rahway HS; Rahway, NJ; (Y); 48/264; Am Leg Boys St; JA; Band; Concert Band; Jazz Band; Mrchg Band; Orch; Pep Band; Symp Band; Hon Roll; Pres Acad Ftns Awd 86; Hghst Avrg Instmntl Music Awd 86; Howard U; Brdcst Prod.

DIZENZO, DENISE; Passaic Valley HS; Little Falls, NJ; (Y); Bus.

DO CAMPO, ORLANDO; Emerson HS; Union City, NJ; (Y); Am Leg Boys St; Yrbk Bus Mgr; Bsbl; Ftbl; Hon Roll; NHS.

DOBJAN, SUZANNE; North Brunswick Township HS; North Brunswick, NJ; (Y); Church Yth Grp; Spanish Clb; Church Choir; Rep Frsh Cls; Rep Soph Cls; Rep Jr Cls; Rep Stu Cncl; JV Crs Cntry; Hon Roll; Intl Bus.

DOBROWOLSKI, JILLIAN; Toms River HS East; Toms River, NJ; (Y); Art Clb; Camera Clb; Dance Clb; PAVAS; Science Clb; Stage Crew; OCC Art Cntst 2nd Pl Wnr 85; OCC; Elem Ed.

DOBROWOLSKI, SUZANNE J; Hopewell Valley Central HS; Pennington, NJ; (S); Var DECA; Hon Roll; Prfct Atten Awd; Free Enterprise Proj Awd 85; Elizabeth Gas Energy Consrvtn Pgm Awd 85; Safety Belt Campaign Awd 85; Advrtsng Desgn.

DOBSON, TRENIERE; Marylawn Of The Oranges; Newark, NJ; (Y); 20/51; 4-H; Girl Scts; Spanish Clb; Yrbk Stf; Rep Soph Cls; Rep Sr Cls; Bsktbl; Vllybl; 4-H Awd; Duguesne U; Mgnt Info Sys.

DODDS, MATT; Christian Brothers Acad; Little Silver, NJ; (Y); 50/217; Math Tm; Im Ftbl; Im Ice Hcky; Im Tennis; High Hon Roll; Hon Roll; Im Ftbll Champ 85-86; Strat-O-Matic Bsbll Club 84-85; Bus.

DOE, RENEE; Bayonne HS; Bayonne, NJ; (Y); Computer Clb; Dance Clb; French Clb; Spanish Clb; Church Choir; School Play; Var Cheerleading; High Hon Roll; NHS; Chem Cert From St Peters Clgs; Fshn Byng.

DOEHM, DENISE; Saint Aloysius HS; Jersey City, NJ; (Y); 27/30; Computer Clb; Exploring; Yrbk Stf; Rep Jr Cls; Hon Roll; Awd Comptrs 85; Awd Missn Rep 86 Tobe; Fshn Merch.

DOELFEL, SUSAN JOAN; E P Memorial HS; Elmwood Park, NJ; (Y); 2/160; Library Aide; Math Clb; Spanish Clb; Concert Band; School Musical; School Play; Bsktbl; Tennis; NHS; Spanish NHS; Gdn ST Dstngshd Schlrs Awd 86; 1st Pl NJ Mth Lg 86; Douglass Coll Schlrs Pgm; Douglass Coll; Mth.

DOERFLEIN, DENISE; Middletown South HS; Leonardo, NJ; (Y); 4-H; Girl Scts; Library Aide; Teachers Aide; Variety Show; Nwsp Ed-Chief; Nwsp Rptr; Nwsp Stf; Fld Hcky; Powder Puff Ftbl; Bus Mgmt.

DOERFLER, KIRK; Bridgewater-Raritan HS West; Bridgewater, NJ; (Y); Hon Roll; Somerset Cnty Coll.

DOERR, DIANE; East Brunswick HS; E Brunswick, NJ; (Y); Church Yth Grp; Varsity Clb; Chorus; Church Choir; Variety Show; Var Crs Cntry; JV Gym; JV Var Trk; Middlesex; Psych.

DOERRE, GEOFFREY O; Mtn Lakes HS; Mtn Lakes, NJ; (Y); Drama Clb; FHA; GAA; JCL; Latin Clb; Math Clb; Office Aide; Science Clb; Spanish Clb; Orch; Natl Merit Schlrshp Semifnlst 85; Biochem Engrng.

DOHERTY, DAVID; St Joseph Reg HS; Northvale, NJ; (Y); 7/167; Bsbl; Capt Bsktbl; Capt Socr; Capt Trk; Hon Roll; Jr NHS; NHS; VP Spanish NHS.

DOHERTY, SHEILA; Elizabeth HS; Elizabeth, NJ; (Y); Band; Score Keeper; Var Capt Socr; Var Sftbl; Cmnrl Psych.

DOHERTY, TERESA; Williamstown HS; Williamstown, NJ; (Y); 11/267; Nwsp Rptr; Hon Roll; Acad Achvt Awd 86; Pres Acad Fitness Awd 86; Acad Excllnce Fitness Awd 86; Douglass Coll; Bus Mgt.

DOHM, DIANNE; Pascack Hills HS; Montvale, NJ; (Y); Church Yth Grp; Chorus; Color Guard; Stu Cncl; Twrlr; French Hon Soc; Hon Roll; GA ST; Law.

DOKTORSKI, JOE; Steinert HS; Hamilton Sq, NJ; (Y); 150/330; Var Bsbl; Bsktbl; Var Ftbl; Var Ice Hcky; Var Trk; HUN Schlof Princeton; Engrng.

DOLAN, JAMES; Don Bosco Prep; Mahwah, NJ; (S); 4/174; Math Clb; Model UN; Bsbl; Var L Trk; Ntl Merit Schol; High Hon Roll; NHS; Computer Clb; Science Clb; Natl Ldrshp Merit Awd; Schl Schlrshp; SR Liturgy Cmmttee; Bus Adm.

DOLAN, JULIE; Mt St Dominic Acad; North Arlington, NJ; (Y); JCL; Latin Clb; Lit Mag; Hon Roll; NHS; 2nd Hnrs 83-86; Rcgntn Amrgncy Fd Yth Cmmtee 84-85; SRA Tstng 90% 83; U Of NH; Anml Sci.

DOLAN, KELLY; Jackson Memorial HS; Jackson, NJ; (S); 23/431; FBLA; Band; Concert Band; Mrchg Band; Var Socr; Var Sftbl; High Hon Roll; NHS; Bus Mgmt.

DOLAN, MICHAEL K; Northern Burlington Co Regionl HS; Columbus, NJ; (Y); 4/227; Am Leg Boys St; Band; Var JV Ftbl; Var JV Trk; French Hon Soc; High Hon Roll; Hon Roll; NHS.

DOLAN, PETE; West Morris Mendham HS; Mendham, NJ; (Y); 35/305; FBLA; Yrbk Stf; Sec Frsh Cls; Rep Soph Cls; Pres Jr Cls; JV Var Wrstlng; High Hon Roll; Hon Roll; NHS; Finance.

DOLAN, RAYMOND; Christian Brothers Acad; River Plaza, NJ; (Y); 55/213; Math Tm; Stage Crew; Var L Bowling; Im Ftbl; Im Sftbl; Hon Roll; Stage Crew Awd 86; Manhattan Coll; Hstry Tchr.

DOLAN, SUZANNE K; Villa Walsh Acad; Bernardsville, NJ; (Y); Hosp Aide; Math Tm; Lit Mag; Var Capt Bsktbl; Var Capt Trk; NHS; Ntl Merit Ltr; Pres Schlr; Art Clb; Church Yth Grp; US Army Reserve Ntl Schlr-Athlete Awd 86; NJ Star Ledger Prep All St 1st Tm Bsktbll 86; U Of Scranton; Phys Thrpst.

DOLBERRY, CHRIS; Paul Vi Regional HS; Clifton, NJ; (Y); Art Clb; Ski Clb; PA ST; Law.

DOLD, DIANE; Highland HS; Clementon, NJ; (S); 25/326; Office Aide; Stu Cncl; Im Bowling; Stat Sftbl; Stat Swmmng; Hon Roll; Rutgers; Law.

DOLD, JAMES; Highland Regional HS; Glendora, NJ; (S); 1/326; Aud/Vis; German Clb; Service Clb; High Hon Roll; NHS; Ntl Merit Ltr; St Schlr; Rutgers Deans Smmr Schlrs Pgm 85; Grdn ST Dsgngshd Stus Schlrshp 85; Walt Whitman Potry Cntst Awd 85; MA Inst Of Tech; Elec Engr.

DOLLBERG, DAVE; West Essex SR HS; Fairfield, NJ; (Y); 68/380; Key Clb; Var L Crs Cntry; Var L Trk; High Hon Roll; Hon Roll; Winter Track 84-85; NJIT; Arch.

DOLLINGER, BETSY L; Newark Acad; Randolph, NJ; (Y); AFS; Key Clb; School Musical; School Play; Ed Nwsp Stf; Lit Mag; NHS; St Schlr; Pres Frsh Cls; JV Fld Hcky; Williams Coll Almn Assn Awd 85; Headmstrs List 82-86; Govrnr Schl Arts Altrnt 85.

DOLSON, ANITA; Buena Regional HS; Vineland, NJ; (S); Drama Clb; Math Clb; Ski Clb; Pres Frsh Cls; Trs Soph Cls; Rep Jr Cls; Sec Stu Cncl; Var Fld Hcky; Var Sftbl; Jr NHS; Hnr Rl 84-85; Hotel Mgmt.

DOMALEWSKI, CRAIG; Hawthorne HS; Hawthorne, NJ; (Y); Am Leg Boys St; Model UN; Pres Jr Cls; Pres Stu Cncl; Var Capt Ftbl; Var Trk; Var Capt Wrstlng; Hon Roll; Boys Clb Am; SADD; Govrnr Schl Of Pblc Issues 86; Peer Cnslr; Pltcl Sci.

DOMBECK, MICHELLE; Brurian HS; Hillside, NJ; (Y); Drama Clb; Temple Yth Grp; School Play; Yrbk Stf; Im Sftbl; NHS.

DOMBROWSKI, TED; Westfield SR HS; Westfield, NJ; (Y); Church Yth Grp; Ski Clb; Spanish Clb; SADD; JV Bsktbl; Coach Actv; Vllybl; Hon Roll; Law.

DOMINGO, ERNANI; St Peters Preparatory Schl; Jersey City, NJ; (Y); 4/206; Chess Clb; Cmnty Wkr; Dance Clb; Science Clb; Pres Frsh Cls; Var Trk; Hon Roll; St Peters Coll Smmr Schlr Prg 86; 2nd Hnrs Cert Spnsh Lang Cntst 86; Bio & Spnsh Gold Medal 85; Biology.

DOMINGUES, ROSA; Kearny HS; Kearny, NJ; (Y); Spanish Clb; Hon Roll; Prfct Atten Awd; Spanish NHS.

DOMINGUEZ, ELIZABETH; St Joseph Of Palisades HS; Dumont, NJ; (S); 6/120; Math Clb; Spanish Clb; Var Tennis; Hon Roll; Spanish NHS.

DOMINIC, LISA; Holy Cross HS; Medford, NJ; (Y); Am Leg Aux Girls St; Ski Clb; Spanish Clb; School Musical; Yrbk Stf; Rep Frsh Cls; Rep Jr Cls; Tennis; Hon Roll; NHS.

DON, COURTNEY T; Holy Cross HS; Medford Lakes, NJ; (Y); 75/397; Model UN; Service Clb; Ski Clb; Nwsp Rptr; Ed Nwsp Stf; Hon Roll; Internatl Reltns.

DONAHOWER, JOHN; Delsea Regional HS; Franklinville, NJ; (Y); 34/201; Science Clb; Stage Crew; Nwsp Stf; Yrbk Phtg; Trs Jr Cls; VP Sr Cls; Tennis; NHS; Chess Clb; SADD; Drexel; Bus.

DONAHUE, STEPHANIE; St John Vianney HS; Colts Neck, NJ; (Y); 121/275; Church Yth Grp; Cmnty Wkr; Yrbk Stf; Sec Sr Cls; Var Stat Bsktbl; Var L Mgr(s); Var L Sftbl; Hon Roll; Prfct Atten Awd; Service Clb; Gold & White Svc Awd 86; All-Cnty Sftbl Hon Mntn 86; Sprts Med.

DONAR, PAMELA; Roselle Catholic HS; Roselle, NJ; (Y); Cmnty Wkr; Ski Clb; Swmmng; Tennis; French Hon Soc; Hon Roll.

DONATO, LESLIE; Paul VI HS; Turnersville, NJ; (S); 6/546; Math Clb; Var Capt Tennis; French Hon Soc; High Hon Roll; Hon Roll; All Parochial Tennis Singles 84 & 85; Math Awd 84; MVP Tennis 84 & 85; Bus Math.

DONDERO, DIANA; Kinnelon HS; Riverdale, NJ; (Y); 28/180; Art Clb; Sftbl; Hon Roll; NHS; Spanish NHS; Cmrcl Art.

DONDERO, JAMES; Arthur P Schalick HS; Bridgeton, NJ; (Y); Cmnty Wkr; Math Tm; Ski Clb; Var Bsbl; Bsktbl; Rep Frsh Cls; Trs Soph Cls; Engrng.

DONDERO, LISA; Sacred Heart HS; Vineland, NJ; (S); Church Yth Grp; French Clb; Girl Scts; Chorus; School Musical; School Play; Yrbk Stf; Var Swmmng; Hon Roll; 3rd Pl Sci Fair 84; Bio.

DONELAN, STACEY; Belvidere HS; Belvidere, NJ; (S); 2/119; Am Leg Aux Girls St; Quiz Bowl; Chorus; VP Sr Cls; Rep Stu Cncl; Sftbl; Im Vllybl; Pres NHS; St Schlr; French Clb; Engl, Hstry, & Frnch II Outstndng Achvt; Hugh O Brian Yth Fndtn Prtcptn Awd; Rtgrs Schlr; Mrthwstrn U; Bio-Chem.

DONER, LENORE; Hackettstown HS; Hackettstown, NJ; (Y); Church Yth Grp; Hosp Aide; Key Clb; Nwsp Rptr; Ltr & Pin Outstndng Acadmc Achvt 85 & 86; Pre-Med.

DONIA, JEFF; Eastern Regional HS; Berlin, NJ; (Y); 13/325; Yrbk Stf; Hon Roll; Achvt Awd Frnch 85; Psych.

DONIA, SANTO; Paul VI HS; Sewell, NJ; (S); 24/557; NFL; Spanish Clb; Mrchg Band; VP Soph Cls; VP Jr Cls; High Hon Roll; Hon Roll; Church Yth Grp; Stu Cncl; Bowling; Meteorlgy.

DONLEY, ROBERT; Cherry Hill High Schl West; Cherry Hill, NJ; (Y); 7/380; Boy Scts; Computer Clb; Office Aide; Jazz Band; Variety Show; High Hon Roll; NHS; Presdntl Ftns Awd; Mock Trial Tm-NJ ST Chmpnshp Wnr; U Of PA; Comps.

DONLIN, MARGARET; Mt St Dominic Acad; Livingston, NJ; (Y); Chorus; Church Choir; Madrigals; School Musical; High Hon Roll; Hon Roll; NHS; Pres Schlr; JCL; NEDT Awd; Music Eductrs Assn 84-85; Piano Tchrs Soc Amer 86; Marywood Coll; Prfrmng Arts.

DONLON, MARK; Red Bank Catholic HS; Monmouth Bch, NJ; (Y); Socr; Wt Lftg; Coast Guard Acad; Marketing.

DONNELLY, BERNARD JAY; Shawnee HS; Medford, NJ; (Y); 10/540; Math Tm; NHS; MD Acad Sci Smnrs 85; Life Grd Cls 85; Gde Spcl Olympcs 85; Spnsh Awd Hghst Avg Cls 85; Rutgers U; Bus Adm.

DONNELLY, JOHN T; Atlantic Christian Schl; Ventor, NJ; (S); 1/15; Chess Clb; School Play; Var Co-Capt Bsktbl; Var L Socr; High Hon Roll; Math.

DONNELLY, KEITH R; Christian Brothers Acad; Parlin, NJ; (S); Boy Scts; Church Yth Grp; Jazz Band; School Play; Nwsp Stf; Im Socr; Hon Roll; NHS; Ntl Merit SF; Im Bowling.

DONNELLY, PATRICK; Notre Dame HS; Princeton, NJ; (Y); Red Cross Aide; Ski Clb; Varsity Clb; Capt Crs Cntry; Var Trk; Stu Athlt Trnr; Bus.

DONNELLY, WILLIAM; Bishop George Ahr HS; Colonia, NJ; (Y); 42/277; Intnl Clb; Model UN; Thesps; School Musical; School Play; Im Vllybl; Hon Roll; Ntl Merit Ltr; NEDT Awd; ROTC; Cadet Yr 83-84; Most Promising Newcomer Drama 84-85; Most Dedctd Drama 85-86.

DONOFRIO, GINA; Oak Knoll HS; Union, NJ; (Y); Aud/Vis; Cmnty Wkr; Pep Clb; Stat Mgr Bsktbl; Mgr(s); Score Keeper; Var Trk; Im Vllybl; Hon Roll; Bus.

DONOFRIO, KAREN; Hillsborough HS; Belle Mead, NJ; (Y); 17/293; Office Aide; SADD; Rep Sr Cls; Rep Stu Cncl; JV Stat Bsktbl; Var Capt Fld Hcky; Powder Puff Ftbl; Var Sftbl; Hon Roll; NHS; Penn ST U; Acctg.

DONOGHUE, GERALD F; Middletown HS South; Red Bank, NJ; (Y); 65/423; Boy Scts; VP L Socr; Hon Roll; Rutgers Coll Of Engrg; Elec Eng.

DONOHOE, HEIDI; Ridge HS; Basking Ridge, NJ; (Y); Off Ski Clb; Var Capt Civic Clb; Powder Puff Ftbl; Sftbl; Swmmng; JV Trk; Safe Rides Ofcr 85-86; Leadership 86-87; Meredith Modeling Agency Teen Band 84.

DONOHUE, DENISE; Delran HS; Delran, NJ; (Y); 15/189; Am Leg Aux Girls St; VP Soph Cls; VP Jr Cls; Stu Cncl; Var Capt Cheerleading; Var Capt Lcrss; High Hon Roll; Lion Awd; Pres Schlr; Stu Cncl Awd 86; Brd Of Educ Awd 86; Scl Stds Awd 86; Rutgers Coll Of Engrng; Engr.

DONOHUE, JENNIFER; North Warren Regional HS; Blairstown, NJ; (Y); 35/131; Church Yth Grp; FBLA; Ski Clb; Band; Stat Bsktbl; Var Fld Hcky; Stat Sftbl; Hon Roll; Rotary Awd; Var Cheerleading.

DONOHUE, LYNN MARIE; Saint Aloysius HS; Jersey City, NJ; (Y); 9/130; Library Aide; Spanish Clb; Stage Crew; Nwsp Stf; Yrbk Stf; Tennis; Hon Roll.

DONOHUE, MATTHEW D; Don Bosco HS; Mahwah, NJ; (Y); 9/200; Yrbk Stf; Lit Mag; High Hon Roll; NHS; Scholl Worldwide Schlrshp; Scherine-Plough Merit Schlrshp Prgm; Boston Coll; Lit.

DONOVAN, LORI; Piscataway HS; Piscataway, NJ; (Y); Varsity Clb; Color Guard; Drill Tm; Flag Corp; Mrchg Band; Stat L Bsbl; High Hon Roll; Hon Roll; Jr NHS; NHS; Sprchf Bnd-Drl Tm Cmndr 86-87; Stvns Inst Of Tech Wmn In Engrng Prog 86; Adv Studnt Math Exam 86; Penn ST; Engrng.

DONOVAN, SHANNON; Maple Shade HS; Maple Shade, NJ; (Y); French Clb; Band; Concert Band; Jazz Band; Mrchg Band; High Hon Roll; Hon Roll; Jr NHS.

DONOVAN, THOMAS; Plainfield HS; Plainfield, NJ; (S); 1/500; Boy Scts; Math Tm; Capt Scholastic Bowl; Trs Science Clb; Capt Swmmng; Tennis; High Hon Roll; NHS; Ntl Merit Ltr; St Schlr; Rensslr Medl 85; Rutgrs Schlr 85; Brown U; Math.

DOODY, PATRICK A; St Joseph Regional HS; Haworth, NJ; (Y); 84/167; Church Yth Grp; Crs Cntry; Socr; Tennis; Trk; Hon Roll.

DOOLEY, PAULINE; Morris Knolls HS; Green Pond, NJ; (Y); 90/391; Ski Clb; JV Capt Cheerleading; Hon Roll.

DOORLY, SEAN J; Seton Hall Preparatory Schl; Caldwell, NJ; (Y); Art Clb; Science Clb; Nwsp Stf; Yrbk Stf; JV Socr; High Hon Roll; JETS Awd; Computer Clb; German Clb; Intnl Clb; Ntl Sci Olympd 85; Verona Art Assoc 84; W Essex Art Assoc 84; Cmmrcl Art.

DORAI, VIDYA; Wayne Hills HS; Wayne, NJ; (Y); 75/315; Math Clb; Model UN; Science Clb; Spanish Clb; Nwsp Ed-Chief; Ed Nwsp Rptr; Nwsp Stf; Lit Mag; Stu Cncl; Hon Roll; 1st Pl In Literary Contest 86; Bio.

DORATO, JON; Audubon HS; Audubon, NJ; (Y); Church Yth Grp; Computer Clb; DECA; Mathletes; Math Clb; Varsity Clb; Crs Cntry; Trk; Camden County Coll; Comp.

DORATO, PAUL; Red Bank Catholic HS; Tinton Falls, NJ; (Y); Ski Clb; JV Ftbl; Im Wt Lftg.

DOREY, JAMES; West Orange HS; West Orange, NJ; (Y); Church Yth Grp; Rep Varsity Clb; Nwsp Rptr; Nwsp Sprt Ed; Rep Frsh Cls; Var Bsbl; Var Wrstlng; Bus Adm.

DORI, RAVIT; Lakewood HS; Woodbridge, NJ; (Y); English Clb; French Clb; Hosp Aide; Library Aide; Spanish Clb; Nwsp Stf; Yrbk Stf; Bsktbl; Fld Hcky; Trk; ST U NY; Law.

DORN, CASSANDRA; Red Bank Regional HS; Little Silver, NJ; (Y); 2/221; Quiz Bowl; Ski Clb; Band; Yrbk Sprt Ed; VP Sr Cls; JV Var Sftbl; NHS; Sal; Yrbk Rptr; JV Fld Hcky; Vrsty Lttr-For Ftbll Mascot 85; Grdn St Distgshd Schlr 86; Duke U.

DORNER, DEBRA ANN; West Essex SR HS; Fairfield, NJ; (Y); Acpl Chr; Chorus; Madrigals; School Musical; School Play; Frsh Cls; Soph Cls; Var Sftbl; Hon Roll; NHS; Prsdntl Physcl Ftnss Awd.

DOROFEE, CHERYL; Highland Regional HS; Sicklerville, NJ; (Y); Cmnty Wkr; Var JV Cheerleading; Pom Pon; Glassboro ST Coll; Tchr.

DORSCHLER, RICHARD C; Hackettstown HS; Hackettstown, NJ; (Y); Cmnty Wkr; JV Trk; Hon Roll; Schlrshp Smmr Art Inst 85; Art.

DORVAL, ROGER; Wayne Valley HS; Wayne, NJ; (Y); 12/311; Am Leg Boys St; Boy Scts; Computer Clb; FBLA; JV Crs Cntry; JV Trk; Var Wrstlng; High Hon Roll; Hon Roll; Hst NHS; Engrng.

DOSCHER, MARK E; Don Bosco Prep; Waldwick, NJ; (Y); 30/200; Science Clb; Varsity Clb; Yrbk Stf; Rep Frsh Cls; JV Var Ftbl; JV Var Trk; Hon Roll; Art Clb; Stage Crew; Wildernss Advntr Pgm VP 86; Spnsh Clb 84; Schl Mascot 85; Rutgers U; Bus Adm.

DOSSENA, COLLEEN; Hackettstown HS; Great Meadows, NJ; (Y); GAA; Teachers Aide; Varsity Clb; Yrbk Stf; Sr Cls; Bsktbl; Cheerleading; Sftbl; Hon Roll; Prfct Atten Awd; Most Imprvd Vrsty Chrldr Awd 85; E Stroudsburg U; Frech Tcher.

DOSTIE, YVETTE; Jackson Memorial HS; Jackson, NJ; (Y); 17/405; 4-H; High Hon Roll; Engl Awd 85; Mock Trl Tm Awd-Ocean Cnty Cmpns 86; Law.

DOTCH, ERICA; Plainfield HS; Plainfield, NJ; (Y); Aud/Vis; Church Yth Grp; Capt Pep Clb; VP Spanish Clb; Yrbk Stf; Pres Frsh Cls; Rep Jr Cls; Var Capt Cheerleading; Hon Roll; NHS; Pre Law.

DOTHARD, DAWN; Washington Township HS; Sewell, NJ; (Y); French Clb; Ski Clb; High Hon Roll; Hon Roll; NHS.

DOTSIS, VIVIAN; Atlantic City HS; Ventnor, NJ; (Y); Drama Clb; Model UN; Office Aide; High Hon Roll; Hon Roll; Spanish NHS; Art Clb; Cmnty Wkr; Dance Clb; Girl Scts; Christopher Columbus Awd 86; Brown Bk Awd 86; Middlebury; Lang.

DOTTER, KATHERINE; Bergenfield HS; Bergenfield, NJ; (Y); Art Clb; English Clb; German Clb; Math Clb; Spanish Clb; Band; Lit Mag; Hon Roll; NHS; Art.

DOUGHER, ELIZABETH; Ramapo HS; Wyckoff, NJ; (Y); 20/329; Art Clb; Drama Clb; French Clb; Hosp Aide; Lit Mag; High Hon Roll; Hon Roll; Ntl Merit Ltr.

DOUGHERTY, ELIZABETH; West Milford TWP HS; West Milford, NJ; (Y); 2/360; Am Leg Aux Girls St; Intnl Clb; Sec Latin Clb; Model UN; Var Tennis; Elks Awd; NHS; Ntl Merit Ltr; Sal; NJ Dstngshd Schlr Awd 85-86; Natl Hstry Day Awd Excllnc 84-85; Natl Hstry Day Awd Supr 85-86; Cornell U; Spc Sci.

DOUGHERTY, KEVIN; Paul VI HS; Haddonfield, NJ; (S); 43/475; Math Clb; Rep Soph Cls; L Bsbl; L Bsktbl; Hon Roll; NHS; Drexel U; Ind Engrng.

DOUGHERTY, LEA M; Paul VI HS; Runnemede, NJ; (Y); 35/474; Math Clb; Spanish Clb; SADD; Stat Bsktbl; JV Var Fld Hcky; Mgr(s); Score Keeper; JV Var Sftbl; Hon Roll; NHS; IHM Schlrshp Mrywd Coll 86; Wmns Clb Schlrshp 86; Mrywd Coll; Elem Ed.

DOUGHTY, TERRI IRENE; Burlington Township HS; Burlington Twp, NJ; (Y); 13/125; Am Leg Aux Girls St; Pres VP Church Yth Grp; Drama Clb; Math Tm; Varsity Clb; Madrigals; Cit Awd; NHS; Hosp Aide; Library Aide; Internatl Order-Rainbow Grls Wrthy Advsr-Grand Ofcr 85-86; Highst Avrg In Music 86; Modl Cngrs 85-86; IN U Of PA; Accntng.

DOUGLAS, MICHELLE; Clifford J Scott HS; E Orange, NJ; (Y); Church Yth Grp; FHA; Intnl Clb; Stu Cncl; Hon Roll; Prfct Atten Awd; Rutgers U; Pol Sci.

DOUGLAS, STACIA; Clifford J Scott HS; E Orange, NJ; (Y); 49/297; Dance Clb; DECA; Hosp Aide; JA; Teachers Aide; Variety Show; Yrbk Stf; Rep Frsh Cls; Sec Sr Cls; Var Co-Capt Cheerleading; Hmpton U; Acctg.

DOUGLASS, MICHELLE; Hackettstown HS; Hackettstown, NJ; (Y); Exploring; Hosp Aide; Math Tm; Acpl Chr; Chorus; School Musical; Rep Stu Cncl; High Hon Roll; Hon Roll; Key Clb; Fencing-Vrsty Lttr 81-86; Fencing Capt 85-86; Stevens Inst Of Tech; Engrng.

DOVE, DONNA; Red Bank Regional HS; Red Bank, NJ; (Y); 13/220; Rep Sr Cls; Var JV Bsktbl; Var JV Mgr(s); Var JV Score Keeper; Bausch & Lomb Sci Awd; High Hon Roll; Hon Roll; Masonic Awd; NHS; James Dickinson Carr Schrlshp 86; Ntl Negro Womens Clb Schlrshp 86; Rutgers Coll; Chem Engr.

DOW, SUSAN E; Red Bank Catholic HS; Tinton Fls, NJ; (Y); 6/270; Q&S; Nwsp Sprt Ed; Var Capt Crs Cntry; Var Capt Trk; Elks Awd; Lion Awd; VP NHS; NJ Distngshd Schlr, St Anthony Padua Schlrhsp 86; Chem, Span II, US Hist II Awds 83-85; Villanova U; Acctg.

DOWD, JAMES; Passaic Valley Regional HS; Boca Raton, FL; (Y); Chess Clb; Science Clb; Ski Clb; JV Ftbl; JV Socr; Var Trk; Hon Roll; Ntl ST Sci Awd; Passaic Vly Sci Awd; NY Sci Day; U FL; Chem.

DOWLEY, TAMMY; Camden HS; Camden, NJ; (S); 3/408; French Clb; Library Aide; Model UN; Radio Clb; Rep Frsh Cls; Rep Soph Cls; Pres Jr Cls; Pres Stu Cncl; Stat Bsktbl; Sftbl; Rutgers Essy Cntst Wnr 83 & 85; WDAS Radio 1st Pl Essy Cntst Wnr 84-85; Cmnctns.

DOWNES, ANNE; Dwight-Englewood Schl; Englewood, NJ; (Y); Dance Clb; School Play; Yrbk Stf; Capt Gym; Hon Roll.

DOWNES, WILLIAM F; Montclair HS; Montclair, NJ; (Y); Chess Clb; Pres Debate Tm; French Clb; Model UN; Science Clb; School Play; JV Var Ftbl; JV Var Wrstlng; Hon Roll; St Schlr; Engrng.

DOWNEY, TRICIA; Manalapan HS; Manalapan, NJ; (Y); Exploring; Girl Scts; SADD; Yrbk Stf; Socr; Art.

DOWNING, CHRIS; Don Bosco Preparatory HS; Ringwood, NJ; (Y); 12/185; Church Yth Grp; Model UN; Science Clb; Yrbk Stf; Var JV Socr; High Hon Roll; Hon Roll; NHS; Chess Clb; Drama Clb; 1st Pl Chem Don Bosco Prep Sci Fair 85; Med.

DOXEY, KERRY; Red Bank Catholic HS; Red Bank, NJ; (Y); Spanish Clb; Acdmc All Amer At Lrg 86; Intl Forgn Lang Awd 86.

DOYLE, BRIAN; Wayne Valley HS; Wayne, NJ; (Y); Cmnty Wkr; Ski Clb; Stage Crew; Bsbl; Bowling; Hon Roll; Bio.

DOYLE, JOSEPH; Bricktownship Memorial HS; Brick, NJ; (Y); Cmnty Wkr; JV Bsktbl; High Hon Roll; Hon Roll; Prfct Atten Awd; Soc Sci Awd 86; PBA Awd 86; Ocean County Coll; Crim Justice.

DOYLE, KATHLEEN; Sayreville War Memorial HS; Parlin, NJ; (Y); Camera Clb; Church Yth Grp; French Clb; Spanish Clb; Band; Flag Corp; Stage Crew; Yrbk Phtg; Spanish NHS; Sayrvl Polc Benevlt Assn Schlrshp 86; Drexel U; Dsgn Arts.

DOYLE, MICHELE; Roselle Catholic HS; Elizabeth, NJ; (Y); Church Yth Grp; Girl Scts; Service Clb; Ski Clb; Lit Mag; Var L Socr; Commnctns.

DOYLE, THERESA; Mount Saint Mary Acad; Scotch Plains, NJ; (Y); French Clb; GAA; Latin Clb; Pep Clb; Nwsp Rptr; Lit Mag; Bsktbl; Fld Hcky; Sftbl; Vllybl; Scotch Plains Fanwood Inter City Sccr Assn 84 & 85; Girls Div Garden ST Games Field Hcky Event 86.

DOYLE, THOMAS; Bishop George Ahr HS; Plainfield, NJ; (Y); German Clb; JV Ftbl; Im Mgr Wt Lftg; JV Wrstlng; 4th NJ ADFPA Bench Press Champ 86; Sprts Med.

DRABANT, SUE; Indian Hills HS; Oakland, NJ; (Y); 15/274; Church Yth Grp; Cmnty Wkr; Varsity Clb; Stat Bsktbl; Var JV Vllybl; CC Awd; High Hon Roll; NHS; Pres Schlr; Rotary Awd; Oakland Womens Clb Schlrshp 86; Oakland PBA Schlrshp 86; LA ST U; Crmnl Just.

DRADDY, NINA; Lacey Twp HS; Forked River, NJ; (Y); 32/236; Church Yth Grp; Var Capt Bsktbl; Var Capt Crs Cntry; Var Fld Hcky; Var Powder Puff Ftbl; Var Socr; Var Capt Trk; Hon Roll; NHS; Rotary Awd; LTHS Coaches Shlrshp 86; LTHS SR & Athlt Of The Mnth 86; All Cnty & All Conf Bsktbl 85; George Mason U; Elem Ed.

DRAGER, LAURA; Wood-Ridge HS; Wood-Ridge, NJ; (S); 11/91; GAA; Science Clb; Spanish Clb; Nwsp Rptr; Lit Mag; Stat Bsktbl; Stat Ftbl; JV Trk; High Hon Roll; NHS; Fairleigh Dickinson U; Adv.

DRAGHI, NANCY; Paul VI Regional HS; Clifton, NJ; (S); 11/147; Church Yth Grp; French Clb; Ski Clb; Varsity Clb; Var L Cheerleading; French Hon Soc; Hon Roll; NHS; Villanova; Sci.

DRAGOS, DENISE C; Colonia HS; Colonia, NJ; (Y); 8/287; Debate Tm; French Clb; Key Clb; Band; Concert Band; Yrbk Stf; Co-Capt Twrlr; NHS; U Of DE; Accntng.

DRAIN, NANCY; Washington Township HS; Turnersville, NJ; (Y); Drama Clb; French Clb; Yrbk Sprt Ed; Yrbk Stf; Off Frsh Cls; Off Soph Cls; Off Jr Cls; Stu Cncl; Bsktbl; Cheerleading; William & Mary Coll; Law.

DRAINA, BONNIE; S Hunterdon Reg HS; Lambertville, NJ; (S); 1/70; Varsity Clb; Pres Chorus; Drm Mjr(t); Madrigals; School Musical; Yrbk Ed-Chief; Rep Stu Cncl; Ntl Merit Ltr; Val; Concert Band; Piano Schlrshp-Solebury Schl 84-85; Sen Bill Bradley Ldrshp Smnr 86.

DRAKE, KEVIN; Freehold Township HS; Freehold, NJ; (Y); Chess Clb; Computer Clb; Nwsp Stf; Sec Frsh Cls; Stu Cncl; Var Bowling; Var Tennis; Capt Trk; Rutgers Coll.

DRAKE, MELISSA; Hackettstown HS; Hackettstown, NJ; (Y); 1/250; Concert Band; Jazz Band; Rep Stu Cncl; Var L Trk; Wrstlng; Cit Awd; Gov Hon Prg Awd; High Hon Roll; NHS; St Schlr; Rutgrs Schlr 86; Top Rnkng Key Awd 86; Lbrl Arts.

DRANGULA, DREW; Holy Cross HS; Roebling, NJ; (Y); Ski Clb; Var Ftbl; Var Wt Lftg; Arch.

DRAPKIN, PAOLA T; Ocean Township HS; Ocean, NJ; (Y); 22/333; Key Clb; Office Aide; Spanish Clb; SADD; Band; Concert Band; Mrchg Band; Pep Band; School Musical; NHS; Spartan Schlr Awd 83-85; Music Awd 85-86; Ed.

DRAUCIK, EILEEN; Holy Family Acad; Bayonne, NJ; (Y); Art Clb; Cmnty Wkr; Computer Clb; Nwsp Rptr; Hon Roll; Ntl Ldrshp & Svc Awd 85; St Ptrs Coll Smmr Schlr 85&86; Acdmc All-Amrcn Schlr 84; Grphc Art.

DRAVIS, STEPHEN; Roselle Catholic HS; Roselle, NJ; (S); 1/207; Debate Tm; Math Tm; Service Clb; Speech Tm; Lit Mag; Hon Roll; Voice Dem Awd; Essy Cntst 84; Am Legn Oratrcl Cntst 85; Brdcst Jrnlsm.

DRAYTON, LISA; Red Bank Catholic HS; Tinton Falls, NJ; (Y); 59/294; Latin Clb; Political Wkr; Acpl Chr; School Musical; Ed Lit Mag; Drama Clb; Science Clb; Yrbk Stf; Powder Puff Ftbl; High Hon Roll; NY Young Playwrt Assoc 84; 1st Rnnr Up Govrns Schl Vclst 85; Oberlin Coll; Psychlgy.

DREHER, PAM; Southern Regional HS; Waretown, NJ; (Y); Ski Clb; Sthrn Rgnl Hnr Roll 84-86; Georgian Ct Clg; Accntng.

DREISS, STEVEN; Secaucus HS; Secaucus, NJ; (Y); Band; Bowling; Hon Roll; Grphc Arts.

DREW, TODD; Msgr Donovan HS; Bayville, NJ; (Y); Am Leg Boys St; Cmnty Wkr; Var L Bsktbl; Var L Socr; Hon Roll; NHS.

DREXLER JR, HARRY J; Lacey Tgownship HS; Forked River, NJ; (Y); 20/288; Rep Frsh Cls; Trs VP Stu Cncl; Ftbl; High Hon Roll; Hon Roll; Pres NHS; Ldrshp Training Conf Rep 85; Acad Achvt Awd Eng 85-86; Close Up Rep 84-85; Pol Sci.

DREYER, MARY KATHERINE; Steinert HS; Hamilton Sq, NJ; (Y); 24/329; AFS; FBLA; Intnl Clb; Key Clb; Yrbk Stf; Trs Stu Cncl; Fld Hcky; Trk; Hon Roll; NHS; American U WA DC; Bus Mgmt.

DREYER, SUSAN; Toms River High School East; Toms River, NJ; (Y); 10/461; Color Guard; Mrchg Band; Var Swmmng; JV Trk; NHS; Math Tm; Science Clb; Concert Band; Toms River Tchr Assn Schlrshp 86; Booster Clb Schlrshp-Athlts 86; U Of DE; Engrng.

DRINGUS, MICHELLE; Southern Regional HS; Barnegat, NJ; (Y); 57/391; Church Yth Grp; Dance Clb; Ski Clb; School Musical; Yrbk Stf; Rep Jr Cls; Hon Roll; NHS; Ldrshp Awd 83; Mnsgnr Donnovan Schlrshp 86.

DRISCOLL, CHERYL; Pinelands Regional HS; Pakertown, NJ; (Y); Church Yth Grp; Cmnty Wkr; Hosp Aide; Varsity Clb; Band; Church Choir; Concert Band; Jazz Band; Mrchg Band; Variety Show; Accptd U S Music Ambssdrs Go On Tour Europe 85; Schlrshp West Chester Band Camp 86; ST Teen Arts 85; Duquenne U; Music.

DRISCOLL, DEBORAH; Pinelands Regional HS; Tuckerton, NJ; (Y); #12 In Class; Art Clb; Fld Hcky; Socr; Trk; Hon Roll; Sec NHS; Vet.

DRISCOLL, SUSAN; Gloucester Catholic HS; Bellmawr, NJ; (Y); 23/168; Cmnty Wkr; Pep Clb; Stage Crew; Yrbk Stf; Rep Stu Cncl; Var Capt Cheerleading; JV Trk; Hon Roll; NHS; Stu Of Mnth 84-85; Miss Bellmawr Pgnt-Miss Congenlty 86; Stockton ST Coll; Hotl Mgmt.

DRISCOLL, TIM; Mt Olive HS; Budd Lake, NJ; (Y); Var Bsbl; Var Ftbl; Var Ice Hcky; Wt Lftg; Hon Roll; Woodworking 3rd Pl And Grandprize 87.

DRIVER, AUDREY M; Hopewell Vly Central HS; Pennington, NJ; (Y); #44 In Class; AFS; Art Clb; Church Yth Grp; Girl Scts; Office Aide; Spanish Clb; Rep Sr Cls; Rep Stu Cncl; Hon Roll; NHS; Intl Rltns.

DRIZING, STEVEN; Passaic Valley HS; Totowa, NJ; (Y); Pres Chess Clb; Computer Clb; German Clb; Science Clb; Ski Clb; Y-Teens; Hon Roll; Comp Sci.

DROSOS, EVA; Dover HS; Dover, NJ; (Y); Church Yth Grp; Variety Show; Capt Cheerleading; Socr.

DROSOS, HELEN; Dover HS; Dover, NJ; (Y); 33/230; Am Leg Aux Girls St; Church Yth Grp; Ski Clb; Spanish Clb; Variety Show; Capt Cheerleading; Socr; Ahepa Schlrshp 86; Syracuse U.

DRUCK, MATT; Chatham Township HS; Chatham, NJ; (Y); 45/135; Chess Clb; Ftbl; Chem.

DRUCKMAN, STEVEN E; West Windsor Plainsboro HS; Princeton Junctn, NJ; (Y); AFS; Am Leg Boys St; French Clb; Concert Band; Trs Jr Cls; Stu Cncl; Bsbl; Ftbl; High Hon Roll; NHS; Wash Smnr 85; Frnch Exchng NACEL 86.

DRZIK, E KEVIN; Cinnaminson HS; Cinnaminson, NJ; (Y); Am Leg Boys St; Trs Church Yth Grp; Cmnty Wkr; SADD; Chorus; VP Frsh Cls; Pres Soph Cls; Trs Jr Cls; Pres Stu Cncl; JV Capt Socr; Bus Adm.

DU BOIS, BERNARD; Gloucester City HS; Gloucester, NJ; (Y); Cmnty Wkr; JA; Science Clb; Teachers Aide; Ftbl; Wt Lftg; Cit Awd; High Hon Roll; Hon Roll; NHS; Technel Engr.

DU BOIS, JEFFREY T; Cumberland Christian Schl; Estell Manor, NJ; (S); 1/33; Church Yth Grp; Trs Frsh Cls; Pres Soph Cls; Pres Jr Cls; Trs Stu Cncl; Var Mgr(s); Var Socr; Hon Roll; Sprtsmnshp Awd/Soccer 84-85; Arch.

DU BOIS, LISA; Maranatha Christian Acad HS; Freehold, NJ; (S); 1/6; Church Yth Grp; Chorus; Church Choir; School Play; Yrbk Stf; Rep Stu Cncl; High Hon Roll; Hstry Eng & Bible Awds 83 & 84; Elem Ed.

DUBLIN, TARA; Raritan HS; Hazlet, NJ; (Y); 50/312; VP Drama Clb; French Clb; School Musical; School Play; Stage Crew; Hosp Aide; Intnl Clb; Temple Yth Grp; Chorus; Variety Show; Emerson Coll Boston; Actrss.

DUBROSKI, ALISON M; Union Catholic Regional HS; Roselle, NJ; (Y); 93/399; Hosp Aide; Service Clb; Ski Clb; SADD; School Musical; Rep Sr Cls; Stu Cncl; Var Cheerleading; Hon Roll.

DUCUSIN, DONATO; Dickinson HS; Jersey City, NJ; (Y); Computer Clb; Scholastic Bowl; Science Clb; Hon Roll; NHS; Prfct Atten Awd; NJ Inst Of Tech; Elec Engr.

DUDAK, MARYALICE; East Brunswick HS; East Brunswick, NJ; (Y); Drama Clb; FBLA; German Clb; Color Guard; CC Awd; NHS; German Hnr Socy 84-86; German Hnr Socy-Treas 85-86; Miami U; Mktg.

DUDDY, PATRICK; Red Bank Catholic HS; Red Bank, NJ; (Y); Pres Aud/Vis; Boy Scts; Chess Clb; Cmnty Wkr; Exploring; Science Clb; Hon Roll; Egl Sct 86; Rutgers; Comp.

DUDZINSKI, PATRICIA; Sparta HS; Sparta, NJ; (Y); Key Clb; Concert Band; Mrchg Band; Yrbk Stf; JV Bsktbl; High Hon Roll; NHS; Pres Schlr; Coll Of Holy Cross.

DUERK, CHRISTINE; Parsippany HS; Parsippany, NJ; (Y); Cmnty Wkr; Exploring; FBLA; Hosp Aide; Pep Clb; Rep Stu Cncl; High Hon Roll; Hon Roll; NHS; Ntl Merit Ltr.

DUESPOHL, KRISTEN; Overbrook Regional SR HS; Pine Hill, NJ; (Y); 4-H; Hosp Aide; Band; Concert Band; Mrchg Band; Cheerleading; Twrlr; NHS.

DUFFIELD, C STEWART; Clearview Regional HS; Mullica Hill, NJ; (Y); 9/180; Am Leg Boys St; Spanish Clb; Pres Band; Chorus; Pres Concert Band; Jazz Band; Mrchg Band; Stat Bsktbl; Hon Roll; JP Sousa Awd; Drexel U; Bus Admn.

DUFFUS, KEVIN; St Joseph Regional HS; Northvale, NJ; (Y); 33/210; Service Clb; JV Bsbl; JV Bsktbl; JV Var Ftbl; Hon Roll; NHS; Spanish NHS; Mst Imprvd Bsktbl 84; MVP Ftbll 86; U Of Scranton; Physcl Thrpy.

DUFFY, DIANE; Central Regional HS; Bayville, NJ; (Y); Var Bsktbl; Powder Puff Ftbl; Var Sftbl; Trk; Social Work.

DUFFY, KERRY; Middletown HS South; Navesink, NJ; (S); 38/436; Pres 4-H; Variety Show; Nwsp Rptr; Rep Jr Cls; Rep Sr Cls; Rep Stu Cncl; Powder Puff Ftbl; Sftbl; Trk; 4-H Awd; Pony Clb C-2 Rtng; 4-H Eques Yr 85; 1st Rnnr-Up 4-H Queen Cntst 85; Cornell U; Pre-Law.

DUGAN, JENNIFER; Toms River HS East; Toms River, NJ; (Y); 33/480; VP French Clb; Chorus; Yrbk Ed-Chief; Stat Ftbl; Mgr(s); Powder Puff Ftbl; JV Socr; JV Tennis; High Hon Roll; Hon Roll; T R Educnl Assoc Schlrshp 86; Frank & Irene Papines Schlrshp 86; Garden ST Schlrshp; Drew U; Bio Sci.

DUGAN, KELLY; Holy Cross HS; Marlton, NJ; (Y); Church Yth Grp; Hosp Aide; Rep Soph Cls; Cheerleading; High Hon Roll; Hon Roll.

DUGAN, TERESA ANN; Holy Cross HS; Cinnaminson, NJ; (Y); 109/385; Church Yth Grp; French Clb; Mrchg Band; School Musical; Nwsp Stf; Yrbk Stf; Rep Soph Cls; Cheerleading; Fld Hcky; Sftbl; St Joes U; Elem Ed.

DUGGAN, DORIS; Mount Saint Dominic Academy; Bloomfield, NJ; (Y); Scholastic Bowl; Rep Soph Cls; Rep Jr Cls; Rep Sr Cls; Stu Cncl; JV Var Bsktbl; Var Capt Crs Cntry; Capt Var Trk; Hon Roll; NHS; Math.

DUHNOSKI, CARL; Hamilton H S West; Yardville, NJ; (Y); Aud/Vis; Church Yth Grp; Key Clb; Stage Crew; Stu Cncl; Diving; Swmmng; Trk; Hon Roll; Kiwanis Awd; Mrktng.

DUKE, LISA; Clifton HS; Clifton, NJ; (S); 44/583; Am Leg Aux Girls St; Key Clb; Math Clb; Ski Clb; Speech Tm; Var Capt Trk; Var Capt Vllybl; Hon Roll; Jr NHS; Ntl Merit Ltr; 1st Tm NNJIL Passaic-Essex Vlybl 85; 2nd Tm Passaic Cnty Vlybl 85; Cmmnctns.

DUKES, KIMBERLY; Mother Seton Regional HS; Linden, NJ; (Y); Church Yth Grp; Debate Tm; Drama Clb; Stage Crew; Lit Mag; Kiwanis Awd; Pres NHS; Voice Dem Awd; Scholastic Bowl; Hon Roll; Acad All Amer; Ladies Aux KOC Scholar; Polc Benevolent Assoc Unden Scholar; Columbia U; Spn.

DUKIET, LINDA; John P Stevens HS; Edison, NJ; (Y); 20/488; Art Clb; Church Yth Grp; Math Tm; Model UN; Science Clb; Orch; Nwsp Bus Mgr; Powder Puff Ftbl; French Hon Soc; NHS.

DULOG, MAX; St Pius X HS; Edison, NJ; (Y); Computer Clb; Trs Math Clb; Off Frsh Cls; Var Bsktbl; Var Ftbl; Var Socr; Var Trk; Architecture.

DUMAS II, JIMMY E; Morristown HS; Morristown, NJ; (Y); 21/449; Am Leg Boys St; Church Yth Grp; VP Church Choir; Concert Band; Jazz Band; Var L Bsktbl; Var L Trk; Hon Roll; Trs NHS; Ntl Merit Ltr; U S Mltry Acad Acdmc Wrkshp At West Point 86; Archtctr.

DUMOND, LORI; Hackettstown HS; Hackettstown, NJ; (Y); Church Yth Grp; Cmnty Wkr; Key Clb; Pep Clb; Chorus; Church Choir; School Musical; Rep Stu Cncl; Hon Roll; NHS; Crmnlgy.

DUNCAN, STEVE; Holy Cross HS; Mount Laurel, NJ; (Y); 130/400; Trs Church Yth Grp; Ski Clb; Varsity Clb; Var Tennis; High Hon Roll; Hon Roll; James Madison; Bus Mgmt.

DUNHOUR, TINA; Cinnaminson HS; Cinnaminson, NJ; (Y); 98/250; Church Yth Grp; Pep Clb; Spanish Clb; Sec Frsh Cls; Off Soph Cls; Off Jr Cls; Off Sr Cls; Stu Cncl; Var Capt Fld Hcky; Sftbl; U Of DE; Lbrl Arts.

DUNICH, JENNIFER; South River HS; S River, NJ; (Y); 27/130; Sftbl; Hon Roll; Graphic Desgn.

DUNIGAN, MARY BETH; Mother Seton Regional HS; Woodbridge, NJ; (Y); 16/116; Trs Church Yth Grp; GAA; Math Tm; Science Clb; Nwsp Rptr; Nwsp Stf; Yrbk Stf; Lit Mag; Rep Jr Cls; JV Capt Bsktbl; Yth Ministry Awd 84-85 & 85-86; Cert Recruitment 86; Law.

DUNKIEL, BRIAN; Pascack Valley Regional HS; Rivervale, NJ; (Y); AFS; Nwsp Bus Mgr; Nwsp Rptr; Rep Sr Cls; JV Bsktbl; JV Socr; Var Swmmng; Mst Imprvd Swmr 84; 1st & 2nd Pl NJ Grdn ST Gms 85; Qualfr YMCA Natls 85-86; Bus Ec.

DUNLEAVY, PETER; Manalapan HS; Englishtown, NJ; (Y); 50/440; JCL; Latin Clb; Stu Cncl; Var Bsktbl; Var Socr; NHS; Latin Awd 85; Poltcl Sci.

DUNN, ANNMARIE; Queen Of Peace HS; North Arlington, NJ; (S); 10/243; Church Yth Grp; Cmnty Wkr; Drama Clb; PAVAS; SADD; School Musical; High Hon Roll; NHS; Thesps; Chorus; Semi-Fin Govnrs Schl Arts 85; Summr Schlr Pgm St Peters Coll 85; Garden ST Dstngshd Schlr 85; Comm.

DUNN, BILL; Hunterdon Central HS; Stockton, NJ; (Y); Boy Scts; Ski Clb; Bsbl; JV Ftbl; JV Var Wt Lftg; Bench Press Compttn At Local Hlth Clb 86; U Sthrn CA; Bus Mgmt.

DUNN, COLLEEN; Nutley HS; Nutley, NJ; (Y); 30/338; Office Aide; Ski Clb; Spanish Clb; Rep Soph Cls; Stu Cncl; Cheerleading; Mgr(s); High Hon Roll; NHS; Womans Club-Maureen Marion Mem Awd 86; Rutgers U; Pre-Med.

DUNN, KERRI; Long Branch HS; Elberon, NJ; (Y); 20/214; Computer Clb; Drama Clb; English Clb; Pres French Clb; Key Clb; Pep Clb; PAVAS; Varsity Clb; School Musical; School Play; Vrsty Schlr 85-86; St Thomas U Schlrshp 86; PA Coll; Crmnl Justc.

DUNN, WAYNE; High Point Regional HS; Sussex, NJ; (Y); 15/234; CAP; Computer Clb; Pres Debate Tm; Trs Am Leg Aux Girls St0; Latin Clb; Model UN; Quiz Bowl; Capt Scholastic Bowl; Science Clb; Im Trk; Coaches Awd 86; Aersp Engrg.

DUNNE, CHRISTINE; Pompton Lakes HS; Pompton Lakes, NJ; (Y); OEA; Spanish Clb; Teachers Aide; Chorus; Nwsp Stf; Hon Roll; Bus Adm.

DUNNE, ERIC M; Montclair HS; Upr Montclair, NJ; (Y); 24/432; Quiz Bowl; JV Var Lcrss; JV Var Computer Clb; NHS; Ntl Merit SF; St Schlr; Engrng.

DUNSON, NATALYNN; University HS; Newark, NJ; (Y); 2/59; Church Yth Grp; JA; Chorus; School Musical; Nwsp Ed-Chief; Nwsp Rptr; Pres Soph Cls; Pres Jr Cls; Pres Sr Cls; Var Capt Bsktbl; Stu Rep Bd Of Ed 85-86; Acadmc All Am 85-86; Stu Of Yr Schlrshp 86; U Of PA Wharton; Ecnmcs.

DUNTON, WAYNE; River Dell Regional HS; River Edge, NJ; (S); Boy Scts; Church Yth Grp; Band; Concert Band; Jazz Band; Mrchg Band; Orch; School Musical; Symp Band; NJ Rgn 1 Cncrt & Jazz Band 84; Class Musician 84-85; Pro Musician.

DUPRE, DARREN; Shore Regional HS; Oceanport, NJ; (Y); Var Ftbl; Var Wt Lftg; High Hon Roll; Elec Engrng.

DUPREE JR, FRANK L; Middletown HS North; Middletown, NJ; (Y); 91/420; Band; Concert Band; Jazz Band; Mrchg Band; Symp Band; Variety Show; High Hon Roll; Hon Roll; All Shore Jazz Band 83-86; Regn Jazz Band 83-86; All ST Jazz Band 85; Music.

DUPREE, JEFFREY; Hudson Catholic HS; Jersey Cty, NJ; (Y); 208/280; Boys Clb Am; Rep Frsh Cls; Pres Jr Cls; Pres Sr Cls; Capt Crs Cntry; Capt Trk; Im Vllybl; Hon Roll; X-Cntry Hawk Awd 85; Accntg.

DUPUIS, PATRICIA; Pascack Hills HS; Hillsdale, NJ; (Y); Bsktbl; Socr; Sftbl; Hon Roll; Fshn Dsgnr.

DUQUE, D ALEJANDRO; Toms River HS; Pine Beach, NJ; (Y); 10/297; Math Clb; Math Tm; Scholastic Bowl; Science Clb; Band; Concert Band; Jazz Band; Mrchg Band; School Musical; Variety Show; NE Awd Excllnc Lang Stdy Frgn Lang 86; Pres Acad Ftnss Awd 86; Papr Carr Schlrshp 84; Le High U; Elec Engrng.

DURAN, ROSALBA; Mary Help Of Christians Acad; Paterson, NJ; (S); Art Clb; Cmnty Wkr; Computer Clb; Hosp Aide; Latin Clb; Math Clb; Drill Tm; Hon Roll; Awd In Spanish, Engl & W Hist 85; Rutgers; Engnr.

DURAND, CARRIE; Scotch Plains-Fanwood HS; Scotch Pl, NJ; (Y); Dance Clb; FBLA; VP Soph Cls; Sec Sr Cls; Rep Stu Cncl; Cheerleading; Im Vllybl; Civil Engrng.

DURELL, ALAN; Dumont HS; Dumont, NJ; (Y); 3/205; FBLA; Math Tm; Pres Sr Cls; JV Ftbl; Var Golf; Bausch & Lomb Sci Awd; High Hon Roll; Mu Alp Tht; Opt Clb Awd; Pres Schlr; All Cnty Golf 86; Clinton-Suburbanite Sprtsmnshp Awd 86; Grdn ST Dstngshd Schlr Awd 85; Cornell U; Engrng.

DURHAM, CHRIS; Hopewell Valley Central HS; Hopewell, NJ; (Y); 7/202; Am Leg Boys St; Var Ice Hcky; Socr; Var Tennis; NHS; Pre-Med.

DURHAM JR, EDDIE L; John F Kennedy HS; Willingboro, NJ; (Y); 29/339; Chess Clb; Church Yth Grp; Computer Clb; Hosp Aide; Science Clb; Ftbl; Hon Roll; NHS; Air Force Rotc 4 Yr Schlrhsp 85; AFNA Stu 82-85; Rutgers Coll Engrs; Bio Engr.

DURHAM, LINDA; Paulsboro HS; Gibbstown, NJ; (Y); Church Yth Grp; Office Aide; Band; Church Choir; Concert Band; Mrchg Band; Symp Band; Variety Show; High Hon Roll; Hon Roll; Nrsng.

DURKAC, DAVID; Neptune SR HS; Neptune, NJ; (Y); Camp Fr Inc; Varsity Clb; Rep Soph Cls; Rep Jr Cls; JV Capt Bsktbl; Var L Socr; Hon Roll; Stckbrkr.

DURKIN, DEIDRE; North Arlington HS; N Arlington, NJ; (Y); French Clb; Trs Frsh Cls; Trs Soph Cls; Trs Jr Cls; Trs Sr Cls; Rep Stu Cncl; Mgr Crs Cntry; Sftbl; Hon Roll; $100 Schlrshp NAHS Schlrshp Fund; Montclair ST Coll.

DURSO, THOMAS; Deptford Township HS; Deptford, NJ; (Y); 1/300; Am Leg Boys St; Church Yth Grp; Nwsp Ed-Chief; Nwsp Rptr; Yrbk Stf; Pres Stu Cncl; Bsbl; Jr NHS; NHS; Rutgers Schlrshp 86; Englsh.

DURST, CHRISTINE; Red Bank Catholic HS; Spring Lake, NJ; (Y); French Clb; Yrbk Stf; Lit Mag; Hon Roll; Cert Of Awd For Hon Roll 86; Business.

DUSCIO, THERESA; Jackson Memorial HS; Jackson, NJ; (Y); 50/411; Sec PAVAS; SADD; Yrbk Ed-Chief; Ed Lit Mag; High Hon Roll; Hon Roll; Ntl Art Hnr Soc Sec 86; Rider Coll Frgn Lang Comp Wnnr 85-86; Outstndng Stu Awd-Ltrary Mgzn Edtr 86; Comm Prodctn.

DUSEK, JENNIFER; Haddon Township HS; Westmont, NJ; (Y); VP Girl Scts; Flag Corp; Yrbk Stf; Camden County Coll; Bus.

DUSHECK, BRIAN; Toms River High School East; Toms River, NJ; (Y); 51/587; Intnl Clb; Var L Bsktbl; Hon Roll; Boostr Assoc Mst Supptv Plyr Bsktbl 85-86; Prsnll Mgmt.

DUTHALER, TODD; Don Bosco Prep HS; Maywood, NJ; (Y); Boy Scts; Stage Crew; Mgr Ftbl; Hon Roll; NHS; Egl Sct 85; Sci.

DUTKIEWICZ, STEPHEN; St Peters Prep Schl; Jersey City, NJ; (Y); 31/209; Aud/Vis; Pres Camera Clb; School Play; Stage Crew; Nwsp Phtg; Yrbk Phtg; Lit Mag; Hon Roll; NHS; Pres Schlr; Pres Schlrshp Prep 82-86; Stevens Inst; Elec Engr.

DUTKO, PAUL W; Passaic Valley Regional HS; Little Falls, NJ; (Y); Am Leg Boys St; Chess Clb; Debate Tm; Science Clb; Rep Stu Cncl; Crs Cntry; Ftbl; Trk; NHS; Biomed.

DUTTON, TERESA; Pennsauken HS; Pennsauken, NJ; (Y); 8/365; Concert Band; Yrbk Stf; Hon Roll; NHS; Spanish NHS; Pres Ftns Awd 86.

DUVE, MARK F; Warren Hill Regional SR HS; Washington, NJ; (Y); Am Leg Boys St; Boy Scts; Ski Clb; Var Crs Cntry; JV Socr; Hon Roll; NHS; Eagl Sct; Sci.

DVORAK, LORI A; St Joseph Of The Palisade; North Bergen, NJ; (S); 4/128; Cmnty Wkr; Math Clb; Teachers Aide; Variety Show; Nwsp Ed-Chief; Ed Lit Mag; Capt Bowling; High Hon Roll; NHS; Spanish NHS; NJ Garden ST Schlrs Prog Hnbl Mntn 85-86; Ntl Ldrshp & Svc Awd 85-86; Dartmouth Bk Clb Awd 84-85; Accntng.

DVORKIN, HEIDI; Toms River North; Toms River, NJ; (Y); 10/430; FBLA; Spanish Clb; Mrchg Band; Yrbk Stf; Off Stu Cncl; Stat Bsktbl; Fld Hcky; Sftbl; High Hon Roll; Hon Roll; Liberal Arts.

DWORKIN, DAVID; The Wardlaw-Hartridge Schl; Piscataway, NJ; (Y); 32/53; Aud/Vis; Camera Clb; VP Debate Tm; Key Clb; Office Aide; Yrbk Stf; JV Socr; JV Tennis; JV Var Wrstlng; Bus.

DWYER, JOSEPH; Westfield SR HS; Westfield, NJ; (Y); French Clb; Nwsp Rptr; Nwsp Stf; Bus Finance.

DYCHKOWSKI, PAUL; Toms River HS South; Beachwood, NJ; (Y); Im Bsktbl; JV Var Ftbl; JV Var Trk; Widener U; Comp.

DYER, NADINE; St Aloysius HS; Jersey City, NJ; (Y); 5/113; Exploring; SADD; Teachers Aide; Yrbk Stf; High Hon Roll; Sec NHS; Outstndng Achvt-Frnch Cert 84-85; Outstndnt Achvt-Rlgs Studies Cert 85-86; Outstndnt Achvt-Rel Studies.

DYGOS, RICHARD; West Milford HS; West Milford, NJ; (Y); Am Leg Boys St; SADD; VP Frsh Cls; VP Soph Cls; Var L Bsbl; Var L Bsktbl; Var L Socr; High Hon Roll; NHS; Acctg.

DYITT, MARLON; Pleasantville HS; Pleasantville, NJ; (S); 4/150; Spanish Clb; Rep Soph Cls; Rep Jr Cls; Var Bsbl; Var Bsktbl; Var Ftbl; Wt Lftg; Jr NHS; NHS; Ntl Merit Ltr; Cert For Nrs Aide Red Cross Bld Dr 85; All-Sci Stu Trphy 82; Temple; Chem Engr.

DZIEDZIC, JANINE; Bishop George A H R HS; Fords, NJ; (Y); Ski Clb; Spanish Clb; Cheerleading; Crs Cntry; Acctng.

DZIEZAWIEC, JOY; Mary Help Of Christians Acad; Paterson, NJ; (Y); Church Yth Grp; Cmnty Wkr; Latin Clb; Orch; Yrbk Stf; Ntl Merit Ltr; NEDT Awd; Hnr Cls; Rutgers; Psych.

DZUBERA, JOHN; Butler HS; Bloomingdale, NJ; (Y); 2/197; Math Tm; High Hon Roll; Sal; Quiz Bowl; Scholastic Bowl; NHS; Ntl Merit Ltr; St Schlr; Drew U; Bus.

DZULA, SUE; W Essex HS; N Caldwell, NJ; (Y); 84/350; Cmnty Wkr; Var Jr Cls; Mat Maids; Rutgers U.

DZUREK, MICHAEL; Pope John XXIII HS; Hackettstown, NJ; (Y); Church Yth Grp; Ski Clb; Bsbl; Ftbl; High Hon Roll; Cert Of Hnr-Scl Stds 84; Cert Of Hnr-Alg & Hstry 86; Comp Engrng.

DZURKOC, JEFF; Hamilton HS West; Trenton, NJ; (Y); 12/360; Math Clb; Stage Crew; Hon Roll; NHS; Drexel COLL; Elect Engrng.

EACHUS, BARBARA; Washington Township HS; Sewell, NJ; (Y); Spanish Clb; Trk; Hon Roll; Rutgers U; Bio.

EALER, JAMES G; Hunterdon Central HS; Whitehouse Statn, NJ; (Y); 3/560; Math Tm; Lit Mag; Im Vllybl; Gov Hon Prg Awd; High Hon Roll; NHS; Ntl Merit Ltr; Computer Clb; Hon Roll; Rusain Hnr Soc 85-86; Russain II,III,Geramn I Lang Awds 85-86.

EARLE, WHITNEY; Lakewood HS; Lakewood, NJ; (Y); 86/240; Church Yth Grp; Civic Clb; Girl Scts; Office Aide; Chorus; Church Choir; Lit Mag; Var Crs Cntry; Var Trk; Wt Lftg; Lizzie Dunn Schrlshp Ad 86; Ntl Seacoast Schrlshp Awd 86; PTSA Awd 86; Rutgers; Law.

EASLEY, NANCY-CAROL; Immaculate Conception HS; Orange, NJ; (Y); 5/65; Computer Clb; Math Clb; PAVAS; Acpl Chr; Chorus; Yrbk Bus Mgr; Cheerleading; Capt Trk; High Hon Roll; Church Yth Grp; Paine Coll Augusta GA; Elec En.

EASTERDAY JR, BOB; Victory Christian Schl; Williamstown, NJ; (Y); 3/17; Church Yth Grp; Pres Soph Cls; JV Var Bsbl; Var Capt Bsktbl; Var Capt Socr; Hon Roll; Savings Bond From Womens Club Of Williamstown 86; Pensacola Chrstn Coll; Accntng.

EASTERLING, KIM; East Orange HS; E Orange, NJ; (S); Church Yth Grp; French Clb; FNA; Band; Concert Band; Mrchg Band; Nwsp Rptr; Nwsp Stf; Yrbk Stf; JV Sftbl; Mrktng.

EASTMOND, PATTI; St John Vianney HS; Union Beach, NJ; (Y); 116/298; Dance Clb; Girl Scts; School Musical; Lit Mag; Rep Jr Cls; Var L Cheerleading; Powder Puff Ftbl; Var Trk; Hon Roll; Teen Arts 1st Jazz 83; Showstopper Natl Dance Comp 4th 83; Gold/Whtie Awd 87; INTL Bus.

EATON, TODD; Haddon Township HS; Westmont, NJ; (Y); Am Leg Boys St; German Clb; Acpl Chr; Jazz Band; School Play; Variety Show; Var Swmmng; West Point; Engrng.

EBEDE, UCHECHI; Piscataway HS; Piscataway, NJ; (Y); Church Yth Grp; Computer Clb; Key Clb; Math Clb; Science Clb; Nwsp Stf; Yrbk Stf; Rutgers U; Pedtrcn.

EBELING, MARY; Burlington Co Vo Tech Schl; Willingboro, NJ; (Y); 10/177; Church Yth Grp; FBLA; VICA; Yrbk Stf; JV Var Bowling; Im Socr; High Hon Roll; Hon Roll; NHS; Accntng.

EBERLE, ROBERT; Gloucester JR SR HS; Gloucester, NJ; (Y); Am Leg Boys St; Aud/Vis; Pres Science Clb; Rep Stu Cncl; Var Bsktbl; Hon Roll; NHS; Prfct Atten Awd; Marine Engrg.

EBERSOLE, SEAN; Brick Twp HS; Brick Town, NJ; (Y); 27/410; Debate Tm; Drama Clb; Math Tm; Stage Crew; Bsbl; Bowling; High Hon Roll; NHS; Comp Engrng.

ECCLESTON, MARY ELLEN; Our Lady Of Mercy Acad; Cherry Hill, NJ; (Y); SADD; Chorus; Church Choir; VP Stu Cncl; Var Cheerleading; Var Sftbl; NHS; Church Yth Grp; 4-H; Im Diving; Rutgers Schlr Awd 86; Pres Phys Fit Awd 84-86; Intr Dsgn.

ECHO, JENNIE; Brick Memorial HS; Brick Town, NJ; (Y); 92/307; Cmnty Wkr; JA; Chorus; Church Choir; School Musical; School Play; Variety Show; VP Frsh Cls; Hon Roll; Hnrs Awd Pins & Ltr 84-86; Relgs Awd & Mst Respctd Awd 82; M/S 1st Awd 83; Big Sistr & Hrt Fnd Vlntr; Ocean Cnty Coll; Psysc.

ECKERT, KEVIN; Brick Twp HS; Brick, NJ; (Y); 39/329; Boy Scts; Drama Clb; Thesps; Band; Concert Band; Jazz Band; Mrchg Band; Stage Crew; High Hon Roll; Pres Acadmc Ftnss Awd; Ocean County Clg; Comptr Sci.

ECKSTEIN, DAVID; Christian Brothers Acad; Middletown, NJ; (Y); 7/230; Church Yth Grp; FCA; Var Letterman Clb; Math Tm; Varsity Clb; Var L Bsbl; Im Bsktbl; High Hon Roll; Mst Valbl Plyr Awd Monmouth Cnty CYO Bsktbll Leag 85-86.

EDELBACH, DOUGLAS; Hunterdon Central HS; Ringoes, NJ; (Y); 25/548; Am Leg Boys St; Boy Scts; Church Yth Grp; Ski Clb; Rep Jr Cls; Rep Stu Cncl; JV Trk; Im Vllybl; Hon Roll; NHS.

EDELSTEIN, ANDREA B; Scotch Plains-Fanwood HS; Scotch Plns, NJ; (Y); Key Clb; Temple Yth Grp; Concert Band; Mrchg Band; Symp Band; Hon Roll; Wmn In Mngmnt Semnr At Stvns Inst 86; Bus Admn.

EDGAR, JACQUELINE; Hamilton HS West; Yardville, NJ; (Y); Math Clb; JV Fld Hcky; JV Trk; Hon Roll; Pre-Med.

EDMOND, BOBBI; Holy Spirit HS; Pleasantville, NJ; (Y); Jrnlsm.

EDMONDSON, BEN; Schalick HS; Bridgeton, NJ; (Y); 18/140; Varsity Clb; JV Bowling; Var Score Keeper; JV Var Socr; Var Tennis; Cit Awd; VFW Awd; Howard U; Politcl Sci.

EDWARDS JR, JAMES; Bridgewater-Raritan HS East; Bridgewater, NJ; (Y); Pres Church Yth Grp; Jr Cls; Im Bowling; JV Socr; Hon Roll; Lbrl Arts.

EDWARDS, JONATHAN D; Hackensack HS; Hackensack, NJ; (Y); 1/475; Am Leg Boys St; Ski Clb; Spanish Clb; Lit Mag; Var L Tennis; High Hon Roll; NHS; Ntl Merit Ltr; Spanish NHS; Val; 3rd Pl Spnsh Oratory Cmptn ST-WD 86; Nmrs Awds Clsscl Piano 84-86; Ctznshp Awd Cty 86; Physcs.

EDWARDS, LAURA; Paramus HS; Paramus, NJ; (Y); Cmnty Wkr; Pres Drama Clb; French Clb; PAVAS; Pres Trs Chorus; School Musical; School Play; Yrbk Bus Mgr; Rep Sr Cls; Twrlr; Catholic U; Theatre.

EDWARDS, LEAH; Rutherford HS; Rutherford, NJ; (Y); 59/185; Drama Clb; French Clb; Key Clb; Spanish Clb; Chorus; Flag Corp; School Musical; School Play; Stage Crew; Variety Show; Coll Experience Pgm, Outstndng Vocalist Awd 86; Farleigh Dickinson U.

EDWARDS, PAUL; Glassboro HS; Pitman, NJ; (Y); Science Clb; Varsity Clb; Var Bsbl; Var Socr; Hon Roll; NHS; Hnrb Mntn All Conf Socr 85-86; Tri-Cnty Conf Clssc Div All Star Bsbl 85-86.

EDWARDS, ROBIN; Plainfield HS; Plainfield, NJ; (Y); 2/486; Hst FBLA; Model UN; Concert Band; Sec Capt Mrchg Band; Rep Stu Cncl; JV Vllybl; High Hon Roll; Hon Roll; Sec NHS; Mst Indstrs JR New Horizons Coll Outreach 86; Duke U; Vet.

EDWARDS, SHEILA A; Millville HS; Woodbine, NJ; (Y); Church Yth Grp; Computer Clb; Office Aide; Red Cross Aide; Acpl Chr; Church Choir; Variety Show; Nwsp Rptr; Sec Stu Cncl; Var Capt Cheerleading; Hmcmng Queen 85-86; Ldrs Club Awd Outstndg Ldr Yr 83-84; U Of DE; Crmnl Jstc.

EDWARDS, VICTORIA; Maranatha Christian Acad; Hillside, NJ; (S); 1/6; VP Church Yth Grp; Band; Chorus; Mrchg Band; Nwsp Ed-Chief; Yrbk Stf; Hon Roll; Hghst Grdpnt Avrge 84; Stu Yr 84; Bio Awd 85.

EDZENGA, LYNN ANN; Pompton Lakes HS; Pompton Lakes, NJ; (Y); 5/152; Am Leg Aux Girls St; Hosp Aide; Math Clb; Teachers Aide; Color Guard; Mrchg Band; High Hon Roll; JP Sousa Awd; NHS; St Schlr; Alumni Schlrshp Trntn ST Coll 86; Hnrs In Hstry 84-85; Hnrs In Englsh & Hmnts 85-86; Trntn ST Coll; Nrs.

EELMAN, KEVIN; Lakewood HS; Lakewood, NJ; (Y); 11/294; Am Leg Boys St; Boy Scts; Chess Clb; German Clb; Math Tm; High Hon Roll; Hon Roll; Grmn Hnr Scty 85; Ordr Of Arrow 85; High Scr Math Team 86.

EFFENBERGER, KRISTIN; West Essex HS; Roseland, NJ; (Y); Church Yth Grp; Hosp Aide; Ski Clb; Chorus; Var L Bsktbl; Var L Cheerleading; Gym; JV Socr; JV Sftbl; Hon Roll; Elem Ed.

EFROM, MICHELE; Matawan Regional HS; Aberdeen, NJ; (S); 3/290; Math Tm; VP Concert Band; VP Mrchg Band; Orch; Bowling; Trk; High Hon Roll; NHS; Mth Hnr Soc 84-86; U DE; Acctg.

EGAN, JACK; Hunterdon Central HS; Whitehouse Sta, NJ; (Y); 100/539; Computer Clb; Ski Clb; Rep Frsh Cls; Rep Soph Cls; Im Bsktbl; Sec Ftbl; JV Trk; Lockheed Mgmt Awd 86; All Arnd Stu Awd 82; Villanova; Bio.

EGAN, KATHLEEN; Parsippany Hills HS; Morris Plains, NJ; (Y); 20/302; Var Chrmn Church Yth Grp; VP FBLA; Chrmn Varsity Clb; Variety Show; Nwsp Rptr; Rep Stu Cncl; Var L Bsktbl; Var L Socr; Var L Sftbl; Var L Tennis; Var Clb Scholar 86; US Army Stu Achvt Awd 86; Polc Ath Lg Scholar 86; Lehigh U; Engrng.

EGAN, PATRICK; Christian Bros Acad; Spring Lake Hts, NJ; (Y); 22/220; Dance Clb; Math Tm; Nwsp Rptr; Var L Bsktbl; Im Ftbl; Var L Golf; High Hon Roll; Bus.

EGENTON, BRIAN; Bishop George Ahr HS; Plainfield, NJ; (Y); German Clb; Sec Frsh Cls; Sec Soph Cls; Pres Jr Cls; JV Var Ftbl; Var Wt Lftg; Hon Roll; U S Stu Cncl Awds 85; Accntng.

EGER, DEANA; Mainland Regional HS; Somers Pt, NJ; (Y); 112/250; Pep Clb; SADD; Yrbk Stf; Mgr(s); Stat Trk; 2-Yr Vrsty Ltr Wnr, Boys Trck Mgr 84-86; Pblc Rltns.

EGGENHOFER, KARA; A P Schalick HS; Centerton, NJ; (Y); Church Yth Grp; Ski Clb; Pres SADD; Chorus; Concert Band; Flag Corp; Rep Soph Cls; Stat Bsktbl; Var L Cheerleading; Golf; Beautician.

EGGER, AMY S; West Essex SR HS; Roseland, NJ; (Y); 2/356; Pres Latin Clb; High Hon Roll; NHS; Ntl Merit SF; Pres Schlr; Spanish NHS; St Schlr; Computer Clb; Pres JCL; Hon Roll; Rutgers Pres Schlr 85; Roseland Borough Outstndg Achvt Awd 85; U PA; Psych.

EHLENBERGER, CAROL; Hightstown HS; E Windsor, NJ; (Y); Drama Clb; Intnl Clb; Ski Clb; Band; Mrchg Band; Yrbk Phtg; Rep Frsh Cls; Stu Cncl; Var Trk; Hon Roll; Lawyr.

EHRHARDT, JULIA; Mother Seton Redgional HS; Springfield, NJ; (Y); 1/103; Scholastic Bowl; Yrbk Ed-Chief; Yrbk Rptr; VP Jr Cls; Stat Sftbl; Bausch & Lomb Sci Awd; High Hon Roll; NHS; Ntl Merit Ltr; St Schlr; Gov Schl SF 86; Rutgers Schlr 86; Physics.

EHRLICH, MARK F; Paramus Catholic Boys HS; Wood Ridge, NJ; (Y); 12/178; Am Leg Boys St; Boy Scts; Co-Capt Debate Tm; School Musical; French Hon Soc; Hon Roll; Ntl Merit Ltr; Drama Clb; VP French Clb; Math Tm; Outstndg Srv Awd Var Letter Debate Tm 86; OSA/Ul Lead Schl Musical Fiddler On The Roof 86; Dartmouth; Marine Bio.

EHROLA, ALIX; Pt Pleasant Boro HS; Pt Pleasant Boro, NJ; (S); 16/243; Sec VP Girl Scts; Keywanettes; Chorus; Madrigals; Sec Soph Cls; Rep Stu Cncl; JV Var Cheerleading; JV Sftbl; High Hon Roll; Hon Roll; Grl Scts Slvr Awd & Ldrshp Awd 83-84; Pltcl Sci.

EICHLER, MARIA; Paramus Catholic HS; Cliffside Pk, NJ; (Y); Computer Clb; Church Choir; Lit Mag; William Patterson Coll; Commnct.

EICHLER, SUSAN; St Pius X Regional HS; Kendall Park, NJ; (Y); 4/91; Trs Girl Scts; Library Aide; Math Tm; ROTC; Spanish Clb; Sftbl; Capt Twrlr; High Hon Roll; NHS; NEDT Awd; Prsdntl Acad Ftns Awd 86; Yth Ldrshp Awd 86; Am Lgn Brnz Awd Acad Exclnc 86; Catholic U Of Am; Bimdcl Engr.

EICHNER, KAREN; Absegami HS; Egg Hbr City, NJ; (Y); 32/200; Church Yth Grp; FBLA; Socr; Sftbl; Hon Roll; Phila Bible Coll; Nrsng.

EICK, GEORGE; South Hunterdon Regional HS; Lambertville, NJ; (Y); FFA; Varsity Clb; Ftbl; Wt Lftg; Wrstlng; Ind Art.

EINSTEIN, ANDREW J; W Orange HS; W Orange, NJ; (Y); 4/176; Cmnty Wkr; Computer Clb; Math Tm; Quiz Bowl; Spanish Clb; Concert Band; Nwsp Stf; Lit Mag; Gov Hon Prg Awd; Jr NHS; Rensellaer Medal 85; Wm Patterson Coll Math Test Wnnr 85; Math.

EISELE, JOANNE; Mainland Regional HS; Northfield, NJ; (Y); Art Clb; Computer Clb; Badmtn; Mgr(s); Pres Sftbl; Swmmng; Vllybl; Rep Stu Cncl; Mrt Rl 83-85; Physcl Ftns Awd 83-84; Advrtsng.

EITZEN, JOHN; Notre Dame HS; Kendall Pk, NJ; (Y); 50/380; Key Clb; Off Ski Clb; Varsity Clb; Var L Ftbl; Var L Golf; Wt Lftg; High Hon Roll; Hon Roll; NHS; Ftbl-12th Man TD Clb 85-86; Ftbl-All Cnty Hnrb Mntn 85-86; Arch Engrng.

EKBERG, LISA; Blair Acad; Danville, PA; (Y); 2/117; Church Yth Grp; French Clb; Latin Clb; Ski Clb; Rep Stu Cncl; Var Capt Cheerleading; Im Gym; Var Mgr(s); Var Tennis; Var Trk; UNH; Frnch.

EL, SAMARIA; South Plainfield HS; S Plainfield, NJ; (Y); Teachers Aide; Band; Nwsp Stf; Lit Mag; Law.

EL-KHARBOUTLY, TAREK; Toms River HS; Toms River, NJ; (Y); 151/412; Chess Clb; Ski Clb; Var Trk; Hon Roll; Acad Ltr 86; Rutgers U; Engrng.

ELAMIN, SEMADRA; Dwight Morrow HS; Englewood, NJ; (Y); Dance Clb; Girl Scts; Model UN; Pep Clb; Pep Band; Variety Show; Rep Frsh Cls; Stu Cncl; Var Cheerleading; Sftbl; Pre-Law.

ELASHEWICH, JEANNINE; Hunterdon Central HS; Edinburg, VA; (Y); 150/550; Church Yth Grp; 4-H; Band; Chorus; Church Choir; Orch; School Musical; Symp Band; Sr Cls; Stu Cncl; Flmngtn Chptr Sweet Adlns Schlrshp 86; Cincinnati Cnsrvtry Music Annual Tlnt Schlrshp 86; U Cincinnati; Music.

ELBAZ, JENNIFER; Toms River High School North; Toms River, NJ; (Y); Dance Clb; Temple Yth Grp; Nwsp Stf; Lit Mag; Trk; High Hon Roll; Hon Roll; Rutgers U; Cmnctns.

ELCHAK, TONYA; Hillsborough HS; Bellemead, NJ; (Y); 61/300; Band; Mrchg Band; Tennis; Trk; High Hon Roll; Hon Roll; SADD; Pep Band; Off Frsh Cls; Off Soph Cls; Mth Tchr.

ELDER, BILL; Parsippany HS; Parsippany, NJ; (Y); Model UN; JV Bsktbl; Var Capt Bowling; Var Capt Golf; Hon Roll; NHS.

ELDER, ELAINE; Pinelands Regional HS; Mystic Island, NJ; (Y); Church Yth Grp; Band; Church Choir; High Hon Roll; Hon Roll; NHS; Nrs.

ELDER, JANET; Pinelands Regional HS; Tuckerton, NJ; (Y); 8/192; Church Yth Grp; Band; Church Choir; Concert Band; High Hon Roll; Hon Roll; NHS; Nrsng.

ELDER, LORI; High Point Regional HS; Sussex, NJ; (Y); 44/260; Debate Tm; German Clb; Color Guard; Mrchg Band; Im Gym; JV Trk; Im Vllybl; High Hon Roll; Hon Roll.

ELDRIDGE, PATRICK; South River HS; South River, NJ; (Y); 25/140; French Clb; Math Tm; Scholastic Bowl; Im Bsktbl; Var Golf; Var Capt Socr; Im Vllybl; NHS; Drexel U; Arch Engrng.

ELENBARK, DIANA; Deptford HS; Deptford, NJ; (Y); 3/275; Am Leg Aux Girls St; Dance Clb; Hosp Aide; Teachers Aide; VP Jr Cls; Stu Cncl; Var Capt Cheerleading; Gym; Cit Awd; High Hon Roll; Rep HOBY Ldrshp Sem 85; Physical Therapy.

ELIAS, ANABEL; Perth Amboy HS; Perth Amboy, NJ; (Y); Var Socr; Law.

ELLERBEE, ANGELIQUE; Pleasantville HS; Pleasantville, NJ; (Y); Btcn.

ELLERBUSCH, GARY; Roselle Park HS; Roselle Park, NJ; (Y); 2/129; Am Leg Boys St; Church Yth Grp; Math Tm; Bsbl; Bausch & Lomb Sci Awd; Pres NHS; Sal; German Clb; 1st Pl Telephone Pioneers Amer Essay Noise Poll 85; Union Cnty Outstndg Schltc Achvt Awd 86; N J I T; Engrng.

ELLERSICK, ED; Hudson Catholic HS; North Bergen, NJ; (Y); Hon Roll; St Peters.

ELLIOTT, BERNADETTE; Abraham Clark HS; Roselle, NJ; (Y); 20/195.

ELLIOTT, CHRISTINA S; Cinnaminson HS; Cinnaminson, NJ; (Y); Art Clb; Church Yth Grp; SADD; Nwsp Stf; Stu Cncl; JV Mgr(s); JV Score Keeper; Socr; Houghton Coll; Elem Ed.

ELLIOTT, KATHY; Jackson Memorial HS; Jackson, NJ; (Y); 28/405; Church Yth Grp; JA; Mrchg Band; Symp Band; Sftbl; High Hon Roll.

ELLIOTT, TEAL J; High Point Regional HS; Branchville, NJ; (Y); VP Exploring; School Play; Nwsp Rptr; Yrbk Stf; Var Capt Cheerleading; Im Gym; Stat Trk; Im Wt Lftg; High Hon Roll; Hon Roll; Foothill Coll; Intl Bus.

ELLIS, APRIL; Weequahic HS; Newark, NJ; (Y); 50/400; Exploring; Nwsp Stf; Rep Stu Cncl; French Hon Soc; VA Intermont; Chld Psych.

ELLIS, CHERYL; Pleasantville HS; Pleasantville, NJ; (Y); Church Yth Grp; Computer Clb; 4-H; Girl Scts; Math Clb; Band; Church Choir; Concert Band; Mrchg Band; Nwsp Stf; Nrs.

ELLIS, GLENN; Teaneck HS; Teaneck, NJ; (Y); Church Yth Grp; Library Aide; SADD; Band; Concert Band; Mrchg Band; Rep Jr Cls; Rep Stu Cncl; Socr; Hon Roll; Acdmc All-Amer 86; U Of Vermont; Biolgy.

ELLIS, THOMAS B; Immaculata HS; Martinsville, NJ; (Y); 1/213; Am Leg Boys St; Math Tm; Model UN; Jazz Band; Mrchg Band; School Musical; Socr; Gov Hon Prg Awd; Pres NHS; French Clb; 1st Pl Natl Oratorical Cont 86; Delegate Hugh O Brian Yth Ldrshp Sem 85; Gen Excllnc Medals Acadmc; Liberal Arts.

ELLISON, KIMBERLY SHERLY; Hillside HS; Hillside, NJ; (Y); 99/201; Church Yth Grp; Cmnty Wkr; Girl Scts; Chorus; Church Choir; Color Guard; JV Bsktbl; Var Trk; 1st Tm Union Cnty Hon Mntn Trck 85; Mtn Vly Conf Chmp Trck 86; 1st Tm Union Cnty Trck & Fld 86; U Of NC; Bus.

ELLISON, LISA; Bishop George Ahr/St Thomas HS; Edison, NJ; (Y); Hosp Aide; Model UN; Ski Clb; Spanish Clb; Capt Color Guard; Mgr School Musical; Stage Crew; Nwsp Stf; Hon Roll; NEDT Awd; MS Spllng Bee Awd 85-86; Attrny.

ELLSWORTH, ERIK; Marlboro HS; Marlboro, NJ; (Y); 78/528; Chess Clb; German Clb; Ski Clb; JV Trk; Hon Roll; Ntl Merit SF; US Naval Acad; Nuclear Engr.

ELMO, CHARLES; Lodi HS; Lodi, NJ; (Y); Key Clb; Leo Clb; Spanish Clb; Stage Crew; JV Wrstlng; PTA Outstndng Stu Schlrshp 86; Rutgers U.

ELSEY, MICHELLE; Lower Cape May Regional HS; Villas, NJ; (Y); 51/225; Pep Clb; Varsity Clb; VICA; Sftbl; Trk; Hon Roll; Prfct Atten Awd; 1st Pl In Hairsylng Cmptn 85, 2nd Pl 86; Hairstylist.

ELTORA, MICHAEL R; Hackettstown HS; Hackettstown, NJ; (Y); 32/200; Exploring; Q&S; School Play; Nwsp Phtg; Nwsp Rptr; Nwsp Stf; Hon Roll; NHS; Pres Schlr; Muhlenberg Coll; Pre-Med.

ELWELL, JEFFREY; Salem HS; Quinton, NJ; (Y); 7/150; Am Leg Boys St; Church Yth Grp; JA; VP Jr Cls; VP Sr Cls; Var Capt Tennis; Hon Roll; Pres NHS; Chess Clb; Computer Clb; Claude G Aikens Schrslhp 86; John J Kavanaugh Mem Schlrshp 86; Susquehanna U; Acctng.

ELY, PAM; Manalapah HS; Coltsneck, NJ; (Y); 62/445; Temple Yth Grp; Rep Soph Cls; Rep Jr Cls; Rep Sr Cls; Stu Cncl; JV Trk.

EMBLEY, GREG; Hamilton High West; Trenton, NJ; (Y); Am Leg Boys St; Aud/Vis; Key Clb; Varsity Clb; Tennis; Bus Mgmt.

EMBRICH, JANN; Mary Help Of Christians Acad; Paterson, NJ; (Y); Drama Clb; School Play; Nwsp Stf; Gym; Prfct Atten Awd; Perfect Attdnc Awd 84; Montclair.

EMEL, DEVEREAUE; Salem HS; Salem, NJ; (Y); Sec Am Leg Aux Girls St; Exploring; Pres Hosp Aide; Sec Soph Cls; Co-Capt Cheerleading; High Hon Roll; Hon Roll; NHS; Candystrpr Of Yr 86; Nrsng.

EMENECKER, GARY; Maple Shade HS; Maple Shade, NJ; (Y); 16/150; Am Leg Boys St; DECA; Yrbk Stf; Pres Frsh Cls; Pres Soph Cls; Pres Jr Cls; Var Bsbl; JV Bsktbl; Var Ftbl; Socr; Natl GA Commp Dist Educ Clbs Of Amer 86; Rider Coll; Bus Admin.

EMERSON, MICHAEL; Delaware Valley Regional HS; Frenchtown, NJ; (Y); 11/165; Science Clb; Trs Soph Cls; Off Stu Cncl; JV Bsktbl; Var Socr; JV Trk; Hon Roll; Altrnte Amrcn Leg Boys State 86; Political Sci.

EMERSON, WENDY; Deptford Township HS; Sewell, NJ; (Y); Debate Tm; GAA; JA; Office Aide; Chorus; Yrbk Bus Mgr; Rep Stu Cncl; Stat Bsktbl; Im Fld Hcky; Score Keeper.

EMILIANI, NANCY; East Brunswick HS; E Brunswick, NJ; (Y); Hosp Aide; Ski Clb; Variety Show; High Hon Roll; Hon Roll; Silv & Brnz Mdl Piano Plyng 84; Montclair; Bus Mngmnt.

EMILIO, BRAD; Edison HS; Edison, NJ; (Y); 56/430; Im Bsbl; JV L Socr; Engrng.

EMMER, ROBERT A; Lacey Township HS; Forked River, NJ; (S); 70/208; DECA; Sec Sr Cls; Var Capt Bsbl; Var Capt Socr; Hon Roll; Science Clb; 1st Fd Mrktng Evnt Regions & ST, 15th Natl 86; Soccer Golden Paw Awd 86,1st All Conf 86,3rd Tm 86; Kean Coll; Bus Adm.

EMMERT, BONNIE; Toms River Hgh Schl North; Toms River, NJ; (Y); 7/420; Ski Clb; VP Spanish Clb; SADD; Var Capt Bsktbl; Var Tennis; High Hon Roll; NHS; MVP Bsktbl 85; All-Cnty Scnd Dbls Tns 84; Sprts Med.

EMMOLO, RENEE; Paul VI Regional HS; Cedar Grove, NJ; (Y); 21/147; Church Yth Grp; GAA; Service Clb; Rep Soph Cls; Rep Jr Cls; Rep Stu Cncl; Var Bsktbl; Var Sftbl; French Hon Soc; Hon Roll; Sci.

ENG, GORDON W; Cliffside Park HS; Cliffside Park, NJ; (Y); Chess Clb; Hosp Aide; Latin Clb; Spanish Clb; Concert Band; Jazz Band; Mrchg Band; Stu Cncl; Bsktbl; Var Tennis; Amer Legion Boys ST 86.

ENG, MICHAEL; North Brunswick Township HS; N Brunswick, NJ; (Y); German Clb; Key Clb; Mathletes; Rep Stu Cncl; Capt Crs Cntry; Var Swmmng; JV Trk; Hon Roll.

ENGEL, MICHELLE C; Union Catholic Regional HS; Rahway, NJ; (Y); School Play; Stage Crew; Montclair ST NJ; Art.

ENGEL, TRACY; Cherry Hill HS; Cherry Hill, NJ; (Y); Intnl Clb; Spanish Clb; Teachers Aide; Temple Yth Grp; Chorus; Stage Crew; Nwsp Stf; Ed Yrbk Stf; Hon Roll; NHS; Hm & Schl Assn Awd 85; NJ Grdn ST Schlrshp 86; Pres Acad Ftnss Awd 86; Rutgers U; Doc.

ENGELBERT, KEITH P; Collingswood HS; Collingswood, NJ; (Y); Am Leg Boys St; Church Yth Grp; School Play; JV Bsktbl; Var Socr; Var Tennis; Bus.

ENGELHARDT, DARA; Sayreville War Memorial HS; S Amboy, NJ; (Y); 150/389; Sec Church Yth Grp; French Clb; GAA; SADD; Varsity Clb; Cheerleading; Mgr(s); Score Keeper; Trk; Hon Roll; Kutztown U; Telecomm.

ENGELS, GLENN K; Sussex County Vo-Tech; Montague, NJ; (Y); Am Leg Boys St; Band; Mrchg Band; Stage Crew; Hon Roll; NHS; Peer Cnslg; Crpntry.

ENGLAND, KIMBERLEY; Delaware Valley Regional HS; Asbury, NJ; (Y); 40/190; Art Clb; Ski Clb; Yrbk Stf; High Hon Roll; Hon Roll; Art Awd 85-86; Bus Mgt.

ENGLEHART, BRIAN; Hackettstown HS; Hackettstown, NJ; (Y); Var L Bsbl; Var L Bsktbl; Hon Roll; NHS; Psych.

ENGSTROM, KRISTIN; Mercer Christian Acad; Hightstown, NJ; (S); 1/14; Church Yth Grp; Teachers Aide; Band; Chorus; School Musical; School Play; Yrbk Ed-Chief; High Hon Roll; Val; Extraordnry Chrstn Stdnts Of Amer 85-86; Dean Schlr Awd 87; Philadelphia Coll Bible; Elem.

ENRIGHT, JACKIE; Red Bank Catholic HS; Middletown, NJ; (Y); 2/225; Exploring; French Clb; SADD; Sec Concert Band; Pres Mrchg Band; Nwsp Stf; Yrbk Stf; Hst Score Keeper; Im Sftbl; Trk; Scranton U; Pre-Med.

ENTIN, PAUL; Hightstown HS; E Windsor, NJ; (Y); Ski Clb; Spanish Clb; Varsity Clb; Var Ice Hcky; High Hon Roll; Hon Roll; Bus.

ENTWISTLE, SUZANNE; Clifton HS; Clifton, NJ; (Y); 37/637; Cmnty Wkr; Pres Key Clb; Chorus; School Musical; Nwsp Ed-Chief; JV Mgr(s); Hon Roll; Jr NHS; Opt Clb Awd; Drama Clb; Hugh O Brien Yth Ldrshp Fndtn Ambsdr 84-85; TAG/Rogate 83-87; Femls Engrng Methds Motvtn & Exprnc 84.

ENWRIGHT, JOANNE; James Caldwell HS; W Caldwell, NJ; (Y); French Clb; Key Clb; High Hon Roll; Hon Roll; Accntng.

EPHRAT, DINA; Cliffside Park HS; Cliffside Pk, NJ; (Y); 47/255; Color Guard; Flag Corp; Yrbk Phtg; Pres Stu Cncl; Score Keeper; Swmmng; Vllybl; High Hon Roll; Awf Dplma Dept Hm Econ 86; William Patterson Coll; Bus Mng.

EPPS, DENISE; Malcolm X Shabazz HS; Newark, NJ; (S); Girl Scts; Yrbk Stf; VP Jr Cls; Hon Roll; NHS; Acad All-Amer 86; Accntng.

EPPS, SHARICE; Orange HS; Orange, NJ; (Y); Pep Clb; Varsity Clb; Nwsp Rptr; Sec Frsh Cls; Rep Jr Cls; JV L Cheerleading; Chorus; Var Pom Pon; Hnr Rl 81-83; Psychlgy.

EPSTEIN, CRAIG; Fair Lawn HS; Fair Lawn, NJ; (Y); Political Wkr; Band; Chorus; Concert Band; Mrchg Band; School Musical; School Play; Stu Cncl; Socr; Bus Mgmt.

EPSTEIN, JEFF; Manalapan HS; Englishtown, NJ; (Y); 38/450; Latin Clb; Temple Yth Grp; Bsbl; Ftbl; NHS; Bus.

ERBRECHT, JOHN; Christian Brothers Acad; Colts Neck, NJ; (Y); 6/200; Math Tm; Rptr Yrbk Bus Mgr; Im Ftbl; Im Sftbl; High Hon Roll; Architect.

ERCOLINO, GINO; Shore Regional HS; W Long Branch, NJ; (Y); Ski Clb; Var Ftbl; Im Ice Hcky; Var Trk; Hon Roll; Prfct Atten Awd; Pre-Law.

ERD, CHRISTOPHER ARVIN; Cresskill HS; Cresskill, NJ; (Y); 19/130; Ski Clb; Concert Band; Jazz Band; Mrchg Band; School Musical; Var Ftbl; Var Trk; NHS; Crum & Forster Schlrshp 86; Mst Musicl Instrumntl Music Dept Awd 86; Cook Coll; Bio.

ERHARD, PATRICIA; Mt St Mary Acad; Brant Beach, NJ; (Y); Art Clb; Debate Tm; Drama Clb; Office Aide; Ski Clb; Spanish Clb; School Musical; School Play; Stage Crew; Fld Hcky; Art Natl Hnr Soc 85-86; Art Inst Of Pgh; Interior Dsgn.

ERICKSEN, SHARON; Bridgewater Raritan HS East; Pluckemin, NJ; (Y); SADD; Chorus; School Musical; Variety Show; Pres Frsh Cls; Pres Soph Cls; Pres Jr Cls; Rep Stu Cncl; Im Powder Puff Ftbl; JV Sftbl; Girls Ctznshp Inst 86; Music.

ERICKSON, JOSEPH W; Palmyra HS; Palmyra, NJ; (Y); 2/107; Am Leg Boys St; Drama Clb; Key Clb; Yrbk Stf; Rep Stu Cncl; High Hon Roll; NHS; Aud/Vis; School Play; Stage Crew; Brlngtn Cnty Yth Orgnztn 85 & 86; NJ Dstngshd Schlr 86; Trntn ST Coll Schlrshp 86; Trnton ST Coll; Arntcl Engrng.

ERICKSON, WENDY NYE; Wall HS; Sea Girt, NJ; (Y); Drama Clb; Pep Clb; Ski Clb; Spanish Clb; School Musical; Var Fld Hcky; Stat Wrstlng; High Hon Roll; Womans Clb, Boosters Schlrshps 86; U DE; Bus.

ERICSON, JOHN T; High Point Regional HS; Branchville, NJ; (Y); Am Leg Boys St; Pres 4-H; Rep Frsh Cls; Rep Soph Cls; Rep Stu Cncl; Socr; Var Tennis; Cit Awd; 4-H Awd; Hon Roll; Sussex Cnty Equestrian Of Yr 85; Ctznshp WA Focus Dlgt 85; Ntl Clb Cngrs 86; Bus.

ERICSON, KELLYANN; Kittatinny HS; Newton, NJ; (Y); Debate Tm; Girl Scts; Spanish Clb; Band; Chorus; School Play; Sec Frsh Cls; Var Cheerleading; Powder Puff Ftbl; 4-H Awd; Hnr Roll 86; Pre-Law.

ERNST, JOSEPH; Northern Valley Regional HS; Norwood, NJ; (Y); 81/313; AFS; Church Yth Grp; Ski Clb; Rep Stu Cncl; JV Bsbl; Bsktbl; Golf; Socr; Hon Roll; NHS; Amer Can Co Schlrp Wnr 85-86; Boston Coll; Finance.

ERRICHETTL, LISA; West Essex HS; Fairfield, NJ; (Y); 17/350; Am Leg Aux Girls St; Girl Scts; Band; Concert Band; Mrchg Band; Rep Stu Cncl; Capt Swmmng; High Hon Roll; Hon Roll; Jr NHS; Frfld Schlrshp Fnd 86; West Essx Wmns Clb 86; Dglss Coll; Med.

ERRICO, JOSEPH P; Delbarton HS; Far Hills, NJ; (Y); Cmnty Wkr; Math Tm; Quiz Bowl; Chorus; Orch; School Musical; Ed Lit Mag; Off Sr Cls; Swmmng; Wt Lftg; Mst Valubl JV Wrstlr 85; Engrng Physcs.

ERSIN, DENNIS; Holy Cross HS; Marlton, NJ; (Y); Ski Clb; Ftbl; Wt Lftg; Hon Roll; Engr.

ESANDRIO, MERYL; Kinnelon HS; Riverdale, NJ; (Y); 48/176; French Clb; FBLA; Hosp Aide; Library Aide; Spanish Clb; Hon Roll; Spanish NHS; Accntng.

ESCURRA, MONICA; Paterson Catholic Regional HS; Paterson, NJ; (Y); 4/100; Science Clb; Yrbk Ed-Chief; Yrbk Phtg; High Hon Roll; NHS; Natl Hispanic Schlr Awds Semifnlst 85-86; Socl Studies Schlr Awd 85; Psych.

ESKILSON, PATRICIA; Washington Twp HS; Turnersville, NJ; (Y); Girl Scts; Chorus; Yrbk Stf; Dirs Awd Chr 86; Stockton ST Clg; Crmnl Just.

ESMURDOC, CAROLINA FRANCES; Oak Knoll Schl; Elizabeth, NJ; (Y); Art Clb; Church Yth Grp; Dance Clb; Hosp Aide; Service Clb; Church Choir; Nwsp Rptr; Nwsp Stf; High Hon Roll; Chem.

ESPINOSA, ROSARIO; Millburn SR HS; Short Hills, NJ; (Y); AFS; JA; Swmmng; Hon Roll; Hnr Roll 84-86; Hotl Mgmt.

ESPIRITU, ALEXANDER; Bayonne HS; Bayonne, NJ; (Y); 80/360; Art Clb; Trs Aud/Vis; Ski Clb; Spanish Clb; Ftbl; Lion Awd; Art Awd Lions Clb 86; Culinary Inst Am; Culnry Arts.

ESPOSITO JR, ANTHONY; Highland HS; Laurel Springs, NJ; (S); 30/326; Ice Hcky; Im Socr; High Hon Roll; Acctng.

ESPOSITO, CHRISTINE; Northwarren Regional HS; Blairstown, NJ; (Y); Sec 4-H; FBLA; Nwsp Stf; Yrbk Stf; 4-H Awd; Blairstown Twp Sftbl All Star 83-85; 1st Pl Essay Cont 84; Bus.

ESPOSITO, FRANK; Passaic Valley HS; Little Falls, NJ; (Y); Boys Clb Am; Boy Scts; Church Yth Grp; Cmnty Wkr; Computer Clb; Key Clb; Ski Clb; Chorus; Bowling; Hon Roll; Elec Engr.

ESPOSITO, JANICE; Bergenfield HS; Bergenfield, NJ; (Y); 55/308; Exploring; Ski Clb; Nwsp Phtg; VP Church Yth Grp; VP Jr Cls; Pres Sr Cls; Rep Stu Cncl; Fld Hcky; Lion Awd; Mayor For Day 86; U DE.

ESPOSITO, JOHN; Manchester Regional HS; Haledon, NJ; (Y); DECA; Engr.

ESPOSITO, MIKE; Parsippany HS; Lk Hiawatha, NJ; (Y); Bsbl; Wrstlng; High Hon Roll; Hon Roll; Bus.

ESPOSITO, RENEE; Jackson Mem HS; Jackson, NJ; (Y); 58/417; Girl Scts; Hosp Aide; Gym; Powder Puff Ftbl; Sftbl; High Hon Roll; Hon Roll; Monmouth Coll; Bus.

ESPOSITO, TAMARA LOUISE; Hackettstown HS; Hackettstown, NJ; (S); Cmnty Wkr; VP Key Clb; Office Aide; Color Guard; Mrchg Band; Stage Crew; Ed Yrbk Phtg; Stu Cncl; Hon Roll; Vrsty Ltrs 83-86; Salisbury ST Coll; Psych.

ESQUIVEL, LETICIA; Mother Seton Regional HS; Elizabeth, NJ; (Y); 12/95; Debate Tm; Drama Clb; GAA; Hosp Aide; Stage Crew; Rep Sr Cls; Hon Roll; Douglas.

ESSER, MONICA; Oak Knoll Schl; Verona, NJ; (Y); Intnl Clb; Pep Clb; Stage Crew; Yrbk Phtg; Var Bsktbl; Var Crs Cntry; Im Vllybl; High Hon Roll; Hon Roll; Ntl Merit Ltr; Latin Awd 85, Advanced Bio 86, Math & Alg II 86.

ESSERMAN, MATTHEW; Manalapan HS; Manalapan, NJ; (Y); Band; Concert Band; Jazz Band; Mrchg Band; School Musical; Symp Band; Variety Show; 2nd Annual Daily Sunday Register Tlnt Showcase Awd 84; All Shore Jazz Ensmbl 86 & 84; Engineering.

ESSOKA, JONATHAN D; Columbia HS; South Orange, NJ; (Y); Boy Scts; Church Yth Grp; Drama Clb; Quiz Bowl; School Play; Nwsp Bus Mgr; Nwsp Rptr; Rep Frsh Cls; Rep Sr Cls; Rep Stu Cncl; Electrcl Engrng.

ESTELLE, EDDIE; Lakewood HS; Lakewood, NJ; (Y); 51/294; FFA; Key Clb; Spanish Clb; Badmtn; Bsbl; Bsktbl; Ftbl; Vllybl; Hon Roll; Spanish NHS.

ESTLACK, JENNIFER; Pitman HS; Pitman, NJ; (Y); 18/145; Teachers Aide; Stat Mgr(s); Var L Sftbl; Hon Roll; NHS; Law.

ESTLER, MELISSA; Dover HS; Dover, NJ; (Y); 36/186; Church Yth Grp; French Clb; Band; Concert Band; Mrchg Band; Stage Crew; Hon Roll; Nyack Coll; Elem Ed.

ESTLOW, BERT; Holy Spirit HS; Brigantine, NJ; (Y); French Clb; Latin Clb; JV Bsbl; Im Sftbl; Var Trk.

ESTRUCH, RAMON; Memorial HS; West New York, NJ; (Y); Boy Scts; Bsktbl; Hon Roll; NJ Inst Tech; Electrncs.

ESWEIN, GLENN; Boonton HS; Boonton, NJ; (Y); Am Leg Boys St; French Clb; Math Tm; VP Band; Concert Band; Jazz Band; Mrchg Band; School Musical; Nwsp Ed-Chief; High Hon Roll; Engrng.

ETHEREDGE, MICHAEL; Dwight Morrow HS; Englewood, NJ; (Y); 37/275; Cmnty Wkr; Varsity Clb; Band; Var Capt Bsbl; Var Coach Actv; Var Capt Ftbl; High Hon Roll; NHS; Urbn Lg Brgn Cnty Blk Schlrs Awd 86; Stu Orgnztn Srv Awd 86; Steel Drm Band Awd 86; Jacksonvill U; Bus Admin.

ETTER, KERRYLEA; Cherry Hill HS East; Cherry Hill, NJ; (Y); Church Yth Grp; Exploring; Quiz Bowl; Band; Chorus; Church Choir; Madrigals; Mrchg Band; School Musical; Symp Band; Fleet Rsrv Assoc-Reg-Amer Essay 1st Pl 86; All Region Choir TX 1st Soprano 83-84; All S Jersey 85-86; Archaolgy.

EVANGELISTA, BETH; Shawnee HS; Medford Lakes, NJ; (Y); 22/537; Camera Clb; Church Yth Grp; Var Capt Gym; Hon Roll; NHS; 4 Yrs Brlngtn Cnty All St Tm 82-85; 4th Pl Brs USALGC Ntnls 86; Otstndng SR Awd 86; William & Mary Coll.

EVANISH, DAWN; Holy Cross HS; Medford, NJ; (Y); 11/369; Trs Spanish Clb; Church Choir; Ed Nwsp Stf; Ed Yrbk Stf; JV Sftbl; High Hon Roll; NHS; Church Yth Grp; Trs Drama Clb; Library Aide; NEDT Awd 84; Mock Trial Tm; Lancers For Life Pro-Life Grp Sec; Phrmclgy.

EVANOUSKAS, KAREN; Madison Central HS; Old Bridge, NJ; (Y); 27/356; Quiz Bowl; Scholastic Bowl; School Musical; School Play; Ed Lit Mag; PTSA Schlrshp 86; Otstndng Drm Stu Awd 86; Rutgers U; Prdctn Mngmnt.

EVANS, BONNIE; Central Regional HS; Bayville, NJ; (Y); Varsity Clb; Var L Bsktbl; Coach Actv; Var L Sftbl; Var L Tennis; High Hon Roll; Hon Roll; NHS; Ath Acad Achvt Sftbl 84-86; Def Awd Bsktbl 84 & 85, Sftbl 85; Outstndng Product Berkley Bsktbl 84; Med.

EVANS, CECELIA; Gloucester HS; Gloucester, NJ; (Y); Church Yth Grp; Computer Clb; Hosp Aide; Science Clb; Spanish Clb; Pom Pon; JV Vllybl; Hon Roll; Jr NHS; Bio.

EVANS, JOHN M; Cherokee HS; Marlton, NJ; (Y); Am Leg Boys St; Church Yth Grp; French Clb; Pres Soph Cls; Pres Jr Cls; Pres Sr Cls; Stu Cncl; Coach Actv; Var Ftbl; Capt Wrstlng.

EVANS, KATHLEEN M; Williamstown HS; Williamstown, NJ; (Y); 23/262; Nwsp Stf; Distngushd Schlrs Schlrshp 86; Pres Awd Acad Ftns 86; Faclty Awd 86; Glassboro ST Coll; Comm.

EVANS, KIM; Holy Cross HS; Burlington, NJ; (Y); 24/394; Ski Clb; Color Guard; Drill Tm; Stage Crew; Mgr(s); Var JV Tennis; High Hon Roll; Hon Roll; Jr NHS; Ntl Merit SF; Hnr & Advncd Plcmnt Courses; Mrn Bio.

EVANS, LAURA; Holy Cross HS; Florence, NJ; (Y); 33/369; Hosp Aide; Concert Band; Sec Mrchg Band; Stage Crew; High Hon Roll; Hon Roll; NHS; Peds Nrsg.

EVANS, MARK; Hamilton HS East; Hamilton Sq, NJ; (Y); 68/327; Varsity Clb; Var L Bsktbl; Sci Awd 86; Drexel U; Elec Engrng.

EVANS, RITA; Paul VI HS; Blackwood, NJ; (Y); French Clb; Rep Frsh Cls; Rutgers U; Math.

EVANS, SANDRA; Frank H Morrell HS; Irvington, NJ; (Y); #9 In Class; Spanish Clb; High Hon Roll; NHS; Katharine Gibbs Schlrshp 86-87; Spnsh Achvt Awd 86; Katharine Gibbs Schl; Bilgl Sec.

EVANS, SHERI; Randolph HS; Randolph, NJ; (Y); Dance Clb; Girl Scts; Varsity Clb; Band; Mrchg Band; Symp Band; Var Fld Hcky; Var Sftbl; Hon Roll; Prfct Atten Awd; MVP Varsity Fld Hcky 86; St Chmps For North Jrsy Fld Hcky Assoc 86; Gold Mdlst Fld Hcky 86; VA Polytech; Comp Sci.

EVANS, TIFFANY; Hillsborough HS; Bel Air, MD; (Y); 36/303; Dance Clb; Mrchg Band; Powder Puff Ftbl; Trk; Hon Roll; Cert Of Voltr Wrk At Baltamore VA Hosp 83; Sthrn CA; Mrktng.

EVEN, RON; Livingston HS; Livingston, NJ; (Y); Computer Clb; Exploring; Key Clb; Math Clb; Math Tm; French Hon Soc; High Hon Roll; Pres Jr NHS; Ntl Merit Ltr; Band; Am Comp Sci League Cntst 84.

EVERARD, STEVEN; Oratory Prep; S Orange, NJ; (Y); 20/50; Boy Scts; Church Yth Grp; Ski Clb; Var Capt Bsbl; Stat Bsktbl; Var Crs Cntry; Mgr(s); Var Tennis; Var Trk; Hon Roll; Bus Mgmt.

EVERETT, WILLIAM; North Brunswick Twp HS; N Brunswick, NJ; (Y); 80/310; Key Clb; Latin Clb; Mathletes; Varsity Clb; Band; Concert Band; Mrchg Band; Var L Crs Cntry; Var L Diving; JV L Tennis; Pre-Med.

EVERLY JR, DON H; Cumberland Regional HS; Bridgeton, NJ; (Y); 16/369; Church Yth Grp; Trs Exploring; Trs Science Clb; Ski Clb; High Hon Roll; Hon Roll; NHS; Ursinus; Pre-Med.

EVERTS, HELEN; Hightstown HS; E Windsor, NJ; (Y); Drama Clb; Ski Clb; Concert Band; Mrchg Band; Socr; Sftbl; Swmmng; Hon Roll; NHS; Band; Music Boosters Orgnztn Awd 86; PA ST U; Pre Med.

EWALD, STACY; So Plainfield HS; S Plainfield, NJ; (Y); Church Yth Grp; Band; Mrchg Band; Hon Roll; Rutgers Coll; Accntng.

EWING, ANTHONY P; Somerville HS; Somerville, NJ; (Y); 4/225; Drama Clb; Model UN; Scholastic Bowl; VP Thesps; VP Band; Drm Mjr(t); CC Awd; Elks Awd; Gov Hon Prg Awd; Kiwanis Awd; Yale U; Pol Sci.

FABER, LORINDA; Eastern Christian HS; Midland Park, NJ; (S); 2/100; Church Yth Grp; Chorus; Church Choir; Orch; Yrbk Stf; JV Bsktbl; High Hon Roll; Jr NHS; NHS; St Schlr; Assoc Degree Trinty Coll Music 83-85; Music Ed.

FABIAN, ELAINE; Immaculate Conception HS; Bloomfield, NJ; (Y); Art Clb; Church Yth Grp; VP Spanish Clb; Nwsp Rptr; Ed Nwsp Stf; Mgr(s); High Hon Roll; Hon Roll; NHS; Prfct Atten Awd; 7th Pl Hnrb Mntn Natl Spn Achvt Tst; Liturgy Choir; Pre-Law.

FABIAN, MARK; Mount Olive HS; Flanders, NJ; (Y); 13/300; Math Clb; Variety Show; L Bsktbl; Wt Lftg; High Hon Roll; Hon Roll; Rotary Awd; Mst Dedctd Awd Bsktbl, Acad All Amercn 84-85; Pres Phy Ftnss Awd 3 Yrs; Syracuse; Law.

FABIJANIC, MICHAEL; Lakeland Regional HS; Ringwood, NJ; (Y); 11/303; Math Clb; Math Tm; Quiz Bowl; Var L Crs Cntry; Var L Ice Hcky; Im Vllybl; GA Inst Of Tech; Engr.

FABRICANT, STACEY; Boonton HS; Boonton, NJ; (Y); Drama Clb; Math Clb; Math Tm; Spanish Clb; Temple Yth Grp; School Musical; School Play; Variety Show; Var L Cheerleading; Var L Trk.

FACCONE, JOHN; Bishop George Ahr HS; Scotch Plains, NJ; (Y); 1/258; Am Leg Boys St; Nwsp Sprt Ed; Ftbl; Capt Swmmng; Tennis; Gov Hon Prg Awd; NHS; NEDT Awd; St Schlr; Val; Close Up 85; Schlr Athl 86; Franklin & Marshall Coll; Bio.

FACEMYER, BRIAN; Salem HS; Hancocks Bdg, NJ; (Y); Am Leg Boys St; Computer Clb; Math Clb; Ski Clb; Varsity Clb; Rep Stu Cncl; Var Bsbl; Var Capt Ftbl; Boys ST Delg 86; All-Tri-Cnty Bsbl Plyr 86; Bus Mgmt.

FADEN, NEIL S; John P Stevens HS; Edison, NJ; (Y); 36/478; Drama Clb; VP Model UN; Thesps; Pres School Play; Mgr Stage Crew; Variety Show; Sec Stu Cncl; Var Cheerleading; Pres NHS; Scholastic Bowl; Awd Excllnc-Natl HS Modl UN 85; FRGN Svc.

FADER, ROBIN SUE; Freehold Boro HS; Freehold, NJ; (Y); 14/275; Sec Soph Cls; Sec Jr Cls; Rep Sr Cls; Rep Stu Cncl; Stat Bsktbl; Score Keeper; French Hon Soc; NHS; Aud/Vis; French Clb; Shield & Key; Mathmtic.

FAGANS, MICHAEL; Woodstown HS; Elmer, NJ; (Y); Am Leg Boys St; Church Yth Grp; Drama Clb; English Clb; Band; Concert Band; Orch; School Musical; Symp Band; Var Socr; Hnrbl Mtn DE Vly Sci Fair 86; Altnt Yth Dlgt Gen Assmbly Presb Ch USA 86; Dlgt Trienium 86; Coll Of Wooster; Archtr.

FAGANS, MICHELLE; Southern Regional HS; Barnegat, NJ; (Y); 23/400; Dance Clb; Ski Clb; Spanish Clb; Jr Cls; Socr; DAR Awd; High Hon Roll; Hon Roll; NHS; Intl Mrktng.

FAGGELLO, JOHN; St Jposephs Regional HS; Teaneck, NJ; (Y); 42/170; Church Yth Grp; Cmnty Wkr; Teachers Aide; Var Bsbl; Var Bsktbl; Hon Roll; Bsktbl Second Tm Cnty 86; Boston U; Law.

FAGGELLO, LISA; Teaneck HS; Teaneck, NJ; (Y); 110/420; Office Aide; Var Bowling; JV Var Sftbl; High Hon Roll; NHS; Church Yth Grp; Cmnty Wkr; Teachers Aide; Nrsng Scholar Am Leg Axt Fund 86; Holy Name Schl Nrsng; Nrsng.

FAGLEY, DIANE; Palmyra HS; Riverton, NJ; (Y); 54/130; Am Leg Aux Girls St; Church Yth Grp; German Clb; Sec Jr Cls; Sec Sr Cls; Rep Stu Cncl; Var Capt Cheerleading; JV Fld Hcky; JV Socr; JV Sftbl; Accntnt.

FAHEY, SEAN; Point Pleasant Boro HS; Point Pleasant, NJ; (Y); 33/243; Trs Key Clb; Latin Clb; Varsity Clb; School Play; Sec Frsh Cls; Trs Stu Cncl; JV Var Bsktbl; JV Var Ftbl; Hon Roll; NHS; Kiwanis Ldrshp Trnng Conf 85; Key Clb Intrl Convntn 86; Iron Man Awd Ftbll 84-85; 100 Pct Attndnc 84-85; Poli Sci.

FAHEY, TIMOTHY F; Holy Cross HS; Burlington, NJ; (Y); 97/390; Ski Clb; Band; Concert Band; Mrchg Band; Stage Crew; Hon Roll; Ltr Marchng Band 84-85; Comp Sci.

FAHY, SCOTT J; Don Bosoo Prep; Ridgewood, NJ; (Y); 25/190; German Clb; Model UN; Science Clb; Tennis; Trk; High Hon Roll; Hon Roll; NHS; 1st Pl Sci Fair Chem 85; Gld Mdl Ntl Piano Audtns 83.

FAICHNEY, ROBERT; Glen Rock HS; Glen Rock, NJ; (Y); 40/152; Drama Clb; Math Tm; Spanish Clb; Thesps; School Musical; School Play; Nwsp Stf; Hon Roll; JV Rugby 83-84; Intl Thespian Soc 84-86; Comp Sci.

FAILLA, DANIELA; Indian Hills HS; Oakland, NJ; (Y); 69/274; Office Aide; Teachers Aide; Chorus; Nwsp Rptr; Nwsp Stf; Yrbk Stf; Frsh Cls; Trk; High Hon Roll; Hon Roll; Chr 3 Yr Awd 86; Spnsh Merit Awd 86; Supts List-Hgh Hon Rl 86; William Paterson Coll; Law.

FAIRBANKS, HILLARY; Lenape Valley Regional HS; Stanhope, NJ; (Y); 5/265; Key Clb; SADD; Chorus; Madrigals; School Play; Crs Cntry; Trk; High Hon Roll; NHS; Spanish NHS; Rutgers Dean Smmr Schlr 86.

FAIRBANKS III, MARSHALL L; Manchester Twp HS; Lakehurst, NJ; (S); Nwsp Rptr; Nwsp Sprt Ed; Var L Ftbl; Var L Trk; Im Wt Lftg; South Jersey Grp II Champ Pole Vlt 85; 4 Yr Vrsty Ltr Wnnr Trck & Fld 82-86; Comp Sci.

FAIRFIELD, RICHARD D; Saint Peters Preparatory Schl; Newark, NJ; (Y); Lit Mag; Hon Roll; Jr NHS; Ntl Merit Ltr; Pres-Rfole Plyng Gms Clb 85-86; Anthrplgy.

FAIS, DONNA; Pascack Valley HS; River Vale, NJ; (S); 20/260; French Clb; Spanish Clb; Chorus; Madrigals; Yrbk Stf; Capt Var Cheerleading; Hon Roll; NHS; 1st Pl Frgn Lang Frnsc Tournmnt 85; Spnsh.

FAJARDO, JOSE; Saint Peters Prep Schl; Jersey City, NJ; (Y); Aud/Vis; Dance Clb; Pep Clb; Mgr Stage Crew; Var Socr; Var Swmmng; Schl Spirt Awd; Euchristc Mnstr; Smr Tutor-Hghr Achvt Pgm; Law.

FALCO, DENNIS; West Orange HS; W Orange, NJ; (Y); JV Bsbl; Var Crs Cntry; JV Trk; Var Wt Lftg; JV Wrstlng; Itl Frgn Lng Hnr Scty 86; Otstndng Lftr 86; Bus.

FALCO, NOEL ELIZABETH-JANE; Collingswood SR HS; Oaklyn, NJ; (Y); 1/240; Pres French Clb; Capt Color Guard; Yrbk Ed-Chief; Var Trk; NHS; Ntl Merit SF; Pres Schlr; St Schlr; Val; Am Leg Aux Girls St; Phi Beta Kappa 86; Gldn Glln 86; Bst Of The Cls 86; Villanova.

FALCONER, SAMANTHA; Clifford J Scott HS; E Orange, NJ; (Y); 3/250; Intnl Clb; Math Clb; Math Tm; Concert Band; Jazz Band; Mrchg Band; Golf; Mgr Socr; High Hon Roll; Mu Alp Tht; T L Smith Schlrshp; Otis Mens Shop Awd; Swrthmr Coll.

FALCONI, ANTOINETTE; Edgewood Regional SR HS; Waterford, NJ; (Y); 8/370; Girl Scts; Chorus; High Hon Roll; Hon Roll; Pres Jr NHS; NHS; Prfct Atten Awd; Sci Awd 83; Spnsh Awd 83; Burlington CC; Medcl Asst.

FALISI, LYNN; Clayton HS; Clayton, NJ; (Y); 13/70; JA; Science Clb; Nwsp Rptr; Nwsp Stf; Yrbk Stf; VP Sr Cls; Var Fld Hcky; Var Sftbl; Hon Roll; Bus.

FALJEAN, LARRY; Monsignor Donovan HS; Bayville, NJ; (Y); 56/218; Civic Clb; Drama Clb; Math Tm; Thesps; Varsity Clb; School Musical; School Play; JV Var Wrstlng; Hon Roll; Prfct Atten Awd; Rutgers U; Lbrl Arts.

FALK, MEGAN; Hunterdon Central HS; Flemington, NJ; (Y); 70/548; Church Yth Grp; Ski Clb; Spanish Clb; Nwsp Stf; Sec Stu Cncl; Fld Hcky; NHS; Spanish NHS; YFU Summer Exchange Stu To The Netherlands 86; Sociology.

FALKIEWICZ, MONICA; Hunterdon Central HS; Rosemont, NJ; (Y); Church Yth Grp; Off Cmnty Wkr; Off SADD; Off Frsh Cls; Off Jr Cls; Off Sr Cls; Stu Cncl; Im Bsktbl; Im Sftbl; JV Trk; Optometry.

FALKOWSKI, DEBORAH A; Northern Burlington Co Reg HS; Columbus, NJ; (Y); 13/296; Pres 4-H; Math Tm; Rep Jr Cls; Rep Sr Cls; JV Bsktbl; Var Fld Hcky; Cit Awd; French Hon Soc; 4-H Awd; Hon Roll; Livingston Coll; Bus.

FALLAHEE, KEVIN; Christian Brothers Acad; Middletown, NJ; (Y); 42/225; Am Leg Boys St; CAP; Cmnty Wkr; Science Clb; Band; Jazz Band; Var Bowling; Socr; Sftbl; High Hon Roll; Avtn.

FALLAN, KRISTEN; Bishop George Ahr HS; Perth Amboy, NJ; (Y); 52/277; Pres Church Yth Grp; Capt Cmnty Wkr; French Clb; Hosp Aide; Ski Clb; Capt Drill Tm; Sftbl; High Hon Roll.

FALLETTA, SALVATORE; Memorial JR-SR HS; Elmwood Park, NJ; (Y); 1/159; Am Leg Boys St; Band; Yrbk Phtg; Pres Soph Cls; VP Pres Stu Cncl; Var Capt Bsktbl; Var Capt Socr; High Hon Roll; NHS; Pre Med.

FALLON, KERRIE; Phillipsburg HS; Phillipsburg, NJ; (Y); 41/334; Yrbk Rptr; Var L Bsktbl; NHS; Marine Bio.

FALLON, KEVIN; Christian Brothers Acad; Ocean Twnshp, NJ; (Y); 30/250; Pres Church Yth Grp; Stage Crew; Yrbk Stf; Im Bowling; Im Ftbl; Im Sftbl; Im Swmmng; Hon Roll; Dance Clb; Hosp Aide; MD Coll Park; Arch.

FALLON, LISA; Immaculate Conception HS; Ridgefield Pk, NJ; (Y); 17/88; Cmnty Wkr; Library Aide; Pres Service Clb; Teachers Aide; Chorus; Yrbk Stf; Lit Mag; Prfct Atten Awd; Natl Art Hnr Scty 85-86; Smmr Schlrs Felician Coll; Elem Educ.

FALS, JAIME; Hudson Catholic HS; Union City, NJ; (Y); 12/179; Math Clb; Science Clb; Pres Spanish Clb; SADD; NHS; Acad All Am; U Of MI; Elec Eng.

FALZONE, ALEXANDER P; Collingswood SR HS; Collingswood, NJ; (Y); 8/230; Am Leg Boys St; Key Clb; Trs Soph Cls; Trs Jr Cls; Rep Stu Cncl; Chrmn Capt Crs Cntry; Var Capt Trk; High Hon Roll; NHS; US Air Frc Acad Wst Pt; Fghtr.

FALZONE, JEFFREY; Bridgeton HS; Bridgeton, NJ; (Y); High Hon Roll; Prfct Atten Awd; Engnrng.

FAMA, MARIA; Pennsauken HS; Pennsauken, NJ; (Y); Varsity Clb; Chorus; School Musical; Off Frsh Cls; Cheerleading; Hon Roll; Maison De Paris; Cosmtlgy.

FAMBRO, LIN; Lincoln HS; Jersey, NJ; (Y); Off Jr Cls; Sftbl; Vllybl; FIT Coll; Dsngr.

FAN, RICHARD; The Peddie Schl; East Windsor, NJ; (Y); 6/140; Am Leg Boys St; Cmnty Wkr; French Clb; Hosp Aide; Science Clb; Chorus; Nwsp Rptr; Nwsp Stf; Var Bsktbl; JV Ftbl; Yale; Med.

FANAROFF, JASON; Pascack Valley HS; River Vale, NJ; (Y); Camera Clb; Cmnty Wkr; French Clb; Hosp Aide; Temple Yth Grp; Yrbk Ed-Chief; JV Bsktbl; JV Trk; Hosp Apprctn Awd 84; Teenarts Prog Photo 1st Pl 86; Nrth Jersey Stu Crftsmns Fair Photo 3rd Pl 86; Lib Arts.

FANELLI, MICHAEL W; Triton Regional HS; Glendora, NJ; (Y); #26 In Class; Am Leg Boys St; Key Clb; Political Wkr; Band; Chorus; Concert Band; Mrchg Band; School Musical; School Play; Stu Cncl; Tchng.

FANNING, EDWARD; Seton Hall Prep; Springfield, NJ; (Y); 14/200; Boys Clb Am; Pres Church Yth Grp; Var L Swmmng; Hon Roll; 2dn Hon Rl; 1st Hon Rl; Law.

FANO, LAURA; James Caldwell HS; W Caldwell, NJ; (Y); Key Clb; Bowling; Acctnt.

FANO, STEVE; West Essex HS; N Caldwell, NJ; (Y); Im Wt Lftg; Var JV Wrstlng; Outstndng Wrstlr Reg Trnmnt 86; Engrng.

FANTINI, ANTHONY; Bridgeton HS; Bridgeton, NJ; (Y); 15/250; Am Leg Boys St; Boy Scts; VP Church Yth Grp; Cmnty Wkr; Drama Clb; Chorus; Mrchg Band; School Musical; Nwsp Phtg; Pres Sr Cls; Eagle Scout 86; Naval Acad; Aero Space.

FANTUZZI, LYNN; Toms River South HS; Toms River, NJ; (Y); 8/350; Math Tm; Powder Puff Ftbl; High Hon Roll; Hon Roll; NHS; Sec Frsh Cls; Sec Soph Cls; Sec Jr Cls; Mgr Bsbl; Acad Ltr 84-86; Vrsty Ltr 84-86; Comp Sci.

FARAHMANDIAN, DORA; Pascack Valley HS; River Vale, NJ; (Y); French Clb; Temple Yth Grp; School Play; Hon Roll.

FARATRO, ANTHONY; Hudson Catholic HS; Jersey City, NJ; (Y); Science Clb; SADD; Stage Crew; Ftbl; Wt Lftg; Hon Roll; Ramapo Coll; Bio.

FARESE, JOSEPH; Clifton HS; Clifton, NJ; (Y); 64/637; French Clb; Var Ftbl; Var Trk; Var Wt Lftg; High Hon Roll; Jr NHS; NHS; Rutgers U; Actng.

FARINA, CARLA; Lakeland Regional HS; Wanaque, NJ; (Y); 4/350; English Clb; Off Soph Cls; Rep Jr Cls; JV Bsktbl; Powder Puff Ftbl; JV Vllybl; High Hon Roll; Pres NHS; Frgn Lang Awd 84-86; Bio.

FARINA, TERRI L; Phillipsburg HS; Phillipsburg, NJ; (Y); 47/292; Ski Clb; VP Jr Cls; VP Sr Cls; Rep Stu Cncl; Var JV Sftbl; Hon Roll; NHS; Bruce Lawrence Mem Schlrshp 86; Jacob Dilts Mem Schlrshp 86; U RI; Phrmcy.

FARINELLA, MICHELLE; Newton HS; Newton, NJ; (Y); Dance Clb; Drama Clb; Pres Thesps; Madrigals; School Musical; School Play; 4-H; Chorus; Variety Show; Var Cheerleading; Performing Arts.

FARIS, AMY; Red Bank Catholic HS; Tinton Falls, NJ; (Y); Art Clb; Church Yth Grp; Cmnty Wkr; Service Clb; Church Choir; Art Awd 84; Govrs Schl Of Art Altrnte 86; Comm.

FARLEY, CHRISTOPHER; Bishop AHR HS; Iselin, NJ; (Y); Boy Scts; Church Yth Grp; German Clb; ROTC; Varsity Clb; Rep Frsh Cls; Rep Soph Cls; Rep Jr Cls; Var Ftbl; Wt Lftg; Comp Sci.

FARLEY, MATTHEW; Hillsborough HS; Belle Mead, NJ; (Y); 63/300; School Musical; School Play; Rep Soph Cls; Rep Jr Cls; Rep Sr Cls; Rep Stu Cncl; Hon Roll; HAM Magic Club; Math Acctg.

FARLEY, THOMAS; Don Bosco Preparatory HS; Upper Saddle Riv, NJ; (Y); Chess Clb; Church Yth Grp; Drama Clb; Model UN; School Musical; Nwsp Rptr; JV Crs Cntry; High Hon Roll; Hon Roll; NHS; TV Jrnlst.

FARMER, WILLIAM; Cumberland Regional HS; Bridgeton, NJ; (Y); 17/400; Intnl Clb; Ski Clb; Var Ftbl; JV Trk; Var Wrstlng; High Hon Roll; Hon Roll; Jr NHS; Bys ST Altrnt; Rtry Yth Ldrshp Awd; ST Sci Dy Physcs; VA Polytech Insti; Aero Engrng.

FARMIGA, NESTOR; Clifton HS; Clifton, NJ; (Y); Rep German Clb; Math Clb; Math Tm; Science Clb; Ski Clb; Rep Soph Cls; High Hon Roll; Ntl Merit Ltr; JV Trk; 1st Pl Stu Cat Art Sq 85; Soccr Trophy & Awds 83-85; Physics.

FARNSWORTH, ELIZABETH; Middlesex HS; Middlesex, NJ; (Y); French Clb; Ski Clb; Spanish Clb; Band; Color Guard; Mrchg Band; CO ST; Bus.

FARRAH, MICHAEL; Millville HS; Millville, NJ; (Y); Computer Clb; SADD; Variety Show; Ed Lit Mag; Badmtn; Bowling; Hon Roll; FTA 86; U S Navy; Advncd Elctrncs.

FARRAR, SUSAN; Rahway SR HS; Rahway, NJ; (Y); Am Leg Aux Girls St; Church Yth Grp; Girl Scts; Hosp Aide; Library Aide; Spanish Clb; Color Guard; Mrchg Band; Yrbk Stf; Rep Jr Cls; Silv Awd Grl Scouts 84; Gold Ldrshp Awd Grl Scouts 86; Med.

FARRELL, SHAWN R; Lenape HS; Mt Laurel, NJ; (Y); Am Leg Boys St; Ski Clb; Varsity Clb; Bsktbl; Socr; Trk.

FARREN, MARY; St Rose HS; Spring Lake, NJ; (Y); Church Yth Grp; Key Clb; JV Cheerleading; JV Var Mgr(s); Hon Roll; Sec NHS; NEDT Awd; Engl II Awd Hghst Grade Avg 84-85; Bus.

FARRO, THERESA; Woodstown HS; Woodstown, NJ; (Y); Art Clb; SADD; VP Band; JV Bsktbl; JV Sftbl; Var Capt Sftbl; Hon Roll; Concert Band; Mrchg Band; Hussians Schl Art Postr Cntst Schlrshp Smmr Course 85; H S Postr Cntst 85; Art.

FARRUGGIO, JAMI LOWY; Ocean Township HS; Wanamassa, NJ; (Y); 118/309; Ski Clb; Spanish Clb; Stage Crew; Mgr Gym; Sftbl; Monmouth Coll; Bus.

FARRY, WILLIAM; Manchester Regional HS; Haledon, NJ; (Y); Am Leg Boys St; Debate Tm; Nwsp Rptr; Lit Mag; Rutgers U; Archaeology.

FARSCHON, TODD; Woodstown HS; Bridgeton, NJ; (Y); Ski Clb; Band; Concert Band; Mrchg Band; Symp Band; Swmmng; Marine Biol.

FATA, JANE; Bayley Ellard Regional HS; E Hanover, NJ; (Y); Church Yth Grp; Service Clb; Chorus; Yrbk Stf; Stat Bsbl; JV Bsktbl; JV Cheerleading; Powder Puff Ftbl; High Hon Roll; Hon Roll; Math.

FATOVIC, TED; North Bergen HS; North Bergen, NJ; (Y); 20/404; VP German Clb; Key Clb; Political Wkr; Yrbk Stf; JV Bsbl; Var Tennis; Gov Hon Prg Awd; High Hon Roll; JETS Awd; NHS; Scty Acad Achvmnt 86; Prncpls 1200 SATS Clb 86; US Air Frc Sci Fr Awd 85; Rutgers Coll Of Engr; Chmcl Eng.

FATUM, JUDI; Pemberton Twp HS; Browns Mills, NJ; (Y); 20/420; Drama Clb; Hosp Aide; Teachers Aide; Capt Drill Tm; Stu Cncl; Capt Pom Pon; Hon Roll; Acadmc Achvt Awd 84-85; Cert Peer Facilitator 83-86; Publ Rel.

FAUBERT, JEFF; Phillipsburg HS; Phillipsburg, NJ; (Y); 72/334; Office Aide; Nwsp Rptr; Rep Soph Cls; Rep Jr Cls; Rep Stu Cncl; Coach Actv; Mgr(s); Mat Maids; Score Keeper; Timer; Wrstlng Ltr 85-86; Grp Iv St Champs Wrstlng 85-86; Teacher.

FAUCI, CHRISTINE; Middletown HS South; Middletown, NJ; (Y); 88/436; Church Yth Grp; Intnl Clb; Political Wkr; Ski Clb; SADD; Band; School Play; Stage Crew; Symp Band; Variety Show; Northeastern U.

FAUNDE, YSAEL; Memorial HS; W New York, NJ; (Y); Boy Scts; French Clb; Off Frsh Cls; Sec Soph Cls; Rep Jr Cls; Rep Stu Cncl; Hon Roll; NJ Inst Tech; Archit.

FAUSEY, LAURA; Middle Township HS; Cape May C H, NJ; (Y); 18/187; Mrchg Band; Stu Cncl; Cheerleading; 4-H Awd; High Hon Roll; NHS; St Schlr; Pres Sec 4-H; Band; Rep Soph Cls; Cape May Co Miss 1st Pl Talnt 85; Cape May Co Equstrn Yr 85-86; Fnlst Miss Teen NJ 86; Stockton ST Coll; Bio.

FAVA, JENNIFER; Notre Dame HS; Trenton, NJ; (Y); Key Clb; Ski Clb; Varsity Clb; Yrbk Stf; Var JV Fld Hcky; JV Sftbl; Trk; Hon Roll; Psych.

FAVATELLA, SUZANNE; Maple Shade HS; Maple Shade, NJ; (Y); 3/150; Trs Drama Clb; School Musical; Variety Show; JV Var Bsktbl; High Hon Roll; NHS; Computer Clb; VP Spanish Clb; Chorus; Rep Jr Cls; Schlstc Achvt Awd 86; Princpls Awd 86; Bond From Chptr 82 Disabled Amer Vets 86; Burlington Cnty Coll; Accntng.

FAVILLA, DAN; Edgewood SR HS; Hammonton, NJ; (Y); 5/400; Exploring; Varsity Clb; Rep Jr Cls; JV Bsbl; JV Ftbl; Var Trk; High Hon Roll; Hon Roll; Jr NHS; NHS; Wnr Edgewood Spllng Bee 82; Rutgers U; Engrg.

FAVORITO, DAWN; Paramus Catholic Girls Rgnl HS; Maywood, NJ; (Y); Church Yth Grp; Cmnty Wkr; Hosp Aide; Library Aide; Spanish Clb; Teachers Aide; JV Sftbl; Cit Awd; Dance Clb; Debate Tm; Amrcn Lgn Sfty Essay 3rd 83; Amrcn Lgn Schl Awd 83; Amrcn Lgn Cncr Soc Awd Of Aprctn 83; Pre-Med.

FAVRETTO, LISA M; Vineland HS; Vineland, NJ; (Y); 1/628; VP French Clb; Off Key Clb; Pres Stu Cncl; Elks Awd; Gov Hon Prg Awd; NHS; St Schlr; Val; Bill Bradley Young Ctzns Awd 86; Teen Corrspndt-Vineland Times Jrnl 83-86; Rutgers Coll/Phrmcy; Phrmcy.

FAY, JAMES; North Bergen HS; North Bergen, NJ; (Y); 5/470; German Clb; Key Clb; Spanish Clb; Stu Cncl; Hon Roll; Jr NHS; NHS; Spanish NHS; Chem Engrng.

FAY, JAMIE; Holy Cross HS; Florence, NJ; (Y); Cmnty Wkr; Ski Clb; Crs Cntry; Trk; Hon Roll.

FAZIO, KARI; De Paul HS; Kinnelon, NJ; (Y); 1/172; Pres Latin Clb; Science Clb; Service Clb; Var L Cheerleading; Var Fld Hcky; Dnfth Awd; High Hon Roll; VP NHS; Val; JCL; Grdn ST Dstngshd Schlr Schlrshp 85; AIM Prgm 85; Grgtwn U.

FEARS, CHRISTOPHER; Scotch Plains-Fanwood HS; Scotch Plains, NJ; (S); Church Yth Grp; Key Clb; Capt Quiz Bowl; ROTC; JV Bsbl; JV Ftbl; JV Trk; Hon Roll; Ntl Merit Ltr; Foster Bio Test Schl Team 85; Stu Ldrshp Conf 84-85; Vet.

FEBINGER, RHONDA; South River HS; South River, NJ; (Y); 9/160; Am Leg Aux Girls St; VP Church Yth Grp; Trs French Clb; German Clb; Library Aide; Mrchg Band; Symp Band; Yrbk Stf; Pres Sr Cls; Rep Stu Cncl; Fshn Inst Tech; Mrchndsng.

FEBRES, GLORIA I; Morris Knolls HS; Denville, NJ; (Y); 2/22; High Hon Roll; Hon Roll; NHS; Flnt Spnsh & Inln; Cert Achvt Supr Achvt; Excllnc Perfmnc & Awd Algbr II; Finance.

FEDELI, LISA; Toms River North HS; Toms River, NJ; (Y); 154/407; Cmnty Wkr; Yrbk Ed-Chief; Yrbk Stf; Rep Stu Cncl; Swmmng; Hon Roll; Educ.

FEDERAL, NATALIE; Emerson JR SR HS; Emerson, NJ; (Y); 2/96; French Clb; Chorus; School Play; Stage Crew; Pres Soph Cls; Pres Jr Cls; Pres Sr Cls; Rep Trs Stu Cncl; Vllybl; Hon Roll; Girls C Itizenship Inst 86; Fashion Inst Of Tech; Fshn Dsgn.

FEDERICO, ROBERT; Clifton HS; Clifton, NJ; (Y); Pres Art Clb; German Clb; Library Aide; Teachers Aide; Capt Ftbl; NJIT Div Cntng Educ Crtfct 86; Aero Engr.

FEDORCZYK, JANICE; Nutley HS; Nutley, NJ; (Y); #41 In Class; Debate Tm; Ski Clb; Spanish Clb; Speech Tm; Orch; Sec Jr Cls; Sec Sr Cls; Rep Stu Cncl; JV Capt Bsktbl; Var Socr; Frdhm U; Advrtsng.

FEDOROW, NATASHA; Immaculate Conception HS; W New York, NJ; (Y); Cmnty Wkr; Debate Tm; English Clb; NFL; Rep Jr Cls; Trs Stu Cncl; Hon Roll; NHS; Ntl Merit Ltr; Natl Merit Awd Ldrshp 86; Vol CCD Tchr 85 & 86; NYU; Pre-Law.

FEENEY, CAROLINE; Chatham Township HS; Chatham, NJ; (Y); 20/140; Church Yth Grp; GAA; Key Clb; Pep Clb; Varsity Clb; Chorus; School Musical; School Play; Variety Show; Yrbk Stf.

FEENEY, ELLEN ANNE; Mount Saint Dominic Acad; W Caldwell, NJ; (Y); 4/53; Church Yth Grp; Debate Tm; JCL; NFL; Service Clb; School Musical; Nwsp Stf; Lit Mag; Pres Stu Cncl; Var Bsktbl; Engrng.

FEERY, DANIEL; Toms River HS; Toms River, NJ; (Y); 108/412; Wt Lftg; Rutgers U; Bus Mgmt.

FEHN, KRISTINA; Morristown HS; Morristown, NJ; (Y); Key Clb; JV Lcrss; JV Tennis; Hon Roll; Boston Coll; Cprt Law.

FEIN, THOMAS; Wayne Hills SR HS; Wayne, NJ; (Y); 19/305; Math Tm; Socr; Trk; Hon Roll; NHS; One To One 83-84; U Of VA; Engrg.

FEINBLATT, SUSAN JILL; Hightstown HS; E Windsor, NJ; (Y); 119/400; Girl Scts; SADD; Hon Roll; Econ.

FEINMAN, ANDREA; Wayne Hills HS; Wayne, NJ; (Y); Spanish Clb; Y-Teens; Band; Mrchg Band; Orch; School Musical; School Play; Symp Band; Hon Roll; Mus.

FEINTUCH, DEBBIE; Bruriah HS; W Orange, NJ; (Y); Temple Yth Grp; Y-Teens; Sec Frsh Cls; Pres Soph Cls; VP Jr Cls; Chptr Pres-NCSY 85-86; Coord Of Chptrs For NCSY 86-87; VP-CHPTR Pgmng NCSY 84-85; Phys Thrpy.

FEIT, JEFFREY; Wayne Valley HS; Wayne, NJ; (Y); 1/329; JCL; Model UN; Yrbk Ed-Chief; Lit Mag; Rep Stu Cncl; NHS; Ntl Merit Schol; Latin Clb; Temple Yth Grp; Yrbk Rptr; NJ Garden ST Schlr 86; Cane Schlrshp 86; Princeton U; Pol Sci.

FEITH, KAREN; Howell HS; Howell, NJ; (Y); 62/373; Lit Mag; Socr; Hon Roll; NHS; Coaches Awd; Pres Acad Achvt Awd; VA Wesleyan.

FEKETE, DAVID; Holy Cross HS; Willingboro, NJ; (Y); Ski Clb; Spanish Clb; Varsity Clb; Ftbl; Trk; Wt Lftg; Hon Roll; Homecoming Committee 84-86.

FEKETE, KATHLEEN; South River HS; South River, NJ; (Y); 7/150; French Clb; Math Clb; Jazz Band; Mrchg Band; Pep Band; Nwsp Stf; Bsktbl; Fld Hcky; Hon Roll; Pres NHS; Pres Acdmc Fit Awd 86; Altrnt Grls Ctznshp Inst 85; FL ST U; Cmmnctns.

FEKETE, ROBERT; St Joseph HS; Piscataway, NJ; (Y); 4/215; Model UN; Ski Clb; Ed Lit Mag; JV Swmmng; Gov Hon Prg Awd; NHS; Ntl Merit Ltr; Trs Spanish NHS; Math Tm; Quiz Bowl; Chrstn Sci Mntr Essy Cntst Hnrbl Mntn 85; NJAATSP ST Spnsh Tm 7th Hnrbl Mntn Lvl IV 86; Pre-Med.

FELCONE, THOMAS; Ewing HS; Trenton, NJ; (Y); Am Leg Boys St; Key Clb; Stage Crew; Yrbk Stf; Var Bsbl; Crs Cntry; Trk; Hon Roll; Arch.

FELDMAN, ALISSA; Glenrock JR SR HS; Glen Rock, NJ; (Y); AFS; Intnl Clb; Latin Clb; Spanish Clb; VP Sec Temple Yth Grp; Nwsp Stf; High Hon Roll; Hon Roll; Certfct Hnr For Serv Usy 85; U Of MD; Child.

FELDMAN, DANA; Shore Regional HS; W Long Branch, NJ; (Y); Temple Yth Grp; Stage Crew; Nwsp Rptr; Rep Frsh Cls; Stat Bsktbl; Stat Gym; Powder Puff Ftbl; High Hon Roll; Hon Roll; Prfct Atten Awd; Fshn Coord.

FELDMAN, DAVID MARTIN; Bridgewater-Raritan H S West; Bridgewater, NJ; (Y); Math Clb; Science Clb; Band; Concert Band; Jazz Band; Mrchg Band; Bsbl; NHS; Ntl Merit Ltr; St Schlr; Gdn St Schlr, Outstndng Musician Awd 86; Ldrshp Awd 85; Coll William & Mary; Bio.

FELDMAN, JOY; Abraham Clark HS; Roselle, NJ; (Y); 33/185; Spanish Clb; Nwsp Rptr; Nwsp Stf.

FELDMAN, LISA; Weehawken HS; Weehawken, NJ; (Y); 2/92; Church Yth Grp; Yrbk Bus Mgr; VP Stu Cncl; Bausch & Lomb Sci Awd; NHS; Sal; St Schlr; Chess Clb; Math Clb; School Play; Brwn Bk Awd; Brd Of Educ Achvt Awd; Lang Arts Awd; Swarthmore Coll; Bio.

FELEDY, M MELIA; Villa Walsh Acad; Morristown, NJ; (Y); Ski Clb; Stat Lcrss; Var Capt Socr; Math Clb; Math Tm; Nwsp Rptr; Yrbk Stf; Trs Stu Cncl; Hon Roll; All ST NJ Soccr 86; MVP Soccr ROTC Awd 86; U Scranton; Acctng.

FELICE, MELISSA; Toms River HS East; Toms River, NJ; (Y); 30/500; SADD; Rep Soph Cls; Rep Jr Cls; Rep Sr Cls; Rep Stu Cncl; Var L Socr; NHS; Dance Clb; Debate Tm; Chorus; U DE; Bus.

FELICIA, GLADYS; Essex Catholic Girls HS; Irvington, NJ; (Y); Art Clb; Drama Clb; English Clb; Church Choir; School Play; Variety Show; Yrbk Stf; Pres Sr Cls; Capt Vllybl; NHS; Eng,Relgn Awd 86; Ntl Spch Drama Awds 86; Rugers U; Pol Sci.

FELICIANO, DENISE; North Bergen HS; North Bergen, NJ; (Y); #23 In Class; Iona Coll Lang Cntst Awd 86; Physcl Educ Awd 84; Crtfct Italian Ptry Cntst 85.

FELL, PAUL; Newton HS; Newton, NJ; (Y); 41/219; Am Leg Boys St; DECA; German Clb; Latin Clb; Rep Stu Cncl; Var Socr; JV Trk; Coaches Awd Scr 85; All Area Sccr Team 85; Ldrshp Trng Cmp 84; Bus.

FELLNER, MARY; Lenape Valley Regional HS; Netcong, NJ; (Y); Key Clb; Red Cross Aide; Chorus; Concert Band; Mrchg Band; Stu Cncl; Cheerleading; High Hon Roll; Hon Roll; JP Sousa Awd; Pre-Med.

FENDRICK, LAUREN; Hightstown HS; East Windsor, NJ; (Y); Cmnty Wkr; French Clb; FBLA; Ski Clb; Temple Yth Grp; Chorus; School Musical; Yrbk Stf; Hon Roll; Ntl Merit Ltr; USNMA Awd Alg II 86; Penn ST; Lawyr.

FENNELL, DOREEN; Abraham Clark HS; Roselle, NJ; (Y); 7/200; Church Yth Grp; Chorus; Yrbk Stf; Vllybl; High Hon Roll; NHS; Pre-Coll Pgm NJIT 85; Nrsng.

FENNELL, HOLLY ANN; Hackensack HS; Hackensack, NJ; (Y); 46/400; Am Leg Aux Girls St; Key Clb; Temple Yth Grp; High Hon Roll; NHS; Prfct Atten Awd; Spanish NHS; Mexican Schlrshp Club 85; Cornell U.

FENNELLY, LOUISE; Southern Regional HS; Manahawkin, NJ; (Y); Dance Clb; Ski Clb; Mgr(s); Powder Puff Ftbl; Socr; Hon Roll; Pratt Inst; Design.

FENNER, LISA; Bridgewater-Raritan HS West; Bridgewater, NJ; (Y); Pres Service Clb; Var Mgr(s); JV Var Tennis; Elks Awd; High Hon Roll; Hon Roll; Kiwanis Awd; NHS; Pres Schlr; Church Yth Grp; MVP Grls Vrsty Tnns 84; Albright; Med Technlgy.

FENSTER, MITCHELL; Bridgewater-Raritan H S East; Martinsville, NJ; (Y); French Clb; Math Tm; Temple Yth Grp; Var JV Wrstlng; Hon Roll; NHS.

FENSTER, ROBERT; Parsippany HS; Parsippany, NJ; (Y); Computer Clb; FBLA; Office Aide; Lit Mag; Hon Roll; Rep Doehlr Assoc Phila Comp Semnr 86; Nwsltr Edtr Morris Area Commodore Usrs; Rutgers U; Comp Prgrmg.

FENWICK, CRAIG; Toms River High School East; Toms River, NJ; (S); Camera Clb; Q&S; Ski Clb; Nwsp Phtg; Nwsp Rptr; Nwsp Stf; Yrbk Phtg; Var JV Crs Cntry; Ocean Cnty Coll.

FERARA, ELIZABETH; Holy Crosds HS; Mt Laurel, NJ; (Y); Cmnty Wkr; Band; Mrchg Band; JV Fld Hcky; DAR Awd; Hon Roll; Journlsm.

FERDINAND, JUDITH T; St Peter HS; Milltown, NJ; (Y); 5/110; Cmnty Wkr; French Clb; Hosp Aide; Lit Mag; JV Trk; High Hon Roll; Hon Roll; NHS; Intl Studies.

FERET, LILI; Highland Regional HS; Blenheim, NJ; (S); 32/332; Girls Interact; Camdon Cnty Coll; X-Ray Tech.

FERGUS, TROY E; University HS; Newark, NJ; (Y); 18/59; Church Yth Grp; JA; Rep Jr Cls; Hon Roll; Martin Luther King Essay Awd 83; Cmmnd Stu Natl Achvt Schlrshp Pgm 85; 3rd Annl HS Schlrs Day Awd 85; Bus.

FERGUSON, LISA; Snyder HS; Jersey City, NJ; (Y); Computer Clb; Dance Clb; Debate Tm; Drama Clb; FBLA; ROTC; Nwsp Rptr; Yrbk Rptr; Cheerleading; Trk; Law.

FERLANTI, ERIK SCOTT; Morris Knolls HS; Denville, NJ; (Y); 10/367; Bsbl; Bsktbl; Ftbl; High Hon Roll; Pres Schlr; Summa Medallion 86; Patrick Caruso Hist Awd 86; Denville Hist Soc Awd 86; IN U; Tele Cmmnctns.

FERMIN, CARLOS M; Emerson HS; Union City, NJ; (Y); Am Leg Boys St; Boy Scts; CAP; Var Capt Bowling; JV Ftbl; Hon Roll; VFW Awd; Sci.

FERNANDEZ, ELEANOR; Glassboro HS; Glassboro, NJ; (Y); Dance Clb; Concert Band; Jazz Band; Trs Orch; Rep Stu Cncl; Var Cheerleading; Var Fld Hcky; Var Trk; Hon Roll; NHS; Perfrmd In Vido 84; 3rd Am Math Test 85; 2nd Pl Wnnr Kybd Yths Audtns 86.

FERNANDEZ, FREDDY; Memorial HS; West New York, NJ; (Y); Elec Engrg.

FERNANDEZ JR, LORENZO; Sayreville War Memorial HS; Parlin, NJ; (Y); Spanish Clb; Rep Stu Cncl; JV Ftbl; JV Golf; Var Wrstlng; Hon Roll; SF Ntl Hisp Schlr Awd 86; Rutgers U; Landscpng.

FERNANDEZ, ROSA; St Aloysius HS; Jersey City, NJ; (Y); 1/102; Church Yth Grp; School Musical; School Play; Nwsp Rptr; Yrbk Stf; Jr Cls; Capt Bowling; High Hon Roll; NHS; Val; Rutgrs Schlr 86; Govs Schl Of NJ 86; Bus Adm.

FERNANDEZ, ROSCEL; Woodbridge HS; Pt Reading, NJ; (Y); 18/420; Chorus; Stage Crew; Nwsp Rptr; Yrbk Stf; Lit Mag; Pres Jr Cls; Pres Sr Cls; Mgr(s); Hon Roll; NHS; Engl.

FERNANDEZ, SANTIAGO; Seton Hall Prep; Newark, NJ; (Y); Church Yth Grp; English Clb; Pep Clb; Pres Spanish Clb; Ed Nwsp Stf; Yrbk Stf; Lit Mag; High Hon Roll; Hon Roll; Natl Hispanic Schlr Awds Program-Semi Fnlst 86; Rifle Team Letter 85-86; Boys Club-Outstndng Teen 82; Columbia Coll; Engl.

FERNANDEZ, VERONICA; Raritan HS; Hazlet, NJ; (Y); Dance Clb; Ski Clb; Band; Mrchg Band; Symp Band; JV Var Fld Hcky; JV Var Socr; Trk; Prfct Atten Awd; Spanish NHS; Frgn Lang.

FERNANDEZ, VIVIAN; Memorial HS; W New York, NJ; (Y); 91/365; French Clb; FBLA; Chorus; Yrbk Stf; Stu Cncl; Hon Roll.

FERRAIOLI, ALFRED; Holy Cross HS; Moorestown, NJ; (Y); Golf; Wrstlng; Hon Roll; Bus.

FERRALASCO, EILEEN; Lakeland Regional HS; Ringwood, NJ; (Y); 16/303; Math Clb; School Play; Off Soph Cls; Off Jr Cls; Chrmn Sr Cls; Gym; Socr; Sftbl; NHS; NEDT Awd; Passaic Cnty Schl Brd Scholar 86; JR Wmns Clb Ringwood Scholar 86; Trenton ST Coll; Spec Ed.

FERRANTE, LOUIS; Hackensack HS; Hackensack, NJ; (Y); 11/410; Aud/Vis; Cmnty Wkr; Ski Clb; Stage Crew; Bsbl; Ftbl; Hon Roll; NHS; Itln Ntl Hnr Soc 86; Franklin & Marshall; Bio.

FERRARA, CATHY-JO; Kearny HS; Kearny, NJ; (Y); Cheerleading; Gym; Sftbl; Hon Roll; Church Yth Grp; French Clb; Teachers Aide; Nrs.

FERRARA, FRANCES; Roselle Catholic HS; Elizabeth, NJ; (Y); Church Yth Grp; Cmnty Wkr; NFL; Speech Tm; Teachers Aide; Lit Mag; Hon Roll; NHS; Spanish NHS; Engl.

FERRARA, LISA; Passaic Valley HS; Upr Montclair, NJ; (Y); GAA; Key Clb; Letterman Clb; Varsity Clb; Sec Frsh Cls; Var Capt Cheerleading; Edward Williams Coll; Bus.

FERRARA, MARIA; Bloomfield SR HS; Bloomfield, NJ; (Y); 153/689; Computer Clb; FBLA; Chorus; Yrbk Stf; Sftbl; Prfct Atten Awd; Usher-Usherette Clb Awd; Bergan County JC; Comp Sci.

FERRARA, NOELLE; Pope John XXIII HS; Oak Ridge, NJ; (Y); French Clb; GAA; Cheerleading; Stat Trk; Gym.

FERRARI, MARK; Seton Hall Prep Schl; S Orange, NJ; (Y); 21/191; Political Wkr; Yrbk Stf; JV Trk; High Hon Roll; NHS; Holy Cross Coll; Bus Admin.

FERRARI, MICHAEL; Roselle Catholic HS; Roselle, NJ; (Y); 2/186; Math Tm; Lit Mag; Im Bsktbl; JV Wrstlng; Hon Roll; NHS; Spanish NHS; Engrng.

FERRARI, MICHELLE J; Roselle Catholic HS; Roselle, NJ; (Y); 23/152; Hosp Aide; Ski Clb; Hon Roll; Spanish NHS; Awd Being Peer Grp Cnslr 85-86; Ntl Engl Merit Awd 84-85; Kean Coll; Child Psychlgst.

FERRARI, TERRI; Cresskill HS; Cresskill, NJ; (Y); 13/125; Ski Clb; Rep Stu Cncl; Capt Var Cheerleading; Capt Var Sftbl; High Hon Roll; NHS; Lehigh U; Bus.

FERRARO, ANNE MARIE; Sayreville War Memorial HS; Parlin, NJ; (Y); 2/385; Pres Science Clb; Mrchg Band; Yrbk Stf; Sr Cls; Capt Swmmng; Trk; VP French Hon Soc; NHS; Sal; St Schlr; Dante Alghri Schlrshp 86; Grdn ST Distgshd Schlr 86; Mddlsx Cnty Outstndng Stud Awd 86; Rensselaer Poly Inst; Comp Sci.

FERRARO, CATHERINE; Union HS; Union, NJ; (Y); Dance Clb; Chrmn Pep Clb; Ski Clb; Spanish Clb; Nwsp Stf; Yrbk Stf; Off Jr Cls; Stu Cncl; Var L Fld Hcky; Hon Roll; Outstndng Cntrbtns Extra Crr Actvties 84; Kiwanis Awd Outstndng Cntrbtns To Schl Cmnty 84; Acctg.

FERRARO, NICK; St Mary HS; Keansburg, NJ; (Y); 27/115; Church Yth Grp; Letterman Clb; Spanish Clb; Rep Jr Cls; Var Bsbl; Var Bsktbl; JV Socr; Hon Roll; Amercn Legn Awd 83; Paul Fecskovicks Awd Outstndng Frshmn Bsktbll Plyr 84; Schlrshp St Mary HS 83.

FERRARO, RICHARD A; Manalapan HS; Englishtown, NJ; (Y); 97/390; Cmnty Wkr; Spanish Clb; SADD; Varsity Clb; Im Bsbl; Im Bsktbl; Var Ftbl; Var Golf; Im Ice Hcky; Im Sftbl; Bus.

FERREIRA, DINA; Wayne Hills HS; Wayne, NJ; (Y); 88/306; Sec Soph Cls; Sec Jr Cls; Var Capt Cheerleading; Var Pom Pon; Hon Roll; Coachs Awd For Vrsty Chrldng 86; Hmcmng Qn 84-85; Law.

FERREIRA, ISABEL; St Patricks HS; Elizabeth, NJ; (S); Boys Clb Am; Drama Clb; Science Clb; Ski Clb; School Musical; School Play; Nwsp Phtg; Nwsp Rptr; Nwsp Stf; Lit Mag; Fash Inst Of Tech; Intr Dsgn.

FERRER, GINA; Our Lady Of Good Counsel; Newark, NJ; (Y); 15/121; Pep Clb; Church Choir; NHS; Montclare ST Coll; Psych.

FERRIER, ELISE; H P Becton Regional HS; E Rutherford, NJ; (Y); 40/120; Chorus; Concert Band; School Play; Nwsp Stf; Yrbk Stf; Capt Var Pom Pon; Tchng Engl.

FERRO, ANN MARIE; Jackson Memorial HS; Jackson, NJ; (Y); 32/405; Yrbk Stf; High Hon Roll; Hon Roll; NEDT Awd; Georgian CT Coll; Mngmnt.

FERRY, EVELYN; South Brunswick HS; Kendall Pk, NJ; (Y); Church Yth Grp; Ski Clb; Powder Puff Ftbl; Score Keeper; Socr; High Hon Roll; Hon Roll; U Of DE.

FERRY, FAITH; Buena Regional HS; Williamstown, NJ; (Y); 27/200; Church Yth Grp; Hon Roll; Jr NHS; Presdntl Acad Fitness Awd 86; Vrsty Schlr Lttr 86; Acad Rcgntn Pgm 86; Phys Thrpst.

FERRY, MARY ANN; Dover HS; Dover, NJ; (Y); 19/160; Hon Roll; NHS; Cntry 21 Acctng Awds 85 & 86.

FERRY, SHERYL; Kingsway Reg HS; Clarksboro, NJ; (Y); Office Aide; Trs Frsh Cls; Trs Soph Cls; Rep Stu Cncl; Var JV Bsktbl; Var JV Cheerleading; Var Crs Cntry; Var Sftbl; Hon Roll; Accntng.

FESENKO, JOHN; Hamilton HS West; Trenton, NJ; (Y); Key Clb; VP Ski Clb; SADD; Madrigals; School Musical; School Play; Lit Mag; Rep Stu Cncl; Hon Roll; Semi-Fnlst Intl Chem Olympd 86; Biochem.

FETTER, TIM; Holy Spirit HS; Brigantine, NJ; (Y); 52/368; Pres Soph Cls; Var Ftbl; JV Swmmng; Wt Lftg; High Hon Roll; NHS.

FETTERS, ROGER; Overbrook HS; Pinehill, NJ; (Y); Spanish Clb; Bsbl; Ftbl; Wrstlng; Hon Roll; Acctng.

FETTNER, HOLLY; Spotswood HS; Spotswood, NJ; (S); Hosp Aide; Intnl Clb; VP Soph Cls; VP Jr Cls; High Hon Roll; NHS; Bnai Brith Yth Orgnztn Chptr Sec 85; Law.

FEUERSTEIN, MONICA; Deptford Twp HS; Wenonah, NJ; (Y); 20/275; Quiz Bowl; Stu Cncl; Bsktbl; Socr; Sftbl; Hon Roll; Jr NHS; NHS; Prfct Atten Awd; UCLA; Systems Analyst.

FEZZUOGLIO, TONI; Cherry Hill HS West; Cherry Hill, NJ; (Y); 27/372; Am Leg Aux Girls St; French Clb; Intnl Clb; PAVAS; Nwsp Rptr; French Hon Soc; Gov Hon Prg Awd; Hon Roll; NHS; Pres Schlr; Chrry Hll Twp Schlrshp Awd 86; Chrry Hll Twp Cmmndtn Awd 85; Dickinson Coll; Poltlcs.

FICARRA, GLENN; St John Vianney HS; Matawan, NJ; (Y); School Musical; School Play; Stage Crew; Lit Mag; NY U; Flm Dir.

FICCA, KRISTIN J; Hawthorne HS; Hawthorne, NJ; (Y); 17/155; Church Yth Grp; Cmnty Wkr; Dance Clb; Drama Clb; French Clb; Pep Clb; SADD; Yrbk Phtg; NHS; Rotary Awd; IN U; Dance.

FIDLER, DONNAMARIE; Edgewood HS; Waterford, NJ; (Y); 27/400; Latin Clb; Drill Tm; Yrbk Stf; High Hon Roll; Hon Roll; Jr NHS; NHS; Prfct Atten Awd; Schl Svc Awd 83-84; Vrsty Ltr Drill Tm 84-85; Gold Star Drill Tm 85-86; Acctg.

FIDLON, JENNIFER; Middletown H S South; Middletown, NJ; (Y); VP Pres Temple Yth Grp; School Musical; Variety Show; Yrbk Ed-Chief; Yrbk Stf; Tennis; Trs French Hon Soc; Hon Roll; NHS; Govnrs Schl 86.

FIEDLER, MICHELE; Washington Township HS; Sicklerville, NJ; (Y); French Clb; Ski Clb; Yrbk Stf; NHS; Trenton ST Coll; Crmnl Jsct.

FIEDLER, TRACY; Atlantic City HS; Margate, NJ; (Y); Key Clb; Latin Clb; Sec Jr Cls; Sec Sr Cls; L Var Bsktbl; Var L Sftbl; High Hon Roll; Hon Roll; NHS.

FIELD, CYNTHIA; Bridgewater-Raritan HS West; Bridgewater, NJ; (Y); Church Yth Grp; French Clb; Pres Mrchg Band; Var Cheerleading; Var Capt Sftbl; DAR Awd; JP Sousa Awd; Hosp Aide; Church Choir; Pres Concert Band; RCA Comm Srvc Schlrshp 86; Natl Hnr Soc Schlrshp 86; Offcr NJ Assoc Stu Carcils 85-86; PA ST U; Intl Bus.

FIELD, JENNIFER ANNE; Wall HS; Wall, NJ; (S); 1/263; Ski Clb; Band; Concert Band; Drm Mjr(t); Mrchg Band; Rep Jr Cls; Trs Stu Cncl; Trk; Bausch & Lomb Sci Awd; NHS; Rutgers Schlr 85; Mst Lkly Sccd 85; Chem Engrng.

FIELD, SHAWN; Sayreville War Memorial HS; Sayreville, NJ; (Y); 17/450; Sec Math Clb; Sec Science Clb; High Hon Roll; St Schlr; NJ Garden St Distgshd Schlr Award 85-86; Natl Sci Olympd 1st Wnnr Bio 85; Otstndng Achvt Schltc 83-86; Rutgers Clg Of Eng; Biomed Engr.

FIELDS, DELVONNA; West Side HS; Newark, NJ; (Y); Church Yth Grp; Sec Church Choir; Stage Crew; Stu Cncl; Cit Awd; High Hon Roll; Jr NHS; Rep Sr Cls; Marie B Moses Schlrshp 86; VA ST U; Accntng.

FIGEL, CAROLYN; Matawan Regional HS; Matawan, NJ; (Y); Sftbl; Gov Hon Prg Awd; Hon Roll; Arch.

FIGLER, CINDY; Raritan HS; Hazlet, NJ; (Y); French Clb; Ski Clb; Temple Yth Grp; Hon Roll; NHS; Corp Law.

FIGUEIREDO, JOHN J; Garfield HS; Garfield, NJ; (Y); 11/175; Am Leg Boys St; Drama Clb; Varsity Clb; Drm Mjr(t); Mrchg Band; School Musical; Nwsp Stf; Yrbk Stf; Rep Soph Cls; Rep Jr Cls; Rutgers U; Comms.

FIGUEROA, BILL; Piscataway HS; Piscataway, NJ; (Y); Am Leg Boys St; Key Clb; Varsity Clb; Rep Sr Cls; Capt Bsktbl; Ftbl; Trk; Govt Alive Wth Stu 84; Bus.

FIGUEROA, CRISTINA; Bishop George Ahr St Thomas HS; Perth Amboy, NJ; (Y); French Clb; Spanish Clb; Drill Tm; Nwsp Stf; Im Vllybl; High Hon Roll; Hon Roll; NHS; Schlrshp 86; Ithaca Coll; Sports Med.

FIGUEROA, MARIETTE; Lakewood HS; Lakewood, NJ; (Y); Am Leg Aux Girls St; Church Yth Grp; Cmnty Wkr; Dance Clb; FBLA; Hosp Aide; Church Choir; Hon Roll; NHS; Spanish NHS; Future Bus Ldrs Amrc Hon 86; Hosp Aide Hon 86.

FIJALKOWSKI, JOYMICHELE; Holy Cross HS; Florence, NJ; (Y); Girl Scts; Scholastic Bowl; Yrbk Stf; Hon Roll; Pfeiffer Coll; Comp Sci.

FILIPOW, NANCY; Chatham HS; Chatham, NJ; (Y); Pres Camera Clb; Church Yth Grp; Cmnty Wkr; VP Key Clb; Pep Clb; Stu Cncl; Var L Socr; Var L Trk; Peer Awarenss Cnslng Ldr 86; Town Cty Swim Leag 82; Coaches Awd 85; VISUAL Arts.

FILIPOWSKI, JOAN; Cinnaminson HS; Cinna, NJ; (Y); Am Leg Aux Girls St; Church Yth Grp; Rep Stu Cncl; Var Bsktbl; Var Fld Hcky; Var Lcrss; Hon Roll; NHS; Rotary Awd; 1st Tm Burlington Co Schlstc Leag & 2nd Tm Sioux Div & 2nd Tm All S Jersey La Cross 86; Bus.

FILIPPELLO, MICHAEL P; Seton Hall Prep; Roseland, NJ; (Y); Church Yth Grp; German Clb; Hosp Aide; Math Tm; Quiz Bowl; Church Choir; Concert Band; School Play; Hon Roll; NHS; Duke U; Bus.

FILLIMAN, LISA; Passaic Valley HS; Little Falls, NJ; (S); 9/359; Am Leg Aux Girls St; Church Yth Grp; Spanish Clb; Concert Band; Drm Mjr(t); School Musical; Yrbk Stf; Tennis; High Hon Roll; NHS; Lib Art.

FILONE, ANDREA; Pope John XXIII HS; Milford, PA; (Y); 60/147; Cmnty Wkr; Computer Clb; 4-H; French Clb; Ski Clb; SADD; Chorus; Variety Show; Yrbk Stf; Lit Mag; Marywood Coll; Fshn Mrchndsng.

FILUS, JULIE; Hackettstown HS; Hackettstown, NJ; (Y); Art Clb; 4-H; Key Clb; Letterman Clb; JV Sftbl; Pres Phy Ftnss Awd; Art Fshn.

FINAMORE, DE ANNE; Wayne Hills HS; Wayne, NJ; (Y); 36/310; GAA; Service Clb; Spanish Clb; Varsity Clb; Stat Bsktbl; Capt Socr; Sftbl; Cit Awd; DAR Awd; Hon Roll; Hghst GPA FBLA Awd Merit 85; Perservrnce FBLA Awd Merit 85.

FINCH II, LESTER G; Hamilton West HS; Trenton, NJ; (Y); 10/307; Am Leg Boys St; Exploring; Band; Mrchg Band; Symp Band; Hon Roll; NHS; Hmltn Twp PTA Cmmtee Awd Schlrshp 86; Prsdntl Acdmc Ftnss Awd 86; Rutgers Coll; Hstry.

FINCH, SANDY; John F Kennedy HS; Avenel, NJ; (Y); 28/279; Ski Clb; SADD; Rep Stu Cncl; JV Var Bsktbl; Stat Sftbl; Hon Roll; NHS; Phys Thrpy.

FINCHLER, TODD; Parsippany HS; Parsippany, NJ; (Y); 63/320; Chess Clb; Computer Clb; FBLA; Math Clb; Hon Roll; NHS; Pres Schlr; St Schlr; Grdn ST Dstngshd Schlr Awd 86; Prsdntl Acdmc Ftns Awd 86; Schlrshp Hbrw Exclnc; SUNY Binghamton; Pltcl Sci.

FINCKEN, HEIDI; Kittatinny HS; Newton, NJ; (Y); 20/228; Am Leg Aux Girls St; Sec Church Yth Grp; Sec Trs 4-H; Intnl Clb; VP Spanish Clb; Nwsp Ed-Chief; Cheerleading; 4-H Awd; High Hon Roll; NHS; Acad All Am Schlr 86; Chrldr Achvt Awd 86; NJ Girls Citznshp Awd 86; Intl Law.

FINDLEY, BARRY; Lenape Valley Regional HS; Stanhope, NJ; (Y); 48/255; Chorus; Madrigals; Comp.

FINE, MICHELLE; Bruriah HS; Matawan, NJ; (Y); Drama Clb; Hosp Aide; Off Temple Yth Grp; School Play; Nwsp Rptr; VP Frsh Cls; Sec Soph Cls; VP Jr Cls; Sec Stu Cncl; NHS; Fnlst Time Lf Ed Prog Expstry Wrtg 86; Barnard Coll.

FINEGAN, WENDY; Hopewell Valley Central HS; Pennington, NJ; (Y); 8/202; AFS; Service Clb; Sec Spanish Clb; Yrbk Ed-Chief; Capt Fld Hcky; High Hon Roll; Chrmn NHS; Ntl Merit Ltr; PAVAS; Rep Soph Cls; Fnlst Gvrnrs Schl Sci 86; Rice U; Econ.

FINGAL, INGA; Hillside HS; Hillside, NJ; (Y); 5/196; Math Clb; Science Clb; Band; Church Choir; Concert Band; Mrchg Band; Pep Band; High Hon Roll; Jr NHS; NHS; Grls Ctznshp Inst 86; Mnrts Engr 83-86; New Jerseys JR Miss 86; Pre-Med.

FINK, CAROLYN; Westfield SR HS; Westfield, NJ; (Y); 59/529; Hosp Aide; Latin Clb; Spanish Clb; Temple Yth Grp; Rep Stu Cncl; Sftbl; Swmmng; High Hon Roll; NHS; Smng ST Grp Chmpnshp 79-85; Smng Rgnl 85; Natl JR Olmpcs Smng 84; Physcl Thrpy.

FINK, MONICA; Riverside HS; Delanco, NJ; (S); Key Clb; Rep Frsh Cls; Rep Soph Cls; Hon Roll; Alg Awd; Moore Coll Of Art; Artst.

FINKELSTEIN, JEFF; Montville HS; Montville, NJ; (Y); 2/269; Cmnty Wkr; Key Clb; Math Clb; Science Clb; SADD; Temple Yth Grp; Stu Cncl; JV Socr; JV Var Tennis; High Hon Roll; Sci.

FINKELSTEIN, MARK; Highstown HS; E Windsor, NJ; (Y); Boy Scts; Pres Computer Clb; Math Tm; Ski Clb; High Hon Roll; NHS; VFW Awd; Prfct Atten Awd; US Natl Mathmtcs Awd 86; Garden ST Distgshd Schlr 86; Presdntl Acadmc Ftnss Awd 86; WA U; Comp Engr.

FINLAY, SHANNON; Brick Township HS; Brick Town, NJ; (Y); 2/400; Math Tm; Band; Rep Frsh Cls; Rep Soph Cls; JV Bsktbl; JV Crs Cntry; Var L Tennis; JV Trk; High Hon Roll; NHS.

FINN, LUCI; Middletown HS South; Leonardo, NJ; (S); 6/436; Yrbk Stf; Sftbl; DAR Awd; High Hon Roll; Hon Roll; Sec NHS; Acad Ltr 83; 2nd Pl Trphy Career Exploration Pgm 85.

FINN, THOMAS; St Peters Prep; Jersey City, NJ; (Y); 25/205; Pep Clb; School Play; Yrbk Ed-Chief; Rep Stu Cncl; JV Im Bsktbl; Im Ftbl; Im Vllybl; High Hon Roll; Prep Spirit Awd 85; Bus.

FINNEY, SONYA; Essex County Voc & Tech HS; Newark, NJ; (Y); FBLA; Atten Awd 83-85; Doc.

FINVER, STACY; Paramus HS; Paramus, NJ; (Y); Drama Clb; FBLA; Ski Clb; Yrbk Stf; Lib Arts.

FIORE, MICHELLE; Montville HS; Towaco, NJ; (Y); 95/265; Pres Art Clb; Church Yth Grp; Hosp Aide; Latin Clb; Color Guard; Mrchg Band; School Play; Mgr(s); JV Powder Puff Ftbl; Im Sftbl; Catholic U Of Amer; Arch.

FIORENTINO, SUSAN; Edgewood SR HS; Hammonton, NJ; (Y); 12/300; Varsity Clb; Var Socr; High Hon Roll; Hon Roll; Jr NHS; NHS; Prfct Atten Awd; Reitger U; Phrmcy.

FIORESI, VICTOR; Vineland HS; Vineland, NJ; (Y); Boy Scts; Church Yth Grp; Key Clb; Rep Soph Cls; Bsbl; Var Tennis; JV Wrstlng; Merit Roll; PA ST U.

FIORITO, DINA; Clifton HS; Clifton, NJ; (Y); Church Yth Grp; Girl Scts; Library Aide; Band; Mrchg Band; Hon Roll; Ed.

FIRESTONE, SCOTT; Somerville HS; Somerville, NJ; (S); 10/253; Aud/Vis; Drama Clb; Letterman Clb; Math Tm; Thesps; Varsity Clb; Chorus; Stage Crew; Rnsslr Plytchnc Mth & Sci Awd 86; MIT; Elctrcl Engr.

FISCH, JONATHAN; Managquan HS; E Brunswick, NJ; (Y); 41/238; Drama Clb; Spanish Clb; Stage Crew; Yrbk Stf; High Hon Roll; Hon Roll; School Musical; School Play; Var Trk; Ecology Clb; Prom, Float Cmmttee; U Of S FL; Bus.

FISCHBEIN, DARA; Ocean Township HS; Oakhurst, NJ; (Y); 79/336; French Clb; Ski Clb; Varsity Clb; Variety Show; Sec Trs Stu Cncl; Stat Socr; Var Sftbl; JV Swmmng; Phys Ther.

FISCHER, CHRISTINE; Passaic Valley HS; Little Falls, NJ; (Y); Am Leg Aux Girls St; Church Yth Grp; Trs French Clb; Yrbk Stf; Sec Stu Cncl; Sftbl; Tennis; Hon Roll; Wmns Clb Girls Ctznshp Inst Awd 86; Bus.

FISCHER, ERIC; Hillsborough HS; Neshanic, NJ; (Y); 21/300; Latin Clb; Mathletes; Math Tm; JV Var Crs Cntry; JV Var Ftbl; Mgr Var Tennis; High Hon Roll; Hon Roll; NHS; U Of Miami; Pre Med.

FISCHER, JENNIFER; Holy Family Acad; Jersey City, NJ; (Y); 16/150; Computer Clb; Dance Clb; Ed Lit Mag; Score Keeper; High Hon Roll; Hon Roll; Dstngshd Hnrs 86; Merit Awd Math, Bio 85; Rutgers U; Accntng.

FISCHER, JENNIFER; Toms River North HS; Toms River, NJ; (Y); 17/420; Var Fld Hcky; Socr; JV Sftbl; High Hon Roll; Hon Roll; NHS; Acdmc Lttr 84; Acdmc Pin 85; Bus.

FISH, TIMOTHY; St Josephs Prep Seminary; Titusville, NJ; (S); 2/15; Cmnty Wkr; Hosp Aide; Sec Service Clb; Spanish Clb; Stage Crew; Yrbk Stf; VP Frsh Cls; Pres Soph Cls; Pres Sr Cls; VP Stu Cncl; Sci.

FISHBURN, JAMES R; Lenape Regional HS; Mount Laurel, NJ; (Y); Am Leg Boys St; Math Tm; Spanish Clb; Band; Jazz Band; School Musical; Variety Show; High Hon Roll; Hon Roll; NHS; NJ Gvnrs Schl Poly Sci 86; Chem Engr.

FISHBURN, PAUL T; Lenape Regional HS; Mount Laurel, NJ; (Y); Am Leg Boys St; Math Tm; Spanish Clb; Band; Jazz Band; Mrchg Band; School Musical; Variety Show; High Hon Roll; Hon Roll.

FISHER, APRIL LEE; Brick Twp High; Brick Town, NJ; (Y); 6/322; Church Yth Grp; JV Bsktbl; Var Powder Puff Ftbl; Var Capt Sftbl; Var Tennis; Cit Awd; High Hon Roll; Church Choir; Schlr Athlete Awd 86; Big A Awd Sftbl 86; Brick Exc Clb Awd 86; Messiah Coll.

FISHER, JIM; Mainland Regional HS; Somers Point, NJ; (Y); 13/270; Ski Clb; Rep Stu Cncl; JV Bsbl; Var L Golf; Im Vllybl; High Hon Roll; Course On Genetic Engr Coll Credits 85.

FISHER, JOSEPH P; Delaware Valley HS; Frenchtown, NJ; (Y); 37/160; Am Leg Boys St; VP Key Clb; Pep Clb; Varsity Clb; Yrbk Stf; Stu Cncl; Var JV Bsbl; Var Capt Bsktbl; Var Capt Socr; Hon Roll.

FISHER, SHERI LYNN; Neptune SR HS; Neptune, NJ; (Y); 9/309; Am Leg Aux Girls St; Sec Pres Church Yth Grp; GAA; Church Choir; Sec Concert Band; Mrchg Band; Capt Var Bowling; JV VP Sftbl; High Hon Roll; NHS; Outstndg SR-BWLG 85-86; Schlrshp Recig Awd 82-84; Phila Coll/Phrmcy/Sci; Phrmcy.

FISHMAN, ERIC; Wayne Hills HS; Wayne, NJ; (Y); 40/301; Model UN; VP Spanish Clb; Temple Yth Grp; Nwsp Rptr; Nwsp Sprt Ed; Var Crs Cntry; JV Golf; Hon Roll; Bus.

FISHMAN, TODD; Clifton HS; Clifton, NJ; (Y); 27/637; Am Leg Boys St; Ski Clb; JV Socr; JV Var Tennis; Pres Jr NHS; Opt Clb Awd; Spanish NHS; Hstry.

FISKE, JASON; Chatham Twp HS; Chatham, NJ; (Y); 40/140; Key Clb; Model UN; Political Wkr; Bsbl; Ftbl; Wt Lftg; Hon Roll; Ntl Merit Ltr; Lawyer.

FITTIPALDI, SUSAN; Franklin HS; Somerset, NJ; (Y); French Clb; Scholastic Bowl; Trs SADD; Color Guard; Concert Band; Mrchg Band; School Musical; Yrbk Stf; Trs Jr Cls; Trs Sr Cls; 1st Rnnr-Up USA Miss NJ Schlrshp Pgnt 85.

FITZER, MARY; Holy Cross HS; Riverton, NJ; (Y); 81/385; JV Trk; High Hon Roll; Hon Roll; Rutgers ST U.

FITZGERALD, BRIAN; Christian Brothers Acad; Ft Monmouth, NJ; (Y); 42/238; Boy Scts; Pres Church Yth Grp; Dance Clb; Varsity Clb; Var Capt Crs Cntry; Var Trk; Hon Roll; VFW Awd; Citatn ST NJ 84; Amer Lgn-Good Ctzn Citatn 84; Marine Corp Leag Cert Rcgntn 84; West Point; Aerospc Aerntcl Eng.

FITZGERALD, COLLEEN; Oak Knoll HS; Short Hills, NJ; (Y); Church Yth Grp; Cmnty Wkr; Dance Clb; Ski Clb; Chorus; Nwsp Rptr; Var Tennis; Hon Roll; Visual Arts Awd For Outstndng Achvt 86; Tm Dedctn Awd For Vrsty Tnns Tm 86; Boston Coll; Fine Arts.

FITZGERALD, ERIC; Memorial HS; Cedar Grove, NJ; (S); 1/125; Math Tm; Pres Stu Cncl; Var Bsbl; Var Bsktbl; Capt Socr; NHS; Ntl Merit Ltr; St Schlr; Val.

FITZGERALD, SCOTT; St James HS; Salem, NJ; (S); Trs Jr Cls; Stu Cncl; JV Var Bsktbl; Hon Roll; Ntl Merit Ltr; Natl Engl Merit Awd 85; Natl Sci Merit Awd 84.

FITZGERALD, SHAWN; Kittatinny Regionial HS; Newton, NJ; (Y); 79/228; Church Yth Grp; Band; Concert Band; Mrchg Band; School Musical; Nwsp Phtg; Lit Mag; Var Socr; JV Trk; Var Wt Lftg; Johnson & Wales; Htl Mgmt.

FITZGERALD, TRACY; Pitman HS; Pitman, NJ; (S); #2 In Class; Chorus; Concert Band; Mrchg Band; JV Bsktbl; Var Crs Cntry; Hon Roll; NHS; Church Yth Grp; Trk; Modrn Music Mstrs Soc-Sec 85-86; NJ All ST Chrs 85; S Jersey Chrs; Pre-Law.

FITZGIBBONS, MOIRA; Pope John XXIII HS; Ogdensburg, NJ; (Y); 1/137; Am Leg Aux Girls St; Political Wkr; Scholastic Bowl; Service Clb; Thesps; School Musical; School Play; Lit Mag; Sec Frsh Cls; Pres Soph Cls; Frnch, Theolgy, Engl Acadmc Awds; 2nd Pl Rider Coll Essy Cont; 1st Pl Paterson Diocese Essy Cont; Lib Arts.

FITZHENRY, DANIEL; St Peters Prep; Bayonne, NJ; (Y); 99/207; Boy Scts; Ski Clb; Yrbk Stf; Stu Cncl; Ftbl; Ice Hcky; Wt Lftg; Bus.

FITZHENRY, STEPHANIE ERIN; Mt St Dominic Acad; N Caldwell, NJ; (Y); Cmnty Wkr; Intnl Clb; Model UN; VP Service Clb; Variety Show; Nwsp Rptr; Var Socr; Hon Roll; Notre Dame.

FITZMAURICE, KAREN; Washington Twnshp HS; Turnersville, NJ; (Y); French Clb; Color Guard; Drill Tm; Mrchg Band.

FITZMORRIS, SEAN; Central Regional HS; Bayville, NJ; (Y); 60/289; Church Yth Grp; Letterman Clb; Pep Clb; JV Bsbl; JV Var Bsktbl; High Hon Roll; Hon Roll; Jr NHS; Schlr-Athlete Awd Bsktbl 86; Peer Cnclng Grp Ldr; Mgr Schl Bookstore; Lawyer.

FITZPATRICK, ANN; St Aloysius HS; Jersey City, NJ; (Y); 5/110; Nwsp Rptr; Yrbk Stf; Var JV Cheerleading; Stat Socr; Var Swmmng; Im Vllybl; CC Awd; Hon Roll; VP NHS; Pres Schlr; Daemen Coll; Physcl Thrpy.

FITZPATRICK, DANIEL; De Paul Diocesan HS; Wayne, NJ; (S); Am Leg Boys St; Aud/Vis; Chess Clb; JCL; Latin Clb; Nwsp Rptr; Var Ftbl; Wt Lftg; Hon Roll; Ltn Clb-Consl 85-86; Soc Stud Awd 85; Boys ST-SEC Ntl Prty 85; Ltn Qz Bwl Tm 86; PA ST U; Intl Stud.

FITZSIMMONS, CAROLE ANN; Mahwah HS; Mahwah, NJ; (Y); 34/187; Sec Soph Cls; Sec Jr Cls; VP Sr Cls; Var Bsktbl; Var Sftbl; High Hon Roll; Hon Roll; Math.

FLAHERTY, DAN; Neptune SR HS; Neptune, NJ; (Y); #39 In Class; Drama Clb; Exploring; Stage Crew; Yrbk Phtg; Yrbk Stf; Hon Roll; Jr NHS; Ntl Merit Ltr; Flm Mkg.

FLAHERTY, DIANNA-JEAN; Palisades Park JR SR HS; Palisades Pk, NJ; (Y); Drama Clb; Swing Chorus; Rep Frsh Cls; Rep Stu Cncl; JV Cheerleading; L Stat Ftbl; Im Wt Lftg; Var Crs Cntry; Letterman Clb; Lit Mag; Ms Phtgenc 84; Ms Touchdwn 82-83; 2 Rls Mtn Pctrs; 1st Rnnr Ms NJ Shore; NYU; Chrprctcs.

FLAHERTY, JAMES; Christian Brothers Acad; Jackson, NJ; (Y); Boy Scts; Off Church Yth Grp; Cmnty Wkr; Yrbk Rptr; Yrbk Stf; Im Bsktbl; Im Bowling; Im Fld Hcky; Im Socr; Hon Roll; Physcl Thrpy.

FLAHERTY, MEGAN; Mount Saint Dominic Acad; West Orange, NJ; (Y); Intnl Clb; VP Service Clb; Var Bsktbl; Var Trk; High Hon Roll; Hon Roll; NHS; Acadmc Schlrshp Coll St Elizabeth 86; Outstndng Achvt 400 Meter 84; Recrtmnt Prog Awd 85; St Elizabeth; Librl Arts.

FLAMM, STEPHEN; Chatham Township SR HS; Chatham Twp, NJ; (Y); #9 In Class; Boy Scts; Computer Clb; Key Clb; Math Tm; Model UN; Yrbk Stf; JV Trk; High Hon Roll; NHS; Band; Olympcs Of Mind-1st Pl Rgnl, 4th Pl ST 84-85; Elec Engrng.

FLANAGAN, SCOTT; West Milford HS; West Milford, NJ; (Y); 32/390; Am Leg Boys St; Varsity Clb; JV Bsbl; Var Capt Ftbl; Im Trk; Im Vllybl; High Hon Roll; Hon Roll; NHS; Pres Phys Fitness Awd 85-87; Tell-A-Peer Peer Cnslng-2 Yrs 86-87; Crim Law.

FLANIGAN, ERROLL; East Orange HS; East Orange, NJ; (S); Computer Clb; Pep Clb; Yrbk Stf; Stu Cncl; Bsktbl; Cheerleading; Coach Actv; High Hon Roll; Hon Roll; Cmmnctns.

FLASCHNER, DEAN A; Sparta HS; Sparta, NJ; (Y); Math Tm; Var Bsbl; Var Capt Bsktbl; Var Ftbl; High Hon Roll; Hon Roll; FL ST U; Law.

FLATTERY, AMY; Scotch Plains-Fanwood HS; Scotch Plains, NJ; (Y); 4/311; Math Tm; Science Clb; Band; Jazz Band; Mrchg Band; JV Bsktbl; Var L Sftbl; High Hon Roll; Ntl Merit Ltr; Bio Tm ST Sci 84; Chem Tm Sci Day 85; Physcs Tm ST Sci Day 86; Cornell U; Vet Med.

FLECK, ROBERT L; North Hunterdon HS; Clinton, NJ; (Y); 161/298; VP Chess Clb; JCL; Latin Clb; Nwsp Rptr; Ntl Merit SF; Comp Sci.

FLECKENSTEIN, DONNA; Woodstown HS; Woodstown, NJ; (Y); FBLA; Hosp Aide; Band; Glassboro ST Coll; Elem Teach.

FLEHER, LAURA; Bayonne HS; Bayonne, NJ; (Y); Sec Drama Clb; VP German Clb; Band; Concert Band; Mrchg Band; Orch; School Musical; School Play; Stage Crew; Lit Mag.

FLEISCHER, LISA; Ocean Twp HS; Wayside, NJ; (Y); 51/333; Hosp Aide; Spanish Clb; Temple Yth Grp; Yrbk Stf; JV Stat Bsbl; High Hon Roll; Sprtn Schlr Awd 84; SPCH Educ.

FLEMING, LEE ANN; Hamilton HS West; Trenton, NJ; (Y); Aud/Vis; Band; Concert Band; Mrchg Band; Pep Band; Symp Band; Jr Cls; Bsktbl; Sftbl; Tennis; 2nd Tm All Cnty Sftbl 86; Hnrb Mntn All Cnty Sftbl 86; Spn.

FLEMING, MORGAN; Boonton HS; Boonton, NJ; (Y); Off Church Yth Grp; Quiz Bowl; Var Crs Cntry; Var Trk; Ofcr Chrch Yth Grp 85-86; Vrsty Indr Trck 85-86; Arch.

FLEMING, PAMELA; John F Kennedy HS; Willingboro, NJ; (Y); 17/295; Computer Clb; Girl Scts; Nwsp Stf; Hon Roll; NHS; Rutgers U; Bus Mgmnt.

FLEMMING, WILLIAM L C; Haddon Twp HS; Haddonfield, NJ; (Y); 14/170; Am Leg Boys St; Capt Chess Clb; Var L Swmmng; High Hon Roll; Hon Roll; NHS; St Schlr; Certfd Peer Facltr 85-86; Full Schlrshp St Peters Coll 86; Pres Of S J Yth Comm 86; St Peters Coll; Philsphy.

FLETCHER, BRUCE; Morris Catholic HS; Morris Plains, NJ; (Y); 55/155; Church Yth Grp; Cmnty Wkr; Dance Clb; FBLA; JA; Letterman Clb; Library Aide; Mathletes; Math Clb; Ski Clb; Contntl Math Leag 82-83; County Coll Morris; Bus.

FLETCHER, CONNIE; Madison Central HS; Old Bridge, NJ; (Y); Drama Clb; FBLA; German Clb; Chorus; Color Guard; Drill Tm; Flag Corp; School Play; Stu Cncl; Hon Roll; Scndry Educ.

FLETCHER, JACKIE; Dover HS; Dover, NJ; (Y); 66/185; Girl Scts; Library Aide; Office Aide; Ski Clb; Spanish Clb; Band; Color Guard; Mrchg Band; Yrbk Stf; Sftbl; Cert Prof Century 21 Acctg 85 & 86; Acctg.

FLETCHER, JANICE; East Brunswick HS; E Brunswick, NJ; (Y); Cmnty Wkr; Hosp Aide; Johnson & Wales Coll; Htl Mgt.

FLICKER, MICHAEL T; Ocean City HS; Ocean City, NJ; (Y); 17/298; Am Leg Boys St; VP Church Yth Grp; FCA; Math Clb; JV Var Socr; Mgr Sftbl; Mgr Swmmng; NHS; Rotary Awd; Rsrch.

FLINT, MELISSA; St John Vianney HS; Colts Neck, NJ; (Y); Hosp Aide; SADD; Off Jr Cls; Bsktbl; JV Sftbl; Var Tennis; Var Trk; JV Pres Schlr; Yellow & White Awd 85-86; Regnl Fin Teens Great Modl Srch 85; Bus Mgmt.

FLINT, MICHAEL; Sparta HS; Sparta, NJ; (Y); 24/233; Camera Clb; Ftbl; Swmmng; Tennis; Hon Roll.

FLOCCO, CHRISSY; Mt Olive HS; Flanders, NJ; (Y); Dance Clb; Ski Clb; Variety Show; Yrbk Stf; Stat Socr; High Hon Roll; Hon Roll; Jr NHS; NHS; Prfct Atten Awd; Dance Schlrshp NJ Schl Ballet 85-86; Talent Show 2(d Dance 86; Radford U; Bus Mgt.

FLORENTO, VERONI C; St Mary HS; Jersey City, NJ; (Y); Am Leg Boys St; Chorus; School Play; Pres Stu Cncl; High Hon Roll; John Hopkins; Med.

FLORES, BILL; South Hunterdon Regional HS; Lambertville, NJ; (Y); Church Yth Grp; FBLA; JA; Varsity Clb; Chorus; School Play; Variety Show; Nwsp Rptr; Frsh Cls.

FLORES JR, LAMBERTO O; Union Catholic Reg HS; Elizabeth, NJ; (Y); 25/332; Church Yth Grp; French Clb; Math Tm; Science Clb; Service Clb; Tennis; High Hon Roll; Hon Roll; NHS; Prfct Atten Awd; Rutgers Coll; Pre-Med.

FLORIO, MARY; Lakeland Regional HS; Wanaque, NJ; (Y); 6/303; FBLA; Math Clb; Teachers Aide; Rep Frsh Cls; Rep Soph Cls; Rep Jr Cls; Rep Sr Cls; Var Capt Cheerleading; Gym; Powder Puff Ftbl; Calculus League 2nd Pl Awd 86; Pres Acadmc Fitness Awd 86; Douglass Coll; Med Technlgy.

FLORIO, PEGGY; Waldwick HS; Waldwick, NJ; (Y); Church Yth Grp; Drama Clb; Math Tm; Red Cross Aide; Nwsp Ed-Chief; Mgr Jr Cls; NHS; Exploring; Girl Scts; Stage Crew; Mddl Coll Prog Fairlgh Dcknsn U 85-87; Flcn Coll Smr Schlrs 86; Grl Sct Gld Awd 84; Spec Educ.

FLOWERS, CHRISTINA; Kingsway Regional HS; Mickleton, NJ; (Y); Art Clb; Model UN; Office Aide; Science Clb; Ski Clb; Spanish Clb; JV Fld Hcky; Im Powder Puff Ftbl; Var Sftbl; Im Wt Lftg; U Of CO.

FLOYD, DEBBIE; Clearview Regional HS; Sewell, NJ; (Y); 11/149; Church Yth Grp; Hosp Aide; Concert Band; Off Frsh Cls; Off Soph Cls; JV Var Bsktbl; Var Cheerleading; High Hon Roll; Hon Roll; NHS; Phy Thrpy.

FLYNN, KIMBERLY; Hackettstown HS; Hackettstown, NJ; (S); Church Yth Grp; Hosp Aide; Key Clb; Band; Concert Band; Drm Mjr(t); Jazz Band; Mrchg Band; Jr Cls; Var Cheerleading; Econ.

FLYNN, MIKE; Toms River HS East; Toms River, NJ; (Y); German Clb; Ski Clb; SADD; Law.

FODER, MATTHEW JOSEPH; Eastern Regional HS; Berlin, NJ; (Y); 1/321; Church Yth Grp; Trs Sr Cls; Rep Stu Cncl; Var Socr; Bausch & Lomb Sci Awd; High Hon Roll; Trs NHS; Ntl Merit Ltr; Val; Garden ST Distngshd Scholar 85-86; NJ Schlr/Ath 86; Camden Cnty Prncpls P Supv Awd 86; Princeton U; Chem Engrng.

FODERARO, TROY; Red Bank Catholic HS; Long Branch, NJ; (Y); JV Bsbl; Var Ftbl; Var Ice Hcky; Acctnt.

FOGARTY, ALLISON; Mt St Mary Acad; Berkeley Hts, NJ; (Y); Church Yth Grp; French Clb; Pep Clb; Chorus; Variety Show; Latin Awd Magna Cum Laude 83-84; Providence Coll; Bus.

FOGARTY, LORI; Monsignor Donovan HS; Howell, NJ; (Y); 19/253; SADD; Stat Bsbl; Stat Bsktbl; Score Keeper; Hon Roll; NHS; Law.

FOGARTY, MARGARET; East Brunswick HS; E Brunswick, NJ; (Y); Cmnty Wkr; Pres VP 4-H; Hosp Aide; Key Clb; SADD; Varsity Clb; Variety Show; Im Bsktbl; Var L Swmmng; Wmns Clb Awd-Nrsng 86; William Patterson; Nrsng.

FOGEL, PAUL; Teaneck HS; Teaneck, NJ; (Y); SADD.

FOGLER, KATHY; East Side HS; Newark, NJ; (Y); Civic Clb; Cmnty Wkr; Ski Clb; Yrbk Phtg; Yrbk Stf; Var Capt Sftbl; Hon Roll; Phtgrphy.

FOLAN, DONNA; Wayne Hills HS; Wayne, NJ; (Y); French Clb; GAA; Ski Clb; JV Bsktbl; JV Socr; JV Sftbl; JV Trk; Int Dsgn.

FOLEY, DE ANNA L; Cinnaminson HS; Cinnaminson, NJ; (Y); 88/257; Sec Trs DECA; German Clb; Key Clb; Ski Clb; SADD; Nwsp Ed-Chief; JV Cheerleading; Var Capt Trk; Yrbk Stf; Sthrn IL U Trck & Fld Schlrshp 86; Zuckerman Memrl Awd 86; Mst Verstl Athl 85; Southern IL U; Cmmnctns.

FOLEY, DEANNA; Cinnaminson HS; Cinnaminson, NJ; (S); 88/257; DECA; SADD; Nwsp Ed-Chief; Stu Cncl; Var Trk; Cmnty Wkr; German Clb; Key Clb; JV Cheerleading; Im Vllybl; Mrktng Educ Pgm Awd 86; Most Verstl Athlt/Athlt Of Wk 86; Reg ST Natl Gld Mdls At DECA 86; S IL U; Commnctns.

FOLEY, KELLY; Holy Cross HS; Medford, NJ; (Y); VP Church Yth Grp; Exploring; VP French Clb; VP JA; Math Clb; Science Clb; Ski Clb; SADD; Stage Crew; Yrbk Stf; JR Exec Yr 85; JR Achvr Yr 85; Douglass Coll; Biomth.

FOLIO, KIM; St John Vianney HS; Colts Neck, NJ; (Y); 50/283; Art Clb; Hosp Aide; SADD; Yrbk Ed-Chief; Trs Soph Cls; Rep Jr Cls; VP Stu Cncl; High Hon Roll; Hon Roll; Chnl 13 Art Awd 84-85; Law.

FOLKER, JUDY; Waldwick HS; Waldwick, NJ; (Y); Church Yth Grp; Intnl Clb; Math Clb; Math Tm; Ski Clb; Chorus; School Musical; Stat Ftbl; Powder Puff Ftbl; Var Socr; Wmns Clb Alt Grls Ctznshp Awd Douglass Coll 86; Rutgers; Engrng.

FOLKERTS, JOHN; Eastern Christian HS; Oakland, NJ; (S); 1/92; Drama Clb; Concert Band; Orch; School Play; Yrbk Stf; Var Crs Cntry; NHS; Ntl Merit Ltr; St Schlr; Val; Rutgers Schlr 85; Sprtsmnshp Awd 84-85; Physics.

FOLLIS, LUCILLE; Audubon HS; Audubon, NJ; (Y); Pres Aud/Vis; Boy Scts; Church Yth Grp; Exploring; Spanish Clb; Church Choir; Flag Corp; Nwsp Bus Mgr; Var Swmmng; Im Vllybl; Sea Explrr Of Yr 86; Md.

FOLTZ, LISA; Southern Regional HS; Manahawkin, NJ; (Y); Church Yth Grp; Computer Clb; Hosp Aide; Red Cross Aide; Service Clb; Ski Clb; JV Socr; Knigts Of Columbs Essy Cntst 81; Chem.

FONG, CLINTON; Parsippany HS; Parsippany, NJ; (S); Computer Clb; Concert Band; Var L Tennis; High Hon Roll; Hon Roll; Prfct Atten Awd; N Jersey Area Band 83-84 & 84-85; N Jersey Rgnl Band 84-85; Asian Clb Pres 85-86; Engrng.

FONG, KIM; Academic HS; Jersey City, NJ; (Y); Art Clb; Chess Clb; Quiz Bowl; Scholastic Bowl; Nwsp Stf; Lit Mag; Var Vllybl; Hon Roll; Sec NHS; Geo Awd, Alg II Hon Ment & Humanities Awd 84-86; Boston U; Med.

FONSECA, DARREN; Pinelands Regional HS; Tuckerton, NJ; (Y); Aud/Vis; CAP; Library Aide; Science Clb; Drill Tm; Stage Crew; Yrbk Phtg; Rep Frsh Cls; Stu Cncl; Hon Roll; Mitchell Awd Cvl Air Ptrl 85; Air Force; Comp Engnrng.

FORAN, EDWARD; Susses County Vo-Tech; Vernon, NJ; (Y); Church Yth Grp; Library Aide; Varsity Clb; Church Choir; Var Capt Crs Cntry; Var Swmmng; Var Trk; High Hon Roll; Hon Roll; Athltc Awds Crss Cntry Swmmng And Trk85-86; County Clg Morris; Electnc Engr.

FORAN, SHEILA K; Verona HS; Verona, NJ; (Y); 8/210; Church Yth Grp; Drama Clb; 4-H; Girl Scts; Hosp Aide; Intnl Clb; Library Aide; Pep Clb; PAVAS; Varsity Clb; Outstndng Jr Muscn 85; Natl Essy Comptn 85; WA Wrkshp Schlrshp; Pres Clssrm Schlrshp 85-86; Band Dir Aw; Lafayette Clg; Vet Med.

FORBES, FRANK; Linden HS; Linden, NJ; (Y); German Clb; Ski Clb; Hon Roll; Bus.

FORD, CARLA; Camden HS; Camden, NJ; (Y); Church Yth Grp; FCA; 4-H; Office Aide; Pep Clb; Cheerleading; Pom Pon; Sftbl; Twrlr; Vllybl; BSA Modeling 83-85; Doctor.

FORD, CAROL; Clearview Regional HS; Mullica Hill, NJ; (Y); 35/162; Sec Band; Sec Concert Band; Sec Mrchg Band; Yrbk Stf; Bsktbl; Prfct Atten Awd; Elem Educ.

FORD, CAROLYN; Kearny HS; Kearny, NJ; (Y); 86/386; Boys Clb Am; Cmnty Wkr; FBLA; Hosp Aide; Red Cross Aide; SADD; Hon Roll; NHS; Annl Engrng Scintfc Techns Schlrshp 86; Hnr Awd 86; PTA Bond 86; Bergeon CC; Radiographic.

FORD, DARLENE; Westfield HS; Westfield, NJ; (Y); 138/514; Church Yth Grp; Key Clb; Spanish Clb; Teachers Aide; Church Choir; Orch; Yrbk Phtg; Var Fld Hcky; Hon Roll; Kiwanis Awd; Statue Liberty Awd 86; Spn.

FORD, ERIC; Passaic Valley HS; W Paterson, NJ; (Y); Am Leg Boys St; Pres Church Yth Grp; VP German Clb; Var L Crs Cntry; Var L Trk; JV Wrstlng; High Hon Roll; Kiwanis Awd; Passaic Vly Hnr Soc 86; West Point.

FORD, JEROD; Newton HS; Newton, NJ; (Y); 30/190; Am Leg Boys St; Computer Clb; Math Clb; Math Tm; SADD; Varsity Clb; Rep Frsh Cls; Rep Soph Cls; Rep Jr Cls; Rep Sr Cls; PTA Bk Schlrshp 83; NDSL 84-85; MVP All Cnty All Area 1st Sngls Tnns 86; Penn ST U; Bus.

FORDYCE, JANE; Livingston HS; Livingston, NJ; (Y); Church Yth Grp; Sftbl; Hon Roll; Jr NHS.

FORESTA, VITA; Garfield HS; Garfield, NJ; (Y); 8/170; Drama Clb; Band; Concert Band; Nwsp Rptr; Rep Soph Cls; Rep Jr Cls; Crs Cntry; Trk; High Hon Roll; NHS; Pre-Law.

FORESTER, MATTHEW L; Millville SR HS; Millville, NJ; (Y); 7/468; Debate Tm; FBLA; Key Clb; Ski Clb; Mrchg Band; Yrbk Phtg; VP Jr Cls; Stu Cncl; JV Bsbl; Im Bowling; NJ Govrs Schlr & NJ Govrs Schl In Public Issues 85; NJ Debat Champ 86; Natl Schlstc Writing Awd 83; Wharton U Of PA; Econ.

FORESTER, PETER; Livingston HS; Livingston, NJ; (Y); 34/500; Key Clb; Nwsp Stf; Rep Stu Cncl; JV Socr; High Hon Roll; Hon Roll; Jr NHS; NHS; Ntl Merit Ltr; Spanish NHS; Nrthwstrn U.

FORHEZ, CHRIS; Ramsey HS; Waldwick, NJ; (S); DECA; JV Bsktbl; L Fld Hcky; CC Awd; Hon Roll; Mktg Stu Of Yr 86; DECA Cls Pres 84-86; NJ Nrthrn Reg DECA VP 86; Fld Hocky Team Capt 86; Mary Mt Coll; Mjr Bus.

FORLENZA, ROBERT; Toms River East HS; Toms River, NJ; (Y); 91/585; Church Yth Grp; Var L Ftbl; Powder Puff Ftbl; Wt Lftg; Hon Roll; Excllnc Mechanical Drwng 85 & 86; 200 Clb Weight Lftng 86; Grove City Coll; Mech Engr.

FORMICA, MIMMA; North Brunswick Township HS; N Brunswick, NJ; (Y); 17/385; Key Clb; Spanish Clb; Hon Roll; Italian Hnr Soc 85-86; Rugers-Cook Coll; Bio.

FORQUER, BETH A; Haddonfield Memorial HS; Haddonfield, NJ; (S); Am Leg Aux Girls St; Church Yth Grp; French Clb; Intnl Clb; Teachers Aide; Church Choir; Yrbk Stf; French Hon Soc; High Hon Roll; NHS; Pol Sci.

FORREST, CAULINE; Essex Catholic Girls HS; Irvington, NJ; (Y); 5/70; Am Leg Aux Girls St; Drama Clb; Science Clb; Spanish Clb; Nwsp Rptr; Yrbk Stf; Pres Jr Cls; Pres Sr Cls; Hon Roll; NHS; Schlrshp Awd 83; Pre Med.

FORRESTER, ANN; Freehold Township HS; Freehold, NJ; (Y); FBLA; Band; Yrbk Stf; Sec Sr Cls; Im Coach Actv; JV Var Socr; Pres Schlr; 1st Team All Dist Sccr; Bryant Coll; Acctg.

FORTE, DAVID; Holy Cross HS; Willingboro, NJ; (Y); Ski Clb; Rep Jr Cls; Var Ftbl; JV Trk; Hon Roll.

FORTE, KENNETH; Voorhees HS; Glen Gardner, NJ; (Y); 25/274; Boy Scts; Latin Clb; JV Socr; Capt Vllybl; Hon Roll; NHS; Ntl Merit Ltr; Computer Clb; JCL; Math Tm; Fncng JV; Ntl Latin Hnr Scty; USAFA Smr Scnc Smnr; US Air Frc Acad; Arnvtcl.

FORTIS, STEPHEN F; Absegami HS; Egg Harbor City, NJ; (Y); 15/250; Am Leg Boys St; FTA; Model UN; Ski Clb; Teachers Aide; VP Jr Cls; Pres Sr Cls; Bsbl; JV Capt Ftbl; Var Wrstlng; Stu Of Mnth 86; 2nd Pl Soc Sci Fair 85; Hstry.

FORTNA, CARL; Elizabeth HS; Elizabeth, NJ; (Y); Pres Church Yth Grp; Pres Science Clb; Stage Crew; Var Crs Cntry; Var Trk; High Hon Roll; NHS; Prfct Atten Awd; Spanish NHS; Var Bsktbl; 3rd Pl Sci Fair 84; 1st Pl Ten Trnmnt 84; Vet Med.

FORTUNA, LISA; Immaculate Conception HS; Newark, NJ; (Y); VP French Clb; Service Clb; Ed Nwsp Stf; Yrbk Stf; Off Frsh Cls; VP Jr Cls; Crs Cntry; French Hon Soc; High Hon Roll; NHS; Natl Sci Lg Awd 86; Outstndg Achvt Biol 85; Cert Wmn In Sci St Elizabeths Coll 86; Princeton U; Med.

FORTUNATO, JOHN; St Peters Prep; Jersey City, NJ; (Y); 68/204; Hosp Aide; Intnl Clb; Var Ftbl; Var Tennis; Var Wt Lftg; Hon Mntns 85-86; Rutgers New Brusnwick; Psyclgy.

FORTUNATO, JOHN E; Christian Brothers Acad; Freehold, NJ; (S); 2/235; Math Tm; Hon Roll; NHS; Church Yth Grp; Band; Jazz Band; Orch; Tennis; Med.

FOSTER, BRYAN; Mount Olive HS; Flanders, NJ; (Y); AFS; Church Yth Grp; FBLA; Science Clb; Ski Clb; Var Tennis; Ntl Merit Ltr; FBLA-NW Rgnl Bus Math 6th Pl 85; Bus.

FOSTER, DENISE; Cumberland Regional HS; Seabrook, NJ; (Y); Exploring; Intnl Clb; JCL; Varsity Clb; Church Choir; Capt Var Crs Cntry; Hon Roll; Jr NHS; Physcl Thrpst.

FOSTER, DOUGLAS; Cherry Hill High School West; Cherry Hill, NJ; (Y); French Clb; Intnl Clb; Mrchg Band; School Play; Rep Sr Cls; JV Var Crs Cntry; JV Tennis; High Hon Roll; Hon Roll; NHS; U Of Rochester; Lbrl Arts.

FOSTER, HELEN L; Lenape Valley Regional HS; Andover, NJ; (Y); Hosp Aide; Key Clb; SADD; Mrchg Band; School Musical; Mgr School Play; Symp Band; Ed Nwsp Stf; Trk; Hon Roll; USNB Awd 85-86; USNS Awd 85-86; CCM; Physcl Therpy.

FOSTER, KENNY; Paramus HS; Paramus, NJ; (Y); Cmnty Wkr; Computer Clb; Debate Tm; JA; Pep Clb; Spanish Clb; Temple Yth Grp; Varsity Clb; Nwsp Stf; Bsktbl; Lead Grad Clss 86; Accntng.

FOSTER, KIM; Toms River North HS; Toms River, NJ; (Y); French Clb; FBLA; Hosp Aide; Library Aide; Yrbk Stf; Sec Frsh Cls; JV Cheerleading; JV Sftbl; JV Swmmng; JV Tennis; Fairleigh Dickinson U; Pre-Med.

FOTIOU, BILL; Mainland Regional HS; Linwood, NJ; (Y); 28/250; Church Yth Grp; JV Var Ftbl; Im Vllybl; Im Wt Lftg; Var L Wrstlng; High Hon Roll; Hon Roll; NHS.

FOULKE, KIM; Absegami HS; Cologne, NJ; (Y); 19/287; Computer Clb; Math Clb; Spanish Clb; Var Jr Cls; Sec Sr Cls; Rep Stu Cncl; Var Cheerleading; Var Gym; JV Trk; Var Sftbl; Glassboro; Math.

FOURNEY, JULIE; Holy Cross HS; Willingboro, NJ; (Y); 120/360; French Clb; SADD; Rep Frsh Cls; JV Fld Hcky; U Of Scranton; Scl Wk.

FOURNIER, MICHELLE; St John Vianney HS; Colts Neck, NJ; (Y); Church Yth Grp; Cmnty Wkr; SADD; Varsity Clb; Nwsp Stf; Yrbk Stf; Cheerleading; Socr; Trk; High Hon Roll; Wilkes Coll; Bio.

FOWLER, CHRISTOPHER; North Brunswick Township HS; N Brunswick, NJ; (Y); 46/300; Boy Scts; Key Clb; Nwsp Sprt Ed; Nwsp Stf; Var Golf; Capt Socr; Hon Roll; Rutgers.

FOWLER, JANET; Hamilton High School West; Trenton, NJ; (Y); Church Yth Grp; SADD; Drill Tm; School Play; Var Capt Bsktbl; Var Fld Hcky; Sftbl; Vllybl; Wt Lftg; All Tourney-Spartan Tip Off Tourney-Bsktbl 85; All Tourney Tm-Bsktbl 85; All Cnty-Hrbl Mntn-Fld Hcky; Comp Pgmr.

FOWLER, KIM; Woodstown HS; Woodstown, NJ; (Y); Church Yth Grp; Dance Clb; FBLA; German Clb; Flag Corp; Mrchg Band; Stu Cncl; Cheerleading; Hon Roll; Katharine Gibbs Ldrshp Awd Future Secrs 86; Sci Fair Awds 83-85; Katharine Gibbs Schl; Bus Exec.

FOWLER, STEPHEN; Bayonne HS; Bayonne, NJ; (Y); Church Yth Grp; Computer Clb; Band; Hon Roll; RETS Schl; Tech Engr.

FOX, CARRIE; Belvidere HS; Phillipsburg, NJ; (Y); 18/118; Library Aide; Red Cross Aide; Chorus; JV Sftbl; Vllybl; Wt Lftg; Hon Roll; Teen Arts Prtcptn Awd 84; Chorus Prtcptn Awd 84; Frleigh Dcknsn U; Comp Sci.

FOX, ED; West Morris Central HS; Long Valley, NJ; (Y); 20/300; Latin Clb; Math Tm; Nwsp Rptr; JV Bsbl; JV Bsktbl; JV Var Socr; High Hon Roll; Hon Roll; NHS; Ntl Merit SF; Slvr Mdl For Natl Latin Tst 86; 2nd Pl Rbbn In Art Show 85; Most Vlbl Plyr Awd For Sccr 84.

FOX, HEATHER; Wall HS; Manasquan Park, NJ; (S); 16/263; AFS; Drama Clb; German Clb; Pres Key Clb; Chorus; School Musical; Socr; Hugh O Brian Yth Ldrshp Fndtn NJ Semnr 84-85; Olympcs Of Mnd 83-84; Intl Rel.

FOX, HEATHER ANNE; Northern Valley Regional HS; Haworth, NJ; (Y); 11/250; Am Leg Aux Girls St; Spanish Clb; VP Temple Yth Grp; Band; Concert Band; School Musical; Yrbk Sprt Ed; Rep Stu Cncl; Var L Sftbl; JV Var Tennis; NV Tchrs Assn Schlrshp 86; Hwrth Home & Schl Assn Schlrshp 86; Vassar; Psych.

FOX, KENNETH; Morris Knolls HS; Rockaway, NJ; (Y); 170/343; Pre Med.

FOX, MERYL; Point Pleasant Beach HS; Pt Pleasant Bch, NJ; (Y); 2/105; Church Yth Grp; Band; Jazz Band; VP Sr Cls; Var Bsktbl; Var Socr; JP Sousa Awd; NHS; Pres Schlr; Sal; Wmns Clb Acadmc And Musc Awds 86; Shenandoahs Pres Schlrshp 86; Louis Armstrong Jazz Awd 86; Shenandoah Clg; Jazz Commcl.

FOX, PAULETTE; Lakewood HS; Oakhurst, NJ; (Y); 17/275; French Clb; Girl Scts; Hosp Aide; Library Aide; Temple Yth Grp; Band; Mrchg Band; Lit Mag; French Hon Soc; NHS; Rutgers; Bio Chem.

FOX, WAYNE; Cumberland Regional HS; Bridgeton, NJ; (S); 7/342; Am Leg Boys St; Science Clb; Var L Ftbl; Var Capt Trk; Im Wt Lftg; Gov Hon Prg Awd; High Hon Roll; Jr NHS; NHS; Rotary Awd; Mech Engrng.

FOXSON, JENNIFER; Wallkill Valley Regional HS; Hamburg, NJ; (Y); SADD; Varsity Clb; Band; Rep Stu Cncl; Var Capt Bsktbl; Var L Tennis; Var L Trk; Cit Awd; Hon Roll; NHS; Lady Rngr Awd 86; Hugh O Brien Ldrshp 85; Grls Ctznshp Inst 86.

FOY, JASON; Dwight Morrow HS; Englewood, NJ; (Y); 53/247; Band; Concert Band; Drm Mjr(t); Jazz Band; Mrchg Band; Variety Show; JV Var Bsbl; Hon Roll.

FOY, REGINA; Mount Saint Mary Acad; Murray Hill, NJ; (Y); Rep Frsh Cls; VP Soph Cls; Rep Jr Cls; VP Stu Cncl; Tennis; High Hon Roll; Hon Roll; NHS; Gftd And Tlntd 85; Mktg.

FOYS, MARTIN; Pope Paul VI HS; Audubon, NJ; (Y); 7/474; Drama Clb; Jazz Band; School Play; Stage Crew; Variety Show; Soph Cls; Hon Roll; NHS; St Schlr; Drew Distngushd Merit Schlrshp 86; Drew U; Bio.

FRABIZIO, KERRY; Villa Victoria Acad; Stockton, NJ; (Y); Drama Clb; Pep Clb; Service Clb; Acpl Chr; Chorus; School Musical; Lit Mag; Mgr(s); Score Keeper; Socr; Vocl Perfrmnc.

FRALINGER, NANCY; Cumberland Regional HS; Bridgeton, NJ; (S); 2/340; VP Church Yth Grp; Pres 4-H; Pres Girl Scts; Office Aide; Yrbk Stf; Stu Cncl; JV Tennis; High Hon Roll; NHS; Georgetown Swim Clb Smmr Leag Most Dpndbl & Bst Sprtsmnshp 83; Psych.

FRANCE, FRANK; Sussez Vo-Tech; Franklin, NJ; (Y); Aud/Vis; Ski Clb; SADD; Rep Jr Cls; Rep Sr Cls; Rep Stu Cncl; JV Var Ftbl; JV Var Wt Lftg; JV Var Wrstlng; Hon Roll; OH Diesel Tech Inst; Dsl Mech.

FRANCESCO, GINA; Riverside HS; Riverside, NJ; (Y); Dance Clb; Drama Clb; FTA; Library Aide; PAVAS; Ski Clb; School Play; Nwsp Rptr; Nwsp Stf; Off Frsh Cls; Rutgers Coll; Elelm Educ.

FRANCESE, MARIA; Colonia HS; Avenel, NJ; (Y); 18/287; Ski Clb; Varsity Clb; Band; Mrchg Band; Sec Soph Cls; Stu Cncl; Var Co-Capt Cheerleading; Hon Roll; NHS; Pep Clb; Trenton ST Coll; Acctg.

FRANCHINA, CAROLE; Immaculate Conception HS; Lyndhurst, NJ; (Y); Sec Art Clb; PAVAS; Ski Clb; Chorus.

FRANCHINO, CHERYL L; Butler HS; Bloomingdale, NJ; (Y); 25/197; Hon Roll; Upsala Coll Hnrs Pgm 86; Bloomingdale Polc Assn 86; Charles K Payne Scholar 86; Upsala Coll; Acctng.

FRANCIS, LUCRETIA; Orange HS; Orange, NJ; (Y); Computer Clb; Girl Scts; Ski Clb; Y-Teens; Nwsp Sprt Ed; Mgr(s); Sftbl; Tennis; Vllybl; Hon Roll; MVP Tennis 85-86; 2nd Hon Sftbll Plyr 86; Law.

FRANCKOWIAK, RICHARD M; Bordentown Regional HS; Bordentown, NJ; (Y); 6/132; Am Leg Boys St; Key Clb; Math Clb; Ski Clb; Bsbl; Bsktbl; Socr; High Hon Roll; Hon Roll; Jr NHS; HS Schlr Athlt 86; Acadmc All Amrcn Awd Bsktbll 85; NJ Inst Ot Tech; Engr.

FRANCONERI, MARC; Bayonne HS; Bayonne, NJ; (Y); 59/362; Sr Cls; Hon Roll; NHS; Rutgers; Pol Sci.

FRANK, AMY; Pascack Hills HS; Woodcliffe Lake, NJ; (Y); Cmnty Wkr; Hosp Aide; Temple Yth Grp; Drill Tm; Stage Crew; Hon Roll; U Of NC; Nrsg.

FRANK, DEANNA; Buena Regional HS; Milmay, NJ; (S); 2/191; Math Clb; Political Wkr; Ski Clb; Spanish Clb; Concert Band; Jazz Band; Mrchg Band; Rep Frsh Cls; Rep Soph Cls; Rep Stu Cncl; Grdn ST Distngshd Schlr 85; Vrsty Ltr Schltc Achvt 85; Dedctn 3 Yrs Band Awd 84; Rutgers Coll Of Phrmcy; Phrmcy.

FRANK, DEIRDRE; James Caldwell HS; Caldwell, NJ; (Y); French Clb; Science Clb; Orch; Ed Nwsp Stf; Stu Cncl; Hon Roll; Engl.

FRANK, LINDA; St Marys HS; East Rutherford, NJ; (S); FNA; Spanish Clb; Nwsp Rptr; Yrbk Stf; High Hon Roll; Hon Roll; Dentl Hyg.

FRANK, PAULETTE; Wall HS; Wall Twp, NJ; (S); 2/265; Ski Clb; Band; Mrchg Band; Nwsp Rptr; Yrbk Stf; Rep Jr Cls; Sec Stu Cncl; Score Keeper; High Hon Roll; Kiwanis Awd; Biophyscs.

FRANK, RAYMOND; Northern Valley Reg HS; Old Tappan, NJ; (Y); 80/287; AFS; Ski Clb; Socr; Trk; High Hon Roll; Hon Roll; Bus.

FRANKEL, JONATHAN; Ocean Township HS; Ocean, NJ; (Y); 1/337; Am Leg Boys St; Capt Debate Tm; NFL; Quiz Bowl; Capt Speech Tm; Trs Frsh Cls; Soph Cls; Pres NHS; Ntl Merit SF; Val; Monmouth Coll Gvrnmnt Inst 86; Mdrtr Ocn Twnshp Pltcl Frm 85; Rutgers Schlr 86; Psychlgy.

FRANKEL, MOLLISSA; Montville HS; Pine Brook, NJ; (Y); Key Clb; Ski Clb; SADD; JV Fld Hcky; Var Lcrss; Powder Puff Ftbl; Hon Roll; Phys Ther.

FRANKET, MOLLISSA; Montville HS; Pinebrook, NJ; (Y); Cmnty Wkr; Key Clb; Ski Clb; SADD; Stage Crew; JV Fld Hcky; Var Lcrss; Powder Puff Ftbl; Hon Roll; Bus.

FRANKIE, BRIAN; Hopewell Valley Central HS; Pennington, NJ; (Y); 16/202; Boy Scts; Church Yth Grp; Math Tm; Science Clb; Var Trk; High Hon Roll; Engrng.

FRANKLIN, BRYON ANTHONY; Plainfield HS; Plainfield, NJ; (S); 75/539; Boy Scts; CAP; Debate Tm; Y-Teens; Yrbk Sprt Ed; Rep Stu Cncl; Capt Bsktbl; Var Crs Cntry; Var Ftbl; JV Trk; Hampton U; Finance.

FRANKLIN, CALLISTA; Vineland HS; Millville, NJ; (Y); Library Aide; Teachers Aide; Yrbk Stf; Bus.

FRANKLIN, MELISSA; Belvidere HS; Belvidere, NJ; (S); 1/120; French Clb; Quiz Bowl; Varsity Clb; Trs Frsh Cls; Trs Soph Cls; Trs Stu Cncl; Fld Hcky; Stat Ftbl; Lcrss; NHS; Mth.

FRANKLIN, STACIA; Parsippany HS; Parsippany, NJ; (Y); 14/318; Church Yth Grp; VP Chorus; Church Choir; School Musical; Ed Yrbk Stf; Lit Mag; High Hon Roll; NHS; Ntl Merit Ltr; Pres Hnr Schlrshp 86; Nelson F Peterson Schlrshp Merit Special Schlrshp 86; VFW Demcrcy Dist Awd; Wheaton Coll; Communications.

FRANKO, SUSAN; Hamilton High West; Trenton, NJ; (Y); 73/330; Church Yth Grp; Cmnty Wkr; Key Clb; Stat Diving; Stat Swmmng; Var Trk; Hon Roll; Trenton ST Coll; Erly Educ.

FRANKS, CONNI; Spotswood HS; Spotswood, NJ; (S); Rep Stu Cncl; JV Sftbl; Art.

FRANKS, RALPH ROBERT; Highland Regional HS; Blackwood, NJ; (S); 5/332; Chess Clb; Nwsp Rptr; Pres Jr Cls; VP Stu Cncl; Var Ftbl; Var Wrstlng; NHS; Bio Tm NJ ST Sci Leag 83-84; U Of PA; Med.

FRANKS, STEPHANIE; Holy Cross HS; Medford, NJ; (Y); 99/396; Ski Clb; Rep Frsh Cls; Rep Soph Cls; Rep Jr Cls; JV Var Socr; JV Sftbl; JV Trk; Im Wt Lftg; Hon Roll; Yth & Poly Systm 86; Sprts Med.

FRANZONI, SCOTT; Pinelands Regional HS; Tuckerton, NJ; (Y); 18/196; Exploring; Wrstlng; High Hon Roll; NHS; US Coast Guard Acad; Engr.

FRASER, JUSTINE; Hawthorne HS; Hawthorne, NJ; (Y); 8/155; Math Clb; Ski Clb; Yrbk Ed-Chief; Sec Jr Cls; Rep Stu Cncl; Capt Twrlr; High Hon Roll; NCTE Awd; NHS; U Of MA; Fshn Mrktng.

FRASIER, MARVA VICTORIA; Dwight Morrow HS; Englewood, NJ; (Y); 52/247; Chrmn Church Yth Grp; Drama Clb; Sec Y-Teens; Pres Church Choir; Mrchg Band; VP Bsktbl; Trk; Hon Roll; Jr NHS; Black Sci Fair 84; Ulysses Kay Musc Inctv Awd 86; Chld Psych.

FRATELLO, DONNA; Linden HS; Linden, NJ; (Y); Key Clb; Band; Concert Band; Mrchg Band; School Play; Yrbk Stf; Rep Frsh Cls; Rep Soph Cls; Rep Jr Cls; Hon Roll; Mrn Bio.

FRAYNE, STEVE; Bishop Eustace Prep; Turnersville, NJ; (Y); 10/200; Chess Clb; Math Clb; Spanish Clb; SADD; Var L Crs Cntry; Var L Trk; High Hon Roll; Hon Roll; NHS; Yale; Med.

FRAZEE, STEPHEN; St Mary HS; Keansburg, NJ; (Y); 20/132; Church Yth Grp; JV Bsbl; Var Socr; High Hon Roll.

FRAZIER, ANGELA; Penns Grove HS; Carneys Point, NJ; (Y); 65/225; Am Leg Aux Girls St; JA; JCL; Latin Clb; Church Choir; Nwsp Sprt Ed; Sec Jr Cls; Stat Bsktbl; Mgr(s); Co-Capt Tennis; Lincoln Tech; Comp Prgrmr.

FRAZIER, LISA; Barringer HS; Newark, NJ; (Y); Drama Clb; Red Cross Aide; Chorus; Color Guard; Mrchg Band; VP Jr Cls; VP Sr Cls; Rep Stu Cncl; Bsktbl; Hon Roll; #10 Frshmn Cls Smll Awd 84; Pepsi Cola Chllnge 86; Admn Mngmnt.

FREDA, ANTHONY; Newton HS; Newton, NJ; (S); 16/210; German Clb; Math Tm; Science Clb; Rep Jr Cls; Stu Cncl; Var Bsktbl; Var Socr; JV Trk; Hon Roll; NHS; Sci.

FREDA, ROBERT; Raritan HS; Hazlet, NJ; (Y); 25/312; Exploring; Ski Clb; Spanish Clb; JV Socr; JV Trk; High Hon Roll; Hon Roll; NHS; Engrng.

FREDENBURGH, LAURA; Holy Family Acad; Bayonne, NJ; (Y); 3/130; Church Yth Grp; French Clb; Hosp Aide; Key Clb; Chorus; Orch; School Musical; Ed Nwsp Rptr; High Hon Roll; NHS; Schlrshp Hotch Kiss 85; Cert NJ Inst 86; 2nd Hghst Avg Engl II, Frnch II, Chem, Hghst Avg Latin 85; Med.

FREDERICK, FAREN; New Brunswick HS; New Brunswick, NJ; (Y); VP Church Yth Grp; Dance Clb; Girl Scts; Library Aide; Pep Clb; Teachers Aide; Church Choir; Yrbk Stf; Rep Frsh Cls; Var Co-Capt Cheerleading; Peer Ldr 86-87; Brandywine Coll; Hairstylist.

FREDERICK, FRANCES; Salem HS; Salem, NJ; (Y); Am Leg Aux Girls St; Church Yth Grp; FBLA; Office Aide; Pep Clb; Spanish Clb; Church Choir; Yrbk Stf; Rep Stu Cncl; JV Var Bsktbl; Rznn Dns Dlbw Mem Awd 86; Bus Awd 86; Schlr Athlt Of Mnth 86; Outstndg Bus Stu Of Mnth 86; Salem CC; Htl & Rest Mgmt.

FREDERICK, KATHLEEN SHARON; Toms River HS East; Toms River, NJ; (Y); 75/489; Am Leg Aux Girls St; Intnl Clb; Political Wkr; SADD; Rep Jr Cls; Rep Sr Cls; Rep Stu Cncl; Co-Capt Crs Cntry; Powder Puff Ftbl; Var Trk; Phil Cittadino Memrl & Gelzer-Kelaher-Shea-Novy-Karr Pre Legl Schlrshps 86; Drew U; Poltcl Sci.

FREDERICKS, JEFF; Pop John XXIII HS; Stanhope, NJ; (Y); Church Yth Grp; Varsity Clb; Ftbl; Hon Roll; Comp Sci.

FREDERIQUE, HENRI; Orange HS; Orange, NJ; (S); Hosp Aide; Var Crs Cntry; Hon Roll; NHS; Rutgers; Bio.

FREED, LAURENCE T; Highland Park HS; Highland Park, NJ; (Y); 3/140; Ntl Merit SF; St Schlr; Stu Cncl; Socr; Tennis; High Hon Roll; Hon Roll; Natl Cncl Tchrs Engl 85; Rutgers Pres Scholar 86; Rutgers U.

FREELY, ANN; Immaculate Conception HS; Lyndhurst, NJ; (Y); 22/99; Q&S; Nwsp Rptr; Hon Roll; NEDT Awd; Prfct Atten Awd; Pres Acdmc Ftns Awd Pgm, SADD VP 86; Natl Hnr Rl 85; Seton Hall U; Pre-Law.

FREEMAN, DANA L; Indian Hills HS; Oakland, NJ; (Y); 89/264; Church Yth Grp; Dance Clb; Radio Clb; Nwsp Rptr; Nwsp Stf; Yrbk Rptr; Lit Mag; JV Trk; Hon Roll; Brdcst Jrnlsm.

FREEMAN, ERIC; Clifton SR HS; Clifton, NJ; (Y); #86 In Class; Y-Teens; Stage Crew; Variety Show; L Bsktbl; Var Ftbl; Wt Lftg; Hon Roll; Jr NHS; NHS; Spanish NHS; Awd All Star Tms Bsbl And Ftbl 84-86.

FREEMAN, NERETTA; Garfield HS; Garfield, NJ; (Y); Rep Sr Cls; Var Capt Trk; Hon Roll; Am Leg Aux Girls St; Teachers Aide; Varsity Clb; Variety Show; Rep Jr Cls; Trs Stu Cncl; L Mgr(s); Trck Mst Outstndg Plyr 85&86; ST Grp II Chmpn 100 Mtrs 86; Rutgers U; RN.

FREESTONE, FRED; Point Pleasant Boro HS; Point Pleasant, NJ; (Y); 17/215; JV Var Bowling; JV Golf; High Hon Roll; Hon Roll.

FREI, ERIKA; Parsippany HS; Parsippany, NJ; (Y); FBLA; GAA; Letterman Clb; Varsity Clb; JV Cheerleading; Sftbl; L Tennis; High Hon Roll; Hon Roll; Jr NHS; Fordham U; Math.

FREIDEL, DIANE; Washington Twnshp HS; Sewell, NJ; (Y); Trs French Clb; German Clb; Yrbk Stf; JV Fld Hcky; Sftbl; High Hon Roll; Hon Roll; NHS; Intl Bus.

FREIS, JEAN; Bishop George Ahr HS; Metuchen, NJ; (Y); Church Yth Grp; German Clb; Ski Clb; Teachers Aide; School Musical; School Play; Stage Crew; Swing Chorus; Yrbk Rptr; Yrbk Stf; Grmn Awd 85; Math.

FRENCH, CRAIG; Colonia HS; Colonia, NJ; (Y); Key Clb; Ski Clb; Varsity Clb; Var Ftbl; Vllybl; Wrstlng; Hon Roll; U Of AZ; Bio.

FRERKS, WILLIAM; Middletown High School South; Middletown, NJ; (Y); Var Trk; Hon Roll.

FRESE, MATTHEW; Holy Cross HS; Mount Holly, NJ; (Y); 97/391; Science Clb; JV Var Ftbl; Wt Lftg; Hon Roll; Penn ST; Metrlgy.

FRETZ, BONNIE; Pennsville Memorial HS; Pennsville, NJ; (Y); 53/210; Art Clb; Church Yth Grp; FBLA; FHA; Ski Clb; VP Soph Cls; Stu Cncl; Bsktbl; Var Capt Cheerleading; Mgr(s); Ns Ntl Tn-Agr NJ 86; Semi Fnlst Teens Mag Mdl Srch 85; Fshn Merch.

FRETZ, PAM; Lower Cape May Regional HS; N Cape May, NJ; (Y); 10/310; Office Aide; Pep Clb; Service Clb; Spanish Clb; Varsity Clb; Rep Stu Cncl; Capt Bsktbl; Var Fld Hcky; High Hon Roll; NHS; Pre-Med.

FREULER, LISA; Delaware Valley Regional HS; Milford, NJ; (Y); 2/167; Am Leg Aux Girls St; Trs Jr Cls; VP Sr Cls; Stu Cncl; Bausch & Lomb Sci Awd; Cit Awd; Pres NHS; Pres Schlr; Sal; NJ Distngshd Schlrs Awd 86; Jenny Haver Awd 86; Rutgers Coll Engrng; Elec Engr.

FREUND, CHERYL; Highstown HS; Cranbury, NJ; (Y); 141/449; Am Leg Aux Girls St; Pres 4-H; Ski Clb; Band; Jazz Band; Mrchg Band; School Musical; Symp Band; Hon Roll; Prfct Atten Awd; Business.

FREUND, HOWARD; Union HS; Union, NJ; (Y); Am Leg Boys St; Service Clb; Temple Yth Grp; Band; Concert Band; Jazz Band; Mrchg Band; Orch; Nwsp Phtg; Golf; Regnl Band; Regnl Jazz Band.

FREY, JULIE; St Joseph HS; Waterford, NJ; (Y); 7/97; Variety Show; Lit Mag; JV Var Cheerleading; High Hon Roll; Hon Roll; Prncpls List; Frnch Cert Of Exclnc; Pre Elem Peduc.

FREY, MATTHEW J; Kearny HS; Kearny, NJ; (Y); Am Leg Boys St; Church Yth Grp; Ski Clb; Varsity Clb; Off Sr Cls; Im Socr; Var L Swmmng; JV Wrstlng; Accntng.

FRIANT, MICHELE L; Pennsgrove HS; Penns Grove, NJ; (Y); 25/161; Church Yth Grp; Band; Mrchg Band; JV Cheerleading; L Sftbl; Prfct Atten Awd; Acad Achvt Bible 84; Acad Achvt Hstry 84; HOSA 85-86; Jefferson U; Nrsg.

FRIBERG, ERIC; Toms River HS South; Toms River, NJ; (Y); 52/365; Church Yth Grp; Math Clb; Church Choir; Rep Jr Cls; Bsktbl; Golf; Socr; Allcnty-All State Grop Iv Scr 84-85; All-Cnty-All State All-Shore Sce 85-86.

FRICKE, LISA; Hunterdon Central HS; Flemington, NJ; (Y); 346/549; Drama Clb; Spanish Clb; Mrchg Band; School Play; Rep Stu Cncl; Im Socr; Var Swmmng; Hon Roll; Assoc Espanola Del Experimento Intl De Convivencia Sum Segovia Spain 84; Studio Prod Engr.

FRICKS, MELINDA; Toms River North HS; Toms River, NJ; (Y); 12/412; Math Tm; Science Clb; Hon Roll; NHS; Ntl Merit Ltr; Acdmc Awd Ltr; 3rd Pl Ocean Cnty Bio Indivdl; Monmouth Sci Sympsm.

FRIE JR, PAUL; Delsea Regional HS; Monroeville, NJ; (Y); Church Yth Grp; ROTC; Spanish Clb; JV Socr; JV Trk; In Hnr Crses Yr 85-87; 2 Yrs Of Gftd & Tlntd Clses; Lehigh; Comp Sci.

FRIEDLAND, HOWARD; Montville Township HS; Pine Brook, NJ; (Y); 24/270; Computer Clb; Key Clb; Speech Tm; Temple Yth Grp; High Hon Roll; NHS; Ntl Merit SF; NJ Dstgshd Schlr Awd; John Hopkins U.

FRIEDMAN, LORI; Manalapan HS; Englishtown, NJ; (Y); 63/431; Drama Clb; Library Aide; Temple Yth Grp; Nwsp Rptr; Off Frsh Cls; Off Soph Cls; Off Jr Cls; Stat Socr; Temple Yth Grp Ldrshp Awd 86.

FRIEDMAN, TODD; Toms River HS; Toms River, NJ; (Y); #17 In Class; Cmnty Wkr; PAVAS; SADD; Pres Temple Yth Grp; School Musical; Stu Cncl; Bsktbl; Socr; High Hon Roll; NHS; Cmnctns.

FRIEDRICH, STEPHEN CHARLES; Sparta HS; Sparta, NJ; (Y); 28/210; Boy Scts; Church Yth Grp; Key Clb; Ski Clb; Im Golf; Im Lcrss; Var Trk; High Hon Roll; Hon Roll; NHS; Womens Club Schlrshp 86; Rookie Yr Awd Ski Tm 85; 1st Giant Slalom Race 86; Clemson U; Comp Engrng.

FRIES, CAROLYN; Bishop George Ahr HS; Metuchen, NJ; (Y); 52/277; Hosp Aide; Cheerleading; Trk; High Hon Roll; Church Yth Grp; Spanish Clb; Crs Cntry; NEDT Awd; Schlr Athl 85; 100 Hr Awd Cndy Strp 86; Vrsty Ltr Crss Cntry & Chrldg 86; Pre-Med.

FRIES, THOMAS; Holy Spirit HS; Ocean City, NJ; (Y); 96/376; JV Swmmng; Rowing Crew Vrsty 84-86; Aerospace Engrng.

FRITSCH, CHRISTINA E; Lenape Valley Regional HS; Stanhope, NJ; (Y); Am Leg Aux Girls St; VP Pres Church Yth Grp; VP Key Clb; Ski Clb; Sec SADD; Chorus; Trs Pres Stu Cncl; Var Tennis; NHS; Spanish NHS; Acad All Am Awd Fr Natl Scndry Educ 86; US Natl Awd Fr US Achvmnt Acad 86.

FRITSCH, JAMES; Parsippany HS; Parsippany, NJ; (S); Boy Scts; Concert Band; Drm & Bgl; Jazz Band; Mrchg Band; Symp Band; Rep Frsh Cls; JV Trk; Hon Roll; Ski Clb; Brd Of Educ Cert Of Cmmndtn 1st Pl Jazz Bnd 85; Brd Of Educ Cert Of Cmmndtn 2nd Pl Concrt Bnd 85.

FROEHLICH, DANIEL R; Princeton HS; Princeton, NJ; (Y); Church Yth Grp; Cmnty Wkr; Exploring; Science Clb; Acpl Chr; Chorus; Church Choir; Orch; School Musical; Lit Mag.

FROHLICH, ALISON; Voorhees HS; Oldwick, NJ; (S); 110/245; FBLA; FFA; Intnl Clb; Key Clb; SADD; Nwsp Rptr; Stat Trk.

FROLE, JEFF; Clifton HS; Clifton, NJ; (Y); Church Yth Grp; German Clb; Science Clb; Band; Concert Band; Jazz Band; Mrchg Band; Symp Band.

FROMKIN, RUSSELL; East Brunswick HS; E Brunswick, NJ; (Y); Latin Clb; Math Clb; VP Temple Yth Grp; Varsity Clb; Stu Cncl; JV Capt Socr; Var Trk; Cptn US Sccr Tm Tel Aviv Cp 83; Asprng Adrndk 46 Mnt Clmbr 86; Cert Scuba Lcnc 84; Astrphyscs.

FRONCKOWIAK, KAREN; Gloucester Catholic HS; Bellmawr, NJ; (Y); Hosp Aide; Pep Clb; Pep Band; School Play; Stage Crew; Variety Show; Var Capt Cheerleading; High Hon Roll; Hon Roll; NHS.

FRUEH, JENNIFER; River Dell HS; Oradell, NJ; (Y); 34/213; GAA; SADD; Varsity Clb; Chorus; Yrbk Stf; JV Cheerleading; Sftbl; Vllybl; Hon Roll; NHS; Bus Adm.

FRY, JENNIFER; Buena Regional HS; Newfield, NJ; (S); Trs Church Yth Grp; Ski Clb; School Play; Rep Stu Cncl; Cheerleading; Pom Pon; Hon Roll; Jr NHS; NHS; Ntl Merit Ltr.

FRY, PAUL; Egg Harbor Township HS; Mays Landing, NJ; (S); 23/266; Church Yth Grp; Key Clb; Ski Clb; Band; School Play; Var Socr; Var Swmmng; Hon Roll; NHS; US Ldrshp Merit Awd; U DE; Cvl Engr.

FRY, RICHARD; Pitman HS; Pitman, NJ; (S); 17/150; Church Yth Grp; Band; Chorus; Jazz Band; Mrchg Band; Pep Band; Stage Crew; Trs Jr Cls; JV Bsktbl; Socr.

FRYAR, VIRGINIA; Mother Seton Regional HS; Newark, NJ; (Y); Art Clb; Church Yth Grp; Computer Clb; Q&S; Scholastic Bowl; Varsity Clb; Chorus; Church Choir; Variety Show; Bsktbl; Kean Coll Union NJ; Bus Mgmt.

FRYE, MICHAEL R; Brick Memorial HS; Brick, NJ; (Y); 83/404; Church Yth Grp; Math Tm; ROTC; Lit Mag; JV Bsktbl; Hon Roll; VFW Awd; Boy Scts; Yrbk Phtg; JV Crs Cntry; Hnrbl Mntn Wrld Poetry Cntst 85; Gldn Poet 86 Awd 86; Embry-Riddle Aerntcl U; Plt.

FUCHS, MICHAEL E; Wayne Valley HS; Wayne, NJ; (Y); 6/320; Computer Clb; Latin Clb; Yrbk Sprt Ed; Capt Socr; Capt Tennis; High Hon Roll; Ntl Merit SF; Rutgers Schlrs Pgm 85; U Of PA; Bus.

FUCHS, ROBYN; Hillsborough HS; Somerville, NJ; (Y); 76/293; DECA; Hosp Aide; Pep Clb; SADD; VP Temple Yth Grp; School Musical; Rep Soph Cls; Off Stu Cncl; Stat Trk; High Hon Roll; Prom Cmt; DECA 1st Pl Rgnl & ST In Aprl & Acsrs; FL ST U; Intl Bus.

FUEHRER, MICHELLE; South River HS; S River, NJ; (Y); Office Aide; Spanish Clb; Nwsp Stf; Yrbk Stf; Sftbl; Tennis; Stat Wrstlng; Hon Roll; NHS; VFW Awd; Rogate Prog 83; Bus.

FUENTES, DAYMA; Memorial HS; W New York, NJ; (Y); Key Clb; Teachers Aide; Drill Tm; Rep Jr Cls; Pom Pon; Pom Pon Squad Bst Newcmr 84-85; US Army; Nrsng.

FUGARO, NICK; Red Bank Catholic HS; Freehold, NJ; (Y); 1/323; Nwsp Stf; Pres Jr Cls; VP Stu Cncl; JV Capt Socr; NHS; US Stu Cncl Awd 86; Comm.

FUGAZZI, MICHELLE; N Hunterdon HS; Flemington, NJ; (Y); 4-H; Socr; Stat Wrstlng; Cit Awd; Girl Scts; Off Stu Cncl; Sftbl; Hunterdon Cnty 4-H Queen 86; 1st In St 4-H Pblc Spkng Pewter Bowl 85-86; Prtcptd In Estrn Natl Cnts 85; Accntng.

FUHRER, CYNTHIA; Clearview Regional HS; Mantua, NJ; (Y); 46/170; Var Capt Bsktbl; Var Capt Cheerleading; Coach Actv; Powder Puff Ftbl; JV Capt Sftbl; VFW Awd; MVP & Bst Dfnsve Plyr Awd 85 & 86; 1st Tm All-Cnfrnse & Coaches Awd 86; Outstngng Atlt R W Mills 86.

FUHRMAN, ANDREW; Glen Rock HS; Glen Rock, NJ; (Y); Temple Yth Grp; Nwsp Rptr; JV Bsbl; JV Bsktbl; Var Socr; Var Tennis; High Hon Roll; Hon Roll; Jr NHS; NHS; DECA ST Fnlst 86; Sprts Mngmnt.

FULCINITI, GARY ANDREW; H G Hoffman HS; South Amboy, NJ; (S); 8/52; Chess Clb; Computer Clb; Yrbk Stf; VP Stu Cncl; Swmmng; Hon Roll; Jr NHS; Arts & Sci Awds 85; ST Sci Day 85; Rutgers U; Phy.

FULDA, KAREN L; Bulleville HS; Belleville, NJ; (Y); 157/380; Art Clb; Hosp Aide; Varsity Clb; Y-Teens; Band; Drill Tm; Coach Actv; Var Sftbl; Var Twrlr; Hon Roll; Pres Acadmc Ftnss Awd; St John Fischer; Mktg Intl.

FULLEN, TRACY; Toms River H S East; Toms River, NJ; (Y); Intnl Clb; Spanish Clb; Yrbk Stf; Stu Cncl; Fld Hcky; Powder Puff Ftbl; Hon Roll.

FULLER, CHRIS; Scotch Plains Fanwood HS; Scotch Plains, NJ; (Y); Church Yth Grp; Nwsp Stf; Yrbk Stf; Lit Mag; Art Awd From Lit Mag; Art.

FULLER, MARC R; Scotch Plains-Fanwood HS; Scotch Plains, NJ; (Y); 54/311; Church Yth Grp; Model UN; Lit Mag; Ntl Merit Ltr; Natl Achvt Scholar Pgm Outstndng Negro Stu SF 85; Pres & Cofndr Yth Soc Actvsm Awrnss 85; Sec Pol Aff; Hstry.

FULLER, TAMIKO; Manasquan HS; Belmar, NJ; (Y); 60/228; Church Yth Grp; FHA; Chorus; Church Choir; JV Trk; Douglass Coll Rutgers; Bus Adm.

FULLILOVE, ANN; Wall HS; Neptune, NJ; (S); 13/279; Ski Clb; Drill Tm; Flag Corp; Capt Var Twrlr; High Hon Roll; Hon Roll; NHS; Ntl Merit Ltr.

FULMORE, BRUCE; Eastside HS; Paterson, NJ; (Y); Art Clb; English Clb; Office Aide; PAVAS; Y-Teens; Hon Roll; St Schlr; Cert Achvt Career Beginnings Pgm 86; UCLA; Art.

FULTON III, BERNARD B; Atlantic Friends Schl; Atlantic City, NJ; (S); Drama Clb; Chorus; Pres Jr Cls; Sec Stu Cncl; Var L Bsktbl; Var L Socr; Cit Awd; NHS; Acad 83-84; Ldrshp 84-85; Dartmouth Coll; Law.

FUNARI, LISA; Monsignor Mc Corristin HS; Trenton, NJ; (Y); 23/225; GAA; Hosp Aide; Pep Clb; School Play; Yrbk Stf; Lit Mag; Capt Var Cheerleading; Capt Var Pom Pon; Var Socr; Hon Roll; Essy Awded By Ancnt Ordr Of 83-84; Poem Pblc Coll Ltrayr Mag 84-85; Mrktng.

FUNG, DIXON; Metuchen HS; Edison, NJ; (Y); 4/143; French Clb; Math Clb; Science Clb; Ski Clb; Yrbk Phtg; Var Tennis; French Hon Soc; High Hon Roll; NHS; Pres Schlr; Metuchen Ed Assoc Schlrshp 86; Metuchen Prnt Tchr Organ Schlrshp 86; Rutgers Coll; Business.

FUNK, KAREN; Hamilton High School East; Hamilton Square, NJ; (Y); 1/302; AFS; VP FBLA; Key Clb; SADD; Varsity Clb; Chorus; Drill Tm; Madrigals; Mrchg Band; School Musical; Rutgers Schlr 86; Semi Finalist NJ Schlrs Prog 86; FBLA ST Ldrshp Conf 85-86; Liberal Arts Coll; Psychlgy.

FURGIUELE, CATHERINE; Lenape Valley Regional HS; Andover, NJ; (Y); 1/253; Church Yth Grp; Hosp Aide; Nwsp Rptr; Var L Bsktbl; Var L Fld Hcky; Var L Trk; High Hon Roll; NHS; Spanish NHS; Ambssdr To Hugh O Brien Ldrshp Semnr 85; Partcpnt In Women In Engrng Prog At Stevens Inst Of Tech 85; Biomed Engrng.

FURLONG, KELLI; Gateway Regional HS; Woodbury Hts, NJ; (Y); 17/188; Sec VP French Clb; Key Clb; Spanish Clb; SADD; Stu Cncl; JV Var Cheerleading; JV Var Sftbl; French Hon Soc; NHS; Spanish NHS; Wilkes Coll; Intl Stds.

FURMAN, LAURIE; Spotswood HS; Spotswood, NJ; (S); 6/189; Intnl Clb; Spanish Clb; Band; Concert Band; Mrchg Band; Yrbk Stf; Stu Cncl; High Hon Roll; Hon Roll; NHS.

FURMANSKI, WILLIAM L; Haddon Hgts HS; Haddon Heights, NJ; (Y); 13/190; Am Leg Boys St; School Musical; Stage Crew; Nwsp Sprt Ed; Yrbk Stf; Mgr Bsbl; JV Socr; Var Trk; VP NHS; Rotary Awd; Garnet & Gold Scty Pres 85-86; Timmy Gideon Schlrshp Awd 86; PSE&G Essay Cntst Schlrshp 86; Seton Hall U; Comm.

FURMICK, TRACY; St Peters HS; Princeton, NJ; (Y); 11/111; French Clb; Ski Clb; Chorus; Color Guard; School Musical; School Play; Lit Mag; JV Sftbl; Var Tennis; NEDT Awd; Mst Impvd On Vrsty Tennis; Criminal Justice.

FURNARI, ROBERT; Spotswood HS; Milltown, NJ; (S); Art Clb; School Play; Yrbk Stf; Socr; Tennis; St Schlr; Frgn Exch Stdnt Austrlia 85; Biogcl Sci.

FUSCO, LAURA LEE; Passaic Valley HS; W Paterson, NJ; (Y); 4/358; Drama Clb; VP French Clb; Science Clb; Yrbk Bus Mgr; Var Bowling; JV Tennis; High Hon Roll; Sec NHS; School Play; JV Crs Cntry; Passaic Vly Hnr Soc 84-87; Ntl Piano Plyng Aud 83-85; Engrng.

FUSSELL, JENNIE; Essex Catholic Gilrs HS; Vailsburg, NJ; (Y); Art Clb; Church Yth Grp; Computer Clb; FBLA; FHA; Model UN; JV Badmtn; JV Fld Hcky; JV Sftbl; Hon Roll; U NC; Comm.

FUSSELL, TRACY; Cinnaminson HS; Cinna, NJ; (Y); JV Chess Clb; Debate Tm; Model UN; Q&S; Concert Band; Mrchg Band; Nwsp Rptr; Im Mgr(s); Im Sftbl; Stat Lcrss; RCA Minorities In Engrng Pgm Cnty Fnlst For The Governors Schlr Pgm; Hamilton Coll; Intl Studies.

FUTCHER, FRANK; River Dell HS; River Edge, NJ; (Y); 20/210; Church Yth Grp; Ski Clb; Spanish Clb; Varsity Clb; Var Golf; Var Capt Socr; Hon Roll; NHS; Spanish NHS; 1st Tm All-Lg Glf & Hnbl Mntn All-Cnty 85-86; Mst Vlbl Plyr Sccr 84-85; 2nd Tm All-Lg BCSL 84-85; Wm & Mary Coll.

FUTEMAN, IRINA; Brick Memorial HS; Lakewood, NJ; (Y); 10/307; Intnl Clb; Key Clb; Science Clb; Temple Yth Grp; High Hon Roll; NHS; Mc Gill U; Polit Sci.

FYE, VIANNA; West Milford HS; Hewitt, NJ; (Y); Exploring; FBLA; JA; Capt Var Fld Hcky; JV Var Sftbl; Hon Roll; Jr NHS; NHS; Spanish NHS; Mech.

GADALETA, LISA; Hoboken HS; Hoboken, NJ; (Y); JA; Spanish Clb; Yrbk Phtg; Yrbk Stf; Hon Roll; Spanish NHS; Cert Typng 60 WPM 86; Coe Pgm 86; Fshn.

GADE, CARLA; James Caldwell HS; Caldwell, NJ; (Y); GAA; Key Clb; Letterman Clb; Varsity Clb; Crs Cntry; Score Keeper; Socr; Sftbl; Trk; Vrsty Ltrs Trck 85-86; JV Sftbl 83-85; Pres Physcl Ftns Awd; Plc Ofcr.

GADSDEN, ROBERT H; Dwight Morrow HS; Englewood, NJ; (Y); Latin Clb; Math Clb; Band; Jazz Band; Mrchg Band; Variety Show; Stu Cncl; JV Socr; Var L Trk; Cit Awd; Bio.

GAFFNEY, JOHN; Parsippany HS; Lake Hiawatha, NJ; (S); 118/318; Church Yth Grp; Dance Clb; Drama Clb; French Clb; NFL; Teachers Aide; Band; Chorus; Church Choir; Color Guard; Critics Awd Acting 85; Amer Musical Fndtn Band Hnrs 85; N Jersey Area & Regn I Band 84-85; Psychology.

GAFFOGLIO, LAURA; N Bruns Twp HS; N Brunswick, NJ; (Y); 13/249; Spanish Clb; Yrbk Stf; Chrmn Stu Cncl; Var Swmmng; Var Trk; Hon Roll; NHS; Ntl Merit Ltr; Brown Boveri Schlrshp; Exc Sci,Math 86; Spnsh Awd; Outstndng Spnsh Stu 86; Lehigh U; Chem.

GAGLIANO, EUGENE; Waldwick HS; Waldwick, NJ; (Y); 15/150; Church Yth Grp; Capt Varsity Clb; Capt Var Ftbl; Hon Roll; Var L Trk; JV Wrstlng; Mltry Acad; Comp Engrng.

GAGLIARDI, STEPHANIE; Palisades Park JR SR HS; Palisades Pk, NJ; (Y); JV Cheerleading; Mat Maids; Hon Roll; Gregg Steno Awd 85; Katherine Gibbs; Bus.

GAHRMANN III, EDWARD H; East Brunswick HS; East Brunswick, NJ; (Y); Spanish Clb; Acpl Chr; Band; Chorus; Concert Band; Drm Mjr(t); Madrigals; Mrchg Band; School Musical; Swing Chorus; Two Ten Schlrshp 86; Keith Allen Raphael Mem Awd 86; EBHS Band Booster Assoc Awd 86; American U; Intl Bus.

GAHWYLER, BRIAN; Mahwah HS; Mahwah, NJ; (Y); Ski Clb; Yrbk Stf; Pres Sr Cls; Bsbl; Ftbl; Wrstlng; NHS; Pres Acad Ftns Awd; Frfld U; Engrng.

GAIBOR, HARRY; St Peters Prep; Jersey City, NJ; (Y); 16/205; Camera Clb; Hosp Aide; Yrbk Phtg; Yrbk Sprt Ed; Yrbk Stf; Wrstlng; Hon Roll; Rotary Awd; Pres Citatn Acad Achvt 86; Pres Schlrshp 83; Stevens Ins Tech; Elect Engr.

GAINES, DERRIK; Neptune SR HS; Neptune, NJ; (Y); Varsity Clb; Var Capt Bsktbl; Var Ftbl; High Hon Roll; Hon Roll; Acctg.

GAINES, JAMES; New Brunswick HS; New Brunswick, NJ; (Y); Boy Scts; NFL; Science Clb; Band; Mrchg Band; Yrbk Stf; Bsbl; High Hon Roll; NHS; Howard; Corp Lawyer.

GAINES, JENNIFER; Lakewood HS; Lakewood, NJ; (Y); 50/300; VP Drama Clb; English Clb; French Clb; Key Clb; Band; Church Choir; School Musical; School Play; Nwsp Rptr; JV Capt Cheerleading; Engl Wrtng Achvt 85; Pre-Schl Educ.

GAINSBURG, ADAM; Ocean Township HS; Wayside, NJ; (Y); VP Key Clb; Ski Clb; Rep SADD; Nwsp Rptr; JV Bowling; Var Golf; JV Im Socr; Rep Soph Cls; Spartn Schlr GPA 3.5 Ovr 83-84; Cmnctns-TV.

GAITA, MARIA; Lodi HS; Lodi, NJ; (Y); 14/135; Key Clb; Varsity Clb; Bsktbl; Sftbl; Hon Roll; NHS; Montclair ST Coll; Tchng.

GAJARSKY, LORI; South Plainfield HS; S Plfd, NJ; (Y); 34/281; Church Yth Grp; Cmnty Wkr; Cheerleading; Var Sftbl; Hon Roll; Jr NHS; Middlesex County Coll; Lib Arts.

GALAIDA, ROBERT; Bishop George Ahr HS; Perth Amboy, NJ; (Y); 149/250; JV Bsktbl; JV Ftbl; Hon Roll; Bus.

GALANG JR, MANUEL T; St Peters Prep; Jersey City, NJ; (Y); 15/201; Computer Clb; Drama Clb; School Play; Lit Mag; High Hon Roll; Hon Roll; Drama Ltr 84-85; Hnr Pin 82/83-85/86; Cert Awd Drama 83/84-84-85; Rutgers Coll; Acctg.

GALATRO, BRYAN; Glen Rock JR SR HS; Glen Rock, NJ; (Y); Church Yth Grp; JCL; Latin Clb; Math Tm; Quiz Bowl; Scholastic Bowl; Science Clb; Varsity Clb; Yrbk Stf; Var Bsktbl; US Naval Acad Smmr Sem 86; Deans Smmr Hons Pgm HS Schlrs 86; US Naval Acad; Electrcl Engrn.

GALBRAITH, AIMEE; Palmyra HS; Beverly, NJ; (Y); 10/120; Art Clb; Key Clb; Sec Teachers Aide; Var Tennis; Hon Roll; NHS; Gld Seal Awd Teen Arts Fstvl 83-84; 1st Pl NJ ST Arts Fstvl 83-84; Bus Admin.

GALDI, KIM; Lakeland Regional HS; Wanaque, NJ; (Y); 29/303; Radio Clb; Rep Sr Cls; Stu Cncl; High Hon Roll; Hon Roll; NHS; Church Yth Grp; Rep Frsh Cls; Rep Soph Cls; Rep Jr Cls; Rutgers Coll Of Arts & Sci; Sci.

GALDIERI, JACQUI; East Brunswick HS; E Brunswick, NJ; (Y); Dance Clb; Key Clb; SADD; Variety Show; Rep Frsh Cls; Var Capt Cheerleading; Mgr(s); Cit Awd; Hon Roll; Rotary Awd; Ltl Schlr/Athlt Awd For Chrldng; Rider Coll; Bus Adm.

GALE, EMILY; Chatham Township HS; Chatham Twp, NJ; (Y); Pep Clb; Band; Concert Band; Yrbk Stf; Var L Bsktbl; Var L Fld Hcky; Mgr(s); Socr; L Sftbl; Hon Roll; Fld Hcky All Morris Cnty Colonial Hlls Conf 85; German Awd & Chldhd Dvlpmnt Awd 86; Alex E Fenik Awd; U SCFELEM Ed.

GALIFI, FRANK; Shore Regional HS; West Long Branch, NJ; (Y); Var L Crs Cntry; High Hon Roll; Hon Roll; Corss Cntry MVP Awd 85; Bus Admn.

GALIK, MARK; Highland HS; Erial, NJ; (Y); Computer Clb; Spanish Clb; Nwsp Stf; Bsbl; Golf; Hon Roll; Carrier Mnth 85; Drexel; Elec Eng.

GALIN, MELISSA; Howell HS; Howell, NJ; (Y); Office Aide; Hon Roll; Psych.

GALL, CINDY; Calvary Christian Schl; Burlington, NJ; (Y); 1/2; Hosp Aide; Yrbk Stf; Var Bsbl; Var Vllybl; High Hon Roll; Hon Roll; NHS; Val; Rep Frsh Cls; Rep Soph Cls; Hghst Avg Awd, Hghst Avg Englsh, Hghst Avg Frnch 85-86; Pensacola Christian Coll; Nrsng.

GALL, JENNIFER E; MT Olive HS; Budd Lake, NJ; (Y); 31/296; FBLA; Ski Clb; SADD; Rep Jr Cls; Rep Stu Cncl; Stat Bsktbl; Trk; High Hon Roll; Hon Roll; Trs NHS; Rcgntn Awd Sci Dept Outstndng Prfrmnce 85; Comp Sci.

GALLAGHER JR, JOHN J; Mainland Regional HS; Northfield, NJ; (Y); 50/300; Cmnty Wkr; Ski Clb; Cit Awd; St Cngrssmn-US Mrchnt Marine Acad 86; USMMA; Med.

GALLAGHER, KATIE; Roselle Catholic HS; Port Reading, NJ; (Y); 52/195; School Musical; Stage Crew; JV Var Cheerleading; Gym; Var Socr; High Hon Roll; Hon Roll; Psych.

GALLAGHER, KEITH; St John Vianney HS; Manalapan, NJ; (Y); Ski Clb; JV Fld Hcky; Var Socr; Var Trk; Pres Physcl Ftns Awd 86; Bus.

GALLAGHER, KELLY; Toms River HS North; Toms River, NJ; (Y); 17/412; Band; Mrchg Band; Rep Stu Cncl; Capt Twrlr; High Hon Roll; Hon Roll.

GALLAGHER, KENDRA ELAINE; Middletown South HS; Lincroft, NJ; (Y); VP Church Yth Grp; Church Choir; School Musical; Swing Chorus; Rep Stu Cncl; Var L Fld Hcky; Hon Roll; Drama Clb; Acpl Chr; Psych.

GALLAGHER, MICHAEL; Bishop George AHR HS; S Plainfield, NJ; (Y); Cmnty Wkr; School Play; Im Bsktbl; Cit Awd; Middle Sex Cnty Co; Crmnl Jstc.

GALLAGHER, MICHELE; Holy Spirit HS; Linwood, NJ; (Y); 76/376; 4-H; Hosp Aide; SADD; Yrbk Stf; JV Bsktbl; JV Coach Actv; Var Mgr(s); NHS; Crs Cntry Awd 84; Bsktbl JV Aawd 84; Crs Cntry Mgr Hnr 85; Med.

GALLAGHER, NANCY; Manalapan HS; Englishtown, NJ; (Y); 137/432; Band; Mrchg Band; Rep Jr Cls; Rep Sr Cls; Capt Twrlr; Bus Mgmt.

GALLAGHER, PATRICK W; Haddon Township HS; Westmont, NJ; (Y); Am Leg Boys St; Church Yth Grp; Letterman Clb; Varsity Clb; Stu Cncl; L Crs Cntry; L Swmmng; L Trk; 3 Vrsty Lttrs For 3 Seasons 85-86; All S Jersey Cross-Cntry Hnbl Mntn 85; All Colonial Conf Trk 86; Crmnl Jstc.

GALLAGHER, PATTI; Paul Vi Regional HS; Bloomfield, NJ; (Y); 6/120; Pres Pep Clb; Rep Jr Cls; Rep Sr Cls; Pres French Hon Soc; High Hon Roll; Hon Roll; NHS; Frnch Hnrs Soc Hnr Awd 85; Educ.

GALLAGHER, TIMOTHY; Toms River HS East; Toms River, NJ; (Y); Band; Concert Band; Mrchg Band; De Vry Tech; Comp Repr.

GALLANT, YVETTE; Southern Regional HS; Waretown, NJ; (Y); 40/350; Var Capt Bsktbl; Var Fld Hcky; Var Socr; Var Trk; NHS; Vrsty Bsktbl Outstndng Dfnsive Plyr MWPL 84-86; Vrsty Hcky MVP Outstndng Offnsive Plryr 84-86; Middle Sex Cnty Coll; Acctg.

GALLENAGH, ELIZABETH; Waldwick HS; Waldwick, NJ; (Y); Church Yth Grp; Drama Clb; Math Tm; Q&S; Orch; Nwsp Ed-Chief; JV Socr; Var Vllybl; Cit Awd; Pres NHS; Grl Sct Gold Awd Recpnt 85; Pltcl Sci.

GALLENGER, LINDA M; Phillisburg HS; Phillipsburg, NJ; (Y); 90/298; SADD; Drill Tm; Mrchg Band; Andover Morris PTA Schlrshp 86; Wm Patterson Coll; Chldhd Ed.

GALLESE, STACY; Sacred Heart HS; Milmay, NJ; (S); 2/68; Spanish Clb; Chorus; School Musical; Yrbk Ed-Chief; Sec Trs Soph Cls; Sec Trs Jr Cls; VP Stu Cncl; High Hon Roll; VP NHS; Cumberland Cnty JR Miss 85-86; Rotary Yth Ldrshp Awd 85; Garden ST Distngshd Schlr 85; Engl.

GALLI, STEPHEN; Northern Highlands Regional HS; Allendale, NJ; (Y); 35/270; Varsity Clb; Nwsp Rptr; Lit Mag; Var Ftbl; Var Trk; Hon Roll; NHS; NJ Acad Dcthln 86.

GALLICCHIO, LISA MARIE; Roselle Park HS; Roselle Park, NJ; (Y); 8/138; Am Leg Aux Girls St; Math Tm; Yrbk Sprt Ed; Trs Sr Cls; Rep Stu Cncl; Cheerleading; Cit Awd; NHS; Pres Schlr; St Schlr; Dist Schlr 86; Rutgers; Pol Sci.

GALLIKER, JENNY; Palisades Park JR/SR HS; Palisades Park, NJ; (Y); 34/122; Rep Stu Cncl; Stat Bsktbl; Var Stat Tennis; Color Guard Capt; JACS; St Peters Coll; Bus.

GALLIN, DARRYL; Jackson Memorial HS; Jackson, NJ; (S); 23/422; FBLA; VP Soph Cls; Im Bsktbl; JV Socr; Var L Tennis; High Hon Roll; NHS; Med.

GALLINA, MICHAEL N; Monroe Township HS; Spotswood, NJ; (Y); 22/180; Am Leg Boys St; Key Clb; Pres Frsh Cls; Pres Soph Cls; Rep Stu Cncl; Hugh O Brien Yth Fndtn Smnr 84; Rider Coll; Finc.

GALLO, ANDREW; Glen Rock JR-SR HS; Glen Rock, NJ; (Y); 10/160; Am Leg Boys St; Debate Tm; Yrbk Sprt Ed; Bsktbl; Socr; Trk; Gov Hon Prg Awd; NHS; Bus.

GALLO, AURA; Eastside HS; Paterson, NJ; (Y); #16 In Class; Church Yth Grp; Cmnty Wkr; Office Aide; Teachers Aide; Temple Yth Grp; Church Choir; High Hon Roll; Hon Roll; Prfct Atten Awd; Acctg.

GALLO, EILEEN; Bayonne HS; Bayonne, NJ; (Y); Boy Scts; Church Yth Grp; Cmnty Wkr; Exploring; Teachers Aide; Chorus; Church Choir; School Play; High Hon Roll; Hon Roll; Christ Hosp Schl Nrsng; Nrsng.

GALLO, JO ANN; Passaic Valley HS; Little Falls, NJ; (Y); 52/358; Sec Art Clb; Intnl Clb; Key Clb; JV Bowling; JV Vllybl; High Hon Roll; Hon Roll; NHS; Passaic Vly Hnr Socty 86.

GALLO, JONATHAN V; Clifton HS; Clifton, NJ; (Y); 97/600; Am Leg Boys St; Chess Clb; Church Yth Grp; Computer Clb; French Clb; Science Clb; Ed Yrbk Stf; Hon Roll; TAG Awd 81-86; Monclair ST Coll Advncd Schlrshp Strng Ensmbl 81-86; Frnsc Pthlgy.

GALLO, SABINA; Cliffside Park HS; Cliffside Pk, NJ; (Y); 2/236; Drama Clb; Math Tm; Band; Nwsp Stf; Trs Frsh Cls; Trs Soph Cls; Trs Jr Cls; Trs Sr Cls; Pres Trs Stu Cncl; Stat Bsbl; Engr.

GALLUZZO, STEVEN; Union Catholic Reg HS; Springfield, NJ; (Y); 75/339; Boy Scts; Church Yth Grp; Red Cross Aide; Yrbk Stf; Hon Roll; Good Citizn Citation 83; Vlbl Srvc Awd 1st Aid Sqd 86; U CRANTON; Chem Bus.

GAMBHIR, MANISHA; Westmilford HS; West Milford, NJ; (S); 26/355; Church Yth Grp; German Clb; Intnl Clb; Ed Nwsp Rptr; Ed Nwsp Rptr; Score Keeper; Var Tennis; JV Trk; Hon Roll; India Day Parade 83; Cert Of Merit-Shankars Int Compttn 84; Learnng Unltd 82 & 83; Intl Mrktng.

GAMBINO, MEREDITH; Watchung Hills Reg HS; Gillette, NJ; (Y); Hon Roll; Bus.

GAMBO, LUANN; South River HS; S River, NJ; (Y); 4/160; Am Leg Aux Girls St; Cmnty Wkr; Trs Spanish Clb; Yrbk Stf; Capt Cheerleading; Trk; Hon Roll; NHS; Pre-Lawd.

GAMMER, CURT; Christian Brothers Acad; Colts Neck, NJ; (Y); 27/230; Crs Cntry; Trk; High Hon Roll; NHS; Lehigh U; Engrng.

GANDHI, KAUSHIK; Emerson HS; Union City, NJ; (Y); Computer Clb; French Clb; French Hon Soc; Foreign Lang Hon Soc French 86; Phrmcy.

GANDY, MICHELLE; Bridgeton HS; Newport, NJ; (Y); Pres Church Yth Grp; Yrbk Stf; Rep Jr Cls; Var Capt Fld Hcky; Var Capt Sftbl; High Hon Roll; Jr NHS; NHS; Yrbk Phtg; Im Bsbl; Sci Day Glassboro Chem Tst 86; Adv Alg/Trig Awd 86; Nuclr Med.

GANGADHARAN, SIDHU P; Parisippany Hills HS; Parsippany, NJ; (Y); 9/302; Var Debate Tm; Math Tm; Political Wkr; School Musical; Pres Sr Cls; Var L Socr; Var L Wrstlng; High Hon Roll; NHS; Ntl Merit SF; Rutgers U Deans Smmr Schlrshp 85; ST Sci-Chem Awd 85; 1st Pl Hanover Prk Dbt Tourn 85; Pre-Med.

GANGE, KIM; Bayley-Ellard HS; Morris Plains, NJ; (Y); Church Yth Grp; Service Clb; Lit Mag.

GANGI, F CRAIG; Northern Valley Regional HS; Demarest, NJ; (Y); 21/260; Math Tm; Science Clb; Nwsp Bus Mgr; Yrbk Bus Mgr; Lit Mag; JV Tennis; NHS; Ntl Merit Ltr; Debate Tm; Ski Clb; Pres Acad Ftnss Awd 86; NJ Distngshd Schlr 86; Williams Coll; Attrny.

GANGONE, PAUL; Don Bosco Prep HS; Monsey, NY; (Y); 62/169; Church Yth Grp; Ski Clb; Varsity Clb; Bsbl; Ftbl; Hon Roll; Athlete Of Week Ftbl 85; 1st Tm All Cnty 3rd Tm All St 85; Prestigious Ironman Awd 86; Albright Coll; Advrtsng.

GANT, ELAINE M; Pennsville Memorial HS; Pennsville, NJ; (Y); School Musical; School Play; Lit Mag; NHS; Office Aide; Q&S; Teachers Aide; Yrbk Stf; Gov Hon Prg Awd; Lit Mag Awds-1st, 2nd, 1st Grd 10-12; Fclty Meml Schlrshp-Drama 86; UCLA; Actg.

GANT, ROBERT L; Red Bank Catholic HS; Elberon, NJ; (Y); Computer Clb; Exploring; Bio.

GANTER, JENNIFER; St John Vianney HS; Holmdel, NJ; (Y); Rep Frsh Cls; Rep Stu Cncl; Var L Bsktbl; Im Powder Puff Ftbl; Var Capt Sftbl; High Hon Roll; Hon Roll; Rep Soph Cls; Natl Hnr Stu Of Amer Awd 85; Mission Awareness Club; Gold & White Awd; Susquehanna U; Acctng.

GARA, STEPHEN; Newark Acad; Morristown, NJ; (Y); Boy Scts; CAP; Pres Exploring; Political Wkr; Var Ice Hcky; Yth Ldrshp Amer Awd Explr Div BSA 85; NJ Wng Cvl Air Patrl, Cadt Yr 85; Eagl Sct Awd 83; Syracuse U; Aerospc Engrng.

GARAY, CAROLYN; Red Bank Catholic HS; Middletown, NJ; (Y); 2/300; Teachers Aide; Hon Roll; Gnrl Acad Excllnc 85-86.

GARBER, LAMI W O; Franklin HS; Kendall Park, NJ; (Y); 35/313; Church Yth Grp; Cmnty Wkr; Computer Clb; SADD; Acpl Chr; Chorus; Church Choir; Madrigals; School Musical; School Play; Govrns Schl Arts Awd 85; Region II Medln 84-85; All ST Chorus 85; Fairleigh Dickinson U; Music.

GARBER, TED R; Edgewood Reg HS; Waterford, NJ; (Y); 22/380; Am Leg Boys St; VP Computer Clb; Drama Clb; Pres German Clb; Nwsp Phtg; Yrbk Phtg; Yrbk Sprt Ed; Yrbk Stf; Var Crs Cntry; Var Trk; The Citadel; B A Chem.

GARBIS, CHRISTINE; Montville Township HS; Montville, NJ; (Y); 23/281; Church Yth Grp; Pres Intnl Clb; Key Clb; Service Clb; JV Trk; High Hon Roll; Jr NHS; NHS; Debate Tm; Mgr Band; Fire Dept Scholar 86; Nrsg Home Volunteer Cert Apprec 83-85; Pres Acad Fit Awd 86; Boston Coll; Law.

GARBOWSKI, CHRISTOPHER; Sayreville HS; Sayreville, NJ; (Y); 6/384; Aud/Vis; Math Clb; Spanish Clb; Varsity Clb; Var L Bsbl; High Hon Roll; NHS; Ntl Merit Ltr; Spanish NHS; St Schlr; Pres Acdmc Fit Awd 86; News Tribune Gold Glove Awd 86; Sentinel All Cnty Tm 86; U Of Richmond; Compu Sci.

GARCES, GLENN V; Franklin HS; Somerset, NJ; (Y); Art Clb; VP Aud/Vis; Cmnty Wkr; Drama Clb; Teachers Aide; School Play; Stage Crew; Nwsp Phtg; Yrbk Phtg; Rep Soph Cls; Art Hnr Rl 86; Somerset Cnty Teen Arts Fest 86.

GARCIA, DELILAH; Red Bank Catholic HS; Oakhurst, NJ; (Y); Debate Tm; Hosp Aide; NFL; Ski Clb; Spanish Clb; L VP Twrlr; Exploring; Color Guard; Yrbk Phtg; Ntl Piano Plyng Adtns; Grad Stdy Corp Law; Bus.

GARCIA, GERARD; Memorial HS; West New York, NJ; (Y); Dance Clb; Co-Capt Debate Tm; FBLA; Key Clb; Church Choir; Yrbk Phtg; Yrbk Stf; Rep Frsh Cls; Rep Soph Cls; Rep Jr Cls; Lehigh U Trstee Schlrshp 86; Lehigh U; Bio.

GARCIA, IRENE; Barringer HS; Newark, NJ; (Y); Camera Clb; GAA; Hosp Aide; Spanish Clb; Chorus; School Play; Yrbk Stf; Sftbl; Vllybl; Cit Awd; Super Hnr Rll; Rutgers U Newark; Pedtrc Nrs.

GARCIA, JEANE; Cherry Hill HS West; Cherry Hill, NJ; (Y); Am Leg Aux Girls St; Intnl Clb; PAVAS; Spanish Clb; Color Guard; Mrchg Band; Off Jr Cls; Capt Pom Pon; Drexel U; Bus Mngmnt.

GARCIA, JOEL; Memorial HS; W New York, NJ; (Y); Aircrft Mech.

GARCIA, LISSETTE; John F Kennedy HS; Paterson, NJ; (Y); 21/438; Hon Roll; NHS; Biocraft Labs Inc Sci Scholar 86; Pres Acad Fit Awd 86; Rutgers U; Chem.

GARCIA, LOURDES; Memorial HS; W New York, NJ; (Y); Art Clb; Computer Clb; Dance Clb; Exploring; Spanish Clb; Diving; Gym; Pom Pon; Sftbl; Swmmng; Pep Squad Awd 84-85; Comp Sci.

GARCIA, MANUELA; St Mary Of The Assumption HS; Elizabeth, NJ; (Y); 3/57; Art Clb; Chess Clb; JA; School Play; Yrbk Stf; Hon Roll; NHS; Religion Awd 86; Natl Guild Piano Tchrs-HS Diploma 85; Rutgers; Bus Admin.

GARCIA, MARIA; Paul VI Regional HS; Clifton, NJ; (Y); 2/130; Church Yth Grp; VP French Clb; Hosp Aide; Sec Pres Key Clb; Band; Sec French Hon Soc; Hon Roll; NHS; 1st Pl WPIX Tv Hs Edtrl Cmptn 85; Fnlst Gvns Schl Of Sci Drw U NJ 86; Pre-Med.

GARCIA, MARISOL; Queen Of Peace HS; Newark, NJ; (Y); Hosp Aide; Ski Clb; School Play; Stage Crew; Nwsp Stf; Yrbk Phtg; Yrbk Stf; Hon Roll; Jr NHS; NY U St Peters; Pre-Med.

GARCIA, MICHAEL; Rahway SR HS; Rahway, NJ; (Y); Am Leg Boys St; Church Choir; Madrigals; School Musical; Yrbk Stf; Stu Cncl; Stu Cncl; French Hon Soc; NHS; MS Phillips Acad Andover MA 84-86; Pre-Law.

GARCIA, NELLY; Memorial HS; West New York, NJ; (S); 4/363; Cmnty Wkr; French Clb; VP Math Clb; Science Clb; CC Awd; High Hon Roll; VP NHS; Minority HS Achvt Awd & St Ptrs Coll Acdmc Schlrshp 86; St Ptrs Coll; Comp Sci.

GARCIA, PATRICIA; Hoboken HS; Hoboken, NJ; (Y); Debate Tm; French Clb; Key Clb; Variety Show; Bsbl; Sftbl; Swmmng; Tennis; Vllybl; Pace U & Stevens Inst Comp Inf.

GARCIA, PATRICK; Ridgefield Park HS; Little Ferry, NJ; (Y); 65/198; Office Aide; Nwsp Sprt Ed; Nwsp Stf; Rep Frsh Cls; Trs Soph Cls; Pres Jr Cls; Sec Stu Cncl; Var Ftbl; Var Trk; Im Wt Lftg; U Scranton; Bus Mgt.

GARCIA, RAMON F; St Marys Of The Assumption HS; Elizabeth, NJ; (S); Chess Clb; English Clb; Hon Roll; NHS; Hnr Rll 83-85; CPR 83-84; Rutgers Coll; Med.

GARCIA, RAUL; Saint Josephs HS; Old Bridge, NJ; (Y); 12/225; JV Swmmng; High Hon Roll; Hon Roll; NHS; St Schlr; Church Yth Grp; Dance Clb; Spanish Clb; Y-Teens; Outstndng Spnsh Stu Cert 83-84; Annual Robert Frost Lit Cntst Hnrbl Ment 84-85; 1st Pl Natl Spnsh Exmn; Frgn Lang.

GARCIA, TRACEY; Dickinson HS; Jersey City, NJ; (Y); Science Clb; Ski Clb; Nwsp Stf; Var Capt Bsktbl; Var Cheerleading; Stat Score Keeper; Var Capt Sftbl; Vllybl 81-82; Trck 81; Hogue Dryer Memorl Trphy 86; Ramapo Coll; Sprts Med.

GARCIA, VIVIAN; John F Kennedy HS; Paterson, NJ; (Y); Hon Roll; NHS; Educ.

GARDENHIRE, BARBARA; Vineland HS; Vineland, NJ; (Y); 131/823; Church Yth Grp; Drama Clb; English Clb; Pep Clb; Spanish Clb; Acpl Chr; School Musical; Nwsp Rptr; Hosp Aide; Navy; Law.

GARDNER, EDWARD; Jackson Memorial HS; Jackson, NJ; (S); 2/332; Science Clb; Ski Clb; Co-Capt Crs Cntry; Trk; High Hon Roll; VP NHS; Ntl Merit Ltr; NEDT Awd; Sal; Rutgers Coll Of Pharmacy; Pharm.

GARDNER, ELIZABETH; Manasquan HS; Manasquan, NJ; (Y); 1/230; Key Clb; Band; Yrbk Stf; Rep Stu Cncl; JV Sftbl; Capt Swmmng; Capt Twrlr; High Hon Roll; NHS; Grls Ctznshp Inst Prtcpnt 86; Kwns Hon Soc 86; Frnch.

GARDNER, ERICA; Vineland HS; Vineland, NJ; (Y); French Clb; French Hon Soc; Law.

GARDNER, GLEN; Washington Township HS; Turnersville, NJ; (Y); Spanish Clb; Variety Show; Var Bsbl; Var Socr; Coin Clb 85-86; Muscns Clb 85-86.

GARDNER, JAMES; Christian Brothers Acad; Colts Neck, NJ; (Y); Ski Clb; Varsity Clb; Var Bsbl; Im Ftbl; JV Socr; Bus.

GARDNER, JEFFREY; Piscataway HS; Piscataway, NJ; (Y); 3/519; Church Yth Grp; Drama Clb; Key Clb; Math Tm; Pres Band; Jazz Band; Rep Stu Cncl; JP Sousa Awd; Pres Schlr; St Schlr; Rutgers Coll; Intl Rel.

GARDNER, JOSEPH; Washington Township HS; Turnersville, NJ; (Y); 61/475; Var Capt Bsbl; Var Capt Socr; Hon Roll; JC Awd; NHS; Army Rsrv Schlr Athlt Awd 86; Branders 1; Pre Law.

GARDNER, LYNN ANN; Dover HS; Mine Hill, NJ; (Y); 1/223; Exploring; French Clb; Yrbk Stf; High Hon Roll; NHS; St Schlr; Val; Coll Clb Dover Scholar 86; Jrnlsm Awd 86; William Hedges Baker Post 27 Am Leg Hnr Awd 86; William Paterson.

GARDNER, PATRICIA; A P Schalick HS; Elmer, NJ; (Y); 2/133; Math Tm; Frsh Cls; Soph Cls; Stu Cncl; Fld Hcky; Swmmng; Close Up Pgm In WA DC 86; Best Defnsv Plyr Awd In Field Hcky 84; Best Defnsv Plyr Awd Fld Hcky 85; Lib Arts.

GARDOS, PETER; Colonia SR HS; Colonia, NJ; (Y); 27/284; Pres French Clb; Library Aide; Temple Yth Grp; Orch; Nwsp Rptr; Ed Lit Mag; Hon Roll; NHS; Hngrn-Amercn Awd/Schlrshp 86; Oberlin Coll; Psychlgy.

GARLAND, DONIELLE; Frank H Morrell I HS; Irvington, NJ; (Y); Debate Tm; Girl Scts; Intnl Clb; Key Clb; Latin Clb; Pep Clb; Band; Color Guard; Mrchg Band; Rep Frsh Cls; Pre-Law.

GARMONT, GLENN; Seton Hall Prep; Newark, NJ; (Y); 10/190; Computer Clb; Math Clb; School Musical; Yrbk Rptr; JV Trk; Hon Roll; NHS; NEDT Awd; Nwrk St Ptrcks Dy Prd Cmmtee Annl Schlrshp Awd 86; Ntl Sci Olympd Cert Dstnctn 85; Aviatn.

GARNER, CHRIS; Burlington City HS; Edgewater Pk, NJ; (Y); Am Leg Boys St; FBLA; JV L Bsbl; Var L Bsktbl; L Ftbl; Slctd Coaches Leag All Str Bsktbl Team 86; Econ.

GARNER, JO ANN; Rancocas Valley Regional HS; Mt Holly, NJ; (Y); French Clb; Hosp Aide; Ski Clb; Yrbk Stf; Lcrss; Occuptn Thrpy.

GARNER, REINA; Freehold Township HS; Freehold, NJ; (Y); Exploring; Spanish Clb; Band; Mrchg Band; Yrbk Phtg; Crs Cntry; Sftbl; Trk; NHS; Rutgers U; Law.

GARNER, SHANTEL; Burlington Township HS; Burlington, NJ; (Y); 59/118; DECA; Office Aide; Spanish Clb; Varsity Clb; Color Guard; Yrbk Stf; Bsktbl; Var Pom Pon; Socr; Trk; Burlington Co Comm; Word Procss.

GAROFALO, MARCIA ANNE; Mary Help Of Christians Acad; N Haledon, NJ; (S); 11/88; Computer Clb; Chorus; Orch; Stage Crew; Rep Jr Cls; Mgr(s); Hon Roll; Ntl Merit Ltr; Yth Mayor 85.

GARONE, WILLIAM; Linden HS; Linden, NJ; (Y); Church Yth Grp; French Clb; Band; Jazz Band; Mrchg Band; Trk; Hon Roll; Jr NHS.

GAROPPO, VALERIE; Delsea Regional HS; Newfield, NJ; (Y); Dance Clb; Drama Clb; PAVAS; School Musical; Pom Pon; Sftbl; Vllybl; Most Outstndg Mjrtt 85; Perfm Arts.

GARRAHAN, ELIZABETH; Pope John XXIII HS; Sussex, NJ; (Y); Church Yth Grp; French Clb; Service Clb; Chorus; Var Crs Cntry; Var Swmmng; High Hon Roll; NHS; Awd Acdmc Excllnc 84-86; Theolgy Awd 84-85; Outstndg HS Athlts Awd 85-86; Bus Mgmt.

GARRANDER, RON; Marist HS; Bayonne, NJ; (Y); 8/120; Scholastic Bowl; Science Clb; Nwsp Rptr; Nwsp Stf; High Hon Roll; Hon Roll; Ntl Merit SF; NY U; Jrnslm.

GARRETSON, KELLI; Queen Of Peace HS; Lyndhurst, NJ; (Y); Cmnty Wkr; Drama Clb; Pep Clb; Varsity Clb; School Musical; Cheerleading; Coach Actv; Gym; Pom Pon; Sftbl; Coachd Cheerg 82 & 86; Elem Ed.

GARRETT, MARJORIE; Pitman HS; Pitman, NJ; (S); 12/139; Teachers Aide; Band; Mrchg Band; Orch; Mgr(s); Score Keeper; Var Tennis; S Jersey Grp I Tennis Tm 84-85; Coaches Awd Tnns Tm 83-85; Hnrb Mntn Gloucester Cnty Au Stars 82-85; Rutgers; Accntng.

GARRETT, MARY MARGARET; Hamilton HS West; Trenton, NJ; (S); Church Yth Grp; Intnl Clb; Key Clb; Band; Chorus; Concert Band; School Musical; Symp Band; Yrbk Stf; Jr Cls; Hugh O Brien Awd; Spec Ed.

GARRICK, GERALYNN D; David Brearley Regional HS; Kenilworth, NJ; (Y); 29/176; Drama Clb; Chorus; School Musical; School Play; Cheerleading; Gym; Hon Roll; Schlrshps Ithaca Coll, Hofstra U & Oral Roberts U 86; Slvr Brnz Mdls Chorl Mus Fstvls 83-84; Mus Thtr.

GARRISON, RENETTA; Plainfield HS; Plainfield, NJ; (S); 4/539; Church Yth Grp; Capt Pep Clb; Yrbk Stf; Rep Frsh Cls; Rep Soph Cls; Rep Jr Cls; Rep Sr Cls; VP Stu Cncl; Gov Hon Prg Awd; NHS; Acadmc All Amercn Schlr 83-84; Ntl Ldrshp & Svc Awd 83-84; Chrch Yng Adlt Ushr Brd-VP 83-84; Elec Engrng.

GARRISON, SANDRA; Lower-Cape May Regional HS; Villas, NJ; (Y); 18/220; Church Yth Grp; Varsity Clb; Lib Band; Chorus; Church Choir; Jazz Band; Mrchg Band; School Musical; Yrbk Stf; NHS; Acdmc All Amer Sci Awd 84-85; All Sth Jrsy Wind Ensmbl 85-86; All Cnty Bnd Awds 82-86; Mnsfld U; Spec Ed.

GARRISON, SCOTT; Hunterdon Central HS; Hopewell, NJ; (Y); 83/550; Camera Clb; Computer Clb; Im Vllybl; Hon Roll; Rutgers; Marine Bio.

GARRY, MICHELLE; Roselle Catholic HS; Elizabeth, NJ; (Y); JA; French Hon Soc; High Hon Roll; Communications Brdcstng.

GARRY, PHILIP; Fair Lawn HS; Fairview, NJ; (Y); 38/335; Nwsp Sprt Ed; JV Bowling; Var Tennis; CC Awd; Hon Roll; Fair Lawn HS Outstndng Prfmnce In Acctg 86; Clumbia Svngs Bus Ed Schlrshp 86; Rutgers; Acctg.

GARRY, ROBERT; St Peters Prep HS; Bayonne, NJ; (Y); Boy Scts; Dance Clb; Ski Clb; School Play; Yrbk Stf; Rep Jr Cls; Var L Socr; Wt Lftg; North Eastern U; Med.

GARVIN, LISA; Paulsboro HS; Paulsboro, NJ; (Y); 4-H; Girl Scts; Hosp Aide; Chorus; Stage Crew; Yrbk Stf; Trk; Hon Roll; NHS; Goldey Beacon Coll; Procssng.

GARWOOD, KATHLEEN; Holy Cross HS; Willingboro, NJ; (Y); 25/397; Yrbk Stf; Wt Lftg; High Hon Roll; Hon Roll; Bnkng.

GARY, LISA; Metuchen HS; Metuchen, NJ; (Y); Scholastic Bowl; Varsity Clb; Nwsp Stf; Yrbk Stf; Var Capt Socr; Var Swmmng; Var Trk; High Hon Roll; NHS; Mathletes; All Cty Schlr Athletic Tm 85-86; SF Girls ST 86; SF Japanese Schlrshp Pgm 86; Arch.

GARZON, ERNESTO; Morris Hills HS; Rockaway, NJ; (Y); 16/198; Math Tm; Natl Beta Clb; NFL; Quiz Bowl; ROTC; Spanish Clb; Varsity Clb; Concert Band; School Musical; School Play; Math Awd Ntnl Math Leg; Englsh Outstndng Achvt Awd; Penn ST; Aerntcl.

GARZON, SANDRA J; St Pius X HS; Edison, NJ; (Y); 10/96; Drama Clb; French Clb; Office Aide; Teachers Aide; Trs Frsh Cls; VP Stu Cncl; Hon Roll; Pres NHS; Frnch Intr Orgnl Wrk 1st 83-84; Rlgn Awd 84-86; 4 Yr Hnr Awd 85-86; Rutgers U; Bus.

GASIS, FAYE; Gateway Regional HS; Woodbury Hts, NJ; (Y); Church Yth Grp; French Clb; GAA; Latin Clb; SADD; Yrbk Stf; Rep Frsh Cls; Sec Rep Soph Cls; Sec Rep Jr Cls; Rep Stu Cncl; Glssbro ST.

GASKINS, JUANITA; Henry Snyder HS; Jersey City, NJ; (S); 13/254; Cmnty Wkr; Dance Clb; FBLA; Hon Roll; Cert Awd Intrnshp Wrk 86; Exec Secy.

GASPARINO, JENNIFER; Paul VI Regional HS; Cedar Grove, NJ; (Y); Nwsp Ed-Chief; Nwsp Rptr; Nwsp Stf; Yrbk Stf; Hon Roll; Spanish NHS; Cmnctns.

GASPERINI, LISA; Shore Regional HS; West Long Branch, NJ; (Y); Drama Clb; Sec French Clb; SADD; Band; Yrbk Stf; Ed Lit Mag; Rep Frsh Cls; Stat Bsktbl; JV Socr; High Hon Roll; Poly Sci.

GASS, ERIC D; Eastside HS; Paterson, NJ; (Y); 17/535; DECA; Var Capt Bsbl; High Hon Roll; Hon Roll; NHS; Rotary Awd; Top 25 Stu Awd; MVP Bsbl Awd; Phia Phi Alpha Schlrshp 85-86; Team Ldr Awd Bsbl 85; Delaware ST Coll; Bus.

GASTON, JERRI; East Orange HS; East Orange, NJ; (S); 55/410; Cmnty Wkr; French Clb; Hosp Aide; Pep Clb; Capt Color Guard; Variety Show; JV Bsktbl; Hon Roll; Homecomg SR Cls Prncss 85; Fshn Mrchndsg.

GATES, CAROLYN; Middletown High School South HS; Middletown, NJ; (Y); Sec Intnl Clb; SADD; Flag Corp; Yrbk Stf; Hon Roll; Ntl Merit Ltr.

GATTO, CARA; Bishop Ahr HS; East Brunswick, NJ; (Y); Church Yth Grp; Church Choir; Concert Band; Mrchg Band; Elks Awd; 4-H Awd; High Hon Roll; NHS; NEDT Awd; Mrt Schlrshp 86; Rep To Gvrnrs Schl Sci Fnlst 85; Hnrd Top 10% Grad Cls 86; Trenton ST Coll; Bio.

GAUDETTE JR, EDWARD J; Seton Hall Prep; Murray Hill, NJ; (Y); Boy Scts; French Clb; Key Clb; Var Socr; High Hon Roll; NHS.

GAUDIOSO, PETER A; West Milford Twp HS; West Milford, NJ; (Y); 23/391; Am Leg Boys St; Model UN; Concert Band; Jazz Band; Mrchg Band; School Musical; Im Bsbl; Im Bsktbl; Im Swmmng; Hon Roll; Law.

GAUGHAN, SEAN A; Northern Burlington County Regional; Allentown, NJ; (Y); Am Leg Boys St; French Clb; Math Clb; Math Tm; Band; Concert Band; Jazz Band; Symp Band; JV Var Bsbl; Var Crs Cntry; Engrng.

GAVAZZI, MELINDA; Bridgewater-Raritan H S West; Bridgewater, NJ; (Y); 79/294; German Clb; Orch; Nwsp Phtg; Off Jr Cls; Off Sr Cls; Stat Bsbl; Powder Puff Ftbl; Var JV Socr; Stat Trk; Hon Roll; JR Prom Comm Publcty Comm Chrprsn 84-85; Scholar Ethicon 86; Kutztown U; Med Tech.

GAVIGAN, KATHLEEN; Vineland SR HS; Vineland, NJ; (Y); 150/820; Art Clb; Church Yth Grp; French Clb; Latin Clb; Pep Clb; Red Cross Aide; Yrbk Stf; Off Stu Cncl; Law.

GAVIN, RACHEL; Brdigewater-Raritan HS West; Bridgewater, NJ; (Y); French Clb; Band; Concert Band; Mrchg Band; Hon Roll; NHS; Lang.

GAVIN, STEPHEN; North Bergen HS; North Bergen, NJ; (Y); 35/470; Pres Key Clb; Sec SADD; Yrbk Stf; Rep Frsh Cls; Rep Soph Cls; Rep Jr Cls; NHS; Mbr Russian Natl Hon Scty 85-86; Accptd Merit Scty 85-86; Med.

GAWEL, LISA; Union Catholic Regional HS; Clark, NJ; (Y); 18/320; Math Clb; Math Tm; Science Clb; Service Clb; Yrbk Stf; Hon Roll; NHS.

GAWRONSKI, JOSEPH C; Colonia HS; Colonia, NJ; (Y); 1/265; Am Leg Boys St; Nwsp Sprt Ed; VP Soph Cls; VP Stu Cncl; Var Capt Socr; NHS; St Schlr; Cmnty Wkr; Math Clb; Political Wkr; 1st Pl Local IUOE Ed Fund Essay Cntst, Rnnr-Up Time Stu Wrtng Cntst 86; 1st Pl NJFPS Bowl 84-85; Pol Sci.

GAWRONSKI, MICHELE; Colonia HS; Colonia, NJ; (Y); 15/287; Cmnty Wkr; Ski Clb; Varsity Clb; Sec Stu Cncl; Stat Bsbl; Socr; Hon Roll; NHS; Pres Schlr; Pres Spanish NHS; Alpha Delta Kappa; Trenton ST Coll; Elem Ed.

GAYNOR, KATE; Ocean City HS; Ocean View, NJ; (Y); 1/280; Drama Clb; Spanish Clb; Ed Yrbk Stf; NHS; Ntl Merit SF; Rotary Awd; Exchng Clb Yth Mth 85; Hopwood Schlr 85; Emergncy Med.

GAZELL, DAWN; Brick Township HS; Brick, NJ; (Y); 17/318; Drama Clb; Key Clb; Sec Band; Concert Band; Mrchg Band; Stage Crew; High Hon Roll; Amer Assn Retired Persns Awd Music 86; U DE.

GAZZARA, DEANNE; Buena Regional HS; Vineland, NJ; (S); 7/199; Cmnty Wkr; Pep Clb; Ski Clb; Band; Rep Frsh Cls; Rep Soph Cls; Rep Jr Cls; Rep Sr Cls; Rep Stu Cncl; Hon Roll; Biol.

GEBELL, THOMAS; Passaic Valley HS; Little Falls, NJ; (Y); Boy Scts; Science Clb; JV Bsktbl; Hon Roll; U Of MN; Aerospc Engr.

GECZIK, LISA; Bishop George Ahr HS; Milltown, NJ; (Y); 10/277; Cmnty Wkr; Spanish Clb; Teachers Aide; Rep Soph Cls; High Hon Roll; NHS; NEDT Awd; Church Yth Grp; Hosp Aide; Raritan Vly Dvng Champ 84; Clss I Gymnstcs Comp 85; KIPS Gym Invtntnl Vltng Fnlst 86; Bus.

GEDDIS, JASON; Hightstown HS; East Windsor, NJ; (Y); #32 In Class; Ftbl; JV Capt Socr; Var Tennis; High Hon Roll; Hon Roll; Bus.

GEDRYS, KRIS; Red Bank Catholic HS; Red Bank, NJ; (Y); Cmnty Wkr; Hosp Aide; Science Clb; Band; Beaver Coll; Lbrl Arts.

GEE, TOM; Holy Cross HS; Maple Shade, NJ; (Y); Am Leg Boys St; School Musical; Rep Soph Cls; Trs Jr Cls; VP Sr Cls; Bsbl; JV Trk; Hon Roll; Outstndng Rep Awd Stu Cncl; SR Cls VP; Bus.

GEHM, HEATHER; West Essex Regional HS; Fairfield, NJ; (Y); Art Clb; French Clb; Girl Scts; Science Clb; Orch; Var Sftbl; Tennis; Hon Roll; Natl Phys Ed Awd 84; Engrng.

GEHOUSKY, DIANE; Maple Shade HS; Maple Shade, NJ; (Y); 16/158; Computer Clb; French Clb; Key Clb; SADD; Nwsp Rptr; Yrbk Stf; Var Capt Cheerleading; Fld Hcky; Jr NHS; NHS; U DE; Fash Merch.

GEHRIG, TINA; Hackensack HS; Maywood, NJ; (Y); #26 In Class; Ski Clb; Nwsp Rptr; Var Crs Cntry; Var Trk; JV Vllybl; French Hon Soc; Hon Roll; NHS; Grmn Hnr Soc 84-85; PA ST; Photo.

GEIB, CHARLES; Kittatinny Regional HS; Newton, NJ; (Y); 12/228; Church Yth Grp; CAP; German Clb; Var L Bsbl; NHS.

GEIGER, JODY; Morristown HS; Morristown, NJ; (Y); Art Clb; Drama Clb; French Clb; JA; Sec Trs Keywanettes; SADD; School Musical; School Play; Mgr(s); Jr NHS; Prsdntl Clssrm 86; Rcvd Outstndg Drama Awd 84.

GEIGER, STEVE; Mt Olive HS; Flanders, NJ; (Y); AFS; Drama Clb; Library Aide; PAVAS; Ski Clb; Stage Crew; Yrbk Phtg; Yrbk Stf; Lit Mag; Trs Soph Cls; Natl Schlstc Photo Awd 85; NJ Govrs Awd In Photogphy 85; Natl Schlstc Photogrphy Awd 86; Advtsn.

GEIGER, THERESA; Cranford HS; Cranford, NJ; (Y); #10 In Class; Church Yth Grp; JCL; Pres Latin Clb; Math Tm; Chorus; Church Choir; Hon Roll; VP NHS; Pres Schlr; Rotary Awd; Pres Acad Fit Awd 85-86; Cum Laude Natl Latin Exam 85-86; Silv Mdl NJJCL Natl Latin Exam 85; Muhlenberg Coll; Elem Schl Tchr.

GEILS, AMY S; Midland Park HS; Midland Park, NJ; (Y); 6/139; VP AFS; Am Leg Aux Girls St; Cmnty Wkr; Debate Tm; FNA; Hosp Aide; Pep Clb; Science Clb; Varsity Clb; Rep Frsh Cls; ITT Schlrshp 86; 1st Tm All League Outstndng Sr Awd Vollybll 85; Springfield Coll; Phys Therapy.

GEISINGER, KIMBERLY; Cumberland Regional HS; Bridgeton, NJ; (Y); 87/357; Church Yth Grp; Exploring; Office Aide; Im Sftbl; Var JV Tennis; Hon Roll; Spcl Educ.

GEISLER, CHRISTINE; Bridgewater-Raritan HS West; Bridgewater, NJ; (Y); Key Clb; Pres Frsh Cls; Pres Soph Cls; VP Stu Cncl; Var Cheerleading; High Hon Roll; Hon Roll; NHS; Ski Clb; Rep Jr Cls; Hoffman La Roche Schlrshp Grant WA Wkshp Found; Ldrshp Trang Camp Delg; Comm Chrman Schl Store.

GEISSLER, WAYNE; St John Vianney HS; Hazlet, NJ; (Y); Cmnty Wkr; Exploring; Math Clb; Math Tm; Hon Roll; NHS; 1st Pl SJV Stu In NJ Chem Cont 85; 12th Pl Cath HS Math Lg JR Var Div A 86; NJ Math Lg Cert 86; Medicine.

GELATO, LISA; Bayonne HS; Bayonne, NJ; (Y); Rep Soph Cls; Rep Jr Cls; Twrlr; High Hon Roll; Hon Roll; Montclair ST Coll; Math.

GELB, JOSEPH; Union HS; Union, NJ; (Y); Boy Scts; Drama Clb; Key Clb; Temple Yth Grp; Concert Band; Nwsp Rptr; Trk; NHS; Voice Dem Awd; AHSME Schl Wnnr 86; Engrng.

GELIN, ABDULLAHAT; Don Bosco Prep; Garfield, NJ; (Y); Science Clb; Sci Fair Awd 2nd Pl 86; Med.

GELORMINI, CAROL; James Caldwell HS; W Caldwell, NJ; (Y); Science Clb; Concert Band; Flag Corp; Mrchg Band; Yrbk Stf; Var Socr; Stat Trk; High Hon Roll; Hon Roll; NHS; Med.

GELS, MICHELLE; Hamilton High Schl West; Trenton, NJ; (S); German Clb; Intnl Clb; Band; Concert Band; Mrchg Band; Symp Band; Stu Cncl; JV Var Fld Hcky; Vet Med.

GEMINO, ERIC; Ridgefield Park HS; Ridgefield Pk, NJ; (Y); Aud/Vis; Chess Clb; Nwsp Stf; Var Capt Trk; Hon Roll; VFW Awd; Wnnr Independence Lodge 76 Hway Safty Local Lodge Poster Cntst 86; Engrng.

GEMMA, FRANK; West Orange HS; W Orange, NJ; (Y); JV Ftbl; Pharm.

GEMSKI, PETER F; West Milford HS; West Milford, NJ; (Y); 5/400; Am Leg Boys St; Math Tm; Varsity Clb; Pres Stu Cncl; Capt Var Bsbl; Capt Var Ftbl; Var Wrstlng; High Hon Roll; NHS; 1st Tm All Confrnc 2nd Tm All Cnty Basebl; Volntr Jr Firemn; Boston U; Med.

GENERALS, DAWN B; Paterson Catholic Regional HS; Paterson, NJ; (Y); 6/100; Chrmn Church Yth Grp; Model UN; Political Wkr; Nwsp Stf; Rep Stu Cncl; Var Trk; Var Vllybl; High Hon Roll; Ntl Merit Ltr; Econ.

GENNARO, ELAINE; Mahwah HS; Mahwah, NJ; (Y); Spanish Clb; Varsity Clb; Chorus; Yrbk Stf; JV Bsktbl; Var Capt Sftbl; High Hon Roll; Hon Roll; Spanish NHS; Pres Acadmc Ftnss Awd 86; Hghst Achvt-Choir 86; Ramapo Coll NJ; Poli Sci.

GENOBLE, LEONA; Montville HS; Montville, NJ; (Y); 16/262; VP French Clb; Hosp Aide; Key Clb; Orch; Rep Soph Cls; Var Bsktbl; NHS; Computer Clb; FBLA; Math Clb; Rgnl Orchstr NJ Cellst 85-86; Karat-Purpl Belt 86; Jr Stsmn Clb-Secy-Treas 86-87; Elec Engr.

GENOESE, JODI; Madison HS; Madison, NJ; (Y); GAA; Service Clb; Spanish Clb; Stu Cncl; Var Cheerleading; Var Gym; Im Powder Puff Ftbl; High Hon Roll; Hon Roll; Spanish NHS; Bus Mgmt.

GENOVESE, ANDREA; West Essex Regional HS; Fairfield, NJ; (Y); German Clb; Pep Clb; Yrbk Stf; Sec Frsh Cls; Rep Stu Cncl; Capt Cheerleading; 2 Jr Vrsty Lttrs; 5 Vrsty Lttrs; Med.

GENOVESE, ANTHONY; Lower Cape May Regional HS; N Cape May, NJ; (Y); 7/250; Math Tm; Swmmng; NHS; Futur Prblm Slvrs 85; Engrng.

GENTHE, DAVID; Spotswood HS; Spotswood, NJ; (S); 5/185; Var Socr; High Hon Roll; NHS; MVP Vrsty Sccr 85; NJ Inst Of Tech; Comp Sci.

GENTHE, THOMAS; Sportsood HS; Spotswood, NJ; (S); Bsbl; Capt Var Socr; Hon Roll; NHS; MVP Var Socr 85; NJIT; Arch.

GENTILE, ANDREW; Washington Township HS; Turnersville, NJ; (Y); 6/500; Civic Clb; German Clb; Im Bsktbl; Var Tennis; Hon Roll; NHS; Ger Hnr Soc 86; Acad All Amer 86; Bus Adm.

GENTILE, CHRISTOPHER; Marine Acad Of Science & Tech; Union Beach, NJ; (S); 1/24; ROTC; Spanish Clb; Nwsp Ed-Chief; Rep Jr Cls; High Hon Roll; VP NHS; Val; Itnl Frgn Lang Awd 85-86; Marine Sci.

GENTILE, KRISTIN; Millville SR HS; Millville, NJ; (Y); VP Church Yth Grp; SADD; Chrmn Stu Cncl; High Hon Roll; NHS; Dance Clb; French Clb; Office Aide; Teachers Aide; Church Choir; Gftd & Tlntd 83-86; Stu Cncl Srv Awd 84-85; Hghst Advncd Eng Avg Awd 85; JR Tste Of Mlvl Lbry Bd 85-86.

GENUS, MICHAEL; Holy Cross HS; Burlington, NJ; (Y); 31/397; Ski Clb; JV Var Bsbl; Im Vllybl; High Hon Roll; Hon Roll; Slctd Garden Sst Bsbll Tm 86; SR Babe Ruth Tournmnt Tm Bsbll 84-86; Math.

GENZALE, THOMAS; Pope John XXIII HS; Oak Ridge, NJ; (Y); Church Yth Grp; Chorus; Var Capt Bsbl; Var Capt Ftbl; Hon Roll; Coaches Mip 86; Wake Forest; Bus Admin.

GEORGE, CHRISTINE; Vineland HS; Vineland, NJ; (Y); Latin Clb; Mrchg Band; Rep Stu Cncl; Mgr(s); Sftbl.

GEORGE, ERIC KENNETH; Union Catholic HS; Newark, NJ; (Y); Boy Scts; Service Clb; SADD; Chorus; Church Choir; Bsbl; Bsktbl; Ftbl; Hon Roll.

GEORGE, GERALYN; Madison Central HS; Old Bridge, NJ; (S); Drama Clb; Spanish Clb; Chorus; Capt Drill Tm; School Musical; School Play; Stu Cncl; Hon Roll; NHS; Sec Spanish NHS; Spnsh Awd 84; Comm.

GEORGE, GINA; Vineland HS; Vineland, NJ; (Y); Chess Clb; 4-H; Library Aide; Office Aide; Pep Clb; RN.

GEORGE, GLYNNIS; Haddon Township HS; W Collingswood Ht, NJ; (Y); 6/170; Band; Chorus; Drm Mjr(t); Madrigals; Orch; JV Swmmng; Cit Awd; High Hon Roll; Sec NHS; Lenoir Rhyne Clg Pres Awd 86; Lenoir Rhyne Coll; Chldhd Ed.

GEORGE, ROBERT; Manchester Regional HS; N Haledon, NJ; (Y); Am Leg Boys St; Boy Scts; Church Yth Grp; Mathletes; Im Bsbl; Im JV Bsktbl; Rotry Career Day 86; Tchr.

GEORGE, ROBERT; Steinert HS; Hamilton Sq, NJ; (Y); Band; Concert Band; Jazz Band; Mrchg Band; School Play; Stage Crew; Var Bsbl; Im Wt Lftg; Prfct Atten Awd; Elec Engr.

GEORGE, STEPHANIE; Ambassador Christian Acad; Turnersville, NJ; (S); 2/8; Church Yth Grp; Hosp Aide; Yrbk Bus Mgr; Pres Stu Cncl; Bsktbl; Var Timer; Hon Roll; NHS; Sal; Voice Dem Awd; Psych.

GERALD, L MONIQUE; Pleasantville HS; Pleasantville, NJ; (S); #6 In Class; Computer Clb; Pres Frsh Cls; Rep Soph Cls; VP Jr Cls; VP Sr Cls; Var Bsktbl; Var Cheerleading; NHS; Chorus; Mrchg Band; Acad Achvt Awde; Englsh Achvt Awd; Modern Sci Achvt Awd; Hampton U; RN.

GERALD, MONIQUE; Pleasantville HS; Pleasantville, NJ; (Y); 4/132; Computer Clb; Pres Frsh Cls; VP Jr Cls; VP Sr Cls; Var Bsktbl; NHS; Mrchg Band; Nwsp Rptr; Nwsp Sprt Ed; Var Cheerleading; Acadmc Achvt Awd 82-86; $1000 Schlrshp-Rotary Clb Of Mainlnd 86; Eng Awd-82; Sci Awd 82; Hampton U; Nrsng.

GERALDO, MARIA; Emerson HS; Union City, NJ; (Y); Cmnty Wkr; SADD; Union County Coll; Dentl Lab.

GERBER, JACKIE; Manalapan HS; Manalapan, NJ; (Y); 140/430; Civic Clb; Dance Clb; Temple Yth Grp; Nwsp Stf; Trk; Bus Mgmt.

GERBMAN, SCOTT; North Brunswick Township HS; N Brunswick, NJ; (Y); 17/300; Cmnty Wkr; Key Clb; Temple Yth Grp; Nwsp Bus Mgr; Nwsp Rptr; Bsbl; Bsktbl; Cit Awd; High Hon Roll; Hon Roll; Engrng.

GERCIE, MELISSA; Phillipsburg HS; Alpha, NJ; (Y); 31/284; Am Leg Aux Girls St; VP FBLA; OEA; Ski Clb; Rep Frsh Cls; Cheerleading; Hon Roll; NHS; Brkly Schl Alumni Assoc Schlrshp 86; Berkeley Schl; Pro Sec.

GERCKENS, JOHN; Northern Valley Regional HS; Old Tappan, NJ; (Y); 57/280; VP Soph Cls; VP Jr Cls; VP Stu Cncl; Var Capt Bsbl; Var Capt Bsktbl; Var Capt Ftbl; NHS; 1st Tm All-NBIL Bsbll 84-86; Bus Adm.

GERDES, MICHELE; St John Vianney HS; Port Monmouth, NJ; (Y); 33/298; Drama Clb; Library Aide; Service Clb; SADD; Hon Roll; Prfct Atten Awd; Vet Sci.

GERHAUSER, JUDE E; Toms River High School South; Beachwood, NJ; (Y); Camera Clb; Spanish Clb; SADD; Band; Concert Band; Stage Crew; Var Fld Hcky; JV Mgr(s); Sftbl; Hon Roll; Georgian Ct Coll; Elem Art Ed.

GERHOLD, GREG; Don Bosco Prep; Tappan, NY; (Y); 18/180; Math Clb; Pep Clb; Red Cross Aide; Varsity Clb; Yrbk Sprt Ed; Yrbk Stf; Var Bsbl; Var L Ice Hcky; Hon Roll; NHS; ST Chmpn Ice Hcky Tm 84-85; ST Chmpn Bsbl Tm 85-86; Ntl Hnr Soc, Hnr Roll 84-87; Finance.

GERKE, CYNTHIA M; Lawrenceville HS; Lawrenceville, NJ; (Y); 1/237; Am Leg Aux Girls St; Church Yth Grp; Service Clb; Madrigals; Nwsp Sprt Ed; Stat Bsbl; Stat Bsktbl; NHS; Ntl Merit SF; Rotary Awd; Wellesley Bk Awd; Distngushd Schlrs Prog; Economics.

GERKENS, FRANCIS; Vernon Township HS; Highland Lks, NJ; (Y); Boy Scts; FBLA; Letterman Clb; Varsity Clb; Chorus; School Musical; Var L Swmmng; Nichols; Mktg.

GERKHARDT, DENNIS; North Warren Regional HS; Columbia, NJ; (Y); Church Yth Grp; Ski Clb; Business Mgmt.

GERLING, WILLIAM; Brick HS; Brick Town, NJ; (Y); German Clb; Math Tm; High Hon Roll; Hon Roll; Frgn Lgn Clb 84-86; Mthmtcs.

GERMANIO, RALPH; Egg Harbor Township HS; Pleasantville, NJ; (S); Var Co-Capt Crs Cntry.

GERMINARIO, ANTHONY T; Bergenfield HS; Bergenfield, NJ; (Y); Am Leg Boys St; Band; Jazz Band; Mrchg Band; Variety Show; Nwsp Sprt Ed; JV Bsbl; Var Bsktbl; Hon Roll; NHS; Penn ST; Cmmnctns.

GERONIMO, VITO; St Joseph Regional HS; Congers, NY; (Y); 14/169; Political Wkr; Ski Clb; Off Soph Cls; Off Jr Cls; VP Sr Cls; VP Stu Cncl; JV Bsbl; Var Capt Socr; NHS; LAB Prg Fndtn Free Entrprs 86; Engrng.

GERULA, CHRISTINE; Clifton HS; Clifton, NJ; (Y); 22/637; French Clb; Math Tm; Office Aide; Science Clb; Spanish Clb; Acpl Chr; Band; Yrbk Stf; Sec Stu Cncl; L Cheerleading; Hgh Achvt Stu VA Music Inst 86; Stu Tlntd & Gftd Prgrm Music & Math 86-87; Biomed Engrnng.

GETZ, BARBARA; Sacred Heart HS; Buena, NJ; (S); 17/67; Y-Teens; Chorus; Variety Show; VP Frsh Cls; JV Var Cheerleading; Var Score Keeper; Var Key Clb; Vllybl; Hon Roll; Jr NHS; Trvl & Toursm.

GEYER, HOWARD L; The Frisch Schl; West Orange, NJ; (Y); Debate Tm; Capt Math Clb; Capt Math Tm; Quiz Bowl; Temple Yth Grp; Yrbk Ed-Chief; Ntl Merit SF; Pres Schlr; Hosp Aide; Scholastic Bowl; 1st Pl Amer H S Mth Exam 85; Cert Svc Montclair Comm Hosp 85; Med.

GEYER, SUSAN; Howell HS; Howell, NJ; (Y); 37/371; French Clb; Key Clb; Rep Soph Cls; Rep Stu Cncl; NHS; Awd In Accntng 85; Stcktn ST Coll; Bus Adm.

GHOSH, ARPAN; Wayne Valley HS; Wayne, NJ; (Y); 33/322; Var Capt Bsbl; Boys Clb Am; Computer Clb; JCL; Latin Clb; Lit Mag; Im Bsktbl; Var Capt Bowling; Im Ftbl; JV Socr; Wayne PTO Schrlshp 86; Vrsty Awd 86; Latin Awd 86; Rutgers U; Engrng.

GHUMMAN, KULWINDER; Mother Seton Regional HS; Carteret, NJ; (Y); Camera Clb; Computer Clb; Math Tm; Science Clb; Service Clb; High Hon Roll; Rukgers Coll Schlrshp 86-87; Rukgers Coll; Comp Sci.

GIACOBBE, NANCY E; Immaculata HS; Neshanic Station, NJ; (Y); 1/211; Math Tm; Pres Band; Jazz Band; Mrchg Band; School Musical; JP Sousa Awd; Pres NHS; Ntl Merit Ltr; Spanish NHS; Val; Govrs Schl Of The Arts 85; Govrs Schl Of The Sci 85; Johns Hopkins U; Biomed Engrng.

GIACOBBEE, DEAN T; Montgomery HS; Skillman, NJ; (Y); Am Leg Boys St; Church Yth Grp; Drama Clb; School Musical; School Play; Stage Crew; Off Frsh Cls; Off Jr Cls; Stu Cncl; JV Bsktbl; HOBY Fndtn Sem.

GIALANELLA, FRANK; Livingston HS; Livingston, NJ; (Y); Key Clb; Math Clb; Math Tm; Ski Clb; Stu Cncl; Ice Hcky; Lcrss; Socr; Sftbl; NHS; Comp Sci.

GIAMPETRO, ANDREW; Eastern HS; Voorhees, NJ; (Y); 72/330; Political Wkr; Service Clb; JV Trk; Hon Roll; Jr NHS; Lttr JV Trck 84-85; Pn JV Trck 85-86; Rutgers U; Engnrng.

GIAMPILIS, MARLENA; The Wilson Schl; Succasunna, NJ; (S); Teachers Aide; Yrbk Phtg; Yrbk Stf; Sec Frsh Cls; Pres Soph Cls; Trs Jr Cls; Var Vllybl; Comp Tech.

GIANGERELLI, JANINE; Bloomfield SR HS; Bloomfield, NJ; (Y); Art Clb; FBLA; High Hon Roll; Hon Roll; Outstndng Achvmnt Awd 84-85; Crt Stngrphr.

GIANGERUSO, ROBERT; Lyndhurst HS; Lyndhurst, NJ; (Y); 8/180; Am Leg Boys St; German Clb; Key Clb; Scholastic Bowl; Science Clb; High Hon Roll; Hon Roll; Jr NHS; NHS; Rutgers ST U; Med.

GIANGIORDANO, RICHARD; Shawnee HS; Medford, NJ; (Y); Am Leg Boys St; Math Tm; Rep Frsh Cls; Rep Soph Cls; Im Bsbl; Var L Ftbl; JV Trk; Im Wt Lftg; High Hon Roll; NHS; Sci Team 1st Pl Cnty Physc 86; Police Athltc Leag Street Hcky 85; Pre Med.

GIANNANTONIO, JOE; Palisades Park HS; Palisades Pk, NJ; (Y); Church Yth Grp; Prfct Atten Awd.

GIANNANTONIO, JOHN P; Lenape Valley Regional HS; Netcong, NJ; (Y); Drama Clb; Chorus; Madrigals; School Musical; School Play; Prfct Atten Awd; NJ ST Teen Art Fstvl Wnnr 86; Recmmnded Rutgers Smmr Music 86; Westminster Chrs Coll; Sngr.

GIANNANTONIO, PAUL; Palisades Park JR SR HS; Palisades Pk, NJ; (Y); Var Ftbl; Var Trk; Var Wt Lftg; Stevens Inst Tech; Elect Engr.

GIANNELLA, DAVID; Manchester Regional HS; N Haledon, NJ; (Y); Boy Scts; Camp Fr Inc; Exploring; Stage Crew; Yrbk Stf; Bsbl; Ftbl; Sftbl; Trk; NJ Inst Tech; Chem Engrng.

GIANNETTI, KRISTEN; Wayne Hills HS; Wayne, NJ; (Y); 82/324; Church Yth Grp; Cmnty Wkr; FBLA; Trs GAA; Math Clb; Trs Spanish Clb; Varsity Clb; Stu Cncl; Capt Tennis; Hon Roll; U Of MA-AMHERST; Bus Mngmnt.

GIANNOBILE, JOAN; Holy Family Acad; Bayonne, NJ; (Y); Church Yth Grp; Computer Clb; French Clb; Im JV Bsktbl; Im Vllybl; NEDT Awd; Lawyer.

GIANNUZZI, LINDA; Rutherford HS; Rutherford, NJ; (Y); 57/186; Pep Clb; Spanish Clb; Trk; Vllybl; High Hon Roll; Hon Roll; Bronze Awd For A Aver 85-86; Fairleigh Dickinson U; Accntng.

GIANSANTI, MADELEINE; Morris Catholic HS; Boonton, NJ; (Y); 37/142; Drama Clb; Pres French Clb; FBLA; Natl Beta Clb; Ski Clb; School Musical; Nwsp Rptr; Rep Stu Cncl; Var Cheerleading; Hon Roll; Bus.

GIARDINA, MATTHEW; Chatham Twp SR HS; Chatham, NJ; (Y); Key Clb; Math Clb; Model UN; Band; Im Bsktbl; Hon Roll; Natl Hnr Rl 85-86; SUNY Stonybrook; Psych.

GIARRANTANO, ANNMARIE; Ramapo HS; Wyckoff, NJ; (Y); 13/329; AFS; Pres French Clb; Science Clb; Lit Mag; Rep Frsh Cls; Rep Soph Cls; VP Stu Cncl; JV Socr; Var Sftbl; JV Trk; Merit Awds.

GIBBONS, PATRICK; West Morris Central HS; Long Valley, NJ; (Y); Drama Clb; FBLA; School Musical; School Play; Lit Mag; Seton Hall Cnty Coll; Ed.

GIBBS, ERIKA; Gloucester City JR SR HS; Gloucester, NJ; (Y); Dance Clb; Hosp Aide; Pep Clb; Chorus; School Musical; Yrbk Stf; Rep Frsh Cls; Stu Cncl; Fld Hcky.

GIBBS, KELLIE; Hackettstown HS; Hackettstown, NJ; (Y); 4-H; Key Clb; Q&S; Band; Jazz Band; Nwsp Phtg; Stu Cncl; Trk; Hon Roll; NHS; Law.

GIBBS, LINDA; West Morris Central HS; Long Va Ley, NJ; (Y); Church Yth Grp; Drama Clb; Band; Concert Band; Mrchg Band; School Musical; School Play; Yrbk Rptr; Yrbk Stf; Fash Merch.

GIBBS JR, RUDOLPH P; Rahway HS; Rahway, NJ; (Y); 30/256; English Clb; Band; Church Chor; Mrchg Band; School Musical; Nwsp Ed-Chief; VP Crs Cntry; VP Trk; Hon Roll; NHS; Natl Scholar Fund Negro Stu 85-86; Comp Sci.

GIBERSON, TAMMY; Southern Regional HS; Manahawkin, NJ; (Y); Service Clb; Spanish Clb; Stage Crew; Hon Roll; Ntl Merit Ltr; Advrtsng.

GIBSON, BRIAN; Atlantic Christian Schl; Northfield, NJ; (Y); Church Yth Grp; Teachers Aide; Yrbk Stf; Var Bsbl; Var Bsktbl; Var Capt Socr; Hon Roll; SJCL All Tourn Tm Sccr 82; MIP Sccr 83; Mst Imprvd Stu Jr Cls 85; Messiah Coll; Bus Admin.

GIBSON, DALE; Central Regional HS; Bayville, NJ; (Y); 58/272; Bsbl; Ftbl; Acad Achvt Awd 86; Acctng.

GIBSON, DONALD; Central Regional HS; Bayville, NJ; (Y); 55/256; Varsity Clb; Bsbl; Ftbl.

GIBSON, ELIZABETH ANNE; Bayley Ellard Regional HS; Milton, NJ; (Y); Church Yth Grp; Cmnty Wkr; Debate Tm; 4-H; Math Clb; NFL; Service Clb; Spanish Clb; School Musical; Symp Band; Rogate Awd; Sci.

GIBSON, JODI; Toms River H S South; Beachwood, NJ; (Y); 85/318; Church Yth Grp; Library Aide; Model UN; Spanish Clb; Teachers Aide; Westchester U; Elem Ed.

GIBSON, MELVIN; Camden HS; Camden, NJ; (S); 18/400; Church Yth Grp; Computer Clb; VP JA; Yrbk Phtg; Rep Sr Cls; Var Wrstlng; Dnfth Awd; NHS; Lehigh U; Acctng.

GIBSON, STACEY; Salem HS; Salem, NJ; (Y); Church Yth Grp; DECA; JA; Office Aide; Church Choir; Fld Hcky; Hon Roll; Norfolk ST U; Bus Ed Tchr.

GIDDENS, GAIL; Metuchen HS; Metuchen, NJ; (Y); 78/178; Church Yth Grp; Ski Clb; Band; Church Choir; Concert Band; Mrchg Band; JV Crs Cntry; Var L Trk; Hon Roll; Athle Of Yr 86; The News Tribune All-Cnty Trck Tm 86; Greater Middlesex Conf Div All-Star Tm 86.

GIERCYK, CHRISTINE F; Parsippany HS; Lake Hiawatha, NJ; (Y); Dance Clb; Drama Clb; French Clb; FBLA; School Musical; Variety Show; High Hon Roll; NHS; Church Yth Grp; Intnl Clb; Danc NJ Schl Ballet 85-86; Danc Mary Lou Hales Schl Danc 83-86; Intr Dsgn.

GIERSBACH, ELIZABETH; Jackson Memorial HS; Jackson, NJ; (Y); 4/411; Art Clb; French Clb; PAVAS; Ski Clb; Spanish Clb; SADD; Yrbk Bus Mgr; Yrbk Ed-Chief; Yrbk Phtg; Yrbk Rptr.

GIGLIO, DAWN; Roselle Catholic HS; Union, NJ; (Y); 4/195; Church Yth Grp; Math Tm; School Musical; Lit Mag; High Hon Roll; NHS; Spanish NHS; Poem Publ In Vox Leonis 86; Seton Hall U; Bio.

GIGLIO, MICHAEL; Westfield HS; Westfield, NJ; (Y); Boy Scts; Red Cross Aide; Band; Concert Band; Mrchg Band; Bsbl; Ftbl; Wt Lftg; Wrstlng; Small Engs Awd 84; VA Mltry Inst; Mech Engr.

GILABERT, DENISE; Assaic Valley Regional HS; W Paterson, NJ; (Y); 31/358; Am Leg Aux Girls St; Cmnty Wkr; Key Clb; Science Clb; Off Spanish Clb; Var Capt Gym; Var L Trk; High Hon Roll; Sec NHS; Stu Athlt Mnth Preview Magzn Gymnstcs Trck 86; Sprts Med.

GILBERT, EILEEN; Montclair HS; Bloomfield, NJ; (Y); Church Yth Grp; Drama Clb; Science Clb; Teachers Aide; Chorus; School Play; Stage Crew; Var L Vllybl; Hon Roll; NJ ST Sci Leag Awd 86; Chem.

GILBERT, EVELYN; Red Bank Catholic HS; Tinton Falls, NJ; (Y); Dance Clb; NFL; Orch; School Musical; Nwsp Stf; Yrbk Stf; JV Cheerleading; JV Crs Cntry; NHS; Ntl Merit Ltr; NJ Schlrs Pgm Recpnt 86-87; Engl Awd 83-84.

GILBERT, MICHAEL W; Palmyra HS; Riverton, NJ; (Y); 1/115; Am Leg Boys St; Var Bsbl; Var L Socr; High Hon Roll; NHS; Ntl Merit SF; Val; Computer Clb; Intnl Clb; Key Clb; NJ Govrnrs Schl Sci Drew U 85; Garden ST Distgnshd Schlr 85; NJ Bowl Team 85; Princeton; Engr.

GILBERT, TIMOTHY C; Middletown HS South; Lincroft, NJ; (Y); Cmnty Wkr; Ski Clb; Concert Band; Variety Show; JV Bsbl; JV Var Ftbl; Var Trk; Im Vllybl; Im Wt Lftg; Wrstlng; Mrt Achvt Awd Sci, Spnsh, Algbra, Englsh 83-84; Fnnc.

GILDENBERG, MICHAEL; Highland Park HS; Highland Park, NJ; (Y); Pres Ski Clb; Acpl Chr; Band; Chorus; Concert Band; Mrchg Band; Socr; Trk; Hon Roll; Sccr Div All-Star Tm 85-86.

GILES, NANCY; Belvidere HS; Phillipsburg, NJ; (Y); 26/118; Letterman Clb; Office Aide; Pep Clb; Ski Clb; Varsity Clb; School Play; Yrbk Stf; Rep Stu Cncl; Var L Cheerleading; Hon Roll; DRC All Str Chrldg 2nd Tm 85; Somerset County Coll; Law Enfrc.

GILIBERTI, GEMMA; Rahway SR HS; Rahway, NJ; (Y); Spanish Clb; Chorus; Var Socr; JV Sftbl; JV Swmmng; High Hon Roll; Hon Roll; Spanish NHS.

GILL, GINA; St James HS; Penns Grove, NJ; (S); 1/79; Trs Church Yth Grp; Girl Scts; School Musical; Yrbk Ed-Chief; VP Stu Cncl; Var Tennis; Gov Hon Prg Awd; NHS; Ntl Merit Ltr; Val; Girl Scout Gold Awd 85; George Washington U Engrng Awd 85; Amer Chemical Soc Chem Awd 85; Georgetown U; Bio.

GILL, HOLLIE; Burlington City HS; Edgewater Pk, NJ; (Y); Am Leg Aux Girls St; Cmnty Wkr; Pres Jr Cls; Var Bsktbl; Im Cheerleading; Im Coach Actv; Var Capt Socr; Var Sftbl; Hon Roll; NHS; Guidance Aid 85-86; Learning Pgm 83-84.

GILL, KATHLEEN; Mary Help Of Christians Acad; Mahwah, NJ; (S); 11/69; NFL; Yrbk Stf; VP Sr Cls; Rep Stu Cncl; Im Bsktbl; JV Var Vllybl; Hon Roll; NHS; Chmstry Awd 85; Ithaca Coll; Physcl Thrpst.

GILL, NISHAT; North Brunswick Township HS; N Brunswick, NJ; (Y); Debate Tm; Drama Clb; French Clb; Key Clb; Model UN; Pres Chorus; School Musical; Swing Chorus; Rep Stu Cncl; Hon Roll; Hnrd NY All-ST Choir 85; Rutgers Coll; Pre-Law.

GILLEECE, DONNA; Roselle Catholic HS; Union, NJ; (Y); Church Yth Grp; Cmnty Wkr; Dance Clb; Drama Clb; Girl Scts; School Musical; Lit Mag; High Hon Roll; Hon Roll; NHS; 3rd Pl Lyrcl Jazz Comptn 86; Fshn Merch.

GILLESPIE, BRIAN K; Bayonne HS; Bayonne, NJ; (Y); Am Leg Boys St; Boy Scts; Exploring; Intnl Clb; Math Tm; School Musical; Rep Stu Cncl; Var Swmmng; High Hon Roll; Jr NHS.

GILLESPIE, CHRISTIAN; River Dell HS; River Edge, NJ; (Y); 21/214; Math Tm; Nwsp Ed-Chief; Var Ftbl; Var Trk; Im Vllybl; Im Wt Lftg; Hon Roll; Ntl Merit Ltr; Pres Schlr; Church Yth Grp; $1000 PTO Schlrshp 86; Rutgers Clg.

GILLESPIE, CHRISTINE; Saint John Vianney HS; Matawan, NJ; (Y); Math Tm; Ski Clb; School Play; Cheerleading; Powder Puff Ftbl; JV Socr; Hon Roll.

GILLESPIE, JOHN A; Hammonton HS; Hammonton, NJ; (Y); 3/191; Am Leg Boys St; Boy Scts; Mrchg Band; Stu Cncl; High Hon Roll; NCTE Awd; NHS; Acdmc Excllnc Awd 85-86; NJ Math Leag Merit Awd 86; NJ Bar Assn Mck Trl Prtcpnt 86; Med.

GILLESPIE, MEGAN; James Caldwell HS; W Caldwell, NJ; (Y); Church Yth Grp; French Clb; Key Clb; JV Bsktbl; Hon Roll; Rlgn Awd Knghts Clmbs 83.

GILLIAM, DAN; Lower Cape May Regional HS; N Cape May, NJ; (Y); 21/310; Key Clb; Band; Concert Band; Drm Mjr(t); Jazz Band; Mrchg Band; Orch; Pep Band; School Musical; School Play; Gvrnrs Schl Perf Arts Trntn ST Coll 85-86; Cape May Cnty Jazz Bnd 83-86; All Cape May Cnty Cncrt Bnd; Berkley Coll Of Music; Msc Tchr.

GILLIARD, DARREL; Hoboken HS; Hoboken, NJ; (Y); Chess Clb; Computer Clb; English Clb; SADD; Yrbk Stf; Ftbl; Wt Lftg; Hnrd Schl Papr Wrtg Poem 86; Rooke Yr Ftbl 86; Hnrd Div All Cnty Ftbl 86; Comp Prgrmr.

GILLIGAN, THOMAS W; Glen Rock SR HS; Glen Rock, NJ; (Y); 2/126; Boy Scts; Capt Debate Tm; Var L Crs Cntry; Var L Trk; High Hon Roll; NHS; Ntl Merit Ltr; Sal; St Schlr; Eagle Scout 86; U S Mltry Acad; Engrng.

GILLIS, SUZANNE L; Washington Township HS; Philadelphia, PA; (Y); Hon Roll; JC Awd.

GILLMAN, HELEN A; Buena Regional HS; Buena, NJ; (Y); 50/151; Cmnty Wkr; Hosp Aide; Ed Nwsp Rptr; Yrbk Rptr; Capt Crs Cntry; Capt Trk; Bond Comm Svc Grp 86; Atlantic Cty Press Tour Explr Post 86; Physcl Ftns Clb Treas 84; Gloucester CC; Jrnlsm.

GILMARTIN, SHAWN; Toms River East HS; Toms River, NJ; (Y); Pres Exploring; 4-H; Sec German Clb; Intnl Clb; SADD; Bowling; Vet.

GILMORE, ELIZABETH; Highland Regional HS; Erial, NJ; (Y); Church Yth Grp; 4-H; FNA; Red Cross Aide; Science Clb; SADD; Band; Concert Band; Drm & Bgl; Jazz Band; PA U; Vet.

GIMON, PATRICIA; Clifton HS; Clifton, NJ; (Y); 92/637; Sec Church Yth Grp; German Clb; SADD; Chorus; Church Choir; Color Guard; Madrigals; JV Crs Cntry; JV Sftbl; Jr NHS; Chem.

GINESTAR, REBECCA; Roselle Park HS; Roselle Pk, NJ; (Y); Drama Clb; French Clb; Pep Clb; Spanish Clb; Speech Tm; Chorus; School Musical; Nwsp Rptr; Nwsp Stf; Rep Frsh Cls; Prfct Attndnc Awd 83; Bst Wrtr Awd 80; Union Cnty Coll; Plc Offcr.

GINGELL, CATHY; Pennsauken HS; Pennsauken, NJ; (Y); 20/368; Math Clb; Spanish Clb; Chorus; Im Church Yth Grp8; Cit Awd; Hon Roll; NHS; Spanish NHS; Pres Ftns Awd; Top 20; Stockton; Spnsh.

GINOUVES, CHRISTINE; Summit HS; Summit, NJ; (Y); GAA; Model UN; Ski Clb; Spanish Clb; Varsity Clb; Band; Church Choir; Orch; School Musical; Yrbk Phtg; Math.

GINSBERG, SUSAN; Piscataway HS; Piscataway, NJ; (Y); 6/519; Mathletes; Radio Clb; Temple Yth Grp; Varsity Clb; Tennis; High Hon Roll; NHS; St Schlr; Voice Dem Awd; Co-Cptn Vrsty Grls Tns; Ststcn, Co-Mgr Boys Tns; Rutghers U; Psychlgy.

GINSBURG, ADAM; Ewing HS; Trenton, NJ; (Y); 4/306; Am Leg Boys St; Computer Clb; Intnl Clb; Key Clb; Math Tm; Quiz Bowl; Scholastic Bowl; Rep Soph Cls; Rep Jr Cls; Trs Sr Cls; Spn Linguistic Comptn Awd 85; Columbia U; Biomed Engrng.

GINSBURG, ILENE; Lakewood HS; Lakewood, NJ; (Y); 51/297; English Clb; Band; Mrchg Band; Prfct Atten Awd; Mrchng Band Ltr 86; Ocean County Coll.

GINSBURG, LYNN; East Brunswick HS; Milltown, NJ; (Y); DECA; Hosp Aide; Model UN; Rtgrs; Spec Ed Tchr.

GIOIOSO, PAUL M; West Essex HS; Fairfield, NJ; (Y); Am Leg Boys St; Capt Ftbl; Wt Lftg; High Hon Roll; Mech Engr.

GIONIS, MICHAEL; Parsippany HS; Parsippany, NJ; (Y); Boy Scts; Teachers Aide; Socr; Amer Cmnty Schls Schlrshp-Athens Greece 81-82; Real Est.

GIORDANO, CHRISTINA; Paul VI HS; Laurel Springs, NJ; (Y); Hon Roll; Bus Mgmt.

GIORGIANNI, NICK; St James HS; Gibbstown, NJ; (Y); 24/84; Exploring; JV Bsbl; Var Ftbl; JV Golf; Var Capt Wrstlng; Hon Roll; Med.

GIOVACCO, TRICIA; Clifton HS; Clifton, NJ; (Y); Am Leg Aux Girls St; Drama Clb; French Clb; Girl Scts; Drm Mjr(t); Mgr(s); Stat Socr; Twrlr; Wrstlng; French Hon Soc; Intl Rltns.

GIOVETIS, PETE; Cherokee HS; Atco, NJ; (Y); Am Leg Boys St; Capt Debate Tm; German Clb; Trs Frsh Cls; Trs Soph Cls; Trs Jr Cls; Trs Sr Cls; Var JV Ftbl; Var JV Trk; Wt Lftg; Acclrtd Hnrs Crs; Law.

GIOVINAZZI, CONNIE A; Buena Regional HS; Vineland, NJ; (Y); Pep Clb; Pres Varsity Clb; Chorus; Yrbk Stf; Rep Sr Cls; Rep Stu Cncl; Capt Crs Cntry; Capt Trk; Hon Roll; Gloucester Cnty Coll; Spec Ed.

GIRARD, GEOFF; Cherry Hill H S West; Cherry Hill, NJ; (Y); Art Clb; Chess Clb; VP PAVAS; School Play; Nwsp Rptr; Nwsp Stf; Lit Mag; JV Var Trk; Boy Scts; Cmnty Wkr; Cretv Wrtng Cntst Wnnr 83-86; WA Coll; Engl.

GIRARDI, ELLEN; Buena Regional HS; Landisville, NJ; (S); 14/191; Cmnty Wkr; Pep Clb; Ski Clb; Sec Varsity Clb; School Play; Variety Show; Rep Frsh Cls; VP Jr Cls; VP Sr Cls; Rep Stu Cncl; Hmcmng Crt 85-86; Jr Prom Queen 85; Bus Mgt.

GIRARDOT, DAVID A; Cinnaminson HS; Cinnaminson, NJ; (Y); Am Leg Boys St; Pres Church Yth Grp; Rep Frsh Cls; Rep Soph Cls; Rep Jr Cls; Rep Stu Cncl; JV Socr; JV Trk; Hon Roll; NHS.

GIRAUD, BETSY; Perth Amboy HS; Perth Amboy, NJ; (Y); French Clb; ROTC; Drill Tm; Twrlr; High Hon Roll; Hon Roll; Rockers; Lwyr.

GIRSHON, TODD; East Brunswick HS; E Brunswick, NJ; (Y); Debate Tm; Model UN; Pres Spanish Clb; Variety Show; Nwsp Bus Mgr; Rep Stu Cncl; JV Socr; NHS; Pres Spanish NHS; NE Conf Tchng Frg Lang Awd Excllnce Spn 86; Cornell Tradition Honorary Fellowshp 86-87; Cornell U; Indstrl Rltns.

GIRTEN, EILEEN; Msgr Donovan HS; Brant Beach, NJ; (Y); 26/243; Am Leg Aux Girls St; Church Yth Grp; Computer Clb; Hon Roll; NHS; Spnsh Awd 86; Gentc Engrng.

GITTENS, SHARON; Pemberton High HS; Pemberton, NJ; (Y); 9/417; Am Leg Aux Girls St; Cmnty Wkr; FBLA; Bsktbl; Sftbl; Trk; Hon Roll; NHS; Acctng.

GIULIANO, CONCETTA; Vineland SR HS; Vineland, NJ; (Y); 7/734; Cmnty Wkr; Exploring; Key Clb; Orch; Symp Band; Rep Frsh Cls; Rep Jr Cls; Stu Cncl; High Hon Roll; NHS; Smmr Hopwood Schlrshp Lynchburg Coll 86; La Salle U; Med.

GIULIANO, JILL; Middlesex HS; Middlesex, NJ; (Y); 22/160; French Clb; Ski Clb; Nwsp Stf; JV Crs Cntry; JV Trk; Lang.

GIUMETTI, MIKE; Woodstown HS; Woodstown, NJ; (Y); Boy Scts; French Clb; Nwsp Rptr; Hon Roll; SAR Awd; VFW Awd; Im Bsktbl; Var Swmmng; Sci Fair Awds At WHS Glassboro ST & Del Val Sci Fair 85-86; Eagle Scout In Trp 38 Of Woodstown 86; Pre Law.

GIUNCO, MARY; Wall HS; Wall, NJ; (S); 22/350; Church Yth Grp; Ski Clb; Band; Concert Band; Mrchg Band; School Musical; High Hon Roll; Hon Roll; NHS; Ntl Merit Ltr; Bus.

GLADDEN, ROBERT; Westfield HS; Westfield, NJ; (Y); 4-H; Y-Teens; Chorus; Church Choir; Im L Bsbl; Var L Bsktbl; Im L Ftbl; Var L Trk; Im Vllybl; JV Var Wt Lftg; Presdntl Physcl Ftns Awd Wnnr 86; Dr Hubert Humphy Merit Awd Wnnr 86.

GLADDIS, JACQUELINE; Mount St Mary Acad; Rahway, NJ; (Y); 6/85; Pres French Clb; Yrbk Stf; Lit Mag; Rep Soph Cls; Rep Sr Cls; French Hon Soc; Hon Roll; Jr NHS; Trs NHS; St Schlr; Teagle Fdntn Schlrshp 86; Giftd/Talntd Pgm 85-86; Natl Piano Playng Audtns 82-83; U Of VT; Law.

GLASER, LESSIE; Cinnaminson HS; Cinna, NJ; (Y); Dance Clb; JA; SADD; Band; Concert Band; Mrchg Band; Var Bowling; Hon Roll; Chef.

GLASS, ADAM; Middletown South HS; Middletown, NJ; (Y); Stage Crew; Variety Show; Drama Clb; German Clb; ROTC; SADD; Off Sr Cls; Stu Cncl; Swmmng; Hon Roll; Pilot.

GLASS, COLLEENA; Central Regional HS; Bayville, NJ; (Y); Political Wkr; Chorus; Nwsp Rptr; Nwsp Sprt Ed; JV Bsktbl; Var Fld Hcky; JV Sftbl; Var Trk; Var High Hon Roll; Var Hon Roll; Med.

GLEASON, TRACY; Middletown High School South; Middletown, NJ; (S); 1/436; Am Leg Aux Girls St; Church Yth Grp; Concert Band; Orch; Symp Band; Elks Awd; French Hon Soc; Gov Hon Prg Awd; NHS; Ntl Merit SF; NJ Distngsd Schlr 85-86; Scty Of Distngshd Amer H S Stu 86; Psych.

GLEE, BERNARD; West Side HS; Newark, NJ; (Y); 97/239; Pres Church Yth Grp; Co-Capt Debate Tm; Pres Church Choir; Sec Trs Stu Cncl; Bsbl; Hon Roll; Boy Scts; Computer Clb; Library Aide; Speech Tm; Atten Awd 84-85; Alliance Coll; Bus Admin.

GLEMAN, MEG; Toms River HS South; Beachwood, NJ; (Y); Stage Crew; Rep Frsh Cls; Rep Soph Cls; Trs Jr Cls; VP Sr Cls; Stu Cncl; JV Bsktbl; Var Fld Hcky; Stat Ice Hcky; Var Socr.

GLEMSER, MICHELLE; Central Jersey Christian Schl; Asbury Park, NJ; (S); 6/18; Band; Chorus; Rep Sr Cls; Stu Cncl; Var Bsktbl; Var Cheerleading; Co-Capt Var Socr; Var Sftbl; NHS; High Hon Roll; Pre Cep Awd 85; Bst Def Plyr 84; Christn Char Awd 85; Lwyr.

GLEN, JAMES; Bridgewater-Raritan West HS; Bridgewater, NJ; (Y); Math Tm; Capt Var Bsbl; Bowling; Var L Socr; High Hon Roll; Hon Roll; Jr NHS; NHS; St Schlr; 1st Ntl Bnk Cntrl Jersey Schlrshp 86; Pres Acad Ftns Awd 86; Rutgers Coll; Bus Admin.

GLENCAMP JR, TIMOTHY; Plainfield HS; Plainfield, NJ; (Y); Mathletes; Math Clb; Math Tm; Concert Band; Jazz Band; Mrchg Band; Nwsp Stf; High Hon Roll; Jr NHS; Montclair ST Coll; Math.

GLENN, CHRISSY; Point Pleasant Borough HS; Point Pleasant, NJ; (S); 8/240; Varsity Clb; Var Bsktbl; Var Fld Hcky; Var Socr; High Hon Roll; Hon Roll; Rutgers.

GLENN, TOKAR ELIZABETH; Southern Regional HS; Beach Haven, NJ; (Y); School Play; Soph Cls; Jr Cls; Sr Cls; Stu Cncl; Powder Puff Ftbl; Trk; High Hon Roll; NHS; Dlg Nj Ntl Stu Cncl Cnvntn 86.

GLEYZER, JANETTE; New Milford HS; New Milford, NJ; (Y); 17/140; Dance Clb; Drama Clb; Concert Band; School Musical; School Play; Hon Roll; UCLA; Prfrmng Arts.

GLICK, GRETCHEN; Cinnaminson HS; Cinna, NJ; (Y); German Clb; Key Clb; Spanish Clb; SADD; Orch; School Musical; JV Fld Hcky; Var Swmmng; Vllybl; Hon Roll; Grphcs Hnrs 83; 3 Yr Vrsty Swmmr 83-86; Bio.

GLICK, JAY; East Brunswick HS; E Brunswick, NJ; (Y); Debate Tm; Drama Clb; German Clb; Model UN; Chorus; School Musical; School Play; High Hon Roll; Ntl Merit SF.

GLICK, SHANAH D; Cherry Hill HS East; Cherry Hill, NJ; (Y); Camera Clb; PAVAS; Sec Temple Yth Grp; Yrbk Ed-Chief; Yrbk Phtg; High Hon Roll; NCTE Awd; Ntl Merit Schol; NJ Schlrs Pgm 85; JFK Hosp Schlrs Pgm 85-86.

GLICKMAN, SHERRY L; Northern Valley Old Tappan HS; Harrington Park, NJ; (Y); 3/313; VP AFS; Dance Clb; Ski Clb; School Musical; School Play; Nwsp Ed-Chief; Rep Stu Cncl; JV Tennis; High Hon Roll; NHS; Acad Decath Tm 85-86; Sci Jrnlsm.

GLIETZ, ROBERT; Henry Hudson Regional HS; Atlantic Hlds, NJ; (Y); 6/73; Capt Pres Exploring; Band; Yrbk Stf; Pres Sr Cls; Stu Cncl; Var L Bsktbl; JV Socr; Cit Awd; Hon Roll; Lion Awd; Johnson & Wales Coll Acad Schlrshp 86; Silver Congrssnl Awd 86; US Army Resrv Schlr Athlt Awd 86; Johnson & Wales Coll; Htl Mgmt.

GLINKIN, BRUCE; Clifton HS; Clifton, NJ; (Y); 28/530; Am Leg Boys St; Boys Clb Am; Boy Scts; Camera Clb; Sec German Clb; Math Clb; Var Crs Cntry; JV Lcrss; JV Trk; Hon Roll; Rtgrs Coll Of Engrng; Elec Engr.

GLOBIS, CATHERINE; Jackson Memorial HS; Jackson, NJ; (Y); 55/424; Art Clb; Library Aide; Office Aide; PAVAS; Science Clb; Yrbk Phtg; Var Trk; High Hon Roll; Hon Roll; San Francisco Art Inst; Photo.

GLOVER, JIMMY; Metuchen HS; Metuchen, NJ; (Y); 26/165; DECA; FBLA; Ski Clb; Var Capt Bsktbl; Var Capt Socr; Trk; Hon Roll; NHS; MIP Sccr 85-86; 2nd Pl Cntrl Jersey Gnrl Mktng DECA 83-84; UCLA.

GLOVER, TROY; East Orange HS; Irvington, NJ; (S); 60/430; Yrbk Stf; Var Capt Bsktbl; Hon Roll; NHS; Bus Adm.

GLOWIENKA, CYNTHIA; Ocean City HS; Ocean City, NJ; (Y); 28/292; Drama Clb; French Clb; School Play; Nwsp Stf; Yrbk Stf; Hon Roll; Ntl Merit Ltr; Newcomers Clb Treas 86; Usaf Smmr Sci Sem 86; Prom Queen Court 86; Jrnlsm.

GLUECK, RICHRD A; West Milford Township HS; W Milford, NJ; (Y); 52/350; Am Leg Boys St; Church Yth Grp; Drama Clb; Stat Bsktbl; Var Score Keeper; JV Tennis; High Hon Roll; Hon Roll; Jr NHS; NHS; William Paterson Clg.

GLYNN, CATHY; Cresskill HS; Cresskill, NJ; (Y); 45/123; Am Leg Aux Girls St; Band; Chorus; Concert Band; Var Capt Bsktbl; Var Capt Vllybl; Prfct Atten Awd; Girl Scts; HS Athltc Bstrs Schlrshp 86; Chptr Of Unico Ntl Schlrshp 86; 11 Vrsty Sprts Ltrs 86; Dominican Coll Blauvelt; Nrsng.

GLYNN, KEN; Chatham Township HS; Chatham, NJ; (Y); 28/128; Boy Scts; Church Yth Grp; Computer Clb; Math Clb; Math Tm; Varsity Clb; JV Var Socr; Hon Roll; NHS; Pres Schlr; Lehigh U; Comp Sci.

GLYNN, PAMELA; Union Catholic Regional HS; Morganville, NJ; (Y); 33/332; Cmnty Wkr; Service Clb; Spanish Clb; Mgr(s); Hon Roll; Catholic Yth Orgnztn Pres 12; Parish Cncl Yth Rep; Fmly Yth Mass; Douglass Coll.

GLYNN, STACEY; Bridgewater East HS; Bridgewater, NJ; (Y); Intnl Clb; Ski Clb; Spanish Clb; SADD; Concert Band; Drill Tm; Drm & Bgl; Mrchg Band; Yrbk Stf; Hon Roll; Med Tech.

GNATIUK, BARBARA; Abraham Clark HS; Roselle, NJ; (S); 10/189; Science Clb; Band; Chorus; Nwsp Stf; Tennis; High Hon Roll; NHS; Acctg.

GNATOWSKI, STACEY; Parsippany HS; Parsippany, NJ; (Y); Am Leg Aux Girls St; Dance Clb; French Clb; Intnl Clb; Pres Sec Chorus; Jazz Band; School Musical; Swing Chorus; Rep Jr Cls; NHS; Rlgs Ed Tchr 83-86; Bst Soloist HS Jazz Fstvl 86; Prfrmng Arts.

GODFREY, ERIK; Paulsboro HS; Gibbstown, NJ; (Y); 5/150; JV Bsbl; Var Ftbl; Im Wt Lftg; JV Var Wrstlng; Hon Roll; Prfct Atten Awd; Ftbl Awds 84; Wrestlng Awds 83-86; Comptrs.

GODINHO, SUSAN; Queen Of Peace HS; Kearny, NJ; (S); 2/250; Model UN; Pres Service Clb; School Musical; School Play; Ed Nwsp Stf; Rep Stu Cncl; Gov Hon Prg Awd; NHS; Ntl Merit Ltr; SR Immaculate Heart Schlrshp 85-86; Rutgers U Schlr 85; Cmmnctns.

GODISH, ANN; Holy Family Acad; Bayonne, NJ; (Y); 21/129; Lit Mag; Hon Roll; St Francis Schl Nrsng; Nrsng.

GODOWN JR, ARTHUR R; South Hunterdon Regional HS; Lambertville, NJ; (Y); 35/92; Cmnty Wkr; FFA; Red Cross Aide; Varsity Clb; Stage Crew; Capt L Ftbl; Im Wt Lftg; JV Wrstlng; Natl Athltc Mrt Endrsmnt Svcs 86; Lmbrtvlle Hvy Rscu Tm Wrld Chmpns 84-86.

GODOWN, CHARLES; South Hunterdon Regional HS; Lambertville, NJ; (Y); 37/73; FFA; Red Cross Aide; Varsity Clb; JV Ftbl; Var Golf; Wt Lftg; Var Wrstlng; Mercer Cnty Voc Schl; Plumber.

GOELZER, KATHRYN ANN; Millville SR HS; Millville, NJ; (Y); Exploring; FNA; Hosp Aide; Nwsp Rptr; Trs Stu Cncl; Bowling; NHS; Hghst GPA Pathlgy 86; Sci Scholar 86; Cumberland Cnty Coll; RN.

GOERKE, CHRISTINE; Union Catholic Regional HS; Hillside, NJ; (Y); 168/365; Ski Clb; SADD; JV Bowling; Var Mgr(s); Union County Coll; Pltcl Sci.

GOETZE, NEIL; Shore Regional HS; Sea Bright, NJ; (Y); ROTC; Var Ftbl; Wt Lftg; Hon Roll; Prfct Atten Awd; Multi-Co Drafting Cont Schl Rep 86; Engrng.

GOFF JR, MICHAEL J; Woodstown HS; Alloway, NJ; (Y); Accntng.

GOHMAN, KELLY; West Morris Central HS; Long Valley, NJ; (Y); Church Yth Grp; Varsity Clb; JV Bsktbl; JV Ftbl; Var Capt Trk; Pre Med.

GOLBEK, KIM; Pompton Lakes HS; Pompton Lakes, NJ; (Y); GAA; Girl Scts; Spanish Clb; Orch; Nwsp Stf; Var Gym; Mgr(s); Grl Sct Gld Awd; Peer Cnslr; Comm.

GOLD, JENNIFER ANNE; Hunterdon Central HS; Flemington, NJ; (Y); 168/552; Intnl Clb; Ski Clb; SADD; Rep Stu Cncl; NHS; Political Wkr; Varsity Clb; School Musical; School Play; Variety Show; Coachs Awd Chrctr, Ldrshp & Svc 84; Prsdntl Physcl Ftnss Awd 84&85; Smrst Vlly YMCA Ntl Tm 85&86; Boston U.

GOLD, JOHN E; Cherry Hill H S East; Cherry Hill, NJ; (Y); 136/680; Church Yth Grp; FCA; Nwsp Rptr; Rep Stu Cncl; Var Bsbl; Im Ftbl; Var Gym; Var Trk; High Hon Roll; Ntl Merit SF; Pres Afro-Amer Clb 85-86; Elec Engrng.

GOLD, MELISSA; Pascack Valley HS; River Vale, NJ; (Y); 18/260; Cmnty Wkr; Chorus; Madrigals; School Musical; Trs Jr Cls; Trs Stu Cncl; Capt Trk; Cit Awd; Hon Roll; Trs NHS; 1st Prz Frnsc Trnmnt Adv Frnch Skt 84; Trinity Coll Hartford; Bus.

GOLDACKER, JENNIFER; Southern Regional HS; Manahawkin, NJ; (Y); Dance Clb; Hosp Aide; Red Cross Aide; Band; High Hon Roll; Hon Roll; NHS; Prfct Atten Awd; Spanish Clb; Concert Band; Bnd Stf Awd 85; Accntng.

GOLDAY, DAVID CHRISTOPHER; Ocean City HS; Ocean City, NJ; (Y); Drama Clb; Sec Latin Clb; Math Clb; Sec SADD; Trs Chorus; School Musical; Trs Soph Cls; Trs Jr Cls; Trs Sr Cls; Rep Stu Cncl; Elm Ed.

GOLDBERG, AMIE; Cherry Hill HS West; Cherry Hill, NJ; (Y); Aud/Vis; Cmnty Wkr; Intnl Clb; Spanish Clb; SADD; Yrbk Stf; Rep Frsh Cls; Rep Soph Cls; Stu Cncl; Hon Roll.

GOLDBERG, LORI; John P Stevens HS; Edison, NJ; (Y); 50/478; Cmnty Wkr; Drama Clb; Hosp Aide; Science Clb; Spanish Clb; Acpl Chr; Flag Corp; Yrbk Rptr; Cit Awd; Hon Roll; Edison Dem Assoc Awd 86; Syracus U; Law.

GOLDBERG, SCOT; Bayonne HS; Bayonne, NJ; (Y); 30/370; Computer Clb; Rep Jr Cls; Rep Stu Cncl; JV Crs Cntry; JV Trk; Im Wt Lftg; High Hon Roll; Hon Roll; NHS; Pres Schlr; Pre-Med.

GOLDBERG, SCOTT M; James Calswell HS; W Caldwell, NJ; (Y); Key Clb; Band; Concert Band; Jazz Band; Nwsp Phtg; Nwsp Rptr; Yrbk Phtg; Yrbk Stf; Jr Cls; Yrbk Stff Layout Editor; Yrbk Photo; Key Clb; Chrch Yth Grp; Fr Clb; Schl Play Actor; SR & JR Stu Cncl; Law.

GOLDELMAN, ALEX; Jonathan Dayton Regional HS; Springfield, NJ; (Y); 1/232; Am Leg Boys St; Computer Clb; Jazz Band; Lit Mag; French Hon Soc; High Hon Roll; NHS; Opt Clb Awd; Rutgers Scholar 86; Intl Affairs.

GOLDEN JR, ALFRED JAMES; Red Bank Catholic HS; Colts Neck, NJ; (Y); Cmnty Wkr; Rep Jr Cls; Pres Sr Cls; Var Bsktbl; Var Capt Ftbl; Im Wt Lftg; Hon Roll; Law.

GOLDEN, EILEEN; Cranford HS; Cranford, NJ; (Y); 40/275; FBLA; Math Clb; Office Aide; Nwsp Rptr; Sftbl; Stat Wrstlng; Hon Roll; U Of NC-CHAPEL Hill; Math.

GOLDEN, LARISSA; Bayley-Ellard HS; Morris Plains, NJ; (Y); 8/76; Church Yth Grp; Model UN; Service Clb; Church Choir; School Musical; Nwsp Ed-Chief; Yrbk Bus Mgr; Lit Mag; Cheerleading; Ntl Merit Ltr; 1st Pl Diocesan Essay Cmptn 84; Undrstndg Amer Bus Semnr 85; Creatv Wrtg.

GOLDEN, RICH; Delsea Regional HS; Glassboro, NJ; (Y); Am Leg Boys St; Nwsp Ed-Chief; Nwsp Sprt Ed; Yrbk Stf; Pres Frsh Cls; Sec Stu Cncl; Socr; High Hon Roll; Hon Roll; VP NHS; IN U; Law.

GOLDEN, SHERRI; Bishop George Ahr HS; S Plainfield, NJ; (Y); Church Yth Grp; Ski Clb; Pres Frsh Cls; Cheerleading; Hon Roll; Drill Tm; Nwsp Rptr; Pom Pon; Stockton; Paralgl.

GOLDFARB, ERIC; Hightstown HS; E Windsor, NJ; (Y); Cmnty Wkr; FBLA; Ski Clb; Temple Yth Grp; Im Lcrss; JV Trk; JV Wrstlng; Bus Adm.

GOLDMAN, ERIC; Governor Livingston Reg HS; Berkeley Hts, NJ; (Y); 3/194; Drama Clb; JCL; Latin Clb; Math Clb; Capt Quiz Bowl; Science Clb; Ski Clb; Acpl Chr; Band; Jazz Band; Teagle Fndtn Schlrshp 86; NJ Clsscl Leag Awd 86; Garden St Dstngshd Schlr 85; Hamilton Coll.

GOLDMAN, MICHELE; Hanover Park HS; East Hanover, NJ; (Y); 20/279; Rptr 4-H; Sec French Clb; Chorus; Flag Corp; Rptr Lit Mag; Hon Roll; NHS; Library Aide; Quiz Bowl; 4-H Awd; IFYE Netherlands 85; Intl Bus.

GOLDMAN, STEVEN; Fairlawn HS; Fair Lawn, NJ; (Y); 11/340; Am Leg Boys St; Capt Computer Clb; Ski Clb; Jr Cls; Ice Hcky; Capt Socr; Tennis; NHS; HOBY Awd 85; Natl Title Comp 84; Brown; Bus.

GOLDMAN, STEVEN D; Pequannock Township HS; Pompton Plains, NJ; (Y); 15/231; Am Leg Boys St; Pres Chess Clb; Mathletes; Quiz Bowl; Pres Temple Yth Grp; Nwsp Rptr; Var L Tennis; Hon Roll; NHS; Hofstra U; Brdcstng.

GOLDNER, SCOTT; Matawan Regional HS; Aberdeen, NJ; (S); 31/320; Drama Clb; Math Clb; Math Tm; Temple Yth Grp; Chorus; School Musical; School Play; Stage Crew; Hon Roll; Advrtsng.

GOLDRICK, CHRIS; Belleville HS; Belleville, NJ; (Y); Boy Scts; Cmnty Wkr; Key Clb; Orch; Rep Stu Cncl; Bsktbl; Socr; High Hon Roll; NHS; Ntl Merit Ltr; Fnlst Gov Schl Math & Sci 86; Elec Engr.

GOLDSBOROUGH, NICOLE; Bridgeton SR HS; Bridgeton, NJ; (Y); Church Yth Grp; FNA; Church Choir; Color Guard; Flag Corp; Mrchg Band; High Hon Roll; Cmnty Wkr; 4-H; Girl Scts; HOSA Wd 86; HOSA Nrsng Comptn 1st Pl Awd 85; HOSA Nrsng Comptn 2nd Lev 5th Pl Awd 86; RN.

GOLDSMITH, JEFF; Brick Township HS; Brick, NJ; (Y); 9/465; Boy Scts; Pres Exploring; Math Tm; Service Clb; Teachers Aide; JV Bsktbl; High Hon Roll; Eagle Sct BSA 85; Ordr Of Arrow Chf Elect 86; Law.

GOLDSTEIN, ERIC; Mt Olive HS; Flanders, NJ; (Y); AFS; Computer Clb; Tennis; Mst Dedicated Ten Plyr Awd 83-84; Bus.

GOLDSTEIN, MADELAINE; Hightstown HS; East Windsor, NJ; (Y); Cmnty Wkr; Service Clb; Band; Concert Band; Mrchg Band; High Hon Roll; Hon Roll; Teen Arts Fstvl 85-86; Fine Arts.

GOLDSTEIN, ROB; Delran HS; Delran, NJ; (Y); 14/207; Am Leg Boys St; Trs FBLA; Stage Crew; Nwsp Rptr; Ed Yrbk Stf; Rep Soph Cls; Rep Jr Cls; Stu Cncl; Hon Roll; NHS; Principles List 84-85; Interact Clb 84-85; Clss Partcptn 84-86; Bus Ed.

GOLDSTEIN, STACI; Paramus HS; Paramus, NJ; (Y); Art Clb; GAA; Varsity Clb; Var Capt Bsktbl; Im Powder Puff Ftbl; Var L Sftbl; JV Vllybl; Itln Hon Soc 83; AllNNJIL Sftbl Tm 85 & 86; All Bergen Sftbl Tm 86; U DE; Phys Ther.

GOLEMBESKI, CORTLYN E; Central Regional HS; Seaside Park, NJ; (Y); 3/250; Am Leg Aux Girls St; Intnl Clb; Ski Clb; Spanish Clb; Varsity Clb; Nwsp Ed-Chief; Stu Cncl; Capt Fld Hcky; NHS; Spanish NHS; Sara C Merrck Spnsh Schlrshp 85; William Smith Coll; Intl Bus.

GOLHAR, ATUL; Hillsborough HS; Bellemead, NJ; (Y); 78/300; Science Clb; Ski Clb; Socr; Hnrbl Ment All Ctrl Jersey Soccer Tm 85-86; 2nd Tm All Conf 85-86; Comet Halley Bushnell Hry Awd Exc; Rutgers Coll; Bus.

GOLIKERI, SARITA; Northern Valley Regional HS; Old Tappan, NJ; (Y); 30/282; Hosp Aide; Intnl Clb; Library Aide; Model UN; Orch; Nwsp Ed-Chief; Yrbk Stf; Lit Mag; NHS; Voice Dem Awd; Voice Democrcy 85; Med.

GOLIN, KEITH; Cherry Hill West HS; Cherry Hill, NJ; (Y); Temple Yth Grp; Frsh Cls; Soph Cls; Stu Cncl; Badmtn; Stat Fld Hcky; Wrstlng; Hon Roll; Sports Med.

GOLLIDAY, DANIELLE; Bridgewater-Raritan East HS; Bridgewater, NJ; (Y); School Play; Sec Frsh Cls; Sec Soph Cls; Sec Jr Cls; Sec Sr Cls; Rep Stu Cncl; Var Capt Gym; High Hon Roll; NHS; French Clb; Prncpls Cncl 83-85; Girls ST Rep 86; Op Entrp 86; Ecnmcs.

GOLLOGLY, GAYLE; Manchester Township HS; Largo, FL; (S); 58/198; JA; Pep Clb; Spanish Clb; SADD; Nwsp Stf; Lit Mag; Bsktbl; Cheerleading; Fld Hcky; Sftbl; MVP Vrsty Sftbl 83; MIP Vrsty Fld Hcky 85; Engl Stu Mnth Nov 85; St Petersburg JC; Comm Major.

GOLOMBEK, AMY; Scotch Plains Fanwood HS; Scotch Pl, NJ; (Y); Church Yth Grp; Key Clb; SADD; Nwsp Rptr; Tennis; Spanish NHS.

GOLUB, KAREN; Matawan Regional HS; Aberdeen, NJ; (Y); 87/348; Hosp Aide; Office Aide; SADD; Temple Yth Grp; Off Soph Cls; Off Jr Cls.

GOLUBIESKI, KAREN MARIE; Oak Knoll HS; Murray Hill, NJ; (Y); Art Clb; Church Yth Grp; Key Clb; Office Aide; PAVAS; Service Clb; Teachers Aide; Stage Crew; Nwsp Stf; Yrbk Stf; Schl Art Awd 85; Svc Awd For Hrs Of Comm Work 84-86; Rep NJ ST Tenn Arts Fest 85.

GOMBES, PAUL; Steinert HS; Mercerville, NJ; (Y); Computer Clb; Exploring; PAVAS; CAP; Varsity Clb; JV Ftbl; VP Wt Lftg; VP Wrstlng; Law.

GOMEZ, ANA; Mary Help Of Christians Academy; Paterson, NJ; (Y); French Clb; Pep Clb; Teachers Aide; Stage Crew; Score Keeper; Vllybl.

GOMEZ, ELISABETH; Millville SR HS; Millville, NJ; (Y); Church Yth Grp; VP FTA; GAA; Key Clb; Acpl Chr; Church Choir; Concert Band; Orch; School Musical; Nwsp Ed-Chief; Cumberland CC; Elem Schl Tchr.

GOMEZ, GABRIELA; Secaucus HS; Secaucus, NJ; (S); 9/160; Dance Clb; Intnl Clb; Math Clb; Ski Clb; Varsity Clb; Color Guard; JV Sftbl; High Hon Roll; Hon Roll; NHS.

GOMEZ, LELIA; Madison HS; Madison, NJ; (Y); 40/218; AFS; Church Yth Grp; Cmnty Wkr; French Clb; Key Clb; SADD; Chorus; Yrbk Stf; Sec Frsh Cls; Crs Cntry; Hnrb Svc & Outstnding Stu Itln; PA ST; Mrktng.

GOMEZ, STEPHEN; St Peters Prep; Bayonne, NJ; (Y); Ski Clb; Yrbk Stf; Rep Frsh Cls; Im Bsktbl; Wt Lftg; Fin.

GOMINIAK, JOHN P; Notre Dame HS; East Windsor, NJ; (Y); Am Leg Boys St; Ski Clb; Varsity Clb; Nwsp Sprt Ed; Nwsp Stf; Rep Soph Cls; Var L Tennis; High Hon Roll; Hon Roll; NHS.

GOMORY, PAMELA; Abraham Clark HS; Roselle, NJ; (S); 11/187; Science Clb; Band; Chorus; Concert Band; Madrigals; Mrchg Band; Yrbk Stf; Gov Hon Prg Awd; Hon Roll; Prfrmg Arts.

GONCALVES, DEBORAH ANN; Jackson Memorial HS; Morganville, NJ; (Y); Am Leg Aux Girls St; Cmnty Wkr; Teachers Aide; Mrchg Band; High Hon Roll; Hon Roll; Prfct Atten Awd; Span Achvt Awd 83-84; Stu Aide Awd 83-84; Early Admssn Stu Brookdale Coll 85-86; Brookdale; Spec Ed.

GONCALVES, JOSE; East Side HS; Newark, NJ; (Y).

GONSALVES, ANTHONY; Marist HS; Jersey City, NJ; (Y); #38 In Class; Aud/Vis; Exploring; PAVAS; Ski Clb; Spanish Clb; JV Var Ftbl; Wt Lftg; Wrstlng; Hon Roll; Spanish NHS; Johnson & Wales; Rstrnt/Htl Mng.

GONSALVES, MICHELE; Our Lady Of Good Counsel HS; Newark, NJ; (Y); 8/73; Yrbk Ed-Chief; Office Procedures Awd 85-86; 2nd Hnrs 85-86; Berkeley Schls; Bus.

GONZALEZ, ANNA; Moorestown Friends Schl; Pennsauken, NJ; (Y); French Clb; Model UN; Chorus; School Musical; Nwsp Rptr; Yrbk Stf; Lit Mag; Rep Sr Cls; Mgr(s); Ntl Merit SF; Physiology.

GONZALEZ, ANNA; Phillipsburg HS; Phillipsburg, NJ; (Y); 21/296; Hosp Aide; High Hon Roll; NHS; Brown U Schlrshp 86; Brown U.

GONZALEZ, CELESTE; Buena Regional HS; Collings Lks, NJ; (Y); #60 In Class; Church Yth Grp; Band; Church Choir; Concert Band; Jazz Band; Mrchg Band; School Musical; Bd Ed Schlrshp 85-86; Ltr Marchng Band 85-86; Perf Atten Awd 85-86; Music.

GONZALEZ, GRACE; Cherry Hill H S West; Cherry Hill, NJ; (Y); 3/400; French Clb; Intnl Clb; Office Aide; Pres Science Clb; Spanish Clb; SADD; Yrbk Phtg; Rep Jr Cls; Rep Sr Cls; JV Capt Tennis; Grdn ST Dstngshd Schlr 85-86; Ntl Hspnc Schlr 86; Johns Hopkins U; Pre Med.

GONZALEZ, HERMINIA; Bayonne HS; Bayonne, NJ; (Y); 10/348; Computer Clb; Key Clb; Math Tm; Spanish Clb; Jr NHS; VP NHS; Pres Acad Fit Awd 86; Acad Achvt Awd Hudson Cnty Chmbr Comm & Ind 86; Douglass Rutgers.

GONZALEZ, JANET; Mary Help Of Chrisitan Acad; Paterson, NJ; (Y); Art Clb; Computer Clb; English Clb; Math Clb; Chorus; School Musical; High Hon Roll; Hon Roll; Engl & Hist Awd 84-85; Sclgy & Hist Awd 85-86; Theology Hon 85-86; Rutgers; Phrmcy.

GONZALEZ, JULIA M; Camden Catholic HS; Pennsauken, NJ; (Y); French Clb; Teachers Aide; Drill Tm; Wrstlng; Hon Roll; Elem Educ.

GONZALEZ, KENNETH; Perth Amboy HS; Perth Amboy, NJ; (Y); 17/501; Office Aide; ROTC; Stage Crew; VP Soph Cls; Trs Jr Cls; Stu Cncl; Hon Roll; NHS; Perth Amboy ROTC Outstndng Cadet 84-86.

GONZALEZ, LARA; Rutgers Prep Schl; Perth Amboy, NJ; (Y); 1/65; Cmnty Wkr; Hosp Aide; Office Aide; Yrbk Ed-Chief; Yrbk Stf; Var Gym; Var Capt Sftbl; Swmmng; Trk; Gov Hon Prg Awd; Coaches Cup For Mst Coachable Athlt 85; Ntl Hispnc Schlr Prog Smifnl 85; Muhlenberg Coll.

GONZALEZ, LISSETTE; Academic HS; Jersey City, NJ; (Y); Art Clb; Bsktbl; Vllybl; Comp.

GONZALEZ, MARIA TERESA; Columbia HS; Maplewood, NJ; (Y); Rep Drama Clb; Rep French Clb; VP Intnl Clb; Pres Pep Clb; Rep Science Clb; Rep Service Clb; Rep Spanish Clb; Rep Stu Cncl; 1st Pl Spnsh Ntl Tst 84-85; 1st Pl Drma Cntst Rydr Coll 85; U Of Madrid; Econ.

GONZALEZ, MIGUEL; Ramapo HS; Franklin Lakes, NJ; (Y); 30/329; Camera Clb; Computer Clb; Drama Clb; Science Clb; Thesps; School Musical; School Play; Stage Crew; Nwsp Phtg; Yrbk Phtg; Altrnt Acdmc Dcthln Team; Med.

GONZALEZ, NORA; Metuchen HS; Metuchen, NJ; (Y); 34/178; Church Yth Grp; Ski Clb; Spanish Clb; High Hon Roll; Hon Roll; Jr NHS; NHS; Spanish NHS; Schlrshp Awd Spn I, Outstndng Achvt 84; Acad Achvt Spn Ii Awd 85; Rutgers U; Jrnlsm.

GOOD, JUANITA; Overbrook SR HS; Lindenwold, NJ; (Y); Dance Clb; Bsktbl; Var Cheerleading; JV Var Fld Hcky; Var Trk; Hon Roll; Awd Mst Imprvd Chrldr Bsktbl 84-85; Psych.

GOOD, LORI; Burlington Co Vo-Tech Schl; Edgewater Pk, NJ; (Y); 5/200; FBLA; Mgr Bsktbl; Mgr Socr; High Hon Roll; Hon Roll; NHS; Trenton ST Coll; Bus Adm.

GOODALL, MICHELLE; Red Bank Regional HS; Shrewsbury, NJ; (Y); Church Yth Grp; French Clb; Key Clb; Yrbk Stf; Rep Jr Cls; Stat Ftbl; JV Socr; French Hon Soc; Hon Roll; Ntl Merit SF; Lwyr RBRHS Mock Trial Tm Cnty Chmp 84-86; Law.

GOODE, NICOLE; Clifford J Scott HS; E Orange, NJ; (S); 5/285; Library Aide; Math Clb; Ski Clb; Hon Roll; NHS; Prfct Atten Awd; Comp Sci.

GOODE, TAMMY; West Side HS; Newark, NJ; (Y); Church Yth Grp; Exploring; Girl Scts; Church Choir; Drill Tm; Exploring 86; Seton Hall U; Bus.

GOODEN, JUSTINA; Holy Cross HS; Edgewater Park, NJ; (Y); Church Yth Grp; Dance Clb; Service Clb; Yrbk Stf; Lit Mag; Rep Frsh Cls; Cheerleading; Mgr(s); Hon Roll; Mktng.

GOODFELLOW, JOSEPH; Overbrook Regional HS; Clementon, NJ; (Y); Pre-Med.

GOODMAN, AARON; Scotch Plains-Fanwood HS; Fanwood, NJ; (Y); Drama Clb; Chorus; VP School Musical; School Play; Swing Chorus; Ed Nwsp Phtg; Nwsp Stf; Ed Yrbk Phtg; Lit Mag; Im Vllybl; NJ All St Choir 84 & 85; Lit Mag Photo Cntst 2nd Pl 86; Photojrnlsm.

GOODMAN, ALEXIS; Franklin HS; Somerset, NJ; (S); 126/336; DECA; Hon Roll; 2nd Pl For Chapter Actvts Scrapbk For DECA 86; Wrd Prcssng.

GOODMAN, BRETT T; Livingston HS; Livingston, NJ; (Y); 10/498; Trs Key Clb; Spanish Clb; Temple Yth Grp; Nwsp Ed-Chief; Nwsp Rptr; Nwsp Sprt Ed; Nwsp Stf; Lit Mag; Off Stu Cncl; Tennis; 1st Pl ST Of NJ Spnsh Prtgs Soc Schlrshp; Intl Stds Assoc; Rtgrs Schlr; Princeton.

GOODMAN, DAVID J; Gateway Regional HS; Wenonah, NJ; (Y); 9/215; Am Leg Boys St; Science Clb; Yrbk Phtg; French Hon Soc; High Hon Roll; NHS; Ntl Merit Ltr; Boy Scts; Debate Tm; Drama Clb; Hugh O Brien Ldrshp Fndtn Rep; Teen Arts Fstvl Fnlst; Congress Bundestag Pgm Semi-Fnlst; Engrng.

GOODMAN, INDIA; Hackensack HS; Hackensack, NJ; (Y); 7/400; Dance Clb; Pep Clb; Band; Concert Band; Mrchg Band; Off Sr Cls; Sftbl; Hon Roll; NHS; Spanish NHS; Mexican Schlrshp Clb 82-86; U Of DE; Lawyer.

GOODMAN, MARTIN; Freehold Township HS; Freehold, NJ; (Y); 56/317; Letterman Clb; VP Temple Yth Grp; Varsity Clb; Yrbk Stf; Var Bsktbl; Var Crs Cntry; Var Trk; Cit Awd; Congressional Mdl Awd 84; Rutgers; Bio.

GOODREDS, STEPHEN; Montville HS; Pine Brook, NJ; (Y); 85/245; Church Yth Grp; FBLA; Key Clb; JV Trk; Cit Awd; High Hon Roll; Hon Roll; Seton Hall U; Bus Adm.

GOODRIDGE, PHILIP; Washington Township HS; Turnersville, NJ; (Y); Spanish Clb; Var Crs Cntry; JV Socr; Var Trk; Hon Roll; Engrng.

GOODROE, MICHELE; Lower Cape May Regional; N Cape May, NJ; (Y); 9/243; Church Yth Grp; Cmnty Wkr; Band; Concert Band; Mrchg Band; Yrbk Stf; Lit Mag; Sftbl; Gov Hon Prg Awd; Hon Roll; Vet Med.

GOODWIN, CHRISTA; Hamilton W HS; Trenton, NJ; (Y); Key Clb; Political Wkr; SADD; Teachers Aide; Chorus; Drill Tm; Pom Pon; High Hon Roll; Hon Roll; Trenton ST; Crmnl Just.

GOODWIN, DANIEL; St Rose HS; Point Pleasant, NJ; (Y); 26/202; JCL; Latin Clb; Math Clb; Ski Clb; Stage Crew; JV Var Bsbl; Hon Roll; NHS; Ocn Cnty CYO Schlrshp 86; Gldn ST Schlr 86; Ramapo Achvt Schlrshp 86; Ramapo Coll Of NJ; Bus.

GOODWIN, SHARON; Ramsey HS; Ramsey, NJ; (Y); 20/261; Teachers Aide; Var Bsktbl; Var Fld Hcky; Var Sftbl; High Hon Roll; NHS; Hon Roll; Mst Imprvd Schlr Awd St Johns Episcopal Chrch 85; Spec Ed.

GOODWYN, JAMES; Clifford J Scott HS; Newark, NJ; (Y); 11/219; Church Yth Grp; Intnl Clb; Math Clb; Nwsp Sprt Ed; Yrbk Stf; Crs Cntry; Trk; Schlrp New Directions 86; U NC; Bus Adm.

GOONAN, MARIANNE; Williamstown HS; Williamstown, NJ; (Y); Exploring; German Clb; Hosp Aide; Nwsp Stf; Bsktbl; Mgr(s); Tennis; Monroe Twnshp Grls Sftbl 84; Nrsng.

GOPAL, SRIHARI; Roselle Catholic HS; Rahway, NJ; (Y); 6/200; Hosp Aide; Math Tm; Var Tennis; High Hon Roll; Jr NHS; NHS; Rutgers U; Med.

GORALSKI, JAMES; Wayne Hills HS; Wayne, NJ; (Y); Spanish Clb; Nwsp Stf; Var Crs Cntry; JV Trk; Hon Roll; Excllnc Soc Studies 83; 2nd Pl Sparring Karate 81; Clss Champ Speller 83.

GORDER, ERIKA; Middletown South HS; Locust, NJ; (Y); Cmnty Wkr; Office Aide; Political Wkr; Hon Roll; U Of IA; Engl.

GORDON, CHERYL; Wallington HS; Wallington, NJ; (Y); 8/66; Drama Clb; Library Aide; School Play; Yrbk Sprt Ed; Bsktbl; Bowling; Score Keeper; Sftbl; Vllybl; Hon Roll; Hm Schl Schlrsh P86; Rutgers Coll; Nrsng.

GORDON, ERIC; Scotch Plaine-Fanwood HS; Scotch Pl, NJ; (Y); AFS; Model UN; Scholastic Bowl; Temple Yth Grp; Yrbk Stf; Bsbl; Capt Crs Cntry; Hon Roll; Prfct Atten Awd; Spanish NHS; Spnsh Awds 83-85; Cmmnctns.

GORDON, ERICA A; The Peddie Schl; Hamilton Twp, NJ; (Y); Cmnty Wkr; Dance Clb; Drama Clb; French Clb; Hosp Aide; School Musical; Nwsp Rptr; VP French Clb; VP Soph Cls; Mgr Bsbl; Natl Achvt Schlrshp Prog Outstndng Negro Stdnts 85; Boston Coll; Hstry.

GORDON, GLENN; Brich HS; Brick, NJ; (Y); Var Bsktbl.

GORDON, HELEN; Hawthorne HS; Hawthorne, NJ; (Y); 33/155; Drama Clb; Color Guard; Flag Corp; Variety Show; Yrbk Ed-Chief; Rep Frsh Cls; Rep Sr Cls; Rep Stu Cncl; Var L Trk; Var L Twrlr; Chrprsn SR Cls Chrstms Dnc; NJ Inst Of Tech; Engrng.

GORDON, JENNIFER; Teaneck HS; Teaneck, NJ; (Y); Drama Clb; French Clb; Office Aide; SADD; Temple Yth Grp; School Play; Yrbk Stf; Hon Roll; NHS; Art.

GORDON, JOHN; North HS; Toms River, NJ; (Y); Capt Trk; JV Wrstlng.

GORDON, KELLIE; Buena Regional HS; Landisville, NJ; (S); 14/191; Chess Clb; Math Clb; Spanish Clb; Varsity Clb; Concert Band; Jazz Band; Mrchg Band; Nwsp Sprt Ed; Var L Sftbl; Hon Roll; Mus.

GORDON, KIM; Cherry Hill High West; Cherry Hill, NJ; (Y); Key Clb; Office Aide; Pep Clb; Spanish Clb; Teachers Aide; Hon Roll; Rutgers; Phrmcy.

GORDON, LINDA; Kittatinny HS; Newton, NJ; (Y); Church Yth Grp; 4-H; Varsity Clb; Band; Concert Band; JV Bsktbl; Var L Crs Cntry; JV Swmmng; Var L Trk; 4-H Awd; ST Regnl & Natl AAU Champnshps X-Cntry 84; NJ Dairymaid 84-85; Math.

GORDON, LINDEN; Linden HS; Linden, NJ; (Y); FBLA; JA; SADD; VICA; Prfct Atten Awd; Rutgers Coll; Accounting.

GORDON, LOVELL; Hackettstown HS; Hackettstown, NJ; (S); Church Yth Grp; Keywanettes; Band; Concert Band; Jazz Band; Mrchg Band; Stu Cncl; Sftbl; Hon Roll; NHS; JR All Amer Bnd Hnrs Awd 85; Cnty Bnd 84-86; Temple U; Arch.

GORDON, ORA; West Orange HS; W Orange, NJ; (Y); 12/177; Math Clb; Spanish Clb; Temple Yth Grp; Chorus; Yrbk Stf; High Hon Roll; Jr NHS; NHS; Spanish NHS; Hon Grd 85; Grad Cntrl Hebrew HS 81-86; Attnd HS Israel Feb/Mar 86; Rutgers U.

GORDON, ROBERT C; St Marys Hall/Deane Acad; Willingboro, NJ; (Y); Boy Scts; Church Yth Grp; Science Clb; Rep Stu Cncl; Im Mgr(s); High Hon Roll; Ntl Merit SF; School Play; Lit Mag; Eagle Sct; Sci Trnng Pgm 85; Rutgers Pres Schlrshp 86.

GORDON, SHERI; Hightstown HS; East Windsor, NJ; (Y); French Clb; Ski Clb; SADD; Drill Tm; JV Swmmng; U Of FL; Int Dcrtng.

GORDON, STUART; Ocean Township HS; Ocean Twop, NJ; (Y); 37/350; Church Yth Grp; VP Temple Yth Grp; Band; Mrchg Band; Pep Band; Var Crs Cntry; Var Trk; Hon Roll; Outstndng Frshmn Hebrew HS Temple Beth Torah 84.

GORDON, SUSAN; Phillipsburg HS; Phillipsburg, NJ; (Y); 44/365; Chorus; Var Tennis; Hon Roll; NHS.

GORDY, KATHLEEN; Atlantic City HS; Atlantic City, NJ; (Y); 85/455; Church Yth Grp; Dance Clb; Office Aide; Band; Church Choir; Concert Band; Jazz Band; Stu Cncl; Capt L Cheerleading; Hon Roll; Oasis Mem Schlrshp 85-86; MVP Band 85-86; Band Dir Awd Schlrshp 85-86; Glassboro ST Coll; Comm.

GORHAM, CORT; Manasquan HS; Spg Lk, NJ; (Y); Spanish Clb; Varsity Clb; Var Ftbl; Im JV Socr; Hon Roll; Elecd Circlm Dirctr Stu Cncl Day 85-86; U Rhode Island.

GORKA, GREGORY J; Sayreville War Memorial HS; Sayreville, NJ; (Y); Cmnty Wkr; Spanish Clb; Stage Crew; Nwsp Phtg; Nwsp Stf; Yrbk Phtg; Yrbk Stf; JV Var Socr; Wt Lftg; Hon Roll; Rutgers Coll.

GORMAN, BRYAN; Washington Township HS; Turnersville, NJ; (Y); 5/480; Debate Tm; Off Exploring; Pres Math Clb; Math Tm; Q&S; Hon Roll; NHS; Ntl Merit Schol; Pres Schlr; HS Math Exam Awd 85; NJ Sci League Awd In Chmstry 84; FL ST U; Phlsphcl Rsrch.

GORMAN, MICHAEL; Glen Rock JR SR HS; Glen Rock, NJ; (Y); 17/170; Latin Clb; Stu Cncl; Var L Bsktbl; Var L Ftbl; Cit Awd; High Hon Roll; Hon Roll; Jr NHS; NHS; Ntl Merit SF; Athlt Yr 85-86.

GORMAN, STEPHANIE; Steinert HS; Groveville, NJ; (Y); FBLA; Color Guard; NHS; Comp Sci.

GORMAN, TAMELA; Hunterdon Central HS; Flemington, NJ; (Y); Church Yth Grp; Cmnty Wkr; Drama Clb; Girl Scts; Chorus; Church Choir; Flag Corp; Variety Show; Stat Crs Cntry; Hon Roll; Int Design.

GORMLEY, SUE ANN; Scotch Plains Fanwood HS; Scotch Plains, NJ; (S); 1/350; French Clb; Hosp Aide; Model UN; Political Wkr; Quiz Bowl; Mrchg Band; Lit Mag; Var Socr; Var Vllybl; Gov Hon Prg Awd; Pltcl Sci.

GORNEJO, UDO; North Bergen HS; North Bergen, NJ; (Y); 15/400; German Clb; Nwsp Stf; Socr; Hon Roll; Wnnr Iona Coll Lang Cmptn Ntv Grmn 85; Wnnr Rider Coll Lang Cmptn Ntv Grmn 85&86; Med.

GOROSCHKO, EUGENE; Hamilton High School West; Yardville, NJ; (S); Computer Clb; Math Clb; Concert Band; Mrchg Band; Symp Band; Im Vllybl; Amer Muscl Fndtn Outstndg Stu 85; Rutgers U; Comp Engrng.

GORSKI, BRIAN; Lower Cape May Regional HS; Villas, NJ; (Y); Church Yth Grp; Church Choir; Atlantic CC; Chef.

GORSKI, JENNIFER; Red Bank Catholic HS; Rumsson, NJ; (Y); Art Clb; Ski Clb; Spanish Clb; Varsity Clb; Drill Tm; Mrchg Band; Yrbk Ed-Chief; JV Var Trk; High Hon Roll; NHS; Arch.

GOSSELINK, MEGAN; James Caldwell HS; W Caldwell, NJ; (Y); Key Clb; Lit Mag; Rep Jr Cls; Rep Stu Cncl; Ntl Merit SF; Librl Arts.

GOSSETT, ERINN E; Matawan Regional HS; Aberdeen, NJ; (Y); 8/270; Math Tm; Sec Band; Sec Mrchg Band; School Musical; Nwsp Ed-Chief; Yrbk Ed-Chief; Rep Stu Cncl; Gov Hon Prg Awd; High Hon Roll; NHS; Cornell U; Pre-Med.

GOTTFRID, DEREK; Watching Hills Regional HS; Warren, NJ; (Y); Boy Scts; Church Yth Grp; Computer Clb; Drama Clb; Ski Clb; SADD; School Musical; School Play; Stage Crew; Rep Frsh Cls; Theater Art.

GOULD, ALISON; Livingston HS; Livingston, NJ; (Y); Dance Clb; Leo Clb; Model UN; Soph Cls; Jr Cls; Sr Cls; Stu Cncl; Socr; Hon Roll; U Of MI; Bus.

GOULD, DEBRA; Linden HS; Linden, NJ; (S); 51/313; FBLA; Key Clb; Band; Concert Band; Mrchg Band; Rep Stu Cncl; Commercl Trust 86; Outstndng Bus Bond 83; Union Cnty Coll; Off Systm Tech.

GOULD, MARY; Buena Regional HS; Newfield, NJ; (S); 14/195; Debate Tm; Drama Clb; Math Clb; Red Cross Aide; Spanish Clb; Varsity Clb; Band; Concert Band; Jazz Band; Mrchg Band; Stu Of Mnth 85; Outstndg Music Recog 85; Math.

GOVETT, STACY; Pitman HS; Pitman, NJ; (Y); 1/150; Sec Pres Key Clb; Sec Frsh Cls; Sec Soph Cls; Sec Jr Cls; Var Capt Cheerleading; High Hon Roll; NHS; Mod Musc Mstrs 85-86; Rutgrs Schlr 86; Girls ST Altnt 86; Engrg.

GRAASKAMP, MARTHA; Montgomery HS; Princeton, NJ; (Y); 3/130; Am Leg Aux Girls St; Cmnty Wkr; Scholastic Bowl; Band; Chorus; NHS; Church Yth Grp; Science Clb; Acpl Chr; School Musical; Smth Coll Bk Awd Outstndg Engl Stu 85; Gradtd Hgh Hnrs 86; Prsdntl Acdmc Ftnss Awd 86; Mount Holyoke Coll; Bio.

GRABILL, JILL-ALLYSON; Montville Twp HS; Montville, NJ; (Y); 18/272; Exploring; VP Intnl Clb; Key Clb; Church Choir; School Musical; JV Trk; High Hon Roll; Hon Roll; NHS; Ntl Merit Ltr; Grdn ST Dstngshd Schlr 86; Frgn Lang Dept Spnsh Awd 86; NJ Assn Blck Edctrs 86; Princeton U; Pltcl Sci.

GRACE, JENNIFER; Manasquan HS; Manasquan, NJ; (Y); #14 In Class; Spanish Clb; Bowling; Crs Cntry; High Hon Roll; Hon Roll; Pres Acdmc Ftns Awd 86; Alt Girls St 85; Manasquan Elem PTO Schlrshp 86; Randolph-Macon Coll.

GRACE, JONI; Maple Shade HS; Maple Shade, NJ; (Y); DECA; French Clb; Key Clb; Nwsp Stf; JV Bsktbl; Var Lcrss; JV Socr; Prfct Atten Awd; Bus Mngmnt.

GRACE, PAUL; Egg Harbor Township HS; Mckee City, NJ; (S); 17/266; Office Aide; Hst Sr Cls; Var Bsbl; Var Capt Socr; Var Swmmng; High Hon Roll; Hon Roll; Jr NHS; Prfct Atten Awd; Val; Bhvrl Sci.

GRACON, ANNETTE; St John Vianney HS; Englishtown, NJ; (Y); Girl Scts; Intnl Clb; Math Tm; Yrbk Stf; Hon Roll; NHS; Girl Sct Silvr Awd; Gold & White Awd.

GRADY, TONY; Kennedy HS; Paterson, NJ; (S); Chorus; High Hon Roll; Hon Roll; Track & Fielk Awds 83-82; Music Awd 84-85; Art Awd 74-83; Music.

GRAEF, LINDA; Palisades Pk JR SR HS; Palisades Pk, NJ; (Y); Sec Stu Cncl; JV Var Cheerleading; Var Capt Pom Pon; Hon Roll; Acdmc Awd Itlaian III 86; Fshn Merchdsng.

GRAESSLE, CYNTHIA; Toms River H S East; Toms River, NJ; (Y); Trs Ed Key Clb; Teachers Aide; Hon Roll; Spec Ed Outstndng Aid 83-84 & 84-85; 2nd Pl Clb Bulletin NJ Dist Key Clb 85-86; Trenton ST Coll; Elem Ed.

GRAF, JOSEPH; Ridge HS; W Millington, NJ; (Y); 28/215; Drama Clb; German Clb; Ski Clb; Hon Roll; Bus.

GRAF JR, ROBERT; Wall HS; Manasquan, NJ; (Y); 23/250; Band; Concert Band; Mrchg Band; Pep Band; JV Bsbl; Var L Bowling; High Hon Roll; Hon Roll; Power & Electrncs Awd 85-86; Shore Conf High Series-Bowlng 84-85; Rutgers Coll Of Engrng; Elec En.

GRAHAM, ALISA; Willingboro HS; Willingboro, NJ; (Y); 13/317; Capt L Pom Pon; Hon Roll; Prfct Atten Awd; Acadmc All Amer Awd 86; Recog Of Spec Achvt-Yth Ach Com 85; Rutgers U; Acctng.

GRAHAM, ALLISON F; Manchester Regional HS; North Haledon, NJ; (S); 1/160; Am Leg Aux Girls St; Math Clb; Quiz Bowl; Nwsp Stf; Yrbk Stf; Rep Frsh Cls; Rep Soph Cls; Rep Jr Cls; Rep Stu Cncl; Var Socr; Don Quixote Spnsh Awd 85; Gftd & Tlntd Prog; Engr.

GRAHAM, DIANE; Union Catholic Regional HS; Scotch Plains, NJ; (Y); 24/331; Drama Clb; PAVAS; Service Clb; Spanish Clb; Sec Thesps; Chorus; School Musical; Nwsp Stf; Hon Roll; NHS; Fairfield U; Bus.

GRAHAM, DORI LAINE; N Burlington Co Reg HS; Allentown, NJ; (Y); 11/228; SADD; Teachers Aide; Varsity Clb; Chorus; School Musical; JV Cheerleading; JV Var Crs Cntry; Hon Roll; NHS; Spanish NHS; Hugh O Brien Yth Ldrshp Amb 85; OH Northern; Phrmcst.

GRAHAM, JAY; Washington Township HS; Turnersville, NJ; (Y); Spanish Clb; Bsbl; Bus.

GRAHAM, STEPHAN; Lenape HS; Medford, NJ; (Y); 3/410; Math Tm; Varsity Clb; Var Capt Socr; Var Trk; High Hon Roll; NHS; Pres Schlr; Rotary Awd; St Schlr; Cornell U; Engr.

GRAHAM, STEVEN; Parsippany HS; Parsippany, NJ; (Y); Im Bsbl; JV Var Ftbl; Hon Roll; NHS; Acctg.

GRAHAM, TASHAWNA; Snyder HS; Jersey City, NJ; (Y); Girl Scts; Church Choir; School Play; Jr Cls; Cheerleading; Sftbl; Prfct Atten Awd; RutgersSEC.

GRAHAM, TRACEY; Frank H Morrell HS; Irvington, NJ; (Y); School Play; Variety Show; Yrbk Stf; Hon Roll; $1000 Alumni Assn For Morgan St U 86; Medal For Outstndng Stu 86; Morgan ST U; Cvl Engr.

GRAHAM, VICTORIA; Bayonne HS; Bayonne, NJ; (Y); 78/362; Computer Clb; Office Aide; Teachers Aide; Chorus; Vllybl; Hon Roll; NHS; Pres Schlr; Activities Awd 86; Rutgers Coll Art/Sci; Comp Sci.

GRAISER, SEAN; Buena Reginal HS; Mays Landing, NJ; (S); Girl Scts; Pep Clb; Ski Clb; Varsity Clb; Rep Frsh Cls; Rep Soph Cls; Rep Jr Cls; Rep Stu Cncl; Fld Hcky; Var Trk; Mst Dedctd Grls Vrsty Trck 85; Sci.

GRAMEGNA, ANNE; David Brearley HS; Kenilworth, NJ; (Y); 49/186; Church Yth Grp; Pres Key Clb; Chorus; School Play; Stat Bsktbl; JV Sftbl; Var Trk; Hon Roll; St Johns U; Psych.

GRAMLICH, JOCELYN; Sayreville War Mem HS; Parlin, NJ; (Y); 28/367; Church Yth Grp; VP Library Aide; Concert Band; Mrchg Band; School Musical; High Hon Roll; Hon Roll; NHS; Ntl Merit Ltr; Pres Schlr; Rutgers U; Engrng.

GRAMUGLIA, ROSE; Cliffside Park HS; Fairview, NJ; (Y); 15/236; Am Leg Aux Girls St; Nwsp Stf; Yrbk Ed-Chief; Lit Mag; Rep Stu Cncl; High Hon Roll; Hon Roll; NHS; Chess Clb; Jr NHS; Italian Clb Vp; Italian Ntl Honor Scty; Italian Merit Awd.

GRANATA, MARYANN; Spotswood HS; Spotswood, NJ; (Y); 41/186; DECA; Yrbk Stf; Hon Roll; 1st Ovr All Gnrl Merch Awd 86; Vtng Dlgt 85-86; Zookeeping.

GRANDA, ANGELA; Manalapan HS; Englishtown, NJ; (Y); Chorus; Church Choir; Mrchg Band; VP Orch; School Musical; Gov Hon Prg Awd; All ST Orchstr 85-87; New Jrsy Yth Symphy 86-87; Bttlgrnd Yth Orchstr 84-87; Music Prfrmnce.

GRANDBERRY, CINDY; Hillside HS; Hillside, NJ; (Y); Computer Clb; Drama Clb; French Clb; Girl Scts; Model UN; Pep Clb; School Play; Nwsp Stf; Cheerleading; Trk; Arch Engrng.

GRANDILLI, CRISTINA; St John Vianney HS; Marlboro, NJ; (S); 10/232; JCL; Chorus; School Musical; School Play; Rep Soph Cls; Rep Jr Cls; Rep Sr Cls; High Hon Roll; Hon Roll; VP NHS.

GRANELLI, KEVIN R; St Peters Prep; Kearny, NJ; (Y); 25/210; Boys Clb Am; Camera Clb; Cmnty Wkr; Intnl Clb; Pep Clb; Science Clb; Ski Clb; Yrbk Stf; Var L Socr; High Hon Roll; Harvard Mdl Cngrss 86; Psych.

GRANGER, KRISTIN; Saint John Vianney HS; Hazlet, NJ; (Y); SADD; Teachers Aide; Ed Nwsp Phtg; Yrbk Rptr; Var L Bsktbl; Stat Ftbl; Powder Puff Ftbl; Var L Trk; Hon Roll; Intl Bus.

GRANT, CARISSA E; Roselle Catholic HS; Newark, NJ; (Y); Computer Clb; Girl Scts; Chorus; Nwsp Rptr; Yrbk Stf; Bowling; JV Trk; Hon Roll; Prfct Atten Awd; Spanish NHS; USAF; Pharm.

GRANT, DANNY; Montville HS; Towaco, NJ; (Y); 41/260; Yrbk Stf; VP Frsh Cls; Rep Soph Cls; Rep Jr Cls; Var Bsbl; Var Ftbl; Var Wrstlng; High Hon Roll; Hon Roll; NHS.

GRANT, TONY; Edgewood Regional SR HS; Sicklerville, NJ; (Y); Computer Clb; French Clb; Im Trk; Hon Roll; Ntl Sci Merit Awd 85-86; Pltcl Sci.

GRASMICK III, LOUIS F; Haddon Township HS; Westmont, NJ; (Y); Boy Scts; Church Yth Grp; Cmnty Wkr; FCA; Varsity Clb; Rep Sr Cls; Coach Actv; Var L Ftbl; Var L Trk; Wt Lftg; Ftbl All-Str 82; Rutgers U; Law.

GRASSO, KAREN; Hammonton HS; Hammonton, NJ; (Y); 24/184; Key Clb; School Musical; School Play; Ed Yrbk Stf; Off Stu Cncl; Cheerleading; Hon Roll; NHS; Glassboro ST Coll; Home Ec.

GRASSO, TINA; Montville Township HS; Pine Brook, NJ; (Y); 37/276; Church Yth Grp; Intnl Clb; Key Clb; Spanish Clb; SADD; Varsity Clb; Var Bsktbl; Var Fld Hcky; Capt Var Sftbl; High Hon Roll; Conf Champs Fld Hcky 85 & 86, Sftbl 85; NHS Scholar 86; Rutgers; Phrmcy.

GRASTY, CHRISTINE; Pleasantville HS; Pleasantville, NJ; (Y); Merit Rll, Stdnt Mnth, B Aver Awd 86; Johnson & Wales; Chef.

GRATE, GERALDINE; Green Brook HS; Green Brook, NJ; (Y); 2/48; Drama Clb; School Play; Nwsp Stf; Yrbk Stf; Lit Mag; Sec Sr Cls; Tennis; Jr NHS; NHS; St Schlr; NJ Thspn Art Awd 86; Grdn ST Dstnghd Schlr 86; Rutgers Coll; Mrktg.

GRAU, CAROLYN; North Warren Regional HS; Columbia, NJ; (Y); 3/129; Am Leg Aux Girls St; Pres Church Yth Grp; Ski Clb; Chorus; School Musical; Rep Stu Cncl; JV Fld Hcky; High Hon Roll; Hon Roll; NHS; Grls Ctznshp Inst Delg 86; Ec.

GRAU, JOHN; Bishop George Ahr HS; Old Bridge, NJ; (Y); Church Yth Grp; ROTC; Trk; High Hon Roll; Hon Roll; NEDT Awd; Engr.

GRAUER, MELISSA; Fairlawn HS; Fair Lawn, NJ; (Y); 17/387; Debate Tm; Latin Clb; Spanish Clb; Stu Cncl; Gov Hon Prg Awd; Hon Roll; NHS; Ntl Merit Ltr; Pres Schlr; St Schlr; Rtgrs Coll Merit Schlrshp 86; Grdn ST Dstngshd Schlr Awd 86; Rutgers Coll.

GRAUMANN, CHRISTEL M; Kittatinny Regional HS; Newton, NJ; (Y); AFS; Church Yth Grp; Pres German Clb; Hosp Aide; Chorus; Yrbk Stf; Lit Mag; Rep Stu Cncl; Var Cheerleading; NHS; Ocptnl Thrpy.

GRAVATT, JILL KATHRYN; Bordentown Regional HS; Bordentown, NJ; (Y); 30/135; Am Leg Aux Girls St; French Clb; Math Clb; Chorus; Yrbk Rptr; Capt Pom Pon; Hon Roll; NHS; Prfct Atten Awd; Ntl Grd Assoc Of NJ Schlrshp 86; Wilson Coll; Psycho Bio.

GRAVERS, ILONA; Scotch Plains-Fanwood HS; Scotch Plains, NJ; (Y); 29/350; AFS; Model UN; Pep Clb; Flag Corp; George Washington U; Lib Arts.

GRAY, BARRY; Paulsboro HS; Gibbstown, NJ; (Y); 30/133; Rep Stu Cncl; Bsbl; High Hon Roll; Hon Roll; Kiwanis Awd; NHS; Gloucester Cnty Coll; Bus.

GRAY, CHRIS; Manalapan HS; Englishtown, NJ; (Y); 115/435; Varsity Clb; Capt L Bsktbl; Var L Ftbl; Engrng.

GRAY, CHRISTOPHER; Toms River HS East; Toms River, NJ; (Y); Band; Jazz Band; Mrchg Band; School Musical; Symp Band; Variety Show; High Hon Roll; Rutgers Coll; Engl.

GRAY, EVELYN; Warren County Vo-Tech; Washington, NJ; (S); VICA; Hon Roll; Data Entry.

GRAY, KATRICE; Mt St Mary Acad; Newark, NJ; (Y); Church Yth Grp; 4-H; Girl Scts; Spanish Clb; Varsity Clb; Chorus; Church Choir; Yrbk Stf; Var Cheerleading; 4-H Awd; Psych.

GRAY, LISANNE; Shore Regional HS; W Long Branch, NJ; (Y); 42/225; Key Clb; Intnl Clb; Nwsp Ed-Chief; Socr; Hon Roll; NHS; Pres Schlr; Jill Abbey Weiss Mem Awd 86; Long Branch Exchange Club Awd 86; Shore Reg Educ Assoc Schlrshp 86; Boston U; Mass Cmmnctns.

GRAY, LOUIS; Kearny HS; Kearny, NJ; (Y); Boys Clb Am; Boy Scts; German Clb; Im Mgr Bsktbl; Im Mgr Ftbl; Var Capt Golf; Im Mgr Sftbl; Bus Adm.

GRAY, MARK; Parsippany HS; Parsippany, NJ; (Y); Varsity Clb; Ftbl; Wt Lftg; Wrstlng; Hon Roll; Prfct Atten Awd; Marine Bio.

GRAY, MICHELLE A; Morris Knolls HS; Denville, NJ; (Y); 46/337; Hon Roll; Ntl Merit Ltr; Bus Mgmt.

GRAY, NA TASHA; St Cecilai HS; Teaneck, NJ; (Y); 18/42; Hon Roll; Prfct Atten Awd; Hal Jacksons Talented Teen Of Bergen Cnty 85-86funattached Swim Team 83-84; Howard U.

GRAY, SUSAN; Jackson Memorial HS; Jackson, NJ; (S); 118/434; Art Clb; 4-H; Library Aide; Nwsp Ed-Chief; Nwsp Rptr; Nwsp Stf; Pres Jr Cls; Rep Stu Cncl; Var Bsktbl; Var Powder Puff Ftbl; Ms Upwrd Bnd 85; 7 Upwrd Bnd Awds Bst Stu Bio Rea 84-85; ROGATE Englsh, SAT Englsh, Geom, Art 83-84; PA ST U; Art.

GRAY, SUSAN; Monsignor Donovan HS; Toms River, NJ; (Y); 73/319; Civic Clb; Drama Clb; French Clb; FBLA; Ski Clb; SADD; Yrbk Stf; Stat Ftbl; JV Trk; High Hon Roll; St Josephs U; Psych.

GRAY, VICTORIA E; Southern Regional HS; Manahawkin, NJ; (Y); Dance Clb; Drama Clb; Sec Spanish Clb; School Play; Stu Cncl; Var L Cheerleading; Pom Pon; Hon Roll; NHS; Prfct Atten Awd; Liberal Arts.

GRAYBUSH, MARC; Randolph HS; Randolph, NJ; (Y); Computer Clb; Ski Clb; Varsity Clb; JV Var Bsbl; JV Var Socr; Comp Sci.

GRAYSON, ROBERT; Clayton HS; Clayton, NJ; (S); 4/60; Am Leg Boys St; Pres Key Clb; Chorus; School Musical; Nwsp Sprt Ed; VP Frsh Cls; Capt Bsbl; Co-Capt Ftbl; Wt Lftg; Hon Roll; Natl Hnr Soc; Bsebl Coaches Awd; Pre-Law.

GRAZIANO, LISA; Rutherford HS; Rutherford, NJ; (Y); Cmnty Wkr; Hosp Aide; Pep Clb; High Hon Roll; Hon Roll; NHS; Nursing.

GRAZIANO, SUZANNE; River Dell Regional HS; Oradell, NJ; (Y); 40/210; Am Leg Aux Girls St; Am Leg Aux Girls St; Pres Pep Clb; Ski Clb; Pres SADD; Rep Sr Cls; Capt Cheerleading; Stat Ftbl; Var Trk; NHS; Unico Schlrshp 86; Amer Lgn Pst 226 86; Otstndng Pntng Sclptr Awd 86; Fairfield U; Bus.

GREAVES, KIRK; Bishop George Ahr HS; Plainfield, NJ; (Y); Varsity Clb; Trk; Hon Roll.

GREEN, CRYSTAL; Our Lady Of Good Counsel HS; Irvingtn, NJ; (Y); Hon Roll; Montclair ST Coll; Gynclgst.

GREEN, DANIEL; Glen Rock HS; Glen Rock, NJ; (Y); L Band; Jazz Band; Mrchg Band; School Musical; School Play; Nwsp Stf; Yrbk Stf; Pres Frsh Cls; Sec Stu Cncl; Hon Roll.

GREEN, KENNETH L; Teaneck HS; Teaneck, NJ; (Y); Am Leg Boys St; Boy Scts; Church Yth Grp; Drama Clb; Office Aide; SADD; Varsity Clb; Church Choir; Var Crs Cntry; Capt Trk.

GREEN, NOAH; Middletown HS; Middletown, NJ; (Y); Yrbk Ed-Chief; Lit Mag; Sec Pres Drama Clb; Gov Hon Prg Awd; Jr NHS; NHS; Ntl Merit SF; Voice Dem Awd; Exploring; Math Tm; Magna Cum Laude Ntl Ltn Exm 85; 2nd Pl NJ Wrtg Cntst 85; 1st Pl Brkdl CC Holocst Wrtg Cntst 85; Brown U; Med.

GREEN, RICHARD; Manalapan HS; Englishtown, NJ; (Y); JV L Bsbl; Var L Socr; US Cst Gurd Prjctm 86; Comp.

GREENBAUN, JOHN PAUL; Hopewell Valley Central HS; Titusville, NJ; (Y); Boy Scts; Band; Concert Band; Mrchg Band; Crs Cntry; Trk; Boston U; Fincr.

GREENBERG, AMY; Hightstown HS; Hightstown, NJ; (Y); Spanish Clb; Temple Yth Grp; Varsity Clb; Nwsp Rptr; Yrbk Stf; Rep Jr Cls; Sec Sr Cls; Rep Stu Cncl; Var JV Fld Hcky; High Hon Roll; Typng Awd 84.

GREENBERG, CORY; Paramus HS; Paramus, NJ; (Y); 5/343; VP Intnl Clb; NFL; Quiz Bowl; Nwsp Stf; Yrbk Stf; Ed Lit Mag; Elks Awd; NHS; Spanish NHS; Rep Frsh Cls; JCC On The Palisades Schlrshp 86; Psych Cert Of Merit 85; Latin Hnr Soc 84; Duke U; Engl.

GREENBERG, REBECCA ANN; East Brunswick HS; E Brunswick, NJ; (Y); Cmnty Wkr; Drama Clb; Spanish Clb; Temple Yth Grp; Yrbk Stf; Var L Socr; JV Trk; High Hon Roll; Hon Roll; NHS; Rutgers; Phrmcy.

GREENBLATT, BENJAMIN; Atlantic City HS; Atlantic City, NJ; (Y); Boy Scts; Nwsp Phtg; Nwsp Rptr; Swmmng; Hon Roll; Med.

GREENE, BETH; Kittatinny Regional HS; Branchville, NJ; (Y); 22/222; Church Yth Grp; Stage Crew; High Hon Roll; Hon Roll; NHS; Ed.

GREENE, CHANTEL; Plainfield HS; Plainfield, NJ; (Y); DECA; Office Aide; Rep Jr Cls; JV Crs Cntry; Trk; Rutgers Upward Bound 83-86; MD U; Elem Teaching.

GREENE, ERICH; Walowick HS; Waldwick, NJ; (Y); Drama Clb; Capt Math Tm; Spanish Clb; School Musical; School Play; Stage Crew; Nwsp Rptr; Nwsp Sprt Ed; Lit Mag; Gov Hon Prg Awd; 1st Pl Coll Bowl Spnsh Adv Lvl-Rider Coll Forensic Tourn; Grp 1 Champ-Bergen Cnty Math Leag; Phy Sci.

GREENE, JENNIFER; Middletown H S South; Middletown, NJ; (Y); Cmnty Wkr; Office Aide; Ski Clb; Var Cheerleading; Var Swmmng; Var Tennis; Hon Roll; Svc Bus.

GREENE, SUSAN ANN; Freehold Township HS; Freehold, NJ; (Y); 86/389; Pres French Clb; Yrbk Stf; Rep Frsh Cls; Rep Soph Cls; Rep Jr Cls; Rep Sr Cls; Pres Stu Cncl; Powder Puff Ftbl; Var Socr; Physcl Thrpy.

GREENLEAF, PAULA LYN; North Hunterdon HS; Annandale, NJ; (Y); 50/300; Am Leg Aux Girls St; JA; Key Clb; Model UN; Pres Spanish Clb; Nwsp Ed-Chief; VP Soph Cls; Var L Cheerleading; High Hon Roll; Pres Schlr; Boston U; Bnkg.

GREENSPAN, IRA; E Brunswick HS; East Brunswick, NJ; (Y); Drama Clb; Model UN; Science Clb; Off Temple Yth Grp; Variety Show; Yrbk Stf; Hon Roll; NJ S Area Brd For AZA/BBG Tmpl Yth Grp 86-87; E Brnswick Yth Srv Cmmsn 86-87; Pltcl Sci.

GREENSTEIN, MARC; Clifton HS; Clifton, NJ; (Y); 115/687; Spanish Clb; Concert Band; Jazz Band; Mrchg Band; Orch; School Musical; Yrbk Stf; Swmmng; Hon Roll.

GREENWAY, ROBERT; St Joseph Regional HS; Monroe, NY; (Y); 90/200; Library Aide; Model UN; Political Wkr; Ski Clb; Yrbk Stf; JV Tennis; Hon Roll; Prfct Atten Awd; Fnlst-Navy ROTC Full Schlrshp 85; VA Military Inst.

GREENWOOD, TRACEY; Wildwood Catholic HS; Wildwood Crest, NJ; (Y); French Clb; Stage Crew; Yrbk Ed-Chief; Yrbk Stf; Vllybl; French Hon Soc; Equestrion Awds/Own A 1/4 Horse; Bus.

GREER, LISA; Pleasantville HS; Pleasantville, NJ; (S); Pom Pon; NHS; Cert Acadmc Achvt 84-85; Cert Achvt Foods I 84; Cert Achvt Eastrn Cultrs 84; Bus Admin.

GREER, MICHELLE; Gateway Regional HS; Westville, NJ; (Y); 46/204; French Clb; Key Clb; SADD; Var Capt Cheerleading; Hon Roll; Rotary Awd; Law.

GREER, RICHARD; Gateway Regional HS; Westville, NJ; (Y); 52/204; Cmnty Wkr; JV Bsbl; Hon Roll; Prfct Atten Awd.

GREEVES, GABRIELLE; Holy Family Acad; Bayonne, NJ; (Y); Computer Clb; Dance Clb; Math Clb; Pep Clb; Spanish Clb; Stage Crew; Nwsp Phtg; Yrbk Phtg; Rep Frsh Cls; Rep Soph Cls; Villanova U; Comp Sci.

GREGORY, CHICONA; Edison HS; Edison, NJ; (Y); #67 In Class; Spanish Clb; Bsktbl; Johns Hopkins U; Med.

GREGORY, DONNA A; Marlboro HS; Morganville, NJ; (Y); 26/528; German Clb; Red Cross Aide; Hon Roll; Ntl Merit SF; Opt Clb Awd; Church Yth Grp; Shld & Key Awd 84 & 85; 1st Pl Physcs Olympds 86.

GREGORY, WALT; Parsippany HS; Parsippany, NJ; (Y); Concert Band; Jazz Band; School Musical; School Play; Symp Band; Gov Hon Prg Awd; Cltrl Enrchmnt Awd 85; Gvrnrs Schl Of Arts 86; Music.

GREGSON, KRIS; Washington Township HS; Sewell, NJ; (Y); Church Yth Grp; Church Choir; Hon Roll.

GREIF, HAYLEY; Hightstown HS; E Windsor, NJ; (Y); AFS; Cmnty Wkr; Intnl Clb; Service Clb; Spanish Clb; Trs SADD; Lit Mag; Rep Soph Cls; Hon Roll.

GREMLICH, MARIA; Weehawken HS; Weehawken, NJ; (Y); 5/89; Math Tm; Yrbk Stf; VP Sr Cls; Hon Roll; Trs NHS; Pres Schlr; Yetta Groshans Ldrshp Awd 86; Fin Gov Schl NJ 85; Rider Coll; Acctng.

GRENNAN, COLLEEN; Lakeland Regional HS; Ringwood, NJ; (Y); 32/303; Church Yth Grp; French Clb; Ski Clb; Yrbk Stf; Off Jr Cls; Rep Sr Cls; JV Fld Hcky; Powder Puff Ftbl; High Hon Roll; NHS; Prudue U; Rstrnt Mang.

GRESCH, EDWARD; Riverside HS; Riverside, NJ; (Y); 5/84; Chess Clb; Rep Frsh Cls; Rep Soph Cls; Rep Jr Cls; Rep Sr Cls; Rep Stu Cncl; Bsbl; High Hon Roll; Hon Roll; Rep NHS; Rutgers U; Comp Sci.

GRIBBLE, JILL; Sacred Heart HS; Vineland, NJ; (S); 8/67; Church Yth Grp; Spanish Clb; Church Choir; School Play; Co-Capt Yrbk Stf; Rep Sr Cls; High Hon Roll; NHS; Achvt Awd-Hstry 85; CPR Cert 84 & 85; Hlth Careers Clb; Eductn.

GRIECO, ANNAMARIA; Mount Saint Dominic Acad; Bloomfield, NJ; (Y); 3/55; Hosp Aide; Pres Intnl Clb; JCL; VP Latin Clb; Service Clb; Hst Frsh Cls; Hst Soph Cls; Stu Cncl; High Hon Roll; NHS.

GRIECO, DORA; Triton Regional HS; Glendora, NJ; (Y); 10/286; Church Yth Grp; Debate Tm; Yrbk Ed-Chief; Powder Puff Ftbl; Hon Roll; NHS; Rotary Awd; Ntnl Jrnlsm Awd 84; Glassboro ST Coll; Spec Ed.

GRIEFER, BRIAN; Wallington HS; Wallington, NJ; (Y); 5/75; Am Leg Boys St; Ski Clb; Bsbl; Bsktbl; High Hon Roll; NHS; Prsdntl Acdmc Ftnss Awd 85-86; Cook Coll; Pre-Vet.

GRIESSLER, PETER; Hamilton HS East; Robbinsville, NJ; (Y); Boy Scts; Crs Cntry; Swmmng; Trk; Garden ST Schlrshp 86; Trenton ST Coll; Cmptr Sci.

GRIEVES, DANIELLE; Paulsboro HS; Paulsboro, NJ; (Y); 27/140; Cheerleading; Mat Maids; Hon Roll; Office Aide; Fld Hcky; Hnrs Engl.

GRIFFIN, DESMOND; Rahway HS; Rahway, NJ; (Y); Am Leg Boys St; Science Clb; Rep Soph Cls; Var L Ftbl; Var L Trk; High Hon Roll; JETS Awd; Jr NHS; NHS; Trs Spanish NHS; Bucknell U; Engrng.

GRIFFIN, GRETCHEN; Toms River H S East; Toms River, NJ; (Y); German Clb; Intnl Clb; Math Tm; Band; Concert Band; Mrchg Band; Yrbk Rptr; Lit Mag; High Hon Roll; Ntl Merit SF; Acadm Ltr; Vetrn.

GRIFFIN, JENNY; Hotchkiss HS; Englewood, NJ; (Y); Thesps; Varsity Clb; Church Choir; School Play; JV Fld Hcky; Var Lcrss; High Hon Roll; Ntl Frnch Cntst 11th Pl 85-86; Figure Sktng Comptn 84; Brdcst Jrnlsm.

GRIFFIN, KEVIN; Wall HS; Neptune, NJ; (Y); 29/300; Ski Clb; JV Bsbl; Var Socr; High Hon Roll; Hon Roll; Ntl Merit SF.

GRIFFIN, MARY; Red Bank Catholic HS; Little Silver, NJ; (Y); NFL; Yrbk Ed-Chief; VP Jr Cls; NHS; Latin Clb; Math Clb; Trk; High Hon Roll; Hon Roll; Engl I Acad Awd 83-84; Latin Acad Awd 83-84; Amer Lit Awd 84-85; Ltn Ptry Acad Awd 85-86; Acad Excllnce; Engl.

GRIFFIN, RICHARD; Kinnelon HS; Kinnelon, NJ; (Y); 60/190; Boy Scts; Latin Clb; Ski Clb; Nwsp Stf; Im Bsbl; Im Bsktbl; Im Bowling; Im Ftbl; Im Golf; Im Lcrss; Stevens Inst Tech; Electrical.

GRIFFIN, ROSE MARIE; Bayonne HS; Bayonne, NJ; (Y); Dance Clb; Drama Clb; Chorus; Stage Crew; Hon Roll; Bus Mgt.

GRIFFIN, ROSEMARIE; Bayonne HS; Bayonne, NJ; (Y); Drama Clb; Chorus; School Play; Stage Crew; Hon Roll; Bus.

GRIFFIN, WARDELL; Snyder HS; Jersey City, NJ; (Y); JA; Renaissance Pgm 85-87.

GRIFFITH, ADRIENNE; Wall HS; Manasquan, NJ; (S); 23/267; Ski Clb; Concert Band; Mrchg Band; Stat Bsbl; JV Bsktbl; Stat Fld Hcky; High Hon Roll; Hon Roll.

GRIFFITH, CARRIE; Clearview Regional HS; Richwood, NJ; (Y); 6/174; Pres Church Yth Grp; Acpl Chr; Capt Drill Tm; Capt Flag Corp; Madrigals; School Musical; Stage Crew; NHS; Library Aide; Chorus; Grls Ctznshp Inst 85; Virginia Polytechnic Inst.

GRIFFITH, KELLY; Sayreville War Memorial HS; Sayreville, NJ; (Y); 23/380; German Clb; GAA; Var Crs Cntry; Var Trk; Hon Roll; NHS; Ntl Merit Ltr; Pres Schlr; Grmn Hnr Soc; Rtgrs Schlr; Rtgrs Coll; Pysch.

GRIFFITH, PATRICIA; Cumberland Regional HS; Bridgeton, NJ; (Y); 23/342; Drama Clb; Hosp Aide; Pres Red Cross Aide; Acpl Chr; Chorus; Madrigals; Stage Crew; Nwsp Stf; Ed Lit Mag; High Hon Roll; Bridgeton Hosp Ladies Aux-L Rainear RN Schlrshp 86; Sweet Adelines Outstndng Vcl Awd 86; Cumberland Cnty Coll; Nrsng.

GRIGG, ERIC B; Southern Regional HS; Waretown, NJ; (Y); Church Yth Grp; Teachers Aide; High Hon Roll; Jr NHS; NHS; Doc Of Chrprctc.

GRIGNI, LAURA; Carteret HS; Carteret, NJ; (Y); 22/198; Concert Band; Drm Mjr(t); Mrchg Band; Sec Soph Cls; Sec Jr Cls; Pres Sr Cls; Var Cheerleading; Hon Roll; NHS; Legal Asst.

GRIKIS, JAMI; Toms River East HS; Toms River, NJ; (Y); 166/490; DECA; Flag Corp; Mrchg Band; Var JV Bsktbl; Comp Sci.

GRILK, ANDREW H; West Milford HS; West Milford, NJ; (Y); 68/420; Am Leg Boys St; Pres Computer Clb; Varsity Clb; Acpl Chr; Band; Chorus; Church Choir; Concert Band; Jazz Band; Mrchg Band; 1st Tm All Conf Hgh Jmp 86; 3rd Pl JR Olympcs Rgn 1 Chmpnshps 85; Mst Dedctd Bktbl Awd 86; NJIT; Elec Engrng.

GRILLO, VITA; Saint John Vianney HS; Colts Neck, NJ; (Y); Cmnty Wkr; FBLA; Service Clb; Teachers Aide; Bus Adm.

GRIM, KATHERINE; Delaware Valley Regional HS; Milford, NJ; (Y); Am Leg Aux Girls St; Church Yth Grp; Intnl Clb; Key Clb; School Play; JV Cheerleading; High Hon Roll; Hon Roll; Mock Trl Tm 86; Eng.

GRIMES, DAWN MARIE; North Brunswick Township HS; N Brunswick, NJ; (Y); 28/297; Yrbk Stf; High Hon Roll; Hon Roll; NHS; Cert De Merite Pour Les Grands Concours 85; Cert De Merite Pour Les Grands Concours 86; Frnch.

GRIMES, KAROL; St Cecilia HS; Eanglewood, NJ; (Y); 9/42; Hosp Aide; Library Aide; Var Cheerleading; Vllybl; Hon Roll; Prfct Atten Awd; Wesleyan U; Rl Est Brkr.

GRIMES, LISA; Passaic County Tech & Voc HS; Paterson, NJ; (S); Spanish Clb; Teachers Aide; Nwsp Stf; Yrbk Stf; VP Jr Cls; VP Sr Cls; Rep Stu Cncl; JV Cheerleading; 1st Deg Of Excel Sngls 83; Montclair ST; Dnce.

GRIMES, SHAUNDRA; Henry Snyder HS; Jersey City, NJ; (Y); Church Yth Grp; Dance Clb; Girl Scts; Church Choir; Color Guard; Drill Tm; Off Jr Cls; Cheerleading; Hon Roll; Prfct Atten Awd; Parent Cncl Achvt Awd 86; Merit Rll 85-86; Essay Awd 84; Rutgers U; Comp Oper.

GRIMES, TAMI; Essex Catholic Girls HS; East Orange, NJ; (Y); 26/70; Pres Church Yth Grp; Dance Clb; Debate Tm; FHA; Pep Clb; SADD; Chorus; Pres Church Choir; Nwsp Phtg; Nwsp Rptr; Religion,Hist,Stu Cncl Awd 83-86; Lawyer.

GRIMMELL, LISA; Parsippany HS; Lake Hiawatha, NJ; (Y); 18/320; FBLA; Library Aide; Pep Clb; Service Clb; Spanish Clb; Yrbk Stf; Sftbl; Hon Roll; NHS; Drew U Piano Comptn MEA Of NJ 82-83; Montclair ST Gftd & Tlntd Prog; Ecnmcs.

GRINBERG, HEATHER; Shore Regional HS; W Long Branch, NJ; (Y); French Clb; Key Clb; Service Clb; Variety Show; Yrbk Ed-Chief; Yrbk Stf; French Hon Soc; High Hon Roll; Hon Roll; Quiz Bowl; Gen Bus.

GRINER, PAMELA; Cumberland Regional HS; Bridgeton, NJ; (Y); 23/315; Church Yth Grp; Debate Tm; Intnl Clb; JCL; Science Clb; Yrbk Phtg; Yrbk Stf; Var Fld Hcky; Hon Roll; Pres Schlr; Intl Frgn Lang Awd 86; Pres Acad Ftns Awd 86; VA Poly Tech Inst; Landscape.

GRINWIS, JOHN; High Point Regional HS; Sussex, NJ; (Y); Pres Aud/Vis; Cmnty Wkr; Acpl Chr; Band; Chorus; Concert Band; Mrchg Band; School Musical; School Play; Var Bowling; Accntng.

GRIPP, DAVID F; Hamilton High West; Trenton, NJ; (Y); 53/323; JV Var Ftbl; Var JV Trk; Hon Roll; Poetry Pblshd In Aspirations 86; Trenton ST Coll; Elec Engr.

GRISHAM, SARAH; Westfield SR HS; New York, NY; (Y); French Clb; Key Clb; Latin Clb; Chorus; Yrbk Bus Mgr; Yrbk Stf; Ed Lit Mag; High Hon Roll; NHS; Publ-Ntl Stu Poetry Anthlgy 83; New York U; Jrnlsm.

GRISSOM, KAREN; Mt Olive HS; Flanders, NJ; (Y); 18/296; Church Yth Grp; Band; Chorus; Church Choir; Concert Band; Mrchg Band; Orch; Hon Roll; NHS; Ntl Music Hnr Soc Tri-M 86; Elem Ed Tchr.

GRIZMALA, JENNIFER; Middletown High Schl South; Lincroft, NJ; (S); 22/436; Cmnty Wkr; Jr Cls; Sec Sr Cls; JV Crs Cntry; Var Trk; Hon Roll; Bus.

GROBELNY, RICHARD; Perth Amboy HS; Perth Amboy, NJ; (Y); Computer Clb; Library Aide; Mathletes; Stage Crew; Stat Bsbl; Var Score Keeper; High Hon Roll; NHS; Comp.

GROCOTT, HEATHER; Bridgewater-Raritan HS West; Bridgewater, NJ; (Y); Trs German Clb; Hosp Aide; Ski Clb; Flag Corp; Sr Cls; Var Socr; Var Capt Swmmng; Hon Roll; NHS; Pres Schlr; Hgh Actvt In German 86; U Of MA Amherst; Hotl Admin.

GRODER, JILL ELLEN; Middletown HS; Middletown, NJ; (Y); 283/483; Church Yth Grp; Hosp Aide; Library Aide; Office Aide; Teachers Aide; School Musical; School Play; Stage Crew; Lit Mag; Im Badmtn; Chptr Of Right Track Anti-Drug Orgnztn For Stu & Teens-Pres 82-83; Russell Sage Coll; Child Psych.

GRODER, SHARI; Scotch Plains-Fanwood HS; Scotch Plains, NJ; (Y); 57/311; AFS; DECA; Drama Clb; Q&S; Temple Yth Grp; Flag Corp; Mrchg Band; Nwsp Rptr; Nwsp Stf; Lit Mag; Boston U; Brdcstng.

GRODSKY, DAVID S; New Milford HS; New Milford, NJ; (Y); 1/160; Am Leg Boys St; Yrbk Ed-Chief; Elks Awd; French Hon Soc; High Hon Roll; NCTE Awd; NHS; Ntl Merit Schol; St Schlr; Val; Gold Mdlst NJ Acad Decthln Soc Sci 86; Outstndng Stu Engl & Soc Studs 86; Pres Acad Fit Awd 86; Princeton U; Hstry.

GROELLER, MATTHEW; Clifton HS; Clifton, NJ; (Y); 1/687; French Clb; Math Clb; Var L Swmmng; JV Tennis; French Hon Soc; Hon Roll; Jr NHS; Top 5 Pct PSAT 86; Rutgers U Schlrs Day 86; Rensselaer Mth & Sci Awd 86.

GROFF, AMANDA; Wash Twp HS; Pitman, NJ; (Y); 4-H; Girl Scts; JA; Library Aide; Chorus; Fld Hcky; 4-H Awd; Art Awd 84-85; 3rd US Pony Club 85; DVC; Animal Hs.

GROFF, DENISE LYNN; Cumberland Regional HS; Bridgeton, NJ; (S); 22/369; Sec FBLA; Hosp Aide; VP Red Cross Aide; Concert Band; Mrchg Band; Yrbk Bus Mgr; Tennis; High Hon Roll; NHS; Church Yth Grp; Typng I Southern Rgnls 4th Pl 84; Bus.

GROFF JR, RICHARD W; Phillipsburg HS; Phillipsburg, NJ; (Y); 68/292; Church Yth Grp; Im Bowling; Im Vllybl; Hon Roll; Bell & Howell Schlrshp 86; Rose-Hulman Inst Tech; Eng.

GROH, TARA; Clifton HS; Clifton, NJ; (Y); 1/687; Cmnty Wkr; Key Clb; Office Aide; Chorus; Sec Stu Cncl; Cheerleading; Mgr(s); High Hon Roll; Jr NHS; Spanish NHS.

GROHOWSKI, WILLIAM R; Hopatcong HS; Hopatcong, NJ; (Y); 45/173; Ftbl; JV Trk; Hon Roll; Cnty COLL Morris; Lndscpng.

GROMEK, ELIZABETH; North Brunswick Township HS; N Brunswick, NJ; (Y); 59/297; Church Yth Grp; French Clb; School Play; Mgr(s); Var Trk; Art.

GROOKETT, TOM; Wildwood HS; Wildwood, NJ; (Y); Letterman Clb; Varsity Clb; School Play; Rep Jr Cls; Var L Bsbl; Var L Ftbl; Hon Roll; Aud/Vis; Pre-Med.

GROOVER, MICHELE; Immaculate Conception HS; Hasbrouck Heights, NJ; (S); 11/88; Ski Clb; Chorus; School Play; Rep Frsh Cls; Rep Soph Cls; Rep Jr Cls; Hon Roll; Spanish NHS.

GROSJEAN, PAUL; Wayne Hills HS; Wayne, NJ; (Y); Varsity Clb; Var Ftbl; Hon Roll; Engrng.

GROSS, DAVID; Absegami HS; Egg Hbr, NJ; (Y); 65/280; Letterman Clb; Ski Clb; Varsity Clb; Bsbl; Coach Actv; Ftbl; Wt Lftg; Wrstlng; Boy Scts; Trk; Ftbl Capt 86; Capt Wrstlng & Bsbl 86; Atlantic CC; Bus Adm.

GROSS, MICHAEL R; Collingswood SR HS; Collingswood, NJ; (Y); Am Leg Boys St; Capt Aud/Vis; German Clb; SADD; Capt Band; Pep Band; Capt Stage Crew; Stat Bsktbl; Mgr(s); Score Keeper; Exemplar Awd 84; PTA Schl Srv Awd 84; Elec Engr.

GROSS, NANCY L; Holy Spirit HS; Cologne, NJ; (Y); 117/370; Am Leg Aux Girls St; Church Yth Grp; Hosp Aide; School Play; Yrbk Stf; Var L Fld Hcky; Mgr Swmmng; Natl Art Hnr Scty 84-86; Fnlst Miss NJ ST Natl Tngr Pgnt 86; VP Frshmn Hmrm; Syracuse U; Brdcst.

GROSSMAN, LISA; Hillsborough HS; Belle Mead, NJ; (Y); 21/285; Cmnty Wkr; Rep Temple Yth Grp; Band; Mrchg Band; Pep Band; Rep Stu Cncl; Var Tennis; High Hon Roll; Hon Roll; NHS; Psychlgy.

GROSSMAN, SHOSHANA; Toms River HS East; Toms River, NJ; (Y); Var Powder Puff Ftbl; JV Socr; Hon Roll; Educ.

GROVATT, TODD; Rancocas Valley Regional HS; Mt Holly, NJ; (Y); 40/265; Church Yth Grp; Pres Ski Clb; Rep Frsh Cls; Rep Jr Cls; JV Socr; Var Tennis; Hon Roll; U Of Tampa; Busnss Admin.

GROVE, RONALD A; Univeristy HS; Newark, NJ; (Y); Church Yth Grp; Computer Clb; Drama Clb; Exploring; FCA; JA; Leo Clb; Spanish Clb; School Play; Crs Cntry; Law.

GROVE, SCOTT; South Brunswick HS; Kendall Pk, NJ; (Y); 17/244; Boy Scts; Math Tm; Science Clb; Ski Clb; Golf; Socr; Wrstlng; Cit Awd; Hon Roll; Ntl Merit Ltr; Excllnc Am Hstry 86; South Brnswick Educ Assoc Schlrshp 86; U Of MI; Marine Blgy.

GROVEMAN, DANIEL; Gill-St Bernards HS; Chester, NJ; (Y); Debate Tm; 4-H; Library Aide; NFL; Office Aide; Radio Clb; Science Clb; Speech Tm; Stat Bsbl; Hon Roll; Law.

GRUBER, AMY; Pitman HS; Pitman, NJ; (Y); Am Leg Aux Girls St; Church Yth Grp; Drama Clb; Girl Scts; PAVAS; Chorus; Church Choir; Concert Band; Jazz Band; Orch; Miss Pitman 86; Schlrshp To NJ Schl Of Arts 84; Soprano Slst All-ST Chrs 86; Music Prfrmnce.

GRUHLER, DARLENE; Vineland HS; Vineland, NJ; (Y); Csmtlgy.

GRUNGO, JOE; Holy Cross HS; Mount Holly, NJ; (Y); Wt Lftg; Business.

GRUNSTRA, GREGG C; Hackensack HS; Maywood, NJ; (Y); Am Leg Boys St; Office Aide; Rep Stu Cncl; Hon Roll; NHS.

GRUNZA, DAVID; Highland Regional HS; Blackwood, NJ; (S); 3/325; Am Leg Boys St; VP Church Yth Grp; Trs Computer Clb; Trs French Clb; JA; Var Crs Cntry; Var L Trk; Pres NHS; Prfct Atten Awd; St Schlr; Top 10 Chem Awd ST 83; Top 20 Physcs Awd ST 84; Chem Engr.

GRUPE, LAURIE; Cranford HS; Cranford, NJ; (Y); 73/292; Latin Clb; Math Clb; Math Tm; Yrbk Stf; Pres Frsh Cls; VP Soph Cls; VP Jr Cls; VP Sr Cls; Fld Hcky; Hon Roll; Union Cnty Fld Hcky Chmps 85; N Jrsy Sctn 2 Grp Hcky Chmps 85; U Of New Hampshire; Htl Mgmt.

GRYL, VIRGINIA M; Notre Dame HS; E Windsor, NJ; (Y); Debate Tm; Var Drama Clb; French Clb; Key Clb; Red Cross Aide; Off Ski Clb; Varsity Clb; School Play; Nwsp Rptr; Yrbk Stf; Pres Italian Clb 85-87; 1st Pl Princeton Marathn 84; 3rd Pl Swmmng Relay Cnty 85; American U; Lawyer.

GRYSZKA, MICHELLE; Rahway HS; Rahway, NJ; (Y); Key Clb; Pep Clb; Sec Service Clb; Nwsp Rptr; Nwsp Stf; Off Jr Cls; Stu Cncl; Tennis; High Hon Roll; Hon Roll.

GRZYBOWSKI, KATHLEEN L; Montville Twp HS; Montville, NJ; (Y); Church Yth Grp; FBLA; Yrbk Phtg; Ed Yrbk Stf; Fld Hcky; Swmmng; Hon Roll; Key Clb; Ski Clb; Varsity Clb; MVP Swim 84-85; Swim Capt 86-87; Photogrphy Wrk Brd Ed Off 86-87; Comm Advrtsng.

GRZYBOWSKI, MELISSA; Mater Dei HS; Atlantic Highlnds, NJ; (Y); 18/157; Cmnty Wkr; Stage Crew; Lit Mag; Hon Roll; NHS; Archaeology.

GUAGE, JOSEPH; St John Vianney HS; Aberdeen, NJ; (Y); Church Yth Grp; SADD; Trs Jr Cls; Trs Sr Cls; Trs Stu Cncl; Var L Crs Cntry; JV Ftbl; Var Capt Trk; JV Wrstlng; Hon Roll; Prsdntl Physcl Frns Awd; St Bonaventure; Accntng.

GUALTIERI, RICHARD; Washington Township HS; Sewell, NJ; (Y); Boy Scts; Chess Clb; Exploring; 4-H; Radio Clb; Wrstlng; Law.

GUARDIOLA, CONRAD; Franklin HS; Somerset, NJ; (Y); Am Leg Boys St; Var Capt Socr; JV Tennis; High Hon Roll; Hon Roll; NHS; Treas Ntl Hnr Soc 86-87.

GUARI, JASON; Red Bank Catholic HS; Coltsneck, NJ; (Y); Cmnty Wkr; Debate Tm; Latin Clb; Math Clb; Ski Clb; VP Frsh Cls; Im Bowling; JV Diving; Im Ftbl; JV Swmmng; Karate Achvt 85-86; Princeton U; Politcn.

GUARINO, CAROLYN; Elizabeth HS; Westfield, NJ; (Y); 3/847; Dance Clb; Key Clb; Math Clb; School Musical; Yrbk Stf; Lion Awd; Sec NHS; Rotary Awd; Pres Spanish NHS; Sorostmst 2nd Pl 86; Elizabeth Ed Assoc Awd 86; Unico Elizabeth 86; Douglass Coll; Nutrtn.

GUARINO, JOY LYNN; Gill/St Bernards HS; Warren, NJ; (Y); 4/17; Cmnty Wkr; Drama Clb; School Musical; School Play; Yrbk Stf; Rep Soph Cls; Rep Jr Cls; High Hon Roll; Trs Church Yth Grp; Church Choir; Drmtc Arts Schlrshp 83-86; U Of Hartford; Brdcstng.

GUDAITIS, CHRISTINE; Neumann Prep; Ringwood, NJ; (Y); 7/82; Drama Clb; Ski Clb; School Play; Variety Show; Yrbk Stf; Var Fld Hcky; Var Trk; French Hon Soc; NHS; Lns Clb Schlrshp 86; NY U; Actrss.

GUDICELLO, LYNETTE; Shore Regional HS; Oceanport, NJ; (Y); Church Yth Grp; Hosp Aide; Ski Clb; Band; Concert Band; Mrchg Band; Nwsp Stf; High Hon Roll; Hon Roll; Bus.

GUDZ, RICHARD; Hunterdon Central HS; Somervle, NJ; (Y); 19/539; VP Church Yth Grp; FCA; 4-H; Math Tm; Science Clb; Coach Actv; JV Tennis; High Hon Roll; Hon Roll; NHS; NJ Dstngshd Schlrs Prog 86; NJ Inst Of Tech Hnrs Prog; NJ Inst Of Tech; Cvl Engrng.

GUDZIJ, MICHAEL; Clifton HS; Clifton, NJ; (Y); 33/667; Cmnty Wkr; Political Wkr; Science Clb; Ski Clb; Spanish Clb; Lit Mag; Rep Frsh Cls; Gov Hon Prg Awd; Hon Roll; Jr NHS; Duke U; Med.

GUEAR, CHRISTOPHER; Hamilton High Schl West; Trenton, NJ; (S); 39/330; Church Yth Grp; Drama Clb; Thesps; Band; Chorus; Concert Band; Madrigals; Mrchg Band; Orch; Pep Band; Poltcl Sci.

GUEAR, JEFFREY; Hamilton HS West; Yardville, NJ; (Y); Trs Key Clb; Pres Science Clb; Concert Band; Madrigals; Mrchg Band; Symp Band; Variety Show; JV Var Wrstlng; Ntl Merit SF; Key Clb NJ Dist Treas 86-87.

GUELDNER, BERNHARD; Edison HS; Edison, NJ; (Y); Ski Clb; JV Ftbl; JV Trk; Hon Roll; Rutgers Coll.

GUERGUERIAN, CLAUDINE; John P Stevens HS; Edison, NJ; (Y); Art Clb; Church Yth Grp; Debate Tm; French Clb; Model UN; Color Guard; Stage Crew; Key Clb; Pom Pon; French Hon Soc; Art.

GUERIN, TODD; Lakeland Regional HS; Ringwood, NJ; (Y); 18/303; Boy Scts; Cmnty Wkr; Math Tm; Quiz Bowl; Nwsp Rptr; Wrstlng; Cit Awd; High Hon Roll; NHS; SUNY Geneseo; Bio.

GUERRA JR, NICANOR D; Marist HS; Jersey City, NJ; (Y); 3/115; Art Clb; Key Clb; Science Clb; Nwsp Rptr; Im Bsktbl; Im Bowling; Hon Roll; NHS; Acad All-Amer 84; Ntl Merit Sci Awd 84; Pre-Med.

GUERRERO, MANUEL; Roselle Catholic HS; Elizabeth, NJ; (S); 2/153; Math Tm; Yrbk Stf; Rep Frsh Cls; Pres Soph Cls; Pres Jr Cls; Pres Stu Cncl; High Hon Roll; NHS; Ntl Merit SF; Semi Fnlst Ntl Hspnc Schlrs Prgrm 85-86; Garden ST Schlrshp 85-86.

GUERRIERO, SUZANNE; Toms River East HS; Toms River, NJ; (Y); 148/585; Camera Clb; SADD; Art Clb; JV Socr; Hon Roll; Teacher.

GUERTIN, MARY; Mt St Mary Acad; Edison, NJ; (Y); 20/83; French Clb; Ski Clb; Nwsp Stf; Yrbk Stf; Rep Frsh Cls; Rep Jr Cls; Rep Stu Cncl; Hon Roll; Church Yth Grp; GAA; Stonehill College; Acctg.

GUESS, LESTER; Camden HS; Camden, NJ; (Y); JA; ROTC; Band; Concert Band; Jazz Band; Mrchg Band; School Musical; School Play; Rep Stu Cncl; Var Tennis; U S Naval Acad; Bus Mgmt.

GUESS, TERRI; East Orange HS; East Orange, NJ; (S); Dance Clb; Drill Tm; Variety Show; Nwsp Rptr; Ed Yrbk Sprt Ed; VP Sr Cls; Stat Bsktbl; Trk; Hon Roll; Glassboro St Coll; Cmnctns.

GUEST, TRACEY JEAN; Ramapo HS; Wyckoff, NJ; (Y); 118/329; VP Church Yth Grp; German Clb; Radio Clb; Yrbk Stf; Cert Of Merit French 3 & German 2-Undergrad Achvt Awd 85-86; Engl.

GUETHER JR, RICHARD C; Woodbridge HS; Woodbridge, NJ; (Y); 11/414; Am Leg Boys St; Church Yth Grp; Math Clb; Political Wkr; Varsity Clb; Rep Jr Cls; Var Crs Cntry; Var Trk; Hon Roll; Pres NHS; Woodbridge Twp Stu Advsry Committee 84-5; Gftd & Tlntd 84-85; Engrng.

GUGLIOTTA, ANTHONY; Bridgewater-Raritan HS West; Bridgewater, NJ; (Y); Math Tm; Scholastic Bowl; Science Clb; High Hon Roll; Hon Roll; Ntl Merit Spcl Schlrshp 86; PTO Jnt Schlrshp 86; 2-Yr Hnrs Hstry 86; Rutgers Coll; Comp Sci.

GUIDICE, CAREY; Wood-Ridge HS; Wood-Ridge, NJ; (S); 12/100; GAA; Spanish Clb; Yrbk Stf; Pres Frsh Cls; Pres Soph Cls; Pres Jr Cls; Pres Sr Cls; VP Church Yth Grp4; Capt Cheerleading; Cit Awd; Rutgers U; Law.

GUIDRY, DEBORAH; Jackson Memorial HS; Jackson, NJ; (S); 14/334; Church Yth Grp; FCA; French Clb; Church Choir; Yrbk Stf; Bsktbl; Powder Puff Ftbl; High Hon Roll; NHS; Arlington Baptist Coll; Elem Ed.

GUIDRY, KEVIN G; Gloucester Catholic HS; Mantua, NJ; (Y); 20/176; Am Leg Boys St; Boy Scts; Chess Clb; Debate Tm; NFL; Speech Tm; Capt Bsktbl; Capt Crs Cntry; JV Capt Ftbl; Capt Trk; All Cnty 2nd Team Trk 86; Schl Rcrds Intermediate Hrdls & 1600 Meter Rly 86; West Point Mili Acad; Military.

GUIDRY, MARY; Holy Cross HS; Edgewater Park, NJ; (Y); 18/380; Church Yth Grp; French Clb; Political Wkr; Service Clb; School Play; Stage Crew; Yrbk Stf; Gov Hon Prg Awd; High Hon Roll; Hon Roll.

GUILIANO, GERALD; Cliffside HS; Fairview, NJ; (Y); 58/254; Am Leg Boys St; Church Yth Grp; Political Wkr; Ski Clb; Variety Show; Yrbk Ed-Chief; Yrbk Phtg; Yrbk Rptr; Stu Cncl; Var Bsbl; Rutgers U; Mktg.

GUILLEN, EDDY; Memorial HS; West New York, NJ; (Y); Intnl Clb; Spanish Clb; Var Bowling; Hon Roll; Acctng.

GUINAN, JOHN; Paramus Catholic Boys; Hackensack, NJ; (Y); 56/178; JV VP Ice Hcky; Villanova U; Bus.

GUINGON, JENNIFER; Mt Saint Dominic Acad; West Orange, NJ; (Y); 8/57; Trs Latin Clb; School Musical; Ed Yrbk Phtg; Ed Lit Mag; Sec Frsh Cls; Stu Cncl; Mgr Socr; High Hon Roll; VP NHS; Pres Acad Ftns Awd 86; Fairfield; Econ.

GUINTU, DANTE B; Palisades Park JR SR HS; Palisades Pk, NJ; (Y); Aud/Vis; Nwsp Phtg; Yrbk Phtg; Var Tennis; Compu Engrng.

GULLACE, MIKE; Hudson Catholic HS; Jersey City, NJ; (Y); Cmnty Wkr; Political Wkr; SADD; Im Bsktbl; St Peters Coll; Accntnt.

GULLY, DEIDRE; Essex Catholic Girls HS; Newark, NJ; (Y); FHA; Office Aide; Pep Clb; Drill Tm; Mgr(s); Score Keeper; Hon Roll; Comp Prgmg.

GUMIENNY, JILL; John F Kennedy HS; Iselin, NJ; (Y); 38/300; FBLA; Hosp Aide; Mrchg Band; Yrbk Stf; Off Sr Cls; Bowling; Capt Twrlr; Hon Roll; NHS; NJ St Twrlng Titles; Montclair ST; Fashion Merch.

GUNDERMAN, CHRISTINE; Phillipsburg HS; Phillipsburg, NJ; (Y); 32/296; Pres Church Yth Grp; Hosp Aide; SADD; Flag Corp; Rep Stu Cncl; Im Bowling; High Hon Roll; Hon Roll; Jr NHS; NHS; Phillipsburg HS Stu Cncl Schlrshp Awd 85-86; William Paterson Coll; Englsh.

GUNDLAH, CHRISANA; Lakeland Regional HS; Wanaque, NJ; (Y); Ski Clb; Off Jr Cls; Stu Cncl; Var Capt Cheerleading; Coach Actv; Tennis; High Hon Roll; Hon Roll; NHS; NEDT Awd; Bio.

GUNIA, CHRISTINE; Manalapan HS; Manalapan, NJ; (Y); 37/431; Yrbk Stf; Hon Roll; NHS; Acctg.

GUPTA, PRABHAT; John F Kennedy Memorial HS; Iselin, NJ; (Y); 15/273; Hosp Aide; VP Math Tm; Trs SADD; Varsity Clb; Orch; Ed Yrbk Stf; Capt Stu Cncl; Var Crs Cntry; Var Trk; Trs NHS; Rutgers Coll; Pre-Med.

GUPTA, RAJEEW; Franklin Twp HS; Somerset, NJ; (Y); 62/313; Boy Scts; Mathletes; Scholastic Bowl; SADD; Concert Band; Mrchg Band; Yrbk Phtg; Off Frsh Cls; Rep Jr Cls; Rep Jr Cls; Vincent Kaselis Mem Awd 85-86; Rutgers U; Biochem Engrng.

GUPTA, SHILPI; Morristown HS; Morristown, NJ; (Y); 5/449; Key Clb; Latin Clb; Math Clb; Math Tm; Red Cross Aide; Off Frsh Cls; Stu Cncl; JV Var Bsbl; Bsktbl; Gov Hon Prg Awd; Surgeon.

GURFIELD, SHARON; Hightstown HS; East Windsor, NJ; (Y); Drama Clb; Office Aide; Spanish Clb; VP SADD; Thesps; Chorus; School Musical; School Play; Variety Show; High Hon Roll; Jrnlsm.

GURSKIS, GRACE-ANNE J; Toms River East HS; Toms River, NJ; (Y); 107/489; Camera Clb; Stage Crew; Variety Show; Yrbk Phtg; Yrbk Stf; Lit Mag; Sec Soph Cls; Sec Jr Cls; Sec Sr Cls; Stu Cncl; Philadelphia Coll Arts; Art.

GURSKY, DAVID; Passaic Valley HS; Totowa, NJ; (Y); 9/358; Am Leg Boys St; French Clb; Key Clb; School Musical; Yrbk Stf; Lit Mag; High Hon Roll; Pres NHS; Ski Clb; Stage Crew; Accptd Carnegie-Mellon U Smmr Prog 86; Elec Engrg.

GURTCHEFF, GARY; Haddon Twp HS; Westmont, NJ; (Y); 27/170; Am Leg Boys St; Ski Clb; Thesps; School Musical; School Play; Yrbk Stf; Rep Stu Cncl; Var Golf; High Hon Roll; NHS; Ntl Hnr Soc Schlrshp Awd 86; Lead In Mscl 86; Top Stud Awd At Grad Frm Elem Schl 86; IN U; Optmtrst.

GURWICH, TREVOR; Dwight-Englewood HS; Englewood, NJ; (Y); Cmnty Wkr; VP Debate Tm; Nwsp Rptr; Rep Jr Cls; Rep Sr Cls; Var Socr; Var Tennis; Hon Roll; ST Tennis Champ 86; Founder Chrmn Cricket Clb 85-86; Bus.

GUSTAFSON, LAURA; Lakewood HS; Lakewood, NJ; (Y); Art Clb; English Clb; French Clb; JV Crs Cntry; JV Var Socr; Stat Trk; Comp Sci.

GUSTAVSON, SCOTT; Manalapan HS; Manalapan, NJ; (Y); JCL; Latin Clb; Thesps; School Musical; School Play; Stage Crew; Var Trk; Felect Engrg.

GUSTIS, JENNIFER; West Milford HS; W Milford, NJ; (S); 8/400; Church Yth Grp; Ski Clb; Spanish Clb; Varsity Clb; Yrbk Phtg; Yrbk Stf; Rep Stu Cncl; Co-Capt Var Gym; Hon Roll; NHS; Rotary Clb Awd Ded Athl 84.

GUTH, SUE; Victory Christian Schl; Elmer, NJ; (S); 4/17; Church Yth Grp; Chorus; School Musical; Yrbk Bus Mgr; Var Cheerleading; Var Mgr(s); Hon Roll; NHS; Christian Character Awd; Elem Educ.

GUTIERREZ, CHRISTOPHER; St Marys HS; Sayreville, NJ; (Y); Bsktbl; Socr; Mddlsx Coll; Engrng.

GUTIERREZ, JOSEPH; St Peters HS; N Bergen, NJ; (Y); Dance Clb; Pep Clb; Stage Crew; Trk; Pres Schlr; Pres Citation Acad Achvt Jersey Cty 86.

GUTIERREZ, JUAN J; Roselle Catholic HS; Elizabeth, NJ; (Y); Computer Clb; Ski Clb; Yrbk Stf; Var Bsbl; Hon Roll; Spanish NHS; Church Yth Grp; Math Clb; Spanish Clb; Varsity Clb; FL ST U; Acctg.

GUTIERREZ, LORETO; Bayonne HS; Bayonne, NJ; (Y); 1/388; Yrbk Stf; Rep Stu Cncl; Var JV Socr; Jr NHS; NHS; St Schlr; Val; Art Clb; Math Tm; Nwsp Rptr; U PA Club Metropolitan NJ Schlr 86; St Peters Coll Summer Schlr 84-85; Isshinryu Karate 85-86; U PA; Bio.

GUY JR, TERRY R; Freehold Twp HS; Freehold, NJ; (Y); Var JV Ftbl; Im Wrstlng; Clemson U; Cmptr Sci.

GUZMAN, AIDA; Perth Amboy HS; Edison, NJ; (Y); Art Clb; Camera Clb; Computer Clb; French Clb; Ski Clb; JV Sftbl; Hon Roll.

GUZMAN, LUZ; Saint Aloysius HS; Jersey City, NJ; (Y); Church Yth Grp; Library Aide; Spanish Clb; Bowling; Crs Cntry; Trk; Hon Roll; NHS; Reverend Joseph B Bagley Awd 86; Psych.

GUZMAN, SANTOS; New Providence HS; New Providence, NJ; (Y); Ski Clb; Varsity Clb; Rep Soph Cls; Rep Jr Cls; Rep Sr Cls; Rep Stu Cncl; JV Bsbl; Var L Ftbl; Ntl Merit SF; PA ST U; Pre-Law.

GUZZO, MARK A; W Deptford HS; Woodbury, NJ; (Y); 7/250; Am Leg Boys St; Boy Scts; Computer Clb; Color Guard; Concert Band; Drm Mjr(t); Mrchg Band; Hon Roll; NHS; Ntl Merit Ltr; Elec Engr.

GWAL, ANITA; Cherry Hill H S East; Cherry Hill, NJ; (Y); Dance Clb; School Musical; School Play; Var JV Pom Pon; High Hon Roll; NHS; Ntl Merit SF; St Schlr; Drama Clb; Library Aide; JR Miss Fin 85; Rutgers Schlr 85; Pre-Med.

GWYNNE, KELLY; Immaculate Conception HS; Maywood, NJ; (Y); Church Yth Grp; Cmnty Wkr; Hosp Aide; Library Aide; Chorus; Church Choir; School Musical; School Play; Nwsp Stf; Awd Typst Schl Nwspr 86; Svc Awd Chrch Chr 86; Spch Pthlgy.

GYORFI, BRENDA; Belvidere HS; Phillipsburg, NJ; (Y); Spanish Clb; SADD; Off Frsh Cls; Rep Soph Cls; Stu Cncl; Bowling; Mgr(s); Vllybl; Stat Wrstlng; Hon Roll; Sec.

GYURE, RICHARD; Dover HS; Mine Hill, NJ; (Y); Am Leg Boys St; Boy Scts; Computer Clb; Latin Clb; Ski Clb; School Musical; Stage Crew; Bsktbl; Bowling; Ftbl; Engr.

GYURE, RUSSELL; Dover HS; Mine Hill, NJ; (Y); AFS; Am Leg Boys St; Boy Scts; Latin Clb; Ski Clb; School Musical; Stage Crew; Var Ftbl; High Hon Roll; Hon Roll; Wstrn NE Coll; Bus.

HAACK, EDWARD; Seton Hall Prep; Verona, NJ; (Y); 40/200; Boy Scts; Key Clb; Band; Concert Band; Yrbk Stf; JV Ice Hcky; JV Socr; Hon Roll; NEDT High Score 83-84; Acctng.

HAAG, JENI; Point Pleasant Beach HS; Lavallette, NJ; (Y); 16/110; Cmnty Wkr; Sec French Clb; Office Aide; Ski Clb; SADD; Band; Concert Band; Mrchg Band; Symp Band; Nwsp Rptr; Seasd Rtry Clb Schlrshp 86; Georgian Court Coll; Elec Educ.

HAAG, KRISTINE CATHERINE; Westfield SR HS; Westfield, NJ; (Y); 98/504; Pep Clb; Spanish Clb; SADD; Chorus; School Musical; Variety Show; Var Cheerleading; Var Gym; Var Socr; Trk; Vrsty Chrlsng Cptn 85-86; Vrsty Lttrs Trk 85 & 86; NJ YMCA Gym ST Chmpn 82; U Of DE; Spnsh.

HAAS, ED; Absegami HS; Cologne, NJ; (Y); JV Ftbl; Hon Roll; Air Force; Engrng.

HAAS, TARA; Rancocas Valley HS; Mount Holly, NJ; (Y); 75/265; 4-H; Stage Crew; Frsh Cls; Soph Cls; Fld Hcky; Lcrss; Swmmng; Trk; Hon Roll; Wilkes; Psych.

HABER, ALAN; Manalapan HS; Manalapan, NJ; (Y); 90/450; Ski Clb; JV Bsbl; Bsktbl; Crs Cntry; JV Socr; Bus Mgt.

HABER, SUSAN; Linden HS; Linden, NJ; (Y); Hosp Aide; Key Clb; Office Aide; Science Clb; Temple Yth Grp; Rep Soph Cls; Stat Swmmng; Hon Roll; NHS; Rahway Hosp Jnr Vlnteer Mst Hours Wrkd 85; Psych.

HABERLE, FRANK; Rahway HS; Rahway, NJ; (Y); Band; Concert Band; Jazz Band; Mrchg Band; School Musical.

HACKETT, ADRIENNE; Camden HS; Camden, NJ; (S); 5/408; Sftbl; Tennis; Hon Roll; NHS; Trenton ST Coll; Nrsng.

HACKETT, STEVEN; Holy Spirit HS; Absecon, NJ; (Y); 79/350; Am Leg Boys St; Church Yth Grp; Civic Clb; Cmnty Wkr; Political Wkr; Teachers Aide; Rep Jr Cls; JV Bsbl; Hon Roll; NHS; La Salle Coll; Law Enf.

HADDEN, ROBIN; Wayne Hills HS; Wayne, NJ; (Y); 108/315; 4-H; GAA; Math Clb; Ski Clb; Mrchg Band; Yrbk Phtg; Tennis; Dnfth Awd; 4-H Awd; Hon Roll; Purdue U; Phrmcy.

HADDOCK, LIZ; Paulsboro HS; Paulsboro, NJ; (Y); DECA; Hosp Aide; Office Aide; Red Cross Aide; Ski Clb; Pres Frsh Cls; Rep Soph Cls; Rep Jr Cls; Rep Stu Cncl; Hon Roll; Gloucester Cnty Coll; Law Enfrc.

HADDON, JAMES; Cinnaminson HS; Cinnaminson, NJ; (Y); Church Yth Grp; Service Clb; Ski Clb; Spanish Clb; Im Bsktbl; Im Golf; Capt Swmmng; Im Vllybl; Outstndng Spanish Achvt Awd 83-84; Rotary Yth Ldrshp Awds Confrnc 85-86; Arch.

HADELER, LISA; Hawthorne HS; Hawthorne, NJ; (Y); 10/155; Church Yth Grp; Cmnty Wkr; Variety Show; Pres Soph Cls; Stu Cncl; Elks Awd; Hon Roll; NHS; Spanish NHS; Prnts Witht Prtnrs Schlrshp 86; DE U; Mrktng.

HADGINIKITAS, CLARISSA; Passaic Valley HS; W Paterson, NJ; (Y); 14/358; Bowling; Hon Roll; NHS; Ldrshp Awd Displyd Fld Stenogrphy 85-86; Berkeley Schl; Crt Stenogrphr.

HADLEY, CHRISTINE; Raulsboro HS; Gibbstown, NJ; (Y); 7/145; Hosp Aide; Stage Crew; Yrbk Stf; Lit Mag; High Hon Roll; VP NHS; VP Drama Clb; Mat Maids; Hon Roll; Stu Of Mnth 86; Space Shuttle Stu Invlmnt Proj 84; Acad Achvt Awd 85; Golden Poet Awd 86; Catawba Coll; Engl.

HADLEY, DEBORAH; Toms River HS North; Toms River, NJ; (Y); 1/412; Pres Church Yth Grp; Church Choir; School Musical; Yrbk Stf; Rep Jr Cls; Rep Sr Cls; Rep Stu Cncl; Sec NHS; St Schlr; Amer Assn U Wmn Awd; Acad Ltr Dstngshd Hnr Roll; Natl Sci Olympd Awds Biol, Hstry; Rutgers U; Elem Ed.

HADLEY, RAKEIM; The Pennington Schl; Newtonville, NJ; (Y); 3/78; Boy Scts; Pres Church Yth Grp; FCA; VP French Clb; Church Choir; Var JV Bsktbl; Bowling; Vllybl; High Hon Roll; Hon Roll; Biochem.

HAEFNER, SUSAN; Rahway HS; Rahway, NJ; (Y); Band; Mrchg Band; Twrlr; Spanish NHS.

HAEKYUNG, LEE; Palisades Pk JR SR HS; Palisades Pk, NJ; (Y); Church Yth Grp; Library Aide; Teachers Aide; Lit Mag; Tennis; High Hon Roll; AHSME Schl Wnnr 1st Pl 86; French 86; Genetics.

HAELIG JR, FREDERICK WEST; Bridgewater-Raritan HS East; Bound Brook, NJ; (Y); Am Leg Boys St; Church Yth Grp; Ski Clb; SADD; Off Sr Cls; Stu Cncl; NHS; Boy Scts; French Clb; Intnl Clb; Hgh O Brn Yth Fndtn NJLS Ambssdr 85; Sntr Brdlys Ldrshp Smnr 86; Egl Sct 86.

HAGAN, JOSEPH; Gloucester City JR SR HS; Brooklawn, NJ; (Y); Dance Clb; Stage Crew; Variety Show; JV Bsktbl; JV Socr; Hon Roll; Engrng.

HAGAN, WAYNE; Gloucester City JR-SR HS; Gloucester, NJ; (Y); Am Leg Boys St; Math Clb; Stage Crew; Yrbk Stf; JV Bsktbl; JV Ftbl; Hon Roll; NHS; Rutgers; Envrnmntl Sci.

HAGAN, YALONDA; Henry Snyder HS; Jersey City, NJ; (Y); Cmnty Wkr; Teachers Aide; Badmtn; Bsbl; Bsktbl; Gym; Score Keeper; Socr; Vllybl; Wt Lftg; Psychlgst.

HAGENBARTH, MICHAEL; Paulsboro HS; Gibbstown, NJ; (Y); 8/140; Ski Clb; Rep Frsh Cls; Rep Soph Cls; Var Wrstlng; High Hon Roll; Hon Roll; NHS; Regnl Winner NASA NSTA Space Shuttle Proj 84; Karate Belt 86; Paulsboro H S 84; Health Care.

HAGGERTY, BABETTE; Northern Highlands Regional HS; Uppr Saddle Riv, NJ; (Y); AFS; DECA; Drama Clb; Lit Mag; Rgnl Deca Apparel/Access Awds, St Conf Apparel/Access 86; Tobe-Coburn Schl; Fshn Merch.

HAGGERTY, BRIAN; Saint Rose HS; Neptune City, NJ; (Y); 27/202; Var Golf; Socr; High Hon Roll; Hon Roll; NHS; NEDT Awd; Govs Tchng Schlrshp; Outstndng Achvt Natl Spnsh Exm; Partl Acadmc Schlrshp Wesley Coll; U Of DE; Tchr.

HAGGERTY, CYNTHIA; Paul Vi HS; Turnsville, NJ; (Y); 149/486; Dance Clb; Drama Clb; Girl Scts; Math Clb; Spanish Clb; Drill Tm; School Musical; Stage Crew; Pom Pon; Spanish NHS; Glassboro ST Coll.

HAGGERTY, KELLY; Immaculate Conception HS; Wood Ridge, NJ; (S); 13/100; Church Yth Grp; School Musical; School Play; Stage Crew; Yrbk Phtg; Yrbk Stf; Stu Cncl; Stat Bsktbl; Score Keeper; Var Sftbl; Rutgers U; Hstry.

HAGOFSKY, LINDA LOUISE; Jacksmon Memorial HS; Jackson, NJ; (Y); 26/329; Am Leg Aux Girls St; Hosp Aide; Band; Capt Color Guard; Concert Band; Capt Drill Tm; Mrchg Band; Yrbk Phtg; Yrbk Stf; Cheerleading; Sprts Med.

HAGUE, CHRISTOPHER; Don Bosco Prep; North Haledon, NJ; (S); 3/150; Nwsp Stf; Lit Mag; JV Socr; Hon Roll; VFW Awd; Voice Dem Awd; Acad All-Amer 85-86; Natl Hstry & Govt Awd 85-86; Invstmnt Banker.

HAGUE, KRISTINE M; East Brunswick HS; East Brunswick, NJ; (Y); Church Yth Grp; 4-H; Spanish Clb; Chorus; Nwsp Rptr; Lit Mag; 4-H Awd; NHS; Spanish NHS; William Patterson Coll; Engl.

HAGY, MICHELLE; Overbrook Regional HS; Pine Hill, NJ; (Y); Am Leg Aux Girls St; Church Yth Grp; French Clb; Varsity Clb; Chorus; Stu Cncl; Sftbl; Tennis; Hon Roll; Prfct Atten Awd; Grphc Dsgn.

HAHM, W DOUGLAS; Manasquan HS; Manasquan, NJ; (Y); 3/223; Church Yth Grp; Math Clb; Lit Mag; Bsbl; Coach Actv; Ftbl; Elks Awd; High Hon Roll; Kiwanis Awd; NHS; Schlrps Natl & Lcl Elks & Kiwanis 86; Vars Schlr 86; PA ST U; Engrng.

HAHN, DAVID; Seton Hall Prep; S Orange, NJ; (Y); Art Clb; Boy Scts; Church Yth Grp; Hosp Aide; Nwsp Stf; Yrbk Stf; Notre Dame Villanova.

HAHN, SARA; Queen Of Peace HS; Rutherford, NJ; (Y); 80/230; Church Yth Grp; French Clb; Hosp Aide; SADD; Off Soph Cls; Trk; High Hon Roll; La Salle U; Bus.

HAINES, CAROLE LYNN; Toms River HS East; Normandy Bch, NJ; (Y); Model UN; Political Wkr; Spanish Clb; Drill Tm; Flag Corp; Mgr(s); Score Keeper; Hon Roll; Outstndng Poli Ed Stu 86; Model Congrs Chrprsn 86; Brookdale CC; Para-Legl Tech.

HAINES, CHRISTOPHER J; Kingsway Regional HS; Mickleton, NJ; (Y); Am Leg Boys St; Aud/Vis; Key Clb; Model UN; Ski Clb; Socr; NHS.

HAINES, JENNIFER; Absegami HS; Absecon, NJ; (Y); 6/254; Church Yth Grp; Pep Clb; Spanish Clb; SADD; Cheerleading; Mgr(s); Pom Pon; Tennis; High Hon Roll; NHS; Williams Coll; Socl Wrk.

HAINES, MICHELLE; John P Stevens HS; Edison, NJ; (Y); Rep Frsh Cls; JV Var Cheerleading; Powder Puff Ftbl; JV Sftbl; Hon Roll; NHS; Chld Psych.

HAINES, TIM; Hillsborough HS; Bellemead, NJ; (Y); 22/285; Cmnty Wkr; Ski Clb; Band; Drm Mjr(t); Mrchg Band; Symp Band; Gym; Trk; Hon Roll; NHS; Engrng.

HAINTHALER, JOSEPH; Don Bosco Prep HS; N Haledon, NJ; (Y); Church Yth Grp; Pres Debate Tm; Yrbk Stf.

HAKIM, MATTHEW; Manasquan HS; Spring Lk Ht, NJ; (Y); 20/250; Church Yth Grp; Math Clb; JV Socr; Var Capt Tennis; Kiwanis Awd; Pres Schlr; MVP Tnns Tm 86; Drexel U; Elec Engr.

HALAJDIDA, PETER; Hamilton High West; Trenton, NJ; (Y); 16/334; High Hon Roll; Hon Roll; Pres Acad Ftns Awd 86; Donald Clark Mem Schrlshp 86; Rutgers Coll; Biochem.

HALCOMB, LORI; Sayreville War Memorial HS; Parlin, NJ; (Y); 11/379; Spanish Clb; VP Varsity Clb; Capt Crs Cntry; Capt Trk; High Hon Roll; NHS; Spanish NHS; NJ Distngshd Schlrs Awd 85-86; Trenton ST Alumni Assn Schlrshp 86; NJ Soc CPA'S Schlrshp 86; Trenton ST Coll; Accntng.

HALE, KAREN; Parsippany HS; Lake Hiawatha, NJ; (Y); Dance Clb; French Clb; FBLA; Girl Scts; Intnl Clb; OEA; Q&S; Chorus; School Musical; Lit Mag; Lawyer.

HALEN, SUSAN; Rancocas Valley Regional HS; Mount Holly, NJ; (Y); Drama Clb; School Play; Hon Roll; Psych.

HALFIN, ELAN; Chatham Twp HS; Chatham, NJ; (Y); 40/130; Boy Scts; Key Clb; Ski Clb; JV Bsktbl; Var Socr; Var Tennis; Hon Roll; U Of Rchstr; Acctng.

HALIFKO, JODI; Woodbridge HS; Hopelawn, NJ; (Y); 12/396; NFL; Acpl Chr; School Musical; School Play; Mgr Stage Crew; Swing Chorus; VP Stu Cncl; NHS; Mid Atlantic Fstvl Of Chmps-2nd Pl Vcl 86; All St Chorus 86; Tech Theater.

HALISKY, MERLAND; Spotswood HS; Milltown, NJ; (S); 16/189; Boy Scts; Church Yth Grp; French Clb; Yrbk Phtg; Yrbk Stf; Var L Socr; Var L Trk; High Hon Roll; Hon Roll; NHS; Rutgers U.

HALL, CAROLYN; Holy Cross HS; Delran, NJ; (Y); 56/390; Ski Clb; Yrbk Stf; Mgr(s); Score Keeper; Stat Socr; JV Trk; Im Wt Lftg; High Hon Roll; Hon Roll; Psychol.

HALL, CATHERINE; Red Bank Catholic HS; Spring Lake, NJ; (Y); Ski Clb; Yrbk Sprt Ed; JV Sftbl; Var L Tennis; Hon Roll; NHS.

HALL, CHRISTINE; St Peters HS; New Brunswick, NJ; (Y); 1/110; Library Aide; Boy Scts; Stage Crew; Lit Mag; High Hon Roll; NHS; NEDT Awd; Deans Summer Schlrs Pgm Rutgers U 86; Engrng.

HALL, CHRISTINE; Union HS; Union, NJ; (Y); 46/510; Am Leg Aux Girls St; German Clb; Band; Concert Band; Drm Mjr(t); Jazz Band; Mrchg Band; Orch; Symp Band; Gov Hon Prg Awd; All-Eastrn Bnd 85; All-ST Mscl Grps 83-86; Mc Donalds All-Amer Bnd 85; New England Consrvtry Music.

HALL, DEBORAH ANN; Highland HS; Erial, NJ; (Y); Art Clb; Aud/Vis; Church Yth Grp; Cmnty Wkr; VP Drama Clb; French Clb; Thesps; School Musical; School Play; Lit Mag; Hnry Stu Mnth 84; Gvrns Schl; Smmr Art Inst NJ; Philadelp Coll Perf Arts; Thtre.

HALL, JEFFREY; Parsippany HS; Lake Hiawatha, NJ; (Y); Pres Computer Clb; Debate Tm; NFL; Varsity Clb; School Play; Stage Crew; Crs Cntry; Trk; Hon Roll; Litterary Awd For Holocaust Essy 85; No 1 Cnty In 3200 For Soph 84-85; PYSICS.

HALL, JOSEPH; Lenepe Valley Regional HS; Andover, NJ; (Y); 33/253; Boy Scts; Varsity Clb; Swmmng; Hon Roll; Trk; Life Sct 85; Electd-Attnd Wk Comp Crs-LVC 85; US Air Force Acad; Comp Sci.

HALL, JULIE; Delaware Valley Regl HS; Milford, NJ; (Y); Key Clb; Stu Cncl; Sftbl; Prfct Atten Awd; Katherine Gibbs; Secry.

HALL, KARA; Cumberland Regional HS; Chattanooga, TN; (Y); Church Yth Grp; Chorus; Variety Show; Var Crs Cntry; JV Tennis; JV Trk; U Of TX; Crrctns Invstgtns.

HALL, KATHY; Nutley HS; Nutley, NJ; (Y); 41/335; Drama Clb; Chorus; School Play; Nwsp Rptr; Yrbk Stf; Hon Roll; Rutgers; Englsh.

HALL, KIMBERLY; Holy Cross HS; Edgewater Park, NJ; (Y); Model UN; School Musical; School Play; Stage Crew; Yrbk Stf; Lit Mag; Hon Roll; Yrbk Artstc Edtr Achvmnt Awd 86; Beaver Coll Acad Schlrshp 86; Yrbk Artstc Edtr 85-86; Beaver Coll; Scntfc Illstrtn.

HALL, NICHELLE; Memorial HS; West New York, NJ; (Y); 149/396; FHA; Off Sr Cls; Twrlr; Berkeley Schl; Auto Off Tech.

HALL, ROBERT S; Ewing HS; Trenton, NJ; (S); DECA; Political Wkr; SADD; Im Bsktbl; Ftbl; Im Wt Lftg; Wrstlng; Hon Roll; Schlrshp Frm DECA For Outstndn Cntrbtns 86; Cert Of Exc Frm Ntl DECA Hdqtrs 86; TV Cmrcl Drnk Drvng; Johnson & Wales Coll; Fnc.

HALL, SANDY; W M Mendham HS; Mandham, NJ; (Y); Church Yth Grp; Dance Clb; Intnl Clb; Ski Clb; Chorus; Church Choir; Color Guard; Mrchg Band; Stage Crew; Hon Roll; Ldrshp Awd Bus Dept 86; Bus.

HALL, STEPHANIE; Neptune SR HS; Neptune City, NJ; (Y); 35/363; Church Yth Grp; GAA; Office Aide; Ski Clb; Hon Roll; Awds In Sci Fair, Stcktn ST Coll Sci Fair, & Ben Frnkln Sci Fair 84; Bus Mgmt.

HALLER, SCOTT E; St Piusx-Reg HS; Monmouth Jct, NJ; (Y); 3/100; Boy Scts; Computer Clb; Library Aide; Math Tm; Office Aide; Var Wrstlng; Hon Roll; NHS; Ntl Merit SF; St Schlr; Rochester Inst; Btchnlgy.

HALLEY, TRICIA; Toms River HS East; Toms River, NJ; (Y); Cmnty Wkr; Exploring; French Clb; Band; Concert Band; Mrchg Band; Symp Band; Pom Pon; Hon Roll; Mrchng Band Lttr 83-84; Mrchng Band 2nd Yr Lttr & Bar 84-85; Pom Pom Lttr 85-86; Bio.

HALLMAN, BRIAN; Holy Spirit HS; Absecon, NJ; (Y); Church Yth Grp; Culinary Inst; Advrstng.

HALLMAN, DARREN L; Wallkill Valley Regional HS; Budd Lake, NJ; (Y); 1/161; Math Tm; Scholastic Bowl; Science Clb; Jazz Band; Pres Frsh Cls; JV Bsktbl; JV Var Ftbl; NHS; Ntl Merit Ltr; Val; Excllnce Soc Stud, Math 85-86; U Of VA; Mech Engr.

HALLOCK, HELEN ELISABETH; South Plainfield HS; S Plainfield, NJ; (Y); 18/287; Church Yth Grp; French Clb; Ski Clb; Capt Flag Corp; Ed Yrbk Stf; Rep Sr Cls; Hon Roll; NHS; Computer Clb; Hosp Aide; Schlstc Hnr Soc 86; Presdntl Acad Fitness Awd 86; S Plainfield Educ Assn $1000 Schlrshp 86; Gordon Coll MA; Bio.

HALPERIN, LESLIE; Paramus HS; Paramus, NJ; (Y); FBLA; JCL; Latin Clb; Lit Mag; Cmmnctns.

HALPERIN, RACHEL; Middletown HS South; Middletown, NJ; (Y); Drama Clb; Math Clb; Thesps; Acpl Chr; Chorus; School Musical; School Play; Stage Crew; Diving; Vllybl; Theater Dsgn.

HALPERN, LYNN; Bridgewater-Raritan HS West; Bridgewater, NJ; (Y); Pres Temple Yth Grp; Var Capt Tennis; Elks Awd; High Hon Roll; Pres NHS; Walesley Bk Awd; Exchng Clb Yth Mnth; Grdn ST Dstngshd Schlr; U Of PA.

HALPIN, JAMES; Memorial HS; West New York, NJ; (Y); 56/375; Church Yth Grp; Computer Clb; Political Wkr; Hon Roll; NJ Inst Tech; Comp Sci.

HALSEY, MEREDITH; Shore Regional HS; W Long Branch, NJ; (Y); Pres Church Yth Grp; Cmnty Wkr; Girl Scts; Varsity Clb; Drill Tm; Powder Puff Ftbl; Var L Sftbl; Var L Swmmng; Var L Twrlr; Hon Roll; Asbury Pk Press Carrier Of Wk Photo & Artcl In Nwsppr 84; Psych.

HALUSKA, ANN-MARIE; Rahway HS; Rahway, NJ; (Y); Band; Concert Band; Drill Tm; Mrchg Band; Orch; Trs Frsh Cls; Var Capt Cheerleading; JV Coach Actv; Socr; Sftbl; St Johns; Bus Adm.

HAMERSTONE, STEPHANIE; Delaware Valley Regional HS; Milford, NJ; (Y); 22/134; Am Leg Aux Girls St; Church Yth Grp; Key Clb; Ski Clb; Color Guard; Concert Band; Mrchg Band; School Musical; School Play; VP Soph Cls; Somerset County Comm; Acctnt.

HAMILTON, CARRIE; Cumberland Regional HS; Bridgeton, NJ; (S); 5/369; Sec Church Yth Grp; Intnl Clb; Library Aide; Office Aide; Teachers Aide; Nwsp Rptr; High Hon Roll; NHS; JV Swmmng; Hon Roll; Engrng.

HAMILTON JR, HENRY A; Delsea Regional HS; Franklinville, NJ; (Y); Art Clb; Key Clb; VICA; JV Var Ftbl; Var Trk; Im Wt Lftg; JV Var Wrstlng; Prfct Atten Awd; Glassboro ST Coll; Law Enfrcmt.

HAMILTON JR, JEFFREY T; Union Catholic Regional HS; Westfield, NJ; (Y); 40/293; Am Leg Boys St; Church Yth Grp; PAVAS; Service Clb; Pres Thesps; Chorus; School Musical; Rep Stu Cncl; JV Socr; Hon Roll; Soc Sci.

HAMILTON, ROBBIE; Mt Olive HS; Budd Lake, NJ; (Y); 12/296; Var Socr; Var Trk; High Hon Roll; Hon Roll; Bio & Chmstry Strght A Awds 85-86; Tchr.

HAMM, IVY; Washington Township HS; Sewell, NJ; (Y); Church Yth Grp; Debate Tm; Drama Clb; Girl Scts; Teachers Aide; Band; Chorus; Church Choir; Drill Tm; Nwsp Rptr; Temple U:Comm.

HAMMER, FRANK; Parsippany HS; Lake Hiawatha, NJ; (Y); Varsity Clb; Stage Crew; JV Bsbl; Var Ftbl; Wt Lftg; Var Wrstlng; Hon Roll; Comp Sci.

HAMMER, KEITH; Clifton HS; Clifton, NJ; (Y); Boys Clb Am; Church Yth Grp; Ski Clb; Spanish Clb; VICA; Im JV Bsktbl; Im Ftbl; Im JV Trk; Hon Roll; U Of UT; Pre-Med.

HAMMER, MICHAEL; Parsippany HS; Lk Hiawatha, NJ; (Y); 27/320; Am Leg Boys St; Church Yth Grp; Var L Crs Cntry; Var L Trk; Var L Wrstlng; Hon Roll; VP NHS; Pres Schlr; Garden ST Schlrshp 85-86; James E Casey Schlrshp 85-86; U Of MI; Law.

HAMMERICH, DARLENE; New Milford HS; New Milford, NJ; (Y); 22/140; 4-H; Spanish Clb; Thesps; Color Guard; Mrchg Band; Lit Mag; Rep Frsh Cls; Rep Soph Cls; Rep Jr Cls; Rep Stu Cncl; Bergen Cty Outstndg 4-H Grl 85; Sci, Soc Stds Awds 82-83; U Of NH; Pre-Vet.

HAMORY, LARISSA; North Brunswick Twp HS; N Brunswick, NJ; (Y); 13/279; Var Capt Bsktbl; Var Socr; Var Sftbl; High Hon Roll; Hon Roll; NHS; All-Middlesex Cnty Sccr Tm 83-85; All-Conf & 1st Tm Sccr 83-85; All-Acad Tms Sccr, Bsktbl, Sftbl 85-86; Princeton.

HAMPTON, JON; Manasquan HS; Sea Girt, NJ; (Y); 2/285; Church Yth Grp; Math Tm; Science Clb; Spanish Clb; Nwsp Ed-Chief; Yrbk Stf; Lit Mag; Hon Roll; Kiwanis Awd; NHS; NCTE Engl Awd Wrtng 87; Bd Ed Awd Acad Achvt 83-85; Intl Law.

HAMPTON, KELLY; Holy Family Acad; Bayonne, NJ; (Y); Church Yth Grp; Girl Scts; Hon Roll; Prfct Atten Awd; St Peters Clg; Sec.

HAMPTON, KESHA; Henry Snyder HS; Jersey City, NJ; (Y); 5/400; Church Yth Grp; Church Choir; Cheerleading; Clarks Coll; Law.

HAMRICK, SANDRA; Cumberland Regional HS; Bridgeton, NJ; (Y); 30/315; Intnl Clb; Model UN; Yrbk Sprt Ed; JV Bsktbl; Var Capt Fld Hcky; Var Capt Sftbl; Cit Awd; Hon Roll; Robert Keith Pilsbury Awd 86; U DE; Phys Ther.

HAMROCK, LAURA; Shore Regional HS; West Long Branch, NJ; (S); 46/230; Drama Clb; Q&S; SADD; Thesps; Nwsp Sprt Ed; Lit Mag; Var Capt Cheerleading; High Hon Roll; Hon Roll; NHS; Rider Coll Essay Cont 85; Muhlenberg Coll; Cmmnctns.

HANAK, CHERYL; Immaculate Conception HS; Garfield, NJ; (Y); Rep Frsh Cls; Ntl Ldrshp & Serv Awd 86.

HANBICKI, AUBREY; Hunterdon Central HS; Three Bridges, NJ; (Y); 13/539; Chess Clb; Model UN; Varsity Clb; Stat Bsbl; French Hon Soc; High Hon Roll; Hon Roll; Gardn ST Distngshd Schlr 86; Rutgers Coll; Physcs.

HANCLICH, CATHY; Hawthorne HS; Hawthorne, NJ; (Y); VP Church Yth Grp; Math Tm; Ski Clb; Yrbk Stf; Rep Stu Cncl; Var L Sftbl; Hon Roll; NHS; Spanish NHS.

HAND, CHRISTINE; Lower Cape May Regional HS; Villas, NJ; (Y); 50/220; Dance Clb; French Clb; Chorus; High Hon Roll; Hon Roll; J R Powers Schl; Modeling.

HAND, JASON E; Jackson Memorial HS; Jackson, NJ; (Y); 42/322; Band; Mrchg Band; Var Capt Bowling; High Hon Roll; Hon Roll; Jackson PBA Scholar 86; Jackson Band Paretns Scholar 86; Women VWF Jackson Scholar 86; Trenton ST Coll; Crimnl Just.

HAND, JENNIFER; Summit HS; Summit, NJ; (Y); Band; Concert Band; Var L Bsktbl; Var L Socr; Var L Sftbl; Alfred V Swick Meml Awd-Athl 86.

HAND, KYLE; Hunterdon Central HS; Flemington, NJ; (Y); JV Ftbl; JV Wrstlng; Stevens Inst Of Tech; Engrg.

HANDRICH, MARIE; Marlboro HS; Marlboro, NJ; (Y); 69/528; Church Yth Grp; JCL; Latin Clb; Ski Clb; Color Guard; Stage Crew; Yrbk Stf; Frsh Cls; Soph Cls; Jr Cls; Judge Technology Children MIIT Cont 86; Best Show JCL Roman House 86; Liberal Arts.

HANDWORK, ANDREW J; Central Regional HS; Island Heights, NJ; (Y); French Clb; Bsbl; Ftbl; ST Teen Arts Fstvl 84-86; Cmmrcl Art.

HANES, ROBERT; Bihsop AHR HS; Carteret, NJ; (Y); Bowling; Hon Roll; Vry Invlvd Martl Arts & Prvt Guitr Lssns; Art.

HANEY, ELAINE J; Piscataway HS; Piscataway, NJ; (Y); 41/519; Am Leg Aux Girls St; Drama Clb; FHA; Hosp Aide; Sec Latin Clb; Pep Clb; Radio Clb; Chorus; School Musical; School Play; Hnrbl Ment Gov Schl Cert Wrtng 85; Rutgers U; Lib Arts.

HANEY, ELLEN; Metuchen HS; Metuchen, NJ; (Y); 15/178; Key Clb; Spanish Clb; Orch; Lit Mag; Rep Stu Cncl; Var JV Fld Hcky; High Hon Roll; Hon Roll; NHS; Spanish NHS; Psych.

HANEY, REGINA; Holy Cross HS; Marlton, NJ; (Y); 25/392; Am Leg Aux Girls St; Spanish Clb; Yrbk Stf; Rep Frsh Cls; Rep Soph Cls; Rep Jr Cls; Rep Stu Cncl; High Hon Roll.

HANEY, SCOTT A; Middletown South; Red Bank, NJ; (Y); Boy Scts; School Play; Variety Show; Pres Jr Cls; Var L Ftbl; Stu Cncl; Dnfsv MVP Hmcmng Ftbl 85; Bst Actr; Bst Sns Hmr; Penn ST; Math.

HANFORD, KRIS; Cumberland Regional; Bridgeton, NJ; (S); 8/342; Church Yth Grp; Soroptimist; Var Capt Bsktbl; Var L Fld Hcky; JV Var Sftbl; High Hon Roll; NHS.

HANIGAN, BILL; Pompton Lakes HS; Pompton Lakes, NJ; (Y); Am Leg Boys St; French Clb; Latin Clb; Varsity Clb; Pres Stu Cncl; Var L Bsbl; JV Capt Bsktbl; Var L Ftbl; JR Mayor Campgn Chief Polc 85-86; All Lg 2nd Tm Qtrbck 85-86; Paterson News All Area Hnrb Mntn 84-85; Bus.

HANIN, JAMI; Jackson Memorial HS; Jackson, NJ; (Y); GAA; Ski Clb; Yrbk Bus Mgr; Yrbk Stf; Bsktbl; Mgr(s); Socr; High Hon Roll; Hon Roll; Hnrbl Mntn Ocn Cnty Cnsrvtn Dstrcct 86; Awd Supr Achvmnt & Exclnc Wndrs Wtlnds 86; Art Thrpst.

HANISSIAN, JEFFREY; Memorial HS; Cedar Grove, NJ; (S); 1/120; Key Clb; Band; School Musical; Nwsp Stf; Socr; Tennis; Bausch & Lomb Sci Awd; NHS; St Schlr; Val; Med.

HANKE, CRAIG; Waldwick HS; Waldwick, NJ; (S); 4/139; VP Church Yth Grp; Drama Clb; Math Tm; Quiz Bowl; Scholastic Bowl; Yrbk Stf; Ed Lit Mag; Hon Roll; NHS; St Schlr; Natl Mrt Commended Stu; Dartmouth; Bio.

HANKS, EVELYN; Hamilton North HS; Mercerville, NJ; (Y); 5/281; VP AFS; Am Leg Aux Girls St; Color Guard; School Musical; Rep Sr Cls; Powder Puff Ftbl; Pres NHS; ROTC Army Schlrshp 86; Knights Of Clmbs Awd 86; Trenton Coll Clb Schlrshp 86; Boston U; Intl Law.

HANLEIN, JEANETTE MARIE; Vail-Deane HS; Hillside, NJ; (Y); French Clb; Science Clb; Spanish Clb; Chorus; School Play; Stage Crew; Nwsp Ed-Chief; Nwsp Rptr; Yrbk Bus Mgr; Yrbk Stf; Stevens Inst Of Tech; Elec Engr.

HANLEY, CHRIS; Holy Cross HS; Medford, NJ; (Y); 42/370; Nwsp Rptr; JV L Wrstlng; High Hon Roll; Hon Roll; NHS; Med.

HANLEY, KATHLEEN; Mount Saint Dominic Acad; Verona, NJ; (Y); 5/57; Chorus; School Musical; Rep Jr Cls; Hst Sr Cls; Stu Cncl; Cheerleading; Capt Trk; High Hon Roll; Hon Roll; Pres NHS; Mst Oustndg Hgh Jmpr; 4th NJ ST Trck Mt; Boston Coll; Psychlgy.

HANLON, ALICE; St Marys HS; Jersey City, NJ; (Y); Band; Hon Roll; Wrd Prcssng Awd 85-86; Wrd Prcssng.

HANLON, BRIDGET; St Rose HS; West Long Branch, NJ; (Y); 34/275; Sec Key Clb; Ski Clb; School Musical; Nwsp Ed-Chief; Nwsp Rptr; Lit Mag; Rep Frsh Cls; Stat Bsbl; Hon Roll; NHS; Villanova; Ed.

HANLON, TIMOTHY; Union HS; Union, NJ; (Y); Boy Scts; Church Yth Grp; Band; Concert Band; Mrchg Band; Ed Yrbk Sprt Ed; Var JV Bsbl; L Bsktbl; Var L Crs Cntry; Hon Roll; Holy Cross Coll; Pilot.

HANN, TRUDY; South Hunterdon Regional HS; Lambertville, NJ; (Y); 2/73; Red Cross Aide; SADD; Varsity Clb; Stage Crew; Yrbk Stf; JV Bsktbl; Var Mat Maids; JV Var Sftbl; Wt Lftg; Hon Roll.

HANNA, FREDERICK A; St Peters Prep; Jersey City, NJ; (Y); Civic Clb; Cmnty Wkr; Hosp Aide; SADD; Band; Variety Show; Stat Bsktbl; Hon Roll; Mgr(s); Score Keeper; Hghr Achvt Pgm Grant 83-87; Howard U; Dentstry.

HANNA, JOHN; Delsea Regional HS; Franklinville, NJ; (Y); Band; Mrchg Band; School Musical; Socr; Tennis; Wrstlng; NHS; Elect Engr.

HANNAH JR, QUESTER; Dwight Morrow HS; Englewood, NJ; (Y); 25/257; Cmnty Wkr; Varsity Clb; Variety Show; Rep Frsh Cls; Var Bsbl; Capt Bsktbl; Var Capt Ftbl; Var Trk; Hon Roll; Var Ltr Ftbl 83-86; Var Ltr Trck 84-85; Var Ltr Bsbl 85-86; Boston Coll; Bus Admin.

HANNAN, JUDITH E; Haddonfield Memorial HS; Haddonfield, NJ; (Y); 10/150; Am Leg Aux Girls St; Church Yth Grp; Cmnty Wkr; Drama Clb; VP Intnl Clb; Latin Clb; Pep Clb; Q&S; Church Choir; School Musical; Hnrbl Mntn Short Story 83; 3rd Pl Essay Coll Essay Cntst 86; Intl Corporate Law.

HANNON, CHRISTINE; Madison Central HS; Old Bridge, NJ; (Y); Art Clb; SADD; Band; Stage Crew; High Hon Roll; Gld-White Awd 84-85; Chef.

HANNON, MADELINE; Union Catholic Regional HS; Cranford, NJ; (Y); Service Clb; Nwsp Sprt Ed; Jr NHS; Art Clb; Church Yth Grp; Drama Clb; Spanish Clb; School Play; Nwsp Rptr; Yrbk Stf; Mvmnt Bttr Wrld Untd Nations; Girls Ctznshp Inst 86; Cmnctns.

HANNUM, DIANE; Vineland HS; Vineland, NJ; (Y); 113/700; Pres Church Yth Grp; Red Cross Aide; Mrchg Band; Orch; JV Sftbl; Bus Mngmnt.

HANNUSAK, JOHN; Dickenson HS; Jersey City, NJ; (Y); Band; Mrchg Band; Ftbl; Bryant; Bus.

HANS, MARIE; Paul VI HS; Laurel Springs, NJ; (S); 38/470; Sec Drama Clb; French Clb; Hosp Aide; School Musical; Variety Show; Var Cheerleading; Var Pom Pon; French Hon Soc; NHS; Church Yth Grp; JR Miss Fnlst 85-86; Frnch Comp Awd 85; Rutgers U; Lib Art.

HANSELL, JAMES; Paulvi HS; Haddonfield, NJ; (S); 28/474; Math Clb; Im Bowling; JV Golf; Var Socr; High Hon Roll; NHS; Med.

HANSEN, AMY; Middletown South HS; Lincroft, NJ; (Y); 4-H; Library Aide; 4-H Awd; High Hon Roll; Hon Roll; Span Awd Highest Grade Pt Avg 85; Statue Of Liberty Merit Awd 84; Fashion.

HANSEN, DONNA; Chatham Township HS; Chatham Twp, NJ; (Y); #61 In Class; Church Yth Grp; Key Clb; Pep Clb; Variety Show; Yrbk Sprt Ed; Rep Stu Cncl; Var L Bsktbl; Var L Lcrss; Var L Tennis; Hon Roll.

HANSEN, ERIC; Fair Lawn HS; Fair Lawn, NJ; (Y); 130/335; Sr Cls; Stu Cncl; Hon Roll; Full Schlrsp Stn Hl U 86; Seton Hl U; Sci.

HANSEN, ERIC J; Delaware Valley Regional HS; Milford, NJ; (Y); 9/165; Church Yth Grp; Ski Clb; Jazz Band; Nwsp Rptr; Stu Cncl; Bsbl; Ftbl; Trk; High Hon Roll; NHS; NJ Schlr 85; Ftbl Awd 86; Prsdntl Acdmc Ftns Awd 86; Fordham U; Pltcl Sci.

HANSEN, MICHAEL; North Warren Regional HS; Blairstown, NJ; (Y); 5/129; Boy Scts; Scholastic Bowl; Spanish Clb; Nwsp Rptr; Rep Stu Cncl; Pres NHS; Blairstown Rotary Schlrshp 86; Eagle Scout 84; Syracuse U Schlrshp 86; Syracuse U; Aerosp Engrng.

HANSON, CINDY; Immaculate Heart Acad; N Haledon, NJ; (Y); 5/163; Math Tm; Model UN; Quiz Bowl; Science Clb; Yrbk Stf; Lit Mag; Vllybl; Hon Roll; NHS; Schl Rep Hugh O Brien Ldrshp Semnr 84; Rutgers Coll; Lwyr.

HANSON, RYAN A; Pennsville Memorial HS; Pennsville, NJ; (Y); 27/201; Am Leg Boys St; Math Tm; Teachers Aide; Var Golf; Hon Roll; Word Processng Comp Tchr 85-86; 1st Prize Tm Salem CC Comp Cont 85-86; Amer Legn Boys St 86; Comp Elect Engr.

HANUS, MICHAEL; Keansburg HS; Keansburg, NJ; (Y); 1/113; Pres German Clb; Pres Key Clb; Bausch & Lomb Sci Awd; Cit Awd; Elks Awd; NHS; Val; Spanish Clb; Pres Frsh Cls; Pres Soph Cls; Rutgers Distngushd Schlr; Ntl Schlr Athlete Awd; Keansburg Stu Yr; Rutgers; Lawyer.

HANVEY, FORREST R; Norahern Highlands Reg HS; Upper Saddle Rv, NJ; (Y); 70/250; Chorus; Color Guard; Jazz Band; Madrigals; Mrchg Band; School Musical; Symp Band; Ntl Merit Ltr; All St Choir 84; All Estrn Choir 85; Peabody Cnsrvtry; Rcrdng Engrng.

HARAN, SEAN T; Christian Brothers Acad; Middletown, NJ; (S); 17/240; Math Tm; Nwsp Sprt Ed; Var Bsktbl; Var Socr; Trk; High Hon Roll; NHS; Mth Tutor.

HARCH, PATRICIA; Pitman HS; Pitman, NJ; (Y); 22/150; German Clb; Band; Jazz Band; Mrchg Band; Nwsp Rptr; Mgr Nwsp Stf; Lit Mag; Var Crs Cntry; JV Trk; Hon Roll; Frgn Lang.

HARDENBURG, ALAN W; Jefferson Township HS; Wharton, NJ; (Y); 7/232; Am Leg Boys St; VP Trs Church Yth Grp; Computer Clb; Debate Tm; Math Tm; Jazz Band; JV Wrstlng; High Hon Roll; NHS; Ntl Merit Ltr; US Air Force Summer Sci Sem Co 86; Wrld Affrs Sem WI 86; US Air Force Acad; Aerntcl Eng.

HARDMAN, KIM; Colonia SR HS; Colonia, NJ; (Y); SADD; Hon Roll; Pres Phys Fit Awd 84 & 86; Bus.

HARDY, CATHY; Bridgeton Public HS; Bridgeton, NJ; (Y); Cmnty Wkr; Office Aide; Soroptimist; Teachers Aide; Nwsp Rptr; Nwsp Stf; Trs Jr Cls; Sec Sr Cls; Schlrshp Fairleigh Dickinson U 86-87; Cntstnt Miss TEEN 86; Fairleigh Dickinson U; Ballt.

HARDY, DALYN; Memorial HS; W New York, NJ; (Y); Chess Clb; Key Clb; Nwsp Rptr; Rep Frsh Cls; Rep Soph Cls; Rep Jr Cls; Rep Sr Cls; Rep Stu Cncl; Vllybl; Hon Roll; Douglass Coll.

HARDY, KELLY ANN; Morris Catholic HS; Denville, NJ; (Y); 3/156; Cmnty Wkr; Latin Clb; Math Clb; Natl Beta Clb; Service Clb; Nwsp Stf; Lit Mag; High Hon Roll; NHS; Outstndng Achvt Awd 86; Morris Catholic Schlr 86; Muhlenberg Coll; Engl.

HARDY, MARK; Saint Pius HS; New Brnswck, NJ; (Y); Am Leg Boys St; Art Clb; Chess Clb; Church Yth Grp; Civic Clb; CAP; Cmnty Wkr; Computer Clb; Drama Clb; Service Clb; Dstngshd Chem Awd 86; Bsktbll Trphy; Rutgers U; Engnrng.

HARGROVE, TAMICA; Frank H Morrell HS; Vailsburg, NJ; (Y); Church Yth Grp; DECA; Office Aide; Church Choir; Flag Corp; Ed Yrbk Stf; Rep Frsh Cls; Rep Soph Cls; JV Bowling; Score Keeper; NJIT; Cmptr Sci.

HARGUS, SARAH E; Cherokee HS; Marlton, NJ; (Y); 5/380; Church Yth Grp; Scholastic Bowl; Concert Band; Jazz Band; Orch; Yrbk Ed-Chief; Yrbk Stf; NHS; Ntl Merit SF; Pres Schlr; All-South Jrsy Jazz & Symphnc Band; Spch Pthlgy.

HARITON, AMI; East Brunswick HS; E Brunswick, NJ; (Y); Dance Clb; Key Clb; SADD; Yrbk Stf; Hon Roll; NHS.

HARKER, CYNTHIA; Northern Burlington HS; Columbus, NJ; (Y); 40/186; Church Yth Grp; DECA; 4-H; Chorus; Church Choir; Off Soph Cls; Off Jr Cls; Cit Awd; Mrvn Rsnbrg Schlrshp Awd 86; Chstrfld Twnshp PTA Awd 86; Johnson & Wales Coll; Rtl Mgt.

HARKER, KERRY; Cumberland Christian HS; Vineland, NJ; (S); 3/32; Church Yth Grp; Drama Clb; Chorus; Orch; School Play; Capt Cheerleading; Mgr(s); Trk; Hon Roll; NJ All ST Orch 84-85; All S Jersey Orch 84-86; Educ.

HARKINS, WENDY L; Wildwood HS; N Wildwood, NJ; (Y); 3/120; Pres Cmnty Wkr; Var Capt Bsktbl; Stat Ftbl; Var Sftbl; Kiwanis Awd; VP NHS; Pres Schlr; VFW Awd; Chess Clb; VP Frsh Cls; U S Army Reserv Natl Schlr Athl Awd 86; NJ Schlr Athl Awd 86; U Of DE; Math Ed.

HARLAN, ANDREA; Egg Harbor Twp HS; Egg Harbor Twp, NJ; (S); 43/318; Exploring; GAA; Girl Scts; Hosp Aide; Var Fld Hcky; Var Sftbl; Var Trk; JV Vllybl; Hon Roll; Jr NHS.

HARLEY, RODNEY; West Orange HS; W Orange, NJ; (Y); 62/166; French Clb; Im Bsktbl; Im Tennis; JV Trk; Im Vllybl; Im Wt Lftg; Hon Roll; Incentv Grant Penn ST 86; PA ST U; Pre-Law.

HARMATZ, MICHAEL; Ocean Twp HS; Oakhurst, NJ; (Y); 53/360; Boy Scts; Nwsp Stf; Var L Crs Cntry; Var L Trk; Hon Roll; Temple Yth Grp; Chorus; Athlt Wk Lcl Nwspr 86; Attnd Natl Crs Cntry Chmpnshps 86; Engrng.

HARMON, CHRISTOPHER; Bridgewater Raritan HS East HS; Pluckemin, NJ; (Y); Church Yth Grp; Ski Clb; Var JV Lcrss; Var JV Socr; Hon Roll; Bus.

HARNESS, JEFF; Red Bank Catholic HS; Middletown, NJ; (Y); Aud/Vis; Camera Clb; Red Cross Aide; Teachers Aide; Stage Crew; JV Bsbl; Im Bsktbl; Im Ftbl; Im Socr; Brookdale CC; Bus.

HARNETT, JOHN F; Sussex Vo-Tech; Blairstown, NJ; (S); 30/180; 4-H; FFA; Spanish Clb; 4-H Awd; Hon Roll; NHS; Culinary Inst Am; Chef.

HAROUTUNIAN, KAREN; Palisades Park HS; Palisades Park, NJ; (Y); Computer Clb; Dance Clb; French Clb; Girl Scts; Office Aide; Church Choir; Yrbk Stf; Socr; Sftbl; SUNY Binghampton; Dentstry.

HARPER, CYNTHIA; Cumberland Regional HS; Seabrook, NJ; (Y); 32/370; Cmnty Wkr; Hosp Aide; Intnl Clb; Science Clb; Fld Hcky; High Hon Roll; Hon Roll; Frsh Acad Achvt Awd 84; Cmmndtn Chem 85-86; Cmmndtn Biol Alg & Geom 84-85; Genetc Rsrch.

HARPER, KRISTIN; Chatham Twp HS; Chatham Twp, NJ; (Y); Church Yth Grp; Cmnty Wkr; Drama Clb; Key Clb; Pep Clb; Red Cross Aide; Chorus; School Musical; School Play; Stage Crew; CTHS Drama Awd 86; St Lawrence U; Orthopedic Srgn.

HARPIN, KIMBERLY; John F Kennedy HS; Paterson, NJ; (Y); Intnl Clb; Nwsp Rptr; Nwsp Stf; Tennis; Hon Roll; NHS; Med Lab Tech.

HARRELL, TAMMIE; John F Kennedy HS; Paterson, NJ; (S); Church Yth Grp; Computer Clb; Office Aide; Teachers Aide; Chorus; Church Choir; Color Guard; Nwsp Rptr; Nwsp Stf; Rep Jr Cls; Hampton U; Law.

HARRINGTON, CHRISTOPHER; Glen Rock JR SR HS; Glen Rock, NJ; (Y); AFS; Chess Clb; Latin Clb; Library Aide; Nwsp Stf; Hon Roll; Law.

HARRINGTON, LISA; James Caldwell HS; W Caldwell, NJ; (Y); Key Clb; Ski Clb; Hon Roll; Prfct Atten Awd; Bus Mgmt.

HARRINGTON, NICOLE; Lincoln HS; Jersey City, NJ; (Y); English Clb; Hosp Aide; ROTC; Spanish Clb; Chorus; Nwsp Stf; Yrbk Rptr; Yrbk Stf; Lit Mag; Intershlstc Comptn Team 85-86; PA ST; Soc Work.

HARRIS, CHRIS; St James HS; Gibbstown, NJ; (Y); Art Clb; Ftbl; Wt Lftg; Wrstlng; U GA; Archtctr.

HARRIS, COSTAS; Dover HS; Dover, NJ; (Y); 9/190; Am Leg Boys St; Latin Clb; JV Wrstlng; High Hon Roll; Hon Roll; NHS; Prfct Atten Awd; Psych Awd 86; Pre-Med.

HARRIS, DAWN E; Paulsboro HS; Gibbstown, NJ; (Y); 20/145; Church Yth Grp; Sec Frsh Cls; Sec Soph Cls; Sec Jr Cls; Sec Sr Cls; Rep Stu Cncl; Cheerleading; Hon Roll; Jr NHS; NHS; Stu Of Mnth 83-84; ST Fin Miss U S Teen Pgnt 84-85; Spc Shttl Stu Invlvmnt Proj 83-84; U Of VA; Med.

HARRIS, ERIC; Seton Hall Prep; Newark, NJ; (Y); Civic Clb; Computer Clb; Dance Clb; Latin Clb; Stage Crew; Frsh Cls; Wt Lftg; Hon Roll; 2nd Hnrs; Temle U; Psych.

HARRIS, JASON D; Neptune SR HS; Neptune, NJ; (Y); Am Leg Boys St; Boys Clb Am; Cmnty Wkr; DECA; VICA; Variety Show; Nwsp Rptr; Nwsp Stf; Rep Frsh Cls; Rep Soph Cls; Bus Adm.

HARRIS, KELLY; Pemberton Twp HS II HS; Pemberton, NJ; (Y); 28/430; Pres Church Yth Grp; Drama Clb; Science Clb; Church Choir; Yrbk Stf; Stat Bsktbl; JV Fld Hcky; Hon Roll; NHS; Cmmrcl Art.

HARRIS, KORET ANN; Garden State Acad; Amityville, NY; (Y); Church Yth Grp; Church Choir; Drill Tm; VP Frsh Cls; Trs Jr Cls; Sec Stu Cncl; Im Badmtn; Var Bsktbl; Im Ftbl; Hon Roll; Howard U; Bus.

HARRIS, MONICA L; John F Kennedy HS; Willingboro, NJ; (Y); 31/300; Am Leg Aux Girls St; Cmnty Wkr; Trs Intnl Clb; JCL; Flag Corp; Ed Nwsp Rptr; Hon Roll; Rotary Awd; Dance Clb; Girl Scts; Top 7 Pct All Blck Stdnts 84; NJ Girls ST 85; Engl.

HARRIS, NICOLE; Vailsburg HS; Newark, NJ; (Y); Church Yth Grp; FNA; Pres Girl Scts; Color Guard; Crs Cntry; Trk; Military; Nursng.

HARRIS, ODETTE; Mary Help Of Christians Acad; Newark, NJ; (S); 3/88; Pres JCL; Letterman Clb; Quiz Bowl; Chorus; Sec Frsh Cls; Sec Soph Cls; Sec Jr Cls; High Hon Roll; Prfct Atten Awd; Natl Cathlc Fornsc Leag; Yale; Med.

HARRIS, SONYA; Hackensack HS; Hackensack, NJ; (Y); 28/400; Pep Clb; Teachers Aide; Band; Concert Band; Mrchg Band; Nwsp Rptr; Sec Sr Cls; L Cheerleading; High Hon Roll; Hon Roll; Sojourner Trth Achvt Awd 86; James P Coleman Schlrshp 86; Alpha Kappa Alpha Schlrshp 86; Hampton U; Mass Commnctns.

HARRIS, WILLIAM C; Washington Township HS; Turnersville, NJ; (Y); 20/510; German Clb; JA; Var Swmmng; High Hon Roll; Hon Roll; Jr NHS; NHS; NISCA Tp 10 Awd Smmng, Grmn Hnr Soc Awd 86.

HARRISON, BENJAMIN; Dwight Morrow HS; Englewood, NJ; (Y); Band; Mrchg Band; Orch; Variety Show; Socr; Trk; Law.

HARRISON, CAROLINE; Midland Park HS; Midland Park, NJ; (Y); 9/137; Church Yth Grp; FNA; Sec Varsity Clb; Rep Sr Cls; Var L Socr; Var L Trk; High Hon Roll; NHS; Rutgers U; Bio.

HARRISON, DEAN; Atlantic City HS; Margate, NJ; (Y); Bsbl; Am Leg Boys St; Church Yth Grp; Key Clb; Latin Clb; Red Cross Aide; Stu Cncl; Bsktbl; Crs Cntry; High Hon Roll; MVP Vrsty Bsbl 85; Amer Lgn Awd 81; Sports Med.

HARRISON, MICHAEL; East Orange HS; E Orange, NJ; (S); 96/410; Variety Show; Yrbk Sprt Ed; JV Bsbl; Var Ftbl; Hon Roll; Wilkes Coll; Elctrcl Engrng.

HART, DEBRA; Jackson Memorial HS; Jackson, NJ; (Y); 7/405; Yrbk Stf; High Hon Roll; Prfct Atten Awd; VFW Awd; Geirgian Crt Coll; Scndry Educ.

HART, DONNA; Toms River HS East; Toms River, NJ; (Y); French Clb; Flag Corp; Jr NHS; NHS; Rtry Clb Cntrl Ocean Cnty 86; John & Irenes Papines Schlrshp Acad Lttr 85; Rutgers U; Lbrl Arts.

HART, LONNIE; East Brunswick HS; E Brunswick, NJ; (Y); Trs Leo Clb; Var Bsbl; Var Ftbl; 2nd Pl Bourough Sci Fair Brooklyn NY 83; Rutgers U; Law.

HART, MICHELLE; Dwight Morrow HS; Englewood, NJ; (Y); 17/249; Stage Crew; Nwsp Rptr; Rep Jr Cls; Capt Trk; Var Vllybl; High Hon Roll; Hon Roll; NHS; Trck Hon Mntn Long Jump 84-85; Trck, Vllybll Hon Mntn 85-86; Lawyer.

HART, PAMELA M; Notre Dame HS; W Trenton, NJ; (Y); 12/375; Hosp Aide; VP Key Clb; Political Wkr; Red Cross Aide; Var Fld Hcky; High Hon Roll; Hon Roll; VP NHS; Var Sftbl; JV Bsktbl; Hon Eng I Awd 84; MIP Vrsty Sftbll 86; 100 Hrs Awd Vlntr 86.

HARTEM, CLAIRE; Bridgeton HS; Dividing Creek, NJ; (Y); Pres Church Yth Grp; Sec French Clb; Band; Mrchg Band; Pep Band; School Musical; Stu Cncl; High Hon Roll; NHS; Rotary Awd; Ntl Cnfrnc Chrstns & Jews Awd 84; NJ Schl Of Arts Schlrshp 84; Schlrshp Ltrs Hghst Hnrs 85-86; Intl Affrs Frnch.

HARTIGAN, LORI; Toms River HS; Beachwood, NJ; (Y); VP Art Clb; Camera Clb; Drama Clb; Ski Clb; Spanish Clb; SADD; VP Thesps; Chorus; Color Guard; School Musical; Best Supporting Actress 85; Thespian Achvt Vocal Music 85; Visual Art.

HARTLEY, SCOTT R; Bordentown Regional HS; Bordentown, NJ; (Y); 15/114; Am Leg Boys St; Boy Scts; Church Yth Grp; Debate Tm; Band; JV Trk; Mu Alp Tht; NHS; Ntl Merit Ltr; Hon Roll; Olympcs Of Mind Tm 85; Duke U; Elec Engr.

HARTMAN, DIANE; Cinnaminson HS; Cinnaminson, NJ; (Y); 20/257; Church Yth Grp; SADD; Var Capt Cheerleading; JV Lcrss; Stat Socr; High Hon Roll; Hon Roll; NHS; Prfct Atten Awd; Pres Schlr; Trntn ST Coll; Nrsg.

HARTMAN, TIFFANY; Chatham Township HS; Chatham, NJ; (Y); 34/135; Key Clb; Yrbk Rptr; Yrbk Stf; Cheerleading; High Hon Roll; Hon Roll.

HARTMANN, CLAUDIA; Belleville HS; Belleville, NJ; (S); 5/363; Key Clb; Flag Corp; VP Pres Stu Cncl; Mgr(s); High Hon Roll; NHS; Ntl Merit Ltr; Mgr Bsktbl; Mgr Trk; Intl Rel.

HARTNETT, KAREN; Hackettstown HS; Hackettstown, NJ; (Y); Church Yth Grp; Cmnty Wkr; 4-H; Hosp Aide; Pres Key Clb; Q&S; SADD; Band; Concert Band; Mrchg Band; Newspaper Staff Feature Editor; Pre-Law.

HARTSUIKER, ELIZABETH; Clifton HS; Clifton, NJ; (S); Church Yth Grp; Ski Clb; Spanish Clb; Chorus; Capt Swmmng; Hon Roll; Jr NHS; Swmmr Yr 84-85; Nutritn.

HARTUNG, JEANNE; Hightstown HS; East Windsor, NJ; (Y); 10/449; Church Yth Grp; Drama Clb; Hosp Aide; SADD; Band; Mrchg Band; School Musical; High Hon Roll; NHS; Ntl Merit Ltr; Prtcptd Stu Cnsrvtn Assn Pgm 86; Sci.

HARTZ, CHRIS; Washington Twp HS; Turnersville, NJ; (Y); Church Yth Grp; German Clb; Var Crs Cntry; Var Trk; Mscns Clb 85-86; Accntng.

HARTZOG, JOANNE; Warren County Tech Schl; Belvidere, NJ; (S); Library Aide; Ski Clb; Sec VICA; Nwsp Stf; Hon Roll; Graphic Arts.

HARVEY, ALYSSA; Jackson Memorial HS; Jackson, NJ; (S); 10/420; FNA; Concert Band; Mrchg Band; Sec Jr Cls; Rep Stu Cncl; High Hon Roll; NHS; NJ ST Pres Hlth Occptns Stu Of Amer 85-86.

HARVEY, BRYAN; W Orange HS; W Orange, NJ; (Y); Church Yth Grp; Spanish Clb; Orch; Stage Crew; Nwsp Stf; Trk; Hon Roll; Spanish NHS; Mrtkng.

HARVEY, CARLETTA; Plainfield HS; Plainfield, NJ; (Y); 6/500; Office Aide; Church Choir; Pres Jr Cls; Pres Sr Cls; Mgr Bsktbl; Mgr Trk; Hon Roll; Acdmc All Am Schlr Pgm Awd 84; Bus Mgmt.

HARVEY, CYNTHIA ANN; Parsippany Hills HS; Parsippany, NJ; (Y); 11/302; Am Leg Aux Girls St; Pres Art Clb; Church Yth Grp; French Clb; Letterman Clb; Service Clb; Varsity Clb; Variety Show; Lit Mag; Rep Jr Cls; French Awd, PHHS Boster Athl/Acdmc Schlrshp, Amie Hoffman Mem Schlrshp 86; U Notre Dame; Psych.

HARVEY, KEVIN; Bayley-Ellard Rgnl HS; Chester, NJ; (Y); Am Leg Boys St; Model UN; School Musical; School Play; Stage Crew; Yrbk Sprt Ed; Yrbk Stf; Rep Frsh Cls; Rep Sr Cls; JV Var Wrstlng.

HARVEY, KEVIN; Hillsborough HS; Somerville, NJ; (Y); 75/300; Church Yth Grp; Ski Clb; Frsh Cls; Soph Cls; Jr Cls; Ftbl; Hon Roll; PA ST; Comp.

HARVEY, PATRICK; Audubon HS; Audubon, NJ; (Y); Am Leg Boys St; German Clb; Pres Frsh Cls; Pres Soph Cls; Pres Jr Cls; Pres Sr Cls; Rep Stu Cncl; Var Capt Bsktbl; High Hon Roll; Hon Roll.

HARVEY, RANJA; Teaneck HS; Teaneck, NJ; (Y); Cmnty Wkr; Spanish Clb; SADD; Sftbl; Vllybl; DAR Awd; High Hon Roll; NHS; EMT 86; Am Red Crs Lfsvg 85; Med.

HARVEY, ROBERT T; Vineland HS; Vineland, NJ; (Y); 10/812; German Clb; VP Pres Intnl Clb; Key Clb; Math Tm; Nwsp Sprt Ed; Yrbk Stf; Stu Cncl; Tennis; NHS; Garden ST Distngshd Schlrs Pgm 86; Pres Acad Fit Awds Pgm 86; Union Coll; Chem.

HARWOOD, MICHELLE; Salem HS; Salem, NJ; (Y); 30/133; Drama Clb; Office Aide; SADD; Thesps; Chorus; School Play; Stage Crew; Yrbk Rptr; Yrbk Stf; Off Stu Cncl; Exctive Sec.

HASSAN, YASMIN; Hightstown HS; Hightstown, NJ; (Y); 5/361; Pres Debate Tm; VP NHS; Rutgers Coll.

HASSAN, ZUBAIR; Hightstown HS; E Windsor, NJ; (Y); 47/480; Varsity Clb; Var Capt Ftbl; Im Wt Lftg.

HASSE, AMY; Northern Valley Regional HS; Harrington Pk, NJ; (Y); 17/281; AFS; Hosp Aide; Ski Clb; Chorus; Drill Tm; School Play; Trs Sr Cls; Var Sftbl; High Hon Roll; NHS; Phys Thrpy.

HASSEBROEK, DOUG; The Mullica Hill Friends Schl; Medford, NJ; (Y); 1/9; Key Clb; Concert Band; Jazz Band; Mrchg Band; Pep Band; Yrbk Stf; Rutgers U Schlrs Prog 86; NJ Inst Of Tech 3 Certfs 86; Friends Schl Schlrsp 85-86; Arch.

HASSLER, BRIAN; Christian Brothers Acad; Jackson, NJ; (Y); Church Yth Grp; Yrbk Stf; Im Bsktbl; Im Ice Hcky; Im Socr; Engrng.

HASTINGS, JON; Williamstown HS; Williamstown, NJ; (Y); Political Wkr; VP Capt Bsktbl; JV Tennis; Im Wt Lftg; Hon Roll; Am Legn Boys ST Altnt 86; Am Legn Yth Ldrshp 86; Engrg.

HATALA, JOHN; North Hunterdon HS; Lebanon, NJ; (Y); 41/362; Am Leg Boys St; Church Yth Grp; Ski Clb; Yrbk Phtg; Pres Stu Cncl; L Ftbl; Var Lcrss; Im Wt Lftg; Hon Roll; U S Nvl Acad; Hstry.

HATCH, JOHN; Paul VI HS; Oaklyn, NJ; (Y); 10/473; Am Leg Boys St; Math Tm; Var L Crs Cntry; Var L Trk; High Hon Roll; JC Awd; NHS; St Schlr; Hon Roll; J Wood Platt Caddie Schlrp 86-87; Lehigh U; Mech Engrg.

HATCH, WENDY ROSE; Buena Regional HS; Williamstown, NJ; (Y); 41/162; Drama Clb; 4-H; Girl Scts; Varsity Clb; School Musical; School Play; Yrbk Stf; Stu Cncl; Cheerleading; Hon Roll; COE 85-86; Yrbk Svc Awd 86; Atlantic CC; Elem Ed.

HATCHER, SUZANNE; Over Brook Reg SR HS; Berlin, NJ; (Y); Trs Church Yth Grp; Hst DECA; Varsity Clb; Church Choir; Rep Stu Cncl; Capt Trk; Library Aide; Office Aide; Pep Clb; Spanish Clb; Mst Vrstle, Outstndng Athlete & All Cnfrnce Plaque All In Track & Field 85; Howard U; Med.

HATFIELD, CHRISTINE; Matawan Regional HS; Matawan, NJ; (S); 2/292; Church Yth Grp; Girl Scts; Stu Cncl; Var Crs Cntry; Cit Awd; Gov Hon Prg Awd; NHS; Sal; St Schlr; Gld Awd Grl Sctng 85; Intnatl Opprtnty Australia Grl Scts 86; Pres Peer Ldrshp Pgm 85 & 86; Comp Graphcs.

HATKE, DOREL; Bogota HS; Bogota, NJ; (Y); 27/106; Church Yth Grp; Drama Clb; Exploring; Spanish Clb; Teachers Aide; Acpl Chr; Band; Chorus; Church Choir; Concert Band; Hnrs Pgm Upsala Coll 86; Upsala Coll; Comp Sci.

HAUCK, DOUG; Bridgewater-Raritan West HS; Bridgewater, NJ; (Y); Var Bsbl; Var Swmmng; High Hon Roll; Hon Roll; NHS; Dntstry.

HAUG, DIANE; Paramus HS; Paramus, NJ; (Y); Church Yth Grp; Girl Scts; Orch; Nwsp Rptr; Var L Bowling; L Score Keeper; High Hon Roll; NHS; Spanish NHS; Rep Frsh Cls; Grl Sct Gld Awd 86.

HAUGETO, KIRSTIN; Kittatinny Regional HS; Newton, NJ; (Y); 6/227; Pres Church Yth Grp; VP 4-H; Girl Scts; Math Tm; Chorus; Score Keeper; DAR Awd; High Hon Roll; NHS; Ntl Merit SF; Anml Sci.

HAUGETO, NOELLE L; Kittatinny Regional HS; Newton, NJ; (S); 4/164; Church Yth Grp; 4-H; Girl Scts; Var Fld Hcky; High Hon Roll; Hon Roll; NHS; Grl Scts Gld Awd 86.

HAUGHNEY, ANNE; Mount Saint Mary Acad; Cranford, NJ; (Y); GAA; Spanish Clb; Chorus; School Musical; Nwsp Rptr; Lit Mag; Bsktbl; Fld Hcky; Sftbl; Spanish NHS; Jrnlsm.

HAUSEL, DEBRA; Warren Tech; Phillipsburg, NJ; (S); Key Clb; Varsity Clb; Nwsp Stf; Yrbk Stf; Trs Frsh Cls; VP Soph Cls; Sec Jr Cls; JV VP Bsbl; Cheerleading; Scrkpr Crs Cntry; Graphic Arts.

HAUSER, MELISSA; Southern Regional HS; Cedar Run, NJ; (Y); 31/400; Dance Clb; Hosp Aide; Ski Clb; Chorus; Yrbk Stf; Off Frsh Cls; Off Soph Cls; Off Jr Cls; Natl Hnr Soc 86; Drexel U; Intr Dsgn.

HAVENS, ANGELA; Villa Victoria Acad; Browns Mills, NJ; (Y); Church Yth Grp; Drama Clb; Hosp Aide; Chorus; School Musical; Yrbk Stf; Socr; Sftbl; Phys Thrpy.

HAVILAND, AMELIA M; Highland Park HS; Highland Park, NJ; (Y); 10/130; Latin Clb; Political Wkr; Acpl Chr; Sec Church Choir; Mgr Stage Crew; Trs Frsh Cls; Trs Soph Cls; Off Stu Cncl; Crs Cntry; Hon Roll.

HAWKINS, KATHLEEN; Bishop AHR HS; Edison, NJ; (Y); Cmnty Wkr; Spanish Clb; Thesps; Chorus; School Musical; School Play; Hon Roll; Rider Coll Scholar 86; Rider Coll; Lib Arts.

HAWKINS, SABRINA B; Highland Park HS; Highland Park, NJ; (Y); 60/130; Pep Clb; Sec Spanish Clb; SADD; Band; Trk; Hon Roll; Ntl Merit Ltr; Spirit Clb Pres 85-86; ST Champ High Jump 84-85; 6th Pl JR Olympcs High Jump 85; Columbia U; Pol Sci.

HAWKINS, STACY D; Frank H Morrell HS; Irvington, NJ; (Y); 90/500; Church Yth Grp; Girl Scts; Rep Stu Cncl; Var Capt Vllybl; Hon Roll; U Of NC.

HAWTHORNE, SANDY; Central HS; Newark, NJ; (Y); Computer Clb; Dance Clb; JA; Office Aide; Color Guard; Yrbk Stf; Sftbl; Vllybl; Prfct Atten Awd; Rutgers; Bus.

HAY, TRACY L; Central Regional HS; Seaside Park, NJ; (Y); 23/250; Math Clb; Math Tm; Yrbk Bus Mgr; Yrbk Stf; High Hon Roll; Hon Roll; NHS; Rutgers; Pre-Med.

HAYEK, GRACE; Manchester Regional HS; Prospect Park, NJ; (Y); Cmnty Wkr; French Clb; Library Aide; Yrbk Phtg; Yrbk Stf; Powder Puff Ftbl; Hon Roll; Spec Ed Tchr.

HAYEK, MARIA; Manchester Regional HS; Prospect Park, NJ; (Y); Cmnty Wkr; French Clb; Library Aide; Yrbk Phtg; Yrbk Stf; Powder Puff Ftbl; Hon Roll; Spec Ed Tchr.

HAYES, CYNTHIA; Atlantic City HS; Atlantic City, NJ; (Y); 118/454; VP Band; Church Choir; Concert Band; Jazz Band; Mrchg Band; Orch; Hon Roll; Mst Outstndg Bnd Stu 85-86; Foy-Mor-Wee Scholar; Chris Columbo Band Scholar; Glassboro ST Coll; Bus Adm.

HAYES, JENNIE; Lower Cape May Regional HS; Cape May, NJ; (Y); 41/275; Pep Clb; Varsity Clb; Variety Show; Var Bsktbl; Mgr(s); Var Tennis; Var Trk; Hon Roll; Rookie Yr-Bsktbl 84; U Of MD Coll Pk; Psych.

HAYES, KEVIN; Clifton HS; Clifton, NJ; (Y); 95/650; Aud/Vis; VP Math Clb; VP Spanish Clb; SADD; VP Frsh Cls; Rep Soph Cls; Rep Jr Cls; Im Bsktbl; JV Ftbl; Cit Awd; Outstndng Achvt-Electrcty-Electrncs 86; Vrsty Ftbl Ltr 83; Gftd-Tlntd Awds 81-86; NJ Inst Tech; Elec Engrng.

HAYES, SANDRA A; Franklin HS; Somerset, NJ; (Y); 2/313; Church Yth Grp; Trs Band; Drm Mjr(t); Yrbk Stf; Off Sr Cls; Bausch & Lomb Sci Awd; High Hon Roll; NHS; Sal; 86 Rgn II Symphonic Band 86; Frnkln Pride Msc Awd 86; Rtgrs U Deans Smmr Schlr 85; Holy Cross Coll; Bio.

HAYES, SHARON; Millville SR HS; Millvile, NJ; (Y); 21/468; FBLA; GAA; Office Aide; OEA; SADD; Stu Cncl; JV Swmmng; High Hon Roll; NHS; Eudora Radcliff Russel Awd 86; Amer Red Cross VIP Blood Dnr 85-86; Hon Grad 86; Glassboro ST Coll; Elem Ed.

HAYES, TRACY LYN; Overbrook Regional SR HS; Clementon, NJ; (Y); French Clb; Office Aide; Q&S; Chorus; School Play; Variety Show; JV Cheerleading; Hon Roll; Indctd Yng Athrs Amer 3 Ltry Wrks Pblshd Bk; Psych.

HAYES, VINCENT; Saint Joseph HS; Fords, NJ; (Y); Trs Church Yth Grp; Cmnty Wkr; Political Wkr; Service Clb; Ski Clb; Hon Roll; Outstdng Parsh Svc 84-85; Aerontcl Engr.

HAYES, WARREN; Pascack Hills HS; Montvale, NJ; (Y); Camera Clb; Computer Clb; Debate Tm; Model UN; Political Wkr; Yrbk Phtg; Var L Bowling; JV Tennis; Hon Roll; 2nd Pl Tm Spkng Awd Model U N 86; Merit Awd U S Hstry 86; Bnkng.

HAYMAN, FLOYD; Frank H Morrell HS; Irvington, NJ; (Y); Boy Scts; Hon Roll; Air Force; Elec.

HAYNES, PETER D; Green Brook HS; Green Brook, NJ; (Y); 1/47; Am Leg Boys St; Key Clb; Thesps; Band; Nwsp Ed-Chief; Yrbk Ed-Chief; Ed Lit Mag; Bausch & Lomb Sci Awd; NHS; Val; Stevens Inst Of Tech; Engrng.

HAYNES, ROXANNE; St Anthony HS; Jersey City, NJ; (Y); Church Yth Grp; Church Choir; Bowling; Seton Hall U; Cmmnctns.

HAYNES, SHARON TONNETTE; Lincoln HS; Jersey City, NJ; (Y); Church Yth Grp; Cmnty Wkr; 4-H; Chorus; Variety Show; Yrbk Stf; Stu Cncl; 4-H Awd; Hon Roll; Seaton Hall U; Bus Admin.

HAYNOR, KELLY CHRISTINE; Haddonfield Mem HS; Haddonfield, NJ; (Y); Hosp Aide; VP Frsh Cls; Off Stu Cncl; Bsktbl; Var Cheerleading; High Hon Roll; Accntng.

HAYWARD, IRONDA; East Side HS; Newark, NJ; (Y); Boys Clb Am; Capt Drill Tm; Rep Frsh Cls; Rep Soph Cls; Rep Jr Cls; Cheerleading; Score Keeper; Opt Clb Awd; Black Heritage Clb; Rutgers U; Accntnt.

HAYWOOD, DOROTHY; Rahway HS; Rahway, NJ; (Y); JA; Office Aide; Pep Clb; Spanish Clb; Teachers Aide; Church Choir; JV Cheerleading; JV Var Gym; High Hon Roll; Hon Roll; Nrsng.

HAYWOOD, LISA; Egg Harbor Twp HS; Linwood, NJ; (S); 1/266; Church Yth Grp; Hosp Aide; Trs Ski Clb; Band; Concert Band; Jazz Band; Mrchg Band; Var Crs Cntry; High Hon Roll; Hon Roll; Louis Armstrong Jazz Awd 84; Sci.

HAZE, JONATHAN; Randolph HS; Randolph, NJ; (Y); Boy Scts; Church Yth Grp; Ski Clb; Golf; Socr.

HAZELL, JOY; Pinelands Regional HS; Tuckerton, NJ; (S); 10/114; Exploring; FBLA; FHA; Color Guard; Capt Sftbl; High Hon Roll; Hon Roll; NHS; Crmnl Justice.

HAZEN, TIMOTHY J; West Milford Township HS; West Milford, NJ; (Y); Am Leg Boys St; Math Tm; Scholastic Bowl; Band; Jazz Band; Trs Stu Cncl; Var Bsktbl; Var Socr; Var Capt Tennis; NHS; Adm Rickover Inst-Hnrbl Mntn 86; Am HS Math Exam-Natl Merit Roll 86; Sen B Bradleys Ldrshp Semnr 86; Appld Math.

HEACOCK, MARJORI; Lawrence HS; Lawrenceville, NJ; (Y); 28/228; Church Yth Grp; Drama Clb; Hosp Aide; Sec Spanish Clb; Church Choir; Co-Capt Flag Corp; Mrchg Band; School Musical; Var Trk; High Hon Roll; Amer Leg Aux Schlrshp, Temple U Pres, Pres Acad Ftnss Awds 86; Temple U; Ed.

HEADLEY, CHRISTOPHER; Egg Harbor TWP HS; Cardiff, NJ; (S); 3/318; Boy Scts; Nwsp Stf; JV Crs Cntry; JV Wrstlng; Bio.

HEALEY, MARK A; West Morris Central HS; Long Valley, NJ; (Y); 3/250; Church Yth Grp; Var Debate Tm; Drama Clb; School Play; Var Crs Cntry; Var Trk; Gov Hon Prg Awd; Ntl Merit SF; Rotary Awd; St Schlr; NJ Schlrs Prog 85; Rensselaer Mdl 85; Stu Of Year Rnnr Up 83; Engnrng.

HEALY, KEVIN; St Joseph Regional HS; Park Ridge, NJ; (Y); 30/167; Church Yth Grp; Ski Clb; Bsktbl; Golf; Trk; Fnlst Bergen Rcrd Schlrshp Cntst 86; Engrng.

HEALY, LEIGH ANN; Westfield HS; Westfield, NJ; (Y); 90/514; Church Yth Grp; Hst Girl Scts; JCL; Latin Clb; Chorus; Hon Roll; American U; Intl Bus.

HEANEY, CYNTHIA; Oak Knoll HS; Madison, NJ; (Y); French Clb; Service Clb; Ski Clb; Stage Crew; Nwsp Rptr; Nwsp Stf; Ed Lit Mag; Engl.

HEANEY, NICOLE; Manchester HS; North Haledon, NJ; (S); 4/180; Church Yth Grp; Cmnty Wkr; GAA; Hosp Aide; Mathletes; Science Clb; Varsity Clb; Socr; Sftbl; Hon Roll; Hnrbl Ment All Leag Sccr Goalie 85.

HEARN, ADRIENNE; Clayton HS; Glassboro, NJ; (Y); Library Aide; Chorus; Concert Band; Yrbk Stf; NHS; Educ.

HEARN, ROBERT; Point Pleasant Borough HS; Point Pleasant, NJ; (Y); 22/243; Am Leg Boys St; Exploring; JCL; Sec Key Clb; School Musical; Variety Show; Pres Frsh Cls; Pres Stu Cncl; Bsbl; JV Var Bsktbl; Kiwanis Ldrshp Inst 85; New Jersey Assn Of Stdnt Cncls Ldrshp Trning Cnference 86.

HEATH, TIFFANY; Middletown HS South; Lincroft, NJ; (Y); Dance Clb; French Clb; DAR Awd; FBI.

HEATHER, FRANK; Dwight Morrow HS; Englewood, NJ; (Y); 39/274; Spanish Clb; Color Guard; School Play; Rep Stu Cncl; Var Cheerleading; Var JV Mgr(s); Var Trk; JV Vllybl; High Hon Roll; Hon Roll; Bus Adm.

HEBERLEY, LISA; Cinnaminson HS; Cinnaminson, NJ; (Y); 13/257; Am Leg Aux Girls St; Church Yth Grp; Hosp Aide; Thesps; Band; Rep Stu Cncl; Var Tennis; High Hon Roll; NHS; Rotary Awd; NJ Socty Certfd Publc Acctnt Schlrshp 86; Burlington Cnty Yth & Govt Forum 85-86; St Josephs U; Intl Bus.

HECHT, DEBRA; Matawan Regional HS; Aberdeen, NJ; (S); 2/350; Math Tm; Concert Band; Jazz Band; Mrchg Band; School Musical; Variety Show; Trs Soph Cls; Stu Cncl; High Hon Roll; Temple Yth Grp; Schlrshp Israel 85; Psych.

HECHT, LINDA; Fair Lawn HS; Fair Lawn, NJ; (Y); 19/335; Lit Mag; High Hon Roll; NHS; ST NJ Distngshd Schlr 86; 2nd Plc Pscl Comptn Contntl Mathmtcs Leag 86; Brandeis U.

HECK, MICHAEL; Pinelands Regional HS; Tuckerton, NJ; (Y); #10 In Class; Aud/Vis; CAP; Library Aide; Drill Tm; Yrbk Phtg; Yrbk Rptr; JV Bsktbl; JV Crs Cntry; JV Socr; High Hon Roll; Norwich U; Med.

HECK, STEVEN W; Shawnee HS; Tabernacle, NJ; (Y); Am Leg Boys St; VP Frsh Cls; VP Jr Cls; VP Sr Cls; Stu Cncl; JV Bsktbl; High Hon Roll; Hon Roll; NHS; Township Bsbl; ST Sci Fair Champs Chem 86; Librl Arts.

HECKEL, KURT; Toms River South HS; Toms River, NJ; (Y); 46/419; Art Clb; Yrbk Stf; Swmmng; Hon Roll; Gftd Stu Awd TR Bd Of Ed.

HECKLER, MICHAEL J; Seton Hall Prep; Berkeley Hts, NJ; (Y); 4/200; Math Clb; Math Tm; School Musical; High Hon Roll; NHS; Ntl Merit Ltr; Knghts Clmbs Schlrshp 86; U Of Notre Dame; Elctrcl Engr.

HECKMAN, CHRISTINE; Newton HS; Andover, NJ; (Y); Church Yth Grp; French Clb; Latin Clb; Ski Clb; Rep Frsh Cls; Rep Jr Cls; Sec Sr Cls; Rep Stu Cncl; Powder Puff Ftbl; Trk; IBEW & Local Schlrshp 86; Clemson U SC; Pre-Law.

HEDDY, SARA; Montville HS; Montville, NJ; (Y); 111/271; 4-H; Merideth Manor; Eqstrn Inst.

HEDGEMAN, CRISPUS FM; Arthur P Schalick HS; Bridgeton, NJ; (Y); 38/132; Am Leg Boys St; Debate Tm; FCA; Math Tm; Varsity Clb; Band; Pres Sr Cls; Var Bsktbl; Var Capt Ftbl; Var Capt Trk; 1st Tm Trck & Fld All Area 85; 1st Tm Conf Trck & Fld 85-86; Pltcl Sci.

HEDIN, DEBBIE; Middletown HS South; Lincroft, NJ; (Y); Church Yth Grp; Ski Clb; Powder Puff Ftbl; JV Socr; Trk; High Hon Roll; NHS; Cmnty Wkr; Lit Mag; Hon Roll; Lincroft Lttl Leag Sftbl All Stars 84 & 85; Lawyr.

HEETER, GREG; Holy Cross HS; Riverton, NJ; (Y); 99/371; Chess Clb; Drama Clb; German Clb; Quiz Bowl; Stage Crew; Coach Actv; Ftbl; Wt Lftg; Hon Roll; All Star Team Bsbl 77-84; Rlgn Awd 83; U S Mltry Acad:Arntcs.

HEFELFINGER, DAWN; Sayreville War Memorial HS; Parlin, NJ; (S); Am Leg Aux Girls St; Church Yth Grp; Math Clb; Varsity Clb; Chorus; Var L Cheerleading; Var L Sftbl; Hon Roll; CPG Synod Convtn 85; Bus Admn.

HEFFERNAN, RACHEL; Holy Cross HS; Moorestown, NJ; (Y); 89/392; Ski Clb; SADD; School Musical; Rep Frsh Cls; Rep Soph Cls; Rep Jr Cls; Rep Sr Cls; Coach Actv; Tennis; Hon Roll; Outstndng Rep Awd 85.

HEFFRON, KATHLEEN; Manalapan HS; Manalapan, NJ; (Y); Dance Clb; Debate Tm; Science Clb; SADD; School Musical; School Play; Stage Crew; NHS; NJ Gvnrs Schl 86; Schl Hstry Hnrs Awd 86; Law.

HEFLICH, LAURIE; Wood-Ridge HS; Wood-Ridge, NJ; (S); 10/91; Church Yth Grp; Model UN; Service Clb; Nwsp Stf; Yrbk Stf; Lit Mag; Bsktbl; Cit Awd; High Hon Roll; Trs NHS; Rutgers; Polit Sci.

HEGEMAN, WENDI; Morris Knolls HS; Rockaway, NJ; (Y); Church Yth Grp; Varsity Clb; Trk; High Hon Roll; Hon Roll; Acctng.

HEGG, ERIC L; Morristown HS; Morristown, NJ; (Y); Am Leg Boys St; Boy Scts; VP Church Yth Grp; Capt Debate Tm; Key Clb; Red Cross Aide; School Musical; Socr; NHS; Ntl Merit Ltr; Woman Vtrs Schlrshp WA Wrkshp 86; North Jersey Regnl Chorus 86; Head Acolyte St Peters Epis Chrch 86; Liberal Arts.

HEHN, LEA; Kittatinny Regional HS; Newton, NJ; (Y); 6/160; Hosp Aide; Math Tm; Spanish Clb; Teachers Aide; Band; Var Bsktbl; Var Capt Crs Cntry; Var Capt Trk; Hon Roll; NHS; Provost Schlrshp VA Commnwlth 86; Athltc Schlrshp Crs Cntry VA Commonwealth 86; Yth Mrt Awd Rtry 86; VA Commonwealth U; Physcl Thrp.

HEIDELBERGER, KENNETH; Christain Brothers Acad; Middletown, NJ; (Y); 74/230; VP Church Yth Grp; Cmnty Wkr; Variety Show; Rep Frsh Cls; Rep Soph Cls; Im Bsktbl; Im Ftbl; Var L Socr; Im Sftbl; Trk; Physcl Thrpy.

HEIDEN, THERESA; Phillipsburg Catholic HS; Phillipsburg, NJ; (Y); Science Clb; Service Clb; School Musical; Stage Crew; Var Bsktbl; Var Fld Hcky; Gibb Scholar 86; Chrstn Svc Awd 86; Northampton Area CC; Blnd Ed.

HEILWEIL, SHARON; West Essex HS; Fairfield, NJ; (Y); 32/350; Computer Clb; Latin Clb; Temple Yth Grp; Orch; Yrbk Stf; Hon Roll; NHS; NY ST U Bnghmtn; Accntng.

HEIMBERG, LISA; Lenape Valley Regional HS; Stanhope, NJ; (Y); 42/241; Sec Church Yth Grp; Capt Color Guard; Capt Flag Corp; Lit Mag; Rep Jr Cls; Fld Hcky; Hon Roll; Dplms Moore Coll Art Smmr Cls 85; Acdmc All Amer 86; Grphc Artst.

HEIN, CHIP; Newe Milford HS; New Milford, NJ; (Y); 17/141; Political Wkr; Concert Band; Jazz Band; Mrchg Band; Rep Stu Cncl; Var Bowling; Cit Awd; Hon Roll; NHS; Bnd Brass Mst Valuable Sect Ldr & Soloist 83-86; U Buffalo; Engrng.

HEIN, JOANNE; Passaic Cnty Tech & Vocational HS; Paterson, NJ; (S); Hosp Aide; Spanish Clb; Yrbk Stf; Var Cheerleading; Score Keeper; JV Sftbl; Hon Roll; US Chrldr Achvt Awd 85.

HEIN, TIFFANY; Hightstown HS; Colorado Springs, CO; (Y); Temple Yth Grp; Concert Band; Rep Jr Cls; Var Mgr(s); JV Trk; San Diego ST; Bus.

HEIN, TINA; Dover HS; Mine Hill, NJ; (Y); JA; Ski Clb; Variety Show; Lit Mag; Stat Bsktbl; Bowling; Mgr(s); JV Socr; JV Sftbl; Hon Roll; Acctg Awd 85; Engrng.

HEINTZ, MATTHEW; Middlesex HS; Middlesex, NJ; (Y); 56/158; Boy Scts; Astronomy.

HEINZ, DIANE; Morris Catholic HS; Montville, NJ; (Y); 38/142; German Clb; Natl Beta Clb; School Play; Bsktbl; Var Socr; Var Trk; Hon Roll; Bsktbl Par B ST Chmpnshp 86; Sccr Conf Chmps 85.

HEINZE, MARGARET; Bridgewater-Raritan HS West; Bridgewater, NJ; (Y); VP German Clb; Capt Flag Corp; School Musical; Yrbk Ed-Chief; Var Powder Puff Ftbl; Var Socr; Capt Swmmng; Hon Roll; Sec NHS; Vrsty Ltr Wnnr Swmng 86; Excllnc Grmn Awd 86; Pres Acdmc Ftns Awd 86; U MO Columbia; Physcl Thrpy.

HEINZMANN, B KEITH; Hillsborough HS; Somerville, NJ; (Y); 97/292; Drm Mjr(t); Jazz Band; Yrbk Ed-Chief; Lit Mag; Off Soph Cls; Off Jr Cls; JV Bsktbl; Var Crs Cntry; Var Trk; Jrnlsm.

HEITMANN, GWEN GENE; Rutherford HS; Rutherford, NJ; (Y); 4/189; Chess Clb; Capt Debate Tm; German Clb; Science Clb; Var Socr; Capt Trk; Bausch & Lomb Sci Awd; Ntl Merit Schol; Kiwanis Awd; High Hon Roll; NJ Acad Dcthln 1st Pl Sci 2nd L Ecnmcs 2nd Pl Spch 3rd Pl Fne Arts 2nd Ovrll Cmp 86; Ml Sbl Awd 85; Cornell U; Amer Hist.

HELEWA, SANDRA; Marylawn Of The Oranges HS; Newark, NJ; (S); Science Clb; School Play; Nwsp Rptr; Hon Roll; Rutgers U.

HELLER, GARY; Matawan Regional HS; Matawan, NJ; (S); 28/290; Capt Debate Tm; Math Tm; NFL; VP Speech Tm; School Musical; Yrbk Stf; Stu Cncl; JV Bsktbl; NHS; Spanish NHS; NJ ST Stu Congrss Finls 2nd Pl 85; NJ Dist Finls Humerous Intrptn SF 85; Econ.

HELTZMAN, DOROTHY; Middletown H S South; Leonard, NJ; (Y); Church Yth Grp; Cmnty Wkr; Dance Clb; Exploring; Girl Scts; JA; Library Aide; Office Aide; Teachers Aide; Varsity Clb; Mrktng.

HELWIG, DONNA; Lower Cape May Regional HS; N Cape May, NJ; (Y); SADD; Varsity Clb; Chorus; Church Choir; Flag Corp; Yrbk Stf; Hon Roll; Comm Educ.

HEMMES, KIMBERLY; Toms River H S East; Toms River, NJ; (S); 101/488; Pres Church Yth Grp; French Clb; Key Clb; Q&S; Ski Clb; Ed Nwsp Stf; Rep Frsh Cls; Rep Jr Cls; Rep Sr Cls; Stu Cncl; Brdcst Jrnlsm.

HEMPLE, TRACEY; St James HS; Paulsboro, NJ; (Y); Chorus; Drill Tm; Mgr Jazz Band; Nrsng.

HEMSLEY, ALEX; Queen Of Peace HS; N Arlington, NJ; (Y); 29/231; Var L Trk; Hon Roll.

HEMSLEY, MARY ELLEN; Queen Of Peace HS; North Arlington, NJ; (S); 4/243; Cmnty Wkr; French Clb; Hosp Aide; Service Clb; Nwsp Phtg; Nwsp Rptr; Nwsp Stf; JV Var Bsktbl; Hon Roll; NHS; Hghst Engl Avg 82-83; Acad All Amer 84-85; Seton Hall U; Med.

HENBEST, JON; Toms River High School South; Toms River, NJ; (Y); Am Leg Boys St; Church Choir; Church Yth Grp; Band; Church Choir; Mrchg Band; Yrbk Stf; NHS; Yth Sessn Presbytrn Chch 84-85; Yth Wk Mnstr Vistatn 86; Yth Rep Natl Brd Opertn Frndshp 86; Acctg.

HENCKEL, JOANNE; Lyndhurst HS; Lyndhurst, NJ; (Y); 5/163; German Clb; Key Clb; Office Aide; Chorus; Hon Roll; NHS; Pres Schlr; St Schlr; Lyndhurst Chptr Unico Natl Schlrp 86-87; Angela Wisneski Smith Engl Lit Awd 86; Good Fllwshp Awd 86; Rutgers; Psychol.

HENDER, DANIEL JOSEPH; Haddonfield Memorial HS; Haddonfield, NJ; (Y); 24/157; Am Leg Boys St; Cmnty Wkr; Latin Clb; Var Crs Cntry; Var Swmmng; Var Trk; High Hon Roll; Hon Roll; NHS; Ntl Ltn Hnr Soc; Pre Law.

HENDERLONG, MICHAEL; Parisppany Hills HS; Morris Plains, NJ; (Y); Boy Scts; FBLA; Varsity Clb; Stu Cncl; Trk; Wt Lftg; Hon Roll; Avtn Mngmt.

HENDERSON, DANIEL S; Southern Regional HS; Beach Haven, NJ; (S); Model UN; Service Clb; Swing Chorus; Yrbk Bus Mgr; Tennis; Kiwanis Awd; NHS; Ski Clb; Spanish Clb; School Musical; HOBY Fndtn Ldrshp Awd 85; Exch Clb Freedom Shrine Awd 85; Mod Congress Princeton U 85; Hstrc Pres.

HENDERSON, LIESL A; Haddonfield Memorial HS; Haddonfield, NJ; (S); Drama Clb; Sec Intnl Clb; Sec Pres Band; Concert Band; Mrchg Band; School Musical; Pres Soph Cls; VP Pres Stu Cncl; Tennis; Cit Awd; Jr Miss 86; Hmcmng Queen 86; Wake Forest; Bus-Econ.

HENDRICKS, ALICIA; Essex Catholic Girls HS; E Orange, NJ; (Y); 35/70; Art Clb; Pep Clb; Drill Tm; Variety Show; VP Sr Cls; Stu Cncl Awd 85-86; Drill Tm & Pep Sqd Awd 82-86; Art Awd 85-86; Grphc Dsgn.

HENDRICKS, JILL; West Essex Regional HS; Fairfield, NJ; (Y); 87/350; Key Clb; Band; Nwsp Rptr; Nwsp Stf; Rep Stu Cncl; JV Fld Hcky; Rugers Coll; Cmmnctns.

HENDRICKS, TRACY; Wayne Valley HS; Wayne, NJ; (Y); 51/320; Ski Clb; Spanish Clb; Band; Concert Band; Drm Mjr(t); Mrchg Band; Mgr Bsbl; Hon Roll; Z Clb Historian 2 Yrs; Wayne Valley Band Mem Schlrshp; Wayne Valley Majorette Awd; Douglass Coll; Mrktng.

HENDRICKSON, BETH; Manasquan HS; Spg Lk Hts, NJ; (Y); 67/247; Drama Clb; Spanish Clb; Thesps; Chorus; Stage Crew; Yrbk Stf; Sec Soph Cls; Socr; Hon Roll; School Musical; Elem Ed.

HENDRICKSON, L ANDREW; Christian Brothers Acad; Freehold, NJ; (S); Pres Church Yth Grp; Cmnty Wkr; Letterman Clb; Varsity Clb; Rep Sr Cls; VP Capt Bsbl; VP Capt Bsktbl; Hon Roll; VP NHS; Pope John Paul VI Awd Excllnt Ldrshp 84; Hnrb Mntn All Shore Conf Bsktbl 85; Boston Coll; Finance.

HENGELI, LAURI; Hunterdon Central HS; Whitehouse Statio, NJ; (Y); 36/548; Jazz Band; Mrchg Band; Symp Band; Variety Show; Hon Roll; NHS; Spanish NHS; Cntrl Jrsy Rgn 11 N Symphnc Bnd 84; Cntrl Jrsy Rgn 11 Symphnc Bnd 86; Fnlst Gov Schl Arts Prog 86; Music.

HENN, MICHAEL; Roselie Catholic HS; Hillside, NJ; (Y); Church Yth Grp; Stage Crew; JV Bsbl; JV Bsktbl; Hon Roll; Spanish NHS.

HENNE, LAURA; Manalapan HS; Manalapan, NJ; (Y); 33/481; Debate Tm; Math Clb; Math Tm; Science Clb; Lit Mag; NHS; Ntl Merit SF; Mdrn Lang.

HENNE, MICHELE; Montville Twsp HS; Montville, NJ; (Y); Intnl Clb; Key Clb; Office Aide; Stage Crew; Var Crs Cntry; JV Trk; Hon Roll; U Of Miami; Chem.

HENNINGER, LISA; Highstown HS; East Windsor, NJ; (Y); Church Yth Grp; Mgr Drama Clb; Hosp Aide; Ski Clb; Band; Mrchg Band; NHS; Ntl Merit Ltr; SADD; Thesps.

HENNINGER, SUSAN; Union HS; Union, NJ; (Y); Dance Clb; Drama Clb; FBLA; Chorus; Church Choir; School Musical; Stage Crew; Cheerleading; Fld Hcky; Wt Lftg; Vocl Schlrshp Union Brd Educ 84; Dnc Schlrshp Acad Bllt 85; Paralgl.

HENRIKSEN, JANET; West Morris Central HS; Califon, NJ; (Y); 26/259; Church Yth Grp; Var Capt Sftbl; High Hon Roll; Hon Roll; NHS; Lisa A Toleno Mst Dedicated Plyr Awd 86; Long Vly JR Wmns Clb K Avellino Mem 86; W Mrs Cntrl Hlth 86; Kean Coll; Phys Thrpy.

HENRY, JENNIFER; Neptune SR HS; Neptune City, NJ; (Y); 32/343; Dance Clb; GAA; Girl Scts; Varsity Clb; Sec Frsh Cls; Capt Bsktbl; Var Socr; NHS; Senatr Bill Bradleys 6 Annl Ldrshp Semnr & Athl Semnr Rutgers U 86; Glassboro ST Coll; Phy Ed.

HENRY, KELLEY; Egg Harbor Township HS; Linwood, NJ; (Y); 45/317; Art Clb; GAA; Key Clb; Sec Frsh Cls; Sec Soph Cls; Sec Jr Cls; JV Var Cheerleading; Hon Roll; Jr NHS; Ntl Merit Ltr; Natl Merit Schlrshp Engl 86; Art.

HENRY, LIBBY; Randolph HS; Randolph, NJ; (Y); 37/357; Pres AFS; Church Yth Grp; Sec Key Clb; Red Cross Aide; Variety Show; Nwsp Bus Mgr; Nwsp Stf; Rep Soph Cls; Rep Stu Cncl; Stat Bsktbl; Spch.

HENRY, LISA A; Hamilton High East Steinert; Hamilton Sq, NJ; (Y); Am Leg Aux Girls St; French Clb; Varsity Clb; Nwsp Phtg; Lit Mag; Stu Cncl; Var L Fld Hcky; JV Var Sftbl; Var L Swmmng; Hon Roll; GALRE Govt & Law Rltd Exprnc Cls; Gftd & Tlntd; Law.

HENRY, MICHAEL; De Paul Diocesan HS; West Milford, NJ; (S); Boy Scts; Church Yth Grp; School Musical; Bsbl; Bsktbl; Var Ftbl; Var L Trk; Hon Roll; Old Dominion U; Psych.

HENRY, NADINE; Eastsid HS; Paterson, NJ; (Y); 162/500; Church Yth Grp; Science Clb; Hon Roll; Sci Awd 86; Hnr Rl 86; William Paterson Coll; Nrsng.

HENRY, PAIGE; Toms River HS; Toms River, NJ; (Y); 14/412; Sec Frsh Cls; VP Soph Cls; VP Jr Cls; L Var Fld Hcky; Var L Sftbl; Var L Trk; High Hon Roll; Hon Roll; MVP Trck 85; Acad Ltrs 84-86; All Cnty 2nd Tm Sftbl 86; Tchr.

HENRY, SUE; Pennsauken HS; Pennsauken, NJ; (Y); 6/352; Chorus; Cit Awd; High Hon Roll; NHS; Prfct Atten Awd.

HENRY, WINIFRED; John F Kennedy HS; Paterson, NJ; (S); Dance Clb; FBLA; Chorus; Church Choir; Orch; Variety Show; Nwsp Rptr; Off Jr Cls; Upward Bnd 85; Hal Jackson Tlntd Tn Prfrmnc Passaic Cnty 85.

HENSEL, MICHELE; Buena Regional HS; Milmay, NJ; (S); Drama Clb; Math Clb; Ski Clb; School Play; Rep Frsh Cls; VP Soph Cls; Pres Jr Cls; Rep Stu Cncl; Hon Roll; Jr NHS; Villanova U; Ed.

HENSON, CHAVELLA; North Brunswick Township HS; N Brunswick, NJ; (Y); 59/300; AFS; Model UN; Mrchg Band; Pres Soph Cls; JV Var Bsbl; Hon Roll; Mdrn Lng.

HENWOOD, CLAIRE M; Marlboro HS; Marlboro, NJ; (Y); 64/500; Pres Church Yth Grp; Drama Clb; Mgr Chorus; School Musical; Mgr Stage Crew; Stat Ftbl; Hon Roll; NHS; Pres Schlr; German Clb; Jentra Fine Art Gllry Awd Of Excllnc 84; Scarlet Masque Awd-Drama 85; Teen Arts Fstvl 84; Caldwell Coll; Fine Art.

HEPPARD, BRIAN; Riverside HS; Delanco, NJ; (S); 2/90; Am Leg Boys St; SADD; Pres Frsh Cls; Pres Stu Cncl; Var L Crs Cntry; Var L Trk; Hon Roll; NHS; NEDT Awd; Rotary Awd; Pre-Med.

HEPPARD, LORELEI; Riverside HS; Delanco, NJ; (S); 18/65; Am Leg Aux Girls St; Art Clb; Sec Church Yth Grp; Keywanettes; SADD; Band; Church Choir; Concert Band; Jazz Band; Mrchg Band; Gold & Silvr Mdls Art East Regnl Fstvl Of Life 85; Comm Art.

HERBERT, AMY; North Brunswick HS; N Brunswick, NJ; (Y); Church Yth Grp; Cmnty Wkr; Dance Clb; PAVAS; School Musical; Variety Show; Yrbk Stf; 2 Yr Schlrshp Barbados Dance Theatre Co 82-84; Cert Royal Acad Dancing; Rutgers Coll; Engrng.

HERBERT, DANIEL; Cherry Hill High School West; Cherry Hill, NJ; (Y); Aud/Vis; Cmnty Wkr; Pres Drama Clb; Library Aide; PAVAS; Spanish Clb; Pres Thesps; School Musical; School Play; Stage Crew; Ithaca-Cornell.

HERBERT, DARREN; Gloucester City JR SR HS; Gloucester, NJ; (Y); Aud/Vis; Cmnty Wkr; Model UN; PAVAS; Yrbk Stf; Cit Awd; High Hon Roll; Hon Roll; Prfct Atten Awd.

HERBERT, JOHN; Colonia HS; Colonia, NJ; (Y); Math Clb; ROTC; SADD; JV Crs Cntry; Var L Trk; JV Wrstlng; High Hon Roll; NHS; Mil.

HERBSTMAN, AUDRA; Montville Twsp HS; Montville, NJ; (Y); 11/272; Cmnty Wkr; Chrmn Key Clb; Ski Clb; Nwsp Stf; Rep Frsh Cls; JV Fld Hcky; Var Socr; Var Trk; High Hon Roll; Sec NHS; Tulane U; Lib Arts.

HERDMAN, JENNIFER; Monsignor Donovan HS; Lakewood, NJ; (Y); 48/216; Art Clb; Drama Clb; French Clb; Service Clb; Ski Clb; High Hon Roll; NHS; Fashion Inst Tech; Merchdsng.

HERLIHY, TRISTIN; Mahwah HS; Mahwah, NJ; (Y); 77/176; Chorus; Hst Frsh Cls; Rep Soph Cls; Rep Jr Cls; Trk; Vllybl; Hon Roll; Bus Mgmt.

HERLINSKY, TAMMY; Paul VI Regional HS; Clifton, NJ; (S); 1/147; Sec French Clb; School Musical; Nwsp Rptr; French Hon Soc; High Hon Roll; NHS; Ntl Merit Ltr; Rutgers Schlrs Day 86; Miss Natl Teen Essay Fin 85.

HERMAN, BRAD J; Cinnaminson HS; Cinnaminson, NJ; (Y); Am Leg Boys St; Science Clb; Rep Frsh Cls; Rep Soph Cls; Var Bsbl; Var Bsktbl; Hon Roll; NHS; 3rd Tm Burlington Cnty Bsbl 86; Honorable Mention All-Group III Bsbl 86; Engrng.

HERMAN, MARK; Manalapan HS; Englishtown, NJ; (Y); 127/450; Temple Yth Grp; Band; Concert Band; Jazz Band; Mrchg Band; Pep Band; School Musical; School Play; Stage Crew; Symp Band; Engrng.

HERMAN, SANDRA; Vineland HS; Vineland, NJ; (Y); 65/803; Red Cross Aide; SADD; Nwsp Stf; Lit Mag; Chld Devl Psych.

HERNANDEZ JR, DAVID; Orange HS; Orange, NJ; (Y); JA; Spanish Clb; Nwsp Rptr; Nwsp Sprt Ed; Capt Var Socr; Natl Yth Phys Ftnss Pgm-Marine Corps Lge 85; Acadmc All Amer 86; Med.

HERNANDEZ, DIANA DELGADO; Rancocas Valley Regional HS; Mount Holly, NJ; (S); DECA; ROTC; Drill Tm; Mgr(s); Distrbtv Educ Clb Amerc 1st Pl & 3rd Gen Merch 86; Mercer Cnty; Med Tech.

HERNANDEZ, GISELLE E; St Joseph Of Palisades HS; Union City, NJ; (S); 1/128; Math Clb; Model UN; Spanish Clb; Variety Show; Nwsp Ed-Chief; Yrbk Stf; Lit Mag; Bowling; High Hon Roll; NHS; Gardn ST Dstngshd Schlr 86; NJ Girls Ctznshp 85; Natl Achvt Awds 82-86; Pre-Med.

HERNANDEZ, HANSY; Don Bosco Technical HS; Paterson, NJ; (Y); 30/96; Cmnty Wkr; Pep Clb; Var Bsbl; JV Bsktbl; Var Socr; Hon Roll; NHS; Ive Dist 3 Socl Actn Cmmte Schlrshp 86; Fairleigh Dickinson U; Accntng.

HERNANDEZ, IDELSI; Secaucus HS; Secaucus, NJ; (S); 6/160; Church Yth Grp; Computer Clb; Math Clb; Spanish Clb; Church Choir; High Hon Roll; NHS; Spanish NHS; 2nd Span Poetry Rdng Cntst 85; Engrng.

HERNANDEZ, JOHN; Keyport HS; Keyport, NJ; (Y); 38/98; Am Leg Boys St; Bsbl; Var L Bsktbl; Var L Ftbl; Var L Trk; Var L Wt Lftg; Cit Awd; All Shr RB, All Mmth RB, All ST DB & Dly Nws All Str 85-86; Montclair Sst Coll; Indstrl Art.

HERNANDEZ, MARIA; Good Counsel HS; Newark, NJ; (Y); 47/106; FBLA; Spanish Clb; Bowling; Business Administrator.

HERNANDEZ, NANCY; Elizabeth HS; Elizabeth, NJ; (Y); 26/847; Trs Debate Tm; Math Clb; French Hon Soc; NHS; Ntl Merit Ltr; Ntl Hispnc Schlr Awd Semfnlst 86; Histry Clb 85-86; Bio-Chemcl Engr.

HERNANDEZ, NEMOY; Essex Catholic Girls HS; Hillside, NJ; (Y); Chorus; Church Choir; Drill Tm; Yrbk Stf; Frsh Cls; Soph Cls; Jr Cls; Stu Cncl; Cheerleading; Score Keeper; Acad All Am 85; Achvt Awd 84-85; Rutgers U; Law.

HERR, LIZ; Saint John Vianney HS; Holmdel, NJ; (Y); 6/275; Stage Crew; Lit Mag; Rep Frsh Cls; Off Soph Cls; Rep Stu Cncl; Bsktbl; High Hon Roll; Hon Roll; NHS; Religious Studies Awd; Rutgers ST Coll; Psych.

HERRERA, WOOVER; Our Lady Of Good Counsel HS; Newark, NJ; (Y); Off Jr Cls; Stu Cncl; Bsbl; Hnrs 85; U TX; Elect Engr.

HERRIGHTY, SEAN; Roselle Catholic HS; Union, NJ; (Y); Church Yth Grp; JV Var Bsbl; Var Socr; Capt Var Swmmng; Im Vllybl; Hon Roll; MVP-SWM Tm 86; St Peters Coll.

HERRING, DAVID; Spotswood HS; Spotswood, NJ; (Y); 18/189; Am Leg Boys St; Church Yth Grp; Sec Intnl Clb; Rep Soph Cls; High Hon Roll; Hon Roll; NHS.

HERRMANN, CHRISTINE; Middletown High School South; Lincroft, NJ; (Y); Exploring; SADD; Yrbk Stf; Trs Sr Cls; Stu Cncl; Bsktbl; Socr; Trk; Twrlr; Hon Roll; Hnr Rll 85-86; Villanova U; Psychlgy.

HERRMANN, KARIN; Bridgewater HS East; Bound Brook, NJ; (Y); German Clb; Intnl Clb; Ski Clb; Concert Band; Stage Crew; VP L Crs Cntry; JV Swmmng; Timer; High Hon Roll; NHS; Engrng.

HERRMANN, MELANIE; Delran HS; Delran, NJ; (Y); 9/252; Am Leg Aux Girls St; Pep Clb; Stage Crew; Var Bowling; Var Crs Cntry; JV Socr; High Hon Roll; Hon Roll; Sec NHS; Burlington Ctys Yth Gov Pgm; Arch.

HERSCHKOWITZ, LIMOR; Fair Lawn HS; Fair Lawn, NJ; (Y); 93/335; Varsity Clb; Hosp Aide; Off Frsh Cls; Off Soph Cls; Off Jr Cls; Off Sr Cls; Stu Cncl; Score Keeper; Socr; Trk; Hebrew Clb 85-86; Gold Crown Wnnr 86; Free Sons Of Isrl And Hebrw Awd Excllnc Lang 86; William Paterson Clg; Pedtrcn.

HERSLOW, KRIS; Chatham Township HS; Chatham Twp, NJ; (Y); 42/137; Cmnty Wkr; Drama Clb; Hosp Aide; Key Clb; Chorus; Yrbk Ed-Chief; Bsktbl; Score Keeper; Trk; DAR Awd; NJ Schl Of Arts Attdnce 86; Lbrl Arts.

HERWITT, JENNIFER; Cresskill HS; Cresskill, NJ; (Y); 37/150; Drama Clb; Ski Clb; Temple Yth Grp; Chorus; Color Guard; School Play; Yrbk Phtg; Yrbk Sprt Ed; Yrbk Stf; Sftbl; NJ Art Fair 1st & 2nd Pl 85; Syracuse U; Indstrl Dsgn.

HERZ, DENISE; Pennsville HS; Pennsville, NJ; (Y); 7/220; Trs Church Yth Grp; FBLA; Hosp Aide; Orch; School Play; Nwsp Stf; Sftbl; Cit Awd; Gov Hon Prg Awd; NHS; Engl.

HERZIG, VICTORIA; Park Ridge HS; Park Ridge, NJ; (Y); 11/106; Political Wkr; Variety Show; Hon Roll; George Washington U; Law.

HERZOG, JEFF; Bridgewater Raritan East HS; Bridgewater, NJ; (Y); Letterman Clb; Varsity Clb; Score Keeper; Var Tennis; Wt Lftg; Var Wrstlng; All Conf Ten Chmps-Dbls 86; All NJ Midst Ten Chmp-Dbls 86; George Washington; Law.

HESS, EMILY; Bridgewater-Raritan HS East; Pluckemin, NJ; (Y); ST U NY; Vet Tech.

HESS, JAMES; Maple Shade HS; Maple Shade, NJ; (Y); DECA; JV Trk; High Hon Roll; Rutgers U; Bus.

HESTERMAN, CHRIS; Haddon Township HS; Haddonfield, NJ; (Y); 34/178; JV Crs Cntry; High Hon Roll; Hon Roll; Ntl Merit Ltr; Chem.

HETTEL, JASON; Highland Regional HS; Clementon, NJ; (Y); 21/360; AFS; Am Leg Boys St; Art Clb; Drama Clb; Latin Clb; PAVAS; Service Clb; Ski Clb; Thesps; Varsity Clb; Syracuse U Schlrshp 86; Cum Laude Cert; Lab Bio Tm; Syracuse U; Musical Theatre.

HEWITT, CAROL; Lower Cape May Regional HS; N Cape May, NJ; (Y); Church Yth Grp; French Clb; Girl Scts; Key Clb; Office Aide; SADD; Yrbk Stf; Lit Mag; Vllybl; Paralegal.

HEWITT, CHERYLINE; Clifford J Scott HS; East Orange, NJ; (S); 1/289; Math Clb; Math Tm; Office Aide; Spanish Clb; Varsity Clb; Band; Concert Band; Jazz Band; Mrchg Band; VP Soph Cls; Spllng Bee Alt Chmpn 82; Miss, Mr Black Tnage Wrld Schlrshp 84; Hrnbl Ment Career Essay 83; Pre Med.

HEWITT, JENNIFER; Toms River East HS; Toms River, NJ; (S); 57/535; Q&S; Band; Concert Band; Mrchg Band; Nwsp Rptr; Powder Puff Ftbl; JV Trk; Hon Roll; ST Sci Lg 84-85; WA Congrssnl Sem 86; Bio.

HEWITT, MARY; Toms River East HS; Toms River, NJ; (S); 114/489; Church Yth Grp; Q&S; Band; Nwsp Ed-Chief; Nwsp Rptr; JV Crs Cntry; JV Var Trk; Hon Roll; Camera Clb; GAA; Acadmc All Amer 84-85; Coll Of St Elizabeths; Bus.

HEYMAN, RUSSELL; Parsippany Hills HS; Morris Plains, NJ; (Y); Trs Cmnty Wkr; DECA; FBLA; JA; Temple Yth Grp; VP Y-Teens; Yrbk Stf; Wrstlng; Rotary Awd; Rotary Intl Exch Trp Japan 85; YMCA Volntr Mnth 84; Northeastern U; Comms.

HEYNIGER, SALLY; Manasquan HS; Spring Lake, NJ; (Y); 3/262; Key Clb; Sec Frsh Cls; Rep Soph Cls; Rep Stu Cncl; JV Cheerleading; JV Sftbl; Capt Twrlr; High Hon Roll; Kiwanis Awd; NHS; Bd Of Ed Awd 85&86; Engnrng.

HEYWARD, TIMOTHY; Central HS; Newark, NJ; (Y); 29/231; Church Yth Grp; Computer Clb; Exploring; Ftbl; Trk; Hon Roll; Mst Imprvd Stu Yr 85-86; Grt Achvrs Dnce Awd 86; Fayetteville ST; Com Engr.

HICKMAN, SUSAN; Bridgewater-Raritan East HS; Bridgewater, NJ; (Y); Church Yth Grp; Ski Clb; Spanish Clb; Drill Tm; Flag Corp; Mrchg Band; Stat Swmmng; NHS; Bus Admn.

HICKMAN, TOM; Cumberland Christian Schl; Millville, NJ; (S); 5/32; Church Yth Grp; Band; Chorus; Yrbk Phtg; Hon Roll; Outstndng Soph Hugh O Brian Yth Fndtn 85; Elem Ed.

HICKS, MICHAEL; Pleasantville HS; Pleasantville, NJ; (Y); 36/149; Art Clb; Church Yth Grp; Cmnty Wkr; Computer Clb; JA; Teachers Aide; VICA; Church Choir; Concert Band; Bsktbl; Cert Of Achvt-Diesel Vo-Tech 86; Stu Of Mnth Awd 86; Cert Of Achvt 83; Bus.

HICKS, QUINLAN; Central HS; Newark, NJ; (Y); Debate Tm; Exploring; JA; Science Clb; Sec Jr Cls; Sftbl; Cit Awd; Hon Roll; Rugers U; Bio-Med.

HICKS, STACY; Holmdel HS; Holmdel, NJ; (Y); Church Yth Grp; Cmnty Wkr; Hosp Aide; Key Clb; Teachers Aide; Nwsp Stf; Rep Soph Cls; Mgr(s); Var Twrlr; Phi Delta Kappa Scholar 86-87; Chubb & Son Fndtn Scholar 86-87; U DE; Spec Ed.

HICKS, STEPHANIE C; East Orange HS; East Orange, NJ; (S); Church Yth Grp; Computer Clb; Sec Drama Clb; French Clb; Band; Church Choir; Concert Band; School Play; Symp Band; Yrbk Bus Mgr; Comp Sci.

HICKS, YOLANDA; Weequahic Hicks HS; Newark, NJ; (Y); 16/440; Capt Debate Tm; Exploring; Library Aide; Nwsp Rptr; Yrbk Stf; Hon Roll; NHS; Opt Clb Awd; Marie L Villani Hon Partcptn Close-Up Prog 86; Penn St; Law.

HIDALGO, RICHARD; Memorial HS; W New York, NJ; (Y); Fl International U; Bus Admin.

HIEL, DOUGLAS; Clifton HS; Clifton, NJ; (Y); 67/634; Band; Concert Band; Jazz Band; Mrchg Band; Hon Roll; Jr NHS.

HIGGINS, BARBARA; Woodstown HS; Woodstown, NJ; (Y); FBLA; Girl Scts; Spanish Clb; Rep Stu Cncl; Cheerleading; Mgr(s); Score Keeper; Grad Barbizon Modeling Schl 84; Comp.

HIGGINS, BRIDGET; Southern Regional HS; Barnegat Light, NJ; (Y); Hon Roll; TEAM 85-86; Physical Therapist.

HIGGINS, DENISE; Notre Dame HS; Kendall Pk, NJ; (Y); 118/360; Church Yth Grp; Nwsp Stf; Bsbl; Bsktbl; Vrsty Lttr Stu Athltc Trnr; Bus Admin.

HIGGINS, KATHERINE; Pope John XXIII HS; Sparta, NJ; (Y); Church Yth Grp; French Clb; Lit Mag; Trs Soph Cls; Var Cheerleading; Var Fld Hcky; Cit Awd; High Hon Roll; Trs NHS; St Schlr; Trig Awd 86; Awd Outstndng Acadmc Achvt 85; Tufts U; Lawyr.

HIGGINS, THOMAS; Matawaw Regional HS; Cliffwood Beach, NJ; (S); 29/302; High Hon Roll; Hon Roll; Bus.

HIGGINS, WILLIAM; Ocean Twp HS; Ocean, NJ; (Y); 117/375; Boys Clb Am; Boy Scts; Rep Frsh Cls; JV Bsbl; Var Capt Bsktbl; Var Capt Ftbl; Im Wt Lftg; All Mnmth Ftbll 86; Albert F Carelli Mrl Awd 85; Engr.

HIGGS, MARCIA; Wildwood HS; Wildwood, NJ; (Y); Church Yth Grp; Church Choir; Rep Jr Cls; Sftbl; Nrs.

HIGH, STEPHANIE; Linden HS; Linden, NJ; (Y); Church Yth Grp; Cmnty Wkr; DECA; French Clb; FHA; JA; Pep Clb; Band; Concert Band; Mrchg Band; DECA Cmptn Awd Mdl 86; DECA Cmptn 86; FIT; Fshn Mrchnds.

HIGHAM, CLAIRE L; Hopewell Valley Central HS; Pennington, NJ; (Y); 5/204; Capt Scholastic Bowl; Chorus; Orch; School Musical; Yrbk Stf; Pres NHS; Ntl Merit SF; St Schlr; French Clb; Latin Clb; Pres Schlrs Pgm 85; Rutgers Schlr 85; Hist.

HILDEBRAND, WERNER; Parsippany HS; Lake Hiawatha, NJ; (Y); German Clb; Ski Clb; Bsktbl; Mech Engr.

HILDEBRANDT, TARA; Metuchen HS; Metuchen, NJ; (Y); 47/178; Am Leg Aux Girls St; Key Clb; Ski Clb; Varsity Clb; Var L Trk; Hon Roll; Bio.

HILER, DARCIE; Bridgewater-Rariton HS East; Bridgewater, NJ; (Y); Cmnty Wkr; Trs French Clb; Chorus; Concert Band; Mrchg Band; Mgr Stage Crew; Stat Crs Cntry; Stat Swmmng; Hon Roll.

HILER, LINDA; Bishop Eustace Prep; Sewell, NJ; (Y); 15/187; Pep Clb; Spanish Clb; Varsity Clb; Nwsp Rptr; Lit Mag; Trk; Hon Roll; NHS; Spanish NHS; Var Ltrs 86.

HILL, ANDREA; Highland Regional HS; Erial, NJ; (Y); Camera Clb; Church Yth Grp; French Clb; Library Aide; Comps.

HILL, BETH; Manasquan HS; Manasquan, NJ; (Y); 2/230; Trs Key Clb; Math Tm; Band; Var Cheerleading; Var Sftbl; JP Sousa Awd; NHS; Ntl Merit Ltr; Garden St Dstngshd Schlr Schlrshp 86; Douglass Coll Rutgers; Comp Sci.

HILL, CHARLES A; West Essex SR HS; Roseland, NJ; (Y); 3/350; Latin Clb; Math Tm; Capt Quiz Bowl; Co-Capt Science Clb; NHS; Ntl Merit SF; Chess Clb; Church Yth Grp; Computer Clb; High Hon Roll; NJ Gov Schl Sci 85; Yale Book Awd 85; Natl Latin Exam Gold & Silver Medls 84-85; Rutgers Schlr 85; Physcs.

HILL, DOUGLAS B; Dwight Morrow HS; Englewood, NJ; (Y); 18/225; CAP; Computer Clb; Math Tm; Band; Concert Band; Drill Tm; Mrchg Band; JV Bowling; High Hon Roll; NHS; Rtgrs Schlrs Pgm 85; Cntry III Ldrs Pgm Schl Wnnr 85; Natl Soc Stud Olympd 85; Elec Engrng.

HILL, GWYNNE; Red Bank Regional HS; Little Silver, NJ; (Y); Pres Exploring; Hosp Aide; Capt Color Guard; Spanish NHS; Service Clb; Intl Bus.

HILL, KIMBERLY; Sussex County Vo-Tech HS; Newton, NJ; (S); 5/175; Am Leg Aux Girls St; Dance Clb; Library Aide; VP Frsh Cls; Powder Puff Ftbl; High Hon Roll; Hon Roll; VP NHS; Katharine Gibbs Ldrshp Awd; NJ Math Leag; Fashn Merch.

HILL, REBEKAH; Bishop George Ahr HS; Piscataway, NJ; (Y); 10/277; Band; Chorus; Concert Band; Jazz Band; Mrchg Band; School Musical; Symp Band; High Hon Roll; NHS; NEDT Awd; Merit Awd For Outstndg Achvmnt Chorus 83-84; Excllnc Schlrshp Awd 83-86; Dist I HS Choral Fstvl Awd; Orchstrl Cndctr.

HILL, SANDRA; Essex Catholic Girls HS; Irv, NJ; (Y); Pep Clb; Service Clb; Chorus; Variety Show; Stu Cncl; Cheerleading; Pom Pon; Ntl Merit Schol; Ldrshp & Svc Awd 86; All Acad Awd 85; Drake; Comp.

HILL, VINCENT; Frank H Morrell HS; Irvington, NJ; (Y); Var Crs Cntry; Capt Var Trk; Cit Awd; Hon Roll; NHS; Engrng.

HILLA, BRIAN; Manasquan HS; Brielle, NJ; (Y); 68/245; Art Clb; Church Yth Grp; Drama Clb; Spanish Clb; SADD; Lit Mag; Var Ftbl; Var Tennis; Var Trk; Im Wt Lftg; RH School Of Design; Dsgn.

HILLENBURG, KIM; Mount Olive HS; Budd Lake, NJ; (Y); 60/258; AFS; Ski Clb; SADD; Chorus; Yrbk Stf; Var Crs Cntry; Var Trk; Hon Roll; Cmmnctns.

HILTON, RICHARD; Passaic Valley HS; West Paterson, NJ; (S); 58/338; Band; Concert Band; Drm & Bgl; Jazz Band; Mrchg Band; Orch; Pep Band; School Musical; School Play; Hon Roll; William Patterson; Musc.

HILTON, TOM; Kingsway Regional HS; Mullica Hill, NJ; (Y); 2/160; Am Leg Boys St; JV Bsktbl; Im Ice Hcky; Var L Socr; NHS; Ntl Merit Ltr; Sal; Attndd NJ Gvrnrs Schl In Sci 85; Cook Coll; Biochmstry.

HILWAY, VIKKI; Passaic Valley HS; Totowa, NJ; (Y); Chess Clb; French Clb; Var JV Score Keeper; Law.

HINDERMYER JR, R MICHAEL; Millville SR HS; Cedarville, NJ; (Y); 26/465; VP Church Yth Grp; French Clb; Science Clb; SADD; Variety Show; Lit Mag; VP Stu Cncl; High Hon Roll; NHS; Acad Achvt 83-84; Bio Awd 82-83; Kiwanis JR Rep 86; Lenoir-Rhyne Coll; Pre Med.

HINDES, FRANK; Howell HS; Howell, NJ; (Y); Church Yth Grp; German Clb; Bsbl; Socr; Arch.

HINDS, PAULINE; Frank H Morrell HS; Irvington, NJ; (Y); Trs Church Yth Grp; VP Latin Clb; Chorus; Church Choir; Rep Stu Cncl; High Hon Roll; Hon Roll; Hst NHS; Latin Achvt Awd 84-85; Penn ST U.

HINES, GREGORY L; University HS; Newark, NJ; (Y); Boy Scts; Debate Tm; JA; Spanish Clb; School Play; Variety Show; Nwsp Stf; Yrbk Stf; Cit Awd; Boy Scout; NJIT; Bus Info Sys.

HINES, KIMBERLY; Camden HS; Camden, NJ; (S); Church Yth Grp; Girl Scts; JA; Key Clb; Church Choir; Mrchg Band; Yrbk Sprt Ed; NHS; Pharm.

HINES, MICHELLE D; St Marys Hall-Doane Acad; Willingboro, NJ; (Y); 3/16; Am Leg Aux Girls St; Debate Tm; Drama Clb; Library Aide; School Musical; Stage Crew; Yrbk Ed-Chief; Lit Mag; Sftbl; High Hon Roll; Wllngbro Twp Yth Achvt Awd 84; PSAT Cmmnded Negro Stu 85; Bio.

HINES, TAMARA; Hightstown HS; E Windsor, NJ; (Y); 93/343; Church Yth Grp; Ski Clb; Stu Cncl; Cheerleading; Hon Roll; NHS; Prfct Atten Awd; Kufu Scholar 86; Ministers Wives Scholar 86; Minoritys Engrng Pgm 86; Middlebury; Frgn Lang.

HINGHER, JEFF; Franklin HS; Kingston, NJ; (Y); Scholastic Bowl; Ski Clb; JV Var Tennis; Gov Hon Prg Awd; High Hon Roll; Hon Roll; NHS; NJ Gvnrs Schl Cndt 86; Engrng.

HINKLE, MICHELE; Northern Burlington Regional HS; Columbus, NJ; (Y); 66/201; Trs Sftbl; Rep Frsh Cls; Rep Soph Cls; Rep Jr Cls; Rep Sr Cls; Stu Cncl; Var Fld Hcky; JV Sftbl; Var Tennis; Monmouth Coll; Comm.

HINMON, CANDICE; Salem HS; Bridgeton, NJ; (Y); Pres Church Yth Grp; Cmnty Wkr; Chorus; Church Choir; Jazz Band; Pres Frsh Cls; Rotary Awd; FBLA; Office Aide; PAVAS; Outstndng Soloist Awd 83-84 & 85-86; Outstndng Stu 83-84; Jessie Jackson Pres Campgn Singer 84; VA Union U; Musicl Perfrmnce.

HINOJOSA, MONICA; Paramus Catholic HS; Teaneck, NJ; (Y); Hon Roll; Iona Coll; Med.

HINRICHSEN, MARIA; Lakeland Regional HS; Ringwood, NJ; (Y); 1/350; Drama Clb; Math Clb; Quiz Bowl; Yrbk Stf; High Hon Roll; NHS; Ntl Merit Ltr; NEDT Awd; Hon Roll; Rtgrs Schlrs Pgm 86; Rmpo Spcl Incntv Pgm 86; U S Naval Acad Smmr Smnr 86; Sci.

HINTZ, MICHAEL; Dover HS; Mine Hill, NJ; (Y); 25/188; Am Leg Boys St; Computer Clb; German Clb; Latin Clb; Bsbl; Ftbl; Swmmng; Trk; Wt Lftg; Hon Roll; U Penn; ROTC.

HINZE, PETER C; Boonton HS; Lincoln Park, NJ; (Y); 1/220; Am Leg Boys St; Math Tm; Nwsp Stf; JV Bsbl; Var Socr; High Hon Roll; Pres NHS; Rutgers Schlr ST U NJ 86; Rensselear Plytechnic Inst Math & Sci Awd 86; Ralph E Porzion Jrnslm Awd; Engineering.

HIPKO, TRACY; Spotswood HS; Milltown, NJ; (S); 6/189; Church Yth Grp; FBLA; Intnl Clb; Church Choir; Yrbk Stf; Rep Stu Cncl; High Hon Roll; Hon Roll; NHS.

HIRATA, JODY; Cumberland Regional HS; Bridgeton, NJ; (Y); Debate Tm; Intnl Clb; JCL; Latin Clb; Pres Frsh Cls; Pres Soph Cls; Jr Cls; Sr Cls; Var Stu Cncl; JV Bsktbl.

HIRSCH, KEITH; Morris Hills HS; Rockaway, NJ; (Y); 49/269; VP JA; Varsity Clb; Nwsp Rptr; Nwsp Sprt Ed; Nwsp Stf; Stu Cncl; JV Var Bsbl; Stat Bsktbl; Var Ftbl; High Hon Roll; Bus.

HIRSCHMAN, KYM; West Windsor-Plainsboro HS; Princeton Jct, NJ; (Y); 9/236; AFS; Service Clb; Teachers Aide; Church Choir; Stat Diving; Stat Swmmng; CC Awd; High Hon Roll; NHS; St Schlr; Pres Acd Fit Awd 86; Duke U; Mth.

HIRSHFIELD, LISA; Ocean Township HS; Wayside, NJ; (Y); 98/336; French Clb; Sec Temple Yth Grp; Varsity Clb; Variety Show; Nwsp Stf; JV Var Tennis; Optmtry.

HIRSHKIND, KIERA; Academy Of St Elizabth; Morris Plains, NJ; (Y); Swmmng; Trk; Prfct Atten Awd.

HIRST, ELLEN; Florence Twp Mem HS; Burlington, NJ; (Y); VP Mrchg Band; Natl Beta Clb; Varsity Clb; Band; Concert Band; Jazz Band; School Musical; Variety Show; Yrbk Stf; Hon Roll; UNC G; Bus Adm.

HIRST, HEATHER; Pitman HS; Pitman, NJ; (Y); 3/146; Band; Chorus; Drm Mjr(t); Jazz Band; Mrchg Band; Trs Frsh Cls; Vllybl; Hon Roll; NHS; Drama Clb; Olympics Mind Wrld Chmpnshp Tm Sphmr & JR Yrs; Vet.

HISCOCK, JANET; Matawan Regional HS; Aberdeen, NJ; (S); 5/273; Hosp Aide; Math Tm; Sec Chorus; Capt Color Guard; Madrigals; Yrbk Ed-Chief; Trs Frsh Cls; VP French Hon Soc; Pres NHS; Lehigh U; Pre-Med.

HITCH, MARCIUS; Pleasantville HS; Sicklerville, NJ; (Y).

HITCHCOCK, KAREN; Pequannock Township HS; Pequannock, NJ; (Y); 6/230; Yrbk Sprt Ed; Pres Rep Stu Cncl; Cit Awd; Hon Roll; NHS; Spanish NHS; Stat Sftbl; Pres Acadmc Ftnss Awd 86; Pres Clsrm Young Amer 86; FLE-NJ Awd Spanish 86; Bucknell U; Bio.

HITCHINGS, KIMBERLY; Holy Spirit HS; Atlantic City, NJ; (Y); Hon Roll; Rowing Crew 81-85; Bus.

HITCHNER, GRETCHEN; Woodstown HS; Alloway, NJ; (Y); English Clb; German Clb; Library Aide; SADD; Stage Crew; Nwsp Stf; Yrbk Stf; Lit Mag; Bowling; Cmmnctns.

HITTNER, LEIGH; Livingston HS; Livingston, NJ; (Y); 126/496; Temple Yth Grp; Chorus; Capt Color Guard; Stage Crew; Mgr(s); Stat Trk; Hon Roll; Bd Of Educ Schlrp 86; Bnd Frnt Schlrp 86; Syracuse U; Int Dsgn.

HJELMAR, LORI; West Milford Twp HS; West Milford, NJ; (Y); 20/350; Art Clb; VP Sec Exploring; German Clb; Intnl Clb; Stage Crew; Var Tennis; JV Trk; High Hon Roll; Hon Roll; NHS; Alxndr Hmltn Bnk Schlarshp 86; Ntl Art Hon Soc 84-86; Penn ST U; Bus.

HJUL, ELIZABETH; Toms River HS South; Norway; (Y); DECA; Chorus; Coach Actv; Ice Hcky; Mgr(s); Tennis; Vllybl; Hon Roll; Rep NJ Ntl DECA 86; Northeastern U; Bus.

HO, DAVID; Matawan HS; Matawan, NJ; (S); Math Tm; Hon Roll.

HOANG, VIET; Metuchen HS; Metuchen, NJ; (Y); Var Capt Socr; Hon Roll; Rutgers Coll Of Engr; Elec Engr.

HOARE, TIM; Cliffside Park HS; Cliffside Pk, NJ; (Y); 10/236; Spanish Clb; Band; Concert Band; Jazz Band; VP Mrchg Band; School Play; Capt Bsktbl; Tennis; Hon Roll; Lion Awd.

HOARLE, BRIAN M; Nutley HS; Nutley, NJ; (Y); 14/329; Am Leg Boys St; Key Clb; Ski Clb; Yrbk Ed-Chief; Im Bsktbl; Var Ftbl; High Hon Roll; NHS; Engr.

HOBBS, MICHAEL; Lenape Regional HS; Vincentown, NJ; (Y); 1/421; Trs Latin Clb; Math Tm; Capt Scholastic Bowl; Var Capt Bowling; Gov Hon Prg Awd; Pres NHS; Ntl Merit SF; Rotary Awd; JCL; Varsity Clb; Presdntl Clsrm Yng Amercns 86; Rutgers Schlr; Chem Engrng.

HOBLITZELL, MARY; Westfield SR HS; Westfield, NJ; (Y); 1/520; Spanish Clb; Yrbk Stf; Var L Fld Hcky; High Hon Roll; NHS; Ntl Merit Ltr; Spanish NHS; Church Yth Grp; Science Clb; Service Clb; NY Schlrs Prgm; Bk Of Emrld Awd.

HOBOKAN, KLAUDIA; Hackettstown HS; Hackettstown, NJ; (Y); Flag Corp; Sec Sr Cls; Plctcl Sci.

HOCKE, CHRISTINE; Parsippany HS; Lk Hiawatha, NJ; (Y); 72/318; Art Clb; Library Aide; Var L Trk; High Hon Roll; Hon Roll; Natl Art Hnr Scty 86; Prnt Tchr Stu Assc Schlrshp 86; Pres Acad Ftnss Awd 86; Lycoming Coll; Vet.

HOCKINGS, SUSAN; Princeton Day Schl; Princeton, NJ; (Y); French Clb; Hosp Aide; Teachers Aide; Church Choir; Madrigals; Var Fld Hcky; Var Vllybl; Girl Scts; Red Cross Aide; Chorus; Grl Sct Gld Awd 85; Headmstrs List 82-86; Cum Laud 86; ESU Exchng.

HODEN, LISA; Pinelands Regional HS; Manahawkin, NJ; (Y); 30/192; Church Yth Grp; Math Clb; Math Tm; Chorus; Church Choir; Hon Roll; Prfct Atten Awd; Hosp Aide; Rutgers Coll Of Nrsng; Nrsng.

HODER, LISA; Park Ridge HS; Park Ridge, NJ; (Y); 9/110; Art Clb; Church Yth Grp; PAVAS; Lit Mag; Sec Stu Cncl; JV Socr; High Hon Roll; NHS; Drama Clb; Science Clb; Acad Lttr 84; Yrbk Art Edtr 86-87; Art.

HODGINS, BRADLEY; Newton HS; Newton, NJ; (Y); 20/191; Computer Clb; Math Clb; Math Tm; Science Clb; SADD; Rep Stu Cncl; Var JV Ftbl; Var JV Trk; High Hon Roll; Hon Roll; Mbr Newtn Vlntr 1st Aid Sqd 85; Penn ST U; Engrng.

HOEFELE, SUSAN; Colonia HS; Colonia, NJ; (Y); 24/280; Am Leg Aux Girls St; German Clb; Concert Band; Jazz Band; Mrchg Band; Stu Cncl; Hon Roll; NHS; Yrbk Stf; Sr Cls; NJ Rgn II Band; NJ All ST Band; Douglass Coll; Mth.

HOEFLICH, MICHAEL J; Moorestown HS; Moorestown, NJ; (Y); AFS; Church Yth Grp; ROTC; Band; Concert Band; Lngstcs.

HOFF, CATHY; Belvidere HS; Belvidere, NJ; (S); 6/125; Church Yth Grp; 4-H; SADD; Varsity Clb; JV Var Bsktbl; JV Var Fld Hcky; JV Var Sftbl; 4-H Awd; Hon Roll; NHS; Hugh O Brien Yth Fndtn Fnlst 85; Psych.

HOFFMAN, ANDREW; Livingston HS; Livingston, NJ; (Y); Aud/Vis; Ski Clb; School Musical; Stage Crew; Ed Yrbk Phtg; Yrbk Stf; Hon Roll; 1st Pl Lvngstn HS Art Shw Photogrphy 86.

HOFFMAN, CHRISTINE; Kearny HS; Kearny, NJ; (Y); 41/375; German Clb; Hon Roll; NHS; Catherine Crane Envrnmntl Scholar; Rutgers U Scholar; Ecolgy Clb Pres; Rutgers Coll Arts; Bio Sci.

HOFFMAN, DEBBIE; Hamilton HS East; Trenton, NJ; (Y); 8/315; AFS; Church Yth Grp; Exploring; Capt Drill Tm; Stu Cncl; NHS; Gov Tchng Awd 86; Trenton ST Coll; Elem Ed.

HOFFMAN, KAREN; St Rose HS; Neptune City, NJ; (Y); 2/206; Am Leg Aux Girls St; Var Bsktbl; Var Capt Socr; High Hon Roll; NHS; Ntl Merit Ltr; NEDT Awd; Spanish NHS; Schlr/Athlt Awd, Best Female Athlt Awd & Varsity Soccer MVP 86; Coll Of The Holy Cross; Econ.

HOFFMAN, LISA; Absegami HS; Smithville, NJ; (Y); 69/250; Aud/Vis; Office Aide; Teachers Aide; Hst Frsh Cls; VP Soph Cls; Rep Jr Cls; Bsktbl; Cheerleading; Sftbl; Comm.

HOFFMAN, NANCY; Fair Lawn HS; Fair Lawn, NJ; (Y); 47/340; Political Wkr; Band; Chorus; Madrigals; Mrchg Band; School Musical; Symp Band; Var Crs Cntry; Drama Clb; All N Jersey Rgn Band 85; Carl E Zaisser Music Schrlshp 86; Brandeis U; Music.

HOFFMAN, PAUL; Natawan Regional HS; Aberdeen, NJ; (Y); Aud/Vis; Cmnty Wkr; Political Wkr; Temple Yth Grp; JV Socr; Hon Roll; Rutgers U; Tech Engr.

HOFFMAN, ROBIN; Voorhees HS; Califon, NJ; (S); Church Yth Grp; Cmnty Wkr; Pres 4-H; VP FFA; Girl Scts; Color Guard; Hst Frsh Cls; Hst Soph Cls; Hst Jr Cls; FFA Membr Of Mnth 86.

HOFFMAN, STEVE; Highstown HS; East Windsor, NJ; (Y); Art Clb; Boys Clb Am; Ski Clb; Spanish Clb; JV Socr; Ntl Merit Ltr; Merit Awd 83; Channel 13 Rnr-Up Poster 86; Comm Art.

HOFFMAN, SUSAN; Union HS; Union, NJ; (Y); Key Clb; Spanish Clb; VP Temple Yth Grp; Y-Teens; Mgr Fld Hcky; Score Keeper; Mgr Swmmng; Timer; Hon Roll; Bus Mngmt.

HOFFMAN, TAMMY; Belvidere HS; Belvidere, NJ; (Y); Hosp Aide; Teachers Aide; Band; Chorus; Color Guard; Flag Corp; Bowling; Btty Crckr Awd; Hon Roll; Bus.

HOFFMAN, WILLIAM; Point Pleasant Boro HS; Point Pleasant, NJ; (Y); 51/216; Off Jr Cls; Off Sr Cls; Stu Cncl; Ftbl; Powder Puff Ftbl; Wt Lftg; DE Vly Coll; Bus.

HOFFMASTER, MIKE; Point Pleasant Boro HS; Point Pleasant, NJ; (Y); 19/250; Am Leg Boys St; Key Clb; Varsity Clb; VP Frsh Cls; VP Soph Cls; Sec Stu Cncl; Var Crs Cntry; Var Socr; Var Wrstlng; Hon Roll; Wrstlng Acad Awd & MVP; Dentist.

HOFSESS, SCOTT; Waldwick HS; Waldwick, NJ; (Y); Church Yth Grp; Intnl Clb; Math Tm; Concert Band; Mrchg Band; Rep Jr Cls; Var L Crs Cntry; Var L Trk; Hon Roll; Vlntr Amblnc Corps 84-86.

HOGAN, CHRISTOPHER; Lenape Valley Rregional HS; Andover, NJ; (Y); 2/215; Band; Concert Band; Jazz Band; Mrchg Band; School Musical; Var Bsbl; JV Bsktbl; Ntl Merit SF; Pres Schlr; Sal; Acdmc All-Amer 85-86; Rutgers Schlr 85; U Of VA; Med Dctr.

HOGAN, KATIE; Kent Pl HS; Summit, NJ; (Y); Camera Clb; Church Yth Grp; Cmnty Wkr; Chorus; Church Choir; Yrbk Phtg; Yrbk Stf; Pres Sr Cls; JV Fld Hcky; Ice Hcky; La Crosse Sprtsmnshp Awd 85; Tn Arts Fstvl 86; Vassar; Lnge.

HOGAN, RICHARD; Neptune HS; Neptune, NJ; (Y); 19/400; Am Leg Boys St; Debate Tm; Model UN; Ski Clb; School Play; Nwsp Rptr; Rep Stu Cncl; God Cntry Awd; NHS; Rep Soph Cls; WFW Voice Democracy 3rd 86; 3rd Sci Fair 84; Best Model UN Security Cncl 84-87; Comp Sci.

HOGG, GERALYN; Mainland Regional HS; Linwood, NJ; (Y); 17/300; Rep Soph Cls; Rep Jr Cls; Rep Sr Cls; Mgr Bsktbl; Var Capt Cheerleading; JV Fld Hcky; Var Capt Powder Puff Ftbl; Var JV Sftbl; Hon Roll; NHS; Rutgers; Eng.

HOHOLICK, ERICA; Bridgewater-Raritan HS; Bridgewater, NJ; (Y); Am Leg Aux Girls St; Yrbk Stf; Rep Frsh Cls; Rep Soph Cls; VP Jr Cls; VP Sr Cls; Rep Chrmn Stu Cncl; Stat Bsbl; Hon Roll; French Clb; Bridgewater Ctzn Awd Convlscnt Ctr Vlntr.

HOLCOMBE JR, GEORGE; Absegami HS; Absecon, NJ; (Y); 11/226; Pres Church Yth Grp; Debate Tm; Math Clb; Ski Clb; Pres Band; Concert Band; Jazz Band; Mrchg Band; Hon Roll; NHS; Prncpl Awd Scl Stds 86; Mdl Cngrs 85 & 86; Grmn Band Awd 86; MI ST U; Elctrcl Engrng.

HOLDEN, STEPHANIE; Middletown HS South; Middletown, NJ; (Y); Church Yth Grp; Cmnty Wkr; Dance Clb; French Clb; Hosp Aide; Red Cross Aide; Ski Clb; SADD; School Play; Psych.

HOLEMON, ELISSA; Eastern HS; West Berlin, NJ; (Y); Concert Band; Mrchg Band; Jr NHS; NHS; Olympic Conf Hnrs Bnd 84-86; Spec Educ.

HOLL, JON K; Haddonfield Memorial HS; Haddonfield, NJ; (Y); Am Leg Boys St; Cmnty Wkr; Sec Intnl Clb; Model UN; Jazz Band; Socr; Trk; Hon Roll; VP NHS; Ntl Merit Ltr; Hnrs Wrkshp Mdrn Bio 86; Pltcl Sci.

HOLLAND, JAMES; Christian Brothers Acad; Aberdeen, NJ; (Y); Stage Crew; Im Bowling; Im Socr; Im Sftbl; Engrng.

HOLLAND, TIM; Notre Dame HS; Trenton, NJ; (Y); Boy Scts; Political Wkr; Variety Show; Var L Bsktbl; Var Ftbl; Hon Roll; Law.

HOLLANDER, ROBERT; Hopewell Valley Central HS; Hopewell, NJ; (Y); 9/210; German Clb; Latin Clb; Off Frsh Cls; Off Soph Cls; Off Jr Cls; Off Sr Cls; Var Tennis; High Hon Roll; NHS; Ntl Merit SF; Econ.

HOLLERON, ANDREW; South Plainfield HS; S Plainfield, NJ; (Y); Drama Clb; Teachers Aide; Band; Concert Band; Drm Mjr(t); Mrchg Band; Pep Band; School Musical; School Play; Symp Band.

HOLLIDAY, KENDALL; Kittatinny Regional HS; Newton, NJ; (S); 9/164; Math Tm; Office Aide; Science Clb; Var L Bsktbl; Im Wt Lftg; High Hon Roll; Hon Roll; NHS; Boys ST Altrnt 85; Gvnrs Schl; Comp Sci.

HOLLINGER, KIMBERLY; Hopewell Valley Central HS; Titusville, NJ; (Y); 24/202; AFS; Church Yth Grp; Service Clb; Spanish Clb; Chorus; School Musical; School Play; Stat Bsktbl; Mgr(s); Score Keeper; Intl Affairs.

HOLLISTER, BRIDGET; Vineland HS; Vineland, NJ; (Y); 50/808; Key Clb; Latin Clb; Political Wkr; Band; Color Guard; Concert Band; Flag Corp; Mrchg Band; Lit Mag; Stu Cncl; Svc Citatn Vineland Mrchg Band 86; Prelaw.

HOLLOWAY, DERRICK; Hillside HS; Hillside, NJ; (Y); 10/196; Am Leg Boys St; Church Yth Grp; Computer Clb; Math Tm; Political Wkr; ROTC; Science Clb; Ski Clb; Q&S; Church Choir; Jerome Bentley JR 35 Annl ST Sci Day 85; Recvd Cert Outstndng Cmmnty Svc Hope Inc 86; Howard U; Dntstry.

HOLLOWAY, RODRICK; Roselle Catholic HS; Roselle, NJ; (Y); Cmnty Wkr; Computer Clb; Drama Clb; French Hon Soc; High Hon Roll; Hon Roll; Fnlst Mensa Soc 86; Pre Med.

HOLLY, RUSSELL; Freehold Twp HS; Freehold, NJ; (Y); 25/382; JV Ftbl; Var Wt Lftg; NHS; 3rd Pl-Pwrlftng Meet 148 Lbs Tnage Div 85; Engrng.

HOLMES, CAROL; Holy Cross HS; Medford, NJ; (Y); 44/286; JV Var Bsktbl; Crs Cntry; Var Sftbl; Hon Roll; NHS.

HOLMES, GINA; Holy Spirit HS; Atlantic City, NJ; (Y); Cmnty Wkr; Radio Clb; Chorus; School Play; Yrbk Stf; High Hon Roll; Hon Roll; Distinguishe Hnrs 86; Rutgers U; Comp Sci.

HOLMES, IRENE; West Side HS; Newark, NJ; (Y); #2 In Class; Debate Tm; Color Guard; Pep Band; Nwsp Rptr; VP Jr Cls; Var Tennis; High Hon Roll; NHS; Dntstry.

HOLMES, JEFFREY B; Lenape Regional HS; Mt Laurel, NJ; (Y); Am Leg Boys St; Boy Scts; Sec Trs Exploring; Latin Clb; Ski Clb; Stage Crew; JV Capt Socr; Hon Roll; NHS; Engrng.

HOLMES, KAREN; Sussex County Vo-Tech HS; Sussex, NJ; (S); 2/150; Latin Clb; Spanish Clb; Nwsp Stf; Im Gym; Stat Trk; High Hon Roll; NHS.

HOLMES, PATRICIA; Lenape Valley Regional HS; Netcong, NJ; (Y); 4/253; Key Clb; Band; Yrbk Stf; High Hon Roll; Hon Roll; NHS; Spanish NHS; Church Yth Grp; Spanish Clb; Concert Band; Lenape Valley Schlr 83-85; Intl Frgn Lang Awd 86; Acad All Am 86; Math.

HOLMES, SUE; Delsea Regional HS; Newfield, NJ; (Y); Church Yth Grp; Sec Computer Clb; Office Aide; School Musical; Im Tennis; High Hon Roll; Hon Roll; NHS; Olympes Of Mind Tm-1st & 3rd Pl; Fashion Inst/Tech; Fshn Dsgn.

HOLMES, SUSAN; Cranford HS; Cranford, NJ; (Y); 25/269; AFS; French Clb; Latin Clb; Science Clb; Acpl Chr; Madrigals; Orch; Var Bsktbl; Sftbl; Hon Roll; Latin Awd Strght A 85-86; Peer Devlpmnt Faciltr 85-87.

HOLOBOWSKI, WILLIAM F; H G Hoffman HS; S Amboy, NJ; (S); 2/60; Chess Clb; Math Tm; Ski Clb; SADD; Rep Frsh Cls; VP Soph Cls; Pres Jr Cls; Stu Cncl; Var Bowling; Var Socr; Span & Typg Awds 84-85; Rutgers; Comp Sci.

HOLOWACHUK, STACIE; Wayne Hills HS; Wayne, NJ; (Y); 28/297; French Clb; Var Capt Bsktbl; Var Capt Socr; JV Sftbl; Var Trk; Hon Roll; Off NHS; Ecology Clb 85-87; Acctg.

HOLT, DOROTHEA; Edgewood Regional HS; West Berlin, NJ; (Y); 10/371; Dance Clb; 4-H; Hosp Aide; Sec SADD; Varsity Clb; Yrbk Phtg; JV Var Fld Hcky; Hon Roll; Jr NHS; NHS; Excellnc Equal Cost Schlrshp Bard C 86; Bard Coll.

HOLT, KATHRYN M; Middletown High School North; Belford, NJ; (Y); 140/420; Ski Clb; Spanish Clb; Chorus; Nwsp Stf; Yrbk Phtg; Yrbk Rptr; Cheerleading; Trk; Hon Roll; Ntl Merit Ltr; Intl Reltns.

HOLTJE, SCOTT; Hudson Catholic Regional HS; Secaucus, NJ; (Y); Boy Scts; Band; Hon Roll; Peer Ministry 86; Fin.

HOLTZ, DAVID O; Moorestown HS; Moorestown, NJ; (Y); Am Leg Boys St; Capt Debate Tm; Math Tm; NFL; Orch; School Play; Stage Crew; Yrbk Ed-Chief; Lit Mag; Socr; Physics.

HOLUB, THOMAS C; Morristown-Beard Schl; Madison, NJ; (Y); 6/78; Drama Clb; School Musical; School Play; Stage Crew; Nwsp Rptr; Trs Soph Cls; Var Crs Cntry; Hon Roll; Ntl Merit SF; Chess Clb; Harvey Mudd Coll; Comp Sci.

HOLVICK, MICHAEL; Oakcrest HS; Mays Landing, NJ; (Y); 36/245; French Clb; Jr NHS; Glassboro ST Coll; Bio.

HOLZHAUER, MONICA; Matawan Aberdeen Regional HS; Aberdeen, NJ; (S); 8/300; Exploring; Math Clb; Co-Capt Crs Cntry; Capt Trk; NHS; Elec Engrng.

HOMA, SHARON L; Red Bank Catholic HS; Eatontown, NJ; (Y); 8/267; Hosp Aide; Ski Clb; Trs Spanish Clb; Nwsp Stf; Rep Jr Cls; Trs Stu Cncl; Var Capt Cheerleading; Kiwanis Awd; NHS; Dorthy Ann Carroll Trzepacz Schlrshp 85; Locl 1262 Schlrshp 86; Ft Monmouth Armd Frc Schlrshp 86; Boston Coll; Comp Sci.

HONEY, KRISTIN ANN; Manasquan HS; Spring Lake, NJ; (Y); 1/234; Church Yth Grp; VP Drama Clb; FBLA; GAA; Key Clb; Math Clb; PAVAS; Spanish Clb; Thesps; Chorus; Girls ST Awd 86; Georgetown; Acctg.

HONIG, DEIDRE; Cinnaminson HS; Cinna, NJ; (Y); Aud/Vis; Church Yth Grp; Dance Clb; Color Guard; Philadelphia Coll Schltc Art Awd 86; Comm.

HONIGSBERG, MARTINE; Hackettstown HS; Great Meadows, NJ; (Y); 4-H; Key Clb; Temple Yth Grp; Stu Cncl; Stat Socr; 2nd Plc Fncng Mdl; Vrsty Fncr; Bus.

HONNICK, KIMBERLY; Mary Help Of Christians Acad; Paterson, NJ; (Y); Yrbk Stf; Off Sr Cls; Stu Cncl; Var Im Vllybl; Cmnty Wkr; Computer Clb; Drama Clb; GAA; Letterman Clb; Varsity Clb; Chrldng Partcpnt & Coach; Montclair ST Coll; Educ.

HONOHAN, MATTHEW J; Paramus HS; Bayville, NJ; (Y); 18/343; Am Leg Boys St; Var Bsbl; Var Bsktbl; NHS; Ntl Merit Ltr; St Schlr; Math Clb; Orch; Im Socr; Acadmc All Amercn; Boston Coll; Poltcl Sci.

HOOD, KEVIN; Williamstown HS; Williamstown, NJ; (Y); 12/220; JV Bsktbl; Acdmc Exc 83-84; Frstry.

HOOKS, KIESHA; Marylawn Of The Oranges HS; E Orange, NJ; (Y); 18/54; Art Clb; Sec Camera Clb; Chorus; School Musical; Yrbk Stf; Rep Jr Cls; JV Bsktbl; JV Sftbl; Hon Roll; NEDT Awd; Frnch Hnrs Soc 85-86; Cert Of Achvt Sci Enrchmnt Prog 85; Cocours Ntl Defrancais Cert De Merite 85; Med.

HOOLKO, CHERYL; Livingston HS; Livingston, NJ; (Y); Ntl Hnr Rl 84-85; Rutgers U; Bus.

HOOPER, MARLISA; Central Regional HS; Bayville, NJ; (Y); 6/240; Math Clb; Math Tm; Nwsp Stf; Tennis; Cit Awd; French Hon Soc; High Hon Roll; Hon Roll; Jr NHS; NHS; MIT; Engrng.

HOOPER, SANDRA; University HS; Newark, NJ; (Y); Church Yth Grp; JA; Math Clb; ROTC; Teachers Aide; Chorus; Variety Show; Bowling; Hon Roll; Cert Awd Peace Essay Cont 85; Gold Car Acad Achvt Awd 85; Prudentials Actuarial Pgm Awd 85; Hampton U; Bus Mgmt.

HOOVER, DANIEL; Ocean City HS; Ocean City, NJ; (Y); 80/300; Jazz Band; Mrchg Band; Orch; Hst Sr Cls; JV Bsktbl; Var Swmmng; Var Tennis; Church Yth Grp; Drama Clb; French Clb; Capt Beacon SCC Cycling Team 86; Jr Natl Criterium Championships 86; ST Rd Race Championships 86; Music.

HOOVER, GREG; Matawan Regional HS; Aberdeen, NJ; (S); 40/289; Rep Stu Cncl; Capt Socr; High Hon Roll; NHS; Bus Adm.

HOOVER, LYNN CHRISTINE; South River HS; South River, NJ; (Y); 7/146; Off Church Yth Grp; Drm Mjr(t); Jazz Band; Pres VP Mrchg Band; Pep Band; Pres Symp Band; NHS; Voice Dem Awd; German Clb; Scholastic Bowl; Cntrl Jersey Rgnl Band 84, 85 & 86; Yth Am European Concert Tour 85; NJ St Yth Orch 85-86.

HOOVER, SORITTA FAY; Penns Grove HS; Carneys Point, NJ; (Y); Church Yth Grp; Spanish Clb; Meritors Awd Shrthnd II & Bus Math 86; Cert Compltn Bus Ed Currclm 86; Goldey Beacom Coll; Exec Secy.

HOOVER, TERRI; Schalick HS; Elmer, NJ; (Y); Art Clb; Dance Clb; DECA; Girl Scts; Pep Clb; Varsity Clb; Chorus; School Musical; School Play; Variety Show; Glassboro ST; Theatre.

HOPE, KAREN; Clayton HS; Clayton, NJ; (Y); 13/60; Library Aide; Band; Chorus; Concert Band; Drm Mjr(t); Mrchg Band; School Musical; Rep Stu Cncl; Yrbk Stf; Trs Jr Cls; Gld Music Awd For Dstngshd Prfrmnc 82-83; Yth Ftnss Achvt Awd 84; Cert Of Merit-Drm Mjrtt 85; Glassboro ST Coll; Med Lab Tch.

HOPKINS, ANASTASIA; Lower Cape May Regional HS; Cape May, NJ; (Y); 6/234; Drama Clb; French Clb; JCL; Key Clb; Varsity Clb; Chorus; School Musical; Stage Crew; Nwsp Stf; Yrbk Stf; Grls Ctznshp Attndnt 86; Lang Stds.

HOPKINS, KEVIN; Pope John XXIII Regional HS; Sparta, NJ; (Y); Band; Trs Jr Cls; Trs Stu Cncl; Var Bsbl; Var Capt Swmmng; Hon Roll; YMCA Swmmng All Amer 86; All Leag Swmmr 85-86; Htl Mgt.

HOPKINS, LISA; Pt Pleasant HS; Pt Pleasant, NJ; (S); 6/243; Math Clb; Pep Clb; Trs Band; Concert Band; Mrchg Band; School Musical; Stu Cncl; Powder Puff Ftbl; Hon Roll; NHS; Georgian Court Coll; Elem Tchr.

HOPKINS, MICHAEL; Gloucester City HS; Gloucester, NJ; (Y); Model UN; Pep Clb; Chorus; School Musical; School Play; Yrbk Stf; Lit Mag; Cit Awd; Hon Roll; Global Affairs Club; Jr Histrns Club; Interact Club; Accntng.

HOPKINS, MICHELE; Arthur P Schalick HS; Elmer, NJ; (Y); Pep Clb; Political Wkr; VICA; Fld Hcky; Hon Roll; Prfct Atten Awd; NJ VICA Skll Olympc Cert Of Achvt 86; JR SR Prom Ct 86; Bus Adm.

HOPLER, TRACY; Morris Knolls HS; Rockaway, NJ; (Y); Church Yth Grp; Library Aide; Service Clb; Lit Mag; Hon Roll; Adv Engl, Britsh Lit 85-86; Psych.

HOPPER, CINDI; Pinelands Regional HS; Tuckerton, NJ; (Y); 7/200; Church Yth Grp; French Clb; Hosp Aide; Pep Clb; Variety Show; Nwsp Phtg; Sec Frsh Cls; Sec Soph Cls; Sec Jr Cls; Var Cheerleading.

HOPSON, ANGELA; Lenape Regional HS; Mt Laurel, NJ; (Y); Church Yth Grp; FNA; Hosp Aide; Varsity Clb; Variety Show; Rep Frsh Cls; Rep Jr Cls; Cheerleading; Trk; Hon Roll; Pre-Med.

HOPSON, KIMBERLY; Queen Of Peace HS; N Arlington, NJ; (Y); 18/216; Debate Tm; Drama Clb; Spanish Clb; Teachers Aide; Stage Crew; Nwsp Rptr; Socr; Sftbl; Hon Roll; Spanish NHS; Med.

HOPTA, DANIELLE; Manasquan HS; Brielle, NJ; (Y); Church Yth Grp; Exploring; Girl Scts; Library Aide; Pep Clb; Spanish Clb; Concert Band; Cheerleading; Score Keeper; Socr; Bus.

HORACE, RENEE; Deptford Township HS; Deptford, NJ; (Y); Church Yth Grp; FHA; Chorus; Pres Church Choir; Flag Corp; Stat Bsktbl; Var Fld Hcky; Capt Trk; Vllybl; Hon Roll; All-South Jersey Chorus 84-86; 4th Rnr Up Ms Blck Awrnss Pgnt 85.

HORBACEWICZ, CATHY; Roselle Catholic HS; Irvington, NJ; (S); #20 In Class; Church Yth Grp; Math Clb; Ski Clb; Stage Crew; JV Swmmng; Var Trk; Hon Roll; Spnsh Awd 85; Med.

HORNER, KYLE J; Cherokee HS; Hainesport, NJ; (Y); Am Leg Boys St; Church Yth Grp; FCA; Model UN; Chorus; Var Bsbl; Var Ftbl; Pres Clssrm 86; Of Bck Yr 85-86; S Jrsy Schlr Athlt Yr 85-86; U Of TN; Hstry.

HORNER, REBECCA; Pinelands Regional HS; Tuckerton, NJ; (Y); 2/170; Girl Scts; Math Tm; Science Clb; Yrbk Stf; High Hon Roll; NHS; Ntl Merit SF; Spanish NHS; Sen Bill Bradley Young Ctzn Awd 86; Grls Ctznshp Inst Rep 86; Am Leg Aux Grls ST Alt 86; Mth.

HORNER, SHERIE; Burlington City HS; Edgewater Pk, NJ; (Y); FNA; Hon Roll; Nrsng.

HORNER, STEPHANIE; Hightstown HS; Cranbury, NJ; (Y); 26/449; French Clb; Ski Clb; Spanish Clb; Color Guard; Frsh Cls; Soph Cls; Jr Cls; Stu Cncl; High Hon Roll; Hon Roll; Intl Bus.

HORNIACEK, JEAN; Mother Seton Regional HS; Hillside, NJ; (Y); 4/102; Debate Tm; Latin Clb; SADD; Rep Frsh Cls; Rep Soph Cls; Rep Jr Cls; Rep Stu Cncl; Hon Roll; VP NHS; Acdmc Schlrshp Hillsides Bus Womn Leag 86; Rutgers U; Pharm.

HORNSTEIN, DANA; Matawan Regional HS; Aberdeen, NJ; (S); 44/321; Computer Clb; Ski Clb; Spanish Clb; Chorus; School Musical; Yrbk Stf; Rep Soph Cls; Rep Jr Cls; Rep Stu Cncl; JV Bowling; Bus.

HORNYAK, CATHERINE; Rahway HS; Rahway, NJ; (Y); French Clb; Girl Scts; Radio Clb; Concert Band; Ed Yrbk Stf; Rep Stu Cncl; JV Vllybl; French Hon Soc; Jr NHS; NHS; Silv Ldrshp Awd Grl Scouts 83-84; Rutgers; Acctng.

HOROUPIAN, MARK; Old Tappan HS; Stanford, CA; (Y); 42/287; Church Yth Grp; Ski Clb; Varsity Clb; Var Ftbl; Hon Roll; Acdmc All Am 86; Bus.

HOROWITZ, ELANA; Manalapan HS; Englishtown, NJ; (Y); 30/440; Cmnty Wkr; Hosp Aide; Q&S; Nwsp Bus Mgr; Nwsp Rptr; Nwsp Sprt Ed; Nwsp Stf; Var L Mgr(s); NHS; Edtr Awd Page Wad 86; Natl Hnr Soc 86-87; Rutgers U; Engrng.

HOROWITZ, ERICA; Red Bank Regional HS; Red Bank, NJ; (Y); School Play; Pres Frsh Cls; Rep Soph Cls; Rep Stu Cncl; Sec Ftbl; Hon Roll; Temple Yth Grp; Flag Corp; Sec Bsbl; Sec Socr; NJ Bar Assoc Mck Trl 85; NJ Bar Assoc Mck Gtrl 86; Law.

HOROWITZ, MARK; Morris Hills HS; Rockaway, NJ; (Y); 105/270; Science Clb; Temple Yth Grp; Yrbk Phtg; Yrbk Stf; Trk; Var JV Wrstlng; Prjct Ld Ldrshp Pgm 85-87; Stu Expctn Cmmtee 85-86; Nts Edctnl Svc Srch 85-86; AZ ST U; Corp Law.

HORSEY, PAUL; Oakcrest HS; Mays Landing, NJ; (Y); 13/255; Cmnty Wkr; Var Wrstlng; Hon Roll; 2 Vrsty Ltrs Schltc Hnrs 84-85; Engrng.

HORTON, HEATHER; North Hunterdon HS; Hampton, NJ; (Y); 33/350; Pep Clb; Ski Clb; Variety Show; Rep Soph Cls; Sec Stu Cncl; Var Crs Cntry; Var Trk; Hon Roll; UC Davis; Pre-Law.

HORTON, KAREN D; Paterson Catholic Regional HS; Paterson, NJ; (Y); 1/106; Drama Clb; Pep Clb; Science Clb; Sec VP Stu Cncl; Capt Cheerleading; Var Trk; NHS; Ntl Merit Ltr; Mrchg Band; NJ Govr Schlr, Rutgers Schlr 85; Biolgcl Sci.

HORTON, KELLY; Rahway HS; Rahway, NJ; (Y); Rep Stu Cncl; JV Bsktbl; Hon Roll; Acctng.

HORTON, LORI; Delran HS; Delran, NJ; (Y); Bsktbl; Comp.

HORTON, RICHARD C; Parsippany Hills HS; Morris Plains, NJ; (Y); 17/350; Computer Clb; Math Tm; Science Clb; Nwsp Rptr; Nwsp Stf; Rep Stu Cncl; Bsbl; Bsktbl; High Hon Roll; Hon Roll; Middle ST Prep Commtt 86; Comp Sci.

HORVATH, DAWN; Toms River North HS; Toms River, NJ; (Y); FBLA; SADD; JV Bowling; JV Gym; Trk; Hon Roll; Ldrshp Awd Future Sectrys 86; Achvt Awd Girls Bwlng 84-86; Ofc Wrk.

HOSEIN, SALIMA; North Bergen HS; North Bergen, NJ; (Y); 67/400; Art Clb; Aud/Vis; Pres Camera Clb; Debate Tm; French Clb; Girl Scts; Key Clb; Spanish Clb; SADD; Stage Crew; Law.

HOSER, TINA E; Phillipsburg HS; Stewartsville, NJ; (Y); 43/296; Pres Sec 4-H; Hosp Aide; Key Clb; Rep Stu Cncl; Cit Awd; 4-H Awd; Hon Roll; Trs NHS; NJ ST Dry Prncss 85-86; Phllpsbrg Cmmnty Yth Of Mnth 86; IA ST U; Elem Educ.

HOSKINS JR, ROBERT; Lakeland Regional HS; Ringwood, NJ; (Y); 49/303; Letterman Clb; JV Bsktbl; Var L Ftbl; JV Trk; High Hon Roll; Hon Roll; NHS; Ftbll Almuni Schlrshp Hnrbl Mntn All-ST 86; MVP Ftbll Dfnsv 1st Tm All-Cnfrnc & All-Cnty 86; U Of NH; Physcs.

HOSLER, KRISTEN; River Dell Regional HS; River Edge, NJ; (Y); 48/215; Church Yth Grp; GAA; Varsity Clb; Lit Mag; Var L Fld Hcky; Var L Trk; High Hon Roll; Letterman Clb; Office Aide; All-Cnty Fld Hockey Hnrbl Mntn 84-85; 2nd Tm All-Cnty Fld Hockey 85-86; Hnrbl Mentn All-Sub Trck 85-86; Elizabethtown Coll; Bus Admin.

HOTHEM, THOMAS; Park Ridge HS; Park Ridge, NJ; (Y); 8/106; AFS; Boy Scts; Church Yth Grp; Math Clb; Quiz Bowl; Yrbk Bus Mgr; Var JV Bsbl; JV Bsktbl; Var JV Socr; NHS; Ordr Arrow 83; Ldr 1st Vrsty Scout Tm-Bergen Cnty 84-85; Selctn Presbytrn Triennium 86; Envrnmntl Study.

HOU, ALEXANDER; Wall HS; Wall Township, NJ; (Y); #16 In Class; Computer Clb; German Clb; Key Clb; Ski Clb; Orch; Var Trk; High Hon Roll; Kiwanis Awd; NHS; Prfct Atten Awd; MIT; Engrng.

HOUCK, SHARON; Paul VI HS; Turnersville, NJ; (S); 4/474; Math Clb; SADD; Var Capt Bsktbl; Var Capt Fld Hcky; High Hon Roll; Hon Roll; VP NHS; Spanish NHS; St Schlr; Bus.

HOULIHAN, PATRICE; St John Vianney HS; Hazlet, NJ; (Y); Intnl Clb; Stat Ftbl; Acctng.

HOUSLEY, JOHN; Northern Valley Regional HS; Northvale, NJ; (Y); 5/281; VP AFS; Band; Chorus; Concert Band; Jazz Band; Madrigals; Mrchg Band; School Musical; School Play; Symp Band.

HOUSLEY, ROBERT; Northern Valley Regional HS; Northvale, NJ; (Y); 17/281; AFS; Bsktbl; Socr; High Hon Roll; Hon Roll.

HOUSMAN, TAMMY; Monsignor Donovan HS; Lakewood, NJ; (Y); 109/243; SADD; Drm Mjr(t); Mrchg Band; Hon Roll; Art Clb; Drama Clb; Math Clb; Ski Clb; Phrmcy.

HOUSTON, MEGAN; Hackettstown HS; Hackettstown, NJ; (Y); Q&S; Chorus; Nwsp Rptr; Crs Cntry; Hon Roll; NHS; Cmnty Wkr; Hosp Aide; Latin Clb; Ski Clb.

HOUTHUYSEN, TODD; Clifton HS; Clifton, NJ; (Y); 60/564; Science Clb; Spanish Clb; Hon Roll; Pres Schlr; Slvr C 86; Lock Haven U; Bio/Med Tech.

HOWARD, BILL; Holy Cross HS; Bordentown, NJ; (Y); Church Yth Grp; Spanish Clb; JV Trk; Hon Roll; Comp.

HOWARD, JONATHAN; Green Brook HS; Greenbrook, NJ; (Y); 5/51; Am Leg Boys St; VP Key Clb; Concert Band; Jazz Band; Mrchg Band; Pres Stu Cncl; Cit Awd; Hon Roll; Lion Awd; NHS; Good Citzn Dghtrs Of Am Revltn 86; NJ Inst Of Tech; Mech Engrg.

HOWARD, KAREN; Atlantic City HS; Atlantic City, NJ; (Y); 136/473; Hon Roll; Hotel Mgr.

HOWARD, KATHLEEN; Holy Cross HS; Bordentown, NJ; (Y); 34/374; Sec Church Yth Grp; Hosp Aide; Spanish Clb; Church Choir; Stage Crew; Stat Fld Hcky; Stat Swmmng; High Hon Roll; Hon Roll; Pres Schlrshp U Scranton 86; U Scranton; Phys Ther.

HOWARD, LAURA; Vail-Deane HS; Roselle Park, NJ; (Y); Chorus; School Musical; Stage Crew; VP Soph Cls; Stu Cncl; Capt Fld Hcky; Capt JV Sftbl; Dance Clb; Drama Clb; French Clb; Fld Hcky MVP 85-86; NJAIS Stu Ldrshp Cnfrnc 86; Gvrnmt.

HOWARD, NANCY; Burlington City HS; Edgewater Park, NJ; (Y); 2/168; VP Key Clb; Sec Soph Cls; VP Sr Cls; Var JV Yrbk Rptr; Yrbk Phtg; Hon Roll; Pres NHS; Pres Schlr; Sal; Lehigh U; Comp Sci.

HOWD, ERIC; Wall HS; Wall, NJ; (S); 21/286; Am Leg Boys St; Chess Clb; Drama Clb; Key Clb; Band; Concert Band; Jazz Band; Mrchg Band; Orch; Pep Band; U Of Hartford; Music Educ.

HOWELL, CYNTHIA; Linden HS; Linden, NJ; (Y); German Clb; Hon Roll; Farleigh Dickinson; Chem.

HOWELL, LORRAINE; Central HS; Newark, NJ; (Y); Var Co-Capt Bsktbl; Var Sftbl; Hon Roll; Prfct Atten Awd; Mth.

HOWELL, WADE C; Kittatinny Regional HS; Newton, NJ; (Y); Am Leg Boys St; 4-H; PAVAS; Thesps; Madrigals; School Musical; School Play; Nwsp Rptr; Yrbk Stf; Lit Mag; Cnty Choir 85; ST Tn Arts Festvl Wrtng On ST Lvl 86; Law.

HOWELLS, BILL; Sayreville Way Memorial HS; Sayreville, NJ; (Y); 41/381; Math Clb; Science Clb; Spanish Clb; Var Socr; Hon Roll; Spanish NHS; All Acad Socr Tm 85-86; Pres Acad Fit Awd 85-86; TAG 84-86; Villanova U; Chem Engrng.

HOWELLS, BRUCE; Ranway HS; Rahway, NJ; (Y); Office Aide; Radio Clb; Science Clb; Nwsp Stf; Rep Stu Cncl; Var L Mgr(s); High Hon Roll; NHS; Hon Roll; Jr NHS; Cramer Corp Stu Art Sem 85-86; Wnnr Comp Pgmr Cntst 86; Engrng.

HOWELLS, REBECCA; Clayton HS; Clayton, NJ; (Y); 14/63; Church Yth Grp; VICA; Band; Chorus; Stage Crew; Nwsp Stf; Yrbk Stf; Hon Roll; Gloucester Cnty Coll; Comp Sci.

HOWELLS, ROBERT; Edgewood Regional SR HS; Cedarbrook, NJ; (Y); 64/379; Band; Concert Band; Jazz Band; Mrchg Band; Hon Roll; VFW Awd; Glassboro ST Coll.

HOWLAND, ANNE; Southern Regional HS; Barnegat, NJ; (Y); Church Yth Grp; GAA; Girl Scts; Model UN; Ski Clb; Spanish Clb; Mrchg Band; Var Crs Cntry; Var Trk; Hon Roll; Mst Vlbl Frshmn Wntr & Spg Trck 84; Mst Vlbl Crss Cntry & Wntr Trck 84-85; Mst Vlbl JR Crss Cntry 85; Visl Arts.

HOWLETT, ANNE; Bridgewater-Raritan East HS; Bridgewater, NJ; (Y); Church Yth Grp; Intnl Clb; Ski Clb; Socr; Swmmng; Trk; High Hon Roll; Hon Roll; NHS; Pres Schlr; Rutgers U; Engrng.

HOWLETT, DONNA; Paul VI Regional HS; W Orange, NJ; (Y); 15/147; Ed Key Clb; JV Bowling; JV Sftbl; High Hon Roll; Hon Roll; Spanish NHS; Acdmc All Amer 86; Bus Adm.

HOYNAK, PAUL; Cherry Hill HS West; Cherry Hill, NJ; (Y); Aud/Vis; Teachers Aide; Tennis; High Hon Roll; Hon Roll; Temple U; Pre Vet.

HOYT, JUSTIN; Indian Hills HS; Franklin Lakes, NJ; (Y); Art Clb; Church Yth Grp; Exploring; Band; Lit Mag; VFW Awd; RI Schl Of Dsgn; Fine Arts.

HOYT, LORI; Lodi HS; Lodi, NJ; (Y); 3/184; Am Leg Aux Girls St; Key Clb; Science Clb; Varsity Clb; Yrbk Phtg; Yrbk Stf; Var Bsktbl; Var Sftbl; Var Capt Tennis; Hon Roll; Whittier Coll CA; Pre-Med.

HRATKO, THOMAS; Jackson Memorial HS; Jackson, NJ; (Y); 46/405; Boy Scts; Dance Clb; Exploring; ROTC; Color Guard; Drill Tm; High Hon Roll; Hon Roll; Military Order Of Wrld Wars Awd 86; Aerontcl Engrng.

HRICAY, DOREEN; Parsippany HS; Parsippany, NJ; (Y); Yrbk Stf; Lit Mag; Pep Clb; Sec Frsh Cls; Sec Soph Cls; Rep Jr Cls; Rep Stu Cncl; JV Bsktbl; Var JV Cheerleading; JV Tennis.

HRONCICH, LISA; North Bergen HS; N Bergen, NJ; (Y); 59/404; Sec Key Clb; Latin Clb; Spanish Clb; SADD; Rep Soph Cls; Rep Jr Cls; Stu Cncl; Var Crs Cntry; Var Capt Trk; Hon Roll; Crss Cntry Trck All Co Awds; Ruters U; Jrnlsm.

HSIAO, CATHY HUI-YI; James J Ferris HS; Jersey City, NJ; (Y); Art Clb; Camera Clb; Camp Fr Inc; Church Yth Grp; Computer Clb; Dance Clb; Drama Clb; JA; JCL; Math Clb; SAI Schlrshp Smmr Art Inst, Jersey City Brd Of Ed Schlrshp 84; JC Brd Ed & FIT Schlrshp 85; Fash Dsgn.

HSIN, ROBERT; Montville HS; Montville, NJ; (Y); 19/230; Cmnty Wkr; FBLA; Key Clb; JV Bsktbl; JV Var Ftbl; JV Var Trk; High Hon Roll; Hon Roll; NHS; Ntl Merit Ltr; Georgetown; Bio.

HSU, JULIE; De Paul Diocesan HS; Wanaque, NJ; (Y); 23/171; Ski Clb; Band; Chorus; School Musical; Nwsp Stf; Yrbk Stf; Stat Trk; Hon Roll; NHS; Rutgers; Phrmcy.

HSU, LILLIAN; Scotch Plains-Fanwood HS; Scotch Plains, NJ; (S); Model UN; Quiz Bowl; Mrchg Band; Yrbk Stf; French Hon Soc; Cmnty Wkr; French Clb; Concert Band; Symp Band; Lit Mag; Enrllmt Gftd Hnrs Math Course 83-86; Law.

HSU, PETER; Hanover Park HS; E Hanover, NJ; (Y); 1/283; Mgr Chess Clb; Sec Exploring; Hosp Aide; Sec Math Clb; Co-Capt Quiz Bowl; Sec Science Clb; Ed Nwsp Bus Mgr; NHS; St Schlr; Val; Boston U; Medcl Dr.

HU, WINNIE; Wet Windsor-Plainsboro HS; Princeton Jct, NJ; (Y); 7/240; Capt Debate Tm; Orch; Nwsp Ed-Chief; Yrbk Stf; Crs Cntry; High Hon Roll; Jr NHS; NHS; Ntl Merit Schol; Voice Dem Awd; Grdn ST Distgshd Schlr 86; Rtgrs U Schlr 85-86; Princeton U.

HUANG, CATHY; Parsippany HS; Parsippany, NJ; (Y); AFS; French Clb; FBLA; Pep Clb; JV Tennis; JV Trk; Hon Roll; NHS; Asian Club 85-86; U C Berkeley; Engrng.

HUANG, EDMUND; Clifton HS; Clifton, NJ; (Y); 1/590; Am Leg Boys St; VP Key Clb; Math Clb; Madrigals; Off Stu Cncl; Capt Var Tennis; VP NHS; Ntl Merit Ltr; Rotary Awd; Val; Cornell U; Elec Engrg.

HUANG, ELLEN; Parsippany HS; Parsippany, NJ; (Y); FBLA; Math Tm; Pep Clb; Spanish Clb; NHS; Natl Art Hnr Soc Sec 86-87.

HUANG, GENE; Parsippany Hills HS; Lake Hiawatha, NJ; (Y); Chess Clb; Computer Clb; Hosp Aide; Key Clb; Math Tm; Science Clb; Ski Clb; Off Frsh Cls; Off Soph Cls; Off Jr Cls; Hugh O Brian Awd 85; NH Govnr Schl 85; Schlrshp Howard U Summr Actrl Prog 86.

HUANG, MARGARET; John F Kennedy Memorial HS; Iselin, NJ; (Y); 13/279; French Clb; VP Pep Clb; Pres SADD; Stage Crew; Stat Socr; Hon Roll; NHS; Pre-Law.

HUANG, PATRICIA; Sayreville War Memorial HS; Parlin, NJ; (Y); 14/380; Am Leg Aux Girls St; French Clb; Girl Scts; Spanish Clb; VP SADD; Band; Chorus; School Musical; Nwsp Rptr; Yrbk Rptr; Douglass Coll; Accntng.

HUANG, RAYMOND; Matawan Regional HS; Matawan, NJ; (S); 5/400; Boy Scts; Church Yth Grp; Math Tm; Radio Clb; Speech Tm; School Musical; Nwsp Rptr; Nwsp Stf; Yrbk Stf; Crs Cntry; Schlrshp Awd 84; Cntntl Math Leag Awd 84; Eagle Sct 85; Sci.

HUANG, SIHONG; Union Hill HS; Union City, NJ; (Y); Mathletes; Math Soc 86; Acctng.

HUBBARD, BONNIE R; Park Bible Acad; Pennsgrove, NJ; (Y); Church Yth Grp; Drama Clb; VICA; Bsktbl; Cheerleading; Mgr(s); Twrlr; Vllybl; Prfct Atten Awd; Mrchg Band; Hghst Lvl Achvmnt Csmtlgy 86; Crtfct Sclptrd Nls 85; Salem CC; Btcn.

HUBER, CRAIG; Jackson Memorial HS; Jackson, NJ; (Y); Ski Clb; Socr; Tennis; Band; School Play; Bowling; High Hon Roll; Hon Roll; Var Tennis Awd 85-86; Embry-Riddle; Cmrcl Pilot.

HUBERT, JOSEPH; Madison HS; Madison, NJ; (Y); 8/206; Church Yth Grp; Pres Spanish Clb; Band; Symp Band; Cit Awd; High Hon Roll; NHS; Spanish NHS; St Schlr; Garden ST Schlr 86; Rotary Awd; Spnsh Ntl Hnr Soc 86; U Scranton; Elect Engr.

HUDDY, PHILIP; Jackson Memorial HS; Jackson, NJ; (Y); 95/405; L Var Ftbl; JV Trk; JV Wrstlng; Hon Roll; York Coll PA; Hstry Tchr.

HUDSON, JACQUELINE A; Manalapan HS; Manalapan, NJ; (Y); 16/452; Hosp Aide; Nwsp Stf; Yrbk Stf; Rep Frsh Cls; Rep Soph Cls; Var L Bsktbl; JV L Sftbl; Var Capt Tennis; VP NHS; Cmnty Wkr; Cornell U; Psychlgy.

HUEBLER, MARTY; Toms River South HS; S Toms River, NJ; (Y); 42/326; Pres Exploring; Math Clb; Nwsp Rptr; Var L Bowling; Var L Golf; High Hon Roll; Hon Roll; Prfct Atten Awd; Nwsp Stf; JV Crs Cntry; Rgnl Ind Bwlng Chmpn-4th Pl ST Fnls 86; 1/2 Pg Featr Pblshd Asbury Pk Prss Area Nwspr 86; NJ Inst Of Tech; Comp Sci.

HUEBNER, LINDA; New Providence HS; New Providence, NJ; (Y); 28/146; Church Yth Grp; Ski Clb; JV Trk; High Hon Roll; Hon Roll; Salvation Army Scholar 86; Cook; Pre-Vet.

HUEBNER, MATTHEW; Southern Regional HS; Manahawkin, NJ; (Y); 10/398; Computer Clb; Exploring; Math Clb; Math Tm; SADD; Variety Show; Ftbl; High Hon Roll; Hon Roll; NHS; Comp Engrng.

HUEBSCH, JULIE; Boonton HS; Boonton, NJ; (Y); Church Yth Grp; 4-H; French Clb; Jazz Band; VP Pres Mrchg Band; School Musical; High Hon Roll; NHS; Ntl Merit Ltr; Cmnty Wkr; Acdmc Exclnc Awd 85-86; Sci.

HUEGEL, HOLLY; Mary Help Of Christians Acad; Clifton, NJ; (Y); JCL; Chorus; Church Choir; School Musical; School Play; Ed Yrbk Stf; St Marys Stu Dvlpmnt Schlrshp 86; Sprt Amer Mrchng Bnd Canadn Tour 86; INTL Bus.

HUFF, HEATHER; Atlantic Christian Schl; Ocean View, NJ; (S); 3/12; Church Yth Grp; Band; Chorus; Church Choir; Yrbk Stf; VP Jr Cls; VP Sr Cls; Bsktbl; Fld Hcky; Sftbl; Atlantic Comm Coll; Bus.

HUGELMEYER, DONNALEE; Bishop Ahr HS; Woodbridge, NJ; (Y); 37/264; VP Church Yth Grp; Intnl Clb; Model UN; Chorus; School Musical; Var Capt Cheerleading; High Hon Roll; NHS; NEDT Awd; Girls Ctznshp Inst 86; Outstndg Svc & Ldrshp Awd St James CYO 86; Lib Art.

HUGHES, BRIAN; Saint John Vianney HS; Hazlet, NJ; (Y); Church Yth Grp; Band; Concert Band; Var Mrchg Band; Var L Bsbl; JV Bsktbl; Var L Crs Cntry; JV Socr; Architecture.

HUGHES, CHRIS; Lyndhurst HS; Lyndhurst, NJ; (Y); 42/188; JV Var Ftbl; Var Capt Trk; Capt Var Wrstlng; Hon Roll; Prfct Atten Awd; Penn ST; Engrng.

HUGHES, DAVID E; Pope John XXIII Reg HS; Andover, NJ; (Y); Debate Tm; Exploring; Model UN; Quiz Bowl; Scholastic Bowl; Ski Clb; Nwsp Ed-Chief; Yrbk Ed-Chief; Lit Mag; Rep Jr Cls; Highest Acadmc Achvt Theology 85-86; Honry Achvt Frech 85-86; Catholic U Of Am; Lawyer.

HUGHES, DOMINIC; Franklin HS; Somerset, NJ; (Y); Debate Tm; SADD; Varsity Clb; Bsbl; Golf; Vllybl; High Hon Roll; Hon Roll; Outstndng Congrssmn 85-86; Rutgers U; Bus Law.

HUGHES, ERIC; Chatham Township HS; Chatham Township, NJ; (Y); 7/133; Key Clb; Science Clb; Pres Band; Concert Band; Jazz Band; Pep Band; School Musical; Pres Sr Cls; Bsktbl; JV L Socr; All ST Woodwnd Ensmbl 86; All ST Orch 86; All ST Symphnc Band 85; All Amer Hall Fame Band Hnrs 85; Phys Sci.

HUGHES, JASON; Red Bank Regional HS; Shrewsbury, NJ; (Y); Boy Scts; Church Yth Grp; French Clb; Ski Clb; Yrbk Rptr; Yrbk Stf; Lit Mag; French Hon Soc; Hon Roll; Ntl Merit SF; Natl Achvt Schlrshp Prog Outstndng Negro Stdnts 86; Sci.

HUGHES, JEFFREY J; Hanover Park HS; Florham Park, NJ; (Y); 45/310; Am Leg Boys St; Debate Tm; Quiz Bowl; Scholastic Bowl; Spanish Clb; Varsity Clb; Var L Bsbl; Var L Bsktbl; U FL; Bus Adm.

HUGHES, KEVIN; Holmdel HS; Holmdel, NJ; (Y); Church Yth Grp; Computer Clb; VP Key Clb; Nwsp Sprt Ed; Trs Stu Cncl; Var Bsktbl; U Of MI Ann Arbor; Econ.

HUGHES, KEVIN; Middletown HS South; Middletown, NJ; (Y); Cmnty Wkr; Varsity Clb; Variety Show; Pres Frsh Cls; JV Bsktbl; Var Ftbl; Im Wt Lftg; Ftbl All North All Shore All Cnty Lambardi Awd 85-86.

HUGHES, KEVIN R; Paul VI Regional HS; Cedar Grove, NJ; (Y); Cmnty Wkr; Spanish Clb; Rep Soph Cls; Rep Jr Cls; Rep Sr Cls; Stu Cncl; Var Bsbl; Var Bsktbl; Var Ftbl; Spanish NHS; Acad All Amer 86; All Lg, Cnty, Area Hnrs Ftbl, Bsktbll, Bsbl 86.

HUGHES, NICOLE; Cinnaminson HS; Cinnaminson, NJ; (Y); Church Yth Grp; Spanish Clb; SADD; Chorus; JV Cheerleading; Var Sftbl; Var Swmmng; JV Var Tennis; Ed.

HUGHES, PHILIP C; Jefferson Township HS; Lake Hopatcong, NJ; (Y); 10/235; Am Leg Boys St; Math Tm; SADD; Varsity Clb; Rep Stu Cncl; Var Crs Cntry; Capt Var Wrstlng; NHS; 3rd Wrld Sombo Wrstlg Champ Madrid Spain 83; NJ Wrstlg Fed Freestyl & Greco Romn ST Champ 86; Engrng.

HUGHES, SHARON; Clearview Regional HS; Sewell, NJ; (Y); 29/162; VP Band; Concert Band; Drm Mjr(t); Mrchg Band; Orch; School Play; Bsktbl; Trk; NHS; Church Yth Grp; All ST Band 85-86; All South Jersey Wind Ensbml 84-86; All S J Orchstra 86; All S J Long Jump Chmp; Bus.

HUGHES, SONYA L; East Orange HS; E Orange, NJ; (Y); #24 In Class; Computer Clb; German Clb; Teachers Aide; Varsity Clb; Acpl Chr; Chorus; Church Choir; Variety Show; Trs Stu Cncl; Var Sftbl; PA ST U; Aero Engnrng.

HUGHES, TAMI; Pennsville Memorial HS; Salem, NJ; (Y); Mgr School Musical; School Play; Rep Frsh Cls; Rep Soph Cls; Rep Jr Cls; Rep Sr Cls; Hon Roll; Pennsville Ed Assn Schlrshp 86; Garden ST Schlrshp 86; Glassboro ST Coll; Engl.

HUGHES, THERESA; John P Stevens HS; Edison, NJ; (Y); 77/488; VP Art Clb; Model UN; NHS; Cmnty Wkr; Debate Tm; Hosp Aide; School Play; Nwsp Stf; Hon Roll; Law.

HUGHES, TREVOR; West Deptford HS; Woodbury, NJ; (Y); 45/145; Capt Var Trk; Wt Lftg; JA; Model UN; Varsity Clb; JV L Crs Cntry; JV L Ftbl; JV Swmmng; Hon Roll; Kiwanis Awd; Physcs Tchrs Am Awd 86; Blck Blt Tan Soo Do Karte 85; Trck MVP 84-86; Mst Dctd 85 All Cnfrcn 84-86; Orsinus; Physcs.

HUH, JAE WAN; Fort Lee HS; Ft Lee, NJ; (Y); Art Clb; Cmnty Wkr; French Clb; High Hon Roll; Hon Roll; Church Yth Grp; Girl Scts; Intnl Clb; Spanish Clb; Trk; Art.

HUHA, NANCY; Pompton Lakes HS; Pompton Lakes, NJ; (Y); 3/150; Math Clb; Q&S; Service Clb; VP Spanish Clb; Ed Yrbk Stf; Ed Lit Mag; High Hon Roll; Trs NHS; Prfct Atten Awd; Intnl Clb; 1st And 2nd Art Shw Clrd Charcl 86; Hnr Soc Schlrshp 86; Kutztown U; Psych.

HULITT, SHERRI; Bridgeton HS; Bridgeton, NJ; (Y); German Clb; Office Aide; Q&S; Ski Clb; Nwsp Rptr; Yrbk Stf; Stu Cncl; Capt Swmmng; Hon Roll; Trs NHS; Sigma Theta Chi Srty Awd; Acdmc All-Amer; Glassboro ST Coll; Englsh.

HULL, KAMMY; Kittatinny Regional HS; Layton, NJ; (Y); Cmnty Wkr; Spanish Clb; SADD; Varsity Clb; Stat Bsbl; Im JV Bsktbl; Var JV Fld Hcky; Var Powder Puff Ftbl; Im Sftbl; JV Trk; Elem Educ.

HULL, LISA; Phillipsburg HS; Phillipsburg, NJ; (Y); 67/334; Yrbk Stf; Rep Stu Cncl; Var Cheerleading; Hon Roll; Frgn Lang Tchr.

HULSMAN, MICHAEL; Toms River H S South; S Toms River, NJ; (Y); VP Church Yth Grp; Off Soph Cls; Var L Swmmng; High Hon Roll; Hon Roll; Chiropractics.

HULTS, KAREN; Highland Regional HS; Somerdale, NJ; (Y); AFS; Am Leg Aux Girls St; Art Clb; German Clb; Hosp Aide; Service Clb; Stu Cncl; Var L Bsbl; Var L Cheerleading; Stat Trk; Bus Admin.

HULTZ, DAVID; John F Kennedy HS; Willingboro, NJ; (Y); Key Clb; Teachers Aide; Yrbk Stf; Mgr(s); JV Socr; Cit Awd; Hon Roll; VFW Awd; Rider Coll; Acctg.

HUMBERT, PAMELA; Villa Walsh Acad; Randolph, NJ; (Y); Nwsp Ed-Chief; Hosp Aide; Math Tm; NFL; Spanish Clb; Sec Stu Cncl; Stat Lcrss; Hon Roll; NHS; Spanish NHS; Lehigh; Pre Law.

HUMER, MELISSA; J F Kennedy HS; Willingboro, NJ; (Y); 26/270; JV Var Fld Hcky; JV Var Lcrss; Hon Roll; Chem Engnrng.

HUMES, LISA; Overbrook HS; Lindenwold, NJ; (Y); 11/262; Church Yth Grp; French Clb; Varsity Clb; Yrbk Ed-Chief; Fld Hcky; Hon Roll; NHS; Pres Schlr; Lindenwold Lions Clb 86; Sophia K Reeves 86; Sons Of Temperence 86; Nyack; Missions.

HUMMEL, JUDY; Matawan Regional HS; Cliffwood Beach, NJ; (S); 15/273; Church Yth Grp; Math Tm; Church Choir; Nwsp Rptr; Nwsp Stf; Yrbk Stf; Stu Cncl; Hon Roll; NHS; Acadmc Al-Amer Awd; Rutgers U.

HUMMER, THERESA; Toms River HS East; Toms River, NJ; (Y); Church Yth Grp; FBLA; Hosp Aide; Color Guard; Mgr(s); Hon Roll; Moravian Coll; Biolgst.

HUMPHREYS, MICHAEL; Penns Grove HS; Penns Grove, NJ; (Y); #7 In Class; Am Leg Boys St; JA; JCL; School Play; Stage Crew; Var L Socr; Var L Trk; Hon Roll; NHS; Wildlf Cnsrvtn.

HUNT, DAVID S; Princeton HS; Princeton, NJ; (Y); Pres Church Yth Grp; Exploring; French Clb; Chorus; School Musical; Variety Show; Rep Sr Cls; Stu Cncl; JV Trk; Ntl Merit SF.

HUNT, GEORGE; Bogota HS; Bogota, NJ; (Y); Band; Concert Band; Jazz Band; Mrchg Band; Nwsp Rptr; Trk; Montclair ST Coll.

HUNT, JON; Cumberland Christian Schl; Newfield, NJ; (S); German Clb; Pres Frsh Cls; Trs Stu Cncl; Var Bsbl; Capt Bsktbl; Socr; High Hon Roll; Hon Roll; Church Yth Grp; Bsktbl Sprtsmnshp Awd 84-85; Aerontcl Engr.

HUNT, KEITH; Rahway SR HS; Rahway, NJ; (Y); Office Aide; Band; Mrchg Band; JV Bsktbl; JV Bowling; Cit Awd; Hon Roll; Prfct Atten Awd; U Of NC; Radio.

HUNT, NANCY; Hamilton HS East; Hamilton Sq, NJ; (Y); #5 In Class; FBLA; SADD; Sec Frsh Cls; Sec Soph Cls; Sec Jr Cls; Sec Sr Cls; Stu Cncl; Stat Mgr(s); High Hon Roll; NHS; GALRE Select Hstry Grp 87.

HUNT, STEPHANIE; Marylawn Of The Oranges HS; Orange, NJ; (Y); Dance Clb; French Clb; NEDT Awd; Fairleigh Dickenson; Art.

HUNT, STEPHEN; Manasquan HS; Spring Lake, NJ; (Y); 48/227; Ski Clb; Nwsp Stf; JV Bsktbl; JV Ftbl; Trk; U CA Santa Cruz; Jrnlsm.

HUNT, THOMAS; Hunterdon Central HS; Readington, NJ; (Y); 120/548; Ski Clb; Chorus; Mrchg Band; School Musical; Variety Show; Rep Wrstlng; Im Vllybl; Hon Roll; Math Achvt Awd 85; Bio & Chmstry Awds 84-86; Sngng.

HUNTER, GLORIA; Hoboken HS; Hoboken, NJ; (Y); Teachers Aide; Pom Pon; Hon Roll; Morgan ST U ; Cooperate Law.

HUNTER, NANCY; Hightstown HS; East Windsor, NJ; (Y); 33/449; AFS; Drama Clb; Sec French Clb; Hosp Aide; Hon Roll; NHS; Cert Outstndng Schltc Perfrmnce 83-86; Hghst Acad Awd 86; Ltr Commendtn Princeton Hosp Svc 86.

HUNTER, SHARON; Jefferson Township HS; Oak Ridge, NJ; (S); 80/225; Pres DECA; SADD; Varsity Clb; Stat Var Ftbl; JV Var Sftbl; Hon Roll; Schl Store Mgr 85; Persnl Devlpmnt Pgm Leader 85 & 86; Mrktng.

HUNTLEY, BRUCE W; Hunterdon Central HS; Whitehse Sta, NJ; (Y); 41/540; Ski Clb; Concert Band; Jazz Band; Mrchg Band; School Musical; School Play; JV Trk; JV Wrstlng; VP NHS; St Schlr; Class Music 85-86; Hchs Mem Music Schlrshp 86; Govnrs Sch For Arts 85; CO ST U; Bus.

HURAY, KIMBERLY PAM; Pequannock Township HS; Pompton Plains, NJ; (Y); 2/231; Ed Yrbk Stf; Rep VP Stu Cncl; Var Trk; Twrlr; NHS; Ntl Merit Ltr; Spanish NHS; Spnsh, Ltn, Algbr, & Actvts Awds 83; Natl Ltn Exam Awd 83; Chem Awd, Pres Acadmc Ftnss Awds 86; Hamilton Coll.

HURD, DOUG; Chatham Township HS; Chatham, NJ; (Y); Band; Concert Band; Orch; Pep Band; Rep Stu Cncl; Var Ice Hcky; Var Socr; Var Tennis; Hon Roll.

HURD, SCOTT; Highland HS; Blackwood, NJ; (S); Church Yth Grp; Computer Clb; Service Clb; Comp Prog.

HURFF, SANDRA; Paulsboro HS; Gibbstown, NJ; (Y); 23/145; Church Yth Grp; Ski Clb; Drill Tm; Stage Crew; Yrbk Stf; Twrlr; Hon Roll; NHS; Glassboro ST Coll; Elem Ed.

HURFF, STEVE; Kingsway Regional HS; Swedesboro, NJ; (Y); Church Yth Grp; PAVAS; Science Clb; Ski Clb; School Play; Stage Crew; Var Tennis; Aud/Vis; Northeastern; Elec Engrng.

HURLBURT, DEANNA; Rahway HS; Winfield, NJ; (Y); Service Clb; Drill Tm; Nwsp Stf; Yrbk Stf; Var Bsktbl; Hon Roll; Jr NHS; Spanish NHS; Cornell; Vet.

HURLBURT, MARY; Wallington HS; Wallington, NJ; (Y); Chorus; School Play; Stage Crew; JV Sftbl; Hon Roll; Pediatric Nurse.

HURON, DAVID; Dover HS; Mine Hill, NJ; (Y); 10/223; Church Yth Grp; German Clb; Scholastic Bowl; Ski Clb; Var Crs Cntry; High Hon Roll; NHS; German Lang Awd; Whittier Coll; Mathmtcs.

HUSTON, JIM; Montville HS; Montville, NJ; (Y); #59 In Class; Computer Clb; Math Clb; Ski Clb; Hon Roll; 2nd Pl Awd Drftng NJ Arts & Crafts Fair 86; Dsgn Wrk For Non Profit Org 85-86; Engrng.

HUSTON, KELLY ANN; Shawnee HS; Vincentown, NJ; (Y); 135/535; Camera Clb; Pep Clb; Variety Show; Nwsp Rptr; Nwsp Stf; Trs Stu Cncl; Capt Cheerleading; Trk; Hon Roll; NHS; Hnrb Mntn Kodak Snpsht Cntst 85; 5th Burlington Cnty Leag Champ 84; Lcl, St, Rgnl Cmptn AAU JR Olymp; Trenton ST Coll; Comm.

HUSZAR, ROSE ANNA; Phillipsburg HS; Phillipsburg, NJ; (Y); 56/284; Band; Concert Band; Mrchg Band; Orch; Nwsp Rptr; High Hon Roll; Hon Roll; NHS; Muscnshp Awd/Merit Awd 85-86; Pres Acad Ftnss Awd 86; Beauchamp E Smith Memrl Fund 86-87; York Coll; Elem Educ.

HUTCHCRAFT, LISA; Wayne Valley HS; Wayne, NJ; (Y); 33/328; Church Yth Grp; Pres Service Clb; Chorus; Mrchg Band; Nwsp Stf; Yrbk Stf; NHS; Aud/Vis; Cmnty Wkr; French Clb; Stdnt Ldr, Cmpus Life, YFC Intl 83-86; Cnslr PEER Ldr, Spch Tlnt, Sprt Awd 86; Comm.

HUTCHINS, IVY; Imaculate Conception HS; East Orange, NJ; (Y); Church Yth Grp; Drama Clb; Spanish Clb; Church Choir; Nwsp Stf; Yrbk Stf; Var Cheerleading; Im Gym; High Hon Roll; NHS; Rodinos Schrlshp 86; Attrny.

HUTCHINSON, JACK; Palmyra HS; Palmyra, NJ; (Y); 30/126; Pres Art Clb; Teachers Aide; Rep Soph Cls; JV Bsbl; Im Bsktbl; Im Bowling; L Golf; JV Socr; High Hon Roll; Hon Roll; Western MD Coll; Mgmt.

HUTCHINSON, LISA; Lyndhurst HS; Lyndhurst, NJ; (Y); 31/180; Church Yth Grp; Key Clb; 1st Pl Outstndng Crftsmn 86; Fash Designer.

HUTCHINSON, MARIE J; Villa Victoria Acad; Trenton, NJ; (Y); Drama Clb; Hosp Aide; School Musical; Yrbk Ed-Chief; Var Socr; Var Sftbl; Hon Roll; Good Ctzn Awd Am Leg Aux Post 314 86; Seton Hall U; Nrsng.

HUTCHINSON, WILLIAM; Mahwah HS; Mahwah, NJ; (Y); 45/187; Math Clb; Ftbl; Hon Roll; Military.

HUTCHISON, HEIDI; Egg Harbor Twp HS; Mays Landing, NJ; (S); 19/450; Drama Clb; French Clb; School Play; Swing Chorus; Pres Frsh Cls; Fld Hcky; Mgr(s); Sftbl; Trk; NHS; Bus.

HUTCHISON, MONICA; Bloomfield SR HS; Bloomfield, NJ; (Y); 22/442; Sec French Clb; Key Clb; Drill Tm; Nwsp Stf; Yrbk Stf; Rep Soph Cls; Rep Jr Cls; French Hon Soc; Hon Roll; NHS; Boston U; Psych.

HUTNAN, DEBBIE; Camden Catholic HS; Pennsauken, NJ; (Y); Art Clb; French Clb; Fld Hcky; Swmmng.

HUTT, STANLEY; North Warren Regional HS; Blairstown, NJ; (Y); 20/140; Spanish Clb; Nwsp Sprt Ed; Nwsp Stf; Hon Roll; NHS; Pres Schlr; Cook College; Metrlgy.

HUTTER JR, STEPHEN J; Rahway HS; Rahway, NJ; (Y); French Clb; Science Clb; Var Tennis; French Hon Soc; High Hon Roll; Jr NHS; NHS; Rutgers; Acctng.

HUTTON, HOLLY A; Asbury Park HS; Asbury Park, NJ; (Y); 1/150; Chorus; School Play; Stage Crew; Nwsp Ed-Chief; Nwsp Sprt Ed; Var Capt Sftbl; Elks Awd; High Hon Roll; Kiwanis Awd; Pres NHS; 4 Yr Vrsty Schlr 82-86; Garden ST Dstnghsd Schlr 85-86; Rutgers; Phrmcy.

HUTTON, JEANNETTE; Mother Seton Regional HS; Newark, NJ; (Y); 1/102; Debate Tm; Math Tm; Nwsp Stf; Yrbk Stf; Pres Jr Cls; Pres Stu Cncl; Vllybl; NHS; Ntl Achvt Schlrshp Prgm 85-86; Grdn ST Dstnghsd Schlr 85-86; St Peters Coll Smr Schlr 84; Prnctn U; Engrng.

HUYNH, VAN THUY T; Moorestown HS; Delran, NJ; (Y); French Clb; Moorestown Rotary Clb Scholar 86; Drexel U; Archit Engrng.

HWANG, AMANDA; Parsippany HS; Parsippany, NJ; (Y); Church Yth Grp; VP Sec French Clb; FBLA; Yrbk Stf; Var L Fld Hcky; High Hon Roll; NHS; Ntl Merit SF; GAA; Intnl Clb; Deans Smmr Schlrs Pgm Scholar Rutgers U 86; Montclair ST Coll Acad Tlnted Yng Stu Pgm 83-85; Med.

HWANG, HANS; Watchung Hills Regional HS; Warren, NJ; (Y); Mathletes; Math Tm; SADD; JV Crs Cntry; Var Trk; Hon Roll; Ntl Merit SF; Rutgers Summer Schlrs Prog 86; Future Prblm Slvng Prog Alt ST Bowl 84-86; Jan Stu Of The Month 86.

HWU, PEGGY; Hillsborough HS; Belle Mead, NJ; (Y); 4/350; Church Yth Grp; Cmnty Wkr; Hosp Aide; Concert Band; Jazz Band; Trs Jr Cls; Trs Stu Cncl; Tennis; High Hon Roll; NHS; Brdcstng.

HYATT, CAROLYN; Midland Park HS; Midland Park, NJ; (Y); 72/137; AFS; Cmnty Wkr; Drama Clb; Hosp Aide; Mrchg Band; School Musical; School Play; JV Trk; JV Vllybl; L Wrstlng; Woodward Schlrshp 86; Dean Grant 86; Mst Outstndg Actress 86; Dean JC; Child Studies.

HYLAND, SHERRY; Mahwah HS; Mahwah, NJ; (Y); Church Yth Grp; Sec Ski Clb; Nwsp Stf; Yrbk Stf; Var Trk; JV Capt Vllybl; Hon Roll; Stat Wrstlng; Horse Trainer 79; Horse Back Riding Lessons Vlybl Tm 85-86; Equine Studies.

HYLAND, SUSAN; North Plainfield HS; N Plainfield, NJ; (Y); 19/180; Church Yth Grp; Girl Scts; Hosp Aide; Capt Color Guard; Concert Band; Mrchg Band; JV Var Fld Hcky; Trk; Hon Roll; Band.

HYLAND, VICTORIA; South River HS; S River, NJ; (Y); 1/145; Dance Clb; Library Aide; Spanish Clb; Yrbk Stf; Trk; High Hon Roll; NHS; Rutgers Schlr 86; Girls Citizenshp Inst 86; Schlstc Letter 84-86; Bus.

HYMER, LORI; A P Schalick HS; Newfield, NJ; (Y); 23/133; Hosp Aide; Office Aide; Chorus; Color Guard; Flag Corp; Rep Frsh Cls; Rep Soph Cls; Rep Jr Cls; Stat Bsktbl; Score Keeper; Schlstc Awd In Spnsh I 82-83; Elsie M Mrgn Mem Schlrshp For Pnmnshp 86; Camdon Cnty Coll; Nrsg.

HYSON, SUZANNE; Lower Cape May Regional HS; Erma, NJ; (Y); 1/220; Am Leg Aux Girls St; Band; Concert Band; Mrchg Band; School Musical; Yrbk Stf; High Hon Roll; NHS; Rutgers Schlr 86; Psych.

IACONA, MARLO; The Hun School Of Princeto; Trenton, NJ; (Y); 13/110; Cmnty Wkr; Debate Tm; Drama Clb; Hosp Aide; Spanish Clb; Chorus; School Play; Stage Crew; Nwsp Rptr; Yrbk Stf; Knghts Columbus Merit Awd & Svc 79-85; Knghts Columbus Schlrshp Cncl 86; Carnegie Mellon U; Eng.

IACOVELLI, MICHELLE; Queen Of Peace HS; Lyndhurst, NJ; (S); 3/243; Cmnty Wkr; Hosp Aide; Service Clb; Ski Clb; Nwsp Ed-Chief; VP Sr Cls; Var Bowling; High Hon Roll; Sec NHS; Spanish NHS; Stevens Inst Of Tech; Aerosp.

IANNACO, KAMI; Edgewood Regional SR HS; Waterford, NJ; (Y); French Clb; Varsity Clb; Soph Cls; Jr Cls; VP Sr Cls; JV Var Bsktbl; Im Cheerleading; Stat Socr; JV Var Sftbl; Hon Roll; Cmmnctns.

IANNACONI, LAURA; Passaic Valley HS; Totowa, NJ; (Y); 78/275; GAA; Key Clb; Cheerleading; Fash Merch.

IANNAZZONE, AL; North Bergen HS; North Bergen, NJ; (Y); 40/470; Computer Clb; Yrbk Stf; Rep Sr Cls; JV Bsbl; JV Var Bsktbl; Coach Actv; High Hon Roll; NHS; Italn Hon Soc; Merit Soc; Italn Clb.

IANNEILLO, ANDREA L; Kearny HS; Kearny, NJ; (Y); 145/375; Pres FBLA; Ski Clb; Cheerleading; Powder Puff Ftbl; Socr; Sftbl; High Hon Roll; Hon Roll; Kean Coll; Bus Mgmt.

IANNUZZI, MICHELE; Holy Cross HS; Delran, NJ; (Y); 132/347; Dance Clb; Ski Clb; Stage Crew; Yrbk Stf; Mgr(s); Score Keeper; JV Tennis; Trk; High Hon Roll; Hon Roll; Bus.

IATAROLA, STEPHEN A; Paul VI HS; Blackwood, NJ; (S); 59/473; Church Yth Grp; Debate Tm; ROTC; SADD; Variety Show; Nwsp Stf; Pres Sr Cls; NHS; Ntl Merit Ltr; St Josephs U; Law.

IAZZETTA, ROSEMARIE; Holy Family Acad; Bayonne, NJ; (Y); Dance Clb; Yrbk Rptr; Yrbk Stf; JV Cheerleading; High Hon Roll; Hon Roll; NHS; Prfct Atten Awd; Law.

IBANEZ, ISMENIA; Union Hill HS; Union City, NJ; (Y); Math Clb; Spanish Clb; Chorus; Sftbl; Trk; Vllybl; Hon Roll; Jr NHS; Mu Alp Tht; NHS; Vllybl Chmps 86; NJIT; Cmptr Sci.

IBAY, ARSENIO; Dwight Morrow HS; Englewood, NJ; (Y); 10/247; Math Clb; Math Tm; Lit Mag.

IBITOYE, DAVID; Dwight Marrow HS; Englewood, NJ; (Y); 4/247; Church Yth Grp; Hosp Aide; Math Tm; Chorus; Church Choir; High Hon Roll; NHS; Ntl Merit Ltr; Prfct Atten Awd; Vol John Harms Theater Englwd 83-84; Chrch Bd Comm 85; AJY Pianist Chrch 86; Bio.

ICKIAN, SUSAN; Holy Family Acad; Bayonne, NJ; (Y); 15/137; Cmnty Wkr; French Clb; Math Clb; Nwsp Stf; Yrbk Stf; Im Bsktbl; VP Swmmng; Trk; High Hon Roll; Hon Roll; Bio Awd Hghst Avg 84-85; 3rd Pl Hdsn Cnty Athltc Assn Swmmg & Dvng Chmpnshps 85; Pre-Law.

IDELBERGER, ANNE-MARIE; West Essex HS; Roseland, NJ; (Y); 122/350; Church Yth Grp; Cmnty Wkr; FTA; Hosp Aide; Office Aide; Hon Roll; Actng Brgh Crk Admnstr Rslnd 86; Hsptl Aide 150 Vlntr Hrs 86; Hnrs Stngrphy Bus Educ 86; Montclair ST Coll; Accntng.

IDICULA, ANITA; Matawan Regional HS; Matawan, NJ; (S); 21/273; Church Yth Grp; French Clb; Math Tm; Yrbk Stf; Off Stu Cncl; Crs Cntry; French Hon Soc; High Hon Roll; NHS; Grdn ST Schlr 85; Med.

IERONIMO, ANTHONY; Christian Brothers Acad; W Long Branch, NJ; (Y); 6/224; Church Yth Grp; Nwsp Rptr; Im Sftbl; High Hon Roll; Pre-Law.

IGLESIAS, JOSE; Kearny HS; Kearny, NJ; (Y); Am Leg Boys St; Cmnty Wkr; Intnl Clb; Math Tm; Rep Jr Cls; Var Swmmng; High Hon Roll; NHS; Spanish NHS; Hon Guard 85; Principals Hon Roll 83; Natl Sci Olympiad Chemistry 86.

IHASZ, ELIZABETH; Phillipsburg HS; Alpha, NJ; (Y); 30/370; Key Clb; Church Choir; High Hon Roll; Hon Roll; Jr NHS; NHS; Elem Educ.

ILAO, EDEN; Frank H Morrell HS; Irvington, NJ; (Y); Church Yth Grp; Girl Scts; Church Choir; Tennis; High Hon Roll; Hon Roll; NHS.

ILARDI, VANESSA; Mount Saint Dominic Acad; N Caldwell, NJ; (Y); Church Yth Grp; Library Aide; Ski Clb; Spanish Clb; Var Crs Cntry; Var Trk.

ILES, GILBERT; St Peters Prep; Nutley, NJ; (Y); Church Yth Grp; Debate Tm; Hosp Aide; Ski Clb; Mgr(s); Hon Roll; Atty.

ILIFF, ANDREW; Newton HS; Newton, NJ; (Y); 27/210; Am Leg Boys St; Boy Scts; Chorus; Variety Show; Sr Cls; Stu Cncl; Ftbl; Trk; Wrstlng; Cit Awd; Stu Athlete 84; ST Champ Wrestlng 86; Mech Engr.

ILJAS, DAVID; James Caldwell HS; W Caldwell, NJ; (Y); Concert Band; Mrchg Band; Orch; Tennis; Fairleigh Dickinson U; Comp Eng.

ILLY, WALTER; St Peters Prep; Jersey City, NJ; (Y); 35/206; German Clb; Stage Crew; Var Crs Cntry; Var Trk; High Hon Roll; Hon Roll; Pre Law.

ILNSEHER, MICHAEL; Toms River High School South; Toms River, NJ; (Y); 22/314; Am Leg Boys St; Var Swmmng; High Hon Roll; Hon Roll; NHS.

IMBALZANO, MICHELLE; Washington Township HS; Turnersville, NJ; (Y); 4/475; Exploring; French Clb; Hosp Aide; Rep Stu Cncl; Hon Roll; NHS; Rotary Awd; Jos Duke Schlrshp 86; Rtry Yth Ldrshp Awd 85; Amer Chem Soc Chem Awd 86; Franklin & Mary Coll; Bio.

IMBROGNO, MICHELE; Ramapo HS; Franklin Lakes, NJ; (Y); 49/327; Spanish Clb; Drm & Bgl; Mrchg Band; High Hon Roll; Hon Roll; Cert Merit Eng I & Hstry 83-84; Cert Merit Typng I & Engl II 84-85; Cert Merit US Hstry I 85-86; Bus Admin.

IMMENDORF, CHARLES; Burlington Twp HS; Burlington, NJ; (Y); 2/110; Math Clb; Nwsp Rptr; JV Bsbl; Var Wrstlng; NHS; Engrng.

INCARVITO, DOROTHY; Bishop Eustace Preparatory Schl; Delran, NJ; (Y); 5/177; Am Leg Aux Girls St; Hosp Aide; VP Pep Clb; Var Bowling; Sftbl; High Hon Roll; NHS; Math Clb; Spanish Clb; Stage Crew; Band Dir Awd 83; Chem.

INCORVAIA, DENISE; Hopewell Valley Central HS; Hopewell, NJ; (Y); 23/202; Chorus; Lit Mag; Rep Soph Cls; Trs Soph Cls; Rep Jr Cls; Sec Sr Cls; Lcrss; High Hon Roll; NHS; Prfct Atten Awd; Comm.

INDERBITZEN, ROBERT J; Christian Brothers Acad; New Fairfield, CT; (Y); 16/230; Art Clb; Math Tm; Yrbk Rptr; Ed Yrbk Stf; High Hon Roll; Hon Roll; Yrbk Editor Achvt Awd 86; Elect Engr.

INDICK, MICHELLE; Bruriah H S For Girls; Elizabeth, NJ; (Y); Yrbk Stf; Lit Mag; NHS; NEDT Awd; Bus Admin.

INDICO, SANDY; Cumberland Regional HS; Bridgeton, NJ; (S); 12/384; Church Yth Grp; Drama Clb; Intnl Clb; Soroptimist; Stage Crew; JV Fld Hcky; JV Sftbl; Var Swmmng; High Hon Roll; Sec NHS; Phys Ther.

INFANTE, FRANCINE; Howell HS; Farmingdale, NJ; (Y); Nwsp Stf; Yrbk Ed-Chief; Ed Lit Mag; Var Socr; Rcvd The Hghst Lvl Of Rcgntn In NJ Teen Arts Comp 86; Holocaust Fstvl 86; Scndry Edu.

INGARO, MONICA; Roselle Catholic HS; Union, NJ; (S); 32/205; Ski Clb; Stage Crew; Var Trk; Hon Roll; Prcfncy Spnsh Awd 85; Rutgers; Nrsng.

INGERSOLL, LYNDA; Lower Cape May Regional HS; Cape May, NJ; (Y); 26/256; Computer Clb; Key Clb; Band; Concert Band; Mrchg Band; Yrbk Stf; Bsktbl; Hon Roll; NHS; Rotary Awd; Yrbk Sr Sectn Edtr 85-86; Wmns Repblcn Clb Awd 86; Trenton ST Coll; Elem Ed.

INGRAM, SANDY; Triton Regional HS; Blackwood, NJ; (Y); 19/294; Office Aide; VP Jr Cls; Rep Stu Cncl; Var Cheerleading; Im Coach Actv; JV Crs Cntry; Powder Puff Ftbl; Var Trk; Hon Roll; NHS.

INMAN, ELISABETH; Newton HS; Newton, NJ; (Y); 2/195; 4-H; German Clb; Math Tm; Scholastic Bowl; Science Clb; Chorus; Lit Mag; NHS; Sal; Natl Merit Fnlst 86; Johns Hopkins U; Bio.

INNELLA, CATHERINE; Pascack Valley HS; Hillsdale, NJ; (Y); Debate Tm; Drama Clb; 4-H; ROTC; School Play; Cheerleading; 4-H Awd; Physcs.

INNIS, SHIRLEY; Pennsville Memorial HS; Pennsville, NJ; (Y); 13/235; Hosp Aide; School Play; Rep Frsh Cls; Rep Soph Cls; Rep Jr Cls; Rep Sr Cls; Sec Stu Cncl; JV Fld Hcky; Sec NHS; Gvnrs Sch Cnty Fnlst 85; Ctzn Of Mnth 85; VA Polytech Inst; Psych.

INSABELLA, GLENDA M; Union Catholic Regional HS; Fanwood, NJ; (Y); 2/339; Math Tm; Service Clb; Nwsp Rptr; Socr; French Hon Soc; High Hon Roll; NHS; Ntl Merit Ltr; Sal; St Schlr; Wesleyan U; Psych.

INSANA, PHYLLIS; Wood-Ridge HS; Wood-Ridge, NJ; (S); 10/76; Service Clb; Spanish Clb; Lit Mag; Var Cheerleading; Hon Roll; NHS; Fshn.

INSOGNA, CHRISTINE; Bishop Ahr HS; Edison, NJ; (Y); Ski Clb; Drill Tm; Glassboro Coll; Cmmnctns.

INTESO, MICHAEL; Toms River HS East; Toms River, NJ; (Y); Church Yth Grp; Pres Ski Clb; Stage Crew; Rep Stu Cncl; Var Co-Capt Ftbl; Wrstlng; High Hon Roll; Hon Roll; Trs NHS; Phil Cittadino Awd 86; Pop Warner Outstndng Lnmn Awd 86; Tr NHS Schlrshp 86; VA Military Inst; Cvl Engr.

INTRIERI, SANDRA; Mary Help Of Christians Acad; Paterson, NJ; (Y); 14/88; Church Yth Grp; Computer Clb; GAA; Hosp Aide; Letterman Clb; Service Clb; Varsity Clb; Chorus; School Musical; Yrbk Stf; Seton Hall U; Nrsng.

IORI, LORENA; Vineland HS; Vineland, NJ; (Y); 41/803; Hosp Aide; Intnl Clb; Church Choir; Nrsng.

IOVANNICCI, CHRISTINE; Holy Cross HS; Medford, NJ; (Y); 75/393; French Clb; Nwsp Sprt Ed; Yrbk Stf; Rep Jr Cls; JV Trk; Hon Roll; School Musical; Nwsp Rptr; Rep Frsh Cls; Ntl Merit Schol; Pres Interact 86; Psychol.

IOVINO, THOMAS K; De Paul Diocesan HS; Bloomingdale, NJ; (Y); 39/164; Am Leg Boys St; Aud/Vis; Church Yth Grp; School Play; Stage Crew; Nwsp Rptr; Nwsp Stf; High Hon Roll; Hon Roll; Hofstra U; Jrnlsm.

IPPOLITO, JOANN; Bridgewater Raritan West HS; Bridgewater, NJ; (Y); Computer Clb; 4-H; Hosp Aide; Key Clb; OEA; Ski Clb; Varsity Clb; Bsktbl; Var L Bowling; Powder Puff Ftbl; Cntrl Jersey Div Bwlng Champs 85-86; 4-H Fair Dog Clb Trph 83-84; County Coll; Bus.

IPPOLITTO, DARA LEE; Toms River East; Toms River, NJ; (Y); Church Yth Grp; FBLA; OEA; Cheerleading; Gym; Powder Puff Ftbl; Tennis; Trk; Hon Roll; Outstndng Achvt-Typing II 85-86; Outstndng Achvt-Steno II 85-86; FBLA 85-86; Tayler Bus Inst; Legal Secy.

IRACA, KEVIN; Hamilton High West; Trenton, NJ; (Y); 69/364; Key Clb; Political Wkr; Band; Jazz Band; Mrchg Band; Orch; School Musical; Stage Crew; Symp Band; Off Sr Cls; Natl Wind Band 85-86; Boston Coll; Pre-Law.

IRELAN, MICHELLE; Pennsville Memorial HS; Pennsville, NJ; (Y); Color Guard; Concert Band; Drm Mjr(t); Jazz Band; Mrchg Band; Orch; School Musical; Rep Frsh Cls; Rep Soph Cls; JP Sousa Awd; Mrchg Band Rookie Of Yr 82-83; U DE; Bio.

IRELAN, STEPHANIE; Freehold Township HS; Freehold, NJ; (Y); Church Yth Grp; Band; Church Choir; Concert Band; Jazz Band; Mrchg Band; Sftbl; Trk; Peer Choice Awd Concert Band 84; Psych.

IRELAND, PATTI; Egg Harbor Twp HS; Mays Landing, NJ; (S); 22/266; Girl Scts; SADD; Yrbk Bus Mgr; Yrbk Ed-Chief; Fld Hcky; Mgr(s); Swmmng; Cit Awd; NHS; Atlantic CC; Exec Secy.

ISAACS, SUSAN; Hillside HS; Hillside, NJ; (Y); Girl Scts; Pres Service Clb; Ski Clb; Yrbk Stf; Var L Socr; Hon Roll; Early Chldhd Ed.

ISAJIW, TAMARA; Kittatinny Regional HS; Newton, NJ; (Y); 37/228; 4-H; Hosp Aide; Band; Concert Band; Mrchg Band; VP Jr Cls; JV Crs Cntry; JV Fld Hcky; JV Swmmng; JV Trk; Grls Ctznshp Awd 86; Htl & Rest Mngmnt.

ISAKOFF, STEVEN; Highland Park HS; Highland Park, NJ; (Y); 1/148; Mathletes; Political Wkr; Science Clb; Nwsp Rptr; Yrbk Stf; Pres Stu Cncl; Var Bsktbll; NHS; Math Tm; Radio Clb; Rutgers Schlr 86-87; Johns Hopkins Tlnt Srch 83; Congrssnl Intrn Cong Robert Torecelli WA DC 86; Mth.

ISIDRO, MARY ROSE B; Parsippany HS; Boonton, NJ; (Y); Art Clb; Cmnty Wkr; French Clb; FBLA; Intnl Clb; Band; Chorus; School Musical; School Play; Stage Crew; Natl Art Hnr Soc 86; Pres Natl Art Hnr Soc Chptr 86-87; Bus Mgmt.

ISRAEL, GARY M; East Brunswick HS; East Brunswick, NJ; (Y); Key Clb; Letterman Clb; Ski Clb; Varsity Clb; Im Bsktbl; Var Socr; JV Tennis; Im Vllybl; Hon Roll; SUNY Binghamton; Pre-Med.

ISRAEL, TIFFANY; Egg Harbor Township HS; W Atlantic City, NJ; (S); 5/317; French Clb; Key Clb; Model UN; Trs Soph Cls; Rep Jr Cls; Rep Stu Cncl; Var Cheerleading; High Hon Roll; Juvnl Conf Cmmttee 85-86; Stu Ldrshp Smnr-Bill Bradley 86; Law.

ISRANI, AJAY; Montville Township HS; Montville, NJ; (Y); Cmnty Wkr; FBLA; Key Clb; Nwsp Ed-Chief; JV Trk; High Hon Roll; Hon Roll; NHS; Math Clb; Science Clb; 4th Pl Hnrs FBLA ST Comptn 85-86; Cert Of Apprctn-Key Clb 85-86.

IULIANO, LUCIA; Garden State Acad; Parrotsville, TN; (Y); Church Yth Grp; Library Aide; Ski Clb; Gym; Hon Roll; Nrsng.

IVESON, DAVID; Arthur P Schalick HS; Elmer, NJ; (Y); 7/68; Library Aide; L Golf; Hon Roll; NHS; Comp Prog.

IVINS, DULCEY; Lakewood HS; Lakewood, NJ; (Y); 90/258; FBLA; Latin Clb; Waynesburg Coll; Geolgst.

IZQUIERDU, MARISOL; Emerson HS; Union City, NJ; (Y); Spanish Clb; Cit Awd; Prfct Atten Awd.

IZZI, ANNMARIE; B R HS East; Bridgewater, NJ; (Y); Art Clb; English Clb; French Clb; Ski Clb; SADD; Stu Cncl; Powder Puff Ftbl; Score Keeper; Hon Roll; Prfct Atten Awd; Prom Chrprsn 86; Art Therapy.

IZZO, ANTHONY; Wall HS; Wall, NJ; (Y); 11/250; Boy Scts; VP Exploring; JCL; Latin Clb; High Hon Roll; Hon Roll; Kiwanis Awd; Ntl Merit Ltr; St Schlr; Stevens Almni Rgnl Schlrshp 86; Stvns Inst Of Tech; Eltrcl Engr.

JABLOW, LEON; St Peters Prep HS; Jersey City, NJ; (Y); 6/200; Mgr Aud/Vis; Chrmn Dance Clb; Var L Drama Clb; French Clb; Pep Clb; School Play; Stage Crew; Var L Swmmng; High Hon Roll; Pres Schlr; Mag Cum Laude Ltn I, Gld Ltn I 83-84; Slvr Mdl Engl, Amer Lit 84-85; Engrng.

JACHNA, BOZENA; Parsippany HS; Parsippany, NJ; (Y); Sec Church Yth Grp; Sec French Clb; Ski Clb; Concert Band; Mrchg Band; Variety Show; Lit Mag; Tennis; NHS; Girls St 86; Chem.

JACIK, TRACY; Rahway HS; Rahway, NJ; (Y); NHS; Muhlenberg Schl Of Nrsg; Matrnl.

JACKIEWICZ, LISA; Roselle Catholic HS; Roselle, NJ; (S); GAA; Girl Scts; Ski Clb; Spanish Clb; Acpl Chr; Var Sftbl; High Hon Roll; NHS; Spanish NHS; Yng Cmnty Ldrs Of Amer 86; Sbrbn Nwspr Orgnl Shrt Stry 2nd Pl Awd 83.

JACKO, VALERIE; Highland Regional HS; Chews Landing, NJ; (S); 31/332; FTA; German Clb; Stu Cncl; Stat Swmmng; Corprt Fiance.

JACKOWSKI, CHRISTINE T; Lower Cape May Regional HS; Bennington, VT; (Y); Political Wkr; Thesps; School Play; Nwsp Bus Mgr; Nwsp Ed-Chief; Nwsp Phtg; Nwsp Rptr; Nwsp Stf; Lit Mag; Hon Roll; Eagly Acceptnc & Admssn Bennington Coll 85; Legal Soc Awd 85; Temple U Stu Pres Awd 83; Bennington Coll; Law.

JACKSON, DAWN MICHELLE; Toms River South HS; Toms River, NJ; (Y); 37/360; OEA; High Hon Roll; Hon Roll; NHS; Ntl Merit Ltr; Prfct Atten Awd; Crtfct Achvmnt Accntng 85; COE; Bus.

JACKSON, ELISHEBA; Neptune SR HS; Neptune, NJ; (Y); 10/25; Church Yth Grp; Computer Clb; Drama Clb; Exploring; GAA; Temple Yth Grp; Chorus; Church Choir; Drill Tm; School Play; Perf Attndnc Awd 83; Mgr Trck Tm Awd 85; Hnr Rl Awd 84; U Dayton; Comp Sci.

JACKSON, ERIC C; Life Center Acad; Willingboro, NJ; (Y); Chess Clb; Jazz Band; Stage Crew; Trs Sr Cls; Capt Var Bsbl; Capt Var Bsktbl; Capt Var Socr; Ntl Merit Schol; Mst Valuable Athlete Of Schl 84-85; I Dare You Awd 85; Elec Engnrng.

JACKSON, HILLARY; West Windsor-Plainsboro HS; Princeton Jct, NJ; (Y); 32/232; NHS; NJ Gvrnrs Arts/Dance Educ Awd 86; Bllt Mrt Awd 86; Pro Dancer.

JACKSON, KEITH R; Teaneck HS; Teaneck, NJ; (Y); 179/420; Church Yth Grp; Computer Clb; FHA; Yrbk Stf; Var Trk; Natl Merit Commended Stu 86; Carnegie-Mellon Scholar 85; NAACP Yth Grp 85-86; Comp Engrng.

JACKSON, KRISTEN; Bridgewater-Raritan HS; Bridgewater, NJ; (Y); Spanish Clb; SADD; Powder Puff Ftbl; Socr; Spnsh Educ.

JACKSON, KURTISS; Plainfield HS; Plainfield, NJ; (Y); Art Clb; Chess Clb; Church Yth Grp; Pres Computer Clb; Exploring; Quiz Bowl; Scholastic Bowl; Church Choir; NHS; Ntl Merit Schol; Sci Resrch 85-86; Sci Sympsm 85-86; Drake Hse Museum Comm Svc Awd 83-84; Rutgers U; Psychlgy.

JACKSON, MARGARET; Garden State Acad; Blairstown, NJ; (Y); Office Aide; Band; School Play; Variety Show; Sec Soph Cls; Var Bsktbl; Gym; Capt Sftbl; Vllybl; High Hon Roll; Schlrshp Columbia Union Coll, Acdmc/Ldrshp Bsktbl 86; Columbia Union Coll; Med Tech.

JACKSON, MARGARET E; Wildwood Catholic HS; N Wildwood, NJ; (Y); 5/89; Exploring; French Clb; Hosp Aide; JV Tennis; Im Vllybl; French Hon Soc; Hon Roll; NHS; Stockton Sci Fair Awd 3rd Pl 83, 2nd Pl 84, Hnrbl Mntn 86; York Coll; Sci.

JACKSON, MARRISSA; Mother Seton Regional HS; Newark, NJ; (Y); 13/92; Church Yth Grp; Debate Tm; JA; Rep Frsh Cls; Rep Soph Cls; Rep Jr Cls; Trs Sr Cls; Rep Stu Cncl; Hon Roll; Lamanda Kappa Mu Sorority 86; Duquesne U; Pharm.

JACKSON, MAUREEN; Nor Val Reg HS; Norwood, NJ; (Y); 10/187; AFS; Church Yth Grp; School Play; Yrbk Ed-Chief; Yrbk Stf; High Hon Roll; Hon Roll; NHS; Engr.

JACKSON, MICHELLE S; New Brunswick HS; New Brunswick, NJ; (Y); 16/123; Church Yth Grp; Library Aide; Pep Clb; Y-Teens; Co-Capt Color Guard; Flag Corp; Stu Cncl; Trk; Hon Roll; Prfct Atten Awd; Hall Educ Fnd Schlrshp 86; Prnt Tchr Assoc Awd 86; Fairleigh Dickinson U; Dntl Hyg.

JACKSON, ROBERT F; The Lawrenceville Sch; Bronx, NY; (Y); Nwsp Stf; VP Sr Cls; Var Bsbl; Var Bsktbl; Var Ftbl; Bus.

JACKSON, SCOTT; Scotch Plains-Fanwood HS; Scotch Pl, NJ; (Y); Boy Scts; Chrmn Church Yth Grp; Concert Band; Jazz Band; Mrchg Band; Symp Band; JV Socr; Var L Trk; Im Vllybl; Cit Awd; Stu Ldrshp Conf 85-86; Vly Forge Conf Schrlshp 86; Discovery Smmr Sci Pgm 86; Engrng.

JACKSON, SHERRY LYNN; Manchester Township HS; Toms River, NJ; (Y); 14/198; Am Leg Aux Girls St; Church Yth Grp; Spanish Clb; Church Choir; Var L Fld Hcky; Var L Trk; Cit Awd; NHS; Rotary Awd; Voice Dem Awd; Trenton ST Coll.

JACKSON, TRACEY LYNN; Hackensack HS; Hackensack, NJ; (Y); Pep Clb; Acpl Chr; Color Guard; Drm & Bgl; Elks Awd; Hon Roll; Hampton Inst; Bus Adm.

JACKSON, TRACY; Orange HS; Orange, NJ; (Y); FBLA; Color Guard; Mrchg Band; Rep Frsh Cls; Sec Soph Cls; Sec Rep Jr Cls; Hon Roll; U Of Daton; Pre-Law.

JACKSON, WILLIAM; Manchester Twp HS; Lakehurst, NJ; (Y); Computer Clb; Debate Tm; Drama Clb; FBLA; Hosp Aide; JA; Library Aide; PAVAS; Speech Tm; Acpl Chr; Harvard U; Engl Prfssr.

JACOBI, ELLEN; Red Bank Regional HS; Little Silver, NJ; (Y); Math Tm; Ski Clb; School Play; Rep Stu Cncl; Stat Socr; Stat Swmmng; Hon Roll; Lehigh U; Busnss.

JACOBS, ANTHONY; Bridgeton SR HS; Bridgeton, NJ; (Y); JA; PAVAS; Church Choir; Art Awd 85-86; Lincln Tech; Art Drftng.

JACOBS, BRUCE; East Brunswick HS; East Brunswick, NJ; (Y); Debate Tm; Model UN; Temple Yth Grp; Varsity Clb; Im Bsbl; Im Ice Hcky; Var L Wrstlng; Hon Roll; Wrstlng Coaches Awd 86; Ntl Hnr Roll Soc 85-86; Carnegie-Mellon U; Law.

JACOBS, CHRIS; Clayton HS; Clayton, NJ; (Y); Boy Scts; Camera Clb; Cmnty Wkr; DECA; VICA; Yrbk Phtg; Prfct Atten Awd; Trustee Clytn Vlntr Amblnc Corps 83-86; Grphc Arts.

JACOBS, GAIL; Clifton HS; Clifton, NJ; (Y); 96/697; Ski Clb; Spanish Clb; Tennis; Vllybl; Jr NHS; Lawyer.

JACOBS, KATHI; Edgewood Regional SR HS; Sicklerville, NJ; (Y); Hosp Aide; Yrbk Ed-Chief; Fld Hcky; Hon Roll; Jr NHS; NHS; VFW Awd; Voice Dem Awd; Pblc Rltns.

JACOBS, KELLY; Hamilton High Schl East; Mercerville, NJ; (Y); 69/320; AFS; Cmnty Wkr; Exploring; GAA; Hosp Aide; Red Cross Aide; Varsity Clb; Var Capt Socr; Cit Awd; Hon Roll; Douglas Clg; Acctg.

JACOBS, MICHAEL; Washington Township HS; Turnersville, NJ; (Y); Model UN; High Hon Roll; Prfct Atten Awd; Rutgers; Math.

JACOBS, ROBERTA; Parsippany HS; Parsippany, NJ; (Y); Church Yth Grp; FBLA; German Clb; Girl Scts; Chorus; Var JV Sftbl; Hon Roll; Acctg.

JACOBSEN, DONNA; Pascack Hills HS; Montvale, NJ; (Y); 84/261; Church Yth Grp; Drama Clb; Thesps; Chorus; Church Choir; School Musical; School Play; Variety Show; Rep Frsh Cls; Socr; Jody Ann Duncan Schlrshp 86; Messiah Coll; Cmmnctns.

JACOBSON, JENNY; Riverdell Regional HS; River Edge, NJ; (Y); 18/214; Am Leg Aux Girls St; Ski Clb; SADD; Nwsp Stf; Var Capt Tennis; Var Capt Trk; NHS; Varsity Clb; Chorus; School Musical; Excel Bio 86; Trck Merit Schlrshp 86; Mst Outstndng Girl Athlt 86; Lehigh U; Frgn Crrs.

JACOBSON, KAREN; Teaneck HS; Teaneck, NJ; (Y); SADD; Temple Yth Grp; Yrbk Stf; L Mgr Bsbl; Mgr(s); L Mgr Tennis; Hon Roll; Business.

JACOBSON, KATHLEEN; Secaucus HS; Secaucus, NJ; (S); 14/160; Math Clb; Varsity Clb; Crs Cntry; Trk; French Hon Soc; High Hon Roll; NHS; 2nd Tm Bergen Cnty Schltc Leag 84-85; 3rd Tm Hudson Cnty Crss Cntry 85; Psychlgy.

JACOBSON, KRISTINE; Burlington City HS; Edgewater Pk, NJ; (Y); Church Yth Grp; Concert Band; Jazz Band; Mrchg Band; Rep Stu Cncl; Var L Fld Hcky; Hon Roll; NHS; Rotary Awd; Chem Engrng.

JACOBUS, JACQUELINE; Belleville HS; Belleville, NJ; (Y); Trs Pep Clb; Chorus; Mrchg Band; Stage Crew; Rep Frsh Cls; Rep Jr Cls; Trk; Belleville Pblc Libry Pctr Bk Cntst; Rutgers U; Chem Lab Tech.

JACOBY, BRIAN; Manalapan HS; Manalapan, NJ; (Y); Concert Band; Mrchg Band; Rep Sr Cls; Var Bsktbl; JV Crs Cntry; JV Trk; Htl Mgmt.

JACOBY, NATALIE G; Solman Schechter Day Schl; West Orange, NJ; (Y); Drama Clb; Nwsp Bus Mgr; Yrbk Stf; Rep Frsh Cls; Rep Soph Cls; Jr Cls; NHS; Hon Volunteer Wrk Harlene Vly Mntl 85; Law.

JACOBY, STACEY; Kittatinny Regional HS; Newton, NJ; (Y); Am Leg Aux Girls St; Debate Tm; Chorus; Nwsp Stf; Pres Jr Cls; JV Fld Hcky; Stat Trk; Boston U; Pre Law.

JACOWITZ, KAREN; East Brunswick HS; E Brunswick, NJ; (Y); Key Clb; Math Clb; SADD; VP Mrchg Band; NHS; Ntl Merit Ltr; St Schlr; Concert Band; School Musical; French Hon Soc; John Bodnar Memrl Awd 86; Band Bstrs Schlrshp 86; Unitd Food-Cmrcl Wrkrs Lcl 1262 Schlrshp 86; Cornell U; Math.

JADWINSKI, STAN J; Sayreville War Memorial HS; Parlin, NJ; (Y); 9/381; Church Yth Grp; Intnl Clb; Scholastic Bowl; Science Clb; Concert Band; Mrchg Band; Stage Crew; Yrbk Ed-Chief; God Cntry Awd; Gov Hon Prg Awd; Olmpcs Of Mnd 86; Govs Sch Sci 85; Pres Acad Achvt Awd 86; Stevens Inst Of Tech; Engrng.

JAEGER, JASON K; Pennsville Memorial HS; Pennsville, NJ; (Y); Am Leg Boys St; Ski Clb; Sec Stu Cncl; Var Capt Crs Cntry; Var Trk; Var Wrstlng; Grmn Exch Stdnt 85.

JAIN, SUSHIL; Parsippany Hills HS; Parsippany, NJ; (Y); 1/360; Key Clb; Var L Tennis; NHS; Am Leg Boys St; Computer Clb; Math Tm; Science Clb; Stu Cncl; Socr; High Hon Roll; NJ Govrs Schl Of Sci 86; AHSME Amer Math Lge Hnr Roll 86; Med.

JAJAL, SANJAY; W L Dickinson HS; Jersey City, NJ; (Y); Art Clb; Chess Clb; Mathletes; Math Clb; Off Sr Cls; Badmtn; Ftbl; Vllybl; Hon Roll; Prfct Atten Awd; Indian Clb 85-86; NJ Inst Of Tech; Electnc Engr.

JAKES, GREGORY; Woodrow Wilson HS; Camden, NJ; (Y); Drama Clb; PAVAS; Chorus; School Musical; Yrbk Rptr; Off Soph Cls; Crs Cntry; Hon Roll.

JAKUB, JAMES; Red Bank Catholic HS; Eatontown, NJ; (Y); Church Yth Grp; JV Var Bsbl; JV Var Wrstlng; Mary Carmody Fndtn Schlrshp 86; Mst Impvd Varsity Wrstlr 85-86; Red Bank Catholic Lifting Cntst 1st Pl; Engrng.

JAKUBOWYC, SUSAN; Bishop George Ahr HS; Carteret, NJ; (Y); Spanish Clb; Score Keeper; JV Socr; High Hon Roll; Excellence Schlrshp Cert Awd 85-86; Rutgers U.

JAMES, BERSHIRIA; Weequahic HS; Newark, NJ; (Y); 42/400; Church Yth Grp; Drill Tm; Variety Show; Hon Roll; Accounting.

JAMES, BETH; Cherry Hill HS West; Cherry Hl, NJ; (Y); Church Yth Grp; 4-H; Office Aide; Teachers Aide; Varsity Clb; Rep Soph Cls; Var Cheerleading; Var Capt Gym; Trk; 4-H Awd; Home & Schl Assoc Awd 84-86; Temple U; Bio.

JAMES, DANYELLE; Rahway HS; Rahway, NJ; (Y); Am Leg Aux Girls St; Office Aide; Teachers Aide; Nwsp Stf; Off Stu Cncl; JV Var Cheerleading; Trk; Hon Roll; Hnr Roll Awd; Hampton U; Law.

JAMES, JACK; Wayne Valley HS; Wayne, NJ; (Y); CAP; Computer Clb; FBLA; Pres German Clb; Model UN; Political Wkr; Nwsp Rptr; Capt Crs Cntry; Var Trk; Most Vlbl Runnr Crss Cntry 85; All Conf Crss Cntry 85; All Cnty Crss Cntry 85; Offcr.

JAMES, KATHRYN; Our Lady Of Mercy Acad; Richland, NJ; (Y); 9/25; Spanish Clb; Chorus; Nwsp Rptr; VP Sr Cls; Var Capt Cheerleading; Hon Roll; Sister Marie Pierre Mem Schlrshp 86; Acad All Am Awd 86; Barry U; Med.

JAMES, KENNETH; Central HS; Newark, NJ; (Y); Yrbk Sprt Ed; Yrbk Stf; Pres Jr Cls; Var Bsbl; High Hon Roll; Hon Roll; Ntl Merit SF; Pepsi Stu Mnth 86; Mth & Sci Awd Rensselaer Polytech Inst 86; Savings Bond 83; Comp Sci.

JAMES, SHANNON R; Paterson Catholic HS; Paterson, NJ; (Y); 29/100; Church Yth Grp; Computer Clb; FBLA; Pep Clb; SADD; Chorus; Church Choir; Pep Band; Yrbk Stf; Jr Cls; Felician Coll; Nrsng.

JAMES, SHERONIA; E Orange HS; E Orange, NJ; (S); 82/410; Church Yth Grp; Acpl Chr; Chorus; Church Choir; Variety Show; Yrbk Sprt Ed; Rep Stu Cncl; Hon Roll; Cls Homecmng Qn 84-85; Early Chldhd Eductn.

JAMES, SHERWIN; Dover HS; Dover, NJ; (Y); 2/183; Computer Clb; Math Tm; Yrbk Stf; Trs Stu Cncl; High Hon Roll; NHS; Prfct Atten Awd; Rensselear Mth/Sci Awd 86; Rogate Critcl Issues Pgm 85; AT&T Bell Labs Summr Sci Pgm 83 & 84; RIT; Comp Sci.

JAMES, TYRONE; Sacred Heart HS; Clayton, NJ; (Y); 17/71; Spanish Clb; Varsity Clb; Rep Stu Cncl; JV Bsktbl; Var Socr; Var Tennis; 2nd Hnrs 84-85; Rotary 86; Drexel; Chem Engrng.

JAMES, VENICE; Camden HS; Camden, NJ; (S); 6/408; DECA; JA; Latin Clb; Library Aide; Teachers Aide; Nwsp Ed-Chief; Nwsp Rptr; Nwsp Stf; Lit Mag; High Hon Roll; Temple U; Cmmnctns.

JAMISON, RICHARD W; J K O Vo Tech; Browns Mills, NJ; (S); #6 In Class; Radio Clb; VICA; Bowling; Hon Roll; Prfct Atten Awd.

JAMPOL, MICHAEL; Middletown High School South; Middletown, NJ; (S); 9/436; Exploring; Math Tm; Capt Science Clb; Lit Mag; Var Socr; Var Capt Swmmng; Var Trk; High Hon Roll; Hon Roll; Ntl Merit Ltr; Pre-Med.

JANCOLA, JEANNETTE; Mt St Mary Acad; Englishtown, NJ; (Y); 19/83; GAA; Key Clb; Ed Yrbk Phtg; Yrbk Sprt Ed; VP Soph Cls; Rep Stu Cncl; Hon Roll; NHS; Mathletes; Prep Clb; Awd Ldrhsp Campus Ministry 86; US Presdntl Acadmc Ftnss Awd 86; Outstndng Achvt Bio 86; Siena Coll; Pre-Med.

JANECZEK, SUSAN; East Brunswick HS; E Brunswick, NJ; (Y); Dance Clb; Hosp Aide; Key Clb; Latin Clb; Math Clb; Pep Clb; Chorus; Hon Roll; NHS; Medicine.

JANISHESKI, JEFFREY; Don Basco Prep; Ramsey, NJ; (S); 7/189; Math Clb; Model UN; Ski Clb; Ed Lit Mag; Var Wrstlng; Hon Roll; NHS; Acad All Amer Awd 86; Art Awd 84; Psychlgy.

JANKOWSKI, CHRISTINE; Brick Township HS; Brick Town, NJ; (Y); Teachers Aide; High Hon Roll; Hon Roll; NHS; Prfct Atten Awd; Johnson & Wales; Fshn Mdse.

JANNS, CATHERINE; Spotswood HS; Spotswood, NJ; (S); 1/189; Math Clb; Science Clb; Yrbk Stf; Socr; Sftbl; Tennis; Trk; High Hon Roll; NHS; Congrssnl Art Exhbt 83.

JANNS, ROBERT; Spotswood HS; Spotswood, NJ; (S); 3/174; Am Leg Boys St; Computer Clb; Math Tm; Science Clb; Bsbl; Socr; Trk; High Hon Roll; Hon Roll; NHS.

JANOCZKIN, MICHELE; South River HS; S River, NJ; (Y); 5/200; Church Yth Grp; Dance Clb; FNA; German Clb; Hosp Aide; Math Clb; Varsity Clb; Fld Hcky; Sftbl; Hon Roll; Vrsty Ltr Fld Hcky 85; Vrsty Ltr Sftbl 86; Rutgers; Accntnt.

JANOSKY, MARK; Newton HS; Newton, NJ; (S); 9/192; Am Leg Boys St; Pres Frsh Cls; Rep Stu Cncl; Var Tennis; High Hon Roll; Hon Roll; NHS; Rotary Awd; Penn ST U; Med.

JANOWITZ, ELIZABETH; Montville Township HS; Montville, NJ; (Y); 37/277; Key Clb; Concert Band; Jazz Band; Mrchg Band; School Musical; Var Capt Trk; NHS; Church Yth Grp; Band; Pep Band; Mst Vlbl Plyr Winter Trck Sprng Trck; Prsdntl Acdmc Ftnss Awd; Mst Imprvd Plyrs Sprng Trck; Gettysburg Coll.

JANUS, ELIZABETH; Holy Cross HS; Delran, NJ; (Y); 47/370; JV Fld Hcky; Hon Roll; Holy Family Coll; Nrsng.

JANUSZ, TIM; Holy Cross HS; Edgewater Park, NJ; (Y); 39/380; School Musical; School Play; Socr; Hon Roll; VFW Awd; NJ Boys ST Conf 86; VFW Boys ST Conf 86; Math.

JANZ, STACEY PATRICIA; Perth Amboy HS; Perth Amboy, NJ; (Y); 39/366; Am Leg Aux Girls St; Church Yth Grp; Civic Clb; SADD; Nwsp Sprt Ed; Yrbk Sprt Ed; Rep Soph Cls; Rep Jr Cls; Rep Jr Cls; Pres Stu Cncl; Pres Acdmc Ftns Awd; Chrsta Mcalffe Mem Awd; Fclty Schlrshp Awd; Prth Amby Almni Schlrshp Awd; U Central Florida; Nrsng.

JARALIM, LISA; Bloomfield HS; Bloomfld, NJ; (Y); 49/460; Hosp Aide; Pep Clb; Spanish Clb; Yrbk Rptr; Yrbk Stf; Cheerleading; Pom Pon; High Hon Roll; Hon Roll.

JARDIM, LISA; Bloomfield HS; Bloomfield, NJ; (Y); 49/460; Intnl Clb; Pep Clb; Spanish Clb; Yrbk Stf; Cheerleading; Pom Pon; High Hon Roll.

JARDINE, MICHELE; Morris Hills HS; Dover, NJ; (Y); 15/298; Art Clb; Varsity Clb; Nwsp Stf; Pres Stu Cncl; Var Capt Fld Hcky; Var Stat Ftbl; High Hon Roll; NHS; Rep Frsh Cls; Rep Soph Cls; 4 Yr Exclsr Awd Mdlln; Pres Acad Excllnce Awd; Rutgers U; Bus.

JAROCKI, KIMBERLY; Ferris HS; Jersey City, NJ; (Y); 25/300; Hosp Aide; Math Clb; PAVAS; Nwsp Ed-Chief; Nwsp Phtg; Nwsp Rptr; Yrbk Phtg; Yrbk Sprt Ed; Tennis; NHS; St Peters Coll; Grphc Arts.

JARRATT, KIRRA L; The Pingry Schl; Westfield, NJ; (Y); French Clb; Acpl Chr; Chorus; Yrbk Ed-Chief; Sec Trs Sr Cls; Sec Stu Cncl; Var Capt Cheerleading; High Hon Roll; Ntl Merit Ltr; Cum Laude Soc 85; Natl Achvt SF 86; Econ.

JARRELL, JOHN; Clauton HS; Clayton, NJ; (Y); 6/75; English Clb; French Clb; Math Clb; Science Clb; Varsity Clb; Nwsp Stf; Yrbk Stf; Sec Soph Cls; L Bsbl; Im Tennis; Georgetown; Pltcl Sci.

JARRELL, WESLEY; Clayton HS; Clayton, NJ; (Y); 2/75; Exploring; French Clb; Science Clb; Nwsp Stf; VP Jr Cls; Var Bsbl; Im Wt Lftg; Hon Roll; NHS; Sal; U Of PA; Frnch.

JARUSZEWSKI, JOSEPH J; Notre Dame HS; Hamilton Sq, NJ; (Y); 55/367; Nwsp Phtg; Nwsp Stf; Yrbk Phtg; Hon Roll; NHS; Natl Bus Hnr Scty; Acolyte Schl Masses; Acctng.

JASAITIS, JOSEPH C; Christian Brothers Acad; Sea Girt, NJ; (Y); Camera Clb; JV Wrstlng.

JASINSKI, MARK; Brick Township HS; Brick, NJ; (S); 12/480; Band; Concert Band; Jazz Band; Mrchg Band; School Play; Bsktbl; High Hon Roll; Hon Roll; NHS; Most Outstndng Soph-Bsktbll 84; Most Outstndng Musician-Band 83-84; Princeton U; Law.

JASKOT, KENNETH; De Paul Diocesan HS; Wayne, NJ; (S); Aud/Vis; Ski Clb; Nwsp Rptr; High Hon Roll; NHS; Sci,Engl Awd; Engnrng.

JAUREGUI, JOSE RODERICK; Marist HS; Bayonne, NJ; (Y); 14/103; Computer Clb; Key Clb; Math Clb; Science Clb; Nwsp Rptr; Nwsp Stf; Rep Stu Cncl; JV Var Tennis; Hon Roll; NHS; Pre-Med.

JAWNY, TATIANA; Oak Knoll Schl; Essex Fells, NJ; (Y); Ski Clb; Nwsp Stf; VP Capt Crs Cntry; Var Trk; Hon Roll; Pltcl Sci.

JAY, KATHLEEN; Kent Place Schl; Chatham, NJ; (Y); Art Clb; Cmnty Wkr; Intnl Clb; Concert Band; Yrbk Phtg; Trs Soph Cls; Off Jr Cls; JV Fld Hcky; Im Ice Hcky; JV Lcrss.

JEAN BAPTISTE, DIDIER P; The Lawrenceville Schl; Newark, NJ; (Y); French Clb; Math Tm; JV Crs Cntry; Im Socr; JV Trk; High Hon Roll; Turrell Schlrshp Lawrenceville 84; Outstndng Negro Stu 85.

JEDZINAK, JENNIFER; Roselle Catholic HS; Roselle, NJ; (S); Drama Clb; Ski Clb; School Musical; School Play; Stage Crew; Rep Soph Cls; Var Capt Cheerleading; Var Sftbl; Var Swmmng; Var Tennis; Frnch Awd 84-85; Gym Club 85-86; Math Lge 85-86; Oceanography.

JEFFERDS, DAVID; Moorestown Friends Schl; Mt Holly, NJ; (Y); Church Choir; Trs Jr Cls; Pres Sr Cls; Trs Stu Cncl; Var Capt Bsktbl; Var Capt Socr; NHS; Ntl Merit Ltr; Garden ST Distngshd Schlr 86.

JEFFERS, CHRIS; Toms River East HS; Toms River, NJ; (S); German Clb; GAA; Q&S; Quiz Bowl; Ski Clb; Mrchg Band; Nwsp Stf; Yrbk Stf; Rep Frsh Cls; Rep Soph Cls.

JEFFERS, W JAMES; Delsea Regional HS; Glassboro, NJ; (Y); Am Leg Boys St; Chess Clb; Capt Debate Tm; Exploring; Band; Nwsp Stf; Yrbk Stf; Tennis; Hon Roll; Best Dbtr Awd Jr St Rgnl Debt At Prnctn 85-86; Rutgers U; Law.

JEFFERY, HEATHER; Middletown H S South; Red Bank, NJ; (Y); 82/436; Church Yth Grp; School Play; Nwsp Rptr; Nwsp Stf; Var Capt Fld Hcky; Trk; Hon Roll; MVP For Fld Hockey 86; Homecoming Queen 86; Montclair ST; Bus Accntng.

JEFFRIES, PATRICK; Atlantic City HS; Margate, NJ; (Y); Latin Clb; Var Crs Cntry; JV Golf; 2nd Pl-Bus Law Symposium Atlantic CC 86; Nvl Avaitor.

JEFFRIES, PAUL C; Montville Township HS; Pine Brook, NJ; (Y); 11/275; Pres Computer Clb; Pres Debate Tm; Math Tm; Pres Science Clb; Nwsp Ed-Chief; Gov Hon Prg Awd; Ntl Merit Schol; Church Yth Grp; FBLA; Key Clb; Columbia U Sci Hnr Prog 85; Johns Hopkins Ctr Acdmcly Tlntd Yth 84; NJ Stdnt Cngrss Champ 85; Princeton U; Physcs.

JELINEK, MARGARET; Freehold Township HS; Freehold, NJ; (Y); Drama Clb; Band; Jazz Band; Mrchg Band; Orch; School Musical; School Play; Ed Lit Mag; NHS; Trs Frsh Cls; Bst Grmn Stu 84; Mst Tlntd Muscian 86; Frgn Lang.

JELINSKY, JEFF; Wayne Valley HS; Wayne, NJ; (Y); FBLA; Pres Frsh Cls; VP Soph Cls; Pres Jr Cls; Pres Sr Cls; Stu Cncl; JV Bsktbl; Socr; Hon Roll; NHS; BUS.

JELISIJEVIC, ZORICA; Sayreville War Memorial HS; Sayreville, NJ; (Y); 1/379; Debate Tm; Drama Clb; NFL; Spanish Clb; Thesps; Stage Crew; Nwsp Sprt Ed; Yrbk Rptr; Lit Mag; Sec NHS; Boston U; Med.

JENERSON, CAPRICE; E Orange HS; E Orange, NJ; (S); 3/410; JA; Drill Tm; Mrchg Band; Ed Yrbk Stf; Ed Lit Mag; Pres Frsh Cls; VP Soph Cls; Bausch & Lomb Sci Awd; Hon Roll; Pres NHS; Minority Achvt Awd 86; PA ST U; Chem Engr.

JENGEHINO, SUSAN; Cumberland Regional HS; Bridgeton, NJ; (Y); Church Yth Grp; Hosp Aide; Intnl Clb; Mrchg Band; Yrbk Stf; Hon Roll.

JENKIN, TED; Hightstown HS; E Windsor, NJ; (Y); 21/458; Cmnty Wkr; French Clb; FBLA; Temple Yth Grp; Nwsp Bus Mgr; Trs Frsh Cls; Trs Soph Cls; Trs Jr Cls; VP Sr Cls; Rep Stu Cncl; ST Champs Bsbl 83; ST Comptn FBLA 3rd Pl 85; Dist Comptn FBLA 3rd And 7th Pl 85-86; Actrl Sci.

JENKINS, ANGELA; Linden HS; Linden, NJ; (Y); FHA; German Clb; Var Bsktbl; U Of NC; Bus Admin.

JENKINS, DENISE; Holy Spirit HS; Absecon, NJ; (Y); 124/369; Bsktbl; Socr; Sftbl; Kiwanis Awd; Phys Ther.

JENKINS, LINDA E; Hunterdon Central HS; Flemington, NJ; (Y); 272/546; Intnl Clb; Ski Clb; Varsity Clb; Stat Lcrss; Socr; Gov Hon Prg Awd; Hon Roll; Jack Connell Schlrshp 85; Summer Arts Inst NJ Schl Of The Arts 84; Govrnrs Arts Awd In Art Educ 85; Philadelphia Coll Of Arts; Dnc.

JENKINS, TINA; Cherokee HS; Marlton, NJ; (Y); SADD; Varsity Clb; Rep Soph Cls; Rep Jr Cls; VP Stu Cncl; Capt Bsbl; JV Var Cheerleading; JV Sftbl; High Hon Roll; Hon Roll; Glassboro ST; Tchr.

JENKINSON, JAMES; Pascack Hills HS; Montvale, NJ; (Y); Church Yth Grp; Computer Clb; Math Tm; Hon Roll; NHS; Part Schlrshp To Bucknell U 86; Local BMW Schlrshp 86; 1st Pl Tm Am Computer Sci Lg 86; Bucknell U; Computer Science.

JENNESS, WALTER; Delaware Valley Regional HS; Milford, NJ; (Y); Boy Scts; Rep Stu Cncl; Im Ftbl; Im Trk; Hon Roll; Emergncy Med Tech 86; Life Scout Wrkng Eagle 86; Pre-Med.

JENNINGS, DAVID; Queen Of Peace HS; N Arlington, NJ; (Y); 121/229; Pres Ski Clb; SADD; Capt Ice Hcky; JV Score Keeper; Hon Roll; Rutgers; Ldnscp Arch.

JENNINGS, PAUL; Lower Cape May Rgnl HS; N Cape May, NJ; (Y); Boy Scts; Chorus; School Musical; School Play; Stage Crew; Radio Tv Thtr.

JENNINGS, SHERRY ELENA; Rutherford HS; Rutherford, NJ; (Y); 34/185; Cmnty Wkr; Ski Clb; Color Guard; Rep Frsh Cls; Rep Soph Cls; Rep Jr Cls; Sec Stu Cncl; Var Trk; German Clb; Key Clb; 1st Pl Cty ST PTA Culturl Arts Exhbt 85; Capt Awd Music Booster Clb 84-86; C Patn Rutherfrd Amb; Rutgers; Econ.

JENSEN, HEIDI; Belvidere HS; Belvidere, NJ; (Y); 14/118; Office Aide; Chorus; Stage Crew; Nwsp Phtg; JV Fld Hcky; Im Vllybl; Hon Roll; Rotary Awd; Stu Dir Of Schl Ply 86; Beaver Coll; Psychlgy.

JENSEN, KURT; Lower Cape May Regional HS; Cape May, NJ; (Y); 73/242; Ski Clb; Varsity Clb; JV Bsktbl; JV Socr; Var Trk; Hon Roll; Pre Law.

JENSEN, SCOTT; Vorhees HS; Lebanon, NJ; (Y); 90/274; JCL; Key Clb; Latin Clb; Rep Stu Cncl; Ftbl; Golf; Ice Hcky; Lcrss; NHS; Intl Rltns.

JENSSEN, KEVIN; Don Bosco Prep; Oakland, NJ; (Y); Boy Scts; Church Yth Grp; Drama Clb; Model UN; School Musical; School Play; Yrbk Stf; JV Wrstlng; Cit Awd; Hon Roll; Eagle Scout 84; UM Machias; Marine Bio.

JERNEE, DEBRA; Neptune SR HS; Neptune City, NJ; (Y); 15/398; Church Yth Grp; GAA; SADD; Teachers Aide; Stage Crew; Yrbk Stf; Lit Mag; JV Fld Hcky; High Hon Roll; NHS; Omega Psi Phi Frtrnty Schlrshp & Ctznshp Awd 84; Actvts Awd 86; Schlrshp Vrsty Ltr 84; Chld Psychlgst.

JEROLAMON, CINDY; Shore Regional HS; W Long Branch, NJ; (Y); Church Yth Grp; DECA; Pep Clb; Ski Clb; Band; Concert Band; Drm & Bgl; Mrchg Band; Stage Crew; Crs Cntry; Culinary Inst Of Amer; Chef.

JERROW, JANET; Bridgewater-Raritan East HS; Bridgewater, NJ; (Y); French Clb; Latin Clb; Nwsp Rptr; Yrbk Bus Mgr; Sr Cls; High Hon Roll; NHS; Pres Schlr; St Schlr; Amer Assoc U Wmn Frnch Awd 86; Amer Assoc Frnch Tchrs 16th Pl Cntst 83; Wellesley Coll.

JESSEN, LAUREN; Bayonne HS; Bayonne, NJ; (Y); Church Yth Grp; Drama Clb; School Musical; School Play; Variety Show; Nwsp Stf; Lit Mag; Rep Frsh Cls; Rep Soph Cls; Rep Jr Cls; Rutgers U; Pol Sci.

JEWEL, ANDREW; Mountain Lakes HS; Mtn Lakes, NJ; (Y); 10/98; Math Clb; Math Tm; Political Wkr; Quiz Bowl; Scholastic Bowl; Temple Yth Grp; Nwsp Stf; Var Tennis; High Hon Roll; Ntl Merit Ltr; All-ST Tnns 3rd Sngls 1st Tm 85; All-Conf 1st Tm 84-85.

JEWELL, ELWIN; Atlantic Christian HS; Ventnor, NJ; (S); School Play; VP Frsh Cls; VP Soph Cls; VP Jr Cls; Var L Bsbl; Var L Bsktbl; Var L Socr; Hon Roll; Hnr Soc Amer Assn Chrstn Schls 84; Engrng.

JIBRIL, AL-QIYAMAH; Rahway HS; Rahway, NJ; (Y); Am Leg Boys St; Crs Cntry; Trk; High Hon Roll; Hon Roll; Jr NHS; NHS; Spanish NHS; Engrng.

JIMENEZ, FARAH M; Bridgewater-Raritan East HS; Bridgewater, NJ; (Y); Church Yth Grp; Debate Tm; Pres NFL; School Musical; Nwsp Stf; Soph Cls; Sr Cls; NHS; Natl Hnr Rl 84-85; Natl Hispnc Merit Semi-Fnlst 85; Biol.

JIMENEZ, ROMILDA; Bishop George AHR HS; Pembrooke Pines, FL; (Y); Ski Clb; Varsity Clb; Yrbk Phtg; JC Awd; JV Var Sftbl; Broward CC; Arch.

JIMENEZ, WILFREDO; East Side HS; Newark, NJ; (Y); Am Leg Boys St; Yrbk Sprt Ed; Yrbk Stf; Var Ftbl; Var Trk; Achvt Awd Field Indstrl Arts 84-85; Engrng.

JO, ANNA; Burlington City HS; Edgewater Park, NJ; (Y); Am Leg Aux Girls St; Key Clb; Trs Jr Cls; Fld Hcky; Score Keeper; High Hon Roll; NHS; Principals Number One Clb; Fash Merch.

JOANNIDIS, NICKOLAS; Saddle Brook HS; Saddle Brook, NJ; (Y); 1/120; Am Leg Boys St; Latin Clb; Q&S; Nwsp Stf; Yrbk Stf; Stu Cncl; Var L Crs Cntry; Var L Trk; High Hon Roll; NHS; Adv Math Awd 86; Spnsh II Awd 86; Physics Awd 86; Rutgers; Accntng.

JOBSON, STEPHANIE; Palmyra HS; Palmyra, NJ; (Y); 3/120; Drama Clb; English Clb; School Play; Stage Crew; Nwsp Ed-Chief; Yrbk Rptr; Yrbk Stf; High Hon Roll; Hon Roll; Sec NHS; Burlington Cty Times MV Staffer Awd 86; Sec.

JOE, GWYNETTA; Benedictine Acad; Newark, NJ; (Y); 8/26; Church Yth Grp; GAA; Church Choir; Stage Crew; Nwsp Stf; Pres Sr Cls; Pres Stu Cncl; Bsktbl; NHS; Prncpls Awd Otstndng SR 86; The Eliane Monticello Mrl Awd 86; All-N Jersey Catholic Grls Bstkbll 886; Hampton U; Spch Cmmnctns.

JOELSON, LAINE; Westfield HS; Westfield, NJ; (Y); Key Clb; Spanish Clb; SADD; Temple Yth Grp; Acpl Chr; Chorus; School Musical; Rep Frsh Cls; Hon Roll; Fnlst Miss Co Ed Pagnt 85; Psych.

JOFFE, ELLIOTT; Watchung Hills Regional HS; Watchung, NJ; (Y); 4/300; Debate Tm; Math Tm; Nwsp Stf; Soph Cls; Hon Roll; Ntl Merit SF; Opt Clb Awd; Voice Dem Awd; Bus.

JOHANESSEN, HAROLD; Paramus Catholic HS; Hackensack, NJ; (Y); 83/178; Computer Clb; Math Clb; JV Var Bsktbl; Med.

JOHANSEN, ERIC; Oratory Catholic Prep; Madison, NJ; (Y); 22/50; Boy Scts; Nwsp Ed-Chief; Nwsp Rptr; Nwsp Stf; Hon Roll; Order Arrow 86; Feature Edtr Omega Schl Nwsp 85; Cmmnctns.

JOHN, MARY; St Pius X Regional HS; Edison, NJ; (Y); Art Clb; Church Yth Grp; Hosp Aide; Library Aide; Church Choir; Mrchg Band; Co-Capt Pom Pon; Hon Roll; Med.

JOHNSON, ALISA D; Plainfield HS; Plainfield, NJ; (Y); 3/539; Pres Science Clb; High Hon Roll; Hon Roll; Sec NHS; Natl Achvt Schlrshp Pgm; Cornell U Smmr Pgm; Natl Sci Merit Awd; Cornell U; Engr.

JOHNSON, AMY D; Asbury Park HS; Asbury Park, NJ; (Y); 3/175; Church Yth Grp; Debate Tm; Pres Key Clb; Math Clb; Band; Church Choir; Concert Band; Mrchg Band; Nwsp Rptr; Yrbk Rptr; Cngrssnl Awd Slvr 86; Blck Prfsnl Bus Schlr 86; Rutgers U; Math.

JOHNSON, BARBARA E; Madison Central HS; Old Ridge, NJ; (Y); 45/364; Church Yth Grp; Hosp Aide; SADD; Y-Teens; Chorus; Madrigals; Swing Chorus; Yrbk Stf; Hon Roll; Choir Spnsr Schlrshp 85-86; Russian Hnr Soc Awd; Russian Clb Awd; Muhlenberg Coll; Comm.

JOHNSON, BRIAN; Vineland HS; Vineland, NJ; (Y); 51/803; Debate Tm; Stu Cncl; Socr; Engrng.

JOHNSON, BRIDGETT; Malcolm X Shabazz HS; Newark, NJ; (S); 5/263; Aud/Vis; Boys Clb Am; Computer Clb; Coach Actv; Hon Roll; NHS; Montclair ST Coll; Chem.

JOHNSON, CARLA; Snyder HS; Jersey City, NJ; (Y); Dance Clb; Variety Show; Gym; Rutgers U; Comp Sci.

JOHNSON, CARRIE; Morris Knolls HS; Rockaway, NJ; (Y); Church Yth Grp; Band; Chorus; Church Choir; Mrchg Band; Stage Crew; Yrbk Stf; Oral Roberts U.

JOHNSON, CHRISTINE; Vailsburg HS; Newark, NJ; (Y); Computer Clb; Dance Clb; Debate Tm; Drama Clb; SADD; Band; Color Guard; School Play; Yrbk Stf; Off Jr Cls; Gold Card 85-86; Bio Awd 85; NYU; Med.

JOHNSON, CHRISTINE A; Our Lady Of Mercy Acad; Brigantine, NJ; (Y); 11/41; Church Yth Grp; Cmnty Wkr; Computer Clb; SADD; Nwsp Rptr; Nwsp Stf; Yrbk Stf; Lit Mag; Im Badmtn; Im Bsktbl; Hugh O Brien Ldrshp Ambsdr & Dir Prog 85-86; Beautfctn Cmmtee Dir; Cambridge; Arch.

JOHNSON, CHRYSTAL; Lacordair Acad; E Orange, NJ; (Y); Intnl Clb; NFL; School Play; Nwsp Stf; Mgr Lit Mag; Var Vllybl; High Hon Roll; Hon Roll; PA ST U; Bus.

JOHNSON, CLINT; Ridge HS; Basking Ridge, NJ; (Y); 53/205; Church Yth Grp; Drama Clb; Ski Clb; Acpl Chr; Chorus; Church Choir; Madrigals; School Musical; School Play; Stage Crew; All ST Chorus 86; Ltr Drama Clb 86; Drama.

JOHNSON, CRAIG; Hawthorne HS; Hawthorne, NJ; (Y); French Clb; School Play; Variety Show; Yrbk Ed-Chief; Gov Hon Prg Awd; High Hon Roll; Sci & Comp Sci Prog 85-86; Excptnl Prfrmnc Frnch II & Advncd Plcmnt Bio 85-86; NY U; Drm.

JOHNSON, CRAIG A; Plainfield HS; Plainfield, NJ; (Y); DECA; Acpl Chr; Jazz Band; Mrchg Band; Orch; School Musical; Yrbk Stf; Rep Soph Cls; Rep Jr Cls; JV Mgr(s); Peer Ldrshp 85-87; Economics.

JOHNSON, CRISTINA; Mary Help Of Christians Acad; Paterson, NJ; (Y); Art Clb; Computer Clb; Service Clb; Teachers Aide; Yrbk Rptr; Badmtn; Bsbl; Bsktbl; Gym; Sftbl; William Paterson Coll.

JOHNSON, DAVID; Howell HS; Howell, NJ; (Y); 102/450; VP Church Yth Grp; VP 4-H; German Clb; Spanish Clb; Yrbk Bus Mgr; Yrbk Phtg; Hon Roll.

JOHNSON, DEBBIE; St John Vianney; Morganville, NJ; (Y); JCL; Latin Clb; Color Guard; School Play; Nwsp Phtg; Nwsp Rptr; Yrbk Phtg; Lit Mag; VP Frsh Cls; Sec Sr Cls; Hnr Rll; Gld & White Awd; Vrsty Ltr Awd Wnnr; Comm.

JOHNSON, DEBORAH; Vineland HS; Vineland, NJ; (Y); Church Yth Grp; English Clb; Drill Tm; Nwsp Stf; Fld Hcky; Lcrss; Swmmng; Hon Roll; Polt Sci.

JOHNSON, ERIK N; West Windsor-Plainsboro HS; Princeton Jct, NJ; (Y); Am Leg Boys St; Political Wkr; Variety Show; Pres Jr Cls; Capt Bsktbl; L Ftbl; Hon Roll; CAP; Cmnty Wkr; Math Tm; Wghtlftg Clb GRUNTS 85-87; Pallbearer Guid Cnslr 86; WA Seminar 85.

JOHNSON, FRANCIS; Phillipsburg HS; Phillipsburg, NJ; (Y); 123/350; Ski Clb; Im Vllybl; Northampton Cnty Area; Comp Sci.

JOHNSON, GREGORY; Glen Ridge HS; Glen Ridge, NJ; (Y); Church Yth Grp; French Clb; Model UN; Nwsp Stf; Lit Mag; Ntl Merit Ltr; Comp Pgmmng.

JOHNSON, JAMES R; Pennsville Memorial HS; Pennsville, NJ; (Y); 1/201; Am Leg Boys St; Church Yth Grp; Concert Band; Jazz Band; Mrchg Band; High Hon Roll; NHS; Ntl Merit Ltr.

JOHNSON, JENNIFER M; Ocean City HS; Marmora, NJ; (Y); 8/278; French Clb; Hosp Aide; JA; Model UN; Ski Clb; Nwsp Rptr; Yrbk Stf; Trs Stu Cncl; Var L Cheerleading; Var L Tennis; Stu Cncl Awd 86; Fr Clb Awd 86; Boston Coll; Intl Fin.

JOHNSON, JENNY; South Hunterdon Regional HS; Lambertville, NJ; (Y); 4/71; Drama Clb; VP Acpl Chr; Band; Chorus; VP Madrigals; School Musical; School Play; Variety Show; Ed Nwsp Stf; Ed Yrbk Stf; Mck Trl Comptn Lwyr 86; Advrtsng.

JOHNSON, JILL L; Plainfield HS; Plainfield, NJ; (Y); 2/535; Band; Yrbk Stf; Rep Wrstlng; Capt Tennis; Var Trk; Gov Hon Prg Awd; NHS; Sal; St Schlr; Natl Achvt Cmmnded Stu 85; Mod Congress Outstndg Chrprsn & Dely 84 & 85; Rutgers Schlr 85.

JOHNSON, JOHN C; Dunelle HS; Dunellen, NJ; (Y); 16/70; French Clb; Key Clb; Office Aide; Ski Clb; Nwsp Rptr; Nwsp Sprt Ed; Nwsp Stf; Lit Mag; Frsh Cls; Soph Cls; AZ ST U; Phys Ed.

JOHNSON, KARYN SUZANNE; Northern Valley Regional HS; Old Tappan, NJ; (Y); 1/313; Sec AFS; Latin Clb; Pres Math Tm; Sec Trs Concert Band; Mrchg Band; NHS; Ntl Merit SF; JCL; Ski Clb; School Musical; NJ Govnrs Schl Sci 85; NJ Dstngshd Schlr 85; Acad Decath 85; Biol.

JOHNSON, KEITH; De Paul HS; Lincoln Pk, NJ; (Y); 64/164; Chess Clb; Church Yth Grp; Hon Roll.

JOHNSON, KIMBERLY; Buena Regional HS; Vineland, NJ; (S); 1/192; Church Yth Grp; Var Debate Tm; Drama Clb; Math Tm; Pep Clb; Mrchg Band; Rep Frsh Cls; Rep Soph Cls; Trs Sec Stu Cncl; Pom Pon; Exch Clbs Stdnt Mnth 85; Rutgers Schlr 85; Garden ST Distngshd Schlr 85; Ursinus; Biochem.

JOHNSON, LAINE; Bordentown Regional HS; Bordentown, NJ; (Y); 11/119; Drama Clb; French Clb; FBLA; Ski Clb; School Play; Yrbk Stf; Cheerleading; Hon Roll; NHS.

JOHNSON, LISA; Holy Cross HS; Willingboro, NJ; (Y); Hosp Aide; Library Aide; SADD; Hon Roll; Ntl Merit Ltr; Hnrb Mntn 85-86; Mst Imprvd Chem Stu 85-86; 2 Typg Awds Spd/Accrcy 84-85; Rutgers; Elem Ed.

JOHNSON, LYNN; Burlington City HS; Burlington, NJ; (Y); 20/168; Band; Concert Band; Mrchg Band; Lit Mag; Sec Stu Cncl; Mgr(s); Hon Roll; Rotary Awd; Extnd Lrng Pgm; Old Dominion U.

JOHNSON, MARK R; Millburn HS; Millburn, NJ; (Y); 31/246; Am Leg Boys St; Chess Clb; Pres Church Yth Grp; Cmnty Wkr; Computer Clb; Spanish Clb; Crs Cntry; Golf; Trk; Ntl Merit SF; Rutgers Schlr, Volntr Wrk Proj Read 85; Arch.

JOHNSON, MICHAEL; Maple Shade HS; Maple Shade, NJ; (Y); VP Church Yth Grp; Computer Clb; SADD; High Hon Roll; Hon Roll; Prfct Atten Awd.

JOHNSON, MICHELLE; Eastside HS; Paterson, NJ; (Y); 3/500; Trs Computer Clb; Science Clb; Yrbk Stf; Hon Roll; Jr NHS; VP NHS; Rutgers U; Comp Sci.

JOHNSON, MONICA; Mother Seton Regional HS; Plainfield, NJ; (Y); GAA; Varsity Clb; Nwsp Sprt Ed; Yrbk Stf; Tennis; Editor Awd 86; Yrbk Staff Awd 86; Captn Yr 86; Clark Coll; Physcl Thrpy.

JOHNSON, OLA; Red Bank Catholic HS; Neptune, NJ; (Y); Aud/Vis; Church Yth Grp; VP Exploring; FCA; SADD; Church Choir; Lit Mag; Pres Frsh Cls; Wt Lftg; Wrstlng; Howard U; Bus Adm.

JOHNSON, PATTIE; Middlesex HS; Middlesex, NJ; (Y); Ski Clb; SADD; Yrbk Stf; Hon Roll; Middlesex Cnty Coll; Fshn Byr.

JOHNSON, PRINCESS R; Malcolm X Shabazz HS; Newark, NJ; (S); 5/263; Ed Yrbk Ed-Chief; Soph Cls; Jr Cls; Sr Cls; Hon Roll; NHS; Rutgers U; Elem Ed.

JOHNSON, REGINA; Wesequahic HS; Newark, NJ; (S); 30/530; Exploring; Church Choir; Yrbk Stf; Stu Cncl; Hon Roll; NHS; Law.

JOHNSON, RICHARD W; Midland Park HS; Ho Ho Kus, NJ; (Y); Am Leg Boys St; Church Yth Grp; Math Tm; Ski Clb; Stage Crew; Var Socr; Var Trk; High Hon Roll; NHS.

JOHNSON, ROBERT; Arthur P Schalick HS; Elmer, NJ; (Y); 16/131; Am Leg Boys St; Var Bsbl; Hon Roll; S Jersey Bsbl Tm Hnrbl Mntn 86; Salem Cty Allstar Bsbl Tm 85-86; Athl Of Wk 86; Sprts Med.

JOHNSON, SABRINA; John F Kennedy HS; Paterson, NJ; (Y); Church Yth Grp; GAA; Band; Church Choir; Mrchg Band; Rep Soph Cls; Rep Jr Cls; Var JV Bsktbl; Mrchng Band Trophy 85-86; Cert Bsktbl 84-85; 5 Bsktbl 85-86; Harvard U; Med.

JOHNSON, SHEILA; Malcolm X Shabazz HS; Newark, NJ; (S); #1 In Class; Computer Clb; Nwsp Rptr; Nwsp Sprt Ed; Yrbk Ed-Chief; Rep Jr Cls; Crs Cntry; Tennis; Trk; High Hon Roll; NHS; Math.

JOHNSON, STEPHANIE; Mt Olive HS; Flanders, NJ; (Y); 2/330; Pres Civic Clb; Concert Band; Mrchg Band; School Musical; Nwsp Stf; Ed Lit Mag; Mgr(s); High Hon Roll; NHS; Ntl Merit Ltr; Frshman Band Awd; Frgn Lang.

JOHNSON, STEPHANIE; Pleasantville HS; Pleasantville, NJ; (Y); Exploring; VICA; Church Choir; Drill Tm; Rep Frsh Cls; Capt Pom Pon; Vllybl; Cnvrstnl Spnch & Frnch Awd; Bst Pom Pom Yr Awd; Stu Mnth Awd; Temple U; Law.

JOHNSON, SUSAN L; Bridgewater-Raritan East HS; Bridgewater, NJ; (Y); AFS; Hosp Aide; Spanish Clb; Concert Band; Mrchg Band; High Hon Roll; Hon Roll; NHS; Ntl Assn Of Accntnts Awd 86; Amer Assn Of U Wmn Awd 86; Pace U; Mngmnt Info Systems.

JOHNSON, TAMMY L; Camden Catholic HS; Camden, NJ; (Y); 105/295; Art Clb; French Clb; FBLA; Science Clb; Rep Frsh Cls; JV Cheerleading; Im Var Tennis; Var Trk; Bus Mngmt.

JOHNSON, THADDEUS R; Union HS; Vauxhall, NJ; (Y); ROTC; Yrbk Stf; Hon Roll; Instrctr Ldrshp Awd ROTC 84; Cmmndtn Ribbn ROTC 84; Penn ST; Physcn.

JOHNSON, TRECIA; Vailsburg HS; Newark, NJ; (Y); Dance Clb; FNA; FTA; Girl Scts; Teachers Aide; Church Choir; Drill Tm; Rep Jr Cls; Im Twrlr; Cit Awd; Otstndng Thrghot Yr 83.

JOHNSON, TRISHA; Calvary Acad; Brick, NJ; (S); Church Yth Grp; Pres Jr Cls; JV Bsktbl; Mgr(s); JV Sftbl; Capt Vllybl; High Hon Roll; GAA; Hnr Stu 84; Highest Average In Math, Engl & Spanish 84; Vet.

JOHNSON, YASMIN; Weequahic HS; Newark, NJ; (Y); 22/150; Girl Scts; Hosp Aide; Library Aide; School Play; Nwsp Stf; Cheerleading; Trk; Cit Awd; NHS; FL A & M; Lwyr.

JOHNSTON, ANDREW; Middletown HS South; Red Bank, NJ; (Y); Am Leg Boys St; Boy Scts; German Clb; Math Clb; Band; Concert Band; Jazz Band; Mrchg Band; Pep Band; School Musical; All-Shore Jazz & All-Shore Band 86; U Of VA; Engrng.

JOHNSTON, ANDREW; Washington Township HS; Turnersville, NJ; (Y); German Clb; Science Clb; Band; Concert Band; Nwsp Stf; JV Trk.

JOHNSTON, ANNMARIE; Eastern Regional HS; Gibbsboro, NJ; (Y); Var Capt Socr; JV Sftbl; Wt Lftg; NHS; Women In Engrng Pgm At Stevens Inst Of Tech 86; Gifted & Talented Pgm 86-87; Aeronautical.

JOHNSTON, BLAINE E; Princeton Day Schl; Skillman, NJ; (Y); Math Tm; Orch; Hon Roll; Ntl Merit Schol; Pres Schlr; Cert Merit Awd Mth Assn Amer 84; CTY Smmr Pgm Scholar 84; Physcs.

JOHNSTON, CAROLYN; St John Vianney HS; Englishtown, NJ; (Y); 70/283; Church Yth Grp; Cmnty Wkr; Intnl Clb; Office Aide; Stage Crew; Yrbk Phtg; Lit Mag; Powder Puff Ftbl; Hon Roll; Blgcl Sci.

JOHNSTON, JAMES; Frank H Morrell HS; Irvington, NJ; (Y); Church Yth Grp; Exploring; Spanish Clb; Church Choir; Hon Roll; Robert Walsh Schl Bus; Airline.

JOHNSTON, KIMBERLY; Mahwah HS; Mahwah, NJ; (Y); Sec Pres JCL; Pres Latin Clb; School Play; JV L Sftbl; High Hon Roll; Drama Clb; Color Guard; Stage Crew; Variety Show; Nwsp Stf; Sml Twn & Fncy Plyrs Schlrshp 86; Cum Laude 84-85; Jr Clsscl Lge Prd & Sprt 84-86; Montclair ST Coll; Tchng.

JOHNSTON, PETER L; Highstown HS; E Windsor, NJ; (Y); 17/441; Church Yth Grp; Nwsp Rptr; Nwsp Stf; Crs Cntry; Trk; High Hon Roll; Hon Roll; NHS; Edtr Church Yth Grp Nwslttr; Mbr Mdl Cngrss Clb; Hist.

JOHNSTON, PHILIP; Kearny HS; Kearny, NJ; (Y); Am Leg Boys St; Aud/Vis; Computer Clb; Nwsp Ed-Chief; Swmmng; High Hon Roll; Hon Roll; NHS; U Richmond; Bus Mgmt.

JOHNSTON, WENDY; Camden Catholic HS; Pennsavken, NJ; (Y); 41/301; Dance Clb; Pep Clb; Ski Clb; Spanish Clb; Yrbk Stf; Cheerleading; Tennis; Hon Roll.

JOHO, BRIAN; Abraham Clark HS; Roselle, NJ; (S); 8/220; FHA; Science Clb; Chorus; Im Bowling; High Hon Roll; Hon Roll; NHS; Olympcs Of Mnd 83-84; Gftd & Tlntd Prog 83.

JOINER, KATHLEEN; River Del SR HS; River Edge, NJ; (Y); 50/213; Yrbk Stf; Hon Roll; Delhi SUNY; Htl Mgmnt.

JONES, ALONZO J; Penns Grove HS; Carneys Point, NJ; (Y); Am Leg Boys St; Church Yth Grp; Computer Clb; Band; Concert Band; Mrchg Band; Rep Soph Cls; Rep Jr Cls; Rep Stu Cncl; Var L Socr; Us Air Force.

JONES, AMY; Dwight Morrow HS; Englewood, NJ; (Y); AFS; Camera Clb; Latin Clb; Service Clb; Concert Band; Drm Mjr(t); Mrchg Band; Hon Roll; Prfct Atten Awd; Rutgers; Psych.

JONES, ANTONIO; University HS; Newark, NJ; (Y); Debate Tm; NFL; Radio Clb; School Musical; School Play; Stage Crew; Variety Show; Im Cheerleading; JV Trk; 1st Pl Peace Essay Cntst 85; Mbr NJ Tlnt Clb 85; Math Advnd Plcmnt 83-87; Engrng.

JONES, CANDICE STARR; Union HS; Union, NJ; (Y); Church Yth Grp; Letterman Clb; Yrbk Phtg; Yrbk Sprt Ed; VP Frsh Cls; Rep Soph Cls; VP Jr Cls; Pres Stu Cncl; Capt Bsktbl; Hon Roll; 3rd Rnnr Up Mis Black Teengr NJ 85; Recog Mst Outstndng Ldr Union Cnty 85; FIT; Photo Fash.

JONES, CARLA; Clifton HS; Clifton, NJ; (Y); 73/681; Church Yth Grp; French Clb; SADD; Church Choir; Rep Frsh Cls; Stat Bsktbl; Var Trk; French Hon Soc; Hon Roll; Jr NHS; Grls Ctznshp; Phrmcy.

JONES, CAROL; Alma Prep; Somerville, NJ; (Y); Church Yth Grp; Ski Clb; Band; Concert Band; Mrchg Band; Symp Band; Yrbk Stf; Score Keeper; Hon Roll; Yrbk Phtg; Phys Thrpst.

JONES, DEBORAH; Dwight Morrow HS; Englewood, NJ; (Y); 41/260; Am Leg Aux Girls St; Church Yth Grp; FBLA; Trs Jr Cls; VP Sr Cls; Rep Stu Cncl; Var Trk; Hon Roll; Xinos Of Phi Delta Kappa 85-86; Yth Flctrs Unit 4 Queen Of Sheeba 79-86; Pstve Image PSI DMH 85-86; Accntng.

JONES, DONNA; Raritan HS; Hazlet, NJ; (Y); 33/314; Bsktbl; Socr; Sftbl; Sues Schlrshp St Peters Coll 86; St Peters Coll; Chld Psych.

JONES, FRANZIE; Piscataway HS; Piscataway, NJ; (Y); 176/521; ROTC; Church Choir; Drill Tm; Orch; Rep Sr Cls; Hon Roll; 1st Pl Awd Forensic Spkng/Frnch 84; 2nd Pl Music Awd/Piano 84; MD U; Pre Dntstry.

JONES, HARRIET D; Sterling HS; Somerdale, NJ; (Y); DECA; Pep Clb; Band; Color Guard; Ed Yrbk Ed-Chief; Yrbk Sprt Ed; Stu Cncl; Mgr Trk; Hon Roll; Ntl Merit Ltr; Bus Admin.

JONES, HOLLY; Rahway HS; Rahway, NJ; (Y); 3/256; Am Leg Aux Girls St; Church Yth Grp; Band; Pres Chorus; School Musical; Yrbk Ed-Chief; Pres Stu Cncl; Elks Awd; Ntl Merit Ltr; Pres Schlr; A J Gov Tchng Schlrshp 86; Daily Journal Outstndg Ctzn Of Future Awd 86; Rahway High Srv Awd 86; Shenandoah Coll; Music.

JONES, JACKIE; Northern Burlington Co Reg HS; Willingboro, NJ; (Y); Red Cross Aide; Chorus; Church Choir; Mrchg Band; Pep Band; School Musical; Yrbk Stf; Off Frsh Cls; Off Soph Cls; Mgr(s); Spelman Coll; Mrktng.

JONES, JOHN; Lower Cape May Regional HS; N Cape May, NJ; (Y); 20/250; Boy Scts; Church Yth Grp; Red Cross Aide; Color Guard; Trk; Ntl Merit Ltr; Future Prob Solvers 86; US Navy Armed Frcs; Metrlgst.

JONES, JOHN R; Ewing HS; Trenton, NJ; (Y); 2/306; Am Leg Boys St; Key Clb; Math Clb; JV Socr; JV Trk; Hon Roll; VP NHS; Sal; Computer Clb; Physics & Bio Awd 84&86; SR Sci Awd Hghst Avg Grade 86; U Of VA; Elec Engrng.

JONES, KARLA; Hillside HS; Hillside, NJ; (Y); Church Yth Grp; Cheerleading; Var Socr; U Medicine Dentistry; Med.

JONES, KRIS; Mt St John Acad; Basking Ridge, NJ; (S); Church Yth Grp; Cmnty Wkr; VP Drama Clb; Thesps; Drill Tm; Nwsp Phtg; Nwsp Rptr; Yrbk Phtg; Pres Soph Cls; Hon Roll; Child Psych.

JONES, KRISTYN MARIE; Garden State Acad; Tranquility, NJ; (Y); German Clb; Office Aide; Concert Band; Yrbk Ed-Chief; Sec Soph Cls; Sec Jr Cls; High Hon Roll; Southern Coll; Offc Adm.

JONES, LYNNETTE; Egg Harbor Township HS; Mays Landing, NJ; (S); 10/317; French Clb; Ski Clb; Jr NHS; Hst Frsh Cls; Hst Soph Cls; Hst Jr Cls; Mgr Trk; Acadmc Awd 85.

JONES, MARGARET; Linden HS; Linden, NJ; (Y); Church Yth Grp; Medcl Spllng Comptns 3rd Pl Rgnl, 2nd Pl St & 17th Pl Natl 86; Neurlgst.

JONES, PAMELA; Clifford J Scott HS; E Orange, NJ; (Y); 4/245; Church Yth Grp; Varsity Clb; Nwsp Phtg; Stu Cncl; Var Capt Bsktbl; High Hon Roll; Hon Roll; Masonic Awd; NHS; JR Deacon 85-86; Trenton ST Clg; Advtsg Dsgn.

JONES, RANDOLPH L; Piscataway HS; Piscataway, NJ; (Y); Pres Church Yth Grp; Capt CAP; ROTC; Varsity Clb; Color Guard; Drill Tm; Rep Stu Cncl; Coach Actv; Var Trk; Wt Lftg; Stu Of Brd Of Educ 86-87; Amer Lgn Mltry Excell Mdl 86; Chrstn Ldrshp Awd 86-87; MD U; Hist.

JONES, RAQUEL; Dwight Morrow HS; Englewood, NJ; (Y); 16/279; AFS; Aud/Vis; Girl Scts; Hosp Aide; Spanish Clb; Color Guard; VP Jr Cls; Pres Sr Cls; JV Vllybl; NHS; Howard WA DC; Law.

JONES, ROBERT; Woodrow Wilson HS; Camden, NJ; (Y); Drama Clb; JA; Band; Concert Band; Mrchg Band; School Musical; Off Jr Cls; Socr; Prfct Atten Awd; NYU; Theatre.

JONES, SCOTT; Bishop George Ahr/St Thomas Aquinas; Edison, NJ; (Y); 88/297; Boy Scts; Intnl Clb; Model UN; Concert Band; Mrchg Band; School Play; Symp Band; Vllybl; Hon Roll; Boy Scts-Egl Sct 85; Old Dominion U; Crmnlgy.

JONES, STEPHANIE A; Dwight-Englewood HS; Hackensack, NJ; (Y); Acpl Chr; Chorus; Madrigals; School Musical; Rep Soph Cls; Sec Jr Cls; Rep Sr Cls; Var Capt Cheerleading; Cit Awd; Hon Roll; Rwn Awd Music 86; Cum Laude Soc 86; NJ Pro Music Tchrs Gld Schlrshp 86; Amherst Coll; Clsscs.

JONES, WENDY L; Rancocas Valley Reginal HS; Medford, NJ; (Y); 65/259; Church Yth Grp; Hosp Aide; Pres Sec Band; Concert Band; Jazz Band; Mrchg Band; Orch; Yrbk Stf; Instrmntlst Magnze Merit Awd 86; Wesley Clg Dover DE; Nrsng.

JORDAN, AMY; Sacred Heart HS; Elmer, NJ; (S); Sec 4-H; Spanish Clb; Variety Show; Yrbk Stf; Lit Mag; 4-H Awd; Hon Roll; NHS; Ntl Merit Schol; ST 4h Food/Nutrtn Proj Wnnr 85; Cumberland Cnty 4h Queen 86; ST Dairy Food Demo Wnnr 85; Secndry Ed.

JORDAN, CARRIE; Central Regional HS; Bayville, NJ; (Y); 1/228; Am Leg Aux Girls St; Cmnty Wkr; Library Aide; Math Tm; Q&S; Ski Clb; Varsity Clb; Nwsp Sprt Ed; Trs Stu Cncl; Capt Crs Cntry; 3rd Tm All ST High Jmp 85; Georgian Court Coll; Mth.

JORDAN, LESLIE; St Pius X Reg HS; Jamesburg, NJ; (Y); Pres Church Yth Grp; Computer Clb; Library Aide; ROTC; Church Choir; Pom Pon; Socr; Rutgers U Sccr Cmp Mst Imprvd ; Metronomes Inc Blck Debutante Soc 86; Pub Rltns.

JORDAN, MAUREEN; Haddon Township HS; Oaklyn, NJ; (Y); Am Leg Aux Girls St; Chorus; Madrigals; School Musical; School Play; Stu Cncl; NHS; Church Yth Grp; Acpl Chr; Swing Chorus; Modern Music Mstrs; Stu Athletic Trnr; Marine Corps Phys Fitness Tm; Phys Thrpy.

JORDAN, RAYMOND; Bridgeton HS; Bridgeton, NJ; (Y); Drama Clb; Model UN; School Musical; Nwsp Bus Mgr; Stu Cncl; Hon Roll; Bst Actor-Drama 84; Outstndng Jrnlst-Model UN Conf 85; Mktng.

JOSE, STEPHANIE; Manalapan HS; Englishtown, NJ; (Y); 180/400; Drama Clb; School Musical; School Play; Stage Crew; Fine & Prfrmng Arts Ctr-Freehold 86; Theatre.

JOSEPH, MARLENE; Plainfield HS; Plainfield, NJ; (Y); Dance Clb; Drama Clb; FBLA; Mrchg Band; School Musical; School Play; Yrbk Stf; Rep Soph Cls; Rep Jr Cls; Var Trk; Howard U; Pltcl Sci.

JOSEY, KIM; Columbia HS; S Orange, NJ; (Y); VP Church Yth Grp; Band; Concert Band; Mrchg Band; Symp Band; Yrbk Stf; JV Crs Cntry; JV Var Trk; Douglass Coll; Bio.

JOSHI, NIMISH; Morris Hills HS; Rockaway, NJ; (Y); 11/272; Chess Clb; Cmnty Wkr; Computer Clb; JA; Spanish Clb; High Hon Roll; NHS; Spanish NHS; Achvt Awd Blck Ed; LEAD; Pre-Med.

JOST, AMANDA; Sacred Heart HS; Vineland, NJ; (S); 4/70; German Clb; School Musical; Rep Frsh Cls; Off Jr Cls; Off Sr Cls; Var JV Cheerleading; JV Sftbl; Hon Roll; NHS; Dietics.

JOST, DANIEL; Manasquan HS; Manasquan, NJ; (Y); 14/256; Boy Scts; Church Yth Grp; Drama Clb; French Clb; JA; Key Clb; Math Clb; Science Clb; Band; Concert Band; Elem PTO Schlrshp 86; Mark C Thompson Meml Schlrshp 86; Bd Of Ed Acad Achvt Awds 83-86; William & Mary; Fin.

JOST, WILLIAM; Dover HS; Mine Hill, NJ; (Y); Boy Scts; German Clb; Ski Clb; Bowling; Crs Cntry; High Hon Roll; Vrsty Ltr In Track.

JOURNETT, AILEEN; Emerson HS; Union City, NJ; (Y); 11/277; English Clb; Spanish Clb; Nwsp Rptr; Nwsp Stf; NHS; Spanish NHS; Stu Of Pan-Amer Clb; Rutgers U; Pre-Med.

JOYCE, JEANMARIE; Cliffside Park HS; Cliffside Park, NJ; (Y); 14/236; Dance Clb; Trs Spanish Clb; Yrbk Stf; Stu Cncl; JV Var Cheerleading; Hon Roll; Jr NHS; Pres NHS; St Peters Coll Summer Schlr 86; William & Mary; Psychlgy.

JOYCE, MAUREEN; Paul VI Regional HS; Cedar Grove, NJ; (Y); Pep Clb; SADD; Yrbk Stf; Rep Soph Cls; Rep Jr Cls; Rep Stu Cncl; Capt Bsktbl; Var Cheerleading; Var Sftbl; Hon Roll.

JOYNER, TRACY; Long Branch HS; Long Branch, NJ; (S); 18/214; Math Tm; Band; Mrchg Band; Symp Band; Nwsp Stf; Cheerleading; Cit Awd; VP NHS; Var Schlr Awd 83-86; Omega Psi Phi 86; James Dickinson Carr Schlrshp 86; Rutgers Coll Of Engrng; Elec En.

JUAREZ, GABRIELA; Marylawn Of The Oranges HS; Orange, NJ; (Y); Art Clb; French Clb; Trnsltr.

JUDSON, STAN; South River HS; South River, NJ; (Y); 43/127; VP Band; Concert Band; VP Jazz Band; VP Mrchg Band; VP Pep Band; VP Symp Band; Brookdale; Mechanic.

JUELIS, JOHN J; Westfield SR HS; Westfield, NJ; (Y); 171/500; Am Leg Boys St; Pres Sr Cls; Var Capt Ftbl; Var L Lcrss; Hon Roll; Hobart Coll.

JUMAN, ROBERT C; J P Stevens HS; Edison, NJ; (Y); 4/471; Model UN; Thesps; School Play; Variety Show; Yrbk Bus Mgr; Cheerleading; Gov Hon Prg Awd; NHS; Ntl Merit SF; Frnch Hnr Soc 86; Pres Schlr 86; Harvard.

JUNG, MICHELLE; Dwight-Englewood HS; Harrington Park, NJ; (Y); AFS; Church Yth Grp; Dance Clb; Drama Clb; Ski Clb; Chorus; Church Choir; Nwsp Rptr; Nwsp Stf; Yrbk Stf; Comm.

JURGENSEN, DAVID; Palisades Park JR SR HS; Palisades Pk, NJ; (Y); VP Computer Clb; Var Ftbl; Var Trk; Hon Roll; Adv Placemnt Pascal Awd 85-86; Comptr Sci.

JURSCA, RICHARD; Christian Brothers Acad; Holmdel, NJ; (Y); 73/220; Im Ftbl; JV Wrstlng; Hon Roll; VA Tech; Bio.

JUSTIS, GLENN P; Henry P Becton Regional HS; E Rutherford, NJ; (Y); 13/110; Am Leg Boys St; Aud/Vis; Boy Scts; Key Clb; Math Tm; ROTC; Drill Tm; Trk; Elks Awd; Pres Schlr; ROTC Army, Kiwanis Schlrshps, Meritrus Achvt ROTC 86; The Citadel; Army Intel Ofcr.

KACPEROWSKI, LISA ANN; Roselle Catholic HS; Roselle, NJ; (Y); 20/152; Am Leg Aux Girls St; Debate Tm; Drama Clb; Girl Scts; NFL; Political Wkr; Service Clb; Speech Tm; School Play; Stage Crew; Ntl Bus Hnr Soc; Acctg Prfcncy Awd; College House Most Dsrvg SR Band; Montclair ST Coll; Acctg.

KADAR, ANNE; Kitlatinny Regional HS; Newton, NJ; (Y); 45/228; Church Yth Grp; Science Clb; Chorus; Church Choir; Nwsp Stf; Lit Mag; Nuclear Convocation 84; Sussex Cnty Chorus 85; Bio.

KADEZABEK, LAUREN; Hunterdon Central HS; Flemington, NJ; (Y); 112/548; Ski Clb; Im Fld Hcky; Stat Lcrss; Hon Roll; Pre Law.

KAEPPLER, SUZANNE; Cumberland Christian HS; Millville, NJ; (S); Church Yth Grp; Drama Clb; German Clb; VP Frsh Cls; VP Soph Cls; VP Jr Cls; L Sftbl; High Hon Roll; Hon Roll; Scripture Mastery Awd; Messiah; Ed.

KAFKA, CHRISTINE; Bridgewater-Raritan HS West; Bridgewater, NJ; (Y); Science Clb; Ski Clb; Flag Corp; Nwsp Phtg; Yrbk Phtg; Var Crs Cntry; Im Powder Puff Ftbl; Var Trk; Hon Roll; NHS; Prsdntl Acdmc Ftnss Awd 86; Lafayette Coll; Elec Engnrng.

KAFKA, JOEYANN; East Brunswick HS; East Brunswick, NJ; (Y); Cmnty Wkr; FFA; Hosp Aide; Pep Clb; Yrbk Stf; Rep Frsh Cls; Mgr(s); Score Keeper; Im Trk; Hon Roll; Rutgers; Med.

KAFTON, DIANE; Perth Amboy HS; Perth Amboy, NJ; (Y); 77/501; Pres Sec Key Clb; Letterman Clb; Nwsp Stf; Yrbk Stf; Trs Stu Cncl; Var L Bowling; Var Mgr(s); Var L Tennis; Hon Roll; Kiwanis Awd; Athlt Of Wk-Jan 85-86; #1 2nd Dbls Tm-Mddlsx Grtr Tnns Conf 85-86; Schl Schlr; Accntng.

KAHLENBERG, DAVID; Hun School Of Princetn; Yardley, PA; (Y); 25/107; Ski Clb; Teachers Aide; Yrbk Ed-Chief; JV Capt Bsktbl; VP Trk; High Hon Roll; Hon Roll; Schlrshp Trip To Israel 85; Dickinson Clg; Libl Arts.

KAHN, ALLEN; Perth Amboy HS; Perth Amboy, NJ; (Y); 10/357; Computer Clb; Pres German Clb; Hon Roll; NHS; Pres Schlr; St Schlr; NJ Dist Schlr 86; Rutgers U; Elec Engrng.

KAIN III, PHILIP G; Bridgewater-Raritan High Schl West; Bridgewater, NJ; (Y); Am Leg Boys St; Pres Spanish Clb; VP Band; Ed Nwsp Stf; Rptr Yrbk Stf; Sec Stu Cncl; Drama Clb; Library Aide; Thesps; Acpl Chr; Hugh Obrian Ldrshp Semnr Ambssdr 85-86; Schlstc Magzn Natl Wrtng Contst Hnr Mntn 84; Poltcl Sci.

KAISER, JOHN; Southern Regional HS; Barnegat, NJ; (Y); 20/400; Pres Math Clb; Capt Math Tm; Model UN; Spanish Clb; Church Choir; Rep Stu Cncl; Var Tennis; JV Trk; Gov Hon Prg Awd; High Hon Roll; Am Chem Soc Awd; NJ Govnrs Schl Adv Sci & Math 86; Engrg.

KAISER, KEVIN; Dept Ford Twsp HS; Dept Ford, NJ; (Y); FHA; Bowling; Hon Roll; Prfct Atten Awd; Mst Imprvd Bwlr Of Yr 85-86; Atlntc Co Cmnty-Sth Jrsy; Clnry.

KALAS, MELINA; Oak Knoll HS; Summit, NJ; (Y); 1/37; PAVAS; Ski Clb; Lit Mag; Gov Hon Prg Awd; High Hon Roll; Ntl Merit Ltr; St Schlr; Val; ST Awd Poetry 86; NJ ST Schrlshp 86; Lang Exc Spnsh Awd 86; Brown; Cosmetc Surgeon.

KALISCH, KIMBERLY; Bishop George Ahr HS; Woodbridge, NJ; (Y); 13/277; French Clb; Science Clb; Teachers Aide; Lit Mag; High Hon Roll; NHS; Intl Frgn Lang Awd 85; US Natl Ldrshp Merit Awd 86; Bio Chem.

KALLER, RICHARD P; Morristown HS; Convent Station, NJ; (Y); Rep Church Yth Grp; German Clb; Church Choir; Rep Jr Cls; JV Var Socr; Hon Roll; NHS; Cmnty Wkr; Latin Clb; Scholastic Bowl; Gina Bachauer Piano Schlrshp 84; Hannah & Leonard Stone Fndtn Awd 85.

KALLOPOULOU, CHRISTINA; North Bergen HS; Guttenberg, NJ; (Y); 94/450; Am Leg Aux Girls St; Church Yth Grp; German Clb; Key Clb; Chorus; Rep Frsh Cls; Rep Soph Cls; JV Crs Cntry; JV Trk; Cit Awd; Excllnce Awd Greek Lang Culture 81; Bill Brunner Humanitrn Awd 83; Germn Hnr Soc 86; Pol Sci.

KALMA, CHRIS; Manalapin HS; Manalapan, NJ; (Y); Band; Concert Band; Mrchg Band; Symp Band; JV Bsktbl; Var Crs Cntry; Var Trk; Most Imprvd Field Awd Trk 86; 3 Trk Vrsty Ltrs 84-86; Vrsty Ltr Wind Ensemble 85; Pol Sci.

KALNINS, ANDIS; Wood-Ridge HS; Wood-Ridge, NJ; (S); 3/76; Computer Clb; Latin Clb; Math Clb; Model UN; Mrchg Band; Nwsp Rptr; Var Capt Crs Cntry; Var Trk; NHS; Eagle Scout 85; Engrng.

KALOLA, BINA; Parsippany Hills HS; Morris Plains, NJ; (S); Debate Tm; VP FBLA; Math Tm; NFL; JV Socr; Hon Roll; Hugh O Brian Yth Ldrshp ST Awd 84-85; NFL 3rd Pl ST Debt 84-85; FBLA ST Cmptn Awd 84-85; Corp Law.

KALTSAS, MARIA; Dover HS; Dover, NJ; (Y); 23/225; Computer Clb; Drama Clb; Office Aide; School Musical; Variety Show; Yrbk Stf; Tennis; Hon Roll; NHS; Prfct Atten Awd; Dover Womns Clb Schlrshp 86; Stockton ST Clg; Bus Admn.

KAM, AGNES; Matawan Regional HS; Aberdeen, NJ; (S); 11/293; Q&S; Spanish Clb; Stage Crew; Nwsp Ed-Chief; Yrbk Ed-Chief; Sec Stu Cncl; Hon Roll; NHS; Spanish NHS; Columbia Schlstc Press Awd 85-86; Jrnlsm.

KAMINSKI, EDWARD; Linden HS; Linden, NJ; (Y); Church Yth Grp; FBLA; German Clb; Key Clb; Quiz Bowl; Var Socr; Var Wrstlng; Hon Roll; NHS; Delta Epsln Phi Grmn Hnrs Clb 85; All Metro Wrstlng Tm 86; Bus.

KAMINSKI, LISA; Eastern HS; Voorhees, NJ; (Y); Office Aide; Chorus; School Musical; School Play; Variety Show; Yrbk Stf; VP Sr Cls; Sec Rep Stu Cncl; Var Cheerleading; Lcrss; Rotary Yth Ldrshp Awd 86; S Jersy Choir 84; Spec Educ.

KAMINSKI, PATRICIA; Paul VI HS; Sicklerville, NJ; (S); 7/474; Pres VP 4-H; Math Clb; JV Crs Cntry; L Pom Pon; Cit Awd; Dnfth Awd; 4-H Awd; Sec NHS; Drama Clb; Gardn ST Dstngshd Schlr-Schlrshp; JR Miss Fnlst; Princeton; Biomed Engrng.

KAMP, KELLY; Palisades Park JR SR HS; Palisades Pk, NJ; (Y); Dance Clb; Pep Clb; Chorus; School Musical; Swing Chorus; Variety Show; Nwsp Rptr; Sec Stu Cncl; JV Var Cheerleading; Var Sftbl; U MD; Jrnlsm.

KANA, MICHELE; Mount Olive HS; Flanders, NJ; (Y); 22/309; Dance Clb; Hosp Aide; Math Tm; Ski Clb; Rep Stu Cncl; Cheerleading; Fld Hcky; Sftbl; Hon Roll; NHS; 3rd Tm All Area Fld Hcky Awd 83; Villanova U; Mktg.

KANACH, TOM; Oratory Prep; Gillette, NJ; (Y); 5/41; 4-H; Math Tm; Capt Quiz Bowl; Concert Band; Yrbk Ed-Chief; Var Tennis; Dnfth Awd; 4-H Awd; High Hon Roll; NHS; Ntl 4-H Cngrs For Seeing Eye Prjct 85; Purdue U; Vtrnry Med.

KANE, AILEEN; Mount Olive HS; Flanders, NJ; (Y); 23/290; AFS; Math Tm; Ski Clb; Fld Hcky; High Hon Roll; Hon Roll; NHS; Bus.

KANE, DAN; Millville SR HS; Millville, NJ; (Y); Latin Clb; Bowling; Var Tennis; Hon Roll; Economics.

KANE, EMILY; Asbury Park HS; Bradley Bch, NJ; (Y); French Clb; High Hon Roll; Hon Roll; NHS; Outstndng Bus Awd 86; Katherine Gibbs Ldrshp Awd 86; Vrsty Schlr 86; Ex Sec.

KANE, JACKIE; Holy Cross HS; Moorestown, NJ; (Y); 4/390; School Musical; Nwsp Stf; Rep Frsh Cls; Rep Soph Cls; Rep Jr Cls; Tennis; High Hon Roll; NHS; Lwyr.

KANE, PATRICK; Cherry Hill High School West; Cherry Hill, NJ; (Y); 55/370; Var Capt Bsbl; Var Capt Ftbl; Cit Awd; Hon Roll; Thomas Bottalico Awd-Ldrshp & Dedctn Ftbl 85; Cherry Hill Schlrshp Fndtn-Cherry Hill W Qtrbk Clb 86; Drexel U; Engrng.

KANE, STEVEN; Cherry Hill HS West; Cherry Hill, NJ; (Y); 4/338; Art Clb; Camera Clb; Drama Clb; French Clb; Intnl Clb; JCL; PAVAS; Quiz Bowl; School Play; Stu Cncl; Bst Drctr Awd 86; Wnr Ntl Frnch Cntst 83-86; Wnr Englsh Wrtng Cntst 84 & 86; Intl Bus.

KANTOR, DEBBIE; Palmyra HS; Palmyra, NJ; (Y); French Clb; Co-Capt Color Guard; Stat Bsbl; Mgr(s); Score Keeper; Hon Roll; Prfct Atten Awd; Bus.

KANTRA, AMY; Toms River HS North; Toms River, NJ; (Y); Pres Church Yth Grp; French Clb; Spanish Clb; Church Choir; Flag Corp; School Musical; Yrbk Stf; Rep Frsh Cls; Rep Soph Cls; Rep Jr Cls; Chrmn SR Prom 87; Good Ctzns Cnfrnce 1st Rnr Up 86; Mngmt.

KAPADIA, VARSA; N Bergen HS; North Bergen, NJ; (S); 33/405; French Clb; Hosp Aide; Intnl Clb; Office Aide; VP Spanish Clb; Chorus; Variety Show; Yrbk Stf; Trs Frsh Cls; Trs Soph Cls; Rutgers U; Psychlgy.

KAPLAN, ALYSSA; River Dell SR HS; River Edge, NJ; (Y); 12/213; Temple Yth Grp; Nwsp Rptr; Nwsp Stf; High Hon Roll; Hon Roll; NHS; Spanish NHS; Paramus Red Wave & Ridgewood Y Brkrs Swim Tms 83-85; Red Cross Lifegrd 85-86; Cmmnctns.

KAPLAN, BRIAN; East Brunswick HS; E Brunswick, NJ; (Y); 4/600; Key Clb; Spanish Clb; SADD; Rep Stu Cncl; Var L Tennis; Hon Roll; VP NHS; Spanish NHS.

KAPLAN, ERIC J; Paramus HS; Paramus, NJ; (Y); 4/347; Debate Tm; Math Tm; NFL; Quiz Bowl; Science Clb; Lit Mag; NHS; Ntl Merit SF; Opt Clb Awd; Camera Clb; Germ NHS; Elec Engrng.

KAPLAN, KRISTY; Middle Township HS; Dennisville, NJ; (Y); 45/224; Church Yth Grp; FNA; Hosp Aide; Model UN; JV Var Bsktbl; Var Fld Hcky; Var Sftbl; High Hon Roll; Hon Roll; Air Force; Phys Therapy.

KAPLAN, LISA; Manalapan HS; Englishtown, NJ; (Y); Temple Yth Grp; Bsktbl; Sftbl.

KAPLAN, MARC; Highstown HS; East Windsor, NJ; (Y); Model UN; Political Wkr; Nwsp Phtg; Nwsp Rptr; Nwsp Stf; Hon Roll; Stock Mrkt Game Tm Capt 85-86; Mdl Congress 85-86; Schl T V News Reprtr 85-86.

KAPLAN, PAUL; Freehold Township HS; Freehold, NJ; (Y); Varsity Clb; Variety Show; Nwsp Sprt Ed; Nwsp Stf; Yrbk Stf; JV Var Bsbl; Var Bsktbl; Ftbl; Wt Lftg; U Of S FL; Med.

KAPLAN, TAMARA MICHELLE; Bruriah HS; Staten Isl, NY; (Y); 6/52; NHS; Ntl Merit Schol; NEDT Awd; Special Ed.

KAPPELMEIER, LORRAINE; Pope John XXIII HS; Lafayette, NJ; (Y); Girl Scts; Varsity Clb; JV Bsktbl; Capt Cheerleading; Var Sftbl; Hon Roll; Educ.

KAPPMEIER, GREGORY; Hudson Catholic HS For Boys; N Bergen, NJ; (Y); 48/182; Dance Clb; Chrmn Pep Clb; SADD; Trs Stu Cncl; JV Var Bsbl; Im Bsktbl; Im Bowling; Im Ftbl; JV Var Ice Hcky; Im Trk; Peer Minstr Prgm; Chrmn Of Chrstms Toy Dr; Secaucus Hcky Leag-Capt, All Stars 86; Crmnlgy.

KAPUSCINSKI, GREGG; Montville Township HS; Montville, NJ; (Y); 32/262; Art Clb; Church Yth Grp; Drama Clb; Key Clb; Ski Clb; Mrchg Band; School Musical; School Play; NHS; Ntl Merit SF; Arch.

KARABINUS, MATT T; Phillipsburg HS; Stewartsville, NJ; (Y); 79/344; Am Leg Boys St; Model UN; JV Var Socr; Engrng.

KARADIS, PAULINE; Villa Victoria Acad; Wrightstown, NJ; (Y); Computer Clb; Math Clb; School Musical; School Play; Stage Crew; Variety Show; Yrbk Stf; Rep Trs Stu Cncl; Var Sftbl; Hon Roll; Schlstc Olympics Awd 83; Sftbl MVP & Good Sprtsmnshp 83; Bst Slsprsn 84-86; Seton Hall; Elem Educ.

KARAGIAS, DIMITRA; Manasquan HS; Brielle, NJ; (Y); 15/250; Art Clb; Church Yth Grp; Drama Clb; Exploring; French Clb; FBLA; Hosp Aide; Key Clb; Latin Clb; Math Clb; Brd Ed Awd 84-85; Brd Ed Awd 85-86; Psych.

KARATY, RAY; Clifton HS; Clifton, NJ; (Y); Hon Roll; Jr NHS; Montclair ST Coll; Bus.

KARBANE, MARCI; Morris Knolls HS; Rockaway, NJ; (Y); Dance Clb; JA; Math Clb; Rep Stu Cncl; Swmmng; High Hon Roll; NHS; Summs Awd 85-86; Lawyer.

KARCHER, ELKE; Fair Lawn HS; Fair Lawn, NJ; (Y); 70/335; Acpl Chr; School Musical; Off Sr Cls; Acad Scholar 86; Johnson & Wales; Travel Mgmt.

KARG, JANET; Neumann Prep; Riverdale, NJ; (Y); 2/83; Sec Art Clb; Church Yth Grp; Yrbk Stf; Ed Lit Mag; Var Trk; High Hon Roll; NHS; Sal; Garden ST Distngshd Schlr Awd 86; Cook Coll Hnrs Stu 86; Cook Coll; Plant Sci.

KARIDES, MARINA; New Milford HS; New Milford, NJ; (Y); 20/144; Mrchg Band; Orch; School Play; Nwsp Ed-Chief; Yrbk Bus Mgr; VP Sr Cls; Var Bsktbl; Var Sftbl; Var Vllybl; NHS; New Milford HS Coaches Awd Excllnce Bsktbll 85-86; US Army Resrv Natl Schlr Athlt Awd 85-86; Wmns Cl; Northeastern U; Advrtsng.

KARIM, ASHRAFUL; Eastside HS; Paterson, NJ; (Y); 1/559; Am Leg Boys St; Pres Computer Clb; Capt Math Tm; Pres Science Clb; Yrbk Phtg; Var Capt Tennis; Dnfth Awd; Gov Hon Prg Awd; NHS; Val; Stevens Inst Tech; Elec Engrng.

KARKOWSKI, ANDREA; Toms River H S North; Toms River, NJ; (Y); Sec Pres 4-H; German Clb; Hosp Aide; Capt Drill Tm; Lit Mag; Stu Cncl; Mgr(s); Hon Roll; NHS; Ntl Merit SF; Lockhaven U; Psych.

KARNS, GENNIFER; Lenape Valley Regional HS; Stanhope, NJ; (Y); 7/255; Church Yth Grp; Drama Clb; Madrigals; School Musical; Sec Frsh Cls; Sec Jr Cls; Rep Stu Cncl; French Hon Soc; Sec NHS; Prfct Atten Awd; Comm.

KARP, JEFFERY; Belvidere HS; Phillipsburg, NJ; (S); #10 In Class; Aud/Vis; Chess Clb; Varsity Clb; Var Bsktbl; Var Socr; Im Vllybl; Hon Roll; NHS; St Sci Day 1st County; Var Ltr Bsktbl.

KARRAS, THOMAS; Hudson Catholic HS; Jersey City, NJ; (Y); 15/196; Camera Clb; Dance Clb; Stu Cncl; JV Var Bsktbl; Im Ftbl; Var Ice Hcky; High Hon Roll; NHS; Savings Clb; De La Salle Svc Adw; Seton Hall U; Comm.

KARRER, LOUIS; Pope John XXIII Regional HS; Augusta, NJ; (Y); 68/131; Art Clb; German Clb; Hon Roll; Anmtn.

KARSEVAR, DANNY; Atlantic City HS; Margate, NJ; (Y); Key Clb; Library Aide; Office Aide; SADD; Teachers Aide; Temple Yth Grp; Yrbk Rptr; Lit Mag; Rep Jr Cls; Rep Sr Cls; Sci.

KASAKS, TARA; Westfield SR HS; Westfield, NJ; (Y); 12/515; French Clb; Latin Clb; Trs Jr Cls; L Socr; L Sftbl; Var Tennis; Hon Roll; NHS; 2 Yrs Magna Cum Lauda Natl Latin Exam 85-86.

KASCIK, KITTY A; South Hunterdon Regional HS; Lambertville, NJ; (Y); Chorus; Pres Frsh Cls; Hon Roll; Jennie M Nesta Mrl Schlrshp; Rider Coll.

KASPER, JENNIFER; Hackettstown HS; Hackettstown, NJ; (Y); 68/199; Church Yth Grp; 4-H; Girl Scts; Hosp Aide; Ski Clb; Church Choir; H S Trade Assn Awd 86; Johnson & Wales Coll; Clnry Art.

KASSAK, KATHRYN; Union HS; Union, NJ; (Y); Drama Clb; FBLA; Trs Intnl Clb; Key Clb; Chorus; Yrbk Stf; Hon Roll; Kiwanis Awd; Prfct Atten Awd; Bus.

KASSOUF, EVELYN; Holy Spirit HS; Absecon, NJ; (Y); Church Yth Grp; Pres French Clb; School Musical; Hon Roll; NHS.

KATCHEN, DEBORAH; Mount Olive HS; Budd Lake, NJ; (Y); 38/296; Church Yth Grp; FBLA; OEA; Yrbk Stf; JV Im Fld Hcky; Var JV Sftbl; Hon Roll; Ntl Merit Ltr; Cert Of Awd-Achvt In Bio 85; Cert Of Awd-Achvt In Typing 86; Cnty Coll-Morris; Med Lab.

KATTAS, PAUL; Chatham Twp HS; Chatham, NJ; (Y); FBLA; Key Clb; Model UN; Ski Clb; Varsity Clb; Nwsp Phtg; Var Tennis.

KATTERMANN, EMIL A; High Point Regional HS; Sussex, NJ; (Y); Am Leg Boys St; Aud/Vis; Debate Tm; German Clb; Office Aide; Spanish Clb; Teachers Aide; Band; Concert Band; Jazz Band.

KATZ, MICHAEL; Freehold Twp HS; Freehold, NJ; (Y); 3/380; Boy Scts; Lit Mag; Rep Frsh Cls; Rep Soph Cls; Rep Jr Cls; JV Socr; NHS; Ntl Merit Ltr; Bus Adm.

KATZ, NEAL; Ocean Township HS; Wayside, NJ; (Y); Temple Yth Grp; Nwsp Phtg; Med.

KAUFER, CHRISTINA; Secaucus HS; Secaucus, NJ; (S); 23/160; Pres Church Yth Grp; Math Clb; Office Aide; Spanish Clb; Var JV Cheerleading; Swmmng; JV Tennis; High Hon Roll; Hon Roll; Mu Alp Tht; Aerontcl Engr.

KAUFFMAN, KEVIN; Middletown HS South; Redbank, NJ; (Y); Teachers Aide; Concert Band; Jazz Band; Pep Band; Symp Band; JV Bsktbl; Var Capt Ftbl; Var Wt Lftg; High Hon Roll; Hon Roll; Wldlf Mgmt.

KAUFFMAN, KIMBERLY S; Hopewell Valley Central HS; Titusville, NJ; (Y); 2/202; AFS; Art Clb; French Clb; Chrmn Service Clb; Nwsp Rptr; Yrbk Stf; High Hon Roll; Ntl Merit SF; St Schlr; Pedtrcn.

KAUFHOLD, CYNTHIA; Livingston HS; Livingston, NJ; (Y); Hosp Aide; Key Clb; Band; Capt Color Guard; Mrchg Band; Hon Roll; Candy Striper 86; Pre Law.

KAUFMAN, DANIEL; Academic HS; Jersey City, NJ; (Y); 10/70; Boy Scts; Computer Clb; Exploring; Math Tm; Quiz Bowl; Scholastic Bowl; Bowling; Capt Swmmng; Hon Roll; Rutgers; Engrngh.

KAUFMAN, IAN; Glen Rock JR SR HS; Glen Rock, NJ; (Y); 2/155; Pep Clb; Spanish Clb; Nwsp Stf; Var L Socr; Var L Tennis; High Hon Roll; Jr NHS; NHS; Accntng.

KAUFMAN, MIKE; Shore Regional HS; Red Bank, NJ; (Y); 7/227; Boy Scts; Cmnty Wkr; Computer Clb; Key Clb; Math Tm; Q&S; Science Clb; Temple Yth Grp; School Play; Nwsp Rptr; Ntl Hnr Soc Jrnlsts; Rutgers; Bus.

KAUFMAN, SHARON; Livingston HS; Livingston, NJ; (Y); French Clb; Temple Yth Grp; Nwsp Rptr; Yrbk Ed-Chief; Lit Mag; Gym; Pres French Hon Soc; High Hon Roll; Jr NHS; Law.

KAUFMANN, TAMMY; Brick Memorial HS; Brick, NJ; (Y); 56/307; Pres Church Yth Grp; Drama Clb; FBLA; Chorus; School Musical; School Play; Rep Soph Cls; Sftbl; High Hon Roll; Voice Dem Awd; Relgn.

KAUR, DVINDER; Indian Hills HS; Franklin Lks, NJ; (Y); 33/279; AFS; Church Yth Grp; Chorus; Yrbk Stf; Hon Roll; NHS; Ntl Merit Ltr; Med.

KAWALEC, JILL; Immaculata HS; N Plainfield, NJ; (Y); 20/226; Band; Concert Band; Mrchg Band; Symp Band; VP Sftbl; High Hon Roll; NHS; Church Yth Grp; Math Tm; Acad All Amer; All Cnty Sftbl 1st Tm; Excllnce Spn III; Biomed Engrng.

KAWANAKA, YOSUKE; Cresskill HS; Oradell, NJ; (Y); 6/120; Math Tm; Ski Clb; Var Crs Cntry; JV Socr; Var Tennis; High Hon Roll; Hon Roll; NHS; Bergen Cnty Math League/Grp VI 1st Pl 86; Intl Bus.

KAY, HONAIRE; Roxbury HS; Princeton Jct, NJ; (Y); 1/309; Math Tm; Scholastic Bowl; Wt Lftg; Gov Hon Prg Awd; NHS; Val; Acdmc All-Amer 85; NJ Nets Schlrshp Awd 85; Rtry Clb Schlrshp 86; U Of FL; Biomed Engr.

KAYAL, JOHN; Don Bosco Prep; Mahwah, NJ; (S); 12/180; Chess Clb; Church Yth Grp; Computer Clb; Math Tm; Model UN; Capt Crs Cntry; Trk; High Hon Roll; Ltn II Awd 84; Thlgy I Awd 83; Engl I Awd 82; Bio.

KAYE, LISA; Red Bank Catholic HS; Freehold, NJ; (Y); Art Clb; Church Yth Grp; Dance Clb; Drama Clb; Hosp Aide; Vllybl; Hon Roll; Ntl Merit SF; Frnch IV 86; US Hstry II 86.

KAYLE, JENNIFER; Hamilton HS East; Hamilton Sq, NJ; (Y); Varsity Clb; Chorus; Madrigals; School Musical; Lit Mag; Var L Diving; Var L Fld Hcky; Hon Roll; NHS; Liberal Arts Coll; Psychlgy.

KAYLOR JR, WILLIAM E; Holy Cross HS; Roebling, NJ; (Y); Debate Tm; JA; Political Wkr; High Hon Roll; Hon Roll; Yth In Pltcl Systm 86; Mck-Trl Cnty Chmpnshp Tm 86; Wshngtn DC Ldrshp Inst 86; Bus.

KAYS, MONICA; Hunterdon Central HS; Felmington, NJ; (Y); 171/548; Acpl Chr; Chorus; School Musical; School Play; Bowling; Trk; JR Grange Sec 84; JR Grange ST Princess; Musician.

KAYSER, KIM; Pitman HS; Pitman, NJ; (Y); Var Ftbl; Var Sftbl; Glasboro ST Coll; Acctng.

KAZAN, BARRY; Hightstown HS; East Windsor, NJ; (Y); Drama Clb; Mathletes; Chorus; School Play; Stage Crew; Nwsp Phtg; Nwsp Rptr; Rep Jr Cls; Var Trk; High Hon Roll; Law.

KAZELLA, STEVE; Don Bosco Prep; N Haledon, NJ; (Y); Boy Scts; Exploring; German Clb; Ski Clb; Var Bsktbl; JV Socr.

KAZOKAS, RENEE; Piscataway HS; Piscataway, NJ; (Y); Dance Clb; JA; Anml Sci.

KEANE, ANNE; Manasquan HS; Spring Lake Hts, NJ; (Y); Art Clb; Key Clb; Latin Clb; Ski Clb; Spanish Clb; School Play; Crs Cntry; Lib Arts.

KEANE, TIM; South Plainfield HS; S Plainfield, NJ; (Y); 25/210; Radio Clb; Ski Clb; Hon Roll; Bus.

KEARNEY, JAMES; Oratory Preparatory Schl; Livingston, NJ; (Y); 2/40; Math Clb; Math Tm; Var Bsbl; Var Capt Bsktbl; Var Socr; Im Vllybl; NHS; Bucknell U.

KEARNEY, PAMELA; Malcolm X Shabazz HS; Newark, NJ; (S); 4/263; Cmnty Wkr; Teachers Aide; Hon Roll; Trs NHS; Black Achvrs Awd 84; William Paterson Coll; Nrsng.

KEARNEY, SUSAN; Red Bank Regional HS; Little Silver, NJ; (Y); 60/223; Teachers Aide; Capt Color Guard; Mrchg Band; Rep Frsh Cls; Rep Stu Cncl; Stat Fld Hcky; JV Socr; Hon Roll; Red Bank Rep Booster Clb Awd 86; Sally Smigler Awd 86; York Coll; Bus Adm.

KEARNS JR, PAUL C; Bergen Catholic HS; Teaneck, NJ; (Y); Church Yth Grp; Exploring; Ski Clb; School Musical; School Play; Stage Crew; Nwsp Rptr; Nwsp Sprt Ed; Im Bsktbl; Im Fld Hcky; Syracuse; Acctng.

KEDIAN, KERRY; Hillsborough HS; Somerville, NJ; (Y); 21/287; Cmnty Wkr; Dance Clb; School Musical; School Play; Yrbk Stf; Lit Mag; Rep Stu Cncl; JV Trk; Hon Roll; NHS; Bus.

KEENAN, CHRISTINE; Chatham Borough HS; Chatham, NJ; (Y); Church Yth Grp; Pep Clb; Chorus; Nwsp Rptr; Yrbk Ed-Chief; Trs Frsh Cls; Rep Stu Cncl; JV Var Socr; Stat L Tennis; Kiwanis Awd.

KEENAN, KIM; Rahway HS; Rahway, NJ; (Y); Drama Clb; Chorus; School Musical; School Play; Hon Roll; John Robert Powers; Csmtlgy.

KEENAN, LAURA; James Caldwell HS; W Caldwell, NJ; (Y); French Clb; Pres Key Clb; Varsity Clb; Yrbk Bus Mgr; Trs Jr Cls; Var Bsktbl; Var Capt Socr; Var Sftbl; Var Tennis; High Hon Roll; Gridiron Schlrshp 86; Unico Awd 86; US Armys Ntl Sccr Coachs Assoc Of Amer MVP 86; Fairfield U; Bus.

KEENAN, MARIE; Lenape Valley Reg HS; Stanhope, NJ; (Y); 18/256; Am Leg Aux Girls St; Church Yth Grp; Trs Frsh Cls; Trs Soph Cls; Trs Jr Cls; Rep Stu Cncl; Capt Cheerleading; Trk; French Hon Soc; NHS; Engr.

KEENAN, SHERRI; West Essex Regional HS; N Caldwell, NJ; (Y); Church Yth Grp; Dance Clb; Quiz Bowl; Spanish Clb; Band; Chorus; Concert Band; Drm & Bgl; Jazz Band; Mrchg Band; Coaches Awd Trophy Swim Tm 82; Tv Anchrwmn Broadcstr.

KEENE, ELIZABETH; Middletown HS South; Navesink, NJ; (Y); Church Choir; JV Capt Bsktbl; Stat Fld Hcky; Powder Puff Ftbl; Im Socr; JV Var Sftbl; DAR Awd; Hon Roll; Sprtsmnshp Awd 83-84; Phy Ed.

KEENEY, MICHAEL; Pinelands Regional HS; Tuckerton, NJ; (Y); 4/192; Varsity Clb; Var Bsbl; Var Capt Bsktbl; Var Capt Ftbl; Im Wt Lftg; High Hon Roll; Hon Roll; VP NHS.

KEES, SUE; Depaul HS; Wayne, NJ; (Y); 27/171; Service Clb; Rep Frsh Cls; Rep Soph Cls; VP Jr Cls; Rep Sr Cls; Rep Stu Cncl; JV Var Cheerleading; JV Sftbl; High Hon Roll; Hon Roll; U Of Richmond; Bus Admn.

KEGEL, WILLIAM B; Lenape Valley Reg HS; Stanhope, NJ; (Y); 90/256; Church Yth Grp; CAP; Bowling; Hon Roll; Engr.

KEHOE, MAUREEN; Holy Cross HS; Cinnaminson, NJ; (Y); 4/380; Church Yth Grp; French Clb; Model UN; Ski Clb; Thesps; Chorus; School Musical; School Play; Nwsp Ed-Chief; Nwsp Stf; Jrnlsm.

KEHOE, PATRICK; Bishop George Ahr HS; Perth Amboy, NJ; (Y); Im Bsbl; Im Bsktbl; Im Bowling; Im Sftbl; Capt Vllybl; Seton Hall U; Jrnlsm.

KEILL, SUSAN; Watchung Hills Reg HS; Stirling, NJ; (Y); 20/315; Drama Clb; SADD; Thesps; Chorus; Color Guard; Flag Corp; Mrchg Band; School Musical; School Play; Stage Crew; Drama.

KEISER, BENJAMIN; Central Regional HS; Bayville, NJ; (Y); 4/360; Computer Clb; Off Ski Clb; Nwsp Stf; Stu Cncl; Crs Cntry; L Trk; High Hon Roll; NHS; Ntl Merit SF; Spanish NHS; Engrng.

KEITH, JONATHAN; West Essex HS; N Caldwell, NJ; (Y); Church Yth Grp; Latin Clb; Science Clb; JV Capt Bsbl; Hon Roll; NHS; Bus.

KEITH, SHARONDA; Central HS; Newark, NJ; (Y); Hosp Aide; Co-Capt Jr Cls; Var Cheerleading; Var Trk; High Hon Roll; Hon Roll; NHS; Goal Card Holder-Hnr Stu Only 85-86; Schlrs Day Awd 85-86; Newark Educ Awd 85-86; U Of PA; Med.

KELL, GARY; Mainland Regional HS; Linwood, NJ; (Y); JCL; Band; Concert Band; Mrchg Band; Nwsp Stf; JV Golf; Im Vllybl; U VA; Bus Admin.

KELLER, EDWARD; Toms River High School East; Toms River, NJ; (S); 162/585; Boy Scts; Q&S; Nwsp Sprt Ed; Var Ftbl; Var Trk; Im Wt Lftg; JV Wrstlng; Ski Clb; Band; Concert Band; Eagle Scout 85; Secndry Schl Tchr.

KELLER, JIM; Overbrook Regional SR HS; Pine Hill, NJ; (Y); 16/275; French Clb; Trs Stu Cncl; JV Bsbl; Mgr(s); High Hon Roll; Hon Roll; Rutgers; Comp Sci.

KELLER, JOHN R; Absegami Regional HS; Smithville, NJ; (Y); 15/265; Art Clb; Cmnty Wkr; German Clb; Key Clb; Model UN; Ski Clb; Rptr Lit Mag; Rep Sr Cls; JV Tennis; Im Mgr Vllybl; Ithica Coll Schlrshp; Absegami/Presdnts Awd & Acad Achvt 82-83 & 84-85; Ithica Coll; Finance.

KELLER, LAURA; Manasquan HS; Belmar, NJ; (Y); 27/257; Church Yth Grp; Dance Clb; Band; Concert Band; Drill Tm; Drm Mjr(t); Jazz Band; Mrchg Band; Orch; Pep Band; All Shore Band 86; Fine Arts.

KELLER, LAUREN; Memorial HS; Cedar Grove, NJ; (Y); 21/120; Nwsp Stf; Yrbk Stf; Sec Frsh Cls; Sec Soph Cls; Sec Jr Cls; Sec Sr Cls; Rep Stu Cncl; Var Capt Cheerleading; High Hon Roll; Hon Roll; Coll Wmns Clb Of Montclair 86; Trenton ST Coll; Bus Mgmt.

KELLER, RICHARD C; Red Bank Catholic HS; Oceanport, NJ; (Y); VP Ski Clb; Yrbk Phtg; Yrbk Stf; Rep Frsh Cls; VP Socr; Im Wt Lftg; Econ.

KELLEY, COLLEEN; Scotch Plains-Fanwood HS; Fanwood, NJ; (Y); Dance Clb; FBLA; Cheerleading; Co-Capt Gym; Hon Roll; Stu Ldrshp Conf 84-85; Fractrd Fmly Comm 84-85; Clb Gymnstc; Bus.

KELLEY, JAK; Jackson Memorial HS; Jackson, NJ; (Y); 95/405; VP Church Yth Grp; Ski Clb; JV Bsbl; Var Ftbl; Wt Lftg; High Hon Roll; Cls Finalist Boys ST 86.

KELLIGREW, SUSAN BOUTON; Summit HS; Summit, NJ; (Y); 9/268; Art Clb; Model UN; Pres Soph Cls; Pres Jr Cls; Pres Sr Cls; JV Bsktbl; Var Lcrss; Hon Roll; NHS; Unitd Way Ctznshp Awd 86; Certfd Laubach Litrcy Tutr 86; Socl Sci.

KELLNER, STEPHEN; Mainland Regional HS; Linwood, NJ; (Y); Intnl Clb; Church Choir; Comm.

KELLUM, TRACY LYNN; Salem HS; Salem, NJ; (Y); 8/200; Am Leg Aux Girls St; Computer Clb; Office Aide; Red Cross Aide; Spanish Clb; SADD; Rep Stu Cncl; Var Cheerleading; Hon Roll; Jr NHS; HOSA 83-87; Med Explrs 83-87; Blck Linkg 84-87; Coll Clb 83-87; Time 83-87; Pre-Med.

KELLY, ANGELA; Dumont HS; Dumont, NJ; (Y); Church Yth Grp; Hosp Aide; SADD; Teachers Aide; Band; Mrchg Band; Variety Show; JV Cheerleading; Var Capt Crs Cntry; Var Trk; Tchg.

KELLY, BRENDA; Mary Help Of Christians Acad; Clifton, NJ; (S); 6/88; GAA; JCL; Quiz Bowl; Service Clb; Teachers Aide; School Play; JV Vllybl; High Hon Roll; Hon Roll.

KELLY, CATHERINE; Northern Valley HS Olds Tappan; Old Tappan, NJ; (Y); 59/350; AFS; Chorus; Concert Band; Stu Cncl; Bsktbl; Fld Hcky; Trk; High Hon Roll; Hon Roll; NHS; Phys Ther.

KELLY, CHRISTINE; Paul SI HS; Runnemede, NJ; (Y); 285/530; Church Yth Grp; Cmnty Wkr; Pep Clb; Spanish Clb; SADD; Varsity Clb; Rep Frsh Cls; Var L Cheerleading; Im Coach Actv; Pom Pon; Chrldg Coach Awd 86; Vrsty Chrldg Ltr 86; Sftbl Trvlg Tm Awd 84; Jrnlsm.

KELLY, GREGORY J; Ocean City HS; Marmora, NJ; (Y); 4/291; Am Leg Boys St; VP Math Clb; Spanish Clb; Var Capt Crs Cntry; Var L Trk; High Hon Roll; NHS; Rotary Awd; US Military Acad Invttnl Acdmc Wrkshp 86; Engrng.

KELLY, JANINE Y; Fort Lee HS; Fort Lee, NJ; (Y); Pres Art Clb; Sec FTA; Pres PAVAS; Spanish Clb; Chorus; Flag Corp; Stage Crew; Ed Lit Mag; Hon Roll; Awd Of Excellnc Edtr Of Vc Mgzn 86; Artst Of Mnth 86; Pres Of Sadd 85-86; Schl Of Vsl Arts; Media Arts.

KELLY, JOHN J; St Joseph Regional HS; Garnerville, NY; (Y); Church Yth Grp; Ski Clb; Var L Crs Cntry; Var L Trk; Cardinal Spellman Yth Svc Awd 86; Law.

KELLY, KATHY; Lacordaire Acad; Essex Fells, NJ; (Y); Pep Clb; Ski Clb; Spanish Clb; School Musical; School Play; Nwsp Stf; Yrbk Bus Mgr; VP Jr Cls; VP Sr Cls; Capt Var Bsktbl; Boston Coll.

KELLY, KEVIN A; Verona HS; Verona, NJ; (Y); 1/174; Chrmn Intnl Clb; School Musical; Nwsp Ed-Chief; Yrbk Ed-Chief; French Hon Soc; Pres NHS; Ntl Merit SF; Val; Chess Clb; Church Yth Grp; NJ Govnrs Schl Sci 85; Rutgers Pres Scholar 86; Rutgers U; Mth.

KELLY, LARISSA; Teaneck HS; Teaneck, NJ; (Y); Church Yth Grp; Chorus; Im Powder Puff Ftbl; JV Sftbl; Hon Roll; NHS.

KELLY, LAURA; Washington Township HS; Turnersville, NJ; (Y); Bsbl; Fld Hcky; Sftbl; Hon Roll; Child Care.

KELLY, LISA; Audubon HS; Audubon Park, NJ; (Y); German Clb; Hon Roll; Rider Coll; Germn.

KELLY, NANCY; Roselle Catholic HS; Hillside, NJ; (S); Church Yth Grp; Math Clb; Stage Crew; Var Bsktbl; Var Socr; Var Trk; Hon Roll; Frnch Awd 85; Parish Cncl 86; Pre Med.

KELLY, SEAN; Bishop George AHR HS; Belle Mead, NJ; (Y); 131/273; Band; Mrchg Band; Orch; Pep Band; Symp Band; Hon Roll; Crmnl Jstc.

KELLY, SUZANNE; Toms River HS East; Toms Rvr, NJ; (Y); 69/575; Church Yth Grp; Cmnty Wkr; Computer Clb; 4-H; PAVAS; Political Wkr; Mgr(s); Powder Puff Ftbl; Hon Roll; Jr NHS; Bus Admin.

KELLY, TARA; Holy Cross HS; Medford, NJ; (Y); 175/400; Ski Clb; Rep Frsh Cls; Trs Soph Cls; Rep Jr Cls; Rep Sr Cls; Sec Stu Cncl; JV Socr; JV Swmmng; JV Tennis; Hon Roll; Nrsg.

KELLY, TONYA; Delsea HS; Williamstown, NJ; (Y); JV Bsktbl; JV Capt Fld Hcky; Mgr(s); Advtsg.

KELNER, SAUL; Nanalapan HS; Manalapan, NJ; (Y); 14/430; Chess Clb; Debate Tm; Science Clb; Temple Yth Grp; NHS; Crtfcte Of Hnr Advncd Algbra & Trignmtry 86; Coll; Bus Admin.

KELSHAW, JENNIFER; Morris Hills HS; Wharton, NJ; (Y); 43/269; FBLA; Prfct Atten Awd; Kthrn Gibbs Outstndng JR In Bus 86; 1st Hnrs Cmptns For Typng 86; Exec Secy.

KELSO, JEAN; Triton Regional HS; Glendora, NJ; (Y); 57/297; AFS; Hosp Aide; Ntl Merit SF; Ldrshp Awd AFS 86; Bsktbl Champs 85; Hnr Rl 86; Bio.

KEMME, GAIL; Hunterdon Central HS; Flemington, NJ; (Y); 88/550; Church Yth Grp; Cmnty Wkr; Church Choir; Stage Crew; Hon Roll; NHS; Recgntn Pgm Svc Achvt 84-85; Recgntn Pgm Mth II Achvt 84-85.

KEMP, MELISSA; Central HS; Newark, NJ; (Y); Yrbk Stf; Trk; Hon Roll; Montclair ST; Comp Pgmmr.

KEMPLE, SUSAN; Mt Olive HS; Budd Lake, NJ; (Y); 60/300; Concert Band; Jazz Band; Mrchg Band; Lit Mag; Drama Clb; Ski Clb; SADD; Band; Orch; School Musical; Scholar Westchester U Band Camp 86; Mst Imprvd Musicn Band 86; Psych.

KENAH, KARA; Immaculate Conception HS; West Orange, NJ; (Y); 4/80; Ed Yrbk Stf; Rep Soph Cls; Rep Jr Cls; Rep Sr Cls; Rep Stu Cncl; Var Capt Bsktbl; Capt Crs Cntry; Sftbl; High Hon Roll; NHS; Spnsh Achvt Test; Hgst Stu Avg; Bus.

KENDEIGH, ANDREW E; Westfield HS; Westfield, NJ; (Y); 130/530; Am Leg Boys St; SADD; Nwsp Stf; Pres Frsh Cls; Pres Stu Cncl; Var Bsbl; JV Bsktbl; Var Capt Ftbl; Im Wt Lftg; Hon Roll; All Union Cnty Ftbll Offnsv Tckl 85; All Metro Hon Ment Bsbll 1st Bse 85; Sec Stu Cncl & Pres 85-86; Cmmnctns.

KENDIG, LESLIE T; S Hunterdon Regional HS; Lambertville, NJ; (S); 3/68; 4-H; FBLA; Key Clb; Library Aide; SADD; Teachers Aide; Band; Chorus; Yrbk Stf; Sec Frsh Cls; Garden ST Distngshd Shlrs 85; Jrnlsm.

KENDZIERSKI, BRIAN; Paul VI HS; Barrington, NJ; (Y); Boy Scts; Math Clb; Spanish Clb; SADD; Bsktbl; Wrstlng; Rutgers U; Bus.

KENERSON, KARA JEAN; Hawthorne HS; Hawthorne, NJ; (Y); Pep Clb; Ski Clb; School Play; Variety Show; Yrbk Stf; Var Bsktbl; Cheerleading; Var Socr; Var Sftbl; Hon Roll; NYU; Fshn Mrktng.

KENIA, KEVIN J; Hackettstown HS; Hackettstown, NJ; (Y); 55/210; Pres Church Yth Grp; Band; Jazz Band; Mrchg Band; Bsbl; Bsktbl; Hon Roll; Cnty Coll Of Morris; Acctng.

KENNEDY, ANTOINETTE; Pleasantville HS; Pleasantville, NJ; (Y); Sec Church Yth Grp; Sec FCA; SADD; Teachers Aide; Band; Sec Church Choir; VP Jr Cls; Sftbl; Vllybl; Prfct Atten Awd; Prfct Atten Sunday Schl 84-86, Schl 85; 1st Aid Comptn 85; Pedtrcn.

KENNEDY, BEVERLY; Penns Grove HS; Carneys Point, NJ; (Y); 2/166; Sec German Clb; Chorus; School Musical; Yrbk Ed-Chief; Rep Stu Cncl; Capt Sftbl; Elks Awd; High Hon Roll; NHS; Sal; Douglass Coll; Indstrl Engrng.

KENNEDY, BRIAN; Manalapan HS; Englishtown, NJ; (Y); Boy Scts; Exploring; Latin Clb; Pres Nwsp Phtg; Yrbk Phtg; Rep Jr Cls; Trs Sr Cls; Phy Thrpy.

KENNEDY, KAREN; Piscataway HS; Piscataway, NJ; (Y); 1/475; Band; Concert Band; Mrchg Band; Orch; School Musical; Gov Hon Prg Awd; High Hon Roll; Hon Roll; NHS; Gov Awd Natl HS Hons Orchestra 86; Orchestra Awd 86; Rutgers U; Med.

KENNEDY, KAREN; St John Vianney HS; Hazlet, NJ; (Y); 18/260; Rep Frsh Cls; Rep Jr Cls; Rep Stu Cncl; Stat Bsbl; Var L Cheerleading; Trk; High Hon Roll; Hon Roll; NHS; Gold And White Awd 84-86; Prom Comm 86; Bus Reltd.

KENNEDY, SUSAN; Bishop George Ahr HS; Fords, NJ; (Y); Church Yth Grp; Cmnty Wkr; Ski Clb; Spanish Clb; Bowling; Hon Roll.

KENNEDY-JANSEN, THOMAS; Paul VI HS; Deptford, NJ; (Y); 100/500; Science Clb; Lit Mag; Ntl Merit Ltr; Rutgers-Camden Coll/Arts & Sci.

KENNEY, CHRISTOPHER; Middletown South HS; Middletown, NJ; (Y); Ski Clb; Ftbl; Gym; Wt Lftg; Wrstlng; Hon Roll; Engrng.

KENNEY, KEVIN; Steinert HS; Hamilton Sq, NJ; (Y); 46/326; Aud/Vis; Drama Clb; Exploring; FBLA; Varsity Clb; Stu Cncl; JV Capt Bsktbl; Var Capt Socr; Hon Roll; FBLA Schlrshp 86; Mr FBLA Cmptn 4th Hnrs ST 86; Widener U; Htl Mgmt.

KENNEY, MARGARET L; Cinnaminson HS; Cinnaminson, NJ; (Y); Drama Clb; Key Clb; Thesps; Band; Chorus; Yrbk Ed-Chief; Mgr(s); High Hon Roll; NHS; Ntl Merit Ltr; Bus Mngmnt.

KENNIE, SONJA; Washington Township HS; Turnersville, NJ; (Y); French Clb; Bsktbl; Fld Hcky; Capt Trk; Hon Roll; Most Imprvd Plyr Bsktbl 85-86; Acctng.

KENNY, JAMES; Piscataway HS; Piscataway, NJ; (Y); Church Yth Grp; Key Clb; Varsity Clb; Yrbk Phtg; Var L Golf; Hon Roll; Bio Sci.

KENNY, MICHAEL; Toms River HS South; Pine Beach, NJ; (Y); FBLA; Nwsp Ed-Chief; JV Tennis; Columbia Schlstc Press Comptn 1st Pl 86; Journlsm.

KENSICKI, KERRILYN; Toms River HS East; Toms River, NJ; (Y); 191/585; Capt Varsity Clb; L Var Chorus; Variety Show; Capt L Gym; JV Powder Puff Ftbl; Bus Adm.

KENT, ELIZABETH R; Shawnee HS; Medford, NJ; (Y); 74/537; Acpl Chr; Chorus; Jazz Band; Madrigals; School Musical; Variety Show; Stu Cncl; L Gym; Hon Roll; NHS; Bucks Cnty Playhouse Cameo Role Awd 85; Temple U; Music Perf & Ed.

KENT, TARA ANNE; Pop John XXIII HS; Vernon, NJ; (Y); 35/131; Hosp Aide; Chorus; Var Capt Fld Hcky; Var Trk; High Hon Roll; NHS; Drama Clb; Red Cross Aide; Ski Clb; NJ ST HS Ski Tm Rnkd 3rd NJ 86; Outstndng Achvt Awd 84 & 86; Miss Teen NJ Pagnt Prsnl Devlpmt 86; Cornell U; Sprts Med.

KEPHART, SHELLEY; Voorhees HS; Lebanon, NJ; (Y); 4/245; Exploring; 4-H; Radio Clb; Varsity Clb; Hst Sr Cls; Rep Stu Cncl; Var L Fld Hcky; 4-H Awd; High Hon Roll; NHS; Yale U; Liberal Arts.

KERBAGE, TAREK; Ferris HS; Jersey City, NJ; (Y); Am Leg Boys St; Boys Clb Am; Math Clb; Science Clb; Var Bowling; JV Tennis; Hon Roll; NHS; Stevens Step Prg Alg III Awd 85; Readg Lab Awd 85-86; Advncd Humnt Awd 86; Rutgers Clg; Elect Engrg.

KERDOCK, DIANE; Howell HS; Howell, NJ; (Y); Speech Tm; Capt Color Guard; Nwsp Rptr; Nwsp Stf; NHS; Opt Clb Awd; Armed Forces Career Explo Engrng/Sci 1st Grp Proj 85; Monmouth Coll Govt Inst-Rsrch Paper Awd 86.

KERISH, JOHN F; Vineland HS; Vineland, NJ; (Y); Exploring; Key Clb; Math Tm; Varsity Clb; Rep Stu Cncl; Var Socr; JV Tennis; French Hon Soc; NHS; St Schlr; US Miltry Acad Wst Pnt; US Military Acad; Aro Spc Engr.

KERLEVSKY, ALEXANDRA; Randolph HS; Randolph, NJ; (Y); 120/363; Art Clb; Political Wkr; Ski Clb; Temple Yth Grp; Yrbk Stf; Coach Actv; Powder Puff Ftbl; Tennis; Poli Sci.

KERN, EDWARD; Bridgewater-Raritan West HS; Bridgewater, NJ; (Y); 48/268; School Play; Stage Crew; Art Clb; JV Ftbl; Im Powder Puff Ftbl; Im Wt Lftg.

KERN, KIMBERLY A; Millville SR HS; Millvlle, NJ; (Y); Church Yth Grp; French Clb; Hosp Aide; Office Aide; Political Wkr; SADD; Variety Show; Lit Mag; Stu Cncl; Bowling; Norwich U; Mdrn Lang.

KERN, LORI J; Wall HS; Manasquan, NJ; (Y); 28/265; Powder Puff Ftbl; High Hon Roll; Hon Roll; Natl Physcl Educ Awd 86.

KERN, TINA; Morris Knolls HS; Denville, NJ; (Y); 2/398; Rep Church Yth Grp; FBLA; Math Clb; Math Tm; Chorus; Church Choir; JV Sftbl; High Hon Roll; NHS; Summa Wad 84-86; Eastern Nazarene Coll; Engrng.

KERR III, FRANCIS; Bridgewater-Raritan West HS; Bridgewater, NJ; (Y); Exploring; Math Tm; Science Clb; Ski Clb; Socr; Trk; High Hon Roll; Hon Roll; NHS; Pres Acadmc Ftnss Awd 86; Lehigh ; Elec Engrg.

KERR, TRACY; Central Regional HS; Seaside Park, NJ; (Y); 3/240; Math Clb; Nwsp Stf; Var L Trk; French Hon Soc; High Hon Roll; VP NHS; Cntrl Reg High Sch Math Clb Individual High Scorer 86.

KERRIGAN, CAROLYN; St John Vianney HS; Aberdeen, NJ; (Y); Church Yth Grp; Cmnty Wkr; Exploring; Hosp Aide; Intnl Clb; SADD; Lit Mag; Hon Roll; Vlntr Awd 84-85; Mltpl Sclrs Citn Awd 85-86; Gld & Wht Awd 85; Rutgers Coll; Law.

KERRIGAN, KELLIE; Holy Cross HS; Moorestown, NJ; (Y); 31/390; Church Yth Grp; Ski Clb; JV Var Cheerleading; High Hon Roll; Yth & Amer Pol Systm 86; Bus.

KERSHAW, ROBERT; Lower Cape May Regional HS; N Cape May, NJ; (Y); 50/220; Computer Clb; Library Aide; Math Tm; SADD; Yrbk Stf; Tennis; Hon Roll; Rutgers New Brunswick; Phrmcy.

KERSTNER, CHRISTINE; Newton HS; Andover, NJ; (S); 7/210; Church Yth Grp; Latin Clb; Math Tm; Thesps; Chorus; Madrigals; School Play; Stage Crew; Hon Roll; Communctns.

KERWIN, BETSEY; Kinnelon HS; Riverdale, NJ; (Y); Art Clb; PAVAS; Band; Concert Band; Mgr Jazz Band; Mrchg Band.

KERZIC, CATHERINE; Kearny HS; Kearny, NJ; (Y); Am Leg Aux Girls St; German Clb; Varsity Clb; Yrbk Stf; Var Bsktbl; Var Socr; Var Sftbl; Vllybl; Soccr, Bsktbl & Sftbl Vrsty Ltrs 84-87; Cert JV & Vrsty Sccr, Bsktbl & Sftbl 83-87; Acctng.

KESH, WENDI; Manalapan HS; Englishtown, NJ; (Y); Cmnty Wkr; Hosp Aide; Office Aide; Temple Yth Grp; Nwsp Stf; Tennis; NHS; SUNY; Psychlgy.

KESSEL, MICHAEL H; Bayonne HS; Bayonne, NJ; (Y); Am Leg Boys St; Intnl Clb; Math Tm; VP Temple Yth Grp; Nwsp Rptr; Lit Mag; High Hon Roll; Jr NHS; JV Socr; Montclair ST Coll Acad Tlnted Young Stu Pgm Grad 84; Red Crs Cert Adv Lifesaver 85; Bio Sci.

KESSLER, DOUGLAS; Pascack Hills HS; Montvale, NJ; (Y); 30/232; Computer Clb; Science Clb; Temple Yth Grp; Y-Teens; JV Bsbl; JV Bsktbl; JV Var Bowling; Var L Socr; JV Trk; Hon Roll; Lehigh U.

KESSLER, EMILY ROBIN; Manalapan HS; Manalapan, NJ; (Y); Drama Clb; Rep Sr Cls; NHS; CT Coll.

KETTLE, DAN; Kittatinny Regional HS; Newton, NJ; (Y); 12/160; Ftbl; Wt Lftg; Wrstlng; High Hon Roll; Hon Roll; NHS; Booster Club Schlrshp 86; Presdntl Acad Fitness Awd 86; Rutgers Coll Eng; Mechncl Eng.

KEY, MARK; New Brunswick HS; New Brunswick, NJ; (Y); Civic Clb; Cmnty Wkr; Debate Tm; Drama Clb; Pep Clb; Ski Clb; School Play; Nwsp Rptr; Yrbk Stf; Off Frsh Cls; Rutgers.

KEYWORTH, CHRISTINE; Bishop Ahr St Thomas HS; Rahway, NJ; (Y); ROTC; Ski Clb; Pres Sec Band; Concert Band; Mrchg Band; Gym; High Hon Roll; Hon Roll; U Sthrn CA Trjn Merit Awed; U Sthrn CA U Schlrshp; U Southern CA.

KHALIL, AMCAD; Dickinson HS; Jersey City, NJ; (Y); Boy Scts; Computer Clb; Math Clb; NJIT; Engrng.

KHALIL, ROBERT; Secaucus HS; Secaucus, NJ; (S); 9/164; Computer Clb; Math Clb; Varsity Clb; Var Bsbl; JV Bsktbl; Var Tennis; French Hon Soc; High Hon Roll; NHS; Engnrng.

KHAN, EKRAMUL; Paterson Catholic Regional HS; Paterson, NJ; (Y); 7/130; Am Leg Boys St; Hosp Aide; Nwsp Phtg; Nwsp Rptr; Yrbk Phtg; Pres Stu Cncl; Capt L Crs Cntry; Capt L Wrstlng; High Hon Roll; NHS; HOBY Fndtn 85; Soc Stud Awd 85; Excllnce In Math Awd 85; Columbia U; Med.

KHAN, SAIRA; Academic HS; Jersey City, NJ; (S); 4/70; Math Clb; Hon Roll; Jr NHS; NHS; 25 Pct Schlrshp Frm St Peters Coll 86; Rutgers Coll Arts & Sci; Pharm.

KHAN, SHAFI; Hamilton High East Steinert; Hamilton Square, NJ; (Y); 3/322; Am Leg Boys St; Pres Debate Tm; NFL; Quiz Bowl; Science Clb; School Play; Var Tennis; JV Trk; NHS; Ntl Merit SF; Engrng.

KHAN, SHAMAILA; Teaneck HS; Teaneck, NJ; (Y); Hon Roll; Bus.

KHATIWALA, BHARAT; Sacred Heart HS; Vineland, NJ; (Y); 24/62; Computer Clb; French Clb; Math Clb; Math Tm; ROTC; Varsity Clb; Im Bsktbl; Var Tennis; Im Vllybl; Hon Roll; Electrical Engineering.

KHAWAJA, AZIM; St Peters Prep; Jersey, NJ; (Y); Computer Clb; French Clb; Im Bsbl; Im Bsktbl; Im Ftbl; Im Socr; Im Sftbl; Im Vllybl; Im Hon Roll; Iona Lang Cntst 86; Pre-Med.

KICERA, MICHAEL J; Hillside HS; Hillside, NJ; (Y); 13/200; Am Leg Boys St; Math Tm; Ski Clb; Var Bsbl; Var Bsktbl; Var Ftbl; Sports Med.

KICZULA, SABINA; Bishop George Ahr HS; Perth Amboy, NJ; (Y); 86/276; Church Yth Grp; Spanish Clb; Var Bsktbl; Var Trk; High Hon Roll; Hon Roll; Lawyer.

KIELTY, JOHN; St John Vianney HS; Holmdel, NJ; (Y); 17/280; Computer Clb; Library Aide; Math Clb; Math Tm; Service Clb; Teachers Aide; High Hon Roll; Hon Roll; NHS; Bowling Awds 84-87; Northwestern Coll Engrng Pgm 86; Camp Cnslr 85; Engrng.

KIESELOWSKY, DEBBIE; Sayreville War Memorial HS; Parlin, NJ; (Y); 18/384; Church Yth Grp; Spanish Clb; Concert Band; Mrchg Band; High Hon Roll; Hon Roll; Prfct Atten Awd; Pres Schlr; Spanish NHS; Laurel Park Civic Assc $200 Awd Schlrshp & Civic Awrnss 86; Spnsh Hon Soc 86; Montclair ST Coll; Accntng.

KIESSLING, LAURA; Pt Pleasant Borough HS; Pt Pleasant, NJ; (Y); Church Yth Grp; English Clb; Exploring; 4-H; Girl Scts; Band; Church Choir; Concert Band; Lit Mag; Var Powder Puff Ftbl; U New England; Physcl Thrpy.

KIESZNOWSKI, SHERI ANNE; St John Vianney HS; Freehold, NJ; (Y); 38/280; Church Yth Grp; Intnl Clb; Church Choir; Concert Band; Mrchg Band; Yrbk Stf; Hon Roll; NHS; Gold & White Awd 83-86; Yth For Life Pres 85-86; Bus.

KIETLINSKI, WANDA; Wallington HS; Wallington, NJ; (Y); 4/72; Am Leg Aux Girls St; Varsity Clb; Yrbk Bus Mgr; Rep Stu Cncl; Var Bsktbl; Im Var Sftbl; Var Capt Vllybl; Hon Roll; NHS; Voice Dem Awd; US Army Rsrv Ntl Schlr/Athlt Awd 86; US Mrn Corps Dstngshd Athlt Awd 86; Pres Acad Ftns Awd 86; Rtgrs Coll Of Arts & Sci.

KIEVIT, JENNIFER L; Saint Rose HS; Point Pleasant, NJ; (Y); 8/226; Sec Trs Church Yth Grp; Key Clb; Lit Mag; Rep Jr Cls; Hon Roll; NHS; Sst Fnlst NJ ST Teen Arts Fest 85; Ocean Cnty CYO Chrldng Champ 86; Art Fld.

KIGER, GRETCHEN; Egg Harbor Township HS; Pleasantville, NJ; (S); 7/265; Spanish Clb; Lib Concert Band; Sec Mrchg Band; Sec Stu Cncl; Var Crs Cntry; High Hon Roll; Jr NHS; Hst NHS; Engrng.

KIJEK, GINA; Bridgewater Raritan HS East; Bridgewater, NJ; (Y); 97/270; Ski Clb; VP Spanish Clb; Yrbk Stf; Trs Sr Cls; Rep Stu Cncl; Var JV Cheerleading; Powder Puff Ftbl; High Hon Roll; NHS; Trs Frsh Cls; Pres Acadmc Ftnss Awd 86; Bucknell; Acctg.

KILBURGH, KAREN; Eastern HS; Voohees, NJ; (Y); Cmnty Wkr; Girl Scts; Office Aide; Score Keeper; Stat Socr; Sftbl; Hon Roll; Phys Thrpy.

KILGORE, JENNIFER; Franklin HS; Somerset, NJ; (Y); Key Clb; Ski Clb; SADD; Sec Chorus; School Musical; Yrbk Stf; Capt Tennis; Hon Roll.

KILLEEN, JOHN; Westfield HS; Westfield, NJ; (Y); Church Yth Grp; Cmnty Wkr; Key Clb; Latin Clb; Political Wkr; Ntl Merit Ltr; Jaycees Schlrshp 86-87; Rtry Schlrshp 86-90; Vanderbilt U; Engr.

KILLEEN, RICHARD; Glen Ridge HS; Glen Ridge, NJ; (Y); 20/130; Am Leg Boys St; Boy Scts; VP JA; Concert Band; Mrchg Band; Bsbl; Capt Bsktbl; Capt Trk; NHS; $100 Sales Clb Jr Achvt 84-85; Jv Bsktbl Mst Outstndng Plyr 84-85; 1st Pl Cnfrnc Pole Vauld Rly 85-86; Arch.

KILLERI, MICHELLE; Pinelands Regional HS; Parkertown, NJ; (Y); Business.

KILROY, JENNIFER L; Palmyra HS; Palmyra, NJ; (Y); 10/112; Am Leg Aux Girls St; Drama Clb; Capt Quiz Bowl; Sec Band; School Play; Nwsp Stf; Yrbk Ed-Chief; Rep Frsh Cls; Rep Soph Cls; Rep Jr Cls; Seton Hall U; Crmnl Just.

KIM, CHOONG; St Peters Preparatory HS; Rutherford, NJ; (Y); Off Church Yth Grp; Exploring; FCA; Science Clb; SADD; Varsity Clb; Lit Mag; JV Bsktbl; Im Ftbl; JV Var Socr; Outstndng In Soccer 84; Ecnmcs.

KIM, CHRISTINA; St Cecilia HS; Alpine, NJ; (Y); Hosp Aide; Math Clb; Yrbk Stf; Rep Jr Cls; Stu Cncl; Var Capt Cheerleading; Vllybl; Ntl Merit SF; Business.

KIM, DAN; Garden State Acad; Piscataway, NJ; (Y); 2/36; Stu Cncl; Im Badmtn; Im Bsktbl; Im Ftbl; Im Sftbl; Im Vllybl; Hon Roll; Hon Roll, Prfct Attnd Awd 86; Andrews U; Engrng.

KIM, ELLEN; Scotch Plains-Fanwood HS; Scotch Plains, NJ; (S); German Clb; Model UN; Quiz Bowl; Band; Chorus; Mrchg Band; Orch; School Musical; Symp Band; Lit Mag; NJ All ST Orch & Band 85; NJ Yth Govt Convtn 85; NJ Yth Symph 85.

KIM, EUSUN; Dwight Morrow HS; Englewood, NJ; (Y); 22/250; VP Church Yth Grp; Debate Tm; JA; Ski Clb; Jazz Band; Lit Mag; Sec Frsh Cls; JV Tennis; Hon Roll; NHS.

KIM, IN-SOOK; Lakeland Regional HS; Haskell, NJ; (Y); 22/103; Teachers Aide; Band; Capt Color Guard; Ed Nwsp Ed-Chief; JV Bsktbl; Var L Crs Cntry; Capt Var Trk; NHS; Rotary Awd; Math Clb; Spirit Awd-Track 84; Garden St Schlrshp 86; Rutgers Coll; Engrng.

KIM, JEAN; Montville HS; Montville, NJ; (Y); 10/276; Church Yth Grp; Key Clb; Ski Clb; Nwsp Rptr; VP Frsh Cls; VP Soph Cls; Pres Jr Cls; Pres Sr Cls; JV Lcrss; Capt Powder Puff Ftbl; Distngshd Schlr 85-86; Ntl Merit Commnd Schlr 85-86; U Of CA Riverside; Med.

KIM, JIYOUNG; Waldwick HS; Waldwick, NJ; (Y); Computer Clb; Hosp Aide; Intnl Clb; Math Tm; Orch; Nwsp Rptr; Yrbk Stf; Lit Mag; Var Tennis; Var High Hon Roll; Awd Vol-Svc Valley Hosp 86.

KIM, JUNG H; Bridgewater-Raritan East HS; Bridgewater, NJ; (Y); Church Yth Grp; German Clb; Hosp Aide; Mathletes; Math Tm; Quiz Bowl; Scholastic Bowl; Service Clb; Nwsp Stf; Yrbk Stf; Rutgers Deans Summer Schlrs Pgm 86; Frgn Lang Co Pres 84-86; Med.

KIM, RICHARD; Palisades Park HS; Palisades Pk, NJ; (Y); Cmnty Wkr; Math Clb; Nwsp Stf; Lit Mag; Ftbl; Tennis; Wt Lftg; Hon Roll; NHS; Prfct Atten Awd; Engr.

KIM, SUN JUNG; Robert Mcnaire Academic HS; Jersey City, NJ; (S); English Clb; PAVAS; Gov Hon Prg Awd; Kiwanis Awd; NHS; Frnds Of Music & Art Awds 3rd Pl 86; Smmr Arts Inst Schlrshps 84; Fash Inst Tech Smmr Schlrshp 85; Parsons; Artst.

KIM, YOUNG NANCY; Cresskill HS; Cresskill, NJ; (Y); 1/125; Debate Tm; Political Wkr; Nwsp Ed-Chief; Yrbk Ed-Chief; VP Stu Cncl; Var Crs Cntry; St Schlr; Drama Clb; Ski Clb; Spanish Clb; U S Congrssnl Page 85; Chrch Yth Grp Trea 86; Mdl Cngrss Rnkng Mnrty Mbr Comm On Armed Svcs 85; Engl.

KIM-ANH, NGUYEN THI; Fair Lawn HS; Fair Lawn, NJ; (Y); 6/332; Cmnty Wkr; Science Clb; Spanish Clb; Off Sr Cls; Capt Tennis; Cit Awd; Gov Hon Prg Awd; High Hon Roll; NHS; Ntl Merit Schol; Fisher Sci Awd 86; Achvt Frgn Lang Awd 86; Natl Sci & Hymanits Sympsm 86; Harvard; Biochem.

KIMBALL, DARREN; East Brunswick HS; E Brunswick, NJ; (Y); Trs Math Clb; Pres Science Clb; Pres Spanish Clb; Ed Nwsp Stf; Rep Stu Cncl; High Hon Roll; NHS; Pres Spanish NHS; Key Clb; Pep Clb; Amer Invtnl Mth Exam Hnr Rl 86; Lawyer.

KIMBALL, MICHAEL; Marist HS; Bayonne, NJ; (Y); Science Clb; Var Trk; Pace U; Bus.

KIMBLE, LINDA; Gloucester HS; Gloucester, NJ; (Y); DECA; Pep Clb; Stage Crew; Rep Stu Cncl; JV Bsktbl; Var Fld Hcky; Var Capt Sftbl; High Hon Roll; Hon Roll; NHS; Hockey Unsung Hero 85.

KIMMEL, MICHAEL; Piscataway HS; Piscataway, NJ; (Y); Letterman Clb; Temple Yth Grp; Thesps; Variety Show; Rep Stu Cncl; Socr; Wrstlng; High Hon Roll; Hon Roll; Wrstlng,Soccer 83-86; US Naval Acad; Engrng.

KINDDON, JENNIFER; Central Regional HS; Ocean Gate, NJ; (Y); 30/285; Church Yth Grp; Varsity Clb; Nwsp Rptr; Rep Jr Cls; JV Bsktbl; Var Fld Hcky; Var Trk; Pre-Law.

KING, CHRISTINE; Eastern HS; Berlin, NJ; (Y); Church Yth Grp; Cmnty Wkr; French Clb; Girl Scts; Hosp Aide; Im JV Bsktbl; JV Im Lcrss; Hon Roll; Trvld Throughout Europe 86; Nrsng.

KING, DANIEL; High Point Regional HS; Sussex, NJ; (Y); 4/250; Church Yth Grp; Cmnty Wkr; Letterman Clb; Scholastic Bowl; Thesps; Varsity Clb; Band; Concert Band; Jazz Band; School Musical; Rotary Club 86; Trenton ST Coll; Mech Engrng.

KING, DOREEN; Toms River East; Toms River, NJ; (Y); Drama Clb; Key Clb; Chorus; School Musical; Off Jr Cls; JV Swmmng; Hon Roll; NHS; Theatre Arts.

KING, GLENN R; Lacey Twp HS; Forked River, NJ; (S); CAP; DECA; Var Golf; DECA Svc Sta Retailg 1st Pl NJ & Top 20 Natl 86; Stockton St Coll; Mrktng.

KING, GREG; Ramapo Regional HS; Wyckoff, NJ; (Y); 9/339; Capt Chess Clb; Trs Spanish Clb; Jazz Band; Ed Nwsp Stf; Ed Yrbk Stf; Lit Mag; NHS; Math Clb; Math Tm; Pep Clb.

KING, JENNIFER; Holy Spirit HS; Brigantine, NJ; (Y); 71/400; Chorus; School Musical; Trenton ST.

KING, LESLEE; Mary Help Of Christians Acad; Paterson, NJ; (Y); Dance Clb; Math Tm; Pep Clb; Service Clb; Varsity Clb; School Play; Variety Show; Capt Var Cheerleading; Ftbl; Essex Cnty CC; Optician.

KING, LINDA; Roselle Catholic HS; Roselle Pk, NJ; (Y); 50/210; Church Yth Grp; Drama Clb; Red Cross Aide; Church Choir; School Musical; French Hon Soc; High Hon Roll; Hon Roll; 1st Yrf Prfcncy Frnch; Fairleigh Dcknsn; Dntstry.

KING, PATRICIA; Mount Saint Dominic Acad; Livingston, NJ; (Y); 20/54; Church Yth Grp; Spanish Clb; Chorus; School Musical; VP Frsh Cls; Hon Roll; Prfct Atten Awd; U DE; Cmmnctns.

KING, PATRICK; St John Vianney HS; Union Beach, NJ; (Y); 25/269; Boy Scts; Church Yth Grp; Variety Show; Nwsp Sprt Ed; Var L Crs Cntry; Var L Trk; Hon Roll; VP NHS; VFW Awd; Vigil Hnr In Ordr Of Arrow 86; Acmndtn Frm Gvnr & Cngrsmn For Eagle Scout 85.

KING, REBECCA; Paramus HS; Paramus, NJ; (Y); Intnl Clb; Math Tm; Temple Yth Grp; Rep Jr Cls; Rep Sr Cls; Var Capt Crs Cntry; Var Capt Trk; Sec NHS; Spanish NHS; 1st Tm Al-Cnty Crs Cntry 85; Anthrplgy.

KING, RUSSELL; Delaware Valley Regional HS; Frenchtown, NJ; (Y); 27/165; Boy Scts; Bsbl; Hon Roll; Indstrl Arts Awd-Wood I 85; Indstrl Arts Awd-Wood II 86; Elec Engrng.

KING, SARAH; East Brunswick HS; E Brunswick, NJ; (Y); Hosp Aide; Mrchg Band; Orch; School Musical; Yrbk Stf; Lit Mag; Hon Roll; NHS; Cmnty Wkr; Latin Clb; Rutgers Dean Summer Schlr Prog 86; Natl Guild Auditions Winner 84-85.

KING, TARA; Howell HS; Howell, NJ; (Y); 35/370; Drama Clb; Band; Trk; Chle Psych.

KINNEALLY, KARA J; St Rose HS; Brielle, NJ; (Y); 5/202; Chess Clb; Sec Church Yth Grp; French Clb; Key Clb; Math Tm; French Hon Soc; High Hon Roll; VP NHS; Garden St Schlr Drew Schlr II Awd Drew U 85-86; Manasquan Elks Schlrshp 86; U Of Notre Dame; Bus.

KINNEY, JOHN; Ramapo HS; Franklin Lakes, NJ; (Y); 17/329; Computer Clb; Radio Clb; Science Clb; Spanish Clb; Nwsp Phtg; Rep Soph Cls; Rep Stu Cncl; JV Var Bsktbl; JV Socr; Hon Roll; Spnsh IV Merit Awd 85-86; Pre-Med.

KINNEY, KERRY; Kittatinney Regional HS; Newton, NJ; (Y); 19/240; Girl Scts; Stage Crew; Nwsp Stf; Lit Mag; High Hon Roll; Hon Roll; Vsl Arts 84; Crftmns Fair Visl Art 86; Med Ill.

KINNEY, RICKY W; Sussex County Vo Tech HS; Montague, NJ; (Y); 39/169; Wt Lftg; High Hon Roll; Hon Roll; Prfct Atten Awd; Outstndng SR Shp Awd In Crpntry 86; Crpntry.

KINSEY, ELEANOR; Glassboro HS; Glassboro, NJ; (Y); Church Yth Grp; Girl Scts; Pres Spanish Clb; Color Guard; Drill Tm; Mrchg Band; School Musical; Yrbk Stf; Bowling; Sftbl; Med.

KINSEY, LATRICE SHARELL; University HS; Newark, NJ; (Y); Church Yth Grp; Girl Scts; JA; Chorus; Church Choir; Cit Awd; Hon Roll; Jr NHS; Bus Adm.

KINZLER, DEBBIE; Manalapan HS; Manalapan, NJ; (Y); 28/431; Church Yth Grp; Library Aide; SADD; Band; Concert Band; Mrchg Band; Yrbk Rptr; Yrbk Stf; NHS; Music Awd 86; Cert Ms Fund Raising 84-86.

KIPP, AMY; Scotch Plains-Fanwood HS; Scotch Plains, NJ; (S); Model UN; Quiz Bowl; Concert Band; Mrchg Band; High Hon Roll; Spanish NHS; Biol Tm 84-85; Psych.

KIRALY, TRACY; Wayne Valley HS; Wayne, NJ; (Y); GAA; Yrbk Stf; Vllybl; Cit Awd; High Hon Roll; Hon Roll; Hnr Guard; Acctng.

KIRBY, ADRIANNE; Woodbridge HS; Woodbirdge, NJ; (Y); Pres Girl Scts; SADD; Acpl Chr; Chorus; Concert Band; Mrchg Band; School Play; Yrbk Stf; Stat Sftbl; NHS; Marian Mdl 84; Bio Rsrch.

KIRBY, BRIAN; Middlesex HS; Middlesex, NJ; (Y); 12/157; Key Clb; Ski Clb; SADD; School Musical; Var Socr; Var L Trk; Hon Roll; NHS; 3rd Plc Trenton ST Coll NJ Wrtrs Cntst 85; NY U; Drmtc Wrtng.

KIRBY, JOHN; Toms River HS East; Toms River, NJ; (Y); 17/585; Chorus; Church Choir; School Musical; Variety Show; Yrbk Stf; Var Tennis; Im Wt Lftg; NHS; Ntl Merit Ltr; Mrktng.

KIRBY, MICHELE; Delran HS; Moorestown, NJ; (Y); Hosp Aide; Spanish Clb; Band; Church Choir; Concert Band; Jazz Band; Mrchg Band; Orch; Pep Band; School Musical; OB Nrsng.

KIRCH, LISA; Egg Harbor Township HS; Linwood, NJ; (S); 3/266; Pres AFS; Art Clb; French Clb; VP German Clb; Key Clb; Model UN; Ed Yrbk Stf; High Hon Roll; Pres NHS; Ntl Merit Ltr; Garden St Dstngshd Schlr 85; US Natl Ldrshp Merit Awd 85-86; Natl Sci Merit Awd 85-86; Intl Rltns.

KIRCHNER, BILL; Delran HS; Delran, NJ; (Y); 8/197; Var Math Tm; Var Stage Crew; NHS; Prfct Attndnc; Drexel; Engrng.

KIRCHNER, DOREEN; Matawan Regional HS; Cliffwood Bch, NJ; (Y); 39/320; Art Clb; Camera Clb; Chorus; Nwsp Phtg; Yrbk Phtg; Yrbk Stf; Fashion Inst Of Tech; Phtgrphy.

KIRCHOFER, LAURA; Morris Catholic HS; Randolph, NJ; (Y); 6/142; Hosp Aide; Math Clb; Natl Beta Clb; Nwsp Stf; Stat Socr; Var Swmmng; Stat Trk; Trs NHS; Bus.

KIRK, BONNIE; Union HS; Union, NJ; (Y); Church Yth Grp; Cmnty Wkr; FCA; Concert Band; JV Bsktbl; Var L Fld Hcky; JV Capt Sftbl; Hon Roll; NHS; Pep Band; Bst Female Ath Awd 84; Phys Ed.

KIRK, KAREN; South River HS; S River, NJ; (Y); Church Yth Grp; FNA; German Clb; Spanish Clb; Chorus; Church Choir; School Musical; School Play; Var Fld Hcky; JV Sftbl; Music Thrpst.

KIRKLAND III, WALTER; Lincoln HS; Jersey City, NJ; (Y); Off Jr Cls; Air Force; Comp Sci.

KIRMSE, KRISTINA; Hightstown HS; E Windsor, NJ; (Y); 2/343; AFS; Drama Clb; Capt Math Tm; Concert Band; Mrchg Band; High Hon Roll; NHS; Sal; School Musical; School Play; Stephen Silverman Mem Mth Awd 86; Chmps Incntv Awd 86; Grdn ST Schlr 86; Carnegie-Mellon U; Arch.

KIRSCH, LORI; Ocean Township HS; W Deal, NJ; (Y); Hosp Aide; Spanish Clb; SADD; VP Temple Yth Grp; Chorus; Rep Jr Cls; Stat Bsktbl; Score Keeper; U S Congressional Awd Bronze 84; Adelfi Girls Cmmnty Srv Clb; Med.

KIRSCHENBAUM, GAYLE; Pascack Valley Regional HS; Hillsdale, NJ; (S); 17/260; Math Clb; Spanish Clb; Concert Band; Mrchg Band; School Musical; Nwsp Rptr; Hon Roll; NHS; Ntl Merit Ltr; St Schlr; Franklin & Marshall Coll; Biol.

KIRSCHNER, BRIAN S; Lenape HS; Medford, NJ; (Y); Am Leg Boys St; Varsity Clb; Var Crs Cntry; Var Trk; Hon Roll; Med.

KIRSCHNER, SUSAN; Mt Olive HS; Flanders, NJ; (Y); 20/287; Hosp Aide; Science Clb; Ski Clb; Yrbk Stf; Ed Lit Mag; Stat Bsktbl; JV Sftbl; High Hon Roll; Hon Roll; NHS; Achvmnt Awd Chem 86; Vrsty Awd Bsktbl 84-85; Candy Striper Svc Awd 85; Pre Law.

KIRSH, ELIZABETH; Immaculate Conception HS; Garfield, NJ; (S); 7/100; English Clb; Scholastic Bowl; Chorus; School Musical; Nwsp Rptr; Lit Mag; VP NHS; Ntl Merit Ltr; Pres Spanish NHS; Art Natl Hnr Soc 83-86; Excllnt Rtng Piano Solo Ntl Fed JR Fest 84; Ntl Piano Plyng Audtns Supr Scrng.

KIRSH, MICHAEL A; Tenafly HS; Tenafly, NJ; (Y); Cmnty Wkr; Math Clb; Model UN; Political Wkr; Yrbk Stf; Rep Frsh Cls; Rep Soph Cls; Trs Jr Cls; Rep Stu Cncl; Ntl Merit Ltr; Engrng.

KIRSTEIN, LAURIE; Dwigght Englewood HS; Fort Lee, NJ; (Y); Debate Tm; Yrbk Stf; Cheerleading; Ntl Merit Ltr; Vlntr Psychtrc Hosp; Natl Frnch Cntst 84-85; Psych.

KISHEL, LORI A; Immaculate Conception HS; Clifton, NJ; (S); 9/103; NFL; Sec Spanish Clb; VP Chorus; School Musical; School Play; Hon Roll; Prfct Atten Awd; Spanish NHS; Coll Of St Elizabeth; Englsh.

KISLY, JEANNE MARIE; Middlesex HS; Middlesex, NJ; (Y); 24/163; Am Leg Aux Girls St; Hosp Aide; Sec Key Clb; School Musical; School Play; Sec Sr Cls; Var Capt Cheerleading; Church Yth Grp; Ski Clb; Chorus; MIDLSX Athl Boostrs Assoc Awd Outstndng Part Pop Warner 86; AAUW Awd Acdmc & Svc Schl & Cmmnty 86; Douglass Coll; Lwyr.

KISS, BRUNO; Bloomfield HS; Bloomfld, NJ; (Y); Art Clb; School Musical; Stage Crew; Variety Show; High Hon Roll; Hon Roll; Rutgers Coll; Audio Engr.

KISS, ILDIKO; Sussex Vo-Tech; Franklin, NJ; (S); #4 In Class; SADD; Chorus; High Hon Roll; NHS; Prfct Atten Awd; Wrd Proc.

KITTRELL, DOUG; Florence Tnp Memorial HS; Roebling, NJ; (Y); DECA; Band; Concert Band; Jazz Band; JV Bsbl; JV Ftbl; Principals Lst Acad Achvmnts 83-86; Mercer Cnty; Cmptr Oprtns.

KIZIAH, JENNIFER; Hunterdon Central HS; Flemington, NJ; (Y); 64/539; Key Clb; Thesps; Acpl Chr; Chorus; Jazz Band; School Musical; Variety Show; Off Stu Cncl; French Hon Soc; Hood Coll; Music.

KLAPPERICH, MARY; Mt Olive HS; Budd Lake, NJ; (Y); Dance Clb; Drama Clb; Intnl Clb; Science Clb; Ski Clb; SADD; School Play; Yrbk Stf; Stu Cncl; Score Keeper; Bus.

KLATSKY, CARL; Matawan Regional HS; Aberdeen, NJ; (S); 33/302; Chess Clb; Math Clb; Math Tm; VP Radio Clb; Hon Roll; Aud/Vis; Socr; Wrstlng; Matawan Reg Math Hnr Soc 85-86; Cooper Union; Comp Sci.

KLAUBER, LINDA; Cresskill HS; Cresskill, NJ; (Y); 40/130; Ski Clb; Stage Crew; Yrbk Ed-Chief; Yrbk Phtg; Yrbk Stf; Rep Stu Cncl; Stat Socr; JV Sftbl; JV Trk; Hon Roll; SUNY New Paltz; Comp Sci.

KLAUBER, LISA; Cresskill HS; Cresskill, NJ; (Y); Art Clb; DECA; Drama Clb; Ski Clb; Spanish Clb; Temple Yth Grp; Chorus; School Play; Yrbk Phtg; Yrbk Stf; Bus.

KLEIMAN, DENNIS; Cherry Hill HS West; Cherry Hill, NJ; (Y); 50/380; VP Camera Clb; VP Intnl Clb; SADD; Temple Yth Grp; School Musical; Nwsp Phtg; Yrbk Phtg; Rep Jr Cls; JV Tennis; Hon Roll; Wrtng Cntst 1st Pl 86; Wrtng Cntst In Ptry 2nd Pl 84; Brnds U; Pre-Med.

KLEIN, BARRIE; Madison Central HS; Old Bridge, NJ; (S); 4/382; French Clb; Chorus; Color Guard; School Musical; Stage Crew; Stat Trk; French Hon Soc; High Hon Roll; Hon Roll; NHS.

KLEIN, CRAIG; Hamilton HS East; Hamilton Sq, NJ; (Y); 111/317; Church Yth Grp; FBLA; SADD; Varsity Clb; JV Bsbl; Var Golf; Var L Socr; Hon Roll; All ST Grp III Socr 85; All Cnty OCR SR Socr 85; Vrsty Ltr 83-85; Mercer Cnty CC; Bus Adm.

KLEIN, DAVID; Egg Harbor Township HS; Linwood, NJ; (S); 27/270; Drama Clb; School Musical; School Play; Variety Show; Hst Frsh Cls; Pres Soph Cls; Pres Jr Cls; Var Capt Ftbl; Hon Roll; NHS; Temple U; Librl Arts.

KLEIN, DAVID; Parsippany HS; Parsippany, NJ; (Y); Am Leg Boys St; Debate Tm; Exploring; Pres German Clb; Acpl Chr; Mrchg Band; JV Bsbl; Hon Roll; NHS; Prfct Atten Awd; Govt.

KLEIN, DEENA; Highstown HS; East Windsor, NJ; (Y); 50/449; AFS; Drama Clb; French Clb; Intnl Clb; Service Clb; Variety Show; Hon Roll; NHS; Schrlshp CO U Summer 86.

KLEIN, KEVIN; Morris Catholic HS; Denville, NJ; (Y); 40/155; Aud/Vis; Cmnty Wkr; FBLA; German Clb; Political Wkr; Ski Clb; Var Socr; Wt Lftg; High Hon Roll; Hon Roll; U Scranton; Acctg.

KLEIN, LAWRENCE J; East Brunswick HS; E Brunswick, NJ; (Y); Hosp Aide; Temple Yth Grp; Concert Band; Mrchg Band; Bowling; God Cntry Awd; U DE; Sci.

KLEIN, LEIANN; Manalapan HS; Manalapan, NJ; (Y); #125 In Class; Cmnty Wkr; Dance Clb; Drama Clb; Girl Scts; Ski Clb; Temple Yth Grp; Varsity Clb; Chorus; Drill Tm; Swing Chorus; Art.

KLEIN, MARGARET; St Pius X Regional HS; Parlin, NJ; (Y); Art Clb; Church Yth Grp; French Clb; Varsity Clb; Church Choir; Hon Roll; NHS; Svc Awd CYO Newlttr Chairperson 85-86; Ldrshp Awd For CYO 85-86.

KLEIN, MICHELLE; Atlantic City HS; Ventnor, NJ; (Y); Key Clb; Office Aide; VP SADD; Yrbk Stf; Rep Soph Cls; Rep Jr Cls; Rep Stu Cncl; High Hon Roll; Hon Roll; NHS.

KLEIN, TAMARA; Washington Township HS; Turnersville, NJ; (Y); 42/480; French Clb; Office Aide; Stage Crew; Var Tennis; Hon Roll; NHS; Rutgers U; Ag Engrng.

KLEIN, THOMAS; North Warren Regional HS; Newton, NJ; (Y); 5/140; Quiz Bowl; Scholastic Bowl; Ski Clb; Nwsp Ed-Chief; VP Soph Cls; VP Jr Cls; Pres Stu Cncl; Var Socr; Hon Roll; St Schlr; Golden Soroll Awd 86; Essy Pblshd In US News & Wrld Rpt 86; Engl.

KLEIN, TIMOTHY E; Freehold Regional HS; New Egypt, NJ; (Y); 13/175; Am Leg Boys St; VP Trk; Secretary; Law.

KLEIN, WALTER; Saint Joseph Regional HS; Park Ridge, NJ; (Y); 12/180; Church Yth Grp; Cmnty Wkr; Var Capt Bsbl; Var Capt Ftbl; Trk; Hon Roll; Jr NHS; NHS; Spanish NHS; Hon Carrier Bergen Record Nwspr 84; Business.

KLEINMAN, JONATHAN; West Windsor-Plainsboro HS; Plainsboro, NJ; (Y); Am Leg Boys St; Chorus; School Musical; Rep Stu Cncl; Bsbl; Var Ftbl; Wt Lftg; Var Wrstlng; High Hon Roll; NHS; Mvp Baseball; Sportsmanship Award Football.

KLELE, MICHAEL; Secaucus HS; Secaucus, NJ; (S); Math Clb; Hon Roll; Med.

KLEMM, LINDA; Bridgewater-Raritan East HS; Bridgewater, NJ; (Y); German Clb; Science Clb; JV Bsktbl; Im Bowling; Stat Swmmng; High Hon Roll; Hon Roll; NHS.

KLEVA, GREG; Central Regional HS; Seaside Park, NJ; (Y); 16/225; Am Leg Boys St; Trs Church Yth Grp; Trs Exploring; Letterman Clb; Ski Clb; Var Capt Crs Cntry; Var Capt Trk; High Hon Roll; Jr NHS; VP NHS; Acad Schlrshp Merrimack Coll 86; NJSIAA Schlr/Athltc Awd 86; US Army Rsrv Ntl Schlr/Athltc Awd 86; Merrimack Coll; Bus.

KLEVA, JENNIFER; Central Regional HS; Seaside Park, NJ; (Y); Church Yth Grp; Exploring; Letterman Clb; Ski Clb; Varsity Clb; Sec Stu Cncl; Var Fld Hcky; Var Trk; Hon Roll; Springfield Coll; Sports Traine.

KLIMASKI, JEFFREY S; Bloomfield HS; Bloomfield, NJ; (Y); 103/440; French Clb; Key Clb; Ski Clb; Yrbk Ed-Chief; Rep Soph Cls; Rep Jr Cls; Rep Stu Cncl; JV Trk; Hon Roll.

KLIMEK, ANDREW J; Pennsauker HS; Pennsauken, NJ; (Y); #5 In Class; Am Leg Boys St; Church Yth Grp; Pres French Clb; Leo Clb; Lit Mag; Var Socr; French Hon Soc; Hon Roll; Pres NHS; Math Tm; NE Conf Frgn Lang Awd 84; Cmmnctns.

KLIMEK, KAREN LEIGH; Lakeland Regional HS; Ringwood, NJ; (Y); 13/303; Math Clb; Off Jr Cls; Off Sr Cls; Var JV Socr; JV Sftbl; Cit Awd; High Hon Roll; NHS; Ntl Merit Ltr; NEDT Awd; Natl Sci Merit Awd Physics 86; Girls Ctznshp Inst 85; Acdmc All Am 86; Mihlenberg Coll; Nuc Physics.

KLINE, CRAIG; Howell HS; Howell, NJ; (Y); 50/400; Chess Clb; Computer Clb; Debate Tm; 4-H; NFL; Band; Jazz Band; Symp Band; Tennis; All Shore Jazz; Corprt Law.

KLING, ELIZABETH; Abraham Clark HS; Roselle, NJ; (S); 1/210; Debate Tm; French Clb; Science Clb; Chorus; Nwsp Phtg; High Hon Roll; NHS; 3rd Pl Wnr Scenario Wrtg Cont 84; Law.

KLIPPLE, KAREN; Phillipsburg HS; Phillipsburg, NJ; (Y); 55/334; Ski Clb; Off Frsh Cls; Rep Jr Cls; Rep Stu Cncl; Var L Cheerleading; Var L Trk; Hon Roll; Giftd & Talntd Clb 83-86; H S Hgh Jmp & Trpl Jmp Rcrds 84 & 85; Psych.

KLOTZ, TAMMY; Bordentown Regional HS; Cookstown, NJ; (Y); 8/119; FBLA; Hosp Aide; Q&S; Nwsp Bus Mgr; Nwsp Rptr; Cheerleading; Sftbl; Hon Roll; NHS; Med.

KLOTZEK, NANETTE; St Peters HS; Piscataway, NJ; (Y); 3/106; Band; Concert Band; Lit Mag; High Hon Roll; Hon Roll; Mst Prfcnt Engl 85; Mst Prfcnt Spnsh I, II, III 84-86; Agri.

KLUEG, BETH; Holy Spirit HS; Absecon, NJ; (Y); 22/410; Pep Clb; Yrbk Stf; Stu Cncl; Cheerleading; High Hon Roll; Hon Roll; NHS; Phys Thrpy.

KLUG, DAVID; Kittatinny Regional HS; Newton, NJ; (Y); 10/222; CAP; Math Tm; Scholastic Bowl; Var Crs Cntry; Var Trk; High Hon Roll; NHS; Merit Achvmnt Awd 86; U Of IL; Engrng.

KLUKOSOSKI, LISA; South Plainfield HS; S Plainfield, NJ; (Y); 28/250; Am Leg Aux Girls St; Yrbk Stf; Sec Soph Cls; Sec Jr Cls; Pres Sr Cls; Trs Stu Cncl; Var Cheerleading; Var Sftbl; Hon Roll; Trs NHS.

KLUMPP JR, EUGENE J; Marist HS; Bayonne, NJ; (Y); #30 In Class; Rep Stu Cncl; JV Var Bsbl; JV Var Bsktbl; Dance Clb; Science Clb; Nwsp Rptr; Wt Lftg; Natl Hnr Soc 85; Capt & MVP For JV Bsbl Tm 84; U Of Charleston; Bus.

KLUMPP, JANET; Union HS; Union, NJ; (Y); FBLA; Girl Scts; Chorus; Church Choir; Stat Tennis; Hon Roll; Merit Awd For Typing 85; NJ Bus Educ Assn 85 & 86; Seton Hall U; Business Admin.

KLUTH, FRED; Clifton HS; Clifton, NJ; (Y); Church Yth Grp; Drama Clb; German Clb; Thesps; Wrstlng; Cmmnctns.

KMECH, KENDRA; Secaucus HS; Secaucus, NJ; (S); Key Clb; Political Wkr; Ski Clb; Mrchg Band; High Hon Roll; Hon Roll; Elem Tchr.

KNAPP, KELLY; Clifton SR HS; Clifton, NJ; (Y); Key Clb; Math Clb; Spanish Clb; Teachers Aide; Sftbl; Hon Roll; Jr NHS; Mthmtcs.

KNAPP, KIRSTINA D; Union HS; Union, NJ; (Y); Hosp Aide; Band; Yrbk Phtg; Yrbk Stf; Off Jr Cls; Off Sr Cls; Stat Bsbl; Stat Bsktbl; Hon Roll; NHS; Exmplry Achvt Awd 84-85; Chem.

KNAPP, LAURA; Pinelands Regional HS; Tuckerton, NJ; (Y); 29/196; VP Frsh Cls; VP Soph Cls; Stu Cncl; Var Bsktbl; Var Fld Hcky; Var Sftbl; Hon Roll; Sprtsmnshp Awd Field Hcky 85-86; MVP Bsktbl 86; Sprtsmnshp Awd Sftbl 86; Phys Ed.

KNAPP, WAYNE; Pembewrton Twp HS Ii; Pemberton, NJ; (Y); Math Tm; Science Clb; Nwsp Rptr; High Hon Roll; Prfct Atten Awd; Engrng.

KNAUSS, LIANE; Hightstown HS; E Windsor, NJ; (Y); Ski Clb; SADD; Varsity Clb; Drill Tm; Yrbk Stf; Rep Jr Cls; Stu Cncl; Fld Hcky; Swmmng; Business Management.

KNEIS, MICHAEL; Wayne Hills HS; Wayne, NJ; (Y); 16/370; Boy Scts; German Clb; Mathletes; Nwsp Phtg; Var Crs Cntry; Var Trk; High Hon Roll; Trs NHS; Engrng.

KNEZEVIC, MICHAEL; Roselle Catholic HS; Roselle, NJ; (Y); Church Yth Grp; JA; Band; Church Choir; Im Bsktbl; Var L Socr; Im Vllybl; High Hon Roll; NHS; Rutgers-Camden; Vet.

KNIGHT, AMY; Manasquan HS; Belmar, NJ; (Y); 1/250; Hosp Aide; Key Clb; Thesps; Band; Chorus; Capt Flag Corp; Rep Stu Cncl; Bowling; High Hon Roll; Trs NHS; Kiwanis Hnr Soc 85&86; Japan-US Sen Schlrshp YFU Alt 86; All Shore Band 85; MUS Ther.

KNIGHT, STEPHANIE; East Orange HS; E Orange, NJ; (Y); JA; Office Aide; Pep Clb; Sec Church Choir; Mrchg Band; Yrbk Stf; Trs Sr Cls; Capt Pom Pon; Hon Roll; Acctg.

KNIGHT, TONYA; Toms River South; Beachwood, NJ; (Y); 27/360; Church Yth Grp; Cmnty Wkr; Debate Tm; French Clb; Math Tm; NFL; Science Clb; Band; Church Choir; Concert Band; Hnrs Schlrshp-Early Admssns Peace Coll Raleigh NC 86-87; Peace Coll; Comp Sci.

KNIPFELBERG, DEBORA; John P Stevens HS; Edison, NJ; (Y); 89/485; Ski Clb; School Play; Rep Jr Cls; Var Cheerleading; Powder Puff Ftbl; Hon Roll; NHS; Dance Clb; Drama Clb; Chorus; Mddlsx Cnty Arts HS 84; HS Vrsty Awd Chrldng 84-86; Mtchn Dance Cntr Outstndng Prfmr 85; Rutgers U; Mktg.

KNITOWSKI, DENNIS; Bridgewater-Raritan East HS; Bridgewater, NJ; (Y); Ski Clb; Ftbl; Wt Lftg; Hon Roll; Finance.

KNOBE, JENNIFER; East Brunswick HS; East Brunswick, NJ; (Y); Debate Tm; Exploring; Key Clb; VP Pep Clb; SADD; Temple Yth Grp; Chorus; Rep Stu Cncl; Hon Roll; NHS; Gov Schlr 85; Schlrshp Smmr Travel Pgm 85; SUNY; Pol Sci.

KNOLMAYER, DAVID; Hillsborough HS; Neshanic, NJ; (Y); 37/272; Computer Clb; Science Clb; Ski Clb; Ftbl; Var Golf; Trk; Wt Lftg; Hon Roll; NHS; Temple U; Mech Engr.

KNOP, ROBERT; Glen Rock JR & SR HS; Glen Rock, NJ; (Y); 18/122; Church Yth Grp; Debate Tm; Exploring; 4-H; Model UN; Spanish Clb; Hon Roll; Jr NHS; Pres NHS; Pres Schlr; The Spnsh Awd 86; VA Tech; Pltcl Sci.

KNOWLES, JAMIE; Highland Regional HS; Clementon, NJ; (S); Computer Clb; FTA; Spanish Clb; NHS; Elem Ed.

KNOWLES, JANIE; Highland Regional HS; Clementon, NJ; (Y); Computer Clb; FTA; Spanish Clb; Stu Cncl; Hon Roll; NHS; Elem Ed.

KNOWLES, JOHN; Dover HS; Mine Hill, NJ; (Y); Am Leg Boys St; Exploring; Latin Clb; Hon Roll; Airforce Nvgtr.

KNUTELSKY, STEPHEN P; Wallkill Valley Regional HS; Franklin, NJ; (Y); 28/161; Am Leg Boys St; FBLA; SADD; Concert Band; Jazz Band; Var Ftbl; Var Trk; Wt Lftg; Hon Roll; NHS; Richard C Mirshak Memrl Schlrshp 86; Englsh Schlr Awd 86; Schlr/Athlt Awd 86; Montclair ST Coll; Bus Adm.

KNUTELSKY, THOMAS G; Wallkill Valley Regional HS; Franklin, NJ; (Y); 8/170; Am Leg Boys St; Math Tm; SADD; Concert Band; Jazz Band; Var Bsbl; Var Ftbl; High Hon Roll; Hon Roll; NHS; Engrng.

KNUTSEN, MARK; Abraham Clark HS; Roselle, NJ; (S); #1 In Class; Pres Chess Clb; Church Yth Grp; Acpl Chr; Chorus; Jazz Band; Gov Hon Prg Awd; NHS; Ntl Merit Ltr; Computer Clb; Library Aide; Rutgers U Pres Scholar 85-86; NJ Future Prob Slvg Bowl ST Wnrs 83; Columbia Sci Hnrs Pgm 84-86; Comp Sci.

KOBELO, EVA; Oakcrest HS; Mays Landing, NJ; (Y); 46/212; 4-H; French Clb; Key Clb; Rep Stu Cncl; Mgr(s); Score Keeper; Sftbl; Tennis; DAR Awd; 4-H Awd.

KOBERNICK, GARY; Clifton HS; Clifton, NJ; (Y); Aud/Vis; Computer Clb; Political Wkr; Ski Clb; Spanish Clb; VP Soph Cls; JV Bsbl; JV Crs Cntry; JV Ftbl; Elec Engrng.

KOBIK, HENRY; Lower Cape May Regional HS; Cape May, NJ; (Y); 33/242; Am Leg Boys St; Concert Band; Drm Mjr(t); Jazz Band; Mrchg Band; Golf; Socr; Trk; Hon Roll; Prfct Atten Awd; Tchng.

KOBLIS, KRIS; Hillsborough HS; Bellemead, NJ; (Y); 87/274; VP Latin Clb; Pep Clb; Science Clb; SADD; Stu Cncl; Im Powder Puff Ftbl; JV Trk; Elks Awd; Carrier Fndtn Schlrshp 86; Fncl Awd From Northeastern U 86; Northeastern U; Pharm.

KOBYLINSKI, JOHN B; Cherry Hill East HS; Cherry Hill, NJ; (Y); Orch; School Musical; Gym; Hon Roll; Ntl Schl Orch Awd 86; Assoc Schrlshp 86; E Stroudsburg U; Comp Sci.

KOCH, BONNIE; North Brunswick Twp HS; N Brunswick, NJ; (Y); 25/309; Sec German Clb; Key Clb; Yrbk Stf; Var Tennis; Hon Roll; NHS; Voice Dem Awd.

KOCH, JENNIFER; Glen Ridge HS; Montclair, NJ; (Y); French Clb; Hosp Aide; Ski Clb; Chorus; Concert Band; Jazz Band; Mrchg Band; Trk; High Hon Roll; Hon Roll.

KOCHANSKY, KRISSY; Monmouth Regional HS; Tinton Falls, NJ; (Y); 41/225; Ski Clb; Yrbk Phtg; Var Cheerleading; Var Socr; High Hon Roll; Hon Roll; Deptmntl Awd-Excllnc In Photo 86; Trenton ST Coll; Advtsng.

KOCHKA, THOMAS; Wayne Valley HS; Wayne, NJ; (Y); 31/320; Model UN; Service Clb; Spanish Clb; Var Crs Cntry; Var Capt Golf; Hon Roll; Ntl Merit Ltr; Boy Scts; Church Yth Grp; Cmnty Wkr; Otstndng Sr Mdl Untd Ntns 86; Otsdndng Spnch Stu 86; John Hopkins U; Intl Stds.

KOCHMAR, JENNIFER; St Marys HS; Wallington, NJ; (S); Mgr Drama Clb; FBLA; FNA; School Musical; School Play; Stage Crew; L Var Cheerleading; Hon Roll; NHS; Ntl Hstry Govt Awd 84-85; Art.

KOCHON, JULIANN; Bergenfield HS; Bergenfield, NJ; (Y); Art Clb; Church Yth Grp; Chorus; Capt Color Guard; Concert Band; Mrchg Band; Orch; School Musical; Opt Clb Awd; Art Hnr Scty 86; Fash Inst Tech; Intr Dsgn.

KOCISCIN, MARK; St Pius X Regional HS; Piscataway, NJ; (Y); Computer Clb; Exploring; JA; Math Tm; Office Aide; Ski Clb; Teachers Aide; Nwsp Stf; Hon Roll; NHS; Comp Sci.

KOCORNIK, JAMES; James Caldwell HS; Caldwell, NJ; (Y); Boy Scts; VP Bsktbl; JV Tennis; Hon Roll; NHS; Ntl Merit Ltr; Lehigh Coll; Accntng.

KOCSIS, LORI ANNE; Sayreville War Memorial HS; S Amboy, NJ; (Y); Hosp Aide; Pres Science Clb; Pres Spanish Clb; Capt Flag Corp; Nwsp Ed-Chief; NHS; Prfct Atten Awd; Spanish NHS; English Clb; Library Aide; Voice Demcrcy Schl Wnnr 86; Phys Therpy.

KOCZAN, CHRIS; St Rose HS HS; Brick, NJ; (Y); Latin Clb; Letterman Clb; Varsity Clb; VP Stu Cncl; Var Socr; Vllybl; Archtctr.

KOEHLER, SUZANNE; Manalapan HS; Manalapan, NJ; (Y); 56/431; Church Yth Grp; Dance Clb; SADD; Yrbk Stf; Rep Sr Cls; Stu Cncl; Var VP Cheerleading; Socr; NHS.

KOENIG, DEBBIE; Paul VI HS; Audubon, NJ; (Y); Yrbk Stf; Capt Var Cheerleading; Coach Actv; Var Trk; Bus.

KOERNER, BONNI; Memorial HS; Cedar Grove, NJ; (S); 11/120; Pres Church Yth Grp; Chorus; Ed Nwsp Stf; Yrbk Sprt Ed; Var Fld Hcky; Var Trk; NHS; Trs French Clb; Outstndng Achvt Physcl Ed 84; Hlth.

KOESTER, JOHN; Kittatinny Regional HS; Newton, NJ; (Y); 43/222; Concert Band; Jazz Band; Var Bsbl; Var Bsktbl; Var Ftbl; Var Tennis; Im Wt Lftg; Hon Roll; MVP Bsbl & Bsktbl 86; 1st Tm All West Jrsy Bsbl 86; Bus.

KOETTING, JACQUELYN; Paramus HS; Paramus, NJ; (Y); Church Yth Grp; Cmnty Wkr; Drama Clb; Intnl Clb; Library Aide; Teachers Aide; Flag Corp; Orch; School Musical; Ed Nwsp Stf.

KOHARCHIK, PAM; Jackson Memorial HS; Jackson, NJ; (S); 15/416; Cmnty Wkr; Concert Band; Mrchg Band; Lit Mag; High Hon Roll; NHS; Voice Dem Awd; Church Yth Grp; French Clb; Acad All Amer 85-86; HOSA 84-86; Engl Tchr.

KOHLER, SCOTT; Seton Hall Prep; Eatontown, NJ; (Y); 37/200; Key Clb; Pep Clb; JV Ftbl; High Hon Roll; Pop Warner Schlr Athl 82; US Naval Acad; Nvl Archtctr.

KOJAC, CRAIG; Emerson HS; Union City, NJ; (Y); Am Leg Boys St; Trs Jr Cls; Var JV Ftbl.

KOLANOVIC JR, ZDENKO; Rutherford HS; Rutherford, NJ; (Y); 25/250; Sec Chess Clb; Computer Clb; Math Tm; School Play; Rep Frsh Cls; Bsktbl; Socr; Hon Roll; John Hopkins; Pre-Med.

KOLARSICK, JENNIFER; Red Bank Catholic HS; Spring Lake, NJ; (Y); French Clb; Math Clb; Ski Clb; Yrbk Stf; Var L Crs Cntry; Mgr(s); Var L Trk; Hon Roll; Bus.

KOLBA, MICHAEL; Union HS; Union, NJ; (Y); Computer Clb; Ski Clb; JV Bowling; Var Golf; Hon Roll; Bus.

KOLBUSH, RICHARD; Burlington Twp HS; Burlington, NJ; (Y); 10/127; Am Leg Boys St; Chess Clb; Math Clb; Varsity Clb; Concert Band; Stu Cncl; Crs Cntry; Cit Awd; NHS; Pres Schlr; Rutgers Coll Engrng; Elctrcl.

KOLE, ALEXANDRA S; Lawrence HS; Lawrenceville, NJ; (Y); 6/240; VP Cmnty Wkr; Trs French Clb; Math Tm; Pres Service Clb; Temple Yth Grp; School Musical; Var Tennis; High Hon Roll; NHS; Ntl Merit SF; Rutgers Pres Schlr 85; Grdn ST Dstngshd Schlr 85; Outstndng Ldr & Ctzn 84; Linguistics.

KOLECKI, CHRIS; Gateway Regional HS; Woodbury Hts, NJ; (Y); 45/180; Dance Clb; Exploring; Girl Scts; Key Clb; JV Bsktbl; Hon Roll; Ntl Merit Ltr; Prfct Atten Awd; Natl Ldrshp And Serv Awd 86; Acctnt.

KOLESAR, STEPHEN; Bloomfield SR HS; Bloomfield, NJ; (Y); 101/442; Hon Roll; Montclair ST Coll.

KOLLAR, KEVIN; Morris Catholic HS; Denville, NJ; (Y); Ski Clb; Var JV Ftbl; Var Golf; Var JV Wrstlng; Am Leg Schl Awd 83; Corp Mgmt.

KOLLER, SHELLE; Cumberland Regional HS; Shiloh, NJ; (Y); Exploring; Cabrini Coll; Englsh.

KOLODIJ, CHRISTINE; St Aloysius HS; Jersey City, NJ; (Y); 12/115; Church Yth Grp; Cmnty Wkr; Co-Capt Bowling; Hon Roll; Trs NHS; Prfct Atten Awd; St Peters Coll; Bus.

KOLWICZ, TRACY; Palmyra HS; Palmyra, NJ; (Y); Am Leg Aux Girls St; Color Guard; School Play; Stage Crew; Rep Frsh Cls; VP Jr Cls; Fld Hcky; High Hon Roll; Hon Roll; NHS; Marine Bio.

KOMAR, KEITH; Westfield HS; Westfield, NJ; (Y); 101/520; Capt L Tennis; Hon Roll; Wstfld Bstr Assoc Schlrshp 86; U Of Vt; Bus Adm.

KOMAZEC, CHRISTY; Red Bank Catholic HS; Tinton Falls, NJ; (Y); Cmnty Wkr; Math Tm; Pep Clb; Red Cross Aide; Ski Clb; Yrbk Phtg; Var JV Cheerleading; Bio.

KOMOROWSKI, DENISE; Lenape Valley Regional HS; Stanhope, NJ; (Y); 36/257; Intnl Clb; Sec Key Clb; Concert Band; Yrbk Stf; Stu Cncl; French Hon Soc; Hon Roll; NHS; John Hopkins U GATE.

KOMPA, JILL; Woodstown HS; Woodstown, NJ; (Y); 1/250; Sec German Clb; Sec Band; VP Jr Cls; Rep Stu Cncl; Var Socr; High Hon Roll; NHS; English Clb; Exploring; Concert Band; Rtgrs Schlr 86; Amer Chmcl Scty Exclnc Chmstry 85-86; S Jersey Grls Sccr All-Conf 2nd Tm 85-86; Med.

KOMSA, RENE; Paul VI Regional HS; Belleville, NJ; (Y); French Clb; Key Clb; SADD; Yrbk Stf; High Hon Roll; Hon Roll; NHS; Fash Merch.

KONCELIK, ROBERT W; Bergen Catholic HS; Dumont, NJ; (Y); Am Leg Boys St; Boy Scts; Chess Clb; Church Yth Grp; Stage Crew; Im Bsktbl; Mgr(s); Var Trk; Im Vllybl; JV Wrstlng; NY U; Bus.

KONDEK, JOSEPH; Matawan Regional HS; Matawan, NJ; (S); 31/273; Math Clb; Math Tm; Stu Cncl; JV Bsbl; Hon Roll; NHS; Math Hnr Socty 85-86; Comp Sci.

KONEK, JAMES TIMOTHY; Spotswood HS; Spotswood, NJ; (S); 19/189; Science Clb; Rep Stu Cncl; JV Bsbl; Var Socr; Hon Roll; Engrng.

KONNICK, MARK; Paulsboro HS; Gibbstown, NJ; (Y); 20/196; Varsity Clb; Rep Stu Cncl; Var Wrstlng; Hon Roll; NHS; Hgh Hnrs Engl Cls 85 & 86; U MO Columbia; Bus Mgmt.

KONOPSKY, LISA M; Howell HS; Howell, NJ; (Y); 56/356; Dance Clb; Stat Bsbl; Socr; Hon Roll; Law.

KOPAZ, ROBERT; Highland Regional HS; Blackwood, NJ; (Y); Art Clb; Church Yth Grp; FCA; French Clb; School Musical; School Play; Stage Crew; Ftbl; Wt Lftg; Wrstlng; U Of PA; Doctor.

KOPER, SHARON; Montville Township HS; Pine Brook, NJ; (Y); Key Clb; Ski Clb; Yrbk Stf; VP Stu Cncl; JV Var Cheerleading; Powder Puff Ftbl; Sftbl; High Hon Roll; Hon Roll; NHS; NJ Dance Theat Gld 84.

KOPIT, STEPHANIE; Sparta HS; Sparta, NJ; (Y); 23/237; Key Clb; Ski Clb; Var JV Cheerleading; High Hon Roll; Hon Roll.

KOPP, STEVEN; Marlboro HS; Colts Neck, NJ; (Y); Boy Scts; Exploring; German Clb; Ski Clb.

KOPPENAL, MICHAEL R; Hawthorne HS; Hawthorne, NJ; (Y); School Musical; Am Leg Boys St; Boy Scts; Variety Show; VP Jr Cls; VP Stu Cncl; Var Ftbl; Var Trk; Var Wrstlng; Hon Roll; Eagle Scout; Intl Rltn.

KOPYCINSKI, ANDREW; St Peters Prep; Bayonne, NJ; (Y); 72/210; French Clb; Letterman Clb; Science Clb; Teachers Aide; Yrbk Phtg; Yrbk Stf; Mgr(s); Trk; Hon Roll; Ftbl; Ltr Pin Track; Yrbk Pin; Crmnlgy.

KORACH, STACY; Weehawken HS; Weehawken, NJ; (S); 1/147; Math Clb; Q&S; Nwsp Ed-Chief; Yrbk Stf; Lit Mag; Hon Roll; NHS; Jrnlsm Awd 86; Acad All Amer 86; Physics.

KORBIN, RONEE FAYE; Cherry Hill West HS; Cherry Hill, NJ; (Y); 56/370; Cmnty Wkr; Drama Clb; French Clb; Intnl Clb; Letterman Clb; Library Aide; Pep Clb; Aud/Vis; Spanish Clb; SADD; Indctee Chrry Hll Wst Hll Of Fame 86; OH ST U; Music.

KORCHICK, ROBYN; Mc Corristin Catholic HS; Yardley, PA; (Y); 15/290; GAA; Rep Frsh Cls; Rep Soph Cls; Var L Bsktbl; Var L Sftbl; High Hon Roll; NHS; Bsktbl 1st Tm Coachs Choice All-Strs 86; Bsktbl 2nd Tm All-Mercr Cnty 86; Sftbl 2nd Tm All-Mercr 86.

KORDOGHLI, RIMA; JR SR HS; Palisades Pk, NJ; (Y); Library Aide; Tennis; Frnch Math Geo 86; Phrmcst.

KORINCHOCK, JO ANN; South Plainfield HS; S Plainfield, NJ; (Y); 5/287; Church Yth Grp; Computer Clb; Mrchg Band; Ed Yrbk Stf; Rep Frsh Cls; Rep Soph Cls; High Hon Roll; Hon Roll; Trs NHS; Pres Schlr; Schlstc Hon Scty 86; Jerseymen Histrcl Scty 84-86; Cook Coll; Bio.

KORINKO, JEFFERY; Florence Twp Memorial HS; Roebling, NJ; (Y); Teachers Aide; Varsity Clb; Stage Crew; JV Var Bsbl; Var JV Ftbl.

KORN, KIRSTIN; Oak Knoll Schl; Scotch Plains, NJ; (Y); Key Clb; Pep Clb; Ski Clb; Spanish Clb; Yrbk Stf; Pres Frsh Cls; Pres Soph Cls; VP Jr Cls; VP Stu Cncl; Var Lcrss.

KORNEK, DON; Clayton HS; Clayton, NJ; (Y); #6 In Class; Am Leg Boys St; Church Yth Grp; Key Clb; Trs Science Clb; Rep Jr Cls; Var Capt Bsbl; Var Capt Ftbl; Hon Roll; NHS; Med.

KORSHALLA, PAULA; South River HS; S River, NJ; (Y); 20/110; German Clb; Library Aide; Sec Frsh Cls; Sec Soph Cls; Var Bsktbl; Var Fld Hcky; Var Sftbl; All Sntl & All Hm Nws Hnbl Mntn 86; All Acad Tm Bsktbl 8; All Sntnl Outstndng Sphmr 85; Sprts Med.

KORTREY, NANCY; Bogota HS; Bogota, NJ; (Y); 12/100; Sec Drama Clb; Sec Frsh Cls; Sec Soph Cls; VP Pres Stu Cncl; Var L Crs Cntry; Var L Trk; Hon Roll; NHS; Prfct Atten Awd; Church Yth Grp; Altrnte NJ Grls St; Mst Creative Prose Awd; Excel Spanish III; Douglass Coll; Educ.

KOSCIENSKI III, WALTER F; St Thomas Aquinas/Bishop Georg Ahr; Edison, NJ; (Y); 18/236; Am Leg Boys St; Nwsp Ed-Chief; Gov Hon Prg Awd; High Hon Roll; NHS; Chess Clb; Hosp Aide; Math Clb; Math Tm; Yrbk Rptr; Jostens Ldrshp Awd 86; Phelps Dodge Fndtn Merit Scholar 86; Seton Hall U; Chem.

KOSSON, NATALIE; Cliffside Park HS; Cliffside Pk, NJ; (Y); 7/239; Pres French Clb; Yrbk Ed-Chief; Pres Frsh Cls; Pres Soph Cls; Pres Jr Cls; Pres Sr Cls; VP Stu Cncl; Capt Cheerleading; Lion Awd; NHS; Grdn ST Arts Cntr Tlnt Expo Wnr 1st Pl 85; Vsn Cable Chrldng Comptn 3rd Pl 86; Swngrs Comptn 2nd Pl; Northwestern; Perfrmng Arts.

KOT, KEVIN; Parsippany HS; Lk Hiawatha, NJ; (Y); FBLA; Ski Clb; Rep Soph Cls; JV Var Ftbl; Comp Engr.

KOTCH, TROY; Bridgewater-Raritan H S East; Bridgewater, NJ; (Y); 84/271; Varsity Clb; Var L Ftbl; Hon Roll; Presdntl Acad Fitness Awd 86; PTO Acad-Chrtr Schlrshp; Rutgers Coll; Liberal Arts.

KOTKIN, JEFFREY H; Ridgefield Memorial HS; Ridgefield, NJ; (Y); Am Leg Boys St; Rep Frsh Cls; Trs Stu Cncl; JV Var Bsbl; Var Crs Cntry; Cit Awd; Hon Roll; Acadmc Decathln 85.

KOTLIAR, ANDREW; Toms River High Schl South; Toms River, NJ; (Y); 2/313; Boy Scts; Church Yth Grp; Math Clb; Math Tm; Model UN; Quiz Bowl; Band; JV Tennis; High Hon Roll; NHS; NJ Dstngshd Schlr 86; Rutgers U; Engrng.

KOTSEN, STEPHEN; Kinnelon HS; Kinnelon, NJ; (Y); 1/180; Pres FBLA; Lit Mag; Pres Frsh Cls; Pres Trs Stu Cncl; Var Capt Bsktbl; Var Capt Ftbl; Powder Puff Ftbl; VP NHS; Opt Clb Awd; Rotary Awd; Hugh O Brien Yth Ldrshp Awd 84-85; Ldrshp Training Conf 83-84; German Hnr Soc 85-86; Intl Studies.

KOTSIRIS, LISA; Arthur P Schalick HS; Bridgton, NJ; (Y); 12/140; Teachers Aide; Band; Concert Band; Mrchg Band; Orch; VP Jr Cls; JV Tennis; Hon Roll; NHS; Ntl Merit Ltr; Photo.

KOTTAKIS, STEVE A; North Plainfield HS; N Plainfield, NJ; (Y); 3/188; Am Leg Boys St; Boy Scts; Key Clb; SADD; Jazz Band; JV Var Bsktbl; L Ftbl; Bausch & Lomb Sci Awd; God Cntry Awd; NHS; Mech Engrg.

KOTULICH, DEBORAH; Bridgewater-Raritan West HS; Bridgewater, NJ; (Y); Pres German Clb; Chrmn Stu Cncl; Capt Bsktbl; Capt Socr; Capt Sftbl; Var Tennis; Hon Roll; NHS; Prncpls Awd Feml Athlt Of Yr 86; Steuben Awd 86; Intl Rel.

KOURLAS, ANNA; Lenape Valley Regional HS; Stanhope, NJ; (Y); 6/253; FBLA; Intnl Clb; Key Clb; Library Aide; Lit Mag; French Hon Soc; High Hon Roll; NHS; Schlr Ad 85-86; Accntng.

KOUTOUZAKIS, PAUL; James Caldwell HS; W Caldwell, NJ; (Y); Am Leg Boys St; Boy Scts; VP Church Yth Grp; Key Clb; Church Choir; Stu Cncl; JV Wrstlng; High Hon Roll; Jr NHS; NHS.

KOVACS, DEBORAH ANN; Lanape Valley Regional HS; Netcong, NJ; (Y); French Clb; Key Clb; SADD; Color Guard; JV Var Cheerleading; JV Trk; French Hon Soc; High Hon Roll; Hon Roll; NHS; Rutgers Coll; Psych.

KOVACS, MARIA A; Paul VI HS; Waterford, NJ; (Y); 89/477; French Clb; SADD; Rep Frsh Cls; Im Bowling; Ntl Merit Ltr; Drexel U; Elec Comp Engrng.

KOVAR, LANCE; Clifton HS; Clifton, NJ; (Y); 27/637; Am Leg Boys St; Math Clb; Science Clb; Spanish Clb; Rep Frsh Cls; Rep Soph Cls; JV Tennis; High Hon Roll; Jr NHS; Spanish NHS; Rogate 83-86; NJ Sci Day 85; Gftd-Tlntd Pgm 83-86; Pre-Med.

KOVATCH, DEBRA; Newton HS; Andover, NJ; (S); 24/200; Varsity Clb; Rep Stu Cncl; Var Bsktbl; Var Fld Hcky; Var Sftbl; Cit Awd; Hon Roll; NHS; All ST 2nd Tm Fld Hcky 85; MIP Sftbl 84; All Leag Fld Hcky 1st Tm 85; U Of DE; Bus.

KOVATCH, JEFF; Wayne Hills HS; Wayne, NJ; (Y); Aud/Vis; FBLA; Spanish Clb; Pres Varsity Clb; Stu Cncl; JV Var Ftbl; JV Var Trk; JV Var Wrstlng; Hon Roll; One-One Orgnztn 83-87; 3 Yr Lttr Wrstlng & One Yr JV Cptn 83-87; Bus Admin.

KOVITZ, ADAM JAY; Hightstown HS; East Windsor, NJ; (Y); 23/450; AFS; Drama Clb; Spanish Clb; Thesps; Chorus; School Musical; School Play; Yrbk Stf; NHS; Arch.

KOVSHUK, HEATHER; Washington Twp HS; Turnersville, NJ; (Y); 56/478; Art Clb; Spanish Clb; Band; Mrchg Band; Yrbk Stf; Stu Cncl; High Hon Roll; Hon Roll; Glassboro ST Clg; Art Ed.

KOWALCZYK, ELIZABETH; Clifton HS; Clifton, NJ; (Y); French Clb; Library Aide; Office Aide; School Play; Nwsp Ed-Chief; Mgr Crs Cntry; French Hon Soc; Hon Roll; Jr NHS; Merit Cert Natl Frnch Cont 86; Cert Achvt Outstndng Perfrmnce Typwrtng I 84; Mth.

KOWALSKI, ELLEN; Paul VI Regional HS; Cedar Grove, NJ; (S); Key Clb; Service Clb; Var Cheerleading; JV Sftbl; Stat Vllybl; French Hon Soc; High Hon Roll; NHS; Bus.

KOWALSKI, JILL; Hopewell Valley Central HS; Hopewell, NJ; (Y); 10/202; French Clb; Service Clb; Chorus; School Musical; School Play; Nwsp Rptr; Yrbk Stf; Rep Stu Cncl; JV Var Tennis; High Hon Roll; Bio.

KOWALSKI, TED; Summit HS; Summit, NJ; (Y); 36/290; Pres Church Yth Grp; Trs Drama Clb; Pres French Clb; Math Tm; Model UN; School Musical; School Play; Socr; High Hon Roll; NHS; Cornell U; Engrng.

KOWALSKY, VICKY; Freehold Township HS; Freehold, NJ; (S); 9/317; Math Tm; Band; Yrbk Rptr; Stu Cncl; Im Powder Puff Ftbl; Jr NHS; Hst NHS.

KOYEN, JEFF; Parsippany HS; Parsippany, NJ; (Y); Lit Mag; Hon Roll; NHS.

KOZA, MARGIE; Passaic Valley HS; Totowa, NJ; (Y); Am Leg Aux Girls St; Church Yth Grp; Dance Clb; Pres Trs 4-H; Hosp Aide; Key Clb; Spanish Clb; Var Cheerleading; 4-H Awd; Hon Roll; Finslt Miss Co-Ed Pgnt 86; William Paterson Coll; Nursing.

KOZAK, MICHAEL J; Hamilton HS West; Trenton, NJ; (Y); Art Clb; Aud/Vis; SADD; Stage Crew; JV Var Bsbl; Exhbtd Artwrk At Teens Arts Fest 85; Artwk Pblshd In Menagerie 85-87; Created Pster For Schl SADD 86; Art.

KOZENIEWSKI, KIM; Highland Regional HS; Somerdale, NJ; (Y); 64/365; German Clb; Spanish Clb; Var Cheerleading; Var Stat Ftbl; Var Stat Score Keeper; Var Capt Socr; Capt Sftbl; Hon Roll; Ntl Merit Schol; Ntl Merit Schlr 84-85; Schlr Athlete Awd 86; Grant Coca Cola Schlr Athl 86; Appalachian ST U; Fash Merch.

KOZERADSKY, JEANNE; Montville Township HS; Towaco, NJ; (Y); 63/265; Church Yth Grp; FBLA; Key Clb; Ski Clb; Color Guard; High Hon Roll; Hon Roll; FBLA Prlmntry Tm 3rd St 86; Hotel/Rstrnt Mngmnt.

KOZLER, LESLIE; Lakeland Regional HS; Ringwood, NJ; (Y); 25/332; Acpl Chr; Jazz Band; Madrigals; School Musical; Var Socr; High Hon Roll; NHS; Gld Crfct Wnr Excllnc WJMA 84-87; Vrsty Fncng Ltr 85-86; Gld Mdl Wnrs Chrl Chmbr Sngrs 85-86; Pltcl Sci.

KOZLOW, ALEXANDRIA; Vailsburg HS; Newark, NJ; (Y); Computer Clb; Debate Tm; Rep Stu Cncl; Sftbl; High Hon Roll; Jr NHS; NHS; Bio Awd 85; Seton Hall; Nrsng.

KOZLOWSKI, DAWN; Wall HS; Wall, NJ; (S); 22/263; Exploring; Ski Clb; Nwsp Rptr; Var Fld Hcky; High Hon Roll; Cmmnctns.

KOZLOWSKI, KEVIN; John P Stevens HS; Edison, NJ; (Y); 12/469; Art Clb; Debate Tm; Key Clb; Capt Bsbl; Bsktbl; Socr; High Hon Roll; NHS; Spanish NHS; Lafayette Coll; Pre-Med.

KOZUB, DEANNA; Holy Cross HS; Burlington, NJ; (Y); 108/389; Ski Clb; Rep Stu Cncl; JV Stat Bsktbl; Var Stat Score Keeper; Var L Socr; Var Sftbl; Im Vllybl; Im Wt Lftg; Hon Roll; Bus Admn.

KOZZI, JON; Monsignor Donovan HS; Toms River, NJ; (Y); 15/226; Drama Clb; Math Tm; Science Clb; SADD; Thesps; Variety Show; High Hon Roll; NHS; Ntl Merit Ltr; Am Leg Boys St; Pine Bch Clb Laser Sailing Trphys 83-85; Engrng.

KRACHE, EVELYN; Piscataway HS; Piscataway, NJ; (Y); 30/519; Girl Scts; Church Choir; Madrigals; School Musical; Symp Band; NHS; Ntl Merit Schol; Am Leg Aux Girls St; Quiz Bowl; Band; Rtgrs U Dns Smr Schlrshp Awd 85; Grdn ST Dstngshd Schlr 86; Pres Acdmc Ftns Awd 86; Tufts U; Englsh.

KRACHUK, COLEEN; Paul VI HS; Laurel Springs, NJ; (S); 2/544; Drama Clb; French Clb; Math Clb; Spanish Clb; School Musical; School Play; French Hon Soc; High Hon Roll; Hon Roll; Spanish NHS; Intl Law.

KRAFT, ANDREAS W; Hamilton H S East; Hamilton Square, NJ; (Y); Cmnty Wkr; Debate Tm; Exploring; Hosp Aide; Quiz Bowl; Chorus; Madrigals; School Musical; Tennis; Bio.

KRAFTS, ANDREW; Roxbury HS; Succasunna, NJ; (Y); 10/435; Math Tm; Ski Clb; Varsity Clb; Nwsp Rptr; Rep Soph Cls; Stu Cncl; JV Crs Cntry; Var L Tennis; High Hon Roll; NHS; Iren Hills Math Lge NJ Merit Awd 85; Rosbury HS Acad Awd 84 & 85 & 86; Marshal Hghst Rnkng Bdy 86; Finance.

KRAJEWSKI, TERRI; Cumberland Regional HS; Bridgeton, NJ; (S); 4/342; Hosp Aide; Science Clb; Soroptimist; Capt Color Guard; Concert Band; Capt Drill Tm; Drm Mjr(t); Jazz Band; Mrchg Band; High Hon Roll; Ntl Merit Schlrshp Ltr Commndtn 84; Outstndng Mbr Awd Mrchng Band & Indoor Guard 85; Phys Thrpy.

KRAMARCHUK, ROMAN A; Clifton HS; Clifton, NJ; (Y); 5/583; Math Tm; Science Clb; Mrchg Band; Frsh Cls; Var Tennis; High Hon Roll; Ntl Merit SF; Am Leg Boys St; German Clb; Key Clb; NJ Govr Schl Public Issues & Future Of NJ 85; Hgh Hnr Grad Ukranian Stud Schl 85.

KRAMER, KATHLEEN; Highland Regional HS; Clementon, NJ; (Y); 20/332; Computer Clb; GAA; Girl Scts; Sec Spanish Clb; Varsity Clb; Sec Stu Cncl; Var Sftbl; Var Capt Tennis; NHS.

KRAMPS, RONALD F; Scotch Plains-Fanwood HS; Scotch Plains, NJ; (Y); 6/311; Am Leg Boys St; Boy Scts; Model UN; Drm Mjr(t); Jazz Band; US Nvl Acad; Ocn Engrng.

KRANICK, CYNTHIA; Linden HS; Linden, NJ; (Y); Cmnty Wkr; Exploring; FBLA; Rep Stu Cncl; Var Socr; Var Trk; Hon Roll; Accntng.

KRAPOHL, CHERYL; Wayne Hills HS; Wayne, NJ; (Y); 10/306; French Clb; Hosp Aide; Library Aide; Chorus; School Musical; Stage Crew; High Hon Roll; NHS; NJ All ST Chr Stu 86; Yrbk SR Edtr 87; Bio.

KRASOWSKI, MATT; Wall Twp HS; Manasquan, NJ; (Y); Spanish Clb; Varsity Clb; Tennis; Hon Roll; Prk Rngr.

KRASSOW, KIMBERLY; Woodstown HS; Monroeville, NJ; (Y); Pres Church Yth Grp; Concert Band; Drill Tm; Mrchg Band; Yrbk Ed-Chief; Rep Stu Cncl; JV Sftbl; Band; Variety Show; Nwsp Rptr; Principals Advsry Committee 85-86; Child Dvlpmnt.

KRATOCHVIL, PAUL; Bayley Ellard HS; Chester, NJ; (Y); 18/90; Letterman Clb; Varsity Clb; Var Capt Ftbl; Lcrss; Wt Lftg; Var L Wrstlng; High Hon Roll; Bus.

KRATOCHVIL, TAMMY; Northern Burlington HS; Mc Guire AFB, NJ; (Y); Church Yth Grp; Girls ST Alternate 84-85; Burlington Cnty Coll; Edu Deaf.

KRAUS, KATHRYN L; Scotch Plains-Fanwood HS; Fanwood, NJ; (S); AFS; VP FBLA; German Clb; Pres Key Clb; Quiz Bowl; Ski Clb; Nwsp Rptr; Rep Stu Cncl; Var Capt Cheerleading; High Hon Roll; Intl Rel.

KRAUS, KRISTINE M; S Plainfield HS; S Plainfield, NJ; (Y); 11/200; Church Yth Grp; Cmnty Wkr; Spanish Clb; Chorus; Var Capt Crs Cntry; Var Stat Mgr(s); Var Capt Trk; High Hon Roll; Hon Roll; Spanish NHS; Phys Thrpy.

KRAUS, MARK; Audubon HS; Audubon, NJ; (Y); Church Yth Grp; Scholastic Bowl; Spanish Clb; Varsity Clb; Var L Bsbl; Var L Bsktbl; Im Wt Lftg; Hon Roll; Pres NHS; Al-Colonl Conf Bsbl 86.

KRAUSE, GLENN; Hillsborough HS; Bellemead, NJ; (Y); 28/365; Church Yth Grp; Hon Roll; NHS; Engrng.

KRAUSE, KIMBERLY; Matawan Regional HS; Matawan, NJ; (Y); Varsity Clb; VICA; Chorus; Bsktbl; Score Keeper; Sftbl; Crtv Wrtng Chsn Rprsnt Schl Teen Arts 85-86; Cert Awd Rcgntn Spnsh 83-84; Psych.

KRAUSE, PATTY; Millville SR HS; Millville, NJ; (Y); Church Yth Grp; Band; Church Choir; Concert Band; Mrchg Band; German Clb; Girl Scts; Chorus; School Musical.

KRAUSER, SHERYL; Morris Knolls HS; Denville, NJ; (Y); Dance Clb; SADD; Temple Yth Grp; VP Frsh Cls; Rep Stu Cncl; Var Cheerleading; Sftbl; Hon Roll; Educ.

KRAUSS, THOMAS; Holy Cross HS; Cinnaminson, NJ; (Y); 65/390; Chess Clb; German Clb; School Musical; School Play; Trk; Hon Roll.

KRAUT, DANIEL; Ocean Twp HS; Ocean, NJ; (Y); 7/330; Am Leg Boys St; Pres Chess Clb; Mathletes; Math Tm; Temple Yth Grp; Im Bsktbl; High Hon Roll; 1st Pl NJ HS Math Cntst 85; 1st Pl Cntntl Math Leag Comptn.

KRAUT, MERYL LEE; Hillel Yeshiva HS; Englishtown, NJ; (Y); Dance Clb; Drama Clb; JCL; Latin Clb; Teachers Aide; Temple Yth Grp; Nwsp Ed-Chief; Yrbk Stf; Trs Soph Cls; Kssr Shem Tov Awd 83; Blmnthl Schlrshp Awd 85; NCS Yer Tear 86; Reg Brd NCSY 86; Stern Coll For Woman.

KRAVETZ, JEFF; Livingston HS; Livingston, NJ; (Y); 175/500; Trs Leo Clb; Stu Cncl; Bsbl; Var Socr; Var Capt Wrstlng; Drexel U; Bus.

KRAWITZ, MICHAEL; Montville Township HS; Pine Brook, NJ; (Y); 1/265; Pres Computer Clb; Trs FBLA; Key Clb; NFL; Nwsp Bus Mgr; JV Golf; NHS; Ntl Merit SF; Cmnty Wkr; Math Clb; Rutgers Schlr 86; 1st Pl In Pblc Spkng In NJ FBLA 86; 1st Pl In Ortrcl Cmptn In NJ Dist Key Clb 86.

KRAYNANSKI, LEA; Delaware Valley Regional HS; Milford, NJ; (Y); Church Yth Grp; Varsity Clb; Yrbk Stf; Off Frsh Cls; Sec Soph Cls; Sec Jr Cls; Sec Sr Cls; Stu Cncl; Bsktbl; Var Fld Hcky; Boyd Schl; Travel.

KREIPKE, ANETTE E; Ramapo HS; Franklin Lakes, NJ; (Y); 41/315; AFS; Chrmn French Clb; Math Tm; Teachers Aide; Orch; Yrbk Stf; Var Trk; NHS; Ntl Merit SF; Church Yth Grp; Vol Ambulance Corps 85-86; Med.

KREITZMAN, ELISA; East Brunswick HS; E Brunswick, NJ; (Y); Key Clb; Pep Clb; Acpl Chr; Band; Chorus; School Musical; Hon Roll; Natl Hon Roll 84-85; Manufacturers Hanover Qtr Century Clb Schlrshp 85; Rutgers Coll; Math.

KRELL, JUSTINE; Passaic Valley Regional HS; Little Falls, NJ; (S); 1/359; Science Clb; Concert Band; Mrchg Band; Var Trk; Cit Awd; Gov Hon Prg Awd; NHS; Hon Roll; High Hon Roll; Schlr Of Chem 86; Stevens Tech; Chem Engrng.

KRENC, BRIAN; H G Hoffman HS; South Amboy, NJ; (Y); 13/49; Letterman Clb; Science Clb; SADD; Varsity Clb; Stu Cncl; Bsbl; Ftbl; Wrstlng; Cit Awd; Dnfth Awd; Ramapo Coll Of NJ; Bus.

KRESS, MARY; St John Vianney HS; Freehold, NJ; (Y); 36/200; Church Yth Grp; Intnl Clb; VP Service Clb; SADD; Teachers Aide; Drill Tm; Mrchg Band; Yrbk Stf; Var Twrlr; Hon Roll; Gold/White Awd 86; Var Ltr Twirling 86; Rutgers U; Bio.

KRESSLER III, WALTER M; Burlington County Vo Tech; Delanco, NJ; (Y); 16/152; Am Leg Boys St; VICA; Yrbk Stf; Pres Frsh Cls; VP Rep Stu Cncl; Var L Bsbl; JV Bsktbl; Var Capt Socr; Hon Roll; VP NHS; Ntl Eng Meri Awd 84; Ntl Ldrshp Awd 86; Embry Riddig; Aviation.

KRETIV, BETH ANN; Toms River H Schl North; Toms River, NJ; (Y); 49/420; Sec Key Clb; Chorus; School Musical; Variety Show; Stat Golf; JV Socr; High Hon Roll; NHS; Acad Ltr 84; Adv Chorus Ltr 85; Child Psychlgy.

KREZEL, KENNETH W; Bayley Ellard HS; Whippany, NJ; (Y); School Musical; School Play; Stage Crew; Nwsp Ed-Chief; Yrbk Stf; Lit Mag; Engl.

KRICENA, SUSIE; Midland Park HS; Midland Park, NJ; (S); 39/137; Church Yth Grp; Dance Clb; DECA; Pep Clb; School Play; Yrbk Stf; Cheerleading; Gov Hon Prg Awd; High Hon Roll; FBLA; Performng Arts.

KRICK, DIANNE; Toms River HS South; Beachwood, NJ; (Y); 8/350; Drama Clb; French Clb; Band; Flag Corp; Mrchg Band; School Musical; Stage Crew; Symp Band; Off Frsh Cls; Off Soph Cls; Rutgers; Med.

KRIEGEL, JENNIFER; Dover HS; Dover, NJ; (Y); Church Yth Grp; Office Aide; Spanish Clb; Teachers Aide; Chorus; Drill Tm; Vllybl.

KRIP, LAURA; Benedictine Acad; Winfield, NJ; (S); 1/48; JCL; Sec Latin Clb; Library Aide; Math Clb; Spanish Clb; Church Choir; School Play; Variety Show; Nwsp Rptr; Pres Jr Cls.

KRIPALANI, ANIL; Glen Rock JR SR HS; Glen Rock, NJ; (Y); 14/126; High Hon Roll; Rensselaer Math & Sci Awd 85; Comptr & Sci Awds 86; Pres Acad Fit Awd 86; Comp Prog.

KRIVOSHIK, ANDREW P; The Pingry Schl; Elizabeth, NJ; (Y); Camera Clb; Chess Clb; German Clb; Key Clb; Math Tm; Band; Yrbk Phtg; JV Jr Cls; Var Wrstlng; Ntl Merit SF; Cum Laude Soc 84-86; RPI Mdl, Whitlock Prz & Sci Prz 85; GWU Sci Mdl Hnrb Mntn NJ St Sci Day 83-85; Engnrng.

KRIZOVSKY, THERESA; Wallington HS; Wallington, NJ; (Y); 11/82; Chess Clb; Girl Scts; Red Cross Aide; Service Clb; Chorus; Church Choir; School Play; Stage Crew; Nwsp Stf; Yrbk Stf; Bio.

KROGH, BOB; Edgewood Regional SR HS; Atco, NJ; (Y); 3/373; Exploring; Quiz Bowl; Bsbl; Var Socr; Hon Roll; Jr NHS; NHS; Questor Awd 84-85; Aero Engr.

KROOK IV, FREJ NILS; St Rose Of Belmar HS; Asbury Park, NJ; (Y); Band; Chorus; Church Choir; Concert Band; Jazz Band; Orch; Hon Roll; Ntl Merit SF; Prfct Atten Awd; Bus Amdin.

KRUCZEK, LISA; Woodbridge HS; Fords, NJ; (Y); 40/350; Art Clb; VP Church Yth Grp; Library Aide; PAVAS; Band; Chorus; Socr; Sftbl; Hon Roll; Comm.

KRUEGER, TRICIA LYNN; Mc Corristin HS; Trenton, NJ; (Y); Church Yth Grp; GAA; Key Clb; Pep Clb; Drill Tm; Variety Show; Var Capt Socr; JV Sftbl; Hon Roll; NHS; Psych.

KRUITWAGEN, ANTOINETTE; Bridgeton SR HS; Bridgeton, NJ; (Y); Church Yth Grp; Political Wkr; Varsity Clb; Yrbk Phtg; Yrbk Stf; Var Fld Hcky; Mgr(s); JV Sftbl; Bus Adm.

KRUMM, ERIK; Mariset HS; Bayonne, NJ; (Y); #13 In Class; Key Clb; Scholastic Bowl; L Nwsp Rptr; Nwsp Stf; Score Keeper; Hon Roll; Spanish NHS; St Johns U; Law.

KRUS, SUSAN; West Essex HS; Fairfield, NJ; (Y); 50/350; Drama Clb; Office Aide; Orch; School Play; Stage Crew; Fld Hcky; Hon Roll; Rutgers Coll.

KRYNICKI, DIANE S; Middletown High School South; Lincroft, NJ; (Y); Office Aide; Teachers Aide; Lit Mag; Rep Soph Cls; Rep Stu Cncl; Var Cheerleading; Stat Fld Hcky; High Hon Roll; Hon Roll; BOTTLECAPPERS 85-86; Psych.

KU, ANTHONY; Tenafly HS; Tenafly, NJ; (Y); Pres Computer Clb; Math Clb; Math Tm; SADD; VP Frsh Cls; JV Trk; Hon Roll; Awd Of Exc Yrkr Dgtl Hstry Cntst 85; 1st Pl Bellmore Monick JH Sci Fr 84; Ctznshp & Srvc Awd 84; Cmptr Prgm.

KUBU, TERRI; Manasquian HS; Manasquan, NJ; (Y); 25/220; Key Clb; SADD; Nwsp Bus Mgr; Fld Hcky; Sftbl; High Hon Roll; NHS; French Clb; GAA; Latin Clb; Band Of Ed Awd 84-86; Pre-Law.

KUCHER, STEPHANIE; Vineland HS; Vineland, NJ; (Y); Church Yth Grp; Letterman Clb; Pep Clb; Varsity Clb; Nwsp Ed-Chief; Yrbk Stf; Lit Mag; Rep Frsh Cls; Rep Soph Cls; Var Swmmng; Newspaper Most Valuable Staff Member 85; Communications.

KUCHERA, MICHELE; High School East; Toms River, NJ; (Y); Church Yth Grp; Ski Clb; School Musical; Stage Crew; Nwsp Stf; Var Capt Cheerleading; Hon Roll; Trenton ST; Bus Admin.

KUCHLER, KATHRYN; East Brunswick HS; E Brunswick, NJ; (Y); French Clb; Science Clb; Orch; Bsktbl; Fld Hcky; Tennis; French Hon Soc; NHS; Ntl Merit Ltr; Jr Athlete Yr Awd 85; Cornell U; Engrng.

KUCZYKOWSKI, DAVID M; Pennsauken HS; Pennsauken, NJ; (Y); 15/374; Am Leg Boys St; Math Clb; Science Clb; VP Sr Cls; Ftbl; Hon Roll; Pres NHS.

KUDA, JANICE M; Paramus Catholic HS; North Haledon, NJ; (Y); 36/157; Cmnty Wkr; Hosp Aide; Library Aide; Variety Show; Lit Mag; Hon Roll; Dancing Awds 82-86; Cert Apprctn Amer Heart Assoc 86; Cert Apprctn 85; Seton Hall U; Mngmnt.

KUDRIAVETZ, C MARIE; Holy Cross HS; Mount Holly, NJ; (Y); Church Yth Grp; High Hon Roll; Hon Roll; Cpmtd-Ntl Fnls Horse Jumpng; Marywood Coll; Bio.

KUEHN, JEFFREY S; Sussex County Vo-Tech HS; Vernon, NJ; (S); JV Ftbl; High Hon Roll; Hon Roll; NHS; NAVY Nuclr Fld Qualif Tst 84-85; U S Navy; Nuclr Electrncs Tech.

KUEHNER, DANIEL; Timothy Christian Schl; N Plainfield, NJ; (S); 1/32; Church Yth Grp; Computer Clb; Chorus; School Musical; Bsbl; Score Keeper; High Hon Roll; Trs NHS; Ntl Merit SF; Stevens Inst Of Tech; Chem Engr.

KUENY, DOUGLAS; John F Kennedy HS; Willingboro, NJ; (Y); Camera Clb; Key Clb; Pep Clb; Radio Clb; Ski Clb; Spanish Clb; Stage Crew; Yrbk Sprt Ed; Yrbk Stf; Jr Cls; Providence Coll; Lbrl Arts.

KUGIT, KELLY; Freehold Township HS; Freehold, NJ; (Y); Speech Tm; Chorus; School Play; Psych.

KUGLER, CRAIG W; Woodstown HS; Woodstown, NJ; (Y); 13/164; Church Yth Grp; German Clb; Pres Key Clb; School Musical; Var L Bsbl; Var L Bsktbl; Var L Ftbl; Hon Roll; Kiwanis Awd; All Grp II Bsbl 85-86; Schlr/Ath South Jersey 86; All South Jersey Bsbl 85 & 86; Coll William & Mary; Pre-Med.

KUHL, DONNA; Middletown South HS; Lincroft, NJ; (Y); Church Yth Grp; Girl Scts; Hosp Aide; Flag Corp; Jr Cls; Mgr(s).

KUHLES, TINA; River Dell Regional HS; River Edge, NJ; (Y); 15/215; Latin Clb; Nwsp Rptr; Ed Nwsp Stf; French Hon Soc; High Hon Roll; NHS; Njaau ST Karate Champ 2nd Pl 84-85; Rider Coll Frgn Lang Fornscs 1st Pl 84-85; Latin Hnr Soc 86; Douglass Coll; Frnch.

KUHN, KRISTIN M; Westwood Regional HS; Washington Twp, NJ; (Y); 17/251; French Clb; Office Aide; Chorus; School Musical; Variety Show; Stu Cncl; Cheerleading; Score Keeper; French Hon Soc; High Hon Roll; Am Mus&drafting Acad; Perf Arts.

KUHN, ROGER; H G Hoffman HS; South Amboy, NJ; (S); Chess Clb; SADD; Var Bsbl; Var Bsktbl; Hon Roll; NHS; Spanish NHS.

KUKOWSKI, WENDY; Holy Family Acad; Bayonne, NJ; (Y); 2/130; Pres Band; Nwsp Stf; Yrbk Stf; Rep Jr Cls; Capt Tennis; Cit Awd; Pres NHS; NEDT Awd; Natl Stu Cncl Awd Wnnr 85-86; Georgetown U; Medicine.

KULAGA, MARK; St Rose HS; Spring Lake, NJ; (Y); Chess Clb; Cmnty Wkr; Drama Clb; JCL; Latin Clb; Nwsp Bus Mgr; Nwsp Rptr; Nwsp Stf; Rep Soph Cls; Sec Trs Jr Cls; Essy Cntst 81; Slvr Mdl Ntl Ltn Exm 84; Cert Schlstc Achvmnt Awd 85; Mst Indstrs Awd 83; U Of PA; Sci.

KULBACK, EDWARD M; Matawan Regional HS; Aberdeen, NJ; (S); 16/273; Math Tm; Thesps; Trs Stu Cncl; JV Socr; High Hon Roll; NHS; Trs Soph Cls; Hist & Govmnt Clb; Math Hnr Society; Union Coll; Med.

KULBERDA, CAROLYN; Linden HS; Linden, NJ; (Y); Church Yth Grp; Key Clb; High Hon Roll; Hon Roll; NHS; Italian Clb 85-86; Union Cnty Coll; Bus Mgmt.

KULEBA, THEODORE J; Middletown HS North; Belford, NJ; (Y); Am Leg Boys St; Intnl Clb; Pres Frsh Cls; Rep Soph Cls; Rep Jr Cls; Pres Stu Cncl; Bsktbl; L Golf; Hon Roll; Jr NHS; Intrntl Stds.

KULICK, AARON; St John Vianney HS; Holmdel, NJ; (Y); 21/283; FBLA; Math Tm; Ski Clb; Nwsp Rptr; Trs Frsh Cls; Rep Soph Cls; Trs Stu Cncl; Ftbl; Trk; NHS; Vrsty Frbl Ltr 84-85; Vrsty Trck Ltr 83-85; Pre-Med.

KUMAGAI, TOMOMI; Indian Hills HS; Oakland, NJ; (Y); 9/276; Math Tm; Science Clb; Chorus; High Hon Roll; Hon Roll; VP NHS; Mus Cmptn Awd NJ Symphny 84; R Hafstdter Schlrshp 84; E J Noble Fndtn Schlrshp 85; Harvard U; Math.

KUNCKEN, RICHARD D; Lenape Valley Regional HS; Stanhope, NJ; (Y); 17/204; Am Leg Boys St; Red Cross Aide; Yrbk Stf; Rep Stu Cncl; JV Capt Socr; Var L Trk; Lion Awd; NHS; Pres Schlr; St Schlr; Susquehanna U; Math.

KUNICKI, THOMAS; Overbrook SR HS; Pine Hill, NJ; (Y); Var JV Ftbl; JV Wrstlng; Hon Roll.

KUNST, SUSAN; Nutley HS; Nutley, NJ; (Y); Cmnty Wkr; Var Socr; High Hon Roll; Hon Roll; Kean Coll NJ; Spcl Ed.

KUNZ, KEVIN; De Paul HS; Wayne, NJ; (Y); Aud/Vis; Boy Scts; Church Yth Grp; Computer Clb; FBLA; Im Vllybl; Hon Roll; Cert Comp Pompton Schl Indstrl Drftng 85; Var Awds Comp Sand Sculpture 85-86; Arch.

KUNZE, GRETCHEN; Shore Regional HS; Sea Bright, NJ; (Y); Church Yth Grp; Debate Tm; Q&S; Concert Band; School Musical; Ed Nwsp Stf; High Hon Roll; Trs NHS; Dist Chmpn JV Oxford Debate 85; 2nd Pl Intl Wmns Day Essy Cont 86; Law.

KUO, PENNY; Parsippany Hills HS; Boonton, NJ; (Y); Computer Clb; Sec Intnl Clb; Key Clb; Math Tm; Science Clb; Service Clb; Yrbk Stf; Trk; High Hon Roll; NHS; Iron Hills Conf Champnshp Mth Tm 83-84 & 85-86; NJ Inst Tech; Comp Sci.

KUPERSMITH, ROSEANNE; Ocean Township HS; Oakhurst, NJ; (Y); 112/333; Exploring; Ski Clb; Temple Yth Grp; Rep Band; Mrchg Band; School Play; Rep Frsh Cls; Rep Stu Cncl; Var Swmmng; Var Trk; Bronze Congrssnl Awd 84; SUNY Cortland; Phys Ed.

KURI, IVETTE; Passaic Valley HS; Totowa, NJ; (Y); Lit Mag; Hon Roll; Cmmnctns.

KURIAWA, JOHN; David Brearley HS; Kenilworth, NJ; (Y); 4/176; Church Yth Grp; Lit Mag; Bsktbl; Hon Roll; Spanish NHS; PTA Schlrshp 86; Rutgers Coll; Econ.

KURLEY, CHRISTEN; Clifton HS; Clifton, NJ; (Y); 127/637; Key Clb; Office Aide; Band; Chorus; JV Var Cheerleading; Var Fld Hcky; JV Var Pom Pon; Hon Roll; Hnr Gurd; Comm Svc Safety Town; Law.

KURLYCHEK, ANTHONY; Manchester Regional HS; Prospect Pk, NJ; (Y); 14/150; Bsbl; Boys Clb Am; Band; Chorus; Concert Band; Mrchg Band; Yrbk Stf; Ftbl; Score Keeper; Hon Roll; GATE Pgm 85-86; All Amer Acad Achvt Awd 86; K Of C Freethrw Champ 84; Bsbl Hstry Clb 85-86; Georgetown; Intl Law.

KURMAN, SHERI; Woodstown HS; Alloway, NJ; (Y); Key Clb; Math Tm; Pep Clb; Ski Clb; Teachers Aide; Color Guard; Mrchg Band; Stu Cncl; Twrlr; Hon Roll; Bus.

KUROKAWA, SHIN; Holy Spirit HS; Margate, NJ; (Y); Computer Clb; Math Clb; Math Tm; Science Clb; Teachers Aide; Band; Orch; School Musical; NHS; Physcs Awd, 1st Pl Annl ST Sci Day, Chem Crvn, 3rd Pl AHSME 86; Physcs.

KUROWSKY, MELISSA; Wall HS; Manasquan, NJ; (S); 4/296; Pres Church Yth Grp; Key Clb; Church Choir; Concert Band; Jazz Band; Mrchg Band; High Hon Roll; Central Jersey Symphnc Band 85; Armed Forces Explrtn Engr Sci 1st Pl 84; Tutorng Clb 84-85; Phrmcy.

KURPICKI, JANCINE LYNN; Collingswood SR HS; Collingswood, NJ; (Y); Am Leg Aux Girls St; Church Yth Grp; Key Clb; Office Aide; Capt Color Guard; Yrbk Stf; Stu Cncl; Stat Bsktbl; Glassboro ST Coll; Law.

KURTA, YVONNE; Mahwah HS; Mahwah, NJ; (Y); 64/176; JCL; Chorus; Trk; Hon Roll; MVP Spring Track Team 86.

KURTH, ERIK; Passaic Valley HS; Totowa, NJ; (Y); Am Leg Boys St; Chess Clb; Key Clb; Varsity Clb; Band; Stage Crew; Yrbk Ed-Chief; Rep Stu Cncl; Capt Bsbl; Var Bsktbl; Engnr.

KURTZ, JEANNE; Elmwood Park Memorial HS; Elmwood Pk, NJ; (Y); 14/160; Am Leg Aux Girls St; Var Capt Bsktbl; Var JV Cheerleading; Var Sftbl; Var Vllybl; NHS; Montcalir ST Coll; Elem Tchr.

KURTZ, JEFF; Cresskill HS; Cresskill, NJ; (Y); 55/120; Am Leg Boys St; Ski Clb; Off Frsh Cls; Off Soph Cls; Off Jr Cls; Stu Cncl; L Bsktbl; Var Ftbl; Capt Tennis; Hon Roll; Bus.

KURTZ, JENNY; Pompton Lakes HS; Pompton Lakes, NJ; (Y); Intnl Clb; Office Aide; Bsktbl; Sftbl; High Hon Roll; Hon Roll; Katherine Gibbs Ldrshp Awd 86; Wrd Procssng.

KURTZ, LAURA; Woodstown HS; Woodstown, NJ; (Y); Church Yth Grp; Spanish Clb; Nwsp Rptr; Nwsp Stf; Yrbk Stf; Rep Soph Cls; Hon Roll; S Jersey Sci Fair-2nd Pl 84 & 85; DE Vly Sci Fair-Hnrb Mntn 84 & 85; Olympcs Of Mind 85 & 86; Psych.

KURUNTHOTTICAL, ZUBIN; Manchester Regional HS; Prospect Park, NJ; (S); 7/156; Mathletes; Science Clb; Band; Concert Band; Mrchg Band; JV Bsbl; JV Var Crs Cntry; Hon Roll; NHS; Gftd & Tlntd 83-85; Aerosp Engrng.

KUSHNER, MELISSA; Central Regional HS; Island Hgts, NJ; (Y); Hosp Aide; Off Office Aide; Temple Yth Grp; Nwsp Ed-Chief; Nwsp Rptr; French Hon Soc; High Hon Roll; Hon Roll; NHS; Law.

KUSHNIRSKY, ALLA; Solomon Schechter Day Schl; Irvington, NJ; (Y); Cmnty Wkr; Library Aide; School Play; Stage Crew; Yrbk Stf; Sci Fair; Bus.

KUSZEWSKI, JOHN J; Delbarton Schl; Warren, NJ; (Y); Boy Scts; Computer Clb; Math Tm; Quiz Bowl; Science Clb; Church Choir; Yrbk Bus Mgr; High Hon Roll; Ntl Merit SF; VFW Awd; Excllnc In Comp Sci; A P Comp Sci Tchng Asst; Yale U; Moleclar Bio.

KUZIEMKO, THOMAS; Bayonne HS; Bayonne, NJ; (Y); Computer Clb; Hon Roll.

KUZNITZ, KIM; Arthur L Johnson Regional HS; Clark, NJ; (S); 18/214; School Musical; Variety Show; Pres Soph Cls; Stu Cncl; French Hon Soc; Hon Roll; Dance Schlrshp 80; Dance Awds 80-81; Thtre.

KVEGLIS, ANN; Montville Township HS; Pine Brook, NJ; (Y); 37/262; Church Yth Grp; Key Clb; Ski Clb; JV Cheerleading; Mgr(s); Stat Mat Maids; Stat Score Keeper; Var JV Sftbl; High Hon Roll; Hon Roll; Hotel Mgmt.

KWAAK, KATHRYN; Red Bank Catholic HS; Englishtown, NJ; (Y); Ski Clb; Capt Flag Corp; Mrchg Band; Capt Twrlr; Natl Piano Gld Auditns ST Wnr Intrmdt Cls 85; Natlpinao Gld Socl Music Tst 84; Georgetown U; Music.

KWAK, SOOJI; Rutherford HS; Rutherford, NJ; (Y); 7/185; Pres Church Yth Grp; Key Clb; Pres NFL; Trs Spanish Clb; Acpl Chr; Nwsp Ed-Chief; Var Tennis; Capt Trk; Sec NHS; Voice Dem Awd; Pres Clssrm Yng Amer 84-85; Becton & Dickenson Schlrshp Prog 86; Barnard Coll; Invstmt Bnkr.

KWAN, KAREN; Matawan Regional HS; Aberdeen, NJ; (Y); 58/320; Hosp Aide; Band; Concert Band; Jazz Band; Mrchg Band; Diving; Hon Roll; Jr NHS; Guild Adtns Piano Awds 84-86; Piano Cmpttns 84-85; Teen Artts Fstvl Awd 84; Phrmcy.

KWIATKOWSKI, MICHELLE; Woodbridge HS; Fords, NJ; (Y); 114/404; Church Yth Grp; SADD; Chorus; Orch; School Play; Nwsp Stf; Rep Soph Cls; Rep Jr Cls; Rep Stu Cncl; Hon Roll; Psychol.

KWON, DAPHNE; Freehold Twp HS; Freehold, NJ; (Y); 5/292; Church Yth Grp; Yrbk Stf; Off Frsh Cls; Capt Crs Cntry; Mgr(s); Capt Trk; VP NHS; Ntl Merit Ltr; Local Union 1262 Schlrshp 86; U MI Alumni Giving 86; Garden ST Distingshd Schlr 86; U MI; Med.

KWON, HELEN; West Essex SR HS; N Caldwell, NJ; (Y); Radio Clb; Nwsp Ed-Chief; Nwsp Rptr; Ed Nwsp Stf; Yrbk Stf; NHS; Ntl Merit SF.

KYLE, JOSEPH M; Hackensack HS; Rochelle Park, NJ; (Y); 32/387; Am Leg Boys St; Computer Clb; Ski Clb; Rep Frsh Cls; Rep Soph Cls; Rep Stu Cncl; Tennis; Hon Roll; NHS; Cert Recgntn Apprectn 85; SUNY; Sci.

KYLE, KATHRYN; Cresskill HS; Cresskill, NJ; (Y); Church Yth Grp; Debate Tm; DECA; Spanish Clb; Chorus; School Musical; JV Socr; JV Stat Sftbl; JV Vllybl; Sec Ed.

L HOMMEDIEU, ARTHUR; Kihatinny Regional HS; Newton, NJ; (Y); 19/222; PAVAS; Stage Crew; Nwsp Rptr; Nwsp Stf; Lit Mag; Gov Hon Prg Awd; High Hon Roll; Hon Roll; NHS; Govnrs Schl Art Trenton ST Coll 86; ST & Locl Symp Art; Pratt Inst; Illus.

LA, LOUIS; Belleville HS; Belleville, NJ; (Y); Var Bsktbl; JV Socr; Var Trk; Hon Roll; NHS; Vrsty Let Trk & Fld 84; Vrsty Let Trk & Bsktbl 85-86; NJIT-RUTGER; Technlgy.

LA BADIA, JILL; Indian Hills HS; Oakland, NJ; (Y); Dance Clb; French Clb; Teachers Aide; Ed Nwsp Rptr; Lit Mag; Rep Soph Cls; Stat Bsktbl; Cit Awd; Hon Roll; NHS; Womens Clb Citznshp Inst 86.

LA BAR JR, RICHARD S; Pope John XXIII HS; Vernon, NJ; (Y); 14/131; Church Yth Grp; French Clb; Scholastic Bowl; Teachers Aide; Lit Mag; Var L Bsbl; JV Bsktbl; Var L Ftbl; High Hon Roll; VP NHS; Alg & Hlth Achvt Awds 83-84; 1st Pl Hstry Pjct/Culture Wknd 84; Agrnmy.

LA BRUNA, BETH; West Deptford HS; Woodbury, NJ; (Y); 20/240; Church Yth Grp; Mrchg Band; Symp Band; Yrbk Stf; Trs Jr Cls; Trs Sr Cls; Rep Stu Cncl; Var Stat Bsktbl; Hon Roll; Pres NHS; Olympics Of The Mind Renatra Fusca Awd Regnl Champs 85 & 86; Business.

LA BRUNO, DAVID; St Peters Prepatory HS; Bayonne, NJ; (Y); 50/202; Aud/Vis; Computer Clb; French Clb; Science Clb; Nwsp Rptr; Nwsp Stf; JV Ice Hcky; Chess Clb; Church Yth Grp; Pep Clb; Knghts Of Clmbs Schlrshp; Intrmrl Chmpnshp Ftbl-Bsktbl 85-86; Rtgrs U Coll-Engrng; Chmcl Engr.

LA COUTURE, TAMARA; Holy Cross HS; Lumberton, NJ; (Y); 7/383; Cmnty Wkr; Girl Scts; Ski Clb; Chorus; Var L Color Guard; Var L Mrchg Band; Stage Crew; Nwsp Rptr; Twrlr; Im L Vllybl; St Josephs U PA Pres Schlrshp 86; Regional ST Awd Natl Hstry Day NJ 83 84; St Josephs U; Bio.

LA MARMORA, JOY DENISE; Ridgefield Memorial HS; Ridgefield, NJ; (Y); 20/104; Drama Clb; Pep Clb; PAVAS; School Musical; School Play; Stage Crew; Variety Show; JV Var Cheerleading; High Hon Roll; Prfct Atten Awd; Fordham U; Acctg.

LA PORTE, KIMBERLY; Washington Twp HS; Blackwood, NJ; (Y); Art Clb; Stu Cncl; Hon Roll; Archtctl Rndrng 84; Stu Govt 84; Cmmrcl Art.

LA ROCCA, JOSEPH; Mc Corristin HS; New Egypt, NJ; (Y); Key Clb; SADD; Stage Crew; Bsbl; Hon Roll; NEDT Awd; Prfct Atten Awd; Bus.

LA ROSA, ANTHONY; Bishop George Ahr HS; Perth Amboy, NJ; (Y); 35/275; Bowling; Socr; High Hon Roll; Hon Roll; Excllnce Scholar 84; Engrng.

LA ROSA, CHRISTOPHER M; Bishop Evstace Prep; Bellmawr, NJ; (Y); Am Leg Boys St; Church Yth Grp; Drama Clb; Science Clb; Church Choir; School Musical; Pres Sr Cls; Hon Roll; NHS; Spanish NHS; Pre-Med.

LA ROSA, MICHELE; Westfield HS; Westfield, NJ; (Y); 90/555; Church Yth Grp; Chorus; Yrbk Stf; Hon Roll; Mus Educ Assoc Awd 84; Bus.

LA STELLA, JESSICA; Passaic Valley HS; Little Falls, NJ; (Y); Drama Clb; Girl Scts; Key Clb; Band; Concert Band; Jazz Band; School Play; Yrbk Stf; Cheerleading; Diving; Yrbk Stff 85-86; Chrldng 85-86; Hnr Rll 83-84; Accntng.

LA TERRA, VINCE; Mainland Regional HS; Northfield, NJ; (Y); 17/320; Var L Bowling; Hon Roll; Jr NHS; NHS; Acad/Phy Educ Awd 86; Cert Of Hnr Excel In Schlrshp 85; Rutgers Coll; Adv.

LA TORRE, JOSEPH; Roselle Catholic HS; Elizabeth, NJ; (Y); 77/195; Am Leg Boys St; Rep Soph Cls; Var Bsbl; JV Bsktbl; Hon Roll; Natl Bus Hnr Soc 86; Crtfct Prfcncy Accntng 86; Bus.

LA VECCHIA, CATHERINE; Marylawn Of The Oranges HS; S Orange, NJ; (S); 1/54; Church Yth Grp; Dance Clb; Pep Clb; Service Clb; Chorus; School Musical; Nwsp Rptr; Nwsp Sprt Ed; Nwsp Stf; Lit Mag; 1st-Art Cls, Physcl Sci, Hstry & Alg; Vrsty Ltr-Tnns; Vrsty Tnns Pin; Parish Cncl; Elem Educ.

LA VELLE, DANIELLE MARIE; Lacey Township HS; Forked River, NJ; (Y); 8/210; Math Tm; Service Clb; Yrbk Sprt Ed; Yrbk Stf; High Hon Roll; Hon Roll; NHS; SADD; Nwsp Stf; Yrbk Rptr; Outstndng Wrtr Awd 85; Itln Am Clb Schlrshp 86; Awd Vlntry Tutr Natl Hnr Soc 86; Livingston Clg; Psych.

LA VORGNA, LOUISE; Paul VI Regional HS; Totowa, NJ; (Y); Key Clb; School Musical; Yrbk Stf; Hon Roll; Fashion Inst Tech; Boutique Own.

LABORDE, WIDMA JO; Essex Catholic Girls HS; Orange, NJ; (Y); 4/71; Computer Clb; Dance Clb; Drama Clb; Math Clb; Cheerleading; Hon Roll; NHS.

LABRUM, JOSETTE A; Lenape Valley HS; Sparta, NJ; (Y); Dance Clb; Drama Clb; French Clb; FBLA; Intnl Clb; Key Clb; SADD; Thesps; Chorus; Natl Dance Champ 83-85; NY U Schrlshp $8000 86; Manhattan Clg; Crmnl Physchlgy.

LACAMERA, SUSAN; Hunterdon Central HS; Somerville, NJ; (Y); Cmnty Wkr; Drama Clb; Key Clb; School Play; Yrbk Rptr; Rptr Yrbk Stf; Cheerleading; Tennis; Twrlr; 4-H Awd; Davis Cup Tnns Awd Of Hntrdn Cnty 83-84; Miss NJ Teen USA Awd 85-86; Tnns Awds; Frlgh Dcknsn U; Bus.

LACAP, ANSEL; Bergenfield HS; Bergenfield, NJ; (Y); Drama Clb; Spanish Clb; School Musical; School Play; Stage Crew; Spanish NHS; Cmptr Sci.

LACATENA, MICHELE; Kinnelon HS; Kinnelon, NJ; (Y); 17/176; Art Clb; Camera Clb; Girl Scts; Spanish Clb; Stage Crew; Lit Mag; Hon Roll; NHS; Ntl Merit SF; Spanish NHS; Anmal Sci.

LACAVA, GREG; Middletown South HS; Middletown, NJ; (Y); FCA; Letterman Clb; SADD; Band; Nwsp Sprt Ed; Yrbk Sprt Ed; Capt Ftbl; Cit Awd; High Hon Roll; Hon Roll; All Schltc Ftbl Camp Outstndg Off Back 86; Holy Cross; Rest Mgmt.

LACAVA, LYNN; De Paul Diocesean HS; Wayne, NJ; (Y); 36/171; JCL; Latin Clb; Math Tm; Trs Sr Cls; Var L Fld Hcky; Var L Sftbl; High Hon Roll; Hon Roll; U Of Scraton; Finance.

LACCITIELLO, DAWN; Nutley HS; Nutley, NJ; (Y); 30/336; Cheerleading; High Hon Roll; Hon Roll; NHS; Montclair ST Coll.

LACHER, BRITT; Franklin HS; Somerset, NJ; (Y); Hosp Aide; Key Clb; VP Temple Yth Grp; Varsity Clb; Band; Color Guard; School Musical; Yrbk Stf; Rep Frsh Cls; Rep Soph Cls; Hnr Rl Awds 83-85; Exclnc In Chrldg 85-86; Pre-Med.

LACHMANN, JUSTINE; Immaculate Conception HS; Ridgefield Pk, NJ; (Y); Pres Cmnty Wkr; Math Clb; Science Clb; Yrbk Stf; Rep Frsh Cls; Tennis; NEDT Awd; Attended Lebanon Vly Coll Yth Schlr Prog 86; Attended ; Chime Program At ; Njit 86; Doctor.

LACHTMAN, DAVID; Manalapan HS; Englishtown, NJ; (Y); 19/456; Latin Clb; Spanish Clb; SADD; Temple Yth Grp; VP Frsh Cls; Rep Soph Cls; Rep Jr Cls; Rep Sr Cls; Rep Stu Cncl; Var L Bsbl; Law.

LACIVITA, ERNEST; Hudson Catholic HS; Union Cty, NJ; (Y); 33/180; Art Clb; Spanish Clb; Band; School Musical; School Play; Variety Show; Trk; Hon Roll; Pratt U; Comm Art.

LACY, MICHAEL; Cumberland Regional HS; Bridgeton, NJ; (Y); 11/315; Stage Crew; Hon Roll; NHS; Ntl Merit Schol; Rotary Awd; St Schlr; Rutgers U; Elec Engrng.

LACZHAZY, ROBERT S; Phillipsburg Catholic HS; Phillipsburg, NJ; (Y); Pres Science Clb; Chorus; Capt Mrchg Band; Mgr School Musical; Nwsp Ed-Chief; Yrbk Stf; Lit Mag; JV Var Socr; Hon Roll; Ntl Merit Ltr; PA ST U; Aero Sp Engr.

LAFAZIA, CHRISTINE; Fair Lawn HS; Fair Lawn, NJ; (Y); Cmnty Wkr; Girl Scts; Hosp Aide; Office Aide; SADD; Chorus; Church Choir; School Musical; School Play; Swing Chorus; Fair Lawn Plc Dept Hnr 82-83; Vly Hosp Axlry Awd 84; Mntclr ST Coll; Tchr.

LAFFERTY, DAWN; Overbrook SR HS; Pine Hill, NJ; (Y); Band; Concert Band; School Play; Capt Var Cheerleading; Powder Puff Ftbl; Capt Socr; JV Sftbl; Glassboro ST Coll; Psych.

LAFFERTY, LIZ; Holy Cross HS; Mount Laurel, NJ; (Y); Church Yth Grp; Ski Clb; High Hon Roll; Librl Arts.

LAGER, JEFFREY T; Gill/St Bernards HS; Bridgewater, NJ; (Y); 1/16; Capt Quiz Bowl; Trs Temple Yth Grp; Yrbk Ed-Chief; Sec Stu Cncl; Var Capt Golf; Var Capt Socr; Cit Awd; High Hon Roll; Ntl Merit SF; Cmnty Wkr; Ambssdr To Hugh O Brian Yth Ldrshp Sem 1984; Harvard Bk Prize; St Fnlst-Japan Us Senate Schlrshp Pgm; Engrng.

LAGERMASINI, PAUL; Saint Peters Prep; Upr Montclair, NJ; (Y); Pep Clb; Nwsp Rptr; Nwsp Sprt Ed; Nwsp Stf; Var Capt Socr; Var Wt Lftg; Hon Roll; Eucharistic Mnstr; Law.

LAHIFF, MICHAEL; Cresskill HS; Cresskill, NJ; (Y); Art Clb; Chess Clb; Ski Clb; Spanish Clb; Mgr(s); Hon Roll; Aerosp Engrng.

LAHNEMAN, EILEEN M; Florence Twp Memorial HS; Florence, NJ; (Y); 11/93; French Clb; FTA; Band; Concert Band; Jazz Band; Pres Mrchg Band; School Musical; Symp Band; Variety Show; Nwsp Stf; 1st Pl Wrtng Pgm 84; US Collgt Winds Band 85; Al-Amer Hl Fm Hnrs 85; Lock Haven U; Elem Ed.

LAINO, KELLY A; East Brunswick HS; E Brunswick, NJ; (Y); French Clb; Hosp Aide; Key Clb; Library Aide; Pep Clb; SADD; Yrbk Stf; High Hon Roll; NHS.

LAKE, ELLEN; North Plainfield HS; N Plainfield, NJ; (Y); 67/189; Hosp Aide; Key Clb; Spanish Clb; Chorus; Pom Pon; Powder Puff Ftbl; Sftbl.

LAKE, JOHN; Notre Dame HS; Belle Mead, NJ; (Y); Band; Concert Band; Jazz Band; Mrchg Band; Orch; Pep Band; Hon Roll.

LAKE, MARGARET; Sayreville War Memorial HS; South Amboy, NJ; (Y); 21/387; French Clb; Spanish Clb; Drill Tm; Yrbk Stf; Stu Cncl; Mgr(s); French Hon Soc; Hon Roll; Lion Awd; NHS; Stdnt Cncl Awd 86; Boston U.

LAKE, VANESSA; Dwight Morrow HS; Englewood, NJ; (Y); Camera Clb; Color Guard; Flag Corp; Yrbk Stf; Sftbl; Hon Roll; Fash Mechndsng.

LAKE, WALTER; Warren County Vo-Tech; Phillipsburg, NJ; (S); Yrbk Stf; Hon Roll; Comp Pgmmr.

LAKSONO, DICKY; Lakeland Regional HS; Ringwood, NJ; (Y); Boy Scts; Math Tm; SADD; Nwsp Phtg; Nwsp Rptr; Yrbk Phtg; Yrbk Rptr; Yrbk Stf; JV Tennis; Hon Roll; Elect Engr.

LAL, SANGEETA; Glen Rock JR SR HS; Glen Rock, NJ; (Y); Am Leg Aux Girls St; Pres Church Yth Grp; Hosp Aide; Spanish Clb; Varsity Clb; Chorus; Madrigals; School Musical; Nwsp Stf; Vllybl; Rutgers U; Psych.

LALA, VINOD; Don Bosco Prep HS; Allendale, NJ; (Y); Math Tm; Model UN; Political Wkr; Scholastic Bowl; Ski Clb; Lit Mag; Rep Frsh Cls; Pres Soph Cls; JV Crs Cntry; Var Trk; Garden ST Schlr 86; Acdm All Amer 85; Prncpls List 86; Cornell U; Economics.

LALBAHADUR, VIDESH; Academic HS; Jersey City, NJ; (Y); Math Clb; Math Tm; Scholastic Bowl; Science Clb; Band; Bsbl; Swmmng; Awd Merit Pres Political Clb 84-85; Councilman Lawrence Clayton Assoc; NJ Inst Tech; Biomed Engrng.

LALLI, CANDICE M; Highland Regional HS; Clementon, NJ; (S); 21/326; Cmnty Wkr; Spanish Clb; Nwsp Rptr; Lit Mag; Stu Cncl; Im Cheerleading; Hon Roll; NHS; Rutgers U; Pre-Law.

LALLY, KEVIN; Seton Hall Prep; Verona, NJ; (Y); 2/200; Key Clb; Pres Pep Clb; Varsity Clb; Nwsp Rptr; Ed Yrbk Stf; Rep Stu Cncl; Capt Swmmng; High Hon Roll; NHS.

LAM, DAVID; Chatham Township HS; Chatham, NJ; (Y); Key Clb; Var Bsbl; Im Trk; High Hon Roll; Hon Roll.

LAMAN, EDWARD; Manchester Regional HS; Prospect Park, NJ; (S); 1/175; Church Yth Grp; German Clb; Mathletes; Science Clb; Yrbk Stf; Rep Frsh Cls; Rep Soph Cls; Rep Jr Cls; Rep Stu Cncl; JV Bsktbl; ST Sci Day; ST Sci Pgm Sci & Comp Sci; Mech Engnrng.

LAMANNA, MARIA; Secaucus HS; Secaucus, NJ; (S); 4/160; Math Clb; Yrbk Stf; High Hon Roll; Hon Roll; NHS; Spanish NHS; Educ.

LAMB, BOB; Maple Shade HS; Maple Shade, NJ; (Y); Am Leg Boys St; Drama Clb; Key Clb; SADD; School Musical; Nwsp Stf; Yrbk Ed-Chief; High Hon Roll; NHS; Prfct Atten Awd; Doctor Of Med.

LAMB, COLLEEN; Highland Regional HS; Laurel Springs, NJ; (S); Girl Scts; JA; Pres Service Clb; Coach Actv; Stat Var Ftbl; Var Mat Maids; Var Stat Wrstlng; Hon Roll; NHS.

LAMBERSON, MICHAEL; South Brunswick HS; Kendall Pk, NJ; (Y); Church Yth Grp; Im Mgr Bsbl; Im Mgr Ftbl; Meterology.

LAMBERT, JODI; Clifton HS; Clifton, NJ; (Y); 85/637; Drama Clb; 4-H; Spanish Clb; Stage Crew; Yrbk Stf; Hon Roll; Comm.

LAMBERT, KATHLEEN; Notre Dame HS; Trenton, NJ; (Y); 26/340; Sec Key Clb; Latin Clb; Ski Clb; Varsity Clb; JV Sftbl; Var L Swmmng; Var L Tennis; High Hon Roll; Hon Roll; NHS; MVP-GIRLS Vrsty Ten 85-86; Latn Hon Soc 84-87; 1st Tm All Cnty-1st Dbls-Girls Vrsty Ten 85-86.

LAMBERT, MICHELLE; North Warren Regional HS; Blairstown, NJ; (Y); 27/150; Hosp Aide; Band; Concert Band; Mrchg Band; Nwsp Rptr; Rep Stu Cncl; Var L Cheerleading; Hon Roll; Montclair ST Clg; Psych.

LAMBERTON, JIM; Waldwick HS; Waldwick, NJ; (Y); Aud/Vis; Pres Church Yth Grp; Pres 4-H; Yrbk Phtg; Cit Awd; 4-H Awd; Natl 4-H Conf 85; Ctznshp WA Focus 84; Hugh Obrian 2nd Rnnr Up 84; U S Coast Guard Acad.

LAMBORNE, RENEE; Holy Cross HS; Marlton, NJ; (Y); 11/391; Church Yth Grp; Ski Clb; Spanish Clb; Sec Soph Cls; Rep Stu Cncl; JV Bsktbl; JV Var Fld Hcky; High Hon Roll; Hon Roll; Pres NHS; Math.

LAMBUSTA, GINA; Brick Township HS; Brick Town, NJ; (Y); Exploring; Hosp Aide; Math Tm; Band; Concert Band; Mrchg Band; Yrbk Stf; JV Var Bowling; Stat Socr; NHS; Bio Med Engr.

LAMONT, MARGARET; Woodstown HS; Woodstown, NJ; (Y); GAA; Key Clb; Spanish Clb; SADD; Church Choir; Yrbk Phtg; Rep Frsh Cls; Var L Bsktbl; Var L Socr; 4-H Awd; Bio.

LAMOTTA, CARIANNE; North Warren Regional HS; Blairstown, NJ; (Y); 11/135; Pep Clb; Rep Stu Cncl; Stat Bsbl; Var Fld Hcky; Hon Roll; Rotary Awd; Pre-Law.

LAMOUR, KRISTINA; Montville Twp HS; Towaco, NJ; (Y); Art Clb; Church Yth Grp; Debate Tm; Key Clb; Yrbk Stf; Lit Mag; Lcrss; ST Recog NJS Teen Art Fstvl 84; Mustang Assn Purchase Prz Vis Art 86; Savannah Coll Art; Illus.

LAMPARELLO, MICHAEL J; Rutherford HS; Rutherford, NJ; (Y); Chess Clb; Computer Clb; Debate Tm; Math Tm; Band; Concert Band; Drm Mjr(t); Jazz Band; Boy Scts; NFL; Louis Armstrong Jazz Awd 86; Mst Promisng Comp Stu 86; Rutgers; Comp Sci.

LAMPE, CARYN; St John Vianney HS; Marlboro, NJ; (Y); 6/286; Church Yth Grp; Church Choir; Capt Color Guard; Drill Tm; Mrchg Band; JV Powder Puff Ftbl; JV Sftbl; High Hon Roll; Hon Roll; Kiwanis Awd; St John Vianney Gold & White Awd 84-86; Math.

LAMPMANN, WALTER D; Becton Regional HS; East Rutherford, NJ; (Y); Am Leg Boys St; Computer Clb; Math Tm; Science Clb; Bsbl; Bowling; Ntl Merit Ltr; NJ Physcs Olympcs 85; Comp Sci.

LAMPSON, DAMON K; Pleasantville HS; Pleasantville, NJ; (S); 3/132; Art Clb; SADD; Stu Cncl; Var Swmmng; JV Trk; Hon Roll; NHS; Comp Oper.

LAMZAKI, DIMAS; Palisades Park JR SR HS; Palisades Park, NJ; (Y); Church Yth Grp; Letterman Clb; Library Aide; Science Clb; Spanish Clb; Yrbk Ed-Chief; Lit Mag; Var Capt Bowling; DAR Awd; NHS; Acad Decthln Tm 85-86; Bst Hstry Stu Awd 85-86; NYU Trst Schlrshp 86-90; NYU; Pre Law.

LAN, VIVIAN; New Milford HS; New Milford, NJ; (Y); 4/140; Math Tm; Nwsp Ed-Chief; Yrbk Stf; Lit Mag; Sec Jr Cls; Var Capt Tennis; Cit Awd; Hon Roll; VP Jr NHS; Pres NHS; Eileen Enright Awd 86; Salvtn Army Schlrp; Johns Hopkins U; Med.

LANCASTER JR, ALLEN; Lenape Valley Regional HS; Andover, NJ; (Y); 31/250; Bsbl; Bsktbl; Ftbl; Trk; Wt Lftg; Wrstlng; Hon Roll; Comp Sci.

LANCE, ALICE; Hun Schl Of Princeto; High Bridge, NJ; (Y); Ski Clb; Spanish Clb; Varsity Clb; Chorus; School Musical; Variety Show; Cmnty Wkr; Drama Clb; GAA; Key Clb; Ldrshp Awd Clss Pres; Pre-Law.

LANCERO, REUEL; Red Bank Regional HS; Red Bank, NJ; (Y); 32/223; Am Leg Boys St; Church Yth Grp; Dance Clb; Church Choir; School Musical; School Play; Stage Crew; Lit Mag; Var Trk; NHS; Rutgers U; Comp Sci.

LAND, FRED; Linden HS; Linden, NJ; (Y); Engine City; Auto Mechnc.

LAND, KEVIN; Kittatinny Regional HS; Newton, NJ; (Y); 19/228; Math Tm; Science Clb; Teachers Aide; Var Bsbl; Var Bsktbl; Var Capt Ftbl; High Hon Roll; Hon Roll; NHS; Slctd Natl Yng Ldrs Conf WA 86; Liberal Arts.

LANDAU, DOUGLAS; Glen Rock HS; Glen Rock, NJ; (Y); 83/170; Camera Clb; DECA; Pep Clb; Ski Clb; Ftbl; Tennis; U Of ME; Mgmt.

LANDEN, ALEXANDRA E; Hightstown HS; East Windsor, NJ; (Y); 31/343; Drama Clb; Band; Chorus; Church Choir; Mrchg Band; School Musical; Stage Crew; Symp Band; Hon Roll; Hartt Schl Of Music; Msc Educ.

LANDINI, LEE C; Randolph HS; Randolph, NJ; (Y); Band; Chorus; Church Choir; Concert Band; Drm Mjr(t); Mrchg Band; School Musical; School Play; Hon Roll; Ntl Merit Ltr; Piano Perfrmnc.

LANDIS, KIMBERLY; Camden Catholic HS; Cherry Hill, NJ; (Y); Art Clb; FBLA; Spanish Clb; Var Crs Cntry; JV Fld Hcky; JV Lcrss; Var Mgr(s); Var Trk; Psychol.

LANDIS, STEVE; Pennsville Memorial HS; Pennsville, NJ; (Y); 4/226; Boy Scts; Church Yth Grp; Computer Clb; Debate Tm; Drama Clb; Office Aide; Ski Clb; Band; Concert Band; Drm & Bgl; W Chester U; Mus Educ.

LANDMESSER, LAURIE; Belvidere HS; Belvidere, NJ; (Y); Hosp Aide; Band; Chorus; Concert Band; Jazz Band; Madrigals; Mrchg Band; Rep Stu Cncl; JV Var Sftbl; Hon Roll; Kutztown U; Early Chldhd Ed.

LANDRIGAN, KATHY; North Bergen HS; North Bergen, NJ; (Y); 29/404; Office Aide; Yrbk Stf; Capt Cheerleading; High Hon Roll; NHS; Coach Actv; Rutgers Coll NJ; Accntnt.

LANE, DAVID A; Union Catholic Regional HS; Fanwood, NJ; (Y); SADD; Rep Frsh Cls; Rep Soph Cls; Rep Jr Cls; Rep Sr Cls; Stu Cncl; Var JV Bsktbl; Hon Roll; Seton Hall U Acad Schlrshp 86; Merrimack Coll Acad Schrlshp 86; Merrimack Coll; Engl.

LANE, GREGORY LEON; Dickinson HS; Jersey City, NJ; (Y); Boy Scts; Church Choir; Rep Frsh Cls; Rep Soph Cls; Rep Stu Cncl; JV Bsbl; Stat Bowling; JV Crs Cntry; Var Ftbl; Var Trk; Acctnt.

LANE, JENNIFER; Mater Dei HS; Highlands, NJ; (Y); 53/151; Church Yth Grp; Cmnty Wkr; Girl Scts; Pep Clb; Var Cheerleading; Powder Puff Ftbl; Hon Roll; Acad Achvt Hstry 84-85; Fine Arts.

LANE, JOANNE; Middletown High School South; Red Bank, NJ; (Y); Am Leg Aux Girls St; Cmnty Wkr; Band; Jazz Band; Mrchg Band; Var L Socr; Gov Hon Prg Awd; High Hon Roll; NHS; Ntl Merit Ltr.

LANE, KATIE; Chatham Twp HS; Chatham, NJ; (Y); 13/128; Trs VP Church Yth Grp; Pep Clb; Sec Varsity Clb; Yrbk Stf; VP Frsh Cls; Sec Stu Cncl; Var JV Bsktbl; Var Capt Fld Hcky; Var Capt Lcrss; High Hon Roll; All ST Grp I Fld Hockey 1st Tm 84-85; All Cnty Fld Hcky 1st Tm 84-85; 1st Tm All Stars Fld Hcky 84-85; Lafayette Coll; Psych.

LANE, TOM; Montville HS; Montville, NJ; (Y); 62/262; Art Clb; FBLA; Nwsp Rptr; Nwsp Stf; Ftbl; High Hon Roll; Hon Roll; Finc.

LANG, CHRIS; Middletown HS S HS; Middletown, NJ; (Y); Var L Socr; High Hon Roll; Hon Roll; Mst Imprvd Athlt 85.

LANG, JEANNETTE; Middlesex HS; Middlesex, NJ; (Y); 18/169; Girl Scts; Model UN; Scholastic Bowl; Ski Clb; SADD; Trs Frsh Cls; Rep Stu Cncl; JV Var Bsktbl; JV Sftbl; Var Capt Tennis; Coll; Lbrl Arts.

LANGAN, JAMES; Perth Amboy HS; Perth Amboy, NJ; (Y); 69/503; Church Yth Grp; German Clb; Key Clb; Library Aide; Mathletes; Math Tm; Quiz Bowl; Scholastic Bowl; Cit Awd; Hon Roll; Rutgers U NJ; Hstrn.

LANGBEIN, TAMMY; Edgewood SR HS; Sicklerville, NJ; (Y); Cmnty Wkr; Capt Flag Corp; Yrbk Stf; Hon Roll; Jr NHS; NHS; Bus Adm.

LANGE, LAURIE; MSGR Donovan HS; Toms River, NJ; (Y); Trs Exploring; Hosp Aide; Ski Clb; SADD; Yrbk Stf; JV Var Trk; Hon Roll; Nrsng.

LANGE, STACEY; Union HS; Union, NJ; (Y); French Clb; Rep Soph Cls; Rep Jr Cls; Pres Sr Cls; Pres Stu Cncl; Capt Cheerleading; Gym; Cit Awd; French Hon Soc; Hon Roll; Fash Inst Of Tech.

LANGEL, HEATHER; Livingston HS; Livingston, NJ; (Y); French Clb; Hosp Aide; Leo Clb; Sec Rep Temple Yth Grp; Yrbk Stf; Lit Mag; Off Stu Cncl; Stat Fld Hcky; Stat Socr; JV Var Swmmng.

LANGERMAN, SHERI; Ocean Township HS; Ocean, NJ; (Y); 17/335; Science Clb; SADD; Nwsp Stf; Yrbk Rptr; Var JV Fld Hcky; Var JV Swmmng; Ntl Merit Ltr; Varsity Clb; NJ ST Sci Day Bio Exm; Rider Coll Lang Frnsc Cmptn-1st Pl Russn; VP, Pres Russn Clb; U Of CA; Marn Bio.

LANGFORD, VIRGINIA; Lower Cape May Regional HS; W Cape May, NJ; (Y); Pep Clb; Chorus; Flag Corp; Mrchg Band; Yrbk Stf; Hon Roll; Atlantic CC; Soclgy.

LANGLEY, GEORGE; Cumberland Regional HS; Rosenhayn, NJ; (Y); Hon Roll; Art Clb; English Clb; French Clb; Lwyr.

LANGLEY, KAREN; Weequahic HS; Newark, NJ; (S); Art Clb; Drama Clb; School Play; Vllybl.

LANGMAN, BARRY; Holmdel HS; Holmdel, NJ; (Y); Pres Temple Yth Grp; Nwsp Ed-Chief; Gov Hon Prg Awd; Hon Roll; NHS; Ntl Merit SF; Pres Schlr; Sci Mrchnds Schlrshp 86; Grdn ST Dstngshd Schlrshp 86; Prnss Awd 86; Princeton U.

LANGTON, JENNIFER; St John Vianney HS; Matawan, NJ; (Y); 36/286; Church Yth Grp; JCL; SADD; Yrbk Phtg; Rep Soph Cls; Rep Sr Cls; JV Bsktbl; Var Stat Ftbl; Var Mgr(s); Capt Powder Puff Ftbl; Bus.

LANIER, ALBERT; Asbury Park HS; Asbury Park, NJ; (Y); 3/250; Am Leg Boys St; Key Clb; Math Tm; Varsity Clb; JV Capt Bsbl; L Crs Cntry; High Hon Roll; Kiwanis Awd; NHS; Omega Psi Phi Frat Achvt Awd 85; U Of FL; Chem Engrg.

LANNI, JEREMY D; Bayonne HS; Bayonne, NJ; (Y); Am Leg Boys St; Art Clb; Science Clb; Nwsp Rptr; Nwsp Stf; Lit Mag; Rep Frsh Cls; Rep Soph Cls; Rep Jr Cls; High Hon Roll; H O Brien Ldrshp Cnfrnc Delgt 85; Jrnlsm.

LANPHEAR, LESLIE; Willingboro HS; Willingboro, NJ; (Y); 1/312; Am Leg Aux Girls St; Scholastic Bowl; High Hon Roll; Hon Roll; Pres NHS; St Schlr; Val; Intnl Clb; JCL; Band; Excellnc In Soc Stud & Engl Awd 86; Outstndg Acadmc Achvmnt Awd 86; William & Mary Coll; Hist.

LANUTE, MICHELLE; Edgewood SR HS; Sicklerville, NJ; (Y); Exploring; Latin Clb; Spanish Clb; Hon Roll; Latn Awd 83-84; Glassboro ST Coll; Math.

LANZ, SABRINA; Chatham Township HS; Chatham Twp, NJ; (Y); Dance Clb; Key Clb; Nwsp Ed-Chief; Lit Mag; JV Var Fld Hcky; High Hon Roll; NHS; Hosp Aide; Var Lcrss; Prfct Atten Awd; Gftd & Tlnted Pgm 84; US Olympc Fld Hcky Dvlpmnt Cmp 84-86; NJ Teen Arts Fstvl 86; Englsh.

LANZA, DANIELLE; Manalapan HS; Englishtown, NJ; (Y); Church Yth Grp; 4-H; Intnl Clb; VICA; Nwsp Rptr; Hon Roll; Cmmtee Coordntr, Rspndng Scrtry & Envrnmntlst Yr Look Toward Life 84-86; Jersey Shore Med Ctr; Med.

LANZA JR, JOHN; James Caldwell HS; Caldwell, NJ; (Y); School Play; Nwsp Ed-Chief; Yrbk Ed-Chief; Bowling; Socr; High Hon Roll; Hon Roll; NHS; Med.

LANZA, RALPH; Memorial HS; West New York, NJ; (Y); Boy Scts; Church Yth Grp; Computer Clb; Bsbl; Hon Roll.

LANZA, ROBERT; North Brunswick Twp HS; N Brunswick, NJ; (Y); 30/300; Boy Scts; Church Yth Grp; Jazz Band; Mrchg Band; School Musical; Var Socr; Var Swmmng; God Cntry Awd; Hon Roll; NHS; Eagle Scout 84; Engrng.

LANZEROTTI, LOUIS D; Madison HS; New Vernon, NJ; (Y); 6/200; Am Leg Boys St; Science Clb; School Musical; Ed Yrbk Phtg; Ed Lit Mag; French Hon Soc; Pres NHS; Exploring; JA; Math Tm.

LANZISERA, ROSA; Toms River H S East; Toms River, NJ; (Y); 45/550; Boy Scts; Exploring; French Clb; Key Clb; Hon Roll; NHS; Med.

LAPIDUS, JACK; Steinert HS; Hamilton Square, NJ; (Y); Am Leg Boys St; VP Debate Tm; NFL; Quiz Bowl; VP Speech Tm; School Musical; Bowling; Hon Roll; NHS; Ntl Merit Ltr; Law.

LAPIDUS, LISA; Bridgewater-Raritan East HS; Bridgewater, NJ; (Y); Cmnty Wkr; Drama Clb; German Clb; Math Clb; Science Clb; Speech Tm; Band; Chorus; Concert Band; Jazz Band; WA Wrkshps-Hoffmann La Roche Schlrshp 86; Smmr Arts Inst 85-86.

LARACY, RICH; Point Pleasant Boro HS; Point Pleasant, NJ; (Y); 15/245; Am Leg Boys St; Exploring; VP Key Clb; Variety Show; VP Stu Cncl; Var Ftbl; Trk; High Hon Roll; Hon Roll; NHS; Pediatrics.

LARAMEE, MICHELLE; Camden Catholic HS; Cherry Hill, NJ; (Y); 64/234; French Clb; Hosp Aide; Drill Tm; Yrbk Stf; Off Jr Cls; Off Sr Cls; Var Cheerleading; French Hon Soc; Hon Roll; Frnch Awd Achvd A For 2 Yrs Stght 82-84; NJ ST Chrldg Champs 85-86; Jrnlsm.

LARDIERI, ANTHONY; Montville HS; Montville, NJ; (Y); Church Yth Grp; Drama Clb; VP Key Clb; Pres Concert Band; Drm Mjr(t); Jazz Band; Mrchg Band; School Musical; Lit Mag; High Hon Roll; Bride Awd 86; Loyola Scholar 86; Prfmg Art Awd 86; Loyola Coll.

LARGEY, JAMES P; Red Bank Catholic HS; Port Monmouth, NJ; (Y); 1/280; Model UN; Political Wkr; School Play; Nwsp Stf; Rep Frsh Cls; Var L Bsktbl; High Hon Roll; NHS; Ntl Merit SF; St Schlr; Pol Sci.

LARKIN, MAURA; Summit HS; Summit, NJ; (Y); Church Yth Grp; Ski Clb; Spanish Clb; Stage Crew; Yrbk Stf; Fld Hcky; Trk; Typing Awd; Bus.

LARRAURI, ILEANA; Red Bank Catholic HS; Shrewsbury, NJ; (Y); Cmnty Wkr; Hosp Aide; NFL; Ski Clb; SADD; Flag Corp; JV Sftbl; Var Trk; NHS; Intnl Foreign Lang Awd 86; Acdmc All Amer 86; Pre Dntstry.

LARSEN, ROBBY; Lenape Valley Regional HS; Stanhope, NJ; (Y); Var L Bsbl; Var L Ftbl; Bus.

LARSON, DANA; Lakeland Reg HS; Wanaque, NJ; (Y); 31/303; Letterman Clb; Math Clb; Var Ftbl; Var Trk; Hon Roll; Ftbll Hll Fame Schlr Athlt 86; All Conf Area Ftbll 85; 3rd Plc NJ Crftsmn Fr 83; Hamline U; Engr.

LARSON, PATRICIA; Mater Dei HS; Hazlet, NJ; (Y); 29/151; Pep Clb; Political Wkr; Variety Show; Lit Mag; Var Trk; Hon Roll; NHS; Awd Wnning Irish Step Dancer 83-86; Georgian Court Coll; Math.

LARUE, YOLETTE; Roselle Catholic HS; Roselle, NJ; (Y); Church Yth Grp; French Clb; French Hon Soc; Hon Roll; Pace U; Chld Psych.

LARWA, REGINA M; Camden Catholic HS; Audubon Pk, NJ; (Y); 55/263; French Clb; Off Frsh Cls; Off Soph Cls; Stu Cncl; Cheerleading; Coach Actv; Mgr(s); Sftbl; Hon Roll; Comptr Sci.

LASALLE, JOANNE; Overbrook Regional SR HS; Clementon, NJ; (Y); Cmnty Wkr; Hosp Aide; OEA; Red Cross Aide; Spanish Clb; Bsktbl; Mgr(s); Socr; Sftbl; Ntl Merit Ltr; Bus.

LASCHIVER, IGOR; Academic HS; Jersey City, NJ; (S); Cmnty Wkr; Hosp Aide; NHS; Prfct Atten Awd; NY Inst Of Tech; Engrng.

LASPATA, SUSANNE; Delsea Regional HS; Monroeville, NJ; (Y); Exploring; Office Aide; Yrbk Stf; Tennis; Hon Roll; NHS; Office Aide; Science Clb; Flag Corp; Gym.

LASSER, SANDY; Bayley Ellard HS; Morristown, NJ; (Y); Drama Clb; School Play; Cheerleading; Gym; Powder Puff Ftbl; CPA.

LASSITER, MICHAEL J; Northern Burlington Co Reg HS; Mc Guire Afb, NJ; (Y); 5/229; Am Leg Boys St; Spanish Clb; Var L Ftbl; JV Trk; Var Wrstlng; High Hon Roll; Hon Roll; VP NHS; Spanish NHS; Most Outstndg Wrstlr J V 86; Law.

LASTNA, ANA; Memorial HS; West New York, NJ; (Y); 8/200; Church Yth Grp; FBLA; Hosp Aide; Key Clb; SADD; Orch; Swmmng; Hon Roll; NHS; Intnl Clb; Piano Awd 83-86; Rutgers ST Coll N Brunswick.

LASTRA, ANA; Memorial HS; West New York, NJ; (Y); 8/200; Intnl Clb; Key Clb; Hon Roll; 3 Piano Awds 1st Pl 83-86; Rutgers ST Coll.

LASVAL, JULIO; Memorial HS; West New York, NJ; (Y); Boy Scts; Science Clb; Var Bsbl; Var Ftbl.

LATHBURY, GREG; Lower Cape May Rgnl HS; N Cape May, NJ; (Y); 41/250; Church Yth Grp; Political Wkr; Church Choir; Stage Crew; Nwsp Stf; JV Socr; Trk; Prfct Atten Awd; Mock Trl Awd NJ St Bar Assoc, Rotary Ldrshp Camp Interview 86; Comp Sci.

LATONA, CHRIS; Manalapan HS; Englishtown, NJ; (Y); Latin Clb; Ski Clb; VP Jr Cls; VP Stu Cncl; Var JV Bsktbl; JV Socr; Bus.

LATOUR, RICHARD; North Bergen HS; North Bergen, NJ; (Y); Boy Scts; Camera Clb; Nwsp Phtg; Nwsp Stf; Bowling; Hon Roll; Outdrs Clb 84-85; Hudson Cnty Hi Ave Bwlng 84-85; NJSYABA Champ Tournmnt Bwlng 1st Pl 85-86; UCLA; Med.

LATRONICA, JOSEPH E; West Milford Twp HS; West Milford, NJ; (Y); Am Leg Boys St; Cmnty Wkr; Band; Chorus; Concert Band; Drm & Bgl; Jazz Band; Mrchg Band; Pep Band; School Musical; 3rd Pl Comp Clb Cntst 86; Arch Law.

LATZ, GLEN; Pascack Valley HS; River Vale, NJ; (Y); Camera Clb; Cmnty Wkr; Ski Clb; JV Bsbl; Im Bsktbl; L Ftbl; Hon Roll; Str Carrier Paperby Brgn Evng Rcd 82-85; Ownr Gln Ltz Lndscp Dsgn & Mntnc Co 86; Vlntr Hndcppd Chldrn; Bus Admin.

LAU, DONNA; Kearny HS; Kearny, NJ; (Y); 9/375; Pres Exploring; Hosp Aide; Math Tm; Science Clb; VP Spanish Clb; Trs Stu Cncl; Hon Roll; VP NHS; PTA Schlrshp, Stu Govt Schlrshp 86; Cook Coll; Bio-Chem.

LAUER, HEIDI; Belvidere HS; Belvidere, NJ; (S); 9/120; Am Leg Aux Girls St; Chorus; Nwsp Rptr; Stat Sftbl; Hon Roll; Sec NHS; Olympia Ntl Schlstc Typng 84; Comp Info Sys.

LAUFER, GLENN; Central Regional HS; Seaside Pk, NJ; (Y); 28/242; Ski Clb; Rep Stu Cncl; Var L Ftbl; Var L Trk; High Hon Roll; Jr NHS; NHS.

LAUGHERY, CARROLL; Academic HS; Jersey City, NJ; (Y); 40/100; Art Clb; Drama Clb; French Clb; SADD; Chorus; School Play; Variety Show; Cheerleading; Powder Puff Ftbl; Swmmng; 1st Pl Wnnr Cty Teen Arts Fstvl 85; 3rd Pl Wnnr Cnty Teen Arts Fstvl 85; Bus.

LAURICE, CLAUDINE; Lodi HS; Lodi, NJ; (Y); Key Clb; Spanish Clb; High Hon Roll; Hon Roll; NHS.

LAVALLE, EDWARD; Manchester Township HS; Lakehurst, NJ; (Y); 36/198; Bsbl; Jr NHS; Ocean Cnty Coll; Pre-Med.

LAVAN, MICHELE; St John Vianney HS; Hazlet, NJ; (Y); 91/286; Church Yth Grp; FBLA; Girl Scts; Hosp Aide; Intnl Clb; Political Wkr; Ski Clb; Stage Crew; Hon Roll; Awd 50 Hrs Comm Ser 85; Law.

LAVANI, SURESH; Hoboken HS; Hoboken, NJ; (Y); Key Clb; Spanish Clb; Off Sr Cls; Elec Engr.

LAVELLE, ANNMARIE; North Bergen HS; N Bergen, NJ; (Y); Crs Cntry; Sftbl; Trk.

LAVENDER, JAMIE; Lakewood HS; Lakewood, NJ; (Y); 4/330; Am Leg Boys St; VP FBLA; JCL; Latin Clb; Temple Yth Grp; Band; Concert Band; Mrchg Band; Nwsp Stf; Yrbk Stf; Psychol.

LAVENDER, JOSHUA; North Brunswick Twp HS; N Brunswick, NJ; (Y); Spanish Clb; JV Trk; High Hon Roll; Hon Roll; Law.

LAVIN, CAROLYN; River Dell SR HS; River Edge, NJ; (Y); 27/213; SADD; JV Bsktbl; JV Var Sftbl; JV Var Vllybl; High Hon Roll; Hon Roll; NHS; Spanish NHS; MVP JV Vllybl 86; Rutgers; Bus.

LAVINE, JOSH; Montville HS; Towaco, NJ; (Y); 30/268; FBLA; JV Golf; High Hon Roll; Hon Roll; Computer Clb; Key Clb; Math Clb; Spanish Clb; Temple Yth Grp.

LAVINSON, MELISSA; Princeton Day Schl; Princeton, NJ; (Y); Camera Clb; Teachers Aide; Yrbk Phtg; Chrmn Jr Cls; Var L Ice Hcky; Var L Lcrss; Var L Socr; Hon Roll; Ntl Merit Ltr; Vrsty Hockey MIP Awd; Vrsty Soccer Dfnsv Awd; Princeton Packet Photo Awd; Lawyer.

LAW, CHRISTINE; De Paul Diocesan HS; Ringwood, NJ; (S); 14/164; Ski Clb; Nwsp Rptr; Nwsp Stf; Bsktbl; High Hon Roll; NHS; Math.

LAW, COLLEEN; Villa Victoria Acad; W Trenton, NJ; (Y); Computer Clb; Math Clb; School Musical; Stage Crew; Yrbk Stf; Lit Mag; Var L Bsktbl; Var L Socr; Var L Sftbl; St Schlr; Mount Holyoke Coll; Chem.

LAW, PATRICIA; Middle Township HS; Avalon, NJ; (Y); 28/180; Teachers Aide; Band; Concert Band; School Play; Symp Band; Yrbk Bus Mgr; Yrbk Rptr; Yrbk Sprt Ed; Yrbk Stf; Rep Frsh Cls; Acad Achvt Awd Engl; Cert Awd Bnd; Grad Wth Hnrs; Stockton St Coll; Engl.

LAWLESS, MICHAEL; St Peters Preparatory Schl; Rutherford, NJ; (Y); 5/210; Boy Scts; Camera Clb; Pres Church Yth Grp; Hosp Aide; Band; Capt Crs Cntry; Im Ftbl; Mgr(s); Capt Trk; Ntl Merit SF; Hall Fm Cr The Bergen Record 85; Bio.

LAWLOR, CHRISTOPHER; Union Catholic Regional HS; Fanwood, NJ; (Y); 18/308; Cmnty Wkr; Science Clb; Sec Service Clb; Var Swmmng; High Hon Roll; NHS; Ntl Merit Ltr; Acdmc All Amer 87.

LAWRENCE, DAVID; Oratory Prep Schl; Short Hills, NJ; (Y); Quiz Bowl; Ski Clb; Yrbk Phtg; Var L Ftbl; Var L Trk; Hon Roll; Vet-Med.

LAWRENCE, DAVID C; Kittatinny Regional HS; Newton, NJ; (Y); 2/168; Am Leg Boys St; Scholastic Bowl; Science Clb; Madrigals; School Musical; Trs Stu Cncl; Swmmng; Boy Scts; Church Yth Grp; Computer Clb; Jostens Fndtn Ldr Schlrshp 86; Air Force ROTC Schlrshp 86; U S Sec Of Educ Intl Yth Yr Awd 85; Rensselaer Polytechnic Inst.

LAWRENCE, DAVID J; Jeferson Twp HS; Milton, NJ; (Y); 13/235; Am Leg Boys St; Church Yth Grp; SADD; Pres Varsity Clb; Nwsp Stf; Pres Stu Cncl; Var Bsbl; Var Crs Cntry; Hon Roll; NHS; Prjct Aim US Cst Grd Acad 86; Arntcs.

LAWRENCE, SHARON; Dover HS; Dover, NJ; (Y); 29/183; AFS; Church Yth Grp; Cmnty Wkr; Pres Dance Clb; Drama Clb; Pres Chorus; Church Choir; Capt Color Guard; Pep Band; Pres Soph Cls; Howard U; Bus.

LAWRENSON, ANNE; Oakcrest HS; Hammonton, NJ; (Y); Nwsp Ed-Chief; Bsktbl; Capt Tennis; Capt Trk; High Hon Roll; Jr NHS; NHS; MVP Ten 85; MVP Trk 85-86; Jrnlsm Awd 85-86; Quill & Scroll 85-86; All Conf Discus & Shot Put 85-86; Jrnlsm.

LAWSON, AVA M; Kingsway Regional HS; Swedesboro, NJ; (Y); Church Yth Grp; Debate Tm; Capt Band; Church Choir; Mrchg Band; School Musical; Var Capt Cheerleading; Parsons Schl Dsgn; Fash Dsgn.

LAWSON, DAVID R; East Brunswick HS; E Brunswick, NJ; (Y); Boy Scts; Church Yth Grp; SADD; Crs Cntry; Trk; Hon Roll; Phys Ed Awd EBHS 86; All Conf Wntr & Sprng Track 85-86; All Cnty Wntr Track 85-86; Lenoir Rhyne Coll; Sports Mgmt.

LAWSON JR, EMORY; Orange HS; Orange, NJ; (S); Exploring; Yrbk Stf; Stu Cncl; Hon Roll; Prfct Atten Awd; TV Prod-Comm.

LAWSON JR, ERVIN V; Cumberland Regional HS; Bridgeton, NJ; (Y); Boy Scts; CAP; Variety Show; Rep Frsh Cls; Rep Soph Cls; Rep Stu Cncl; Var JV Ftbl; Var Trk; Wt Lftg; Hon Roll; Psychlgy.

LAWTON, CLARK; Wall HS; Manasquan, NJ; (S); 26/350; Computer Clb; Math Tm; Im Crs Cntry; JV Socr; Im Vllybl.

LAYCOCK, HOLLI; Mt Olive HS; Flanders, NJ; (Y); 5/300; Hosp Aide; Ski Clb; Yrbk Stf; Stu Cncl; Fld Hcky; High Hon Roll; Hon Roll; NHS; Child Psychg.

LAYMAN, MELISSA; Matawah Regional HS; Matawan, NJ; (S); 14/290; Sec Girl Scts; Temple Yth Grp; Nwsp Rptr; Rep Stu Cncl; French Hon Soc; High Hon Roll; NHS; Ntl Merit Ltr; French Clb; Garden Sst Distinguished Schlr Awd 86; Psych.

LAYTON, BRITTANY; Woodstown HS; Woodstown, NJ; (Y); VP English Clb; VP German Clb; Nwsp Stf; Lit Mag; Var Capt Cheerleading; Cit Awd; Hon Roll; Church Yth Grp; 4-H; Key Clb; Germn Natl Hnr Socty 84-85; Rider Coll Lang Tourn 1st Pl Grmn 85; South Jersey Sci Fair 2nd Chem 85; Cmmnctns.

LAZAR, BEN; Dwight Englewood Schl; Teaneck, NJ; (Y); Spanish Clb; Trk; Wrstlng.

LAZAR, MICHAEL; Queen Of Peace HS; North Arlington, NJ; (S); 1/231; Computer Clb; Math Clb; Model UN; Quiz Bowl; Nwsp Rptr; JV Bsktbl; NHS; Science Clb; Service Clb; Ski Clb; Smmr Schlrp St Peters Coll JC NJ, Comp Progmg 85; Rutgers Schlr 86; Amer Red Crs Adv Lf Svng 84.

LAZZARA, JANELLE; Paramus Catholic HS; Teaneck, NJ; (Y); Church Yth Grp; Cmnty Wkr; Hosp Aide; Nwsp Rptr; Rep Frsh Cls; Bowling; Hon Roll; JR Vlntr Hackensack Med Ctrs Awd 84; 1st Tm All Bergen Cnty Bwlng 85; Nrsng.

LE BLANC, DARYL; Wayne Valley HS; Wayne, NJ; (Y); 40/311; Boys Clb Am; Ski Clb; Band; Concert Band; Jazz Band; Mrchg Band; School Musical; L Golf; Hon Roll; NHS; Archtctr.

LE BOR, SHELLEY; Bayonne HS; Bayonne, NJ; (Y); 24/362; Spanish Clb; JV Var Cheerleading; JV Var Socr; Hon Roll; Phy Thrpst.

LE BORGNE, CHRIS; Paul VI Regional HS; Bloomfield, NJ; (Y); Church Yth Grp; Hosp Aide; Cheerleading; Sftbl; High Hon Roll; Hon Roll; Bus.

LE BORGNE JR, WILLIAM; Wallington HS; Wallington, NJ; (Y); 4/84; Am Leg Boys St; Varsity Clb; School Musical; Nwsp Ed-Chief; Stu Cncl; JV Var Bsktbl; L Trk; Bausch & Lomb Sci Awd; NHS; Voice Dem Awd; Physcs.

LE FUR, JESSICA; Scotch Plains-Fanwood HS; Scotch Plains, NJ; (Y); AFS; French Clb; Trs German Clb; OEA; Chorus; Mrchg Band; School Musical; Trk; High Hon Roll; Hon Roll; Recmmd For Gvrnrs Schl Hnr Pgrm 86; Surgeon.

LE GRAND, SELINA; Clifford J Scott HS; E Orange, NJ; (Y); Drama Clb; Trs FBLA; JA; Pep Clb; L Var Bsktbl; Acctng.

LEACH, DIANNA S; Arthur P Schalick HS; Norma, NJ; (Y); 5/148; VP Church Yth Grp; JA; Church Choir; Concert Band; Drm Mjr(t); Mrchg Band; Nwsp Rptr; Var L Bsktbl; Hon Roll; NHS; Natl Achvt Schlrshp Pgm Outstndg Negro Stus 85; Syracuse U; Jrnlsm.

LEACH, JOSEPH J; Hackettstown HS; Hackettstown, NJ; (Y); High Hon Roll; Hon Roll; NHS; Part Time Job 85-86; Acctg.

LEACH, LAURA E; Hackensack HS; Rochelle Park, NJ; (Y); 82/386; Art Clb; Ed Yrbk Ed-Chief; Yrbk Stf; Hon Roll; Ski Clb; Variety Show; Yrbk Phtg; 2nd Pl Waterclr Vogue Art Gllry 86; Drama.

LEAFEY, ELIZABETH ANN; Paul VI HS; Audubon, NJ; (Y); 104/466; Drama Clb; French Clb; School Musical; School Play; Lit Mag; St Schlr; Lbrl Arts.

LEAHY, ALLISON; Spotswood HS; Spotswood, NJ; (S); 12/189; Dance Clb; Concert Band; Yrbk Stf; VP Crs Cntry; VP Trk; High Hon Roll; Hon Roll; NHS; Columbia U; Law.

LEAHY, DENNIS; Wilwood Catholic HS; Avalon, NJ; (Y); Church Yth Grp; Science Clb; Varsity Clb; School Play; Var Golf; Var Socr; All Parochial B All Str 1st Tm Sccr 85-86; Cape Atlntc Leag All Str 1st Tm Sccr 85-86; Sci.

LEAHY, JOHN; Maple Shade HS; Maple Shade, NJ; (Y); 30/150; Computer Clb; French Clb; Key Clb; Spanish Clb; Nwsp Rptr; Yrbk Bus Mgr; Yrbk Rptr; High Hon Roll; Spnsh Clb Schlrshp 85-86; PTSA Schrlshp 85-86; American U.

LEAK, RISHIE; Lincoln HS; Jersey Cty, NJ; (Y); #1 In Class; Church Yth Grp; JA; Office Aide; Teachers Aide; Church Choir; Im Trk; Hon Roll; Jr NHS; NHS; Prfct Atten Awd; Law.

LEAR, MARISSA; Roselle Catholic HS; Elizabeth, NJ; (S); Church Yth Grp; Ski Clb; Acpl Chr; Church Choir; Stage Crew; High Hon Roll; Hon Roll; Med.

LEARCH, RICHARD; Passaic Valley HS; Little Falls, NJ; (Y); Wt Lftg; JV Wrstlng; Hon Roll; Sccr 83-84; Ski Clb 84-85; Wght Lftng 84-85; Nutrtn.

LEARY, HEATHER; Mainland Regional HS; Somers Point, NJ; (Y); 25/300; Ski Clb; Band; Concert Band; Mrchg Band; Yrbk Ed-Chief; Yrbk Sprt Ed; Yrbk Stf; Jr Cls; Sr Cls; Stu Cncl; Schl Spirit Schlrshp 86; Eva Anderson Schlrshp Awd; VA Tech; Arch.

LEBOVITZ, BRIAN L; Princeton Day Schl; Yardley, PA; (Y); Jazz Band; Orch; School Musical; Lit Mag; Hon Roll; Ntl Merit SF; Wesleyan U; Physcs.

LEBOWITZ, JANINE; Cherry Hill West HS; Cherry Hill, NJ; (Y); Office Aide; Teachers Aide; Temple Yth Grp; Hon Roll; Ctznshp Awd Bnai Brith 82-836; Schltc Awds; Elem Ed.

LEDDEN, RACHEL; Clearview Regional HS; Pitman, NJ; (Y); 30/170; Pres DECA; Drama Clb; Thesps; Acpl Chr; Chorus; School Play; Rep Stu Cncl; Var Fld Hcky; Lion Awd; NHS; Girls ST Alt 86; Hockey Awds, Mst Imprvd Plyr & Good Sprtsmnshp 85-86; Pblc Rltns.

LEDDY, DENISE; Wall HS; Manasquan, NJ; (S); 18/263; Ski Clb; JV Fld Hcky; High Hon Roll; Hon Roll; Bus Adm.

LEDNEV, OLGA; Mater Dei HS; Middletown, NJ; (Y); 29/150; Pep Clb; School Musical; Hon Roll; NHS; Val Alexander Nevsky Russian Schl 85; Publc Rltn.

LEDUC, RICHARD; John F Kennedy HS; Paterson, NJ; (Y); Cmnty Wkr; JV Bsbl; Hon Roll; NHS; Mini Course Sci & Comp Sci 86; Rutgers U; Elec Enrng.

LEE, ADRIENNE; Middletown H S South; Middletown, NJ; (Y); Church Yth Grp; 4-H; Ski Clb; Variety Show; Nwsp Stf; Lit Mag; Capt Cheerleading; Fld Hcky; Powder Puff Ftbl; Score Keeper; Communctns.

LEE, ALAN; Monroe Twp HS; Englistown, NJ; (Y); Am Leg Boys St; Cmnty Wkr; Varsity Clb; Off Frsh Cls; Ftbl; Capt Wt Lftg; Hon Roll; Hm Schl Assn Excllnc Arch 86; Lcl 23-25 Txtbk Schlrshp 86; Rutgers Coll Engrng; Mech Engr.

LEE, BARBARA; Parsippany HS; Parsippany, NJ; (Y); Intnl Clb; Pep Clb; Spanish Clb; Concert Band; Jazz Band; School Musical; Stage Crew; Yrbk Stf; Hon Roll; NHS; Vrsty Ltr Mrchng Pep Bnd; Mxcn Govt Mdl For Music.

LEE, BRUCE; Haddonfield Memorial HS; Haddonfield, NJ; (Y); 1/143; Am Leg Boys St; Capt Scholastic Bowl; Nwsp Ed-Chief; Rptr Yrbk Phtg; L Tennis; Bausch & Lomb Sci Awd; Val; Intnl Clb; Latin Clb; Capt Quiz Bowl; Ntl Merit Fnlst 86; Rutgers Pres Schlr 85; Amer Chmcl Soc Awd 86; Amer Assoc Physcs 86; Harvard U; Math.

LEE, CATHERINE A; Hunterdon Central HS; Flemington, NJ; (Y); Art Clb; Church Yth Grp; Hosp Aide; Latin Clb; Ski Clb; Chorus; Church Choir; School Play; Stage Crew; Variety Show; Lamp Awd 86; Mt Holyoke Coll; Bio.

LEE, CHO; N V R H S Old Tappan HS; Harrington Pk, NJ; (Y); 15/291; Ski Clb; Lit Mag; Sec Soph Cls; Rep Stu Cncl; Var Ftbl; High Hon Roll; NHS; Bus.

LEE, CHRISTINE; Bridgeton HS; Bridgeton, NJ; (Y); Mrchg Band; Capt Pom Pon; High Hon Roll; Hon Roll; Glassboro ST Coll; Elem Educ.

LEE, DAMON; Absegami HS; Smithville, NJ; (Y); 35/250; Debate Tm; Drama Clb; French Clb; School Play; Capt Socr; All Cnfrnce, Cnty, Press, All ST Hon Mntn Sccr 85-86; All Cnfrnce Trck 85-86; Bst Actr Awd 83-84; Law.

LEE, ED; Chatham Twp SR HS; Chatham, NJ; (Y); Boys Clb Am; Latin Clb; Var Bsbl; Im Socr; High Hon Roll; Hon Roll; Prfct Atten Awd; Ntl Latin Awd 85; Biology.

LEE, ERIN; Brick HS; Brick Town, NJ; (Y); 22/400; Hosp Aide; Band; Concert Band; Mrchg Band; Rep Frsh Cls; Crs Cntry; Mgr(s); Socr; Trk; High Hon Roll; Mst Imprvd JV Sccr 86.

LEE, EUGENIA; Rutherford HS; Rutherford, NJ; (Y); Art Clb; Church Yth Grp; French Clb; Ski Clb; Band; Tennis; Hon Roll; Fnlst Modelng Cntst 85; Design.

LEE, EUN YOUNG; Perth Amboy HS; Perth Amboy, NJ; (Y); 2/500; Mathletes; Model UN; Band; Pres Soph Cls; Pres Jr Cls; VP Sr Cls; Rep Stu Cncl; Var Tennis; Mu Alp Tht; NHS; Phrmcy.

LEE, HARVEY; Bishop Eustace Prep; Ewan, NJ; (Y); Political Wkr; Spanish Clb; Varsity Clb; Hon Roll; Spanish NHS; Var Crs Cntry; JV Golf; Im Sftbl; Var Trk; Im Vllybl; American U; Intl Bus.

LEE, JAE; Westfield SR HS; Westfield, NJ; (Y); Chess Clb; Computer Clb; Math Clb; Science Clb; Spanish Clb; Church Choir; JV Socr; Hon Roll; NHS; Spanish NHS; Rensselaer Polytech Inst Math & Sci Awd 86; MA Inst Of Tech; Physicist.

LEE, JAISON C; Mater Dei HS; Middletown, NJ; (Y); 24/167; JA; Latin Clb; Math Clb; Math Tm; Ftbl; Hon Roll; NHS; Armd Forcs Cmmnctns & Electrncs Assn 86; Bryant Coll; Comp Sci.

LEE, JANE; Kent Place Schl; Warren, NJ; (Y); Church Yth Grp; Hosp Aide; Red Cross Aide; Orch; Ed Nwsp Stf; Trs Jr Cls; Ntl Merit Ltr; Admssn Cum Laude Scty Knt Plc Chptr 86; Dstngshd Schlr Awd 84-87; Admssn All-ST Orch NJ Vlnst 83.

LEE, JANE M; New Brunswick HS; New Brunswick, NJ; (Y); 1/123; Mathletes; Nwsp Ed-Chief; Yrbk Ed-Chief; Ed Lit Mag; Trs Stu Cncl; Tennis; Bausch & Lomb Sci Awd; Elks Awd; Pres NHS; Val; Gvrnrs Schlr; Grdn St Dist Schlr; Ntl Hnr Scty Schlrshp; Rutgers; Pharm.

LEE, JAY; Northern Valley Regional HS; Norwood, NJ; (Y); AFS; Church Yth Grp; Capt Wrstlng; Hon Roll; Frgn Langs.

LEE, JOHN; Ocean Township HS; Ocean, NJ; (Y); 3/333; VP Church Yth Grp; Key Clb; Scholastic Bowl; Nwsp Stf; Im Bsktbl; Im Vllybl; NHS; Prncpls Merit Schlrshp 84; Princeton U; Aero Engr.

LEE, JUNG MIN; West Windsor-Plainsboro HS; Princeton Jct, NJ; (Y); 11/236; Am Leg Aux Girls St; Art Clb; Model UN; Lit Mag; Rep Stu Cncl; JV Var Fld Hcky; Gov Hon Prg Awd; High Hon Roll; NHS; Ntl Merit Ltr; NJ Dstngshd Schlr 85-86; Crnl Ntl Schlr 86; Ntl Art Hnr Scty 84-86; Crnl U; Apparel Desn.

LEE, KENNETH; North Bergen HS; North Bergen, NJ; (Y); 8/405; German Clb; Key Clb; Math Tm; Science Clb; Band; Variety Show; Rep Sr Cls; Var Capt Trk; NHS; German Clb; Brian Guashino Trck Awd 86; Westnghse Sci Tlnt Srch 300 Hnrs List 85; Outstndng H S Athl Amer 86; Johns Hopkins U; Biomed Engrng.

LEE, LISA; Dover HS; Dover, NJ; (Y); Ski Clb; Variety Show; Stat Bsbl; Stat Bsktbl; Bowling; JV Cheerleading; Powder Puff Ftbl; Score Keeper; Var Socr; Hon Roll; Psych.

LEE, MARK T; Whippany Park HS; Whippany, NJ; (Y); 25/175; Am Leg Boys St; Church Yth Grp; Varsity Clb; Church Choir; Socr; Trk; Hon Roll; NHS.

LEE, MORRIS S; Millburn HS; Short Hills, NJ; (Y); 15/255; Computer Clb; PAVAS; Band; Chorus; Orch; Yrbk Phtg; Yrbk Stf; Gov Hon Prg Awd; High Hon Roll; St Schlr; Prz Wng Fnlst NJ Symphny Orchestra Anl Yng Arts Cmptn 86; 1st Plc Wnr Smt Symphny Yng Arts Cmptn 84; Princeton U.

LEE, NANCY; Parsippany HS; Parsippany, NJ; (Y); Church Yth Grp; Cmnty Wkr; Computer Clb; Debate Tm; FBLA; German Clb; Hosp Aide; Intnl Clb; Latin Clb; Math Clb; 1st Aid 84-86; Peer Cnslg 85-86; Interact 84-86; Columbia U; Pre-Med.

LEE, OLIVE; Marylawn Of The Oranges; Orange, NJ; (S); 1/51; Science Clb; Stage Crew; Nwsp Ed-Chief; Pres Jr Cls; Sec Sr Cls; Var Bsktbl; Var Capt Tennis; Sec NHS; Pres Spanish NHS; St Schlr; Rutgers U Schlr 85; New Jersey Grvnrs Schl Schlr 85.

LEE, SHAWN; Hillsborough HS; Somerville, NJ; (Y); #9 In Class; Computer Clb; Math Tm; Quiz Bowl; Rep Soph Cls; JV Trk; High Hon Roll; Hon Roll; NHS; Math.

LEE, STEVE; West Essex SR HS; Fairfield, NJ; (Y); 9/350; Church Yth Grp; Computer Clb; Trs Latin Clb; Math Tm; Science Clb; Trs Spanish Clb; JV Crs Cntry; High Hon Roll; Jr NHS; NHS; Garden St Schlrshp 85-86; UC Berkeley; Bio Sci.

LEE, SUZANNE; Gloucester Catholic HS; Bellmawr, NJ; (Y); 21/166; Dance Clb; Pep Clb; PAVAS; Chorus; School Musical; School Play; Stage Crew; Var Capt Cheerleading; Var Capt Pom Pon; Hon Roll; Pre-Law.

LEE, SYLVIA; Lincoln HS; Jersey City, NJ; (S); 2/249; VP FBLA; Pres FHA; JA; VP Jr Cls; Off Stu Cncl; Sec Jr NHS; Ntl Merit Ltr; Church Yth Grp; Cmnty Wkr; Library Aide; Usher; Busnss Mgr; Chrmn Means & Ways Comm; Chrmn Of Dropout Comm; Fshn Dsgnr.

LEE, TZU-JUNG; Mount St Mary Acad; Clifton, NJ; (Y); Art Clb; French Clb; Spanish Clb; Chorus; Lit Mag; Hon Roll; Outstdng Boarder Awd 85; Hnr Rll Awds 86; U Of MA Boston; Chem.

LEE, VIVIAN; Indian Hills HS; Franklin Lakes, NJ; (Y); 20/269; AFS; Church Yth Grp; Hosp Aide; JCL; Latin Clb; Ski Clb; Ed Yrbk Stf; Lit Mag; NHS; Ntl Merit Ltr.

LEE, WM; Bloomfield HS; Bloomfield, NJ; (Y); 8/440; Math Tm; Quiz Bowl; Chorus; JV Socr; High Hon Roll; NHS; Ntl Merit Ltr.

LEEDS, DANIEL D; Boonton HS; Lincoln Park, NJ; (Y); 2/240; Am Leg Boys St; Capt Math Tm; L Socr; L Trk; High Hon Roll; NHS; Capt Indr Sccr Tm 85-86; Ltr Wnr Indr Trck 85-86; Mst Imprvd Swmr Lncln Prk Swm Tm 84; Comp Sci.

LEEDS, DAWN; Absegami HS; Egg Hbr, NJ; (Y); Church Yth Grp; Hosp Aide; Library Aide; Bus.

LEEDS, JENNIFER; Mount Olive HS; Budd Lake, NJ; (Y); 12/300; AFS; Math Tm; Science Clb; Ski Clb; Temple Yth Grp; Yrbk Stf; Stat Fld Hcky; JV Socr; NHS; Cornell U; Gntc Engrng.

LEEGWATER-KIM, JULIE REBECCA; Stuart Country Day Schl; Skillman, NJ; (Y); 1/32; Pres Science Clb; Acpl Chr; Orch; Ed Lit Mag; Bausch & Lomb Sci Awd; Gov Hon Prg Awd; High Hon Roll; Cmnty Wkr; Latin Clb; Teachers Aide; Anna B Stokes Music Schlrshp, Violin, Viola Div $500 85; Smith Coll Awd & Rutgers Chlr 86; Molecular Bio.

LEEK, MICHELE; Pinelands Regional HS; Parktown, NJ; (Y); Art Clb; FHA; Science Clb; Ski Clb; Teachers Aide; Flag Corp; Var Cheerleading; JV Sftbl; Hon Roll; Fshn.

LEER, MARK; Cinnaminson HS; Cinna, NJ; (Y); Math Tm; Science Clb; JV Crs Cntry; Wt Lftg; Mech Engr.

LEFKOWITZ, TOVA; Burlington Township HS; Burlington, NJ; (Y); Am Leg Aux Girls St; Camera Clb; Political Wkr; Stage Crew; Yrbk Stf; Mgr(s); Hon Roll; NHS; Cmnty Wkr; Church Choir; Olympics Of The Mind Tm 83-86; Yth Schlrs Prog At Lebanon Vlly Coll 86; Bus Admin.

LEGG, KIM; Spotswood HS; Spotswood, NJ; (S); 8/189; Church Yth Grp; Concert Band; JV Var Cheerleading; High Hon Roll; Hon Roll; NHS; Cmrnl Lwyr.

LEGGIN, JULIANNE S; Lenape Valley Regional HS; Stanhope, NJ; (Y); 17/253; Key Clb; Powder Puff Ftbl; Var L Swmmng; High Hon Roll; Hon Roll; NHS; Spanish NHS; Mst Vlbl Swmmr 85-86; Ntl Swmmr 83-86; Mrrs Cnty Swm Invtnl Hi Pnt 79-86; Cornell U; Hmn Eclgy.

LEGGIN, PATRICIA; Hillsborough HS; Belle Mead, NJ; (Y); 14/300; Latin Clb; Teachers Aide; Im Bsktbl; Im Swmmng; High Hon Roll; Hon Roll; NHS; Prfct Atten Awd; Biol.

LEHMAN, CHRISTINE; Belleville HS; Belleville, NJ; (S); 26/400; Hosp Aide; Key Clb; Band; Concert Band; Rep Frsh Cls; Off Sr Cls; JV Bsktbl; Sftbl; Hon Roll; NHS; Natl Engl Merit Awd 85; Acad All Amer 86; Cmmnd Stu AwdPSAT Scrs 85; Mktg.

LEHMAN, WILLIAM B; Delran HS; Delran, NJ; (Y); 7/182; Am Leg Boys St; Pres German Clb; Science Clb; Bsktbl; Capt Crs Cntry; Powder Puff Ftbl; Trk; Hon Roll; NHS; Engrg.

LEHMANN, ALISON; Cresskill HS; Cresskill, NJ; (Y); 13/111; Drama Clb; Ski Clb; Temple Yth Grp; Sec Chorus; Concert Band; School Musical; School Play; Yrbk Stf; High Hon Roll; NHS; Edward H Bryan Schl Ctznshp Awd 86.

LEHMANN, PAUL; Riverside HS; Riverside, NJ; (Y); 4/70; Am Leg Boys St; Concert Band; Jazz Band; Mrchg Band; JV L Bsbl; JV Var Socr; Var L Wrstlng; High Hon Roll; Hon Roll; Unsung Hero Wrstlng 85-86; Outstndng Musicianshp 84; Comp Inf Sys.

LEHN, CHRISTOPHER; Scotch Plains-Fanwood HS; Fanwood, NJ; (Y); 80/311; Science Clb; Jazz Band; Mrchg Band; Orch; Symp Band; Yrbk Phtg; Var Trk; Im Vllybl; Stevens Inst Tech; Mchncl Engr.

LEHNER, BARBARA; Freehold Regional HS; Marlboro, NJ; (Y); Intnl Clb; Office Aide; Political Wkr; Service Clb; Ski Clb; Yrbk Phtg; Pom Pon; Hon Roll.

LEHNER, LINDA; Cranford HS; Cranford, NJ; (Y); 19/300; Church Yth Grp; Drama Clb; Teachers Aide; Thesps; Acpl Chr; Chorus; Church Choir; School Musical; Sec Jr Cls; VP Stu Cncl; 1st Presbytrn Chrch Deacon 85-86.

LEHR, SHERRY; Toms River HS South; Toms River, NJ; (Y); 15/313; Science Clb; Mrchg Band; High Hon Roll; Hon Roll; NHS; Pres Acad Ftnss Awd 86; NJ Frgn Lang Tchrs Assoc Achmnt Frgn Lang 86; NE Conf Tchng Frgn Lng Stds 86; U Of San Diego.

LEHRER, JEFF; South Brunswick HS; Kendall Pk, NJ; (Y); 6/250; Am Leg Boys St; Boy Scts; Math Tm; Political Wkr; Scholastic Bowl; Ski Clb; Temple Yth Grp; Orch; French Hon Soc; Hon Roll; NJ Gov Schl Pblc Issues 86; JR Statesmn Amer 84-86; Piano Stds & Prfrmncs 75-86.

LEHRHAUPT, LIESEL E T; West Essex Regional HS; N Caldwell, NJ; (Y); Sec Key Clb; Band; Concert Band; Jazz Band; Mrchg Band; Orch; Symp Band; Ntl Merit Ltr; Wmns Vrsty Fncr 84-87; Magna Cm Ld Awd Ntl Ltn Exm 85; Bio.

LEIB, DAVID; Mt Olive HS; Flanders, NJ; (Y); AFS; Science Clb; Temple Yth Grp; Ntl Merit Ltr; Bus.

LEIB, MICHAEL; Paramus HS; Paramus, NJ; (Y); Debate Tm; Drama Clb; Math Tm; Political Wkr; Temple Yth Grp; School Play; Yrbk Stf; Tennis; NHS; Natl Hebrew Hnr Soc 85 & 86.

LEIBOWITZ, EVAN H; Madison Central HS; Old Bridge, NJ; (Y); 12/368; Am Leg Boys St; Temple Yth Grp; Band; Concert Band; Mrchg Band; Orch; School Musical; Hon Roll; NHS; Spanish NHS; Pre-Med.

LEIDENFROST, STEVE; Paramus Catholic Boys HS; Hasbrouck Hts, NJ; (Y); 43/178; Church Yth Grp; Ski Clb; Stage Crew.

LEIF, FREDERIC; Paramus HS; Paramus, NJ; (Y); Temple Yth Grp; Band; Concert Band; Jazz Band; Mrchg Band; Stage Crew; Yrbk Stf; Accntng.

LEIFER, STEPHANIE; Cranford HS; Cranford, NJ; (Y); 11/292; Sec AFS; Am Leg Aux Girls St; VP French Clb; Sec German Clb; Pres Spanish Clb; Concert Band; Nwsp Ed-Chief; Trs French Hon Soc; Sec NHS; Spanish NHS; Grdn ST Dstngshd Schlr 85-86; Georgetown U; Brdcst Jrnlsm.

LEININGER, KIMBERLY; Colonia HS; Iselin, NJ; (Y); 60/298; Pres Art Clb; Hosp Aide; Key Clb; Concert Band; Drm Mjr(t); Mrchg Band; Yrbk Phtg; Yrbk Stf; Hon Roll; NHS; Jacob Morgan Achvt Awd-Art 86; Mrchng Units/Band Prnts Schlrshp Awd 86; Mrchng Band/Unts Aprctn Awd 86; Parsons Schl Of Dsgn; Intr Dsgn.

LEISECA, EDWARD; Memroail HS; West New York, NJ; (Y); 41/450; Church Yth Grp; Debate Tm; Exploring; Radio Clb; Teachers Aide; Orch; Stu Cncl; Hon Roll; Hnr Rl 85; Judo; Stevens; Cvl Engr.

LEISER, KAREN A; Spotswood HS; Spotswood, NJ; (Y); 25/168; Am Leg Aux Girls St; Camera Clb; Drama Clb; Math Tm; Office Aide; PAVAS; Ski Clb; Band; Color Guard; Concert Band; Dr Jerome Ulan Mem Trust Awd-Excllnc Socl Studies 86; Glassboro ST Coll; Comm.

LEISHMAN, JAMES; Don Bosco Technical HS; Paterson, NJ; (Y); Stage Crew; Nwsp Ed-Chief; Var Bsbl; Im Bsktbl; Im Fld Hcky; Im Vllybl; Hon Roll; VP NHS; Montclr ST Coll; Bus.

LEITCH, DENISE; Jackson Memorial HS; Jackson, NJ; (Y); Church Yth Grp; Law.

LEIVA, MICHAEL J; Ridgefield Park HS; Little Ferry, NJ; (Y); 7/195; Am Leg Boys St; Rep Frsh Cls; Rep Soph Cls; Pres Stu Cncl; Im Bsbl; Cit Awd; Elks Awd; Hon Roll; NHS; VFW Awd; John Weiss Awd 86; Tngr Of Mnth 86; Penn ST U; Ec.

LELESI, JULIANNE; Mater Dei HS; Belford, NJ; (Y); 19/156; Drama Clb; Pep Clb; JV Cheerleading; High Hon Roll; Hon Roll; NHS; Hist,Spnsh Dept Awd 84-85; Rutgers U; Ed.

LEMAIRE, JEAN CYRIL; Don Bosco Prep HS; Allendale, NJ; (S); 13/168; Chess Clb; Computer Clb; Math Tm; Ski Clb; Yrbk Stf; Lit Mag; JV Trk; Hon Roll; NHS; Garden ST Distngshd Schlr 84-85; Finance.

LEMAIRE, JEAN-CYRIL; Don Bosco Prer HS; Hilton Head Is, SC; (Y); 14/175; Chess Clb; Math Tm; Service Clb; Ed Yrbk Stf; Ed Lit Mag; JV Trk; Hon Roll; NHS; Grdn ST Distngshed Schlr Awd; Boston Coll; Fin.

LEMASTERS, JENNIFER LYNN; Hackettstown HS; Hackettstown, NJ; (S); Church Yth Grp; Cmnty Wkr; Key Clb; Office Aide; Band; Concert Band; Jazz Band; Mrchg Band; Hon Roll; Bus.

LEMBO, NICHOLAS; Don Bosco Prep; Franklin Lakes, NJ; (S); 30/200; Boys Clb Am; Nwsp Stf; Rep Stu Cncl; JV Ftbl; Var Wrstlng; Hon Roll; NHS; Law.

LEMING, EMILY; Summit HS; Summit, NJ; (Y); 136/274; Church Yth Grp; Library Aide; Band; School Play; Stage Crew; Stat Bowling; Stat Ftbl; Twrlr; Pntngs Shown At Vrs Art Shows 85-86; Hist.

LEMISCH, VALERIE; Cherry Hill West HS; Cherry Hill, NJ; (Y); Art Clb; Camera Clb; DECA; Drama Clb; PAVAS; School Musical; School Play; Stage Crew; Lit Mag; Cit Awd; Cls Artist 86; Hm & Schl Assn Awd Art 86; 1st Rgnl DECA Conf 86; Philadephia Coll Art; Grphc.

LEMM, SANDRA; West Essex Regional HS; Fairfield, NJ; (Y); 48/350; GAA; Band; Chorus; Boy Scts; Mrchg Band; Orch; Symp Band; Stu Cncl; Capt Fld Hcky; Capt Var Sftbl; 3rd Tm All St, 2nd Tm Co Fld Hcky 84; 1st Tm All St, 1st Tm Co Fld Hcky 85; Co Schlr Athl Awd 86; Boston U; Dntstry.

LEMMA, BRIAN; Overbrook Regional SR HS; Clementon, NJ; (Y); Var Crs Cntry; Var Trk; Most Dedctd Awd Cross Cty,Track 85-86; Comm.

LEMON, BENJAMIN C; Teaneck HS; Teaneck, NJ; (Y); 45/420; Pres Church Yth Grp; Computer Clb; Yrbk Stf; Trk; DAR Awd; Hon Roll; NHS; Comm Stu NAP 86; Engr.

LEMP, DEBRA; St John Vianney HS; Hazlet, NJ; (Y); 68/287; Hosp Aide; Intnl Clb; JCL; Trs Service Clb; Band; Yrbk Stf; Twrlr; Hon Roll; Church Yth Grp; Girl Scts; Grl Scout Gold Awd 84; Gold & White Awd 85 & 86; Biochem.

LEMP, KATHRYN; St John Vianney HS; Hazlet, NJ; (Y); 65/287; Exploring; Sec Intnl Clb; Sec Service Clb; Ski Clb; Drill Tm; Mrchg Band; Ed Yrbk Stf; Hon Roll; Girl Scts; Gold & White Awd 85-86; GS Slvr Awd 84; Comp Engrng.

LENAHAN, THOMAS; Carteret HS; Carteret, NJ; (Y); 15/218; Am Leg Boys St; Latin Clb; Bsbl; Bowling; Ftbl; Hon Roll; NHS.

LENART, JOHN; Toms River HS East; Toms River, NJ; (Y); 125/550; Aud/Vis; CAP; Dance Clb; French Clb; Political Wkr; Radio Clb; Ski Clb; Pres SADD; School Play; Stage Crew; Excllnce In Lghtng Crw 85-86; Excptd Into Pltcl Lgl Ed; PA ST Weslyan; TV Brdcstng.

LENAS, ATHENA; Wayne Hills HS; Wayne, NJ; (Y); 24/300; Church Yth Grp; FBLA; Math Clb; Spanish Clb; Teachers Aide; Nwsp Phtg; Crs Cntry; Vllybl; High Hon Roll; NHS; Piano Cmpttn Awd 84; Intl Bus.

LENCZYCKI, NICOLE; Atlantic Friends Schl; Linwood, NJ; (S); Pep Clb; Spanish Clb; Drill Tm; Yrbk Stf; NHS; St Schlr; Med.

LENEHAN, MICHAEL; Roselle Catholic HS; Roselle, NJ; (S); Pres Church Yth Grp; Cmnty Wkr; NFL; Science Clb; Speech Tm; Rep Stu Cncl; Capt Var Socr; Var Trk; High Hon Roll; Emrgncy Med Tech 85-86; Knights Pythias Spch Wrtng Cntst Wnnr 85; St Peters Coll; Bio.

LENGA, KIRK; Manalapan HS; Westfield, NJ; (Y); 62/438; Political Wkr; Temple Yth Grp; JV Golf; U S Coast Gd AIM Prgm Fnlst 86; Ecnmcs.

LENGENFELDER, JEANNIE; Villa Victoria Acad; Hamilton, NJ; (Y); Drama Clb; Hosp Aide; Chorus; School Musical; School Play; Lit Mag; Var L Socr; Hon Roll; Acadmc Al-Amer Awd-Schlr 86; Acadmc Al-Amer At Large 86; Psych.

LENGYEL, PETER A; Ewing HS; Trenton, NJ; (Y); Am Leg Boys St; Political Wkr; Ski Clb; Nwsp Sprt Ed; Off Stu Cncl; Var Socr; Var Tennis; WA Wrkshp Evluatr 86.

LENIHAN, MEG; St John Vianney HS; Manalapan, NJ; (Y); #26 In Class; JCL; Nwsp Rptr; Lit Mag; Sec Soph Cls; Sec Jr Cls; Pres Sr Cls; JV Bsktbl; Var Crs Cntry; Var Trk; Hon Roll; Most Points Track Tm 84, 85&86; 3rd Tm All Shore X-Cntry Tm 85; Eng.

LENNART, JEAN; Immaculate Conception HS; Ridgefield Park, NJ; (S); 3/98; NFL; Quiz Bowl; Trs Spanish Clb; Church Choir; School Musical; Trs NHS; Spanish NHS; NJS Dstngshd Schlr Hnr Mntn 86; Stevens Inst Of Tech; Engrng.

LENNON, WINOKA; Camden HS; Camden, NJ; (S); Cmnty Wkr; Model UN; Political Wkr; Y-Teens; Jr NHS; Ntl Merit Ltr; Yth Secrtrt For Model U N 85; NJ Model Congress 86; Knowledge Bowl 85; Duke U; Econ.

LENOSKY, LARISSA; West Essex HS; Fairfield, NJ; (Y); 59/350; Ski Clb; Teachers Aide; Sftbl; Tennis; Cit Awd; Hon Roll; Womens Clb Fairfield Schrlshp 86; Douglass Coll.

LENOX, KEVIN P; West Windsor-Plainsboro HS; Princeton Jct, NJ; (Y); 26/236; Capt Debate Tm; Model UN; Sec NFL; Service Clb; Hon Roll; NHS; Ntl Merit SF; Natl Young Ldrs Conf 85; Biomedcl Engrng.

LENTINE, MICHELLE; Our Lady Of Mercy Acad; Wmstown, NJ; (Y); 5/38; Girl Scts; SADD; Nwsp Rptr; Yrbk Phtg; Yrbk Rptr; High Hon Roll; Hon Roll.

LENZ, CHERYL; Morris Knolls HS; Denville, NJ; (Y); FBLA; Hosp Aide; High Hon Roll; Hon Roll; Fairleigh Dickinson U; Psych.

LENZ, JARED; W Milford TWP HS; W Milford, NJ; (Y); 19/373; Boy Scts; Drama Clb; FTA; Band; Concert Band; Jazz Band; Mrchg Band; School Musical; JV Bsbl; JV Wrstlng; Lioness Clb Of W Milford Schlrp 86; Dr Somerville Sr Rotary Schlrp 86; Dr Harold Geiger Mem Schlrp 86; Rutgers U; Biol.

LENZ, SCOTT; Secaucus HS; Secaucus, NJ; (Y); Computer Clb; Math Clb; Ski Clb; Varsity Clb; Var Capt Ftbl; Trk; Hon Roll; Mu Alp Tht; All ST Ftbl 85-86; All Cnty Trck Hnrbl Mntn 86; Arch.

LENZO, CHRIS; Watchung Hills Regional HS; Warren, NJ; (Y); 5/315; Church Yth Grp; Scholastic Bowl; JV Trk; Gov Hon Prg Awd; High Hon Roll; NHS; Ntl Merit SF; Opt Clb Awd; Gld Mdl Amer Clsscl Lg Lvl I Latin Exm 86; Recog 93rd Prcntl Scrng Amer Assc Tchrs German Tst 86; Poli Sci.

LEO, GERALD; Monsignor Donovan HS; Brick, NJ; (Y); Ski Clb; Varsity Clb; Bsktbl; Var Crs Cntry; Var Trk; Mt St Marys Coll; Acctg.

LEOBOLD, KAREN; Union HS; Union, NJ; (Y); Dance Clb; Girl Scts; Teachers Aide; Rep Stu Cncl; Cheerleading; CPA.

LEON, IRENE; Paterson Catholic Regional HS; Paterson, NJ; (Y); 2/98; Yrbk Ed-Chief; Var Crs Cntry; Cit Awd; Gov Hon Prg Awd; High Hon Roll; NHS; Pres Schlr; Rotary Awd; Sal; Amherst Coll.

LEON, PAMELA; Memorial HS; W New York, NJ; (Y); French Clb; Key Clb; Math Clb; Trk; High Hon Roll; NHS; Comp Sci.

LEONARD, ANTOINETTE; St John Vianney HS; Hazlet, NJ; (Y); 104/283; Intnl Clb; Library Aide; SADD; Nwsp Rptr; Nwsp Stf; Score Keeper; Tennis; Hon Roll; Law.

LEONARD, CHRISTINA; Passaic County Tech/Voc HS; Paterson, NJ; (Y); 2/283; Church Yth Grp; Spanish Clb; VICA; Rep Stu Cncl; Var Tennis; Hon Roll; VP Sec NHS; Sal; Pres Acdmc Ftns Awd 86; Grdn ST Dstngshd Schlr 86; High Acdmc Acht Awd 86; MD Inst Of Art; Grphc Dsgn.

LEONARD, KATHRYN; Monsignor Donovan HS; Howell, NJ; (Y); 19/217; High Hon Roll; Hon Roll; Engl IV Hnrs Achvt Awd, Grad Hgh Hnrs 86; US Hist Awd 84; Trenton ST Coll; Bus.

LEONARD, NATALIE; J F K Memorial HS; Colonia, NJ; (Y); 1/277; Am Leg Aux Girls St; Drama Clb; Mathletes; Ed Lit Mag; Sec Stu Cncl; NHS; Ntl Merit Schol; Val; Church Yth Grp; French Clb; Gov Schl Sci, Union Carbide Wash Wrkshps Schlr 85; Princeton U; Math.

LEONARD, OPAL; Toms River HS East; Toms River, NJ; (S); Church Yth Grp; Exploring; Q&S; Nwsp Bus Mgr; Nwsp Rptr; Nwsp Stf; Im Powder Puff Ftbl; Var Trk; U Of Loma Linda; Pedtrcn.

LEONARD, ROBERT; Don Bosco Prep HS; Hillsdale, NJ; (Y); Chess Clb; Cmnty Wkr; Computer Clb; Band; Concert Band; Mrchg Band; Boy Scts; Boys Scouts Rank Of Eagle Scout 86; HS Alumni Awd 86; Stevens Inst Of Tech; Compu Sci.

LEONARD, RONALD A; Morris Knolls HS; Denville, NJ; (Y); 20/450; Suma Awd 84-85; Cedar Lake Sftbl Tm.

LEONARD, SUSAN; Immaculate Conception HS; Secaucus, NJ; (Y); School Musical; School Play; Stage Crew; Girls Citizenship Inst 86.

LEONETTI, KAREN; Washington Twp HS; Turnersville, NJ; (Y); Ski Clb; Spanish Clb; Bsktbl; JV Sftbl; Hon Roll; Bus.

LEONETTI, MICHELE; Arthur P Schalick HS; Elmer, NJ; (Y); Art Clb; Math Clb; Ski Clb; Spanish Clb; Chorus; Capt Flag Corp; Rep Stu Cncl; Hon Roll; NHS.

LEONHARD, BETH; Manchester Regional HS; N Haledon, NJ; (Y); GAA; Sftbl; Hon Roll; Schlstc Awd 84-85; Jv Sports Awd-Sftbll 82-83; Vrsty Sports Awd-Sftbll 84-85; Accntng.

LEPELIS, JANIS; North Burlington Reg HS; Jobstown, NJ; (Y); 19/200; Church Yth Grp; Teachers Aide; Symp Band; JV Var Mgr(s); Mgr Wrstlng; Hon Roll; NHS; Bus Dept Awd 84; Trenton ST; Acctng.

LEPORE, JOSEPH; Toms River South HS; Pine Beach, NJ; (Y); 16/329; Math Tm; Model UN; Jazz Band; Mrchg Band; Symp Band; Bsktbl; High Hon Roll; Hon Roll; NHS; Prfct Atten Awd; Amer Chem Soc Chem Awd 84; All S Jersey Band 85-86; Rutgers Coll; Elec Engrng.

LEPORE, SUZANNE; South Plainfield HS; S Plainfield, NJ; (Y); 17/281; Band; Concert Band; Jazz Band; Mrchg Band; Orch; Pep Band; Symp Band; NHS; Pres Schlr; Spanish NHS; Attndg Girls Ctznshp Inst At Douglass Coll 85; U Of Scranton; Rsrch Chmst.

LERCH, CHARLES F; Clearview Regional HS; Mantua, NJ; (Y); 1/154; Camera Clb; Cmnty Wkr; Yrbk Stf; VP Stu Cncl; Var L Ftbl; Wt Lftg; High Hon Roll; NHS; Prfct Atten Awd; S Jersey Yth Cmsn 85-86; Bus Mgmt.

LERNER, JAMES; West Morris Central HS; Long Valley, NJ; (Y); Camera Clb; Ski Clb; Temple Yth Grp; Stage Crew; Nwsp Phtg; Yrbk Phtg; High Hon Roll; Hon Roll; NHS; Pres Schlr; Yth For Undrstndng-Wrnr Lmbrt Schlrshp-Exchng Stu 85; U Of VT; Bus.

LERRO, MELISSA SUSAN; Washington Twp HS; Turnersville, NJ; (Y); Girl Scts; Library Aide; Q&S; Chorus; Lit Mag; Rep Stu Cncl; Drexel; Chld Psych.

LESH, NEAL; Montville HS; Montville, NJ; (Y); Computer Clb; VP Pres Debate Tm; VP DECA; Pres Math Clb; VP Pres NFL; Science Clb; NHS; Exploring; FBLA; Key Clb; SEER 1st Pl; Stu Expstn Enrgy Res 86; Sci Hnrs Pgm 86; WA Wrkshps 86.

LESKY, KATHLEEN M; Cranford HS; Cranford, NJ; (Y); 32/292; French Clb; VP JA; Math Clb; Math Tm; Science Clb; Nwsp Rptr; L Bsktbl; Hon Roll; Ntl Merit SF; Rutgers Schlrs Pgm 85; Gov Schl Sci 84; U PA; Bioengrng.

LESNIEWSKI, ERIC; Hopewell Valley Central HS; Hopewell, NJ; (Y); Church Yth Grp; Crs Cntry; Hon Roll; Arch.

LETT, MICHELLE; Hillside HS; Hillside, NJ; (Y); #16 In Class; Girl Scts; Nwsp Stf; Var Sftbl; OH ST; Acctg.

LETTER, JENNIFER; Wardlaw Hartridge HS; Fanwood, NJ; (Y); Drama Clb; SADD; Chorus; Nwsp Ed-Chief; Yrbk Bus Mgr; Pres Jr Cls; Var Bsktbl; Var Tennis; Gov Hon Prg Awd; NHS; Elizabeth O Horne Drama Awd 86; Latin Awds Gld & Brnz Mdls 84-86; Govs Schl Fnlst 86.

LEUNG, AMOS; Hanover Park HS; Florham Pk, NJ; (S); 2/280; Sec Debate Tm; Capt Scholastic Bowl; Science Clb; Nwsp Ed-Chief; Sec Sr Cls; Var L Tennis; NHS; Ntl Merit SF; St Schlr; Chess Clb; Acad Excllnce 85; Rutgers U Schlr 85; Engr.

LEUSNER, SCOTT; Palmyra HS; Palmyra, NJ; (Y); 7/121; Am Leg Boys St; Intnl Clb; Key Clb; Band; Rep Soph Cls; Rep Jr Cls; Off Stu Cncl; JV Bsbl; JV Socr; Var Wrstlng; JR All Amer Band 85; West Point; Mech Engrng.

LEUZZI, MARC; Toms River HS North; Toms River, NJ; (Y); 19/420; Am Leg Boys St; Chess Clb; Math Clb; Math Tm; Science Clb; Rep Stu Cncl; JV Bowling; Hon Roll; Rep NHS; Acdmc Lttr; Comp Engnrng.

LEV, ELI; Wayne Hills HS; Wayne, NJ; (Y); 9/305; Chess Clb; Computer Clb; Math Clb; Nwsp Stf; Yrbk Stf; Crs Cntry; Hon Roll; NHS; Ntl Merit Ltr; Essay Cont Wnr 86; Ecology Clb; Stevens Inst Tech; Elec Engr.

LEVENE, DANIEL; Cherry Hill West; Cherry Hill, NJ; (Y); Computer Clb; PAVAS; Temple Yth Grp; Mrchg Band; School Musical; Nwsp Phtg; Rep Sr Cls; JV Tennis; Hon Roll; Spanish Clb; All S Jersey Symphonic Band 85-86; NJ Mock Trl St Champ Tm 86; PA ST U.

LEVENSTEIN, MICHAEL; Glen Rock JR SR HS; Glen Rock, NJ; (Y); 20/160; Drama Clb; Letterman Clb; Spanish Clb; Varsity Clb; Bsbl; Var Capt Socr; Im Sftbl; Var Capt Tennis; High Hon Roll; Hon Roll.

LEVENTIS, JIM; Don Bosco Prep; Monroe, NY; (Y); Ski Clb; Band; Concert Band; Flag Corp; Jazz Band; Mrchg Band; Pep Band; Symp Band; Im Crs Cntry; JV Golf; Ski Team 84-85; Bus.

LEVERINGTON, TOMLYN; Dover HS; Dover, NJ; (Y); 6/183; Aud/Vis; Spanish Clb; Yrbk Stf; Trs Stu Cncl; Var Bsktbl; Var Socr; Var Sftbl; High Hon Roll; Hon Roll; NHS; Acctg.

LEVI, JEANINE; Morris Catholic HS; Parsippany, NJ; (Y); Cmnty Wkr; French Clb; Hosp Aide; Red Cross Aide; Teachers Aide; Chorus; JV Powder Puff Ftbl; JV Sftbl; Mtkg.

LEVIN, SABINA; Highland Regional HS; Laurel Springs, NJ; (S); 12/332; Computer Clb; German Clb; Sec Science Clb; Stu Cncl; Var Fld Hcky; NHS.

LEVINE, AMY; South Hunterdon Regional HS; Stockton, NJ; (Y); 7/71; Church Yth Grp; SADD; Concert Band; School Play; Variety Show; Nwsp Rptr; Nwsp Stf; Rep Jr Cls; Rep Sr Cls; Rep Stu Cncl; Cert Honr Mock Trial 85-86; Varsity Awd Letter Cheerleading 86; Political Sci.

LEVINE, EVAN; Manchester Township HS; Toms River, NJ; (S); Political Wkr; Nwsp Bus Mgr; Nwsp Ed-Chief; Nwsp Rptr; Nwsp Sprt Ed; Bsktbl; JV Crs Cntry; Hon Roll; VFW Awd; Cert Outstndng Accplshmnt Jrnlsm 85; Asbury Park Press Corrspndnt 85-86; Boys ST Dlgt 86; Temple U; Sports Jrnlst.

LEVINE, JEFF; South Brunswick HS; Dayton, NJ; (Y); 40/250; VP Church Yth Grp; Cmnty Wkr; Intnl Clb; Service Clb; Ski Clb; Nwsp Stf; JV Socr; Im Vllybl; Cit Awd; Hon Roll; Yng Ctzns Awd From Senator Bill Bradley Of New Jersey 86.

LEVINE, JEFFREY S; Morris Hills HS; Rockaway, NJ; (Y); 1/269; Am Leg Boys St; French Clb; Math Clb; JV Bsktbl; Var Tennis; French Hon Soc; High Hon Roll; NHS; St Schlr; Chorus.

LEVINE, JUDY D; East Brunswick HS; E Brunswick, NJ; (Y); Key Clb; SADD; Stu Cncl; Mgr Bsktbl; Yrbk Phtg; Rutgers U; Bus.

LEVINE, KAY; Northern Valley Regional HS; Demarest, NJ; (Y); 5/251; Art Clb; Temple Yth Grp; Color Guard; Stu Cncl; Capt Cheerleading; DAR Awd; Gov Hon Prg Awd; High Hon Roll; NHS; Italian Clb 86; Model Congress 85; Duke U; Law.

LEVINE, SARITA; Washington Twp HS; Turnersville, NJ; (Y); 52/470; Art Clb; Hosp Aide; School Musical; Yrbk Stf; Rep Stu Cncl; High Hon Roll; Hon Roll; Pres Acad Fit Awd 86; Hnr Grad Awd 86; Part In 86 NJ Teen Arts Fest 86; Glassboro ST Coll; Art.

LEVINE, STEPHANIE; Newark Acad; Mountainside, NJ; (Y); Cmnty Wkr; Hosp Aide; Nwsp Stf; Yrbk Stf; Lit Mag; Ntl Merit Ltr; NJ Govrs Schl Of Arts-Crtv Wrtg Div 85; Magna Cum Laude Natl Latn Exm; Brown U.

LEVITT, CHERYL; John P Stevens HS; Edison, NJ; (Y); 62/489; Drama Clb; Science Clb; Ski Clb; Y-Teens; Flag Corp; School Musical; School Play; Variety Show; Nwsp Rptr; Yrbk Phtg; Bus.

LEVITZ, JENNI; West Essex SR HS; Roseland, NJ; (Y); 72/350; Pep Clb; Varsity Clb; Chorus; Madrigals; Stu Cncl; Cheerleading; Shw Choir 86; Cncrt Choir 84; Le High U; Arts.

LEVY, ANDREW; Woodbridge HS; Fords, NJ; (Y); 25/390; Debate Tm; Hosp Aide; Pres Temple Yth Grp; Band; Concert Band; Mrchg Band; Im Bowling; High Hon Roll; NHS; Busnss Admin.

LEVY, BETH; Mount Olive HS; Flanders, NJ; (Y); 120/300; AFS; Drama Clb; Hosp Aide; Temple Yth Grp; Yrbk Bus Mgr; Yrbk Stf; JV Bsktbl; JV Var Fld Hcky; Im Vllybl; School Play; 2nd Pl Wnnr Grls Div NW Jrsy Clsc Race 85-86; Pres Physcl Ftns Awd 85-86; Bio.

LEVY, DAWN; Parsippany HS; Parsippany, NJ; (Y); Pep Clb; Speech Tm; Varsity Clb; Color Guard; Nwsp Stf; Yrbk Stf; Gym; Twrlr; NHS.

LEVY, ERIC; Matawan Regional HS; Matawan, NJ; (Y); Ski Clb; Temple Yth Grp; JV Var Ftbl; JV Wrstlng; Hnrs Engl, U S Hstry 84-85; Hnrs Adv Bio 85-86.

LEVY, MARC; Cherry Hill HS East; Cherry Hill, NJ; (Y); Band; Chorus; Symp Band; Variety Show; Var JV Bsktbl; High Hon Roll; Hon Roll; Athltc Schlrshp To Amer U 86; Crimson Shild 83-86; American U; Bus Adm.

LEVY, MARK; Manalapan HS; Manalapan, NJ; (Y); 49/431; JV Im Trk; NHS; Outstndng Achvt Geo 85; Statesmn Am Clb 85-86; Rutgers U; Engrng.

LEVY, MICHAEL I; The Peddie School; East Windsor, NJ; (Y); 19/130; Am Leg Boys St; VP Chess Clb; Nwsp Ed-Chief; JV Bsktbl; Var Crs Cntry; Im Sftbl; Var Trk; High Hon Roll; Pre Dentl.

LEVY, STEVEN; Manalapan HS; Englishtown, NJ; (Y); 68/465; JCL; Latin Clb; Rep Soph Cls; Rep Jr Cls; JV Bsktbl; Var Ftbl; Var Trk; Bus Mgmnt.

LEWANDOWSKI, KAREN; Florence Twp Mem HS; Roebling, NJ; (Y); Drama Clb; Latin Clb; Scholastic Bowl; Band; Mrchg Band; School Play; Yrbk Ed-Chief; Yrbk Stf; Fld Hcky; Mgr(s); Nursing.

LEWANDOWSKI, MICHAEL; Marist HS; Bayonne, NJ; (Y); #9 In Class; Boy Scts; Computer Clb; English Clb; JA; Key Clb; Science Clb; Spanish Clb; Teachers Aide; Nwsp Rptr; Nwsp Stf; Schlstc Achvt Schlrshps 84-86.

LEWANDOWSKI, SUZANNE; East Brunswick HS; E Brunswick, NJ; (Y); Dance Clb; Drama Clb; Pep Clb; School Musical; School Play; Variety Show; Hon Roll; NHS; Gvrnrs Schl Arts 86; Drama Clb Awd 85; Dance.

LEWIN, GLENN; Paterson Catholic Regional HS; Paterson, NJ; (Y); Bsbl; Wrstlng; High Hon Roll; Hon Roll; Bus Adm.

LEWIS, ANDREA; Clifford J Scott HS; E Orange, NJ; (S); 5/289; Drama Clb; FBLA; Hosp Aide; Math Clb; Scrkpr Quiz Bowl; School Play; Nwsp Stf; Lit Mag; Hon Roll; Sec NHS; Pre-Med.

LEWIS, BRENDA; Cumberland Regional HS; Bridgeton, NJ; (Y); Church Yth Grp; Library Aide; Bsktbl; Trk; Prfct Atten Awd; Cook Coll; Math.

LEWIS, BRIAN T; Morris Knolls HS; Long Valley, NJ; (Y); Am Leg Boys St; JA; Varsity Clb; Nwsp Ed-Chief; Trk; Ntl Merit Ltr; Chorus; Yrbk Stf; Lit Mag; Crs Cntry; Natl Merit Blck Semi-Fin 85; All Area Selctn 400m Run 85; Amatr Athltc Union Regnl Chmp Natl JR Olmpc; Rutgers; Jrnlsm.

LEWIS, CHRISTINE; West Morris Central HS; Port Murray, NJ; (Y); Church Yth Grp; Church Choir; JV Fld Hcky; Stat Sftbl; High Hon Roll; Hon Roll; Berkley Bus Awd 86; SUNY Cobleskill; Exec Sec.

LEWIS, CRYSTAL; Atlantic City HS; Atlantic City, NJ; (Y); Cmnty Wkr; Dance Clb; Teachers Aide; Band; Church Choir; Color Guard; Mrchg Band; Pep Band; Bsktbl; Pom Pon; Comm.

LEWIS, DARREN; West Side HS; Newark, NJ; (Y); 31/197; Art Clb; JA; SADD; Teachers Aide; Variety Show; Yrbk Sprt Ed; Bsktbl; Ftbl; Hon Roll; Prfct Atten Awd; Art Skll Awd 84-85; Comp Math Awd 83-84; San Diego ST Coll; Electrncs.

LEWIS, DIANE; Rancocas Valley Regional HS; Lumberton, NJ; (Y); 21/220; Am Leg Aux Girls St; Art Clb; Var Capt Trk; Hon Roll; Jr NHS; Lion Awd; NHS; Montclair ST Coll; Fine Arts.

LEWIS, HEATHER; Southern Regional HS; Manahawkin, NJ; (Y); Art Clb; Church Yth Grp; Latin Clb; Ski Clb; Spanish Clb; SADD; Chorus; Rep Frsh Cls; Stat Var Bsktbl; Stat Var Crs Cntry; Peatt; Design.

LEWIS, HELENA D; Orange HS; Orange, NJ; (S); Co-Capt Color Guard; Yrbk Stf; Rep Stu Cncl; Var Sftbl; Hon Roll; Fishing Club VP; Psych.

LEWIS, JACQUELINE; Holy Cross HS; Medford, NJ; (Y); 2/361; Model UN; Ski Clb; Pres Spanish Clb; Ed Nwsp Rptr; Gov Hon Prg Awd; High Hon Roll; VP NHS; Ntl Merit Ltr; U S Mltry Acad Invit Acad Wrkshp 86; Yth & Polit Systm Sem La Salle U 86.

LEWIS, JAMES S; Hopewell Valley Central HS; Pennington, NJ; (Y); 12/202; VP Pres AFS; Am Leg Boys St; Nwsp Ed-Chief; Nwsp Phtg; Yrbk Phtg; Trs Jr Cls; Trs Sr Cls; Swmmng; Var Capt Trk; High Hon Roll; Engnrng.

LEWIS, JULIANNE; James Caldwell HS; W Caldwell, NJ; (Y); Art Clb; Key Clb; Nwsp Rptr; Rep Frsh Cls; Hon Roll; Rutgers Coll; Advrtsg.

LEWIS, KELLY; Holycross HS; Burlington, NJ; (Y); Spanish Clb; Drill Tm; Stat Bsbl; JV Mgr(s); JV Score Keeper; Sftbl; JV Tennis; Hon Roll; Hmcmg Flt Prep 83-86; Lncrs For Life 85-86; Dnc Prep Cmmtee 83-86; Hstry.

LEWIS, MARYANNE A; Willingboro HS; Willingboro, NJ; (Y); 8/317; Church Yth Grp; Hosp Aide; Intnl Clb; Latin Clb; Service Clb; Mrchg Band; JV Socr; Hon Roll; Natl Achvts Schlrshp Pgm Sem-Fnlst 86; Sem-Fnlst Tn Grt Covr Modl Srch Cntst 85; Princeton U; Pre-Med.

LEWIS, MONIQUE; Lacordaire Acad; Newark, NJ; (Y); School Play; Stage Crew; Yrbk Sprt Ed; Yrbk Stf; Var Bsktbl; Im Sftbl; Hon Roll; Vrsty Bsktbl Trphys 83-86; NJ Inst Or Tech; Archtctr.

LEWIS, PETER; Gill St Bernard HS; Basking Ridge, NJ; (Y); Cmnty Wkr; Computer Clb; Drama Clb; Radio Clb; Spanish Clb; SADD; School Musical; School Play; Stage Crew; Variety Show.

LEWIS, REBECCA; Woodstown HS; Woodstown, NJ; (Y); Church Yth Grp; French Clb; Hosp Aide; Band; Church Choir; Concert Band; Mrchg Band; Pep Band; Sci Fair Awds 2nd Pl 84-85; Sec Yth Grp 84; VP Candystriping 85-86; Nrs.

LEWIS, STEVE; Brick HS; Brick Town, NJ; (Y); 123/400; Ski Clb; Varsity Clb; Capt Bsbl; Var Capt Bsktbl; Var Ftbl; Hon Roll; Penn ST; Acct.

LEWIS, SUSAN MICHELLE; Hackensack HS; Maywood, NJ; (Y); 18/400; Am Leg Aux Girls St; Girl Scts; Hosp Aide; Intnl Clb; Letterman Clb; Ski Clb; Spanish Clb; Teachers Aide; Varsity Clb; Band; Mywd Rtry & Athlt Clb Schlrshp 86; Bill Bradley Young Ctznshp Awd 86; Frdhm U; Intl Bus.

LEWIS, TRACEE; Union Catholic Regional HS; Newark, NJ; (Y); Drama Clb; Math Tm; Pep Clb; Science Clb; Service Clb; SADD; Church Choir; Rep Frsh Cls; Rep Soph Cls; Hon Roll; Psych.

LEWIS, YVETTE; Teaneck HS; Teaneck, NJ; (Y); Church Yth Grp; Dance Clb; Chorus; Lit Mag; Gov Hon Prg Awd; High Hon Roll; Jr NHS; Prfct Atten Awd; Gymnstcs Acad 85; The Erly Lrng Ctr 85-86; Jrnlsm.

LEWKOWITZ, DEBRA; East Brunswick HS; East Brunswick, NJ; (Y); Key Clb; Service Clb; Spanish Clb; Temple Yth Grp; Lit Mag; Hon Roll.

LEYFMAN, YELENA; Bruriah HS; Elizabeth, NJ; (Y); Computer Clb; Dance Clb; Yrbk Stf; Trs Frsh Cls; Trs Soph Cls; Sci Fair Awd 84-85; Physcl Thrpy.

LEYVA, MARIA; St Marys HS; Elizabeth, NJ; (S); Art Clb; Church Yth Grp; Service Clb; School Play; Sec Stu Cncl; Var Bsktbl; Var Score Keeper; Bus Mgmt.

LI, TONGYING ESTHER; Parsippany Hills HS; Parsippany, NJ; (Y); Bsktbl; Trk; Hon Roll; Rutgers U; Architecture.

LIAUW, JULITA; Ramapo HS; Wyckoff, NJ; (Y); 9/329; AFS; Camera Clb; French Clb; Latin Clb; Yrbk Phtg; JV Socr; High Hon Roll; Hon Roll; NHS; Ntl Merit SF; Hnr Guard 86; Photo Publictn 86.

LIBES, MICHAEL; Montville Twp HS; Montville, NJ; (Y); 10/260; VP Computer Clb; Pres DECA; Scholastic Bowl; Science Clb; Rptr Nwsp Rptr; Hon Roll; NHS; Ntl Merit Ltr; Bio Sci.

LIBIEN, JENNY; Glen Rock HS; Glen Rock, NJ; (Y); 6/153; Am Leg Aux Girls St; Trs Latin Clb; Science Clb; Pres Temple Yth Grp; School Play; Var JV Socr; Im Swmmng; Jr NHS; NHS; AFS; Dorothy Parish Mem Awd 85; Coaches Awd 83; Sci Hnrs Pgm 84-86; Med.

LIBONATI, DANA; Freehold Twp HS; Farmingdale, NJ; (Y); Chorus; JV Socr; Soclgy.

LIBRIZZI, ROY; Pinelands Regional HS; Tuckerton, NJ; (S); 2/147; Am Leg Boys St; Art Clb; Chess Clb; French Clb; Band; Mrchg Band; JV Var Socr; French Hon Soc; Hon Roll; NHS; Garden ST Distngushd Schlr Awd 85; Rutgers U; Sci.

LIBROJO, DONATA; Academic HS; Jersey City, NJ; (S); Art Clb; Lit Mag; Var L Bowling; Var L Vllybl; NHS; Ntl Merit Ltr; Prfct Atten Awd; Rotary Awd; Cnty Sci Awd 84; Fine Arts Hnr Paint Awd 86; U S Marine Corp Achvt Awd 84; Stevens Inst Tech; Engr.

LICCIARDIELLO, DONA; Mount Olive HS; Budd Lake, NJ; (Y); AFS; Drama Clb; FBLA; Ski Clb; Yrbk Stf; High Hon Roll; Hon Roll; Jr NHS; NHS.

LICHTENSTEIN, AMY; Northern Valley Regional HS; Harrington Park, NJ; (Y); 67/281; AFS; Drama Clb; Temple Yth Grp; School Play; Stage Crew; Nwsp Stf; Lit Mag; JV Sftbl; Hon Roll; Cornell U Summer Coll Prog 86.

LICHTENSTEIN, TIM; South River HS; South River, NJ; (Y); 16/130; German Clb; Band; Drm Mjr(t); Jazz Band; Im Badmtn; Im Bsktbl; Im Bowling; Im Gym; Wrstlng; Hon Roll; Jazz Band 85-86; Hnr Roll 84-86; Wrstlng 83-84; PIT; Bus.

LIEBER, JONATHAN; Livingston HS; Livingston, NJ; (Y); Computer Clb; Key Clb; Math Clb; Temple Yth Grp; High Hon Roll; Hon Roll; Spanish NHS; Frnkln & Mrshl; Acctng.

LIEBERMAN, BRIAN; Freehold Township HS; Freehold, NJ; (Y); 22/382; Var Bsbl; Var Ftbl; NHS; Mst Imprvd Plyr Basebl 86; Grp III ST Champ Basebl 86; Civil Engr.

LIEBERMAN, WENDY A; Edgewood Regional SR HS; Waterford, NJ; (Y); 2/400; Church Yth Grp; VP French Clb; Pres SADD; Trs Jr NHS; NHS; Ntl Merit Schol; Cmnty Wkr; Girl Scts; Office Aide; Intl Frgn Lang Awd 83-85; Grdn ST Distngshd Schlr 85; Questor Awd 85.

LIEBIG, MICHELLE DEANNA; Sussex Cty Voc Tech Schl; Sussex, NJ; (S); #1 In Class; Church Yth Grp; Science Clb; Spanish Clb; SADD; Varsity Clb; Yrbk Stf; Rep Frsh Cls; VP Soph Cls; Rep Jr Cls; Rep Sr Cls; Stu Of Mnth 85; Rutgers Schlr; NJ Grdn ST Dstngshd Schlr; Math Tchr.

LIEDL, JEFFREY M; Hillsborough HS; Somerville, NJ; (Y); 20/285; JV Bsktbl; Var Crs Cntry; Hon Roll; NHS; Bus.

LIEDTKA, KARL; Notre Dame HS; Trenton, NJ; (Y); Varsity Clb; Ftbl; Hon Roll; Psych.

LIESS, WILLIAM; Passaic Valley Regional HS; Little Falls, NJ; (Y); Am Leg Boys St; Band; Mrchg Band; Pres Sr Cls; JV Bsktbl; NHS; Ntl Merit Ltr; Eagle Sct 86; Boys ST Mayor 86; US Air Force Acad; Arntcl Engr.

LIFSHEY, ADAM; Cherry Hill HS West; Cherry Hill, NJ; (Y); PAVAS; Scholastic Bowl; Nwsp Ed-Chief; Off Frsh Cls; Off Soph Cls; Off Jr Cls; Off Sr Cls; Var Socr; Var Capt Tennis; Gov Hon Prg Awd; Hugh O Brien NJ Yth Ldrshp Smnrs 85; Wnnr 5 Wrtg Cont 84-86; Fndr & Edtr Mnthly Cls Nwspr 83-87; Astrnmy.

LIFSHITZ, DEBRA; Howell HS; Howell, NJ; (Y); 20/379; Pres German Clb; Color Guard; Stage Crew; Nwsp Rptr; Lit Mag; JV Socr; Hon Roll; NHS; Bio.

LIGERALDE, DAVIDSON; Glen Ridge HS; Glen Ridge, NJ; (Y); Trs AFS; JA; Model UN; Spanish Clb; VP Frsh Cls; JV Trk; Elks Awd; High Hon Roll; Ntl Merit SF; Rotary Awd; Comp Sci.

LIGGETT, ROBERT W; Bishop George Ahr HS; Edison, NJ; (Y); Am Leg Boys St; Boy Scts; ROTC; Science Clb; Nwsp Ed-Chief; Rep Frsh Cls; Hon Roll; Exploring; Color Guard; Drill Tm; Vigil Hnr Narraticong 86; Hnr Cadet 84-85.

LIGHT, CYNTHIA L; Penns Grove HS; Carneys Point, NJ; (Y); 12/170; Church Yth Grp; JCL; Band; Mrchg Band; School Musical; Yrbk Stf; Stu Cncl; Stat Sftbl; Hon Roll; Trenton ST Coll; Elem Ed.

LIGHTCAP, KRISTINE; Belvidere HS; Phillipsburg, NJ; (Y); 11/118; Church Yth Grp; Pres VP 4-H; French Clb; Red Cross Aide; Varsity Clb; Yrbk Stf; Var Capt Bsktbl; Var Fld Hcky; JV Sftbl; 4-H Awd; Kutztown U; Envrnmtl Sci.

LIGHTCAP, RICH; Warren County Vo-Tech; Buttzville, NJ; (S); Key Clb; Rep Sr Cls; Stu Cncl; Socr; Hon Roll; Stu Mnth 85; Welding Engr.

LIGOS, MARK; West Morris Central HS; Long Valley, NJ; (Y); Church Yth Grp; Pres Jr Cls; Stu Cncl; Capt Ftbl; Capt Lcrss; Capt Wrstlng; Hon Roll; NHS; Ftbl Awd 86; Mst Outstndng Wrstlr 86; Vrsty Ltrs; U Of PA; Law.

LIGUORI, MICHELE; Toms River East HS; Toms River, NJ; (Y); 23/350; High Hon Roll; Hon Roll; Academic Letter 84; Ocean County Coll.

LILLEY, MICHELLE; Freehold Boro HS; Freehold, NJ; (Y); Yrbk Stf; VP Jr Cls; Rep Stu Cncl; Capt Var Crs Cntry; Cit Awd; French Hon Soc; High Hon Roll; NHS; Cmnty Wkr; SADD; PTSO Schlrshp 86; Loyola Grnt 86; NJ C Sth CC Team Chmpshp 86; Loyola Coll Baltimore; Bus.

LILLIE, SANDRA; North Brunswick Township HS; New Brunswick, NJ; (Y); 127/395; Cmnty Wkr; Spanish Clb; Nwsp Stf; JV Capt Sftbl; Hon Roll.

LILORE, JENNIFER; Parsippany HS; Parsippany, NJ; (Y); FBLA; Var Cheerleading; Var Sftbl; Var Tennis; High Hon Roll; NHS; Rep Jr Cls; Sec Stu Cncl; Nwsp Stf; Spanish Clb; 1st Singles; Girls Sftbl St Champ.

LIM, EUGENE; Hillsborough HS; Somerville, NJ; (Y); Chess Clb; Computer Clb; Spanish Clb; Rep Frsh Cls; Rep Soph Cls; Var Trk; Hon Roll; NHS; Im Wt Lftg; Rider Coll Cert Of Merit Outstndng Achvt In Drmtc Intrprtn 84; Elctrcl Engrng.

LIM, TOM; Academic HS; Jersey City, NJ; (S); Am Leg Boys St; Chess Clb; Scholastic Bowl; Gov Hon Prg Awd; NHS; Prfct Atten Awd; 1st Prize In Rotary Club Peace Letter Contest 86; Chess Club Awd 84; Columbia U; Corp Lawyer.

LIM, VICKI; Delran HS; Delran, NJ; (Y); Am Leg Aux Girls St; Computer Clb; FBLA; Math Tm; Science Clb; SADD; Chorus; Jazz Band; School Musical; Nwsp Ed-Chief; Music Prnt Assoc Schlrshp 84-86; Cmmnctns.

LIN, CINDY; Livingston HS; Livingston, NJ; (Y); AFS; Mathletes; Math Clb; Band; Concert Band; Mrchg Band; Hon Roll; Phrmcy.

LIN, DAVID Y; Paramus HS; Paramus, NJ; (Y); Am Leg Boys St; Computer Clb; Math Tm; Science Clb; Ed Yrbk Stf; Var L Socr; High Hon Roll; NHS; Ntl Merit SF; Debate Tm; German Natl Hnr Scty 86.

LIN, DOROTHY; Parsippany Hills HS; Morris Plains, NJ; (Y); Church Yth Grp; Hosp Aide; Key Clb; Math Tm; NFL; Yrbk Stf; Im Bsktbl; Var Trk; Hon Roll; NHS; Music Ed Assn Gold Awd, Cert Muscl Achvtmnt 86; Golden Poet Awd 85; Engrng.

LIN, EDWARD; Wall HS; Wall, NJ; (S); 15/263; Sec Aud/Vis; Chess Clb; Pres German Clb; Key Clb; Math Clb; Math Tm; High Hon Roll; Ntl Eng Merit Awd 85; Brkdle CC Sci Pgm 1st Pl 85; Engrng.

LIN, GEORGE; Wall HS; Seagirt, NJ; (Y); Art Clb; Trs Aud/Vis; Chess Clb; Computer Clb; Drama Clb; Exploring; Sec Key Clb; Trk; High Hon Roll; Hon Roll; Natl Art Hnrs Soc, Natl Hnrs Tutoring Soc 86; 2nd Engrng Prjct Pgm 85; Engrng.

LIN, JULIE; Howell HS; Howell, NJ; (Y); Mathletes; Bowling; Accntng.

LIN, THOMAS; Bishop Eustace Prep Schl; West Berlin, NJ; (Y); Art Clb; Chess Clb; Pres Math Clb; Math Tm; VP Science Clb; Spanish Clb; Yrbk Stf; NHS; Spanish NHS; Rutgers U; Industrl Engr.

LIN, TINA; Northern Valley Regional HS; Norwood, NJ; (Y); AFS; Art Clb; Cmnty Wkr; Intnl Clb; Science Clb; Yrbk Stf; Rep Stu Cncl; High Hon Roll; Trk; OLVA Gnrl Exc Schlrshp 84; Hgh Hnr Roll 86; NYU.

LIND, JEANNE S; Westfield HS; Westfield, NJ; (Y); 159/525; Cmnty Wkr; Key Clb; Spanish Clb; Teachers Aide; Concert Band; High Hon Roll; Hon Roll; Cert Of Achievement Science 84; Northwestern U; Education.

LIND, KRISTEN; Maple Shade HS; Maple Shade, NJ; (Y); Computer Clb; Dance Clb; French Clb; Trs Key Clb; Rep Frsh Cls; Stat Var Bsbl; Capt Cheerleading; Hon Roll; Acdmc All Amer 86; Psychlgy.

LINDBERG, ROBERT; Hightstown HS; Hightstown, NJ; (Y); 43/396; Church Yth Grp; Radio Clb; Ski Clb; High Hon Roll; Hon Roll; NHS; Pres Acadmc Ftnss Awd 86; Worcester Poly Tech Inst; Elec.

LINDENFELSER, KIM; Kearney HS; Kearny, NJ; (Y); Pres Cmnty Wkr; German Clb; Office Aide; Teachers Aide; Yrbk Stf; JV Capt Cheerleading; Powder Puff Ftbl; Cit Awd; Hon Roll; Ger Hnr Soc 86.

LINDER, MARK; Clifton HS; Clifton, NJ; (Y); 90/637; Church Yth Grp; German Clb; Math Clb; Ski Clb; Band; Jazz Band; Mrchg Band; JV Var Golf; JV Socr; Var Swmmng; PA ST; Aerontcl Engnrng.

LINDERMUTH, DAVID T; Woodstown HS; Woodstown, NJ; (Y); Am Leg Boys St; Church Yth Grp; Spanish Clb; Varsity Clb; Var L Bsktbl; Im Bowling; Var Capt Ftbl; High Hon Roll; Hon Roll; NHS; Engrng.

LINDSAY, KATHLEEN MARY; Lyndhurst HS; Lyndhurst, NJ; (Y); 3/167; Am Leg Aux Girls St; Church Yth Grp; Key Clb; Variety Show; Yrbk Ed-Chief; Jr Cls; Stu Cncl; Bsktbl; High Hon Roll; NHS; Hghst Ranking Stu Awd 86; Sally Gentile Mem Awd 86; Rutgers Newark Coll; Acctng.

LINDSEY, LUCINDA M; St Dominic Acad; Jersey City, NJ; (Y); 41/131; Art Clb; Church Yth Grp; Drama Clb; Science Clb; Spanish Clb; Chorus; Church Choir; Lit Mag; Hon Roll; Ntl Merit Ltr; Bio.

LINDSEY, MICHELE; Holy Cross HS; Mapleshade, NJ; (Y); 172/384; Church Yth Grp; Hon Roll; Glassboro ST Coll; Home Ec.

LINENBERG, KAREN ANN; Westfield SR HS; Westfield, NJ; (Y); Art Clb; Band; Lit Mag; Off Sr Cls; Var Swmmng; Var Trk; French Hon Soc; Hon Roll; NHS; Asst Sports Trainer 85-86; Art Awd 86; Cornell; Sports Nutrition.

LINFANTE, CINDY; Secaucus HS; Secaucus, NJ; (S); 14/160; Key Clb; Math Clb; Ski Clb; Spanish Clb; Varsity Clb; Yrbk Rptr; Vllybl; Hon Roll.

LINFANTE, STEVEN L; Belleville HS; Belleville, NJ; (Y); Capt Var Ftbl; Pres Schlr; Schlr Ath Awd 85.

LINK, JEFF; Clearview Regional HS; Mullica Hill, NJ; (Y); 32/146; Band; Concert Band; Mrchg Band; Yrbk Stf; Bsbl; Bsktbl; Socr; Tennis; Wt Lftg; Rutgers; Accntng.

LINK, MICHELE; St Peters HS; Highland Park, NJ; (Y); 8/109; Spanish Clb; Stage Crew; Yrbk Stf; Lit Mag; JV Var Cheerleading; JV Var Trk; Hon Roll; NHS; Ntl Merit Ltr; Prfct Atten Awd; Tchr.

LINNEHAN, MARY JANE; Marlboro HS; Morganville, NJ; (Y); Cmnty Wkr; Pres Exploring; Hosp Aide; Library Aide; Office Aide; Stage Crew; Ed Lit Mag; VP Pres Service Clb; Cngrssnl Awd 85; Achvmnt Citatn Cert NJ 12th Cngrssnl Dist 86; Hlth Care Admin.

LINNEMANN, ANDREW; St Joseph Regional HS; Upper Saddle Rive, NJ; (Y); 45/175; Boys Clb Am; Church Yth Grp; Model UN; Varsity Clb; Yrbk Stf; Var L Socr; Hon Roll; Notre Dame; Law.

LINTZ, JENNIFER; Delran HS; Delran, NJ; (Y); 3/181; School Musical; Yrbk Stf; Sec Sr Cls; JV Bowling; Powder Puff Ftbl; NHS; Ntl Merit Ltr; St Schlr; Pres Acadmc Ftns Awd 86; Bst Of Cls-TV Awd 86; Acadmc All Amer 86; U Of VA; Engrng.

LIOI, ANTHONY F; Bishop Eustace Prep; Marlton Lakes, NJ; (Y); 2/183; Church Yth Grp; Drama Clb; Pres Science Clb; Church Choir; School Musical; Ed Lit Mag; NHS; Ntl Merit SF; French Clb; Math Clb; Engl.

LIPARI, PATRICIA; St Mary HS; Passaic, NJ; (Y); 9/44; FBLA; Letterman Clb; Yrbk Stf; Var Capt Sftbl; Hon Roll; Montclair ST.

LIPINSKI, BEATA; Linden HS; Linden, NJ; (Y); Church Yth Grp; FBLA; Rep Frsh Cls; Sec Soph Cls; Sec Jr Cls; Sec Sr Cls; Rep Stu Cncl; Capt Cheerleading; High Hon Roll; NHS; Ambsdr Hly Yth Smnr 84-85.

LIPINSKI, LINDA; Lenape Valley Regional HS; Stanhope, NJ; (Y); 66/269; Var L Frsh Cls; Var L Fld Hcky; Score Keeper; Var L Sftbl; Hon Roll; Fld Hockey Offnsv Awd 85-86; Hotel Rest Mgmt.

LIPKO, CHRISTINE; Audubon HS; Audubon, NJ; (Y); Am Leg Aux Girls St; Art Clb; Church Yth Grp; Cmnty Wkr; SADD; Yrbk Stf; Var Cheerleading; JV Score Keeper; Hon Roll; Drill Tm; 1st Pl Essay For SADD 86; Arch.

LIPNICK, OWEN; Parsippany Hills HS; Morris Plains, NJ; (Y); Cmnty Wkr; Service Clb; Tennis; Hon Roll; NHS; Ntl Merit Ltr.

LIPPAI, KAREN J L; South Plainfield HS; S Plainfield, NJ; (Y); 17/275; Yrbk Stf; Rep Sr Cls; Var L Cheerleading; JV Capt Sftbl; High Hon Roll; Hon Roll; JV Spanish NHS; Furman U; Commnctns.

LIPPAI, STEPHEN P; Woodbridge HS; Fords, NJ; (Y); Church Yth Grp; Off Jr Cls; JV Socr; Hon Roll; Prfct Atten Awd.

LIPPINCOTT, LESA; Woodstown-Pilosgrove HS; Woodstown, NJ; (Y); Church Yth Grp; 4-H; Spanish Clb; Diving; Hon Roll; NHS; Spanish NHS; Awds Equestrn Shwg; Equestn Stds.

LIPSYTE, SAMUEL P; Northern Valley Regional HS; Closter, NJ; (Y); 42/250; Quiz Bowl; Nwsp Ed-Chief; Ed Lit Mag; Capt Trk; Hon Roll; NCTE Awd; NHS; Ntl Merit Ltr; Arts Recgntn & Talnt Srch-Fnlst 86; Writer.

LISA, CATHERINE; St James HS; Swedesboro, NJ; (Y); 15/76; Church Yth Grp; Sec Hosp Aide; Yrbk Stf; JV Bsktbl; JV Sftbl; Var Tennis; Cit Awd; NHS; SCRTRL Stdies.

LISK, RICHARD; St John Vianney HS; Union Beach, NJ; (Y); Cmnty Wkr; Off Sr Cls; Var JV Bsbl; Cit Awd; VFW Awd; Monmouth Coll; Law.

LISKIEWICZ, LORI; Queen Of Peace HS; N Arlington, NJ; (Y); 19/229; Church Yth Grp; Drama Clb; Hosp Aide; Service Clb; Spanish Clb; School Musical; Mgr School Play; Stage Crew; Hon Roll; Cert Of Merit Spnsh 83-84; Soph Hnr Soc 84-85; Rutgers U; Hist.

LISOTTA, CHRISTOPHER; Pope John XXIII Regional HS; Belvidere, NJ; (Y); Art Clb; Scholastic Bowl; Thesps; Chorus; School Musical; School Play; Yrbk Bus Mgr; Lit Mag; Hon Roll; NHS; Cnty Quiz Bowl Tm Champ 85; Commncnts.

LISOWSKI, CHERYL; Clifton HS; Clifton, NJ; (Y); Church Yth Grp; Girl Scts; Mrchg Band; Stat Bsktbl; JV Sftbl; Vllybl; Hon Roll; Jr NHS; Hnr Guard Grad 86.

LISOWSKI, DIANE; Holy Spirit HS; Linwood, NJ; (Y); 8/345; French Clb; Hosp Aide; Pres Frsh Cls; JV Cheerleading; Capt Fld Hcky; JV Sftbl; Hon Roll; Kiwanis Awd; NHS; Miss NJ Amer Co-Ed 85; Mock Trl Tm Attrny 85-86; Duke U; Law.

LISTA, ANGLEO; Manalapan HS; Englishton, NJ; (Y); Art Clb; Drama Clb; SADD; Socr; Trk; Art Awd Prvnt Smkng 79.

LISTON, VICKI; Manalapan HS; Manalapan, NJ; (Y); Church Yth Grp; Office Aide; Varsity Clb; Var Socr; Hon Roll; Rutgers; Psych.

LISZEWSKI, MARGE; Eastern HS; Voorhees, NJ; (Y); #10 In Class.

LITTERER, JIM; Seton Hall Prep; Elizabeth, NJ; (Y); Key Clb; Ftbl; Hon Roll; Futr Lwyrs Clb.

LITTLE, DENISE; Edgewood Regional SR HS; Atco, NJ; (Y); 6/373; Am Leg Aux Girls St; Cmnty Wkr; French Clb; Latin Clb; Rep Jr Cls; High Hon Roll; Hon Roll; Jr NHS; NHS.

LITTLE, KAROLEE; High Point Regional HS; Sussex, NJ; (Y); Dance Clb; 4-H; German Clb; Band; Concert Band; Mrchg Band; Symp Band; Swmmng; Vllybl; Hon Roll; Htl Mngmnt.

LITTLE, MICHELLE FRANCINE; Madison Avenue Baptist Acad; Mahwah, NJ; (S); Band; Chorus; Church Choir; Orch; School Play; Stat Bskthl; Score Keeper; Stat Socr; Vllybl; 1st Pl Bible Tchng NJ ST Comptn 85; 1st Pl Classcl Key Brd NJ ST Comptn 86; Hyles-Anderson Coll; Secndry Ed.

LIU, LISA; Watchung Hills Regional HS; Warren, NJ; (Y); 31/315; Pres German Clb; Hosp Aide; Nwsp Ed-Chief; Nwsp Rptr; Nwsp Stf; JV Fld Hcky; JV Trk; Cit Awd; Hon Roll; NHS; 1st Dgre Blck Blt Karat 1st Feml Blck Blt Pgm 76-86; Mert Schlrshp-Dean Smr Schlrs Pgm Rutgers U 86; Wellesley Coll; Medcl Dr.

LIU, MINETTA; Kent Place Schl; Florham Park, NJ; (Y); Math Tm; Teachers Aide; Orch; Nwsp Ed-Chief; Sec Stu Cncl; Cit Awd; Ntl Merit Ltr; St Schlr; Hosp Aide; Nwsp Rptr; US Achvmt Awd For Physcl Fit; Hugh O Brien Yth Ldrshp Conf Rep; Cum Laude Soc For Outstndng Acdmc Ach; Sci.

LIU, VICTOR; Parsippany Hills HS; Morris Plains, NJ; (Y); Aud/Vis; Key Clb; Pres Science Clb; Symp Band; Frsh Cls; JV Tennis; JV Wrstlng; Bausch & Lomb Sci Awd; Hon Roll; NHS; Dly Rcrd Nwspr Hnr Crrier 84; Pres Olympcs Of Mind Tm-4th Pl In ST 86; Elec Engrng.

LIVANIS, JASON L; NVR H S At Demarest; Closter, NJ; (Y); 57/259; Drama Clb; PAVAS; Radio Clb; Thesps; Acpl Chr; Chorus; Madrigals; School Musical; School Play; Gov Hon Prg Awd; Tom Connor Memrl Grant Fund Vocal Awd 82-86; Amer Lgn Awd 82; Green C-Outstdng Commnty Svcs 82; Carnegie Mellon; Opera.

LIVINGOOD, WENDY; Hunterdon Central HS; Flemington, NJ; (Y); 104/550; Art Clb; Church Yth Grp; German Clb; PAVAS; Stage Crew; Var Gym; Var Sftbl; Var Trk; Hon Roll; Mason Gross; Visual Arts.

LIVINGSTON, RANDY; Raritan HS; Hazlet, NJ; (Y); 13/312; Socr; High Hon Roll; Hon Roll; 2dn Engr Soc Mfg Engr 86; Archtctr.

LIVINGSTON, ROBERT B; Northern Valley Regional HS; Haworth, NJ; (Y); 66/250; Am Leg Boys St; Church Yth Grp; Cmnty Wkr; French Clb; Political Wkr; Chorus; Concert Band; Mrchg Band; School Musical; Hon Roll; Tom Cnnr Mem Schlrshp Bnd 84; Hwrth Fire Co Schlrshp 86; Hwrth Wmns Clb Schlrshp 86; Hamilton Coll; Govt Svc.

LLANO, CINDY; Hunterdon Central HS; Whitehouse Sta, NJ; (Y); Church Yth Grp; Spanish Clb; JV Bsktbl; Im Socr; Hon Roll; Bus Admin.

LLEWELLYN, ROSANNE; Hackensack HS; Rochelle Park, NJ; (Y); 80/386; French Hon Soc; Hon Roll; Jackson U Florida.

LLOYD, DOUG; Freehold Township HS; Freehold, NJ; (Y); 50/325; Church Yth Grp; Var Im Socr; Hon Roll; Dntrstry.

LLOYD, EILEEN E; Roxbury HS; Succasunna, NJ; (Y); 61/350; Drama Clb; Varsity Clb; Lit Mag; Var Sftbl; Var Swmmng; AFS Clb 84-86; Acad Excllnce Soc Studs 86; Cnty Coll Morris; Humanities.

LLOYD, KEVIN; Pennsville Memorial HS; Salem, NJ; (Y); Am Leg Boys St; JA; Teachers Aide; Stat Bsktbl; Var Golf; High Hon Roll; Hon Roll; NHS; Rutgers; Engrng.

LO, STEPHEN; Metuchen HS; Metuchen, NJ; (Y); 16/160; French Clb; Hosp Aide; Scholastic Bowl; Science Clb; Ski Clb; Ed Yrbk Phtg; Var Capt Crs Cntry; Var Capt Trk; Hon Roll; NHS; Middlesex Cnty Schlr-Athlt 86; Booster Clb Schlr-Athlt 86; Rutgers Coll; Engrng.

LO CASCIO, ANTHONY J; Lakeland Regional HS; Haskell, NJ; (Y); 7/303; Debate Tm; Nwsp Rptr; Rep Stu Cncl; Var L Crs Cntry; Var Trk; High Hon Roll; NHS; Pres Schlr; Math Clb; SADD; Boston U Schlrp 86-87; Wanaque Police Assoc Awd 86; Boston U; Bus Mgmt.

LO CASCIO, FRANK; Arthur L Johnson HS; Clark, NJ; (Y); 8/195; High Hon Roll; NHS; Chem.

LO CICERO, RICHARD; Pascack Valley HS; River Vale, NJ; (Y); Ski Clb; Var Ftbl; JV Trk; Hon Roll.

LO GIUDICE, MARIA D; North Brunswick Township HS; N Brunswick, NJ; (Y); Drama Clb; Sec Girl Scts; Pres Key Clb; SADD; Concert Band; Jazz Band; Mrchg Band; School Musical; School Play; Stage Crew; Outstndg Stu Awd Key Clb 84; 10 Yr Girls Sct Awd 86; Dntst.

LO MARRO, LISA; Clifton HS; Clifton, NJ; (Y); 11/618; Church Yth Grp; Hosp Aide; Math Clb; Ski Clb; Spanish Clb; SADD; Chorus; Hon Roll; Jr NHS; Spanish NHS; Nrsng.

LO PRESTI, NICK; Holy Cross HS; Mount Laurel, NJ; (Y); Pep Clb; School Musical; Pres Frsh Cls; Rep Soph Cls; Rep Stu Cncl; Hon Roll; La Salle U; Med.

LO RE, LARA; Glen Ridge HS; Glen Ridge, NJ; (Y); Art Clb; Spanish Clb; Var Cheerleading; JV Fld Hcky; Hon Roll; Natl Art Hnr Socty 85-87; Vrsty Chrldg Ltr 85-87; Advrtsg.

LO RICCO, MARIA; Hillsborough HS; Belle Mead, NJ; (Y); 20/297; Hosp Aide; Intnl Clb; Office Aide; SADD; Off Sr Cls; Stu Cncl; JV Var Socr; High Hon Roll; Hon Roll; NHS; Rutgers Coll.

LO SCRUDATO, ANGELO; Marist HS; Bayonne, NJ; (Y); 38/134; Camera Clb; Church Yth Grp; Drama Clb; Intnl Clb; Pep Clb; Ski Clb; Rep Frsh Cls; Rep Soph Cls; Off Jr Cls; Rep Sr Cls; Champagnat Awd 86; U S Army MVP Sccr Awd 86; Philadelphia Coll Of Text & Sc.

LOATMAN, LORI; Cumberland Regional HS; Bridgeton, NJ; (Y); 120/369; Intnl Clb; Chorus; Hon Roll; Nrsg.

LOBB, SHERRY; Buena Regional HS; Newfield, NJ; (S); 5/191; Cmnty Wkr; Debate Tm; School Play; Trs Frsh Cls; Rep Soph Cls; Sec Sr Cls; Sec Stu Cncl; JV Capt Cheerleading; JV Var Sftbl; Var Capt Tennis; Hrbl Mntn-Wrld Of Poetry 85; Stu Of Mth 86; Eng.

LOBODA, SUSAN; Mount Saint Dominic Acad; Livingston, NJ; (Y); 19/62; Dance Clb; Intnl Clb; Chorus; School Musical; Capt Sftbl; Vllybl; Hon Roll; NHS; Cert 99 Pct SRA Testng Pgm; Pres Physcl Ftns Awd; Loyola Coll; Bio.

LOBODA, TRACY; Mt St Dominic Acad; Livingston, NJ; (Y); Ski Clb; School Musical; School Play; Yrbk Stf; Off Sr Cls; JV Var Sftbl; Church Yth Grp; Library Aide; Chorus; Yrbk Phtg; Parsons Schl Of Dsgn; Art.

LOCASCIO, JOSEPH; North Brunswick Township HS; N Brunswick, NJ; (Y); 6/300; Church Yth Grp; Latin Clb; Rep Stu Cncl; Var Bsbl; Var Bsktbl; Var Ftbl; High Hon Roll; NHS; All Conf Ftbl Plyrs 85; Pre Law.

LOCASCIO, MICHAEL; Westfield SR HS; Westfield, NJ; (Y); 31/514; Church Yth Grp; Key Clb; Yrbk Ed-Chief; Sec Frsh Cls; Rep Stu Cncl; Var Lcrss; JV Socr; Hon Roll; NHS; Crisis Mgmt Tm 85-86.

LOCASCIO, TINA; Freehold Township HS; Freehold, NJ; (Y); Capt Var Bsktbl; Stat Gym; Capt Var Sftbl; Phy Ed.

LOCASTRO, FLORENCE; Mary Help Of Christians Acad; Mahwah, NJ; (Y); 15/88; GAA; Letterman Clb; Stage Crew; Rep Jr Cls; Var Bsktbl; Stat Gym; Im Vllybl; Hon Roll; NHS; Sci Awd 83-84; Grad Spec Sci Pgm 85-86; Comp Awd 85-86; Rutgers; Sci.

LOCKHART, ANTOINETTE; Snyder HS; Jersey City, NJ; (Y); Church Yth Grp; Computer Clb; English Clb; FBLA; FHA; FTA; Math Clb; SADD; Yrbk Stf; Trk; Achvmnt Rl 86; Mrt Rl 86; Wntr Trck Awds 84-85; Comp Prog.

LOCKO, DANA; Hamilton High West; Trenton, NJ; (Y); Band; Concert Band; Mrchg Band; Symp Band; Rep Stu Cncl; Stat Bsbl; Mgr(s); Sftbl; Stat Wrstlng; Hon Roll; Trenton ST Coll; Acctnt.

LODOUICE, MICHAEL; Millville SR HS; Millville, NJ; (Y); 78/500; Cumberland Cnty Coll; Acctg.

LOEBER, KAREN; Mary Help Of Christians Acad; Mahwah, NJ; (Y); Church Yth Grp; Computer Clb; Letterman Clb; Pep Clb; Stage Crew; Frsh Cls; Pres Jr Cls; Stu Cncl; Var Bsktbl; Var Vllybl.

LOEHREN, TARA; Jackson Memorial HS; Jackson, NJ; (Y); 26/422; French Hon Soc; High Hon Roll; Fshn Mrchndsng.

LOFRANO, MICHELE; Academy Of St Hoysius; Jersey City, NJ; (Y); Service Clb; Nwsp Stf; Sec Stu Cncl; CC Awd; NHS; Prfct Atten Awd; Spanish NHS; St Schlr; Cmnty Wkr; FBLA; Math Leag JA Awd 84; Natl Latn Exm Slvr & Gld Medls 83-84; Schlrshp St Peters Coll 86; Douglass Coll; Psych.

LOFTUS, KRISTIN; Wayne Hills HS; Wayne, NJ; (Y); 86/400; Drama Clb; GAA; OEA; PAVAS; Spanish Clb; School Musical; School Play; Bsktbl; Cheerleading; Hon Roll.

LOFTUS, PATRICIA; St Marys HS; Old Bridge, NJ; (Y); 5/140; GAA; Spanish Clb; Yrbk Stf; Bsktbl; Socr; High Hon Roll; NHS; Spanish NHS; Alt Wmns ST 86.

LOGAN, LAURA; Freehold Township HS; Freehold, NJ; (Y); Pres Church Yth Grp; Drama Clb; Hosp Aide; Concert Band; Madrigals; Mrchg Band; School Musical; Yrbk Stf; Outstndng Achvt Awd Best Vlclst 86; Top Score In All-Shore Chorus 86; Mbr Of All-ST Chorus 85; Capital U Cols Oh; Bus.

LOGAN, MARY-FRANCES; Red Bank Catholic HS; Neptune, NJ; (Y); Church Yth Grp; Intnl Clb; SADD; Teachers Aide; Chorus; School Play; JV Var Socr; Johnson & Whales; Travel.

LOGAN, ORINTHAL; Pleasantville HS; Pleasantville, NJ; (Y); Dance Clb; Math Clb; Spanish Clb; SADD; Stage Crew; Yrbk Sprt Ed; Rep Stu Cncl; JV Var Bsbl; JV Var Bsktbl; JV Var Crs Cntry; Real Estate.

LOGOTHETIS, KORI C; Haddonfield Memorial HS; Haddonfield, NJ; (Y); VP Drama Clb; VP Band; VP Concert Band; VP Mrchg Band; Orch; School Musical; School Play; Stage Crew; Variety Show; Yrbk Stf; VA Commonwealth U; Comm Art.

LOGOYDA, DEBBIE; H G Hoffman HS; South Amboy, NJ; (Y); 8/60; Ski Clb; Band; Jazz Band; Pep Band; Im Bsktbl; Var Capt Cheerleading; Var Capt Crs Cntry; Im Capt Vllybl; Hon Roll; Jr NHS; Highest Av Foods, Cntrl Ersey St Champs, St Grp I Rnnr Up, Blue Div Champs 86; All Conf X-Cntry 84; Nutrition.

LOH, BENJAMIN; Cliffside Park HS; Cliffside Pk, NJ; (Y); 5/200; Math Tm; Bowling; Fld Hcky; High Hon Roll; NHS; Ntl Merit Ltr; Polytech Rensalior Awd 86; Pre Med.

LOHM, FELICITY; Glen Ridge HS; Glen Ridge, NJ; (Y); French Clb; Hosp Aide; Key Clb; Nwsp Rptr; Nwsp Stf; Im JV Bsktbl; Var JV Sftbl; High Hon Roll; Hon Roll; Ntl Merit Ltr; Ltr Commendtn Mountanside Hosp 86; Super Sportsmnshp Awd Sftbl 85; Best Effort Awd Bsktbl 85; Psychlgy.

LOHNES, JENNY; Wall Township HS; Wall Neptune, NJ; (S); 7/256; Trs German Clb; Key Clb; Acpl Chr; Band; Chorus; Church Choir; Concert Band; Mrchg Band; School Musical; Rep Stu Cncl; NJ Al-Shor Chorus 85-86; Accntncy.

LOIZEAUX, NICHOLAS; Scotch Plains-Fanwood HS; Scotch Plains, NJ; (S); German Clb; Model UN; Quiz Bowl; Nwsp Rptr; Var L Trk; Gov Hon Prg Awd; High Hon Roll.

LOKICH, DESIREE; Holy Cross HS; Mcguire Afb, NJ; (Y); French Clb; Hosp Aide; Model UN; Ski Clb; Trk; High Hon Roll; Hon Roll; Intract Clb Secy.

LOMAURO, AMY; Fair Lawn HS; Fair Lawn, NJ; (Y); 86/335; Chorus; Var L Trk; MVP Trck 86; 1st Tm Trck Bergen Cnty 86; Trenton ST Coll.

LOMBARDI, JODI; Cherry Hill HS; Cherry Hill, NJ; (Y); Office Aide; PAVAS; Hon Roll; Art.

LOMBARDI, LINDA C; Buena Regional HS; Newfield, NJ; (S); 7/191; Debate Tm; Office Aide; Spanish Clb; Chorus; Rep Jr Cls; Rep Stu Cncl; High Hon Roll; Hon Roll; Jr NHS; Futr Secy Assn 85-86; Recptnst.

LOMBARDO, AMY; Sacred Heart HS; Vineland, NJ; (Y); Cmnty Wkr; Dance Clb; French Clb; Pep Clb; Teachers Aide; Chorus; School Musical; School Play; Stage Crew; Yrbk Bus Mgr; Prfmng Arts.

LOMBARDO, CAROLYN; Monsignor Donovan HS; Lakewood, NJ; (Y); 56/218; Dance Clb; French Clb; Ski Clb; High Hon Roll; Hon Roll; Stockton ST Coll; Bus Adm.

LOMBARDO, FRANK; St Josephs HS; N Brunswick, NJ; (Y); 15/224; Church Yth Grp; Cmnty Wkr; Dance Clb; Yrbk Stf; JV Trk; Im Wt Lftg; High Hon Roll; NHS; Garden St Schlr 86; Summa Cum Laude Hnrs 86; William Perdue Mem Sci Awd 86; Cook Coll; Pre-Med.

LOMBARDY, DAWN M; Bridgewater Raritans HS West; Raritan, NJ; (Y); Am Leg Aux Girls St; Sec Church Yth Grp; Girl Scts; Spanish Clb; Jr Cls; High Hon Roll; Hon Roll; NHS; Hghst Achvmnt 6 Yrs Of Spnsh 85-86; NJ Gvrnrs Tchng Schlrshp Ln Rcpnt 86; Pres Eastrn Crct Lthr Lge; Muhlenberg Coll; Spnsh.

LONARD JR, KENNETH; Central Regional HS; Chicopee, MA; (Y); Church Yth Grp; Computer Clb; French Clb; Band; Concert Band; Jazz Band; Mrchg Band; Pep Band; Hon Roll; NJ ST Teen Art Fstvl 86; MIT; Cmptrs Engrng.

LONDON, SCOTT; Lakewood HS; Lakewood, NJ; (Y); 65/295; Am Leg Boys St; Key Clb; Latin Clb; Temple Yth Grp; Nwsp Sprt Ed; Stu Cncl; JV Var Bsbl; Hon Roll.

LONDONER, COREY; River Dell SR HS; Oradell, NJ; (Y); 79/213; GAA; Pep Clb; Ski Clb; SADD; Teachers Aide; Temple Yth Grp; Varsity Clb; Chorus; Score Keeper; Mgr Tennis; Emerson; Mass Cmmnctns.

LONEGAN, STACEY; Spotswood HS; Spotswood, NJ; (S); 24/181; Am Leg Aux Girls St; Sec Camera Clb; Model UN; Ski Clb; Color Guard; Nwsp Stf; Rep Frsh Cls; Rep Soph Cls; Rep Sr Cls; Comm.

LONER, RHONDA P; Saddle Brook HS; Saddle Brook, NJ; (Y); 3/115; Yrbk Ed-Chief; Lit Mag; Hst Stu Cncl; Bausch & Lomb Sci Awd; High Hon Roll; NHS; Ntl Merit Ltr; Latin Clb; Band; Concert Band; Ntl Latn Exm Slvr Medl & Maxima Cum Laude Cert 82-84; Ntl Latn Exm-Magna Cum Laude Cert 84-85; Union Coll; Med.

LONG, CYNTHIA; Middlesex HS; Middlesex, NJ; (Y); 7/170; Sec Trs Church Yth Grp; Girl Scts; Chorus; School Musical; High Hon Roll; Hon Roll; NHS; H S Rsrv Squad Cdts; YMCA Yth In Govt; H S Law Clb.

LONG, DONALD; Monsignor Onovan HS; Toms River, NJ; (Y); 11/243; Am Leg Boys St; Var Capt Bsbl; Var Bsktbl; High Hon Roll; NHS; Engrg.

LONG, JEFFREY; Camden Catholic HS; Cherry Hill, NJ; (Y); 41/259; Am Leg Boys St; FBLA; SADD; Rep Jr Cls; Rep Sr Cls; Var L Bsktbl; Var L Crs Cntry; Var L Trk; Hon Roll; NHS; Capt H S Ushers 85-87.

LONG, THERESA; Holy Cross HS; Cinnaminson, NJ; (Y); Hosp Aide; Var JV Fld Hcky; Church Yth Grp; Rep Frsh Cls; Nrsng.

LONGAKER, DEBBIE; Westfield HS; Westfield, NJ; (Y); 18/514; French Clb; Key Clb; Ski Clb; Socr; French Hon Soc; Hon Roll; Sci Semnry Lectr Svc 86; Psych.

LONSKI, MEGAN A; Princeton HS; Princeton, NJ; (Y); Jazz Band; Orch; Symp Band; Yrbk Sprt Ed; Fld Hcky; Ntl Merit SF; St Schlr; Science Clb; Band; Concert Band.

LOOKABAUGH, ANDREA S; Millville SR HS; Millville, NJ; (Y); 68/500; Science Clb; Var Capt Fld Hcky; Var Capt Sftbl; NHS; FBLA; Office Aide; Spanish Clb; Mgr(s); Fmle Schlr Athlt 86; MVP Fld Hcky 86; Coachs Awd 86; Delaware U; Bio.

LOONAM, PATRICIA A; Immaculate Conception HS; Lodi, NJ; (Y); Chorus; Church Choir; School Musical; School Play; Nwsp Rptr; Sftbl; Natl Art Hnr Soc 85 & 86; Montclair ST Coll; Int Dsgn.

LOONEY, STACEY; Ramapo HS; Wyckoff, NJ; (Y); 56/329; AFS; Church Yth Grp; French Clb; Band; Symp Band; Yrbk Sprt Ed; Lit Mag; Crs Cntry; Trk; High Hon Roll; 1st Team All Srbn, 2nd Team All Cnty X-Cntry 85; Hon Mntn All Cntry Mi & 2 Mi Trck 86; Vrsty Ltr Wnnr; Cmnctns.

LOPERFIDO, GABRIELLE J; Bishop Evstace Prep Schl; Haddonfield, NJ; (Y); 3/183; Drama Clb; JCL; Latin Clb; Spanish Clb; Stat Bsktbl; High Hon Roll; NHS; Ntl Merit SF; Spanish NHS; St Schlr; Spn.

LOPES, ANA; St Vincent Acad; Newark, NJ; (Y); 3/66; Church Yth Grp; Girl Scts; Office Aide; Mrchg Band; School Play; Stage Crew; Hon Roll; Jr NHS; Pres Schlr; Rutgers U; Pharm.

LOPES, CHRISTINA; Benedictine Acad; Elizabeth, NJ; (Y); Cmnty Wkr; French Clb; Chorus; Church Choir; Nwsp Rptr; Hon Roll; Var NHS; School Play; Outstndng Achvt Cert Of Music 84; Alg I Achvt 85; Educ.

LOPEZ, BEATRIZ; Frank H Morrell HS; Irvington, NJ; (Y); Flag Corp; Mgr(s); Score Keeper; Sftbl; Hon Roll; Essex County Coll; Comp Oper.

LOPEZ, DAVID; Glassboro HS; Glassboro, NJ; (Y); Exploring; Nwsp Stf; Var L Bsbl; Bsktbl; Var L Ftbl; High Hon Roll; Hon Roll; Hnrbl Mntn Scrd Hrt HS Sci Fair 83-84; Outstndg Acdmc & Brthrhd Schlrshp 85-86; Temple U; Med.

LOPEZ, HENRY; Woodbridge HS; Keasbey, NJ; (Y); Boy Scts; Speech Tm; Badmtn; Bsktbl; Wt Lftg; Hon Roll; Prfct Atten Awd; Med.

LOPEZ, JULIO; Hudson Catholic HS; North Bergen, NJ; (Y); Exploring; Lit Mag; Boy Scts; Dance Clb; FBLA; Political Wkr; Varsity Clb; Im Bsktbl; Im Vllybl; Hon Roll; St Peters Coll; Bus.

LOPEZ, LYDIA; Woodrow Wilson HS; Camden, NJ; (Y); Art Clb; Pres Drama Clb; English Clb; Library Aide; VP PAVAS; Ski Clb; School Musical; School Play; Lit Mag; Rep Jr Cls; Rutgers U; Mtrlgy.

LOPEZ, MARIA CRISTELA; Memorial HS; North Bergen, NJ; (S); 28/650; Intnl Clb; Math Clb; Spanish Clb; Hon Roll; NHS; Montclair ST Coll; Dentist.

LOPEZ, MARTHA; Hoboken HS; Hoboken, NJ; (Y); Spanish Clb; Teachers Aide; Yrbk Stf; Sci Fair Cert 83; Asst Nurse Opertr.

LOPEZ, MICHELE; Hightstown HS; East Windsor, NJ; (Y); Spanish Clb; High Hon Roll; Hon Roll.

LOPEZ, ROBERT; St John Vianney HS; Matawan, NJ; (Y); 135/283; Rep Frsh Cls; JV Var Ftbl; Hon Roll; Glassboro ST Coll; Acctng.

LOPEZ, ROBERTO; Teaneck HS; Teaneck, NJ; (Y); 68/420; Church Yth Grp; Hon Roll; NHS; Sol Greene Schlrshp Awd $1000 86-87; Rutgers Coll; Ec.

LOPEZ, ROSA; Hoboken HS; Hoboken, NJ; (Y); Debate Tm; Hosp Aide; JA; Key Clb; Service Clb; Spanish Clb; Teachers Aide; Yrbk Phtg; Yrbk Stf; CC Awd; Hghst Avg Engl As A 2nd Lang 83; Rutgers; Doc.

LOPEZ, ROSE; Emerson HS; Jersey City, NJ; (Y); Dance Clb; Spanish Clb; Chorus; Stu Cncl; Bsktbl; Co-Capt Cheerleading; Powder Puff Ftbl; Sftbl; Vllybl; Stevens Inst Of Tech; Elec Engr.

LOPEZ, SANDRA; Saint Dominic Acad; N Bergen, NJ; (Y); 7/131; French Clb; Model UN; Science Clb; Yrbk Rptr; High Hon Roll; NHS; WSUC Schlrshp 86; Rlgs Stds Awd 86; Pres Acad Ftnss Awds Prgrm 86; NY U; Biochmstry.

LOPEZ, STEVEN; Elizabeth HS; Elizabeth, NJ; (Y); Church Yth Grp; VICA; Hon Roll; NJ Inst Of Tchnlgy; Arch.

LOPEZ, WILLIAM; Memorial HS; W New York, NJ; (Y); Chess Clb; Sec Computer Clb; Key Clb; Math Clb; Science Clb; Sec Jr Cls; High Hon Roll; NHS; Hlth Clb; Engrng.

LOPIPARO, SUSAN; Freehold Township HS; Freehold, NJ; (Y); 33/382; Drama Clb; Ed Yrbk Stf; Lit Mag; Sec Stu Cncl; Stat Bsbl; NHS; Natl Piano Tchrs Guild Adtns 83-87; Lwyr.

LOPUS, NANCY; West Essex SR HS; Essex Fells, NJ; (Y); 40/350; Church Yth Grp; Concert Band; Drm Mjr(t); Jazz Band; Mrchg Band; Symp Band; JV Var Fld Hcky; Hon Roll; NHS; Prfct Atten Awd; Wst Essx Bnd Boostr Awd 86; VA Polytechnic Inst; Bus.

LORD, DAVID; Hightstown HS; E Windsor, NJ; (Y); 3/449; Var JV Bsbl; Var JV Trk; High Hon Roll; Hon Roll; Prfct Atten Awd; Engr.

LORDI, JOELLE; Clifton HS; Clifton, NJ; (Y); 47/564; Am Leg Aux Girls St; Civic Clb; Sftbl; Hon Roll; NHS; Spanish NHS; Clifton Coll Womns Clb 86; Rutgers Coll; Phrmcy.

LORENTZ, ALISON; Voorhees HS; Califon, NJ; (Y); 84/274; Church Yth Grp; French Clb; Ski Clb; Varsity Clb; Jr Cls; Sr Cls; Stu Cncl; Cheerleading; Hon Roll; NHS; Psych.

LORENTZ, PAMELA; A P Schalick HS; Elmer, NJ; (Y); Sftbl; Tennis; Hon Roll; Cumberland Coll; Bus.

LORENZ, DIANE; Holy Cross HS; Willingboro, NJ; (Y); 157/364; School Musical; School Play; Rep Frsh Cls; Rep Soph Cls; Rep Jr Cls; Rep Sr Cls; Rep Stu Cncl; Var Crs Cntry; Var Trk; Hon Roll; George Mason U; Bus Adm.

LORENZ, MICHAEL; Weehawken HS; Weehawken, NJ; (Y); Boy Scts; Math Tm; Yrbk Stf; Hon Roll; Wmns Clb Awd Wrtng 86; Jersey City ST Coll; Comm Art.

LORENZO, GISELA; Barringer HS; Newark, NJ; (Y); Church Yth Grp; Dance Clb; Office Aide; Church Choir; NCTE Awd; Achvt Awd Comp Prog 84; Activities Awd 83.

LORENZO, MARILYN; Dover SR HS; Dover, NJ; (Y); Church Yth Grp; FBLA; High Hon Roll; Cnty Coll Morris; Exec Sec.

LORENZO, MICHELLE; North Bergen HS; North Bergen, NJ; (Y); Trs German Clb; La Roche Coll; Psych.

LOSCALZO, TONIANN; Holy Family Acad; Bayonne, NJ; (Y); Computer Clb; JV Cheerleading; Prfct Atten Awd; Bus Adm.

LOSQUADRO, CHRIS; Seton Hall Prep HS; Cedar Grove, NJ; (Y); Computer Clb; French Clb; FBLA; Key Clb; Ski Clb; Var L Ftbl; Pre-Law.

LOTKE, MARK; East Brunswick HS; East Brunswick, NJ; (Y); Math Clb; Stu Cncl; Im Bsktbl; JV Socr; JV Tennis; French Hon Soc; High Hon Roll; NHS; Ntl Merit Ltr; St Schlr; Pyscs I Tm; Chmstry II Tm; #11 NJ ST Sci Day Chmstry Tst; U Of PA; Econ.

LOTT, KATHRYN; Voorhees HS; Lebanon, NJ; (Y); Latin Clb; Orch; Varsity Clb; Var Capt Tennis; Im Vllybl; Hon Roll; Cert Hnr Outstndng Musicnshp Yth Symph 86; MVP Soph & JR Yr Tennis 85-86; Mst Imprvd Tennis Plyr 85.

LOTT, VIRGINIA D; Wayne Hills HS; Wayne, NJ; (Y); Cmnty Wkr; Latin Clb; Office Aide; Acpl Chr; Church Choir; Trk; Ecology Club 85-86; Bus Admin.

LOUGHLIN, FLORENCE; Central Regional HS; Ocean Gate, NJ; (Y); Thtre Prfrmr 14 Plys; Trng Music & Dance; Brookdale CC; Thtre Arts.

LOUGHRAN, PATRICIA L; St Rose HS; Spring Lake Hts, NJ; (Y); 16/206; Lit Mag; Crs Cntry; High Hon Roll; Hon Roll; NHS; St Schlr; Douglass Coll; Eng.

LOUIE, DAVID; Cinnaminson HS; Cinnaminson, NJ; (Y); Chess Clb; Sec Computer Clb; Drama Clb; Key Clb; Thesps; Chorus; Mrchg Band; Stu Cncl; Trk; NHS; John Hopkins; Bio.

LOUIS, KELLY; Middletown South HS; Lincroft, NJ; (Y); Girl Scts; Latin Clb; SADD; Variety Show; Lit Mag; Rep Stu Cncl; Bsktbl; Score Keeper; Var L Trk; Hon Roll; Excptnl Scorng ASVAB 86; Trvl Abrd.

LOURENCO, LORI; Carteret HS; Carteret, NJ; (Y); 28/198; Church Yth Grp; Drama Clb; Intnl Clb; Ski Clb; Capt Band; Concert Band; Capt Mrchg Band; Trs Soph Cls; Sec Sr Cls; Mgr Bsbl.

LOUX, J HOLLY; John P Stevens SR HS; Edison, NJ; (Y); 50/500; Sec Church Yth Grp; Yrbk Stf; Rep Sr Cls; Var Capt Cheerleading; High Hon Roll; NHS; Ntl Merit Ltr; Pres Schlr; Spanish NHS; Dstngshd Mrt Scty 83; Villanova U; Engr.

LOVE, KIM; Central Regional HS; Bayville, NJ; (Y); 49/225; Drama Clb; Girl Scts; Office Aide; Chorus; School Musical; School Play; Stage Crew; Yrbk Stf; High Hon Roll; Hon Roll; Ocean Cnty Coll; Librl Arts.

LOVE, THOMAS; Clearview Regional HS; Sewell, NJ; (Y); 3/152; 4-H; SADD; VP Stu Cncl; Var Ftbl; Wt Lftg; Var Wrstlng; 4-H Awd; Hon Roll; NHS; Med.

LOVELL, CHRISTOPHER; Arthur P Schalick HS; Elmer, NJ; (Y); 1/150; Debate Tm; Band; Concert Band; Mrchg Band; Nwsp Stf; Stu Cncl; High Hon Roll; NHS; St Schlr; Val; Tp 5 Stdnt Awd 86; U PA; Soclgy.

LOVELL, LUKE; Governor Livingston HS; Berkeley Heights, NJ; (Y); 25/195; Church Yth Grp; FCA; Latin Clb; Band; Yrbk Rptr; Crs Cntry; Trk; Hon Roll; NHS; Ntl Merit Ltr; Berkeley Hts Wmns Clb Schlrp 86; U Notre Dame; Bus.

LOVETT, MARYBETH; Holy Cross HS; Burlington, NJ; (Y); 97/400; Church Yth Grp; Exploring; Ski Clb; Spanish Clb; Band; Mrchg Band; Stage Crew; Var Mgr(s); Im Vllybl; Hon Roll; Engrng.

LOWE, CATHERINE; Schalick HS; Newfield, NJ; (Y); Cmnty Wkr; Hosp Aide; SADD; Sftbl; NHS; Teens Art Fest Awd Outstndng Pntng 86; 6 Sftbl Trophies 80-86; Bus Mgt.

LOWE, CHRISTINE M; Wardlaw-Hartridge HS; Plainfield, NJ; (Y); 5/46; Band; Chorus; Yrbk Stf; JP Sousa Awd; NHS; Yale U; Econ.

LOWE, DIONNA; Burlington County Vocation Tech; Beverly, NJ; (Y); Chorus; Drill Tm; Variety Show; Yrbk Stf; Bsktbl; Ftbl; Gym; Powder Puff Ftbl; Sftbl; Tennis; FHA Hero Clb 86; Beverlys Cmnty Day 85; Burlington Cnty Coll; Acctg.

LOWE, SCOTT; Phillipsburg HS; Phillipsburg, NJ; (Y); 104/292; Ski Clb; Rep Stu Cncl; Var L Crs Cntry; Var L Golf; Var L Trk; Im Vllybl; Crs Cntry Champ Jacket 84; Trk Champ Jacket 85; NC ST U; Textile Engrng.

LOWERY, KATHY; Henry Snyder HS; Jersey City, NJ; (Y); 10/300; Church Yth Grp; Dance Clb; GAA; Rep Frsh Cls; Rep Soph Cls; Rep Jr Cls; Rep Stu Cncl; Var Capt Cheerleading; Var Sftbl; Rutgers U; Nrsng.

LOYAS, DONALD; Don Bosco Prep; Waldwick, NJ; (Y); Hon Roll; Philadelphia Coll; Phrmcy.

LOYD, PATRICK; St Peters/Christian Ctr; Lorton, VA; (Y); FCA; French Clb; Bsktbl; Ftbl; Wt Lftg; SAR Awd; OH ST U; Engrng.

LOZA, STEPHANIE; Cinnaminson HS; Cinnaminson, NJ; (Y); 13/254; Church Yth Grp; Sec Drama Clb; Key Clb; Sec Thesps; Acpl Chr; Band; Color Guard; Orch; School Musical; Var Swmmng; Orchstr Awd 86; Intl Thespn Soc 84-86; Catholic U Of Amer; Music Ed.

LOZEA, SCOTT; Freehold Township HS; Freehold, NJ; (Y); 92/386; Drama Clb; Spanish Clb; Temple Yth Grp; School Musical; School Play; Stage Crew; Im Bowling; Var Gym; Ntl Merit Ltr; 1st Pl Trophy Bowling Lg 86; 2nd Pl Gym JR Olympics 85; Communications.

LUBENOW, ANNE; Overbrook Regional HS; Lindenwold, NJ; (Y); 4/350; French Clb; Chorus; Jr Cls; Crs Cntry; Powder Puff Ftbl; Trk; NHS; Air Force Acad; Aero Engr.

LUCAS, DENENE; Teaneck HS; Teaneck, NJ; (Y); Sec Church Yth Grp; Dance Clb; Girl Scts; Hosp Aide; Acpl Chr; Chorus; Church Choir; Madrigals; Cheerleading; Mgr(s); Cheney; Psych.

LUCAS, JEFF; Hightstown HS; Cranbury, NJ; (Y); Chess Clb; Cmnty Wkr; Computer Clb; Exploring; Teachers Aide; High Hon Roll; NHS; Coast Grd Acad; Engr.

LUCAS, MICHELE; Lodi HS; Lodi, NJ; (Y); Camera Clb; Key Clb; Pep Clb; Science Clb; Chorus; Color Guard; Pep Band; Yrbk Phtg; Pre Med.

LUCAS, MYRON; Irvington HS; Irvington, NJ; (Y); Latin Clb; Ftbl; Trk; Hon Roll.

LUCAS, NICHOLAS; Bricktown HS; Brick Town, NJ; (Y); 40/400; Church Yth Grp; German Clb; JV Var Bowling; High Hon Roll; Boston U; Arspc.

LUCAS, TED; Hollycross HS; Maple Shade, NJ; (Y); Church Yth Grp; Hosp Aide; Hon Roll; Engrng.

LUCCA, CAROLYN; Hammonton HS; Hammonton, NJ; (Y); 1/176; Key Clb; Trs Soph Cls; Trs Jr Cls; Trs Sr Cls; JV Bsktbl; Var Sftbl; High Hon Roll; NHS; Pres Schlr; St Schlr; NJ Dstngshd Schlr 85-86; Rtgers Schlr 85; Fairleaigh Dickinson U; Mgmnt.

LUCCA, TRACY; St Joseph HS; Hammonton, NJ; (Y); Chorus; School Play; Trs Jr Cls; Var Cheerleading; JV Coach Actv; Stat Tennis; Drama Clb; PAVAS; Ski Clb; Spanish Clb; St Joseph U; Pol Sci.

LUCCHESI, ARTHUR; Washington Township HS; Sewell, NJ; (Y); Stage Crew; Prnt Tchr Orgntn Hon Mntn 84-85; 2nd Pl All Arnd Prnt Tchr Orgnztn Bst Tech 85-86; Drexel; Drftng Engr.

LUCCHESI, ERIC; Ridgefield Park HS; Cliffside Park, NJ; (Y); 40/187; Chess Clb; Yrbk Stf; Hon Roll; Arch.

LUCCHESI, JOE; Woodstown HS; Woodstown, NJ; (Y); Bsktbl; Cmptr Sci.

LUCIA, JOSEPH R; Red Bank Catholic HS; Eatontown, NJ; (Y); Church Yth Grp; Cmnty Wkr; Math Clb; Ski Clb; Teachers Aide; Varsity Clb; Jazz Band; Variety Show; Off Frsh Cls; Off Soph Cls; Acctng.

LUCIANO, MARIA; Frank H Morrell HS; Irvington, NJ; (Y); JA; ROTC; Off Frsh Cls; Off Soph Cls; Off Jr Cls; Mgr(s); Sftbl; Hon Roll; Rutgers; Nrsng.

LUCIANO, TERRY; Lyndhurst HS; Lyndhurst, NJ; (Y); 16/163; Key Clb; Drm Mjr(t); Twrlr; Amjts Mem Schlrshp 86; Amer Lgn Axlry Amer Essy Cntst 82; Mntclr ST Coll; Hm Ec.

LUCIVERO, PHILIP; Parsippany HS; Parsippany, NJ; (Y); FBLA; Varsity Clb; Rep Stu Cncl; JV Var Bsbl; JV Var Ftbl; Hon Roll; Bsbl Boosters Assn Scholar 86; Susquehanna U; Bus Adm.

LUCKENBACH, RICHARD A; Lyndhurst HS; Lyndhurst, NJ; (Y); 42/163; German Clb; Var Capt Crs Cntry; JV Trk; Lyndhurst Emblem Clb Art Schlrshp 86; William Paterson Coll; Art.

LUCKEY, ANNE MARIE; Passaic HS; Little Falls, NJ; (Y); Hon Roll; Comp.

LUDVIGSEN, MARK; Voorhees HS; Pottersville, NJ; (Y); 4/274; Var Crs Cntry; JV Trk; JV Wrstlng; French Hon Soc; High Hon Roll; Hon Roll; Ntl Merit Ltr; French Clb; Yrbk Stf; Prfct Atten Awd; Voorhees Acad Achvt Soc 84-86; Engrng.

LUDWICK, MELISSA; Gloucester City JR R HS; Gloucester, NJ; (Y); #1 In Class; Am Leg Aux Girls St; Chorus; School Musical; School Play; Rep Stu Cncl; Var Cheerleading; Var Fld Hcky; Var Capt Sftbl; High Hon Roll; NHS; Vet.

LUDWIG, JAMES D; Toms River HS North; Toms River, NJ; (Y); 7/400; Computer Clb; FBLA; Ski Clb; VP Sr Cls; Rep Stu Cncl; Var Capt Ftbl; Wt Lftg; Elks Awd; High Hon Roll; Hon Roll; Am Leg Hstry Awd 86; ETS NJSIAA Schlr Athlt Awd 86; Schlr Athlt Tm Ocn Cty Tms Obsrv 86; VA Tech; Arspc Engr.

LUDWIG, JENS O; Lenape HS; Mt Laurel, NJ; (Y); 10/421; Am Leg Boys St; German Clb; SADD; School Play; Variety Show; Stu Cncl; JV Var Socr; NHS; Ntl Merit Ltr; Pres Schlr; Rutgers Coll; Bus.

LUEDER, DAVID; Ambassador Christian Acad; Aura, NJ; (S); 1/8; Drama Clb; Orch; VP Sec Sr Cls; Var Co-Capt Bsktbl; Var Co-Capt Socr; High Hon Roll; NHS; Val; Art Clb; Church Yth Grp; Garden ST Distngshd Schlr Awd; Rutgers Schlr Awd.

LUEDER, LUCIANO J; Ambassador Christian Acad; Aura, NJ; (S); Bsktbl; Socr; High Hon Roll; Hon Roll; NHS; Ecnmcs.

LUETHI, GABRIELA; Monsignor Donovan HS; Toms River, NJ; (Y); 41/243; Drama Clb; Exploring; Intnl Clb; Ski Clb; High Hon Roll; Engl, Sci Awds 84; Lang.

LUGIANO, DARREN; Vineland HS; Vineland, NJ; (Y); Pep Clb; Ski Clb; Varsity Clb; Rep Frsh Cls; Rep VP Soph Cls; Rep Jr Cls; Var L Ftbl; Var L Trk; Var L Wrstlng; Prfct Atten Awd; Ftbl All Area, Cnty, Conf And Press 85; Wrstlg All Area, Conf, Hnrbl Mntn 85-86; Trk Champ 86; C W Post; Psych.

LUGO, SANDRA; Abbegami HS; Absecon Hlds, NJ; (Y); Sec Drama Clb; Key Clb; Yrbk Stf; Hon Roll; NHS; Ntl Merit Ltr; Stockton ST Coll; Marine Bio.

LUGO, VIVIAN; Bogota HS; Bogota, NJ; (Y); 1/100; Am Leg Aux Girls St; Drama Clb; Spanish Clb; Acpl Chr; Chorus; School Musical; Lit Mag; Pres Frsh Cls; Pres Church Yth Grp; Pres Jr Cls; Rutgers Schlr 86; ROGATE 84; Frgn Lgs.

LUKACS, TIMOTHY; Bound Brook HS; Bound Brook, NJ; (Y); 6/130; French Clb; Concert Band; Jazz Band; Mrchg Band; Tennis; Wrstlng; NHS; Med.

LUKAS, DIANE; Clifton HS; Clifton, NJ; (Y); 27/637; Girl Scts; Library Aide; SADD; Capt Var Bowling; Capt Var Fld Hcky; Var Socr; Var Sftbl; Twrlr; Hon Roll; NHS; Grl Sctng Slvr Awd 84; Vlntr Pbl Lbry 85; Bus Accntng.

LUM, LINDA; Cherry Hill HS West; Cherry Hill, NJ; (Y); Church Yth Grp; Intnl Clb; JCL; Spanish Clb; Chorus; Flag Corp; Stage Crew; Yrbk Ed-Chief; Yrbk Stf; Stu Cncl; Phrmcy.

LUM, LINDA; Hackensack HS; Maywood, NJ; (Y); Cmnty Wkr; Office Aide; Teachers Aide; Yrbk Stf; Off Jr Cls; Var L Vllybl; Cit Awd; High Hon Roll; Awd For Steno Comp 85; Boston U; Bio.

LUMADVE, MARK; St Marys Hall/Doane Acad; Burlington, NJ; (Y); Aud/Vis; Drama Clb; Library Aide; Lit Mag; Nwsp Rptr; Yrbk Stf; Burlngtn Tn Arts Poetry 1st Pl 85; Trentn ST Drama Fstvl 86; Wrtng.

LUMBY, JEFFREY S; Rancocas Valley Regional HS; Mt Holly, NJ; (Y); Am Leg Boys St; Varsity Clb; Pres Frsh Cls; Pres Soph Cls; Rep Jr Cls; Rep Sr Cls; Rep Stu Cncl; Var Socr; Hon Roll; Quiz Bowl; Stu Rep Middle ST Eval Comm 85-86; Aeronautical Engrng.

LUMBY, JULIE; Rancocas Valley Regional HS; Mount Holly, NJ; (Y); 1/271; Pres VP FBLA; Concert Band; Jazz Band; Mrchg Band; Orch; Sftbl; High Hon Roll; NHS; Swmmng; JR All Amer Hall Of Fame Band Hnrs 85-86.

LUMIQUINGA, NELSON; Frank H Morrell HS; Irvington, NJ; (Y); Art Clb; Boy Scts; Church Yth Grp; Dance Clb; Key Clb; Latin Clb; Library Aide; Spanish Clb; Teachers Aide; School Play; Montclair SR; Pre-Law.

LUMPKIN, BETH ANN; Paul VI HS; Haddonfield, NJ; (S); 41/474; Hosp Aide; Math Clb; SADD; Rep Soph Cls; Var Capt Cheerleading; Var Trk; Hon Roll; NHS; Villanova; Nrsng.

LUNA, PEARLIE; Lyndhurst HS; Lyndhurst, NJ; (Y); 1/180; German Clb; Library Aide; Office Aide; Scholastic Bowl; Yrbk Stf; Var L Mgr(s); JV Var Sftbl; L Capt Vllybl; High Hon Roll; NHS; Spllng Bee Awd 83; Art Shw Awd 82; Bus.

LUND, CHRISTIAN; Hackettstown HS; Belvidere, NJ; (Y); #20 In Class; Church Yth Grp; 4-H; Nwsp Rptr; Var Crs Cntry; Swmmng; Var Wrstlng; Dnfth Awd; 4-H Awd; Ski Clb; School Musical; USMA Invtnl Acdmc Wrkshp 86; Ntl 4-H Conf Dlgt 86; 4-H Ldrshp Awds 84-85; Engrng.

LUND, SUZANNE DENISE; Teaneck HS; Teaneck, NJ; (Y); 19/420; Am Leg Aux Girls St; Quiz Bowl; Madrigals; Nwsp Stf; Yrbk Stf; God Cntry Awd; Ntl Merit Ltr; St Schlr; Scl Stds Awd; Yth Ldrshp Awd; Wellesley Coll; Art Hstry.

LUNDGREN, GENI; Brick Township HS; Brick Town, NJ; (Y); 34/413; Pres Church Yth Grp; Math Tm; Teachers Aide; Flag Corp; Variety Show; JV Bowling; High Hon Roll; Hon Roll; NHS; Phrmcy.

LUNDHOLM, ROBERT; Lower Cape May Reg HS; Cape May, NJ; (Y); Varsity Clb; VICA; Rep Stu Cncl; Ftbl; Golf; Hon Roll; Prfct Atten Awd; Cape Atlantic Leag Glf All Str 85-86; Indstrl Arts Exhbt Awd Wnnr 86; FL ST; Crmnl Jstc.

LUNGARI, GINA; Central Regional HS; Bayville, NJ; (Y); Kean Coll NJ; Elem Ed.

LUNNEY, KELLY P; Middletown HS South; Leonard, NJ; (Y); Art Clb; Spanish Clb; Vllybl; Hon Roll.

LUONGO, LISA; Belleville HS; Belleville, NJ; (Y); Key Clb; Ski Clb; Spanish Clb; Trs Jr Cls; Trs Sr Cls; Bsktbl; JV Var Mgr(s); Hon Roll; Bus.

LUPO, MELISSA; Bishop George Ahr HS; Colonia, NJ; (Y); Church Yth Grp; French Clb; Girl Scts; Color Guard; Lit Mag; Hon Roll; Vet Med.

LUPPINO, CATHY; Bayonne HS; Bayonne, NJ; (Y); Church Yth Grp; Library Aide; Office Aide; Political Wkr; SADD; Teachers Aide; Nwsp Rptr; Rep Frsh Cls; Rep Stu Cncl; Rutgers; Nrsg.

LUSTIG, MIKE; Pascack Valley HS; River Vale, NJ; (Y); Var Socr; Var Tennis; Var Trk; Hon Roll; Sci.

LUSZCZ, DANIEL; Linden HS; Linden, NJ; (Y); Chess Clb; Church Yth Grp; German Clb; Varsity Clb; JV Var Wrstlng; NHS; Pre Med.

LUTHE, SHANNON; Lower Cape May Regional HS; N Cape May, NJ; (Y); French Clb; Pep Clb; Varsity Clb; VP Frsh Cls; VP Soph Cls; VP Jr Cls; Stu Cncl; Cheerleading; Mgr(s); Hon Roll; Acdmc Achvt Awd 84-86; Intl Byr.

LUTHER, KAY; Woodstown HS; Merchantville, NJ; (Y); 17/162; German Clb; Band; School Musical; Nwsp Stf; Yrbk Ed-Chief; Trs Stu Cncl; JV Bsktbl; JV Golf; Kiwanis Awd; Cmnty Wkr; Wmns Club Litry Awd 86; Grls Citznshp Inst 85; American U; Comm.

LUTTGENS, PAMELA; Linden HS; Linden, NJ; (Y); Am Leg Aux Girls St; Cmnty Wkr; Office Aide; Service Clb; Stage Crew; Off Jr Cls; VP Stu Cncl; Cheerleading; Hon Roll; NHS; Fshn Inst; Fshn Merch.

LUTTON, DEBORAH; Egg Harbor Township HS; Mays Landing, NJ; (S); 5/269; Spanish Clb; Trs Chorus; Mgr School Musical; Yrbk Stf; Jr NHS; Ntl Merit Ltr; St Schlr; Drama Clb; US Nvl Acad Smr Smnr 85; Ocngrphy.

LUTTRELL, JAMES; Ridgefield Memorial HS; Ridgefield, NJ; (Y); Cmnty Wkr; JV Bsbl; JV Bsktbl; Jornalism.

LUTZ, KEVIN; Millville SR HS; Millville, NJ; (Y); Merit Roll 83-86; Ldrs Clb 83-87; GATE 83-87; Pennco Tech; Comp.

LUTZ, KIMBERLY; Rancocas Valley Regional HS; Mt Holly, NJ; (Y); 16/259; Spanish Clb; Trs Varsity Clb; Yrbk Ed-Chief; Lit Mag; Sec Soph Cls; Sec Jr Cls; Sec Sr Cls; Var Diving; Var Gym; Var Swmmng; Acadmc Achvmnt Awd; U Of DE; Chem Engr.

LUTZ, MICHELE; Watdhung Hills Regional HS; Warren, NJ; (Y); 5/315; Church Yth Grp; SADD; Drill Tm; Yrbk Rptr; Var L Swmmng; High Hon Roll; Hon Roll; Trs NHS; Voice Dem Awd; Off Soph Cls; Mst Imprvd Swmmr Vrsty Swim Team 84; Coaches Awd Vrsty Swm Team 86; Adv.

LUTZ, NICHOLAS; Verona HS; Verona, NJ; (Y); French Clb; French Hon Soc; Hon Roll; Comptr Sci.

LUWISH, JUDY; Bruriah HS; Hillside, NJ; (Y); 3/48; Cmnty Wkr; School Musical; School Play; Nwsp Rptr; VP Frsh Cls; NHS; NEDT Awd; Drama Clb; Awds Merit Music 78-84; Sci Fair Wnnr 85; Schlsrhp Alfred U Smmr Music Inst 85; Columbia U; Psych.

LUYANDO, ALFREDO; Hoboken HS; Hoboken, NJ; (Y); ROTC; Spanish Clb; Bsbl; Bsktbl; Coach Actv; Ftbl; Sftbl; Swmmng; Wt Lftg; Hon Roll.

LUZAR, TINA; Middlesex HS; Middlesex, NJ; (Y); Capt Color Guard; Capt Drill Tm; Capt Flag Corp; Off Mrchg Band; School Musical; Hon Roll; Future Sec Honorable Mention Ldrshp Awd 86; Typing Awd 85-86; Nice Kid Awd 85; BUS Edu.

LUZKY, DANA; Toms River HS North; Toms River, NJ; (Y); Ski Clb; Pres Spanish Clb; Rep Stu Cncl; JV Sftbl; JV Swmmng; Hon Roll; Acadmc Ltr 85-86; Acctng.

LUZURIAGA, YANDRY; Our Lady Of Good Counsel HS; Newark, NJ; (Y); 27/106; Capt Socr; Prfct Atten Awd.

LYDEN, JOHN; Msgr Donovan HS; Ocean Gate, NJ; (Y); Cmnty Wkr; Computer Clb; Drama Clb; French Clb; Variety Show; Hon Roll; Englsh.

LYDON, JENNIFER; Westwood HS; Westwood, NJ; (Y); 10/230; German Clb; Library Aide; Office Aide; Band; Concert Band; Mrchg Band; NHS; Ntl Merit Ltr; U DE Ntl Schlr Awd 86; Grdn ST Dstngshd Schlr Awd 86; U Of DE; Bio Sci.

LYLES, DANETTA L; Eastside HS; Paterson, NJ; (Y); 55/800; Chorus; Rep Soph Cls; Stat Sftbl; Hon Roll; Prfct Atten Awd; Cert Achvt Chem 85; Stu Comndtn 85; Upward Bound Pgm-Fairleigh Dickinson U 85; U NC; Comp Sci.

LYNCH, BRIAN P; Midland Park HS; Midland Park, NJ; (Y); Am Leg Boys St; Church Yth Grp; Computer Clb; FBLA; Letterman Clb; Radio Clb; Ski Clb; Stage Crew; Yrbk Stf; Var Crs Cntry; Providence Coll.

LYNCH, DENISE; Ocean City HS; Sea Isle City, NJ; (Y); 55/291; Church Yth Grp; Debate Tm; FNA; Hosp Aide; Intnl Clb; Spanish Clb; Band; Concert Band; Drill Tm; Jazz Band; Mount St Marys; Acctg.

LYNCH, JENNIFER; Toms River North HS; Toms River, NJ; (Y); 37/364; Red Cross Aide; Ski Clb; Capt Var Bsktbl; JV Sftbl; JV Tennis; Var L Trk; High Hon Roll; NHS; MVP Bsktbl 85-86; Best Defnse Trophy Sftbl 83-84; Lady Mariner Bsktbl Schlrshp Awd 83-84; Sports Med.

LYNCH, JILL; Rancocas Valley Regional HS; Hainesport, NJ; (Y); #53 In Class; Am Leg Aux Girls St; Church Yth Grp; Cmnty Wkr; Spanish Clb; Chorus; Yrbk Ed-Chief; Yrbk Stf; JV Golf; JV Sftbl; High Hon Roll; Natl Luth Yth Conv 86; Hotl Mgmt.

LYNCH, KEVIN; Roselle Catholic HS; Roselle, NJ; (S); Frsh Cls; Stu Cncl; JV Bsbl; Var Bsktbl; High Hon Roll; Hon Roll; Med.

LYNCH, MICHELE; Red Bank Catholic HS; Red Bank, NJ; (Y); Church Yth Grp; GAA; PAVAS; Ski Clb; School Musical; School Play; Mgr(s); Stat L Socr; JV Var Sftbl; Swmmng; Schl Ad Drive Wnnr & Rep 85-86; Vly Forge Christain Coll; Tchr.

LYNCH, NORENE; Franklin HS; Somerset, NJ; (Y); French Clb; Key Clb; SADD; School Play; Nwsp Sprt Ed; Trs Stu Cncl; Stat Bsbl; JV Capt Fld Hcky; NHS; VP Soph Cls; Bus.

LYNCH, SARAH; Oak Knoll Schl; Chatham, NJ; (Y); Teachers Aide; Yrbk Ed-Chief; JV Fld Hcky; Var Lcrss; High Hon Roll; NCTE Awd; Ntl Merit Ltr; Key Clb; Pep Clb; Ski Clb; Cornelian Schlrshp 83; 3rd Trenton ST Coll Annl NJ Wrtrs Cont 86; Hnrbl Mntn 9th Annl NJ Poetry 86.

LYNCH, TIMOTHY W; Montclair HS; Montclair, NJ; (Y); 4/438; Chess Clb; Math Tm; Quiz Bowl; School Play; Lit Mag; Rep Frsh Cls; Hon Roll; NHS; Ntl Merit SF; Pres Schlr; Rnsslr Medal 85; Mock Trial Team 85-86; Cornell U; Astro.

LYNES, DAVID; St Marys Hall-Doane Acad; Cherry Hill, NJ; (Y); 7/18; Am Leg Boys St; Stage Crew; VP Frsh Cls; VP Soph Cls; Stu Cncl; Var L Bsbl; Var L Socr; Hon Roll; ST NJ Bar Assoc Mock Trail Comptn 86.

LYNN, DOREEN; Holy Cross HS; Mount Laurel, NJ; (Y); Church Yth Grp; Ski Clb; Varsity Clb; Yrbk Stf; Stu Cncl; JV Var Fld Hcky; Stat Socr; Im Sftbl; Im Vllybl; Hon Roll; E Stroudsburg U; Ecnmcs.

LYNSKEY, MELISSA; Triton Regional HS; Bellmawr, NJ; (Y); 75/294; DECA; Office Aide; Yrbk Stf; Rep Jr Cls; Powder Puff Ftbl; Hon Roll; Accntnt.

LYONS, BETH; Ramapo Regional HS; Wyckoff, NJ; (Y); 18/329; Am Leg Aux Girls St; Church Yth Grp; French Clb; Stage Crew; Var JV Bsktbl; Var L Sftbl; High Hon Roll; Hon Roll; NHS.

LYONS, KAREN; Manasquan HS; Brielle, NJ; (Y); 47/238; Drama Clb; French Clb; Spanish Clb; Acpl Chr; Band; Chorus; Concert Band; Flag Corp; Mrchg Band; Swing Chorus; Mens Clb Brielle Schlrshp 86; Douglass Coll; Frnch.

LYONS, LISA; Toms River High School East; Toms River, NJ; (Y); 61/479; Debate Tm; Drama Clb; French Clb; Political Wkr; Chorus; Drill Tm; School Musical; School Play; Variety Show; Stat Bsbl; Jim Furlong Memrl Schlrshp Jersey Shr Irish Amer Clb 86; Bst Actrss Bucks Co Plyhse Drama Fest 86; NY U; Actg.

LYONS, SCOTT; Paramus Catholic Boys HS; Fair Lawn, NJ; (Y); 6/178; Computer Clb; SADD; Lit Mag; Sr Cls; Stu Cncl; Var Ftbl; Var Trk; Hon Roll; NHS; Ntl Merit Ltr; Engr.

LYTLE, LINDA; Paulsboro HS; Paulsboro, NJ; (Y); 3/145; Am Leg Aux Girls St; School Musical; School Play; Pres Sec Stu Cncl; Mat Maids; Var Co-Capt Tennis; Stat Wrstlng; Cit Awd; Hon Roll; Trs NHS.

MAAT, STACEY ANN; Hackensack HS; S Hackensack, NJ; (Y); 22/400; Var Bsktbl; Capt Var Vllybl; Hon Roll; Cptn Bergen Vllybl Elito Tm 85-86; All Cnty Vllybl 1st Tm 2 Yrs 85; Atlc Schrlshp Frlgn Dcknsn U 86; Fairleigh Dickinson U; Bus.

MAC DONALD, JOELL; Lower Cape May Regional HS; Cape May, NJ; (Y); 15/235; Cmnty Wkr; Political Wkr; Varsity Clb; JV Sftbl; Var Tennis; High Hon Roll; Hon Roll; NHS; Law.

MAC DONNELL, TIMOTHY W; Saint Joseph Regional HS; Westwood, NJ; (Y); 9/250; Art Clb; Aud/Vis; Chess Clb; Spanish NHS; NJ Schl Of Arts 86.

MAC DUFF, HEATHER L; Eastern HS; Berlin, NJ; (Y); 2/330; Church Yth Grp; Stu Cncl; JV Bsktbl; Var JV Fld Hcky; Var JV Sftbl; High Hon Roll; NHS; Fnlst NJ Gov Schl Public Issues; Highest Av Hnrs Hist; Highest Av Phys Educ; Qldr Gftd/Tlntd Pgm; Bus Acctg.

MAC FARLAND, DARREN; Toms River High School East; Toms River, NJ; (Y); 11/585; Chess Clb; Church Yth Grp; Teachers Aide; Band; Concert Band; Drm & Bgl; Jazz Band; Mrchg Band; Symp Band; High Hon Roll; Chem.

MAC FARLANE, JENNIFER; Southern Regional HS; Manahawkin, NJ; (Y); Ski Clb; Spanish Clb; Chorus; JV Bsktbl; JV Sftbl; Coaches Awd-Bsktbll 86; Hotel Mgt.

MAC FARRAN, CARRIE A; Mahwah HS; Mahwah, NJ; (Y); Drama Clb; Band; Chorus; Concert Band; Jazz Band; School Play; Var Cheerleading; Var Sftbl; Hon Roll; Poly Sci.

MAC KINNON, WENDY; Nutley HS; Nutley, NJ; (Y); 40/349; Drama Clb; Science Clb; Ski Clb; School Musical; School Play; Stage Crew; Nwsp Phtg; Yrbk Phtg; Stu Cncl; Stat Crs Cntry; Glassboro.

MAC MILLAN, ERIC W; Mendham HS; Chester, NJ; (Y); Church Yth Grp; Cmnty Wkr; FBLA; Ski Clb; Varsity Clb; Concert Band; Jazz Band; Mrchg Band; Orch; Pep Band; All ST Rochstr & Wnd 84-86; Ust Altrnt Gvrnrs Schl 86; Med.

MAC NEIL, JOCELYN; Chatham Township HS; Chatham, NJ; (Y); 36/130; Key Clb; Pep Clb; Varsity Clb; Yrbk Stf; Var Bsktbl; JV Fld Hcky; Var Lcrss; Hon Roll; Lehigh U.

MAC TAGGART, ETHAN; Seton Hall Prep; S Orange, NJ; (Y); Boy Scts; Hosp Aide; School Play; Lit Mag; JV Var Wrstlng; Hon Roll; Church Choir; Natl Sci Olympd 85-86; NJ Inst Of Tech; Comp Engr.

MACALISTER, HEATHER; Northern Valley Regional HS; Demarest, NJ; (Y); 15/235; Science Clb; Ski Clb; Spanish Clb; High Hon Roll; Hon Roll; NHS; Ntl Merit Ltr; JV Fld Hcky; Dstngshd Schlr 86; Pres Acadmc Ftns Awd 86; Bronfman Schlrshp 86; Smith Clg.

MACALUSO, ROBERT; Westfield HS; Westfield, NJ; (Y); 127/519; Art Clb; Computer Clb; Key Clb; Science Clb; Ski Clb; Spanish Clb; Varsity Clb; Acpl Chr; Chorus; School Musical; Holy Cross Coll; Pre-Med.

MACAULAY, MELISSA; Phillipsburg HS; Phillipsburg, NJ; (Y); Ski Clb; Band; Concert Band; Jazz Band; Fld Hcky; JV Capt Sftbl; Hon Roll; NHS; Chem.

MACAULEY, SHERI; Central Regional HS; Seaside Park, NJ; (Y); 4/214; Am Leg Aux Girls St; Varsity Clb; Nwsp Rptr; Cheerleading; Var L Crs Cntry; Var L Trk; French Hon Soc; High Hon Roll; NHS; Pres Schlr; Berkeley Township Tchrs Assoc Schlrshp 86; Amer Chem Soc Achvt Awd 84; Mst Vlble Rnnr Crs Cnty 84; Cedart Crest Coll.

MACAVOY JR, ROBERT FRANCIS; Arthur L Johnson Reg HS; Clark, NJ; (Y); 8/217; VP Thesps; School Musical; School Play; Yrbk Stf; VP Jr Cls; NHS; SAR Awd; St Schlr; Drama Clb; German Clb; Delta Epsilon Phi Natl Ger Hnr Soc Awd Pres 85-86; U DE Advncd Stud Pgm Scholar 85; Clrk Ed Assn Schl; Rutgers Coll.

MACCHERONE, AMY; Clearview Regional HS; Mantua, NJ; (Y); 23/180; DECA; Rep Stu Cncl; Fld Hcky; NJ DECA ST Cmptn-1st Pl Ind Evnt 86; NJ DECA ST Cmptn-1st Pl Ind Evnt 85; 1st Pl DECA Cmptn 86; Widener U; Hotl-Restrnt Adm.

MACCHIAVERNA, MICHAEL; Toms River HS South; Toms River, NJ; (Y); 119/360; Computer Clb; Ski Clb; Im Golf; Im Lcrss; JV Socr; Var Swmmng; JV Trk; Spanish Clb; Varsity Clb; Var Powder Puff Ftbl; Villinova; Mchnl Engrn G.

MACCIACHERA, DEBBIE; Roselle Catholic HS; Elizabeth, NJ; (S); High Hon Roll; Hon Roll; NHS; St Elizabeths Coll; Bus.

MACCO, LISA; Parsippany HS; Parsippany, NJ; (Y); 122/318; Sec French Clb; Sec Intnl Clb; Ski Clb; Chorus; Ldrshp Awd Marymount Coll 86; Marymount Coll.

MACDONALD, ANDREW; Wildwood HS; Wildwood, NJ; (Y); 15/130; Boy Scts; Church Yth Grp; Cmnty Wkr; Drama Clb; Library Aide; PAVAS; Band; Concert Band; Drill Tm; Jazz Band; Cnty Bandk 84-86; Teen Arts Fstvl 86; Bus Admn.

MACDONALD, ELLEN; Mahwaah HS; Mahwah, NJ; (Y); 45/178; Church Yth Grp; JCL; Math Clb; Church Choir; High Hon Roll; Hon Roll; Soclgy.

MACDONALD, JEROME; Lower Cape May Regnl HS; Cape May, NJ; (Y); Boy Scts; Band; Jazz Band; Mrchg Band; Orch; Pep Band; School Musical; Symp Band; Golf; Socr; Music.

MACDONALD, MICHELLE; Delaware Valley Regional HS; Milford, NJ; (Y); Church Yth Grp; Band; Concert Band; Mrchg Band; Hon Roll.

MACHADO, CRISTINA; St John Vianney HS; Manalapan, NJ; (Y); Var Crs Cntry; Powder Puff Ftbl; Var Socr; Hon Roll; NHS; Teachers Aide; Band; Mrchg Band; Yrbk Stf; Var Trk; All Shore Sccr Tm 84-85; All Shore Crss Cntry Tm 85-86; All Mnmth Sccr Tm 85-86.

MACHADO, ELIZABETH; Piscataway HS; Piscataway, NJ; (Y); 67/519; Pres Church Yth Grp; Key Clb; Spanish Clb; Nwsp Stf; Yrbk Stf; High Hon Roll; Hon Roll; NHS; Scholar Schor Middle Schl 86; Pres Acad Fit Ad 86; Rutgers Coll; Mth.

MACHERE, MICHAEL; Lyndhurst HS; Lyndhurst, NJ; (Y); 10/180; Am Leg Boys St; Camera Clb; Cmnty Wkr; Math Clb; Pres Science Clb; Varsity Clb; Var Trk; Hon Roll; NHS; NJ Acad Dcthln 85-86; Elec Engr.

MACHESKA, DAVID; Belleville HS; Belleville, NJ; (Y); 49/387; Stage Crew; Nwsp Rptr; Lit Mag; High Hon Roll; Pres Schlr; Crtv Wrtng Awd Belleville HS 86; Upsala Coll; Art.

MACIAG, GRACE; Immaculate Conception HS; Wallington, NJ; (S); Drama Clb; Hosp Aide; Spanish Clb; SADD; Tennis; Prfct Atten Awd; Spanish NHS; Rtgrs U Newrk.

MACIOCH, CHERYL; Woodbridge HS; Woodbridge, NJ; (Y); 32/395; Varsity Clb; Var Crs Cntry; Var Trk; Hon Roll; NHS; Ntl Merit Ltr; Pres Physcl Ftns Awd 80-85; Rutgers U; Mrktng.

MACIURAK, M STEPHANIE; Bishop George Ahr HS; Perth Amboy, NJ; (Y); Church Yth Grp; Hosp Aide; Intnl Clb; Spanish Clb; School Musical; Lit Mag; Co-Capt Socr; JV Sftbl; Cert Of Partcptn Awd-Lit Mag 86; Psych.

MACK, BRIAN; Williamstown HS; Williamstown, NJ; (Y); 2/240; Scholastic Bowl; Spanish Clb; Nwsp Rptr; Nwsp Stf; Yrbk Stf; Off Frsh Cls; NHS; Ntl Merit SF; Sal; VFW Awd; Garden ST Dstngshd Schlrshp 86; Glassboro ST Coll; Comp Sci.

MACK, COLLETTE; Secaucus HS; Secaucus, NJ; (S); 18/164; Computer Clb; Math Clb; Math Tm; Spanish Clb; Varsity Clb; Band; Color Guard; Mrchg Band; Score Keeper; Hon Roll; Vrsty Awd For Band 85; Rutgers-Newark; Accntng.

MACKEWICH, MARIA; Washington Township HS; Turnersville, NJ; (Y); 74/467; French Clb; Church Yth Grp; Math Clb; Band; Church Choir; Mrchg Band; Orch; School Musical; Im Sftbl; High Hon Roll; Hnr Grad Top 15 Pct Cls; Drexel U; Acctng.

MACKEY, MURAE; Red Bank Catholic HS; Manalapan, NJ; (Y); Church Yth Grp; Girl Scts; Spanish Clb; Teachers Aide; High Hon Roll; Hon Roll; NEDT,Spnsh Awd 84; Rutgers; Math.

MACKIE, JENNIFER; Middlesex HS; Middlesex, NJ; (Y); 35/175; Intnl Clb; Ski Clb; SADD; Varsity Clb; Rep Stu Cncl; Cheerleading; Trk; Girl Scts; Pep Clb; Spanish Clb; Bus.

MACKIEWICZ, ANN MARGARET; John F Kennedy HS; Iselin, NJ; (Y); 6/286; Am Leg Aux Girls St; French Clb; FBLA; Yrbk Stf; Hon Roll; Top 20; Seton Hall U Bus; Bus Mgmt.

MACKINTOSH, VICTORIA E; Burlington County Vocational HS; Pemberton, NJ; (S); 7/250; 4-H; FFA; Varsity Clb; Pres Stu Cncl; Bowling; 4-H Awd; Hon Roll; Coast Guard Acad; Marine Bio.

MACLEAN, BARRY; New Milford HS; New Milford, NJ; (Y); 28/150; Church Yth Grp; JV Bsbl; Bio.

MACNAMARA JR, JAMES F; Haddon Township HS; Westmont, NJ; (Y); 1/180; Am Leg Boys St; Boy Scts; Varsity Clb; Crs Cntry; Wt Lftg; Wrstlng; Bausch & Lomb Sci Awd; High Hon Roll; NHS; Chem Engr.

MACOR, JEFFREY; Piscataway HS; Pisc, NJ; (Y); Radio Clb; Wrstlng; Culnry Stdy.

MACPHERSON, PAUL; Mahway HS; Mahwah, NJ; (Y); Drama Clb; JA; PAVAS; Political Wkr; Service Clb; Speech Tm; School Play; Stage Crew; Sec Frsh Cls; VP Soph Cls; Petty Ofcr 1st Cls Royal Canadian Sea Cadets 82-86; Pres Stu Actvts Cmmttee Of Mahwah 86; Comp Sci.

MACZKO, KRISTIE; Montville Township HS; Towaco, NJ; (Y); 38/236; Key Clb; Ski Clb; Color Guard; Stage Crew; Nwsp Phtg; Var Trk; High Hon Roll; Hon Roll; NHS; Ntl Merit Ltr; Rutgers; Econ.

MADALONE, CATHY; Middletown South HS; Middletown, NJ; (Y); Var Capt Bsktbl; Capt Powder Puff Ftbl; Var L Sftbl; Hon Roll; Educ.

MADAMBA, AARON; Pinelands Regional HS; Mystic Island, NJ; (Y); VP Aud/Vis; CAP; VP Science Clb; Stage Crew; Yrbk Phtg; JV Var Tennis; Comp Pgmng.

MADARA, JAMIE; Overbrook SR HS; Berlin, NJ; (Y); Hon Roll; Camden Cty Coll; Law Enfrcmnt.

MADDOCKS, BRIAN K; Pennsville Memorial HS; Pennsville, NJ; (Y); 1/208; Am Leg Boys St; CAP; Pres Ski Clb; Off Soph Cls; Off Jr Cls; Stu Cncl; Var L Ftbl; Bausch & Lomb Sci Awd; NHS; JV L Trk; NJ Govrnrs Schlr Math & Sci 86; US Air Force Acad; Aerospace.

MADDOX, PATRICIA; St Mary HS; Spotswood, NJ; (Y); 10/127; Church Yth Grp; Library Aide; Spanish Clb; Yrbk Stf; Cheerleading; High Hon Roll; NHS; Spanish NHS.

MADDUX, ERICA; Franklin Twp HS; Somerset, NJ; (Y); 44/313; Chrmn Am Leg Aux Girls St; Pres Church Yth Grp; Rep Stu Cncl; Capt Bowling; Stat Sftbl; JV Stat Tennis; Stat Trk; Frnkln Twp Repblcn Cmmtee Schlrshp Awd 86; Jck & Jll Of Amrca Inc Crl Rbrtsn Awd 86; Hmptn U Schlrs; Hampton U; Poly Sci.

MADERA, PRISCILLA; Cliffside Park HS; Cliffside Pk, NJ; (Y); 11/236; French Clb; Lit Mag; Stu Cncl; JV Crs Cntry; JV Trk; High Hon Roll; Hon Roll; NHS; Slvr, Brnz Mdl Sprng Trck 86; Mdl X-Cntry 86; Cert Hon Soc, Hon Roll 86; Law.

MADIA, JOSEPH; Pt Plsnt Boro HS; Manasquan, NJ; (Y); 25/229; Am Leg Boys St; Drama Clb; Band; Pres Chorus; Concert Band; Madrigals; Mrchg Band; School Play; Variety Show; Lit Mag; Womens Club Drama & Music Schlrshp 86; Old Guard Music Schlrshp 86; U S Best Male Sngr & Actor 86; Beaver Coll; Thtr Arts.

MADNICK, JULIE; Ocean Township HS; Wayside, NJ; (Y); 41/315; French Clb; Key Clb; Ski Clb; Temple Yth Grp; Pres Varsity Clb; Drill Tm; Yrbk Stf; Var Twrlr; High Hon Roll; NHS; Sprtn Schlr-Acadmc Awd 83-86; U Of DE; Bio.

MADURSKA, ELIZABETH; Wallington HS; Wallington, NJ; (Y); Dance Clb; Bergen CC; Bus Compu.

MAESER, KARI; Audubon HS; Mt Ephraim, NJ; (Y); Cheerleading; Sftbl; Hon Roll; Art Awd; Drnk Drvng Cntst 86; Elene Fuld School Nursing; Nrsg.

MAGAZENO, JULIANNE; Wayne Hills HS; Wayne, NJ; (Y); 55/350; FBLA; GAA; Math Clb; Red Cross Aide; Co-Capt Swmmng; Hon Roll; Coaches Awd Swmmng 86; Awd Merit FBLA 86; Cert Recgntn 86; Bus.

MAGBALON, MICHAEL J; Camden Catholic HS; Cherry Hill, NJ; (Y); 1/300; Am Leg Boys St; Computer Clb; English Clb; FBLA; German Clb; VP Spanish Clb; Stage Crew; Var Tennis; JV Trk; Hon Roll; Am Leg Jersey Boys ST 85-86; Engrng.

MAGEE, AMY LYNN; Wayne Hills HS; Wayne, NJ; (Y); 42/310; Pres Church Yth Grp; Dance Clb; Drama Clb; GAA; Girl Scts; Library Aide; Math Clb; Ski Clb; Spanish Clb; School Musical; Grl Sct Gold Awd 84; Willits Fdtn, Untd Meth Wmns Schlrshps 86; Gettysburg Coll; Ed.

MAGEE, BRIAN; Glassboro HS; Glassboro, NJ; (Y); Office Aide; Hon Roll; NHS; Drexel U; Comp Sci.

MAGEE, SEAN; Marine Acad Of Science & Tech; Linden, NJ; (S); 4/24; Boy Scts; Pres Church Yth Grp; Hosp Aide; Key Clb; ROTC; Band; Chorus; Church Choir; Drill Tm; Mrchg Band; Bst Metl Shop Stu 83; Bst Hstry Stu 85; Eagle Sct 85; Naval Acad; Navl Ofcr.

MAGENHEIMER, PATRICIA; Pinelands Regional HS; Tuckerton, NJ; (Y); 5/192; Am Leg Aux Girls St; Science Clb; Spanish Clb; Sec Stu Cncl; JV Cheerleading; Var Capt Tennis; Hon Roll; NHS; Action Word Procssng Prod Mgr 85-86; JR Exec Committee 85-86; Engrng.

MAGI, JILL KARIN; Garden State Acad; Allamuchy, NJ; (Y); 2/25; Church Yth Grp; Pres Ski Clb; Nwsp Ed-Chief; Yrbk Bus Mgr; VP Soph Cls; Rep Sr Cls; Stu Cncl; Capt Gym; High Hon Roll; Pres Schlr; Columbia Union Coll Acad Achvmnt Schlrshp 86; Columbia Union Coll; Mrktng.

MAGLIARO, LORI ANN; Pompton Lakes HS; Pompton Lks, NJ; (Y); 20/150; Cmnty Wkr; Service Clb; Varsity Clb; School Musical; Rep Stu Cncl; Var L Cheerleading; High Hon Roll; Hon Roll; Drama Clb; Spanish Clb; Long Is U CW Pst Acadmc Achvt Awd 86; Safe Rides 86; Long Is U.

MAGNABOUSCO, ROBERT; Hackensack HS; Maywood, NJ; (Y); 106/400; Am Leg Boys St; Boys Clb Am; Golf; Cit Awd; DAR Awd; SAR Awd; VFW Awd; Key Clb; Ski Clb; Varsity Clb; Natl Eagle Scout Assoc 83; Maywood Athltc Clb Schlrshp 86; Unico Natl Schlrshp 86; Marist Coll; Pre-Med.

MAGNANI, KAREN; Metuchen HS; Metuchen, NJ; (Y); RISA Olmzr Mem Schlrshp; Ntl Assoc Of Acctnts Awd; Rider Coll; Bus Admin.

MAGNUSEN, JOAN; Pope John XXIII HS; Wharton, NJ; (Y); Drama Clb; Hosp Aide; Thesps; Band; School Musical; School Play; Lit Mag; High Hon Roll; Hon Roll; Stat Bsktbl; Mst Imprvd Swmmr 85-86; Nrsng.

MAGOS, DEANNA; Washington Twp HS; Sewell, NJ; (Y); Art Clb; Church Yth Grp; Dance Clb; FHA; Hosp Aide; Model UN; Q&S; Spanish Clb; Chorus; JV Cheerleading; Widener U; Htl Mngmnt.

MAGUIRE, CHRISTINE; Hopewell Valley Central HS; Pennington, NJ; (Y); AFS; Church Yth Grp; French Clb; Latin Clb; Church Choir; Lit Mag; JV Gym; JV Tennis; High Hon Roll; Hon Roll.

MAGUOCCHETTI, CATHERINE; Dover HS; Dover, NJ; (Y); 1/190; Am Leg Aux Girls St; Trs Band; Drm Mjr(t); Orch; Yrbk Sprt Ed; VP Stu Cncl; Var L Trk; High Hon Roll; NHS; AFS; Rogate-Toward Satori Awd 84-85; All Area Grls Trck Team 86; All Area Grls Trck Team Hrnb Mntn 85-86; Chem Engr.

MAHABIR, ROBINDRA; Academic HS; Jersey City, NJ; (Y); Art Clb; Spanish Clb; Rep Jr Cls; Rep Stu Cncl; Var Trk; Hon Roll; Acad Interschlstc Tm 85-86; Math.

MAHAFFEY, JENNIFER; Howell HS; Howell, NJ; (Y); 7/371; Var L Bsktbl; Var Capt Sftbl; High Hon Roll; NHS; Wt Lftg; Pres Schlr; Coachs Awd Sftbl 86; Pres Acadmc Fit Awd 86; Omega 13 Schlrshp 86; Rutgers Coll; Engrng.

MAHER, EILEEN; Harrison HS; Bloomfield, NJ; (Y); 16/155; Computer Clb; Co-Capt Crs Cntry; Hon Roll; NHS; Club Awd Span 86; Sanford L Kahn Lds Auxlry 86; Montclair ST Coll.

MAHER, KATHLEEN; Mt St Dominic Acad; Livingston, NJ; (Y); 1/56; Church Yth Grp; Ski Clb; Nwsp Rptr; Sec Soph Cls; Pres Jr Cls; Bausch & Lomb Sci Awd; NHS; St Schlr; St Peters Summr Schlr 85-86; George Washington U Engrg Mdl 86.

MAHER, KRIS; Glen Rock HS; Glen Rock, NJ; (Y); Latin Clb; Science Clb; Ski Clb; Band; Mrchg Band; School Musical; JV Bsktbl; High Hon Roll; Hon Roll; Jr NHS; Pre Med.

MAHER, MAUREEN; Bishop George Ahr HS; Edison, NJ; (Y); French Clb; Girl Scts; Hosp Aide; JV Var Cheerleading; Capt Coach Actv; Hon Roll; Engl.

MAHER, WENDY; Westfield HS; Westfield, NJ; (Y); Latin Clb; Concert Band; Nwsp Stf; Socr; Hon Roll; All ST & All Cnty In Soccer 84-85; Colgate U.

MAHESHWARI, PRAMOD; Manalapan HS; Manalapan, NJ; (Y); 155/417; CAP; Computer Clb; Mrchg Band; Stage Crew; Comp Prgmng.

MAHMOOD, ARSAD; Ferris HS; Jersey City, NJ; (Y); Am Leg Boys St; Boys Clb Am; Computer Clb; Library Aide; Math Clb; Quiz Bowl; Scholastic Bowl; Science Clb; Spanish Clb; Teachers Aide; Sci Awd 83; Hnr Rl Awds 85; Rutgers U; Med.

MAHN, KEVIN; James Caldwell HS; W Caldwell, NJ; (Y); Variety Show; Bsbl; Var Bsktbl; Ftbl; Im Sftbl; High Hon Roll; Hon Roll; Bus Mktg.

MAHON, DEBBIE; Notre Dame HS; Trenton, NJ; (Y); Var L Crs Cntry; Var L Trk; High Hon Roll; Hon Roll; NHS; Ntl Bus Hnr Soc Sec 86-87.

MAHON, MEREDITH; Central Regional HS; Bayville, NJ; (Y); FHA; High Hon Roll; Pre-Med.

MAHONEY, BRIAN; Teaneck HS; Teaneck, NJ; (Y); 72/420; Boy Scts; Church Yth Grp; Hon Roll; NHS; Villanova U; Elec Engnrng.

MAHONEY, KEVIN; Hillsborough HS; Somerville, NJ; (Y); 8/340; Math Tm; Quiz Bowl; ROTC; Science Clb; Rep Jr Cls; Tennis; NHS; Ntl Merit Ltr; Bnkg.

MAHONEY, MAURA; Oak Knoll School Of The Holy Child; Chatham, NJ; (Y); 5/55; Cmnty Wkr; Hosp Aide; Pep Clb; Chorus; Nwsp Stf; Off Jr Cls; Off Sr Cls; Fld Hcky; Lcrss; Hon Roll; All Star Laenosse Fam 86; Oustndng Laenosse Player 86; Biochemistry.

MAHONY, DANNY; Queen Of Peace HS; Rutherford, NJ; (Y); 90/235; Church Yth Grp; Letterman Clb; SADD; Varsity Clb; Rep Jr Cls; Stu Cncl; JV Var Bsbl; JV Var Bsktbl; JV Var Ftbl; Wt Lftg; All Lg Running Back Ftbl 86; Hnrb Mntn Lg Catcher Bsbl 86; Bio.

MAHURTER, LARRY; St Joseph Regional HS; Westwood, NJ; (Y); JV Bsbl; Var Capt Ice Hcky; Criminal Justice Tm; Law.

MAIA, VICTOR; Seton Hall Prep; Hillside, NJ; (Y); French Clb; Key Clb; Im Var Socr; Hon Roll; Engr.

MAIELLO, THOMAS; Bayonne HS; Bayonne, NJ; (Y); Band; Concert Band; Drm & Bgl; Drm Mjr(t); Jazz Band; Mrchg Band; Orch; Drum Majr 83; Rookie Of Yr 83-84; Musc Educ.

MAILLARO, KATHLEEN; Holy Spirit HS; Brigantine, NJ; (Y); 120/400; PAVAS; SADD; Chorus; School Musical; School Play; Stage Crew; Nwsp Bus Mgr; DAR Awd; Wall Street Wiz Awd 82; Cath Dghtrs Amer 83; Knights Of Columbia 83; Rutgers; Comm.

MAIN, LYNNAIA; Egg Harbor Township HS; Cardiff, NJ; (S); 4/317; French Clb; GAA; Ski Clb; Color Guard; Nwsp Rptr; Sec Jr Cls; Rep Stu Cncl; Jr NHS; Acad Ltr 85; Intl Affairs.

MAINIERO, JOHN; Sacred Heart HS; Vineland, NJ; (Y); Camera Clb; Church Yth Grp; Dance Clb; School Musical; School Play; Yrbk Phtg; Yrbk Rptr; Yrbk Stf; Tennis; Bus Admin.

MAIO, KRISTIN; Paramus HS; Paramus, NJ; (Y); 180/360; FBLA; Spanish Clb; Yrbk Stf; Rep Frsh Cls; Rep Soph Cls; Rep Jr Cls; Rep Sr Cls; Stu Cncl; Var Capt Sftbl; Vllybl; 1st Tm All Leg Sftbl 86; 2nd Tm All Brgn Co; 1st Tm All Subrn Mst Vlbl Plyr Tm MVP; Quinnipiac Coll; Mrktng.

MAJEWSKI, CHET; Woodbridge HS; Fords, NJ; (Y); 36/396; Quiz Bowl; Band; Concert Band; Jazz Band; Mrchg Band; Pep Band; Rep Soph Cls; Rep Jr Cls; Var Socr; VP NHS; Engr.

MAJEWSKI, DAVID W; Christian Brothers Acad; Leonardo, NJ; (Y); 98/220; Church Yth Grp; Varsity Clb; JV Bsktbl; Var L Trk; Hon Roll; First Aid Sqd.

MAJMUDAR, KAUSHAL; St Peters Prep; Jersey City, NJ; (Y); 6/250; Chess Clb; Pres Church Yth Grp; Computer Clb; Science Clb; High Hon Roll; Ntl Merit Ltr; Prfct Atten Awd; Smmr Copm Based Physics Pgm Schrlshp; MA Inst Tech; Comp Engr.

MAJMUDAR, PARAG; Bloomfieldd HS; Bloomfield, NJ; (Y); 2/442; Am Leg Boys St; Hosp Aide; Key Clb; Quiz Bowl; Scholastic Bowl; Temple Yth Grp; Chorus; Trk; Gov Hon Prg Awd; NHS; Med.

MAJOR, VICTORIA; Waldwick HS; Waldwick, NJ; (Y); Church Yth Grp; Spanish Clb; Variety Show; Rep Stu Cncl; Var JV Cheerleading; Powder Puff Ftbl; Var JV Socr; Bus Awd Typng II Clss; Sprts Queen Rnnr-Up; Bus.

MAJURY, KIMBERLEY S; Brick Memorial HS; Brick, NJ; (Y); 10/307; Am Leg Aux Girls St; Pres Church Yth Grp; VP Frsh Cls; Sec Stu Cncl; Stat Bsbl; Var Tennis; High Hon Roll; VP NHS; Voice Dem Awd; Key Clb; Natl Presbyterian Schlr; ST Stu Cncl Exec Brd; Eckerd Coll; Bus Law.

MAKAROW, TIM; Millville SR HS; Millville, NJ; (Y); Chess Clb; PAVAS; Concert Band; Jazz Band; Variety Show; Hon Roll.

MAKO, EVA; Burl Co Vo-Tech HS; Roebling, NJ; (Y); 1/200; Am Leg Aux Girls St; Pres Exploring; Scholastic Bowl; Speech Tm; VP VICA; Im Socr; Im JV Sftbl; Tennis; Im Vllybl; Cit Awd; Rtgrs Schlr Pgm 86; Explr Achvmnt Awd 86; 3rd Pl Stu Crftsmn Fr 86; VO-TAG 86; Drexel U; Engnrng.

MAKOWSKI, KIM; Weehawken HS; Weehawken, NJ; (S); Flag Corp; Nwsp Stf; Yrbk Stf; Lit Mag; Rep Frsh Cls; Pres Soph Cls; Pres Jr Cls; Rep Stu Cncl; Var Twrlr; Hon Roll; Fashion Inst Of Tech; Fshn Buyr.

MALANGA, JOHN; Immaculate Conception HS; Neward, NJ; (Y); Boy Scts; School Musical; Var Bsbl; Var Ftbl; Im Gym; Im Wt Lftg; Capt Var Wrstlng; Hon Roll; Acctng.

MALATESTA, ALICIA; Neumann Prep HS; Paterson, NJ; (Y); 5/82; Church Yth Grp; SADD; Church Choir; Yrbk Stf; Lit Mag; Capt Var Bsktbl; Capt Var Vllybl; Pres Schlr; Spanish NHS; Duquesne, Hofstra, Coll Mt ST Vincnt Schlrshps 86; Excllnc Spnsh Awd 86; Acadmc Al-Amercn Schlr 84-86; Duquesne U; Intl Bus.

MALDONADO, IVETTE; John F Kennedy HS; Paterson, NJ; (S); Church Yth Grp; Girl Scts; Hosp Aide; Library Aide; Chorus; Church Choir; Valley Hosp Schl Of Radlgy; Rad.

MALDONY, MAURA; Mother Seton Reg HS; Edison, NJ; (Y); 21/120; Art Clb; Hosp Aide; School Play; Yrbk Stf; Lit Mag; Rep Soph Cls; Art.

MALDONY, STEVE; Sayreville War Memorial HS; S Amboy, NJ; (Y); 33/379; Math Clb; Band; Stage Crew; NHS; Blue Bdg Assn #1 86-87; U Of DE; Comp Info Sci.

MALESICH, RICHARD C; Camden Catholic HS; Cherry Hill, NJ; (Y); 80/295; Am Leg Boys St; Computer Clb; German Clb; Political Wkr; Science Clb; Stage Crew; Hon Roll; Villanova; Bus.

MALESKI, KARINA; Weehawken HS; Weehawken, NJ; (Y); 3/90; Band; Rep Soph Cls; Rep Sr Cls; CC Awd; Hon Roll; Masonic Awd; NHS.

MALETTO, JAMES; Shore Regional HS; W Long Branch, NJ; (Y); Var Bsbl; James Maletto.

MALINCHAK, TRICIA; John F Kennedy HS; Paterson, NJ; (Y); Nwsp Rptr; Nwsp Sprt Ed; Yrbk Rptr; Yrbk Stf; Rep Frsh Cls; Rep Soph Cls; Rep Jr Cls; Rep Sr Cls; Hon Roll; NHS; Montclair St Coll.

MALINOWSKI, ROBERT A; Piscatoway Vocational & Tech HS; Piscataway, NJ; (Y); Teachers Aide; Var Bsbl; Var Bsktbl; Var Socr; Hon Roll; Grtr Middlesex Conf All-Acad Hnr Rl 85-86; MVP Bsbl Vrsty 84-85; Hnrbl Mnth Judges Acad Culinry 84-85; Atlatnic CC; Culinary Arts.

MALISOFF, MICHAEL; Vail-Deane Schl; Elizabeth, NJ; (Y); 1/14; Teachers Aide; Concert Band; School Musical; High Hon Roll; French Clb; Math Tm; Rptr Nwsp Rptr; Nwsp Stf; Yrbk Stf; Hstry Awd-Excllnc 85-86; Hghst Avg Awd 83-85; French Awd 84-86; Wstrn Cvlztn Awd-Excllnc 84-85; Kean Coll; Musician.

MALLEK, GREGORY S; Bernards HS; Bernardsville, NJ; (Y); Church Yth Grp; Varsity Clb; Mrchg Band; Orch; School Musical; Symp Band; Ftbl; Trk; Hon Roll; Gov Schl NJ Arts Div 85; Goldblatt Comptn Winds Brass 85; Awardee Ntl Found Adv Arts 86; Northwestern; Music.

MALLETT JR, ARTHUR N; Middletown North HS; Port Monmouth, NJ; (Y); Am Leg Boys St; Band; Concert Band; Jazz Band; Mrchg Band; Var Swmmng; High Hon Roll; NHS; Hgh Hnrs Acad Awd 84; Engrng Sci.

MALLETT, PETER; Cinnaminson HS; Cinna, NJ; (Y); Church Yth Grp; DECA; FBLA; Ski Clb; SADD; Trk; Hon Roll; 3rd Pl Wnnr Ovrll In ST Shplftng Cmpgn 86; Dist Ectn Clbs Of Amer Awd 86; Bus Adm.

MALLON, JOHN; Hightstown HS; E Windsor, NJ; (Y); 77/149; Church Yth Grp; Cmnty Wkr; Ski Clb; Ftbl; JV Socr; High Hon Roll; Hon Roll; Cabinet Making.

MALLON, WILLIAM; Roselle Catholic HS; Roselle, NJ; (S); Boy Scts; Drama Clb; Math Clb; Ski Clb; School Musical; School Play; Stage Crew; Var Capt Golf; Var Swmmng; Hon Roll.

MALONE, AMY C; De Paul Diocesan HS; Pompton Plains, NJ; (S); 18/170; JCL; Science Clb; Pres Jr Cls; Var Capt Bsktbl; Var Capt Sftbl; Im Vllybl; High Hon Roll; NHS; Pres Schlr; St Schlr; Cert Outstndng Achvt Eng Lit 85; Acad All Am Schlr 86; Loyola Coll Pres Schlrshp 86; Loyola Coll; Pre-Med.

MALONE, BETH; Camden HS; Camden, NJ; (Y); 89/400; Variety Show; Rep Stu Cncl; Im Bsktbl; Im Vllybl; Hon Roll; FBLA Awd 86; Rutgers U; Bus Mgmt.

MALONE, JENNIFER; Marylawn Of The Oranges HS; W Orange, NJ; (Y); 10/53; Art Clb; School Musical; Stage Crew; Lit Mag; High Hon Roll; NHS; Natl Educ Dev Tests Awd 84-85; Hghst Cls Avg Art, Rlgn & Alg II 86.

MALONE, STEVEN A; Triton Regional HS; Glendora, NJ; (Y); 3/310; Am Leg Boys St; Science Clb; Im Capt Bowling; High Hon Roll; NHS; Ntl Merit Ltr; St Schlr; Rtry Clb Schlrshp 86; Natl Hnr Soc Schlrshp 86; Vtd-Mst Studious By Cls 86; Drexel U; Elec Engrng.

MALONEY, BARBARA; Immaculate Conception HS; Wood-Ridge, NJ; (Y); Church Yth Grp; Girl Scts; Hosp Aide; Trs SADD; Church Choir; School Musical; Stage Crew; Outstndng Svc As A JR Vlntr 85; William Paterson Clg; Nrsng.

MALONEY, CATHY; Lodi HS; Lodi, NJ; (Y); Key Clb; VP Leo Clb; Pep Clb; Varsity Clb; Mgr Variety Show; Rep Frsh Cls; Rep Soph Cls; Rep Jr Cls; Var JV Cheerleading; Stat Trk; SOC Sci.

MALONEY, CHRIS; Paul VI HS; Haddon Field, NJ; (Y); 224/530; Boy Scts; Church Yth Grp; Var Co-Capt Crs Cntry; Var Trk; Effort Awd 85; Temple U; Hstry-Ed Tchr.

MALONEY, CHRISTINE; Toms River HS South; Pine Beach, NJ; (Y); Band; Mrchg Band; Symp Band; Yrbk Stf; JV Var Bsktbl; High Hon Roll; Hon Roll; NHS; Elem Ed.

MALONEY, PATRICIA; Queen Of Peace HS; Wood Ridge, NJ; (Y); 14/231; Hosp Aide; Math Clb; School Musical; School Play; Nwsp Rptr; Yrbk Stf; Rep Jr Cls; Var Socr; High Hon Roll; NHS; Hghst Hnrs; Biotechnlgy.

MALOY, MARCY; Wayne Valley HS; Wayne, NJ; (Y); 80/320; FBLA; JCL; Latin Clb; Temple Yth Grp; JV Bsktbl; Var L Crs Cntry; Var L Trk; Hon Roll; Ntl Merit Ltr; Ntl Ltn Hrn Soc 83-86; All Cnf Trk 85; Cum Laude Cert Ntl Latn Exm 86; Boston U; Pre Law.

MALOY, RICHARD; Matawan Regional HS; Matawan, NJ; (S); 26/302; Cmnty Wkr; Ski Clb; Spanish Clb; Var Bsbl; Var Ftbl; JV Trk; Im Wt Lftg; Hon Roll; Baseball.

MALSBURY, ANN; Hamilton HS; Trenton, NJ; (Y); 8/307; Aud/Vis; Key Clb; Nwsp Ed-Chief; Stu Cncl; Sec NHS; Pres Schlr; Rotary Awd; St Schlr; Cmnty Wkr; Chorus; Induction Into Rutgers Hnrs Prgm 86; Elma R Borden Schlrshp; IASC Schlrshp; Rutgers U; Engl.

MALTESE, MARGARET ANN; Bridgewater-Raritan HS West; Raritan, NJ; (Y); 90/294; Church Yth Grp; Math Tm; Pres Science Clb; Nwsp Stf; Ed Yrbk Sprt Ed; Jr Cls; Sr Cls; JV Tennis; High Hon Roll; Hon Roll; Pres Acadmc Ftnss Awd 85-86; Sci Leag Cert Of Partcptn 85-86; Math Leag Cert Of Merit 85-86; Rutgers College; Phrmcy.

MALTOSZ, RENATA; Linden HS; Linden, NJ; (Y); Camera Clb; Key Clb; Spanish Clb; Church Choir; Yrbk Phtg; Yrbk Sprt Ed; Yrbk Stf; Debate Tm; Yrbk Rptr; Wt Lftg; Montclair.

MALVASIA, DAWN; Paramus Catholic HS; Little Ferry, NJ; (Y); 46/157; Church Yth Grp; Var Cheerleading; JV Sftbl; Hon Roll; Ring Ceremony Comm Photo Section; Dream Clb; William Paterson Coll; Hlth Sci.

MALZONE, ROSANNA; Hawthorne HS; Hawthorne, NJ; (Y); 13/157; Intnl Clb; Yrbk Phtg; Lit Mag; Rep Stu Cncl; High Hon Roll; Hon Roll; NHS; Prfct Atten Awd; Distngushd Engl Stu Awd 86; Soc Studies Dept Awd 86; Congrsnl Sem 86; William Paterson Coll; Psychlgy.

MAMMANA, TINA; Freehold Township HS; Freehold, NJ; (Y); Dance Clb; School Play; Swing Chorus; Sftbl; Hon Roll; Dance.

MAMOLA, NINA; Mahwah HS; Mahwah, NJ; (Y); French Clb; Key Clb; Pep Clb; Teachers Aide; Yrbk Stf; Cheerleading; Score Keeper; Trk; Wt Lftg; High Hon Roll; Phy Ed Achvt Awd 86; Chrldng Awds 85; FIT; Fshn.

MAMOLA, RACHELA; Toms River HS East; Toms River, NJ; (Y); 2/586; Math Clb; Spanish Clb; Concert Band; Drm Mjr(t); Mrchg Band; Powder Puff Ftbl; JV Trk; High Hon Roll; NHS; Acad All Amer 86; Comp Sci.

MANABIANCO, MANNY; Emerson HS; Union City, NJ; (Y); Ski Clb; Teachers Aide; School Play; Stage Crew; Variety Show; Stu Cncl; Bsbl; Bowling; Ftbl; Mgr(s).

MANCINELLI, DIANA; Washington Township HS; Turnersville, NJ; (Y); DECA; High Hon Roll; Hon Roll; Bus.

MANCINI, LEIGH; Wall HS; Wall, NJ; (S); 10/256; German Clb; Ski Clb; School Musical; Stage Crew; Var Capt Tennis; High Hon Roll; Hon Roll; NHS; St Schlr.

MANCUSO, WILLIAM; Parsippany HS; Lk Hiawatha, NJ; (Y); 31/320; Am Leg Boys St; Church Yth Grp; Pres FBLA; SADD; Var L Bsktbl; Hon Roll; NHS; Pres Schlr; Natl Assn Accountants 86; Mr Future Bus Ldr Am 2nd 86; FBLA Awd 86; Trenton ST Coll; Acctg.

MANDAK, GREGORY; Clifton SR HS; Clifton, NJ; (Y); 1/687; Am Leg Boys St; Trs Computer Clb; Math Clb; Office Aide; Science Clb; Var Capt Lcrss; Hon Roll; Jr NHS; Tlntd & Gftd Prgm 84-86; Rogate Prgm 84; Engrng.

MANDEL, ALYSE; Montville HS; Pine Brook, NJ; (Y); Key Clb; Ski Clb; Temple Yth Grp; Yrbk Stf; Rep Frsh Cls; Off Soph Cls; Rep Jr Cls; Rep Sr Cls; Stu Cncl; Cheerleading; Bus.

MANDEL, GLENN; Fairlawn HS; Fairlawn, NJ; (Y); Off Frsh Cls; Off Soph Cls; Off Sr Cls; JV Socr; JV Tennis; Hon Roll; Law.

MANDEL, WENDY; Parsippany HS; Lake Hiawatha, NJ; (Y); FBLA; Pep Clb; Service Clb; Spanish Clb; Temple Yth Grp; Lit Mag; JV Bsktbl; JV Tennis; JV Trk; Hon Roll.

MANETTA, THERESA; Bishop Ahr St Thomas HS; Carteret, NJ; (Y); Band; Concert Band; Drm Mjr(t); Jazz Band; Mrchg Band; School Musical; Symp Band; Girl Scts; Hosp Aide; ROTC; Otstndng Perf By A Dancer Drama Awd 86; 2nd Pl In Gold Cup Schlrshp Dncng Achvt 86; Dancing.

MANGALICK, ANOOP; Livingston HS; Livingston, NJ; (Y); 16/496; Chrmn Debate Tm; Math Clb; Math Tm; Trk; CC Awd; NHS; Cornell U; Comp Sci Mjr.

MANGAN, JENNIFER; Roselle Catholic HS; Roselle, NJ; (Y); 32/195; Drama Clb; Church Choir; Lit Mag; French Hon Soc; High Hon Roll; NHS; School Musical; Stage Crew; Hon Roll.

MANGAN, SEAN; Washington Twp HS; Sewell, NJ; (Y); Model UN; Var Crs Cntry; Var Trk.

MANGER, DIANE A; West Orange HS; W Orange, NJ; (Y); 50/177; French Clb; Pep Clb; Chorus; Variety Show; Yrbk Stf; Frsh Cls; Soph Cls; Stu Cncl; French Hon Soc; Hon Roll; Sci Expo Awd 85; Fash Inst Tech; Intr Desgn.

MANGIERI, LISA; Bergerfield HS; Bergenfield, NJ; (Y); 90/306; Spanish Clb; Mat Maids; Stat Trk; JV Vllybl; Hon Roll; Berkeley; Exec Sec.

MANGO, WAYNE J; Triton HS; Blackwood, NJ; (Y); 59/350; Rutgers U; Comp Prog.

MANGONE, CHRISTOPHER A; Hillsborough HS; Belle Mead, NJ; (Y); 23/300; Church Yth Grp; 4-H; Ski Clb; Trk; 4-H Awd; Hon Roll; NHS; Math.

MANIGLIA, ANN; Penns Grove HS; Carneys Point, NJ; (Y); 10/145; Church Yth Grp; Band; Chorus; School Play; Yrbk Stf; Stu Cncl; Sftbl; Co-Capt Tennis; Hon Roll; Pres NHS; Old Dominion U; Physcl Thrpy.

MANION, BARRY; Sussex County Vo-Tech; Stockholm, NJ; (Y); School Musical; School Play; Stage Crew; Recdng Artst.

MANISCALCO, MARY M; Freehold Boro HS; Freehold, NJ; (Y); 1/208; Girl Scts; Hosp Aide; Nwsp Ed-Chief; Trs Jr Cls; Stat Ftbl; Pres NHS; Val; Exploring; Yrbk Stf; Off Stu Cncl; Japan-Us Senate Exchng Schlrsp 85; Girl Scout Gold Awd 85; Silver Congrssnl Awd 86; Duke U; Pblc Policy Hlth.

MANKOWSKI, KEN; Delran HS; Delran, NJ; (Y); 46/214; Computer Clb; FBLA; Hon Roll; Prfct Atten Awd; Comp Sci.

MANLEY JR, JAMES LAWRENCE; Oratory Prep; Berkeley Hts, NJ; (Y); Service Clb; Ski Clb; Nwsp Rptr; Yrbk Stf; Var L Bsktbl; Var Capt Golf; Hon Roll; Bus.

MANLULU, CONSTANTINE; St John Vianney HS; Freehold, NJ; (Y); Computer Clb; Library Aide; Camp Fr Inc; Mrchg Band; Hon Roll; Med.

MANN, EDWARD; River Dell SR HS; Oradell, NJ; (S); Temple Yth Grp; Band; Concert Band; Jazz Band; Mrchg Band; Orch; Symp Band; High Hon Roll; Hon Roll; JP Sousa Awd.

MANNING, DAWN F; E Orange HS; E Orange, NJ; (S); 15/404; Debate Tm; Math Clb; Band; Nwsp Rptr; VP Stu Cncl; JV Var Bsktbl; Capt Var Sftbl; Hon Roll; Prfct Atten Awd; Pres Schlr; Pol Sci.

MANNING, DIANA; Wayne Valley HS; Wayne, NJ; (Y); 30/323; Church Yth Grp; French Clb; Model UN; Ski Clb; Nwsp Stf; Yrbk Sprt Ed; High Hon Roll; NHS; Ntl Merit Schol; St Schlr; Rutgers Coll; Polit Sci.

MANNING, GREGORY; Bayley Ellard HS; Whippany, NJ; (Y); 15/91; Am Leg Boys St; Church Yth Grp; Model UN; Capt L Socr; Var L Wrstlng; Hon Roll; Coaches Awd Soccr 86; Engrng.

MANSKOPF, BRITTA; Rutherford HS; Rutherford, NJ; (S); Key Clb; Varsity Clb; Yrbk Stf; Rep Frsh Cls; Rep Soph Cls; Rep Jr Cls; Var JV Bsktbl; Var Capt Crs Cntry; High Hon Roll; JV Capt Sftbl.

MANSONET, ALEXANDRA; Perth Amboy HS; Perth Amboy, NJ; (Y); 20/200; Sec Church Yth Grp; Dance Clb; Drama Clb; Office Aide; Spanish Clb; Chorus; Church Choir; Rep Jr Cls; Cit Awd; Hon Roll; Psych.

MANTEAU, JOANN; Toms River High School North; Toms River, NJ; (Y); 89/398; VP Key Clb; Q&S; Science Clb; SADD; Stage Crew; Yrbk Stf; Lit Mag; Hon Roll; Glassboro ST Coll; Fine Art.

MANTEN, KAREN; Highland Regional HS; Blackwood, NJ; (Y); Hon Roll; Cmdn Cnty Lgl Sectys Schlrshp 86; Omega Institute; Secty.

MANTZAVINOS, SPIROS G; James Caldwell HS; Caldwell, NJ; (Y); 58/266; Am Leg Boys St; Church Yth Grp; Band; Concert Band; Orch; Stage Crew; Var Trk; Hon Roll; St Johns Dist Oratorical Fest Hon Men 85; AHEPA Schlrshp 86; Ladys Scty Sts Constantine & Helen 86; Muhlenberg Coll; Bus.

MANUTTI, JACQUELINE; St Rose HS; Belmar, NJ; (Y); 30/206; Art Clb; Key Clb; School Play; Nwsp Stf; Ed Yrbk Stf; Lit Mag; Kiwanis Awd; NHS; Rep Frsh Cls; Rep Soph Cls; Alternate Delegate Girls Ctznshp Prgm 85; Artwork Chosen For The Teen Arts Fstvl 84-86; U Of DE; Visual Comm.

MANZELLA, DAWN; John F Kennedy HS; Willingboro, NJ; (Y); Hosp Aide; Office Aide; Hon Roll; Nrsg.

MANZO, JOSEPH M; Roselle Park HS; Roselle Park, NJ; (Y); Am Leg Boys St; Radio Clb; SADD; Band; Concert Band; Jazz Band; Mrchg Band; School Musical; Var L Tennis; Hon Roll; Princeton; Law.

MANZONI, DIANNA; Paulsboro HS; Paulsboro, NJ; (Y); 1/135; Pres VP Stu Cncl; L Capt Crs Cntry; Capt L Trk; NHS; Val; Drama Clb; Office Aide; Soroptimist; Band; Church Choir; NJ Schlr 85; Hmcmng Qn 85; NJ Schlr Athl Awd 86; Naval Ofcr.

MARABLE, JAMEELA; Frank H Morrell HS; Irvington, NJ; (Y); FBLA; GAA; Girl Scts; VP Key Clb; Pres SADD; Teachers Aide; Capt Drill Tm; Rep Frsh Cls; Rep Soph Cls; Rep Jr Cls; Twnshp Offcl Awd 86; Vllybl Awd 86; Engr.

MARANDINO, GINA; Sacred Heart HS; Minotola, NJ; (S); 15/67; French Clb; Sec FNA; Hosp Aide; School Play; Yrbk Stf; Cheerleading; Crs Cntry; High Hon Roll; Hon Roll; 1st Pl Millville Run Wmns Div 85; Nrs.

MARANDINO, PAM; Sacred Heart HS; Vineland, NJ; (S); 3/67; VP Spanish Clb; Yrbk Stf; Rep Jr Cls; Trs Stu Cncl; Cheerleading; Crs Cntry; Sftbl; Trs NHS; Ntl Hist Gov Awd; Acad All Am; Ldrshp Merit Awd; Glassboro ST Coll; Ed.

MARANO, JAMES P; David Brearley Reg HS; Garwood, NJ; (Y); 9/165; Am Leg Boys St; Bsbl; Bowling; Crs Cntry; Trk; Vllybl; Hon Roll; VFW Awd; Athl Adm.

MARAZITI, DEBORAH; Morris Catholic HS; Boonton, NJ; (Y); 1/150; Drama Clb; Girl Scts; Hosp Aide; Chorus; Capt Color Guard; School Musical; School Play; High Hon Roll; Pres NHS; Ntl Merit Ltr; Astrophyscs.

MARAZITI, JACQUELINE; Chatham Township HS; Chatham Twp, NJ; (Y); 20/137; Girl Scts; Key Clb; Model UN; Pep Clb; Yrbk Bus Mgr; Stat Bsktbl; JV Lcrss; JV Trk; Hon Roll; NHS.

MARBLESTONE, ALAN; Parsippany HS; Parsippany, NJ; (S); Boy Scts; NFL; Concert Band; Drm & Bgl; Drm Mjr(t); Jazz Band; Mrchg Band; School Musical; Trk; Hon Roll; PTA NJ Cultural Enrichmnt Awd 85; NJ Area Band 85.

MARCAZZO, JULIET REBECCA; Marylawn Of The Oranges HS; Hoboken, NJ; (Y); Drama Clb; Service Clb; Chorus; School Musical; Stage Crew; Lit Mag; Rep Jr Cls; Sec Sr Cls; Intl Stu Ldrshp Inst Notre Dame 85; Schlrshp Oberlin Thetre Inst 86; Cmpl Intl Stu Ldrshp Inst 86; Arts.

MARCEL, JOSEPH R; Kittatinny Regional HS; Newton, NJ; (Y); 26/229; Math Tm; Scholastic Bowl; JV Var Bsktbl; Var Capt Socr; Var Trk; High Hon Roll; Hon Roll; NHS; MVP Track 86; All Leag Trck & Sccr 84-86; Comp Sci.

MARCHESELLO, ANNA; Sussex County Vo-Tech HS; Hamburg, NJ; (S); 16/178; Drama Clb; Spanish Clb; Varsity Clb; School Play; Yrbk Ed-Chief; Yrbk Stf; Pres Soph Cls; Rep Jr Cls; Rep Sr Cls; Rep Stu Cncl; Mip Vrsty Sftbl 85; Intl Bus.

MARCHETTI, DENISE L; Kingsway Regional HS; Clarksboro, NJ; (Y); 10/163; GAA; Pres Sr Cls; Var Bsktbl; Capt Powder Puff Ftbl; Var Capt Sftbl; Var Capt Tennis; Cit Awd; Hon Roll; Pres NHS; Womens Guild Pre-Med Schlrshp; Seton Hall Acdmc Schlrshp; Seton Hall U; Pre-Med.

MARCI, LYNN; Carteret HS; Carteret, NJ; (Y); 38/198; English Clb; Science Clb; Acpl Chr; Concert Band; Mrchg Band; Bsktbl; Crs Cntry; Mgr(s); Trk; Hon Roll; Coaches Assoc Awd Wntr Trk 86; Gtr Mdlsx Cnfrnc All Acad Hnr Rl 85-86; Nj Intrschlstc Athltc Assoc 86; Med.

MARCINCZYK, MARTIN J; Toms River HS; Beachwood, NJ; (Y); 18/362; Math Tm; Science Clb; Ski Clb; Im Bsbl; Var Capt Ice Hcky; NHS.

MARCOU, MARIA; West Orange HS; W Orange, NJ; (Y); Church Yth Grp; Dance Clb; Drama Clb; Yrbk Stf; Ed.

MARCOZZI, DAVID E; Bishop Eustace Prep; Cinnaminson, NJ; (Y); Am Leg Boys St; Church Yth Grp; Spanish Clb; Pres SADD; Nwsp Sprt Ed; VP Jr Cls; Golf; Socr; Trs NHS; Nwsp Phtg; Med.

MARCUS, NINA; Hightstown HS; E Windsor, NJ; (Y); 51/343; Ski Clb; Yrbk Stf; Rep Frsh Cls; Rep Soph Cls; Rep Jr Cls; Rep Sr Cls; Rep Stu Cncl; L Mgr(s); Powder Puff Ftbl; Rutgers Coll; Orthpdc Surgeon.

MARCUSSEN, JENNIFER; Roselle Catholic HS; Roselle, NJ; (S); Drama Clb; Ski Clb; Socr; Swmmng; Hon Roll; Profcncy Span Awd 85; Biol.

MARDER, MELISSA; Holy Cross HS; Browns Mills, NJ; (Y); Drama Clb; Spanish Clb; Band; Jazz Band; School Musical; Lit Mag; Vllybl; Wt Lftg; Hon Roll; AAHPER Awd Phy Fitnss 83-84; Outstndng Pgm Ms Amer Co-Ed, ST Fnlst 85; Rutgers; Marine Bio.

MAREK, ANNEMARIE; St Dominic Acad; Jersey City, NJ; (Y); 3/135; Computer Clb; Pres GAA; Ski Clb; Chorus; Yrbk Bus Mgr; Pres Frsh Cls; Var Capt Swmmng; Var Capt Tennis; High Hon Roll; VP NHS; Boston Coll; Bus.

MARESCA, JAMES; Holy Cross HS; Marlton, NJ; (Y); Boy Scts; Church Yth Grp; Art Clb; Letterman Clb; Ski Clb; Varsity Clb; Rep Frsh Cls; Var Ftbl; Stat Wt Lftg; Hon Roll; Bench Press Champ 86; Rutgers; Bus.

MARESCA, KAREN; Secaucus HS; Secaucus, NJ; (Y); Var Cheerleading; Hon Roll; Rutgers U; Nrsng.

MARGOLIES, TRACIE; Collegiate Schl; W Paterson, NJ; (S); 1/17; Math Tm; Stat Bsktbl; Var Vllybl; High Hon Roll; Chess Clb; French Clb; Quiz Bowl; Teachers Aide; Yrbk Stf; Bowling; NJ Dstngshd Schlr 86-87; Congrssnl Schlr 85-86; Rutgers U; Indstrl Engrng.

MARGOLIS, MICHAEL ARAM; Livingston HS; Livingston, NJ; (Y); 17/496; Model UN; Orch; Symp Band; Yrbk Stf; Wt Lftg; High Hon Roll; Jr NHS; NHS; Ntl Merit Schol; Stanford U.

MARHOEFER, MICHELLE; A L Johnson Regional HS; Clark, NJ; (Y); 61/200; German Clb; Band; Concert Band; Stu Cncl; Var Bsktbl; Var Swmmng; High Hon Roll; Phy Ftnss Awd; AATG Natl Ger Tst Lvl III; Delta Epsilon Phi; Frgn Lang.

MARIANI, FRANCESCA; Hillsborough HS; Neshanic, NJ; (Y); Church Yth Grp; Latin Clb; Yrbk Stf; Var Trk; Hon Roll; NHS; Biolgcl Sci.

MARIANI, ROBERT; Don Bosca Prep HS; Thiells, NY; (Y); 48/250; Boy Scts; Ftbl; Eagle Scout 86; Fordham U; Engrng.

MARICHAK, DANICA; Hillsborough HS; Flemington, NJ; (Y); 92/300; Sec Trs 4-H; Library Aide; Pep Clb; Quiz Bowl; 4-H Awd; Smrst Cnty 4-H Eqstrn Of Yr 86; ST Chmpn Hrs Jdgng Tm 86; NJ Rep-2 Ntl Hrs Jdgng Comptitns 85; Douglass Coll; Bus Adm.

MARIE, CATHERINE JEAN; Vaislburg HS; Newark, NJ; (Y); Church Yth Grp; Drama Clb; Teachers Aide; Chorus; Church Choir; Cazenovia Coll; Bus Mgmt.

MARIN, GLADYS M; Essex County Voc-Tech HS; Newark, NJ; (Y); FBLA; Rep Jr Cls; Stu Cncl; Sftbl; Best Defns Sftbl 86; Glassboro ST Clg; Comm.

MARINACCIO, LISA; Toms River H S North; Toms River, NJ; (Y); 59/412; Pres VP 4-H; Key Clb; Ski Clb; Spanish Clb; Chorus; School Musical; School Play; Yrbk Stf; Off Soph Cls; Off Jr Cls.

MARINELLI, JON; Hackettstown HS; Hackettstown, NJ; (Y); Boy Scts; Ski Clb; Chorus; Rep Stu Cncl; JV Ftbl; JV Capt Socr; JV Trk; JV Capt Wrstlng; Hon Roll; NHS; Yale; Crpt Law.

MARINHO, ROSELINDA; Harrison HS; Harrison, NJ; (Y); 14/167; Art Clb; Computer Clb; Drama Clb; Science Clb; Ski Clb; Stage Crew; Swmmng; High Hon Roll; NHS; Prfct Atten Awd; PTA Ed Grnt 86; E Nwrk Blue Td Bstr Clb Grnt 86; Mst Valuable Plr For Grls V Swm Tm 86; Rutgers Coll New Brnswck; Bio.

MARINKOVIC, PETRIJA; Mary Help HS; Paterson, NJ; (S); 16/88; Computer Clb; Hosp Aide; Nwsp Stf; Var Vllybl; Hon Roll; Prfct Atten Awd; Ltrmn Sweater 85; Span Awd Span I & II 84 & 85; Wrld Hist I & II 84 & 85.

MARINO, CHRISTOPHER; Cherry Hill West HS; Cherry Hill, NJ; (Y); 1/325; Am Leg Boys St; Thesps; Drm Mjr(t); School Musical; Symp Band; Nwsp Ed-Chief; Off Frsh Cls; Off Soph Cls; Off Jr Cls; Off Sr Cls; All ST Orch/Oboe-NJ 85-86; Engrng.

MARINO, FRANK; Toms River HS East; Toms River, NJ; (Y); Church Yth Grp; Stage Crew; Socr; Hghst Subj Avr Math 82-83, Sci, Spnsh II 83-84; De Vry; Elec Engrng.

MARINO, JOSEPHINE; Nutley HS; Nutley, NJ; (Y); 20/335; Church Yth Grp; Spanish Clb; Yrbk Phtg; Bsktbl; Hon Roll; NHS; Chem Engrng.

MARINO, MARC; Cumberland Regional HS; Bridgeton, NJ; (S); 10/369; Intnl Clb; Var Bsbl; Var Ftbl; Im Wt Lftg; High Hon Roll; NHS; Engrng.

MARINO, MICHAEL; West Essex SR HS; Fairfield, NJ; (Y); Pres Band; Concert Band; Drm Mjr(t); Jazz Band; Pres Mrchg Band; Pres Frsh Cls; Stu Cncl; Hon Roll; Herald News Carrier Yr 83; Bus.

MARINO, PAUL; Saint John Vianney HS; Matawan, NJ; (Y); 91/270; Bsbl; Bsktbl; Golf; Hon Roll; Bus.

MARINO, SUSAN; Pascack Hills HS; Woodcliff Lk, NJ; (Y); Church Yth Grp; Cmnty Wkr; Office Aide; Chorus; Lit Mag; Bsktbl; Hon Roll; Intl Fince.

MARINO, THERESA; Summit HS; Morristown, NJ; (Y); Pres Art Clb; Church Yth Grp; Drama Clb; French Clb; Chorus; School Musical; School Play; Nwsp Rptr; Nwsp Stf; Lit Mag; Awd Mntng 4.0 Avrg Bio 85.

MARINZOLI, ANTHONY R; Madison Central HS; Old Bridge, NJ; (Y); 1/360; Scholastic Bowl; Varsity Clb; School Play; Yrbk Phtg; Pres Stu Cncl; Trk; Elks Awd; Gov Hon Prg Awd; NHS; Val; Festa Italiana Schlrp 86; Walter Gural Mem Schlrp 86; Georgetown Sch Frgn Svc; Law.

MARION, ELLEN; Middletown H S South; Lincroft, NJ; (Y); Cmnty Wkr; French Clb; Math Clb; Flag Corp; Yrbk Stf; Rep Jr Cls; French Hon Soc; High Hon Roll; NHS; Stage Crew.

MARION, JOHN; Buena Regional HS; Dorothy, NJ; (S); 21/200; JV Bsbl; Hon Roll; Stockton ST Coll; Elec Engr.

MARIUS, ROBERT E; Seton Hall Prep; Union, NJ; (Y); Chess Clb; Civic Clb; Stage Crew; Hon Roll; Ntl Merit Ltr; Natl Achvt Schlrshp 85; Sci.

MARKERT, BRIAN T; Dumont HS; Dumont, NJ; (Y); 66/209; Art Clb; PAVAS; Var Trk; JV Wrstlng; Lit Mag; USM Acad; Military Sci.

MARKHAM, JEFFERY; Paramus HS; Paramus, NJ; (Y); Prntg.

MARKIEWICZ, KERI; Middletown South HS; Middletown, NJ; (Y); Church Yth Grp; French Clb; Math Tm; Quiz Bowl; Stage Crew; Off Soph Cls; Off Jr Cls; L Var Tennis; Hon Roll.

MARKLE, NICOLE; Middlesex HS; Middlsex, NJ; (Y); 33/169; Girl Scts; Hosp Aide; Ski Clb; Spanish Clb; Variety Show; Rep Frsh Cls; Var Bsktbl; Var Fld Hcky; Var Sftbl; Hon Roll; Grl Sct Slvr Awd 83; Cook Coll Smmr Career Voctnl Enrchmnt Prog Animal Sci 84; Grl Sct Ledrshp Awd 83; Hotel & Restaurant Mngmnt.

MARKLEY, CHRISTOPHER; Washington Township HS; Sewell, NJ; (Y); FCA; Chorus; Socr; Cmptr Prgrmr.

MARKOFF, JULIE S; J P Stevens HS; Edison, NJ; (Y); 21/478; Art Clb; Debate Tm; Nwsp Stf; Yrbk Sprt Ed; Var Tennis; French Hon Soc; Hon Roll; NHS; Ntl Merit SF; St Schlr; Hist.

MARKOVIC, MARK; Audubon HS; Mt Ephraim, NJ; (Y); Am Leg Boys St; Church Yth Grp; Chorus; Madrigals; Var L Bsbl; JV L Bsktbl; Var L Socr; Wt Lftg; VFW Awd; Math.

MARKOVICH, MICHAEL; Toms River North HS; Toms River, NJ; (Y); 118/422; Var Capt Ftbl; Var Wt Lftg; JV Bsbl; JV Bsktbl; Hon Roll; PA ST; Tchng.

MARKOWITZ, ERIC; Arthur L Johnson HS; Clark, NJ; (Y); 9/200; Aud/Vis; Service Clb; Spanish Clb; Band; Concert Band; Jazz Band; Mrchg Band; Yrbk Stf; Stu Cncl; Score Keeper; Comp Edtr Of Yrbk 87; Sci Rsrch.

MARKOWSKI, DIANE; Bayonne HS; Bayonne, NJ; (Y); 11/350; Am Leg Aux Girls St; Church Yth Grp; Cmnty Wkr; Drama Clb; English Clb; French Clb; Math Tm; Q&S; Nwsp Bus Mgr; Nwsp Ed-Chief; WA Wrkshps Cngrrsnl Sem 85; Bennington July Pgm Bennington Coll 85; Columbia Press Assn 1st Pl Awd; NYU; Polit Sci.

MARKOWSKI, VICTORIA; Audubon HS; Audubon Park, NJ; (Y); Am Leg Aux Girls St; Library Aide; Office Aide; Spanish Clb; Drill Tm; Mrchg Band; Rep Frsh Cls; Rep Soph Cls; Off Jr Cls; Hon Roll.

MARKS, DAVE; Mahwah HS; Mahwah, NJ; (Y); Cmnty Wkr; JCL; Pres Latin Clb; Teachers Aide; Lit Mag; VP Stu Cncl; JV Socr; Var Tennis; Stdnt Actvts Comm Hd Of Secrty 85-86; 1st Tm All Leag Tennis Tm 85-86; Achvt Awd Drftg 84-85.

MARKS, E MICHELLE; Cumberland Regional HS; Bridgeton, NJ; (Y); 130/360; Sec Trs Church Yth Grp; Exploring; Church Choir; Color Guard; Capt Flag Corp; Mrchg Band; Hon Roll; Commendbl Achvt Lang Arts I,II 83-85; Speed Reading 85-86; Pre-Med.

MARKS, ROBIN; East Brunswick HS; E Brunswick, NJ; (Y); Varsity Clb; Var L Gym; Hon Roll; GAA; Temple Yth Grp; Chorus; Psychlgy.

MARKULIC, LORI A; Sayreville War Memorial HS; Sayreville, NJ; (S); Spanish Clb; Varsity Clb; School Musical; Cheerleading; Hon Roll; Church Yth Grp; Cmnty Wkr; Drama Clb; School Play; Coach Actv; Rutgers ST U; Ansthlgst.

MARKUS, DEBBIE; High Point Regional HS; Sussex, NJ; (Y); Chorus; School Play; Var JV Cheerleading; Var Capt Pom Pon; JV Stat Score Keeper; Hon Roll; Clincl Psych.

MARLOW, RICH; Washington TWP HS; Turnersville, NJ; (Y); Church Yth Grp; Band; Concert Band; Jazz Band; Mrchg Band; Var Trk; Rutgers.

MARMARAS, IRENE; Belleville HS; Belleville, NJ; (Y); Church Yth Grp; FBLA; Girl Scts; Key Clb; Yrbk Stf; Hon Roll; Greek Schl Equivlncy Diplma 82; AHEPA Cert Achvt 82; 2nd Hnrs FBLA ST Bus Engl 86; Berkeley Schl; Paralgl.

MARMORA, JOSEPH B; St Joseph Regional HS; Upper Saddle Rive, NJ; (Y); 59/170; Cmnty Wkr; Drama Clb; Political Wkr; School Musical; School Play; Variety Show; Var JV Socr; Hon Roll; Spanish NHS; NJ Close-Up Rep Trenton & Wash DC 83-85; Peer Cnslr 85-86; Finance.

MAROTTA, DAVID; Highland Reg HS; Blackwood, NJ; (S); 6/332; Computer Clb; Key Clb; Spanish Clb; Ed Nwsp Rptr; Capt Bsbl; NHS; Prfct Atten Awd; Stu Of Mnth 84; U Of PA; Sci.

MARQUES, ANABELA; East Side HS; Newark, NJ; (Y); Church Yth Grp; Computer Clb; Office Aide; Teachers Aide; NHS; Gold Card Awd 84-85; Talnt Srch Awd 86.

MARQUES, JOSEPH; Ste James HS; Carneys Point, NJ; (S); Stage Crew; High Hon Roll; Hon Roll; Soc Of Dstngshd Amer HS Stu 85; Exclince In Spanish 84; Stevens Inst Of Tech; Elec Engr.

MARRAMA, LOUIS; Middletown South HS; Ft Mancock, NJ; (Y); Nwsp Bus Mgr; Nwsp Phtg; Nwsp Rptr; Hon Roll; Ntl Merit Ltr; Prfct Atten Awd; Library Aide; Teachers Aide; Perfect Attndnc 83; Outstndng Svc Natl Park Svc 84; U Of NM; Accntng.

MARRELLA, JACQUELYN; Holy Cross HS; Marlton, NJ; (Y); Church Yth Grp; Acpl Chr; Chorus; Drm & Bgl; Yrbk Stf; Hon Roll; Villanova; Cmnctns.

MARRERO, NICOLE; South Hunterdon HS; Lambertville, NJ; (Y); 19/70; Cmnty Wkr; Drama Clb; Key Clb; Library Aide; SADD; VICA; Band; Variety Show; Hon Roll; Nwsp Stf; Mrktng.

MARROCCO, MONICA; Immaculate Conception HS; Passaic, NJ; (S); 7/100; Drama Clb; FCA; L Science Clb; Trs Spanish Clb; School Musical; Yrbk Stf; Lit Mag; Var Hon Roll; Prfct Atten Awd; Trs Spanish NHS; Art Natl Hnr Soc; Pre-Med.

MARRONI, BETH; Toms River H S East; Toms River, NJ; (Y); Church Yth Grp; Band; Church Choir; Concert Band; Mrchg Band; Hon Roll; Library Aide; Soc Of Dstnghsd Amer HS Stu 84; HS Ltr; Bus Merchndzng.

MARSDEN, CINDY; Lower Cape May Regional HS; Erma Park, NJ; (Y); 3/220; Church Yth Grp; Sec Spanish Clb; Varsity Clb; Yrbk Stf; High Hon Roll; NHS; Acdmc All Am Awd 85-86.

MARSEGLIA, MICHAEL F; Hackensack HS; Hackensack, NJ; (Y); Am Leg Boys St; Aud/Vis; Ski Clb; Stage Crew; Var Bsbl; Var Ftbl; Im Vllybl; Hon Roll; Jr NHS; NHS; Engrng.

MARSEILLE, PHILIPPE; Linden HS; Linden, NJ; (Y); FBLA; Var Socr; Var Tennis; Var High Hon Roll; Accountant.

MARSH, AMY; Neptune SR HS; Neptune City, NJ; (Y); 18/400; Exploring; GAA; Ski Clb; Varsity Clb; Bsktbl; Fld Hcky; Socr; High Hon Roll; Hon Roll; NHS; Bus Adm.

MARSH, JENNIFER; Timothy Christian HS; Rahway, NJ; (S); Church Yth Grp; Drama Clb; School Play; VP Jr Cls; Rep Stu Cncl; Var Bsktbl; High Hon Roll; Jr NHS; NHS; Val; Mertrs Svc Awd 84; Erly Chldhd Educ.

MARSHALL, ALTERIC; Essex Co Vo-Tech/Bloomfield Tech; Newark, NJ; (Y); Computer Clb; Debate Tm; Exploring; Chorus; Cit Awd; Hon Roll; NHS; Prfct Atten Awd; FL Inst Of Tech; Elec Engr.

MARSHALL, DAVID; St James HS; Salem, NJ; (S); 2/76; Am Leg Boys St; Drama Clb; Chorus; School Play; NHS; Ntl Merit Ltr; Sal; Grdn ST Schlrshp 85; Ldrshp Merit Awd 85; Natl Eng Merit Awd 85; Biochem.

MARSHALL, DINI; Lakewood Prep; Lanoka Harbor, NJ; (Y); Chorus; Concert Band; Nwsp Stf; Var Cheerleading; Capt L Socr; Math Hons Soc 85; College Communications Pgm.

MARSHALL, KIMBERLY; James Caldwell HS; Caldwell, NJ; (Y); Church Yth Grp; Concert Band; Flag Corp; Yrbk Sprt Ed; Var Vllybl; High Hon Roll; NHS.

MARSHALL, PAUL W; Holy Spirit HS; Absecon, NJ; (Y); 1/338; Pres Aud/Vis; School Musical; Yrbk Stf; Pres Stu Cncl; Crs Cntry; L Trk; NHS; Ntl Merit SF; St Schlr; Trs Church Yth Grp; Mock Trial Tm; Math Awd; Physics Awd.

MARSICO, LYNANNE; Pennsville Memorial HS; Pennsville, NJ; (Y); School Play; Var Capt Cheerleading; Drama Clb; FBLA; FHA; Off Frsh Cls; Off Soph Cls; Off Jr Cls; Off Sr Cls; Stu Cncl; Wilma Boyd Travel Schl; Trvl.

MARSICO, TONY; West Essex HS; Fairfield, NJ; (Y); Church Yth Grp; Model UN; Science Clb; Ftbl; Hon Roll; Georgetown U; Pltcl Sci.

MARTENS, ANNEMARIE; Indian Hills HS; Oakland, NJ; (Y); 59/278; French Clb; Yrbk Stf; Stat Bsktbl; Hon Roll; Bus.

MARTIN, ALYSON; Hunterdon Central HS; Whitehouse Sta, NJ; (Y); 41/570; Model UN; Pres SADD; Ed Yrbk Stf; Rep Jr Cls; Rep Sr Cls; Rep Stu Cncl; JV Crs Cntry; JV Trk; NHS; Ntl Merit Ltr; NJ Govrs Schl Public Issues Fnlst 86; Hugh O Brien Yth Fndtn Smnr Ambssdr 85; Intl Rel.

MARTIN, DOUGLAS M; Neptune SR HS; Neptune, NJ; (Y); 117/500; Church Yth Grp; Drama Clb; Exploring; School Play; Var Capt Golf; Var Capt Socr; Capt Vllybl; JV Capt Wrstlng; God Cntry Awd; 10 Sci Fair Awds 80-85; Socr ST Chmps 80; Regnl Socr Tm Rep NJ 81; West Point; Nuclr Engrng.

MARTIN, EDWARD; Westfield HS; Westfield, NJ; (Y); 62/525; Chess Clb; Science Clb; Spanish Clb; Nwsp Phtg; Nwsp Rptr; Nwsp Stf; JV Bsktbl; JV Socr; Var Trk; Hon Roll; Lehigh U; Engrng.

MARTIN JR, ELLIOTT B; St Josephs HS; E Brunswick, NJ; (Y); 3/225; Cmnty Wkr; Dance Clb; Debate Tm; Math Tm; Model UN; Band; Jazz Band; Nwsp Rptr; Ed Nwsp Stf; Yrbk Rptr; Columbia U; Sports Psych.

MARTIN, FELICIA; Eastside HS; Paterson, NJ; (S); #5 In Class; Camera Clb; Science Clb; Church Choir; Jazz Band; Mrchg Band; Stu Cncl; Dnfth Awd; NHS; AL ST; Law.

MARTIN, JESSE; Edgewood SR HS; Sicklerville, NJ; (Y); Computer Clb; Crs Cntry; Trk; Hon Roll; Comp.

MARTIN, JOHN; Toms River HS East; Toms River, NJ; (Y); Church Yth Grp; French Clb; Stage Crew; Var L Bsbl; Var Ice Hcky; Var L Socr; JC Awd; Pres Schlr; Soc Of Dstngushed Americn High Schl Studnts 85; Med.

MARTIN, JOSLYN; Hightstown HS; East Windsor, NJ; (Y); Am Leg Aux Girls St; Drama Clb; Sec French Clb; Thesps; Band; Jazz Band; School Musical; School Play; Variety Show; Hon Roll; Deaf Ed.

MARTIN, KATHY A; Kittatinny Regional HS; Newton, NJ; (S); Am Leg Aux Girls St; Sec Church Yth Grp; Chorus; Nwsp Rptr; Rep Stu Cncl; Var Crs Cntry; Var Capt Trk; NHS; Vrsty Capt-Winter Track; Mock Trial Tm; Sussex Cnty Jr Miss 86; Pre-Med.

MARTIN, KIM; Our Lady Of Mercy Girls Acad; Millville, NJ; (Y); Sec Jr Cls; Sec Stu Cncl; Hon Roll; Pres Schlr; Drexel U; Psych.

MARTIN, KRISTIE; Northern Valley Regional HS; Closter, NJ; (Y); 84/256; Yrbk Stf; Sec Soph Cls; JV Fld Hcky; Hon Roll; NHS; Major Doton Schlrshp 86; Hnr Soc 85-86; Quality Circle 82-86; Quinnipiac Coll; Occu Ther.

MARTIN, MELISSA; Lenape Valley HS; Stanhope, NJ; (Y); 10/212; JA; Math Clb; SADD; Nwsp Rptr; Yrbk Ed-Chief; Yrbk Rptr; Vllybl; High Hon Roll; Hon Roll; NHS; Syracuse U; Cmmnctns.

MARTIN, OLIVEE; Weequahic HS; Newark, NJ; (S); 11/354; Boys Clb Am; Exploring; Hosp Aide; Pres Church Choir; Drill Tm; Sec Pep Band; Ed Yrbk Stf; Rep Sr Cls; Hon Roll; NHS; Drexel U; Acctng.

MARTIN, SANDRINE; Oak Knoll School Of The Holy Child; South Orange, NJ; (Y); Church Yth Grp; Cmnty Wkr; Dance Clb; Debate Tm; Drama Clb; English Clb; Girl Scts; Hosp Aide; Library Aide; Service Clb; NYU; Lawyer.

MARTIN, SHERRI; Notre Dame HS; Hamilton Sq, NJ; (Y); 43/348; Drama Clb; Spanish Clb; Chorus; Madrigals; School Musical; School Play; Stage Crew; Off Frsh Cls; Off Soph Cls; High Hon Roll; Soph Cls Am Lit Awd 85; Soph Cls Spd Typng Awd 85; Trntn ST Coll; Sec Ed.

MARTIN, STACY; Plainfield HS; Plainfield, NJ; (Y); FBLA; Spanish Clb; SADD; Chorus; Drill Tm; Pep Band; Variety Show; Yrbk Stf; Off Frsh Cls; Off Soph Cls; Morgan ST; Pre Law.

MARTIN, STEVE; Wardlaw-Hartridge HS; Plainfield, NJ; (Y); 17/53; Debate Tm; Pres Key Clb; Ski Clb; JV Bsktbl; Mgr(s); Var Capt Tennis; DAR Awd; High Hon Roll; Hon Roll; WA & Lee U; Bus.

MARTINEAU, GALE; Manalapan HS; Englishtown, NJ; (Y); 7/356; Hst Drama Clb; Am Leg Boys St; Thesps; School Musical; School Play; Stage Crew; Rptr Lit Mag; French Hon Soc; NHS; Fine & Perf Arts Video Awd 86; Grdn ST Distngshd Schlr Awd 86; Jack Gldfn Cvcc Awd 86; SUNY Purchase; Lghtng Dsgn.

MARTINELLI, ANGELA; Sacred Heart HS; Vineland, NJ; (S); 13/78; Art Clb; Hosp Aide; Spanish Clb; School Play; Yrbk Rptr; Hon Roll; NHS; Natl Ldrshp & Merit Awd 85; Natl Sci Awd 85; Acctg.

MARTINELLY, MICHELLE; Red Bank Regional HS; Shrewsbury, NJ; (Y); Pres Church Yth Grp; French Clb; VP Key Clb; Ski Clb; Rep Frsh Cls; Rep Soph Cls; Rep Jr Cls; Var Socr; French Hon Soc; High Hon Roll; Bus.

MARTINEZ, ESPERANZA; Ridgefield Park HS; Little Ferry, NJ; (Y); 32/182; French Clb; Spanish Clb; NYU; Comp Sci.

MARTINEZ, GIL; Dumont HS; Dumont, NJ; (Y); 59/210; Varsity Clb; Band; Concert Band; Mrchg Band; Bsbl; Score Keeper; Socr; Timer; Trk; Wt Lftg; Sci.

MARTINEZ, GRISEL; Dover HS; Dover, NJ; (Y); 4/183; Am Leg Aux Girls St; French Clb; Math Tm; Band; Yrbk Ed-Chief; Bsktbl; Bausch & Lomb Sci Awd; High Hon Roll; NHS; All Amer Acad Schlr 86; Engr.

MARTINEZ, HUMBERTO; St Joseph Of The Palisades HS; West New York, NJ; (S); 6/118; Spanish Clb; Nwsp Stf; Hon Roll; Spanish NHS; Acad All-Amer 84; Natl Ldrsp & Svc Awd 85; Mrktng.

MARTINEZ, MARIA; North Bergen HS; North Bergen, NJ; (Y); 91/410; Color Guard; Variety Show; Mat Maids; French Hon Soc; Engl Off Aid Awd 86; Montclair ST Coll; Cmptr Sci.

MARTINEZ, MARIA; Our Lady Of Good Counsel; Newark, NJ; (Y); 20/73; Church Yth Grp; Hosp Aide; Office Aide; Pep Clb; Teachers Aide; Church Choir; Yrbk Stf; Soclgy, Ecnmcs Awd 86; Acadmc Al-Amrcn 86; Rutgers U; Sociolgy.

MARTINEZ, MICHELLE; Rancocas Valley Regional HS; Mount Holly, NJ; (Y); 37/270; Am Leg Aux Girls St; Varsity Clb; Rep Soph Cls; Rep Jr Cls; VP Stu Cncl; Var Fld Hcky; Var Lcrss; JV Trk; High Hon Roll; Hon Roll; Lacrosse 3rd Tm Builng 2nd Tm Mohawk Div 86; Air Force Acad; Pilot.

MARTINEZ JR, SAMUEL; Our Lady Of Good Counsel HS; Newark, NJ; (Y); Boy Scts; Rep Jr Cls; Var Bsbl; JV Bsktbl; Var Socr; Mst Imprvd JV Bsktbl Plyr 85; Mst Imprvd Socr Plyr 86.

MARTINEZ, VIVIAN; North Bergen HS; N Bergen, NJ; (Y); 54/400; German Clb; Key Clb; William Paterson Coll; Spch.

MARTINI, JULIA; Notre Dame HS; Lawrenceville, NJ; (Y); Latin Clb; Red Cross Aide; Ski Clb; Varsity Clb; Socr; Hon Roll; Lat Hon Soc 85-87; Boston Coll; Business.

MARTINI, NICK; Palisades Park JR SR HS; Palisades Pk, NJ; (Y); 20/115; Trk; NJ ST U; Comptr Sci.

MARTINKA, LAURIE; De Paul Diosecan HS; Bloomingdale, NJ; (S); 10/173; Church Yth Grp; JA; Latin Clb; Capt Quiz Bowl; Band; Chorus; Nwsp Rptr; Mgr(s); High Hon Roll; NHS; Hstry & Ltn Awd; Pr Cnslng; Vassar Coll; Pre-Med.

MARTINO, ANGELINA; Woodbridge HS; Port Reading, NJ; (Y); 25/400; Quiz Bowl; Ski Clb; Chorus; Capt Flag Corp; Stage Crew; Hon Roll; Sec NHS; Ntl Merit Ltr; Spanish NHS; Gifted & Tlntd Open House Presntatns 84-86; JR Cotillion Comm 85-86; Ed.

MARTINO, CHERI-ANN; Middlesex HS; Middlesex, NJ; (Y); 24/170; Drama Clb; SADD; Color Guard; School Musical; School Play; Cheerleading; Fld Hcky; Score Keeper; Sftbl; Cmmnctns.

MARTINO, JAMES; Cherry Hill West HS; Cherry Hill, NJ; (Y); DECA; Office Aide; JV Bsbl; Var Ftbl; Var Wrstlng; Ntrtion.

MARTINO, JENNIFER; Arthur L Johnson Reg HS; Clark, NJ; (Y); 2/198; Am Leg Aux Girls St; Sec Art Clb; Yrbk Stf; High Hon Roll; NHS; Ntl Merit Ltr; Spanish NHS; Voice Dem Awd; 1st Pl Voice Dem 85-86; Cert Sci League Bio,Physcis 84-86; Am Math Ex 86; Sci Resrch.

MARTINS, MICHAEL; Woodstown HS; Woodstown, NJ; (Y); English Clb; French Clb; Key Clb; Lit Mag; Bsbl; Var Capt Crs Cntry; Var L Trk; Hon Roll; Aerspc Engr.

MARTIRANO, MICHAEL; Queen Of Peace HS; Kearny, NJ; (S); 2/231; Model UN; Rep Soph Cls; VP Jr Cls; High Hon Roll; Hon Roll; NHS; Sal; Math Clb; Service Clb; Nwsp Rptr; Top 3 Rank Awd 84; Awds-Relgn, Engl, Top 2 Rank 85; Top 2 Rank Awd 86.

MARTOPANA, TERESA; Notre Dame HS; Trenton, NJ; (Y); JV Socr; Trenton Sst Coll; Phys Ther.

MARTORELL, KEVIN; Carteret HS; Carteret, NJ; (Y); 21/200; Drama Clb; Math Tm; Pep Clb; Stage Crew; Bowling; Tennis; Hon Roll; Pres Schlr; All Cnty Bwlng 86; 2nd Team All Cnty Bwlng 85; HS MVP Bwlng 85-86; Acctng.

MARTZ, MICHELLE MARIE; Hun Schl Of Princetn; Frederick, MD; (Y); AFS; Debate Tm; Latin Clb; Science Clb; Orch; Rep Frsh Cls; Trs Soph Cls; Rep Jr Cls; Stu Cncl; Var Capt Fld Hcky; Boston U; Pol Sci.

MARULLO, TARA; Toms River High School South; Beachwood, NJ; (Y); VP Cmnty Wkr; Dance Clb; SADD; Variety Show; Erly Chldhd Ed.

MARZANO, LISA; Montville HS; Towaco, NJ; (Y); Church Yth Grp; Hosp Aide; Key Clb; Ski Clb; Yrbk Phtg; Yrbk Stf; Rep Frsh Cls; Rep Soph Cls; Var Capt Cheerleading; JV Lcrss; Accntng.

MARZEC, EDWARD; St John Vianney HS; Englishtown, NJ; (Y); Boy Scts; Ski Clb; SADD; Teachers Aide; Band; Mrchg Band; JV Score Keeper; Var JV Socr; Var Tennis; Hon Roll; Engrng.

MARZO, DONNA; Nutley HS; Nutley, NJ; (Y); 12/359; Am Leg Aux Girls St; Political Wkr; Capt Bsktbl; Capt Crs Cntry; Capt Sftbl; Cit Awd; High Hon Roll; Hon Roll; NHS; Drr Amttia Awd 86; AMVET Awd 86; Jackman Mem Awd 86; Dickinson Coll; Med.

MASCELLINO, ANN MARIE; Montville Township HS; Montville, NJ; (Y); 53/276; 4-H; Key Clb; Concert Band; Lit Mag; JV Mgr Sftbl; High Hon Roll; Hon Roll; NHS; St Elizabeth Bio Schlrshp; ST Elizabeth; Bio.

MASCHAL, LYNN; Bishop Ahr HS; Carteret, NJ; (Y); Church Yth Grp; Intnl Clb; Model UN; Drill Tm; Lit Mag; High Hon Roll; Vet Med.

MASCHKE JR, ROBERT; Edgewood Regional SR HS; Hammonton, NJ; (Y); 3/375; French Clb; Varsity Clb; Yrbk Phtg; Var Capt Socr; Var Capt Trk; High Hon Roll; Hon Roll; Jr NHS; NHS; Ntl Schlr Athlt Awd 86; NJ Schlr Athltc Awd 86; Wanslow Twp Rtry Clb Awd 86; Westpoint Mltry Acad; Nclr Engr.

MASCIA, JACQUELINE; St John Vianney HS; Marlboro, NJ; (Y); Church Yth Grp; Intnl Clb; Stage Crew; Lit Mag; Rep Stu Cncl; JV Mgr(s); Capt Powder Puff Ftbl; Stat Var Score Keeper; Var L Sftbl; Hon Roll; Gold & White Achvt Awd; Pre-Law.

MASCOLO, ARTHUR; Pope Paul VI HS; Haddon Heights, NJ; (S); 60/474; Math Clb; Rep Frsh Cls; Rep Soph Cls; Rep Jr Cls; Rep Sr Cls; Var Capt Bsktbl; Jr NHS; NHS; All Parochial Bsktbl Plyr 85; PA Inquirer Boys Bsktbl Plyr Wk 85; Bus.

MASCONE, SUSAN; Clifton HS; Clifton, NJ; (Y); Drama Clb; Key Clb; Spanish Clb; SADD; VP Chorus; Madrigals; School Musical; Variety Show; Twrlr; Govs Schl Of Arts 86; Lead In Schl Musical 86; SADD Chptr 85; Music.

MASCOTT, PAIGE; Middletown HS South; Middletown, NJ; (S); 3/436; Ski Clb; Thesps; School Musical; School Play; VP Soph Cls; Elks Awd; French Hon Soc; NHS; Am Leg Aux Girls St; 4-H; Rutgers Schlr 85; Garden ST Distngshd Schlr 85; Yale U; Intl Bus.

MASELLA, JOE; Fair Lawn HS; Fair Lawn, NJ; (Y); Boy Scts; French Clb; Ski Clb; JV Lcrss; Trk; Business.

MASILANG, MARIA B; Holy Rosary Acad; Jersey City, NJ; (Y); Art Clb; JA; Nwsp Ed-Chief; Nwsp Stf; Yrbk Phtg; Yrbk Stf; Tennis; Ntl Merit Ltr; NEDT Awd; Art Awd 86; Fash Edit Cert Awd 86; Cert Of Svc 86; Fairleigh Dickinson U; Advrtsng.

MASS, MONIQUE E; Montclair HS; Montclair, NJ; (Y); 66/469; Sec French Clb; FBLA; Chrmn Service Clb; Chorus; Yrbk Stf; DAR Awd; High Hon Roll; Hon Roll; Ntl Merit SF.

MASSARI, JOHN; Vineland HS; Vineland, NJ; (Y); 37/801; Aud/Vis; Trs Church Yth Grp; Computer Clb; Drama Clb; Science Clb; School Musical; School Play; VP Stage Crew; Im Vllybl; Aero Engrng.

MASSARO, TRICIA; Southriver HS; South River, NJ; (Y); Church Yth Grp; Y-Teens; Spanish Clb; Band; Chorus; Fshn Cnslnt.

MASSENGILL, JAMES; Bogota HS; Bogota, NJ; (Y); 25/113; Am Leg Boys St; Boy Scts; Church Yth Grp; Cmnty Wkr; Drama Clb; Quiz Bowl; Thesps; Band; Chorus; Concert Band; Bus.

MASSEY, TIMIKA; Henry Snyder HS; Jersey City, NJ; (Y); Dance Clb; FBLA; Pres Frsh Cls; Rep Soph Cls; VP Jr Cls; Pres Sr Cls; Pres Stu Cncl; Capt Cheerleading; Prfct Atten Awd; Achvmnt Rl 86; Mst Dpndbl Sqd 85-86; Rutgers ST U; Pre-Med.

MASSIMINO, MARIA; Monsignor Donovan HS; Toms River, NJ; (Y); 16/243; Drama Clb; Hosp Aide; Service Clb; Ski Clb; SADD; Yrbk Stf; Capt Cheerleading; Trk; High Hon Roll; NHS; Villanova U; Lbrl Arts.

MASSIMO, MICHAEL; Bishop Ahr HS; Edison, NJ; (Y); 40/270; Am Leg Boys St; Boy Scts; Science Clb; Jazz Band; Mrchg Band; School Musical; Symp Band; Lit Mag; Hon Roll; Garden ST Arts Ctr Talent Expo 86; Eagle Sct 87; Natl Sci Merit Awd 84; Bus.

MASSO, JESSICA ANN; St Joseph HS; Atco, NJ; (Y); Am Leg Aux Girls St; Church Yth Grp; Civic Clb; Hosp Aide; Church Choir; School Play; Yrbk Stf; Rep Frsh Cls; Rep Soph Cls; Rep Jr Cls; Chestnut Hill Coll; Ed.

MASTANDO, ANTHONY; Lyndhurst HS; Lyndhurst, NJ; (Y); 27/180; German Clb; JA; Varsity Clb; Stage Crew; Var L Bsbl; Var L Bsktbl; Lyndrst Bstr Clb Cert Awd Vrsty Ltr Bsbl, Bsktbl 86-87.

MASTELLON, MEGHAN; Waldwick HS; Waldwick, NJ; (S); 2/140; Drama Clb; Math Tm; Nwsp Ed-Chief; Yrbk Phtg; Lit Mag; Off Jr Cls; Off Sr Cls; High Hon Roll; NHS; Church Yth Grp; Most Imprvd Writer Awd-Eng Dept 84; Outstndng Writer-Eng Dept 85; Prose Wnnr-Lit Magzn Cntst 84 & 85; Commnctn Arts.

MASTERSON, BRIAN; Northern Valley Reg HS; Old Tappan, NJ; (Y); 125/283; Church Yth Grp; Letterman Clb; Ski Clb; SADD; Varsity Clb; Sec Stu Cncl; JV Var Bsbl; JV Bsktbl; JV Var Ftbl.

MASTERSON, BRIAN; Sacred Heart HS; Cedarville, NJ; (Y); 35/87; Art Clb; Boy Scts; Chess Clb; Computer Clb; Science Clb; Spanish Clb; Varsity Clb; Chorus; Church Choir; Capt Bsbl; Elctrncs.

MASTERSON, STEPHANIE; Spotswood HS; Milltown, NJ; (Y); Cmnty Wkr; 4-H; Library Aide; Office Aide; Bsktbl; Hon Roll; Glassboro ST; Tchg.

MASTIN, JANET; Florence Twp Mem HS; Florence, NJ; (Y); Church Yth Grp; French Clb; Math Clb; Science Clb; Stage Crew; Yrbk Stf; Pres Stu Cncl; 1st Plc Wrtng Cmptn 85; Slvr Pin Accntng 85; Intl Bus.

MASTRODIMOS, JOHN; Hackettstown HS; Hackettstown, NJ; (Y); Church Yth Grp; German Clb; JV Bsbl; Hon Roll; Morris Co Coll; Bus Admin.

MASTROGIOVANNI, MARK; Washington Twp HS; Turnersville, NJ; (Y); Science Clb; Lasalle U; Bus.

MASTROPAOLO, FRANCES; Lodi HS; Lodi, NJ; (Y); 1/127; Trs Art Clb; Sec Key Clb; Color Guard; JV Bsktbl; Var Trk; Gov Hon Prg Awd; High Hon Roll; NHS; Ntl Merit Ltr; Italian Club VP 85-86.

MASUCCI, MARIA; Immaculate Conception HS; Newark, NJ; (Y); Chorus; Church Choir; Spanish NHS; Transltr.

MATACONIS, DOUGLAS; Piscataway HS; Piscataway, NJ; (Y); 180/519; Band; Concert Band; Mrchg Band; Pep Band; Symp Band; Prfct Atten Awd; Rutgers U; Pltcl Sci.

MATARAZZO, CHRISTINE; Manchester Regional HS; North Haledon, NJ; (S); Cmnty Wkr; Pep Clb; Chorus; Powder Puff Ftbl; Var Socr; JV Trk; Hon Roll; NHS; Rutgers Coll; Bus Mngmnt.

MATARAZZO, JIM; West Essex HS; N Caldwell, NJ; (Y); Rep Stu Cncl; Im Bsbl; Var L Bsktbl; Im Sftbl; Hon Roll; MVP Rgnl Baseball League 85; Rgnl Baseball Champs 82-5; Vrsty Bsktbll Chamber Of Commerce 1st Pl 85; Bus.

MATCHOK, MICHELLE S; Hackensack HS; Rochelle Park, NJ; (Y); 37/386; Am Leg Aux Girls St; Art Clb; Church Yth Grp; Drama Clb; English Clb; French Clb; Girl Scts; Key Clb; Ski Clb; Chorus; Grls St 85; Cert NEDT Tstng 83-84; Ntl Art Hnr Scty 84-86; Parsons Schl Dsgn; Art.

MATEO, LISSETTE; Ferris HS; Jersey City, NJ; (Y); Am Leg Aux Girls St; Boys Clb Am; Church Yth Grp; Jr Cls; Pres Stu Cncl; Mgr(s); Sftbl; Swmmng; Mntclr ST Coll.

MATEOS, ARTHUR; Notre Dame HS; E Windsor, NJ; (Y); 1/350; Nwsp Ed-Chief; Off Jr Cls; Off Sr Cls; Var Swmmng; Var Tennis; Pres NHS; French Clb; Math Tm; Varsity Clb; JV Trk.

MATERA JR, JAMES J; Senior HS; Kenilworth, NJ; (Y); 7/168; Art Clb; German Clb; Lit Mag; High Hon Roll; Pres Schlr; Var L Socr; JV Trk; Soc Stud Awd; Cert Of Achvt 86; U Of MD; Engrg.

MATHERS, BRENT; Schalick HS; Elmer, NJ; (Y); Church Yth Grp; FCA; Letterman Clb; Ski Clb; Varsity Clb; Nwsp Rptr; Nwsp Stf; Soph Cls; Sr Cls; Bsbl; Untd ST Swmmng All-Amer 85; Natl Rookie Yr 85; 1 Rndkng 400 IM Midlantc All Str Tms Wrld Gms Trls.

MATHIS, DONNA; Franklin HS; Kingston, NJ; (Y); 165/313; Church Yth Grp; Dance Clb; Spanish Clb; Teachers Aide; VP Frsh Cls; Rep Jr Cls; Rep Sr Cls; Mgr(s); Var Trk; First Baptst Church Princeton Bk Schlrshp 86; 4 Yr Manager Awd 86; Towson ST U; Bus Mgmt.

MATHIS, ROBIN; John F Kennedy HS; Willingboro, NJ; (Y); Camera Clb; Church Yth Grp; Cmnty Wkr; Dance Clb; Hosp Aide; Intnl Clb; Ed Yrbk Stf; Rep Jr Cls; Stu Cncl; JV Mgr(s); Bus Adm.

MATHUR, ATUL D; Boonton HS; Lincoln Park, NJ; (Y); Am Leg Boys St; Cmnty Wkr; Ski Clb; Nwsp Rptr; Rep Stu Cncl; Var Bsbl; High Hon Roll; Hon Roll; Sgt Arms Jackson Cty NJ Boys ST 86; Engrng.

MATIC, MIRA; Manchester Regional HS; Prospect Park, NJ; (S); Cmnty Wkr; Yrbk Stf; Rep Frsh Cls; Rep Soph Cls; Rep Jr Cls; Var Socr; Var Sftbl; Hon Roll; NHS; Brown; Mth.

MATIS, VALERIE; Mother Seton Regional HS; Maplewood, NJ; (Y); 35/93; Art Clb; Computer Clb; Drama Clb; Chorus; School Play; Stage Crew; Bowling; Montclair ST Coll; Grphc Arts.

MATLACK, JACQUELINE; Glassboro HS; Glassboro, NJ; (Y); Church Yth Grp; Drama Clb; Exploring; Q&S; Thesps; Chorus; School Musical; School Play; Hon Roll; Prncpls Hnr List 85-86.

MATLOCK, DIANE; Belvidere HS; Hope, NJ; (Y); Art Clb; 4-H; Office Aide; Pep Clb; Varsity Clb; Fld Hcky; Sftbl; Hon Roll; Fld Hcky MIP 83; Schlott Dvlpmnt Schl; Rl Est.

MATO, GEORGE; Seton Hall Prep; Newark, NJ; (Y); 17/193; Key Clb; Ski Clb; Ed Nwsp Stf; High Hon Roll; Hon Roll; UCLA; Bus.

MATONIS, LAURA; Mother Seton Reional HS; Edison, NJ; (Y); 6/124; Hosp Aide; Sec Key Clb; Stage Crew; Ed Nwsp Stf; Yrbk Stf; Trs Soph Cls; Var Stu Cncl; Var Tennis; High Hon Roll; NHS; Dancing Awd 85.

MATRISCIANO, TERESA; Rancoras Valley Regional HS; Mt Holly, NJ; (Y); 6/280; Am Leg Aux Girls St; Band; Concert Band; Mrchg Band; Ed Lit Mag; Bsktbl; Fld Hcky; Var Trk; High Hon Roll; NHS.

MATSUDA, HIROKO; River Dell Reg HS; Oradell, NJ; (Y); Teachers Aide; Var Capt Bsktbl; High Hon Roll; Hon Roll; NHS; JV Tennis; JV Stat Vllybl; 3rd Highest Score In AHSME In Palisadeo HS 84; Rutgers U NJ; Chem.

MATT, LISA; Fort Lee HS; Ft Lee, NJ; (Y); French Clb; Teachers Aide; Thesps; School Musical; School Play; Stage Crew; Nwsp Ed-Chief; Nwsp Rptr; Nwsp Stf; Hon Roll; Achvt Awd Thespn Socty 85; Gen Membrshp Thespn Socty 84; Trstee Thespn Socty 84; Jrnlsm.

MATTEI, JEANNE; Notre Dame HS; Lawrenceville, NJ; (Y); 119/380; 4-H; French Clb; Stage Crew; JV Fld Hcky; Score Keeper; Wt Lftg; Hon Roll; Pol Sci.

MATTEO, JOHN; Bishop Eustace Prep; Laurel Springs, NJ; (Y); 17/194; Am Leg Boys St; Art Clb; Science Clb; Spanish Clb; SADD; Rep Soph Cls; Rep Jr Cls; Trk; High Hon Roll; NHS; Notre Dame; Med.

MATTES, ERIC; Passaic Valley HS; Little Falls, NJ; (Y); 35/307; Am Leg Boys St; Drama Clb; Pres German Clb; Key Clb; Ski Clb; School Musical; School Play; Stage Crew; Lit Mag; Jr NHS; Great Notch Assoc 86; Rutgers Cook Coll; Lndscp Arch.

MATTES, GREGORY; Hunterdon Central HS; Whitehouse Sta, NJ; (Y); Church Yth Grp; German Clb; Ntl Merit Ltr; NJ ST Bar Assoc Mck Trl Regn Fnlst 86; Rutgers U; Elec Engr.

MATTHAI, MERU ANN; Belleville HS; Belleville, NJ; (Y); Pres Church Yth Grp; French Clb; Key Clb; Spanish Clb; Nwsp Rptr; Nwsp Stf; Rep Frsh Cls; Rep Soph Cls; Mgr(s); Score Keeper; 2nd Pl Poetry Awd JR Wmns Clb 84; 1st Pl Poetry Awd JR Wmns Clb 85; WA Wrkshps 86; Finance.

MATTHEWS, ADRIENNE; Livingston HS; Livingston, NJ; (Y); Church Yth Grp; VP French Clb; Model UN; Ed Yrbk Stf; Rep Frsh Cls; Rep Soph Cls; Rep Jr Cls; Trs Stu Cncl; Powder Puff Ftbl.

MATTHEWS, ARTHUR C; Edgewood SR HS; Atco, NJ; (Y); Am Leg Boys St; Computer Clb; French Clb; Quiz Bowl; Mrchg Band; Nwsp Phtg; Nwsp Sprt Ed; Upward Bound 81-86; Mr Upward Bound 85; Tuskegee Inst; Arch.

MATTHEWS, CRAIG W; Lakewood HS; Lakewood, NJ; (Y); 35/294; Am Leg Boys St; Art Clb; Church Yth Grp; Drama Clb; PAVAS; School Musical; School Play; Nwsp Rptr; Nwsp Stf; Hon Roll.

MATTHEWS, JEROME; Marist HS; Jc, NJ; (Y); 7/104; Scholastic Bowl; Rep Stu Cncl; Var Bsktbl; Var Ftbl; High Hon Roll; NHS; Bus Mgt.

MATTHEWS, LAURA; Lakewood HS; Lakewood, NJ; (Y); Cmnty Wkr; English Clb; Pres Exploring; German Clb; Hosp Aide; Key Clb; Library Aide; Spanish Clb; SADD; Chorus; Explrer Of Yr 85; Brnz Mdl NJ Assoc For Blnd Trck 85.

MATTHEWS, ROBERT; Southern Regional HS; Barnegat, NJ; (Y); 22/365; Spanish Clb; Rep Frsh Cls; Rep Soph Cls; JV Bsbl; Var Ftbl; High Hon Roll; Hon Roll; NHS; Ntl Merit SF; 1/2 Schlrshp-Philadelphia Coll Of Phrmcy & Sci 86; R Brackman Schlrshp 86; Amer Lgn Schlrshp 86; Phili Coll Phrmcy/Sci; Phys Thr.

MATTHEWS, TARA; Cherry Hill HS East; Cherry Hill, NJ; (Y); Am Leg Aux Girls St; Hosp Aide; JA; Rep Jr Cls; Var Crs Cntry; Var Trk; Hon Roll; NEDT Awd; SR Hall Fame Awd 86; Jr Sptlght Awd 85; U Connecticut; Sprts Med.

MATTICAO, LILLIAN; Linden HS; Linden, NJ; (Y); French Clb; Key Clb; Drill Tm; Mrchg Band; School Play; Yrbk Stf.

MATTICOLA, LEE; Howell HS; Howell, NJ; (Y); Church Yth Grp; FCA; Hosp Aide; JCL; Trs Band; Mrchg Band; JV Bsktbl; Var Sftbl; NHS; Ltn Awd 84; Schlrshp For Smr Bnd Lsns 86; Hon Bnds 85-86.

MATTIELLO, JENNIFER; Clifton HS; Clifton, NJ; (Y); 21/687; French Clb; Office Aide; Sec Sr Cls; Capt Var Cheerleading; Mgr(s); French Hon Soc; Hon Roll; Jr NHS; Chrprctr.

MATTIO, MICHAEL; Highland Regional HS; Blackwood, NJ; (Y); JA; Ftbl; Golf; Score Keeper; Rutgers U; Bus.

MATTLE, JOSEPH; Oakcrest HS; Mays Landing, NJ; (Y); 11/220; Math Clb; Quiz Bowl; Ski Clb; Yrbk Stf; JV Bsbl; JV Var Socr; NHS; French Clb; Im Lcrss; Hon Roll; Var Schlr 83-86; Pres Acad Fit Awd 86; William Collins Mem Scholar 86; Drexel U; Civil Engrng.

MATTO, LINDA A; Belleville HS; Belleville, NJ; (Y); 30/387; Church Yth Grp; Key Clb; Spanish Clb; High Hon Roll; Hon Roll; NHS; Pres Schlr; Montclair ST Coll; Psych.

MATTONE, JOHN; St John Vianney HS; Aberdeen, NJ; (Y); Var Capt Bsbl; Var Capt Bsktbl; Ftbl.

MATTSON, MICHELLE; Burlington Twp HS; Burlington, NJ; (Y); 20/118; Key Clb; Ski Clb; Varsity Clb; Rep Jr Cls; Rep Sr Cls; Rep Stu Cncl; Fld Hcky; Vrsty Fld Hcky Ltr 83-85; Home Ec Hi Avg 86; Stu Snt Awd 86; Rider Coll; Bus Mgt.

MATVIAK, IVAN; Gill St Bernards HS; Plainfield, NJ; (Y); 2/45; Boy Scts; Church Yth Grp; Radio Clb; Scholastic Bowl; Variety Show; Nwsp Rptr; Rep Frsh Cls; Rep Soph Cls; Pres Jr Cls; VP Stu Cncl; Mrdth Pyne Ctznshp & Achvmnt Schlrshp; Hstry Dpt Schlrshp; Thomas A Conover Cop; Aero Engr.

MATYAS, ATTILA; Franklin HS; Somerset, NJ; (Y); Boy Scts; Ski Clb; Band; Concert Band; Drm & Bgl; Mrchg Band; Intrntl Bus.

MATYAS, SHARON; St Elizabeths Acad; Watchung, NJ; (Y); 4/58; French Clb; Ski Clb; Lit Mag; Rep Jr Cls; JV Bsktbl; Score Keeper; Sftbl; High Hon Roll; Math Clb; Annual Shanely Schlrshp; Bryant Coll; Bus Mktg.

MATYSCZAK, BERNARD; Matawan Regional HS; Cliffwood Beach, NJ; (S); 34/280; Concert Band; Jazz Band; Mrchg Band; Nwsp Ed-Chief; Ftbl; Hon Roll; NHS; Spanish NHS; Band; Math Natl Hnr Socty 85-86.

MAURER, FRANK; St James HS; Salem, NJ; (Y); 12/88; School Play; Stage Crew; Yrbk Stf; Stu Cncl; JV Golf; Hon Roll; NHS; Prfct Atten Awd; Anml Sci.

MAURER, JAMES; Phillipsburg Catholic HS; Phillipsburg, NJ; (Y); Art Clb; Stage Crew; Lit Mag; Ftbl; Wt Lftg; CC Awd; JC Awd; Rgnl, ST Teen Arts Fstvl 85; Rgnl Tn Art 86; Art Inst Ft Ldrdale; Adv Dsgn.

MAURO, MICHELE; Linden HS; Linden, NJ; (Y); Pres Church Yth Grp; Hosp Aide; Yrbk Stf; VP Frsh Cls; Var Capt Cheerleading; High Hon Roll; Hon Roll; NHS; Math Assoc Awd 86; Var Sport Awd Chrldng 85-86; Rutgers; Nrsng.

MAURO JR, ROBERT D; St John Vianney HS; Hazlet, NJ; (S); 19/298; Computer Clb; Math Tm; SADD; Nwsp Sprt Ed; Var Bsbl; Var Mgr Bsktbl; Gov Hon Prg Awd; Hon Roll; NHS; Most Outstndng Frnch Awd 84; Engrng.

MAURO, SUSAN; Cresskill HS; Cresskill, NJ; (Y); 28/119; Ski Clb; Band; Chorus; Concert Band; Drm Mjr(t); Jazz Band; Mrchg Band; School Musical; Crs Cntry; High Hon Roll; NJ Stu Crftmn Fair 3rd Pl Awd Archit 86; Archit.

MAURONE, BRENDA; Vineland HS; Millville, NJ; (Y); English Clb; Latin Clb; Political Wkr; Lit Mag; Hon Roll; Vnlnd Jvnl Cnfrnc Cmt 85-87; Lawyer.

MAUTE, MICHELLE; Holy Cross HS; Cinnaminson, NJ; (Y); 4/369; Church Yth Grp; Ski Clb; Pres Spanish Clb; JV Bsktbl; Var Fld Hcky; Capt Var Sftbl; High Hon Roll; Hon Roll; NHS; Ntl Merit Ltr; Sftbl JV MVP 85; Sftbl 2nd Tm All Liberty Div Honr Ment 86.

MAWHINNEY, DOUG; Nutley HS; Nutley, NJ; (Y); 10/320; Computer Clb; German Clb; Math Clb; Rep Jr Cls; Im Wrstlng; Hon Roll; NHS; Ntl Merit Ltr; Garden St Schlr 86; Marquette U; Chem.

MAXLOWE, THOMAS; Wildwood HS; N Wildwood, NJ; (Y); #7 In Class; Quiz Bowl; Spanish Clb; Bsbl; Ftbl; Hon Roll; Pre-Med.

MAXWELL, JENNIFER; Arthur P Schalick HS; Elmer, NJ; (Y); 14/142; Art Clb; Math Tm; Pres Ski Clb; Capt Flag Corp; Stu Cncl; JV Var Cheerleading; Pom Pon; U S Achvmnt Acad Chrldr Awd 85-86; Prsdntl Acdmc Ftnss Awd 85-86; Rutgers U; Pre-Med.

MAY, ARNOLD P; Cherry Hill HS East; Cherry Hill, NJ; (Y); Am Leg Boys St; Rep Frsh Cls; Rep Soph Cls; Rep Jr Cls; Rep Sr Cls; Rep Stu Cncl; Gym; Trk; Wrstlng; Hon Roll; NJ Dstngshd Schlr 86; Natl Cncl Jewish Wmn Achvt Awd 86; Grad Magna Cum Laude 86; Rutgers U; Biomed Engrng.

MAY, DAVID P; Bishop Eustace Prep Schl; Medford Lakes, NJ; (Y); Am Leg Boys St; Teachers Aide; Nwsp Stf; Var Capt Crs Cntry; Var Capt Trk; Hon Roll; NHS; Spanish NHS; MVP Crs Cntry Trk & Indoor Trk 85-86; All Olympic Conf Trk Crs Cntry 85-86; Pre Vet.

MAY, JOSEPH C; South River HS; S River, NJ; (Y); 15/131; German Clb; Im Bsktbl; JV Var Ftbl; Var L Golf; Am Leg Boys St; Mech Engrng.

MAY, KELLY; Newton HS; Newton, NJ; (S); 22/194; Cmnty Wkr; FNA; Hosp Aide; Teachers Aide; JV Var Mgr(s); JV Score Keeper; JV Sftbl; Hon Roll; NHS; Stu Trnr; JR Vlntr 400 Hr Awd; Sptrs Med.

MAY, LORIE; Woodstown Pilesgroove HS; Salem, NJ; (Y); FFA; Church Choir; Var Sftbl; Hon Roll; Am Legion Awd Medal 82-83; Ruritan Hnr Plque; Psychlgy.

MAY, MICHELE; Vineland SR HS; Vineland, NJ; (Y); 29/845; Cmnty Wkr; Service Clb; Spanish Clb; Lit Mag; Rep Jr Cls; High Hon Roll; Hon Roll; Spanish NHS; Spec Ed.

MAY, ROBIN; Belvidere HS; Blairstown, NJ; (Y); Art Clb; Cmnty Wkr; English Clb; Library Aide; Office Aide; Pep Clb; Spanish Clb; SADD; Varsity Clb; Pep Band; Tp 5 Spnsh I Awd 83; Chrldng Cert 83-86; E Straudsburg U; Htl Mngr.

MAY, SHAWN; High Point Regional HS; Lafayette, NJ; (Y); 12/230; Boy Scts; Debate Tm; Exploring; 4-H; Spanish Clb; Im JV Socr; High Hon Roll; Hon Roll; Sec NHS; Arch.

MAYER, CONRAD J; Haddonfield Memorial HS; Haddonfield, NJ; (Y); Am Leg Boys St; Church Yth Grp; Rep Stu Cncl; Capt Var Bsbl; JV Bsktbl; Var Socr; French Hon Soc; Hon Roll; NHS; Ntl Merit SF.

MAYER, DOROTHY; Mc Corristin Catholic HS; Trenton, NJ; (Y); 50/280; Church Yth Grp; Variety Show; Stu Cncl; Var L Bsktbl; Var L Socr; Var L Sftbl; Hon Roll; NHS; Pep Clb; Rep Frsh Cls; Ladies Aux Acient Order Hiberians Essay; Schl Sci Fair 2nd.

MAYER, LISA; Linden HS; Linden, NJ; (Y); Hst FBLA; Ski Clb; Yrbk Ed-Chief; Yrbk Phtg; Yrbk Stf; Cheerleading; Hon Roll; Bus Adm.

MAYER, NICHOLAS; Hudson Catholic Schl; Secaucus, NJ; (Y); Church Yth Grp; Hosp Aide; SADD; Ed Nwsp Sprt Ed; Rep Frsh Cls; Rep Soph Cls; Var Ftbl; Wt Lftg; Wrstlng; Bus Mgmt.

MAYER, PAM; Westwood HS; Westwood, NJ; (Y); 30/220; Ski Clb; Yrbk Stf; Trs Frsh Cls; Trs Soph Cls; Trs Jr Cls; Trs Sr Cls; Rep Stu Cncl; Co-Capt Cheerleading; VP French Hon Soc; NHS; Grls ST Altrnt 86; Lang.

MAYERS, GLEN; St Marys HS; Cliffwood Bch, NJ; (Y); Yrbk Phtg; Yrbk Stf; Var Socr; Hon Roll; Olympics Of Mind 86; Psychlgy.

MAYERS, KENNETH B; St Marys HS; Cliffwood Beach, NJ; (Y); 7/119; Am Leg Boys St; Yrbk Stf; Var Capt Socr; High Hon Roll; NHS; Pres Schlr; St Schlr; German Clb; Hon Roll; NEDT Awd; NJ Schlr/Ath 86; Pres Acad Fit Awd 86; Greater Middlesex Conf All Acad Tm 86; U Scranton; Biol.

MAYES, KAREN; St Anthony HS; Jersey City, NJ; (Y); Art Clb; Church Yth Grp; Cmnty Wkr; Computer Clb; Dance Clb; Pep Clb; Teachers Aide; Im Bowling; High Hon Roll; Hon Roll; Cert Awd 2nd Hnrs 84-86, 1st Hnrs 85; Outstndng Schltc Achvt Scholar 86; Shrthnd Cert; Type Cert.

MAYES JR, THOMAS D; Lenape Valley Regional HS; Sparta, NJ; (Y); 18/241; Church Yth Grp; CAP; Ski Clb; Church Choir; Yrbk Phtg; Var Trk; High Hon Roll; Pilot.

MAYES, TOM; Dover HS; Dover, NJ; (Y); 18/187; Am Leg Boys St; FCA; Ski Clb; Var Capt Ftbl; High Hon Roll; NHS; Latin Clb; Letterman Clb; Varsity Clb; JV Bsbl; Ftbl MVP Awd 85; Psych Awd 85-86; U Of FL; Bus.

MAYFIELD, DANIEL; Woodrow Wilson HS; Camden, NJ; (Y); Church Yth Grp; Dance Clb; Scholastic Bowl; Band; Church Choir; Variety Show; Rep Jr Cls; Hon Roll; Stu Of Mnth 85-86; NY Schl Of Arts Schlrshp 86; Vsl Art.

MAYHEW, KENNY; Cumberland Regonal HS; Bridgeton, NJ; (Y); 4-H; FFA; Ski Clb; 4-H Awd; Hon Roll; Greenhnd Awd 84; Farming.

MAYNARD, MARK; Newton HS; Andover, NJ; (S); 14/195; Boy Scts; Latin Clb; Math Tm; Lit Mag; Rep Stu Cncl; Socr; High Hon Roll; NHS; Pres Clsrm Young Amer 85; Hugh O Brien Ldrshp Sem 84; NJ Distngshd Schlr 86; Econ.

MAYRINA, KATHRINE M; Hillside HS; Hillside, NJ; (Y); Drama Clb; ROTC; Ski Clb; Spanish Clb; School Play; Stage Crew; Sftbl; Hon Roll; Rutgers U; Engrng.

MAYS, KEVIN; E Orange HS; E Orange, NJ; (S); 3/410; Math Tm; Yrbk Ed-Chief; Lit Mag; Var Stat Bsktbl; Hon Roll; NHS; Prfct Atten Awd; Mnrty HS Achvt Awd 86; Elec Engrng.

MAZOR, TANYA; Bruriah HS; Staten Isl, NY; (Y); Dance Clb; Temple Yth Grp; Variety Show; Yrbk Stf; Pres Soph Cls; Rep Jr Cls; NHS; Hnrary Mntn Sci Fair; Bus.

MAZUR, LISA; Manville HS; Manville, NJ; (Y); Dance Clb; Drama Clb; Pep Clb; Ski Clb; Stage Crew; Variety Show; Var Co-Capt Cheerleading; Powder Puff Ftbl; Hon Roll; St Teen Arts For Dnc 82; Perform Dance Champs-Grdn St Art Ctr 82; Hlpd MS Assn 85-86; Wilma Boyd Career Schl; Toursm.

MAZURKIEWICZ, STAN; Sayreville War Memorial HS; Parlin, NJ; (Y); Spanish Clb; Concert Band; Jazz Band; Mrchg Band; Orch; School Musical; JV Var Fld Hcky; Wt Lftg; JV Var Wrstlng; Hon Roll; Middlesex Cnty Arts-Music 86; PA ST; Bus.

MAZUROWSKI, PETER; North Warren Regional HS; Edmond, OK; (Y); 26/129; Ski Clb; Hon Roll; Psych.

MAZZA, ANTHONY; Roselle Catholic HS; Elizabeth, NJ; (Y); 80/210; Boy Scts; Ski Clb; Bsktbl; Crs Cntry; Socr; Wrstlng; Hon Roll; Engrng.

MAZZA, LISA; Toms River HS North; Toms River, NJ; (Y); 68/410; SADD; Band; Rep Jr Cls; Rep Stu Cncl; JV Bsktbl; JV Socr; Var Tennis; Wt Lftg; Obsrvr All Ocean Cnty & All Shore Tennis Tm Awd 84; Flagler U; Engl.

MAZZA, STEPHANIE; Millville SR HS; Millville, NJ; (Y); Camera Clb; Cmnty Wkr; SADD; Color Guard; Flag Corp; Nwsp Rptr; Sec Sr Cls; Rep Stu Cncl; Hon Roll; NHS; Psych.

MAZZALONI, JACKI; Clifton HS; Clifton, NJ; (Y); 11/564; JA; Spanish Clb; Capt Cheerleading; Mgr(s); Score Keeper; Cit Awd; High Hon Roll; Jr NHS; NHS; Spanish NHS; Montclair ST Coll; Bus.

MAZZARELLA, STEPHEN; Livingston HS; Livingston, NJ; (Y); Church Yth Grp; Hosp Aide; Key Clb; Jazz Band; Variety Show; Var L Tennis; High Hon Roll; Hon Roll.

MAZZELLA, DONNA; Lakeland Regional HS; Ringwood, NJ; (Y); Church Yth Grp; Hosp Aide; Math Tm; SADD; Yrbk Phtg; Rep Jr Cls; Rep Sr Cls; Rep Stu Cncl; Bowling; Powder Puff Ftbl; Human Awareness Day 85; Lock Haven U; Math.

MAZZELLA, ELAINE; Hillsborough HS; Bellemead, NJ; (Y); 33/297; Dance Clb; NFL; Pep Clb; Science Clb; Spanish Clb; Variety Show; Powder Puff Ftbl; High Hon Roll; NHS; Cert Awd Eng 86; Cook Coll; Meteorlgy.

MAZZELLA, PAUL; St Mary HS; Keansburg, NJ; (Y); 10/125; School Play; Yrbk Stf; Pres Frsh Cls; Pres Soph Cls; Pres Jr Cls; Pres Sr Cls; Pres Stu Cncl; Socr; High Hon Roll; Boy Scts; Bus.

MAZZERINA, KEITH; Passaic Valley Regional HS; West Paterson, NJ; (Y); 88/310; JV Bowling; Im Golf; Hon Roll; Montclair ST Coll; Bus.

MAZZILLI, MICHAEL; St Joseph Reg HS; Norwood, NJ; (Y); 60/200; Boy Scts; Ski Clb; JV Var Socr; JV L Trk; High Hon Roll; Hon Roll; Opt Clb Awd; Montvale Police Benevolent Assoc Schlrshp 86; Life Scout Awd 84; William Paterson Coll; Pblc Adm.

MAZZONI, DOREEN; Vineland HS; Vineland, NJ; (Y); 21/628; French Clb; Math Tm; Pep Clb; Political Wkr; Stat Bsktbl; NHS; Garden ST Schlrshp 86; Rutgers U; Med Technlgy.

MAZZONI, RANDALL; Vineland HS; Vineland, NJ; (Y); 36/800; Trs German Clb; Math Clb; Crs Cntry; JV Ftbl; NHS; Pres Schlr; St Schlr; Appntmnt US Air Force Acad; Appntmnt US Navl Acad; Navy ROTC Schlrshp Air Force ROTC Schlrshp; US Air Force Acad CO; Engr.

MC ADAM, FAITH; Egg Harbor Township HS; Pleasantville, NJ; (S); 13/266; GAA; Key Clb; Spanish Clb; Mrchg Band; JV Sftbl; Var Capt Tennis; Jr NHS; NHS; Office Aide.

MC ADAMS, JAMES; Paul VI HS; Clementon, NJ; (Y); 230/492; JV Ftbl; JV Trk; Camden Cnty Coll; Law Enfrcmnt.

MC ADAMS, JOHN; Queen Of Peace HS; N Arlington, NJ; (Y); 76/229; Church Yth Grp; Computer Clb; Science Clb; Im Fld Hcky; Hon Roll.

MC ADAMS, KENNETH; Hopatcong HS; Hopatcong, NJ; (Y); Church Yth Grp; Ski Clb; Varsity Clb; Var Golf; Var Capt Socr; Hon Roll; NHS; Sccr Sprtsmnshp Awd 85; Glf Mst Imprvd Awds 85 & 86; Bus.

MC ALVANAH, SUZANN; Bloomfield SR HS; Bloomfield, NJ; (Y); 37/442; Drama Clb; Girl Scts; Key Clb; Pres Spanish Clb; Chorus; Madrigals; Yrbk Stf; VP Pres Stu Cncl; NHS; Opt Clb Awd; Hugh O Brian Yth Fndtn Ambssdr 85; WA Wrkshp Sem 86; Outstndng Stu Ctzn Awd 84; Bus Admin.

MC ANDREW, MARK; Don Bosco Prep; Upper Saddle Rivr, NJ; (S); 7/210; Church Yth Grp; Model UN; Var Golf; JV Ice Hcky; JV Socr; High Hon Roll; Acad All Amer 85-86.

MC ANDREW, PATRICK J; Freehold Township HS; Freehold, NJ; (Y); 4/350; Cmnty Wkr; Ftbl; Var L Trk; Wt Lftg; NHS; Engrng.

MC ANENY, JOHN; James Caldwell HS; W Caldwell, NJ; (Y); Am Leg Boys St; Science Clb; Pres Jr Cls; Var Bsktbl; JV Ftbl; High Hon Roll; NHS; Yale Bk Awd 86; Med.

MC ANENY, MEG; Oak Knoll HS; Summit, NJ; (Y); Camera Clb; Church Yth Grp; Dance Clb; Key Clb; Pep Clb; Service Clb; Ski Clb; Chorus; Nwsp Ed-Chief; Nwsp Stf; Adv Plcmnt European Hist,Am Hist 85-87; Dedctn Awd Tennis 85-86; Hist.

MC AULEY, MARGARET; Oak Knoll Schl; S Orange, NJ; (Y); Art Clb; English Clb; French Clb; School Musical; Nwsp Ed-Chief; Pres Frsh Cls; VP Soph Cls; Ntl Merit Ltr; Cmnty Wkr; Hosp Aide; Oak Knoll Book Awd Schlrshp 82-86; Fairfield U; Communications.

MC AULIFFE, AMY; Bishop Ahr-St Thomas HS; Milltown, NJ; (S); 5/240; Cmnty Wkr; French Clb; Math Tm; Service Clb; Trk; High Hon Roll; Intl Frgn Lang Awd 84; Ntl Ed Dvlpmnt Tst Awd 84; Jrnlsm.

MC AULIFFE, CHRIS; Don Bosco Prep; Franklin Lakes, NJ; (Y); Model UN; Quiz Bowl; Ed Yrbk Stf; Lit Mag; Bsktbl; Coach Actv; High Hon Roll; Acad Schlrshp 82-83; Hghst Aver Brtsh Lit Gld Mdl 84-85; Coll Holy Cross.

MC AVEETY, MARK; Holy Cross HS; Riverton, NJ; (Y); Aud/Vis; Church Yth Grp; JA; Spanish Clb; Stage Crew; Hon Roll; Rutgers; Engrng.

MC BREEN, KELLEY; St John Vianney HS; Freehold, NJ; (S); 6/275; Hosp Aide; SADD; Stage Crew; Yrbk Stf; Stat Ftbl; Var L Trk; High Hon Roll; Hon Roll; VP NHS; Prfct Atten Awd; Picture Teen Arts Festival 84; Chem Cntst 86; Gold & White Awd Inter-Intra-Extra Crrclr Actvtcs 84-85; Pre Med.

MC BRIDE, D ANDRE M; Oakcrest HS; Mays Landing, NJ; (Y); 39/244; Boys Clb Am; Boy Scts; Cmnty Wkr; Computer Clb; French Clb; Political Wkr; Stu Cncl; Swmmng; Tennis; Hon Roll; Peter Francis Egnor Mem Fdtn Schlrshp 86; U Of Maryland; Pre Med.

MC BRIDE, ELLEN; Wildwood Catholic HS; Cape May, NJ; (Y); #29 In Class; Church Yth Grp; Spanish Clb; Nwsp Rptr; Nwsp Stf; Var Bsktbl; Sftbl; Hon Roll; Voaches Awd Varsty Bsktbl 85-86; Hournalsm.

MC CABE, JENNIFER; Kinnelon HS; Kinnelon, NJ; (Y); Camera Clb; Spanish Clb; Stat Bsbl; Stat Bsktbl; JV Cheerleading; Powder Puff Ftbl; Stat Socr; Hon Roll; NHS; Spanish NHS; Math.

MC CABE, MICHELE; Egg Harbor Twp HS; Linwood, NJ; (S); 29/317; GAA; Rep Stu Cncl; JV Bsktbl; Golf; Var Tennis; Hon Roll; Prfct Atten Awd; All Area, Star Ten Tm 83 & 85; Eductnl Lamp Learning 84-85; William & Mary; Econ.

MC CAFFREY, EILEEN; Morris Catholic HS; Denville, NJ; (Y); 7/142; Church Yth Grp; Girl Scts; Math Clb; Natl Beta Clb; Thesps; School Musical; High Hon Roll; NHS; Ntl Merit SF; German Clb; Bill Bradley Yng Ctzns Awd 86; Elem Educ.

MC CAHILL, JAY W; Dover HS; Dover, NJ; (Y); 8/220; Math Tm; Ski Clb; Pres Jr Cls; Pres Sr Cls; Bausch & Lomb Sci Awd; High Hon Roll; Hon Roll; Kiwanis Awd; NHS; Garden ST Distngushd Schlr; Rensselaer Math,Sci Awd; Rutgers U; Mech Engr.

MC CAHILL, SHEILA; St Aloysius HS; Jersey City, NJ; (Y); 7/107; Church Yth Grp; Nwsp Phtg; Yrbk Stf; Rep Stu Cncl; Bowling; Var Capt Cheerleading; Hon Roll; NHS; Friendly Sons St Patrick Soc Schlrshp 86-87; JC ST Coll Pres Citation Acad Achvt Awd 86; Montclair ST Coll; Cmmnt.

MC CALL, NAN; Camden Catholic HS; Pennsauken, NJ; (Y); 20/270; Sec Spanish Clb; School Musical; Yrbk Stf; Rep Jr Cls; Stu Cncl; Var Cheerleading; JV Fld Hcky; Hon Roll; Sec NHS; Spanish NHS; Engl Hnr Soc 85-86; Hist Hnr Soc 85-86; Pre Law.

MC CANN, BRYAN D; Northern Highlands Regional HS; Mahwah, NJ; (Y); Scholastic Bowl; Band; Lit Mag; Pres Jr Cls; Rep Stu Cncl; Var Socr; Var Trk; Ntl Merit SF; Pres Schlr; Stu Forum 85; Arts Symposum 85; Sec Guard.

MC CANN, CAROLYN; Scotch Plains Fanwood HS; Scotch Plains, NJ; (Y); Drama Clb; German Clb; School Play; Stage Crew; Var L Bsktbl; Var L Socr; Var L Sftbl; MVP Bsktbl Tm 83-84; MVP Vrsty Sccr 85-86; Landscp Dsgnr.

MC CANN, EILEEN; West Orange HS; W Orange, NJ; (Y); Church Yth Grp; Cmnty Wkr; GAA; Office Aide; Service Clb; Spanish Clb; Chorus; Church Choir; Nwsp Stf; Yrbk Stf.

MC CANN, MICHAEL T; Washington Twp HS; Sewell, NJ; (Y); Pres Spanish Clb; Thesps; School Musical; School Play; La Salle U; Crmnl Law.

MC CANTS, KELLY L; Marylawn HS; E Orange, NJ; (Y); 7/51; Spanish Clb; School Play; Nwsp Stf; Ed Yrbk Stf; Lit Mag; Capt Cheerleading; NHS; Ntl Merit Ltr; NEDT Awd; Princeton U.

MC CARDELL, JANE; Mainland Rgnl HS; Somers Point, NJ; (Y); #7 In Class; JV Fld Hcky; High Hon Roll; NHS; Ntl Merit SF; Archlgy.

MC CARRON, DIANA; Asbury Park HS; Bradley Beach, NJ; (Y); 1/140; Nwsp Ed-Chief; Stat Sftbl; Bausch & Lomb Sci Awd; High Hon Roll; NHS; Val; German Clb; Chorus; Stat Bowling; Kiwanis Hnr Soc 85-86; Distngushd Schlrs Schlrshp 86; Garden ST Schlrshp 86; Trenton ST Coll; Ed.

MC CARRON, KATHLEEN; East Brunswick HS; E Brunswick, NJ; (Y); Cmnty Wkr; Key Clb; Latin Clb; JV Crs Cntry; Var L Trk; Hon Roll; Rtgrs Coll.

MC CARTER, CHRISTINA; High Point Regional HS; Sussex, NJ; (Y); 8/260; Debate Tm; German Clb; Science Clb; Im Sftbl; Var Capt Swmmng; High Hon Roll; NHS; Church Yth Grp; Am Leg Aux Girls ST Alt 86; Swm Tm Ldrshpa Wd 86; Vet Med.

MC CARTHY, KERRY; Waldwick HS; Waldwick, NJ; (Y); Church Yth Grp; Cmnty Wkr; Math Tm; Ski Clb; Nwsp Rptr; Yrbk Rptr; JV Socr; JV Sftbl; Var Capt Tennis; Hon Roll; Hon Roll 84-86.

MC CARTHY, SHARON; Red Bank Regional HS; Little Silver, NJ; (Y); Nwsp Bus Mgr; French Hon Soc; High Hon Roll; Hon Roll; NHS.

MC CARTHY, STEPHEN G; Dwight Englewood Schl; Englewood, NJ; (Y); Am Leg Boys St; Rep Soph Cls; Rep Jr Cls; Rep Sr Cls; Var Ice Hcky; Var Lcrss; Var Socr; Hon Roll; HOBY Sem Atten; Wnnr Paul Ketting Photo Cont.

MC CARTHY, SUSAN; Arthur L Johnson HS; Clark, NJ; (S); 17/222; Sec Key Clb; Chorus; Yrbk Stf; Sec Stu Cncl; Trk; Hon Roll; Trs Spanish NHS; Quiz Bowl; Spanish Clb; School Play; 3rd Pl Music Educ Cncl Piano Cmptn 83-86; Hgh Hnrs Gld Auditns Clsscl Piano 82-86; Pltcl Sci.

MC CARTNEY JR, JAMES P; Egg Harbor Township HS; Scullville, NJ; (S); 30/270; Exploring; Key Clb; Varsity Clb; Band; Concert Band; Jazz Band; Mrchg Band; School Musical; Socr; VP NHS; Law.

MC CARTNEY, MEGHAN; Rutherford HS; Rutherford, NJ; (Y); Key Clb; Varsity Clb; Yrbk Stf; Rep Frsh Cls; Rep Soph Cls; Rep Sr Cls; JV Var Crs Cntry; Var JV Trk; Hon Roll; Ntl Merit Ltr.

MC CARTNEY, SCOTT; Egg Harbor Township HS; Scullville, NJ; (S); Boy Scts; Church Yth Grp; Key Clb; Concert Band; Mrchg Band; Pres Sr Cls; Rep Stu Cncl; Var Capt Socr; Jr NHS; NHS; Vrsty Schlr Awd, All Cnty, All Star Sccr Tm 84; Ntl Ldrshp, Merit Awd 85; West Point; Arch Engr.

MC CASKILL, ERIC; Long Branch HS; Long Branch, NJ; (S); FBLA; Pep Clb; Varsity Clb; Yrbk Stf; Sr Cls; Ftbl; Trk; Wt Lftg; Elks Awd; Hon Roll; 1600 Meter Rly Tm Chmpns 84; 800 Yrd Rlty Chmpn 85; Trck Rly Chmpns 84; Bus Mngmnt & Adm.

MC CAULEY, ALYSON M; Roselle Park HS; Roselle Pk, NJ; (Y); 36/129; FTA; Hosp Aide; JA; Office Aide; Spanish Clb; Band; Color Guard; Drill Tm; Mrchg Band; Twrlr; Ftr Tchr Of Amer Awd 86; Kean Coll; Spcl Educ Hrng.

MC CAULEY, JENNIFER; St John Vianney HS; Freehold, NJ; (Y); Church Yth Grp; JCL; Service Clb; Fld Hcky; Powder Puff Ftbl; Sftbl; Vllybl; DAR Awd; Bus.

MC CAULEY, JOHN; Hillsborough HS; Bellemead, NJ; (Y); 3/320; Math Tm; School Musical; Pres Soph Cls; Pres Stu Cncl; Var Crs Cntry; Var Trk; NHS.

MC CAULLEY, PATRICE; Holy Spirit HS; Longport, NJ; (Y); 28/394; Yrbk Ed-Chief; Hon Roll; NHS; Law.

MC CLAMMY, JAMES I; West Windsor-Plainsboro HS; Princeton, NJ; (Y); Off Am Leg Boys St; Off Model UN; Band; Jazz Band; Orch; School Musical; Yrbk Phtg; High Hon Roll; Ntl Merit Ltr; Computer Clb; Govnrs Schl Pub Issues & Future Of NJ 86; Corp Law.

MC CLANE, JAMES; Park Ridge HS; Park Ridge, NJ; (Y); 1/120; Math Clb; Quiz Bowl; Science Clb; Varsity Clb; Var Bsbl; Var Capt Bsktbl; JV Ftbl; High Hon Roll; Pres NHS; Val; Rnslr Math & Sci Awd 86; NJAATSP Outstndng Stu Cert 86; Amer Lgn Jrsy Boys St 86; Bio Med Engrng.

MC CLEAN, BONNIE; Pual VI HS; Haddonfield, NJ; (Y); 201/521; Math Clb; SADD; Capt Bsktbl; Capt Fld Hcky; Sftbl; Lycoming.

MC CLELLAN, STEVEN; Vailsburg HS; Newark, NJ; (Y); Am Leg Boys St; Art Clb; Band; Stu Cncl; Var Bsbl; JV Bsktbl; JV Ftbl; Hon Roll; Rutgers; Comp Engr.

MC CLENAHAN, JOHN; St John Vianney HS; Aberdeen, NJ; (Y); Math Tm; Bsktbl; Capt Crs Cntry; Capt Trk; High Hon Roll; Hon Roll; Sec NHS; Prfct Atten Awd; Indoor Track Captn 84-86; Appalacian Svc Proj Vol 85-86; Engrng.

MC CLOSKEY, DAWN; Burlington County Vo- Tech; Edgewater Pk, NJ; (Y); Nwsp Rptr; Nwsp Stf; Yrbk Stf; Mgr(s); Hon Roll; Burlington CC; Child Psych.

MC CLOSKEY, MARGARET; Monsignor Donovan HS; Beachwood, NJ; (Y); Drama Clb; Hosp Aide; Ski Clb; SADD; Yrbk Stf; Stat Bsktbl; School Musical; Bus.

MC CLOUGH, KIMBERLY; Cumberland Regional HS; Bridgeton, NJ; (Y); Church Yth Grp; Chorus; JV Var Bsktbl; High Hon Roll; Hon Roll; Air Force.

MC CLOY, TAMMY; Lower Cape May Regional HS; W Cape May, NJ; (Y); 4/242; Math Tm; Pep Clb; Spanish Clb; Varsity Clb; Yrbk Stf; Rep Stu Cncl; JV Bsktbl; Var Fld Hcky; Hon Roll; Jr NHS; Athltc Schlrs Awd 84-86; Marine Phy Ftns Awd 84-86; Prfct Attndnc 84-86; Pre-Law.

MC COMBS, TYRONE; Palmyra HS; Palmyra, NJ; (Y); 11/121; Drama Clb; German Clb; Church Choir; Yrbk Stf; Pres Jr Cls; Pres Stu Cncl; Hon Roll; Pres NHS; Sec Church Yth Grp; Dist Gov Of DIRC 86-87; Ed.

MC CONNELL, KEVIN; Columbia HS; Maplewood, NJ; (Y); Aud/Vis; Boy Scts; Drama Clb; Math Clb; SADD; Capt Stage Crew; JV Wrstlng; Lion Awd; Marquette U; Biomed Engr.

MC CONNELL, STACEY; Middlesex HS; Middlesex, NJ; (Y); 22/160; Girl Scts; Key Clb; Spanish Clb; Varsity Clb; Concert Band; Jazz Band; Mrchg Band; Crs Cntry; Trk; Girl Scout Gold Ldrshp Awd 85-86; Stu Mnth 85; Bloomsburg U.

MC COOL, JANET; Washington Twp HS; Grenloch, NJ; (Y); Art Clb; French Clb; Hon Roll; Cmrcl Art.

MC CORKELL, LISA; Oakcrest HS; Hammonton, NJ; (Y); 14/244; Key Clb; Stat Bsbl; Stat Socr; Stat Wrstlng; Hon Roll; VP NHS; Schlr 84-86; Mgmt.

MC CORMACK, MARY; Wardlaw Hartridge Schl; Edison, NJ; (Y); 9/51; Church Yth Grp; Drama Clb; Hosp Aide; Pres SADD; Chorus; School Musical; School Play; Yrbk Stf; High Hon Roll; NHS; Key Clb VP 86-87; Field Hcky 85-86; Vllybl 86; Vocal Msc.

MC CORMACK, RENE; Scotch Plains-Fanwood HS; Fanwood, NJ; (Y); AFS; Church Yth Grp; DECA; French Clb; FBLA; Key Clb; Chorus; Var Sftbl; French Hon Soc; Bus Adm.

MC CORMICK, ANNMARIE; Nutley HS; Nutley, NJ; (Y); Sftbl; High Hon Roll; Chem.

MC COY, JAMES; Southern Regional HS; Waretown, NJ; (Y); Aud/Vis; Chess Clb; Computer Clb; Math Clb; Math Tm; Hon Roll; NHS; Prfct Atten Awd; Sci Sympsium 85; Sci Day Comptn 85-86; Comp Sci.

MC CRACKEN, KELLY; Roselle Catholic HS; Elizabeth, NJ; (S); 20/210; Mgr Church Yth Grp; Girl Scts; Var Socr; High Hon Roll; Hon Roll; Spn Proficiency Awd 85; Champ Sftbl Lg Tm 85; Hnr Clsses 83; U GA; Law.

MC CRAE, WANDA; East Orange HS; East Orange, NJ; (S); Pres Girl Scts; Hosp Aide; Math Tm; Church Choir; Cit Awd; High Hon Roll; Hon Roll; Jr NHS; Prfct Atten Awd; Montclair ST Coll Music Prep Div Schlrshp 83; Outstndng Ctznshp & Acad Bio Achvt Awd 85; Elec Engrng.

MC CRAY, JOYCE; Central Jersey Christian Schl; Wall, NJ; (S); 9/18; Church Yth Grp; Office Aide; Ski Clb; Yrbk Ed-Chief; Sec Trs Jr Cls; VP Sr Cls; Cheerleading; Stat Score Keeper; Socr; High Hon Roll; Schlrp Johnson & Wales Coll 86-87; Johnson & Wales Coll; Hotel-Res.

MC CREA, BILLY; South Hunterdon Regional HS; Lambertville, NJ; (Y); 5/72; Am Leg Boys St; FBLA; Key Clb; Chorus; VP Frsh Cls; Pres Soph Cls; Rep Jr Cls; Rep Sr Cls; Trs Stu Cncl; L Bsbl; U Of PA; Finance.

MC CREARY, LORI; Washington Twp HS; Turnersville, NJ; (Y); Am Leg Aux Girls St; Church Yth Grp; Cmnty Wkr; French Clb; Model UN; Capt Color Guard; Mrchg Band; Yrbk Ed-Chief; Yrbk Stf; Hon Roll; Intl Bus.

MC CUE, KEITH; Washington Township HS; Sewell, NJ; (Y); Church Yth Grp; Mathletes; Var Trk.

MC CUE, MARTHA; Holy Cross HS; Riverton, NJ; (Y); Stage Crew; JV Bsktbl; JV Var Trk; High Hon Roll; Hon Roll; NHS; Engrg.

MC CULLAGH, PAUL; Don Bosco Prep HS; Garnerville, NY; (S); 8/180; VP Model UN; Nwsp Ed-Chief; Hon Roll; NHS; Wrld Hist Awd 83; Amer Hstry Awd 84; Pre-Calcls Awd 85.

MC CULLOCH, HEATHER; Middletown HS South; Lincroft, NJ; (Y); Dance Clb; Drama Clb; Hosp Aide; Stage Crew; Nwsp Rptr; Nwsp Stf; Powder Puff Ftbl; Hon Roll; Jrnlsm.

MC CURDY, PAULA; Delsea Regional HS; Franklinville, NJ; (Y); 1/200; Am Leg Aux Girls St; Debate Tm; Drama Clb; Yrbk Ed-Chief; Mgr(s); Tennis; High Hon Roll; NHS; St Schlr; Amer Chem Soc Cert Excllnc 86; Rutgers; Optmtrst.

MC CUSKER, STEVE; Egg Harbor Township HS; Mays Landing, NJ; (S); 41/266; Key Clb; Ski Clb; Trs Soph Cls; Crs Cntry; Ftbl; Trk; Hon Roll; Merit Awds-Ntl Ldrshp & Ntl Sci 85.

MC DANIEL, MICHAEL D; University HS; Newark, NJ; (Y); 5/80; Civic Clb; Cmnty Wkr; Debate Tm; Exploring; JA; Library Aide; Radio Clb; Yrbk Rptr; JV Trk; High Hon Roll; Vrsty Lncln Dglss Dbt 86; Comp.

MC DANIEL, SHEILAREE; Academic HS; Jersey City, NJ; (Y); Chorus; Church Choir; Powder Puff Ftbl; High Hon Roll; Prfct Atten Awd; Cert Svc JR Nrs Aide 84; Cert Recog U S Navys Sec 85; Bus Adm.

MC DANIELS, KAREN; Overbrook Regional SR HS; W Berlin, NJ; (Y); Church Yth Grp; Drama Clb; German Clb; Band; Color Guard; Concert Band; Mrchg Band; Hon Roll; NHS; Cmmnctns.

MC DERMOTT, GEORGE; Queen Of Peace HS; Kearny, NJ; (Y); 112/242; Cmnty Wkr; Drama Clb; Letterman Clb; SADD; School Musical; School Play; Var Socr; Capt Im Vllybl; Hon Roll; Opt Clb Awd; Publc Rltns.

MC DERMOTT, MICHAEL; Monsignor Donovan HS; Bayville, NJ; (Y); 29/243; Church Yth Grp; Hon Roll; Religion III Awd 85-86; Accntng.

MC DERMOTT, SEAN P; Don Bosco Prep HS; Stony Pt, NY; (Y); CAP; Ski Clb; Band; Nwsp Ed-Chief; Rep Jr Cls; Civil Air Patrol Cert Recgntn Life Savng 85; Cadet Officer 86; Air Force; Pilot.

MC DERMOTT, VIRGINIA; Riverside HS; Riverside, NJ; (S); 3/90; Varsity Clb; Nwsp Stf; Rep Jr Cls; Var Capt Cheerleading; JV Sftbl; Hon Roll; NEDT Awd 84; Govs Schl 85; Bus.

MC DEVITT, JOHN; Bishop George AHR HS; Scotch Plains, NJ; (Y); Am Leg Boys St; German Clb; Math Tm; Band; Nwsp Rptr; Rep Stu Cncl; Var Bsbl; Var Bsktbl; Var Capt Socr; High Hon Roll.

MC DEVITT, JOHN; Hackettstown HS; Hackettstown, NJ; (Y); Aud/Vis; Latin Clb; Q&S; Spanish Clb; Teachers Aide; Yrbk Bus Mgr; Yrbk Stf; VP Sr Cls; Var Crs Cntry; Var Trk; U Of Notre Dame; Engrng.

MC DEVITT, TARA; Bayonne HS; Bayonne, NJ; (Y); 15/362; Computer Clb; Drama Clb; French Clb; Math Tm; Crs Cntry; Trk; High Hon Roll; Jr NHS; NHS; Manhattan Coll Schlrshp & Grant 86; Manhattan Coll; Phy Thrpy.

MC DONALD, DANIELLE; Gloucester JR-SR HS; Gloucester, NJ; (Y); French Clb; Q&S; Band; Chorus; Concert Band; Mrchg Band; Orch; Pep Band; Lit Mag; JV Sftbl; Music.

MC DONALD, KEELEY; Roxbury HS; Landing, NJ; (Y); 40/436; AFS; Political Wkr; Ski Clb; Orch; Rep Soph Cls; Sec Jr Cls; Capt Fld Hcky; L Sftbl; Hon Roll; NHS; Pres Physcl Ftnss Awd 85; European Touring Choir 84; Govnrs Schl Of Music 86; Pol Sci.

MC DONALD, LISA; Immaculate Conception HS; Newark, NJ; (Y); 3/62; Yrbk Stf; Var Sftbl; Bausch & Lomb Sci Awd; High Hon Roll; NHS; Spanish NHS; Shlrshp Coll Wnms Club Mntclr 86; Carmen Orechio NJ ST Senate 86; Catholic Daughters 86; Rutgers U; Biology.

MC DONALD, MARC; Dwight Morrow HS; Englewood, NJ; (Y); Church Yth Grp; Cmnty Wkr; FCA; FBLA; Nwsp Stf; Prfct Atten Awd; Rep Jr Cls; JV Ftbl; JV Trk; Ntl Amer Studys Awd; Bst Mdl Cngrss Prjct 86; Rutgers U; Grphc Dsgn.

MC DONALD, PATRICK; Christian Brothers Acad; Springlake, NJ; (Y); Cmnty Wkr; Dance Clb; Varsity Clb; Chorus; Var L Bsbl; Im Bsktbl; Im Ftbl; JV L Mgr(s); Im Socr; Hon Roll; Spirit Comm-Chrmn/Athltc Comm 2 Yrs/Dance Comm 2 Yrs 87; Ump-Babe Ruth Lge, 2 Yrs Ump Little Lge; Sociology.

MC DONALD, RAYANNE; Edgewood Regional SR HS; Sicklerville, NJ; (Y); FBLA; Office Aide; Stat Socr; JV Sftbl; Hon Roll; Jr NHS; Bus Admin.

MC DONALD, RENFORD; Clifford J Scott HS; E Orange, NJ; (Y); Boy Scts; Church Yth Grp; Computer Clb; 4-H; Intnl Clb; Math Clb; Red Cross Aide; Stage Crew; Socr; Trk; Cert Most Imprvd Engl 85-86; Boston U; Engrng.

MC DONNELL, ROBERT; Hillsborough HS; Somerville, NJ; (Y); 68/285; Boy Scts; Rep Frsh Cls; Mgr Bsktbl; Stat Ftbl; Var Golf; Mgr(s); Score Keeper; SAR Awd; VFW Awd; Eagle Scout 85; Wilkes Coll; Envrnmntl Engr.

MC DONNELL, STACEY; Mount Saint Mary Acad; Spotswood, NJ; (S); 10/90; Church Yth Grp; Computer Clb; Ski Clb; Chorus; School Play; Nwsp Sprt Ed; Nwsp Stf; Yrbk Stf; Hon Roll; Cert NJ Spcl Olympcs 84-85; Brdcst Jrnlsm.

MC DONOUGH, JAMES; Manasquan HS; Freehold, NJ; (Y); 67/234; Computer Clb; Math Clb; JV Ftbl; JV Trk; High Hon Roll; Hon Roll; Monmouth College; Fnce.

MC DOWELL, CHRISTA; Millville SR HS; Millville, NJ; (Y); 3/435; Am Leg Aux Girls St; Trs Church Yth Grp; SADD; Color Guard; Rep Stu Cncl; Var Fld Hcky; JV Sftbl; Var Trk; NHS; Prfct Atten Awd; Compu Sci.

MC DUFFIE, LOUISE; Malcomn X Shabazz HS; Newark, NJ; (S); 7/268; Computer Clb; Yrbk Stf; Sec Jr Cls; Trs Sr Cls; Capt Sftbl; Cit Awd; Hon Roll; Jr NHS; VP NHS; Comp Sci.

MC DYER, SHARON; Camden Catholic HS; Cherry Hill, NJ; (Y); 31/265; French Clb; School Play; Ed Yrbk Stf; Rep Jr Cls; Rep Sr Cls; Var Capt Cheerleading; High Hon Roll; Hon Roll; NHS; Gym; Sci Hnr Socty 84; Knghts Clmbus Essy Cntst 1st Pl 83; S Jrsy ST Chrldg Champ 86; Chem.

MC ELFISH, DONNA; Trinton Regional HS; Somerdale, NJ; (Y); 15/295; Sec AFS; French Clb; Science Clb; Nwsp Rptr; NHS; Schlrshp Ltr 83-84; Cert Recog Outstndng Achvt Chem 84-85; Cert Recog Outstndng Achvt Physcs 85-86; Baylor U; Engrng.

MC ELNEA, CHRIS; West Essex HS; Essex Fells, NJ; (Y); Hon Roll; Rutgers; Phrmcst.

MC ELROY, EILEEN; Cinnaminson HS; Cinna, NJ; (Y); Church Yth Grp; SADD; Rep Frsh Cls; Rep Soph Cls; Rep Jr Cls; JV Var Civic Clb; JV Var Lcrss; High Hon Roll; Hon Roll; NHS; Lacrosse 3rd Tm B C S L 86.

MC ELROY, MARY ERIN; Cinnaminson HS; Cinnaminson, NJ; (Y); 7/252; Church Yth Grp; Science Clb; Rep Soph Cls; Rep Jr Cls; Rep Sr Cls; Rep Stu Cncl; JV Capt Fld Hcky; JV Capt Lcrss; High Hon Roll; NHS; Fld Hcky & La Crosse Clb Schlrshps 86; Pepsi-Cola Schlr/Athltc Schlrshp 86; Grl Athltc Of Yr & Frnlst 86; William & Mary Coll; Bio.

MC ELWAIN, JOHN; Bishop George AHR HS; Edison, NJ; (Y); 81/250; Bowling; Rutgers.

MC ENERY, JOHN; Pitman HS; Pitman, NJ; (Y); 37/140; Spanish Clb; Var Bsbl; Gloucester Cnty Coll; Bus Mgmt.

MC FADDEN, DAMON; Eastside HS; Paterson, NJ; (Y); Mrchg Band; Bsbl; High Hon Roll; Hon Roll; Tlnt Shw; Awd Print Shp, Wood Shp; Marines; Comp.

MC FADDEN, DENISE; Mother Seton Regional HS; Roselle Pk, NJ; (Y); 27/124; Exploring; Hosp Aide; Science Clb; Service Clb; Drill Tm; School Play.

MC FADDEN, SANDY; Williamstown HS; Williamstown, NJ; (Y); French Clb; Girl Scts; Service Clb; Yrbk Stf; Off Frsh Cls; Off Soph Cls; Stu Cncl; NHS; Prfct Atten Awd; Rainbw Svc Awd 86; Acdmc Excllnc Awd 84 & 86.

MC FILLIN, TERRI; Holy Spirit HS; Margate, NJ; (Y); Cit Awd; Hon Roll; Lawyer.

MC GARRY, JEANNE; South Plainfield HS; S Plainfield, NJ; (Y); 55/281; Computer Clb; French Clb; Latin Clb; Ski Clb; Varsity Clb; Nwsp Rptr; Yrbk Stf; Capt Var Crs Cntry; Capt Trk; Elks Awd; Marietta Coll; Comp Sci.

MC GARRY, ROSEMARIE; St Joseph Of The Palisades HS; North Bergen, NJ; (S); Spanish Clb; Variety Show; Nwsp Stf; Yrbk Stf; Sftbl; Swmmng; Tennis; Hon Roll; Spanish NHS; Med.

MC GEARY, KERRY ANNE; Westfield SR HS; Westfield, NJ; (Y); 71/529; Church Yth Grp; Key Clb; Spanish Clb; Chorus; Church Choir; Stage Crew; JV Socr; JV Sftbl; High Hon Roll; Hon Roll; YFU Awd For Exch Stu 86; Hgh Hons Awd 84; Law.

MC GEE, KIMBERLY; Memorial HS; Cedar Grove, NJ; (S); 18/118; Church Yth Grp; Key Clb; Spanish Clb; Band; Color Guard; Orch; School Musical; School Play; Stage Crew; Nwsp Rptr; Bio.

MC GEE, SECORA; Passaic Valley Regional HS; Totowa, NJ; (Y); VP Debate Tm; Drama Clb; Radio Clb; Chorus; School Musical; Nwsp Stf; Lit Mag; Cheerleading; Cit Awd; Ntl Merit SF; US Naval Academy; Test Pilot.

MC GEEHAN, CAROLE; Lower Cape Mey Regional HS; N Cape May, NJ; (Y); 7/250; Church Yth Grp; French Clb; Key Clb; Nwsp Rptr; Yrbk Rptr; Cheerleading; French Hon Soc; High Hon Roll; NHS; Pol Sci.

MC GHEE, VICTORIA A; Kent Place Schl; Roselle, NJ; (Y); Chorus; School Musical; Stage Crew; Ed Nwsp Phtg; Rep Sr Cls; Var Sftbl; Cit Awd; St Schlr; Natl Achvt Schlrshp 85-86; Cum Laude 85-86; Yale U.

MC GILL, GRETCHEN ANN; Bloomfield SR HS; Bloomfld, NJ; (Y); 28/442; GAA; VP Key Clb; Capt Drill Tm; Yrbk Stf; Rep Soph Cls; Rep Jr Cls; Rep Sr Cls; Rep Stu Cncl; Var Trk; High Hon Roll.

MC GILL, SUSAN; Penns Grove HS; Carneys Point, NJ; (Y); Spanish Clb; Crs Cntry; Mgr(s); Hon Roll; Diploma De Merito 85-86; Sr Athlt Awd 84-86; Air Force.

MC GINLEY, EILEEN; Mount St Dominic Acad; Fairfield, NJ; (Y); Dance Clb; GAA; JCL; Latin Clb; Library Aide; Pep Clb; Service Clb; Ski Clb; Spanish Clb; Varsity Clb; Essex Country JR Miss 85; Mt Saint Dominic Recrtmnt Awd 85-86; MIP Var Sccr 84; Business Administration.

MC GINLEY, MICHAEL; Marist HS; Bayonne, NJ; (Y); 5/120; Key Clb; Im Bsktbl; Im Vllybl; High Hon Roll; Spanish NHS; Partial Schlrshp $200 HS 84-87.

MC GINNITY, KERRY; Keansburg HS; Keansburg, NJ; (Y); 2/110; German Clb; Trs Key Clb; Yrbk Phtg; Yrbk Stf; Trs Frsh Cls; Trs Soph Cls; Trs Jr Cls; VP Stu Cncl; Stat Ftbl; Var JV Tennis; Athlt Schlr Awd; Georgetown-Schuller; Intl Rltns.

MC GINTY, JAMES; Toms River HS North; Toms River, NJ; (Y); 6/412; Am Leg Boys St; Science Clb; Yrbk Sprt Ed; Pres Jr Cls; Pres Sr Cls; Rep Stu Cncl; JV Var Bsktbl; JV Var Ftbl; Var Trk; High Hon Roll; Acdmc Awd 84-86.

MC GIVERN, CHRIS; Ocean Township HS; Oakhurst, NJ; (Y); 140/333; Boy Scts; Church Yth Grp; Var Capt Crs Cntry; Var Capt Trk; Cngrssnl Awd Brnz 85.

MC GLINCHY, COLLEEN; Triton Regional HS; Somerdale, NJ; (Y); 39/296; Hosp Aide; Office Aide; Chorus; School Musical; Nwsp Stf; Yrbk Stf; Off Frsh Cls; Off Soph Cls; Off Jr Cls; Mgr Crs Cntry.

MC GLYNN, CHRISTY; Mainland Regional HS; Northfield, NJ; (Y); Church Yth Grp; Girl Scts; Radio Clb; Ski Clb; SADD; Capt Mrchg Band; Ed Yrbk Stf; Rep Stu Cncl; Crs Cntry; Swmmng; Save Our Chldrn Prgm 84-85; Mst Outstndng In Bndfrnt 83-85; Intl Bus.

MC GLYNN, PATRICK; Passaic Valley HS; Little Falls, NJ; (Y); Ski Clb; Varsity Clb; Yrbk Sprt Ed; Socr; Tennis; Hon Roll; Accntng.

MC GOVERN, BRIAN; Roselle Catholic HS; Elizabeth, NJ; (Y); 90/195; Church Yth Grp; Cmnty Wkr; Computer Clb; FBLA; Math Tm; Science Clb; Ski Clb; Im Bsktbl; Hon Roll; Natl Bus Hnr Soc 85-86; Bookkpng/Acctng Profcncy Awd 85-86; Accntnt.

MC GOVERN, BRIAN; Union Catholic Regional HS; Fanwood, NJ; (Y); 40/360; Boy Scts; Latin Clb; Service Clb; Ski Clb; Cit Awd; Hon Roll; SAR Awd; Eagl Sct 84; Acadmc Al-Amer 86; Rquetbl 84-86.

MC GOWAN, SHAWN; Holy Spirit HS; Absecon, NJ; (Y); #46 In Class; School Play; JV Var Tennis; High Hon Roll; Hon Roll; NHS; Bus Admin.

MC GOWAN, TRACEY ANN; Wildwood HS; W Wildwood, NJ; (Y); 1/121; Trs Civic Clb; Ed Lit Mag; Trs Frsh Cls; Pres Soph Cls; Trs Jr Cls; Sec Sr Cls; Mgr Bsktbl; Sec Trs NHS; Val; Am Leg Aux Girls St; Gvnrs Tchng Schlrshp Prgm 86; Douglass Coll; Tchr.

MC GRATH, CATHERINE; Middletown HS South; Lincroft, NJ; (Y); 75/436; Band; Concert Band; Mrchg Band; School Musical; School Play; Symp Band; Crs Cntry; Trk; Hon Roll; NEDT Awd; Pres Schlrshp 86; U DE; Psychlgst.

MC GRATH, KEVIN; Jonathan Dayton Regional HS; Mountainside, NJ; (Y); 78/222; VP Church Yth Grp; Spanish Clb; Chorus; Madrigals; Mrchg Band; Ftbl; Boy Scts; CAP; Varsity Clb; Concert Band; Thomas J Riccardi Schlrshp 86; Myrs Dy Glfrm Schlrshp 86; Montclair St Coll; Physcl Educ.

MC GRATH, ROBERT B; West Deptford HS; Woodbury, NJ; (Y); 1/232; Am Leg Boys St; Cmnty Wkr; Exploring; Red Cross Aide; Var Bsktbl; Var Crs Cntry; Var Capt Tennis; Bausch & Lomb Sci Awd; Elks Awd; High Hon Roll; PA Inqurer Nwspr Crrr 86; Fnlst Gvrnrs Schl Sci 85; West Deptford Mnccpl Yth Cmsn 85; Dickinson Coll; Blgy.

MC GRATH, SHANNON; North Bergen HS; N Bergen, NJ; (Y); 94/470; Art Clb; Rep Frsh Cls; Rep Soph Cls; VP Jr Cls; Var Cheerleading.

MC GRAW, CHRISTINE; Triton Regional HS; Bellmawr, NJ; (Y); AFS; Drama Clb; Sec French Clb; Sec FHA; Office Aide; Speech Tm; School Play; Var Cheerleading; Mgr(s); JV Trk; Bst Sprtng Actrs 85; NY U; Drama.

MC GROGAN, WILLIAM; Parsippany Hills HS; Parsippany, NJ; (Y); FBLA; Temple Yth Grp; Band; Symp Band; Variety Show; Ftbl; Score Keeper; Wt Lftg; Wrstlng; Hon Roll; Rutgers; Pharmacy.

MC GUINNES, DAVID; Hamilton High School East; Trenton, NJ; (Y); Boy Scts; Exploring; ROTC; JV Socr; Trenton ST Coll; Acctng.

MC GUIRE, JAMES; Wayne Valley HS; Wayne, NJ; (Y); 80/320; Church Yth Grp; Latin Clb; Stage Crew; Lit Mag; JV Bsbl; JV Crs Cntry; Hon Roll; Ntl Merit Ltr; Ntl Latin Exam Magna Cum Laude Awd 83; Montclair ST Coll; History.

MC GUIRE, JOHN; Red Bank Catholic HS; Red Bank, NJ; (Y); FCA; Q&S; Nwsp Sprt Ed; Nwsp Stf; JV Var Bsbl; Im JV Bsktbl; High Hon Roll; Hon Roll; NHS; Bus Admn.

MC GUIRE, KEVIN; Roselle Catholic HS; Roselle, NJ; (S); JV Bsbl; Var Bsktbl; Socr; High Hon Roll.

MC GUIRE, MICHAEL; Toms River East HS; Toms River, NJ; (Y); 81/585; Var Capt Ftbl; Powder Puff Ftbl; Var Capt Trk; Wt Lftg; Ocean Cnty Obsrvr 1st Tm All Cnty Nose Tackle 85; US Mrchnt Mrne Acad; Mrne Eng.

MC GUIRE, PETER; St Peters Prep; Union City, NJ; (Y); 12/206; Camera Clb; Church Yth Grp; Cmnty Wkr; Dance Clb; High Hon Roll; Gold Mdl Latin 84; Bio.

MC GUIRE, RICHARD; Clifton HS; Clifton, NJ; (Y); Church Yth Grp; Ski Clb; Crs Cntry; Golf; Swmmng; High Hon Roll; Jr NHS.

MC GUIRE, STEPHEN; South Hunterdon Regional HS; Lambertville, NJ; (S); 5/68; Am Leg Boys St; Yrbk Stf; Bsbl; Bsktbl; Ftbl; Hon Roll; VP NHS; Mst Imprvd Bsbl 85; Bobby Godown Bsktbl 85; 2nd Tm All W Jersey Bsbl 85; Bus Adm.

MC GUIRE, TRACY; Overbrook SR HS; Clementon, NJ; (Y); Spanish Clb; Varsity Clb; VP Jr Cls; Stat Bsktbl; Stat Ftbl; Mgr(s); Var Sftbl; Stat Wrstlng; Hon Roll; Rep Frsh Cls; Cls Pres.

MC GUIRL, MICHELE; St Aloysius HS; Jersey City, NJ; (Y); Yrbk Stf; Bowling; Hon Roll; Rutgers U.

MC GURK, COLLEEN; Maple Shade HS; Maple Shade, NJ; (Y); VP DECA; Rep Frsh Cls; Rep Soph Cls; Rep Jr Cls; JV Cheerleading; Var JV Socr; High Hon Roll; Jr NHS; 1st Pl Finc & Credt Wrttn Evnt NJ ST DECA Conf 86; 5th Pl Finc & Credt Wrttn Natl DECA Conf 86; Penn ST; Bus.

MC HUGH, STEVEN ELLIOT; Hackettstown HS; Hackettstown, NJ; (Y); 93/207; Am Leg Boys St; Camera Clb; Dance Clb; Drama Clb; FFA; Varsity Clb; VP Chorus; School Musical; Variety Show; Socr; 4 Yr Mbr Awd Chorus; Cnty Coll-Morris; Mngr Bus.

MC HUGH, TERRY; James Caldwell HS; W Caldwell, NJ; (Y); Rep Stu Cncl; JV Bsbl; Ftbl.

MC INDOE, KATHY; Bogota HS; Bogota, NJ; (Y); 32/105; Radio Clb; Ski Clb; Teachers Aide; Chorus; Yrbk Stf; Rep Stu Cncl; JV Var Cheerleading; JV Var Pom Pon; Hon Roll; Schl Muscl Cstum Commt 85-86; Prom 86-87; Typng Awd 85; Phtgrphy.

MC INERNEY, SUSAN D; Central Jersey Christian Schl; Elberon, NJ; (S); 11/18; Church Yth Grp; Drama Clb; Ski Clb; Band; Chorus; Church Choir; Pep Band; School Musical; School Play; Nwsp Stf; Cheerleading-Joy Awd 83-84; Music.

MC INTOSH, NICOLE; Malcolm X Shabazz HS; Newark, NJ; (S); GAA; Varsity Clb; Rep Jr Cls; Var Crs Cntry; Var Trk; NHS; Comp Sci.

MC INTOSH, TARA; Buena Regional HS; Buena, NJ; (S); Ski Clb; Stage Crew; Rep Soph Cls; Rep Jr Cls; Rep Stu Cncl; Tchng.

MC INTYRE, ELIZABETH; Westfield SR HS; Westfield, NJ; (Y); 38/514; Church Yth Grp; Chorus; Church Choir; School Musical; Rptr Nwsp Stf; Hon Roll; NHS; Spanish NHS; Spanish Clb; School Play; NJ All ST Chorus 85-86; Westfld JR Music Clb Pres 86-87.

MC INTYRE, LAUREN; Bishop Eustace Prep; Cherry Hill, NJ; (Y); 8/200; Cmnty Wkr; Debate Tm; French Clb; Math Clb; Science Clb; School Play; Stage Crew; Ed Lit Mag; Hon Roll; NHS.

MC IVER, DELENIA; Clifford J Scott HS; E Orange, NJ; (S); #2 In Class; Hosp Aide; Math Clb; Aud/Vis; Spanish Clb; Nwsp Stf; Sec Soph Cls; Sec Jr Cls; Hon Roll; Hst NHS; Mayor E Orange 85 For Day 85; Aero Sp Engr.

MC IVER, ROGER; Barringer HS; Newark, NJ; (Y); Boy Scts; Stage Crew; Rep Jr Cls; JV Var Bsktbl; Trk; Newark Muncpl Councl Bsktbl 85-86; Cmmnctn.

MC KAY, DOUG; Timothy Christian Schl; Piscataway, NJ; (S); 1/32; Church Yth Grp; Var L Bsbl; Var Capt Socr; VP NHS; Ntl Merit SF; Pres Schlr; St Schlr; Val; Computer Clb; Drama Clb; Wheaton Coll.

MC KEAN, JULIE; Red Bank Catholic HS; Middletown, NJ; (Y); Civic Clb; Cmnty Wkr; 4-H; Pep Clb; Political Wkr; Ski Clb; Chorus; School Musical; Twrlr; 4-H Awd; 3rd Pl Yr Equitatn Champ MCHSA; 1st Pl Slvr Bwl Oral Presntn Rutgers U; 2nd NJ Pony & Hrse Assoc 86; Villanova; Pre-Law.

MC KEEVER, KATHLEEN; Lyndhurst HS; Lyndhurst, NJ; (Y); 15/180; Am Leg Boys St; Pres Key Clb; Office Aide; Var Trk; Var Vllybl; Hon Roll; Bsktbl; Pres Clsrm Yng Amers 86; Hopwood Smmr Schlrs Prog 86; Slppry Rck Smmr Acad 86; Fndtn Free Entrpz Lab 86; Engrg.

MC KEEVER, TODD R; Delran HS; Delran, NJ; (Y); Aud/Vis; Stage Crew; Var Crs Cntry; Var Trk; Prfct Atten Awd; Audio Visual Awd 84-86; Livingston; Arch.

MC KEGNEY, KRISSY; River Dell Reg HS; River Edge, NJ; (Y); 60/213; Church Yth Grp; Pep Clb; Ski Clb; SADD; Varsity Clb; Cheerleading; Crs Cntry; Sftbl; Vllybl; Hon Roll.

MC KENDRICK, DINA MARIE; North Brunswick Township HS; North Brunswick, NJ; (Y); 121/330; Key Clb; Spanish Clb; Nwsp Ed-Chief; Nwsp Rptr; Nwsp Stf; Stat Timer; Bus Admn.

MC KENNA, DAVID; Queen Of Peace HS; N Arlington, NJ; (Y); Art Clb; Church Yth Grp; Drama Clb; Chorus; Church Choir; School Musical; School Play; Stage Crew; Nwsp Stf; Hon Roll.

MC KENNA, JAMES; Oratory Catholic Prep; Millburn, NJ; (Y); 8/48; Boy Scts; Ski Clb; High Hon Roll; NHS; Eagle Scout 86; Bus.

MC KENNA, KATHLEEN; Saint Rose HS; Brick Town, NJ; (Y); 14/225; Hosp Aide; Cit Awd; French Hon Soc; High Hon Roll; Hon Roll; Trs NHS; NEDT Awd; Physcn.

MC KENNA, KEVIN; Christian Brothers Acad; Belford, NJ; (Y); 16/230; Church Yth Grp; Math Tm; Quiz Bowl; Nwsp Rptr; Im Bsktbl; JV Crs Cntry; Var Chess Clb; High Hon Roll; NHS; 4-H; All Conf Tm 600 Yd Run NJ Cathlc Trk 86; West Point; Mech Engrng.

MC KENNA, RACHEL; St John Vianny HS; Keyport, NJ; (Y); Cmnty Wkr; Spanish Clb; High Hon Roll; Hon Roll; NHS; Eng.

MC KENZIE, JACQUELINE E; Essex Valley Schl; East Orange, NJ; (Y); Art Clb; Church Yth Grp; Speech Tm; Teachers Aide; Chorus; Church Choir; School Musical; School Play; Nwsp Rptr; High Hon Roll; Spllg Bee Awd 81; Common Entrnce Exam 81; Spch & Bst Prfrmnce Flk Dncg 82; Poet Writer Art & Read 81-82; Marietta Coll; Med Psych.

MC KENZIE, KRISTA S; Vineland HS; Vineland, NJ; (Y); 135/628; Sec FHA; Sec Concert Band; Ed Lit Mag; Rep Stu Cncl; L Bsbl; L Stat Bsktbl; L Stat Trk; High Hon Roll; Hon Roll; NHS; High Avrg Home Ec 84; Messiah College; Dietcs.

MC KENZIE, MICHAEL; Hunterdon Central HS; Flemington, NJ; (Y); 23/548; Am Leg Boys St; Church Yth Grp; Pres FBLA; Ski Clb; Spanish Clb; Nwsp Stf; Var L Bsbl; Var L Socr; NHS; Best Stu Spnsh II 83-84; All Mid ST Soccr 85-86; Ecnmcs.

MC KENZIE, MICHAEL; Woodstown HS; Alloway, NJ; (Y); Spanish Clb; Fld Hcky; JV Wrstlng; PENN ST U; Bus Admin.

MC KERNAN, PATRICIA; Paul VI HS; Somerdale, NJ; (S); 59/495; German Clb; SADD; Variety Show; Nwsp Rptr; Nwsp Stf; Yrbk Stf; Pres Jr Cls; Rep Sr Cls; Bowling; Hon Roll; Trenton ST; Psych.

MC KEVITT, DANIEL; Hudson Catholic HS; Secaucus, NJ; (Y); Dance Clb; Pep Clb; Political Wkr; SADD; JV Capt Bsktbl; Score Keeper; De Lasalle Schrlshp 83; Peer Ministry Pgm 86; Exec Bus.

MC KINLEY, LEON; Henry Snyder HS; Jersey City, NJ; (S); Hon Roll; NHS; Stu Achvt Awd 83 & 84; Phys Ther.

MC KINNEY, ALYTHEA W; Absegami HS; Pomona, NJ; (Y); 1/220; Pres Church Yth Grp; Drama Clb; Girl Scts; Hosp Aide; Yrbk Stf; Rep Stu Cncl; High Hon Roll; NCTE Awd; NHS; Val; Grdn ST Dstngshd Schlr Schlrshp.

MC KINNEY, ROBIN CYLINTHIA; Burlington Twp HS; Burlington, NJ; (Y); 9/146; Am Leg Aux Girls St; Pres FBLA; FNA; Hosp Aide; Band; Color Guard; Mrchg Band; Nwsp Rptr; Yrbk Stf; Bsktbl; Pres SAE 86; Treas SURE 85; Montclair; Med.

MC KNIGHT, KERRY; St Rose HS; Neptune City, NJ; (Y); 22/265; Hosp Aide; Latin Clb; Nwsp Rptr; Rep Frsh Cls; High Hon Roll; Hon Roll; NHS; CCD Tchr 86-87; Bus.

MC KNIGHT, SEAN; Voorhees HS; High Bridge, NJ; (Y); 91/274; Math Tm; Ski Clb; Yrbk Phtg; Yrbk Stf; Lit Mag; Im Lcrss; Var Socr; JV Trk; German Clb; Varsity Clb; Natl Bio Olympd 84; Intl Kartg Fed 85; Ice Racg 85-86; Rochester Inst Of Tech; Img Sci.

MC LAIN, SUSAN; Bricktownship HS; Brick Town, NJ; (Y); 46/415; Drama Clb; Band; Concert Band; Mrchg Band; Stage Crew; High Hon Roll; Hon Roll; Band Ofc Sec 86-87.

MC LANE, MADELINE; St John Vianney HS; Hazlet, NJ; (Y); 75/233; FBLA; SADD; Yrbk Stf; Off Frsh Cls; Stat Bsktbl; Hon Roll; M S Awd Spnsrshp; Vrsty Lttr; Trenton ST Coll.

MC LAREN, MICHAEL J; Delaware Vly Reg HS; Milford, NJ; (Y); Am Leg Boys St; Church Yth Grp; Key Clb; Pep Clb; Varsity Clb; VP Jr Cls; Var Golf; Var Socr; Swmmng; JV Wrstlng; Engnrng.

MC LAREN, TAMMY; Washington Township HS; Sewell, NJ; (Y); Ski Clb; Swmmng.

MC LAUGHLIN, BRIAN; Edgewood SR HS; Sicklerville, NJ; (Y); 12/330; Cmnty Wkr; Exploring; Scholastic Bowl; Nwsp Rptr; Socr; High Hon Roll; Hon Roll; NHS; Acadmc Excllnc Algbr I.

MC LAUGHLIN, CHRISTOPHER B; New Milfrod HS; New Milford, NJ; (Y); 4/141; Am Leg Boys St; Ski Clb; Varsity Clb; Nwsp Stf; Yrbk Stf; VP Frsh Cls; Rep Jr Cls; Var L Socr; Var Capt Trk; Jr NHS; Acad Top Ten 84-86; Otstndng Eng Stu 85-86; Otstndng Cmptr Sci 85; Jrnlsm.

MC LAUGHLIN, COLETTE; Bayonne HS; Bayonne, NJ; (Y); Church Yth Grp; Library Aide; Nwsp Stf; Frsh Cls; Rutgers U; Psych.

MC LAUGHLIN, DAWN; Bloomfield HS; Bloomfield, NJ; (Y); 52/456; Key Clb; Band; Chorus; Mrchg Band; Orch; Crs Cntry; Trk; High Hon Roll; Hon Roll; Band Council Pres 86-87; Marine Bio.

MC LAUGHLIN, JOSEPH; Holy Spirit HS; Atlantic City, NJ; (Y); 22/386; French Clb; Hon Roll; NHS; Holy Spirit Crew Tm 84-87; Acctng.

MC LAUGHLIN, LORI; Holy Cross HS; Willingboro, NJ; (Y); 4/389; Debate Tm; Model UN; Nwsp Rptr; Ed Nwsp Stf; Lit Mag; Capt Vllybl; Gov Hon Prg Awd; High Hon Roll; Jr NHS; NHS; Knights Of Columbus Outstndng Stu Awd 86; Sci Awd 86; Christian Brthrs Schrshp 86; La Salle U; Engl.

MC LEISH, NYRON A; Seton Hall Prep; East Orange, NJ; (Y); French Clb; Rep Varsity Clb; Rep Soph Cls; Rep Stu Cncl; Var Crs Cntry; Var L Trk; Hon Roll; Hnr Rl Awd 86; Bus.

MC LEOD, BRUCE; Holmdel HS; Holmdel, NJ; (Y); 2/210; Boy Scts; Drama Clb; Key Clb; Jazz Band; Trs Jr Cls; Trs Sr Cls; JP Sousa Awd; NHS; Sal; Church Yth Grp; NJ All ST Orch 86; U Of MI; Elec Engrng.

MC LEOD, JOAN; Spotswood HS; Helmetta, NJ; (S); 15/174; Am Leg Aux Girls St; Intnl Clb; School Musical; Rep Jr Cls; Rep Sr Cls; Stu Cncl; Cheerleading; Twrlr; Hon Roll; NHS; Rutgers Coll; Telecomm.

MC MAHON, JOHN; Marist HS; Jersey City, NJ; (Y); 35/140; Key Clb; Science Clb; St Peters Coll; Acctg.

MC MAHON, PATRICK; West Morris Central HS; Long Valley, NJ; (Y); 1/300; Camera Clb; Mathletes; Bsbl; JV Trk; High Hon Roll; Hon Roll; NHS; Ntl Merit Ltr; Rutgers Schlr 86.

MC MAHON, THERESA; Bishop George Ahr HS; Colonia, NJ; (Y); Spanish Clb; JV Capt Bsbl; Var Bsktbl; Var Mgr(s); Var Score Keeper; Var Sftbl; Hon Roll.

MC MANUS, DANIELLE; Pope Paul VI HS; Stratford, NJ; (S); Math Clb; Sec Stu Cncl; Var Capt Crs Cntry; Var Capt Trk; Hon Roll; Nwsp Rptr; Nwsp Stf; Im Bowling; All S Jersey Cross Cnty 84-85; All S Jersey Trck 84.

MC MANUS, HEATHER; St James HS; Salem, NJ; (Y); VP Sr Cls; Bsktbl; Fld Hcky; Sftbl; Hon Roll; All Salem Cnty Field Hockey 85; Law.

MC MANUS, MAJELLA; Paul VI Regional HS; Bloomfield, NJ; (S); Church Yth Grp; Hosp Aide; Key Clb; High Hon Roll; Hon Roll; NHS; Spanish NHS; Montclair ST.

MC MARTIN, BETH; Hunterdon Central HS; Flemington, NJ; (Y); 11/548; VP Church Yth Grp; Math Tm; Church Choir; Jazz Band; Mrchg Band; School Musical; Symp Band; Trs French Hon Soc; NHS; Variety Show; NJ Region II Symphnc Bnd 85-86; Cert Awd Frnch II 85.

MC MENAMIN, DONNA; Bishop Ahr HS; E Brunswick, NJ; (Y); Drama Clb; Red Cross Aide; Ski Clb; Teachers Aide; Band; JV Bsktbl; Hon Roll; Nrsng.

MC MENIMEN, KATHERINE; Mt St Mary Acad; South River, NJ; (S); 5/83; Sec Church Yth Grp; Library Aide; Spanish Clb; Nwsp Rptr; Nwsp Sprt Ed; Lit Mag; Tennis; High Hon Roll; NHS; VP Spanish NHS; Natl Latin Exam-Magna Cum Laude 84; Natl Spnsh Exam-Hnrb Mntn 84; Schl Awd Hghst Avg Spnsh I-III; Jrnslm.

MC MICHAEL, MARIA M; Audubon HS; Audubon, NJ; (Y); French Clb; Scholastic Bowl; Ed Lit Mag; Stu Cncl; Capt Twrlr; High Hon Roll; Pres NHS; Ntl Merit Schol; Pres Schlr; St Schlr; Jr Miss 85-86; Mst Likely To Succeed 86; Westmont Cmnty Orchstra 82-86; Chestnut Hill Coll; Eng.

MC MILLAN, ERIC; Orange HS; Orange, NJ; (S); Boy Scts; Yrbk Stf; Rep Stu Cncl; Capt Wrstlng; Hon Roll; Mech Engrng.

MC MILLIAN, TONYA S; Mary Help Of Christian Acad; Paterson, NJ; (Y); Girl Scts; Chorus; Drill Tm; Rep Frsh Cls; VP Soph Cls; Rep Jr Cls; Rep Stu Cncl; Im Bsktbl; JV Vllybl; Corporate Lwyr.

MC NAIR, JACKIE; Ewing HS; Trenton, NJ; (S); Cmnty Wkr; VP DECA; Chorus; Church Choir; Drill Tm; Im Trk; Black Hstry Awd Trenton Alumnae Chptr Delta Sigma Theta Sorority 84; DE ST Coll; Bus Adm.

MC NALLY, GWENDOLEN; Northern Highlands HS; Allendale, NJ; (Y); AFS; Drama Clb; Trs Chorus; Madrigals; Mrchg Band; Nwsp Bus Mgr; Nwsp Rptr; Lit Mag; Wrstlng; Hon Roll; Rutgers U; Bio.

MC NALLY, MAUREEN; Red Bank Regional HS; Little Silver, NJ; (Y); Church Yth Grp; Band; Drm Mjr(t); Jazz Band; School Musical; Rep Stu Cncl; High Hon Roll; NHS; Sec Spanish NHS; VA Tech; Cmnctns.

MC NAMARA, HEATHER; Haddon Heights HS; Barrington, NJ; (Y); 70/190; Office Aide; Pep Clb; VP Frsh Cls; Capt Var Bsktbl; Capt Var Fld Hcky; JV Var Sftbl; Cit Awd; Garnet-Gold Honry Soc 83-86; Mst Athltc Grl Stu 86; MVP Bsktbl Awd 86; Ball ST U; Phys Ftns Spclst.

MC NAMARA, JEFFREY; Arthur P Schalick HS; Centerton, NJ; (Y); 25/144; Library Aide; Math Clb; Sec Sr Cls; Ftbl; Trk; Ftbll 1st Tm Tri-Cnty All-Area Df Bck 85; Trck 1st Tm Salem Cnty Mst Pts Awd 84-85; Trck Brnz Mdl 86; Cmmnctns.

MC NAMEE, KELLY J; Riverside HS; Delanco, NJ; (Y); Church Yth Grp; DECA; ST Prtcpnt Awd DECA 86; Omega Tech; Trvl Agnt.

MC NEIL, LAURA; Mt St Mary Acad; Edison, NJ; (Y); Pres Frsh Cls; Pres Stu Cncl; Var L Bsktbl; Im Golf; Capt Socr; Capt Sftbl; Im Tennis; Im Trk; Im Vllybl; Church Yth Grp; Medicine.

MC NERNEY, JEAN; Paul VI Regional HS; Clifton, NJ; (Y); Church Yth Grp; Ski Clb; Church Choir; Var Cheerleading; Spanish NHS; Z-Club Hstrn 86-87; Spnsh Hon Soc Pres 86-87; Acdmc All Amrcn 86.

MC NULTY, MAUREEN; Saint Mary HS; Keansburg, NJ; (Y); 8/130; Church Yth Grp; Office Aide; Stage Crew; Yrbk Stf; Lit Mag; High Hon Roll; Spanish NHS; CDA Scholar 83-86; Elem Ed.

MC PEAK, KEVIN; Highland Regional HS; Blackwood, NJ; (Y); Cmnty Wkr; VP German Clb; Voice Dem Awd.

MC PEEK, ROBERT; Hopewell Valley Central HS; Pennington, NJ; (Y); 4/220; German Clb; Math Tm; Quiz Bowl; Science Clb; School Play; NHS; Ntl Merit SF; High Hon Roll; Hon Roll; Mth Crs At Prnctn U 85-86; Outstndng Physics Stu Awd Amer Assoc Of Physics Tchrs 85-86; Mth.

MC PHERSON, SHIGERU; Maple Shade HS; Maple Shade, NJ; (Y); Am Leg Aux Girls St; Computer Clb; Key Clb; Rep Stu Cncl; Var Fld Hcky; JV Var Lcrss; High Hon Roll; NHS; Ntl Merit SF; Schlstc Achvt Awd 86; 1st Pl NJ Stu Crftsmn Fair 83-84; Acad All-Amer 85-86; Columbia U; Elctrcl Engrng.

MC QUAID, KATHLEEN; Southern Regional HS; Barnegat, NJ; (Y); 48/340; Aud/Vis; Trs Church Yth Grp; Bsktbl; Capt Cheerleading; Hon Roll; NHS; Temple U; TV/Radio Brdcstng.

MC SHANE, SARAH; Mahwah HS; Mahwah, NJ; (Y); Church Yth Grp; Drama Clb; Ski Clb; Spanish Clb; Chorus; School Musical; School Play; Lit Mag; Hon Roll; Spanish NHS; Elem Educ.

MC VEIGH, COLLEEN; West Essex SR HS; Fairfield, NJ; (Y); English Clb; 4-H; GAA; 4-H Awd.

MC VEY, KARA; Middle Township HS; Cape May, NJ; (Y); 20/220; Sec VP Key Clb; Quiz Bowl; SADD; Rep Stu Cncl; Capt Bsktbl; Capt Tennis; Capt Trk; Hon Roll; Kiwanis Awd; NHS; Hon Ment All Cape Atlantic Leag Bsktbll & Tennis 87; Dstngshd Clb Sec Key Clb Intl NJ Dist 87; Law.

MEADE, CURT; Overbrook Regional HS; Lindenwold, NJ; (Y); Spanish Clb; JV Tennis; Hon Roll; NHS; Elec Engrng.

MEADE JR, PAUL; Oratory Prep; Cranford, NJ; (Y); Spanish Clb; Varsity Clb; Variety Show; Bsbl; Socr; Hon Roll; Mt St Marys; Acctng.

MEADOWS, TYRETTA; Essex Catholic Girls HS; Hillside, NJ; (Y); Pep Clb; Science Clb; Chorus; Co-Capt Drill Tm; Variety Show; Ed Yrbk Stf; Rep Jr Cls; VP Sr Cls; High Hon Roll; Schlstc Awd 84; Accntng.

MEALHA, CHRISTINA; Rahway HS; Rahway, NJ; (Y); VP Key Clb; Mrchg Band; Stage Crew; Yrbk Bus Mgr; Ed Yrbk Stf; Rep Soph Cls; Rep Jr Cls; Trs Sr Cls; Mgr(s); JV Capt Vllybl; Intr Desgn.

MEANDRO, DEBRA; Millville SR HS; Millville, NJ; (Y); 61/450; Church Yth Grp; Model UN; Office Aide; Nwsp Rptr; Nwsp Stf; Rep Stu Cncl; Var Capt Cheerleading; Fld Hcky; Sftbl.

MEARA, JACQUELINE; Hamilton High West; Trenton, NJ; (Y); Rep Trs Exploring; Key Clb; Office Aide; Political Wkr; School Play; Stat Bsbl; Var Capt Cheerleading; Var JV Trk; Mercer Explrtng Outstndng PO 85; 8th Vrsty Ltr 86; Nrs.

MEARS, MARY BETH; Glassboro HS; Glassboro, NJ; (Y); 1/163; French Clb; Sec Flag Corp; Var L Mrchg Band; Im L Bsktbl; Bausch & Lomb Sci Awd; High Hon Roll; NHS; English Clb; Im L Fld Hcky; Hon Roll; Achvt For Inro To Phy Sci 84; Achvt Awds For Frnch III, Pre Calculs & AP Amer Hist 86; Math.

MECHLER, ROBERT T; New Milford HS; New Milford, NJ; (Y); Am Leg Boys St; Ski Clb; Band; Concert Band; Jazz Band; Capt Mrchg Band; VP Sr Cls; Rep Stu Cncl; JV Trk; Cit Awd; Engrng.

MEDEIROS, MARY JANE; Williamstown HS; Williamstown, NJ; (Y); Sec.

MEDINA, DAVID; Elizabeth HS; Elizabeth, NJ; (Y); Boys Clb Am; Computer Clb; Bsbl; Wt Lftg; Comp Elctrncs.

MEDURI, STEVEN M; Pitman HS; Pitman, NJ; (Y); Am Leg Boys St; Key Clb; Pres Frsh Cls; Pres Soph Cls; VP Jr Cls; Pres Sr Cls; Stu Cncl; Bsbl; Capt Ftbl; Var Capt Wrstlng; Athlete Awd 86; All Star Tm Ftbl,Wrestlng 85-86; George Mason U; Bus.

MEEHAN, BARBARA ANN; Bishop George Ahr HS; Edison, NJ; (Y); Church Yth Grp; Ski Clb; Var L Cheerleading; Im Gym; Hon Roll.

MEEHAN, JENNIFER; St Rose HS; Bradley Beach, NJ; (Y); 52/206; Key Clb; Rep Jr Cls; Var Mgr Trk; NHS; NEDT Awd; Fac Schlrshp Monmouth Coll 86-87; Top Schl Speller MS Spelling Bee 86; Monmouth Coll; Cmmnctns.

MEEHAN, JOHN; East Brunswick HS; E Brunswick, NJ; (Y); German Clb; Latin Clb; Hon Roll; NHS; Acadmc All Am 84; Germ Hnr Soc 85-86; Hist.

MEEK, AMANDA SUE; Lyndhurst HS; Lyndhurst, NJ; (Y); 17/180; French Clb; High Hon Roll; Hon Roll; Fndtn For Free Entrprs 86; Fshn Inst Of Tech; Fshn.

MEEKS, MARCY A; Howell HS; Farmingdale, NJ; (Y); Church Yth Grp; Office Aide; Church Choir; School Play; Nwsp Rptr; Lit Mag; Pblctn Asbury Pk Press Artcls, 2 Shrt Strs 85-86; Asst Chrprsn Ntl Cnf Chrstns-Jews 86; Wrtr.

MEENAN, BERNIE; Holy Cross HS; Riverside, NJ; (Y); 55/369; Boy Scts; Model UN; Stage Crew; Hon Roll; Engrng.

MEGLAUGHLIN, DANIELLE; Westfield SR HS; Westfield, NJ; (Y); 77/529; Cmnty Wkr; Spanish Clb; SADD; Chorus; Church Choir; School Musical; School Play; Score Keeper; Hon Roll; NHS; Cert Of Outstndng Achvt In Englsh 84; Anl Audtns Awd In Piano 83; U DE; Fshn Merch.

MEHAFFEY, EDWARD; Woodstown HS; Salem, NJ; (Y); 40/230; Embry-Riddle Aerontcl U; Engnrn.

MEHL, SCOTT P; Rancocas Valley Regional HS; Mt Holly, NJ; (Y); Church Yth Grp; French Clb; Office Aide; Quiz Bowl; VP Band; Chorus; VP Mrchg Band; Ed Lit Mag; Diving; Swmmng; Elizabethtown Coll; Accntng.

MEHTA, NIMISH; Hasbrouck Heights HS; Hasbrouck Heights, NJ; (Y); Am Leg Boys St; Trs German Clb; Key Clb; Letterman Clb; Trs Temple Yth Grp; Nwsp Phtg; VP Jr Cls; Off Stu Cncl; Ftbl; Trk; Wall Street Smnr 86; NJ Acad Decthln 86; Acctg.

MEICKE, LISA; Secaucus HS; Secaucus, NJ; (Y); 35/169; Dance Clb; Key Clb; Chorus; Color Guard; Mrchg Band; Yrbk Stf; JV Bsktbl; Var Mgr(s); JV Vllybl; Hon Roll; Montclair ST; Htl Mgmt.

MEIDENBAUER, LAURA; Wayne Hills HS; Wayne, NJ; (Y); 49/310; Hosp Aide; Ski Clb; Spanish Clb; Capt Variety Show; Nwsp Stf; Yrbk Sprt Ed; Lit Mag; Hon Roll; Catholic U; Nrsng.

MEIER, CHRIS; Middletown HS South; Leonardo, NJ; (Y); Hon Roll; Cmntr HS Fshn Shw 86; Rutgers; Cmnctns.

MEIER, CYNTHIA L; Glenr Ock HS; Glen Rock, NJ; (Y); Pres AFS; Church Yth Grp; Debate Tm; Drama Clb; Letterman Clb; Ski Clb; Chorus; School Musical; School Play; Rep Stu Cncl; Soc Sci.

MEISEL, JOHN; Wayne Hills HS; Wayne, NJ; (Y); 14/350; Am Leg Boys St; Cmnty Wkr; Latin Clb; Mathletes; Y-Teens; Stage Crew; Yrbk Ed-Chief; Yrbk Stf; Capt Crs Cntry; Trk; Capt Ushers Grad 86; Bio.

MEISELMAN, JAMIE; Westfield HS; Westfield, NJ; (Y); 27/529; Ski Clb; Temple Yth Grp; Nwsp Ed-Chief; Rep Stu Cncl; JV Bsbl; Var L Ftbl; Var Lcrss; Hon Roll; NHS.

MEISNER II, THOMAS D; Lakewood HS; Lakewood, NJ; (Y); 14/295; Am Leg Boys St; German Clb; Math Tm; Soroptimist; VP Sr Cls; High Hon Roll; Hon Roll; Bus.

MEIXNER, PAUL; South Plainfield HS; S Plainfield, NJ; (Y); JV Bsbl; Var L Ftbl; Var Lttrmn Ftbl 85-86.

MEJIA, YANIRA; Abraham Clark HS; Roselle, NJ; (Y); French Clb; Spanish Clb; Hlth & Sci Fair 85-86; ESL Prgrm 83-84; Hlth Ocptn 85-86; Comp Wrd Prcsr.

MELE, STACI; Monsignor Donovan HS; Lakewood, NJ; (Y); 127/252; Cmnty Wkr; Dance Clb; SADD; Yrbk Stf; Var Cheerleading; Hon Roll; Psych.

MELENDEZ, LISSETTE; Academic HS; Jersey City, NJ; (Y); Spanish Clb; Church Choir; Vllybl; Acctnt.

MELENDEZ, MADELINE; William L Dickinson HS; Jersey City, NJ; (Y); Prfct Atten Awd; Actg.

MELIKIAN, NAIRI; New Milford HS; New Milford, NJ; (Y); Church Yth Grp; Dance Clb; Girl Scts; Library Aide; Political Wkr; Quiz Bowl; Spanish Clb; Band; Chorus; Concert Band; Physcl Educ Hi Acad Achvt Citation 83-84, 85-86; NY U; Drama.

MELILLO, LORI; Wayne Hills HS; Wayne, NJ; (Y); 112/305; Var Socr; JV Sftbl; JV Trk; Hon Roll; Itln Clb 85-86; Fshn.

MELLBERG, LAURA; Voorhees HS; Pottersville, NJ; (Y); 5/276; Debate Tm; Girl Scts; VP Key Clb; Pres SADD; Mrchg Band; High Hon Roll; NHS; Ntl Merit Ltr; Jazz Band; Swing Chorus; Girls Ctznshp Inst 86; Hugh O Brien Ldrshp 85; Engrng.

MELLOR, DENNIS J; Milville SR HS; Millville, NJ; (Y); 1/468; Camera Clb; Debate Tm; Drama Clb; Key Clb; Model UN; Science Clb; SADD; Stage Crew; Yrbk Phtg; Stu Cncl; U PA; Apld Sci.

MELNICK, MELISSA; Wall HS; Sea Girt, NJ; (S); 8/259; Exploring; Spanish Clb; Capt Drill Tm; Rep Jr Cls; Rep Sr Cls; Powder Puff Ftbl; JV Sftbl; Hon Roll; Kiwanis Awd; Trs NHS; Mst Outstndng Lncr 83; Chem.

MELOCCHI, MICHAEL; Burlington Township HS; Burlington, NJ; (Y); 8/110; Am Leg Boys St; Rep Stu Cncl; Var Bsbl; JV Var Ftbl; High Hon Roll; Hon Roll; NHS; Mech Engrng.

MELOGRANA JR, LOUIS F; Rumson-Fair Haven Regional HS; Fair Haven, NJ; (Y); 21/234; Am Leg Boys St; Debate Tm; Crs Cntry; Hon Roll; 1st, 2nd, 3rd Pl Karate Trnmnts 85-86; Asst Instrctr Karate 85-86; Comp.

MELSKY, MICHAEL; South Hunterdon Regional HS; Lambertville, NJ; (Y); 19/75; FBLA; Ski Clb; Varsity Clb; JV Bsbl; Var Capt Ftbl; Im Wt Lftg; Var Wrstlng; Hon Roll; Ftbll 1st Tm-De Rvr Conf, All ST Grp 1, All W Jersey, All Area & All Ctrl Jersey 84-85; Eagle Awd 85; Moravian Coll.

MELTON, GARY P; Absegami HS; Egg Harbor City, NJ; (Y); 27/265; Am Leg Boys St; Aud/Vis; Church Yth Grp; French Clb; Church Choir; Nwsp Stf; Pres Jr Cls; VP Sr Cls; Bsktbl; Ftbl; Amer Lgn Oratorical St Fnlst 85; St Hnrbl Mntn Ftbl & Bsktbl 85-86; I Dare You Schlrshp Awd 86; Penn ST; Pre-Med.

MELTON, KIRSTEN; Mainland Regional HS; Northfield, NJ; (Y); 17/256; Hosp Aide; Ski Clb; Yrbk Sprt Ed; Yrbk Stf; L Mgr(s); Hon Roll; NHS; Asst Editor Yrbk 86-87; Psych.

MELZAK, LORI; Raritan HS; Hazlet, NJ; (Y); Drama Clb; Nwsp Rptr; Nwsp Stf; Child Physcology.

MELZER, SUSAN E; Triton Regional HS; Somerdale, NJ; (Y); Band; Color Guard; Concert Band; Mrchg Band; Nwsp Rptr; Nwsp Stf; Lit Mag; Prfct Atten Awd; Chess Clb; JA; Gldn Poet Awd Of 85; Gldn Poet Awd Of 86; Hnrbl Ment In Great Poetry Cntst 85; Comm.

MELZL, SUSAN; Midland Park HS; Midland Park, NJ; (Y); 17/137; Pres FBLA; Math Tm; Color Guard; Stage Crew; Rep Soph Cls; Rep Jr Cls; Rep Sr Cls; Vllybl; Cit Awd; High Hon Roll; Fordham U; Acctg.

MENAPACE, CHRISTINE; Red Bank Regional HS; Shrewsbury, NJ; (Y); Ski Clb; School Musical; School Play; Lit Mag; JV Crs Cntry; High Hon Roll; Hon Roll; NHS; Spanish NHS; Stu To Stu Grp Ldr 85-86; Perf Arts Crtve Wrtng 84-85; NJ ST Teen Arts Fest Wrtng 85; Advrtsng.

MENCK, CHRISTINA; Lakewood HS; Lakewood, NJ; (Y); English Clb; German Clb; Letterman Clb; Chorus; Color Guard; Ger Hnr Soc.

MENDELSON, DAVE; Hightstown HS; E Windsor, NJ; (Y); 141/441; Boy Scts; SADD; Teachers Aide; Temple Yth Grp; Varsity Clb; Stage Crew; Nwsp Rptr; Nwsp Stf; Rep Frsh Cls; Rep Soph Cls; Boston U; Brdcstng.

MENDEZ, LEONIDES; Eastside HS; Paterson, NJ; (S); 11/700; Cmnty Wkr; Rep Frsh Cls; Rep Soph Cls; JV Bsbl; JV Socr; High Hon Roll; Hon Roll; NHS; Merit Awd 84; 2dn Pl Mayor Frank Graves Yth Mnth Art Cntst 84; Comp Sci.

MENDEZ, LOURDES; Memorial HS; W New York, NJ; (Y); French Clb; FBLA; FHA; Spanish Clb; Chorus; Swing Chorus; Lit Mag; Rep Frsh Cls; Rep Soph Cls; Rep Stu Cncl; Bus Mrktng.

MENDEZ, OSVALDO M; Eastside HS; Paterson, NJ; (Y); 79/477; Computer Clb; Pres FBLA; Library Aide; Yrbk Phtg; Yrbk Stf; Var Tennis; Hon Roll; Science Clb; Cert Apprctn Vlbl Cntrbtn Yrbk 85-86; Stu Mth-Bus 85; Prfct Attndnc 85; William Paterson Coll; Bus Adm.

MENDEZ, WILLIAM; Vineland SR HS; Vineland, NJ; (Y); Aud/Vis; Church Yth Grp; Key Clb; Library Aide; Stu Cncl; Hon Roll; Centruy 21 Awd 86; Hofstra U; Law.

MENDONCA, FRANCISCO M; East Side HS; Newark, NJ; (Y); Am Leg Boys St; Civic Clb; Cmnty Wkr; FBLA; Intnl Clb; Stage Crew; Yrbk Rptr; Yrbk Stf; Church Yth Grp; Library Aide; Cert Apprctn 85; 3rd Pl Sci Fair 84; City Newark Cert 86.

MENDOZA, MARIA; Oak Knoll Schl Of The Holy Child; Livingston, NJ; (Y); Pep Clb; Spanish Clb; Rep Soph Cls; Var Bsktbl; JV Fld Hcky; Var Sftbl; High Hon Roll; Camera Clb; Ski Clb; Im Vllybl; Rensselaer Medal Exc Math,Sci 86; Cornelian Schrlshp 83; Med Soc Yth Ldrshp Awd 84.

MENDOZA, MERCEDES; Memorial HS; Union City, NJ; (Y); Boy Scts; Stage Crew; Trk; Cit Awd; Citation Of Apprctn From Amer Legn 85; Outstndg Achvmnt Cert HS 85; Marksman 1st Clss Qlfctn Cert 84; CO Schl Of Mining; Ptrlm Engr.

MENDOZA, RIA; Notre Dame HS; Robbinsville, NJ; (Y); Math Clb; Red Cross Aide; Service Clb; SADD; Stage Crew; Rep Frsh Cls; Rep Soph Cls; Rep Jr Cls; Score Keeper; French Hon Soc; Wellesley Book Awd.

MENDUM, CHARLES; Lakewood HS; Lakewood, NJ; (Y); Cmnty Wkr; Hon Roll; Food Svc Awd 86; YWCA Awd 86; PSAT Scholar 86; Ocean Cnty Coll.

MENEGHELLO, LAURA; St Aloysius HS; Jersey City, NJ; (Y); Office Aide; Spanish Clb; Hon Roll; Jr NHS; Cert Hon Excllnc Hstry 85-86; Jersey City ST Coll; Bus Admn.

MENENDEZ, ALEX; Secaucus HS; Secaucus, NJ; (Y); 38/169; Am Leg Boys St; Key Clb; Off Math Clb; Varsity Clb; Stage Crew; Variety Show; VP Frsh Cls; VP Soph Cls; VP Jr Cls; Pres Stu Cncl; Acctg.

MENENDEZ, CHRISTINE; Secavcus HS; Secaucus, NJ; (S); 13/160; Math Clb; Spanish Clb; Varsity Clb; Var Cheerleading; High Hon Roll; NHS; Spanish NHS; Pre-Med.

MENENDEZ, J LYLE; Princeton Day Schl; Princeton, NJ; (Y); Var L Tennis; Hon Roll; Natl All Amer 86; ST Prep Champ Cls A & B Tennis 85-86; Natl USTA No 62 85; Middle ST Tennis Assoc; Princeton U.

MENEREY, LAURIE ANNE K; Glassboro HS; Glassboro, NJ; (Y); Drama Clb; Thesps; Chorus; Mrchg Band; School Musical; School Play; Crs Cntry; Hon Roll; Cmnty Wkr; Latin Clb; Wrtg Clb; Close Up; Sch Of Arts 86; Ped.

MENGUCCI, GENA M; Phillipsburg HS; Alpha, NJ; (Y); 62/300; Ski Clb; Sec Rep Stu Cncl; High Hon Roll; NHS; Psych.

MENON, LAKSHMI; South Brunswick HS; Kendall Park, NJ; (Y); Cmnty Wkr; FHA; Hosp Aide; Pep Clb; Service Clb; Band; Concert Band; Lit Mag; Vllybl; Hon Roll; Rutgers U; Pre Med.

MENZ, MICHAEL; Jackson Memorial HS; Jackson, NJ; (Y); 45/405; Aud/Vis; Computer Clb; FBLA; JV Bsbl; Im Bsktbl; Im Ice Hcky; High Hon Roll; Hon Roll.

MEOLA, JAMIE; Shore Regional HS; W Long Branch, NJ; (Y); Nwsp Rptr; Nwsp Sprt Ed; Yrbk Ed-Chief; VP Stu Cncl; Powder Puff Ftbl; Socr; Swmmng; High Hon Roll; Hon Roll; VP NHS; Bus Admin.

MERANDINO, ANN MARIE; Clifton HS; Clifton, NJ; (Y); 44/687; Band; Drm Mjr(t); Mrchg Band; Var Bsktbl; JV Sftbl; Hon Roll; Jr NHS.

MERCADO, JERRY B; Our Lady Of Good Counsel HS; Newark, NJ; (Y); 19/106; Yrbk Phtg; Rep Frsh Cls; Rep Soph Cls; Rep Jr Cls; Pres Sr Cls; Stu Cncl; Bsbl; Bsktbl; Socr; NHS; Ntl Physcl Ed Awd 85; Ltr 86; Hofstra U; Industrl Engr.

MERCADO, JOSE; Lakewood HS; Lakewood, NJ; (Y); 85/294; Am Leg Boys St; Boy Scts; ROTC; Jazz Band; School Musical; VP Jr Cls; Pres Sr Cls; Var Bsbl; Var Socr; Spanish NHS; US Naval Acad; Engr.

MERCEDES, JEANETTE; Holy Family Acad; Bayonne, NJ; (Y); 21/129; Spanish Clb; Hon Roll; Computer Clb; Psychtrst.

MERCER, CRYSTAL; Mc Corristin Catholic HS; Trenton, NJ; (Y); Hosp Aide; Pep Clb; Church Choir; Color Guard; Hon Roll; Smmr Pgm Math Comp Sci 86; Norfolk ST Coll; Comp Techncn.

MERCHAK, JOSEPH; Dover HS; Mine Hill, NJ; (Y); Hon Roll; NHS; Elec Tech.

MERCOGLIANO, FRANK; North Bergen HS; North Bergen, NJ; (Y); 7/400; Cmnty Wkr; Key Clb; Nwsp Stf; Rep Soph Cls; Rep Jr Cls; Rep Stu Cncl; Hon Roll; Jr NHS; NHS; Ntl Merit Ltr; Sci & Chem Fnlst Cmptn 86; Cornell; Vet.

MERCURIO, MICHELE; Livingston HS; Livingston, NJ; (Y); Church Yth Grp; Hosp Aide; Leo Clb; Lit Mag; Var Mgr(s); Hon Roll; Computer Clb; Girl Scts; Var Stat Socr; Im Vllybl; Bus.

MERIGHI, LISA; Buena Regional HS; Richland, NJ; (S); 10/191; Math Tm; Service Clb; Ski Clb; SADD; Band; Concert Band; Drm Mjr(t); Jazz Band; Sec VP Mrchg Band; School Musical; Phil Col Phrm & Sci; Phrmcy.

MERIGHI, STEPHANIE; Sacred Heart HS; Vineland, NJ; (Y); Sec Spanish Clb; Pres Frsh Cls; Stat Im Bsktbl; Var L Sftbl; Var L Tennis; Im Vllybl; Hon Roll; Coachs Awd Tennis 85-86; Math.

MERINGOLO, DENISE; Shore Regional HS; Oceanport, NJ; (Y); 19/225; Drama Clb; Q&S; Pres Thesps; School Musical; School Play; Nwsp Rptr; Ed Nwsp Stf; High Hon Roll; NHS; J Capoferi Crtv Wrtng Awd 86; Shore Schlr 86; Pres Acdmc Ftns Awd 86; Geo Wshngtn U; Jrnlsm.

MERINGOLO, PETER; Shore Regional HS; Oceanport, NJ; (Y); 5/200; Church Yth Grp; SADD; Pres Jr Cls; Pres Sr Cls; JV Bsbl; JV Socr; High Hon Roll; Shore Area Shop Tchrs Engr 2nd Pl 85; Notre Dame; Arch.

MERINGOLO, PHILIP; Paramus Catholic Boys HS; Paramus, NJ; (Y); 105/178; Camera Clb; Nwsp Phtg; JV Bsktbl; Var Tennis; Archtctr.

MERKLE, DIANE; Sparta HS; Sparta, NJ; (Y); Capt Color Guard; Drm & Bgl; School Play; Siena Coll; Comp Sci.

MERKLE, ROBERT; Oratory Prep; New Providence, NJ; (S); 5/50; Math Tm; Varsity Clb; Nwsp Stf; Yrbk Phtg; Var Bsktbl; Var Socr; High Hon Roll; NHS; Outstndng Alg Awd 84; Engr.

MERLO, STEPHEN; Don Bosco Preperatory HS; Hillsdale, NJ; (S); 15/205; Cmnty Wkr; Model UN; Pep Clb; Ski Clb; Spanish Clb; Rptr Nwsp Rptr; Yrbk Stf; Im Bsbl; Im Var Bsktbl; JV Var Golf; Hgst Avg Eng 83-85; Bus Mgmt.

MERLY JR, PEDRO JUAN; James J Ferris HS; Jersey City, NJ; (Y); Boys Clb Am; Church Yth Grp; Church Choir; Ftbl; Prfct Atten Awd; Elect Tech.

MEROLA, STEPHEN; Parsippany Hills HS; Morris Plains, NJ; (Y); Chess Clb; Computer Clb; Key Clb; Math Tm; Science Clb; Band; Mrchg Band; Hon Roll; NHS; Ntl Merit Ltr; Med.

MERRICK, DAVID; North Warren Regional HS; Blairstown, NJ; (Y); Boy Scts; Cmnty Wkr; FBLA; Ski Clb; Nwsp Rptr; Nwsp Stf; Rep Frsh Cls; JV Var Bsbl; Hon Roll; Bus Adm.

MERRIGAN, THOA; Toms River South HS; Beachwood, NJ; (Y); 26/360; JV Fld Hcky; High Hon Roll; Hon Roll; Engl Cls Rep 83; UC Berkeley; Pre-Med.

MERRITS, BRYAN; Metuchen HS; Metuchen, NJ; (Y); Drama Clb; Ski Clb; Varsity Clb; School Musical; Stage Crew; Variety Show; JV Bsktbl; Var Capt Ftbl; Var Trk; 2nd Tm All Cnty In Middlesex Cnty For Ftbl 85; Rutger U; Prof Ftbl Plyr.

MERRITT, CHRISTINE; Delaware Valley Regional HS; Frenchtown, NJ; (Y); 17/176; Intnl Clb; Pres Key Clb; Service Clb; Varsity Clb; Stu Cncl; Mgr(s); Sftbl; Timer; Hon Roll; Kiwanis Awd; U Of Pittsburgh; Bio.

MERRITT, TINA; Montville Township HS; Towaco, NJ; (Y); 40/262; Cmnty Wkr; Rep Sec Intnl Clb; Key Clb; Office Aide; Church Choir; Color Guard; Stage Crew; High Hon Roll; Hon Roll; NHS; Ltr Marchng Band 86; Spnsh.

MERSIER, TRACY; Essex Catholic Girls HS; Newark, NJ; (Y); 3/52; Drama Clb; Pep Clb; Trs Service Clb; School Musical; Yrbk Stf; Pres Frsh Cls; High Hon Roll; Pres NHS; Grnsbr Coll; Psychlgy.

MERTZ, SUZANNE; Mount Saint Mary Acad; Watchung, NJ; (S); 5/90; Church Yth Grp; Chorus; Pres Frsh Cls; Pres Soph Cls; Rep Jr Cls; Fld Hcky; Var Tennis; French Hon Soc; Hon Roll; NHS; ST Ortrcl Cont Wnnr 83; Hugh O Brian Ldrshp-2nd Pl 85.

MESA, ANTOLIN; Roselle Catholic HS; Elizabeth, NJ; (Y); Math Tm; Ed Lit Mag; Im Bsktbl; Var L Wrstlng; Hon Roll; NHS; Spanish NHS; Philos.

MESDAY, MAUREEN; Notre Dame HS; Trenton, NJ; (Y); 5/343; Cmnty Wkr; Key Clb; Latin Clb; JV Socr; High Hon Roll; Hon Roll; NHS; Ntl Ltn Hnr Scty 84-86; Red Cross Clb 85-86; Wolinski Mem Trst Schlrshp 86; St Thomas U; Tourism.

MESNIKOFF, NATHAN; Ocean Twp HS; Wayside, NJ; (Y); 158/333; French Clb; Latin Clb; Science Clb; Stage Crew; Yrbk Phtg; Cum Laude Natl Latin Exams 83-84; Cert Of Devotion & Merit Karate 83-84; Bio Sci.

MESSIEH, RAMSEY; St Aloysius HS; Jersey City, NJ; (Y); 4/109; Chess Clb; Var Socr; Bausch & Lomb Sci Awd; Hon Roll; NHS; Schlr Athl Jersey Cty Sccr Coaches Assn 86; Hudson Cnty Chmbr Commrc & Indstry Awd Acadmc Achvt 86; NJ Inst Of Tech; Engrng.

MESSINA, CHRIS; Voorhees HS; Lebanon, NJ; (Y); #60 In Class; JCL; Key Clb; Latin Clb; Radio Clb; Varsity Clb; Band; Variety Show; Off Stu Cncl; Var Bsbl; Var Bsktbl; 2nd Tm Mid-ST Sccr 85; 3rd Tm All-Wst Jrsey 85; All Mid-ST Bsbl 85; Engr.

MESSINA, LOREN; James Caldwell HS; W Caldwell, NJ; (Y); Key Clb; High Hon Roll; Hon Roll; NHS.

MESSINA, LORI; St Pius X HS; Sayrevle, NJ; (Y); Church Yth Grp; Chorus; Church Choir; School Musical; School Play; Nwsp Stf; Yrbk Stf; Pom Pon; Hon Roll; Mth.

MESSINA, LYNDA; Paramus HS; Paramus, NJ; (Y); Camera Clb; Cmnty Wkr; Hosp Aide; Service Clb; Lit Mag; Bowling; Sftbl; Elks Awd; 4-H; Yrbk Stf; Grl Scout Gold Awd 86; Capt Bowlng Tm; Phys Thrpy.

MESSNER, ALISA; Red Bank Regional HS; Interlaken, NJ; (Y); 28/223; Pres Exploring; Hosp Aide; NFL; Stage Crew; High Hon Roll; Hon Roll; Rutgers Coll; Lib Arts.

MESZAROS, JENNIFER; Parsippany Hills HS; Morris Plains, NJ; (Y); Cmnty Wkr; VP Girl Scts; Hosp Aide; Political Wkr; Spanish Clb; Concert Band; School Musical; Variety Show; Swmmng; Hon Roll; Bus Adm.

MESZAROS, KENNETH; Hamilton HS East; Hamilton Sq, NJ; (Y); 23/322; Boy Scts; Concert Band; Jazz Band; Mrchg Band; Hon Roll; NHS; Pres Schlr; Trenton ST Coll Alumni Schlrshp; Trenton ST Coll; Comp Sci.

MESZAROS, LORI; Hoepwell Valley Central HS; Lambertville, NJ; (Y); Trs Church Yth Grp; Trs 4-H; Hosp Aide; Chorus; Church Choir; School Musical; Var Ltr Stu Ath Trainer 86; Nrsng.

METALLO, VICTOR N; Seton Hall Preparatory Schl; Montclair, NJ; (Y); Boy Scts; Church Yth Grp; Cmnty Wkr; Key Clb; Cit Awd; High Hon Roll; Outstndg Stu Awd For Go-Ju Ryu Krte 83; Blck Blt 84; 4th Dgree Knghts Of Clmbs Ctznshp Awd 83; Seton Hll U; Med.

METHFESSEL, DONNIE; Gill Saint Bernards HS; Warren, NJ; (Y); Aud/Vis; VP Golf; VP Socr; Hon Roll; MVP Sccr 84, 85 & 86; 2nd Tm All St Sccr 86; Law.

METTEE, GAYLE; Clifton HS; Clifton, NJ; (Y); Cmnty Wkr; Drama Clb; Key Clb; Spanish Clb; Band; Chorus; Var Gym; Sftbl; Hon Roll; NHS; Gym Hnrbl Ment 85-86; Ntl Hnr Soc 83-84; Comm Wrk 83-84; Nrsng.

MEYER, MELANIE; Hunterdon Central HS; White House Stati, NJ; (Y); 55/560; Pres Church Yth Grp; Sec Key Clb; Band; Concert Band; Mrchg Band; Pep Band; Symp Band; Variety Show; Hon Roll; Band Vrsty Band 86; Spnsh.

MEYER, RICHARD; Belleville SR HS; Belleville, NJ; (Y); 39/378; Computer Clb; Ski Clb; Band; Chorus; Jazz Band; Orch; Capt Stage Crew; Rep Sr Cls; High Hon Roll; Comp Sci Awd 84-85; Theatre Awd 85-86; Hnrs Group 85-86; NJ Inst Of Tech; Comp Sci.

MEYERS, BRAD; Fair Lawn HS; Fairlawn, NJ; (Y); Am Leg Boys St; Computer Clb; Temple Yth Grp; Varsity Clb; Band; Mrchg Band; Off Jr Cls; Ntl Merit SF; Political Wkr; Concert Band; 1st Pl Ntl Comptn Am Comp League 84; Capt Fencng Tm 86.

MEYERS, CARL; Overbrook HS; Clementon, NJ; (Y); German Clb; Var JV Ftbl; Acctng.

MEYERS, LYNNE; Pt Pleasant Borough HS; Point Pleasant, NJ; (Y); Chrmn Church Yth Grp; Sec Band; Chorus; Church Choir; Concert Band; VP Madrigals; Mrchg Band; School Musical; School Play; Variety Show; Natl Choral Awd 85-86; Bst Sr Perf 85-86; Natl Hnr Scty Wrtng Awd 84-86; Syracuse U; Theatre.

MEYERSON, JOSEPH; Secaucus HS; Secaucus, NJ; (S); 8/163; Key Clb; Math Clb; Ski Clb; Score Keeper; High Hon Roll; Mu Alp Tht; NHS; Comp Sci.

MEZZANOTTE, CHRISTOPHER; North Warren Regional HS; Blairstown, NJ; (Y); 8/130; Cmnty Wkr; Office Aide; Spanish Clb; Varsity Clb; Off Frsh Cls; Bsbl; JV Var Bsktbl; Crs Cntry; Socr; Hon Roll; West Point Prep; Engrng.

MIAH, KAHLU A; Eastern Regional HS; West Berlin, NJ; (Y); Acad All-Amer 85; GA Tech; Comp Engrg.

MICELI, ROSINA; Essex Catholic Girls HS; Irvington, NJ; (Y); Art Clb; Camera Clb; Service Clb; Yrbk Phtg; Bowling; Socr; Sftbl; Vllybl; Hon Roll.

MICHAEL, BANGE; Ridgefield Park HS; Little Ferry, NJ; (Y); 30/186; Computer Clb; Ski Clb; Concert Band; Stage Crew; Hon Roll; NJIT; Comp Engnrng.

MICHALIK, KEN; Bishop George Ahr HS; Fords, NJ; (Y); Church Yth Grp; Math Clb; Var L Golf; Hon Roll; NEDT Awd; All Conf & Middlesex Cnty Golf Team 85-86; World Seris JR Golf Regnl Tour 86.

MICHALSKI, MARIA; Freehold Township HS; Freehold, NJ; (Y); 11/317; PAVAS; Thesps; Madrigals; School Musical; NHS; Ntl Merit SF; St Schlr; Drama Clb; Rtgrs Coll Alumni Schlrshp 86; NJ Grdn ST Dstngshd Schlr 85; Rutgers Coll; Psychlgy.

MICHEL, ERICH; Bogota HS; Bogota, NJ; (Y); Am Leg Boys St; Aud/Vis; Church Yth Grp; Cmnty Wkr; Drama Clb; Library Aide; Aud/Vis; Trs Pres Science Clb; Spanish Clb; Teachers Aide; Stu Myrs Cmnty Hnds Across Amer 85-86; Comp Sci.

MICHELLE, MC FARLAND; Delsea Reg HS; Newfield, NJ; (Y); VICA; Fld Hcky; Nrsng.

MICHELUCCI, PIETRO; North Warren Regional HS; Fairport, NY; (Y); Boy Scts; Church Yth Grp; Rep Frsh Cls; Rep Stu Cncl; JV Socr; Hon Roll; Accptd As A Rtry Intl Exchnge Stud 85-86 1st & 2 Time Awd Wnnr Rogates Twrd Stri Awd 83-85; Comp Sci.

MICHURA, LISA; Neumann Prep; North Caldwell, NJ; (Y); 7/82; Church Yth Grp; Dance Clb; Variety Show; Nwsp Stf; Yrbk Stf; Var Cheerleading; High Hon Roll; NHS; Spanish NHS; Ntl Hnr Roll 85-86; Dnc Awds 75-82; Bus Admin.

MICKENS, FELIX; Plainfield HS; Plainfield, NJ; (Y); Art Clb; Aud/Vis; Camera Clb; Cmnty Wkr; Science Clb; Spanish Clb; School Play; Howfird Orrutgers U; Systms Anl.

MICKLE, SESILY MARIE-GREEN; Roselle Catholic HS; Roselle, NJ; (Y); Chorus; Bowling; Var Trk; Fshn Inst Tech HS Pgm Awd 86; Fashion Inst Tech; Buying.

MICKUS, SHAUN; Abraham Clark HS; Roselle, NJ; (S); 7/208; Debate Tm; Chorus; School Play; Nwsp Rptr; Nwsp Stf; Stu Cncl; High Hon Roll; Hon Roll; NHS; Olymp Of Mind ST Fnlst 83-84; Futr Prblm Slvng Tm 85-86; Comms.

MIDDENDORF, CHERYL; Ramapo HS; Wyckoff, NJ; (Y); 112/329; Church Yth Grp; Cmnty Wkr; Drama Clb; French Clb; Band; Stage Crew; Yrbk Ed-Chief; Stat Ice Hcky; Var Socr; JV Sftbl; APTS Cert Of Merit Accntng I, Comp Prog I & U S Hstry I; Accntng.

MIDDINGS, CHRIS; West Morris Central HS; Chester, NJ; (Y); Hon Roll; 1st, 2nd & 3rd Pl Arch Drwng Cmptn; PA ST U; Arch.

MIECZKOWSKI, JOHN W; Marist HS; Bayonne, NJ; (Y); 22/110; Science Clb; Spanish Clb; JV Bsbl; Im Bsktbl; Im Vllybl; Hon Roll; Spanish NHS; Bro Leo Sylvius & Marist Acadmc Schlrshp 83-84; St Johns U; Lwyr.

MIELKE, MARIANNE; Lyndhurst HS; Lyndhurst, NJ; (Y); 5/185; GAA; Girl Scts; Hosp Aide; Drm Mjr(t); Sftbl; Twrlr; NHS.

MIFFLIN, BRITTANY; Salem HS; Salem, NJ; (Y); Church Yth Grp; Computer Clb; Math Clb; Spanish Clb; Trs Frsh Cls; Trs Soph Cls; Rep Stu Cncl; Var Cheerleading; Hon Roll; NHS; Acctg.

MIGLIAZZA, MISSY; Red Bank Catholic HS; W Long Branch, NJ; (Y); Girl Scts; Ski Clb; Spanish Clb; Yrbk Stf; Pres Jr Cls; Socr; Swmmng; Wt Lftg; Fordham U; Lwyr.

MIGLIORE, JOSEPHINE; Cliffside Park HS; Fairview, NJ; (Y); 36/239; Spanish Clb; Color Guard; Yrbk Ed-Chief; Stu Cncl; High Hon Roll; Hon Roll; Speech Tm; Salvatn Army Frvw Chap Schlrshp 86; Englewood Hosp Schl Radi; Radio.

MIGNOGNA, MARISSA; Camdden Catholic HS; Bellmawr, NJ; (Y); 7/260; Drill Tm; Rep Soph Cls; Off Sr Cls; Stu Cncl; Bsktbl; Var Cheerleading; Wrstlng; High Hon Roll; Hon Roll; NHS; Emerald Socty Engl Hnr Socty 85; Sci & Math Hnr Soctys 84; NJ ST Champ Chrldg Sqd 85-86; Math.

MIHALEK, LYDIA; Toms Rivers HS North; Toms River, NJ; (Y); 31/700; FBLA; Intnl Clb; Spanish Clb; Band; Mrchg Band; School Musical; Stu Cncl; Capt Bsktbl; High Hon Roll; NHS; Brdcst Cmmnctns.

MIHALENKO, GEOFF; North Brunswick Township HS; N Brunswick, NJ; (Y); Spanish Clb; Band; Concert Band; Jazz Band; Mrchg Band; School Musical; Bsbl; Var L Crs Cntry; Var L Trk; Hon Roll; Grtr Middlesex Conf All Acad Tm 86; Band Cncl Treas 85.

MIHALK, DENISE; Piscataway HS; Piscataway, NJ; (Y); Pres Church Yth Grp; Sec Chorus; Madrigals; School Musical; Sftbl; NHS; Hugh O Brien Yth Fndtn Ldrshp Smnr 85; Arts HS 86; All Cnty 85-86; Msc Perf.

MIHLON, JEFFREY; Jackson Memorial HS; Jackson, NJ; (Y); 44/363; French Clb; Band; Concert Band; Drm & Bgl; Jazz Band; Mrchg Band; Symp Band; Im Bsktbl; Capt Powder Puff Ftbl; Var Tennis; Christa A Mc Auliffe Mem Schlrshp 86; CA U PA; Elem Educ.

MIICK, SEAN; Bricktown HS; Brick Town, NJ; (Y); Boy Scts; Political Wkr; Ski Clb; SADD; Variety Show; Nwsp Phtg; Nwsp Stf; Yrbk Phtg; Yrbk Stf; Rep Frsh Cls; Rutgers; Elctrnc Engnrng.

MIKESELL, CORINNE; Parsippany HS; Parsippany, NJ; (Y); Church Yth Grp; Debate Tm; Rep DECA; Exploring; French Clb; FBLA; Hosp Aide; NFL; Pep Clb; Q&S; DECA NJ Advrts Cmptn 1st Pl & NJ ST 4th Pl 86; Advrtsg.

MIKHAIL, SAMMY; Hudson Catholic HS; Jersey City, NJ; (Y); 40/180; Camera Clb; Church Yth Grp; Computer Clb; SADD; Acpl Chr; Church Choir; Nwsp Phtg; Nwsp Rptr; Nwsp Sprt Ed; Nwsp Stf; Cert Apprctn Nwspr Stff, Athl Awds Phy Ed 85-86; Rutgers Coll; Engrng.

MILAN, SUSAN; Holy Family Acad; Bayonne, NJ; (Y); 10/140; Cmnty Wkr; Hosp Aide; Service Clb; Spanish Clb; Orch; Ed Yrbk Stf; High Hon Roll; NHS; NEDT Awd; Chrstn Svc Awd 84; Music Awd 84; St Peters Coll Smr Schlr 85-86; Vetrnry Mdcn.

MILANE, JOSEPH E; Marist HS; Bayonne, NJ; (Y); Sec GAA; Scholastic Bowl; Spanish Clb; Stage Crew; Yrbk Stf; Rep Stu Cncl; High Hon Roll; Hon Roll; NHS; Spanish NHS; Brother Leo Sylvius Mem Schlrshp 83-86; Acad Schlrshp 83-86; Smmr Schlr St Peters Coll 85-86; Accntnt.

MILEY, FRANCIS; Sacred Heart HS; Vineland, NJ; (Y); 3/67; Am Leg Boys St; Chorus; School Play; Sec Sr Cls; Var Tennis; Hon Roll; Ntl Merit Ltr; Rotary Awd; Hugh O Brien Yth Ldrshp 85; Natl Hnr Socty 85.

MILIOTE, ANTHONY; Manalapan HS; Manalapan, NJ; (Y); 128/451; JV Bsbl; Bsktbl; Bowling; Var Ftbl; Golf; Vllybl; Wt Lftg; Clemson U SC; Bus Mgmt.

MILLAR, MICHAEL; Holy Spirit HS; Ocean City, NJ; (Y); Swmmng; Hon Roll; Crew Crowing Y Lttr 84-87; Real Estate.

MILLAR, MINETTE; The Pilgrim Acad; Port Republic, NJ; (Y); 2/14; Drama Clb; Orch; Yrbk Bus Mgr; Co-Capt Cheerleading; High Hon Roll; NHS; Sal; VFW Awd; Hdmstrs Ltrary Awd 86; Chncllrs Schlrshp For Klbrty U 86; Lbrty U; Hmn Eclgy.

MILLEMANN, MIKE; Jackson Memorial HS; Jackson, NJ; (Y); Computer Clb; Ski Clb; JV Var Powder Puff Ftbl; Var L Trk; Var Vllybl; Var Wt Lftg; High Hon Roll; Hon Roll; U Of S CA; Arch.

MILLER, ADAM; Mt Olive HS; Flanders, NJ; (Y); 15/296; Ski Clb; VP Temple Yth Grp; School Play; Nwsp Ed-Chief; Pres Stu Cncl; JV Socr; Var Swmmng; NHS; Math Clb; SADD; NFTY Socl Actn Netwrk 86-87; Pol Sci.

MILLER, ADAM M; Hanover Park HS; East Hanover, NJ; (Y); 18/285; Am Leg Boys St; School Musical; Nwsp Sprt Ed; Off Jr Cls; Off Sr Cls; Stu Cncl; Socr; NHS; Tommy Markowski Mem Schlrshp 86; Kane Lodge Awd 86; Boston U; Med.

MILLER, ADINAH; Solomon Schechter Day Schl; E Windsor, NJ; (Y); Cmnty Wkr; VP Drama Clb; VP Temple Yth Grp; Nwsp Stf; Ed Yrbk Stf; Sec Rep Stu Cncl; Mgr(s); Pres NHS; St Schlr; School Play; NJ Israel Tst 85.

MILLER, ANDREA; Pitman HS; Pitman, NJ; (Y); Office Aide; Spanish Clb; Rep Frsh Cls; Rep Soph Cls; Rep Jr Cls; Rep Stu Cncl; Mgr(s); Pom Pon; Score Keeper; Phil Coll Of Phrmcy; Phrmcy.

MILLER, BENJAMIN S; Killatinny Regional HS; Hainesville, NJ; (Y); Chorus; Concert Band; Madrigals; Mrchg Band; Orch; School Musical; Symp Band; Teachers Aide; Acpl Chr; Band; Cnty Choir & Band 83-85; NJ All ST Choir 83; Mt Union Music Prof Schlrshp 85-86; Mt Union Coll; Music Ed.

MILLER JR, CLINTON W; Neptune HS; Neptune City, NJ; (Y); 67/400; Drama Clb; Thesps; School Musical; School Play; Stage Crew; Nwsp Stf; Yrbk Stf; Lit Mag; Cit Awd; Lucas Film.

MILLER, CRISTINA; Waldwick HS; Waldwick, NJ; (Y); Church Yth Grp; Cmnty Wkr; Drama Clb; Letterman Clb; Teachers Aide; Varsity Clb; Nwsp Stf; L Var Trk; Theatre Awd 86; Schl Paper Awd 86; Vrsty Ltr In Trk 86; Art.

MILLER, DEBRA; Highland HS; Blackwood, NJ; (S); Art Clb; Spanish Clb; Concert Band; Mrchg Band; Socr; Trk; NHS.

MILLER, DERRICK; Park Ridge HS; Park Rigdge, NJ; (Y); 21/106; Boy Scts; Political Wkr; Quiz Bowl; Varsity Clb; Band; Jazz Band; Bsktbl; Socr; Ntl Merit SF; Mech Engr.

MILLER, DONALD; Bridgewater-Raritan HS; Bridgewater, NJ; (Y); Church Yth Grp; Ski Clb; Bsktbl; Capt Var Lcrss; Socr; High Hon Roll; Hon Roll; NHS; Hnrbl Ment All Cty Soccer Sq 85; 1st Tm Garden ST League Attack 86; Mech Engr.

MILLER, ELIZABETH; Randolph HS; Randolph, NJ; (Y); Church Yth Grp; Chorus; Fld Hcky; High Hon Roll; Hon Roll; 1st Pl-Somerset Rgnl Stu Art Shw-Ceramics 85.

MILLER, ERIC; Williamstown HS; Williamstown, NJ; (Y); Am Leg Boys St; Varsity Clb; Stu Cncl; Var Socr; Var Capt Tennis; Cit Awd; NHS; Frsh Cls; Hon Roll; Male Soph Athlt Of Yr 84-85; Male JR Athlt Of Yr 85-86; Tenns Grp III 1st Tm 85-86; Acctg.

MILLER, FAITH; Pleasantville HS; Pleasantville, NJ; (Y); 10/120; Drama Clb; VP FBLA; SADD; Church Choir; Yrbk Stf; Rep Stu Cncl; NHS; Alpha Bette 86; Town & Cntry 86; Johnson & Wales; Bus Adm.

MILLER, GERI; Our Lady Of Good Counsel HS; Irvington, NJ; (Y); 46/106; Cmnty Wkr; Girl Scts; Teachers Aide; Chorus; Rep Sr Cls; Rep Stu Cncl; Cert Apprectn 86; Psychlgy.

MILLER, HENRY L; Somerville HS; Neshanic Station, NJ; (Y); 1/235; Math Tm; Scholastic Bowl; Rep Stu Cncl; Var L Tennis; High Hon Roll; NHS; Ntl Merit SF; St Schlr; Val; Exchg Clb Yth Mnth 85; Tnnis Tm MVP 84; Pre-Law.

MILLER, JACK J; Hillsborough HS; S Somerville, NJ; (Y); 4/300; Boy Scts; Latin Clb; Math Clb; Math Tm; JV Golf; Im JV Socr; Hon Roll; Ntl Merit SF; Eagle Sct Brnz Palm; Rutgers Schlr; Philsphy.

MILLER, KATHY; Union Catholic Regional HS; Irvington, NJ; (Y); 23/308; Church Yth Grp; Service Clb; SADD; Yrbk Stf; Acdmc All-Amrcn 86.

MILLER, KIMBERLY MARIA; North Warren Regional HS; Johnsonburg, NJ; (Y); 34/148; Church Yth Grp; 4-H; Spanish Clb; School Musical; Trs Sr Cls; Rep Stu Cncl; Swmmng; Pres Acdmc Fit Awd 86; George Van Campen Awd 86; U Of DE; Apprl Dsgn.

MILLER, KOREY B; Saddle Brook HS; Saddle Brook, NJ; (Y); 3/116; Am Leg Boys St; Math Clb; Q&S; Quiz Bowl; Nwsp Phtg; Nwsp Sprt Ed; Var Ftbl; Var L Trk; High Hon Roll; NHS; Prncpls Hnr Roll Awd 84-86; Hstry Wrld Stud Amer Stud Awds 85-86; Enrchd Alg II-GEOM Awds 85; Aero Engr.

MILLER, KRISTEN; Red Bank Catholic HS; Manasquan, NJ; (Y); Church Yth Grp; Cmnty Wkr; Latin Clb; NFL; Yrbk Stf; Pres Frsh Cls; Chrmn Jr Cls; Pres Stu Cncl; Var L Cheerleading; Hon Roll; Catholic Coll.

MILLER, KRISTIN; Pual VI HS; Laurel Spgs, NJ; (Y); SADD; JV Crs Cntry; Var Trk; Cmnty Wkr; Chorus; JV Var Mgr(s); JV Sftbl; Host Hostess Club PTA; Trenton ST; Speech Pathlgy.

MILLER, LEANNE; Riverside HS; Riverside, NJ; (Y); Am Leg Aux Girls St; FTA; Rep Sr Cls; Rep Stu Cncl; High Hon Roll; Hon Roll; Garden ST Schlrshp 86; Trustee Schlrshp 86; Alumni Schlrshp 86; Rider Clg; Sec Eng Tchr.

MILLER, LYNN; Essex Catholic Girls HS; Newark, NJ; (Y); Pep Clb; Chorus; Capt Drill Tm; Yrbk Stf; Hon Roll; Rep Frsh Cls; Berkely; Exec Secy.

MILLER, MELISSA; Burlington City HS; Burlington, NJ; (Y); Church Yth Grp; Chorus; JV Cheerleading; Acctng.

MILLER, MELISSA; Oak Knoll Schl; Summit, NJ; (Y); Pres Art Clb; Service Clb; Ed Lit Mag; Rep Jr Cls; Var Crs Cntry; Swmmng; Hon Roll; Art Awd 83-86; Art.

MILLER, MICHELLE; Hamilton West HS; Yardville, NJ; (Y); Am Leg Aux Girls St; Rep Church Yth Grp; Co-Capt Drill Tm; Variety Show; Rep Jr Cls; Rep Sr Cls; Rep Stu Cncl; Hon Roll; Mercer Cnty Teen Arts Fest 84-86; Qualf Prfrmd NJ ST Teen Arts Fest 85-86; Dance Thrpy.

MILLER, NEAL; Hightstown HS; Hightstown, NJ; (Y); 13/450; Trs Church Yth Grp; Church Choir; Var Crs Cntry; Var Trk; High Hon Roll; Hon Roll; Sec NHS; Ntl Merit SF; Tri Cnty Shrt Stry Wrtrs Hon Mntn 85; Sci.

MILLER, NICHELLE; Kingsway Regional HS; Woodstown, NJ; (Y); Pres Church Yth Grp; Model UN; Pres Church Choir; Trs Jr Cls; Trs Sr Cls; Rep Stu Cncl; Var Capt Cheerleading; Var Trk; Hon Roll; NHS; Gloria Miller Mem Awd 85.

MILLER, PATTI; Gateway Regional HS; Westville, NJ; (Y); Church Yth Grp; Girl Scts; Library Aide; SADD; Band; Chorus; Flag Corp; Yrbk Stf; Cheerleading; Sftbl; Schlrshp Moore Coll Of Art Sprng Cls 85; Glassboro ST Coll; Lbrl Arts.

MILLER, PETER; Montville Township HS; Pine Brook, NJ; (Y); 155/283; Key Clb; Varsity Clb; Var Capt Lcrss; Var Capt Socr; Im Tennis; Mst Imprvd Plyr Lacrss 84; Jimmy Miller Awd Sccr 84; Bus.

MILLER, ROBIN; Middletown HS South; Lincroft, NJ; (Y); Sec French Clb; Chorus; Var Trk; French Hon Soc; High Hon Roll; Ntl Merit SF; Psych.

MILLER, SANDEE; Middletown H S North; Leonardo, NJ; (Y); SADD; Thesps; Color Guard; School Musical; School Play; Lit Mag; Sec Church Yth Grp; Cmnty Wkr; Drama Clb; US Congressional Awd Brnz Mdl 84; Golden Poet Awd 86; Acadm All Am 84; Art.

MILLER, SCOTT; Delran HS; Delran, NJ; (Y); Capt Ftbl; Var L Trk; JV Capt Wrstlng; S Jersey Cham Group II 400 Im Hurdls 86; 1 Clb Delran HS 86; Freedom Div Cham 400 Im Hurdls 86; Pilot.

MILLER, SCOTT; Toms River HS North; Toms River, NJ; (Y); 38/412; Am Leg Boys St; German Clb; Ski Clb; Off Stu Cncl; Mgr(s); Stat Score Keeper; Hon Roll; NHS; VFW Awd; Voice Dem Awd; William & Mary; Bus Adm.

MILLER, SEAN; Holy Cross HS; Edgewater Park, NJ; (Y); 64/369; Cmnty Wkr; Computer Clb; Church Choir; Concert Band; Drm Mjr(t); Mrchg Band; Hon Roll; Latin Clb; Teachers Aide; Bio-Chem.

MILLER, SHARON; Shore Regional HS; Oceanport, NJ; (Y); 3/222; Am Leg Aux Girls St; Drama Clb; Thesps; School Musical; Yrbk Stf; Mgr(s); High Hon Roll; Lion Awd; NHS; Pres Schlr; Long Branch Exch Clb Awd 86; Frank & Louise Groff Schlrp Med 86; Dr Santo Trufulo Thespn Schlrp; Boston Coll; Med.

MILLER, SHERRY; Orange HS; Orange, NJ; (S); Church Yth Grp; Cmnty Wkr; Pep Clb; Nwsp Stf; High Hon Roll; Hon Roll; NHS; H S Schlrs Prog NJ Inst Of Tech 85; NJIT; Comp Engrng.

MILLER, STACE; Garden State Acad; Andover, NJ; (Y); Church Yth Grp; 4-H; Pep Clb; Band; Concert Band; Nwsp Ed-Chief; Nwsp Rptr; Nwsp Sprt Ed; Rep Jr Cls; Sftbl; Columbia Union Coll; Psych.

MILLER, STEPHANIE; Lower Cape May Regional HS; Cape May, NJ; (Y); 35/239; Pres Girl Scts; SADD; Concert Band; Jazz Band; Mrchg Band; School Play; Stage Crew; Nwsp Ed-Chief; Yrbk Stf; Lit Mag; Producer.

MILLER, THAD; Mt Olive HS; Flanders, NJ; (Y); 27/310; AFS; Math Clb; Math Tm; Varsity Clb; Trs Stu Cncl; Var L Bsbl; Var L Bsktbl; Var L Ftbl; Im Wt Lftg; High Hon Roll; Bus Admin.

MILLER, TRACY T; Chatham Twp HS; Chatham, NJ; (Y); 13/138; VP Church Yth Grp; Girl Scts; Key Clb; Model UN; Service Clb; JV Fld Hcky; Var JV Sftbl; High Hon Roll; Hon Roll; Sec NHS.

MILLER, WILLIAM; Wildwood HS; North Wildwood, NJ; (Y); Latin Clb; ROTC; Color Guard; Drill Tm; Tennis; Hon Roll; Prfct Atten Awd; Cadet Of Mo Of April ROTC 85; Cadet Of Mo Of March ROTC 86.

MILLET, MARIA; Marylawn HS; Harrison, NJ; (Y); 17/60; Hosp Aide; Library Aide; Spanish Clb; School Musical; Twrlr; Hon Roll; Prfct Atten Awd; Spanish NHS; 1st Pl Spanish Cntst 85; Rutgers U; Pre-Law.

MILLEY, RODNEY; Williamstown HS; Williamstown, NJ; (Y); JV Bsbl; JV Ftbl; JV Trk; Wt Lftg; Hon Roll; Stockton ST Coll; Comp.

MILLILO, RICHARD; Holy Cross HS; Cinnaminson, NJ; (Y); Chess Clb; Rep Church Yth Grp; Math Clb; Ski Clb; Lit Mag; Rep Sr Cls; Im Bsbl; Im Bsktbl; Coach Actv; JV Crs Cntry; Garden ST Schlrshp 86; C Mu Schlrshp 86; St Josephs Schlrshp 86; Carnegie Mellon U; Med.

MILLIRON, RICK; South Hunterdon Regional HS; Lambertville, NJ; (Y); 31/98; Church Yth Grp; Rep Frsh Cls; JV Bsbl; Fld Hcky; Var L Ftbl; Im Wt Lftg; Capt L Wrstlng; 2 Letters Wrstlng & Ftbll 85-86; Penn ST; Mrtng.

MILLMAN, MARK J; Milburn SR HS; Short Hills, NJ; (Y); 7/260; Capt Quiz Bowl; Teachers Aide; Temple Yth Grp; Lit Mag; Gov Hon Prg Awd; High Hon Roll; Ntl Merit SF; St Schlr; Rensselaer Poly-Tech Inst Awd Mdl 85; Capt-Letter Mens Fncng 85-86; 1st Bio-St Sci Day Comp 84; Harvard U; Genetic Engr.

MILLS, DAVID; Hunterdon Central HS; Fletcher, NC; (Y); 223/548; Art Clb; FFA; U Of NC; Engrng.

MILLS, ERIN; Morris Knolls HS; Denville, NJ; (Y); 158/383; Ski Clb; Chorus; School Play; Yrbk Stf; Diving; Swmmng.

MILLS, GEORGE; Holy Cross HS; Browns Mills, NJ; (Y); Ski Clb; Trk; Hon Roll; Comp Sci & Engr.

MILLS, KEN; Delran HS; Delran, NJ; (Y); 20/210; Aud/Vis; Drama Clb; Ski Clb; School Musical; Stage Crew; JV Var Crs Cntry; JV Var Trk; Hon Roll; Engrng.

MILNE, JOHN; Hoboken HS; Hoboken, NJ; (Y); VP Key Clb; Chorus; School Musical; School Play; Variety Show; Nwsp Rptr; Trs Jr Cls; Trs Stu Cncl; Var Cheerleading; Swmmng; Actng.

MILORA, DONALD; Atlantic City HS; Ventnor, NJ; (Y); 38/455; Ski Clb; Art Clb; JV Bsbl; Im Capt Bsktbl; Im Capt Ice Hcky; High Hon Roll; Jr NHS; 86 Pres Ftnss Awd 86:Columbus Schlrshp Awd Hnrbl Mntn $200 86; 2 Star Grad Credit 86; Florida Inst Of Tech; Bus.

MILORDO, LOUIS; Eastside HS; Paterson, NJ; (S); 13/600; Var Ftbl; Var Trk; Var Wt Lftg; NHS; Ntl Merit Schol.

MILTON, KARLA; Henry Snyder HS; Jersey City, NJ; (Y); Sr Cls; Social Wrkr.

MILTON, LAMARR J; Trenton Central HS; Trenton, NJ; (Y); Boys Clb Am; Cmnty Wkr; FBLA; Science Clb; SADD; Chorus; Stage Crew; Rep Frsh Cls; Rep Soph Cls; Rep Jr Cls; Norfold ST U; Bus Admin.

MIN, CHARLEENE; Hopewell Valley Central HS; Princeton, NJ; (Y); Cmnty Wkr; Debate Tm; Latin Clb; Spanish Clb; Lit Mag; Rep Stu Cncl; Swmmng; High Hon Roll; Hon Roll; NHS; M S Gindhart Piano Comp 2nd 84-85; Cert Swmmng, Mem Day Spch Wnnr 86.

MIN, JOHN; Middlesex HS; Middlesex, NJ; (Y); 2/156; Am Leg Boys St; Off Church Yth Grp; Key Clb; Math Tm; Model UN; SADD; Nwsp Ed-Chief; Pres Stu Cncl; NHS; Ntl Merit Ltr; Harvard U; Biomed Engr.

MINAR, MARYANN; Hamilton High West; Trenton, NJ; (Y); 29/330; Am Leg Aux Girls St; Church Yth Grp; Dance Clb; Key Clb; Teachers Aide; Color Guard; Nwsp Rptr; Yrbk Stf; VP Stu Cncl; JV Fld Hcky; Glassboro ST Coll; Eng.

MINASIAN, LARRY; Seton Hall Prep; Orange, NJ; (Y); Church Yth Grp; Intnl Clb; Pep Clb; Ski Clb; High Hon Roll; Ntl Sci Achvmnt Awd; Bus.

MINDNICH, GRETCHEN; Red Bank Regional HS; Little Silver, NJ; (Y); Key Clb; Pres Ski Clb; Rep Soph Cls; Rep Jr Cls; Var L Socr; JV L Sftbl; Var L Swmmng; Var L Tennis; Spanish NHS; All Shore Hnrb Mntn Tnns 84.

MINERVINI, ANNA; Emerson HS; Weehawken, NJ; (Y); Art Clb; Library Aide; Office Aide; Teachers Aide; Yrbk Stf; Jr Cls; Stu Cncl; Hon Roll; Jr NHS; NHS; Natl H S Italn Cntst Hnbl Mntn 84-86; Italn Hnr Socty 86; Fashn Merch.

MINERVINI, FRANK A; Hudson Catholic HS; Hoboken, NJ; (Y); 65/186; Church Yth Grp; Cmnty Wkr; Pep Clb; Pres SADD; JV Var Bsktbl; Hon Roll; Peer Minstry Awd; De La Salle Svc Awd; St Peters Coll; Bus.

MINERVINI, LUCIA; Secaucus HS; Secaucus, NJ; (S); 5/160; VP Computer Clb; Key Clb; VP Math Clb; Varsity Clb; Nwsp Rptr; Rep Soph Cls; Rep Jr Cls; Var Tennis; High Hon Roll; Mu Alp Tht; 1st & 2nd Pl Itln Ptry Cntst; Itln Natl Hnr Soc.

MINERVINI, TINA; St John Vianney HS; Englishtown, NJ; (Y); 77/259; Intnl Clb; JCL; Stage Crew; Yrbk Bus Mgr; Hon Roll; Gld Wht Merit Awd St John Vianney 85; Int Dsgn.

MINERVINI, VINCENT; Wood-Ridge HS; Wood-Ridge, NJ; (S); 20/91; Computer Clb; Latin Clb; Pres Math Clb; Math Tm; Model UN; Science Clb; Pres VP Service Clb; Trs Stu Cncl; High Hon Roll; NHS; Actrl Sci.

MINGO, RYAN JAMES; Red Bank Regional HS; Little Silver, NJ; (Y); 16/232; Pres Ski Clb; School Play; Trs Frsh Cls; Trs Soph Cls; Trs Jr Cls; Capt Diving; Socr; Capt Swmmng; NHS; Spanish NHS; VA Polytech Inst; Arch.

MINICHIELLO, GABRIEL; Hudson Catholic HS; Jersey City, NJ; (Y); Art Clb; Boy Scts; SADD; Band; School Play; JV Trk; Im Wt Lftg; Hon Roll; Im Bsktbl; Im Ftbl; Boy Scouts 1st Cls Rank 83; Bsktbl Trophy Cnty Champs 82; Rutgers U; Comp Pgmmr.

MINICUCCI, PATRICIA ANNE; De Paul Diocesan HS; Pompton Lakes, NJ; (S); Chess Clb; Church Yth Grp; Spanish Clb; Mrchg Band; Nwsp Stf; Yrbk Rptr; Var Cheerleading; Trk; High Hon Roll; NHS; Ms Teen-Ager NJ 84; Ms Teen-Ager Pgnt STS 4th Rnr-Up 84; Natl Hnr Scty Tlnt Shw Mst Tlntd 85; SUNY Binghampton; Pre-Med.

MINIERI, MICHAEL A; Union HS; Union, NJ; (Y); 3/500; Am Leg Boys St; Church Yth Grp; Var Bsktbl; JV Socr; Var Trk; NHS; Ntl Merit Ltr; Pres Clssrm Young Amer 86; Outstndng Achvt Germn 84.

MINITEE, TABRINA; Hillside HS; Hillside, NJ; (Y); Pep Clb; Ski Clb; School Play; Nwsp Rptr; Hon Roll; Hampton U; Lawyer.

MINK, ALBERT; Buena Regional HS; Mays Landing, NJ; (S); 1/240; Boy Scts; Church Yth Grp; Political Wkr; High Hon Roll; Hon Roll; Mdcl.

MINORE, DOMINICA; Washington Township HS; Turnersville, NJ; (Y); Spanish Clb; Cheerleading; AZ ST U; Bus.

MINTZ, NEIL A; Wayne Hills HS; Wayne, NJ; (Y); 15/310; Math Tm; Spanish Clb; Jazz Band; Bsktbl; High Hon Roll; Hon Roll; NHS; Ntl Merit Ltr; St Schlr; Rutgers Coll; Comp Sci.

MINTZ, STEPHEN; Teaneck HS; Teaneck, NJ; (Y); Cmnty Wkr; SADD; Stage Crew; Yrbk Stf; Trs Sr Cls; Im Fld Hcky; JV Tennis; Im Vllybl; Hon Roll; NHS; Bus.

MIRAGLIA, WANDA; Northern Valley Regional HS; Norhvale, NJ; (Y); Art Clb; Ski Clb; Dsgng Fshn Inst Of Tech; Dsgn.

MIRAGLIOTTA, TINA; Kittatinny Regional HS; Newton, NJ; (Y); 5/240; Science Clb; Spanish Clb; Teachers Aide; Nwsp Rptr; Nwsp Stf; High Hon Roll; NHS; Area Achvt Awd Eng,Math,Chem 85-86; Med.

MIRANDA, ANTONIO; Roselle Catholic HS; Elizabeth, NJ; (Y); 18/195; Ski Clb; Im Bsktbl; Spanish NHS; NJIT; Lzr Physcst.

MIRANDI, VINCENT; Whippany Park HS; Whippany, NJ; (Y); Am Leg Boys St; Debate Tm; Thesps; Jazz Band; Yrbk Ed-Chief; Yrbk Stf; Pres Frsh Cls; Pres Soph Cls; Hon Roll; NHS; Graphic Design.

MIRON, JAIME; Memorial HS; West New York, NJ; (Y); French Clb; Hon Roll; Spllng Bee Awd 82; NJIT; Chem Engr.

MIRSKY, ANDREW T; Millburn SR HS; Short Hills, NJ; (Y); 18/247; Cmnty Wkr; Spanish Clb; Temple Yth Grp; Acpl Chr; Band; Chorus; Concert Band; Jazz Band; School Musical; Rptr Nwsp Phtg; Garden ST Dstngshd Schlr 85; Rutgers U Schlr 85; Essex Cnty Zoo Photo Cntst Grnd Prz 84; Harvard U; Music.

MIRZAI, HOSSEIN; Washington Township HS; Sewell, NJ; (Y); French Clb; Hon Roll; Elect Engrng.

MISCHAK, DANA LYNN; Villa Victoria Acad; Yardley, PA; (Y); Trs Church Yth Grp; Hosp Aide; School Musical; Yrbk Stf; Sec Trs Frsh Cls; Sec Trs Soph Cls; Var Bsktbl; Var Socr; Var Sftbl; Hon Roll; US Army Rsrv Natl Schlr/Athlt Awd 86; Hghst Avg Englsh 2nd Hghst Avg Math 86; Ursinus Coll; Econ.

MISIAG, HELEN; Spotswood HS; Spotswood, NJ; (S); FBLA; Ski Clb; Yrbk Stf; Pres Stu Cncl; JV Var Cheerleading; High Hon Roll; Hon Roll; Ntl Merit SF; School Musical; Brd Educ 85-87; Wrld Hungr Pgm 85; FBLA 3rd Pl Rgnl Cmptv Evnts-Wrd Prcsng, Mach Trnscrptn 86.

MISKE, FRANCINE; Toms River HS North; Toms River, NJ; (Y); 28/440; VP German Clb; Hosp Aide; Intnl Clb; Fld Hcky; Hon Roll; NHS; Physcs Tm 85; Advanced Plcmnt Bio Tm 86; NJ Natl Guard Assc Schlrshp 86; Roger Williams Coll; Archtctr.

MISKO, SUSAN; Belleville HS; Belleville, NJ; (Y); Chorus; High Hon Roll; Hon Roll; NHS.

MISYAK, PATTI; Dover HS; Mine Hill, NJ; (Y); 2/183; Am Leg Aux Girls St; Concert Band; Mrchg Band; Yrbk Ed-Chief; Bsktbl; High Hon Roll; Hon Roll; NHS; Latin Clb; Band; CCD Tchr Chch 84-86; JR Art Awd 86; Intr Decrtr.

MITCHEL, ROBERT D; Watching Hills Regional HS; Gillette, NJ; (Y); 5/330; Church Yth Grp; Math Tm; Capt Scholastic Bowl; Nwsp Stf; Var L Crs Cntry; Var L Swmmng; Var L Trk; NHS; Ntl Merit SF; NJ Gov Schl Sci 85; Engr.

MITCHELL, AUDRA; Southern Regional HS; Manahawkin, NJ; (Y); Dance Clb; Band; Concert Band; Jazz Band; Hon Roll; Music.

MITCHELL, BRENDA; Jackson Memorial HS; Jackson, NJ; (Y); 38/322; Am Leg Aux Girls St; Church Yth Grp; 4-H; ROTC; Rep Soph Cls; Bowling; Sftbl; Vllybl; Cit Awd; High Hon Roll; Military Order World Wars Awd 84-85; Am Leg Scholar Awd 85-86; Dayton W Elyra III Mem Scholar 85-86; Travel.

MITCHELL, DENISE L; Delaware Valley Regional HS; Milford, NJ; (Y); Church Yth Grp; Yrbk Stf; Trk; Wt Lftg; Hghst Avg, Hghst Tst Grds Math Awd 84; Trenton ST Coll; Chld Care.

MITCHELL, ERIC D; The Lawrenceville Schl; Trenton, NJ; (Y); JV Bsbl; JV Bsktbl; Var L Ftbl; Var JV Trk; Bausch & Lomb Sci Awd; Art.

MITCHELL, KRISTI; Arthur P Schalick HS; Elmer, NJ; (Y); 1/137; Math Tm; Sec Frsh Cls; Sec Soph Cls; Rep Stu Cncl; JV Bsktbl; JV Var Fld Hcky; Var Stat Score Keeper; JV Var Sftbl; Hon Roll; NHS; Spllg Bee Champ 82; Top 5 Cls 86; Bus Adm.

MITCHELL, LAURA; Millville SR HS; Millville, NJ; (Y); Church Yth Grp; Drama Clb; French Clb; Office Aide; PAVAS; Radio Clb; Ski Clb; Speech Tm; Orch; School Musical; Cumberland Plyrs Comm Theatre; U Of DE; Flm Prod.

MITCHELL, MARTIN; Cherokee HS; Marlton, NJ; (Y); 35/431; Am Leg Boys St; Church Yth Grp; Debate Tm; Math Tm; Nwsp Rptr; Lit Mag; Rep Jr Cls; Var Trk; Yth Advsry Brd Rcrdng Sec 83-87; Peer Adolescent Lstnng Spprt Grp 85-87; Chem.

MITCHELL, MICHELLE; Shore Regional HS; Oceanport, NJ; (Y); Girl Scts; Key Clb; Spnsh.

MITCHELL, ROMONITA; Eastside HS; Paterson, NJ; (Y); 54/398; Art Clb; Church Yth Grp; Pep Clb; Chorus; Pres Church Choir; Yrbk Stf; Rep Stu Cncl; High Hon Roll; Hon Roll; NHS; Rutgers Coll; Computer Sci.

MITCHELL, SOPHIA; Eastside HS; Paterson, NJ; (Y); 47/500; Hon Roll; NHS; Ntl Merit Ltr; Natl Englsh Merit Awd 86; Fourleigh Dickinson U; Pol Sci.

MITCHELL, SUZANNE; Middletown HS South; Middletown, NJ; (Y); Ski Clb; Yrbk Phtg; Rep Jr Cls; Var Stat Bsbl; Bsktbl; Cheerleading; Powder Puff Ftbl; Score Keeper; High Hon Roll; Hon Roll; Natl Hnr Rl 86; Acctg.

MITCHENER, LORI; Passaic Valley HS; Paterson, NJ; (Y); Intnl Clb; Sftbl; Hon Roll; Berkley; Fshn Merch.

MITKUS, ROBERT; Holy Cross HS; Medford, NJ; (Y); 11/369; Debate Tm; Varsity Clb; Var L Socr; High Hon Roll; Hon Roll; Prfct Atten Awd; Biochmstry.

MITZNER, DAWN; Watchung Hills Regional HS; Watchung, NJ; (Y); Debate Tm; Sec Key Clb; VP Frsh Cls; High Hon Roll; Jr NHS; NHS; Ntl Merit SF; Spanish NHS; Quiz Bowl; Pres Election Bd 86-87; Gov Schl Sci 86; Genetics.

MIX, SUSANNE; Hamilton High School East; Hamilton Sq, NJ; (Y); 39/326; Church Yth Grp; Band; Concert Band; Mrchg Band; Mgr Stage Crew; JV Sftbl; Mrchng Unit Schlrshp 86; Natl Hnr Soc 85; Various Awds & Cert In The Mrchng Unit 82-86; Vrsty Let 85; Trenton ST Clg; Art.

MIX, TRACY; Howell HS; Howell, NJ; (Y); 14/392; Exploring; Intnl Clb; Nwsp Rptr; Nwsp Stf; Lit Mag; Stat Bsktbl; Bowling; Im Crs Cntry; Im Socr; NHS; Phys Thrpy.

MIZAK, JOHN; Colonia HS; Avenel, NJ; (Y); Am Leg Boys St; Varsity Clb; Var Capt Crs Cntry; Var Capt Trk; Hon Roll; NHS; Jrnlsm.

MIZEL, ADAM M; Morristown HS; Convent Station, NJ; (Y); 2/449; Sec Am Leg Boys St; Cmnty Wkr; Trs Exploring; Mgr Radio Clb; Nwsp Ed-Chief; Var JV Wrstlng; High Hon Roll; NHS; Political Wkr; Q&S; Cruma Forster Schlrshp 85; Schlrshp WA Wrkshp Cngrsnl 86; Ecnmcs.

MIZESKI, DENISE; Queen Of Peace HS; Lyndhurst, NJ; (Y); 86/229; Church Yth Grp; Girl Scts; Ski Clb; Rep Stu Cncl; L Var Bowling; Im Powder Puff Ftbl; L Var Sftbl; L Var Trk; Hon Roll; Nrsng.

MIZOV, DEBRA; Bridgewater-Ranten HS East; Bridgewater, NJ; (Y); Pres Church Yth Grp; German Clb; Science Clb; High Hon Roll; Hon Roll; NHS; Aid Assn For Lutherans All-Clg Schlrshp 86; Case Western Reserve U; Biomed.

MOBLEY, KELLIE; Eastern HS; Sewell, NJ; (Y); 54/480; Girl Scts; Chorus; Rep Frsh Cls; Rep Stu Cncl; Trk; High Hon Roll; Hon Roll; Black Awareness Club; Rutgers U; Corp Law.

MOCCARO, ROSE; St John Vianney HS; Hazlet, NJ; (Y); L Var Socr; Hon Roll; GAA; Yrbk Stf; SPCH Thrpy.

MOCHI, MANISHA; Hoboken HS; Hoboken, NJ; (Y); Spanish Clb; Rep Stu Cncl; High Hon Roll; NHS; 1st Pl Schl Spllg Bee 83; 5th Pl Hdsn Cnty Spllg Bee 83; Sprvsrs & Admnstrtn Awd 83.

MODI, VIRAL; Wardlaw Hartridge HS; Colonia, NJ; (Y); Aud/Vis; Computer Clb; Debate Tm; Hosp Aide; Sec SADD; Band; Yrbk Stf; JV Var Socr; JV Trk; Var Capt Wrstlng; Med.

MOFFATT, JOY; Red Bank Catholic HS; Oceanport, NJ; (Y); Library Aide; School Play; Stage Crew; Nwsp Rptr; Nwsp Stf; Stu Cncl; Var Crs Cntry; Var Trk; Hon Roll; NHS; Exclinc Awd-Art.

MOFFITT, ROBERT; Matawan Reg HS; Cliffwood Bch, NJ; (Y); ROTC; VICA; Ftbl.

MOGLIN, DOUGLAS; Morristown HS; Morristown, NJ; (Y); Speech Tm; Pres Y-Teens; PWP Schlrshp 86; Rutgers; Comptr Sci.

MOHL, ANNA P; Solomon Schechter Day Schl; Summit, NJ; (Y); Temple Yth Grp; Nwsp Ed-Chief; Yrbk Rptr; Stu Cncl; Tennis; Pres NHS; NEDT Awd; Drama Clb; Teachers Aide; School Play; Abraham Joshua Heschel Hnr Soc 84-86; Delg Columbia U Schltc Pass Assn 85; 1st Sci Fair 83; Barnard Coll.

MOHN, WENDY; South Hunterdon Regional HS; Lambertville, NJ; (S); 6/70; Am Leg Aux Girls St; Key Clb; VP Frsh Cls; VP Soph Cls; VP Jr Cls; Pres Sr Cls; Sec Stu Cncl; Capt Fld Hcky; Var Sftbl; Hon Roll.

MOHRHAUSER, MARY; T R High Schl East; Toms River, NJ; (Y); Stat Bsktbl; Mgr(s); Score Keeper; Hon Roll; Acctng.

MOIR, DENNIS; Collingswood HS; Oaklyn, NJ; (Y); Am Leg Boys St; Quiz Bowl; Scholastic Bowl; Rep Frsh Cls; Rep Soph Cls; Rep Sr Cls; Rep Stu Cncl; Var Crs Cntry; Var Trk; Hon Roll; Law.

MOJARES, RICHARD; Oratory Catholic Prep; New Providence, NJ; (S); 4/50; Math Tm; Nwsp Rptr; Pres Frsh Cls; Pres Soph Cls; Sec Stu Cncl; Var L Bsktbl; Var L Socr; Var L Tennis; High Hon Roll; NHS; Cert Of Achvt In Gmtry & Latin I 83-84; Med.

MOLINA, ANNABELLA; Hoboken HS; Hoboken, NJ; (Y); Dance Clb; Key Clb; Spanish Clb; Variety Show; Rep Frsh Cls; Rep Soph Cls; Rep Jr Cls; Var Pom Pon; High Hon Roll; NHS; Miss Pom Pon Hudson Cath Cmptn 86; Aspira Clb; Emcee Mdlng Clb Show 86; Comp Sci.

MOLINA, CECILIA; Memorial HS; W New York, NJ; (Y); French Clb; Math Clb; Rep Frsh Cls; Rep Soph Cls; Rep Jr Cls; Hon Roll; Sci Gifted & Tlntd Prog 86; Bio.

MOLINA, HELEN A; Belleville SR HS; Belleville, NJ; (Y); Camera Clb; French Clb; FTA; Tennis; Twrlr; 1st Hnrs Cls Standing 84; Princeton U; Frnch.

MOLINARI, BRIAN; Christian Brothers Acad; Neptune, NJ; (Y); 8/240; Math Tm; Varsity Clb; Yrbk Sprt Ed; Yrbk Stf; Var L Bsbl; Im Ftbl; NHS; Dance Comm Chairman.

MOLLEN, JUDY L; Union HS; Union, NJ; (Y); 77/560; English Clb; Band; Concert Band; Jazz Band; Orch; Nwsp Ed-Chief; Yrbk Stf; Bsktbl; Hon Roll; U MD College Pk.

MOLLER, JAMES V; Bayonne HS; Bayonne, NJ; (Y); 80/342; Ski Clb; Ftbl; Swmmng; High Hon Roll; Hon Roll; Devry Tech Inst; Electron Engr.

MOLNAR, ALYSSA; Chatham Township HS; Chatham Twp, NJ; (Y); 3/137; AFS; Key Clb; Model UN; Science Clb; Concert Band; Yrbk Rptr; Stat Crs Cntry; JV Trk; High Hon Roll; NHS; 3rd Pl Sktng Clb-Morris Showcase Comp 85; Spnsh Achvt Awd 84; 1st Pl Dramatic Intrprttn-SCOM 85.

MOLOUGHNEY, KRISTEN; St Marys HS; Secaucus, NJ; (Y); 9/44; Am Leg Aux Girls St; Spanish Clb; Sftbl; Vllybl; High Hon Roll; Hon Roll; Spanish NHS; Acadmc Achvt Awd Religion 85; Cert Hnr Schlrshp Geom 85; Cert Awd Hist Acvties 86; Cert Recogntn Span; Med.

MONACO, AMY; Riverdell Regional HS; Oradell, NJ; (Y); Hosp Aide; Pep Clb; SADD; High Hon Roll; Hon Roll; NHS; Spanish NHS; Bus.

MONACO, ANTHONY; Toms River HS North; Toms River, NJ; (Y); 12/412; Am Leg Boys St; Model UN; Band; Trs Soph Cls; Trs Sr Cls; Stu Cncl; Capt Crs Cntry; Capt Trk; High Hon Roll; NHS; NJ Yth & Govmt Sen; Empire ST Games Bronze Medlst; All Shore & All County Cross Country; US Naval Acad; Polit Sci.

MONAGLE, KEVIN D; Camden Catholic HS; W Berlin, NJ; (Y); 55/295; Am Leg Boys St; Science Clb; Band; Concert Band; Jazz Band; Mrchg Band; Pres Frsh Cls; Capt Tennis; Hon Roll; NHS; Jrnlsm.

MONAGLE, LARRY; Bridgewater-Raritan HS East; Bridgewater, NJ; (Y); Am Leg Boys St; Intnl Clb; Math Tm; Spanish Clb; Rep Frsh Cls; Rep Soph Cls; Rep Jr Cls; Pres Sr Cls; Stu Cncl; Var Lcrss.

MONAH, CINDY; Roselle Catholic HS; Roselle, NJ; (Y); #101 In Class; Church Yth Grp; Cmnty Wkr; French Clb; Girl Scts; JA; Band; Var Socr; JV Trk; Hon Roll; NHS; Flght Attndt.

MONAHAN, BRIAN; Rutherford HS; Rutherford, NJ; (Y); Office Aide; Chorus; School Play; Stage Crew; Suprior Vcl Achvmnt 86; Engnrng.

MONAHAN, DANIEL; St Josephs Prep Seminary; Philadelphia, PA; (S); Cmnty Wkr; Latin Clb; Spanish Clb; Speech Tm; Chorus; School Play; Lit Mag; Im Bsktbl; Im Sftbl; Im Vllybl.

MONAHAN, JENNIFER; Hunterdon Central HS; Three Bridges, NJ; (Y); 36/539; Pres Church Yth Grp; 4-H; Band; Church Choir; Mrchg Band; School Musical; Symp Band; Nwsp Rptr; High Hon Roll; Spanish NHS; Trenton ST Coll; Jrnlsm.

MONAHAN, PEGGY; Freehold Township HS; Cumberland, RI; (Y); 4/317; VP Drama Clb; Thesps; Band; Madrigals; School Musical; Stage Crew; Variety Show; Gov Hon Prg Awd; NHS; Pres Schlr; Natl Soc Of Pro Engrs 86; Boston U; Engrg.

MONCRIEF, CRAIG; Holy Spirit HS; Ocean City, NJ; (Y); Computer Clb; Teachers Aide; Rotary Yth Ldrshp Awd 85; U DE.

MONCRIEF, ERICA; Toms River HS South; Beachwood, NJ; (Y); 52/320; Concert Band; Flag Corp; Capt Sftbl; Hon Roll; Athletic Schlrshp Sftbll 86; Debbie Mc Chesney Mem Awd 86; GA Court Coll; Hist.

MONEGO, CARL; Pope John XXIII HS; Hewitt, NJ; (Y); JV Bsbl; Hon Roll; Cert Hnr 84.

MONG, JESSICA; Holy Spirit HS; Absecon, NJ; (Y); 11/350; Church Yth Grp; French Clb; Red Cross Aide; Rep Frsh Cls; Rep Soph Cls; Rep Jr Cls; High Hon Roll; Jr NHS; NHS; Med.

MONIER, JILIAN; North Plainfield HS; N Plainfield, NJ; (Y); Church Yth Grp; Key Clb; Ski Clb; Chorus; Var L Fld Hcky; Stat L Ftbl; Var Powder Puff Ftbl; JV Sftbl; Hon Roll; All Co & All Conf Fld Hcky Hnbl Mntn 85.

MONIER, KIRSTEN; Red Bank Regional HS; Little Silver, NJ; (Y); 76/221; Cmnty Wkr; Pres Ski Clb; Rep Stu Cncl; Capt Fld Hcky; Socr; Yrbk Stf; Variety Show; Pep Clb; Dance Clb; Stu To Stu Cnclr; Susquehanna U.

MONINGHOFF, LARA; Belvidere HS; Belvidere, NJ; (S); 3/131; Cmnty Wkr; English Clb; Red Cross Aide; Scholastic Bowl; Nwsp Rptr; Hon Roll; Gftd & Tlntd Prgm 84-86; Outstndng Achvt In Spnsh II Awd 84-85; Pdtrc Srgry.

MONITZER, DIANE; Overbrook SR HS; Lindenwold, NJ; (Y); FBLA; Var Sftbl; Cit Awd; DAR Awd; Hon Roll; Lion Awd; Pres Schlr; Bus.

MONROE, VANCE; Hamilton HS West; Trenton, NJ; (Y); SADD; Rep Frsh Cls; Rep Soph Cls; Rep Jr Cls; Rep Sr Cls; Rep Stu Cncl; Var Bsktbl; Var Ftbl; Elec Engr.

MONROY, CHRISTINA; Elizabeth HS; Elizabeth, NJ; (Y); Boy Scts; Hosp Aide; Key Clb; JV Socr; Hon Roll; Psych.

MONSEN, ERIK; Highstown HS; East Windsor, NJ; (Y); 1/450; Trs AFS; Am Leg Boys St; Church Yth Grp; Drama Clb; VP Exploring; Mathletes; Scholastic Bowl; Spanish Clb; School Musical; School Play; Rutgers Schlr 85-86; Aero-Astro Engrng.

MONSON, DAVID A; Scotch Plains-Fanwood HS; Fanwood, NJ; (Y); 13/311; Model UN; Quiz Bowl; Band; Pres Mrchg Band; School Musical; Symp Band; Im Vllybl; Gov Hon Prg Awd; Hon Roll; Yth In Gvt Sntr 86; Lehigh U; Pltcl Sci.

MONTALVO, RICHARD; Hoboken HS; Hoboken, NJ; (Y); Boys Clb Am; Church Yth Grp; Cmnty Wkr; Spanish Clb; SADD; JV Bsktbl; Mr Hstl Awd In Bsktbl 86.

MONTALVO, SAMUEL; Vineland SR HS; Vineland, NJ; (Y); Camera Clb; Chess Clb; FHA; JA; Spanish Clb; Bsktbl; Bowling; Swmmng; Trk; Comp Elctrcn.

MONTANA, JACQUELINE; West Milford HS; Hewitt, NJ; (S); 15/350; French Clb; Ski Clb; Nwsp Stf; Yrbk Rptr; Yrbk Stf; Stat Ftbl; French Hon Soc; Jr NHS; NHS; Math.

MONTANA III, WILLIAM; Vineland HS; Vineland, NJ; (Y); Church Yth Grp; Cmnty Wkr; Concert Band; NRA Clb Trophy 85; Cnslr Order De Molay 84; Cnty Hnrs Band 86.

MONTANARO, LARA; Holy Cross HS; Riverside, NJ; (Y); Am Leg Aux Girls St; Frsh Cls; Soph Cls; Jr Cls; Stu Cncl; Stat Var Bsbl; JV Var Fld Hcky; Var Mgr(s); Gov Hon Prg Awd; High Hon Roll; Outstndng Stdy Hall Rep 83-84; Hmcmng Rep 83; Soclgy.

MONTANE, THOMAS; Park Ridge HS; Park Ridge, NJ; (Y); 22/106; Trs AFS; Boy Scts; Varsity Clb; Yrbk Phtg; Rep Soph Cls; L Crs Cntry; L Trk; Hon Roll; NHS; Eagle Scout 83; Bnkng.

MONTANEZ, ANTONIO; Vineland SR HS; Vineland, NJ; (Y); Church Yth Grp; Cmnty Wkr; Stu Cncl.

MONTANEZ, EVELYN; Eastside HS; Paterson, NJ; (Y); 48/550; Computer Clb; Spanish Clb; Yrbk Stf; Lit Mag; Hon Roll; NHS; Cert Of Prtcptn; Pie Stu; Photo.

MONTAREZ, EVELYN; Eastside HS; Paterson, NJ; (Y); 48/550; Computer Clb; Spanish Clb; Yrbk Stf; Lit Mag; Hon Roll; NHS; Pie Stdnt; Phtgrphy.

MONTEFUSCO, SANDY; Colonia HS; Colonia, NJ; (Y); Varsity Clb; Bowling; Sftbl; Hon Roll; NHS; Spanish NHS; Sftbl Hnbl Mntn All Middlesex Cnty 86; Pres Phy Fit 84-85.

MONTEITH, MARK; Christian Brothers Acad; Tinton Falls, NJ; (Y); Im Sftbl; Monmouth Coll; Bus.

MONTELEONE, JOYCEANN; Ocean City HS; Ocean View, NJ; (Y); 65/278; Church Yth Grp; Sec Band; Capt Color Guard; Drill Tm; Swing Chorus; Stu Cncl; Capt Pom Pon; Drama Clb; French Clb; Pep Clb; Salisbury ST Coll; Educ.

MONTEMURRO, RITA; Toms River H Schl East; Toms River, NJ; (Y); 19/585; Am Leg Aux Girls St; Drama Clb; Acpl Chr; Chorus; Mrchg Band; School Musical; Capt Pom Pon; High Hon Roll; Hon Roll; NHS; Ntl Ldrshp Merit Awd 85-86; Pre-Law.

MONTENARO, LAUREN; Brick Memorial HS; Brick, NJ; (S); 154/310; Drama Clb; Key Clb; Office Aide; Teachers Aide; School Play; Stu Cncl; Var Cheerleading; JV Var Socr; Hon Roll; Eclen Cnty Coll; Scl Wrk.

MONTENARO, LINDA; Brick Twp Memorial HS; Brick, NJ; (S); 155/310; Key Clb; Office Aide; Teachers Aide; Nwsp Ed-Chief; Nwsp Stf; Stu Cncl; Var Cheerleading; JV Var Powder Puff Ftbl; High Hon Roll; Hon Roll; Ocn Cnty Coll; Erly Chldhd Educ.

MONTGOMERY, STACEY; Ridgefield Park HS; Ridgefield Pk, NJ; (Y); 17/184; Am Leg Aux Girls St; Spanish Clb; Lit Mag; Stu Cncl; Var Cheerleading; NHS; Fshn Merch.

MONTILLA, PATRICIA MARIE; Morristown HS; Ann Arbor, MI; (Y); Am Leg Aux Girls St; VP GAA; Pep Clb; Varsity Clb; Sec Stu Cncl; Fld Hcky; Lcrss; JV Trk; High Hon Roll; Pres Acadmc Ftnss Awd 86; Kappa Lambda Ldrshp Awd 86; U Of MI Ann Arbor.

MONTOTO, MICHELE; Secaucus HS; Secaucus, NJ; (S); 17/160; Intnl Clb; Key Clb; Math Clb; Ski Clb; Spanish Clb; Varsity Clb; Ed Nwsp Phtg; Nwsp Rptr; Nwsp Stf; Soph Cls.

MOOCK, JENNIFER; Viiiia Victoria Acad; Yardley, PA; (Y); Art Clb; Church Yth Grp; Drama Clb; GAA; SADD; Varsity Clb; Chorus; School Musical; School Play; Yrbk Stf; Art Awd 85; Sports Awd-Capt 85; Varsty Bsktbl Champns 85; Phys Therpy.

MOODY, LISA; Lakewood HS; Lakewood, NJ; (Y); DECA; Dance Clb; English Clb; Key Clb; Church Choir; Rep Frsh Cls; Rep Soph Cls; Rep Jr Cls; Capt Trk; High Hon Roll; PSAT Hm Econ Ovrl Excell 86; Kean Coll; Bus.

MOODY, SHELLY; Audubon HS; Mt Ephraim, NJ; (Y); Spanish Clb; Yrbk Stf; Rep Sec Jr Cls; Pres Stu Cncl; Powder Puff Ftbl; Sftbl; Vllybl; Wt Lftg; Hon Roll; VFW Awd; Comm.

MOON, CLAIRE T; Toms River North HS; Toms River, NJ; (Y); 32/372; Church Yth Grp; Intnl Clb; Boy Scts; Chorus; Madrigals; Mrchg Band; Orch; Var Badmtn; Capt Fld Hcky; NHS; Lions Club Awd 86; Alpha Phi Alpha Schlrhsp 86; Rutgers Coll; Bus.

MOORE, ANGELA; Frank H Morrell HS; Irvington, NJ; (Y); Art Clb; Church Yth Grp; Exploring; Latin Clb; Library Aide; Flag Corp; Rep Jr Cls; Rep Stu Cncl; Hon Roll; NHS; Artstclly Tlntd Awd 83; Prncpl Awd 83; Stage Crew 81-83; NJIT; Arch.

MOORE, DEZORAY; Burlington City HS; Burlington, NJ; (Y); FBLA; FTA; JA; Drill Tm; Variety Show; Yrbk Stf; Rep Stu Cncl; Cheerleading; Trk; High Hon Roll; RCA Minority Engrng Prg 84-85; Prime Mnrty Tchng Prg 86; Var Sweater & Letter Plaque 84-86; Accntnt.

MOORE, DIANE; Union HS; Union, NJ; (Y); 106/464; Dance Clb; Pres French Clb; GAA; Pres Church Choir; Mrchg Band; Variety Show; Yrbk Stf; Rep Frsh Cls; Rep Soph Cls; Rep Jr Cls; U Of DE; Bus Adm.

MOORE, JEANNIE; Eastside HS; Paterson, NJ; (S); 14/400; Computer Clb; Drama Clb; Math Clb; Band; Church Choir; Concert Band; School Play; Nwsp Stf; Off Frsh Cls; Off Soph Cls; Journlsm Schlrshp 86; Cmpstn Awds 84; Acadmc & Sci Awds 85; Howard U; Reporter.

MOORE, JOHN H; Morristown-Beard Schl; Summit, NJ; (Y); 13/81; Church Yth Grp; Hosp Aide; Yrbk Stf; Sec Soph Cls; Sec Jr Cls; Sec Sr Cls; Stu Cncl; Im Crs Cntry; JV Socr; JV Var Tennis; Hon Roll 84-85; Econ.

MOORE, KIMBERLY; Middletown HS South; Red Bank, NJ; (S); 37/436; Math Tm; Hon Roll; Math.

MOORE, MEGHAN; De Paul Diocesan HS; Kinnelon, NJ; (S); 97/172; Girl Scts; Chorus; Yrbk Stf; Vllybl; Brigade Amer Revltn; 42nd Royal Hghlnd Rgmnt; NY U; Hist.

MOORE, NICOLE J; Lenape HS; Mt Laurel, NJ; (Y); 64/436; Girl Scts; Latin Clb; Varsity Clb; Rep Frsh Cls; Capt Soph Cls; Capt Jr Cls; Capt Sr Cls; Trk; Hon Roll; Ntl Merit Ltr; Rsrch Apprntc Prgrm/U Of VT 86; Smmr Scntfc Smnr P/US Air Frce Acad 86; MVP Grls Wntr Trck Tm 86; Bryn Mawr Coll; Med.

MOORE, RON; Pinelands Regional HS; Tuckerton, NJ; (Y); Chess Clb; Science Clb; Hon Roll; Volunteer Fireman; Navy; Nuclear Prg.

MOORE, RONALD; Cumberland Regional HS; Bridgeton, NJ; (S); 7/369; Science Clb; Ski Clb; VP Soph Cls; VP Jr Cls; Im JV Bsktbl; Im JV Ftbl; Var JV Tennis; Cit Awd; High Hon Roll; Hon Roll; Elec Engr.

MOORE, SANDRA; Woodstown HS; Woodstown, NJ; (Y); 96/203; Trs Church Yth Grp; FBLA; Spanish Clb; Chorus; Church Choir; Rep Stu Cncl; Var Capt Cheerleading; Mgr(s); JV Sftbl; Pre-Dntstry.

MOORE, SUSAN; Lyndhurst HS; Lyndhurst, NJ; (Y); 6/154; Pres Sec Key Clb; Band; Chorus; Yrbk Stf; JV Var Bsktbl; JV Var Trk; JV Var Vllybl; High Hon Roll; Kiwanis Awd; NHS; Womens Clb Schlrshp Nrsng 86; William Paterson Coll; Nrsng.

MOORE, TERESA; Eastside HS; Paterson, NJ; (Y); 24/650; Band; Concert Band; Mrchg Band; Orch; Pep Band; School Musical; Yrbk Stf; Hon Roll; NHS; Mst Outstndng Mrchng Bnd Awd 84; Trphys For Sngng In Tlnt Shws 86; Rtgrs Schl Art & Sci; Pdtrcn.

MOORE, TRACEY; Frank H Morrell HS; Irvington, NJ; (Y); Drama Clb; Key Clb; High Hon Roll; Hon Roll; Jr NHS; NHS; Bus Admn.

MOORE, TRACY; Roms Rivers E HS; Toms River, NJ; (Y); Powder Puff Ftbl; Hon Roll; Tchng.

MOORMAN, JAMES; Northern Valley Regional HS; Harrington Pk, NJ; (Y); Boy Scts; Church Yth Grp; 4-H; Latin Clb; Ski Clb; JV Golf; JV Socr; JV Tennis; Hon Roll; Finance.

MOORZITZ, DIANE; St John Vianney HS; Hazlet, NJ; (Y); 32/260; Library Aide; Yrbk Stf; Sec Frsh Cls; Sec Soph Cls; Hon Roll; Nrsng.

MOOS, VERONICA; Highland Regional HS; Sicklerville, NJ; (Y); 18/332; Pres Art Clb; Camera Clb; Computer Clb; Dance Clb; Civic Clb; Spanish Clb; Yrbk Stf; Rep Soph Cls; Trs Jr Cls; Trs Sr Cls; Drexel; Arch Engrng.

MOOYMAN, CYNTHIA; North Brunswick Township HS; N Brunswick, NJ; (Y); 51/315; JCL; VP Sec Latin Clb; Spanish Clb; Varsity Clb; Y-Teens; Stu Cncl; Var Swmmng; JV Trk; Hon Roll; Church Yth Group; Young Life; Trainers Asst; Dentistry.

MORALES, KEVIN; East Side HS; Paterson, NJ; (Y); Computer Clb; Ftbl; Stu Of Mnth 78; Engl 86; Math 77; PCCC; Accntng.

MORALES, LIZZETTE; Academic HS; Jersey City, NJ; (S); 17/70; Pres Sec Church Yth Grp; Hosp Aide; Library Aide; Office Aide; Spanish Clb; Temple Yth Grp; Chorus; Church Choir; Rep Stu Cncl; Hon Roll; Stu Of Mnth 85; Million Dollar Smile Awd 86; St Peters Coll; Accntng.

MORALES, MARGARET; Matawan Regionall HS; Cliffwood Beach, NJ; (S); 15/302; Church Yth Grp; FBLA; Math Clb; Office Aide; SADD; Nwsp Stf; Yrbk Stf; Trs Frsh Cls; Rep Soph Cls; Rep Jr Cls; Bus Adm.

MORAN, DARREN A; Union Catholic Regional HS; Rahway, NJ; (Y); 41/338; Chess Clb; Trs French Clb; Math Tm; Political Wkr; Scholastic Bowl; Service Clb; Rptr Nwsp Ed-Chief; Nwsp Sprt Ed; Nwsp Stf; Lit Mag; Dickinson Coll; Poli Sci.

MORAN, ELIZABETH N; Teaneck HS; Teaneck, NJ; (Y); Church Yth Grp; Cmnty Wkr; Office Aide; SADD; Nwsp Stf; Yrbk Stf; Var L Sftbl; Var L Swmmng; NHS; Prfct Atten Awd; Mrkng Hnr AwdsSPCL Olympics; Legal Sec.

MORANO, DEBORAH; Highland Regional HS; Clementon, NJ; (S); 26/326; AFS; Church Yth Grp; Computer Clb; Sec Trs Drama Clb; VP FTA; Science Clb; Church Choir; Stu Cncl; Hon Roll; NJ Gvrnrs Schl Fnlst 85; Natl Ldrshp Orgnztn 85; Drexel U; Engrng.

MORANO, DINA; Raritan HS; Hazlet, NJ; (Y); 31/320; Stu Cncl; Sftbl; NHS.

MORANO, JENNIFER; St Thomas Aquinas HS; Plainfield, NJ; (Y); 3/240; Church Yth Grp; 4-H; Hosp Aide; Spanish Clb; 4-H Awd; High Hon Roll; NHS; NEDT Awd; St Schlr; Rutgers Schlr Awd 85; Monmth Fclty Schlrshp 86-90; Garden ST Dstngshd Schlr Awd 86-90; Monmouth Coll; Bus Adm.

MORASH, TIM; Hunterdon Central HS; White House Stati, NJ; (Y); 30/548; FCA; FBLA; Red Cross Aide; Spanish Clb; SADD; Stu Cncl; JV Bsbl; JV Bsktbl; Var L Socr; Hon Roll; Bus Mgmt.

MORCHOWER, MATTHEW B; Millburn HS; Short Hills, NJ; (Y); 6/260; Political Wkr; Ed Nwsp Stf; Ed Lit Mag; JV Bsktbl; Var Trk; High Hon Roll; Ntl Merit SF; St Schlr; Mth & Eng Tutor 84-86; Rutgers Schlr 85.

MORCOM, KIM; Neptune SR HS; Neptune City, NJ; (Y); 38/398; GAA; Science Clb; Ski Clb; Varsity Clb; JV Var Bsktbl; JV Var Fld Hcky; JV Var Socr; Hon Roll; Asbury Park Press All Shore Hockey 85; Star Ledger 3rd Tm 85; Garden ST Hockey Tm 86; Marine Bio.

MORDWIN, DREW; James Caldwell HS; Caldwell, NJ; (Y); FCA; Nwsp Sprt Ed; Nwsp Stf; Var Bsktbl; Var Ftbl; Var Trk; 1st Tm All Conf Bsktbl ST Of NJ 86; Journalism.

MOREA, JOSEPH; Northern Valley Regional HS; Northvale, NJ; (Y); Exploring; Political Wkr; JV Var Ftbl; Trk; Wt Lftg; Ftbl Scholar Awd 86; Ramapo Valley Coll; Acctng.

MOREIRA, VICTOR GEORGE; Queen Of Peace HS; Kearny, NJ; (Y); Drama Clb; Ski Clb; School Play; Stage Crew; Nwsp Rptr; L Bsbl; JV L Mgr(s); JV L Score Keeper; High Hon Roll; Achvt Awd For Charity Bwlng Tourn; Rutgers; Portuquese.

MORELAND, GLORIA L; John F Kennedy HS; Willingboro, NJ; (Y); Dance Clb; Var Cheerleading; JV Sftbl; Hon Roll; Ntl Chrldng Assn Sprt Awd 85-86; JFK 100 Pct Chrldr Awd 86; Kthrn Gibbs Bus Schl; Scrtry.

MORELLI, DAYNA; John P Stevens HS; Edison, NJ; (Y); Art Clb; Drama Clb; School Play; Variety Show; Rep Frsh Cls; Rep Soph Cls; Rep Jr Cls; Rep Sr Cls; Rep Stu Cncl; Powder Puff Ftbl; Actrss.

MORELLI, LUCIANO M; Becton Regional HS; Carlstadt, NJ; (Y); 2/120; Am Leg Boys St; Library Aide; Math Tm; Var Crs Cntry; Var Trk; High Hon Roll; NHS; Physcs Tm No 1 ST Physcs Olmpc 86; Elctrcl Engr.

MORENO, AMPARO; Memorial HS; W New York, NJ; (Y); 58/300; Rep Key Clb; Rep Spanish Clb; Teachers Aide; VP Chorus; Rep Frsh Cls; Rep Soph Cls; Rep Jr Cls; Rep Sr Cls; Rep Stu Cncl; NHS; Tchr.

MORENO, LINDA; Manalapan HS; Englishtown, NJ; (Y); 89/393; Church Yth Grp; Trs Thesps; Trs Chorus; Madrigals; School Musical; School Play; Music Prnts Assn Scholar 86; Thaddeus Lubaczewski Mem Awd 86; Minority Gdn ST Scholar 86; Trenton ST Coll; Comm.

MORENO, RAYMOND; Queen Of Peace HS; Newark, NJ; (S); 1/243; Drama Clb; Model UN; School Play; Nwsp Rptr; Yrbk Bus Mgr; Pres Stu Cncl; Var Trk; Gov Hon Prg Awd; Pres NHS; NJ Govnr Schl Schlr; Brown U; Pre Law.

MORENO, TONY; Kearney HS; Kearny, NJ; (Y); Boy Scts; Camera Clb; Church Yth Grp; Cmnty Wkr; Spanish Clb; Ftbl; Trk; Wt Lftg; Wrstlng; Teterboro Schl; Avtn Mntnce.

MORENO, WANDA; Hoboken HS; Hoboken, NJ; (Y); Trs Church Yth Grp; Key Clb; Hon Roll; St Elizabeth; Tchr.

MORGAN, CHRISTINE; Morris Knolls HS; Denville, NJ; (Y); 63/367; JA; Ski Clb; Pres Chorus; Color Guard; School Musical; School Play; VP Frsh Cls; Sec Stu Cncl; Stat Socr; Hon Roll; Knghts Of Columbus Cncl No 3359 Chrl Awd 86; Morris Knolls Hm & Schl Assn Srvce Awd 86; Bloomsburg U; Cmnctns.

MORGAN, JOY; Williamstown HS; Williamstown, NJ; (Y); Church Yth Grp; Library Aide; Chorus; Yrbk Stf; JV Badmtn; Var Cheerleading; JV Sftbl; JV Tennis; Hon Roll; Gloucester County Coll; Educ.

MORGAN, LAURA; No Bruns Township HS; N Brunswick, NJ; (Y); 30/297; German Clb; Spanish Clb; VP Sec Band; VP Sec Concert Band; VP Sec Mrchg Band; School Musical; Hon Roll; NHS; Ed.

MORGAN, LISA; Midland Park HS; Midland Park, NJ; (S); 2/137; DECA; FBLA; Pep Clb; VP Varsity Clb; Yrbk Stf; Stu Cncl; Var L Cheerleading; Var L Trk; High Hon Roll; NHS; Midland Pk Rutgers Schlr 85; Cert Outstndng Achvmnt Engl II Hnrs 85; Coaches Awd Vrsty Chrldng 85; Psych.

MORGAN, LISA; Northern Valley Old Tappan HS; Harrington Pk, NJ; (Y); 35/281; Drama Clb; Chorus; Capt Color Guard; Madrigals; Mrchg Band; School Musical; Stu Cncl; High Hon Roll; Pres NHS; Yrbk Stf; Stu Acdmc Dcthln Team NJ ST Wnnr 86; Schl Rep Hnds Acrs Amer 86; Cmnctns.

MORGAN, SHARON A; B R High Schl East; Bidgewater, NJ; (Y); 69/287; Drama Clb; SADD; Thesps; School Musical; School Play; Rep Sr Cls; Pres Rep Stu Cncl; Stat Gym; JV Capt Socr; Sftbl; Stu Cncl Schlrshp; Alpha Delta Kappa XI Chptr Schlrshp; Ursinus Coll; Math.

MORGAN, TAWANA A; St Dominic Acad; Jersey City, NJ; (Y); Church Yth Grp; Cmnty Wkr; Drama Clb; Science Clb; Teachers Aide; Chorus; Lit Mag; JV Trk; Hon Roll; Ntl Merit Ltr; Plaque Of Commendation Salv Army 85; Indust Psych.

MORGAN, TONETTE; Weequahic HS; Irvington, NJ; (Y); 30/380; Church Yth Grp; French Clb; Library Aide; Acpl Chr; Pres Chorus; VP Church Choir; Rep Jr Cls; Rep Stu Cncl; Stat Bsktbl; Hon Roll; Choral Awd Donald Payne 85; Rutgers; Jrnlsm.

MORGENSTERN, CYNTHIA; Pope John XXII HS; Sparta, NJ; (Y); Chrmn Hosp Aide; School Play; Yrbk Ed-Chief; Yrbk Stf; Lit Mag; JV Sftbl; Var L Swmmng; High Hon Roll; NHS; Ntl Merit SF.

MORGNER, MELISSA A; Kittatinny Regional HS; Branchville, NJ; (Y); 21/165; Church Yth Grp; Hosp Aide; Chorus; Yrbk Stf; Sec Frsh Cls; Sec Soph Cls; Sec Jr Cls; Chrmn Stu Cncl; Hon Roll; NHS; Iva Valler Scholar 86; Wmns Clb Newton Scholar 86; Bloomsburg U; Secndry Ed.

MORI, NANCY D; Millville SR HS; Millville, NJ; (Y); 64/468; Aud/Vis; German Clb; Office Aide; SADD; Color Guard; Nwsp Ed-Chief; Nwsp Rptr; Nwsp Stf; Yrbk Stf; NHS; Syracuse U; Jrnlsm.

MORIELLO, CARMINE; Linden HS; Linden, NJ; (Y); VICA; Wt Lftg; Hon Roll; Machinist.

MORLEY, DENIS; Don Boxo Prep HS; Allendale, NJ; (S); Model UN; Nwsp Rptr; Trk; Hon Roll.

MORLEY, KEVIN; Pitman HS; Pitman, NJ; (S); 24/150; VP Chess Clb; Church Yth Grp; German Clb; Band; Concert Band; Jazz Band; Mrchg Band; Bsbl; Socr; Wt Lftg.

MORNEWECK, LYNN; Cranford HS; Cranfod, NJ; (Y); 7/292; Trs JCL; Off Thesps; Concert Band; Drm Mjr(t); Madrigals; School Musical; School Play; JP Sousa Awd; Ntl Merit Schol; Math Clb; Cranford Dramatic Clb Awd 86; Oberlin Coll; Physics.

MORONEY, TARA A; St Rose HS; Spring Lake, NJ; (Y); 2/206; Sec Drama Clb; Key Clb; Chorus; School Musical; Var L Trk; French Hon Soc; Pres NHS; Ntl Merit Ltr; NEDT Awd; Ambsdr Hugh O Brien Yth Fndtn 84; Delg Grls Ctznshp Inst 85; Boston Coll; Econ.

MORREALE, MICHAEL G; Roselle Catholic HS; Roselle, NJ; (Y); 59/160; Church Yth Grp; Yrbk Stf; Lit Mag; Im Bsktbl; Im Fld Hcky; JV Var Socr; Var Tennis; Var Wt Lftg; Hon Roll; Prfct Atten Awd; Jrnlsm.

MORRELL, FRANK; Belleville HS; Belleville, NJ; (Y); High Hnr Roll; NJ Lib In Focus; Career Essay Cntst Wnnr; Stevens Inst Tech; Engr.

MORRELL, KIMBERLY LYNN; Rutherford HS; Rutherford, NJ; (Y); 6/180; Am Leg Aux Girls St; Church Yth Grp; Key Clb; Chorus; School Musical; Variety Show; Nwsp Ed-Chief; High Hon Roll; NHS; NFL; WA Wrkshps Cngrssnl Smnr 85; ST Wnr PTA Poetry Cntst 86; William Carlos Williams Poetry Cntst Wnr; Douglass Coll Of Rutgers U.

MORRELL, SHERRI; Delsea Regional HS; Williamstown, NJ; (Y); Boys Clb Am; Exploring; Varsity Clb; Band; Var Capt Bsktbl; Var Capt Fld Hcky; Var Capt Sftbl; Hon Roll; MV Offnsv Plyr Fld Hcky 85; U PA; Law.

MORRIS, ANDREA; James J Ferris HS; Jersey City, NJ; (Y); DECA; Yrbk Stf; Rep Jr Cls; Rep Stu Cncl; Capt Cheerleading; Hon Roll.

MORRIS, APRIL J; Edgewood Reg SR HS; Sicklerville, NJ; (Y); 36/371; Pres Church Yth Grp; Office Aide; Rep Frsh Cls; Rep Soph Cls; Rep Jr Cls; Sec Stu Cncl; Hon Roll; Jr NHS; NHS; US Mrn Crps Phys Achvt Awd 84-86; Cert Of Recgntn 86; Glassboro ST Coll.

MORRIS, CAREN; Teaneck HS; Teaneck, NJ; (Y); Dance Clb; Drama Clb; Yrbk Stf; Trk; Prfct Atten Awd; Med.

MORRIS, CRYSTAL L; Archeray HS; Camden, NJ; (Y); Cmnty Wkr; Library Aide; Chorus; Variety Show; Sec Stu Cncl; Sftbl; Hon Roll; Ntl Soc Mnrty Wrtrs & Artst; Camden CC; Entrepeneru.

MORRIS, DAVE; Hightstown HS; East Windsor, NJ; (Y); Boy Scts; Ski Clb; JV Trk; Prfct Atten Awd; Schl Spirit Awd 83; Arch.

MORRIS, GWENDOLYN S; Cumberland Regional HS; Bridgeton, NJ; (Y); 64/342; Church Yth Grp; Ski Clb; Commndtn Ntc Art I 83; Lang Arts II Cmmndtn Ntc 83; US Hstry Cmmndtn Ntc 3 Tms 84-85; Cumberland Cnty; Wldlf.

MORRIS, JACQUELINE; Paramus HS; Paramus, NJ; (Y); 7/350; Computer Clb; Debate Tm; NFL; Quiz Bowl; Scholastic Bowl; Lit Mag; Rep Sr Cls; Var L Crs Cntry; Var L Trk; NHS; Amer Assn U Wmn Schlrshp 86; Pres Acdmc Ftns Awd 86; Awd Exclinc Engl 86; Hall Fame 86; Johns Hopkins U; Biomed.

MORRIS, JEAN F; Moorestown HS; Moorestown, NJ; (Y); 12/200; Am Leg Aux Girls St; Trs Latin Clb; Orch; Yrbk Stf; Var Fld Hcky; JV Lcrss; Var Capt Swmmng; Cit Awd; Hon Roll; BEA Thomas Swmmng Awd 86; Quakerooters Hall Fame 86; Duke U; Hist.

MORRIS, JOHN; South Plainfield HS; S Plainfield, NJ; (Y); Political Wkr; Jazz Band; Trenton ST Coll; Poltcl Sci.

MORRIS, MARIANNE; Middletown HS South; Middletown, NJ; (Y); Math Tm; Stage Crew; Yrbk Stf; Hon Roll.

MORRIS, MICHELE; Burlington Township HS; Burlington Twp, NJ; (Y); 31/122; Ski Clb; SADD; Capt Mrchg Band; School Play; Yrbk Stf; Rep Stu Cncl; Mgr Crs Cntry; Mgr Tennis; Hon Roll; Highst Aver In Art; Notbl Stud In Art; Glassbr ST Coll; Bus Admin.

MORRIS, MICHELLE; Oakcrest HS; Mays Landing, NJ; (Y); 11/212; Aud/Vis; Key Clb; Mrchg Band; Stat Bsbl; Capt Twrlr; Hon Roll; NHS; Vrsty Schlr 84-86; Miss Loooies 86; Miss Yacht Clb 86; Radio.

MORRIS, RACHEL; Belvidere HS; Phillipsburg, NJ; (S); 1/125; Sec Church Yth Grp; Pep Clb; Ski Clb; Capt Cheerleading; Jr NHS; NHS; St Schlr; Supdt Awd 83; Messiah Coll.

MORRIS, ROBERT; Pt Pleasant Boro HS; Point Pleasant, NJ; (Y); 33/240; Cmnty Wkr; Key Clb; Hon Roll; Civil Engr.

MORRIS, THERESA; Northern Burlington Regional HS; Manassas, VA; (Y); 10/201; Church Yth Grp; Red Cross Aide; Chorus; Var Capt Bsktbl; Bowling; JV Trk; High Hon Roll; Hon Roll; NHS; Spanish NHS; Unsng Hereo Bskbl, Bst Dfnsv Plyr Bskbl 85-86; Pres Schlrshp Messiah 86; Messiah Coll; Nrsng.

MORRISON, CAROL; Academic HS; Jersey City, NJ; (Y); Scholastic Bowl; Spanish Clb; Yrbk Ed-Chief; Lit Mag; VP Stu Cncl; Vllybl; Harvard U; Law.

MORRISON, GREGORY; James Caldwell HS; W Caldwell, NJ; (Y); 10/265; Boy Scts; Var Socr; Var Trk; High Hon Roll; NHS; Ntl Merit Ltr; Grmn Awd, Chem Awd 86; Grdn ST Dstngshd Schlr 85; Cornell; Engrng.

MORRISON, MARTIN; Hunterdon Central HS; Ringoes, NJ; (Y); 96/575; Church Yth Grp; Ski Clb; Im Capt Vllybl; Air Force; Fghtr Pilot.

MORRISON, TONY; Jersey City HS; Jersey City, NJ; (Y); 14/296; Art Clb; Aud/Vis; Camera Clb; Computer Clb; Dance Clb; DECA; Drama Clb; Key Clb; Letterman Clb; Political Wkr; Cls King 83-85; Comp Sci.

MORRISON, WENDY; Marine Acad Of Science & Tech; Red Bank, NJ; (S); 8/25; Sec Spanish Clb; Color Guard; Drill Tm; Yrbk Stf; Rep Stu Cncl; Swmmng; Hon Roll; NHS; Bus Adm.

MORRISSEY, SEAN; Holy Cross HS; Willingboro, NJ; (Y); Var L Swmmng; High Hon Roll; Hon Roll; MVP Swm Tm 83-86; Burlington Cnty Schlstc All Star Swm Tm 83-86; All S Jersey All Star Swim Tm 84-86.

MORRISSEY, SIZEMORE; Bridgeton HS; Bridgeton, NJ; (Y); Yrbk Phtg; Yrbk Rptr; Yrbk Stf; Wt Lftg; Glassboro ST Coll; Bus Admnst.

MORROW, DONNA; Neptune SR HS; Neptune, NJ; (Y); Church Yth Grp; Drama Clb; Exploring; GAA; Office Aide; Stage Crew; Nwsp Rptr; Nwsp Stf; Lit Mag; High Hon Roll; Wesley Coll; Sectrl.

MORSE, CAROLYN; Lower Cape May Regional HS; Cape May, NJ; (Y); 2/215; 4-H; Math Clb; VP Spanish Clb; Varsity Clb; Rptr Lit Mag; Fld Hcky; Gov Hon Prg Awd; High Hon Roll; NHS; Sal; Drew U.

MORSTATT, MARY; Pequannock Township HS; Pompton Plains, NJ; (Y); 12/245; Am Leg Aux Girls St; Sec Church Yth Grp; Varsity Clb; Nwsp Ed-Chief; Yrbk Ed-Chief; Lit Mag; Pres Frsh Cls; Capt L Tennis; High Hon Roll; NHS; Soroptimist Yth Ctznshp Awd 86; George Washington U; Bus.

MORTIMER, DONNA; Holy Cross HS; Maple Shade, NJ; (Y); 4/375; Church Yth Grp; German Clb; Capt Math Tm; Model UN; Nwsp Ed-Chief; Var Pom Pon; Gov Hon Prg Awd; NHS; Ntl Merit Ltr; St Schlr; Disbld Am Vet Awd 86; U Of DE; Chem.

MORTIMER, KEVIN; Gloucester City HS; Gloucester, NJ; (Y); 4/159; Math Clb; Q&S; Ski Clb; School Musical; Nwsp Stf; Stu Cncl; Bsbl; Bowling; Socr; Gov Hon Prg Awd; Campbell Soup Co Schlrshp 86; Monmouth Coll Trustee Schlrshp 86; Garden T Distngushd Schlr 85-86; Monmouth Coll; Math.

MORTMAN, KEITH; Manalapan HS; Manalapan, NJ; (Y); 10/400; Pres Exploring; Science Clb; Rep Frsh Cls; Rep Soph Cls; Pres Jr Cls; VP Stu Cncl; NHS; St Schlr; Yth Yr Freehld Exch Clb 86; WA U; Bio.

MORTON, JOHN R; Camden HS; Camden, NJ; (Y); 1/408; Pres Church Yth Grp; French Clb; Wt Lftg; Var Wrstlng; High Hon Roll; Hon Roll; NHS; Prfct Atten Awd; Medcn.

MOSCINSKI, CHRISTOPHER; Bishop Ahr HS; Pt Reading, NJ; (Y); 26/276; Am Leg Boys St; Boy Scts; Chess Clb; Intnl Clb; Model UN; Thesps; Sec Trs Bowling; NHS; NEDT Awd; Order Of The Arrow Brthhd; Astrophysics.

MOSER, CYNTHIA E; Jonathan Dayton Regional HS; Mountainside, NJ; (Y); 4/236; Church Yth Grp; French Clb; Varsity Clb; Chorus; School Musical; Lit Mag; Var L Crs Cntry; JV Trk; French Hon Soc; Hon Roll; NJ Grls Ctznshp Inst 85; Gftd & Tlntd Pgm 84-85; 1st Pl Oral Amer Assoc Tchrs Frnch Exm 85.

MOSES, DENISE; Essex Catholic Girls HS; Newark, NJ; (Y); 2/60; FBLA; Library Aide; Yrbk Stf; High Hon Roll; Hon Roll; Principals List 85; Pace U; Bus Mgt.

MOSES, KIM; Lakewood HS; Lakewood, NJ; (Y); 64/384; English Clb; JCL; Key Clb; Latin Clb; Pep Clb; Science Clb; Yrbk Stf; Var Gym; Var Socr; Ntl Ltn Hnr Soc 85&86.

MOSES, ROBERT; Northern Valley Reg HS; Northvale, NJ; (Y); 13/300; Science Clb; Varsity Clb; VP Pres Soph Cls; JV Bsbl; Var L Socr; High Hon Roll; Hon Roll; NHS; Phillips Exeter Summr Enrchmnt Sessn 85; Elec Engrng.

MOSES, SHAUNA; Lakewood HS; Lakewood, NJ; (Y); 4/300; Concert Band; Nwsp Ed-Chief; French Hon Soc; NHS; Jr NHS; Cmnty Wkr; French Clb; Band; Nwsp Rptr; Nwsp Stf; S Jersey Symphnc Band 84 & 85; Cmmnctns.

MOSEY, WILLIAM; Morris Catholic HS; Succasunna, NJ; (Y); 30/160; Am Leg Boys St; Church Yth Grp; Pres German Clb; Natl Beta Clb; School Musical; Capt Socr; Trk; High Hon Roll; Hon Roll; Cmnty Wkr; Drexel U; Hotel/Rstrnt Mgmnt.

MOSHINSKY, ALAN; Paul VI HS; Turnersville, NJ; (S); 37/477; German Clb; Math Clb; Jazz Band; Mrchg Band; School Play; Band; Hon Roll; NHS; Engrng.

MOSHO, AMY; Manalapan HS; Englishtown, NJ; (Y); Exploring; Girl Scts; Hosp Aide; Latin Clb; Temple Yth Grp; Thesps; School Musical; School Play; Stage Crew; Yrbk Stf; Hofstra U; Brdcstng.

MOSKOWITZ, DUSTIN; John F Kennedy HS; Willingboro, NJ; (Y); 1/270; Am Leg Boys St; Key Clb; Temple Yth Grp; Jazz Band; Mrchg Band; Yrbk Stf; Cheerleading; Tennis; High Hon Roll; NHS; Rutgers Schlr 86; Loudest Bnd Stu 84; Princeton; Arch.

MOSLEY, ROBERT J; West Windsor Plainsboro HS; Plainsboro, NJ; (Y); Am Leg Boys St; Boy Scts; Computer Clb; Ski Clb; Acpl Chr; Yrbk Stf; High Hon Roll; NHS; Ntl Merit SF; Eagle Sct 86; Future Problm Slvrs Tm 83-86; Math.

MOSQUERA, INES; Mother Seton Regional HS; Elizabeth, NJ; (Y); 3/94; Art Clb; JA; Aud/Vis; Sec Service Clb; Yrbk Stf; High Hon Roll; NHS; Piano Trphys & Dplma 83-86; Math Awds 84-86; Sci Awds In Bio & Chmstry 84-85; Rtgrs-Nwrk Coll; Math.

MOSQUERA, KENNY; Emerson HS; Union City, NJ; (Y); Spanish Clb; Nwsp Rptr; Hon Roll; Jersey City ST Coll; Bus.

MOSS, JOMARIE; Spotswood HS; Spotswood, NJ; (Y); Drama Clb; Color Guard; Orch; Nwsp Stf; Lit Mag; VP Frsh Cls; Var Mgr(s); NYU; Creative Wrtng.

MOSSMAN, TIMOTHY; Pitman HS; Pitman, NJ; (S); 4/180; Chess Clb; German Clb; Scholastic Bowl; Teachers Aide; L Crs Cntry; High Hon Roll; Hon Roll; Olympics Of Mind Wrld Chmpn 85; Engrng.

MOSTELLO, DAVID; West Windsor-Plainsboro HS; Princeton Jct, NJ; (Y); 89/236; Church Yth Grp; Radio Clb; Lit Mag; Rep Jr Cls; Hon Roll; Voice Dem Awd; 1st Pl Amer Lgn Essy Cntst 84; Spcl Featr Dir 84-85; Chf Anncr Schl Radio Sta 85-86; Seton Hall U; Lawyr.

MOSTELLO, DIANE B; West Windsor-Plainsboro HS; Princeton Junct, NJ; (Y); 10/236; Capt Flag Corp; Mrchg Band; Orch; School Musical; Symp Band; Variety Show; Yrbk Stf; NHS; Church Yth Grp; Lit Mag; Wrtng Finlst Arts Recogntn & Talent Search 86; Playwright.

MOSTOFIZADEH, DJAVAD; South Hunterdon HS; Lambertville, NJ; (Y); 21/80; French Clb; Teachers Aide; Chorus; School Musical; Variety Show; Nwsp Stf; Rep Stu Cncl; Capt Crs Cntry; Boy Scts; Camera Clb; Most Imprvd Runner 84-85; Most Vlblr Runner 85-86; Sci.

MOTAMEDI, JOHN; Pinelands Regional HS; Tuckerton, NJ; (S); 6/147; Church Yth Grp; VICA; Nwsp Rptr; Trs Soph Cls; JV Bsbl; JV Socr; Var Trk; Hon Roll; NHS; Amer Chem Soc Chem Awd 84; Knights Columbs Essay Cont Wnnr 82; Princpls List 84; U NM; Intl Affairs.

MOTOMAL, ELAINE; Piscataway HS; Piscataway, NJ; (Y); Debate Tm; Color Guard; Drill Tm; School Play; Yrbk Phtg; Rep Stu Cncl; Stat Bsbl; JV Fld Hcky; Hon Roll; NHS; SR Lg Bnd Season 86; Drl Team Co-Capt 86.

MOTTER, LAURA; Highland HS; Blackwood, NJ; (Y); German Clb; Band; Chorus; Mrchg Band; Stage Crew; Yrbk Stf; Pom Pon; Mrchng Bnd Awd 86; Harris Sch Bus ; Acctng.

MOTTO, HEATHER; Montgomery HS; Belle Mead, NJ; (Y); 52/133; AFS; Church Yth Grp; Sec 4-H; Math Tm; Science Clb; Band; Jazz Band; Yrbk Stf; 1st Natl Bank Cntrl Jersey Schlrshp 86; U Of SC; Sci.

MOTTRAM, KATE; Freehold HS; Colts Neck, NJ; (Y); SADD; Varsity Clb; Var Bsktbl; Var Crs Cntry; Var Socr; Hon Roll; Im Powder Puff Ftbl; All Shore Soccr 1st Tm; Shield & Key Awd; All Dist Crs Cntry & Soccr 1st Tm; Phys Ed.

MOTYKA, DANIELLE; Waldwick HS; Waldwick, NJ; (Y); Drama Clb; Math Tm; Ski Clb; Band; Orch; Mgr Jr Cls; Rep Stu Cncl; JV Vllybl; High Hon Roll; NHS; Engrng.

MOUGAKOS, NICOLE; Millville SR HS; Millville, NJ; (Y); FBLA; Key Clb; SADD; Variety Show; Fld Hcky; Mgr(s); Sftbl; Hon Roll; Prfct Atten Awd; Ldrshp Awd-Future Scrtrs 86; Legal Fld.

MOUNT, DOUG; Lenape Valley Regional HS; Andover, NJ; (Y); Boy Scts; Church Yth Grp; Var Golf; JV Var Wrstlng; Hon Roll; Grove City Coll; Math.

MOUNT, WILLIAM; Hamilton High West HS; Trenton, NJ; (S); Key Clb; Math Clb; Varsity Clb; Band; Concert Band; Drm Mjr(t); Jazz Band; Mrchg Band; Symp Band; VP Stu Cncl; Actg Dir Secndry Ed 85; LTC 85; Pre-Law.

MOUREY, MARY; Burlington City HS; Beverly, NJ; (Y); Red Cross Aide; Chorus; Concert Band; Drm Mjr(t); Jazz Band; Mrchg Band; Nwsp Stf; Rep Stu Cncl; Mgr(s); Score Keeper; NJ ST Tn Arts Fest 86; Jazz Bnd Awd 83-86; U Of Akron; Musc Perf.

MOWEN, JEFF; Point Pleasant Boro HS; Pt Pleasant Bch, NJ; (S); 7/245; Key Clb; JV Bsbl; Ftbl; JV Var Wrstlng; High Hon Roll; Acad Awd Wrstlng 85; Acad Awd 84; Bio.

MOY, MAY; Manalapan HS; Manalapan, NJ; (Y); Debate Tm; Math Tm; Yrbk Ed-Chief; Yrbk Phtg; Yrbk Stf; Cert Of Part In AAA Anl Schl Preg 80; Grolier Intrst Achvt Cert 78; Crm Stppr Cert 79; Pltcl Sci.

MOY, SHANNI LINN; Jackson Memorial HS; Jackson, NJ; (Y); 80/411; Art Clb; VP Church Yth Grp; Office Aide; High Hon Roll; Hon Roll; Cert Of Merit 86; 1st Pl Regional Cmptitn 86.

MRAZ, CAROLE; Paul VI Regional HS; Nutley, NJ; (S); 8/129; Trs Key Clb; NFL; School Play; Yrbk Stf; French Hon Soc; Hon Roll; NHS; NEDT Awd; Voice Dem Awd; Acadmc All Amer Schlr 86; Intl Forgn Lang Awd Wnnr 86; Amer Poetry Assn Poem Accptnc Publctn 86; Felician Coll; Lib Arts.

MUCCHIELLO JR, JOE; Metuchen HS; Metuchen, NJ; (Y); 16/143; Math Tm; Band; Concert Band; Mrchg Band; School Musical; French Hon Soc; NHS; Debate Tm; Ntl Merit SF; Math Clb; NJ Distinguished Schlrshp 86; NJIT Hnrs Schlrshp 86; PTO Cncl Schlrshp 86; NJ Inst Of Tech; Comp Engrng.

MUCCIOLI, DAVID; Roselle Catholic HS; Roselle, NJ; (S); 55/195; Trs Church Yth Grp; Band; Chorus; Church Choir; Concert Band; Orch; JV Socr; Hon Roll; Profcncy Spnsh 84-85; Elect Engr.

MUDRY, THERESA; Mc Corristin Catholic HS; Trenton, NJ; (Y); 35/225; Dance Clb; Yrbk Stf; Hon Roll; NHS; Comp Sci.

MUELLER, CHUCK; Westfield HS; Westfield, NJ; (Y); 135/550; Am Leg Boys St; Church Yth Grp; Var L Bsbl; Var L Ftbl; Hon Roll; Wt Lftg; Ski Clb; Bk Of Emrld Awd 84; 1st Tm-Union Cnty Conf & Metro-Bsbl 86; 3rd Tm-All St Group 4 86.

MUELLER, CLAUDIA; Clifton HS; Clifton, NJ; (Y); SADD; Stat Bsbl; Capt JV Cheerleading; Mgr(s); Score Keeper; Stat Sftbl; Hon Roll; Jr NHS; Kean Coll; Physcl Thrpy.

MUELLER, HAIDEE; Newton HS; Andover, NJ; (S); 13/192; Latin Clb; Math Tm; Trs Chorus; Church Choir; Madrigals; Variety Show; Yrbk Stf; Rep Sr Cls; Rep Stu Cncl; Powder Puff Ftbl; Natl Physcs Olympd Awd 85; Bus.

MUELLER, ROSEMARIE; Teaneck HS; Teaneck, NJ; (Y); Band; Chorus; Concert Band; Mrchg Band; Stu Cncl; Mgr(s); Hon Roll; NHS; Manhattan Coll; Engrng.

MUENCH, MICHELLE; Rancocas Valley HS; Mt Holly, NJ; (Y); DECA; High Hon Roll; Hon Roll; Stu Yr Dstrbtv Educ 86.

MUENCH, NADINE; Rancocas Valley Regional HS; Mt Holly, NJ; (Y); 13/248; Church Yth Grp; Mgr Color Guard; Yrbk Stf; Lit Mag; High Hon Roll; NHS; Pres Schlr; John Jr & Betty Haire Scholar 86; Cls Of 80 Scholar 86; Stetson U; Psych.

MUENZENBERGER, DIANA; Gateway Regional HS; Woodbury Heights, NJ; (Y); 31/206; Church Yth Grp; FCA; German Clb; Hosp Aide; SADD; Church Choir; Yrbk Stf; JV Fld Hcky; Gov Hon Prg Awd; Hon Roll; Nrsng.

MUGGLIN, JOEL; Ocean Township HS; Deal, NJ; (Y); 4/338; Pres Church Yth Grp; Band; Church Choir; Concert Band; Mrchg Band; Symp Band; Ed Yrbk Phtg; Yrbk Stf; NHS; Im Bsktbl; Spartan Schlr 84 & 85; Elec Engr.

MUGNO, ALBERT M; Don Bosco HS; W Paterson, NJ; (Y); 5/71; Am Leg Boys St; Pres Frsh Cls; Pres Soph Cls; Pres Jr Cls; Pres Stu Cncl; Var Bsktbl; Var Socr; Var Capt Trk; NHS; Montclair ST; Indstrl Arts.

MUHAMMAD, AHSONNA; Weequahic HS; Newark, NJ; (Y); Dance Clb; Drama Clb; Chorus; School Play; Variety Show; Nwsp Stf; Lit Mag; Stu Cncl; Trk; Hon Roll; Psych.

MUHLBAIER JR, WILLIAM S; Millville SR HS; Millville, NJ; (Y); 14/400; Church Yth Grp; SADD; Var Bsbl; Im Bsktbl; Var JV Bowling; Var Socr; Im Tennis; High Hon Roll; Hon Roll; NHS; Ldrs Clb 85-86; Comp Sys.

MUHLHAUSER, KRISTIN; Pope John XXIII HS; Milford, PA; (Y); Church Yth Grp; Cmnty Wkr; Red Cross Aide; JV Capt Fld Hcky; Mgr(s); High Hon Roll; Hon Roll; NHS; Skiing Capt V 83-86; Blgy.

MUIA, ANGELA; Bishop Ahr St Thomas Aquinas HS; Sewaren, NJ; (Y); Drama Clb; Chorus; Church Choir; Color Guard; School Musical; Stage Crew; Var Trk; Var Vllybl; Hon Roll; Outstndng Performer Color Guard 84-86; Natl Honor Society Nomiee 86-87; Educ.

MUKODA, PATTY; Cumberland Regional HS; Bridgeton, NJ; (Y); 30/400; Church Yth Grp; Intnl Clb; VP JCL; Ed Yrbk Stf; JV Var Fld Hcky; Stu Cncl; Hon Roll; Jr NHS; Prfct Atten Awd; State Finals On Field Hockey Team 85-86.

MULARZ, JEFFREY; Union Catholic Regional HS; Elizabeth, NJ; (Y); 19/293; Ski Clb; 2nd Hnr Roll 84-86; NJ Inst Tech; Elec Engrng.

MULCOCK, WHITNEY; Kinnelon HS; Bloomingdale, NJ; (Y); 72/216; Church Yth Grp; Sec Frsh Cls; Rep Soph Cls; Rep Jr Cls; Rep Stu Cncl; JV Var Cheerleading; Powder Puff Ftbl; JV Var Sftbl; Fres Class Sec 83-84; Var Ltr Sftbl 86; Comptn Cheering Sqd 3rd 86; Arch.

MULDERRIG, FRANCIS BUDDY; Fair Lawn HS; Glen Rock, NJ; (Y); 48/335; Church Yth Grp; Cmnty Wkr; Math Tm; Science Clb; Coach Actv; JV Var Socr; Var Capt Trk; Im Vllybl; Hon Roll; N J Garden St Schlrshp 86; Fair Lawn Athl Clb Awd 86; N J Crftsmns Fair Wnnr 84; Rutgers U; Mech Engrng.

MULFORD, ROBERT; Glassboro HS; Pitman, NJ; (Y); Church Yth Grp; Trs FBLA; Pep Clb; Trs Science Clb; Varsity Clb; Stu Cncl; JV Bsbl; Var JV Socr; Hon Roll; Pres Physical Fitness Awd 84; Most Valuable Goalkeeper Sccr 84; Kean ST NJ; Physical Edu.

MULFORD, VICTORIA; Woodstown HS; Woodstown, NJ; (Y); Cmnty Wkr; French Clb; FFA; VP German Clb; JV Fld Hcky; Var Socr; Hon Roll; NHS; Vet.

MULHOLLAND, DENISE; St John Vianney HS; Freehold, NJ; (Y); Cmnty Wkr; Ski Clb; U DE; Physcl Ther.

MULHOLLAND, ROBERT; St Peters Prep Schl; Jersey City, NJ; (Y); Computer Clb; JV Bowling; JV Socr; Hon Roll; Cmptr Sci Gld Mdl 86; Stevens Inst Of Tech; Cmptr Eng.

MULLEN, KEVIN; Florence Twp Mem HS; Roebling, NJ; (Y); Am Leg Boys St; Church Yth Grp; FBLA; JV Bsbl; Var Mgr(s); Var Score Keeper; Acctg.

MULLEN, MARIE; Phillipsburg Catholic HS; Phillipsburg, NJ; (Y); 1/77; Science Clb; Chorus; Concert Band; Jazz Band; Mrchg Band; School Musical; Nwsp Stf; Ed Lit Mag; Fld Hcky; Val; Ntl Merit Ltr Commdntn, L Armstrong Jazz Awd, Red Crss Wtr Sfty Instr 86.

MULLEN, TY; Salem HS; Salem, NJ; (Y); 1/135; Am Leg Boys St; Computer Clb; Math Clb; Var Capt Bsbl; Cit Awd; Hon Roll; NHS; St Schlr; Beneficial Hodsedn Schlrshp 86; Rugery Schlr 85; Johns Hopkins U; Mech Engrng.

MULLER, EDWARD; Kittatinny Regional HS; Newton, NJ; (Y); 55/223; Boy Scts; Lit Mag; JV Socr; Im Swmmng; Var Wrstlng; Hon Roll; Am Indstrl Arts Stu Assoc 84-86; Accntng.

MULLER, MARK; St Augustine Prep; Marmora, NJ; (Y); 1/50; Computer Clb; Lit Mag; Pres Sr Cls; Bsktbl; Var JV Socr; High Hon Roll; NHS; Val; Acadmc Schlrshp Villanova 86; Schl Mdl Achvt Hist 86; NJ ST Dstngshd Schlr 86; Villanova U; Mech Engrg.

MULLER, RAYMOND; Burlington City HS; Edgewater Park, NJ; (Y); Am Leg Boys St; Chess Clb; Church Yth Grp; Drama Clb; FTA; Chorus; Rep Stu Cncl; Var Capt Tennis; Rep South Jrsy Annl Cnfrnce; Hstry.

MULLER, SHARON; Paul VI Regional HS; Bloomfield, NJ; (S); Pep Clb; Rep Frsh Cls; Rep Soph Cls; Rep Jr Cls; Sec Stu Cncl; JV Bsktbl; Var Golf; High Hon Roll; NHS; Spanish NHS.

MULLIGAN, JOYCELYN; Shore Regional HS; Sea Bright, NJ; (Y); JV Swmmng; Hon Roll; Mt ST Marys Coll; Bio.

MULLIN, KATHLEEN; Hawthorne HS; Hawthorne, NJ; (Y); Pres Girl Scts; Trs Trs Library Aide; Band; Concert Band; Jazz Band; Mrchg Band; School Play; Yrbk Stf; Mgr(s); 4-H; Girl Scout Gold Awd 86; Math.

MULLINS, STEPHANIE; Clifford J Scott HS; E Orange, NJ; (S); 4/254; Library Aide; Acpl Chr; Chorus; School Musical; Hon Roll; VP NHS; NC Central U; Acctng.

MULROONEY, HELEN; Middlesex HS; Middlesex, NJ; (Y); Ski Clb; Yrbk Bus Mgr; Yrbk Sprt Ed; Yrbk Stf; Stat Bsktbl; Var Stat Trk; Hon Roll; Bus.

MULROONY, KEVIN; Parsippany HS; Parsippany, NJ; (Y); Varsity Clb; Rep Frsh Cls; Rep Soph Cls; Sec Jr Cls; Rep Sr Cls; Pres Stu Cncl; Var Ftbl; JV Trk; Var Wrstlng; Bloomsburg U; Bus.

MUN KIM, CHONG; Long Branch HS; Long Branch, NJ; (S); 2/213; Church Yth Grp; Science Clb; Nwsp Rptr; Trs Jr Cls; Trs Sr Cls; Pres Stu Cncl; Bausch & Lomb Sci Awd; NHS; St Schlr; Elec Engr.

MUND, MARY JEAN; Westfield HS; Westfield, NJ; (Y); 112/524; Art Clb; Off Church Yth Grp; Cmnty Wkr; French Clb; Hosp Aide; Science Clb; Church Choir; JV Trk; High Hon Roll; Hon Roll; PTO Crafts Awd 84-85; Art Purchase Awd 85-86; Bio Sci.

MUNDELL JR, THOMAS; Neptune SR HS; Neptune, NJ; (Y); 4/398; High Hon Roll; Hon Roll; NHS; Med.

MUNDO, GEORGE; Memorial HS; West New York, NJ; (Y); Boy Scts; Var Crs Cntry; Var Trk; Athlt Achvmnt Awd 86; Engr.

MUNECH, TOM; Don Bosco Prep HS; N Haledon, NJ; (Y); Cmnty Wkr; Exploring; Ski Clb; Bsbl; Ftbl; Wt Lftg; Hon Roll; Villanova.

MUNGRO, SANDRA; John F Kennedy HS; Willingboro, NJ; (Y); Church Yth Grp; Cmnty Wkr; Drama Clb; Hosp Aide; Intnl Clb; Stage Crew; Yrbk Phtg; Yrbk Rptr; JV Socr; Lion Awd; PTSA Schlrshp 85-86; E Strdsbrg U; Mass Cmnctns.

MUNIZ, BARBARA; Manchester Regional HS; Haledon, NJ; (S); Trk; High Hon Roll; Hon Roll; NHS.

MUNLEY, ROBERT; Kearny HS; Kearny, NJ; (Y); Ski Clb; Varsity Clb; Concert Band; Var Bsbl; Var Ftbl; Sftbl; Wt Lftg; Rutgers U; Jrnlsm.

MUNOZ, YVETTE; Mother Seton Regional HS; Irvington, NJ; (Y); 5/124; Drama Clb; GAA; Math Tm; Science Clb; Hon Roll; Cert Of Merit In Spnsh 85-86; Rtgrs U.

MUNRO, GLEN; Carteret HS; Cartert, NJ; (Y); 25/225; Computer Clb; Latin Clb; Spanish Clb; Stage Crew; JV Bsbl; Var Bowling; JV Ftbl; Var Socr; Var Tennis; Hon Roll.

MUNROE, KAY; Wacquahic HS; Newark, NJ; (S); Drama Clb; English Clb; FTA; GAA; JA; PAVAS; Acpl Chr; Chorus; School Play; Nwsp Phtg; Bsbl Team Merit Badge 84-85; Good Atndnc Awd 83; Englsh Tchr.

MUNSON, SUSAN; Manasquan HS; Brielle, NJ; (Y); 13/243; Church Yth Grp; French Clb; Key Clb; Latin Clb; Math Clb; Yrbk Ed-Chief; VP Stu Cncl; High Hon Roll; NHS; Pres Schlr; Brielle Wmns Clb Grad Schlrp 86; Amer U Pres Schlrp 86; Villanova U; Law.

MUNSON, T EUGENE; Triton Regional HS; Somerdale, NJ; (Y); 3/294; Am Leg Boys St; Chess Clb; Key Clb; Scholastic Bowl; Yrbk Stf; JV Bsktbl; JV Crs Cntry; Cit Awd; Jr NHS; VP NHS; Cnty Govt Smnr 85; Accntng.

MUNSON, TODD; Washington Twp HS; Turnersville, NJ; (Y); 9/470; Church Yth Grp; German Clb; Chorus; Var Crs Cntry; Var Trk; Im Vllybl; High Hon Roll; Hon Roll; NHS; Pres Schlr; NROTC Schlrshp 86; German Hnr Scty 85-86; Minuteman Awd & Bio Awd 86; Drexel U; Elec Engr.

MUNYON, HILLARY; Bridgeton SR HS; Cedarville, NJ; (Y); Church Yth Grp; 4-H; GAA; Yrbk Stf; Var Fld Hcky; Var Sftbl; Sftbl Bst All Around, Mst Imprvd & All Conf Hnrbl Mntn Catcher 85-86.

MURACCO, STEPHEN; Washington Township HS; Turnersville, NJ; (Y); Church Yth Grp; German Clb; JV Var Mgr(s); JV Var Socr; Hon Roll; Youth & Govt 86; German Honor Socty 86; Bus.

MURDOCH, KAREN; Spotswood HS; Spotswood, NJ; (Y); 52/152; Band; Concert Band; Orch; Symp Band; Rep Stu Cncl; Hon Roll; Middlesex Cnty Arts HS 86; Hstry.

MURIN, CRAIG; Roselle Catholic HS; Roselle, NJ; (S); 14/195; Math Tm; VP Frsh Cls; Rep Soph Cls; Pres Jr Cls; JV Bsbl; Im Bsktbl; Var Socr; Var Capt Swmmng; Hon Roll; St Peters Schlr 85; Math.

MURNANE, PAULA; Morris Knolls HS; Dover, NJ; (Y); 41/383; Girl Scts; Hosp Aide; Ski Clb; Varsity Clb; Yrbk Phtg; Yrbk Stf; Crs Cntry; Score Keeper; Trk; High Hon Roll; Nrsng.

MURPHY, DANIEL L; Bergen Catholic HS; Harrington Park, NJ; (Y); 22/259; Church Yth Grp; Cmnty Wkr; Church Choir; French Hon Soc; NHS; Ntl Merit SF; School Musical; School Play; Stage Crew; Nwsp Stf; Garden ST Dstngushd Schlr 85-86.

MURPHY, DINA; Florence Twp Mem HS; Roebling, NJ; (Y); Am Leg Aux Girls St; French Clb; FBLA; Math Clb; Yrbk Stf; Trs Soph Cls; Trs Stu Cncl; Var Capt Cheerleading; VFW Awd; La Salle U; Law.

MURPHY, EAIN; St Josephs Prep Seminary; Bronx, NY; (S); 3/19; Debate Tm; Hosp Aide; Latin Clb; NFL; Spanish Clb; Speech Tm; Church Choir; Stage Crew; Socr; High Hon Roll; MIT; Physcs.

MURPHY, JAMES; Seton Hall Prep; S Orange, NJ; (Y); Cmnty Wkr; JA; Key Clb; Var Bsbl; JV Trk; Hon Roll; NHS; Prfct Atten Awd; Bsbl 84; Trck-Cnty Chmps 85; Bsbl-1st Tm-All Metro & Prchial, 2nd Tm-All Cnty 86; Pro Basebl.

MURPHY, JESSICA; Mount St Mary Acad; Edison, NJ; (S); 1/85; French Clb; Q&S; Band; Concert Band; Nwsp Rptr; Nwsp Stf; Lit Mag; French Hon Soc; High Hon Roll; NHS; Cntrl Jrsy Rgn II Bnds 84, 85 & 86; Smrst Cnty HS Cncrt Bnd 84, 85 & 86; Frgn Lng.

MURPHY, KAREN; Vailsburg HS; Newark, NJ; (Y); 3/38; Debate Tm; Drama Clb; Exploring; Office Aide; Teachers Aide; Chorus; Color Guard; Drill Tm; Yrbk Stf; Stu Cncl; Cert Awd Bio 83-84, Typwrtng 85-86, Prfct Atten 84-85; Army Res; Adm.

MURPHY, KELLY; Holy Spirit HS; Margate, NJ; (Y); 163/366; Stat Bsktbl; Arch.

MURPHY, KEN; Gateway Regional HS; Wenonah, NJ; (Y); 14/205; Boy Scts; Church Yth Grp; Exploring; JCL; Trs Latin Clb; SADD; Nwsp Stf; Trs Soph Cls; Trs Jr Cls; Rep Stu Cncl; Frgn Lang Hnr Soc; Stu Of Mth; Boston Coll; Pltcl Sci.

MURPHY, MARTIN; Hackettstown HS; Hackettstown, NJ; (Y); Boy Scts; Hon Roll; Pre Med.

MURPHY, MARY JOAN; Oak Knoll HS; S Orange, NJ; (Y); Pep Clb; Chorus; Yrbk Stf; Rep Frsh Cls; Rep Soph Cls; Rep Jr Cls; JV Var Bsktbl; Var Lcrss; Var Tennis; Hon Roll; Rnnr Up For Hugh O Brian Awd 85.

MURPHY, PAMELA; Raritan HS; Hazlet, NJ; (S); 11/314; Drama Clb; Band; Concert Band; Mrchg Band; Orch; School Musical; Socr; High Hon Roll; Hon Roll; NHS; All Shore Symph Band 85; Schlrs Awd 86; Monmouth Coll; Chem.

MURPHY, SHEILA; Jackson Memorial HS; Jackson, NJ; (Y); 100/420; Aud/Vis; Ski Clb; Socr; High Hon Roll; Hon Roll; Cmnctn.

MURPHY, TOM; North Warren Regional HS; Blairstown, NJ; (Y); 7/135; 4-H; Quiz Bowl; School Play; Nwsp Sprt Ed; Nwsp Stf; Bsbl; Socr; Wt Lftg; 4-H Awd; NHS; Micro Comp Tech.

MURRAY, ANGELINE; Lincoln HS; Jersey City, NJ; (Y); Church Yth Grp; FCA; 4-H; JA; SADD; Church Choir; VP Frsh Cls; Bsbl; Gym; Vllybl; Morgan ST U; Acctg.

MURRAY, LESLIE C; Bridgewater-Raritan East HS; Bridgewater, NJ; (Y); 85/271; Drama Clb; French Clb; Ski Clb; SADD; Stu Cncl; Bsktbl; Stat Socr; Trk; High Hon Roll; NHS; Schlrshp PTO 86; NY U; Tele Comm.

MURRAY, MELODY; Colonia HS; Colonia, NJ; (Y); 32/300; Co-Capt Color Guard; Hon Roll; NHS; Amer Assn Of Retired Prsns Awd 86; Douglas Coll; Tchng.

MURRAY, RUSSEL; Don Bosco Prep; Hawthorne, NJ; (Y); Boy Scts; Model UN; Band; Concert Band; Mrchg Band; Nwsp Stf; Var L Trk; Hon Roll; NHS; Eagl Sct 85; Rutgers U; Govt Law.

MURRAY, TIM; Bishop George Ahr HS; Iselin, NJ; (Y); Church Yth Grp; Yrbk Sprt Ed; Bsktbl; JV Var Ftbl; Wt Lftg; Hon Roll.

MURRAY, WILLIAM SEAN; Haddon Twp SR HS; Westmont, NJ; (Y); 17/165; Am Leg Boys St; Pres Aud/Vis; Chess Clb; Church Yth Grp; JCL; Pres Latin Clb; Pres Science Clb; Pres Stage Crew; Rep Jr Cls; Kiwanis Awd; Scottish Rt; Stevens Intl Tech; Engrng Physc.

MURSCHELL, KAREN; Woodstown HS; Woodstown, NJ; (Y); Church Yth Grp; German Clb; Band; Yrbk Stf; Im Socr; Hon Roll; NHS; Engrng.

MURTHA, CHRISTOPHER; Washington Township HS; Turnersville, NJ; (Y); Cmnty Wkr; Exploring; Glassboro ST Coll; Commnctns.

MURTHA, JACK; Deptford Township HS; Deptford, NJ; (Y); Quiz Bowl; Acpl Chr; Band; Chorus; Concert Band; Jazz Band; Mrchg Band; Pep Band; School Musical; Variety Show; Pres Ntl Hon Soc 86-87; Rec Sec Stu Cncl 86-87; Lead Schl Mscl 85-86; Westchester; Music.

MURTHA, THOMAS S; Sayreville HS; Morgan, NJ; (Y); 121/379; Boy Scts; Math Clb; Spanish Clb; Varsity Clb; Yrbk Stf; Var Socr; Hon Roll; Awds Rllr Sktng 1st,2nd,3rd Plcs 82-84; Kean Coll.

MURZENSKI, MICHAEL; Lenape Valley Reg HS; Andover, NJ; (Y); Var Bsbl; Var Bowling; JV Ftbl; Im Wt Lftg; Hon Roll; Law.

MUSCARNERA, REGINA; Westfield Senior HS; Westfield, NJ; (Y); Art Clb; Drama Clb; Spanish Clb; Band; School Play; Yrbk Stf; Swmmng; High Hon Roll; NHS; Spanish NHS; Schlrshp To U Of Madrid Spain 84; Spnsh High Achvmnt Awd 86; Pres Acdmc Ftnss Awd 86; Catholic U Of Amer; Theater Art.

MUSCHERT, GLENN; Holy Cross HS; Cinnaminson, NJ; (Y); Boy Scts; Chess Clb; Exploring; Am Leg Aux Girls St; JA; Model UN; Science Clb; Ski Clb; Band; Concert Band.

MUSSER, ERICA LYNN; Williamstown HS; Williamstown, NJ; (Y); French Clb; Nwsp Stf; JV Var Fld Hcky; French Hon Soc; Hon Roll; NHS; Voice Dem Awd; RYLA 86; Schlrshp Prog JFK Memrl Hosp 86-87; Bio.

MUSSER, JENNIFER LYNN; Penns Grove HS; Carneys Point, NJ; (Y); 33/183; Am Leg Aux Girls St; Drm Mjr(t); School Musical; Yrbk Sprt Ed; Sec Stu Cncl; Capt Sftbl; JCL; Thesps; Band; All ST Chorus 85; Pres Clsrm 86; Juniata Coll; Elem Ed.

MUSTERER, JOHN H; Millburn HS; Short Hills, NJ; (Y); Pres Computer Clb; Teachers Aide; Hon Roll; Ntl Merit SF; Military Acad Invtntl Acad Wrksshp 85; Rutgers Schlr 85; GA Inst Tech; Engrng.

MUSTILLO, DIANA; Mother Seton Regional HS; Union, NJ; (Y); 6/102; Church Yth Grp; Science Clb; Service Clb; Nwsp Rptr; Yrbk Stf; Rep Jr Cls; Pres Sr Cls; Rep Stu Cncl; Hon Roll; NHS; Cert Top Stu Frnch III, Mdrn Euro Hstry, US Hstry I 84-86; Coll St Elizabeth; Chem.

MUSUMECI, GINA; St James HS; Swedesboro, NJ; (Y); 11/78; Church Yth Grp; School Play; Yrbk Rptr; Yrbk Stf; Pres Frsh Cls; Pres Jr Cls; Stat Bsbl; Var JV Cheerleading; Var Tennis; Rotary Awd; Hgh Achvt In Rlgn & Math 84; Hgh Achvt In Comp 86; Bus Mgmt.

MUSUMICI, FRANK; Hoboken HS; Hoboken, NJ; (Y); Boy Scts; Variety Show; Jr Cls; Bsbl; U Rutgers; Engrng.

MUTH, DAVID; West Morris Central HS; Long Valley, NJ; (Y); Sec FBLA; Office Aide; IN ST U; Pilot.

MUTH, ROBERT; Mount Olive HS; Hackettstown, NJ; (Y); 7/296; Math Tm; Science Clb; Band; Concert Band; Drm Mjr(t); Jazz Band; Mrchg Band; School Musical; Hon Roll; Louis Armstrng Jazz Awd 86; Mdrn Msc Mstrs 86; Bnd 85-86; Elec Engr.

MUTSCHLER, BRETT M; North Warren Regional HS; Blairstown, NJ; (Y); Ski Clb; Soph Cls; Bsbl; Golf; Socr; Bus.

MUZAFFAR, AYESHA; Friends Schl; Woodstown, NJ; (Y); 2/9; Cmnty Wkr; Dance Clb; Exploring; Hosp Aide; Model UN; Yrbk Phtg; Yrbk Stf; VP Jr Cls; Stu Cncl; Mgr(s); Hnrd Miss TEEN NJ Cont 86; Bio.

MYERS, ARTHUR SAMUEL; Millville SR HS; Millville, NJ; (Y); 14/468; Science Clb; Band; Jazz Band; School Musical; High Hon Roll; JP Sousa Awd; NHS; Key Clb; SADD; S Polkowitz Schlrshp; Exch Clb; Ntl Sci Olympd; Glassboro ST Coll; Music.

MYERS, DONNA; Roselle Catholic HS; Irvington, NJ; (Y); Hon Roll; Ducret Schl Of Arts.

MYERS, IRENE ROCHELLE; Gloucester City JR SR HS; Gloucester, NJ; (Y); 7/170; Band; Chorus; Concert Band; Drm Mjr(t); Flag Corp; Mrchg Band; School Play; Var Bowling; Stat Trk; NHS; Mst Imprvd Band Frnt 84-85; Brd Ed Awd Bwlg 85-86; Phy Thrpst.

MYERS, JILL SUZETTE; Villa Victoria Acad; Trenton, NJ; (Y); 13/29; Cmnty Wkr; 4-H; School Musical; School Play; Score Keeper; Socr; Sftbl; Swmmng; 4-H Awd; Prfct Atten Awd; ST Am Postal Workers Un Schlrshp 86; Paine Coll Schlrshp 86; Top Teens Am; Paine Coll; Pre-Med.

MYERS, LISA; Our Lady Of Mercy Acad; Wmstown, NJ; (Y); Church Yth Grp; SADD; Chorus; Church Choir; Nwsp Rptr; Nwsp Stf; Yrbk Stf; Cert Recgntn Essay Cont Time Mag 86; Urban Jrnlsm Wrkshp Scholar Rider Coll 86; Radio/TV Cmmnctns.

MYERS, MARCIA; Clayton HS; Clayton, NJ; (Y); Am Leg Aux Girls St; Pres Boys Clb Am; Drama Clb; Sec Key Clb; Sec Science Clb; School Musical; School Play; Nwsp Rptr; Nwsp Stf; Yrbk Rptr; Stu Of Mnth Awd 85; Rutgers Schlr 86.

MYERS, MATT; Delran HS; Delran, NJ; (Y); JV Var Bsbl; JV Var Socr; Bus Fnc.

MYERS, STEPHANIE A; Palmyra HS; Palmyra, NJ; (Y); 3/109; Am Leg Aux Girls St; Church Yth Grp; Drama Clb; French Clb; Office Aide; Quiz Bowl; Band; Church Choir; Concert Band; Mrchg Band; U S Naval Acad; Engrng.

MYHRE, KRISTIN; Delaware Valley Regional HS; Frenchtown, NJ; (Y); 43/150; Church Yth Grp; Intnl Clb; Office Aide; Pep Clb; Varsity Clb; Drill Tm; Var Cheerleading; Letterman Clb; Chorus; Color Guard; All Conf Var Chrldr 1st Tm, St TEEN Arts Fest Cncrt Choir, 6 Flags Choral Fest Overall Exclnt 86; VA Westleyan; Educ.

MYOTT, KIMBERLY; Our Lady Of Good Counsel HS; Newark, NJ; (Y); 53/106; Church Choir; Stu Cncl; Bsktbl; Wt Lftg.

NAAR, MARY; Perth Amboy HS; Perth Amboy, NJ; (Y); Var Socr; Hon Roll; Accntng.

NACHSHEN, COREY; Parsippany HS; Lake Hiawatha, NJ; (Y); Boy Scts; Chess Clb; Drama Clb; Letterman Clb; Ski Clb; Varsity Clb; Stage Crew; Yrbk Stf; Var L Trk; Hon Roll; Aerospc Engr.

NACHT, JEREMY M; Dwight Morrow HS; Englewood, NJ; (Y); 34/225; Chess Clb; Math Tm; Ed Nwsp Phtg; Ed Yrbk Phtg; Lit Mag; Var L Wrstlng; Hon Roll; NHS; Mrt Awd, Arts Recogntn & Tlnt Srch, Natl Fndtn For Advncmt In Arts 86; Summer Arts Inst; Sci.

NACON, MARK; Middletown South HS; Middletown, NJ; (S); 29/450; School Play; Yrbk Phtg; Rep Stu Cncl; Bsbl; JV Capt Socr; High Hon Roll; Hon Roll; NHS; NEDT Awd; PFA-CTZN-SCHLR Awd 82; GA Tech; Elec Engrng.

NADEL, JOHN; Middletown H S North; Belford, NJ; (Y); 14/420; VP Intnl Clb; NFL; Capt Swmmng; High Hon Roll; Hon Roll; NHS; Spanish NHS; St Schlr; Distngshd Quality Schlrshp 86; New Jersey St Distngshd Schlr 86; Natl Hispanic Schlr Awd 86; Purdue U; Accntng.

NADELL, STACEY; Matawan Regional HS; Matawan, NJ; (Y); Drama Clb; GAA; PAVAS; Ski Clb; School Play; Stu Cncl; Cheerleading; Sftbl; Cit Awd; NHS; Thespn Socty Secy; Peer Ldrshp Pres; U Of DE; Bus Adm.

NAFZIGER, JOHN; High Point Reg HS; Lafayette, NJ; (Y); 29/220; JV Bsbl; JV Ftbl; Var JV Socr; Var Tennis; Im Wt Lftg; High Hon Roll; Hon Roll; Ctzsnshp Awd 86; Villanova U; Med Engrng.

NAGLER, ANASTASIA; Ambassador Christian Acad; Gibbstown, NJ; (S); 1/14; 4-H; Yrbk Stf; Off Frsh Cls; Sec Soph Cls; Trs Jr Cls; 4-H Awd; High Hon Roll; NHS; Sci Awd 83-84; U Of PA; Vetrnrn.

NAGY, MATTHEW C; Millburn HS; Short Hills, NJ; (Y); 16/267; Math Clb; Math Tm; Concert Band; Orch; Nwsp Stf; Lit Mag; Gov Hon Prg Awd; High Hon Roll; Ntl Merit SF; St Schlr; No 1 Stu Essex Cnty Math League Alg II; No 1 Tm Essex Cnty Math League Alg; Schl Peer Wrtng Ctr-Tutor; Yale; Engl.

NAGY, PETER; Clifton HS; Clifton, NJ; (Y); 69/687; Math Clb; Science Clb; Band; Concert Band; Jazz Band; Mrchg Band; Orch; High Hon Roll; Jr NHS; Spanish NHS; Cornell U; Chem.

NAIK, BELA; Nutley HS; Nutley, NJ; (Y); 50/350; Spanish Clb; Stu Cncl; Hnr Rl 84; Pre-Med.

NAIK, RAJESH; Bridgewater-Raritan HS West; Bridgewater, NJ; (Y); CAP; 4-H; Math Tm; Science Clb; Band; Concert Band; Mrchg Band; Trk; High Hon Roll; NHS; USAF Acad Appntmnt 86; Air Force Rotc Schlrshp 86; Navy Rotc Schlrshp 86; USAF Acad; Astrntcl Engrng.

NAIMAN, MAUREEN; Union Catholic Regional HS; Linden, NJ; (Y); Church Yth Grp; Drama Clb; PAVAS; Thesps; Chorus; School Musical; School Play; Yrbk Stf; Hon Roll; 2 Str Hnr Thspn 86; Dstngshd SR Prfrmr 86; Lndn Dbutnte Fndtn Schlrshp 86; Lndn Intrafth Schlrshp 86; William Paterson Coll; Nrsng.

NAIPAWER, MICHELE; Immaculate Conception HS; Wallington, NJ; (S); 1/88; Math Tm; NFL; Science Clb; Ed Nwsp Stf; Rep Frsh Cls; Rep Soph Cls; NEDT Awd; Spanish NHS; St Peters Coll Smmr Schlrs 85; Rutgers Schlr 86; Princeton U; Arch.

NALLS, TISH; Henry Snyder HS; Jersey City, NJ; (S); Debate Tm; Drama Clb; Scholastic Bowl; SADD; Drill Tm; School Play; Yrbk Stf; Lit Mag; Rep Frsh Cls; Rep Soph Cls; Rutgers U; Acctnt.

NAM, KYUNG; Freehold Township HS; Freehold, NJ; (Y); 18/340; Hosp Aide; Spanish Clb; Yrbk Stf; Sftbl; NHS; Psych.

NAMVAR, ALI; Ramapo HS; Franklin Lakes, NJ; (Y); 1/329; Math Tm; Science Clb; Band; Stage Crew; Variety Show; High Hon Roll; Ntl Merit Ltr; Rutgers Schlr 86.

NANAYAKKARA, ABIGAIL; Villa Victoria Acad; Ewing, NJ; (Y); Office Aide; Chorus; School Musical; School Play; Yrbk Stf; Lit Mag; Marie H Katzenbach Schl Deaf Vlntr Awd 84; Seton Hall U; Bus.

NANFARA, RALPH JOHN; Holy Spirit HS; Atlantic City, NJ; (Y); 17/340; High Hon Roll; Hon Roll; Jr NHS; NHS; Im Mgr Vllybl; Pres Awd For Acad Ftnss 86; Tmple U Pres Awad 86; Hap Frly Bstrs Clb Awd 86; Temple U; Archtctr.

NAPCHEN, SHERI; East Brunswick HS; E Brunswick, NJ; (Y); German Clb; Variety Show; Rep Frsh Cls; Var L Crs Cntry; Var L Trk; Hon Roll; Sec NHS; Ntl Merit Ltr; Gov Tchg Schlrs 85-86; E Brunswick Educ Assoc Schlrshp 86; U VA Charlottesville; Tchr.

NAPLES, BETHANN; Hamilton High West; Trenton, NJ; (Y); Key Clb; SADD; Band; Concert Band; Mrchg Band; Symp Band; Yrbk Stf; Rep Stu Cncl; Im Bsktbl; Var Trk; Bus Admin.

NAPODANO, GINA; Passaic Valley HS; W Paterson, NJ; (Y); Key Clb; Hon Roll; Hnr Roll 83-86; Italian Clb Trea 83-86; Key Club 84-86; Hill Inst; Ct Rprtng.

NAPOLI, KAREN; St Pius X HS; Milltown, NJ; (Y); 12/118; Sec Dance Clb; Drama Clb; Office Aide; Chorus; School Musical; School Play; Yrbk Stf; Hon Roll; NHS.

NAPOLI, PETER C; Salem HS; Salem, NJ; (Y); 2/180; Am Leg Boys St; VP Jr Cls; VP Sr Cls; Stu Cncl; Bsbl; Ftbl; Wrstlng; High Hon Roll; NHS.

NAPOLITANO, EUGENE; Park Ridge HS; Park Ridge, NJ; (Y); 30/122; Nwsp Stf; Yrbk Stf; High Hon Roll; Hon Roll; Long Island U; Acctg.

NAPOTANO, ROBIN; Lyndhurst HS; Lyndhurst, NJ; (Y); 11/180; Pres FNA; Band; Concert Band; Mrchg Band; Stage Crew; Variety Show; JV Mgr(s); JV Score Keeper; Hon Roll; Trs NHS; Bnd Nmrls JV Ltr Bnd; JV Ltr Bnd; Y Ltrs Bnd; Med Lab.

NAPPEN, LOUIS; Township Of Ocean HS; Ocean, NJ; (Y); Boy Scts; Band; Mrchg Band; Orch; Pep Band; School Musical; Lit Mag; Var Trk; Short Story Contst 1st Pl 86; Poetry Contst 3rd Pl 86; Excell In Drama Awd 85-86; Monmath Coll; Commnctns.

NARDINI, WILLIAM J; Neumann Prep; Totowa, NJ; (Y); 1/84; Am Leg Boys St; Boy Scts; Yrbk Ed-Chief; Var Bowling; Var Trk; Pres French Hon Soc; Gov Hon Prg Awd; Pres NHS; St Schlr; Val; Knghts Of Columbus Yth Exch To Mexico 84; Lwyr.

NARDO, CHRISTINE; Jackson Memorial HS; Jackson, NJ; (Y); 19/322; Art Clb; Debate Tm; 4-H; Ski Clb; Nwsp Rptr; VP Frsh Cls; VP Soph Cls; Sec Jr Cls; Mgr(s); Mat Maids; Grdn St Schlrshp 86; Douglass Coll; Bio.

NARDONE, JOANNE; Morris Catholic HS; Towaco, NJ; (Y); 100/142; Sftbl; Tennis; Ltr Tennis,Sftbl 84-86; Bus.

NARDONE, TOM; Washington Township HS; Turnersville, NJ; (Y); Bsbl; Bsktbl; Ftbl; Ice Hcky; Sftbl; Wt Lftg; Bus Law.

NARITA, WADE; Middletown H S South; Lincroft, NJ; (S); 18/436; VP Church Yth Grp; Band; Concert Band; Jazz Band; Mrchg Band; Pep Band; School Musical; Variety Show; Lit Mag; Var L Diving; Monmouth Conservtry Of Mus Schlrshp 1st Pl 85; Ntl Ldrshp Grp 85-86; Columbia U; Engr.

NASH, KELLY; Hunterdon Central HS; Whitehouse Sta, NJ; (Y); 70/540; FBLA; High Hon Roll; Hon Roll; 7th Central Reg FBLA Acctng II 86; Flemington Lions Clb Schlrshp Wnnr 86; U MD; Bus Adm.

NASSER, BETSY; Chatham Township HS; Chatham, NJ; (Y); 22/135; Girl Scts; Key Clb; Yrbk Sprt Ed; Yrbk Stf; Rep Stu Cncl; Stat Bsktbl; Stat Fld Hcky; Mgr(s); JV Sftbl; High Hon Roll.

NASTA, FRANK; Lodi HS; Lodi, NJ; (Y); Var Ftbl; Var L Trk; Im Wt Lftg; JV Wrstlng; Communications.

NASTASI, BILLY; Wildwood HS; N Wildwood, NJ; (Y); 5/100; Quiz Bowl; SADD; Var Bsktbl; Var Tennis; Hon Roll; NHS; Rotary Awd.

NATALE, FILOMENA; Bridgewater-Raritan HS West; Raritan, NJ; (Y); Spanish Clb; Band; Pep Band; Mgr(s); Hon Roll; NHS; Mrktng.

NATALE, KERRI; Ramsey HS; Ramsey, NJ; (Y); 100/240; Yrbk Stf; Stat Bsbl; Capt Cheerleading; Gym; Bentley Coll; Accntng.

NATALE, LAURA; Shore Regional HS; Oceanport, NJ; (Y); Var L Bowling; Hon Roll; NJ Coll; Acctng.

NATHAN, EDWARD; Manalapan HS; Englishtown, NJ; (Y); Cmnty Wkr; Temple Yth Grp; Madrigals; Variety Show; Nwsp Stf; Ftbl; Wt Lftg; Var JV Wrstlng; Hon Roll; NHS; Rutgers; Engl.

NATHAN, SHARI; South Brunswick HS; Kendall Pk, NJ; (Y); Cmnty Wkr; 4-H; Hosp Aide; Ski Clb; Temple Yth Grp; Score Keeper; 4-H Awd; Hon Roll; Rotary Awd; Glassboro ST Coll.

NATHAN, SUSAN; East Brunsiwck HS; E Brunswick, NJ; (Y); Civic Clb; Hosp Aide; Powder Puff Ftbl; Prom Cmmtte 85; Hands Across Amer 86; Spec Olympics Coachd 86; Rutgers; Bio.

NATOLI, WILLIAM; Highland Regional HS; Erial, NJ; (Y); JV Bsbl; JV Var Ftbl; JV Var Socr; Wrstlng; Sec Rotary Awd; Bys Intrct Sctry; Cvl Engrng.

NAVALLO, DAWN E; N Brunswick Twp HS; N Brunswick, NJ; (Y); 118/309; Drama Clb; German Clb; Radio Clb; Thesps; Varsity Clb; Chorus; Concert Band; Mrchg Band; School Musical; School Play; Law.

NAVARRO, ALEX; Memorial HS; West New York, NJ; (Y); Boy Scts; Church Yth Grp; Cmnty Wkr; Spanish Clb; Fld Hcky; Spllng Bee Cntst 3rd Pl 83; Outstndng Math Achvt Awd 83; Arch.

NAVARRO, JORGE ISAAC; North Bergen HS; West New York, NJ; (Y); 145/404; JV Var Bsktbl; Pace U; Comp Sci.

NAVAS, JULIO C; Ocean Township HS; Ocean, NJ; (Y); 16/337; Chess Clb; Ski Clb; Band; Concert Band; Mrchg Band; Trk; NHS; Spartan Schlr-Schl Awd 83-86; Aerospace Engr.

NAYAK, JAWAHAR; Woodbridge HS; Port Reading, NJ; (Y); 1/357; Boy Scts; Pres Math Clb; Capt Quiz Bowl; Chorus; Var Crs Cntry; Gov Hon Prg Awd; Val; NFL; Sbrbn Cblvsn Schlrshp 86; 9th Pl In NJ ST Sci Day 86; Fnlst In NJ Tlnt Expo 84; Priceton U:Sci.

NAYLOR, BONNIE; Riverside HS; Riverside, NJ; (Y); 21/718; DECA; DECA Modeling Awd 85; Camden Co Coll; Anml Sci Tech.

NAYLOR, CRAIG; Woodstown HS; Woodstown, NJ; (Y); French Clb; Off Jr Cls; Off Sr Cls; Swmmng; Hon Roll; NHS; All-S Jersey Swim Team 86.

NAZARIO, DEAN A; Pompton Lakes HS; Pompton Lakes, NJ; (Y); Boy Scts; Chess Clb; Latin Clb; Science Clb; Teachers Aide; Varsity Clb; Band; Lit Mag; Socr; Hon Roll; Passaic Cnty Cmnty Clg Schlrshp 86; NJAFPA Stu Grant 86; Vrsty Let Vrsty Awd SR Hnr Awd 86; Kent ST U; Aero Engnrng.

NAZARIO, EDWIN; James J Ferris HS; Jersey City, NJ; (Y); Boys Clb Am; Rep Frsh Cls; Rep Soph Cls; Rep Stu Cncl; JV Ftbl; Swmmng; Tennis; Hon Roll; Cert Awd For Bxbl Trnmnt 84-85; Cert From Ceta For Cmpltng 83; Rutgers U; Comp.

NAZARIO, ORLANDO; Academic HS; Jersey City, NJ; (Y); Boys Clb Am; Varsity Clb; School Musical; Stage Crew; Variety Show; Sec Jr Cls; Var Bsbl; L Powder Puff Ftbl; NJIT Urban Engrg Prog 86; Stevens Inst; Astront.

NEAL, JOE; Camden HS; Camden, NJ; (Y); Art Clb; Cmnty Wkr; Computer Clb; JA; Key Clb; Political Wkr; Stage Crew; Variety Show; Nwsp Rptr; Yrbk Rptr; Cmdn Co Coll Prjct Adv 86; Glssbro ST Coll 86; Boys ST Rep 86; Howard U; Psych.

NEALEN, LORI; Bishop George AHR HS; Piscataway, NJ; (Y); Hon Roll; Tchr Elem Educ.

NEALON, JOSEPH; St Joseph Regional HS; Spring Valley, NY; (Y); 52/225; VP Church Yth Grp; Cmnty Wkr; Red Cross Aide; Stu Cncl; JV Bsktbl; Var L Socr; Var L Trk; Hon Roll; Spanish NHS; Law.

NEELY, KRISTIN; Mercer Christian Acad; Hopewell, NJ; (S); 1/14; Church Yth Grp; Pres FCA; Band; Chorus; School Play; Yrbk Stf; Rep Jr Cls; Var Capt Bsktbl; Var Capt Socr; Var Sftbl; Fllwshp Of Christian Athlts-Hudle Offcr Of Yr 86; Distngshd Christian H S Stu 85; Extrordnry Stu Amer; Oral Roberts U.

NEELY, PHEEBE; Weequahic HS; Newark, NJ; (S); 9/355; Boy Scts; Church Yth Grp; Exploring; FBLA; Library Aide; Spanish Clb; Chorus; Cit Awd; NHS; Ms Spring Hmcmg Parade; Rutgers; Acctg.

NEGRON, ANA L; Dover HS; Dover, NJ; (Y); 23/183; Hon Roll; U Of Puerto Rico; Ped Nrs.

NEGRON, EVA M; Frank H Morrell HS; Irvington, NJ; (Y); ROTC; Chorus; FIT; Fashion Designer.

NEGRON, JOSE; Barringer HS; Newark, NJ; (Y); Pres Drama Clb; VP English Clb; Pres Science Clb; Pres Spanish Clb; Chorus; School Play; Pres Frsh Cls; Pres Soph Cls; Rep Tennis; High Hon Roll; 5 Mdls Sci, 1 Trphy & Mdl Spnsh, 1 Mdln Englsh, 1 Hstry & 13 Dplmas 9th Grd Grad 84; Dctr.

NEGRON, MARILYN; Our Lady Of Good Counsel; Newark, NJ; (Y); 4/106; Camera Clb; Drama Clb; PAVAS; Teachers Aide; School Musical; School Play; Hon Roll; NHS; Rlgn Stds Hnr 85; Biomed Engrng.

NEGRON, ROSE; Franklin HS; Somerset, NJ; (Y); 100/313; Church Yth Grp; Cmnty Wkr; Dance Clb; NFL; Office Aide; Political Wkr; Spanish Clb; Teachers Aide; Band; Chorus; Rutgers U; Cmmnctns.

NEIDICH, WENDY; Holy Cross HS; Edgewater Pk, NJ; (Y); Church Yth Grp; Band; Color Guard; Concert Band; Mrchg Band; Swmmng; Hon Roll; Co Cptn Color Grd 85-86; Color Grd Cptn 86-87; Holy Cross Rifle Tm Sprt Awd 86; Physcl Thrpy.

NELL, WILLIAM; Freehold Township HS; Freehold, NJ; (Y); 25/375; Computer Clb; High Hon Roll; NHS; Ntl Merit Ltr; Elec Engr.

NELSEN, GREGG; Red Bank Catholic HS; Red Bank, NJ; (Y); Cmnty Wkr; Math Clb; Math Tm; Political Wkr; Ski Clb; Nwsp Rptr; Nwsp Stf; JV Bsktbl; Socr; Var Trk; Gen Acad Exclince Awd 86; Bus Adm.

NELSON, CHRISTOPHER M; Hopewell Valley Regional HS; Trenton, NJ; (Y); Chorus; School Musical; School Play; Stage Crew; Rep Sr Cls; Rep Stu Cncl; Ntl Merit SF; NY U; Theory Prdctn.

NELSON, ELISSA; Westfield SR HS; Westfield, NJ; (Y); 11/514; Spanish Clb; SADD; Temple Yth Grp; Chorus; Church Choir; School Musical; High Hon Roll; NHS; Spanish NHS; Msc.

NELSON, PIERRE A; Washington Twp HS; Sewell, NJ; (Y); 116/480; Church Yth Grp; Debate Tm; German Clb; Model UN; Office Aide; Nwsp Rptr; Lit Mag; Rep Soph Cls; Rep Sr Cls; Stat Bsktbl; Elem Ed.

NELSON, RAQUEL; Camden HS; Camden, NJ; (Y); German Clb; Pep Clb; Teachers Aide; Church Choir; School Musical; School Play; Hon Roll; Prfct Atten Awd; MBST Awd 82-86; HSPT Mth & Readng Awd 82-83; Lab Tech.

NELSON, SHERRI; Weequahic HS; Newark, NJ; (Y); 18/400; Exploring; Chorus; Rep Stu Cncl; Cit Awd; Hon Roll; NHS; DE ST; Pre-Law.

NELSON, SIMONE; West Essex SR HS; North Caldwell, NJ; (Y); French Clb; Key Clb; Pep Clb; School Play; Nwsp Stf; Rep Stu Cncl; Var Cheerleading; High Hon Roll; NCTE Awd; Amer Acad Dramtc Arts NYC 85-86; Vrsty Comptn Chrldg Sqd 85-86.

NELSON, SUSAN; Holy Cross HS; Edgewater Pk, NJ; (Y); Am Leg Aux Girls St; Church Yth Grp; Yrbk Stf; Trk; Im Vllybl; Hon Roll; Rotary Awd; Rotary Yth Ldrshp Awd 86; Psychlgy.

NELSON, THOMAS; Red Bank Regional HS; Shrewsbury, NJ; (Y); Trs Church Yth Grp; German Clb; Ski Clb; Var JV Bsbl; Var JV Socr; High Hon Roll; Hon Roll; Ger Natl Hnr Soc 85; Amer Chem Soc Awd 85; Actg.

NELSON, TRISHA; Pitman HS; Pitman, NJ; (S); 10/150; Teachers Aide; Chorus; Concert Band; Drm Mjr(t); School Play; VP Frsh Cls; VP Soph Cls; VP Jr Cls; Hon Roll; NHS; S Jersey All ST Chorus 84-85; Olympc Mind Wrld Champs 85; Phy Thrpy.

NEMECKAY, DINA MARIE; Brick Township HS; Brick Town, NJ; (Y); 88/318; Key Clb; JV Sftbl; High Hon Roll; Assoc Human Soc Artwrk Publshd 85; Stockton ST Coll; Comm Art.

NEMETH, ELIZABETH; Our Lady Of Mercy Acad; Vineland, NJ; (Y); 3/25; Exploring; Hosp Aide; Service Clb; SADD; Chorus; Nwsp Stf; Sec Jr Cls; Cit Awd; High Hon Roll; Masonic Awd; Merit Schlrshp Rutgers Dean Smmr Schlr Prgm 85; Pres Acad Achvt Awd 86; Spnsh Excllnc Awd 86; Randolph-Macon Wmns Coll.

NEMETH JR, JOHN ANDREW; St Mary HS; S Amboy, NJ; (Y); 20/120; Quiz Bowl; JV Bsktbl; Var Socr; Stat Wrstlng; Livingston Coll; Comm.

NEMETH, MICHELE; Toms River North HS; Toms River, NJ; (Y); German Clb; Hosp Aide; Key Clb; High Hon Roll; Hon Roll; St Schlr; NJ Distngshd Schlr Awd 86; Drew U Schlr 86-87; Drew U; Chem.

NEPSHA, TINA; Jackson Memorial HS; Jackson, NJ; (Y); Art Clb; Dance Clb; Band; Concert Band; Lit Mag; Ftbl; Gym; Wt Lftg; High Hon Roll; Natl Am Math Achvt Awd 83-84; NY U; Physical Therapy.

NERAL, JOHN; Christian Brothers Acad; Pt Pleasant Bch, NJ; (Y); Cmnty Wkr; Teachers Aide; Chorus; Church Choir; Variety Show; Var L Bowling; Im Tennis; High Hon Roll; Accntng.

NESLER, MARK; Piscataway HS; Piscataway, NJ; (Y); Am Leg Boys St; Church Yth Grp; Varsity Clb; Var Capt Swmmng; Hon Roll; NHS; Accntnt.

NESTA, JULIANNE; Bloomfield SR HS; Bloomfield, NJ; (Y); 51/442; Chorus; Orch; JV Var Cheerleading; Sftbl; High Hon Roll; Hon Roll; Itln Clb 83-86; Straight Avrg Itln 86; Chrldg Cmptn 86.

NESTOR, MICHELE P; Sussex County Vo-Tech HS; Sussex, NJ; (S); #15 In Class; Nwsp Rptr; Nwsp Sprt Ed; High Hon Roll; Hon Roll; Jr NHS; NHS; Diesel Mech.

NEUENDORFF, NANCY; Seaucus HS; Secaucus, NJ; (S); 1/160; Hosp Aide; Math Clb; Ski Clb; Spanish Clb; Varsity Clb; Band; Nwsp Stf; Tennis; NHS; Spanish NHS; Ntl Math Exam Cert Of Hnr 85; Peditrcn.

NEUHAUS, LAUREN; Manalapan HS; Englishtown, NJ; (Y); 92/431; Church Yth Grp; Exploring; Trs 4-H; JCL; Drill Tm; Orch; School Musical; Yrbk Stf; Var Twrlr; 4-H Awd; 4-H Unt Awd Fr Cookng 84; Jr Clsscl Lge 86; Physcl Thrpy.

NEUMANN, MARC; Mt Olive HS; Flanders, NJ; (Y); AFS; Drama Clb; Ski Clb; Varsity Clb; VP Sr Cls; Rep Stu Cncl; Capt Crs Cntry; Var Trk; Hon Roll.

NEVARD, GARY; Clifton HS; Clifton, NJ; (Y); Computer Clb; Science Clb; Teachers Aide; Yrbk Stf; Lcrss; Hon Roll.

NEVES, SANDRA; Piscataway HS; Piscataway, NJ; (Y); Hosp Aide; Yrbk Stf; Pediatrician.

NEVILLE, LAURA J; Ocean Township HS; Oakhurst, NJ; (Y); 26/314; JCL; Latin Clb; Acpl Chr; Concert Band; Jazz Band; Mrchg Band; Pep Band; School Musical; Lit Mag; NHS; All ST Wnd Ensmbl 86; All Shore Chrs 86; All Shore Jaze Ensmbl 84-86; Temple U; Music.

NEVIN, CHRISTINE; Mt St Dominic Acad; Clifton, NJ; (Y); Ed Lit Mag; VP Sr Cls; Church Yth Grp; Hosp Aide; JCL; Quiz Bowl; Ski Clb; School Musical; Nwsp Rptr; Rep Soph Cls; Fordham U; Chmstry.

NEVISTICH, SANDRA; Livingston HS; Livingston, NJ; (Y); Pres AFS; Dance Clb; French Clb; German Clb; Math Clb; Math Tm; Ski Clb; JV Vllybl; Hon Roll; Hnr Rolls; Math Team Awd 86; Art Show Awd 84; Archtctr.

NEWHARD, STEFANIE; St James HS; Pennsville, NJ; (Y); Am Leg Aux Girls St; Pres Sec Hosp Aide; School Musical; Yrbk Stf; Rotary Awd; Nrsng.

NEWHOUSE, STACY; Ramsey HS; Ramsey, NJ; (Y); 46/230; Cmnty Wkr; Political Wkr; Yrbk Stf; Bsbl; Cheerleading; Score Keeper; Hon Roll; Pres Schlr; PA ST; Bus Adm.

NEWMAN, DEREK; Millburn SR HS; Short Hills, NJ; (Y); 1/247; Math Tm; Quiz Bowl; Science Clb; Acpl Chr; School Musical; School Play; High Hon Roll; Ntl Merit SF; Pres Schlr; Val; Stu Consrvtn Assoc H S Wrk Grp 85; Colmba Sci Hnrs Pgm 85; NJ All ST Chrs 85; Socl Scintst.

NEWMAN, GLEN; Toms River HS East; Toms River, NJ; (Y); 125/560; Boy Scts; Dance Clb; 4-H; Ski Clb; Band; Orch; Gym; Wrstlng; Vrsty Lttr Wrstlng 84-86; Vrsty Lttr Gymstcs 83-86; Trenton ST Coll.

NEWMAN, JEFF; Burlington City HS; Burlington, NJ; (Y); 1/202; Am Leg Boys St; Drama Clb; FTA; VP Key Clb; Band; Yrbk Stf; Pres Frsh Cls; VP Stu Cncl; High Hon Roll; NHS; Prncpls Club Of Dstngshd Stu 84, 85 & 86; Ldrshp Trng Camp Of NJ 85; Math Ed.

NEWMAN, KAREN; Long Branch HS; Long Branch, NJ; (Y); 10/267; Keywanettes; Science Clb; Temple Yth Grp; Rep Trs Frsh Cls; Rep Trs Soph Cls; Stat Bsktbl; Var Cheerleading; Capt Gym; Hon Roll; Sec NHS; Natl Hon Socty Sec 86; Vrsty Schlr Awd 83-86; Treas Of Clss 87 83-85; Psychlgy.

NEWMAN, LEIGHANN; Lakewood HS; Lakewood, NJ; (Y); Hosp Aide; Teachers Aide; RN.

NEWMAN, LORI; Union HS; Union, NJ; (Y); 1/550; Hosp Aide; Trs Temple Yth Grp; Nwsp Stf; Yrbk Stf; Tennis; High Hon Roll; Trs Jr NHS; NHS; Ntl Merit Ltr; NEDT Awd; Slctd Rsrch Jackson Lab ME 86; Chsn Rutgers Schlr 86; Biolgy Tm Rnkd #1 NJ 86; Biochmstry.

NEWMAN, PAMELA; Northern Highlands Regional HS; Uppr Saddle Riv, NJ; (Y); Church Yth Grp; Drama Clb; Church Choir; Concert Band; Mrchg Band; School Musical; Symp Band; Variety Show; Yrbk Stf; Lit Mag; Bergen Comm Coll; Dntl Hygn.

NEWMAN, SETH; Teaneck HS; Teaneck, NJ; (Y); Hosp Aide; Political Wkr; Temple Yth Grp; Chorus; Stage Crew; Im Fld Hcky; Hon Roll; NHS; Prfct Atten Awd; Phys Ther.

NEWMAN, TARA; East Brunswick HS; E Brunswick, NJ; (Y); 55/900; Dance Clb; Key Clb; Pep Clb; Spanish Clb; SADD; Temple Yth Grp; Variety Show; Yrbk Stf; Var Cheerleading.

NEWMARK, LORRAINE; Madison Central HS; Old Bridge, NJ; (Y); 28/360; French Clb; Nwsp Rptr; Yrbk Rptr; Frsh Cls; Soph Cls; Jr Cls; Stu Cncl; Stat Mgr Bsbl; Mgr Stat Wrstlng; NHS; Trenton ST Coll; Bus Admn.

NEWSOM, STEVEN; Maple Shade HS; Maple Shade, NJ; (Y); Am Leg Boys St; Cmnty Wkr; Bsbl; Bsktbl; Ftbl; Cit Awd; Hon Roll; Engrng.

NEWTON, LISA MARIE; Haddon Township HS; Westmont, NJ; (Y); School Play; Variety Show; Sec Frsh Cls; Sec Soph Cls; Rep Stu Cncl; JV Var Fld Hcky; Sftbl; JV Swmmng; JV Trk; Hon Roll; Gvrnmnt Day Camden Cnty Delegate 85; NJ ST Stu Cncl Cnvntn Delegate 85; Politcl Sci.

NEZ, VIRGINIA; Cherry Hill HS West; Cherry Hill, NJ; (Y); Dance Clb; Drama Clb; Hosp Aide; French Hon Soc; High Hon Roll; Hon Roll; Lion Awd; NHS; Piano Solo-Philadelphia Orch 83; Piano Solo Monmouth Symph Orch 84; Piano Solo Acad Mus Skipje Yugo 86.

NG, HOLLY; Trenton Central HS; Trenton, NJ; (Y); Aud/Vis; Church Yth Grp; Cmnty Wkr; Computer Clb; Key Clb; Library Aide; ROTC; Spanish Clb; Drill Tm; Orch.

NGUYEN, ANH; Mt St Dominic Academy; Little Falls, NJ; (Y); 2/54; Church Yth Grp; Intnl Clb; Pres JCL; Latin Clb; Library Aide; Chorus; VP Frsh Cls; Jr Cls; Stu Cncl; High Hon Roll; Christopher Columbus Essay Cntst 2nd Pl 83; Project Excel 86; Stevens Inst Of Tech; Math.

NGUYEN, DUY; Oakcrest HS; Hammonton, NJ; (Y); 4/255; French Clb; Math Clb; Var Socr; Var Tennis; High Hon Roll; Hon Roll; Sec NHS; U Of PA; Pre-Med.

NGUYEN, KY; Woodstown HS; Woodstown, NJ; (Y); Am Leg Boys St; Key Clb; Trs Frsh Cls; Trs Soph Cls; Trs Jr Cls; Trs Sr Cls; Rep Stu Cncl; Var Capt Socr; Var L Swmmng; Var L Tennis.

NGUYEN, LOANN; Randolph HS; Randolph, NJ; (Y); AFS; Church Yth Grp; Hon Roll; Fash Dsgn.

NGUYEN, PHONG; Academic HS; Jersey City, NJ; (Y); Art Clb; Spanish Clb; Ntl Merit Ltr; Merit Achvt Awd 85-86; Crdt Roll 85-86; Merit Roll 85-86; Stvns Inst Of Tech; Comp Engr.

NGUYUZA, MC NEAL H; Pascock HS; Montvale, NJ; (Y); JV Socr.

NIBBLING, LAURENCE; Clifton HS; Clifton, NJ; (Y); 111/637; Boys Clb Am; Exploring; Spanish Clb; Mrchg Band; Stage Crew; Bowling; Trk; Hon Roll; Jr NHS; Spanish NHS; Comm.

NIBBS, ANGELA; Notre Dame HS; Trenton, NJ; (Y); Red Cross Aide; SADD; Coach Actv; Mgr(s); JV Im Socr; Im Sftbl; Im Vllybl; Hon Roll; Diploma Of Merit-Spnsh 84-85; Cert Of Awd 86; Amer Coll Of Paris.

NICE, KATHY; Northern Burlington Co Reg HS; Bordentown, NJ; (Y); 35/197; Band; Church Choir; Concert Band; Jazz Band; Mrchg Band; Orch; Pep Band; School Musical; School Play; Symp Band; Louis Armsgrong Jazz Awd 86; Berklee Awd 86; Kathryn Margaret Walter Schlrshp 86; Trenton ST Coll; Music.

NICEFORO, LAURA; Matawan Regional HS; Matawan, NJ; (S); 24/273; Camera Clb; Church Yth Grp; Capt Computer Clb; Hosp Aide; Q&S; Ed Nwsp Phtg; Co-Capt Fld Hcky; Gov Hon Prg Awd; NHS; Math Clb; Monmouth Arts Fndtn, Tn Arts Fstvl, Potry Awd 82; Achv Itln 82-85; Fld Hcky Rook Yr 83; Invstmnt Bnkr.

NICHOLAS, MARK; Central Regional HS; Bayville, NJ; (Y); Ski Clb; Temple Yth Grp; Var Ftbl; JV Tennis; Var Trk; JV Wrstlng.

NICHOLS, BRIAN; Penns Grove HS; Carneys Point, NJ; (Y); 3/192; Am Leg Boys St; Pres Soph Cls; Pres Jr Cls; Pres Sr Cls; Rep Stu Cncl; Stat Bsktbl; Ftbl; Socr; Tennis; NHS; All Amer Schlr Athlt 83-84; Scty Dstngshd Amer HS Stu 84-86; U S Mltry Acad; Engrng.

NICHOLS, CATHERINE; Saint James HS; Mickleton, NJ; (Y); 16/73; Church Yth Grp; Church Choir; School Musical; School Play; Yrbk Stf; Hon Roll; Yth Mnstry Awd; Tampa U; Mrne Sci.

NICHOLS, ROBERT A; Kittatinny Regional HS; Newton, NJ; (S); 5/164; VP Church Yth Grp; Math Tm; Science Clb; Chorus; Church Choir; Jazz Band; Madrigals; High Hon Roll; NHS; St Schlr; Johns Hopkins U; Elec Engrng.

NICHOLSON, YVETTE; South Plainfield HS; S Plainfield, NJ; (Y); 1/260; Am Leg Aux Girls St; Math Tm; Band; Nwsp Sprt Ed; Capt Bsktbl; Capt Sftbl; Sec NHS; Computer Clb; Spanish Clb; Varsity Clb; Natl Achvt Schlrshp; NJ Distngshd Schlr; Princeton U; Bio.

NICKLOW, SHARON; West Side HS; Newark, NJ; (Y); Boy Scts; Color Guard; Nwsp Stf; Yrbk Stf; Rep Frsh Cls; Rep Soph Cls; Rep Jr Cls; Rep Stu Cncl; Centenary Coll; Comp Sci.

NICOL, LIA; Manasquan HS; Brielle, NJ; (Y); 88/227; Drama Clb; Acpl Chr; Chorus; School Musical; School Play; Stage Crew; Mgr(s); Score Keeper; Socr; Vllybl.

NICOLELLA, JENNIFER; Bernards HS; Bernardsville, NJ; (Y); Pres 4-H; Teachers Aide; 4-H Awd; Hon Roll; DE Valley Coll; Anml Hsbndry.

NICOLETTI, RICHARD C; Whippany Park HS; N Ft Myers, FL; (Y); Am Leg Boys St; Boy Scts; Church Yth Grp; Cmnty Wkr; DECA; Letterman Clb; Radio Clb; Ski Clb; Varsity Clb; Var Crs Cntry; Own Auto Svc.

NICOLL, PAMELA R; Middlesex County Voctnl & Tech HS; Spotswood P O, NJ; (Y); Church Yth Grp; Cmnty Wkr; Library Aide; Rep Stu Cncl; Hon Roll; Pastry Arts.

NICOLOSI, JOANNE; De Paul HS; Wayne, NJ; (S); 62/169; Church Yth Grp; Cmnty Wkr; Hosp Aide; Red Cross Aide; Yrbk Ed-Chief; Yrbk Stf; Hon Roll; Aud/Vis; Math Tm; Chorus.

NICOSIA, MARK; Phillipsburg Catholic HS; Phillipsburg, NJ; (Y); Aud/Vis; CAP; Ski Clb; Lit Mag; Var Capt Socr; French Clb; Chorus; Stage Crew; Bowling; JV Co-Capt Golf; DRC Sccr Chmpnshp Tm 85; Mst Vlbl Dfnsv Plyr 85; Easton Exprs Pltcl Cartoon Cntst Wnr 86; NY U; Film.

NIECE, KATHRYN; Warren Hills Reg SR HS; Oxford, NJ; (Y); AFS; German Clb; Key Clb; Var Bsktbl; High Hon Roll; NHS; Bus Mgmt.

NIEDERMAIER, SCOTT; Hamilton West HS; Trenton, NJ; (S); Key Clb; Band; Drm Mjr(t); Madrigals; Mrchg Band; School Musical; Symp Band; Pres Jr Cls; Var Tennis; Drama Clb; Outstndng Frshmn-Band 83-84; Dir Band Awd 83-84; Theatre.

NIELSEN, TRACEY; S Hunterdon Regional HS; Lambertville, NJ; (Y); 11/87; Am Leg Aux Girls St; Key Clb; School Play; Stu Cncl; Hon Roll; Church Yth Grp; Cmnty Wkr; Dance Clb; Teachers Aide; Stage Crew; Elem Ed.

NIEPORTE, WILLIAM; Don Bosco Prep HS; Franklin Lks, NJ; (Y); Chess Clb; Church Yth Grp; Cmnty Wkr; Debate Tm; 4-H; French Clb; Math Clb; Science Clb; Teachers Aide; Band; Physician.

NIERADKA, DAVID J; Clifton HS; Clifton, NJ; (Y); 83/637; Am Leg Boys St; Boy Scts; French Clb; Math Clb; Trs Frsh Cls; Bsktbl; Ftbl; Trk; Hon Roll; Jr NHS; Law.

NIERSTEDT, JANICE; Roselle Catholic HS; Roselle, NJ; (Y); 4-H; Girl Scts; Ski Clb; School Play; Var Cheerleading; Im Gym; Var Socr; JV Swmmng; Hon Roll; Chld Psych.

NIESHALLA, THOMAS; Don Bosco Prep; Oakland, NJ; (S); 1/186; Church Yth Grp; German Clb; Orch; Nwsp Rptr; Socr; Hon Roll; NHS; Don Bosco Prep Schlrshp 84 & 85; Hghst Hstry Avg 85; Engrng.

NIETO, MICHAEL K; Christian Brothers Acad; Hazlet, NJ; (S); 12/247; Church Yth Grp; Civic Clb; School Musical; Coach Actv; Lcrss; NHS; Boy Scts; Im Capt Bsktbl; Im Capt Bowling; Im Socr; Eagle Scout, Ordr Of Arrow, JR Asstnt Sctmstr 85-86; Yrbk Sect Edtr 85-86; Euchrstc Minister 85-86; Pre-Law.

NIETO, PATRICIA; St Marye HS; Parlin, NJ; (Y); Cmnty Wkr; Secr Sci.

NIEVES, CARMEN; Kingsway Regional HS; Swedesboro, NJ; (Y); Church Yth Grp; Drama Clb; Science Clb; Spanish Clb; Mrchg Band; Yrbk Stf; Pres Frsh Cls; Powder Puff Ftbl; Trk; Glassboro ST Clg; Law.

NIEVES, CARMENCITA; Out Lady Of Good Coucel HS; Newark, NJ; (Y); 5/106; Cmnty Wkr; Science Clb; Church Choir; School Musical; School Play; Cheerleading; Twrlr; Hon Roll; NHS; Spnsh Awd 84-85; Natl Soc Mbrshp Awd 85; All-Schl Prod Play Cert Awd 85; Pedtrc Nrs.

NIEVES, GLADYS; James J Ferris HS; Jersey City, NJ; (Y); Science Clb; Teachers Aide; Rep Stu Cncl; Hon Roll; NHS; Pedtrcn.

NIEVES, SONIA; Oakcrest HS; Elwood, NJ; (Y); 19/250; French Clb; GAA; VP Spanish Clb; Trs SADD; Church Choir; Yrbk Ed-Chief; JV Tennis; Var Trk; Hon Roll; Prfct Atten Awd; Vrsty Schlr For B Avrg Yr Rnd; 1st Pl Atlntc Cnty Trck & Fld Relay 85.

NILLA, ERIC; East Brunswick HS; E Brunswick, NJ; (Y); Ski Clb; Spanish Clb; Jazz Band; Nwsp Stf; Fld Hcky; Ice Hcky; Hon Roll; Rutgers; Bus Mgmt.

NILLES, BONNIE; Toms River High School South; Toms River, NJ; (Y); 26/360; Var Mgr(s); Powder Puff Ftbl; Score Keeper; JV Socr; Hon Roll; Rutgers; Sci.

NINE, JENNA; Chatham Township HS; Chatham, NJ; (Y); 58/138; Church Yth Grp; Key Clb; Model UN; Jazz Band; Yrbk Stf; Rptr Stu Cncl; Stat Trk; Cmnty Wkr; Library Aide; Pep Clb; Secy Presbytn SR Hgh Yth Fllwshp 86; Pharm.

NING, ANDREA S; West Essex Regional HS; Escondido, CA; (Y); 7/350; Am Leg Aux Girls St; Church Yth Grp; VP Model UN; Quiz Bowl; Science Clb; Trs Stu Cncl; Ntl Merit SF; Computer Clb; Library Aide; Band; Lib Awd 86; Ntl Fed Of Music Clbs 5 Gold Cups 80-86; Grdn St Dist Schlr 86; Paderewski Mdl 83; Stanford U; Pol Sci.

NISSENBAUM, ROBERT; Manalapan HS; Manalapan, NJ; (Y); 13/400; Chess Clb; Yrbk Rptr; Yrbk Stf; Im Socr; JV Trk; NHS; Intl Bus & Law.

NITTI, TARA; Toms River East HS; Toms River, NJ; (Y); Intnl Clb; Math Tm; Ski Clb; Spanish Clb; Yrbk Stf; Jr Cls; Stat Bsktbl; JV Fld Hcky; Hon Roll; Stck Brkr.

NITTING, THOMAS; Dickinson HS; Jersey City, NJ; (Y); Mrchg Band; Orch; School Play; Cook Coll; Envrnmntl Hlth.

NITTOLO, DINA MARIE; West Essex HS; Roseland, NJ; (Y); Yrbk Stf; Hon Roll; Italn Achvt Awd 85; Htl Mgmt.

NIVISON, KRISTIN; Red Bank Regional HS; Little Silver, NJ; (Y); Key Clb; Ski Clb; Stu Cncl; Crs Cntry; Socr; Trk; Hon Roll; Spanish NHS; Bus.

NIXON, SUSAN; Matawan Regional HS; Matawan, NJ; (Y); 76/286; Sec Trs DECA; Stat Bsbl; Stat Socr; Stat Wrstlng; Presdntl Acadmc Fitness Awd 86; Montclair ST Coll; Bus Admin.

NIZAMOFF, STEVE; Toms River High School North; Toms River, NJ; (Y); Ski Clb; Ftbl; Trk; Wrstlng; High Hon Roll; Arch.

NOBLE, JENNIFER; Northern Highlands HS; Montclair, NJ; (Y); Church Yth Grp; Key Clb; Ski Clb; Stage Crew; Yrbk Stf; Var Cheerleading; 1st Pl Gymnstcs 84; Mssn Clb 84; Montclair ST Coll; Bus.

NOBLEJAS, ANNA; Notre Dame HS; Morrisville, PA; (Y); Service Clb; Chorus; Stage Crew; Yrbk Stf; Hon Roll.

NOCITO, FRANK; Holy Cross HS; Delran, NJ; (Y); Church Yth Grp; Church Choir; School Musical; Yrbk Phtg; Rep Frsh Cls; Pres Soph Cls; Pres Jr Cls; Pres Stu Cncl; Hon Roll; Camera Clb; Johnson & Wales; Chef.

NODARI, GINA; Montville HS; Montville, NJ; (Y); 97/272; Drama Clb; FBLA; Intnl Clb; Key Clb; OEA; Color Guard; Flag Corp; School Musical; Ldrshp Awd Schlrshp Music Dept 86; Frlgh Dcknsn U; Bus Admin.

NOEL, CASSANDRA; East Brunswick HS; E Brunswick, NJ; (Y); Church Yth Grp; Drama Clb; French Clb; Office Aide; SADD; Acpl Chr; Chorus; Color Guard; School Musical; Top 10 Fnlst Mod Miss NJ Scholar Pagnt 85; Rutgers Coll Phrmcy; Phrmcst.

NOL, LINA; Morris Catholic HS; Pine Brook, NJ; (Y); 9/165; Sec French Clb; Math Clb; Natl Beta Clb; Service Clb; Swmmng; High Hon Roll; NHS; Pres Schlr; U CT; Pharm.

NOLAN, COLLEEN; Holy Cross HS; Willingboro, NJ; (Y); 65/370; French Clb; Mgr Bsktbl; Mgr(s); Im Vllybl; Elem Ed Tchr.

NOLAN, GEORGE; St Peters Prep; Westfield, NJ; (Y); 175/210; Cmnty Wkr; Ski Clb; Band; Concert Band; Jazz Band; Yrbk Rptr.

NOLAN, JOHN P; Moorestown HS; Moorestown, NJ; (Y); Am Leg Boys St; Boy Scts; Cmnty Wkr; Latin Clb; JV Bsbl; Var Capt Socr; Var Capt Swmmng; Hon Roll; Pilot Eng Prog HS SRS Temple U 86; NJ ST Swmng Champshps 86; Georgetown; Pol Sci.

NOLAN, MICHAEL; St John Vianney HS; Hazlet, NJ; (Y); Var L Bsbl; Var L Bsktbl; Hon Roll; Commnctns.

NORBY, DENISE; West Morris Mendham HS; Chester, NJ; (Y); 5/307; Dance Clb; Hosp Aide; Library Aide; Math Tm; Concert Band; Jazz Band; Mrchg Band; Symp Band; Bausch & Lomb Sci Awd; High Hon Roll; 1st ST Bio ST Sci Day 86; Area Band Clarinet 83-84; All N Jersey Regn Symphnc Band 85; Davidson Coll; Biochem.

NORDBY, BRITT; Lakeland Reg HS; Ringwood, NJ; (Y); 23/340; Church Yth Grp; Intnl Clb; Ski Clb; Yrbk Stf; Rep Jr Cls; Rep Sr Cls; Rep Stu Cncl; L Var Crs Cntry; High Hon Roll; NHS; BS; Cosmtcl Chem.

NORDMAN, GLENN; Park Ridge HS; Park Ridge, NJ; (Y); 91/108; Socr; Franklin Pierce Coll; Bus.

NORIEGA, SAMIR; Hackensack HS; Hakcnesack, NJ; (Y); 5/375; Am Leg Boys St; Pres French Clb; Nwsp Rptr; Nwsp Sprt Ed; Capt Socr; Capt Wrstlng; Pres French Hon Soc; High Hon Roll; Jr NHS; NHS; Acad Decthlt-B Grp-Mth Brnz Mdlst 86; MIT; Chem Engrng.

NORIN, SCOTT; West Morris Mendham HS; Chester, NJ; (Y); Church Yth Grp; Radio Clb; Ski Clb; Band; Concert Band; Drm Mjr(t); Jazz Band; Mrchg Band; Var Trk; Im Mgr Vllybl; Engrng.

NORMAN, BENJAMIN E; Rancocas Valley Regional HS; Mt Holly, NJ; (Y); Am Leg Boys St; Church Yth Grp; Var Capt Bsktbl; JV Tennis; JV Trk; High Hon Roll; Bus Mgmt.

NORMAN, JULIE; Ocean Township HS; Wayside, NJ; (Y); Drama Clb; Ski Clb; SADD; Thesps; School Musical; Rep Jr Cls; Stu Cncl.

NORMAN, MICHELE; Governor Livingston HS; Bradenton, FL; (Y); 1/195; Church Yth Grp; Frsh Cls; Soph Cls; Jr Cls; Stu Cncl; Cheerleading; NHS; Ntl Merit Schol; St Schlr; Val; Schrlshp Amu Assoc U Women 86; Schl Math,Hist Awd; U VA; Bus.

NORMANN, HOLLY; Howell HS; Freehold, NJ; (Y); 17/400; German Clb; JV Sftbl; Monmouth Coll; Bus Admin.

NOROWSKI, RAYMOND; Glen Rock SR HS; Glen Rock, NJ; (Y); 47/153; DECA; French Clb; Band; Hon Roll; Jr NHS; Rutgers U; Bus.

NORRIS, KRISTIN; Pineland Regional HS; Tuckerton, NJ; (S); 6/160; Am Leg Aux Girls St; Drama Clb; Yrbk Stf; Lit Mag; VP Jr Cls; VP Sr Cls; JV Capt Cheerleading; Var Tennis; NHS; Mst Outstndng Stu 85; NJ Gov Tchng Schlrs Pgm Alt 86; GEORGIAN Court Coll; Ed.

NORRIS, PAUL; Bridgewater Raritan HS East; Bridgewater, NJ; (Y); Math Tm; Sr Cls; Golf; Hon Roll; NHS; Lehigh U; Bus.

NORTH, CINDY; Columbia HS; Maplewood, NJ; (Y); Aud/Vis; Cmnty Wkr; Hosp Aide; Spanish Clb; SADD; Nwsp Rptr; Rep Frsh Cls; Rep Soph Cls; Rep Jr Cls; Rep Sr Cls.

NORTHOVER, DWIGHT; Grank H Morrel HS; Irvington, NJ; (Y); Socr; Hon Roll; NJIT; Cvl Engr.

NORTON, DANIEL; Roxbury HS; Mt Arlington, NJ; (Y); High Hon Roll; JC Awd; NHS; Morris County Coll; Mech Engrng.

NORWOOD, BETH; Scotch Plains-Fanwood HS; Scotch Pl, NJ; (Y); SADD; Flag Corp; Hon Roll; Comm Art.

NORWOOD, HUGH D; Toms River East HS; Toms River, NJ; (Y); 27/484; Chess Clb; Church Yth Grp; Math Tm; Model UN; Quiz Bowl; Band; Concert Band; Jazz Band; Mrchg Band; Orch; Law.

NOSEK, SHARON; Woodstown HS; Woodstown, NJ; (Y); Key Clb; Spanish Clb; Yrbk Phtg; Yrbk Rptr; Yrbk Stf; Stat Bsktbl; Var Score Keeper; JV Swmmng; Hon Roll; NHS; Hgh Schl Sci Fair 1st Pl 84-85; Thomas Edison Sci Fair 1st Pl 84-85; Del Valley Sci Fair 3rd Pl 85; Slgy.

NOTARE, ROBERT; Bloomfield HS; Bloomfield, NJ; (Y); Hon Roll; Rutgers; Ecnmcs.

NOTHACKER, CHRISTINE; Paulsboro HS; Gibbstown, NJ; (Y); 4/130; Church Yth Grp; Library Aide; Nwsp Stf; Mat Maids; Co-Capt Sftbl; Capt Tennis; Wt Lftg; High Hon Roll; Hon Roll; Kiwanis Awd; Schlrshp Trste Frnk Flwrs Trst 86; Grdn ST Schlrshp 86; Glassboro ST Coll; Elem Educ.

NOVAK, CHRISTINE; Toms River South HS; Beachwood, NJ; (Y); 37/300; Band; Concert Band; Mrchg Band; Symp Band; Var Sftbl; High Hon Roll; NHS; Prfct Atten Awd; Grgn Crt Coll; Elem Ed.

NOVAK, KAREN; Spotswood HS; Spotswood, NJ; (Y); 31/189; Rep Cmnty Wkr; Intnl Clb; Office Aide; Band; Concert Band; Mrchg Band; Orch; Ed Yrbk Stf; Var Mgr(s); Hon Roll; Mgmt.

NOVAK, MARGO; Columbia HS; S Orange, NJ; (Y); 49/541; Church Yth Grp; Cmnty Wkr; Intnl Clb; Latin Clb; Chorus; Concert Band; Mrchg Band; Symp Band; Yrbk Stf; Im Sftbl; Lib Arts.

NOVAK, MICHELLE D; Indian Hills HS; Oakland, NJ; (Y); Art Clb; Pres Camera Clb; Drama Clb; Q&S; Band; Drm & Bgl; Mrchg Band; Nwsp Phtg; Yrbk Phtg; Lit Mag; PTSO Awds 83-84; RI Schl Of Design; Grphcnt.

NOVELLA, JOSEPH; Pennsauken SR HS; Pennsauken, NJ; (Y); 8/365; Boy Scts; Church Yth Grp; French Clb; Math Clb; Model UN; School Musical; Var Bowling; JV Tennis; NHS; Pres Schlr; Govnrs Tchg Schlrs Pgm NJ 86; Hofstra U; Sec Ed.

NOVELLINO, GINA; Woodbridge HS; Fords, NJ; (Y); 28/400; Church Yth Grp; Library Aide; Acpl Chr; Chorus; Swing Chorus; Hon Roll; NHS; Spanish NHS.

NOVEMBRE, CARMINE; Morris Catholic HS; Flanders, NJ; (Y); 47/142; Church Yth Grp; Hosp Aide; Rep Stu Cncl; Hon Roll; Peer Counselng 85; Interact Clb Pres 85.

NOVEMBRE, ROBT; Lenape Valley Regional HS; Netcong, NJ; (Y); 22/260; Church Yth Grp; Civic Clb; French Clb; Intnl Clb; Key Clb; Latin Clb; Pep Clb; Service Clb; SADD; Nwsp Ed-Chief; Lenape Schlr Awd 85; Boston U; Pre-Med.

NOVINA, JULIA; Northern Valley Reginal HS; Harrington Pk, NJ; (Y); AFS; Ski Clb; Chorus; Color Guard; Jazz Band; School Musical; Stage Crew; Nwsp Rptr; Lit Mag; Qlty Cir Clb Ldrshp Cmmtee 86-87; Englsh.

NOWACKY, NICOLE; Clifton HS; Clifton, NJ; (Y); 6/259; Office Aide; Chorus; Rep Frsh Cls; Rep Stu Cncl; Var Bowling; JV Crs Cntry; Pom Pon; Hon Roll.

NOWAKIWSKY, LISA; Mount St Dominic Acad; S Orange, NJ; (Y); VP Church Yth Grp; Civic Clb; Cmnty Wkr; Hosp Aide; Intnl Clb; Spanish Clb; Teachers Aide; Nwsp Phtg; Nwsp Rptr; Yrbk Stf; William & Mary; Comm.

NOWICKI, KATIE; Toms River HS South; Toms River, NJ; (Y); 27/375; Am Leg Aux Girls St; Ski Clb; Trs Frsh Cls; Stu Cncl; Cheerleading; Hon Roll; NHS; Voice Dem Awd; Cultrl Olympcs Awd 1st Pl-Art Div; Villanova U; Bus.

NUGENT, EDWARD; Paramus HS; Paramus, NJ; (Y); Sec Am Leg Boys St; VP Church Yth Grp; Lit Mag; Im Bsktbl; Capt Crs Cntry; Im Socr; Capt Trk; Im Vllybl; Corporal Christn Svc Brigade 84; Messiah Coll; History.

NUGENT, KEVIN; Oratory Catholic Prep HS; Livingston, NJ; (Y); Church Yth Grp; Nwsp Ed-Chief; Nwsp Phtg; Nwsp Rptr; Im Bsktbl; Im Ftbl; Im Vllybl; High Hon Roll; Hon Roll; Farleigh Dickensn NJ; Dntstry.

NUGENT, VALERIE; Parsippany HS; Lk Hiawatha, NJ; (S); Church Yth Grp; Intnl Clb; Ski Clb; Varsity Clb; Pres Concert Band; Drm Mjr(t); Jazz Band; Mrchg Band; School Musical; Symp Band; Outstndg Drum Major Awd 85; Lynchburg Coll; Advrtsg.

NUGUID, MARIEPAZ; Marylawn Of The Oranges HS; Maplewood, NJ; (Y); 15/52; Camera Clb; French Clb; French Hon Soc; Hon Roll; Seton Hall U; Pre Law.

NUKK, RANDY; Mahwah HS; Mahwah, NJ; (Y); 49/190; Latin Clb; Math Clb; Ski Clb; Yrbk Stf; Trs Sr Cls; Coach Actv; Var Ftbl; JV Trk; Wt Lftg; Hon Roll.

NUNER, JENNIFER C; Kittatinny Regional HS; Newton, NJ; (S); Hosp Aide; Spanish Clb; Capt L Swmmng; Trk; High Hon Roll; Hon Roll; NHS; Rotary Awd; Rtry Yth Exchng S Africa 84-85; Hood Coll.

NUNES, KENNETH J; Raritan HS; Keyport, NJ; (Y); 1/300; Am Leg Boys St; Art Clb; Math Clb; Science Clb; Var Tennis; Bausch & Lomb Sci Awd; High Hon Roll; NHS; Val; 3rd Pl Ntl Chmpn In Artistic Roller Skating 85.

NUNES, SEAN; Frank H Morrell HS; Irvington, NJ; (Y); 51/500; Yrbk Sprt Ed; Bsbl; Socr; Hon Roll; Embry Riddle Aeron U; Aeronatcl.

NUNEZ, CRIS; Mother Seton Regional HS; Union, NJ; (Y); 29/118; Mgr Church Yth Grp; Mgr Cmnty Wkr; Mgr Girl Scts; Mgr Hosp Aide; Mgr SADD; School Musical; Stage Crew; Rep Frsh Cls; Rep Soph Cls; Rep Jr Cls; Rutgers; Scl Wrk.

NUNEZ, HARRY S; Memorial HS; West New York, NJ; (Y); Chess Clb; Wt Lftg; Comp Tech.

NUNZIATO, CHRIS P; Cliffside Park HS; Cliffside Pk, NJ; (Y); 17/236; Boys Clb Am; Math Clb; Spanish Clb; Stu Cncl; Crs Cntry; Trk; NHS; Rutgers; Engrg.

NURSE, NONA; Frank H Morrell HS; Irvington, NJ; (Y); Am Leg Aux Girls St; VP Church Yth Grp; Cmnty Wkr; Debate Tm; Latin Clb; Church Choir; VP Frsh Cls; High Hon Roll; NHS; Cornell U; Psychol.

NUSSBAUM, MINDY RAE; Parsippany Hills HS; Parsippany, NJ; (Y); 39/317; Cmnty Wkr; Temple Yth Grp; Thesps; Pres Chorus; Jazz Band; School Musical; Variety Show; DAR Awd; Hon Roll; NHS; Thomas J Bradley Vocal Achvt Awd 86; John E Sheehy Scholar 86; Players Awd 86; U Hartford; Music Mgmt.

NUSZ, NANCI; West Essex Regional HS; N Caldwell, NJ; (Y); 23/350; Sec AFS; Church Yth Grp; German Clb; Hosp Aide; Model UN; Var L Swmmng; High Hon Roll; Jr NHS; NHS; U DE; Lang.

NUTLAY, PAMELA; Hunterdon Central HS; Ringoes, NJ; (Y); 13/548; Hosp Aide; Scholastic Bowl; Temple Yth Grp; Chorus; Nwsp Ed-Chief; Ed Nwsp Stf; French Hon Soc; NHS; Hon Roll; Library Aide; ST Teen Arts Fstvl Piano; Mck Trail Team Lwyr; Pre-Law.

NUTT, BRIAN; Holy Cross HS; Columbus, NJ; (Y); Computer Clb; Ski Clb; Mgr Ftbl; Cit Awd; Elks Awd; Hon Roll; Vet Med.

NYERGES, MARK J; Steinert Hamilton HS East HS; Hamilton Sq, NJ; (Y); Band; Concert Band; Jazz Band; Mrchg Band; Orch; Pep Band; School Musical; Symp Band; Msc Schlrshp From Widener U & Hs 86; Widener U; Engrng.

O BANION, SUE; Bayonne HS; Bayonne, NJ; (Y); Art Clb; Ski Clb; SADD; Hon Roll; Commercl Art.

O BOYLE, BRIAN F; Union HS; Union, NJ; (Y); Aud/Vis; Church Yth Grp; Stage Crew; Yrbk Ed-Chief; Var L Ftbl; L Trk; Wt Lftg.

O BOYLE, JEFFREY M; Morris Knolls HS; Denville, NJ; (Y); 43/367; Quiz Bowl; Nwsp Rptr; Ed Nwsp Stf; Ftbl; High Hon Roll; Hon Roll; Pres Schlr; Morris Knolls Summa Awd Acdmc Excllnc 90 Or Bttr Avg 84; SR Lttl Leag 84; Seton Hall U; Engl.

O BOYLE, TIMOTHY F; West Orange HS; W Orange, NJ; (Y); 38/400; Aud/Vis; Drama Clb; Varsity Clb; Band; School Musical; Nwsp Bus Mgr; Yrbk Stf; L Var Trk; CC Awd; Voice Dem Awd; Princlpls Aid Awd; Rutgers Coll; Pharmacy.

O BRIEN, AMY; Northwest Christian Schl; Hamburg, NJ; (Y); 2/7; Church Yth Grp; Hosp Aide; Teachers Aide; Yrbk Ed-Chief; Vllybl; Cnty Coll Of Morris; Nrsng.

O BRIEN, COLLEEN; Villa Victoria Acad; Yardley, PA; (Y); English Clb; Acpl Chr; School Musical; Yrbk Ed-Chief; Yrbk Phtg; Lit Mag; Bsktbl; Socr; Sftbl; Hon Roll; Syracuse; Communications.

O BRIEN, DAVID; Morris Catholic HS; Morris Plains, NJ; (Y); 3/159; Church Yth Grp; Letterman Clb; Nwsp Sprt Ed; Trs Sr Cls; JV Var Ftbl; JV Var Trk; High Hon Roll; NHS; Ntl Merit Schol; Cmnty Wkr; Emerson Elctrc Schlrshp 86; Boston U; Cmmnctns.

O BRIEN, JAMES; Paramus Catholic Boys HS; Ridgefield Pk, NJ; (Y); Boy Scts; Bsbl; Ftbl; Wt Lftg; English.

O BRIEN, KATHIE; Mainland Regional HS; Somers Pt, NJ; (Y); 60/320; Trs Jr Cls; Stu Cncl; Mgr(s); Sftbl; Trk; Hon Roll; Bus.

O BRIEN, KEVIN; Westfield SR HS; Westfield, NJ; (Y); 15/511; Boy Scts; VP Chess Clb; Spanish Clb; Nwsp Phtg; Nwsp Stf; Hon Roll; NHS; Spanish NHS; Eagle Scout 85.

O BRIEN, MICHAEL; Northern Burlington HS; Mc Guire AFB, NJ; (Y); Boy Scts; Church Choir; School Musical; Rep Jr Cls; Rep Sr Cls; Rep Stu Cncl; Gym; Swmmng; Egl By Sct 86 Offcrs Wvs Clb Schlrshp; St Edwards U; Hstry Tchr.

O BRIEN, MOLLIE; Morristown HS; Convent Station, NJ; (Y); 100/404; Church Yth Grp; Cmnty Wkr; GAA; JCL; Key Clb; Latin Clb; Lit Mag; Stat Bsktbl; Var Fld Hcky; Var Lcrss; Fairfield U; Engl.

O BRIEN, SHAUN; Southern Regional HS; Manahawkin, NJ; (Y); 2/380; French Clb; Model UN; Bowling; Bausch & Lomb Sci Awd; High Hon Roll; NHS; Ntl Merit Ltr; Cert Of Excllnc Frm Fed Of Alliances Francaises; Cert Of Merit-Rider Coll Frgn Lang Frnsc Trnmnt.

O BYRNE, PATRICIA G; Red Bank Catholic HS; West Long Branch, NJ; (Y); 13/300; Cmnty Wkr; NFL; Spanish Clb; Lit Mag; Pres Jr Cls; Pres Stu Cncl; Var Tennis; High Hon Roll; Kiwanis Awd; Powder Puff Ftbl; Cook Coll Hnrs Pgm 86-87; U Of Ntre Dm.

O CONNELL, BRIAN; Red Bank Catholic HS; Tinton Falls, NJ; (Y); Var Bsktbl; Var Socr; Principl Awd Excel In Gym 84-85; Math.

O CONNELL, JOAN M; Ramapo HS; Wyckoff, NJ; (Y); 63/310; Church Yth Grp; Ed Yrbk Stf; Lit Mag; Gym; High Hon Roll; Hon Roll; 2nd Pl NJ Dept Enrgy Expo Awds Cmpttn 86; Cert Of Merit Accntng I 85; Pres Acdmc Fit Awd 86; U Of Hartford; Fine Arts.

O CONNOR, CHRIS; Hackettstown HS; Belvidere, NJ; (Y); Letterman Clb; Bsbl; Bsktbl; Ftbl; All Conf Ftbl & Bsbl 86; Bus.

O CONNOR, CLAIRE E; Neumann Prep; Lincoln Park, NJ; (Y); 10/83; Am Leg Aux Girls St; Cmnty Wkr; Hosp Aide; Stage Crew; Nwsp Stf; Cit Awd; High Hon Roll; NHS; Creighton U; Med.

O CONNOR, KEVIN; Hudson Catholic HS; Secaucus, NJ; (Y); 67/182; Cmnty Wkr; Exploring; Hon Roll; Rutgers; Engr.

O CONNOR, PATRICIA; Manalapan HS; Englishtown, NJ; (Y); 72/431; Cmnty Wkr; Drill Tm; Mrchg Band; Yrbk Phtg; Yrbk Stf; Im Socr; Psych.

O CONNOR, RAYMOND; Northern Burlington HS; Juliustown, NJ; (Y); Church Yth Grp; Drama Clb; Var Bsbl; Var Bsktbl; Var Capt Ftbl; Hon Roll; Hnrd Ftbl Unsung Hero 85-86; Mercer Cnty CC; Bus Admin.

O DELL, ERIC J; Cherry Hill East HS; Cherry Hill, NJ; (Y); Am Leg Boys St; PAVAS; Jazz Band; Mrchg Band; Orch; School Musical; Variety Show; Hon Roll; JP Sousa Awd; NHS; Music Boosters Scholar Outstndg Svc 86; All S Jersey Wnd Ens & Orch 85 & 86; Bucknell U; Bus.

O DELL JR, JOHN; North Bergen HS; North Bergen, NJ; (Y); 72/475; Political Wkr; Ski Clb; SADD; Nwsp Stf; Rep Jr Cls; Trs Sr Cls; Var Ftbl; Var Tennis; Hon Roll; JV Bsbl; Rsn Hnr Soc 85-86; Iona Coll; Bus Admin.

O DOM, DENISE; Frank H Morrell HS; Irvington, NJ; (Y); Art Clb; Church Yth Grp; CAP; Debate Tm; Drama Clb; School Play; JV Bsktbl; Trk; Compete For Entrnce To West Pointe 86; Seton Hall U; Comp Sci.

O DONALD, COLLEEN; Penns Grove HS; Penns Grove, NJ; (Y); JCL; Latin Clb; Mrchg Band; Yrbk Stf; Rep Jr Cls; Rep Stu Cncl; Var Mgr(s); JV Sftbl; Twrlr; Sec Frsh Cls; Lawyer.

O DONNELL, COURTNEY; Middletown HS South; Lincroft, NJ; (Y); Dance Clb; Girl Scts; Ski Clb; Yrbk Stf; Rep Jr Cls; Powder Puff Ftbl; Sftbl; Hon Roll.

O DONNELL, DAVID; Bridgeton HS; Bridgeton, NJ; (Y); 4/210; Am Leg Boys St; Boy Scts; Science Clb; SADD; Yrbk Stf; Var L Tennis; NHS; Church Yth Grp; Math Clb; Math Tm; Olympics Of Mind 84-85; Schlrshp Lttr Awd 84-85 & 85-86; Am Chem Soc Awd For Excllnt Chem Achvt 85-86; US Marine Corps; Elec Engrng.

O DONNELL, JAMES; St Josephs Regional HS; Oakland, NJ; (Y); 19/167; Church Yth Grp; Hon Roll; Engineering.

O DONNELL, MARK C; Oratory Prep; Mountain Lakes, NJ; (Y); Boy Scts; Chess Clb; Political Wkr; Band; Nwsp Rptr; Vllybl; Wrstlng; Pres Clssrm 85; Eagle Sct Awd 85; Plcd & Won Indiv Bagpipe Comp 86; Catholic U; Pol Sci.

O DONNELL, SEAN; Lower Cape May Regional; Villas, NJ; (Y); Cmnty Wkr; Office Aide; Pep Clb; Ski Clb; Spanish Clb; Teachers Aide; Varsity Clb; Drm & Bgl; Mrchg Band; Off Jr Cls; Wnnr Stck Mrkt Gm 85-86; Trenton ST; Engnrng.

O DONOHUE, GWEN; Egg Harbor Township HS; Mays Landing, NJ; (S); 13/277; Cmnty Wkr; JA; Key Clb; Keywanettes; Leo Clb; Math Clb; Math Tm; Ski Clb; SADD; Teachers Aide; Phy Thrpy.

O DONOHUE, JENNIFER; Egg Harbor Township HS; Mayslanding, NJ; (S); 40/253; GAA; JA; Key Clb; Teachers Aide; Var Capt Crs Cntry; Im Gym; Im Swmmng; Im Tennis; Var Capt Trk; Ntl Merit Ltr; X-Cntry & Track Co Champ 85-86; Grp III St Meet 77th 85; Qlfr Meet Of Champs 85; Westchester; Phys Ther.

O DOWD, BRIAN; Morris Catholic HS; Montville, NJ; (Y); 11/165; Church Yth Grp; Pres Natl Beta Clb; VP Jr Cls; Capt Ftbl; Trk; NHS; Letterman Clb; Varsity Clb; Wt Lftg; Hon Roll; U S Army Rsrv Natl Schlr/Athlt Awd 86; Mst Courageous Atlt Awd 86; All Area Ftbl/Offnsv Constncy Mem; Muhlenberg Coll; Bus.

O DRISCOLL, MAUREEN A; West Windsor-Plainsboro HS; Princeton Jct, NJ; (Y); 22/232; Sec Church Yth Grp; Acpl Chr; Church Choir; School Musical; School Play; Yrbk Stf; Rep Stu Cncl; Stat Ftbl; JV Trk; High Hon Roll; NE Conf Awd Excllnce Spn 86; Schl Scholar 86; Bucknell U; Spn.

O DWYER, MICHELE; Highstown HS; Hightstown, NJ; (Y); Church Yth Grp; Pres Intnl Clb; VICA; Hon Roll; Prfct Atten Awd; Teen Arts Fest 85-86; MD Coll Art & Dsgn; Comm Art.

O GRADY, TOM; Notre Dame HS; Trenton, NJ; (Y); 74/380; Aud/Vis; French Clb; Ski Clb; Nwsp Rptr; French Hon Soc; High Hon Roll; Hon Roll; Poly Sci.

O HARA, DANIEL P; Pemberton Township HS; Browns Mills, NJ; (Y); 41/438; Am Leg Boys St; Aud/Vis; Camera Clb; Science Clb; Nwsp Phtg; Yrbk Phtg; Im Tennis; JV Trk; Im Vllybl; Hon Roll; Rotary Intl Spnsrd Interact Clb Pres 86; Grelvance Cmmtte; Aerospc Engrng.

O HARE, MICHELE; Sayreville War Memorial HS; Sayreville, NJ; (S); 12/376; Spanish Clb; Varsity Clb; Cheerleading; High Hon Roll; NHS; Spanish NHS; U S Chrldr Achvt Awd 86; Rutgers U.

O HEARN, ELIZABETH; Holy Cross HS; Mount Laurel, NJ; (Y); Ski Clb; Yrbk Stf; Sftbl; High Hon Roll; Computer Clb; Pro-Life Grp; Mth.

O KEEFE, KAREN; Notre Dame HS; Mercerville, NJ; (Y); 25/359; Drill Tm; Yrbk Stf; Capt Pom Pon; High Hon Roll; Hon Roll; NHS; Spanish NHS; Rep Stu Cncl; Statue Of Liberty Drill Tm 86; Law.

O KEEFE, MARY LYNNE; Lacordaire Acad; Upper Montclair, NJ; (Y); Church Yth Grp; Ski Clb; School Musical; School Play; Variety Show; Nwsp Bus Mgr; Nwsp Rptr; Nwsp Stf; Lit Mag; Cheerleading; Math.

O LEARY, HEATHER; Cranford HS; Cranford, NJ; (Y); 1/295; VP AFS; Sec Acpl Chr; Madrigals; School Musical; Nwsp Rptr; Sec Stu Cncl; Val; French Clb; Math Tm; Spanish Clb; Engl Awd 86; Watchung Mounted Troops SR Champ & JR Hunt Clb Treas 85-86; Williams Coll; Vet Med.

O LEARY, JUDITH; Central Regional HS; Bayville, NJ; (Y); Band; Chorus; Drm Mjr(t); School Musical; Rptr Nwsp Rptr; JV Bsktbl; French Hon Soc; High Hon Roll; NHS; Ntl Merit Ltr.

O LEARY, JUNE; St Marys HS; S Amboy, NJ; (Y); 35/140; Church Yth Grp; Cmnty Wkr; Hosp Aide; SADD; Yrbk Bus Mgr; Lit Mag; Bsktbl; Crs Cntry; Sftbl; Hon Roll; Holy Name Essay Cntst Wnnr 83; Rutgers U; Med.

O LEARY, KATHI-ANN; Waldwick HS; Waldwick, NJ; (Y); Dance Clb; Ski Clb; Yrbk Phtg; Stat Bsbl; Var Cheerleading; Powder Puff Ftbl; Hon Roll.

O LOUGHLIN, KATHLEEN; Cresskill HS; Cresskill, NJ; (Y); Pres French Clb; Ski Clb; Band; Concert Band; Var Cheerleading; Hon Roll; Law.

O MALLEY, MARK FRANCIS; Emerson HS; Union City, NJ; (Y); Church Yth Grp; Cmnty Wkr; Debate Tm; Political Wkr; Pblc Rltns.

O MALLEY, MATTHEW P; Warren Hills Regional SR HS; Washington, NJ; (Y); Am Leg Boys St; Trs Band; Jazz Band; Mrchg Band; Lit Mag; Jr NHS; Ntl Merit SF; St Schlr; Aud/Vis; Church Yth Grp; Mdl Orgnztn Of Amer States; Yrbk St Lf Edtr; Law.

O MARA, DEBRA; Highland Regional HS; Blackwood, NJ; (Y); Band; Concert Band; Jazz Band; Mrchg Band; Bowling; Berklee Coll; Music.

O NEILL, KELLY; Manasquan HS; S Belmar, NJ; (Y); 6/228; Teachers Aide; Yrbk Stf; Mgr Bsktbl; Mgr Socr; German Clb; Latin Clb; Math Tm; Var Stat Crs Cntry; Stat Wt Lftg; High Hon Roll; Gvnrs Tchng Schlrshp 86; Brd Of Ed Acdmc Achvt Awd 85-86; Pres Acdmc Ftns 86; Rtgrs-Dgls; Ed.

O NEILL, MICHAEL; Saint Josephs Prep Seminary; Philadelphia, PA; (Y); Boy Scts; Church Yth Grp; Speech Tm; VP Bsbl; VP Socr; Cit Awd; Variety Show; Im Bsktbl; Im Sftbl; Im Vllybl; Eagle Scout 84; Ad Altare Dei Religious Awd 83; Pope Pius XII Religious Awd 84; St Johns U; Roman Catholic Prst.

O ROURKE, COLLEEN; Dover HS; Dover, NJ; (Y); 10/224; Ski Clb; Im Bowling; Var Socr; Var Sftbl; High Hon Roll; NHS; Prfct Atten Awd; North Dover PTA Schlrshp 86; Cook Lyons Math Schlrshp 86; Coaches Awd Sftbl 82; Rutgers Schl Of Pharm; Pharm.

O ROURKE, MARY; Montville Township HS; Towaco, NJ; (Y); Church Yth Grp; Girl Scts; Chorus; High Hon Roll; Hon Roll; Tchr.

O ROURKE, MOLLY; Summit HS; Summit, NJ; (Y); Model UN; Pres Soph Cls; VP Jr Cls; Rep Sr Cls; Pres Stu Cncl; Capt Lcrss; NHS; Hosp Aide; Nwsp Stf; Trs Frsh Cls; Summit HS Initial Wnnr Stu Mnth Awd 86; Six Super Stu 86; Ntl Merit Schlrshp 85; Brown U; Intl Affairs.

O SHAUGHNESSY, KATHLEEN; St John Vianney HS; Freehold, NJ; (Y); 3/280; Hosp Aide; SADD; Yrbk Stf; Rep Soph Cls; High Hon Roll; Hon Roll; NHS; Art Clb; Ski Clb; Stage Crew; Gold & White Awd; Merit Awd Englsh; Merit Awd Spnsh.

O SHEA, MICHELE; John P Stevens HS; Edison, NJ; (Y); 40/469; GAA; Socr; Sftbl; NHS; Letterman Clb; Science Clb; Varsity Clb; Acpl Chr; Chorus; Madrigals; Girls Schlr Athlete 83-86; John F Kennedy 83; Rutgers Coll; Phrmcy.

O SULLIVAN, KATHERINE; Lacordaire Acad; Bloomfield, NJ; (Y); Intnl Clb; Service Clb; Stage Crew; Nwsp Ed-Chief; Lit Mag; Pres Soph Cls; French Hon Soc; Hon Roll; Prfct Atten Awd; Fordham U; Pre Med.

O TOOLE, KIMBERLY; Paul Vi HS; Bellmawr, NJ; (S); 20/477; Math Clb; Lit Mag; Sec Frsh Cls; Sec Soph Cls; Sec Jr Cls; Bowling; Trk; Hon Roll; NHS; Drexel U; Comp Engr.

OAKES, EILEEN; Mainland Regional HS; Northfield, NJ; (Y); 37/360; Ski Clb; SADD; Varsity Clb; Nwsp Bus Mgr; Nwsp Stf; Off Frsh Cls; Off Soph Cls; Off Jr Cls; Stu Cncl; Var L Cheerleading; Adlgy.

OAKLEY, CRISTIN; Phillipsburg HS; Phillipsburg, NJ; (Y); Church Yth Grp; Cmnty Wkr; Key Clb; Office Aide; Chorus; Church Choir; School Musical; Nwsp Stf; BUS Mngmnt.

OBAL, KATHLEEN; Pascack Valley HS; Hillsdale, NJ; (Y); Art Clb; Yrbk Stf; Hon Roll; Comm Art.

OBAL, PATRICIA; East Brunswick HS; E Brunswick, NJ; (Y); Key Clb; Sec Math Clb; VP Mrchg Band; French Hon Soc; NHS; Commended Natl Merit 85; Grdn ST Distngshd Schlr 85-86; Sci Leag 84-86; MA Inst Of Tech; Engrng.

OBERTI, FELICIA; Toms River HS East; Toms River, NJ; (Y); 13/550; French Clb; Hosp Aide; VP Key Clb; Political Wkr; SADD; Chorus; Powder Puff Ftbl; High Hon Roll; Kiwanis Awd; NHS; Teens Edctng Alchl Misuse Merit Awd 85-86; Poli Sci.

OBERTUBBESING, MARY ANN; Middletown South HS; Leonardo, NJ; (Y); Trs Cmnty Wkr; Hosp Aide; Teachers Aide; Sec Band; Concert Band; Mrchg Band; School Musical; Symp Band; Fld Hcky; Hon Roll; Awd Of Commndtn Riverview Hosp JR Vol 84-86; Nrsng.

OBFENDA, TONY; Holy Cross HS; Mount Laurel, NJ; (Y); Church Choir; Var Trk; Hon Roll; Engrng.

OBNEY, MICHAEL; Lower Cape May Regional HS; Cape May, NJ; (Y); Boy Scts; Webbs Inst; Engrng.

OBREGON, ISABEL; St Josephs Of The Palisades HS; Rutherford, NJ; (S); 10/115; Pep Clb; Spanish Clb; Yrbk Stf; Spanish NHS; Fordham U; Adol Psych.

OBUDHO, LESLIE; Florence Twp Memorial HS; Florence, NJ; (Y); 18/99; Camera Clb; Church Yth Grp; FBLA; GAA; Letterman Clb; Library Aide; Math Clb; ROTC; Teachers Aide; Varsity Clb; Elctrncs.

OCASIO, ALEXIS; Woodrow Wilson HS; Camden, NJ; (Y); Ski Clb; Teachers Aide; Off Frsh Cls; Socr; Vllybl; Spanish NHS; Bus.

OCCHIPINTI, BRIDGET; Butler HS; Butler, NJ; (Y); Church Yth Grp; Hosp Aide; Varsity Clb; Rep Soph Cls; Rep Jr Cls; Sec Stu Cncl; Var JV Cheerleading; Var JV Fld Hcky; JV Sftbl; Hon Roll.

OCCHIPINTI, NATALIE M; Paterson Catholic R H HS; Paterson, NJ; (Y); Church Yth Grp; JA; Church Choir; Variety Show; Yrbk Stf; Rep Stu Cncl; Var Capt Sftbl; JV Capt Vllybl; Cit Awd; High Hon Roll; Coll New Rochelle; Med.

OCHINEGRO, BEN; Matawan Regional HS; Cliffwood, NJ; (Y); #72 In Class; Camera Clb; Chess Clb; Computer Clb; Exploring; Red Cross Aide; Service Clb; SADD; Var L Ftbl; Golf; Bus.

OCHN, STEVEN; Montville Twnshp HS; Montville, NJ; (Y); 150/280; Computer Clb; FBLA; Key Clb; Ski Clb; Hon Roll; Castleton; Acctng.

OCONNOR, JASON; Wall HS; Wall, NJ; (Y); 6/264; Am Leg Boys St; Trs Aud/Vis; Exploring; German Clb; JCL; VP Key Clb; Trs Latin Clb; Trk; High Hon Roll; NHS; Amer Clscl League Natl Latin Awd; Elec Engrng.

OCONNOR, SHIVAUN; Immaculate Conception HS; Secaucus, NJ; (Y); Art Clb; Stage Crew; Swmmng; Hon Roll; Natl Art Hon Soc 84-86.

ODELL, KATHY; Middlesex HS; Middlesex, NJ; (Y); 33/160; Church Yth Grp; Key Clb; Ski Clb; Spanish Clb; School Musical; Yrbk Stf; Var Pom Pon; JV Trk; Stat Wrstlng; Accntng.

ODEN, DEREK; Hudson Catholic HS; Jersey City, NJ; (Y); Church Yth Grp; Computer Clb; 4-H; Latin Clb; Math Clb; Ski Clb; SADD; Bsbl; Var L Bowling; Wt Lftg; Comp Sci.

ODENWALD, PATRICIA; Bergenfield HS; Bergenfield, NJ; (Y); 18/303; Hon Roll; VA Tech; Hmn Ntrtn.

ODES, REBECCA; West Orange HS; W Orange, NJ; (Y); 27/197; French Clb; Ski Clb; Temple Yth Grp; Chorus; School Play; Nwsp Stf; Yrbk Stf; Stu Cncl; French Hon Soc; NHS; 2nd Prize Frnch Postr Cntst 86; Stu Cncl Publcty Chairprsn Awd 86; Societe Honorire De Francais Awd 86; Vassar Coll; Art.

OEHLER, KIM; Edgewood SR HS; Berlin, NJ; (Y); 30/385; VP French Clb; FBLA; Girl Scts; Varsity Clb; Rep Frsh Cls; Rep Soph Cls; JV Sftbl; JV Var Tennis; Hon Roll; Jr NHS; PYJU & Michele Gordy Schlrshps 86; Vrsty Pin 86; Douglass Coll; Acctg.

OESE, MADELINE; Toms River High School South; S Toms River, NJ; (Y); 35/300; Church Yth Grp; Hosp Aide; Quiz Bowl; Science Clb; Capt Drill Tm; Orch; Swmmng; Tennis; High Hon Roll; NHS; Mentclair ST Coll; Ed Tchr.

OESKOVIC, SUE L; Middlesex HS; Middlesex, NJ; (Y); 14/159; Sec Frsh Cls; JV Bsktbl; Stat Fld Hcky; Var JV Sftbl; High Hon Roll; Hon Roll; J E Mc Gowan Schlrshp 86; Bond For Secy Fld 86; Cittone Inst; Ct Rprtg.

OESTERLE, KAREN; Middletown HS; Middletown, NJ; (Y); 200/460; Church Yth Grp; Ski Clb; Yrbk Stf; Seton Hall U; Erly Educ.

OGANDO, ROBERT; West Essex SR HS; N Caldwell, NJ; (Y); Boy Scts; Latin Clb; Var L Ice Hcky; Rutgers U; Law Enfrcmnt.

OGENESKI, CHRIS; Clifton HS; Clifton, NJ; (Y); Church Yth Grp; German Clb; Letterman Clb; JV Bsbl; JV Bsktbl; Var Ftbl; Im Vllybl; Im Wt Lftg; Hon Roll; Mech Engrg.

OGRINZ, MIKE; High Point Regional HS; Sussex, NJ; (Y); Computer Clb; Debate Tm; German Clb; Latin Clb; Quiz Bowl; Scholastic Bowl; Teachers Aide; Acpl Chr; Chorus; School Musical; Manhatenville Coll; Comp.

OHARA, STEVE; B-R High School West; Bridgewater, NJ; (Y); Varsity Clb; Nwsp Stf; Rep Stu Cncl; JV Var Bsktbl; Coach Actv; Var Tennis; NHS; Accntng.

OHARRIZ, MERCHE; Pennesville Memorial HS; Pennsville, NJ; (Y); 51/216; JA; Spanish Clb; SADD; Rep Stu Cncl; Cheerleading; Im Gym; Var L Trk; Im Vllybl; Hon Roll; Spanish NHS; ST Fin Trk; Schl Rcrd 200 M Trk 83; IADE Spain; Fash Merch.

OHLE, COLLEEN; Hightstown HS; Hightstown, NJ; (Y); 16/441; Am Leg Aux Girls St; Drama Clb; VP French Clb; Trs FBLA; Intnl Clb; Off Jr Cls; Stu Cncl; JV Stat Socr; High Hon Roll; NHS; Katherine Gibbs Awd Ldrsp Fut Secrtrs 86; 5th Pl Awd FBLA Regnl Comptn Typng II 86; 8th Pl Acct I 85; Bus.

OHTSU, BEN; West Essex SR HS; N Caldwell, NJ; (Y); Key Clb; Latin Clb; Science Clb; JV Trk; Hon Roll; VP NHS; Engrng Fld.

OJEDIRAN, IRETI; Frank H Morrell HS; Irvington, NJ; (Y); French Clb; Hon Roll; Law.

OKSAS, NURDANE; John F Kennedy HS; Paterson, NJ; (Y); 15/360; Computer Clb; French Clb; Nwsp Ed-Chief; Nwsp Rptr; Yrbk Phtg; Hon Roll; NHS; Outstndng Acadmc Achvt Awd 82-86; Pres Acadmc Fit Awd 85-86; William Paterson Coll.

OLAH, ANISSA; Lower Cape May Regional HS; N Cape May, NJ; (Y); 19/245; Am Leg Aux Girls St; French Clb; Varsity Clb; Rep Stu Cncl; Var Capt Cheerleading; Pom Pon; JV Sftbl; Hon Roll; NHS; Chrldng Awds Mst Sprtd & Bst All Arnd 84-85; Prom Queen 86; NJC Ncl Of Ec Educ 86.

OLAH, JENNIFER; Mount Olive HS; Budd Lake, NJ; (Y); PAVAS; Chorus; Color Guard; Stat Socr; Twrlr; Natl Art Hnr Soc 86.

OLANDER, DALE; Wall HS; Wall, NJ; (S); 25/263; Chess Clb; ROTC; Crs Cntry; Trk; High Hon Roll; Hon Roll; Cross Cnty Vrsty Lrt 85; Chess Ltr 85; US Naval Acad; Marine Corp Ofc.

OLDMAN, MARK; Bridgewater-Raritian HS East; Martinsville, NJ; (Y); French Clb; Math Tm; Ski Clb; Nwsp Stf; Rep Stu Cncl; JV Var Tennis; Im Wt Lftg; Var L Wrstlng; High Hon Roll; Hon Roll; Wghtlftng Clb 85; Pingry Wrstlng Cmp Trnmnt 1st Pl 85.

OLDROYD, MICHAEL; Oakcrest HS; Mays Landing, NJ; (Y); Boy Scts; Exploring; 4-H; SADD; Lit Mag; Socr; Military.

OLESNICKI, ANNETTE; Union HS; Union, NJ; (Y); Church Yth Grp; French Clb; Key Clb; Church Choir; Nwsp Stf; Yrbk Stf; Off Soph Cls; Intl Rel.

OLHOVSKY, SERGE; Hamilton High School West; Trenton, NJ; (S); 5/330; Math Clb; Band; Mrchg Band; Nwsp Rptr; Nwsp Stf; Yrbk Stf; Swmmng; Hon Roll; Trs NHS; Arch.

OLITSKY, AMY; Union HS; Union, NJ; (Y); French Clb; Girl Scts; Key Clb; Temple Yth Grp; Thesps; Drill Tm; Flag Corp; Orch; Symp Band; Hon Roll; Symphony Orch Plyd Violin 85-86; Israel Trip Schlrshp 85; Nghbrhd Playhs Drama Schl NY 84; DE U; Nrs.

OLIVE, SANDRA; E Orange HS; E Orange, NJ; (S); 11/410; Hosp Aide; Capt Pep Clb; Yrbk Stf; Crs Cntry; Hon Roll; Jr NHS; NHS; Stockton ST Coll; Bus Adm.

OLIVEIRA, TAMMY; Highland Reg HS; Somerdale, NJ; (Y); 77/370; Church Yth Grp; Dance Clb; French Clb; German Clb; Church Choir; Var Cheerleading; Mgr(s); Score Keeper; Hon Roll; Catawba Coll; Sprts Med.

OLIVER, ALBERT C; Burlngton Township HS; Burlington, NJ; (Y); Am Leg Boys St; SADD; Band; Capt L Bsbl; L Bsktbl; Capt L Ftbl; Cit Awd; Chess Clb; Church Yth Grp; FCA; Dem Commtte Awd 86; Grace Cathedral 1st Born Chrch Schlrshp 86; All Cty Bsbl 86; U Miami; Acctng.

OLIVER, ERIN; Spotswood HS; Spotswood, NJ; (S); #4 In Class; Church Yth Grp; Cmnty Wkr; French Clb; Intnl Clb; Math Clb; Science Clb; Color Guard; Drm Mjr(t); Mrchg Band; Yrbk Stf; Sci.

OLIVER, HONORA ANN; Newton HS; Newton, NJ; (Y); French Clb; German Clb; Latin Clb; Ski Clb; Concert Band; Mrchg Band; Stu Cncl; High Hon Roll; NHS; U Of KS; Russian Frnch.

OLIVER, KATHLEEN; Lower Cape May Regional HS; Cape May, NJ; (Y); Key Clb; Office Aide; Varsity Clb; Yrbk Phtg; Yrbk Stf; Mgr(s); Mgr Tennis; High Hon Roll; Hon Roll; Prfct Atten Awd; Cape May County Voc Tech; Dentl.

OLIVER, KELLY; Maple Shade HS; Maple Shade, NJ; (Y); Am Leg Aux Girls St; Church Yth Grp; French Clb; Intnl Clb; Key Clb; SADD; VP Frsh Cls; Var Cheerleading; Jr NHS; Prfct Atten Awd.

OLIVER, KIMBERLY; Maple Shade HS; Maple Shade, NJ; (Y); 15/180; Am Leg Aux Girls St; Pres Key Clb; Fld Hcky; Lcrss; Mgr(s); Hon Roll; Wheelock Coll; Spcl Ed.

OLIVER, WILLIAM; Wall HS; Manasquan, NJ; (S); 4/268; Aud/Vis; Boy Scts; Drama Clb; Key Clb; Ski Clb; Tennis; NHS; St Schlr; Church Yth Grp; Spanish Clb; Am Chem Socty Awd 84-85; Garden ST Distngushd Schlr 85-86; Engrng.

OLIVERAS, LUIS; Bridgeton HS; Bridgeton, NJ; (Y); CAP; Off Jr Cls; Bsbl; Bsktbl; Swmmng; Hon Roll; Engrng.

OLIVERI, JOSEPH; Wayne Valley HS; Wayne, NJ; (Y); 21/323; Var L Bsktbl; Var L Golf; Hon Roll; NHS; Bus.

OLIVERI, MARY E; Saint James HS; Gibbstown, NJ; (Y); Cmnty Wkr; Exploring; Red Cross Aide; Church Choir; Hon Roll; Pope Pius Vi 85; Miss VFW Beauty Pgnt 1st Rnr-Up 86; Merit Awd Outstndg Effrt Sci 84; Glassboro ST Coll; Elem Ed.

OLIVERO, NOEL; Toms River HS North; Toms River, NJ; (Y); 24/424; Boy Scts; Pres German Clb; Orch; Swmmng; Trk; Wt Lftg; High Hon Roll; NHS; Dntstry.

OLIVETO, GERARDO; Paul VI Regional HS; Bloomfield, NJ; (S); 3/125; JV Bsbl; High Hon Roll; Hon Roll; NHS; MA Inst Of Tech; Engnrng.

OLIVO, CHARLES; Cherry Hill HS West; Cherry Hill, NJ; (Y); Aud/Vis; Boy Scts; Orch; Var Ftbl; Drexel U; Bus Admns.

OLKIEWICZ, MARK; Southern Regional HS; Ship Bottom, NJ; (Y); 7/350; Church Yth Grp; German Clb; Spanish Clb; Stu Cncl; JV Bsbl; Var Bsktbl; Var Capt Crs Cntry; Var Golf; JV Trk; High Hon Roll; Stu Ath Awd 86; Beach Haven Exch Clb Yth Mnth 86; US Army Res Natl Schlr/Ath Awd 86; U Notre Dame; Engrng.

OLLIE, ANGELO; Orange HS; Orange, NJ; (S); Hon Roll; NJIT; Engrng.

OLSEN, BARBARA ANN; Sparta HS; Sparta, NJ; (Y); 4/208; Capt Scholastic Bowl; Mgr Nwsp Bus Mgr; Ed Yrbk Sprt Ed; Var Capt Socr; Trk; High Hon Roll; NHS; Ntl Merit Ltr; St Schlr; VP Church Yth Grp; Soroptomst Ctznshp Awd; Spartan Clb Schlrshp; JR Womens Clb Schlrshp; Cornell U; Med.

OLSEN, SHANNON; Matawan Regional HS; Matawan, NJ; (S); 7/305; Hosp Aide; SADD; Band; Color Guard; Concert Band; Mrchg Band; Sec Frsh Cls; Pres Soph Cls; VP Jr Cls; Stu Cncl; Most Dedicated & Responsible Guard 83; Nicest Persnlty 84; Hnr Rl Awd 84; Comm.

OLSON, ERIC S; Neumann Prep; Ringwood, NJ; (Y); Am Leg Boys St; Cmnty Wkr; Stage Crew; Nwsp Stf; Lit Mag; JV Bsbl; JV Socr; French Hon Soc; High Hon Roll; NHS.

OLSON, STEPHEN; Atlantic City HS; Atlantic City, NJ; (Y); Art Clb; Band; Concert Band; Jazz Band; Mrchg Band; Orch; Pep Band; School Musical; Variety Show; Hon Roll; Vp-Atlantic City HS Band 85-87; Philadelphia Inst-Art; Comm Art.

OLSON, TAMMY; Manasquan HS; Boynton Beach, FL; (S); Art Clb; Camp Fr Inc; Church Yth Grp; Civic Clb; Cmnty Wkr; Debate Tm; Drama Clb; English Clb; FCA; FBLA; Hall Fame Awd Sprts 84-85; Baseball, 2 Track Awds 84-85; Elem Grade Schl Tutor 84-85; Palm Beach JC; Elem Educ.

OLSSON, KAREN; Mainland Regional HS; Linwood, NJ; (Y); #13 In Class; Ski Clb; Yrbk Stf; Var L Bsktbl; JV Capt Fld Hcky; Var L Sftbl; Hon Roll; NHS; Bus.

OLTMER, CHRISTINA; Lakeland Regional HS; Ringwood, NJ; (Y); 15/303; Church Yth Grp; FBLA; SADD; Nwsp Rptr; Rep Stu Cncl; JV Var Bsktbl; Powder Puff Ftbl; JV Trk; High Hon Roll; Hon Roll; U NH; Bus Adm.

OMBALSKY, SANDRA; Belleville HS; Belleville, NJ; (Y); Am Leg Aux Girls St; FBLA; Key Clb; Spanish Clb; Pres Sr Cls; Var Cheerleading; JV Sftbl; High Hon Roll; NHS; Acctng.

OMENSON, LYNNE; Cherry Hill East HS; Cherry Hill, NJ; (Y); Camera Clb; Hosp Aide; Red Cross Aide; Spanish Clb; Band; Concert Band; Mrchg Band; Nwsp Phtg; Yrbk Stf; JV Var Sftbl; Towson ST U; Tchng.

ONACILLA, SUSAN; Shore Regional HS; Oceanport, NJ; (Y); Yrbk Stf; Rep Stu Cncl; Var L Bsktbl; JV Fld Hcky; Var L Sftbl; Hon Roll.

ONEILL, KELLY; Mainland Regional HS; Somers Point, NJ; (Y); 11/350; Band; Pres Soph Cls; Pres Jr Cls; Cheerleading; Var Diving; JV Sftbl; Trk; Hon Roll; NHS; Ski Clb.

ONEILL, MIKE; Seton Hall Prep; Morristown, NJ; (Y); French Clb; Key Clb; Nwsp Rptr; Bsbl; Coach Actv; Ftbl; Swmmng; Capt Wrstlng; Hon Roll; MVP Wrstlng, Ftbl; Penn ST; Law.

ONORATO, MICHELE; Bloomfield SR HS; Bloomfld, NJ; (Y); 20/435; Key Clb; Yrbk Rptr; Sec Jr Cls; Sec Sr Cls; Var Cheerleading; Cit Awd; High Hon Roll; Hon Roll; NHS; Ntl Merit SF; WA Wrkshp Smnr 86; Bus Admin.

ONOREVOLE, KEVIN; Nutley HS; Nutley, NJ; (Y); 120/332; Yrbk Phtg; Hon Roll; Church Yth Grp; Office Aide; Orch; Stage Crew; Variety Show; Stu Cncl; Accntng.

ONORI, JAMES; Hudson Catholic HS; Jersey City, NJ; (Y); SADD; Bowling; JV Var Ftbl; Gym; Swmmng; Wt Lftg; Vrsty Lttr Crtfct Achvmnt Ftbll 86; Crtfct Fr Hghst Wgthlftn 85; St Peters Coll; Psychlgy.

ONTELL, LAUREN; Wayne Hills HS; Wayne, NJ; (Y); 30/305; French Clb; Math Clb; Temple Yth Grp; Stage Crew; Nwsp Rptr; Nwsp Stf; JV Fld Hcky; JV Socr; Hon Roll; NHS; Ski Tm Var Letters 85-86.

ONTKO, CAROL; Delaware Valley Regional HS; Milford, NJ; (Y); 6/165; Key Clb; JV Cheerleading; JV Fld Hcky; JV Sftbl; High Hon Roll; NHS; Phys Thrpy.

ONTKO, MARY; Delaware Valley Regional HS; Milford, NJ; (Y); 3/165; Key Clb; Stat Bsktbl; Stat Crs Cntry; Stat Socr; Stat Sftbl; High Hon Roll; Pres NHS; Chem Engrng.

ONUFROW, MICHAEL J; Kinnelon HS; Kinnelon, NJ; (Y); 5/176; Am Leg Boys St; Church Yth Grp; Varsity Clb; Band; Capt Swmmng; Trk; Hon Roll; NHS; Spanish NHS; Cmnty Wkr; Engnrs Local 68 Essay Cntst-Hnrb Mntn 84; Math.

OPPENHEIM, DAVID; Manalapan HS; Englishtown, NJ; (Y); 19/470; JCL; Latin Clb; Ski Clb; Varsity Clb; Stu Cncl; Var Capt Socr; Cit Awd; NHS; Lawyer.

OPPENHEIM, ROBERT; Watchung Hills Regional HS; Warren, NJ; (Y); 1/315; Church Yth Grp; Scholastic Bowl; Orch; Gov Hon Prg Awd; High Hon Roll; NHS; Physcs.

OQUENDO, VIRGINIA; Camden HS; Camden, NJ; (S); Church Yth Grp; Cmnty Wkr; FHA; Hosp Aide; Teachers Aide; Church Choir; High Hon Roll; Hon Roll; NHS; Rutghers; Obstetrician.

ORAM, RICKI; John F Kennedy HS; Willingboro, NJ; (Y); Intnl Clb; Color Guard; Mrchg Band; Var Pom Pon; Var JV Timer; Hon Roll; Para Lgl.

ORCIUOLI, KIM; Livingston HS; Livingston, NJ; (Y); Key Clb; Math Clb; Math Tm; Spanish Clb; Variety Show; Yrbk Stf; Rep Stu Cncl; High Hon Roll; Hon Roll; Spanish NHS; Med.

ORDEN, RICHARD; Lenape Valley Regional HS; Netcong, NJ; (Y); Am Leg Boys St; Boy Scts; Pres SADD; Orch; Nwsp Phtg; Lit Mag; Rep Stu Cncl; Crs Cntry; Trk; NHS.

ORDONEZ, CHARLES; St Peters Prep; N Bergen, NJ; (Y); Church Yth Grp; Cmnty Wkr; SADD; Im Bsbl; Im Bsktbl; Im Fld Hcky; JV Im Ftbl; Im Score Keeper; Im Wt Lftg; Pre Med.

ORDONEZ, IVAN; North Bergen HS; North Bergen, NJ; (Y); 72/405; Key Clb; ROTC; Var Gym; Var Score Keeper; JV Socr; Im Wt Lftg; JV Wrstlng; High Hon Roll; Hon Roll; NJROTC Area No 4-Annual Inspect Outstdng Cadel 86; Natl Russian Olympiada Gold & Slvr 84-86; Med.

ORELLANO, DAYANA; Mary Help Of Christians Acad; Paterson, NJ; (Y); Computer Clb; Dance Clb; Hosp Aide; Latin Clb; Variety Show; Badmtn; Vllybl; Hon Roll; Prfct Atten Awd; Engl & Comptr Certfcts 86; Med Tech.

ORFANAKOS, GEORGE; Wayne Valley HS; Wayne, NJ; (Y); Aud/Vis; Church Yth Grp; FCA; Acpl Chr; Chorus; Church Choir; Madrigals; School Musical; School Play; Hon Roll; 2 Yr Natl Oratorcl Fstvl Fnlst 85-86; Pres-Chrch Yth Grp 85-87; Champ-Vllybl Tm 83-85; Hellenic Coll; Pre Theology.

ORIA, JILL P; St Josephs Of The Palisade; West New York, NJ; (S); 4/200; Church Yth Grp; Dance Clb; Girl Scts; Science Clb; Ski Clb; Teachers Aide; Variety Show; Sec Frsh Cls; Score Keeper; High Hon Roll; Georgtown; Med.

ORLANDO II, JOSEPH M; Parsippany HS; Parsippany, NJ; (Y); Intnl Clb; JV Capt Socr; Trk; Hon Roll; Prfct Atten Awd; Hugh O Brian Yth Fndtn Outstndng Prsn 85; Itln Clb.

ORMSBY, THOMAS; St John Vianney HS; Englishtown, NJ; (Y); Im Bsbl; Im Bsktbl; Var Ftbl; Im Trk; Im Vllybl; Var Wt Lftg; Hon Roll; Vrsty Ltr Ftbl; Road Schlr.

OROS, REBECCA; Northern Burlington Co Reg HS; Bordentown, NJ; (Y); 3/197; Am Leg Aux Girls St; Math Tm; Nwsp Stf; Rep Jr Cls; Rep Sr Cls; Mgr Fld Hcky; Mgr Var Trk; French Hon Soc; NHS; Pres Schlr; Rutgers; Math.

OROZCO, JUAN CARLOS; Roselle Catholic HS; Elizabeth, NJ; (Y); #5 In Class; Church Yth Grp; Lit Mag; Stu Cncl; Im Bsktbl; Im Vllybl; Im Wt Lftg; Hon Roll; NHS; Spanish NHS; Rutgers U; Gyneclgy.

ORRICK, ANNEMARIE; Middletown HS; Red Bank, NJ; (Y); Church Yth Grp; Concert Band; Jazz Band; Mrchg Band; Pep Band; School Musical; Nwsp Rptr; Rep Stu Cncl; Hon Roll; Vrsty Ltrs Marching Bnd 85-86; Comm.

ORRICO, JOHN; Bloomfield HS; Bloomfield, NJ; (Y); 140/425; Var Bsbl; Var Ftbl; JV Wrstlng; Kean Coll; Criminal Justice.

ORSINI, DANA; Voorhees HS; Glen Gardner, NJ; (S); Debate Tm; 4-H; FFA; GAA; Girl Scts; Drm & Bgl; JV Bsktbl; JV Crs Cntry; 4-H Awd; Cert Hnr Outstndng Achvt Voctnl Ag I 85; H O Sampson Achvt Awd 85; FFA Judgng Cntst Achvt Awds 85.

ORSZEWSKI, DAWNE; St Marys HS; S Amboy, NJ; (Y); 13/125; Library Aide; Spanish Clb; SADD; High Hon Roll; Spanish NHS; Stage Crew; Variety Show; Yrbk Stf; Lit Mag; Hon Roll; Ballgrl Bsktbl; Lipp Sync Cntst; Lab Tech.

ORTEGA, AMARILIS; East Side HS; Newark, NJ; (Y); Cmnty Wkr; French Clb; Nwsp Stf; Rep Jr Cls; Schlrshp Trng Chldrn 87.

ORTEGA, ARNEL V; St Peters Prep Schl; Jersey City, NJ; (Y); 19/206; Intnl Clb; Letterman Clb; Varsity Clb; Im Bsktbl; Im Ftbl; Var L Socr; Im Vllybl; Var Wt Lftg; High Hon Roll; Hnr Pin.

ORTEGA, JOHN; Dickinson HS; Jersey City, NJ; (Y).

ORTEGA, JULIA LUISE; Northern Burlington Regional HS; Marlton, NJ; (Y); 90/197; Civic Clb; Cmnty Wkr; Dance Clb; Drama Clb; Hosp Aide; Library Aide; Office Aide; Pep Clb; Radio Clb; Red Cross Aide; Read Mrtn Lthr Kngs Spch To Stu Bdy 85-86; Chf Mrng Anncr 84-86; Spelman Coll; Mss Cmmnctns.

ORTEGA, LAURIE; Clifton HS; Clifton, NJ; (Y); 241/526; Art Clb; Church Yth Grp; English Clb; Office Aide; Im Cheerleading; Bergen CC; Comp Prgrmg.

ORTIZ, IRIS; Our Lady Of Good Counsel HS; Newark, NJ; (Y); Nwsp Stf; Yrbk Stf; Hon Roll; NHS; Prfct Atten Awd; St Peters Coll; Bio.

ORTIZ, JUDITH; Hoboken HS; Hoboken, NJ; (Y); French Clb; Chorus; Sftbl; Nursng.

ORTIZ, MARCOS; Our Lady Of Good Counsel HS; Newark, NJ; (Y); 73/123; Pres Aud/Vis; Boy Scts; Chess Clb; Computer Clb; Exploring; Chorus; Mgr Stage Crew; Bsktbl; Socr; Prfct Atten Awd; Eagle Scout 85; Junior Assistant Scout Master 85; Pres Of Altar Boys 83-86; Comp Sci.

ORTIZIO, MARIANNE; Union HS; Union, NJ; (Y); Church Yth Grp; Dance Clb; Sec FBLA; Key Clb; Yrbk Stf; Rep Frsh Cls; Rep Soph Cls; Rep Jr Cls; Off Sr Cls; Stu Cncl; Rutgers; Bus Mgmt.

ORTLOFF, CHERYL; Highland Regional HS; Blackwood, NJ; (S); 1/325; Pres Church Yth Grp; Hosp Aide; Trs Spanish Clb; Mrchg Band; Orch; Stu Cncl; VP NHS; Voice Dem Awd; Chess Clb; Olympia Conf Hnr Band 82-84; S Jersey Bnd 83-84; Glassboro Yth Orcehstra 85-86; Cedarville Coll; Med.

ORTOLF, KIRSTEN; Cumberland Regional HS; Bridgeton, NJ; (Y); Intnl Clb; JCL; Ski Clb; Yrbk Stf; VP Frsh Cls; Pres Jr Cls; Fld Hcky; JV Sftbl; Intl Bus.

ORTON, ADAM; Central Regional HS; Seaside Hgts, NJ; (Y); Ski Clb; Band; Concert Band; Ftbl; Var Tennis; High Hon Roll; Hon Roll.

ORZECHOWSKI, DENISE; Gloucester Catholic HS; Deptford, NJ; (Y); 4/166; Pep Clb; Stage Crew; Yrbk Stf; Stu Cncl; Var Cheerleading; Hon Roll; NHS; Fncng.

OSBORN, CATHERINE; Mt St Dominic Acad; Kearny, NJ; (Y); Ski Clb; Spanish Clb; Nwsp Stf; Yrbk Phtg; VP Sr Cls; JV Cheerleading; SRA Achvt Awd; Mrktng.

OSBORN, ROBINLYNN; Brick Township HS; Brick Town, NJ; (Y); 21/415; Drama Clb; SADD; Thesps; Nwsp Ed-Chief; Rep Frsh Cls; Rep Stu Cncl; Gov Hon Prg Awd; High Hon Roll; NHS; Church Choir; Katherine Gibbs Ldrshp Awd 86; Acctng.

OSBORNE, DAVID; Franklin Twp HS; Somerset, NJ; (Y); Band; Concert Band; Jazz Band; Mrchg Band; Pres Frsh Cls; Stat Bsktbl; Gov Hon Prg Awd; NHS; Ntl Merit Ltr; All Rgn Orchestra 1st St 86; All ST Symphonic Band 1st St 86; Journ.

OSBORNE, RICHARD; Pompion Lakes HS; Pompton Lakes, NJ; (Y); 25/125; Var Bsktbl; Var Socr; Accntg.

OSBORNE, WENDY; Vineland HS; Vineland, NJ; (Y); Cmnty Wkr; Debate Tm; Pep Clb; Political Wkr; Service Clb; Teachers Aide; Pres VP Temple Yth Grp; JV Fld Hcky; Yrbk Phtg; Rep Soph Cls; Womans Clb Vineland Schrlshp 86; Womans Clb Awd Civic Ach 86; Douglass Coll; Psychlgy.

OSBUN, LISA; Jefferson Township HS; Oak Ridge, NJ; (Y); Drama Clb; French Clb; GAA; Stage Crew; Hon Roll; Presdntl Acad Ftns Awd 86; Spanish Excllnc Awd 86; IFLA For French & Spanish 86; Ramapo Coll; Accntng.

OSEKAVAGE, CHUCK; Mahwah HS; Mahwah, NJ; (Y); JV Socr; JV Trk; Clemson U; Archtctr.

OSES, KATHERINE; N Bergen HS; N Bergen, NJ; (Y); 35/404; French Clb; Hon Roll; NHS; Rutgers Coll; Comp Sci.

OSHVA, PHIL; Bridgewater Raritan HS East; Martinsville, NJ; (Y); Boy Scts; Debate Tm; Intnl Clb; Math Tm; Spanish Clb; Speech Tm; Orch; Nwsp Ed-Chief; Hon Roll; NHS; Chem.

OSIECKI, CHERYL; Villa Walsh Acad; Budd Lake, NJ; (S); Church Yth Grp; Math Tm; Chorus; Church Choir; Orch; Lit Mag; Sftbl; NHS; 1st Plc Natl Essy Cntst 86; 1st Plc NJ ST Tn Arts Fstvl 86; 2nd Plc Dlbrtn Crtv Arts Fstvl 86.

OSLICK, JEFFREY; Westfield HS; Westfield, NJ; (Y); Intnl Clb; Scholastic Bowl; VP Science Clb; Spanish Clb; VP Temple Yth Grp; Chorus; Orch; Nwsp Phtg; Yrbk Phtg; Lit Mag; US Pwr Sqdrn Publ Boatng Crse 85; Engr.

OSOWSKI, JOSEPH; Middletown HS South; Leonardo, NJ; (S); 33/436; Am Leg Boys St; Cmnty Wkr; Var L Socr; High Hon Roll; Hon Roll; Jr NHS; NHS; Outstndng Athlt Awd 85; 2nd Tm All Conf Soccer 85; MVP Soccer 85; Connecticut U; Engr.

OSSOWSKI, DAVID; Jackson Mrmotial HS; Jackson, NJ; (Y); 94/417; Var L Socr; Hon Roll.

OSTAPOVICH, LYNN; Bound Brook HS; S Bound Brook, NJ; (Y); French Clb; Girl Scts; Sec Key Clb; Mrchg Band; Symp Band; Sec Frsh Cls; Hon Roll; NHS; Ntl Merit Ltr; Grls Ctznshp Isnt Delg Spnsrd NJ Fed Wmns Clbs 86; Wmn Engr Stevens Inst Of Tech; Engr.

OSTUNI, NICHOLAS; Palisades Park JR SR HS; Palisades Pk, NJ; (Y); Lit Mag; Bsbl; Bsktbl; Ftbl; Wt Lftg; Hon Roll; Bus.

OSUCH, THERESA; Linden HS; Linden, NJ; (Y); High Hon Roll; Trvl Agnt.

OTANI, ROBERT K; Pascack Valley HS; River Vale, NJ; (Y); 35/262; Var Capt Ftbl; Hon Roll; NHS; Var Trk; Rutgers Coll Of Engr; Engr.

OTCHET, FELICIA; Rantan HS; Hazlet, NJ; (Y); 8/280; French Clb; Math Tm; Science Clb; Temple Yth Grp; Mrchg Band; Rep Frsh Cls; Pres Soph Cls; Bsktbl; Var L Tennis; NHS; Wrk At Spcl Olympcs & Trnmnt Of Chmpns 85-86; Pre-Med.

OTERO, SUSAN; St John Vianney HS; Marlboro, NJ; (Y); Church Yth Grp; Off Trs Intnl Clb; Drm Mjr(t); Nwsp Sprt Ed; Yrbk Ed-Chief; Socr; 1st Hons 2nd Marking Period 86 & 85; St John Vianney Gold & White Awd 86; 2nd Hons 84-86; Phsy Therapy.

OTT, BRIAN; Gloucester Co Christian Schl; Turnersville, NJ; (S); 1/16; Debate Tm; Chorus; Yrbk Stf; Var L Bsbl; Var L Socr; High Hon Roll; NHS; Ntl Merit SF; Val; English Clb; Awana Yth Ldr 82-83; Pensacola Chrstn Coll; Mech Eng.

OTT, CHRISTINE N; Howell HS; Howell, NJ; (Y); 42/400; VP Church Yth Grp; French Clb; Office Aide; Chorus; Church Choir; Stage Crew; Variety Show; Nwsp Stf; Hon Roll; NHS; Eagle Of Cross Awd 85; Scl Psychlgy.

OTT JR, ROY J; James Caldwell HS; W Caldwell, NJ; (Y); Pres Trs Key Clb; Nwsp Stf; Rep Frsh Cls; Rep Soph Cls; Rep Jr Cls; Rep Sr Cls; Var JV Socr; High Hon Roll; NHS; Bio Awd 84.

OTT, THERESA; Saint James HS; Mantua, NJ; (S); 13/78.

OTTAVIANO, CHARLES; Maple Shade HS; Maple Shade, NJ; (Y); Am Leg Boys St; Pres DECA; French Clb; Key Clb; SADD; Variety Show; Var Ftbl; JV Trk; Var Wrstlng; Hon Roll; ST Fnlst Gnrl Mrktg NJ DECA 86; 1st Pl X-Mas Wrstlng Trnmnt 86; 4th Pl Dist Wrstlng Trnmnt 86; Sprts Med.

OTTEN, JILL; Paulsboro HS; Paulsboro, NJ; (Y); Ski Clb; Rep Jr Cls; JV Trk; Im Wt Lftg; Gloucester Cty Tn Art Fstvl-Hnrbl Mntn/Orgnlty 85-86; Phldlphia Schl Art; Cmrcl Art.

OTTEN, PATRICK; Bloomfield SR HS; Bloomfield, NJ; (Y); 176/447; Boy Scts; Church Yth Grp; German Clb; Key Clb; JV Var Crs Cntry; JV Socr; Var Trk; Aerospc.

OTTEN, THEODORE; St James HS; Paulsboro, NJ; (S); 6/79; VP Jr Cls; Var Bsbl; Var Bsktbl; JV Ftbl; Hon Roll; Class Merit Awd Social Studies & Spanish 83-85; Med Doctor.

OTTERBEIN, LYNNE; Mt St Dominic Acad; Cedar Grove, NJ; (Y); Cmnty Wkr; Hosp Aide; Library Aide; NFL; Ski Clb; Varsity Clb; Chorus; JV Bsktbl.

OUELLETTE, MISS; Washington Township HS; Sewell, NJ; (Y); Church Yth Grp; French Clb; Band; Concert Band; Mrchg Band; Off Soph Cls; Rotary Awd; Rotary Yth Ldrshp Awds 86; Archit.

OUGHOURLI, DIANA; Manchester Reg HS; Prospect Pk, NJ; (Y); Cmnty Wkr; Yrbk Phtg; JV Var Vllybl; Hon Roll; GATE Pgm 84-86; Hnrs Engl,Hist,Math 84-86; Rutgers U; Bus.

OVERN, DOUGLAS; Indian Hills HS; Oakland, NJ; (Y); 28/280; Church Yth Grp; Varsity Clb; Band; Yrbk Stf; Var Ftbl; Var Trk; Hon Roll; NHS; Ntl Merit Ltr; All-Leag Ftbl 85; Cornell; Engrng.

OWCHARIW, SONIA; Abraham Clark HS; Roselle, NJ; (S); Church Yth Grp; Band; Chorus; Drm Mjr(t); Jazz Band; Madrigals; Mrchg Band; Nwsp Rptr; Pres Frsh Cls; Pres Soph Cls; Oral Roberts U; Music.

OWEN, VALERIE; Keyport HS; Keyport, NJ; (Y); 3/89; Trs French Clb; Pres SADD; Yrbk Ed-Chief; Sec Sr Cls; VP Stu Cncl; Var Cheerleading; Var Capt Trk; High Hon Roll; Sec NHS; Voice Dem Awd; Athlt Yr Awd; Grls Ctznshp Ist Delegt; Hghst Avg Awd Alg II, Geom, Frnch I; Elon Coll NC.

OWENS, ANITA; Irvington HS; Irvington, NJ; (Y); 7/350; Drama Clb; FBLA; Key Clb; Library Aide; Spanish Clb; Yrbk Stf; Lit Mag; Pres Stu Cncl; Hon Roll; Pres NHS; Girl Mnth 86; Fellowshp WA Wk 86; Schlrshp BPW 86; Rutgers; Comm.

OWENS, GAY; Bridgeton HS; Dividing Creek, NJ; (Y); Sec Church Yth Grp; Civic Clb; Teachers Aide; Yrbk Stf; Rep Soph Cls; Rep Jr Cls; Gov Hon Prg Awd; High Hon Roll; Jr NHS; NHS; Schlrshp Ltr B Hghst Hnrs Fr 3 Rprt Prds 83-85; George Washngtn U Mdl Sci & Math 85-86; Phrmcy.

OWENS, RICH; Gloucester County Vocational Schl; Franklinville, NJ; (Y); 4/22; Gloucester County Voc; Crpntr.

OWENSBY, JENNIFER; Weehawken HS; Weehawken, NJ; (S); 5/104; Hosp Aide; Q&S; Band; Color Guard; Nwsp Ed-Chief; Yrbk Stf; Lit Mag; High Hon Roll; NHS; 3rd Pl Trenton ST Wrtng Cntst 85; Medcn.

OXLEY, LARRY; Toms River North HS; Toms River, NJ; (Y); FBLA; Math Clb; Gym; Wrstlng; Jr NHS.

OXLEY, RENAE; Gateway Reginal HS; National Park, NJ; (Y); Church Yth Grp; FHA; Latin Clb; SADD; Yrbk Stf; Stu Cncl; Stat Bsktbl; Cheerleading; FHA Mdl-Cnsmr Awrns-ST Cnvntn 86; Hmcmmng Rep 82; Compltd Mdlng & LO Cmmrcl Crses; Psyclgy.

OZER, ESRA; Hopewell Valley Central HS; Pennington, NJ; (Y); AFS; Am Leg Aux Girls St; French Clb; Pres FBLA; School Play; Nwsp Phtg; Nwsp Rptr; Nwsp Stf; Yrbk Stf; Hon Roll; FLBA Awd Regl Comptn 85; Intl Finance.

PABST, CAROL; Abraham Clark HS; Roselle, NJ; (S); 3/200; DECA; Chorus; Concert Band; Jazz Band; Mrchg Band; Sec Frsh Cls; Var Cheerleading; Hon Roll; Sec NHS; Music Theatr.

PACCIONE, JOHN; Holy Spirit HS; Margate, NJ; (Y); 52/360; Stage Crew; Nwsp Rptr; Bsktbl; Im Ftbl; Im Vllybl; High Hon Roll; Hon Roll; Bus Law Awd 86; U Dayton OH; Accntngh.

PACE, BRIAN; Parsippany Hills HS; Morris Plains, NJ; (Y); Chess Clb; Church Yth Grp; Political Wkr; U Of CA Canta Cruz; Comp Sci.

PACE, FRANK; Linden HS; Linden, NJ; (Y); Church Yth Grp; Drama Clb; Capt Quiz Bowl; JV Bsbl; JV Bsktbl; JV Bowling; High Hon Roll; Hon Roll; Seton Hall; Hotel Mgmt.

PACE, HILARY; Clifton HS; Clifton, NJ; (Y); 33/687; Church Yth Grp; French Clb; Key Clb; SADD; Nwsp Stf; Ed Yrbk Stf; Mgr Lcrss; Im Mgr(s); Twrlr; French Hon Soc; Honor Guard 86; Acctng.

PACE, JOHN C; Passaic Valley HS; Little Falls, NJ; (Y); 34/309; Am Leg Boys St; Church Yth Grp; VP Key Clb; Yrbk Stf; Rep Jr Cls; Rep Sr Cls; Var Bsbl; Var Capt Ftbl; Hon Roll; Jr NHS; Muhlenberg Coll.

PACELLI, DAN; Colonia HS; Avanel, NJ; (Y); Nwsp Rptr; Nwsp Stf; Ice Hcky; Hon Roll; Accntng.

PACHANA, JOANN; Oak Knoll Schl; Newark, NJ; (Y); Cmnty Wkr; French Clb; Hosp Aide; Service Clb; Spanish Clb; Varsity Clb; Stage Crew; Nwsp Stf; Lit Mag; Im Vllybl; Supr Wrk Comp BASIC Awd 86; Comp Engrng.

PACHTMAN, CORI; Freehold Twp HS; Freehold, NJ; (Y); 62/319; French Clb; Nwsp Rptr; Stu Cncl; JV Gym; Var JV Socr; Hon Roll; Geo Wshngtn U; Bus Adm.

PACIORKOWSKI, PATRICK; Bayonne HS; Bayonne, NJ; (Y); Boy Scts; Cmnty Wkr; High Hon Roll; Hon Roll; Math Hnrs 84-86; Stvns Inst Of Tech; Stllite Cmn.

PACIORKOWSKI, THOMAS; Bayonne HS; Bayonne, NJ; (Y); Boy Scts; High Hon Roll; Hon Roll; Ntl Merit Ltr; Bayonne Prof Wmns Schlrshp 85-86; Alex Bordon Schlrshp; Principl Hnrs; Stevens Inst; Elec Engnrng.

PADDOCK, CATHY; Kinnelon HS; Kinnelon, NJ; (Y); German Clb; Bsktbl; Trk; Hon Roll; Physcl Thrpst.

PADDON, ERIC; Chatham Twp HS; Chatham, NJ; (Y); Key Clb; Model UN; Radio Clb; Concert Band; Jazz Band; Hist.

PADILLA, MAYRA; Holy Family Acad; Bayonne, NJ; (Y); Church Yth Grp; Cmnty Wkr; Pres French Clb; School Play; Rep Soph Cls; Rep Jr Cls; VP Stu Cncl; Cit Awd; Hon Roll; NHS; Maria Limon Mem Awd 85; Tchr Handicppd Chldrn 84-86; Frnch Lang.

PADLLA, MICHELE; Piscataway HS; Piscataway, NJ; (Y); Varsity Clb; Fld Hcky; Sftbl; Trk; Elem Ed.

PAGANO, ARMAND V; Saint Aloysius HS; W Palm Beach, FL; (Y); 21/165; Boy Scts; Exploring; School Play; Rep Stu Cncl; Im Bowling; Hon Roll; Chiro Engrng.

PAGE, DAVID; Haddon Township HS; Westmont, NJ; (Y); Am Leg Boys St; Boy Scts; Church Yth Grp; Office Aide; Varsity Clb; Var L Bsbl; Var L Socr; Hon Roll.

PAGE, GLENN; Mater Dei HS; Red Bank, NJ; (Y); 23/151; Church Yth Grp; Debate Tm; JV Crs Cntry; Hon Roll; Philosphy.

PAGE, GLENN; Pascack Hills HS; Woodcliff Lk, NJ; (Y); Boy Scts; Computer Clb; Im Bsbl; Im Bsktbl; Im Coach Actv; Im Golf; JV Var Tennis; Hon Roll; Thomas Alva Edison Foundtn 85-86; Max Mc Graw Foundtn 85-86; Law.

PAGE, TANYA; Rancocas Valley Reg HS; Mt Holly, NJ; (Y); 173/350; Am Leg Aux Girls St; Church Yth Grp; FBLA; Girl Scts; JA; Chorus; Capt Co-Capt Cheerleading; Coach Actv; Powder Puff Ftbl; JV Sftbl; Awd Outstndng Chrldng Awd 85-86; VA ST U; Pre-Law.

PAGELS, JOSEPH; Hamilton East; Trenton, NJ; (Y); 28/315; Trs AFS; Var Capt Golf; Var L Socr; Hon Roll; NHS; Pres Schlrshp Clarion U PA 86; Clarion U PA; Cmmnctns.

PAGLIONE, MIKE; Toms River H S East; Toms River, NJ; (Y); 26/585; Ski Clb; Socr; Trk; Hon Roll; Comp Engr.

PAGLIUCA, CAROLYN; Cresskill HS; Cresskill, NJ; (Y); 30/111; Ski Clb; Spanish Clb; Stage Crew; Pres Jr Cls; VP Sr Cls; Cheerleading; Sftbl; Vllybl; High Hon Roll; God Cntry Awd; Highest Hnrs 82-83; Intramural Sports 79-83; Schl Band 79-83; Bus.

PAGLIUGHI, MARTY; Holy Spirit HS; Brigantine, NJ; (Y); 70/330; Key Clb; Pep Clb; Ski Clb; Var Ftbl; JV Golf; Im Gym; Im Vllybl; High Hon Roll; Hon Roll; NHS; Big Brothrs 86-87; Rutgers; Med.

PAGTALUNAN, HONESTO; Woodbridge HS; Fords, NJ; (Y); 11/400; Computer Clb; Debate Tm; Quiz Bowl; Band; Concert Band; Orch; Lit Mag; JV Tennis; High Hon Roll; Outstndg Achvt Awd-Fndtn Of Philippine 85; Amer Med Soc Of NJ Inc; Rutgers U; Elec Engrng.

PAIK, EDWARD Y; Glen Rock HS; Glen Rock, NJ; (Y); 6/153; Am Leg Boys St; Pres Church Yth Grp; Trs Hosp Aide; VP Latin Clb; Science Clb; Band; School Musical; Nwsp Stf; Var Trk; NHS; Grad Andover Smmr Sessn 85; Grad Ramapa Coll Sci Prog 86; Grad Cornell U Summer Coll 86; Pre-Med.

PAIZ, BRIGITTE; Millville SR HS; Millville, NJ; (Y); Office Aide; SADD; Color Guard; Rep Stu Cncl; Var Capt Crs Cntry; JV Sftbl; Var Trk; Hon Roll; NHS; SR Fml Athlt/Grls Crs Cntry 86; Chmstry Awd 84; Thndrblt Awd 86; Frlgh Dcknsn; CPA.

PAK, JOO; Lincoln HS; Jersey Cty, NJ; (Y); Church Yth Grp; Drama Clb; FHA; Hosp Aide; Spanish Clb; Prfct Atten Awd; Pvt Invstgr.

PALARG, KIM; Hightstown HS; E Windsor, NJ; (Y); Spanish Clb; Stat Crs Cntry; Stat Trk; Trenton ST.

PALESCHIC, CAMI; Pennsville Memorial HS; Pennsville, NJ; (Y); 86/235; FBLA; Hosp Aide; Office Aide; Teachers Aide; Concert Band; Capt Flag Corp; Mrchg Band; Orch; Var Cheerleading; MV Flg Tm Membr 84-85; Brandywine Coll; Fashn Merch.

PALESCHIC, CHRISTOPHER; Woodstown HS; Woodstown, NJ; (Y); 15/235; Church Yth Grp; English Clb; German Clb; Nwsp Rptr; Stu Cncl; Golf; Socr; USAA Natl Ldrshp & Svc Awd 85-86; USAA Frgn Lang Awd 85-86; Acad Exclnce In Olympics Of Mind 86; Ursinus; Lawyer.

PALEY, DONNA; Piscataway HS; Piscataway, NJ; (Y); 46/519; Key Clb; Varsity Clb; Var Fld Hcky; Var Capt Sftbl; Stat Wrstlng; Hon Roll; NHS; Yrbk Stf; Schlrshp Itln-Amercn Clb 86; Mike Capasso Memrl Schlrshp 86; Schlr-Athlt 86; Rutgets Coll; Bus.

PALISI, DAMIAN; Columbia HS; Maplewood, NJ; (Y); German Clb; Pres Intnl Clb; Pres Pep Clb; Science Clb; Spanish Clb; Rep Frsh Cls; Rep Soph Cls; Stat Fld Hcky; Spanish NHS; Frgn Exchng Stu Austrla 85; Bryn Mawr Coll; Govt.

PALITTO, JAMES A; Roselle Park HS; Roselle Park, NJ; (Y); 24/175; Am Leg Boys St; Political Wkr; School Musical; School Play; Stage Crew; JV Ftbl; Var Socr; Var L Trk; JV Wrstlng; Hon Roll; Announcer WVTP Schl Radio Statn; Yth Mayors Advsr Comm; Pre Law.

PALLANTE, JIM; Montville HS; E Hanover, NJ; (Y); Art Clb; Church Yth Grp; Key Clb; Ski Clb; SADD; Var JV Ftbl; Var Lcrss; Hon Roll; Soph Clss Essy Cont Natl Acid Rain Comp 84-85; Soph Clss Collg 1st 84-85; Art Exhibit Prize 84-85; Rutgers U; Pre-Law.

PALLEN, ANDREW; Toms River North HS; Toms River, NJ; (Y); Ski Clb; Nwsp Phtg; Nwsp Rptr; Nwsp Stf; Golf; Socr; High Hon Roll; Hon Roll.

PALMA, ANTHONY; Bloomfield HS; Bloomfield, NJ; (Y); 70/450; JV Var Bsbl; JV Var Golf; Var Socr; Arch.

PALMA, DOUGLAS; Rancolas Valley Regional HS; Mount Holly, NJ; (Y); 4/330; Am Leg Boys St; Science Clb; Ski Clb; Varsity Clb; Var Golf; Var Socr; Var Swmmng; High Hon Roll; NHS; Phys Thrpy.

PALMBERG, KAREN; Parsippany HS; Lake Hiawatha, NJ; (Y); Chorus; Stage Crew; Ed.

PALMER, ANNE WHITNEY; West Morris Mendham HS; Mendham, NJ; (Y); 51/304; Pres VP 4-H; Intnl Clb; Quiz Bowl; Ski Clb; Dnfth Awd; 4-H Awd; High Hon Roll; Hon Roll.

PALMER, MICHAEL; Southern Regional HS; Manahawkin, NJ; (Y); 1/380; Model UN; Yrbk Sprt Ed; Var Crs Cntry; Var Golf; High Hon Roll; NHS; Corp Admin.

PALMIERI, CYNTHIA; West Essex HS; Fairfield, NJ; (Y); Key Clb; Pep Clb; Capt Var Cheerleading; Hon Roll.

PALMIERI JR, VINCENT J; Southern Regional HS; Barnegat, NJ; (Y); 17/400; Church Yth Grp; Model UN; Variety Show; Rep Stu Cncl; JV L Bsbl; Var L Bowling; JV L Crs Cntry; Gov Hon Prg Awd; High Hon Roll; NHS; 1st Essy Cntst 85; Villa Nova; Bus.

PALMISANO, JOE; Middle Township HS; Rio Grande, NJ; (Y); Art Clb; VICA; Band; Mrchg Band; Yrbk Stf; Hon Roll; Hnr Rll-Cmmrcl Art 84-86; Atlantic CC; Cmmrcl Art.

PALMISANO, PAIGE; Parsippany HS; Parsippany, NJ; (Y); 63/318; FBLA; Office Aide; Pep Clb; Political Wkr; Service Clb; Spanish Clb; High Hon Roll; NHS; Pres Schlr; Trenton ST; Bus.

PALOMBINI, DENISE; Toms River North HS; Toms River, NJ; (Y); Concert Band; Mrchg Band; Orch; School Musical; Stu Cncl; Jr NHS; NHS; 7th Annual William H Sattern Mem Awd Achvt Music 86; Rutgers U; Bus.

PALOMBINI, MATT; Toms River North HS; Toms River, NJ; (Y); 14/412; Ski Clb; Stage Crew; Socr; Tennis; High Hon Roll; Hon Roll; NHS; Ntl Merit Ltr.

PALUMBO, ANGELO; Central Regional HS; Bayville, NJ; (Y); Bsbl; Hon Roll; NHS; George Washington U; Elec.

PALUS, MARK; Indian Hills HS; Franklin Lks, NJ; (Y); 12/279; Am Leg Boys St; Cmnty Wkr; Debate Tm; Math Tm; Science Clb; Rep Stu Cncl; JV Bsbl; High Hon Roll; Ntl Merit Ltr; IBM Yth Ldrshp Prg 86; Engrng.

PANCHAL, JYOTI; Cherry Hill High Schl West; Cherry Hill, NJ; (Y); Drama Clb; Hosp Aide; Intnl Clb; Library Aide; Science Clb; Spanish Clb; School Play; Yrbk Bus Mgr; Hon Roll; NHS; Temple U; Bio.

PANCIONE, DANIELLE; Mt St Mary Acad; Piscataway, NJ; (Y); 35/90; Dance Clb; Office Aide; Spanish Clb; School Play; VP Frsh Cls; Rep Soph Cls; Rep Jr Cls; Stu Cncl; Hon Roll; Spanish NHS; Bus.

PANDISCIA, ANNE; Hopatcong HS; Hopatcong, NJ; (Y); 45/211; Scholastic Bowl; Band; Concert Band; Mrchg Band; School Musical; Stage Crew; Nwsp Rptr; Yrbk Rptr; Hon Roll; Art Awd 83; Phrmcy.

PANDYA, PIYUSH; Clifton HS; Clifton, NJ; (Y); 90/564; Jr NHS; Rtgrs U; Comp Engr.

PANDYA, RUPAM; Metuchen HS; Metuchen, NJ; (Y); 33/178; French Clb; Math Tm; Science Clb; JV Fld Hcky; Hon Roll; NHS; Biochem.

PANELLA, TERRI; Sacred Heart HS; Milmay, NJ; (Y); School Play; Yrbk Rptr; Yrbk Stf; Var L Crs Cntry; German Clb; Hosp Aide; Chorus; Accntng.

PANICO, MICHAEL A; Fair Lawn HS; Fair Lawn, NJ; (Y); 1/325; Am Leg Boys St; Math Tm; Science Clb; SADD; Varsity Clb; Capt Wrstlng; High Hon Roll; NHS; St Schlr; Val; All Cnty Wrstlng Tm 85; Rutgers Schlr 86; Ntl Mrt Commnd 86.

PANICUCCI, RICHARD; Montville HS; Pine Brook, NJ; (Y); 21/262; Key Clb; Ski Clb; SADD; Rep Frsh Cls; Rep Soph Cls; Rep Jr Cls; JV Lcrss; Wt Lftg; High Hon Roll; Hon Roll; PRE-DNTSTRY.

PANKAVICH, KATHY; Villa Victoria Acad; Hamilton Sq, NJ; (Y); Camera Clb; School Musical; Yrbk Stf; Lit Mag; VP Jr Cls; Stu Cncl; JV Var Bsktbl; Var Fld Hcky; Var Sftbl; NEDT Awd; Grtr Trntn Sci Fair 83-84; Schl Sprt Awd $100 Bond 86; Red & Gry Schlrshp OH ST U $1100 86; OH ST U.

PANKOW, AMY; Pompton Lakes HS; Pompton Lks, NJ; (Y); 46/153; German Clb; Intnl Clb; Math Tm; Q&S; Teachers Aide; Color Guard; Stage Crew; Ed Yrbk Phtg; Ed Lit Mag; Hon Roll; Ntl Hstry Day NJ ST Chmpns 86; Ntl Hstry Day NJ Rgnl Chmpns 85; Montclair ST Coll; Phrmcy.

PANNER, MICHELLE; Pitman HS; Pitman, NJ; (S); 7/141; Teachers Aide; Chorus; Rep Stu Cncl; JV Var Bsbl; JV Var Cheerleading; Var Mgr(s); Var Mat Maids; Stat Wrstlng; Hon Roll; NHS; Modern Mus Masters Soc.

PANNULLO, BARBARA JEAN; Paul VI Regional HS; Clifton, NJ; (Y); 38/129; Key Clb; Library Aide; Service Clb; French Hon Soc; High Hon Roll; Hon Roll; Montclair ST Coll.

PANZERA, PAUL; Hillsborough HS; Belle Mead, NJ; (Y); 1/300; Math Tm; Co-Capt Quiz Bowl; Science Clb; Rep Frsh Cls; Rep Soph Cls; VP Jr Cls; Var JV Bsbl; High Hon Roll; NHS; Ntl Merit Ltr; Stu Ldrshp Smnr By US Sntr Bill Bradley 86; Engrng.

PANZITTA, THERESA; St Elizabeth Acad; W Caldwell, NJ; (Y); Camera Clb; Cmnty Wkr; Spanish Clb; Yrbk Stf; Lit Mag; Trs Sr Cls; Seton Hall U; Bus.

PAOLILLO, NADINE; St John Vianney HS; Morganville, NJ; (Y); Art Clb; Church Yth Grp; Computer Clb; Office Aide; Ski Clb; Yrbk Stf; Rep Jr Cls; Mgr(s); Powder Puff Ftbl; Hon Roll.

PAOLINE, JOSEPH; Paul VI HS; Runnemede, NJ; (S); Math Clb; Spanish Clb; Hon Roll; Acad All Amer 84; Natl Ldrshp & Svc Awd 85; Phrmcy.

PAOLINI, DAVE; Holy Cross HS; Palmyra, NJ; (Y); Church Yth Grp; Ski Clb; Yrbk Phtg; JV L Bsbl; Hon Roll; Med.

PAPA, FRANCINE; Southern Regional HS; Barnegat, NJ; (Y); 7/375; Trs Frsh Cls; Trs Soph Cls; Trs Jr Cls; Trs Sr Cls; JV Var Fld Hcky; High Hon Roll; Hon Roll; NHS; St Schlr; NJ Schlr Athlt Awd 86; Walter C Sharp Schlr Schlrshp 86; Cls Of 86 Schlrshp 86; MA Schl Of Pharmacy; Phrmcy.

PAPADAKIS, FANNY; William L Dickinson HS; Jersey City, NJ; (Y); 1/38; Church Yth Grp; Computer Clb; Dance Clb; Girl Scts; Math Clb; Pres Frsh Cls; Swmmng; Tennis; Vllybl; High Hon Roll; Dncng Awd 83; Tchng Dnc Awd 86; Rutgers ST U; Dntstry.

PAPADAKIS, GEORGE; Ferris HS; Jersey City, NJ; (Y); 15/300; Computer Clb; Math Clb; High Hon Roll; Hon Roll; Hnr, Merit, Achvt Cert 83 & 85-86; Merit P Achvt Cert 84; Rutgers; Engrng.

PAPADELIAS, KATHY; East Brunswick HS; E Brunswick, NJ; (Y); Church Yth Grp; Dance Clb; Hosp Aide; Key Clb; Pep Clb; SADD; High Hon Roll; Hon Roll; Cert Outstndg Creat Comp 81; 100 Hr Bar Volunteer Wrk Candystrpr 84; Miss JR Goya 85; Rutgers U; Psych.

PAPAGELOPOULOS, MARIA; Dover HS; Dover, NJ; (Y); 14/183; VP Pres Church Yth Grp; French Clb; German Clb; Office Aide; VP Spanish Clb; Nwsp Stf; Lit Mag; Hon Roll; NHS; Prfct Atten Awd; Law.

PAPALEO, BETSY; Cherry Hill HS East; Cherry Hill, NJ; (Y); Drama Clb; French Clb; Letterman Clb; Model UN; Pep Clb; Speech Tm; Cheerleading; Pom Pon; Tennis; Hon Roll; IN U; Psych.

PAPANIKOLAS, ANASTASIOS; Neptune SR HS; Neptune, NJ; (Y); 30/390; Church Yth Grp; Math Tm; Science Clb; Yrbk Rptr; Yrbk Stf; Rep Soph Cls; Rep Jr Cls; Bsktbl; Hon Roll; NHS; Intl Business.

PAPARO, DOMINIC; Overbrook Regional HS; Pine Hill, NJ; (Y); Var Ftbl; Var Wt Lftg; Hon Roll; Prfct Atten Awd; Natl Latin Exam Magna Cum Laude 84-85; Penn ST; Bio.

PAPAZOGLOU, JOHN; North Brunswick Township HS; N Brunswick, NJ; (Y); 31/210; Church Yth Grp; Model UN; Band; Concert Band; Jazz Band; Mrchg Band; JV Swmmng; Hon Roll; NHS.

PAPE, ED; Pitman HS; Pitman, NJ; (Y); 26/153; Boy Scts; Trs Exploring; VP Concert Band; VP Mrchg Band; Rep Stu Cncl; JV Bsktbl; Var L Crs Cntry; L Trk; Im Vllybl; God Cntry Awd; Bus Adm.

PAPP, ALBERT; Columbia HS; Maplewood, NJ; (Y); Chess Clb; Computer Clb; German Clb; Band; Concert Band; Jazz Band; Mrchg Band; Orch; Symp Band; Im Vllybl; Delta Epsilon Phi 86; Elec Engrng.

PAPPALARDO, VINCENT; Lenade Valley Regional HS; Sparta, NJ; (Y); 12/253; Pres Frsh Cls; Pres Jr Cls; Stu Cncl; JV VP Ftbl; JV Var Trk; Wt Lftg; High Hon Roll; Hon Roll; NHS; Lenape Schlr 85.

PAPPAS, ELENI; St Dominic Acad; Bayonne, NJ; (Y); 8/149; Art Clb; Computer Clb; French Clb; GAA; JCL; Sec Latin Clb; Service Clb; Spanish Clb; Teachers Aide; Acpl Chr; Excllnc Hstry, Frnch; Aerntcl Engr.

PAPPAS, PAUL; Atlantic City HS; Ventnor, NJ; (Y); Boy Scts; Church Yth Grp; FCA; Key Clb; Church Choir; Ftbl; Wt Lftg; L Wrstlng; Hon Roll; Archt Engr.

PARABOSCHI, STEVEN; Montville HS; Towaco, NJ; (Y); 68/265; Boy Scts; Church Yth Grp; Varsity Clb; Sec Frsh Cls; Sec Soph Cls; Rep Jr Cls; JV Ftbl; Swmmng; Wt Lftg; Wrstlng; Bio Sci.

PARADA, MARIA; Queen Of Peace HS; Newark, NJ; (Y); Church Yth Grp; Cmnty Wkr; Dance Clb; French Clb; Hosp Aide; Library Aide; Service Clb; SADD; Hon Roll; Spanish NHS; Folklore Dancing Awd 86; Rutgers; Intl Bus.

PARADISE, SCOTT; Life Center Acad; Croydan, PA; (S); Pres Church Yth Grp; Drama Clb; Hosp Aide; Church Choir; Nwsp Stf; Concordia Coll NY; Thlgy.

PARCELLS, TRISH; Boonton HS; Lincoln Park, NJ; (Y); Am Leg Aux Girls St; Drama Clb; GAA; Chorus; Church Choir; Drill Tm; School Musical; Stage Crew; Capt Twrlr; Hon Roll; Sclgy.

PARDO, DANIELLE A; Hanover Park HS; Florham Park, NJ; (Y); 7/283; Am Leg Aux Girls St; Pres Debate Tm; NFL; Pres Spanish Clb; Pres Speech Tm; Nwsp Rptr; Yrbk Ed-Chief; Rep Soph Cls; Rep Jr Cls; JV Cheerleading; U VA; Hstry.

PARDUCCI, JUDITH; Edgewood Regional SR HS; Berlin, NJ; (Y); 52/410; Sec FNA; Hosp Aide; Red Cross Aide; Band; Rptr Lit Mag; Rep Stu Cncl; Jr NHS; Loren Esposito Mem Schlrshp 86; Mary G Middleman Mem Schlrshp 86; Esther Dietz Mem Schlrshp 86; U Delaware; Nrsng.

PAREDES, ALESSIO JOSEPH; Paul VI HS; Passaic, NJ; (Y); VP Computer Clb; Ski Clb; Trk; High Hon Roll; Hon Roll; MECH Engr.

PAREDES, EMIGDIO; Garden State Acad; N Bergen, NJ; (Y); Cmnty Wkr; Exploring; Red Cross Aide; SADD; Church Choir; Yrbk Sprt Ed; Sec Soph Cls; Rep Jr Cls; Capt Bsktbl; Cit Awd; NY U; Radiation Ther.

PAREJO, MARIA; Northern Burlington County Reg HS; Wrightstown, NJ; (Y); Church Yth Grp; Cmnty Wkr; Spanish Clb; SADD; Chorus; Rep Frsh Cls; Rep Soph Cls; Rep Jr Cls; Rep Sr Cls; Rep Stu Cncl; Glassboro ST.

PARENT, CLIFFORD; Hamilton High School West; Trenton, NJ; (Y); 5/307; Church Yth Grp; Hosp Aide; Key Clb; Radio Clb; Pres Chorus; Church Choir; Madrigals; School Musical; School Play; Variety Show; Gov Tchng Schlrshp 86; Foreign Lang Awd Spn 86; Nat Schlstc Choral Awd 86; Seton Hall U; Sec Math Ed.

PARETTI JR, JAMES A; West Milford Twp HS; W Milford, NJ; (Y); 1/350; Am Leg Boys St; Model UN; Capt Quiz Bowl; Nwsp Ed-Chief; Yrbk Ed-Chief; Pres Sr Cls; NHS; Ntl Merit SF; Val; Rep Stu Cncl; Mdl Congrs 86; Govn Keans Ldrshp Smnr 86; Sen Bradley Convoctn 86; Harvard U; Govnmt.

PARGAS, ILEANA; Elizabeth HS; Elizabeth, NJ; (Y); Dance Clb; School Musical; School Play; Stage Crew; Rep Frsh Cls; Rep Soph Cls; Rep Jr Cls; Princpls Schlr Awd 83; Superintndts Schlr Awd 83; Fash Inst Tech; Fash Merch.

PARIKH, NEETA; Madison Central HS; Old Bridge, NJ; (Y); 20/342; French Clb; Math Tm; Yrbk Stf; Mgr(s); Score Keeper; Timer; French Hon Soc; NHS; Rutgers U; Econ.

PARIKH, SETUL; Shore Regional HS; West Long Branch, NJ; (Y); Boys Clb Am; Church Choir; Chess Clb; Temple Yth Grp; Stage Crew; Yrbk Stf; Bsbl; Crs Cntry; Swmmng; Wt Lftg; Ctznshp Awd 83; Hon Rl 85-86; Bus.

PARIKH, VIRAJ; Lodi HS; Lodi, NJ; (Y); English Clb; Key Clb; Math Clb; Spanish Clb; Hon Roll; Stu Cncl Scholar 86; Bergen CC; Phrmcy.

PARILLO, CHRISTINE; Sayreville War Memorial HS; Parlin, NJ; (Y); 85/379; French Clb; Chorus; School Musical; Swing Chorus; Hon Roll; Hnrs Chorus 85; 1st Brian Farias Vcl Music Schlrshp 86; Cultrl Arts Cncl Music Awd 86; Douglass Coll; Music Ed.

PARISE, CHRIS; Jackson Memorial HS; Jackson, NJ; (Y); Computer Clb; German Clb; Varsity Clb; Mrchg Band; Var Capt Socr; Hon Roll; Band; Concert Band; 4 Yr Vrsty Scr SR Yr Cptn; Rutges Schl Of Engr; Engrng.

PARISE, LORI; Mount Saint Mary Acad; Plainfield, NJ; (Y); Church Yth Grp; GAA; Math Clb; Pep Clb; Service Clb; Rep Frsh Cls; Jr Cls; Cum Laude Natl Latn Exam 83; Outstndng Svc Acad 85.

PARISI, ANTHONY; Washington Twp HS; Blackwood, NJ; (Y); Church Yth Grp; Cmnty Wkr; Dance Clb; Drama Clb; ROTC; Chorus; Church Choir; School Musical; Stage Crew; Nwsp Rptr; V P & P SC; Cmpgn Cnclmnn; Camden Cnty Coll.

PARISI, DAVID; Ridgefield Park HS; Little Ferry, NJ; (Y); 19/183; Chess Clb; Debate Tm; Band; Yrbk Stf; Var Capt Crs Cntry; Var Trk; Hon Roll; NHS; NJ Boys ST Altrn Dele 86; Naval Acad; Aero Engrng.

PARISI, MARIA; Lodi HS; Lodi, NJ; (Y); Key Clb; Pep Clb; Chorus; Color Guard; Rep Frsh Cls; Rep Soph Cls; Stu Cncl; JV Sftbl; High Hon Roll; Hon Roll; Berdan Inst; Mecl Assist.

PARISI, PAUL; Don Bosco Prep; Mahwah, NJ; (S); 20/178; Service Clb; Ski Clb; Yrbk Stf; Rep Stu Cncl; Var Trk; VP NHS; 1st Hnrs 82-84; Prncpls Lst 84-85; Coll William & Mary; Engrng.

PARK, DAVID; Burlington City HS; Burlington, NJ; (Y); 15/200; Am Leg Boys St; Camera Clb; Var Bsbl; Var Ftbl; Var L Wrstlng; Hon Roll; Wrestlng Christmas Tour 1st Pl 85; Bus.

PARK, GRACE H; Cherry Hill HS East; Cherry Hill, NJ; (Y); 9/680; Am Leg Aux Girls St; Church Yth Grp; French Clb; Model UN; Off Chorus; Ed Yrbk Stf; Lit Mag; High Hon Roll; Ntl Merit SF; NEDT Awd; Amercnsm Essay Awd-2nd Pl Ntl 85; Frnch Ntl Cont Awd-2nd Pl Ntl 85; New Jersey Dstngshd Schlr Awd 86.

PARK, HYUNG; East Brunswick HS; East Brunswick, NJ; (Y); 32/360; Computer Clb; Hosp Aide; Latin Clb; Hon Roll; Hsptl Vlntrng Awd 85; Karate Cls Awds 84; Jhns Hpkns U; Pre-Med.

PARK, JANE; Eastern HS; Voorhees, NJ; (Y); Church Yth Grp; Chorus; Stu Cncl; Hon Roll; Prfct Atten Awd; S Jrsy Music Tchrs Assoc 85; Panache Tlnt Shw 85; Phil Music Tchrs Assoc 85; Rutgers; Bus.

PARK, ROBERT K; Christian Brothers Acad; West Long Branch, NJ; (S); 1/223; Hosp Aide; Math Tm; Quiz Bowl; Nwsp Stf; Yrbk Stf; Var Trk; High Hon Roll; Sec NHS; Debate Tm; US Congrssnl Awd 85; Nwsppr Featr Ed 85-86.

PARKE, MARK; Kittatinny Reg HS; Newton, NJ; (Y); 54/228; Boy Scts; Teachers Aide; Bsbl; Socr; Trk; Wrstlng; Hon Roll; Wrestling Hnrs 80-86; Bsbl Hnrs; Rutgers.

PARKER, BRIAN; Audubon HS; Mt Ephraim, NJ; (Y); Art Clb; Band; Mrchg Band; Var Socr; Var Trk; Hon Roll; 2nd Prz Clnl Cnfrnc Art Cntst 86; Cmmrcl Artst.

PARKER, CARLA; Henry Snyder HS; Jersey City, NJ; (Y); FBLA; FHA; Library Aide; Rep Stu Cncl.

PARKER, EDWARD; Pinelands Regional HS; Tuckerton, NJ; (Y); Hon Roll; Ducks Unlimited; Comp Repair Tech.

PARKER, GEORGE; Saint Rose HS; Belmar, NJ; (Y); Nwsp Rptr; Lit Mag; Pres Soph Cls; Rep Jr Cls; Sec Stu Cncl; Var Tennis; High Hon Roll; Ntl Merit Ltr; NEDT Awd; Im Bsktbl; Hnrbl Merti Awd Ntl Latin Ex 84; Law.

PARKER, JANETTE LEE; Northern Burlington CR HS; Wrightstown, NJ; (Y); 11/183; Am Leg Aux Girls St; Math Tm; Q&S; Ski Clb; Yrbk Ed-Chief; Pres Frsh Cls; Var L Fld Hcky; L Trk; NHS; Spanish NHS; Rotry Yth Ldrshp Actvities Alt 84-85; Villanova U; Chem Engrg.

PARKER, JENNIFER; North Arlington HS; N Arlington, NJ; (Y); 3/130; VP French Clb; Sec Ski Clb; Yrbk Stf; Hst Stu Cncl; Trk; Elks Awd; Pres NHS; NEDT Awd; Gardn ST Dstngshd Schlr 85-86; Donald And Flora Borg Merit Schlrshp 86; Cornell U; Engr.

PARKER, JUSTINA; Dover HS; Dover, NJ; (Y); 8/183; Dance Clb; Ski Clb; Mrchg Band; School Musical; School Play; VP Soph Cls; VP Jr Cls; VP Sr Cls; Co-Capt Cheerleading; NHS; Bio.

PARKER, KELLY; Wggquahic HS; Newark, NJ; (Y); Hosp Aide; Chorus; School Play; Off Jr Cls; Vllybl.

PARKER, SHARON; Summit HS; Summit, NJ; (Y); 59/284; Drama Clb; Concert Band; Mrchg Band; School Musical; Yrbk Stf; Rep Stu Cncl; JV Sftbl; Var Swmmng; Hon Roll.

PARKES, CHRIS; Mater Dei HS; Middletown, NJ; (Y); 30/152; Trs VP Church Yth Grp; Model UN; School Musical; School Play; Nwsp Stf; Yrbk Stf; Trs Stu Cncl; Var Golf; JV Socr; Hon Roll; Pares Soc Sci Fed, Hist Clb 86-87; Exec Bd Mater Dei 85-86; Fin.

PARKMAN, KATRINA; Hamilton West HS; Trenton, NJ; (Y); 37/307; Church Yth Grp; Sec FBLA; Pep Clb; Church Choir; JV Var Cheerleading; Fld Hcky; Mgr(s); Hon Roll; Brkly Bus Schl Achvt Awd; Cert Of Merit-Prdctn Typng-NJ Bus Educ Assn; Hampton U; Bus Mngmt.

PARKS, JOSEPH; John F Kennedy HS; Paterson, NJ; (Y); FCA; Varsity Clb; Yrbk Rptr; Yrbk Sprt Ed; Capt Bsbl; Capt Bsktbl; Capt Ftbl; Capt Powder Puff Ftbl; Rep Sftbl; Pres Wt Lftg; Ftbl Schlrshps 86; Most Athltc Awd 87; MN U; Arch.

PARKS, KATHLEEN; Bishop George Ahr HS; Edison, NJ; (Y); Cmnty Wkr; VP Model UN; Science Clb; Lit Mag; Swmmng; Vllybl; High Hon Roll; NHS; Ntl Merit Ltr; Decthln Knwldg 85-86; Grls ST SF 85-86; Top 10 Pct Clss 83-86; Rsrch Gentcst.

PARKS, STACEY; Waldwick HS; Waldwick, NJ; (Y); Church Yth Grp; Spanish Clb; Lit Mag; Rep Soph Cls; Off Jr Cls; Sec Stu Cncl; Var Tennis; Prfct Atten Awd; 1st & 2nd Tm All Lg Vrsty Tnns 84 & 85; Bus Mngmnt.

PARKS, YOLANDA; Frank H Morrell HS; Irvington, NJ; (Y); Cheerleading; JV Vllybl; Hon Roll; Cheerldng Awd 86; UCLA; Acctng.

PARRILLO, CHRISTINE; Wayne Valley HS; Wayne, NJ; (Y); 17/325; Capt Color Guard; Yrbk Stf; High Hon Roll; Hon Roll; NHS; Adv Plcmnt Calc Exam 86; Math.

PARRINELLO, MARIA; Paul VI Regional HS; Passaic, NJ; (Y); Pres French Clb; Key Clb; Service Clb; SADD; Church Choir; School Musical; School Play; Nwsp Stf; Yrbk Stf; French Hon Soc; Peer Cnslr Trng Prgm 86; Fash Inst Of Tech; Fash Dsgnr.

PARRISH, THOMAS J; Roselle Catholic HS; Union, NJ; (Y); Am Leg Boys St; Boy Scts; Church Yth Grp; Stage Crew; Var L Swmmng; Hon Roll; NJ Inst Of NJ; Elect Engrng.

PARRISH, VALERIE; Vineland HS; Vineland, NJ; (Y); 15/630; Pres Varsity Clb; Rep Stu Cncl; Var Swmmng; Var Tennis; Var Capt Trk; NHS; Trs Spanish NHS; Math Clb; Pep Clb; Spanish Clb; Pres Acdmc Fit Awd 86; Nicandro Cifaloglio Memrl Schlrshp 86; James Madison U; Bus Adm.

PARRY, DEBRA; Bishop George Ahr HS; Colonia, NJ; (Y); Church Yth Grp; Capt Cmnty Wkr; Ski Clb; SADD; Sec Trs Jr Cls; Sec Trs Sr Cls; Stu Cncl; Capt Cheerleading; Coach Actv; Hon Roll; Phys Thrpy.

PARSIO, ANTHONY; Penns Grove HS; Carneys Point, NJ; (Y); 4/225; German Clb; Trs JA; Mrchg Band; School Musical; School Play; Rep Stu Cncl; Var Socr; Hon Roll; NHS; Engrng.

PARSLEY, CRAIG; Salem HS; Salem, NJ; (Y); Am Leg Boys St; Computer Clb; Pres JA; Pep Clb; Band; Color Guard; Mrchg Band; Bsbl; Bsktbl; Ftbl; Schlr Athl Mnth Exch Clb 85-86; Lnmn Wk Tchdwn Clb 85-86; All Salem & All Tri Cnty Lnbckr 85-86; Athl Mgmt.

PARSON, PAMELA; Hillside HS; Hillside, NJ; (Y); Band; Church Choir; Cheerleading; Score Keeper; Trk; Hon Roll; Penn ST; Nrsng.

PARSONS, ALLEANA; A P Schalick HS; Bridgeton, NJ; (Y); Hon Roll; Cmbrlnd Cmnty Coll; Lbrl Arts.

PARSONS, ELIZABETH; Schalick HS; Elmer, NJ; (Y); 12/131; Art Clb; Spanish Clb; Rep Soph Cls; Stat Ftbl; Var Trk; Hon Roll; NHS; Psych.

PARSONS, SANDRA S; Somerville HS; Somerville, NJ; (Y); 1/300; Drama Clb; Math Clb; Model UN; Spanish Clb; Band; Color Guard; School Play; High Hon Roll; NHS.

PARTHASARATHY, MADHAVAN; Paterson Catholic Regional HS; Fair Lawn, NJ; (Y); 1/119; Am Leg Boys St; Computer Clb; Science Clb; Nwsp Rptr; VP Stu Cncl; JV Trk; JV Wrstlng; High Hon Roll; NHS; Rtgrs Schlr Awd 86; MA Inst Of Tech; Comp.

PARTLOW, MACKENZIE R; Shawnee HS; Medford Lakes, NJ; (Y); Am Leg Boys St; Church Yth Grp; Rep Jr Cls; Var Co-Capt Ftbl; Var L Wrstlng; Hon Roll; JV Trk; All-Lg Wrstlng Coaches All-Str Tm 86; Pre-Med.

PARTNOW, PHILIP; The Lawrenceville Schl; Moorestown, NJ; (Y); VP Debate Tm; Mgr Model UN; Nwsp Rptr; Jr Cls; Im Socr; Im Tennis; High Hon Roll; Ntl Merit SF; WA U Engrg Awd 85; Dartmouth Clb Of Princeton Bk Awd 85; Head Of Tutrng Prog 85-86.

PARTRIDGE, WILLIAM M; The Lawrenceville Schl; Princeton, NJ; (Y); Church Yth Grp; German Clb; Hosp Aide; Chorus; Bowling; Ftbl; Sftbl; Ntl Merit SF; Frederick P King Prz Accmplshmnt In Frgn Lgs 85; Norval F Bacon Jr Prz Bst Hist Trm Ppr 85; Dist Schlr; Hist.

PASCIULLO, MICHELE T; Maple Shade HS; Maple Shade, NJ; (Y); 5/150; Am Leg Aux Girls St; Pres French Clb; Pres Spanish Clb; Nwsp Stf; Yrbk Ed-Chief; Sec Jr Cls; Trs Stu Cncl; Lcrss; Socr; Gov Hon Prg Awd; Rutgers U; Lbrl Arts.

PASCUAL, JENARO; Frank Morrel HS; Irvington, NJ; (Y); 3/30; Am Leg Boys St; Tennis; NHS; NJH; Engrng.

PASKIN, LEWIS; Shore Regional HS; W Long Beach, NJ; (Y); Computer Clb; Frsh Cls; Jr Cls; Sr Cls; Bsktbl; Socr; High Hon Roll; Scholastic Bowl; 1st Pl Stockton ST Coll Sci Fair 86; Comp.

PASQUA, JOHN ANTHONY; Oratory Catholic Prep; Madison, NJ; (S); 5/44; Chess Clb; Math Clb; Math Tm; Quiz Bowl; Service Clb; Im Bsktbl; Im Golf; High Hon Roll; NHS; Lat I II 83 & 84; Geom 84; Phys Sci 84; Drew U; Astrnmy.

PASQUINI, CHRIS; New Milford HS; New Milford, NJ; (Y); 40/150; Ftbl; Var Trk; JV Wrstlng; Pre-Dentl.

PASSADOR, MARYANN; Lodi HS; Lodi, NJ; (Y); #1 In Class; Intnl Clb; Key Clb; Math Tm; Science Clb; Drill Tm; L Stat Socr; Var L Trk; Bausch & Lomb Sci Awd; NHS; Math Clb; Renssalear Math & Sci Awd 87; Rutgers U; Bio Chem.

PASSAMONTI, ADAM; St Josephs Regional HS; Chestnut Ridge, NY; (Y); 29/200; Cmnty Wkr; Letterman Clb; Pep Clb; SADD; Varsity Clb; Off Sr Cls; Stu Cncl; Bsbl; Ice Hcky; High Hon Roll; ST Hock Champs 83-85; SUNY; Bus.

PASSANANTE, JANE E; Middlesex HS; Middlesex, NJ; (Y); 19/170; Debate Tm; Hosp Aide; Model UN; Nwsp Rptr; Rep Frsh Cls; Hon Roll; NHS; Acad Achvt Awd 86; Mst Crtv & Bst Wrtr Awd 86; U Of DE; Lbrl Arts.

PASSANO, CHERIE; Hawthorne HS; Hawthorne, NJ; (Y); Pep Clb; Pres SADD; Pres Sr Cls; Rep Stu Cncl; JV Cheerleading; Var Sftbl; Hon Roll; Pedtrctn.

PASSARELLI, DANIEL F; N Plainfield HS; N Plainfield, NJ; (Y); Boy Scts; Church Yth Grp; Band; Concert Band; Jazz Band; Mrchg Band; Ftbl; Wt Lftg; Ad Altar Dei By Sct Cathlc Relgs Mdl 81; By Sct Yr Awd 84; Engl.

PASSERELLA, DEBORAH; Kearny HS; Kearny, NJ; (Y); 88/375; Dance Clb; Sftbl; Hon Roll; Flght Attndnt.

PASSERELLA, SUSAN; Hamilton West HS; Trenton, NJ; (Y); 54/350; Church Yth Grp; Key Clb; Pep Clb; Band; Concert Band; Mrchg Band; Orch; Pep Band; School Musical; Symp Band; Mst Imprvd Plyr Awd Ten 85; Hall Fame All Amer Band Hnrs 84-85; Band Parents Scholar Awd 86; Trenton ST Coll; Music Ed.

PASSI, VIKAS; Hudson Catholic HS; Jersey City, NJ; (Y); 1/200; Debate Tm; Math Clb; Science Clb; Nwsp Rptr; High Hon Roll; NHS; Val; Yrbk Rptr; NJ Distngshd Schlrshp 85; Hghst Avg Awds Math, Engl, Sci 86; Mst Lkly Succd 86; Stevens Inst Tech; Elec Engr.

PASSMORE, CALVIN; East Orange HS; E Orange, NJ; (Y); 47/496; Spanish Clb; Var Bsbl; Var Ftbl; Var Trk; Lincoln U; Indstrl Engrng.

PASTAKIA, HETTLE; Colonia HS; Colonia, NJ; (Y); 5/280; SADD; Orch; Yrbk Stf; Trs Lit Mag; Trs Sr Cls; Rep Stu Cncl; Hon Roll; NHS; Spanish NHS; Phrmcy.

PASTELAK, DEANNA; Linden HS; Linden, NJ; (Y); Church Yth Grp; Pres FBLA; Office Aide; Ski Clb; Teachers Aide; Rep Jr Cls; Cheerleading; Trk; Hon Roll; NHS; Berkeley Schl Of Bus; Exec Sec.

PASTERNAK, JEFFREY; Union Catholic Reg HS; Elizabeth, NJ; (Y); Math Tm; Science Clb; Service Clb; Spanish Clb; Teachers Aide; Rep Frsh Cls; Stu Cncl; Hon Roll; Livingston Coll; Biol.

PASTOR, BERNIE; St Josephs Of The Palisdes; North Bergen, NJ; (Y); 25/128; Church Yth Grp; Cmnty Wkr; Political Wkr; Spanish Clb; Variety Show; Nwsp Ed-Chief; VP Jr Cls; Pres Stu Cncl; Var Bsbl; NHS; Fordham U; Law.

PASTOR, TARA; Kittatinny Reg HS; Layton, NJ; (Y); 71/227; Church Yth Grp; SADD; Boy Scts; School Musical; School Play; Jr Cls; Stu Cncl; JV Var Cheerleading; Powder Puff Ftbl; Trk; Prsh Cncl Teen Rep 84-86; DWI Stu Task Frc 85-86; Spcl Olympcs Vlntr-Sprng Field Day 83-86; Comm.

PATEL, AMAL; Middletown South HS; Lincroft, NJ; (Y); Boy Scts; Varsity Clb; High Hon Roll; Hon Roll; Var Tennis; Accntng.

PATEL, BHAVIKA; Highland Regional HS; Blackwood, NJ; (S); Library Aide; Hon Roll; NHS; Troph Natl Multpl Sclerosis Outstndng Achvt 83-84; Engrng Sci.

PATEL, HINA; Middletown South HS; Lincroft, NJ; (S); 7/436; Acpl Chr; Chorus; School Musical; Rep Jr Cls; Rep Sr Cls; Trk; High Hon Roll; NHS; St Schlr; Spnsh Merit Awd Prfct A Rcrd 84-85; Med.

PATEL, HITESH; Sayreville Wm HS; Parlin, NJ; (Y); 43/379; Math Clb; Science Clb; Spanish Clb; Varsity Clb; Var Socr; Hon Roll; Rutgers Coll; Engrng.

PATEL, KAMLESH; Hudson Catholic HS; North Bergen, NJ; (Y); 9/180; Computer Clb; Math Clb; Science Clb; High Hon Roll; Boston U; Med.

PATEL, KAUSHIK; Wm L Dickinson HS; Jersey City, NJ; (Y); 7/400; VP Computer Clb; Scholastic Bowl; Hon Roll; NHS; Acad Achvt Awd Hudson Cnty Chmbr Cmmrc 86; Rutgers; Pre-Med.

PATEL, KETAN; Piscataway HS; Piscataway, NJ; (Y); Boy Scts; Math Clb; Hon Rl; Jr NHS; NHS; Ntl Merit Schol; St Schlr; 1st Pl Publc Spch India 79; 1st Pl Bike Race India 80; Awd Hghst Grd Engl India 84; Rutegers U; Elec Engr.

PATEL, LEENA; East Brunswick HS; E Brunswick, NJ; (Y); Dance Clb; FBLA; Girl Scts; Key Clb; SADD; Chorus; Concert Band; Mrchg Band; Yrbk Stf; Hon Roll; 1st Pl Danc Comptn Toronto Canada 84; 2nd Pl ST Poetry Cntst 86; Fnlst Natl Poetry Cntst 86; Rutgers Coll Pharm; Pharm.

PATEL, MAYUR; Union HS; Union, NJ; (Y); Computer Clb; German Clb; Hon Roll; Hstry Clb 85-86; NJIT; Biomdcl Engrng.

PATEL, MONA; Cranford HS; Cranford, NJ; (Y); 12/295; Math Clb; Spanish Clb; Yrbk Stf; Bsktbl; Tennis; French Hon Soc; High Hon Roll; Trs NHS; Pres Acad Ftns Awd 86; Govrs Tchg Schlrshp 86; Rutgers Coll; Scndry Educ Tchr.

PATEL, MUKESH; North Bergen HS; North Bergen, NJ; (Y); 1/480; Speech Tm; Band; School Musical; Var JV Socr; High Hon Roll; NHS; Prfct Atten Awd; Camera Clb; Computer Clb; Drama Clb; Math & Sci Awd Rensselaer Polytec Inst 85-86; Natl Rssn Olymp Awd 83-85; Rutgers Schlr 85-86; Math.

PATEL, NILESH P; Sayreville War Memorial HS; Parlin, NJ; (Y); Boy Scts; Trs Sec Math Clb; Varsity Clb; Band; Yrbk Rptr; JV Bsktbl; Var Socr; Hon Roll; NHS; Spanish NHS; All Cnty Acad Soccr 86; 2nd Pl Indian Grp Dance FOGA 85; Eagle Scout 85; Rutgers Coll Engrng; Engrng.

PATEL, NIMESH; E Brunswick HS; E Brunswick, NJ; (Y); Hosp Aide; Band; Concert Band; Hon Roll; NHS; Lehigh U; Med.

PATEL, PARAG; Hamilton HS East; Hamilton Sq, NJ; (Y); 29/301; Cmnty Wkr; Math Clb; Math Tm; Office Aide; Temple Yth Grp; High Hon Roll; Hon Roll; Prfct Atten Awd; Highest Physics Avg Physics Clsses 85 & 86; Sci Awd 85; Rutgers Coll Of Engr; Engr.

PATEL, PINKI; BRHS East; Bridgewater, NJ; (Y); Hosp Aide; Intnl Clb; SADD; Orch; Nwsp Stf; Yrbk Stf; Im Bowling; Sftbl; Var Swmmng; High Hon Roll; Sci.

PATEL, RAKESH; Memorial HS; W New York, NJ; (Y); 2/360; Math Clb; Spanish Clb; High Hon Roll; Hon Roll; NHS; Sal; Grden ST Dstngshd Schlr 85-86; Acad Achvt Awd Hudson Cnty Chmbr Cmmrc & Indstry 86; Med.

PATEL, SACHIN; Paul VI Regional HS; Wayne, NJ; (Y); Am Leg Boys St; Var JV Bsbl; High Hon Roll; NHS; Spanish NHS; Hartford; Sci.

PATEL, SNEHAL; Union HS; Union, NJ; (Y); Computer Clb; Drama Clb; Red Cross Aide; Science Clb; Spanish Clb; School Play; Yrbk Phtg; Yrbk Stf; Ice Hcky; Hon Roll; At&t Bell Lab Smmr Yth Emplymnt Pgm 83-85; Hofstra U; Pre-Med.

PATEL, VIP; Cinnaminson HS; Cinnaminson, NJ; (Y); 51/257; Computer Clb; Yrbk Stf; Var Capt Bowling; Hon Roll; Alcan Awd Intrnl Undrstnd 85-86; Pres Awd Acad Ftns 85-86; Drexel U; Accntng.

PATEL, VISHAL; North Bergen HS; North Bergen, NJ; (Y); 12/412; Computer Clb; Key Clb; Trs Spanish Clb; Stu Cncl; High Hon Roll; NHS; Trs Spanish NHS; Acad All Am Awd 85; Intrntl Frgn Lang Awd 85; Natl Ldrshp Srv Awd 85; Pre-Med.

PATERNOSTER, JOSEPH; St Marys Of The Assumption HS; Elizabeth, NJ; (S); Chess Clb; JV Bsbl; Hon Roll; Seton Hall; Stck Brkr.

PATERNOSTER, PAMELA; Passaic Valley HS; Totowa, NJ; (Y); Var Bsktbl; Var Sftbl; Hon Roll; Hlth Physcl Ed Awd; Health.

PATERSON, GEORGE J; Brick Memorial HS; Brick, NJ; (Y); 6/350; Am Leg Boys St; Chess Clb; Key Clb; Math Clb; Math Tm; JV Crs Cntry; JV Trk; Bausch & Lomb Sci Awd; High Hon Roll; NHS; Rutgers; Psych.

PATRICK, BETH; Holy Spirit HS; Northfield, NJ; (Y); 31/336; Church Yth Grp; French Clb; Church Choir; School Musical; Nwsp Stf; Hon Roll; NHS; Nwspr Lay-Out Edtr; Douglass Coll; Jrnlsm.

PATRICK, KARA; Manville HS; Manville, NJ; (Y); Rep Frsh Cls; Sec Rep Soph Cls; Sec Rep Jr Cls; Rep Stu Cncl; JV Var Bsktbl; Hon Roll; Bsktbl 2 Plqs & Ltr JV 84; Vrsty Bsktbl Ltr 85; Bus.

PATRICK, PAUL; Spotswood HS; Spotswood, NJ; (S); 20/189; Band; Concert Band; Jazz Band; Mrchg Band; Orch; Symp Band; JV Var Ftbl; Var Trk; JV Var Wrstlng; Karate 82; Comp Pgrmng.

PATRICOLA, CHRIS; Red Bank Regional HS; Little Silver, NJ; (Y); 39/225; FBLA; Math Tm; Spanish Clb; JV Bsbl; JV Socr; High Hon Roll; Hon Roll; Ntl Merit Ltr; Bowman Ashe Schlrshp 86; U Of Miami; Accntng.

PATRUZNICK, MICHAEL; West Morris Central HS; Long Valley, NJ; (Y); 11/300; Cmnty Wkr; Debate Tm; Math Clb; Math Tm; Radio Clb; Science Clb; Temple Yth Grp; High Hon Roll; Hon Roll; NHS; Law.

PATTABHI, RUTH; John F Kennedy Memorial HS; Colonia, NJ; (Y); 7/279; Church Yth Grp; Hosp Aide; Science Clb; Spanish Clb; SADD; Color Guard; Nwsp Rptr; Stat Bsktbl; Hon Roll; Jr NHS; Elctd V-Pres Sr Cls 86-87; Pre-Med.

PATTEN, CYNTHIA M; Passaic Valley Regional HS; Totowa, NJ; (Y); 70/309; Church Yth Grp; Cmnty Wkr; Computer Clb; Hosp Aide; Office Aide; Teachers Aide; Concert Band; Lit Mag; Stu Cncl; High Hon Roll; Totowa Womens Clb 86; PVHS Alumni 86; Bergern CC; Med Ofc Asst.

PATTEN, THOMAS; Christian Brothers Acad; Freehold, NJ; (Y); 60/225; Ski Clb; Im Bsktbl; Var L Trk; Hon Roll.

PATTEN, WENDY; Clearview Regional HS; Mullica Hill, NJ; (Y); 2/180; Pres 4-H; Yrbk Ed-Chief; Sec Stu Cncl; Capt Fld Hcky; 4-H Awd; NHS; Sal; St Schlr; Bst Clss 86 Prog; Amer Legn Awd; Cook Coll; Bio.

PATTERSON, BONITA; Henry Snyder HS; Jersey City, NJ; (Y); Church Yth Grp; Hosp Aide; Pres Church Choir; Capt Vllybl; NHS; Magna Cum Laude Natl Latin Exam 83-85; Acad Achvmnt Awd 85-86; Bus Mngmnt.

PATTERSON, CAROL; Highland Regional HS; Laurel Springs, NJ; (S); 11/291; Church Yth Grp; Drama Clb; Spanish Clb; Chorus; Capt Flag Corp; Capt Mrchg Band; Nwsp Rptr; Lit Mag; Rep Stu Cncl; Hon Roll; Pre-Med.

PATTERSON, ELIZABETHANN; Lakewood HS; Lakewood, NJ; (Y); 34/294; French Clb; Sec FBLA; Hosp Aide; Chorus; Stat Mgr Crs Cntry; Var L Trk; French Hon Soc; Hon Roll; Asbury Park Press Hon Carrier 86; Physical Therapy.

PATTERSON, ERIKA PATRICE; Union HS; Vauxhall, NJ; (Y); Church Yth Grp; Dance Clb; Pep Clb; Chorus; Pres Church Choir; Drill Tm; Mrchg Band; Rep Frsh Cls; Var Capt Cheerleading; JV Mgr(s); Coaching In Chrldng Awd 85; Tuskegee Inst; Psychlgy.

PATTERSON, JOHN D; Middletown South HS; Red Bank, NJ; (Y); 3/434; Boy Scts; Mrchg Band; Swmmng; Cit Awd; DAR Awd; French Hon Soc; High Hon Roll; NHS; Pres Schlr; Asbury Pk Press Grnt 85; Goldn Nugnt Schlrshp 86; Osborne Schlrshp 86; Duke; Bio.

PATTERSON, MICHAEL; Hackensack HS; Hackensack, NJ; (Y); 70/386; Hon Roll; Prncpls Hnr Rll 86; Mary Mccleod Bethune Schlrshp 86; Alpha Phi Alpha Frtnty Schlrshp 86; U Of SC; Elec Engrng.

PATTERSON III, ROBERT C; Wildwood HS; Wildwood Crest, NJ; (Y); 2/122; Am Leg Boys St; Nwsp Ed-Chief; Var Capt Bsktbl; Mgr Var Bowling; Mgr Var Vllybl; Bausch & Lomb Sci Awd; Pres NHS; Sal; St Schlr; Civic Clb; Pres Acdmc Ftns Awd 86; VA Tech; Comp Engrng.

PATTERSON, RODNEY; Barringer HS; Newark, NJ; (Y); Aud/Vis; Boys Clb Am; Boy Scts; Camera Clb; Dance Clb; PAVAS; Rep Frsh Cls; Stu Cncl; JV Bsktbl; PA ST U; Math.

PATTON, GLENN; Northern Valley Reg At Old Tappan; Old Tappan, NJ; (Y); 5/280; AFS; JV Var Bsktbl; JV Tennis; High Hon Roll; NHS; Ntl Merit Ltr.

PATTON, LORI; Northern Burlington Co Reg HS; Mc Guire A F B, NJ; (Y); 8/197; Church Yth Grp; Math Tm; Model UN; Varsity Clb; VP Soph Cls; Var Capt Bsktbl; French Hon Soc; High Hon Roll; NHS; SADD; Intl Honor Choir 83-84; Councl For Eductn In World Citznshp 84; NC ST; Vet.

PATTON, MELISSA; Tenafly HS; Tenafly, NJ; (Y); Pres JA; Color Guard; Var Trk; High Hon Roll; Hon Roll; IN U; Pltcl Sci.

PATTON, PENNI; Toms River HS South; Toms River, NJ; (Y); 3/365; Church Yth Grp; Exploring; Church Choir; Flag Corp; VP Frsh Cls; JV Sftbl; Var Capt Swmmng; L High Hon Roll; Jr NHS; Voice Dem Awd; Mst Vlbl Swmr 84-86; TV Brdcstng.

PATTON, TALRYN; Bridgewater-Raritan HS West; Bridgewater, NJ; (Y); Sec Church Yth Grp; Math Tm; Thesps; Stage Crew; JV Bsktbl; High Hon Roll; NHS; Drama Clb; French Clb; Frnch Exch Clb 85; Chrch Nrsry Schl Asst Tchr 83-86; Chldrns Daycare Ctr Hlpr 86.

PAUER, DIANE; St Patricks HS; Elizabeth, NJ; (S); 2/40; Science Clb; School Musical; Yrbk Ed-Chief; Trs Frsh Cls; Off Soph Cls; Stu Cncl; Co-Capt Cheerleading; Trs NHS; Natl Sci Merit Awds 85; Rutgers; Educ.

PAUGH, JUDITH; St Mary HS; Sayreville, NJ; (Y); Library Aide; Pep Clb; Spanish Clb; SADD; Chorus; Lit Mag; Var JV Cheerleading; Var JV Pom Pon; High Hon Roll; Hon Roll; Awd Outstndg Ldrshp Ability Presented By Katherine Gibbs Schl 86; Berkeley; Bus Admin.

PAUL, JAMES; Trenton Central HS; Trenton, NJ; (Y); 95/536; Computer Clb; Church Choir; Variety Show; Trk; Hon Roll; Lincoln Tech Inst; Htng Sys Tch.

PAUL, MELANIE; Hamilton HS East; Hamilton Sq, NJ; (Y); 33/311; Key Clb; JV Im Bsktbl; Var Crs Cntry; Var Fld Hcky; Var Capt Trk; NHS; MVP Wntr & Sprng Trck 84-85; Stockton ST Coll; Comp.

PAULA, VINCENT; Bridgeton HS; Brideton, NJ; (Y); 28/209; Art Clb; French Clb; GAA; Yrbk Stf; VP Frsh Cls; Sec Soph Cls; Sec Jr Cls; JV Bsktbl; Var Fld Hcky; NHS; Babe Ruth Sprtsmnshp Awd 86; BHS Art Almni Awd 86; Canvs Bag Futr Artsts Awd 86; Glassboro ST Coll; Art.

PAULDING, TAMMY; Paul VI Regional HS; Passaic Pk, NJ; (Y); Cmnty Wkr; DECA; Red Cross Aide; Chorus; Yrbk Bus Mgr; Vllybl; High Hon Roll; Hon Roll; Bergan CC; Fashion Merch.

PAULLIN, LISA; Deptford Township HS; Deptford, NJ; (Y); 22/300; Spanish Clb; Band; Concert Band; Sec Mrchg Band; Rep Stu Cncl; Var Tennis; Jr NHS; Prfct Atten Awd; Rutgers; Phrmcy.

PAVINCICH, MARILYN; St Rose HS; Spring Lake, NJ; (Y); 2/230; Church Yth Grp; Cmnty Wkr; Red Cross Aide; Teachers Aide; NEDT Awd; Elem Ed.

PAVLIK, DONNA; Clifton HS; Clifton, NJ; (Y); 18/590; Am Leg Aux Girls St; Church Yth Grp; Key Clb; Chrmn Math Clb; Hon Roll; Jr NHS; NHS; Seton Hl U Acad Schlrshp 86-90; Seton Hall U; Hstry.

PAVLOV, KAREN; Perth Amboy HS; Perth Amboy, NJ; (Y); German Clb; JA; Rep Jr Cls; Bsktbl; Sftbl; High Hon Roll; Hon Roll; Rutgers U; Bus Mgmt.

PAVONE, BEN; Westfield HS; Westfield, NJ; (Y); 24/475; Spanish Clb; Var L Bsbl; Im Wt Lftg; Hon Roll; NHS; Ntl Merit Ltr; Pres Schlr; Teagle Scholar; Cornell U; Comp Sci.

PAVONE, RICHARD A; St Josephs Regional HS; River Vale, NJ; (Y); 17/167; Am Leg Boys St; JV Ice Hcky; Hon Roll; Spanish NHS.

PAWELEK, JOSEPH E; St Pius X Regional HS; So Rvr, NJ; (Y); Church Yth Grp; Computer Clb; ROTC; Stage Crew; JV Bsbl; Pre-Med.

PAWLAK, CHRISTOPHER T; Burlington Co Vo Tech HS; Browns Mills, NJ; (S); 2/152; Radio Clb; VICA; Wt Lftg; High Hon Roll; Pres NHS; Prfct Atten Awd; Monmouth Coll Trstee Full Schlrshp 86; Amer Legn Boys ST 85; NJ Distngshd H S Schlr 85; Monmouth Coll; Elctrncs Engr.

PAWLISH, CYNTHIA; Ocean Township HS; Wayside, NJ; (Y); 83/337; Camera Clb; Cmnty Wkr; Keywanettes; Spanish Clb; Trk; Secy & Treas Chldrn Of Amer Rev 82-84; VP & ST Ofcr Govt Stds Chldrn Amer Rev 84-86.

PAWLOWSKI, PAUL; St Peters Prep; Jersey City, NJ; (Y); 78/205; Yrbk Stf; Lit Mag; Var L Bsktbl; Cit Awd; Art Clb; Im Ftbl; Im Vllybl; Cmmnctns.

PAWLUS, DAWN; South River HS; South River, NJ; (Y); 16/139; Library Aide; Yrbk Stf; Hon Roll; Lib Cncl Clb Awd 86; Sec.

PAWSON, DAVID J; Lawrence HS; Lawrenceville, NJ; (Y); 20/239; Civic Clb; Math Tm; Trs Service Clb; Rep Stu Cncl; Var Bsbl; Hon Roll; VP NHS; Ntl Merit SF; St Schlr; Letterman Clb; Rene Marques Spnsh Awd 84; Gabriel Garcia Marques Spnsh Awd 83; Write-Up Intl Jugglers Assn 85; Mech Engrng.

PAYLOR, KARLA; Bishop George Ahr HS; Plainfield, NJ; (Y); 15/277; Teachers Aide; Band; Concert Band; Mgr(s); Trk; High Hon Roll; Hon Roll; Mst Vlbl Chrldr Boys Sprtsmn Lge 83-84; Pre-Med.

PAYNE, DWIGHT; Kingsway Regional HS; Swedesboro, NJ; (Y); 8/163; Boy Scts; Church Yth Grp; Concert Band; Mrchg Band; Var L Trk; Var L Wrstlng; Hon Roll; NHS; Band; Stage Crew; Bill Bradley Young Citzns Awd 86; Eagle Scout 86; Rutgers U; Biochem.

PAYNE, JACQUELINE ANN; Wayne Valley HS; Wayne, NJ; (Y); Capt GAA; Office Aide; JV Capt Cheerleading; Stat Ftbl; Trainr.

PAYNE, PATRICIA; Highland Regional HS; Blackwood, NJ; (S); #19 In Class; High Hon Roll; Hon Roll; Med Lab Tech.

PAYNE, SANDRA L; Delaware Valley Regional HS; Bloomsbury, NJ; (Y); Church Yth Grp; Intnl Clb; Key Clb; Varsity Clb; Yrbk Stf; Stu Cncl; Var Capt Cheerleading; JV Fld Hcky; Hon Roll.

PAZ, CATHY; Clifton HS; Clifton, NJ; (S); 1/687; Drama Clb; Science Clb; Var Swmmng; Var Trk; High Hon Roll; Jr NHS; Opt Clb Awd; Spanish NHS; Key Clb; Spanish Clb; 2nd Team All-St Crss-Cntry 84; 1st Team All-Cnty Crss-Cntry 84-85; Med.

PEACE, LINDA; Orange HS; Orange, NJ; (S); 31/182; Hosp Aide; Church Choir; Yrbk Stf; Pres Jr Cls; Pres Sr Cls; Rep Stu Cncl; Sftbl; Tennis; Hon Roll; Sci Pgm NJ Inst Tech 85; Chld Psych.

PEACH, CYNTHIA; The Pilgrim Acad; Northfield, NJ; (Y); Sec Church Yth Grp; FTA; Hosp Aide; Office Aide; Teachers Aide; Church Choir; Nwsp Ed-Chief; Nwsp Phtg; Yrbk Phtg; High Hon Roll; Liberty U; Spec Edu.

PEACOCK, BRYAN; Williamstown HS; Williamstown, NJ; (Y); Am Leg Boys St; Math Tm; Pres Frsh Cls; Pres Soph Cls; Pres Jr Cls; Pres Sr Cls; Rep Stu Cncl; Var Socr; JV Trk; NHS.

PEARCE, CHRISTOPHER; Manasquan HS; Manasquan, NJ; (Y); 30/241; Church Yth Grp; Math Tm; Band; Concert Band; Jazz Band; Mrchg Band; Crs Cntry; Hon Roll; PTO Scholar 86; Library Aux Scholar 86; Ladies Aux Vlntr Equine Co No 2 Scholar 86; Catholic U Amer; Mech Engrng.

PEARCE, KEVIN; Point Pleasant Boro HS; Pt Pleasant, NJ; (Y); Debate Tm; Math Tm; ROTC; Drill Tm; Nwsp Stf; Yrbk Sprt Ed; Var Ftbl; Im Wt Lftg; Gov Hon Prg Awd; High Hon Roll; US Naval Sea Cadet Of Yr 82; Natl Chem Soc Awd 86; Gardn ST Distngshd Schlr 86; Webb Inst; Engrg.

PEARIS, KIRSTEN; Washington Township HS; Turnersville, NJ; (Y); Aud/Vis; Rep Stu Cncl; Var Trk; Hon Roll; Indr Trk Long Jmp Rcd; Sprng Trk Long Jump Rcd; Hampton U; Bus Adm.

PEARSON, WENDY; Delsea Regional HS; Ewan, NJ; (Y); Art Clb; Debate Tm; Pres 4-H; Rep Sr Cls; Stu Cncl; JV Trk; 4-H Awd; Mgr(s); Communications.

PEASE, WHITNEY; Eastern Regional HS; Berlin, NJ; (Y); 17/350; Var Pep Clb; Variety Show; Nwsp Stf; Yrbk Stf; Stu Cncl; Cheerleading; Lcrss; High Hon Roll; Hon Roll; NHS.

PECCI, LISA; Mary Help Of Christians Acad; Paterson, NJ; (Y); Service Clb; Varsity Clb; School Play; Im Var Cheerleading; Gym.

PECK, KELLY; Lodi HS; Lodi, NJ; (Y); French Clb; Key Clb; Letterman Clb; Varsity Clb; Band; Nwsp Phtg; Yrbk Phtg; Yrbk Stf; Stat Socr; Var Trk; Bus Admin.

PECK, TIMOTHY; St James HS; Gibbstown, NJ; (S); 5/73; Drama Clb; School Play; Stage Crew; Bsbl; Ftbl; Wrstlng; High Hon Roll; Hon Roll; Ntl Merit Ltr; All Acdmc South Jersey Ftbl Tm 85; Engrng.

PECK, WILLIAM F; Toms River High School South; Beachwood, NJ; (Y); 69/360; Church Yth Grp; JV Bsbl; JV Var Socr; Beachwd JR Yacht Clb Srgnt Arms 84; Rcqtbl Clb; Crmnl Justc.

PEDANA, BRYAN; Academic HS; Jersey City, NJ; (Y); Chess Clb; U NC; Law.

PEDERSEN, CAROLINE M; Middletown High School South; Lincroft, NJ; (Y); Church Yth Grp; Church Choir; Flag Corp; French Hon Soc; Hon Roll; NHS; Hand-Bell Chr-Perfmd At White House & Chrystal Cathedral,Garden Grv CA 86; Engl.

PEDERSEN, DAN; Clearview HS; Richwood, NJ; (Y); 32/153; Ftbl; Wt Lftg; Hon Roll; NHS; Sprts Med.

PEEK, EMILY; Millville SR HS; Millville, NJ; (Y); FNA; Im JV Fld Hcky; Im Trk; Cumberlnd Cnty; Nrsg.

PEEK, PATRICIA; North Bergen HS; North Bergen, NJ; (S); 14/404; Yrbk Stf; Rep Frsh Cls; Rep Jr Cls; Rep Sr Cls; Stu Cncl; French Hon Soc; High Hon Roll; NHS; Prfct Atten Awd; Biologist.

PEEPLES, JULIE ANNE; Highland HS; Sicklerville, NJ; (Y); Drama Clb; FTA; JA; Latin Clb; Library Aide; Band; Chorus; Capt Drill Tm; Mrchg Band; Pep Band; Camden Cnty Coll; Mgt Csmtlgy.

PEHOWSKI, TODD; Hackettstown HS; Hackettstown, NJ; (Y); #3 In Class; Am Leg Boys St; Exploring; VICA; Stu Cncl; Im Bsktbl; Var Capt Crs Cntry; Var Capt Trk; Gov Hon Prg Awd; High Hon Roll; Hon Roll; NJ Gov Schl Sci 86; Bst Chem Stu 85; Boys ST 86; USAF Acad; Aerontcl Engrng.

PEIFFER, JONATHAN; Shore Regional HS; Oceanport, NJ; (Y); Chess Clb; Pres Church Yth Grp; Math Tm; Science Clb; Band; Concert Band; Jazz Band; Mrchg Band; Nwsp Stf; High Hon Roll; Del Luth Natl Yth Convention 86; Arch.

PELLE, LARA; Passaic Valley HS; Little Falls, NJ; (Y); 120/310; Camera Clb; French Clb; Key Clb; Yrbk Bus Mgr; Yrbk Stf; Mgr(s); Var L Wrstlng; Hon Roll; William Paterson Coll; Bus.

PELLIGRA, NICOLE; North Brunswick Township HS; N Brunswick, NJ; (Y); Sec Latin Clb; Rep Church Yth Grp; Var L Swmmng; High Hon Roll; Hon Roll; NHS; Cnty Chmp Swmmng 84-86; YWCA Natl Chmp Swmmng 85; Capt Cntrl Jrsey YWCA Smw Tm 86.

PELLINO, DARYL ANN; Delaware Valley Regional HS; Milford, NJ; (Y); Sec Church Yth Grp; Cmnty Wkr; FBLA; Key Clb; Capt Pep Clb; Ski Clb; Trs Varsity Clb; Sec Sr Cls; JV Var Cheerleading; Capt Pom Pon; Michael J Thorpe Mem Awd 86; Vrsty Blnkt Awd 86; U Of Tampa; Bus Admin.

PELLOT, BRAULIO; East Side HS; Aguadiua, PR; (Y); Church Yth Grp; Cmnty Wkr; French Clb; Library Aide; Math Clb; Math Tm; Science Clb; Spanish Clb; Teachers Aide; Church Choir; Dist & Fed Medls-Ntl Spllg Bee 84; Govt Schlrshp In Puerto Rico 84; Neighbrhd Recog Awd 83; USAF Acad; Astronautcs.

PELOSI, GILDA; Manchester Regional HS; Haledon, NJ; (Y); French Hon Soc; Hon Roll; William Paterson Coll; Bio.

PELOSI, MONICA; Oak Knoll Schl; Murray Hill, NJ; (Y); Camera Clb; Cmnty Wkr; Pep Clb; Ski Clb; Spanish Clb; Teachers Aide; Varsity Clb; Hon Roll; Spnsh III Acadmc Excllnc 85-86; Psychlgy.

PELTZMAN, STEVE; Hackensack HS; Maywood, NJ; (Y); 1/400; Am Leg Boys St; Nwsp Stf; Trk; Gov Hon Prg Awd; Spanish NHS; St Schlr; Val; Cmnty Wkr; Spanish Clb; Socr; Best In Show Vogue Art Gllry Art Show 86; US Air Force ROTC Schlrshp 86; Tm Mbr-N J Acad Decthln 86; Mass Inst Of Tech; Arspce Engrn.

PELUSO, MARLO; Watchung Hills Regional HS; Gillette, NJ; (Y); 99/321; Church Yth Grp; Key Clb; Yrbk Stf; Off Jr Cls; Off Sr Cls; Powder Puff Ftbl; Hon Roll; Outstndng Achvt Acctg 83-86; U Rhode Island; Bus.

PELUSO, ROSEANN; Cliffside Park HS; Fairview, NJ; (Y); 15/230; Church Yth Grp; Nwsp Stf; Yrbk Ed-Chief; Yrbk Phtg; Lit Mag; Stu Cncl; Hon Roll; NHS; Itln Natl Hnr Soc; Rutgers; Phrmcy.

PEMBERTON, ROBERT; Orange HS; Orange, NJ; (S); Computer Clb; English Clb; French Clb; Library Aide; Math Clb; Math Tm; Science Clb; Spanish Clb; SADD; High Hon Roll; Math.

PEMBERTON, RON; Highland Regional HS; Somerdale, NJ; (Y); Latin Clb; Spanish Clb; Varsity Clb; Var Capt Bsktbl; Var Bowling; JV Ftbl; Var Tennis; Spanish NHS; Spn Clb 84-85; Pre-Med.

PENA, BECKI; Memorial HS; West New York, NJ; (Y); Church Yth Grp; French Clb; Library Aide; Office Aide; Spanish Clb; Band; Concert Band; Mrchg Band; Symp Band; Lit Mag; Prtcptn Teen Arts Fstvl; Cntrbtr Mltpl Schlrs Soc; Rutgers; Mharmcy.

PENDLETON, DESIREE; Lakewood HS; Lakewood, NJ; (Y); 81/252; Key Clb; Color Guard; Mrchg Band; Rider Coll.

PENN, TAMMATHA LOUISE; Cumberland Regional HS; Bridgeton, NJ; (Y); Office Aide; Teachers Aide; Capt Bowling; JV Mgr(s); JV Score Keeper; Var Sftbl; Swmmng; High Hon Roll; Hon Roll; Prfct Atten Awd; De Vry Inst; Comp Pgmr.

PENNA, CHRISTINE DELLA; Rancocas Valley Regional HS; Mt Holly, NJ; (Y); 4/240; Church Yth Grp; Mrchg Band; Orch; Yrbk Bus Mgr; Bausch & Lomb Sci Awd; DAR Awd; NHS; Ntl Merit SF; Pres Schlr; Rotary Awd; MA Inst Of Tech.

PENNA, JUDY; Rutherford HS; Rutherford, NJ; (Y); Church Yth Grp; Chorus; Church Choir; Color Guard; Rep Jr Cls; Twrlr; High Hon Roll; Hon Roll; NHS; Engr.

PENNA, MADELINE; Passaic Valley HS; Totowa, NJ; (Y); Spanish Clb; Hon Roll; Med.

PENNA, MARK; Parsippany HS; Parsippany, NJ; (Y); Aud/Vis; Nwsp Stf; Lit Mag; Hon Roll; Ntl Merit SF; Morris Cnty Arts Sympsm 85 & 86; Montclair 83; Jrnlsm.

PENNA, SABRINA; Middlesex HS; Middlesex, NJ; (Y); 19/158; German Clb; Hosp Aide; Band; Concert Band; Mrchg Band; Pep Band; Ntl Merit Ltr; Ltr Marchng Band 85.

PENNELL, ARTHUR; Toms River H S South; South Toms River, NJ; (Y); Med.

PENNIMAN, DAWN E; Vernon Twsp HS; Glenwood, NJ; (Y); 28/219; German Clb; Scholastic Bowl; Trs Chorus; Church Choir; Madrigals; French Hon Soc; Hon Roll; Syracuse U; Cvl Engr.

PENNISE, PAULA; Holy Cross HS; Burlington, NJ; (Y); Ski Clb; Trk; Hon Roll.

PENNISE, THERESA; Holy Cross HS; Burlington, NJ; (Y); Hosp Aide; Service Clb; Stage Crew; Nwsp Stf; Yrbk Stf; Trk; Hon Roll; St Josephs U; Accntng.

PENQUE, THOMAS D; Hackensack HS; Maywood, NJ; (Y); 30/375; Am Leg Boys St; Boy Scts; Pres Key Clb; Pep Band; Nwsp Stf; Yrbk Stf; VP Jr Cls; VP Sr Cls; CC Awd; Cit Awd; Hugh O Brian Ldrshp Smnr 85; Wrld Affars Smnr 86; Exchng Stu Mexico 86; Sons Of Theamer Revolution Awd; Bus.

PENSABENE, CYNTHIA; Cherry Hill HS West; Cherry Hill, NJ; (Y); 19/370; Am Leg Aux Girls St; French Clb; Intnl Clb; Bsktbl; Co-Capt Fld Hcky; Sftbl; NHS; Lehigh Trustee Schlrp 86; Sch-Ath Awd 86; Fld Hcky Olym Conf, All Grp 4, S Jrsy Sr All-Str Tm 86; Lehigh U; Biomed Engrg.

PENSWATER, JOHN J; Holy Cross HS; Delran, NJ; (Y); Am Leg Boys St; Rep Frsh Cls; Rep Soph Cls; Rep Jr Cls; Rep Stu Cncl; Im Var Bsbl; JV Im Socr; Hon Roll; Outstndng Rep 86; Rutgers U; Lwyr.

PEPPER, LAWRENCE; Sacred Heart HS; Vineland, NJ; (Y); 20/69; Computer Clb; Drama Clb; French Clb; Science Clb; School Play; Bsbl; Bsktbl; Mgr(s); Score Keeper; Hon Roll; Beta Sigma Phi Schlrshp 86; Villanova; Bus.

PERAINO, RENEE; Toms River High School North; Toms River, NJ; (Y); Dance Clb; Drama Clb; Chorus; Mrchg Band; School Musical; Variety Show; Yrbk Stf; Pom Pon; Hon Roll; 2nd Pl Photo Cont-Tlnt Cmptn 86; 3rd Pl Duo Tap Cmptn 86; Danc Cls Schlrshp-Muscl Cmdy 86; Dntl Hygnst.

PERAZZA, GINA; Holy Cross HS; Medford, NJ; (Y); Cmnty Wkr; Stage Crew; Yrbk Stf; Mgr(s); High Hon Roll; Hon Roll; Bus.

PERCARIO, NANCY; East Brunswick HS; E Brunswick, NJ; (Y); Key Clb; JV Bsktbl; Var Fld Hcky; Var Trk; NHS; Grmn Hon Soc 85; Arch.

PERCIVAL, DEBORAH; Audubon HS; Audubon, NJ; (Y); Am Leg Aux Girls St; Art Clb; Spanish Clb; Teachers Aide; School Play; Stage Crew; Yrbk Stf; Stat Bsbl; Engrng.

PERDOMO, EDISON; Perth Amboy HS; Perth Amboy, NJ; (Y); 9/305; Am Leg Boys St; German Clb; ROTC; Scholastic Bowl; Key Clb; Mathletes; Math Clb; Math Tm; Model UN; Quiz Bowl; US Navy Acad; Prtcl Phscst.

PERDOMO, PEDRO; Perth Amboy HS; Perth Amboy, NJ; (Y); Computer Clb; German Clb; Mathletes; Im Vllybl; Natl Hispnc Schlr 86; Rutgers U; Agrnmy.

PEREIRA, DIEGO; Gill/St Bernards HS; Mendham, NJ; (Y); Ski Clb; Band; Concert Band; Mrchg Band; Nwsp Rptr; Rep Frsh Cls; Rep Soph Cls; Var Bsbl; Var Socr; Hon Roll.

PEREIRA, ISABEL; Immaculate Conception HS; Newark, NJ; (Y); Cmnty Wkr; French Clb; Science Clb; Nwsp Rptr; Yrbk Stf; Rep Stu Cncl; French Hon Soc; NHS; Chorus; Yrbk Rptr; Mxma Cum Laude Slvr Mdl Ntl Ltn Exm 85; Cum Laude Cert Ntl Ltn Exm 86; Ntl Frnch Cntst 86; Intrntl Law.

PEREIRA, PIERRE; Ridge HS; Basking Ridge, NJ; (Y); Boy Scts; Pep Clb; Ski Clb; VP Frsh Cls; Hon Roll; Church Yth Group 85-86; Life Saving CPR Cert 85; Float Comm; ST U Of NY; Intl Bus.

PEREIRA, RICKEY; Roselle Catholic HS; Elizabeth, NJ; (Y); Boy Scts; Church Yth Grp; Wt Lftg; Wrstlng.

PERETTI, BRENDA; Vineland SR HS; Vineland, NJ; (Y); 69/815; Aud/Vis; Key Clb; Pep Clb; Yrbk Phtg; Yrbk Stf; Italian Clb Ctznshp Awd; Wallsholm Clb Awd; Trenton Coll; Math Educ.

PEREZ, AIDA; Emerson HS; Union City, NJ; (Y); Montclair ST Coll; Art Tchr.

PEREZ, ARTHUR; Jackson Memorial HS; Jackson, NJ; (Y); 96/405; Jazz Band; School Play; Yrbk Stf; Pres Soph Cls; Sec Jr Cls; Sec Sr Cls; Sec Stu Cncl; Hon Roll; Rutgers U; Msc.

PEREZ, JACQUELINE; Emerson HS; Union City, NJ; (Y); 27/275; Hon Roll; NHS; Fclty Schlrshp Bus Educ 86; Union Cty Assoc Schlrshp 86; Berkeley Schl Schlrshp 86; Berkeley Schl; Acctnt.

PEREZ, LIZETTE; St Joseph HS; Union City, NJ; (Y); FCA; French Clb; Variety Show; Yrbk Stf; Bsktbl; French Hon Soc; Hon Roll; Jr NHS; NHS; NY U; Law.

PEREZ, NANCY; Washington Township HS; Turnersville, NJ; (Y); 8/480; Am Leg Aux Girls St; Spanish Clb; Stu Cncl; JV Bsktbl; Var Fld Hcky; Hon Roll; NHS; BC Schlrshp 86; Boston Coll.

PEREZ, NIURKA; Memorial HS; West New York, NJ; (Y); Church Yth Grp; Computer Clb; FBLA; Teachers Aide; Stu Cncl; Var Cheerleading; Var Pom Pon; Var Score Keeper; High Hon Roll; Hon Roll; Rutgers U-Miami; Accntng.

PERFILIO, JULIE; Scotch Plains Fanwood HS; Scotch Plains, NJ; (Y); Drama Clb; French Clb; Girl Scts; Pep Clb; Chorus; School Musical; School Play; Variety Show; Var Cheerleading; Hon Roll; Child Dev.

PERINCHIEF, ALISON; Holy Cross HS; Mount Holly, NJ; (Y); Pres Church Yth Grp; Rep Stu Cncl; JV Var Bsktbl; JV Var Socr; Hon Roll; Sec NHS; Phys Ther.

PERKINS, CHARLES; Pinelands Regional HS; Manahawkin, NJ; (Y); Ski Clb; Golf; Hon Roll; Frstry.

PERKINS, DAWNE; Southern Regional HS; Cedar Run, NJ; (Y); 96/348; Model UN; Spanish Clb; Frsh Cls; Soph Cls; Jr Cls; Cheerleading; Crs Cntry; Hosp Aide; Trk; Hon Roll; Model UN Outstndg Delegate In Crisis Situation 85-86; Intl Business Mgmt.

PERKINS II, EDDIE L; Burlington City HS; Burlington, NJ; (Y); 20/165; Am Leg Boys St; Church Yth Grp; Civic Clb; Cmnty Wkr; JV Ftbl; Hon Roll; Accptd Hofstra U 86; Hofstra U; Comm.

PERKINS, KEITH; Henry Snyder HS; Jersey City, NJ; (S); 1/256; Bsbl; Bsktbl; Hon Roll; NHS; St Schlr; Acadmc Achvt Awds 83-85; Accntng.

PERLMUTTER, KAMI; Wayne Hills HS; Wayne, NJ; (Y); 27/314; Cmnty Wkr; GAA; Math Tm; Pres Spanish Clb; Temple Yth Grp; JV Fld Hcky; Var JV Trk; High Hon Roll; Hon Roll; NHS; Rutgers Coll; Bio.

PERONE JR, NICK P; Manasquan HS; Manasquan, NJ; (Y); 61/235; Key Clb; Pres Band; Concert Band; Jazz Band; L Ftbl; JP Sousa Awd; Drama Clb; Mrchg Band; School Musical; Recd Grdn ST Schlrshp 86-87; Music Awd Old Gurd Grtr Pt Plsnt Area 86-87; Slctd Reg II Symphnc Bnd; Montclair ST Coll; Math.

PEROSA, SCOTT; South River HS; S River, NJ; (Y); Aud/Vis; Cmnty Wkr; Debate Tm; Drama Clb; Trs Library Aide; Science Clb; Spanish Clb; Speech Tm; Band; Mrchg Band; Lttrs In Trk & Mrchng Band 83-85; Lab Tech.

PERRI, DAWN; Bricktownship HS; Brick Town, NJ; (Y); 53/400; Drama Clb; French Clb; Pep Clb; Q&S; Ski Clb; Thesps; Band; Chorus; Concert Band; Mrchg Band; Bst Supprtng Actrss Awd 86; Treas Drama Clb 86-87; Rutgers Coll; Engl.

PERRICONE, PAM; Mater Dei HS; Union Beach, NJ; (Y); 42/151; Pep Clb; Variety Show; JV Powder Puff Ftbl; Hon Roll; NHS; Task Force SADD 84-85; Church Prog Shut Ins 83; Brookdale CC; Prim Educ.

PERRIN, REBECCA; West Orange HS; W Orange, NJ; (Y); Church Yth Grp; Office Aide; Chorus; Schl Offc Awd 84; Kean Coll; Phys Thrpy.

PERRINE, DINA; Hackettstown HS; Hackettstown, NJ; (Y); Key Clb; Band; Concert Band; Jazz Band; Mrchg Band; JV Gym; JV Trk; Hon Roll; NHS; Sec Church Yth Grp.

PERRINE JR, FREDERICK L; South Plainfield HS; S Plainfield, NJ; (Y); 18/210; Boy Scts; Church Yth Grp; Computer Clb; Ski Clb; Band; Mrchg Band; Stu Cncl; Var JV Bsbl; Var JV Bowling; Hon Roll; Bus Adm.

PERRINO, DINA; St John Vianney HS; Matawan, NJ; (S); 5/234; Cmnty Wkr; Hosp Aide; JCL; Office Aide; Service Clb; Yrbk Stf; Rep Stu Cncl; Crs Cntry; Powder Puff Ftbl; Trk; Gold & White Awd 84-86; Latin Awd For Highest Schlstc Avg In Latin 84-86; Franklin & Marshall Coll; Phys.

PERRON, KELLEY; Garden State Adac; Hackettstown, NJ; (Y); Church Yth Grp; Office Aide; Teachers Aide; School Play; Stage Crew; Nwsp Ed-Chief; Nwsp Rptr; Swmmng; High Hon Roll; Hon Roll; Loma Linda Schl Med; Pedatrcn.

PERRY, DEAN; Bishop Eustace Prep; Medford, NJ; (Y); Art Clb; Drama Clb; French Clb; Science Clb; Ski Clb; Var L Socr; Hon Roll; Ntl Merit Ltr; Rutgers U; Engrng.

PERRY, LAURA; Holy Cross HS; Willingboro, NJ; (Y); Cheerleading; Im Pom Pon; Hon Roll.

PERRY, ODESSA; Long Branch HS; Long Branch, NJ; (S); 74/216; Church Yth Grp; Exploring; Pep Clb; Varsity Clb; Drill Tm; Yrbk Ed-Chief; Cheerleading; Mgr(s); Score Keeper; Twrlr; Temple U; Nrsg.

PERRY, ROBERT; Ramapo Regional HS; Wyckoff, NJ; (Y); 3/329; Trs AFS; Math Tm; Science Clb; VP Spanish Clb; Concert Band; Jazz Band; School Musical; Trk; Bausch & Lomb Sci Awd; High Hon Roll; Record Carrier Schlrshp 86; Engr.

PERRY, THOMAS W; Christian Brothers Acad; W Keansburg, NJ; (Y); 21/221; JV Var Crs Cntry; JV Var Trk; High Hon Roll; Engrng.

PERSAUD, PADMALA; Bishop Georgeahr HS; Metuchen, NJ; (Y); Dance Clb; Pres French Clb; Trs Intnl Clb; Model UN; ROTC; Church Choir; School Musical; Nwsp Stf; CC Awd; Hon Roll; Rfl Sqd Capt Grls Mrchng Unt 85-87; Frgn Lang Awd 86; Leadership Awd 86; Intl Rltns.

PERSEL, KENNETH; Monsignor Donovan HS; Toms River, NJ; (Y); 9/243; French Clb; Math Tm; Thesps; Mrchg Band; School Musical; School Play; Rep Sr Cls; JV Crs Cntry; Hon Roll; NHS.

PERSICHETTI, MICHAEL; Hamilton High West; Trenton, NJ; (Y); 34/370; Computer Clb; Key Clb; VP Math Clb; Varsity Clb; Mrchg Band; Pep Band; Symp Band; Var Crs Cntry; Var Capt Trk; Hon Roll; Kiwanians Boy Mth 86; Mst Imprvd Athlt Trck 86; Drexel U; Acctng.

PERSICO, JILL; Paramus HS; Paramus, NJ; (Y); Pres Intnl Clb; Yrbk Stf; Lit Mag; Stat Bsktbl; JV Capt Cheerleading; NHS; Spanish NHS; Pres Phy Ftnss Awd 83-85; Pre Med.

PERUCKI, MATTHEW; Monsignor Donovan HS; Barnegat, NJ; (Y); 13/243; SADD; JV Var Socr; Var Tennis; Hon Roll; NHS; VA Cmmnwlth; Phrmcy.

PERUGINI, LAURA; Buena Regional HS; Richland, NJ; (S); Girl Scts; Intnl Clb; Pep Clb; Political Wkr; Ski Clb; Varsity Clb; Stage Crew; Pres Frsh Cls; Rep Soph Cls; Trs Jr Cls.

PESCHERINE, MIKE; Parsippany HS; Parsippany, NJ; (Y); Varsity Clb; VP Jr Cls; VP Sr Cls; JV Capt Bsbl; Var L Wrstlng; High Hon Roll; Hon Roll; NHS; Finance.

PESCI, CHRISTINE; Union Catholic Regional HS; Roselle Park, NJ; (Y); 2/339; Pres Service Clb; Spanish Clb; SADD; Nwsp Stf; Hon Roll; NHS; Sal; Spanish NHS; NJ Dstngshd Schlr 85-86; Rutgers Coll; Compu Sci.

PESSANO, JOYCE; Gateway Regional HS; Woodbury Hts, NJ; (Y); #40 In Class; Church Yth Grp; Spanish Clb; SADD; Chorus; Gassboro St Coll; Bus Admin.

PESTRITTO, JOS; Washington Twp HS; Turnersville, NJ; (Y); Hon Roll.

PETERLA. BRIAN; Hamilton High East; Hamilton Sq, NJ; (Y); 144/340; Church Yth Grp; Varsity Clb; Ice Hcky; 7th Pl Plymouth Trouble Shootng ST Cntst 86; Mercer County CC; Arch.

PETERMAN, JEFFREY P; Washington Township HS; Grenloch, NJ; (Y); 48/480; Church Yth Grp; Exploring; French Clb; Ski Clb; Band; Concert Band; Jazz Band; Mrchg Band; School Musical; Var Socr; U Of Louisville; Pre-Med.

PETERMANN, LAURA; Rutherford HS; Rutherford, NJ; (Y); Band; Concert Band; Drm Mjr(t); Mrchg Band; School Musical; JV Tennis; High Hon Roll; Hon Roll; NHS; Phrmcy.

PETERS, ANDREW; Howell HS; Howell, NJ; (S); #27 In Class; Band; Chorus; Jazz Band; Madrigals; Nwsp Ed-Chief; Trk; Hon Roll; School Musical; School Play; Symp Band; Al-Shore Band 85; Rgn Band 84; Al-ST Band 85; Music Ed.

PETERS, BONNIE; Riverside HS; Delanco, NJ; (S); #6 In Class; Hosp Aide; Teachers Aide; Rep Stu Cncl; Mgr Fld Hcky; Mgr(s); Score Keeper; Mgr Sftbl; Vllybl; Hon Roll; Child Care.

PETERS, BRIAN; Holy Spirit HS; Linwood, NJ; (Y); Var Capt Socr; Var Capt Trk; Hon Roll; JV Bsktbl; MVP Soccer 86; Blue Gold Awd Track 86; Comp Sci.

PETERS, COLLEEN; Lodi HS; Lodi, NJ; (Y); Intnl Clb; Key Clb; Leo Clb; JV Sftbl; High Hon Roll; Hon Roll; Montclair ST Coll; Psychlgy.

PETERS, DANIEL; St Peters Prep; Jersey City, NJ; (Y); 50/208; Boy Scts; Dance Clb; Drama Clb; French Clb; Stage Crew; L Gym; Var Trk; Hon Roll; Man Hattanville.

PETERS, MARIA; Eastern Regional HS; Marlton, NJ; (Y); 25/346; Rep Church Yth Grp; Intnl Clb; Service Clb; Band; Capt L Sftbl; Hon Roll; NHS; German Acadmc Awd 85-86; JV Sftbl Sprtmnshp & Dedctn Awd 86; Vet Sci.

PETERS, MICHELE; Randolph HS; Randolph, NJ; (Y); 138/358; Church Yth Grp; Var Bsktbl; Var Capt Powder Puff Ftbl; Var Capt Socr; Var Sftbl; Acctng.

PETERS, STACEY; Park Ridge HS; Park Ridge, NJ; (Y); 16/125; Drama Clb; Varsity Clb; School Musical; School Play; Yrbk Stf; Sec Trs Sr Cls; Stu Cncl; Var Capt Cheerleading; High Hon Roll; Acdmc Ltr; Chsn Fr Grls ST Douglass Coll; Rutgers; Psych.

PETERSEN, KARL; Colonia SR HS; Colonia, NJ; (Y); Varsity Clb; JV Var Bsbl; JV Bsktbl; Var Wt Lftg; Elks Awd; Hon Roll; Bus.

PETERSEN, MICHAEL; Toms River HS S HS; Beachwood, NJ; (Y); 42/310; VP Trs 4-H; Band; Concert Band; Mrchg Band; Variety Show; Socr; Swmmng; Trk; 4-H Awd; Hon Roll; 7th Pl Nation 4-H Elec Prjct Awd 85; Rtry Schlrshp 86; Kutztown U; Cvl Engrng.

PETERSON, AMY; Cherry Hill HS West; Cherry Hill, NJ; (Y); Cmnty Wkr; Drama Clb; Chrmn Red Cross Aide; Science Clb; SADD; Pres Stu Cncl; JV Cheerleading; JV Tennis; Var Trk; ARS Medica Clb 85-86; Head Pathlgist Aide JFK Hosp 85-86; Pre-Med.

PETERSON III, CARL E; Dover HS; Mine Hill, NJ; (Y); 4/223; Church Yth Grp; Math Tm; Ski Clb; School Musical; Lit Mag; Capt Bowling; High Hon Roll; NHS; German Clb; Math Clb; Garden ST Dist Schlrs Awd 85; Ust Pl Poetry Awd 86; Math Tm Awds 84 & 85 &86; Rutgers U; Engrng.

PETERSON, CHRISTINE; Atlantic City HS; Ventnor, NJ; (Y); Var Crs Cntry; Hon Roll; Vrsty Ltr Crss Cntry 85; Vet.

PETERSON, DAWN MARIE; Millville SR HS; Millville, NJ; (Y); 80/470; Variety Show; Yrbk Phtg; Bowling; Var Cheerleading; Hon Roll; Cumberland Cnty Coll; Bus Mgmt.

PETERSON, DOUGLAS A; Nutley HS; Nutely, NJ; (Y); 58/335; Am Leg Boys St; Camera Clb; Key Clb; Ski Clb; Spanish Clb; Rep Stu Cncl; Var L Bsbl; Im Bsktbl; Var L Ftbl; Im Sftbl; Pre-Med.

PETERSON, EDWARD; Middle Township HS; Cape May C H, NJ; (Y); 2/187; Am Leg Boys St; Ski Clb; Varsity Clb; Drm Mjr(t); Mrchg Band; Capt Trk; High Hon Roll; NHS; Opt Clb Awd; Sal; MVP Trck 85; TOB Chptr I Chmpnshp Bst Drum 85; Harry S Eldredge Schlrshp 86; U Of DE; Bus.

PETERSON, ERIC JOHN; Don Borco Tech HS; Clifton, NJ; (Y); 29/96; Boy Scts; Rep Frsh Cls; Rep Soph Cls; Cit Awd; Elks Awd; Hon Roll; NHS; SAR Awd; VFW Awd; Sci Fr 1st, 3rd & 4th Pl 83-85; William Paterson Coll; Comp Sci.

PETERSON, KATY; West Milford Twp HS; West Milford, NJ; (S); 15/390; Exploring; French Clb; Ski Clb; Ed Yrbk Stf; Cheerleading; French Hon Soc; NHS; Doc.

PETERSON, PAMELA; Monsignor Donovan HS; Brick, NJ; (Y); Cmnty Wkr; French Clb; Latin Clb; Nwsp Rptr; Yrbk Stf; Lit Mag; Ntl Merit Ltr; Drama Clb; Hosp Aide; L Trk; Natl Hnr Roll 84; Acad All Amer 84; Natl Ldrshp & Serv Awd 85; Med.

PETERSON, STEVEN; Elizabeth HS; Elizabeth, NJ; (Y); Church Yth Grp; Rep Frsh Cls; Rep Soph Cls; JV Bsbl; Hon Roll; Prncpls Hnr Roll 85; Bus.

PETERSON, TARA LEE; De Paul HS; Butler, NJ; (S); 50/164; Yrbk Phtg; Bsktbl; Var Cheerleading; Var Pom Pon; JV Capt Socr; JV Sftbl; Var Trk; Hon Roll; Art Shw 3rd Plc Chalk Pstl 85; Med.

PETERSON, TONYA; Bridgeton HS; Bridgeton, NJ; (Y); Dance Clb; FBLA; JA; Spanish Clb; SADD; Yrbk Stf; Badmtn; Bsktbl; Vllybl; NHS; Glassboro Coll; Acctnt.

PETITT, JEAN; James Caldwell HS; West Caldwell, NJ; (Y); 19/255; Key Clb; Color Guard; Yrbk Stf; Rep Frsh Cls; Stu Cncl; Bsktbl; High Hon Roll; Hon Roll; Kiwanis Awd; NHS; Engrng.

PETNER, GINA; Manalapan HS; Englishtown, NJ; (Y); SADD; Acpl Chr; Chorus; Church Choir; Lit Mag; Poetry Awds 85-86; Poem Yr Awd 84; Trenton ST; Psych.

PETRACCA, DAWN; St Patricks HS; Elizabeth, NJ; (S); #5 In Class; JA; Pep Clb; Science Clb; Yrbk Bus Mgr; VP Jr Cls; VP Sr Cls; Hon Roll; Sec NHS; Accntng.

PETRANTONAKIS, HELEN; Middlesex HS; Middlesex, NJ; (Y); French Clb; Ski Clb; Band; Color Guard; Concert Band; Pres Mrchg Band; Psych.

PETRAS, REBECCA; Manville HS; Manville, NJ; (Y); 4/113; Co-Capt Color Guard; Yrbk Ed-Chief; Yrbk Stf; Stat Bsktbl; JV Var Sftbl; Hon Roll; VP NHS; Greensboro Coll; Bus Adm.

PETRAZIO, JOEL K; Northern Burlington HS; Mcguire Afb, NJ; (Y); 60/240; Am Leg Aux Girls St; Boy Scts; Church Yth Grp; Chorus; Church Choir; School Musical; Trs Stu Cncl; JV Bsbl; Studnt Cncl Pres 86-87.

PETRECCA, KAREN; Queen Of Peace HS; Newark, NJ; (S); 5/231; Model UN; Pres NFL; Service Clb; School Musical; School Play; Nwsp Rptr; Pres Jr Cls; Rep Stu Cncl; NHS; Opt Clb Awd; Spn Awd 85; Forn Awd 1st Pl Vrsty Reading 84 & 85.

PETRI, RICHARD; Christian Bros Acad; Middletown, NJ; (Y); 70/230; Boys Clb Am; Im Ice Hcky; Im Sftbl; Hon Roll; Lib Arts.

PETRO, JANE; Holy Spirit HS; Pleasantville, NJ; (Y); Am Leg Aux Girls St; Sec 4-H; Hosp Aide; Quiz Bowl; Church Choir; Concert Band; School Musical; 4-H Awd; Hon Roll; Prfct Atten Awd; Kean Coll; Occptnl Thrpy.

PETRO, ROBERT; Washington Twp HS; Turnersville, NJ; (Y); 35/470; Pres Debate Tm; Model UN; Spanish Clb; Im Bowling; JV Golf; Im Socr; Hon Roll; NHS; Air Frc ROTC Schlrshp 86; U DE; Mech Engrng.

PETROCELLA, THOMAS J; Audubon HS; Audubon, NJ; (Y); Computer Clb; Concert Band; Mrchg Band; Lincoln Tech; Comp Pgmng.

PETRON, ELENA; Verona HS; Verona, NJ; (Y); Cmnty Wkr; Rep Frsh Cls; Rep Soph Cls; Var Cheerleading; French Hon Soc; Sci.

PETROSKI, EILEEN; Bishop George Ahr HS; Carteret, NJ; (Y); 46/244; Hosp Aide; Jazz Band; Pres Mrchg Band; Pep Band; School Musical; Symp Band; Nwsp Stf; Hon Roll; NEDT Awd; Pres-Mrchng Band 86-87; Treas-Mrchng Band 85-86; Mrchng Band Ldrshp Awd 86; Mst Imprvd Musicn 85; Jrnlsm.

PETROVIC, JUSTINE; Manville HS; Manville, NJ; (Y); 11/111; Cmnty Wkr; Girl Scts; Band; Yrbk Stf; Stu Cncl; Cheerleading; Hon Roll; NHS; Chorus; Concert Band; Tn Arts 84-86; Dncng 84-86; Gymnstc Cmptn Sqd 84; Bus.

PETRUCCELLI, MICHAEL; Cresskill HS; Cresskill, NJ; (Y); 2/115; Am Leg Boys St; Aud/Vis; Church Yth Grp; Nwsp Rptr; Nwsp Stf; Rep Stu Cncl; Var L Socr; Var L Trk; High Hon Roll; NHS; Ed.

PETRUZZI, DEBORAH; Washington Township HS; Sewell, NJ; (Y); Church Yth Grp; Ski Clb; Drill Tm; Mrchg Band; Yrbk Stf; Stu Cncl; Hon Roll; Glassboro ST; Bus Law.

PETRY, DAVID; Spotswood HS; Milltown, NJ; (S); #19 In Class; Am Leg Boys St; Church Yth Grp; FBLA; Ski Clb; Var L Bsbl; Im Bowling; Im Coach Actv; Im Ftbl; Im Golf; Capt Im Ice Hcky; Rutgers U; Engrng.

PETRY, HEIDI; Spotswood HS; Milltown, NJ; (S); 26/189; Girl Scts; Political Wkr; Chorus; Color Guard; Flag Corp; Mrchg Band; Nwsp Bus Mgr; Nwsp Rptr; Nwsp Stf; Rutgers; Phrmcst.

PETRYCKI, JOHN V; Holy Cross HS; Moorestown, NJ; (Y); Am Leg Boys St; Ski Clb; Rep Stu Cncl; Var Golf; Hon Roll; Bus.

PETSCHENIK, ANDREW; Manalapan HS; Manalapan, NJ; (Y); Aud/Vis; Camera Clb; Computer Clb; Drama Clb; Math Clb; Thesps; Madrigals; School Musical; School Play; Hon Roll; Bio.

PETTERUTI, JEANNE; Waldwick HS; Waldwick, NJ; (Y); Spanish Clb; Rep Stu Cncl; Cheerleading; Powder Puff Ftbl; Socr; Awd Excllnce Stdy Chld Dev 86; Acctg.

PETTEWAY, JASON; Bound Brook HS; So Bound Brook, NJ; (Y); 27/170; Am Leg Boys St; Drama Clb; Latin Clb; NFL; VP Thesps; Band; Mrchg Band; School Play; Rep Stu Cncl; Hon Roll; Creatv Wrtng Awd 85-86; Spch & Theater Trophies 83-86; Jrnlsm.

PETTI, BRIAN; Don Bosco Prep; Highland Mills, NY; (Y); Nwsp Ed-Chief; Rptr Nwsp Rptr; Nwsp Stf; Lit Mag; Im Ftbl; Im Trk; Hon Roll; NHS; Jrnlsm.

PETTI, CATHY A; Nutley HS; Nutley, NJ; (Y); 1/350; VP AFS; Am Leg Aux Girls St; Drama Clb; Key Clb; Spanish Clb; Band; School Play; Rep Stu Cncl; Var Capt Tennis; Var Trk; Rnslr Polytech Inst Awd 86; Rtgrs Schlr 86; NY Gvnrs Schl 86.

PETTIFORD-CHANDLER, AARON; Hillside HS; Hillside, NJ; (Y); Boy Scts; Symp Band; Var Crs Cntry; Var Trk; Vars Ltrs 85-86; Bnd Ltr 83-84; Lebanon Vly Coll; Comp Sci.

PETTINELLI, GINA; Phillipsburg HS; Alpha, NJ; (Y); 98/335; Band; Chorus; Concert Band; Jazz Band; Mrchg Band; Orch; Symp Band; Nwsp Stf; Yrbk Stf; Rep Stu Cncl; Psychlgst.

PETTIS, SONIA; Lincoln HS; Jersey City, NJ; (S); Drama Clb; Girl Scts; JA; Rep Frsh Cls; Rep Soph Cls; Hst Sr Cls; Stu Cncl; Co-Capt Cheerleading; Swmmng; Prfct Atten Awd; Rutgers U; Nrs.

PEYKO, MARC; Lodi HS; Lodi, NJ; (Y); 65/150; Leo Clb; Spanish Clb; Varsity Clb; Pres Soph Cls; Pres Jr Cls; Pres Stu Cncl; Var Bsbl; Var Ftbl; Var Wrstlng; Hon Roll.

PEZZUTI, DEBORAH; West Essex SR HS; Fairfield, NJ; (Y); Art Clb; Drama Clb; Chorus; Madrigals; Stage Crew; JV Sftbl; Hon Roll; Masquers Brd Of Dir 86-87; Vis Arts.

PEZZUTI, VICKI; Fair Lawn HS; Fairlawn, NJ; (Y); Church Yth Grp; Dance Clb; Chorus; Variety Show; Off Jr Cls; Sftbl; Trk; High Hon Roll; Hon Roll; NHS; Schlrshp In Dance Lorraine Victorias SOPA 84-85; Early Childhood Educa.

PFEIFFER, ANN; Cinnaminson HS; Cinna, NJ; (Y); Am Leg Aux Girls St; Rep Frsh Cls; Rep Soph Cls; Rep Jr Cls; Rep Stu Cncl; Var Bsktbl; Var Lcrss; Var Socr; Hon Roll; Prfct Atten Awd; Bus Adm.

PFEIFFER, CONSTANCE; Spotswood HS; Spotswood, NJ; (S); 1/189; Church Yth Grp; Intnl Clb; Model UN; Science Clb; Mrchg Band; Yrbk Stf; Var Socr; High Hon Roll; NHS; JV Sftbl; ST Sci Day Bio Compet 7th NJ ST 84; Rutgers Schl Phrmcy; Phrmcst.

PFENNINGER, PEGGY; South Hunterdon Regional HS; Lambertville, NJ; (S); 9/72; Am Leg Aux Girls St; Art Clb; Key Clb; SADD; School Play; Nwsp Rptr; Yrbk Ed-Chief; Rep Stu Cncl; Cheerleading; Hon Roll; Graphic Desgn.

PFISTERER, DAVID; Toms River H S North; Toms River, NJ; (Y); 45/412; Pres Church Yth Grp; Math Tm; Yrbk Stf; Off Sr Cls; Stu Cncl; Bsktbl; Sports Med.

PFIZENMAIER II, DAVID H; Delsea Regional HS; Franklinville, NJ; (Y); 2/193; Am Leg Boys St; Mrchg Band; School Play; Yrbk Stf; Pres Soph Cls; Pres Jr Cls; Pres Stu Cncl; Capt Bsktbl; VP NHS; Sal; Dghtrs Of Amer Rvltn Schlrshp 86; Mst Imprvd Bsktbl Plyr 84-85; Fclty Bwl Otstndng Grad 5-86; Rutgers U; Pre-Med.

PFLAUM, WENDY; Oak Knoll Schl; Scotch Plns, NJ; (Y); Pep Clb; Ski Clb; Chorus; Nwsp Phtg; Nwsp Rptr; Nwsp Stf; Var JV Fld Hcky; Im Vllybl; Intr Dsgn.

PFUELB, PAMELA S; Chatham HS; Chatham, NJ; (Y); 22/126; Hosp Aide; Acpl Chr; Sec Pres Chorus; School Musical; Nwsp Rptr; Nwsp Stf; VP Jr Cls; Trk; Twrlr; High Hon Roll; Lynchburg Coll Hnr Schlrshp 86; Librl Arts.

PHAM, DU; Dover HS; Dover, NJ; (Y); 12/232; Am Leg Boys St; Varsity Clb; Bowling; Socr; Tennis; Hon Roll; NHS; Soccr Mst Imprvd Plyr 84-85; Soccr Mst Desired 85-86; Mth Awd 85-86; Physics Awd 85-86; Bowling Champ; Rutgers U; Elec Engr.

PHAN, PHAT; Bound Brook HS; Bound Brook, NJ; (Y); 29/130; Var Socr; Engr.

PHANDER, JOHN; Toms River South HS; S Toms River, NJ; (Y); Church Yth Grp; SADD; Band; Church Choir; Concert Band; Mrchg Band; JV Bsbl; Hon Roll; Comp Sci.

PHARES, JOEL; Cinnaminson HS; Cinna, NJ; (Y); Church Yth Grp; Drama Clb; Thesps; Acpl Chr; Chorus; Church Choir; School Musical; Rep Soph Cls; Hon Roll; NHS; All S Jersey Tenor Sectn Ldr 85-86; Bell Choir Dir 87; Med.

PHELPS, LAURA; James Caldwell HS; Caldwell, NJ; (Y); Art Clb; French Clb; Pres Orch; Nwsp Phtg; Ed Yrbk Ed-Chief; Yrbk Phtg; Stu Cncl; High Hon Roll; VP NHS; Smith Clg Bk Awd 86; Bus Comm.

PHILBIN, KELLY; Bishop Eustace Prep; Blackwood, NJ; (Y); 28/182; Cmnty Wkr; Pep Clb; Spanish Clb; Nwsp Rptr; Nwsp Stf; Lit Mag; Capt Cheerleading; Hon Roll; NHS; Spanish NHS; Lib Arts.

PHILIPPE, SHEILA; St Mary Of The Assumpti; Elizabeth, NJ; (S); 6/59; Hosp Aide; Math Clb; Chorus; School Musical; School Play; Yrbk Ed-Chief; Sec Jr Cls; Hon Roll; Rutgers Coll; Nrsng.

PHILIPPS, KAREN; Paul VI HS; Laurel Springs, NJ; (S); 4/477; Math Clb; Drill Tm; Variety Show; Nwsp Rptr; Ed Nwsp Stf; Lit Mag; Pom Pon; French Hon Soc; High Hon Roll; NHS; Engrng.

PHILLIPS, DEBRA LYNN; Toms River HS East; Toms River, NJ; (Y); 70/425; Var Capt Socr; Hon Roll; Bus Adm.

PHILLIPS, JULIE; Summit HS; Summit, NJ; (Y); Pres AFS; Cmnty Wkr; Hosp Aide; Thesps; Sec Chorus; School Musical; JV Diving; High Hon Roll; Hon Roll; English.

PHILLIPS, KURT; Hopewell Valley Central HS; Pennington, NJ; (Y); Tennis; Trk; Northeastern; Arch.

PHILLIPS, LISA; Mount Olive HS; Budd Lake, NJ; (Y); AFS; Art Clb; DECA; Office Aide; Yrbk Stf; Natnl Art Hnr Socty 86; Art Educ.

PHILLIPS, LOUIS; Paulsboro HS; Gibbstown, NJ; (Y); 24/145; Hon Roll; Brotherhd Awd 83; Hnbl Mntn S Jersey Sci Fair 83; Cert Acadmc Achvt 86; Rutgers; Wldlf Mgmt.

PHILLIPS, MICHELLE E; East Brunswick HS; East Brunswick, NJ; (Y); 69/700; Dance Clb; Debate Tm; Key Clb; Model UN; Variety Show; Rutgers U; Pol Sci.

PHILLIPS, RANDI; Fair Lawn SR HS; Fair Lawn, NJ; (Y); Hosp Aide; Science Clb; VP Sec Temple Yth Grp; Nwsp Phtg; Yrbk Phtg; Off Jr Cls; Off Sr Cls; Hon Roll; Office Aide; Off Frsh Cls; Alexander Lamport Hebrew Achvt Awd 86; Livingston Coll; Bio.

PHILLIPS, ROBERT; Manville HS; Manville, NJ; (Y); 5/100; Var Capt Bsbl; Var Capt Bsktbl; Var Capt Ftbl; Gov Hon Prg Awd; Hon Roll; Jr NHS; NHS; 2nd Tm All-Cnty Bsbll 2nd Bs 86; 3rd Tm Group 1 All-St 86; Eng.

PHILPOTT, STEPHEN; Overbrook Regional SR HS; Lindenwold, NJ; (Y); 2/350; Am Leg Boys St; Church Yth Grp; Drama Clb; Science Clb; Concert Band; Drm Mjr(t); Mrchg Band; School Play; Crs Cntry; Var Capt Tennis; US Naval Acad; Aerospace Engr.

PHISTER, FRED; Sussex County Vo-Tech; Stanhope, NJ; (Y); Teachers Aide; Yrbk Stf; Rep Jr Cls; Rep Sr Cls; Stu Cncl; Ftbl; Wrstlng; High Hon Roll; De Vry Inst Tech; Engrng.

PHY, GEORGE; Oakcrest HS; Mays Landing, NJ; (Y); Exploring; Ski Clb; SADD; Teachers Aide; Rep Frsh Cls; Var Bsbl; JV Bsktbl; Var Socr; Hon Roll; Jr NHS; Engrng.

PIANO, JOANN; River Dell SR HS; Oradell, NJ; (Y); 41/217; Church Yth Grp; Cmnty Wkr; Hosp Aide; Yrbk Bus Mgr; Sec French Hon Soc; Hon Roll; NHS; Amer Legn Auxlry Schlrshp 86; 1st Pl ST Frnsc Meet Frnch Drmtc Intrprtn 85; Rutgers Coll; Ec.

PICART, XENIA; Henry Snyder HS; Jersey City, NJ; (Y); Church Yth Grp; Church Choir.

PICCONE, ANTHONY; Paul VI HS; Atco, NJ; (Y); 180/500; Cmnty Wkr; Political Wkr; Spanish Clb; SADD; Bsbl; Ftbl; Wt Lftg; Wrstlng; Temple Univ Awd 86; La Salle Univ Awd 86; Temple U; Corp Lawyer.

PICHINSON, DANIEL L; Highland Park HS; Highland Park, NJ; (Y); 18/130; Cmnty Wkr; Trs French Clb; Mathletes; Radio Clb; Science Clb; Band; Yrbk Stf; NHS; Ntl Merit SF; Rugers U Dean Summr Schlr 85; Hstry.

PICKELS, ANGELA; Mary Help Of Christians Acad; Paterson, NJ; (Y); SADD; Nwsp Rptr; Yrbk Stf; Hon Roll.

PICKER, TRACY; Mt Olive HS; Flanders, NJ; (Y); Dance Clb; Drama Clb; Exploring; Science Clb; Teachers Aide; Chorus; School Musical; School Play; Stage Crew; Variety Show; NJ Schl Ballet Schlrshp 84-85; NJSAM Schlrshp 86; Twice Invtd Morris Co & NJ St Teen Art Fest 85-86; Dance Tchr.

PICONE, ALLISON; St Marys HS; Lyndhurst, NJ; (Y); Trk.

PICONE, RACHAEL; Hunterdon Central HS; Whitehouse Sta, NJ; (Y); 133/548; Thesps; Capt Color Guard; Jazz Band; School Musical; Variety Show; Yrbk Stf; Off Frsh Cls; Off Soph Cls; Off Jr Cls; Off Stu Cncl; Rcgntn Prg Extra Curricular Actvts 84-85; Rcgntn Prg Outstndg Achvmnt 85-86; Giftd/Tlntd Vsl Art 85-86; Prfrmng Arts.

PIDANE, DONNA; Holy Family Acad; Bayonne, NJ; (Y); 1/130; Church Yth Grp; French Clb; Nwsp Ed-Chief; Nwsp Rptr; High Hon Roll; NHS; St Petres Coll Summer Schlr 85 & 86; Rutgers Schlr 86; Essay Wnr 86; Rutgers U; Pre-Med.

PIEKARZ, SUZANNE; Clifton HS; Clifton, NJ; (S); 139/637; Drama Clb; Key Clb; SADD; Varsity Clb; School Musical; School Play; Stage Crew; Yrbk Stf; Bsktbl; Trk; Trck & Fld Athlt Yr 86; All Area Discs 86; All CO Shtpt & Discs 86; Spcl Educ.

PIELA, SUZANNE; Pope John XXII HS; Sparta, NJ; (Y); Church Yth Grp; Debate Tm; Drama Clb; Math Tm; Pep Clb; Spanish Clb; Speech Tm; Teachers Aide; Varsity Clb; Band.

PIERCE, ANDREA; Cumberland Regional HS; Bridgeton, NJ; (Y); 154/500; JA; Stat Socr; Stat Trk; Chem Engrng.

PIERCE, PAMELA; Eastside HS; Paterson, NJ; (S); #21 In Class; Yrbk Stf; Stu Cncl; Co-Capt Twrlr; Hon Roll; NHS; Accntng.

PIERCE, PAULA; Pt Pleasant Beach HS; Pt Pleasant Bch, NJ; (Y); 26/100; Key Clb; NFL; Ski Clb; Sec Spanish Clb; Varsity Clb; Cheerleading; Crs Cntry; Socr; Trk; Rotary Awd; Ciba Geigy Sci Awd 86; Purdue U; Comp Sci.

PIERCE, TERESA; Phillipsburg HS; Phillipsburg, NJ; (Y); 75/334; Bsktbl; Crs Cntry; Fld Hcky; Trk; Hon Roll; E PA Grls X-Cntry All-Str 85-86; Schl Rcd 1600 Mtrs & 1500 Mtrs 85; Art.

PIERRE, BEATRICE; Linden HS; Linden, NJ; (Y); Art Clb; Dance Clb; French Clb; FBLA; GAA; Math Clb; SADD; Variety Show; Yrbk Stf; Business Administration.

PIERRE, GINIA; Abraham Clark HS; Roselle, NJ; (S); Drama Clb; French Clb; Library Aide; Chorus; Rep Jr Cls; Rep Stu Cncl; JV Bsktbl; JV Crs Cntry; Hon Roll; Bio.

PIERSON, GARY; Sayreville War Memorial HS; Parlin, NJ; (Y); Am Leg Boys St; Spanish Clb; Varsity Clb; JV Bsbl; Var Capt Ftbl; Var Trk; Im Wt Lftg; Hon Roll; NHS; Spanish NHS; Engrng.

PIESTOR, DANIEL W; Steinert HS; Hamilton Square, NJ; (Y); AFS; Am Leg Boys St; Pres Church Yth Grp; DECA; Pres Key Clb; Pres SADD; Concert Band; Mrchg Band; Stu Cncl; Kiwanis Awd; Kiwanis Schlrshp 86; Bus Adm.

PIETKEWICZ, MELISSA; Matawan Regional HS; Matawan, NJ; (Y); 76/302; Church Yth Grp; Cmnty Wkr; Math Clb; Office Aide; Ski Clb; Chorus; School Musical; School Play; Rep Frsh Cls; Var JV Bsktbl; Hnrs Chem 84-85; Adv Bio Hnrs 85-86; Pres Ftns Awd 83-84.

PIETRO, LAURA; Central Regional HS; Bayville, NJ; (Y); 38/241; Am Leg Aux Girls St; VP Church Yth Grp; Pres Key Clb; Pep Clb; Varsity Clb; Chorus; Sec Soph Cls; Sec Jr Cls; Sec Sr Cls; Rep Stu Cncl; Comm.

PIETROWICZ, STANLEY; Hudson Catholic HS; Jersey City, NJ; (Y); 2/188; Science Clb; Yrbk Bus Mgr; Yrbk Rptr; Im Socr; Im Vllybl; CC Awd; Elks Awd; High Hon Roll; Prfct Atten Awd; Ntl Hstry & Govt Awd; U S Bus Educ Awd; Soc Dstngshd Amercn H S Stu; U S Jrnlsm Awd; 5-AP Chem Exam; Stevens Inst/Tech; Elec Engrng.

PIETRUSKA, DANNY; St Peters Prep; Bayonne, NJ; (Y); Computer Clb; High Hon Roll; Hon Roll; Rutgers U; Cmptr Engr.

PIETRYKOSKI, ELIZABETH; Bloomfield SR HS; Bloomfield, NJ; (Y); Band; Chorus; School Play.

PIETSCH, JOSEPH; Lodi HS; Lodi, NJ; (Y); VP Key Clb; Leo Clb; Varsity Clb; Variety Show; Tennis; Accntg.

PIGAGE, JOY; Long Branch HS; Long Branch, NJ; (S); 22/300; Yrbk Ed-Chief; Lit Mag; Sec Jr Cls; Socr; Twrlr; Vrsty Schlr 85; Jrnlsm.

PIGHINI, MARK; Cliffside Park HS; Cliffside Pk, NJ; (Y); 29/236; Pres Church Yth Grp; Math Tm; Hon Roll; Rotary Awd; Stdnts Intl Rel Smnr 84; NJ Isnt Tech; Engrng.

PIIZZI, DONNA; Cranford HS; Cranford, NJ; (Y); 40/269; FBLA; JA; Teachers Aide; Varsity Clb; Chorus; Yrbk Bus Mgr; Stu Cncl; Crs Cntry; Trk; Hon Roll; Katherine Gibbs Awd 86; Rutgers U Of Med; Med.

PILEWSKI, KIMBERLY; Linden HS; Linden, NJ; (Y); Art Clb; Computer Clb; GAA; Girl Scts; Nwsp Rptr; Pom Pon; Rutgers U; Accntng.

PILIGNO, AMY N; Williamstown HS; Williamstown, NJ; (Y); 12/261; French Clb; Hosp Aide; Rep Frsh Cls; Rep Soph Cls; Rep Jr Cls; Rep Sr Cls; Sec Trs Stu Cncl; Var Capt Tennis; Trs NHS; Pres Schlr; NJ Schlr-Athlt Awd 86; JR Miss Pgnt 85; Frnch Pin; Rutgers U; Intl Bus.

PILONG, EILEEN; Haddon Heights HS; Hadon Heights, NJ; (S); 17/188; Church Yth Grp; Drama Clb; Chorus; Church Choir; Madrigals; School Musical; School Play; Variety Show; Nwsp Rptr; Lit Mag; Music & Drama Awds 83; Haddon Honors Choir 85; NJ All-ST Chorus 85; Trenton ST Coll; Music.

PINDAR, CAROL; Mahwah HS; Mahwah, NJ; (Y); 17/178; Cmnty Wkr; Red Cross Aide; Chorus; Yrbk Stf; Lit Mag; Socr; Var Swmmng; High Hon Roll; Accntng.

PINELLI, LISA; Hopewell Valley Central HS; Pennington, NJ; (Y); 20/202; School Musical; Var JV Fld Hcky; High Hon Roll; Hon Roll; NHS; Bio.

PINEROS, LUCIA; Elizabeth HS; Elizabeth, NJ; (Y); 5/900; Dance Clb; Drama Clb; VP French Clb; Math Clb; NFL; PAVAS; Speech Tm; Chorus; School Musical; Lit Mag; Princpls Schlr/Supt Schlr 82-86; Boston U; Pre-Med.

PINGA, VICTOR; Academic HS; Jersey City, NJ; (S); 3/70; Chess Clb; Exploring; Scholastic Bowl; School Play; VP Frsh Cls; Rep Stu Cncl; Var Tennis; Hon Roll; NHS; Bard Coll; Engrng.

PINIAK, ANDREW; Red Bank Regional HS; Red Bank, NJ; (Y); Nwsp Sprt Ed; Bsbl; Var L Trk; Hon Roll; Lab Asst 84-85; BU; Bus.

PINIZZOTTO, ANTHONY; Paulsboro HS; Paulsboro, NJ; (Y); 25/135; Pres Drama Clb; Acpl Chr; Drm Mjr(t); Mrchg Band; School Musical; Nwsp Rptr; Ed Lit Mag; Stu Cncl; Hst NHS; Voice Dem Awd; NJSMA Awd 83; Glassboro ST Coll; Musical.

PINKOWITZ, DAVID A; Madison Central HS; Old Bridge, NJ; (Y); 3/342; Math Tm; Band; School Play; Yrbk Ed-Chief; VP Stu Cncl; NHS; Ntl Merit SF; German Clb; Hosp Aide; SADD; Page U S House Rep 84-85; 1st Aid Squad; German Hon Soc 83-84; Pol Sci.

PINNELLA, KEVIN; Toms River HS North; Toms River, NJ; (Y); Math Tm; Stage Crew; Hon Roll; Ntl Merit SF; Rep Schl In County Art Competition 86.

PINOSKI JR, PAUL; Wash Twp HS; Sewell, NJ; (Y); 1/70; Church Yth Grp; Computer Clb; Spanish Clb; Nwsp Rptr; Var Capt Crs Cntry; Var JV Trk; High Hon Roll; Hon Roll; Val; Art Clb; Mst Outstndg Dstnc Rnnr 84-86; 99.9 Prcnt ST Achvmnt Tst 84; 2nd Pl Pstr Cntst 83; MIT; Comp Engnrng.

PINTO, LYNN; Cranford HS; Cranford, NJ; (Y); 90/300; Pres Thesps; Band; Chorus; Church Choir; Madrigals; School Musical; School Play; Pres Jr Cls; Hon Roll; Westfield Jr Musical Clb Schlrp 86; All St Chorus & Bnd 83-86; All-Eastrn Chorus 85; Carnegie-Mellon U; Voice.

PINTO, ROB; Holy Cross HS; Mount Laurel, NJ; (Y); 55/391; Boy Scts; Cmnty Wkr; Debate Tm; Ski Clb; Y-Teens; Nwsp Rptr; Tennis; High Hon Roll; Hon Roll; U Of Scrntn; Pre-Med.

PINTO, ROWENA; Morris Catholic HS; Parsippany, NJ; (Y); 2/142; Math Clb; Math Tm; Natl Beta Clb; NFL; Scholastic Bowl; Service Clb; Hon Roll; NHS; Ntl Merit Ltr; Church Yth Grp; Ntl Arts Olympd 1st Pl 83; Rtgrs Schlr 86; Diocesan Essy Cntst 2nd Pl 84; Dartmouth; Physcs.

PIPPI, MICHELE; Kittatinny Regional HS; Newton, NJ; (Y); Chorus; Capt Flag Corp; School Musical; School Play; Stage Crew; Stat Swmmng; Hon Roll; Psych.

PIRONE, JAMES; North Bergen HS; North Bergen, NJ; (Y); Boy Scts; French Hon Soc; Accntnt.

PIROZZI, ANTHONY; Notre Dame HS; Trenton, NJ; (Y); 37/360; Varsity Clb; School Play; Nwsp Phtg; Nwsp Stf; Off Frsh Cls; Off Soph Cls; Off Jr Cls; VP Sr Cls; Golf; Hon Roll.

PIROZZI, DONNA; Hillsborough HS; Bellemead, NJ; (Y); Girl Scts; Var Capt Cheerleading; Powder Puff Ftbl; Hon Roll; Chrprsn Prm Cmmtte; Mdrn Danc Cls SC Teen Arts Fstvl Fnlst; Crmnlgy.

PISACK, ROBERT; Bridgewater Raritan HS West; Bridgewater, NJ; (Y); Boy Scts; 4-H; Ski Clb; Im Bowling; JV Ftbl; Var L Lcrss; Hon Roll; Bus Mgmt.

PISAURO, ERIC D; Ewing HS; Trenton, NJ; (Y); 1/306; Trs Key Clb; Math Clb; Concert Band; Mrchg Band; Orch; School Musical; Ntl Merit SF; Bio Awd 83-84; Alg III Awd 84-85; Finc.

PISCATORE, LAURENE; S Plainfield HS; S Plainfield, NJ; (Y); Drama Clb; Color Guard; Nwsp Ed-Chief; Yrbk Sprt Ed; Lit Mag; Rep Stu Cncl; Stat L Ftbl; Art Clb; VP French Clb; Letterman Clb; Attnd Middlesex Cnty Arts HS Creative Wrtng 84-85; Alternate Govnrs Schl Or Arts Creative Wrtng 86; Engl.

PISCITELLO, MICHELLE; Livingston HS; Livingston, NJ; (Y); French Clb; Varsity Clb; Yrbk Stf; Var Cheerleading; Powder Puff Ftbl; Hon Roll; Athletic Trng & Coaching.

PISINSKI, KIM; West Morris Central HS; Long Valley, NJ; (Y); French Clb; FBLA; Math Clb; Var Crs Cntry; French Hon Soc; Hon Roll; Bus.

PISKADLO, BRYAN; Ramapo Regional HS; Wyckoff, NJ; (Y); 95/329; Camera Clb; Hon Roll; Cert Merit Eng I And Sci 84; Cert Of Merit Alge II 86; Rutgers Sch Phrmcy; Phrmcst.

PISSALIDIS, LAKY; James Caldwell HS; W Caldwell, NJ; (Y); JV Socr; JV Swmmng; JV Tennis; JV Trk; High Hon Roll; Hon Roll; Science.

PITCHER, BRIAN S; Pemberton HS; Pemberton, NJ; (Y); 40/411; Am Leg Boys St; Church Yth Grp; Math Clb; ROTC; Science Clb; Im Bsbl; Im Ftbl; Hon Roll; Schl Rep Hugh O Brien Ldrshp Sem NC 85; USAFA; Aero Engrng.

PITCHERELLO, LORI; Northern Burlington HS; Jobstown, NJ; (Y); Drama Clb; Exploring; FFA; Concert Band; School Musical; Symp Band; Cheerleading; Burlington County Coll; Elem Ed.

PITCHFORD, SHEREE; James J Ferris HS; Jersey City, NJ; (Y); Am Leg Aux Girls St; Church Yth Grp; Debate Tm; GAA; Model UN; PAVAS; Scholastic Bowl; SADD; Capt Var Cheerleading; Trk; Pres Citation 86; Elec Engrng.

PITTAKAS, MINA; Wildwood Catholic HS; N Wildwood, NJ; (Y); 2/87; Church Yth Grp; Debate Tm; French Clb; NFL; SADD; Church Choir; School Musical; School Play; Stage Crew; Yrbk Ed-Chief; Trenton ST Full Scholar 86; U Tampa Pres Scholar 86; AHEPA Scholar 86; U S FL; Ind Engrng.

PITTMAN, BRIAN; Lakeland Regional HS; Ringwood, NJ; (Y); 42/303; Chess Clb; Math Clb; Varsity Clb; JV Var Bsbl; JV Var Socr; JV Var Wrstlng; Hon Roll; NHS; St Schlr; Ramapo Achvt Schlrshp 86; Cupsaw Lk Athltc Schlrshp 86; Ramapo Coll; Math.

PITTMAN, JODY; Vailsburg HS; Newark, NJ; (Y); Church Yth Grp; Cmnty Wkr; Pep Clb; Drill Tm; Pres Frsh Cls; Rep Soph Cls; Coach Actv; High Hon Roll; Hon Roll; Awd Profcncy-Offc Prctc 86; Pre-Mdcn.

PITTMAN, LINDA; Hopewell Valley Central HS; Pennington, NJ; (Y); 6/202; Church Yth Grp; Service Clb; Chorus; School Musical; JV Bsktbl; High Hon Roll; NHS.

PITTS, CAROLYN; Salem HS; Bridgeton, NJ; (Y); Church Yth Grp; Hosp Aide; Library Aide; Spanish Clb; Cheerleading; Hon Roll; Nrsng.

PIZZA, GLORIA; Wildwood Catholic HS; N Wildwood, NJ; (Y); Cheerleading; Tennis; Hon Roll; Elec Engrng.

PIZZI, LISA; Pascack Hills HS; Montvale, NJ; (Y); Church Yth Grp; Library Aide; SADD; Nwsp Bus Mgr; Hon Roll; Acctng.

PIZZO, GINA; Cumberland Regional HS; Bridgeton, NJ; (Y); Intnl Clb; Ski Clb; Pres Stu Cncl; Cheerleading; Bus.

PIZZULLI, LYNN; Mount St Marys Acad; Edison, NJ; (Y); Computer Clb; Dance Clb; Sec GAA; VP Jr Cls; Pres Stu Cncl; Var Bsktbl; Var Tennis; Hon Roll; Catholic U; Bus.

PIZZUTO, JULIE; Gateway Regional HS; Woodbury Heights, NJ; (Y); 29/205; Church Yth Grp; French Clb; JCL; Key Clb; Spanish Clb; SADD; Rep Stu Cncl; JV Cheerleading; High Hon Roll; Hon Roll; Drexel; Mrktng.

PLACA, DONNA; Monsignor Donovan HS; Brick Town, NJ; (Y); Debate Tm; Ski Clb; SADD; Hon Roll; Acadmc Excllnc Chem Awd 85-86; Law.

PLACIDE, CARLENE; Academic HS; Jersey City, NJ; (S); Drama Clb; Girl Scts; Hosp Aide; Quiz Bowl; Scholastic Bowl; Science Clb; Band; Concert Band; Variety Show; JV Cheerleading; 2nd Pl Hudson County Sci Fair 84-85; US Airforce Sci Awd 84-85; Am Musicl Found Awd 84-85; Law.

PLADDYS, LAUREEN; N Bergen HS; N Bergen, NJ; (Y); 33/470; Key Clb; Spanish Clb; Pres Soph Cls; Stat Bsbl; Cheerleading; Gov Hon Prg Awd; High Hon Roll; Prfct Atten Awd; Spanish NHS; Rep Frsh Cls; Schlrshp HB Studio NYC 85-87; Drama.

PLANCEY, HOWARD D; Solomon Schechter Day Schl; New Providence, NJ; (Y); 5/21; Pres Chess Clb; VP Temple Yth Grp; Bsbl; Socr; NHS; Frsh Cls; Soph Cls; Jr Cls; Stu Cncl; Frisbee Tm Capt; U PA; Engrg.

PLANCHARD, STEVEN; Chatham Twp HS; Chatham, NJ; (Y); 1/137; Trs AFS; Church Yth Grp; Sec Model UN; Quiz Bowl; Concert Band; Jazz Band; Pep Band; NHS; Val; Band; Georgetown; Intl Rltns.

PLANK, JENNIFER; Montgomery HS; Belle Mead, NJ; (Y); 10/131; AFS; Church Yth Grp; Hosp Aide; Library Aide; Band; Concert Band; Mrchg Band; Cheerleading; Gym; High Hon Roll; PTSA Schlrshp 86; Awd-Vlntrng Princetn Mdcl Ctr Emer Rm 85 & 86; Athltc Awd-Gymnstcs, Chrldng 86; Dickinson Coll; Medcn.

PLASTINE, LAURA; Secaucus HS; Secaucus, NJ; (S); 9/170; Dance Clb; Math Clb; Ski Clb; Spanish Clb; Varsity Clb; Concert Band; Mrchg Band; Ed Yrbk Stf; Rep Sr Cls; NHS.

PLATT, JOHN; Freehold Township HS; Freehold, NJ; (Y); 20/300; Aud/Vis; Computer Clb; VP Spanish Clb; Lit Mag; NHS; Ntl Merit Ltr; TV 39 Sta Mem; Radio/Tv Brdcstng.

PLATT, SHERYL; Cherry Hill HS East; Cherry Hill, NJ; (Y); Aud/Vis; Stage Crew; Nwsp Rptr; Rep Jr Cls; Rep Sr Cls; Rep Stu Cncl; Var Powder Puff Ftbl; High Hon Roll; Hon Roll; NHS; SR Hall Of Fame 86; Stu Congrs Partctpn Awd 86; Cls Govt Partcpnt Awd 86; Syracuse U; Brdcst Jrnlsm.

PLATZ, PHILIP; Don Bosco Prep; Nanuet, NY; (Y); Boy Scts; Trk; Chess Clb; Church Yth Grp; Civic Clb; Cmnty Wkr; Debate Tm; Pep Clb; Political Wkr; Ski Clb; Accntng.

PLAXE, DONNA; South Plainfield HS; S Plainfield, NJ; (Y); 13/286; Church Yth Grp; Hosp Aide; High Hon Roll; Hon Roll; Spanish NHS; Schltc Hnr Soc 85-86; Schlrshp Ladies Aux 86; Pres Acadmc Ftnss Awd 86; E Stroudsburg U; Nrsg.

PLAZA, CHRISTIAN E; Christian Brothers Acad; Tinton Falls, NJ; (S); 13/216; Hosp Aide; JA; Math Tm; Quiz Bowl; Teachers Aide; Ed Nwsp Rptr; Im Wrstlng; High Hon Roll; Pres NHS; Ntl Merit Ltr; Brwn U; Med.

PLEMENOS JR, GEORGE J; Paul VI HS; Laurel Spgs, NJ; (Y); Im JV Wrstlng; Engr.

PLESNIARSKI, ERIC; Southern Regional HS; Barnegat, NJ; (Y); Model UN; Stu Cncl; Hon Roll; NJ ST Sci Cmptn 86; Rd Crss Crtfd Basic Frst Aid & CPR 86.

PLEVYAK, SANDRA P; Phillipsburg Catholic HS; Phillipsburg, NJ; (Y); 3/78; Cmnty Wkr; Hosp Aide; Science Clb; Concert Band; Stage Crew; Nwsp Stf; Fld Hcky; Score Keeper; Sftbl; Hon Roll; Phllpsbrg Cthlc HS Schlr Athlt 86; Stu Recogntn Awd 86; Merit Awd 85; U Of Notre Dame; Chem.

PLOCEK, MICHELLE; Watchung Hills Regional HS; Warren, NJ; (Y); 10/315; Ski Clb; SADD; Chorus; Color Guard; Orch; Yrbk Stf; Hon Roll; Ntl Merit SF; Key Clb; Swmmng; Stu Of Mnth 86; Sci.

PLUMMER, CATHY; Hillside HS; Hillside, NJ; (Y); Art Clb; Church Yth Grp; Spanish Clb; Chorus; Church Choir; Color Guard; School Play; Hon Roll; Medical.

PNESAR, SANDALY; Howell HS; Howell, NJ; (Y); Nwsp Rptr; Nwsp Stf; Yrbk Stf; Rep Frsh Cls; Rep Soph Cls; Tennis; Fshn Merch.

PO, GENALYN; Union Catholic RHS; Hillside, NJ; (Y); 25/308; Hosp Aide; Latin Clb; Service Clb; Spanish Clb; Nwsp Rptr; Yrbk Stf; Hon Roll; Spanish NHS; Acadmc All Am 86; Pre Med.

POAT, ROBBIN; West Milford Twp HS; W Milford, NJ; (S); 40/350; French Clb; Sec Latin Clb; VP Varsity Clb; Nwsp Stf; Yrbk Sprt Ed; Var L Bsktbl; Var L Trk; Hon Roll; Jr NHS; Grls Trck & Fld Mst Dedctd Awd 85; Clemson U; Bus.

POBLETE, CHRISTINE; St John Vianney HS; Marlboro, NJ; (Y); Church Yth Grp; Cmnty Wkr; Intnl Clb; Service Clb; SADD; Nwsp Rptr; Yrbk Stf; Soph Cls; Im Cheerleading; Hon Roll; Outstndng Awd Hist,Comm Invl 84-85; Bio.

POCCIA, CATERINA; Parsippany Hills HS; Morris Plains, NJ; (Y); FBLA; Yrbk Phtg; Off Jr Cls; High Hon Roll; Hon Roll; NHS; Prfct Atten Awd; Camera Clb; Key Clb; Pep Clb; Tres Itln Clb; Hnr Cert Fluncy 86; Hugh O Brian Yth Ldrshp Fndtn Cert 85; Proj ROLE Recmntn 86; Rutgers U; Bus Admn.

POCKELL, LORI ANN; Eastern HS; West Berlin, NJ; (Y); VP Church Yth Grp; Speech Tm; SADD; Acpl Chr; School Musical; Yrbk Stf; Sr Cls; High Hon Roll; NHS; Ntl Merit SF; Psych.

POCKLEMBO, ANN MARIE E; John P Stevens HS; Edison, NJ; (Y); 68/469; Acpl Chr; Chorus; Madrigals; Orch; School Musical; Variety Show; French Hon Soc; High Hon Roll; Hon Roll; NHS; SMU Meadows Artistic Schlrshp 86-90; Ssmu U Schlr 86-90; Southern Meth U; Violinist.

PODURGIEL, GERALDINE; Paul VI Regional HS; Belleville, NJ; (S); French Clb; Key Clb; School Play; Var Trk; French Hon Soc; High Hon Roll; NHS; Rutgers U; Sci.

POGGI, MATTHEW A; Cresskill HS; Cresskill, NJ; (Y); 3/111; Am Leg Boys St; Nwsp Sprt Ed; Nwsp Stf; Yrbk Stf; JV Var Bsktbl; Stat Ftbl; High Hon Roll; NHS; Ntl Merit SF; Prtcptd ST Sci Day Bio 86; Bus.

POGUE, KERRY; Abraham Clark HS; Elizabeth, NJ; (Y); Church Yth Grp; Girl Scts; Service Clb; Chorus; Yrbk Stf; Var Capt Bsktbl; Var Trk; Hon Roll; Coe Awd 86; Rutgers; Engl.

POH, KRISTY; Chatham Twp HS; Chatham Twp, NJ; (Y); 7/128; Key Clb; Model UN; Pep Clb; Yrbk Stf; Stu Cncl; Fld Hcky; Stat L Ice Hcky; NHS; St Schlr; PTO Schlrshp 86; Grdn ST Dstngshd Schlr Pgm 86; Accntng Awd 86; Villanova U; Eco.

POINT, TERESA; Woodstown HS; Woodstown, NJ; (Y); Church Yth Grp; English Clb; German Clb; Nwsp Rptr; Yrbk Stf; Lit Mag; Socr; High Hon Roll; NHS; Grmn Hon Soc 85; Engl.

POINT-DU-JOUR, MARIE A; Abraham Clark HS; Roselle, NJ; (Y).

POINTER, JAMIE; Monsignor Donovan HS; Lanoka Harbor, NJ; (Y); VP Drama Clb; Intnl Clb; VP Thesps; Nwsp Rptr; School Play; Yrbk Stf; High Hon Roll; NHS; Theology Award 85-86; $2000 Schlrshp To Westmnstr Choir Clg 86; $500 Garden St Schlrshp 86; Westminster Choir Clg; Music Ed.

POINTON, GREGG; Hamilton HS; Yardville, NJ; (S); Band; Concert Band; Mrchg Band; Orch; JV Socr; Hon Roll; Math Awd-Us Achvmnt Acad 86; Drexel; Engnrng.

POIRIER, ALANNA; Mount Olice HS; Budd Lake, NJ; (Y); 8/300; JV Bsktbl; Var Crs Cntry; Var Fld Hcky; Var Trk; High Hon Roll; Hon Roll; NHS; Morris Co Trck Coaches Assn All-Co Tm 85 & 86; Sci Tchrs Recgntn Awd-Hnrs Bio 85.

POIST, ANDREA; Voorhees HS; High Bridge, NJ; (Y); 9/276; Am Leg Aux Girls St; Varsity Clb; Lit Mag; Rep Jr Cls; Bsktbl; Fld Hcky; Sftbl; High Hon Roll; NHS; Spanish NHS; Acdmc Achvmnt Soc; MVP Sftbll; Sci Awds; Law.

POIST, MICHAEL J; Voorhees HS; High Bridge, NJ; (Y); 22/240; Am Leg Boys St; Varsity Clb; Var Crs Cntry; Ftbl; Capt Var Wrstlng; Hon Roll; NHS; Spanish NHS; Acdmc Achvt Socty 82-85; U S Army Rsrv Schlr Athl Awd 85-86; U Of VA.

POLACK, ERIC; St Peters Prep HS; Bayonne, NJ; (Y); Boy Scts; Trs Church Yth Grp; Concert Band; Jazz Band; Pep Band; Hon Roll; Cathlc Sct Awd 84; Talnt Shw 1st Musc Catgry 86; Eclgy.

POLAK, ALICIA; Cinnaminson HS; Cinnaminson, NJ; (S); DECA; English Clb; FBLA; SADD; Nwsp Stf; Stu Cncl; Swmmng; Nat Cnfrnc Ldr 86; Sst Wn Ust Pl 86; Rgnls 5th Pl 86; Jrnlsm.

POLANIN, JOSEPH; Carteret HS; Carteret, NJ; (Y); 1/175; Am Leg Boys St; Capt Quiz Bowl; Science Clb; Nwsp Ed-Chief; Off Stu Cncl; Var L Trk; Bausch & Lomb Sci Awd; NHS; Pres Schlr; St Schlr; Middlesex Cnty Assoc Sec Schl Prncpls & Advsrs Outstndng Stu Ad 86; Rutgers Deans Schlr 85; Trck Divis; US Naval Acad; Offcr.

POLASKI, MICHELLE L; Camden Catholic HS; Pennsauken, NJ; (Y); #24 In Class; Spanish Clb; VP Sr Cls; Hon Roll; NHS; Spanish NHS; French Clb; Hosp Aide; Mat Maids; Socr; Hlth Crs Clb; Engrng.

POLASKY, CHRISTOPHER; Howell HS; Howell, NJ; (Y); 54/260; SADD; JV Bsktbl; Wt Lftg; Hon Roll; Bus.

POLE, NNAMDI; Hightstown HS; E Windsor, NJ; (Y); 9/449; Am Leg Boys St; Pres Drama Clb; Pres Thesps; Acpl Chr; School Musical; School Play; Nwsp Stf; Rep Jr Cls; Trk; NHS; Deans Summer Schlr 86; Psychtry.

POLESE, MARY; Brick Memorial HS; Brick, NJ; (S); 30/385; Drama Clb; Intnl Clb; Math Clb; Stage Crew; Nwsp Rptr; Yrbk Phtg; Yrbk Rptr; Powder Puff Ftbl; High Hon Roll; NHS; Marist; Fash Desgn.

POLESUK, ERIC; Parisppany HS; Parsippany, NJ; (Y); Chess Clb; German Clb; Math Tm; Ski Clb; Var Socr; JV Wt Lftg; Hon Roll; Jr NHS; NHS; Engrng.

POLICANO, MARIANNE; Paramus Catholic Girls Regionl HS; Elmwood Pk, NJ; (Y); Church Yth Grp; Drama Clb; Political Wkr; School Play; Nwsp Rptr; Nwsp Stf; Var Cheerleading; Sftbl; Trk; Merit Awd Euchanistic Mnstry 85-86; Right To Life Club Geniology Club 86; CYO Natl Champ St Annes Bish; Dominican Coll; Pol Sci.

POLICAR, DAVID; N Bergen HS; N Bergen, NJ; (Y); 7/404; Q&S; Nwsp Ed-Chief; VP Stu Cncl; Hon Roll; Ntl Merit SF; Prfct Atten Awd; Voice Dem Awd; Rep Frsh Cls; Rep Soph Cls; Rep Jr Cls; MA Inst Of Tech; Physcs.

POLICE, CHERIE; Dover HS; Dover, NJ; (Y); 5/160; AFS; Sec Latin Clb; VP Concert Band; VP Mrchg Band; School Musical; Lit Mag; Var Capt Cheerleading; JV Score Keeper; Hon Roll; NHS; Penn ST; Chem.

POLIDORI, LAURA; Sayreville War Memorial HS; Parlin, NJ; (Y); 62/379; FBLA; OEA; Spanish Clb; Varsity Clb; Crs Cntry; Trk; High Hon Roll; Hon Roll; NHS; Spanish NHS; FSA Bond 86; Kean; Acctg.

POLING, JEFFREY M; Keyport HS; Keyport, NJ; (Y); 6/120; Am Leg Boys St; Cmnty Wkr; Letterman Clb; Varsity Clb; Var Bsbl; Var Capt Ftbl; Var L Trk; Var Wt Lftg; Hon Roll; All Cnfrnc Lnbckr In Ftbl; All Mnmth Cnty Ftbl Lnbckr; Sprts Med.

POLINIAK, SUSAN; Holy Cross HS; Willingboro, NJ; (Y); 11/369; Chess Clb; Scholastic Bowl; Science Clb; Chorus; School Musical; Stage Crew; Lit Mag; High Hon Roll; Rutgers Smmr Schlr 86; Physics.

POLITO, BETH; Scotch Plains Fanwood HS; Scotch Plains, NJ; (Y); SADD; Chorus; Var JV Sftbl; Co-Capt Tennis; Hon Roll; Spanish NHS; Athltc Trainr 85-86; Varsty Tnns Awd 83; Varsty Sftbl Awd 86; Health.

POLITZINER, LOREE; North Brunswick Township HS; N Brunswick, NJ; (Y); 11/300; Hosp Aide; Key Clb; Sec Temple Yth Grp; Variety Show; Trs Frsh Cls; Rep Soph Cls; VP Jr Cls; VP Sr Cls; Rep Stu Cncl; Var Capt Tennis; All Conf All Div Tennis Plyr 85; Bus.

POLK, SYLVIA S; Glen Rock JR SR HS; Glen Rock, NJ; (Y); Cmnty Wkr; Debate Tm; Science Clb; Ed Nwsp Stf; Lit Mag; Jr NHS; NHS; Pres Stu Cncl Brgn Cnty HS Of Jwsh Stds 86-87; Stu Cncl Rep Of BCHSJS 83-86; Schlrshp U Madrid 86; Eng.

POLKOWITZ, GARY; J P Stevens HS; Edison, NJ; (Y); 65/485; Debate Tm; Chrmn Model UN; Band; Nwsp Rptr; Rep Soph Cls; Rep Stu Cncl; Var Bsbl; Hon Roll; NHS; Spanish NHS; Pres Acad Fit Awd 85-86; U DE; Accntnt.

POLL, DENISE; Central Regional HS; Bayville, NJ; (Y); 44/280; L Capt Cheerleading; JV Var Fld Hcky; High Hon Roll; Hon Roll; Chem.

POLLACK, JOAN; East Brunswick HS; E Brunswick, NJ; (Y); French Clb; Key Clb; SADD; Orch; Yrbk Bus Mgr; French Hon Soc; High Hon Roll; NHS; ST Sci Day 11th ST 86; Sci League Chem Tm 86; Rutgers Schl Phrmcy; Phrmcy.

POLLACK, SUZANNE; Westfield SR HS; Westfield, NJ; (Y); 5/491; Am Leg Aux Girls St; Hosp Aide; Orch; Yrbk Stf; French Hon Soc; NHS; Pres Schlr; Science Clb; Concert Band; Lit Mag; Union Carbide Awd Chem 86; Engl/Sci Awd 86; Jack E Von Roesgen Calculus/Chem Awd 86; Stanford U; Natl Sci.

POLLAK, DEBORAH; Bridgewater-Raritan HS East; Bridgewater, NJ; (Y); Am Leg Aux Girls St; SADD; Trs Soph Cls; Trs Jr Cls; Trs Sr Cls; Rep Stu Cncl; Var JV Bsktbl; Var JV Fld Hcky; Var Stat Ftbl; Var JV Sftbl; Spcl Olympcs; Prm Cmmttee; Wrld Hungr Cmmttee; Cmmnctns.

POLLARD, CHERISE; Howell HS; Howell, NJ; (Y); 30/380; French Clb; Intnl Clb; Trs SADD; Color Guard; Stage Crew; Nwsp Rptr; Nwsp Stf; NHS; Opt Clb Awd; Math.

POLLARO, FELICIA; Lodi HS; Lodi, NJ; (Y); 7/147; Church Yth Grp; Key Clb; Office Aide; Pep Clb; Sec Spanish Clb; Co-Capt Color Guard; Flag Corp; High Hon Roll; Hon Roll; NHS; Montclair ST Rutgers.

POLLARO, NICK; Wallington HS; Wallington, NJ; (Y); Office Aide; School Play; Stage Crew; Trs Jr Cls; Trs Stu Cncl; Var L Bsbl; Var L Bowling; Var L Ftbl; Hon Roll; NHS; Bus.

POLLOCK, FELICIA; Atlantic City HS; Ventnor, NJ; (Y); Library Aide; Office Aide; Red Cross Aide; Chorus; Nwsp Rptr; Ed Nwsp Stf; Insgnia Crw 84; Brdcstng.

POLLOCK, HILLEL DAVID; Edgewood SR HS; Atco, NJ; (Y); Boy Scts; Latin Clb; JV Trk; Hon Roll; NHS; BSA Photo Schlrshp Awd 83; BBYO Re Ut Chptr Trea 85; Prntng Brd Waterfrd Twsp Libr 85-86; Cmmnctn.

POLONIO, SUZANNE; Red Bank Catholic HS; Neptune, NJ; (Y); Church Yth Grp; Gym; Crimnl Justc.

POLYMEROPOULOS, MARC; Highland Park HS; Highland Park, NJ; (Y); 14/148; Am Leg Boys St; Stu Cncl; Var L Crs Cntry; Im Ice Hcky; Var L Tennis; Var L Trk; Hon Roll; Frgn Svc.

POMANELLI, DIANE; Madison HS; Madison, NJ; (Y); Rep Soph Cls; Rep Jr Cls; Rep Stu Cncl; Var Cheerleading; Powder Puff Ftbl; Sftbl; Fshn Mdse.

POMERANTZ, JENNIFER; Newton HS; Newton, NJ; (S); 4/210; Church Yth Grp; Trs French Clb; Math Tm; Science Clb; Concert Band; Mrchg Band; Yrbk Bus Mgr; Rep Stu Cncl; Stat Tennis; NHS; Chem.

POMPA, MICHELLE; Hightstown HS; East Windsor, NJ; (Y); Art Clb; Band; Chorus; Concert Band; Var Capt Bsktbl; Hon Roll; Art.

POMPEO, MARIO; James Caldwell HS; W Caldwell, NJ; (Y); 15/250; Ski Clb; Yrbk Bus Mgr; Yrbk Ed-Chief; Stu Cncl; Socr; Tennis; High Hon Roll; NHS; Prfct Atten Awd; Pres Ftns Awd 84; Pre-Law.

PONSTINGEL, LAURA; Mary Help Of Christians Acad; Paterson, NJ; (Y); Cmnty Wkr; Computer Clb; English Clb; Girl Scts; Quiz Bowl; Science Clb; Service Clb; Nwsp Stf; Im Badmtn; Im Bsktbl; Hnr Pin Wrld Hstry 84-85; Hnr Awd Us Hstry 85-86; Music.

PONTE, ANTHONY; Hackensack HS; Hakcensack, NJ; (Y); 80/400; Art Clb; Computer Clb; FBLA; Teachers Aide; Fairleigh Dickinson U; Accntng.

PONTORIERO, ANTONETTA; Mother Seton Regional HS; Union, NJ; (Y); Cmnty Wkr; Drama Clb; Hosp Aide; Intnl Clb; Math Tm; Science Clb; Chorus; Stage Crew; Yrbk Stf; Hon Roll; Douglass Coll; Accntnt.

PONTORIERO, JOSEPH; Seton Hall Prep; Newark, NJ; (Y); 23/260; Boys Clb Am; Church Yth Grp; Computer Clb; Key Clb; Pep Clb; Ski Clb; Nwsp Rptr; Yrbk Phtg; Off Frsh Cls; Off Soph Cls; Parochial A ST Bsktbl Champs 86; Law.

POOLE, BRENT; Watchung Hills Regional HS; Millington, NJ; (Y); Cmnty Wkr; Key Clb; SADD; Concert Band; Variety Show; Bsbl; Coach Actv; Ftbl; Vllybl; Hon Roll; 1st Prz Bnd Cntst 86; Ecmncs.

POOLE, WILIAM; Middletown HS South; Red Bank, NJ; (Y); Pres Church Yth Grp; Ski Clb; Crs Cntry; Golf; Bus Admn.

POONIAN, VANEETA; James Caldwell HS; West Caldwell, NJ; (Y); Yrbk Stf; Trk; Hon Roll; Engr.

POPE, YVETTE; East Orange HS; E Orange, NJ; (Y); Computer Clb; Teachers Aide; Hon Roll; Prfct Atten Awd; Taylor Inst; Comp Pgmg.

POPECK, TOM; Wallington HS; Wallington, NJ; (Y); #5 In Class; Chess Clb; Letterman Clb; Ski Clb; Concert Band; School Musical; Nwsp Rptr; Yrbk Stf; Var Bowling; Var Ftbl; Var Trk; Natl French Awd 85; Elec Engr.

POPIEL, KATARZYNA; Vernon Twp HS; Hamburg, NJ; (Y); Boy Scts; Exploring; Chorus; Nwsp Stf; Yrbk Stf; Lit Mag; Hon Roll; NHS; Ntl Merit Ltr; Med.

POPLAWSKI, LORRAINE; Cresskill HS; Cresskill, NJ; (Y); 9/111; Am Leg Aux Girls St; Var Debate Tm; Band; Chorus; Co-Capt Color Guard; Rep Stu Cncl; Var Trk; Church Yth Grp; Ski Clb; Extraordinary Stu Of Amer 86; Psych.

POPLAWSKI, WALTER; Clifton HS; Clifton, NJ; (Y); 102/637; Boys Clb Am; Boy Scts; Chess Clb; Science Clb; Rutgers Coll; Engrng.

POPOLA, JENNIFER; Middletown S HS; Lincroft, NJ; (Y); Church Yth Grp; GAA; Ski Clb; Varsity Clb; Flag Corp; Var Powder Puff Ftbl; JV Var Sftbl; Capt Twrlr; Var Sftbl 86; Bus.

POPPE, CHRIS; Ramapo HS; Franklin Lakes, NJ; (Y); Symp Band; Nwsp Rptr; Nwsp Stf; Rep Frsh Cls; VP Soph Cls; VP Jr Cls; Rep Stu Cncl; Var Ftbl; Capt L Ice Hcky; NHS.

POPPER, MINDY; Toms River High School North; Toms River, NJ; (Y); Cmnty Wkr; Key Clb; Ocean County Coll; Spokesprsn.

PORCELLI, JOSEPH; Toms River HS East; Toms River, NJ; (Y); 7/585; Am Leg Boys St; Computer Clb; DECA; FBLA; Intnl Clb; Mathletes; Math Tm; Scholastic Bowl; Science Clb; Spanish Clb; Cornell U; Bio Med Engr.

PORCH JR, BARRY; Bridgeton HS; Bridgeton, NJ; (Y); DECA; Yrbk Phtg; Rotary Awd; Elec Engrng.

PORCH, WENDY; Cresskill HS; Cresskill, NJ; (Y); 22/111; French Clb; Hosp Aide; Yrbk Sprt Ed; Var JV Sftbl; Hon Roll; NHS; West Point; Mltry.

POREDA, STANLEY; Burlington County Vo-Tech; Riverside, NJ; (Y); Am Leg Boys St; Quiz Bowl; Scholastic Bowl; VICA; Yrbk Bus Mgr; Ice Hcky; Im Socr; Im Sftbl; Im Vllybl; Hon Roll; 2nd Pl VICA Comptn Schl Comp 86; De Vry; Comp Oprtr.

PORFANO, DAWN; Hackensack HS; Hackensack, NJ; (Y); Am Leg Aux Girls St; Yrbk Sprt Ed; Yrbk Stf; Var L Swmmng; Var Trk; Hon Roll; Grmn Hnr Scty 85-86.

PORMANN, ALISON; West Morris Central HS; Hackettstown, NJ; (Y); 25/280; Mrchg Band; Yrbk Stf; Tennis; High Hon Roll; Hon Roll; Art.

PORRO, JEANINE; Rutherford HS; Rutherford, NJ; (Y); VP Varsity Clb; Pres Frsh Cls; Pres Soph Cls; Pres Jr Cls; Pres Sr Cls; Var Bsktbl; Var Sftbl; Capt Var Vllybl; High Hon Roll; NHS; Hugh O Brian Outstdng-Ldrshp 85; Girls Ctznshp Inst At Douglass Coll; Stu Asst To Towns Teen Nght Clb; Law.

PORTALES, RAFAEL; N Bergen HS; North Bergen, NJ; (S); 15/404; Q&S; Band; Ed Nwsp Rptr; Yrbk Ed-Chief; Stu Cncl; NHS; Rep Frsh Cls; Rep Soph Cls; Rep Jr Cls; Rep Sr Cls; Natl Hspnc Schlr Awd Fnlst 85-86; Mrt Soc 85-86; Prncpls 1200 Clb 86.

PORTER, JUDY; Wall HS; Wall Township, NJ; (Y); 81/314; Church Yth Grp; German Clb; Church Choir; Co-Capt Var Fld Hcky; Var Sftbl; High Hon Roll; Hon Roll; Hnr For Teach Vctn Bible Schl 85-86; Rcvd Hnr For Ldng Chrch Girls In Action Msn Group 86; OK Baptist U; Rlgn.

PORTER, KENT R; Frank H Morrell HS; Irvington, NJ; (Y); Am Leg Boys St; Church Yth Grp; Computer Clb; Political Wkr; Chorus; Church Choir; Yrbk Sprt Ed; Trs Frsh Cls; High Hon Roll; Marketing.

PORTER, KISHA; Hoboken HS; Hoboken, NJ; (Y); Debate Tm; Sec FHA; Pres Key Clb; Church Choir; Capt Color Guard; Rep Jr Cls; VP Stu Cncl; Swmmng; NHS; Chorus; Aspira Achvmnt Awd 86; ANJ ST Inst; RN.

PORTER, MICHAEL N; Shawnee HS; Medford, NJ; (Y); Am Leg Boys St; Church Yth Grp; Math Tm; Variety Show; Lit Mag; Trs Jr Cls; Trs Sr Cls; JV Var Crs Cntry; Hon Roll; NHS; Hstry.

PORTILLA, PEDRO J; Passaic HS; Passaic, NJ; (Y); Am Leg Boys St; Chess Clb; Pres Computer Clb; Math Clb; Spanish Clb; Socr; Tennis; Hon Roll; NHS; Comp Sci.

PORTLOCK, NANCY; Matawan Regional HS; Matawan, NJ; (S); 24/302; French Clb; Ski Clb; Thesps; School Musical; School Play; Rep Stu Cncl; JV Fld Hcky; JV Sftbl; Hon Roll.

PORTO, DOREEN; Montville Twsp HS; Montville, NJ; (Y); 48/270; FBLA; Key Clb; Varsity Clb; Mrchg Band; VP Capt Cheerleading; JV Sftbl; High Hon Roll; Hon Roll; MIP Chrldg 85; MVP Chrldg 86; St Johns U; Acctnt.

PORTO, JOSEPH; Marist HS; Jersey City, NJ; (Y); 27/103; Chess Clb; Computer Clb; Key Clb; Nwsp Rptr; Bowling; Hon Roll; NHS; Comp Tech.

POSSA, CYRILLE; West Essex SR HS; North Caldwell, NJ; (Y); 112/350; Computer Clb; French Clb; Science Clb; Var Ice Hcky; Im Socr; Im Tennis; Hon Roll; Outstndng Achvt Boys Physcl Ed Awd 86; NJ Inst Of Tech; Elec Engrng.

POSSERT, DEENA; Roxbury HS; Kenvil, NJ; (Y); 17/378; Rep Chorus; Swing Chorus; Rep Stu Cncl; Var Cheerleading; Coach Actv; High Hon Roll; NHS; Chrldg Mst Cooprtv 84-85; Roxbury Chrldrs Parents Assn Schlrshp 85-86; Mst Vlubl Chrldr 85-86; County Coll Of Morris; Bus Adm.

POST, LAUREN T; Sayreville War Memorial HS; Parlin, NJ; (Y); 61/379; Am Leg Aux Girls St; Chorus; Capt Drill Tm; School Musical; Gov Hon Prg Awd; NHS; English Clb; Spanish Clb; Band; Mrchg Band; Rhythmic Sym Cls Ntl Champ 5 Golds 85; Gov Schl Seque Artist 86; Pres Acad Ftns Awd 86; James Madison U; Dance.

POST, MEGAN ANNE; Our Lady Of Mercy Acad; Marmora, NJ; (Y); Art Clb; Library Aide; School Play; Yrbk Stf; Sec Frsh Cls; Pres Sr Cls; Rep Stu Cncl; Bsbl; Cheerleading; Sftbl; Stu Of Yr 83-84; Pittsburgh U; Spcl Ed.

POST, MICA; Morris Catholic HS; Parsippany, NJ; (Y); 2/160; Service Clb; School Play; Nwsp Rptr; Ed Lit Mag; High Hon Roll; VP NHS; Sal; Ntnl Mrt Fnlst 86; 1st Pl Cthlc Frnsc Lg Grnd Trnmnt 86; Oldhm Schlrshp U Of Rchmnd 86; U Of Richmond.

POTENZA, VALERIE A; Livingston HS; Livingston, NJ; (Y); 6/498; Church Yth Grp; Band; High Hon Roll; Jr NHS; Spanish NHS; Ntl Merit Semifnlst 85; Chrch Folk Grp; 3rd Ntl Assn Tchrs Spnsh 85; Law.

POTTER, KELLEY; Williamstown HS; Williamstown, NJ; (Y); Hosp Aide; Chorus; School Musical; Variety Show; Off Soph Cls; Off Jr Cls; Off Sr Cls; Stu Cncl; Crmnl Justc.

POTTS, KIMBERLY; Middletown High School South; Middletown, NJ; (S); 19/436; VP Trs Girl Scts; Science Clb; Teachers Aide; High Hon Roll; Hon Roll; Ntl Merit SF; Girlscout Silver Awd 84; Vet Med.

POVLICK, JOANN; North Brunswick Twp HS; N Brunswick, NJ; (Y); 17/240; Drill Tm; Rep Stu Cncl; Var Gym; Stat Swmmng; Hon Roll; NHS; Lafayette Coll; Comp Sci.

POWELL, ALBERT; Audubon HS; Audubon, NJ; (Y); Computer Clb; German Clb; Var Capt Tennis; Im Vllybl; Hon Roll; Comp Engrng.

POWELL, TRACI; St James HS; Salem, NJ; (Y); 8/76; Church Yth Grp; Hosp Aide; Chorus; Church Choir; School Play; Stage Crew; Yrbk Stf; High Hon Roll; NHS; Natl Ldrshp Merit Awd 85; Natl Engl Merit Awd 85; Anderson Coll; Comp.

POWELL, VICKIE; Central HS; Newark, NJ; (Y); 8/141; JA; Math Clb; Office Aide; Nwsp Stf; Yrbk Stf; Hon Roll; Jr NHS; NHS; Prfct Atten Awd; Top Ten 86; Rutgers U; Accntng.

POWERS, BARBARA; Paul VI Regional HS; Upper Montclair, NJ; (S); 12/147; French Clb; Service Clb; Orch; School Musical; School Play; Nwsp Rptr; French Hon Soc; High Hon Roll; NHS; Intl Frgn Lang Awd Wnnr 86; Acad All Amer 86.

POWERS, DENISE; Pascack Valley HS; Hillsdale, NJ; (S); 25/265; Color Guard; Madrigals; High Hon Roll; NHS; Church Choir; School Musical; Yrbk Stf; Sec Frsh Cls; Merit Awd Bus Ed 83-84; Mst Imprvd Band Frnt Stu 84-85; Bloomsburg U PA; Deaf Interptr.

POWERS, KELLY; Middletown S HS; Highlands, NJ; (Y); 51/468; Band; Concert Band; Mrchg Band; Orch; Symp Band; Powder Puff Ftbl; Sftbl; Hon Roll; Vrsty Lttr Mrchng Band 84-85; Seton Hall; Accntng.

POWERS, SCOTT W; Pequannock Township HS; Pompton Plains, NJ; (Y); 13/217; Am Leg Boys St; Spanish Clb; Varsity Clb; JV Bsbl; JV Bsktbl; Var Capt Ftbl; Var Golf; Hon Roll; NHS; Bus.

PRACHAR, CYNTHIA ANN; Bishop George Ahr HS; Iselin, NJ; (Y); 94/277; Drama Clb; French Clb; Ski Clb; Spanish Clb; Thesps; Capt Color Guard; School Musical; School Play; Stage Crew; Hon Roll; Mktg.

PRACHTHAUSER, JONATHAN D; Morris Town HS; Morristown, NJ; (Y); Boy Scts; Exploring; Stage Crew; Trk; High Hon Roll; Hon Roll; Tri Cnty Asphalt Awd 84-86; Grad 1st Cls Firefighter 1 ST NJ 86; Morris Cnty Fire Trnng; Firefgh.

PRADHAN, AMRUTA B; Kearny HS; Kearny, NJ; (Y); 53/375; Computer Clb; French Clb; Chorus; Yrbk Stf; NHS; Newark Coll Of Art & Sci; Psych.

PRAGER, STACEY; Hightstown HS; Cranbury, NJ; (Y); Church Yth Grp; Drama Clb; Spanish Clb; Band; Chorus; Church Choir; Concert Band; Mrchg Band; School Play; Sftbl; Monmouth Coll; Accntng.

PRASAD, ALOK; Sayreville War Memorial HS; Parlin, NJ; (Y); 2/400; Boy Scts; German Clb; Intnl Clb; Math Clb; Quiz Bowl; Scholastic Bowl; Science Clb; Hon Roll; NHS; Sal; Grmn Hnr Society 85; U Of MI Ann Arbor; Elec Engr.

PRASAD, SUDHES; Jackson Memorial HS; Jackson, NJ; (Y); High Hon Roll; Hon Roll; Rutgers; Bio.

PRATE, ROCCO; Maple Shade HS; Maple Shade, NJ; (Y); Am Leg Boys St; Computer Clb; French Clb; Varsity Clb; VP Soph Cls; Ftbl; Trk; High Hon Roll; NHS; Prfct Atten Awd; Yth Merit Awd Stu Govrnmnt Day.

PRATER, HILLARY L; Neptune SR HS; Neptune, NJ; (Y); 32/300; Office Aide; Science Clb; Spanish Clb; Concert Band; High Hon Roll; Hon Roll; Jr NHS; NHS; Pres Schlr; Scroll Of Hon From Omega Psi Phi Frtrnty Phi Upsilon Chptr Of Neptune NJ 85; Douglass Coll; Business Admin.

PRATT, DAVID; Hopatcong HS; Hopatcong, NJ; (Y); Church Yth Grp; Im JV Bsbl; JV Socr; JV Wrstlng; Hon Roll; Stockton ST; Envrnmntl Sci.

PRECKAJLO, JOSEPH; St Peters Preparatory Schl; Elizabeth, NJ; (Y); 91/206; Camera Clb; Dance Clb; Intnl Clb; Library Aide; Stage Crew; Yrbk Stf; Lit Mag; Hon Roll; Pol Sci.

PREHN, DAWN; St Pius X Regional HS; Dunellen, NJ; (Y); Sec Church Yth Grp; Hon Roll; NHS; Accntng.

PREHODKA, BETHANY; North Warren Regional HS; Blairstown, NJ; (Y); Church Yth Grp; Hosp Aide; Intnl Clb; Ski Clb; Yrbk Stf; Trs Frsh Cls; Var Cheerleading; Var Fld Hcky; Score Keeper; Hon Roll; Bus.

PREKOPA, CHRIS; Lakeland Regional HS; Ringwood, NJ; (Y); 33/303; High Hon Roll; Road Show 85-86; U Of CA; Bus Mgt.

PRENDERGAST, SEAN; Vernon Twp HS; Glenwood, NJ; (Y); 18/287; French Clb; FBLA; Ski Clb; JV Bsbl; Var Bsktbl; Im Wt Lftg; FBLA Bus Math Awd 85; Georgetown; Bus.

PRENTICE, BRIAN; Rutherford HS; Rutherford, NJ; (Y); Key Clb; Ski Clb; Varsity Clb; Var Bsbl; JV Im Bsktbl; Im Socr; Im Vllybl; Im Wt Lftg; Hon Roll; Fordham U.

PRENTISS, CATHY; Chatham Township HS; Chatham, NJ; (Y); 29/130; Church Yth Grp; Key Clb; Model UN; Pep Clb; Band; Pep Band; Bsktbl; Fld Hcky; Ice Hcky; Sftbl.

PRESCOTT, RANCE; Oratory Prep; Union, NJ; (Y); Variety Show; Hon Roll; Interclss Vllybl-1st Pl 85; Millburn Mens Sftbl Leag 86; Cardlgy.

PRESCOTT, SARAH; Pleasantville HS; Absecon, NJ; (Y); 6/120; Sec SADD; Trs Sr Cls; Stu Cncl; Tennis; Hon Roll; Acad Achvt 82-86; Acad Achvt Gen & Modrn Sci 84; Accntg.

PRESCOTT, WILLIAM; Don Bosco HS; Hawthorne, NJ; (Y); Church Yth Grp; Computer Clb; Debate Tm; SADD; Teachers Aide; Yrbk Phtg; Yrbk Stf; Hon Roll; NHS; Natl Hnr Soc 83-86; Sci Fair Bio Awd 84; Rugers; Comp Sci.

PRESS, MICHELE; Pennsville Memorial HS; Pennsville, NJ; (Y); 27/220; Am Leg Aux Girls St; FBLA; Band; Concert Band; Drm Mjr(t); Mrchg Band; Rep Stu Cncl; Cheerleading; Pom Pon; Hon Roll; Suprntndnt Stu Cmte 84-85; Persnl & Lbr Rltns.

PRESS, PAM; Manalapan HS; Manalapan, NJ; (Y); Nwsp Rptr; Nwsp Stf; JV Trk; Mst Imprvd In Trck 85-86.

PRESSIMONE, DOREEN; Vernon Twp HS; Vernon, NJ; (Y); 1/221; Cmnty Wkr; Teachers Aide; Rep Frsh Cls; Sec Soph Cls; Sec Stu Cncl; Elks Awd; High Hon Roll; NHS; Prfct Atten Awd; St Schlr; Intl Yth Yr Awd 86; Rutgers Schlr 85; Congrssnl Yth Ldrshp Cncl 86; William Paterson Coll; Chld Ed.

PRESSLER, ESTHER; Ridgefield Park HS; Little Ferry, NJ; (Y); 7/183; Church Yth Grp; Debate Tm; Math Tm; Science Clb; Rep Stu Cncl; Hon Roll; NHS; Voice Dem Awd; Computer Clb; Ski Clb; Art Edtr & Crtnst For Schl Nwspr; Engrng.

PRESTIFILIPPO, ELIZABETH; James Caldwell HS; W Caldwell, NJ; (Y); Nurtn.

PRESTIS, ALISA; Sacred Heart HS; Vineland, NJ; (S); 12/67; Cmnty Wkr; Office Aide; Spanish Clb; Yrbk Stf; Hon Roll; NHS; Mrktng-Fshn Merch.

PRESTON, DOREEN; Arthur P Schalick HS; Elmer, NJ; (Y); Church Yth Grp; Debate Tm; Office Aide; Band; Church Choir; Color Guard; Concert Band; Mrchg Band; Yrbk Ed-Chief; Baptist Bible Coll Of PA.

PRESTON, EDWIN W; Riverside HS; Delanco, NJ; (Y); 16/84; Dance Clb; Trs Drama Clb; Band; Concert Band; Jazz Band; Mrchg Band; School Play; Stage Crew; Nwsp Rptr; Yrbk Rptr; Trch Unsng Hero Awd; Rams Bstr Clb Awd; Stockton ST Coll; Acctng.

PRETTYMAN, CHRIS; Mother Seton Regional HS; Carteret, NJ; (Y); Church Yth Grp; GAA; Hosp Aide; Science Clb; Var Sftbl; HS Recruiter Cert 85-86; JR Sci Symposium Fairleigh Dcknsn U Cert 86; Tri Beta Cnvntn Cert 85; Chem.

PREVITE, MELISSA; North Brunswick Twp HS; N Brunswick, NJ; (Y); AFS; German Clb; Key Clb; Drill Tm; Lit Mag; Rep Stu Cncl; Var Gym; Hon Roll; Awd For Outstndng Achvt Ntl Stndrdzd Grmn 84; Achvt Awd Excllnce Frgn Lang 86; Schrlshp Stud Plng 86; Rutgers Coll; Lwyr.

PREZIOSI, DAMIAN; Voorhees HS; Califon, NJ; (Y); 81/274; Church Yth Grp; French Clb; Key Clb; Latin Clb; Math Clb; Varsity Clb; Rep Stu Cncl; Capt Socr; Hon Roll; St Bonaventure; Med.

PRICE JR, GEORGE A; Dwight Englewood HS; Saddle River, NJ; (Y); Math Tm; JV Bsktbl; Bowling; Var L Lcrss; Var L Socr; Im Wt Lftg; Ntl Merit Ltr; Supr Achvt NJ Math Leag 86; Natl Hnr Rl 86.

PRICE, JEANNIE; Westside HS; Newark, NJ; (Y); Computer Clb; Montclair ST Coll; Bus Admin.

PRICE, JENNIFER; Middletown HS South; Middletown, NJ; (Y); Stage Crew; Variety Show; JV Powder Puff Ftbl; French Hon Soc; Hon Roll; Psych.

PRICE, JIM; Montville Twp HS; Towaco, NJ; (Y); Boy Scts; Church Yth Grp; JV Ftbl; Var Lcrss; Var Wrstlng; Hon Roll; Medcl Technlgy.

PRICE, JUDITH; Secaucus HS; Secaucus, NJ; (S); 7/160; Sec Math Clb; Varsity Clb; Var Sftbl; Var Capt Vllybl; Stat Wrstlng; High Hon Roll; Sec Mu Alp Tht; NHS; Spanish NHS; Vllybl Hon Men All Lg 84; Vllybl ST Sec Chmps 83 & 84; Vllybl BCSL Chmps 85; Mth.

PRICE, MICHELLE; Raritan HS; Hazlet, NJ; (Y); 21/314; Spanish Clb; Concert Band; Mrchg Band; Symp Band; Yrbk Stf; JV Bsktbl; Hon Roll; NHS; AZ ST U; Comp Engrng.

PRICE, PAMELA; Bridgeton HS; Bridgeton, NJ; (Y); Church Yth Grp; Computer Clb; 4-H; GAA; JA; Spanish Clb; Varsity Clb; Band; Church Choir; JV Bowling; Mgr Boys Trck & Fld 84-85; Grls JV Trck 83-84; Comp.

PRICE, SUSAN; Westfield HS; Westfield, NJ; (Y); 70/515; Church Yth Grp; Spanish Clb; Chorus; School Musical; School Play; Hon Roll; NHS; Spanish NHS; Math Tchr.

PRICE, WILLIAM; St Peters Prep; Jersey City, NJ; (Y); 1/203; Church Yth Grp; Dance Clb; Pep Clb; Nwsp Sprt Ed; Rep Frsh Cls; Rep Soph Cls; Rep Jr Cls; Pres Sr Cls; Pres Stu Cncl; High Hon Roll; Rutgrs Schlr; St Peters Coll Smmr Schlr; Holy Cross Bk Awd; Georgetown; Lib Arts.

PRICHARD, DEBBI; Highstown HS; East Windsor, NJ; (Y); 4/441; Church Yth Grp; French Clb; German Clb; High Hon Roll; NHS; Prfct Atten Awd; Cngrs Bndstg Schlrshp Wst Grmny 86-87; Wheaton Coll; Mdrn Lng.

PRIEBE, JOANN; North Arlington HS; N Arlington, NJ; (Y); 6/131; Varsity Clb; Ed Yrbk Stf; Trs Jr Cls; Trs Sr Cls; Rep Stu Cncl; Var L Bsktbl; JV Sftbl; JV Vllybl; NHS; VP Spanish NHS; Natl Sci & Spnsh Merit Awds 85; Bus.

PRIEST, KIMBELRY; Audubon HS; Audubon, NJ; (Y); Varsity Clb; Cheerleading; Fld Hcky; Med Sec.

PRIEST, MARC; Pennsville Memorial HS; Pennsville, NJ; (Y); 6/222; Am Leg Boys St; Off Sr Cls; Var Socr; High Hon Roll; NHS; St Schlr; Fairleigh Dickinson U Pres Schlr Awd 86; Garden ST Distngshd Schlr Awd 86; L G Balfour Co Awd 86; VA Polytech Inst; Engrng.

PRIEST, PATRICIA; Our Lady Of Mercy Acad; Wmstown, NJ; (Y); 10/35; Cmnty Wkr; GAA; Variety Show; Yrbk Phtg; Yrbk Rptr; Yrbk Stf; Hon Roll; Prfct Atten Awd; Im Badmtn; Im Bsktbl; Id Photographer 85-86; Comp Bus.

PRIETO, HECTOR; Memorial HS; West New York, NJ; (Y); Key Clb; Science Clb; Stu Cncl; Hon Roll; U Miami; Pre-Dentstry.

PRIETO, LAURA; Mount Saint Mary Acad; Westfield, NJ; (Y); 1/83; Ed Lit Mag; French Hon Soc; Sec NHS; Pres Spanish NHS; St Schlr; Val; Part In Gifted & Tlntd Program At MSMA 85-86; Recipient Of Natl Hispanic Schlr Awd 85-86; Wellesley Coll.

PRILL, SHARON; Montville Twsp HS; Towaco, NJ; (Y); Intnl Clb; Ski Clb; Cheerleading; Lcrss; Mgr(s); Socr; U Of Syracuse.

PRINCIPE, TAMMY; Arthur P Schalick HS; Elmer, NJ; (Y); 15/128; JA; Office Aide; Sec Band; Concert Band; Mrchg Band; Orch; Hon Roll; NHS; Cumberland County Coll; Math.

PRIOLA, STEPHEN J; Parsippany HS; Parsippany, NJ; (Y); Am Leg Boys St; French Clb; Q&S; Yrbk Ed-Chief; Yrbk Phtg; Rep Frsh Cls; Rep Jr Cls; Pres Sr Cls; Hon Roll.

PRIOR, SALLY; Mount St Dominic Acad; W Orange, NJ; (Y); Library Aide; Ski Clb; School Musical; School Play; Hon Roll; Advrtsng.

PRIOR, STEPHANIE B; Wood-Ridge HS; Wood-Ridge, NJ; (S); 1/91; Math Clb; Yrbk Stf; Stat Bsktbl; Stat Ftbl; Var Trk; Im High Hon Roll; NHS; Garden ST Distngshd Schlr 85-86; NJ Inst Of Tech; Engr.

PRIORE, VINCENZA; Belleville HS; Belleville, NJ; (Y); Key Clb; Yrbk Stf; High Hon Roll; Hon Roll; Trs NHS; Vet.

PRITCHETT, CHRISTINE Y; Moorestown HS; Moorestown, NJ; (Y); VP Church Yth Grp; Band; Chorus; VP Church Choir; Madrigals; Stat Bsktbl; JV Lcrss; JV Socr; Var Trk; Teachers Aide; Psych.

PRITSCH, DONNA; Middletown High School South; Lincroft, NJ; (Y); Church Yth Grp; Math Tm; Model UN; Church Choir; Yrbk Ed-Chief; Rep Jr Cls; Cheerleading; Fld Hcky; Gov Hon Prg Awd; High Hon Roll; Math Awd 83-84; Cum Laude 83-84; Supptg Feml Rl 83-84; NY U; Law.

PRIZELL, BRIGID; Union Catholic HS; Westfield, NJ; (Y); Political Wkr; Service Clb; Thesps; Ed Lit Mag; Ntl Merit Ltr; Cmnty Wkr; Drama Clb; School Musical; School Play; Hon Roll; Journalism.

PROANO, ELKE; Hackensack HS; Hackensack, NJ; (Y); 68/500; Church Yth Grp; Cmnty Wkr; Dance Clb; Teachers Aide; Schlrshp From Rotary Clb 86; Schlrshp 86; Mason Gross At Rutgers; Dance.

PROBASCO, BILL; Cumberland Regional HS; Bridgeton, NJ; (S); 5/342; Am Leg Boys St; Church Yth Grp; Drama Clb; JCL; Quiz Bowl; Science Clb; School Play; High Hon Roll; NHS; St Schlr; Elec Engr.

PROBST, ERIC; Don Bosco Prep; Oakland, NJ; (S); Church Yth Grp; Ski Clb; Nwsp Rptr; Nwsp Stf; JV Capt Socr; Trk; High Hon Roll; NHS; Soph Schlrshp 84-85; Villanova.

PROCTOR, TONYA; Burlington City HS; Beverly, NJ; (Y); Pres Church Yth Grp; Drill Tm; Var Capt Bowling; Hon Roll.

PROFETA, BERNADETTE; Highland Regional HS; Clementon, NJ; (S); 4/332; Computer Clb; Service Clb; Spanish Clb; Yrbk Stf; Stu Cncl; Hon Roll; NHS; Pre-Med.

PROFITO, DAVID; Green Brook HS; Green Brook, NJ; (Y); 9/60; Key Clb; Thesps; Chorus; School Play; Nwsp Stf; Var JV Bsktbl; Var JV Ftbl; Var Trk; Pres Jr NHS; NHS; Sprts Mgmt.

PROKOP, KIM; Colonia HS; Colonia, NJ; (Y); Trs Key Clb; Bowling; Sftbl; Hon Roll; NHS; Mercer Cnty Coll; Trvl/Toursm.

PRONGAY, MICHELE; St John Vianney HS; Aberdeen, NJ; (Y); 62/298; Church Yth Grp; Cmnty Wkr; Intnl Clb; SADD; Teachers Aide; Stage Crew; Hon Roll; Gld & Wht Awd Crclr, Intrcrclr, Extrcrclr Actvts 85; Montclair; Psych.

PRONTI, DANIEL; St Peters Prep; Bayonne, NJ; (Y); Aud/Vis; Computer Clb; Latin Clb; Ski Clb; VP Jr Cls; Im Bsktbl; Im Fld Hcky; Im Ftbl; Im Score Keeper; Ntl Merit Schol.

PROTOMASTRO, MARIA; Mt Saint Dominic Acad; Bloomfield, NJ; (Y); Cmnty Wkr; NFL; Chorus; Concert Band; Pres Frsh Cls; Var Crs Cntry; Var Trk; High Hon Roll; NHS; Intnl Clb; Smr Schlr St Ptrs Coll 86; High SRA Scr Awd 84; Saint Peters Coll; Bio.

PROULX, SUZZANNE; Pope John XXIII Regional HS; Andover, NJ; (Y); #11 In Class; French Clb; Teachers Aide; Lit Mag; Bsktbl; Sftbl; High Hon Roll; NHS; Acdmc Achvmnt Awd 84-86; Nuclr Engnrng.

PROUT, MAUREEN; Marylawn Of The Oranges HS; Maplewood, NJ; (Y); 5/51; School Musical; Nwsp Stf; Pres Soph Cls; Trs Jr Cls; Pres Sr Cls; Mgr(s); Pres French Hon Soc; Hon Roll; Jr NHS; NHS; Pres Clssrm 86; Intl Stu Ldrshp Inst 85; Alumnae Clss Agnt 86; Manhattanville Coll; Pol Sci.

PROVDA, JENNIFER; Metuchen HS; Metuchen, NJ; (Y); 20/180; Science Clb; Spanish Clb; Varsity Clb; School Play; Yrbk Phtg; Yrbk Stf; Rep Stu Cncl; JV Var Tennis; Hon Roll; NHS; Law.

PROVOST, ALDEN; Glen Ridge HS; Glen Ridge, NJ; (Y); AFS; Model UN; Off Jr Cls; Var Capt Socr; Var Capt Tennis; High Hon Roll; Hon Roll; 2nd Tm Socr 84; 2nd Cnty Soccr 85; 1st Tm Conf Soccr Ant Tenns 85.

PROVOST, KELLIE; Hackettstown HS; Belvidere, NJ; (Y); 26/198; 4-H; Pres Key Clb; Office Aide; Speech Tm; Rep Stu Cncl; Stat Bsktbl; Capt Cheerleading; Var Score Keeper; Hon Roll; NHS; Bill Bradley Yng Citzns Awd 86; Pres Acadmc Fitnss Awd 86; Prnt & Teach Organztn Schlrshp 86; PA ST U; Bus Adm.

PRUDENTI, DEBORAH; Mt Olive HS; Flanders, NJ; (Y); 38/296; Band; Chorus; Concert Band; Drm Mjr(t); Jazz Band; Mrchg Band; Lit Mag; Gov Hon Prg Awd; Hon Roll; NHS; Outstndng Musicn-Band, Chorus 86; Area, Rgn, Al-ST Band, Chorus 86; Tri-M Music Hnr Soc 85; Profssnl Pianst.

PRUESS, DOUGLAS R; Franklin HS; Somerset, NJ; (Y); Am Leg Boys St; Pres Church Yth Grp; Ski Clb; Chorus; Church Choir; Concert Band; Mrchg Band; Bsbl; Socr; Trk; Natl Conf Of Christians & Jews Schlrshp 85; Engineering.

PRUNK, ROB; Don Bosco Prep HS; Park Ridge, NJ; (Y); Cmnty Wkr; Model UN; Ski Clb; SADD; Nwsp Rptr; Bus Mrktng.

PRUSAKOWSKI, SANDRA; St John Vianney HS; Keyport, NJ; (Y); 26/234; Church Yth Grp; Drama Clb; Political Wkr; Teachers Aide; Church Choir; Flag Corp; School Musical; School Play; Capt Twrlr; High Hon Roll; Gld & Wht Awd; Vrsty Ltr; Pin Chorus; Rutgers U Douglass; Med.

PRYOR, CYNTHIA; Camden HS; Camden, NJ; (Y); Church Yth Grp; JA; Teachers Aide; Church Choir; Hon Roll; Prfct Atten Awd; Katherine Gibbs Schl; Bus Mgmt.

PRYOR, MARCUS L; Vailsburg HS; Newark, NJ; (Y); Am Leg Boys St; Var Bsbl; Var Capt Bsktbl; Var Ftbl; Hon Roll; NHS; All Cty Ftbl, Bsbl, Bsktbl 85-86; Acctg.

PRZECHA, LORIE ANNE; Hamilton H S East Steinert; Hamilton Square, NJ; (Y); 54/326; Debate Tm; Key Clb; NFL; Chorus; Church Choir; Drill Tm; Madrigals; Mrchg Band; School Musical; Nwsp Stf; Douglass.

PRZYBYLINSKI, VINCENT; West Essex SR HS; Fairfield, NJ; (Y); 6/350; Church Yth Grp; Pres Frsh Cls; Pres Soph Cls; Rep Jr Cls; Trs Stu Cncl; L Var Bsbl; L Var Ftbl; NHS; VFW Awd; U Of Notre Dame; Math.

PSEJA, DAVID; Pascack Valley HS; River Vale, NJ; (Y); VP Church Yth Grp; Computer Clb; Drama Clb; French Clb; Stage Crew; Hon Roll; Chem.

PSILLOS, LAUREN; North Plainfield HS; N Plainfield, NJ; (Y); 10/189; Key Clb; Math Tm; Orch; School Musical; Yrbk Stf; JV Capt Cheerleading; Var Fld Hcky; Var Stat Ftbl; Hon Roll; Mtn Valley Conf Fld Hcky 1st Tm, All Cnty 2nd Tm 85; Psych.

PSIROGIANES, JASON; Indian Hills HS; Oakland, NJ; (Y); Cmnty Wkr; FBLA; Varsity Clb; Off Sr Cls; Bsbl; Bsktbl; Ftbl; Cit Awd; High Hon Roll; Hon Roll; U PA.

PUCCI, CLAUDIA; Marylawn HS; S Orange, NJ; (S); 3/60; Art Clb; Hosp Aide; Ed Nwsp Stf; Rep Soph Cls; Pres Sr Cls; Var Capt Cheerleading; Gym; Sftbl; Pres French Hon Soc; High Hon Roll.

PUCCIANI, CAROLINE; Cliffside Park HS; Fairview, NJ; (Y); 18/239; Am Leg Aux Girls St; Stu Cncl; High Hon Roll; Hon Roll; NHS; Leonardo Da Vinci Brnz Medlln Excllnc Itln Lang 86; Itln Hnr Socty 86; Pace U.

PUCCIARELLO, LISA; Nutley HS; Nutley, NJ; (Y); Church Yth Grp; Office Aide; Y-Teens; Stu Cncl; Scholar Anthony Placidos Schl Hair Dsgn 86; Anthony Placidos Dsgn; Csmtlgy.

PUCHALSKI, STEVE; Dover HS; Dover, NJ; (Y); Am Leg Boys St; Latin Clb; Letterman Clb; Varsity Clb; JV Ftbl; Var Wrstlng; High Hon Roll; Hon Roll; Pres Phys Fit Awd 84; U PA; Engrng.

PUCKETT, JENNIFER; North Plainfield HS; N Plainfield, NJ; (Y); 33/160; Church Yth Grp; Math Tm; Ski Clb; Nwsp Rptr; Nwsp Stf; Off Stu Cncl; Var Capt Cheerleading; Powder Puff Ftbl; Hon Roll; NHS; Vrsty Chrldng Ltr 84-86; Outstndng SR Chrldr 86; Moravian Coll; Lawyer.

PUENTES, ADRIANA; Belleville HS; Belleville, NJ; (Y); 43/363; School Play; JV Bsktbl; JV Swmmng; JV Tennis; JV Trk; NHS; $50 Schlrshp Awd Shermans Fshn Awd 86; Pres Foreign Lang Clb 86; Stu SR Senate Clb 86; Fashion Inst Of Tech; Fshn Ills.

PUERLING, CHERYL; Red Bank Regional HS; Little Silver, NJ; (Y); Art Clb; Library Aide; Nwsp Bus Mgr; Nwsp Rptr; Nwsp Stf; French Hon Soc; Hon Roll; Psychlgy.

PUGH, PAMELA; Paterson Catholic Rgnl HS; Paterson, NJ; (Y); 12/123; DECA; FBLA; Vllybl; Hon Roll; Montclair ST Coll; Acctg.

PUGILESE, PAT; Queen Of Peace HS; Newark, NJ; (Y); 124/229; Intnl Clb; Ftbl; Socr; Hon Roll; Montclair ST Coll; Hotel Bus.

PUGLIA, LISA; Northern Burl HS; Columbus, NJ; (Y); Drama Clb; 4-H; FFA; Ski Clb; SADD; Teachers Aide; Varsity Clb; Band; Stage Crew; Yrbk Stf; Juneta Coll PAFC 84; Putgers Coll Dlgt ST FFA Cntn 84; Mercer Comm Coll.

PUGLISI, CATHI LYNN; Wayne Valley HS; Wayne, NJ; (Y); 52/320; Church Yth Grp; GAA; Variety Show; Yrbk Stf; Lit Mag; Hon Roll; Rutgers Coll; Pre-Med.

PUGLISI, SILVIA; Passaic Valley Regfional HS; Totowa, NJ; (Y); Art Clb; Church Yth Grp; French Clb; Key Clb; Spanish Clb; Bowling; Fld Hcky; Hon Roll; Passaic Valley Hnr Scty 86; Accntng.

PULSFORT, DEBBIE; Union Catholic Regional HS; Scotch Plains, NJ; (Y); Pep Clb; Service Clb; Ski Clb; Nwsp Stf; Yrbk Stf; Var L Sftbl; Ntl Hnr Rll 86; Rutgers U.

PUMA, JOYCE; Bridgewater-Raritan H S East; Bound Brook, NJ; (Y); Church Yth Grp; German Clb; Yrbk Stf; Powder Puff Ftbl; Score Keeper; Drama Clb; E Stroudsburg; English Educ.

PUOPOLO, TARA; Jackson Memorial HS; Jackson, NJ; (Y); 26/411; Ski Clb; High Hon Roll; Hon Roll; Ftbl; Powder Puff Ftbl; Grls ST Semifnlst Rydr Coll 86; Stockton Coll; Bus.

PURDUE, KRISTEN; Pinelands Regional HS; Tuckerton, NJ; (Y); Nwsp Ed-Chief; Var Capt Cheerleading; High Hon Roll; Hon Roll; MVP Ftbl Chrldng 85-86; Princpls List Awd All A's 85-86; Chrldng Captn 86-87; Comm.

PURDY, LYNN; Kittatinny Regional HS; Newton, NJ; (Y); 31/164; JV Bsktbl; Var Fld Hcky; Var Trk; OH U; Cmmnctns.

PURI, PUNEET K; Cherry Hill East HS; Cherry Hill, NJ; (Y); Hosp Aide; Library Aide; Science Clb; Im Bowling; Intnl Clb; Temple Yth Grp; Lit Mag; Hon Roll; White Ltr Patch Recgntn Extr Curricular Activities 86; Cum Laude 85-86; Rutgers Coll Of Engrg; Engineer.

PURI, RAJEEV; Vineland HS; Vineland, NJ; (Y); 137/810; Debate Tm; French Clb; Band; Symp Band; Off Sr Cls; Timer; Hon Roll; Bnad Hnrs Awd 86; Dbtng Clb Stu 86; DE U; Thrpy.

PURI, REENA; James Caldwell HS; W Caldwell, NJ; (Y); Dance Clb; Hosp Aide; JV Tennis; JV Vllybl; Hon Roll; Sci.

PUROHIT, BELA; Overbrook SR HS; Lindenwold, NJ; (Y); Dance Clb; Temple Yth Grp; Badmtn; Fld Hcky; Gym; Mgr(s); Tennis; Vllybl; Hon Roll; Prfct Atten Awd; Phrmcst.

PUROHIT, URVASHI; Linden HS; Linden, NJ; (Y); French Clb; ROTC; Band; Chorus; Mrchg Band; Stat Swmmng; Hon Roll; Bus Adm.

PUSCIAN, LISA; Eastern HS; Voorhees, NJ; (Y); 37/300; Office Aide; Concert Band; Mrchg Band; Yrbk Phtg; Yrbk Stf; Fld Hcky; Socr; Trk; Jr NHS; NHS.

PUSHPARAJ, VANITHA; Oak Knoll HS; Summit, NJ; (Y); French Clb; Hosp Aide; Pep Clb; Service Clb; Stage Crew; Nwsp Stf; Lit Mag; Stu Cncl; Var Bsktbl; Hon Roll; St Peters Coll Summr Schlrs Pgm Scholar 86; Rutgers; Psych.

PUSTERLA, MICHAEL; Wayne Hills HS; Wayne, NJ; (Y); 116/312; Aud/Vis; Cmnty Wkr; Varsity Clb; Variety Show; Yrbk Sprt Ed; Yrbk Stf; Var Bsbl; Var Ftbl; Im Wt Lftg; Hon Roll; 2nd Tm Nrthrn Brgn Intrschlstc Lge Bsbl 86; Athlt Of Mnth 86; Ftbl Cptn Of Frshmn 83.

PUTNAM, JILL M; Hightstown HS; E Windsor, NJ; (Y); 8/340; Co-Capt Drill Tm; Stu Cncl; JV Socr; Gov Hon Prg Awd; High Hon Roll; NHS; Pres Schlr; St Schlr; Church Yth Grp; Eli Whitney Sci Awd 86; U Schlrshp Vanderbilt U 86; Vanderbilt U.

PUTNAM, MAI-LINH; Piscataway HS; Piscataway, NJ; (Y); 31/478; Hosp Aide; Key Clb; Nwsp Rptr; Rep Frsh Cls; Rep Soph Cls; Rep Sr Cls; Hon Roll; NHS; Prsdntl Acdmc Ftnss Awd 86; Grdn ST Dstngshd Schlrs Awd 86; Douglass Coll; Hstry.

PUTTBACH, KENNETH; Parsippany HS; Parsippany, NJ; (Y); 110/315; Pres Drama Clb; French Clb; Pres Chorus; School Musical; School Play; Swing Chorus; Hon Roll; Bst Dirctr Awd Drama Fest 85; Bst Ensmble Perfrmnce Drama Fest 86; PTSA Scholar Wnnr 86; Montclair ST Coll; Theatre Art.

PUZZO, MICHAEL; Palisades Pk HS; Palisades Pk, NJ; (Y); Var Bsktbl.

PYLA, JOHN; Pennsville Memorial HS; Pennsville, NJ; (Y); Bsbl; Crs Cntry; Wrstlng; AZ ST U; Comp Sci.

PYLANT, STEPHANIE; Howell HS; Howell, NJ; (Y); 25/370; Cmnty Wkr; Color Guard; Var Vllybl; Hon Roll; NHS; Bus Admn.

PYOTT, LEANNE; Cumberland Regional HS; Millville, NJ; (S); 2/342; Am Leg Aux Girls St; Debate Tm; VP FBLA; Science Clb; Soroptimist; Nwsp Sprt Ed; High Hon Roll; NHS; St Schlr; Grdn ST Dstngshd Schlr 85; Bus Adm.

PYTAL, JENNIFER L; Passaic Valley HS; Little Falls, NJ; (Y); 12/365; Am Leg Aux Girls St; Church Yth Grp; Cmnty Wkr; French Clb; Yrbk Stf; Tennis; High Hon Roll; NHS; Passaic Vlly Hnr Soc 86; Bus Mgmt.

QASIM, KATHY; John P Stevens HS; Edison, NJ; (Y); Key Clb; Model UN; Science Clb; French Hon Soc; Hon Roll; Bus Lwyr.

QAYYUM, BASIT; Roselle Catholic HS; Hillside, NJ; (S); Computer Clb; Debate Tm; Math Clb; School Play; Im Bsktbl; Im Vllybl; High Hon Roll; NHS; Acad All-Amer 85-86; Frnsc Fnlst 85; Columbia Coll; Pre-Med.

QUADIR, DEEPA; Kingsway Regional HS; Swedesboro, NJ; (Y); 14/166; Office Aide; Spanish Clb; Band; Yrbk Ed-Chief; Yrbk Stf; High Hon Roll; Hon Roll; NCTE Awd; Schl Engl Awd 86; Drake U; Med.

QUAGLIANA, HARRY; Passaic Valley HS; Little Falls, NJ; (Y); Am Leg Boys St; Art Clb; Yrbk Rptr; Bsktbl; Tennis; Hon Roll; NHS; Passaic Vly Hnr Soc 85-86; Pre-Law.

QUARLES, VICTORIA L; Pemberton Township HS; Pemberton, NJ; (Y); 1/417; Drama Clb; Math Tm; Science Clb; Drill Tm; Nwsp Ed-Chief; Nwsp Sprt Ed; Yrbk Stf; Mgr(s); High Hon Roll; NHS; Info Sys Mgmnt.

QUARTO, PAUL; Old Tappan Regional HS; Harrington Pk, NJ; (Y); JV Bsbl; Var Ftbl; Cmptr Sci.

QUATRELLA, LISA; Hanover Park HS; E Hanover, NJ; (Y); OEA; Hon Roll; Berkeley Sch Outstndng Achvt 86; Cooperative Office Edu Awd 86; John Brasea Mem COE Awd 86; Stafford Hall; Executive Sec.

QUATTROMINI, CHRISTINE; Immaculate Conception HS; N Arlington, NJ; (Y); Pres Drama Clb; Hosp Aide; Science Clb; Spanish Clb; Varsity Clb; Yrbk Rptr; Stu Cncl; Capt Var Cheerleading; Swmmng; Vllybl; Rutgers; Phrmcy.

QUICK, JIM; South Hunterdon Reg HS; Lambertville, NJ; (Y); 12/73; Camera Clb; Pres Church Yth Grp; VP Computer Clb; Trs FBLA; Key Clb; Office Aide; SADD; School Play; Stage Crew; Yrbk Phtg; Fbla Comp Comptn 5th Pl 86; Bus Admin.

QUIDLEY, SHARON; Trenton Central HS; Trenton, NJ; (Y); Bsktbl; Fld Hcky; Trk; Wt Lftg; Hon Roll; Comp.

QUIGLEY, COLETTE; Shore Regional HS; W Long Branch, NJ; (Y); 73/238; Am Leg Aux Girls St; Church Yth Grp; Key Clb; Stage Crew; Yrbk Stf; Sec Jr Cls; Var Bsktbl; Var Fld Hcky; Var Mgr(s); Im Powder Puff Ftbl; Congressnl Awd 84-86; Boyd Schl; Travel.

QUIGLEY, EDWARD J; Phillipsburg HS; Phillipsburg, NJ; (Y); 8/284; FFA; Ski Clb; Var L Bsbl; Var L Crs Cntry; Wrstlng; High Hon Roll; NHS; St Schlr; Montclair ST Coll Merit Awd 86; Cnty Champ NJ ST Mock Trl Cmptn 86; Pres Acdmc Fit Awd 86; Mont Clair ST Coll; Bus Asdmin.

QUIGLEY, ELLEN M; St Joseph HS; Hammonton, NJ; (Y); 8/86; French Clb; Yrbk Stf; Sftbl; Cit Awd; Hon Roll; Amer Bus Womens Assoc Schlrshp 86; Delegate To Girls Citizenship Inst-Douglas Coll 85; Stockton ST Coll.

QUILL, RONNIE; Somerville HS; Somerville, NJ; (S); 3/210; Am Leg Boys St; French Clb; Orch; Nwsp Sprt Ed; Rep Soph Cls; High Hon Roll; NHS; Rnsslr Mdl 85; Frgn Lang Frnsc Trnmnt Mrt Cert 85; Acad Tm Vrsty Lttr 85; Elec Engr.

QUINDE, ALINA; Benedictine Acad; Elizabeth, NJ; (Y); French Clb; Pres Latin Clb; School Musical; School Play; Variety Show; Trs Frsh Cls; Rep Stu Cncl; JV Cheerleading; High Hon Roll; Hon Roll; Cert Apprctn Cty Elzbth Ofc Agng 84 & 85; LIM; Fshn Coordntr.

QUINN, A ROBYN; Bridgeton HS; Bridgeton, NJ; (Y); 1/219; GAA; Science Clb; SADD; Varsity Clb; Var Bsktbl; Bausch & Lomb Sci Awd; High Hon Roll; NHS; Am Leg Aux Girls St; Cmnty Wkr; HOSA ST Chptr Ofcr 83-86; Ntl Yung Ldrs Cngrssnl, Rutgers Schlr 86; Pre Med.

QUINN, ANDREW; Hillside HS; Hillside, NJ; (Y); Chess Clb; Computer Clb; Stage Crew; Arch.

QUINN, COLLEEN; Holy Family Acad; Bayonne, NJ; (Y); Church Yth Grp; French Clb; Hosp Aide; Spanish Clb; Orch; School Musical; School Play; Education.

QUINN, ERIN; Millville SR HS; Millville, NJ; (Y); SADD; Im Bowling; Var Fld Hcky; JV Sftbl; High Hon Roll; NHS; Prfct Atten Awd; Bsktbl; Chem & Alg Awds Hghst Avg 85; Ldrs Clb 84-86; Commnctns.

QUINN, JOHN; Indian Hills HS; Franklin Lks, NJ; (Y); 57/280; AFS; Radio Clb; Yrbk Sprt Ed; Yrbk Stf; Im Ftbl; Hon Roll; Hstry Awd 84.

QUINN, ROBERT J; Ridge HS; Basking Ridge, NJ; (Y); 2/206; Boy Scts; Church Yth Grp; VP Computer Clb; Trs Key Clb; Math Tm; Ski Clb; Var Swmmng; NHS; Sal; St Schlr; Bernrd Area Schlrshp Asst Fnlst 86; John Mc Mlln Deans Schlrshp 86; Rnsllr Plytchnc Inst Mth Sci Mdl; Cornell U; Electrl Engnrng.

QUINTANA, BRENDA; New Brunswick HS; New Brunswick, NJ; (Y); Church Yth Grp; Intnl Clb; Pep Clb; Spanish Clb; Chorus; Ldrshp Awd Hispnc Cult Clb 86; B A Prg; Math.

QUINTANA, RAUL; Hoboken HS; Hoboken, NJ; (Y); Boy Scts; Church Yth Grp; Variety Show; Var Cheerleading; JV Socr; 4th Pl NJ Natural Bdy Bldng Chmpnshp 86.

QUIRK, JACQUELINE; Middletown HS South; Middletown, NJ; (Y); Church Yth Grp; Drama Clb; Intnl Clb; NFL; Thesps; Acpl Chr; Chorus; Mrchg Band; School Musical; School Play; NJ ST Thspn Fstvl Bst Actrs 85-86; NJ Frnsc Comptn Fnlst 85-86; Bstn U Tnglwd Fstvl Chrs 85-86; Music.

RA, JEANNIE; Woodbridge HS; Woodbridge, NJ; (Y); 66/367; Chorus; Rep Frsh Cls; Rep Soph Cls; Rep Jr Cls; JV Var Cheerleading; NY Inst Tech; Arctctr.

RABB, MELISSA; Metuchen HS; Metuchen, NJ; (Y); VP Key Clb; Spanish Clb; Yrbk Sprt Ed; Sec Soph Cls; Sec Jr Cls; Pres Stu Cncl; Tennis; Hon Roll; Jr NHS; NHS; Law.

RABB, TIHAMDA; Essex County Voc; Newark, NJ; (Y); Boys Clb Am; Church Yth Grp; Cmnty Wkr; Computer Clb; French Clb; Hosp Aide; Chorus; Frsh Cls; Soph Cls; Jr Cls; DE U; Criminal Law.

RABBINO, JASON; Cranford HS; Cranford, NJ; (Y); ROTC; Band; School Musical; School Play; Yrbk Ed-Chief; DAR Awd; Gov Hon Prg Awd; NCTE Awd; Ntl Merit Ltr; St Schlr; George WA U; Intl Reltns.

RABINO, RUBI; Lower Cape Mary Regional HS; N Cape May, NJ; (Y); 13/250; Pep Clb; Concert Band; Mrchg Band; Pep Band; School Musical; Symp Band; Nwsp Rptr; Cheerleading; Hon Roll; NHS; Cst Grd Ofcrs Wvs Clb Schlrshp 86; Brdt Tmln Mem Hosp Axlry Schlrshp 86; Rtgrs Coll Phrmcy; Phrmcy.

RABUANO, LISA; Mary Help Of Christians Acad; Paterson, NJ; (Y); Computer Clb; Math Clb; Yrbk Stf; Im Cheerleading; Im Gym; Hon Roll; Ntl Math Awd; Rutgers; Math.

RACCIATTI, JOANNE; South Hunterdon Regional HS; Lambertville, NJ; (S); 7/68; Trs 4-H; VP Key Clb; Concert Band; Variety Show; Stu Cncl; 4-H Awd; Hon Roll.

RACEK, SARA; Red Bank Catholic HS; Lincroft, NJ; (Y); Church Yth Grp; Church Choir; School Musical; Yrbk Sprt Ed; Twrlr; Accntnt.

RACHESKY, JILL; Clifton HS; Clifton, NJ; (Y); 250/637; Dance Clb; Drama Clb; Girl Scts; Band; Concert Band; Mrchg Band; Mgr(s); Vllybl; Hon Roll.

RACIOPPI, MARLENE; Bloomfield HS; Bloomfield, NJ; (Y); Key Clb; JV Bsktbl; Var Sftbl; Hon Roll; Itlaian Clb 84-86; Montclair ST; Pre Law.

RACO, PATRICIA; Holy Spirit HS; Northfield, NJ; (Y); 115/345; Am Leg Aux Girls St; French Clb; Ski Clb; Yrbk Phtg; Yrbk Sprt Ed; Rep Soph Cls; Fld Hcky; Swmmng; NCTE Awd; NHS; John M Civera Schrlsh P86; Towson ST U; Intl Bus.

RADER, BRIAN; Phillipsburg HS; Bloomsbury, NJ; (Y); 30/294; High Hon Roll; Pres Acdmc Ftns Awd.

RADER, KAREN; North Warren Regional HS; Blairstown, NJ; (Y); 16/130; FBLA; Rep Jr Cls; Rep Stu Cncl; Capt Var Gym; Powder Puff Ftbl; Hon Roll; Katharine Gibbs Awd Future Sec 86; Parlgl.

RADER, MARK A; Burlington Co Voc Tech HS; Medford, NJ; (S); 1/153; Radio Clb; Scholastic Bowl; VICA; High Hon Roll; NHS; Prfct Atten Awd; St Schlr; Gold Medl-Lcl Lvl Elec VICA Cmptn 85; Elec Engrng Tech.

RADIGAN, DEBRA; Notre Dame HS; Cranbury, NJ; (Y); 19/339; Red Cross Aide; Ski Clb; Spanish Clb; Fld Hcky; Sftbl; Hon Roll; NHS; Spanish NHS; Boston Coll; Bus Adm.

RADIGAN, TRACEY; Hightstown HS; Hightstown, NJ; (Y); Am Leg Aux Girls St; Ski Clb; Rep Jr Cls; Var L Bsktbl; Var L Fld Hcky; JV Sftbl; Hon Roll; Prom Comm 85-86.

RADKE, TANYA; Phillipsburg HS; Phillipsburg, NJ; (Y); 69/296; VP Church Yth Grp; Hosp Aide; Flag Corp; Hon Roll; Warren Hosp Hlt Careers Schlrshp 86; Warren Hosp Merit Stat Awd 85; York Coll; Med Techngly.

RADOMSKI, ANNETTE; Manville HS; Manville, NJ; (Y); 5/95; Am Leg Aux Girls St; SADD; Band; Yrbk Stf; Sec Sr Cls; JV Var Bsktbl; JV Var Cheerleading; JV Sftbl; Hon Roll; NHS.

RADOMSKI, CHRISTINE; Manville HS; Manville, NJ; (Y); 1/114; Stat Bsktbl; Var JV Fld Hcky; Bausch & Lomb Sci Awd; High Hon Roll; Hon Roll; NHS; St Schlr; Val; Rtgrs Schlr; Rtgrs Coll Fo Phrmcy; Phrmcy.

RADTKE, LETITIA C; Westfield SR HS; Westfield, NJ; (Y); 70/482; French Clb; Q&S; Ed Nwsp Bus Mgr; Nwsp Rptr; Nwsp Stf; Yrbk Stf; Var Capt Cheerleading; Score Keeper; Hon Roll; NHS; Spec New Stu Awd 83; U Nice ALSG Smmr Pgm 84; Miami U OH; Intl Bus.

RADVANSKI, ROBERT; Hudson Catholic HS; Bayonne, NJ; (Y); 4/188; Computer Clb; Science Clb; Nwsp Rptr; Im Bsktbl; Im Vllybl; CC Awd; Elks Awd; Hon Roll; NHS; Prfct Atten Awd; Pres Citation Acad Excllnce 86; U Scranton; Comp Sci.

RADWANSKI, PATRICIA; St Marys HS; Parlin, NJ; (Y); 1/130; Yrbk Stf; Var L Bsktbl; Var L Crs Cntry; Var L Socr; JV Sftbl; French Hon Soc; High Hon Roll; NHS; Ntl Merit Ltr; French Clb; Rtgrs Schlr 86.

RADZIETA, TONY; Middle Town Ship HS; Cape May Ct House, NJ; (Y); Art Clb; Var Golf; Hon Roll.

RAE, CHRISTOPHER D; Ridgewood HS; Ridgewood, NJ; (Y); Am Leg Boys St; Var Capt Crs Cntry; Var L Trk; High Hon Roll; NHS; 1st Tm All Cnty Indr Trk 85; 3rd Tm All ST Indr Trk 86; Physcs Tm 86.

RAEL, NIKOLAZ; Clayton HS; Clayton, NJ; (S); 1/60; Am Leg Boys St; Pres Trs Key Clb; Madrigals; School Musical; Rep Sr Cls; Ftbl; NHS; Pres Schlr; Church Yth Grp; Drama Clb; Music Theory.

RAFANELLO, CARRIE; Oak Knoll Schl Of The Holy Child; E Hanover, NJ; (Y); Church Yth Grp; Dance Clb; Hosp Aide; Chorus; Lit Mag; Hon Roll; Aud/Vis; Ski Clb; Trk; Music Eductrs Awd 83-84; Mkt Rsrch.

RAFANO, ROBERT; South River HS; S River, NJ; (Y); Aud/Vis; Boy Scts; Debate Tm; Library Aide; Jazz Band; Mrchg Band; JV Socr; Var Tennis; NHS.

RAFELD, DEVRA; Ridge HS; Basking Ridge, NJ; (Y); 8/209; Pres Sec Church Yth Grp; Pres German Clb; Band; DAR Awd; High Hon Roll; Hon Roll; NHS; Bus & Prfsnl Wmns Of Brnrds Twnshp Schlrshp 86; Outstndng German Stu 86; Grmn Hnr Scty 83-86; Wake Frst U; Intl Bus.

RAFFAY, RUSSELL; Lenape Valley Regional HS; Stanhope, NJ; (Y); 49/253; Am Leg Boys St; Boy Scts; Exploring; 4-H; Band; Concert Band; Drm Mjr(t); Jazz Band; Mrchg Band; JV Trk.

RAFFERTY, MARY; Monsignor Donovan HS; Jackson, NJ; (Y); 6/243; Drama Clb; Intnl Clb; Science Clb; Service Clb; Thesps; School Musical; High Hon Roll; NHS; Ntl Merit Ltr; School Play; Merit Awd Frnch I II III 84-86; Hugh Obrien Soph Ldrshp Semnr 85; Mod Lang.

RAGO, CHRISTOPHER; Washington Township HS; Sewell, NJ; (Y); Art Clb; Church Yth Grp; DECA; Drama Clb; Key Clb; Ski Clb; Spanish Clb; School Musical; School Play; Variety Show; 1st Pl Awd Gnrl Mrktng In ST DECA Chmpnshp 86; Stnfrd U CA; Bus.

RAGOLIA, STACIA E; Northern Highlands Regional HS; Upper Saddle Rvr, NJ; (Y); 15/250; Debate Tm; Nwsp Rptr; Yrbk Stf; Lit Mag; Sr Cls; High Hon Roll; Jr NHS; NHS; Ntl Merit SF; St Schlr; Cert Merit Cncl Multiclt rlsm & Mod Wrld; Engl.

RAICHEL, ROBERT; Clifton HS; Clifton, NJ; (Y); 102/690; German Clb; Var L Bsbl; Hon Roll; Jr NHS; Alg Awd 83-84; Bus.

RAIN, KIMBERLY; Woodstown HS; Elmer, NJ; (Y); Spanish Clb; Sec Concert Band; Sec Mrchg Band; Bsktbl; Socr; Sftbl; Hon Roll; NHS; Exploring; Slaem Cty All Star Sftbl Tm 86; 2nd Tm All S Jersey Soccer Tm 85; Sports Med.

RAINEY, TANYA; Edgewood SR HS; Waterford, NJ; (Y); Library Aide; PAVAS; Spanish Clb; Yrbk Stf; JV Socr; High Hon Roll; Hon Roll; Jr NHS; Sec NHS.

RAISCH, JACQUELINE M; Secaveus HS; Secaucus, NJ; (S); 5/164; Math Tm; Spanish Clb; Jazz Band; Gov Hon Prg Awd; High Hon Roll; Mu Alp Tht; NHS; Spanish NHS; FBLA; Grls Ctznshp Inst 85; 5th Pl-NJ Nrthrn Rgn Typng Comptn 85.

RAJCOK, MARK; Toms River HS North; Toms River, NJ; (Y); 1/400; Church Yth Grp; Key Clb; Science Clb; Band; VP Jazz Band; School Musical; High Hon Roll; NHS; Rotary Awd; St Schlr; Natl/Profssnl Engr Schlrshp; Stevens Inst Of Tech; Elec Engr.

RAJEWSKI, ELIZABETH A; Cherry Hill High Schl East; Cherry Hill, NJ; (Y); Church Yth Grp; French Clb; Hosp Aide; Intnl Clb; Latin Clb; Model UN; Science Clb; Acpl Chr; Chorus; Orch; NJ Govrnrs Awd 85 & 86; Ntl HS Hnrs Orchstr 86; Sthrn Mthdst U-Full Schlrshp 86; Eckstn Schlr 86; Northwestern Meth U; Music Prfm.

RAJKOWSKI, DAVID; Cranford HS; Cranford, NJ; (Y); 21/300; Church Yth Grp; French Clb; JA; Math Tm; Quiz Bowl; Science Clb; Band; Concert Band; Mrchg Band; Orch; Fairfield U; Biolgy.

RAK, ANDREW; Morris Catholic HS; Pine Brook, NJ; (Y); 33/147; Church Yth Grp; FBLA; Natl Beta Clb; Varsity Clb; Lit Mag; Crs Cntry; Trk; High Hon Roll; Hon Roll; 1st Tm All Conf Trk 86; Biochem.

RAKOCY, GREG; St Joseph Regional HS; Rochelle Park, NJ; (Y); Bsbl; Ftbl; Trk; Hon Roll; Med.

RAMAKRISHNAN, LAKSHMI; Lodi HS; Lodi, NJ; (Y); Exploring; Science Clb; Spanish Clb; NHS; Rutgers Clg; Phrmcy.

RAMANO, NICOLE; Paul VI HS; Blackwood, NJ; (Y); SADD; School Play; Stat Ftbl; Phys Ther.

RAMELLA, ANTHONY J; Marist HS; Bayonne, NJ; (Y); Am Leg Boys St; Pres Key Clb; Science Clb; Nwsp Rptr; Var Capt Crs Cntry; Cit Awd; Elks Awd; Hon Roll; NHS; Var Capt Trk; Manhattan Coll; Finance.

RAMEN, LESTER; Paul VI Reg HS; Passaic, NJ; (Y); Boy Scts; Church Yth Grp; FBLA; Key Clb; Spanish Clb; Stage Crew; Rep Frsh Cls; Ftbl; Hon Roll; Spanish NHS; Syracuse U; Psychlgy.

RAMIREZ, AINISSA; St Dominic Acad; Rahway, NJ; (Y); 16/131; Computer Clb; Nwsp Stf; Yrbk Stf; Lit Mag; Pres Stu Cncl; Im Vllybl; Hon Roll; Pres NHS; French Clb; Hosp Aide; Ntl Ldrshp Trng Ctr 85-86; Engrng Awd Frm Stevens Inst Of Tech 84-85; NJ Girls ST 85-86; Brown U; Comp Sci.

RAMIREZ, JOSEPH; Asbury Park HS; Bradley Bch, NJ; (Y); JV Bsktbl; Var Crs Cntry; Chorus; School Play; High Hon Roll.

RAMIREZ, LILIANA; Elizabeth HS; Elizabeth, NJ; (Y); Church Yth Grp; Church Choir; Concert Band; Mrchg Band; Cit Awd; Hon Roll.

RAMIREZ, WALTER; South River HS; South River, NJ; (Y); Church Yth Grp; Spanish Clb; Nwsp Rptr; Nwsp Sprt Ed; Ed Nwsp Stf; Rutgers Coll; Jrnlsm.

RAMIZA, KATHERINE M; Boonton HS; Lincoln Park, NJ; (Y); 6/209; Am Leg Aux Girls St; Cmnty Wkr; GAA; Hosp Aide; Ski Clb; Capt Gym; High Hon Roll; NHS; Ntl Merit Ltr; U PA.

RAMJATTAN, ANDRE; Vineland HS; Vineland, NJ; (Y); Own Bus.

RAMOS, BEATRIZ; St Patricks HS; Elizabeth, NJ; (S); #2 In Class; Boys Clb Am; Hosp Aide; JA; Pep Clb; Science Clb; Ski Clb; Chorus; Church Choir; School Play; Stage Crew; All Amer & Ntl Sci Merit Awds 84-85; Rochester Inst Of Tech; Grp Art.

RAMOS, FERNANDO; Elizabeth HS; Elizabeth, NJ; (Y); Church Yth Grp; Computer Clb; Church Choir; Rep Frsh Cls; Rep Soph Cls; Cit Awd; Comp Tech.

RAMOS, GERALDO; Hoboken HS; Hoboken, NJ; (Y); Boy Scts; JV Bsktbl; Rep Trk; Crss Cntry 86; Cmptr Tech.

RAMOS, IDALISSE; Our Lady Of Good Counsel HS; Newark, NJ; (Y); Church Yth Grp; Dance Clb; Office Aide; Pep Clb; Service Clb; Variety Show; Yrbk Stf; Rep Soph Cls; Rep Jr Cls; Stu Cncl; Mdlng Awd Miss Fashion Teen Schl 84; Mst Likely Succeed, Best Acdmc Awd 85; Rutgers U; Med.

RAMOS, VANESSA; Roselle Catholic HS; South Plainfield, NJ; (Y); Stage Crew; Lit Mag; Mgr(s); Socr; French Hon Soc; Hon Roll; Fshn Coord.

RAMOTH, ERIC; Wayne Hills HS; Wayne, NJ; (Y); 10/307; Boy Scts; Church Yth Grp; Math Tm; Spanish Clb; Band; Concert Band; School Musical; JV Capt Socr; High Hon Roll; Hon Roll; Egl Sct 86; Spnsh.

RAND, MINDY; Passaic HS; Passaic, NJ; (Y); Cmnty Wkr; FBLA; Hosp Aide; Latin Clb; Library Aide; Office Aide; Political Wkr; Science Clb; Service Clb; Spanish Clb; 1st Pl Sci Fair Cert 85; Cmp Hillel Smmr & Lead 84; Sng Rl Oliver Musicl Prod Excllnt Sngng Voice; Rutgers U; Psych.

RANDAZZO JR, LUDWIG; Passaic HS; Passaic, NJ; (Y); 6/488; Boy Scts; Cmnty Wkr; Political Wkr; Ski Clb; Crs Cntry; Fld Hcky; Trk; Yth Govt Day 86; 3rd Pl Sci Fair Proj 86; Army Res Natl Schlr Athl Awds; Seymour Puckowitz Schlr; Stevens Inst Technlgy; Elec Eng.

RANDLE, BRET; Lower Cape May Regional HS; Cape May, NJ; (Y); #67 In Class; Computer Clb; French Clb; JA; Varsity Clb; Rep Frsh Cls; Rep Soph Cls; Rep Jr Cls; Rep Stu Cncl; Ftbl; Gym; UCLA; Comp Engrng.

RANDOLPH, JILL; Cresskill HS; Cresskill, NJ; (Y); 7/115; VP French Clb; Ski Clb; Chorus; Color Guard; Flag Corp; Hon Roll; NHS; Prtcptd Exchange Prg Frnch Stu 84; Prcptdc Accrdttn Prcss Middle ST Accrdttn 85-86; Bus Mngmnt.

RANDOLPH, MONIQUE; Kent Place Schl; Irvington, NJ; (Y); Art Clb; Intnl Clb; Spanish Clb; Yrbk Stf; Rep Frsh Cls; Trk; Natl Achvt Schlrshp Prog Outstndng Negr Stdnts 84; Kent Pl Schlrshp 83-86; Lwyr.

RANELLI III, FRANK; Bishop Ahr/St Thomas HS; Fords, NJ; (Y); 146/277; Boy Scts; Church Yth Grp; Letterman Clb; Varsity Clb; Var L Socr; Var Trk; Trk; JV Wrstlng; Hon Roll; Air Force.

RANGASWAMY, ROOPA; North Brunswick Twp HS; N Brunswick, NJ; (Y); 15/270; Hosp Aide; Model UN; SADD; Yrbk Ed-Chief; Lit Mag; Rep Stu Cncl; Hon Roll; NHS; Pres Schlr; Amrcn Asso Tchrs Frnch 85; Yrbk Awd Dedctn Yrbk 86; George WA U; Intl Rltns.

RANGEL, LORRAINE; North Arlington HS; N Arlington, NJ; (Y); 19/126; Math Tm; Capt Color Guard; Sec Concert Band; Sec Frsh Cls; Sec Soph Cls; Sec Jr Cls; Trs Pres Stu Cncl; Cheerleading; Hon Roll; Sec Pres Spanish NHS; Seton Hall 1; Psych.

RANGER, BOBLYN; Eastside HS; Paterson, NJ; (Y); Church Yth Grp; Debate Tm; 4-H; Science Clb; Speech Tm; Church Choir; Stu Cncl; Swmmng; High Hon Roll; Hon Roll; Rutgers; Cvl Engr.

RANIERI, SHERRY; Rancocas Valley Regional HS; Mt Holly, NJ; (Y); 16/240; Library Aide; Quiz Bowl; Scholastic Bowl; Speech Tm; Flag Corp; School Play; Stage Crew; Yrbk Stf; Lit Mag; Hon Roll; PTA Schlrshp 86; Outstndng Spnsh Stu Awd 86; Presdntl Acadmc Ftns Awd 86; Rutgers Coll; Psych.

RAO, BENJAMIN; Park Ridge HS; Park Ridge, NJ; (Y); 4/107; AFS; Math Clb; Science Clb; Varsity Clb; Yrbk Sprt Ed; JV Bsbl; Var L Socr; High Hon Roll; NHS; Quiz Bowl; Acadmc Ltr 84; Acadmc Pin 85; Electrncs Engr.

RAO, DEANNA; Park Ridge HS; Park Ridge, NJ; (Y); 16/115; Sec AFS; Math Clb; Science Clb; Varsity Clb; Yrbk Stf; Var L Sftbl; JV Vllybl; High Hon Roll; Hon Roll; NHS; Outstndg Achvt Awd Soc Stud 86; PEP Schlrshp 86; Rutgers U; Engrng.

RAPHAEL, FLORENCE; East Orange HS; E Orange, NJ; (Y); French Clb; School Play.

RAPP, CLAIRE; Glen Rock JR SR HS; Glen Rock, NJ; (Y); 22/123; Dance Clb; Spanish Clb; Church Choir; Var Capt Gym; High Hon Roll; Hon Roll; NHS; Pres Schlr; Bus Awd 86; Activities Awd 86; Gymnastics St Meet-1st Pl Uneven Bars 82; Juniata Coll; Phys Thrpy.

RAPP, DAVID G; Wallkill Valley Regional HS; Franklin, NJ; (Y); 3/160; Am Leg Boys St; Scholastic Bowl; SADD; Nwsp Rptr; Lit Mag; Bsktbl; Ftbl; Trk; Gov Hon Prg Awd; NHS; Sussex Cnty Round Tbl Awd 83; Clemson U; Engr Analysis & Bus.

RAPP, ILANA; Sayreville War Memorial HS; Sayreville, NJ; (Y); Cmnty Wkr; Drama Clb; Library Aide; OEA; Spanish Clb; Mrchg Band; School Play; Hon Roll; Am Fdrtn TV/Radio Artists Awd, Flynn & Son Essay Wnnr 86; Prof Actress Brdwy-Film-TV 82-88; SUNY Stony Brook; Bio.

RAPP, TAMMY; Woodbridge HS; Keasbey, NJ; (Y); 33/400; Church Yth Grp; Hosp Aide; Spanish Clb; Band; Flag Corp; Nwsp Stf; Lit Mag; NHS; Spec Ed.

RAPPORT, HOLLY; Cherry Hill HS West; Cherry Hill, NJ; (Y); Intnl Clb; Spanish Clb; Yrbk Stf; Comm.

RAPSON, MARIA; Delran HS; Willingboro, NJ; (Y); Band; Concert Band; Mrchg Band; Orch; Pep Band; School Musical; JV Fld Hcky; Hon Roll; Jr NHS; Schlrshps 2 Colls 86; Catawba Coll; Optometry.

RAQUET, EVELYN; Wayne Hills HS; Wayne, NJ; (Y); 8/305; Hst FBLA; Math Clb; High Hon Roll; Hon Roll; NHS; 2nd,3rd Hnrs Bus Math FBLA Conf 84-86; Bus.

RASCIO, MARK CARL; Manchester Regional HS; North Haldon, NJ; (Y); 4/156; Am Leg Boys St; Church Yth Grp; Trs Intnl Clb; Mathletes; Acpl Chr; Band; Concert Band; Jazz Band; Madrigals; Wt Lftg; Rcrd Schlrshp 86; Pres Acad Ftnss Awd 86; Appntmnt US Air Frc Acad 86; Clrksn U Schlrshp 86.

RASKAS, ROBERT; East Brunswick HS; E Brunswick, NJ; (Y); Key Clb; Temple Yth Grp; Yrbk Phtg; JV Wrstlng; NHS.

RASMUSSEN, KAREN; Sparta HS; Sparta, NJ; (Y); 2/221; Capt Debate Tm; Concert Band; Jazz Band; Mrchg Band; Nwsp Rptr; Yrbk Stf; Socr; High Hon Roll; NHS; Sal; U PA; Med.

RASTELLI, ROB; Chatham Township HS; Chatham, NJ; (Y); 6/128; CAP; FFA; Girl Scts; Mathletes; ROTC; VICA; Jazz Band; Powder Puff Ftbl; Btty Crckr Awd; Run-DMC Rap Awd 86; Coltec; Engrng.

RATHBONE, LARRY J; Woodstown HS; Alloway, NJ; (Y); Boy Scts; Drama Clb; English Clb; School Musical; School Play; Nwsp Rptr; Lit Mag; Var Crs Cntry; Var Trk; Hon Roll; Nmntd Govrnrs Schl Arts 86; Rcgnzd Perf NJ ST Tn Arts Fest 85; Rcgnzd Perf Cumberld Cnty Tn Art Fest; Liberal Arts.

RATHBUN, ROLLIN; Manville HS; Manville, NJ; (Y); Boy Scts; Church Yth Grp; Stage Crew; Nwsp Phtg; Yrbk Phtg; Bsktbl; Ftbl; Golf; Trk; Embry Riddle Aero U; Pilot.

RATHJE, ADRIENNE; John F Ennedy Memorial HS; Colonia, NJ; (Y); 11/274; German Clb; Pres SADD; School Musical; Yrbk Ed-Chief; Chrmn Stu Cncl; JP Sousa Awd; NHS; All ST And Regl Orch And Sympnc Band 85-86; Yth Advsry Delg Genl Assmbly 86; Muhlenberg College.

RATLIFF, SHERRY D; Woodrow Wilson HS; Camden, NJ; (Y); Church Yth Grp; FBLA; Chorus; Church Choir; Color Guard; Rep Jr Cls; Var Trk; Capt Wt Lftg; Hon Roll; NHS; Outstndng Perfrmnc Cls Ofc; Acctng.

RATTAY, DAN; Morris Catholic Schl; Rockaway, NJ; (Y); 42/142; Varsity Clb; Var L Bsbl; Var L Bsktbl; Var L Ftbl; Hon Roll; Dream Tm Def Back Ftbl; Dream Tm Outfldr Bsbl; Bus.

RATTAY, TOM; Morris Catholic HS; Rockaway, NJ; (Y); 28/142; Varsity Clb; Var L Bsbl; Var L Bsktbl; Var L Ftbl; Wt Lftg; Hon Roll; Christopher Thomas Mem Schlrshp 83; Bus.

RATYCZ, CHRISTINA; Bishop George AHR HS; Edison, NJ; (Y); Church Yth Grp; German Clb; Girl Scts; Hosp Aide; Ski Clb; SADD; Varsity Clb; Drill Tm; School Musical; School Play; Ukrainian Yth Orgnztn Awd 86; Ukrainian Dance Ensmble 83-86.

RAU, FRANK; Red Bank Regional HS; Little Silver, NJ; (Y); High Hon Roll; Hon Roll; NHS; Spanish NHS; George Washington U Awd 86; 3rd Pl HS Math Exm 86; Karate 2nd NJ ST Tourmnt.

RAUF, JENNIFER; Point Pleasant Borough HS; Pt Pleasant Bch, NJ; (S); 18/241; Drama Clb; Intnl Clb; Chorus; Camp Fr Inc; School Play; Lit Mag; High Hon Roll; Hon Roll; Prfct Atten Awd.

RAUH III, GEORGE A; Piscataway HS; Piscataway, NJ; (Y); Cmnty Wkr; Key Clb; Varsity Clb; JV Bsbl; Var Bsktbl; Coach Actv; Sftbl; Var Trk; Wt Lftg; Hon Roll; PA ST; Envrnmntl Sci.

RAUSCH, SUSAN; Matawan Regional HS; Matawan, NJ; (Y); 67/350; Band; Mrchg Band; Var Bsktbl; Var Fld Hcky; Var Sftbl; Hon Roll.

RAUSCHENBERGER, SHARON; Voorhees HS; Glen Gardner, NJ; (Y); 21/274; German Clb; Key Clb; SADD; Hon Roll; NHS.

RAVEN, KAREN; Overbrook Regional SR HS; Berlin, NJ; (Y); VP French Clb; Hosp Aide; Pres Concert Band; Drm Mjr(t); Mrchg Band; Stu Cncl; Sftbl; Hon Roll; NHS; VFW Awd; Stu Dirc Concrt Band 86-87; Mrktng.

RAVEN, SHARON; Bruriah HS For Girls; Old Bridge, NJ; (Y); Pres Temple Yth Grp; Ed Yrbk Stf; Trs Soph Cls; Awd 2nd Plc In Sci Fair 86; Rutgers U; Polit Sci.

RAVO, TINA; Kitatinny Regional HS; Branchville, NJ; (Y); 34/224; Spanish Clb; Chorus; High Hon Roll; Hon Roll; NHS; Ldrshp Awd Fut Secy 86; Dover Bus Coll; Exec Secy.

RAY, KIMBERLEY L; Eastside HS; Pompton Lakes, NJ; (Y); Church Yth Grp; Dance Clb; Drama Clb; French Clb; Spanish Clb; Acpl Chr; Chorus; Church Choir; High Hon Roll; Soc Of Distngushd Amrcn HS Studnts 84-86; Presdntl Phy Ftns Awd; Chpl Of Four Chldrn Schlrshp 86; The Juilliard Schl; Dance.

RAY, MICHELLE; Franklin HS; Somerset, NJ; (Y); 102/313; Church Yth Grp; Girl Scts; Varsity Clb; Acpl Chr; Chorus; Church Choir; Nwsp Stf; Yrbk Stf; Rep Frsh Cls; Rep Soph Cls; Delta Sigma Theta Scholar Awd 86; Hampton U; Mgmt.

RAYAUSKAS, MARIA ANNE; Wildwood Catholic HS; Wildwood Crest, NJ; (Y); Spanish Clb; SADD; School Play; Yrbk Stf; Mgr(s); Hon Roll; Villanova U; Bus Adm.

RAYMOND, KEN; Watchung Hills Regional HS; Gillette, NJ; (Y); 200/320; Boy Scts; Church Yth Grp; Im Bsbl; Im Ice Hcky; Hon Roll; Prfct Atten Awd; Johnson & Wales Culinary Inst.

REAGAN, MICHELLE; Toms River High School East; Toms River, NJ; (Y); 68/585; Art Clb; Jr Cls; Stu Cncl; JV Fld Hcky; JV Powder Puff Ftbl; JV Swmmng; Wt Lftg; Hon Roll; Bus.

REAGLE, DEBRA; Central Regional HS; Bayville, NJ; (Y); 56/240; Church Yth Grp; Pres Band; Concert Band; Jazz Band; Mrchg Band; School Musical; JV Bsktbl; JV Var Sftbl; Im Wt Lftg; Westchester U; Music.

REALMUTO, GREG; Ratitan HS; Hazlet, NJ; (Y); 10/312; Pres Latin Clb; Ski Clb; Stage Crew; Yrbk Rptr; Yrbk Stf; Stu Cncl; Socr; High Hon Roll; Hon Roll; NHS; Rutgers Coll; Math.

REAMER III, RAYMOND V; Don Bosco Preparatory HS; Fairlawn, NJ; (Y); 85/170; Church Yth Grp; Cmnty Wkr; Letterman Clb; Pep Clb; Varsity Clb; Bsbl; Bsktbl; Coach Actv; Ftbl; Socr; Crmnl Jstc.

REARDON, EILEEN; Red Bank Regional HS; Little Silver, NJ; (Y); Church Yth Grp; Key Clb; Sec Frsh Cls; Trs Sr Cls; Rep Stu Cncl; Var Tennis; High Hon Roll; Hon Roll; Pres NHS; Spanish NHS; Outstndng Ltn Stu 84-85; Ntl Piano Plyng Adtn 83-85; All Shore Tnns Team, NJ ST Tnns Trnmnt 83-86; Econ.

REASNER, GEORGE; Pitman HS; Pitman, NJ; (S); 9/150; German Clb; Sec Key Clb; Concert Band; Jazz Band; Mrchg Band; Pres Jr Cls; Pres VP Stu Cncl; Bsktbl; NHS; Modern Music Masters Hnr Scty 84-86; Senate Ldrshp Training Semnr 86; Wake Forest U; Bus Adm.

RECCHION, MICHELE; Toms River HS South; Pine Beach, NJ; (Y); 12/360; Math Tm; JV Bsktbl; Sftbl; Var L Tennis; High Hon Roll; Hon Roll; NHS; Acdmc Letter 83-84; JV Bsktbll MVP 84-85; Var Sftbll Overall Clutch Awd 85-86.

RECH, WENDY; Edgewood SR HS; Sicklerville, NJ; (Y); 28/410; Spanish Clb; Stage Crew; Lit Mag; Im Sftbl; Hon Roll; Jr NHS; NHS; La Salle U; Cmnctns.

RECTO, ANNALISA; Pompton Lakes HS; Pompton Lakes, NJ; (Y); Math Clb; PAVAS; Spanish Clb; School Play; Nwsp Rptr; Lit Mag; Trs Soph Cls; Trs Stu Cncl; Var Cheerleading; Hon Roll; Muhlenberg Coll; Bio.

RECTOR, KIM; Piscataway HS; Piscataway, NJ; (Y); Church Yth Grp; Varsity Clb; Concert Band; Drm Mjr(t); Mrchg Band; JV Bsktbl; Var L Trk; Hon Roll; NHS; Bus Mgmt.

REDAVID, JOHN; Morris Catholic HS; Succasunna, NJ; (Y); 4/155; Church Yth Grp; Cmnty Wkr; French Clb; FBLA; Math Tm; SADD; Nwsp Stf; French Hon Soc; High Hon Roll; NHS; Seton Hall U; Math.

REDD, DANA; Bishop Eustace Prep; Camden, NJ; (Y); 38/170; Latin Clb; Spanish Clb; Yrbk Stf; Hon Roll; NHS; Spanish NHS; Peirce JR Coll; Prlgl.

REDDICK IV, WILLIAM J; Seton Hall Prep Schl; Union, NJ; (Y); 108/193; Church Yth Grp; Cmnty Wkr; JV Var Bsbl; Trk; Hon Roll; Parish Cncl 86-87; Seton Hall Bsbl Camp JR Cnslr 85-87; Treas Cath Yth Orgnztn 86-87; Seton Hall U; Coach.

REDDINGTON, RITA; Clifton HS; Clifton, NJ; (Y); 61/637; Cmnty Wkr; Girl Scts; Band; Jazz Band; Mrchg Band; Var L Bsktbl; Stat Ftbl; Stat Sftbl; Hon Roll; Jr NHS; Grl Sct Slvr Awd 84.

REED, BRENT; Lenape Valley Regional HS; Stanhope, NJ; (Y); 16/250; JV Bsbl; Var Ftbl; Im Wt Lftg; High Hon Roll; Hon Roll; Lenape Vly Schlr 85.

REED, ELIZABETH; Shore Regional HS; W Long Branch, NJ; (Y); Ski Clb; SADD; VP Soph Cls; VP Jr Cls; VP Sr Cls; Diving; Fld Hcky; Gym; Powder Puff Ftbl; Socr; Fshn Merchandising.

REED, JOHN; Overbrook Regional HS; Pine Hill, NJ; (Y); 20/340; Church Yth Grp; French Clb; Var Crs Cntry; Socr; Var Trk; Hon Roll; NHS; Trgrs Cmdn Deans Sumr Schlr; Phila Coll; Phar.

REED, JOY; A P Schalick HS; Bridgeton, NJ; (Y); Art Clb; SADD; Band; Color Guard; Concert Band; Mrchg Band; JV Bsktbl; JV Cheerleading; Sftbl; Stat Trk; Bst Sect Awd For Clarinet 85; Cumberland Cnty Coll; Intr Dsgn.

REED, KEITH; East Orange HS; East Orange, NJ; (S); Pres Jr Cls; Bsktbl; Ftbl; Hon Roll; Rep German Clb; Rep Spanish Clb; Mst Outstndng Stu Bio 83-84; Monmouth Coll; Accntnt.

REED, KENNETH; Spotswood HS; Spotswood, NJ; (S); 24/175; Nwsp Stf; Ed Lit Mag; Var Capt Wrstlng; Hon Roll; VFW Awd; USMC.

REED, KIMBERLY; Toms River HS North; Toms River, NJ; (Y); Church Yth Grp; French Clb; Band; Chorus; Church Choir; Mrchg Band; Rep Jr Cls; Rep Sr Cls; Pres Frnch Clb 85-86; Frgn Affairs.

REED, MELISSA; Hopewell Valley Central HS; Hopewell, NJ; (Y); School Musical; Rep Stu Cncl; JV Crs Cntry; Wrkshp Schlrshp 85; Prof Aviatn.

REED, MICHAEL; Paulsboro HS; Paulsboro, NJ; (Y); 14/145; Band; Chorus; Concert Band; Jazz Band; Mrchg Band; School Musical; School Play; Stage Crew; Symp Band; Hon Roll; Natl Music Awd-Tenor Sax Solo 86; Goldy-Beecom; Accntnt.

REED, MICHAEL; Vineland HS; Newfield, NJ; (Y); 100/823; Var Crs Cntry; Bio Chem.

REED, MONIQUE; Eastside HS; Paterson, NJ; (Y); #20 In Class; Science Clb; Church Choir; Stu Cncl; Cheerleading; Bausch & Lomb Sci Awd; Cit Awd; Hon Roll; Rory Sparrow Found Ldrshp Pgm 86; Sci Fair Wnnr 86; Outstndng Acad Achvt Sci 86; Trenton ST; Ped Nrs.

REED, PATRICK; Overbrook SR HS; Pine Hill, NJ; (Y); 21/247; German Clb; Socr; High Hon Roll; Hon Roll; NHS; Accntng.

REED, PENNY; Holy Spirit HS; Absecon, NJ; (Y); Pep Clb; Yrbk Stf; Cheerleading; NHS; Stocton; Sci.

REED, ROBBIN; Overbrook Regional SR HS; Berlin, NJ; (Y); 23/260; Office Aide; Varsity Clb; Chorus; Rep Jr Cls; Trs Sr Cls; Var Stat Bsbl; JV Fld Hcky; Hon Roll; Jr NHS; NHS; La Salle U; Psychlgy.

REEDER, BILL; Bridgewater-Raritan HS East; Bridgewater, NJ; (Y); Ski Clb; Concert Band; Jazz Band; Orch; Var Socr; High Hon Roll; NHS; MVP Sccr Cmp; Bst Trombn Solo At Jazz Cmptn; Comp Sci.

REEDER, MARY R; Academy Of Saint Elizabth; Chatham, NJ; (Y); Church Yth Grp; Cmnty Wkr; Ski Clb; Varsity Clb; Pep Band; Nwsp Rptr; Nwsp Stf; Trs Frsh Cls; Rep Sr Cls; Stu Cncl; Teagle Fndtn Fnlst Schlrshp 86; Providence Coll; Reprtng.

REEDER, YOLANDA; Plainfield HS; Plainfield, NJ; (Y); Chorus; Drill Tm; Yrbk Stf; Hon Roll; Business Administration.

REEDY, LANCE; The Pennington Schl; Rocky Hill, NJ; (Y); Chess Clb; Latin Clb; Library Aide; Nwsp Rptr; Nwsp Stf; Var L Crs Cntry; Var L Trk; Hon Roll; Tennis; Wt Lftg; Hue Chen & Chris Lawson Penntonian Awd 85-86; Embry-Riddle Aero U; Aero Engr.

REEVES, DOROTHY; Parsippany HS; Parsippany, NJ; (Y); Church Yth Grp; Stage Crew; Lit Mag; Trk; Hon Roll; TX Wesleyan Coll; Vet.

REEVES, FAITH; Bridgeton HS; Bridgeton, NJ; (Y); 4/209; 4-H; Girl Scts; Q&S; SADD; Nwsp Ed-Chief; Yrbk Stf; Tennis; Hon Roll; Ntl Merit Ltr; Glassboro ST Coll; Jrnlsm.

REFANO, MICHELE; Sayreville War Memorial HS; Parlin, NJ; (Y); Church Yth Grp; French Clb; Spanish Clb; SADD; Band; Color Guard; Flag Corp; Stage Crew; Hon Roll; Rutgers Coll; Phrmcy.

REGAL, MARY; Memorial HS; West New York, NJ; (Y); Cmnty Wkr; Spanish Clb; Band; Concert Band; Mrchg Band; Pep Band; Rep Frsh Cls; Pres Soph Cls; Hon Roll; Hnr Roll 83-86; Dntstry.

REGAN, LINDA; James Caldwell HS; West Caldwell, NJ; (Y); Nwsp Stf; Yrbk Stf; Rep Jr Cls; Var Cheerleading; Var Capt Trk; Hon Roll; Elem Tchr.

REGAN, MARGARET; Immaculate Conception HS; E Orange, NJ; (Y); 14/77; Office Aide; Nwsp Rptr; Yrbk Ed-Chief; Rep Jr Cls; Pres Stu Cncl; Sftbl; Cit Awd; Hon Roll; NHS; Chorus; Shakespearean Essy Cont 85; Eng Class Awd 85; English.

REGECI, KRISTEN; Arthur L Johnson Regional HS; Clark, NJ; (S); 95/295; Pres French Clb; School Play; Stage Crew; Variety Show; Nwsp Rptr; Nwsp Stf; Yrbk Stf; Trs Pres Stu Cncl; Stat Bsktbl; JV Cheerleading; Govt.

REGENYE, CHRIS; Brick HS; Brick Town, NJ; (Y); Chess Clb; Debate Tm; German Clb; Intnl Clb; Math Tm; Band; Mrchg Band; High Hon Roll; Hon Roll; Robotics.

REGINA, SHARI A; Parsippany HS; Lake Hiawatha, NJ; (Y); 19/318; Cmnty Wkr; Drama Clb; Hosp Aide; Red Cross Aide; Chorus; School Musical; School Play; Cit Awd; High Hon Roll; NHS; JR Vlntry Actn Ctr Awd 86; Prsdntl Acad Ftnss Awd 86; Drama Awd 86; E Stroudsburg U; Nrsng.

REGUER, RAFI; North Bergen HS; Guttenberg, NJ; (Y); 1/404; Am Leg Boys St; Debate Tm; Capt Quiz Bowl; Nwsp Stf; Yrbk Stf; Stu Cncl; Tennis; Val; Amer Lgn Ortrcl Cntst St Wnr 84; NJ Govrs Schl Schlr-Sci 85; U Of PA.

REGULA, WALTER; Don Bosco Prep; Wallington, NJ; (Y); Chess Clb; Church Yth Grp; Bsktbl; Hon Roll; Engineering.

REHBERG, MICHAEL; Don Bosco Prep HS; Wyckoff, NJ; (Y); Boy Scts; Cmnty Wkr; Computer Clb; Science Clb; High Hon Roll; Hon Roll; NHS; Comp Sci.

REHMAN, MARC; Hunterdan Central HS; Three Bridges, NJ; (Y); 167/539; Boy Scts; VICA; Eaglt Sct Boy Scts Amerca 83; Syracuse U; Arch.

REHMAN, TRACY; Williamstown HS; Williamstown, NJ; (Y); French Clb; Mgr(s); Var Tennis; Hon Roll; NHS; All Glcstr Cnty Girls Tnns Tm Hon Ment 85; Intl Bus.

REHO, JAMES; St Josephs Preparatory Seminary; Staten Island, NY; (S); 1/19; Latin Clb; VP NFL; Spanish Clb; Church Choir; School Play; Yrbk Ed-Chief; Crs Cntry; High Hon Roll; NHS; Spanish NHS; Intrdctry Phy Sci Awd 83-84; St Josephs Awd Hghst Avg 83-85; Philsphy.

REHSE, DENIS; Lenape Valley Regional HS; Stanhope, NJ; (Y); JV Ftbl; JV Trk; Im Wt Lftg; High Hon Roll; Hon Roll; NHS; Spanish NHS; Lenape Vlly Schlr 85; Engrng.

REICH, ANDREW L; Morristown HS; Morristown, NJ; (Y); 5/399; JCL; Quiz Bowl; Temple Yth Grp; School Play; Stu Cncl; Var Swmmng; Gov Hon Prg Awd; NHS; Ntl Merit SF; Pres Schlr; Grdn ST Dstgnshd Schlr 85; Lib Arts.

REICH, BRIAN; West Orange HS; West Orange, NJ; (Y); Am Leg Boys St; Math Tm; Nwsp Rptr; Nwsp Sprt Ed; JV Socr; Var Tennis; Var Wrstlng; High Hon Roll; VP Computer Clb; Var Ski Clb; NJ Ambasdr HOBY Intl Ldrshp Smnr 85; NJ Govrns Schl Sci 86.

REICH, ROBERT; Pequannock Twp HS; Pequannock, NJ; (Y); 1/225; VP German Clb; VP Latin Clb; Mathletes; Quiz Bowl; School Play; Capt Tennis; Gov Hon Prg Awd; NHS; Pres Schlr; Val; NJ Gvrnrs Schl Pblc Iss 86; Hugh Obrien Yuth Fndtn Smnr 85; NJ Bys ST 86.

REICHARDT, JENIFER; Ramsey HS; Ramsey, NJ; (Y); 55/240; Church Yth Grp; JA; Orch; School Musical; Yrbk Stf; Hon Roll; Cert Awd For Acad Achvt 84; Intl Fstvl Prgm 85; Augustana Coll; Educ.

REID, AMEE; Kingsway Regional HS; Mullica Hill, NJ; (Y); Church Yth Grp; 4-H; Key Clb; Ski Clb; Yrbk Stf; Fld Hcky; High Hon Roll; Teen Arts Fest Prog Dsgn Hnbl Mntn 86; Stff Awd Positv Attitd; Arch Intr Dsgn.

REID, JULIET; East Side HS; Wyckoff, NJ; (Y); Art Clb; Pres Church Yth Grp; Cmnty Wkr; Girl Scts; VP Intnl Clb; Church Choir; School Musical; Variety Show; Nwsp Phtg; Swmmng; Chrst Chrch Untd Mthdst Acdmc Achvt 85; Trrnt Scndry Schl 2nd Pl 81; Ramapo Coll; Brdcstng.

REID, KAREN; Essex Catholic Girls HS; Hillside, NJ; (Y); Church Yth Grp; Pep Clb; Service Clb; Church Choir; Yrbk Stf; Var Bowling; Var L Cheerleading; Var Trk; High Hon Roll; Hon Roll; Acdmc All Amer 85-86; Natl Hon Soc 84-86; Kutztown U; Crmnl Jstc.

REID, KIM; Henry Snyder HS; Jersey City, NJ; (S); 5/256; Office Aide; Stage Crew; Yrbk Stf; Lit Mag; Hon Roll; NHS; Parents Cncl Achvt Awd 85; Accntng.

REID III, MEL; Jackson Memorial HS; Jackson, NJ; (Y); 12/411; Computer Clb; French Clb; Math Tm; Ski Clb; High Hon Roll; Rutgers Deans Sumr Schlr, Olympcs Of The Mnd 3rd Pl ST & Physcs Tm 86; Rutgers; Engrng.

REID, MONEE; Vailsburg HS; Newark, NJ; (Y); Exploring; Hosp Aide; Chorus; Color Guard; Yrbk Stf; Rep Jr Cls; Rep Stu Cncl; Cit Awd; High Hon Roll; Hon Roll; Seton Hall U; Pol Sci.

REID, RICHARD; St Marys HS; Lyndhurst, NJ; (S); Drama Clb; FBLA; SADD; Nwsp Ed-Chief; Yrbk Bus Mgr; VP Frsh Cls; Sec Soph Cls; Trs Jr Cls; Var Capt Bsktbl; School Musical; Mdl Stu Awd 86; Otstndng Algbra Awd 83; Bus Adm.

REID, SCOTT D; Haddon Heights HS; Cherry Hill, NJ; (Y); Pres Church Yth Grp; Computer Clb; ROTC; SADD; Band; VP Church Choir; Variety Show; Bsktbl; Trk; Hon Roll; VA ST U; Hstry.

REID, SHAWNISE; Snyder HS; Jersey City, NJ; (Y).

REIDEL, LAURIE; Ridgefield Park HS; Little Ferry, NJ; (Y); 6/158; Spanish Clb; Rep Stu Cncl; Var Capt Bsktbl; Score Keeper; Trk; Var Capt Vllybl; High Hon Roll; Hon Roll; NHS.

REIDENBAKER, RICHARD; Faith Christian Schl; Merchantville, NJ; (S); Yrbk Ed-Chief; Pres Stu Cncl; Var L Bsktbl; Capt L Bsktbl; JV Coach Actv; Capt L Socr; High Hon Roll; NHS; Sci, Math, & Hstry Awds 84-85; Rutgers U-Camden; Engrng.

REIFENHEISER, ROBERT; Toms River High School North; Toms River, NJ; (Y); Band; Concert Band; Jazz Band; Mrchg Band; School Musical; Stu Cncl; Gym; Wt Lftg; Wrstlng; Hon Roll; Bus.

REILLY III, CHARLES JOSEPH; Overbrook SR HS; Pine Hill, NJ; (Y); Am Leg Boys St; ROTC; Crs Cntry; Prfct Atten Awd; US Army Cadet Yr Awd 85-86; US Army Rsrve Natl Essay Cntst Awd 86; Bus Admin.

REILLY, CHRISTOPHER; Toms River H S South; S Toms River, NJ; (Y); Band; Jazz Band; Mrchg Band; Orch; School Musical; Symp Band; JV Tennis; NHS; Band 85-86; Ntl Arion Awd Music 85-86; Rutgers Deans Smmr Schrls Pgm Merit Schlrshp 86.

REILLY, KELLY; Pope John XXIII HS; Ogdensburg, NJ; (Y); Lit Mag; Stat Bsbl; Cheerleading; High Hon Roll; Hon Roll; NHS; Typng I Awd 84-85.

REILLY, WILLIAM; Cherry Hill West HS; Cherry Hill, NJ; (Y); Diving; Socr; Swmmng; Hon Roll.

REIM, JOHN T; Delsea Regional HS; Franklinville, NJ; (Y); 3/201; Am Leg Boys St; Trs Key Clb; Pres Sr Cls; Stu Cncl; Cit Awd; High Hon Roll; NHS; Pres Schlr; Touchdown Clb; All Acad Tm 85; Wachman Awd; Cumberland Paper Sply Co Awd; Chem.

REINHART, KIM; Princeton Day Schl; Lawrenceville, NJ; (Y); 4-H; French Clb; Hosp Aide; Chorus; Stage Crew; Nwsp Phtg; Yrbk Phtg; Bsktbl; Capt Socr; 4-H Awd; Achvt In Art Awd Photo 86; U Of DE; Bio.

REINHOLD, ROBYN; Pinelands Regional HS; Tuckerton, NJ; (Y); SADD; JV Socr; DAR Awd; Hon Roll.

REINKE, MICHAEL G; Secancus HS; Secaucus, NJ; (Y); Am Leg Boys St; Aud/Vis; Cmnty Wkr; German Clb; Key Clb; Varsity Clb; Stage Crew; Yrbk Stf; Crs Cntry; Var Capt Trk; Grp II ST Hgh Hrdls 86; Hudson Bergen Cnty Leag Champ Hrdls 86; Amer Legn Jrsy Boys ST As Aid 86; Seton Hall; Crmnl Jstc.

REISER, JOSH; James Caldwell HS; W Caldwell, NJ; (Y); Key Clb; Temple Yth Grp; Band; Jazz Band; Mrchg Band; Lit Mag; Rep Jr Cls; Rep Stu Cncl; High Hon Roll; NHS; Ina Wolfe Endwmnt Fnd Schlrp 85; Mrn Sci.

REISMAN, GARRETT; Parsippany HS; Lake Hiawatha, NJ; (Y); 1/315; Am Leg Boys St; Intnl Clb; Concert Band; Var Capt Wrstlng; NHS; Ntl Merit SF; Val; Boys Clb Am; Chess Clb; Computer Clb; Golden Nugget Schlrshp 86; Rensselaer Medal Math,Sci 85; Am Def Preprdns Assoc Schlrshp 86; U PA; Engr.

REISTLE, JACK; Woodstown HS; Woodstown, NJ; (Y); 20/235; Var Capt Socr; NHS; Drama Clb; German Clb; Key Clb; School Musical; School Play; VP Frsh Cls; JV Golf; Var Tennis; Boys St Altnt 86; W Pt Summer Invtl Acad Wrkshp 86; Bus.

REITER, LORNE; Sayreville War Memorial HS; Sayreville, NJ; (Y); Spanish Clb; SADD; Stu Cncl; Ftbl; Trk; Hon Roll.

REITMEYER, LYNNE; Absegami HS; Pomona, NJ; (Y); 10/300; Church Yth Grp; French Clb; Girl Scts; Band; Church Choir; Mrchg Band; School Play; Nwsp Rptr; Lit Mag; Voice Dem Awd; Acad Ltr Of Achvts; Engl.

REIZISS, PHYLLIS; Freehold Township HS; Howell, NJ; (Y); Hosp Aide; Temple Yth Grp; Capt Color Guard; JV L Socr; Var L Twrlr; Sec, VP, Pres 1st Aid Sqd Cadts 83-85; Trophy And Plaq Var Rifl Sqd 85-86; Outstndng Achvt Bes Band; Kean College; Elem Ed.

REJRAT, SUSAN A; Roselle Catholic HS; Roselle, NJ; (Y); 32/160; High Hon Roll; Hon Roll; Un Cnty Clg Full Fndtn Schlrshp 86; Union County Clg; Bus.

REJTERADA, IRENE; Rahway HS; Rahway, NJ; (Y); Hosp Aide; Key Clb; Service Clb; Spanish Clb; Nwsp Stf; Yrbk Stf; Socr; Jr NHS; Spanish NHS; Bio.

RELIGIOSO, DEOGRACIAS; Hudson Catholic HS; Jersey Cty, NJ; (Y); Nwsp Ed-Chief; Hon Roll; NHS; Med Tech.

RELOTA, JOSIP; Bayley-Ellard Regional HS; Chatham, NJ; (Y); Am Leg Boys St; Church Yth Grp; Drama Clb; Model UN; Varsity Clb; Yrbk Stf; Var Socr; High Hon Roll; NHS; Pre Med.

RELOVSKY, DAN; Holy Cross HS; Mount Laurel, NJ; (Y); Church Yth Grp; Church Choir; Concert Band; Stage Crew; Rep Stu Cncl; JV Bsbl; JV Var Bsktbl; Hon Roll; Aerontcl Engrng.

REMAZOWSKI, LISA; Queen Of Peace HS; N Arlington, NJ; (Y); 77/229; Spanish Clb; SADD; Yrbk Phtg; Hon Roll; Allied Hlth.

REMENTOV, TAMARA; Kings Christian HS; Cherry Hill, NJ; (Y); 3/40; Church Yth Grp; Latin Clb; Teachers Aide; Chorus; Yrbk Ed-Chief; Yrbk Stf; Fld Hcky; Sftbl; High Hon Roll; MACSA Art Awd Gold And Silvr 84-86; Bio.

REMSTER, LISA; Woodstown HS; Woodstown, NJ; (Y); VP English Clb; 4-H; Trs French Clb; Key Clb; Ski Clb; Trs Rep Stu Cncl; Var Capt Cheerleading; High Hon Roll; Hon Roll; NHS; Pre-Med.

RENCHER, KELLY; Hunterdon Central HS; Flemington, NJ; (Y); 110/548; Church Yth Grp; 4-H; German Clb; Ski Clb; Band; Church Choir; Color Guard; Concert Band; Mrchg Band; Intl Stds.

RENDE, MICHELLE; Gateway Regional HS; Woodbury Hts, NJ; (Y); 20/200; JCL; Key Clb; Latin Clb; Science Clb; SADD; Stu Cncl; Var Fld Hcky; Var Trk; Stat Wrstlng; NHS; Pres Acdmc Ftns Awd, Ctznshp Awd 86; Trenton ST Coll; Bio.

RENDEIRO, MARIA; Queen Of Peace HS; Lyndhurst, NJ; (Y); 33/229; Church Yth Grp; Cmnty Wkr; VP SADD; Yrbk Stf; Stat Bsktbl; Powder Puff Ftbl; Var Trk; High Hon Roll; Score Keeper; Hon Roll; Amrcl Allianc Hlth, Phys Ed, Recrtn & Dnce Achvt Aed 86; Phys Thrpy.

RENDON, SHIRLEY; Mary Help Of Christians Acad; Paterson, NJ; (Y); 21/85; Chess Clb; Computer Clb; French Clb; Hosp Aide; Off Frsh Cls; Off Jr Cls; Rep Stu Cncl; Im Mgr Cheerleading; Vllybl; Hon Roll; Hstry; Engl; Frnch; Pre Med.

RENDUELES, ANDREA; Toms River North HS; Toms River, NJ; (Y); 74/412; Church Yth Grp; 4-H; Mrchg Band; Orch; Yrbk Ed-Chief; Stu Cncl; 4-H Awd; Hon Roll; Al-S Jersey Symphnc Band 85; Garden ST Philhrmnc Yth Orch 83-86; H Mann Memrl Awd Outstnd Presntn 85; Elem Ed.

RENGEPIS, JOHN; Clearview Regional HS; Mantua, NJ; (Y); 7/182; VP Band; VP Concert Band; VP Mrchg Band; Yrbk Stf; Var L Golf; Elks Awd; High Hon Roll; Hon Roll; NHS; Prfct Atten Awd; Am Leg Robt W Mills Post Awd 86; Drexel U; Engrng.

RENK, LAURA J; Pt Pleasant Buro HS; Point Pleasant, NJ; (Y); 28/240; Band; Chorus; Church Choir; Concert Band; Madrigals; Mrchg Band; School Musical; Church Yth Grp; Cmnty Wkr; Ntl Prsbytrn Schlrshp 86; Beaver Coll; Phy Thrpy.

RENN, THERESA; Egg Harbor Township HS; Scullville, NJ; (S); 19/317; SADD; Hon Roll; Jr NHS; Schlstc Lttr Awd 84-85; Acctng.

RENOLDS, THOMAS G; Hackensack HS; Hackensack, NJ; (Y); 25/421; Am Leg Boys St; Letterman Clb; Ski Clb; Spanish Clb; Varsity Clb; Yrbk Sprt Ed; Yrbk Stf; Var L Bsktbl; Hon Roll; NHS; Engrng.

RENSHAW, APRIL; Overbrook Regional HS; Pine Hill, NJ; (Y); Sec French Clb; Band; Concert Band; Mrchg Band; Symp Band; Rep Stu Cncl; Im Bsktbl; Var Sftbl; Hon Roll; Jr NHS; U Of Miami; Oceanogrphy.

RENTERIA, LUISA; James J Ferris HS; Jersey City, NJ; (Y); Am Leg Aux Girls St; Computer Clb; Math Clb; Math Tm; Scholastic Bowl; Nwsp Phtg; Nwsp Stf; Yrbk Ed-Chief; Yrbk Phtg; Jr Cls; Rutgers Schlr 86; Chem Engrng.

RENTON, SANDRA; Newton HS; Newton, NJ; (S); 6/210; Pres 4-H; Latin Clb; Math Tm; Acpl Chr; Yrbk Stf; Rep Stu Cncl; 4-H Awd; Hon Roll; NHS; Mt St Mary Coll-NY; Medcl Tech.

RENWICK, IAN; Wayne Hills HS; Wayne, NJ; (Y); 25/305; Math Tm; Pres Concert Band; Jazz Band; Pres Mrchg Band; School Musical; School Play; Gov Hon Prg Awd; Hon Roll; NHS; Orch; Rcgntn Prtcptn NJ Area, Rgnl & All ST Bands 84-86; Engrng.

RENZ, PATRICIA; Holy Cross HS; Cinnaminson, NJ; (Y); French Clb; High Hon Roll; Hon Roll.

REPERT, JOHANNA; Red Bank Catholic HS; Freehold, NJ; (Y); 47/264; Band; Concert Band; Jazz Band; Mrchg Band; High Hon Roll; Hon Roll; NEDT Awd; Scholar Marquette U 86; Boston U; Psych.

REPOZA, ANDREW; St Peters Pres; Morehead City, NC; (Y); 7/206; Boy Scts; Chess Clb; Science Clb; Hon Roll; Ntl Merit Ltr; 1st Hnrs Lang Cntst Spnsh 86; Cum Laude Ntl Latin Ex 85; Pres Schlrshp St Peters Prep 83; Harvard; Sci.

REPSHER, NANCY L; Haddonfield Memorial HS; Haddonfield, NJ; (S); 8/141; Drama Clb; Lib 4-H; Service Clb; Concert Band; Mrchg Band; Yrbk Stf; Var Capt Swmmng; 4-H Awd; NHS; Var St Schlr.

RESCH, LORI; Wayne Hills HS; Raleigh, NC; (Y); 68/310; GAA; Ski Clb; Spanish Clb; Varsity Clb; Mrchg Band; Capt Var Cheerleading; Hon Roll; U NC; Engrng.

RESH, CHRISTIAN; Christian Brothers Acad; Colts Neck, NJ; (Y); 30/225; Math Tm; Stage Crew; Yrbk Rptr; Yrbk Stf; Lit Mag; Im Bowling; High Hon Roll; Hon Roll; Ntl Merit Ltr; Asst Edtr In Chief Yrbk.

RESIDE, ROBIN; Hopewell Valley Central HS; Titusville, NJ; (Y); Sec FBLA; Service Clb; Chorus; School Play; Stage Crew; Var JV Mgr(s); Var JV Score Keeper; 3rd Pl Clerk Typist I Central Rgnl FBLA Comp 86; Merce Co CC Litry Jrnl Aspirations 86; Court Reporter.

RESLER, EUGENE; Elizabeth HS; Elizabeth, NJ; (Y); Chess Clb; Nwsp Rptr; Jrnlsm.

RESNICK, HELAINE; Levingston HS; Livingston, NJ; (Y); Leo Clb; Model UN; Temple Yth Grp; Hon Roll; Svc Awd 84; Bus.

RESNICK, ROBERT; Glen Rock HS; Glen Rock, NJ; (Y); 16/166; Debate Tm; Drama Clb; JCL; Political Wkr; Varsity Clb; Band; Mrchg Band; Nwsp Ed-Chief; Lit Mag; Trs Soph Cls; Jrnlsm.

RESTAINO, GARY; Metuchen HS; Metuchen, NJ; (Y); 2/143; Pres Church Yth Grp; Yrbk Sprt Ed; Var L Socr; JP Sousa Awd; NHS; Sal; Spanish NHS; Boy Scts; Cmnty Wkr; Quiz Bowl; Eagle Scout 86; NJ Regional & All ST Bands 84-86; Hstry Depart Awd 86; Haverford Coll; History.

RESTIVO, FRANK; Christian Brothers Acad; Long Branch, NJ; (Y); VP Church Yth Grp; Cmnty Wkr; Var L Bsbl; Im Bsktbl; Im Ftbl; Wt Lftg; High Hon Roll; Hon Roll; T Rntn Diocs Yth Of Yr Awd 86; Elctn As Euchrstc Mnstr-H S 86; Bus.

RETTAS, GEORGE; Dover HS; Dover, NJ; (Y); 22/250; Church Yth Grp; FCA; Concert Band; Mrchg Band; Orch; School Musical; JV Bsbl; Capt L Bsktbl; Capt Var Ftbl; Hon Roll; Coaches Awd Bsktbl; MVP Bsktbl; Bus Mgn & Adm.

RETTIG, LISA; Manalapan HS; Englishtown, NJ; (Y); Orch; ASVAB Awd 86; Brookdale CC.

REUTER, STEFANIE; Union Catholic HS; Berkeley Hts, NJ; (Y); Church Yth Grp; French Clb; Latin Clb; Art Clb; Math Clb; Science Clb; Service Clb; Ski Clb; Chorus; Yrbk Stf; Natl Latin Game Wnr 85; Natl Physics Olympiad Wnr 86; Pre-Med.

REUTTER, T R CHRISTIAN; Woodbury HS; Woodbury, NJ; (Y); 5/115; Am Leg Boys St; Boy Scts; Varsity Clb; Pres Chorus; Rep Frsh Cls; Rep Soph Cls; Sec Stu Cncl; Capt Var Swmmng; High Hon Roll; NHS.

REVER, SCOTT; Unio HS; Union, NJ; (Y); Cmnty Wkr; FBLA; Key Clb; Service Clb; Temple Yth Grp; Nwsp Sprt Ed; Nwsp Stf; Yrbk Stf; Rep Frsh Cls; Rep Stu Cncl; Statu Lib Essy Cntst 1st Pl 86; Law.

REYES, DEANA; Central Reyes HS; Ocean Gate, NJ; (Y); 85/350; Church Yth Grp; Letterman Clb; Ski Clb; Varsity Clb; Var Fld Hcky; Var Socr; Var Trk; Rotary Awd; Business.

REYNIK, LAURA S; Ramsey HS; Ramsey, NJ; (Y); Art Clb; Church Yth Grp; 4-H; Girl Scts; Library Aide; PAVAS; SADD; Teachers Aide; School Play; Nwsp Stf; Rutgers U Smmr Arts Schl Schlrshp 85; Pratt Coll; Grphc Dsgn.

REYNOLDS, JENNIFER; Burlington City HS; Edgewater Pk, NJ; (Y); Am Leg Aux Girls St; Var JV Fld Hcky; Hon Roll; Ntl Merit Ltr; Smmr Schlrshp Moore Coll 85; Olymcs Of Mind 1st Pl Rgnl & 2nd Pl ST 85-86; Stu Extndd Lrnng Prg 83-86; Pre Med.

REYNOLDS, L BENTLEY; High Point Regional HS; Branchville, NJ; (Y); Am Leg Boys St; Church Yth Grp; Drama Clb; Thesps; Varsity Clb; Band; Chorus; School Musical; School Play; Louis Armstrong Jazz Awd 86; U IA; Vocl Music.

REYNOLDS, LORI; Rancocas Valley Regional HS; Mt Holly, NJ; (Y); 58/248; Aud/Vis; Spanish Clb; Band; Concert Band; Jazz Band; Mrchg Band; Stage Crew; Yrbk Stf; Mgr(s); Hon Roll; S Jersey SF Phila Inquirer Spllg Bee 82; Central PA Bus Schl; Mass Meda.

REYNOLDS, MICHELLE; Central HS; Newark, NJ; (Y); Math Clb; Hon Roll; Law.

REYNOLDS, ROSEANN; Orange HS; Orange, NJ; (S); 82/182; Boy Scts; Exploring; Hosp Aide; Math Tm; Speech Tm; Nwsp Rptr; Hon Roll; Masonic Awd; Cert Partcptn 85; Dance Awd 84; Lincoln U; Crimnl Justc.

REYNOLDS, SANDI; Cinnaminson HS; Cinnaminson, NJ; (Y); Pres Church Yth Grp; Service Clb; SADD; Church Choir; Rep Frsh Cls; Rep Soph Cls; Rep Jr Cls; JV Fld Hcky; JV Lcrss; JV Swmmng; Economics.

RHATIGAN, DEBORAH; Chatham Twp HS; Chatham, NJ; (Y); Drama Clb; Girl Scts; Key Clb; Model UN; Chorus; School Musical; Swing Chorus; Yrbk Stf; High Hon Roll; Hon Roll.

RHOADES, BETH; Parsippany Hills HS; Boonton, NJ; (Y); AFS; Am Leg Aux Girls St; French Clb; Political Wkr; Teachers Aide; Church Choir; Yrbk Bus Mgr; Yrbk Phtg; Yrbk Stf; Debate Tm; James Madison; Pre-Law.

RHODE, MARK; Toms River HS East; Toms River, NJ; (Y); 65/585; Boy Scts; German Clb; Science Clb; Varsity Clb; Lit Mag; Crs Cntry; JV Swmmng; Hon Roll; NHS; Arspc Engr.

RHODES, LAURA; Bridgewater Raritan W HS; Raritan, NJ; (Y); Pres Church Yth Grp; Capt Flag Corp; Mrchg Band; Jr Cls; L Var Bsktbl; Hon Roll; NHS; Instrmntlst Mgzn Merit Awd 86; Stature Lbrty Drl Team 86; PTO Schlrshp 86; Brghm Yng U; Psychlgy.

RHODES, WENDY; Govenor Livingston Regional HS; Berkeley Hts, NJ; (Y); 41/198; Drama Clb; French Clb; Chorus; School Musical; School Play; Hon Roll; Syracuse U; Intr Dsgn.

RIAD, AMIRA; North Brunswick Township HS; N Brunswick, NJ; (Y); 40/250; French Clb; Key Clb; Pres Spanish Clb; Ed Yrbk Stf; Ed Soph Cls; Ed Jr Cls; Sftbl; Hon Roll; NHS; Rutgers U; Dntstry.

RIBARDO, MICHAEL; Seton Hall Prep; S Orange, NJ; (Y); Cmnty Wkr; Band; School Musical; Im Bsktbl; Coach Actv; JV Ftbl; Engnrng.

RIBAUDO, GINA; Saint Rose HS; Oakhurst, NJ; (Y); JCL; Key Clb; Latin Clb; Ski Clb; Rep Soph Cls; Pres Jr Cls; Cheerleading; High Hon Roll; Hon Roll; Pres NHS; Pfrct Attndnc 84; Athltc Awd 84; Carer Explrtn Prjct 3rd Pl 84.

RIBEIRO, MARIA; Riverside HS; Riverside, NJ; (S); #2 In Class; Cmnty Wkr; FTA; Off Soph Cls; Off Jr Cls; Hon Roll; Algbra I Awd 83-84; Stu Mnth Awds 83-86; Nrsng.

RIBEIRO, NANCY; Kearny HS; Kearny, NJ; (Y); Am Leg Aux Girls St; French Clb; Color Guard; Mrchg Band; Var Capt Crs Cntry; Var Capt Trk; French Hon Soc; High Hon Roll; Hon Roll; NHS; Law.

RICARDO, ALEX; Freehold Township HS; Freehold, NJ; (Y); 44/382; Church Yth Grp; Computer Clb; Drama Clb; French Clb; Thesps; Madrigals; School Musical; Stage Crew; NHS; Rep Tv 39 86-87; Aero Sp Engr.

RICCARDI, CLAIRE; Princeton Day Schl; Skillman, NJ; (Y); Drama Clb; Thesps; Madrigals; School Musical; School Play; Stage Crew; Lit Mag; JV Vllybl; Gov Hon Prg Awd; NCTE Awd; U Of CA-SANTA Cruz; Ctrv Wrtng.

RICCARDI, JERRY; Burlington City HS; Edgewater Pk, NJ; (Y); Am Leg Boys St; Cmnty Wkr; JA; Var Crs Cntry; JV Socr; Var Trk; JV Wrstlng; Hon Roll; Olympc Of Mind 2nd Pl ST Comp 84-86; Arts.

RICCIARDI, MICHAEL; Lakewood HS; Lakewood, NJ; (Y); 74/294; CAP; French Clb; FBLA; Latin Clb; JV Bsktbl; Comm.

RICCIO, CLARK; Bloomfield HS; Belleville, NJ; (Y).

RICCITIELLO, GINA M; Pleasantville HS; Pleasantville, NJ; (Y); SADD; Yrbk Stf; Sec Jr Cls; Rep Stu Cncl; Cheerleading; Swmmng; Hon Roll; Ntl Merit SF; Am Lgn Awd 84; NC U; Law.

RICCO, DEBBIE; John F Kennedy Memorial HS; Iselin, NJ; (Y); 75/275; Church Yth Grp; Dance Clb; Trs FBLA; Spanish Clb; Yrbk Stf; Rep Jr Cls; Hon Roll; Bus.

RICE, ANGELA; Jackson Memorial HS; Jackson, NJ; (Y); 3/405; Concert Band; Mrchg Band; High Hon Roll; NEDT Awd; VFW Awd; Voice Dem Awd; Leukemia Soc Type-A-Thn Cert Merit 86; Enrchmt Pgm 83-86; Elem Ed.

RICE, LAVONNE; Pleasantville HS; Pleasantville, NJ; (Y); 33/104; Computer Clb; FBLA; FNA; SADD; Varsity Clb; Yrbk Sprt Ed; Yrbk Stf; Bsktbl; Coach Actv; Sftbl; MVP Bsktbl 85-86; VA ST U; Accntng.

RICE, NICKO; East Side HS; Newark, NJ; (Y); Boy Scts; JCL; Red Cross Aide; SADD; Chorus; Church Choir; Jr Cls; Stu Cncl; Bowling; Cheerleading; Aspira Clb 84; Army.

RICE, SHELLY; Bridgeton HS; Bridgeton, NJ; (Y); Aud/Vis; French Clb; Q&S; Nwsp Rptr; VP Soph Cls; Pres Jr Cls; High Hon Roll; Jr NHS; VFW Awd; Voice Dem Awd; Schlstc Schl Ltr B 84,85,86; Hugh Obrian Ldrshp Rep 85; Presdntl Clsrm Rep 86; Engrng.

RICH, MICHAEL; Glen Ridge HS; Glen Ridge, NJ; (Y); AFS; Trs French Clb; Model UN; JV Socr; JV Tennis; High Hon Roll; Rotary Awd; Hnr Guard; Most Enthusistc Soccer.

RICH, SETH I; Hightstown HS; East Windsor, NJ; (Y); Cmnty Wkr; Library Aide; Math Clb; Office Aide; Teachers Aide; Band; Chorus; Church Choir; Mrchg Band; NHS; Rutgrs Smmr Schlrs Prog 86; Math.

RICH, STEPHEN J; Voothees HS; Califon, NJ; (Y); Am Leg Boys St; Varsity Clb; Jr Cls; Sr Cls; Stu Cncl; Hon Roll; Jr NHS; Jr Cls Athlete Awd 86.

RICHARDS, KELLY; Shore Regional HS; Oceanport, NJ; (Y); Church Yth Grp; Yrbk Stf; Var Capt Bsktbl; Var Fld Hcky; Var Socr; Var Sftbl; High Hon Roll; Sccr Clss C-South Hon Mntn 86; Bus Adm.

RICHARDS, MICHELLE; Bishop George Ahr/St Thomas HS; Plainfield, NJ; (Y); Church Yth Grp; Stat Bsktbl; High Hon Roll; High Hon Roll; Crtfct Awd Exclnc Schlrshp; Psych.

RICHARDS, SCOTT; Highland HS; Laurel Spgs, NJ; (Y); Chess Clb; German Clb; Latin Clb; Science Clb; Spanish Clb; Varsity Clb; Nwsp Stf; JV L Bsbl; Var L Bsktbl; Var L Socr; Accntg.

RICHARDS, SHARON; Bloomfield SR HS; Bloomfld, NJ; (Y); 46/442; Var L Trk; JV Vllybl; DAR Awd; High Hon Roll; Hon Roll; Elec Engrg.

RICHARDS, VANESSA C; Jackson Memorial HS; Jackson, NJ; (Y); Band; Concert Band; Mrchg Band; Yrbk Stf; Hst Jr Cls; Rep Stu Cncl; Capt L Bsktbl; Powder Puff Ftbl; Capt Var Trk; Hon Roll; Band & Bsktbl Var Ltr 84 & 86; Dancing Awds 81-84; HOSA 83-87; NYU; Psych.

RICHARDS JR, VERNON G; Seton Hall Prep Schl; Newark, NJ; (Y); Chess Clb; Church Yth Grp; Computer Clb; French Clb; Nwsp Rptr; Yrbk Rptr; Yrbk Sprt Ed; Pres Jr Cls; Rep Sr Cls; Rep Stu Cncl; Bus Admin.

RICHARDSON, AMY; North Plainfield HS; N Plainfield, NJ; (Y); 16/150; Church Yth Grp; Drill Tm; Nwsp Stf; Pres Frsh Cls; Pres Soph Cls; JV Var Bsktbl; Capt Pom Pon; Im Powder Puff Ftbl; JV Var Sftbl; Cit Awd; Erly Chldhd Ed.

RICHARDSON, DANA; Hackettstown HS; Great Meadows, NJ; (Y); Office Aide; Spanish Clb; Stage Crew; Sftbl; Hon Roll; Prfct Atten Awd; U Of Sthrn CA; Law.

RICHARDSON, JOYCE; West Side HS; Newark, NJ; (Y); Math Clb; Yrbk Stf; Rep Jr Cls; Rep Stu Cncl; Mgr(s); High Hon Roll; Tennis; Hon Roll; NHS; Ntl Merit Schol; Outstndng Frshmn 83-84; Humn Rghts Awd 85-86; Blck Achvrs 85-86; Dntstry.

RICHARDSON, KEVIN A; St Marys Hall Doane Acad; Willingboro, NJ; (Y); 4/16; Am Leg Boys St; Drama Clb; Pres Jr Cls; Pres Sr Cls; Stu Cncl; Var Bsktbl; Var Socr; Cit Awd; High Hon Roll; Bst Actor-Drama Fstvl86; Wesleyan U; Pre Med.

RICHARDSON, KRYSTAL; Eastside HS; Paterson, NJ; (Y); DECA; Church Choir.

RICHARDSON, PAMELA; Camden HS; Camden, NJ; (Y); Dance Clb; Sec Frsh Cls; Sec Soph Cls; Var Cheerleading; Pom Pon; Acctnt.

RICHARDSON, SHANNON; Memorial HS; Cedar Grove, NJ; (S); Pres Sec Church Yth Grp; Drama Clb; Key Clb; Ski Clb; Chorus; School Musical; School Play; Rep Sr Cls; Stu Cncl; Var Cheerleading; Acad Achvt In Art Fndtns 83; Var Lettr In Chrldng 86.

RICHICHI, MICHAEL; Millville SR HS; Millville, NJ; (Y); 10/448; Boy Scts; Church Yth Grp; Drama Clb; Science Clb; School Musical; School Play; Hon Roll; NHS; Ntl Merit SF; Key Clb; Gov Schl Sci 86; Physics.

RICHIE JR, WILLIAM; Salem HS; Salem, NJ; (Y); Am Leg Boys St; Chess Clb; Computer Clb; Latin Clb; Math Clb; Ski Clb; Tennis; Trk; Cit Awd; Hon Roll; Navy; Elec.

RICHMAN, BETH; Montville Township HS; Montville, NJ; (Y); 4/260; Drama Clb; NFL; Sec VP Speech Tm; School Musical; School Play; Nwsp Rptr; Lit Mag; Rep Stu Cncl; High Hon Roll; NHS; NJ ST Champ Humorous Intrprttn 86; Gov Schl Of Arts 86; Cmmnty Prfrmnc Prg 86.

RICHMOND, CHRISTINE; Haddon Twp HS; Collingwood, NJ; (Y); Aud/Vis; German Clb; Girl Scts; Hosp Aide; Office Aide; SADD; Chorus; Drill Tm; School Play; Stage Crew; Germ Hnr Soc 86; Thomas Jefferson U; Med Tech.

RICHMOND, FREDRICK; Teaneck HS; Teaneck, NJ; (Y); SADD; Varsity Clb; School Play; Nwsp Sprt Ed; Yrbk Sprt Ed; Sec Sr Cls; Var L Swmmng; Var L Tennis; Hon Roll; Sec NHS; Acad All Amer 86; Bus Admin.

RICHMOND, KELLY; Hightstown HS; E Windsor, NJ; (Y); Ski Clb; SADD; Rep Jr Cls; JV Fld Hcky; Var Swmmng; Var Trk; Hon Roll.

RICHMOND, MARK; Pennsville Memorial HS; Pennsville, NJ; (Y); 40/243; Am Leg Boys St; Nwsp Stf; Jr Cls; Stu Cncl; Var Capt Crs Cntry; Var Capt Trk; Hon Roll; Rotary Awd; Geneva Coll; Chem Engrng.

RICHMOND, NANCY; Red Bank Regional HS; Shrewsbury, NJ; (Y); Sec Sr Cls; Rep Stu Cncl; JV Stat Socr; Stat Tennis; High Hon Roll; NHS; Spanish NHS; St Schlr; Temple Yth Grp; Var Mgr(s); Outstndng Wrld Hstry Stu 83-84; Vrsty Lttr Hgh Hnr Rll 5 Mkng Prds 83-84; Rutgers U Schlr 85-86.

RICHMOND, SANDRA; Red Bank Regional HS; Shrewsbury, NJ; (Y); Temple Yth Grp; Var Crs Cntry; Var Trk; Hon Roll; NHS; Spanish NHS.

RICHMOND, SUSAN; Wall Township HS; Wall, NJ; (S); 5/270; German Clb; Ski Clb; Concert Band; Mrchg Band; High Hon Roll.

RICHTER, KENDRA; Chatham Township HS; Chatham Tup, NJ; (Y); GAA; Key Clb; Pep Clb; Varsity Clb; Yrbk Phtg; Yrbk Stf; Lcrss; Socr; Tennis; Hon Roll; Acctng.

RICKANSRUD, KYLE; Eastern Regional HS; Voorhees, NJ; (Y); 47/306; Pres Church Yth Grp; Hosp Aide; Church Choir; Drm Mjr(t); Mrchg Band; School Musical; All ST Symphonic Band 83-85; All S Jersey Symphonic Band 83-86; Music Medallian Recpnt 83-85; Sci.

RICKE, THOMAS; Morris Catholic HS; Bridgewater, NJ; (Y); 35/142; JV Socr; JV Wrstlng; Church Yth Grp; French Clb; German Clb; Natl Beta Clb; Scholastic Bowl; Hon Roll; Bus Admin.

RICKENS, KEN; Don Bosco Prep; Wayne, NJ; (Y); Drama Clb; Model UN; Quiz Bowl; School Musical; School Play; Yrbk Ed-Chief; Lit Mag; Var Crs Cntry; JV Trk; Le Moyne Coll; Pre-Law.

RICKERT, CAROLYN; Vineland HS; Vineland, NJ; (Y); 127/804; 4-H; Key Clb; JV Fld Hcky; Stat Wrstlng; 4-H Awd; Phys Thrpy.

RICKERT, DAVID; Toms River HS East; Toms River, NJ; (Y); Boy Scts; Chess Clb; Church Yth Grp; Exploring; Ski Clb; Yrbk Stf; Var L Swmmng; Eagle Sct 86; Ocean County Coll; Vet.

RICUCCI, JILL; Paul VI Regional HS; Clifton, NJ; (Y); 25/130; School Musical; Bsktbl; Score Keeper; High Hon Roll; Hon Roll; Spanish NHS; Comm.

RIDER, JOAN; Riverside HS; Riverside, NJ; (Y); Key Clb; Stu Cncl; Var Capt Bsktbl; Stat Ftbl; Var Sftbl; Sec.

RIDGWAY, PAUL H; Cumberland Regional HS; Bridgeton, NJ; (Y); Church Yth Grp; Hon Roll; Prfct Atten Awd; Rutgers; Elctrcl Engrng.

RIDOLFO, ROD; Montville Township HS; Montville, NJ; (Y); 120/263; Computer Clb; Key Clb; JV Var Bsbl; Im L Bsktbl; Hon Roll; AZ ST U; Bus.

RIEBEL, CHRISTINE; Camden Catholic HS; Pennsauken, NJ; (Y); FBLA; Temple Yth Grp; Drill Tm; Sftbl; Hon Roll; Leadership Award For Future Secretaries 86; Elem Educ.

RIECK, KRISTINA; Millville SR HS; Millville, NJ; (Y); Exploring; FTA; SADD; Jazz Band; Mrchg Band; Rep Stu Cncl; Bsktbl; NHS; Church Yth Grp; Pep Clb; Drum Capt Marchng Band 85-86; Phys Ed Ldrs Clb 83-84 & 85-86; Cumberland Cnty Coll Wind Symphny 84-86; Norwich U; Pol Sci.

RIEDER, ELIZABETH; Union HS; Union, NJ; (Y); 59/450; Church Yth Grp; Ski Clb; Spanish Clb; L Stat Ftbl; L Var Sftbl; Hon Roll; Jr NHS; VFW Awd; FBLA; Girl Scts; Outstndg Am Hist Stud 86; Union HS Schl PTA Schlrshp 86; Union County Coll; Dental Hyg.

RIEGER, LORI; Cumberland Regional HS; Bridgeton, NJ; (S); 9/369; Art Clb; Church Yth Grp; Drama Clb; Pres Intnl Clb; School Play; Stage Crew; Yrbk Rptr; High Hon Roll; Jr NHS; NHS; Pol Sci.

RIEGLER, DAVID; Toms River HS North; Toms River, NJ; (Y); Chess Clb; Debate Tm; Math Tm; Science Clb; Ntl Merit Ltr; Mth.

RIEHLE, LEILANI; Edgewood Regional HS; Sicklerville, NJ; (Y); #1 In Class; Pres Latin Clb; Library Aide; Stage Crew; Nwsp Rptr; Yrbk Stf; Rep Jr Cls; JV Socr; High Hon Roll; NHS; Ntl Merit SF; Rutgers Schlr 85-86; Schl Nom Senate-Japan Exchg Pgm 85.

RIEHMAN, EILEEN; Holy Cross HS; Mount Laurel, NJ; (Y); 33/375; School Musical; Rep Stu Cncl; JV Crs Cntry; Mgr(s); Hon Roll; Most Imprvd Crss Cty 84-85; Outstndng Rep Awd 85-86.

RIESER, TERRI; Middle Township HS; Avalon, NJ; (Y); Am Leg Aux Girls St; Computer Clb; Exploring; Sec Key Clb; Stage Crew; Nwsp Ed-Chief; Hon Roll; NHS; Ntl Merit Ltr; Vet Med.

RIGBERG, LORI; Cherry Hill H S West; Cherry Hill, NJ; (Y); Drama Clb; PAVAS; School Play; Nwsp Stf; Lit Mag; Soph Cls; Sr Cls; Cheerleading; NHS; Ntl Merit SF; NYU; Comm.

RIGGI, JOHN; John P Stevens HS; Edison, NJ; (Y); JV Bsbl; Var L Ftbl; Spanish NHS; U DE; Bus.

RIGGINS, DANIEL A; Williamstown HS; Williamstown, NJ; (Y); 56/163; Rep Frsh Cls; Var Capt Bsktbl; Var Capt Socr; Carini Awd Soccr; MVP Soccr 86; Most Imrpvd Bsktbl Coach Awd 86; Glassboro ST Clg.

RIGGIONE, GINA; Sacred Heart HS; Vineland, NJ; (S); 9/67; VP French Clb; Hosp Aide; School Play; Yrbk Stf; Mgr Sftbl; Co-Capt Tennis; Hon Roll; Pres NHS; Ms Sprt Grls Tnns Awd 82-83; Hlth Creers Clb Treas 83-86; Phy Thrpst.

RIGSBEE, AUDREY; Camden HS; Camden, NJ; (Y); 29/408; Hosp Aide; VP JA; Model UN; Chorus; Church Choir; Mrchg Band; Ed Nwsp Stf; Ed Yrbk Stf; Mgr(s); Tennis; MBS Readers Awd 81-82; Engl Merit Acknwldgmnt 84-85; Drew U; Engl.

RIKER, TAMMY; Passaic Valley HS; Little Falls, NJ; (Y); Key Clb; Ski Clb; Spanish Clb; Hon Roll; E Stroudsburg U; Elem Ed.

RILEY, ANN; Pennsauken HS; Pennsauken, NJ; (Y); Aud/Vis; DECA; Sec Library Aide; Spanish Clb; Chorus; Hon Roll; Prfct Atten Awd; Lacrs Mngr 82-84; Secr Lbry Cncl 82-85; Awd Outstndng Prfrmnc Lbry Cncl 86.

RILEY, CHRISSY; Eastern HS; West Berlin, NJ; (Y); 68/380; Civic Clb; Cmnty Wkr; SADD; Varsity Clb; Variety Show; Cheerleading; Trk; Hon Roll; Outstndng Weight Persn Awd Javelin Thrower & Trk 85; Marine Phy Fitns Awds 84-86; Nrsng.

RILEY, JOHN; North Warren Regional HS; Columbia, NJ; (Y); 10/128; CAP; Ski Clb; JV Crs Cntry; JV Wrstlng; Hon Roll; NHS; Navy; Pilot.

RILEY, KIMBERLY; Red Bank Catholic HS; Neptune, NJ; (Y); Cmnty Wkr; Service Clb; L Flag Corp; L Stat Crs Cntry; L Swmmng; L Trk; NEDT Awd; Exploring; Math Clb; Political Wkr; Girls Ctzns Inst Dely NJ ST Fed Wmns Clbs 86; Stockton ST Sci Fair 2dn Pl Med Sci 85; Intl Rltns.

RILEY, LEAH; Hillside HS; Hillside, NJ; (Y); 7/223; Cmnty Wkr; Math Tm; Var Capt Bsktbl; Var Capt Sftbl; Var Trk; High Hon Roll; Hon Roll; NHS; 1st Tm All ST Bsktbl, All Cnty Bsktbl 86; 1st Tm All Metro 85 & 86; Rutgers Coll Engrng; Engr.

RILEY, SUSAN; Cumberland Regional HS; Bridgeton, NJ; (S); 6/403; Yrbk Stf; JV Fld Hcky; Var L Sftbl; High Hon Roll; Hon Roll; NHS.

RILVERIA, MARJORIE; St Marys HS; Sayreville, NJ; (Y); 31/130; Library Aide; Spanish Clb; Var JV Cheerleading; Hon Roll; Bus.

RIMILI, DAVID; Hamilton High West; Yardville, NJ; (S); 40/340; Computer Clb; Exploring; Math Clb; Concert Band; Mrchg Band; Pep Band; Var Co-Capt Swmmng; Elctrcl Engrng.

RINALDI, CHRISTOPHER J; River Dell SR HS; Oradell, NJ; (Y); Am Leg Boys St; Ski Clb; SADD; Varsity Clb; Var Capt Ftbl; Im Vllybl; 1st Tm All Lg BCSL Ftbl 85-86; Hon Mntn All Cnty 85-86; All Sbrbn Ftbl 85-86.

RINALDI, SERENA; Middletown South HS; Lincroft, NJ; (S); 27/440; SADD; Nwsp Rptr; Yrbk Phtg; Lit Mag; Rep Frsh Cls; Stat Fld Hcky; Mgr(s); Stat Sftbl; High Hon Roll; Hon Roll; Outstndg Achvt Awds Hnrs Bio & Spnsh III; Rutgers Coll; Optmtrst.

RINALDI, STEVEN; Union HS; Union, NJ; (Y); Church Yth Grp; Ski Clb; Band; Church Choir; Yrbk Stf; Var Tennis; Exmplry Achvt Awd Arch 85-86; NJ Crftsmns Fair 2nd Pl Mdl 85-86; Sci.

RINCON, MARIA E; Paterson Catholic HS; Paterson, NJ; (Y); Art Clb; English Clb; French Clb; Sftbl; Hon Roll; Berkely Bus Schl; Bus Admin.

RING, SHEILA; Red Bank Cath; Colts Neck, NJ; (Y); 17/300; Church Yth Grp; French Clb; Stage Crew; Nwsp Sprt Ed; Nwsp Stf; Var Crs Cntry; Var Trk; Hon Roll; NHS; NEDT Awd; Exchng Stu Yth For Undrstndng Corp Schlrshp 86; Cross Cnty 100 PCT Coach Awd 84.

RINGLE, JEFF; West Essex SR HS; Fairfield, NJ; (Y); Science Clb; Acpl Chr; Chorus; Swing Chorus; Variety Show; Im JV Bsbl; Im Bsktbl; Im JV Ftbl; Im Vllybl; Hon Roll; U Of FL; Vet Med.

RINKE, JOAN; Palisades Park HS; Palisades Pk, NJ; (Y); Yrbk Stf; Trs Stu Cncl; Stat Bsbl; Mat Maids; Stat Wrstlng.

RINKEL, PATRICIA A; Sussex County Vo-Tech; Montague, NJ; (S); #19 In Class; Drama Clb; Library Aide; SADD; School Play; Stage Crew; Yrbk Stf; Rep Frsh Cls; Rep Soph Cls; Rep Jr Cls; Rep Sr Cls; 3rd Pl Cty WIDE Essay Cntst 85.

RINKOWSKI, KIM; Pinelands Regional HS; Tuckerton, NJ; (Y); 10/192; JV Sftbl; Hon Roll; NHS; Physcl Thrpy.

RIOLA, CHERYL; Union Catholic Regional HS; Hillside, NJ; (Y); Chess Clb; Dance Clb; Drama Clb; French Clb; PAVAS; Red Cross Aide; Service Clb; Spanish Clb; Teachers Aide; School Musical; Italn Natl Hnr Socty 86; Italn Awd 86; Pres Law Clb 86; Rutgers U; Intl Law.

RIOS, LILLIAN; Barringer HS; Newark, NJ; (Y); Boy Scts; Dance Clb; Exploring; FNA; Hosp Aide; Library Aide; Science Clb; SADD; Teachers Aide; Temple Yth Grp; Rutgers Coll; Nrsg.

RIOS, NANCY; West Side HS; Newark, NJ; (Y); Computer Clb; Dance Clb; Debate Tm; JA; Spanish Clb; Bausch & Lomb Sci Awd; Cit Awd; Hon Roll; NHS; Music Awd 83; Outstndng Soph 84-85; Rutgers U; Paralegal.

RIPPON, NAOMI; West Orange HS; W Orange, NJ; (Y); JV L Bsktbl; Var L Mgr(s); Var L Score Keeper; Var L Sftbl; Hon Roll; Schlr Athl Awd 83-84.

RISE, WENDY; Shore Regional HS; Oceanport, NJ; (Y); Science Clb; School Musical; Var Cheerleading; Var Tennis; Capt Var Trk; High Hon Roll; Pres NHS; Cmnty Wkr; Math Clb; Stage Crew; SF Japan US Senate Scholar Pgm 86; HOBY Fndtn Ldrshp Sem Ambssdr 85; Congrssnl Awd 86; SGA Hnr 85; U VA; Sci.

RISELEY, MITZI K; Barnstable Acad; Hawthorne, NJ; (Y); Cmnty Wkr; Dance Clb; Ski Clb; Teachers Aide; Wt Lftg; High Hon Roll; Val; Math,Engl Lit,Frnch Awds 83-86; Barnstable Acad Schrlshp Awd 86.

RISLEY, DAWN MARIE; Egg Harbor Township HS; Cardiff, NJ; (S); 6/317; Ski Clb; Rep Stu Cncl; JV Bsktbl; Var Crs Cntry; JV Trk; High Hon Roll; Jr NHS; Ntl Ldrshp Merit Awd; Schlstc Ltr Awd; Corp Lawyer.

RISPOLI, VICTOR; Arthur L Johnson HS; Clark, NJ; (S); 148/226; Drama Clb; Chorus; School Musical; School Play; Stage Crew; JV Bsktbl; Var Bowling; Bowlng State Chmps 84-85; St Peters Coll.

RISSMEYER, DONALD J; West Milford Twp HS; West Milford, NJ; (Y); 3/350; Am Leg Boys St; Debate Tm; Model UN; Quiz Bowl; Varsity Clb; Trs Stu Cncl; Var Capt Socr; Var Capt Trk; High Hon Roll; NHS; U VA; Engrng.

RITCHIE, JENNIFER; Lakewood HS; Lakewood, NJ; (Y); Dance Clb; English Clb; French Clb; Keywanettes; Chorus; School Musical; Var Co-Capt Cheerleading; Var Socr; MD U; Intrnatl Rel.

RITTENHOUSE, ELIZABETH; Point Pleasant Borough HS; Point Pleasant, NJ; (S); 9/250; VP Keywanettes; Varsity Clb; Chorus; Pres Soph Cls; Pres Jr Cls; Stu Cncl; Cheerleading; Fld Hcky; Powder Puff Ftbl; NHS; GS Slvr Awd 84; MVP Fld Hocky 85.

RITZ, JAMES; Hamilton High West; Yardville, NJ; (Y); CAP; School Musical; School Play; Hon Roll; Berkley Coll Of Music; Mscn.

RIVA, RICHARD; Seton Hall Prep; Millburn, NJ; (Y); 8/245; Church Yth Grp; Key Clb; Nwsp Rptr; VP Stu Cncl; Wt Lftg; Var Wrstlng; High Hon Roll; Pres NHS; Med.

RIVERA JR, ANGEL DAVID; Westfield HS; Westfield, NJ; (Y); Lit Mag; Im Bsbl; Ntl Merit SF; Piano Stu; Greenblt Karate 84; Engrng.

RIVERA, EDDIE; Hoboken HS; Hoboken, NJ; (Y); 31/303; Church Yth Grp; DECA.

RIVERA, ELIZABETH; Our Lady Of Good Counsel HS; Newark, NJ; (Y); 12/77; Church Yth Grp; Church Choir; School Play; Hon Roll; Trs NHS; Val; Stage Crew; Sci Awd 84; FL Stheastrn Coll.

RIVERA, JOHN J; Memorial HS; W New York, NJ; (Y); 63/367; Cmnty Wkr; Rep Stu Cncl; Capt Bsbl; Capt Bsktbl; Capt Ftbl; Cit Awd; Hon Roll; Masonic Awd; Alumni Awd 86; Barry Sherman Mrl Awd 86; Mr Hunanity Awd 86; Rutgers U; Cmmnctns.

RIVERA, KATHERINE; Emerson HS; Union City, NJ; (Y); 112/277; Cmnty Wkr; Political Wkr; Chorus; Color Guard; Lit Mag; Rep Jr Cls; Rep Sr Cls; Twrlr; Am Leg Aux Girls St; Intnl Clb; Rifles & Silks-Outstnding Mbr 84-85; Coord Committee Union City 60th Annvrsry Celebration 86; Rutger U; Polit Sci.

RIVERA, LUIS; Manalapan HS; Englishtown, NJ; (Y); Boy Scts; Church Yth Grp; Comp Sci Meteorology.

RIVERA, MIKE; Our Lady Of Good Counsel HS; Newark, NJ; (Y); 22/106; Boy Scts; Church Yth Grp; Cmnty Wkr; Debate Tm; Drama Clb; Red Cross Aide; Acpl Chr; Church Choir; Var Bsktbl; NHS.

RIVERA, TONY; River Dell SR HS; River Edge, NJ; (S); Boy Scts; Church Yth Grp; Cmnty Wkr; SADD; Teachers Aide; Band; Chorus; Church Choir; Concert Band; Jazz Band; CYO Rep 85-86; CCD Tchr 85-86; Music Minster 80-86; Prof Musicn.

RIVERS, MARILYN; Lincoln HS; Jersey City, NJ; (Y); Dance Clb; Drama Clb; JA; Key Clb; Mgr Bsktbl; Capt Pom Pon; Cit Awd; Prfct Atten Awd; Rotary Awd; Blck Unity Soc Clb 84-87; Strutters Sqd 84-87; Stu Cousely Homeroom Rep 84-86; Drama.

RIVERS, TIFFANY; University HS; Newark, NJ; (Y); Church Yth Grp; Cmnty Wkr; Dance Clb; Debate Tm; Drama Clb; Girl Scts; JA; Leo Clb; Math Clb; Model UN; Colr Purpl Awd, JR Achvt Awd & Hlth Awd 86; Fshn Inst Of Tech Awd 86; Cnslr In Trng Awd 85; Fshn Inst Of Tech; Fshn Buyng.

RIZZA, MICHELLE; Clifton HS; Clifton, NJ; (Y); Key Clb; Chorus; Yrbk Stf; Sec Jr Cls; Mgr Ftbl; Stat Mgr(s); Score Keeper; Hon Roll; Jr NHS; Stockton ST Pamona; Cmnctns.

RIZZO, CHRISTINE; Ocean City HS; Sea Isle City, NJ; (Y); Church Yth Grp; French Clb; Rep Stu Cncl; Var Crs Cntry; Mgr(s); Capt Powder Puff Ftbl; JV Var Trk; Wt Lftg; Cape May Cnty Art Lge 2nd Pl Wnnr 86; Teene Hmsphre Model Of Cape May Cnty 86; Crmnl Lawyer.

RIZZO, FRANK; St James HS; Gibbstown, NJ; (Y); Varsity Clb; Trs Frsh Cls; JV Bsbl; Var Bsktbl; JV Var Ftbl; Villanova U; Psych.

RIZZUTO, GLORIA; Gateway Regional HS; Wenonah, NJ; (Y); 16/197; French Clb; Key Clb; Rep Stu Cncl; Capt Var Cheerleading; JV Fld Hcky; French Hon Soc; Hon Roll; NHS; Church Yth Grp; Dance Clb; Glassboro ST Coll; Frnch Educ.

ROA, HELEN; Memorial HS; West New York, NJ; (Y); Teachers Aide; Nwsp Stf; Var Bowling; Var Sftbl; Var Tennis; Hon Roll; All Cnty Grls Tnns 85-86; Cert Achvt Entrng Wll Wrttn Edtrl To TV Sttn Cntst 86; Engl.

ROACH, GARY; Middle Township HS; Rio Grande, NJ; (Y); 18/250; Am Leg Boys St; Boy Scts; Exploring; Quiz Bowl; Mrchg Band; Var L Socr; Hon Roll; NHS; Engrng.

ROANE, VALVIN; Paulsboro HS; Paulsboro, NJ; (Y); Art Clb; JA; Chorus; School Musical; School Play; Stage Crew; JV Var Bsktbl; JV Var Ftbl; Hon Roll; Stu Of Mth 84; South Jersey Chorus 83-86; All St Chorus 84; Elec Engrng.

ROARKE, SUSAN; Cumberland Regional HS; Bridgeton, NJ; (Y); 17/390; Hosp Aide; Latin Clb; Office Aide; Ski Clb; Sec Soph Cls; Sec Jr Cls; High Hon Roll; Hon Roll; NHS; Med.

ROAYAIE, KAYVAN; Hightstown HS; Cranbury, NJ; (Y); Church Yth Grp; Var Crs Cntry; Var Trk; High Hon Roll.

ROBART, FORREST; Linden HS; Linden, NJ; (S); Key Clb; Science Clb; Ski Clb; Madrigals; Mrchg Band; School Musical; Rep Soph Cls; Swmmng; High Hon Roll; NHS; Chem.

ROBE, SUSAN; Bridgewater-Paritan HS East; Basking Ridge, NJ; (Y); 13/266; German Clb; Intnl Clb; Off Jr Cls; Off Sr Cls; Powder Puff Ftbl; Var L Sftbl; NHS; Ntl Merit Ltr; Pres Schlr; St Schlr; Seton Hall U; Finance.

ROBERSON, TRAVELON; Weequahic HS; Newark, NJ; (S); 2/354; Exploring; French Clb; Teachers Aide; Yrbk Stf; French Hon Soc; Hon Roll; NHS; Sal; Rutgers U; Elec Engr.

ROBERSON, VERONICA; Lincoln HS; Jersey City, NJ; (Y); Key Clb; Var Cheerleading; Christ Hosp; Nrsng.

ROBERTO, MICHELLE ANN; Watchung Hills Regional HS; Stirling, NJ; (Y); 46/315; Church Yth Grp; French Clb; GAA; Key Clb; SADD; Nwsp Rptr; Nwsp Stf; Lit Mag; Off Jr Cls; JV Bsktbl; Intl Rel.

ROBERTO, STEVEN; Passaic Valley Regional HS; Totowa, NJ; (Y); 75/360; Bsktbl; Var L Ftbl; Var L Trk; Passaic Valley Hon Soc 86; Bio.

ROBERTS, AMY; Deptford HS; Deptford, NJ; (Y); Church Yth Grp; Girl Scts; Chorus; Stage Crew; Socr; High Hon Roll; Hon Roll; Jr NHS; NHS; Bus Adm.

ROBERTS, AUDREY; Newton HS; Newton, NJ; (S); 17/200; German Clb; Varsity Clb; Band; Yrbk Ed-Chief; Rep Soph Cls; Rep Jr Cls; Rep Sr Cls; Trs Stu Cncl; Var Capt Bsktbl; Var Crs Cntry; Hmcmng Crt 85; Rutgers; Bus.

ROBERTS, BEVERLY; Plainfield HS; Plainfield, NJ; (Y); Dance Clb; Thesps; Mrchg Band; School Musical; School Play; Lit Mag; Rep Jr Cls; Hon Roll; Jr NHS; Prfct Atten Awd; Minor Engrg 82-86; New Horizons Clg Clb 85-86; Hampton U; Bus Adm.

ROBERTS, CAROLE MELISSA; Middletown HS North; Belford, NJ; (Y); 25/420; Am Leg Aux Girls St; Variety Show; Nwsp Phtg; Nwsp Rptr; Cheerleading; Crs Cntry; NHS; Acadmc All Am 86; Osborne Schlrshp 86; Marist Coll; Communications.

ROBERTS, CHARLENE; Hillside HS; Hillside, NJ; (Y); Concert Band; Mrchg Band; Trk; Hon Roll; NHS; Dlgt Grls Ctznshp Inst 86; Prtcpnt Rtgrs Smmr Engnrng 86; Rutgers; Bus.

ROBERTS, COLIN A; Hillside HS; Hillside, NJ; (Y); 3/214; Church Yth Grp; Computer Clb; Math Tm; Science Clb; School Play; Trs Stu Cncl; Elks Awd; Lion Awd; NHS; Ntl Merit Ltr; Pa Rizzuto, Tp 5 Hnr Stdnt Awds, Cngrssnl Smnr 86; Brown U; Pre Med.

ROBERTS, JENEE; Essex County Vocational HS; Newark, NJ; (Y); #22 In Class; FBLA; FHA; Yale U; Acctnt.

ROBERTS, JENNIFER; Morris Knolls HS; Rockaway, NJ; (Y); FBLA; Chorus; Katherine Gibbs Ldrshp Awd 86; Intr Dectr.

ROBERTS, LISA; Elmwood Park Memorial HS; Elmwood Pk, NJ; (Y); Girl Scts; Hon Roll; Cmptr Prcssr.

ROBERTS, RENE L; St Patricks HS; Elizabeth, NJ; (Y); 1/45; Science Clb; Chorus; School Musical; Nwsp Stf; Yrbk Stf; Lit Mag; VP Stu Cncl; Capt Cheerleading; Hon Roll; NHS; NJ Distngshd Schlr 85; Cmmnded Stu Natl Mert Schlrshp-Ngro Stus 85; Med.

ROBERTS, SHERYL; Pennsville Memorial HS; Pennsville, NJ; (Y); 15/210; Office Aide; Rep Jr Cls; Hon Roll; NHS; U Of Cntrl FL; Acctng.

ROBERTS, STEVE; Newark Central HS; Newark, NJ; (Y); Bsktbl; Ftbl; Trk; Hon Roll; Rugters New Brunswick; Engrng.

ROBERTS, TINA J; Middle Township HS; Dennisville, NJ; (Y); 32/189; Dance Clb; Concert Band; Mrchg Band; Sr Cls; Stu Cncl; Socr; Wt Lftg; Hon Roll; Roay A Kroc Ytha Cad Achvt Awd 86; Polish Amer Clb Savgs Bnd Awd 86; Cape May Cnty Ed Sec Svgs Bnd 86; Goldeny Beacom Coll; Legl Sec.

ROBERTS, WANDA; Orange HS; Orange, NJ; (S); 22/182; Church Yth Grp; Drama Clb; Chorus; Church Choir; Sec Frsh Cls; Rep Soph Cls; Rep Jr Cls; Rep Sr Cls; Rep Stu Cncl; Bowling; Bus Admin.

ROBERTSON, CORWIN; Dwight Morrow HS; Englewood, NJ; (Y); Exploring; Hosp Aide; Math Tm; Spanish Clb; Lit Mag; VP Frsh Cls; Trs Soph Cls; Var Crs Cntry; NHS; Latin Clb; Bst Bill Modl Congrss 86; Law Clb Sec 86-87; Med.

ROBERTSON, HEATHER; Kearny HS; Kearny, NJ; (Y); Art Clb; German Clb; GAA; Hosp Aide; Latin Clb; Nwsp Phtg; JV Cheerleading; Powder Puff Ftbl; JV Var Socr; Hon Roll; V Wesleyan Coll; Photo Journlsm.

ROBERTSON, JANET; A P Schalick HS; Bridgeton, NJ; (Y); 5/131; Math Tm; Band; Concert Band; Mrchg Band; Rep Soph Cls; Rep Jr Cls; Stu Cncl; High Hon Roll; Hon Roll; NHS; Math.

ROBERTSON, PAMELA; Haddon Twp HS; Haddonfield, NJ; (Y); Am Leg Aux Girls St; Debate Tm; Chorus; Madrigals; School Musical; Var Gym; High Hon Roll; Sec NHS; Ntl Merit Ltr; Rutgers U Smmr Schlr 86; S Jersey Chorus 85-86; Modern Music Masters 86.

ROBERTSON, SCOTT C; The Pingry Schl; Scotch Plains, NJ; (Y); Chess Clb; German Clb; Ski Clb; Acpl Chr; Jazz Band; Orch; Var L Crs Cntry; Var L Trk; Hon Roll; Ntl Merit SF; Ctr Advncmnt Acadmclly Tlntd Yth Spnsrd J Hopkins U 83-85; Physcs.

ROBICHAUD, MICHAEL; Verona HS; Verona, NJ; (Y); Band; Concert Band; Drm Mjr(t); Jazz Band; Mrchg Band; School Play; Swmmng; Tennis; All N Jersey HS Symphnc Bnd 86; NJ All State HS Symphnc Bnd 86; US Naval Acad; Naval Ofcr.

ROBINETTE, SHARON; Morris Knolls HS; Branchville, NJ; (Y); 27/383; Latin Clb; High Hon Roll; Hon Roll; Awds In Algebra I & Latn 83-84; Germn Awd 85-86.

ROBINS, STEVE; James Caldwell HS; W Caldwell, NJ; (Y); Am Leg Boys St; Yrbk Ed-Chief; VP Jr Cls; Pres Sr Cls; JV Trk; High Hon Roll; NHS; Cmnty Wkr; Nwsp Rptr; Rep Frsh Cls; Mst Outstndg Stu Awd 84; Pres Phys Fit Awd 84; Pres Mar Biol Clb 87; Ivy Lg Schl; Radlgy.

ROBINSON, BRETT; Dwight Englewood Schl; Englewood, NJ; (Y); Church Yth Grp; Nwsp Stf; Var Trk; Var Wrstlng; Hon Roll; Ntl Merit SF; Jnthn Wedeck Mem Schlrshp 86; Brown U; Med.

ROBINSON, BRIAN; Colonia SR HS; Avenel, NJ; (Y); Chess Clb; French Clb; SADD; Hon Roll; U Hartford; Sci.

ROBINSON, CAROLE D; Burlington City HS; Edgewater Park, NJ; (Y); Am Leg Aux Girls St; Cmnty Wkr; Stu Cncl; Cheerleading; Mgr(s); Score Keeper; Timer; Albrght Coll; Lawyer.

ROBINSON, CIAN; Newton HS; Andover, NJ; (S); 9/210; Latin Clb; Math Tm; Science Clb; Symp Band; JV Bsbl; JV Bsktbl; L Socr; Hon Roll; NHS; Ntl Sci Olympd 1st Bio 83-84; Engr.

ROBINSON, CLARENCE; Woodstown HS; Elmer, NJ; (Y); Spanish Clb; Nwsp Rptr; Yrbk Bus Mgr; Yrbk Rptr; Yrbk Stf; Im Vllybl; High Hon Roll; Hon Roll; NHS; Vllybl Chmpns 84-85; Comp.

ROBINSON, HEIDI; Middle Twp HS; Dennisville, NJ; (Y); Church Yth Grp; Band; Concert Band; Mrchg Band; Yrbk Stf; Exec Secretary.

ROBINSON, JANELLE A; Pascack Valley Regional HS; Hillsdale, NJ; (Y); 86/256; French Clb; Thesps; Band; Chorus; Capt Color Guard; Concert Band; Drill Tm; Madrigals; School Musical; School Play; Garden ST Tlnt Expo Fnlst 86; Tlnt Schlrshp Hartt Schl Mus 86; PFO Tlnt Awd 85; Hartt Schl Music; Mus Theatre.

ROBINSON, JOEL D; Haddon Heights HS; Haddon Heights, NJ; (Y); Am Leg Boys St; Church Yth Grp; Chorus; Church Choir; Mrchg Band; School Musical; Hon Roll; NHS; Drama Clb; French Clb; Jack Robinson Meml Awd 83; Summer Abrd France 86; Sen Bill Bradley Citznshp Awd 86; Bus.

ROBINSON, KAREN; Pope Paul VI HS; Turnersville, NJ; (S); 128/500; Sec Jr Cls; Rep Stu Cncl; Var L Bsktbl; Var L Crs Cntry; JV Fld Hcky; All S Jersey Bsktbl Hon Men 85; All Parochial Bsktbl 2nd Tm 85; Street & Smiths H S All Amer Hon Men; Spts Med.

ROBINSON, KELLI; Delran HS; Delran, NJ; (Y); 13/214; Cmnty Wkr; Pres French Clb; School Musical; School Play; Lit Mag; Tennis; Hon Roll; SW ST U; Bio.

ROBINSON, KELLY; Academic HS; Jersey City, NJ; (Y); Off Am Leg Aux Girls St; English Clb; Scholastic Bowl; Nwsp Rptr; Yrbk Stf; Pres Stu Cncl; Vllybl; Hon Roll; Jr NHS; Voice Dem Awd; Knghts Pyths Awd Pstv Thnkng Spch 86; Boston U; Cmnctns.

ROBINSON, KELLY; Roselle Catholic HS; Carteret, NJ; (S); 10/207; Ski Clb; Yrbk Stf; Rep Frsh Cls; Rep Soph Cls; Sec Stu Cncl; Var Crs Cntry; Var Trk; High Hon Roll; St Peters Smmr Schlr 85; Gentc Engr.

ROBINSON, KIER; Woodstown HS; Woodstown, NJ; (Y); Computer Clb; Varsity Clb; Var L Socr; Var L Swmmng; Var Capt Tennis; High Hon Roll; Hon Roll; NHS.

ROBINSON, KIMBERLY; Woodrown Wilson HS; Pennsauken, NJ; (Y); Dance Clb; FBLA; JA; Office Aide; Teachers Aide; Hon Roll; NHS; Chorus; Rep Frsh Cls; Schlstc Recog Awd 86; Bus.

ROBINSON, LEANNE; Southern Regional HS; Surf City, NJ; (Y); 70/317; Dance Clb; Frsh Cls; Soph Cls; Jr Cls; Sr Cls; Stu Cncl; DAR Awd; Hon Roll; Sec Bsbl; Var Ftbl; OCC; Phrmcy.

ROBINSON, MARY; Middle Twp HS; S Seaville, NJ; (Y); Band; Concert Band; Mrchg Band; Hon Roll; Acctg.

ROBINSON, MICHELLE RENEE; Kingsway Regional HS; Swedesboro, NJ; (Y); Key Clb; VICA; Flag Corp; Mrchg Band; Mgr(s); Comp Info Sys.

ROBINSON, OLGA; Woodstown HS; Woodstown, NJ; (Y); Church Yth Grp; French Clb; Office Aide; Teachers Aide; Hon Roll; NHS; JV Var Mgr(s); JV L Socr; JV Swmmng; Var L Tennis; Sci Fair 84-85; Early Childhd Educ.

ROBINSON JR, ROBERT; Camden HS; Camden, NJ; (S); 9/409; Capt Aud/Vis; Boy Scts; Church Yth Grp; Cmnty Wkr; Key Clb; Red Cross Aide; Concert Band; Ed Nwsp Rptr; High Hon Roll; NHS; Pres Fndr Cmnty Svc Clb 82; Theolgy.

ROBINSON, ROBYN; Middletown South HS; Middletown, NJ; (Y); Church Yth Grp; JV Var Coach Actv; Im Powder Puff Ftbl; Im Socr; Im Sftbl; Capt L Swmmng; Capt L Trk; Im Vllybl; Im Wt Lftg; Hon Roll; Wake Forest NC ST; Pre-Med.

ROBINSON, STEFANIE; Parsippany HS; Parsippany, NJ; (Y); FBLA; Pep Clb; Spanish Clb; Varsity Clb; Trs Frsh Cls; Trs Soph Cls; Capt Var Cheerleading; JV Sftbl; Hon Roll; NHS; Acad All Amer 86; Bus.

ROBINSON, TRACY; Brick Twp HS; Brick Town, NJ; (Y); 130/430; Key Clb; Yrbk Stf; Stu Cncl; Socr; Tennis.

ROBINSON, VICKI RENEE; Bridgeton SR HS; Bridgeton, NJ; (Y); Church Yth Grp; Cmnty Wkr; Drama Clb; Hosp Aide; Spanish Clb; Chorus; Church Choir; School Musical; Trk; Hon Roll; Glassboro ST Coll; Comp Sci.

ROBISON, BILL; Northern Burlington C R HS; Bordentown, NJ; (Y); 4-H; FFA; Var Bsbl; Var L Ftbl; Var L Tennis; Var L Wrstlng; 4-H Awd; Hon Roll; NBC Bus Drivers Awd 86; Marlin Essay Awd-1st St 82-83; NHS Spec Ag & Ind Arts Awd 83-85; U Of AR; Ind Arts.

ROBLES, ROSEMARIE; Abraham Clark HS; Roselle, NJ; (Y); FNA; Hosp Aide; Rep Jr Cls; RN.

ROBSON, ALICIA; Nutley HS; Nutley, NJ; (Y); 30/350; Trs VP Church Yth Grp; Sec French Clb; Key Clb; Ski Clb; Rep Stu Cncl; Stat Bsktbl; JV Mgr(s); JV Score Keeper; Hon Roll; Health Sci.

ROCCA, MARIA DELLA; Immaculate Conception HS; Lodi, NJ; (Y); 15/90; Chorus; School Musical; Yrbk Stf; JV Sftbl; High Hon Roll; Hon Roll; Prfct Atten Awd; Cert NEDT 84; NYU; Denstry.

ROCCATO, DARIA; Washington Township HS; Turnersville, NJ; (Y); Spanish Clb; Varsity Clb; Var Cheerleading; Im Gym; JV Mgr(s); JV Score Keeper; Hon Roll; Photo.

ROCCO, JAMES; Holy Cross HS; Edgewater Park, NJ; (Y); 43/392; Am Leg Boys St; Ski Clb; Capt Swmmng; High Hon Roll; Hon Roll; NHS; Swmmng Ntl Jr Olympics 85; Pre-Law.

ROCCO, MARY CATHERINE; Bricktownship HS; Brick, NJ; (Y); VP Girl Scts; SADD; Prfct Atten Awd; Gld Awd Gnl Scts Am 86; Hosa Hlth Org Stu Am 84-85; Nrsng.

ROCCO, RAFFAELE; John F Kennedy HS; Paterson, NJ; (Y); Am Leg Boys St; Church Yth Grp; Nwsp Ed-Chief; Nwsp Sprt Ed; Yrbk Stf; Rep Jr Cls; Capt L Socr; Var L Trk; High Hon Roll; NHS.

ROCHA, MARIA; East Side HS; Irvington, NJ; (Y); 64/420; Civic Clb; Office Aide; Chorus; Hon Roll; Sndy Schl Tchr 85-86; Rcgntn Awd Strdy Acad 85-86; Outstndng Stu Cvcs Clb 84-86; Hood; Bio.

ROCHA, MARIA; South River HS; S River, NJ; (Y); #20 In Class; Church Yth Grp; Pres French Clb; FNA; JV Bsktbl; Cit Awd; Dnfth Awd; Hon Roll; Awd Wrtg Essay On What Ctznshp Means To Me 86; Kean Coll; Phys Ther.

ROCHE, DONNA MARIE; Metuchen HS; Metuchen, NJ; (Y); 13/178; Church Yth Grp; DECA; French Clb; Mathletes; JV Var Fld Hcky; French Hon Soc; High Hon Roll; Hon Roll; NHS; Tourn Exclnce TOE Tm 85-86; Genetic Engrng.

ROCHE, KRISTEN; Paul VI HS; Clementon, NJ; (S); 12/476; Hosp Aide; Math Clb; Mrchg Band; Variety Show; Sec Sr Cls; Bowling; Trk; Hon Roll; NHS; Politics.

ROCK, LISA; Howell HS; Howell, NJ; (Y); 8/347; Math Clb; Rep Sr Cls; Stat Bsktbl; Score Keeper; JV Sftbl; High Hon Roll; Hon Roll; NHS; Rutgers Clg; Nrsg.

ROCKER, BRANDON F; Memorial HS; Leonia, NJ; (Y); Tennis; Hon Roll.

ROCKHOLD, KIM; Absegami HS; Absecon, NJ; (Y); 40/237; Church Yth Grp; French Clb; SADD; Band; Mrchg Band; Yrbk Stf; High Hon Roll; Hon Roll; Ntl Hnr Roll 83-84; Pncpls Hrn Roll 83-84; IN Inst; Chem Engrng.

ROCKLIFF, MARA; Solomon Schechter Day Schl; Cranford, NJ; (Y); Capt Chess Clb; Nwsp Ed-Chief; Ed Lit Mag; NHS; Ntl Merit SF; NEDT Awd; Drama Clb; Temple Yth Grp; Church Choir; School Play; NJ Poetry Cont HS Div-1st Pl ,K, Hon Mntn 86; Schltc Wrtg Awds 3rd Pl 86; Merit Schlrshp Rutgers 86; Oberlin Coll; Engl.

ROCKMAN, DAVID A; Jonathan Dayton Regional HS; Springfield, NJ; (Y); #3 In Class; Boy Scts; Cmnty Wkr; Sec Computer Clb; Rep Key Clb; Sec Radio Clb; Science Clb; Hon Roll; NHS; Ntl Merit SF; St Schlr; Ger Hnr Soc 83; Semi-Fnlst Cngrss Bundestag Exch Pgm 84; 3rd Pl Chem Mth Day 82; Sci.

ROCOURT, MARISSA; East Orange HS; East Orange, NJ; (S); 1/403; French Clb; Nwsp Stf; Yrbk Stf; Lit Mag; Bowling; Capt Tennis; High Hon Roll; Hon Roll; Val; Garden ST Schlr; Rutgers U; Phy.

RODAMMER, STACEY; High Point Reg HS; Branchville, NJ; (Y); 21/215; 4-H; Ski Clb; SADD; Band; Concert Band; Jazz Band; Mrchg Band; School Musical; Stage Crew; Symp Band; Schrlshp 86; U UT; Phrmcy.

RODDA, RANDALL D; Immaculata HS; Green Brook, NJ; (Y); Boy Scts; Church Yth Grp; Cmnty Wkr; Computer Clb; Letterman Clb; Ski Clb; Spanish Clb; JV Bsbl; Var Ftbl; Var Wt Lftg; Mrktng.

RODDY, BRIAN J; Christian Brothers Acad; Little Silver, NJ; (S); 3/225; Boy Scts; Camera Clb; Church Yth Grp; Math Tm; Stage Crew; Im Socr; High Hon Roll; NHS; High Scorer Am Math Cntst; Outstndng Achvt Catholic Math Leag; Engrng.

RODEN, ANNE; Oak Crest HS; Mays Landing, NJ; (Y); 1/250; Aud/Vis; Yrbk Ed-Chief; Yrbk Stf; Rep Soph Cls; Rep Jr Cls; Rep Stu Cncl; Var Capt Cheerleading; Bausch & Lomb Sci Awd; High Hon Roll; NHS; Phy Thrpy.

RODEN, PAUL; Oakcrest HS; Mays Landing, NJ; (Y); 7/300; Var L Bsbl; Var L Socr; Hon Roll; Jr NHS; NHS; Trenton St Coll; Elec Engr.

RODESCHIN, STEPHEN EDWARD; Holy Cross HS; Medford, NJ; (Y); 2/374; Model UN; Spanish Clb; Var Capt Tennis; High Hon Roll; Sal; US Military Acad; Poli Sci.

RODGERS, CHERYL; St Aloysius HS; Jersey City, NJ; (Y); 2/109; Church Choir; Yrbk Bus Mgr; Bsktbl; Coach Actv; High Hon Roll; Pres NHS; Ntl Merit Schol; Sal; St Schlr; Douglass Clg; CPA.

RODI, MARK; Bridgeton HS; Bridgeton, NJ; (Y); Cmnty Wkr; Letterman Clb; Political Wkr; Varsity Clb; Bsbl; Bsktbl; Socr; Hon Roll; MVP Bsbll; Coachs Awd Bsbll; Ldng Httr; U Of DE; Athltc Trnr.

RODLAND, CAROL E; Ridgewood HS; Ridgewood, NJ; (Y); 15/498; Church Yth Grp; PAVAS; Chorus; Church Choir; Orch; Cit Awd; Gov Hon Prg Awd; High Hon Roll; Jr NHS; NHS; Bergen Cnty Wrtng Cntst 1st Pl 85; Brown U Bk Awd Exclnc In Engl 85; Julian Paul Darby Engl Prize 86; The Juilliard Sch; Music.

RODRIGUES, ROSA; East Side HS; Newark, NJ; (Y); #8 In Class; NHS.

RODRIGUES, TONY; Elizabeth HS; Elizabeth, NJ; (Y); VP Political Wkr; Sprntndt Of Schls Schlr Awd 85-86; Prncpls Schlr Awds 1st & 2nd Mrkg Prds 85-86; Rutgers U; Elctrncl Engnr.

RODRIGUEZ, ANA; Orange HS; Orange, NJ; (S); 1/182; JA; Band; Mrchg Band; Rep Stu Cncl; High Hon Roll; Hon Roll; NHS; Val; Geomtry Awd 84; Inroads/NNJ Inc Hghst GPA & Perfect Attndnc 85; Finance.

RODRIGUEZ, ANTHONY L; Bishop George Ohr HS; Colonia, NJ; (Y); Art Clb; Computer Clb; Comp Sci.

RODRIGUEZ, CARMELA TRUEBA; East Side HS; Newark, NJ; (Y); 34/430; Civic Clb; Band; Concert Band; Orch; Nwsp Phtg; Nwsp Rptr; Yrbk Stf; Rep Jr Cls; Rep Sr Cls; Hon Roll; Montcalir ST Coll; Bus Adm.

RODRIGUEZ, CARMEN; Vineland HS; Vineland, NJ; (Y); Gregg Shrthnd Awd-90 WAM 86; Cert Of Prfcncy-Typwrtng 84.

RODRIGUEZ, ELSA; Union Hill HS; Union City, NJ; (Y); Math Clb; Science Clb; Spanish Clb; SADD; Flag Corp; JV Gym; Twrlr; High Hon Roll; Hon Roll; Spanish NHS; Bus Adm.

RODRIGUEZ, ENRIQUE; Oakcrest HS; Hammonton, NJ; (Y); 3/221; Sec Church Yth Grp; Civic Clb; Computer Clb; French Clb; Math Clb; Spanish Clb; Church Choir; School Play; Rep Stu Cncl; Jr NHS; Excllnc Math 86; U Of PA; Chem Engrng.

RODRIGUEZ, HECTOR; Good Counsel HS; Newark, NJ; (Y); 11/32; Art Clb; Chess Clb; FCA; Library Aide; SADD; Varsity Clb; Band; Concert Band; School Musical; Yrbk Phtg; Sprtsmnshp & Schl Helpr Awds 85; Arch.

RODRIGUEZ, JESSICA; Dover HS; Dover, NJ; (Y); Church Yth Grp; French Clb; Varsity Clb; Church Choir; Cheerleading; Hon Roll; Prfct Atten Awd; Psychlgy Hnr Stu 86; Typng Awd 85; Med.

RODRIGUEZ, JOSEPH; Vineland High School HS; Newfield, NJ; (Y); Art Clb; Library Aide; Spanish Clb; Rutgers Engrng Coll; Archit Eng.

RODRIGUEZ, LINDA; Emerson HS; Union City, NJ; (Y); Art Clb; Model UN; Co-Capt Color Guard; Yrbk Stf; Var Cheerleading; Hon Roll; Med.

RODRIGUEZ, MARIA; Bayonne HS; Bayonne, NJ; (Y); Spanish Clb; Teachers Aide; Katharine Gibbs; Sec.

RODRIGUEZ, MARIBEL; Trenton HS; Trenton, NJ; (Y); 16/400; Hon Roll; DE Vly Bus Co Scholar Awd 86; Puerto Rican Congress Awd 86; U Bridgeport; Law.

RODRIGUEZ, MINERVA; Vineland HS; Vineland, NJ; (Y); Church Yth Grp; Church Choir; Stage Crew; La Juventud Hispnc Tngrs Tkdng Actn 86; Coll Of St Elizabeth; Bus.

RODRIGUEZ, MORENA; Woodbridge HS; Keasbey, NJ; (Y); 79/350; French Clb; Spanish Clb; Badmtn; Golf; Sftbl; Tennis; Vllybl; French Hon Soc; Hon Roll; Comp Pgmng.

RODRIGUEZ, RAYMOND; Monsignor Donovan HS; Lakewood, NJ; (Y); 43/226; Hosp Aide; Ski Clb; Band; Church Choir; Jazz Band; Orch; School Musical; Var Bsbl; Im Ftbl; Hon Roll.

RODRIGUEZ JR, SAMUEL; Vineland HS; Vineland, NJ; (Y); Band; Concert Band; Drill Tm; Mrchg Band; Frsh Cls; Soph Cls; Stu Cncl; Law.

RODRIGUEZ, SUNEN; W L Dickinson HS; Jersey City, NJ; (Y); French Clb; Nwsp Bus Mgr; Tennis; Vllybl; St Peters Coll; Lawyer.

RODRIGUEZ, THEODORE; North Bergen HS; North Bergen, NJ; (S); Trs German Clb; Key Clb; Chorus; Nwsp Rptr; Yrbk Stf; Rep Frsh Cls; Rep Soph Cls; Rep Jr Cls; Stu Cncl; Trk; Princeton; Comp Sci.

ROE, STEPHEN; Manalapan HS; Englishtown, NJ; (Y); Church Yth Grp; JV Ftbl; Engrng.

ROEGGE, DAVID; Hightstown HS; Cranbury, NJ; (Y); AFS; JV Lcrss; JV Wrstlng.

ROG, MARGARET; South River HS; South River, NJ; (Y); Cmnty Wkr; German Clb; Yrbk Stf; JV Fld Hcky; Comm.

ROGALSKI, ELLIE; MSGR Donovan HS; Island Heights, NJ; (Y); 24/217; Art Clb; Church Clb; High Hon Roll; NHS; Trooper P Lamonaco Fund Schlrshp 86; Isl Hts Cmmnty Clb Schlrshp 86; Isl Hts Tchrs Assn Schlrshp 86; Boston U; Pre-Law.

ROGERS, ANGIE; Holy Spirit HS; Absecon, NJ; (Y); Red Cross Aide; Yrbk Stf; Im Powder Puff Ftbl; Crew Adw 86; Boston U.

ROGERS, ELIZABETH; Manasquan HS; Belmar, NJ; (Y); 48/250; Dance Clb; Drama Clb; Hosp Aide; Latin Clb; Political Wkr; Spanish Clb; Acpl Chr; Church Choir; Var Socr; Cit Awd; Soccr Awd 84-85; Acappella Choir 83-84; Rutgers; Psych.

ROGERS, HEIDI; Jackson Memorial HS; Jackson, NJ; (Y); Chorus; Yrbk Stf; Bsktbl; Mgr(s); Powder Puff Ftbl; High Hon Roll; Hon Roll; Jackson Twp Comm Schlrshp 86; Ocean Co Coll; Bus.

ROGERS, KRISTINE; Toms River East HS; Toms River, NJ; (Y); 61/584; French Clb; Chld Psych.

ROGERS, LINDA; Bishop George Ahr HS; Perth Amboy, NJ; (Y); 127/277; ROTC; Band; Concert Band; Mrchg Band; Symp Band; Yrbk Phtg; Lit Mag; Rep Frsh Cls; Rep Soph Cls; Rep Jr Cls; 4th Pl Knockout Drill Comptn 84; Ltr Marchng Band 85-86; Schl Visual Arts; Photo.

ROGERS, MONICA; Neptune SR HS; Neptune, NJ; (Y); 14/368; Cmnty Wkr; Varsity Clb; Variety Show; Crs Cntry; Pom Pon; Trk; High Hon Roll; Hon Roll; Trs Jr NHS; NHS; Spartan Schlr Ocean Twnshp HS 84 & 85; Principals Hon Roll 85; Rutgers U.

ROGERS, SCOTT; Ridge HS; Basking Ridge, NJ; (Y); 34/230; Church Yth Grp; VP Trs German Clb; Ski Clb; Yrbk Phtg; Yrbk Stf; Im JV Bsktbl; Var L Golf; Mgr(s); Hon Roll; NHS; Grmn Natl Hnr Soc; Hugh O Brien Ldrshp.

ROGERS, STEPHEN W; Seton Hall Prep; Orange, NJ; (Y); 40/201; Drama Clb; French Clb; Lit Mag; Rep Sr Cls; Im Golf; Hon Roll; Pres Schlr; 2nd Hnr Awd 82-86; Mt St Marys Coll; Bus.

ROGOZINSKI, DIANE; Manville HS; Manville, NJ; (Y); Ski Clb; High Hon Roll; Hon Roll; Grgg Shrthnd Awd; Cttn Inst Awd; Cittone Inst; Ct Rprtr.

ROHRS, SABRINA C; Matawan Regional HS; Aberdeen, NJ; (S); Dance Clb; Concert Band; Drm Mjr(t); Mrchg Band; School Musical; Variety Show; Yrbk Stf; Rep Stu Cncl; Hon Roll; NHS.

ROJAS, CATALINA; Mary Help Of Chrst Acad; Paterson, NJ; (S); 2/88; French Clb; Letterman Clb; Band; School Musical; Pres Soph Cls; Off Jr Cls; Rep Stu Cncl; High Hon Roll; Hon Roll; Ntl Merit Ltr; Hgh Merit Awds Fr II Biol & Hstry 84-85; Merit Cert Theol Geom Fr I & Eng 83-85; Cert Lfe Grd 84 & 85; Psych.

ROJAS, GIOVANNI; Eastside HS; Paterson, NJ; (Y); Art Clb; Boys Clb Am; Boy Scts; Wrstlng; Hon Roll; Comm Art.

ROJEK, JEFF; Lodi HS; Lodi, NJ; (Y); 20/180; Leo Clb; Science Clb; Varsity Clb; Bsbl; Bsktbl; Ftbl; Wt Lftg; Hon Roll; NHS; Alld Hlth.

ROKICKI, BARBARA; Hackensack HS; Maywood, NJ; (Y); Latin Clb; Ski Clb; Spanish Clb; Teachers Aide; Rep Frsh Cls; Rep Soph Cls; Rep Stu Cncl; JV Var Vllybl; Cit Awd; High Hon Roll; Girls Ctznshp Inst 86; Bio.

ROLLER, PAMELA; Cumberland Regional HS; Bridgeton, NJ; (S); 10/342; Soroptimist; Yrbk Stf; Lit Mag; NHS; Cmrcl Art.

ROLLER, RHONDA C; Lenape Valley Regional HS; Sparta, NJ; (Y); Bowling; Hon Roll; Hnrb Mntn 86 Ldrshp Awd Future Sec 86.

ROLON, NICK; North Bergen HS; North Bergen, NJ; (Y); 49/405; Key Clb; Nwsp Stf; Var Ftbl; High Hon Roll; St Schlr; Church Yth Grp; Cmnty Wkr; FCA; Intnl Clb; Q&S; Grdn ST Schl, Bst Prsnlty, Mst Frndly & Hppy-Go-Lcky 86; ST Chmpn-Ftbl NJ 85-86; John Jay Schl-Crmnl Jstc; Law.

ROMAGLIA, GINA; North Bergen HS; North Bergen, NJ; (Y); FBLA; Off Soph Cls; Off Jr Cls; Off Sr Cls; Sec.

ROMAN, DAVID; Franklin HS; Franklin Pk, NJ; (Y); 11/313; Pres Band; Concert Band; Jazz Band; Mrchg Band; Orch; Symp Band; Var Golf; Hon Roll; NHS; Rep Stu Cncl; FAA Prvt Pilots Lcnse 85; Auburn U; Prfsnl Pilot.

ROMAN, LAURA; Raritan HS; Hazlet, NJ; (Y); 25/342; Yrbk Stf; Var Fld Hcky; Socr; Hon Roll; NHS; Psych.

ROMAN, MARIA MERCEDEZ; Essex Co Vo Tech HS; Newark, NJ; (Y); #21 In Class; FBLA; Office Aide; Variety Show; Rep Jr Cls; Sec Sr Cls; VP Stu Cncl; Bsktbl; Sftbl; Hon Roll; Jr NHS; Montclair ST Coll; Comp Sci.

ROMANCHIK, JOELLE; Holy Cross HS; Delran, NJ; (Y); Aud/Vis; VP Church Yth Grp; Spanish Clb; Band; Chorus; Concert Band; Mrchg Band; Orch; Hon Roll; NHS; Instrmntl Music Awd 84; Vrsty Ltr 84; Dietcs.

ROMANELLO, THERESA; St John Vianney HS; Matawan, NJ; (Y); 15/237; Art Clb; Intnl Clb; SADD; Stage Crew; Yrbk Stf; Powder Puff Ftbl; High Hon Roll; Hon Roll; NHS; Prfct Atten Awd; Gold & White Awd 85; Excllnc In Art 84; Awd Cmmnty Serv & Mdl For High Hons 86; Monmouth Coll; Bus Admin.

ROMANIW, JANIS; James Caldwell HS; West Caldwell, NJ; (Y); Church Yth Grp; Key Clb; Office Aide; Teachers Aide; Concert Band; Orch; School Musical; Variety Show; Stu Cncl; Capt Cheerleading; Elem Schl Teacher.

ROMANO, FRANCES MARIE; Bayonne HS; Bayonne, NJ; (Y); 20/348; Computer Clb; Drama Clb; Math Tm; Spanish Clb; Stage Crew; Hon Roll; NHS; VP Italian Club 86; NJ Inst Of Tech; Compu Sci.

ROMANO, JOHN; Bayley-Ellard Regional HS; Morristown, NJ; (Y); High Hon Roll; Hon Roll; Prfct Atten Awd; Outstndg Achvmnt Awd French & Chem 84-86.

ROMANO, MARIA; Ramapo HS; Wyckoff, NJ; (Y); Art Clb; Chorus; Church Choir; School Play; Stage Crew; Powder Puff Ftbl; Tennis; Vllybl; Hon Roll; Eng Awd 83; Bergen Comm Coll; Mdcl Offc Ast.

ROMANOWSKI, WILLIAM; Gloucester JR-SR HS; Gloucester, NJ; (Y); Computer Clb; DECA; Nwsp Stf; Bowling; Vllybl; Hon Roll; Vlybl 87; Grphc Arts.

ROMERO, RAFAEL; Memorial HS; West New York, NJ; (Y); 85/385; FBLA; Var Trk; Hon Roll; Montclair ST Coll; Acctng.

RONAN, KATHLEEN; Immaculate Conception HS; Secaucus, NJ; (Y); #24 In Class; Political Wkr; Chorus; School Musical; Nwsp Rptr; Rep Frsh Cls; Cheerleading; Pres Clssrm Yng Am 86; Seton Hall U; Poltc Sci.

RONKOVITZ, ANN; Toms River HS East; Toms River, NJ; (Y); French Clb; Chorus; Cheerleading; Hon Roll; Bus Mgmt.

ROOD, HAL; West Morris Central HS; Long Valley, NJ; (Y); 81/280; Radio Clb; Nwsp Rptr; Pres Jr Cls; Pres Sr Cls; Trs Stu Cncl; Bsbl; Tennis; Pres Clsrm Yng Amer 86; Amer HS Bys & Grls Bsktbl 85-86; Brdcstr WRNJ HS Ftbl Brdcsts 85-86; Comm.

ROOKS, JULI; Essex Catholic Girls HS; Orange, NJ; (Y); 12/63; Cmnty Wkr; Dance Clb; Drama Clb; Y-Teens; Stage Crew; Yrbk Stf; Hon Roll; Bus Admin.

ROONEY, BRIAN P; Morris Hills HS; Wharton, NJ; (Y); 64/290; Am Leg Boys St; Exploring; Rep Soph Cls; Var Bsbl; Var Ftbl; Mathews Mcmyne Ftbl Awd 85; Amer Legn Schlrshp 86; Fordham Coll.

ROONEY, JOHN; Notre Dame HS; Plainsboro, NJ; (Y); Key Clb; Math Clb; Math Tm; Varsity Clb; Nwsp Rptr; Nwsp Stf; Lit Mag; Socr; Var Tennis; Im Vllybl.

ROONEY, JOHN PATRICK; Bridgewater-Rariton East HS; Martinsville, NJ; (Y); Church Yth Grp; FCA; Math Tm; Quiz Bowl; Mrchg Band; Nwsp Rptr; Var Capt Bsktbl; Hon Roll; NHS; Pres Schlr; Hnrb Mntn In Bsktbl 85-86; Frtrnl Ordr Of Eagles Schlrshp 86; NY Inst Of Tech; Elec Engrng.

ROONEY, SCOTT; Hamilton HS East; Hamilton Sq, NJ; (Y); 14/326; AFS; Art Clb; Computer Clb; Math Tm; Scholastic Bowl; Varsity Clb; Yrbk Ed-Chief; Var Bsbl; JV Bsktbl; Hon Roll; Yardville Band Scholar 86; U Richmond; Comp Grphcs.

ROONEY, SEAN; Northern Burlington Regional HS; Trenton, NJ; (Y); Var L Bsktbl; Var L Ftbl; Im Sftbl; Im Trk; Im Vllybl; Hon Roll; Ftbl Athltc Scholar Hackley Prep Schl 86.

ROORK, MICHELLE; Cumberland Regional HS; Bridgeton, NJ; (S); 21/369; Church Yth Grp; Drama Clb; Sec 4-H; Intnl Clb; JCL; 4-H Awd; High Hon Roll; Hon Roll; Jr NHS; NHS; Vet Sci.

ROOTH, MICHELE; Holy Family Acad; Bayonne, NJ; (Y); French Clb; Orch; School Play; Yrbk Stf; Tennis; Hon Roll; NHS; NEDT Awd; Acctg.

ROQUE, ALDRIN; Clifton HS; Clifton, NJ; (Y); 64/637; Band; Ftbl; Tennis; Hon Roll; NHS; Med.

RORK, HEATHER; Lakewood HS; Lakewood, NJ; (Y); Church Yth Grp; Pres Dance Clb; Drama Clb; English Clb; French Clb; JCL; Key Clb; Latin Clb; Var Socr; Fshn Mrchndsng.

RORRO, MARY; Villa Victoria Acad; Trenton, NJ; (Y); 5/31; Orch; Nwsp Ed-Chief; Lit Mag; Stu Cncl; DAR Awd; Gov Hon Prg Awd; High Hon Roll; Lion Awd; Spanish NHS; US Marine Corps Sci Fair Wnnr 86; Pardoe String Scholar Wnnr 85 & 86; Interlhcn Natl Music Scholar 85; Physician.

ROSA, BLANCA; Garden State Acad; Tampa, FL; (Y); Church Yth Grp; German Clb; Hosp Aide; Red Cross Aide; Science Clb; Spanish Clb; Spanish NHS; Med Explrrs In Alexian Bros Hosp NJ 84-85; Loma Linda U; Ped.

ROSA, EDITH; Camden HS; Camden, NJ; (S); 12/408; Sec Church Yth Grp; Cmnty Wkr; FBLA; Hosp Aide; Library Aide; Chorus; Church Choir; High Hon Roll; Hon Roll; NHS; Rutgers U; Bus Adm.

ROSA, NOEMI; Hoboken HS; Hoboken, NJ; (Y); Church Yth Grp; French Clb; Hon Roll; Bus Adm.

ROSADO, JANE; Peth Amboy HS; Perth Amboy, NJ; (Y); 6/357; Rep French Clb; Rep Key Clb; Rep Mathletes; Office Aide; Band; Nwsp Rptr; Rep Jr Cls; Rep Stu Cncl; High Hon Roll; Mu Alp Tht; Soc Sec Writng Awd 85; John Burke Mem Awd.

ROSADO, JULIAN; Essex County Voc & Tech; Newark, NJ; (Y); FBLA; Jr Cls; Stu Cncl; Bsbl; Bsktbl; Coach Actv; Score Keeper; Citzns Scholar Fndtn Amer Inc 85-86; Mth Scholar Awd 83; Montclair ST Coll; CPA.

ROSALES, IGNACIO; Cresskill HS; Cresskill, NJ; (Y); 1/121; Am Leg Boys St; Ski Clb; VP Jr Cls; Pres Sr Cls; VP Stu Cncl; JV Bsbl; Var Capt Socr; High Hon Roll; NHS; Ntl Merit SF; Hugh O Brien Ldrshp Smnr 84; U Of PA; Bus.

ROSALES, PABLO; Good Counsel HS; Newark, NJ; (Y); Boy Scts; Score Keeper; Socr; Med Dr.

ROSAMILIA, SALVATORE N; Kearny HS; Kearny, NJ; (Y); Am Leg Boys St; Cmnty Wkr; Var Bsbl; Var Bsktbl; Capt Socr; Hon Roll; NHS; All St Soccer Team By SCA 85; Comm.

ROSANDER, DAVID; Timothy Christian Schl; Piscataway, NJ; (S); 1/35; Cmnty Wkr; Computer Clb; Political Wkr; Radio Clb; Chorus; Stage Crew; JV Bsbl; JV Socr; High Hon Roll; NHS; Natl Hnr Soc 84-85; Chem Awd, Alb II Awd & Attendance Awd 84-85; Geom, High Hnrs & Soccer Ltr 83-84; Engrng.

ROSANIA, JEWEL; Scotch Plains Franwood HS; Scotch Plains, NJ; (Y); 169/311; Aud/Vis; Drama Clb; Leo Clb; SADD; School Musical; Yrbk Phtg; Yrbk Stf; Rep Jr Cls; Var Cheerleading; Stu Ldrshp Conf Rep 84-86; Frsh Capt Vrsty Chrldr; E Stroudsburg U; Chldhd Ed.

ROSARIO, ONEIDA; Warren County Vo-Tech; Washington, NJ; (S); VICA; Rep Frsh Cls; Sec Soph Cls; Pres Jr Cls; Rep Stu Cncl; High Hon Roll; Hon Roll.

ROSASCO, JOHN; Neptune SR HS; Neptune, NJ; (Y); #28 In Class; Latin Clb; Science Clb; Ed Yrbk Stf; Rep Frsh Cls; JV Socr; Hon Roll; Jr NHS; NHS; Cmnctns.

ROSATELLI, GUY; North Berge HS; North Bergen, NJ; (Y); SADD; Varsity Clb; Drm & Bgl; Variety Show; Var Bsbl; Im JV Bsktbl; Im Ftbl; Im Lcrss; Im Vllybl; Im Wrstlng; U Of NC; Law.

ROSATI, PATRICIA; Ocean Township HS; Oakhurst, NJ; (Y); 44/333; Mgr Ed Nwsp Rptr; VP Stu Cncl; Sec NHS; Church Yth Grp; SADD; Variety Show; High Hon Roll; Tchr.

ROSCHER, JEFFREY A; Hunterdon Central HS; Flemington, NJ; (Y); 5/539; Key Clb; Math Tm; Ski Clb; High Hon Roll; Hon Roll; NHS; Ntl Merit SF; Grdn ST Dstngshd Schlrshp 86; Rutgers Coll; Engrng.

ROSE, ABIGAIL L; Princeton HS; Roosevelt, NJ; (Y); AFS; Dance Clb; School Musical; Nwsp Stf; Pres Frsh Cls; VP Stu Cncl; Cmnty Wkr; Drama Clb; French Clb; Q&S; Gld Key Awd-Svc, Ldrshp & Chrctr 85; Smth Coll Book Awd 85; Wrtng Awd-Tmpl U Press Trnmnt 85; Cornell U.

ROSE, ALAN; East Brunswick HS; East Brunswick, NJ; (Y); Key Clb; Temple Yth Grp; Chorus; School Musical; School Play; Nwsp Rptr; Nwsp Stf; Jr NHS; NHS; Ntl Merit Ltr; Rutgers Shlr 85-86; Garden ST Schlr 85-86; Commnd Ntl Merit Schlr 85-86; Haverford Coll; Engl.

ROSE, BRANDON; Brick Township HS; Brick, NJ; (Y); 57/412; German Clb; Trs Varsity Clb; JV Var Ftbl; Var Trk; Wt Lftg; JV Wrstlng; High Hon Roll; Hon Roll; Lwyr.

ROSE, DEBORAH; Freehold Township HS; Freehold, NJ; (Y); 15/350; Yrbk Ed-Chief; Yrbk Stf; Var Tennis; NHS; Bus.

ROSE, LISA BETH; Governor Livingston Regional HS; Berkeley Hts, NJ; (Y); 49/194; Ski Clb; School Musical; Nwsp Rptr; Nwsp Stf; Ed Lit Mag; JV Var Cheerleading; JV Var Fld Hcky; High Hon Roll; Hon Roll; Mtn Vlly Conf Hnrbl Mntn Fld Hockey 85; All Union Cnty 3rd Tm Fld Hockey 85; Clmba Schlstc Press Assn; Syracuse U; Comm.

ROSE, MICHAEL; Bishop Eustace Preparatory Schl; Cherry Hill, NJ; (Y); 7/187; Spanish Clb; Rep Frsh Cls; Pres Soph Cls; Var Bsbl; Var Capt Ftbl; Wt Lftg; Var Wrstlng; Hon Roll; NHS; Acdmc All-Amrcn 86; All-Cnfrnc Ftbll 86; All-Parochl Ftbll 86; Sprts Med.

ROSEBERRY, JANEL; Gloucester Co Christian HS; Monroeville, NJ; (S); 3/13; Sec Soph Cls; Sec Jr Cls; Sec Sr Cls; Capt Bsktbl; Stat Fld Hcky; Capt Sftbl; Capt Vllybl; High Hon Roll; Natl Christian Honor Soc 84; Messiah Coll; Nursng.

ROSELLI, KENNETH D; Williamstown HS; Williamstown, NJ; (Y); 1/261; Key Clb; Scholastic Bowl; Varsity Clb; Rep Soph Cls; Var Capt Bsbl; Var Bsktbl; Var Crs Cntry; High Hon Roll; VP NHS; Rotary Awd; U Of NC; Indstrl Engrng.

ROSEN, ADAM; James Caldwell HS; Caldwell, NJ; (Y); Computer Clb; Drama Clb; French Clb; Math Tm; School Play; Variety Show; Var Crs Cntry; High Hon Roll; Pres NHS; Biomed Engrng.

ROSEN, ELIZABETH; North Brunswick Township HS; N Brunswick, NJ; (Y); 45/350; Drama Clb; Key Clb; Spanish Clb; Chorus; School Musical; School Play; Variety Show; Hon Roll; Rep Frsh Cls; Rep Soph Cls; Lawyer.

ROSEN, HEIDI; Memorial HS; Cedar Grove, NJ; (S); 14/119; Trs Ed Key Clb; Concert Band; Mrchg Band; School Musical; Variety Show; Yrbk Stf; Trs Frsh Cls; VP Fld Hcky; Hon Roll; NHS.

ROSEN, RENEE; Freehold Township HS; Freehold, NJ; (Y); 59/319; Exploring; Trs French Clb; Office Aide; Rep Stu Cncl; Var Capt Bsktbl; Powder Puff Ftbl; Var Trk; Bsktbl 1st Team All-Monmouth & 1st Team All-District 85-86; Bsktbl All Tournmnt Team 84-86; Gettysburg Coll.

ROSEN, STEVEN; Asbruy Park HS; Avon By The Sea, NJ; (Y); 9/134; JV Bowling; Hon Roll; Trenton ST Coll; Acctg.

ROSENBAUM, MATT; Montville HS; Montville, NJ; (Y); 30/262; FBLA; Key Clb; Math Clb; Pres Ski Clb; SADD; VP Stu Cncl; JV Golf; JV Socr; High Hon Roll; NHS; 3rd Pl Sprng Arts Fstvl 84-85; 2nd Pl Sprng Arts Fstvl 85-86; Cert Apprctn YVA 85-86; IL Inst Tech; Arch.

ROSENBERG, LINDA DIANE; Cresskill HS; Cresskill, NJ; (Y); 23/111; Drama Clb; French Clb; Hosp Aide; VP Temple Yth Grp; Band; Mrchg Band; Ed Yrbk Stf; JV Cheerleading; Var JV Sftbl; NHS; Bus Admin.

ROSENBERG, RACHEL; Morris Knolls HS; Denville, NJ; (Y); 52/383; Computer Clb; Ski Clb; SADD; Church Choir; Yrbk Bus Mgr; Yrbk Phtg; Yrbk Stf; VP Stu Cncl; High Hon Roll; Hon Roll; Miss Indn Lk 86; Cert Of Apprctn For Vlntr Srv 86; Slvr Awd Grl Scts 84; Sci.

ROSENBERG, RHONDA; Tenafly HS; Tenafly, NJ; (Y); Nwsp Bus Mgr; Nwsp Rptr; Swmmng; Tennis; Trk; Dartmouth Coll.

ROSENBERGER, LYNN; Freehold Boro HS; Freehold, NJ; (Y); 6/241; French Clb; Key Clb; Rep Frsh Cls; Rep Jr Cls; Sec Sr Cls; Rep Stu Cncl; JV Bsktbl; JV Sftbl; Var L Tennis; French Hon Soc.

ROSENBLATT, ROBERT; Piscataway HS; Piscataway, NJ; (Y); 132/516; Drama Clb; School Play; Im Socr; Ntl Merit Ltr; Outstndng Prfmnc Awd Mdlsx Co Per Arts Fstvl 85 & 86; Achvt Awd Mdlsx Co Arts HS; Phlsphy Awd; Rutgers Coll; Thtr Arts.

ROSENFARB, JASON; Randolph HS; Randolph, NJ; (Y); 74/358; Am Leg Boys St; Exploring; Ski Clb; Temple Yth Grp; Im Wt Lftg; Var Wrstlng; Hon Roll; Amer Hstry.

ROSENFELD, RICHARD; Cherry Hill High School West; Cherry Hill, NJ; (Y); 24/333; PAVAS; Pres Temple Yth Grp; Rptr Nwsp Stf; Lit Mag; Off Soph Cls; Var Tennis; Gov Hon Prg Awd; NHS; Ntl Merit Schol; Art Clb; Rtgrs Dean Smr Shlrs Awd 86; Hm & Schl High Hon Awd 86.

ROSENGREN, JOHN; Wayne Valley HS; Wayne, NJ; (Y); 52/320; JV Socr; Capt L Swmmng; High Hon Roll; Ntl Merit Ltr; Rutgers Coll.

ROSENKRANTZ, PAMELA; Bloomfield HS; Bloomfield, NJ; (Y); 44/437; French Clb; Key Clb; Temple Yth Grp; VP Yrbk Stf; Cheerleading; NHS.

ROSENSWEIG, SARA; Highstown HS; E Windsor, NJ; (Y); 31/343; Pres French Clb; Political Wkr; Temple Yth Grp; Ed Yrbk Stf; VP Sr Cls; Stu Cncl; Capt Cheerleading; Tennis; Cit Awd; High Hon Roll; New Jersey Grls Ctznshp Awd; U MA; Prof Law.

ROSENTHAL, GLENN; Fair Lawn HS; Fair Lawn, NJ; (Y); Computer Clb; Math Tm; Pep Clb; Band; Concert Band; Mrchg Band; Off Jr Cls; Hon Roll; Ntl Merit Ltr; Pep Band; Nrthwstrn NHSI Tech Stu 86; MIT; Comp.

ROSENZWEIG, LISA BETH; Fair Lawn HS; Fair Lawn, NJ; (Y); 20/335; Art Clb; Cmnty Wkr; Spanish Clb; Temple Yth Grp; Yrbk Stf; High Hon Roll; Hon Roll; NHS; Grdn ST Distngshed Schlr 86; Jwsh Comm Cncl Palsdes 86; Fair Lwn PTA 86; Rutgers.

ROSERO, BELKYS; Saint Anthony HS; Jersey City, NJ; (Y); 6/63; Computer Clb; NFL; School Musical; Bowling; JV Cheerleading; Hon Roll; Natl Sci Merit Awd 86; St Peters Coll; Comp.

ROSIAK, JENNIFER ANNE; Rutherford HS; Rutherford, NJ; (Y); Band; Concert Band; Mrchg Band; School Musical; High Hon Roll; DECA; Pep Band; Johnston & Wales; Culnary Arts.

ROSLAN, CHRIS; Kittatinny Reg HS; Newton, NJ; (Y); 45/228; PAVAS; Band; Jazz Band; School Musical; Variety Show; Hon Roll; Summr Art Inst Rutgers Coll 84; NJ ST Teen Arts Fest 84; Recitals & Perfrmnce; Jazz Music.

ROSNER, FRANK; New Milford HS; New Milford, NJ; (Y); 41/141; Boy Scts; Varsity Clb; Var Bsbl; Ftbl; Cit Awd; Marn Biol.

ROSNER, WILLIAM; Ocean Twp HS; Ocean, NJ; (Y); 46/333; Drama Clb; Ski Clb; Spanish Clb; Thesps; School Musical; School Play; Hon Roll; NHS; NEDT Awd; Rep HOBY Ldrshp Sem 85; Engrng.

ROSS, ALESE; Cherry Hill HS West; Cherry Hill, NJ; (Y); Stage Crew; Socr; Trk; Frnch Lang Pgm Switzerland 86.

ROSS, BRUCE EVAN; Paramus HS; Paramus, NJ; (Y); Am Leg Boys St; Debate Tm; Drama Clb; NFL; VP Temple Yth Grp; Chorus; Mrchg Band; School Musical; School Play; Stage Crew; NJ All ST Chrs, NJ Reg I Chrs 84-85; VP Jrsy Fed Tmpl Yth 85-86; Pres Jsry Fed Tmpl Yth 86-87; Music.

ROSS, DANI; Freehold Township HS; Freehold, NJ; (Y); 35/317; Drama Clb; Temple Yth Grp; Thesps; NHS; U Of MA; Bus.

ROSS, JAMES; Hamilton H S West; Trenton, NJ; (S); 13/345; Church Yth Grp; Key Clb; Math Clb; Concert Band; Mrchg Band; Symp Band; Nwsp Ed-Chief; Nwsp Sprt Ed; Rep Stu Cncl; Var Bsbl; Hugh O Brian Yth Ldrshp Awd 84; All Amer Band 85-86; Elec Engr.

ROSS, KELLY; Eastside HS; Paterson, NJ; (Y); Hampton U; Lwyr.

ROSS, MICHAEL P; River Dell HS; Oradell, NJ; (Y); 8/214; Am Leg Boys St; Capt Chess Clb; Debate Tm; Pres Math Tm; Model UN; Quiz Bowl; SADD; Concert Band; Nwsp Ed-Chief; Im Tennis; Renssalaer Medl 85; Rutgers Schlr 85; Amnesty, Rotary & Projections Wrtng Awds 86; U Of PA.

ROSS, PATRECIA ANN; Deptford Twp HS; Wenoah, NJ; (Y); NFL; Chorus; School Musical; JV Fld Hcky; JV Sftbl; Hon Roll; Ucla; Nrsng.

ROSS, PATRICIA; Union Catholic Regional HS; Rahwall, NJ; (Y); 64/350; Church Yth Grp; Service Clb; Spanish Clb; SADD; Yrbk Stf; Capt Cheerleading; Hon Roll; Rutgers Coll.

ROSS, SCOTT; Bridgewater-Raritan E HS; Bridgewater, NJ; (Y); Church Yth Grp; Ski Clb; Stu Cncl; Var Bsbl; JV Bsktbl; Var Ftbl; High Hon Roll; NHS; Mth.

ROSS, SCOTT; Sussex County Vocational Tech Schl; Montague, NJ; (Y); Var Swmmng; Var Tennis; Var Trk.

ROSS, STACY; Holy Cross HS; Delran, NJ; (Y); 1/396; Am Leg Aux Girls St; Letterman Clb; Ski Clb; Rep Frsh Cls; Rep Soph Cls; Rep Jr Cls; Trs Stu Cncl; Var Tennis; High Hon Roll; NHS; 3rd Rnnr Up Miss Teen NJ 85; All Parochl Dbls In S Jersey 84; All Parochl Sngls S Jersey 85; Bus.

ROSS, STEPHANIE; E Orange HS; E Orange, NJ; (S); GAA; Chorus; Variety Show; Capt Crs Cntry; Capt Trk; Cit Awd; Prfct Atten Awd; Var Track Awds 85-86; Stu Gov Day Essay Wnnr 85; JR Class Prncss 85; Sclgy.

ROSSELL, LISA; Notre Dame HS; Trenton, NJ; (Y); 7/380; Cmnty Wkr; Hosp Aide; Red Cross Aide; Service Clb; Teachers Aide; Rep Frsh Cls; Rep Soph Cls; Cit Awd; High Hon Roll; NHS; Pre-Med.

ROSSETER, CATHY M; Asbury Park HS; Belmar, NJ; (Y); Aud/Vis; Key Clb; Varsity Clb; Drm Mjr(t); Stage Crew; Nwsp Stf; Hon Roll; Var Sftbl; Var Tennis; Chld Psych.

ROSSI, ANNE MARIE; Riverside HS; Delanco, NJ; (S); Dance Clb; VP Jr Cls; Stu Cncl; Var Cheerleading; JV Sftbl; Glassboro ST Coll; Art.

ROSSI, CARL; Clifton HS; Clifton, NJ; (Y); 13/630; Math Clb; JV Socr; JV Trk; Hon Roll; Jr NHS; Spanish NHS; Stevens Inst Of Tech; Engrng.

ROSSI, LISA; St Peters HS; Somerset, NJ; (Y); 2/110; French Clb; Hosp Aide; Chorus; School Musical; Yrbk Ed-Chief; Pres Frsh Cls; VP Jr Cls; Var L Tennis; High Hon Roll; NHS; Rutgers Deans Smmr Schlr Prg 86; Acdmc All Amer Schlr Awd 86; Educ.

ROSSI, LOUISE; Clifton HS; Clifton, NJ; (Y); 17/750; Church Yth Grp; French Clb; Key Clb; Library Aide; Math Clb; Ski Clb; Chorus; Nwsp Rptr; French Hon Soc; Hon Roll; Carrier Of Mnth 84; Carrier Of Yr 85; Girls Ctznshp Inst Douglass Coll 86; Intl Law.

ROSSI, MICHELE; Bloomfield SR HS; Bloomfield, NJ; (Y); 43/463; FBLA; Yrbk Stf; Stu Cncl; Var Capt Cheerleading; Cit Awd; High Hon Roll; NHS; Rotary Awd; VP Frsh Cls; PBA Schlrshp 86; AM Bus Acadmy Schlrshp 86; Rtry Clb Schlrshp 86; AM Bus Acad; Crt Rprtng.

ROSSO, PAOLA; Marylawn Of The Oranges HS; E Orange, NJ; (Y); Art Clb; Math Clb; Spanish Clb; Teachers Aide; Hon Roll; Ntl Merit SF; Spanish NHS; Spn Awd 84 & 85; Psych.

ROSTOKER, DAWN; Pompton Lakes HS; Pompton Lakes, NJ; (Y); Am Leg Aux Girls St; Hosp Aide; VP Latin Clb; Q&S; Spanish Clb; Teachers Aide; Temple Yth Grp; Nwsp Bus Mgr; Nwsp Stf; High Hon Roll; Peer Cncslng Awd; U Of DE; Consmr Econ.

ROSWECH, MARC; Toms River HS South; Beachwood, NJ; (Y); 15/360; Am Leg Boys St; Hosp Aide; Math Tm; Bsbl; JV Bsktbl; Socr; High Hon Roll; Hon Roll; NHS; Prfct Atten Awd.

ROTANTE, JAMES; St Josephs Regional HS; Wyckoff, NJ; (Y); 8/180; Camera Clb; Church Yth Grp; Computer Clb; Mathletes; Math Clb; Math Tm; Ski Clb; Rep Soph Cls; Rep Jr Cls; Rep Stu Cncl; Engrng.

ROTBERG, TAMARA LEE; Washington Township HS; Turnersville, NJ; (Y); Cmnty Wkr; Spanish Clb; Chorus; Color Guard; Mrchg Band; Var Coach Actv; Pom Pon; Var Swmmng; High Hon Roll; Hon Roll; Tchr/Cnslr.

ROTELLA, JANET; Holy Family Acad; Bayonne, NJ; (Y); Am Leg Aux Girls St; French Clb; Pep Clb; Orch; School Musical; Yrbk Stf; Religious Retreat Comm 84-86; Soph Dance Comm-Jr Prom Comm 85-86; Jr Ring Ceremony 86; Psych.

ROTH, JOSEPH R; Montclair HS; Upper Montclair, NJ; (Y); 6/436; Lit Mag; Var L Lcrss; Hon Roll; NHS; Ntl Merit SF; Garden ST Dstngshd Schlr 85.

ROTH, SANDRA LEE; Bayley Ellard Reg HS; Whippany, NJ; (Y); Cmnty Wkr; Hosp Aide; Service Clb; Yrbk Ed-Chief; Yrbk Stf; Rep Frsh Cls; Rep Soph Cls; VP Jr Cls; Stu Cncl; JV Score Keeper; Hugh O Brien Ldrshp Awd 84-85; U DE; Bus Mgmt.

ROTHBERG, MATTHEW I; Highland Park HS; Highland Park, NJ; (Y); Am Leg Boys St; Chorus; Stage Crew; Nwsp Ed-Chief; NJ Gvrnrs Schl Of Pblc Issues 86; Pltcl Action.

ROTHERY, RICHARD; Wall HS; Wall, NJ; (S); 11/269; JV Var Bsbl; Var L Crs Cntry; High Hon Roll; Hon Roll.

ROTHSCHILD, BRADFORD; Solomon Schechter Day Schl; Plainfield, NJ; (Y); School Play; Nwsp Sprt Ed; Rep Stu Cncl; Var Bsbl; JV Bsktbl; JV Socr; Merit Schlrshp/Temple Beth.

ROTHSTEIN, DONNA; West Milford Township HS; West Milford, NJ; (Y); 8/350; Model UN; Lib Concert Band; Mrchg Band; Elks Awd; High Hon Roll; NHS; Pres Schlr; Spanish NHS; Chess Clb; Band; Delg Girls Citznshp Inst 85; Pres Physcl Ftns Awd 82-86; ASQC Schlrshp 86; Bryn Mawr Coll; Econ.

ROTHSTEIN, JILL; Lakewood HS; Lakewood, NJ; (Y); English Clb; French Clb; Key Clb; Chorus; Color Guard; Mrchg Band; Yrbk Stf; Pre-Law.

ROTHSTEIN, SHAWN; Dwight Englewood HS; Franklin Lakes, NJ; (Y); Math Tm; JV Socr; Var L Trk; Bausch & Lomb Sci Awd; Hon Roll; Rtgrs Schlr 86; Engrng.

ROTOLO, JOHN; Cherry Hill H S West; Cherry Hill, NJ; (Y); 39/350; Intnl Clb; Spanish Clb; Hon Roll; Elec Engrng.

ROTONDO, ANTHONY; Raritan HS; Hazlet, NJ; (Y); Ski Clb; Var JV Socr; Pres Itln Clb 86-87; Rutgers; Comp.

ROTONDO, DANIEL; Raritan HS; Hazlet, NJ; (Y); Computer Clb; Ski Clb; Wrstlng; Comp.

ROTONDO, MARK; NVR HS; Harrington Pk, NJ; (Y); 52/283; AFS; Concert Band; Mrchg Band; School Musical; Rep Stu Cncl; Bus.

ROTTER, KENNETH; Lenape Valley Regional HS; Andover, NJ; (Y); #1 In Class; Trs Key Clb; Quiz Bowl; Pres Temple Yth Grp; Nwsp Stf; Rep Stu Cncl; JV Swmmng; Var Tennis; NHS; Ntl Merit Ltr; Hgh Hnr Rl.

ROTTINGHAUS, KEVIN; Middletown High School South; Middletown, NJ; (Y); JA; Spanish Clb; Im Golf; Im Socr; Hon Roll; Prfct Atten Awd; Bus Mgt.

ROTUNDA, DOMENICA; West Essex Regional HS; Fairfield, NJ; (Y); 44/350; Debate Tm; Key Clb; Political Wkr; Color Guard; Ntl Merit SF; Johns Hopkins U; Intl Studies.

ROTUNDO, FAUSTO; North Bergen HS; North Bergen, NJ; (Y); 26/400; DECA; Socr; Trk; High Hon Roll; Hon Roll; NHS; Prfct Atten Awd; Rutgers; Acctg.

ROUDCULP, MATTHEW; Jackson Memorial HS; Jackson, NJ; (Y); 20/405; Am Leg Boys St; Church Yth Grp; Letterman Clb; Ski Clb; Varsity Clb; Stu Cncl; Ftbl; Trk; Wt Lftg; Wrstlng; Acadmc All Amer 86; Pre-Med.

ROUDEZ, KIM; Immaculate Conception HS; Newark, NJ; (Y); Sec Church Yth Grp; Pep Clb; Red Cross Aide; Chorus; Church Choir; School Play; Variety Show; Rep Jr Cls; Trk; Ntl Spnsh Achvt Test 85; Psychlgy.

ROUGHNEEN, THOMAS; Roselle Catholic HS; Union, NJ; (S); 17/207; Church Yth Grp; Orch; School Musical; Im Bsktbl; Var Wrstlng; High Hon Roll; Hon Roll; KC Essay Awd 84; Violin Cmptn 85; Spnsh Awd 85; Syracuse U; Comms.

ROUSCULP, MATT; Jackson Memorial HS; Jackson, NJ; (S); 24/417; Science Clb; Ski Clb; Varsity Clb; VP Stu Cncl; Capt Ftbl; JV Trk; JV Wrstlng; High Hon Roll; NHS; Pre-Med.

ROUSE, TAMIKA D; Camden Catholic HS; Camden, NJ; (Y); 21/285; FBLA; Spanish Clb; Color Guard; Rep Jr Cls; Stat Bsktbl; Hon Roll; NHS; Ntl Merit Ltr; Sci Hnr Soc 83-84; Soc Sci Hnr Soc 84-85; Natl Achvt Schlrp Prog Cmmnded Stu 85-86; Bus Adm.

ROUX, LISA; Pennsville Memorial HS; Pennsville, NJ; (Y); Am Leg Aux Girls St; FBLA; Band; Chorus; Concert Band; Mrchg Band; Rep Frsh Cls; Rep Soph Cls; Stu Cncl; Var Mgr Ftbl; Actg.

ROUX, MICHELE ANN; Rancocas Valley Regional HS; Mt Holly, NJ; (Y); 28/248; Am Leg Aux Girls St; Varsity Clb; Rep Jr Cls; Trs Sr Cls; Sec Stu Cncl; Var Bsktbl; Var Fld Hcky; Stat Ftbl; Var Capt Sftbl; NHS; Phlps Schlr Athlt Awd 86; Bloomsburg U; Acctg.

ROVELLO, ZULMA; Memorial HS; West New York, NJ; (Y); Office Aide; Spanish Clb; Capt Color Guard; Rep Frsh Cls; Rep Jr Cls; Most Likely To Succeed 83; Most Likely To Get Along 83; Psych.

ROVICK, PETER; Chatham Twp HS; Chatham Twp, NJ; (Y); 125/139; Political Wkr; Sec Soph Cls; VP Jr Cls; Trs Sr Cls; Rep Stu Cncl; Var Crs Cntry; Var Trk; Hon Roll; NHS.

ROWAN, COLLEEN M; Holy Cross HS; Burlington, NJ; (Y); 31/394; Church Yth Grp; Cmnty Wkr; Hosp Aide; Spanish Clb; Band; Church Choir; Capt Color Guard; Concert Band; Mrchg Band; High Hon Roll; Varsty Let Band 84-86; Elem Educ.

ROWAND, DONNA; Egg Harbor Township HS; Mays Landing, NJ; (Y); Exploring; French Clb; Girl Scts; Ski Clb; Mrchg Band; Nwsp Rptr; Hst Stu Cncl; Hon Roll; Jr NHS; Glassboro ST Coll; Bio Tchr.

ROWAND, MELINDA; Sterling HS; Laurel Springs, NJ; (Y); 6/242; Pep Clb; SADD; Nwsp Rptr; Im Bowling; Var Capt Crs Cntry; Var Capt Trk; Im Vllybl; High Hon Roll; Hon Roll; NHS; Pres Acdmc Fit Awd 86; NJ Schlr Athlete 86; Full Athletic Schlrshp Trck U Of MI 86; U Of MI; Physcl Thrpy.

ROWAND, SUSAN; Overbrook Regional SR HS; Berlin, NJ; (Y); French Clb; Varsity Clb; Band; Concert Band; JV Var Bsktbl; High Hon Roll; Hon Roll; NHS; Comp Sci.

ROWE, MICHAEL J; Don Bosco Prep; N Haldeon, NJ; (Y); Church Yth Grp; Model UN; Pep Clb; Ski Clb; Yrbk Stf; JV Var Ftbl; Wt Lftg; Fndtn For Free Entrprs-Free Mrkt Stud Crs 86; Smmr Time Yth Ldrshp Exprnc 85-86; Nvl Aviatr.

ROWLEY, MICHAEL; Highstown HS; E Windsor, NJ; (Y); Church Yth Grp; French Clb; Intnl Clb; Yrbk Stf; Pres Jr Cls; Pres Stu Cncl; Crs Cntry; Trk; Hon Roll; Med.

ROY, GARRY; Middlesex HS; Middlesex, NJ; (Y); 62/175; Varsity Clb; Var Bsbl; Var Ftbl; Var Wrstlng; Bus.

ROY, MICHELLE; South Hunterdon Regional HS; Lambertville, NJ; (Y); FBLA; Stat Fld Hcky; Mgr(s); Score Keeper; Hon Roll; Stat Sftbl; Cazenovia; Acctng.

ROY, SUSAN; Howell HS; Howell, NJ; (Y); 36/370; Hon Roll; NHS; VFW Awd; Voice Dem Awd; Comp Sci.

ROYCE, LAURA; Kittatinny Regional HS; Newton, NJ; (Y); 18/250; Pres Sec Church Yth Grp; Sec Chorus; School Musical; Sec Jr Cls; Rep Stu Cncl; Var Bsktbl; JV Socr; Gov Hon Prg Awd; High Hon Roll; NHS; Drama Tchr.

ROYSTER JR, JAMES; Lincoln HS; Jersey City, NJ; (Y); Camera Clb; Computer Clb; FBLA; Badmtn; Var Bausch & Lomb Sci Awd; JV Bsktbl; JV Bowling; Var Ftbl; Sftbl; Vllybl; Comp Sci.

ROZAS III, RAMON; Butler HS; Butler, NJ; (Y); Am Leg Boys St; Debate Tm; Math Clb; Quiz Bowl; Chorus; Concert Band; Mrchg Band; Hon Roll.

ROZELL, FRED; Brick HS; Brick Town, NJ; (Y); Varsity Clb; JV Ftbl; Var Ice Hcky; Ocean Cnty Coll; Bus.

ROZO, TERESA; Butler HS; Butler, NJ; (Y); Spanish Clb; Varsity Clb; Chorus; Var Cheerleading; Var JV Mgr(s); Var JV Score Keeper; Hon Roll; Engrng.

RUANE, LESLIE; Nutley HS; Nutley, NJ; (Y); 42/338; Church Yth Grp; French Clb; Girl Scts; Concert Band; Mrchg Band; Stu Cncl; Trk; Hon Roll; NHS; Hofstra U; Bus Acctng.

RUBERTO, MICHAEL; North Bergen HS; North Bergen, NJ; (S); 4/404; Church Yth Grp; Trs Key Clb; Latin Clb; Trs Stu Cncl; Capt Trk; Wt Lftg; High Hon Roll; Hon Roll; VP NHS; NJ Marine Ed Assn Sci Contst Champ 86; Rensselaer Medl-Sci/Math 85; Amer Legn Jersey Boys ST Delg 85; Pre-Med.

RUBIN, CHERYL; Jonathon Dayton Reg HS; Springfield, NJ; (Y); 17/230; Band; Concert Band; Mrchg Band; Sftbl; Pres Schlr; Spanish NHS; 7 Gold Awds-Piano-Gvn By NJ Music Edctrs; Brandeis U.

RUBIN, ERIC; Union HS; Union, NJ; (Y); 61/464; Boy Scts; Key Clb; Band; Concert Band; Jazz Band; Mrchg Band; Orch; Pep Band; Crs Cntry; Wrstlng; Rutgers U; Lawyer.

RUBIN, MARK; Manalapan HS; Englishtown, NJ; (Y); 3/401; Computer Clb; Debate Tm; Math Tm; Model UN; NHS; St Schlr; Natl Merit Fnlst 86; Olympics Of The Mind NJ Shore Conf Chmpnshp Tm & Spntns Respns Awds 84 & 85; Princeton U; Law.

RUBIN, NANCY; Colonia SR HS; Colonia, NJ; (Y); FTA; Teachers Aide; Temple Yth Grp; Varsity Clb; Yrbk Stf; Stat Bsktbl; Im Bowling; Im Sftbl; Var Capt Tennis; Var Capt Trk; All Conf All Acad Tennis 85; Close Up Cert Of Pgm Prtcptn 86; Educ.

RUBIN, RACHELLE; West Orange HS; Livingston, NJ; (Y); Hosp Aide; Library Aide; Office Aide; Pep Clb; Service Clb; Temple Yth Grp; Orch; Nwsp Rptr; Nwsp Stf; Yrbk Stf; Essay Awd 85; Candystripng Awd 83-85; HS Inst 85; Rutgers; Acctng.

RUBIN, STEPHANIE; Livingston HS; Livingston, NJ; (Y); FBLA; Key Clb; Office Aide; Temple Yth Grp; Yrbk Ed-Chief; Rep Soph Cls; Rep Jr Cls; Stat Wrstlng; High Hon Roll; Hon Roll; Bus.

RUBIN, THOMAS S; Hunterdon Central HS; Flemington, NJ; (Y); 4/540; Chess Clb; Math Clb; Math Tm; Quiz Bowl; Nwsp Ed-Chief; Nwsp Stf; High Hon Roll; Hon Roll; NHS; Ntl Merit SF; Dartmouth Clb Bk Awd; Garden ST Dstngshd Schlr.

RUBINO, CHRIS; Marist HS; Jersey City, NJ; (Y).

RUBIO, A LIZ; Roselle Catholic HS; Roselle, NJ; (Y); 19/230; Spanish Clb; Var Socr; High Hon Roll; Spanish NHS.

RUBIO, RAMON; Mon Mouth Regional HS; Eatontown, NJ; (Y); Bsbl; Ftbl; Wt Lftg; Wrstlng; Rutgers U; Elec Engr.

RUBULOTTA, KELLY; Shore Regional HS; W Long Branch, NJ; (Y); Cmnty Wkr; Girl Scts; SADD; Thesps; Stage Crew; Cheerleading; Fld Hcky; Gym; Sftbl; Trk; Prfct Atten Awd 83-84; Pop/Warner Chrldng Coach Cert 83-85; Brookdale CC; Intr Decrtr.

RUDDY, JAMES; Jackson Memorial HS; Jackson, NJ; (Y); 1/362; Am Leg Boys St; Science Clb; Stu Cncl; Bsktbl; Ftbl; Trk; High Hon Roll; NHS; Pres Schlr; St Schlr; Princeton; Engrng.

RUDE, JOE; Wayne Valley HS; Wayne, NJ; (Y); 79/310; Ski Clb; Badmtn; Bsbl; JV Ftbl; Ice Hcky; JV Trk; Vllybl; Im Wt Lftg.

RUDE, KELLY; Newton HS; Newton, NJ; (Y); Cmnty Wkr; DECA; Latin Clb; SADD; Stu Cncl; Hon Roll; U Of NC; Bus.

RUDEN, ELAINE; Freehold Township; Freehold, NJ; (Y); Cmnty Wkr; Hosp Aide; Office Aide; Yrbk Stf; Lit Mag; NHS; Brandeis U.

RUDING, JENNIFER; Neptune SR HS; Ocean Grove, NJ; (Y); Lit Mag; Rep Jr Cls; High Hon Roll; Hon Roll; Jr NHS; NHS; Mertrious Achvmnt Contrbtn Triton Ltry Magzn 83-84; Cmpltn Div Cntng Ed NJ Inst Tech 86; Crdt Drftng; Archtr.

RUDISILL, MARK; Egg Harbor Township HS; West Atlantic, NJ; (S); 28/266; Nwsp Rptr; Capt L Ftbl; Jr NHS; Ntl Merit Schol; All Conf Offnsv Guard 85.

RUDITSKY, SUE; Mt Olive HS; Budd Lake, NJ; (Y); Drama Clb; Science Clb; Chorus; School Musical; School Play; Lit Mag; Rep Frsh Cls; JV Swmmng; Medcn.

RUDNICK, HOLLY; Union HS; Union, NJ; (Y); Rep Key Clb; Pres Temple Yth Grp; Band; Concert Band; Orch; Symp Band; Mgr(s); Capt Twrlr; NHS; Opt Clb Awd; Union Twnshp Schlrhsp 86; NBA Natl Hnrs Bnd 86; Holocst Rmbrnce Cmmtee Essy Awd 85.

RUDOLPH, LINDA; Howell HS; Howell, NJ; (Y); 40/371; VP School Musical; Yrbk Ed-Chief; Pres Stu Cncl; Stat Ftbl; L Socr; L Tennis; Cit Awd; Hon Roll; NHS; Pres Schlr; Estrn NM U; Educ.

RUDOLPH, STEVEN A; Collingswood HS; Collingswood, NJ; (Y); Am Leg Boys St; Aud/Vis; Camera Clb; Key Clb; Office Aide; Band; Yrbk Phtg; High Hon Roll; Hon Roll; Deans Summer Schlr Pro Rutgers U 85; 2nd Yr Awd; Rutgers U; Elec Engr.

RUEDA, EMILY; Mary Help Of Christians Acad; Prospect Park, NJ; (S); 1/67; Church Yth Grp; Letterman Clb; Chorus; Church Choir; School Musical; High Hon Roll; NHS; NEDT Awd; Prfct Atten Awd; Ntl Ldrshp Orgnztn 84-85; 7th Pl Cathlc HS Math Leag 84; William Paterson Coll; Elem Ed.

RUEDIGER, ARTHUR; Cumberland Regional HS; Bridgeton, NJ; (Y); Boy Scts; Var L Crs Cntry; JV Socr; Var Trk; JV Wrstlng; Hon Roll; Cross Cntry 2nd In State 84; Mdl Cngrs Tm 86; Sprng Trck 84-85; DE Vly Coll Of Sci & Ag; Bio.

RUELA, ANTHONY J; Carteret HS; Carteret, NJ; (Y); 11/198; Am Leg Boys St; Pres Ski Clb; School Play; Yrbk Stf; Pres Frsh Cls; VP Jr Cls; Off Sr Cls; Var Bsbl; Var Ftbl; NHS; Greatr Middlsx Cnty Conf All Acdmc Ftbl Tm 85-86; Sci.

RUELAN, ROBERT; Williamstown HS; Williamstown, NJ; (Y); Spanish Clb; School Musical; School Play; Variety Show; Yrbk Stf; Tennis; Hon Roll; NHS; Rotary Awd; Rutgers ST U; Comp Pgmr.

RUGARBER, CATHY; St John Vianney HS; Freehold, NJ; (Y); 35/236; Church Yth Grp; Cmnty Wkr; Political Wkr; Drill Tm; Stage Crew; Hon Roll; Trenton ST Coll.

RUGGIERO, GLEN A; Watchung Hills Regional HS; Stirling, NJ; (Y); 105/321; Am Leg Boys St; Church Yth Grp; Ski Clb; Band; Concert Band; Mrchg Band; Yrbk Stf; Var Trk; Wt Lftg; Var Wrstlng; FL ST U; Acctng.

RUIZ, ELVIRA; Hillside HS; Hillside, NJ; (Y); 11/200; Church Yth Grp; Science Clb; Nwsp Ed-Chief; Nwsp Rptr; U SFL; Occ Thrpy.

RUIZ, GLADYS; Memorial HS; West New York, NJ; (Y); Camera Clb; Chorus; Variety Show; 2nd Photo Awd 85; Para-Legal.

RUIZ, NORMA; Perth Amboy HS; Perth Amboy, NJ; (Y); 4/358; Chorus; Capt Color Guard; School Musical; Nwsp Ed-Chief; Pres Sr Cls; Var Bowling; Gov Hon Prg Awd; NHS; Art Clb; Girls ST Delg 86; Gov Schl; Bus Mgmt.

RUIZ, RAOUL; Bloomfield SR HS; Bloomfield, NJ; (Y); 15/442; Math Tm; Science Clb; Chorus; Orch; JV Bowling; Trk; High Hon Roll; Hon Roll; NHS; Sci Hnr 85-86; Columbia U; Biomed Engre.

RUMSON, MARK; Washington HS; Turnersville, NJ; (Y); 21/480; Debate Tm; Model UN; Spanish Clb; Hon Roll; NHS; Drexel U; Elec Engrg.

RUNYON, KERRY; Point Pleasant Boro HS; Point Pleasant, NJ; (S); 12/250; Chorus; Church Choir; School Musical; JV Fld Hcky; JV Trk; High Hon Roll; Hon Roll; Chrstr Guild Awd; Art.

RUOCCO, TARA; Morris Knolls HS; Rockaway, NJ; (Y); 197/383; Boys Clb Am; Exploring; Hosp Aide; Ski Clb; Chorus; Yrbk Bus Mgr; Yrbk Stf; JV Socr; 100 Hrs Candy Striping 85-86; Uof MD; Lwyr.

RUOPP, ALAN; Belleville HS; Belleville, NJ; (Y); 96/400; Var Capt Bsbl; Hon Roll; Eckerd Coll; Bus.

RUOTOIO, CHRISTINE; James Caldwell HS; Caldwell, NJ; (Y); Band; Concert Band; Jazz Band; Mrchg Band; Orch; Symp Band; Nwsp Rptr; High Hon Roll; NHS; Secy Natl Hnr Socty 86-87.

RUPP, KRISTIN; North Brunswick Twp HS; N Brunswick, NJ; (Y); Church Yth Grp; Cmnty Wkr; Drama Clb; Key Clb; Latin Clb; Mathletes; Math Tm; Model UN; School Musical; School Play; Itln Clb 83-84; Sundy Sch Tchr 86; Middl ST Evltn Comm 86; Ecnmcs.

RURA, TRACY; Hamilton High North; Trenton, NJ; (Y); 29/281; Key Clb; Pep Clb; Chorus; School Musical; School Play; Var L Cheerleading; JV Fld Hcky; High Hon Roll; Hon Roll; NHS.

RUSCAVAGE JR, JOSEPH V; Red Bank Catholic HS; Tinton Falls, NJ; (Y); 81/267; Q&S; Nwsp Sprt Ed; Var Ftbl; Var Trk; Qll & Scrll Natl Hnr Socty 86; Robert Connors Spirit & Sprtsmnshp Schlrshp Awd 86; Villanova U; Elctrcl Engrng.

RUSCIANI, LISA; Paul VI HS; Berlin, NJ; (S); 3/474; Jazz Band; Mrchg Band; School Musical; Variety Show; Lit Mag; Sftbl; NHS; Ntl Merit Ltr; St Schlr; Rutgers Smmr Schlr 85; Psychlgy.

RUSCINGNO, DONNA; Ridgefield Park HS; Little Ferry, NJ; (Y); 41/183; Church Yth Grp; Debate Tm; Math Tm; Ski Clb; Spanish Clb; Nwsp Stf; Yrbk Stf; Stu Cncl; Capt Coach Actv; Montclair ST; Actg.

RUSCONI, SHERYL; Clifton HS; Clifton, NJ; (Y); 29/687; French Clb; Key Clb; Mrchg Band; Mgr(s); French Hon Soc; Hon Roll; Jr NHS; Accntng.

RUSH, DARYN E; Phillipsburg HS; Stewartsville, NJ; (Y); 2/292; Pres VP 4-H; L Ftbl; L Trk; High Hon Roll; Pres NHS; Ntl Merit Ltr; Sal; St Schlr; U MD Chncllrs Schlr 86-87; Bell & Howell Natl Spec Scholar 86-87; Phillipsburg Exch Clb Yth Yr 85-86; U MD College Pk; Govt.

RUSH, HOLLY; Bridgewater Raritan HS; Bridgewater, NJ; (Y); Rep Frsh Cls; Rep Soph Cls; Rep Jr Cls; Rep Sr Cls; JV Cheerleading; Powder Puff Ftbl; Capt Swmmng; Hon Roll; Full Swmmng Schlrshp 86; WV U; Pre-Med.

RUSIN, JILL C; Hopewell Valley Central HS; Pennington, NJ; (Y); 8/199; AFS; Dance Clb; School Musical; Nwsp Rptr; Ed Yrbk Stf; Rep Stu Cncl; Var Cheerleading; Ntl Merit SF; St Schlr; French Clb; Girls St Alternate 85; Liberal Arts.

RUSMAN, JARED; St Peters Prep; Jersey City, NJ; (Y); 13/218; Capt Debate Tm; German Clb; Political Wkr; Capt Speech Tm; SADD; High Hon Roll; Ntl Merit Ltr; Capt NFL; Germn Lang Gold Mdl 85; Schl Hnr Pins 84-86; Stu Exch W Germny 85; Intl Bus.

RUSSANO, MICHELE; Pascack Valley HS; Hillsdale, NJ; (S); 14/260; Computer Clb; Math Tm; Lit Mag; Var Capt Bsktbl; High Hon Roll; Hon Roll; NHS; All Leag Bsktbl Hnrble Ment 86; Bus Educ & Phy Educ Prnt Fclty Orgnztn Mrt Awds 84-85; Fairfield U.

RUSSEK, DAVE; Lakewood HS; Lakewood, NJ; (Y); Boy Scts; Drama Clb; Key Clb; PAVAS; Chorus; School Play; Stage Crew; Variety Show; Var JV Bsbl; Var Ftbl; Perfrmng Arts.

RUSSELL, CARL; Hightstown HS; Hightstown, NJ; (Y); Church Yth Grp; Cmnty Wkr; French Clb; Chorus; Hon Roll; NHS; Ntl Merit Ltr; Prfct Atten Awd; Stdnt Advsry Comm 83-85; Engrng Physcs.

RUSSELL, CHRISTINE; Morris Knolls HS; Denville, NJ; (Y); Ski Clb; Chorus; School Musical; High Hon Roll; Hon Roll; Lbrl Arts.

RUSSELL, DAWN; Central Jersey Christian Schl; Manasquan, NJ; (S); Church Yth Grp; Band; Chorus; Var Bsktbl; Var Capt Socr; Var Sftbl; High Hon Roll; Sec Trs NHS; Eastern Mennonite Coll; Intl Ag.

RUSSELL, HEATHER; St Peters HS; New Brunswick, NJ; (Y); Church Yth Grp; Drama Clb; Church Choir; School Musical; Lit Mag; L Var Trk; Hon Roll; Bus Adm.

RUSSELL III, LYMAN; Parsippany Christian Schl; Landing, NJ; (Y); 1/17; Trs Sr Cls; Var Capt Bsbl; Var Capt Bsktbl; Cit Awd; High Hon Roll; Val; Pres Frsh Cls; Pres Soph Cls; VP Jr Cls; Soc Of Distngsdh Am H S Stu 83-86; Chancllrs Schlrshp 86; Liberty U; Poltcl Sci.

RUSSELL, MARYLYNN; Randolph HS; Randolph, NJ; (Y); Church Yth Grp; Chorus; Capt Drill Tm; Trs Jr Cls; Trs Sr Cls; Rep Stu Cncl; Powder Puff Ftbl; Hon Roll; Antioch Tm Ldr 86; Jr & Sr Prm Cmmtee 86.

RUSSELL, MELISSA; Woodstown HS; Woodstown, NJ; (Y); Church Yth Grp; FBLA; Hosp Aide; Spanish Clb; Church Choir; Rep Frsh Cls; JV VP Bsktbl; JV VP Cheerleading; Hon Roll; Candy Striper Of The Month 84; Bus Major.

RUSSELL, MINETTE; Linden HS; Linden, NJ; (Y); French Clb; Minorities Engrng; NYU.

RUSSELL, STEVE; Salem HS; Salem, NJ; (Y); Computer Clb; Spanish Clb; Varsity Clb; Bsbl; Ftbl; Frshnmn Ftbl Awd.

RUSSELL, STEVEN; High Point Regional HS; Sussex, NJ; (Y); 81/216; Church Yth Grp; Band; Concert Band; Jazz Band; Mrchg Band; L Var Bsbl; Var Ftbl; Hon Roll; Prfct Atten Awd; Seton Hall U; Bus.

RUSSELL, TARIQ; Rahway HS; Rahway, NJ; (Y); Art Clb; Computer Clb; Y-Teens; VP Frsh Cls; Stu Cncl; Bsktbl; Ftbl; Wt Lftg; Hon Roll; NHS; Pres Phy Ftns Awd 84; Achvng Hnrs Acad Studies 82; Marksmn 1st Cls Natl Rifle Assoc 82; Math.

RUSSELLO, CAROLYN; Gateway Regional HS; Woodbury Hts, NJ; (Y); 1/215; Cmnty Wkr; Hosp Aide; Office Aide; Scholastic Bowl; VP Spanish Clb; SADD; Var Swmmng; High Hon Roll; NHS; Spanish NHS; Rutgers Coll 86; Hghst Avg In Hist & Spanish In Jr Yr 85-86; Pharm.

RUSSO, COLUMBIA; North Arlington HS; N Arlington, NJ; (Y); Off Jr Cls; High Hon Roll; Hon Roll; Montclair ST Coll; Bus.

RUSSO, GINA; Toms River H S East; Toms Rvr, NJ; (Y); 42/545; Trs French Clb; Mrchg Band; Off Jr Cls; Stu Cncl; Var Fld Hcky; Var Pom Pon; Powder Puff Ftbl; Var Socr; Var Swmmng; Hon Roll; Acctg.

RUSSO, JEANA; Lodi HS; Lodi, NJ; (Y); 1/176; Trs Key Clb; Math Tm; Mrchg Band; Yrbk Phtg; Rep Stu Cncl; Bausch & Lomb Sci Awd; Pres Jr NHS; Val; Distngshd Schlr NJ; Rutgers Coll; Pharmacist.

RUSSO, JOANN; Phillipsburg HS; Phillipsburg, NJ; (Y); 59/334; Drama Clb; Ski Clb; Church Choir; Color Guard; Concert Band; Flag Corp; Mrchg Band; Nwsp Stf; Rep Stu Cncl; Hon Roll; Comm.

RUSSO, KAREN; Pequannock Twsp HS; Pompton Plains, NJ; (Y); 5/230; Am Leg Aux Girls St; Drama Clb; School Musical; Yrbk Rptr; VP Frsh Cls; Rep Stu Cncl; Gov Hon Prg Awd; NHS; Pres Schlr; Chorus; Pequannock Twsp Mem Post No 450 Amer Lgn $200 86; Rutgers Schlrs Prog 86-90; Rgn Choir NJ 84-86; Rutgers U; Pre-Med.

RUSSO, MARICLAIRE; Sacred Heart HS; Vineland, NJ; (S); 1/67; German Clb; Rep Frsh Cls; Sec Trs Soph Cls; Pres Jr Cls; Pres Sr Cls; Bsktbl; Cheerleading; Socr; Sftbl; Vllybl; Rutgers Schlr Awd 86; Bio.

RUSSOMAN, DANIEL; Bloomfield SR HS; Bloomfield, NJ; (Y); 117/447; Chess Clb; Nwsp Rptr; Nwsp Stf; Var Ftbl; High Hon Roll; Hon Roll; Journalism.

RUSSOMANNO, SAMANTHA; Belleville HS; Belleville, NJ; (Y); JV Var Sftbl; Hon Roll; Vrsty Letter Sftbll 86; Rutgers U; Bio.

RUSSONIELLO, CHRISTOPHER; St Rose HS; Point Pleasant, NJ; (Y); 24/226; Capt Chess Clb; Drama Clb; Thesps; School Musical; School Play; Lit Mag; Var Crs Cntry; Ntl Merit Schol; Bio.

RUST, TARA; Woodstown HS; Alloway, NJ; (Y); Sec French Clb; Office Aide; Teachers Aide; School Play; Yrbk Stf; Rep Stu Cncl; Var Cheerleading; Var Fld Hcky; Var Mgr(s); Var Score Keeper; U DE; Bus Adm.

RUSZALA, GREG; St Thomas Aquinas/Bishop Ahr; Colonia, NJ; (Y); Nwsp Rptr; Hon Roll; Antrhrplgy.

RUTECKI, KAREN; Fair Lawn HS; Fair Lawn, NJ; (Y); 37/325; VP Spanish Clb; Off Frsh Cls; Off Soph Cls; Jr Cls; JV Trk; Hon Roll; Bus.

RUTH, KEITH; Elmwood Park Memorial HS; Elmwood Pk, NJ; (Y); 20/160; Church Yth Grp; School Musical; Pres Jr Cls; Pres Sr Cls; Rep Stu Cncl; Var Capt Ftbl; Var Capt Wrstlng; Hon Roll; Drama Clb; Math Clb; Yth Wk Bd Ed Pres 85-86; Bd Ed Athletc Polcy Commtte 84-86; Prom Commtte Pres 85-86.

RUTNIK, TRACEY; Ramapo Regional HS; Wyckoff, NJ; (Y); 47/329; Sec VP Spanish Clb; Yrbk Stf; Rep Frsh Cls; Off Soph Cls; VP Jr Cls; Stu Cncl; Hon Roll; NHS; Merit Awd Outstndng Achvmnt Engl 83-84; Mert Awd Spnsh III 84-85; Merit Awd Soclgy 85-86.

RUTOWSKI, THOMAS SCOTT; Secaucus HS; Seacaucus, NJ; (Y); Am Leg Boys St; Key Clb; Var Bsktbl; Var Ftbl; Law.

RUTTER, JENNIFER; Deptford Township HS; Deptford, NJ; (Y); 3/283; FBLA; GAA; Band; Yrbk Bus Mgr; Yrbk Stf; VP Stu Cncl; JV Tennis; Trk; Hon Roll; VP NHS; Prncpls Lst Awd 83; Secy.

RUVO, SCOTT J; Pope John XXIII HS; Sparta, NJ; (Y); 30/150; Drama Clb; German Clb; Ski Clb; Varsity Clb; Chorus; School Play; Stage Crew; Rep Stu Cncl; NHS; Sussex Cnty All-Lg Awd In Wrstlng 86; Outstndng Srv Awd 86; Gettysburg Coll.

RUYAK, CRAIG; Hamilton High East; Hamilton Sq, NJ; (Y); 71/327; Key Clb; Varsity Clb; Rep Stu Cncl; Var Capt Bsbl; Var L Ftbl; Var L Wrstlng; Elks Awd; Hon Roll; 1st Team All Cnfrce, 2nd Tream All Cnty Ftbl 85-86; 2nd Team All Cnfr, All Cnty Wrstlng 85-86; Coll William & Mary.

RYAN, BECKY; Delsea Regional HS; Monroeville, NJ; (Y); Var Cheerleading; Var Fld Hcky; Var Sftbl; High Hon Roll; Hon Roll; NHS; Sftbl Athlete Of Wk 86; All Star 1st Team Tri-County Field Hockey 84-85; All Star Sftbl Tri Cnty 85-86; Glassboro ST Coll; Bus.

RYAN, BRIDGET; Manasquan HS; Spring Lake Hts, NJ; (Y); 30/241; Church Yth Grp; Drama Clb; Girl Scts; Key Clb; Spanish Clb; School Musical; School Play; Var Socr; High Hon Roll; Pres Schlr; Cngrsnl Awd Bnze 85; Internl Thspn Soc 86; Frst Aid Cdt Cptn 86; Clemson U; Mcrblgy.

RYAN, DONNA; Rumson-Fair Haven Regional HS; Rumson, NJ; (Y); 17/260; Cmnty Wkr; Band; School Play; Nwsp Rptr; Var Capt Cheerleading; High Hon Roll; JETS Awd; NHS; Grdn ST Dstngshd Schlr 86; Engrng Aide 85-86; U VA; Chem Engrng.

RYAN, JENNIFER; Manasquan HS; Manasquan, NJ; (Y); 1/244; Church Yth Grp; Drama Clb; Science Clb; Spanish Clb; Stage Crew; Lit Mag; Var Trk; High Hon Roll; Kiwanis Awd; NHS; Brd Educ Awd 85 & 86; Rutgers; Medcn.

RYAN, JIM; Middletown High School South; Middletown, NJ; (Y); 190/460; Latin Clb; Office Aide; Stage Crew; Variety Show; L Capt Bsbl; L Capt Ftbl; L Capt Trk; Hon Roll; Outstndg Athlt Mddltwn 85; Rider Coll; Bus Admin.

RYAN III, JOHN T; Seton Hall Prep; New Providence, NJ; (Y); 23/193; Church Yth Grp; Key Clb; Varsity Clb; Var L Socr; High Hon Roll; NHS.

RYAN, KRISTINE; Marylawn Of The Oranges HS; West Orange, NJ; (S); 6/52; VP Service Clb; Spanish Clb; Stage Crew; Nwsp Rptr; Sec Soph Cls; VP Sftbl; High Hon Roll; NHS; Spanish NHS.

RYAN, MELISSA; Essex Catholic Girls HS; Irvington, NJ; (Y); 8/60; Am Leg Aux Girls St; FHA; Church Choir; Drill Tm; Nwsp Stf; Yrbk Bus Mgr; Rep Jr Cls; Cheerleading; NHS; Prfct Atten Awd.

RYAN, SARAH; Mother Seton Regional HS; Elizabeth, NJ; (Y); Church Yth Grp; Drama Clb; GAA; Pep Clb; School Musical; School Play; Stage Crew; Variety Show; Nwsp Ed-Chief; Nwsp Phtg; Drama.

RYAN, WILLIAM; Parsippany HS; Parsippany, NJ; (Y); 117/367; Church Yth Grp; Stage Crew; Var Capt Socr; Hon Roll; Engrng.

RYBACKI, ROBERT; Indian Hills HS; Oakland, NJ; (Y); 93/273; Church Yth Grp; Ski Clb; JV Bsbl; JV Ice Hcky; JV Socr; High Hon Roll; Hon Roll; Spanish NHS; William Patterson Coll; Bus Adm.

RYBICKI, PAMELA; Triton Regional HS; Runnemede, NJ; (Y); 49/286; Spanish Clb; Band; Chorus; Concert Band; Jazz Band; Orch; Bowling; Socr; Hon Roll; Yrbk Stf; Louis Armstrong Awd Jazz Band 86; Olympc Conf Hnrs Band 81-85; Katherine Gibbs; Sec.

RYDER, SCOTT; Lyndhurst HS; Lyndhurst, NJ; (Y); 33/189; German Clb; Var Bsbl; Var Capt Bsktbl; Hon Roll; HOBY Fndtn 84-85; Med.

RYERSON, ANNE; Morris Catholic HS; Boonton, NJ; (Y); 10/142; Church Yth Grp; Natl Beta Clb; Pep Clb; Varsity Clb; VP Jr Cls; Pres Sr Cls; Var Sftbl; High Hon Roll; NHS; Pres Latin Clb; Natl Lang Arts Olympiad 3rd Pl 84; Grphc Arts.

RYKIEL, DAWN; Wall HS; Wall, NJ; (S); 17/269; German Clb; Ski Clb; Sftbl; Trk; High Hon Roll; Hon Roll.

RYSINSKI, ROBERT; N Brunswick Twp HS; N Brunswick, NJ; (Y); 59/265; Boy Scts; JV Bsktbl; Var Socr; Business Mgmt.

SAAM, BILL; Voorhees HS; Hampton, NJ; (Y); 25/274; German Clb; JCL; Latin Clb; Varsity Clb; Var Crs Cntry; Var Trk; Hon Roll; NHS; Natl Sci Chem 85; Natl Sci Physcs 86; Engr.

SAARI, RONALD; Manasquan HS; Spring Lake Hgts, NJ; (Y); Computer Clb; Band; Mrchg Band; Comp Pgmr.

SABARESE, TED; Christian Brothers Acad; Colts Neck, NJ; (Y); 52/220; Cmnty Wkr; Dance Clb; Red Cross Aide; Rep Jr Cls; Sec Stu Cncl; JV L Crs Cntry; Im Capt Socr; Var L Trk; Hon Roll; FIFA Affltd Sccr Referee 80-86; Volntr Wrk Awd 86; William & Mary; Bus Mngmnt.

SABATINO, ANTHONY; Metuchen HS; Metuchen, NJ; (Y); Am Leg Boys St; Boy Scts; Math Tm; Band; Jazz Band; Mrchg Band; Trs Jr Cls; Hon Roll; NHS; Math & Sci Rensselaes Medal 86.

SABBATH, JOSEPH W; Pequannock Township HS; Pompton Plains, NJ; (Y); 60/204; Am Leg Boys St; Church Yth Grp; FBLA; Hosp Aide; Latin Clb; Acpl Chr; Band; Mrchg Band; School Play; Stat Bsktbl; NJ Boys ST Dely 86; Comm.

SABER, KRISTINE L; Williamstown HS; Williamstown, NJ; (Y); Cmnty Wkr; Stat Score Keeper; Frgn Lang Awd Spanish 83-84; Elem Educ.

SABINE, GARY; Sayreville War Memorial HS; Parlin, NJ; (Y); 56/367; Am Leg Boys St; VP Varsity Clb; VP Stu Cncl; Socr; Trk; Cit Awd; DAR Awd; Hon Roll; Lion Awd; NHS; Bd Educ Awd Bst Srvd Schl Thrgh Stu Cncl 86; Pres Acdmc Ftns Awd 86; Rtry Clb Ctznshp Awd 86; Rider Coll; Bus Admn.

SABLON, CYNDI; West Orange HS; W Orange, NJ; (Y); 14/168; Service Clb; Spanish Clb; Yrbk Stf; Cheerleading; High Hon Roll; Hon Roll; Jr NHS; NHS; Spanish NHS; St Schlr; Cornell U.

SABO, PATRICIA; Holy Family Acad; Bayonne, NJ; (Y); High Hon Roll; Psych.

SABO, STEPHANIE ANN; Morris Hills Regional HS; Wharton, NJ; (Y); 70/290; Am Leg Aux Girls St; Pres JA; Nwsp Ed-Chief; Lit Mag; Sec Frsh Cls; Sec Soph Cls; Sec Jr Cls; Sec Sr Cls; Stu Cncl; Fld Hcky; Am Leg Aux Schlrshp 86; U AZ; Pre-Law.

SACCO, AMIE ELIZABETH; Holy Spirit HS; Margate, NJ; (Y); 58/329; Yrbk Stf; Rep Stu Cncl; Hon Roll; NHS; La Salle U; Communications.

SACCO, LOUIS W; Buena Regional HS; Richland, NJ; (S); Math Clb; Ski Clb; Varsity Clb; Var Bsbl; Var Bsktbl; Var Crs Cntry; Hon Roll; Jr NHS; Visl Arts Awd; Muscl Awd; Engr.

SACCO, MARK; South Plainfield HS; S Plainfield, NJ; (Y); 71/287; Letterman Clb; Varsity Clb; Rep Frsh Cls; Rep Soph Cls; Rep Jr Cls; Rep Sr Cls; Rep Stu Cncl; Ftbl; Wrstlng; Hon Roll; Drew Frgsh Schlrshps 86; NJ ST Wrstlng Trnmnt 85-86; Rutgers U.

SACCO, STEPHANIE; Shore Regional HS; W Long Branch, NJ; (Y); French Clb; SADD; Mrchg Band; Rep Frsh Cls; Capt Twrlr; High Hon Roll; Hon Roll; Stage Crew; Stat Trk; Awd Rcgnzng Outstndg Ldrshp Qualities 86; Sci Fair Prtcptn Awd 84-85; Lttrs Of Apprctn Art Crrclm 86.

SACKS, ALLISON; Lakewood HS; Lakewood, NJ; (Y); English Clb; Hosp Aide; JCL; Key Clb; Latin Clb; Mrchg Band; Yrbk Stf; Stu Cncl; Socr; Latin Hnr Scty 85-87.

SACKS, JOEL D; Triton Regional HS; Bellmawr, NJ; (Y); Am Leg Boys St; Capt Debate Tm; Science Clb; Pres Frsh Cls; Pres Stu Cncl; Hon Roll; NHS; Chess Clb; Computer Clb; Drama Clb; Pres Sth Jrsy Yth Cmsn 86-87; Hugh O Brian NJ Altrnt Intl Cnvtn 85; Law.

SACRO, FAYE; Westfield SR HS; Westfield, NJ; (Y); 55/514; French Hon Soc; High Hon Roll; Hon Roll; NHS; Cert Rcgntn Alg I 84; Pre-Med.

SADHAR, AMRIT; Mother Seton Regional HS; Hillside, NJ; (Y); 8/93; Cmnty Wkr; Hosp Aide; Math Tm; Science Clb; VP Service Clb; Stage Crew; Yrbk Stf; Stu Cncl; High Hon Roll; NHS; Douglass Coll.

SADLER, ELISE; Woodrow Wilson SR HS; Camden, NJ; (Y); Aud/Vis; Computer Clb; Drama Clb; JA; Science Clb; VICA; Chorus; School Play; Mgr(s); Tennis; Afro Am Club 86; Glassboro ST Col6; Cosmetology.

SADOVY, DAVID J; Hamilton HS North; Trenton, NJ; (Y); Am Leg Boys St; FBLA; VP Key Clb; Pres Math Clb; Lit Mag; Rep Stu Cncl; JV Bsbl; JV Trk; Bausch & Lomb Sci Awd; NHS; ST Champ Future Problem Slvng 86; 3rd Pl NJ Fuure Prblm Slvng 85; Semi Fnlst Gov Schl Of Sci 86; Physics.

SADOW, AUDREY; Freehold Township HS; Freehold, NJ; (Y); 55/382; French Clb; Temple Yth Grp; Varsity Clb; Rep Frsh Cls; Rep Soph Cls; Rep Jr Cls; Rep Sr Cls; Rep Stu Cncl; Mgr(s); Var L Socr; Psych.

SADOWSKI, CHERYL; Toms River H S South; Toms River, NJ; (Y); 73/360; Rep Frsh Cls; Rep Soph Cls; Rep Jr Cls; Rep Sr Cls; Rep Sec Stu Cncl; Var Capt Crs Cntry; Var Trk; TEAM 84-86; Trenton ST; Crmnl Jstc.

SADOWSKI, DOUGLAS J; Fair Lawn HS; Fair Lawn, NJ; (Y); 36/324; Am Leg Boys St; Im Coach Actv; Var Socr; Mech Engrng.

SADOWSKI, MARY BETH; Union Catholic Regional HS; New Providence, NJ; (Y); 30/308; Church Yth Grp; French Clb; Service Clb; Ski Clb; SADD; Rep Stu Cncl; Var Bsktbl; Var Capt Socr; Var Capt Vllybl; Hon Roll; Acadmc All Am 86; MVP Soccr Tm 86.

SADUSKY, VALARIE; Passaic Valley HS; Little Falls, NJ; (Y); 80/300; GAA; Hosp Aide; Key Clb; Letterman Clb; Ski Clb; Spanish Clb; Varsity Clb; School Play; Var Bsktbl; Var Sftbl; 1st Tm All Lg Ten 85; 1st Tm All Lg Sftbl, 2nd Tm All Cnty 85-86; 2nd Tm All Lg Bsktbl 85-86; Coll FL Atlantic; Bus Mgmt.

SAFFICI, CHRIS; Overbrook SR HS; Pine Hill, NJ; (Y); 26/270; Church Yth Grp; Spanish Clb; Band; Concert Band; Mrchg Band; Stage Crew; Nwsp Sprt Ed; Nwsp Stf; Rep Stu Cncl; Socr; Pine Hill Yth Assn & Philadelphia Police & Fire Hero Schlrshp 86; Temple U; Hstry.

SAGRESTANO, KENNETH; Bridgewater-Raritan East HS; Bridgewater, NJ; (Y); Boy Scts; Pres Church Yth Grp; Chorus; Concert Band; Drm & Bgl; Mrchg Band; Wt Lftg; Var Capt Wrstlng; NHS; Pres Schlr; Natl Hnr Roll 84-86; Syracuse U; Bus.

SAKATOS, NANCY; Red Bank Catholic HS; Wayside, NJ; (Y); Church Yth Grp; VP Debate Tm; Off NFL; Ski Clb; Drill Tm; Yrbk Stf; Tennis; Twrlr; Capt Stck Mrkt Gm Clss 86; Acad Awd Gym Grds 85-86; Coll Ruhich.

SAKS, JEFFREY; Abraham Clark HS; Roselle, NJ; (S); 9/210; Temple Yth Grp; Hon Roll; NHS; Camera Clb; French Clb; Latin Clb; Science Clb; Nwsp Rptr; Nwsp Stf; Yrbk Stf; Communal Rltns Coordntr ETZ Chaim NJ NCSY 84-85, Regnl VP 85-86.

SALAGA, MARIANNE; Burlington City HS; Burlington, NJ; (Y); VP Church Yth Grp; Hosp Aide; Rep Sec Stu Cncl; Var L Cheerleading; JV Var Fld Hcky; Var L Trk; High Hon Roll; NHS; Varsity Clb; Variety Show; Stu Frgn Exc Pgm 86; Sci Sympsum 86; Princpls Clb Awd 85; Pre-Med.

SALAS, ERIC; Morristown-Beard Schl; Mendham, NJ; (Y); 1/89; Church Yth Grp; Pres Intnl Clb; Model UN; Science Clb; Chorus; Nwsp Stf; Lit Mag; Trs Stu Cncl; Mgr(s); JV Tennis; Tri-M Music Hnr Soc 86.

SALAS, WILLIAM; Senior HS; Jersey City, NJ; (Y); NHS; Hon Cert, Achvmnt Cert & Merit Cert 85-86; Jersey City ST Coll; Compu Sci.

SALAYI, JENNIFER; Mater Dei HS; Middletown, NJ; (Y); 42/154; Pep Clb; Powder Puff Ftbl; Score Keeper; Cert Of Hnr In Bio 85; Astrmny.

SALERNO, ANN MARIE; Roselle Catholic HS; Roselle, NJ; (Y); Rep Soph Cls; JV Var Cheerleading; Stat Mgr(s); Stat Sftbl; Var Tennis; High Hon Roll; Hon Roll; Spanish NHS; Bus.

SALERNO, MIKE; Union HS; Union, NJ; (Y); Am Leg Boys St; Boy Scts; Service Clb; Trs Stu Cncl; JV Socr; Var L Swmmng; JV Trk; Hon Roll; Jr NHS; NHS; Engrg.

SALES, TAWANA; Frank H Morrell HS; Irvington, NJ; (Y); 19/400; Debate Tm; Spanish Clb; Chorus; Am Leg Boys St; JV Var Mgr(s); JV Var Timer; High Hon Roll; Hon Roll; Prfct Atten Awd; Guidance Schlrshp 86; Comp Prcsng Inst; Ofc Info Spec.

SALGADO, CARLO; Ocean Twp HS; Ocean, NJ; (Y); 151/336; Camera Clb; Nwsp Stf; Im Bsktbl; Rutgers; Pol Sci.

SALGADO JR, FERNANDO; Watchung Hills Regional HS; Gillette, NJ; (Y); Church Yth Grp; Ski Clb; Im Bsktbl; JV Socr; Tennis; Im Vllybl; Hon Roll.

SALGADO, MARGARIT; Perth Amboy HS; Perth Amboy, NJ; (Y); Drama Clb; Mrchg Band; Stu Cncl; Twrlr; High Hon Roll; Hon Roll; Dance Clb; French Clb; School Play; Top 25 Prcnt Cls 86; Intl Bus.

SALITER, KAREN; Villa Walsh Acad; Morris Plains, NJ; (S); Hosp Aide; Trs NFL; School Musical; Nwsp Stf; Lit Mag; Crs Cntry; Trk; High Hon Roll; Pres Spanish NHS; Paterson Dioce Frnsc Grnd Tnmnt; Natl Yng Ldrs Conf Sch Rep; Wheat Awd.

SALKO, THOMAS; Bayley-Ellard HS; Whippany, NJ; (Y); Am Leg Boys St; Boy Scts; Ski Clb; Church Choir; Stage Crew; Yrbk Phtg; Yrbk Stf; Lit Mag; Prfct Atten Awd; Eagle Sct Awd 85; Outstndng Cntrbtn Stg Crew 84-86; Rcvd Outstndng Acdmc Awd Bus 86; U Of Scranton; Med.

SALLA, GERALD DELLA; Bayley Ellard Reg HS; E Hanover, NJ; (Y); Cmnty Wkr; Letterman Clb; Varsity Clb; JV Var Bsbl; JV Var Ftbl; Wt Lftg; Hon Roll; No Absenties Awd 83; Phys Ed.

SALLATA, SUZANNE; Atlantic City HS; Ventnor, NJ; (Y); Dance Clb; Office Aide; Var Cheerleading; Var Capt Diving; Capt Swmmng; Hon Roll; Rotary Awd; CREW-2 Yr Lttrmn-Lghtwght 8 84-85; VP-FASH Show Clb 86.

SALLEE, PAUL W; Middletown HS South; Middletown, NJ; (Y); Church Yth Grp; Band; Chorus; Jazz Band; Mrchg Band; Hon Roll; NHS; Office Aide; Acpl Chr; Church Choir; Julliard Schl Of Mus Schlrshp 84-86; 1st Pl Monmouth Arts Cmptns Piano & Orgn 86; SMU.

SALLEROLI, CHRISTIAN MARK; Bergen Catholic HS; River Vale, NJ; (Y); 32/257; Am Leg Boys St; Chrmn Drama Clb; Capt Math Tm; School Musical; Rptr Nwsp Stf; VP Stu Cncl; High Hon Roll; NHS; Ntl Merit Ltr; Spanish NHS; Pres Phy Ftnss Awd 86; Bowdoin Coll; Plstc Surgn.

SALLIS, YOLANDA; Passaic County Tech; Paterson, NJ; (S); 21/445; Hosp Aide; Spanish Clb; Varsity Clb; Var Cheerleading; Var Pom Pon; Trk; High Hon Roll; NHS; Camera Clb; Dance Clb; Rutgers Coll.

SALM, ROBERT; Oratory Prep; Fanwood, NJ; (S); Boy Scts; Chess Clb; Computer Clb; Math Clb; Math Tm; Nwsp Stf; Im Vllybl; High Hon Roll; NHS; Eagle Scout 85.

SALMANOWITZ, JANIE; Pompton Lakes HS; Pompton Lakes, NJ; (Y); DECA; Ski Clb; Band; Chorus; Mrchg Band; Stu Cncl; Cheerleading; Gym; Sftbl; Hon Roll; Bergen CC; Mfg Agent.

SALMON, LAURA DIANE; Pompton Lakes HS; Pompton Lakes, NJ; (Y); French Clb; Varsity Clb; Band; Mrchg Band; Bsktbl; Crs Cntry; Tennis; High Hon Roll; Hon Roll; Prfct Atten Awd; Rcgntn Mdl Band 84-85; Bst In Clss Mdl Band 85-86; Stdy Abrd Amrcn Inst Frgn Stdy 86-87; Scl Sci.

SALOMAN, DEBBIE; N Brunswick Township HS; N Brunswick, NJ; (Y); Hosp Aide; Temple Yth Grp; JV Cheerleading; Var Capt Gym; Hon Roll; NHS.

SALTER, MICHELLE; Trenton Central HS; Trenton, NJ; (Y); 85/520; Sec Intnl Clb; Sec Spanish Clb; Hon Roll; Outstndng Ability In Art Fld 83; Peer Ldrshp Awd 86; 100 Behavior Crdts Awd 86; PA ST U; Commrcl Art.

SALTERS, AUDRA; Linden HS; Linden, NJ; (Y); French Clb; Girl Scts; Chorus; School Musical; School Play; Hon Roll; NHS; Minrties-Engrng; NY U.

SALVAGGIO, RALPH J; Dwight Morrow HS; Englewood, NJ; (Y); Church Yth Grp; Letterman Clb; Varsity Clb; JV Var Bsbl; Var Crs Cntry; JV Var Ftbl; Var Socr; JV Wrstlng; Hon Roll; Gltst Lkng Dfndnt 86; 1st Pl Tnns Dbls 84-85; Smmr Bsbll MVP 85-86; Bus.

SALVATORE, ALLISON; Clayton HS; Clayton, NJ; (Y); 8/74; Drama Clb; Key Clb; Chorus; School Musical; Yrbk Stf; Cheerleading; Fld Hcky; Sftbl; NHS; Exploring; Rep Hugh O Brien Yth Fndtn Semnr 85; Theatr Arts.

SALVATORE, ANN; De Paul HS; Wayne, NJ; (S); SADD; God Cntry Awd; Hon Roll; Glassboro ST Coll; Lawyer.

SALVATORE, MARY BETH; Bishop Ahr HS; Belle Meade, NJ; (Y); JV Sftbl; High Hon Roll; Phrmcy.

SALZ, ANDRE; Pascack Hills HS; Woodcliff Lake, NJ; (Y); Computer Clb; Model UN; Ski Clb; Band; Concert Band; Jazz Band; Mrchg Band; School Musical; Cit Awd; Hon Roll; Bus.

SAMALIS, JENNIFER; Red Bank Catholic HS; Loch Arbour, NJ; (Y); Church Yth Grp; French Clb; SADD; Teachers Aide; Chorus; Var Drill Tm; JV Var Mgr(s); JV Socr; Capt Var Twrlr; Stat L Wrstlng; Ed.

SAMBHU, MOHIT; Montville Township HS; Towaco, NJ; (Y); Computer Clb; DECA; Math Clb; Nwsp Rptr; Nwsp Stf; High Hon Roll; Hon Roll; Bio I Sci Tm 2nd NJ Sci Leag.

SAMITT, ALISON; Parsippany HS; Parsippany, NJ; (Y); French Clb; Hosp Aide; Math Tm; Pres Science Clb; Temple Yth Grp; Flag Corp; Yrbk Stf; High Hon Roll; NHS; Gvrnrs Schlr Sci 86; Med.

SAMMON, KATHY M; High Point Regional HS; Sussex, NJ; (Y); 60/235; SADD; Band; Drill Tm; Mrchg Band; High Hon Roll; Rep Frsh Cls; Rep Soph Cls; Trs Jr Cls; Trs Sr Cls; Rep Stu Cncl; Kutztown U; Accntng.

SAMPERS, KIMBERLEY; Lacordaire Acad; Montclair, NJ; (Y); 5/39; Art Clb; Computer Clb; FNA; Spanish Clb; Band; Chorus; Yrbk Phtg; VP Sr Cls; Var Tennis; Hon Roll; Troph Mst Imprvd Tnns 85-86; Distngshd Amer H S Stus 85-86; Archtctr.

SAMPSON, TRACY A; Pennsville Memorial HS; Pennsville, NJ; (Y); 25/222; Band; Color Guard; Concert Band; Mrchg Band; Orch; Hon Roll; NHS; Trenton ST Coll; Bio.

SAMRA, DAVID; Sayreville War Memorial HS; Sayreville, NJ; (Y); Church Yth Grp; Spanish Clb; Hon Roll; UCLA.

SAMUEL, ANTHONY; Orange HS; Orange, NJ; (S); 5/182; High Hon Roll; NHS; Rotary Clb Stu Of Mnth 85; Wesley; Bus.

SAMUEL, LOLETA; Lincoln HS; Jersey City, NJ; (Y); JA; Speech Tm; Color Guard; Bsktbl; Coach Actv; Capt Sftbl; Vllybl; NHS; Prfct Atten Awd; Most Likely To Succeed-Edkot Ctr Dvlpmnt Corp 85; Nrsng.

SAMUELSON, ALEXANDER I; Montclair HS; Montclair, NJ; (Y); 49/438; Aud/Vis; Cmnty Wkr; Jazz Band; Nwsp Stf; Hon Roll; High Avrg Itln 85; Syracuse U; Newhouse Schl.

SANABRIA, ANTHONY; Hudson Catholic HS; Jersey Cty, NJ; (Y); 9/185; Am Leg Boys St; Boy Scts; Hosp Aide; Hon Roll; NHS; Prtcptd Amrcn Chem Socs 9 Hr Crs 85; Prtcptd Hghr Achvt Prgm 82; Chem.

SANCHEZ, ANA; Camden HS; Camden, NJ; (S); Church Yth Grp; Dance Clb; Hosp Aide; Nwsp Rptr; Nwsp Stf; Score Keeper; Sftbl; High Hon Roll; Hon Roll; Sec.

SANCHEZ, BEATRICE; Eastside HS; Paterson, NJ; (Y); Vllybl; Hon Roll; Prfct Atten Awd; Sec.

SANCHEZ, BENJAMIN; Hillside HS; Hillside, NJ; (Y); 1/215; Computer Clb; Math Tm; Science Clb; Service Clb; Concert Band; Mrchg Band; High Hon Roll; Jr NHS; NHS; B Steisel Chem Awd 85-86; Gvrnrs Schl Sci85-86; Rutgers Schlrs Prgm 85-86; Rutgers U; Chem.

SANCHEZ, CELSO; Highland Park HS; Highland Park, NJ; (Y); 6/131; Cmnty Wkr; Pres German Clb; Concert Band; Mrchg Band; Var Bsbl; Var Bsktbl; Var Capt Socr; Lion Awd; NHS; St Schlr; Ntl Hspnc Schlr Schlrshp 85-86; Ntl Merit Fnlst 85-86; US Army Rsrv Ntl Schlr Athlt Awd 85-86; Dartmouth.

SANCHEZ, HECTOR; Eastside HS; Queens, NY; (Y); 35/556; Boy Scts; Church Yth Grp; Math Tm; Radio Clb; Spanish Clb; Band; Nwsp Phtg; Nwsp Rptr; Off Frsh Cls; Rep Soph Cls; MVP Spnsh Sccr Leag 85; MVP Indr Sccr Semi Profssnl T 85; Athetic Schlrshp Sccr FDU 86; Fairleigh Dickinson U; Brdsctng.

SANCHEZ, IGMARA; Our Lady Of Good Counsel; Newark, NJ; (Y); 1/73; Hosp Aide; Science Clb; CC Awd; High Hon Roll; JC Awd; Masonic Awd; NHS; Prfct Atten Awd; Val 86; Cert Tchr Natl Guild Piano Tchrs 86; Grdn St Dstngshd Schlrs Awd 86; Cornell U; Pre Med.

SANCHEZ, PEDRO; St Joseph Of The Palisades HS; Union City, NJ; (S); Art Clb; DECA; FCA; JA; Yrbk Phtg; Ftbl; Swmmng; Cit Awd; Hon Roll; JETS Awd; Archtctr.

SANCHEZ, REBECCA; Bishop Ahr/St Tghomas HS; Colonia, NJ; (Y); Pres VP Leo Clb; VP Spanish Clb; Chorus; Yrbk Stf; High Hon Roll; Hon Roll; Lion Awd; Dance Awd Ballet 83-86; Awd Flamenco Dancing 84-86; Bus.

SANCHEZ, SANDRA; Immaculate Conception HS; Passaic Pk, NJ; (Y); Church Yth Grp; VP Drama Clb; Ski Clb; Spanish Clb; Teachers Aide; High Hon Roll; Hon Roll; Bus.

SANDERS, BRIAN; Lakewood HS; Lakewood, NJ; (Y); 4/252; Am Leg Boys St; FBLA; Mrchg Band; Orch; Nwsp Sprt Ed; High Hon Roll; NHS; Temple Yth Grp; Nwsp Rptr; Hon Roll; H S Mrchng Band Schlrshp 86; Physcl Sci Awd 86; LHSPTSA Awd-Engl 86; Lehigh U; Engrng.

SANDERS, DAWN; Lenape Valley Regional HS; Stanhope, NJ; (Y); PAVAS; Teachers Aide; Chorus; Var Stu Cncl; Var L Sftbl; Hon Roll; NHS; Prfct Atten Awd; Spanish NHS; Spnsh Awd-Excllnc 84-86; Grgg Typng Awd 83-84; 12 Yrs Piano Lssns 84; 2 Yrs Accomp For Chrus 86-87; Rutgers; Psyclgy.

SANDERS, ELIZABETH; Parsippany Hills HS; Mt Tabor, NJ; (S); NFL; Thesps; Chorus; School Musical; School Play; Variety Show; VP Soph Cls; Hon Roll; Acpl Chr; Band; U S Congrssnl Pg 86; NJ All ST Chorus 84-86; Outstndng Ovr All Chrprsn NJ Modl Congrss 85.

SANDERS, ROBERT M; Monmouth Regional HS; Eatontown, NJ; (Y); 7/253; Cmnty Wkr; Ski Clb; Bowling; VP Socr; Hon Roll; Ntl Merit SF; St Schlr; ST Sci Day Rep 83-85; Sci Sympsm Rep 85; Comp Sci.

SANDERSON, JOE; Gloucester City JR SR HS; Gloucester, NJ; (Y); Chorus; School Musical; School Play; Socr; Hon Roll; Photographer.

SANDFORD, RICHARD; Wall HS; Manasquan, NJ; (S); 3/250; Church Yth Grp; VP German Clb; Key Clb; Ski Clb; VP Socr; High Hon Roll; Kiwanis Awd; Kiwanis Hon Soc 85; Engrng.

SANDHAM, AIMEE; Notre Dame HS; Kendall Pk, NJ; (Y); Office Aide; Pep Clb; Rep Frsh Cls; Rep Soph Cls; Var Capt Swmmng; Im Vllybl; Wt Lftg; High Hon Roll; Hon Roll; Excllnc Art Awd 84; Swmmng 84-85; Am H S Athlt 85; Libl Arts.

SANDLER, AMY; Hightstown HS; E Windsor, NJ; (Y); 81/449; Cmnty Wkr; French Clb; FBLA; Intnl Clb; Yrbk Stf; Off Jr Cls; Hon Roll; Reg Typing Cmpttn Awd 86; Chldhd Educ.

SANDMANN, RONALD J; Hackensack HS; Rochelle Park, NJ; (Y); Am Leg Boys St; Aud/Vis; Radio Clb; Lit Mag; Hon Roll; Dplm Grad Amer Lgn Jersey Bys ST 86; Plt.

SANDONATO, PATTY; Linden HS; Linden, NJ; (Y); Rep Soph Cls; Rep Jr Cls; Rep Stu Cncl; Var Cheerleading; High Hon Roll; Hon Roll; NHS; Sec/Trsr Natl Hnr Scty 86-87.

SANDRO, MARY; Paul VI HS; Berlin, NJ; (S); 10/544; Math Clb; SADD; JV Fld Hcky; JV Trk; Hon Roll; Sci.

SANDRUE, DARRELL; Hackettstown HS; Long Valley, NJ; (Y); Church Choir; Lit Mag; JV Ftbl; Hon Roll; Cmrcl Advrtsg.

SANDS, STACI; Gateway Regional HS; National Park, NJ; (Y); Church Yth Grp; French Clb; Hosp Aide; SADD; Im Sftbl; Student Of Month 84; Acctng.

SANFILIPPO, DONNA; East Brunswick HS; East Brunswick, NJ; (Y); Dance Clb; French Clb; German Clb; Key Clb; SADD; Band; Mrchg Band; Hon Roll; Adult & Continuing Ed Awd; Diplomat.

SANFORD, RICHARD J; Wall HS; Manasquan, NJ; (Y); 3/300; Am Leg Boys St; VP German Clb; Ski Clb; Var JV Socr; Kiwanis Awd; NHS; Natl Eng Merit Awd, Acdmc All Am; Engrng.

SANG, JANSEW; Memorial HS; W New York, NJ; (Y); Computer Clb; Key Clb; Sec Math Clb; Science Clb; Band; School Play; Twrlr; High Hon Roll; Hon Roll; Jr NHS; Sci.

SANNEY, STACIE; Hopewell Valley Central HS; Hopewell, NJ; (S); DECA; FBLA; German Clb; Hon Roll; DE ST Comp 1st Pl Fin & Credit Wrttn Evnt 86; Feb Bus Stu Mnth 86; Hon Men Awd Ldrshp Awd Fut Sec; Rider Coll; Bus Adm.

SANPHILIP, LORI; Holy Family Acad; Bayonne, NJ; (Y); Church Yth Grp; Pep Clb; Variety Show; Bsktbl; Vllybl; Villa Nova; Psych.

SANTA LUCIA, DIANE; Fair Lawn HS; Fairlawn, NJ; (Y); Color Guard; Hon Roll; Penn ST; Engrng.

SANTANA, JULISSA KATHERINE; Paul VI Regional HS; Passaic, NJ; (S); Computer Clb; FBLA; Key Clb; SADD; Ed Nwsp Stf; Stu Cncl; JV Mgr(s); High Hon Roll; NHS; Voice Dem Awd; Prlmntry Prcdr 2nd Pl 84-85; Engrng.

SANTANA, YOLANDA; Dover HS; Dover, NJ; (Y); Computer Clb; Spanish Clb; Varsity Clb; Chorus; Variety Show; Nwsp Stf; Rep Sr Cls; Crs Cntry; Trk; Hon Roll; Rutgers; Comp Sci.

SANTANELLO, TRACY; St Rose HS; Bradley Beach, NJ; (Y); Am Leg Aux Girls St; JV Bsktbl; JV Var Crs Cntry; JV Var Trk; French Hon Soc; High Hon Roll; Hon Roll; NHS; ROTC Schlrshp 86; US Air Force Acad 86; US Mltry Acad 86; US Military Acad.

SANTANGELO, DONNA; Sacred Heart HS; Vineland, NJ; (S); Cmnty Wkr; Drama Clb; Hosp Aide; Spanish Clb; Chorus; School Play; Off Frsh Cls; Rep Soph Cls; Rep Jr Cls; Off Sr Cls; Law.

SANTANGELO, KELLEY L; Sussex County Vo-Tech Schl; Franklin, NJ; (S); #3 In Class; Library Aide; Yrbk Stf; High Hon Roll; Hon Roll; NHS; Katherine Gibbs Ldrshp Awd Futr Secys Hnbl Mntn 85.

SANTANNA, MARGARET; Bishop George AHR; Edison, NJ; (Y); 40/277; Hosp Aide; Intnl Clb; Math Tm; Model UN; Science Clb; Service Clb; Band; Concert Band; Mrchg Band; Nwsp Stf.

SANTANTONIO, SHERI; Parsippany HS; Parsippany, NJ; (Y); 81/318; Concert Band; Jazz Band; Mrchg Band; Var JV Socr; JV Sftbl; High Hon Roll; Varsity Clb; Band; Hon Roll; Pres Schlr; MVP JV Sccr Tm 83; Pres Acdmc Fit Awd 86; Montclair ST; Tchg.

SANTIAGO, ROBERTO; Lincoln HS; Jersey City, NJ; (Y); Art Clb; DECA; Key Clb; Spanish Clb; Rep Frsh Cls; Badmtn; Bsbl; Gym; Swmmng; Arch.

SANTIAGO, SALLY; Vineland HS; Vineland, NJ; (Y); CAP; Spanish Clb; Vineland Acad; Cosmtlgst.

SANTILLI, LYNN; Rancocas Valley Regional HS; Mount Holly, NJ; (Y); 12/296; Church Yth Grp; Church Choir; Orch; School Musical; Sec Stu Cncl; Var JV Fld Hcky; Var JV Lcrss; Stat Wrstlng; High Hon Roll; Hon Roll; Pre-Med.

SANTINO, JANINE; Emerson JR SR HS; Emerson, NJ; (Y); Church Yth Grp; Pres FNA; Hosp Aide; Pep Clb; Spanish Clb; Band; Concert Band; Mrchg Band; School Musical; Yrbk Stf; UNICO Ntl Schlrshp 86; Rssll Sage Coll Schlrshp 86; Dstngshd & Praiswrthy Hnr Rll 85-86; Russell Sage Coll; Physcl Thrpy.

SANTO, RACHEL; Spotswood HS; Milltown, NJ; (S); Hosp Aide; Intnl Clb; Science Clb; School Play; Yrbk Stf; Mgr(s); Stat Tennis; High Hon Roll; Hon Roll; NHS.

SANTONASTASO, RALPH; North Plainfield HS; N Plainfield, NJ; (Y); Church Yth Grp; Ski Clb; JV Bsbl; Coach Actv; VP Ftbl; Wt Lftg; VP Wrstlng; Hon Roll; Prfct Atten Awd; Engrng.

SANTORA, ANTHONY; Hudson Catholic HS; Jersey City, NJ; (Y); Boy Scts; Bsbl; Ftbl; Trk; Bus.

SANTORA, ROBIN; Our Lady Of Good Counsel; Newark, NJ; (Y); 1/106; Science Clb; Teachers Aide; Chorus; School Musical; Yrbk Stf; Hon Roll; NHS; Prfct Atten Awd.

SANTORA, SCOTT; Wayne Hills HS; Wayne, NJ; (Y); 138/305; PAVAS; Radio Clb; Varsity Clb; Chorus; Concert Band; Jazz Band; School Musical; Capt Ftbl; Trk; Hon Roll; 2nd Team All Cnty, All Leag Ftbl 85; 2nd Team All Leag Trck 86; Bus.

SANTORELLI, MICHAEL; Morristown HS; Morristown, NJ; (Y); 130/449; Varsity Clb; Rep Frsh Cls; Rep Soph Cls; Var Ftbl; Var Lcrss; Var Wt Lftg; Hon Roll.

SANTORIELLO, MARIANNE; Roselle Catholic HS; Hillside, NJ; (Y); Dance Clb; JA; Math Tm; Variety Show; Var Tennis; High Hon Roll; Bst Chrstn Awd 83.

SANTORO, CHUCK; Paramus HS; Paramus, NJ; (Y); Am Leg Boys St; VP Drama Clb; PAVAS; VP Chorus; School Musical; School Play; Yrbk Ed-Chief; Rep Jr Cls; Stu Cncl; Thtr Schlrshp Hmptn Plyhs 84 & 85; Brgn Cnty Chr 85.

SANTORO, TERRY; Eastern Regional HS; Gibbsboro, NJ; (Y); 38/330; Var Cheerleading; Var Hon Roll; Church Yth Grp; Rotary Ldrshp Awds Seminar 86; Physical Ther.

SANTOS, MANOLITA; Bishop Ahr HS; Carteret, NJ; (Y); 86/246; Cmnty Wkr; Hosp Aide; Spanish Clb; Hon Roll; Spanish NHS; Excllnc In Span; Seton Hall U; Polit Sci.

SANTOS, NUNO; St Peters Prep; Newark, NJ; (Y); 71/218; Boys Clb Am; Letterman Clb; ROTC; Spanish Clb; Stage Crew; Nwsp Stf; Yrbk Stf; Rep Soph Cls; Sec Jr Cls; Var L Socr; All ST Parochl A Tm 85; All Hudson Cnty Tm 85; 2nd Hnrs H S 83-86; Bus.

SANTOS, REGINA; Red Bank Regional HS; Union Bch, NJ; (Y); FHA; PAVAS; SADD; Nwsp Rptr; Nwsp Stf; Rep Frsh Cls; Sec Soph Cls; Hon Roll; Spanish NHS; 1st Pl In A Future Hmemkrs Of Amer Pstr Cntst 84-85; Achvt Awd Frm Rd Mgzine 84-85; Jrnlsm Awd 85-86; Cmnctns.

SAPARA, MARK; Howell HS; Howell, NJ; (Y); 14/379; Temple Yth Grp; Nwsp Rptr; High Hon Roll; NHS; Acdmc Excllnce Awd Eng 84, 85 & 86; Cert Highest Fund Raiser MS Work Encounter 85; Rutgers U; Chld Psych.

SAPERSTEIN, LYLE; Manalapan HS; Englishtown, NJ; (Y); 132/450; Science Clb; Temple Yth Grp; Sci.

SAPONARO, ELIZABETH; Paul VI HS; Berlin, NJ; (S); 6/470; Church Yth Grp; Math Clb; Variety Show; Nwsp Ed-Chief; Yrbk Stf; High Hon Roll; NHS; Italian Clb; Hst, Hstss; Rutgers U; Pre-Med.

SAPORITO, GRACE MARIE; Atlantic City HS; Ventnor, NJ; (Y); 66/456; Church Yth Grp; Cmnty Wkr; Drama Clb; Exploring; SADD; School Play; Stu Cncl; Hon Roll; Library Aide; Trk; Clmbs Day Schlrshp Cmmtee Itln Awd 83-86; Glassboro ST Coll.

SAPORITO, MARIA; Clifton HS; Clifton, NJ; (Y); 37/637; Key Clb; Math Clb; Office Aide; Spanish Clb; Cheerleading; Hon Roll; Jr NHS; Spanish NHS; Chld Psych.

SARABIA, TANIA; Memorial HS; West New York, NJ; (Y); Concert Band; Flag Corp; Stu Cncl; Var Twrlr; Hon Roll; Piano Guild Fndrs Medal NGPT 84; Accntnt.

SARACENI, FRANK; North Bergen HS; North Bergen, NJ; (Y); 4/470; Rep Frsh Cls; Rep Jr Cls; Im Bsktbl; Var JV Ftbl; Var Wt Lftg; Hon Roll; NHS; Merit Society 87; Engrng.

SARACINO, MICHOLENE; Pinelands Regional HS; Tuckerrton, NJ; (Y); Art Clb; French Clb; Hosp Aide; Nwsp Ed-Chief; Nwsp Rptr; Frsh Cls; Sr Cls; Sftbl; Accounting.

SARACO, ARLENE; Bishop Ahr/St Thomas HS; Colonia, NJ; (Y); Art Clb; Church Yth Grp; Drama Clb; Ski Clb; Yrbk Stf; JV Sftbl; JV Var Trk; Hon Roll; Comm.

SARDANA, SEEMA; Cedar Ridge HS; Old Bridge, NJ; (Y); 9/378; Computer Clb; Trs FBLA; Key Clb; Chorus; Orch; Yrbk Stf; Cit Awd; French Hon Soc; High Hon Roll; NHS; 1st Pl Girls Div Schl Decthln 84; 6th Pl Acctg I FBLA Regnl, 2nd Pl ST Comptv Evnts 86; Sci.

SARDEIRA, SILVIA; Colonia HS; Colonia, NJ; (Y); Chess Clb; Computer Clb; Drama Clb; French Clb; SADD; Chorus; Church Choir; Orch; Nwsp Rptr; Vllybl; Diplmcy.

SARGEANT, JAMIE; Pope John XIII Regional HS; Oak Ridge, NJ; (Y); French Clb; Teachers Aide; Yrbk Rptr; Lit Mag; Var L Bsktbl; Im Crs Cntry; Var L Ftbl; High Hon Roll; Hon Roll; Jr NHS; Pre-Vet.

SARIC, NEDA M; Audubon HS; Mt Ephraim, NJ; (Y); 13/119; Quiz Bowl; Scholastic Bowl; Spanish Clb; Drill Tm; Mrchg Band; School Play; Yrbk Stf; Rep Stu Cncl; Cit Awd; Hon Roll; Sons Of Amer Rvltn Good Ctznshp Awd 86; Elzbthtwn Coll; Intl Bus.

SARKAR, MOUSUMI; Bridgewater-Raritan HS West; Bridgewater, NJ; (Y); French Clb; Quiz Bowl; Science Clb; Off Jr Cls; High Hon Roll; Hon Roll; NHS; Pres Acad Fit Awd 86; PTO Coll Scholar 86; Soc Studies Awd 86; Rutgers Coll; Bus Adm.

SARNO, DENISE; Bloomfield HS; Bloomfield, NJ; (Y); 74/442; GAA; Varsity Clb; Im Badmtn; Var Bsktbl; Capt Var Fld Hcky; Sftbl; High Hon Roll; Hon Roll; Prfct Atten Awd; All ST Sftbll Essx Cnty All Area Sftblltms 84-85; All Mtrpltn Sftbll Tm 85-86; MVP Awd 85.

SAROKAS, CHRISTINE; Clifton HS; Clifton, NJ; (Y); 139/637; Computer Clb; Hosp Aide; Office Aide; Science Clb; Thesps; School Play; Nwsp Ed-Chief; Nwsp Rptr; Hon Roll; Jr NHS; Nrsg.

SASS, KIRSTEN; North Warren Regional HS; Johnsonburg, NJ; (S); Trs Pres 4-H; VP FFA; 4-H Awd; FFA Mst Actv Ofcr 84-85; 1st Pl FFA ST Frts & Vgtbls Jdgng 84; 2nd Pl FFA ST Lvestck Jdgng 85; Alfred Coll; Vet Asst.

SASS, STEVE; Don Bosco Prep; Franklin Lks, NJ; (Y); 80/180; Church Yth Grp; Model UN; Ski Clb; School Play; Stage Crew; Yrbk Rptr; Rep Frsh Cls; Im Bsktbl; Capt Coach Actv; Crs Cntry; Prsh Cncl Rep; Law.

SASSAMAN, JO ANN; Burlington City HS; Beverly, NJ; (Y); 16/168; Am Leg Aux Girls St; FNA; Office Aide; Lit Mag; Rep Stu Cncl; Im Sftbl; Gov Hon Prg Awd; Hon Roll; Garden ST Schlrshp; Ratgers U; Bus Adm.

SASSO, ROBERT; Lodi HS; Lodi, NJ; (Y); 20/148; Boys Clb Am; Math Clb; Math Tm; Var L Bsbl; Hon Roll; NHS; Math.

SASSO, THERESA; Egg Harbor Twp HS; Mays Landing, NJ; (S); 4/266; French Clb; GAA; JV Var Fld Hcky; High Hon Roll; NHS; Ntl Merit Ltr; SADD; Rep Frsh Cls; Jr NHS; Natl Ldrshp Merit Awd; Natl Merit Awd-Chem; World Affairs Clb; American U; Intl Rltns.

SATOLA, BRIAN; St Joseph Regional HS; Upper Saddle Rive, NJ; (Y); 26/163; Church Yth Grp; Math Clb; Rep Frsh Cls; Hon Roll; NHS; Spanish NHS; Var Capt Bsbl; JV Bsktbl; Var Capt Ftbl; Nnsl 2nd Tm All-Leag Ftbl Qtrbck,Bsbl Otfld 85-86; Soph & JR Athlete Of The Yr 85-86.

SATTERTHWAITE, CHRISTINE L; Sussex County Vo-Tech HS; Stanhope, NJ; (S); #6 In Class; Girl Scts; Spanish Clb; Rep Jr Cls; Trs Sr Cls; Stu Cncl; JV Bsktbl; Cit Awd; High Hon Roll; NHS; St Schlr; County Coll Of Morris; Comp Prg.

SAUCHELLI, CHRISTINE; Morris Catholic HS; Rockaway, NJ; (Y); 13/142; Nwsp Sprt Ed; Score Keeper; High Hon Roll; NHS.

SAUER, NEIL; Toms River HS North; Toms River, NJ; (Y); School Musical; Stage Crew; Variety Show; Stu Cncl; JV Var Trk; Hon Roll; NHS; Voice Dem Awd; Shore Shp Crftmns Fair 1st Pl 83-84 2nd Pl 84-85; Cnty Trck Chmpnshp 2nd Pl 82-83; NJ Inst Of Tech; Arch.

SAUERS, AMANDA; Williamstown HS; Williamstown, NJ; (Y); Varsity Clb; Band; Concert Band; Drill Tm; Flag Corp; Orch; School Play; Fld Hcky; Mgr(s); Trk; Stockton ST Coll; Scndry Educ.

SAUL, FAYE; Immaculate Conception HS; East Orange, NJ; (Y); 9/62; Hosp Aide; School Musical; Nwsp Rptr; Yrbk Stf; Sec Frsh Cls; Pres French Hon Soc; High Hon Roll; Hon Roll; Prfct Atten Awd; Pres French Clb; Acdmc All Am 85; Natl Ldrshp/Svc Awd 86; Cum Laude/Magna Cum Laude Awd-Natl Latin Exam 83 & 84; Rutgers U; Pre-Law.

SAUL, KEVIN M; St Joseph Regional HS; Westwood, NJ; (Y); 41/192; Art Clb; Varsity Clb; Var Bsbl; JV Bsktbl; Capt Var Socr; Pascack Vly Police Wives Schlrshp 86; Westwood Fire Dept Schlrshp 86; Fred Witte 86; Rutgers U; Bus Adm.

SAUL, MELISSA; Arthur P Schalick HS; Elmer, NJ; (Y); Art Clb; JA; Var Bsktbl; JV Sftbl; Hon Roll; Psych.

SAULOG, AIMEE E; St Pius X Regional HS; Piscataway, NJ; (Y); 1/115; Library Aide; Quiz Bowl; Speech Tm; School Musical; Nwsp Rptr; Off Frsh Cls; Capt Tennis; High Hon Roll; NHS; Natl Ed Develpmnt Awds 84-85; Natl Sci Olympd Awd Distgshd Comptn 85; St Pius X Awds Engl Mathmtcs 85; Biochem.

SAUMS, KATHRYN; Hunterdon Central HS; Flemington, NJ; (Y); 33/539; Computer Clb; Key Clb; Spanish Clb; Hon Roll; Spanish NHS; Garden St Dstngshd Schlr 86; Rider Coll; Actrl Sci.

SAUNDERS, KIM; Elizabeth HS; Elizabeth, NJ; (Y); 14/840; Key Clb; Yrbk Stf; High Hon Roll; NHS; Ntl Merit Ltr; Spanish NHS; WA Wrkshps Cngrssnl Smnr 86; Yth Cty Gvrnmt 86; George Washington U; Lbrl Arts.

SAUNDERS, MARYANN; Woodbridge SR HS; Woodbridge, NJ; (Y); 100/425; Ski Clb; Chorus; School Musical; School Play; Var Capt Cheerleading; Score Keeper; Stat Sftbl; UCLA; Spch Thrpst.

SAUTER, DAVID; Sparta HS; Sparta, NJ; (Y); 18/210; Chess Clb; Pres Church Yth Grp; Scholastic Bowl; Varsity Clb; Concert Band; Mrchg Band; Var Crs Cntry; Var Trk; Hon Roll; NHS; Blmsbrg U Mitrani Schlrshp 86; Psdntl Acad Ftns Awd 86; Bloomsburg U; Bus Mgmnt.

SAUTER, LUISA P; Holy Family Acad; Bayonne, NJ; (Y); 23/119; Art Clb; Church Yth Grp; Cmnty Wkr; Dance Clb; Teachers Aide; Chorus; School Musical; Variety Show; Lit Mag; Hon Roll; NJS Teenarts Rep 82-83; NJ Mus Tchrs Assn Piano Comp 1st 83; Holy Fmly Acad Hnr Schlstc Achvt 85, 86; Westminster Choir Coll; Piano P.

SAVA, ROBERT; Hightstown HS; E Windsor, NJ; (Y); JV Trk; Hon Roll; Bus.

SAVAGE, AMY; South Plainfield HS; S Plainfield, NJ; (Y); Spanish Clb; Chorus; Mrchg Band; Orch; School Musical; Yrbk Stf; Stu Cncl; JV Bsktbl; Hon Roll; Rutgers; Psych.

SAVERY II, CHARLES; Haddonfield Memorial HS; Haddonfield, NJ; (Y); AFS; Cmnty Wkr; Intnl Clb; Teachers Aide; Stu Cncl; Var L Socr; Var L Trk.

SAVIANO, NICOLETTE; Toms River HS East; Toms River, NJ; (Y); 60/450; SADD; Variety Show; Rep Frsh Cls; Rep Soph Cls; Rep Jr Cls; Rep Sr Cls; Rep Stu Cncl; Var Capt Cheerleading; Powder Puff Ftbl; Hon Roll; Mst Outstndng Stu Cncl Scholar 85-86; Trenton ST Coll; Elem Ed.

SAVITSKY, ANNE P; Pascack Valley HS; River Vale, NJ; (Y); Church Yth Grp; Red Cross Aide; Spanish Clb; Concert Band; Mrchg Band; School Musical; Variety Show; Yrbk Stf; Bowling; Ltr Concert Marchng Band 85; L Bowlng 86; Bus.

SAVONIJE, NICOLE T; Rutherford HS; Rutherford, NJ; (Y); Ski Clb; Flag Corp; Off Jr Cls; Var Swmmng; Var Trk; Rutgers U; Stckbrkr.

SAWAGED, RAID; Hudson Catholic HS; Jersey Cty, NJ; (Y); Church Yth Grp; Math Clb; VP Spanish Clb; SADD; School Musical; Nwsp Rptr; Im Vllybl; Hon Roll; NHS; Joseph V Monaco Mem Schlrshp 85-86; Martin Luther King Jr Schlrshp; St John Baptist Acad Schlrshp; Seton Hall U; Pre-Med.

SAWCZUK, JOSEPH M; Edgewood Regional HS; Atco, NJ; (Y); Church Yth Grp; VP Varsity Clb; Rep Frsh Cls; Rep Soph Cls; Rep Jr Cls; Hon Roll; Jr NHS; NHS; Var Capt Socr; Comp Sci.

SAWEY, JOSEPH; Palisades Park HS; Palisades Pk, NJ; (Y); Q&S; Nwsp Ed-Chief; Nwsp Rptr; Nwsp Stf; JV Bowling; Hon Roll; Trs NHS; NY U; Cmmnctns.

SAWHNEY, ROGER ANU; Wardlaw-Hartridge HS; Edison, NJ; (Y); 3/53; Civic Clb; Debate Tm; Hosp Aide; SADD; Acpl Chr; School Musical; School Play; Nwsp Rptr; Yrbk Rptr; Chrmn Stu Cncl; Fin Gov Schl Sci NJ 86; Natl Latin Exam Magna Cum Laude 84, Cum Laude 85; Smmr Inst Gftd 85; Sci.

SAWN, DIANE; Washington Township HS; Turnersville, NJ; (Y); 20/470; JA; Var L Swmmng; Var L Trk; Cit Awd; High Hon Roll; NHS; Pres Schlr; Cmnty Wkr; Girl Scts; Hosp Aide; Danny Greenblatt Schlrshp 86; Mst Courageous Swimmer In S Jersey Awd 86; RYLA Conferee 85; Trenton ST Coll; Bio.

SAWYER, YVETTE; Parsippany HS; Parsippany, NJ; (Y); 46/322; FBLA; GAA; Stu Cncl; Bsktbl; Sftbl; Tennis; High Hon Roll; Hon Roll; NHS; Pep Clb; Rutgers U; Acctg.

SAYA, ANTONINO; Paulsboro HS; Paulsboro, NJ; (Y); JV Ftbl; Im Socr; Hon Roll; Bus Admin.

SAYA, NICHOLAS; Manchester Regional HS; N Haledon, NJ; (S); Band; Chorus; Concert Band; Jazz Band; Mrchg Band; Orch; Jr All Amer Hall Of Fame 83-84; Schlrshp-Berklee Coll 85; Band Person Of The Yr 82; Berklee Coll Of Music; Music.

SAYEGH, ROBERT B; Fair Lawn HS; Fair Lawn, NJ; (Y); Am Leg Boys St; Varsity Clb; Yrbk Stf; Rep Frsh Cls; Rep Soph Cls; Trs Jr Cls; Pres Sr Cls; Var Crs Cntry; Var Capt Trk; Hon Roll; 2nd Tm All Cnty Trck/Mile Rly 86; 400 M 2nd Tm All Lgu 86; West Point VA Mltry Inst.

SAYLOR, DEBRA; Washington Township HS; Turnersville, NJ; (Y); 1/500; Am Leg Aux Girls St; French Clb; Pep Clb; Yrbk Stf; Stu Cncl; Cheerleading; Hon Roll; NHS; Acad All-Amer Schlr Prog 84; U Of PA Phila; Bus.

SAYRE, BEVERLY; Lower Cape May Regional HS; Cape May, NJ; (Y); 113/222; JV Fld Hcky; Var Trk; Stockton ST Coll; Envrn Stud.

SCACCIA, JACQLENE; Red Bank Regional HS; Little Silver, NJ; (Y); Key Clb; Pep Clb; SADD; Var L Bsktbl; Var L Tennis; Var Wt Lftg; Hon Roll; Indstrl Psych.

SCAGLIONE, KRISTIN; St Pius Regional HS; Dunellen, NJ; (Y); 7/130; Dance Clb; JA; Chorus; School Musical; Nwsp Rptr; Rep Soph Cls; JV Capt Cheerleading; Hon Roll; NHS; NEDT Awd; Cmmnctns.

SCAGNELLI, JAMES; Buena Regional HS; Vineland, NJ; (S); #7 In Class; Hon Roll; Jr NHS.

SCAGNELLI, LEIGH; Warren County Vo-Tech; Alpha, NJ; (S); Key Clb; VICA; Nwsp Stf; Yrbk Stf; Pres Soph Cls; VP Sr Cls; Mgr Bsbl; Capt Cheerleading; Var Sftbl; High Hon Roll; Grphc Art.

SCALA, DANTE J; Union Catholic Regional HS; N Plainfield, NJ; (Y); Church Yth Grp; Quiz Bowl; Thesps; School Musical; Nwsp Ed-Chief; Var Tennis; High Hon Roll; NHS; Spanish NHS; Pres Schlrshp To Villanova U 86; Villanova U; Lbrl Arts.

SCALA, JOSEPH; Secaucus HS; Secaucus, NJ; (S); 1/169; Math Clb; Varsity Clb; Yrbk Stf; Var Capt Bsbl; High Hon Roll; Mu Alp Tht; NHS; Spanish NHS; Contntl Math Leag Awd 85; Comp Leag Awd 85.

SCALA, MARY; Franklin HS; Somerset, NJ; (Y); Chorus; Spec Educ.

SCALA, ROSINA; St Aloysius HS; Jersey City, NJ; (Y); #13 In Class; Boy Scts; Exploring; Pep Clb; Spanish Clb; Hon Roll; Coburn; Fash Ind.

SCALERA, MELISSA M; Verona HS; Verona, NJ; (Y); 13/178; PAVAS; JV Bsktbl; Var Gym; High Hon Roll; Ntl Merit SF; Spanish NHS; Grdn ST Distngshd Schlr 86; NJ Govrnrs Schl Semi-Fnlst 85; Diplomcy.

SCALES, TARA; Marylawn Of The Oranges HS; E Orange, NJ; (S); 11/54; Service Clb; Spanish Clb; Chorus; School Musical; Trs Jr Cls; High Hon Roll; NEDT Awd; Spanish NHS; Ntl Spnsh Ex 3rd Hnrbl Ment 85; Ntl Latin Ex Magna Cum Laude 85; Bus Mgmt.

SCALES, VALERIE; East Orange HS; E Orange, NJ; (S); Nwsp Rptr; Nwsp Stf; Crs Cntry; Trk; Prfct Atten Awd; Church Yth Grp; Debate Tm; Girl Scts; Rep Soph Cls; Prfct Atten Awd; Stu Of Yr In Bio 85; Bio.

SCALOBIN, MARK; Northern Valley Regional HS; Northvale, NJ; (Y); Drama Clb; Latin Clb; Science Clb; SADD; School Play; Var Ftbl; Hon Roll.

SCALPATI, CARROLL; Ocean Township HS; Ocean, NJ; (Y); Cmnty Wkr; SADD; Stat Bsktbl; Powder Puff Ftbl; Score Keeper; Italn Awd & Mdl Grd Pt Avg 85-86; Italn Clb Pres 86-87; US Hist II Awd 86; Widener U; Htl & Restrnt Mgt.

SCALZO, LESLIE; Bogota HS; Bogota, NJ; (Y); 24/96; Cmnty Wkr; French Clb; Ski Clb; Mrchg Band; School Musical; Yrbk Stf; Var Trk; Twrlr; DAR Awd; U Of DE; Vsl Cmmnctns.

SCALZO, STACEY L; Lakewood HS; Lakewood, NJ; (Y); 30/337; Dance Clb; Key Clb; School Musical; Yrbk Stf; Trs Soph Cls; Trs Jr Cls; Trs Sr Cls; Var Socr; Drama Clb; Ger Hnr Soc 86; PA ST U.

SCANLAN, BETH; Holy Cross HS; Riverside, NJ; (Y); Church Yth Grp; Cmnty Wkr; Mgr(s); Score Keeper; Socr; Sftbl; Bus.

SCANLON JR, ROBERT A; Don Bosco Prep HS; Fairlawn, NJ; (Y); 48/180; VP Aud/Vis; Trs Science Clb; Varsity Clb; Stage Crew; Yrbk Phtg; Yrbk Stf; Trk; Wt Lftg; Wrstlng; Hon Roll; Ldrshp Tourn 86; Pre-Med.

SCANLON, TOM; East Side HS; Newark, NJ; (Y); Bsbl; Ftbl; High Hon Roll; Hon Roll; NHS; Schlr Athl J V Baseball 84; Rutgers Coll; Sports Mgnt.

SCANZERA, BETH; Bloomfield HS; Bloomfield, NJ; (Y); 39/442; Key Clb; Var L Bsktbl; Var L Tennis; High Hon Roll; Hon Roll; NHS; Bus.

SCARANI, GIA; Sacred Heart HS; Bridgeton, NJ; (Y); Cmnty Wkr; German Clb; Stat Bsktbl; Var L Crs Cntry; JV Sftbl; Prfct Atten Awd; Intl Rltns.

SCARANI, MISHEL; Vineland SR HS; Vineland, NJ; (Y); 34/800; Art Clb; Church Yth Grp; Dance Clb; Drama Clb; Key Clb; Ski Clb; Varsity Clb; Chorus; Rep Frsh Cls; Rep Soph Cls; Vet.

SCARBROUGH, STEPHANIE; Vineland SR HS; Vineland, NJ; (Y); Church Yth Grp; Mathletes; Color Guard; Var Mgr(s); Prfct Atten Awd; Bus.

SCARDUFFA, ERIC; Don Bosco Technical HS; Clifton, NJ; (Y); 18/95; Pres Church Yth Grp; 1st Pl Drftg; 2nd Pl Elctrncs; Embry-Riddle Aero U; Aero Engr.

SCARINGELLA, REGINA; Mount Saint Dominic Acad; Fairfield, NJ; (Y); Intnl Clb; VP JCL; Ed Nwsp Stf; Ed Lit Mag; High Hon Roll; NHS; Italian Lng Awd 86; Caldwell Coll Prjct Excel 84-86; Schl Of Lngs & Linguistcs; Itln.

SCAROLA, LISA; Point Pleasant Boro HS; Pt Pleasant Boro, NJ; (S); 10/240; VP SADD; Band; Powder Puff Ftbl; Trk; High Hon Roll; Hon Roll; NHS; Grls ST Alt 86; Grls Ctznshp Alt 86.

SCATURO, JENNIFER; Roselle Catholic HS; Elizabeth, NJ; (S); Drama Clb; Math Clb; Ski Clb; School Musical; School Play; Cheerleading; Tennis; High Hon Roll; Hon Roll; Psych.

SCAVRON, ROBIN; Morris Knolls HS; Rockaway, NJ; (Y); 56/431; Science Clb; Band; Concert Band; Jazz Band; School Musical; School Play; Yrbk Phtg; Stu Cncl; Mgr(s); Art Clb; George WA U; Cardlgst.

SCERBO, KEITH; Don Bosco Prep; Ramsey, NJ; (Y); 74/175; Boy Scts; Pep Clb; Political Wkr; Service Clb; Ski Clb; Coach Actv; Bus.

SCHAEDEL, DARIN; Warren County Vo Tech; Hope, NJ; (S); 6/75; 4-H; Hosp Aide; Spanish Clb; VICA; Church Choir; Yrbk Bus Mgr; Yrbk Phtg; Yrbk Sprt Ed; Rep Sr Cls; Score Keeper; Northampton Cty Area CC; Comp.

SCHAEFER, JENNIFER; Hunterdon Central HS; Whitehouse Sta, NJ; (Y); Hosp Aide; Stu Cncl; Var Cheerleading; Gym; Hon Roll; Comp.

SCHAFER, DEAN J; Seton Hall Prep; Kenilworth, NJ; (Y); 3/228; Capt Chess Clb; Capt Math Tm; Im Bsktbl; Var L Bowling; Gov Hon Prg Awd; High Hon Roll; JETS Awd; NHS; Computer Clb; Capt Mathletes; Indl 1st Pl Math League NJ 85-86; Indl 2nd Pl Math Cont 85; Indl 1st Pl Tri ST Math League 85-86.

SCHAFER, GENE; Paramus Catholic Boys HS; Rochelle Pk, NJ; (Y); Church Yth Grp; Hon Roll; Spanish NHS; Med.

SCHAFER, GWEN; Paul VI HS; Cupertino, CA; (S); 20/474; Math Clb; Im Bowling; Var Crs Cntry; Var Trk; Hon Roll; NHS; U Of CA; Psycho-Bio.

SCHAFFER, MICHAEL F; Randolph HS; Randolph, NJ; (Y); 50/360; Am Leg Boys St; Ski Clb; Temple Yth Grp; Orch; Nwsp Rptr; Var Ice Hcky; Var Socr; Hon Roll; Regn HS Orchestra 83-84; Mid NJ Yth Sccr Assoc 83-84.

SCHAIRER, HENRY; Highstown HS; Hightstown, NJ; (Y); Drama Clb; Band; Chorus; Concert Band; Jazz Band; Mrchg Band; School Musical; School Play; JV Wrstlng; Hon Roll; Outstndng Schltc Perf Cert 83-85; Govnrs Sch Arts 85-86; Temple U; Musc.

SCHALICK, MISSY; Arthur P Schalick HS; Bridgeton, NJ; (Y); Computer Clb; Sec Ski Clb; Varsity Clb; Flag Corp; Nwsp Stf; Stu Cncl; Stat Bsktbl; Score Keeper; Var Sftbl; Hon Roll; Gettysburg; Poli Sci.

SCHANZLIN, TODD; Hopewell Valley Central HS; Pennington, NJ; (Y); 40/202; AFS; Am Leg Boys St; 4-H; Trs Spanish Clb; Rep Jr Cls; Rep Sr Cls; Var L Socr; JV Swmmng; High Hon Roll; Hon Roll; Air Frc ROTC Schlrshp 87-90; Lehigh U; Engrng.

SCHARPF, ERIC; Christian Brothers Acad; Colts Neck, NJ; (Y); 30/230; Church Yth Grp; Cmnty Wkr; Band; Yrbk Stf; Socr; Co-Capt Tennis; High Hon Roll; Hon Roll; 3rd Singles Plyr Cnty & ST Cath Champ Ten; Bus.

SCHARR, DONNA; Overbrook SR HS; Pine Hill, NJ; (Y); French Clb; Chorus; Stat Bsktbl; Cheerleading; Var L Crs Cntry; Var L Trk; Hon Roll; Acctg.

SCHAUBACH, KURT R; Indian Hills HS; Oakland, NJ; (Y); 20/274; Am Leg Boys St; Science Clb; Church Choir; School Musical; Nwsp Bus Mgr; Nwsp Rptr; Socr; Trs NHS; Garden ST Dstngshd Schlr 86; C Clamke Flson Mrl Schlrshp 86; VA Plythchnc Inst; Elec Engr.

SCHAUM, MATTHEW; North Bergen HS; North Bergen, NJ; (Y); 37/440; Boy Scts; German Clb; Band; Concert Band; Mrchg Band; Symp Band; Bowling; Hon Roll; Hstry.

SCHECHTER, KIM; Bridgewater Raritan H S East HS; Bridgewater, NJ; (Y); Ski Clb; SADD; VP Rep Frsh Cls; Chrmn Rep Soph Cls; Trs Stu Cncl; Var Tennis; Stat Lcrss; Hon Roll; Hnrb Mntn Midstate Conf Grls Ten 84-85; Rnnr Up Singles Somerset Cnty Coll Trnmnt Ten 84; Fash Merch.

SCHECHTERMAN, JILL; East Brunswick HS; E Brunswick, NJ; (Y); Drama Clb; Key Clb; Ski Clb; Temple Yth Grp; School Musical; School Play.

SCHEIDELER, DAWN; Howell HS; Howell, NJ; (Y); 42/350; Hosp Aide; Band; Mrchg Band; Var Crs Cntry; Stat Socr; Hon Roll; NHS; Rutgers Schl Nrsng; Nrsng.

SCHEIDERMAN, KIMBERLY; Toms River High Schl South; Toms River, NJ; (Y); Art Clb; Cmnty Wkr; DECA; FBLA; Hosp Aide; SADD; Band; Chorus; Concert Band; Nwsp Stf; Ocean Co JC; Resp Ther.

SCHEINTHAL, LISA; Montville Township HS; Pine Brook, NJ; (Y); 83/262; Art Clb; Drama Clb; Hosp Aide; Chrmn Key Clb; SADD; Teachers Aide; Temple Yth Grp; School Musical; School Play; Nwsp Stf; Saferides-VP-PLNNG 86-87; Art Show-2 1st Pl Awds 83-84; Drug Abuse Cncl 84-85; Mass Cmnctns.

SCHELLSCHEIDT, KARL; Roselle Catholic HS; Union, NJ; (S); 6/153; Boys Clb Am; Church Yth Grp; Ed Lit Mag; Capt Socr; Capt Tennis; Ntl, All State & County Soccr 85-86; Princeton; Engr.

SCHENONE, EDWARD; Saint Joseph Regional HS; Maywood, NJ; (Y); 35/167; Computer Clb; Math Tm; JV Bsktbl; Bsktbl MVP Awd 84-85; Mth.

SCHEURER, JOSEPH; St Peters Prep; Bayonne, NJ; (Y); 101/240; German Clb; JV Capt Bsbl; Var L Bsktbl; Vrsty Ltrs Bsktbl 86; Irsh Clb Sec 86; JR Prm Comm VP 85; U Of Scranton; Ecnmcs.

SCHEY, MARCY; Parsippany HS; Parsippany, NJ; (Y); FBLA; Pep Clb; Varsity Clb; Rep Frsh Cls; Rep Soph Cls; Rep Jr Cls; Var Co-Capt Cheerleading; JV Sftbl; High Hon Roll; Hon Roll.

SCHIER, NEIL; J P Steven HS; Edison, NJ; (Y); 18/469; Debate Tm; Drama Clb; French Clb; Hosp Aide; Math Tm; Model UN; Political Wkr; Science Clb; Stage Crew; Nwsp Phtg; Gvrnrs Schlr 85; Dlgt YMCA Yth Cncl Natl Affrs 85; Muhlenberg Coll; Pre-Law.

SCHIETTINO, ANTOINETTE; Cliffside Park HS; Cliffside Pk, NJ; (Y); 29/264; Camera Clb; Intnl Clb; Pep Clb; Nwsp Stf; Yrbk Phtg; Yrbk Stf; Lit Mag; Stu Cncl; Cheerleading; High Hon Roll; Glass Boro; Teachng.

SCHILL JR, JAMES M; Holy Cross HS; Riverton, NJ; (Y); German Clb; Stage Crew; Hon Roll; NHS; Elec Engrng.

SCHILLING, CHRISTOPHER; Hightstown HS; Hightstown, NJ; (Y); 8/327; Church Yth Grp; Service Clb; Stu Cncl; JV Var Bsbl; JV Var Ftbl; Cit Awd; High Hon Roll; Lion Awd; NHS; Pres Schlr; Merit Schlrshp Widener U 86; Rams Athltc Cncl Awd 86; DE Vly Umprs Schlrshp 86; Widener U; Htl Mngmnt.

SCHILLING, JULIE; North Waren Regional HS; Columbia, NJ; (Y); 9/138; Church Yth Grp; Spanish Clb; Color Guard; Mrchg Band; Nwsp Stf; Yrbk Stf; Sec Stu Cncl; Stat Bsktbl; Hon Roll; Sec NHS; Stu Cncl Schlrshp 86; Blair Womens Clb Schlrshp 86; Warren Cnty Parent-Tchr Assc Schlrshp 86; Rider Coll; Journlsm.

SCHILLING, KENT W; Moorestown HS; Mt Laurel, NJ; (Y); Am Leg Boys St; Church Yth Grp; Teachers Aide; Varsity Clb; Chorus; School Musical; Var Ftbl; Var Trk; Var Wrstlng; Secndry Ed.

SCHIMMINGER, THOMAS; Bayley Ellard HS; E Hanover, NJ; (Y); Var Capt Ftbl; Var Capt Wrstlng; MVP Wrstlng; Acctng.

SCHINA, MICHELE; Washington Township HS; Sewell, NJ; (Y); Rep Frsh Cls; JV Fld Hcky; Hon Roll; JC Awd; Intr Dcrtng.

SCHINELLER, CRISTA; Park Ridge HS; Park Ridge, NJ; (Y); 2/106; AFS; Church Yth Grp; Girl Scts; Math Clb; Math Tm; Quiz Bowl; Scholastic Bowl; Science Clb; Varsity Clb; Band; Stu Of Mnth 85; NJ Acad Dcthln Brnz Mdl For Essy 86; 8th Pl Age Grp Cnty Ntl Chmpnshps Hltn Hd; Lng.

SCHININA, JOANNE; Immaculate Conception HS; Lodi, NJ; (Y); Hon Roll; Psych.

SCHIPSI, LISA; Paul VI HS; Somerdale, NJ; (Y); GAA; Ski Clb; SADD; VP Frsh Cls; JV Var Trk; Middlebury Coll VT; Frgn Lang.

SCHIPSKE, MONICA P; Delsea Regional HS; Franklinville, NJ; (Y); 20/201; Church Yth Grp; Office Aide; School Play; Rep Sr Cls; Var Mgr Fld Hcky; NHS; Drama Clb; PAVAS; Teachers Aide; Var Bsktbl; South Jersey Hcky Mgr 85; Dstngshd Athletc Schlr Awd 86; Catawba Coll; Educ.

SCHITO, LISA; Middletown South HS; Middletown, NJ; (Y); GAA; Varsity Clb; Rep Stu Cncl; JV Cheerleading; Powder Puff Ftbl; High Hon Roll; Hon Roll.

SCHLANGER, ILENE; Mount Olive HS; Flanders, NJ; (Y); 4/296; AFS; Dance Clb; Temple Yth Grp; Nwsp Stf; JV Fld Hcky; High Hon Roll; Hon Roll; NHS; Schlrshp NJ Schl Ballet 85-86; Psychlgst.

SCHLATE, INGEBORG; Morristown Beard HS; Morristown, NJ; (Y); 6/85; French Clb; Intnl Clb; Model UN; Spanish Clb; Teachers Aide; Yrbk Bus Mgr; Var Bsktbl; Var Fld Hcky; Var Lcrss; Hon Roll; Georgetown U; Intl Studies.

SCHLATMANN, RAYMOND; Lakewood HS; Lakewood, NJ; (Y); 18/22; SADD; VICA; Bsktbl; Ftbl; Reading Awd 86; OH Diesel Tech Inst; Diesel.

SCHLEIDER, JOANNE; Edgewood Regional SR HS; Sicklerville, NJ; (Y); 18/364; Yrbk Stf; High Hon Roll; Hon Roll; NHS; JFK Hosp Med Schlrs Pgm 86; Frlgh Dcknsn Prsdntl Schlrshp 86; Cmdn Cnty Coll Merit Schlrshp 86; Thomas Jefferson U; Nrsng.

SCHLEIFMAN, SHARI; Highstown HS; E Windsor, NJ; (Y); French Clb; Girl Scts; Key Clb; Var Sftbl; Var Tennis; Var Trk; Hon Roll; MVP Ten 85; Sportsmnshp Awd Ten 85; CVC Hnrb Mntn Ten 85.

SCHLETTER, ANJA; Toms River East HS; Toms River, NJ; (S); Art Clb; Church Yth Grp; Dance Clb; Drama Clb; 4-H; Intnl Clb; Key Clb; Q&S; Ski Clb; Chorus; Lang.

SCHLOSSBERG, MICHELE; Marlboro HS; Morganville, NJ; (Y); Debate Tm; Drama Clb; PAVAS; School Musical; School Play; Stage Crew; Variety Show; 3rd Ranked Humorus Interp 85; 2 Yrs Fine & Perfoming Arts Ctr HS Dist 84-55 & 85-86; Am Acad Of Dramatic Arts; Actg.

SCHLOSSER, LAURA; Middletown HS South; Lincroft, NJ; (Y); Girl Scts; Science Clb; Hon Roll; Ntl Merit SF; Psych.

SCHLOSSER, SANDRA; Timothy Christian Schl; Warren, NJ; (S); 4/33; Church Yth Grp; Drama Clb; Service Clb; Teachers Aide; Chorus; Church Choir; High Hon Roll; VP NHS; St Schlr; Var Sftbl; Messiah Coll Acad Scholar 86-87; Messiah Coll; Music.

SCHMERSAL, STEVEN; Vineland HS; Vineland, NJ; (Y); Pres Church Yth Grp; Capt Debate Tm; English Clb; German Clb; Political Wkr; Nwsp Stf; Lit Mag; Rep Jr Cls; Rep Stu Cncl; Swmmng; Gvnrs Schlr 85; U DE; Bus Adm.

SCHMIDHEISER, MARK; Clearview Reginal HS; Mullica Hill, NJ; (Y); 11/180; Trs Stu Cncl; Var Capt Bsktbl; Socr; Wt Lftg; Lion Awd; NHS; Ntl Merit Ltr; St Schlr; Voice Dem Awd; Srptmst Intl Yth Ctznshp Awd 86; Stu Cncl Schlrshp 86; U Of Richmond; Pre-Med.

SCHMIDIG, BRIAN; Henry P Becton Reg HS; East Rutherford, NJ; (Y); Band; Stage Crew; Hon Roll; Bergen CC; Med Field.

SCHMIDT, CHRISTY A; St John Vianney HS; Bricktown, NJ; (Y); 13/257; Intnl Clb; Math Tm; Trs SADD; Capt Flag Corp; Stage Crew; Powder Puff Ftbl; Hon Roll; Accptnc To Mensa 86; Douglass Coll Sch Rshp 86-87; Douglass Coll; Law.

SCHMIDT, DONNA; Highland Regional HS; Clementon, NJ; (Y); Spanish Clb; Yrbk Bus Mgr; Yrbk Rptr; Yrbk Stf; Sr Cls; Trk; DE U; Commnctns.

SCHMIDT, DONNA MARIE; Mount Saint Mary Acad; Somerset, NJ; (Y); 15/83; Computer Clb; Trs Girl Scts; Yrbk Stf; Hon Roll; NHS; Cum Laude; Girl Scout Silver Awd; Lehigh U; Arch.

SCHMIDT, GRETA; South Hunterdorz Regional HS; Lambertville, NJ; (Y); 16/73; Am Leg Aux Girls St; Art Clb; Library Aide; Yrbk Stf; Rep Stu Cncl; ILLSTRTN.

SCHMIDT, KRISTEN A; Marlboro HS; Marlboro, NJ; (Y); Drama Clb; Pep Clb; Spanish Clb; SADD; Nwsp Stf; Ed Lit Mag; Off Jr Cls; Off Sr Cls; JV Socr; Var Tennis; U MO; Bus Mgmt.

SCHMIDT, LINDA; South River HS; S River, NJ; (Y); 14/150; German Clb; Library Aide; Yrbk Stf; JV Fld Hcky; NHS; GATE Pgm; Biol Sci.

SCHMIDT, MICHAEL; Woodbridge HS; Woodbridge, NJ; (Y); Boy Scts; Camera Clb; Office Aide; Radio Clb; School Musical; Nwsp Phtg; Yrbk Phtg; Cit Awd; Hon Roll; Devry Inst; Elec Tech.

SCHMIDT, SHERRY; Cherry Hill H S West; Cherry Hill, NJ; (Y); Church Yth Grp; Cmnty Wkr; Hosp Aide; Intnl Clb; Library Aide; Socr; Sftbl; Jeanne Lisowski Schlrshp 86; Cherry Hill W Home & Schl Asso Awd 86; Trenton ST Coll; Nrsg.

SCHMITT, ROBERT; Northern Valley-Old Tappan HS; Old Tappan, NJ; (Y); JV Capt Socr; High Hon Roll; Hon Roll; AFS; Church Yth Grp; Cmnty Wkr; Ski Clb; Stage Crew; JV Bsbl; JV Wrstlng; NJ Pool Mgrs Assn Swm & Dvng Champshps 84 & 86; Coaches Awd Swm Clb 86.

SCHMOTOLOCHA, DANIEL A; Seton Hall Prep; Livingston, NJ; (Y); Boy Scts; Cmnty Wkr; Exploring; German Clb; Intnl Clb; Science Clb; Nwsp Rptr; Yrbk Stf; Off Jr Cls; VP Stu Cncl; Rutgers; Elec Engrng.

SCHNABEL, GREG; E Brunswick HS; E Brunswick, NJ; (Y); Chess Clb; FBLA; Key Clb; Pep Clb; Ski Clb; Rep Jr Cls; JV Bsktbl; Rochester U; Economics.

SCHNABOLK, HOWARD; Red Bank Catholic HS; Ocean, NJ; (Y); Cmnty Wkr; JV Bsktbl; Var L Trk.

SCHNECK, THOMAS W; Camden Catholic HS; Medford, NJ; (Y); 92/275; Church Yth Grp; Drama Clb; Nwsp Stf; Yrbk Stf; Ice Hcky; Socr; Tennis; Seton Hall U; Bus.

SCHNEIDER, BRIAN; Hackettstown HS; Hackettstown, NJ; (Y); Var JV Ftbl; Var JV Wrstlng.

SCHNEIDER, CHRISTOPHER; Don Bosco Prep HS; Wyckoff, NJ; (S); 2/180; Ski Clb; SADD; Rptr Nwsp Rptr; Rptr Yrbk Rptr; Yrbk Stf; Crs Cntry; Ice Hcky; JV Socr; JV Tennis; High Hon Roll; Soph Rep HOBY Ldrshp Conf 85; Columbia U Sci Schlr Prog 86; Rep To Cath Schl Conf Bergen Cnty 86; Sci.

SCHNEIDER, DAVID; Hightstown HS; Hightstown, NJ; (Y); 46/347; Chess Clb; French Clb; FBLA; NFL; Ski Clb; Bowling; French Hon Soc; NHS; Ntl Merit SF; Bwlng 200 Clb; Cook Coll.

SCHNEIDER, DIANE; Colonia HS; Colonia, NJ; (Y); SADD; Varsity Clb; Yrbk Phtg; Var Bsktbl; Var Crs Cntry; JV Sftbl; NHS; All Acad Tm-Bsktbl-Grtr Middlesex Conf 85-86; Athl Trng.

SCHNEIDER, DORON; Summit HS; Summit, NJ; (Y); 28/290; Science Clb; Spanish Clb; Varsity Clb; Concert Band; Jazz Band; Var L Socr; Var L Tennis; High Hon Roll; NHS; Ntl Merit Schol; NJ Distngshd Schlr 86; Emory U.

SCHNEIDER, FREDERICK; Secaucus HS; Secaucus, NJ; (Y); 43/161; Math Clb; Hon Roll; Chem.

SCHNEIDER, JILL; Parsippany HS; Parsippany, NJ; (Y); 11/318; Cmnty Wkr; FBLA; Intnl Clb; Pep Clb; Political Wkr; Spanish Clb; Chorus; High Hon Roll; Hon Roll; NHS; Expstry Wrtng Awd 86; Pres Acad Ftnss Awd; Buckwnell; Acctg.

SCHNEIDER, MARK; Lower Cape May Regional HS; Villas, NJ; (Y); Church Yth Grp; Drama Clb; Trs French Clb; Letterman Clb; Pep Clb; Varsity Clb; School Musical; School Play; Ftbl; Capt Golf; WV U; Theatre.

SCHNEIDER, MICHELE; Middlesex HS; Middlesex, NJ; (Y); Girl Scts; Ski Clb; Spanish Clb; Varsity Clb; Bsktbl; Crs Cntry; Trk; Hon Roll.

SCHNEIDER, NANCY; Butler HS; Bloomingdale, NJ; (Y); 15/197; Varsity Clb; Lit Mag; Rep Frsh Cls; Rep Soph Cls; Trs Jr Cls; VP Stu Cncl; JV Var Cheerleading; Var Capt Gym; Hon Roll; NHS; Hnrb Mntn All Cnfrnc In Gymnstcs 85; Stu Of Mnth In Hstry 85; Stu Of Mnth In Frgn Lng 86; Syrcs U; Lbrl Arts.

SCHNEIDER, RISA; Fairlawn HS; Fair Lawn, NJ; (Y); 40/325; Science Clb; Acpl Chr; Chorus; Madrigals; Orch; School Musical; 3rd Tm Natl Sci Olympd 86; Pre Med.

SCHNEIDERMAN, AMY; Manalapan HS; Englishtown, NJ; (Y); Dance Clb; SADD; Yrbk Stf; Psych.

SCHNEIDERMAN, CORI; East Brunswick HS; E Brunswick, NJ; (Y); Cmnty Wkr; Hosp Aide; Intnl Clb; Key Clb; Pep Clb; SADD; Band; Drill Tm; Yrbk Stf; Hon Roll; Occptnl Thrpy.

SCHNELL, BRIAN; Ridgefeld Park HS; Ridgefield Pk, NJ; (Y); 8/183; Math Tm; Pres Stu Cncl; Hon Roll; NHS; Am Leg Boys St; Cmnty Wkr; Computer Clb; Off Soph Cls; Cmptr Sci.

SCHNEPP, LIBBY; Bishop Eustace Prep; Pennsauken, NJ; (Y); 20/186; Pep Clb; Spanish Clb; L Var Cheerleading; Hon Roll; NHS; Spanish NHS.

SCHNITZER, LORI; Linden HS; Linden, NJ; (Y); Drama Clb; Office Aide; Spanish Clb; School Play; Im Fld Hcky; Rutgers Coll Phrmcy; Phrmcy.

SCHNITZIUS, CHERYL; Monsignor Donovan HS; Toms River, NJ; (Y); 17/224; Band; Concert Band; Rep Frsh Cls; Rep Soph Cls; Rep Jr Cls; Rep Sr Cls; Stu Cncl; Var Cheerleading; Stat Sftbl; Hon Roll; Physcl Thrpy.

SCHNOLL, RACHEL; Summit HS; Summit, NJ; (Y); Drama Clb; Model UN; VP Temple Yth Grp; Thesps; Chorus; School Musical; School Play; Nwsp Bus Mgr; Nwsp Stf; Stat Sftbl; Intl Rltns.

SCHOBER, SCOTT; Edison HS; Edison, NJ; (Y); Computer Clb; Ski Clb; Rutgers; Comp Pgmmg.

SCHOCH, GAIL; Washington Twp HS; Turnersville, NJ; (Y); Chorus; School Play; Worthy Advisor Of Mystic No 5 86; JR Grand Exec Committee NJ 86; HS Chorus Pin & Letter 85-86; Med Lab.

SCHOCKET, ANDREW M; Mountain Lakes HS; Mountain Lakes, NJ; (Y); 8/110; School Play; Nwsp Ed-Chief; Var Capt Crs Cntry; JV Capt Trk; French Hon Soc; High Hon Roll; NHS; Ntl Merit SF; CC Awd; St Schlr; Rutgers U Pres Schlr 85; Century III Ldrshp Awd 85; Brown U Bk Awd 85.

SCHOEMER, SHERRI; Toms River HS South; Beachwood, NJ; (Y); Var Socr; Hon Roll.

SCHOENBERGER, WENDI; Fair Lawn HS; Fair Lawn, NJ; (Y); 20/325; Drama Clb; Exploring; Spanish Clb; School Musical; School Play; Off Frsh Cls; Off Soph Cls; Off Jr Cls; Hon Roll; NHS; Princpls List 83-86; Prim Educ.

SCHOENEWOLF, BARBARA JANE; Manasquan HS; Spring Lake, NJ; (Y); 18/234; Hosp Aide; Key Clb; Spanish Clb; Pres Stu Cncl; Capt Twrlr; Cit Awd; High Hon Roll; Hon Roll; Jostens Ldrshp & Srv Awd 86; Pres Acdmc Fit Awd 86; Colgate U; Pre Med.

SCHOENWALD, ELLEN; Colonia HS; Colonia, NJ; (Y); #5 In Class; Ski Clb; Trs SADD; Temple Yth Grp; Yrbk Ed-Chief; Yrbk Stf; Bowling; Hon Roll; Jr NHS; NHS; Spanish NHS; Bus.

SCHOLZ, ROBERT; Don Bosco Prep; Ringwood, NJ; (Y); 5/170; Chess Clb; Pres German Clb; Ftbl; Wt Lftg; 1st Hnrs; Bucknell; Bus Admin.

SCHONENBERGER, SIMONE; Park Ridge HS; Park Ridge, NJ; (Y); 7/100; Nwsp Ed-Chief; Nwsp Stf; Rep Jr Cls; High Hon Roll; VP NHS; Amer Assn Tchrs Germn Inc Cert Of Merit 85; NJAATSP Outstndng Stdnt Cert Spnsh 85; Pltcl Sci.

SCHONFELD, DANNY; Livingston HS; Livingston, NJ; (Y); VP Computer Clb; French Clb; Pres Math Clb; Concert Band; Jazz Band; Bsbl; Bsktbl; Var Socr; Var Trk; Cit Awd; 1st Plc Calc Essec Cnty 86.

SCHOOLER, MARCELLUS; Clifford J Scott HS; E Orange, NJ; (Y); 32/264; Intnl Clb; Nwsp Ed-Chief; Lit Mag; Socr; Trk; Hon Roll; Penn ST U; Geogrphy.

SCHOONMAKER, JACK; Brick HS; Brick, NJ; (Y); 7/340; Var Capt Crs Cntry; Var Capt Trk; Dnfth Awd; High Hon Roll; VP NHS; All Ocean Cnty X-Cntry Team 84-85; MVP Trck, X-Cntry 84-85; Bd Ed Sci Awd; Seton Hall U; Pre-Med.

SCHOONOVER, REGINA; Papa John XXIII HS; Lake Hoptacong, NJ; (Y); Church Yth Grp; Drama Clb; German Clb; Hosp Aide; School Musical; School Play; Lit Mag; Cheerleading; Trk; NHS; Pre Med.

SCHOR, SARA; Toms River High Schl North; Toms River, NJ; (Y); 26/412; Cmnty Wkr; FBLA; JA; Key Clb; Ski Clb; Spanish Clb; Stu Cncl; Fld Hcky; High Hon Roll; Hon Roll; Bus.

SCHORR, HEATHER; West Morris Mendram HS; Brookside, NJ; (Y); Intnl Clb; Radio Clb; Band; Concert Band; Flag Corp; Mrchg Band; Symp Band; High Hon Roll; Hon Roll; NHS.

SCHORR, LOUANN; Glen Rock JR SR HS; Glen Rock, NJ; (Y); Church Yth Grp; Cmnty Wkr; DECA; Girl Scts; Chorus; Sftbl; Trk; Twrlr; Casanova; Chld Care.

SCHOTT, DARLENE; Mahwah HS; Mahwah, NJ; (Y); 25/185; Drama Clb; Hosp Aide; Red Cross Aide; Spanish Clb; Yrbk Phtg; Yrbk Stf; Stu Cncl; Capt Var Cheerleading; Gym; Pom Pon; Schl Spirt Awd Chrldng Comp 85; HS Rep Douglass Coll 86; Rutgers; Crmnl Just.

SCHOTT, PATTI; Red Bank Catholic HS; Colts Neck, NJ; (Y); 86/280; Cmnty Wkr; Exploring; JA; Ski Clb; Stage Crew; VP Frsh Cls; VP Soph Cls; VP Jr Cls; Powder Puff Ftbl; Socr; Douglass Coll; Bus.

SCHOWN, JOHN; Piscataway HS; Piscataway, NJ; (Y); 19/475; Boy Scts; VP Church Yth Grp; Varsity Clb; Chorus; Swmmng; Hon Roll; NHS; Ntl Merit Ltr; Acad Summer Sem 86; Alliance Action Essay Awd Wnnr 85; US Naval Acad; Naval Arch.

SCHRANK, MARNI; St Mary HS; Passaic, NJ; (Y); 16/44; FBLA; FNA; Variety Show; Yrbk Stf; Rep Stu Cncl; Cheerleading; Trk; Hon Roll; Cosmtlgst.

SCHREIBER, KIMBERLY; Lakeland Regional HS; Haskell, NJ; (Y); 110/303; Church Yth Grp; Nwsp Rptr; Nwsp Stf; Trk; High Hon Roll; Hon Roll; NYACK Coll; Engl.

SCHREIER, MARY; Central Regional HS; Bayville, NJ; (Y); 17/250; Teachers Aide; Band; Concert Band; Jazz Band; Mrchg Band; Orch; Var Tennis; Var Trk; High Hon Roll; Sec NHS.

SCHREIN, AARON M; St Joseph Regional HS; River Vale, NJ; (Y); 28/167; Chrmn Am Leg Boys St; Boy Scts; Nwsp Rptr; JV Bsbl; Var Ftbl; Var Wrstlng; Hon Roll; Jr NHS; NHS; Spanish NHS; ST & Rgnl Champ-Sandy Kaufax Leag Bsbl Tm 84; Eagle Scout 85; Comm.

SCHREUDERS, KIM; Paramus Catholic Girls HS; Teaneck, NJ; (Y); Art Clb; Church Yth Grp; Computer Clb; Service Clb; Teachers Aide; Lit Mag; Hon Roll; Ntl Merit SF; Paramus Cthlc Art Awd & Chrctr Awd 84-85; Comm Art.

SCHREYER, LAURA; Middletown H S South; Middletown, NJ; (Y); Letterman Clb; Varsity Clb; Yrbk Phtg; Yrbk Stf; JV Fld Hcky; Im Powder Puff Ftbl; Var Sftbl; Im Vllybl; Im Wt Lftg; High Hon Roll.

SCHROEDER, SUSAN; Point Pleasant Beach HS; Bay Head, NJ; (Y); Church Yth Grp; Drama Clb; Hosp Aide; Ski Clb; Spanish Clb; Chorus; School Play; Stage Crew; Cit Awd; Sec NHS; Seton Hll U; Bus.

SCHROETTER, THOMAS; Mater Dei HS; Hazlet, NJ; (Y); 42/152; Boy Scts; French Clb; Variety Show; Rep Frsh Cls; Rep Soph Cls; Trs Jr Cls; Off Sr Cls; Rep Stu Cncl; Bowling; Var Golf; Eagl Sct Trp 86; Twnshp, Schl & Cmmnty Awds 83-86; No 1 Man Schl Golf Tm; NJ Tri ST; Bus Mgmt.

SCHUBEL, LIAM; Freehold Township HS; Freehold, NJ; (Y); Boy Scts; Church Yth Grp; Hosp Aide; Spanish Clb; Rep Stu Cncl; Var Crs Cntry; Var Trk; NHS; Brnz Cngrssnl Awd 84; Hugh O Brian Yth Fndtn Outstndg Soph 85; Compu Sci.

SCHUBIGER, SCOTT; Lacey Township HS; Forked River, NJ; (Y); 14/211; Math Tm; Science Clb; Nwsp Rptr; Yrbk Rptr; JV Capt Bsbl; Bsktbl; Co-Capt Ftbl; High Hon Roll; NHS; Prfct Atten Awd; Vince Lombardi Outstndng Lineman Awd 85; Bowdoin Coll; Chem.

SCHUELER, BETH; Middletown H S North; Middletown, NJ; (Y); Trs Church Yth Grp; Trs Ski Clb; School Play; Variety Show; Nwsp Phtg; Yrbk Phtg; Yrbk Stf; VP Jr Cls; Var Gym; Sftbl; Bus.

SCHUESSLER, THERESA; Ramapo HS; Riverside, CT; (Y); 21/311; AFS; French Clb; Trs Sr Cls; Var Capt Cheerleading; Cit Awd; High Hon Roll; NHS; Lafayette Coll; Elec Engrng.

SCHUGG, STACEY; Westfield HS; Westfield, NJ; (Y); 100/485; Hosp Aide; SADD; Varsity Clb; Chorus; Nwsp Rptr; Bsktbl; Cheerleading; Mgr(s); Powder Puff Ftbl; Timer; Awd In The Ntl Frnch Cntst 85; U Of WI; Brdcst.

SCHUJKO, LINDA; Hamilton HS West; Yardville, NJ; (Y); 9/320; FBLA; Math Clb; Color Guard; Im Vllybl; High Hon Roll; Ntl Merit SF; St Schlr; Full Schlrshp Trntn ST Coll 86; Yrdvl Hghts Almni Schlrshp 86; Trntn ST Coll; Fnc.

SCHULDES, FELICIA; Notre Dame HS; Trenton, NJ; (Y); Church Yth Grp; Cmnty Wkr; Hosp Aide; Yrbk Rptr; Koinonia Clb 85-86; Horticltr Bus.

SCHULER, HELEN; No Brunswick Twsp HS; N Brunswick, NJ; (Y); 34/325; Church Yth Grp; French Clb; Latin Clb; Varsity Clb; VP Frsh Cls; Rep Soph Cls; Rep Jr Cls; Pres Sr Cls; Pres Stu Cncl; Stat Bsktbl.

SCHULER, KRISTIN; Scotch Plains-Fanwood HS; Fanwood, NJ; (Y); 70/311; Chorus; Concert Band; Jazz Band; Mrchg Band; Symp Band; JV Bsktbl; Capt Var Socr; JV Var Sftbl; High Hon Roll; Hon Roll; Quinnipiac Coll; Phys Thrpy.

SCHULTE, DAVID C; Pope John HS; Sparta, NJ; (Y); 5/175; Am Leg Boys St; Spanish Clb; Church Choir; School Musical; School Play; Lit Mag; Off Frsh Cls; Bsktbl; Ftbl; Golf; Am Legion Boys ST 86; Golf Varsty Four Yrs 84-87; Spn Clb 86-87; Finance.

SCHULTZ, ANNE MARIE; Matawan Regional HS; Matawan, NJ; (S); 9/273; Computer Clb; French Clb; Math Tm; Capt Color Guard; Madrigals; School Musical; French Hon Soc; NHS; St Schlr; Biomed Engrng.

SCHULTZ, CHERYL; East Brunswick HS; East Brunswick, NJ; (Y); SADD; Sftbl; Vllybl; Hon Roll; San Diego ST; Bus Admin.

SCHULTZ, DANIEL A; Paramus Catholic Boys HS; Woodridge, NJ; (Y); 2/165; Math Tm; Nwsp Stf; Im Bowling; Lion Awd; NHS; Sal; Spanish NHS; Am Leg Boys St; Computer Clb; Science Clb; Garden ST Dstngshd Schlr 85-86; Rutgers Coll Gen Hnrs Schlrshp 85-86; Wood Ridge Mem Fndtn Fiesta I; Rutgers Coll; Med.

SCHULTZ, JEFFREY; James Caldwell HS; Caldwell, NJ; (Y); German Clb; Key Clb; Jazz Band; Off Soph Cls; Off Jr Cls; Trs Sr Cls; Bsbl; Bsktbl; Golf; Sftbl; Emplyee Of Mth-Roy Rogers 86.

SCHULTZ, PETER; Oratory Prep; Lake Hopatcong, NJ; (S); 4/41; Computer Clb; French Clb; VP Math Clb; Math Tm; Quiz Bowl; Scholastic Bowl; Service Clb; Ski Clb; Im Bsktbl; Im Tennis; Commnded Stu PSAT 85; Pre Law.

SCHULTZE, JILL; Hawthorne HS; Hawthorne, NJ; (Y); French Clb; Math Tm; Science Clb; Yrbk Stf; Rep Frsh Cls; Rep Jr Cls; Rep Stu Cncl; Var Bsktbl; Powder Puff Ftbl; High Hon Roll.

SCHULTZE, WENDY; High School East; Toms Rvr, NJ; (Y); Church Yth Grp; Cmnty Wkr; Dance Clb; SADD; Chorus; Mrchg Band; Pom Pon; Hon Roll; Rutgers U; Prof Dncr.

SCHULZ, JAMES; Hamilton HS; Yardville, NJ; (Y); Am Leg Boys St; Cmnty Wkr; Key Clb; Political Wkr; Varsity Clb; Var Golf; Var Socr; Intl Lawyer.

SCHUMACHER, JANE; St John Vianney HS; Freehold, NJ; (Y); 6/280; Art Clb; Church Yth Grp; Girl Scts; SADD; Church Choir; Mrchg Band; Mgr Stage Crew; Hon Roll; NHS; Gold White Awd 84-86; Physcl Thrpy.

SCHUYLER, CHERYL; St John Vianney HS; Woodbridge, NJ; (Y); 132/269; Computer Clb; Mgr Score Keeper; Bartending.

SCHUYLER, DEBORAH; East Orange HS; E Orange, NJ; (S); 20/410; Exploring; Science Clb; Spanish Clb; Yrbk Stf; Lit Mag; Rep Frsh Cls; Sec Soph Cls; VP Jr Cls; Stat Bsktbl; Stat Ftbl.

SCHWAID, MATTHEW; Christian Brothers Acad; Middletown, NJ; (Y); Lit Mag; Var L Tennis; Hon Roll; Art.

SCHWARTZ, ABBE; Hackettstown HS; Hackettstown, NJ; (Y); 4/250; Hosp Aide; JA; School Musical; Swing Chorus; Chrmn Jr Cls; Socr; Sftbl; High Hon Roll; Hon Roll; NHS; Grgtwn U; Intl Bus.

SCHWARTZ, CORINNE E; Gateway Regional HS; Wenonah, NJ; (Y); 3/190; Pres French Clb; Science Clb; Chorus; Stu Cncl; Capt Cheerleading; French Hon Soc; High Hon Roll; Sec NHS; Westville Wmns Clb Schlrshp 86; Garden ST Schlrshp 86; Bnd Gatewy Chptr Natl Hnr Soc 86; Rutgers U; Commnctns.

SCHWARTZ, DAVID A; Millburn SR HS; Short Hills, NJ; (Y); 29/245; Acpl Chr; Band; Chorus; Concert Band; Mrchg Band; Orch; School Musical; Symp Band; Hon Roll; Ntl Merit SF.

SCHWARTZ, HOWIE; MT Olive HS; Flanders, NJ; (Y); Hst Drama Clb; Math Clb; SADD; Teachers Aide; Temple Yth Grp; Varsity Clb; School Play; JV Var Socr; Var Wrstlng; Hon Roll; Outstndng Wrstlr 83-86; Pre-Law.

SCHWARTZ, ILYSSA; Montville Township HS; Pine Brk, NJ; (Y); FBLA; Ski Clb; Pep Band; Powder Puff Ftbl; Hon Roll; Sec Frsh Cls; Rep Soph Cls; JV Cheerleading; JV Fld Hcky; Stat Mgr(s); Syracuse; Lawyer.

SCHWARTZ, JENNIFER; Watching Hills Regional HS; Watchung, NJ; (Y); Am Leg Aux Girls St; Key Clb; Rep Stu Cncl; Capt JV Bsktbl; Capt Fld Hcky; Capt JV Sftbl; High Hon Roll; Hon Roll; NHS; Opt Clb Awd; NY U; Mrktng.

SCHWARTZ, JOEL; Cherry Hill HS West; Cherry Hill, NJ; (Y); 1/362; Aud/Vis; Computer Clb; JCL; JV Bsktbl; Var Capt Golf; High Hon Roll; Masonic Awd; NHS; Rensselaer Mdl Math & Sci 85; NJ Dstngshd Schlr 86; Natl Cncl Jewish Wmn Schlrshp 86; U Of PA; Engrng.

SCHWARTZ JR, JOHN A; Holmdel HS; Holmdel, NJ; (Y); Lit Mag; Var JV Bsbl; JV Bsktbl; JV Ftbl; NHS; Pres Schlr; Govnrs Schlrshp-Bstn U 86; Boston U; Physcl Thrpy.

SCHWARTZ, MELISSA; No Burl Co Reg HS; Wrightstown, NJ; (Y); 11/200; Drama Clb; Scholastic Bowl; Chorus; School Musical; School Play; Yrbk Phtg; Var Tennis; Rotary Awd; St Schlr; Math Tm; Joseph A Sakach Memrl Engl Awd 86; Springfield Hm & Schl Assn Awd 86; NYT Cable TV Qz Bwl Awd 86; Vassar Coll; Theatr Arts.

SCHWARTZ, MICHELE; Jackson Memorial HS; Jackson, NJ; (S); 7/343; Chrmn Cmnty Wkr; VP FNA; Hosp Aide; Office Aide; Drill Tm; High Hon Roll; NHS; Voice Dem Awd; Hugh O Brian Yth Fllwshp Awd-Outstndg Stu 84; Modern Miss Acad Schlrshp Pgnt 85; Century 3 Ldrshp Awd; William Paterson Coll; Nrsg.

SCHWARTZ, NAOMI; Holy Cross HS; Maple Shade, NJ; (Y); 73/385; Church Yth Grp; Cmnty Wkr; German Clb; Library Aide; Service Clb; Teachers Aide; Stage Crew; Yrbk Phtg; Lit Mag; Hon Roll; Trenton ST Coll; Elem Tchr.

SCHWARZ, CATHY; Franklin HS; Princeton, NJ; (Y); 29/389; Church Yth Grp; Girl Scts; Band; Concert Band; Mrchg Band; Sftbl; High Hon Roll; Hon Roll; NHS; Rider Coll; Bus Mgmt.

SCHWARZ, KENNETH; Somerset County Vo Tech; Princeton, NJ; (Y); Boy Scts; Hon Roll; Achvt, Excllnc Vo-Tech Shop Pgm 86.

SCHWARZMAN, MARK; Metuchen HS; Metuchen, NJ; (Y); Var Bsbl; Var Ftbl; Hon Roll; Ftbl Hnr-All Star Tm Conf 85.

SCHWEIKER, ERIC; Overbrook Regional HS; Lindenwold, NJ; (Y); 1/350; Trs French Clb; Science Clb; Pres Stu Cncl; Bsktbl; Var Capt Ftbl; Var Trk; High Hon Roll; NHS; Ntl Merit Ltr.

SCHWIETERING, BARBRA; Colonia HS; Colonia, NJ; (Y); 29/296; Am Leg Aux Girls St; Band; Concert Band; Mrchg Band; School Play; Yrbk Stf; Hon Roll; NHS; Art Clb; Church Choir; Home & Schl Assoc Schlrshp 86; Kean Coll Alumni Assoc Schlrshp 86; Claremont Ave Schl PTO Awd 86; Kean Coll; Commercl Art.

SCHWORN, LISA; Brick Township HS; Brick Town, NJ; (Y); Pres Girl Scts; Hosp Aide; Sec Key Clb; Math Tm; SADD; Drill Tm; Bausch & Lomb Sci Awd; High Hon Roll; NHS; Gld Awd GS 86; Pre Med.

SCIALABBA, JOHN; Freehold Twp HS; Freehold, NJ; (Y); American U; Intl Bus.

SCIALLA, GINA T; Ridge HS; Brookside, NJ; (Y); Off Ski Clb; Capt Cheerleading; High Hon Roll; Hon Roll; NHS; Sec Boy Scts; Church Yth Grp; German Clb; Powder Puff Ftbl; Score Keeper; German Hnr Soc; U VT; Bus.

SCIANCALEPORE, LAWRENCE; Hoboken HS; Hoboken, NJ; (Y); 1/300; Aud/Vis; Computer Clb; SADD; Varsity Clb; Stage Crew; Nwsp Rptr; Yrbk Stf; Stu Cncl; Bsktbl; Capt Ftbl; Rutgers Scholar 86; Accelerated First Honors 84-86; Engrng.

SCIARABBA, AMY M; Toms River High School East; Toms River, NJ; (Y); Church Yth Grp; Cmnty Wkr; 4-H; Hosp Aide; Key Clb; Off Frsh Cls; Off Soph Cls; Capt JV Cheerleading; Mgr(s); Powder Puff Ftbl; Nursing.

SCIARRONE, DENISE; Passaic Valley HS; Little Falls, NJ; (Y); Ski Clb; Varsity Clb; Cheerleading; Score Keeper; Hon Roll; Girls Show 85-86&86-87; Bus.

SCILLIERI, JANICE; Lyndhurst HS; Lyndhurst, NJ; (Y); 2/180; German Clb; JV Sftbl; JV Vllybl; High Hon Roll; Hon Roll; VP NHS; Comp Sci.

SCILLIERI, JOSEPH J; Pompton Lakes HS; Pompton Lakes, NJ; (Y); 1/134; Am Leg Boys St; Pres Math Tm; Capt Quiz Bowl; Sec Band; Concert Band; Drm Mjr(t); Sec Mrchg Band; VP NHS; Church Yth Grp; Spanish Clb; Rensselaer Poly Tech Ins Mathard Sci Awd 85-86; Fncng Team; Spcl Awd Essay Wrtng A Vision Of Peace; Arspc Engrng.

SCIMECA, BETTY; Lodi HS; Lodi, NJ; (Y); Church Yth Grp; Girl Scts; VICA; Band; Concert Band; Mrchg Band; Orch; Yrbk Stf; Socr; Trk.

SCIMECA, ELIZABETH JO; Notre Dame HS; Kendall Pk, NJ; (Y); Dance Clb; French Clb; Varsity Clb; Bsbl; Ftbl; Score Keeper; French Hon Soc; Hon Roll; Psychlgy.

SCIMENE, DORIANN; Bishop G Ahr/St Thomas Aquinas HS; Milltown, NJ; (Y); 22/277; Pres Service Clb; Band; Concert Band; School Musical; High Hon Roll; Hon Roll.

SCIRETTA, MICHAEL SCOTT; Bishop George AHR HS; Old Bridge, NJ; (Y); 29/250; Off ROTC; Rep Sr Cls; Var L Bsbl; Var L Ftbl; Var L Golf; High Hon Roll; NHS; Cmnty Wkr; Spanish Clb; Varsity Clb; NROTC Scholar 86; Edison Exch Clb Yth Yr 86; Outstndng Cadet Rotc 85-86; PA ST U; Aerontcl Engrng.

SCOLA, ROBIN M; Mahwah HS; Mahwah, NJ; (Y); 61/176; Hosp Aide; Ski Clb; Variety Show; Yrbk Stf; Trs Soph Cls; Trs Jr Cls; Stu Cncl; JV Var Crs Cntry; Mgr(s); JV Sftbl; Mst Imprvd Crss Cntry 85.

SCOTT, CHRISTOPHER P; Abseyami HS; Oceanville, NJ; (Y); French Clb; Band; Concert Band; Jazz Band; Mrchg Band; Var Tennis; Hon Roll; Jr NHS; Acadmc Lttr 3.5 & Above Avg 85 & 86; Chemical Engnrng.

SCOTT, DEXTER L; Florence Twp Memorial HS; Florence, NJ; (Y); Am Leg Boys St; Church Yth Grp; Cmnty Wkr; DECA; FBLA; Varsity Clb; Nwsp Rptr; Pres Sr Cls; Var Capt Trk; VP Jr Cls; Ntl Bus Hnr Soc 86-87; Bus Admin.

SCOTT, DONNA; St Aloysius HS; Jersey City, NJ; (Y); Church Yth Grp; Exploring; Church Choir; Capt Bowling; Hon Roll; NHS; Acctng.

SCOTT, GEORGE; St Peters Prep; Bayonne, NJ; (Y); 19/205; Cmnty Wkr; Letterman Clb; Red Cross Aide; Ski Clb; Varsity Clb; Pres Frsh Cls; Im Bsktbl; Var L Ftbl; Var Wt Lftg; High Hon Roll; Rutgers; Bus.

SCOTT, GREGORY A; Holmdel HS; Holmdel, NJ; (Y); 20/210; Am Leg Boys St; Boy Scts; Drama Clb; Pres Keywanettes; Rep Stu Cncl; Var Socr; High Hon Roll; NHS; Chess Clb; French Clb; Sen Bradleys Ldrshp Semnr 86; USNA.

SCOTT JR, JAMES H; Trenton Central HS; Trenton, NJ; (Y); Boys Clb Am; Chess Clb; Church Yth Grp; Computer Clb; Chorus; Rep Stu Cncl; Im Bsktbl; JV Var Socr; Drexel U; Engnrng.

SCOTT, JEFFREY R; Sayreville War Memorial HS; Parlin, NJ; (Y); 35/378; Sec Spanish Clb; Trs Varsity Clb; School Musical; Sec Sr Cls; Rep Stu Cncl; Var Socr; Var Trk; Gov Hon Prg Awd; VP NHS; Olympcs Mind 2nd ST 83-86; Presdnts Acadmc Ftns Awd 86; Al-Acadmc Cnfrnc Tm Sccr 86; Drexel U; Bus Mgmt.

SCOTT, JENNIFER KAY; Memorial HS; Cedar Grove, NJ; (S); 5/118; Church Yth Grp; Cmnty Wkr; Pres Key Clb; Church Choir; Yrbk Bus Mgr; High Hon Roll; NHS; French Clb; Girl Scts; Garden ST Dstngshd Schlr 85; Bus.

SCOTT, KATHLEEN; Kingsway Regional HS; Swedesboro, NJ; (Y); 29/165; Key Clb; Office Aide; Rep Stu Cncl; Hon Roll; Cadmen Cnty Coll; Cmnctns.

SCOTT, KIMBERLY; Midland Park HS; Midland Park, NJ; (Y); 40/136; AFS; Church Yth Grp; Debate Tm; Girl Scts; Quiz Bowl; Chorus; School Musical; Nwsp Rptr; Lit Mag; Score Keeper; Moravian Coll; Psychlgy.

SCOTT, LISA; Columbia HS; S Orange, NJ; (Y); Yrbk Stf.

SCOTT, LISA; Piscataway HS; Piscataway, NJ; (Y); Church Yth Grp; Comp Prog.

SCOTT JR, ROBERT M; Belvidere HS; Belvidere, NJ; (Y); 7/118; Drama Clb; Varsity Clb; Band; Chorus; Madrigals; School Musical; Pres Stu Cncl; Capt Bsbl; Colby Coll; Music.

SCOTT, SHARON A; Queen Of Peace HS; North Arlington, NJ; (Y); 10/250; Drama Clb; Model UN; NFL; Ski Clb; Spanish Clb; Chorus; School Musical; Nwsp Sprt Ed; Capt Var Trk; Ntl Merit SF; Mst Imprvd Plyr Trck & Bsktbl; Sprts Sptlght In Schl Paper; Bst Sprtng Actrs In Drama; Intl Rltns.

SCOTT, STEPHANIE; Monsignor Donovan HS; Bayville, NJ; (Y); 10/243; Church Yth Grp; French Clb; JV Trk; High Hon Roll; Hon Roll; NHS; Fnlst Govnrs Schl NJ 86.

SCOTT, TAMARA; St Marys Hall-Doane Acad; Medford, NJ; (Y); 4/18; Cmnty Wkr; Hosp Aide; Library Aide; Pep Clb; Sec Sr Cls; JV Socr; Var Sftbl; Var Trk; High Hon Roll; Band; Grls Intrmrl Champ 86.

SCOTT, TRACEY; Hillside HS; Hillside, NJ; (Y); #29 In Class; Pres Church Yth Grp; ROTC; Color Guard; School Play; Rep Jr Cls; Pres Stu Cncl; Cheerleading; Trk; Psych.

SCOTTI, ANNE; Shore Regional HS; W Long Branch, NJ; (Y); Debate Tm; Ski Clb; SADD; Flag Corp; Yrbk Stf; Co-Capt Gym; Powder Puff Ftbl; Socr; Twrlr; Hon Roll; Seton Hall U; Poli Sci.

SCOTTON, MARY; Hillsborough HS; Belle Mead, NJ; (Y); 7/289; Girl Scts; Math Tm; Ski Clb; Nwsp Bus Mgr; Nwsp Ed-Chief; Rep Stu Cncl; Var Capt Fld Hcky; JV Var Sftbl; NHS; Ntl Merit Ltr; Star Ledgers All Somerset Cnty Fld Hockey 85; N Jersey All Star Group III 2nd Tm 85.

SCRIBELLITO, DAVID; Toms River HS East; Toms River, NJ; (Y); 66/585; Computer Clb; Intnl Clb; Math Tm; Science Clb; Spanish Clb; Bsbl; Hon Roll; Intl Piano Recrdng Comptn 83-86; Natl Piano Plyng Auditions 83-86; Amer Music Schlrshp Assn 83-86; Comp Sci.

SCROFINE, SUZANNE; Toms River HS East; Toms Rvr, NJ; (Y); 31/585; Intnl Clb; Spanish Clb; Teachers Aide; Yrbk Stf; Stu Cncl; JV Fld Hcky; Hon Roll; Off Jr Cls; Hrts Assoc 86; Blgy.

SCRUGGS, ANNA; Highland Park HS; Highland Park, NJ; (Y); 57/143; German Clb; SADD; Var Capt Bsktbl; Var Cheerleading; JV Crs Cntry; Var Trk; Hon Roll; Chld Psychlgy.

SCUDERI, JENNIFER; Washington Township HS; Sewell, NJ; (Y); Tchr.

SCULTHORPE, ARLENE; Neptune HS; Neptune, NJ; (Y); 27/380; Church Yth Grp; GAA; Yrbk Stf; JV Fld Hcky; JV Socr; High Hon Roll; Hon Roll; NHS.

SCUORZO, CHRIS; Howell HS; Howell, NJ; (Y); Chess Clb; German Clb; Band; Concert Band; Jazz Band; Mrchg Band; Pep Band; Symp Band; Smmr Music Lsn Schlrshp 85; Wind Ensemble 85-86; Brookdale CC; Elec Engr.

SEABROOK III, CHARLES F; Cumberland Regional HS; Bridgeton, NJ; (Y); FBLA; Teachers Aide; NHS; Pres Schlr; U Richmond; Bus.

SEABROOKS, JIMMIE; Eastside HS; Paterson, NJ; (Y); Boy Scts; 4-H; Rep Jr Cls; JV Ftbl; 4-H Awd; PSAT Achvt Awd 86; Accptnce Naval Acad 86; Howard U; Pre-Med.

SEAGRAVES, MICHELLE; Pennsville Memorial HS; Pennsville, NJ; (Y); 38/216; Ski Clb; Teachers Aide; Var Fld Hcky; Var Capt Sftbl; Hon Roll; Player Of Yr Sftbl 86; Plyr Of Week 85 & 86; All-Tri Cnty Tm 85 & 86; Westchester U; Elem Ed.

SEALE, JENNIFER; Hamilton HS West; Trenton, NJ; (Y); 40/322; Church Yth Grp; Pres FBLA; Office Aide; Rep Frsh Cls; Rep Soph Cls; Stat Bsktbl; Stat Trk; Hon Roll; ETE Schlrshp 86; Alpha Kappa Alpha Srty Schlrshp 86; Drexel U; Intr Dsgn.

SEALS, HEATHER; Mt Olive HS; Budd Lake, NJ; (Y); 27/312; Art Clb; Camera Clb; Dance Clb; Model UN; Yrbk Phtg; Yrbk Stf; Hon Roll; US Natl Art Awd 86; Intrnatl Drctry Dstngshd Yng Ldrshp 86; N Jersey Stu Crtfsmn Fiar Otstndng Awd 86.

SEAMAN, TOM; Bloomfield SR HS; Bloomfld, NJ; (Y); 21/452; Key Clb; Var L Bsktbl; JV Ftbl; Socr; Var Tennis; Im Wt Lftg; Cit Awd; High Hon Roll; Hon Roll; NHS; Aero-Sp Engr.

SECCO, MICHELE; Dover HS; Dover, NJ; (Y); 14/185; Am Leg Aux Girls St; Ski Clb; Sec Band; Mrchg Band; Yrbk Stf; Sec Stu Cncl; Var Socr; JV Capt Sftbl; Hon Roll; NHS; Phy Ther.

SECOOLISH, SHELLEY; Wall HS; Allenwood, NJ; (S); 12/276; German Clb; Ski Clb; Cheerleading; Score Keeper; DAR Awd; High Hon Roll; Hon Roll; NHS; MD U; German.

SEDA, AWILDA; Our Lady Of Good Counsel HS; Newark, NJ; (Y); 18/77; Camera Clb; Pep Clb; Teachers Aide; School Play; Stage Crew; Variety Show; Nwsp Stf; Yrbk Stf; Bowling; Hon Roll; Aspira Clb Awd 85-86; St Peters Coll; Accntng.

SEDLOCK, CRAIG; Lyndhurst HS; Lyndhurst, NJ; (Y); 26/180; Church Yth Grp; Office Aide; Pep Clb; Ski Clb; Stage Crew; Variety Show; Bsbl; Bsktbl; Hon Roll; Pres Clsrm Alumni; Pre-Law.

SEDLOCK, TRACY; Egg Harbor Township HS; Mays Landing, NJ; (S); 1/317; Spanish Clb; Nwsp Rptr; Nwsp Stf; Yrbk Rptr; Yrbk Stf; Trs Jr Cls; Stat Bsktbl; Mgr(s); Score Keeper; Hon Roll.

SEE, JENNIFER; Mother Seton Regional HS; Carteret, NJ; (Y); 54/101; Art Clb; Pres Church Yth Grp; Computer Clb; GAA; Rep Jr Cls; Rep Sr Cls; Var Capt Tennis; Prtcptd With Dstnctn In Ntl Sci Olympd, & Ntl Lang Arts Olympd 84; Supr Achmnt & Exllnce Algebra II; Math.

SEESINK, ANTONIUS F; North Warren Regional HS; Blairstown, NJ; (Y); 1/129; Am Leg Boys St; School Musical; School Play; Bausch & Lomb Sci Awd; Dnfth Awd; NHS; Pres Schlr; Val; Computer Clb; Scholastic Bowl; Natl Young Ldrs Conf Delegate 85; O M Chevron Schlrshp 86; N J Teen Arts St Competitor 86; WV U; Aerosp Engrng.

SEESSEL, BEN; Hopewell Valley Regional HS; Hopewell, NJ; (Y); 60/210; Pres AFS; Drama Clb; Capt Quiz Bowl; Chorus; School Musical; School Play; Nwsp Rptr; Rep Jr Cls; Rep Sr Cls; Im Bsktbl; Jack Rees Awd Dramtc Talnt 86; Kenyon Coll; Pol Sci.

SEGAL, HEIDI J; Paramus HS; Fort Lee, NJ; (Y); 19/350; Capt Math Tm; Pres Model UN; NFL; Chrmn Stu Cncl; Var L Trk; NHS; Spanish NHS; Off Frsh Cls; Off Soph Cls; Off Jr Cls; William E Remmington Mem Awd 85-86; Gardn ST Schlr 86; Natl Afrs Conf 85-86; Vassar Coll; Law.

SEGAL, ROBYN; Bridgewater-Raritan HS East; Martinsville, NJ; (Y); Ski Clb; Temple Yth Grp; Rep Frsh Cls; Rep Soph Cls; Rep Jr Cls; Rep Sr Cls; Rep Stu Cncl; Powder Puff Ftbl; Hon Roll; Pres Schlr; Lehigh; Bus.

SEIB, LORRAINE; Holy Spirit HS; Brigantine, NJ; (Y); Cmnty Wkr; French Clb; Hosp Aide; SADD; Teachers Aide; Concert Band; Orch; Fld Hcky; Sftbl; High Hon Roll; Neonatlgy Srgn.

SEIBERT, KERRY; Newton HS; Newton, NJ; (S); 21/210; Latin Clb; Ski Clb; SADD; Concert Band; Mrchg Band; Symp Band; Bowling; Trk; Hon Roll; NHS; Crmnl Justc.

SEIDENGLANZ, ELIZABETH; Notre Dame HS; Trenton, NJ; (Y); Hosp Aide; Key Clb; Office Aide; Red Cross Aide; SADD; Varsity Clb; Stage Crew; Rep Soph Cls; Rep Jr Cls; Fld Hcky.

SEIJAS, CARLOS; St Joseph Of The Palisades HS; West New York, NJ; (S); 5/110; Spanish Clb; Variety Show; Nwsp Rptr; Var Tennis; High Hon Roll; NHS; Spanish NHS; Mgmt.

SELBY, ALESHIA; Weequahic HS; Newark, NJ; (Y); 50/360; Cmnty Wkr; SADD; NHS; Ntl Merit Schol; Val; Voice Dem Awd; Boys Clb Am; Debate Tm; Exploring; Ldrshp Awds 85-86; Outstndng Avc Awd 85-86; Pub Rel.

SELFRIDGE, PAT; Haddonfield Memorial HS; Haddonfield, NJ; (Y); Pep Clb; Var Ftbl; Var Trk; Im Wt Lftg; Hon Roll; Crim Law.

SELIGER, RAYMOND; Wildwood Catholic HS; Avalon, NJ; (Y); Aud/Vis; Boy Scts; Chess Clb; Church Yth Grp; Cmnty Wkr; Carpntry.

SELIGMAN, ERIK; Ranapo HS; Wyckoff, NJ; (Y); 2/319; Pres Math Tm; Lit Mag; High Hon Roll; NHS; Chess Clb; Cmnty Wkr; Computer Clb; Library Aide; Science Clb; Rptr Nwsp Rptr; Comp Tm-Capt 85-86; RPI Awd 86; Govs Schlr-86 Govs Schl In Sci 86.

SELINGER, MARC; East Brunswick HS; E Brunswick, NJ; (Y); Debate Tm; Model UN; VP Temple Yth Grp; Concert Band; Jazz Band; Pres Mrchg Band; Symp Band; Nwsp Bus Mgr; NHS; Ntl Merit Ltr; Garden St Distngshd Schlr 85; E Brnswck Hstrcl Soc Awd 86; E Brnswck Band Bstrs Assn Awd 86; U Of MI; Poli Sci.

SELLECK, JOHN; Don Bosco Prep; Suffern, NY; (S); 5/190; Cmnty Wkr; Mathletes; Service Clb; Var Tennis; Var Trk; High Hon Roll; NHS; Bus Mgmt.

SELLNER, SAMANTHA; Parsippany HS; Parsippany, NJ; (Y); Dance Clb; FBLA; GAA; Pep Clb; Varsity Clb; Var L Cheerleading; Im Gym; Im Tennis; JV Trk; Rep Frsh Cls; Mst Imprvd Chrldr 85; Dance Awds 84-86.

SEMENTA, PINA; Mainland Regional HS; Somers Pt, NJ; (Y); Hosp Aide; Intnl Clb; SADD; Soph Cls; Stu Cncl; Future World Problm Solvers 84; Rotary Yth Ldrshp Awds 86; Politial Sci.

SEMITSCHEW, SHARON; Bridgewater-Rariton H S West; Raritan, NJ; (Y); Drama Clb; JV Cheerleading; Powder Puff Ftbl; Hon Roll; Intr Dectr.

SEMS, CYNTHIA L; Wayne Hills HS; Wayne, NJ; (Y); 23/313; Aud/Vis; Church Yth Grp; German Clb; Capt GAA; Ski Clb; Yrbk Stf; Var Socr; High Hon Roll; Lion Awd; NHS; Eclgy Clb Schlrshp 86; Shawn Richter Shclrshp 86; Natl Hnr Scty Schlrshp 86; La Fayette Coll; Chem Engnrng.

SEN, APARUP; Waldwick HS; Waldwick, NJ; (Y); 5/147; Chess Clb; Math Tm; JV Ftbl; High Hon Roll; Ntl Merit Ltr; Amer Legn Schl Awd 83.

SENATORE, ANDREA; Paul VI HS; Bellmawr, NJ; (S); Trs Frsh Cls; Trs Soph Cls; Trs Jr Cls; Stu Cncl; JV Var Cheerleading; Powder Puff Ftbl; La Salle; Accntng.

SENDAD, JACK; St Marys HS; Newark, NJ; (Y); Yrbk Bus Mgr; Rep Sr Cls; Ftbl; St Johns U; Bus Admin.

SENDZIA, DONNA; Lower Cape May Regional HS; N Cape May, NJ; (Y); 45/213; Cmnty Wkr; Girl Scts; Trs Library Aide; Spanish Clb; Band; Yrbk Stf; Hon Roll.

SENICO, THERESA L; Lower Cape May Regional HS; Villas, NJ; (Y); 15/225; Key Clb; Pep Clb; Ski Clb; Bsktbl; Trk; High Hon Roll; Hon Roll; NHS; Intrntnl Frgn Lng Awd 84-86; Acad Achvmnt Awd 86; Vrsty Ltr Schlrshp 84-86; Rutgers Coll; Pre Law.

SENKOVICH, MICHAEL H; Elmwood Park Memorial HS; Elmwood Park, NJ; (Y); 5/180; Am Leg Boys St; Band; School Musical; Rep Stu Cncl; Var L Trk; French Hon Soc; Hon Roll; NHS; American HS Math Exam-Hnrb Mntn-Elmwood Pk HS 86; Engrng.

SENNER, SUSAN; Paul VI HS; Williamstown, NJ; (S); 9/544; Hosp Aide; Math Clb; Trk; High Hon Roll; Hon Roll; Bus.

SENTNOR, DAVID; Hightstown HS; East Windsor, NJ; (Y); 45/441; FBLA; Stu Cncl; Var Crs Cntry; JV Socr; Var Trk; High Hon Roll; Hon Roll; Accntng.

SEPANIC, JENNIFER; Audubon HS; Audubon, NJ; (Y); 16/120; School Play; Yrbk Bus Mgr; Ed Lit Mag; VP Stu Cncl; Var Cheerleading; Var Tennis; Cit Awd; Hon Roll; NHS; Natl Hon Soc Srv Awd 86; Rutgers U; Bus.

SEPETJIAN, JOANNE; Palisades Park JR SR HS; Palisades Pk, NJ; (Y); 2/116; Pres Concert Band; Nwsp Bus Mgr; Stu Cncl; Tennis; Twrlr; NHS; VP Church Yth Grp; Band; Mgr School Musical; Nwsp Stf; NJ Distngushd Schlr 85; Aermenian Relief Soc Schrlshp 86; PTA Schrlshp 86; Hofstra U; Finance.

SEPINWALL, ALYSSA; Montville Township HS; Pine Brook, NJ; (Y); 7/262; Cmnty Wkr; Trs Drama Clb; Capt FBLA; NFL; Political Wkr; Trs VP Speech Tm; VP Temple Yth Grp; Nwsp Rptr; Gov Hon Prg Awd; Ski Clb; Dstrct NJ Chmpn US Extmprns Spkng 85 & 86; ST Chmp FBLA Imprmpt Spkng 86; Pltcl Sci.

SEPULVEDA, EVELYN; Frank H Morrell HS; Irvington, NJ; (Y); 15/480; Exploring; Hst FBLA; Key Clb; Library Aide; Nwsp Rptr; Yrbk Stf; Off Stu Cncl; High Hon Roll; Hon Roll; NHS; Cook Coll; Pre Med.

SERAD, SONIA; Delsia Regional HS; Vineland, NJ; (Y); Am Leg Aux Girls St; Aud/Vis; Cmnty Wkr; Exploring; Sec Girl Scts; School Musical; Yrbk Stf; JV Crs Cntry; JV Fld Hcky; Stat Mgr(s); Vet Med.

SERAFIN, TODD; Vineland HS; Vineland, NJ; (Y); 19/720; Church Yth Grp; Key Clb; Band; High Hon Roll; Hon Roll; Prfct Atten Awd; Sec Spanish NHS; Math Clb; Spanish Clb; Church Choir; Awd Part In Lebbanon Vly Coll Smr Chem Prgm 85; Smi Fnlst Gvnrs Schl Prgm For NJ 85; Hon Grad 86; VA Tech; Engrng.

SEREIKA, LYNDA; Colonia SR HS; Colonia, NJ; (Y); Latin Clb; Pres VP SADD; Co-Capt Drill Tm; Ed Yrbk Sprt Ed; Yrbk Stf; Lit Mag; Rep Jr Cls; Var JV Mgr(s); Stat Trk; Montclair ST Coll; Rcrtnl Ther.

SERI, ANGELA; Pinelands Regional HS; Egg Harbor, NJ; (Y); French Clb; Yrbk Bus Mgr; Yrbk Ed-Chief; French Hon Soc; Frnch Natl Hon Soc 86; Frgn Affairs.

SERIL, PETER; Bishop George AHR HS; Plainfield, NJ; (Y); Nwsp Stf; Yrbk Stf; Lit Mag; Hon Roll; Hon Mntn St Peters HS Art Cntst 86; Cmmrcl Art.

SERIO, ALEX; Rutherfird HS; Rutherford, NJ; (Y); Science Clb; Ftbl; Cmnty Wkr; Hon Roll; Pilot.

SEROCK, CHRISTIAN DAVID; Notre Dame HS; Trenton, NJ; (Y); 3/385; SADD; Lit Mag; French Hon Soc; High Hon Roll; Hon Roll; NHS; Prfct Atten Awd; Hnrs Awds Of Excllnc Engl III, Frnch III & Algbra II Trig 86; U Of GA; TV Cmmnctns.

SERPICO, DOREEN; Middletown HS South HS; Middletown, NJ; (Y); 71/468; School Play; Stage Crew; Rep Sr Cls; Rep Stu Cncl; High Hon Roll; Hon Roll; Ntl Merit Ltr; Yrbk Phtg; Yrbk Stf; JV Stat Bsktbl; Achvt Awd Math; Hnrbl Ment Art Work; Fash Design.

SERRANO, STEPHANIE; Sayreville War Memorial HS; Parlin, NJ; (Y); 69/380; Drama Clb; French Clb; FBLA; Spanish Clb; Band; Color Guard; Concert Band; Mrchg Band; School Musical; School Play; 5th Pl-FBLA Rgnl Comptn 83-84; Rutgers U; Acctng.

SERVELLO, CLAIRE; Holy Family Acad; Bayonne, NJ; (Y); Church Yth Grp; Cmnty Wkr; Hosp Aide; Lit Mag; Hon Roll; Jrnlsm.

SERVIDIO, LINA; Waldwick HS; Waldwick, NJ; (Y); Spanish Clb; Yrbk Rptr; Yrbk Stf; Powder Puff Ftbl; Prfct Atten Awd; Spanish NHS; Attnded Rdr Coll-Spnsh Comptn 85-86; Tutrd Spnsh 84-86; Awd-Art 84-85; Bus.

SESSA, SANDRA; Columbia HS; Maplewood, NJ; (Y); Dance Clb; Red Cross Aide; Teachers Aide; Variety Show; Kiwanis Awd; S Orange-Mplwd Ed Assn, HS Schlrshps 86; Mplwd 1st Aid Sqd 86; Montclair ST Coll; Ed.

SESSOMES, DARCELLA A; Monroe Township HS; Jamesburg, NJ; (Y); Church Yth Grp; Cmnty Wkr; Dance Clb; DECA; Girl Scts; SADD; School Play; Rep Frsh Cls; Rep Soph Cls; Rep Jr Cls; NYU; Mrktng Mgmnt.

SETAR, KEVIN; Rahway HS; Rahway, NJ; (Y); Church Yth Grp; Hon Roll; Jr NHS; De Vry; Comp Sci.

SETRAKIAN, ANAHID; Fair Lawn HS; Fairlawn, NJ; (Y); 3/325; Church Yth Grp; Girl Scts; Teachers Aide; Church Choir; Off Soph Cls; Off Jr Cls; Sftbl; Trk; High Hon Roll; Hon Roll.

SETTER, CATHERINE; Haddonfield Memorial HS; Haddonfield, NJ; (Y); 84/152; Cmnty Wkr; Rep Stu Cncl; JV Bsktbl; Var Stat Socr; French Hon Soc; High Hon Roll; Pres NHS; Bus.

SEVERINO, JOHN; Toms River HS; Toms River, NJ; (Y); Wt Lftg; Hon Roll; Hnr Role 82-83; Ltr Commendtn 82-83; Brick Computer Inst; Comp Tech.

SEVERINO, WILLIAM; North Bergen HS; Ridgefield, NJ; (Y); 35/404; Boy Scts; VICA; Concert Band; Mrchg Band; Hon Roll; PTA Schlrshp, BSA Eagle 86; NJ Inst Tech; Arch.

SEVERS, BARBARA; Paul VI Regional HS; Montclair, NJ; (Y); Ski Clb; Stage Crew; JV Trk; French Hon Soc; Hon Roll; Rutgers U; Psych.

SEWALL, LINDSEY D; Haddon Township HS; Haddonfield, NJ; (Y); 2/177; VP Band; Church Choir; Var Tennis; Kiwanis Awd; NHS; Sal; St Schlr; Concert Band; Madrigals; Orch; All Eastern Chorus 85; Natl Presbytrn Schlr 86; Natl Schl Choral Awd 86; Westminster Coll.

SEWDASS, INDIRA; Howell Regional HS; Howell, NJ; (Y); Church Yth Grp; Hosp Aide; Spanish Clb; Color Guard; Hon Roll; M S Word Encounters Cit Cert Multi Sclerosis 85 & 86; Rutegers; Acctg.

SEXTON, MICHELE; Saint Rose HS; Spring Lake Hgts, NJ; (Y); Cmnty Wkr; Drama Clb; Soroptimist; School Musical; School Play; Rep Frsh Cls; Rep Jr Cls; Rep Stu Cncl; Var Cheerleading; NEDT Awd; Top Prz & Accptnce ST Teen Arts Fstvl CPP Pgm 85; Sngng Conc With Eugenio Fernandi 86; Comm.

SEYMOUR, CARLA; Plainfield HS; Plainfield, NJ; (Y); 12/647; DECA; Science Clb; Concert Band; Mrchg Band; L Mgr(s); Timer; Capt JV Vllybl; High Hon Roll; Hon Roll; NHS; Pres Ntl Hnr Scty 86-87; Trphy For Apparel & Acc Instrctr 85; 3yr Hnr Roll 83-84; Accntng.

SGAMBELLONE, BRUNO; Palisades Park JR SR HS; Palisades Park, NJ; (Y); Drama Clb; Math Clb; School Play; Variety Show; Yrbk Stf; Ftbl; Trk; Wt Lftg; Wrstlng; Prfct Atten Awd.

SHABABB, ROBERT; Emerson HS; Union City, NJ; (Y); Am Leg Boys St; Sec Church Yth Grp; Cmnty Wkr; Yrbk Bus Mgr; Yrbk Phtg; Yrbk Rptr; Yrbk Stf; Capt Tennis; Amrcn Lgn Boys St 86; Cptn Tns Tm 85-86; Yrbk Bus Mgr 86-87; Bus.

SHADY, KATHRYN; Point Pleasant Beach HS; Lavallette, NJ; (Y); 13/110; Am Leg Aux Girls St; Concert Band; Jazz Band; Mrchg Band; Sr Cls; JP Sousa Awd; Debate Tm; Band; Variety Show; Yrbk Stf; Lavallette Elm Schl Rtrd Tchrs Assoc Schlrshp 86; Seaside Italian Am Clb Schlrshp 86; Old Grd Schlrshp; Trenton ST Coll; Music.

SHAFFER, KENNETH; Roselle Catholic HS; Roselle, NJ; (Y); 21/195; Ski Clb; Chrmn SADD; Church Choir; Lit Mag; Rep Frsh Cls; Rep Stu Cncl; Var Trk; Hon Roll; Jr NHS; Du Cret Art Schl; Grphc Dsgnr.

SHAFFER, MARY K; Roselle Catholic HS; Roselle, NJ; (S); 2/152; Ski Clb; Church Choir; Hon Roll; NHS; Prfct Atten Awd; Spanish NHS; St Peters Coll Smr Schlr 84-86; Ed.

SHAFFER, RONALD; Overbrook Regional HS; Berlin, NJ; (Y); Boy Scts; Church Yth Grp; Trs 4-H; 4-H Awd; Bus Admin.

SHAFFERY, LISA; Toms River North HS; Toms River, NJ; (Y); 64/480; Drama Clb; French Clb; German Clb; Key Clb; Chorus; Rep Frsh Cls; Rep Soph Cls; Rep Jr Cls; JV Capt Socr; Hon Roll; Frgn Affrs Admin.

SHAH, INA; North Bergen HS; North Bergen, NJ; (Y); 9/470; Sec Key Clb; Office Aide; Spanish Clb; SADD; Yrbk Stf; VP Soph Cls; Stu Cncl; Hon Roll; Sec NHS; Spanish NHS; Guidance Off Awd; Rutgers Coll Phrmcy; Phrmcy.

SHAH, MANOJ N; Passaic HS; Passaic, NJ; (Y); 6/600; Am Leg Boys St; Computer Clb; Science Clb; Rep Soph Cls; Rep Sr Cls; Tennis; Hon Roll; Pres NHS; FBLA; Hosp Aide; Centry III Cntst Stu Jdg 86; Hodel Cngrs-Treas 85-86; Acadmc Decathln A-Tm 85-86; Cornell 1; Comp Sci.

SHAH, MINESH; Bound Brook HS; S Bound Brook, NJ; (Y); 2/133; Am Leg Boys St; French Clb; Math Clb; NFL; Speech Tm; Tennis; High Hon Roll; NHS; Sal; St Schlr; Lehigh U; Cvl Engr.

SHAH, MITESH; Emerson HS; Union City, NJ; (Y); Computer Clb; Hon Roll; Rutgers U.

SHAH, PINKIE; Dickinson HS; Jersey City, NJ; (Y); French Clb; Hosp Aide; Math Clb; Q&S; Science Clb; Nwsp Rptr; Nwsp Stf; Yrbk Stf; High Hon Roll; Hon Roll; Rtgrs Schlrs Awd 85-86; Candy Strpr Awd 85; Med.

SHAH, PRASANT; Hoboken HS; Hoboken, NJ; (Y); Chess Clb; French Clb; Nwsp Rptr; Nwsp Stf; Off Frsh Cls; Off Soph Cls; Jr Cls; Off Sr Cls; Off Stu Cncl; NHS; Comp Sci.

SHAH, RAKESH; South Brunswick HS; Kendall Pk, NJ; (Y); 15/250; Cmnty Wkr; Mathletes; Ski Clb; Temple Yth Grp; Im Sftbl; Im Vllybl; Hon Roll; NHS; Rotary Awd; Computer Clb; Grdn ST Dstngshd Schlr 85-86; S Brnswck PTA Schlrshp 86; Rutgers U; Engnrng.

SHAH, RITA; North Bergen HS; N Bergen, NJ; (Y); 40/404; French Clb; Hosp Aide; Intnl Clb; Office Aide; Spanish Clb; SADD; Hon Roll; NHS; Outstndng Achvt Stu Cncl Schlrshp 86; Fairleigh Dickinson U; Accntng.

SHAH, SONAL; Dickinson HS; Jersey City, NJ; (Y); CC Awd; Hon Roll; Comp Sci.

SHAH, SUDIP; Parippany HS; Cedar Knolls, NJ; (Y); 100/318; Computer Clb; Science Clb; Spanish Clb; SADD; Bsbl; Ftbl; Tennis; Hon Roll; Comp Clb 84-85; NJ Inst Tech; Engrng.

SHAH, SUKEN A; Cherry Hill HS East; Cherry Hill, NJ; (Y); Am Leg Boys St; Var Debate Tm; Pres Temple Yth Grp; Off Sr Cls; Rep Stu Cncl; JV Var Tennis; High Hon Roll; NHS; Rep Jr Cls; Hosp Aide; Med Schlrs Prog Kennedy Hosp 86-87; Bio & Hlth Profssns Cornell U 86; Med.

SHAH, SWATI S; Montville Township HS; Pine Brook, NJ; (Y); 11/280; Capt Dance Clb; FBLA; Hosp Aide; Intnl Clb; Key Clb; Capt Gym; High Hon Roll; NHS; Ntl Merit SF; Cnty Teen Arts Fstvl Essay Wnnr 85; Med.

SHAH, TAJEL; Bridgewater Rariten East HS; Bridgewater, NJ; (Y); FBLA; Intnl Clb; Pep Clb; PAVAS; SADD; Rep Stu Cncl; Var Fld Hcky; Var Stat Lcrss; Powder Puff Ftbl; Poltcs.

SHAHROKH, LALEH; Wayne Hills HS; Wayne, NJ; (Y); 21/305; French Clb; Math Clb; Trk; Hon Roll; NHS; Rutgers Coll; Pdtrcn.

SHAIR, WENDY; Colinia HS; Colonia, NJ; (Y); Art Clb; Chorus; School Musical; Hon Roll; Hnr Acadmc & Attitd Hnr Rlls 84-85; Awd Poetry 85; Awd Fnlst Miss TEEN NJ Pagnt 86; FIT NY; Fashn Dsgnr.

SHAKKOUR, GHADA; John F Kennedy HS; Paterson, NJ; (Y); 5/403; Nwsp Rptr; Secy Skills 2nd Pl Typing II 86; Outstndng Acad Achvt 82-86; Pres Acad Ftnss Awd 86; US Navy; Engrng.

SHALAWAY, STACEY; Pitman HS; Pitman, NJ; (S); 11/141; Pres Church Yth Grp; Teachers Aide; JV Bsktbl; JV Fld Hcky; Var Sftbl; Hon Roll; NHS; Phy Thrpy.

SHALFOROOSH, SORAYA; Waldwick HS; Waldwick, NJ; (Y); Intnl Clb; Nwsp Rptr; Lit Mag; High Schl Netwrk 85-86; Minds Eye Editor 85-87; CARE Fundrsr 85-86.

SHALLCROSS, WILLIAM; St James HS; Elmer, NJ; (Y); 9/85; CAP; Cmnty Wkr; Red Cross Aide; Stage Crew; Hon Roll; Prfct Atten Awd; St NJ Gnrl Asmbly Citation For OEM Srv 85; CAP Awd For Slm Cnty Dstr Drill 85.

SHAND, EILEEN; Toms River East HS; Toms River, NJ; (Y); 45/587; Church Yth Grp; Drama Clb; French Clb; Band; Concert Band; Orch; School Play; Var Stat Bsbl; Var Mgr(s); High Hon Roll; ST Fnlst Modern Miss Schrlshp Cntst 85; Lawyer.

SHANDOR, JENNIFER; Belvidere HS; Phillipsburg, NJ; (S); 11/125; Varsity Clb; JV Var Bsktbl; JV Var Fld Hcky; JV Sftbl; NHS; HOBY Fndtn Fin 85; Mst Outstndng Stu Frnch I 84.

SHANEMAN, CHERIE; Wildwood Catholic HS; Wildwd Crst, NJ; (Y); French Clb; Office Aide.

SHANKAR, ANJE; Parsippany HS; Parsippany, NJ; (Y); Hosp Aide; ROTC; Varsity Clb; Badmtn; Bsktbl; Diving; Socr; Swmmng; Var L Tennis; Vllybl; NY U; Bus Admin.

SHANLEY, LORI; Secaucus HS; Secaucus, NJ; (Y); Church Yth Grp; Cmnty Wkr; Computer Clb; Key Clb; Math Clb; Chorus; Color Guard; Mrchg Band; Hon Roll.

SHANNON, THOMAS; Rutgers Prep; Berkeley Hts, NJ; (Y); Boy Scts; VP Pres Exploring; Spanish Clb; Exmplry Scout 84; Eagle Scout 86; Outstndng Svc To Oper USA & Lewisham Nrth-London BSA 85; Rutgers U; Cvl Engrng.

SHAPIRO, DAVID; Haddonfield Memorial HS; Haddonfield, NJ; (S); Cmnty Wkr; French Clb; Band; Concert Band; Mrchg Band; Orch; Var Tennis; French Hon Soc; Hon Roll; NHS; 2nd Pl Rgnl Cmptn Olympcs/Mnd 83; U Of DE; Bio Sci.

SHAPIRO, IGOR; Union HS; Union, NJ; (Y); 39/457; Chess Clb; Computer Clb; Math Tm; Hon Roll; Stevens Inst Of Tech; Com Engr.

SHAPIRO, LAWRENCE; Shore Regional HS; W Long Branch, NJ; (Y); Am Leg Boys St; Lit Mag; Pres Frsh Cls; Pres Soph Cls; Var L Bsbl; Hon Roll; NHS; Var L Socr; Lit Wrk Published Teen Arts Fest Booklet 86; Lit Wrk Pblshd Shore Lines Lit Booklet 86; Bus.

SHAPIRO, MICHAEL S; Union HS; Union, NJ; (Y); FBLA; Key Clb; Service Clb; Ski Clb; Temple Yth Grp; Chorus; School Play; Stu Cncl; Co-Capt JV Socr; Hon Roll; H S PTA Schlrshp 86; Soc Of Dstngshd H S Stu 84-85; Long Island U; Bus Adm.

SHAPIRO, TRACY L; Millville SR HS; Millville, NJ; (Y); 14/470; Trs French Clb; FBLA; Key Clb; Science Clb; SADD; Rep Stu Cncl; JV Fld Hcky; High Hon Roll; Sec NHS; Pres Schlr; Hnr Soc Svc Awd 86; Outstndng Sci Stu Awd 86; Trenton ST Coll; Bus Adm.

SHARAR, LINDA DOROTHY; Glen Rock HS; Glen Rock, NJ; (Y); 13/163; Pres Church Yth Grp; DECA; Drama Clb; English Clb; GAA; Latin Clb; Library Aide; Pep Clb; Varsity Clb; Trs Sr Cls; Ath Yr 84; 2nd Tm All Lg Soccr & Sftbl 86; 3rd Pl Advrtsng DECA ST Comptn 86; Rep Meth Chrch Missn 85; Psych.

SHARKEY, GREG; Toms Rive HS North; Toms River, NJ; (Y); Art Clb; School Musical; School Play; Stage Crew; Lit Mag; Hon Roll; Fnlst & Altrnte Gov Schl For The Arts 85-86; NY U Film Schl; Cinematography.

SHARKEY, KATHLEEN; Pope John XXIII Regional HS; Oak Ridge, NJ; (Y); 28/133; Church Yth Grp; Sec Stu Cncl; Var Bsktbl; NHS; Drama Clb; Hosp Aide; Latin Clb; SADD; Varsity Clb; Church Choir; Acad Awd Spn 86; All Area Awd Bsktbl, Trk 87; Phys Ther.

SHARKEY, KIM; Brick Township HS; Brick, NJ; (Y); Hosp Aide; Key Clb; Powder Puff Ftbl; Im Stat Sftbl; Hon Roll; Lock Haven U; Physcl Thrpy.

SHARLOW, REGINA; Mt Saint Mary Acad; Edison, NJ; (S); 2/90; Church Yth Grp; GAA; Latin Clb; Service Clb; Varsity Clb; Rep Soph Cls; Fld Hcky; High Hon Roll; Hon Roll; NHS; Stu Atty Cnty Champ Mock Trial Tm 86; Peer Minister 86.

SHARMA, PRIYA; Mater Dei HS; Matawan, NJ; (Y); 9/151; Cmnty Wkr; Model UN; Pep Clb; Nwsp Ed-Chief; Yrbk Ed-Chief; Powder Puff Ftbl; Hon Roll; NHS; Gentc Engrng.

SHARP, BRIAN; Washington Township HS; Turnersville, NJ; (Y); Church Yth Grp; Cmnty Wkr; Hon Roll; Acctg.

SHARP, DAWN; Vineland HS; Vineland, NJ; (Y); High Hon Roll; Hon Roll; Cumberland Cnty Coll; Legl Sec.

SHARP, GREGORY W; Edgewood SR HS; Atco, NJ; (Y); German Clb; Stage Crew; Hon Roll; Jr NHS; NHS; Rutgers U Smmr Schlrs Pgm 85; Rutgers U Camden; Acctg.

SHARP, JESSICA; James Caldwell HS; Caldwell, NJ; (Y); Key Clb; Score Keeper; Hon Roll; Cert Grad Baribzon 86; Bus.

SHARP, MARTHA JOY; Hunterdon Central HS; Grand Rapids, MI; (Y); 69/539; Church Yth Grp; Pres Key Clb; Thesps; Mrchg Band; Sec Jr Cls; NHS; FCA; 4-H; Ski Clb; Intrntl Yth Achvt 85; NJ Gvrnrs Tchng Schlrs Pgm Rcpnt 86; NJ Grls Ctznshp 85; Hope Coll; Elem Ed.

SHARPE, RHONDA; Cumberland Regional HS; Bridgeton, NJ; (Y); Drama Clb; FBLA; Yrbk Stf; Church Yth Grp; Intnl Clb; Hon Roll; Glassboro ST Coll.

SHARRY, AUDRA; Wayne Hills HS; Wayne, NJ; (Y); 49/302; Church Yth Grp; Cmnty Wkr; French Clb; Lit Mag; Stu Cncl; Var Capt Bsktbl; JV Socr; JV Trk; Var Vllybl; Hon Roll; Peer Cnclng Ldr 86-87; County Fnlst Gov Schl Arts 85-86; Teen Fash Bd Modelng 85-86; Visual Comm.

SHAUGHNESSY, MAUREEN; Bishop George Ahr HS; Colonia, NJ; (Y); 37/291; Dance Clb; Ski Clb; Yrbk Stf; Stu Cncl; Var L Crs Cntry; Var L Trk; High Hon Roll; NHS; Rep Frsh Cls; Rep Soph Cls; Miss Amer Irish 86; Natl & Wrld Dance Comp 83-86; Cnty & ST Trck Mts Indiv & Relay Tms 83-86; Rutgers U; Pharm.

SHAUGHNESSY, SARA; St Rose HS; Point Pleasant, NJ; (Y); 12/222; Pres Church Yth Grp; Drama Clb; Exploring; Hosp Aide; Key Clb; Church Choir; Variety Show; Nwsp Rptr; Nwsp Stf; Yrbk Stf; Armed Forces Career Exploratn Engrng & Sci 1st Pl Spch 84, Project 84; Bio.

SHAW, DEBORAH JEAN; Haddonfield Memorial HS; Haddonfield, NJ; (Y); Intnl Clb; Spanish Clb; Drm Mjr(t); Mrchg Band; Orch; Rep Stu Cncl; Var Capt Bowling; Capt Twrlr; Hon Roll; Spanish NHS; Acctng.

SHAW, JANE; Neumann Prep; Kinnelon, NJ; (Y); 3/80; Ski Clb; Lit Mag; JV Var Tennis; Var Trk; French Hon Soc; Hon Roll; NHS; Excllnc In Sci 86; Alg II & Trig, ACC Engl & US Hist II Awd 85; Cornell U; Vet Med.

SHAW, JOHN; Midland Park HS; Midland Park, NJ; (Y); 45/137; AFS; Aud/Vis; Drama Clb; French Clb; Model UN; Political Wkr; VP Chorus; School Musical; School Play; Stage Crew; Trustee Schlr NYU; Natl Choral Awd; NYU; Drama.

SHAW, KELLY; Manalapan HS; Manalapan, NJ; (Y); Church Yth Grp; Exploring; Girl Scts; Hosp Aide; Mrchg Band; Stage Crew; Acctg.

SHAW, LINDA; Gloucester City JR SR HS; Gloucester, NJ; (Y); FBLA; Pep Clb; Chorus; School Musical; Stu Cncl; Cheerleading; Fld Hcky; Lcrss; Hon Roll; Prfct Atten Awd; Mst Imprvd Lacrs 83; 7th Pl Regnl Comptn Steno I 86; 3rd Pl ST Comptn Steno I 86; Stenogrphr.

SHAW, LINDA; Manalapan HS; Englishtown, NJ; (Y); Color Guard; School Play; Stage Crew; Rep Frsh Cls; NHS; NJ Distngshd Schlr 85-86; Garden ST Schlrp 85-86; E R Voorhees Schlrp 85-86; Rutgers U.

SHAW, MATT; Pt Pleasant Boro HS; Pt Pleasant Bch, NJ; (S); 31/244; Key Clb; Varsity Clb; VP Socr; Var Tennis; Hon Roll; NHS; Sprts Mgmt.

SHAW, REBECCA; Passaic Valley HS; Little Falls, NJ; (Y); Church Yth Grp; Dance Clb; Key Clb; Color Guard; Mrchg Band; Variety Show; Nwsp Rptr; Nwsp Stf; Cheerleading; Englsh.

SHAW, TRACEE; Freehold Township HS; Freehold Twp, NJ; (Y); 23/384; Aud/Vis; Church Yth Grp; Hosp Aide; Spanish Clb; Mrchg Band; Stat Bsktbl; Var Trk; Capt Twrlr; NHS; Accntnt.

SHEA, JOE; Woodbridge SR HS; Fords, NJ; (Y); School Play; Ftbl; U Of MD; Pre-Law.

SHEA, MICHAEL; Christian Brothers Acad; Brielle, NJ; (Y); 82/222; Camera Clb; Pep Clb; Nwsp Phtg; Nwsp Rptr; Lit Mag; Var Crs Cntry; Gym; Var Trk; Hon Roll; Vrsty Ltr Crss Cntry, Indr Trck, Outdr Trck; Bus Adm.

SHEARD, ROBERT; Central Regional HS; Bayville, NJ; (Y); 79/249; Art Clb; JA; Pep Clb; Varsity Clb; Yrbk Phtg; Yrbk Sprt Ed; Off Stu Cncl; JV Bsbl; Var Capt Bsktbl; Bus Admn.

SHEARS, TRACEY; Holy Cross HS; Browns Mills, NJ; (Y); 20/380; Cmnty Wkr; Exploring; Hosp Aide; Red Cross Aide; Spanish Clb; Yrbk Stf; High Hon Roll; Hon Roll; Rtgrs Undrgrad Mnrty Merit Schlrshp, NJ Grdn ST Schlrshp, 86; Rutgers U; Med.

SHEEHAN, COLLEEN; Newton HS; Newton, NJ; (S); 2/218; Sec French Clb; Girl Scts; Math Tm; Science Clb; Madrigals; School Musical; Var Cheerleading; Stat Ftbl; Hon Roll; NHS.

SHEEHAN, DANIEL; Matawan Feednao HS; Cliffwood Beach, NJ; (S); 7/770; Math Clb; Var L Socr; French Hon Soc; Hon Roll; NHS; Ntl Merit SF; Hstry Govt Clb; Engrng.

SHEEHAN, JENNIFER; Indian Hills HS; Oakland, NJ; (Y); 87/287; Trs AFS; Debate Tm; French Clb; Hosp Aide; Hon Roll; Bus.

SHEEHAN, JOHN P; Christian Brothers Acad; Colts Neck, NJ; (S); 8/216; Math Tm; Service Clb; Yrbk Stf; Im Ftbl; Var Im Socr; High Hon Roll; Trs NHS; Hlth Cr Adm.

SHEEHAN, KATHERINE; Pequannock Township HS; Pequannock, NJ; (Y); 11/231; Pres Latin Clb; Band; Mrchg Band; Orch; School Musical; Nwsp Stf; Yrbk Stf; Hon Roll; Sec Yrbk Stf; Pres Schlr; Garden ST Distngshd Schlr 86; Rutgers U.

SHEEHY, SUSAN; Westfield HS; Westfield, NJ; (Y); 75/480; French Clb; Political Wkr; Red Cross Aide; Chorus; JV Fld Hcky; JV Trk; Hon Roll; NHS; Ntl Merit Ltr; Wellesley Coll; Intl Rltns.

SHEETZ, AMY; Kings Christain HS; Haddon Hts, NJ; (Y); Cmnty Wkr; Drama Clb; Hosp Aide; Varsity Clb; Band; Chorus; School Play; Sec Frsh Cls; Pres Jr Cls; Fld Hcky; 1st Pl Macsa Fin Arts Fstvl 85-86; Cmmnctns.

SHEETZ, SANDRA; The Kings Christian HS; Somerdale, NJ; (Y); Drama Clb; Red Cross Aide; Chorus; School Play; Pres Soph Cls; Pres Stu Cncl; Capt Cheerleading; High Hon Roll; NHS; Mildred Shrdr Msc Awd 85-86; Parent Tchr Fllwshp Schlrshp 85-86; Liberty U; Englsh Educ.

SHEFFIELD, DIANE LYNN; Salem HS; Salem, NJ; (Y); 6/140; Computer Clb; Drama Clb; Trs 4-H; Math Clb; Concert Band; Sec Sr Cls; Rep Stu Cncl; Hon Roll; VP NHS; Rotary Awd; Achvt Commndtns Acctg 84-86; Ordr Of Eastern Star Schlrshp 86; W M Lawrence Jr Schlrshp 86; Elizabethtown Clg; Acctg.

SHEFT, MICHAEL; West Essex SR HS; N Caldwell, NJ; (Y); Am Leg Boys St; Boy Scts; Bsktbl; Golf; High Hon Roll; Hon Roll; Brd Dir Stu Voice; Bus.

SHEIKH, MUHAMMAD; Dickinson HS; Jersey, NJ; (Y); Computer Clb; Hosp Aide; Off Sr Cls; Vllybl; Boys Clb Am; Off Soph Cls; Comp Pmgr.

SHEILS, CAROLYN; Villa Walsh Acad; Morristown, NJ; (S); Church Yth Grp; Drama Clb; SADD; Orch; Lit Mag; Var Socr; French Clb; Chorus; Church Choir; Hnrb Mntn-Chrstphrs Essy Cntst 86; $800 Schlrshp Irish Amercn Cltrl Inst 86; Jrnlsm Awd Lcl Cnty Nwspr; Comm.

SHEILS, JULIE; Villa Walsh Acad; Morristown, NJ; (Y); 3/34; Church Yth Grp; Hosp Aide; Math Clb; School Musical; Yrbk Stf; Capt L Crs Cntry; Dnfth Awd; NHS; Spanish NHS; Judy Baratte Mem Schlrshp 86; James Madison U; Math.

SHELAT, SURESH G; Emerson JR SR HS; Emerson, NJ; (Y); 1/98; Am Leg Boys St; Boys Clb Am; Pres Spanish Clb; Chorus; Ed Spanish Clb; Ed Nwsp Stf; Ed Yrbk Stf; Trs Sr Cls; Var Capt Tennis; Var L Trk; 1st Prize B Franklin Reinauer II Free Enterprise Awd 85; Rutgers U Schlr 86; US Military Scholar 86; Engrng.

SHELDON, DAN; Paul VI HS; Haddon Hgts, NJ; (Y); Church Yth Grp; SADD; Villanova; Real Estate.

SHELTON, LISA; Toms River North HS; Toms River, NJ; (Y); 4/412; Am Leg Aux Girls St; Hosp Aide; Trs Spanish Clb; Stu Cncl; Stat Ftbl; High Hon Roll; NHS; Amer Assn Of U Wmn Hnr 85-86; Lehigh U; Lawyer.

SHELTON, SONYA E; Univeristy HS; E Orange, NJ; (Y); 6/70; Color Guard; School Play; High Hon Roll; Hon Roll; Psych.

SHELTON, TANYA; Pennsauken HS; Delair, NJ; (Y); Church Choir; Var Mgr Bsktbl; Var Mgr Ftbl; Lcrss; Hon Roll; Goldey Beacom Coll; Accounting.

SHEN, VIVIAN; Parsippany Hills HS; Morris Plains, NJ; (Y); 10/309; AFS; FBLA; Key Clb; Band; High Hon Roll; Hon Roll; NHS; Ntl Merit Ltr; PRNT-TCHR-STU Assn Acadmc Achvt Awd 86; NE Conf Tchng Frgn Lang Awd-Grmn 86; Stu Guide Awd 86; U Of MI; Bus.

SHENEKJI, CHRISTINE; Wayne Hills HS; Wayne, NJ; (Y); Church Yth Grp; Dance Clb; Drama Clb; Ski Clb; Spanish Clb; Chorus; Church Choir; School Musical; School Play; Stage Crew; 1st Plc Vcl Ctgry Ryl Strs Tlnt Cmptn 85; 1st Plc Vcl Shwstpprs Natl Tlnt Cmptn 86; Amer Acad Dramatic Arts; Dncr.

SHENKER, KARYN; Teaneck HS; Teaneck, NJ; (Y); Dance Clb; SADD; Acpl Chr; Chorus; Madrigals; School Play; Yrbk Ed-Chief; Sec Jr Cls; Capt Cheerleading; Capt Gym; TABS Awd For Outstndng Plyr 84-86; Lawyer.

SHENTON, PHILIP; Millville HS; Millville, NJ; (Y); 18/430; Church Yth Grp; Debate Tm; Drama Clb; German Clb; Band; Church Choir; Concert Band; Mrchg Band; School Musical; School Play; Amer Legion Bnd.

SHEPARD, MICHAEL; Wayne Hills HS; Wayne, NJ; (Y); Math Tm; Stu Cncl; Crs Cntry; JV Tennis; Var Capt Wrstlng; Ath Of Mnth 85; Bio-Engrng.

SHEPARD, RENEE; Lincoln HS; Jersey, NJ; (Y); Dance Clb; FBLA; FHA; Key Clb; Yrbk Stf; Off Jr Cls; Stu Cncl; Mgr(s); Score Keeper; Vllybl; Temple U; Nrsng.

SHEPHERD, KIMBERLY; Delaware Valley Regional HS; Milford, NJ; (Y); Cmnty Wkr; VP Intnl Clb; Key Clb; VP Thesps; School Musical; School Play; Yrbk Rptr; High Hon Roll; Hon Roll; Ntl Merit Ltr; Pltcl Sci.

SHEPLER, JANET; Passaic Valley HS; Totowa, NJ; (Y); 69/358; Key Clb; Spanish Clb; Score Keeper; Trk; Vrsty Trck Ltr; Bio.

SHEPPARD, EDWARD; Hudson Cath; Jersey Cty, NJ; (Y); Boy Scts; SADD; Yrbk Stf; L Ftbl; Trk; Wt Lftg; Relgs Grp Peer Mnstry 85-86; Bus.

SHEPPARD, GRETCHEN; Cumberland Ragional HS; Bridgeton, NJ; (Y); Camera Clb; Computer Clb; 4-H; GAA; Hosp Aide; Ski Clb; Nwsp Ed-Chief; Sftbl; 4-H Awd; Lion Awd; Jrnlsm.

SHEPPARD, MICHAEL E; Jefferson Twp HS; Lake Hopatcong, NJ; (Y); Am Leg Boys St; Debate Tm; Drama Clb; PAVAS; Chorus; Jazz Band; School Musical; School Play; Rep Soph Cls; Rep Jr Cls; Union Coll; Pol Sci.

SHEPPARD, MIGNON; Lacordaire Acad; Newark, NJ; (Y); Office Aide; Spanish Clb; SADD; Acpl Chr; Chorus; Madrigals; School Musical; Variety Show; Diving; Var Swmmng; Vailsburg Cmnty Schl Art Music Awd 84-85; Yth Orgnztn PASE 86; Howard U; Bus Adm.

SHEPPARD, SEAN P; Notre Dame HS; Kendall Park, NJ; (Y); 76/342; Boy Scts; Church Yth Grp; Key Clb; Pep Clb; Varsity Clb; Yrbk Stf; Ftbl; Wt Lftg; Hon Roll; Cath Scholar Negroes Inc 86; Southland Corp 86; Alpha Phi Alpha Frat Inc 86; Georgetown U; Bio.

SHERIDAN III, EDWARD FRANCIS; Seton Hall Prep; Whippany, NJ; (Y); 58/219; Church Yth Grp; FBLA; Key Clb; Pep Clb; SADD; School Musical; Yrbk Stf; Golf; Ice Hcky; Mgr(s); Fairfield U; Acctng.

SHERIDAN, JOSEPH; Highland Regional HS; Erial, NJ; (S); 16/332; VP Chess Clb; Latin Clb; Band; Concert Band; Mrchg Band; Im Socr; Hon Roll; NHS; Olympic Conf Band 85 & 86.

SHERIDAN, KELLIANNE; Bishop George Ahr HS; S Plainfield, NJ; (Y); 37/277; Trs French Clb; Model UN; Service Clb; Ski Clb; Stage Crew; Lit Mag; Hon Roll; Excllnc Schlrshp Awd 84; Poltc Sci.

SHERIDAN, RICHARD; Linden HS; Linden, NJ; (Y); VP German Clb; Ski Clb; Band; Jazz Band; Capt Mrchg Band; School Musical; Var Golf; Im Ice Hcky; Hon Roll; NHS.

SHERMA, SHIRVAN MARIE; Our Lady Of Mercy Acad; Mays Landing, NJ; (Y); Drama Clb; 4-H; Pres SADD; Nwsp Ed-Chief; Nwsp Rptr; Ed Lit Mag; Pres Jr Cls; Pres Sr Cls; Rep Stu Cncl; High Hon Roll; Ldrshp, Journlsm & Schl Spirit Awd; San Diego ST U; Spch Cmmnctns.

SHERMAN, JEANINE; St John Vianney HS; Matawan, NJ; (Y); Church Yth Grp; Ski Clb; Stage Crew; Nwsp Rptr; Nwsp Stf; Yrbk Stf; Diving; Swmmng; Trk; Wt Lftg; Pres Phys Ftnss Awd 83-87; Phys Ed Dept Awd 84; Govt.

SHERMAN, JOHN; Bridgeton HS; Cedarville, NJ; (Y); Boy Scts; Church Yth Grp; Ski Clb; Hrtcltrl.

SHERMAN, JONATHAN M; Livingston HS; Livingston, NJ; (Y); Drama Clb; Radio Clb; Chorus; School Musical; School Play; Nwsp Rptr; Rep Stu Cncl; Mgr(s); Ntl Merit SF; Lit Cont Schl Nwsp Wnnr 85; Bennington Coll; Theater.

SHERMAN, NADINE; Immaculate Conception HS; Kearny, NJ; (Y); Sec Cmnty Wkr; Hosp Aide; Q&S; Pres Science Clb; VP Chorus; School Play; Nwsp Rptr; Ed Nwsp Stf; Trs Sr Cls; Hon Roll; Chem.

SHERRIER, WILLIAM; Rahway HS; Rahway, NJ; (Y); Chess Clb; Ski Clb; Bsbl; Var Socr; Wrstlng; Hon Roll.

SHERROD, KEISHA; West Side HS; Newark, NJ; (Y); Boys Clb Am; Church Yth Grp; Debate Tm; Drama Clb; Church Choir; Color Guard; Mrchg Band; Stage Crew; Trs Jr Cls; Trs Sr Cls; Accntng.

SHERRY, COLLEEN; Holy Cross HS; Medford Lakes, NJ; (Y); Church Yth Grp; Cmnty Wkr; GAA; Mrchg Band; Yrbk Stf; Rep Frsh Cls; Rep Jr Cls; Rep Stu Cncl; Bsktbl; JV Mgr(s); Towson ST U; Mass Commnctns.

SHESTAKOW, VALERIE; Monsignor Donovan HS; Jackson, NJ; (Y); 21/218; Church Yth Grp; Intnl Clb; Library Aide; Nwsp Rptr; High Hon Roll; NHS; Rotary Awd; Century III Ldrs Comp Schlrshp 2nd Pl 86; Nom Girls ST; Trenton ST Coll; Pol Sci.

SHEVCHUK, NATALIE; Hamiton High Schl West; Trenton, NJ; (Y); VP Church Yth Grp; Pres Science Clb; SADD; Ed Lit Mag; Stat Bsktbl; Fld Hcky; Mgr(s); Hon Roll; NHS.

SHICK, HUBERT; Cinnaminson HS; Cinnaminson, NJ; (Y); Am Leg Boys St; Key Clb; Math Tm; Science Clb; Orch; Yrbk Stf; JV Bowling; JV Trk; Trs NHS; Ntl Merit Ltr; Hnr Rll 84-86; Prfct Attndnc Awd 84&86; Med.

SHIEH, BRYAN; East Brunswick HS; E Brunswick, NJ; (Y); VP German Clb; Hosp Aide; Key Clb; Lit Mag; Rep Jr Cls; Var Socr; Var Swmmng; Var Tennis; Hon Roll; NHS; Grmn Hon Soc 85-86; MIP Swmmr 85-86.

SHIELDS, KEITH; Bloomfield HS; Bloomfield, NJ; (Y); 34/442; Drama Clb; Chorus; Madrigals; School Play; L Crs Cntry; Var Trk; High Hon Roll; Hon Roll; NHS; All N NJ Choir 85-86; Sci.

SHIELDS, SCOTT ALLEN; Highland Regional HS; Clementon, NJ; (S); 13/332; Computer Clb; Spanish Clb; Socr; Wrstlng; Hon Roll.

SHIFFMAN, SCOTT; Jackson Memorial HS; Jackson, NJ; (S); 6/422; Bsktbl; Socr; High Hon Roll; Jr NHS; NHS; Ntl Merit Ltr; Prfct Atten Awd.

SHIGGS, SEBRINA; Atlantic City HS; Atlantic City, NJ; (Y); Bradford Schl; Business.

SHIH, FLORENCE; Bridgewater-Raritan HS East; Bridgewater, NJ; (Y); French Clb; Hosp Aide; Intnl Clb; Ski Clb; Chorus; Nwsp Stf; Yrbk Stf; Im Bowling; Hon Roll; NHS; 2nd Pl Tnns Camp 85; Frnch Schl Of Music Stu 83-86.

SHILLITO, KRISTIN; East Brunswick HS; E Brunswick, NJ; (Y); Church Yth Grp; Dance Clb; Drama Clb; Hosp Aide; Trs Chorus; School Musical; School Play; Stage Crew; Swing Chorus; Hon Roll; Athltc Trnr.

SHIMOMURA, KARIN; Bridgewater-Raritan H S East; Bridgewater, NJ; (Y); Church Yth Grp; German Clb; Ski Clb; SADD; Varsity Clb; VP Jr Cls; Bsktbl; Var Fld Hcky; JV Gym; Im Powder Puff Ftbl; Ath Of Wk Nwpr 86; MVP Trk 85 & 86; Phys Engrng.

SHIMP, CINDY; Woodstown HS; Woodstown, NJ; (Y); English Clb; German Clb; Band; Nwsp Rptr; Lit Mag; Sec Frsh Cls; JV Var Socr; JV Sftbl; Hon Roll; NHS; Comp Sci.

SHIMP, WILLIAM; Woodstown HS; Woodstown, NJ; (Y); Aud/Vis; Cmnty Wkr; English Clb; Exploring; Spanish Clb; Stage Crew; Socr; High Hon Roll; NHS; Olympcs Of The Mnd 85-86; Emrgny Med Tech 86-89; Pre-Med.

SHIMSHAK, RANDI; Bayonne HS; Bayonne, NJ; (Y); 9/400; Nwsp Stf; Yrbk Stf; Lit Mag; Tennis; CC Awd; High Hon Roll; Jr NHS; NHS; Aud/Vis; Computer Clb; Presntl Acadmc Fitness Awd 85-86; Dance Acad NJ 82-86; Bayonne HS Schl Activities Awd 86; Fsh Inst Of Tech; Merchandsng.

SHIN, EUNG-YONG; Cherry Hill HS West; Cherry Hill, NJ; (Y); Pres Church Yth Grp; French Clb; Nwsp Stf; Yrbk Bus Mgr; JV Trk; French Hon Soc; High Hon Roll; NHS; Intnl Clb; JCL; Schlrshp & Awd Frm Korean-Amer Assn Of Sthrn NJ 85; Fndr & Pres Of Asian Clb 86-87; Pre-Med.

SHIN, SOON KYU; Kittatinny Regional HS; Newton, NJ; (Y); 5/222; Boy Scts; Church Yth Grp; Math Tm; SADD; Chorus; School Musical; Pres Frsh Cls; Pres Stu Cncl; Swmmng; Cit Awd; Bill Bradley Young Ctzns Awd 86; Sussex Cnty Music Fndtn SR Piano Hnrb Mntn 84; Princeton; Math.

SHINDLER, CAROL; Bridgeton HS; Bridgeton, NJ; (Y); Am Leg Aux Girls St; Cmnty Wkr; VP French Clb; GAA; Ski Clb; Soroptimist; Varsity Clb; Yrbk Ed-Chief; Yrbk Phtg; Yrbk Rptr; Drexel U; Acctng.

SHINGELO, LISA; Palisades Park HS; Palisades Pk, NJ; (Y); 7/120; Nwsp Rptr; Nwsp Stf; Yrbk Stf; Lit Mag; Sec Jr Cls; Sec Sr Cls; Sec Stu Cncl; Stat Bsbl; Capt Var Cheerleading; Score Keeper; French III Awd; Elem Tchng.

SHINN, BILL; Wildwood Catholic HS; Erma, NJ; (Y); French Clb; Golf; Hon Roll; Accntng.

SHINN, TIMOTHY; Williamstown HS; Williamstown, NJ; (Y); Boy Scts; JV Socr; Comp Sci.

SHIPLEY, HELENE; Spotswood HS; Spotswood, NJ; (S); 14/189; FBLA; Chorus; Capt Color Guard; Hon Roll; NHS; FBLA 5th Hnrs ST Comptn 85; CPA.

SHIPLEY JR, JOHN C; Cherry Hill HS East; Cherry Hill, NJ; (Y); 4/730; Am Leg Boys St; Aud/Vis; Debate Tm; Model UN; Political Wkr; Im Bsktbl; Var L Tennis; High Hon Roll; NHS; Ntl Merit SF; Princeton; Law.

SHIPMAN, TYRA; Lincoln HS; Jersey City, NJ; (Y); Pres DECA; Drama Clb; Hosp Aide; Key Clb; Office Aide; Spanish Clb; Yrbk Phtg; Yrbk Stf; Rep Stu Cncl; Montclair St Coll; Bus Admn.

SHIREMAN, TIMOTHY; Paulsboro HS; Gibbstown, NJ; (Y); 9/168; Art Clb; L Tennis; Computer Clb; Band; Mrchg Band; High Hon Roll; Hon Roll; Acad Awd Excel 84-86; Cmmrcl Art.

SHISSLER, JANINE E; Haddonfield Memorial HS; Haddonfield, NJ; (Y); 99/156; Q&S; Pres Service Clb; Nwsp Sprt Ed; Yrbk Sprt Ed; Ed Lit Mag; Var Capt Tennis; NHS; Rensselaer Mdl/Math & Sci 86; Bio.

SHIUEY, YI CHIEH; Nutley HS; Nutley, NJ; (Y); 1/320; Math Tm; Scholastic Bowl; Capt Crs Cntry; Var Trk; Bausch & Lomb Sci Awd; High Hon Roll; NHS; Ntl Merit Schol; Val; Chess Clb; Chem Sci Awd 86; Rensellear Medal Achvt Sci 85; Garden ST Schlr 86; Columbia Coll; Chem.

SHIVERS, SUSAN; Holy Family Acad; Bayonne, NJ; (Y); 45/136; Pep Clb; Ski Clb; Drm & Bgl; Rep Stu Cncl; Bowling; Im Mgr(s); Hon Roll; Father Hue O Brien Schlrshp 83-87; Jersey City ST Coll; Acctng.

SHKLYAREVSKY, ELLEN; Hamilton HS West; Trenton, NJ; (Y); 9/330; Am Leg Aux Girls St; Debate Tm; Pres French Clb; Pres Intnl Clb; Yrbk Stf; Stu Cncl; Tennis; French Hon Soc; Hon Roll; NHS; Tnns Var Lttr 85; French Awd 84; Debate Awd 85; Rutgers; Psychlgy.

SHOCKLEY, ANN; St Joseph HS; Atco, NJ; (Y); Cmnty Wkr; School Play; Yrbk Phtg; Lit Mag; Var Cheerleading; High Hon Roll; Hon Roll; Honors-Eng II, Spn II, Relgn II, Eng II & Alg II; ST Cheerldng Champs; 2nd Pl Ntl Chrldng Comptn; Stockton ST Coll; Eductn.

SHOEMAKER, SUE; A P Schalick HS; Clayton, NJ; (Y); 18/130; Art Clb; Math Clb; Band; Yrbk Stf; High Hon Roll; Hon Roll; NHS; Mrchg Band; Yrbk Phtg; Math Lg Wnr 86; Pres Acad Ftns Awd 86; Top 10 Of Grd 12 86; Drexel U; Cmptr Sci.

SHONTZ, KAREN; Northern Burlington Co Reg HS; Vincentown, NJ; (S); Cmnty Wkr; Pres 4-H; Pres FFA; Teachers Aide; Chorus; Church Choir; Cit Awd; 4-H Awd; Hon Roll; Jr NHS; Burlington Co Farm Fair Qn 85-86; Delg Ctznshp WA Focus 86; ST Rep 4-H Natl Clb Cngrss 85; Ag.

SHOOLBRAID, BETH; Bridgewater-Raritan HS East; Bridgewater, NJ; (Y); Ski Clb; Off Frsh Cls; Off Soph Cls; Chrmn Jr Cls; VP Sr Cls; Stu Cncl; JV Var Bsktbl; Var Stat Lcrss; Capt Powder Puff Ftbl; Hon Roll; Spec Olympcs Clwn 86; Dnky Bsktbl Tm Mbr 86; Comp Fun Chrprsn 85-86; Psych.

SHOPLAND, SARAH; Kittatinny Regional HS; Newton, NJ; (Y); 59/222; SADD; School Play; Rep Stu Cncl; Cheerleading; Hon Roll; Rotry Frgn Exchng Stu Nw Zlnd 85-86.

SHORNOCK, SHANNON; Perth Amboy HS; Perth Amboy, NJ; (Y); Dance Clb; Model UN; Varsity Clb; Chorus; School Musical; Yrbk Stf; Sec Stu Cncl; Var Cheerleading; JV Sftbl; High Hon Roll; Chem.

SHORT, ARTHUR; Triton Regional HS; Somerdale, NJ; (Y); 21/307; Computer Clb; Capt Bowling; Vllybl; Hon Roll; NHS; Prfct Atten Awd; Trenton ST Coll; Comp Sci.

SHORT, KRISTINE; Manalapan HS; Manalapan, NJ; (Y); 86/412; Church Yth Grp; Color Guard; School Play; Nwsp Stf; Psychlgy.

SHORTAL, PATRICK; Hudson Catholic HS; Hoboken, NJ; (Y); 8/171; SADD; Bsktbl; Vllybl; High Hon Roll; Hon Roll; Pres Of Peer Ministry 86-87; Acad All-Amer 86-87; U Of Miami; Arch Engrng.

SHREKGAST, GREG; Wall HS; Wall Twp, NJ; (Y); Cmnty Wkr; Varsity Clb; Im Bsktbl; Var L Ftbl; Im Ice Hcky; Hon Roll; Plyd Lttle Leag Bsbl 81-82; Plyd In A Biddy Bsktbl Leag 82-83; Rcvd Ftbl Awds 82-83; Acctng.

SHROPSHIRE, LESLIE; Cherry Hill HS East; Cherry Hill, NJ; (Y); Church Yth Grp; PAVAS; Acpl Chr; Band; Chorus; Church Choir; School Musical; High Hon Roll; Hon Roll; James Madison U; Math Educ.

SHUBACK, HARRY J; Morris Hills HS; Wharton, NJ; (Y); Am Leg Boys St; Letterman Clb; Ski Clb; Varsity Clb; Ftbl; Dance Clb; Hon Roll.

SHUE, JOHN MADISON; Columbia HS; South Orange, NJ; (Y); 54/541; Rep Am Leg Boys St; Boy Scts; Chrmn Cmnty Wkr; Church Choir; Nwsp Rptr; Lit Mag; Var L Bsbl; Var L Socr; Pres Vlntr Awd For Stu Srvng SR Orgnztn By Pres Reagan 86; Pltcl Sci.

SHUE, SUSANNA G; Phillipsburg HS; Phillipsburg, NJ; (Y); 3/294; Church Choir; Sec Stu Cncl; Var Capt Fld Hcky; Var Trk; Elks Awd; High Hon Roll; NHS; Pres Schlr; VFW Awd; Voice Dem Awd; Phillipsburg NJ Schlr Athlete Awd 86; All Star Tms Fieldhcky 85; Womens Facuety Schrlshp 86; Elizabethtown Coll.

SHUGAR, SETH; Howell HS; Howell, NJ; (Y); 20/380; Math Tm; Temple Yth Grp; Crs Cntry; Mtrlgy.

SHUGARD, DEBBIE; Governor Livingston Regional HS; Berkeley Hts, NJ; (Y); Yrbk Rptr; Yrbk Stf; Var L Cheerleading; Im Powder Puff Ftbl; Var L Sftbl; Var L Swmmng; Hon Roll; George Mason U; Accntng.

SHUKLA, NIPURNA; Cedar Ridge HS; Matawan, NJ; (Y); 21/378; Dance Clb; Pres FBLA; Hosp Aide; Temple Yth Grp; Hon Roll; NHS; Spanish NHS; Cmnty Wkr; Pep Clb; Lit Mag; Rutgers U; Comp Sci.

SHULER, KRISTA; Holy Family Acad; Bayonne, NJ; (Y); 9/130; Socr; High Hon Roll; Varsity Clb; Bsktbl; Valedctrn 83; Hgh Hon Rl 82-83; Math.

SHULTIS, MICHELE; North Warren Regional HS; Blairstown, NJ; (Y); 28/130; Church Yth Grp; Yrbk Ed-Chief; Yrbk Stf; Rep Stu Cncl; Comm.

SHULTZ, JULIE; Kittatinny Regional HS; Middleville, NJ; (Y); Church Yth Grp; Exploring; Math Tm; Science Clb; Ski Clb; Spanish Clb; Var Fld Hcky; Var Sftbl; High Hon Roll; Hon Roll; 1st Tm All Area Fld Hockey 85-86; 2nd Tm All North Jersey 85-86; Comp.

SHULTZ, ROBERT E; Willingboro HS; Willingboro, NJ; (Y); 6/309; Am Leg Boys St; Boy Scts; Drama Clb; Latin Clb; Band; Jazz Band; Mrchg Band; Stage Crew; Hon Roll; Jr NHS; Phila Inqurr Schlrshp Awd 84-86.

SHUPACK, MICHELLE L; South Plainfield HS; So Plainfield, NJ; (Y); Drama Clb; Temple Yth Grp; Band; Chorus; Concert Band; Mrchg Band; Orch; School Musical; School Play; Cheerleading; Ffnlstt Miss US Teen Pagnt 86; Clss Actress & Vocalist 86; Amer Music Drmtc Acad; Actress.

SHURR, VINCENT; Kearny HS; Kearny, NJ; (Y); 4/375; German Clb; Ski Clb; Socr; Tennis; Elks Awd; High Hon Roll; Hon Roll; NHS; Opt Clb Awd; Hnr Grd; Grmn Natl Hnr Scty; Acad Excllnc Awd; Boston Coll; Bus.

SHUSTACK, KIMBERLY; Colonia HS; Colonia, NJ; (Y); Hosp Aide; Varsity Clb; Socr; High Hon Roll; Spanish NHS; Archry 83-84; Physcl Ftns Awd 83-84.

SIBER, LISA; Wallington HS; Wallington, NJ; (Y); 3/84; Am Leg Aux Girls St; Ski Clb; Varsity Clb; Drm Mjr(t); Yrbk Bus Mgr; Bsktbl; Capt Trk; Capt Twrlr; High Hon Roll; NHS.

SICA, MATTHEW; North Arlington HS; N Arlington, NJ; (Y); 4/131; Varsity Clb; Yrbk Stf; Pres Stu Cncl; Var L Bsbl; Var Bsktbl; Var L Ftbl; Hon Roll; NHS; NEDT Awd; Spanish NHS; All Amer Acdmc Awd 86; Intl Forgn Lang Awd 85; Natl Ldrshp Awd 86.

SICCONE, PATRICIA; Bloomfield SR HS; Bloomfield, NJ; (Y); #139 In Class; French Clb; Librl.

SICKELS, DAWN M; Matawan Regional HS; Matawan, NJ; (S); 20/309; Cmnty Wkr; Hosp Aide; Rep Frsh Cls; Stu Cncl; Var Crs Cntry; Stat Trk; Hon Roll; Pharm.

SICOLI, ANTHONY G; Union HS; Union, NJ; (Y); 3/450; Am Leg Boys St; Exploring; Ski Clb; Off Spanish Clb; Trk; High Hon Roll; Hon Roll; NHS; Spanish NHS; Hgh Scores NEDT Test Awd 85; Frgn Lang Awd 86.

SIDAROS, MAGED; Marist HS; Jersey City, NJ; (Y); Church Yth Grp; Cmnty Wkr; Key Clb; Science Clb; School Play; Stage Crew; Nwsp Rptr; Var Crs Cntry; Var Trk; Hon Roll; 5 Vrsty Lttrs 83-85; St Peters Coll; Bus.

SIDDIQUI, NASEEM; Vineland HS; Vineland, NJ; (Y); French Clb; Pep Clb; Stage Crew; Rep Stu Cncl; Var Trk; French Hon Soc; Pre Med.

SIDEROWICZ, AMELIA; Bridgewater-Raritan-West HS; Raritan, NJ; (Y); Cmnty Wkr; Acpl Chr; Chorus; Stage Crew; Yrbk Stf; Library Aide; Nrsng.

SIEBEN, LAURA; Red Bank Regional HS; Sea Bright, NJ; (Y); JA; Math Tm; Jazz Band; School Musical; NHS; St Schlr; Presdntl Acad Fitness Awd 85-86; Mt Holyoke Coll; Intl Rltns.

SIEBENLIST, BRIAN; Voorhees HS; Glen Gardner, NJ; (Y); 42/365; Key Clb; Varsity Clb; Sec Frsh Cls; Sec Soph Cls; VP Jr Cls; Sec Sr Cls; Var Capt Socr; JC Awd; NHS; Spanish NHS; Fncn Vrsty Cptn 85-87; Bus.

SIEGEL, JEFF; East Brunswick HS; E Brunswick, NJ; (Y); Cmnty Wkr; Hosp Aide; Key Clb; Ski Clb; Nwsp Rptr; Rep Jr Cls; Im Ice Hcky; JV Socr; Hon Roll; Coaches Awd Soccr 84.

SIEGEL, JENNIFER; Millburn HS; Short Hills, NJ; (Y); 24/247; Chorus; Orch; School Play; Yrbk Ed-Chief; JV Var Bsktbl; Cit Awd; Ntl Merit SF; St Schlr; Drama Clb; Temple Yth Grp; Co-Princpl Viola-NJ Yth Symphony 81-86; Franklin & Marshall Bk Awd 85; Yale U.

SIEGER, MARC J; Westwood HS; Westwood, NJ; (Y); Ski Clb; Yrbk Stf; Ftbl; Socr; High Hon Roll; Hon Roll; NHS; Syracuse U; Mgnt Animation Sys.

SIEGERMAN, CYNTHIA; Pascack Hills HS; Hillsdale, NJ; (Y); Hosp Aide; SADD; Temple Yth Grp; Color Guard; Flag Corp; Mrchg Band; Hon Roll; Bio.

SIEH, LUI; Glen Ridge HS; Glen Ridge, NJ; (Y); French Clb; JA; Pres Model UN; Nwsp Stf; Rep Stu Cncl; Bsktbl; Hon Roll; Charlotte Rubinow Awd 84; Adell Williams Awd Yng Artst Wnnr & Mstr Cls Prfmr 85 & 86; Jnrlsm.

SIEIRA, MARIA; Howell HS; Farmingdale, NJ; (Y); 7/371; School Musical; School Play; Nwsp Bus Mgr; NHS; Ntl Merit SF; Prfct Atten Awd; Drama Clb; French Clb; Math Tm; Speech Tm; Fine & Perfrmg Arts Awd 85; Stdnt Wk; ST Teen Arts Fest; Hmcmg Ct; Perfrmg Arts Own Bus.

SIFFORD, VANESSA; Clifford J Scott HS; E Orange, NJ; (S); 7/289; Pep Clb; Flag Corp; Cit Awd; Gov Hon Prg Awd; Hon Roll; NHS; Temple U; Psych.

SIGGINS, LISA; High Point Regional HS; Branchville, NJ; (Y); 16/252; Debate Tm; German Clb; Var Stat Bsktbl; Score Keeper; Var Stat Trk; High Hon Roll; Hon Roll; Acctg.

SIGNORELLA, GINA M; Roselle Park HS; Roselle Park, NJ; (Y); 6/140; Church Yth Grp; JA; Key Clb; Band; Concert Band; Drm Mjr(t); Jazz Band; Mrchg Band; Rep Stu Cncl; NHS; U Of DE; Bio.

SILBAHAR, BANU; Clifton SR HS; Clifton, NJ; (Y); 134/637; Key Clb; Math Clb; Spanish Clb; SADD; Chorus; Stat Bsktbl; Jr NHS; Spanish NHS; Fashion Desgnr.

SILBER, MIRIAM; Bruriah HS For Girls; Paterson, NJ; (Y); Temple Yth Grp; Nwsp Stf; Yrbk Stf; Sec Frsh Cls; NHS; NEDT Awd; School Play; Nwsp Phtg; Nwsp Rptr; Yrbk Phtg; Sci Awd 84; NCSY Lrng Prog Awd 86; Adv.

SILBERT, JACK; West Windsor Plainsboro HS; Plainsboro, NJ; (Y); Am Leg Boys St; Computer Clb; Math Tm; Model UN; School Play; Variety Show; VP Jr Cls; Pres Sr Cls; NHS; NJ Schlrs Pgm; Cmnctns.

SILGHIGIAN, CHARLENE; Scotch Plains-Fanwood HS; Scotch Plains, NJ; (Y); 31/311; Band; Concert Band; Jazz Band; Mrchg Band; Orch; Symp Band; Gov Hon Prg Awd; High Hon Roll; Hon Roll; Spanish NHS; Gov Schl Arts 85; Joseph Checcio Mwic Schlrshp 86; Trenton ST Col; Music.

SILIKOVITZ, HARVEY; W Orange HS; W Orange, NJ; (Y); 35/177; Political Wkr; Temple Yth Grp; Nwsp Sprt Ed; Lit Mag; VP Stu Cncl; Mgr Bsbl; Stat Ftbl; French Hon Soc; Ntl Merit Ltr; Johns Hopkins U; Law.

SILLETTI, JASON J; Bergen Catholic HS; Bogota, NJ; (Y); 45/261; Am Leg Boys St; Church Yth Grp; Computer Clb; Ski Clb; Im JV Bsktbl; Im Tennis; Im Vllybl; High Hon Roll; Spanish NHS; Hnrs Courses Engl, Hist, Sci, Spnsh 84-86; Ofc CCA 85; Stanford; Engr.

SILVANIO, DIANE; Haddan Heights HS; Haddon Heights, NJ; (Y); 12/190; Chorus; School Musical; School Play; Lit Mag; Stat Ftbl; Hon Roll; Var Lttr; Homerm Sen; Rutgers U.

SILVERGOLD, ROGER; Matawan Regional HS; Aberdeen, NJ; (S); 17/302; CAP; Debate Tm; Exploring; Math Clb; Math Tm; NFL; Ski Clb; Speech Tm; Hon Roll.

SILVERMAN, ERIKA; St Peters HS; Kendall Park, NJ; (Y); Cmnty Wkr; Intnl Clb; Ski Clb; Stage Crew; Lit Mag; Stat Bsbl; Stat Bsktbl; Stat Crs Cntry; JV Sftbl; NHS; Mst Imprvd Engl 85-86; Law.

SILVERSMITH, ELISSA; Jackson Memorial HS; Jackson, NJ; (Y); 114/337; Yrbk Stf; Hosp Aide; High Hon Roll; Hon Roll; William Paterson NJ.

SILVERSTEIN, JODI; Paramus HS; Paramus, NJ; (Y); 68/345; French Clb; Chorus; Var Tennis; French Hon Soc; Exc Frnch 86; Douglass Coll.

SILVERSTEIN, LAURI; Columbia HS; Maplewood, NJ; (Y); Sec Spanish Clb; Temple Yth Grp; Band; Capt Color Guard; School Musical; Yrbk Stf; Rep Jr Cls; Rep Sr Cls; Cheerleading; NHS; Bus.

SILVESTRE, ISABEL; Riverside HS; Riverside, NJ; (S); 5/66; Am Leg Aux Girls St; Trs Keywanettes; Var Fld Hcky; JV Trk; High Hon Roll; Hon Roll; NHS; Church Yth Grp; VP FTA; Stu Govt Awd 85; Mst Imp Hcky Awd 84; Nrsng.

SIM MONS, CHE; Deptford Township HS; Wenonah, NJ; (Y); 40/275; VP JA; Library Aide; School Musical; Yrbk Bus Mgr; JV Socr; JV Tennis; Hon Roll; Jr NHS; Voice Dem Awd; Bryant Coll; Accntng.

SIMER, LORI; Holy Cross HS; Delran, NJ; (Y); 60/380; Ski Clb; Rep Stu Cncl; Var Swmmng; Var Tennis; Var Trk; High Hon Roll; Hon Roll; NHS; Rutgers U; Finance.

SIMMONDS, DALE; Orange HS; Orange, NJ; (Y); Church Yth Grp; Church Choir; Socr; Tennis; High Hon Roll; Hon Roll; Tnns Hnr Awd; Secton Hall; Dntst.

SIMMONS, ANN; Lake Land Regional HS; West Milford, NJ; (Y); 52/303; Pres Camera Clb; VP DECA; SADD; School Play; Nwsp Phtg; Yrbk Phtg; High Hon Roll; Hon Roll; NHS; NEDT Awd; Cert Awd JV Fncng 83-84; Cert Awd Photo 86.

SIMMONS, FAITH C; Edgewood Regional SR HS; Berlin, NJ; (Y); 16/374; French Clb; Quiz Bowl; Pres Spanish Clb; Rep Frsh Cls; High Hon Roll; Hon Roll; Rep Sec Jr NHS; NHS; Ntl Sority Phi Delta Kappa Schlrshp 86; Sophia K Reeves Found Schrlshp 86; Pres Clsrm Yng Am 86; U VA-CHARLOTTESVILLE; Psychlgy.

SIMMONS, JULIE; Belvidere HS; Belvidere, NJ; (Y); Varsity Clb; Var Capt Bsktbl; Var Capt Fld Hcky; Var Sftbl; Hon Roll; Hlth & Phys Educ & Hmn Ecolgy Achvt Awds 86; Mst Outstndng Fml Athlt 86; West Chester U; Hlth-Phys Educ.

SIMMONS, LISA; Howell HS; Howell, NJ; (Y); Library Aide; PAVAS; Nwsp Rptr; Ed Nwsp Stf; Ed Lit Mag; Tennis; Trk; NHS; Pres Schlr; NY U Trustee Schlrshp, Richard Roberts Jrnlsm Schlrshp 86; NY U; Jrnlsm.

SIMMONS, MARCIA; Northern Valley Reg HS; Harrington Pk, NJ; (Y); 80/320; Church Yth Grp; PAVAS; SADD; Band; Concert Band; Jazz Band; Orch; School Musical; Hon Roll; Music Edu.

SIMMS, ELIZABETH; Notre Dame HS; Mercerville, NJ; (Y); 19/360; Service Clb; Stage Crew; Yrbk Stf; Rep Frsh Cls; Rep Jr Cls; Var Fld Hcky; Var Sftbl; High Hon Roll; NHS; Phys Thrpy.

SIMMS, LIIMU; Princeton Day Schl; Trenton, NJ; (Y); Drama Clb; Madrigals; School Musical; School Play; JV Bsktbl; Chorus; Stage Crew; Ntl Merit Ltr; Expermnt Intl Living Pgm Scholar 86; ABC Princeton Day Scholar 83-87; Actress.

SIMMS, SHERI; Orange HS; Orange, NJ; (Y); FBLA; Office Aide; Sec Soph Cls; High Hon Roll; Hon Roll; Columbia Union Coll; Accntng.

SIMON, COLLEEN; Audubon HS; Audubon, NJ; (Y); Sec Sr Cls; Var Cheerleading; Var Fld Hcky; Hon Roll; Psych.

SIMON, DANIEL; East Brunswick HS; E Brunswick, NJ; (Y); Boy Scts; Drama Clb; VP Chorus; Church Choir; Orch; Rep Stu Cncl; Trk; Hon Roll; Church Yth Grp; German Clb; Nj All St Orchestra 85-86; Cntrl Jrsy Rgn II Orchestra 84-86; Math.

SIMON, DAVID; River Dell Regional HS; River Edge, NJ; (Y); 3/213; Am Leg Boys St; Yrbk Ed-Chief; High Hon Roll; Hon Roll; NHS; Ntl Merit Ltr; Spanish NHS; Outstndng Achvt In Sci 84; Acdmc Decathalon 86; Estrn Coll; Lawyer.

SIMON, HEIDI; Matawan Regional HS; Hazlet, NJ; (S); 19/273; Math Tm; Ski Clb; Yrbk Phtg; JV Crs Cntry; JV Var Sftbl; JV Trk; Hon Roll; NHS; Spanish NHS; NJ Sci Acad Stu 84; Math Hnr Soc 85-86.

SIMON, ILYSE; Montville Twnshp HS; Montville, NJ; (Y); 31/269; Art Clb; Drama Clb; FBLA; VP Key Clb; NFL; Speech Tm; SADD; Chorus; School Musical; Swing Chorus; Hugh O Brien Yth Ldrshp Hnr 85; Gldn Poet Awd 86; Schlrshp NJ Arts Fndntn Summer Arts Inst 86.

SIMON, JODI; Saddle Riber Day HS; Monsey, NY; (Y); 10/69; Key Clb; School Musical; School Play; Yrbk Bus Mgr; Lit Mag; Var Capt Socr; Var Capt Sftbl; Hon Roll; Sec Frsh Cls; VP Soph Cls; Outstndg Cmmnty Svc Awd 86; Cum Laude Soc 86; CT Coll.

SIMONELLI, EMILIA; Shore Regional HS; W Long Branch, NJ; (Y); Church Yth Grp; Hosp Aide; Key Clb; Stage Crew; Im Powder Puff Ftbl; High Hon Roll; Hon Roll; Frgn Serv.

SIMONELLI, JAMES; High School East; Toms River, NJ; (Y); 36/529; Boy Scts; Church Yth Grp; Math Tm; Orch; School Musical; School Play; Variety Show; Lit Mag; JV Bowling; NHS; Prtcpnt Sci Leag 85-86; Rutgers U; Vet Med.

SIMONELLI, JILL; Metuchen HS; Metuchen, NJ; (Y); 51/177; Church Yth Grp; Church Choir; JV Var Bsktbl; Var L Sftbl; Hon Roll; Drftng.

SIMONETTI, MICHELLE; Toms River HS East; Toms River, NJ; (Y); Off Sr Cls; JV Crs Cntry; JV Fld Hcky; JV Trk; Hon Roll; Comp.

SIMONS, GREGORY; East Brunswick HS; East Brunswick, NJ; (Y); English Clb; FBLA; Key Clb; VP Pep Clb; Sec Ski Clb; Spanish Clb; SADD; Temple Yth Grp; Varsity Clb; Lit Mag; Jewish Thlgcl Sem Stu 82.

SIMPKINS, BARBARA; Riverside HS; Delanco, NJ; (Y); Church Yth Grp; Var Color Guard; Hon Roll; Ctznshp Awd 82; Glassboro; Elem Ed.

SIMPKINS, FIONA; Chatham Twp HS; Chatham Twp, NJ; (Y); Key Clb; Nwsp Stf; Yrbk Stf; Rep Stu Cncl; JV Var Cheerleading; JV Fld Hcky; Var Trk; Hon Roll; Smith College.

SIMPSON, ANDREA; Essex Catholic Girls; Newark, NJ; (Y); 42/75; Church Yth Grp; FBLA; Girl Scts; Pep Clb; Service Clb; Chorus; Church Choir; Yrbk Stf; Mgr Bsktbl; Cit Awd; Servc Awd Gospel Chorus 82-86; Merit Awd Varty Show 86; Rutgers; Bus Mgmt.

SIMPSON, SUSAN; St James HS; Salem, NJ; (Y); Math Tm; Spanish Clb; Band; Chorus; Jazz Band; Pres Soph Cls; Rep Stu Cncl; Barbizon Schl Mdlng 83; Engl & Geogrphy Commndtns 83; Bus Mgmt; Cosmotology.

SIMS, ELIZABETH; Red Bank Regional HS; Little Silver, NJ; (Y); Church Yth Grp; Key Clb; Varsity Clb; Rep Soph Cls; JV Var Bsktbl; JV Capt Tennis; Hon Roll; Snapsht Awds; Natl Guild Of Piano 83-84; Hnrbl Mntn Regstrs 85; Wrtg Cntst 85; Poltc Sci.

SIN QUEE, KAREN; Hmailton High West; Trenton, NJ; (Y); FBLA; Badmtn; Stat Bsktbl; JV Var Fld Hcky; JV Var Mgr(s); JV Var Timer; Stat Trk; Vllybl; Air Force; Cmptr Pgrmgn.

SINATRA, ROCCO; Lacey Township HS; Forked River, NJ; (Y); 11/211; Math Clb; Math Tm; Capt Bsbl; Var Capt Bsktbl; Var Capt Ftbl; High Hon Roll; Hon Roll; NHS; Ftbl Unsung Hero Awd 85; Sci Fair Awds 85-86; Am Chem Soc Awd 86; U Of DE.

SINCLAIR, JENNIFER; Vernon Township HS; Vernon, NJ; (Y); 30/239; Dance Clb; Sec Exploring; Trs Intnl Clb; Pep Clb; Yrbk Stf; Hon Roll; Jr NHS; Outstndng Perfrmnce Mech Drawng 83; Clarkson U; Elec Engrng.

SINCLAIR, MATTHEW W; Summit HS; Summit, NJ; (Y); 63/290; Church Yth Grp; Math Clb; Science Clb; Jazz Band; Nwsp Sprt Ed; Nwsp Stf; Var Bsbl; Coach Actv; Hon Roll; Math Tm; Summit First Aid Squad; La Fayette; Math.

SINGER, RANDALL; Matawan HS; Matawan, NJ; (S); 13/310; Nwsp Rptr; Yrbk Ed-Chief; VP Frsh Cls; Rep Soph Cls; Rep Jr Cls; Rep Stu Cncl; Stat Bsktbl; Stat Ftbl; Hon Roll; Georgetown U Stu Sci Trng Prog 85.

SINGER, SCOTT; Raritan HS; Hazlet, NJ; (Y); 19/300; Exploring; JV Var Ftbl; Im Vllybl; Wt Lftg; Wrstlng; Elks Awd; Hon Roll; NHS; Pigskin Awd 86; 1st Tm Schlr/Athlt 86; NJ Schlr/Athlt 86; Rutgers Coll; Econ.

SINGH, ANUDEEP; Highland Regional HS; Laural Springs, NJ; (S); 9/330; AFS; Computer Clb; Pres French Clb; Science Clb; Nwsp Rptr; Yrbk Stf; Rep Stu Cncl; Tennis; Hon Roll; NHS; Blackwood Lions Club Awd 83; Frnch Hnr Socy 86; U Of PA; Med.

SINGH, DINAKAR; Livingston HS; Livingston, NJ; (Y); 2/498; Pres Chess Clb; Computer Clb; Hosp Aide; Key Clb; Mathletes; Math Clb; Math Tm; Pres Model UN; Orch; Nwsp Stf; Columbia U Sci Hnrs Prog 85; Doc.

SINGH, JASBINDER; Rancocas Valley Reg HS; Mount Holly, NJ; (Y); Nwsp Rptr; Nwsp Stf; Lit Mag; JV Lcrss; Hon Roll; Caldwell Coll.

SINGH, RAJ R; Moorestown Friends Schl; Willingboro, NJ; (Y); Am Leg Boys St; Model UN; Science Clb; Varsity Clb; Chorus; School Musical; Yrbk Stf; Rep Stu Cncl; Var Bsktbl; Var Tennis; LEAD Program In Bus 86; Princeton; Arch.

SINGH, RITU; John P Steven HS; Edison, NJ; (Y); French Clb; Ski Clb; Yrbk Stf; Rep Frsh Cls; Rep Soph Cls; Rep Jr Cls; Powder Puff Ftbl; Clmba U; Bus.

SINHA, PARAKH; Wardlaw-Hartridge HS; Colonia, NJ; (Y); Drama Clb; 4-H; Hosp Aide; Key Clb; Red Cross Aide; SADD; Chorus; School Play; Stage Crew; Lcrss; Bio.

SININSKI, CHARLES; Saint Peters Prep; Jersey City, NJ; (Y); 49/205; Chess Clb; Cmnty Wkr; Hon Roll; Accntg.

SINKLERIS, ANDY; Riverside HS; Riverside, NJ; (S); 1/87; Drama Clb; SADD; School Play; Nwsp Ed-Chief; Nwsp Phtg; Nwsp Rptr; Nwsp Sprt Ed; Nwsp Stf; Pres Jr Cls; Bsbl; Acting.

SINNEMA, PATRICIA; Arthur P Schalick HS; Elmer, NJ; (Y); 4/144; Math Tm; VP Frsh Cls; VP Soph Cls; Var Bsktbl; Var Sftbl; Hon Roll; NHS; Sftbl JV Mst Vlbl Plyer 84; Bskbl V Unsng Hero 85; Douglass Coll; Elem Educ.

SINNOTT, ADRIENNE; Academic HS; Jersey City, NJ; (Y); Am Leg Aux Girls St; Art Clb; Stu Cncl; Bsktbl; Rotary Awd; Math.

SINNWELL, PATRICIA; Northern Burlington County Reg HS; Jobstown, NJ; (Y); 5/200; Flag Corp; Mrchg Band; Pep Band; Rep Soph Cls; Rep Jr Cls; L Mgr(s); L Trk; High Hon Roll; NHS; Spanish NHS; Mst Otstndng Comp & Englsh Stu 84-86; Hnr Hstry & Englsh Pgms 83-86; Rutgers Coll; Engrng.

SINOPOLI, CHERYL; Rutherford HS; Rutherford, NJ; (Y); Hosp Aide; Office Aide; Pep Clb; Yrbk Stf; Rep Sr Cls; Stat Bsbl; Trk; High Hon Roll; NHS; Brown U; Phrmcy.

SIPER, BETH; West Essex SR HS; Roseland, NJ; (Y); FTA; Key Clb; Latin Clb; Teachers Aide; Temple Yth Grp; Hon Roll; Vrsty Fencng Tm 86; Psyclgy.

SIPP, DOUGLAS; Overbrook Regional HS; Lindenwold, NJ; (Y); Quiz Bowl; Chorus; Stage Crew; JV Crs Cntry; Var Trk; JV Wrstlng; Hon Roll; Ntl Merit SF.

SIPPIO, FAUSTINA; Glassboro HS; Glassboro, NJ; (Y); 4/130; Off Sr Cls; Var Mgr(s); Hon Roll; VP NHS; Gdn ST Scholar 86; NHS Awd & Scholar 86; Pres Acad Fit Awd 86; Engl Awd 86; Glassboro ST Coll; Comp Sci.

SIRACUSA, CHRISTINE; Red Bank Catholic HS; Middletown, NJ; (Y); Cmnty Wkr; Exploring; School Musical; VP Soph Cls; NHS; French Clb; Ski Clb; Chorus; Pres Stu Cncl; Hon Roll; Alt Govnrs Schl Art 86; Comm.

SIRAGUSA, MARY ELLEN; Lacordaire Acad; Bloomfield, NJ; (Y); Spanish Clb; Chorus; School Play; Nwsp Stf; Yrbk Stf; Lit Mag; High Hon Roll; Hon Roll; NHS; Pres Schlr; Untd Food & Cmmrcl Wrkrs Union Schlrshp 86-87; Montclair ST Coll; Accntng.

SIRAK, STACIE A; Holy Cross HS; Beverly, NJ; (Y); 80/375; Church Yth Grp; Rep Frsh Cls; Rep Soph Cls; Rep Stu Cncl; JV Cheerleading; Hon Roll; Rotary Awd; Frgn Exchng Stu-Brzl; U Of Scranton; Accntng.

SIRANGELO, MARY; St Marys HS; Parlin, NJ; (Y); 12/120; Church Yth Grp; French Clb; High Hon Roll; Hon Roll; Prfct Atten Awd; Pre-Med.

SIRKIN, JILL; Manalapan HS; Manalapan, NJ; (Y); 61/420; SADD; Temple Yth Grp; JV Socr; Comp Pgmg.

SISCO, KHRIS L; Newton HS; Newton, NJ; (Y); Church Yth Grp; German Clb; Hosp Aide; Ski Clb; SADD; Stage Crew; Stat Fld Hcky; Timer; Vrsty Awd Mgr; Tech Thtre Awd GPA; Htl-Mtl Food Mngmt.

SISK, MAIA; Vail-Deane Schl; Westfield, NJ; (Y); 1/14; Pres French Clb; School Play; Yrbk Ed-Chief; Trs Jr Cls; VP Sr Cls; Rep Stu Cncl; Var Fld Hcky; Var Sftbl; Math Tm; Spanish Clb; Prnts Assoc Awd 84-86; Chem Awd 86; Hstry Awd 85-86; Coll; Engnrng.

SITEK, KIM; Toms River HS East; Toms River, NJ; (Y); 27/585; Exploring; FBLA; Intnl Clb; Spanish Clb; SADD; Varsity Clb; Yrbk Phtg; Yrbk Rptr; Yrbk Sprt Ed; Yrbk Stf; Var Girls Tennis 84-87; All County Girls Tennis 86; Accounting.

SITLER, PAMELA; Phillipsburg HS; Phillipsburg, NJ; (Y); 71/341; Exploring; Chorus; Color Guard; Nwsp Stf; Trvl.

SIVOLELLA, JENNIFER; Wood-Ridge HS; Wood-Ridge, NJ; (S); 3/78; Art Clb; Political Wkr; Y-Teens; Off Jr Cls; Bsktbl; Trk; NHS; Montclair ST Coll; English.

SIWY, CHERISH; S Hunterdon Regional HS; Lambertville, NJ; (Y); 11/71; Am Leg Aux Girls St; Drama Clb; Band; Chorus; Concert Band; Drm & Bgl; Jazz Band; Mrchg Band; School Play; Nwsp Rptr; Susquehanna U; Cmmnctns.

SIZER, CARLA; Weequahic HS; Newark, NJ; (S); 20/300; Nwsp Stf; Var Capt Bsktbl; Sftbl; NHS; Merit Awd For Womens Vrsty Bsktbll In Acad 85; 2 Vrsty Letters 84-85; Math.

SKEENS, SCOTT J; Warren Hills Regional SR HS; Broadway, NJ; (Y); Am Leg Boys St; Church Yth Grp; Exploring; Ski Clb; Powder Puff Ftbl; Var L Socr; Var Trk; JV Wrstlng; Hon Roll.

SKEVNICK, MONICA KRISTINE; Toms River HS South; Pine Beach, NJ; (Y); 29/329; Art Clb; Cmnty Wkr; Dance Clb; Debate Tm; Key Clb; Math Clb; Model UN; Science Clb; Spanish Clb; Orch; VA Tech; Chemstry.

SKEWES, WILLIAM A; Ridgewood HS; Ridgewood, NJ; (Y); Am Leg Boys St; Church Yth Grp; Ski Clb; Varsity Clb; Jazz Band; Stu Cncl; L Ftbl; Trk; L Wrstlng; Dmstc Exchng 85-86; Acctg.

SKIFIC, ELENOR; Cliffside Park HS; Cliffside Park, NJ; (Y); 6/236; French Clb; Nwsp Ed-Chief; Lit Mag; Stu Cncl; Bsktbl; Trk; Vllybl; High Hon Roll; Hon Roll; NHS; Atlantic Pacific Math Tem Awd 85-86; Frgn Lang Cert Merit 85-86; Columbia U; Jrnlst.

SKIRBST, HENRY M; Belvidere HS; Washington, NJ; (Y); 3/117; Am Leg Boys St; Church Yth Grp; CAP; Co-Capt Quiz Bowl; Lit Mag; VP Jr Cls; Var Trk; Var Wrstlng; High Hon Roll; NHS; Outstndg Achvmnt Physcs 86; Excllnc Engl 86; Outstndg Achvmnt Math Alg I & II, Geo, Adv Math, Cacl 86; Stockton ST Coll; Envrmntl Sci.

SKLADANY, JOHN; Morris Catholic HS; Morris Plains, NJ; (Y); 7/155; Math Clb; Mrchg Band; Nwsp Rptr; Im Bsktbl; JP Sousa Awd; NHS; Acdmc Schlrshp Seton Hall U 86-90; Seton Hall U; Comp Sci.

SKLAR, STUART; Cherry Hill H S West; Cherry Hill, NJ; (Y); 6/300; Am Leg Boys St; Drama Clb; Trs French Clb; Intnl Clb; Office Aide; PAVAS; Teachers Aide; Trs Thesps; School Musical; School Play.

SKLAVOUNOS, STEVE; Rutherford HS; Rutherford, NJ; (Y); Computer Clb; Varsity Clb; Stage Crew; Capt Socr; Var Swmmng; Hon Roll; Pre-Med.

SKLENAR, MARK J; Wayne Valley HS; Wayne, NJ; (Y); 12/330; Boy Scts; Cmnty Wkr; Model UN; Lit Mag; JV Ftbl; JV Wrstlng; High Hon Roll; Hon Roll; NHS; Ntl Merit SF; Grdn ST Distgnshd Schlr; Wimmer Schlrshp; Rutgers Schlr; Engrng.

SKOLLER, FRAN; Hightstown HS; Hightstown, NJ; (Y); 92/449; Ski Clb; Teachers Aide; Temple Yth Grp; Yrbk Stf; Rep Jr Cls; Rep Stu Cncl; Cheerleading; Hon Roll; 10 Yr Dnc Awd 84; Bus.

SKONDRAS, GUS; Lodi HS; Lodi, NJ; (Y); Boys Clb Am; Church Yth Grp; French Clb; Key Clb; Leo Clb; Letterman Clb; Math Clb; Math Tm; Quiz Bowl; Scholastic Bowl; Stevens Inst Tech; Engrng.

SKORCH, KIM; Holy Cross HS; Marlton Lakes, NJ; (Y); Church Yth Grp; Spanish Clb; Hon Roll; La Salle; Physcl Thrpy.

SKORUK, GINA; Pope Paul VI HS; Bellmawr, NJ; (S); 150/500; VP Sr Cls; Stu Cncl; Var Capt Cheerleading; Powder Puff Ftbl; Miss Chrldr 81; St Josephs U; Bus.

SKOVIAK, JOHN; Delran HS; Delran, NJ; (Y); 41/215; Chess Clb; Debate Tm; FBLA; Ski Clb; Var Bsbl; Var Bsktbl; Im Ftbl; Var Socr; Im Vllybl; Hon Roll; Vrsty Ltr Awd Wnr 85-86; MVP Smmr League Bsbl Trnmnt 84; U Of NC; Bus Admin.

SKOWRONSKI, JOHN; Hawthorne HS; Hawthorne, NJ; (Y); Am Leg Boys St; Ski Clb; Rep Jr Cls; Var L Golf; Var L Tennis; Hon Roll; 1st Team All-Leag Ftbl BPSL Offnsive Tckle 85-86; Engrng Sci Coll; Bio Engrng.

SKRENTA, ELIZABETH ANN; Wallington HS; Wallington, NJ; (Y); 4-H; Varsity Clb; Yrbk Stf; Trk; Hon Roll.

SKROCE, MERI; Cliffside Park HS; Cliffside Pk, NJ; (Y); 19/260; Cmnty Wkr; Dance Clb; Scholastic Bowl; Spanish Clb; Nwsp Ed-Chief; Nwsp Stf; Yrbk Ed-Chief; Yrbk Stf; Sec Frsh Cls; Sec Soph Cls; Grp Mdrtr Stu Annl Intl Rltns Smnr 86; Acad Dcthln Tm 86; Jrnlsm.

SKURAT, TOM; Brick Township HS; Brick Town, NJ; (Y); 19/423; VP Jr Cls; JV Trk; High Hon Roll.

SKURBE, SUZANNE; East Brunswick HS; E Brunswick, NJ; (Y); FBLA; Key Clb; Model UN; Chorus; Drill Tm; Variety Show; Rep Stu Cncl; Otstndng Srv Awd 15th Annual Mdl Cngrss 84lcl 464 A Schlrshp Awd 86; SR Bnd Awd 86; PA ST U; Fnc.

SLACK, AMY; Delsea Regional HS; Ewan, NJ; (Y); Drama Clb; Rep Jr Cls; VP Stu Cncl; Mgr Trk; Hon Roll; NHS; Prfct Atten Awd; Bus.

SLACK, THOMAS H; Cherry Hill HS East; Cherry Hill, NJ; (Y); Drm Mjr(t); Jazz Band; Mrchg Band; Orch; Symp Band; High Hon Roll; Ntl Merit SF; German Clb; Math Tm; Band; Cum Laude Soc; Mech Engrng.

SLATE, JASON; Ocean Township HS; Oakhurst, NJ; (Y); Key Clb; Office Aide; Ski Clb; Thesps; School Play; Variety Show; Ftbl; Gym; Physician.

SLATER, GLENN E; E Brunswick HS; E Brunswick, NJ; (Y); Lit Mag; VP Frsh Cls; Pres Soph Cls; Pres Jr Cls; Pres Sr Cls; Var Socr; Var Trk; NCTE Awd; NHS; Ntl Merit SF; Wnnr Phelps Dodge Full Schlrshp Grnt Adv Stds 85; Altrnt Govnrs Schl Of Art Creative Wrtng 85; Engl.

SLATER, KRISTINE; Lakeland Regional HS; Ringwood, NJ; (Y); 37/328; Am Leg Aux Girls St; Church Yth Grp; FBLA; JA; SADD; Teachers Aide; Varsity Clb; Yrbk Bus Mgr; Yrbk Stf; Pres Frsh Cls; Trenton ST U; Ed.

SLATER, TODD; James Caldwell HS; W Caldwell, NJ; (Y); Art Clb; Boy Scts; Band; Variety Show; Yrbk Stf; Im Bowling; Im Var Socr; High Hon Roll; NHS; Ntl Merit SF.

SLATTERY, STEPHEN; Morris Catholic HS; Succasunna, NJ; (Y); Boy Scts; Bus.

SLEAR, DAVID; Newton HS; Newton, NJ; (S); 14/210; Latin Clb; Math Tm; Science Clb; JV Ftbl; JV Trk; Im Wt Lftg; Hon Roll; JETS Awd; NHS; Mech Engrng.

SLICKMEYER, TINA; Highland Regional HS; Erial, NJ; (S); 1/332; AFS; Computer Clb; VP Key Clb; Spanish Clb; Varsity Clb; Stu Cncl; Var Cheerleading; Stat Crs Cntry; Stat Trk; NHS; Rutgers New Brunswick; Acctng.

SLIKER, MICHAEL JOHN; Dover HS; Dover, NJ; (Y); 46/183; AFS; Pres Church Yth Grp; Computer Clb; VP 4-H; Ski Clb; Yrbk Stf; Im Bowling; JV Ftbl; Wt Lftg; Mgr Wrstlng; Bus Adm.

SLIM, SHARON; Cherry Hill H S West; Cherry Hill, NJ; (Y); Cmnty Wkr; 4-H; Science Clb; Symp Band; Var Bsktbl; JV Sftbl; 4-H Awd; Hon Roll; Bio.

SLIMM, SUZANNE MARIE; Point Pleasant Beach HS; Pt Pleasant Bch, NJ; (Y); 20/103; Drama Clb; Key Clb; Office Aide; Ski Clb; Spanish Clb; Color Guard; Stage Crew; Ed Yrbk Stf; Twrlr; Outstndng Key Clb 85-86; Rtry Schlrshp 86; Rotry Voctnl Awd 86; Taylor Bus Inst; Trvl.

SLOAN, COLEEN; Wood Ridge HS; Wood-Ridge, NJ; (S); 13/91; Spanish Clb; Yrbk Stf; Sec Frsh Cls; Sec Soph Cls; Sec Jr Cls; Sec Sr Cls; Stu Cncl; Capt Cheerleading; Sftbl; Sec NHS; Rutgers U.

SLOAN, DEBRA; Cherry Hill West HS; Cherry Hill, NJ; (Y); Cmnty Wkr; Drama Clb; PAVAS; Spanish Clb; SADD; Sec Thesps; Chorus; School Musical; Variety Show; Cheerleading; CHW Home & Schl Assn Awd 86; Nj St Teen AAS Fstvl 86.

SLOAN, JENNIFER; Rutherford HS; Rutherford, NJ; (Y); Pep Clb; Varsity Clb; Rep Frsh Cls; Rep Soph Cls; Rep Jr Cls; Rep Sr Cls; Var JV Sftbl; Var Capt Vllybl; Stat Wrstlng; Hon Roll; Girls ST 86; Girls Ctznshp 86; Bus Admin.

SLOAT, GEORGETTE; Overbrook Reg SR HS; Albion, NJ; (Y); Art Clb; Church Yth Grp; Spanish Clb; Church Choir; Fld Hcky; JV Socr; Hon Roll; Bus Mgt.

SLOBODIEN, JANET; Metuchen HS; Metuchen, NJ; (Y); French Clb; Key Clb; Ski Clb; Temple Yth Grp; Ed Nwsp Stf; Var Fld Hcky; French Hon Soc; High Hon Roll; Hon Roll; NHS.

SLOJKOWSKI, STEVEN; Oratory Catholic Prep; Morris Plains, NJ; (S); 2/55; Mathletes; Nwsp Phtg; Im Tennis; Im Vllybl; Hon Roll; NHS; Brtsh Lit Awd 85.

SLONIM, JENNIFER; Shawnee HS; Medford Lakes, NJ; (Y); Ski Clb; Rptr Frsh Cls; Rep Soph Cls; Rep Stu Cncl; Var Socr; JV Sftbl; Im Vllybl; Im Wt Lftg; Hon Roll; Awd Of Excllnce In Frnch 86; Psych.

SLOSS, MARK A; Neptune SR HS; Neptune, NJ; (Y); 42/340; Am Leg Boys St; Science Clb; Var Capt Bowling; Hon Roll; Outstndng SR Athlt Bwlng 86; Rider College; Bus Adm.

SLUKE, EDWARD; W Essex Regional HS; Fairfield, NJ; (Y); 52/356; Computer Clb; Stu Cncl; Var Crs Cntry; JV Trk; Hon Roll; NJ ST Schlrshp 86; Cook Coll; Envrnmtl Ecnmcs.

SLY, JENNIFER; Notre Dame HS; Morrisville, PA; (Y); Art Clb; Cmnty Wkr; Variety Show; Yrbk Stf; High Hon Roll; Hon Roll; US Marine Athltc Awd 85-86; Fshn Merch.

SMALL, JACKIE; Linden HS; Linden, NJ; (Y); Girl Scts; Hosp Aide; Sec Key Clb; Service Clb; Yrbk Stf; Hon Roll; NHS.

SMEDLEY, CYNTHEA M; Pitman HS; Pitman, NJ; (S); 10/140; Spanish Clb; Yrbk Phtg; Sec Stu Cncl; Var Cheerleading; French Hon Soc; High Hon Roll; Jr NHS; NHS; Church Yth Grp; Computer Clb; Mdrn Msc Mstrs Pres 85-86; Natl Hnr Soc Sec 85-86; MBA; Frgn Lang.

SMELAS, MATTHEW; Metuchen HS; Metuchen, NJ; (Y); 26/176; Am Leg Boys St; Varsity Clb; JV Bsktbl; Var Ftbl; JV Trk; Wt Lftg; French Hon Soc; Hon Roll; NHS; Bus.

SMETANA, DEBORAH; Pope John Xx111 HS; Andover, NJ; (Y); 3/124; Am Leg Aux Girls St; Hosp Aide; Band; Var Bsktbl; Var Capt Fld Hcky; Var Trk; High Hon Roll; Pres NHS; Ntl Merit Ltr; MIP Fld Hockey & Bsktbl 85-86; Acadmc Awds French, Pre-Calculus, Hist, Theology, Phys Ed 85-86; US Naval Acad; Engr.

SMETANA, MATTHEW J; Pope John XXIII HS; Andover, NJ; (Y); Art Clb; Math Tm; Spanish Clb; Chorus; Nwsp Sprt Ed; Yrbk Ed-Chief; Im JV Bsbl; Var Trk; Hon Roll; NHS; Mth Lg Awd 86; Roger Williams Coll; Arch.

SMIALOWICZ, THOMAS; Point Pleasant Bord HS; Pt Pleasant, NJ; (S); 2/243; Key Clb; Varsity Clb; French Clb; Rep Stu Cncl; Var L Socr; Var L Trk; JV Wrstlng; High Hon Roll; NHS; Sal; Engrng.

SMITH, ALISSA; Hamilton High School North; Trenton, NJ; (Y); 26/281; Key Clb; Chorus; Rep Sr Cls; Var Capt Cheerleading; Powder Puff Ftbl; Gftd & Talntd Prog; Garden ST Distgshd Schlr; Vlntr Intnshp Prog Psychtry; Bio.

SMITH, ALLAN C; Warren Hills Regional HS; Oxford, NJ; (Y); Im Badmtn; Im Vllybl; High Hon Roll; NHS; Ntl Merit Ltr; Pres Schlr; St Schlr; William Paterson Coll; Bus Adm.

SMITH, ANITA; Abraham Clark HS; Roselle, NJ; (S); Stu Cncl; Co-Capt Cheerleading; Sftbl; Hon Roll; Jr NHS; Ms JR 85-86; Med.

SMITH, ASIA; Frank H Morrell HS; Irvington, NJ; (Y); Aud/Vis; ROTC; Hon Roll; Robert Walsh Bus Schgl; Bus.

SMITH, BRIAN; Notre Dame HS; Lawrenceville, NJ; (Y); Am Leg Boys St; Boy Scts; Church Yth Grp; Varsity Clb; Nwsp Phtg; Stat Bsktbl; L Var Crs Cntry; Var Trk; Im Vllybl; Hon Roll; Excllnc US Hstry I 85-86; Chem Engrng.

SMITH, BRIAN C; Penns Grove HS; Carneys Point, NJ; (Y); 10/792; Nwsp Sprt Ed; Yrbk Sprt Ed; Capt Var Ftbl; Var L Golf; Var L Wrstlng; Voice Dem Awd; Temple U Pres Awd 86; Donald C Haines Mem Awd 86; Temple U; Brdcstng.

SMITH, CARLTON; Westside HS; Newark, NJ; (Y); Boy Scts; Ftbl; Socr; Boy Scout Yr 80.

SMITH, CAROLYN; De Paul Diocesan HS; W Milford, NJ; (Y); 13/168; Church Yth Grp; JV Var Bsktbl; Capt Var Crs Cntry; Sftbl; High Hon Roll; NHS; Pres Schlr; Garden St Distngshd Schlr 86; Seton Hall U Acad Schlrshp 86-90; Awd For Outstndng Achvt In Engl 86; Seton Hall U; Accntng.

SMITH, CAROLYN; Lincoln HS; Jersey Cty, NJ; (Y); Tchng.

SMITH, CATHRYN; Plainfield HS; Plainfield, NJ; (Y); 4/517; Computer Clb; FBLA; Library Aide; Quiz Bowl; Science Clb; Nwsp Stf; Hon Roll; NHS; Accntng.

SMITH, CHRIS; Freehold Twp HS; Freehold, NJ; (Y); 100/375; Cmnty Wkr; French Clb; Htl/Rest Mgmt.

SMITH, CHRISTINA; Maple Shade HS; Maple Shade, NJ; (Y); Spanish Clb; SADD; Prfct Atten Awd; Trs FBLA; Rep Stu Cncl; Stat Bsktbl; JV Socr; Var Sftbl.

SMITH, CHRISTINE; Monsignor Donovan HS; Lavallette, NJ; (Y); 22/243; Science Clb; Ski Clb; JV Socr; JV Trk.

SMITH, CHRISTINE L; Neptune HS; Neptune City, NJ; (Y); 8/309; Church Yth Grp; Trs GAA; Rep Soph Cls; Rep Jr Cls; Var Cheerleading; JV Socr; Var Swmmng; Hon Roll; NHS; Pres Acad Ftnss Awd 86; E Elizabeth Adams Mem Schlrshp 86; Neptune City Wmns Clb Schlrshp 86; U Of DE.

SMITH, CHRISTOPHER; Haddonfield Memorial HS; Haddonfield, NJ; (Y); 31/163; Chess Clb; 4-H; Hon Roll; NHS; Air Force; Aerontcl Engnr.

SMITH, COLEEN; Roselle Catholic HS; Hillside, NJ; (Y); Ski Clb; Stage Crew; Var JV Bsktbl; Var Socr; JV Trk; Natl Bus Hnr Scty 85-86; Typng Prof Cert 85-86; NJ Bus Educ Assoc 85-86; Art.

SMITH, CRAIG; Christian Brothers Acad; Red Bank, NJ; (Y); 53/221; Band; Jazz Band; Orch; School Musical; School Play; Variety Show; Nwsp Stf; Yrbk Rptr; Yrbk Stf; Lit Mag; Cert Cardplmnry Resscttn AM Red Crss 86; Cert Com SR Lfsvng YMCA 86; Part Awd Orchstra 84-85; Fairfield U; Eng.

SMITH, CRAIG D; Teaneck HS; Teaneck, NJ; (Y); Am Leg Boys St; Aud/Vis; Band; Concert Band; Mrchg Band; School Musical; Im Sftbl; Var Capt Trk; Im Vllybl; Hon Roll; Rollin D Wilber Band Awd 84; Outstndng Sci Stu Awd 84; Eugene Storins Meml Awd 84; Mgmt Acctg.

SMITH, DAWN; Phillipsburg HS; Phillipsburg, NJ; (Y); 69/334; Variety Show; Rep Soph Cls; VP Cheerleading; Coach Actv; Trk; Hon Roll; East Stroudsburg U; Spanish.

SMITH, DONALD; Holy Cross HS; Delran, NJ; (Y); 170/369; Church Yth Grp; JA; Ski Clb; JV Ftbl; Var Swmmng; Var Trk; Hon Roll; Trainer For Var & JV Ftbl Tms 85; Villanova U; Bus.

SMITH, DORAL; Weequaltic HS; Newark, NJ; (S); 6/345; Dance Clb; Exploring; Math Clb; Math Tm; Mrchg Band; Gym; Score Keeper; Hon Roll; Howard U; Acctg.

SMITH, DORI; Paul Vi HS; Turnsville, NJ; (Y); 81/467; Math Clb; Spanish Clb; Swmmng; Hon Roll; NHS; 2nd Hnrs 83-84 & 85-86; Chstnt Hl Coll; Chmstry.

SMITH, DOUG; Brick Township HS; Brick Town, NJ; (Y); 40/400; Ski Clb; Nwsp Bus Mgr; Trs Frsh Cls; Rep Soph Cls; Rep Jr Cls; VP Sr Cls; Rep Stu Cncl; Bsbl; Var Bsktbl; Var Tennis; Most Improved Varsity Tn Player Awd 86; Bus Finance.

SMITH, EARLYNE; Weequahic HS; Newark, NJ; (Y); 25/497; Church Yth Grp; Dance Clb; Sec Debate Tm; Church Choir; Nwsp Ed-Chief; Lit Mag; Rep Stu Cncl; NHS; Exploring; Awd Of Partcpn Close Up Fndtn 86; City Cncl 86; Stockton ST Clg; Crmnl Just.

SMITH, ELIZABETH; Chatham Twp HS; Chatham, NJ; (Y); 18/140; Key Clb; Model UN; Pep Clb; Stage Crew; Yrbk Stf; Stat Bsktbl; Stat Socr; High Hon Roll; Hon Roll; NHS.

SMITH, ERNEST NATHANIEL; Teaneck HS; Teaneck, NJ; (Y); Am Leg Boys St; Boy Scts; Debate Tm; NFL; Speech Tm; Pres Church Choir; Jazz Band; Pres Church Yth Grp; Exploring; Band; Grnd Mstr Cnslr Ordr Of Pythgrns In ST Of NJ 86; Keynote Spkr At Cmncmt Exc 86; Alchl & Drg Abs Tsk; Syracuse Ufpltcl Sci.

SMITH, ESTELLE M; Delaware Valley Regional HS; Milford, NJ; (Y); Cmnty Wkr; Intnl Clb; Red Cross Aide; Ski Clb; Band; Mrchg Band; Pep Band; Nrsng.

SMITH, GREGORY; Bridgeton HS; Bridgeton, NJ; (Y); Boy Scts; Crs Cntry; Ftbl; Gym; Trk; Wt Lftg; Acctg.

SMITH, HEATHER; Manchester Regional HS; Haledon, NJ; (Y); GAA; Off Frsh Cls; Off Soph Cls; Off Jr Cls; Stu Cncl; Cheerleading; Trk; Ldrshp Trng Conf; Accntng.

SMITH, HOLLY; Garden ST Acad; Andover, NJ; (Y); Church Yth Grp; Band; Chorus; Andrews U; Elem Educ.

SMITH, JANET; Newton HS; Newton, NJ; (Y); Art Clb; Church Yth Grp; Girl Scts; Hosp Aide; Pep Clb; Spanish Clb; Chorus; Color Guard; School Musical; Stage Crew; Pratt Art Schl; Art.

SMITH, JEANNETTE; Kittatinny Regnl HS; Newton, NJ; (Y); 32/238; Office Aide; Hon Roll; Natl Hgh Point Yth 85; Champ Wstrn Pleasure Wnnr 85; Natl Champ Wstrn Riding Wstrn Pleasure 85; Vet.

SMITH, JEFFREY; Montville Township HS; Montville, NJ; (Y); 34/290; Church Yth Grp; Key Clb; SADD; Varsity Clb; Bsktbl; Socr; Tennis; High Hon Roll; NHS; Prfct Atten Awd; Schltt Rltr Schlrshp 86; Ctzn Dream Tm Tnns 86; All ST Grp 3 Tnns 84-86; La Fayette Coll; Elec Engr.

SMITH, JEFFREY; South Plainfield HS; S Plainfield, NJ; (Y); 1/250; Am Leg Boys St; Church Yth Grp; Computer Clb; Math Tm; Crs Cntry; Trk; High Hon Roll; Ntl Merit Ltr; Spanish NHS; Gvrnrs Schl Of Sci Drew U 86; MA Inst Of Tech; Elctrcl Engr.

SMITH, JENNIFER; Toms River N HS; Toms River, NJ; (Y); 11/412; French Clb; Band; Capt Drill Tm; Mrchg Band; Orch; Yrbk Stf; Stu Cncl; Var L Trk; High Hon Roll; NHS; Dntstry.

SMITH, JUDITH; Lakewood HS; Lakewood, NJ; (Y); #26 In Class; Pres Church Yth Grp; Cmnty Wkr; Drama Clb; English Clb; Pres German Clb; Key Clb; Stat Bsktbl; Capt Fld Hcky; Hon Roll; Cert Apprctn Lakewood Bd Educ 85; Intl Rel.

SMITH, JULIA M; Jonathan Dayton Reg HS; Mountainside, NJ; (Y); 1/226; Church Yth Grp; Pres 4-H; French Clb; JCL; School Musical; Nwsp Ed-Chief; Var Swmmng; 4-H Awd; NHS; Ntl Merit SF; Mlclr Bio.

SMITH, JULIE; Bridgewater Raritan HS East; Martinsville, NJ; (Y); Church Yth Grp; French Clb; Ski Clb; Off Soph Cls; Off Jr Cls; Capt Crs Cntry; Stat Ftbl; Powder Puff Ftbl; Trk; Hon Roll; Boston Coll; Pre-Med.

SMITH, JUSTINE; Washington Twp HS; Turnersville, NJ; (Y); French Clb; Yrbk Stf; Rep Frsh Cls; Rep Stu Cncl; Jr NHS; Glassboro ST Coll; Tchr.

SMITH, KAREN; Burlington Township HS; Burlington, NJ; (Y); 19/118; Varsity Clb; Bsktbl; Socr; Hon Roll; Burlington Cnty Coll; Acctng.

SMITH, KATHY; Toms River HS North; Toms River, NJ; (Y); French Clb; FBLA; Rptr Stu Cncl; Fld Hcky; Hon Roll; 6th Steno At 26th FBIA ST Ldrshp Conf 86; Ldrshp Awd Future Secy Katharine Gibbs Bus Schl 86; Secy.

SMITH, KEITH; Henry Snyder HS; Jersey City, NJ; (Y); 8/25; Art Clb; Boy Scts; Math Clb; SADD; Band; Chorus; Jazz Band; School Play; Stage Crew; Nwsp Stf; NJIT; Engrng.

SMITH, KENNETH; Hudson Catholic HS; Jersey City, NJ; (Y); Church Yth Grp; Computer Clb; Science Clb; Im Stat Bsktbl; JV Bowling; Mgr(s); Im Vllybl; NY Inst Tech; Elect Tech.

SMITH, KIMBERLY; Hackettstown HS; Great Meadows, NJ; (Y); Trs FFA; Girl Scts; Office Aide; Spanish Clb; Stage Crew; Trk; Hon Roll; Hnr Rl Badge 83-84; Bus.

SMITH, KIMBERLY; Voorhees HS; Glen Gardner, NJ; (Y); 29/274; Key Clb; Red Cross Aide; SADD; Concert Band; Mrchg Band; Lit Mag; French Hon Soc; Hon Roll; Pediatrcn.

SMITH, LANCE; Wall HS; Manasquan, NJ; (S); 19/254; Bsktbl; Bowling; Crs Cntry; Trk; High Hon Roll; Hon Roll; 2nd Pl Shore Shop Tchr Crftsmn Fair 84-85; Mech Engr.

SMITH, LISA V; Hackettstown HS; Hackettstown, NJ; (Y); Band; Concert Band; Jazz Band; Cheerleading.

SMITH, LORA JANE; Mount Olive HS; Budd Lake, NJ; (Y); 53/296; Church Yth Grp; Drama Clb; Acpl Chr; Chorus; Flag Corp; Mrchg Band; School Musical; School Play; Yrbk Stf; Hon Roll; Optmtry.

SMITH, LORI; Ocean Township HS; Oceantwp, NJ; (Y); 5/337; VP Cmnty Wkr; Drama Clb; Key Clb; Spanish Clb; SADD; Color Guard; School Play; JV Sftbl; Capt Twrlr; NHS; Sprtn Schlr 84 & 85; Med.

SMITH, LYNNE; Mainland Regional HS; Hatfield, PA; (Y); 71/250; Dance Clb; Ski Clb; Yrbk Stf; Rep Frsh Cls; Rep Soph Cls; Rep Jr Cls; Rep Sr Cls; Rep Stu Cncl; Var L Cheerleading; JV Fld Hcky; All Amer Chrldr Fnlst 85; East Carolina U.

SMITH, MARGARET E; Union Catholic Reg HS; Fanwood, NJ; (Y); 16/320; Girl Scts; Hosp Aide; Service Clb; Sec Spanish Clb; Nwsp Rptr; Lit Mag; Rep Frsh Cls; Hon Roll; NHS; Spanish NHS; Union Catholic Reprrsntv Movemnt For Better World 86-87.

SMITH, MARK; Schalick HS; Elmer, NJ; (Y); Ski Clb; Teachers Aide; Rep Frsh Cls; Rep Soph Cls; Pres Jr Cls; Rep Stu Cncl; Ftbl; Trk; Wrstlng; Mst Imprvd 1st Team Dfns, All Stars, Salem Cnty, Vinland Times Jrnl-Ftbl 85-86; Crmnl Jstc.

SMITH, MICHAEL; Kearny HS; Kearny, NJ; (Y); 33/375; Church Yth Grp; Computer Clb; German Clb; Band; Concert Band; Mrchg Band; Pep Band; Var Golf; High Hon Roll; NHS; Rutgers U Newark.

SMITH, MICHAEL; Toms River HS South; Pine Beach, NJ; (Y); 27/360; Math Tm; Spanish Clb; Band; Concert Band; Mrchg Band; Mth Ltr 85; Band Ltr 84-86; Ed.

SMITH, MONICA; Metuchen HS; Metuchen, NJ; (Y); 7/175; French Clb; Orch; Nwsp Rptr; Fld Hcky; French Hon Soc; Hon Roll; NHS; Golden Poet Awd 85; Slvr Poet Awd 86.

SMITH, NANETTE; Linden HS; Linden, NJ; (Y); Am Leg Aux Girls St; Art Clb; Key Clb; Band; Church Choir; Concert Band; Mrchg Band; Cheerleading; High Hon Roll; Hon Roll; Cert PREFACE Engrng Pgm Purdue U; 85; Cert Teen Arts Fstvl 86; Engrng.

SMITH, NOREEN; Pope John XXIII HS; Hackettstown, NJ; (Y); 20/155; Debate Tm; French Clb; Latin Clb; Model UN; Teachers Aide; Lit Mag; Cheerleading; High Hon Roll; English Clb; Pep Clb; Frnch Awd 84-85; Spec Acadmc Achvt Awd 85-86; FL Intl U; Intl Rel.

SMITH, PAMELA; Immaculate Conception HS; Saddle Brook, NJ; (S); 9/99; Art Clb; Q&S; Ed Lit Mag; Stu Cncl; Hon Roll; Art Natl Hnr Scty Pres; Natl Engls Mrt Awd; William Paterson Coll; Erly Chl.

SMITH, PAMELA M; Plainfield HS; Plainfield, NJ; (Y); Aud/Vis; Computer Clb; Girl Scts; Office Aide; Sec Science Clb; Chorus; Lit Mag; Rep Jr Cls; Hon Roll; Prfct Atten Awd; Trenton ST Coll; Accntng.

SMITH, PETER; Haddonfield HS; Haddonfield, NJ; (Y); Var Capt Bsktbl; Var Capt Tennis; Bsktbll Coaches Awd MVP 85-86; All S Jersey Bsktbll & Tennis 85-86; Bus.

SMITH, RAYMOND SCOTT; Burlington County Vo-Tech Schl; Riverside, NJ; (Y); VICA; Hon Roll; De Molay Yth Grp Master Cnclr 85-86; Burlington Cnty Coll; Compu Sci.

SMITH JR, ROBERT H; Hamilton High School East; Allentown, NJ; (Y); 30/326; Boy Scts; Pres Church Yth Grp; Hon Roll; NHS; Stevens Inst Of Tech; Cvl Engr.

SMITH, ROGER; Bayonne HS; Bayonne, NJ; (Y); Math Tm; Rep Stu Cncl; Im Ftbl; Im Trk; Hon Roll; Jr NHS; NY U; Comp.

SMITH, SARA; Our Lady Of Mercy Acad; Vineland, NJ; (Y); 16/40; Cmnty Wkr; SADD; Trs Soph Cls; Trs Stu Cncl; Im Badmtn; Im Bsktbl; Im Swmmng; Im Vllybl; Hon Roll; Chem.

SMITH, SELINA; Camden HS; Pensauken, NJ; (Y); 32/408; Pres Church Yth Grp; Hst FBLA; JA; Sec Church Choir; Hon Roll; Upward Bnd Acad Adhvt 85; Rutgers U; Med.

SMITH, SHAWN W; Bishop Eustace Prep; Deptford, NJ; (Y); Jrnlsm.

SMITH, SHERRY L; Paul VI HS; Paterson, NJ; (Y); Church Yth Grp; SADD; Chorus; Library Aide; Church Choir; Concert Band; School Musical; School Play; Stage Crew; Variety Show; Berkleys Bus Schl; Wrd Process.

SMITH, STACEY; St Joseph HS; Collingslakes, NJ; (Y); Church Yth Grp; Hosp Aide; School Play; Sec Jr Cls; Capt Cheerleading; Crs Cntry; Mgr(s); Capt Sftbl; Hon Roll; Prncpls Lst/ST Chrldng Chmps; 2nd Rnr Up JR MS Pgnt Altnc Cnty & Tlnt Awd; Glsbro ST Coll; Tchr.

SMITH, STEVE; Toms River HS South; Beachwood, NJ; (Y); Art Clb; Key Clb; Model UN; Ski Clb; Var L Socr; Var L Trk; Prestigeous Fclty Schlrshp 86; Navy ROTC Schlrshp 86; Rochester Inst/Tech; Elec Engr.

SMITH, SUSAN; Audubon HS; Audubon, NJ; (Y); Am Leg Aux Girls St; French Clb; Yrbk Stf; VP Frsh Cls; VP Soph Cls; VP Jr Cls; Var Sftbl; Var Tennis; Hon Roll; West Chester U; Elem Educ.

SMITH, SUSAN; Edgewood Regional SR HS; Atco, NJ; (Y); Hosp Aide; Model UN; Scholastic Bowl; Nwsp Stf; Yrbk Phtg; Fld Hcky; Sftbl; High Hon Roll; Jr NHS; NHS; Earth Sci Awd 84; Mrchng Bnd Awd 85; Phil Coll Pharm & Sci; Pharm.

SMITH, TERRI; Essex Catholic Girls HS; E Orange, NJ; (Y); Pep Clb; Ed Nwsp Stf; Ed Yrbk Stf; Rep Jr Cls; Capt Cheerleading; High Hon Roll; NHS; Cmnctns.

SMITH, TERRY A; Kearny HS; Kearny, NJ; (Y); Trs FBLA; Trk; Rutgers U; Accntng.

SMITH, WILLIAM; Chatham Twp HS; Chatham, NJ; (Y); Boy Scts; Church Yth Grp; Model UN; Quiz Bowl; Concert Band; Jazz Band; Pep Band; High Hon Roll; Hon Roll; NHS.

SMITH, WILLIAM; Cinnaminson HS; Cinnaminson, NJ; (Y); 90/300; Drama Clb; Spanish Clb; SADD; Thesps; Band; Concert Band; Mrchg Band; Pep Band; School Play; Spnsh Study For Smmr 85 & 86; Excllnc Spnsh 86; NE Conf Tchng Of Foreign Langs For Spnsh 86; Misericordia Coll; Intl Bus.

SMITS, ALEXANDRA; South River HS; South River, NJ; (Y); 30/138; Band; Capt Color Guard; Concert Band; Jazz Band; Pep Band; Symp Band; NHS; Phila Coll/Txtl/Sci; Txtl Tech.

SMOLEN, HEATHER L; Bishop George Ahr HS; Edison, NJ; (Y); Drama Clb; French Clb; Drill Tm; School Play; Rep Jr Cls; Pom Pon; Hon Roll; Hmcmng Princess 84; Poetry Alive For Young Teens 86; Drama.

SMTIH, DARIN S; Wayne Hills HS; Sandusky, OH; (Y); 18/310; Am Leg Boys St; Math Clb; NFL; Speech Tm; School Play; Var L Bsktbl; JV Ftbl; JV Golf; High Hon Roll; NHS; 2nd Plc Nthrn IN Regnl Sci Fr; Spcl Marine Corps Awd Nthrn IN Regnl Sci Fr; IN U Bloomington IN; Bio.

SMYTH, JEFF; Millville SR HS; Millville, NJ; (Y); Pres JA; VP Jr Cls; Rep Stu Cncl; Stat Ftbl; Var L Trk; Jr NHS; NHS; NEDT Awd; AZ Math Cntst Top 10 Pct 84; Sci League 85; Engr.

SMYTH, LAURA; Immaculate Conception HS; Lyndhurst, NJ; (S); 7/89; Math Tm; NFL; Q&S; Nwsp Sprt Ed; VP Frsh Cls; Pres Soph Cls; Pres Jr Cls; Hon Roll; NEDT Awd; Hugh O Brian Ldrshp Sem Rep 85; Summr Schlr St Peters Coll Jersey City 85; English Educ.

SNEAD, NANCY LYNN; Essex Catholic Girls HS; Irvington, NJ; (Y); Church Yth Grp; FHA; Pep Clb; Church Choir; Nwsp Rptr; Yrbk Phtg; Yrbk Stf; Rep Stu Cncl; Hon Roll; Prfct Atten Awd; Prfct Attndnc 83-87; Mst Sprtd 4-86; Chld Psychlgy.

SNEDEKER, SCOTT; Middletown HS South; Middletown, NJ; (Y); Ski Clb; JV Capt Socr; Var L Trk; Bus.

SNENSKY, MARK S; Saint Josephs HS; Milltown, NJ; (Y); Church Yth Grp; German Clb; Var L Swmmng; NHS; 1st 100 Yd Butterfly Brown U & Natl Cath Invtnl Villanova U, 3rd Butterfly NJ St Wmin Chmpnshps 86; FL ST U; Rsrch Bio.

SNIDER, KATHLEEN; Memorial HS; Cedar Grove, NJ; (S); 16/118; Pres Church Yth Grp; Drama Clb; Pres Intnl Clb; Mrchg Band; School Musical; School Play; Nwsp Stf; Yrbk Stf; NHS; Pres Schlr; Seton Hall Schlrshp 86; Douglass Coll Merit Schlrshp 86; Bio Awd 84; St Lawrence U; Acting.

SNIDER, LISA; Toms River High School North; Toms River, NJ; (Y); 51/412; Church Yth Grp; Ski Clb; Capt Cheerleading; High Hon Roll; Hon Roll; Academic Letter 84; Advertising.

SNIVELY, DIANA; Delsea Regional HS; Vineland, NJ; (Y); Debate Tm; School Musical; Yrbk Phtg; Rep Soph Cls; Trs Jr Cls; Pres Stu Cncl; High Hon Roll; Hon Roll; NHS; Ntl Merit Schol; Pre/Law.

SNOVER, KATHLEEN; Belvidere HS; Belvidere, NJ; (S); 13/125; Drama Clb; Scholastic Bowl; SADD; Varsity Clb; Madrigals; School Musical; Lit Mag; Cheerleading; Hon Roll; French Clb; Hugh O Brian Yth Ldrshp Awd 85; Cntry II Ldrshp Awd 85; Frnch II Awd 85; Douglas Coll; Bus Law.

SNYDER, CINDY; Bishop Ahr HS; Metuchen, NJ; (Y); Church Yth Grp; Drama Clb; Spanish Clb; Thesps; Stage Crew; Hon Roll.

SNYDER, KERRI; Mount Saint Mary Acad; Dunellen, NJ; (Y); 15/80; French Clb; GAA; Office Aide; Chorus; Var L Cheerleading; French Hon Soc; Hon Roll; Magna Cum Laude In Natl Latin Exam 85; Acctng.

SNYDER, MATT; Cherry Hill HS West; Cherry Hill, NJ; (Y); Boy Scts; PAVAS; Mrchg Band; Orch; School Musical; Symp Band; God Cntry Awd; Eagle Scout Awd 86; Home & Schl Assoc Awd For Music 86; All ST Wind Ens 86 Rutgers Coll.

SNYDER, TERRI; Millville SR HS; Heislerville, NJ; (Y); 30/352; FBLA; SADD; Natl Sci Olympiad 84; Secretarial.

SOBCZAK, MARGIE; Washington Township HS; Turnersville, NJ; (Y); Exploring; VP German Clb; Color Guard; Mrchg Band; Im Ice Hcky; Socr; Sftbl; Im Vllybl; Hon Roll; German Hnr Soc 85-86; La Salle U; Genetic Engrng.

SOBOCINSKI, ADRIANNE; Spotswood HS; Spotswood, NJ; (S); 6/180; Am Leg Aux Girls St; Cmnty Wkr; Intnl Clb; Concert Band; Mrchg Band; Symp Band; Stu Cncl; High Hon Roll; Hon Roll; NHS; Phy Thrpy.

SOCHA, TED; Roselle Catholic HS; Linden, NJ; (S); 8/207; Church Yth Grp; Cmnty Wkr; Computer Clb; JA; Math Clb; Lit Mag; Wrstlng; High Hon Roll; Hon Roll; NHS; Bio Sci.

SODANO, ANGELA; Madison HS; Madison, NJ; (Y); 29/220; Pep Clb; Varsity Clb; Yrbk Sprt Ed; Var Capt Cheerleading; Powder Puff Ftbl; French Hon Soc; High Hon Roll; NHS; Stat Ftbl; Stat Socr; Italian Natl Hnr Soc; PA ST U; Law.

SODORA, GARY; Don Bosco Tech HS; N Arlington, NJ; (Y); Camera Clb; Computer Clb; SADD; Nwsp Ed-Chief; Rep Frsh Cls; Rep Soph Cls; Rep Jr Cls; Rep Sr Cls; Rep Stu Cncl; JV Socr; Seton Hall Univ; Political Sci.

SOECHTING, CHRISTINE; Matawan Regional Hs; Matawan, NJ; (S); 12/350; SADD; Chorus; Madrigals; School Musical; Off Jr Cls; Stu Cncl; JV Fld Hcky; Hon Roll.

SOETY, JOHN J; Monroe Township HS; Spotswood, NJ; (Y); Art Clb; Church Yth Grp; Drama Clb; School Musical; School Play; Stage Crew; Hon Roll; Jr NHS; 2nd Pl Knghts Of Phythias Pstr Cntst 85.

SOFFEL, WENDY LYNN; River Dell SR HS; Oradell, NJ; (Y); 88/216; Ski Clb; Teachers Aide; Chorus; School Musical; Stage Crew; Rep Soph Cls; Stat Bsbl; Cheerleading; Stat Ftbl; Stat Ice Hcky; Hofstra U; Comm.

SOFIELD, KEVIN; Ocean Township HS; Oakhurst, NJ; (Y); 5/333; Nwsp Rptr; Sr Cls; Bsbl; Bsktbl; Ftbl; Socr; NHS; Spartan Schlr; Engrng.

SOFKA, CAROLYN; Woodbridge HS; Woodbridge, NJ; (Y); 1/396; Am Leg Aux Girls St; French Clb; Scholastic Bowl; Chorus; Concert Band; Drm Mjr(t); Mrchg Band; Swing Chorus; High Hon Roll; NHS; Regn II Orch 86; Fin Gov Schl Mth & Sci 86; Chem & Physics ST Sci Day 85-86; Chem.

SOFRONAS, KATHERINE; Red Bank Catholic HS; Lincroft, NJ; (Y); Var Capt Crs Cntry; Var Capt Trk; High Hon Roll; Hon Roll; NHS; 4 Yr Var Awd Wnnr Crsscntry 83-86; MVP Awd Wnnr Outdoor Trck 84-87; Cmmnctns.

SOFRONEY, SANDRA; Atlantic Christian Schl; Ocean View, NJ; (Y); Hosp Aide; Library Aide; Spanish Clb; Chorus; Yrbk Stf; Trs Jr Cls; Trs Sr Cls; Stat Bsktbl; Mgr(s); Sftbl; St Cmptn 2nd Spelling Bee 86; Yrk Coll Of PA; Nrsng.

SOKALSKI, ELIZABETH; Union HS; Unin, NJ; (Y); 15/500; FBLA; Chorus; Trk; Hon Roll; SAR Awd; Pres Acad Awd 86; Union Township Educ Awd 86; Nick Dispenzier Mem Awd 86; Seton Hall U; Psych.

SOKOLIC, ROBERT; Solomon Schechter Day Schl; Elizabeth, NJ; (Y); Math Tm; Nwsp Rptr; Yrbk Stf; Lit Mag; Rep Soph Cls; Stu Cncl; JV Var Bsktbl; JV Socr; VP NHS; Philosphy.

SOKOLOWSKI, CAROL; St John Vianney HS; Morganville, NJ; (Y); Sec Intnl Clb; Office Aide; Yrbk Stf; Powder Puff Ftbl; Vllybl; GA Court Coll; Sci.

SOLAN, JOE A; Mount Olive HS; Flanders, NJ; (Y); 14/279; Pres Computer Clb; Var VP Socr; Var VP Trk; Church Yth Grp; Science Clb; High Hon Roll; NHS; Prfct Atten Awd; St Schlr; H S Soccr Club Awd 83; Cert Of Awd-Math 82-83; Sci Teachrs Recgntn Awd 84-85; Harvard U; Comptr.

SOLANKI, GIRIRAJ; Hoboken HS; Hoboken, NJ; (Y); Off Jr Cls; Crs Cntry; Tennis; Engr.

SOLEM, JON ERIK; Woodbury HS; Woodbury, NJ; (Y); 9/101; Scholastic Bowl; Ski Clb; Varsity Clb; Stu Cncl; JV Var Tennis; JC Awd; Ntl Merit SF; Computer Clb; Math Tm; JV Ftbl; Rutgers Schlr 85; NJ ST Bio Awd 82; Military Acad Invtnl Wrkshp 85; West Point; Engrng.

SOLETTO, MICHELLE; Watchung Hills Regional HS; Warren, NJ; (Y); Church Yth Grp; SADD; School Play; Yrbk Sprt Ed; Ed Lit Mag; Mgr(s); Var Trk; Voice Dem Awd; Drama Clb; 4-H; Spec Art Awd Du Cret Art Cntst 86; Cert Apprctn Mc Dougal Littel Annl 86; U Of FL; Soclgy.

SOLIMENE, PATRICIA; Hackettstown HS; Hackettstown, NJ; (Y); Church Yth Grp; Cmnty Wkr; 4-H; Red Cross Aide; Ski Clb; SADD; Acpl Chr; Band; Chorus; Concert Band; Phys Thrpy.

SOLIMENE, SANDRA L; Hackettstown HS; Hackettstown, NJ; (Y); 29/210; Drama Clb; Concert Band; Jazz Band; School Play; Var Capt Cheerleading; Hon Roll; NHS; Aud/Vis; Band; Stage Crew; Mst Imprvd Band Stu 86; Top 10 Bio Stu 84; Drm Clb 86; DE Vly Coll; Flrst.

SOLLECITO, VINCENT T; Christian Brothers Acad; Colts Neck, NJ; (S); Church Yth Grp; Math Tm; Nwsp Rptr; Sec Ed Yrbk Stf; Im Capt Fld Hcky; Im Capt Ftbl; Im Tennis; NHS; Pltcl Sci.

SOLLITTI, DANIEL; William L Dickinson HS; Jersey City, NJ; (Y); Art Clb; Civic Clb; VP Exploring; Lit Mag; Rep Frsh Cls; Kiwanis Awd; Appntd Jvnl Cnfrnce Cmmttee 86; Outstndng Art Stu 84; NJ ST Bar Assn Mcktrl Cert Hon 86; John J Coll Crmnl Jstc; Law.

SOLLOG II, JOHN JOSEPH; Middletown HS; Red Bank, NJ; (Y); Chess Clb; Church Yth Grp; Cmnty Wkr; Library Aide; Political Wkr; Band; Concert Band; Drm & Bgl; Jazz Band; Mrchg Band; Awd Crt Brd Educ Cmmnty Srv 85-86; Boston U; Law.

SOLOMON, JONATHAN; Freehold Twp HS; Farmingdale, NJ; (Y); 31/382; Computer Clb; Spanish Clb; Capt Bowling; NHS; Tutor Alg Chem 85-86.

SOLOMON, STEVE; Highstown HS; East Windsor, NJ; (Y); 138/359; Ski Clb; Varsity Clb; Rep Stu Cncl; Var Bsbl; Hnrs Distngshd Bus Achvt 86; NY Dept Ladies Aux Of Jewish War Vets Schlrp 86; Trenton ST Coll; Bus.

SOLOMON, TANYA; Frank H Morrell HS; Irvington, NJ; (Y); Church Yth Grp; Dance Clb; Hosp Aide; Key Clb; Pep Clb; Spanish Clb; Yrbk Stf; Rep Frsh Cls; Vllybl; Hon Roll; Hnr Rl 86; Rutgers New Brunswick; Comp Sci.

SOLTESZ, SUSAN; Woodbridge HS; Woodbridge, NJ; (Y); 32/394; French Clb; Acpl Chr; Chorus; Rep Frsh Cls; Rep Soph Cls; Rep Jr Cls; Var JV Bsktbl; Var JV Sftbl; Jr NHS; NHS; Frgn Lang.

SOLTYS, MICHAEL; Cinnaminson HS; Cinnaminson, NJ; (Y); Church Yth Grp; Math Tm; Science Clb; SADD; Bsbl; Bsktbl; Hon Roll; JV Bsbl Mst Potntl 85.

SOMERVILLE, STACEY; Abraham Clark HS; Roselle, NJ; (Y); 19/180; Chess Clb; Cmnty Wkr; Debate Tm; Science Clb; Service Clb; Chorus; Sftbl; Var Tennis; Var Vllybl; Hon Roll; James Dixon Carr Schlrshp 86; Rtgrs Coll; Pre-Med.

SOMERVILLE, TINA; Wall HS; Sea Girt, NJ; (S); 21/263; Latin Clb; Ski Clb; Rep Frsh Cls; Rep Soph Cls; Rep Stu Cncl; Var Fld Hcky; Stat Gym; JV Socr; High Hon Roll; Hon Roll; Bus.

SOMMER JR, JOSEPH; James Caldwell HS; Caldwell, NJ; (Y); JV Bsbl; Im JV Bsktbl; JV Ftbl; Im Mgr(s); Im Sftbl; Im Wt Lftg; Hon Roll; Prfct Atten Awd; Montclare ST Coll; Bus Mang.

SOMOGYI, SANDI; Florence Twp Memorial HS; Roebling, NJ; (Y); DECA; FBLA; Hosp Aide; Library Aide; Teachers Aide; Hon Roll; Hghst Acdmc Prgrss 86; Prncpls Lst For Imprvmnt 84-86; Katharin Gibbs-Phila; Exec Sec.

SONDEY, LIZ; Summit HS; Summit, NJ; (Y); 24/271; Cmnty Wkr; GAA; Ski Clb; Band; NHS; Var Fld Hcky; JV Lcrss; Hstry.

SONG, EUNJOO; Hillside HS; Hillside, NJ; (Y); 5/240; Church Yth Grp; 4-H; Intnl Clb; Math Tm; Science Clb; Spanish Clb; Chorus; Church Choir; Nwsp Rptr; Nwsp Stf; Schlrshp Dr Wayne T Branom Awd 86; Plq Awd Outstndng Acdmc Achvt 86; Rutgers U; Bus Adm.

SONI, RITA; Mt Olive HS; Flanders, NJ; (Y); 42/297; Cmnty Wkr; Dance Clb; Math Tm; Ski Clb; SADD; Chorus; School Musical; Hon Roll; NHS; Prfct Atten Awd; Choral Awds; Engrng.

SONZ, LORRETTA; Union Catholic Regional HS; Scotch Plains, NJ; (Y); Church Yth Grp; Hosp Aide; Latin Clb; Ski Clb; Spanish Clb; SADD; Nwsp Rptr; Var Swmmng; Var Tennis; Hon Roll.

SOOKRAM, ELISE I; Paramus HS; Paramus, NJ; (Y); Art Clb; Church Yth Grp; English Clb; French Clb; JCL; Ed Nwsp Stf; Lit Mag; Mgr(s); Sftbl; Mgr Tennis; Latin Hnr Soc, Slvr Svc Awd HS 86; Fshn Illus.

SOONG, ADAM; Parsippany HS; Parsippany, NJ; (Y); Latin Clb; Trk; Hon Roll; Magna Cm Ld Awd For Ntl Ltn Exm; Envrnmntl Sci Dvlpmnt.

SOOS, JEFF; St Josephs HS; Edison, NJ; (Y); Church Yth Grp; Cmnty Wkr; Political Wkr; Service Clb; Ski Clb; Var Tennis; Hon Roll; Bus Adm.

SOOY, KAREN; Parsippany Hills HS; Denville, NJ; (Y); AFS; Church Yth Grp; Hosp Aide; Mrchg Band; JV Fld Hcky; Hon Roll; Pre-Med.

SORACCO, MICHAEL P; Morris Hills HS; Rockaway, NJ; (Y); 8/306; Band; Concert Band; Jazz Band; Mrchg Band; Symp Band; High Hon Roll; NHS; Church Yth Grp; Debate Tm; Math Tm; ROTC Schlrshp 86; GA Inst Of Tech; Aerntcl Engr.

SORENSEN, ERIC; Lacey Township HS; Forked River, NJ; (Y); 1/209; Math Clb; Rptr Nwsp Rptr; Yrbk Rptr; Bsbl; Bsktbl; High Hon Roll; NHS; St Schlr; Val; Wake Forest U; Bus.

SORI, TARA; Washington Township HS; Sewell, NJ; (Y); Church Yth Grp; Dance Clb; Key Clb; Ski Clb; Spanish Clb; Lit Mag; Off Jr Cls; Stu Cncl; Cheerleading; Hon Roll; Rutgers U; Bus Mgmt.

SOROCHEN, WILLIAM; Banonne HS; Bayonne, NJ; (Y); Im Vllybl; Hon Roll; Prfct Atten Awd; Finance.

SORRENTINO, SUSAN; East Brunswick HS; E Brunswick, NJ; (Y); Dance Clb; Drama Clb; Key Clb; Pep Clb; Chorus; JV Capt Cheerleading; Jrnlsm.

SOSA, MARIE; Lakewood HS; Lakewood, NJ; (Y); 48/298; Drama Clb; English Clb; Exploring; Hosp Aide; Stage Crew; Hon Roll; Lwyr.

SOSDORF, RICHARD; Holy Cross HS; Delran, NJ; (Y); Stage Crew; Arch Engr.

SOSIK, SUE; Delsea Regional HS; Franklinville, NJ; (Y); Dance Clb; Var JV Cheerleading; Var Gym; Church Yth Grp; 4-H; Girl Scts; Science Clb; Church Choir; Sftbl; 4-H Awd; Dance Gymnstcs Ribbons Medals Trophies 82, 85-86; Beautcn.

SOSIS, STACI; Toms River South HS; Toms River, NJ; (Y); 35/318; Keywanettes; Temple Yth Grp; Yrbk Stf; Lit Mag; Crs Cntry; NHS; Schlrshp Svc Awd 86; U Of MD; Psych.

SOTNYCHUK, STEVEN; Vineland HS; Vineland, NJ; (Y); Ftbl; Contrctn.

SOTO, EVELYN; Camden HS; Camden, NJ; (S); Cmnty Wkr; Sec FHA; Hosp Aide; High Hon Roll; Hon Roll; NHS; Math & Sci Awd 83; Schlrshp To Phillips Acad-Math & Sci 84-8; Med.

SOUCEK, CRISTIN; Edison HS; Edison, NJ; (Y); Church Yth Grp; Girl Scts; Band; Church Choir; Jazz Band; Mrchg Band; Symp Band; Yrbk Stf; Soph Cls; Jr Cls; Dstngshd Merit Soc 84; Engl.

SOUDER, STEPHEN; Lower Cape May Regional HS; Cape May, NJ; (Y); Math Tm; Band; Concert Band; Jazz Band; Mrchg Band; School Musical; Nwsp Rptr; Bsktbl; Hon Roll; NHS; Sound Engrng.

SOULI, NEELI; Bruriah HS For Girls; Staten Island, NY; (Y); Church Yth Grp; NHS; NY U; Pre-Law.

SOUS, TERRI; Wayne Hills HS; Wayne, NJ; (Y); 60/328; Aud/Vis; FBLA; Pep Clb; Radio Clb; Spanish Clb; Cheerleading; High Hon Roll; Ntl Merit Ltr; Schl Lttr Chrldng 83; Hghst GPA-COOKING Cls 85; Hon Mntn Natl Merit Schlrshp 85; William Paterson Coll; Psych.

SOUVEREIN, GARY; Lakeland Reg HS; Ringwood, NJ; (Y); 18/380; Math Clb; Service Clb; Ski Clb; Var Capt Socr; Var Capt Trk; High Hon Roll; Hon Roll; NHS; Track Field Hnrbl Ment All Passaic Cty 85; All Conf 85-86; Soccer Hnrbl Ment All Conf 86; UT ST U; Civil Engr.

SOUZA, DAWN; Matawan Regional HS; Matawan, NJ; (Y); FNA; Hosp Aide; Red Cross Aide; Spanish Clb; SADD; Badmtn; Bowling; Swmmng; Vllybl; Hon Roll; Nrsng.

SOVA, PAUL; De Paul HS; Wayne, NJ; (S); Var L Ftbl; Trk; Wt Lftg; High Hon Roll; Hon Roll; Cochs Awd 85; Al-Conf Ftbl Tm 85; Al-Cnty Ftbl Tm 85; PA ST U; Vet Medcn.

SOVIERO, JIM; Red Bank Catholic HS; Red Bank, NJ; (Y).

SOWA, JENNIFER; Villa Victoria Acad; Yardville, NJ; (Y); Camera Clb; Church Yth Grp; Cmnty Wkr; Pep Clb; Political Wkr; Ski Clb; Chorus; Rep Sr Cls; Hon Roll; Math Awd 84; Pre-Med.

SOWELL, RYAN; Washington Township HS; Sewell, NJ; (Y); Q&S; Ftbl; JC Awd; Prfct Atten Awd; Drexel; Arch.

SOWERS, TRACY; Mainland Regional HS; Linwood, NJ; (Y); Church Yth Grp; Dance Clb; Drama Clb; Girl Scts; SADD; School Play; Stu Cncl; Mgr(s); Score Keeper; Socr; Polit Science.

SPADAVECCHIA, KRIS ANN; High Point Regional HS; Sussex, NJ; (Y); 7/215; Chorus; Drm Mjr(t); Jazz Band; School Musical; Rep Jr Cls; Capt Var Crs Cntry; NHS; Church Yth Grp; German Clb; PAVAS; Rcpnt Arts Cncl & Sussex Womens Clb Art Awd 86; US Army Schlr Athlete 86; 1st Tm All Cnty Xc Rnng; West Point Prep; Foreign Rltns.

SPAETH, DANA; Hopewell Valley Central HS; Hopewell, NJ; (Y); 29/202; Art Clb; Drama Clb; French Clb; PAVAS; School Musical; School Play; Rep Frsh Cls; Rep Soph Cls; Rep Jr Cls; Rep Sr Cls; Awd Schlrshp Mre Coll Art 85-86; Art Wnr Cnty & ST Tn Arts 85-86; Wnr Hssn Pstr Cntsts 85-86; Cornell U; Fine Arts.

SPAFFORD, MARYANN; Matawan Regional HS; Aberdeen, NJ; (Y); Exploring; Hosp Aide; Crs Cntry; Trk; Hon Roll; Hnr Rl 83-85; Rutgers; Accntng.

SPAGES, JASON B; Paterson Catholic HS; Paterson, NJ; (Y); Am Leg Boys St; Letterman Clb; Varsity Clb; Yrbk Phtg; JV Bsbl; Var Ftbl; Var Trk; Var Wt Lftg; Var Wrstlng; Bus.

SPAGNOLA, DAWN; Brick Twp HS; Brick Town, NJ; (Y); Dance Clb; Drama Clb; Key Clb; Band; Concert Band; Mrchg Band; Yrbk Phtg; Yrbk Stf; Stu Cncl; Powder Puff Ftbl; Varsity Letters Soccer 85 86; Music Achvt Awd 84; Rutgers Coll; Corporate Law.

SPAHR, RENEE; Secaucus HS; Secaucus, NJ; (Y); Hosp Aide; Intnl Clb; PAVAS; Ski Clb; Acpl Chr; Chorus; Church Choir; Madrigals; School Musical; School Play; Aux Riverside Gen Hosp Scholar 86; Vocal Awd 86; Rutgers SAI Pgm 83; Manhattan Schl Music Div 85; Shenandoah Coll; Psych.

SPAIS, CHRYSANTHE; Hopewell Valley Central HS; Pennington, NJ; (Y); 11/202; AFS; French Clb; Service Clb; School Musical; School Play; Stat Bsktbl; Var Capt Gym; High Hon Roll; NHS; Church Yth Grp; Gymnastics MVP 86; Rutgers U; Bio Sci.

SPAN, HENRY A; Westfield SR HS; Westfield, NJ; (Y); 28/450; Nwsp Rptr; Nwsp Sprt Ed; Stat Ftbl; JV Trk; High Hon Roll; Sec NHS; Ntl Merit SF; Quiz Bowl; Spanish Clb; Temple Yth Grp; Garden St Distngshd Schlr $1000 Yr Each Yr At NJ Coll 86; Pol Sci.

SPANGLER, LAURA; Ramapo HS; Franklin Lakes, NJ; (Y); 103/329; Dance Clb; Drama Clb; Radio Clb; Spanish Clb; School Musical; School Play; Yrbk Stf; Powder Puff Ftbl; Hon Roll; Cert Of Merit For Spanish 85-86; Bus.

SPANIER, JONATHAN E; Mainland Regional HS; Linwood, NJ; (Y); 2/300; Drama Clb; Math Clb; Temple Yth Grp; Jazz Band; Nwsp Stf; Rep Stu Cncl; Tennis; High Hon Roll; Kiwanis Awd; VP NHS; Grdn ST Dstngshd Schlr 86; HOBY Ldrshp Semifnlst 85; Mst Outstndng Wdwnd-Band-Sxphnst 85; Drew U; Chem.

SPANN, KATHRYN; Phillipsburg Catholic HS; Lebanon, NJ; (Y); French Clb; Stage Crew; Lit Mag; VP Soph Cls; Pres Jr Cls; Pres Stu Cncl; Co-Capt Cheerleading; JV Fld Hcky; Stu Cncl Ldrshp Awd 86; Le Moyne.

SPANO, MICHAEL; Ocean Township HS; Oakhurst, NJ; (Y); 80/333; Boy Scts; Debate Tm; Ski Clb; JV Trk; Comp Sci.

SPANO, ROB; East Brunswick HS; E Brunswick, NJ; (Y); 92/600; Key Clb; Spanish Clb; SADD; Nwsp Rptr; Nwsp Sprt Ed; Yrbk Stf; Tennis; High Hon Roll; Spanish NHS; Bus Adm.

SPARACIO, CHRISTINE; Vineland HS; Vineland, NJ; (Y); 32/800; Am Leg Aux Girls St; Church Yth Grp; Cmnty Wkr; English Clb; French Clb; Girl Scts; Latin Clb; Political Wkr; Rep Frsh Cls; Hon Roll; Girls State Rep 86; Mdl Cngrss Awd Bst Legsltn 85; Law.

SPARACO, PETER; Raritan HS; Hazlet, NJ; (Y); 60/300; Intnl Clb; Ski Clb; Nwsp Sprt Ed; Rep Frsh Cls; Rep Soph Cls; Trs Jr Cls; Trs Sr Cls; Rep Stu Cncl; Im Bsbl; Var Bsktbl; Springfield Coll; Phys Educ.

SPARKES, GINA; Red Bank Catholic HS; Red Bank, NJ; (Y); U Miami; Bus.

SPARKS, CHRISTY; Lower Cape May Regional HS; Cape May, NJ; (Y); Church Yth Grp; Pres 4-H; Rep Frsh Cls; Tennis; 4-H Awd; NJ Opn Wrkng Hunter Chmp 84; 4-H Vrstlty Chmpn 85; Co-Fndr Ust Equestrn Clb NJ-HS Lvl 86; Ferrum Coll; Recreatn-Leisur.

SPARMAKER, CHRISTINA; Highland Regional HS; Blackwood, NJ; (S); 33/332; Gym; Hon Roll; Glassboro ST Coll; Gym Tchr.

SPARROCK, ANNE; Ocean Twp HS; Wayside, NJ; (Y); 76/333; Church Yth Grp; French Clb; Key Clb; SADD; Varsity Clb; Color Guard; Flag Corp; Variety Show; Swmmng; Twrlr; Spartan Schlr Awd 83-84; Vet.

SPARROW, DAVID; Plainfield HS; Plainfield, NJ; (Y); Mrchg Band; Hon Roll; Jr NHS; NHS; Opt Clb Awd; Rensselaer Math And Sci Awd 86; Sci Day 86; Elect Engrg.

SPARTA, KAREN; West Milford Township HS; Hewitt, NJ; (S); 104/350; Am Leg Aux Girls St; French Clb; Varsity Clb; Nwsp Stf; Yrbk Stf; Rep Stu Cncl; Stat Bsktbl; Var Capt Fld Hcky; Var Sftbl; Rotry Clb Awd Mst Dedctd Athl 84-85; Jrnlsm.

SPATOLA, DALE G; Middletown HS; Leonardo, NJ; (Y); Off Sr Cls; Stu Cncl; Bsktbl; Powder Puff Ftbl; Sftbl; Hon Roll.

SPATOLA, MARY ANN; Bishop ARH/St Thomas HS; Rahway, NJ; (Y); 23/277; Service Clb; Yrbk Ed-Chief; JV Socr; JV Trk; High Hon Roll; NHS; Advertising.

SPAULDING, HAZEL; Middle Township HS; Cape May C H, NJ; (Y); 5/163; Pres Church Yth Grp; Church Choir; Mrchg Band; Trs Sr Cls; Stat Bsktbl; High Hon Roll; VP NHS; Opt Clb Awd; Rotary Awd; JV Tennis; Schrlshp 86; Soc Annual Comptn Magna Cum Laude 85; Trenton ST Coll; Ed.

SPEAKMAN, GEORJEAN; Paulsboro HS; Paulsboro, NJ; (Y); 37/150; Church Yth Grp; Office Aide; Pep Clb; Cheerleading; Sftbl; Bus Admn.

SPEARS, BARBARA; Middletown HS South; Leonard, NJ; (Y); Church Yth Grp; Concert Band; Capt Cheerleading; Var Crs Cntry; Var Trk; French Hon Soc; High Hon Roll; Hon Roll; Intl Bus.

SPEARS, TINA LA SHARNE; Abraham Clark HS; Roselle, NJ; (S); 17/188; Church Yth Grp; FBLA; FHA; Office Aide; Service Clb; SADD; Chorus; Church Choir; Color Guard; Madrigals; Rutgers U; Bus Admin.

SPEED, BONNIE; Lakeland Regional HS; Ringwood, NJ; (Y); Church Yth Grp; Chorus; School Musical; School Play; Yrbk Stf; Var Socr; High Hon Roll; Hon Roll; NHS; Dance Masters Am 1st 83&84; Montreal Intl Mus Fest Gld Mdl 85; Toronto Intl Mus Fest Gld Mdl 84; Trenton ST Coll; Acctg.

SPEED, LA-SHANNA D; Vailsburg HS; Newark, NJ; (Y); Church Yth Grp; FHA; Pep Clb; Teachers Aide; Lit Mag; Hon Roll; Comp Pgrmng.

SPEED, MARGARET; Bloomfield SR HS; Bloomfld, NJ; (Y); 1/447; Math Tm; Chorus; Church Choir; Jazz Band; School Musical; Gov Hon Prg Awd; High Hon Roll; VP NHS; Prfct Atten Awd; Val; Louis Armstrong Jazz Awd 84; Rutgers Schlr 86; Princeton U; Chem Engr.

SPEED, WILLIAM C; Bloomfield SR HS; Bloomfield, NJ; (Y); 1/468; Math Tm; Science Clb; Chorus; Church Choir; School Musical; Gov Hon Prg Awd; High Hon Roll; NHS; Ntl Merit SF; Biochemst.

SPEER, KAREN; Hightstown HS; Hightstown, NJ; (Y); Church Yth Grp; Drama Clb; French Clb; Intnl Clb; Sec Ski Clb; Chorus; Drill Tm; Mrchg Band; School Musical; School Play; Shwstppr Natl Tlnt Cmptn Awds 84-86.

SPEKTOR, MARK; Solomon Schechter Day Schl; Elizabeth, NJ; (Y); Chess Clb; Yrbk Stf; Bsbl; Bsktbl; Fld Hcky; Socr; Blue Blt 84; NEDT Awds 84-85; Rutgers U; Pre Med.

SPELLER, CRYSTAL D; Union Catholic Regional HS; Newark, NJ; (Y); 18/341; Library Aide; Math Tm; Pep Clb; Service Clb; Ski Clb; SADD; High Hon Roll; Hon Roll; Jr NHS; NHS; H S 4 Yr Schlrshp 82-86; 2nd Pl Ntn Spnsh Comptn 85; 1st Pl NJ Spnsh Comptn 84; NY U ; Pre Med.

SPELLMAN, MARISA A; Immaculate Conception HS; Hasbrouck Hts, NJ; (Y); 23/86; Art Clb; Spanish Clb; Stage Crew; Yrbk Stf; Var Capt Cheerleading; JV Sftbl; Hon Roll; Pep Clb; Church Choir; Variety Show; 2nd Degree Excllnce In NJ ST Chrldng Comp 85-86; Hnrbl Mntn Chrldng Vrsty Capt 86; Fash Inst Tech; Fash Dsgn.

SPENCE, ANDREA; Pleasantville HS; Pleasantville, NJ; (Y); Computer Clb; Math Clb; Science Clb; SADD; Band; Nwsp Rptr; Yrbk Stf; Stu Cncl; Gym; Swmmng; Stockton ST Coll; Crmnl Jstc.

SPENCE, STACEY D; Pleasantville HS; Pleasantville, NJ; (S); Cit Awd; Hon Roll; Acctng.

SPENCE, ZELDA; Buend Regional HS; Newtonville, NJ; (S); 25/200; Church Yth Grp; Pep Clb; Varsity Clb; Church Choir; Variety Show; Var Crs Cntry; Stat Mgr(s); Stat Tennis; Var Trk; Hon Roll; Cape Atlantic Leag All-Star Trck 85; Howard U; Psych.

SPENCER, SLADE; Clearview Regional HS; Mantua, NJ; (Y); Cmnty Wkr; VP Band; Concert Band; Jazz Band; VP Mrchg Band; Stage Crew; Hon Roll; Prfct Atten Awd; Mrchng Band Awd For Srvc 85; Mrchng Band Mgr 85; Vp Clrvw Band & Brd Cncl; Grove City Coll; Engr.

SPENCER, TANYA; Lenape Valley Regional HS; San Francisco, CA; (Y); 30/200; FBLA; Intnl Clb; Key Clb; Latin Clb; Yrbk Stf; JV Cheerleading; Var Tennis; NHS; Pres Schlr; USC Schlrshp 86; UC Berkeley; Engr.

SPENGEL, DONNA; East Brunswick HS; E Brunswick, NJ; (Y); GAA; Ski Clb; Capt Var Bsktbl; Var L Socr; JV Sftbl; Var Trk; Vllybl; Hon Roll; NHS; Middlesex Cty Athletic Dir Assn; Female Schlr Athlete Awd 85-86; Ntl Schlr 86; Lock Haven U; Athlete Trng.

SPENGER, GREGG W; Bound Brook HS; Bound Brook, NJ; (Y); Am Leg Boys St; Aud/Vis; Cmnty Wkr; Key Clb; Latin Clb; Science Clb; Capt L Socr; L Var Tennis; Hon Roll; NHS; GA Inst Tech; Engrng.

SPERA, EMMA; Villa Victoria Acad; Trenton, NJ; (Y); Am Leg Aux Girls St; Computer Clb; Spanish Clb; Stage Crew; Sec Trs Jr Cls; Pres Sr Cls; Rep Stu Cncl; Bsktbl; Sftbl; Hon Roll; Seton Hall; Math.

SPERRY, ALIZA; Wall Twp HS; Wall Township, NJ; (Y); 31/263; Aud/Vis; Band; Concert Band; Drm Mjr(t); Jazz Band; Mrchg Band; Orch; Symp Band; Var Trk; Hon Roll; Drum Major Scholar 85; Mst Outstndg Fld Ath 84-86; Mst Outstndg Musician 84-85; National Guard; Mltry.

SPEXARTH, SUSAN; Freehold Township HS; Freehold, NJ; (Y); Stat Bsktbl; Sftbl; JV Var Trk; U Of CA San Diego; Film Stdy.

SPIDALETTO, TRISTA; Academic HS; Jersey City, NJ; (Y); Nwsp Rptr; Rep Soph Cls; Rep Jr Cls; Capt Var Crs Cntry; Var Trk; Hon Roll; Smith College Bk Awd 86.

SPIEGEL, RICHARD; Bridgewater East HS; Bridgewater, NJ; (Y); Debate Tm; German Clb; Quiz Bowl; Band; Concert Band; Drm Mjr(t); Jazz Band; Mrchg Band; School Play; Var Bsktbl; US Naval SEA Cadet Of Yr & Chf Petty Ofcr 85-86; Outstndng Band Stu 86; Rutgers U; Army Offcr.

SPIEGELMAN, JENNIFER; Wayne Hills HS; Wayne, NJ; (Y); 12/303; French Clb; GAA; Math Tm; Varsity Clb; Concert Band; Yrbk Sprt Ed; Var Fld Hcky; High Hon Roll; Hon Roll; NHS; 3rd Tm All-Lg Fld Hcky 85-86; Hnrbl Mntn All Passaic Fld Hcky 85-86; Bus.

SPIGAI, CHRISTINE; Roselle Catholic HS; Elizabeth, NJ; (S); Am Leg Aux Girls St; French Clb; Rep Jr Cls; Rep Stu Cncl; Var L Bsktbl; Mgr Crs Cntry; Var L Trk; Hon Roll; Schlrshp; Fnlst Ms Itln Amercn; Pr Grp Cnsllr; Cmnctns.

SPIGNER, CHARLENE; Hillside HS; Hillside, NJ; (Y); Civic Clb; Hosp Aide; Church Choir; Var Bsktbl; Stat Ftbl; Var Score Keeper; Cit Awd; Hon Roll; FBLA; OEA; VA ST U; Acctg.

SPILEWSKI, THOMAS; Northern Valley Reg HS; Norwood, NJ; (Y); 56/281; AFS; Var Bowling; JV Trk; Hon Roll; Penn ST; Bus.

SPILL, RORIE; East Brunswick HS; E Brunswick, NJ; (Y); Key Clb; Pep Clb; Ski Clb; Drill Tm; Nwsp Phtg; Ntl Merit Ltr; Pol Sci.

SPILLANE, ELLEN; Northern Valley Regional HS; Harrington Pk, NJ; (Y); 78/313; Church Yth Grp; Capt Pep Clb; Capt Var Cheerleading; Coach Actv; Diving; Swmmng; Hon Roll; NHS; U Of DE; Cmnctns.

SPILLANE, PATRICIA; Belleville HS; Belleville, NJ; (Y); Intnl Clb; Key Clb; Ski Clb; Orch; Sec Jr Cls; Sec Sr Cls; Hon Roll.

SPILMAN, DARIN; Bridgewater Raritan West HS; Bridgewater, NJ; (Y); German Clb; Key Clb; Letterman Clb; Ski Clb; JV Var Ftbl; Trk; Gov Hon Prg Awd; High Hon Roll; NHS; Cornell; Engrng.

SPINA, MICHAEL; Delsca Regional HS; Franklinville, NJ; (Y); Cmnty Wkr; Debate Tm; Nwsp Rptr; Nwsp Stf; Yrbk Rptr; Yrbk Stf; Hon Roll; Prof Engrng Soc Of Sthrn NJ; Drexel U; Engrng.

SPINELLI, ANTHONY; Bridgewater-Raritan HS East; Martinsville, NJ; (Y); Boy Scts; Var L Ftbl; Var L Lcrss; Var L Socr; Var L Swmmng; Hon Roll; Notre Dame; Aero Engrg.

SPINELLO, ERIN; Queen Of Peace HS; Kearny, NJ; (S); 9/250; VP PAVAS; Sec Spanish Clb; SADD; School Musical; School Play; Nwsp Rptr; Sec Sr Cls; High Hon Roll; NHS; Spanish NHS; Alt In Govrns Schl Of Dance-Trntn 85; Pres-Soc Stu Clb 85-86; Bst Spprtng Actrss In Grease 85; Cmnctns.

SPINO, MICHELE E; Sussex County Vo-Tech HS; Andover, NJ; (S); 30/175; FFA; Spanish Clb; Varsity Clb; Yrbk Stf; Rep Soph Cls; Rep Jr Cls; Rep Sr Cls; Var Bsbl; Var Cheerleading; Powder Puff Ftbl; FFA Pres, VP, Secy 3 Yrs; Grnhd Degr FFA; Schls Peer Cnslg Prog; Schl Floral Design; Flrl Dsgn.

SPINOGATTI, DANIEL; Christian Brothers Acad; Freehold, NJ; (Y); 52/220; Im Tennis; Marine Bio.

SPIRKO, CAROL; Colonia HS; Colonia, NJ; (Y); Church Yth Grp; Girl Scts; Office Aide; Ski Clb; SADD; Varsity Clb; Var Bsktbl; Var Socr; Var Sftbl; All-Dnty Sftbl 84-86; Athltc Trnng.

SPIRO, AMY; Middletown H S South; Middletown, NJ; (Y); Hosp Aide; Red Cross Aide; SADD; VP Sec Temple Yth Grp; School Musical; Nwsp Stf; Rep Jr Cls; Sec Sr Cls; Mgr(s); Mgr Tennis; Vlntr Awd 85; Law.

SPIRT, MELISSA; Livingston HS; Livingston, NJ; (Y); Debate Tm; NFL; VP Frsh Cls; Sec Sr Cls; Rep Stu Cncl; JV VP Cheerleading; Hon Roll; Jr NHS; Ntl Merit Ltr; Spanish NHS.

SPITALETTA, ALEX; Emerson HS; Union City, NJ; (Y); Var Capt Ftbl; Var Capt Trk; Var Wt Lftg; Hon Roll; Kiwanis Awd; Accntng.

SPITZBERG, ERIN; East Brunswick HS; Watchung, NJ; (Y); Art Clb; Dance Clb; Drama Clb; Key Clb; Pep Clb; Ski Clb; Temple Yth Grp; School Musical; School Play; Trk; Temple Schlrshp Israel 85; Psych.

SPITZER, MATTHEW C; Millburn SR HS; Short Hills, NJ; (Y); 5/247; Pres Temple Yth Grp; Jazz Band; Ed Nwsp Stf; Var L Socr; Var L Trk; High Hon Roll; Ntl Merit Schol; Math Tm; Band; Mrchg Band; Rutgers & Grdn ST Dstngshd Schlr 85; 2nd Tm All Conf Goalkeeper Sccr 85-86; Sccr Schlr/Athl 85-86; Bio.

SPIVEY, ANDREA; Ashbury Park HS; Neptone, NJ; (Y); 35/228; Cmnty Wkr; Hosp Aide; Color Guard; Co-Capt Var Cheerleading; Rutgers U; Sociolgy.

SPIZZUCO, DANIEL; Toms River High School East; Toms River, NJ; (Y); Stage Crew; Variety Show; Ftbl; Trk; Hon Roll; Pres Fitnss Awd; Comp Sci.

SPOONER, ERICA; Lakewood HS; Lakewood, NJ; (Y); English Clb; French Clb; Key Clb; Political Wkr; Lit Mag; Ed Lit Mag; Mgr(s); Socr; Lit Awd For Poetry 86; Intl Rltns.

SPOTO, GLENN; Montville Township HS; Montville, NJ; (Y); 73/266; Church Yth Grp; FBLA; Var Bsbl; Var Ftbl; Business Administration.

SPRAGUE, JOHN; Pinelands Regional HS; Tuckerton, NJ; (S); 5/150; Boy Scts; Church Yth Grp; Varsity Clb; Band; Concert Band; Jazz Band; Mrchg Band; School Musical; Var Bsbl; Bsktbl; Eagl Sct 83; Stu Govt VP 85-86; Al-Amer Hll Fm Band Hnrs, MVP Band 85; US Nvl Acad; Engrng.

SPRAGUE, LINDA; Nottingham HS; Wrightstown, NJ; (Y); Pres Church Yth Grp; Drama Clb; French Clb; FBLA; FNA; Hosp Aide; Office Aide; Yrbk Stf; Cheerleading; Hon Roll; 1st 3rd Pl Rbbns Swmmng 76-77; Chrldng Plq 76; Burlington Cnty CC; Ofc Sys Te.

SPRAUER, SCOTT; Ridge HS; Basking Ridge, NJ; (Y); 37/212; Church Yth Grp; Key Clb; Off Sr Cls; Var Capt Bsktbl; Im Ftbl; Im Wt Lftg; Hon Roll; NHS; Invstmnt Bnkng.

SPRECHER, KRISTA; Holy Cross HS; Mount Laurel, NJ; (Y); 14/400; German Clb; Quiz Bowl; Scholastic Bowl; Nwsp Rptr; Lit Mag; Rider Coll Frgn Lang Frnsc Trnmnt Germn Coll Band Wnnr 86; Eugene Long Coll; Engl.

SPREEN, JULIE K; Hawthorne HS; Hawthorne, NJ; (Y); JA; Pep Clb; Spanish Clb; School Musical; Yrbk Stf; VP Sr Cls; Sec Stu Cncl; Capt Var Sftbl; High Hon Roll; NHS; Acdmc All Amer Schlrshp 86; Stu Cncl Ldrshp Awd 86; U DE; Nrs.

SPRICIGO, ELIZABETH; Roselle Catholic HS; Roselle, NJ; (Y); Ski Clb; School Play; Stage Crew; Yrbk Stf; Lit Mag; High Hon Roll; Hon Roll; Natl Bus Hnr Soc 85; Mt Saint Marys Coll.

SPRIGGS, JOHN; Lower Cape May Regional HS; Cape May, NJ; (Y); 16/250; Church Yth Grp; Band; Chorus; Church Choir; Concert Band; Jazz Band; School Musical; Ed Yrbk Stf; NHS; Boy Scts; Eagle Scout 86; Summer Band; Japan Essay Cntst; Comp Sci.

SPRINGER, ADAM; Montville HS; Montville, NJ; (Y); 15/262; Computer Clb; Key Clb; VP Math Clb; Spanish Clb; Nwsp Rptr; Lit Mag; Var Trk; High Hon Roll; NHS; Mntvl Twsp 1st Aid Squd Stu 86-87; Pltcl Sci.

SPULER, ALBERT; Washington Township HS; Sewell, NJ; (Y); Church Yth Grp; Civic Clb; Spanish Clb; School Musical; Yrbk Stf; Trs Frsh Cls; High Hon Roll; NHS; Ntl Merit SF; Intl Rltns.

SPULER, STEVE; Delran HS; Delran, NJ; (Y); 8/181; Church Yth Grp; FCA; Church Choir; School Musical; Nwsp Ed-Chief; Yrbk Rptr; Bsktbl; Var L Socr; High Hon Roll; Pres NHS; Whitesls Entrps Schlrshp 86; Dstngshd H S Chrstn Stu Awd 86; Temple U; Bus Admn.

SPYCH, DAVID; Hamilton High School West; Trenton, NJ; (S); 97/380; Computer Clb; Exploring; Varsity Clb; Band; Concert Band; Mrchg Band; Symp Band; Var Golf; Hon Roll; Vrsty Glf Lttr 85; US Cllgte Wnd Bnds 84; Rochester Inst Of Tech; Rbtcs.

SQUICCIMARRA, LYNN; Spotswood HS; Spotswood, NJ; (S); 25/225; Drama Clb; Band; Concert Band; Orch; School Musical; Nwsp Stf; Lit Mag; Mgr(s); Hon Roll; Lib Arts.

SQUIER, STEVEN; Kittatinny Regional HS; Newton, NJ; (Y); 21/228; Var Capt Bsktbl; Var Capt Trk; High Hon Roll; Hon Roll; NHS.

SRAGOW, HOWARD M; Jewish Educational Ctr; East Brunswick, NJ; (Y); 6/16; Chess Clb; Computer Clb; Drama Clb; Math Tm; Temple Yth Grp; Nwsp Ed-Chief; Nwsp Rptr; Nwsp Stf; Yrbk Rptr; Yrbk Stf; Rutgers Schlr; Engnrng.

SRAY, MARK; Cumberland Regional HS; Bridgeton, NJ; (S); Trs Church Yth Grp; JCL; Ski Clb; Church Choir; Yrbk Sprt Ed; Ftbl; Tennis; High Hon Roll; Jr NHS; NHS; Math Leag Awd 83; PA ST U; Nclr Engrng.

SRIBAR, VALENTIN T; John P Stevens HS; Edison, NJ; (Y); Pres Debate Tm; Drama Clb; Pres Model UN; Ski Clb; Speech Tm; Stage Crew; Variety Show; Nwsp Phtg; Yrbk Phtg; Ntl Merit SF; Elctrcl Engrng.

SRIKONDA, SUSHEEL; Hawthorne HS; Hawthorne, NJ; (Y); 6/155; Am Leg Boys St; Scholastic Bowl; School Musical; School Play; Stage Crew; Variety Show; Trs Jr Cls; Trs Sr Cls; Stu Cncl; JV Var Socr; Grdn ST Dsdtngshd Schlr 86; Natl Engl Merit Awd 85-86; Pres Acdmc Fit Awd 85-86; Boston U; Compu Engrng.

SROKA, RONALD; Phillipsburg HS; Alpha, NJ; (Y); 90/360; Church Yth Grp; Ski Clb; JV Im Bsktbl; Rose-Hulman Inst Tech; Elec Eng.

SROLOVITZ, STEVEN R; Willingboro HS; Willingboro, NJ; (Y); 2/208; Am Leg Boys St; Key Clb; Quiz Bowl; Science Clb; Temple Yth Grp; Mgr(s); Var Tennis; Hon Roll; NHS; Ntl Merit Ltr; Ntl Hbrw Hnr Soc 82-85; U Of CA-BERKELEY; Chmstry.

STA MARIA, MARISSA; Immaculate Conception HS; Ridgefield Pk, NJ; (Y); 8/32; Rep Soph Cls; Rep Jr Cls; Rep Stu Cncl; Var Cheerleading; Vllybl; Hon Roll; Nrsng.

STABILE, MARK; Montville HS; Pine Brook, NJ; (Y); Bsbl; Ftbl; Trk; High Hon Roll; NHS; St Schlr; Garden ST Distngshd Schlrs 86; Pres Acad Fit Awd 86; West Point; Mth.

STABILE, WENDY; Paul VI HS; Newark, NJ; (Y); Key Clb; SADD; Yrbk Stf; Rep Stu Cncl; Var Cheerleading; French Hon Soc.

STADINSKI, DAVID; Clifton HS; Clifton, NJ; (Y); 58/637; Boys Clb Am; Church Yth Grp; Computer Clb; Office Aide; Science Clb; Bsbl; Bsktbl; Ftbl; Jr NHS; TAG 83-85; Engrng.

STAGLIANO, THERESA; Bishp Ahr-St Thomas Quinas HS; Perth Amboy, NJ; (Y); 5/239; Spanish Clb; Yrbk Stf; High Hon Roll; Stanley Britski Schlrshp Awd 86; Tutrd Chrstn Socl Actn Clb 86; Monmouth Coll; Bus Mgmt.

STAHL, ARTHUR; Central Jersey Christian HS; Brielle, NJ; (S); 2/17; Pres Church Yth Grp; Drama Clb; Chorus; Nwsp Stf; Yrbk Bus Mgr; High Hon Roll; Pres NHS; St Schlr; Frnch Awd; Monmouth Coll; Med.

STAHL, MATTHEW; Bordentown Regional HS; Bordentown, NJ; (Y); 4/114; Am Leg Boys St; Computer Clb; Math Clb; Math Tm; Var Im Bsktbl; Var Capt Golf; Wt Lftg; High Hon Roll; Mu Alp Tht; Ntl Merit SF; Olympcs Of Mnd Fnlst 86; Gftd & Tlntd 83-87; U NC Chpl Hl; Systms Anlyst.

STAHLBERGER, WILLIAM H; Bridgeton HS; Bridgeton, NJ; (Y); French Clb; Ski Clb; Bsbl; Bsktbl; Ftbl; Golf; Wt Lftg.

STALEY, CRIS; Riverside HS; Riverside, NJ; (Y); Drama Clb; Hosp Aide; Ski Clb; School Play; Nwsp Rptr; Yrbk Rptr; Yrbk Stf; Bsktbl; Fld Hcky; Score Keeper.

STALLINGS, MARY; Brick Twsp HS; Brick Town, NJ; (Y); 14/415; Drama Clb; Latin Clb; Yrbk Sprt Ed; Yrbk Stf; Var Bsktbl; Im Powder Puff Ftbl; Var Capt Socr; High Hon Roll; Tourn Soccer 84-85; Most Imprvd Soccer Plyr 84; MV Soccer Plyr 86; Psychbio.

STALLINGS, SHERRY; Scotch Plains-Fanwood HS; Scotch Plains, NJ; (S); Cmnty Wkr; Debate Tm; German Clb; Girl Scts; Hosp Aide; Library Aide; Model UN; Quiz Bowl; SADD; Temple Yth Grp; John Hopkins Talent Srch 83; Minorities In Engrng; Med.

STAMOS, BRUCE; Pt Pleasant Boro HS; Pt Pleasant, NJ; (S); 5/250; Key Clb; Variety Show; Stu Cncl; JV Capt Socr; High Hon Roll; NHS; Prfct Atten Awd.

STAMOS, DEIDRE; Red Bank Catholic HS; Brielle, NJ; (Y); Cmnty Wkr; Hosp Aide; Political Wkr; Trs SADD; Stu Cncl; Crs Cntry; Trk; Hon Roll; NHS; French Clb; Hgh Obrn Ldrshp Smnr 85; Pre-Coll Pgm Duke U 86; Pre-Med.

STAMP, SCOTT; Manalapan HS; Manalapan, NJ; (Y); 4/360; Hosp Aide; NHS; Ntl Merit Ltr; Garden ST Dist Schlrs; Soc Stud Awd; Rutgers Schl Engr; Indus Engr.

STAMPALIA, ANDREA M; Emerson HS; Union City, NJ; (Y); 4/277; Am Leg Aux Girls St; Church Yth Grp; Hosp Aide; Ski Clb; High Hon Roll; NHS; Spanish NHS; Hudson Cnty Chmbr Cmmrc Acdmc Exclnc Awd 86; Fclty Schlrshp Englsh 86; St Peters Coll.

STAMPES, JEFF; Summit HS; Summit, NJ; (Y); Model UN; Nwsp Stf; Lit Mag; Cmnctns.

STAMPONE, RAPHAEL; West Essex HS; Fairfield, NJ; (Y); 112/355; Boy Scts; Band; Concert Band; Mrchg Band; Var Bsbl; Eagle Sct; Yth Awd Cmnty Svc; NJ Inst Tech; Elec Engrng.

STANIVUKOVICH, GEORGIA; Clifton HS; Clifton, NJ; (Y); 75/546; Office Aide; OEA; Spanish Clb; Teachers Aide; School Play; Stat Crs Cntry; Score Keeper; Hon Roll; Jr NHS; NHS; Hnr Intrdctry Algebra 81; Insrnc Agnt.

STANKIEWICZ, MICHAEL D; Millburn HS; Short Hills, NJ; (Y); 5/250; Am Leg Boys St; Math Tm; Concert Band; Orch; Symp Band; Ed Nwsp Stf; Var L Bsktbl; High Hon Roll; Band; Chorus; Schl Mscn Yr 84; Jr Statsmn WA Smmr Schl Grad 86.

STANLEY, DEBBIE; Wall HS; Wall, NJ; (Y); Exploring; JCL; Key Clb; Latin Clb; Ski Clb; Spanish Clb; High Hon Roll; Hon Roll; NHS; Acctng.

STANLEY, LINN; Memorial HS; Cedar Grove, NJ; (Y); 16/118; Church Yth Grp; Chorus; Mrchg Band; School Musical; Yrbk Stf; Trs Stu Cncl; Var Crs Cntry; Capt Trk; High Hon Roll; NHS; Jean Stanley Merit Awd 86; Coll Wmns Clb Montclair Schlrshp 86; Boston U; Lbrl Arts.

STANLEY, TAWANNA; Plainfield HS; Piscataway, NJ; (S); Dance Clb; Rep Frsh Cls; Rep Soph Cls; Rep Jr Cls; Rep Sr Cls; Capt Socr; Var Trk; Hon Roll; 2dn Tm All Cty Trck 85; ST Trck Meet Champ 84; Ntl Awd Dancing Tap 80; Hampton U; Acctng.

STANZ, BRIAN; Washington Township HS; Sewell, NJ; (Y); Am Leg Boys St; Band; Concert Band; Drm Mjr(t); Jazz Band; Mrchg Band; Flag Corp; JV Golf; Rotary Awd.

STANZIANO, DARREN; St Peter's Prep; Jersey City, NJ; (Y); 103/206; French Clb; Im Bsktbl; Im Fld Hcky; Im Ftbl; Im Score Keeper; Hon Roll; Chem Engr.

STANZIONE, JENNIFER; Toms River HS East; Toms River, NJ; (Y); 81/585; Am Leg Aux Girls St; Intnl Clb; Key Clb; Political Wkr; Ski Clb; Cheerleading; Var Fld Hcky; Hon Roll; NHS; Sec Trs Stu Cncl; Delg Natl Conv Of Stu Cncls NJ 85; NJ Govrnrs Schl Of Pblc Issues 86; Georgetown Smmr Prog JRS 86; Pol Sci.

STAPLAR, ERICA; Neptune SR HS; Neptune, NJ; (Y); Chorus; Church Choir; Pres Frsh Cls; VP Stu Cncl; Mgr Cheerleading; Mgr(s); Twrlr; Council Award 83-84; Student Council Awd 83-84; Law.

STARACE, LISA A; River Dell Regional HS; River Edge, NJ; (Y); 16/214; Church Yth Grp; Pep Clb; Ski Clb; SADD; Varsity Clb; Chorus; Nwsp Rptr; Nwsp Sprt Ed; Rep Sr Cls; JV Cheerleading; Excllnce Lit & Wrtng 86; Fred Witte Mem 86; 3rd Pl Amnestry Intl Term Paper 86; Cornell U; Cmmnctns.

STARACE, TRISHA; Morris Knolls HS; Denville, NJ; (Y); #60 In Class; Q&S; Science Clb; Chorus; Nwsp Rptr; Lit Mag; High Hon Roll; Hon Roll.

STARK, JOSEPH; Highland Regional HS; Blackwood, NJ; (Y); Pres AFS; Drama Clb; Band; Chorus; Pep Band; School Play; Nwsp Rptr; Stu Cncl; Crs Cntry; Trk; Rutgers; Bus.

STARKEY, BETH; Steinert HS; Hamilton Square, NJ; (Y); 3/300; Concert Band; Mrchg Band; Orch; School Musical; Symp Band; Lit Mag; Stu Cncl; Hon Roll; NHS; Smmr Art Wrkshp Schlrshp-Hssn Schl Of Art 86; Advrtsng Dsgn.

STARR, CYNTHIA; Fair Lawn HS; Fair Lawn, NJ; (Y); 31/343; Pres Drama Clb; VP Temple Yth Grp; Chorus; School Musical; School Play; Stage Crew; Off Sr Cls; Hon Roll; NHS; Class Scholar; Boston U; Cmnctns.

STARR, KELLI; Egg Harbor Twp HS; Pleasantville, NJ; (S); 7/317; Ski Clb; Nwsp Rptr; JV Bsktbl; Var Crs Cntry; Var Trk; High Hon Roll; Ntl Merit Ltr; Phy Ther.

STARR, STEVEN; West Orange HS; West Orange, NJ; (Y); Am Leg Boys St; Trs Jr Cls; Rep Stu Cncl; Var Ftbl; Powder Puff Ftbl; Var Trk; Var Wrstlng; Hon Roll; Rotary Awd; Ski Clb; Carniege Mellon U; Chem.

STARUCH, TODD; Union HS; Union, NJ; (Y); 31/467; Aud/Vis; Cmnty Wkr; VP Computer Clb; Spanish Clb; Band; Stage Crew; Hon Roll; Jr NHS; NHS; Humanitarn Scholar Awd 86; Rensselaer Polytech; Elec Engr.

STASEY, BRIAN; Glen Rock HS; Glen Rock, NJ; (Y); Church Yth Grp; French Clb; JA; Office Aide; Var Crs Cntry; Im Ftbl; JV Var Trk; Hon Roll; Engrng.

STASI, EVAMARIE; Roselle Catholic HS; Elizabeth, NJ; (Y); Tennis; Hon Roll; Spanish NHS; Profcncy-Spnsh Awd 84-85.

STASKEWICZ, SHERIDAN; Newton HS; Andover, NJ; (S); 9/200; Latin Clb; Madrigals; Pres Jr Cls; Rep Stu Cncl; Var Cheerleading; Gov Hon Prg Awd; High Hon Roll; NHS; Chorus; Amer Legn Awd 83-84; Govs Schl 85-86; Yng Ctzn Awd 85-86; Rutgers; Law.

STAUFENBERG, LYNN E; Mater Dei HS; Middletown, NJ; (Y); 4/167; French Clb; Keywanettes; Stage Crew; Nwsp Stf; Lit Mag; Cheerleading; High Hon Roll; NHS; Pres Schlr; Voice Dem Awd; Hnrb Mntn NJ Distngshd Schlrs Pgm 85; Summa Cum Laude Awd Natl Latine Exam 84; Quill & Scroll 86; Bervy Coll; Cmmnctns.

STAUFFER, RICKY; Vineland HS; Vineland, NJ; (Y); Cmnty Wkr; Radio Clb; Y-Teens; Band; Concert Band; Jazz Band; Mrchg Band; Stage Crew; Rep Soph Cls; Rep Stu Cncl; Penn ST; Elec Engr.

STEAD, KARA; North Brunswick Township HS; N Brunswick, NJ; (Y); 51/300; French Clb; Teachers Aide; Stu Cncl; Var Capt Tennis; JV Trk; Hon Roll; Pol Sci.

STEADMAN, ROBERT F; Montclair HS; Upper Montclair, NJ; (Y); 5/438; FCA; Latin Clb; Lit Mag; Stu Cncl; Var Capt Swmmng; Trk; Hon Roll; NHS; Ntl Merit SF; Cosmopolitan Clb Awd 85.

STEBNER, LAURA; Bishop George Ahr HS; Rahway, NJ; (Y); 50/240; Church Yth Grp; Band; Concert Band; VP Mrchg Band; Pep Band; School Musical; Symp Band; High Hon Roll; JP Sousa Awd; Sectn Lr Music Awds 85-86; Excllnc In Music; Siemper Fidelis Band Awd; Trenton ST Coll; Early Chldhd.

STEED, DEIRDRE; St John Vianney HS; Colts Neck, NJ; (Y); 18/293; Intnl Clb; Teachers Aide; Yrbk Stf; Bsktbl; Sftbl; High Hon Roll; Hon Roll; NHS; Prfct Atten Awd; Gold White Awd 85-86.

STEELE, BRAD; Johnson Regional HS; Clark, NJ; (Y); 22/200; JV Var Bsbl; JV Var Bsktbl; Im Socr; High Hon Roll; Hon Roll; St Sci Day Tm 86; Engrg.

STEELE, KIM; Clifford J Scott HS; E Orange, NJ; (Y); 31/257; Aud/Vis; Camera Clb; Camp Fr Inc; Church Yth Grp; Computer Clb; Dance Clb; Drama Clb; English Clb; Exploring; French Clb; Merit Achvt Awd Jrsy Cty ST Coll 84-86; Trenton ST Coll; Law.

STEELE, LINDA; Lower Cape May Regional HS; N Cape May, NJ; (Y); Mgr(s); Hon Roll; Prfct Atten Awd; Compu.

STEERE, CHRISTINA; Glassboro HS; Glassboro, NJ; (Y); Church Yth Grp; Office Aide; Science Clb; Teachers Aide; Band; Concert Band; Mrchg Band; JV Fld Hcky; Var Trk; Hon Roll; Med.

STEFAN, ANTON CHRISTOPHER; Jackson Memorial HS; Jackson, NJ; (Y); 72/405; Boy Scts; Cmnty Wkr; Ski Clb; Teachers Aide; Jazz Band; Mrchg Band; School Musical; Rep Stu Cncl; High Hon Roll; Founded Own Rock Bnd Nmd Alliance; Art Hon Soc Indctn Cerem Pianist; Music.

STEFANCHIK, JOHN A; Princeton HS; Princeton, NJ; (Y); Am Leg Boys St; Church Yth Grp; Jazz Band; Orch; JV Lcrss; Var Socr; Cmnty Wkr; Pre-Med.

STEFANICS, ROBERT AUGUST; Hamilton HS West; Trenton, NJ; (Y); Boy Scts; JV Var Bsktbl.

STEFANSKI, SABINA A; Bridgewater-Raritan West HS; Bridgewater, NJ; (Y); German Clb; Office Aide; Science Clb; Ski Clb; Varsity Clb; Nwsp Stf; Yrbk Stf; Rep Frsh Cls; Rep Soph Cls; Stat Lcrss; Pres Acad Ftnss Awd 86; Acad Excllnc Awd 86; Ortho Phrmctcl Co Sci Schlrshp Awd 86; Cornell U; Bio.

STEGER JR, THOMAS R; Wall Township HS; Wall, NJ; (S); 7/256; Aud/Vis; Chess Clb; Service Clb; Spanish Clb; Yrbk Stf; High Hon Roll; Tutorial Soc 85; Shore Shop Stu Crftsmns Fair-1st Pl-Tech Drwg 84; Kiwanis Hnr Soc 85; U Of FL; Mech Engrng.

STEGLITZ, BRIAN D; Columbia HS; South Orange, NJ; (Y); Am Leg Boys St; Cmnty Wkr; Var L Socr; Var L Tennis; Gov Hon Prg Awd; Ntl Merit Ltr; St Schlr; Aaron Selenfriend Memrl Awrd 86; Cmnty Svc Awrd 86; Yale U.

STEIGER, ANDREW; Glassboro HS; Glassboro, NJ; (Y); Art Clb; Exploring; French Clb; Q&S; Chorus; Orch; School Musical; School Play; Nwsp Stf; Lit Mag; Artist.

STEIN, JENNIFER ANN; Toms River High School East; Toms River, NJ; (Y); 3/585; FBLA; Intnl Clb; Quiz Bowl; Trs Spanish Clb; Off Jr Cls; Stu Cncl; Powder Puff Ftbl; JV Tennis; High Hon Roll; NHS; Amer Assn U Wmn 84-86; Acad Lttr 83-86; Cmmnctns.

STEIN, VALARIE A; Belvidere HS; Phillipsburg, NJ; (Y); #91 In Class; Var Letterman Clb; Varsity Clb; JV Bsktbl; Var Mgr(s); Var Score Keeper; Var Sftbl; Im Vllybl; Hon Roll; Teen Arts Prog 82-85; Taylor Bus; Exec Sec.

STEINBAUM, SUZANNE; Livingston HS; Livingston, NJ; (Y); 48/500; Dance Clb; Debate Tm; Science Clb; Varsity Clb; Sec Jr Cls; Off Sr Cls; JV Var Cheerleading; Powder Puff Ftbl; NHS; Spanish NHS; Stephen Gillock Sprt And Dedctn Awd 86; Clss 79 Spirt Awd 86; Tufts U; Pre Med.

STEINBERG, DAVID; East Brunswick HS; E Brunswick, NJ; (Y); Key Clb; Rep Frsh Cls; Stu Cncl; Hon Roll; NHS; Engineering.

STEINER, ANITA; John P Stevens HS; Edison, NJ; (Y); Computer Clb; French Clb; Math Clb; Hon Roll; NHS; Ntl Merit Ltr; Sci.

STEINER, ISABELLE; Paul VI Regional HS; Cedar Grove, NJ; (Y); 23/129; French Clb; Pres Sec Key Clb; Library Aide; Service Clb; Chorus; School Musical; School Play; Nwsp Stf; Yrbk Stf; 4-H Awd; Trinity Coll Of VT.

STEINHAUER, MARY; Bridgeton HS; Newport, NJ; (Y); 1/217; Trs Church Yth Grp; Nwsp Rptr; Yrbk Bus Mgr; Var Capt Fld Hcky; Var Capt Sftbl; Bausch & Lomb Sci Awd; High Hon Roll; Pres NHS; St Schlr; Val; Rensselar Polytchnc Inst Mdl For Math & Sci 85; NJ Distgshd Schlr 85; Century III Ldrshp Awd 85; Glassboro ST Coll; Acctng.

STELEVICH, JENNIFER GERMAINE; Monsignor Donovan HS; Jackson, NJ; (Y); 50/214; Drama Clb; SADD; Thesps; School Musical; School Play; Nwsp Ed-Chief; Yrbk Rptr; Lit Mag; High Hon Roll; NHS; Faculty Staff Schrlshp 86; Montclair ST Coll; Spch.

STELTZER, JODI; Parsippany Hills HS; Parsippany, NJ; (Y); Varsity Clb; Symp Band; Trs Sr Cls; Stu Cncl; Coach Actv; Var Fld Hcky; Powder Puff Ftbl; JV Sftbl; Stat Wrstlng; Hugh O Brien Yth Ldrshp Nomnee 84; Mst Imprvd Plyr Fld Hcky 84; Televsn.

STEMMER, TAMMY LYNN; Rancocas Valley Regional HS; Mount Holly, NJ; (Y); 30/260; Hosp Aide; Trs Key Clb; Ski Clb; Yrbk Stf; Rep Soph Cls; Rep Jr Cls; Sec Sr Cls; Trs Stu Cncl; Var Bsktbl; Var Sftbl; Mt Holly Wmns Lg Scholar 86; Stu Cncl Scholar 86; Mip Sftbl 86; Rutgers Schl Phrmcy; Phrmcy.

STEPHANS, LORI; Belvidere HS; Hope, NJ; (Y); 26/118; French Clb; GAA; Ski Clb; Varsity Clb; Yrbk Stf; Bowling; Fld Hcky; Lcrss; JV Var Sftbl; Girls ST Alternate 85; E Stroudsburg U; Bio Chem.

STEPHENS, LOU; Westfield HS; Westfield, NJ; (Y); 75/513; Crs Cntry; Trk.

STEPHENSON, CAREN; Union Catholic Regional HS; Fanwood, NJ; (Y); 49/450; Church Yth Grp; GAA; Varsity Clb; Socr; St Josephs U; Humanities.

STEPHENSON, ELLEN; Mc Corristin Catholic HS; Trenton, NJ; (Y); Church Yth Grp; Drama Clb; GAA; Chorus; School Musical; School Play; Stage Crew; Yrbk Stf; Bsktbl.

STEPHENSON, LAUREL; Hunterdon Central HS; Flemington, NJ; (Y); 35/548; Chorus; Church Choir; Juniata Coll; Law.

STEPHENSON, MICHAEL C; Lenape HS; Medford, NJ; (Y); 10/450; Am Leg Boys St; SADD; Varsity Clb; Variety Show; Var L Socr; Var Capt Swmmng; Var L Trk; High Hon Roll; Hon Roll; VP NHS; Senate Maj Ldr NJ Boys St 86; VP Natl Hnrs Soc 86; Outstndg Plyr Awd Rutgers Sccr Cmp 85; Engr.

STEPHENSON, OMAR; Eastside HS; Paterson, NJ; (Y); High Hon Roll; Hon Roll; Bus Adm.

STEPIKURA, TRACY ANN; Manalapan HS; Englishtown, NJ; (Y); 22/431; Church Yth Grp; 4-H; Girl Scts; Science Clb; Nwsp Rptr; Im Socr; NHS; Brnz Cngrssnl Awd 86; Grl Sct Gld Awd 84; Psych.

STERLING, CRAIG; Freehold Township HS; Freehold, NJ; (Y); 42/382; VP Computer Clb; Exploring; Math Tm; Ski Clb; VP Temple Yth Grp; Trk; NHS; Freehold Twp Lttl Leag Mgr; Accnt.

STERLING JR, FRANCIS X; Morris Knolls HS; Dover, NJ; (Y); Am Leg Boys St; Varsity Clb; Var Stat Bsbl; Var Ftbl; Var Wt Lftg; Merit Hnr Roll, 2nd Tm All Co Bsbl 85-86; Schl Rec Hits 86; MIP Bsbl Var 86; UNC Chapel Hill; Pro-Bsbl.

STERLING, LLOYD; Vineland HS; Vineland, NJ; (Y); NFL; Spanish Clb; Hon Roll; Prfct Atten Awd; Spanish NHS; Mech Engrng.

STERLING, RENEE; Plainfield HS; Plainfield, NJ; (S); 30/539; Office Aide; Chorus; Variety Show; VP Frsh Cls; VP Soph Cls; VP Jr Cls; VP Sr Cls; Rep Stu Cncl; Stat Bsktbl; Mgr(s); Blck Achvrs Lnkg Pgm 85-86; Stockton ST Coll; Bus Admn.

STERN, ALETHEA M; Lodi HS; Lodi, NJ; (Y); Varsity Clb; Chorus; Capt Color Guard; Madrigals; Trk.

STERN, JOSHUA; Cherry Hill H S West; Cherry Hill, NJ; (Y); 19/345; Am Leg Boys St; Nwsp Stf; Rep Frsh Cls; Pres Soph Cls; Rep Jr Cls; Var Socr; Hon Roll; NHS; Chry Hll HS W Hm Schl Assoc Awd 85-86; Psychlgy.

STERN, LAWRENCE; Madison Central HS; Old Bridge, NJ; (S); 27/378; Math Tm; Spanish Clb; Temple Yth Grp; Chorus; Concert Band; Mrchg Band; School Musical; Hon Roll; NHS; Spanish NHS; Mth.

STEVENS, BRIAN; Middletown High School South; Red Bank, NJ; (Y); Ski Clb; Varsity Clb; Yrbk Stf; JV Socr; Var L Tennis; Im Vllybl; Hon Roll; MVP Of Tnns Tm 86; Comp Sci.

STEVENS, CHRISTY A; Haddonfield Memorial HS; Haddonfield, NJ; (S); Latin Clb; Acpl Chr; Concert Band; Mrchg Band; Yrbk Stf; Lit Mag; NHS; Ntl Merit Ltr; St Schlr; Knndy Hosp Schlrs Pgm 85-86; Oglethorpe U; Opthmlgst.

STEVENS, MARY ANN; Wall Twp HS; Manasquan Park, NJ; (S); 13/289; German Clb; Key Clb; Ski Clb; Concert Band; Mrchg Band; Rep Stu Cncl; Var Trk; High Hon Roll; Natl Eng Merit Awd 85-86.

STEVENS, SCOTT; Hamilton HS North; Mercerville, NJ; (Y); Church Yth Grp; Cit Awd; Hon Roll; NJ Boatmns Sfty Crse Awd 81; Amer Leg Awd, Awd Merit Outstndng Schlrshp Awd 80; Rutgers; Acctnt.

STEVENSON, CHARLOTTE; Teaneck HS; Teaneck, NJ; (Y); French Clb; Variety Show; Ed Nwsp Stf; Yrbk Stf; Cit Awd; Hon Roll; NHS; Talent America Awd 84; Natl Fdrtn Music 84; Comp Sci.

STEVENSON, JOE ANTHONY; Camden HS; Camden, NJ; (S); Church Yth Grp; VICA; JV Bowling; JV Mgr(s); JV Socr; Hon Roll; Prfct Atten Awd; Rutgers U; Elect Engr.

STEVENSON, JOSEPH P; Cedar Ridge HS; S Amboy, NJ; (Y); 35/388; Sec Computer Clb; Hon Roll; NHS; Spanish NHS; St Schlr; Chem Yth Schlrs Pgm Lebnon Vly Coll 85; Mddlsx Cnty Coll Prjct Gftd 85; Chmcl Engrng.

STEWARD, KAREN; Manchester Township HS; Toms River, NJ; (S); 61/198; Hosp Aide; Spanish Clb; Capt Color Guard; Capt Flag Corp; School Play; Stage Crew; Variety Show; Nwsp Rptr; Nwsp Stf; Var Socr; Geogrphcl Studs Awd 82-83; Elon Coll; Mass Cmmnctns.

STEWART, ALLAN; Queen Of Peace HS; North Arlington, NJ; (S); 2/234; Boy Scts; Church Yth Grp; Cmnty Wkr; Computer Clb; Drama Clb; French Clb; Model UN; Science Clb; Service Clb; Ski Clb; Johns Hopkins U; Cardio Srgry.

STEWART, EDW; Washington Township HS; Sewell, NJ; (Y); Var JV Ftbl; Im Wt Lftg.

STEWART, HEATHER; Red Bank Regional HS; Shrewsbury, NJ; (Y); 5/223; Scholastic Bowl; Orch; Ed Yrbk Stf; Var Lcrss; JV Var Socr; Hon Roll; Kiwanis Awd; Lion Awd; Pres NHS; Spanish NHS; Grdn ST Shlr 85; Smith Col.

STEWART, JANUARY; Holy Spirit HS; Oceanville, NJ; (Y); 69/386; Hon Roll; Ntl Art Hnr Soc 85; Grls Crw Tm Rwng 84; Philadelphia Coll; Stdy Grphic.

STEWART, JEFFREY A; Moorstown HS; Moorestown, NJ; (Y); Am Leg Boys St; Aud/Vis; Var Debate Tm; Off JA; Latin Clb; Var Speech Tm; School Play; Stage Crew; Yrbk Bus Mgr; Var Trk; Otstndng Spkr Princeton U Mdl Cngrs 85; Spkr Awd Novic Debater Ridgewood 85; Pole Vltng Awd 86.

STEWART, JOHN; Salem HS; Salem, NJ; (Y); 1/150; Am Leg Boys St; Math Clb; Spanish Clb; Trs Jr Cls; Trs Sr Cls; Rep Stu Cncl; Var Bsbl; Var Ftbl; Gov Hon Prg Awd; High Hon Roll; Engrng.

STEWART, KATHLEEN; Clearview Regional HS; Mantua, NJ; (Y); 42/146; Pres DECA; Rep Frsh Cls; Sec Soph Cls; Sec Jr Cls; Sec Sr Cls; Rep Stu Cncl; JV Var Bsktbl; Var Cheerleading; JV Var Sftbl; Hnrbl Mntn ST DECA 86.

STEWART, KATHY; Paulsboro HS; Paulsboro, NJ; (Y); 43/180; Trs VICA; Bsktbl; Mgr Fld Hcky; Gym; Var Mgr(s); Trk; Badge Gym Cert 84-85; Vrsty Ltrs & Cert Trck & Hcky 85-86; Phtgrphy.

STEWART, KELLY; Saint James HS; Woodstown, NJ; (Y); 27/75; Hosp Aide; Temple Yth Grp; School Musical; School Play; Sec Stu Cncl; Var Score Keeper; JV Sftbl; Var Tennis; Hon Roll; Sci Achvmnt Awd Chem 85-86; Law.

STEWART, KRISSY; Ocean Twp HS; Ocean, NJ; (Y); 166/332; Pres Church Yth Grp; Drama Clb; Office Aide; Ski Clb; SADD; School Play; Variety Show; Cheerleading; Sftbl; American U; Crimnlgy.

STEWART, MARK; Dwight Morrow HS; Englewood, NJ; (Y); Boy Scts; Socr; Wrstlng; Hon Roll; Prfct Atten Awd; Stevens Tech; Math.

STEWART, MICHELE; Carteret HS; Carteret, NJ; (Y); 94/198; Drama Clb; Latin Clb; Ski Clb; Spanish Clb; Capt Color Guard; Concert Band; Mrchg Band; Stage Crew; Rep Stu Cncl; Var Trk.

STEWART, PAMELA; Camden HS; Camden, NJ; (Y); Church Yth Grp; Key Clb; Variety Show; Yrbk Stf; Pres Frsh Cls; Pres Soph Cls; Pres Jr Cls; Cheerleading; Hon Roll; Prfct Atten Awd; Acdmc Achvmnt Awd 86; Rl Mdl Awd Blck Hstry 86; Mss Blck Teenage Wrld Of Cmdn Cnty 86; Pltcn.

STGERARD, EVANS; Elizabeth HS; Elizabeth, NJ; (Y); Band; Color Guard; Drm & Bgl; Flag Corp; Mrchg Band; Capt Twrlr; Med.

STIBITZ, DAVID M; Southern Regional HS; Manahawkin, NJ; (Y); 13/350; German Clb; Stat Bsbl; High Hon Roll; Hon Roll; NHS; St Schlr; Rutgers U; Comp Engr.

STIBITZ, RUSS; Southern Regional HS; Manahawkin, NJ; (Y); 70/385; Chess Clb; Church Yth Grp; French Clb; Model UN; Church Choir; Im Crs Cntry; JV Trk; Hon Roll; NHS; Rutgers U; Biblcl Stud.

STILE, GEMMA; Passaic Valley HS; Totowa, NJ; (Y); Church Yth Grp; Drama Clb; Office Aide; Acpl Chr; Chorus; Church Choir; School Musical; School Play; Lit Mag; Mgr(s); Passaic Cnty; Sectrl.

STILES, MICHAELE; Linden HS; Linden, NJ; (Y); Church Yth Grp; FBLA; Girl Scts; Hosp Aide; Key Clb; Hon Roll; Minority Engrng 84; Bus Mgmt.

STILL, YOLANDA; Overbrook Regional SR HS; Lindenwold, NJ; (Y); 8/400; Spanish Clb; Teachers Aide; Bsktbl; Fld Hcky; Trk; High Hon Roll; Hon Roll; Jr NHS; Rutgers U; Math.

STIRITZ, SARAH; Bloomfield HS; Bloomfield, NJ; (Y); 32/440; Camera Clb; Cmnty Wkr; French Clb; Chorus; French Hon Soc; High Hon Roll; Hon Roll; NHS; Elem Ed.

STISO, MICHELE; Colonia HS; Colonia, NJ; (Y); Key Clb; Office Aide; Rep Soph Cls; Rep Stu Cncl; Mgr(s); Var Swmmng; High Hon Roll; Hon Roll.

STITES, CHERYL; Bridgeton HS; Bridgeton, NJ; (Y); Aud/Vis; French Clb; Office Aide; Ski Clb; Spanish Clb; Varsity Clb; Capt Cheerleading; Stat Score Keeper; Hon Roll; Accntng.

STIZZA, LISA; Toms River HS North; Toms River, NJ; (Y); French Clb; Stage Crew; High Hon Roll.

STOCKER, GERARD; Toms River East HS; Toms River, NJ; (Y); 49/479; Exploring; Intnl Clb; Spanish Clb; Socr; Hon Roll; Ntl Merit SF; Carnegie-Mellon U; Bus.

STOCKER, KAREN; Rancocas Valle Regional HS; Mount Holly, NJ; (Y); Church Yth Grp; Pres Key Clb; Science Clb; Yrbk Stf; Var Mgr(s); Var Score Keeper; High Hon Roll; NHS; Psych.

STOECKER, MICHAEL; North Bergen HS; Guttenberg, NJ; (Y); Drama Clb; PAVAS; School Play; Variety Show; Hon Roll; NY U; Actor.

STOERR, HEIDI; Midland Park HS; Ho-Ho-Kus, NJ; (S); 53/137; Camera Clb; DECA; Pep Clb; Ski Clb; Varsity Clb; JV Bsktbl; Capt Var Tennis; JV Trk; Hon Roll; Bus.

STOERRLE, MARGIE; Sacred Heart HS; Vineland, NJ; (Y); French Clb; School Play; Sec Frsh Cls; Rep Soph Cls; Jr Cls; Sec Stu Cncl; Hnr Frshmn Treas Stu Cncl 83-4; Finance.

STOJAKOVIC, LUCY; Mary Help Of Christians Acad; Haledon, NJ; (S); 3/68; Computer Clb; Latin Clb; Service Clb; Stage Crew; High Hon Roll; Hon Roll; NHS; Comp Awd 84-85; Chem Awd 84-85; Analysis 84-85; Montclair ST Coll; Accntng.

STOJALOWSKY, LASZLO J; St Josephs Preparatory Seminar HS; Trenton, NJ; (S); 1/16; Boy Scts; Hosp Aide; Pres Spanish Clb; Yrbk Stf; Lit Mag; NHS; Spanish NHS; Nwsp Stf; St Josephs Mdl Hghst Cls Avg 83-85; VP Of Bread For The Wrld Clb 84-85; Poli Sci.

STOKES, BERNADETTE; Hillside HS; Hillside, NJ; (Y); Church Yth Grp; ROTC; Soph Cls; Cheerleading; Sftbl; Penn ST; Phy Thrpy.

STOKES JR, ROBERT J; Bergen Catholic HS; River Vale, NJ; (Y); 24/257; Ski Clb; Stage Crew; Nwsp Rptr; Stu Cncl; Var L Ftbl; Var L Trk; French Hon Soc; High Hon Roll; Ntl Merit SF; Grdn ST Dstngshd Schlr 86.

STOLLER, SCOTT; Paramus HS; Paramus, NJ; (Y); 1/343; Am Leg Boys St; Chess Clb; Computer Clb; Pres German Clb; Math Clb; Quiz Bowl; Band; Concert Band; Mrchg Band; Lit Mag; Princeton U; Physcs.

STOLTE, SUSAN; Bridgewater-Rariton HS East; Bridgewater, NJ; (Y); Church Yth Grp; French Clb; Girl Scts; Science Clb; Church Choir; Nwsp Stf; Lit Mag; Hon Roll; VP NHS; Pres Schlr; Awd Outstndng Achvt Eng 86; Garden ST Distngshd Schlr 86; Cert Achvt Socl Stud 86; U Of PA; Eng.

STOLZ, DANIEL; Jackson Memorial HS; Jackson, NJ; (S); 4/411; Camp Fr Inc; Church Yth Grp; FBLA; Pres Math Clb; Science Clb; SADD; Nwsp Stf; High Hon Roll; NHS; State Parlimentarian-NJ Chptr FBLA 86-87; Comps.

STOMBAUGH, MELISSA; East Brunswick HS; E Brunswick, NJ; (Y); Teachers Aide; Chorus; School Musical; School Play; Gym; JV Mgr(s); JV Score Keeper; Hon Roll; Hme Econ Schlrshp 86; Gym Awds 81-83; Kean Coll; Educ.

STONE, JONATHAN; Hackettstown HS; Allamuchy, NJ; (S); 44/236; Boy Scts; Chess Clb; Band; Concert Band; Jazz Band; Mrchg Band; Hon Roll; NHS.

STONE, JONATHAN; Manalapon HS; Englishtown, NJ; (Y); Computer Clb; Math Tm; Science Clb; Ski Clb; Bausch & Lomb Sci Awd; NHS; Trs Soph Cls; Brown U; Research.

STONE, KEVIN; Red Bank Catholic HS; Freehold, NJ; (Y); Cmnty Wkr; Letterman Clb; SADD; Varsity Clb; JV Var Ftbl; JV Var Trk; Hon Roll; NHS; Middl ST Evltn 85; Schlr Athlt Awd 86; Engrg.

STONE, KIMBERLY; Franklin HS; Somerset, NJ; (Y); Pres Intnl Clb; Key Clb; Office Aide; VP Varsity Clb; Color Guard; Nwsp Rptr; Rep Jr Cls; Co-Capt Cheerleading; Trk; Hon Roll; Hmcmng Princess 83 & 85; Hnrb Mntn NJ Press Wmns Assn 86.

STONEBRAKER, DAVE; Christian Brothers Acad; Bricktown, NJ; (Y); Cmnty Wkr; Trs Stu Cncl; Var Capt Crs Cntry; Var Trk; Psych.

STONER, JENNIFER; Salem HS; Salem, NJ; (Y); 13/133; Am Leg Aux Girls St; Teachers Aide; School Play; Cheerleading; Hon Roll; NHS; Rtry Stu Of Mnth 86; West Chester U; Erly Chldhd Dev.

STOOR, SHELLIE; Holy Cross HS; Willingboro, NJ; (Y); Hosp Aide; JA; Library Aide; Office Aide; Mrchg Band; Twrlr; High Hon Roll; Hon Roll; Accntng.

STORCH, AMI; Scotch Plains-Fanwood HS; Westfield, NJ; (Y); Dance Clb; French Clb; Quiz Bowl; Chorus; French Hon Soc; High Hon Roll; Hon Roll; Rep Frsh Cls; Med.

STORCH, SUSAN; Manalapan HS; Manalapan, NJ; (Y); 53/383; Drama Clb; Temple Yth Grp; Pres Sec Thesps; VP Chorus; Drill Tm; Mrchg Band; School Musical; School Play; Swing Chorus; NHS; Chrs Awd 83; Chrs Ltr 84; 3rd & 4th Yr Music Awds 85-86; Douglass Coll; Psych.

STORCK, COLLEEN; Paterson Catholic Regional HS; Paterson, NJ; (Y); 7/122; Church Yth Grp; Cmnty Wkr; Church Choir; Nwsp Stf; Yrbk Stf; Rep Stu Cncl; High Hon Roll; Sec NHS; Office Aide; K Gibbs Ldrshp Awd 85-86; 2nd Pl Poetry Cntst Elks Clb 85-86; Hon Mntn Chrstphrs Wrtng Cntst 85-86; St Johns U; Statistics.

STRACCO, KERRI; Lenape Valley Regional HS; Stanhope, NJ; (Y); Am Leg Aux Girls St; Key Clb; VP Frsh Cls; VP Soph Cls; VP Jr Cls; Rep Stu Cncl; Stat Crs Cntry; Powder Puff Ftbl; Stat Trk; French Hon Soc; Bus Admn.

STRACHAN, SHARON; Lodi HS; Lodi, NJ; (Y); 25/143; Art Clb; French Clb; Key Clb; Leo Clb; Office Aide; Pep Clb; Yrbk Stf; Hon Roll; NHS; Fashn Dsgnr.

STRACK, ANN; Villa Victoria Acad; Titusville, NJ; (Y); Art Clb; Church Yth Grp; Hosp Aide; Pep Clb; Chorus; School Musical; School Play; Lit Mag; VP Frsh Cls; Chrmn Stu Cncl; Typg Awd 85; Engl, Hstry Awds 86; Fashion Inst/Tech; Fash Mdsg.

STRAHLE, ROBERT E; West Windsor-Plainsboro HS; Robbinsville, NJ; (Y); 59/240; Am Leg Boys St; Church Yth Grp; French Clb; Ski Clb; Varsity Clb; Rep Stu Cncl; Var L Socr; Var L Swmmng; Hon Roll; NHS; All Cnty Area ST 1st Tm Swmmng Hon; VA Tech; Aerospc Engrng.

STRALEY JR, JOHN G; Matawan Regional HS; Matawan, NJ; (Y); 25/360; Church Yth Grp; Computer Clb; Math Clb; Math Tm; Ski Clb; Stu Cncl; Crs Cntry; Rutgers U.

STRAMAGLIA, CHRISTOPHER; Saddle River Day Schl; Cliffside Park, NJ; (Y); Art Clb; Drama Clb; Key Clb; Ski Clb; Teachers Aide; School Play; Yrbk Phtg; Yrbk Stf; Bsbl; Socr; MVP Bsbl 84; MIP Sccr 84; Radford U; Art.

STRANG, CHRISTOPHER; Manchester HS; Toms River, NJ; (Y); 8/175; Am Leg Boys St; French Clb; Math Clb; French Hon Soc; Gov Hon Prg Awd; High Hon Roll; Hon Roll; JETS Awd; Jr NHS; NHS; Natl Ftns Awd 86; U Of S FL; Chem Engr.

STRANG, SCOTT; Buena Regional HS; Newfield, NJ; (S); Church Yth Grp; Debate Tm; Math Tm; Varsity Clb; Nwsp Stf; Yrbk Ed-Chief; Rep Frsh Cls; Pres Soph Cls; Rep Jr Cls; Var Bsktbl; Mech Engrng.

STRANO, STEPHEN; Highland Regional HS; Blackwood, NJ; (S); 3/332; Sec Chess Clb; Latin Clb; Trs Science Clb; Service Clb; Stu Cncl; Bowling; Var Tennis; Hon Roll; NHS; Stu Actvties Cert 85; Engrng.

STRATEN, THOMAS; Hoboken HS; Hoboken, NJ; (Y); Boy Scts; Camera Clb; Yrbk Phtg; Yrbk Stf; Var Bowling; Swmmng; JV Tennis; Hon Roll.

STRATTON, TRINA; Pleasantville HS; Pleasantville, NJ; (S); Art Clb; Math Clb; Varsity Clb; Stage Crew; Nwsp Stf; Var Capt Bsktbl; Var Sftbl; Var L Trk; Wt Lftg; NHS; MVP Bsktbl; Cmmnctns.

STRAUB, KEN; Arthur P Schalick HS; Elmer, NJ; (Y); Scrt Svc Man.

STRAUCH, KAREN D; Colonia HS; Colonia, NJ; (Y); Hon Roll; Seled U; Bus Adm.

STRAUP, RENEE; Overbrook Reg SR HS; Lindenwold, NJ; (Y); French Clb; FBLA; Letterman Clb; Varsity Clb; Mgr(s); JV Socr; Mgr Stat Trk; French Hon Soc; High Hon Roll; Hon Roll; Med.

STRAUSS, JON; West Orange HS; W Orange, NJ; (Y); 123/177; Ski Clb; Chorus; Im Bsbl; Capt JV Ftbl; Var Wt Lftg; Rider Coll; Pre-Med.

STRAUT, THERESA; Waldwick HS; Waldwick, NJ; (Y); Church Yth Grp; Computer Clb; Drama Clb; French Clb; Intnl Clb; Math Tm; Quiz Bowl; Varsity Clb; School Musical; School Play; Pres Acdmc Ftns Awd 86; Grdn ST Dstngshd Schlr 85; SUNY Bnghmtn.

STRAVALACCI, PETER; Franklin HS; Somerset, NJ; (Y); Math Clb; Math Tm; Office Aide; Teachers Aide; JV Capt Bsbl; Im Lcrss; Im Tennis; Im Vllybl; Hon Roll; Carpenter.

STRAWLEY, KARYN; Wildwood Catholic HS; Cape May, NJ; (Y); Spanish Clb; Stage Crew; Yrbk Stf; Stat Bsbl; Var Stat Bsktbl; Var Mgr(s); JV Tennis; Hon Roll; Sec NHS; Spanish NHS; Int Dsgn.

STREELMAN, JODY; Union HS; Union, NJ; (Y); French Clb; Hosp Aide; Key Clb; Yrbk Stf; Im Fld Hcky; Mgr(s); Hon Roll; Hotl/Bus Mgmt.

STREHLE, MELISSA; Jackson Memorial HS; Jackson, NJ; (Y); 182/405; Powder Puff Ftbl; Hon Roll.

STREKER, CLIFF; Parsippany HS; Lake Hiawatha, NJ; (Y); Hon Roll; Comp Sci.

STRELEC, VICTORIA G; Bayley-Ellard Regnl Catholic HS; Morristown, NJ; (Y); Church Yth Grp; Capt Cheerleading; Powder Puff Ftbl; Physcl Educ.

STRICKER, SHERRY I; Cherry Hill HS East; Cherry Hill, NJ; (Y); 85/700; Band; Jazz Band; Mrchg Band; School Musical; Var Capt Sftbl; Hon Roll; Concert Band; Orch; Symp Band; JV Bsktbl; Serv Awd And Crimson Shld 83-86; SR Hall Of Fame 86; Cum Laude 86; Douglass Clg; Bus.

STRICKLAND, SALLIE; Delaware Valley Regional HS; Milford, NJ; (Y); Church Yth Grp; Dance Clb; Hosp Aide; Church Choir; Stat Bsktbl; JV Var Fld Hcky; Sftbl; Hon Roll; Phys Therapy.

STRICKLAND, TAMIKA L; Edgewood HS; Sicklerville, NJ; (Y); Sec FBLA; Office Aide; OEA; Pep Clb; Spanish Clb; Varsity Clb; Var Mgr(s); Var Score Keeper; JV Sftbl; Im Tennis; Distngshd Person Awd 85-86; Accntng Awd 86; Office Prctc Awd 86; VA ST U; Accntnt.

STRICKLAND, YVETTE; St Vincent Acad; Newark, NJ; (Y); Church Yth Grp; Yrbk Stf; Cheerleading; Kean Coll; Bus Adm.

STROHLEIN, KATHLEEN; Cinnaminson HS; Cinnaminson, NJ; (Y); Church Yth Grp; Key Clb; SADD; Off Frsh Cls; Off Soph Cls; Off Jr Cls; Pres Sr Cls; Stu Cncl; Capt Fld Hcky; Capt Lcrss.

STROLI, DANIELLE; Brurian HS For Girls; Passaic, NJ; (Y); Debate Tm; Pep Clb; Sec Temple Yth Grp; Y-Teens; School Play; Variety Show; Ntl Merit Ltr; NEDT Awd; Yrbk Humor Editr 86 & 87; Schoolwide Poet Cont Wnr 86; Visit The Elderly Clb 86; Columbia; Actrss.

STROLLO, CARLA; Shore Regional HS; W Long Branch, NJ; (Y); Drama Clb; SADD; Thesps; Capt Flag Corp; School Musical; School Play; Stage Crew; Yrbk Stf; Off Sr Cls; Stat Bsktbl.

STRONG, MARY LOUISE; Hunterdon Central HS; Flemington, NJ; (Y); 157/539; Trs Key Clb; Ski Clb; Band; Concert Band; Mrchg Band; Symp Band; Variety Show; Im Gym; JV Sftbl; Superior Marching Band Awd 84-85; OH ST U; Elec Engrng.

STRONG, PENELOPE; Hopewell Valley Central HS; Pennington, NJ; (Y); AFS; Camera Clb; Cmnty Wkr; Chorus; School Play; Nwsp Rptr; Yrbk Phtg; Yrbk Stf; Bsktbl; Sftbl; Jrnlsm.

STROOL, HEIDI FAITH; Paramus HS; Paramus, NJ; (Y); Hosp Aide; Rep Band; Rep Chorus; Concert Band; Drm & Bgl; Jazz Band; Mrchg Band; Orch; School Musical; Symp Band; Rgnl Orchstra 84-86; All St Orchstra 85-86; Douglass U Schlrshp 86; Rutgers U; Music.

STROUT, ELLEN; West Morris Central HS; Long Valley, NJ; (Y); 32/253; Art Clb; Drama Clb; Band; Mrchg Band; School Play; Yrbk Stf; Var Socr; Var Trk; High Hon Roll; NHS; MIP-TRCK & Fld 85-86; 2-1st Pl & 1-2nd Pl-Art Wrk Schl Art Fstvls 84-86; Art.

STRUMOLO, TRACY; Raritan HS; Hazlet, NJ; (Y); Drama Clb; Girl Scts; Office Aide; SADD; Chorus; JV Bsktbl; Im Sftbl; Im Vllybl; Im Wt Lftg; Hon Roll; Nrsng.

STRZEMINSKI, MARK; Saddle Brook HS; Saddle Brook, NJ; (Y); Am Leg Boys St; Cmnty Wkr; Stu Cncl; Var Capt Ftbl; JV Trk; Hon Roll; Athltc Cert JR Lttr Ftbll & Trk 83-84; Cert Of Merit Frnch I 83-84; 3rd Tm All Cnty Ftbll 84-85; Pre-Med.

STUART, CRAIG; Princeton Day Schl; Princeton, NJ; (Y); VP Drama Clb; Model UN; School Musical; School Play; Stage Crew; Nwsp Ed-Chief; Trs Frsh Cls; Trs Soph Cls; Hon Roll; Nwsp Rptr; Pltcl Sci.

STUART, JASON; Hightstown HS; East Windsor, NJ; (Y); 70/449; Letterman Clb; Varsity Clb; Bsbl; Var Capt Ftbl; Var Trk; Var Wrstlng; Hnrb Mntn-Wrestling 86; Bus.

STUART, KEITH; Cinnaminson HS; Cinnaminson, NJ; (Y); Var Ftbl; JV Socr; Prfct Atten Awd; FIT; Fsh Byng.

STUBBS, ELLA; Cumberland Regional HS; Bridgeton, NJ; (Y); 4-H; FBLA; GAA; Hosp Aide; Intnl Clb; Math Clb; Pep Clb; Science Clb; SADD; Varsity Clb; Accntnt.

STUBIN, ERIC; Cresskill HS; Cresskill, NJ; (Y); 41/111; Am Leg Boys St; Cmnty Wkr; Varsity Clb; JV Bsbl; Capt Ftbl; Bus.

STUDENKO, NICK; Howell HS; Farmingdale, NJ; (Y); 72/363; Math Tm; JV Var Socr; Hon Roll; NHS; AATSEEL H S Cert Excllnc Russn 85-86; Mst Imprvd Plyr 84-85; Rssn Clb 84-85; U Of NC; Engrng.

STURDIVANT, JACQUELINE; Union HS; Union, NJ; (Y); Drama Clb; VP French Clb; School Play; Ed Yrbk Stf; Rep Frsh Cls; Rep Jr Cls; Rep Stu Cncl; Var Crs Cntry; High Hon Roll; NHS; Physcs Prog 5 Wks NJIT 86.

STUTZ, RAY; Mc Corristin Catholic HS; Trenton, NJ; (Y); Computer Clb; Letterman Clb; Varsity Clb; Yrbk Stf; Ftbl; Wrstlng; Church Yth Grp; FCA; German Clb; Key Clb; Engrng.

STYLES, SANDRA; Clayton HS; Clayton, NJ; (Y); Key Clb; Library Aide; Chorus; Mrchg Band; Stage Crew; Yrbk Stf; NHS; Gloucester Cnty Clg.

SU, CHRISTINE; Mount Olive HS; Flanders, NJ; (Y); 6/296; Sec FBLA; Band; Chorus; Concert Band; Mrchg Band; High Hon Roll; NHS; AFS; Science Clb; Pep Band; 2nd Plc Clrk Typst Cmptn 84; 4th Plc Bus Englsh Cmptn 86; Awd Exclnc Frnch 85; Msc Hnr Scty; Intl Stdies.

SUAREZ, ANGELIQUE; Mount Saint Mary Acad; Spring Lk, NJ; (Y); 21/86; Dance Clb; French Clb; Rep Soph Cls; Stu Cncl; French Hon Soc; Magna Cum Laude Ntl Ltn Exam 82-83; NY U; Bus Admin.

SUAREZ, DANIELLE; Holy Family Acad; Bayonne, NJ; (Y); 23/130; Hosp Aide; Spanish Clb; Im Bsktbl; Var Swmmng; Hon Roll; NHS; School Play; Yrbk Phtg; Yrbk Stf; Ntl Hnr Soc; Adv.

SUAREZ, HELEN; Palisades Park JR SR HS; Palisades Pk, NJ; (Y); Nwsp Rptr; Nwsp Stf; Yrbk Stf; Stat Trk; NHS; Rutgers U; Pre-Law.

SUAREZ, JOYCEANN; Lodi HS; Lodi, NJ; (Y); 10/143; Church Yth Grp; Sec Hosp Aide; Key Clb; Leo Clb; VP Spanish Clb; Cit Awd; Hon Roll; Nrsng.

SUAREZ, LINDA; Mount St Mary Acad; Fanwood, NJ; (Y); Cmnty Wkr; Dance Clb; Debate Tm; Drama Clb; GAA; Band; Concert Band; School Play; Stage Crew; Hon Roll; HOPE Clb Rep 85-86; Peer Mnstr 86; Rutgers; Prelaw.

SUAREZ, MARGARET; Palisades Park JR SR HS; Palisades Pk, NJ; (Y); Nwsp Stf; Yrbk Stf; Stat Trk; High Hon Roll; Hon Roll; NHS; NY U; Fshn Merch.

SUBOURNE, JOELLE; Hunterdon Central HS; Flemington, NJ; (Y); Am Leg Aux Girls St; Ski Clb; SADD; Chorus; Color Guard; Mrchg Band; School Musical; Rep Jr Cls; Sec Stu Cncl; JV Trk; Stu Cncl Ldrshp Training Conf; Chld Psych.

SUDNIK, VICTORIA; Passaic Valley HS; Little Falls, NJ; (Y); 13/358; Key Clb; Concert Band; Mrchg Band; Ed Nwsp Stf; Ed Yrbk Stf; Var Bowling; Timer; Var Trk; Var Vllybl; High Hon Roll.

SUFFEL, LISA; St John Vianney HS; Manalapan, NJ; (Y); Cmnty Wkr; Hosp Aide; Intnl Clb; JCL; Service Clb; Teachers Aide; Yrbk Stf; Hon Roll; Cert Merit Awd Ltn; Gld & Wht Awd; Phrmcy.

SUGERMAN, ETHAN; Middletown High Schl South; Lincroft, NJ; (Y); Chess Clb; Math Clb; Math Tm; Variety Show; Lit Mag; Trk; Hon Roll; Rutgers Univ; Blgy.

SUH, RYUNG; West Orange HS; W Orange, NJ; (Y); 7/250; Band; Jazz Band; Ed Yrbk Stf; Trs Soph Cls; Pres Stu Cncl; Var Socr; Wrstlng; NHS; Ntl Merit Ltr; Spanish NHS; W Point US Miltry Acad; US Of.

SUILLIVAN, BARBARA; Morris Catholic HS; Lk Hiawatha, NJ; (Y); 54/142; Church Yth Grp; Varsity Clb; Var L Bsktbl; Var L Socr; Var L Sftbl; Hon Roll; All ST Soccr Tm 2nd Tm 85; All Conf 2nd Tm Bsktbl, 1st Tm Soccr & Sftbl 86; Radiolgy.

SUKHDEO, ROMESH; Montclair HS; Upper Montclair, NJ; (Y); Church Yth Grp; Cmnty Wkr; Hosp Aide; Model UN; Ftbl; Trk; Intl Rel.

SULLIVAN, ANN; Dumont HS; Dumont, NJ; (Y); 25/209; Church Yth Grp; Office Aide; Spanish Clb; Stage Crew; Nwsp Rptr; Yrbk Rptr; Lit Mag; Off Frsh Cls; Off Soph Cls; Off Jr Cls; PA ST U; Avtg.

SULLIVAN, BERNADETTE; Roselle Catholic HS; Elizabeth, NJ; (S); 26/151; Drama Clb; Acpl Chr; School Musical; Yrbk Stf; Hon Roll; Spanish NHS; St Peters Coll; Ed.

SULLIVAN, CHANDRA YVETTE; Vailsburg HS; Newark, NJ; (Y); FBLA; Office Aide; Teachers Aide; Rep Frsh Cls; Rep Soph Cls; NHS; Prfct Atten Awd; Cert Of Achvmnt Sec FBLA 85-86; NC A&T; Bus Adm.

SULLIVAN, CHRISTINE E; Eastern HS; Voorhees, NJ; (Y); 21/321; Church Yth Grp; Exploring; Hosp Aide; Intnl Clb; Scholastic Bowl; Yrbk Stf; Hon Roll; NHS; Ntl Merit SF; Hugh O Brian Yth Ldrshp Conf 84; MIT; Physics.

SULLIVAN, JOANNE; Freehold Township HS; Freehold, NJ; (Y); French Clb; FBLA; Yrbk Ed-Chief; Yrbk Stf; Rep Frsh Cls; Rep Soph Cls; Rep Jr Cls; Rep Sr Cls; JV Capt Socr; Widener U; Bus.

SULLIVAN, JOHN; Christian Brothers Acad; Manalapan, NJ; (Y); 6/222; Cmnty Wkr; Math Tm; Nwsp Rptr; Rep Frsh Cls; Rep Soph Cls; Rep Jr Cls; Var L Bsktbl; Hon Roll; Ntl Merit Ltr.

SULLIVAN, JONATHAN P; Ewing HS; Trenton, NJ; (Y); 5/312; Am Leg Boys St; Church Yth Grp; Cmnty Wkr; VP Debate Tm; Nwsp Stf; Crs Cntry; Hon Roll; NHS; Eng And Fornsc Awd 86; Dartmouth Clg.

SULLIVAN, KATE; Holy Cross HS; Vincentown, NJ; (Y); Sec Church Yth Grp; Wrstlng; Chorus; Lit Mag; Var L Fld Hcky; Var L Sftbl; High Hon Roll; Hon Roll; Spch Thrpy.

SULLIVAN, KATHLEEN; Red Bank Catholic HS; Tinton Falls, NJ; (Y); Church Yth Grp; School Musical; Yrbk Rptr; JV Crs Cntry; Trk; NHS; Pres Soph Cls; Gnrl Acdmc Excllnc 86; Parochl A ST Shtpt Chmpn 86.

SULLIVAN, KATHLEEN; Wall HS; Sea Girt, NJ; (S); 26/263; Ski Clb; Nwsp Stf; JV Bsktbl; Var Score Keeper; Var Timer; High Hon Roll; Hon Roll; Ntl Englsh Merit Awd 85.

SULLIVAN, KELLI; Union Catholic HS; Linden, NJ; (Y); Church Yth Grp; Pep Clb; Ski Clb; Church Choir; Fash Ind.

SULLIVAN, KENNETH C; Florence Twp Mem HS; Roebling, NJ; (Y); Am Leg Boys St; Rep Stu Cncl; JV Bsbl; Im Bsktbl; Hon Roll; Bus Adm.

SULLIVAN, MATT; Ocean City HS; Ocean City, NJ; (Y); 1/276; Math Clb; Ftbl; High Hon Roll; NHS; Ntl Merit SF; Pediatrician.

SULLIVAN, MICHAEL T; West Windsor Plainsboro HS; Princeton Junctio, NJ; (Y); 1/242; Am Leg Boys St; Capt Debate Tm; Trs Model UN; Ed Nwsp Stf; Stu Cncl; Var L Wrstlng; CC Awd; NHS; Val; Quiz Bowl; Garden ST Distngshd Schlr, Century III Schl Wnnr 85-86; Geo Wash U Engrng Mdl 84-85; Duke U; Pol Sci.

SULLIVAN, PATRICIA; Passaic Valley HS; Totowa, NJ; (Y); Art Clb; Key Clb; High Hon Roll; Hon Roll; Med.

SULLIVAN, TALMADGE; Dwight Morrow HS; Englewood, NJ; (Y); Boy Scts; Varsity Clb; Band; Var L Bsbl; Capt Var Ftbl; Var Trk; Im Mgr Wrstlng; Hon Roll; NC A&T ST U; Poly Sci.

SULLIVAN, TANYA; Frank H Morrell HS; Irvington, NJ; (Y); Church Yth Grp; Exploring; Hosp Aide; ROTC; Church Choir; Mrchg Band; Trk; Hon Roll; Pre-Med.

SULLIVAN, TARA; Paramus HS; Paramus, NJ; (Y); 15/343; Trs Band; Yrbk Sprt Ed; Stu Cncl; Var Capt Socr; Var Capt Trk; Lion Awd; NHS; Ntl Merit Ltr; NFL; Orch; German Hnr Soc Treas 84-86; Garden ST Distngushd Schlr 85-86; Rutgers Coll; Pol Sci.

SULLIVAN, TIM; Paul VI Regional HS; Clifton, NJ; (Y); Computer Clb; DECA; FBLA; Political Wkr; Ski Clb; Rep Frsh Cls; Rep Stu Cncl; Bsktbl; Ftbl; UCLA; Movie Mkr.

SULZINSKY, JOHN G; St Joseph HS; Milltown, NJ; (Y); Cmnty Wkr; Math Tm; Political Wkr; Ski Clb; Yrbk Stf; Lit Mag; High Hon Roll; NHS; Ntl Merit SF; Boy Scts; Robert Frost Litrcy Cntst Hnrb Mntn 83-84; Monitor Essay Cntst Hnrb Mntn; Bus Adm.

SULZMANN, JACQUELINE; Toms River North HS; Toms River, NJ; (Y); 68/412; Var Bsktbl; Var Socr; Cit Awd; High Hon Roll; Hon Roll; Bsktbll Awd Smmr Camp Rutgers 85; Pres Physcl Fit Awd; Rutgers; Tchr.

SUMALA, RILEY; Teaneck HS; Teaneck, NJ; (Y); Drama Clb; School Play; Nwsp Stf; Yrbk Stf; Lit Mag; Hon Roll; Bus.

SUN, EDMOND; Jackson Memorial HS; Jackson, NJ; (Y); 30/322; Computer Clb; French Clb; Ski Clb; Concert Band; Mrchg Band; Var L Bowling; JV Tennis; High Hon Roll; Hon Roll; Erly Admssn Prgrmn Ocean Cnty Coll 85-86; Archt.

SUNDARARAJ, SUJA; South Brunswick HS; Kendall Park, NJ; (Y); Church Yth Grp; FHA; Hosp Aide; Nwsp Rptr; Nwsp Stf; Lit Mag; Powder Puff Ftbl; Sftbl; Vllybl; Hon Roll; S Brunswick Adm Awd Schrlshp 85-86; Rutgers U; Pre-Med.

SUNSHINE, AMY; Matawan Regional HS; Aberdeen, NJ; (S); 33/273; French Clb; Math Clb; SADD; Yrbk Stf; Off Frsh Cls; Off Soph Cls; Off Jr Cls; Off Sr Cls; Sec Stu Cncl; Var Fld Hcky.

SUNSHINE, IAN; Matawau Regional HS; Aberdeen, NJ; (Y); Aud/Vis; JCL; Ski Clb; Varsity Clb; Yrbk Phtg; Yrbk Stf; Frsh Cls; Soph Cls; Jr Cls; Sr Cls; Bus.

SUPCHAK, KRISTEN; Bloomfield SR HS; Bloomfld, NJ; (Y); 36/442; Drama Clb; Girl Scts; Key Clb; Capt Flag Corp; Mrchg Band; Stage Crew; Rep Stu Cncl; NHS; Camera Clb; SADD; Bnd Frnt Capt 86-87; Girl Scts Gld Awd 86; Villanova U; Chem.

SUPEL, JANET; Secaucus HS; Secaucus, NJ; (Y); French Clb; Chorus; Vllybl; French Hon Soc; High Hon Roll; Hon Roll; Jr NHS; Phychlgst.

SUPOWIT, STEVE; Delaware Vly Regional HS; Milford, NJ; (Y); 30/200; Exploring; Im Sftbl; Im Tennis; JV Trk; Im Vllybl; High Hon Roll; Hon Roll; Rutgers U; Acctg.

SUPPA, STEPHANIE; Ocean Township HS; Ocean Township, NJ; (Y); 15/309; Am Leg Aux Girls St; Exploring; French Clb; Key Clb; Ski Clb; Yrbk Ed-Chief; Yrbk Stf; Trk; NHS; Ocean Twsp Tchrs Assn Ed Scholar 86; Coll William & Mary.

SUPPA, SUSAN; Our Lady Of Mercy Acad; Vineland, NJ; (Y); SADD; Chorus; School Musical; Nwsp Rptr; Sec Soph Cls; JV Var Cheerleading; Hon Roll; Mrn Bio.

SURACE, ROBERT J; Millville HS; Millville, NJ; (Y); 3/500; Am Leg Boys St; Trs FCA; French Clb; Bsbl; Bsktbl; Capt Ftbl; Wt Lftg; Dnfth Awd; Elks Awd; Gov Hon Prg Awd; Schlr Ath S Jersey 86; Jewish War Veta Schlr Ath 86; Princeton U; Pre-Med.

SURBRUG, AMY; Union Catholic Regional HS; Scotch Plains, NJ; (Y); 74/319; Church Yth Grp; Service Clb; Ski Clb; JV Sftbl; Psychlgy.

SURMAN, LORI; Lenape HS; Indian Mills, NJ; (Y); 3/421; Church Yth Grp; Spanish Clb; Yrbk Stf; Var Capt Cheerleading; High Hon Roll; NHS; Rotary Awd; Spanish NHS; SADD; Varsity Clb; Presdntl Clssrm For Yng Amercns; Garden ST Distngshd Schlr; Math.

SURRETTE, DANIELLE; Wall HS; Wall, NJ; (S); 12/267; Ski Clb; Band; School Play; Nwsp Stf; Score Keeper; Socr; High Hon Roll; Piano Hbbysts Of Wrld 85.

SUSHKO, PETER; Our Lady Of Good Counsel HS; Newark, NJ; (Y); 19/137; Boy Scts; Computer Clb; Socr; Ctznshp Awd 84; Boy Scout Life Rank Awd 84; Alumni Asstnce Awd 85-86; Comp Sci.

SUSSNA, TRACY; Lakewood HS; Lakewood, NJ; (Y); Am Leg Aux Girls St; English Clb; Pres Key Clb; Spanish Clb; Var Capt Bowling; Gym; High Hon Roll; Hon Roll; Jr NHS; Spanish NHS; Marin Bio.

SUTER, CATHERINE; Princeton Day Schl; Princeton, NJ; (Y); AFS; Model UN; Teachers Aide; Church Choir; Madrigals; School Musical; Yrbk Phtg; High Hon Roll; Hon Roll; Drama Clb; Cum Laude 86; Vrsty Fncg 85-86; Bikg Clb 86.

SUTTER, JANICE A; Clifton HS; Clifton, NJ; (Y); 109/637; Ski Clb; Chorus; Var Capt Crs Cntry; Trk; Spanish NHS; Cmnty Wkr; Spanish Clb; Hon Roll; Hnr Guard 86 Commncmnt 86; Comm.

SUTTON, RITA; Mainland Regional HS; Northfield, NJ; (Y); 9/250; Church Yth Grp; Computer Clb; Exploring; Ski Clb; Vllybl; High Hon Roll; Intl Martial Arts Fed Cert Of Merit 86; Attnd Blaie Acad Summr Inst For Giftd & Talented 84-85; Sci.

SUTTON, STACEY; Hamilton H S East; Hamilton Sq, NJ; (Y); 16/311; Church Yth Grp; Debate Tm; Key Clb; Political Wkr; Speech Tm; SADD; Mgr(s); Hon Roll; Jr NHS; Pres Schlr; Trenton ST Coll.

SUYDAM, NICOLE; Overbrook Rgnl SR HS; Pinehill, NJ; (Y); JV L Bsktbl; JV L Crs Cntry; Hon Roll; Law.

SVENNINGSEN, SUSANNE; Watchung Hills Regional HS; Watchung, NJ; (Y); 6/315; Intnl Clb; Key Clb; SADD; Var L Fld Hcky; Var L Swmmng; High Hon Roll; Hon Roll; NHS; Safe Rides; Intl Rltns.

SVETLOV, MARINA; North Brunswick Township HS; N Brunswick, NJ; (Y); 5/300; AFS; French Clb; Key Clb; Latin Clb; Library Aide; Mathletes; Nwsp Stf; Sftbl; High Hon Roll; Hon Roll; Columbia Coll; Intl Affrs.

SWAAK, DERRICK; Chatham Township HS; Chatham, NJ; (Y); Key Clb; Science Clb; Dr Scholl Wrldwd Schlrshp 86; Cornell U; Htl Mgmt.

SWAIN, JOHN; Toms River South HS; Toms River, NJ; (Y); 16/365; Capt L Ftbl; L Trk; JV L Wrstlng; Hon Roll; NHS; Perfct Attnd 83-85; Bio Team 83; Dntstry.

SWALINA, CAROLYN; Middlesex HS; Middlesex, NJ; (Y); 48/170; Spanish Clb; SADD; Hon Roll; Artstcly Tlntd Crtv Wrtg 86; Jrnlsm.

SWALUK, JEFFREY D; East Brunswick HS; Spotswood, NJ; (Y); AFS; Church Yth Grp; Orch; Gov Hon Prg Awd; High Hon Roll; NJ Gvrnrs Schl Strng Qrtet 85; All ST Orchstra 82-85; Natl HS Hnrs Orchstra 86; Viola Prfrmnc.

SWANICK, CHRISTINE L; Hackettstown HS; Hackettstown, NJ; (Y); 1/200; Cmnty Wkr; Q&S; School Play; Ed Nwsp Stf; Trs Pres Stu Cncl; Var Capt Crs Cntry; Var Capt Trk; NHS; Val; Key Clb; Hugh O Brien Yth Fndtn Smnr 84; NY Schlrs Prog 85; Boston Coll; Pre Law.

SWANK, MEREDITH; Cumberland Regional HS; Shiloh, NJ; (Y); Debate Tm; Intnl Clb; JCL; High Hon Roll; Hon Roll; Ornmntl Hortcltr.

SWARD, GREG; Hanover Park HS; Florham Park, NJ; (S); 5/280; Trs Frsh Cls; Soph Cls; Jr Cls; Sr Cls; JV Bsktbl; L Ftbl; Capt L Trk; High Hon Roll; Hon Roll; NHS; HP Trck Spirit Awd 85; Hornet Awd JV Bsktbl For Spirit, Hustl & Attitd 84; Chem.

SWARTZ, CHRISTINE L; Whippany Park HS; Morris Plains, NJ; (Y); 3/198; VP Church Yth Grp; Trs Pres Drama Clb; Band; Church Choir; Mrchg Band; Var L Tennis; Gov Hon Prg Awd; Ntl Merit SF; Hosp Aide; Rutgers Schlr 85; Ntl Hnr Scty; Bates Coll; Hstry.

SWARTZ JR, HAROLD J; Pleasantville HS; Pleasantville, NJ; (S); #1 In Class; Pres Computer Clb; Math Clb; Capt Mrchg Band; Nwsp Ed-Chief; Yrbk Phtg; Trs Jr Cls; Tennis; Hon Roll; Sec NHS; Comp Sci Awd 84; Rutgers Schlr 86.

SWAYZE, BILL; Dover HS; Dover, NJ; (Y); 6/220; Am Leg Boys St; Letterman Clb; Ski Clb; Nwsp Rptr; Yrbk Stf; Ftbl; Powder Puff Ftbl; Trk; Wt Lftg; High Hon Roll; MVP Ftbl Tm 86; John Roach Jr Meml Schlrshp 86; All Cnty Coachs Ftbl Tm 86; Recd 1st Tm Ftbl; Advnc 1st; U Of DE; Pre Law.

SWEENEY, DONALD; Franklin HS; Somerset, NJ; (Y); 17/306; Math Clb; Math Tm; Hon Roll; NHS; Pres Schlr; St Schlr; Natl Assoc Accntnts Gold Key Awd 86; Bucknell U; Accntng.

SWEENEY, KATHLEEN; Holy Cross HS; Riverside, NJ; (Y); 35/400; Spanish Clb; Yrbk Stf; High Hon Roll; Hon Roll; 2nd NJ ST Rllr Sktng Chmpshp 86; 5th NJ ST Estrn Rgnl Sktng Chmpshp 86.

SWEET, JENNIFER; Pennsville Memorial HS; Pennsville, NJ; (Y); 22/224; Am Leg Aux Girls St; FBLA; Band; Mrchg Band; Rep Frsh Cls; Rep Soph Cls; Rep Jr Cls; Rep Sr Cls; Rep Stu Cncl; Mgr(s); U Delaware; Txtl Mktg.

SWEETEN, KATHLEEN; Paulsboro HS; Gibbstown, NJ; (Y); 3/130; Trs Jr Cls; Rep Sr Cls; Rep Stu Cncl; Mat Maids; Stat Trk; Stat Wrstlng; Bausch & Lomb Sci Awd; High Hon Roll; Hon Roll; NHS; Amer Chem Socy Awd 86; Pres Acad Ftnss Awd 86; Frank Flowers Mem Fund-Schlrshps 86; PA ST U.

SWEETWOOD, DAWN; Oakcrest HS; Hammonton, NJ; (Y); 8/250; Hosp Aide; SADD; Teachers Aide; Band; Concert Band; Mrchg Band; Ed Yrbk Stf; Hon Roll; Jr NHS; Helene Fuld Schl Of Nursing.

SWEITZER, JOSEPH H; The Pilgrim Acad; Northfield, NJ; (Y); 6/14; Am Leg Boys St; Church Yth Grp; Yrbk Bus Mgr; Yrbk Stf; Bsbl; Bsktbl; Mgr(s); Im Socr; Hon Roll; Keith Chrstiana Memrl Sccr Awd; Taylor U; Cmptr Sci.

SWENSON, INGRID; Indian Hills HS; Oakland, NJ; (Y); 95/279; Lit Mag; Var Capt Socr; Hon Roll; Office Aide; Varsity Clb; Chorus; Var JV Bsktbl; Var Stat Sftbl; Spec Educ.

SWETZ, GEOFFREY O; Seton Hall Prep; Cedar Grove, NJ; (Y); Boy Scts; VP Church Yth Grp; Ski Clb; School Musical; Nwsp Stf; Yrbk Stf; Crs Cntry; Wrstlng; High Hon Roll; NHS; MSGR Thomas J Tuohy Awd 86; Villanova U; Bus Adm.

SWEZEY, WAYNE W; Midland Park HS; Midland Park, NJ; (Y); Am Leg Boys St; Concert Band; Drm Mjr(t); School Musical; JV Capt Socr; Gov Hon Prg Awd; NHS; Band; Chorus; All ST Chrs 85 & 86; Regn I Symph Band 86; Westminister Chrs Coll Vocal Camp Scholar 85; Music Comp.

SWIATEK, EDWARD; Bishop George HS; S Plainfield, NJ; (Y); Computer Clb; Drama Clb; Pep Clb; Band; Concert Band; Jazz Band; Mrchg Band; Pep Band; School Musical; Symp Band; Comp Sci.

SWIECONEK, APRIL; Delaware Valley Regional HS; Milford, NJ; (Y); Key Clb; Radio Clb; Thesps; Band; Concert Band; Drm Mjr(t); Mrchg Band; Orch; School Musical; School Play; Theatr.

SWIFT, PATRICK; Hudson Catholic HS; Jersey City, NJ; (Y); 120/183; Var L Bsbl; Capt Bsktbl; Var L Ftbl; Most Improved Awd Ftbl 85; All Cnty Ftbl 85; Ftbl 5th Qtr Club Hnrbl Mntn 85; U Of Louisville; Prof Baseball.

SWIGART, DAN; Warren Co Vo-Tech; Hackettstown, NJ; (S); Boy Scts; Key Clb; Ski Clb; VICA; Hon Roll; Comp Pgmmr.

SWINGLE, DEBRA LEE; Newton HS; Newton, NJ; (Y); 62/210; Girl Scts; Hosp Aide; Spanish Clb; Color Guard; Concert Band; Mrchg Band; Twrlr; God Cntry Awd; Gld Awd 86, Slvr 84 GS; Nrsg.

SWINGLE, LISA; Mahwah HS; Mahwah, NJ; (Y); 17/174; High Hon Roll; Exec Inst For Travel; Travel.

SWINT, SONYA; Woodrow Wilson HS; Camden, NJ; (Y); Computer Clb; FTA; Math Clb; Office Aide; Spanish Clb; Vllybl; Temple; Comp.

SWINTON, PAUL; Schalick HS; Bridgeton, NJ; (Y); 19/132; JV Bsbl; JV Ftbl; Var Trk; U Of Hartford; Compu Sci.

SWISHER, KIRSTEN; Egg Harbor Township HS; Pleasantville, NJ; (S); 10/266; GAA; Key Clb; SADD; School Play; Var Crs Cntry; Var Fld Hcky; High Hon Roll; NHS; Opertn Entrprs 85; Ntl Ledrshp Merit Schlrshp Awd 84-85; Vrsty Schlr Awd 83-85; Villanova U; Bus Admn.

SWON, KIMBERLY A; West Morris Mendham HS; Brookside, NJ; (Y); 72/311; Dance Clb; Chorus; Yrbk Stf; Var Cheerleading; Hon Roll; Comptv Ice Skater; ST Fin Miss TEEN 86; ST Fin Outstndng Young Amer 84; Fash Merch.

SWOPE, NANCY ANN; Mahwah HS; Mahwah, NJ; (Y); 7/138; Capt Math Tm; JV Sftbl; JV Tennis; High Hon Roll; NHS; Pres Schlr; Spanish NHS; Gdn ST Dstngshd Schlr Awd 86; Hnry Kng Stnfrd Schlrshp 86; HS Thndrbrd Schlrshp 86; U Of Miami; Mrn Bio.

SYDLOWSKI, BARB; BRHS-WEST HS; Bridgewater, NJ; (Y); French Clb; SADD; Rep Frsh Cls; Rep Soph Cls; Rep Jr Cls; Rep Sr Cls; Rep Stu Cncl; Cheerleading; Hon Roll; NHS; Purdue U; Dsgn.

SYKES, K; Orange HS; Orange, NJ; (Y); PAVAS; Band; Concert Band; Mrchg Band; School Musical; Sr Cls; Stu Cncl; Mgr(s); Swmmng; Band Pres 85-86; Stu Council Rep 82-86; Designers Club Awd 83-86; Cheyney U; Bus.

SYLVESTER, KATHRYN; Our Lady Of Mercy Acad; Williamstown, NJ; (Y); 5/26; Exploring; Pres 4-H; Nwsp Stf; Yrbk Stf; Ed Lit Mag; VP Soph Cls; Dnfth Awd; 4-H Awd; Hon Roll; Nato Political Sci Awd 86; Pres Acdmc Fit Awd 86; NEDT Tst Awd 83; Rosemont Coll; Attrny.

SYRACUSE, ALBERT; Pompton Lakes HS; Pompton Lakes, NJ; (Y); Cmnty Wkr; Letterman Clb; OEA; Varsity Clb; Off Jr Cls; Var Ftbl; Wt Lftg; Wrstlng; High Hon Roll; Hon Roll; Schlrshp Pompton Lks Athltc Booster Clb 86; ST Grnt 86; Montclair ST Coll; Comp Sci.

SYREK, JENNIFER ROSE; East Brunswick HS; E Brunswick, NJ; (Y); Hosp Aide; Chorus; Jazz Band; Orch; Yrbk Ed-Chief; French Hon Soc; Gov Hon Prg Awd; NHS; French Clb; School Musical; All Estrn Symphny Orchstr 85; Ntl HS Hnrs Orchstr 86; Rutgers Coll; Med.

SYRON, JENNIFER ANN; Wayne Valley HS; Wayne, NJ; (Y); 8/321; Am Leg Aux Girls St; Red Cross Aide; Lit Mag; Var Crs Cntry; Var Capt Swmmng; Var Trk; NHS; Cmnty Wkr; JCL; Latin Clb; Bill Bradley Yng Ctzn Awd 86; US Army Res Natl Schlr Athlt Awd 86; NJ Garden ST Distgshd Schlr 85; Rutgers Coll; Pol Sci.

SZABO, GABRIELLA; North Warren Regional HS; Delaware, NJ; (Y); 9/141; Spanish Clb; Teachers Aide; Nwsp Ed-Chief; Nwsp Rptr; Nwsp Sprt Ed; Nwsp Stf; Yrbk Stf; Bsktbl; Im Powder Puff Ftbl; Hon Roll; World Affirs Sem 86; Biomed Engr.

SZALGA, STACY; Lakewood Prep; Rick, NJ; (Y); Art Clb; German Clb; JA; Library Aide; Math Clb; Science Clb; Ski Clb; Spanish Clb; Band; Chorus; Georgetown U; Pre-Med.

SZALONY, AMY E; Lawrence HS; Lawrenceville, NJ; (Y); 41/228; Art Clb; Church Yth Grp; VP Frsh Cls; Bsktbl; Var Sftbl; Moore Coll Stu Gnt 86; Moore College Of Art; Med Illst.

SZAP, MATTHEW; Toms River HS East; Toms River, NJ; (Y); 27/585; Math Tm; Quiz Bowl; Science Clb; Band; Concert Band; Pres Mrchg Band; School Musical; Variety Show; Trk; VP NHS; Hlth.

SZATKOWSKI, SEAN; North Plainfield HS; N Plainfield, NJ; (Y); 41/190; Church Yth Grp; Letterman Clb; Ski Clb; SADD; Coach Actv; Var L Ftbl; Var L Trk; Hon Roll; Villanova.

SZCZEPANIAK, NANCY; Matawan Regional HS; Matawan, NJ; (Y); French Clb; Latin Clb; Library Aide; Office Aide; Teachers Aide; Chorus; School Musical; French Hon Soc; Hon Roll; Natl Lang Arts Olympiad 84; Allegheny Coll; Med.

SZEKERES, JOLANDA; Notre Dame HS; Trenton, NJ; (Y); Yrbk Stf; JV Cheerleading; Var Score Keeper.

SZEP, KRISTINA; Franklin HS; Somerset, NJ; (Y); Varsity Clb; Var Tennis; Vrsty Ltr Wnnr Tennis 83-85; Sport Psychology.

SZEWCZUK, JOHN; Toms River HS; Toms River, NJ; (Y); 12/412; Chess Clb; FBLA; Math Tm; JV Bowling; High Hon Roll; Hon Roll; Acad Ltr 83-86; Math.

SZILASSY, PAUL; Washington Twp HS; Turnersville, NJ; (Y); VP French Clb; Q&S; Var L Crs Cntry; JV L Tennis; High Hon Roll; Hon Roll; NHS; Prfct Atten Awd; Priv Violn & Vocl Stdy; Arch.

SZOSTAK, ELIZABETH; Chatham Township HS; Chatham, NJ; (Y); 42/128; Church Yth Grp; Key Clb; Library Aide; Stage Crew; Rep Frsh Cls; Rep Soph Cls; Rep Jr Cls; Var Crs Cntry; Var Trk; Hon Roll; U NH; Frnch.

SZUCHY, MATTHEW; Highland Regional HS; Laurel Springs, NJ; (S); 6/326; Latin Clb; Service Clb; Nwsp Ed-Chief; Nwsp Phtg; Nwsp Rptr; Nwsp Stf; High Hon Roll; Hon Roll; NHS; Magna Cum Laude Latn Awd; Cum Laude Latn Awd; Pre-Med.

SZUMSKI, CINDY; South River HS; South River, NJ; (Y); 6/140; Sec Spanish Clb; Nwsp Stf; Yrbk Stf; Var Capt Cheerleading; Var L Sftbl; DAR Awd; Hon Roll; NHS; German Clb; Chorus; Brkly Awd Outstndng Bus Stu 86; Mddlsx Cnty Coll Schlrshp 86; Bd Educ Spec Acdmc Awd 86; Middlesex County Coll; Ofc Syst.

SZYMANSKI, ELLEN; Oak Knoll School Of Hly Chld; Bedminster, NJ; (Y); Aud/Vis; Drama Clb; Key Clb; Service Clb; Chorus; Stage Crew; Nwsp Stf; Lit Mag; Swmmng; Hon Roll; Vlntr Ldrshp Awd 85.

SZYMANSKI, PAUL; Highstown HS; E Windsor, NJ; (Y); Church Yth Grp; Trs Ski Clb; Var Socr; Gettysburg Coll; Acctg.

TABACCHI, MICHAEL; Manalapan HS; Englishtown, NJ; (Y); Rtgrs U; Bus.

TABAKA, JOELLE L; Clifton HS; Clifton, NJ; (Y); 188/564; DECA; Office Aide; SADD; Sr Cls; Mgr(s); Hon Roll; Rider Coll.

TABAR, JEFFREY; A P Schalick HS; Bridgeton, NJ; (Y); 35/132; Red Cross Aide; Ski Clb; Nwsp Rptr; Rep Frsh Cls; Rep Sr Cls; Var L Ftbl; Var L Trk; Engrng.

TABOR, MARY; Paramus HS; Paramus, NJ; (Y); Art Clb; Church Yth Grp; Off Jr Cls; Sftbl; Teterboro Schl Aeronaut; Arplns.

TABOR, ROBERT; Arthur L Johnson Regional HS; Clark, NJ; (Y); 11/196; Var Golf; Hon Roll; Spanish NHS; Villanova U; Comp Sci.

TABS, DANIEL; West Essex SR HS; N Caldwell, NJ; (Y); Debate Tm; Temple Yth Grp; Nwsp Bus Mgr; Nwsp Rptr; Mgr Nwsp Stf; Rep Stu Cncl; Hon Roll; Cum Laude Cert The Natl Latin Exmntn; Bus.

TAFARO, MARIA; West Essex Regional HS; N Caldwell, NJ; (Y); Key Clb; Pep Clb; Varsity Clb; Capt Cheerleading; Trk; Hon Roll; Bus.

TAFT, SUZANNE; Buena Regional HS; Vineland, NJ; (S); 20/200; Church Yth Grp; Drama Clb; 4-H; GAA; Pep Clb; Varsity Clb; Acpl Chr; Chorus; Church Choir; Madrigals; Stdnt Wk 86; NJ Schl Perfrmg Arts 85-86; Immaculata Coll; Ed.

TAFURI, SANDRA; Manchester Regional HS; N Haledon, NJ; (S); Hosp Aide; Yrbk Stf; Rep Jr Cls; Rep Stu Cncl; Stat Bsktbl; Socr; Trk; Hon Roll; NHS.

TAGLIERI, PAUL; Hudson Catholic HS; Hoboken, NJ; (Y); 19/188; SADD; Variety Show; JV Var Bsbl; Im Bsktbl; JV Var Bowling; Swmmng; Hon Roll; Schlrshp St Francis Grmmr Sch 83; St Johns U; Bus.

TAGUE, INGRID H; Madison HS; Madison, NJ; (Y); 1/218; Church Yth Grp; School Play; Ed Lit Mag; NHS; Ntl Merit SF; Val; Science Clb; French Hon Soc; High Hon Roll; Grdn ST Dstngshd Schlr, Rutgers Schlr 86.

TAHAN, MICHELLE; Paul VI Regional HS; Clifton, NJ; (Y); 23/147; JV Bsktbl; Var Sftbl; Hon Roll; Spanish NHS; Sftbl Hnrbl Mntn All Leag, Cnty 86; Montclair ST.

TAHANEY, KRISTEN; Bishop Eustace Prep; Atco, NJ; (Y); 39/182; Church Yth Grp; Trs French Clb; Pep Clb; Teachers Aide; Stat Bsbl; Stat L Bsktbl; L Mgr(s); Stat L Socr; Hon Roll; NHS; Psych.

TAHMOOSH, SUSAN; John F Kennedy HS; Paterson, NJ; (Y); German Clb; Orch; Nwsp Rptr; Nwsp Stf; Yrbk Rptr; Yrbk Stf; Hon Roll; NHS; 1st Plc Alcoa Can Co Pstr Cntst 86; Natl Piano Plyng Adtns; Supr Rtng Natl Fed Jr Festvls Piano 85-86; Montclair ST Coll; Comm Art.

TAILOR, MAMTA; Clifton HS; Clifton, NJ; (Y); 120/753; Camera Clb; Key Clb; Spanish Clb; Yrbk Ed-Chief; Yrbk Stf; Var Crs Cntry; Var Trk; Hon Roll; Spanish NHS; Nrsng.

TAILOR, REKHA; Dickinson HS; Jersey City, NJ; (Y); Computer Clb; French Clb; Key Clb; Math Clb; Quiz Bowl; Scholastic Bowl; Science Clb; Nwsp Rptr; Yrbk Stf; Lit Mag; NJIT; Comp.

TAKACS, CHRISTINE; Hopewell Valley Central HS; Titusville, NJ; (Y); 89/202; AFS; Church Yth Grp; FBLA; Service Clb; Spanish Clb; Stage Crew; Im Badmtn; Im Swmmng; Hon Roll; Accntng.

TAKAKI, FREDRICK; Vineland HS; Vineland, NJ; (Y); Police Sci.

TAKAKJIAN, AMY; Hasbrouch Heights HS; Hasbrouck Heights, NJ; (Y); 21/124; Trs Drama Clb; Trs Key Clb; Trs Spanish Clb; Band; Chorus; Concert Band; Mrchg Band; School Musical; Hon Roll; Voice Dem Awd; Armenian Gen Ath Union Scholar 86; Publc Spkng Awd 86; Instrmntl Music Scholar 86; Douglass Coll; Child Psych.

TALARICO, MARIA; North Bergen HS; North Bergen, NJ; (Y); 143/400; DECA; Key Clb; Capt Color Guard; Yrbk Stf; Modeling Clb 4th Pl Awd 85; Homerm Rep 84-87; Italian Clb & Stu Cncl 85-87; Fashion Inst Tech; Fash Merch.

TALBERT, RUBY; University HS; Newark, NJ; (Y); JA; Church Choir; Hon Roll; Elec Engr.

TALBOT, CHRISTINE; Red Bank Catholic HS; Oceanport, NJ; (Y); Hosp Aide; Teachers Aide; Stage Crew; JV Coach Actv; Crs Cntry; Powder Puff Ftbl; JV Sftbl; Nazareth Col6; Spc Ed Tchr.

TALESA, CLAUDIA; V Ineland HS; Vineland, NJ; (Y); 153/816; Office Aide; OEA; Yrbk Stf; Fld Hcky; Cit Awd; NHS; ILGWU Schrlshp 86-90; Stockton ST Coll; Bus Adm.

TALIAFERRO, JAMES; Trenton Central HS; Trenton, NJ; (Y); Debate Tm; Latin Clb; Band; Concert Band; Jazz Band; Mrchg Band; Orch; Pep Band; School Musical; Yrbk Rptr; FL A&M U; Music Educ.

TALIAFERRO, JEFF; The Wardlaw-Hartridge Schl; Plainfield, NJ; (Y); 10/53; Debate Tm; Drama Clb; Chorus; School Musical; School Play; Sec Stu Cncl; Stat Ftbl; Mgr(s); Stat Swmmng; High Hon Roll; Law.

TALLARIDA, VALERIE; Maple Shade HS; Maple Shade, NJ; (Y); DECA; French Clb; GAA; Key Clb; Nwsp Stf; Pres Frsh Cls; Rep Soph Cls; Rep Jr Cls; Rep Stu Cncl; Var Cheerleading; Psychlgy.

TALONE, PAUL J; Triton Regional HS; Runnemede, NJ; (Y); 22/286; Am Leg Boys St; Church Yth Grp; Chorus; Church Choir; VP Stu Cncl; Crs Cntry; Trk; Hon Roll; NHS; Prfct Atten Awd; Presdntl Acadmc Ftns Awd 85-86; Stu Cncl Schlrshp 86; Prncpls Svc Awd 86; Cedarvl Coll OH; Pre-Med.

TALPAS, CHRIS; Phillipsburg HS; Phillipsburg, NJ; (Y); Ftbl; Wt Lftg; Var L Wrstlng; Hon Roll.

TALTY, CARA; Parsippany Hills HS; Boonton, NJ; (Y); Trs Drama Clb; French Clb; PAVAS; Trs Thesps; Chorus; School Musical; Stage Crew; Lit Mag; Rep Stu Cncl; Hon Roll; Semi Fnlst NJ ST Gvrnrs Prfrmng Arts 86; NJ Rgn J Choir 85-86; Carng Mlln Pre Coll Prfrmng Arts 86; Music.

TALVACCHIA, PAMELA; Queen Of Peace HS; Kearny, NJ; (Y); 89/230; Hosp Aide; Ski Clb; SADD; JV Cheerleading; JV Sftbl; Hon Roll; Accntng.

TAM, MARGARET; Linden HS; Linden, NJ; (Y); Key Clb; Stage Crew; Rep Soph Cls; Rep Stu Cncl; Hon Roll; NHS; Bus.

TAMBONE, MICHAEL; Middlesex HS; Middlesex, NJ; (Y); 4/160; Am Leg Boys St; Church Yth Grp; VP Key Clb; SADD; School Musical; Rep Stu Cncl; Var Vllybl; Var Tennis; NHS; St Schlr; YMCA Yth Conf Natl Affrs Delg 85; Kiwanis Yth Ldrshp Training Conf 84; YMCA Yth & Govt Conf 86; Engrng.

TAMBURRO, MARINA; Mother Seton Regional HS; Irvington, NJ; (Y); 44/124; Art Clb; Church Yth Grp; Science Clb; Service Clb; Chorus; Church Choir; Lit Mag; Inerprtr.

TAMMARU, KATY; Middleton High School South; Middletown, NJ; (Y); Teachers Aide; Yrbk Stf.

TANG, SYLVIA; Parsippany HS; Denville, NJ; (Y); AFS; Cmnty Wkr; Key Clb; Band; Symp Band; Pres Frsh Cls; Hon Roll; NHS; Rutgers U.

TANGALOS, JOHN; Red Bank Catholic HS; Red Bank, NJ; (Y); JA; Trk; High Hon Roll; Hon Roll; 2 Awds-Bus Law Cls 85-86; JV Awd-Trck 84; Law.

TANSLEY, WALTER; Toms River HS East; Toms River, NJ; (Y); 175/525; Boy Scts; Exploring; Ocean Cnty Coll; Law Enfrcmnt.

TAORMINA, DANIEL; Rutherford HS; Rutherford, NJ; (Y); 48/187; FBLA; Science Clb; Ftbl; Wt Lftg; Acad Dcthln; Rutgers Newark.

TAPE, KRISTINA; Belvidere HS; Gt Meadows, NJ; (S); 10/118; Camera Clb; Spanish Clb; Yrbk Phtg; Stat Bsktbl; High Hon Roll; Hon Roll; JR Soc Studys Psychlgy Awd 85; Erly Chldhd Educ.

TAPPER, BRENDA; Edgewood Reg HS District No 1; Atco, NJ; (Y); VP Church Yth Grp; Office Aide; JV Cheerleading; Stat Ftbl; JV Sftbl; Hon Roll; Flrst Dsgnr.

TAPPER, ROB; Lakewood HS; Lakewood, NJ; (Y); 29/300; Am Leg Boys St; English Clb; French Clb; Science Clb; Trs Mrchg Band; Var Golf; French Hon Soc; Hon Roll; NHS; Prfct Atten Awd; Most Imprvd Plyr Golf 85; Marchng Band Pres,Trea 84-85.

TARABOLA, JEAN; Leonia HS; Edgewater, NJ; (Y); 41/165; Church Yth Grp; Cmnty Wkr; Journalism.

TARANTINO, COLLEEN; Newton HS; Newton, NJ; (S); 12/210; Hosp Aide; Latin Clb; SADD; Varsity Clb; Chorus; Madrigals; VP Soph Cls; Rep Stu Cncl; Stat Bsktbl; Var Fld Hcky; Physcl Thrpy.

TARANTINO, ERIC; Columbia HS; Maplewood, NJ; (Y); Band; Concert Band; Jazz Band; Mrchg Band; Orch; School Musical; Band, Jzz Band & Orchstr Outstndng Awd 82-86; Frshmn Cnslr Prjct 88 85-86; The Citadel-Charleston; Pol Sci.

TARANTO, MARY; Ramapo Regional HS; Wyckoff, NJ; (Y); 52/325; Church Yth Grp; French Clb; Yrbk Stf; Lit Mag; Stat Bsktbl; Coach Actv; Powder Puff Ftbl; Cit Awd; Hon Roll; NHS; Hnr Gd 86; Cert Merit Frnch & Hstry 86; Grls Ctznshp Dlgt 86; Engl.

TARASEVITSCH, NINA L; Woodbridge SR HS; Iselin, NJ; (Y); Am Leg Aux Girls St; SADD; Chorus; Flag Corp; Yrbk Ed-Chief; Yrbk Stf; Hon Roll; NHS; Hugh O Brien Yth Fndtn Smnr Ldrshp; Prjct Gftd Mddlsx Cnty Coll; Engrng.

TARDIFF, DEAN; Notre Dame HS; Hamilton Sq, NJ; (Y); 90/367; Nwsp Stf; Envrnmtl Sci.

TARGONSKI, ROBERTA; Sayreville War Memorial HS; Sayreville, NJ; (Y); 8/380; Pres VP German Clb; Spanish Clb; High Hon Roll; Lion Awd; NHS; German Hon Soc; Rutgers U; Engrg.

TARLACH, GEMMA; Moutn St Mary Acad; Perth Amboy, NJ; (S); Pres German Clb; Chorus; School Play; Nwsp Ed-Chief; Yrbk Stf; Lit Mag; NHS; Drama Clb; Nwsp Rptr; Nwsp Stf; Outstndg Sen Awd Congress 86; Natl Guitar Summer Wrkshp Scholar Recip 85; Somerset Cnty Chrs 85.

TARLOW, ELISHA M; Solomon Schechter Day Schl; W Orange, NJ; (Y); 2/21; Drama Clb; VP Temple Yth Grp; Nwsp Rptr; Ed Nwsp Stf; Ed Yrbk Phtg; Stu Cncl; Var Tennis; Sec NHS; NEDT Awd; Sal; Garden ST Dstngshd Scholar 86; Fnlst Metrowest Isreal Tst 85; Stu Abraham J Heschel Hon Soc 85-86; Barnard Coll; Psychlgy.

TARRADELLAS, CLAUDIA; Westfield SR HS; Westfield, NJ; (Y); 83/514; Cmnty Wkr; French Clb; Spanish Clb; Band; JV Fld Hcky; French Hon Soc; High Hon Roll; Hon Roll; Jr NHS.

TARRANT, CAROLYN; Ocean Township HS; Oakhurst, NJ; (Y); 181/336; JCL; Latin Clb; SADD; Yrbk Stf; Sftbl; Accntng.

TARSITANO, JIM; Passaic Valley HS; Totowa, NJ; (Y); Church Yth Grp; Bsktbl; Crs Cntry; Hon Roll; Accntng.

TARTAGLIA, DEBORAH; Immaculate Conception HS; Hasbrouck Hts, NJ; (Y); Drama Clb; PAVAS; Teachers Aide; Pep Band; School Play; Yrbk Stf; Sec Sr Cls; Var Sftbl; Var Capt Vllybl; Hon Roll; Most Outstndng Choreography 85-86; Most Valuable Player Varsity Vllybl 84-85; Natl Art Hnr Soc 86-87.

TARZY, JAMES B; Cherokee HS; Marlton, NJ; (Y); 10/400; Am Leg Boys St; FCA; Varsity Clb; Nwsp Sprt Ed; L Var Socr; L Var Wrstlng; High Hon Roll; Hon Roll; NHS; Yth In Cnty Govt 86; Engrng.

TASSY, LEONARD F; Montclair HS; Montclair, NJ; (Y); 37/438; Nwsp Stf; JV Var Lcrss; Hon Roll; Acadmc-Athltc Achvt Awds 83-85; Ocean Explrs Clb 83-84.

TATEM, LINDA; Haddon Township HS; Westmont, NJ; (Y); Am Leg Aux Girls St; Varsity Clb; Stu Cncl; JV Bsktbl; Var Fld Hcky; Var Sftbl; High Hon Roll; Hon Roll; Trs NHS; Genetics.

TATKOW, RICHARD; Wayne Valley HS; Wayne, NJ; (Y); 75/320; FBLA; Trk; U Of RI; Bus Adm.

TATTER, TRACEY; Bridgewater-Rarhan HS East; Bridgewater, NJ; (Y); Church Yth Grp; Ski Clb; Nwsp Stf; Rep Stu Cncl; Stat Bsktbl; Mgr Fld Hcky; Stat Lcrss; High Hon Roll; Hon Roll; Varsity Clb.

TATULLI, LISA; Paul VI Regional HS; Clifton, NJ; (Y); 2/130; Pep Clb; SADD; Nwsp Ed-Chief; Rep Stu Cncl; Var Cheerleading; French Hon Soc; High Hon Roll; Pres NHS; Sal; NJ Prof Womn Schlrshp 86; Bucknell U; Med.

TAVENAS, HAYDEE; Northbergen HS; North Bergen, NJ; (Y); French Clb.

TAYLOR, AMY SUZANNE; Kittatinny Regional HS; Newton, NJ; (S); 10/164; Service Clb; Concert Band; Jazz Band; Pres Jr Cls; Stu Cncl; Var Capt Crs Cntry; Trk; Hon Roll; NHS; Ski Clb; Mst Lkly Sccd 85; Lbrl Arts.

TAYLOR, BARBARA; Elmwood Pk Memorial HS; Elmwood Pk, NJ; (Y); Q&S; Chorus; Drill Tm; Nwsp Stf; Mgr(s); Score Keeper; Hon Roll; Grad Modlng Schl 85; Comp Prgrmr.

TAYLOR, CINDY; West Morris Central HS; Chester, NJ; (Y); Dance Clb; Drama Clb; Band; Concert Band; Drm Mjr(t); Mrchg Band; Orch; School Musical; Yrbk Stf; Hon Roll; North Jersey Area Symphonic Band 84-86; NJ Region I Wind Ensemble 86; Math.

TAYLOR, DAVID; West Morris Central HS; Tyrone, GA; (Y); 61/260; French Clb; Var Golf; Var Socr; Hon Roll; Prfct Atten Awd; Partl Sccr Schlrshp 86; Eckerd Coll; Pltcl Sci.

TAYLOR, DENISE LA VERNE; University HS; Newark, NJ; (Y); Cmnty Wkr; VP JA; Political Wkr; VP Spanish Clb; Teachers Aide; Yrbk Phtg; Sec Jr Cls; Rep Stu Cncl; Capt Pom Pon; Spanish NHS; Pres Nrth Jrsy Yth Clb Ntl Assn Negro Bus & Prfsnl Wmns Clbs 83-87; Rutgers U; Law.

TAYLOR, DIANE LYN; Ramsey HS; Ramsey, NJ; (Y); 9/241; Church Yth Grp; Varsity Clb; Nwsp Sprt Ed; Bsktbl; Socr; Hon Roll; NHS; St Schlr; Penn ST U; Bio Mdcl Engrng.

TAYLOR, HOLLY; Wildwood HS; N Wildwood, NJ; (Y); 4/121; Pep Clb; School Musical; Rep Sr Cls; Rep Stu Cncl; Cheerleading; Hon Roll; U Of DE; Elem Ed.

TAYLOR, JENNIFER; Westfield HS; Westfield, NJ; (Y); 28/519; French Clb; Sec Latin Clb; Chorus; School Play; Yrbk Stf; Var Trk; High Hon Roll; Bio.

TAYLOR, JEROME; Cumberland Regional HS; Bridgeton, NJ; (Y); Library Aide; Office Aide; Band; Chorus; Concert Band; Jazz Band; Mrchg Band; Pep Band; Var Bsktbl; JV Crs Cntry; Elctrcn.

TAYLOR, JO ANN; Plainfield HS; Plainfield, NJ; (Y); Band; Trs Frsh Cls; Trs Soph Cls; Trs Jr Cls; Rep Stu Cncl; Stat Bsktbl; Var JV Score Keeper; Var Trk; Hon Roll; Busnss Admin.

TAYLOR, JOHN; Gill/St Bernards HS; Madison, NJ; (Y); Am Leg Boys St; Camp Fr Inc; Chess Clb; Church Yth Grp; Computer Clb; Drama Clb; Exploring; French Clb; Office Aide; Pep Clb; Bus.

TAYLOR, KELLY; Delsea Regional HS; Franklinville, NJ; (Y); Art Clb; Dance Clb; Drama Clb; French Clb; FTA; School Play; Yrbk Rptr; Yrbk Stf; Tennis; Tchr.

TAYLOR, LEN; Holy Cross HS; Burlington, NJ; (Y); 11/385; Am Leg Boys St; Chrmn Dance Clb; Nwsp Sprt Ed; Rep Jr Cls; Rep Sr Cls; Im Mgr Vllybl; High Hon Roll; Hon Roll; NHS; St Schlr; Acdmc Schlrhsp Monmouth Coll, Schl Nwspr Awd-Assoc Editor 86; Outstndng Stu Cncl Rep 85-86; Monmouth Coll; Crmnl Just.

TAYLOR, MAURICE; Weequahic HS; Newark, NJ; (Y); 19/159; Exploring; Bsbl; Math.

TAYLOR, MICHELLE; Kings Christian HS; Medford, NJ; (Y); 11/33; Church Yth Grp; Chorus; Yrbk Stf; VP Jr Cls; Rep Sr Cls; Var Bsktbl; Var Capt Fld Hcky; Hon Roll; NHS; Houghton Coll; Psychlgy.

TAYLOR, ROBERT; East Brunswick HS; E Brunswick, NJ; (Y); Aud/Vis; Boy Scts; Lit Mag; Trk; Rutgers; Pre-Law.

TAYLOR, SHARON; Gill/St Bernards HS; Plainfield, NJ; (Y); Rep Frsh Cls; Rep Soph Cls; Rep Stu Cncl; Var Bsktbl; Var Socr; Var Sftbl; JV Tennis; High Hon Roll; Hon Roll; Mrgrt D Jffrsn Cup-Mst Otstndng Grl 85; Engnrng.

TAYLOR, SHARON; Millville SR HS; Millville, NJ; (Y); Office Aide.

TAYLOR, TANYA M; Newark Acad; S Orange, NJ; (Y); Hosp Aide; Key Clb; Pep Clb; JV Bsktbl; Var Fld Hcky; Powder Puff Ftbl; Hon Roll; Ntl Merit Ltr; Ntl Merit Schlrshp, Distngher Schlr Hrn Ment ST NJ 85-86; Bio.

TAYLOR, VERONICA; Harrison HS; E Newark, NJ; (Y); Girl Scts; Yrbk Stf; Rep Stu Cncl; Powder Puff Ftbl; Hon Roll; Hon Rl 86; Bergin CC; Motel Rest Mgmt.

TEAT, TANYA; Marylawn Of The Oranges HS; S Orange, NJ; (Y); 12/54; Dance Clb; Latin Clb; Pres Science Clb; Spanish Clb; School Musical; Var Bsktbl; Hon Roll; Prfct Atten Awd; Spanish NHS; Natl Latin Exam Magna Cum Laude 84-85; Phys Fit Awd 84-85; Pre-Law.

TECCO, DARIA; Bishop Eustace Prep; Cherry Hill, NJ; (Y); 27/183; Sec French Clb; Hosp Aide; Latin Clb; Pep Clb; Capt Cheerleading; Mgr(s); Hon Roll; VP NHS; Tlnt Awd ST JR Ms Pagnt 86; 1st Rnnr Up ST JR Ms Pagnt 86; Ped Med.

TEDESCHI, LISA; Cranford HS; Cranford, NJ; (Y); 12/269; JCL; Latin Clb; VP Pres Spanish Clb; Yrbk Stf; Sec Stu Cncl; Var Capt Vllybl; Hon Roll; NHS; Spanish NHS; Band; Slvr Mdlst Natl Ltn Exm 86.

TEDESCO, MICHELLE K; Monsignor Donovan HS; Whiting, NJ; (Y); 11/230; Service Clb; Ski Clb; Flag Corp; Yrbk Stf; Stu Cncl; Var L Twrlr; High Hon Roll; Hon Roll; NHS; Ntl Merit SF; Frnch Hnrs Awd; Pre-Med.

TEEHAN, CATHERINE; Middletown HS North; Belford, NJ; (Y); 35/405; Sec Drama Clb; French Clb; Ski Clb; Nwsp Rptr; Nwsp Stf; Lit Mag; Twrlr; Cit Awd; High Hon Roll; Hon Roll; Middletown Wmns Clb Schlrshp 86; Middletown Ten Assoc Schlrshp 86; Suny Oswego.

TEEL, CYNTHIA; Holy Cross HS; Cinnaminson, NJ; (Y); Church Yth Grp; Rep Frsh Cls; Rep Soph Cls; Rep Jr Cls; VP Sr Cls; Capt L Socr; Wt Lftg; Hon Roll; NHS; Jrnlsm.

TEEVAN, JOHN; Christian Brothers Acad; Holmdel, NJ; (Y); 17/221; Computer Clb; Math Tm; Ski Clb; Im Bsbl; Im Bsktbl; Im Ftbl; Im Sftbl; Var L Wrstlng; High Hon Roll; Hon Roll; 4th Camp Trnmnt 86; Med.

TEEVAN, MARTIN; Christian Brothers Acad; Holmdel, NJ; (Y); 17/220; Debate Tm; Hosp Aide; Math Tm; School Play; Nwsp Sprt Ed; Yrbk Rptr; Lit Mag; Var JV Wrstlng; High Hon Roll; Cngrssnl Awd Brnz 86.

TEGER, MICHAEL R; Morristown HS; Morris Plains, NJ; (Y); 45/525; Am Leg Boys St; CAP; Cmnty Wkr; Exploring; Ski Clb; Rep Frsh Cls; Rep Soph Cls; High Hon Roll; NHS; Amelia Earhart Awd Cvl Ari Patrol 85; Resltn Mayor Morris Plains Cncl Honrng 84; Aerntcl Engr.

TEICH, TAMMY D; Montville HS; Pine Brook, NJ; (Y); FBLA; Key Clb; Temple Yth Grp; Lit Mag; Pres Stu Cncl; Fld Hcky; Sftbl; NHS; Ntl Merit SF; Office Aide; Pres Stu Cncl 87; Aid Vic Prncpl.

TEIPEL, DEBBIE; A P Schalick HS; Bridgeton, NJ; (Y); 10/147; Art Clb; Girl Scts; JA; Hon Roll; NHS; Rep Frsh Cls; Sec Soph Cls; JV Bsktbl; Var L Fld Hcky; JV Trk; Clse-Up Cert 86; Sci Exhbt Rbn Of Mrt 85; U DE; RN.

TEJANI, SHAMIN; Paul Vi HS; Williamstown, NJ; (S); 2/544; Math Clb; Spanish Clb; Trk; High Hon Roll; Med.

TELESCA, CHRISTINA; St John Vianney HS; Colts Neck, NJ; (S); 4/284; SADD; Yrbk Stf; Mgr(s); Var Socr; NHS; Prfct Atten Awd; Outstndng Spnsh Achvt Awd 84; Engl.

TELESH, JOHN; Hopatcong HS; Hopatcong, NJ; (Y); Church Yth Grp; Nwsp Rptr; Ed Nwsp Stf; Yrbk Rptr; Yrbk Stf; Hon Roll; Bus.

TELLER, DENNIS N; Hopatcong HS; Hopatcong, NJ; (Y); Aud/Vis; Boy Scts; Computer Clb; English Clb; Yrbk Stf; Lit Mag; Var Bowling; Mgr(s); JV Socr; Hon Roll; Comp Tp Of Cls 84; Glassboro ST; Bus.

TELLIS, TAMMI; Mother Seton Regional HS; Newark, NJ; (Y); 13/93; Church Yth Grp; Cmnty Wkr; Debate Tm; GAA; Intnl Clb; Office Aide; Acpl Chr; Chorus; Pres Church Choir; Variety Show; M L King Jr Schlrshp 86; Otpmst Clb-1st Ortrcl Cntst Wnr 86; Yth Choirs Fthfl Dedication Awd 84; Seton Hall U; Lawyer.

TEMPLE, PATRICK; Jefferson Township HS; Oakridge, NJ; (Y); Debate Tm; Drama Clb; FCA; Ski Clb; Chorus; School Play; Rep Frsh Cls; Rep Soph Cls; JV Var Ftbl; Swmmng; Sprts Med Tm 84-85; U Of FL; Med.

TEMPRANO, MICHELLE; Immaculate Conception HS; Lodi, NJ; (Y); Hosp Aide; Spanish Clb; Hon Roll; Acdmc All Amer Awd 86; Chld Psych.

TENCZA, WILLIAM; St Ros HS; Neptune City, NJ; (Y); 57/206; Latin Clb; Ski Clb; Spanish Clb; Socr; High Hon Roll; U Of St Joseph; Bus.

TEPLITZKY, DEBRA; Paramus HS; Paramus, NJ; (Y); Art Clb; Temple Yth Grp; Band; Yrbk Stf; Lit Mag; Sftbl; Johns Hopkins Talent Search 82; Ecnmcs.

TEPPER, ALAN; Mt Olive HS; Flanders, NJ; (Y); 45/296; Math Clb; Stage Crew; Lit Mag; Hon Roll; Math.

TERI, ANTHONY; Bayonne HS; Bayonne, NJ; (Y); Cmnty Wkr; Key Clb; Yrbk Rptr; Yrbk Stf; Pres Soph Cls; Pres Jr Cls; Pres Stu Cncl; Coach Actv; Hon Roll; Prfct Atten Awd; Audio Engrng.

TERNAY, JENNIFER; Sacred Heart HS; Elmer, NJ; (S); VP Pres German Clb; School Musical; Yrbk Stf; Hon Roll; NHS; US Natl Math Awd 85-86; Govnrs Schl 84-85; Garden St Dstngshd Schlr 85-86; Bus.

TERRELL, BRENDA SHEREE; Red Bank Catholic HS; Neptune, NJ; (Y); Cmnty Wkr; VP Service Clb; Spanish Clb; Band; Concert Band; Mrchg Band; Pep Band; Trk; Duke U; Med.

TERRIZZI, SANTI; Saint Peters HS; New Brunswick, NJ; (Y); 14/121; Stage Crew; Lit Mag; JV Bsbl; Prfct Atten Awd; Acad All Am Hnr 85-86.

TERRY, SHARON; Paul VI Regional HS; Clifton, NJ; (Y); Am Leg Aux Girls St; Art Clb; Dance Clb; Chorus; School Musical; School Play; Nwsp Rptr; Nwsp Stf; Yrbk Stf; Stu Cncl; Girls St 86; Ringwood Art Assn 1st Pl Awd 83; Comm.

TESTA, FRANK C; Vineland HS; Vineland, NJ; (Y); 15/720; Key Clb; Latin Clb; Jr Cls; Sr Cls; Stu Cncl; Trk; High Hon Roll; NHS; LAW.

TESTA, JENNIFER; Bishop Eustace Prep; Berlin, NJ; (Y); Dance Clb; Pep Clb; Spanish Clb; Var Cheerleading; Var Trk; All Amer Fnlst Chrldg 84 & 85.

TESTA, SUSAN E; Buena Regional HS; Landisville, NJ; (S); 10/190; Drama Clb; Pep Clb; Ski Clb; Varsity Clb; School Play; Trs Sr Cls; Stu Cncl; Var Co-Capt Cheerleading; Hon Roll; NHS; Gregg Shrthnd Awd 83-84; Stockton ST Coll; Bus Mgt.

TESTORI, JEANNE; Pascack Hills HS; Montvale, NJ; (Y); Service Clb; SADD; Hon Roll; NHS; Yrbk Bus Mgr; 1st Plc Orgnl Dsgn Nrth Jrsey Stu Crftsmn Fr 86; 2nd Plc Illstrtn 86; PFA Hm Ec Awd 85-86; Fshn Dsgn.

TETER, THOMAS; St Augustine Prep; Vineland, NJ; (Y); Boy Scts; Pres Church Yth Grp; Pres Science Clb; Concert Band; Jazz Band; Mrchg Band; Hon Roll; NHS; Hstry Bwl 86; Brigham Young U; Bus.

TETI, DONNA MARIE; Pennsauken HS; Pennsauken, NJ; (Y); 168/368; Dance Clb; Drama Clb; Pep Clb; Chorus; Capt Color Guard; Mrchg Band; School Musical; Bsktbl; Cit Awd; Hon Roll; 2 Marching Band Awds 86.

TETLEY, KIM; Egg Harbory Township HS; Mays Landing, NJ; (S); 24/317; Hst French Clb; Sec Band; Concert Band; Mrchg Band; School Musical; Nwsp Rptr; Rep Jr Cls; Ntl Merit Ltr; Rutgers; Frnch.

THAL, JULIE; Toms River HS East; Toms River, NJ; (Y); Church Yth Grp; Cmnty Wkr; Hon Roll; Outstndng Partcptn Awd 84; Mentlly Retrtd Cls Aide 85; Spcl Ed Tchr.

THALER, ROBERTA; Sacred Heart HS; Vineland, NJ; (Y); 25/75; Spanish Clb; SADD; Nwsp Stf; Yrbk Stf; Lit Mag; Hon Roll; Bus Awd-Bst In Bus Sbjcts 86; Hnr Rll 84-86; Cumberland County Coll; Bnkng.

THAPAR, SAMITA; Boonton HS; Boonton, NJ; (Y); 2/270; Computer Clb; Dance Clb; Sec French Clb; Variety Show; Lit Mag; High Hon Roll; NHS; ST SF Poetry Morris Cnty Arts Fest 86; 3rd Pl Natl Frnch Exm 84; Cert Apprctn Frnch Clb Secy 86; Rutgers ST U; Bus Adm.

THAXTON, CHERYL; Immaculate Conception HS; East Orange, NJ; (Y); 17/181; Computer Clb; Dance Clb; French Clb; Pep Clb; Variety Show; Nwsp Rptr; Nwsp Sprt Ed; Stu Cncl; JV Crs Cntry; Var Score Keeper; Harvard U; Pre-Med.

THAYER, KAREN; Freehold Township HS; Freehold, NJ; (Y); Spanish Clb; Yrbk Bus Mgr; Lit Mag; Rep Frsh Cls; Rep Soph Cls; Trs Stu Cncl; Var Gym; Var Trk; NHS; Ntl Merit Ltr; Middlebury Coll; Math.

THERIAULT, MARK; Holy Cross HS; Riverton, NJ; (Y); Swmmng; Wrstlng; Hon Roll; Schlrshp Cok Coll Rugers U 86-90; Cook Coll; Pre-Vet.

THIEMANN, JILL L; Toms River HS North; Toms River, NJ; (Y); 4/412; Sec French Clb; Drill Tm; Co-Capt Flag Corp; Stat Ice Hcky; Trk; High Hon Roll; NHS; Clarkson Schl; Math.

THIES, GINA; Hillsborough HS; Belle Mead, NJ; (Y); 60/300; Art Clb; Church Yth Grp; Ski Clb; Lit Mag; JV Powder Puff Ftbl; Im Sftbl; St Lawrence U.

THIESE, KRITI; Sparta HS; Sparta, NJ; (Y); 1/220; Church Yth Grp; Jazz Band; Mrchg Band; Nwsp Ed-Chief; Chrmn Stu Cncl; Capt Socr; High Hon Roll; NHS; Ntl Merit SF; Val; Egne Dpnt Mem Schlrshp; NJ Gov Schlr 85; Chmbr Cmmrce Schlrshp 86; U Delaware; Frgn Lang.

THINSCHMIDT, JILL; Mainland Regional HS; Northfield, NJ; (Y); 26/285; Church Yth Grp; 4-H; German Clb; GAA; Ski Clb; Band; Mrchg Band; Crs Cntry; Trk; NHS; Mst Imprvd Rnnr Cr Cntry 85; Zoology.

THOELE, VICKI; West Morris Central HS; Long Valley, NJ; (Y); 12/300; Pres Church Yth Grp; Concert Band; Mrchg Band; Nwsp Stf; Capt Var Tennis; Hon Roll; NHS; Intl Bus.

THOMAS, CAROL; Westfield SR HS; Westfield, NJ; (Y); Church Yth Grp; French Clb; Ski Clb; Soroptimist; Chorus; Rep Stu Cncl; L Cheerleading; NJ Govrnrs Schl Of Pblc Issues & Future Of NJ 85; Yth In Bus & Govt; Kids On Black Puppeteers; Bucknell U; Psych.

THOMAS, CHRISTINE; Bayonne HS; Bayonne, NJ; (Y); French Clb; Variety Show; Crs Cntry; Trk; 3rd All Cnty Trck Awd 84; F I T.

THOMAS, DENNE; John F Kennedy HS; Willingboro, NJ; (Y); 15/298; Dance Clb; Drama Clb; Chorus; Church Choir; Color Guard; Drill Tm; Mrchg Band; School Musical; School Play; Yrbk Stf; Pre-Med.

THOMAS, MICHELLE M; Orange HS; Orange, NJ; (Y); Band; Color Guard; Mrchg Band; Rep Jr Cls; Rep Stu Cncl; Stat Wrstlng; Hon Roll; Elizabethtown; RN.

THOMAS, PAMELA; Clifford J Scott HS; E Orange, NJ; (Y); #9 In Class; Mathletes; Office Aide; Mrchg Band; Nwsp Stf; Hon Roll; NHS; Mst Outstndng Stdnt Sci Enrchmt Prog 85; Hgh Hnrs Math, Sci, Spnsh & Fine Arts 85-86; Rutgers U Coll Of Pharm; Pharm.

THOMAS, RHONDA; Mc Corristin HS; Trenton, NJ; (Y); Cmnty Wkr; Hon Roll; Lgl Sec.

THOMAS, SEAN; Millville SR HS; Millville, NJ; (Y); 29/435; Computer Clb; Var Trk; Hon Roll; Aerontcl Engr.

THOMAS, SHARON; Red Bank Regional HS; Little Silver, NJ; (Y); 9/223; Concert Band; Jazz Band; Sec Mrchg Band; Orch; School Musical; School Play; Gov Hon Prg Awd; NHS; Spanish NHS; Monmth Arts Fndtn Awd 86; Ltl Slvr Ed Assn Schlrshp 86; VA Tech Music Dpt Schlrshp 86; VA Polytech Inst; Music.

THOMAS, SHEILA; Holy Cross HS; Willingboro, NJ; (Y); School Musical; Yrbk Phtg; Yrbk Stf; Trk; Hon Roll; Crtfct Achvmnt N & Bar Assoc Mck Trl 86; Hd Hall Dcrtng Cmmtt Hmcmng 83; Lbrl Arts.

THOMAS, VAUGHAN L; Paul VI HS; Somerdale, NJ; (Y); Drama Clb; German Clb; NFL; Chorus; Jazz Band; School Musical; Bowling; Natl Negro Schlrshp Search Semi-Fnlst 85; Fin.

THOMAS, WENDY S; Watchung Hills Regional HS; Warren, NJ; (Y); 8/325; VP 4-H; Hosp Aide; Var L Trk; Hon Roll; Ntl Merit SF; St Schlr; Review Edtr-Newsletter For NJ Gftd & Tlntd Stu 81; Rutgers U; Enviro & Forst Bio.

THOMPSON, ANN; Metuchen HS; Metuchen, NJ; (Y); Church Yth Grp; Cmnty Wkr; Dance Clb; Drama Clb; Varsity Clb; Church Choir; Var Trk; Hon Roll; NHS; Music.

THOMPSON, CAROL; Eastside HS; Paterson, NJ; (Y); 66/600; Church Yth Grp; Cmnty Wkr; Drama Clb; Chorus; Church Choir; School Musical; School Play; Variety Show; Nwsp Bus Mgr; Nwsp Rptr; Cngrssnl Salute & Cert Mrt 86; Rutgers U; Hstry.

THOMPSON, CHRISTINE; Hunterdon Central HS; Flemington, NJ; (Y); 46/546; Church Yth Grp; Yrbk Stf; Var Cheerleading; French Hon Soc; Hon Roll; NHS; Gftd & Tlntd Art I & II; Hmcmt Qn; Interact; Advtg.

THOMPSON, CHRISTINE; Toms River HS North; Toms River, NJ; (Y); 9/412; Drama Clb; Hosp Aide; Spanish Clb; School Musical; Rep Sr Cls; VP Stu Cncl; High Hon Roll; Hon Roll; Trs NHS; Intnl Clb; Cmmnctns.

THOMPSON, COLLEEN; Gateway Regional HS; Woodbury Hts, NJ; (Y); 21/197; French Clb; Hosp Aide; JCL; Key Clb; Latin Clb; SADD; Capt Var Cheerleading; Var Fld Hcky; Cit Awd; High Hon Roll; Soroptimist Yth Citznshp Awd 86; 1st Pl Gloucester Co Cultural & Heritage Comm Essay Cntst 86; Penn ST; Librl Arts.

THOMPSON, CORRINE; Cliffside Park HS; Cliffside Pk, NJ; (Y); 60/240; Cmnty Wkr; VP French Clb; Sec Latin Clb; Chorus; Rep Stu Cncl; Var Cheerleading; Coach Actv; Var Sftbl; Stat Tennis; Masonic Awd; Masonic Fndtn Schlrshp 86; Unico Schlrshp 86; Bergen Cnty Dmcrtc Clb Schlrshp 86; Old Dominion U; Nrsng.

THOMPSON, ELDA; Vailsburg HS; Newark, NJ; (Y); VP Sec JA; Rep Nwsp Stf; VP Jr Cls; Rep Stu Cncl; JV Bsktbl; Hon Roll; Chrldr Awd 83; Gld Crd 85; Accptnc Inroads 85; Elec Engr.

THOMPSON, PRISCILLA; Lincoln HS; Jersey City, NJ; (S); Cmnty Wkr; JA; Key Clb; Church Choir; Yrbk Stf; Ntl Merit Ltr; Prfct Atten Awd; Church Yth Grp; FBLA; Library Aide; Trenton Engl, Hstry Awd 84-85; Mrt And Achvt Awd 82-85; Jersey City ST; Bus Admin.

THOMPSON, SANDY; James Caldwell HS; W Caldwell, NJ; (Y); Sec Jr Cls; Sec Sr Cls; Var Cheerleading; JV Gym; JV Sftbl.

THOMPSON, SHEILA; Scotch Plains-Farwood HS; Scotch Pl, NJ; (Y); Pres VP Church Yth Grp; German Clb; Model UN; SADD; Drm Mjr(t); Capt Flag Corp; Yrbk Stf; Stu Cncl; Sftbl; Grmn Hnr Soc 86-87; Stu Ldrshp Cnfrnc 84-85; Poli Sci.

THOMPSON, TINA; Middletown South HS; Highlands, NJ; (Y); VP Church Yth Grp; Sec Church Choir; Drill Tm; Bsktbl; Gym; Hon Roll; Dance Clb; GAA; Girl Scts; Variety Show.

THOMPSON, WILLIAM; Toms River North HS; Toms River, NJ; (Y); 42/421; Pres Chess Clb; 4-H; German Clb; Key Clb; Math Clb; Math Tm; Science Clb; Stage Crew; 4-H Awd; Prfct Atten Awd; Coll Of S FL; Dentist.

THOMSON, BARBARA; Sacred Heart HS; Vineland, NJ; (S); 2/63; Art Clb; Dance Clb; Spanish Clb; School Musical; School Play; Stage Crew; Variety Show; Vllybl; High Hon Roll; Hon Roll; NSMA Ntl Sci Merit Awd 85; Math.

THOMSON, MICHAEL P; Raritan HS; Hazlet, NJ; (Y); 25/350; Am Leg Boys St; JV Bsbl; JV Ftbl; High Hon Roll; NHS; Bus Adm.

THOR, MELISSA; Wall Twp HS; Manasquan, NJ; (S); 1/277; AFS; Church Yth Grp; GAA; JCL; Latin Clb; SADD; Varsity Clb; Rep Jr Cls; Coach Actv; Var Co-Capt Gym; Occptnl Thrpy.

THORNE, CHARLES; Notre Dame HS; Trenton, NJ; (Y); Political Wkr; Nwsp Rptr; Bowling; Socr; Hon Roll.

THORNE, LISA; Shore Regional HS; Oceanport, NJ; (Y); Church Yth Grp; Im Powder Puff Ftbl; Var L Trk; Hon Roll; Prfct Atten Awd; Grphc Art.

THORNER, LARRY; Howell HS; Howell, NJ; (Y); 36/361; Boy Scts; FCA; JCL; Latin Clb; Bowling; Golf; Socr; Wrstlng; Hon Roll; NHS; Trenton ST Coll; Acctg.

THORNTON, AUDREY; Hillside HS; Hillside, NJ; (Y); Band; Concert Band; Drm Mjr(t); Mrchg Band; School Play; Pres Jr Cls; VP Sr Cls; Stat Bsktbl; Score Keeper; Hon Roll.

THORNTON, SHAWNA L; Vailsburg HS; Newark, NJ; (Y); Church Yth Grp; Cmnty Wkr; English Clb; FBLA; JA; Political Wkr; Teachers Aide; Church Choir; Color Guard; Flag Corp; Hnr Awds Typg, Steno & Career Ed Clss 85-86; VA ST U; Acctg.

THORNTON SMITH, VALERIE; Washington Twp HS; Sewell, NJ; (Y); JCL; Latin Clb; Ski Clb; Spanish Clb; Chorus; Pres Soph Cls; Pres Jr Cls; Off Stu Cncl; JV Bsktbl; JV Fld Hcky; Rutgers U New Brunswick; Bus.

THORP, GEORGE; Cloucester Catholic HS; Brooklawn, NJ; (Y); Camp Fr Inc; Scholastic Bowl; Spanish Clb; Var JV Bsbl; Var JV Wrstlng; High Hon Roll; Hon Roll; Jr NHS; NHS; Spanish NHS; York Coll; Pre-Med.

THORPE, JENNIFER; Toms River East HS; Toms River, NJ; (Y); 29/580; French Clb; Key Clb; Rep Stu Cncl; High Hon Roll; Hon Roll; Rider Coll; Mktg.

THORPE, TOM; Hunterdon Central HS; Flemington, NJ; (Y); 210/565; Computer Clb; Band; Concert Band; Mrchg Band; Orch; Pep Band; School Musical; Symp Band; JV Ftbl; JV Lcrss; Comp.

THROM, COLIN C; Montgomery HS; Skillman, NJ; (Y); 12/131; Drama Clb; School Play; Lit Mag; Var JV Trk; Hon Roll; NHS; Ntl Merit Ltr; Colby Coll Bk Awd 85; Rutgers; Phrmcy.

THURSTON, PORTIA; Delsea Reginal HS; Franklinville, NJ; (Y); Dance Clb; Spanish Clb; Varsity Clb; Variety Show; Rep VP Frsh Cls; Sec Sr Cls; Var Capt Cheerleading; JV Fld Hcky; High Hon Roll; Hon Roll; One Of Mst Prominent Stus 85-86; Trophy For Jazz Dncng 85-86; Rutgers U; Lawyer.

TICE, JANET; Burlington City HS; Burlington, NJ; (Y); 5/168; Am Leg Aux Girls St; Church Yth Grp; Nwsp Rptr; Hon Roll; VP NHS; Extended Lrning Prog 82-86; Olympics Mind 83-86; Pres Acad Fitness Awd 86; Douglass Coll; Pre-Law.

TICE, SHARON; Clearview Regional HS; Sewell, NJ; (Y); 14/146; GAA; Ski Clb; Yrbk Stf; Rep Stu Cncl; JV Bsktbl; Im Powder Puff Ftbl; Var L Sftbl; Var L Tennis; Hon Roll; NHS.

TIDWELL, JAY; Ridge HS; Basking Ridge, NJ; (Y); Boy Scts; Church Yth Grp; Computer Clb; Drama Clb; Key Clb; Ski Clb; Chorus; Church Choir; School Play; Stage Crew; Lf Sct 85; Elec Engnrng.

TIEMAN, TAMARA; Souhern Regional HS; Barnegat, NJ; (Y); 5/389; Band; Yrbk Stf; Rep Frsh Cls; Rep Soph Cls; Rep Jr Cls; Rep Sr Cls; Rep Stu Cncl; JV Var Fld Hcky; Socr; High Hon Roll; Monmouth JR Sci Symp; Hopwood Smmr Schlrs Prog 86; Duke U; Mktg.

TIENCKEN, DENISE; High Point Regional HS; Sussex, NJ; (Y); 49/209; Church Yth Grp; 4-H; Pep Clb; PAVAS; Ski Clb; SADD; Thesps; Varsity Clb; Band; Chorus; Sussex Cty Police Chfs Crmnlgy Schlrshp 86; Upsala Coll; Crmnlgy.

TIERNEY, MICHAEL; Holy Spirit HS; Ventnor, NJ; (Y); SADD; School Play; Rep Jr Cls; Rep Sr Cls; Rep Stu Cncl; L Bsbl; L Ftbl; Hon Roll; NHS; Sprt Med.

TIGHE, COLEEN P; Linden HS; Linden, NJ; (S); French Clb; Trs Key Clb; Science Clb; Ski Clb; Band; Concert Band; Mrchg Band; School Musical; High Hon Roll; NHS.

TIGHE, KEVIN; St John Vianney HS; Hazlet, NJ; (Y); 150/300; Exploring; Office Aide; Service Clb; SADD; VP Soph Cls; VP Jr Cls; VP Sr Cls; Rep Stu Cncl; Coach Actv; Var L Trk; St John Vianney Gold & White Srvc Awd 84-86; Fclty Stu Discpln Brd 84-87; LA Salle U; Hlth Care Adm.

TILLER, MICHELE; Washington Township HS; Turnersville, NJ; (Y); 89/470; Capt Var Tennis; Var Trk; Tennis Mst Imprvd 84; Tennis Sprtsmnshp Awd 85; Rutgers U; Bus.

TILLMAN, CARLA; Middlesex HS; Middlesex, NJ; (Y); Church Yth Grp; Ski Clb; Church Choir; Variety Show; Bsktbl; Cheerleading; Fld Hcky; Gym; Sftbl; Mst Vly Plyr Slftbl 83; 2nd Cntry Tm Bsktbl 86; VP & Dir Yth Choir 84-85.

TILLMAN, DIANE; North Warren Regional HS; Columbia, NJ; (Y); Church Yth Grp; Church Choir; Rep Stu Cncl; Var Cheerleading; Var Coach Actv; Var Capt Gym; Pom Pon; Powder Puff Ftbl; Vrsty Gym MVP Awd & Schlrshp 84-85; Vrsty Chrldg All Star-Fall 2nd Tm & Wntr 1st Tm 85-86; MOG Awd; East Stroudsburg U; Gymstcs.

TILTON, CORI; Woodstown HS; Elmer, NJ; (Y); 4-H; German Clb; Key Clb; School Play; Var Fld Hcky; 4-H Awd; Hon Roll; NHS; Prfct Atten Awd; Med.

TILTON, MONICA; Red Bank Catholic HS; Old Bridge, NJ; (Y); Church Yth Grp; Cmnty Wkr; 4-H; Gym Mem Awd 85-86; 4-H Camp Cnslr 85.

TIMBROOK, TODD; Holy Spirit HS; Northfield, NJ; (Y); Letterman Clb; Ski Clb; SADD; Varsity Clb; Var JV Ftbl; Var Swmmng; Im Vllybl; Wt Lftg; Prfct Atten Awd; Ntl Chmps, Ltr Rowng 85-86; Art Awds 81-82; Phrmst.

TIMKO, DONNA; Spotswood HS; Milltown, NJ; (Y); Art Clb; Dance Clb; Library Aide; Church Choir; JV Socr; JV Trk; Hon Roll; Mason Gross; Cmrcl Art.

TIMKO, SUSAN; Mt St Marys HS; Scotch Plains, NJ; (Y); Church Yth Grp; Drama Clb; Service Clb; Hon Roll; Spanish NHS; Natl Latin Exam Maxima Cum Laude 85; George Washington U; Marketing.

TIMKO, TED; Rahway HS; Rahway, NJ; (Y); Aud/Vis; Pres Church Yth Grp; Band; Concert Band; Jazz Band; School Musical; Variety Show; Nwsp Stf; Soph Cls; Jr Cls; Arch.

TIMONERA, MAYDA; Washington Township HS; Sewell, NJ; (Y); Church Yth Grp; Hosp Aide; Ski Clb; Spanish Clb; Color Guard; Mrchg Band; Hon Roll; JC Awd; Prfct Atten Awd; Rotary Yth Ldrs Awd-S NJ 86; Outstndg Female Karate Awd-Brwn Belt 84; Piano-Bst Plyr; Phila Coll/Phrmcy/Sci; Phy Ther.

TINDELL, SHANNAN; Benedictine Acad; Newark, NJ; (Y); Church Yth Grp; French Clb; Math Clb; Chorus; Sec Church Choir; Nwsp Rptr; Nwsp Sprt Ed; Nwsp Stf; Rep Frsh Cls; Twrlr; Awd For Volntrng Svcs SR Ctzns 84-85; Awd For Outstdng Perf Phy Ftnss Tst 86; Spcl Educ Tchr.

TING, STEVEN; Arthur L Johnson Reg HS; Clark, NJ; (Y); 18/195; Computer Clb; Exploring; Lit Mag; Hon Roll; Spanish NHS; Elec Engrng.

TIPPENS, BROOKE; Weequahic HS; Hillside, NJ; (S); 1/435; Sec Church Yth Grp; Debate Tm; Exploring; NFL; Drill Tm; Nwsp Ed-Chief; Lit Mag; NHS; Black Mnrty Ldr; Amherst; Finance.

TIRELLA, MICHAEL; Butler HS; Butler, NJ; (Y); Church Yth Grp; Cmnty Wkr; Drama Clb; Spanish Clb; School Play; Ftbl; Wt Lftg; Wrstlng; Stu Mnth Hnrbl Ment Hist 86; Hortwich; Comp Sci.

TIRENIN, MICHAEL; Hopewell Valley Central HS; Trenton, NJ; (Y); 42/202; Art Clb; Science Clb; Spanish Clb; High Hon Roll; Hon Roll; Teen Arts 85; Hussian Coll Summer Schlrshp 86; Pre-Dentistry.

TIROCKE, JOANNE; Cherry Hill HS West; Cherry Hill, NJ; (Y); 11/132; Spanish Clb; SADD; Rep Soph Cls; Rep Jr Cls; Rep Sr Cls; Stu Cncl; Var Fld Hcky; Var Lcrss; Mgr Wrstlng; NHS; Home & Schl Awd For Svc; Grdn St Dstngshd Schlr Awd; Recgntn-Natl Spnsh Exam; Phy Ed.

TIROLY, DAVID; Point Pleasant Boro HS; Point Pleasant, NJ; (Y); Trk; Rider Coll; Bus Adm.

TIRONI, MICHAEL J; North Warren Regional HS; Blairstown, NJ; (Y); Am Leg Boys St; Ski Clb; Band; Concert Band; Mrchg Band; Bsbl; Bsktbl; Ftbl; Golf; Tennis; Amer Legion NJ Boys St 86; Pratt Inst; Indus Dsgn.

TIRRELL, LORI; Belleville HS; Belleville, NJ; (Y); Key Clb; Spanish Clb; Drill Tm; Var Tennis; High Hon Roll; Hon Roll; NHS; 1st Pl-Poetry Cntst-Jnr Wmns Clb 83-84; Montclair ST; Illstrtn.

TIRRI, CARMELINA; Mary Help Of Christians Acad; Paterson, NJ; (S); 1/88; Church Yth Grp; JCL; Teachers Aide; High Hon Roll; NHS; NEDT Awd; Prfct Atten Awd; Amer Legn Awd 83; Paterson Diocesn Essy 1st Pl 84.

TITOLO, ANGIE; St Marys HS; Perth Amboy, NJ; (Y); 20/160; Yrbk Stf; Sec Soph Cls; VP Pres Jr Cls; Off Sr Cls; Stu Cncl; High Hon Roll; Hon Roll; Jr NHS; NHS; Fshn Mrchndsng.

TITTLE, DAWN M; Paul VI HS; Laurel Springs, NJ; (S); 15/474; French Clb; Math Clb; SADD; Nwsp Stf; Lit Mag; Var Pom Pon; French Hon Soc; Hon Roll; NHS; Rutgers U; Bio.

TIWARI, SUDHA; Cherry Hill HS West; Cherry Hill, NJ; (Y); Library Aide; Nwsp Rptr; Nwsp Stf; Capt Lcrss; Hon Roll; NHS; Pres Schlr; Ntl Merit Ltr; High Hon Roll; Swmmng; SR All Star Team S Lacrosse 86; Hme & Schl Awd 85; Brd Of Ed Awd For Lacrosse 86; Rtgrs U; Law.

TJALMA, MICHELE; Belvidere HS; Phillipsburg, NJ; (S); 4/128; Pres Church Yth Grp; Library Aide; JV Var Sftbl; Hon Roll; NHS; Elem Eductn.

TKACZ, JAROSLAW; Clifton HS; Clifton, NJ; (Y); Library Aide; Yrbk Stf; Hon Roll; Jr NHS; Schl Ukranian Studs Compltn & Grad 76-86; Med Careers Clb Beth Israel Hosp 86; Pre-Med.

TOBEY, JOANNE; Holy Family Acad; Bayonne, NJ; (Y); 6/136; Teachers Aide; Rep Frsh Cls; Rep Stu Cncl; Stat Bsktbl; JV Cheerleading; Capt Score Keeper; Stat Sftbl; JV Swmmng; Stat Trk; Capt Vllybl; Law.

TOBEY, MICHELE; Holy Family Acad; Bayonne, NJ; (Y); 34/129; Computer Clb; Off Frsh Cls; Off Soph Cls; Cheerleading; Hon Roll; Comp Sci.

TOBEY, PATRICK; Marist HS; Bayonne, NJ; (Y); 32/103; Science Clb; Yrbk Stf; Im JV Bsktbl; Im Coach Actv; Im Vllybl; Hon Roll; Schlrshp Marist 83; Johnson & Wales Coll; Clnry Art.

TOBIA, CHRISTOPHER J; Paul VI HS; Laurel Springs, NJ; (Y); 47/519; Am Leg Boys St; Mathletes; Math Clb; Var L Bsbl; Bsktbl; NHS; Intl Bnkg.

TOBIASSEN, CHERYL; Howell HS; Howell, NJ; (Y); 13/371; Church Yth Grp; Hosp Aide; Spanish Clb; Color Guard; Hon Roll; NHS; Farmingdale Fortnightly Clb Schlrshp Grnt 86; Typg Awd 85; Acctg Awd 86; Trenton ST Coll.

TOBIO, EDIT; Kearney HS; Kearny, NJ; (Y); 3/375; Am Leg Aux Girls St; French Clb; Band; Drm Mjr(t); Mrchg Band; Gym; Trk; NHS; Law.

TOCCI III, LOUIS J; Christian Brothers Acad; Monmouth Bch, NJ; (Y); Im Ftbl; JV Trk; Eucharistc Mnstr 85-86.

TODD, DEBORAH M; Florence Twp Mem HS; Roebling, NJ; (Y); #34 In Class; DECA; FBLA; FTA; Concert Band; Drm & Bgl; Mrchg Band; Trs Sr Cls; Hon Roll; Mrktng.

TODD, JEFFREY; Linden HS; Linden, NJ; (Y); Chess Clb; Church Yth Grp; Cmnty Wkr; French Clb; Yrbk Stf; JV Var Ftbl; Im Ice Hcky; Trk; Wt Lftg; Hon Roll; Hnr Algbr & Trig 85-86; Accntng.

TODD, MARGARET; Lower Cape May Regional HS; N Cape May, NJ; (Y); 27/222; Am Leg Aux Girls St; Key Clb; Pep Clb; Varsity Clb; Flag Corp; Rep Soph Cls; Rep Jr Cls; Rep Sr Cls; Rep Stu Cncl; CC Awd; Outstndg Bus Stu 86; Prac Art Outstndg Stu 86; Atlantic CC; Fin.

TOFFENETTI, GINA; Buena Regional HS; Vineland, NJ; (S); 3/191; Dance Clb; Ski Clb; JV Cheerleading; High Hon Roll; Hon Roll; Jr NHS; Natl Hnr Socty 84-86; U Of DE; Bio.

TOIGO, MARK; Piscathaway HS; Piscataway, NJ; (Y); Mathletes; Math Clb; Math Tm; Science Clb; Chrmn NHS; Ntl Merit Ltr; Pres Schlr; RCA Schlrshp, PTEA Schlrshp, GA Glf Schlrshp 86; Johns Hopkins U; Chem Engrng.

TOIVONEN, TANYA; Glen Rock HS; Glen Rock, NJ; (Y); 20/169; AFS; Civic Clb; Drama Clb; French Clb; Latin Clb; PAVAS; Varsity Clb; Acpl Chr; Band; Chorus; Ballet Co-Kalamazoo MI; Hstry.

TOLAND, KIMBERLY; Holy Spirit HS; Atlantic City, NJ; (Y); Drama Clb; Political Wkr; School Musical; Nwsp Stf; Rep Frsh Cls; Rep Stu Cncl; Hon Roll; Rutgers Mason Gross Schl; Music.

TOLBERT, VALENCIA NINETTE; Trenton Central HS; Trenton, NJ; (Y); 16/529; Pep Clb; Church Choir; Yrbk Ed-Chief; Off Sr Cls; Mgr(s); JV Sftbl; Hon Roll; Spanish NHS; Hmcmng Queen 85-86; RCA MEP Pgm 85-86; Acdmc All Am 85-86; Spelman Coll; Elec Engrng.

TOLEDO, EVELYN; Hoboken HS; Hoboken, NJ; (Y); Tchr.

TOLENTINO, CARMEN; St Anthonys HS; Jersey City, NJ; (Y); 3/60; JV Bowling; High Hon Roll; Hon Roll.

TOLMAYER, ROBERT J; Rancocas Valley Regional HS; Mt Holly, NJ; (Y); 9/270; Am Leg Boys St; Key Clb; Band; Var Capt Bsktbl; Var Capt Socr; JV Tennis; Var Trk; Hon Roll; NHS; Rutgers U Deans Smmr Schlrs Pgm Scholar 86.

TOMARCHIO, BRIAN; Washington Township HS; Turnersville, NJ; (Y); Aud/Vis; Spanish Clb; Pres Band; Pres Mrchg Band; Stage Crew; Rep Stu Cncl; Var Ftbl; Hon Roll; Comp Sci.

TOMASELLO, ANNETTE; Matawan Regional HS; Matawan, NJ; (S); 21/311; Nwsp Sprt Ed; Rep Jr Cls; Var Bsktbl; Var Sftbl; Hon Roll; MVP Sftbl, Bsktbl 84; Physcl Thrpy.

TOMASELLO, RONALD; Edgewood Regional SR HS; Elm, NJ; (Y); Aud/Vis; Boy Scts; Drama Clb; School Play; Stage Crew; Nwsp Rptr; Rep Jr Cls; Hon Roll; Jr NHS; NHS; Cmmnctns.

TOMASULA, LINDA; Newton HS; Newton, NJ; (Y); French Clb; GAA; Pep Clb; Ski Clb; Teachers Aide; Varsity Clb; Band; Concert Band; Mrchg Band; Stat Bsbl; Cmmndtns Typng 82-83; Cmmndtns Accntng Hsry 84-85; Cmmndtns Mrtrus Acad Achvmnt 885-86; Kathern Gibbs Schl; Infrmnt Prc.

TOMKOVICH, CELESTE; Manalapan HS; Manalapan, NJ; (Y); Church Yth Grp; Hosp Aide; Chorus; Nwsp Stf; JV Capt Cheerleading; Tchng.

TOMKOVICH, SUSAN; Toms River North HS; Toms River, NJ; (Y); 13/414; Color Guard; Rep Frsh Cls; Rep Soph Cls; Rep Jr Cls; Rep Sr Cls; JV Var Bowling; High Hon Roll; Hon Roll; NHS; Stat Trk; Kean Coll Of NJ.

TOMLINSON, AMY; Parsippany Hills HS; Morris Plains, NJ; (Y); VP AFS; Am Leg Aux Girls St; Debate Tm; Pres French Clb; Girl Scts; Hosp Aide; NFL; Variety Show; Yrbk Stf; Stat Tennis; Intl Rltns.

TOMLINSON, JUSTIN; Union Catholic Regional HS; Hillside, NJ; (Y); Chess Clb; French Clb; Office Aide; Service Clb; Hon Roll; Columbia U; Acctng.

TOMMINELLI, LORI; Toms River H S East; Toms River, NJ; (Y); FBLA; Intnl Clb; Hon Roll; Bus Admin.

TONER, EILEEN; Roselle Catholic HS; Roselle, NJ; (Y); Drama Clb; Chorus; Church Choir; School Musical; School Play; Stage Crew; Lit Mag; High Hon Roll; Hon Roll; Grls Ctznshp Inst Alt 86; Rutgers U; Thtre.

TONEY, QUANDAL; Abraham Clark HS; Roselle, NJ; (S); 16/187; FHA; OEA; Service Clb; Chorus; Church Choir; Yrbk Stf; Hon Roll; NHS; Piano Hnr-Plyd For 6 Yrs 84-85; Piano Hnr-Being Sndy Schl Musicn 85-86.

TONGES, SANDRA; Middlesex HS; Middlesex, NJ; (Y); 3/170; German Clb; Quiz Bowl; Ski Clb; SADD; Stat Bsktbl; JV Var Fld Hcky; High Hon Roll; Hon Roll; NHS; Bus Admin.

TOOHEY, SUZANNE; Highland Regional HS; Blackwood, NJ; (Y); 52/332; GAA; Var L Bsktbl; Var L Socr; Var L Sftbl; Contrbtn Awd Sftbl 86; Comp Sci.

TOOL, KRISTINA; Southern Regional HS; Beach Haven, NJ; (S); 5/370; Cmnty Wkr; Pres Ski Clb; Yrbk Ed-Chief; Rep Soph Cls; Rep Jr Cls; Rep Sr Cls; High Hon Roll; Trs NHS; French Clb; Model UN; Grdn ST Dstngshd Schlr 85; Brwn U Bk Awd 85; Bch Haven Exchng Clb 86.

TOOLAN, JOHN; Christian Brothers Acad; Rumson, NJ; (Y); Model UN; School Play; Stage Crew; Ed Yrbk Phtg; Yrbk Stf; High Hon Roll; Hon Roll; Trap Skeet Shootng Champ 85-86.

TOOLE, CONOR G; Seton Hall Prep; Livingston, NJ; (Y); 82/198; Boy Scts; Cmnty Wkr; Science Clb; Hon Roll; Computer Clb; Exploring; Intnl Clb; Yrbk Stf; Socr; JETS Awd; U MI; Aerontcl Engrng.

TOOLE, KERRY; Burlington City HS; Edgewater Park, NJ; (Y); 1/200; Cmnty Wkr; VP Jr Cls; Var Fld Hcky; Var Sftbl; High Hon Roll; NHS; Rutgers Schlr 86; Youth For Outstndng Japa US Sen Schlrshp Finalist 85; Principals #1 Clb 84-86; Bus.

TOOLE, LESLEY; Mt Olive HS; Budd Lake, NJ; (Y); Dance Clb; Ski Clb; JV Cheerleading; Hon Roll; Boca Raton; Fshn Mrchndsng.

TOPOLENSKI, GAIL; Clifton HS; Clifton, NJ; (Y); Key Clb; Sec Chorus; Madrigals; Variety Show; Yrbk Stf; Twrlr; Hon Roll; Outstndng Chrl Awd 85-86.

TOPPER, KIMBERLY; Notre Dame HS; Trenton, NJ; (Y); 14/324; Debate Tm; Drama Clb; NFL; PAVAS; SADD; Madrigals; School Musical; School Play; High Hon Roll; NHS; Boston U; Thtre.

TORCHY, SUSAN; Bridgewater Raritan H S East; Martinsville, NJ; (Y); Ski Clb; Spanish Clb; Yrbk Stf; Off Sr Cls; Powder Puff Ftbl; High Hon Roll; Hon Roll; NHS; Honorarium Awd 86; Pres Acdmc Ftns Awd 86; St Elzbth Coll; Ed.

TORIGIAN, DREW A; Paramus HS; Paramus, NJ; (Y); Am Leg Boys St; French Clb; Math Clb; Science Clb; Ski Clb; Pres Band; French Hon Soc; High Hon Roll; NHS; NJ All St Band, 1st Frgn Lang Poster Cntst 86; MIT; Math.

TORRES, ALEXANDER; St John Vianney HS; Freehold, NJ; (Y); Var Tennis; Hon Roll; Bus Mgmt.

TORRES, BETHZAIDA; Paterson Catholic Regnl HS; Wayne, NJ; (Y); Pep Clb; Chorus; School Play; Yrbk Ed-Chief; Rep Frsh Cls; Rep Soph Cls; Sftbl; Vllybl; Hon Roll; William Patterson Coll; Nrsng.

TORRES, CLAUDIA; Camden HS; Camden, NJ; (Y); Office Aide; Cit Awd; French Hon Soc.

TORRES, EDWIN; Christian Brothers Acad; Freehold, NJ; (Y); 10/265; Math Tm; Teachers Aide; Yrbk Stf; Im Fld Hcky; High Hon Roll; Acctng.

TORRES, GEORGE; Morris Catholic HS; Denville, NJ; (Y); 9/142; Math Clb; School Play; Stu Cncl; L Var Bsktbl; L Var Socr; High Hon Roll; Hon Roll; NHS; Rep Soph Cls; Trs Jr Cls; MIP Soccer 85-86.

TORRES, JESUS; Harold G Hoffman HS; S Amboy, NJ; (Y); 8/49; Computer Clb; ROTC; Yrbk Stf; Trs Frsh Cls; Rep Stu Cncl; Var Crs Cntry; JV Val; High Hon Roll; Pres Schlr; Spanish NHS; Prfct Attndnc; Hnd In Hnd Svc Awd; Pilot.

TORRES, LISA MARIE; Paramus Catholic Girls Regionl HS; Fair Lawn, NJ; (Y); 3/157; Dance Clb; School Play; Rep Stu Cncl; Var Capt Cheerleading; Var L Socr; Trk; Math Clb; Math Tm; Science Clb; Service Clb; Hugh O Brien Ldrshp Ambssdr 84; Bergen Cnty Recruitor For Ldrs 85; Miss Congeniality/Miss Amity 84-85; Lawyr.

TORRES, RAQUEL; James J Ferris HS; Jersey City, NJ; (Y); DECA; Science Clb; Spanish Clb; Chorus; School Musical; Rep Jr Cls; Rep Stu Cncl; Var Cheerleading; Var Swmmng; Hon Roll; 1st Pl Frgn Lang Poster Cont 85; Coll Atlantic; Marine Bio.

TORRES, SANTOS; Perth Amboy HS; Perth Amboy, NJ; (Y); Model UN; Teachers Aide; Chorus; Rep Jr Cls; Rep Stu Cncl; Tennis; Vllybl; Hon Roll; NHS; Cert Rcgntn Acdmc Exclnc 86; Vrsty Tns Ltr 86; Hofstra; Bus.

TORRES, THERESA; Kearny HS; Kearny, NJ; (Y); German Clb; Ski Clb; Yrbk Stf; Rep Sr Cls; Rep Stu Cncl; Cheerleading; Gym; Gov Hon Prg Awd; High Hon Roll; NHS; Grmn Ntl Hnr Soc; Pre Med.

TORRES, TY A; Point Pleasant Beach HS; Point Pleasnt Bch, NJ; (Y); 11/100; Am Leg Boys St; Cmnty Wkr; Debate Tm; Drama Clb; Pep Clb; Variety Show; Nwsp Sprt Ed; Rep Frsh Cls; Rep Soph Cls; Var L Bsbl; Math.

TORRES, VICTOR; Emerson HS; Union City, NJ; (Y); Boy Scts; Math Clb; Service Clb; Teachers Aide; Chorus; Pep Band; Variety Show; Capt Bsbl; Bsktbl; Capt Ftbl; Co Tutrng Awd, Presdntl Fitnes Awd & All Co Bsebll 84-86; U Of Bridgeport; Accntnt.

TORRUELLAS, MADELINE R; Camden County Voc Trade Schl; Camden, NJ; (S); Dance Clb; DECA; Stu Cncl; Sftbl; DECA Pres Awd 85-86; 2nd Gld Div Sales Demo Sthrn Rgnl Cnfrnc 86; Retail.

TORSIELLO, BRYON; Rutherford HS; Rutherford, NJ; (Y); Cmnty Wkr; Service Clb; Im Socr; JV Trk; Im Wt Lftg; Comp Sci.

TORSIELLO, GINA; West Essex HS; Fairfield, NJ; (Y); 76/350; Pep Clb; VP Soph Cls; VP Jr Cls; VP Sr Cls; VP Stu Cncl; Var Capt Cheerleading; Hon Roll; Stu/Fclty Cmmte Chrprsn; Stu Voice; Prm Qun, Bst Lkng, Frndlst; Franklin & Marshall; Pre-Med.

TORTORELLI, RAYMOND; Audubon HS; Mt Ephraim, NJ; (Y); 2/119; Am Leg Boys St; Jazz Band; Pres Sr Cls; Crs Cntry; Wrstlng; Bausch & Lomb Sci Awd; JP Sousa Awd; Ntl Merit Ltr; Sal; Mltry Trng Cert Rppllng 85; Choir Pres 85-86; Bnd Pres 85-86; Annapolis; Engr.

TORTORIELLO, JERRI; East Brunswick HS; East Brunswick, NJ; (Y); Cmnty Wkr; Girl Scts; Key Clb; Band; Mrchg Band; Stage Crew; Yrbk Stf; Bowling; Grl Scout Silv Awd 85; Art Hnr 86.

TOSCANO, ANGELO; Passaic Valley HS; W Paterson, NJ; (Y); 6/350; Computer Clb; Science Clb; Rep Soph Cls; Im Bsbl; High Hon Roll; NHS; 1st Pl Math Cntst; Olympcs Mnd Comptn; NJ Sci Leag; Engrng.

TOSCANO, BENJAMIN; Passaic Valley HS; Totowa, NJ; (Y); 67/303; Am Leg Boys St; Im Bsktbl; NJ Inst Of Tech; Mech Engr.

TOSI, LOREN; Middletown Hgh Schl South; Leonard, NJ; (Y); Latin Clb; Pep Clb; Flag Corp; Rep Frsh Cls; Var L Swmmng; Hon Roll; Magna Cum Laude Ntl Latn Exam.

TOSSOUNIAN, NORA; Montville Township HS; Pine Brook, NJ; (Y); 12/268; Trs Church Yth Grp; Hosp Aide; Key Clb; Red Cross Aide; Ed Nwsp Stf; Lit Mag; Sec NHS; Art Clb; FBLA; Math Clb; Europn Yth Fest Music 85; N Jersey HS Orch 85-86; NJ All ST Orch 86; Med.

TOTA, MICHAEL; Cliffside Park HS; Fairview, NJ; (Y); 72/236; Chess Clb; Varsity Clb; Church Choir; Coach Actv; Socr; Hon Roll; MVP Sccr 83; Law Enfrcmnt.

TOTH, EVELYNNE; Toms River HS East; Toms River, NJ; (S); 103/576; Band; Concert Band; Jazz Band; Mrchg Band; Orch; Pep Band; School Musical; Symp Band; Sftbl; Gov Hon Prg Awd; Garden ST Yth Orch 85-86; S Jersey Symph Bnd Dist 85-86; Engrng.

TOTH, JACQUELINE; St John Vianney HS; Union Beach, NJ; (Y); Hosp Aide; Rep Soph Cls; Rep Jr Cls; Socr; Hon Roll.

TOURTELLOTTE, SHANE M; Westfield SR HS; Westfield, NJ; (Y); 50/450; Chess Clb; Library Aide; Science Clb; Trs Soph Cls; Trs Stu Cncl; Gov Hon Prg Awd; JC Awd; NHS; Ntl Merit Schol; St Schlr; Cornell; Engrng.

TOVAR, ADRIANNE; Bayonne HS; Bayonne, NJ; (Y); 9/362; Art Clb; VP Church Yth Grp; Pres Spanish Clb; Nwsp Stf; Yrbk Ed-Chief; Rep Sr Cls; Rep Stu Cncl; Sec NHS; Lit Mag; Hon Roll; Natl Hipsnc Schlrs Awd 86; Mnrty Achvt Awd 86.

TOWEY, CARA L; Northern Valley HS; Harrington Park, NJ; (Y); 112/311; VP Art Clb; French Clb; Intnl Clb; Political Wkr; Spanish Clb; Concert Band; Stage Crew; Nwsp Stf; Ed Lit Mag; Hon Roll; Languages.

TOWEY, JOHN; Riverside HS; Delanco, NJ; (S); 12/66; Am Leg Boys St; Church Yth Grp; Ski Clb; Varsity Clb; Band; Concert Band; Jazz Band; Mrchg Band; JV Bsbl; Capt JV Bsktbl; Outstdng Band Mbr Hnr 84-85; Aviation.

TOWEY, JOYCELYN; Bishop George Ahr HS; S Plainfield, NJ; (Y); Rep Church Yth Grp; Ski Clb; Drill Tm; Mrchg Band; Stage Crew; Crs Cntry; Pom Pon; Trk; High Hon Roll; Hon Roll; Mgmt.

TOWNSEND, CHRISTINE; St Rose HS; Spring Lake, NJ; (Y); Cmnty Wkr; Drama Clb; JCL; School Musical; Variety Show; JV Var Cheerleading; French Hon Soc; Hon Roll; NHS; NEDT Awd; Talnt Expo Wnnr Dance 86; ST Teen Arts Festvl 85; Theatre.

TOWNSEND, CHRISTY; Hackettstown HS; Hackettstown, NJ; (Y); 4-H; Hosp Aide; Sec Key Clb; Ski Clb; Spanish Clb; Score Keeper; Montclau ST; Acctng.

TOZOUR, LAUREN; Gloucester County Christian Schl; Sewell, NJ; (S); 5/16; Church Yth Grp; Chorus; Trs Frsh Cls; Trs Soph Cls; Trs Jr Cls; Var Capt Bsktbl; Var Capt Fld Hcky; Var Sftbl; Var Trk; Vllybl; All Star Tm-Sftbl 85; Elem Educ.

TRACEY, MARY FRANCES; Pope John XXIII HS; Stanhope, NJ; (Y); Am Leg Aux Girls St; Church Yth Grp; Drama Clb; Teachers Aide; Drill Tm; School Musical; School Play; High Hon Roll; Hon Roll; NHS; Acad Achvt Awd Scholar Notre Dame 86; Paterson Dioscese Essay Cont 84-85; Prfrmg Art Dir Awd Pope 86; Coll Notre Dame; Bus.

TRAEGER, GEOFFREY; Lenape Valley Regional HS; Andover, NJ; (Y); 44/241; Am Leg Boys St; Cmnty Wkr; German Clb; JV Bsbl; JV Socr; Hon Roll; Mltry Aviator.

TRAFICANT, LISA; Central Regional HS; Bayville, NJ; (Y); 31/240; Church Yth Grp; GAA; Intnl Clb; Varsity Clb; Y-Teens; JV Bsktbl; Coach Actv; Mgr(s); Var Capt Socr; Var Capt Tennis.

TRAINOR, MICHAEL; Jackson Memorial HS; Jackson, NJ; (Y); 141/405; DECA; Hon Roll; Reg DECA Comptn Role Plyng Mrktng & Mgmt 3rd Pl, Wrttn & Over All 1st Pl & ST Hnrbl Mntn Rbn 86; Rutgers; Law Enfrcmnt.

TRAN, THAO; Dickinson HS; Jersey City, NJ; (Y); FNA; Girl Scts; Hon Roll; Rutgers U; Bio.

TRAPP, TONJA; Cherry Hill East HS; Cherry Hill, NJ; (Y); Church Yth Grp; Cmnty Wkr; Church Choir; Var L Trk; Hon Roll; Cherry Hill Minorities Civic Assn Scholar 86; Cls Clown 86; Howard U; Lawyer.

TRASFERINI, ROBERT; Buena Regional HS; Minotola, NJ; (S); Math Clb; Varsity Clb; Var Capt Crs Cntry; Var L Trk; Var L Wrstlng; Cit Awd; Hon Roll; Jr NHS; USN Acad; Aeronaut Engrng.

TRAUGER, GEORGE; Paul VI HS; Barrington, NJ; (S); 140/474; SADD; Pres Frsh Cls; Pres Soph Cls; VP Jr Cls; Pres Sr Cls; Pres VP Stu Cncl; Bsbl; Ftbl; Capt Wrstlng; NHS; Liberal Arts.

TRAVAGLIO, TONI; Toms River High School East; Toms River, NJ; (Y); 103/585; French Clb; Intnl Clb; Letterman Clb; Spanish Clb; Teachers Aide; Varsity Clb; Frsh Cls; Soph Cls; Sr Cls; Stu Cncl; Forensc Pathlgy.

TRAVERS, CHRISTOPHER; Cedar Grove Memorial HS; Cedar Grove, NJ; (S); 14/120; Church Yth Grp; Pres Intnl Clb; Spanish Clb; Nwsp Rptr; Yrbk Stf; Capt Bsktbl; Ftbl; High Hon Roll; Hon Roll; NHS; Natl Sci Olympd 83; Admin Asst Twnshp Mgr 85; Co-Fndr Current Affrs Clb 85; Acctg.

TRAVERSO, AL; Leonia HS; Leonia, NJ; (Y); Drama Clb; FBLA; Band; School Musical; Crs Cntry; Trk; Trenton ST; Acctng.

TREACY, SHELLEY ANN; Shore Regional HS; Oceanport, NJ; (Y); 60/225; Drama Clb; Pres Key Clb; Thesps; School Musical; Stage Crew; Yrbk Sprt Ed; Stat Bsktbl; JV Socr; Hon Roll; US Schltc Fit Awd 86; Hofstra U; TV Prodctn.

TREDICI, FRANK; Bishop AHR HS; Edison, NJ; (Y); Boy Scts; FBLA; JA; Ski Clb; JV Bsbl; JV Var Bowling; High Hon Roll; Hon Roll; Syracuse U; Accntng.

TREDY, DENNIS; Southern Regional HS; Barnegat, NJ; (Y); 4/358; VP Math Tm; Yrbk Stf; Sr Cls; Stu Cncl; JV Socr; JV Trk; Im Vllybl; Gov Hon Prg Awd; High Hon Roll; NHS; Toms Rvr Chmcl Sci Awd 86; Outstndng Sci Sr 86; Gvnrs Schl Schlr Awd 85; Rnslr Polytech Inst; Chem.

TRENDLER, CHRISTINA; Holy Spirit HS; Brigantine, NJ; (Y); 24/420; Church Yth Grp; Civic Clb; Cmnty Wkr; French Clb; Hosp Aide; Stage Crew; Trk; French Hon Soc; Hon Roll; NHS; U Scranton; Nrsng.

TRENERY, LORI; Memorial HS; Cedar Grove, NJ; (S); 9/120; Dance Clb; VP Chorus; Trs Mrchg Band; Orch; School Musical; Rep Stu Cncl; Var Cheerleading; Capt Crs Cntry; Capt Trk; NHS; PA ST U; Fine & Prfrmng Arts.

TREOLE, KATHLEEN M; Clifton HS; Clifton, NJ; (Y); 30/687; Girl Scts; Library Aide; Band; Concert Band; Mrchg Band; Symp Band; Yrbk Stf; Mgr Bsktbl; Hon Roll; Jr NHS; Hnr Grd; Spch Pathlgy.

TRETINA, MARCEL; Mater Dei HS; Union Beach, NJ; (Y); 73/170; Ski Clb; Lit Mag; Crs Cntry; Ec & Sci Awds; Rochester Inst; Grphc Arts.

TRIANO, EDWIN; Queen Of Peace HS; Kearny, NJ; (Y); Aud/Vis; Computer Clb; Varsity Clb; Nwsp Rptr; Yrbk Rptr; Yrbk Stf; Im Bsbl; Im Bowling; Im Ftbl; Im Sftbl; Rutgers U; Accntng.

TRICHON, BENJAMIN H; Delron HS; Delran, NJ; (Y); 20/220; Am Leg Boys St; Aud/Vis; French Clb; Science Clb; Ski Clb; Band; Concert Band; Mrchg Band; Sr Cls; Swmmng; Pre-Med.

TRIFARI, CAROLEE; Montville Township HS; Montville, NJ; (Y); 56/272; Church Yth Grp; Key Clb; Varsity Clb; Stu Cncl; Bsktbl; Var Capt Fld Hcky; Var Score Keeper; Var Sftbl; High Hon Roll; Hon Roll; U Of MA; Legl Stds.

TRIFOLI, GEORGE; Manchester Regional HS; N Haledon, NJ; (S); 9/156; Am Leg Boys St; Church Yth Grp; Mathletes; Nwsp Bus Mgr; Pres Stu Cncl; Var Bsktbl; Var Crs Cntry; Trs NHS; NC ST U; Engrng.

TRILONE, DONNA; Manville HS; Manville, NJ; (Y); 17/93; Church Yth Grp; Library Aide; Rdlgy.

TRILONE, KELLY A; Manville HS; Manville, NJ; (Y); 2/115; AFS; Scholastic Bowl; Co-Capt Var Sftbl; High Hon Roll; Hon Roll; NHS; Pres Schlr; Sal; Garden ST Dist Schlr 86; Mountain Valley Conf & Somerest Cnty Schlr Athl 86; Sftbl All ST 85; Fairleigh Dickinson U; Bus Adm.

TRIMMER, KATHLEEN; Brick Twon HS; Brick Town, NJ; (Y); 157/400; VP Church Yth Grp; Hosp Aide; Key Clb; SADD; Nwsp Stf; JV Sftbl; Hon Roll; Marine Bio.

TRINCA, CHRISTOPHER; Passiac Valley HS; Totowa, NJ; (Y); Aud/Vis; Church Yth Grp; Rep Soph Cls; Rep Jr Cls; Pres Stu Cncl; JV Crs Cntry; Var Trk; Hon Roll; Bus.

TRINH, HOA; Linden HS; Linden, NJ; (Y); Camera Clb; German Clb; Key Clb; Library Aide; Band; Mrchg Band; Orch; Yrbk Phtg; Yrbk Stf; High Hon Roll; Smmr Orchestra Awd 83; Peer Ldrshp 85-86; Rugers; Mech Engr.

TRINKLE, JANE F; Villa Walsh Acad; Morris Plains, NJ; (Y); 1/34; Pres Pres Church Yth Grp; Girl Scts; Math Tm; NFL; School Musical; Nwsp Rptr; Var Capt Crs Cntry; Bausch & Lomb Sci Awd; Pres NHS; Val; JR Sci & Humnties Symp 86; Natl Cath Forn Lg Awd 82-86; NJ JR Acad Sci Awd 86; U PA.

TRIOLA, STACEY; Bridgewater-Raritan H S East; Bridgewater, NJ; (Y); Cmnty Wkr; Intnl Clb; Ski Clb; SADD; Yrbk Stf; Rep Sr Cls; Rep Stu Cncl; High Hon Roll; NHS; AFS; Pres Acadmc Ftnss Awd 86; Spcl Olympc Vlntr 82-86; Chrmn Of Prom Comm 85; Rutgers U; Pol Sci.

TRIOLO, MAUREEN; Toms River High School East; Toms River, NJ; (Y); Dance Clb; Hon Roll; Rutgers U; Law.

TRIVEDI, SUNIL J; West Milford HS; West Milford, NJ; (Y); 2/375; Am Leg Boys St; Math Tm; Quiz Bowl; VP Sr Cls; JV Wrstlng; NHS; Olympics Of Mnd; Pre-Med.

TROGDON, MELISSA; Overbrook SR HS; Ceementon, NJ; (Y); 9/350; Girl Scts; Band; Mrchg Band; School Play; JV Bsktbl; Var L Crs Cntry; Var L Trk; High Hon Roll; Hon Roll; NHS; Corp Mngmnt.

TROIANO, LAURIE; North Bergen HS; N Bergen, NJ; (Y); 15/400; Church Yth Grp; Key Clb; Hon Roll; NHS; Italian Poetry Cntst Awds 2nd,3rd Plc 85-86; Italian Hon Soc 85; Merit Socty 86; Early Chldhd Ed Tchr.

TROIKE, TISHA; Hopewell Valley Central HS; Pennington, NJ; (Y); 5/202; AFS; Church Yth Grp; Dance Clb; Drama Clb; Hosp Aide; Spanish Clb; Chorus; School Musical; Socr; High Hon Roll; U Of NC; Pre-Med.

TROISI, MICHAEL; Cherry Hill HS West; Cherry Hill, NJ; (Y); Art Clb; Aud/Vis; Boy Scts; Camera Clb; CAP; Exploring; French Clb; Ski Clb; Band; Drm & Bgl; Embry Riddle; Aviation.

TROLLER, MARK; Wallington HS; Wallington, NJ; (Y); 6/81; Am Leg Boys St; Boy Scts; Chess Clb; Church Yth Grp; Office Aide; School Play; Nwsp Stf; Yrbk Stf; Ftbl; Hon Roll; Wallington JR Var Ftbll Tm; Chess Clb; Schl Newspr Stff; Schl Play; Ofc Aide; Stud Of Wk; Altern Boys ST; Bio Med.

TROLLER, SCOTT; Wallington HS; Wallington, NJ; (S); 9/75; Boy Scts; VICA; VP Sr Cls; Var Ftbl; Swmmng; Hon Roll; NHS; Nova Awd-Trck Diesel-Brnz Lvl 84, Slvr Lvl 85 & Gld Lvl 86.

TROPP, BETH; Parsippany HS; Parsippany, NJ; (Y); GAA; Temple Yth Grp; Varsity Clb; Bsktbl; Var Socr; JV Sftbl; High Hon Roll; Hon Roll; NHS; Parsippany Vrsty Sftbl-ST Chmpns 86.

TROTMAN, VALERIE; Toms River High School North; Toms River, NJ; (Y); 15/391; Bsktbl; Var Capt Fld Hcky; Var Capt Socr; Var Trk; High Hon Roll; Hon Roll; Kiwanis Awd; NHS; All-Cnty All-Shr & 3rd Tm All-ST Fld Hcky 84-85; MVP Fld Hcky 85; Army Schlr Athlt Awd Mrns Schlr 86; U Of CT; Nrsg.

TROTT, MARGO KAREN; Manalapan HS; Manalapan, NJ; (Y); 9/383; SADD; Nwsp Rptr; Lit Mag; Rep Jr Cls; Rep Sr Cls; Var Socr; Jr NHS; Pres NHS; Variety Show; Nwsp Stf; Jrnlsts Awd 86; Math & Spnsh Excel Awds 83; Mark Lederman Memrl Schlrshp 86; Muhlenberg Coll; Cmmnctns.

TROTT, RICHARD; Manalapan HS; Englishtown, NJ; (Y); 25/447; Debate Tm; Math Tm; Sr Cls; NHS; Ntl Merit SF.

TROTTA, FRANK; Ridgefield Memorial HS; Ridgefield, NJ; (Y); Boy Scts; Var Bsktbl; Var Ftbl; Hon Roll; Bus.

TROTTER, NICOLE; Glen Ridge HS; Glen Ridge, NJ; (Y); 6/125; Sec Pres AFS; Sec Soph Cls; Gym; Var Trk; High Hon Roll; Hon Roll; 4th Pl Cls III NJ ST Gymnstcs 84; 2nd Pl Gardn ST Opn Optnl Mt Gymnstcs 85; Awerospc Engrng.

TROTTER, SANDRA; Paul VI HS; Collingswood, NJ; (Y); 55/480; 4-H; Math Clb; SADD; Varsity Clb; Stage Crew; Var Cheerleading; Swmmng; 4-H Awd; NHS; Spanish NHS; Natl 4-H Clb Cngrs Fashion Revue 86; Camden Cnty 4-H Queen 85-86; Marymount Coll; Fash Design.

TROTTER, WILLIAM; Indian Hills HS; Franklin Lks, NJ; (Y); 6/279; Math Tm; Science Clb; Teachers Aide; Lit Mag; Ftbl; Trk; Wt Lftg; High Hon Roll; NHS; Ntl Merit Ltr; Pre-Med.

TROTTIER, NICOLE; Roselle Park HS; Roselle Pk, NJ; (Y); 3/129; Am Leg Aux Girls St; Drama Clb; JA; Trs Key Clb; Radio Clb; Pres Spanish Clb; Concert Band; Jazz Band; Mrchg Band; School Play; Bnd Schlrshp 82; J C Simigan Mem 86; Stvns Inst Of Tech; Engrng.

TROUMEES, LINDA; Cumberland Regional HS; Bridgeton, NJ; (Y); Debate Tm; German Clb; Girl Scts; Intnl Clb; Latin Clb; Office Aide; Ski Clb; Lit Mag; Cheerleading; Swmmng; Natl JR Hnr Soc 82; Musc Ed Cncl Awd 84-85; Swmmg Awd 85; Poltc Sci.

TROUNG, HUNG; North Bergen HS; North Bergen, NJ; (Y); 107/450; Boy Scts; Computer Clb; French Clb; Tennis; French Hon Soc; Stevens Inst Tech; Engrng.

TROUTON, SUSAN; Eastern HS; Gibbsboro, NJ; (Y); 38/330; French Clb; Office Aide; Var Cheerleading; Acctg.

TROVATO, SANDRA; Morris Knolls HS; Dover, NJ; (Y); Hosp Aide; Chorus; Nwsp Stf; Lit Mag; Stat Bsbl; Var Fld Hcky; Var Swmmng; High Hon Roll; Hon Roll; Home Safe Vlntr; Penn ST U; Lwyr.

TRUDEAU, MICHAEL; Oakcrest HS; Mays Landing, NJ; (Y); 10/250; Quiz Bowl; JV Bsbl; Var Crs Cntry; Ice Hcky; JV Socr; High Hon Roll; Hon Roll; Jr NHS; Pres Schlr; Vrsty Schlr Acad Ltr 86; Gtd Tlntd; U Of DE; Psychlgy.

TRUEMAN, JENNIFER P; Sussex Co Vo-Tech; Hamburg, NJ; (S); 27/152; Pres Chorus; Nwsp Sprt Ed; Nwsp Stf; Yrbk Ed-Chief; Yrbk Stf; Pres Frsh Cls; Pres Jr Cls; Pres Sr Cls; Var Capt Bsktbl; Var Swmmng; Sports Schlrshp 85-86; Muhlenburg; Comm Artist.

TRUGLIO, RUTH; Hopewell Vly Cntrl HS; Hopewell, NJ; (Y); 30/225; Art Clb; Church Yth Grp; Drama Clb; Hosp Aide; Spanish Clb; Chorus; Church Choir; School Play; Yrbk Ed-Chief; Yrbk Stf; PSYCH.

TRUITT, SUE; West Morris/Mendham HS; Mendham, NJ; (Y); 16/327; Church Yth Grp; Varsity Clb; Stat Var Ftbl; High Hon Roll; Bus Mgmt.

TRUJILLO, LILLIAN; North Bergen HS; North Bergen, NJ; (S); 2/470; Key Clb; Nwsp Rptr; Nwsp Stf; Yrbk Stf; Rep Jr Cls; Stu Cncl; Var Crs Cntry; Var Trk; French Hon Soc; High Hon Roll; Princeton U; Engrng.

TRUONG, TRI M; Monroe Township HS; Spotswood, NJ; (Y); Am Leg Boys St; Computer Clb; Key Clb; Mathletes; Quiz Bowl; Science Clb; JV Socr; Im Tennis; Im Wt Lftg; Gov Hon Prg Awd; Engrng.

TSOMOS, EVANGELIA; Memorial HS; W New York, NJ; (Y); Church Yth Grp; French Clb; Hosp Aide; Key Clb; Math Clb; Science Clb; Yrbk Stf; High Hon Roll; NHS; Piano Awd; AHEPA Medal Schlstc Exc; Study Greek Lang Hellenic Cultr; Pre-Med.

TUCCI, CONCETTA; Clayton HS; Clayton, NJ; (Y); Band; Mrchg Band; Yrbk Stf; VP Bsktbl; Trk; Hon Roll; NHS.

TUCCINO, PETER A; Rutherford HS; Rutherford, NJ; (Y); Am Leg Boys St; High Hon Roll; NHS; Rcvd Brnz Mtl 85; Slvr Mtl 86; Psych.

TUCKER, LLOYD A; Hopewell Valley Central HS; Hopewell, NJ; (Y); 44/200; AFS; Church Yth Grp; Pres French Clb; Yrbk Sprt Ed; Sec Stu Cncl; Var Bsktbl; High Hon Roll; Hon Roll; NHS; Ntl Merit Ltr; Bio.

TUCKER, LYNN; Washington Twp HS; Sewell, NJ; (Y); Church Yth Grp; Csmtlgy.

TUCKER, TARA; Manasquan HS; Spg Lk Hts, NJ; (Y); Drama Clb; French Clb; Thesps; Chorus; School Play; Stage Crew; JV Swmmng; Var Trk; DAR Awd; Hon Roll; Business.

TUERS, JODY; Shore Regional HS; W Long Branch, NJ; (Y); Chess Clb; Pres Key Clb; Q&S; Thesps; School Musical; Ed Nwsp Stf; Rep Stu Cncl; High Hon Roll; Church Yth Grp; Cmnty Wkr; Olympics Of Mind 3rd & 1st 85-6; Sci Fair 84-6; Newspaper Feature Edtr 85; Drftng Trnmnt 86; Arch.

TUERS, KIPP; Shore Regional HS; W Long Branch, NJ; (Y); Chess Clb; Key Clb; Q&S; Thesps; Nwsp Stf; High Hon Roll; NHS; Prfct Atten Awd; Church Yth Grp; Cmnty Wkr; Sci Fair 1st Teen Arts Festvl 84; Gftd & Tlntd Teen Arts Fstvl, Sci Fair 1st, Stck Mrkt Clb 3rd 85; Arts.

TUGMAN, BRILLIA; Paterson Catholic Regional HS; Paterson, NJ; (Y); 30/120; DECA; Capt Pep Clb; Chorus; Church Choir; Color Guard; School Play; Variety Show; Var Cheerleading; Hon Roll; Prfct Atten Awd; Howard U; Ped Med.

TULIG, CRAIG; Pope John XXIII Regional HS; Sparta, NJ; (Y); 16/150; Am Leg Boys St; Computer Clb; Chorus; Stage Crew; Var Ftbl; Var Ftbl; Presdntl Acadmc Ftns Awd; Cert Of Hnr-Comp Pgmmng; Outstndng Acadmc Achvt Awd; Syracuse U; Comp Engrng.

TULL, WENDY; Holy Spirit HS; Ventnor, NJ; (Y); 5/366; Stage Crew; Trk; Hon Roll; NHS; Fnlst-Govrnrs Schl-Sci 86; Rtry Yth Ldrshp Confrnc 86.

TULLIO, MICHELLE; Union Catholic HS; Scotch Plns, NJ; (Y); 106/386; Church Yth Grp; Ski Clb; SADD; Yrbk Stf; Tennis; Trk; Hon Roll; Mullenberg Coll.

TUMSER, KEITH; Fair Lawn HS; Fair Lawn, NJ; (Y); 56/330; Am Leg Boys St; JV Bsbl; Var Ftbl; Hon Roll; STAIRS Ramapo Coll 86; Montclair ST; Actg.

TUNISON, AUDRA; Hunterdon Central HS; Whitehouse Sta, NJ; (Y); 157/548; Art Clb; Church Yth Grp; Chorus; Stage Crew; Phy Therapy.

TUOHY, JOHN; Christian Brothers Acad; Aberdeen, NJ; (Y); 63/221; Math Tm; Stat Bsktbl; Wrstlng; High Hon Roll; Hon Roll; Ntl Merit Schol; Comp Sci.

TUOHY, THOMAS; St Peters Prep; Jersey City, NJ; (Y); 23/206; JA; Pres Soph Cls; Stu Cncl; JV Bsbl; Capt Var Ftbl; Wt Lftg; High Hon Roll; Prep Spirit Awd 86; Ftbl Outstndng Def, Prfrmnc Awd 85; West Point; Bus Admnstn.

TURANICK, TRACY; West Essex HS; Fairfield, NJ; (Y); Computer Clb; Key Clb; Ski Clb; Var Socr; Var JV Sftbl; Hon Roll; Comp.

TURCZAK, NADINE; Bound Brook HS; S Bound Brook, NJ; (Y); 32/143; Latin Clb; VP Spanish Clb; VP Chorus; Var JV Bsktbl; JV Tennis; Educ.

TURIEL, KAREN; Westfield HS; Westfield, NJ; (Y); Teachers Aide; Temple Yth Grp; Band; Nwsp Rptr; Yrbk Stf; High Hon Roll; Hon Roll; Amer U; Comm.

TURNER, BILL; Atlanitc Christian Schl; Mays Landing, NJ; (S); 1/12; Church Yth Grp; Drama Clb; German Clb; Intnl Clb; Bsbl; Mgr(s); Score Keeper; Socr; NHS; Presdntl Clsrm Yng Amer 86; Hghtst Acadmc Avg; Vrsty Ltr/Acadmcs; Stockton ST Coll; Law.

TURNER, JAYNE; Clifton HS; Bricktown, NJ; (Y); 27/564; Trs Chorus; Stage Crew; JV Var Tennis; Twrlr; French Hon Soc; High Hon Roll; Hon Roll; Jr NHS; NHS; Pres Schlr; Hnr Guard 85; Douglass Coll; Pol Sci.

TURNER, JOHN; Middletown South HS; Atl Highlands, NJ; (Y); Var L Ftbl; Asst Coach Pee-Wees & Jr Pee-Wees & Pop Warner Ftbll Leaque At Highlands 83-86; Springfield Coll; Phys Thrpy.

TURNER, JONATHAN M; Toms River High School East; Toms River, NJ; (Y); Boy Scts; 4-H; Key Clb; Math Clb; Math Tm; Ski Clb; Band; Chorus; Concert Band; Madrigals; Embry Riddle; Flight Engrng.

TURNER, KAREN; The Pilgrim Acad; Absecon, NJ; (Y); 1/14; Art Clb; Church Yth Grp; Drama Clb; Orch; Nwsp Stf; Yrbk Stf; Var Cheerleading; Cit Awd; High Hon Roll; VFW Awd; Chancellors Schrlshp 86-87; Acad Awd 86; German Awd 86; Liberty U; Chrch Minstries.

TURNER, MATTHEW; Morris Catholic HS; Flanders, NJ; (Y); 19/142; Boy Scts; Church Yth Grp; Cmnty Wkr; Hosp Aide; Natl Beta Clb; High Hon Roll; Hon Roll; Pre-Med.

TURNER, NANCY; Scotch Plains Fanwood HS; Westfield, NJ; (Y); German Clb; Swmmng; Capt Tennis; Hon Roll; Grmn Ntl Hon Soc 86; Outstndng Erth Sci Stu 84; Outstndng Grmn Stu 86; Boston U; Wrtr.

TURNER, STEVE; Sacred Heart HS; Vineland, NJ; (S); 6/63; German Clb; Chorus; School Musical; School Play; Stage Crew; Variety Show; Yrbk Rptr; High Hon Roll; Hon Roll; NHS; Archtctr.

TURNER, TERRY; Cherry Hill HS; Cherry Hill, NJ; (Y); PAVAS; SADD; Mrchg Band; Yrbk Stf; Lit Mag; Rep Jr Cls; Pom Pon; Hon Roll; NHS; Ntl Merit Ltr; Marktng.

TUROCZI, LORI; Atlantic Christian Schl; Ocean City, NJ; (S); 2/12; Church Yth Grp; Chorus; Pres Sr Cls; Var L Fld Hcky; Var L Sftbl; High Hon Roll; Yrbk Stf; Rep Frsh Cls; Rep Soph Cls; Pres Jr Cls; Amrcn Chrstn Hnr Soc 84-86; Bsktbl Vrsty Awd 85-86; Messian Coll; Art.

TURPYN, GREGORY; Burlington Township HS; Burlington, NJ; (Y); 18/120; French Clb; Bowling; Lcrss; Finance.

TURQMAN, LOUISA; Watchung Hills Regional HS; Millington, NJ; (Y); Church Yth Grp; Drama Clb; Girl Scts; Teachers Aide; PAVAS; Ski Clb; SADD; Chorus; Flag Corp; Madrigals; Cnty Rnkd 7 Javln 85; Fndng Safe Rides 85-86; Sec Ed.

TURRELL, MIKE; Mahwah HS; Mahwah, NJ; (Y); Aud/Vis; Teachers Aide; Nwsp Phtg; Nwsp Rptr; Yrbk Phtg; Yrbk Stf; Syracuse U; Journlsm.

TUSTION, CHRISTINE; South Hunterdon Regional HS; Lambertville, NJ; (Y); 3/74; FBLA; JV Sftbl.

TUTTLE, APRIL; Middletown HS South; Leonard, NJ; (Y); Church Yth Grp; JV Cheerleading; Var Powder Puff Ftbl; JV Sftbl; Var Trk; Hosp Aide; Hon Roll; Messiah Coll; Dietetics.

TUTTLE, STEVE; Don Bosco Prep; Ringwood, NJ; (Y); Ski Clb; NHS; Rngwd Vrsty Hcky Tm.

TWARDOWSKY, JERRY; Union HS; Union, NJ; (Y); SADD; Var Socr; Var Trk; Hon Roll; Cmnty Wkr; Wt Lftg; NJ Inst Technlgy; Engrng.

TWEED, JOANN; Clayton HS; Clayton, NJ; (Y); Trs FFA; Girl Scts; Rep Soph Cls; Sec Jr Cls; Twrlr; Hon Roll; NHS; Wason FFA NJ 1st Pl Floriculture Team 86; 8th Pl Individual FFA Floriculture Contest 86; Floriculture.

TWEED, VERONICA; Notre Dame HS; Mercerville, NJ; (Y); 31/360; Dance Clb; Red Cross Aide; Stu Cncl; Var Stat Bsbl; Hon Roll; NHS; Spanish NHS.

TWOHY, MARY SUE; St John Vianney Regional HS; Aberdeen, NJ; (S); 6/258; Church Yth Grp; Office Aide; Jazz Band; Mrchg Band; School Musical; Nwsp Stf; Stu Cncl; Capt Vllybl; Hon Roll; NHS; Cert Musicnshp Awd Brkle Coll Of Music 85; Mrchng Band Vrsty Ltr 83-85; Gld & Wht Awd 83-85; U Of Notre Dame; Bus.

TYAS, MIKE; Clearview HS; Mantua, NJ; (Y); 16/176; Cmnty Wkr; Dance Clb; Varsity Clb; Rep Soph Cls; Rep Jr Cls; Trs Stu Cncl; Var JV Ftbl; Var Wt Lftg; Var Wrstlng; Hon Roll.

TYHANIC, KURT; Pinelands Regional HS; Tuckerton, NJ; (S); JV Bsbl; JV Ftbl; Var Golf; Var Tennis; JV Wrstlng; Hon Roll; NHS; PA ST U; Film Studies.

TYLER, PHILIP; Clifford J Scott HS; E Orange, NJ; (S); 22/289; Hosp Aide; Math Clb; Varsity Clb; Concert Band; Mrchg Band; Rep Stu Cncl; VP Bowling; Hon Roll; Trs Jr NHS; NHS; Comp Engr.

TYLICKI, DONNA; Linden HS; Linden, NJ; (Y); Trs French Clb; Pres Key Clb; Science Clb; Ski Clb; Drm Mjr(t); Mrchg Band; High Hon Roll; NHS; Quiz Bowl; School Play; Key Clb Distgshd Pres Awd 86; Best Drum Majrt 2nd Annl Marchng Band Comptn 85.

TYLKA, KATHLEEN SHAWN; West Morris Central HS; Long Valley, NJ; (Y); 40/280; Cmnty Wkr; Capt Flag Corp; Lit Mag; VP Soph Cls; VP Jr Cls; VP Sr Cls; Rep Stu Cncl; Bsktbl; JV Var Powder Puff Ftbl; NHS; Cmmnctns.

TYMKOW, TAMMY MARIE; Toms River South HS; Beachwood, NJ; (Y); 4-H; Model UN; Ski Clb; Variety Show; Var Capt Cheerleading; Powder Puff Ftbl; Capt L Sftbl; Hon Roll; Schl Mascot, Indian Princess & Hmcmng Queen 86; Sftb Comeback Plyr Fo Yr Awd 86; Sftbl MVP 83; Monmouth Coll; Lbrl Arts.

TYNES, LINZIE; Kennedy HS; Paterson, NJ; (S); 240/480; Aud/Vis; Boys Clb Am; Camera Clb; Church Yth Grp; FCA; French Clb; JA; Math Clb; Temple Yth Grp; Band; Govnrs Awd 84-85; All Eastrn Chrs 84; All ST Opera Fstvl; Westminster Chrs Coll.

TYRE, ROSLYN; Dwight Morrow HS; Englewood, NJ; (Y); 7/247; Cmnty Wkr; Debate Tm; Hosp Aide; Library Aide; Math Tm; Model UN; Color Guard; School Musical; School Play; High Hon Roll; Prom Hostess SR Prom 86; Delegate Attnd Annual Girls Citizenship Inst 86; Ithaca Coll; Prod.

TYSEN, LISA; Dwight Morrow HS; Englewood, NJ; (Y); 13/270; Church Yth Grp; Drama Clb; JA; School Play; Variety Show; High Hon Roll; NHS; Art.

TYSON, JAMES; Howell HS; Howell, NJ; (Y); 6/371; Math Clb; Quiz Bowl; Band; Jazz Band; Mrchg Band; School Musical; Symp Band; NHS; Pres Schlr; Dean Schlrshp 86; William J Hanrahan Schlrshp 86; Bst Male Mrcher 84 & 85; Missiah; Math.

TZOUANOS, LARRY; Burlington City HS; Edgewater Pk, NJ; (Y); Aud/Vis; NY Inst Of Tech; Comp Engrng.

UBER, MYRA ANN; Vineland HS; Vineland, NJ; (Y); 203/803; Camera Clb; Church Yth Grp; Key Clb; Pep Clb; Socr; Swmmng; Wt Lftg; Crmnl Psychlgy.

UBHAUS, SUE; Bishop George Ahr HS; Edison, NJ; (Y); 99/277; French Clb; Mgr(s); Socr; Hon Roll; Bus.

UDDO, PETER; Lenape Valley Regional HS; Andover, NJ; (Y); 2/265; Trs Key Clb; Capt Quiz Bowl; Nwsp Rptr; Sec Soph Cls; Sec Stu Cncl; Capt Socr; Tennis; High Hon Roll; Pres NHS; Spanish NHS; Pre-Med.

UETZ, DAWN; Lower Cape May Regional HS; N Cape May, NJ; (Y); 27/240; Pep Clb; Varsity Clb; Flag Corp; Bsktbl; Mgr(s); Sftbl; Tennis; Hon Roll; NHS; Memor JC; Dental Hygiene.

UGALDE, MARISA; Dover HS; Dover, NJ; (Y); Pres AFS; Church Yth Grp; Exploring; Office Aide; Science Clb; Spanish Clb; Color Guard; Bowling; Cheerleading; Natl All Amer Acad 86; Spn Awd 85.

UHER, BRIAN; Paul VI HS; Gibbsboro, NJ; (S); 13/520; Church Yth Grp; Drama Clb; VP German Clb; Math Clb; Scholastic Bowl; Lit Mag; Hon Roll; St Schlr.

UHL, TRISHA MARIE; Ocean Township HS; Wayside, NJ; (Y); 81/333; Bsktbl; Hon Roll; Magna Cum Laude Natl Latin Exams 84-8; Spartan Schlr 85; U Deleware; Anml Sci.

UHRBROCK, CHRISSY B; Wayne Hills SR HS; Wayne, NJ; (Y); 14/310; German Clb; Hosp Aide; Latin Clb; Math Clb; Nwsp Ed-Chief; Cit Awd; DAR Awd; High Hon Roll; NHS; Prnt Tchr Organ Acad Awd 86; Grdn ST Dist Schlrshp 85; Rutgers Coll; Med.

UHRIG, CRAIG; Abraham Clark HS; Roselle, NJ; (Y); Pep Clb; JV Var Bsbl; Ftbl; Prntr.

UIBELHOER, DENISE; Roselle Catholic HS; Roselle Park, NJ; (Y); Church Yth Grp; Stage Crew; Yrbk Stf; Trk; Hon Roll; Kean Coll; Pre Schl Ed.

ULASHKEVICH, PAUL; Saint John Vianney HS; Marlboro, NJ; (Y); Intnl Clb; Service Clb; Yrbk Ed-Chief; Var Tennis; High Hon Roll; Hon Roll; Outstndng Achvt Spnsh Cert Merit 86; Pre-Med.

ULBRICH, JO ANN; Millville SR HS; Millville, NJ; (Y); 9/470; Office Aide; Variety Show; Bowling; Cheerleading; High Hon Roll; NHS; Psychlgy.

ULRICH, SHEILA; Secaucus HS; Secaucus, NJ; (Y); 30/169; Varsity Clb; Var Capt Bsktbl; Var Sftbl; Var Capt Vllybl; High Hon Roll; Hon Roll; NY Daily News All Star Sftbll Tm 86; 1st Tm All Leag & All Cnty Vllybll & Sftbll 86.

UMALI, RODRIGO; St Peters Prep; Jersey City, NJ; (Y); Computer Clb; Nwsp Ed-Chief; Pres Jr Cls; Var L Socr; High Hon Roll; NHS; Ntl Merit Ltr; French Clb; Pres Jr Cls; Pres Ftnss Awd 85-86; Prep Spirit Awd 85-86; Newspaper Writing Awd 85-86; Rensselaer Polytech Inst; Comp.

UMANZOR, SAUL; Union Catholic Regional HS; Elizabeth, NJ; (Y); French Clb; Scholastic Bowl; Science Clb; Band; Jazz Band; Trk; Hon Roll; Bus Admin.

UMLAND, DAWN; Cliffside Park HS; Cliffside Pk, NJ; (Y); 13/233; French Clb; Nwsp Stf; Frsh Cls; Soph Cls; Jr Cls; Rep Stu Cncl; Trk; Vllybl; Hon Roll; NHS; Frnch Schlrshp Merit; 1st Team All Leag Dscs; Gurdn Chrctr Ntl Hon Soc; Law.

UMSTEAD, KELLY; Burlington Township HS; Burlington, NJ; (Y); 4/125; French Clb; Ski Clb; Varsity Clb; Yrbk Stf; Var Fld Hcky; Hon Roll; NHS; Hghst Avg-Frnch Awd 86; NJ Grdn ST Schlrshp 86; Rutgers U; Poli Sci.

UMSTETTER, PATTI; Paul VI HS; Turnersville, NJ; (Y); 188/467; Teachers Aide; Glassboro ST Coll; Ed.

UNDERDUE, TOWANDA; St Vincent Acad; Newark, NJ; (Y); 1/68; Cmnty Wkr; Yrbk Ed-Chief; Ed Lit Mag; Cit Awd; NHS; St Schlr; Val; School Play; Variety Show; High Hon Roll; Dow Jones News Fund Schlrshp, Advocate Of E Orange News Correspondent 85; Schl Outstndng Svc Awd 86; CW Post LIU; Jrnlsm.

UNDERWOOD, LORRAINE; Matawan Regional HS; Cliffwood, NJ; (Y); Sec Church Yth Grp; Trs FNA; Sec Church Choir; RN.

UNGAR, TRACEY; Lodi HS; Lodi, NJ; (Y); 13/140; Boys Clb Am; Exploring; Key Clb; Scholastic Bowl; Pres Spanish Clb; Acpl Chr; Chorus; Yrbk Stf; High Hon Roll; NHS; Span Clb Schlrp 86; Med.

UNGARTEN, DOREEN; Middletown HS South; Middletown, NJ; (Y); Debate Tm; Letterman Clb; Office Aide; Red Cross Aide; Spanish Clb; SADD; Teachers Aide; Varsity Clb; Variety Show; Yrbk Stf; Outstanding Achievement In Spanish & French; FIT; Fashion Design.

UNIPAN, CHRISTINA B; Highland HS; Blackwood, NJ; (Y); Civic Clb; Nwsp Phtg; Nwsp Rptr; Nwsp Stf; Lit Mag; Bsktbl; Ltr Of Merit; Med.

UNTERBERGER, BRIAN; Metuchen HS; Metuchen, NJ; (Y); JV Crs Cntry; JV Trk; Hon Roll; Rutgers; Comp.

URBAN, BONNIE; John F Kennedy Memorial HS; Iselin, NJ; (Y); 22/279; VP FBLA; Spanish Clb; SADD; Yrbk Stf; Stat Bsktbl; Capt Trk; Hon Roll; NHS; Sec.

URBAN, BONNIE; Pitman HS; Pitman, NJ; (Y); Hosp Aide; Office Aide; JV Crs Cntry; Var Capt Trk; Hon Roll; Nrsng.

URBAN, DAWN; Gateway Reginal HS; Westville, NJ; (Y); Library Aide; Color Guard; Nwsp Stf; Yrbk Phtg; Yrbk Stf; Wmns Clb Wstvl Hm Ec Awd 85-86; SR Awd Wrk On Plrs Nwspr 85-86; Antonelli Inst Photo; Photo.

URBAN, TRACY; Linden HS; Linden, NJ; (Y); JA; Teachers Aide; VICA; Hon Roll; Prfct Atten Awd; Dntl.

URBANO, FRANK L; Toms River H S East; Toms River, NJ; (Y); 3/479; VP FBLA; Scholastic Bowl; Pres Band; Pres Mrchg Band; School Musical; Symp Band; Gov Hon Prg Awd; High Hon Roll; NHS; Pres Schlr; NJS Sci Lg 83-86; Iltn Amer Cult Soc Scholar 86; Ciba-Geigy H S Amer Chem Soc Awds Chem Sci 84-86; Cook Coll; Pre-Med.

URBANO, MICHAEL A; Passaic HS; Passaic, NJ; (Y); Am Leg Boys St; Ski Clb; Im Bsbl; Hon Roll; SAR Bronze Good Ctznshp Mdl 86; Hamilton Essay Cntst 2nd Pl 86; Wrk Study With Hoffman La Roche Pharm.

URBANOWICZ, EILEEN; Toms River High Schl North; Toms River, NJ; (Y); 41/420; Cmnty Wkr; Exploring; Hosp Aide; Ski Clb; SADD; Band; Chorus; Flag Corp; School Musical; School Play; $500 Schlrshp-TEAM 86; Sales.

URBANSKI, PAUL; Arthur L Johnson HS; Clark, NJ; (Y); Computer Clb; Exploring; German Clb; Hon Roll; Engrng.

URBAY, OLIVETTE; Memorial HS; West New York, NJ; (Y); 95/450; Church Yth Grp; JA; Office Aide; Varsity Clb; Church Choir; Color Guard; Nwsp Rptr; Rep Stu Cncl; Capt Cheerleading; Var Pom Pon; Outstndng Achvt Chrldng 86; Exc Achvt Resrch Bio 85; Pre-Law.

URENA, ROSA; Hoboken HS; Hoboken, NJ; (Y); Key Clb; Office Aide; OEA; Chorus; Rep Frsh Cls; Rep Soph Cls; Rep Jr Cls; Rep Sr Cls; Off Stu Cncl; High Hon Roll; Bus Adm.

URICH, DEBORAH; Chatham Township HS; Chatham, NJ; (Y); 2/125; Church Yth Grp; Key Clb; Sec Band; Pep Band; Var Fld Hcky; JV Sftbl; High Hon Roll; NHS; RPI Math & Sci Awd 86; Smith Coll Clb Bk Awd 86.

URIGUEN, CYNTHIA; Essex Catholic Girls HS; Irvington, NJ; (Y); 2/65; FBLA; FHA; Library Aide; Yrbk Ed-Chief; High Hon Roll; Hon Roll; Cert Of Awd For Outstndg Schlstc Achvmnt 86; Rutgers U; Comp Sci.

URION, ALICE; Woodstown HS; Woodstown, NJ; (Y); Art Clb; Drama Clb; English Clb; French Clb; Key Clb; Band; Yrbk Ed-Chief; Stu Cncl; Im Socr; Rotary Poster Pearl Cont 86; Psych.

URON, REBECCA M; Edgewood Regional SR HS; Waterford, NJ; (Y); 101/376; Boy Scts; Computer Clb; Exploring; Latin Clb; Red Cross Aide; ROTC; Varsity Clb; Coach Actv; JV Fld Hcky; Stat Ftbl; Grants In Aide Schlrshp NCJC 86; U S Marn Corps Phys Achvt Awds 85; Vrsty Clb Pin Questr Awd 86; Camden County Coll; Nrsg.

USARZEWICZ, MARK J; St Peters Prep; Bayonne, NJ; (Y); 62/206; Am Leg Boys St; Boy Scts; VP Church Yth Grp; Rep Jr Cls; Rep Sr Cls; Rep Stu Cncl; JV Bsktbl; Im Ftbl; Hon Roll; Parish Deanery Yth Cncl 86-87; Restrnt Owner.

USCHAK, ROMAN JOHN; Union HS; Union, NJ; (Y); Am Leg Boys St; Band; Concert Band; Rep Stu Cncl; Var L Socr; High Hon Roll; Hon Roll; Orch; Newspaper Features Editor 84; Cty Sponsrd Ice Hcky Tm 85-86; Most Imprvd Awds; ST Sci League Bio 85; Ivy League Coll; Pre-Med.

USCINSKI, JANET; Red Bank Catholic HS; Coltsneck, NJ; (Y); Cmnty Wkr; Ski Clb; Spanish Clb; SADD; Band; Chorus; Concert Band; Jazz Band; Trk; Acctng.

USSHER, KERRI; Pascack Valley Rgnl; Hillsdale, NJ; (Y); French Clb; Letterman Clb; Spanish Clb; JV Socr; JV Sftbl; Im Timer; Hon Roll; Sftbl MVP & All Star 84; Phy Ed Awd 84-86; Intrmrl Trck 1st Pl Yumi & 2nd Pl 100 Yrds 85; Corp Law.

USTIN, KAREN; Montville Township HS; Pine Brk, NJ; (Y); Art Clb; Off FBLA; Ski Clb; SADD; Stu Cncl; Lcrss; Mgr(s); Hon Roll; Key Clb; Score Keeper; Ldrshp Trng Cmp Stu Cncl 84; Nmrs FBLA Trnng Smnrs Cnfrnc; Grls Ctznshp Inst Of NJ 86.

UTH, RICHARD P; Holy Cross HS; Medford, NJ; (Y); Boy Scts; Cmnty Wkr; Debate Tm; Stage Crew; Yrbk Stf; Cit Awd; God Cntry Awd; Hon Roll; Rept To Cnty Govt 86; Polt Sci.

VACANTE, ROSELYN; Monsignor Donovan HS; Lakehurst, NJ; (Y); Am Leg Aux Girls St; JA; Orch; Yrbk Stf; Hon Roll; NHS; Ntl Piano Plyng Adtns 85; Ntl Piano Plyng Adtns 86; Med.

VACCA, ROBERT; Linden HS; Linden, NJ; (Y); Ski Clb; Yrbk Stf; Rep Soph Cls; Rep Jr Cls; Rep Sr Cls; Pres Stu Cncl; Bsbl; JV Ftbl; Capt Var Golf; Var Socr; Rutgers U; Comp Sci.

VACCARO, ANNE MICHELE; Red Bank Catholic HS; Sea Bright, NJ; (Y); 115/265; Art Clb; Hosp Aide; Latin Clb; Ski Clb; SADD; Teachers Aide; School Play; Off Frsh Cls; Off Soph Cls; Off Jr Cls; Brookdale CC; Nrsg.

VACCARO, FRANCO; North Bergen HS; Guttenberg, NJ; (S); SADD; Stu Cncl; VFW Awd; Rutgers; Acctnt.

VACCHIO, MELISSA; South River HS; South River, NJ; (Y); German Clb; GAA; Library Aide; Office Aide; Varsity Clb; Yrbk Stf; Pres Jr Cls; Rep Stu Cncl; Var L Bsktbl; Var L Crs Cntry; All Cnty Hnrbl Mtn Bsktbl,Sftbll 85-86; All Sntnl All Star Sftbl 86; Montclair ST; Phys Ed.

VACLAVICEK, RENEE; Immaculate Conception HS; Little Falls, NJ; (Y); Exploring; Spanish Clb; Bowling; Sftbl; Vllybl; Acctng.

VAICUS, REGINA; Kittatinny Reg HS; Newton, NJ; (Y); 86/260; 4-H; Hosp Aide; Varsity Clb; Band; Mrchg Band; Powder Puff Ftbl; JV Swmmng; Var Trk; Hon Roll; Bus Mgmt.

VAJO, MICHELE BARBARA; Edison HS; Edison, NJ; (Y); 19/330; French Clb; Rep Sr Cls; Rep Stu Cncl; NHS; Assoc PTA Schlrshp; Rtgrs U; Psychlgy.

VALATKA, MICHELE; Notre Dame HS; Trenton, NJ; (Y); 18/365; Drama Clb; Math Tm; Red Cross Aide; Service Clb; School Musical; School Play; Hon Roll; NHS; Med.

VALAVERIS, ANNA; Hackensack HS; Hackensack, NJ; (Y); Church Yth Grp; Cmnty Wkr; French Clb; Hosp Aide; Office Aide; Red Cross Aide; Teachers Aide; Im Trk; French Hon Soc; Hon Roll; Chrstn Lectrs 2nd Prz-Greek Orthdx Chrstn Socty Amer 86; NJ ST Chmpnshp Vllybl-GOYA Tms 85; Pre-Med.

VALDES, JOHN; Red Bank Catholic HS; Middletown, NJ; (Y); Yrbk Sprt Ed; Rep Frsh Cls; Im Bsbl; Im Tennis; Im Var Wt Lftg; Var Wrstlng; NHS; NEDT Awd; Orange Blt Karate; Comp Sci.

VALDES, RICHARD; Memorial HS; West New York, NJ; (Y); Computer Clb; Bowling; Fld Hcky; Pom Pon; Socr; Sftbl; Trk; Vllybl; High Hon Roll; Hon Roll; Comp Tech.

VALDEZ, ABIGAIL JEANNE; Paramus HS; Paramus, NJ; (Y); 52/343; Church Yth Grp; Church Choir; Color Guard; Co-Capt Flag Corp; Jazz Band; Orch; Lit Mag; Nat Soc Stds Olympd 85; Columbia Bible Coll; Blbe.

VALENCIA, JUAN; Hillside HS; Hillside, NJ; (Y); 11/249; Am Leg Boys St; Math Clb; Var Capt Crs Cntry; Var Capt Trk; Var Capt Wrstlng; Hon Roll; Rutgers; Elec Engrng.

VALENTE, JOSEPH; St Peters Prep; Bayonne, NJ; (Y); Hosp Aide; Ski Clb; Jazz Band; Yrbk Stf; Soph Cls; Stu Cncl; Trk.

VALENTE, MICHAEL; Sayreville War Memorial HS; Parlin, NJ; (Y); 50/379; Cmnty Wkr; Mathletes; Math Clb; Spanish Clb; Nwsp Rptr; Hon Roll; NHS; Portugese Am Schlrshp 86; PBA Sayreville Schlrshp 86; Rider Coll; Accounting.

VALENTIEN, DAWN; Bogota HS; Bogota, NJ; (Y); 21/100; Church Yth Grp; Drama Clb; Band; Church Choir; Color Guard; School Musical; Sec Frsh Cls; Pres Soph Cls; Pres Jr Cls; Hon Roll; Drama Awd 86; USNBA Band Awd 86; Rampapo ST Clg; Fine Arts.

VALENTIN, JANET; James J Ferris HS; Jersey City, NJ; (Y); Science Clb; Jr Cls; Sr Cls; JV Var Cheerleading; Swmmng; Merit Awd 86; St Francis Schl Nrsng; Nrsng.

VALENTIN, MARIA D; Our Lady Of Good Council HS; Newark, NJ; (Y); Dance Clb; Pep Clb; School Musical; School Play; Stage Crew; Yrbk Stf; Bsktbl; Gym; Sftbl; Vllybl; Rutgers U; Bus Admn.

VALENTIN, NANCY; Eastside HS; Paterson, NJ; (S); #21 In Class; Church Yth Grp; Office Aide; Church Choir; High Hon Roll; Hon Roll; NHS; Scl Wrkr.

VALENTINE, JOSEPH M; Livingston HS; Livingston, NJ; (Y); Am Leg Boys St; Var Bsbl; JV Ftbl; JV Wrstlng; Hon Roll; Rider Coll; Acctg.

VALENTINE, MICHAEL; Pope John XXIII HS; Oak Ridge, NJ; (Y); 8/140; French Clb; Quiz Bowl; Scholastic Bowl; Varsity Clb; Var Co-Capt Bsbl; Var Ftbl; High Hon Roll; NHS; Bsbl-MVP Al-Leag,Al-Area,Al-Nrth Jrsey 86; Yale U; Pre-Med.

VALENTINE, TARA; Lenape Valley Regional HS; Andover, NJ; (Y); 52/250; Pres Soph Cls; Rep Jr Cls; Rep Stu Cncl; Powder Puff Ftbl; JV Capt Sftbl; JV Swmmng; Timer; Hon Roll; Spanish NHS; MVP Sftbl 84; Childhd Ed.

VALENTINO, LEONARD; St John Vianney HS; Middletown, NJ; (Y); 106/300; SADD; Ftbl; Wt Lftg; Hon Roll; St Bonaventure; Acctng.

VALERIO, PAUL; Bayley-Ellard Regional HS; Morristown, NJ; (Y); School Play; Rep Soph Cls; Rep Jr Cls; Rep Sr Cls; Var Bsktbl; Var Socr; High Hon Roll; NHS; Hugh O Brien Yth Ldrshp Semnr 85; Church Yth Grp 83-86; Engrng.

VALIAN, DAVID; Linden HS; Linden, NJ; (Y); German Clb; Ski Clb; Acpl Chr; Chorus; Im Bsbl; Im Bsktbl; Var L Ftbl; Var L Trk; Var Wt Lftg; Ftbl ST Chmpnshp Grp III 85-86; Mdgrgls 86; VP Of Cncrt Choir 86.

VALIAVEEDAN, MARIA; Saint John Vianney HS; Freehold, NJ; (Y); 6/236; Cmnty Wkr; Hosp Aide; Intnl Clb; Math Tm; Service Clb; Yrbk Bus Mgr; Yrbk Stf; JV Powder Puff Ftbl; High Hon Roll; Hon Roll; French Awd 82-83; Gold & White Awd 83-84; Lehigh U; Bus.

VALLABHANENI, SURENDRA; East Brunswick HS; E Brunswick, NJ; (Y); Camp Fr Inc; FBLA; Key Clb; Math Clb; Nwsp Rptr; Rep Stu Cncl; 4-H Awd; NHS; Prfct Atten Awd; Spanish NHS; Med.

VALLANDINGHAM, TRACI; Paulsboro HS; Swedesboro, NJ; (Y); Office Aide; Var JV Cheerleading; JV Fld Hcky; Stat Wrstlng; Cit Awd; High Hon Roll; Hon Roll; Prfct Atten Awd; JV Bsktbl; Var JV Mat Maids; 2 2nd Pl Cooking Cont Awds 86; Self Def Awd 86; Excllnt Hlth & Fitness Awd 86; Gloucester County Coll; Nursng.

VALLE, CHRISTINA; Triton Regional HS; Runnemede, NJ; (Y); 17/286; Band; Chorus; Color Guard; Concert Band; Drm Mjr(t); Mrchg Band; JP Sousa Awd; NHS; Latin Clb; Math Clb; Olympc Conf Hnrs Band; S Jersey Orch; Semper Fidelis Awd; Glassboro ST Coll; Spec Ed.

VALLILA, ANDREW; Don Bosco Prep; Lyndhurst, NJ; (Y); Chess Clb; Church Yth Grp; Cmnty Wkr; Science Clb; Im Bsbl; Im Bowling; Hon Roll; Don Bosco Sprt Clb 85; Prlw.

VALVERDE, KENNETH DAVID; Perth Amboy HS; Perth Amboy, NJ; (Y); Trs Chorus; Madrigals; School Musical; Rep Stu Cncl; JV Ftbl; Im Wt Lftg; Kiwanis Awd; Nj All St Chorus 83-85; All Eastern Coast Chorus 84; Yth Of Amer Chorus Eur Cncrt Tour 86; Glassboro ST Coll; Music Ed.

VAN BLARCOM, JENNIFER; Immaculate Conception HS; Rutherford, NJ; (S); 5/87; Debate Tm; Drama Clb; English Clb; Q&S; Science Clb; School Musical; Nwsp Ed-Chief; Pres Frsh Cls; Sec Soph Cls; Rep Stu Cncl; John Hopkins Stu 84-86; St Peters Coll Smmr Schlr 85-86; Rep Stu Cncl-Bergen Co Cthlc HS Frm 84-86; Princeton; Arch.

VAN BLARCOM, KRISTINA; Toms River East HS; Toms River, NJ; (S); 65/489; Drama Clb; Q&S; Thesps; Chorus; Jazz Band; School Musical; Nwsp Rptr; Hon Roll; NHS; French Clb; Arion Awd 85-86; Outstndg Voclst Awd 84-85; Mod Congress 84-86; Music.

VAN BLOEM, KRISTINE; Red Bank Catholic HS; Oceanport, NJ; (Y); Boys Clb Am; Cmnty Wkr; Ski Clb; Varsity Clb; JV Var Bsktbl; JV Var Crs Cntry; Var L Socr; Var L Trk; Hon Roll; NHS; Physcl Ther.

VAN BLOEN, KRISTINE; Red Bank Catholic HS; Oceanport, NJ; (Y); Boys Clb Am; Cmnty Wkr; Math Clb; Science Clb; Ski Clb; Varsity Clb; Var L Bsktbl; Var L Crs Cntry; Var L Socr; JV L Trk; Physcl Thrpy.

VAN BRUMMELEN, JAMES B; Calvary Acad; Toms River, NJ; (S); Church Yth Grp; VP Jr Cls; Var Bsbl; Var Bsktbl; Hon Roll; Accntng.

VAN BUREN, KENNETH R; Vineland HS; Vineland, NJ; (Y); 10/730; Am Leg Boys St; Pres Aud/Vis; Chess Clb; Debate Tm; Key Clb; Library Aide; Math Tm; Science Clb; Spanish Clb; Stu Cncl.

VAN BURK JR, GERRIT J; Governor Livingston Regional HS; Berkeley Hts, NJ; (Y); 53/160; Boy Scts; Pres Church Yth Grp; Var Tennis; Hon Roll; Lwyr.

VAN BUSKIRK, TEDD; Bernards HS; Basking Ridge, NJ; (Y); 30/180; Boy Scts; Church Yth Grp; French Clb; Science Clb; Band; Concert Band; Jazz Band; Mrchg Band; School Musical; School Play; Eagle Sct BSA 86; Edward P Buchanan Svc Awd 85-86; New Theatr Drama Svc Awd; Rutgers Coll Engrng; Mech Engrg.

VAN DAM, LEONARDUS; Cliffside Park HS; Cliffside Pk, NJ; (Y); Boy Scts; Church Yth Grp; Band; Yrbk Phtg; Rep Stu Cncl; Bowling; Golf; Socr; Wrstlng; All League Golf 85-86; Italian Clb; Fifty Miler Afoot; U Of RI; Accntnt.

VAN DER VLIET, DANIEL G; Sussex County Tech HS; Franklin, NJ; (S); 12/150; Am Leg Boys St; Church Yth Grp; Spanish Clb; Trs Frsh Cls; Rep Soph Cls; Rep Jr Cls; Capt Var Bsbl; Pres NHS; Arch.

VAN DIEN, STEPHEN; Voorhees HS; Pottersville, NJ; (Y); 1/274; Boy Scts; Math Tm; Ski Clb; Var Golf; JV Socr; Bausch & Lomb Sci Awd; High Hon Roll; NHS; Ntl Merit Ltr; Spanish NHS; Mth-Sci Tm Outstndng Stu Awd 85; Spn III Awd 86; Natl Spn Cont 86; Natl Chem & Physics Cont 85; Chem Engrng.

VAN DOREN, JACQUELINE; James Caldwell HS; W Caldwell, NJ; (Y); Church Yth Grp; Cmnty Wkr; Science Clb; Chorus; Church Choir; Orch; School Musical; Swmmng; JV Trk; High Hon Roll.

VAN DRIGHT, KARI SUE; Kittatinny Regional HS; Blairstown, NJ; (Y); 85/287; Ski Clb; Trvl.

VAN DYKE, CAROLINE; Shore Regional HS; Oceanport, NJ; (Y); Var Fld Hcky; Stat Mgr(s); Powder Puff Ftbl; JV Sftbl; Var Swmmng; Hon Roll; Hstry.

VAN DYKE, TRACY; Ramapo HS; Franklin Lakes, NJ; (Y); Church Yth Grp; Drama Clb; Radio Clb; Thesps; School Musical; School Play; Stage Crew; Frsh Cls; VP Soph Cls; VP Jr Cls; NJ Miss Teen 85-86; Extraord Stu Of Am 86; Stu Of Mnth 84; Hnr Rll; Natl Hnr Soc; Sch Rado Anncr; TV Anchr Persn.

VAN EMBURG, WILLIAM S; Kinnelon HS; Kinnelon, NJ; (Y); 2/156; Am Leg Boys St; Boy Scts; Chess Clb; German Clb; PAVAS; Scholastic Bowl; Science Clb; Varsity Clb; Band; Concert Band; Grmn Hnr Soc; Rtgrs Schlr; Rnsslr Mdl Wnnr For Math & Sci; Rutgers Coll; Elec Engrng.

VAN ES, KIM; Secaucus HS; Secaucus, NJ; (S); 6/175; Church Yth Grp; Computer Clb; Key Clb; VP Math Clb; Math Tm; Ski Clb; VP Spanish Clb; Varsity Clb; Co-Capt Color Guard; Stage Crew; 2nd Natl Tst Mu Alpha Theta 83; 2nd Comp Lg Natn Mu Alpha Theta 85; Bus Adm.

VAN GRONIGEN, JOSEPH; Paul VI HS; Glendora, NJ; (Y); 197/516; Computer Clb; Math Clb; SADD; U PA Wharton; CPA.

VAN GROUW, DOROTHY; Manchester Regional HS; North Haledon, NJ; (S); 3/156; GAA; Quiz Bowl; Yrbk Stf; Rep Stu Cncl; Powder Puff Ftbl; Score Keeper; Vllybl; High Hon Roll; Hon Roll; NHS; Intl Frgn Lang Awd 85-86; Natl Hnr Soc Pres 85-86; Frgn Lang Hnr Soc 84-86; Fairleigh Dcknsn U; Dntl Hygne.

VAN HASSEL, STEPHEN; Glen Rock JR SR HS; Glen Rock, NJ; (Y); 2/160; Church Yth Grp; Latin Clb; Science Clb; Spanish Clb; Yrbk Stf; Var JV Bsbl; JV Socr; High Hon Roll; Jr NHS; NHS.

VAN HORN, DENISE; Delsea Regional HS; Franklinville, NJ; (Y); Cmnty Wkr; Yrbk Stf; JV Sftbl; Hon Roll; Accntng.

VAN HORN, HEATHER; James Caldwell HS; Caldwell, NJ; (Y); Science Clb; Band; Concert Band; Mrchg Band; Orch; Crs Cntry; Socr; Trk; High Hon Roll; NHS; Montclair St Coll Hnrs Wind Ensmble Bassoon 86; Pre-Med.

VAN HORN, SHARI; Manasquan HS; Pt Pleasant, NJ; (Y); 38/242; Dance Clb; Girl Scts; Spanish Clb; Varsity Clb; JV Var Socr; E Strudsburg U.

VAN HOUTEN, DAWN; Nutley HS; Nutley, NJ; (Y); AFS; Drama Clb; FBLA; Key Clb; Ski Clb; Band; Color Guard; Yrbk Ed-Chief; Sec Frsh Cls; Rep Stu Cncl; Bryan Coll; Hotel Mgmt.

VAN MEIR, VICKIE; Secaucus HS; Secaucus, NJ; (S); 30/160; Key Clb; Pres Ski Clb; Varsity Clb; School Musical; Rep Jr Cls; Var L Trk; JV Capt Vllybl; High Hon Roll; Hon Roll; Dance Clb; Gftd & Tlntd Prgm; Hnr Cls; Engr.

VAN METER, LORI; Garden State Acad; Andover, NJ; (Y); 1/25; Church Yth Grp; Girl Scts; Ski Clb; Band; Concert Band; School Play; Stage Crew; Variety Show; Nwsp Rptr; Trs Frsh Cls; Columbia Union Coll; Engr.

VAN NOSTRAN, KIRSTEN; Lenapo Valley Regional HS; Stanhope, NJ; (Y); 24/240; SADD; Band; Orch; School Musical; School Play; Stage Crew; Symp Band; Hon Roll; NHS; German Hnr Socy 86; Music.

VAN OFDEN, RICHARD; Lenape Valley Regional HS; Netcong, NJ; (Y); 42/241; Am Leg Boys St; Boy Scts; Pres SADD; Orch; Nwsp Phtg; Lit Mag; Rep Stu Cncl; Crs Cntry; Trk; NHS.

VAN ORDEN, ANN MARIE; Dover HS; Mine Hill, NJ; (Y); 15/220; AFS; Am Leg Aux Girls St; Key Clb; Office Aide; Band; Concert Band; Mrchg Band; Orch; School Musical; Var Bsktbl; Arion Awd Most Outstndng Musician 86; Mine Hill PTA Schrlshp 86; Dover Band Booster Schrlshp 86; Trenton ST Coll; Psychlgy.

VAN ORDEN, PAUL J; St Peters Prep; Kearny, NJ; (Y); Am Leg Boys St; Boy Scts; Pres Church Yth Grp; Dance Clb; German Clb; Science Clb; School Play; Rep Soph Cls; Envrnmntl Engrng.

VAN PAMEL, LAURA; Hawthorne HS; Hawthorne, NJ; (Y); SADD; Chorus; Off Color Guard; School Play; Church Yth Grp; 4-H; Concert Band; Stage Crew; Rutgers; Drama.

VAN RIPER, LISA; Newton HS; Andover, NJ; (Y); Spanish Clb; Drill Tm; School Play; Cheerleading; Powder Puff Ftbl; Trk; Twrlr; DAR Awd; Gd Ctznshp Awd 83; Morris Cnty Coll; Sec.

VAN SCIVER, MICHELLE; Burlington Co Vo Tech; Beverly, NJ; (Y); Yrbk Stf; 3rd Pl Dnc Cmptn ITDI 84; 2nd Pl Dnc Cmptn ITDI 85; Dnc.

VAN STEEN, LESLIE; Pemberton Township H S II; Browns Mills, NJ; (Y); 69/400; Camera Clb; Dance Clb; Key Clb; Teachers Aide; Band; Chorus; Concert Band; High Hon Roll; Schl Ltr Awd Tchrs Aid 86; Crtfct Awd Fr Tchrs Aid 86; Choir Awd 86; Trenton ST Coll; Accntng.

VAN SYCKLE, MARIA T; Manasquan HS; Spring Lake, NJ; (Y); 2/250; Church Yth Grp; Key Clb; Math Tm; Science Clb; Spanish Clb; JV Capt Bsktbl; JV Im Sftbl; High Hon Roll; Kiwanis Awd; Sec NHS; Bd Educ Awd 85&86; Math.

VAN TASSELL, HARRY L; Watchung Hills Regnional HS; Watchung, NJ; (Y); 24/315; Am Leg Boys St; Trs Ski Clb; SADD; Trs School Musical; Stage Crew; Rep Frsh Cls; Rep Soph Cls; Bus.

VAN TOL, INGRID; Montville Township HS; Montville, NJ; (Y); 27/262; Church Yth Grp; GAA; Hosp Aide; Key Clb; Ski Clb; Concert Band; Stage Crew; Var Capt Gym; Var Trk; High Hon Roll; MVP Gymnstcs 84-85; 1st Tm All Conf & All Arnd 85-86; 1st Pl On Beam, Bars, Vlt, All Arnd Conf 85-86; Pre-Med.

VAN WINKLE, DEBBY; Passaic Valley HS; W Paterson, NJ; (Y); 10/359; Am Leg Aux Girls St; Pres Debate Tm; Pres Drama Clb; Pres Thesps; School Musical; School Play; Ed Yrbk Rptr; Trs Sr Cls; Trs Stu Cncl; NHS; Bst Dirctr Secndry Schl Drama Comptn 86; WA Wrkshps 86; JR Statesmn Amer 85-86; Summr Schl Scholar; Med.

VAN WINKLE, JAMES; Hudson Catholic HS; Secaucus, NJ; (Y); 45/200; Church Yth Grp; Cmnty Wkr; Dance Clb; Rptr Key Clb; Pep Clb; SADD; Yrbk Phtg; Rptr Soph Cls; VP Stu Cncl; Var JV Bsbl; Civic Engrng.

VANAMAN, ROBERT; Millville SR HS; Millville, NJ; (Y); Church Yth Grp; Key Clb; Math Clb; SADD; JV Bsbl; Bowling; JV Var Ftbl; Wt Lftg; Hon Roll; NHS; Chemical Engineering.

VANBERGEN, SUSAN; St John Vianney HS; Freehold, NJ; (Y); 21/259; Art Clb; Church Yth Grp; Library Aide; Ski Clb; SADD; Stage Crew; Nwsp Stf; Yrbk Stf; Rep Stu Cncl; Score Keeper; Congrssnl Schlr Awd 86; Penn ST; Law.

VANCE, BONNIE; Holy Spirit HS; Margate, NJ; (Y); 120/238; Letterman Clb; Varsity Clb; Cit Awd; 2nd Ntl Schlboy Regata 84-85; Frostbite Regatta 84-85; Psychlgy.

VANDENBERG, LORETTA; Monteville Township HS; Towaco, NJ; (Y); 9/262; Key Clb; Quiz Bowl; Concert Band; Mrchg Band; School Musical; Crs Cntry; Var Capt Trk; High Hon Roll; NHS; Ntl Merit Ltr; US St Naval Acad.

VANDENBURG III, JAMES; Clifton HS; Clifton, NJ; (Y); 37/564; Science Clb; Band; Concert Band; Jazz Band; Mrchg Band; Nwsp Rptr; High Hon Roll; Jr NHS; NHS; Pres Acad Ftns Awd 86; Gladys G Mickelven Mem Schlrshp 86; Green Belt Tue Kwon Do 86; Rutgers U; Biochem.

VANDER MEER, DEBBIE; Toms River High School South; Toms River, NJ; (Y); Church Yth Grp; Girl Scts; Science Clb; JV Bsktbl; Mgr Fld Hcky; JV Socr; High Hon Roll; NHS; Acad Ltr 85-86.

VANDER MOLEN, KEN; Manchester Regional HS; Prospect Park, NJ; (S); Church Yth Grp; German Clb; Band; Concert Band; Mrchg Band; Coach Actv; Hon Roll.

VANDERBEEK, TRACIE; North Begen HS; North Bergen, NJ; (Y); 4/490; Church Yth Grp; German Clb; Key Clb; Library Aide; Band; Capt Twrlr; CC Awd; High Hon Roll; NHS; Gvrnrs Schlr Pgm 86; Nrma Stnwld Schlrshp 86; Schlrs Schlrshp NYU 86; NYU; Elem Educ.

VANDERMARK, ANNE; Hightstown HS; Cranbury, NJ; (Y); Aud/Vis; Drama Clb; GAA; Service Clb; Spanish Clb; Thesps; Varsity Clb; Band; Concert Band; Mrchg Band; Bus.

VANDERSTARRE, CORINA; Rutherford HS; Rutherford, NJ; (Y); 70/179; Debate Tm; Key Clb; Acpl Chr; Band; Chorus; Concert Band; Orch; Socr; Spr Musicnshp Awd, Judge NBCDL 85-86; Montclair ST Coll; Bus Admn.

VANDZUNA, PAULA; Our Lady Of Mercy Acad; Minotola, NJ; (Y); 3/30; Chorus; Yrbk Stf; JV Var Cheerleading; Hon Roll.

VANGREJ, CLIFF; Union HS; Union, NJ; (Y); Var JV Ftbl; Var Wt Lftg; Graphic Arts Studnt Of The Yr 86; North Jersey Art Fair 1st Pl 86; Fashion Inst Of Tech; Graph Art.

VANN, ROGER; Woodstown HS; Elmer, NJ; (Y); Spanish Clb; Chorus; Hon Roll; Spanish NHS.

VANNEST, AYMEE; Secaucus HS; Secaucus, NJ; (S); 29/160; Computer Clb; FBLA; Hosp Aide; Key Clb; Office Aide; Mrchg Band; Sec Frsh Cls; Cheerleading; Sftbl; High Hon Roll; Typg Awd 1st Pl 85.

VANNOTE, TATIA L; Hopewell Valley C HS; Trenton, NJ; (Y); 12/199; Math Clb; Science Clb; Service Clb; Church Choir; Sec Sr Cls; High Hon Roll; NHS; Ntl Merit SF; Off Frsh Cls; Rep Soph Cls; Cnty Ltry Magzn Pblctn 85; Garden ST Schlr 85; Peeer Ldr 85-86.

VANORDEN, RICHARD; Lenape Valley Regional HS; Netcong, NJ; (Y); 24/253; Am Leg Boys St; Boy Scts; Pres SADD; Band; Nwsp Phtg; Lit Mag; Stu Cncl; Crs Cntry; Trk; NHS.

VANSTEENACKER, JEANINE; Holy Cross HS; Maple Shade, NJ; (Y); Church Yth Grp; Band; Concert Band; Mrchg Band; Pep Band; Stage Crew; High Hon Roll; Hon Roll; Nursing.

VANVOURELLIS, JOYCE; Colonia HS; Colonia, NJ; (Y); Girl Scts; JA; Nwsp Stf; Yrbk Stf; High Hon Roll; Jr NHS; NHS; Prfct Atten Awd; Bus.

VARA, MANUEL; Union Catholic HS; Rahway, NJ; (Y); Scholastic Bowl; Service Clb; Spanish Clb; Teachers Aide; JV Wrstlng; High Hon Roll; Hon Roll; NHS; Law Clb 86; NJ AATSP Levl II 2nd Pl 84 & 85; Raqtbll Clb 85; Seton Hall; Poltcl Sci.

VARELA, YVONNE; Madison Ave Baptist Acad; Paterson, NJ; (S); Church Yth Grp; Church Choir; School Play; Bsktbl; Cheerleading; Vllybl; Hon Roll; Pensacola Chrstn Coll; Bus Adm.

VARGA, JULIA; Villa Victoria Acad; Trenton, NJ; (Y); 1/31; Am Leg Aux Girls St; Acpl Chr; School Musical; Lit Mag; Pres Soph Cls; Pres Stu Cncl; High Hon Roll; Spanish NHS; Wllsly Bk Awd 86; Rtgrs Schlr 86; Cornell U; Htl Mngmt.

VARGAS, NURIA M; Paul VI Reg HS; Passaic, NJ; (Y); 4-H; Key Clb; Office Aide; Spanish Clb; 4-H Awd; Hon Roll; Spanish NHS; Tourism.

VARGAS, RICHARD; Hoboken HS; Hoboken, NJ; (Y); Band; Concert Band; Mrchg Band; Pep Band; Bus.

VARGAS, YADIRA; Memorial HS; W New York, NJ; (Y); Girl Scts; Hosp Aide; Drm Mjr(t); Twrlr; Hlth Club 86; Med.

VARRELLA, JOHN; Washington Township HS; Turnersville, NJ; (Y); 200/470; Boy Scts; Church Yth Grp; Exploring; Ski Clb; Hon Roll; U Cntrl FL; Elec Engrng.

VASQUEZ, ANDRES; John F Kennedy HS; Paterson, NJ; (Y); Boys Clb Am; Intnl Clb; Spanish Clb; Socr; Hon Roll; Cmptr Sci.

VASSALLO, MARY; Villa Victoria Acad; Yardley, PA; (S); Drama Clb; School Musical; Lit Mag; Rep Stu Cncl; Socr; High Hon Roll; Mu Alp Tht; Church Yth Grp; Math Clb; Chorus; 4-Yr Acad Schlrshp 83-87; Hghst Avg Sbjct Awd-Sci, Typng, Rlgn 83-84.

VASSER, EDWARD; Holy Spirit HS; Margate, NJ; (Y); 35/340; Mathletes; Yrbk Stf; Var L Bsktbl; Im Vllybl; NHS; Ntl Hon Rl 85; Big Brothers 85; U Of DE; Bus Adm.

VATH, FREDERICK; Oratory Prep; Watchung, NJ; (Y); Boy Scts; Chess Clb; Church Yth Grp; Math Clb; Ski Clb; Pres Jr Cls; VP Trs Stu Cncl; Var Crs Cntry; Var Trk; Hon Roll; BSA Eagle; US Mltry Acad; Engrng.

VAUGHAN, MARNIE; Hightstown HS; East Windsor, NJ; (Y); 25/450; AFS; Pres French Clb; German Clb; Pres Intnl Clb; Pres Spanish Clb; Teachers Aide; High Hon Roll; Hon Roll; NHS; Middlebury; Intrprtr Itln.

VAUGHAN, PATRICK; St Peters Prep; Jersey City, NJ; (Y); Boy Scts; Church Yth Grp; German Clb; Hosp Aide; Speech Tm; Thesps; Church Choir; Variety Show.

VAUGHN, JOEL; Freehold Twp HS; Freehold, NJ; (Y); 97/385; Var Capt Bsktbl; Var Capt Ftbl; Hon Roll; Bill Bradley Awd 84-85; All Dist Kickr 1st Tm 85-86; All Dist Bsktbl 85-86; Htl/Rest Mgmt.

VAUGHN, MARCEL; Essex Catholic Girls HS; Irvington, NJ; (Y); 6/72; School Musical; VP Soph Cls; Trs Jr Cls; Trs Sr Cls; High Hon Roll; Hon Roll; NHS; Church Yth Grp; Drama Clb; Actvts Edtr Yrbk 85-86; 1st Pl Sci Fair 83-84; Rutgers; Pre-Dntstry.

VAZQUEZ, BETTY; Mary Help Of Christians Acad; Paterson, NJ; (S); Computer Clb; Drama Clb; Math Clb; Chorus; School Musical; High Hon Roll; Hon Roll; Prfct Atten Awd; Camp Cnslr 85.

VAZQUEZ, JULIO; St Anthonys HS; Jersey, NJ; (Y); 10/60; JV Var Bsbl; JV Bsktbl; Hon Roll; Acctng.

VAZQUEZ, WALTER J; Union Hill HS; Union City, NJ; (Y); Am Leg Boys St; Stage Crew; JV Ftbl; Navy ROTC; Comp Tech.

VECCHIONE, BRIAN; Emerson HS; Union City, NJ; (Y); French Clb; Science Clb; Yrbk Rptr; Yrbk Stf; Lit Mag; VP Jr Cls; VP Sr Cls; Rep Stu Cncl; Var Tennis; Hon Roll; Math.

VECCHIONE, PAUL; Toms River HS South; So Toms River, NJ; (Y); 32/360; Math Tm; Scholastic Bowl; Spanish Clb; Var Capt Bsbl; Var L Ftbl; Im Wt Lftg; High Hon Roll; JV Mst Dedctd Awd Bsbll 85; U Of DE; Corp Law.

VEGA, ADELIA; Mary Help Of Christians Acad; Paterson, NJ; (Y); Computer Clb; French Clb; JCL; Latin Clb; Pep Clb; Variety Show; Rep Jr Cls; Gym; Vllybl; Hon Roll; Natl Hnr Socty 85-86.

VEGA, DAISY; Franklin HS; Somerset, NJ; (Y); JV Mgr(s); Rutgers U; Pre Med.

VEGA, JUANITA; Arts HS; Newark, NJ; (Y); 23/130; Drama Clb; School Play; NJ ST Drama Comp 1st Pl 85, 2nd Pl 86; Gov Awd Outstndg Achvt Arts 85; Mason Gross Schl Arts; Drama.

VEGA, MELISSA; Columbia HS; Maplewood, NJ; (Y); 98/446; Church Yth Grp; Office Aide; Pres Sec Spanish Clb; Chorus; Lit Mag; Stu Cncl; High Hon Roll; Hon Roll; Jr NHS; Spanish NHS; Mnrty Grdn ST Schlr 86; Ntl Rcgntn Intl Yth Yr Awds 85; Inter-Amer U Puerto Rico; Psych.

VEGA, NATALIA; Mary Help Of Christians Acad; Paterson, NJ; (Y); Vllybl; Upsala Coll; Intl Mgmt.

VEIT JR, RICHARD F; South Plainfield HS; So Plnfld, NJ; (Y); 12/280; Drama Clb; Mrchg Band; Symp Band; Im Bowling; NHS; Ntl Merit SF; Pres Schlr; Church Yth Grp; German Clb; Hosp Aide; Outstndng Band Member Schlrshp 85-86; Jerseyman Schlsrhp 86; German Hnr Scty Drew Schlr Schlrsp 86; Drew U; Anthropology.

VEITH, JENNIFER; Paul Vi HS; Atco, NJ; (Y); 22/511; Am Leg Aux Girls St; Drama Clb; German Clb; Math Clb; SADD; School Musical; School Play; Stage Crew; Yrbk Stf; High Hon Roll; Ntl Grmn Hnr Soc 85-86; Amer Lgn Essy 83-84; Tutor In Grmn & Mth 84-86; Comm.

VELARDI, JOE; Lodi HS; Lodi, NJ; (Y); Am Leg Boys St; Leo Clb; Varsity Clb; Var L Ftbl; Var L Trk; Wt Lftg; Hon Roll; NHS; Law.

VELARDI, RONICA; Toms River High School South; Toms River, NJ; (Y); 7/315; Cmnty Wkr; Math Clb; Math Tm; Var Fld Hcky; Var L Sftbl; High Hon Roll; NHS; Prfct Atten Awd; Pres Schlr; Spanish Clb; Ruth Cline Applegate Awd Exclnc 86; Prsdntl Acdmc Ftns Awd 86; Natl Hnr Scty Top 10 Awd 86; Penn ST U; Math.

VELASCO, JULIAN; Bishop Ahr St Thomas Aquinas HS; Perth Amboy, NJ; (Y); 15/277; Am Leg Boys St; Boy Scts; Drama Clb; Model UN; Thesps; School Musical; School Play; High Hon Roll; NHS; Intnl Clb; Drama Mst Promsng Newcomer.

VELASQUEZ, BRENDA; Middletown H S South; Lincroft, NJ; (Y); Drama Clb; PAVAS; SADD; Temple Yth Grp; Thesps; School Musical; Yrbk Stf; Trk; High Hon Roll; Prfct Atten Awd; 1st Prize Middletown Art/Crft Show 84; Copellia Dancing & Ballet Corps 84; Psych.

VELAZQUEZ, DIONISIO D; North Bergen HS; North Bergen, NJ; (Y); Key Clb; Spanish Clb; SADD; Color Guard; Var Ftbl; Socr; Wt Lftg; Wrstlng; Hon Roll; Mchncl Engrng.

VELE, LINDA; East Brunswick HS; East Brunswick, NJ; (Y); Dance Clb; Varsity Clb; Var Cheerleading; Rutgers U; Advrstng.

VELEBER, ALLISON; Eastern Christian HS; Towaco, NJ; (Y); 10/91; Church Yth Grp; Hosp Aide; Chorus; Nwsp Rptr; Yrbk Stf; Hon Roll; Pres Schlr; Drew U; Math.

VELECHKO, SCOTT; Paul VI Regional HS; Clifton, NJ; (S); Computer Clb; Math Tm; Nwsp Rptr; Off Soph Cls; Rep Jr Cls; Trs Stu Cncl; JV Crs Cntry; Var L Socr; NHS; VFW Awd; Bys ST 85; Engrng.

VELEZ, ARACELIS; Burlington City HS; Edgewater Pk, NJ; (Y); Drama Clb; FTA; Band; Chorus; Concert Band; Mgr Jazz Band; Mrchg Band; School Musical; JV Fld Hcky; Mgr Wrstlng.

VELEZ, DEBORAH; Pennsville Memorial HS; Pennsville, NJ; (Y); 3/235; Nwsp Ed-Chief; Yrbk Ed-Chief; Trs Soph Cls; Rep Stu Cncl; Mgr Socr; Cit Awd; NHS; St Schlr; Church Yth Grp; Cmnty Wkr; Supertndnts Stu Liason Comm 84-86; Girls Citznshp Inst 85; Intl Bus.

VELEZ, ELSIE; Frank H Morrell HS; Irvington, NJ; (Y); 13/550; Library Aide; OEA; Band; Concert Band; Mrchg Band; High Hon Roll; NHS; Cnty Essex Awd Excllnce 85; Cert Awd Hnrb Mntn Katerhine Gibbs 85; Schl Ldrshp Awd Fut Sec 85; Union Cnty Coll; Actg.

VELEZ, KIM; Clifton HS; Clifton, NJ; (Y); 58/687; Church Yth Grp; Office Aide; Ski Clb; Spanish Clb; High Hon Roll; Jr NHS; NHS; Spanish NHS; Bus Awd 84; Rutgers; Bus Admin.

VELEZ, MARY JO G; West Orange HS; W Orange, NJ; (Y); Ski Clb; Spanish Clb; Chorus; Concert Band; Yrbk Stf; Sec Sr Cls; Rep Stu Cncl; Hon Roll; Jr NHS; Mgr(s); Miss Ldrshp 86.

VELKE, KATHY; Howell HS; Howell, NJ; (Y); Girl Scts; Chorus; Gym; Vllybl; Typing Awd 86; Chaimber Choir Awd 85; Bus.

VELLANTI, DEBBIE; Saint Mary HS; S Amboy, NJ; (Y); Library Aide; Sec Frsh Cls; Sec Soph Cls; Rep Jr Cls; Rep Sr Cls; Stu Cncl; Var Socr; Montclair; Bus.

VELLUTO, MIKE; Wildwood Catholic HS; Avalon, NJ; (Y); High Hon Roll; Hon Roll; Rutgers U; Frstry.

VELTRE, ADAM JOHN; Bishop George AHR HS; Old Bridge, NJ; (Y); 135/277; Cmnty Wkr; ROTÇ; JV Bsbl; Var L Ftbl; Wrstlng; Hon Roll; Hnbl Mntn All Cnty Ftbl 85-86; Acctg.

VELTRI, GREGORY; Lodi HS; Lodi, NJ; (Y); Boy Scts; Key Clb; Leo Clb; Math Clb; Math Tm; Science Clb; Band; Drm & Bgl; Jazz Band; Orch; U Of RI; Phrmclgy.

VENA, VALERIE; Sacred Heart HS; Glassboro, NJ; (Y); VP Art Clb; Spanish Clb; Teachers Aide; School Play; Stage Crew; Yrbk Rptr; Yrbk Stf; 2nd Pl Sci Fair Awd; Hlth Careers Clb; Glassboro ST Coll; Cmnctns.

VENACCIO, CHRIS; Holy Cross HS; Cinnaminson, NJ; (Y); 2/384; Chess Clb; Church Yth Grp; German Clb; Scholastic Bowl; Science Clb; Stage Crew; Ed Yrbk Bus Mgr; Yrbk Phtg; Yrbk Stf; High Hon Roll; Math.

VENCIUS, LORRAINE; Deptford Township HS; Wenonah, NJ; (Y); Var Capt Bsktbl; Var Fld Hcky; Var Socr; Var Sftbl; Var Trk; Var Vllybl; Hon Roll; Mst Dedctd Bstktbl Plyr 84-85; 2nd Grp III Con & All Gloucester Cnty 85-86; MVP Grls Trck Tm 85-86; Sprts Physcn.

VENDITTI, KATIE; Hunterdon Central HS; Flemington, NJ; (Y); Off French Clb; Hosp Aide; Teachers Aide; School Musical; Lit Mag; Rep Soph Cls; Stu Cncl; JV Var Cheerleading; Hon Roll; Church Yth Grp; Amer Merit Ldrshp Awd 86.

VENEZIA, NANCY; West Essex SR HS; Fairfield, NJ; (Y); 63/350; Computer Clb; VP FTA; Hon Roll; Italian Hnr Soc 83-85; Schrlshp Am Assoc Women Caldwell Brnch 86; Newark Coll.

VENOUZIOU, SILVANA; Manalapan HS; Manalapan, NJ; (Y); 21/431; Debate Tm; Exploring; JCL; Mgr Temple Yth Grp; Nwsp Bus Mgr; Nwsp Rptr; Yrbk Ed-Chief; Yrbk Phtg; Yrbk Stf; NHS; Lee Jaccoca Sls Awd 86; Magna Cum Laude Latin II Awd 85; Business.

VENTOLA, JOSEPH; Immaculate Conception HS; Newark, NJ; (Y); Spanish Clb; Spanish NHS; Chsn NJ ST Sci Lg 86.

VENUTO, DIANA; Highland Regional HS; Blackwood, NJ; (S); 34/326; Sec Spanish Clb; Im Art Clb; Hon Roll; Frgn Lang.

VERBEL, DEBORAH; Mount Olive HS; Flanders, NJ; (Y); 65/360; AFS; Ski Clb; SADD; Dance Clb; Girl Scts; Temple Yth Grp; Nwsp Stf; Yrbk Stf; Fld Hcky; Score Keeper; Rutgers U; Jrnlsm.

VERDISCO, SAREH; Westfield HS; Westfield, NJ; (Y); 182/537; German Clb; Latin Clb; Band; Orch; Gym; Wt Lftg; Hon Roll; Lbrl Arts.

VERENICIN, TANIA; Red Bank Catholic HS; Monmouth Beach, NJ; (Y); 2/450; Ski Clb; SADD; School Play; Yrbk Stf; VP Jr Cls; Stat Socr; Hon Roll; Hnr Rll 81-83; Cmmnctns.

VERGANO, SCOTT T; Newark Acad; Randolph, NJ; (Y); Teachers Aide; Orch; Symp Band; Nwsp Rptr; Var Swmmng; High Hon Roll; Ntl Merit SF; Math Clb; Science Clb; Yrbk Stf; Ram Page Most Val Mbr Awd; Math Dept Awd; Lang Dept Awd Excell Frnch.

VERGEL, JESENIA; Memorial HS; W New York, NJ; (Y); French Clb; Key Clb; Math Clb; Rep Soph Cls; Rep Jr Cls; Rep Stu Cncl; High Hon Roll; NHS; Voice Dem Awd; Computer Clb; Sci Gftd & Tlntd Prog 85-86; Med.

VERHILLE, LORI; Washington Township HS; Sewell, NJ; (Y); Church Yth Grp; Drama Clb; Spanish Clb; Stu Cncl; Var Stat Ftbl; Var L Mgr(s); Var L Trk; Phldlpha Inqrs Athlt Wk 86; Glvcstr Cnty Tms All Str Grls Trck 86; CB Wests Grls Trck Team MVP 85.

VERHOEVEN, MICHELLE; Mahwah HS; Mahwah, NJ; (Y); Math Tm; Orch; School Play; Rep Soph Cls; Sec Sr Cls; Var Cheerleading; Swmmng; JV Trk; French Hon Soc; High Hon Roll; Bus Admin.

VERISH, SANDRA; Delaware Valley Regional HS; Milford, NJ; (Y); #2 In Class; Sec Key Clb; JV Bsbl; Stat Crs Cntry; High Hon Roll; Trs NHS; Prfct Atten Awd; Bus.

VERMILYEA, LAURA J; North Brunswick Twp HS; No Brunswick, NJ; (Y); 41/249; AFS; Library Aide; Drill Tm; Mrchg Band; Yrbk Phtg; Trk; Hon Roll; VP NHS; Beaver Coll Schlrshp 86; Beaver Coll; Cmnctns.

VERNAZA, ZORAYA; Elizabeth HS; Elizabeth, NJ; (Y); 169/846; Dance Clb; Key Clb; Ski Clb; Spanish Clb; Yrbk Stf; Rep Frsh Cls; Rep Soph Cls; Rep Jr Cls; Rep Sr Cls; Hon Roll; Montclair; Psych.

VERNY, GAIL; Union HS; Union, NJ; (Y); FBLA; Hosp Aide; Key Clb; Math Clb; Office Aide; Science Clb; Spanish Clb; Teachers Aide; Chorus; Cit Awd; Attrny Gen Triple C Awd 84; Certf Hon Engl 84; Princ Hon Roll 85; Med.

VERSACI, FREDERICK; Hudson Catholic HS; Hoboken, NJ; (Y); 40/183; Dance Clb; Intnl Clb; Pep Clb; SADD; Nwsp Sprt Ed; Rep Jr Cls; Var L Bsktbl; Var L Trk; Hon Roll; Peer Mnstry 85-86; Rutgers; Hstry.

VESEY, JOSEPH; Hudson Catholic HS; Jersey Cty, NJ; (Y); Political Wkr; Ski Clb; SADD; Varsity Clb; Capt Var Ice Hcky; MI Awd Ic Hockey 84-85; 1st Tm All Conf Ice Hockey 85-86.

VESLEY, ALYSIA; Wayne Hills HS; Wayne, NJ; (Y); 135/310; Ski Clb; Mrchg Band; Orch; Fld Hcky; Socr; Hon Roll; Lycoming Coll; Pre-Law.

VESPOLI, CHRISTINE; Rutherford HS; Rutherford, NJ; (Y); Pep Clb; Ski Clb; Chorus; Color Guard; Variety Show; Var JV Tennis; Stat Trk; Comp Sci.

VESTERGAARD, KAREN; West Windsor Plainsboro HS; Princeton Jct, NJ; (Y); Art Clb; Badmtn; Coach Actv; Socr; Tennis; Trk; NHS; Most Imprvd Player Awd Track & Tennis 85-86; Gold Key & Finlst Philadelphia Schlstic Art Show 86; U DE; Vet.

VETERI, JOHN J; Passaic Valley HS; Little Falls, NJ; (Y); Debate Tm; FBLA; Nwsp Stf; Golf; Hon Roll; Law Accntng.

VEYTSMAN, PETER; Washington Twp HS; Sewell, NJ; (Y); French Clb; Math Clb; Varsity Clb; JV Ftbl; JV Swmmng; JV Wrstlng; 1st Pl Indstrl Drftg Show 85; Engrng.

VICENTE, MIKE; Washington Township HS; Turnersville, NJ; (Y); Red Cross Aide; Band; Concert Band; Jazz Band; Yrbk Stf; Var Bsbl; Var Score Keeper; Var Trk; Hon Roll; NHS.

VIDRO, CARMEN; Paul VI Regional HS; Passaic, NJ; (Y); Key Clb; Fairleigh Dickinson U; Nrsng.

VIDUCIC, ANTHONY; Dumont HS; Dumont, NJ; (Y); 21/210; Bsktbl; High Hon Roll; NYU; Law.

VIEIRA, ISABEL; Benedictine Acad; Newark, NJ; (Y); Church Yth Grp; French Clb; GAA; Latin Clb; Math Clb; Nwsp Stf; Yrbk Phtg; Stu Cncl; Sftbl; Vllybl; Fshn Inst Tech; Mrchndsg.

VIERECK, CHARLES A; Paulsboro HS; Gibbstown, NJ; (Y); Off CAP; JA; School Play; Var L Golf; Socr; Hon Roll; Aerosp Engrng.

VIGORITO, STEVEN J; Morris Hills HS; Wharton, NJ; (Y); 100/296; Am Leg Boys St; Cmnty Wkr; Varsity Clb; Var Bsbl; Var Bsktbl; Var Ftbl; Cit Awd; Hon Roll; Bsktbl Awd 85.

VIJ, ANIL; Hudson Catholic HS; Jersey City, NJ; (Y); Ftbl.

VILACHA, BOBBI; Union HS; Union, NJ; (Y); Dance Clb; FBLA; Outstnd Achvt FBLA ST Ldrshp Conf Resolution 86; Montclair ST Coll; Bus.

VILARDI, GREG M; Red Bank Catholic HS; Middletown, NJ; (Y); Boy Scts; Cmnty Wkr; Letterman Clb; Varsity Clb; Var Bsbl; JV Scrkpr Ftbl; Wt Lftg; Wrstlng; Dntstry.

VILLA, DAVID; Middletown HS South; Lincroft, NJ; (Y); Ski Clb; Varsity Clb; JV Bsbl; Im Bsktbl; Im Ftbl; Var L Socr; High Hon Roll; Hon Roll; Prfct Atten Awd.

VILLA, JOHN; St Joseph Regional HS; Pearl River, NY; (Y); 2/180; Church Yth Grp; Cmnty Wkr; Rep Jr Cls; Var L Bowling; Var L Trk; High Hon Roll; Jr NHS; NHS; Spanish NHS; Pep Clb; Intl Yth In Achvt 3rd Edition 86; Sci.

VILLADOLID, LAARNI; Bloomfield HS; Bloomfield, NJ; (Y); 24/424; FHA; Girl Scts; Math Clb; Spanish Clb; Chorus; High Hon Roll; NHS; Math Wizard Philippines 85; Comp Sci.

VILLAMARIA, EDWARD N; Teaneck HS; Teaneck, NJ; (Y); Computer Clb; Office Aide; Concert Band; School Musical; Hon Roll; NHS; Prfct Atten Awd; Carnegie Mellon U; Computer.

VILLANI, ANNA; Marylawn HS; Orange, NJ; (Y); 25/54; VP Art Clb; Church Yth Grp; French Clb; Servc Awd ATT Clb VP 86; Berkeley Schl; Fshn Merch.

VILLANI, CHERYL; Middlesex HS; Middlesex, NJ; (Y); 24/158; French Clb; Hosp Aide; Chorus; Church Choir; Nwsp Rptr; Score Keeper; Var JV Tennis; High Hon Roll; Hon Roll; Voice Dem Awd; Natl Piano Plyng Audtns-ST 85 & 86; Artstcly Tlntd-Keybrd 84-86.

VILLANI, GINALYN; Piscataway HS; Piscataway, NJ; (Y); Cmnty Wkr; Key Clb; Varsity Clb; Drill Tm; Flag Corp; Stat Bsbl; JV Fld Hcky; Var Gym; Commrcl Art.

VILLANI, SUSAN; Toms River H S East; Toms River, NJ; (Y); Camera Clb; Intnl Clb; Pep Clb; Spanish Clb; Chorus; Powder Puff Ftbl; JV Socr; Hon Roll; Art Design.

VILLANO, LISA; Linden HS; Linden, NJ; (Y); Yrbk Stf; Rep Frsh Cls; Pres Soph Cls; Pres Jr Cls; Pres Sr Cls; Rep Stu Cncl; Var Socr; High Hon Roll; Hon Roll; NHS; Var Soccr & Sftbl Cert; Bus Adm.

VILLASENOR, ANNE P; Bishop Eustace Prep Schl; Seaford, DE; (Y); Cmnty Wkr; Pep Clb; Spanish Clb; Nwsp Rptr; Ed Nwsp Stf; Var Trk; Hon Roll; NHS; Spanish NHS; Tutor In Spnsh 84-85; U DE; Accntng.

VILLIERE, LINETTE; Ridge HS; Basking Ridge, NJ; (Y); 39/202; Ski Clb; Band; Concert Band; Mrchg Band; JV Var Cheerleading; Powder Puff Ftbl; French Hon Soc; Hon Roll; NHS; Emory U.

VILORD, KIMBERLY; Washington Twp HS; Turnersville, NJ; (Y); Am Leg Aux Girls St; Church Yth Grp; French Clb; Ski Clb; Band; Color Guard; Flag Corp; Mrchg Band; Rep Frsh Cls; Rep Soph Cls; Rotary Yth Ldrshp Awd 85; Girls ST 86; Philadelphia Coll; Fshn Mrchnds.

VINCENT, MARK; Orange HS; Orange, NJ; (S); Pres Church Yth Grp; Trs Frsh Cls; Var Bsbl; JV Var Bsktbl; Capt Crs Cntry; High Hon Roll; NHS.

VINDEL, MARIA L; Wm L Dickinson HS; Jersey City, NJ; (Y); Library Aide; Science Clb; NHS; U Of Notre Dame; Psych.

VINKMAN, VICTOR OLAV; Parsippany HS; Parsippany, NJ; (Y); 31/316; Latin Clb; Ski Clb; Ftbl; Trk; High Hon Roll; Hon Roll; NHS; Pres Schlr; Rutgers Coll; Bus Admnstrtn.

VINTIGAN, ABRIELLE; Nutley HS; Nutley, NJ; (Y); 38/338; Drama Clb; FBLA; Yrbk Ed-Chief; Rep Stu Cncl; Stat Trk; French Hon Soc; Hon Roll; NHS; Church Yth Grp; Cmnty Wkr; Acad Schlrshp Seton Hall U 86; SR Music Achvmnt Awd 86; Seton Hall U; Corp.

VIOLA, MARIA; Marylawn Of The Oranges HS; Orange, NJ; (Y); 2/54; Hosp Aide; Service Clb; Chorus; School Musical; Nwsp Rptr; Pres Soph Cls; Var Stu Cncl; NHS; NEDT Awd; Spanish NHS; Pre Med.

VIRGIL, KARIN; Immaculate Conception HS; East Orange, NJ; (Y); Rep Frsh Cls; Stu Cncl; Prfct Atten Awd; Spanish NHS; Montclair ST Coll; Bus.

VISCEGLIA, DAWN; Lakeland Reg HS; Ringwood, NJ; (Y); Church Yth Grp; FCA; French Clb; Pep Clb; Stu Cncl; Hon Roll; Pre-Law.

VISCIDO, STEVEN; Columbia HS; S Orange, NJ; (Y); Chess Clb; Library Aide.

VISCONTI, DANNY; North Bergen HS; N Bergen, NJ; (Y); Ski Clb; Var L Bsktbl; Im Ftbl; Im Socr; Im Vllybl; Italian Amer Clb 86; Hotel/Rest Mgmt.

VISICH, NED; Dumont HS; Dumont, NJ; (Y); 23/210; Math Clb; Var Capt Socr; High Hon Roll; NHS; NYU; Elctrnc Engnrng.

VISSCHER, LISA; Clifton HS; Clifton, NJ; (S); 15/587; Math Clb; Science Clb; Var Capt Swmmng; Var Trk; Jr NHS; Spanish NHS.

VISSCHER, THEODORE; Clifton HS; Clifton, NJ; (Y); 35/637; CAP; Key Clb; Science Clb; High Hon Roll; Hon Roll; Aero Eng.

VISWAMBHARAN, MANOJ; William L Dickinson HS; Jersey City, NJ; (Y); 2/400; Pres Camera Clb; Capt Chess Clb; Pres Computer Clb; Pres Exploring; Library Aide; Q&S; Capt Scholastic Bowl; Pres Science Clb; Nwsp Rptr; Yrbk Phtg; Stevens Tech; Engr.

VITA JR, ANDREW S; Don Bosco Prep; Hawthorne, NJ; (Y); 15/172; Church Yth Grp; Ski Clb; Off Frsh Cls; Off Soph Cls; Off Jr Cls; Off Stu Cncl; Bsktbl; Var Capt Ftbl; Var Trk; High Hon Roll; Acctg.

VITALE, DEBORAH; St Rose HS; Spring Lake, NJ; (Y); 81/214; Church Yth Grp; French Clb; Hosp Aide; Key Clb; Ski Clb; Yrbk Stf; Swmmng; Hon Roll; Variety Show; Nwsp Rptr; Marymount; Nutritn.

VITALE, HEATHER; Spotswood HS; Helmetta, NJ; (Y); 70/200; Camera Clb; Model UN; Office Aide; Ski Clb; SADD; School Musical; School Play; Stage Crew; Nwsp Rptr; Nwsp Stf; Lbrl Arts.

VITALE, VIRGINIA; Mary Help Of Christians Acad; Paterson, NJ; (S); 17/68; Art Clb; Church Yth Grp; Computer Clb; Dance Clb; Hosp Aide; Math Clb; Math Tm; Service Clb; Teachers Aide; Chorus; Englsh, Comp, Hstry, Alg II & Theolgy 84-85; Monclair ST; Acctng.

VITALETTI, LORI; Bloomfield SR HS; Bloomfield, NJ; (Y); 81/437; Key Clb; Office Aide; Science Clb; Chorus; Sftbl; Vllybl; Hon Roll; Physcl Thrpsy.

VITALI, DOMINIQUE; Glen Ridge HS; Glen Ridge, NJ; (Y); 24/114; Art Clb; Cmnty Wkr; French Clb; Hosp Aide; Nwsp Stf; Art Clb; Yrbk Stf; Lit Mag; JV Cheerleading; High Hon Roll; Schlrshp Art Stu 83-85; Hnrbl Ment Schlstc Mag Comp 84; 2nd Prize Illustrtn 85; Illustrtn.

VITALI, TINA; Woodbridge HS; Fords, NJ; (Y); 80/400; Church Yth Grp; French Clb; Ski Clb; Varsity Clb; Mrchg Band; Stage Crew; Rep Stu Cncl; Hon Roll; Band; Chorus; Teens Growing In Faith Awd 86, Spirit Awd 86; Cmmnctns.

VITULLO, MICHELLE; Parsippany HS; Parsippany, NJ; (Y); FBLA; Spanish Clb; Teachers Aide; Varsity Clb; Var L Sftbl; Hon Roll; NHS; Bus Adm.

VIVENZIO, AUGIE; St John Vianney HS; Morganville, NJ; (Y); Varsity Clb; Rep Frsh Cls; Rep Soph Cls; Rep Jr Cls; Var L Bsbl; JV Bsktbl; L JV Ftbl; Im Powder Puff Ftbl; Var Wt Lftg; Bsbl All-Mnmth, All-Shr & All-ST 86; Brk 3 Schl Rcrds Bsbl 86; Miami U.

VIVONA, DAVID; St John Vianney HS; Colts Neck, NJ; (Y); 46/283; JV Math Tm; Nwsp Rptr; Rep Frsh Cls; Rep Soph Cls; Rep Jr Cls; JV Bsbl; JV Bsktbl; JV Ftbl; Var Golf; Hon Roll; Bus Adm.

VOEGELI, CHRISTINE; Hightstown HS; Cranbury, NJ; (Y); Church Yth Grp; Intnl Clb; Service Clb; Spanish Clb; Nwsp Rptr; Ed Nwsp Stf; Yrbk Stf; High Hon Roll; Hon Roll; NHS.

VOGEDING, MARK EDWARD; Paulsboro HS; Paulsboro, NJ; (Y); 45/140; JA; Library Aide; Office Aide; Band; Concert Band; Drm & Bgl; Jazz Band; Mrchg Band; VP Rep Frsh Cls; Rep Soph Cls; Hnrbl Mntn All-Cnty & All-Grp ISJ Ftbll 85; Crmnl Jstc.

VOGEL, DEBORAH A; Highstown HS; East Windsor, NJ; (Y); 67/343; French Clb; Service Clb; SADD; Band; Concert Band; Flag Corp; Mrchg Band; Symp Band; Yrbk Stf; Stu Cncl; Miami U.

VOGEL, JEFFREY; Manasquan HS; Brielle, NJ; (Y); #12 In Class; Math Tm; Spanish Clb; Concert Band; Jazz Band; Mrchg Band; School Musical; Socr; High Hon Roll; NHS; Brd Of Educ Awd; Engr.

VOGEL JR, ROBERT A; Randolph HS; Randolph, NJ; (Y); 17/366; Am Leg Boys St; VP Jr Cls; Pres Sr Cls; Var Socr; High Hon Roll; Hon Roll; VP NHS; Ldrshp Cncl 85-86; Rng Scr Clb 84-86; Sccr Offcl 84-86; Dntstry.

VOGEL, SUZANNE; Hightstown HS; East Windsor, NJ; (Y); 132/449; Sec 4-H; French Clb; Letterman Clb; Drill Tm; Stage Crew; Var L Crs Cntry; Mgr(s); Score Keeper; Mgr Sftbl; L Trk; Cross Cntry MVP 85-86; Sprng Trck Mst Imprvd Athlt 85-86; Mercer Cnty 4-H Hrs Shw 2 4ths & 1 3rd 85; Bus.

VOGELSANG, CHRISTA; Dwight-Englewood Schl; Fairview, NJ; (Y); Church Yth Grp; Hosp Aide; Ntl Merit Ltr; Gettysburg Coll.

VOGT, CHARLTON; Paul VI HS; Barrington, NJ; (Y); 86/468; Chess Clb; Drama Clb; Math Clb; SADD; Thesps; School Play; High Hon Roll; Hon Roll; NHS; Schlstc Schlrshp Awd To VA Wslyn Coll 86-87; VA Wslyn Coll; Comp Sci.

VOGT, PAM; Bridgewater Raritan High Schl West; Bridgewater, NJ; (Y); Sec Church Yth Grp; Ski Clb; Church Choir; Rep Frsh Cls; Sec Soph Cls; Rep Jr Cls; Rep Stu Cncl; Stat Bsbl; JV Bsktbl; JV Var Cheerleading; Intr Dsgn.

VOGT, TRACEY; Passaic Valley HS; Little Falls, NJ; (Y); Debate Tm; Drama Clb; Key Clb; Political Wkr; School Musical; School Play; Stage Crew; Nwsp Stf; Yrbk Stf; Lit Mag; Passaic Vly Hnr Scty 85-86; Cert Hnr Mock Trial Comptn 85-86; Advncd Hnr Eng Course PU 85-86; Communctns.

VOGT III, WILLIAM; Hamilton High East; Trenton, NJ; (Y); 47/327; Varsity Clb; Lit Mag; Var Ftbl; Wt Lftg; Wrstlng; Elks Awd; Hon Roll; Pblshd Aspirations Lit Mag 84; All Cnty Ftbl Offnse Grd 86; Montclaire ST Bus Schl; Bus.

VOIT, BETH; St James HS; Pennsville, NJ; (Y); 30/76; Cmnty Wkr; Exploring; Letterman Clb; Office Aide; Pep Clb; Thesps; Varsity Clb; Chorus; School Musical; School Play; Thespian Awd Outstndg Work At Acting 86; Mt St Marys Emmistburg.

VOLPITTA, RICHARD; Paramus Catholic Boys HS; Wood Ridge, NJ; (Y); 17/178; Am Leg Boys St; Boy Scts; VP Computer Clb; Debate Tm; Hosp Aide; Var Swmmng; Hon Roll; NHS; Spanish NHS; Lafayette Coll.

VOLZ, MATT; Southern Regional HS; Waretown, NJ; (Y); Church Yth Grp; German Clb; Ski Clb; Varsity Clb; Coach Actv; Wt Lftg; Hon Roll; NJIT; Engrng.

VON METER, KRISTIN; Garden State Acad; Andover, NJ; (Y); Church Yth Grp; Band; Nwsp Rptr; Trs Soph Cls; Hon Roll; Columbia Union Coll; Drm.

VOORHEES, JAMES; Secaucus HS; Secaucus, NJ; (S); 4/168; Am Leg Boys St; Key Clb; Math Clb; Math Tm; Spanish Clb; Varsity Clb; Variety Show; Yrbk Sprt Ed; VP Frsh Cls; Sec Soph Cls; Al Co, All Lg X-Cntry 84-85; All Co Spg Track 85; Hugh O Brien Yth Org 84; Pre-Med.

VOORHEES, KIM; Toms River HS East; Toms River, NJ; (Y); 56/587; Church Yth Grp; Girl Scts; Key Clb; Library Aide; Cheerleading; Fld Hcky; Mgr(s); Hon Roll; NHS; Egl Of Crss Awd Ntl Awd For Outstndg Ldrshp & Svc Chrch 84; Vrsty Lttrs Bsbll Mgr & Fld Hcky; Acctg.

VOORHIS JR, KENT; St Josephs Regional HS; West Nyack, NY; (Y); 91/169; Cmnty Wkr; Political Wkr; Ice Hcky; Hon Roll; Lbrl Arts.

VOSBURGH, DAVID; Toms River HS North; Toms River, NJ; (Y); 39/371; Boy Scts; Church Yth Grp; Q&S; Science Clb; Band; Concert Band; Mrchg Band; Lit Mag; JV Socr; JV Trk; TREA Ed Schlr 86; Eagle Sct Awd 86; FL Inst Tech; Cvl Engng.

VOSSELLER, DAVID; Middlesex HS; Middlesex, NJ; (Y); 17/158; Boy Scts; Pres Church Yth Grp; German Clb; Var L Trk; Hon Roll; Hstry.

VOSSHALL, NICOLE K; Kinnelon HS; Kinnelon, NJ; (Y); 6/155; Church Yth Grp; Sec German Clb; Girl Scts; Sec Varsity Clb; School Musical; Nwsp Stf; Yrbk Stf; Lit Mag; Lcrss; VP NHS; Hmcmng Qun 85; 4-Yr Vrsty Awd 86; Franklin-Marshall Coll; Psychlg.

VOULGARIS, DOROTHEA; Fair Lawn HS; Fair Lawn, NJ; (Y); 103/335; Church Yth Grp; Acpl Chr; Chorus; Madrigals; School Musical; School Play; Yrbk Phtg; Yrbk Stf; Off Jr Cls; Off Sr Cls; AHEPA Scholar 86; AHEPA Scholar Awd 84; Simmons Coll; Math Ed.

VOVCHIK, VICTORIA; Northern Valley Regional HS; Harrington Pk, NJ; (Y); 21/313; Ski Clb; SADD; Yrbk Phtg; Ed Yrbk Stf; JV Cheerleading; NHS; WA Coll; Pre-Med.

VOZEH, CHRISTIAN; Paramus Catholic HS; Elmwood Pk, NJ; (Y); 69/179; Art Clb; Camera Clb; Nwsp Stf; Lit Mag; Var Ftbl; JV Var Trk; Comms.

VREELAND, JOHN; Wayne Hills HS; Wayne, NJ; (Y); Yrbk Ed-Chief; Hon Roll; Law.

VRICELLA, MARILYN; Passaic Valley HS; Totowa, NJ; (Y); 9/367; Art Clb; Debate Tm; Science Clb; Ski Clb; JV Bsktbl; Var Crs Cntry; Var Trk; Hon Roll; NHS; Prfct Atten Awd; Optmtry.

VRSALOVIC, TANJA; Wallington HS; Wallington, NJ; (Y); Church Yth Grp; Dance Clb; Service Clb; Ski Clb; Varsity Clb; Chorus; Flag Corp; School Musical; Nwsp Stf; Yrbk Stf; 1st Team All League Awd In Vlybl 85; 2nd Team Hnrb Mntn In Track 85; Coaches Awd In Vlybl 85; Mntclr ST Coll; Bus Mngmnt.

VYDRO, CAROLEE; St Mary HS; Passaic, NJ; (S); 2/45; Hosp Aide; NFL; SADD; School Musical; Nwsp Rptr; Bsktbl; Crs Cntry; Trk; NHS; Marian Mdl 84; Thms Dffly Memrl Schlrshp 83; Bio.

WAAS, JACK; Bridgewater-Raritan H S West; Bridgewater, NJ; (Y); Mathletes; Science Clb; Concert Band; Mrchg Band; Orch; NHS; Ntl Merit Ltr; 4-H; German Clb; Ntl Hnr Soc Schlrshp 86; Ortho Phrmctcls Corp Schlrshp 86; Swrthmr Coll; Chem.

WACHTER, MARK; St James HS; Repaupo, NJ; (S); 8/73; Am Leg Boys St; School Play; Stage Crew; Nwsp Rptr; Yrbk Rptr; VP Soph Cls; Var Bsktbl; JV Ftbl; Var Golf; High Hon Roll; Geometry Merit Awd 85; Phy Ed Merit Awd 85; Chmcl Engrng.

WADDELL, BERNADETTE E; Kingsway Regional HS; S Beckett, NJ; (Y); 34/168; Church Yth Grp; Debate Tm; Key Clb; Science Clb; Yrbk Stf; Hon Roll; Ntl Merit Schol; Gvrnr Schl Schlr 85; Stu/Mnth; Lwyr.

WADDELL, EMMA; Montville Township HS; Montville, NJ; (Y); 33/262; FBLA; Hosp Aide; Key Clb; Lit Mag; Lcrss; High Hon Roll; Hon Roll; NHS.

WADDINGTON, MIKE; Pennsville Memorial HS; Pennsville, NJ; (Y); 11/215; Am Leg Boys St; VP JA; Trs Stu Cncl; JV L Bsbl; Golf; Var Capt Socr; Cit Awd; Hon Roll; Pres NHS; Rotary Awd; Roy Rogers Schlr Athlete Yr 86; Army Resrve Schlr Athlete Soccer 86; Firefighter Heroism Awd; Virginia Tech; Bio.

WADDY, GENE C; Neptune SR HS; Neptune, NJ; (Y); 35/310; Cmnty Wkr; Band; Concert Band; Drm & Bgl; Mrchg Band; Variety Show; L Bsbl; High Hon Roll; Hon Roll; NHS; Omega Psi Phi Hgh Achvt Awd 85; Armd Forces Awd 83; Cornell U; Mech Engrng.

WADE, ANTHONY; Saint Anthony HS; Jersey City, NJ; (Y); Boys Clb Am; Church Choir; Nwsp Rptr; Nwsp Stf; Yrbk Rptr; Bowling; Trk; Vllybl; Hon Roll; Juv Conf Comm Awd NJ 86; Jersey Jrnl Stu Jrnlsm Awd NJ 84; Police Firearm Trnng Course Awd UCNJ 85; Media Comm.

WADE, GRETCHEN; Shore Regional HS; Monmouth Beach, NJ; (Y); 52/225; SADD; Band; Stage Crew; Stu Cncl; Powder Puff Ftbl; Sftbl; High Hon Roll; Hon Roll; Pres Acad Ftns Awds Pgm 86; Brooksdall Comm Coll; Lbrl Arts.

WADE, KIM; St John Vianney HS; Colts Neck, NJ; (Y); Church Yth Grp; Cmnty Wkr; Ski Clb; Teachers Aide; Varsity Clb; Var L Bsktbl; JV Coach Actv; JV Mgr(s); JV Score Keeper; Var L Socr; Educ.

WADE, SUSAN; St Rose HS; Spring Lake, NJ; (Y); 48/208; Cmnty Wkr; Key Clb; Nwsp Stf; Yrbk Stf; Rep Stu Cncl; Coach Actv; Score Keeper; Hon Roll; Lasalle U; Mrktng.

WADE, TRACY LYNN; Immaculata HS; Middlesex, NJ; (Y); 14/214; Camera Clb; Library Aide; Science Clb; Spanish Clb; Lit Mag; Spanish NHS; Ski Clb; Bowling; Hon Roll; Prfct Atten 84-85; Engrng.

WADE, TROY; Ferris HS; Jersey City, NJ; (Y); Am Leg Boys St; Band; Ftbl; Hon Roll; NCU; Engrng.

WADE, YOLANDA C; Kent Place Schl; Newark, NJ; (Y); Cmnty Wkr; French Clb; PAVAS; Variety Show; Yrbk Stf; Stu Cncl; Ntl Merit SF; Art Clb; Sec Computer Clb; Ski Clb; Cable Show Talk Show Host 83-85; Natl Achvt Scholar Outstndng Negro Stu 85; Publctn Poetry 81; Bio.

WADSACK, JENNIFER; Chatham Twp HS; Chatham Twp, NJ; (Y); Am Leg Aux Girls St; Pres Church Yth Grp; Drama Clb; Sec Girl Scts; Model UN; Sec Chorus; School Musical; Swing Chorus; High Hon Roll; NHS; Al-Nrthrn NJ Rgnl Choir 85-86; Semi-Fnls NJ Mock Trial Cmptn 85; Olympcs Mind 2nd, 3rd Pl 85 & 86; Law.

WAER, CAROLYN SUSAN; Audubon HS; Audubon, NJ; (Y); Aud/Vis; Church Yth Grp; German Clb; Girl Scts; Acpl Chr; Band; Chorus; Church Choir; Concert Band; Madrigals; Ortary Yth Ldrs Awd 86; All ST Chorus 84-86; All S Jersey Chorus 85-86; Elem Ed.

WAGNER, AMANDA; Memorial HS; Cedar Grove, NJ; (S); 12/121; Church Yth Grp; Drama Clb; Key Clb; Ski Clb; Spanish Clb; Chorus; Mrchg Band; Nwsp Stf; Sec Stu Cncl; Var Trk; Tempera Paintg 1st Pl Somerset Regnl Art Shw 85; Comm Art.

WAGNER, BARBARA D; Fair Lawn HS; Fair Lawn, NJ; (Y); 97/379; Chorus; School Musical; Yrbk Ed-Chief; Rep Soph Cls; Rep Jr Cls; Rep Sr Cls; Stat Lcrss; Mgr Wrstlng; Hon Roll; Yrbk Phtg; Svc Awd JR Cls Cncl; RI Schl Of Design.

WAGNER, CHRIS; Toms River HS East; Toms River, NJ; (Y); 114/585; Var Bsbl; Ftbl; Wt Lftg; 3rd Tm All-Cnty Bsbl Ptchr 84-85; 2nd Tm All-Cnty Bsbl Ptchr 85-86; Farch.

WAGNER, EDWARD W; Westwood HS; Westwood, NJ; (Y); 40/230; Am Leg Boys St; Art Clb; Church Yth Grp; Varsity Clb; Var Crs Cntry; Var Trk; Hon Roll; Jr NHS; 1T Pl Nrth Jrsy Stu Crftsmn Fair 86.

WAGNER, HEATHER; Wall Township HS; Wall, NJ; (S); 10/260; Latin Clb; Ski Clb; Var Bsktbl; Powder Puff Ftbl; Var Socr; High Hon Roll; Hon Roll; Cmmrcl Art.

WAGNER, JEANINE; Central Jersey Christian Schl; W Long Branch, NJ; (S); 5/18; Church Yth Grp; Drama Clb; German Clb; Chorus; Church Choir; Yrbk Stf; Rep Stu Cncl; Var Socr; High Hon Roll; NHS; 7 Yrs Clsscl Piano Lssns 79-86; Elem Ed.

WAGNER, JEANNINE; Union Catholic Regional HS; Garwood, NJ; (Y); Pep Clb; Service Clb; Ski Clb; SADD; Yrbk Stf; JV Var Cheerleading; Coach Actv.

WAGNER, KATHERINE; West Morris Mendham HS; Mendham, NJ; (Y); 104/307; Dance Clb; Intnl Clb; Fld Hcky; Hon Roll; VFW Awd; Artist Of Mnth 85; Portfolio Schlrshp 86; Atlanta Coll; Advrtsng Dsgn.

WAGNER, KATHLEEN; Cherry Hill High School West; Cherry Hill, NJ; (Y); PAVAS; Spanish Clb; Capt Color Guard; Hon Roll; NHS; Sci.

WAGNER, KIRSTEN; Watching Hills Regional HS; Warren, NJ; (Y); Aud/Vis; Key Clb; Cheerleading; Coach Actv; Gym; Vllybl; Bus Mngmnt.

WAGNER, PATRICIA M; Egg Harbor Township HS; Mays Landing, NJ; (S); 12/266; Model UN; Trs Spanish Clb; Var Cheerleading; Hon Roll; Jr NHS; NHS; US Natl Ldrshp Merit Awd; Psych.

WAGNER, WILLIAM; Ridge HS; Millington, NJ; (Y); Church Yth Grp; German Clb; Yrbk Rptr; Yrbk Stf; High Hon Roll; Hon Roll; NHS.

WAHLBERG, SUSAN; Midland Park HS; Ho-Ho-Kus, NJ; (S); Church Yth Grp; DECA; French Clb; FBLA; Girl Scts; Pep Clb; Science Clb; Church Choir; Yrbk Stf; Cheerleading; Ctznshp Inst Del 85; Slvr Awd GSA 82; Lasell JC; Fshn Merch.

WAIN, MARY FRANCES; Newton HS; Newton, NJ; (S); 14/250; Sec French Clb; FTA; SADD; Pres Frsh Cls; Rep Jr Cls; Rep Stu Cncl; JV Fld Hcky; Hon Roll; NHS; Engl Awd; Wrld Geogrphy Awd.

WAINWRIGHT, BRIAN; Toms River East HS; Toms River, NJ; (Y); Band; Concert Band; Jazz Band; Mrchg Band; Symp Band; Hon Roll; Band Ltr 83-84; Mercer Cnty; Arch.

WAINWRIGHT, SCOTT; Christian Brothers Acad; Brielle, NJ; (Y); Church Yth Grp; Cmnty Wkr; Varsity Clb; JV Socr; Var JV Trk; Hon Roll; MVP Track; BA Colt Champ 85.

WAITERS, KATRINA; Marylawn HS; Irvington, NJ; (Y); Dance Clb; French Clb; Math Clb; Service Clb; Chorus; School Musical; Rep Frsh Cls; Rep Soph Cls; French Hon Soc; High Hon Roll; Gld Medl Summa Cum Laude Latn Awd 85; Penn ST U; Acctg.

WAKEFIELD, WENDY LEIGH; Hanover Park HS; E Hanover, NJ; (Y); 10/283; NFL; Band; Mrchg Band; Co-Capt Socr; Co-Capt Trk; Jr NHS; Masonic Awd; NHS; Church Yth Grp; West Point Militry Acad 86; Band Dir Awd 86; 3 Yr Army ROTC Schlrshp 86; Prudential Asset Mgmt Awd 86; Military Coll Of VT; Engrng.

WALBURN, MARYANN; Union Catholic HS; Rahway, NJ; (Y); Church Yth Grp; Debate Tm; Science Clb; SADD; Nwsp Stf; Coach Actv; Capt Swmmng; Chrprsn Schl Blood Drv 86; Kean Coll; Sprts Med.

WALCH, BETH; Glen Ridge HS; Glen Ridge, NJ; (Y); 8/120; AFS; Girl Scts; Model UN; Nwsp Rptr; Nwsp Stf; Yrbk Stf; High Hon Roll; Hon Roll; Law.

WALD, URSULA R; Sussex County Vo-Tech Schl; Montague, NJ; (S); 14/150; Drama Clb; Hosp Aide; Spanish Clb; SADD; School Play; Stage Crew; Stu Cncl; Tennis; Morris County Coll; Bus.

WALDEN, JAMES; John F Kennedy HS; Willingboro, NJ; (Y); 39/389; Band; Concert Band; Mrchg Band; Var Bsbl; Var Ftbl; Var Wt Lftg; Hon Roll; Syracuse U; Finance.

WALDEN, ROBIN; Overbrook Regional SR HS; Lindenwold, NJ; (Y); 13/270; Church Yth Grp; French Clb; FBLA; Nwsp Ed-Chief; Nwsp Rptr; Rep Stu Cncl; JV Var Cheerleading; Jr NHS; NHS; Messiah Coll Deans Scholar 86; Messiah Coll; Soclgy.

WALDMAN, BETH; Bruriah HS Girls; Elizabeth, NJ; (Y); Art Clb; Camera Clb; Cmnty Wkr; Computer Clb; Girl Scts; Mathletes; Math Clb; Stage Crew.

WALDMAN, MELISSA A; Haddonfield Memorial HS; Haddonfield, NJ; (S); Intnl Clb; Model UN; Red Cross Aide; Church Choir; Yrbk Stf; Pres Frsh Cls; Stu Cncl; Var Swmmng; French Hon Soc; NHS; Futgers Hnr Schlr 85; Grls ST 85; Intl Rltns.

WALDRON, PATRICIA; St Pius X Regional HS; Piscataway, NJ; (Y); 26/120; Church Yth Grp; Dance Clb; Teachers Aide; Varsity Clb; Nwsp Stf; Yrbk Stf; Hon Roll; Elem Ed.

WALDRON JR, WILLIAM F; Holy Cross HS; Medford, NJ; (Y); Aud/Vis; Boy Scts; Ski Clb; Spanish Clb; Thesps; Band; Jazz Band; Mrchg Band; School Musical; Off Soph Cls; Eagle Sct 85; U Of Scranton; Pre Law.

WALENCIAK, MATT; Wayne Hills HS; Wayne, NJ; (Y); 29/304; Boy Scts; Church Yth Grp; Var Bsbl; Bsktbl; Var Ftbl; CC Awd; Cit Awd; Elks Awd; Hon Roll; NHS; Mth Lg 83-86; Engrng.

WALIGORE, MARK; Clayton HS; Clayton, NJ; (S); 13/70; Church Yth Grp; Political Wkr; Nwsp Ed-Chief; Yrbk Rptr; Yrbk Stf; Rep Stu Cncl; L Bsktbl; Hon Roll; Rutgers; Jrnlsm.

WALK, LOUISE E; Kinnelan HS; Kinnelon, NJ; (Y); 22/154; Drama Clb; PAVAS; Thesps; Chorus; Church Choir; School Musical; School Play; Stat Bsktbl; Powder Puff Ftbl; Hon Roll; NJ Regin Choir; Trenton ST Coll; Elm Tchr.

WALKER, AMY; Mother Seton Regional HS; Rahway, NJ; (Y); 60/154; Am Leg Aux Girls St; GAA; JA; SADD; Yrbk Stf; Var Capt Vllybl.

WALKER, ANITA; Trenton Central HS; Trenton, NJ; (Y); Camera Clb; Dance Clb; GAA; Color Guard; Drill Tm; Yrbk Phtg; Crs Cntry; Pom Pon; Trk; Rutgers U; Bus Acctg.

WALKER, BRET; Pitman HS; Pitman, NJ; (Y); Church Yth Grp; 4-H; Chorus; Concert Band; Mrchg Band; Jazz Band; Orch; Yrbk Phtg; Yrbk Rptr; 4-H Awd; All S Jersey Band & Chorus & All ST Band & Chorus 85-86; Yth Orch Glassboro ST Coll 84-86; Berkley Coll Music; Prfrmnc.

WALKER, ISABELLA; Secaucus HS; Secaucus, NJ; (S); 18/169; Hosp Aide; Key Clb; Ski Clb; Spanish Clb; Chorus; Church Choir; School Musical; Swing Chorus; Rep Frsh Cls; Rep Soph Cls; Nrs.

WALKER, KEN; Clearview Regional HS; Sewell, NJ; (Y); Dance Clb; Drama Clb; Varsity Clb; Nwsp Sprt Ed; JV Bsktbl; Var Socr; Var Tennis; Meteorlgy.

WALKER, ROBERT; Chatham Township HS; Chatham, NJ; (Y); 11/140; Key Clb; Math Tm; Model UN; Concert Band; Jazz Band; Var L Bsbl; JV Socr; High Hon Roll; NHS; Boy Scts; Alt-NJ Govrs Schl Of Arts 86; All-Area Jazz & Cncrt Bands 84-86; Alt-N Jersey Rgnl Band 84.

WALKER, RONNIE; Marist HS; Newark, NJ; (Y); 45/104; Church Yth Grp; Computer Clb; Key Clb; Science Clb; SADD; Lit Mag; Var Tennis; Im Vllybl; Ntl Merit Schol; Prfct Atten Awd; Bus Mgmt.

WALKER, TAMMY; Toms River North HS; Toms River, NJ; (Y); 106/424; Nwsp Rptr; Nwsp Stf; Yrbk Stf; Lit Mag; Stu Cncl; Cmmnctns.

WALKER, TRACY; Edison Vocational & Technical HS; Elizabeth, NJ; (Y); Pres Church Yth Grp; Cmnty Wkr; Dance Clb; Pres VICA; Variety Show; Stu Cncl; Bsktbl; Cit Awd; Hon Roll; Prfct Atten Awd; Princpls Schlrp Certs 85-86; Hnr Rl Certs 83-86; Genl Bus.

WALKO, JOANNE; Linden HS; Linden, NJ; (Y); Church Yth Grp; Key Clb; Science Clb; Rep Frsh Cls; Rep Stu Cncl; Var Sftbl; Var Capt Tennis; High Hon Roll; NHS; Rutgers U.

WALL, LINDA; St Rose HS; Spring Lake, NJ; (Y); 3/200; Church Yth Grp; Dance Clb; Key Clb; Math Clb; VP Sr Cls; Rep Stu Cncl; Var Cheerleading; French Hon Soc; High Hon Roll; NHS; Western Cltr Awd Outstndng Excllnc 84; Outstndng Perfrmc NEDT Tstng 84-85; Attnd Monmouth Coll Jr Sci; Nutrition.

WALL, MONICA T; Pitman HS; Pitman, NJ; (Y); 5/140; Dance Clb; VP French Clb; Teachers Aide; Sec Frsh Cls; Trs Jr Cls; Rep Stu Cncl; Var JV Cheerleading; Hon Roll; NHS; Bruce Rslr Esqr Schlrshp 86; Sara Knkd Mem Schrlshp 86; Kwns Clb Schlrshp 86; Penn ST U; Bus Admn.

WALLACE, CHARLES; Palmyra HS; Palmyra, NJ; (Y); 27/121; Scrkpr Quiz Bowl; Im L Ftbl; Capt L Socr; Hon Roll; Astrnmy.

WALLACE, CHRIS; Lower Cape May Regional HS; Cape May, NJ; (Y); Spanish Clb; Church Choir; School Musical; School Play; Yrbk Stf; Lit Mag; Hon Roll; NHS; Salisbury; Bus Adm.

WALLACE, LYNN; Central Regional HS; Bayville, NJ; (Y); 91/241; Pep Clb; Rep Frsh Cls; Rep Stu Cncl; Var Stat Bsktbl; Score Keeper; Var Stat Socr; Var L Sftbl; High Hon Roll; Hon Roll; Dentistry.

WALLACH, KENNETH; Summit HS; Summit, NJ; (Y); 12/290; Cmnty Wkr; Model UN; Capt Quiz Bowl; Capt Scholastic Bowl; Gov Hon Prg Awd; NHS; Ntl Merit Ltr; Chess Clb; French Clb; Temple Yth Grp; Union Cnty Hstrcl Socty Awd 86; Rtry Yth Ldrshp Cmp 84; Amer Jewish Socty Svc 85; Duke U; Hstry.

WALLEN, AMY SUSAN; Millville SR HS; Millville, NJ; (Y); 5/468; Am Leg Aux Girls St; Drama Clb; FBLA; German Clb; Soroptimist; Acpl Chr; Yrbk Phtg; NHS; Camera Clb; Church Yth Grp; Ntl Affirs Delg Yth Gov 85; 2nd Pl Econ 86; Lafayette Coll; Engrng.

WALLEN, STEPHANIE; Cumberland Regional HS; Bridgeton, NJ; (Y); 2/315; JCL; Soroptimist; Nwsp Ed-Chief; Yrbk Ed-Chief; NHS; Rotary Awd; Sal; Mock Trial Tm 86; Pres Schlrshp 86-87; Ntl Latin Ex Magna Cum Laude 86; American U; Attrny.

WALLER, SABRINA; Ewing HS; Trenton, NJ; (S); DECA; Office Aide; Teachers Aide; Chorus; Drill Tm; Rep Frsh Cls; Rep Soph Cls; Stu Cncl; Cheerleading; Fld Hcky; ST Pres DECA 86-87; Hnrbl Mntn Apprl & Accrs Cntrl Rgn Comptn DECA 86; FIT NY City; Fshn Dsgnr.

WALLERSTEIN, JOLIE; Scotch Plains-Fanwood HS; Fanwood, NJ; (Y); 113/350; AFS; Key Clb; Mrchg Band; School Musical; Yrbk Rptr; Rep Frsh Cls; Rep Soph Cls; Rep Jr Cls; Gldn Poet Awd 85; Hon Mntn Ptry 84; Amrcn U; Cmnctns.

WALLING, THERESA; Middletown High School South; Red Bank, NJ; (Y); Church Yth Grp; Teachers Aide; Church Choir; Rep Stu Cncl; JV Var Socr; Hon Roll; MVP For JV Sccr 84-85; Schl Msct 86-87; Stockton ST U; Phtgrphr.

WALLS, KATHLEEN; Mainland Regional HS; Linwood, NJ; (Y); 52/300; Ski Clb; Cheerleading; Trk; Glassboro ST Coll; Psych.

WALLS, RENATE C; Clayton HS; Clayton, NJ; (Y); 4/70; FBLA; Science Clb; NHS; Cert Acad Achvtr Voc Tech 85-86; Culinary Arts.

WALMSLEY, LISA; Gloucester City JR SR HS; Gloucester City, NJ; (Y); 9/152; Church Yth Grp; Nwsp Stf; Yrbk Stf; Rep Stu Cncl; JV Crs Cntry; NHS; Prfct Attndnc 86; Profcncy Grphcs 86; Lions Clb Svc 86; Portland CC; Anml Caretkr.

WALSH, AIMEE; Glen Rock HS; Glen Rock, NJ; (Y); Church Yth Grp; Band; Chorus; Church Choir; Concert Band; Madrigals; Mrchg Band; Orch; School Musical; Score Keeper; HS Musical 86; Elem Educ.

WALSH, CHRISTINE; Sparta HS; Sparta, NJ; (Y); Church Yth Grp; Key Clb; Nwsp Rptr; Nwsp Stf; Lit Mag; Rep Stu Cncl; Capt JV Cheerleading; Stat Ftbl; Trk; Hon Roll; Jrnlsm.

WALSH, CYNDY; Toms River H S North; Toms River, NJ; (Y); 86/412; Q&S; Band; Concert Band; Jazz Band; Mrchg Band; Symp Band; Lit Mag; Tennis; Hon Roll; Psych.

WALSH, DAVID B; Sussex County Vo-Tech Schl; Branchville, NJ; (S); 16/150; Am Leg Boys St; Church Yth Grp; Drama Clb; School Play; Stage Crew; Rep Soph Cls; Pres Trs Stu Cncl; Var Bsktbl; Var Tennis; High Hon Roll.

WALSH, JIM; St Josephs Regional HS; Congers, NY; (Y); Chrmn Church Yth Grp; Cmnty Wkr; Exploring; Ski Clb; Bsktbl; Rockland CC; Psych.

WALSH, KELLEY; Chatham Township HS; Chatham, NJ; (Y); Chrmn Church Yth Grp; Key Clb; VP Pep Clb; Chorus; School Musical; Variety Show; Yrbk Stf; Capt Var Cheerleading; JV Var Fld Hcky; Hon Roll; Psych.

WALSH, KELLY; Matawan Regional HS; Matawan, NJ; (S); 30/315; Math Tm; SADD; Nwsp Sprt Ed; Off Jr Cls; Stu Cncl; Hon Roll; John Hpkns Gftd & Tlntd Stu; Monmth Cnty Teen Arts Fstvl Awd; Jrnlsm.

WALSH, KELLY ANN; Kinnelon HS; Riverdale, NJ; (Y); 13/160; VP Varsity Clb; Nwsp Ed-Chief; Yrbk Ed-Chief; Var Capt Bsktbl; Var Sftbl; Pres NHS; VFW Awd; A Bolles Sprtsmnshp Awd; NJSIAA Stdnt Athl Awd; Soroptmst Intl Ctznshp Awd; Barnard Coll; Pol Sci.

WALSH, LAURA; Hackettstown HS; Hackettstown, NJ; (Y); 114/236; Chorus; Color Guard; Mrchg Band; Hon Roll.

WALSH, LORI ELIZABETH; Toms River North HS; Toms River, NJ; (Y); 27/385; Am Leg Aux Girls St; Church Yth Grp; Quiz Bowl; Ski Clb; Spanish Clb; Concert Band; Mrchg Band; Pres Stu Cncl; High Hon Roll; NHS; Jstns Stu Ldrshp & Srv Awd 86; Drew U.

WALSH, MAUREEN; Arthur L Johnson Regional HS; Clark, NJ; (S); 31/217; Am Leg Aux Girls St; Drama Clb; Key Clb; Pres PAVAS; Nwsp Ed-Chief; Sec VP Stu Cncl; Hon Roll; Spanish NHS; Thesps; Chorus; Hmcmng Queen Ct; Un Cty Mental Hlth Plyrs; Comm.

WALSH, MEGHAN; Chatham Twp HS; Chatham Twp, NJ; (Y); 66/136; 4-H; Key Clb; Yrbk Stf; JV Fld Hcky; JV Var Sftbl; Psych.

WALSH, SUSAN; Atlantic City HS; Brigantine, NJ; (Y); 60/456; Church Yth Grp; Spanish Clb; Nwsp Ed-Chief; Nwsp Phtg; Nwsp Rptr; Nwsp Stf; Lit Mag; High Hon Roll; Hon Roll; NHS; Earth Sci Awd 86; Crew Insignia 83-84; Stockton ST Coll; Lbrl Arts.

WALSH, SUSAN; West Morris Mendham HS; Chester, NJ; (Y); Church Yth Grp; 4-H; Girl Scts; Teachers Aide; Hon Roll; Im Badmtn; Stat Ftbl; Im Vllybl; Chld Psych.

WALSTROM, MARY; Central Regional HS; Bayville, NJ; (Y); 20/240; Nwsp Rptr; Nwsp Stf; Yrbk Stf; Lit Mag; Var L Tennis; High Hon Roll; NHS; Church Yth Grp; Mrchg Band; Var L Pom Pon; Tennis Awd Most Imprvd 85-86; Hnr Short Story Ocean Cty Festvl 85-86; Comm.

WALTER, CHRISTOPHER D; North Bergen HS; Guttenberg, NJ; (S); 62/470; Computer Clb; French Clb; Library Aide; SADD; Nwsp Stf; Yrbk Phtg; Yrbk Stf; Rep Soph Cls; Rep Soph Cls; Stu Cncl; U Of NC; Mktg.

WALTER, TINA; Hamilton West HS; Trenton, NJ; (S); 4/330; Exploring; FBLA; Key Clb; Band; Concert Band; Drm Mjr(t); Mrchg Band; Symp Band; Jr Cls; Sr Cls; Band Dir Awd 83; All Am Hall Fame Band Hnrs 85; Nrsng.

WALTERS, JOSEPH T; Maple Shade HS; Maple Shade, NJ; (Y); Am Leg Boys St; Church Yth Grp; Cmnty Wkr; FBLA; Political Wkr; SADD; Yrbk Phtg; Pres Jr Cls; Pres Sr Cls; Rotary Awd; Maple Shade Democ Clb 86; Jaycee Town Watch 86; Maple Shade Jaycees 86; Bus.

WALTERS, ROBERTA; Manville HS; Manville, NJ; (Y); Church Yth Grp; Yrbk Rptr; Ed Yrbk Stf; JV Sftbl; Hon Roll; Sprts Med.

WALTERS, THOMAS; Maranatha Christian Acad; Marlboro, NJ; (S); 1/2; Church Yth Grp; Yrbk Stf; Val; Dstngshd Chrstn HS Stdnt ACSI 85-86; Nrthwstrn Coll; Pre-Law.

WALTERS, TRACY; Vineland HS; Vineland, NJ; (Y); 29/856; Sec German Clb; Ski Clb; Rep Jr Cls; L Capt Fld Hcky; JV Sftbl; NHS; German Ntl Hnr Soc 84-86; Stockton ST Coll; Bio.

WALTZ, CHRISTOPHER; West Essex SR HS; N Caldwell, NJ; (Y); Math Tm; Model UN; Varsity Clb; Band; Concert Band; Mrchg Band; Var L Socr; High Hon Roll; NHS; Ntl Merit SF; Engineering.

WALTZ, SHARI L; Hunterdon Central HS; Flemington, NJ; (Y); 94/539; Art Clb; Drama Clb; FHA; Library Aide; Spanish Clb; Hon Roll; Bowling Green ST U; Acctng.

WALTZER, SHARI; Manalapan HS; Manalapan, NJ; (Y); Dance Clb; Ski Clb; SADD; Yrbk Stf.

WAMPLER, PAUL; Westfield SR HS; Westfield, NJ; (Y); 32/514; Am Leg Boys St; Chorus; Lit Mag; Rep Stu Cncl; Var L Ftbl; Var Lcrss; Var L Trk; Var Wrstlng; Hon Roll; NHS; Book Of Gold Awd; MVP Ftbl, Male Vocal Awd; Pre-Med.

WANAMAKER, BRENDA; Pennsville Memorial HS; Pennsville, NJ; (Y); Exploring; Band; Mrchg Band; Sftbl; Elon Coll; Med Tech.

WANG, HOWARD T; W Windsor-Plainsboro HS; Plainsboro, NJ; (Y); AFS; Am Leg Boys St; Math Tm; Model UN; Spanish Clb; Teachers Aide; Orch; High Hon Roll; Hon Roll; NHS; Medicine.

WANG, HUI; St Dominic Acad; Jersey City, NJ; (Y); #6 In Class; Intnl Clb; Lit Mag; Bausch & Lomb Sci Awd; High Hon Roll; Masonic Awd; NHS; Prfct Atten Awd; Sci Awd 86; NY U Trstee Schlr 86; NY U.

WANG, JOHN; Ramapo HS; Franklin Lakes, NJ; (Y); Camera Clb; Church Yth Grp; Science Clb; Spanish Clb; Symp Band; Nwsp Phtg; Bsktbl; High Hon Roll; NHS; Arch.

WANG, LINDA; Watchung Hills Regional HS; Warren, NJ; (Y); Intnl Clb; Band; Concert Band; Drm Mjr(t); Jazz Band; Mrchg Band; Symp Band; Variety Show; Rep Frsh Cls; Rep Soph Cls; Govs Schl Arts Music 86; NJ All-ST Symph Band 85-86; Cntrl Jersey Regnl Band 84-85; Bio Sci.

WANG, MARJORIE; Summit HS; Summit, NJ; (Y); 2/276; Hosp Aide; Science Clb; Orch; School Musical; Ed Nwsp Phtg; Rptr Nwsp Rptr; Yrbk Phtg; Ed Lit Mag; High Hon Roll; NHS; NJ Govs Schl Arts 86; All ST, Regnl Orchs 85-86; NJ Yth Symph 82-85; Med.

WAPLES, JOY; Teaneck HS; Teaneck, NJ; (Y); Spanish Clb; Chorus; Yrbk Stf; L Mgr(s); Hon Roll; Ntl Merit Ltr; Prfct Atten Awd; Journalism.

WARD, CHRISTOPHER; Linden HS; Linden, NJ; (Y); Church Yth Grp; Acpl Chr; Var JV Bsbl; Var JV Ftbl; NHS; Marine Bio.

WARD, MARLENE; Eastside HS; Paterson, NJ; (Y); Chorus; Drill Tm; Mrchg Band; Rep Stu Cncl; Var Trk; Twrlr; Hon Roll; Prfct Atten Awd; Nrsng.

WARD, MICHAEL; West Dept Ford HS; Elmer, NJ; (Y); JV Socr; JV Tennis; Hon Roll; Grad Glou Vo Tech 86; Bldg Trds.

WARD, RENEE; Egg Harbor Twp HS; Linwood, NJ; (S); 20/266; Cmnty Wkr; Rep Band; Color Guard; Concert Band; Jazz Band; Mrchg Band; Nwsp Rptr; Hon Roll; NHS; Comm.

WARD, RUSSELL S; Randolph HS; Randolph, NJ; (Y); 80/365; Am Leg Boys St; Church Yth Grp; Band; Concert Band; Mrchg Band; Pep Band; Var Tennis; Pol Sci.

WARD, VICTORIA E; Kinnelon HS; Kinnelon, NJ; (Y); 4/150; Church Yth Grp; Pres German Clb; Nwsp Bus Mgr; Yrbk Stf; Lit Mag; Var Swmmng; Trs NHS; Ntl Merit Ltr; Am Leg Aux Girls St; Exploring; Gov Schl Public Issues & Future Of NJ 85; H O Brian Yth Ldrshp Smnr 84; German Hnr Scty; Yale U; Intl Econ.

WARDELL, CHARLES; West Orange HS; W Orange, NJ; (Y); Church Yth Grp; Computer Clb; Ski Clb; Spanish Clb; Nwsp Stf; VP Jr Cls; VP Stu Cncl; JV Bsktbl; JV Socr; Hon Roll; U Of VA; Bus Admin.

WARFIELD, CHARLES; Penns Greove HS; Carneys Point, NJ; (Y); JCL; Band; Concert Band; Mrchg Band; Nwsp Stf; JV Var Bsbl; JV Var Socr; All Salem Cnty Cncrt Bnd; Cls Exec Cmmtte; Engrng.

WARGO, KEITH A; West Morris Mendham HS; Mendham, NJ; (Y); 23/310; Am Leg Boys St; Church Yth Grp; Cmnty Wkr; Radio Clb; Ftbl; High Hon Roll; Hon Roll; NHS; Intnl Clb; Pres Acad Ftns Awd 86; Boston Coll; Econ.

WARGO, TAMARA; Holy Cross HS; Willingboro, NJ; (Y); Spanish Clb; JV Bsktbl; Var Score Keeper; Stat Socr; Var JV Trk; High Hon Roll; Hon Roll; Engrg.

WARNER, MARC D; Lawrence HS; Lawrenceville, NJ; (Y); AFS; Computer Clb; English Clb; Spanish Clb; School Play; Tennis; Trk; Ntl Merit SF; Bus.

WARNICK, ELIZABETH A; West Orange HS; West Orange, NJ; (Y); Church Yth Grp; Cmnty Wkr; Spanish Clb; Varsity Clb; Band; Yrbk Stf; Trs Frsh Cls; Trs Sr Cls; Var Bsktbl; Var Sftbl; 2nd Tm All Conf Sftbl 3rd Bse 86; 1st Tm All Oranges Sftbl 3rd Bse 86; Outstndng Stdnt 84.

WARR, STACEY M; Southern Regional HS; Manahawkin, NJ; (Y); 2/380; Church Yth Grp; Model UN; Church Choir; Jr Cls; Stu Cncl; Stat Bsbl; Var Cheerleading; High Hon Roll; NHS; Prfct Atten Awd; Mdl UN Rep Argntina Awd 86; Gnrl Assmbly Outstndg Dlgtn In Crisis Situatn 86; Lynchbrg Coll Hpwd Smmr; Acctg.

WARREN, COLIN T; Wall HS; Neptune, NJ; (Y); 38/240; Am Leg Boys St; Church Yth Grp; Ski Clb; Spanish Clb; Teachers Aide; Band; Church Choir; Concert Band; Jazz Band; Mrchg Band; Bryant Coll; Hotel Mngmnt.

WARREN, JOSH; Cherry Hill HS West; Cherry Hill, NJ; (Y); Aud/Vis; ROTC; Audio Visual Aide Awd 82-83; Brown Blt Karate 83-86; Comp.

WARREN, MARIANETTE; Manalapan HS; Englishtown, NJ; (Y); Mgr(s); Score Keeper; Var Trk; Black Awareness Clb Pres & VP 83-86; Montclair ST Coll; Bus Mgmt.

WARREN, MELISSA; Abraham Clark HS; Roselle, NJ; (S); Hosp Aide; Spanish Clb; Band; Chorus; School Play; Hon Roll; Phy Thrpy.

WARSING, NANCY LYN; Triton Regional HS; Blackwood, NJ; (Y); 65/307; Pep Clb; Spanish Clb; Rep Stu Cncl; Stat Bsktbl; Var Powder Puff Ftbl; Stat Sftbl; Stat Trk; Hon Roll; Lady Of Lourdes Schl Of Nursng.

WARTMAN, JOSEPH JOHN; Paul VI HS; Collingwood, NJ; (Y); 108/470; Math Clb; Villanova; Civil Engr.

WASACZ, MARGARET; St Rose HS; Avon By The Sea, NJ; (Y); 25/226; Service Clb; Ski Clb; Nwsp Rptr; Nwsp Stf; Yrbk Stf; Hon Roll; Trenton ST Coll; Edu.

WASHINGTON, CHRIS; Westside HS; Newark, NJ; (Y); DECA; Exploring; Spanish Clb; Drm Mjr(t); Nwsp Stf; Stu Cncl; CC Awd; Cit Awd; Ntl Merit SF; Bus Mgnt.

WASHINGTON, DONNA; Clifford J Scott HS; E Orange, NJ; (Y); 11/219; Pres Church Yth Grp; Pres DECA; Drill Tm; Nwsp Rptr; Sec Nwsp Stf; Yrbk Stf; Rep Jr Cls; Var Cheerleading; Cit Awd; Hon Roll; Q-Ettes Awd 86; Bethany Bapt Chrch Academc Awd 86; Mt Olive Bapt Chrch Yth Awd 86; VA ST U; Comm.

WASHINGTON, EVA; Henry Snyder HS; Jersey City, NJ; (S); Sec Church Yth Grp; Sec Church Choir; Rep Stu Cncl; Co-Capt Cheerleading; VP NHS; FBLA; Trk; Achvmnt Roll 84-85; Merit Roll 82-84; Rutgers; Nrsng.

WASHINGTON, KASSANDRA J; Pemberton Twp HS No 2; Pemberton, NJ; (Y); 5/435; Church Yth Grp; Cmnty Wkr; Chorus; Concert Band; Mrchg Band; Stage Crew; Hon Roll; NHS; VFW Awd; Voice Dem Awd; Explrs; Concessn Stnd; Currclm Aid; Engrng.

WASIK, MIKE; Bridgewater-Raritan East HS; Bridgewater, NJ; (Y); German Clb; Letterman Clb; Ski Clb; Varsity Clb; Stage Crew; Var Bsbl; Var Coach Actv; Var Ftbl; Var Powder Puff Ftbl; JV Wt Lftg; Somerset County Coll.

WASNER, CATHERINE; Essex Catholic Girls; Colonia, NJ; (Y); FBLA; Hosp Aide; Sec Library Aide; Ed Yrbk Stf; Bus Mgmt.

WASSERMAN, MARC J; Lawrence HS; Lawrenceville, NJ; (Y); 85/215; Am Leg Boys St; FBLA; JA; Varsity Clb; Off Soph Cls; Stu Cncl; Socr; Wt Lftg; Wrstlng; Hon Roll; Acctg.

WASTELL, CHARLOTTA; Bridgeton HS; Bridgeton, NJ; (Y); Cmnty Wkr; GAA; Ski Clb; Var Sftbl; Var Swmmng; Var Tennis; High Hon Roll; NHS; SADD; Varsity Clb; HOSA; Clss Rep; Ped Nrse.

WASZAK, JEANNINE; St John Vianney HS; Hazlet, NJ; (Y); 65/283; Var JV Bsktbl; Im Ftbl; Im Powder Puff Ftbl; Im Vllybl; Hon Roll; Loyola Coll; Law.

WATERS, JENNIFER; Scotch Plains Fanwood HS; Scotch Pl, NJ; (Y); Key Clb; Leo Clb; Off Frsh Cls; Off Soph Cls; Off Jr Cls; Cheerleading; Tennis.

WATERS, NICHELLE; Camden HS; Camden, NJ; (S); Church Yth Grp; Cmnty Wkr; Nwsp Rptr; Trs Frsh Cls; Rep Soph Cls; JV Var Cheerleading; High Hon Roll; NHS; Prfct Atten Awd; Girl Scts; Schlrshp-Phllps Acad Preprtn Schl 83-86; Indvdl Achvt Awd Scrng 99.9 NJ Bsc Sklls Tst-Rdng 84; Psychtry.

WATERS, PAMELA; Plainfield HS; Plainfield, NJ; (Y); Cmnty Wkr; Rep Jr Cls; JV Mgr(s); JV Score Keeper; Hon Roll; Fairleigh Dickinson U; Bus Adm.

WATERS, SHARON A; Red Bank Regional HS; Little Silver, NJ; (Y); 19/223; Variety Show; Yrbk Ed-Chief; Sec Frsh Cls; Sec Soph Cls; Sec Sr Cls; Var L Swmmng; Sec French Hon Soc; Hon Roll; NHS; Ski Clb; 1st Pl Awd-Columbia Schlstc Prs/Yrbk 85; Howard Whitfield Schlrshp 86; Rosa Weiss Schlrshp 86; Villanova U; Bus.

WATERS, TARIFF; E Orange HS; E Orange, NJ; (S); 95/438; Boys Clb Am; Boy Scts; Church Yth Grp; Church Choir; Bsbl; Capt Ftbl; Wt Lftg; All Conf Ftbl 85; All Ornge Cnty Ftbl 85; Springfield Coll; Bus Admin.

WATERS, TUTASI; Marylawn Of The Oranges; Newark, NJ; (S); 5/54; Math Clb; Stage Crew; Ed Quiz Bowl; Lit Mag; Rep Jr Cls; Var Sftbl; French Hon Soc; High Hon Roll; Trs NHS; Prfct Atten Awd; Cum Laude Cert Natl Lat Exm 83-84fmaxima Cum Laude Cert W/Silvr Mdl Natl Lat Exm 84-85; Pre-Med.

WATKINS, DERRICK; Eastside HS; Paterson, NJ; (Y); Church Yth Grp; Computer Clb; Rep Jr Cls; Stu Cncl; High Hon Roll; Hon Roll; Ntl Merit SF; Elec Engrng.

WATROUS, DEANNE L; East Brunswick HS; East Brunswick, NJ; (Y); Computer Clb; Concert Band; Drill Tm; Var L Mrchg Band; Hon Roll; JP Sousa Awd; E Brunswick Band Bstr Schlrshp Awd 86; Trenton ST; Bio.

WATSON, DAWN; Paulsboro HS; Gibbstown, NJ; (Y); 13/145; Office Aide; Var Capt Cheerleading; Var Mat Maids; JV Sftbl; Hon Roll; NHS; Voice Dem Awd; Americansim Essy Cont 84.

WATSON, DEE MARIE; Overbrook SR HS; Clementon, NJ; (Y); Spanish Clb; Band; Concert Band; Crs Cntry; Trk; Hon Roll; NHS; Spanish NHS; Temple; Med.

WATSON, EDW; Washington Township HS; Sewell, NJ; (Y); Ftbl; Hon Roll; Tech Engrng.

WATSON, LOVIE; Overbrook Regional SR HS; Berlin, NJ; (Y); Office Aide; Capt Color Guard; Concert Band; Jazz Band; Mrchg Band; Rep Frsh Cls; Rep Soph Cls; Rep Jr Cls; Hon Roll; Prfct Atten Awd; Duke U; Dietary Ntrtn.

WATSON, RICHARD F; Edgewood Regional HS; Sicklerville, NJ; (Y); 24/374; ROTC; Varsity Clb; Bsbl; Ftbl; Hon Roll; Jr NHS; NHS; Most Dedctd Plyr Ftbl Awd 82; Most Dstngshd Cadet Awd For Acad Excllnc JROTC 86; Ftbl Schlrshp 86; Glassboro ST Coll; Phys Educ.

WATSON, SHERRELL; Franklin HS; Somerset, NJ; (Y); Drama Clb; FBLA; FNA; Office Aide; SADD; Yrbk Stf; Rep Frsh Cls; Gov Hon Prg Awd; Rtgrs Schl Of Nrsg; Nrsg.

WATT, GLEN; Brick Township HS; Brick Town, NJ; (Y); Key Clb; Math Tm; SADD; Ftbl; Hon Roll.

WAUGH, ALEXANDER J; Ewing HS; West Trenton, NJ; (Y); 62/306; Am Leg Boys St; Intnl Clb; Key Clb; School Play; Nwsp Stf; Rep Stu Cncl; Mgr(s); Socr; Co-Capt Tennis; Co-Capt Wrstlng; US Nvl Acad Fndtn Spnrshp 86; US Air Force Acad Appmtmnt 86; US Nvl Acad; Engrng.

WAVERSHAK, ROSE; Toms River HS East; Toms River, NJ; (Y); English Clb; Intnl Clb; Key Clb; Spanish Clb; SADD; Drill Tm; Mrchg Band; Pom Pon; Hon Roll; NHS; NHS 86-87; Rider; Bus Adm.

WAWRA, FEDOR; Secaucus HS; Secaucus, NJ; (S); 9/164; Boy Scts; Computer Clb; Off Math Clb; Ski Clb; Band; Concert Band; Jazz Band; Mrchg Band; Var Tennis; French Hon Soc; Aerntcl Engr.

WEADOCK, MARGARET; St John Vianney HS; Marlboro, NJ; (Y); Ski Clb; SADD; Nwsp Stf; Yrbk Stf; Stu Cncl; Gym; Powder Puff Ftbl; Socr; Trk; Hon Roll; Stu Agnst Drnk Drvng 85; Pwdr Pf Ftbl 85; Bus.

WEATHERBY, BARBARA; Overbrook Reg SR HS; Albion, NJ; (Y); 26/273; Church Yth Grp; Trs Pres 4-H; Office Aide; Spanish Clb; Trs Sec Chorus; Capt Var Cheerleading; Powder Puff Ftbl; JV Var Trk; Hon Roll; Jr NHS; Glsbro ST Coll; Elem Ed.

WEATHERLY, BARBARA; Overbrook Reg SR HS; Albion, NJ; (S); 26/273; VP Sec 4-H; Trs Sec Chorus; JV Var Cheerleading; Powder Puff Ftbl; JV Var Trk; Hon Roll; Jr NHS; Office Aide; Spanish Clb; Glassboro ST Coll; Elem Ed.

WEATHERS, ESTHER B; Montville Twp HS; Montville, NJ; (Y); 7/275; Cmnty Wkr; Key Clb; Concert Band; School Play; Sec Frsh Cls; Elks Awd; High Hon Roll; Kiwanis Awd; NHS; St Schlr; Acad Achvt Acctng Awd 86; Rutgers Coll; Lib Arts.

WEBB, BELINDA; Eastside HS; Paterson, NJ; (Y); 165/600; Bsktbl; Sftbl; MVP Bsktbl 86; NJ ST Interschltc Ath Assn Cert 84-85; Comp Tech.

WEBB, CAROLYN; Wall HS; Wall, NJ; (S); 15/250; AFS; Key Clb; Leo Clb; Ski Clb; Mgr(s); Powder Puff Ftbl; Hon Roll; Kiwanis Awd; Amer Chem Soc Comp Chem Exm 85; Ntl Engl Merit Awd 84-85.

WEBB III, EDMUND B; Middle Twp HS; Cape May Court Hs, NJ; (Y); 2/225; Computer Clb; Key Clb; Math Clb; Math Tm; SADD; School Musical; Pres Frsh Cls; Pres Soph Cls; Pres Stu Cncl; Socr; Engrng.

WEBB, JENNIFER; Vineland HS; Vineland, NJ; (Y); DECA; Sec Soph Cls; Sec Jr Cls; Sec Sr Cls; Bsktbl; Poly Sci.

WEBB, KATRINA; Florence Twp Memorial HS; Roebling, NJ; (Y); 42/87; French Clb; FNA; Hosp Aide; Rep Soph Cls; Rep Stu Cncl; Cit Awd; Hon Roll; Voice Dem Awd; Nrsng.

WEBB, LISA; Eastside HS; Paterson, NJ; (Y); Sec Church Yth Grp; Capt Pep Clb; Acpl Chr; Sec Church Choir; Capt Drill Tm; School Play; Rep Stu Cncl; Bus Admin.

WEBB, MICHAEL; Middle Township HS; Cape May Ct Hse, NJ; (Y); Hon Roll; Atlantic CC; Bus Adm.

WEBB, MICHELLE; Scotch Plains-Fanwood HS; Scotch Plains, NJ; (S); Cmnty Wkr; Spanish Clb; Band; Mrchg Band; Stu Cncl; JV Cheerleading; Var Gym; Var Sftbl; Hon Roll; Spanish NHS; Elec Engrng.

WEBER, ANNE MARIE; Monsignor Donovan HS; Toms River, NJ; (Y); #1 In Class; Am Leg Aux Girls St; Yrbk Stf; Rep Stu Cncl; Stat Bsktbl; Val; Math Tm; Flag Corp; Bausch & Lomb Sci Awd; Lion Awd; NHS; Am Chem Soc Awd 84-85; Rotary Distngushed Stu 85-86; Schl Spirit Awd 86; Drew U; Chem.

WEBER, CAROLYN; Monsignor Donovan HS; Toms River, NJ; (Y); 1/243; Drama Clb; Math Clb; Math Tm; Science Clb; Service Clb; Teachers Aide; Thesps; Stage Crew; High Hon Roll; VP NHS; Amercn Asso U Women Awd 84-86; Teacher.

WEBER, CHRISTY; Waldwick HS; Waldwick, NJ; (Y); Cmnty Wkr; Math Tm; Ski Clb; Stage Crew; Yrbk Ed-Chief; Mgr Soph Cls; Mgr Jr Cls; Var L Vllybl; Hon Roll; NHS; Ballet Co Mbr.

WEBER, ELIZABETH; Cinnaminson HS; Cinnaminson, NJ; (Y); Am Leg Aux Girls St; Sec German Clb; Concert Band; Mrchg Band; Orch; Var Swmmng; JV Trk; NHS; Ntl Merit Ltr; Key Clb; Duke U; Bus.

WEBER, ERICK; Cresskill HS; Cresskill, NJ; (Y); #48 In Class; Bsktbl; Ftbl; Im Ice Hcky; JV Var Trk; Im Wt Lftg; Hon Roll; Boston U; Blgy Dntst.

WEBER JR, JOHN M; West Windsor-Plainsboro HS; Princeton Jct, NJ; (Y); Church Yth Grp; Radio Clb; Church Choir; Jazz Band; Variety Show; JV Socr; Var Swmmng; Hon Roll; 1st Pl NJ ST B Div Swim 84-85 & 85-86; 10th ST Freestyle & 1st ST Free Relay Indvdl.

WEBER, RENATA; Memorial HS; Cedar Grove, NJ; (S); 10/120; Pres Church Yth Grp; Key Clb; School Musical; Nwsp Bus Mgr; High Hon Roll; NHS.

WEBER, SANDY; Paulsboro HS; Gibbstown, NJ; (Y); 1/145; Drill Tm; Flag Corp; Rep Jr Cls; Var Capt Cheerleading; JV Sftbl; High Hon Roll; NHS; George WA U Mth/Sci Awd 86; Amer Chem Soc Cert Excllnce 86.

WEBER, SANDY; Paulsboro HS; Sandy, UT; (Y); 1/145; Drill Tm; Flag Corp; Rep Jr Cls; Rep Stu Cncl; Var Capt Cheerleading; JV Sftbl; High Hon Roll; Hon Roll; NHS; St Schlr; George Washington U Math Sci Awd 86; Cert Of Hon Am Chem Soc 86.

WEBER, SUSAN; New Milford HS; New Milford, NJ; (Y); 43/146; Church Yth Grp; Var L Bsktbl; Var L Sftbl; JV Vllybl; Cit Awd; Atten Awd 83-86; Educ.

WEBER, TAMMY; Cumberland Regional HS; Bridgeton, NJ; (S); 14/369; Intnl Clb; JCL; Teachers Aide; Var Cheerleading; High Hon Roll; Jr NHS; NHS; Brd Of Educ Awd 83; Med.

WEBSTER, JOHN CLAY; Highland Park HS; Highland Park, NJ; (Y); 15/150; Computer Clb; Ski Clb; Lit Mag; JV Tennis; JV Trk; Hon Roll; U Of Miami; Arch.

WECKLER, MICHAEL; Newton HS; Newton, NJ; (S); 11/210; German Clb; Math Clb; Science Clb; Rep Stu Cncl; JV Socr; JV Trk; Hon Roll; NHS; Prfct Atten Awd; Sci Leag 83-84; Altrnt Physcs Leag 85-86; Rutgers; Dentstry.

WEED, MARK; Union HS; Union, NJ; (Y); Computer Clb; Pres 4-H; Bsbl; Hon Roll; Ntl Merit SF; Eximplary Achvt Awd 85-86; N Jersey Stu Crftsmns Fr 1st Plc 86; Kean Coll Union NJ; Indust Art.

WEEDON, EARL; Red Bank Catholic HS; Neptune, NJ; (Y); Boy Scts; Varsity Clb; Var L Bsktbl; JV Crs Cntry; Var L Trk; Im Wt Lftg.

WEEKS, MARIE; North Bergen HS; Ridgefield, NJ; (Y); 21/404; French Clb; Yrbk Stf; Stu Cncl; Twrlr; High Hon Roll; Hon Roll; NHS; Merit Soc 85-86; Pres Acad Ftns Awd 86; Soc For Acad Achvt 86; PA ST; Comp Sci.

WEEMS, MICHAEL; South River HS; S River, NJ; (Y); 24/128; German Clb; Rep Stu Cncl; Var Bsbl; Var Ftbl; Var Capt Wrstlng; Hon Roll; Al-Acadmc Hnr Roll 86; Guts Desire Awd-Wrstlng 86; Bus.

WEEMS, RICHARD K; Atlantic City HS; Ventnor, NJ; (Y); 25/500; Aud/Vis; Computer Clb; Drama Clb; School Play; Lit Mag; Var Capt Wrstlng; Hon Roll; Latin Clb; 3rd Pl Schl Wrtng Cont 85; 2-3rd Pl & 2nd Pl In Wrstlng Tourn 83-84; Hnrbl Mntn Shrt Stry Cnt Teen Art; Stockton ST U; Englsh.

WEGENER, MARGARET A; Memorial HS; W New York, NJ; (Y); 13/400; Band; Church Choir; Concert Band; Mrchg Band; Capt Bsktbl; Capt Vllybl; Hon Roll; Jr NHS; Mst Vlbl Plyr Vlybl & Bsktbl 86; Rtgrs; Crprt Lwyr.

WEGMANN, SUE; Newton HS; Newton, NJ; (S); 20/190; German Clb; Madrigals; Variety Show; Lit Mag; Stu Cncl; Hon Roll; NHS; Band; Chorus; Concert Band; Mrktng.

WEGNER, CANDACE; Ramapo HS; Wyckoff, NJ; (Y); 57/329; Church Yth Grp; Church Choir; Mrchg Band; Symp Band; Nwsp Ed-Chief; Yrbk Stf; Hon Roll; NHS; Yth Grp Awd For Practical & Courageous Faith 85.

WEHRENBERG, ALAN; Saint John Vionney HS; Freehold, NJ; (Y); Hon Roll; Art Awd Homdel Polc Sfty Pstr 84; U Of NC; Acctg.

WEI, VIRGINIA; Hopewell Valley Central HS; Pennington, NJ; (Y); AFS; Tennis; High Hon Roll; Pres NHS; French Clb; Math Tm; Service Clb; Concert Band; School Play; JV Bsktbl; ST Fin Optomist Clb Oratorical Cntst 85; ST Fin Mercer Cnty Teen Arts Fest 85; Afs Merit Schlrshp 86; Engrng.

WEIDMAN, AMY; Maple Shade HS; Maple Shade, NJ; (Y); Am Leg Aux Girls St; Computer Clb; French Clb; Var Mgr Bsktbl; Var Socr; High Hon Roll; Jr NHS; NHS; Yth Burlington Cnty Cnty Clrk 86; Acad All Amer Math; Math.

WEIGAND, DAVID; Piscataway HS; Piscataway, NJ; (Y); Varsity Clb; Chorus; Madrigals; School Musical; Rep Soph Cls; Bsbl; Bsktbl; Ftbl; Hon Roll; Vet Med.

WEIGEL, DANA; Piscataway HS; Piscataway, NJ; (Y); Varsity Clb; Yrbk Phtg; Var Bsktbl; Var Socr; Var Sftbl; High Hon Roll; NHS; Camera Clb; Stat Score Keeper; Hon Roll; Horsebckrdng Shows 83-86 & Drill Tm Ldr 83; Head Groom 85-86; Envrnmntl Sci.

WEIL, JILL STACIE; Union HS; Union, NJ; (Y); Pres Drama Clb; FBLA; Key Clb; Sec Spanish Clb; Mrchg Band; Co-Capt L Twrlr; Hon Roll; Jr NHS; NHS; Twrlng Assoc Cert Tchr 85; FBLA Rgnl Comptn 1st Pl Clcl Typng II 86; 1st Pl Gold Mdl US Dance Trnmt; Rutgers U; Dietitian.

WEIL, SUZANNE; Westfield HS; Westfield, NJ; (Y); 157/550; Cmnty Wkr; Spanish Clb; SADD; Temple Yth Grp; Chorus; Nwsp Rptr; Nwsp Stf.

WEILER, MOLLY; Bound Brook HS; Bound Brook, NJ; (Y); 15/143; Trs Key Clb; Band; Trs Soph Cls; VP Stu Cncl; Bsktbl; Tennis; Trk; Capt Twrlr; Hon Roll; Phy Thrpy.

WEILER, ROY; Holy Spirit HS; Pleasantville, NJ; (Y); 61/366; Am Leg Boys St; Computer Clb; Chem & Physics Lab 84-86; Boston U; Aerospace Engr.

WEINBERG, LISA; Glen Rock JR SR HS; Glen Rock, NJ; (Y); 8/122; Sec Debate Tm; Pres French Clb; Sec Concert Band; Mrchg Band; Ed Yrbk Stf; JV Var Bsktbl; High Hon Roll; Jr NHS; Sec NHS; St Schlr; Am Legn Am Hist Awd 86; Natl Schlr And Athlt Awd 86; Pres Acadmc Ftnss Awd 86; Tufts U; Polt Sci.

WEINBERGER, BETH; Overbrook Regional HS; Berlin, NJ; (Y); Teachers Aide; Yrbk Stf; Rep Soph Cls; Capt Var Cheerleading; Powder Puff Ftbl; Mgr Trk; Stat Wrstlng; Hon Roll; Librl Arts.

WEINDORF, SUSAN; Toms River High School East; Toms River, NJ; (Y); Intnl Clb; Key Clb; Spanish Clb; SADD; Chorus; Off Frsh Cls; Off Soph Cls; Off Jr Cls; Off Sr Cls; L Stat Bsktbl; Slvr Physcl Ftns Awd 86; U Of NC; Med.

WEINER, DAVID M; Westfield SR HS; Westfield, NJ; (Y); Computer Clb; French Clb; Science Clb; JV Socr; Var Tennis; JV Trk; JV Wrstlng; High Hon Roll; NHS; Sci Awd Recognition Bio 84; Westfield Tennis Assoc WTA Schlrshp 84; Pre-Med.

WEINER, JILL; Lakeland Regional HS; Wanaque, NJ; (Y); Math Clb; Ski Clb; SADD; Rep Soph Cls; Rep Jr Cls; Rep Stu Cncl; JV Var Cheerleading; High Hon Roll; NHS; Ntl Merit Schol; Achvt Acad Awd 86; Acad All Am 86.

WEINFELD, ANDREA; John P Stevens HS; Edison, NJ; (Y); 39/475; Debate Tm; Drama Clb; Service Clb; Temple Yth Grp; Color Guard; School Musical; School Play; Variety Show; Nwsp Stf; Yrbk Stf; SUNY; Child Psychrst.

WEINREB, NEIL; Memorial HS; Elmwood Pk, NJ; (Y); Political Wkr; Temple Yth Grp; JV Var Bsbl; JV Var Bsktbl; Bus Mgt.

WEINSTEIN, BRIAN; Clayton HS; Clayton, NJ; (S); Art Clb; Cmnty Wkr; Drama Clb; Band; Concert Band; Mrchg Band; School Musical; Nwsp Rptr; Trk; Hon Roll; Bio.

WEINSTEIN, GARY; Manalapan HS; Englishtown, NJ; (Y); 54/354; Var Ftbl; Var Tennis; Var Trk; NJ Inst Of Tech; Cvl Engrng.

WEINSTEIN, HOPE; Westfield HS; Westfield, NJ; (Y); Drama Clb; Spanish Clb; Chorus; School Musical; School Play; Variety Show; Govrnrs Awd-Arts Educ 86; 1st Pl Scene Comptn NJ Dramtc Comptn 86; NJ All ST Chrs 85-86; Theatr.

WEINSTEIN, JULIE; Lenape Valley Regional HS; Stanhope, NJ; (Y); 22/240; Am Leg Aux Girls St; Drama Clb; Key Clb; SADD; Mrchg Band; Nwsp Ed-Chief; Wt Lftg; NHS; Val; Mss Teen Schlrshp & Rcgntn Pgnt 86; IFLA Awd 86; Rydr Coll Frnsc Trnmnt 1st Pl Spnsh 86; Chapel Hill; Poly Sci.

WEINSTEIN, KENNETH; West Essex SR HS; Fairfield, NJ; (Y); 144/350; Boy Scts; Camera Clb; French Clb; Science Clb; Var Crs Cntry; Var Trk; Relgs Sch 85; Recog Achvts In Sci 86; Syracuse; Ecnmcs.

WEINSTEIN, MICHAEL; Gill St Bernards HS; New Vernon, NJ; (Y); Variety Show; Rep Soph Cls; Rep Jr Cls; Rep Stu Cncl; Var L Bsbl; Var L Bsktbl; Var L Socr; Var L Trk; High Hon Roll; Hon Roll; Amer HS Athlt 84; Arch.

WEIR, DAWN; John P Stevens HS; Edison, NJ; (Y); Drama Clb; Thesps; School Musical; School Play; Stage Crew; Im Bsktbl; Var L Socr; Var L Sftbl; Hon Roll; NHS; Mst Vlbl Plyr Sftbl 84; Bst Offns Sftbl 86; All-Conf All-Cnty Sftbl 86.

WEIR, KAYLENE; Garden State Acad; Teaneck, NJ; (Y); Spanish Clb; Chorus; Yrbk Rptr; Stat Gym; Stat Score Keeper; Stat Vllybl; High Hon Roll; Hon Roll; Outstndng Acdmc Achvt Awd 86; Oakwood CollPEDTRCS.

WEIS, ANDREW; Woldwood Catholic HS; Wildwood Crest, NJ; (Y); 5/98; Spanish Clb; Var Golf; Var Socr; Hon Roll; NHS; Accntng.

WEIS, CHRISTINA; Lenape Valley Regional HS; Andover, NJ; (Y); Key Clb; Nwsp Sprt Ed; Lit Mag; Rep Stu Cncl; JV Var Fld Hcky; Var L Trk; High Hon Roll; Pres Schlr; Spanish NHS; Intnl Clb; All Area Awd Trck & Field Hockey 85-876; Bloomsburg U Schlrshp 86; Bloomsburg U; Pre Med.

WEISBURG, JEFFREY; Ranney Schl; Aberdeen, NJ; (S); #10 In Class; NFL; Spanish Clb; Speech Tm; Thesps; School Play; Nwsp Sprt Ed; JV Var Mgr(s); JV Var Score Keeper; L Socr; Hon Roll; Bio Chmstry.

WEISEL, HOLLY; Hightstown HS; Hightstown, NJ; (Y); Church Yth Grp; Cmnty Wkr; Ski Clb; Var Mgr(s); Seton Hall U; Nrsng.

WEISENBERG, RONALD; South Brunswick HS; Kendall Pk, NJ; (Y); 21/241; Boy Scts; Debate Tm; Exploring; Math Tm; Ski Clb; Pres Temple Yth Grp; JV Bsktbl; Var Trk; Hon Roll; Ecnmcs.

WEISERT, THOMAS; Seton Hall Prepartory Schl; Hillside, NJ; (Y); 1/180; Pres Church Yth Grp; Cmnty Wkr; Key Clb; Mathletes; Political Wkr; Var Im Bsbl; High Hon Roll; NHS; Ftur Lwyrs Clb; Attrny-Mck Trl Tm.

WEISMAN, LAWRENCE J; Jame Caldwell HS; W Caldwell, NJ; (Y); Key Clb; Library Aide; Office Aide; Teachers Aide; Temple Yth Grp; Nwsp Rptr; Nwsp Stf; Rep Frsh Cls; Var Bowling; Hon Roll; N Hlls Cnfrnc Hndcp Bwlg Trnmnt Sngls Chmpn 85; Med.

WEISS, EDWARD V; Monroe Township HS; Spotswood, NJ; (Y); Church Yth Grp; Civic Clb; Key Clb; Ski Clb; SADD; Teachers Aide; Varsity Clb; Nwsp Sprt Ed; Yrbk Sprt Ed; Off Frsh Cls; Middlesex Cnty Outstndng Ptchr Awd; Schlr/Athlt 85-86; Dlgt-Boys St 84-85; GMC-ALL Acadmc Sccr 85-86; WV U; Phy Ed.

WEISS, HEATHER L; Millville HS; Millville, NJ; (Y); Drama Clb; French Clb; GAA; Pep Clb; Ski Clb; School Musical; Nwsp Rptr; Nwsp Stf; Yrbk Stf; Var Swmmng; JR Miss Schlrshp 85; Frst Untd Mthdist Chrch Schlrshp 86; Elon Coll; Pltcl Sci.

WEISS, KAREN; Spotswood HS; Milltown, NJ; (S); 23/174; FBLA; Intnl Clb; Temple Yth Grp; Nwsp Stf; Stu Cncl; Capt Var Crs Cntry; Capt Var Trk; Hon Roll; Mktg.

WEISS, KIMBERLY; Bayonne HS; Bayonne, NJ; (Y); Trs German Clb; Math Tm; Hon Roll; Jr NHS; French Clb; Key Clb; Lit Mag; Off Soph Cls; Off Jr Cls.

WEISS, KIMBERLY; Parsippany HS; Parsippany, NJ; (Y); FBLA; Spanish Clb; Rep Frsh Cls; Rep Soph Cls; Rep Jr Cls; Rep Stu Cncl; JV Socr; JV Sftbl; Hon Roll; NHS.

WEISS, MARTIN; Middletown South HS; Middletown, NJ; (Y); Boy Scts; Chess Clb; Band; Mrchg Band; High Hon Roll; Hon Roll; NHS; Engrng.

WEISS, MICHAEL; Pascack Valley HS; Rivervale, NJ; (Y); Debate Tm; Drama Clb; Spanish Clb; Stage Crew; Hon Roll.

WEISS, MICHELLE; Abraham Clark HS; Roselle, NJ; (Y); #112 In Class; Bus Adm.

WEISS, NINA; Red Bank Regional HS; Little Silver, NJ; (Y); 21/240; Lit Mag; High Hon Roll; Hon Roll; NHS; Prfct Atten Awd; Pres Acad Ftns Awd 86; Hofstra U Merit Schlrshp 86; Teen Arts Festvl Cert Exc Visual Art 84; U DE; Graphic Design.

WEISS, TODD; Wayne Hills HS; Wayne, NJ; (Y); Hosp Aide; PAVAS; Spanish Clb; Jazz Band; School Musical; Stu Cncl; Wrstlng; Hon Roll; One To One 84-86; Bryant Clg; Htl/Rest Mgmt.

WEISS, WENDY; Washington Township HS; Grenloch, NJ; (Y); Art Clb; Church Yth Grp; Band; Color Guard; Concert Band; Mrchg Band.

WEISSBEIN, DANIEL A; Bridgewater-Paritan H S East; Bridgewater, NJ; (Y); Teachers Aide; Temple Yth Grp; Band; Ftbl; Wrstlng; High Hon Roll; NHS; Ntl Outdoor Ldrshp Schl Adv Course 84; Temple Sholom Hebrew HS Hnrs Degree 87.

WEISSMAN, GARY; Fair Lawn HS; Fair Lawn, NJ; (Y); 40/350; Nwsp Ed-Chief; Ed Lit Mag; Brown U Schlrshp 86; Sal Rubino Jrnlsm Awd Cosmos Clb 86; Brown U; Crtv Wrtng.

WEITZMAN, RICHARD; Glen Rock HS; Glen Rock, NJ; (Y); 2/155; Cmnty Wkr; Debate Tm; Math Tm; Science Clb; High Hon Roll; NHS; Ntl Merit Ltr; Sal; NJ Debate Lg 1st Pl Novice Spkr 84; U PA Awd Merit 86; Lib Arts.

WELCH, ANTHONY S; Willingboro HS; Willingboro, NJ; (Y); 1/339; Am Leg Boys St; Key Clb; Scholastic Bowl; Science Clb; JV Bsktbl; Capt Trk; High Hon Roll; Jr NHS; NHS; Rtgrs Schlr 86; Rensselaer Polytech; Biomed.

WELISCHEK, KIM; Delsea Regional HS; Franklinville, NJ; (Y); Mrchg Band; Stat Bsktbl; JV Fld Hcky; Pom Pon; Var Sftbl; Hon Roll; NHS; Prfct Atten Awd; Rutgers U; Med.

WELKER, ANDREA L; Eastern HS; Gibbsboro, NJ; (Y); 32/321; Intnl Clb; JV Fld Hcky; High Hon Roll; Hon Roll; NHS; Ntl Merit SF; Pres Schlr; St Schlr; Sophia K Reeves Schlrshp 86; Am Legion Awd 86; Acad Awd 84-86; Drexel U; Mech Engr.

WELLER, HEIDI; Hillsborough HS; Somerville, NJ; (Y); Girl Scts; Rep Frsh Cls; Rep Soph Cls; Rep Jr Cls; Sr Cls; Rep Stu Cncl; Stat Bsktbl; Crs Cntry; JV Fld Hcky; Var Trk; James Langdon Schlrp 86-87; Outstndg Germn Stu 86; Rutgers U; Bus Adm.

WELLER, KATHLEEN; Riverside HS; Delanco, NJ; (Y); Off Stu Cncl; Law.

WELLER, MICHELLE; Eggharbor HS; Pleasantville, NJ; (Y); Teachers Aide; Sftbl; High Hon Roll; SUNY Buffalo; Dntl Hygn.

WELLS, DAWN; Plainfield HS; Plainfield, NJ; (Y); Church Yth Grp; Dance Clb; Drama Clb; Mrchg Band; Rep Jr Cls; Hon Roll; NHS; Comp Sci.

WELLS, JESSICA; Vail Deane Prep; Millburn, NJ; (Y); French Clb; Nwsp Rptr; Nwsp Stf; Yrbk Stf; Swmmng.

WELLS, KIM; Lower Cape May Regional HS; N Cape May, NJ; (Y); 8/230; Key Clb; Spanish Clb; High Hon Roll; Hon Roll; NHS; Ntl Merit SF; Rotary Awd; St Schlr; Intl Rltns.

WELSEY, MARISA; Highland HS; Blackwood, NJ; (S); 27/330; Pres Spanish Clb; Off Sr Cls; Stat Bsbl; Capt Cheerleading; Sftbl; Hon Roll; Contrbtn Awd-Chrldng 84-85; U Of DE; Pre Law.

WELSH, MARGARET; Mary Help Of Christians Acad; Suffern, NY; (Y); Drama Clb; French Clb; JCL; Latin Clb; Quiz Bowl; School Play; Nwsp Stf; Yrbk Stf; Hon Roll; NHS; Coll Holy Cross; Acctg.

WELSH, MICHAEL P; Mater Dei HS; Highlands, NJ; (Y); 36/160; Am Leg Boys St; Drama Clb; SADD; School Play; Nwsp Stf; Lit Mag; Pres Stu Cncl; JV Bsktbl; Ftbl; Hon Roll; Otstndng Achvmnt Catholic HS Math Lg 86; US Nvl Acad; Engr.

WELSH JR, RONALD; Buena Regional HS; Minotola, NJ; (S); 18/191; Drama Clb; Math Clb; Pep Clb; Ski Clb; Spanish Clb; Varsity Clb; Chorus; School Play; Stu Cncl; JV Ftbl; Comp Sci.

WENDT, LAURIE; Jackson Memorial HS; Jackson, NJ; (Y); 78/450; Art Clb; Ski Clb; Varsity Clb; Yrbk Stf; Pres Frsh Cls; Sec Soph Cls; Sec Jr Cls; Pres Sr Cls; Cheerleading; Fld Hcky; Natl Art Hon Soc 85-86; Int Dsgn.

WENTZELL, DEBORAH; Woodstown HS; Woodstown, NJ; (Y); Cmnty Wkr; English Clb; 4-H; VP Hosp Aide; Office Aide; Spanish Clb; Teachers Aide; Nwsp Rptr; Lit Mag; Hon Roll; Candystrpr Of The Yr 85; Woodstown Pilesgrove JR Hist Soc VP 84; Rep Woodstwn Cndy Strprs 85; Mrktng.

WENTZELL, VICKI; Arthur P Schalick HS; Elmer, NJ; (Y); 14/131; Art Clb; Church Yth Grp; Ski Clb; Chorus; Flag Corp; JV Capt Cheerleading; Var Pom Pon; JV Sftbl; Hon Roll; Soclgy.

WENZ, MIKE; Toms River HS East; Toms River, NJ; (Y); 148/592; Im Bsbl; L Ftbl; NJ Stu Crftmns Fair Awd 85; Shore Shop Stu Crftmns Fair Awd 86; Pratt; Arch.

WENZ, TIM; Holy Spirit HS; Absecon, NJ; (Y); 35/350; Am Leg Boys St; Church Yth Grp; Stage Crew; Yrbk Stf; Rep Stu Cncl; Hon Roll; Jr NHS; NHS; Pres Schlr; Glassboro ST Coll; Pub Rel.

WERDER, MATTHEW; Parsippany HS; Parsippany, NJ; (Y); Aud/Vis; Camera Clb; FBLA; Office Aide; Stage Crew; Hon Roll; Audio Vis Asst Awd 86; Bnkng.

WESCOTT, JULIE; Bishop George Ahr HS; Edison, NJ; (Y); Trs Exploring; Off ROTC; Color Guard; Drill Tm; Stage Crew; Rifle Tm Mrksmn Shrpshtr Bar 1,2 Knlng 84-86; ROTC Distngshd Cadt Conduct Aptitd Apprnc Partcptn83-6; Chem.

WESLER, NICHOL; Toms River E HS; Toms River, NJ; (Y); Crs Cntry; Wt Lftg; FIT; Fshn.

WESLEY, RYAN; Arthur L Johnson Regional HS; Clark, NJ; (Y); 42/195; Computer Clb; JV Socr; Var Trk; Hon Roll; Spanish NHS; NCTE Achvt Awd 86.

WESSLING, ROBIN; Red Bank Catholic HS; Lincroft, NJ; (Y); Church Yth Grp; Science Clb; Service Clb; Chorus; Hon Roll; St Schlr; Intl Frgn Lang Awd In Frnch 85; Bio Scis.

WESSNER, GREGORY; Burlington City HS; Edgewater Park, NJ; (Y); Am Leg Boys St; Key Clb; Pres Rep Stu Cncl; JV Tennis; High Hon Roll; NHS; Princpls #1 Clb Awd; Bio Lab Asstnt; Extnd Lrng Pgm; Arch.

WEST, BETH; Southern Regional HS; Barnegat, NJ; (Y); 64/380; Trs Church Yth Grp; Library Aide; Spanish Clb; Stockton ST Coll; Elem Ed.

WEST, CAROLYN; Shore Regional HS; W Long Branch, NJ; (Y); Trs Church Yth Grp; SADD; Church Choir; Yrbk Stf; VP Stu Cncl; Capt Fld Hcky; Powder Puff Ftbl; Sftbl; High Hon Roll; Hon Roll; Knights Of Pythias 86; Beaver Coll; Intr Dsgn.

WEST, STEVE A; Hackettstown HS; Hackettstown, NJ; (Y); 39/200; Church Yth Grp; Q&S; Chorus; Swing Chorus; Nwsp Rptr; Nwsp Sprt Ed; JV Var Bsktbl; Hon Roll; NHS; WV U; Engrng.

WESTON, MELISSA; Kinnelon HS; Kinnelon, NJ; (Y); 45/179; Camera Clb; Dance Clb; Girl Scts; Rep Stu Cncl; Bsktbl; Var L Cheerleading; Hon Roll; Bus Admin.

WESTON, RENEE; Maple Shade HS; Maple Shade, NJ; (Y); Sec Aud/Vis; DECA; Drama Clb; GAA; Sec Library Aide; Spanish Clb; SADD; Flag Corp; School Musical; School Play; Won 3rd Pl DECA ST Cmptns 85; Burlington Cnty Coll; Acctg.

WESTRA, SUZANNE; Wayne Hills HS; Wayne, NJ; (Y); 50/400; Church Yth Grp; Hosp Aide; Spanish Clb; Teachers Aide; Swmmng; Hon Roll; Volntrng 4000 Hrs; Ed.

WETTERAU, LAWRENCE; Toms River E HS; Toms River, NJ; (Y); 1/585; Pres Church Yth Grp; Exploring; VP Intnl Clb; Math Tm; Trs Sr Cls; JV Var Gym; JV Wrstlng; Bausch & Lomb Sci Awd; High Hon Roll; NHS; Acad Letter 83-86; Med.

WETZ, RYAN; Middletown South HS; Middletown, NJ; (Y); Art Clb; Aud/Vis; Computer Clb; JV Bsbl; Ntl Merit Ltr; Art.

WETZEL, PAMELA; Paul VI Regional HS; Passaic, NJ; (Y); Spanish NHS; Nrsng.

WHALEN, DANIEL; Bridgewater-Raritan HS East; Bridgewater, NJ; (Y); Capt Var Bowling; Ftbl; MVP Bwlng 85-86; Var Bwlng Tm 83-86; Ftbl SR Awd 85; Stevens Inst Tech; Engrng.

WHALEN, KEN; Audubon HS; Audubon, NJ; (Y); Church Yth Grp; Varsity Clb; VICA; Var L Bsktbl; JV Ftbl; Var Mgr(s); Im Sftbl; Im Vllybl; Im Wt Lftg; 2nd Pl Stu Crftmns Fair Woodshp, Grphc Art 86; Indstrl Art Tchr.

WHALEN, KIM ANN; Abraham Clark HS; Roselle, NJ; (Y); 7/180; Art Clb; Drama Clb; French Clb; Ski Clb; Nwsp Ed-Chief; Nwsp Rptr; Yrbk Ed-Chief; Sftbl; High Hon Roll; NHS; Robert B Barlow Schlrshp 86; Top 10 Pct Of Cls 86; U Of DE; Intl Rltns.

WHALEN, LACHLAN; Kittatinny Regional HS; Stillwater, NJ; (Y); 11/228; Quiz Bowl; Scholastic Bowl; Science Clb; JV Socr; Var Trk; High Hon Roll; Hon Roll; NHS; Ntl Merit SF; 1st Pl NJ Amer Indstrl Arts Stu Assn 84-86; Jrnlst.

WHALEN, SUZANNE PATRICIA; Morris Knolls HS; Denville, NJ; (Y); 60/387; Am Leg Aux Girls St; Pres Drama Clb; NFL; Chorus; School Musical; School Play; JV Crs Cntry; High Hon Roll; Rtry Yth Ldrshp Awd 84-85; U Of Scranton; Ec.

WHALEY JR, JAMES C; Camden HS; Camden, NJ; (S); Band; Concert Band; Jazz Band; Mrchg Band; Hon Roll; Prfct Atten Awd; Cert Recgntn Teen Arts Fest 83-84; Glassboro ST Coll; Music.

WHELAN, PETER; Morris Catholic HS; Denville, NJ; (Y); 52/153; Varsity Clb; Var Capt Socr; Hon Roll; All ST, All Conf, All Area, All County 85-86; Accounting.

WHETSTONE, BRIAN; High Point Regional HS; Sussex, NJ; (Y); 53/250; Rep Stu Cncl; Var L Bsbl; Var L Ftbl; Athlt Of Mnth 85; 2nd Tm All-Area Offns Ftbll 85; Music.

WHITCHURCH, JANE ANN; Bogota HS; Bogota, NJ; (Y); 9/101; Am Leg Aux Girls St; Nwsp Rptr; Trs Jr Cls; Trs Sr Cls; Rep Stu Cncl; Cit Awd; DAR Awd; Trs NHS; Pres Schlr; Voice Dem Awd; Jrnlsm Awd Exc 86; Douglas Coll; Law.

WHITCOMB, BRADFORD P; Randolph HS; Randolph, NJ; (Y); 6/315; Am Leg Boys St; Church Yth Grp; Computer Clb; Rep Jr Cls; JV Var Bsbl; Var Ice Hcky; High Hon Roll; NHS; Engelhard Inc, Army ROTC 4 Yr & Randolph Booster Clb Schlrshps 86; Washington & Lee U; Chmstry.

WHITE, ADRIENNE LIESL; Hunterdon Central HS; Whitehouse Statio, NJ; (Y); 40/540; Am Leg Aux Girls St; VP 4-H; Thesps; Orch; Sec Frsh Cls; Sec Soph Cls; Trs Jr Cls; NHS; Spanish NHS; Church Yth Grp; Jennie Haver Mem Schlrshp 86; Nat Schl Orcstr Ad 86; Moravian Coll; Phrmcy.

WHITE, ANDREW; Howell HS; Howell, NJ; (Y); 4/400; Boy Scts; Exploring; NFL; Science Clb; Ftbl; Socr; Trk; Hon Roll; NHS; No 1 Acctng I Stu Schl 85-86; Bus.

WHITE, BONNIE; Lakeland Regional HS; Ringwood, NJ; (Y); AFS; SADD; Rep Frsh Cls; Rep Soph Cls; Rep Jr Cls; Stu Cncl; High Hon Roll; NHS; 1st Sem Stu Spain; Gordon Coll; Psych.

WHITE, CHERYL; Abraham Clark HS; Roselle, NJ; (Y); GAA; Hosp Aide; Library Aide; Spanish Clb; Sec Jr Cls; JV Capt Cheerleading; Var L Sftbl; Var Capt Trk; Rutgers U; Comp Sci.

WHITE, CINDY; Livingston HS; Livingston, NJ; (Y); 44/496; AFS; Sec German Clb; Var Socr; French Hon Soc; Jr NHS; NHS; German Hnr Soc 86; Prevntn Of Abuse PALS 86; Unico Schlrshp 86; Richmond U; Psychlgy.

WHITE, CLINT; Christian Brothers Acad; Oceanport, NJ; (Y); 44/222; Cmnty Wkr; Computer Clb; Ski Clb; Jazz Band; Nwsp Rptr; Nwsp Stf; Im Fld Hcky; Hon Roll; U S Air Force Acad; Astrntcl En.

WHITE, CURTIS; Bridgewater High School East; Bound Brook, NJ; (Y); Math Tm; Band; Drm & Bgl; Mrchg Band; Swmmng; JV Tennis; Hon Roll; Trs NHS; Pres Schlr; Glenn Robert Johnson Mem Schlrshp 86; Lafayette Coll Easton PA; Chem.

WHITE, FELICIA; Burl. Co-Vo Tech; Willingboro, NJ; (Y); FBLA; Chorus; Nwsp Ed-Chief; Yrbk Stf; Rep Stu Cncl; Var Cheerleading; Vllybl; Gov Hon Prg Awd; NHS; Prfct Atten Awd; FBLA/YFU Schlrshp To Japan Exhng Stu 85; Stcktn ST Coll; Bus Mgmt.

WHITE, FRANCINE; Burlington City HS; Edgewater Park, NJ; (Y); Am Leg Aux Girls St; Church Yth Grp; FTA; Band; Chorus; Church Choir; Concert Band; Mrchg Band; School Musical; Hon Roll; Bio.

WHITE, HEATHER; Woodstown HS; Elmer, NJ; (Y); Drama Clb; English Clb; Sec 4-H; Sec French Clb; Band; Chorus; Church Choir; School Musical; Sec Soph Cls; JV NHS; Grls Ctznshp Cnfrnc 86; Bus Adm.

WHITE, JEANNE K; Morris Catholic HS; Parisippany, NJ; (Y); 11/142; Church Yth Grp; Hosp Aide; Math Clb; Chorus; Color Guard; Lit Mag; Hon Roll; NHS; Pin For Hon Roll 85; 1st Pl In Piano Rctl 85; Elec Engr.

WHITE, JENNIFER; Shore Regional HS; Oceanport, NJ; (Y); 18/225; Drama Clb; SADD; Stage Crew; Ed Yrbk Stf; Capt Bsktbl; Capt Im Sftbl; High Hon Roll; Church Yth Grp; GAA; Girl Scts; KY Centre Coll SRS Schlr Pgm 86; Physcl Thrpy.

WHITE, JONATHAN; Belvidere HS; Phillipsburg, NJ; (Y); Am Leg Boys St; CAP; Pres Drama Clb; Letterman Clb; Chorus; Madrigals; School Musical; Yrbk Phtg; Var L Bsbl; Hon Roll; Bst Thespian Awd 86; Seton Hall U; Pre-Law.

WHITE, JONATHAN; Timothy Christian Schl; Millington, NJ; (S); 4/46; Church Yth Grp; Hosp Aide; JV Socr; High Hon Roll; Hon Roll; NHS; Prfct Atten Awd; Comp Sci.

WHITE, KATHY; Weeauahic HS; Newark, NJ; (Y); 33/357; Debate Tm; Exploring; Girl Scts; Sftbl; NHS; Uppr Bnd Pgm At Blmfld Coll 83-86; Bloomfield Coll; Nrsng.

WHITE, LESLIE; Edison HS; Edison, NJ; (Y); Camera Clb; Church Yth Grp; Civic Clb; Cmnty Wkr; Girl Scts; Teachers Aide; Stage Crew; Variety Show; Yrbk Phtg; Yrbk Stf; Radcliffe Coll; Pblc Rltns.

WHITE, MICHELLE; Hamilton High School West; Trenton, NJ; (S); 27/330; Church Yth Grp; Band; Drm Mjr(t); Mrchg Band; Pep Band; Symp Band; Stat Bsktbl; Var L Tennis; Var Hon Roll; All Cnty, All CVC Hon Ment Sftbl 85; SR All Amer Hall Fame Band 85; Trenton ST Coll; Elem Educ.

WHITE, RACHEL; Hightstown HS; Cranbury, NJ; (Y); Ski Clb; Concert Band; Mrchg Band; Rep Stu Cncl; Capt Socr; Capt Trk; High Hon Roll; NHS; Girls Ctznshp Inst-Altrnt 86; Robbie Miller Sccr Awd 86.

WHITE, RANDY; Paulsboro HS; Paulsboro, NJ; (Y); Church Yth Grp; Computer Clb; Stage Crew; Yrbk Stf; JV Bsbl; JV Var Bsktbl; JV Var Ftbl; Hon Roll; Engr.

WHITE, ROBERT; Marist HS; Bayonne, NJ; (Y); 15/108; Cmnty Wkr; VP Key Clb; Band; Nwsp Rptr; Nwsp Stf; Hon Roll; NHS; Spanish NHS; Drama Clb; Science Clb; Engrng.

WHITE, ROSS; Edgewood Regional SR HS; Sicklerville, NJ; (Y); Band; Concert Band; Drm Mjr(t); Jazz Band; Mrchg Band; Rep Frsh Cls; Im Wt Lftg; JV Wrstlng; Hon Roll; Jr NHS; NHS; Johns Hopkins U; Med.

WHITE, SHARI; Wall HS; Wall Township, NJ; (Y); Church Yth Grp; Ski Clb; Yrbk Stf; High Hon Roll; Hon Roll; Bus.

WHITE, TRICIA; Pemberton Twp Campus II HS; Browns Mills, NJ; (Y); VP Trs Church Yth Grp; SADD; Church Choir; VP Soph Cls; Rep Jr Cls; Rep Sr Cls; Rep Stu Cncl; Var Capt Cheerleading; Coach Actv; Hon Roll; Seton Hall U; Crmnl Jstc.

WHITE, VALERIE DENISE; Millville SR HS; Millville, NJ; (Y); 140/500; Church Yth Grp; Civic Clb; DECA; FBLA; OEA; Variety Show; Var L Mgr(s); Var L Trk; Jack Jill Am Inc Debutante 1st Hnrs 86; Millvile Modeling Clb Miss Grace 84; Lincoln U; Hosp Adm.

WHITE, WILLIAM; Don Bosco Prep; Sloatsburg, NY; (Y); Gld Mdl Drwng & Clr 84.

WHITE, WILLIAM; Wall HS; Beielle, NJ; (S); 19/275; Chess Clb; Math Tm; Spanish Clb; L Bsktbl; L Crs Cntry; Capt Golf; High Hon Roll; Fin.

WHITESALL, BOB; Bridgeton HS; Bridgeton, NJ; (Y); Aud/Vis; Camera Clb; Science Clb; JV Bsbl; JV Trk; Driver Ed 86; Mchncl.

WHITESIDE, KELLY; Bishop Ahr HS; East Brunswick, NJ; (S); 15/240; French Clb; Nwsp Ed-Chief; Rep Frsh Cls; Rep Soph Cls; Capt Bsktbl; Capt Socr; Sftbl; Trk; High Hon Roll; NHS; Cmmnctns.

WHITING, TERRI; Clayton HS; Clayton, NJ; (Y); Church Yth Grp; Trs Key Clb; Teachers Aide; Mrchg Band; Stage Crew; Yrbk Stf; Rep Stu Cncl; Mgr(s); Capt Pom Pon; Score Keeper; Gifted & Talented 84-87; Elem Educ.

WHITMAN, SHERRY; Arthur L Johnson Regional HS; Clark, NJ; (Y); 34/200; Spanish Clb; Varsity Clb; Yrbk Rptr; Yrbk Stf; Rep Frsh Cls; Rep Soph Cls; Rep Jr Cls; Var Capt Cheerleading; Hon Roll; Spanish NHS; Lib Arts.

WHITNEY, LISABETH; Watchung Hills Regional HS; Watchung, NJ; (Y); 79/369; Church Yth Grp; Drama Clb; French Clb; Girl Scts; Hosp Aide; Latin Clb; SADD; Thesps; Acpl Chr; Chorus; Yng Citizens Awd By Bill Bradley; Pol Sci.

WHITNEY, PAUL; Hightstown HS; East Windsor, NJ; (Y); Cmnty Wkr; Ski Clb; Yrbk Stf; JV Socr; Var Tennis; Hon Roll; Bus.

WHITTLE, ROSLYN; Frank H Morrell HS; Irvington, NJ; (Y); 1/500; Drama Clb; Sec Latin Clb; Chorus; Rep Jr Cls; Var Capt Sftbl; Var Twrlr; High Hon Roll; NHS; St Schlr; Val; Latn Hnr Soc 85-86; Med.

WHOOLEY, JOHN; Morris Catholic HS; Boonton, NJ; (Y); 20/155; Cmnty Wkr; Computer Clb; English Clb; Letterman Clb; Math Clb; Math Tm; Natl Beta Clb; Varsity Clb; Var L Bsbl; Var L Bsktbl; Rutgers; Phrmctcl.

WHYTE, ANDREA; East Orange HS; E Orange, NJ; (Y); Cmnty Wkr; Exploring; FNA; Hosp Aide; Library Aide; Spanish Clb; Rep Stu Cncl; Tennis; Hon Roll; NHS; Chem.

WHYTE, PAULA; East Orange HS; East Orange, NJ; (S); Sec FBLA; VP JA; High Hon Roll; Hon Roll; NHS; JR Achvt VP Awd Prodctn 85; Rep Stdnt Cncl 86; Navy; Acctg.

WICELINSKI, THERESE; St John Vianney HS; Hazlet, NJ; (Y); 1/283; VP Intnl Clb; Math Tm; Office Aide; Service Clb; L Twrlr; High Hon Roll; Hon Roll; NHS; Gld & White Awd; Engrng.

WICHTNER, KRISTEN L; W Milford Twp HS; W Milford, NJ; (Y); 13/370; Sec Church Yth Grp; Sec German Clb; Office Aide; Church Choir; Drill Tm; Mrchg Band; Variety Show; Rep Frsh Cls; Twrlr; High Hon Roll; German Hnr Soc; Natl Art Hnr Soc; Hofstra U; Comp Sci.

WICKE, ROBERT; Bishop Ahr HS; Edison, NJ; (S); 4/300; Model UN; Thesps; School Musical; School Play; Nwsp Rptr; Nwsp Stf; Lit Mag; Var Tennis; High Hon Roll; Scholastic Bowl; Trenton ST Drama Fest Bst Chrctr Actng 85; Mst Promsng New Cmr Drama 83; Spec Acvt Awd Drama 85; Comp Pgmmr.

WICKHAM, ROBERT; Dwight-Englewood HS; Englewood, NJ; (Y); Exploring; Math Tm; Yrbk Phtg; Aerosp Engrng.

WIDDIFIELD, DARA; Arthur P Schalick HS; Elmer, NJ; (Y); Band; Color Guard; Concert Band; JV Bsktbl; Var Pom Pon; Art Clb; Church Yth Grp; Pep Clb; Ski Clb; JV Fld Hcky; Cumberland County Coll; Arts.

WIDEMAN, MILO; Henry Snyder HS; Jersey City, NJ; (Y); Mgr Var Ftbl; Prfct Atten Awd; Snyders Rnassnce Pgm 83-86; Elec Engr.

WIECEK, URSULA; Hawthorne HS; Hawthorne, NJ; (Y); Science Clb; Ski Clb; Chorus; School Play; Variety Show; Yrbk Stf; Var Trk; Gov Hon Prg Awd; Hon Roll; Bus Adm.

WIECZOREK, CYNTHIA; Frank H Morrell HS; Irvington, NJ; (Y); Church Yth Grp; Flag Corp; Sftbl; Swmmng; Hon Roll; NHS; Child Psyclgy.

WIECZOREK, LISA; Middlesex HS; Middlesex, NJ; (Y); Ski Clb; SADD; Yrbk Stf; Var Crs Cntry; Im Swmmng; Var Trk; Hon Roll; Fshn Merch.

WIEDMANN, JAMES; Hillsborough HS; Belle Mead, NJ; (Y); 30/267; Church Yth Grp; Stage Crew; Lit Mag; Tennis; JV Trk; Im Wt Lftg; Hon Roll; Cert Of Merit-Sci 86; Rutgers U; Elec Engrng.

WIEGAND, WENDY; Pompton Lakes HS; Pompton Lakes, NJ; (Y); 11/147; Church Yth Grp; Math Tm; Teachers Aide; Chorus; Stage Crew; Nwsp Rptr; High Hon Roll; NHS; 20 Hr Pin Zonta Clb 86; Pst Wrthy Advsr Ordr Rnbw Grls & Grnd Trsr 86.

WIELAND, KRISTINE D; The Peddie Schl; E Windsor, NJ; (Y); 12/150; Library Aide; Spanish Clb; Nwsp Rptr; Yrbk Stf; Rep Soph Cls; Off Stu Cncl; Capt Cheerleading; Hon Roll; Ntl Merit SF; Engl.

WIELAND, RUTH M; Pascack Valley HS; Hillsdale, NJ; (Y); Church Yth Grp; Girl Scts; Library Aide; Spanish Clb; Chorus; Yrbk Stf; Hon Roll; Masonic Awd; Debate Tm; 4-H; Home Edon 83; Ledrshp Awd 85; Columbia; Pre Med.

WIELANDT, AMY; Msgr Donovan HS; Jackson, NJ; (Y); FBLA; Ski Clb; Rep Stu Cncl; Capt Cheerleading; Trk; Ocean County Coll; Dctr Chirop.

WIELICZKO, MEGAN A; Haddonfield Memorial HS; Haddonfield, NJ; (Y); 10/139; Drama Clb; Hosp Aide; Political Wkr; School Musical; School Play; Stage Crew; Var Cheerleading; Hon Roll; NHS; Rep Frsh Cls; Hugh O Brian Yth Ldrshp Smnr Dlgt 84; NJ ST Teen Arts Fstvl Crtve Wrtng Fnlst 84; Grls ST 85; NY U; Thtre Arts.

WIEMER, MICHAEL J; Atlantic City HS; Ventnor, NJ; (Y); Boy Scts; 4-H; Key Clb; Service Clb; SADD; Varsity Clb; Var Ftbl; Crmnl Just.

WIENER, ANDREW; Ocean Township HS; Ocean, NJ; (Y); 34/333; Pres Key Clb; Ski Clb; Stu Cncl; JV Ftbl; Hon Roll; NHS; Spanish Clb; Temple Yth Grp; Lcrss; Wt Lftg.

WIENER, ELLEN; Bruriah HS; Staten Island, NY; (Y); Bsktbl; NHS; NEDT Awd.

WIENER, KIM; Glen Rock JR SR HS; Glen Rock, NJ; (Y); Dance Clb; Drama Clb; Girl Scts; Library Aide; Office Aide; Spanish Clb; Acpl Chr; Chorus; Color Guard; Madrigals; Psych.

WIENER, LIZABETH; Ridgewood HS; Ridgewood, NJ; (Y); Mathletes; Pres NFL; Temple Yth Grp; Capt Color Guard; Variety Show; Yrbk Stf; Ed Lit Mag; High Hon Roll; NHS; Peer Cnslr 85-86; Physcs.

WIERCISZEWSKI, EDWARD; Secaucus HS; Secaucus, NJ; (S); 10/175; Key Clb; Band; Concert Band; JV Bsbl; Mgr Bsktbl; JV Bowling; Hon Roll; Pres NHS; Spanish NHS; Hofstra; Bus Admin.

WIESEL, SABRINA E; Central Regional HS; Bayville, NJ; (Y); 58/228; Key Clb; Q&S; Varsity Clb; Nwsp Rptr; Nwsp Stf; Socr; Wrstlng; NJ Mock Trial Cmptn-2nd Pl ST 84-85; Hugh O Brian Ldrshp Fndtn Essy Cont Wnnr 82-83; Fairleigh Dickenson U; Cmmnctns.

WIESING, CAROLINE; North Warren Regional HS; Blairstown, NJ; (Y); 13/126; Hosp Aide; Yrbk Stf; Sec Frsh Cls; Sec Soph Cls; Sec Jr Cls; JV Fld Hcky; Im Powder Puff Ftbl; JV Capt Sftbl; Hon Roll; NHS; Internl Bus.

WIGGINS, ADRIENNE; Essex Catholic Girls HS; East Orange, NJ; (Y); 16/60; Trs Church Yth Grp; Trs Pep Clb; Drill Tm; Variety Show; Nwsp Rptr; Yrbk Stf; Rep Soph Cls; Trs Jr Cls; Var Cheerleading; Hnr Rll 84-85; Rutgers U; Bus Mgmnt.

WIKANDER, KELLY; Newton HS; Newton, NJ; (S); 8/210; French Clb; Latin Clb; Sec Trs Ski Clb; Band; Rep Jr Cls; JV Bsktbl; JV Fld Hcky; Var Sftbl; NHS; Rep Frsh Cls.

WILBUR, DANIEL; Highstown HS; E Windsor, NJ; (Y); AFS; French Clb; German Clb; Library Aide; Frsh Cls; Stu Cncl; Hon Roll; NYU; Comm Art.

WILCE, GERALD; Morris Knolls HS; Denville, NJ; (Y); 108/367; Concert Band; Jazz Band; Mrchg Band; Hon Roll; Home & Schl Assn Awd 86; Frostburg ST Coll MD; Bus Adm.

WILCZYNSKI, ALINA C; Perth Amboy HS; Perth Amboy, NJ; (Y); Pres Art Clb; German Clb; Key Clb; Model UN; School Play; Rep Sr Cls; JV Sftbl; Var Tennis; High Hon Roll; Jr NHS; 2nd Pl Ntl Arts Comp 85; 1st Pl Wmns Clb Art Comp 83 & 85; All Acad Tennis Team 85; Montclair ST Coll; Fine Arts.

WILDER, LISA M; Willingboro HS; Willingboro, NJ; (Y); Drama Clb; Trs Intnl Clb; Service Clb; Thesps; School Musical; School Play; Stage Crew; Var L Tennis; Rotary Awd; Latin Clb; Carnegie Mellon U Schlrshp 85; Middle Aston Fine Arts Conf Awd 83; Persnl Develpmt Awd 84; Hofstra U; Cmmnctn Arts.

WILEY, REGINALD D; Westfield HS; Westfield, NJ; (Y); 75/469; Pres Church Yth Grp; Band; Concert Band; Jazz Band; Pres Mrchg Band; Pres Symp Band; Var L Trk; High Hon Roll; Hon Roll; JP Sousa Awd; Co Club Natl Assoc Negro Bus & Womens Club Inc, Band Parents Assoc, Westfield Negro Hist Club 86; Rutgers Coll Engrng; Chem Engr.

WILINSKY, JENNIFER; Freenold Township HS; Freehold, NJ; (Y); 10/307; Yrbk Ed-Chief; Yrbk Stf; Rep Frsh Cls; Rep Soph Cls; Rep Jr Cls; Sec Stu Cncl; Var Sftbl; NHS; U Of Richmond.

WILKERSON, LESHA; Plainfield HS; Plainfield, NJ; (Y); Camera Clb; FBLA; Library Aide; Office Aide; Quiz Bowl; VP Stu Cncl; Hon Roll; NHS; Rutgers U; Acctg.

WILKES, DAWN; Teaneck HS; Teaneck, NJ; (Y); Dance Clb; Rep Soph Cls; Rep Jr Cls; Rep Sr Cls; Trs Stu Cncl; Capt Var Bsktbl; Coach Actv; NHS; Bucknell; Acctng.

WILKIE, JENNIFER; Holy Cross HS; Cinnaminson, NJ; (Y); 63/374; Political Wkr; Red Cross Aide; Chorus; School Musical; Stage Crew; Nwsp Stf; Ed Lit Mag; Fld Hcky; Hon Roll; NHS; Yth In Govt 85-86; NJ ST U Rutgers; Zoology.

WILKINS III, JOHN W; Overbrook Regional SR HS; Pine Hill, NJ; (Y); Am Leg Boys St; French Clb; Science Clb; Sec Stu Cncl; Stat Ftbl; Mgr(s); Var L Tennis; Drexel Schl Business; Finc.

WILKINSON, LISA M; Gloucester Catholic HS; Woodbury Hts, NJ; (Y); 3/163; Hosp Aide; JV Cheerleading; L Socr; Trk; Bausch & Lomb Sci Awd; Elks Awd; High Hon Roll; NHS; Pres Schlr; St Schlr; Gloucester Cty Hstry Awd 86; Rutgers U; Pre Med.

WILKINSON, MATT; Freehold Township HS; Freehold, NJ; (Y); 13/375; Cmnty Wkr; Var L Socr; Var L Trk; NHS; Chem Achvt Monmarth Coll 84-85; Trvlng Soccer USYSA Tm Camp 84-85; Physical Therapy.

WILL, CAROLYN; Washington Township HS; Turnersville, NJ; (Y); Art Clb; Ski Clb; Spanish Clb; Var Crs Cntry; Var Trk; High Hon Roll; NHS; Gloucester Cnty Teen Arts Fest, Outstndng Art Achvt Awd 84-86; Gloucester Cnty Artwk ST Fnls 85-86; Bio Med.

WILLARD, RANDY; North Waren Regional HS; Blairstown, NJ; (Y); Boy Scts; Church Yth Grp; Letterman Clb; Varsity Clb; Band; Stu Cncl; Bsbl; Ftbl; Ice Hcky; Wrstlng; Phrmcy.

WILLARD, RANDY; South Hunterdon Regional HS; Lambertville, NJ; (Y); 3/72; Camp Fr Inc; Key Clb; Band; Concert Band; Jazz Band; Mrchg Band; Stage Crew; Nwsp Stf; Crs Cntry; Hon Roll; X-Cntry Mst Imprvd 86; Engrng.

WILLBERGH, DONNA; Brick Township HS; Brick, NJ; (Y); 23/318; Keywanettes; Ski Clb; SADD; Teachers Aide; Color Guard; Drill Tm; Yrbk Stf; Powder Puff Ftbl; Twrlr; High Hon Roll; NJ Assoc Pblc Acctnts & IRS 86; Susquehanna U; Acctg.

WILLEVER, SEAN; Nottingham HS; Trenton, NJ; (Y); 96/265; JV Bsbl; JV Socr; Law Enfrcmnt.

WILLEY, LINDA; Lincoln HS; Jersey City, NJ; (Y); Computer Clb; FHA; FNA; FTA; Hosp Aide; Office Aide; Political Wkr; ROTC; SADD; Yrbk Stf; Comp Prgmng.

WILLIAMS, ALBERT; Cherry Hill HS West; Cherry Hill, NJ; (Y); Teachers Aide; Nwsp Stf; Ftbl; Bus.

WILLIAMS, ANGELA D; Holy Cross HS; Willingboro, NJ; (Y); Cmnty Wkr; SADD; Chorus; Yrbk Stf; Sec Soph Cls; Crs Cntry; Cit Awd; Hon Roll; Hnr Top Ten Fnlst Mdrn Mss Pgnt 85; JR Exec Awd 85; Farleigh Dickinson U; Ind Psych.

WILLIAMS, CARLA; Marylawn Of The Oranges; E Orange, NJ; (Y); 30/56; Church Yth Grp; Cmnty Wkr; Dance Clb; FNA; Red Cross Aide; Service Clb; Chorus; School Play; Vllybl; Hon Roll; Seton Hall U; Bio.

WILLIAMS, CHERYL; Roselle Catholic HS; Roselle Park, NJ; (S); 7/153; Girl Scts; Yrbk Rptr; Cheerleading; Vllybl; Hon Roll; NHS; Ntl Merit SF; Spanish NHS; Mthrs Clb Schlrshp 82-86; Acadmc All Am Schlr 85-86.

WILLIAMS, CHRISTINE; Henry Snyder HS; Jersey City, NJ; (Y); Cmnty Wkr; Bsktbl; Prfct Atten Awd; Bloomfield; Computer Pgrmmg.

WILLIAMS, CHRISTOPHER W; Holy Cross HS; Edgewater Park, NJ; (Y); 137/388; Am Leg Boys St; Boy Scts; French Clb; School Musical; Ftbl; Capt Trk; Masonic Awd; Unsung Hero Ftbl, 2nd Tm S Jersey Parochial Ftbl Dfnsve Back 85; 2nd All Co Track 800 M 86; Howard U; Comp Info.

WILLIAMS, DAVID DAKIN; The Lawrenceville Schl; Cranford, NJ; (Y); Cmnty Wkr; Computer Clb; Science Clb; Spanish Clb; Lit Mag; Im Trk; Hon Roll; Ntl Merit SF; St Schlr; Im Bsktbl; Lawrencvl Eng Awd-Gen Excllnc 82; Lib Arts.

WILLIAMS, DINA; St Marys Hall-Doane Acad; Pemberton, NJ; (Y); Am Leg Aux Girls St; Drama Clb; Stage Crew; Lit Mag; Rep Frsh Cls; Rep Soph Cls; Rep Jr Cls; Off Stu Cncl; Library Aide; Yrbk Stf; Brdcst Jrnlsm.

WILLIAMS, DIONNE; East Orange HS; East Orange, NJ; (S); 2/410; Lit Mag; Rep Stu Cncl; High Hon Roll; Hon Roll; NHS; Prfct Atten Awd; Sal; Nwsp Rprtr 86; Fclty Edtr 86; Tnns 84-86; Rutgers U; Orthpdst.

WILLIAMS, GARY; Shawwee HS; Medford, NJ; (Y); 21/535; Am Leg Boys St; Church Yth Grp; Intnl Clb; Jr Cls; Sr Cls; Stu Cncl; JV Var Ftbl; JV Var Trk; Hon Roll; NHS; Pres Clssrm 86; Outstndng SR Dist 86; Franklin Clg; Bus.

WILLIAMS, JACQUELINE; Rahway HS; Rahway, NJ; (Y); Church Yth Grp; Hosp Aide; French Hon Soc; Hon Roll; Prfct Atten Awd; Its Acad Clb Awd 83; Retail Buyer.

WILLIAMS, JEAN; Morris Knolls HS; Denville, NJ; (Y); 15/369; FBLA; High Hon Roll; Morris & Somerset Bldrs Assn Schlrshp 86; Pres Acadmc Fit Awd 86; 2nd Pl FBLA ST Comptn Acctg II 86; U Of Scranton; Acctg.

WILLIAMS, JEANA; University HS; Newark, NJ; (Y); Church Yth Grp; Math Tm; Teachers Aide; Chorus; Timer; Hon Roll; U Notre Dame; Elem Ed.

WILLIAMS, JEFFREY JAMES; University HS; Newark, NJ; (Y); 46/59; Computer Clb; JA; Trk; Vllybl; Comp Sci.

WILLIAMS, JO ANNE; Piscataway HS; Piscataway, NJ; (Y); Dance Clb; Variety Show; Gym; High Hon Roll; Hon Roll; NHS; Trophies Dance Cmptns 83-86; Frgn Lang Cert Itln 85; Miss JR Am Candt 86; Dance.

WILLIAMS, KAMILI; Immaculate Conception HS; East Orange, NJ; (Y); Dance Clb; Pep Clb; Yrbk Stf; High Hon Roll; Hon Roll; Spelman; Bus Admin.

WILLIAMS, KATHERINE; Neptune SR HS; Neptune, NJ; (Y); Trs Church Yth Grp; Dance Clb; Library Aide; Teachers Aide; Church Choir; Drill Tm; Variety Show; Yrbk Stf; Lit Mag; High Hon Roll; Religious Ed Tchr 84-86; Ed.

WILLIAMS, KERRI; Highland HS; Erial, NJ; (Y); 36/330; Camera Clb; Spanish Clb; JV Cheerleading; Stat Crs Cntry; JV Sftbl; Hon Roll; Rutgers; Acctng.

WILLIAMS, LARRY; Jackson Memorial HS; Jackson, NJ; (Y); 49/424; Political Wkr; Ski Clb; Band; Chorus; VP Frsh Cls; Stu Cncl; Cheerleading; Mgr(s); Socr; Wt Lftg; Trenton ST Coll; Pre-Med.

WILLIAMS, LESLEY; Wardlaw Hartridge HS; Scotch Plains, NJ; (Y); 2/53; Camera Clb; Drama Clb; Key Clb; Ski Clb; VP SADD; Chorus; School Musical; Stage Crew; Nwsp Sprt Ed; Yrbk Sprt Ed; Ntnl Latin Exam Slvr Brnz Brnz Awds 84-86.

WILLIAMS, LESLIE; Glassboro HS; Glassboro, NJ; (Y); Civic Clb; Varsity Clb; Stat Bsktbl; Var Fld Hcky; Stat Ftbl; Sftbl.

WILLIAMS, LESLIE; Gloucester City JR SR HS; Gloucester, NJ; (Y); 11/180; Am Leg Aux Girls St; Trs FBLA; VP Pep Clb; Sec Science Clb; School Musical; Yrbk Stf; Stu Cncl; Var Capt Cheerleading; NHS; Chorus; Governors Schl Fnlst 86; 2nd Pl Imprmpt Comp-ST Lvl 86.

WILLIAMS, LORI; Neptune SR HS; Neptune, NJ; (Y); Church Yth Grp; Cmnty Wkr; French Clb; GAA; Hosp Aide; Church Choir; Lit Mag; Hon Roll; Lion Awd; Tn Arts Fest Wnnr 86; Intr Dec.

WILLIAMS, LUCETTE ANN; Ramsey HS; Ramsey, NJ; (Y); 35/243; Sec Church Yth Grp; Girl Scts; Math Tm; Chorus; Yrbk Stf; Rep Frsh Cls; High Hon Roll; Hon Roll; NHS; Schlstc R 84 & 85; Presdntl Acadmc Ftns Awd 86; Acolyte 84-86; Moravian Coll; Comp Sci.

WILLIAMS, MARCIA Y; Lawrence HS; Lawrenceville, NJ; (Y); Sec VP AFS; Cmnty Wkr; Drama Clb; French Clb; Lit Mag; Rep Sr Cls; Rep Stu Cncl; Var Capt Trk; Hon Roll; Ntl Merit SF; Le Petit Prince Frnch III Achvt Awd; Lawrence Twp Dist Nwsltr; Bus.

WILLIAMS, R KEITH; Bishop Eustace Prep; Atco, NJ; (Y); 18/182; Am Leg Boys St; Drama Clb; School Musical; Sec Soph Cls; Var Bsbl; Var Bsktbl; Var Socr; French Hon Soc; Hon Roll; NHS; All Parochial Honorable Mention Basebell 86; 2nd Team All Conf Soccer 85; Engr.

WILLIAMS, RACHEL; Garden State Acad; Paterson, NJ; (Y); Trs Concert Band; Off Frsh Cls; Off Soph Cls; Off Stu Cncl; Hon Roll; Merit Schlrshp Frm Columbia Union Coll 86; Columbia Union Coll; Acctg.

WILLIAMS, SANDRA LYNN; Lodi HS; Lodi, NJ; (Y); Spanish Clb; Rep Soph Cls; Stu Cncl; Essy Schlrhsp $1000-St Thomas U FL 86; Farleight Dickinson U; Poli Sci.

WILLIAMS, SONIA; Lincoln HS; Jersey City, NJ; (Y); #5 In Class; FHA; Church Choir; Off Frsh Cls; Sec Soph Cls; Stu Cncl; Mgr Socr; Hon Roll; NHS; Prfct Atten Awd; St Peters Coll; Tchr.

WILLIAMS, STACI; Hackensack HS; Hackensack, NJ; (Y); Church Yth Grp; Spanish Clb; Band; Jazz Band; Mrchg Band; Rep Stu Cncl; Var Bsktbl; Hon Roll; Ped.

WILLIAMS, SUSAN; Hopewell Valley Central HS; Hopewell, NJ; (Y); VP DECA; Stu Cncl; Hon Roll; NJ ST DECA Schlrshp 85-86; Joann Amison Achvt Awd 85-86; U Of RI; Mrchndsng.

WILLIAMS, TARA; Kent Place Schl; Newark, NJ; (Y); Church Yth Grp; French Clb; Model UN; Church Choir; Rep Frsh Cls; VP Soph Cls; Bsktbl; Gym; Schlrshp A Better Chance Inc 83-87; Duke U; Indust Engrgn.

WILLIAMS, TAWANA; Plainfield HS; Plainfield, NJ; (Y); 19/469; Cmnty Wkr; Debate Tm; Band; Concert Band; Jazz Band; Mrchg Band; Nwsp Rptr; Yrbk Rptr; Lit Mag; JV Bsktbl; Rutgers-Douglas; Music.

WILLIAMS, TAWANNA M; Pope Paul VI HS; Lawnside, NJ; (Y); Cmnty Wkr; Spanish Clb; Stage Crew; Yrbk Stf; Rep Jr Cls; Rep Sr Cls; Bsktbl; Bowling; Fld Hcky; Lcrss; Villanova Univ; Nursing.

WILLIAMS, TERI; Pennsville Memorial HS; Pennsville, NJ; (Y); 58/216; Drama Clb; JA; Office Aide; Q&S; School Play; Stage Crew; Stat Bsktbl; Var Socr; Var Sftbl; Hon Roll; Pennsville Soccer Assn Schlrshp 86; W Chester U; Speech Crrctn.

WILLIAMS, THOMAS; St Peters Prep; Jersey City, NJ; (Y); 70/210; French Clb; Capt Gym; JV Wrstlng; Bus.

WILLIAMSON, GREGG; West Essex SR HS; N Caldwell, NJ; (Y); 50/350; VP Debate Tm; Key Clb; Var L Socr; Hon Roll; Soccer 3rd Tm All ST Group 3 85-86; Wake Forest U; Bus.

WILLIAMSON, JAMAL; East Orange HS; E Orange, NJ; (S); Civic Clb; Var Capt Bsktbl; Var Capt Ftbl; Hon Roll; Comp Sci.

WILLIS, ALLEN; Bridgeton HS; Bridgeton, NJ; (Y); 42/209; Art Clb; Church Yth Grp; Ski Clb; Varsity Clb; Nwsp Rptr; Nwsp Stf; Yrbk Stf; JV Var Bsbl; Var Wrstlng; Cit Awd; Bsbl Awd 86; R L Johnson Meml Awd Wrstlng 86; Gene Matalucci Meml Awd 86; WV Tech; Arch.

WILLIS, JOESPH; Morris Catholic HS; Lk Giawatha, NJ; (Y); Math Clb; L Var Wrstlng; Hon Roll; Bus.

WILLIS, JOYCE; Vineland HS; Newfield, NJ; (Y); 152/816; Cmnty Wkr; Sec Red Cross Aide; Spanish Clb; Chorus; Swmmng; Hon Roll; Spanish NHS; Wm Simpson Schlrshp Awd 86; Elizabethtown Coll; Spnsh.

WILLISTON, PETER; Pinelands Regional HS; Tuckerton, NJ; (Y); 44/196; Varsity Clb; JV Var Bsbl; Bsktbl; Var Ftbl; Im Lcrss; JV Socr; Im Wt Lftg; Hon Roll; VMI; Pre-Med.

WILLMAN, CHRIS; Oakcrest HS; Mays Landing, NJ; (Y); 2/221; French Clb; Math Clb; Band; Yrbk Stf; Var Wrstlng; Gov Hon Prg Awd; NHS; Ntl Merit Ltr; Sal; Bausch & Lomb Sci Awd; NJ Gov Schl Sci 85; US Military Acad; Biochem.

WILSON, AMY; Ridge HS; Liberty Corner, NJ; (Y); 30/210; Church Yth Grp; Ski Clb; Spanish Clb; Chorus; Drill Tm; Yrbk Stf; Cheerleading; Pom Pon; High Hon Roll; Hon Roll; Bus.

WILSON, CHANEL; East Orange HS; East Orange, NJ; (S); Church Yth Grp; FBLA; Pep Clb; Church Choir; Pep Band; Cit Awd; Hon Roll; Attend Awd 82; Berkeley Bus Schl; Comp Oper.

WILSON, CYNTHIA J; Phillipsburgh HS; Phillipsburg, NJ; (Y); 28/284; Drama Clb; Key Clb; SADD; Church Choir; Stage Crew; Nwsp Rptr; Nwsp Stf; High Hon Roll; Hon Roll; Jr NHS; Bell Howell Schlrshp 86; Unico Schlrshp 86; VA Poly Inst; Arch Engr.

WILSON, DARNELL ANTHONY; Lincoln HS; Jersey City, NJ; (S); 7/233; Church Yth Grp; Pres Stu Cncl; Dnfth Awd; NHS; Ntl Merit Ltr; Prfct Atten Awd; JA Clb Treas 85; Martin; Acctg.

WILSON, DEBRA; Southern Regional HS; Barnegat, NJ; (Y); Civic Clb; Dance Clb; Hosp Aide; Ski Clb; Spanish Clb; Rep Soph Cls; Pom Pon; Hon Roll; Medcl.

WILSON, DENISE; Hamilton HS West; Trenton, NJ; (Y); 3/330; Key Clb; Drill Tm; Nwsp Rptr; Var Sftbl; High Hon Roll; VP NHS; Pres Schlr; St Schlr; Rider Coll; Accntng.

WILSON, DENNIS; Absegami HS; Absecon, NJ; (Y); 40/223; JV Ftbl; JV Trk; JV Wrstlng; B Hnr Rll Nat Hnr Soc 84-85; Physcl Ftns Awd 85-86.

WILSON, DONALD; St Peters Prep; Jersey City, NJ; (Y); 156/251; Chess Clb; Dance Clb; Exploring; Science Clb; SADD; Var L Bsktbl; Var L Ftbl; Var Mgr(s); Var Score Keeper; Comp Sci.

WILSON, EDWARD S; Eastside HS; Paterson, NJ; (Y); 41/655; Am Leg Boys St; Boy Scts; Nwsp Sprt Ed; Yrbk Stf; Rep Sr Cls; Rep Stu Cncl; Ftbl; Trk; NHS; Ntl Merit Schol; Cert Of Merit Home Ec 85; Engrg.

WILSON, ERIC; Saint James HS; Pennsvile, NJ; (Y); 14/75; Varsity Clb; Frsh Cls; Var L Bsbl; Capt Var Ftbl; Im Wt Lftg; VP Hon Roll; VP Prfct Atten Awd; Mathmtcs Awd 84-85; Span Awd 84-86; Physcl Ed Awd 85-86; Hotel/Motel Mgmt.

WILSON, JANET; Edgewood Regional SR HS; Atco, NJ; (Y); Church Yth Grp; Cmnty Wkr; Latin Clb; Pep Clb; Political Wkr; Teachers Aide; High Hon Roll; Hon Roll; Jr NHS; NHS; Comp Tech.

WILSON, JONATHAN D; Kings Christian HS; Somerdale, NJ; (Y); Church Yth Grp; Ski Clb; Varsity Clb; Pres Frsh Cls; Rep Soph Cls; Rep Stu Cncl; L Var Bsbl; Var Stat Bsktbl; L Var Mgr(s); Var L Socr; Liberty U; Bus Admin.

WILSON, KELLY; Burlington City HS; Burlington, NJ; (Y); Am Leg Aux Girls St; Office Aide; Rep Stu Cncl; JV Var Fld Hcky; Hon Roll; Kiwanis Awd; Med Tech.

WILSON, LISA; Warren County Vo-Tech; Belvidere, NJ; (S); Library Aide; VICA; AAA Natl Schl Traffic Safety Poster Pgm 84; Data Entry.

WILSON, LYNDA; North Brunswick Township HS; New Brunswick, NJ; (Y); 99/385; Spanish Clb; Yrbk Stf; Hon Roll; Jrnlsm.

WILSON, MICHELLE; Eastside HS; Paterson, NJ; (Y); DECA; Bus Adm.

WILSON, RACHAEL; Warren County Tech Schl; Belvidere, NJ; (S); High Hon Roll; Hon Roll; NHS; Stu Mnth.

WILSON, ROBIN; Columbia HS; Maplewood, NJ; (Y); Dance Clb; JA; Pep Clb; Spanish Clb; Yrbk Phtg; Off Frsh Cls; Cheerleading; Trk; Hon Roll; JC Awd; Hal Jckns Tlntd Teen NJ 82; 2nd Rnr Up USA Teen NJ 84; Coll Schlrshp Essex Cnty JR Miss Pgnt 86; Cornell U; Chem Engr.

WILSON, SHERI; Lower Cape Mary Regional HS; N Cape May, NJ; (Y); 83/175; Hosp Aide; Library Aide; Mrchg Band; Pom Pon; Atlantic CC Comptn Typng 86; Natl Lang Arts Olympiad Awd 85; Bus.

WILSON, TRACY; Holy Spirir HS; Absecon, NJ; (Y); 25/360; School Play; Yrbk Ed-Chief; Stat Var Bsktbl; Mgr(s); NHS; Glassboro ST Coll; Mktg.

WILSON JR, WILLIAM L; Wayne Hills HS; Wayne, NJ; (Y); 42/310; Computer Clb; FCA; Spanish Clb; Varsity Clb; Bsbl; Var Ftbl; JV Wrstlng; Hon Roll; NHS; Bus Adm.

WILSTED, JEFF; Wardlaw-Hartridge HS; Westfield, NJ; (Y); 12/53; Church Yth Grp; Key Clb; Ski Clb; Band; Chorus; Church Choir; School Musical; School Play; Stage Crew; Stat Socr.

WIMBERG, JOHN; Egg Harbor Township HS; Pleasantville, NJ; (S); 13/262; French Clb; Office Aide; JV Bsktbl; Var Socr; Hon Roll; NHS; Ntl Ldrshp Merit Awd 85-86; Ntl Sci Merit Awd 85-86; Acctng.

WIMBUSH, SHONTAE; Abraham Clark HS; Roselle, NJ; (Y); Church Yth Grp; Office Aide; Service Clb; Chorus; School Musical; Rep Stu Cncl; Gibbs Sch Of Bus; Bus Admin.

WIMMER, ANGELA; Westfield HS; Westfield, NJ; (Y); 4/498; Am Leg Aux Girls St; Girl Scts; Spanish Clb; Chorus; Var Crs Cntry; Var Scrkpr Trk; Cit Awd; NHS; Ntl Merit Ltr; St Schlr; Kiwahis Schlrshp 86; Grl Scts Slvr Awd 83; Cand For Army ROTC 86; Notre Dame; Med.

WIMMER, STEPHANIE; Columbia HS; S Orange, NJ; (Y); Radio Clb; Orch; Gov Hon Prg Awd; Seton Hall U; Communications.

WINANS, LORI; Morris Knolls HS; Denville, NJ; (Y); 30/398; Church Yth Grp; Drama Clb; NFL; Speech Tm; School Musical; School Play; Stage Crew; High Hon Roll; NHS; Summa Awd 84; Educ.

WINEGARDNER, WILLIAM; Gloucester City JR SR HS; Gloucester, NJ; (Y); #4 In Class; Am Leg Boys St; Chorus; Concert Band; Jazz Band; Mrchg Band; School Musical; Nwsp Rptr; Var Socr; Hon Roll; NHS; Actor.

WINGFIELD, CHRISTINE; Benedictine Acad; Orange, NJ; (Y); Art Clb; JCL; Latin Clb; Library Aide; Spanish Clb; School Play; Ed Nwsp Stf; Ed Yrbk Stf; NHS; Seton Hall U; Pre-Med.

WINKELMANN, CATHRIN; Pt Pl Bch HS; Mantoloking, NJ; (Y); 6/100; Am Leg Aux Girls St; Nwsp Ed-Chief; Trs Stu Cncl; NHS; High Hon Roll; Voice Dem Awd; Trs Frsh Cls; Tennis; Chem Soc Awd 85; Pres Acad Actress Awd 86; Voice Democracy Spch Cont 1st Pl 85.

WINKLER, SUZANNE; Bridgewater Raritan HS; Bridgewater, NJ; (Y); Church Yth Grp; French Clb; Intnl Clb; Ski Clb; Band; Color Guard; Concert Band; Mrchg Band; Crs Cntry; Powder Puff Ftbl; Acctng.

WINSICK, JODY; Secaucus HS; Secaucus, NJ; (S); 26/160; Band; Chorus; Concert Band; Mrchg Band; Hon Roll; Bus Admin.

WINT, ANTHONY A; Teaneck HS; Teaneck, NJ; (Y); 67/420; Aud/Vis; Church Yth Grp; Computer Clb; Hon Roll; NHS; Prfct Atten Awd; Natl Merit Commended Stu 85; Comp Sci.

WINTER, CATHERINE; Summit HS; Summit, NJ; (Y); 28/279; Yrbk Stf; Sec Frsh Cls; VP Soph Cls; Capt Cheerleading; Var JV Fld Hcky; Var JV Lcrss; Im Powder Puff Ftbl; Capt Var Swmmng; Hon Roll; NHS; Maxima Cum Laude Ntl Latin Ex 84; 3rd Tm All Cty Field Hockey 85; Most Imprvd 86.

WINTERS, DOUG; Monsignor Donovan HS; Jackson, NJ; (Y); 100/243; SADD; Rep Jr Cls; Rep Stu Cncl; Var L Bsktbl; Var L Ftbl; Wt Lftg; Hon Roll; JV Trk; NROTC Schlrshp Fnlst 86; Naval Acad; Engrng.

WINTERS, LARA; Bishop Ahr St Thomas HS; E Brunswick, NJ; (Y); Band; Concert Band; Jazz Band; Mrchg Band; Pep Band; School Musical; Symp Band; Hon Roll; Outstndng Ldrshp Music Awd 85; Sci.

WINTERS, ROBIN E; Livingston HS; Livingston, NJ; (Y); 1/498; Hosp Aide; Chrmn Key Clb; Model UN; Quiz Bowl; Nwsp Ed-Chief; Ed Yrbk Rptr; Rep Stu Cncl; VP French Hon Soc; High Hon Roll; Jr NHS; Essay Contst; Mock Trial 1st Pl; Merit Awd For Service-Candystriping; Pol Sci.

WINTERSTELLA, JUDY; Manasquan HS; Manasquan, NJ; (Y); 17/227; French Clb; Math Tm; Color Guard; Yrbk Phtg; Stu Cncl; JV Stat Bsbl; Twrlr; High Hon Roll; NHS; Brd Of Ed Awd 84-85; Math.

WISE, LORETTA; Cinnaminson HS; Cinna, NJ; (Y); Church Yth Grp; Off Soph Cls; Off Jr Cls; JV Fld Hcky; JV Lcrss; Hon Roll; Psych.

WISER, MARK; Wayne Valley HS; Wayne, NJ; (Y); 20/320; FBLA; Capt Ftbl; Capt Trk; Im Vllybl; Im Wt Lftg; Var Wrstlng; NHS; USAFA Schlrshp 86-90; USAF Acad; Aerontcl Engr.

WISHART, KIMBERLY; Buena Regional HS; Milmay, NJ; (Y); 27/160; Church Yth Grp; Drama Clb; 4-H; Political Wkr; Chorus; School Musical; Crs Cntry; 4-H Awd; Gov Hon Prg Awd; Hon Roll; NJ Schl Of The Arts 84-86; All South Jersey Chorus 82-86; Duke U; Comm.

WISK, KEVIN; Overbrook SR HS; Lindenwold, NJ; (Y); 9/270; DECA; Nwsp Rptr; Var Capt Tennis; NHS; MVP Tennis 85-86; Alumni Schlrshp Rutgers U 86; Garden ST Distngushd Schlrshp Awd 86; Rutgers U; Bus.

WITAS, BARBARA; Clifton HS; Clifton, NJ; (Y); 187/637; Band; Yrbk Stf; Spanish NHS; Rutgers U; Jrnlsm.

WITHAM, GRETCHEN; Hamilton High East HS; Mercerville, NJ; (Y); Band; Concert Band; Mrchg Band; Var Capt Diving; Hon Roll; U ME Orono; Bus Adm.

WITHAM, MARIE GRACE; Neumann Prep; Prospect Park, NJ; (Y); 2/83; Hosp Aide; Mrchg Band; Rptr Nwsp Stf; VP Trk; French Hon Soc; High Hon Roll; NHS; Spanish NHS; VFW Awd; Voice Dem Awd; Amer Lg Schl Awd 86; Dr Angelo A Guariglia Scholar 86; MASS-APCA Scholar 86; Gdn ST Dstnshd Schlr 86; Muhlenberg Coll; Bio.

WITHERS, DONNA; Williamstown HS; Williamstown, NJ; (Y); 6/250; Ed Nwsp Rptr; Hon Roll; Prsdntl Acdmc Ftnss Awd 86; Outstndg Grmn I & II Stu 82-84; Glassboro ST Coll; Law.

WITHKA, TOM; Bishop George Ahr HS; Milltown, NJ; (Y); Church Yth Grp; Var Ftbl; Hon Roll; All-St Ftbl 1st Tm 85; All-Amer 85; Pharm.

WITTEN, ALLAN; Lakewood HS; Lakewood, NJ; (Y); 97/297; German Clb; Key Clb; Rep Frsh Cls; Rep Soph Cls; Trs Jr Cls; Var L Ftbl; Var Wt Lftg; Var L Wrstlng; Pres Phy Ftnss Awd 84-85; U Of MD C P; Crmnl Jstc.

WITTLINGER, LINDA; Hopewell Valley Central HS; Pennington, NJ; (Y); 31/209; AFS; Sec Latin Clb; Chorus; School Musical; School Play; Yrbk Stf; Stu Cncl; Mgr Fld Hcky; Var JV Socr; NHS; Babson Coll; Mngmnt.

WITZE, PAMELA; Bernards HS; Bernardsville, NJ; (Y); 9/186; Q&S; Mrchg Band; Orch; School Musical; NHS; Cmnty Wkr; French Clb; Intnl Clb; Latin Clb; Band; Natl Mrt Fnlst 86; Yrbk SR Edtr 86; Nspr Lyot Ed 86; Stanford U; Eng.

WLAZLOWSKI, JUDITH; Notre Dame HS; Englishtown, NJ; (Y); 43/367; Band; Chorus; Church Choir; Drill Tm; Mrchg Band; School Musical; School Play; Pom Pon; High Hon Roll; Hon Roll; Bus.

WNOROSKI, THEODORE; Lenape Valley Reg HS; Netcong, NJ; (Y); Art Clb; Pep Clb; Red Cross Aide; Ski Clb; Bowling; Ftbl; Trk; Wt Lftg; Cnty Coll Of Morris; Drftng Eng.

WO, HONG-FU; Lakewood HS; Lakewood, NJ; (Y); 18/297; Am Leg Boys St; Capt Chess Clb; JCL; Trs Latin Clb; Hon Roll; NHS; Im Bsbl; Comp Sci.

WODZIAK, JOHN R; Clifton HS; Clifton, NJ; (Y); 140/650; Am Leg Boys St; Church Yth Grp; Computer Clb; Math Tm; Pres Ski Clb; Concert Band; Mrchg Band; Var L Golf; Jr NHS; Spanish NHS; Talntd Giftd Pgm; Engr.

WOELFLE, CHRIS; Monsignor Donovan HS; Jackson, NJ; (Y); 96/218; Boy Scts; Exploring; German Clb; Ski Clb; Yrbk Stf; Trk; Seton Hall U; Pre-Law.

WOHL, DEBRA; Bridgewater High School West; Bridgewater, NJ; (Y); 8/285; French Clb; Science Clb; Ski Clb; Pres Temple Yth Grp; Concert Band; Mrchg Band; Frsh Cls; Soph Cls; Hon Roll; Trs NHS; Pres Acdmc Fit Awd 86; Hnry Fclty Schlrshps Acdmc Excllnc 86; U Of MI; Sci.

WOHLAND, SUSAN; Indian Hills HS; Oakland, NJ; (Y); 64/279; Cmnty Wkr; Dance Clb; Concert Band; Hon Roll.

WOHR, PAMELA; St Peters HS; New Brunswick, NJ; (Y); 6/111; Lit Mag; JV Cheerleading; High Hon Roll; Hon Roll; Engrg.

WOJCIECHOWICZ, KELLY; Howell HS; Howell, NJ; (S); 18/324; Rep Band; Drm Mjr(t); Jazz Band; Mrchg Band; Orch; Symp Band; Rep Jr Cls; JV Bsktbl; Var Sftbl; Church Yth Grp; Rookie Of Yr-Mrchng Band 83-84; Music.

WOJIE, SCOTT; Oratory Catholic Prep Schl; Scotch Plains, NJ; (S); 3/45; Computer Clb; Math Tm; Ski Clb; Varsity Clb; Nwsp Rptr; VP Soph Cls; VP Jr Cls; Rep Stu Cncl; Var Bsktbl; Var Socr; Harvard; Bus.

WOJNAR, MELISSA; Hunterdon Central HS; Flemington, NJ; (Y); 177/548; Art Clb; Rptr 4-H; SADD; Fld Hcky; 4-H Awd; Hon Roll; Auburn; Marine Bio.

WOLANSKI, DEBORAH; Rancocas Valley Regional HS; Mount Holly, NJ; (Y); French Clb; Spanish Clb; Varsity Clb; Nwsp Phtg; Yrbk Phtg; Var Stat Mgr(s); JV Var Tennis; Hon Roll; Stu Of Dstnctn 84; Coaches Chocie Awd In Tennis 85; Fash Inst Tech; Phtgrphr.

WOLCOTT, JANET; Central Regional HS; Bayville, NJ; (Y); Drama Clb; Library Aide; Chorus; School Musical; School Play; Stage Crew; Yrbk Stf; High Hon Roll; Peer Counslng SHOP; Psych.

WOLF, BARRY F; Pascack Hills HS; Woodcliff, NJ; (Y); Am Leg Boys St; Camera Clb; Debate Tm; Band; Trk; Hon Roll; Ntl Merit Ltr; Awds For Achvmnt In Bio 85/Chem 86; Smfnlst AAAS Sci Photgrphy Contst 86.

WOLF, DEBORAH; Bridgewater Rantan East HS; Bridgewater, NJ; (Y); AFS; French Clb; Intnl Clb; Ski Clb; Temple Yth Grp; Var Bowling; Var Trk; NHS; U Of WI.

WOLF III, ROBERT D; Christian Brothers Acad; Interlaken, NJ; (Y); Cmnty Wkr; Political Wkr; Spanish Clb; Bsbl; Bsktbl; Im Socr; Hnrs Awd 85; Liberal Arts.

WOLFBERG, MARK; Montville Township HS; Towaco, NJ; (Y); 64/263; FBLA; Key Clb; Ski Clb; Spanish Clb; Rep Frsh Cls; Rep Soph Cls; Rep Jr Cls; JV Var Tennis; JV Wrstlng; High Hon Roll; NJ ST Compitor 5th Bus & Math 84; NJ ST Competor 3rd Bus Engl 85; Awds Recgntn NJ FBLA 84-86; Bus Adm.

WOLFE IV, EDWARD I; Whippany Park HS; Whippany, NJ; (Y); 3/200; Am Leg Boys St; Church Yth Grp; Exploring; JA; Letterman Clb; Science Clb; JV Var Ftbl; Var L Golf; Var L Tennis; High Hon Roll; Sci.

WOLFE, STEVE; Phillipsburg HS; Alpha, NJ; (Y); 84/340; Var Ftbl; Var Wt Lftg; Var Wrstlng; Prfct Atten 83-84; Cmptr.

WOLFRAM, JOHN; Paul VI HS; Westmont, NJ; (S); 2/480; Math Clb; Math Tm; Ed Lit Mag; Capt Crs Cntry; Var L Trk; High Hon Roll; NHS; Ntl Merit Ltr; Engrng.

WOLFROM, STACY; Gloucester City JR SR HS; Gloucester, NJ; (Y); 3/161; Church Yth Grp; Math Clb; Chorus; School Musical; Nwsp Rptr; Var Capt Bowling; Lcrss; Cit Awd; DAR Awd; NHS; Helen Ameisan Scholar 86; Rotary Scholar 86; PTA Scholar 86; Kean Coll NJ; Phys Thrpy.

WOLFSEN, JULIE; St John Vianney HS; Keyport, NJ; (Y); Church Yth Grp; Drama Clb; Red Cross Aide; Chorus; Church Choir; School Musical; Swing Chorus; JV Powder Puff Ftbl; Var Trk; Hon Roll; Psychtrst.

WOLLMAN, GWEN; Phillipsburg HS; Bloomsbury, NJ; (Y); Drama Clb; FBLA; Thesps; Chorus; School Play; Stage Crew; Vllybl; 2nd Pl Acctg FBLA Rgnl Amptn 85; Chrstn Clwn 84; JR Rescue Sqd 84-85.

WOLLOCK, AMY; Wayne Hills HS; Wayne, NJ; (Y); 90/303; GAA; Math Clb; Spanish Clb; Temple Yth Grp; Yrbk Stf; Hon Roll; Var Stat Bsbl; Var Mgr(s); Var Stat Vllybl; 4 Yrs Vrsty Catp Fncng Tm; New York U; Bus Admn.

WOLMAN, KEITH; Matawan HS; Matawan, NJ; (S); 33/325; Debate Tm; Im Bsbl; Var Socr; Im Sftbl; Var Tennis; High Hon Roll; NHS; Soccer Ref; Mth Hon Soc.

WOLSKI, BRUCE; Sayreville War Memorial HS; Sayreville, NJ; (Y); Church Yth Grp; English Clb; Spanish Clb; Varsity Clb; Yrbk Stf; Rep Sr Cls; Crs Cntry; Capt Trk; Cit Awd; Hon Roll; Sayreville Trk Clb 86; Bd Of Ed Plq 86; Bd Of Ed Plqs Outstndng Wntr Trk, Best Male Athlt Trk 86; Trenton ST Clg; Advtsg Dsgn.

WOLSTROMER, ELLEN; River Dell Regional HS; River Edge, NJ; (Y); 14/214; Church Yth Grp; Exploring; Chorus; Var L Sftbl; Stat Vllybl; High Hon Roll; Hon Roll; NHS; Rutgers Coll Engrng; Mech Engr.

WOMACK, ANITA; Eastside HS; Paterson, NJ; (S); 4/560; Computer Clb; Dance Clb; Drama Clb; Chorus; School Play; Yrbk Stf; Sec Sr Cls; Tennis; Trk; Pres NHS; Frances R North Outstndng Sr Awd 86; Anonymous Schlrshp Awd 86; Socl Studies Awd 86; Hampton U; Bio.

WONG, BETTY; Cherry Hill HS West; Cherry Hill, NJ; (Y); PAVAS; Chorus; Color Guard; Concert Band; Drm & Bgl; Mrchg Band; School Musical; School Play; Stage Crew; Hon Roll; Outstndng Cntrbtn & Dedctn Mrchg Band 86; Hm & Schl Awd Theatr & Music 86; Rutgers U; Bilngl Corp Lwyr.

WONG, WING KAM; Academic HS; Jersey City, NJ; (S); French Clb; Math Clb; NHS; Music Awd Vocal; Rutgers Coll; Bus.

WONH, RICHARD; Paramus HS; Paramus, NJ; (Y); Chorus; Var Jr Cls; Var Sr Cls; Var Socr; Trk.

WOO, DANNY; Hillsborough HS; Bellemead, NJ; (Y); 1/300; Church Yth Grp; Math Tm; Science Clb; Ski Clb; Orch; Ftbl; Trk; NHS; Tp 10% NJ ST Sci Chmstry Exam 85; Engr.

WOOD, JEFFREY; South Henterdon Regional HS; Lambertville, NJ; (Y); 5/80; Church Yth Grp; FBLA; Key Clb; Rep Stu Cncl; Var L Bsbl; Var L Ftbl; Hon Roll; NHS; Physics.

WOOD II, JOHN W; Edgewood Reg SR HS; Berlin, NJ; (Y); 4/381; VP NHS; Am Leg Boys St; Exploring; Ski Clb; Varsity Clb; Lit Mag; Socr; Trk; High Hon Roll; Jr NHS; Phila Coll Of Phrmcy & Sci Pres Schlrshp 86-90; Tgle Fndntn Schlrshp 86; Hm & Schl Assoc Awd 86; Phila Coll Of Phrmcy; Txclgst.

WOOD, KRISTEN E; Hopewell Valley Central HS; Pennington, NJ; (Y); 1/199; Church Yth Grp; Math Tm; Science Clb; Service Clb; Yrbk Stf; VP Socr; High Hon Roll; NHS; Ntl Merit SF; Opt Clb Awd; Biochem.

WOOD, MELISSA; Chatham HS; Chatham, NJ; (Y); Church Yth Grp; Latin Clb; Spanish Clb; Yrbk Stf; Var L Bsktbl; JV Sftbl; High Hon Roll; Drama Clb; NHS; Ntl Merit Ltr; Schl Bell Awd Chem Achvt 86; Schl Bell Awd Lang Achvt 85; Cert Excllnce Advncd Lat 86.

WOOD, MICHELLE; Holy Cross HS; Willingboro, NJ; (Y); 63/360; Chess Clb; Color Guard; Drill Tm; Stage Crew; Yrbk Stf; Im Vllybl; Hon Roll.

WOOD, PAMELA; Manville HS; Manville, NJ; (Y); Church Yth Grp; Girl Scts; Hosp Aide; Office Aide; SADD; JV Var Cheerleading; JV Sftbl; NRSNG.

WOOD, ROBYN; Linden HS; Linden, NJ; (Y); Church Yth Grp; FBLA; German Clb; Hosp Aide; Acpl Chr; Cheerleading; Gym; 2nd Hnrs Bus Math NC Regnl Comptve Events 85; CPA.

WOOD, SCOTT; Deptford Township HS; Deptford, NJ; (Y); 29/275; Boy Scts; Exploring; JV Bowling; Var Socr; Jr NHS; NHS; Elec Engrng.

WOOD, SHAWN; Bridgewater Rariton HS; Pluckemin, NJ; (Y); Ski Clb; Varsity Clb; Yrbk Stf; Coach Actv; Ftbl; Wt Lftg; Ind Eng.

WOOD, TONY; Hackettstown HS; Hackettstown, NJ; (Y); 25/247; Var Capt Socr; Hon Roll; NHS; 2nd Tm DRC Soccr; 2nd Yr Var; Engrg.

WOODLAND, PAULETTE; Lakewood HS; Lakewood, NJ; (Y); 47/294; Am Leg Aux Girls St; English Clb; Hosp Aide; JCL; Key Clb; Mrchg Band; Rep Jr Cls; Stat Sftbl; Hon Roll; Church Yth Grp; NAACP Yth Grp Treas 85-87; Howard U; Med.

WOODMAN, JAMES; Hamilton High East; Hamilton Sq, NJ; (Y); 21/315; Pres Church Yth Grp; Pres Exploring; Math Tm; Red Cross Aide; Hon Roll; NHS; Rutgers Coll; Math.

WOODRING, COREY; Wallington HS; Cranford, NJ; (Y); FCA; Leo Clb; SADD; Varsity Clb; Stage Crew; Rep Stu Cncl; Im Coach Actv; Var L Ftbl; Var L Trk; JV Var Wrstlng; Mgmt.

WOODRUFF, HILLARY; Woodstown HS; Elmer, NJ; (Y); 12/170; Church Yth Grp; French Clb; PAVAS; Band; Chorus; Concert Band; Mrchg Band; Orch; Nwsp Stf; VP Frsh Cls; Gov Schl Arts 85; Dickinson; Mus.

WOODWORTH, STEPHEN; Northern Valey Regional HS; Old Tappan, NJ; (Y); 1/285; Boy Scts; Math Tm; Science Clb; Ski Clb; Band; Trk; Bausch & Lomb Sci Awd; Gov Hon Prg Awd; NHS; Ntl Merit Ltr; Hghst Scr In ST Blgy I 84; 7th Hghst Scr Blgy II 86; 11th Hghst Scr Blgy ST Sci Lge 86; Sci.

WOODY, LISA; Camden HS; Camden, NJ; (S); FHA; Church Choir; Capt JV Bsktbl; Pre-Law.

WOOLF, KATHLEEN; Cinnaminson HS; Cinna, NJ; (Y); VP Bowling; Capt JV Socr; JV Sccr MVP 84; High Avg Bwlng 84; Mst Imprvd Bwlr 85; Westchester; Tchr.

WOOLLUMS, MICHELLE; Kearny HS; Kearny, NJ; (Y); 11/375; German Clb; Latin Clb; Science Clb; JV Bsktbl; High Hon Roll; Hon Roll; NHS; Stn Hll U Schlrshp 86; Ntl Hnr Scty Schlrshp 86; Washington Schl PTA Awd 86; Seton Hall U; Eng.

WOOLSTON, TINA MARIE; Burl Co Vo-Tech; Edgewater Pk, NJ; (Y); 56/177; Library Aide; Teachers Aide; Variety Show; VP Jr Cls; Mgr Bsktbl; Cosmetologist.

WOOTTEN, MICHELE; Lenape Valley Regional HS; Stanhope, NJ; (Y); 26/256; Key Clb; Yrbk Stf; Powder Puff Ftbl; Hon Roll; NHS.

WORKMAN, DANIELLE; Vineland HS; Vineland, NJ; (Y); Orch; Gregg Shrthnd Awd 85-86; Sec.

WORMACK, COREY A; S Plainfield HS; South Plainfield, NJ; (Y); 8/194; Am Leg Boys St; CAP; Math Tm; Band; Var Capt Trk; High Hon Roll; NHS; Spanish NHS; Schlr Athlt 85-86; U S Air Frc Acad; Pilot.

WORMANN, JACQUELINE; Lenape Valley Regional HS; Stanhope, NJ; (Y); Am Leg Aux Girls St; Hosp Aide; Intnl Clb; Key Clb; Yrbk Sprt Ed; Trs Jr Cls; Trs Sr Cls; JV Var Fld Hcky; Powder Puff Ftbl; Sftbl; Myrs Awd Outstndng Ctznshp 85; Pffrr Agncy Awd Chrctr Ctznshp 86; Cls Awd Mst Cls Soc Schl 86; Trntn ST Coll; Erlychld Ed.

WOROBEL, STEVE; Morris Catholic HS; Denville, NJ; (Y); 23/147; French Clb; Math Clb; Natl Beta Clb; Ski Clb; JV Bsbl; JV Var Socr; Hon Roll; Engrg.

WORONIECKA, JULITA; Wm L Dickinson HS; Jersey City, NJ; (Y); Computer Clb; Exploring; Math Clb; Math Tm; Scholastic Bowl; Hon Roll; NHS; Jersey City Rotary Club Schlrshp 86; Awd Of Merit Achvt ST Sci Day 86; Stevens Inst; Engnrng.

WORTH, KEVIN; Scotch Plains-Fanwood HS; Scotch Plains, NJ; (S); Key Clb; Quiz Bowl; Temple Yth Grp; JV Bsktbl; JV Socr; JV Tennis; Cit Awd; Gov Hon Prg Awd; High Hon Roll; Hon Roll; Merit Awd Wnr Apple Comp Clbs Intl 85; Engrng.

WORTHINGTON JR, GARY; Overbrook Regional HS; W Berlin, NJ; (Y); Art Clb; Varsity Clb; Var Capt Bsbl; Var Capt Ftbl; Var Capt Wrstlng; Cit Awd; Prfct Atten Awd; All Conf Ftbl 85; 2nd Tm All S Jersey Ftbl 85; All Grp III NJ Ftbl 85; Wrstlg All Conf 84 & 85; Prof Spts.

WORTHINGTON, MARJORIE G; Hopewell Valley Central HS; Pennington, NJ; (Y); 32/208; AFS; German Clb; School Play; Yrbk Stf; Var Fld Hcky; Var Lcrss; Hon Roll; Ntl Merit SF; Pres Schlr; NHS.

WORTHY, BRIDGET; Lakewood HS; Lakewood, NJ; (Y); DECA; JCL; Latin Clb; Pep Clb; Varsity Clb; Nwsp Rptr; Rep Frsh Cls; Rep Soph Cls; Rep Jr Cls; Trk; 1st Prz Wnnr Blck Hstry Mnth Essy Cntst 86; Pres Afro Amrcn Soc 86; Engnrng.

WOZNEY, KIM; Waldwick HS; Waldwick, NJ; (Y); Art Clb; Spanish Clb; Cheerleading; Powder Puff Ftbl; Socr; High Hon Roll; Hon Roll; Syracuse; Graphic Desgnr.

WOZNICKI, TRICIA; Johnson Regional HS; Clark, NJ; (S); Church Yth Grp; Cmnty Wkr; Dance Clb; GAA; Pep Clb; Ski Clb; Varsity Clb; Band; Concert Band; Jazz Band; Hmcmng Queen 85; Mst Vlbl Athlete Gymnstc Team 83-85; Ntl Phy Ed Awd Wnnr 86; Pharm.

WOZUNK, BOBBIE NADINE; A P Schalick HS; Bridgeton, NJ; (Y); Art Clb; Church Yth Grp; DECA; Var L Cheerleading; JV Fld Hcky; Var JV Sftbl; Hon Roll; NJ Bus Ed Assn Typg Awd 86; Glassboro ST Coll; Wrd Proc.

WRANICH, ROBERT; Bridgeton HS; Bridgeton, NJ; (Y); Drama Clb; SADD; School Play; Nwsp Bus Mgr; Nwsp Stf; Yrbk Stf; Hon Roll; Sci Awd Lab Tech; HOSA 2 Yrs; Ed.

WRIGHT, ANTHONY; West Side HS; Newark, NJ; (Y); Church Yth Grp; Drama Clb; Band; Chorus; Church Choir; Concert Band; Mrchg Band; Off Soph Cls; Crs Cntry; Hon Roll; Rutgers; Crpt Law.

WRIGHT, BRIAN; Chatham Township HS; Chatham, NJ; (Y); Pres AFS; Boy Scts; Model UN; Band; Concert Band; Jazz Band; Pep Band; Hon Roll; NHS; Asn Stu.

WRIGHT, CHRISTINA MOON; James Caldwell HS; Caldwell, NJ; (Y); Art Clb; Church Yth Grp; PAVAS; Chorus; Church Choir; Orch; Yrbk Stf; Lit Mag; Gov Hon Prg Awd; NJ Govrnr Schlr Arts Ed 86; NJ Schl Arts 86; NFAA Arts Awd 86; MD Inst; Fine Artst.

WRIGHT, DANIEL; Westfield HS; Westfield, NJ; (Y); 35/497; Boy Scts; Math Tm; Temple Yth Grp; Band; Orch; Var Crs Cntry; Var Trk; NHS; St Schlr; Northwestern U.

WRIGHT, DAVID P; Montgomery HS; Belle Mead, NJ; (Y); 17/110; Am Leg Boys St; Church Yth Grp; Cmnty Wkr; VP Drama Clb; School Musical; School Play; Nwsp Stf; VP Stu Cncl; Crs Cntry; Trk; Bst Character Actor 85-86; Bst Supportng Actor 85-86; Comp Sci.

WRIGHT, DONNA; Lincoln HS; Jersey City, NJ; (S); 3/232; Am Leg Aux Girls St; Hst FBLA; Nwsp Sprt Ed; Lit Mag; VP Jr Cls; Capt Cheerleading; Dnfth Awd; VP NHS; Ntl Merit SF; Kean Coll; Acctg.

WRIGHT, JAMES; Linden HS; Linden, NJ; (Y); French Clb; Key Clb; ROTC; Rep Sr Cls; Rep Stu Cncl; High Hon Roll; Hon Roll; NHS; Howard U; MD.

WRIGHT, LISA A; Mainland Regional HS; Somers Point, NJ; (Y); 7/300; Science Clb; Nwsp Rptr; Hst Yrbk Stf; Trs Stu Cncl; Trk; High Hon Roll; Trs NHS; Hghst Acad Avg Soc Sci 86; Eva Anderson Scholar 86; Bud Kern Mem Scholar 86; VA Polytech Inst; Chem Engrng.

WRIGHT, LISA R; Northern Burlington Co Reg HS; Wrightstown, NJ; (Y); 111/211; VP Exploring; Hosp Aide; Red Cross Aide; Comp Sci Excel Awd 86; Burlington Cnty Coll; Zlgy.

WRIGHT, NEIL; Fairlawn HS; Fair Lawn, NJ; (Y); 42/330; Civic Clb; Cmnty Wkr; ROTC; Varsity Clb; Stu Cncl; Var L Ftbl; Var Capt Lcrss; Var Capt Wrstlng; Hon Roll; Frshmn, Soph Yr Ridgewood News Wrstlng 83-84; NJ St Wrstlng Tourn 85; U S Military Acad; Military Sci.

WRIGHT, R JEFFREY; Glen Rock JR-SR HS; Glen Rock, NJ; (Y); 6/155; Church Yth Grp; Debate Tm; Math Tm; Science Clb; Spanish Clb; Bsktbl; Gov Hon Prg Awd; High Hon Roll; Jr NHS; NHS; Renssalear Mth/Sci Awd 86; U VA; Bus.

WRIGHT, RAYMOND; Bayonne HS; Bayonne, NJ; (Y); Lit Mag; Im Bsktbl; Im Crs Cntry; JV Var Ftbl; Im Gym; Im Socr; Im Sftbl; Im Tennis; Im Vllybl; Var Wt Lftg; Physcl Educ Awd 83; Bsktbll Cert Awd 83; Chr Cert Awd 83; Compu Sci.

WRIGHT, SUSAN; Delran HS; Delran, NJ; (Y); 34/207; Spanish Clb; SADD; Varsity Clb; Band; Yrbk Stf; Rep Sr Cls; Var Fld Hcky; Var Lcrss; JV Sftbl; Var Swmmng; Chem.

WRIGHT, TYRONE; Bridgeton SR HS; Bridgeton, NJ; (Y); Art Clb; Boy Scts; Church Yth Grp; 4-H; Band; Concert Band; Jazz Band; Mrchg Band; Pep Band; School Musical; MTA; Truckng Co.

WRIGHT, VICTORIA; John F Kennedy HS; Willingboro, NJ; (Y); Intnl Clb; Keywanettes; Chorus; Church Choir; Drm Mjr(t); Orch; Hon Roll; UCLA; Psych.

WU, GEORGE; Freehold Township HS; Freehold, NJ; (Y); Computer Clb; French Clb; Math Tm; Bowling; High Hon Roll; NHS; Ntl Merit Ltr; Elect Engr.

WU, JEANNIE; Monmouth Regional HS; Eatontown, NJ; (Y); 19/225; Pres French Clb; German Clb; Latin Clb; Math Clb; Trs Spanish Clb; Yrbk Ed-Chief; Stu Cncl; Sftbl; Var Tennis; High Hon Roll; Pres Acdmc Ftns Awds Pgm, Awd Exclnce Lang Study, Phys Educ Awd 86; Rutgers Coll; Bus.

WU, JENNIFER; Cherry Hill Hgh Schl West; Cherry Hill, NJ; (Y); JCL; PAVAS; Jazz Band; Mrchg Band; Yrbk Stf; Off Jr Cls; Off Sr Cls; Var Lcrss; NHS; Bsktbl; Pres Bio Clb 86-87.

WULFF, LYNN; High School South; Beachwood, NJ; (Y); 3/360; Math Clb; Science Clb; SADD; Orch; School Musical; Var Gym; Var Swmmng; High Hon Roll; NHS; Cncrt Mstrs Grdn ST Yth Orchstra 86 & 87; U Of Virginia; Mtlrgcl Engr.

WUNDER, TRACY; Hunterdon Central HS; Flemington, NJ; (Y); 104/554; FCA; SADD; Cheerleading; Diving; Pom Pon; Swmmng; Hon Roll; NHS; Natl H S Chrldg Comp 84 & 85; Interact Clb Treas 86; Miami U; Psych.

WURM, LAURIE; The Friends Schl; Malaga, NJ; (Y); PAVAS; Teachers Aide; Yrbk Stf; Lit Mag; Hon Roll; NJ Poet Awd ST Teen Art Fstvl Summer Art Inst 84; Govnrs Awd ST Teen Arts Summer Art Inst 86; Creat Wrtg.

WURST, EILEEN; Clifton HS; Clifton, NJ; (Y); 122/637; Church Yth Grp; Hosp Aide; Spanish Clb; Chorus; Church Choir; Cit Awd; High Hon Roll; Hon Roll; NHS; Spanish NHS; Bio.

WURZBURGER, WALTER; Roselle Catholic HS; Roselle, NJ; (Y); Drama Clb; Church Choir; School Musical; French Hon Soc; Hon Roll; Soc Actn Clb Coord 85-87; Cmmnctn.

WYCHE, TODD B; Rancocas Valley Regional HS; Mt Holly, NJ; (Y); 6/295; Am Leg Boys St; Science Clb; Ski Clb; Pres Stu Cncl; JV Socr; JV Swmmng; JV Tennis; High Hon Roll; NHS; Govnrs Sch NJ On Public Issues Smmr 86; Economics.

WYLOT, MIKE; Washington Township HS; Sewell, NJ; (Y); Church Yth Grp; JV Var Ftbl; JV Wrstlng; Acctng.

WYLUPEK, JENNIFER; Audubon HS; Audubon, NJ; (Y); Drama Clb; Exploring; Girl Scts; Band; Jazz Band; Mrchg Band; Stage Crew; Im Coach Actv; JV Im Sftbl; Rutgers North Jersey; Elem Ed.

WYMBS, BRIAN; Wood-Ridge HS; Wood-Ridge, NJ; (S); 7/85; VP Frsh Cls; VP Soph Cls; VP Jr Cls; Var Capt Ftbl; Var Wrstlng; High Hon Roll; NHS.

WYMBS, KEVIN; Middletown HS South; Red Bank, NJ; (Y); Church Yth Grp; Church Choir; Variety Show; Nwsp Rptr; Var Golf; Svc VP Church Yth Grp 84-85; Activities VP Church Yth Grp 85-86; Pres Church Yth Grp 86-87; Sci.

WYNNE, STEVE; Holy Spirit HS; Linwood, NJ; (Y); 21/386; Computer Clb; School Musical; School Play; Nwsp Rptr; Nwsp Stf; Hon Roll; NHS; Jr Vrsty Catholic Math Lge Wnnr 86; Aero Engr.

WYROUGH, KELLY E; Hamilton High West; Trenton, NJ; (Y); 72/350; GAA; Varsity Clb; Var Bsktbl; Stat Ftbl; Hon Roll; Rider Coll; Pol Sci.

XANTHACOS, ATHENA; Lakewood HS; Lakewood, NJ; (Y); 34/306; English Clb; French Clb; Key Clb; Office Aide; Mrchg Band; Lit Mag; Mgr(s); Vllybl; French Hon Soc; Miss NJ Natl Teen Ager Pageant 86; Rutgers U; Pre Law.

XHERAJ, HASTRIT; Lodi HS; Lodi, NJ; (Y); Key Clb; Math Clb; Math Tm; Band; Concert Band; Jazz Band; Mrchg Band; Frnk Slpo Schrlshp 86; Hofstra U; Finance.

YABLONSKI, JANET; Bridgewater-Raritan High Schl West; Bridgewater, NJ; (Y); Girl Scts; Ski Clb; Acpl Chr; Flag Corp; Yrbk Sprt Ed; Soph Cls; Var Trk; Hon Roll; NHS; Htl Mgmnt.

YABLONSKY, LEEDRA; Cranford HS; Cranford, NJ; (Y); 29/299; Chess Clb; Trs German Clb; VP Trs JA; Capt Flag Corp; School Play; NHS; Ntl Merit Ltr; Drama Clb; Math Clb; Science Clb; Garden :St Distngshd Schlr 85-86; Treas & Prsctng Attrny Law Clb 85-86; Mcgill U; Psychlgy.

YACCARINO, CHRYSSA; Ocean Township HS; Wayside, NJ; (Y); 132/314; Latin Clb; Ski Clb; Varsity Clb; Nwsp Stf; Stat Bsktbl; Crs Cntry; Gym; Var Sftbl; Mgr(s); Monmouth Coll; Bus Ed.

YACULLO, DENISE; Bloomfield SR HS; Bloomfld, NJ; (Y); 44/445; Key Clb; Chorus; Rep Soph Cls; Rep Jr Cls; Rep Stu Cncl; Var Cheerleading; Var Pom Pon; Hon Roll; NHS.

YAEDE, KELLY; Hamilton HS North; Trenton, NJ; (Y); 32/281; Am Leg Aux Girls St; FBLA; Hosp Aide; Chorus; School Play; Pres Jr Cls; Pres Sr Cls; Capt Cheerleading; Trk; High Hon Roll; Hmcmng Queen 85; Swthrt Couple 85; Prom Queen 86; Polt Sci.

YAGED, JONATHAN; Manalapan HS; Manalapan, NJ; (Y); 20/436; Exploring; Capt Crs Cntry; NHS; Merit Awd A Avg US Hist II 86; Presdnt Manalapan HS Radio Cntrl Clb 85-86; Law.

YAGOZINSKI, STEVEN; Pope John XXIII HS; Lk Hopatcong, NJ; (Y); Church Yth Grp; Varsity Clb; Band; Mrchg Band; Var VP Bowling; Hon Roll; Jr NHS.

YAGUEZ, OLGA; Voorhees HS; Hampton, NJ; (Y); 34/274; Am Leg Aux Girls St; GAA; Varsity Clb; Var Bsktbl; Var Capt Fld Hcky; JV Sftbl; Hon Roll; NHS; Prfct Atten Awd; Spanish NHS; Acad Achvt Awd 84-86; Dntl Hygn.

YAKER, REBECA; Teaneck HS; Teaneck, NJ; (Y); 32/420; French Clb; VP Spanish Clb; SADD; Stu Cncl; French Hon Soc; Hon Roll; NHS; Spanish NHS; Hebrew U Jerusalem; Law.

YALLOWITZ, LAURIE; Highstown HS; E Windosr, NJ; (Y); AFS; Hosp Aide; Service Clb; Spanish Clb; Rep Soph Cls; Stu Cncl; Var Trk; High Hon Roll; Hon Roll; NHS; Med.

YALONG, MARIA FIDES P; Bayonne HS; Bayonne, NJ; (Y); 26/362; Sec Church Yth Grp; Cmnty Wkr; Drama Clb; Key Clb; Library Aide; Math Tm; Office Aide; PAVAS; Science Clb; Spanish Clb; Math Awd 86; Cook Coll; Vet.

YAMAGUCHI, NAOKI; Northern Highlands HS; Allendale, NJ; (Y); 31/249; Cmnty Wkr; Computer Clb; Hosp Aide; Science Clb; Var L Socr; JV Tennis; Var L Trk; High Hon Roll; Hon Roll; NHS; CHIME 85; ST Biol Teest NJ Sci Day 85; Columbia Smmr Schl Engrng Pgm 85; Le High U; Engrng.

YAMASAKI, DARIN; Cumberland Regional HS; Bridgeton, NJ; (Y); 29/357; Pres Church Yth Grp; JCL; Latin Clb; Science Clb; Ski Clb; Yrbk Sprt Ed; Im Crs Cntry; Hon Roll; Jr NHS; Cum Laude Ntl Latin Ex 85; Phrmcy.

YAMBAO, EDELWINA; Dickinson HS; Jersey City, NJ; (Y); Debate Tm; Library Aide; Science Clb; Trk; Twrlr; Var Vllybl; Hon Roll; Trs NHS; Pres Citation Awd 86; Nrsng.

YAMIN, ELI B; Highland Park HS; Highland Park, NJ; (Y); 28/130; Political Wkr; Radio Clb; Acpl Chr; Band; VP Chorus; Concert Band; Jazz Band; School Musical; School Play; Stu Cncl; Gvrnrs Awd Arts & Educ 86; Jazz Pnst.

YANEGA, HOLLY; Union Catholic Regional HS; Elizabeth, NJ; (Y); 41/335; French Clb; Sec Trs Library Aide; Service Clb; SADD; Hon Roll; NHS; Pres Schlrshp Allentown Coll 86-87; U Of Scranton Schlrshp 86-87; U Of Scranton; Bus.

YANG, ARLENE; Livingston HS; Livingston, NJ; (Y); Key Clb; Band; Mrchg Band; Stage Crew; Yrbk Phtg; Var Capt Fld Hcky; Twrlr; High Hon Roll; Kiwanis Awd; Ntl Merit SF.

YANG, IRENE; E Brunswick HS; E Brunswick, NJ; (Y); Hosp Aide; Key Clb; Orch; Yrbk Phtg; Var Fld Hcky; French Hon Soc; NHS; Church Yth Grp; French Clb; Yrbk Stf; NJ All-State Orchestra 84-85; NJMTA Nrs Awd 83-86; Cntrl Jersey SR Regnl Orchestra 83-84; Duke U.

YANG, JEONGA; Matawan Regional HS; Cliffwood, NJ; (S); 4/273; Church Yth Grp; Library Aide; Math Tm; Nwsp Stf; Yrbk Stf; Stu Cncl; Hon Roll; NHS.

YANG, JING; Neptune SR HS; Neptune, NJ; (Y); 20/400; Church Yth Grp; French Clb; Office Aide; Tennis; High Hon Roll; Prfct Atten Awd; Omega Psi Phi Frtrnty-Schlrshp & Ctznshp Awd 83; Rutgers Coll; Bus.

YANG, NATALIE; Leonia HS; Edgewater, NJ; (Y); 63/150; Girl Scts; Jr NHS; Bus Adm.

YANG, SOPHIA SHENG HUI; Livingston HS; Livingston, NJ; (Y); Leo Clb; Math Clb; Capt Drill Tm; Mrchg Band; Orch; Stage Crew; Yrbk Ed-Chief; Yrbk Stf; Var Vllybl; Jr NHS; NY U; Econ.

YANKALUNAS, PAUL; Belvidere HS; Columbia, NJ; (S); 5/123; Am Leg Boys St; Varsity Clb; Trs Jr Cls; Trs Sr Cls; Stu Cncl; Var Wrstlng; French Hon Soc; Hon Roll; NHS; St Schlr; Cnrl U; Physcs.

YANOFSKY, LISA; Brurian HS; Staten Isl, NY; (Y); Cmnty Wkr; Office Aide; Chorus; School Musical; Stage Crew; Variety Show; Ed Yrbk Stf; Trs Frsh Cls; Trs Soph Cls; NEDT Awd; 2nd Pl Sci Fair-Psych 85; Law.

YANOWITZ, TRACEY; Asbury Park HS; Asbury Park, NJ; (Y); 14/196; Office Aide; Band; Yrbk Stf; JV Sftbl; Glassboro ST Coll.

YARD, ERIN; Hamilton H S West; Yardville, NJ; (Y); Key Clb; Yrbk Rptr; Im Ice Hcky; Var Capt Socr; Tennis; Im Vllybl; Old Dominion; Marine Engrng.

YARIS, MICHAEL; Florence Twp Memorial HS; Roebling, NJ; (Y); 14/93; Church Yth Grp; Drama Clb; Math Clb; Science Clb; Varsity Clb; Rep Stu Cncl; JV Bsbl; Var Ftbl; Hon Roll; Rutgers Coll Of Engineering.

YAROSH, ANTHONY J; Spotswood HS; Milltown, NJ; (S); 21/174; Am Leg Boys St; Model UN; Science Clb; JV Bsbl; Var L Bsktbl; Var L Crs Cntry; Hon Roll; NHS; Engrng.

YARUSI, STEPHANIE; Central Regional HS; Seaside Park, NJ; (Y); FHA; High Hon Roll; Peer Cnslng 85-86; Spcl Ed.

YARUSO, JOANNE; Bridgewater Ruritan West HS; Raritan, NJ; (Y); Am Leg Aux Girls St; Spanish Clb; JV Sftbl.

YASKULKA, TAMMI; Manalapan HS; Manalapan, NJ; (Y); 191/431; Cmnty Wkr; SADD; VP Temple Yth Grp; Chorus; Drill Tm; Stage Crew; Nwsp Rptr; Nwsp Stf; Rep Jr Cls; Rep Sr Cls; Chaptr Ded Navy 84-85; Chaptr Achvt NAVY 85-86; Bus.

YATCILLA, JUDY; Delran HS; Delran, NJ; (Y); 47/250; Am Leg Aux Girls St; Drama Clb; Chorus; Sec Frsh Cls; Rep Stu Cncl; Fld Hcky; Trk; Ski Clb; Cheerleading; Powder Puff Ftbl; Cls Sprt, Vrsty & Stu Cncl Awds 85-86; Bd Ed Rcgntn, Drama Clb Awds Arts Fest 85-86; All Star 85-86; Mngmnt.

YATES, MAGGIE; Rancocas Valley Regional HS; Mt Holly, NJ; (Y); Key Clb; Acpl Chr; Chorus; School Musical; Yrbk Stf; Lit Mag; Hon Roll; Jr NHS; All S Jersey ST Chr 86; William Paterson Coll; Bus Mgmt.

YATKO, STEVE; Pascack Hills HS; Montvale, NJ; (Y); Computer Clb; Band; Jazz Band; Mrchg Band; Var L Bsbl; JV L Ftbl; Hon Roll; Merit Awd Comp Sci 85; 1st Pl Am Comp Sci League 86; Comp Sci.

YAYAC, CINDY; Mohsignor Ddonovan HS; Jackson, NJ; (Y); Am Leg Aux Girls St; Church Yth Grp; Drama Clb; Thesps; School Play; NHS; Arch.

YAZDAN, DAVID; Saint Rose HS; Mansquan, NJ; (Y); 45/250; Latin Clb; Var L Bsktbl; Var L Crs Cntry; Var L Trk; Catholic U; Arch.

YEAGER, JENNY; Piscataway HS; Piscataway, NJ; (Y); 79/519; Key Clb; Jazz Band; Yrbk Stf; Lit Mag; Douglass Coll; Nrsng.

YEARICKS, VALERIE; Lower Cape May Regional HS; Villas, NJ; (Y); Band; Concert Band; Mrchg Band; Pep Band; School Musical; Fshn Merch.

YEARSLEY, ANNE; Hackettstown HS; Hackettstown, NJ; (Y); 14/212; Church Yth Grp; Cmnty Wkr; Key Clb; SADD; High Hon Roll; Hon Roll; NHS; Pres Schlr; SR Hghst Avg Frnch 86; Grdn ST Schlr 86; Rose Memrl Schlrshp Drew U 86; Drew U; Psych.

YEH, DAVID M Y; Tenafly HS; Tenafly, NJ; (Y); Sec Chess Clb; Computer Clb; Intnl Clb; Sec VP Math Clb; Math Tm; Sec Trs Stage Crew; Sec Lit Mag; High Hon Roll; Ntl Merit SF; St Schlr.

YEH, RUBINA; Dwight-Englewood Schl; Norwood, NJ; (Y); AFS; Art Clb; Hosp Aide; VP Intnl Clb; Sec Service Clb; Trk; U Of MI.

YEN, NORMAN; Livingston HS; Livingston, NJ; (Y); Chess Clb; VP Trs Computer Clb; Library Aide; Math Clb; Hon Roll; Comp Engnrng.

YERGEAU, LESLIE; Bishop George Ahr HS; Perth Amboy, NJ; (Y); Cmnty Wkr; Hosp Aide; Spanish Clb; Lit Mag; High Hon Roll; Hon Roll; Distinguished Awd 86; Excellence Schlrshp 86; Rutgers Coll; Pharmacist.

YERMAN, ARTHUR; Monsignor Donovan HS; Toms River, NJ; (Y); 24/240; Church Yth Grp; Math Tm; Ski Clb; JV Bsbl; Hon Roll; NHS; Cert Prtcptn Stu Govt Day; Mech Engrng.

YESENOSKY, MIKE; Passaic Valley Reg HS; West Patterson, NJ; (S); 33/303; Chorus; Concert Band; Mrchg Band; School Musical; High Hon Roll; Passaic Valley Hnr Soc 85; Berklee Coll Music; Music Rec.

YESUVIDA, JOHN; Linden HS; Linden, NJ; (S); 153/304; Band; Concert Band; Jazz Band; Mrchg Band; Orch; School Musical; School Play; JV Bowling; JP Sousa Awd; Stockton ST Coll; Cmptr Prgrmr.

YEZUITA, DENISE; Lakeland Regional HS; Haskell, NJ; (Y); Cmnty Wkr; Hosp Aide; SADD; Rep Frsh Cls; Rep Soph Cls; Rep Jr Cls; Rep Sr Cls; Rep Stu Cncl; Powder Puff Ftbl; Cit Awd; Girls Citznshp Awd 86; Nrs.

YI, CHU JULIE; Cliffside Park HS; Cliffside Park, NJ; (Y); 2/239; Intnl Clb; Math Tm; Orch; Gov Hon Prg Awd; High Hon Roll; Jr NHS; NHS; Pres Schlr; Sal; St Schlr; Merit Awds 1st & 2nd Stuart Hl Schlstc Cmpttn 85 & 86; Merit Cert Supvr Achvt NJ Math League 85 & 86; U Of PA; Law.

YI, HEIDI; Matawan Regional HS; Matawan, NJ; (Y); 50/322.

YIN, MARK T; Rumson-Fair Haven Reg HS; Rumson, NJ; (Y); 7/230; Am Leg Boys St; Math Clb; Var Bsbl; Im Wt Lftg; Hon Roll; Hnrb Mntn Natl Sci Olympd 83-84; Boy Scout Electrncs Pst 84-85; Yellow Blt Karate 85-86; Engrng.

YOBOOD, DENISE; Parsippany HS; Lake Hiawatha, NJ; (Y); Girl Scts; JV Var Bsktbl; Var L Socr; Var L Sftbl; NJ ST Chmpns In Sftbl Var 86; Bus Adm.

YOCKEL, TIM; Westfield SR HS; Westfield, NJ; (Y); 55/514; Boy Scts; French Clb; Chorus; School Musical; Var L Crs Cntry; Var L Trk; Hon Roll; NHS; MVP-SPRING Track 84; Med.

YOCUM, JEFFREY S; Moorestown HS; Moorestown, NJ; (Y); Am Leg Boys St; Church Yth Grp; Latin Clb; Sec Jr Cls; JV Var Bsbl; JV Var Bsktbl; Im Vllybl; High Hon Roll; Ntl Merit Ltr; Ofcr-Intrct Clb 85-86; Jr Rotarian-Rtry Clb Of Moorestwn 86.

YOKOYAMA, TAKASHI; Fort Lee HS; Fort Lee, NJ; (Y); Trs FBLA; Stat Bsktbl; High Hon Roll; Hon Roll; NHS; Ntl Merit Ltr; Spanish NHS; Brwrd Cnty Fr Drftng 1st Pl 83; Brwrd Cnty Fr Drftng 1st & 2nd Pl 84; Indstrl Arts Clb Trsr 84-85.

YONKER, DIANE; Ridge HS; Basking Ridge, NJ; (Y); 65/205; Office Aide; SADD; Teachers Aide; Var Bsktbl; Var Capt Fld Hcky; Capt Powder Puff Ftbl; Var Capt Sftbl; Hon Roll; Chrstphr J Zckmn Mem Awd 86; All ST Fldhcky 85; Lock Haven U; Physcl Thrpy.

YOON, CATHERINE S; East Brunswick HS; North Brunswick, NJ; (Y); Hosp Aide; Intnl Clb; Key Clb; Library Aide; Pep Clb; Band; Nwsp Stf; Stu Cncl; Boston U.

YOON, SUSAN; Scotch Plains-Fanwood HS; Fanwood, NJ; (S); AFS; Sec Trs Key Clb; Rep Soph Cls; Var Capt Cheerleading; High Hon Roll; Prfct Atten Awd.

YORIO, DIANA; Highland Park HS; Highland Park, NJ; (Y); 47/148; Church Yth Grp; Civic Clb; German Clb; Pep Clb; SADD; Flag Corp; Var Bsktbl; Crs Cntry; JV Var Sftbl; Hon Roll; Middlesex CC; Bus Adm.

YOUMANS, KELLY; Hopatcong HS; Savannah, GA; (S); Spanish Clb; Varsity Clb; School Play; Yrbk Stf; Rep Stu Cncl; Var Cheerleading; Var Crs Cntry; Var Trk; Var Vllybl; Hon Roll; GA Southern Coll; Crmnl Jstc.

YOUNG, ALAN S; Burlington Co Vo-Tech; Vincentown, NJ; (S); 9/280; 4-H; Radio Clb; VICA; Var Bsbl; JV Socr; High Hon Roll; 1st Pl VICA Comptn Printing.

YOUNG, AUDREY; Central HS; Newark, NJ; (Y); 31/300; Drama Clb; Nwsp Ed-Chief; Yrbk Phtg; Yrbk Stf; Pres Frsh Cls; VP Jr Cls; Stu Cncl; Var Cheerleading; Sftbl; Trk; Acctnt.

YOUNG, FAYE; Delsea Regional HS; Glassboro, NJ; (Y); Library Aide; Office Aide; Spanish Clb; Hon Roll; Air Force; Computers.

YOUNG, KARIN; Morris Knolls HS; Denville, NJ; (Y); 20/383; Art Clb; Church Yth Grp; Cmnty Wkr; High Hon Roll; Hon Roll; Summa Awd 84-85; Art.

YOUNG, KELLY; Dickinson HS; Jersey City, NJ; (Y); Ftbl; ROTC; SADD; Var Sftbl; Swmmng; Trk; GAA; Hon Roll; Prfct Atten Awd; Comp.

YOUNG, LARRY; Ridge HS; Basking Ridge, NJ; (Y); Latin Clb; Ski Clb; Yrbk Stf; Bsktbl; Trk; Aud/Vis; Church Yth Grp; Computer Clb; 1st Pl Rdg Drftng Cntst 85; Outstndng CJCF 85; U DE; Bio.

YOUNG JR, ROBERT E; Union Catholic Regional HS; N Plainfield, NJ; (Y); 22/319; Church Yth Grp; Math Tm; Service Clb; Spanish Clb; Nwsp Rptr; Swmmng; Hon Roll.

YOUNG, STEVEN; Holy Spirit HS; Northfield, NJ; (Y); 7/364; French Clb; Yrbk Stf; High Hon Roll; Hon Roll; NHS; Prfct Atten Awd; Advrtsng.

YOUNG, SUSAN; Middletown High School South; Middletown, NJ; (Y); Sec Soph Cls; VP Jr Cls; VP Sr Cls; Cheerleading; Var Trk; Cit Awd; French Hon Soc; High Hon Roll; NHS; Ntl Merit Ltr; MVP Awds In Track 86; Advncd Life Svng Cert Amer Red Cross 84; Bus.

YOUNGER III, EUGENE L; Arts HS; Newark, NJ; (Y); Drama Clb; Band; Concert Band; Drm & Bgl; Flag Corp; Jazz Band; Mrchg Band; Orch; Stage Crew; Trs Jr Cls; Essex Cnty Coll Perfrmng Awd 85.

YOUNGLOVE, CATHERINE; Holy Cross HS; Willingboro, NJ; (Y); 56/368; Church Yth Grp; Spanish Clb; Trs Sr Cls; JV Bsktbl; JV Capt Sftbl; Hon Roll; Elem Educ.

YOUNUS, ZAINAB N; Washington Township HS; Sewell, NJ; (Y); French Clb; Math Clb; Math Tm; Science Clb; Service Clb; Nwsp Ed-Chief; Hon Roll; Intnl Clb; PA JR Acad Of Sci 2nd Pl 84; Hnrb Mntn Mntgmry Cnty Sci Rsrch Cmptn 84; NY Sci League/Chmstry 86; Math Tchr.

YOUST, SUSAN; Wildwood HS; Wildwood, NJ; (Y); 3/100; Spanish Clb; Nwsp Stf; Yrbk Stf; Rep Jr Cls; Hon Roll; NHS; Advncd Plcmnt Engl III Awd 86; Educ.

YU, CECILIA; Montville HS; Montville, NJ; (Y); 61/262; Sec Trs Art Clb; FBLA; NFL; Speech Tm; Chorus; School Play; Sec Church Yth Grp; Drama Clb; Mgr Office Aide; Acpl Chr; Schl Store Mgr FBLA; Cert Recog NJ ST Teen Arts Fest 86; Outstndng Achvt Lang Chnese; Rutgers; Cmmnctns.

YU, DAVID; Rutherford HS; Rutherford, NJ; (Y); High Hon Roll; Hon Roll; Pre Med.

YU, ELEANOR; East Brunswick HS; E Brunswick, NJ; (Y); Cmnty Wkr; Nwsp Sprt Ed; Ed Nwsp Stf; Ed Lit Mag; Rep Stu Cncl; Trs French Hon Soc; NHS; Ntl Merit SF; St Schlr; French Clb; Telluride Assn Smmr Pgm Cornell U 85.

YU, ERIC T; Wayne Valley HS; Wayne Township, NJ; (Y); 1/311; Am Leg Boys St; Pres Computer Clb; Hosp Aide; Trs Latin Clb; Model UN; Quiz Bowl; Scholastic Bowl; Yrbk Stf; High Hon Roll; JCL; Rensselaer Polytech Inst Mth & Sci Awd 86; Latin Nwsp Co Edtr In Chief; Boston U Rsrch Intrnshp 86; Engrng.

YU, MICHELLE; Vineland HS; Vineland, NJ; (Y); Camera Clb; Ski Clb; Spanish Clb; Var Trk; Drexel; Fash Merch.

YU, YOUNG; Deptford Township HS; Deptford, NJ; (Y); Church Yth Grp; Bowling; Socr; Tennis; Hon Roll; Jr NHS; Prfct Atten Awd; Drexel U; Elec Engrng.

YUASA, YOSHIAKI; West Essex SR HS; N Caldwell, NJ; (Y); 28/350; Science Clb; Concert Band; Jazz Band; Mrchg Band; Sec Orch; Var Swmmng; Ntl Schl Orchstr Awd 86; Dprtmnt Awd Music 86; Otstndng Achvt Awd 86; Columbia U; Engr.

YUDOFF, DAVID SETH; Montville HS; Montville, NJ; (Y); 18/262; Drama Clb; Key Clb; Scholastic Bowl; Chorus; Jazz Band; Mrchg Band; School Musical; High Hon Roll; NHS; Ntl Merit Ltr.

YUELL, DANIELLE; East Brunswick HS; E Brunswick, NJ; (Y); Cmnty Wkr; DECA; Key Clb; Hon Roll; Livingston Coll; Bus.

YUN, CHEE HUN; Academic HS; Totowa, NJ; (Y); 17/70; Am Leg Boys St; Church Yth Grp; French Clb; JV Bsbl; Var Bowling; Var Socr; Var Tennis; Engr.

YUN, SOOJIN; Linden HS; Linden, NJ; (Y); Hosp Aide; Office Aide; Rep Jr Cls; Var Socr; NHS; German Clb; Key Clb; High Hon Roll; Natl Ger Hnr Soc 85-86; Principals Hnr Roll 85-87; Vrsty Girls Scor Athltc Awd 85.

YURECKO, MICHELE; Holy Family Acad; Bayonne, NJ; (Y); Math Clb; Speech Tm; Acpl Chr; Chorus; Orch; School Play; Nwsp Ed-Chief; High Hon Roll; Trs NHS; St Schlr; U Of Georgetown; Math.

YURGATIS, HEIDI; James Caldwell HS; Caldwell, NJ; (Y); Pep Clb; Ski Clb; Off Frsh Cls; Cheerleading; Gym; Trk; Hon Roll; Pres Physcl Ftnss Awd 84; Bus Mngmt.

YURKONIS, DEBBIE; Paul VI HS; Gibbsboro, NJ; (Y); 150/468; Church Yth Grp; Spanish Clb; JV Tennis; Spanish NHS; Rutgers-Camden; Accntng.

ZACCHERIA, LEE FULLAM; Bogota HS; Bogota, NJ; (Y); 11/99; Am Leg Aux Girls St; Nwsp Stf; Var L Trk; Hon Roll; NHS; Sci Awd 84; Typing Awd 84; Design.

ZADIE, DONNA MARIA; Camden Catholic HS; Blackwood, NJ; (Y); 58/320; Pres Church Yth Grp; French Clb; Spanish Clb; Sftbl; VP French Hon Soc; Spanish NHS; Languages.

ZAGER, SCOTT; West Essex HS; Roseland, NJ; (Y); Computer Clb; Temple Yth Grp; Hon Roll; NHS; Ntl Merit Ltr; Ntl Hnr Scty 86-87.

ZAGORSKI, SANDY; Ocean Twp HS; Wayside, NJ; (Y); 93/333; Ski Clb; Var Score Keeper; Var Capt Socr; High Hon Roll; Ed.

ZAHARIADES, CHRISTOPHER; Northern Valley Regional HS; Norwood, NJ; (Y); 102/287; AFS; Boy Scts; Church Yth Grp; Dance Clb; Rep Stu Cncl; Var Capt Socr; JV Wrstlng; Hon Roll; Eagle Scout Awd 85; Alpha Omega Awd 84; Finance.

ZAHLER, ELEZA; Villa Victoria Acad; Lambertville, NJ; (Y); 6/33; Church Yth Grp; Cmnty Wkr; Sec NFL; Political Wkr; Chorus; School Musical; Yrbk Stf; Sec Stu Cncl; Var L Socr; High Hon Roll; American U; Bus Law.

ZAHN, JENNIFER; East Brunswick HS; E Brunswick, NJ; (Y); Church Yth Grp; German Clb; Co-Capt Swmmng; NHS; Ntl Merit Ltr; Grmn Hnr Soc VP 85-86; Stephen A Orlando Memrl Schlrshp 86; U Of NC-CHAPEL Hill; Pol Sci.

ZAHORSKY, MATTHEW J; Wall HS; Allenwood, NJ; (Y); 43/263; Am Leg Boys St; Key Clb; Ski Clb; Spanish Clb; Varsity Clb; Bsbl; Var L Crs Cntry; Var L Wrstlng; Hon Roll; Amer HS Athlete 84; Military Srv Acad; Aviation.

ZAJAC, LAURA; East Brunswick HS; East Brunswick, NJ; (Y); Debate Tm; Key Clb; SADD; Teachers Aide; Temple Yth Grp; Variety Show; Yrbk Stf; Stu Cncl; French Hon Soc; NHS; Yth Fr Undrstndng Stu Exchng Prgrm 84; WA U St Louis; Pre-Med.

ZAK, JUDI; Maple Shade HS; Maple Shade, NJ; (Y); VP Church Yth Grp; Computer Clb; Sec Key Clb; SADD; Varsity Clb; Var Bsktbl; Var Cheerleading; Im Tennis; Gov Hon Prg Awd; NHS; Acadmc All Amer & Chrldr All Amer 84-86; Rutgers; Comp Sci.

ZAKROFF, STEPHEN; Holy Cross HS; Cinnaminson, NJ; (Y); 4/389; Church Yth Grp; Capt Debate Tm; Spanish Clb; JV Trk; High Hon Roll; Hon Roll; Trs NHS; S Jersey Co Champs Debate-Negative Tm 84-85.

ZALESKI, ERIKA; Union HS; Union, NJ; (Y); Cmnty Wkr; Intnl Clb; Key Clb; Service Clb; Sec Spanish Clb; Band; Concert Band; Drm Mjr(t); Flag Corp; Jazz Band; 3rd Drum Majrtte Solo Mid Atlntc 86; Cntrl Jersey Reg II Jazz Ensemble/Orch 84 & 85; Mus Achvt Awd 84.

ZALETA, LISA; Hunterdon Central HS; Hopewell, NJ; (Y); 92/549; Church Yth Grp; Key Clb; Band; Mrchg Band; School Musical; Variety Show; Off Frsh Cls; Off Jr Cls; Hon Roll; NHS; Bilingual Psychlgst.

ZALOUM, ALAN; Paul VI Regional HS; Clifton, NJ; (Y); Aud/Vis; Chess Clb; Church Yth Grp; Cmnty Wkr; Debate Tm; Drama Clb; Key Clb; Library Aide; Thesps; Chorus; Mass Cmmnctn.

ZAMBRANO, ANNA; Villa Victoria Acad; Titusville, NJ; (Y); Cmnty Wkr; Computer Clb; Math Clb; Chorus; School Musical; Pres Soph Cls; Sec Stu Cncl; Bausch & Lomb Sci Awd; High Hon Roll; Hon Roll; 1st Hnrs Englsh 86; 2nd Hnrs Chmstry & Anatmy 86; NJ Assoc Stu Cncls Pin 85; Med.

ZAMORA, DONALD A; Lenape Valley Regional HS; Andover, NJ; (Y); 10/253; Trs Church Yth Grp; Key Clb; VP SADD; Band; Concert Band; Nwsp Stf; High Hon Roll; NHS; Spanish NHS; Lenape Schlr 3 Yrs; Perfect Attndnc 2 Yrs.

ZAMORA, HAYDEE M; St Joseph Of The Palisades HS; North Bergen, NJ; (S); 3/135; Office Aide; Pres Spanish Clb; Nwsp Rptr; Yrbk Stf; Lit Mag; Var Swmmng; Cit Awd; Hon Roll; Spanish NHS; Pace U; Bus Mgmt.

ZAMORA, ROBERT; Columbia HS; Maplewood, NJ; (Y); Chess Clb; Computer Clb; Im Vllybl; Gov Hon Prg Awd; 1st Pl Frgn Lng Pstr Cntst 83-84; Phillips Exeter Smmr Schl 85; Harvard Smmr Schl 86; Cmptr Sci.

ZAMOS, JO ELLEN; Newton HS; Newton, NJ; (S); 17/200; Varsity Clb; Rep Stu Cncl; Var Bsktbl; Var Fld Hcky; Capt Powder Puff Ftbl; Var Capt Sftbl; Wt Lftg; High Hon Roll; NHS; Coachs Sftbl Awd 85; DECA Trphy 85; West Chester U; Math.

ZAMPAGLIONE, FRANCINE; Paulsboro HS; Gibbstown, NJ; (Y); 6/135; Ski Clb; Nwsp Stf; Sec Sr Cls; Var Capt Cheerleading; JV L Trk; Gov Hon Prg Awd; High Hon Roll; Hon Roll; Lion Awd; Sec NHS; Acad Excllnc Awds 83-86; Frank Flowers Mem Fnd Schlrshp 86; Presdntl Acad Ftnss Awd 86; Widener U.

ZANETTI, AMY; West Essex HS; Fairfield, NJ; (Y); Church Yth Grp; Chorus; Church Choir; Orch; JV Fld Hcky; Hon Roll; Varsity Fencing 84-85-86; Capt And A Strip-Fencing 86; Marketing-Sales.

ZANGER, DOUG S; Haddonfield Memorial HS; Haddonfield, NJ; (Y); Am Leg Boys St; French Clb; Intnl Clb; Concert Band; Lit Mag; Pres Jr Cls; Pres Stu Cncl; Socr; Var JV Trk; French Hon Soc; Prncpl Slctn Cmmttee 86; Mddl STS Evltn Strng Cmmttee 85-86; Htl Mgt.

ZANGER, MATTHEW; Westfield HS; Westfield, NJ; (Y); Temple Yth Grp; Concert Band; Symp Band; Trk; Hon Roll; NHS; Med.

ZANIELLO, JAMES; Don Bosco Prep; Mahwah, NJ; (Y); Nwsp Rptr; Ski Clb; NHS; Catholic HS Forum Rep 85-86; St Bonaventue U; Finance.

ZANNA, GERMAINE; Secaucus HS; Secaucus, NJ; (S); Intnl Clb; Key Clb; Math Clb; Ski Clb; Drm Mjr(t); Mrchg Band; Nwsp Phtg; Nwsp Rptr; Yrbk Phtg; Hon Roll.

ZANNI, TERRY; Sacred Heart HS; Vineland, NJ; (S); 11/67; Math Tm; Spanish Clb; School Play; Nwsp Stf; Yrbk Stf; JV Var Cheerleading; High Hon Roll; Hon Roll; Hnrbl Ment Sci Fair; Glee Clb; Ped Nrsg.

ZAPF, EDWARD; Southern Regional HS; Barnegat, NJ; (Y); 19/350; JV Var Crs Cntry; JV Trk; Hon Roll; Jr NHS; Prfct Atten Awd.

ZAPICO, ANTHONY M; Kearny HS; Kearny, NJ; (Y); Am Leg Boys St; Latin Clb; Math Tm; VP Jr Cls; VP Sr Cls; Var Tennis; Var Wrstlng; Hon Roll; Pres NHS; Acadmc Excllnc Awd 86; Phrmclgy.

ZAPOTOCHNY, TERESA; Holy Cross HS; Moorestown, NJ; (Y); 62/385; Hosp Aide; Hon Roll; Rotary Awd; Vlntr Wrk Schlrshp-Zurbrugg Hosp Riverside NJ 86; Trenton ST Coll; Nrsng.

ZAPPOLA, DONNA; Paulsboro HS; Gibbstown, NJ; (Y); Church Yth Grp; Cmnty Wkr; Yrbk Stf; JV Bsktbl; JV Sftbl; Var Tennis; Var Wt Lftg; Johnson & Wales Schlrshp; Karate Green Blt.

ZARELLI, LEIGH; Scotch Plaines Fanwood HS; Scotch Plains, NJ; (S); AFS; Key Clb; Radio Clb; Color Guard; Mrchg Band; Symp Band; Sec Trs Frsh Cls; Stu Cncl; JV Golf; High Hon Roll; ST Sci Day Bio Tm 85; Bus Law.

ZARICZNY, LILY; Holy Family Acad; Bayonne, NJ; (Y); 30/129; Church Yth Grp; Cmnty Wkr; Hosp Aide; School Play; Bowling; Hon Roll; NJ Inst Of Tech; Engrng.

ZARIELLO, GERARD; Don Bosco Prep HS; Thiells, NY; (Y); Ski Clb; Rep Frsh Cls; Rep Soph Cls; Coach Actv; Var Ftbl; Var Ice Hcky; Wt Lftg.

ZAROUNI, ALICIA; Middletown South HS; Middletown, NJ; (Y); Mathletes; Math Clb; Math Tm; JV Capt Fld Hcky; Var L Socr; Var L Sftbl; French Hon Soc; High Hon Roll; Hon Roll; NHS; Acctng.

ZATORSKI, KIM; Bishop George Ahr HS; Edison, NJ; (Y); 73/273; Rep Church Yth Grp; Hosp Aide; Rep Frsh Cls; Rep Soph Cls; Trs Stu Cncl; JV Capt Socr; Sftbl; Hon Roll; U S Stu Cncl Awd 85; Natl Ldrshp & Svc Awd 86; Phys Thrpy.

ZATZARINY, JANEANE; Vineland HS; Vineland, NJ; (Y); 4/628; Sec French Clb; Math Clb; Service Clb; Teachers Aide; Sec Jazz Band; Trs Ed Nwsp Stf; Yrbk Stf; French Hon Soc; Hon Roll; NHS; NJ Gov Tchng Schlrshp 86; SICO Fndtn Schlrshp 86; Durand Frnch Awd & Women Clb Engl Achvmnt Awd 86; U Of DE; Elem Ed.

ZAVOCKI, JOHN M; Setan Hall Prep; Irvington, NJ; (Y); Church Yth Grp; Computer Clb; French Clb; Key Clb; NFL; Pep Clb; Speech Tm; Thesps; School Musical; Hon Roll; MVP Frnsc Scty; Wnr Wngrng Clbs Egg Drop Cntst.

ZAVOLAS, EVA LYNN; Arthur L Johnson HS; Clark, NJ; (Y); 76/196; Dance Clb; Trs French Clb; Chorus; School Musical; School Play; Yrbk Stf; Stu Cncl; Pom Pon; French Hon Soc; Hon Roll; Miss ALJ Pgnt-Tlnt Comp 86; Vrsty Lttr-Chrldng 86; Dance.

ZAWACKI, LISA; Woodstown HS; Woodstown, NJ; (Y); Church Yth Grp; Political Wkr; Spanish Clb; Band; Concert Band; Mrchg Band; School Musical; Rep Stu Cncl; Stat Bsktbl; Im Sftbl; WA Workshps Congressnl Smnr 86; Mock Trl Comptn 86; Law.

ZAWOJSKI, LISA; Delran HS; Delran, NJ; (Y); SADD; Chorus; School Musical; School Play; Nwsp Rptr; Score Keeper; Cit Awd; Rotary Awd; Interact Club 83-86, Cultural Club Pres 83-86; Stu Cmnty Outreach Pgm 86; Psych.

ZDRAVKOVIC, CAROL; Cliffside Park HS; Cliffside Pk, NJ; (Y); 39/236; VP French Clb; Chorus; Nwsp Rptr; Stu Cncl; Hon Roll; Frnch Merit Awd 86; Bus Admin.

ZDRAZIL, JOHN; Wall HS; Wall, NJ; (S); 8/253; German Clb; Ftbl; High Hon Roll; Aerontcl Engr.

ZDZIENICKI, TARA; St Marys HS; S Amboy, NJ; (Y); 1/130; Am Leg Aux Girls St; School Play; Ed Yrbk Rptr; Ed Lit Mag; Var L Tennis; French Hon Soc; Hon Roll; NHS; NEDT Awd; French Clb; Monitor Essay Cont Hnrb Mntn; St Marys Crrspndnt Lcl Nwspr; Mission Clb; Law.

ZEARFAUS, DENISE; Burlington City HS; Burlington, NJ; (Y); Church Yth Grp; Cmnty Wkr; Hosp Aide; JA; Nwsp Ed-Chief; Yrbk Bus Mgr; Yrbk Stf; Tennis; Hon Roll; NHS; Mdcl Pthlgst.

ZEARFAUS, MARK; Gloucester Co Christn; Newfield, NJ; (Y); 2/12; Church Yth Grp; French Clb; Quiz Bowl; Yrbk Stf; Bsbl; Bsktbl; Socr; NHS; Prfct Atten Awd; Sal; Harry S Sink Awd 86; Cedarville Coll OH; Broadcastg.

ZEBICK, ROBERT; Oratory Catholic Prep; Morristown, NJ; (S); 3/44; Chess Clb; Computer Clb; Latin Clb; Math Tm; Service Clb; Ski Clb; Pres Soph Cls; Var Tennis; High Hon Roll; NHS; Grad Chrstn Ldrshp Inst 84; Natl Merit Schlr Hnrb Mntn 85; Mech Engrng.

ZEBLEY, DAWN; Bridgeton HS; Bridgeton, NJ; (Y); JV Var Cheerleading; Hon Roll.

ZEBLEY, KIMBERLY; Bridgeton HS; Bridgeton, NJ; (Y); 6/217; Art Clb; 4-H; French Clb; Capt Bowling; French Hon Soc; 4-H Awd; High Hon Roll; Jr NHS; Prfct Atten Awd; Pres Schlr; Stockton ST Coll; Bus Admin.

ZECCHIN, LUIGI; St Josephs Regional HS; Congers, NY; (Y); 6/170; JV Var Bsbl; JV Var Ftbl; Trk; NHS; Trs Spanish NHS; Engrng.

ZEHL, IVY; Jefferson Township HS; Lake Hopatcong, NJ; (Y); Camp Fr Inc; Girl Scts; Band; JV Cheerleading; JV Sftbl; Hon Roll; Prfct Atten Awd.

ZELAYA, LUISA; Dwight Morrow HS; Englewood, NJ; (Y); 2/247; Church Yth Grp; Hosp Aide; Spanish Clb; Yrbk Phtg; Rep Stu Cncl; Var Crs Cntry; JV Vllybl; High Hon Roll; Jr NHS; NHS; Comm.

ZELHOF, ANDREW; St Joseph Regional HS; Oakland, NJ; (Y); 1/200; Ski Clb; Wrstlng; NHS; Spanish NHS; Med.

ZELLER, HOLLY; Rancocas Valley Regional HS; Medford, NJ; (Y); 56/256; German Clb; JA; Ski Clb; Thesps; Varsity Clb; Band; School Play; Stage Crew; Rep Sr Cls; Var Fld Hcky; Susquehann U; Polit Sci.

ZELLER, LISA; Chatham Township HS; Chatham, NJ; (Y); Key Clb; Pres Pep Clb; Varsity Clb; Rep Stu Cncl; Var Capt Cheerleading; JV Lcrss; Var Sftbl; Hon Roll.

ZELLERKRAUT, DEBBI; Lakewood HS; Lakewood, NJ; (Y); 58/294; Drama Clb; English Clb; French Clb; PAVAS; School Play; Stage Crew; Mgr Crs Cntry; Mgr(s); French Hon Soc; Prfct Atten Awd; Ithaca Coll; Cmmnctns.

ZELLERS, KATHLEEN; Sussex Co Vo-Tech HS; Sussex, NJ; (S); Am Leg Aux Girls St; Varsity Clb; Rep Stu Cncl; Var L Tennis; High Hon Roll; NHS; Katharine Gibbs Ldrshp Awd 85; Hmcmng Queen 85; Bus Adm.

ZEMAITAITIS, DIANE; Woodstown HS; Elmer, NJ; (Y); English Clb; Spanish Clb; Band; Concert Band; Mrchg Band; Nwsp Rptr; Lit Mag; JV Socr; JV Var Trk; Jrnlsm.

ZEMSKY, MICHELLE; Manalapan HS; Englishtown, NJ; (Y); SADD; Temple Yth Grp; Chorus; Capt Flag Corp; Ed Yrbk Stf; Rep Jr Cls; Rep Sr Cls; Mgr Trk; Jr Prm Queen 86; Bus.

ZENO, DANNEEN; Hamilton HS East; Mercerville, NJ; (Y); 14/315; Exploring; JV Bsktbl; Var Socr; Var Sftbl; NHS; Schlrshp Frm Bnk Of Md Jrsy 86; 1st Tm All Mrcr For Trntn For Sftbl 86; Ntl Hon Soc 85 & 86; Clemson U; Engrng.

ZERBE, GEOFF; Ridge HS; Basking Ridge, NJ; (Y); French Clb; German Clb; Hon Roll; Ntl Merit Ltr; Chem Engr.

ZESZOTARSKI, JOSEPH; Green Brook HS; Green Brook, NJ; (Y); 5/63; Church Yth Grp; Trs Jr Cls; Var Capt Bsktbl; Var Ftbl; Var Trk; High Hon Roll; NHS.

ZETTELL, SCOTT; Jackson Memorial HS; Jackson, NJ; (Y); 3/322; Am Leg Boys St; Office Aide; Band; Stu Cncl; Capt Crs Cntry; Capt Trk; High Hon Roll; NHS; Voice Dem Awd; Garden ST Dstngshd Schlr 86; Boston Coll; Invstmnt Anal.

ZGLOBICKI, CHRISTINE; Union Catholic Regional HS; Colonial, NJ; (Y); Church Yth Grp; Girl Scts; Science Clb; Service Clb; SADD; Rep Soph Cls; Off Sr Cls; Stu Cncl; Hon Roll; NHS; Miss Polonia 86; Rutgers U; Business.

ZICK, PATRICIA; Toms River HS East; Toms River, NJ; (Y); Church Yth Grp; Cmnty Wkr; Dance Clb; DECA; FBLA; Hosp Aide; Pres Sec Key Clb; Stage Crew; Outstndng Dedctn, Svc Key Clb 84-86; Outstndng Prfrmnc Key Clb Secy 85-86; Candy Strpr Svc 84-86; Socl Wrk.

ZIEGLER, GREG; Matawon Regional HS; Cliffwood, NJ; (Y); 124/322; Rep Frsh Cls; Ammr Arts Inst 84.

ZIELENSKI, TRACEY; Cliffside Park HS; Cliffside Pk, NJ; (Y); Church Yth Grp; Drama Clb; Science Clb; Ski Clb; Spanish Clb; Stat Ftbl; Stat Wrstlng; Penn ST; Fshn Buyer.

ZIEMIAN, LEIGH E; Phillipsburg HS; Phillipsburg, NJ; (Y); 1/284; Drama Clb; Key Clb; Model UN; School Play; Nwsp Stf; High Hon Roll; NHS; Ntl Merit Ltr; Val; VFW Awd; Vassar Coll Schlrhsp 86; NJ Distinguished Schlr 85; Vassar Coll.

ZIEMSKI, ELIZABETH; Red Bank Catholic HS; W Long Brnch, NJ; (Y); Ski Clb; Gym; Trk; Hon Roll; NHS; Gen Acadmc Achvmnt Awd 86; Outstndng Perfrmnc On NEDT 83-84; Med.

ZIENTEK, MARYBETH; Holy Family Acad; Bayonne, NJ; (Y); 2/119; Church Choir; Pres Orch; School Musical; Nwsp Ed-Chief; CC Awd; Cit Awd; Elks Awd; NHS; Sal; Ambass HOBY Fndtn Ldrshp Sem 84; Georgetown U.

ZIER, LESLIE; Hamilton HS West; Yardville, NJ; (Y); Key Clb; SADD; Band; Concert Band; Mrchg Band; Symp Band; Stu Cncl; Sftbl; Cmptr Prgmng.

ZILAI, MARK; St Rose HS; Brielle, NJ; (Y); Var L Socr; Var L Tennis; Hon Roll; NHS; New Jersey ST Shr Area Slct Sccr Tm 85-86; Shore Bys Clb Trvlng Sccr Tm 83-84-85-86; Asst Coach Sccr; Sprts Med.

ZIMMERMAN, BRIAN; Delran HS; Delran, NJ; (Y); 170/205; Art Clb; Varsity Clb; Lit Mag; Crs Cntry; Golf; Socr; Swmmng; Trk; Hon Roll; Champ Trk 86; Hussoin Sch Art; Art.

ZIMMERMANN, THOMAS; Saint Peters Prep; N Arlington, NJ; (Y); 23/200; Im Ftbl; L Var Trk; Hon Roll; NY U; Bus.

ZIMNY, DAVID; Parsippany HS; Lake Hiawatha, NJ; (Y); Chess Clb; Intnl Clb; Spanish Clb; Hon Roll; NHS; Prfct Atten Awd; 1st Pl Trphy Cmnty Bsbl Tm 84; Bus Adm.

ZIMOLZAK, JOANNE; Pitman HS; Pitman, NJ; (S); 2/139; Church Yth Grp; Cmnty Wkr; Drama Clb; Pres French Clb; Girl Scts; Key Clb; Political Wkr; Quiz Bowl; Teachers Aide; Chorus; Garden ST Distngshd Schlr Awd 85-86; Knowldg Bwl Schlrshp 84; Penn ST U; Pol Sci.

ZINDEL, STEVEN A; Seton Hall Prep; Maplewood, NJ; (Y); 3/196; German Clb; Mathletes; Math Tm; Science Clb; Trk; High Hon Roll; Masonic Awd; NHS; NEDT Awd; Pres Schlr; Lehigh U; Elec Engr.

ZINK, ROBERT C; St John Viannney HS; Colts Neck, NJ; (Y); 36/233; Computer Clb; Red Cross Aide; Service Clb; Ski Clb; Rep Jr Cls; Mgr Bsktbl; Crs Cntry; Swmmng; Trk; NHS; Loyola Grant 86; Commnty Svc Awd 86; Schl Merit Awds 84-86; Loyola Coll; Bus.

ZINN, LISA; Ocean Township HS; Oakhurst, NJ; (Y); 39/333; Ski Clb; Spanish Clb; SADD; Teachers Aide; High Hon Roll; Spartan Schlr Awd 85; Psych.

ZIOBRO, ANDREW; Manalapan HS; Englishtown, NJ; (Y); 44/500; Aud/Vis; Drama Clb; JCL; Science Clb; Thesps; Band; Concert Band; Jazz Band; Mrchg Band; Trs Symp Band; MIT; Elec Engrg.

ZIPP, CHRISTOPHER; Seton Hall Prep; W Orange, NJ; (Y); Computer Clb; Exploring; French Clb; Science Clb; Band; Concert Band; High Hon Roll; NHS; Med Sci.

ZIPPERIAN, DAWN; Toms River High School East; Toms River, NJ; (Y); 70/485; Sec Church Yth Grp; Spanish Clb; Teachers Aide; Band; Co-Capt Color Guard; Mrchg Band; Mgr Swmmng; Hon Roll; Cstdl Schlrshp 86; Ntl Band Assoc Awd 85; Flagler Coll; Elem Ed.

ZIRKES, NEIL B; Livingston HS; Livingston, NJ; (Y); 9/496; Key Clb; SADD; VP Temple Yth Grp; Rep Stu Cncl; Capt Crs Cntry; Capt Trk; Elks Awd; NHS; Ntl Merit Ltr; U Of PA; Econ.

ZIRRILLO, VINCENT; Red Bank Catholic HS; Long Branch, NJ; (Y); Aud/Vis; Church Yth Grp; Cmnty Wkr; Ski Clb; SADD; Band; Im Bsktbl; Im Ftbl; Im Ice Hcky; Im Wt Lftg; Johnson & Wales RI; Bus.

ZIRVI, SUMRA; Fair Lawn HS; Fair Lawn, NJ; (Y); 10/335; Computer Clb; Math Tm; Science Clb; Spanish Clb; Yrbk Stf; Rep Jr Cls; Rep Sr Cls; High Hon Roll; NHS; St Schlr; PTA Schlrshp 86; Valley Hosp Schlrshp 86; PA ST U; Pre Med.

ZISSU, JONATHAN A; Millburn HS; Short Hills, NJ; (Y); 17/247; Math Tm; Teachers Aide; Acpl Chr; Band; Chorus; Jazz Band; Swing Chorus; High Hon Roll; Ntl Merit SF; Rutgers Schlr 85; Engrng.

ZITT, DEANNA; North Bergen HS; N Bergen, NJ; (Y); 45/404; Hon Roll; Pres Schlr; Prncpls 1000 Clb 86; PTA Schlrshp 86; Rutgers; Comp Sci.

ZOBITZ, JED; Columbia HS; S Orange, NJ; (Y); Var Ftbl; Var Lcrss; Im Wt Lftg.

ZOCKS, ADAM; Livingston HS; Livingston, NJ; (Y); Cmnty Wkr; Key Clb; Band; Jazz Band; Mrchg Band; School Musical; JV Var Bsktbl; Var Crs Cntry; JV Tennis; Var Trk; Schlr Ath Awd 84.

ZOLAN, CRAIG; Hightstown HS; East Windsor, NJ; (Y); French Clb; Math Tm; High Hon Roll; Comp Sci.

ZOLANDZ, JOSEPH; Manville HS; Manville, NJ; (Y); 1/99; Yrbk Rptr; Yrbk Stf; High Hon Roll; NHS; Comp Sci.

ZOLDI, MARY; Riverside HS; Delanco, NJ; (S); 3/85; Church Yth Grp; Sec FTA; Pres Keywanettes; Church Choir; School Play; JV Var Fld Hcky; Var Trk; NHS; NEDT Awd; Sec Drama Clb; Amer Lgn Awd 86; Walsh Coll Canton OH; Chld Psy.

ZOLLA, VALERIE; Hightstown HS; E Windsor, NJ; (Y); Spanish Clb; Concert Band; Mrchg Band; Hon Roll.

ZOLLO III, JOHN F; Washington Township HS; Turnersville, NJ; (Y); Church Yth Grp; Var L Swmmng; Var Trk; High Hon Roll; Mst Imprvd Swmr Awd 85-86; Ntl Intrschlstc Swmmrs Coachs Awd Top 10 ST 85-86; Villanova.

ZORNER, DEBORAH; St Rose HS; Jacksonville, NC; (Y); Church Yth Grp; Drama Clb; JCL; Sec Key Clb; Latin Clb; Spanish Clb; School Play; Lit Mag; Rep Soph Cls; High Hon Roll; Lt Gvnr Of Key Clb 86-87; Lngustcs.

ZOROVICH, KENNY; Notre Dame HS; Allentown, NJ; (Y); Art Clb; JV Ice Hcky; Socr; Hon Roll.

ZUBAR, VICTOR W; Sussex Vo-Tech HS; Highland Lakes, NJ; (S); Aud/Vis; Cmnty Wkr; Library Aide; High Hon Roll; Hon Roll; NHS; Elect Engr.

ZUBEL, STACY; Henry P Becton Regional HS; E Rutherford, NJ; (Y); 27/120; Church Yth Grp; Cmnty Wkr; Ski Clb; Yrbk Stf; Stu Cncl; Twrlr; High Hon Roll; Hon Roll; Psych.

ZUCCA, HEATHER; Vineland HS; Vineland, NJ; (Y); 183/803; French Clb; Key Clb; Office Aide; Pep Clb; Yrbk Stf; Rep Soph Cls; Rep Jr Cls; Rep Stu Cncl; Cheerleading; Bus Adm.

ZUCCA, LOUISE ERNESTINE; Lacey Township HS; Forked River, NJ; (Y); FBLA; Math Tm; Science Clb; Chorus; Orch; Nwsp Rptr; Powder Puff Ftbl; High Hon Roll; NHS; Prfct Atten Awd; Mus Awd 86; Drvrs Ed Awd 86; Musc.

ZUCCARINO JR, RALPH; St Augustine Prep; Cardiff, NJ; (Y); Cmnty Wkr; Computer Clb; Nwsp Rptr; Yrbk Rptr; Lit Mag; Off Jr Cls; Capt L Crs Cntry; Hon Roll; Church Yth Grp; Engl Schlrshp 86; Cross Cty All Star 85; Allentown Coll; Engl.

ZUCZEK, BETH ANN; South River HS; South River, NJ; (Y); German Clb; VP Library Aide; Spanish Clb; Capt Color Guard; Score Keeper; Comm.

ZUKOWSKI, GREGORY A; De Paul HS; Wayne, NJ; (Y); 18/165; Am Leg Boys St; JCL; Ski Clb; School Musical; School Play; Variety Show; NHS; Hnrbl Mention Acrylic Painting 86; Hnrbl Mention Water Color Painting 85; Awd R J Prepsters 86.

ZUKOWSKI, KATHRYN; Spotswood HS; Milltown, NJ; (S); 1/174; Am Leg Aux Girls St; Science Clb; School Play; Ed Yrbk Ed-Chief; Yrbk Phtg; Stu Cncl; Var Mgr Bsbl; High Hon Roll; Hon Roll; NHS; Rutgers Schlr 86; NJ Dstnghsd Schlr 86; Rutgers U; Engrng.

ZULIN III, MICHAEL F; Toms River HS East; Toms River, NJ; (Y); Am Leg Boys St; Boy Scts; Exploring; ROTC; Police Explr Acad 86; Stocktn ST Coll; Crmnl Just.

ZULLO, PAUL; Teaneck HS; Teaneck, NJ; (Y); L Var Ftbl; Im Powder Puff Ftbl; JV Trk; Im Vllybl; Im Wt Lftg; Bus.

ZUMPANO, JENNIFER; Mainland Regional HS; Northfield, NJ; (Y); Church Yth Grp; Computer Clb; Exploring; Intnl Clb; Comp Sci.

ZUNIGA, ALEXANDER; Arthur L Johnson Reg HS; Clark, NJ; (Y); French Clb; Var Socr; French Hon Soc; High Hon Roll; Eco.

ZUPKO, JEAN; Gateway Regional HS; Wenonah, NJ; (Y); 22/188; Exploring; French Clb; Hosp Aide; Sec Key Clb; Sec Science Clb; SADD; Capt Cheerleading; Hon Roll; NHS; Gateway Ed Assoc Schlrshp 86; ST Teachers Yr Awd 86; Coll St Elizabeth; Spcl Ed.

ZURLO, JOHN; Belleville HS; Belleville, NJ; (Y); Key Clb; Ski Clb; Rep Stu Cncl; Crs Cntry; Trk; High Hon Roll; Hon Roll; NHS.

ZURLO, LAURA; Highland Reg HS; Blackwood, NJ; (S); 36/326; Office Aide; Hon Roll; Camden Cnty Coll; Bus Mgmt.

ZURZOLO, DOMINICK; Marist HS; Bayonne, NJ; (Y); 17/85; Cmnty Wkr; Yrbk Stf; Im Bsktbl; Im Score Keeper; Im Vllybl; Wt Lftg; Cit Awd; Hon Roll; Schlrshp Keepng 85 AVG Bttr 3 Yrs; Comp Techncn.

ZUSI, NOLA; Summit HS; Summit, NJ; (Y); 78/270; Cmnty Wkr; Off Frsh Cls; Off Sr Cls; Stu Cncl; Var L Cheerleading; Var Gym; JV Lcrss; JV Var Powder Puff Ftbl; High Hon Roll; Hon Roll; Psychlgy.

ZVARA, LAURA; Union Catholic Regional HS; Scotch Plains, NJ; (Y); 15/337; French Clb; Latin Clb; Ski Clb; Nwsp Rptr; French Hon Soc; Hon Roll; NHS; Acadmc Al-Amer; Natl Hnr Rl; Natl Sci Achvt Acad.

ZVARA, PATRICIA; Union Catholic Regional HS; Scotch Plains, NJ; (Y); 116/339; Ski Clb; Var Crs Cntry; Var Trk; Kings Coll Grant 86; Kings Coll; Pre-Vet.

ZYGIEL, LYNEE ANN; Palisades Park HS; Palisades Pk, NJ; (Y); #6 In Class; Nwsp Stf; Yrbk Stf; Sec Soph Cls; Var Capt Cheerleading; Sftbl; High Hon Roll; NHS; Voice Dem Awd; Knights Of Pythias Ortcl Essy Cntst 84-85; Rutgers Coll Phrmcy; Phrmcy.

PENNSYLVANIA

AARON, KELLY LYNN; B Reed Henderson HS; West Chester, PA; (Y); AFS; Debate Tm; German Clb; Chorus; Church Choir; Stu Cncl; Cheerleading; Socr; Hon Roll; NHS; Soc Distinguished Am HS Stu 85; 6 FWC New Century Clb Bk Awd 86; Outstnading Debate 86; PA ST Univ.

AARONS, KIMBERLY; Taylor Allderdice HS; Pittsburgh, PA; (Y); Hosp Aide; Var Sftbl; High Hon Roll; Hon Roll; U Pittsburgh.

ABADILLA, ANGELA; Ambridge Area HS; Baden, PA; (Y); Hosp Aide; Band; Concert Band; Jazz Band; Mrchg Band; School Musical; Symp Band; Variety Show; JV L Crs Cntry; Var Trk; Music.

ABATE, AGNES; Venango Christian HS; Oil City, PA; (Y); Pep Clb; Political Wkr; School Play; Variety Show; Sftbl; High Hon Roll; Hon Roll; NHS.

ABBADINI, ANGELA; Brownsville Area HS; Brownsville, PA; (Y); Drama Clb; Hosp Aide; Intnl Clb; Office Aide; Ski Clb; SADD; Band; Mrchg Band; Gov Hon Prg Awd; Hon Roll; Governors Schl Prjct-Quest 86; Psych.

ABBOTT, JOSEPHINE; Turkeyfoot Valley Area HS; Ursina, PA; (S); Q&S; Chorus; Color Guard; Nwsp Sprt Ed; Yrbk Stf; High Hon Roll; Prfct Atten Awd; Drama Clb; Mrchg Band; School Play; Awds-Typng I, Spnsh I & Coll Prep Engl 84-85; Photo.

ABBOTT, KRISTEN; Uniontown Area HS; Smock, PA; (Y); Letterman Clb; Yrbk Stf; VP Frsh Cls; French Hon Soc; High Hon Roll; French Clb; SADD; Var L Sftbl; L Tennis; Hon Roll; Psychtry.

ABBOUD, ABDO; Freedom HS; Bethlehem, PA; (Y); 93/404; Trs Church Yth Grp; Ski Clb; Rep Frsh Cls; JV Var Wrstlng; Pittsburgh U; Sci.

ABBRUZZI, MIA; Saint Maria Goretti HS; Philadelphia, PA; (Y); Cmnty Wkr; Library Aide; Office Aide; Lit Mag; Hon Roll; Temple U; Bus.

ABDOE, LISA; Snenango HS; New Castle, PA; (Y); 9/119; Varsity Clb; Nwsp Stf; Stu Cncl; Bsktbl; Twrlr; Cit Awd; Hon Roll; NHS; Amer Lg Awd; Duquesne U; Mktng.

ABDULLAH, MAAHI; Frankford HS; Philadelphia, PA; (Y); Boy Scts; Computer Clb; FBLA; JA; JV Var Ftbl; Gym; Trk; Comp Engr.

ABEL, DONNALEE S; Whitehall HS; Whitehall, PA; (Y); 24/293; Sec German Clb; Leo Clb; Band; Chorus; Color Guard; Jazz Band; Mrchg Band; School Musical; Hon Roll; NHS; Excllnt Dedctn Cncrt Choir Awd 86; Germannatl Hon Soc Tst Awd 83; Catawba Coll; Psychlgy.

ABEL, URSULA; Marple Newtown SR HS; Newtown Square, PA; (Y); Drama Clb; Hosp Aide; JA; Library Aide; Ski Clb; Band; Church Choir; Concert Band; Mrchg Band; Orch; 2nd Flute Dist Orch 85; 1st Flute Sch Orch & Band 85; Accpt DE Yth Orch 86.

ABELEDA, MARIA; Cedar Crest HS; Lebanon, PA; (Y); 2/295; French Clb; Pep Clb; Orch; High Hon Roll; Hon Roll; NHS; Hnr Banquet Mdlns 84, 85 & 86; Hnrs Orchstra Mdls 84, 85 & 86; Trphy In Guitar 86; Doctor.

ABELL, CYNTHIA; Neshaminy HS; Levittown, PA; (Y); 17/752; GAA; JV Sftbl; High Hon Roll; Hon Roll; NHS; Merit Awd 84; West Chester; Bus Adm.

ABER, JOHN; Steel Valley HS; Munhall, PA; (S); 4/245; Trs Church Yth Grp; Cmnty Wkr; Pres JCL; Key Clb; Rep Jr Cls; Rep Sr Cls; Rep Stu Cncl; Tennis; High Hon Roll; Hon Roll; Hugh O Brien Ldrshp Conf 83-84; JR Mrshl Grad Clss 85; Hlth.

ABERCROMBIE, SARENE; Aliquippa JR/Sr HS; Aliquippa, PA; (Y); Church Yth Grp; DECA; French Clb; FNA; JA; Band; Church Choir; Concert Band; Mrchg Band; Off Jr Cls; Hnr Roll 79-84; Pre-Med.

ABNER, ERIC MAURICE; Frankford HS; Philadelphia, PA; (Y); Art Clb; Office Aide; School Play; JV Var Ftbl; Var Trk; Hon Roll; Prfct Atten Awd; U Of MD; Bus Ed.

ABPLANALP, EDWARD; Warren Area HS; Warren, PA; (Y); Boys Clb Am; Church Yth Grp; French Clb; Ski Clb; Bsbl; Bowling.

ABRAHAM, BACHU; Pennsbury HS; Fairless Hills, PA; (Y); 11/712; Church Yth Grp; Mathletes; Hon Roll; NHS; Pres Schlr; Pnnsbry Schlrshp Fndtn Grnt 86; Drexel U; Engrng.

ABRAHAM, LESLIE; Brownsville Area HS; Brownsville, PA; (Y); 23/218; Drama Clb; Sec Trs Girl Scts; Math Clb; Office Aide; SADD; Pres Jr Cls; Var Co-Capt Cheerleading; High Hon Roll; Hon Roll; Hnr Chords Grad 86; CA U PA; Elem Ed.

ABRAMASON, LISA; Lower Merion HS; Philadelphia, PA; (Y); JCL; Nwsp Rptr; Rep Soph Cls; Rep Jr Cls; Rep Stu Cncl; JV Cheerleading; JV Fld Hcky; JV Var Lcrss; Hon Roll; U PA; Bio Sci.

ABRAMOWICH, PATRICK; Shanksville-Stonycreek HS; Stoystown, PA; (S); 1/34; Am Leg Boys St; Nwsp Rptr; VP Jr Cls; Stu Cncl; Var L Bsbl; JV Bsktbl; High Hon Roll; NHS; Spanish NHS; Church Yth Grp; Hugh O Brian Yth Ldrshp Semnr 85; Amer Lgn Essay Wnnr For Somerset Cnty 85; Pol Sci.

ABRAMS, KAREN; Akiba Hebrew Acad; Wyndmoor, PA; (Y); Art Clb; Dance Clb; Hosp Aide; Teachers Aide; Sec Temple Yth Grp; Chorus; School Musical; Sec Frsh Cls; Sec Soph Cls; Sec Jr Cls; Chld Psyclgy.

ABRAMS, KAREN; Marple Newtown SR HS; Broomall, PA; (Y); Math Clb; Rep Jr Cls; Stu Cncl; Cheerleading; High Hon Roll; Jr NHS; NHS.

ABRAMS, ROSANNETTE; Sayre Area HS; Sayre, PA; (Y); 2/125; VP SADD; Chorus; Sec Pres Stu Cncl; Capt Var Crs Cntry; Dnfth Awd; High Hon Roll; NHS; PA Govs Schl Arts-Altnt Voic 86; Elmira Coll Key Awd 86; Pre-Med.

ABRAMS, SUSAN; St Maria Goretti HS; Philadelphia, PA; (Y); 86/426; Off Frsh Cls; Off Soph Cls; Hon Roll; Jr NHS; NHS; Prfct Atten Awd; Cosmotlgst.

ABRAMSON, BARB; Hempfield Area SR HS; Greensburg, PA; (Y); 66/647; AFS; French Clb; Letterman Clb; Pep Clb; Ski Clb; Temple Yth Grp; Yrbk Stf; Cheerleading; Capt Swmmng; Trk; OH ST; Bus.

ABRAMSON, MARLA; Lower Moreland HS; Huntingdon Valley, PA; (S); VP FBLA; Yrbk Stf; Rep Soph Cls; Var Capt Cheerleading; JV Trk; Hon Roll; NHS; Bus.

ABRETSKE, GWENDOLYN; Norwin SR HS; North Huntingdon, PA; (Y); German Clb; Pep Clb; Ski Clb; Pres VICA; Off Stu Cncl; Crs Cntry; Trk; Hon Roll; Kiwanis Awd; Excllnc Ldrshp Awd VICA 85-86; Pres Cosmtlgy Shop CWAUTS 85-86; Pres Cntrl Westmoreld Vo-Tech Schl.

ABRUZZO, JOSEPH; Roman Catholic HS; Philadelphia, PA; (S); 2/140; Office Aide; Nwsp Stf; Yrbk Stf; Pres Stu Cncl; Bsktbl; Capt Ftbl; Wt Lftg; High Hon Roll; Hon Roll; Pres NHS; Temple U; Comms.

ABT, EILEEN; The Harrisburg Acad; Hershey, PA; (Y); 3/32; Teachers Aide; Temple Yth Grp; Orch; Nwsp Ed-Chief; Yrbk Phtg; Var Crs Cntry; Tennis; High Hon Roll; Hon Men Schl Sci Fr 86; Semifnlst Govrns Schnl Intl Stds 86; Dist Tnns Dbls.

ABT, SUZANNE; Harrisburg Acad; Hershey, PA; (Y); 2/32; Orch; Ed Nwsp Stf; Yrbk Phtg; Lit Mag; Sec Frsh Cls; Crs Cntry; Co-Capt Tennis; Gov Hon Prg Awd; High Hon Roll; Ntl Merit Ltr; PA Govrn Schl Arts 86; Certfct Merit Natl Achvt Photo 86; Kodak Medallion Excllnc Nominee 86.

ACCIAI, JOANN; Lackawanna Trl HS; Factoryville, PA; (Y); 1/92; Chorus; Yrbk Phtg; Yrbk Stf; Stu Cncl; Bausch & Lomb Sci Awd; High Hon Roll; NHS; Marine Bio.

ACEY, CARLA; Moshannow Valley HS; Brisbin, PA; (Y); School Play; Yrbk Phtg; Yrbk Stf; Scndry Educ.

ACHKIO, KAREN; Trinity HS; Carlisle, PA; (Y); Church Yth Grp; Pep Clb; Spanish Clb; Cheerleading; Trk; High Hon Roll; Hon Roll; Sec Spanish NHS.

ACHRE, NANCY; Hickory HS; Hermitage, PA; (Y); 1/175; Pres Computer Clb; Trs Math Clb; Chorus; Madrigals; Var Capt Bsktbl; Var Capt Trk; DAR Awd; NHS; Ntl Merit Ltr; Val; U S Army Rsrve Natl Schlr/Ath Awd 86; Pres Acad Fit Awds Pgm 86; Mercer Cnty Hall Fame Acad All Str 86; U PA; Comp Sci.

ACHTZEHN, ROBERT; Belle Vernon Area HS; Belle Vernon, PA; (Y); Sec Church Yth Grp; Band; Yrbk Sprt Ed; Trs Frsh Cls; JV Bsktbl; Var L Ftbl; Wt Lftg; High Hon Roll; NHS; Law.

ACHY, CAROLINE; Central Columbia HS; Bloomsburg, PA; (Y); 24/180; Drama Clb; VP Chorus; Church Choir; School Musical; Stage Crew; High Hon Roll; Espy Womens Cvc Clb Schlrshp 86; Pres Acad Ftns Awd 86; Chorus Key Awd-Accpnst 86; Bloomsburg U; Mass Comm.

ACKARD, DIANN M; State College Area SR HS; State College, PA; (Y); Church Yth Grp; French Clb; Acpl Chr; Jazz Band; Mrchg Band; Orch; Swing Chorus; Symp Band; Nwsp Rptr; Hon Roll; Concours Natl De Francais; Power Paws Awds; NEDT Superior Perfrmnc Awd; UC Berkeley; Psych.

ACKER, RON; Manheim Township HS; Lancaster, PA; (Y); Boy Scts; Church Yth Grp; Varsity Clb; Im Fld Hcky; Var L Gym; Var Trk; Im Vllybl; WA Wrkshps Semnr 86; Georgetown Intl Reltns Semnr 86; Intl Reltns.

ACKERMAN, ALAN; Wyoming Area HS; Wyoming, PA; (Y); 12/250; Boy Scts; French Clb; Key Clb; Trs Frsh Cls; Trs Soph Cls; Trs Jr Cls; Var Ftbl; Var Trk; Wt Lftg; God Cntry Awd; Law.

ACKERMAN, BRADLEY; Lower Moreland HS; Huntingdon Valley, PA; (S); Pres FBLA; Key Clb; Science Clb; Rep Stu Cncl; High Hon Roll; Hon Roll; NHS; FBLA 2nd Tm Regn Entrpnrshp I Comp 84; 6th Pl ST Comp Entrprnrshp I 84; 1st Pl Regnl Comp Bus Mth 85; Bus Adm.

ACKERMAN, CHRISTINE; Abington Heights HS; Clarks Summit, PA; (Y); 22/270; Exploring; Sec 4-H; Orch; Symp Band; Yrbk Stf; 4-H Awd; Hon Roll; NHS; 3 Dist & 1 Rgnl Orchstra Fstvl 84-86; 4-H Hrs Clb 85-86; Bio-Chem.

ACKERMAN, CHRISTINE; St Huberts HS; Philadelphia, PA; (Y); 80/367; Hosp Aide; Spanish Clb; Yrbk Stf; Co-Capt Cheerleading; Gym; Hon Roll; Frankford Nrsng Schl; Nrsng.

ACKERMAN, ELIZABETH N; Lower Dauphin HS; Harrisburg, PA; (Y); 12/210; Am Leg Aux Girls St; SADD; Thesps; Chorus; School Musical; Sec Sr Cls; Rep Stu Cncl; Hon Roll; NHS; Pres Schlr; Pres Schlrshp U Of Scranton 86; Musical Ldrshp Awd 86; U Of Scranton; Engl.

ACKERMAN, JOHN; Freedom HS; Easton, PA; (Y); 48/404; Ski Clb; Hon Roll; Pres Schlr; Gifted Prg; Treas Vo Tech Clss; Lehigh U; Elec Engrng.

ACKERMAN, JULIE; Tamaqua HS; Tamaqua, PA; (Y); 1/170; Drama Clb; Band; Chorus; Concert Band; Mrchg Band; Stage Crew; Var L Trk; Hon Roll; NHS; Prfct Atten Awd.

ACKERMAN, LORIE; Berlin Brothersvalley HS; Glencoe, PA; (Y); 21/67; Cmnty Wkr; Trs FBLA; Red Cross Aide; Teachers Aide; Band; Concert Band; Mrchg Band; Yrbk Rptr; Yrbk Stf; Cit Awd.

ACKERMAN, R CHRISTIAN; Danville Area HS; Danville, PA; (Y); Church Yth Grp; Cmnty Wkr; Hosp Aide; Letterman Clb; Spanish Clb; Yrbk Sprt Ed; Yrbk Stf; Pres Stu Cncl; Ftbl; Gym; All PA Wrstlng Tm 84-86; All Amer Wrstlng 84-85.

ACKERT, DAVID; Pennsbury HS; Morrisville, PA; (Y); Band; Concert Band; Mrchg Band; Hon Roll; Engr.

ACKIEWICZ, JOSEPH; Shenandoah Valley HS; Shenandoah, PA; (Y); 5/106; Yrbk Sprt Ed; Hst Sr Cls; L Var Bsbl; Capt L Ftbl; Wt Lftg; Hon Roll; NHS; Mchncl Engrng.

ACKINCLOSE, LORI; Frazier HS; Fayette City, PA; (Y); FNA; Jr NHS; NHS.

ACKINCLOSE, TIM; Frazier HS; Fayette City, PA; (Y); JV Bsktbl; High Hon Roll; Hon Roll; CA U Pennsylvania; History.

ACOSTA, FELIX; The Christian Acad; Chester, PA; (Y); Church Yth Grp; Chorus; Rep Frsh Cls; Rep Soph Cls; Pres Stu Cncl; Stat Bsktbl; Capt Crs Cntry; Capt Trk; Cit Awd; Prfct Atten Awd; VA Military Inst; Law.

ACQUAROLO, MICHAEL; St John Neumann HS; Philadelphia, PA; (Y); 8/350; French Clb; Var L Bowling; French Hon Soc; High Hon Roll; Jr NHS; NHS; Temple; Comm.

ADAIR, JENNIFER; General Mc Lane HS; Edinboro, PA; (Y); 14/220; Church Yth Grp; Model UN; Spanish Clb; Band; Concert Band; Jazz Band; Mrchg Band; Pep Band; Symp Band; Hon Roll; Edinboro U; Secndry Educ.

ADAIR, JOHN; Valley Forge Military Acad; Glen Burnie, MD; (Y); 18/145; Boy Scts; Church Yth Grp; Letterman Clb; Varsity Clb; Chorus; Drill Tm; Var Wrstlng; God Cntry Awd; Hon Roll; NHS; Expermnt In Intl Lvng Swtzrlnd 85; Perry Syst Extnsv Wrstlng Cmp USNA 86; Invstmnt Bnkr.

ADAM, DENISE; Hamburg Area HS; Hamburg, PA; (Y); 4/152; High Hon Roll; Hon Roll; NHS; German Ntl Hnr Soc 85-86; Trig,Alg III Acad Ltr Awd 85; Analysis Acad Ltr Awd 86.

ADAMCZAK, PAUL; Allentown Central Catholic HS; Allentown, PA; (Y); Church Yth Grp; Exploring; FBLA; Service Clb; Rep Jr Cls; VP Sr Cls; Rep Stu Cncl; Capt Var Ftbl; Wt Lftg; Var Wrstlng; CPA.

ADAMECZ, HEIDI ANN; Quakertown Community SR HS; Quakertown, PA; (Y); 2/274; Cmnty Wkr; Dance Clb; Model UN; Ski Clb; Varsity Clb; Chorus; Color Guard; Drill Tm; Flag Corp; School Musical; Bst/Clss, Soc Womns Engrs Awd, Schlrshp Cornell U 86; Cornell U; Engrng.

ADAMETZ, GREG; Belle Vernon Area HS; Belle Vernon, PA; (Y); Exploring; JA; Bowling; Socr; Venture Club Schlrshp Awd 86; Sec & Treas Police Epxlrs; Rober Morris Coll; Bus Admin.

ADAMETZ, KAREN; Richland HS; Wexford, PA; (Y); Dance Clb; Debate Tm; Library Aide; Chorus; School Musical; Sec Swing Chorus; Variety Show; Capt Cheerleading; High Hon Roll; Hon Roll; Accntng.

ADAMO, ANTHONY; Tunkhannock Area HS; Tunkhannock, PA; (S); 5/315; VP Cmnty Wkr; Trs Intnl Clb; Key Clb; Trs Letterman Clb; Off Service Clb; Spanish Clb; Band; Rep Stu Cncl; Var L Crs Cntry; Var L Trk; Var X-Cntry Mst Val Awd 84; U PA; Engrng.

ADAMO, RHONDA; Clearfield HS; Clearfield, PA; (Y); French Clb; FBLA; Key Clb; Sftbl; Hon Roll; Acctg.

ADAMROVICH, DOUGLAS; Mt Pleasant Area HS; Mount Pleasant, PA; (Y); German Clb; L Bsbl; L Ftbl; Im Wt Lftg; Hon Roll.

ADAMS, ABIGAIL; Fairview HS; Fairview, PA; (Y); 11/184; French Clb; Trk; Hon Roll; NHS; Purdue U; Physics.

ADAMS, AIDA M; Phila HS Of Engineering And Sci; Philadelphia, PA; (Y); Drama Clb; JA; Office Aide; School Play; Stage Crew; Nwsp Rptr; Yrbk Stf; Hon Roll; Ntl Merit Ltr; Excllnt Svc Lt Sfty Mrshll 85; Microbio.

ADAMS, AMBER; Bishop Hannan HS; Scranton, PA; (Y); 18/123; Cmnty Wkr; Exploring; Ski Clb; Stage Crew; High Hon Roll; NHS; Pres Schlr; Church Yth Grp; School Musical; School Play; Schlstc Bonus U Of Scrntn 86-87; Mdl Outstndg Achvmnt Art 83-86; Times Blue Ky Awd Art 85; U Of Scranton; Physcl Thrpy.

ADAMS, BECKY; Southern Columbia HS; Elysburg, PA; (Y); 22/91; Key Clb; Varsity Clb; Trs Stu Cncl; Bsktbl; Fld Hcky; Sftbl; DAR Awd; Elks Awd; NHS; Rotary Awd; Wayne Erdman Mem Awd 86; Millersville U.

ADAMS, BERTHAJO; Sullivan County HS; Dushore, PA; (Y); Drama Clb; Ski Clb; Mrchg Band; Bsktbl; Crs Cntry; Sftbl; Vllybl; High Hon Roll; Rotary Awd.

ADAMS, BILL; Greater Latrobe HS; Latrobe, PA; (Y); Army.

ADAMS, CARRIE; Gettysburg SR HS; Gettysburg, PA; (Y); Church Yth Grp; FCA; Varsity Clb; VP Sr Cls; Stat Bsktbl; JV Fld Hcky; Hon Roll; Messiah Coll; Elem Educ.

ADAMS, CHRISTINE; Tunkhannock Area HS; Mehoopany, PA; (S); 43/280; Church Yth Grp; Cmnty Wkr; Girl Scts; Letterman Clb; Band; Concert Band; Mrchg Band; JV Var Bsktbl; JV Var Fld Hcky; Hon Roll.

ADAMS, CHRISTOPHER M; Fairview HS; Fairview, PA; (Y); 58/183; Drama Clb; PAVAS; Ski Clb; Thesps; Band; Concert Band; Jazz Band; Mrchg Band; Pep Band; School Musical; Humboldt ST Coll CA; Ocngrphy.

ADAMS JR, CLAYTON M; Roman Catholic HS; Philadelphia, PA; (S); Var JV Bsktbl; Hon Roll; Ntl Merit Ltr; Depaul; Law.

ADAMS, DAN; Union HS; Rimersburg, PA; (Y); 12/70; Church Yth Grp; Bsbl; Bsktbl; Ftbl; Trk; Wt Lftg; Chem Engr.

ADAMS, DAWNNA; Greater Latrobe SR HS; Pleasant Unity, PA; (Y); DECA; 4-H; Hon Roll; Svc Sta Retailing Comp Wnnr DECA, Svc Sta Rtlng 2nd DECA 86; Acctg.

ADAMS, GEORGE; Rocky Grove HS; Franklin, PA; (Y); Band; Concert Band; Yrbk Stf; Var JV Bsktbl; JV Crs Cntry; Var Golf; Var Tennis; Im Vllybl.

ADAMS, GREGORY; Tunkhannock Area HS; Mehoopany, PA; (S); 4-H; FFA; Chorus; JV Wrstlng; 4-H Awd; Hon Roll; Penn ST U; Ag.

ADAMS, JAY; Franklin HS; Franklin, PA; (Y); 9/213; Radio Clb; Pres Concert Band; Jazz Band; Pres Mrchg Band; Pep Band; Var Trk; DAR Awd; High Hon Roll; Kiwanis Awd; NHS; Notl Merit Semifnlst; Presdnts Acadmc Ftnss Awd; PA Gov Schl Sci 85; Grove City Coll; Elec Engr.

ADAMS, JODI; Hamburg Area HS; Shoemakersville, PA; (Y); Spanish Clb; Crim Jstc.

ADAMS, KELLY; Wyoming Valley West HS; Kingston, PA; (Y); 3/400; Nwsp Rptr; Nwsp Stf; Yrbk Rptr; Yrbk Stf; Lit Mag; Trs Stu Cncl; Cheerleading; Cit Awd; NHS; VFW Awd; U Of PA; Bus.

ADAMS, KEVIN THOMAS; John S Fine SR HS; Nanticoke, PA; (Y); Chess Clb; SADD; Timer; Var Trk; High Hon Roll; Hon Roll; Schls Tp Scor Amer Chemcl Socts Lvl I Tst 85; Kings Coll; Pre-Med.

ADAMS, KIMBERLY; Blacklick Valley JR-SR HS; Twin Rocks, PA; (S); 4/96; Camera Clb; Church Yth Grp; Pep Clb; Ski Clb; Rep Stu Cncl; Var Cheerleading; Score Keeper; Stat Trk; Hon Roll; NHS.

ADAMS, KIMBERLY; Meadville Area SR HS; Meadville, PA; (Y); 30/287; Pres Church Yth Grp; Science Clb; Service Clb; Varsity Clb; Chorus; Concert Band; Rep Stu Cncl; Var Capt Cheerleading; High Hon Roll; Outstndng Chrldr 84-85; Outstndng Acad Achvt 83-85; U Of TN-MARTIN; Psychlgy.

ADAMS, MATTHEW; Rockwood Area HS; Confluence, PA; (S); 17/96; Quiz Bowl; Teachers Aide; Chorus; Nwsp Rptr; Nwsp Stf; Stu Cncl; Var Capt Crs Cntry; Var Capt Trk; Hon Roll; VP NHS; Kent ST U; Hstry Tchr.

ADAMS, MELINDA; Mahoney Area HS; Barnesville, PA; (Y); Church Yth Grp; Cmnty Wkr; Drama Clb; Spanish Clb; Chorus; School Play; Stage Crew; Variety Show; Nwsp Rptr; Nwsp Sprt Ed; Lifeguard & CPR Card Owner 85-86; X-Ray Tech.

ADAMS, OLIVIA A; St Maria Goretti HS; Philadelphia, PA; (Y); 72/402; Church Yth Grp; Debate Tm; Exploring; Intnl Clb; JA; Latin Clb; Math Clb; Pep Clb; Science Clb; Service Clb; Messiah Coll; Law.

ADAMS, PAM; Upper Dauphin Area HS; Lykens, PA; (Y); Trs Church Yth Grp; Computer Clb; Chorus; Concert Band; Drm Mjr(t); School Musical; Swing Chorus; Yrbk Bus Mgr; Trs Jr Cls; Twrlr; Drunk Drvg Slogn Cntst 1st Schlrshp 85; Schltc Achvt Awd 86; Fash Merch.

ADAMS, PAM; West Middlesex JR SR HS; Mercer, PA; (S); 7/125; FBLA; Hosp Aide; Library Aide; High Hon Roll; Hon Roll; NHS; Spanish NHS; Elem Educ.

ADAMS, PHILIP M; Pocono Mountain HS; Tannersville, PA; (Y); 112/315; Am Leg Boys St; Dance Clb; Service Clb; Off Frsh Cls; Off Soph Cls; Pres VP Stu Cncl; Cit Awd; Awd Contrbtngh Most To Schl 84-86; Pol Sci.

ADAMS, REBECCA; Franklin JR SR HS; Harrisville, PA; (Y); 31/213; Band; Chorus; Concert Band; Mrchg Band; High Hon Roll; Hon Roll; NHS; Secy Awd For Outstndng Sr 86; Med Secy.

ADAMS, REBECCA; Marion Center Area HS; Creekside, PA; (Y); Church Yth Grp; FNA; Red Cross Aide; Teachers Aide; VICA; Band; Church Choir; Mrchg Band; Orch; Pep Band; Mt Aloysius; Nrsg.

ADAMS, REBECCA; Portage Area HS; Portage, PA; (Y); 25/150; Church Yth Grp; Cmnty Wkr; Drama Clb; English Clb; Letterman Clb; PAVAS; Ski Clb; Band; Chorus; Church Choir; Schlrshp West Chesker U Vc Prfrmnc 86; West Chester U; Vc Prfrmnc.

ADAMS, RICHARD; Strong Vincent HS; Erie, PA; (Y); 24/200; Var JV Bsbl; Var Bsktbl; Hon Roll; Kent ST U; Accntng.

ADAMS, SARAH; Bishop Shanahan HS; W Chester, PA; (Y); 104/218; School Musical; School Play; Hon Roll; Hist.

ADAMS, SCOTT; Hempfield HS; Lancaster, PA; (Y); 6/430; Rep Church Yth Grp; Church Choir; Mrchg Band; Hon Roll; NHS; Youth Schlrs Prog Chem Schlrshp 86; Arch.

ADAMS, SHARI; Warren Area HS; Warren, PA; (Y); Acpl Chr; Concert Band; Mrchg Band; Orch; School Musical; Yrbk Ed-Chief; Cit Awd; High Hon Roll; NHS; Pres Schlr; Natl Hstry Day Regnl Lvl 1st & 2nd Pl 84-86; Natl Hstry Day ST Lvl 84-86; Med.

ADAMS, SHEMAINE; William Allen HS; Allentown, PA; (Y); Art Clb; Teachers Aide; Chorus; Hon Roll; Temple U; Art Tchr.

ADAMS, STACEY; Somerset Area HS; Somerset, PA; (Y); 24/239; Drama Clb; English Clb; French Clb; Varsity Clb; School Play; Yrbk Stf; Stu Cncl; Cheerleading; High Hon Roll; Hon Roll; Penn ST; Marine Blgy.

ADAMS, TAMARA; Greater Works Acad; Monroeville, PA; (Y); 11/36; Yrbk Stf; Rep Jr Cls; VP Stu Cncl; Var Cheerleading; Var Vllybl; Hon Roll; PA ST U; Acctg.

ADAMS, TAMMY; Canon Mc Millan HS; Strabane, PA; (Y); 1/390; French Clb; Ski Clb; Flag Corp; Im Vllybl; High Hon Roll.

ADAMSKI, JANET; Wyoming Valley West HS; Larksville, PA; (Y); Church Yth Grp; High Hon Roll; Hon Roll; Prfct Atten Awd; Luzerne County CC; Tchr.

ADAMSON, LISA; Marion Center Area HS; Marion Ctr, PA; (Y); Church Yth Grp; FBLA; FHA; Pep Clb; Hon Roll.

ADDIS, JOHN; Bradford Area HS; Derrick City, PA; (Y); Am Leg Boys St; Boy Scts; Key Clb; Ski Clb; Mgr Bsktbl; Var L Ftbl; Var L Trk; Var L Wrstlng; High Hon Roll; Hon Roll; 1st Tm Dist 9 Ftbl All Star 85; Dist 9 Rnnr Up Wrstlng 86; 2nd Pl ST Greco-Roman Wrstlng 86; Pre-Law.

ADDIS, RANDY; Trinity HS; Washington, PA; (Y); Boy Scts; Chess Clb; Exploring; Hosp Aide; Chorus; Ftbl; Cazinovia Coll; Trnsprt.

ADELMANN, DIANA; Notre Dame HS; Stroudsburg, PA; (Y); Stage Crew; Nwsp Stf; Trs Frsh Cls; Pres Soph Cls; Stat Bsbl; Var JV Cheerleading; Var Fld Hcky; Wilkes Coll; Bus Mgt.

ADELSON, SUSAN; Coughlin HS; Laflin, PA; (Y); Office Aide; Temple Yth Grp; Color Guard; Nwsp Stf; Yrbk Stf; Hon Roll; Jr NHS; NHS; Ldrshp Ltr Awd 86; Pres Physcl Awd 86; Typng Awd 84; Lezeune CC; Phrmcy.

ADER, MARGIE; Pennsbury HS; Yardley, PA; (Y); Drama Clb; Intnl Clb; Political Wkr; Service Clb; SADD; Teachers Aide; Pres Temple Yth Grp; Chorus; School Musical; School Play; Tchrs Asstnt Awd 85; Outstndng Achvt Awd In Grmn 86; Cmndtn For Outstndng Achvt In Anlys & Spch 86; Psychlgy.

ADHAM, HOPE; Seneca Valley SR HS; Zelienople, PA; (Y); Letterman Clb; School Play; Nwsp Stf; Off Stu Cncl; L Capt Swmmng; Stat Trk; Hon Roll; David A Ketterer Awd Swmming Hardest Wrkr 85-86; Allegheny Coll PA.

ADKINSON, ERICA; Philadelphia HS For Girls; Philadelphia, PA; (Y); Teachers Aide; Stage Crew; Nwsp Stf; Hon Roll; Jr NHS; Spanish NHS.

ADLER, DAVID; Upper Dublin HS; Dresher, PA; (Y); FBLA; Intnl Clb; Pres Rep JA; Math Tm; Service Clb; Temple Yth Grp; Yrbk Rptr; Yrbk Stf; JV Bowling; NHS; Intl Exchng 84; Muhlenberg Coll.

ADOLF, CINDY; Cardinal O Haro HS; Drexel Hill, PA; (Y); 43/772; Art Clb; Church Yth Grp; Dance Clb; Service Clb; Spanish Clb; Rptr Yrbk Sprt Ed; Yrbk Stf; High Hon Roll; Hon Roll; NHS; Schlstc Awd Art 86; Prncpls Awd 85 & 86; Cmrcl Art.

ADOMAITIS, TERI; Seneca Valley SR HS; Zelienople, PA; (Y); Thesps; School Play; Lit Mag; Twrlr; Church Yth Grp; Hon Roll; Melissa Lang Outstndng Colorguard Awd 86; Mrchng Band Ltr 86; Butler CO CC; Legal Secry.

ADOMITIS, MELISSA; Wyoming Area SR HS; W Wyoming, PA; (Y); French Clb; Ski Clb; Nwsp Stf; Rep Stu Cncl; Crs Cntry; High Hon Roll; Bus Mrktng.

ADSIT, KIPPY; Conneaut Lake HS; Conneaut Lake, PA; (Y); 2/87; Pres Church Yth Grp; Spanish Clb; Band; Church Choir; Concert Band; Mrchg Band; Pep Band; High Hon Roll; NHS; Drama Clb; Greenville Symphny 86; Cedarville Coll.

ADVINCULA, ARNOLD P; Bishop Neumann HS; Lock Haven, PA; (Y); 1/45; Model UN; NFL; Pep Clb; Pres Soph Cls; Pres Stu Cncl; Im Bsktbl; L Socr; High Hon Roll; NHS; Val; Am Legn Sch Awd 83; Exchng Clb Yth Of Yr 86; Supr Delg Awd 86; U Of Scranton; Med.

ADZENTOIVICH, ERNIE; Mahanoy Area HS; New Boston, PA; (Y); Aud/Vis; Ski Clb; Stage Crew; Variety Show; Im Bsktbl; Var L Ftbl; JV Wrstlng; Hon Roll; NHS; Music.

AEBLI, FRED; Scranton Central HS; Scranton, PA; (Y); Church Yth Grp; Band; Trs Sr Cls; Stu Cncl; Hon Roll; Boys Clb Am; Mrchg Band; Orch; Boy Cntrbtd Mst To Cls; Cls Hstrn; Penn ST; Comp Sci.

AFFLERBACH, SUSAN; Pennridge HS; Perkasie, PA; (Y); 101/414; SADD; Chrmn Stu Cncl; Var Capt Cheerleading; Mgr(s); Hon Roll; Kutztown U; Med Tech.

AGATE, DAVID; Penn Hills HS; Pittsburgh, PA; (Y); 60/762; Church Yth Grp; Exploring; German Clb; JV Wrstlng; High Hon Roll; Hon Roll; NHS; U Pittsbgh.

AGATE, JENNIFER; Laurel Highlands HS; Uniontown, PA; (S); 11/400; FBLA; Yrbk Stf; Cheerleading; Sftbl; Vllybl; CC Awd; High Hon Roll; Jr NHS; NHS; PA ST; Accntng.

AGLER, KIMBERLY; Warrior Run HS; Watsontown, PA; (Y); 8/176; Hosp Aide; Trs Spanish Clb; Varsity Clb; Ed Yrbk Ed-Chief; Yrbk Phtg; VP Sr Cls; Rep Stu Cncl; Var Bsktbl; Hon Roll; Pres Schlr; Yung Amercn 85; PA ST U Schlrshp 86; PA ST U; Cmptr Sci.

AGNEW, JON; Penn Hills SR HS; Pittsburgh, PA; (Y); Science Clb; Crs Cntry; Trk; Natl Sci.

AGOSTINELLI, MICHELE; Mt Lebanon HS; Mt Lebanon, PA; (Y); 28/532; Hosp Aide; Sec Soph Cls; VP Jr Cls; VP Sr Cls; Var Crs Cntry; Var Trk; High Hon Roll; Hon Roll; Chem Key 84-85; Penn ST U.

AGOSTO, LISETTE M; St Hubert Catholic HS; Philadelphia, PA; (Y); 36/367; Cmnty Wkr; Spanish Clb; Sr Cls; NHS; Prfct Atten Awd; Pres Schrlshp Wagner Coll 86; Wagner Coll; Bus Adm.

AGOVINO, FRANK; West Catholic HS; Philadelphia, PA; (Y); 35/270; Pep Clb; Varsity Clb; Nwsp Rptr; Nwsp Sprt Ed; Nwsp Stf; Yrbk Stf; Var Capt Bsbl; Stat Ftbl; Var Mgr(s); Hon Roll; Jrnlsm.

AGUILAR, ANNA K; Central Catholic HS; Allentown, PA; (Y); Var JV Cheerleading; Var JV Sftbl; Hon Roll; Prfct Atten Awd; Chrldng Camp 1st Pl 85; U Of CA San Francisco; Pre-Med.

AHLBORN, JENNIFER M; Elizabethtown Area HS; Elizabethtown, PA; (Y); Trs Girl Scts; Model UN; Thesps; Chorus; Capt Drill Tm; Orch; Yrbk Ed-Chief; NCTE Awd; NHS; Ntl Merit SF; Human Rltns Clb Sec; Girl Mnth 85; Engl.

AHLERT, MICHAEL; Moravian Acad; Buttzville, NJ; (Y).

AHLQUIST, RONALD; Kiski Area HS; Apollo, PA; (Y); German Clb; High Hon Roll; Hon Roll; Acad Schlrshp Robert Morris Coll; Robert Morris Coll; Finance.

AHNER, DARRYL; Lehighton Area HS; Palmerton, PA; (Y); Debate Tm; Scholastic Bowl; Chorus; Concert Band; Mrchg Band; Var Bsktbl; Var Trk; Hon Roll; Lion Awd; NHS; Maj Genrl Bert A David Awd 86; US Military Acad; Engrng.

AHNER, TISHA; Lehighton Area HS; Lehighton, PA; (Y); Girl Scts; Hosp Aide; Nwsp Rptr; Nwsp Stf; Hon Roll.

AHRENS, ANDREA; Exeter Township SR HS; Reading, PA; (Y); Varsity Clb; Sec Y-Teens; Concert Band; Mrchg Band; Trs Soph Cls; Pres Jr Cls; Pres Sr Cls; Rep Stu Cncl; Fld Hcky; Jr NHS; U Of Pittsburgh; Bio.

AHRENS, JESSICA M; Jersey Shore Area SR HS; Jersey Shores, PA; (Y); 9/200; Sec VP Church Yth Grp; Letterman Clb; Band; Chorus; Concert Band; Mrchg Band; School Musical; Var Capt Trk; High Hon Roll; NHS; Dist And Regnl Chrs 84-85; IN U PA; Commctns.

AIELLO, JAMES; West Hazleton HS; W Hazleton, PA; (Y); 62/200; Scholastic Bowl; Spanish Clb; JV Var Bowling; PA ST U; Comp Sci.

AIELLO, JOHN; Central Catholic HS; Pittsburgh, PA; (Y); 94/263; Church Yth Grp; Yrbk Rptr; JV Bsbl; Im Bsktbl; Im Ftbl; Im Vllybl; Var Capt Wrstlng; Hon Roll; Capt Vrsty Wrstlng 2nd Yr Lttrmn 86; Cnslr Chrch Grp 86; Hnr Rll 85; U Of Pittsburgh; Bus.

AIELLO, MICHELLE; Bishop Hafey HS; Hazleton, PA; (Y); 35/182; Hosp Aide; Office Aide; Ski Clb; Spanish Clb; Y-Teens; Color Guard; Yrbk Stf; Trk; Hon Roll; NHS; PA ST U; Bus Adm.

AIGLER, JOLENE; West Snyder HS; Beavertown, PA; (Y); 11/93; Pres Church Yth Grp; Rptr FBLA; Sec Band; Concert Band; Mrchg Band; Nwsp Rptr; Nwsp Stf; Hon Roll; Prfct Atten Awd; Acad Ltr 83-84 & 85-86; Acctng I Awd 86.

AIKEN, ADRIENNE; Hollidaysburg SR HS; Hollidaysburg, PA; (Y); Var L Bsktbl; Var L Sftbl; Var L Vllybl.

AIKEY, LAURA; Westmont Hilltop HS; Johnstown, PA; (Y); 25/151; Concert Band; Jazz Band; Orch; Cheerleading; Var Stat Vllybl; High Hon Roll; NHS; IUP Hon Band 86; IN U Of PA; Jrnlsm.

AIKEY, MELINDA SUE; Mifflinburg Area HS; Mifflinburg, PA; (Y); 2/160; Am Leg Aux Girls St; German Clb; Hosp Aide; Key Clb; Yrbk Ed-Chief; Cheerleading; JV Fld Hcky; JV Sftbl; NHS; Geisinger Schl Of Nrsng; Nrsng.

AIKINS, BRENDA; Kiski Area HS; Vandrgrift, PA; (Y); Pep Clb; Chorus; Yrbk Stf; Var L Sftbl; High Hon Roll; Hon Roll; Mercyhurst Clg.

AIKINS, DENISE; Leechburg Area HS; Leechburg, PA; (Y); Drama Clb; Library Aide; Chorus; Yrbk Stf; Score Keeper; Bradford Schl Of Bus; Exec Sec.

AIL, MICHELLE; Palmyra Area SR HS; Palmyra, PA; (Y); 29/200; 4-H; Quiz Bowl; Spanish Clb; Band; Chorus; Mrchg Band; Tennis; 4-H Awd; High Hon Roll; Hon Roll; Acctg.

AIMINO, BARBARA; Punxsutawney Area HS; Rochester Mills, PA; (Y); French Clb; Science Clb; Varsity Clb; Band; Drm Mjr(t); Mrchg Band; Bsktbl; Tennis; Hon Roll; Rotary Awd.

AINSLEY, MARCIA; Connellsville Area HS; Normalville, PA; (Y); Camera Clb; Church Yth Grp; Girl Scts; Ski Clb; Band; Concert Band; Mrchg Band; Pep Band; Sftbl; Hon Roll; Vet.

AITA, KIM; St Marie Goretti HS; Philadelphia, PA; (Y); French Clb; GAA; Mathletes; Stage Crew; Hon Roll; Phila Cthlc Mathletes Leag Cert Of Merit 85-86; Drexel U; Sci Fld.

AITKEN, KIP; Mt Lebanon HS; Pittsburgh, PA; (Y); Key Clb; Science Clb; SADD; Stage Crew; Pres Frsh Cls; Pres Soph Cls; Pres Jr Cls; Pres Stu Cncl; Crs Cntry; Tennis; PA Jnr Acad Of Sci-1st Rgn-1st ST; Buhl Sci Awd-Cash 84 & 86; Pre-Med.

AKAM, THOMAS; Corry Area HS; Spartansburg, PA; (S); 4-H; Spanish Clb; 4-H Awd; Dairy Sci.

AKDOGAN, OZLEM; Exeter HS; Reading, PA; (Y); 9/200; Sec Band; Jazz Band; Orch; Pep Band; School Musical; Rep Sr Cls; JV Fld Hcky; Jr NHS; NHS; Rgn 415 Orch 86; Lehigh U; Elec Engrng.

AKHTAR, SAADIA R; Schenley HS Teachers Center; Pittsburgh, PA; (S); Math Tm; School Play; Ed Yrbk Stf; Rep Jr Cls; Mgr Swmmng; High Hon Roll; NHS; Prfct Atten Awd.

AKINGS, SHARON; Avon Grove HS; West Grove, PA; (Y); Computer Clb; Drama Clb; Spanish Clb; Chorus; School Musical; Variety Show; Nwsp Stf; Bsktbl; Hon Roll; Stu Senate Awd 86; Isiah Smith Mem Awd 85; Outstndg Prfrmnce Pub Spkg 85; U Pittsburgh; Bus Adm.

ALAM, ANTHONY; Quigley HS; Aliquippa, PA; (Y); 61/104; Exploring; Stage Crew; Bus Admin.

ALAMPI, MICHAEL; Bangor Area HS; Bangor, PA; (Y); 8/175; Am Leg Boys St; Computer Clb; Office Aide; Yrbk Stf; Rep Stu Cncl; Var JV Bsktbl; Var Capt Golf; High Hon Roll; Hon Roll; Jr NHS; Bus Admin.

ALBA, KIM; Pittston Area SR HS; Pittston, PA; (Y); Computer Clb; Key Clb; Math Clb; Ski Clb; Yrbk Stf; Pres Stu Cncl; Var Chrmn Cheerleading; Hon Roll; Hmcmng Ct 3rd Rnnr Up 85; Chrldng Co-Capt, Lttr & Trphy 85-86; Luzerne County CC; Bus Adm.

ALBA, PATRICK; Wyoming Area HS; Wyoming, PA; (Y); Aud/Vis; Boy Scts; Band; Concert Band; Jazz Band; Mrchg Band; Bsbl; Bowling; Golf; Hon Roll; Penn ST; Cermc Engrng.

ALBANESE, MICHAEL; Pen Argyl Area HS; Wind Gap, PA; (Y); 36/160; Ski Clb; Varsity Clb; Chorus; Stage Crew; Ftbl; Trk; Wt Lftg; Wrstlng; High Hon Roll; Hon Roll; Bloomsburg U; Sci.

ALBANI, TERESA M; Alberrt Gallatin SR HS; Masontown, PA; (Y); 20/154; Church Yth Grp; 4-H; Pep Clb; Ski Clb; Teachers Aide; Acpl Chr; Band; Chorus; Concert Band; Mrchg Band; St Vincents Coll; Fshn Merch.

ALBANO, CHRISTINE; Mt Lebanon HS; Mt Lebanon, PA; (Y); Dance Clb; Var Trk; Pep Clb; SADD; Mrchg Band; Pep Band; L Pom Pon; Score Keeper; PA ST U; Bus.

ALBAUGH, KAREN; Venango Christian HS; Oil City, PA; (Y); Cmnty Wkr; Drama Clb; Hosp Aide; School Play; Var Bsktbl; JV Vllybl; Hon Roll; Elem Educ.

ALBEE, JACQUELINE M; Cardinal O Hara HS; Broomall, PA; (Y); Church Yth Grp; Hosp Aide; Teachers Aide; School Musical; School Play; Nwsp Rptr; Engl Acad Awd 84-85.

ALBERA, DANA; Pottsgrove HS; Pottstown, PA; (Y); 83/229; Debate Tm; French Clb; Library Aide; Model UN; Pep Clb; Ski Clb; Varsity Clb; Orch; Fld Hcky; Wrstlng; Elizabethtown Coll; Pysch.

ALBERT, CARRIE; Lakeland HS; Jermyn, PA; (S); 10/152; Art Clb; 4-H; JA; Spanish Clb; Yrbk Stf; 4-H Awd; Hon Roll; Scranton U; Bio.

ALBERT, DANETTE; Hamburg Area HS; Hamburg, PA; (Y); Sec Chess Clb; Trs Church Yth Grp; French Clb; German Clb; Library Aide; Ski Clb; Chorus; Church Choir; School Musical; Variety Show; Acadmc Ltr-Hstry; Slct Chrs; Widener; Mech Engrng.

ALBERT, JUDITH; Northern Senior HS; Dillsburg, PA; (Y); 14/209; Church Yth Grp; French Clb; Chorus; Church Choir; High Hon Roll; Hon Roll; Messiah Coll; Nrsng.

ALBERT, MIKE; Greater Latrobe SR HS; Latrobe, PA; (Y); 115/410; Computer Clb; FCA; JCL; Trk; Hon Roll; Prfct Atten Awd; Pre-Med.

ALBERT, MYRNA; Northern HS; Dillsburg, PA; (Y); Pres Church Yth Grp; French Hon Soc; High Hon Roll; Hon Roll.

ALBERT, RUSSELL; Wilson Area HS; Easton, PA; (S); 8/127; Rep Church Yth Grp; JV Bsbl; Var Wt Lftg; High Hon Roll; NHS; MINISTER.

ALBERT, SHERRY; Donegal HS; Marietta, PA; (Y); Var L Cheerleading; Fld Hcky; Wrkng Chldrn.

ALBERTINE, KARA; Hazleton HS; Audenried, PA; (Y); FBLA; Data Proc.

ALBERTSON JR, DENNIS E; Benton Area HS; Orangeville, PA; (Y); 2/41; Pres Church Yth Grp; Yrbk Stf; NHS.

ALBRECHT, LORI; James M Coughlin HS; Wilkes-Barre, PA; (Y); 1/384; Exploring; Color Guard; Yrbk Stf; High Hon Roll; Jr NHS; NHS; Vet Med.

ALBRECHT, LORIANN; West Scranton SR HS; Scranton, PA; (Y); 30/250; Latin Clb; Thesps; Orch; School Play; Stage Crew; Nwsp Stf; Yrbk Ed-Chief; Cheerleading; High Hon Roll; NHS; Penn ST U; Art.

ALBRECHT, PHIL; Montoursville HS; Montoursville, PA; (Y); German Clb; Letterman Clb; Ski Clb; Var Bsbl; Var Ftbl; Wrstlng; Hon Roll; Cornell U; Med.

ALBRIGHT, CHRISTINE; Central HS; E Freedom, PA; (Y); FCA; VP FNA; GAA; Ski Clb; Varsity Clb; Yrbk Stf; Stu Cncl; Bsktbl; Crs Cntry; Trk; Med Asst.

ALBRIGHT, DEB; Central HS; Martnsburg, PA; (Y); GAA; Varsity Clb; Band; Chorus; Color Guard; Soph Cls; Trk; High Hon Roll; Hon Roll; NHS; Hnr Soc Awd Rep Edwin Johnson 86; Vrsty Ltr Trk 86; IN U PA; Elem Ed.

ALBRIGHT, JOHN; Upper Darby SR HS; Upper Darby, PA; (Y); JV Ftbl; Var Capt Trk; Hon Roll; Engrng.

ALCARAZ, LORI; Shenandoah Valley JR SR HS; Shenandoah, PA; (Y); 24/108; Computer Clb; Spanish Clb; Nwsp Stf; Yrbk Stf; Off Frsh Cls; Sftbl; Hon Roll.

ALCARO, ROSEMARY L; Saint Hubert HS; Philadelphia, PA; (Y); Art Clb; Drama Clb; JA; Teachers Aide; Chorus; Stage Crew; Lit Mag; Trk; Hon Roll; NHS; Phila Chptr Knghts Of Clmbs For Svc To Schl Awd 86; Cert Acdmc Merit Art II 85; Phila Coll Txtl & Sci; Philadelphia Coll Txtl & Sci.

ALCENDOR, VINNAE; Steelton-Highspire HS; Steelton, PA; (Y); 44/99; Church Yth Grp; Computer Clb; Library Aide; Pep Clb; Spanish Clb; Speech Tm; Church Choir; Yrbk Stf.

ALCORN, DIANE; Punxsutawney Area SR HS; Mayport, PA; (Y); Hon Roll; Prfct Atten Awd; Bus.

ALDER, TRACEY; Palisades HS; Coopersburg, PA; (Y); 30/150; Sec FBLA; Office Aide; Flag Corp; Mrchg Band; CC Awd; High Hon Roll; Hon Roll; Jr NHS; Cert Of Merit-Sectrl 86; FBLA Rgnl Comptns-1st Pl Offc Prcdrs 86, 2nd Pl Bus Engl 85; Allentown Bus Schl; Exec Scrtl.

ALDERFER, AIMEE; Lower Morland HS; Huntingdon Valley, PA; (S); Church Yth Grp; Drama Clb; French Clb; Key Clb; Church Choir; Madrigals; School Musical; Rep Jr Cls; Rep Stu Cncl; Tennis; Forgn Lang.

ALDERFER, TIFFANY; Souderton Area HS; Harleysville, PA; (Y); Church Yth Grp; Chorus; School Musical; Trs Frsh Cls; Rep Stu Cncl; JV Sftbl; Hon Roll; Jr NHS; Svc Awd 84; Nrs.

ALDERSON, LARRY; Northeast Bradford HS; Lerayville, PA; (Y); Chess Clb; Computer Clb; FBLA; Pres Frsh Cls; Pres Soph Cls; Pres Jr Cls; Pres Sr Cls; High Hon Roll; Hon Roll; Dairy Frmr.

ALDRIDGE, RUDELLE; Lawrence County Area Vo-Tech; New Castle, PA; (Y); 15/245; FBLA; Church Choir; Yrbk Stf; Hon Roll; U Pittsburgh; Exec Sectry.

ALEO, GINAMARIE; G A R Memorial HS; Wilkes Barre, PA; (Y); 31/176; Office Aide; Chorus; Hon Roll; NHS; Wilkes Coll; Hstry.

ALESE, EUGENE; Kiski HS; Vandergrift, PA; (Y); Computer Clb; Pep Clb; SADD; Mrchg Band; Symp Band; Rep Frsh Cls; Rep Jr Cls; Rep Stu Cncl; Var Tennis; Var Trk; Hnr Band 84.

ALESE, GENE; Kiski HS; Vandergrift, PA; (Y); Chess Clb; Computer Clb; Pep Clb; SADD; Mrchg Band; Pep Band; Symp Band; Rep Frsh Cls; Rep Jr Cls; Rep Stu Cncl; Hnr Band 84.

ALEXANDER, CHRISTINA; St Pius X HS; Phoenixville, PA; (Y); 18/161; AFS; Pres Drama Clb; Service Clb; Spanish Clb; School Play; Rptr Nwsp Stf; Stu Cncl; Hon Roll; NHS; Spanish NHS; Acad All Am Exc Awd 86; Pre-Law.

ALEXANDER, COLLEEN; H S Truman HS; Levittown, PA; (Y); Hosp Aide; Political Wkr; Rep Frsh Cls; Rep Soph Cls.

ALEXANDER, DAWN; Halifax Area HS; Halifax, PA; (Y); 51/106; Church Yth Grp; Drama Clb; 4-H; FBLA; Band; Chorus; Church Choir; 4-H Awd; Hon Roll; Gordon Coll; Chld Psych.

ALEXANDER, GWENDOLYN RAE; Warren Area HS; Warren, PA; (Y); French Clb; Math Tm; Ski Clb; Acpl Chr; Hon Roll; Jr NHS; NHS; Pres Acadmc Fitnss Awd 86; G Washington U; Pub/Intl Affrs.

ALEXANDER, JEFFREY W; Upper Merion Area HS; King Of Prussia, PA; (Y); 4/278; Aud/Vis; Pres Computer Clb; Capt Math Tm; Im Vllybl; Hon Roll; Mu Alp Tht; Ntl Merit SF; Pres Acad Fit Awd 86; ARML Comptn 4th Tm Pl 86; Phila Sci Cncl Physcs Awd 86; Carnegie-Mellon U; Comp Engrg.

ALEXANDER, MARJORIE; Riverview HS; Verona, PA; (Y); Am Leg Aux Girls St; Chorus; Yrbk Ed-Chief; Yrbk Stf; Jr Cls; Powder Puff Ftbl; Score Keeper; High Hon Roll; Hon Roll; NHS; Fash Merch.

ALEXANDER, MELISSA; St Clair Area HS; Pottsville, PA; (Y); 7/82; Church Yth Grp; Drama Clb; FHA; School Play; Stage Crew; Nwsp Rptr; Nwsp Stf; Yrbk Rptr; Yrbk Stf; High Hon Roll; Pres Acadmc Ftnss Awd 86; Avrg All 4 Yrs Of H S 86; Millersville KY; Psych.

ALEXANDER, RICHARD; West Scranton HS; Scranton, PA; (Y); Computer Clb; Latin Clb; Pep Clb; Ski Clb; Yrbk Stf; Hon Roll; NHS; PA ST U; Engr.

ALEXANDER, SHANE; Butler SR HS; Butler, PA; (Y); Art Clb; Boy Scts; Spanish Clb; Band; Mrchg Band; Symp Band; Variety Show; Yrbk Stf; Stu Cncl; Aanla Schl Tlnt Cntst 86; Art Cntst 81; Pitt U; Music.

ALEXANDER, TANYA; Creative & Performing Arts; Philadelphia, PA; (S); 14/160; Cmnty Wkr; Teachers Aide; Nwsp Ed-Chief; Yrbk Stf; Rep Frsh Cls; Rep Soph Cls; High Hon Roll; Hon Roll; NHS; Semi-Fin Natl Arts Recog Talent Srch 85; Recip Educ Roundtable Scholar 86; PA Govnrs Schl Art 85; Howard U; Comm Media.

ALEXANDER, TERRI; Northern SR HS; Wellsville, PA; (Y); 123/200; Pres Church Yth Grp; French Clb; Stage Crew; Yrbk Stf; Trs Stu Cncl; Powder Puff Ftbl; High Hon Roll; Spanish Clb; Yrbk Rptr; Young Life Christn Fellowshp 83-86; Peer Counslng 84-85; Lawbach Litrcy Councl Tutor 84-86; West Liberty ST Coll; Dentl.

ALEXANDER, TRACEY; Susquenita HS; Duncannon, PA; (S); 2/184; Drama Clb; Quiz Bowl; Spanish Clb; Chorus; School Musical; School Play; Yrbk Stf; Hon Roll; Penn ST U; Psychlgy.

ALEXANDER, WENDY; Towanda Area HS; Towanda, PA; (Y); Am Leg Aux Girls St; Church Yth Grp; French Clb; Science Clb; SADD; Chorus; Yrbk Stf; Sec Stu Cncl; Hon Roll; NHS; Comp Engrng.

ALEXY, SHERYL; Pennsbury HS; Fairless Hls, PA; (Y); Var Bowling; Hon Roll; NHS; Bucks County CC; Accntnt.

ALEY, WILLIAM T; Seneca Valley SR HS; Evans City, PA; (Y); 34/375; Chrmn SADD; Mrchg Band; School Musical; Symp Band; Yrbk Ed-Chief; High Hon Roll; Hon Roll; NHS; Regn I Band 86; Westminster Hnr Band 85 & 86; Dist V Band 85 & 86; Slippery Rock U; Music Ed.

ALFANO, CHRIS; York Vocational Schl; York, PA; (Y); 5/500; Hosp Aide; JA; Var Bsktbl; JV Score Keeper; Sftbl; High Hon Roll; Hon Roll; Acad Excllnc 86; York Coll; Rn.

ALFER, ANNE; Penn Hills SR HS; Pittsburgh, PA; (Y); FTA; Spanish Clb; Varsity Clb; Nwsp Rptr; Ed Yrbk Stf; Stu Cncl; Bsktbl; High Hon Roll; NHS; Prfct Atten Awd; Chthm; Elem Ed.

ALFORD, TAMMIE; Aliquippa SR HS; Aliquippa, PA; (S); 19/154; Chess Clb; Rptr DECA; Drama Clb; Band; Mrchg Band; Yrbk Phtg; Yrbk Stf; Off Jr Cls; Off Sr Cls; Hon Roll; Outstndng Prfrmnc Drma Clb 85; Actng.

ALFORD, VIVIAN; William Allen HS; Allentown, PA; (Y); 18/557; Dance Clb; VP JA; JCL; Spanish Clb; Nwsp Stf; Rep Stu Cncl; Hon Roll; Jr NHS; NHS; Ntl Merit Ltr; Ntl Ltn Exam-Gld Mdl-Summa Cum Laude 85; Semi-Fnlst Ntl Achvmnt Schlrshp Pgm Outstndng Ngro Stu 86; U Of PA; Nrsg.

ALGAR, DANIEL; Tunkhannock HS; Tunkhannock, PA; (S); Ski Clb; Crs Cntry; Ftbl; Trk; Wt Lftg; Hon Roll; NHS; Engrng.

ALIA, COLLEEN; St Maria Goretti HS; Philadelphia, PA; (Y); 70/420; Camera Clb; Cmnty Wkr; French Clb; Nwsp Phtg; Nwsp Rptr; Nwsp Stf; Tennis; Hon Roll; Phy Thrpy.

ALICEA, ELVIS; Bensalem HS; Bensalem, PA; (Y); 36/564; JV Var Ftbl; Wt Lftg; Var Capt Wrstlng; High Hon Roll; NHS; Outstndng SR Awd 85-86; Stu Of Mnth 81-82; Suburban I All Lg 2nd Tm Awd 85-86; Temple U; Acctng.

ALIMECCO, BETHANN; West Hazleton HS; Conyngham, PA; (Y); Church Yth Grp; French Clb; Pep Clb; Ski Clb; SADD; Color Guard; Physcl Thrpy.

ALISESKY, MARK; Bethel Park HS; Bethel Park, PA; (Y); 37/550; Band; Jazz Band; Mrchg Band; Orch; School Musical; Symp Band; Variety Show; High Hon Roll; NHS; Princpls Awd 84; Engrng.

ALLEGRUCCI, MARK; Lakeland HS; Olyphant, PA; (S); 20/162; French Clb; Hon Roll; Law.

ALLEMAN, FRANCES; Moshannon Valley HS; Glen Hope, PA; (Y); #5 In Class; Sec Church Yth Grp; Red Cross Aide; SADD; Church Choir; High Hon Roll; Hon Roll; NHS; Prfct Atten Awd; Comp Pgmrng.

ALLEMAN, MICHALLE; Susquenita HS; Marysville, PA; (S); 2/152; Trs Church Yth Grp; 4-H; Spanish Clb; Chorus; Church Choir; School Musical; Sftbl; High Hon Roll; Hon Roll; NHS; Exchng Stu To Costa Rica 85; Schl Sci Fair Awds 83 & 85; Engrng.

ALLEN, AMY; W Middlesex HS; New Wilmington, PA; (S); #15 In Class; Concert Band; Mrchg Band; Stu Cncl; Var Bsktbl; Sftbl; Var Vllybl; Hon Roll; 1st Tm All Cnty Bsktbl 84-85; 1st Tm All Cnty Vlybl 84-86; Hnrb Mntn Vlybl 83-84.

ALLEN, DAVID; Franklin Area SR HS; Franklin, PA; (Y); 27/221; L Band; Concert Band; Jazz Band; Mrchg Band; School Musical; School Play; Hon Roll; NHS; Ntl Merit Ltr; PA Gov Schl Arts 85; IN U Pennsylvania; Music.

ALLEN, DAVID; Oxford Area HS; Cochranville, PA; (Y); 19/160; Varsity Clb; Yrbk Stf; Hst Stu Cncl; Var Capt Ftbl; Var Trk; Var Wrstlng; Hon Roll; Lion Awd; Prfct Atten Awd; JV Bsbl; Vtd All Rnd SR Boy Stff 86; Frank J Michaels Schlrshp 86; Schlrly Athl Awd 86; U Of DE; Math.

ALLEN, DONALD R; Redhawk Valley HS; New Bethlehem, PA; (Y); Am Leg Boys St; Church Yth Grp; Speech Tm; Varsity Clb; School Musical; Ftbl; Trk; Wt Lftg; Upward Bound 84-87; Amer Leg Essay Cont Wnr 2nd Pl 86; Med.

ALLEN, ERIC; United HS; Armagh, PA; (Y); Church Yth Grp; Ski Clb; Var Ftbl; Hon Roll; Prfct Atten Awd; Bus Adm.

ALLEN, HEATHER ELIZABETH; Delaware County Christian HS; Newtown Sq, PA; (Y); Church Yth Grp; Drama Clb; Math Tm; Band; Rep Sr Cls; Var JV Fld Hcky; Var L Sftbl; Var L Trk; High Hon Roll; NHS; Social Work.

ALLEN, JANET; Brownsville Area SR HS; E Millsboro, PA; (S); 6/225; Church Yth Grp; Mathletes; Band; Concert Band; Mrchg Band; Yth Educ Assoc Sec; Rotary Stu Month; Compttv Schlrshp & Schl Educ Schlrshp Duquesne U; Duquesne U; Math.

ALLEN, JENNY; Wilson SR HS; Sinking Spgs, PA; (Y); 135/266; Cmnty Wkr; Exploring; German Clb; JA; Concert Band; Drm Mjr(t); Mrchg Band; Orch; School Musical; Hon Roll; Bloomsburg U; Audiology.

ALLEN JR, JOHN J; Neshaminy HS; Langhorne, PA; (Y); Aud/Vis; Computer Clb; Varsity Clb; Ftbl; Trk; Wt Lftg; Wrstlng; Hon Roll; Ftbl & Wrstgl Hnrb Mntn Sub 1 Lg; Trenton ST; Ind Arts Tchr.

ALLEN, KATHY; Lakeland JRSR HS; Jermyn, PA; (S); 14/152; Girl Scts; Ski Clb; Acpl Chr; Band; Church Choir; Concert Band; Mrchg Band; Pep Band; Nwsp Sprt Ed; Lit Mag; Alpha-Omega Religious Awd 84; Dnce.

ALLEN, KERI JO; Northeast Bradford HS; Rome, PA; (Y); 6/80; Varsity Clb; Trs Frsh Cls; VP Jr Cls; Sec Stu Cncl; Cheerleading; Crs Cntry; Capt Twrlr; High Hon Roll; Hon Roll; NHS; U Of Pittsbrgh; Phrmcy.

ALLEN, KRISTIN; Lewisburg Area HS; Lewisburg, PA; (Y); 7/175; Latin Clb; Spanish Clb; Chorus; Yrbk Stf; Tennis; High Hon Roll; Hon Roll; Jr NHS; Sec NHS; Pres Schlr; Dickinson Coll; Bus.

ALLEN, LYNN MARIE; Cardinal Dougherty HS; Philadelphia, PA; (Y); 125/704; Cmnty Wkr; Hosp Aide; Office Aide; SADD; Rep Jr Cls; Stu Cncl; Dietetics.

ALLEN, MARJIE; Clarion-Limestone HS; Toledo, OH; (Y); 13/89; Intnl Clb; Chorus; School Musical; School Play; JV Var Cheerleading; Hon Roll; NHS.

ALLEN, RHONDA; Abington HS; Willow Grove, PA; (Y); Art Clb; Church Yth Grp; Cmnty Wkr; French Clb; Latin Clb; Spanish Clb; School Play; Pres Frsh Cls; JV Bsktbl; JV Fld Hcky; Exec Intl Sec.

ALLEN, ROBERT; Brownsville Area HS; E Millsboro, PA; (S); Boy Scts; Hon Roll.

ALLEN, RONDA; Jefferson-Morgan JR SR HS; Jefferson, PA; (Y); 20/87; Art Clb; French Clb; Varsity Clb; Nwsp Rptr; Nwsp Stf; Yrbk Rptr; Yrbk Stf; Var Trk; Prfct Atten Awd; Edinboro; Jrnlsm.

ALLEN, TAMMY; Seneca HS; Union City, PA; (Y); Art Clb; Boy Scts; Sec Pep Clb; Band; Concert Band; Mrchg Band; Orch; Sec Soph Cls; Sec Jr Cls; VP Cheerleading; Edinboro U Of PA; Elem Ecduc.

ALLEN, VALERIE; Neshaminy HS; Port Allegany, PA; (Y); 38/700; Pres Trs Key Clb; Chorus; School Musical; Stage Crew; Lit Mag; High Hon Roll; Hon Roll; NHS; PA ST U; Secondary Ed.

ALLEN, WILLIAM; Central Catholic HS; Pottstown, PA; (Y); Boy Scts; Church Yth Grp; Letterman Clb; Science Clb; Ski Clb; L Ftbl; L Trk; L Wt Lftg; Bus Mgmnt.

ALLER, CHRISTIE; Mt Pleasant Area HS; Acme, PA; (Y); GAA; Teachers Aide; Nwsp Stf; Mat Maids; Hon Roll; Prom Comm 86; Spcl Olym Coach 85-87; Elem Spec Ed Tchr.

ALLER, VIRGINIA; Tussey Mountain HS; Riddlesburg, PA; (Y); Library Aide; Red Cross Aide; Band; Concert Band; Mrchg Band; Nwsp Phtg; Nwsp Rptr; Nwsp Stf; Sftbl; Hon Roll; Airline Schl.

ALLERSMA, MIRIAM W; Schenley High School Teachers Center; Pittsburgh, PA; (S); Church Yth Grp; Sec French Clb; JA; Math Tm; Mrchg Band; School Musical; Co-Capt Swmmng; Mgr Tennis; High Hon Roll; VP NHS; Outstndng Stu Awd; Prospects Change Essay Cont Wnnr.

ALLEVA, DAVID QUENTIN; Upper Moreland HS; Hatboro, PA; (Y); 5/280; Church Yth Grp; French Clb; Key Clb; Pep Clb; Ski Clb; High Hon Roll; NHS; Rotary Awd; Stearns/Catalytic Inc Schlrshp 86; Ursinus Coll Schlrshp 86; U PA; Doctor.

ALLEY, GLORIA; Nazareth Acad; Philadelphia, PA; (Y); Church Yth Grp; French Clb; Orch; Sec Soph Cls; VP Jr Cls; High Hon Roll; Hon Roll; Katharine Gibbs Schl Future Secs Cntst Hnrb Mntn 86; K Gibbs Sec Schl; Bus.

ALLGEIER, CATHERINE; Brookville Area HS; Brookville, PA; (Y); 25/143; Key Clb; Pep Clb; Band; Concert Band; Jazz Band; Mrchg Band; Bsktbl; Swmmng; Pres Schlr; Clarion U; Bus Adm.

ALLISON, BELINDA; Mc Guffey HS; Claysville, PA; (Y); French Clb; Varsity Clb; Rep Sr Cls; Score Keeper; Trk; Hon Roll; Stu Recog Awd 83-85; Med.

ALLISON, DANIELLE HOPE; The Christian School Of York; York, PA; (Y); Church Yth Grp; JA; Spanish Clb; Varsity Clb; Band; Chorus; Church Choir; Pep Band; School Musical; School Play; Pres Physcl Fitnss 81-86; Calvary Bible Coll; Med.

ALLISON, KATHIE; Carbondale Area JR SR HS; Carbondale, PA; (Y); French Clb; FBLA; Ski Clb; Bus.

ALLISON, LISA; Marion Center Area HS; Dayton, PA; (S); 8/148; FBLA; Pep Clb; Q&S; Varsity Clb; Yrbk Ed-Chief; Yrbk Sprt Ed; Yrbk Stf; Trk; High Hon Roll; NHS; Hmcmng Crt 85; Acctng I Bkpng Clrk Awd 85; Grgg Typng I Awd 84; Du Bois Bus Schl; Medcl Secy.

ALLISON, STEPHANIE; Union Area HS; New Castle, PA; (S); 1/70; Band; Chorus; School Musical; Pres Stu Cncl; Co-Capt Bsktbl; High Hon Roll; NHS; Church Yth Grp; FTA; Pep Clb.

ALLMAN, TAMMY; Millersburg Area HS; Millersburg, PA; (Y); 28/77; Cmnty Wkr; Hon Roll; Bloomsburg U PA; Bus Educ.

ALLSHOUSE, AMY; Bishop Guilfoyle HS; Altoona, PA; (S); Pep Clb; Red Cross Aide; Science Clb; Var Bsktbl; L Vllybl; High Hon Roll; Hon Roll; Med.

ALLSHOUSE, JESSICA; Ringgold SR HS; Donora, PA; (Y); Drama Clb; JA; SADD; School Musical; Sftbl; Hon Roll; Sci, Math Hnr Soc; Coll HS Pgm; Cmptr Sci.

ALLSMAN, FRANCIS; Cardinal O Hara HS; Media, PA; (Y); 400/800; Church Yth Grp; Computer Clb; 4-H; Band; Concert Band; Jazz Band; Mrchg Band; School Musical; School Play; Yrbk Stf; Dlgt Yth Amer Poli Sysm Seminar 86; U Of Scranton; Bus.

ALLSOPP, SHELLEY; South Park HS; Library, PA; (Y); 34/195; Pres Church Yth Grp; Exploring; Hosp Aide; Library Aide; Office Aide; Service Clb; Capt Color Guard; Yrbk Stf; VP Sec Stu Cncl; Hon Roll; Spcl Svc Awd To S Park HS 86; Stu Cncl Awd 86; U Of Pittsburgh; Dental Asstnt.

ALLWARDT, SYLVIA; Conrad Weiser HS; Wernersville, PA; (Y); 10/184; Computer Clb; Drama Clb; Chorus; School Musical; Yrbk Stf; Trs Jr Cls; Stu Cncl; Hon Roll; NHS; Pre-Med.

ALLWEIN, JOHN; Annville Cleona HS; Annville, PA; (Y); Stage Crew; JV Crs Cntry; JV Socr; JV Trk; Im Vllybl; Im Wt Lftg; Embry Riddle U; Mktg.

ALLWES, DEBBIE; Cambridge Springs HS; Cambridge Springs, PA; (Y); Church Yth Grp; French Clb; Pep Clb; Varsity Clb; Stu Cncl; JV Cheerleading; Stat Score Keeper; JV Var Vllybl; Elem Educ Tchr.

ALMES, DARLA; Saltsburg JR-SR HS; Saltsburg, PA; (Y); Church Yth Grp; SADD; Chorus; Nwsp Stf; Yrbk Stf; Score Keeper; High Hon Roll; NHS; New Kensington Bus Schl; Sec.

ALMONY, PATRICIA J; Emmaus HS; Zionsville, PA; (Y); 2/479; VP Trs Church Yth Grp; VP Q&S; Nwsp Rptr; Rep Sr Cls; Rep Stu Cncl; Var Crs Cntry; Var Trk; High Hon Roll; Sec NHS; Ntl Merit SF; Jrnlsm.

ALNER, HOLLI; Blue Mountain Acad; Athol, MA; (Y); Church Yth Grp; Band; Chorus; Church Choir; Concert Band; Nwsp Phtg; Yrbk Phtg; Yrbk Stf; Gym; Cit Awd; Commercial Art.

ALOI JR, FRANCIS J; Penns Manor HS; Clymer, PA; (Y); 4/76; Pres Chess Clb; Quiz Bowl; Stu Cncl; Trk; High Hon Roll; NHS; Cntry III Ldrs Awd 86; PA Mnr Educ Asstnc Schlrshp 86; Ntl Hnr Soc Cert 86; IN U Of PA; Comp Sci.

ALOI, JAMES; Deer Lakes JR SR HS; Tarentum, PA; (Y); 2/182; Church Yth Grp; VP Varsity Clb; School Musical; School Play; Var Capt Crs Cntry; L Capt Trk; DAR Awd; High Hon Roll; Hon Roll; Lion Awd; Stu Athlt Awd 86; Vally News Schlrshp 86; Var Clb Awd 86; PA ST; Engrg.

ALOISIO, JONATHAN; Kennett HS; Kennett Sq, PA; (Y); Boy Scts; Letterman Clb; Pep Clb; Varsity Clb; Coach Actv; Var Capt Wrstlng; PA Wrstlng 85-86; Dist AA Wrstlng Chmpn 85-86; Keystone Qlfr Wrstlng 86; Bus Adm.

ALSDORF, KIM; Corry JR SR HS; Spartansburg, PA; (S); 1/212; Church Yth Grp; Pres SADD; Chorus; Drill Tm; Drm Mjr(t); Rep Jr Cls; Stu Cncl; 4-H Awd; High Hon Roll; WA Wrkshp Congrssnl Sem 86; Stu Forum 85-86.

ALSIPPI, LYNETTE; Kiski Area HS; Avonmore, PA; (Y); FBLA; Varsity Clb; Rep Stu Cncl; Swmmng; High Hon Roll; Hon Roll; Swmng Cptn; Hrdst Wrkr In Swmng; Rookie Of Yr; Clrn U PA; Accntng.

ALSPACH, JENNIFER; Middletown Area HS; Middletown, PA; (Y); Church Yth Grp; Cmnty Wkr; Hosp Aide; Yrbk Stf; Stu Cncl; High Hon Roll; Hon Roll; Jr NHS; NHS; Acad Alla Mer 85-86; Bus.

ALSTON, CRYSTAL; Chester HS; Chester Twp, PA; (Y); Band; Concert Band; Mrchg Band; Orch; Twrlr; High Hon Roll; Hon Roll; NHS; Katherine Gibbs Awd 86; Mst Outstndng Alg II Stu 86; Acctng.

ALTEMOSE, JEFF; Pen Argyl Area HS; Windgap, PA; (Y); 41/129; Soroptimist; Varsity Clb; Var L Bsbl; Im JV Bsktbl; Var L Ftbl; Wt Lftg; Pltcl Sci.

ALTEMOSE, LISA L; North Penn HS; Lansdale, PA; (Y); Ski Clb; Band; Cheerleading; Hon Roll; Bus.

ALTEMUS, JAMES; Tunkhannock Area HS; Tunkhannock, PA; (Y); 54/320; Aud/Vis; Boy Scts; Letterman Clb; Spanish Clb; Varsity Clb; Band; Bsbl; Co-Capt Bsktbl; Trk; Wt Lftg; MVP Bsktbl Trphy 82-84; Mst Imprvd Bsktbl Trphy 83 & 84; Acadmc Al-Amercn, Schlstc Al-Amercn 85-86; Kings Coll; Crmnl Justc.

ALTEMUS, MEGAN; Penns Manor Area HS; Penn Run, PA; (Y); 1/102; Concert Band; Capt Flag Corp; School Musical; Nwsp Rptr; Yrbk Stf; Var Capt Bsktbl; Var Capt Vllybl; Bausch & Lomb Sci Awd; High Hon Roll; NHS; IUP; Pblc Rltns.

ALTERI, DENISE; Sayre Area HS; S Waverly, PA; (Y); Church Yth Grp; Spanish Clb; SADD; Church Choir; Lit Mag; Rep Soph Cls; High Hon Roll; Rotary Awd; Parlgl.

ALTERIO, KELLI; Bellefonte HS; Bellefonte, PA; (Y); 74/219; Office Aide; Spanish Clb; Varsity Clb; Chorus; JV Stat Bsbl; Var Cheerleading; Var Capt Gym; Var Trk; Im Vllybl; Hon Roll; Penn ST U; Sprts Psych.

ALTERIO, MICHAEL J; Bellefonte Area HS; Bellefonte, PA; (Y); Letterman Clb; Pep Clb; SADD; Varsity Clb; Chorus; Bsbl; Bsktbl; Ftbl; Hon Roll; Sprtsmnshp Awd Var Bsktbl 86; Penn ST U; Criminology.

ALTIERI, JOANNE; Aliquippa HS; Aliquippa, PA; (S); 13/156; Aud/Vis; Sec French Clb; SADD; Yrbk Stf; Jr Cls; Sr Cls; High Hon Roll; Hon Roll; Jr NHS; NHS; Sewickley Sch; Radiology.

ALTLAND, ANGELA; Christian Schl Of York; York, PA; (S); 15/42; Church Yth Grp; JA; Chorus; School Play; Yrbk Sprt Ed; Yrbk Stf; Trs Frsh Cls; Trs Soph Cls; Trs Jr Cls; Trs Sr Cls; Word Of Life.

ALTLAND, MARIANNE; Delone Catholic HS; Mc Sherrystown, PA; (Y); 6/170; JA; Chorus; Yrbk Stf; High Hon Roll; Hon Roll; NHS; Pres Schlr; German Awd; Temple U; Bus Admin.

ALTLAND, TAMMY; New Oxford SR HS; New Oxford, PA; (Y); Drama Clb; Girl Scts; Chorus; School Musical; School Play; High Hon Roll; Hon Roll; Best Home Ec Stu Plaque 84; Best Cameo Actress, Stu Mnth 86; Empire Schl Beauty; Csmtlgy.

ALTMAN, BETH; South Allegheny HS; Elizabeth, PA; (Y); 7/164; Exploring; 4-H; FNA; Pres VP Girl Scts; Library Aide; Office Aide; Spanish Clb; Y-Teens; Chorus; Sr Cls; Penn ST U; Ed.

ALTMAN, DAVID; Shenango JR-SR HS; New Castle, PA; (Y); Aud/Vis; Church Yth Grp; Y-Teens; Nwsp Rptr; JV Ftbl; Hon Roll; NHS; Rotary Awd; Engrg.

ALTMAN, NEITH; Penn Trafford HS; Irwin, PA; (Y); FBLA; VICA; Color Guard; Hon Roll; Prfct Atten Awd; Monroeville Schl Of Bus; Ex Sec.

ALTMANN, GRIFFITH EDWARD; Dunmore HS; Dunmore, PA; (Y); 3/160; Pres Letterman Clb; Scholastic Bowl; Nwsp Rptr; Var Capt Bsbl; Var Capt Ftbl; High Hon Roll; Lion Awd; Trs NHS; Ftbl 1st Tm All Schlstc 85; U Rochester; Chem Engr.

ALTMILLER, COOPER; Lakeland HS; Clarks Summit, PA; (S); 3/152; Computer Clb; French Clb; Var Crs Cntry; Var Trk; Math.

ALTO, SHELBY; Monongahela Valley Catholic HS; Scenery Hill, PA; (Y); 33/83; Church Yth Grp; Cmnty Wkr; Girl Scts; Spanish Clb; Chorus; Powder Puff Ftbl; Hon Roll; Med Asst.

ALTOE, ELAINE; E L Meyers HS; Wilkes Barre, PA; (Y); Cmnty Wkr; FBLA; Sftbl; Hon Roll; Upwrd Bnd Cert Photgrphy 85; Upwrd Bnd Cert Danc, Theatr, Nwsltr, Secy Stdnt Govt 86; Chld Psych.

ALTVATER, KAREN; Seneca Valley HS; Mars, PA; (Y); 15/356; Church Yth Grp; Girl Scts; Var Crs Cntry; High Hon Roll; Hon Roll; Prfct Atten Awd; Schrlsh Pawd 86; 1st Pl Awd Poem Scars 86; Fight Attendnt.

ALTZMAN, JERRY; Strath Haven HS; Wallingford, PA; (Y); CAP; Exploring; Quiz Bowl; Band; Concert Band; Jazz Band; Mrchg Band; Orch; Pep Band; School Musical; Amer Chem Soc Awd 86; Regn Band 86; Columbia U; Physcs.

ALUNNI, LEE A; Valley View HS; Jessup, PA; (Y); 22/198; Latin Clb; Spanish Clb; Varsity Clb; Yrbk Stf; Stu Cncl; Cheerleading; Vllybl; High Hon Roll; Hon Roll; NHS; PA Gov Schl Arts Scholar 85; Fred Astaire Dance Comptn Fin 85; U Scranton; Nrsng.

ALVAREZ, LAURIE; Monongahela Vly Catholic HS; Donora, PA; (Y); FBLA; Ski Clb; Church Choir; Yrbk Stf; Chorus; Rep Frsh Cls; Natl Ldrshp Srv Awd; Acad All Am Natl Hstry Gvrmnt Awd; Elem Educ.

ALVERSON, LEE; Mc Keesport Area HS; Mckeesport, PA; (Y); #108 In Class; Spanish Clb; Acpl Chr; Hon Roll; Penn ST U; Music.

ALVINO, MANDY; Villa Maria Acad; Erie, PA; (S); Ski Clb; Yrbk Stf; Rep Frsh Cls; Trs Soph Cls; Stu Cncl; L Socr; NHS; Sch Sprts Day Chrprsn 84-86.

ALWINE, EUGENE; Conemaugh Township Area HS; Hollsopple, PA; (Y); 14/105; Church Yth Grp; 4-H; Office Aide; Q&S; School Play; Nwsp Phtg; 4-H Awd; Hon Roll; NHS; Physcl Educ Awd 86.

ALWINE, MARCY; Highlands HS; Brackenridge, PA; (Y); 50/280; Church Yth Grp; SADD; Teachers Aide; Stage Crew; Yrbk Stf; Soph Cls; Jr Cls; Sr Cls; 5 Brown Awds Mntn 3.0-3.0 QPA 84-86; Sawyer; Trvl.

ALWOOD, DAVID; Central Columbia HS; Bloomsburg, PA; (Y); 30/177; Church Yth Grp; Ski Clb; Teachers Aide; Bsktbl; Bowling; Ftbl; Hon Roll; Jr NHS; Walter S Carpenter Scholar Engrng 86; Wilkes Coll; Elec Engrng.

ALWORTH, GLYNIS; Gateway SR HS; Monroeville, PA; (S); Dance Clb; Drama Clb; Sec NFL; PAVAS; School Play; Nwsp Bus Mgr; Nwsp Stf; Highland Scttsh Gms Vrs Mdls 83-85; Brtsh Dncng Tchrs Assoc Awd 83; Engl.

AMADEI, TAMMY; Northern Cambria HS; Edensburg, PA; (Y); Ed Yrbk Phtg; Yrbk Stf; Stu Cncl; High Hon Roll; Hon Roll; NHS; IN U Of PA; Sclgy.

AMALONG, CATHY; Shenango JR-SR HS; New Castle, PA; (S); 1/112; Varsity Clb; Var L Gym; Sftbl; Var L Trk; Var L Vllybl; Hon Roll; NHS; NEDT Awd; Math Tm; Natl Merit Sci Awd-Chem 86; Veternry Med.

AMANN, PAMELA; Cowanesque Valley HS; Sabinsville, PA; (S); Letterman Clb; Stat Bsktbl; Ftbl; Sec NHS; Camera Clb; Church Yth Grp; German Clb; Girl Scts; Quiz Bowl; Dstngshd Yng Ldrshp Awd 85.

AMANN, STEPHANIE; Villa Maria Acad; Erie, PA; (Y); Church Yth Grp; Computer Clb; Intnl Clb; Cmnty Wkr; Im Bsktbl; Mgr(s); JV Score Keeper; JV Sftbl; Im Vllybl; Hon Roll; Rcqtbl Clb.

AMANULLAH, CAROLYNE; Harrisburg Acad; Harrisburg, PA; (Y); Political Wkr; Chorus; School Play; Nwsp Bus Mgr; Rep Stu Cncl; Var Crs Cntry; Var Trk; High Hon Roll; Hon Roll; Drama Clb; Journalisn.

AMAROSA, DEAN; Wellsboro SR HS; Wellsboro, PA; (Y); Chess Clb; Church Yth Grp; FFA; Nwsp Stf; Capt Socr; Temple U; Rstrnt Mgmt.

AMATO, JONNA; Big Spring SR HS; Newville, PA; (Y); FBLA; Chorus; School Musical; Off Soph Cls; Rep Jr Cls; Rep Stu Cncl; Gym; Trk; Studnt Cncl Spec Recog Awd 85-86; Govs Sch For The Arts In Dnce Finals 86; Achvt Awd In Phy Ed 84-86; The Juilliard Schl; Dance.

AMBROSE, CINDY; Crestwood HS; Mountaintop, PA; (Y); 3/223; Sec VP Church Yth Grp; Debate Tm; Key Clb; Math Clb; Math Tm; NFL; Spanish Clb; High Hon Roll; Hon Roll; Nrsg.

AMBROSE, DANA; Bentworth HS; Cokeburg, PA; (Y); Am Leg Aux Girls St; FHA; Concert Band; Drill Tm; Yrbk Ed-Chief; Sec Stu Cncl; NHS; Acad All Amer 84-85 & 85-86.

AMBROSE, ELEANOR; Tamaqua Area SR HS; Tamaqua, PA; (Y); Cmnty Wkr; Girl Scts; Band; Chorus; Church Choir; Concert Band; Mrchg Band; Adv Germn Cls; Top 10 Nwsp Carriers Cnty; Acctng.

AMBROSE, MARY ANN; Butler Area HS; Butler, PA; (Y); 78/777; AFS; Sec Spanish Clb; Thesps; Nwsp Rptr; Hon Roll; Prm Cmt; Spch & Dbt Clb; Ntl Jr Hnr Scty; Vlntr Physcl Thrpy Dept Btlr Cnt Mem Hosp; Btlr Cnty CC; Physcl Thrpst.

AMBROSE, TRACY; Charleroi Area HS; Charleroi, PA; (Y); Sec French Clb; Science Clb; Concert Band; Nwsp Sprt Ed; Yrbk Stf; Stu Cncl; Twrlr; High Hon Roll; Hon Roll; NHS; PA St Baton Twrlng Awd 82-85; Pre-Pharm.

AMBROZEVITCH, VALERIE; North Pocono HS; Moscow, PA; (Y); Art Clb; Church Yth Grp; Ski Clb; Cheerleading; Trk; Cit Awd; Hon Roll; Gftd Stu Pgm 84-86; Bus Adm.

AMBRUSO, KATHLEEN; Bishop O Reilly HS; Wyoming, PA; (Y); Science Clb; Ski Clb; Spanish Clb; School Musical; Stage Crew; Yrbk Phtg; Sftbl; High Hon Roll; NHS; Spanish NHS; Ntl Hnr Soc, Spnsh Hnr Soc 85-87; Bio Awd 85; Vet.

AMEDURE, CARMELA; West Allegheny HS; Oakdale, PA; (Y); 42/203; Debate Tm; GAA; Girl Scts; Spanish Clb; Varsity Clb; Nwsp Rptr; Yrbk Rptr; Yrbk Stf; Rep Stu Cncl; L Crs Cntry; Physcl Ftnss Awd 84; Slippery Rock; Phy Ed.

AMELOTTE, STACIE; Eastern York HS; York, PA; (Y); PAVAS; Ski Clb; Chorus; Drill Tm; School Musical; Yrbk Stf; Var JV Cheerleading; Powder Puff Ftbl; Twrlr; Hon Roll.

AMEND, EDWARD; Laurel Highlands HS; Uniontown, PA; (S); 6/365; JA; Capt Math Tm; Var L Bsbl; Var L Swmmng; CC Awd; High Hon Roll; Jr NHS; NHS.

AMENDOLA, HEATHER; St Marys Area HS; Saint Marys, PA; (Y); 23/301; Pres Camera Clb; Trs Church Yth Grp; Sec Computer Clb; Yrbk Phtg; Trs Yrbk Stf; Rep Stu Cncl; Hon Roll; NHS; Cmmnctns.

AMENT, BRENDA; Mt Pleasant HS; Stahlstown, PA; (Y); 21/254; GAA; Latin Clb; Color Guard; Hon Roll; NHS; Pres Schlr.

AMENT, DAVID; Penncrest HS; Media, PA; (Y); Church Yth Grp; Drama Clb; Library Aide; Thesps; Chorus; School Musical; School Play; Yrbk Stf; Ntl Merit Schol; Penn ST; Engl Prfssr.

AMENT, SANDRA; Highlands SR HS; Natrona Hts, PA; (Y); 60/279; Hosp Aide; Concert Band; Mrchg Band; High Hon Roll; Jr NHS; NHS; Rep Frsh Cls; Stu Cncl; Church Yth Grp; Jazz Band; Brown Awd 86; U Ptsbrgh; Physch Thrpy.

AMENT, SHERRI; Kiski Area HS; Leechburg, PA; (Y); Church Yth Grp; Color Guard; Mgr(s); High Hon Roll; Hon Roll; Acad Ltr & Awd 85; Ctzns Gen Hosp Schl; RN.

AMERSHEK, NEIL; Our Lady Of Lourdes HS; Elysburg, PA; (Y); Aud/Vis; Church Yth Grp; Cmnty Wkr; Key Clb; Ftbl; Wt Lftg; Phrmcy.

AMES, GARY S; Central York Senior HS; York, PA; (Y); 50/208; Varsity Clb; JV Capt Bsbl; Bsktbl; L Golf; Comm.

AMES, MARY JO; Crestwood HS; Mountaintop, PA; (Y); 25/187; Art Clb; Hosp Aide; Ski Clb; Band; Concert Band; Mrchg Band; Var Mgr(s); Hon Roll; Kutztown U Of PA; Comm Dsgn.

AMES, WILLIAM; Tamaqua Area HS; New Ringgold, PA; (Y); 22/170; Chess Clb; Drama Clb; Pep Clb; Band; Chorus; Yrbk Stf; Var Trk; French Hon Soc; Ntl Merit Ltr; Pres Schlr; Forrest Vcl Schlrshp 85; Dist 10 & Regn V ST Chorus 85 & 86; Top Vocal & Instrmntl Music Stu 86; PA ST U; Elec Engineers.

AMICI, JOHN; William Allen HS; Allentown, PA; (Y); Exploring; Off Frsh Cls; Off Soph Cls; Off Jr Cls; JV Socr; Wrstlng; Law.

AMICO, PHIL; Pittston Area HS; Pittston, PA; (Y); French Clb; Key Clb; Ski Clb; Capt Bsktbl; Capt Golf; Im Wt Lftg; High Hon Roll; Hon Roll; NHS; Golf All-Star 85; Penn ST Worthington; Engrng.

AMMATURO, ADRIANA; Saint Basil Acad; Philadelphia, PA; (Y); Church Yth Grp; Pres Drama Clb; French Clb; Latin Clb; Thesps; Chorus; School Play; Stage Crew; Variety Show; Cheerleading; La Salle U; Med.

AMMERMAN, JUDY; Sayre Area HS; Athens, PA; (Y); Band; Chorus; Concert Band; Mrchg Band; French Clb; Church Choir; Pep Band; High Hon Roll; Hon Roll; The Instrumentalist Mag Merit Awd 84 & 85; Music.

AMMON, MICHELE F; Souderton Area HS; Schwenksville, PA; (Y); 75/391; Aud/Vis; Dance Clb; Drama Clb; School Musical; School Play; Nwsp Rptr; Lit Mag; Bsktbl; Powder Puff Ftbl; Sftbl; Stu Fdrtn 85-86; Stu Advsry Cncl 85-86; Gvrnrs Arts Schl Audtns 85; Temple U; Thtre.

AMODEI, DAWN; Frankford HS; Philadelphia, PA; (Y); 3/744; Am Leg Aux Girls St; Sec Service Clb; School Play; Nwsp Ed-Chief; Nwsp Rptr; Co-Capt Cheerleading; High Hon Roll; Hon Roll; NHS; Prfct Atten Awd.

AMON, STEPHANIE; Fortle Boeuf HS; Waterford, PA; (Y); Church Yth Grp; Dance Clb; Cheerleading; High Hon Roll; Hon Roll; Jamestown Business Coll; Acctg.

AMOROSO, ROBERT CARL; Ambridge Area SR HS; Baden, PA; (Y); Sec Exploring; Spanish Clb; SADD; Pres Band; Pres Concert Band; Pres Jazz Band; Pres Mrchg Band; Pres Pep Band; School Musical; Pres Symp Band; Mc Donalds Marching Band 86; Westminster Honors Band; Pilot.

AMOROSO, SCOTT A; Bethel Park SR HS; Bethel Park, PA; (Y); Capt Math Tm; Bausch & Lomb Sci Awd; High Hon Roll; NHS; Pres Schlr; Exclnc Frnch 85; Jr Engrs; U Of Pittsburgh; Chem.

AMORTEGUI, CLAUDIA I; North Allegheny SR HS; Allison Pk, PA; (Y); 301/605; Camera Clb; Church Yth Grp; Hosp Aide; Office Aide; Ski Clb; Band; Concert Band; Mrchg Band; Variety Show; Rep Frsh Cls; U South Carolina; Intl Bus.

AMORY, MICHAEL A; Whitehall HS; Whitehall, PA; (Y); 45/300; Am Leg Boys St; Trs Leo Clb; Church Choir; Concert Band; Jazz Band; Mrchg Band; School Musical; Hon Roll; JP Sousa Awd; NHS; Amer Fedrtn Of Musicns 84-86; Dist 10 PMEA Band 85-86; Pres Acad Ftnss Awd 86; Coll Misericordia; Occptnl Thrp.

AMOS, JULIE; Burgettstown JR SR HS; Slovan, PA; (Y); Band; Concert Band; Mrchg Band; Symp Band; Pres Frsh Cls; VP Soph Cls; VP Sec Stu Cncl; High Hon Roll; Jr NHS; NHS; ACCTNG.

AMOS, LISA; Trinity HS; Washington, PA; (Y); FHA; JA; Political Wkr; Trs Sec VICA; Vllybl; Outstndng Voctnl Stu Awd 85-86; Safety Chrmn Awd 84-86; Ldrshp Awds 84-86; Johnson & Whales; Voctnl Ed.

AMOS, LORI; Conneaut Lake HS; Conneaut Lake, PA; (Y); JA; Spanish Clb; Mrchg Band; Var Sftbl; Hon Roll; Sec.

AMOS, SHELLY; West Green Md SR HS; Sycamore, PA; (S); 5/70; Hst Church Yth Grp; Dance Clb; Drama Clb; Band; Sec Trs Chorus; Concert Band; Drm Mjr(t); Pep Band; School Musical; Nwsp Rptr; HS Coll Prog Comp Crdts 84; Elem Ed.

AMOS, SHERRY; West Greene Md SR HS; Sycamore, PA; (S); Pres Sec Church Yth Grp; Capt Dance Clb; Drama Clb; Office Aide; Band; Pres Chorus; Drm Mjr(t); Yrbk Stf; Stu Cncl; High Hon Roll; HS Coll 3 Coll Crdts 83-84; Music Bus.

AMOW, CHRIS; Pleasant Valley HS; Saylorsburg, PA; (Y); Exploring; Math Tm; Ski Clb; Concert Band; Jazz Band; Mrchg Band; Pep Band; Nwsp Phtg; Bsktbl; Hon Roll; PA ST U; Comp Pgmmng.

AMSLER, BETTY; Keystone JR/SR HS; Knox, PA; (Y); 8/120; Acpl Chr; Nwsp Rptr; Yrbk Stf; Stu Cncl; High Hon Roll; Hon Roll; NHS; Prfct Atten Awd; Clarion U; Acctg.

AMSLER, TRACI; Sheffield JR SR HS; Clarendon, PA; (Y); FCA; Sec SADD; Trs Varsity Clb; Concert Band; Jazz Band; VP Mrchg Band; Var Sftbl; Var Vllybl; NHS.

AMSPACHER, WENDY; Central York SR HS; York, PA; (Y); Hosp Aide; Varsity Clb; Band; Yrbk Stf; Mgr Bsbl; Mgr Ftbl; Hon Roll; Dc Clinton Ruby Schlrshp 86; Onyx Schrlshp 86; Outstndng Hm Ec 86; Cedar Crest Coll; Nrsng.

ANAWALT, CATHLEEN; North Hills SR HS; Pittsburgh, PA; (S); 21/502; AFS; Trs Church Yth Grp; Girl Scts; Keywanettes; Thesps; School Musical; School Play; Stage Crew; High Hon Roll; NHS; Thiel Coll.

ANCERAVIGE, PAULA; Marian HS; Mahanoy, PA; (Y); 33/121; Office Aide; Pep Clb; School Play; Rep Soph Cls; Rep Jr Cls; Rep Sr Cls; Rep Stu Cncl; Var Capt Cheerleading; Stat Sftbl; Mahanoy Cty Womens Clb Awd 86; Bloomsbsurg U.

ANCHORS, JANET; Mt Lebanon SR HS; Pittsburgh, PA; (Y); Church Yth Grp; Ski Clb; SADD; Acpl Chr; Band; Chorus; Church Choir; Capt Drill Tm; Mrchg Band; Symp Band; Dist Band Fest 86; Tripl Trio 86-87; Southmnstr Ringers 86; Jrnlsm.

ANDEREGG, MARIA B; Faith Community Christian HS; Pittsburgh, PA; (S); 2/40; Church Yth Grp; Cmnty Wkr; Office Aide; Chorus; Church Choir; Cit Awd; Ntl Hnr Rll 85; U Of Pittsburgh; Engr.

ANDERER, STACY; Archbishop Kennedy HS; Philadelphia, PA; (Y); 2/200; Cmnty Wkr; Drama Clb; Office Aide; Service Clb; Nwsp Rptr; Nwsp Stf; Yrbk Rptr; Yrbk Stf; Fld Hcky; High Hon Roll; Eng Awd 84-85; Sci Awd 86; Spn Awd 85.

ANDERLINE, TINA; Bishop Hannan HS; Scranton, PA; (Y); Chorus; Variety Show; Hon Roll; NHS; Hnbl Mntns Bio, Spnsh, Wrld Cultr, Typg I, Soclgy & Chorus; 9 Bwlg Troph & 1 Bsktbl; Bus.

ANDERS, DEBBY; St Marys Area HS; Kersey, PA; (Y); Hon Roll.

ANDERS, KIMBERLY; Ringgold HS; Monongahela, PA; (Y); Am Leg Aux Girls St; Church Yth Grp; Office Aide; Rep Frsh Cls; Rep Stu Cncl; Hon Roll; Law.

ANDERS, REED; Ringgold HS; Monongahela, PA; (Y); JV Var Bsbl; Sci-Math Hnr Soc 85-86; IUP; Crmnl Jstc.

ANDERSEN, CINDY LEE; Sheffield Area JR-SR HS; Warren, PA; (Y); FBLA; Pep Clb; SADD; Chorus; Color Guard; Nwsp Stf; Yrbk Stf; Var Trk; Var Twrlr; JV Vllybl; Jamestown Bus Coll; Sectrl.

ANDERSEN, STEPHEN M; Red Lion Area SR HS; Red Lion, PA; (Y); 4/327; Jazz Band; Mrchg Band; Symp Band; High Hon Roll; VP NHS; Ntl Merit Ltr; Prfct Atten Awd; Pres Schlr; Orch; Pep Band; Modern Music Masters Prs 85-86; Louis Armstrong Jazz Awd 86; U DE; Engrng.

ANDERSON, ALENA; West Allegheny HS; Oakdale, PA; (Y); Church Yth Grp; Drama Clb; Spanish Clb; Chorus; Nwsp Rptr; Yrbk Rptr; Pom Pon; High Hon Roll; NHS; VFW Awd; Eastern Star Awd 86; Northwestern U Grant 86; Northwestern U; Cmmnctns.

ANDERSON, ANDY; Central SR HS; York, PA; (Y); VP Varsity Clb; Pres Frsh Cls; Pres Soph Cls; Pres Jr Cls; Pres Sr Cls; Rep Stu Cncl; JV Bsktbl; Var Ftbl; Var Vllybl; Hon Roll; Schl Brd Rep 86; Psych.

ANDERSON, ANNETTE; Seneca Valley HS; Zelienople, PA; (Y); Church Yth Grp; Ski Clb; Band; Chorus; Church Choir; Rep Stu Cncl; Hon Roll; Trk; Stat Wrstlng; Socl Wrk.

ANDERSON, CHARLENE; Trinity HS; Washington, PA; (Y); 53/374; Mltry Polc.

ANDERSON, CHARLES R; Uniontown Area HS; New Salem, PA; (Y); 5/330; Math Clb; Science Clb; Pres Sr Cls; Var Bsktbl; CC Awd; DAR Awd; High Hon Roll; Ntl Merit Ltr; Rotary Awd; PA Govnrs Schl For Sci 86; CMU; Genetic Engrng.

ANDERSON, CHRISTINE L; South Park HS; Library, PA; (S); 34/207; Drama Clb; Political Wkr; Thesps; Chorus; Stage Crew; Hon Roll; NEDT Awd; Pres Mimi Troupe 85-86 & 86-87; BSA Ex Plorers Post 951 Law 85-86; AIU Excptnl Pgm Gftd/Tlntd Pgm; Law.

ANDERSON, DANIELLE; Laurel Highlands HS; Uledi, PA; (Y); 40/345; Art Clb; Vllybl; High Hon Roll; Hon Roll; Sign Lang Clb Awd 82; Sign Lang.

ANDERSON, DAWN; Central Dauphin East HS; Harrisburg, PA; (Y); 5/271; Acpl Chr; Chorus; Flag Corp; Stage Crew; Rep Soph Cls; Rep Jr Cls; Mgr(s); NHS; Ntl Merit Ltr; Rotary Ldrshp Conf 86; Dauphin Cnty Teen-Age Repblcn Clb-Vice Chrmn 85.

ANDERSON, DIANA; West Mifflin Area HS; W Mifflin, PA; (Y); 3/340; Pres Church Yth Grp; Hosp Aide; Trs Science Clb; Band; Rep Sr Cls; Rep Stu Cncl; High Hon Roll; NHS; Sec FTA; Concert Band; Pres Acad Ftns Awd 86; Seton Hill Ldrshp Dev; Slippery Rock; Elem Ed.

ANDERSON, DOREEN; Villa Maria Acad; Erie, PA; (Y); 53/133; Hon Roll; Edinboro U; Mth.

ANDERSON, FALECE; Pine Forge Acad; Camp Springs, MD; (S); Debate Tm; Office Aide; Teachers Aide; Church Choir; School Play; Nwsp Rptr; Sftbl; Vllybl; Cit Awd; Hon Roll; Howard U; Nrsng.

ANDERSON, GEORGE; Bentworth HS; Bentleyville, PA; (Y); 10/103; Varsity Clb; School Play; Trs Sr Cls; L Church Yth Grp8; L Ftbl; High Hon Roll; Lion Awd; NHS; Band; Mrchg Band; Thomas Vaira Mem Awd 86; Outstanding Defensive Ftbl Plyr 85; U Pittsburgh; Pharmacy.

ANDERSON, HARRY; Shaler Area HS; Allison Park, PA; (Y); Band; PA ST; Engrng.

ANDERSON, HEATHER; Valley HS; New Kensington, PA; (Y); 14/376; Dance Clb; FNA; Chorus; School Musical; Nwsp Stf; Sec Soph Cls; Cheerleading; Trk; Cit Awd; French Hon Soc.

ANDERSON, HOLLY; St Pauls Cathedral HS; Pittsburgh, PA; (Y); Camera Clb; Drama Clb; French Clb; Science Clb; School Play; Nwsp Rptr; Hon Roll; NEDT Awd; Schlrshp-Chthm Coll-Logic 86; Schlrshp-Chthm Coll-Hstry & Engl 86-87; NEDT Awd-2 Yrs.

ANDERSON, JEREMY; Tunkhannock Area HS; Dalton, PA; (S); Spanish Clb; Mrchg Band; Var Bsbl; Var Bsktbl; Im Ftbl; Hon Roll; NHS; Acctg.

ANDERSON, JILL; Bethlehem Catholic HS; Bethlehem, PA; (Y); Key Clb; Ski Clb; Rep Jr Cls; Im Fld Hcky; Hon Roll; Lehigh U; Eng.

ANDERSON, JON; Punxsutawney Area HS; Punxsutawney, PA; (Y); Math Tm; Varsity Clb; Capt L Bsbl; L Ftbl; Wt Lftg; DAR Awd; Hon Roll; Rotary Awd; Ind Engrng.

ANDERSON, JULI; Rocky Grove HS; Franklin, PA; (S); Church Yth Grp; Science Clb; Band; Chorus; Church Choir; Pep Band; Var Bsktbl; Var Golf; Sec NHS; Girl Scts; Futr Prblm Slvng 3rd, 5th PA 84 & 85.

ANDERSON, KAREN; Connellsville Area SR HS; Connellsville, PA; (Y); 5/470; Computer Clb; 4-H; Hosp Aide; Office Aide; Yrbk Stf; DAR Awd; 4-H Awd; High Hon Roll; Prfct Atten Awd; Spanish NHS.

ANDERSON, KAREN; Monteau JR-SR HS; Boyers, PA; (Y); Band; Chorus; Church Choir; Concert Band; Drm Mjr(t); Jazz Band; Mrchg Band; Pep Band; Variety Show; Im Socr; Outstndng Cmpr-Chrch Cmp 84; Slippery Rock U; Psychlgy.

ANDERSON, KAREN; Northern Cambria HS; Spangler, PA; (Y); 5/126; Hosp Aide; Red Cross Aide; Spanish Clb; Chorus; Color Guard; Stage Crew; Yrbk Stf; High Hon Roll; Hon Roll; NHS; ID U; Psych.

ANDERSON, KAYLYNN; Kennedy Christian HS; Sharon, PA; (Y); Art Clb; Dance Clb; French Clb; FBLA; Latin Clb; Pep Clb; Chorus; School Musical; Var Cheerleading; NHS; Edinboro U PA; Psychlgy.

ANDERSON, KELLY; Churchill HS; Braddock, PA; (Y); 85/224; Art Clb; Church Yth Grp; Teachers Aide; Accntng.

ANDERSON, KRISTINE; Greater Works Acad; Murrysville, PA; (Y); 5/36; Church Yth Grp; Drama Clb; Chorus; School Play; Nwsp Rptr; Yrbk Stf; Stu Cncl; High Hon Roll; Awd Distinction Span 85; Oral Roberts U; Drama.

ANDERSON, KRISTINE; Mon Valley Catholic HS; Donora, PA; (Y); 23/97; Camp Fr Inc; Letterman Clb; Spanish Clb; Chorus; Drill Tm; Mrchg Band; Yrbk Stf; Var Capt Bsktbl; Score Keeper; Swmmng; Amrcn Lgn Awd 83; St Vincent Coll; Ln Offcr.

ANDERSON, LEE; Ambridge SR HS; Ambridge, PA; (Y); Boy Scts; Pres Church Yth Grp; Pep Clb; JV Var Ftbl; Stat Vllybl; Hon Roll; Pittsburgh Inst; Pwrplnt Mechnc.

ANDERSON, LENNI; California Area SR HS; California, PA; (Y); Drama Clb; VP FBLA; Ski Clb; Concert Band; Mrchg Band; Yrbk Stf; Hon Roll; CA U Of PA.

ANDERSON, LORI; Strong Vincent HS; Erie, PA; (Y); French Clb; Spanish Clb; Hon Roll; Amrcn Strlzr Schrlshp 86-87; PA ST Grnt 86-87; PA ST Behrend; Nrsng.

ANDERSON, MARJORIE; Merion Mercy Acad; Phila, PA; (Y); JA; Spanish Clb; Acpl Chr; Chorus; School Play; Im Bsktbl; Im Vllybl; Hon Roll; Outstndg Achvt NEDT Stndrdzd Tst 84; Accntg.

ANDERSON, MARK; Dover Area HS; Dover, PA; (Y); VP Church Yth Grp; VP FFA; School Musical; Hon Roll; FFA York Cnty Vp 85-86; ST FFA Pub Spkng 5th Pl 85-86; ST FFA Interview Cntst 5th Pl 84-85; PA ST U; Ag.

ANDERSON, MARY; Lancaster Christian Schl; Lancaster, PA; (Y); VP Church Yth Grp; Teachers Aide; Stage Crew; Yrbk Stf; Sftbl; Chet Bitterman III Schlrshp Awd 86; Spanish Schlr Awd 86; Philly Coll Of Bible; Bible.

ANDERSON, MARYJO; Burgettstown Area JR SR HS; Burgettstown, PA; (Y); 1/172; Pres Mrchg Band; Pres Symp Band; VP Stu Cncl; Var Stat Bsktbl; Capt Sftbl; High Hon Roll; NHS; Val; Im Vllybl; Cit Awd; Willm Harold Malone Memrl Schlrshp 86; Eugene & Neil Petrucci Schlrshp 86; Cmptv Schlrshp 86; Duquesne U; Phrmcy.

ANDERSON, MELANIE; Lancaster Christian Schl; Lancaster, PA; (Y); Church Yth Grp; Yrbk Stf; Stat Bsktbl; Var Cheerleading.

ANDERSON, MELISSA; Coatesville SR HS; Downingtown, PA; (Y); 108/550; Cmnty Wkr; French Clb; Spanish Clb; Band; Concert Band; Mrchg Band; Pep Band; Lang.

ANDERSON, MELISSA; Phil-Mont Christian Acad; Lock Haven, PA; (Y); 6/41; Church Yth Grp; Lit Mag; VP Sr Cls; JV Var Bsktbl; Var Fld Hcky; JV Var Sftbl; High Hon Roll; NHS; Pres Schlr; Natl Hon Roll 84; Acdmc All Amer Schlr 84; Pres Schlrshp Gordon Coll 86; Gordon Coll; Bio.

ANDERSON, MELISSA; St Marys Area HS; Kersey, PA; (Y); Hon Roll; Arln Mech.

ANDERSON, MICHELE L; Red Lion Area SR HS; Red Lion, PA; (Y); 2/327; Mrchg Band; School Musical; Symp Band; High Hon Roll; Lion Awd; NHS; Prfct Atten Awd; Pres Schlr; Sal; Church Yth Grp; Acdmc All Stars 86; Cmmncmnt Spkr 86; Juniata Coll; Chem Tchr.

ANDERSON, MICHELLE; Penn Hills SR HS; Pittsburgh, PA; (S); 236/708; Church Yth Grp; French Clb; Science Clb; Yrbk Stf; Stu Cncl; Vllybl; Hon Roll; Slippery Rock U; Elem Educ.

ANDERSON, MICHELLE L; Mc Guffey HS; Washington, PA; (Y); JA; Spanish Clb; Color Guard; Mrchg Band; High Hon Roll; Hon Roll; NHS; Stu Recgntn Awd 84-86; Achvt Schlrshp 86; Cls Hnr Grad 86; U Pittsburgh; Chem.

ANDERSON, MOLLY; Newport HS; Newport, PA; (Y); JV Fld Hcky; Capt Twrlr; Tri M Mdrn Music Mstrs 83-86; Elem Educ.

ANDERSON, NICCOLA; Phila H S For Girls; Philadelphia, PA; (Y); Church Yth Grp; Drama Clb; Library Aide; Varsity Clb; Chorus; Var L Tennis; Cmmnctns.

ANDERSON, PATRICIA; Pocono Central Catholic HS; Mt Pocono, PA; (Y); 8/22; Art Clb; Ski Clb; Nwsp Rptr; Nwsp Sprt Ed; Nwsp Stf; Yrbk Rptr; Yrbk Stf; Fld Hcky; High Hon Roll; Hon Roll; AP Engl Awd 85-86; Pocono Lions Schlrshp 86; Scranton U; Secndry Engl Educ.

ANDERSON, REGINA; St Maria Goretti HS; Philadelphia, PA; (Y); 64/390; Camp Fr Inc; Cmnty Wkr; Mathletes; Orch; School Musical; Hon Roll; U PA; Pre-Med.

ANDERSON, RHONDA; Bradford Area HS; Bradford, PA; (Y); Art Clb; French Clb; Comp Drftng.

ANDERSON, ROBERT; Penn-Trafford HS; Irwin, PA; (Y); Varsity Clb; Var Bsktbl; Var L Socr; Im Swmmng; Im Vllybl; Hon Roll; Clemson U; Mchncl Engrng.

ANDERSON, SCOTT; Sharon HS; Hermitage, PA; (Y); 55/175; Art Clb; French Clb; Bsbl; Sci.

ANDERSON, SHARON; Lincoln HS; Ellwood City, PA; (Y); 7/163; AFS; Church Yth Grp; Drama Clb; Hosp Aide; Spanish Clb; Y-Teens; Chorus; School Musical; School Play; Powder Puff Ftbl; Westminster Coll All Strs Hnr Pgm & Hnr Chrs 85 & 86; Dstrct & Rgnl Chrs 85 & 86; Educ.

ANDERSON, SHAWN; Clearfield Area HS; Clearfield, PA; (Y); Church Yth Grp; Drama Clb; French Clb; Key Clb; School Play; Nwsp Rptr; Var L Bsbl; Var JV Bsktbl; Hon Roll; NEDT Awd; Phrmcy.

ANDERSON, SHEILA; St Francis Acad; Pittsburgh, PA; (S); #2 In Class; Red Cross Aide; Nwsp Rptr; Rep Frsh Cls; VP Soph Cls; Stu Cncl; Bsktbl; Vllybl; High Hon Roll; NHS; Hugh O Brien Yth Fndtn Semnr 85; Med.

ANDERSON, TAUNYA; Ringgold HS; Monongahela, PA; (Y); Exploring; Hosp Aide; Nwsp Rptr; Nwsp Stf; Yrbk Stf; Tour Gd.

ANDERSON, TRACI; Penn-Trafford HS; Harrison City, PA; (Y); JCL; Latin Clb; Service Clb; Capt Color Guard; Mrchg Band; Lit Mag; High Hon Roll; NHS; Prfct Atten Awd; Physical Thrpst.

ANDERSON, WAYNE; Hershey SR HS; Hummelstown, PA; (Y); Church Yth Grp; Church Choir; Variety Show; Trk; Wrstlng; Cert Awd Svc MX Teen Mission 83.

ANDERSON, WENDY; Sheffield Area JR SR HS; Sheffield, PA; (Y); Drama Clb; French Clb; FHA; Pres VP Library Aide; Pep Clb; Color Guard; School Musical; School Play; Cheerleading; Score Keeper; Clarion U PA; Elem Ed.

ANDERSON MILLER, GREGORY; Kutztown Area HS; Kutztown, PA; (Y); 15/126; Chess Clb; Capt Quiz Bowl; School Play; Im Badmtn; Var L Bsbl; High Hon Roll; NHS; Ntl Merit Ltr; Pres Schlr; Commonwealth PA Higher Ed Asst Agncy Cert Of Merit 85; U Of DE; Chem.

ANDERTON, DEBORAH; Oil City HS; Oil City, PA; (Y); 64/273; Varsity Clb; Variety Show; Trs Jr Cls; Trs Sr Cls; Rep Stu Cncl; Var JV Cheerleading; Var Trk; Var JV Vllybl; Wt Lftg; Hon Roll; Vllybl 2nd Tm All-Strs 85; IN U Of PA; Dietetics.

ANDES, JENNIFER; Danville SR HS; Danville, PA; (Y); Cmnty Wkr; Latin Clb; Chorus; Color Guard; Var JV Mat Maids; Med.

ANDO, SUSAN; Blacklick Valley HS; Nanty Glo, PA; (Y); Office Aide; Ski Clb; Varsity Clb; Flag Corp; Yrbk Stf; Trk; Track Letter 86; Med Sec.

ANDRACA, PATRICIA; Cardinal O Hara HS; Broomall, PA; (Y); 3/750; Dance Clb; Spanish Clb; School Musical; Cheerleading; Diving; Pom Pon; High Hon Roll; Hon Roll; NHS; Opt Clb Awd; Scott Hi-Q Tm 85-87; 2nd NAATSP Pan Cntst 85; Awds PJAS Speech Cntst 85 & 86; Comp Sci.

ANDRACHICK, KIMBERLY; Bentworth HS; Bentleyville, PA; (Y); Cmnty Wkr; PAVAS; Ski Clb; Band; Concert Band; Drill Tm; Mrchg Band; School Play; Pom Pon; Hon Roll; Scholar Awd B Avg 82-86; Bus & Prof Wmn Grl Mnth 86; Superstar Drill Tm Grl 84; Robert Morris Coll; Mktng.

ANDRAE, REBECKA; Jeannette SR HS; Jeannette, PA; (Y); Pres Church Yth Grp; CAP; Hosp Aide; SADD; Band; Chorus; Church Choir; Concert Band; Mrchg Band; High Hon Roll; ROTC.

ANDRALIS, JIM; Freedom HS; Bethlehem, PA; (Y); 99/445; Art Clb; Ski Clb; School Play; Variety Show; Yrbk Phtg; Bus.

ANDRASCIK, ANN; Homer Center HS; Homer City, PA; (Y); Sec FNA; Varsity Clb; Sec Band; Sec Concert Band; Jazz Band; Mrchg Band; L Var Sftbl; Hon Roll; Jr NHS; Cambria-Rowe Bus Coll; Exec Sec.

ANDRE, RICNARD; North Clarion HS; Leeper, PA; (Y); 1/86; French Clb; Band; Pep Band; Pres Frsh Cls; Pres Soph Cls; VP Jr Cls; Var L Bsbl; Var Bsktbl; Hon Roll; NHS.

ANDREANI, CLYDE; California Area HS; Coal Center, PA; (Y); Computer Clb; PAVAS; Spanish Clb; Rep Band; Concert Band; Jazz Band; Rep Mrchg Band; Pep Band; VP Stu Cncl; High Hon Roll; Am Leg Essay Cont 1st Pl 86; Arion Awd Music 86; Frsh Soph & JR Rep Bnd 84-86; CA U PA; Optom.

ANDRETTI, BARBIE; Nazareth SR HS; Nazareth, PA; (Y); Drama Clb; Key Clb; Chorus; Pep Band; School Musical; Variety Show; Capt Cheerleading; Cit Awd; Apprectn Awd; Equestrian Sci.

ANDREUZZI, RICHARD; West Hazleton HS; Tresckow, PA; (Y); 62/189; Church Yth Grp; Var L Ftbl; Var Wrstlng; Hon Roll; MVP Ftbl 83; Penn ST U; Bus Adm.

ANDREWLEVICH, VALERIE; Shikellamy HS; Sunbury, PA; (Y); 7/304; French Clb; Chorus; School Musical; Sec Soph Cls; Sec Jr Cls; Rep Stu Cncl; Capt Cheerleading; Hon Roll; Dist Chorus 86.

ANDREWS, CATHERINE; Bethel Park SR HS; Bethel Park, PA; (Y); Church Yth Grp; Letterman Clb; Science Clb; Varsity Clb; L Crs Cntry; Var Golf; Im Powder Puff Ftbl; L Swmmng; Hon Roll; PIAA ST Champshp Qlfr 84-85; WPIAL Champshp Qlfr 84-86; Law.

ANDREWS, CHRISTOPHER; Quaker Valley HS; Sewickley, PA; (Y); 14/165; Debate Tm; Key Clb; Rep Soph Cls; Rep Jr Cls; Var Socr; High Hon Roll; Cont Trip Wnnr To NYC & Wall St 86; Completed 50 Manhrs Key Clb 86; Investments.

ANDREWS, COLLEEN M; Bishop Mc Devitt HS; Roslyn, PA; (Y); 32/355; Church Yth Grp; Hon Roll; NHS; Prfct Atten Awd; Archdiocese Philadelphia Bus Cntst 85-86; Bronze Mdl Bus Cls; Hghst Avg Sec Stds Cls; Temple U; Comm.

ANDREWS, DEAN; West Mifflin Area HS; Pittsburgh, PA; (Y); 30/400; Cmnty Wkr; Library Aide; VP Science Clb; Rep Band; Concert Band; Jazz Band; Mrchg Band; Orch; Pep Band; Nwsp Stf; Rep West Mifflin Dist I Band 86-87; Awd MVP Hon & Var Tnns Tm 86-87; Named Sectn Ldr Trmpts Band 86; WV U; Phrmcy.

ANDREWS, HARRY; Our Lady Of The Sacred Heart HS; Aliquippa, PA; (Y); Boy Scts; SADD; Mgr Bsktbl; Eagle Scout Awd 86.

ANDREWS, JENNIFER; Trinity HS; Washington, PA; (Y); 52/374; French Clb; Ski Clb; Concert Band; Jazz Band; Mrchg Band; High Hon Roll; Hon Roll.

ANDREWS, JILL; Pottsgrove HS; Sanatoga, PA; (Y); 21/278; German Clb; Latin Clb; Pep Clb; Science Clb; Ski Clb; Varsity Clb; Rep Stu Cncl; JV Capt Cheerleading; Var L Trk; NHS; Psych.

ANDREWS, JOHN; St Pius X HS; Phoenixville, PA; (S); Pres JA; Rep Stu Cncl; Var L Ftbl; Var Trk; Hon Roll; Jr NHS; Ftbl All Chesmont-All Suburbn 85; Engr.

ANDREWS, JOY; Garden Spot HS; New Holland, PA; (Y); Chorus; Nwsp Stf; Trs Frsh Cls; Trs Soph Cls; Trs Jr Cls; Trs Sr Cls; Var Capt Cheerleading; Var JV Fld Hcky; Im Powder Puff Ftbl; Fshn Mrchndsng.

ANDREWS, JOY; Parkland HS; Orefield, PA; (Y); 52/415; Church Yth Grp; Cmnty Wkr; Band; Chorus; School Musical; Var Capt Crs Cntry; Var Capt Trk; Hon Roll; JC Awd; NHS; Miss Teen PA Semi Fnlst 85-86; Outstndng SR Fml Athlt Crss Cnty 86; Outstndng SR Fml Athlt Trck 86; Coll William & Mary; Bus Adm.

ANDREWS, KELLY J; Upper Dublin HS; Ambler, PA; (Y); 1/307; Intnl Clb; Nwsp Rptr; Ed Yrbk Stf; Ed Lit Mag; NHS; Prfct Atten Awd; Hnrbl Mntn Schltc Wrtg Awds 85; Cert Of Merit Am Assoc Tchrs Of Spnsh And Protgs 85; Acadmc All Am 85.

ANDREWS, KENYA; South Philadelphia HS; Philadelphia, PA; (Y); English Clb; JA; Office Aide; OEA; Scholastic Bowl; Service Clb; Teachers Aide; Hon Roll; Outstndng Achvt In Bus Typng 84; Hmn Rltns Awd 84; Cert Of Apprctn Essay Cntst 85; Exec Sec.

ANDREWS, LAURA; Phil-Mont Christian Acad; Blue Bell, PA; (Y); 5/41; Church Yth Grp; Yrbk Stf; VP Jr Cls; Trs Sr Cls; Var L Bsktbl; Var L Fld Hcky; Var L Sftbl; Hon Roll; NHS; Stu Cncl Awd 85-86; Vrsty Fld Hcky Plyr Of Yr 85-86; Vrsty Sftbl Plyr Of Yr 85-86; Grdn Coll; Phy Ed.

ANDREWS, MELISSA; Bishop Guilfoyle HS; Altoona, PA; (S); 30/150; Hosp Aide; Science Clb; Yrbk Stf; Coach Actv; Var L Vllybl; High Hon Roll; Hon Roll; Prfct Atten Awd; Blair Cnty Vllybl All Star Tm 85; Art Awd-Altoona Wmns Clb Of Amer 85; PA ST; Bio.

ANDREWS, NORMAN; Upper Darby HS; Drexel Hill, PA; (Y); Var Bsktbl; Hon Roll; Drexel U; Engrng.

ANDREWS, SCOTT; Sullivan County HS; Laporte, PA; (Y); 1/92; VP Church Yth Grp; Scholastic Bowl; Pres Soph Cls; Pres Jr Cls; Pres Sr Cls; Cit Awd; NHS; Pres Schlr; Val; Guthrie Clinic Hlth Prof Scholar Awd 86; PA ST Renaissance Scholar 86; Nrthrn Cntrl Bank Scholar 86; PA ST U; Pre-Med.

ANDREWS, SEAN; Girard Collge; Philadelphia, PA; (Y); Band; Nwsp Sprt Ed; Pres Sr Cls; Var L Bsktbl; Computer Clb; Office Aide; Jazz Band; School Musical; Yrbk Stf; Most Imprvd Plyr Bsktbl 84-85; Hnr Rll Girard Clg 84-85; 1st Instrmntl Solo Cntst 85-86; U Of PA; Acctg.

ANDREWS, SHAWN; Greenwood HS; Millerstown, PA; (S); 1/62; Chorus; School Musical; School Play; Rep Frsh Cls; Rep Stu Cncl; Var Socr; Trk; High Hon Roll; Hon Roll; NHS; Athletic Awd 84-85; PA U; Comp Sci.

ANDREWS, TIFFANY; Bald Eagle Area HS; Bellefonte, PA; (S); 35/204; Cmnty Wkr; Pres French Clb; Office Aide; Sec SADD; Mrchg Band; Variety Show; Nwsp Stf; Yrbk Stf; Trs Frsh Cls; Trs Soph Cls; PA ST U; Humn Serv.

ANDREZZE, MARINA; Berwick Area SR HS; Berwick, PA; (Y); Capt Dance Clb; Sec FBLA; Library Aide; Hon Roll; NHS; Bloomsburg U Of PA; Bus Adm.

ANDRIS, MATTHEW; Cardinal Dougherty HS; Phila, PA; (Y); 100/748; Cmnty Wkr; Pres Sr Cls; Var Bsbl; Var Capt Ftbl; Var Wrstlng; Cit Awd; Hon Roll; Kiwanis Awd; Opt Clb Awd; Robert W Maxwell Awd Ftbl Plyr Wk 85; MVP Ftbl 85; Most Popluar Guy Cls 85-86; Lebanon Valley Coll; Sci.

ANDRUKAITIS, LAURA; West Scranton HS; Scranton, PA; (Y); 9/260; Trs Boys Clb Am; Cmnty Wkr; Dance Clb; Letterman Clb; Red Cross Aide; Service Clb; Ski Clb; Spanish Clb; Drill Tm; Yrbk Stf; U Scranton; Med.

ANDRYCZYK, MARK; Devon Preparatory Schl; Westover Woods, PA; (Y); Cmnty Wkr; Computer Clb; Math Tm; Political Wkr; Nwsp Stf; Off Soph Cls; JV Socr; JV Trk; High Hon Roll; NHS; Distngshd Soc Of Am HS Stu 85.

ANELLA, DAVE; Archbishop Wood For Boys; Holland, PA; (Y); Church Yth Grp; Im Bsbl; Var Bsktbl; Im Vllybl; Hon Roll.

ANFUSO, THOMAS D; Freedom HS; Bethlehem, PA; (Y); 43/465; Pep Clb; Var Crs Cntry; JV Ftbl; Wt Lftg; JV Wrstlng; High Hon Roll; Hon Roll; JETS Awd; Ntl Merit Ltr; 3rd Pl Ntl Hstry Dy Cmptn 86; Pre-Med.

ANGEL, DON; Mt Lebanon HS; Pittsburgh, PA; (Y); Var L Bsktbl; Var L Golf; Var L Tennis; Cit Awd; High Hon Roll; Hon Roll; NEDT Awd; SAR Awd; Mt Lebanon Rep 86-87; Acctnt.

ANGELL, JOSEPH; W B Saul HS Of Agricultural Science; Philadelphia, PA; (Y); 59/175; FFA; Stage Crew; Off Frsh Cls; Off Soph Cls; Off Jr Cls; JV Bsktbl; JV Fld Hcky; Golf; Sftbl; Wt Lftg; Military; Aqua Culturlist.

ANGELLO, THOMAS; Trinity HS; Camp Hill, PA; (Y); French Clb; Science Clb; Ski Clb; Socr; Hon Roll.

ANGELO, ANTHONY; St John Neuman HS; Philadelphia, PA; (Y); 41/338; Church Yth Grp; Spanish Clb; Nwsp Stf; Mktng.

ANGELO, PHILIP; Downingtown SR HS; Downingtown, PA; (Y); French Clb; JA; Teachers Aide; Nwsp Stf; Var Ftbl; Im Vllybl; High Hon Roll; NHS; Ntl Merit Ltr; NEDT Awd; Aerspc Engr.

ANGELO, SAM; Coughlin HS; Plains, PA; (Y); Ski Clb; Hon Roll; NHS; Penn ST; Civil Engineering.

ANGELUCCI, CHRISTOPHER B; St Josephs Prep; Philadephia, PA; (Y); Office Aide; Spanish Clb; Stage Crew; Lit Mag; High Hon Roll; Hon Roll; Ntl Arts Pgm Schlrshp Tmpl U 85-86; St Jsphs Prep Schlrshp & Grnt; Phldph Coll Art Prcoll Pgm; Philadelphia Coll Art; Art.

ANGELUCCI, MARGARET A; Norristown Area HS; Norristown, PA; (Y); 64/400; DECA; Key Clb; Service Clb; Nwsp Stf; Rep Soph Cls; Rep Jr Cls; Rep Stu Cncl; Hon Roll; Ntl Merit Ltr; Pres Schlr; Thomas Dugan Schlrshp 86; Bloomsburg U Schlrshp 86; Vlly Frg Optmst Clb Essy Cntst 3rd Pl 86; Bloomsburg U.

ANGELUCCI, ROSEMARIE; Merion Mercy Acad; Phila, PA; (Y); 6/81; Quiz Bowl; Sec Science Clb; Service Clb; VP Spanish Clb; Im Vllybl; Hon Roll; NHS; Spanish NHS; Immculta Aastp Spnsh Cntst 84-86; Immculta Sci Bwl 84-86; Drexel U; Sci.

ANGENY, BARRY; Downingtown SR HS; Downingtown, PA; (S); 18/550; Boy Scts; VP German Clb; Letterman Clb; Ski Clb; Varsity Clb; Band; Pres Soph Cls; Pres Jr Cls; Rep Stu Cncl; Var Socr; Engrng.

ANGERMANN, KATHERINE; New Hope-Solebury HS; New Hope, PA; (Y); 6/66; AFS; Ski Clb; Chorus; Rep Stu Cncl; Crs Cntry; Sftbl; High Hon Roll; Hon Roll; Home Ec Awd 83; Frnch Awd 85; CA Niece Lmbr Awd 86; Syracuse U; Frgn Lang.

ANGERMIER, DEANA; Ephrata SR HS; Ephrata, PA; (Y); JV Bsktbl; Mgr Socr; Hon Roll; Greg Shrthnd Awd 60 & 70 WPM 85-86; Bus.

ANGIOLELLI, VINCIE; Shenango HS; New Castle, PA; (S); 4/112; Hosp Aide; Band; Concert Band; Jazz Band; Mrchg Band; Pep Band; Stu Cncl; Cit Awd; Hon Roll; NHS; Amercn Legn Awd; Red Crss Svc Awd; Med.

ANGLE, JEFF; Wissahickon HS; Norristown, PA; (S); 4/280; Math Clb; Spanish Clb; Var L Bsbl; Var L Ftbl; DAR Awd; NHS; Subrbn I Amer Cnfrnc 2nd Tm Defnsv Bck 85; Outstndng Dfnsv Bck Awd 85; Penn ST U; Chem Engr.

ANGLE, STEPHEN J; Carlisle Area SR HS; Carlisle, PA; (Y); 35/362; Am Leg Boys St; Church Yth Grp; High Hon Roll; Prfct Atten Awd; 1st Pl-Regnl Hstry Day 86; Civl War Inst Schlrshp 86; Completed Adv Placemnt Course 85-86; Amer Hstry.

ANGRADI, DAMIAN; John S Fine HS; Glen Lyon, PA; (Y); Letterman Clb; Varsity Clb; Variety Show; Yrbk Stf; Bsktbl; Crs Cntry; Trk; Tchr.

ANITA, YODER; Rockwood Area HS; Somerset, PA; (Y); 12/95; Church Yth Grp; Computer Clb; Band; Chorus; Church Choir; JV Var Bsktbl; Var Sftbl; Hon Roll; NHS; Hlth Educ.

ANKER, STEFANIE ANNE; Harrisburg Academy; Camp Hill, PA; (Y); 10/31; Art Clb; GAA; Office Aide; Yrbk Ed-Chief; Sec Jr Cls; Var L Bsktbl; Var L Fld Hcky; Var L Sftbl; Camera Clb; Ski Clb; Schltc Art Awd 85-86.

ANKNEY, CHRISTY; Jefferson-Morgan HS; Mather, PA; (Y); Am Leg Aux Girls St; Varsity Clb; Nwsp Stf; Yrbk Stf; Rep Stu Cncl; Var JV Cheerleading; Hon Roll; Church Yth Grp; Dance Clb; Letterman Clb; Cinderella 84; May Day Attndnt 84-86; Jr Hmcmng Attndnt 85.

ANNABEL, KATHRYN; Sayre Area HS; Sayre, PA; (Y); Cmnty Wkr; Drama Clb; Hosp Aide; Library Aide; Spanish Clb; School Play; Stage Crew; Nwsp Ed-Chief; Nwsp Stf; Lit Mag; Robert Packer Schl; Nrsng.

ANNIS, ANDREA; North Clarion HS; Tionesta, PA; (Y); Church Yth Grp; Computer Clb; Sec 4-H; French Clb; Library Aide; Varsity Clb; Band; Chorus; Var Bsktbl; Var Trk; Penn ST U; Physcl Thrpy.

ANSARI, NENA; Westinghouse HS; Pittsburgh, PA; (Y); Library Aide; Chorus; NHS; Hampton U; Med.

ANSELL, JUDY; Mary Fuller Frazier HS; Dawson, PA; (S); Church Yth Grp; Band; Church Choir; Color Guard; Mrchg Band; Pep Band; Yrbk Ed-Chief; Yrbk Stf; Rep Soph Cls; Sftbl; Bradford Sch Bus; Lgl Sec.

ANSPACH, KIMBERLY; Cedar Crest HS; Lebanon, PA; (Y); 149/350; German Clb; Latin Clb; Capt Drill Tm; Mrchg Band; Nwsp Stf; Yrbk Phtg; Rep Sr Cls; Hon Roll; NHS; Press Clb VP 85-86; Temple U; Brdcst Jrnlsm.

ANSPACH, SCOTT; Northern Lebanon HS; Palmyra, PA; (Y); Church Yth Grp; Science Clb; Forestry.

ANSWINI, DOMINICK; Wyoming Area HS; W Wyoming, PA; (S); French Clb; Ski Clb; Band; Concert Band; Jazz Band; Mrchg Band; Hon Roll; NHS; Dist Band 85-86; Rgnl Band 85.

ANTEL, AMY; West Allegheny HS; Mc Donald, PA; (Y); Camera Clb; Drama Clb; Hosp Aide; Library Aide; Spanish Clb; Capt Color Guard; Capt Flag Corp; Capt Mrchg Band; Lit Mag; High Hon Roll; Winter Guard 85-86; Teen Inst Clb 85-86; U Pittsburgh; Phys Thrpy.

ANTES, JAMES; West Catholic HS; Philadelphia, PA; (Y); 30/265; Art Clb; Library Aide; Math Clb; Math Tm; Spanish Clb; Stage Crew; Nwsp Ed-Chief; Nwsp Phtg; Nwsp Rptr; Yrbk Stf; Prfct Conduct 83-84; Prfct Atten 83-84; NHS Awd 86; PA ST; Attrny.

ANTHONY, CHRISTINE; Cowanesque Valley HS; Westfield, PA; (Y); Computer Clb; Dance Clb; Red Cross Aide; SADD; Chorus; Stage Crew; Hon Roll; Cntrl PA Bus Schl; Court Sten.

ANTHONY, CRIS; Lenape Vo Tech; Worthington, PA; (Y); Trs Church Yth Grp; SADD; VICA; Band; Concert Band; VP Frsh Cls; Sec Stu Cncl; Var Capt Cheerleading; Arch.

ANTHONY, DENISE; Bishop Guilfoyle HS; Altoona, PA; (S); 11/168; Chess Clb; Pres Science Clb; Service Clb; Speech Tm; Rep Soph Cls; Rep Sr Cls; Rep Stu Cncl; JV Cheerleading; Rotary Awd; Voice Dem Awd; Rotry Intl Frgn Exchg Stu 84-85; Intl Rel.

ANTHONY IV, EDWARD MASON; Hampton HS; Allison Park, PA; (Y); 23/205; Ski Clb; Spanish Clb; Nwsp Ed-Chief; Rep CAP; Im Bsbl; JV Bsktbl; Im Tennis; High Hon Roll; NHS; Pres Schlr; Penn ST; Law.

ANTHONY, JENNIFER; Bishop Shanahan HS; Kennett Sq, PA; (Y); 93/218; Church Yth Grp; Dance Clb; Chorus; Madrigals; Yrbk Stf; Socr; Pre-Law.

ANTHONY, MARGARET; G B G Central Catholic HS; Greensburg, PA; (Y); 12/240; Pres Church Yth Grp; Ski Clb; JV Crs Cntry; JV Trk; Im Vllybl; High Hon Roll; NHS; Ntl Merit Ltr; U PA; Vet Med.

ANTHONY, RAY; Northampton Area SR HS; Northampton, PA; (Y); AFS; Boy Scts; Cmnty Wkr; Chorus; Stage Crew; Rep Stu Cncl; Hon Roll; Vp & Pres Emergncy Respnse Tm 85-87; Vp Of Hm Rm; Asstnt Trnr For Fall Sprts; U S Air Force; Paramedic.

ANTHONY, SHELLY A; High Schl Of Engineering & Science; Philadelphia, PA; (Y); 28/198; Pres Church Yth Grp; Capt Cheerleading; Hon Roll; NHS; Prfct Atten Awd; Actrl Sci.

ANTIDORMI, JOAN; North Pocono HS; Moscow, PA; (Y); FBLA; Sec Frsh Cls; Var Capt Cheerleading; Var Trk; Most Congenial 85; Lackawanna JC; Bus Mgmt.

ANTIS, DAVID MARTIN; Yough SR HS; W Newton, PA; (Y); 28/227; Church Yth Grp; Ski Clb; Spanish Clb; Band; Trs Chorus; Concert Band; Jazz Band; VP Mrchg Band; Pep Band; Stage Crew; NHS Schlrshp 86; Music Hnr Awd 86; U Of Pittsburgh; Blgy.

ANTKOWIAK, REBECCA; Venango Christian HS; Oil City, PA; (Y); 13/36; Variety Show; Nwsp Stf; Rep Stu Cncl; JV Var Bsktbl; Stat Wrstlng; Hon Roll; NHS; Prfct Atten Awd; PA Free Enterprise Wk 85.

ANTOLIC, MIKE; Ambridge HS; Baden, PA; (Y); Pep Clb; Var L Gym; Gymnstcs Tm ST Champs 84; Teacher.

ANTONACCI, MICHELLE; Valley HS; New Kensington, PA; (Y); 11/202; AFS; French Clb; JA; Key Clb; Library Aide; Color Guard; Concert Band; High Hon Roll; NHS; Pres Schlr; Clarion U Of PA; Elem Ed.

ANTONETTI, MICHAEL; Buryettstown Jr Sr HS; Burgettstown, PA; (Y); Ski Clb; High Hon Roll; Hon Roll; Jr NHS.

ANTONINI, MICHELLE; Hopewell HS; Aliquippa, PA; (Y); 25/245; Trs Computer Clb; Spanish Clb; Band; Trs Soph Cls; Var JV Bsktbl; Capt Powder Puff Ftbl; Var L Sftbl; Var L Vllybl; Hon Roll; NHS; All-Star Team 85-86; Raccoon Boys Clb Champ Team SR Div 85-86; U San Diego; Comp Sci.

ANTOSH, JOSEPH J; North Pocono HS; Moscow, PA; (Y); 7/250; JV Golf; High Hon Roll; NHS; U Scrntn; Comp Sci Prgmr.

ANTUS, KATHY; Hickory HS; W Middlesex, PA; (Y); 37/175; German Clb; JA; Chorus; Orch; NHS; Hermitage Ed Assc Schlrshp 86; JR Achvmnt Schlrshp 86; Bradford Schl; Sec.

ANUSZEWSKI, BEVERLY; Mid-Valley HS; Dickson City, PA; (Y); Yrbk Stf; Surgcl Tech.

ANWEILER JR, JAMES C; Churchill HS; East Pittsburgh, PA; (Y); Boy Scts; Church Yth Grp; Cmnty Wkr; Ski Clb; Chorus; Var L Bsbl; Var L Bsktbl; Im Bowling; JV Im Ftbl; Hon Roll; IN U Of PA; Mktg.

APEL, CHALICE; Apollo-Ridge HS; Saltsburg, PA; (Y); 4/150; Drama Clb; German Clb; Madrigals; School Play; Nwsp Stf; Yrbk Ed-Chief; Stu Cncl; Hon Roll; NHS; Pres Schlr; Carnegie U; Crtv Wrtng.

APGAR, ANDERS; Manheim Twp HS; Lancaster, PA; (Y); 5/350; VP JA; Lit Mag; Var Bsbl; JV Wrstlng; High Hon Roll; NHS; VP Mrktng Yr 86; Slsmn Yr 86; Rotary Intrnl Ldrshp Cnfrnc 86; Med.

APGAR, JOSEPH; Louis E Dieruff HS; Allentown, PA; (Y); 15/321; Boy Scts; Church Yth Grp; Letterman Clb; Vllybl; High Hon Roll; Hon Roll; Jr NHS; NHS; Prfct Atten Awd; Pres Schlr; Louis E Dieruff Schlrshp 86; Allentown Schlmns Clb Awd 86; DE ST Coll; Sci Ed.

APOLINARIO, ETHEL E; Abington SR HS; Rydal, PA; (Y); 48/535; School Musical; Off Sr Cls; JV Var Socr; JV Sftbl; High Hon Roll; Hon Roll; Jr NHS; NHS; Pres Ftnss Awd 86; Ctznshp & Svc Awd 86; Acad Decthln Plaq 86; Temple U; Bio.

APONTE, CARMELO; Thomas A Edison HS; Philadelphia, PA; (Y); Office Aide; Bsbl; Crs Cntry; Ftbl; Trk; Wrstlng; Prfct Atten Awd; Bus Awd 86; Temple; Accntng.

APPEL, KIMBERLEE; Mid Valley HS; Throop, PA; (Y); Art Clb; Spanish Clb; Chorus; Empire Beauty Schl; Csmtlgy.

APPLE, CHRYSTI; East Juniata HS; Millerstown, PA; (Y); 7/86; Band; Concert Band; Mrchg Band; Yrbk Sprt Ed; Yrbk Stf; Var L Fld Hcky; Var L Sftbl; Prfct Atten Awd; Outstndg Sftbll Plyr Awd ,6.

APPLE, ED; East Juniata HS; Richfield, PA; (Y); 15/95; Church Yth Grp; 4-H; Concert Band; Mrchg Band; Pep Band; Var L Bsbl; Var Socr; Im Vllybl; Hon Roll; Mansfield U; Cmnctns.

APPLEBAUM, LISA; Bensalem HS; Philadelphia, PA; (Y); Nwsp Rptr; Nwsp Stf; Yrbk Ed-Chief; Yrbk Rptr; Yrbk Stf; Tennis; Hon Roll; Fashion Inst Of Tech; Fshn Dsgn.

APPLEBEY, TRACY; John S Fine SR HS; Nanticoke, PA; (Y); Library Aide; Nwsp Stf; Yrbk Stf; Hon Roll; Bloomsburg U; Psych.

APPLEBY, JIM; Mechanicsburg Area SR HS; Mechanicsburg, PA; (Y); Pres German Clb; Ski Clb; Chorus; School Play; Symp Band; Yrbk Stf; VP Frsh Cls; NHS; Ntl Merit Ltr; Boy Scts; Order Of Arrow 84; Coll NYC; Pre Med.

APPLETON, HEATHER; St Francis Acad; Whitehall, PA; (Y); 4/20; Cmnty Wkr; Drama Clb; JA; Pep Clb; Spanish Clb; School Musical; Cheerleading; Hon Roll; PA Jr Acad Sci.

APPLEYARD, DONNA; Downingtown SR HS; Exton, PA; (Y); 111/501; Church Yth Grp; GAA; Teachers Aide; Chorus; Orch; School Musical; Yrbk Stf; Stat Tennis; JV Trk; Hon Roll; U Of Pittsburgh; Chem Engr.

APRIL, KEN; Attoona Area HS; Altoona, PA; (S); Computer Clb; Math Tm; Ski Clb; SADD; Var Diving; Var Socr; Var Swmmng; JV Tennis; High Hon Roll; Hon Roll; Comp Sci.

ARACO, DEANA; Saint Maria Goretti HS; Philadelphia, PA; (Y); #79 In Class; Cmnty Wkr; French Clb; Service Clb; Teachers Aide; Orch; School Musical; Variety Show; Lit Mag; Hon Roll; Charles E Ellis Schlrshp 84-87; Communications.

ARACRI, JOSEPH; Canevin HS; Pittsburgh, PA; (Y); 39/200; Aud/Vis; Drama Clb; VP FBLA; NFL; Pres Speech Tm; School Musical; School Play; Var Capt Socr; Hon Roll; Natl Qualfr NFL 85-86; Nalt Catholic Forensic Qualfr 86; Allegheny; Med.

ARAGON, BRYON; Bethlehem Catholic HS; Bethlehem, PA; (Y); Ski Clb; Var Crs Cntry; Im Wt Lftg; JV Wrstlng; Aerosp Engrng.

ARBOGAST, JOHN E; Hollidaysburg Area SR HS; Hollidaysburg, PA; (Y); 18/367; Church Yth Grp; Latin Clb; Var L Ftbl; Im Capt Vllybl; High Hon Roll; Hon Roll; NHS; Acad H Awd 84-86; Juniata Coll; Bus Adm.

ARBUTISKI, THOMAS; St Joseph HS; Natrona Hgts, PA; (Y); 4/55; French Clb; Math Clb; Math Tm; Yrbk Bus Mgr; Yrbk Stf; Bsktbl; Tennis; Math Schlrshp To U Ptsbrgh 85-86; Minnie Hymen Schlrshp To PA ST U 86; Ntl Hstry Day Awds 86; PA ST U; Aerospace Engrng.

ARCANGEL, ANNA MAY; Little Flower HS; Philadelphia, PA; (Y); 56/413; Aud/Vis; Cmnty Wkr; Orch; School Musical; School Play; Var Vllybl; Jr NHS; NHS; Prfct Atten Awd; Pres Acad Ftnss, TV Arts, Sci Awds 86; Temple U; Nrsg.

ARCH, STEPHANIE; North Catholic HS; Pittsburgh, PA; (Y); 44/255; German Clb; Hosp Aide; JA; Ski Clb; Chorus; Hon Roll.

ARCHAMBO, CYNTHIA; Keystone Oaks HS; Pittsburgh, PA; (Y); German Clb; Red Cross Aide; Rep Frsh Cls; U Of MT; Pharm.

ARCHER, LIONEL; St John Neumann HS; Philadelphia, PA; (Y); 30/321; Art Clb; Chess Clb; Computer Clb; Varsity Clb; Nwsp Stf; Yrbk Stf; Rep Soph Cls; Rep Jr Cls; Rep Sr Cls; Rep Stu Cncl; Ldrshp Silvr Mdl Awd 86; Temple Tyler; Grphc Dsgn.

ARCHER, OLIVER B; Blue Mountain Acad; Brooklyn, NY; (Y); Church Yth Grp; Varsity Clb; Chorus; Church Choir; Color Guard; Bsktbl; Ftbl; Sftbl; Trs Wt Lftg; Hon Roll; Prncpls List 85-86; Educ.

ARCHER, PATRICIA A; Council Rock HS; Holland, PA; (Y); 95/845; Church Yth Grp; Cmnty Wkr; SADD; Thesps; Church Choir; Capt Flag Corp; Mrchg Band; Nwsp Rptr; Hon Roll; 2nd Yr Pin & Ltr Marching Band 87; Penn ST; Communications.

ARCHER, ROB; Emmaus HS; Macungie, PA; (Y); 45/490; Computer Clb; Latin Clb; Service Clb; School Play; Var L Swmmng; High Hon Roll; Hon Roll; Jr NHS; NHS; Rotary Awd; 1st Pl Indstrl Arts Fair For Intaglio 83-84; Rotary Ldrshp Cmp 86; Modl UN; Aerosp Engrng.

ARCHIBALD, SUSAN; Parkland HS; Schnecksville, PA; (Y); 28/415; Exploring; Key Clb; Band; Flag Corp; Stu Cncl; Mgr(s); NHS; Spanish NHS; Lehigh Cnty CC; Mathmtcs.

ARDINI, LEE A; Central Cambria HS; Nanty-Glo, PA; (S); 13/209; Cmnty Wkr; Science Clb; Hon Roll; Amer Dstngshd HS Stu 86; U Fo Pittsburgh; Biolgcl Sci.

ARDIZZONE, KATHI; Bishop Guilfoyle HS; Altoona, PA; (Y); Church Yth Grp; Hosp Aide; Drill Tm; Yrbk Stf; Army.

ARDOLINO, KARI L; Emmaus HS; Allentown, PA; (Y); 18/463; Hosp Aide; Key Clb; SADD; VP Chorus; School Musical; School Play; Stage Crew; Rep Soph Cls; Rep Jr Cls; Sec Sr Cls; Dir Awd Choir; Crtvty Lang Arts Drama Awd; Coll Wm & Mary; Theatre.

ARDREY, JACQUELINE; Bensalem HS; Bensalem, PA; (Y); Cmnty Wkr; Chorus; Capt Color Guard; Rep Frsh Cls; Rep Soph Cls; JV Fld Hcky; JV Capt Sftbl; Hon Roll; NHS; Mrchg Band; Rider Coll Forensic Lang Tourn Frnch 85-86; Elem Educ Tchr.

ARDRON, THERESA; St Huberts High School For Girls; Philadelphia, PA; (Y); 218/367; Church Yth Grp; Chorus; School Musical; Hon Roll; Philadelphia Cmnty Clg; Scl Wrk.

ARENSBERG, LAURA K; South Hills HS; Pittsburgh, PA; (Y); Stage Crew; Yrbk Rptr; High Hon Roll; Hon Roll; Miss Talnt Unltd Of OH 82; CC Allegheny Cnty; CPA.

ARENZ, WARREN; Lebanon Catholic HS; Jonestown, PA; (Y); 3/67; School Play; Nwsp Rptr; Off Jr Cls; Off Sr Cls; Stu Cncl; Bsktbl; Ftbl; Trk; High Hon Roll; NHS; Rotary Boy Of The Mnth 85; Natl Engl Merit Awd 85; Awd For Best Math & Econ Stu 86; U Of HA; Engrng.

ARGENZIO, RENEE; Swissvale HS; Rankin, PA; (Y); #12 In Class; Spanish Clb; Yrbk Stf; Sec Stu Cncl; High Hon Roll; NHS; Hmcmng Queen 85-86; Comp Sci.

ARGOT JR, ROBERT G; Pleasant Valley HS; Saylorsburg, PA; (Y); 4/233; Boy Scts; Math Tm; Band; Off Jr Cls; Var L Golf; God Cntry Awd; Jr NHS; Trs NHS; Church Yth Grp; Scholastic Bowl; Eagle Scout Awd 85; Alternate Fnlst PA Gov Schl Sci 86; Renssalaer Poly Inst; Sci.

ARHANGELSKY, BARBARA; J S Fine SR HS; W Nanticoke, PA; (S); 10/244; Key Clb; Red Cross Aide; Chorus; Yrbk Stf; Rep Sr Cls; High Hon Roll; NHS; NEDT Awd; Acad All Amer Schlr Prog 86; Acad Ftnss Awd 86; Bio.

ARISON, TRACY; Fairchance Georges HS; Smithfield, PA; (Y); Exploring; Jr Cls; Cit Awd; Hon Roll; Law.

ARKWRIGHT, PAMELA; Palmyra SR HS; Palmyra, PA; (Y); 46/200; Drama Clb; French Clb; Pep Clb; Spanish Clb; Stat Bsktbl; Var Fld Hcky; Stat Ftbl; JV Var Sftbl; Trk; High Hon Roll; Penn ST; Fshn Mrchndsng.

ARLINGTON, VINCENT; Tech Memorial HS; Erie, PA; (Y); 34/367; Stage Crew; Swmmng; Hon Roll; NHS; Air Force.

ARMAGOST, LINDA; Du Bois Area HS; Reynoldsville, PA; (Y); 22/275; Varsity Clb; Capt Swmmng; Tennis; Psych.

ARMAGOST, MICHELE; Clarion Area HS; Sligo, PA; (Y); Sec Church Yth Grp; FCA; VICA; Chorus; Drm Mjr(t); Hon Roll; Penn ST Parlmntrn VICA 85-86; Edinboro CollNRS.

ARMBRUST, DONALD; Penn Trafford HS; Irwin, PA; (Y); Varsity Clb; Var L Bsbl; Var L Bsktbl; JV Ftbl; AZ ST U; Engr.

ARMBRUSTER, JOHN; Lehighton HS; Lehighton, PA; (Y); 42/247; Church Yth Grp; Nwsp Stf; Var Bsktbl; Var Golf; Var Trk; Golf MVP 86.

ARMBRUSTER, LAURA; Upper Dublin HS; Dresher, PA; (Y); Church Yth Grp; Hosp Aide; Varsity Clb; Rep Stu Cncl; Var JV Bsktbl; Var JV Lcrss; NHS; Ntl Merit Ltr; JV Tennis; Im Wt Lftg; Eastern Coll; Bio.

ARMITAGE, KEVIN; Wyalusing Area HS; Laceyville, PA; (Y); Church Yth Grp; Spanish Clb; Bsbl; Bsktbl; Coach Actv; Ftbl; Hon Roll; Ftbl All Str Tm 85; Bsbl All Str Tm 86.

ARMITAGE, VICKI; Wyalusing Valley HS; Wyalusing, PA; (Y); Letterman Clb; Pep Clb; Spanish Clb; Mrchg Band; Var Co-Capt Cheerleading; Var Twrlr; High Hon Roll; Hon Roll; Penn ST U; Educ.

ARMOLD, MELISSIA; Donegal HS; Marietta, PA; (Y); 17/168; Latin Clb; Spanish Clb; Varsity Clb; Pres Stu Cncl; Var L Cheerleading; Var L Sftbl; Hon Roll; Ntl Merit Ltr; Spanish NHS; Phrmcst.

ARMOUR, JULIE; Meadville SR HS; Meadville, PA; (Y); Pep Clb; Spanish Clb; Varsity Clb; Trs Jr Cls; Trs Stu Cncl; Capt Co-Capt Cheerleading; DAR Awd; Elks Awd; Hon Roll; Outstndg Chrldr 85; Crim Just.

ARMSTRONG, CATHY; Chester HS; Chester, PA; (S); 18/384; Cmnty Wkr; Library Aide; Pep Clb; Soroptimist; Nwsp Stf; Pres Stu Cncl; Hon Roll; Prfct Atten Awd; Rotary Awd; 1st Rnnr Up Hmcmng Cntst 85-86; Millersville U; Chemcl Engrng.

ARMSTRONG, DAVID; Rockwood Area HS; Rockwood, PA; (S); 29/98; Trs Chess Clb; Var L Bsbl; Bsktbl; Hon Roll; NHS; Pensacola U; Law Enfrcmnt.

ARMSTRONG, DLYNN FAITH; Butler SR HS; Butler, PA; (Y); 22/752; Am Leg Aux Girls St; VP Church Yth Grp; French Clb; JA; Thesps; Mrchg Band; School Play; Rep Stu Cncl; Jr NHS; NHS; Bio.

ARMSTRONG, MICHELE; Unionville HS; Chadds Ford, PA; (Y); 55/300; GAA; Spanish Clb; Band; Orch; Ftbl; Stat Lcrss; Stat Wrstlng; High Hon Roll; Hon Roll; Jr NHS; Athltc Trng.

ARMSTRONG, NORA; Northern HS; Wellsville, PA; (Y); 139/209; Elmntry Educ.

ARMSTRONG, PAUL; Brookville HS; Sigel, PA; (Y); Var Church Yth Grp; Var Cmnty Wkr; FCA; Math Tm; SADD; Church Choir; JV Bsbl; JV Ftbl; Sftbl; Hon Roll; Bible Coll; Pastor.

ARMSTRONG, REBECCA; Chief Logan HS; Yeagertown, PA; (Y); Computer Clb; Key Clb; Letterman Clb; Pep Clb; Soroptimist; Spanish Clb; Varsity Clb; Band; Chorus; Concert Band; Geolgst.

ARMSTRONG, ROGER; Solance HS; Willow St, PA; (Y); 5/276; Trs VP Church Yth Grp; Concert Band; Mrchg Band; Yrbk Stf; JV Capt Socr; Wrstlng; High Hon Roll; Jr NHS; Trs NHS; Aerospc Engr.

ARNDT, CHRIS; Emmaus HS; Emmaus, PA; (Y); 5/493; German Clb; Latin Clb; Model UN; Scholastic Bowl; Im Bsktbl; JV Var Ftbl; Im Wt Lftg; High Hon Roll; Hon Roll; NHS; Lib Arts.

ARNDT, PATRICE; Lebanon SR HS; Lebanon, PA; (Y); Exploring; German Clb; Hon Roll; Navy.

ARNDT, STACEY; East Pennsboro HS; Enola, PA; (Y); GAA; Latin Clb; Spanish Clb; Nwsp Rptr; JV Bsktbl; JV Fld Hcky; Var L Sftbl.

ARNDT, VICTORIA L; Susquehanna Township HS; Harrisburg, PA; (Y); 7/165; GAA; Key Clb; Model UN; Nwsp Stf; Ed Yrbk Stf; Capt Var Cheerleading; High Hon Roll; Hon Roll; VP NHS; Am Yth Fndtn Awd 86; Progress PTO Awd 86; Lehigh U; Engrng.

ARNER, CAROL; Apollo-Ridge HS; N Apollo, PA; (Y); 32/157; Church Yth Grp; Girl Scts; Varsity Clb; Band; Concert Band; Madrigals; Mrchg Band; Gym; Var Sftbl; Hon Roll; Louis V Nelson Schlrshp 86; Athltc Awds 84-86; Bradford Schl Of Bus; Accntng.

ARNER, EDWARD; Panther Valley HS; Coaldale, PA; (Y); 39/106; VICA; Stage Crew; Yrbk Stf; Lit Mag; Stat Trk; Wrstlng; Fndmntls Of Fire Fghtg 84; Fire & Arson Detctn 85; Emerg Med Tech 86; Lincoln Tech Inst; Drftg.

ARNER, MARK; Minersville Area HS; Pottsville, PA; (Y); French Clb; Band; Concert Band; Jazz Band; Mrchg Band; Pep Band; School Musical; French Hon Soc; Hon Roll; Musician.

ARNOLD, ALLISON; Central SR HS; York, PA; (Y); 29/248; Church Yth Grp; Cmnty Wkr; Exploring; Hosp Aide; Pep Clb; Band; Chorus; Concert Band; Mrchg Band; Orch; PTSA Rflctns Cntst ST Phtgrphy Wnnr 86; Dist VII Band Fstvl Prtcpnt 84-85; PA Ambssdrs Music 84; Lehigh County CC; Physcl Thrpy.

ARNOLD, ANGIE; South Williamsport Area HS; S Williamsport, PA; (Y); 21/140; Church Yth Grp; French Clb; Intnl Clb; Sftbl; French Hon Soc; Hon Roll; Phy Thrpy.

ARNOLD, CAROL; Northern Chester County Tech Schl; Pottstown, PA; (Y); 10/137; FBLA; Yrbk Stf; High Hon Roll; Hon Roll; VICA Comptn 1st Plc Advncd Typng 85-86; Comm Art.

ARNOLD, CATHY; Annville-Cleona HS; Annville, PA; (S); 8/130; Sec French Clb; Girl Scts; Red Cross Aide; Varsity Clb; Chorus; Yrbk Ed-Chief; Tennis; NHS; Frnch.

ARNOLD, GREG; Cedar Crest HS; Lebanon, PA; (Y); 4/320; Key Clb; Latin Clb; Pep Clb; Spanish Clb; Var L Bsbl; Var L Bsktbl; Var L Golf; Im Vllybl; High Hon Roll; NHS; Rtry Ldrshp Conf Dstrct 739 86; MVP Myerstwn Bsktbl Trnmnt 82-83; Cdr Crst Hnr Bnqt 84-86; Engr.

ARNOLD JR, JAMES R; Lebanon Catholic HS; Hershey, PA; (Y); 20/68; School Play; Off Jr Cls; Off Sr Cls; Stu Cncl; Bsbl; Bsktbl; Ftbl; Dstrct All Str Bsbl Tm 86; Lebanon Cthlc Athlt Of Yr 86; Otstndng Bsbll Plyr Of Yr 86; U Of Richmond.

ARNOLD, KRISTEN; Cedar Crest HS; Lebaon, PA; (Y); Camera Clb; Drama Clb; VP French Clb; Key Clb; Pep Clb; School Musical; Yrbk Ed-Chief; Var Socr; Im Vllybl; High Hon Roll; Eng Comm.

ARNOLD, LISA; Trinity Christian HS; Pittsburgh, PA; (S); 4/16; VP JA; Band; Yrbk Stf; Sec Stu Cncl; Var L Bsktbl; High Hon Roll; Trs Jr NHS; NHS; NEDT Awd; Civil Engr.

ARNOLD, LORI; Tyrone Area JR SR HS; Tyrone, PA; (Y); Key Clb; VP Spanish Clb; Pres SADD; Band; Chorus; Concert Band; Mrchg Band; JV Var Bsktbl; Hon Roll; Prfct Atten Awd.

ARNOLD, LORI; Upper Dauphin Area HS; Lykens, PA; (Y); 41/105; German Clb; Hon Roll; Co-Op Awd 86.

ARNOLD, MICHELLE; Northern Lebanon HS; Lebanon, PA; (Y); Church Yth Grp; 4-H; Spanish Clb; Color Guard; Fld Hcky; Sftbl; 4-H Awd; Hon Roll; Harrisburg Area CC; Bus Adm.

ARNOLD, STACEY; Elk County Christian HS; St Marys, PA; (Y); 19/80; Ski Clb; VP Frsh Cls; Score Keeper; Trk; High Hon Roll; Nrsg.

ARNOLD, STEPHANIE; Lebanon Christian Acad; Jonestown, PA; (S); Yrbk Stf; Sec Frsh Cls; Sec Soph Cls; Sec Jr Cls; Bsktbl; Sftbl; High Hon Roll; Prfct Atten Awd; Pres Acadmc Ftns Awd 85; Outstndng GPA Alg II 85; Hgst GPA Englsh 8 83; Med Sec.

ARNOLD, TROY; Red Lion Area SR HS; Red Lion, PA; (Y); 43/337; Am Leg Boys St; Varsity Clb; School Play; Stage Crew; JV Var Bsktbl; JV Var Ftbl; Mgr(s); JV Var Trk; Aud/Vis; Cmnty Wkr; Ntl Athletic Schrlsh Psoc 84-85; Stu Mnth 86; York Coll; Engrng.

ARNOLD, WILLIAM V; Bishop Mc Devitt HS; Wyncote, PA; (Y); 1/359; Cmnty Wkr; German Clb; Mathletes; Political Wkr; Nwsp Ed-Chief; Trs Stu Cncl; Hon Roll; Trs NHS; Ntl Merit Ltr; Rensselaer Medal-Math & Sci 85; Natl Fnlst-Natl Cncl Of Teachers Of Englsh 85; St Josephs U; MD.

ARNOUT, ERIC R; Nativity B V M HS; St Clair, PA; (Y); 1/98; Church Yth Grp; Pres Band; Chorus; Variety Show; Rep Stu Cncl; Gov Hon Prg Awd; High Hon Roll; NHS; Prfct Atten Awd; U Of CA Santa Crum Bk Awd 86; Schl & ST Sci Fair 83-86; Stu Of The Mnth Mar 86; Saint Charles Sem; Cathlc Prist.

ARONE, ERIC; Homer Center HS; Homer City, PA; (Y); Boy Scts; Varsity Clb; Band; Concert Band; Jazz Band; Frsh Cls; Soph Cls; Bsbl; Bsktbl; Ftbl; Juniata Coll; Bus.

ARORA, SANJAY; Downingtown SR HS; Downingtown, PA; (S); 15/544; Boy Scts; Intnl Clb; Spanish Clb; Trs SADD; Rep Stu Cncl; Im Lcrss; High Hon Roll; NHS; NEDT Awd; Pre Med.

ARPINO, MICHELE; Bishop Carroll HS; Portage, PA; (S); 30/110; Drama Clb; Ski Clb; Trs Jr Cls; Rep Stu Cncl; Bsktbl; Im Bowling; Crs Cntry; Hon Roll; Prfct Atten Awd; MI ST; Phys Thrpy.

ARQUILLO, MARIA; Charleroi Area HS; Charleroi, PA; (Y); French Clb; Science Clb; Varsity Clb; VP Band; Concert Band; Drm Mjr(t); Jazz Band; Mrchg Band; JV Var Bsktbl; CA U Of PA; Clncl Psych.

ARRIETA, TONY; Unionville HS; W Chester, PA; (Y); Boy Scts; Church Yth Grp; Computer Clb; Exploring; Ski Clb; Pres Frsh Cls; JV Var Socr; JV Var Tennis; Hon Roll; All Leag MVP Soccer 83-84; Bus Adm.

ARRIGO, CHUCK; Carlynton JR SR HS; Pittsburgh, PA; (Y); German Clb; High Hon Roll; Hon Roll; NHS; Carnegie Mellon U; Aerontcl Eng.

ARRIGO, LARRY; Bethel Park HS; Bethel Park, PA; (Y); Spanish Clb; Band; Concert Band; Drm Mjr(t); Jazz Band; Mrchg Band; Symp Band; Stu Cncl; JV Ftbl; Var Wrstlng; John Carroll U; Intl Bus.

ARRIGO, PHILIP; Penn Hills HS; Pittsburgh, PA; (Y); French Clb; Rep Stu Cncl; Stat Bsbl; Im Ftbl; Hon Roll; U Pittsburgh; Bus.

ARRINGTON JR, LARRY G; Carver HS Of Engineering & Science; Philadelphia, PA; (Y); 18/240; Church Yth Grp; Chorus; Church Choir; Hon Roll; NHS; Drexel U; Engrng.

ARRISON, DANIEL P; Lansdale Catholic HS; Lansdale, PA; (Y); Church Yth Grp; Mathletes; Math Clb; Bsktbl; Wrstlng; High Hon Roll; Hon Roll; Physics PSSC 86.

ARSENBERGER, LISA; Connellsville Area HS; Mill Run, PA; (Y); Camera Clb; Church Yth Grp; SADD; Band; Concert Band; Mrchg Band; Pep Band; School Play; Sec Soph Cls; VP Sr Cls; Flight Attndnt.

ARSENIU, ANN; Lewistown Area HS; Lewistown, PA; (Y); 17/256; Pres AFS; French Clb; Sec Pep Clb; Science Clb; Ski Clb; Band; School Musical; Var JV Cheerleading; Var Trk; High Hon Roll; Amer Assn Of U Womn 86; Pres Acadmc Fit Awds Prog 86; Panther Schlr Athls 86; Friends World Coll; Marn Sci.

ARTELLO, KRISTY; Villa Maria Acad; Erie, PA; (Y); 37/132; NFL; Pres PAVAS; School Musical; High Hon Roll; Hon Roll; Adv Plc Stu Gannon U 85-86; Rosemont Coll; Mod Lang.

ARTH, BRIAN; Clarion Area HS; Clarion, PA; (Y); Band; Chorus; Concert Band; Jazz Band; Mrchg Band; School Musical; Ftbl; Trk; Wt Lftg; Hon Roll; Pres Fit Awd 85.

ARTH, NANCY; St Francis Acad; Bethlehem, PA; (Y); Church Yth Grp; Drama Clb; Red Cross Aide; Chorus; School Musical; School Play; Nwsp Rptr; Yrbk Rptr; Yrbk Stf; Lit Mag; Engl.

ARTHUR, CHRISTINE; Susquehanna Comm HS; Lanesboro, PA; (Y); Church Yth Grp; Ski Clb; Band; Chorus; Church Choir; Concert Band; Var Cheerleading; Powder Puff Ftbl; Hon Roll; Bloomsburg Coll; Libl Arts.

ARTIM, DAVID; Freedom HS; Bethlehem, PA; (Y); Sec Trs Church Yth Grp; Trs Drama Clb; French Clb; JA; Chorus; Capt Mrchg Band; School Musical; School Play; Lit Mag; Hon Roll; U Scranton; Finance.

ARTMONT, DIANA; Pittston Area SR HS; Pittston, PA; (Y); Church Yth Grp; Girl Scts; Spanish Clb; Band; Hon Roll; CCD Prfct Attndnc Awd 83; Pre-Med.

ARTUR, TONY; Central Bucks East HS; Wycombe, PA; (Y); Aud/Vis; School Play; Stage Crew; Lit Mag; Trk; Hon Roll; Ntl Merit Ltr; Jornlst.

ARTURO, RENEE; Fox Chapel Area HS; Cheswick, PA; (Y); French Clb; Hosp Aide; Key Clb; Chorus; School Musical; High Hon Roll; Hon Roll; Ohio St U; Pre-Vet Med.

ARTYMOWICZ, RICHARD; Chichester SR HS; Linwood, PA; (Y); 8/270; Scholastic Bowl; Band; Concert Band; Drm Mjr(t); Var Bsbl; Hon Roll; NHS; Rotary Awd; Spanish NHS; Sen Bells Stu Advsry Bd 85-86; Century III Ldrs Awd Schl Wnr 85; Anna M Vincent Scholar 86; Philadelphia Coll Phrmcy; Txclg.

ARTZ, SHAIN; Willaims Valley HS; Williamstown, PA; (Y); 21/108; Computer Clb; Office Aide; Teachers Aide; Chorus; Church Choir; Color Guard; Yrbk Stf; Rep Stu Cncl; Var L Cheerleading; Capt Powder Puff Ftbl; Most Outstndng Chorus 86; Best Defense Ftbl 84-85; Impulse Beauty Cntst 3rd Prx 84; Elem Ed.

ARUSKEVICIUS, ANDY; Marion Ctr; Ernest, PA; (S); Church Yth Grp; Mgr Bsktbl; Trk; High Hon Roll; Hon Roll; Hlth.

ASBELL, LYNN; Wyomissing Area HS; Wyomissing Hls, PA; (Y); Art Clb; French Clb; Chorus; Capt Flag Corp; Trk; Hon Roll; Reading Museum Stu Art Show 2nd Pl 86; Arch.

ASCHENBRENNER, ALAN; Scranton Prep Schl; Laplume, PA; (Y); 115/298; Boy Scts; Rep Church Yth Grp; Dance Clb; Drama Clb; Speech Tm; Thesps; Band; Sec Chorus; Pep Band; Hon Roll; Drma.

ASCHENBRENNER, JOHN P; Scranton Preparatory Schl; Laplume, PA; (Y); 86/190; Boys Clb Am; Boy Scts; Church Yth Grp; Cmnty Wkr; Crs Cntry; Hon Roll; St Joseph U; Inf Sys.

ASH, RENA; Harrisburg Christian Schl; Marysville, PA; (Y); Chorus; School Play; Nwsp Stf; Yrbk Stf; Trs Jr Cls; Var Cheerleading; Socr; Sftbl; Hon Roll; Bus.

ASHBAUGH, GINA; Clarion Limeston HS; Strattanville, PA; (Y); FNA; Spanish Clb; Yrbk Stf; VP Frsh Cls; VP Soph Cls; Pres Jr Cls; Pres Sr Cls; Natl Hist Day Hon Ment 85; Clarion U; Elem Educ.

ASHBERRY, ERIC; Halifax Area HS; Halifax, PA; (Y); 53/108; Drama Clb; Pep Clb; Band; Chorus; School Musical; School Play; Variety Show; Rep Stu Cncl; JV L Ftbl; Wt Lftg; District Chorus Medal 85; Slippery Rock U; Music.

ASHBY, MATTHEW; Kiski Area HS; Leechburg, PA; (Y); Computer Clb; Science Clb; SADD; Chorus; Yrbk Sprt Ed; Yrbk Stf; Rep Soph Cls; JV Var Crs Cntry; Var Trk; High Hon Roll.

ASHBY, TOM; Central Bucks H S West; Warrington, PA; (Y); 16/497; Computer Clb; Chorus; Var L Bsbl; Hon Roll; Jr NHS; Prfct Atten Awd; 1st Pl Ntl Sci Olympc 84; Elec Engrng.

ASHFORD, NINA; Freedom HS; Bethlehem, PA; (Y); 30/445; Church Yth Grp; Drama Clb; French Clb; Pres Trs Science Clb; Trs SADD; Church Choir; School Play; Rptr Nwsp Stf; Rep Stu Cncl; Capt Pom Pon; Pstrl Cnslng.

ASHMAN, LAURA; Westmont Hilltop HS; Johnstown, PA; (Y); Church Yth Grp; Drama Clb; Thesps; Band; Concert Band; Mrchg Band; School Play; Var L Tennis; High Hon Roll; Hon Roll; Law.

ASHMORE, TODD; Trinity HS; Washington, PA; (Y); Spanish Clb; Ntl Merit Ltr; PA ST; Strctrl Engrng.

ASHOFF, REBECCA; Steel Valley HS; Munhall, PA; (Y); 1/207; Church Yth Grp; Varsity Clb; Var Swmmng; Var Tennis; High Hon Roll; NHS; Jr Mrshl At Sr Cmmncmnts 86; Intl Bus.

ASHTON, KIRK; Meadville Area HS; Meadville, PA; (Y); Aud/Vis; Church Yth Grp; Varsity Clb; Var L Ftbl; Var L Trk; Im Vllybl; JV L Wrstlng; Offnsv Plyr Of Yr Ftbl 85-86; 2nd Tm NW Cnfrnc Rnng Bck 85-86; Hnbl Mntn NW Cnfrnc Dfnsv Bck 85-86; Sprts Rltd Med.

ASHTON, SUSAN; Neshaminy HS; Levittown, PA; (Y); 8/720; Church Yth Grp; Sec Church Choir; Concert Band; Jazz Band; Mrchg Band; School Musical; Nwsp Stf; Rep Stu Cncl; High Hon Roll; NHS; PMEA Dist Chrl Fstvl 85 & 86; BCMEA Music Fstvl; Math.

ASKEW, CARLA; Gateway SR HS; Monroeville, PA; (Y); JA; Ski Clb; Chorus; Sec Frsh Cls; Trs Soph Cls; Rep Jr Cls; Rep Sr Cls; Rep Stu Cncl; JV Var Cheerleading; $100 Sls Awd Jr Achvmnt 84.

ASKEY, LORI; Brockway Area HS; Brockway, PA; (Y); Trs Church Yth Grp; Pres Drama Clb; Thesps; Band; Chorus; Drill Tm; School Play; Variety Show; Hon Roll; Dist, Rgnl, Al-ST Chorus 86; Falls Crk Fire Qun 85; Vly Forge Chrstn Coll; Music.

ASKEY, MELISSA; Mechanicsburg Area SR HS; Mechanicsburg, PA; (Y); 9/311; VP Church Yth Grp; Library Aide; Chorus; Mrchg Band; Orch; Symp Band; High Hon Roll; NHS; Ntl Merit Ltr; Amer Music Aboard Hnr Band 86.

ASMAN, DAWN; North East Bradford HS; Rome, PA; (Y); Art Clb; Camera Clb; FHA; Library Aide; SADD; Teachers Aide; Chorus; Vllybl; Hon Roll; Drama Clb; Ursinus Coll; Psyclgy.

ASMAN, SCOTT; Bensalem HS; Bensalem, PA; (Y); Varsity Clb; Var Capt Bsbl; Var Capt Bsktbl; Var Capt Ftbl; Wt Lftg; Hon Roll; 2nd Ldng Pssr-Bck Cnty 85-86; 2nd Tm Bsbl 85-86; Hnrb Mntn Ftbl, Bsktbl 85-86; Pre-Med.

ASPINALL, SUSAN ELAINE; Bethel Park HS; Bethel Park, PA; (Y); 47/519; Church Yth Grp; French Clb; Jazz Band; Sec Mrchg Band; Sec Symp Band; Rep Frsh Cls; Rep Jr Cls; Sftbl; NHS; Sec Ed.

ASSAD, AUDRA; Riverview HS; Oakmont, PA; (Y); 1/98; Key Clb; Band; Jazz Band; School Play; Nwsp Ed-Chief; Stu Cncl; Trk; DAR Awd; High Hon Roll; JP Sousa Awd; Englsh Awd 86; Penn ST; Commnctns.

ASSAL, MARIE; Central Catholic HS; Breiningsville, PA; (Y); 36/210; Church Yth Grp; JA; Math Tm; Q&S; Chem.

ASSENMACHER, THOMAS; Father Judge HS; Philadelphia, PA; (Y); 30/403; German Clb; Service Clb; Nwsp Stf; Hon Roll; NHS; KC Outstndng Svc Schl Comm 86; U Dayton; Criminal Justice.

ASTI, DAWN; St Marys Area HS; Saint Marys, PA; (Y); Office Aide; NHS; PA ST U; Chld Care.

ASTICK, CHRISTINE; Middleburg HS; Middleburg, PA; (Y); 17/108; German Clb; Varsity Clb; Band; Chorus; Nwsp Rptr; Nwsp Stf; Yrbk Stf; Stu Cncl; Var L Cheerleading; Gym; Bloomsburg ST; Bus Adm.

ASTLE, TAMMY; Ringgold HS; Monongahela, PA; (Y); Ski Clb; Varsity Clb; Band; Stat Bsbl; L Var Vllybl; Hon Roll; NHS; Sci & Math Hnr Soc; Interact Clb; Physcl Thrpy.

ASTLEY, AUTUMN; Hempfield Area SR HS; Youngwood, PA; (Y); Rep Church Yth Grp; Science Clb; Trs Spanish Clb; Chorus; School Play; High Hon Roll; Jr NHS; Lion Awd; NHS; Sec Spanish NHS; 3rd Pl Span Drmtc Pres 86; Slctd To Compete NCTE Wrtng Cntst 86; Biol Rsrch.

ASTOLFI, ERIN; Crestwood JR SR HS; Mountaintop, PA; (Y); Y-Teens; Chorus; Nwsp Ed-Chief; JV Socr; L Trk; High Hon Roll; NHS; 4-H; Gov Schl Arts SF 86; PTSSA ST Qlfr 84, 86; JR Olympc Ntl Trk-Fld 85; Art Ed.

ASTON, ADAM; Taylor Allderdice HS; Pittsbugh, PA; (Y); 3/437; Cmnty Wkr; Debate Tm; Mathletes; Math Clb; Math Tm; Q&S; Scholastic Bowl; Ski Clb; Stage Crew; Nwsp Ed-Chief; PA Govnrs Schl For Sci 85; Westnghs Sci Hnrs Inst 85; Soroptmsts Of Pttsbrg Yth Citznshp Awd 86; Princeton U.

ASTORINO, HOLLY; Franklin Area SR HS; Franklin, PA; (Y); French Clb; Radio Clb; Chorus; Stage Crew; Jr Cls; Sr Cls; High Hon Roll; NHS; Schl Dir Awd 84-86.

ASTORINO, JEAN; Punxsutawney Area HS; Walston, PA; (Y); 10/238; Trs Science Clb; Pres Band; Yrbk Stf; Ftbl; Elks Awd; NHS; Spanish NHS; Ftbl Queens Ct 85-86; Co-Rcpnt Cls Hrts 86; Jms V Clnna Bnd Awd 86; Washngtn & Jeffersn Coll; Optmt.

ASTRAB, PATRICIA; Mc Keesport Area HS; Mckeesport, PA; (Y); 29/368; Office Aide; Yrbk Stf; Rep Jr Cls; Trs Stu Cncl; Capt L Bsktbl; L Var Sftbl; L Var Vllybl; Hon Roll; VP NHS; Bus Admin.

ATEN, CHRISTINE; Col-Mont AVTS; Berwick, PA; (Y); Sec Church Yth Grp; Sec Exploring; Pres 4-H; Girl Scts; Library Aide; Red Cross Aide; Church Choir; Var Sftbl; 4-H Awd; Hlth Occ.

ATHANASION, CONSTANCE; St Francis Acad; Bethelehem, PA; (Y); Church Yth Grp; Chorus; Church Choir; School Musical; School Play; Variety Show; Trs Jr Cls; Hon Roll; Interior Design.

ATHERHOLT, JODY; West Hazleton HS; Drums, PA; (S); 17/191; Ski Clb; Thesps; Chorus; Rep Sr Cls; L Crs Cntry; L Trk; High Hon Roll; NHS; Pres Of Schl Spirit Clb 85-86; Bloomsburg U.

ATKINS, ANGELA LYNN; Donegal HS; Maytown, PA; (Y); Am Leg Aux Girls St; Pres FBLA; Pep Clb; JV Trk; Rotary Awd; Zenophile Bnqut Cmmtte-Frgn Lang; Spnsh.

ATKINS, LYNN; Penn Trafford HS; Irwin, PA; (Y); Spanish Clb; Band; Concert Band; Mrchg Band; Var Crs Cntry; Var L Trk.

ATKINS, RAMA; Creative & Performing Arts HS; Philadelphia, PA; (S); 12/146; Drama Clb; Library Aide; Office Aide; Thesps; School Play; Stage Crew; Yrbk Stf; High Hon Roll; Hon Roll; Actg.

ATKINS, SHARON M; Canevin HS; Pittsburgh, PA; (Y); 2/176; Exploring; FBLA; Yrbk Stf; High Hon Roll; NHS; Ntl Merit Ltr; Rotary Awd; Hon Mntn Chmstry Sctn Sci & Engrng Fr 86; SR Chmpnshp Sci Fr 86; Amrcn Inst Of Chem Engrs Pitts Sctn; Engrng.

ATKINS, TIMOTHY; Devon Prep; Wayne, PA; (Y); Cmnty Wkr; Sec Stu Cncl; Socr; JV Trk; Hon Roll; NHS; Ntl Merit Ltr; Math Tm; School Musical; High Genl Avrg 84; Eng Awd 85; Lolty & Sch Spirt Awd 86; Med.

ATKINSON, CLINT; Highlands HS; Tarentum, PA; (Y); 60/265; Cmnty Wkr; Drama Clb; Chorus; School Play; Cit Awd; Nacel Cultural Exch Stu In Great Britain 86; The Studio Schl Of Engl Diploma In Engl Heritage 86; Westminster Coll; Theater.

ATKINSON, CODEE; Marion Center HS; Smicksburg, PA; (Y); Church Yth Grp; FBLA; FNA; Intnl Clb; Library Aide; Office Aide; Science Clb; SADD; JV Trk; High Hon Roll; Bus.

ATKINSON, DAN; Lampeter Strasburg HS; Willow Street, PA; (Y); 25/146; FBLA; Varsity Clb; Chorus; School Musical; Nwsp Rptr; Pres Frsh Cls; VP Soph Cls; VP Stu Cncl; Var L Bsbl; Var L Bsktbl; Stu Of Mnth Paradise Rotary 85; Boy Of Mnth H S 85; Millersville U; Bus Admin.

ATKINSON, TEAGUE; Cumberland Valley HS; Mechanicsburg, PA; (Y); Yrbk Stf; Rep Frsh Cls; Rep Soph Cls; VP Jr Cls; Pres Sr Cls; Pres Sec Stu Cncl; Var Tennis; Var Trk; Hon Roll; Key Clb; Hmcmng Atten; James Madison; Engrng.

ATTARDO, CHARLES; Crestwood HS; Mountaintop, PA; (Y); Computer Clb; Ski Clb; Bsbl; Bsktbl; Socr; Vllybl; High Hon Roll; NHS; Marine Bio.

ATTICKS, BARRY; Central Dauphin HS; Harrisburg, PA; (Y); Band; Chorus; Concert Band; Drm Mjr(t); Jazz Band; Mrchg Band; School Musical; L Trk; High Hon Roll; NHS; Lions Club Music, Kiwanis Acad, & Readers Digest Natl Cntst Wnnr Awds 86; Elizabethtown Coll; Bus Admin.

ATTIG, LISA; Red Lion Area SR HS; Felton, PA; (Y); 44/338; Trs Church Yth Grp; Chorus; Church Choir; Drill Tm; School Musical; High Hon Roll; Prfct Atten Awd; Frederic Chopin Piano Awd 86; WY; Engr.

ATTMAN, MICHAEL E; Archbishop Ryan HS For Boys; Philadelphia, PA; (Y); 5/434; Cmnty Wkr; Computer Clb; Nwsp Rptr; Lit Mag; Capt Swmmng; Cit Awd; High Hon Roll; Sec NHS; Pres Schlr; Princpls Awd Distngushd Hnrs 86; Outstndng Achvt Calculus 86; Sci Schlrshp 86; U DE; Chem Engr.

ATWELL, HOLLY; Sheffield HS; Clarendon, PA; (Y); 18/84; Drama Clb; SADD; Varsity Clb; Chorus; Color Guard; Mrchg Band; Nwsp Stf; Bsktbl; Trk; Hon Roll; Drama.

ATWELL, LAURA; Grove City HS; Grove City, PA; (Y); Church Yth Grp; FHA; Chorus; Trk; Hon Roll; Ntl Merit Ltr; Chrus HS 1st Yr A Crtfct 84; HS Chrus Lttr 2nd Yr 85; 3rd Yr HS Chrus Mtl 86; Bus.

AUBEL, ROBERT; Eastern York HS; Wrightsville, PA; (Y); 20/170; Var Bsbl; Var Bsktbl; Var Socr; High Hon Roll; Hon Roll; Math Sci.

AUCHEY, ANGELA; Littlestown HS; Littlestown, PA; (Y); 10/149; Concert Band; Jazz Band; Mrchg Band; Swing Chorus; High Hon Roll; NHS; Natl Math Exam Awd 85; Presdntl Acad Fitness Awd 86; Arion Fndtn Awd-Music Instrmntl 86; Jacksonville U; Music.

AUDRA, DAVIS; Crestwood HS; Wopwallopen, PA; (Y); 4-H; VICA; Color Guard; Mrchg Band; Vllybl; 4-H Awd; High Hon Roll; Hon Roll; Comp Sci.

AUER, TIM; Connellsville SR HS; Mt Pleasant, PA; (Y); 44/300; Boy Scts; Pres Church Yth Grp; Library Aide; High Hon Roll; Jr NHS; Eagle Sct Awd 86; Elctrncs.

AUFSCHLAG, DAWN L; Bristol JR SR HS; Bristol, PA; (Y); 16/92; VP Church Yth Grp; Pres FFA; Church Choir; Hon Roll; NHS; Highest Avg Tech Schl Crs 86; 1st Pl Harrisburger Frmshw Terarium 86; 2nd Pl Harrisburge Frmshw 86; Horticultural.

AUGUSTINE, BONNIE; Penn Hills SR HS; Pittsburgh, PA; (Y); Drama Clb; JA; Sec Library Aide; Spanish Clb; Crs Cntry; Trk; Hon Roll; NHS; Prfct Atten Awd; MIT; Elctrcl Engrng.

AUGUSTINE, CHRIS; Pocono Mountain HS; Mt Pocono, PA; (Y); 23/325; Chess Clb; Debate Tm; Drama Clb; JA; Library Aide; Model UN; NFL; Quiz Bowl; Scholastic Bowl; Speech Tm; Villanova U; Atty.

AUGUSTINE, GREG; Mid Valley HS; Throop, PA; (Y); Boy Scts; VICA; Eagl Sct 85; Electrncs.

AUGUSTINE, LINDA; Turkeyfoot Valley Area HS; Addison, PA; (Y); 16/47; Church Yth Grp; Q&S; Ski Clb; Varsity Clb; Color Guard; Yrbk Stf; Pres Jr Cls; Pres Stu Cncl; Bsbl; JV Var Bsktbl; Donald B Kaufman Family Good Stu Awd 86; CA U PA; Phys Thrpy.

AUGUSTINE, NICOLE; Pennsbury HS; Yardley, PA; (Y); 98/729; French Clb; Rep Frsh Cls; Pom Pon; Hon Roll; NHS; Interact Clb; FL ST U; Bus Cmnctns.

AUGUSTUS, FAITH; Allentown Central Catholic HS; Allentown, PA; (Y); 20/210; Church Yth Grp; Pres VP Intnl Clb; Math Clb; Pep Clb; Speech Tm; Teachers Aide; Sec Chorus; Flag Corp; Nwsp Ed-Chief; Lion Awd; PA JR Acad Sci 84-86; Princpls Awd Sci & Ldrshp 85; HOBY Ldrshp Awd 85; Pre-Med.

AULENBACH, LISA; Brandywine Hts HS; Mertztown, PA; (Y); 3/130; Church Yth Grp; Band; Chorus; Concert Band; Jazz Band; Mrchg Band; NHS; Regnl Chorus; Contemporary Band Step Beyound; Messengers A Chrch Dram Grp; Lebanon Vly; Music.

AULT, BILL; New Brighton HS; New Brighton, PA; (Y); 42/165; Aud/Vis; Computer Clb; Letterman Clb; Varsity Clb; Stage Crew; L Ftbl; Trk; Wt Lftg; Hon Roll; Trck Awd; Michigan ST; Engrng.

AULTMAN, LORI; Frazier HS; Perryopolis, PA; (Y); Drama Clb; Ski Clb; Mrchg Band; School Play; Rep Stu Cncl; Twrlr; Hon Roll; Prfct Atten Awd; Miss JR PA 86; Law Prg 85-86; Pgnt Coordntr & EMCEE Miss Mid Mon Vly Pgnt 86; U Of Tampa; Pre-Law.

AULTZ, TAMMIE; Somerset Area SR HS; Somerset, PA; (Y); Pres Sec 4-H; Library Aide; Office Aide; Ski Clb; Varsity Clb; Chorus; Yrbk Stf; Stu Cncl; Bsktbl; 4-H Awd; Penn ST; Nrsng.

AUMACK, JAMES; Blue Mt Acad; Hamburg, PA; (S); 14/63; Pres Frsh Cls; Pres Jr Cls; Capt Bsbl; Var Capt Bsktbl; Var Capt Ftbl; Var Capt Sftbl; Var Hon Roll; Nwsp Rptr; Nwsp Sprt Ed; Rep Stu Cncl; Mens Clb Pres O Sigma Kappa; Stu Senate; Columbia Union Coll.

AUMACK, SHERRY; Blue Mt Acad; Hamburg, PA; (S); Church Yth Grp; Office Aide; Chorus; Church Choir; School Musical; VP Frsh Cls; VP Jr Cls; Gym; Hon Roll; Bsktbl; Publc Rltns Sec Stu Assn 84-85; Columbia Union Coll; Dentl Hyg.

AUMAN, LISA; Elk County Christian HS; St Marys, PA; (Y); 19/98; Art Clb; JA; Library Aide; Ski Clb; Spanish Clb; Yrbk Stf; Stat Bsktbl; High Hon Roll; Hon Roll; Penn ST; Acctg.

AUMAN, MIKE; Conrad Weiser HS; Robesonia, PA; (Y); 35/137; JCL; VP Soph Cls; VP Jr Cls; VP Sr Cls; Stu Cncl; Var Capt Bsbl; JV Bsktbl; Var Capt Ftbl; Wt Lftg; Hon Roll; Best All Around Sr Cls 85-86; Old Dominion U; Elec Engrng.

AUMENT, BRENDA; Lampeter Strasburg HS; Strasburg, PA; (S); 43/135; DECA; Trk; Hon Roll; Vo-Tech Awd LS Cmncemnt 86; Mrktng.

AUMENT, MICHAEL; John S Fine HS; Nanticoke, PA; (Y); Trk; PA ST U; Arch Engr.

AUMILLER, SANDRA; West Snyder HS; Beavertown, PA; (Y); 6/78; Varsity Clb; Concert Band; Mrchg Band; Nwsp Sprt Ed; Yrbk Sprt Ed; Trs Stu Cncl; Var Bsktbl; Var Capt Fld Hcky; Var Sftbl; Hon Roll; Physcl Sci Awd 86; Lebanon Valley; Biochem.

AUNGST, STACY; Ephrata SR HS; Hopeland, PA; (Y); 76/250; Church Yth Grp; Cmnty Wkr; Teachers Aide; Chorus; Church Choir; School Musical; Variety Show; Im Fld Hcky; Hon Roll; Typng Awd 86; TX Lutheran Coll; Soclgy.

AURENTZ, DAVID; Lebanon HS; Lebanon, PA; (Y); 26/285; Cmnty Wkr; German Clb; Key Clb; Yrbk Stf; Var L Bsbl; Im Bsktbl; Var L Socr; Im Tennis; Im Wt Lftg; Hon Roll; Engrg.

AUSMAN, MICHELE; S Park HS; Library, PA; (Y); 80/203; Office Aide.

AUSTIN, CHRISTINA; Villa Maria HS; Warren, OH; (Y); 10/63; Cmnty Wkr; Hosp Aide; Science Clb; Spanish Clb; Thesps; Stage Crew; Yrbk Stf; High Hon Roll; NHS; Spanish NHS; 2nd Pl JR Acad Sci Eclgy Day 86; U Of MI; Med.

AUSTIN, DOROTHEA; Wilkinsburg JR SR HS; Wilkinsburg, PA; (Y); Boys Clb Am; Church Yth Grp; FBLA; Library Aide; Spanish Clb; Y-Teens; Acpl Chr; Chorus; Church Choir; Bsktbl; Cmptr Pgrmr.

AUSTIN, HOWARD; University City HS; Philadelphia, PA; (Y); Otstndng Achvt Indstrl Arts 86; Thompson Inst; Accntnt.

AUSTIN, PAUL; Governor Mifflin HS; Shillington, PA; (Y); 8/290; Varsity Clb; School Musical; Stage Crew; Capt Ftbl; Capt Trk; Wt Lftg; Capt Wrstlng; Hon Roll; Rotary Awd; U Of VA; Engrng.

AUSTIN JR, ROY; State College SR HS; State College, PA; (Y); 12/580; Debate Tm; Model UN; Jazz Band; Nwsp Ed-Chief; JV L Socr; Cit Awd; High Hon Roll; Ntl Merit Ltr; Library Aide; Math Clb; PA Gov Schl Intl Studs 85; Law.

AUSTIN, TARA A; Elizabethtown Area HS; Elizabethtown, PA; (Y); Church Yth Grp; 4-H; Ski Clb; Powder Puff Ftbl; U Of DE; Bus Admin.

AUSTIN, TERESA; North Allegheny HS; Ingomar, PA; (Y); 47/605; Church Yth Grp; Band; Church Choir; Concert Band; Hon Roll; NHS; PMEA Dist Bd 85-; PA Musc Edctrs 86; :Pmea Regn 1 86; Distngshd Muscn Awd 86; PA ST U; Comm.

AUTREY, MICHELLE; Bethlehem Catholic HS; Bethlehem, PA; (Y); 20/210; Church Yth Grp; Nwsp Rptr; Nwsp Stf; Rep Jr Cls; VP Sr Cls; Var L Bsktbl; Var Cheerleading; Var L Crs Cntry; Im Fld Hcky; Sec NHS; Schlrp Big 5 Bsktbl Camp 86; Govt.

AUXER, WILLIAM; Archbishop Carroll HS; King Of Prussia, PA; (Y); 21/162; Boy Scts; JV Var Bsbl; Bsktbl; JV Ftbl; High Hon Roll; Cngrssnl Schlr 86; Hstry Awd 86; Egl Sct Rank BSA 86; Archbshp Crrll Hnr Soc 85-86; Envrnmntl Engnrng.

AVEARD, LAURA; Hampton HS; Gibsonia, PA; (Y); Ski Clb; Band; Concert Band; Mrchg Band; Yrbk Stf; Bsktbl; Sftbl; Trk; High Hon Roll; Hon Roll; IN U PA; Finance.

AVERSA, MICHELLE; Bethlehem Catholic HS; Bath, PA; (Y); 25/175; Fld Hcky; High Hon Roll; Hon Roll; Churchmans Bus Sch; Bus.

AVERY, BONNIE; Tunkhannock Area HS; Dalton, PA; (S); 28/320; Sec JA; NHS; Bus Wmn And Sec Of Yr 85; Bloomsburg U; Bus Admin.

AVERY, CONNIE; Tunkhannock HS; Dalton, PA; (S); Church Yth Grp; Computer Clb; Hosp Aide; Spanish Clb; Rep Frsh Cls; Rep Soph Cls; Rep Jr Cls; Stat Bsbl; JV Var Fld Hcky; JC Awd; Aerntcl Engr.

AVERY, DAMON; Farrell HS; Farrell, PA; (Y); 23/95; Church Yth Grp; Computer Clb; French Clb; Letterman Clb; Varsity Clb; Bsbl; Im Bsktbl; Var L Ftbl; Var Trk; Bus Admin.

AVERY, DEBBIE; Wyoming Area HS; Falls, PA; (Y); 62/247; Camera Clb; Computer Clb; Ski Clb; Spanish Clb; Teachers Aide; Y-Teens; Color Guard; Drill Tm; Yrbk Rptr; Yrbk Stf; U Scranton; Comp Sci.

AVERY, JOEL; Blue Mt Acad; Secane, PA; (Y); Aud/Vis; Sec Church Yth Grp; Library Aide; Yrbk Phtg; Rep Soph Cls; Jr Cls; Rep Stu Cncl; Im Sftbl; Im Vllybl; Hon Roll.

AVERY, MICHELLE; Little Flower H S F G; Philadelphia, PA; (Y); 202/395; Temple U; Bio.

AVILA, KAREN; York County Vo-Tech; York, PA; (Y); VICA; JV L Trk; Hon Roll; Psych.

AVVISATO, CHRISTOPHER; Old Forge HS; Old Forge, PA; (S); Bsbl; Wt Lftg; High Hon Roll; NHS; Louisville; Engrng.

AVVISATO, FRANK; Scranton Prep; Old Forge, PA; (Y); 85/190; Var Capt Bsbl; Hon Roll; All Schltc Bsbl 85 & 86; Schl Recrd 221 Var Strikeouts 86; Geo WA Bsbl Scholar 86; Geo WA U; Engrng.

AW, ANDREW; Huntingdon Area HS; Huntingdon, PA; (Y); 27/223; Key Clb; Pres Frsh Cls; VP Soph Cls; Pres Jr Cls; Rep Stu Cncl; L Ftbl; Hon Roll; Avtn.

AXELROD, MICHAEL; Upper Dublin HS; North Hills, PA; (Y); FBLA; JA; Varsity Clb; Variety Show; VP Stu Cncl; Capt Bsktbl; JV Bowling; Var L Socr; Var L Tennis; All Lgu Tnns Awd 86; Stu Actv Awd 86; US Maccabi Trnmnt Canada Tns & Sftbl 86; Tulane U; Bus.

AXLINE, BRENDA; Towanda Area HS; Towanda, PA; (Y); French Clb; Letterman Clb; Band; Drill Tm; Mrchg Band; Yrbk Stf; Score Keeper; Trk; Hon Roll; NHS; Most Imprvd Swmmr Awrd 86; Outstndg Fld Competitr Trck 85-86; Capt Pom Pom Sqd 85-87; Dance.

AYALA, IRIS; J P Mc Caskey HS; Lancaster, PA; (Y); 106/450; Church Yth Grp; 4-H; Library Aide; Office Aide; Chorus; Church Choir; Hon Roll; Music Achvt 80; Volunteer Awd 84; Summer Yth Emplymnt Prog Awd 85; Atten Awd; Central Penn Bus Schl; Bus.

AYERS, MARK; State College Area HS; Boalsburg, PA; (Y); 234/483; CAP; Cmnty Wkr; Ski Clb; Im JV Ftbl; Powder Puff Ftbl; Hon Roll; Penn ST U; Bus Mgmnt.

AYERS, RICHARD; Tyrone Area HS; Tyrone, PA; (Y); Key Clb; Pres Band; Sec Chorus; Church Choir; Pres Concert Band; Jazz Band; Pres Mrchg Band; Pep Band; School Musical; Off Soph Cls; W Paul Price Mem Schrlshp 86; NALC Schrlsh P86; Lisa Lehman Outstndngt Voclst Awd 86; PA ST; Jrnlsm.

AYMONG, NICOLE; Mercyhurst Prep; Erie, PA; (Y); Sec VP Drama Clb; Thesps; School Musical; School Play; Stage Crew; Lit Mag; L Bowling; Im Wt Lftg; High Hon Roll; Hon Roll; Contstnt Mss PA Pagnt; Acad Schlrshp MPS; East Stroudsburg U; Eclgy.

AYOUB, KATHARINE; Forest City Regional HS; Pleasant Mount, PA; (Y); 3/54; Nwsp Ed-Chief; Stu Cncl; JV Var Sftbl; JV Var Vllybl; Dnfth Awd; High Hon Roll; NHS; Ntl Merit Ltr; JV Coaches Awd Vllybl 84-85; 2nd Tm All Strs Vllybl 85-86.

AZAREWICZ, JOYCE; St Huberts HS; Philadelphia, PA; (Y); 196/367; Camera Clb; Dance Clb; Yrbk Stf; Hon Roll; Prfct Atten Awd; Prfct Atten 83-84; Hnr Roll 85-86.

AZEFF, ALTHEA L; Plymouth-Whitemarsh HS; Plymouth Meeting, PA; (S); 68/362; Computer Clb; Sec Intnl Clb; Model UN; Nwsp Ed-Chief; Ed Nwsp Stf; High Hon Roll; Hon Roll; Pol Jrnlsm.

AZER, JANET; Central Bucks HS East; New Hope, PA; (Y); Hosp Aide; Band; Yrbk Stf; Stu Cncl; Var L Fld Hcky; Hon Roll; Pres NHS; Georgetown; Frgn Serv.

AZINGER, TIM; Kiski Area HS; Saltsburg, PA; (Y); 70/365; French Clb; Science Clb; SADD; Var Ftbl; Var Swmmng; High Hon Roll; Hon Roll; Rotary Schlr Awd 85; Engrng.

AZZARELLO, NICHOLAS; Altoona Area HS; Altoona, PA; (Y); Letterman Clb; Ski Clb; Spanish Clb; Varsity Clb; Timer; Trk.

BAAS, WILLIAM; The Mill Schl; Elverson, PA; (Y); Model UN; Capt Color Guard; Capt Drill Tm; Im Capt Gym; Im Socr; Im Tennis; DAR Awd; High Hon Roll; Naval Sea Cadel Ldrshp Awd 86; Naval Sea Cadet Shipmate Awd 85; Military Ofcr.

BABCOCK, CLINT; Monoursville HS; Montoursville, PA; (Y); 32/174; Am Leg Boys St; Dance Clb; French Clb; Letterman Clb; Varsity Clb; Trs Frsh Cls; Trs Soph Cls; Trs Jr Cls; Var Bsbl; JV Bsktbl; Real Estate.

BABETSKI, LINDA; Lake-Lehman HS; Dallas, PA; (Y); 2/140; Ski Clb; Concert Band; Mrchg Band; Yrbk Stf; Golf; Tennis; Cit Awd; High Hon Roll; Jr NHS; NHS; Computers.

BABIARZ, MARY ROSE; Old Forge HS; Old Forge, PA; (S); Church Yth Grp; Drill Tm; Mrchg Band; Hon Roll; NHS; Spanish Awd 85; Typing Awd 86; Phys Thrpst.

BABIK, STEPHANIE; Hopewell SR HS; Aliquippa, PA; (Y); FBLA; German Clb; Band; Chorus; Variety Show; Rep Stu Cncl; Bowling; Bus.

BABINCHAK, JOHN; Shenandoah Valley HS; Shenandoah, PA; (Y); 3/108; Debate Tm; Pres Frsh Cls; Pres Soph Cls; VP Jr Cls; Trs Sr Cls; Rep Stu Cncl; L Bsbl; L Bsktbl; Hon Roll; NHS.

BABINSACK, JOSEPH; Highlands SR HS; Natrona, PA; (Y); 19/277; Boy Scts; Exploring; Rep Sr Cls; Var L Trk; Cit Awd; Jr NHS; NHS; Ntl Merit Ltr; Varsity Clb; Nwsp Stf; Eagle Sct 84; Westinghouse Sci Hnrs Inst 85-86; Top Physcs Stu 86; U Pittsburgh; Chem Engrg.

BABJACK, LISA; Langley HS; Pittsburgh, PA; (Y); 19/270; DECA; Yrbk Stf; High Hon Roll; Hon Roll; OH Vly Schl Nrsng; Nrsng.

BABU, BINDHU; Exeter SR HS; Birdsboro, PA; (Y); 3/226; Hosp Aide; Library Aide; Stage Crew; Off Frsh Cls; Stat Bsktbl; Var Fld Hcky; High Hon Roll; Jr NHS; NHS; M Baver Schlrshp 86-87; Penn ST U; Bio.

BACA, JAMES; Highlands SR HS; Natrona Heights, PA; (Y); Exploring; Science Clb; Socr; Cit Awd; NHS; Prfct Atten Awd; Elec Engr.

BACCAMAZZI, LISA; Windber Area HS; Windber, PA; (Y); Yrbk Stf; Rep Stu Cncl; JV Cheerleading; Hon Roll; Hagerstown Business Schl; Legal.

BACCO, CHRISTINE; Ringgold HS; Monongahela, PA; (Y); Nwsp Stf; Var Mgr(s); Sci,Math Hnr Soc 85-86; Giftd Pgm; Bus.

BACCUS, ANNA; Coiry HS; Columbus, PA; (S); Church Yth Grp; Drama Clb; Model UN; Yrbk Stf; Rep Stu Cncl; Var Cheerleading; High Hon Roll; Hon Roll; Engrng.

BACHER, JOY; New Hope-Solebury HS; New Hope, PA; (S); 1/82; Art Clb; Church Yth Grp; Mathletes; Var JV Bsktbl; Var JV Fld Hcky; Pom Pon; Var Tennis; Twrlr; High Hon Roll; NHS; Spnsh Awd 83-84.

BACHIKE, JESSIE; Pennsbury HS; Yardley, PA; (Y); Spanish Clb; Chorus; Yrbk Stf; Rep Soph Cls; Capt Cheerleading; JV Socr; Im Sftbl; JV Trk; Im Vllybl; Hon Roll; Child Psychlgy.

BACHMAN, ADAM; Milton Area HS; New Columbia, PA; (Y); Spanish Clb; Varsity Clb; Chorus; School Play; Ftbl; Trk; WACC; Transprtatn Tech Engr.

BACHMAN, CRISTEN; Freedom SR HS; Bethlehem, PA; (Y); 108/445; Cmnty Wkr; Nwsp Stf; Hon Roll; Arch.

BACHMAN, NATE; Mt Leabanon SR HS; Mt Lebanon, PA; (Y); Computer Clb; Ski Clb; Var Ftbl; DAR Awd.

BACHMAN, STEPHANIE; Northern Lebanon HS; Lebanon, PA; (Y); 24/200; Spanish Clb; Band; Chorus; Color Guard; Flag Corp; Mrchg Band; School Musical; Sftbl; Twrlr; Hon Roll; Flagler Coll; Accntng.

BACHTLE, BRETT M; Wallenpaupack HS; Newfoundland, PA; (Y); 1/152; Am Leg Boys St; Science Clb; VP Jr Cls; Var Bsktbl; Var Ftbl; Var Trk; Bausch & Lomb Sci Awd; NHS; Ntl Merit Ltr; Varsity Clb; 1st Pl ST Lvl Sci Olympd 86; Aero Engrng.

BACHURA, DEBBIE; Butler HS; Butler, PA; (Y); Exploring; Office Aide; Yrbk Stf; Hon Roll; Jr NHS; Geneva; Elem Ed.

BACIK, MIKE; Fairview HS; Fairview, PA; (Y); Band; Concert Band; Jazz Band; Mrchg Band; Pep Band; School Musical; Louis Armstrong Jzz Awd 86; Dstrct Bnd 86; Rgnl Bnd 86; Gannon U; Elec Engr.

BACKNER, SUSAN; Canon-Mc Millan HS; Canonsburg, PA; (Y); French Clb; Office Aide; Teachers Aide; Chorus; Nwsp Stf; Hon Roll; Engl.

BACON, JENNIFER; Pen Argyl Area HS; Wind Gap, PA; (Y); 16/159; Church Yth Grp; Ski Clb; Spanish Clb; Varsity Clb; Co-Capt Color Guard; JV Stat Bsktbl; Powder Puff Ftbl; Var L Trk; High Hon Roll; Lion Awd; Pres Acdm Ftns Awd 86; Bloomsburg U; Math.

BACZEWSKI, GARY; Hopewell Memorial SR HS; Aliquippa, PA; (Y); 50/270; Drama Clb; VP Exploring; Trs German Clb; Chorus; School Play; Vllybl; U Of Pittsburgh; Pre-Med.

BADAMO, ANTHONY; Hazleton SR HS; Hazelton, PA; (Y); 14/388; Church Yth Grp; Drama Clb; Pres VP Leo Clb; Chorus; School Musical; Stage Crew; Stu Cncl; High Hon Roll; Penn ST U; Engrng.

BADDICK, BRIAN; Marian Catholic HS; Quakake, PA; (Y); Aud/Vis; Boy Scts; Ski Clb; SADD; VP Frsh Cls; JV Bsbl; Stat Bsktbl; Stat Coach Actv; Var L Ftbl; Var L Trk; Villanova U; Law.

BADEN, AMANDA; Cumberland Valley HS; Camp Hill, PA; (Y); 15/541; Art Clb; German Clb; Key Clb; Ski Clb; Mrchg Band; Nwsp Rptr; Hon Roll; NHS; Rotary Awd; Natl Art Hnr Scty 85-86; Arch Engnr.

BADER, KAREN; Ambridge Area HS; Ambridge, PA; (Y); German Clb; Chorus; Sftbl; Hon Roll; Robert Morris; Sec.

BADER, KIM; St Basil Acad; Philadelphia, PA; (S); 4/96; VP Computer Clb; GAA; Math Clb; Spanish Clb; Capt Bsktbl; Socr; Hon Roll; NEDT Awd; Math.

BADGER, TAMMY; Lincoln HS; Wampum, PA; (Y); 18/163; AFS; Drama Clb; Church Choir; Stu Cncl; Tennis; High Hon Roll; NHS; Church Yth Grp; Latin Clb; Y-Teens; Phi Dlta Kppa Awd 86; PSEA Comptitv Schlrshp 86; 3rd Pl-Persuasv Spkng Geneva Coll Frnsc Tourn 86; Grove City Coll; Elem Educ.

BADINGER, KAREN; Daniel Boone HS; Birdsboro, PA; (Y); 51/166; Church Yth Grp; Flag Corp; Stu Cncl; Capt Cheerleading; Fld Hcky; Trk; Hon Roll; Daniel Boone Youth Education Association Pres 85-86; Elem Educ.

BADMAN, CYNTHIA R; Phoenixville Area HS; Phoenixville, PA; (Y); 57/194; VP Key Clb; Varsity Clb; School Musical; School Play; Yrbk Sprt Ed; Rep Soph Cls; Rep Jr Cls; Rep Sr Cls; Rep Stu Cncl; Girl Scts; Stu Mnth 85; Millersville U; Elem Ed.

BADMAN, LUKE; Lebanon Catholic HS; Hummelstown, PA; (Y); Boy Scts; Ski Clb; German Clb; SADD; School Play; Ftbl; Cit Awd; 5 Yrs Bsbl All-Str Tm 80-85; Captl Area Sci Fair Wnr 80.

BADORF, WAYNE; Ephrata SR HS; Ephrata, PA; (Y); 55/234; Boy Scts; Chess Clb; Chorus; Stu Cncl; Im Badmtn; Var Tennis; Im Vllybl; Hon Roll; Eagl Sct Awd 86; Harry Hibschman Schlrshp 86; Millesville U Of PA; Hstry.

BADOWSKI, DIANA; Villa Maria Acad; Erie, PA; (Y); Hosp Aide; Mathletes; Model UN; Science Clb; Spanish Clb; Stu Cncl; Bsktbl; Mgr(s); Score Keeper; Timer; Many Sci & Math Presentatns For Acad Achvt; Penn ST; Math.

BAEHR, MARK; Harborcreek HS; Erie, PA; (Y); 23/200; Var L Tennis; Hon Roll; NHS; Spanish NHS; Edinboro U; Bus.

BAER, BELINDA; Newport HS; Newport, PA; (S); Teachers Aide; Concert Band; Mrchg Band; School Play; Hon Roll; NHS; Tri M Modrn Music Mstrs; PYEA PA Yth Ed Assn; Elem Ed.

BAER, CHRIS; Connellsville Area HS; Connellsville, PA; (Y); 90/528; Ski Clb; SADD; Varsity Clb; Golf; Capt Var Wrstlng; High Hon Roll; Hon Roll; Ptsbrgh U; Physcl Thrpy.

BAER, JEFF; Scranton Tech; Scranton, PA; (Y); JV Bsktbl; Var Ftbl; Capt Swmmng; Var Trk; Rotary Ldrs Camp 85; Biomed Tech.

BAER, LISA; Beaver Area JR SR HS; Beaver, PA; (Y); Office Aide; Teachers Aide; High Hon Roll; Hon Roll; Schlstc Achvmnt Awd 86; U Of MD; Retl Mgmt.

BAER, SCOTT; Somerset Area HS; Friedens, PA; (Y); 55/233; Church Yth Grp; 4-H; French Clb; Church Choir; High Hon Roll; NHS; PA ST U; Anml Sci.

BAER, SUSAN; South Western HS; Hanover, PA; (Y); 2/206; Varsity Clb; Sec Sr Cls; Stu Cncl; Var L Tennis; Elks Awd; High Hon Roll; NHS; Rotary Awd; Sal; Vc Dmcrcy Hnvr Lcl Wnr 85; Untd Pprwrks Intrntnl Uns Coll Schlrshp Awds 86; SICO Fdn Schlrshp 86; Shippensburg U; Fnce.

BAGAMERY, JONATHAN; Beaver Area JR SR HS; Beaver, PA; (Y); Boy Scts; JCL; Nwsp Stf; High Hon Roll; Hon Roll; Cartoonst.

BAGGETT, TIMOTHY; Northeast Catholic HS; Philadelphia, PA; (Y); Jr Cls; Crs Cntry; Trk; Hon Roll; NHS; Rets; Electrncs.

BAGGOTT, MATTHEW J; Msgr Bonner HS; Yeadon, PA; (Y); VP Computer Clb; Debate Tm; Intnl Clb; High Hon Roll; Ntl Merit SF.

BAGINSKI, MICHELLE; Archbishop Kennedy HS; Philadelphia, PA; (Y); 6/185; Hosp Aide; Library Aide; Chorus; Yrbk Stf; High Hon Roll; NHS; Prfct Atten Awd; Pres Schlr; Soc Studies Awd 83-84; Drexel U; Bio.

BAGLEY, TRACEY; Purchase Line HS; Cherry Tree, PA; (Y); FBLA; Pep Clb; SADD; Varsity Clb; Sftbl; Vllybl; Art.

BAGSHAW, RHONDA; Ambridge Area HS; Freedom, PA; (Y); 32/265; Band; Concert Band; Mrchg Band; Pep Band; Symp Band; Off Sr Cls; High Hon Roll; Hon Roll; Schlrshp Beaver Cty Chptr Medcl Assist 86; Prof Sec Intl Awd 86; Co Op Hnrs Pgm Bradfrd Bus Schl 86-87; Bradford Bus Schl; Med Sec.

BAGWELL, BRETT EDWARD; Quaker Valley HS; Sewickley, PA; (Y); 13/167; Am Leg Boys St; Debate Tm; German Clb; Key Clb; NFL; Political Wkr; Nwsp Rptr; Rep Soph Cls; Rep Jr Cls; L Trk; Awd Spr Spkr Stu Cngrs NFL 86; Awd Merit Nat Frnsl Lge 86; US Naval Acad; Poltcl Sci.

BAHARA, ROBBIE; Scranton Prep; Moscow, PA; (Y); Church Yth Grp; German Clb; Letterman Clb; Ski Clb; Varsity Clb; Var L Bsbl; Var L Ftbl; Wt Lftg; Dist Bsbl Champs 86; Am Leg All Star Tm Bsbl 86; Bsbl Leag Champ 85; Sci.

BAHL, MONISH; Riverview HS; Oakmont, PA; (Y); 25/150; AFS; Boy Scts; Dance Clb; Letterman Clb; Ski Clb; Varsity Clb; Band; Stu Cncl; Ftbl; Capt Tennis; Acctng.

BAHNER, JEFFERY; Shikellamy HS; Northumberland, PA; (Y); JV Bsbl; JV Var Bsktbl; Var Golf; Stu Cncl; Law.

BAHR, KRIS; Neshaminy HS; Hulmeville, PA; (Y); 23/252; Chorus; High Hon Roll; NHS; Prfct Atten Awd; Crmnl Just.

BAHRENBURG, TAMMI; Susquenita HS; Duncannon, PA; (Y); FBLA; Flag Corp; Mrchg Band; Yrbk Stf; Hon Roll; Ed Lit Mag; Central Penn Bus Schl; Htl Mgmt.

BAIER, FRANK H; Jersey Shore SR HS; Williamsport, PA; (Y); Trs FBLA; Trs Service Clb; School Musical; School Play; Yrbk Phtg; Yrbk Stf; VP Soph Cls; Trs Stu Cncl; Var L Ftbl; Stat Trk; Rgn 7 Mr Future Bus Ldr Of Amer 86; Outstndng Bus Stu Of Wk 86; Hotel Mgmt.

BAILEY, ANGELA M; Greencastle-Antrim HS; Waynesboro, PA; (Y); 32/198; VP 4-H; Drill Tm; Nwsp Rptr; Nwsp Stf; Rep Stu Cncl; 4-H Awd; High Hon Roll; Hon Roll; NHS; PA ST U; Anml Biosci.

BAILEY, BILL; Pennsbury HS; Levittown, PA; (Y); Sec Sr Cls; Hon Roll; Art Clb; French Clb; Library Aide; Drexel Coll; Arch.

BAILEY, CHRISTOPHER; Du Bois Area SR HS; Luthersburg, PA; (Y); 35/271; Boy Scts; Letterman Clb; Varsity Clb; L Ftbl; Var Trk; Capt Wt Lftg; JV Wrstlng; High Hon Roll; Hon Roll; Engnrng.

BAILEY, DONALD R; Forest Hills HS; Sidman, PA; (Y); 20/160; Trs Church Yth Grp; Hon Roll; Jr NHS; Spanish NHS; U Pittsburgh Johnstown; Sci.

BAILEY, ELIZABETH; Hampton HS; Gibsonia, PA; (Y); VP Trk; High Hon Roll; Hon Roll; Ntl Merit Ltr; Pre Med.

BAILEY, GARY; Clearfield Area HS; Clearfield, PA; (S); 40/325; Debate Tm; FFA; Speech Tm; Chorus; Concert Band; Mrchg Band; Orch; Pep Band; Cit Awd; High Hon Roll.

BAILEY, GREGORY M; Meadville Area SR HS; Meadville, PA; (Y); Church Yth Grp; Key Clb; SADD; Ftbl; Swmmng; Hon Roll.

BAILEY, JIM; North Hills HS; Glenshaw, PA; (Y); Rep Stu Cncl; Var L Bsktbl; Hon Roll; Bus.

BAILEY, KATHLEEN; Neshaming HS; Langhorne, PA; (Y); 9/758; SADD; Rep Stu Cncl; Var Bsktbl; JV Var Fld Hcky; Var Socr; Var Sftbl; Var Trk; High Hon Roll; Hon Roll; Sec NHS; All Area 1st Tm Sccr 85 & 86; Courier Times Gldn 11 Sccr 85; Suburban I All Lg 2nd Tm Hockey 86; Allied Hlth.

BAILEY, KRISTA; Philipsburg-Osceola Area SR HS; Philipsburg, PA; (Y); 21/245; Letterman Clb; Pep Clb; Ski Clb; Var Bsktbl; Var Cheerleading; Var Vllybl; Im Wt Lftg; NHS; NEDT Awd; Erly Chldhd.

BAILEY, LEAH; Freedom HS; Bethlehem, PA; (Y); 46/450; Church Yth Grp; Chorus; Mgr(s); Var Swmmng; Hon Roll; Pace U; Intl Bus.

BAILEY, LEE; Saint Maria Goretti HS; Philadelphia, PA; (Y); 11/426; Sec Church Yth Grp; Mathletes; Model UN; Mrchg Band; Orch; High Hon Roll; Jr NHS; NHS; Pres Admc Ftns Awd 86; Tmpl U Pres Awd 86; Spec Svc Awd Girl Scts 86; Temple U; Bus.

BAILEY, LISA; Northern SR HS; Wellsville, PA; (Y); 30/204; Yrbk Rptr; Yrbk Stf; Rep Stu Cncl; Fld Hcky; Powder Puff Ftbl; Score Keeper; Trk; Hon Roll; Natl Literacy Cncl; Homecoming Queen; PA ST U; Pre Law.

BAILEY, LISA; Overbrook HS; Philadelphia, PA; (Y); Exploring; Science Clb; Teachers Aide; Yrbk Stf; Var Badmtn; Var Bowling; Hon Roll; Sec Teacher.

BAILEY, LISA; Tyrone Area HS; Tyrone, PA; (Y); 21/187; Pres FBLA; Spanish Clb; SADD; High Hon Roll; Hon Roll; NHS; Penn ST; Bus Admin.

BAILEY, MARY ANN; Mars Area SR HS; Valencia, PA; (Y); 29/154; Office Aide; Teachers Aide; Yrbk Stf; High Hon Roll; Hon Roll; NHS; Ntl Merit Ltr; Spanish Clb; Chorus; JV Vllybl; Bus Club Schlrshp 86; Cert For Excllnc Bus Skls 86; Robert Morris Clg; Acctg.

BAILEY, MELISSA; Columbia HS; Columbia, PA; (Y); 5/84; Powder Puff Ftbl; Hon Roll; Bruno Glaesel Schrlshp 86; Ed Assoc Awd 86; Ithaca Coll Schlrshp 86; Ithaca Coll; Physcl Thrpy.

BAILEY, MONICA; Chester HS; Chester, PA; (S); 3/364; Pep Clb; Chorus; School Play; Variety Show; Yrbk Rptr; Var Capt Cheerleading; High Hon Roll; NHS; Prfct Atten Awd; Rensselaer Polytech Inst Math,Sci Awd 85; Most Distngushd Comp Lit,Alg II Stu 85; Temple U; Eng.

BAILEY, NICOLE; West Snyder HS; Beaver Springs, PA; (Y); FBLA; Varsity Clb; Drm Mjr(t); Yrbk Stf; Var Bsktbl; Hon Roll; FBLA 11th Grd Typng Awd 85; Typng Awd 86; Bst Bus Stu Awd 86; S Hills Bus Schl; Leg Sec.

BAILEY, PATRICIA; Laurel JR SR HS; Slippery Rock, PA; (Y); 17/104; Church Yth Grp; Letterman Clb; Ski Clb; Varsity Clb; Nwsp Rptr; Nwsp Stf; Tennis; Vllybl; Hon Roll; Nwsp Phtg; Hghst Pnt Awd Vlybl; Jameson Schl Nrsng; Nrsng.

BAILEY, RONALD; Forest Hills HS; Sidman, PA; (Y); 36/160; Hon Roll; U Pittsburgh Johnstown; Sci.

BAILEY, SHANNON; North Allegheny HS; Pittsburgh, PA; (Y); Church Yth Grp; Spanish Clb; Band; Concert Band; Mrchg Band; Pep Band; High Hon Roll; Hon Roll; Acctg.

BAILEY, SHAWN; Bellwood-Antis HS; Bellwood, PA; (Y); 25/118; Art Clb; Varsity Clb; Chorus; Nwsp Stf; Jr Cls; Stu Cncl; Bsktbl; Ftbl; Trk; Wt Lftg; Engr.

BAILEY, STEVE; Manheim Township HS; Lancaster, PA; (Y); Church Yth Grp; Band; Concert Band; Orch; Pep Band; Variety Show; Crs Cntry; Mgr(s); Swmmng; Trk; Htl/Mtl Mgmt.

BAILEY, TANYA; William Penn HS; Philadelphia, PA; (Y); 4/239; Cmnty Wkr; Dance Clb; Nwsp Phtg; Nwsp Stf; Yrbk Stf; Pres Sr Cls; Tennis; Cit Awd; Hon Roll; Jr NHS; Sen PA Offcl Sen Seal Good Ctznshp 86; Sen Funo Vncnt J Plaqu Awd Ctznshps 86; Bk Awd Excllnc Engl 85; Temple U; Bus & Comm.

BAILEY, TONJA; Harrisburg HS; Harrisburg, PA; (Y); Band; Concert Band; Jazz Band; Orch; Hon Roll; USAA Awd Natl Hnr Rll 86; USAA Awd Frgn Lng 86; Penn ST; Elec.

BAILEY, TRACY; Philipsburg-Osceola Area HS; Philipsburg, PA; (Y); 50/256; Letterman Clb; Pep Clb; Ski Clb; SADD; Flag Corp; Yrbk Stf; Stat Bsktbl; Var Cheerleading; Var L Sftbl; Hon Roll; Duquesne; Pharm.

BAILEY, VALERIE; Cedar Crest HS; Lebanon, PA; (Y); 46/325; FTA; Pep Clb; Spanish Clb; Chorus; School Musical; Hon Roll; NHS; Millersville ST U; Math.

BAILLEY, BRENDA; Norwin HS; North Huntingdon, PA; (Y); 46/550; Exploring; French Clb; Pep Clb; SADD; Color Guard; Nwsp Rptr; Sec Sr Cls; Rep Stu Cncl; Trk; Hon Roll; Westminster Coll; Bio.

BAILOR, JANICE; Altoona Area HS; Altoona, PA; (Y); Chorus; Nwsp Rptr; Nwsp Stf; Lit Mag; VP Soph Cls; Jr Cls; Sr Cls; JV Crs Cntry; JV Trk; Hon Roll; Semi Fnlst Govr Schl Of Arts 85-86; 2nd Pl Wmns Clb Art Comptn For Pen & Ink 85-86; IUP; Art Teach.

BAILS, JAMIE LYNN; Canon Mc Millan SR HS; Canonsburg, PA; (Y); 40/340; French Clb; Office Aide; Chorus; School Musical; Nwsp Ed-Chief; Nwsp Phtg; Nwsp Rptr; Yrbk Phtg; Yrbk Rptr; Mgr(s); Gftd And Tlntd Educ Prog 77-86; Fnlst Govnrs Sch For Arts 85; Advncd Plcmnt Eng Lit 85-86; Chatham College; Eng.

BAILY, ROBERT CARPENTER; Waynesburg Central HS; Waynesburg, PA; (Y); 59/194; VP Spanish Clb; Var L Bsktbl; Hon Roll; Edinboro U Of PA; Bus Adm.

BAIN, KATHY; Highlands SR HS; Natrona Hts, PA; (Y); 61/280; Library Aide; Office Aide; Teachers Aide; Band; Chorus; Schlstc Achvt Awds Brwn Cert 82-83,85, Gld Cert 84; Bus.

BAINES, DAVID; Chief Logan HS; Yeagertown, PA; (Y); Boy Scts; Church Yth Grp; Hon Roll.

BAIR, TAMMY; Elizabethtown Area HS; Rheems, PA; (Y); Teachers Aide; Nwsp Sprt Ed; Cheerleading; Fld Hcky; Powder Puff Ftbl; Hon Roll; Kutztown U; Elem Ed.

BAIRD, KATHY; Bellefonte Area HS; Pleasant Gap, PA; (Y); 47/232; French Clb; Office Aide; Ski Clb; Mrchg Band; JV Var Cheerleading; Var Trk; Im Vllybl; Wt Lftg; Hon Roll; Arts.

BAIRD III, PAUL; Mt Pleasant Area SR HS; Mt Pleasant, PA; (Y); 60/250; Church Yth Grp; VP German Clb; Letterman Clb; Ski Clb; SADD; Varsity Clb; Var L Ftbl; Var Trk; High Hon Roll; Acdmc All Amer 85 & 86; Indiana U PA.

BAJURA, KEITH; West Mifflin Area HS; Pittsburgh, PA; (Y); 1/340; Boy Scts; Church Yth Grp; Computer Clb; Drama Clb; Math Tm; Orch; School Play; High Hon Roll; Jr NHS; NHS; Ad Altare Dei 85; Cltrl Arts Awd-Music 85-86; Carnegie-Mellon; Music.

BAJUS, AMY; Hampton HS; Gibsonia, PA; (Y); Crs Cntry; Trk; High Hon Roll; Powder Puff Ftbl; Hon Roll; Mock Trial Cmptn 86; Gannon U Of PA; Chmnlgy.

BAKER, ADRIENNE; Emmaus HS; Allentown, PA; (Y); Church Yth Grp; Key Clb; Political Wkr; Spanish Clb; SADD; School Musical; Off Jr Cls; Stu Cncl; Var Bsktbl; Hon Roll; Finlst Ms Tn PA Pgnt 86; Stu Exchng Pgm 84; Communctns.

BAKER, AMANDA; Henderson HS; Exton, PA; (Y); 115/350; Church Yth Grp; Drill Tm; Hon Roll.

BAKER, AMY; Phoenixville Area HS; Phoenixville, PA; (Y); Cmnty Wkr; Drama Clb; French Clb; Hosp Aide; Band; School Musical; Nwsp Rptr; Nwsp Stf; Yrbk Ed-Chief; Yrbk Stf; WA Jrnlsm Inst American 1 86; Bst Wrkr Yrbk 84; American U; Jrnlsm.

BAKER, AMY B; Wallenpaupack Area HS; Greentown, PA; (Y); 3/131; Sec Church Yth Grp; Scholastic Bowl; Band; Color Guard; Sec Stu Cncl; Gym; Sftbl; High Hon Roll; Jr NHS; Sec NHS; Mdl $50 Hghst Avg 4 Yrs Frgn Lang 86; Susann Birch Mem Awd Med Fld 86; GA Inst Tech; Biomed.

BAKER, ANN; Bishop Hoban HS; Mountaintop, PA; (Y); 6/187; FBLA; Sec JV Math Clb; Red Cross Aide; Chorus; Color Guard; Concert Band; Socr; Trk; NHS; Advncd Bio, Hstry Awds 86; Presdntl Acadmc Ftns Awd 86; PA ST U; Envrnmntl Rsrc Mgmt.

BAKER, BRIAN; Lewiston HS; Lewistown, PA; (Y); 53/262; AFS; Boy Scts; Church Yth Grp; Computer Clb; Key Clb; Var Golf; Hon Roll; Acad Ltr 83-84; Eagle Scout 84; Engrng.

BAKER, CAROL; Waynesboro Area SR HS; Waynesboro, PA; (Y); Ski Clb; Church Choir; Cit Awd; Prfct Atten Awd.

BAKER, CHRISTINE; Central York SR HS; York, PA; (Y); Cmnty Wkr; Library Aide; Mrchg Band; Symp Band; High Hon Roll; Hon Roll; NHS; Pres Schlr; Ntl Art Hnr Soc 85-86; Librarian.

BAKER, CORRI; Altoona Area HS; Altoona, PA; (Y); 180/683; FBLA; Key Clb; Office Aide; Teachers Aide; Lit Mag; Rep Stu Cncl; Hon Roll; Jr NHS; 2nd Pl Data Proc FBLA 86; Typng Awds 83; Prncpls Advsry Comm; SR Cls Exec Comm; Prtcptd Co-Op Pgm; Katharine Gibbs Bus Schl; Secty.

BAKER, DANIEL S; Big Spring HS; Carlisle, PA; (Y); 8/189; JV Socr; Im Vllybl; High Hon Roll; Hon Roll.

BAKER, DAVID; W Catholic HS For Boys; Phila, PA; (Y); Boys Clb Am; Cmnty Wkr; Varsity Clb; Var L Bsktbl; Hon Roll; Temple U; Bus Admin.

BAKER, GILES; Strath Haven HS; Rose Valley, PA; (Y); Socr; Tennis; High Hon Roll; Hon Roll; NHS; Cornell U; Engrng.

BAKER, GLORIA; Red Land HS; New Cumberland, PA; (Y); 4/275; Quiz Bowl; Rep Stu Cncl; Tennis; Bausch & Lomb Sci Awd; High Hon Roll; NHS; Spanish NHS; Spanish Clb; School Play; Trk; Dickinson Coll HS Schlrshp 86; 1st Pl Spnsh Rdng Lvl II Cntst 86; 1st Pl HS Indstrl Arts Drwng 84; Chmcl Engrng.

BAKER, HOLLY; Scranton Prepatory Schl; Clarks Summit, PA; (Y); 105/192; Girl Scts; JV Bsktbl; High Hon Roll; Hon Roll; Bus.

BAKER, JENNIFER; Mechanicsburg Senior HS; Mechanicsburg, PA; (Y); 38/311; Flag Corp; High Hon Roll; Hon Roll; Elem Educ.

BAKER, JENNIFER; N Clarion HS; Fryburg, PA; (Y); 7/84; French Clb; Band; Chorus; Capt Drill Tm; Hon Roll; TCM School Business; Med Secty.

BAKER, KAREN; Emmaus HS; Emmaus, PA; (Y); Church Yth Grp; Key Clb; Chorus; Church Choir; School Musical; School Play; Nwsp Stf; Hon Roll; H S Rifl Tm; Microbio.

BAKER, KEITH; The Church Farm Schl; N Wales, PA; (Y); School Play; Rep Frsh Cls; Rep Soph Cls; Stu Cncl; Coach Actv; L Var Socr; L Var Trk; L Var Wrstlng; Hon Roll; Pgnt Awd 1st Plc 1 Ml Rly Trck Lge 85-86; Hstry Hnrs 86-87; 2nd Lge Wrstlng Trnmnt 85-86; WA & Jefferson Coll; Hstry.

BAKER, KELLY; Punxsutawney Area HS; Punxsutawney, PA; (Y); Debate Tm; Math Tm; Spanish Clb; Band; Chorus; School Musical; School Play; Nwsp Ed-Chief; Nwsp Rptr; Bsktbl; Upward Bound; 3rd Pl Overall Athltcs 85; Upward Bound Cnslr Aide; Nrsng.

BAKER, KRYSTAL; Cameron County HS; Emporium, PA; (Y); Teachers Aide; Color Guard; Mrchg Band; Yrbk Stf; Rep Soph Cls; Hon Roll; Prfct Atten Awd; Mary Kuhn Mem Schlrshp 86; Lock Haven U; Elem Ed.

BAKER, LESA; North Star HS; Friedens, PA; (Y); Aud/Vis; FCA; 4-H; Sec VICA; Mgr Band; Concert Band; Mrchg Band; Pep Band; Swing Chorus; Cnty Bnd 85-86; Cnty Chrs 85-86; Cmptr Prgrmr.

BAKER, LORI; Slippery Rock Area HS; Portersville, PA; (Y); 9/178; Church Yth Grp; German Clb; Girl Scts; Pep Clb; Teachers Aide; Band; Concert Band; Mrchg Band; Pep Band; Symp Band; Rifle Tm Var Let 86; Air Force Acad; Math.

BAKER, MICHELLE; Hanover Area HS; Wilkes Barre, PA; (Y); 1/179; Nwsp Stf; Var Capt Bsktbl; Var Capt Sftbl; DAR Awd; High Hon Roll; Jr NHS; NHS; NEDT Awd; Val; Stu Mnth 86; Ath Wk 85; Pres Scholar U Scranton 86; U Scranton; Pre-Med.

BAKER, MICHELLE; Valley HS; New Kensington, PA; (Y); 5/225; Drama Clb; JA; Office Aide; Science Clb; Spanish Clb; Nwsp Stf; Yrbk Stf; High Hon Roll; NHS; Val; Stu Mnth Awd 84-85; Grove City Coll; Elec Engrng.

BAKER, MICHELLE; Waynesboro SR HS; Waynesboro, PA; (Y); Yrbk Stf; Rep Frsh Cls; Rep Soph Cls; Co-Capt Cheerleading; JV Fld Hcky; Var Trk; High Hon Roll; NHS; Runnr Up Keystone Awd 86; Acctnt.

BAKER, MIKE; Grove City HS; Volant, PA; (Y); Trs French Clb; Var L Ftbl; Trk; Im Vllybl; Wt Lftg; JV Var Wrstlng; Hon Roll.

BAKER, PAIGEANN; Greater Johnstown SR HS; Johnstown, PA; (Y); Church Yth Grp; German Clb; Intnl Clb; NFL; Red Cross Aide; Speech Tm; Band; Chorus; Concert Band; Mrchg Band; Nrsg.

BAKER, PATTY; Neshaminy HS; Levittown, PA; (Y); Church Yth Grp; Drama Clb; German Clb; Teachers Aide; Band; Chorus; Church Choir; Concert Band; Mrchg Band; Orch; Doc.

BAKER, RAY; Kiski Area HS; Leechburg, PA; (Y); Science Clb; Chorus; Stage Crew; Var Trk; Var Wrstlng; Hon Roll; WPIAL Chmpn In Wrstlng 83-84; Vrsty Ltr In Wrstlng 83-84 & 84-85; Cnty Chorus 83-84; Elec Engrng.

BAKER, RHONDA; Center HS; Monaca, PA; (Y); GAA; Latin Clb; Sec Spanish Clb; Varsity Clb; Im Bowling; JV Cheerleading; Var Crs Cntry; Var Powder Puff Ftbl; Var Trk; NHS; Pre-Med.

BAKER, SANDY; Berlin Brothers Valley HS; Fairhope, PA; (Y); 15/90; French Clb; GAA; Band; Concert Band; Mrchg Band; JV Bsktbl; Var L Sftbl; French Hon Soc; NHS; Ldrsthp Awd Sftbl 86; Chrprctr.

BAKER, SCOTT; Perkiomen Schl; E Greenville, PA; (Y); Pres Varsity Clb; Chorus; Var Bsbl; Capt Var Bsktbl; Capt Var Ftbl; Hon Roll; NHS; Robt J Gottshall Awd Hghst Avg Socl Sci 86; Athl Cncl Awd Sprtsmnshp Prsrvrnc Lylty & Svc 86; Bucknell U; Govt.

BAKER, SHARON M; Conneaut Lake HS; Boulder, CO; (Y); Church Yth Grp; Drama Clb; Band; Mrchg Band; Pep Band; School Play; Twrlr; High Hon Roll; NHS; JETS Acad Tm 86; Ve.

BAKER, SONDRA JO; Central HS; Roaring Spring, PA; (Y); 42/187; JA; Band; Chorus; Stage Crew; Nwsp Rptr; JV Bsktbl; Im Vllybl; Hon Roll; St Francis; Physcn Asst.

BAKER, STEPHANIE JEANINE; Great Valley HS; Malvern, PA; (Y); Am Leg Aux Girls St; Church Yth Grp; Capt Debate Tm; French Clb; Letterman Clb; NFL; Varsity Clb; Chorus; Concert Band; Nwsp Ed-Chief; Syracuse U Outstndng Wrtg 86; Girls ST Am Legn 86; 2nd Dist Spch Comptn 86; Eng.

BAKER, SUZANNE; Canon Mcmillan SR HS; Canonsburg, PA; (Y); 18/371; Chess Clb; French Clb; Office Aide; Ski Clb; Yrbk Stf; Sec Soph Cls; Sec Jr Cls; Sec Stu Cncl; High Hon Roll; NHS; Phrmcy.

BAKER, TAMMY; Lower Dauphin HS; Elizabethtown, PA; (S); Church Yth Grp; VP 4-H; Sec FFA; Hon Roll; Acad All Amer Schlr 84.

BAKER, TERESA; Du Bois Area HS; Dubois, PA; (Y); Church Yth Grp; Intnl Clb; Pep Clb; Chorus; School Musical; Stage Crew; Nwsp Rptr; Nwsp Stf; Hon Roll; Boy Scts; Tp 3 Cmmnctns Clarion Smmr Acad 86; Explrer Of Yr 83; Comp.

BAKER, TRACY LYNN; Penn Trafford HS; Claridge, PA; (Y); 89/322; AFS; Pres FBLA; SADD; Chorus; Color Guard; Mrchg Band; High Hon Roll; Hon Roll; Ms Future Bus Ldr 5th Pl 85-86; Entrprnrshp II 1st Pl Reg 5th Pl St 84-85; Bus Math 3rd Pl Reg 83-84; Westmoreland Cnty CC; Bus Mgmt.

BAKER, WILLIAM; Perry Traditional Acad; Pittsburgh, PA; (Y); Library Aide; Hon Roll; Jr NHS; Millersville ST Coll; Bus.

BAKOWSKI, BRIAN; South Side Catholic HS; Pittsburgh, PA; (S); 7/48; Camera Clb; Chess Clb; Exploring; French Clb; Pres Sr Cls; Stu Cncl; Var Bsbl; JV Bsktbl; Hon Roll; Pittsburgh Tech Inst; Comp Drft.

BALAKONIS, PAULA; Central Dauphin HS; Harrisburg, PA; (Y); 40/389; Church Yth Grp; Varsity Clb; Rep Stu Cncl; Var Capt Bsktbl; Var Capt Sftbl; Im Capt Vllybl; Hon Roll; Chem.

BALANDOVICH, AMIE; Abington HS; Phila, PA; (Y); 6/508; French Clb; Var Socr; Hon Roll; Jr NHS; NHS; Vtrnry Med.

BALASCIO, KIMBERLEY; Mid Valley HS; Dickson, PA; (Y); VICA; High Hon Roll; Hon Roll; VICA Hrstylng Cmptn 1st Pl 84; LCAUTS Soph & JR Hrstlng & Cttng 1st Pl 85-86; Csmtlgy.

BALAWEJDER, JANET; Gateway SR HS; Monroeville, PA; (Y); 47/450; Cmnty Wkr; Girl Scts; Teachers Aide; Chorus; School Musical; Yrbk Ed-Chief; Yrbk Stf; High Hon Roll; NHS; Pres Schlr; U Pittsburgh; Bus Law.

BALCEREK, MICHAEL; Mt Pleasant HS; Mt Pleasant, PA; (Y); 68/246; German Clb; Rep Frsh Cls; JV Bsktbl; Var Golf; Hon Roll; Bus.

BALCH, MAGGIE; Canon-Mc Millan SR HS; Canonsburg, PA; (Y); 81/371; Chess Clb; Church Yth Grp; French Clb; FBLA; Office Aide; Yrbk Bus Mgr; Yrbk Stf; Tennis; Hon Roll; Ed.

BALCUNAS, CHRISTIAN T; Wissahickon HS; Norristown, PA; (Y); Church Yth Grp; VICA; Penn ST; Engrg.

BALDERSON, JEFF; Hoepwell SR HS; Aliquippa, PA; (Y); 4/295; Pres Church Yth Grp; Latin Clb; Rep Frsh Cls; Rep Soph Cls; Rep Jr Cls; VP Sr Cls; Var L Socr; Var L Tennis; Trk; High Hon Roll.

BALDIGA, BRENDA; Wyoming Area SR HS; W Pitston, PA; (Y); 14/247; Hosp Aide; Key Clb; Trs Spanish Clb; Stu Cncl; Trk; High Hon Roll; Hon Roll; NHS; Marywood Coll; Cmmnctns Disordr.

BALDINI, APRIL; Scranton Preparatory HS; Dalton, PA; (Y); 68/190; Dance Clb; Drama Clb; Trk; High Hon Roll; Hon Roll; Church Yth Grp; Cmnty Wkr; Stage Crew; U Of Scranton; Bus Mgmt.

BALDINO, JENNIFER; Merion Mercy Acad; Phila, PA; (Y); 22/81; Church Yth Grp; Dance Clb; French Clb; Office Aide; Q&S; Nwsp Bus Mgr; Lit Mag; Hon Roll; NEDT Awd; Nwsppr Feature Editor 85-87; Temple U; Cmmnctns.

BALDO, CHRISTINA; Mansfield JR & SR HS; Mansfield, PA; (S); 2/98; Church Yth Grp; Drama Clb; FCA; Concert Band; Mrchg Band; Yrbk Ed-Chief; Tennis; NHS; Sal; Bus & Prof Womn Of Mnth April 86; Mansfield U.

BALDO, DENISE; St Huberts HS; Philadelphia, PA; (Y); 125/367; Boys Clb Am; Church Yth Grp; Girl Scts; JCL; Teachers Aide; Rep Soph Cls; Rep Jr Cls; Rep Sr Cls; Rep Stu Cncl; JV Vllybl; Med.

BALDWIN, HOLLY; California Area SR HS; Coal Center, PA; (Y); Drama Clb; FBLA; FNA; Ski Clb; Mrchg Band; Twrlr; Hon Roll.

BALDWIN, JAMES; Mc Keesport Area SR HS; White Oak, PA; (Y); 45/390; AFS; Pres Church Yth Grp; 4-H; French Clb; NFL; Sec Orch; School Musical; VP Stu Cncl; Hon Roll; Acad Games Ntls 1st Pl Mr Pres 86; Pres Schrlshp 86; Villanova; Econ.

BALDWIN, JANICE EILEEN; Southern Lehigh HS; Center Valley, PA; (Y); 15/240; Drama Clb; Q&S; Chorus; School Musical; Nwsp Ed-Chief; Nwsp Rptr; Nwsp Stf; Off Sr Cls; NHS; Pres Schlr; PA ST Wrtng Comptn Awd 85-86; Messiah Coll; Cmmnctns.

BALDWIN, LAURIE S; Western Wayne HS; Waymart, PA; (Y); Art Clb; Church Yth Grp; Exploring; 4-H; FBLA; Library Aide; Pep Clb; SADD; Y-Teens; Flag Corp; Cosmtlgy Schlrshp 86; Empire Beauty Schl; Cosmtlgst.

BALE, HOPE; Freeport Area SR HS; Sarver, PA; (S); 1/170; Church Yth Grp; Drama Clb; Chorus; School Musical; Off Stu Cncl; JV Capt Cheerleading; High Hon Roll; Stu Schl Brd 85-86; Stu Of Mnth 84-85; IUP Marine Bio Pgm 85; Corporate Law.

BALENDY, MICHELLE; Scranton Technical HS; Scranton, PA; (Y); Pep Clb; Ski Clb; Chorus; Variety Show; ROTC; Mst Imprvd Chorus Stu 86; Bst Dancer 86; Red/White Awd Tech HS 86; Schl Lttr Pep Clb & Chorus 86.

BALENOVICH, DENISE; Yough SR HS; W Newton, PA; (Y); 70/253; Pres Church Yth Grp; Cmnty Wkr; French Clb; Chorus; Concert Band; School Play; Twrlr; Hon Roll; Gannon U; Rsprtry Thrpy.

BALENT JR, JAMES S; Washington HS; Washington, PA; (S); #1 In Class; Boy Scts; Church Yth Grp; Math Tm; Ski Clb; Spanish Clb; Band; Mrchg Band; JV Bsktbl; Im Golf; High Hon Roll; Med.

BALESTRIERI, TERESA; Canevin Catholic HS; Pittsburgh, PA; (Y); Pep Clb; Ski Clb; Varsity Clb; VP Frsh Cls; VP Soph Cls; Rep Jr Cls; Rep Sr Cls; Var Capt Cheerleading; High Hon Roll; Hon Roll; Outstndng Achvt JR Engl 85-86; Spr Achvt IA Achvt & Prfcncy Tests 84-85; Med.

BALEWSKI, JOHN; Riverview HS; Oakmont, PA; (Y); 7/110; Var Bsbl; JV Bsktbl; Var Crs Cntry; High Hon Roll; NHS; Engrng.

BALIN, STACEY; Lincoln HS; Ellwood, PA; (Y); 67/143; Cmnty Wkr; FBLA; Key Clb; Y-Teens; Chorus; Bsktbl; Powder Puff Ftbl; Hon Roll; Cert Of Proficiency-Acctng 86; Acctng.

BALL, BARBARA; Meadville Area SR HS; Meadville, PA; (Y); Church Yth Grp; French Clb; Key Clb; SADD; Nwsp Rptr; Nwsp Stf; JV Bsktbl; Socr; Hon Roll; Bus Adm.

BALL, CATHY; Penn Cambria HS; Ashville, PA; (Y); 40/220; Church Yth Grp; Drama Clb; Red Cross Aide; Ski Clb; Spanish Clb; Chorus; Stage Crew; Trs Frsh Cls; Rep Jr Cls; Co-Capt Trk; Most Outstndng Awd-Grammar 84; Track & Fld Awd 84; Slippery Rock; Physcl Thrpy.

BALL, CHRISTOPHER; Father Judge HS; Philadelphi, PA; (S); FBLA; Hon Roll; 2nd Pl FBLA Regnl Comptn Offc Procdrs 85; Pierce JC.

BALL, DENISE; Central York SR HS; York, PA; (Y); Trs Art Clb; Pres Church Yth Grp; Band; Chorus; Church Choir; Concert Band; Mrchg Band; Orch; Pep Band; School Musical; Reflections Cont 86; Intr Dsgn.

BALL, ELIZABETH; Ringgold HS; Monongahela, PA; (Y); Pep Clb; Ski Clb; School Musical; School Play; Variety Show; Pres Frsh Cls; Pres Stu Cncl; Cheerleading; Powder Puff Ftbl; Twrlr; Amer Leg Awd 84; Bus.

BALL, KIMBERLY; Old Forge HS; Old Forge, PA; (S); Dance Clb; Variety Show; Hon Roll; Jr NHS; NHS; Penn ST; Art.

BALL, LORIE; Bishop Carroll HS; Ebensburg, PA; (Y); 45/102; Pep Clb; Ski Clb; SADD; Off Stu Cncl; JV Var Cheerleading; Trk; Hon Roll; IN U Of PA; Fshn Merch.

BALL, MICHELLE; Saint Maria Goretti HS; Philadelphia, PA; (Y); 77/429; Camp Fr Inc; Mathletes; Office Aide; Spanish Clb; Teachers Aide; Rep Stu Cncl; Im Bsktbl; Hon Roll; NHS; Prfct Atten Awd; Drexel U; Bus Adm.

BALL, VALERIE; Conneaut Lake HS; Conneaut Lake, PA; (Y); Church Yth Grp; Spanish Clb; Yrbk Stf; Stat Ftbl; Hon Roll; Jamestown Bus Coll; Lgl Secy.

BALLA, KEVIN W; Gateway HS; Monroeville, PA; (Y); Church Yth Grp; Ski Clb; Band; Concert Band; Jazz Band; Mrchg Band; Orch; JV L Wrstlng; Hon Roll; Achvd Red Belt Tae Kwon Do 86; 5th Pl PA ST Karate Chmpnshp 85; Duqueshe U; Phrmcy.

BALLARD JR, BLAINE E; Elizabethtown Area HS; Elizabethtown, PA; (Y); 42/221; Radio Clb; Ftbl; Golf; Hon Roll; Natl Rifle Assn Awd 85-86; Millersville U; Physcs.

BALLARD, THOMAS; Northeast Catholic HS; Philadelphia, PA; (S); 5/427; Cmnty Wkr; Office Aide; Nwsp Rptr; Nwsp Sprt Ed; Yrbk Rptr; Yrbk Sprt Ed; Yrbk Stf; L Im Bsktbl; High Hon Roll; NHS; Grmn III Hghst Aver; Fin.

BALLAY, KIMBERLY; Nazareth Acad; Philadelphia, PA; (S); 16/120; Spanish Clb; Chorus; Church Choir; School Musical; School Play; Variety Show; Yrbk Stf; Rep Stu Cncl; Hon Roll; Music.

BALLEW, CLARENCE; Mt Pleasant Area SR HS; Mt Pleasant, PA; (Y); VICA; Crs Cntry; Swmmng; Hon Roll; Mechanic.

BALLIET, DEBORAH ANN; Hollidaysburg Area SR HS; Hollidaysburg, PA; (Y); 17/360; Trs VP Exploring; Library Aide; Office Aide; VP SADD; Mrchg Band; Stu Cncl; Capt Twrlr; Vllybl; High Hon Roll; NHS; Plaq & Lttr Top 10 Clss 84; Willamsport Area Comm Coll Schrlshp 86; Top Sr Bus Stu Awd & Typng Awd 86; Williamsport Area Comm; Dentl.

BALLIET, LISA; Hazleton HS; Drums, PA; (Y); 56/388; Church Yth Grp; FBLA; Hosp Aide; Office Aide; Chorus; Nwsp Stf; Yrbk Stf; Capt JV Cheerleading; Hon Roll; Geisinger Nrsng Schl; Nrsng.

BALLONE, DONNA; Brownsville Area HS; Allison, PA; (S); 1/225; Hosp Aide; Math Tm; Drm Mjr(t); Yrbk Stf; Stu Cncl; High Hon Roll; NHS; Opt Clb Awd; Rotary Awd; Schlrshp Duquesne U 86; Martin Faglar Schlrshp 86; Hugh O Brian Outstndg Awd 84; Duquesne U; Pre Law.

BALLUCH, SAMUEL; Sharon HS; Sharon, PA; (Y); 52/196; Church Yth Grp; Varsity Clb; Church Choir; Var L Ftbl; Wt Lftg; Hon Roll; NEDT Awd; Pres Of Sundy Sch Clss 85-86; Nuc Powr Prog.

BALOG, ANDREA; Brownsville Area HS; East Millsboro, PA; (S); 14/221; Trs FBLA; Office Aide; Ski Clb; SADD; Band; Stu Cncl; High Hon Roll; Jr NHS; NHS; Miss FBLA 3rd Pl 84-85; US Bus Ed Awd Shrthnd 84-85; USBEA Accntg 85-86; Natl Travel Schl.

BALOG, JAMES; Highlands HS; Natrona Hts, PA; (Y); 40/274; Yrbk Stf; Rep Stu Cncl; JV Var Bsbl; Jr NHS; NHS; IN U PA; Acctg.

BALOG, JEFFREY; Highlands SR HS; Natrona, PA; (Y); Key Clb; Trs Band; Trs Concert Band; Trs Mrchg Band; Pep Band; Rep Frsh Cls; Rep Soph Cls; Rep Jr Cls; Rep Stu Cncl; Hon Roll; JV Babl Ltr 84; Bus Admin.

BALOGH, CHAZ; Meyers HS; Wilkes Barre, PA; (Y); Var L Ftbl; Var L Wrstlng; CC Awd; Hon Roll; E Stroudsberg; Acctnt.

BALOH, RICKY; Hempfield Area SR HS; Youngwood, PA; (Y); 20/800; Ski Clb; Spanish Clb; Bsktbl; Golf; Socr; Tennis; High Hon Roll; Jr NHS; NHS; Spanish NHS; Duke U; Medicine.

BALSBAUGH, AMY; Central Dauphin HS; Harrisburg, PA; (Y); 20/385; Church Yth Grp; Political Wkr; SADD; Chorus; Madrigals; Variety Show; Off Frsh Cls; Off Soph Cls; Off Jr Cls; Off Sr Cls; Intl Pltcl Sci.

BALSIS, KIMBERLY A; Bethel Park SR HS; Bethel Park, PA; (Y); 105/515; Drama Clb; Library Aide; Acpl Chr; School Musical; School Play; Swing Chorus; Hon Roll; Pres Schlr; Hnr Grad 86; Edinboro U PA.

BALSLEY, MATT; Saltsburg JR/SR HS; Saltsburg, PA; (Y); 4/105; Church Yth Grp; Spanish Clb; Gov Hon Prg Awd; High Hon Roll; Carnegie Mellon U; Bio.

BALTER, KATHERINE; Seneca HS; Erie, PA; (Y); 17/156; Chorus; Stage Crew; Yrbk Rptr; Yrbk Stf.

BALTER, MELISSA; Fort Le Boeuf HS; Erie, PA; (Y); Pres 4-H; Model UN; Quiz Bowl; Ski Clb; JV Trk; 4-H Awd; High Hon Roll; Keystone Grls ST 85; Pres Acad Ftnss Awd 86; Edinboro U PA; Chem.

BALTHASER, BEVERLY; Scotland Schl; Girardville, PA; (Y); 9/26; Art Clb; Drama Clb; Office Aide; ROTC; Flag Corp; Yrbk Phtg; Yrbk Stf; JV Var Fld Hcky; High Hon Roll; Hon Roll; JROTC Awds 84-86; MVP Trk 86; Air Force; Radlgst.

BALTRUSH, MICHAEL J; Neshaminy HS; Langhorne, PA; (Y); Crs Cntry; Socr; Trk; High Hon Roll; Hon Roll; Natl Hnr Soc 86; Achvt Awd 84; Mst Imprvd JV Sccr Plyr 84; Arch.

BALTZER, BRENDA; Greater Johnstown HS; Johnstown, PA; (Y); French Clb; Key Clb; NFL; Church Choir; Concert Band; Jazz Band; Mrchg Band; Rep Jr Cls; Hon Roll; NHS; IN U Of PA; Law.

BALUTA, DAVID; Northwest Area JR SR HS; Shickshinny, PA; (Y); 5/108; Var L Bsbl; Var L Crs Cntry; High Hon Roll; Hon Roll; NHS; JV Bsktbl; Sci Awd Outstdng Acad Achvt 86; Penn ST U; Aerosp Engr.

BALZER, ROBERT; North Hills HS; Pittsburgh, PA; (Y); 49/527; Cert Of Prfct Atndnc 86; Pred Acdmc Ftns Awd 86; Acdmc Schlrshp To Rose Hulman 86; Milw Schl Fo Engrng; Elec Engr.

BAMBERGER, MARC; Southern Lehigh HS; Coopersburg, PA; (Y); 13/233; Boy Scts; VP Exploring; Band; Concert Band; School Musical; God Cntry Awd; High Hon Roll; NHS; Ntl Merit Ltr; Robotic Engr.

BAMBINO, ANTHONY; Greater Johnstown SR HS; Johnstown, PA; (Y); Church Yth Grp; Spanish Clb; Orch; Var Bsbl; JV Var Ftbl; Var Wt Lftg; High Hon Roll; NHS.

BAMFORD, SUSAN; Ringgold HS; Donora, PA; (Y); Band; Concert Band; Mrchg Band; School Play; Nwsp Stf; Yrbk Stf; Hon Roll.

BAMMAN, TERESA; Rockwood Area HS; Markleton, PA; (S); 13/93; Pres Church Yth Grp; Sec NFL; Quiz Bowl; Band; Nwsp Stf; Yrbk Phtg; Chrmn Stu Cncl; High Hon Roll; NHS; NEDT Awd; Somerset All-County Band 81-85; Edinboro U Of PA; Nursng.

BAN, MATTHEW; Steel Valley HS; Munhall, PA; (Y); Spanish Clb; Capt Var Bsbl; JV Ftbl; Var L Golf; Var Wt Lftg; Hon Roll; NHS; Prfct Atten Awd; Athl Schlrshp OH ST 86; MVP Bsbl Tm 86; OH ST; Pre-Med.

BANAS, J MICHAEL; Chartiers Valley HS; Presto, PA; (Y); Pres Church Yth Grp; Ski Clb; Stu Cncl; Scholastic Bowl; Pres Model UN; Kent ST U; Pre-Law.

BANASHEK, CARLA; Pennsbury HS; Levittown, PA; (Y); Var Swmmng; Im Vllybl; Hon Roll; NHS; Stu Of Mnth 84.

BANASZAK, LORI; Churchill HS; Pittsburgh, PA; (Y); Drama Clb; Acpl Chr; Chorus; School Musical; Nwsp Stf; Yrbk Stf; Rep Stu Cncl; Var JV Cheerleading; Awd Cert Athltc Rqurmnts Chrldng 84-86; Spec Educ.

BANCROFT, HARRY; Greenville SR HS; Greenville, PA; (Y); 95/250; Boy Scts; Church Yth Grp; DECA; 4-H; Library Aide; Chorus; Bsktbl; 4-H Awd; Butler CC; Store Mngmnt.

BANDO, DAVID S; Mt Pleasant Area SR HS; Mt Pleasant, PA; (Y); Latin Clb; Varsity Clb; Rep Frsh Cls; Var Ftbl; Wt Lftg; JV Wrstlng; Hon Roll; Auto.

BANE, RONALD; Cardinal Brennan HS; Frackville, PA; (Y); JV Var Bsbl; JV Var Bsktbl; JV Var Ftbl; Im Vllybl; Var Wt Lftg; Prfct Atten Awd; Hlth.

BANE, RUTH; Mapletown JR SR HS; Bobtown, PA; (Y); 4/75; Varsity Clb; Band; Concert Band; Jazz Band; Mrchg Band; Mgr Bsktbl; Var Sftbl; Im Vllybl; Hon Roll; NHS; Dunkard Twnshp Awd 86; CA U PA; Med Tech.

BANE, STEPHANIE; Mcguffey HS; Claysville, PA; (Y); French Clb; Tennis; Poetry Publshd 85-86; Jrnlsm.

BANG, JOHN; Marple Newtown HS; Newton Sq, PA; (Y); Chess Clb; Pres Church Yth Grp; Pres Intnl Clb; Math Clb; Church Choir; Stu Cncl; Wrstlng; Hon Roll; NEDT Awd; Prfct Atten Awd; Bus.

BANGO, LISA; Bishop Mc Cort HS; Johnstown, PA; (Y); German Clb; Pep Clb; Service Clb; Ski Clb; Chorus; School Musical; Vllybl; Hon Roll; Am Inst Frgn Stdy 85; Ger.

BANH, TIN; J P Mc Caskey HS; Lancaster, PA; (Y); Im Socr; Im Tennis; Var Vllybl; Debate Tm; Outstndng Comp Pgm Awd 85-86; De Vry Inst Tech; Elec Engrng.

BANIECKI, JOHN DAVID; Carmichaels Area SR HS; Carmichaels, PA; (S); 1/127; Science Clb; Ski Clb; Spanish Clb; VP Band; Chorus; Concert Band; VP Mrchg Band; Nwsp Rptr; Lion Awd; NHS; All Cnty Band; Engrng.

BANIQUED, LORRAINE; Perkiomen Valley HS; Collegeville, PA; (Y); Church Yth Grp; Red Cross Aide; Ski Clb; High Hon Roll; Hon Roll; Typing Awd, Eng Awd 84.

BANKERT, SHERRY; Spring Grove Area SR HS; Spg Grove, PA; (Y); 17/285; Camera Clb; Yrbk Stf; JV Var Bsktbl; High Hon Roll; Hon Roll; NHS; Schltc Achvt Awd-300 Pnt Pin 85; Accntng.

BANKES, DAVID; Col-Mont Vo-Tech HS; Berwick, PA; (Y); Var Bsbl; Bowling; Hon Roll; Best Penmanship Awd 77; Bsbl Allstar Trophy, Ftbl 82; Marine Corps.

BANKES, MARGARET; Danville SR HS; Danville, PA; (Y); Art Clb; 4-H; Girl Scts; Hosp Aide; Latin Clb; Spanish Clb; Color Guard; School Musical; School Play; 4-H Awd; Elem Ed.

BANKO, ADESTA; Connellsville HS; Connellsville, PA; (Y); Pres FBLA; Ski Clb; Concert Band; VP Soph Cls; DAR Awd; Hon Roll; Arln Stwrds.

BANKS, JADE; Harrisburg HS; Harrisburg, PA; (S); 1/396; Cmnty Wkr; Model UN; Pep Clb; SADD; Band; Stu Cncl; High Hon Roll; Hon Roll; NHS; Val; PA Govr Schl For Sci-Carnegie-Mellon U 84; Smmr Schlrshp To LEAD Pgm Wharton Schl Of Fin U Of PA; Bus Adm.

BANKS, PATRICIA; Harry S Truman HS; Croydon, PA; (Y); High Hon Roll; Hon Roll; Princeton; Pre-Law.

BANKS, TAMMY; Forest Hills SR HS; Salix, PA; (Y); Church Yth Grp; FBLA; VP Y-Teens; Band; Chorus; Church Choir; Concert Band; Mrchg Band; Pep Band; High Hon Roll; Natl JR Hrn Soc 84; Bob Jones U; Accntng.

BANNER, JILL; North Clairon HS; Marble, PA; (Y); Stat Bsktbl; Capt L Vllybl; Hon Roll; ICM; Comp.

BANNER, PAUL; Venango Christian HS; Fryburg, PA; (Y); 6/36; Rep Frsh Cls; Sec Soph Cls; Rep Jr Cls; VP Stu Cncl; Var Bsbl; JV Bsktbl; JV Var Ftbl; Hon Roll; NHS; NEDT Awd; US Nvl Acad; Avtn.

BANNON, ALLISON; Council Rock HS; Wycombe, PA; (Y); Dance Clb; Key Clb; Trenton ST; Nrs.

BANNON, ANNE; Scranton Prep; Clarks Green, PA; (Y); 75/192; Ski Clb; Var Capt Cheerleading; High Hon Roll; Hon Roll; Bus.

BANNON, MICHELE; Carbondale Area HS; Carbondale, PA; (Y); 25/160; French Clb; FNA; Pres Ski Clb; Varsity Clb; Chorus; School Musical; School Play; Variety Show; Sftbl; Capt Tennis; Penn ST U; Psyclgy.

BANSE, SUSAN; Perkiomen Valley HS; Collegeville, PA; (Y); 30/196; Aud/Vis; Chess Clb; Science Clb; Church Choir; School Play; Var Cheerleading; Chorus; School Musical; Yrbk Phtg; Yrbk Stf; Schlrshp To Smmr Wrkshp-Hussian Schl Of Art 86; Messiah Coll Pres Schlrshp 86; Bell Tele Schlrshp 86; Messiah Coll; Art.

BANULL, CHRISTINE; Scranton Central HS; Scranton, PA; (Y); JA; Band; Concert Band; Mrchg Band; Pep Band; Symp Band; Hon Roll; Jr NHS; Girl Scts; Orch; Cert Accomplshmnt JA 86; 100 Pct Atten JA 86; Mth.

BARALE, STEPHANIE; Mt Lebanon HS; Pittsburgh, PA; (Y); 132/509; Cmnty Wkr; GAA; Hosp Aide; Spanish Clb; VP Frsh Cls; JV Capt Socr; L Sftbl; Hon Roll; PA ST Coll; Psychlgy.

BARAN, JOSEPH; Greensburg Central Catholic HS; Latrobe, PA; (Y); 42/264; Chess Clb; Ski Clb; Im Bsktbl; Im Sftbl; Var Trk; Im Vllybl; JV Wrstlng; High Hon Roll; Hon Roll; NHS; Acad Schlrshp 86-87; Oral Roberts U; Comp Sci Engrng.

BARANCHO, TRACEY; Wyoming Valley West HS; Forty Fort, PA; (Y); Key Clb; Chorus; Yrbk Stf; Rep Soph Cls; Rep Stu Cncl; L Cheerleading; Hon Roll; Prfct Atten Awd; Penn ST U; Math.

BARANIEWICZ, WALTER; Northeast Catholic HS; Philadelphia, PA; (Y); 12/369; Teachers Aide; Yrbk Stf; Im Bsktbl; Im Socr; Hon Roll; NHS; Latn Awd; Villansua; Commctn.

BARANOSKI, MATT; Selinsgrove Area HS; Middleburg, PA; (Y); 33/300; Spanish Clb; Nwsp Rptr; VP Stu Cncl; Bsktbl; High Hon Roll; Hon Roll; Crimnlgy.

BARATS, PATTI; Bensalem HS; Bensalem, PA; (Y); 112/543; High Hon Roll; Hon Roll.

BARATTA, ADAM; St Josephs Prep Schl; Huntingdon Vly, PA; (Y); Latin Clb; Letterman Clb; School Musical; School Play; JV Bsbl; Bsktbl; Var Ftbl; High Hon Roll.

BARBACCIA, TRICIA; Catasauqua Area Schl Dist; Allentown, PA; (Y); Church Yth Grp; Girl Scts; Band; Color Guard; Drill Tm; Flag Corp; Mrchg Band; Variety Show; Im Bsktbl; High Hon Roll; Bus Adm.

BARBALINARDO, DARIO; St John Neumann HS; Philadelphia, PA; (Y); 90/365; Temple U; Bnkg.

BARBARA, JOE; East HS; Erie, PA; (Y); 6/125; Boy Scts; Latin Clb; Science Clb; Ski Clb; Stu Cncl; Ftbl; Trk; Hon Roll; NHS; PA ST U; Elec Engrng.

BARBARO, JOE; St John Neumann HS; Philadelphia, PA; (Y); 175/338; Church Yth Grp; JV Bsktbl; Temple U; Lawyer.

BARBARO, PAMELA; General Mc Lane HS; Edinboro, PA; (Y); Sec Model UN; Spanish Clb; Band; Concert Band; Mrchg Band; Stu Cncl; Powder Puff Ftbl; Hon Roll.

BARBER, AMY; Portersville Christian HS; Butler, PA; (Y); 2/7; Church Yth Grp; Chorus; VP Stu Cncl; L Bsktbl; L Sftbl; Capt Vllybl; High Hon Roll; NHS; Sal; ACSI 86; 1st Pl Talents ST Level Piano 85; PA Jr Sci Sympsm At PA ST 85; Cedarville Coll; Bus.

BARBER, DEBBIE; Johnsonburg Area HS; Wilcox, PA; (Y); Church Yth Grp; Computer Clb; JV Var Bsktbl; Stat Ftbl; JV Var Vllybl; Prfct Atten Awd; Mst Vlbl Dfnsv Plyr Awd 86; Bys Bsktbl Ststcn Awd 86; Liberty U; Accntng.

BARBER, GREG DANIEL; Laurel Highland SR HS; Hopwood, PA; (S); 10/345; JA; Math Tm; Chorus; Stage Crew; JV Bsbl; JV Ftbl; Var Golf; High Hon Roll; Jr NHS; VP NHS; Gftd/Tlntd Prgm 86; PA JR Acad Of Sci 83-86; Ski Patrol 85-86; Engrng.

BARBER, MELINDA; Beaver Area HS; Beaver, PA; (Y); 12/212; Pep Clb; Trs Spanish Clb; Trs Soph Cls; Capt Powder Puff Ftbl; Var L Swmmng; Var L Trk; Hon Roll; Comm.

BARBER, NANCI; Ephrata HS; Ephrata, PA; (Y); Church Yth Grp; FBLA; Band; Orch; School Musical; Stage Crew; Rep Sr Cls; Hon Roll; Music Minstry.

BARBER, PETINA; Brownsville Area HS; Grindstone, PA; (Y); Sec Leo Clb; Mathletes; VICA; Spec Recog Awd Data Proc Fayete Area Vo Tech 86; ICM Schl Bus; Comp Mgmt.

BARBER, WILLIAM; Mt Pleasant Area HS; Mt Pleasant, PA; (Y); Cmnty Wkr; Varsity Clb; Nwsp Rptr; JV Ftbl; JV Trk; Pre-Dent.

BARBERICH, MICHAEL WILLIAM; Allentown Central Catholic HS; Allentown, PA; (Y); 19/208; Band; Concert Band; Jazz Band; Mrchg Band; Pep Band; Nwsp Stf; Swmmng; High Hon Roll; Htl Manag.

BARBERY, KENDRA; Southmoreland HS; Scottdale, PA; (Y); 3/245; French Clb; Band; Chorus; Concert Band; Mrchg Band; Stage Crew; Nwsp Stf; Lit Mag; French Hon Soc; Trs NHS; Math & Verbal Tlnt Srch Cndctd By OTID 82; Psych.

BARBIC, CATHY; Springdale HS; Cheswick, PA; (Y); Band; Drm Mjr(t); Mrchg Band; Bsktbl; Sftbl; High Hon Roll; NHS.

BARBIERI, NICK; Pittston Area HS; Duryea, PA; (Y); 86/365; Key Clb; Ski Clb; Spanish Clb; Chorus; Stu Cncl; Ftbl; Trk; Hon Roll.

BARBOLISH, PATRICIA; Mid Valley HS; Throop, PA; (Y); 11/128; Exploring; Letterman Clb; Chorus; Bsktbl; Coach Actv; Score Keeper; Vllybl; High Hon Roll; Hon Roll; Ntl Merit Ltr; Century Clb Schlrshp 86; Intl Foreign Lang Awd 85; Cmnty Med Ctr Schl; Nrsng.

BARBOUR, JON; Central Bucks HS East; Furlong, PA; (Y); Boy Scts; Science Clb; Hon Roll; Var Crs Cntry; JV Golf; Var L Trk.

BARBOUR JR, MICHAEL; Hempfield Area SR HS; Greensburg, PA; (Y); Boy Scts; Camera Clb; Chess Clb; Exploring; French Clb; Science Clb; Variety Show; Mgr(s); Wrstlng; Mrn-Optn NROTC Schlrshp 86; PA ST U; Pilot.

BARBUSH, CHRISTINE; Trinity HS; Mechanicsburg, PA; (Y); 19/121; Drama Clb; Sec French Clb; NFL; Pep Clb; Chorus; School Musical; School Play; Pres Stu Cncl; Im Bsktbl; Capt Var Cheerleading; Peer Cnslr 86.

BARBUTI, MIKE; Hazleton HS; Hazelton, PA; (Y); Nwsp Ed-Chief; Nwsp Sprt Ed; Yrbk Stf; JV Bsktbl; Var L Trk; Hon Roll; VFW Awd; Phys Ther.

BARCASKEY, MITCHELL; Moon Area HS; Coraopolis, PA; (Y); 2/311; Am Leg Boys St; Boy Scts; German Clb; Pres Soph Cls; Pres Rep Stu Cncl; L Bsbl; L Ftbl; L Wrstlng; Bausch & Lomb Sci Awd; High Hon Roll; Chem Olympic Tm 85; Adventure Cl Ub 86-87; USAF Acad; Pre-Med.

BARCHFELD, TERRY; Gateway SR HS; Monroeville, PA; (Y); Church Yth Grp; Band; JV Bsktbl; Var L Ftbl; Hon Roll; Ntl Bible Quz Chmpnshp Team 84-85; Physcs.

BARCLAY, DANA; Uniontown Area SR HS; Uniontown, PA; (Y); Office Aide; Spanish Clb; Drill Tm; Flag Corp; Mrchg Band; High Hon Roll; Hon Roll; Jr NHS; Spanish NHS; Harcum JC; Anml Cntr Mngmnt.

BARCLAY, KAREN; West Perry HS; Loysville, PA; (Y); Church Yth Grp; Varsity Clb; VP Chorus; Concert Band; Mrchg Band; Nwsp Stf; Var Capt Bsktbl; Var Capt Fld Hcky; Var Capt Sftbl; Var L Trk; Elizabethtown Coll; Acctng.

BARCLAY, RITA; Rockwood Area HS; Somerset, PA; (S); 22/95; Pres Church Yth Grp; Drama Clb; Pres 4-H; VP Trs NFL; Speech Tm; Band; Concert Band; Mrchg Band; Nwsp Rptr; Var Stat Wrstlng; Child Psychlgy.

BARCLAY, ROBERT; Moniteau HS; Parker, PA; (Y); 4/141; Drama Clb; Spanish Clb; Varsity Clb; Chorus; Stage Crew; Variety Show; Var L Bsktbl; Var L Ftbl; Var L Trk; NHS; Engr.

BARCZYNSKI, CATHY; Bethelehem Catholic HS; Bethlehem, PA; (Y); Capt Color Guard; Capt Drill Tm; Drm & Bgl; Mrchg Band; Yrbk Stf; Stat Bsktbl; L Mgr(s); Score Keeper; Capt Twrlr; Elem Educ.

BARD, CYNTHIA; Ambridge Area HS; Ambridge, PA; (Y); Church Yth Grp; Pep Clb; Spanish Clb; Off Soph Cls; Off Jr Cls; Mgr Wrstlng; Hon Roll; Chem.

BARE, ROBERT; Northern Lebanon HS; Lebanon, PA; (Y); 5/174; Band; School Musical; Nwsp Ed-Chief; Rep Stu Cncl; Crs Cntry; Wrstlng; Cit Awd; DAR Awd; Kiwanis Awd; NHS; Booster Clb Schlrshp 86; Tri Mi Y Schlrshp 86; Moravian Clg; Chem.

BARE, SEAN; Hershey HS; Hershey, PA; (Y); 40/210; Stage Crew; Yrbk Phtg; VP Jr Cls; Rep Sr Cls; Var Capt Bsktbl; Im Coach Actv; Im Sftbl; Im Vllybl; High Hon Roll; Hon Roll.

BAREFOOT, JEFF; Franklin Area JR SR HS; Utica, PA; (Y); Church Yth Grp; Chorus; Church Choir; Crs Cntry; Tennis; Cit Awd; High Hon Roll; NHS; Acadmc All Am Schlr; Sch Dir Awd 84-86; Electrncs Engrg.

BAREFOOT, TRACY; Chestnut Ridge HS; Alum Bank, PA; (Y); 31/137; Trs FHA; Chorus; Church Choir; Hon Roll; Hist Awd 81-82; Cal U PA.

BAREI, MICHELE; West Phila Catholic Girls; Philadelphia, PA; (Y); 20/263; Church Yth Grp; Hosp Aide; Science Clb; Service Clb; School Play; Nwsp Stf; Yrbk Rptr; Yrbk Stf; Hon Roll; Nrsg.

BARENTINE, ANGELA; Marion Ctr; Creekside, PA; (Y); French Clb; Latin Clb; Ski Clb; Bsktbl; Stat Mgr(s); Hon Roll.

BARGER, BENJAMIN; Halifax HS; Halifax, PA; (S); 5/100; Ski Clb; JV Bsbl; L JV Ftbl; Var Swmmng; High Hon Roll; Hon Roll; NHS; Penn ST U; Engr.

BARGERSTOCK, CATHY A; Central Christian HS; Du Bois, PA; (Y); Cmnty Wkr; Pres Exploring; Band; Chorus; Variety Show; Yrbk Stf; Science Clb; Stat Bsbl; Cheerleading; Dist & Regl Chorus 85-86; Gldn Key Awd Excllnc Music 86; RYLA 85; Berklee Coll Music; Voic Prfrmn.

BARHITE, VERONICA; Sheffield HS; Clarendon, PA; (Y); 13/89; Sec Church Yth Grp; Drama Clb; Varsity Clb; Sec Band; Capt JV Bsktbl; Vllybl; High Hon Roll; NHS; Hosp Aide; Guest Page Rep Curt Bowley House Rep 86; Soclgy.

BARILE, MICHAEL; St John Neumann HS; Philadelphia, PA; (Y); 19/338; Boy Scts; Band; Concert Band; Jazz Band; Pep Band; High Hon Roll; Merit Of Honor 86; Commrcl Art.

BARISH, RICHARD; Hopewell HS; Aliquippa, PA; (Y); 32/296; Church Yth Grp; Computer Clb; Drama Clb; Latin Clb; School Play; VP Jr Cls; Ftbl; Wt Lftg; Wrstlng; High Hon Roll; KDKA Chnnl 2 TV Extr Effrt Awd 85; Pizza Ht Schlstc Athlt Awd 85; PA ST; Nuclr Engr.

BARKAND, AMY; Wilmington Area HS; Volant, PA; (Y); FBLA; Spanish Clb; Band; Concert Band; Jazz Band; Mrchg Band; Pep Band; Nwsp Stf; Trk; Music.

BARKDOLL, MICHAEL; Waynesboro Area SR HS; Waynesboro, PA; (Y); Bowling; Sftbl; Vllybl; Crmnlgy.

BARKDOLL, TY; Waynesboro Area HS; Waynesboro, PA; (Y); Chess Clb; JCL; Chorus; Concert Band; Jazz Band; Mrchg Band; School Musical; Swing Chorus; High Hon Roll; NHS.

BARKER, COLLEEN; West Mifflin Area HS; W Mifflin, PA; (Y); Drama Clb; Ski Clb; Thesps; School Play; Sr Cls; Powder Puff Ftbl; Wt Lftg; Hon Roll; CIA; Culnry Schl.

BARKER, DAVID; East SR HS; West Chester, PA; (Y); 42/385; JA; Hon Roll; NHS; Ntl Merit Ltr; Drexel U; Comp Info Studies.

BARKER, JONATHAN; Emmaus HS; Emmaus, PA; (Y); CAP; Drama Clb; Exploring; Red Cross Aide; SADD; School Play; Stu Cncl; Socr; Gov Hon Prg Awd; Chrprsn Safety Belt Awareness Camp 85-86; Comm Safe Rides Ing 85-86.

BARKER, MAURA; Mount Lebanon HS; Pittsburgh, PA; (Y); 110/467; Church Yth Grp; Cmnty Wkr; Dance Clb; Hosp Aide; Letterman Clb; Ski Clb; SADD; Var Capt Cheerleading; High Hon Roll; Hon Roll; Miami U.

BARKER, TIMOTHY; Muhlenberg HS; Reading, PA; (Y); Boy Scts; Debate Tm; Model UN; School Musical; School Play; Rep Jr Cls; Gov Hon Prg Awd; Hon Roll; NHS; Church Yth Grp; Fnlst & Hon Mntn Wnr In Ntl Essy Cntst 85; PA Gvrnrs Schl 86.

BARKLEY, HELEN; Burgettstown Area HS; Langeloth, PA; (Y); Church Yth Grp; French Clb; Hon Roll; Hnr Schlrshp Waynesburg Coll 86.

BARKLEY, MATTHEW; Mc Keesport SR HS; White Oak, PA; (Y); 34/339; German Clb; Rep Soph Cls; Var L Bsktbl; Var L Ftbl; Var L Trk; Hon Roll; Finc.

BARKLEY, RONALD; Mt Pleasant Area SR HS; Mt Pleasant, PA; (Y); Church Yth Grp; VICA; Hon Roll; Prfct Atten Awd; Viking Rcgntn Awd 84; De Vry; Comp Sci.

BARKMAN, PAUL; Northern Bedford County HS; Hopewell, PA; (Y); Church Yth Grp; Varsity Clb; Ftbl; Trk; Wrstlng; Hon Roll.

BARKMAN, ROBERT; Punxsutawney Area HS; Punxsutawney, PA; (Y); Math Clb; Math Tm; Var L Ftbl.

BARKOCY, GARY; Bishop Egan HS; Washington Cros, PA; (Y); 6/250; Trs Church Yth Grp; Pres Debate Tm; Hosp Aide; Nwsp Ed-Chief; Pres Stu Cncl; Var L Tennis; High Hon Roll; NHS; Sec German Clb; Outstndng Merit Physcs 86; Outstndng Merit Rlgn 82-86; Ntl Sci Olympd Awd Bio 84; Franklin & Marshall Coll; Med.

BARKOS, CARLA; Williams Valley HS; Williamstown, PA; (S); 17/101; Chorus; Yrbk Stf; Stu Cncl; Cheerleading; Powder Puff Ftbl; Hon Roll; Soph Hmcmng Rep 84; Peer Ed Grp 85-86; Erly Chldhood Dev.

BARLAMAS, CONSTANCE; Ambridge Area HS; Ambridge, PA; (Y); Pres Sec Church Yth Grp; JA; Red Cross Aide; Spanish Clb; Church Choir; Concert Band; Mrchg Band; Off Jr Cls; Wrstlng; Hon Roll; Psycht.

BARLEY, DEBORAH; Conestoga Valley HS; Lancaster, PA; (Y); 30/250; Girl Scts; Spanish Clb; Chorus; Mrchg Band; Pep Band; Yrbk Stf; Bsktbl; Var L Fld Hcky; Var L Trk; Hon Roll; Rotary Stu Of Month 86; Silver Ldrshp Awd 83; Phy Thrpy.

BARLOW, JAMES M; Northwestern SR HS; Cranesville, PA; (Y); 19/147; Pres Drama Clb; Thesps; Chorus; School Musical; School Play; Swing Chorus; Hon Roll; NHS; Natl Spch, Drma Awd 85; Natl Choral Awd 86; Edinboro U; Bus Adm.

BARLUP, SCOTT; East Pennsboro HS; Enola, PA; (Y); 10/190; Varsity Clb; Nwsp Rptr; Nwsp Sprt Ed; Var Capt Bsbl; Var Bsktbl; Hon Roll; Hnrb Mntn Patriot News Big 15 Lst Bsktbl 84-86; Mid PA Div II All Star Bsktbl 84-86; Co-MVP Bsktbl; Lebanon Vly Coll; Cmmnctns.

BARNA, BRIAN; North Allegheny SR HS; Pittsburgh, PA; (Y); 177/642; Boy Scts; Debate Tm; Scholastic Bowl; Concert Band; Jazz Band; Mrchg Band; School Musical; Vllybl; Intl Bus.

BARNA, SANDRA; Lakeland HS; Jermyn, PA; (S); 12/152; FBLA; Color Guard; High Hon Roll; Hon Roll; Lackawanna JC; Med Sec Sci.

BARNARD, SHELLY; Meadviulle Area SR HS; Meadville, PA; (Y); Church Yth Grp; SADD; Nwsp Sprt Ed; Yrbk Stf; JV Cheerleading; Capt Gym; NHS; Mercyhurst Coll; Dance.

BARNDT, LORI; Somerset Area HS; Friedens, PA; (Y); Am Leg Aux Girls St; Church Yth Grp; Q&S; Soroptimist; SADD; Band; Chorus; Church Choir; Concert Band; Jazz Band; Maple Prncss Cntstnt 85-86; Grl Mnth May 86; Red Crss Ldrshp Wrkshp 85; Penn ST U; Secdry Ed.

BARNER, AILENA; Bishop Kenrick HS; Norristown, PA; (Y); FBLA; Nwsp Rptr; Hon Roll; Penn ST U; Journlsm.

BARNER, JEFF; Tyrone Area HS; Tyrone, PA; (Y); 19/189; VP Key Clb; Speech Tm; Varsity Clb; Yrbk Phtg; Yrbk Rptr; Yrbk Stf; High Hon Roll; Hon Roll; NHS; Prfct Atten Awd; Tyrone Area PTO Voc Schlrshp Awd 86; Law Day Awd-SADD Radio Comm For Blair Cnty 85; Pttsbrgh Tch Inst; CAD/Cam Dft.

BARNER, JODELL; Sheffield Ares JR-SR HS; Sheffield, PA; (Y); L Drama Clb; Am Leg Boys St; SADD; Varsity Clb; Sec Jr Cls; Rep Stu Cncl; JV Var Cheerleading; JV Capt Vllybl; NHS; Voice Dem Awd; Psych.

BARNER, LAUREN E; Hershey SR HS; Hershey, PA; (Y); 3/189; Chorus; School Musical; Yrbk Bus Mgr; VP Sr Cls; Var L Fld Hcky; DAR Awd; NHS; Church Yth Grp; Math Tm; Pres Pep Clb; Gettysburg Address Essay Cntst 1st 82; Fed Womens Club Girl Mnth 85; AAUW Schlrshp Awd 86; Penn ST U U Park; Cmmnctns.

BARNER, SHERRI; Emmaus HS; Emmaus, PA; (Y); Church Yth Grp; Chorus; VP Frsh Cls; Rep Jr Cls; VP Stu Cncl; Var Sftbl; Hon Roll; Law.

BARNER, TAMMY; Jersey Shore Area SR HS; Jersey Shore, PA; (Y); 2/275; Church Yth Grp; German Clb; Service Clb; Varsity Clb; Rep Soph Cls; Var Sftbl; NHS; Math Educ.

BARNES, BARB; Karns City HS; Petrolia, PA; (Y); Pep Clb; Trk; Duffs Bus Inst; Exec Sec.

BARNES, CHRISTOPHER N; Clearfield SR HS; Clearfield, PA; (Y); Key Clb; Varsity Clb; Y-Teens; Var Bsbl; Capt Var Bsktbl; Wt Lftg; Hon Roll; Accntng.

BARNES, DEBRA; Emmaus HS; Allentown, PA; (Y); 19/495; Church Yth Grp; Hosp Aide; Spanish Clb; Band; Concert Band; Mrchg Band; Orch; High Hon Roll; Hon Roll; NHS.

BARNES JR, DONALD; Peters Twnshp HS; Mcmurray, PA; (Y); JA; School Play; Stage Crew; Hon Roll; Auto Dsgn.

BARNES, J SCOTT; Octorara HS; Parkesburg, PA; (Y); 3/163; Radio Clb; Scholastic Bowl; Concert Band; Mrchg Band; School Musical; Stage Crew; Variety Show; Nwsp Ed-Chief; Nwsp Rptr; Lit Mag; Schrlshp PA Free Enterprise Wk 85; Elect Engr.

BARNES, JENNIFER; Upper Moreland HS; Willow Grove, PA; (Y); 27/276; Church Yth Grp; Service Clb; Teachers Aide; Chorus; Capt Mrchg Band; School Musical; School Play; High Hon Roll; NHS; Pres Schlr; Emma Jane Fish Math Scholar 86; Wheaton Coll; Elem Ed.

BARNES, LISA; St Clair Area HS; Pottsville, PA; (Y); Church Yth Grp; Drama Clb; Ski Clb; Varsity Clb; Bsktbl; Vllybl; Wt Lftg; Hon Roll; Sftbl; Co-Cptn JV Vlybl Tm 83-84; Vlybl Ltr & Vrsty Pin 84-86; Marktng.

BARNES, MARILYN E; Seneca Valley HS; Hendersonville, TN; (Y); Pres JA; Library Aide; Ski Clb; Teachers Aide; Concert Band; Mrchg Band; Pep Band; Mgr(s); Stat Trk; Hon Roll; Sprts Med.

BARNES, MARY; Curwensville Area HS; Curwensville, PA; (Y); Drama Clb; French Clb; Thesps; School Musical; School Play; Nwsp Rptr; NHS; Pres Frsh Cls; Rep Stu Cncl; JR Rep Homecomg Court 85-86.

BARNES, R ANDREW; Mc Guffey HS; West Alexander, PA; (Y); Am Leg Boys St; Boy Scts; Cmnty Wkr; Exploring; Letterman Clb; Coach Actv; Ftbl; Trk; Wt Lftg; DAR Awd; WV ST; Crmnl Jstc.

BARNES, RENEE; Canon Mc Millan SR HS; Eighty Four, PA; (Y); 31/371; Chess Clb; Hosp Aide; Office Aide; Spanish Clb; Chorus; Yrbk Stf; Vllybl; Cit Awd; High Hon Roll; Hon Roll; Westminster Coll; Elem Ed.

BARNES, RHONDA; Mohawk JRSR HS; New Galilee, PA; (S); Pres Church Yth Grp; Pres VP FHA; Girl Scts; Spanish Clb; Concert Band; Mrchg Band; Stat Bsktbl; Powder Puff Ftbl; Stat Trk; NHS; Chem.

BARNES, ROXANNE; Conemaugh Township HS; Johnstown, PA; (S); 21/101; Chrmn Church Yth Grp; Pep Clb; Nwsp Rptr; Nwsp Stf; Rep Stu Cncl; L JV Bsktbl; Var Sftbl; Hon Roll; Accntng.

BARNES, VICKI; Shade HS; Central City, PA; (Y); Trs Letterman Clb; Ski Clb; Trs Varsity Clb; Trs Soph Cls; L Var Bsktbl; Stat Ftbl; Var L Sftbl; Var L Vllybl; All Tourn Team Richland Invtatnl Vllybl 86; :Engrng.

BARNETT, BRIAN; Shippensburg SR HS; Shippensburg, PA; (Y); Teachers Aide; Var Ftbl; Var Wrstlng; High Hon Roll; Jr NHS; NHS; Voice Dem Awd; Tm Capt Wrstlng 84-85; MVP Wrstlng 84-85; Cchs Chc Awd Wrstlng 85-86; Aubrn U Of AL; Vet.

BARNETT, DONNA; Bishop Mc Devitt HS; Jenkintown, PA; (Y); 103/351; Church Yth Grp; GAA; Political Wkr; Spanish Clb; Bsktbl; Ftbl; Sftbl; Vllybl; VFW Awd; Amer Lgn Coats Jrdn Pst Schlrshp 86; La Salle U; Cmntns.

BARNETT, KENDRA; Overbrook HS; Philadelphia, PA; (Y); Rep Soph Cls; Bsktbl; Var Trk; High Hon Roll; Hon Roll; Psych.

BARNETT, MARTHA; Villa Maria Acad; Erie, PA; (Y); Hosp Aide; Service Clb; NHS; Acctg.

BARNETT, MAURICE; Westinghouse HS; Pittsburgh, PA; (Y); Aud/Vis; Exploring; JA; Science Clb; Teachers Aide; Variety Show; Nwsp Rptr; Nwsp Stf; Rep Frsh Cls; Rep Soph Cls; Wstnghs Mex Proj Essy Cont; GA Tech; Engrng.

BARNFATHER, ERIC; Shady Side Acad; Pittsburgh, PA; (Y); Drama Clb; School Play; Stage Crew; Lit Mag; JV Ftbl; Var Trk; Im Wt Lftg; Hon Roll; Theat Clb Awd 86; Trck Ltr 86; Bus Mgmt.

BARNHART, DE ANN; Anneville-Cleona HS; Annville, PA; (Y); 23/105; VP Sec 4-H; FNA; SADD; Mrchg Band; School Musical; Yrbk Bus Mgr; NHS; Ntl Merit Ltr; Vet Tech.

BARNHART, KARL S; Slippery Rock Area HS; Butler, PA; (Y); 1/152; Am Leg Boys St; Trs German Clb; Nwsp Bus Mgr; Nwsp Ed-Chief; High Hon Roll; Pres NHS; Sal; Rtry Yth Ldrshp Awd 85; Clara Sllngr Schlrshp 86; Rtry Wrld Affrs Cncl 85; Carnegie-Mellon U; Crtcl Wrtng.

BARNHART, LINDA; Cedar Crest HS; Lebaon, PA; (Y); 10/295; Drama Clb; Latin Clb; Pep Clb; Chorus; Orch; School Musical; High Hon Roll; Hon Roll; NHS; Church Yth Grp; Boostr Clb Hnrs Bnqt; Messiah; Sec Engl Tchr.

BARNHART, MELISSA; North East HS; North East, PA; (Y); 52/165; Sec Church Yth Grp; Hosp Aide; Latin Clb; Letterman Clb; Pep Clb; Band; Bowling; Capt Cheerleading; Capt Sftbl; Hon Roll; NE Schlrshp 86; Hrtzd Schlrship 86; 2nd Rnnr Up For PA ST Qu 85-86; ST Vincents Schl; Nrsnng.

BARNHART, MICHAEL; Central Catholic HS; Reading, PA; (Y); Aud/Vis; Boys Clb Am; Boy Scts; CAP; Pres Computer Clb; French Clb; Office Aide; Science Clb; Ski Clb; Teachers Aide; Mst Val Stu Math/Comp Dept 82; 3rd Comp Pgmng Co Sci & Engrng Fair 83; Bst Wrk Alg II 86; De Vry Inst Tech; Comp Sys Anal.

BARNHART, NANCY; Lower Dauphin HS; Hershey, PA; (Y); Church Yth Grp; 4-H; Hosp Aide; Teachers Aide; Chorus; Stage Crew; JV Bsktbl; Score Keeper; Socr; JV Sftbl; Empire Bty Schl Schlrshp 86-87; Empire Bty Schl:Csmtlgy.

BARNHART, PAMELA; California HS; Coal Center, PA; (Y); Drama Clb; FBLA; Band; Concert Band; Drm Mjr(t); Mrchg Band; Symp Band; Yrbk Stf; Pres CA Yth Educ Assoc 86-87; Natl Hnr Rl 87; Radlgy.

BARNHART, STEPHEN; Southern Fulton HS; Warfordsburg, PA; (Y); Boy Scts; Church Yth Grp; 4-H; Nwsp Stf; Yrbk Stf; Var Bsbl; JV Var Bsktbl; Score Keeper; Hon Roll; Penn ST U; Engr.

BARNHART, SUSAN; Jersey Shore Area SR HS; Jersey Shore, PA; (Y); French Clb; FBLA; Scndry Educ.

BARNHART II, THOMAS L; Cocalico HS; Denver, PA; (Y); Boy Scts; Church Yth Grp; Concert Band; Pres Frsh Cls; Pres Soph Cls; Pres Jr Cls; Pres Sr Cls; Var Ftbl; Var Capt Trk; Bsbl; HOBY Outstndng Ldrshp Sem 83-84; Stu Mnth 85; Vly Forge Mltry JC; Psych.

BARNINGER, NATALIE; Cumberland Valley HS; Mechanicsburg, PA; (Y); Key Clb; Ski Clb; JV Fld Hcky; Var Trk; Ntl Art Hnr Soc 86; Schltc Art Awd 86; Bloomsburg U.

BARNISHIN, LESLIE A; Gateway SR HS; Monroeville, PA; (Y); Am Leg Aux Girls St; Art Clb; Church Yth Grp; DECA; Exploring; FBLA; Yrbk Stf; Rep Sr Cls; Rep Chrmn Stu Cncl; La Roche Coll; Intr Dsgn.

BARNISKY, JO-LYNN; Tamaqua Area HS; Tamqua, PA; (Y); French Clb; Pep Clb; Yrbk Stf; French Hon Soc; Hon Roll; Mc Cann Schl Of Bus; Bus Admin.

BARNOT, TERRY; Belle Vernon Area HS; Belle Vernon, PA; (Y); 74/276; Pres Band; Pres Frsh Cls; Pres Soph Cls; Pres Jr Cls; Pres Sr Cls; Pres Stu Cncl; DAR Awd; Ski Clb; Trs SADD; Sci Awd, Most Likley Succeed, Best All Round Stu 83; Indiana U PA; Crmnlgy.

BARNOVSKY, RONALD A; New Castle SR HS; New Castle, PA; (S); 17/236; AFS; Cmnty Wkr; SADD; Concert Band; Mrchg Band; Hon Roll; NHS; Youth Page Reporter 82-86; Ofcr Spec Asst SADD 83-85; SADD Advsry Bd 85-86; Millersville U PA; Earth Sci.

BARON, DAWN; Unionville HS; West Chester, PA; (Y); Pep Clb; JV Fld Hcky; Hon Roll; Jr NHS; Fine Arts.

BARON, LEONARD; Laurel Highlands SR HS; Uniontown, PA; (Y); Church Yth Grp; Cmnty Wkr; JA; Band; Concert Band; Drm Mjr(t); Jazz Band; Mrchg Band; Pep Band; JV Crs Cntry; Penn ST U; Multi-Media Jrnlsm.

BARON, TAMARA; Steel Valley HS; Munhall, PA; (Y); Church Yth Grp; Stu Cncl; Cheerleading; NHS; Drama Clb; Spanish Clb; Varsity Clb; Church Choir; School Musical; Variety Show; Choir Solost 83-84; Featrd Prfrmr Song & Danc Natl Theme Pk Kennywood 86; Htl Fd Mgmt.

BARONTI, TANYA L; North Allegheny SR HS; Wexford, PA; (Y); 186/605; Church Yth Grp; Dance Clb; JA; VP Thesps; Chorus; School Musical; School Play; Nwsp Stf; Rep Sr Cls; Hon Roll; Penn ST U; Pre-Law.

BARR, BONNIE; Mohawk JR SR HS; New Castle, PA; (S); Church Yth Grp; Pres 4-H; French Clb; Band; Stat Bsktbl; Stat Crs Cntry; Stat Trk; 4-H Awd; NHS; Vet Med.

BARR, BRIAN; Boyertown SR HS; Bechtelsville, PA; (Y); 37/418; Chess Clb; Trs Church Yth Grp; SADD; Band; Concert Band; Mrchg Band; Trk; Hon Roll; Elect Engr.

BARR, CHRISTINE; Mohawk Area JRSR HS; New Castle, PA; (S); 1/128; Church Yth Grp; Hosp Aide; Pres Latin Clb; Band; Jazz Band; Mrchg Band; School Musical; Pres Sr Cls; Capt Tennis; NHS; Lawrence Cnty Jr Miss Schlrshp Achvmnt 85-86; C Knox Fndtn Schlrshp 86; U Of Pttsbrgh Val Schlrshp 86; U Of Pittsburgh; Physcl Thrpy.

BARR, LESLIE; Pequea Valley HS; Gap, PA; (Y); 13/138; Church Yth Grp; GAA; Varsity Clb; Band; Chorus; Church Choir; Concert Band; Mrchg Band; School Musical; School Play; SW Ridgeway Schlrshp Awd 79-80; Bio.

BARR, PAULA; Marion Center HS; Home, PA; (Y); FHA; Band; Concert Band; Mrchg Band; Orch; Pep Band; Dist Band 86; Regnl Band 86; Music.

BARR, RACHEL; Curwensville Area HS; Curwensville, PA; (Y); AFS; Drama Clb; Ski Clb; Band; Chorus; Concert Band; Mrchg Band; School Play; Nwsp Rptr; NHS; PA ST U; Secndry Educ.

BARR, STEVE; Grove City HS; Grove City, PA; (Y); Church Yth Grp; FFA; Science Clb; Ski Clb; JV Bsktbl; Var L Ftbl; Var Wt Lftg; Hon Roll; Pres Physcl Ftnss Awd 84; PA ST U; Arch.

BARR, SUSAN I; Nazareth Acad; Philadelphia, PA; (Y); 10/120; French Clb; Girl Scts; Q&S; Yrbk Rptr; Yrbk Stf; Lit Mag; DAR Awd; High Hon Roll; NHS; Fordham U.

BARR, TINA; Tyrone Area HS; Tyrone, PA; (Y); Pres Spanish Clb; High Hon Roll; Hon Roll; NHS; Outstndng Food Svc Awd 86; Dietcn.

BARR, TOM; Ridley SR HS; Folsom, PA; (Y); 56/427; Debate Tm; French Clb; Letterman Clb; Speech Tm; Nwsp Rptr; JV Bsbl; Var Bsktbl; NHS; Bus.

BARR, VICKY; Connellsville Area HS; Champion, PA; (Y); 98/550; Cmnty Wkr; Computer Clb; Science Clb; Spanish Clb; Nwsp Stf; High Hon Roll; Hon Roll; Jrnlsm.

BARRACCA, CHRISTINE M; Linden Hall HS; Stevens, PA; (Y); 1/30; Drama Clb; Quiz Bowl; Pres Thesps; School Musical; School Play; Yrbk Phtg; Pres Sr Cls; Dnfth Awd; Gov Hon Prg Awd; High Hon Roll; Long Islnd U.

BARRALL, RICHARD; Liberty HS; Bethlehem, PA; (Y); 112/391; Boy Scts; Exploring; Band; Concert Band; Mrchg Band; Orch; Eagle Scout 86; Kutztown U; Comm Art.

BARRALL, SHARON; Liberty HS; Bethlehem, PA; (Y); 143/417; Hon Roll; VA Intrmnt Coll; Physcl Thrpy.

BARRETT, DAVE; Northern York HS; Grantham, PA; (Y); Band; Chorus; Church Choir; Concert Band; Drm Mjr(t); Jazz Band; Mrchg Band; School Musical; JV Socr; L Var Trk; Tri M Ntl Music Hnr Soc Tres, Yuth Grp Ofcr 86; Dst, Hnr Band 83-86; Engrng.

BARRETT, DONNA LYNN; St Maria Goretti HS; Philadelphia, PA; (Y); Library Aide; Office Aide; Political Wkr; Rep Soph Cls; Rep Jr Cls; Rep Stu Cncl; Capt JV Cheerleading; JV Coach Actv; JV Mgr(s); Prfct Atten Awd; Howard U; Obstetrician.

BARRETT, ERIN; Sacred Heart HS; Munhall, PA; (Y); Rep Drama Clb; Hosp Aide; Scholastic Bowl; Ski Clb; Spanish Clb; Chorus; Mgr School Musical; School Play; Stage Crew; Yrbk Phtg; Queens Ct Prom 86; Psych.

BARRETT, KIM; Pine Forge Acad; Durham, NC; (Y); 15/80; Chorus; Church Choir; Nwsp Ed-Chief; Pres Stu Cncl; JV Var Cheerleading; High Hon Roll; Hon Roll; Howard; Engrng.

BARRETT, ROBERT; Warwick HS; Lititz, PA; (Y); 57/226; Church Yth Grp; Im Socr; Im Vllybl; High Hon Roll; Hon Roll; Physcis.

BARRETT, STACY; Bellefonte SR HS; Bellefonte, PA; (S); 2/219; Model UN; Concert Band; Jazz Band; Mrchg Band; Nwsp Ed-Chief; Nwsp Rptr; Im Powder Puff Ftbl; NHS; Q&S; Band; Dist Band 85-86; Enrichment; OH ST U; Math.

BARRICK, REBECCA; Newport JR/Sr HS; Newport, PA; (Y); Art Clb; FBLA; FTA; Flag Corp; Mrchg Band; Yrbk Stf; Hon Roll.

BARRICK, TIM; Big Spring HS; Carlisle, PA; (Y); Art Clb; Ski Clb; Spanish Clb; Var L Wrstlng; Hon Roll; Gld Key Art Awd 83; Cnsrvtn Clb 84; Envrnmtl Fld.

BARRINGTON, JENNIFER; Unionville HS; Chadds Ford, PA; (Y); Church Yth Grp; Hosp Aide; Pep Clb; Chorus; Church Choir; School Musical; Yrbk Stf; Rep Stu Cncl; High Hon Roll; NHS; Intl Bus.

BARRISH, ANDREW; Mapletown HS; Greensboro, PA; (Y); 3/78; Ski Clb; Varsity Clb; Capt Ftbl; Golf; Hon Roll; NHS.

BARRON, DIANE; Elizabethtown Area HS; Elizabethtown, PA; (Y); Trs VP 4-H; Teachers Aide; Sec Band; Concert Band; Mrchg Band; Orch; Mgr(s); Powder Puff Ftbl; Twrlr; 4-H Awd; Cnty Bnd 86; Millersville U; Elem Ed.

BARRON JR, EDWARD L; Monogahela Valley Catholic HS; Belle Vernon, PA; (Y); 47/102; Mgr Bsktbl; Mgr Ftbl; Mgr(s); Gldn Trgr 3 Cnsctv Qrtrs Trig 85-86; St Vincent Coll; Bio.

BARRON, JUDITH; Central Bucks East HS; Warrington, PA; (Y); Church Yth Grp; Band; Church Choir; Yrbk Stf; Fld Hcky; Mgr(s); Wt Lftg; Hon Roll; Sci.

BARRON, SCOTT; Tamaqua Area SR HS; Tamaqua, PA; (Y); 14/191; Boy Scts; German Clb; Trk; Comp Sci.

BARRON, STEPHEN; Council Rock HS; Churchville, PA; (Y); Church Yth Grp; Chrmn Drama Clb; Chorus; School Musical; School Play; Stage Crew; Rep Jr Cls; Hon Roll; Ntl Merit Ltr; Newtown Arts Co Schlrshp 86; Taylor U; Theatre Arts.

BARRY, CAROLE ANN P; G A R Memorial HS; Wilkes Barre, PA; (S); 25/180; Hosp Aide; Key Clb; Chorus; Rep Stu Cncl; Twrlr; NHS; NEDT Awd; Ski Clb; Color Guard; Outstndng Sci Stu Awd; Typing Awd; Pre Med.

BARRY, ELIZABETH; Council Rock HS; Newtown, PA; (Y); 66/769; Nwsp Stf; Rep Stu Cncl; Capt Var Cheerleading; Fld Hcky; Hon Roll; NHS; Ntl Merit Ltr; Mktg.

BARRY, GAYLE; Northgate JR/SR HS; Pittsburgh, PA; (Y); 36/134; Church Yth Grp; Girl Scts; Hosp Aide; Library Aide; Yrbk Stf; Rep Frsh Cls; Rep Soph Cls; Stat Diving; Mgr(s); Stat Sftbl; ICM; Bus Mgmt.

BARRY, GERALD; New Hope-Soleburg JR SR HS; Lahaska, PA; (S); Mathletes; High Hon Roll; Hon Roll; NHS; Cert Of Mrt Govrnr Of PA 85; Stanford U; Chem Engrng.

BARRY, JOYCE J; Peters Twp HS; Mcmurray, PA; (Y); Intnl Clb; Rep Key Clb; Science Clb; Chorus; Church Choir; Yrbk Phtg; Stu Cncl; High Hon Roll; NCTE Awd; Rotary Awd; PA ST U; Corp Law.

BARRY, MICHELLE; Bishop Hannan HS; Scranton, PA; (Y); Church Yth Grp; Ski Clb; School Play; Rep Frsh Cls; Rep Soph Cls; Rep Stu Cncl; JV Bsktbl; Sftbl; Hon Roll; NHS; Phy Thrpst.

BARRY, MICHELLE; Cardinal Brennan HS; Frackville, PA; (Y); 12/48; Dance Clb; Drama Clb; German Clb; School Musical; Yrbk Ed-Chief; Rep Stu Cncl; Twrlr; NHS; Ski Clb; Chorus; Studnt Of The Mnth 86; Wntr Crnvl Rep 86; Bloomsburg U; Nrsng.

BARRY, STEPHEN; Archbishop Carroll HS; Berwyn, PA; (Y); 19/169; Boy Scts; Exploring; High Hon Roll; Hon Roll; Carroll Hnr Soc 85-86; Bus.

BARRY, TRISHA; Williams Valley JR SR HS; Tower City, PA; (Y); 17/99; Church Yth Grp; Band; Chorus; School Musical; Yrbk Stf; Rep Stu Cncl; Capt Ftbl; God Cntry Awd; Hon Roll; John Hall Fndtn Schlrshp 86; John Travitz Schlrshp 86; Williams Vlly Sngrs Awd 85-86; Outstdng Vclst; Harrisburg Area CC; Polic Adm.

BARSAMELLA, LAINA; St Maria Goretti HS; Philadelphia, PA; (Y); 121/361; Computer Clb; Math Tm; Teachers Aide; Hon Roll; Workng Rcgntn 86; Invstmt Broker.

BARSHINGER, LISA; Central Park SR HS; York, PA; (Y); Church Yth Grp; Var Mgr(s); Mat Maids; Yorktown Bus Inst; Bus Mgmt.

BARSHINGER, RONALD; Tulpehocken HS; Myerstown, PA; (Y); Boy Scts; Church Yth Grp; Pep Clb; Band; Concert Band; Mrchg Band; Pep Band; School Musical; Stage Crew; Trk; Machnst.

BARSOLO, LISA; Deer Lakes JR-SR HS; Cheswick, PA; (Y); 56/210; Exploring; Band; Concert Band; Jazz Band; Mrchg Band; Pep Band; School Play; Yrbk Stf; Hon Roll; Robert Krauland Memrl Schlrshp 85-86; Duquesne U; Phrmcy.

BARSZCZEWSKI, JUDITH; St Maria Goretti HS; Philadelphia, PA; (Y); 88/420; Hon Roll; 2nd Hnrs 84 & 85; Pierce; Sec Sci.

BARTASAVICH, DAVID; Lakeland HS; Jermyn, PA; (S); 23/152; JV Bsbl; JV Bsktbl; Hon Roll.

BARTEK, MARTIN; Frazier JR SR HS; Perryopolis, PA; (Y); Bsbl; Hon Roll; Spanish Clb; Bsbl Let 86.

BARTEL, SCOTT; Reynolds HS; Greenville, PA; (Y); 2/122; Latin Clb; Math Clb; Varsity Clb; Var L Crs Cntry; Var L Trk; Hon Roll; NHS; NEDT Awd; Sal; Church Yth Grp; Gannon U Math & Engnrng Awd; Grove City Coll; Engnrng.

BARTEL, SHELLY A; Commodore Perry HS; Hadley, PA; (S); 2/72; VICA; Var L Bsktbl; Var L Sftbl; High Hon Roll; Hon Roll; Prfct Atten Awd; Chorus; Sec Soph Cls; Sec Jr Cls; Sec Sr Cls; NC ST U; Arch.

BARTELS, BRYAN; Cambridge Springs Joint HS; Cambridge Springs, PA; (Y); 8/112; Key Clb; Pep Clb; Spanish Clb; Stu Cncl; Hon Roll; Layout Editor Of Yrbk 86-87; Engineering.

BARTH, DEBRA; Harry S Truman HS; Levittown, PA; (Y); Church Yth Grp; Drama Clb; Band; Concert Band; Mrchg Band; School Musical; School Play; Stu Cncl; Var Capt Fld Hcky; Var Capt Sftbl; Fld Hcky 1st Tm All Amer Goaltendg 85 & Mst Val JV Playr 84; Trenton ST Coll; Art Ther.

BARTHLOW, THOMAS E; Northern Lehigh HS; Neffs, PA; (Y); 4/144; Am Leg Boys St; Church Yth Grp; Scholastic Bowl; Variety Show; Rep Stu Cncl; Var Trk; High Hon Roll; Hon Roll; Lion Awd; NHS; Phrmcst.

BARTHOLOMAI, TINA; Connellsville Area HS; Cnelvle, PA; (Y); Drama Clb; Science Clb; School Musical; Stage Crew; Soph Cls; French Hon Soc; High Hon Roll; Natl Ed Develpmnt Test.

BARTHOLOMEW, KRISTINA; Bethlehem Catholic HS; Bethlehem, PA; (Y); 93/215; Key Clb; Chorus; Rep Frsh Cls; Rep Stu Cncl; JV Sftbl; Hon Roll; Nrsng.

BARTHOLOMEW, LESLIE; Spring-Ford SR HS; Royersford, PA; (Y); 19/250; Off 4-H; French Clb; Sec Thesps; Yrbk Stf; L Tennis; L Trk; Dnfth Awd; 4-H Awd; NHS; Opt Clb Awd; Dietcs/Ntrtn.

BARTHOLOMEW, MICHAEL; Northampton Area HS; Bath, PA; (Y); Leo Clb; Varsity Clb; Rep Soph Cls; Rep Jr Cls; Rep Stu Cncl; Var VP Bsbl; JV Var Ftbl; Var L Trk; Var Wt Lftg; Var L Wrstlng; 2nd Pl-Dist XI PA Wrstlng 85; 4th Po Rgnls-Nrtheast PA-WRSTLNG 85; 2nd Pl-Chrstms Cty-Wrstlng Tourn; U Of MD; Sprts Med.

BARTIS, SARAH; Peters Township HS; Mc Murray, PA; (S); VP NFL; VP Spanish Clb; Sec SADD; Thesps; School Play; JV Vllybl; High Hon Roll; VP Spanish NHS; 2nd Pl PTA Litry Awds 83-84; PA ST; Comm.

BARTLEBAUGH, CARRIE; Marion Center HS; Rochester Mls, PA; (Y); FBLA; Pep Clb; Teachers Aide; Band; Stu Cncl.

BARTLES, KIMBERLY L; Yough SR HS; Irwin, PA; (Y); Church Yth Grp; French Clb; Girl Scts; Ski Clb; Band; Nwsp Rptr; Nwsp Stf; Hon Roll; Slvr Awd & Sr Ldrshp Girl Scouts 85; Norwin Art League 2nd Pl Ribbon 86; Newsp Corresponding Editor 86; Davis & Elkins; Art.

BARTLETT, ANDREA; John S Fine HS; Wapwallopen, PA; (Y); VP Church Yth Grp; Cmnty Wkr; Chorus; Yrbk Stf; Photo.

BARTLETT, JEFF; Canton JR SR HS; Canton, PA; (Y); Im Wrstlng; High Hon Roll; Rotary Awd; Wllmsprt Coll Vo-Tech Pgm-Auto Bdy Trd 85-87; Veal Frmr.

BARTLETT, MARK; Mt Lebanon HS; Pittsburgh, PA; (Y); 7/500; Church Yth Grp; Bsbl; Bsktbl; High Hon Roll; Cvl Eng.

BARTLEY, ELAINE; Shenango JR SR HS; New Castle, PA; (Y); 27/112; Office Aide; Teachers Aide; Yrbk Stf; Hon Roll; NHS.

BARTLEY, PAUL E; Wyoming Seminary HS; Tunkhannock, PA; (Y); Ski Clb; Var L Ftbl; JV Wrstlng; Hon Roll; NEDT Awd; William & Mary; Bus.

BARTLEY, WADE; Hopewell HS; Aliquippa, PA; (Y); 6/285; French Clb; Math Tm; JV Ftbl; High Hon Roll; Lion Awd; NHS; Ntl Merit Ltr; Pres Schlr; Natl Math Exam Awd 85-86; PA ST U; Elec Engrg.

BARTMAN, JENNIFER; St Paul Cathedral HS; Pittsburgh, PA; (S); 7/65; Art Clb; Hosp Aide; Red Cross Aide; Pres Service Clb; Spanish Clb; Nwsp Rptr; Yrbk Stf; Stu Cncl; Hon Roll; NHS; IN U Of PA; Sociology.

BARTNICK, CARL; Crestwood HS; Mountaintop, PA; (Y); JV Var Ftbl; JV Var Trk; JV Var Wt Lftg; Prfct Atten Awd; PA ST; Med.

BARTNICKI, TARA M; Scranton Preparatory Schl; Old Forge, PA; (Y); 14/192; Drama Clb; Political Wkr; Nwsp Rptr; Yrbk Ed-Chief; Bowling; Crs Cntry; Tennis; Trk; High Hon Roll; Jr NHS.

BARTO, CONNIE; Juniata HS; Mifflintown, PA; (Y); Camera Clb; Church Yth Grp; Computer Clb; Drama Clb; PAVAS; Chorus; JV Var Trk; High Hon Roll; NHS; 4-H.

BARTO, NASREEN; Juniata HS; Mifflintown, PA; (Y); Church Yth Grp; PAVAS; NHS; Camera Clb; Cmnty Wkr; Computer Clb; Dance Clb; 4-H; Spanish Clb; Chorus; Arch.

BARTO, NEIL; Northeastern HS; Manchester, PA; (Y); Church Yth Grp; Cmnty Wkr; SADD; Thesps; Band; Church Choir; Concert Band; Mrchg Band; School Musical; Lit Mag; Penn ST U; Comp Sci.

BARTOCK, KIM; Southmoreland SR HS; Scottdale, PA; (Y); Church Yth Grp; FFA; Pep Clb; Floral Designer.

BARTOE, MICHAEL T; Northwestern HS; Albion, PA; (Y); 20/164; Stu Cncl; JV Bsbl; JV Crs Cntry; JV Trk; Var Wrstlng; Hon Roll; Bus Adm.

BARTOL, STEPHANIE; West Hazelton HS; Weston, PA; (Y); FBLA; Hosp Aide; Office Aide; Teachers Aide; Y-Teens; Nwsp Ed-Chief; Yrbk Ed-Chief; Cheerleading; Pom Pon; Swmmng; Luzerne Cnty CC; Acctng.

BARTOLACCI, PAULETTE; Notre Dame HS; Easton, PA; (Y); 12/88; Church Yth Grp; Church Choir; Yrbk Stf; Cheerleading; High Hon Roll; Hon Roll; Lib Arts.

BARTOLOMEO, ELIZABETH; St Maria Goretti HS; Philadelphia, PA; (Y); Cmnty Wkr; French Clb; Office Aide; Spanish Clb; Chorus; Nwsp Stf; Rep Jr Cls; Rep Sr Cls; Im Stu Cncl; Hon Roll; Acad Hnrs; Rep Mnth Stu Govnmnt; Bus.

BARTON, JILL; Cameron County HS; Emporium, PA; (Y); 24/84; Cmnty Wkr; Spanish Clb; Teachers Aide; Color Guard; Yrbk Stf; Powder Puff Ftbl; Hon Roll; Accntng.

BARTON, KATHY; Northeast Bradford HS; Rome, PA; (Y); Letterman Clb; Varsity Clb; Var Capt Cheerleading; Var Sftbl; High Hon Roll; Hon Roll; FHA; SADD; JV Bsktbl; Bus.

BARTON, LEILA; Harrisburg Christian Schl; Harrisburg, PA; (Y); Church Yth Grp; Drama Clb; Girl Scts; Chorus; School Play; Nwsp Stf; Sec Jr Cls; Hon Roll; Christian Testimony Awd 85-86; Cosmtlgy.

BARTON, MATTHEW; Middletown Area HS; Middletown, PA; (Y); 32/181; Var L Bsbl; Var L Ftbl; Var L Wt Lftg; Cit Awd; Hon Roll; Sprts Med.

BARTON, RUTH; Central Dauphin HS; Harrisburg, PA; (Y); 16/386; Band; Chorus; Concert Band; Mrchg Band; School Musical; Yrbk Stf; JV Fld Hcky; Hon Roll; Jr NHS; NHS; Med.

BARTON, TRACY; Penn-Trafford HS; Trafford, PA; (Y); Swmmng; Tennis; Trk; Drama Clb; FBLA; Ski Clb; Hon Roll.

BARTORONA, KARA M; Albert Gallatin SR HS; Masontown, PA; (Y); 1/152; Math Tm; Ski Clb; Concert Band; Mrchg Band; Ed Nwsp Stf; Stu Cncl; High Hon Roll; Jr NHS; Trs NHS; Val; W PA Mem Scholar Rnnr Up 86; Westminster Coll Pres Scholar 86; Exch Clb Awd Acad Achvt 85-86; Westminster Coll; Engrng.

BARTOS, SUSAN; Blairsville SR HS; Blairsville, PA; (Y); SADD; Varsity Clb; Concert Band; Drm Mjr(t); Mrchg Band; School Musical; Var L Bsktbl; Var L Trk; Var L Vllybl; High Hon Roll; Smith Coll; Psychtrc Med.

BARTOW, SUSAN; Boyertown Area SR HS; Boyertown, PA; (Y); 4/455; Math Tm; Chorus; Rep Stu Cncl; Bsktbl; Var Fld Hcky; Var Sftbl; Cit Awd; High Hon Roll; NHS; Prfct Atten Awd; 2nd Tm All-Ches-Mont Sftbl 85; Pottstown Mercury All-Area Sftbl Tm 85.

BARTUSH, ROSE; Nativity B V M HS; Pottsville, PA; (Y); 12/98; Am Leg Aux Girls St; Cmnty Wkr; Library Aide; SADD; Yrbk Stf; Rep Jr Cls; Bsktbl; Capt Crs Cntry; Hon Roll; VP NHS; U S Achvmnt Acad 84; Acdmc All-Amrcn Schlr Pgm 84; Tulane U; Arch.

BARTYNSKI, MELISSA A; Louis E Dieruff HS; Allentown, PA; (Y); Ski Clb; Yrbk Stf; Co-Capt Twrlr; Hon Roll; Prfct Atten Awd; Prom Cmmtte 86; Penn ST U.

BARYCKI, ANDREA; Old Forge HS; Old Forge, PA; (S); Color Guard; Mrchg Band; Pom Pon; High Hon Roll; Hon Roll; NHS; Gregg Typng Awd; Bus Adm.

BARYCKI, JOSEPH; Old Forge HS; Old Forge, PA; (S); 1/106; Rep Stu Cncl; Var Bsktbl; Var Ftbl; High Hon Roll; NHS.

BARZANTI, LADA; Mapletown JR SR HS; Bobtown, PA; (Y); 5/85; Mrchg Band; Yrbk Bus Mgr; Yrbk Stf; Twrlr; Im Vllybl; High Hon Roll; Hon Roll; NHS; Pre-Law.

BARZDO, AMY; Blacklick Valley JR-SR HS; Twin Rocks, PA; (S); Church Yth Grp; Drama Clb; Girl Scts; Sec NFL; Pres Ski Clb; Spanish Clb; Varsity Clb; School Play; Nwsp Stf; Yrbk Ed-Chief; JR Miss Fnlst 85; U Of Pittsburgh; Comm.

BASAING, MONICA; Spring-Ford HS; Royersford, PA; (Y); 42/237; Church Yth Grp; German Clb; Pep Clb; Ed Yrbk Stf; Var Co-Capt Cheerleading; Lcrss; Hon Roll; Trs Frsh Cls; Trs Soph Cls; Trs Jr Cls; Buckwalter Schrlshp 86; Temple U; Pre-Physcl Thrpy.

BASARAB, AIMEE; E L Meyers HS; Wilkes Barre, PA; (Y); Church Yth Grp; Dance Clb; Key Clb; Ski Clb; Chorus; Color Guard; Spanish NHS; U Scranton.

BASCHOFF, MARY; Upper Merion Area HS; King Of Prussia, PA; (Y); Drama Clb; School Musical; School Play; Nwsp Ed-Chief; Nwsp Rptr; Nwsp Stf; Yrbk Rptr; Yrbk Stf; Lit Mag; Rep Soph Cls; Outstndng Actng Awd 86; Sprts Anncr 85-87; Fnlst Miss PA Ntl Tngr Pgnt 84; Western MD; Cmmnctns.

BASH, KRISTIN ALAINE; Central Bucks H S East; Buckingham, PA; (Y); Nwsp Stf; Sftbl; Pres Schlr; Sci Sem Tlnt Srch 84-85; Barnard Coll; Humanities.

BASH, TRAVIS; J P Mc Caskey HS; Lancaster, PA; (Y); 91/551; AFS; Band; Chorus; Nwsp Stf; Rep Stu Cncl; Var Cheerleading; Hon Roll; All Amer Chrldr Rnnr Up 84-85; Chrldng Excllnc Awd Wnnr 86-87; Bus Admin.

BASHIAN, MICHELLE; Central SR HS; York, PA; (Y); Church Yth Grp; Girl Scts; Chorus; Church Choir; Hon Roll.

BASHIOUM, ROBERTA; Yough SR HS; Sutersville, PA; (Y); FBLA; VICA; Chorus; Color Guard; Hon Roll.

BASHORE, DONNA; Tulpehocken HS; Mount Aetna, PA; (Y); 8/110; Church Yth Grp; Pres Band; Chorus; Church Choir; Concert Band; School Musical; Swing Chorus; Yrbk Bus Mgr; Sec Sr Cls; Var Capt Sftbl; PMEA Al-ST Chorus 86; Natl Choral Awd 86; Music.

BASILE, ANDREW; The Hill Schl; Douglassville, PA; (Y); Radio Clb; Ski Clb; Nwsp Phtg; Yrbk Phtg; Gym; JV Lcrss; Im Socr.

BASILE, BETH; Cardinal O Hara HS; Broomall, PA; (Y); 297/772; Trs Church Yth Grp; Off Dance Clb; Off FNA; Office Aide; SADD; School Play; Nwsp Stf; Yrbk Stf; Gym; Hon Roll; Shippensburg U; Med.

BASILE, MARIA; Downingtown SR HS; Downingtown, PA; (Y); 66/563; High Hon Roll; Hon Roll; Frnch Merit Cert 84; Typng Awd 85; Villanova U; Acctng.

BASINGER, RONNA; Somerset Area HS; Somerset, PA; (Y); 45/211; Pres FHA; Pres JA; Color Guard; Mrchg Band; Var L Trk; Var L Twrlr; Hon Roll; NHS; 1st Pl Pres Awd In JR Achvt 86; Prsdntl Physcl Ftnss Awd 83-86; ICM; Acctg.

BASITS, SUSAN; Belle Vernon Area HS; Belle Vernon, PA; (Y); 33/272; Pep Clb; Nwsp Stf; Yrbk Stf; Capt Twrlr; Hon Roll; NHS; SR Comm 85-86; Stdnt Mnth Awd 86; 1st Pl Spnsh Awd 85; Penn ST U; Bus.

BASKERVILLE, KEYVA L; Dobbins A V T HS; Philadelphia, PA; (S); 52/550; Math Clb; Yrbk Stf; Cheerleading; Hon Roll; JETS Awd; Jr NHS; Mu Alp Tht; Elec Engr.

BASKETTE, SUSAN; York Vo Tech; New Park, PA; (Y); 25/408; German Clb; VICA; JV Fld Hcky; High Hon Roll; Hon Roll; Archtectural Drafting.

BASKIN, MARCY; Radnor HS; Rosemont, PA; (S); VP Debate Tm; VP JA; VP Speech Tm; SADD; Chorus; Capt Drill Tm; Hon Roll; Dist 12 Chorus 2 Times 85-86; Rgn 6 Chorus 1 Time 86; Active Theatre 80-85; Brandeis U.

BASS, GEORGE; Steelton-Highspire HS; Steelton, PA; (Y); 35/99; Var Wt Lftg; Army.

BASSETT, BRIDGET; Brookville Area HS; Brookville, PA; (Y); Chess Clb; Church Yth Grp; French Clb; Hosp Aide; Key Clb; SADD; Chorus; Nwsp Rptr; Nwsp Stf; Yrbk Rptr; Lib Arts.

BASSION, SHAN; North East Bradford HS; Ulster, PA; (Y); Nwsp Stf; Stu Cncl; Tennis; Tutored 85-86; Barry U; Pre Vet.

BASSLER, JANINE M; Hollidaysburg Area SR HS; Hollidaysburg, PA; (Y); Drama Clb; Lit Mag; Exchange Stu To Engl 85-86; Stage Mgr In Drama Prod 86; U Of Pittsburgh; Politics.

BASTAN, JENNIFER; Emmaus HS; Emmaus, PA; (Y); Church Yth Grp; GAA; Var L Sftbl; High Hon Roll; Hon Roll; Jr NHS; NHS; FCA; Teachers Aide; Church Choir; Engrng.

BASTIAN, HARRY; Technical Memorial HS; Erie, PA; (Y); 50/380; German Clb; School Play; Stage Crew; Variety Show; Im Bsktbl; Var Socr; Hon Roll; Jr NHS; NHS; Penn ST; Elctrcl Engrng.

BATCH, RACHEL; Kiski Area HS; Saltsburg, PA; (Y); 24/371; Aud/Vis; Dance Clb; Math Tm; Spanish Clb; Chorus; Variety Show; Nwsp Rptr; Rep Frsh Cls; Im Cheerleading; NHS; Stdy Pgm Inst Spanish Studies Valencia Spain 86; CMU; Intl Bus.

BATCHELOR, ROBERT; Slippery Rock Area HS; Slippery Rock, PA; (Y); 36/180; Nwsp Sprt Ed; Pres Stu Cncl; L Bsktbl; Im Wt Lftg; Pep Clb; Var Bsbl; Hon Roll; Acdmc All-Amer 86; Econ.

BATDORF, HOLLY; Milton SR HS; Milton, PA; (Y); Church Yth Grp; Computer Clb; Band; Chorus; Church Choir; Concert Band; Mrchg Band; Pep Band; School Musical; School Play; Williamsport Schl Comm; Med Sec.

BATDORF, VICKIE; Lebanon Catholic HS; Lebanon, PA; (Y); 15/68; Key Clb; Pep Clb; Spanish Clb; SADD; Stage Crew; Nwsp Stf; Stat Bsktbl; Hon Roll; Alvernia Coll; Bus Mgt.

BATEMAN, FRAN; Merion Mercy Acad; Merion, PA; (Y); 8/73; French Clb; Rep Frsh Cls; Rep Soph Cls; Sec Jr Cls; Pres Sr Cls; Stu Cncl; Stat Bsktbl; Var Fld Hcky; Var Tennis; NHS; Math.

BATES, ANTHONY; Strath Haven HS; Wallingford, PA; (Y); 25/275; Cmnty Wkr; Stu Cncl; Var Bsbl; Var Ftbl; Ice Hcky; Hon Roll; Hnrs Ltr 85-86; Engrng.

BATES, CHRISTOPHER A; Geibel HS; Connellsville, PA; (Y); Church Yth Grp; Computer Clb; Var L Bsbl; Bsktbl; Var L Ftbl; Hon Roll; NEDT Awd; Pres Acad Ftns Awd; CA U Of PA; Comp Sci.

BATES, CINDY; Plmyrfa HS; Palmyra, PA; (Y); 28/196; Band; Chorus; Pres Frsh Cls; Pres Soph Cls; Pres Jr Cls; Rep Stu Cncl; Fld Hcky; Trk; High Hon Roll; Hon Roll; MVP Field Hcky 84; Outstndng Stu 84; Outstndng Employee Wk 85; Elem Ed.

BATES, JILL; Greensburg Central Catholic HS; Greensburg, PA; (Y); Church Yth Grp; Chorus; Hon Roll; St Vincent Coll.

BATES, KEVIN; Derry Area SR HS; Pitcairn, PA; (Y); 67/255; Computer Clb; FFA; Math Clb; Im Badmtn; Im Bsktbl; Im Ftbl; Im Socr; Im Vllybl; High Hon Roll; Hon Roll; Clarion U Of PA; Accntng.

BATES, MATTHEW J; Mansfield JR-SR HS; Mansfield, PA; (S); 4-H; FFA; Ski Clb; VICA; JV Bsktbl; Capt Bowling; Capt Crs Cntry; Var Trk; 4-H Awd; Hon Roll; FFA Grnhnd Dgr 83; FFA Cnty Frmr Dgr 85; FFA Kystone Frmr Dgr 86.

BATH, MANRAJ; Warren Area HS; Warren, PA; (Y); Hosp Aide; Letterman Clb; Temple Yth Grp; Varsity Clb; Chorus; Nwsp Phtg; Nwsp Rptr; Yrbk Phtg; Pres Soph Cls; Pres Jr Cls; Gannon U; Med.

BATRLA, PAMELA; Aliquippa HS; Aliquippa, PA; (S); French Clb; Pom Pon; Hon Roll; U Of Pittsburgh; Pediatrcn.

BATRUS, CAREY; Conemaugh Twp Area HS; Johnstown, PA; (Y); Art Clb; Church Yth Grp; Band; Concert Band; Mrchg Band; School Musical; Rep Stu Cncl; Nrsg.

BATSHON, BRIGITTE S; Valley HS; New Kensington, PA; (Y); AFS; Key Clb; Band; Concert Band; Mrchg Band; High Hon Roll; Hon Roll; NHS; Prfct Atten Awd; Penn ST; Pre Med.

BATT, LISA; Otto-Eldred JR-SR HS; Eldred, PA; (Y); Drama Clb; Pep Clb; Concert Band; Drm Mjr(t); Mrchg Band; Yrbk Rptr; Yrbk Stf; Stat Trk; NHS; Lock Haven U; Psych.

BATTAGLINI, DANEEN; Brownsville Area HS; Republic, PA; (Y); FBLA; Rep Jr Cls; USBE Assn 84 & 86; Acctg.

BATTELLI, LORI; West Mifflin Area HS; W Mifflin, PA; (Y); 65/330; Church Yth Grp; Cmnty Wkr; Exploring; Girl Scts; Hosp Aide; Science Clb; Ski Clb; Nwsp Stf; Vllybl; Hon Roll; Vet Sci I, Sci II 85; Gov Schl 86; U VA; Med.

BATTEN, STEVE; Purchase Line SR HS; Glen Campbell, PA; (Y); Letterman Clb; Spanish Clb; Varsity Clb; Nwsp Stf; Var Bsbl; Var Ftbl; Var Trk; Var Wt Lftg; Hon Roll; IN U PA.

BATTERSON, SEAN; Coudersport HS; Coudersport, PA; (Y); French Clb; FFA; Ski Clb; Varsity Clb; Trk; Wrstlng.

BATTISTA, AMY; Shenango HS; New Castle, PA; (Y); French Clb; Office Aide; Yrbk Stf; Var Capt Cheerleading; Var Gym; Hon Roll; Jr NHS; NHS; Bio.

BATTISTA, BARBARA; Cardinal O Hara HS; Clifton Hts, PA; (Y); Church Yth Grp; Cmnty Wkr; GAA; Hosp Aide; Office Aide; Teachers Aide; Prfct Atten Awd; West Chester; Crmnl Jstc.

BATTLE, CASSANDRA; Roxborough HS; Philadelphia, PA; (Y); 77/328; Church Yth Grp; Cmnty Wkr; Dance Clb; Hosp Aide; SADD; Church Choir; Yrbk Phtg; Stu Cncl; Library Aide; Red Cross Aide; Med.

BATTLES, MACHAEL; Quigley HS; Aliquippa, PA; (S); 13/112; Chess Clb; JA; Math Clb; Math Tm; Chorus; Swing Chorus; Nwsp Rptr; Nwsp Stf; High Hon Roll; Hon Roll; Hnr Schlrshp To Robert Morris Coll 86; Acad Schlrshp To St Vincent Coll 86; Robert Morris Coll; Bus Info Sy.

BATURIN, MADELAINE; Susquehanna Township HS; Harrisburg, PA; (Y); 16/167; AFS; Cmnty Wkr; Drama Clb; Exploring; VP Temple Yth Grp; Nwsp Rptr; Ed Yrbk Stf; Tennis; Cit Awd; Hon Roll; Grad W/ Distngshd Schlrs 85-86; Amer Lgn Wmns Acadmc Essy Contst 1st/2nd 84-86; Spnsh Stu Of Yr 84-85; Dickinson Coll; Law.

BATZ, MICHAEL; Annville-Cleona HS; Annville, PA; (Y); Church Yth Grp; Math Tm; Mgr Bsbl; JV Bsktbl; JV Crs Cntry; Var Mgr(s); Rest Ownr.

BATZ, ROBERT; Hopewell SR HS; Aliquippa, PA; (Y); 2/260; Math Tm; Spanish Clb; Var L Golf; Bausch & Lomb Sci Awd; High Hon Roll; Lion Awd; NHS; Ntl Merit Ltr; Sal; Mrshl Hahn Engrng Schlrshp 86; Virginia Tech; Elec Engrng.

BAUDER, ALEX D; Franklin HS; Franklin, PA; (Y); 25/249; German Clb; Varsity Clb; Wrstlng; Hon Roll; NHS; Ntl Merit SF; Nuclear Engrng.

BAUDUIN, RACHEL; Avella Area JR SR HS; Avella, PA; (Y); Art Clb; Church Yth Grp; French Clb; Ski Clb; Band; Concert Band; Mrchg Band; Yrbk Stf; Twrlr; Hon Roll.

BAUER, CHRISTIAN; St Marys Area HS; St Marys, PA; (Y); L Ftbl; L Trk; Hon Roll; Dist 9 AAA Chmp 200 M Dash & 4 X 100 M Rely 86; Schl Rcrd Hldr 100 M Dash & 4 X 100 M Rely 86; Penn ST; Comp Sci.

BAUER, JIM; Cathedral Prep; Erie, PA; (Y); 150/260; Church Yth Grp; German Clb; Math Clb; Science Clb; Varsity Clb; Bsbl; Bsktbl; Cheerleading; Ftbl; Mgr(s); Slippery Rock U; Bus.

BAUER, KELLY; North Clarion HS; Lucinda, PA; (Y); 3/90; Drama Clb; French Clb; Trs SADD; VP Stu Cncl; Bsktbl; Cheerleading; Hon Roll; NHS; Library Aide; School Play; PA Governors Arts Schl Schlrshp 85; Schlrshp PA Free Entprs Wk 86.

BAUER, PATRICK; Elk County Christian HS; St Marys, PA; (Y); 16/88; Boys Clb Am; Boy Scts; JV Bsktbl; JV Ftbl; High Hon Roll; Mrn Bio.

BAUER, PAUL; Elk County Christiam HS; St Marys, PA; (Y); Boy Scts; Var L Bsktbl; L Var Ftbl; Var L Trk; High Hon Roll; Hon Roll; Coaches Awd In Bsktbl 85-86; Bill Gapinski Awd In Ftbl 85-86; Gannon U.

BAUER, ROGER; Elk County Christian HS; St Marys, PA; (S); Boy Scts; Letterman Clb; Rep Soph Cls; VP Ftbl; VP Trk; Hon Roll; C D Of A Essay Cont 2nd Pl Dist; IVP; Sfty Sci.

BAUER, RUTH; Northampton Area SR HS; Northampton, PA; (Y); Church Yth Grp; Chorus; Rep Frsh Cls; Hon Roll; Activity Ltr 83-84; Northampton Area CC; Photo.

BAUGHMAN, DAVID; Moshannon Valley HS; Houtzdale, PA; (Y); 19/120; Aud/Vis; Boy Scts; Varsity Clb; VP Soph Cls; Pres Jr Cls; Trs Sr Cls; Stu Cncl; JV Var Ftbl; Socr; Hon Roll; PA ST; Engrng.

BAUGHMAN, JENNIFER J; Canon Mc Millian HS; Eight Four, PA; (Y); 11/350; French Clb; Office Aide; Ski Clb; Varsity Clb; Nwsp Stf; Yrbk Ed-Chief; Stu Cncl; Capt Sftbl; High Hon Roll; Keystone ST Games Sftbl 85; Temple U; Finance.

BAUGHMAN, JON S; Upper Dubyn HS; Ft Washington, PA; (Y); 1/345; VP Computer Clb; Pres Capt Math Tm; Church Choir; Pres Mrchg Band; School Musical; NCTE Awd; Ntl Merit SF; Boy Scts; Church Yth Grp; Office Aide; Natl Creatv Wrtng Schltc Awd 84; Chrs Hnrbl Ment 84-85; Dist & Rgnl Bnd 84-85; Princeton U; Elec Engr.

BAUGHMAN, LISA; Franklin Regional HS; Export, PA; (Y); Trs Church Yth Grp; Mgr JA; Band; Concert Band; Var L Sftbl; Var L Tennis; High Hon Roll; NHS; Westinghouse Schlrshp Wmn In Sci & Engrng Carnegie Mellon U 85; Math.

BAUGHMAN, STEVEN; Upper Dubun HS; Ft Washington, PA; (Y); 1/350; Pres Capt Math Tm; Church Choir; Pres Mrchg Band; NCTE Awd; Ntl Merit Schol; Pres Schlr; Val; Boy Scts; Church Yth Grp; VP Computer Clb; Fnlst ISEF 83-84; Westinghouse Tlnt Srch Hnr Grp Wnnr, Ntl Soc Prof Engrs Schlrshp 86; Princeton U; Elec Engrng.

BAUM, JOY ILENE; Big Spring HS; Carlisle, PA; (Y); 4/211; Rep Chorus; Church Choir; School Musical; School Play; Rep Stu Cncl; JV Var Cheerleading; Elks Awd; Lion Awd; NHS; Pres Schlr; SICO Schlrshp 86; Carlisle Exch Clb Yth Of Yr 86; R T & R R Wolfram Vly Times-Star Engl Awd 86; Shippensburg U; Elem Educ.

BAUM, TERRIE; Greater Latrobe SR HS; Latrobe, PA; (Y); Band; Concert Band; Mrchg Band; Symp Band; Mgr(s); Score Keeper; Timer; Awd For Mssng 1 Day Or Less Thru Out Yr 82-83; Awd Asstg Ofc Durng Schl & Summr Days 82-84; Secy.

BAUM-TILLMAN, KELLY ANN; Greater Latrobe HS; Greensburg, PA; (Y); Church Yth Grp; Hosp Aide; JCL; Ski Clb; Teachers Aide; High Hon Roll; Hon Roll; U Pittsburgh; Nrsng.

BAUMAN, CINDY; Christopher Dock Mennonite HS; Souderton, PA; (Y); Pres Church Yth Grp; Pres 4-H; Concert Band; Jazz Band; Orch; School Play; 4-H Awd; Hon Roll; Prfct Atten Awd; Spcl Ed.

BAUMAN, JOHN; Pittston Area HS; Duryea, PA; (Y); 50/330; Computer Clb; French Clb; Key Clb; Math Clb; Science Clb; Chorus; Var L Bsbl; Im Bsktbl; Var L Ftbl; NEDT Awd; PA Higher Educ Cert For SAT 85; Duguesene Schlrshp 86; Kings Clg; Math.

BAUMAN, MIC; Columbia/Montour A V T S HS; Catawissa, PA; (Y); Aud/Vis; Math Tm; Science Clb; Teachers Aide; VICA; Band; Concert Band; Drm & Bgl; Var Bsktbl; Hon Roll; Natl Sci Olympd Brnz 86; Penn ST U; Astrnmy.

BAUMANN, L KIRK; Kennedy Christian HS; Hermitage, PA; (Y); 20/98; Civic Clb; Ski Clb; Spanish Clb; Var Golf; High Hon Roll; Hon Roll; Engrg.

BAUMBACH, ANGELA; Conestoga Valley HS; Leola, PA; (Y); Church Yth Grp; Cmnty Wkr; Dance Clb; Girl Scts; Hosp Aide; Service Clb; Flag Corp; Stat Bsktbl; JV Var Cheerleading; Hon Roll; Med.

BAUMGARDNER, SHERRI; Forest Hills HS; South Fork, PA; (Y); 26/156; Pep Clb; Ski Clb; Y-Teens; Cheerleading; Trk; Hon Roll; Jr NHS; 8th Pl Ntl Chrldng Cmptn 84.

BAUMGARTEN, GAYLE; Philadelphia HS For Girls; Philadelphia, PA; (Y); 31/395; Teachers Aide; Temple Yth Grp; Nwsp Stf; Rep Stu Cncl; Spanish NHS; Law.

BAUMUNK, CARLA; Sullivan County HS; Forksville, PA; (Y); 4-H; Key Clb; Band; Chorus; Concert Band; Jazz Band; Var L Vllybl; Hon Roll; NHS; High Hon Roll; SPEC Ed.

BAUS, LISA; Emmaus HS; Emmaus, PA; (Y); German Clb; Library Aide; Chorus; School Musical; Hon Roll; Jr NHS; Bus Mngmnt.

BAUTTI, DENINA; Quigley HS; Midland, PA; (S); 9/107; Math Clb; Yrbk Stf; Cheerleading; Powder Puff Ftbl; High Hon Roll; NHS; Fr I Awd 83; Fr III Awd 85; Pres Hnr Awd Scholar 86; John Carroll U; Math.

BAUTTI, JOANN; Quigley HS; Midland, PA; (S); 13/110; Pres Girl Scts; Yrbk Rptr; Yrbk Stf; Var Powder Puff Ftbl; L Var Tennis; High Hon Roll; Hstry Awd 83; Grl Sct Awd 83-84; Fshn Mrchndsng.

BAUTZ, AMY; Mon Valley Catholic HS; New Eagle, PA; (Y); Church Yth Grp; Cmnty Wkr; JA; Ed Yrbk Stf; Stat Bsktbl; Score Keeper; Stat Sftbl; Sec French Hon Soc; 1st Jr Cls Art Cntst 85-86; Duquesne U; Educ.

BAXENDELL, JANICE; Carrick HS; Pittsburgh, PA; (S); Math Tm; Office Aide; Q&S; Color Guard; Mrchg Band; Stage Crew; Yrbk Stf; Stu Cncl; High Hon Roll; Hon Roll.

BAXTER, BRENT; Danville HS; Danville, PA; (Y); Church Yth Grp; Computer Clb; Key Clb; Spanish Clb; Band; Ftbl; Hon Roll; Schlrshp PA Free Entrprs Wk 85; Acctg.

BAXTER, JASON; Carlisle SR HS; Carlisle, PA; (Y); Boy Scts; Drama Clb; Letterman Clb; Office Aide; Ftbl; Socr; Tennis; Hon Roll.

BAXTER, KARIN; Harrisburg Acad; Harrisburg, PA; (Y); 4/36; Church Yth Grp; Office Aide; Ski Clb; School Play; Trs Soph Cls; VP Jr Cls; JV Cheerleading; Var Fld Hcky; Var Mgr(s); Var Score Keeper; Amer Coll Music 80-85; Colgate U; Psych.

BAXTER, KERRY; Greater Johnstown HS; Johnstown, PA; (Y); Sec Church Yth Grp; Hosp Aide; Spanish Clb; Chorus; School Musical; Variety Show; Hon Roll.

BAXTER, STEPHANIE L; Monongahela Valley Catholic HS; Monongahela, PA; (S); 12/107; School Play; Stage Crew; Yrbk Stf; Stat Bsktbl; French Hon Soc; CA U Of PA; CPA.

BAYER, JENNIFER; Montour HS; Mckees Rocks, PA; (Y); French Clb; Pres Frsh Cls; Rep Soph Cls; Pres Jr Cls; Rep Stu Cncl; JV Var Cheerleading; Powder Puff Ftbl; Hon Roll; Exploring; Office Aide; Acad Frnch IV Achvt Awd 86; Engl Lit.

BAYER, MICHELE; Cardinal O Hara HS; Drexel Hill, PA; (Y); Pres Church Yth Grp; Cmnty Wkr; Service Clb; Spanish Clb; Nwsp Stf; Prfct Atten Awd; Elem Educ.

BAYLEY, ELIZABETH; Bishop Hoban HS; Mountain Top, PA; (Y); 16/196; FBLA; Latin Clb; Mgr Stage Crew; High Hon Roll; Hon Roll; NHS; NEDT Awd; Highest Religion 83-84; Bloomsburg U; :Spec Educ.

BAYLISS, TODD; Wilson HS; W Lawn, PA; (Y); 68/286; Boy Scts; Church Yth Grp; German Clb; Ski Clb; JV L Bsbl; Im Bsktbl; JV L Bowling; Var L Crs Cntry; JV L Ftbl; Var L Trk; Star Sct 85; VA Tech; Arch.

BAYLOR, ROBYN LORRAINE; Archbishop John Carroll Girls HS; Philadelphia, PA; (Y); 91/216; Church Yth Grp; Library Aide; Thesps; School Musical; School Play; Variety Show; Nwsp Rptr; Lit Mag; Min Ofcrs Clb Awd 85 & 86; Cnslr Aides Awd 86; Soc Justice Action Corp 86; Temple U; Communications.

BAYLY, AMY; West Allegheny HS; Imperial, PA; (Y); 8/208; Spanish Clb; Rep Frsh Cls; Stu Cncl; Crs Cntry; Swmmng; Dnfth Awd; High Hon Roll; NHS; Pres Schlr; Rotary Awd; U PA; Law.

BAYNARD, DION; Pine Forge Acad; Pine Forge, PA; (Y); Ski Clb; JV Bsktbl.

BAYNARD JR, RAYMOND; Pine Forge Acad; Pine Forge, PA; (Y); 1/53; Ski Clb; Chorus; Pres Frsh Cls; Trs Jr Cls; Trs Stu Cncl; Var Bsktbl; Bausch & Lomb Sci Awd; NHS; Val; Oakwood Coll; Accntng.

BAYNES, JOYA Z; Central SR HS; York, PA; (Y); Boy Scts; Church Yth Grp; JA; Church Choir; VP Frsh Cls; Var Trk; Hon Roll; Air Force; Pre Law.

BAYZICK, JOHN; West Hazelton HS; W Hazelton, PA; (Y); 20/244; Church Yth Grp; Letterman Clb; Scholastic Bowl; Varsity Clb; Rep Stu Cncl; Var L Bsbl; Var L Bsktbl; High Hon Roll; VFW Awd; Acad Sci 84; Civil Engr.

BAZALA, STEPHANIE; Marion Center HS; Ernest, PA; (Y); Trs Church Yth Grp; FBLA; Trs FHA; Church Choir; Color Guard; Flag Corp; High Hon Roll; Hon Roll; Bus.

BDYH, MELISSA; West York Area HS; York, PA; (Y); 13/209; Church Yth Grp; French Clb; Band; Chorus; Church Choir; Concert Band; Madrigals; Mrchg Band; Pep Band; School Play; Dist Chrs, Mod Music Masters 84-86; Shiloh Lioness Clb Scholar 86; PA Ambass Music Europe 86; Harcum JC; Anim Tech.

BEACH, JOHN; Franklin HS; Polk, PA; (Y); 2/270; Church Yth Grp; Spanish Clb; Varsity Clb; Band; Concert Band; Yrbk Stf; Var Capt Ftbl; Wt Lftg; High Hon Roll; NHS; PA ST U; Med.

BEACH, JOHN; Troy SR HS; Granville Summit, PA; (S); 40/144; FFA; Degree Keystone Farmer 86; Degree Star Chptr Farmer 86; 1st Clssmn Agri Currclm Grad 86; USAF; Biomed.

BEACHEL, CANDY; Danville SR HS; Milton, PA; (Y); Church Yth Grp; FBLA; FHA; Trs SADD; Chorus; Secrtry.

BEACHELL, BETH; Northern Lebanon HS; Grantville, PA; (Y); 5/179; Model UN; Sec Pres Service Clb; School Play; Ed Nwsp Ed-Chief; Rep Sec Jr Cls; Pres Stu Cncl; Var L Fld Hcky; Var L Trk; High Hon Roll; NHS; Demographics.

BEACHELL, JEFFRY; Susquehanna Township HS; Harrisburg, PA; (Y); 26/154; Band; Concert Band; Jazz Band; Mrchg Band; Orch; Pep Band; Hon Roll; NHS; Music Educ.

BEACHELL, REBECCA L; Mountain View Christian Schl; Hummelstown, PA; (S); Church Yth Grp; Chorus; Church Choir; Nwsp Stf; Yrbk Stf; Hon Roll; Provrbs 31 Awd-Grls Chrstn Chractr Awd 84-85; 1st Pl Art Cntst-Keystone Chrstn Ed Assn Rgnl 84-85; Bob Jones U; Sectrl Stud.

BEACHEM, KELLY; Lincoln HS; Ellwood, PA; (Y); Sec Camera Clb; Key Clb; Y-Teens; Chorus; Powder Puff Ftbl; Hon Roll; Bus.

BEACHY, DEBRA; Mountain View Christian Schl; Meyersdale, PA; (S); 2/9; Church Yth Grp; Hon Roll; Sal; Sec.

BEACHY, OWEN; Rockwood Area HS; Fort Hill, PA; (S); 6/91; Chess Clb; High Hon Roll; Hon Roll; NHS; Pres Phys Ftnss Awd 84-85; Chem Awd 84-85; Johnstwn Invtnl Chess Trnmnt 2nd Pl 81-82; U Of Pittsburgh; Cvl Engrng.

BEADLE, MELISSA; Minersville Area HS; Minersville, PA; (Y); Spanish Clb; School Musical; Stage Crew; Variety Show; Var Crs Cntry; Mgr(s); Hon Roll; Med Tech.

BEAGLE, BRIAN; Linesville HS; Linesville, PA; (Y); 15/87; German Clb; Ski Clb; Yrbk Phtg; Yrbk Rptr; Yrbk Stf; Ftbl; Gym; Wt Lftg; Hon Roll; Boy Scts; Proj Enhance Giftd Pgm; Comp Engr.

BEAHM, JOSEPH; Salisbury HS; Allentown, PA; (Y); 12/138; Exploring; Trs JA; Concert Band; Mrchg Band; JV Socr; Trk; High Hon Roll; Hon Roll.

BEAKEN, STACY; Greater Latrobe SR HS; Latrobe, PA; (Y); Church Yth Grp; Hosp Aide; JA; Teachers Aide; Chorus; Concert Band; Lib Chorus; Concert Band; School Musical; Mat Maids; Choir Ltr 85-86; Sls Clb JR Achvt 84-86; Bus.

BEAL, VIRGINIA L; Biglerville HS; Biglerville, PA; (Y); Camera Clb; Girl Scts; Varsity Clb; Yrbk Phtg; Yrbk Stf; Rep Sr Cls; Stat Bsktbl; Var Capt Fld Hcky; Mgr(s); Trk; MIP Hockey 83-84; PA ST Police Acad.

BEALE, BELINDA MYRA; Downingtown SR HS; Downingtown, PA; (Y); Church Yth Grp; Exploring; Girl Scts; Hosp Aide; Library Aide; SADD; Band; Chorus; Church Choir; Color Guard; Vrsty Lttrs Choir-85, Band-85 & Trck-84; 4 Yr Awd Bar Gld Band 86; 300, 100, 400, 600 Hr Awds Cndystrp; Liberty Baptist U; Erly Elem Ed.

BEALLA, LISA A; Dallas SR HS; Dallas, PA; (Y); 32/217; Key Clb; Chorus; Flag Corp; Rep Stu Cncl; Hon Roll; Ntl Merit Ltr; NEDT Awd; U Scranton; Pre-Med.

BEALS, KRIS; Seneca HS; Waterford, PA; (Y); 5/163; Hosp Aide; Quiz Bowl; Drill Tm; Mrchg Band; School Musical; School Play; Nwsp Rptr; JV Trk; Hon Roll; NHS; Cub Reprtr Awd; Natl Merit Commnded Schlr; Bio.

BEAM, CHERYL; Ambridge Area HS; Ambridge, PA; (Y); 15/265; Sec Trs Church Yth Grp; Pep Clb; Spanish Clb; Drill Tm; Off Soph Cls; Off Jr Cls; Off Sr Cls; High Hon Roll; Hon Roll; NHS; Ambridge Bus & Prof Wmns Clb Grl Mnth 86; Ambridge Wmns Clb Scholar 86; Robert Morris Coll; Word Proc.

BEAM, CHRISTINE LYNN; Twin Valley HS; Morgantown, PA; (Y); 8/162; Am Leg Aux Girls St; German Clb; SADD; Varsity Clb; Drill Tm; School Play; Var Bsktbl; Var Capt Sftbl; High Hon Roll; NHS; Phrmcy.

BEAM, DENNIS; Hazleton SR HS; Hazleton, PA; (Y); Art Clb; Aud/Vis; Church Yth Grp; Cmnty Wkr; Yrbk Stf; Var Bsbl; JV Bsktbl; Frgn Lang Awd Latn; U S Achvt Acad 85-86.

BEAM, JESSE; Newport HS; Liverpool, PA; (S); 6/97; Chess Clb; Stu Cncl; Hon Roll; NHS; Prfct Atten Awd; Crrnt Evnts Qz Awd; Cvl Engrng.

BEAMENDERFER, CHRIS; Lampeter Strasburg HS; Lancaster, PA; (Y); 29/162; Boy Scts; Var Bsbl; Var Ftbl; Wt Lftg; PA ST; Gnrl Engnrng.

BEAMER, AMY; Newport HS; Newport, PA; (Y); 4/101; Am Leg Aux Girls St; Concert Band; Pres Mrchg Band; School Musical; School Play; Yrbk Bus Mgr; Pres Stu Cncl; JP Sousa Awd; Pres NHS; Rotary Awd; Hugh O Brien Ldrshp Awd 84; Amer Can Co Schlrshp 86; Elizabethtown Coll; Bus Admin.

BEAMER, MICHAEL; Freedom HS; Bethlehem, PA; (Y); 25/445; JV Ftbl; Wt Lftg; Hon Roll; NHS; Acdmc Lttrmn Sweater 84; Peace Corps.

BEAMER, ROBIN; Hempfield Area SR HS; Bovard, PA; (Y); Sec Trs Church Yth Grp; Pres Library Aide; Spanish Clb; Band; Church Choir; Mrchg Band; Orch; Symp Band; High Hon Roll; Jr NHS; Milligan Coll; Psychlgst.

BEAN, AMY; Forest City Regional HS; Pleasant Mount, PA; (Y); Spanish Clb; Trs Band; Concert Band; Mrchg Band; Nwsp Rptr; Nwsp Stf; Co-Capt Vllybl; Military; Surgcl Tech.

BEAN, MATTHEW; Saveon Valley HS; Bethlehem, PA; (Y); 30/130; Church Yth Grp; Band; Chorus; Concert Band; Jazz Band; Mrchg Band; Orch; School Musical; School Play; Variety Show; Music Ed.

BEAN, RONALD; Lasalle College HS; Lansdale, PA; (Y); 37/240; Boys Clb Am; Church Yth Grp; Letterman Clb; Varsity Clb; Rep Soph Cls; Var L Trk; High Hon Roll; NEDT Awd; Cathloic Trck 86; PA Rly Mile Rly Chmpns 86; Acad Schlrshp Grnt U Of Miami 86; William & Mary Coll; Mrktng.

BEANS, DEBORAH; Warwick HS; Lititz, PA; (Y); 53/200; Varsity Clb; JV Bsktbl; Var Fld Hcky; High Hon Roll; Hon Roll; Accntng.

BEAR, CATHY; State College SR HS; Boalsburg, PA; (Y); 24/568; Spanish Clb; SADD; Hon Roll; Englsh Achvmnt Awd 86; PA ST U; Secndry Educ.

BEAR, JULIE; Boiling Springs HS; Boiling Spgs, PA; (Y); 10/115; Cmnty Wkr; Drama Clb; Political Wkr; Quiz Bowl; Red Cross Aide; Band; Flag Corp; School Play; Twrlr; Hon Roll; Schlstc Wrtng Awd 85.

BEARD, CHRISTOPHER; Palmyra Area HS; Palmyra, PA; (Y); Church Yth Grp; German Clb; Acpl Chr; Chorus; Var Bsktbl; Var Crs Cntry; Hon Roll.

BEARD, RONALD; Cowanesque Valley HS; Knoxville, PA; (S); 5/90; Boy Scts; Trs Letterman Clb; Trs Ski Clb; Band; Pres Jr Cls; L Ftbl; L Trk; High Hon Roll; NHS; Engrng.

BEARD, STEPHEN K; Milton SR HS; Milton, PA; (Y); 12/226; JV Crs Cntry; Trk; Ntl Merit SF; Pres Schlr; VFW Awd; Voice Dem Awd; Chess Clb; Computer Clb; Hghst PSAT & SAT-SCHL Dist 86; Schltc & Athltc Citatn-PA House Of Reps 86; PA ST U; Aerosp Engr.

BEARINGER, JANE P; Conestoga SR HS; Berwyn, PA; (Y); 33/408; Church Yth Grp; Hosp Aide; Leo Clb; Rep Sr Cls; Stu Cncl; Var Tennis; Hon Roll; JC Awd; NHS; Trinity Coll.

BEARY, JEAN; Keystone HS; Shippenville, PA; (Y); Hosp Aide; Varsity Clb; Band; Drm Mjr(t); Nwsp Stf; Yrbk Stf; Var L Cheerleading; NHS; Arion Awd Band 86; Hist Days Local & Dist 82-85; U Of Pittsburgh; Pharmacy.

BEARY, TINA; North Clarion JR SR HS; Marble, PA; (Y); 9/100; French Clb; Mrchg Band; Im Var Cheerleading; Mgr(s); Stat Vllybl; High Hon Roll; Hon Roll; :Exec Secy.

BEASLEY, LESLIE; Pennsbury HS; Fairless Hills, PA; (Y); Dance Clb; Drama Clb; French Clb; School Play; Stage Crew; Hon Roll; Psych.

BEASTON, ANGIE; Big Spring HS; Newville, PA; (Y); Pres 4-H; Pep Clb; School Musical; School Play; Rep Stu Cncl; JV Var Cheerleading; Powder Puff Ftbl; Trk; Hon Roll; Stu Of Month 85; Beaver Coll; Psychlgy.

BEATTY, ANGIE; Jamestown HS; Jamestown, PA; (Y); VICA; Spanish Clb; Chorus; Flag Corp; Capt Twrlr; Pres Phys Ftnss Awd 84; Commnd Perfrmnc Ldrshp 86; Csmtlgy.

BEATTY, CHRIS; West Middlesex HS; W Middlesex, PA; (S); 4/125; Church Yth Grp; Bsbl; Bsktbl; Ftbl; High Hon Roll; Hon Roll; Jr NHS; Spanish NHS; Natl Sci Acad Awd 82-84; Physcs.

BEATTY, DAVID; Vincentian HS; Allison Park, PA; (Y); Aud/Vis; Drama Clb; Office Aide; Service Clb; SADD; School Play; Yrbk Phtg; Stu Cncl; Hon Roll; Ntl Merit Ltr; Comp Anlyst.

BEATTY, DAWN; Hopewell Area SR HS; Aliquippa, PA; (Y); 22/295; Church Yth Grp; Exploring; French Clb; JA; Latin Clb; Yrbk Stf; High Hon Roll; NHS; Cptl U Rgnts & Bvr Co Cncl PTA Schlrshps 86; Capital U; Bio.

BEATTY, DEBBIE; Greater Latrobe SR HS; Latrobe, PA; (Y); 1/409; Church Yth Grp; Chorus; Church Choir; High Hon Roll; NHS; Physcn Asstnt.

BEATTY, LISA; Punxsutawny Area HS; Punxsutawney, PA; (Y); 6/238; Hosp Aide; Math Tm; Science Clb; Color Guard; Concert Band; Jazz Band; Mrchg Band; Variety Show; High Hon Roll; NHS; IN U PA; Nrsg.

BEATTY, MATT; Grove City Area HS; Grove City, PA; (Y); 11/195; Thesps; Pres Chorus; Concert Band; Mrchg Band; Pep Band; School Play; Stage Crew; Swing Chorus; High Hon Roll; NHS; PMEA Hnrs Dstrct & Rgnl In Choirs 84-86; Snd Of Amer Hnr Chorus 85; Msc.

BEATTY, TODD; Lincoln HS; Ellwood City, PA; (Y); 76/162; Art Clb; Key Clb; Band; Drm & Bgl; Jazz Band; Mrchg Band; Hon Roll; Key Clb ST Ofc-Lt Govnr 86-87; Ushers Clb 84-86; Dist Bnd 86.

BEAUCHAMP, MARIA; Saint Pius X HS; Gilbertsville, PA; (S); 12/139; VP JA; Office Aide; Service Clb; School Musical; Ed Yrbk Stf; Stat L Trk; High Hon Roll; NHS; Regnl & Natl JC Conf 85; Elem Ed.

BEAUMONT, GREGG; West Allegheny SR HS; Oakdale, PA; (Y); Pres Band; Chorus; Pres Concert Band; Jazz Band; Pres Mrchg Band; Pep Band; High Hon Roll; Hon Roll; Mech Engrng.

BEAUMONT, PENNI; Marple-Newtown HS; Broomall, PA; (Y); Church Yth Grp; Capt Co-Capt Debate Tm; Girl Scts; L Trk; Hon Roll; Jr NHS; Dist Hist Dy Fnlst 84; Grl Sct Trp Jamboree England 85; Schl Prtcpt Trip Peoples Rep China 86; Intl Affrs.

BEAVEN, RACHEL; Wilmington Area HS; New Wilmington, PA; (Y); Church Yth Grp; Drama Clb; French Clb; Concert Band; Drill Tm; Flag Corp; Pep Band; School Play; Stage Crew; Nwsp Stf; Penn ST; Writing.

BEAVER, JAMIE; Juniata HS; Mifflintown, PA; (Y); 4/150; Band; Chorus; School Musical; Yrbk Phtg; Hst Jr Cls; Var Capt Bsktbl; Var Capt Fld Hcky; L Tennis; High Hon Roll; NHS; Bd Of Gonvrs Schlrshp 86; SR Wrtg Awd 86; Outstndng Athlt Awd 86; Millersville U; Eng Ed.

BEAVER, LAURA; Waynesboro Area SR HS; Waynesboro, PA; (Y); 32/363; Ski Clb; Rep Stu Cncl; Trk; Hon Roll; NHS.

BEAVER, MELISSA; Milton SR HS; Milton, PA; (Y); 23/200; Hosp Aide; Spanish Clb; Color Guard; Mrchg Band; Nwsp Rptr; Nwsp Stf; Powder Puff Ftbl; Cntral PA Bus Schl; Dsptchr.

BEAVER, WENDY; Wilson Area HS; Easton, PA; (S); 5/150; Drama Clb; Model UN; Scholastic Bowl; Chorus; School Play; Mgr(s); High Hon Roll; Jr NHS; NHS; Voice Lssns 85.

BEAVERS, DEBORAH; Upper Moreland HS; Hatboro, PA; (Y); 68/260; Library Aide; Hon Roll; Sec.

BEAZLEY, EDWARD V; York Catholic HS; York, PA; (Y); 2/140; German Clb; JV Crs Cntry; Var Trk; High Hon Roll; NHS; Ntl Merit SF; Northwestern U; Chem.

BEBENEK, FRANCINE; Lourdes Regional HS; Shamokin, PA; (Y); Drama Clb; PAVAS; Mrchg Band; School Play; Coach Actv; Twrlr; Cert Of Merit Svc To Lourdes Band 85; Apprctn Awd-Hlpng Undrprvlgd 85; Awd For Outstndng Prfrmnc 85; Crmnl Justice.

BEBEY, WENDY; Lake-Lehman HS; Dallas, PA; (S); 29/140; Pres Key Clb; Ski Clb; SADD; School Play; Trs Frsh Cls; Rep Jr Cls; Rep Stu Cncl; JV Bsktbl; Var Fld Hcky; L Sftbl; Wy Vly Yth Ldrshp Salute 86.

BEBKO, ANTHONY; Cathmedral Prep; Erie, PA; (Y); 18/221; Church Yth Grp; French Clb; Band; Concert Band; Mrchg Band; High Hon Roll; Hmcmng Cmmttee; Frgn Lang Comptn 3rd Pl Frnch; Med.

BEBKO, RENEE; Tech Memorial HS; Erie, PA; (Y); 10/349; CAP; Girl Scts; Hosp Aide; Rep Frsh Cls; Trk; Hon Roll; NHS; Ldrshp Awd 86; Nrsng.

BEBOUT, ROB; Trinity HS; Washington, PA; (Y); Chorus; Stage Crew; Penn ST; Naval Pilot.

BECA, MELISSA; Center HS; Monaca, PA; (Y); Spanish Clb; Sec Band; Concert Band; Jazz Band; Mrchg Band; School Musical; Symp Band; Rep Stu Cncl; Hon Roll; Bradford Business Schl; Exe Sec.

BECCARIA, KRISTIN; Upper Dublin HS; Dresher, PA; (Y); Pep Clb; Varsity Clb; JV Fld Hcky; JV Var Lcrss; JV Var Mgr(s); Im Powder Puff Ftbl; JV Var Score Keeper; Swmmng; JV Var Timer; Hon Roll; John E Buckley Mem Awd 86; Persnnl Mgmt.

BECHT, JENNIFER; Lewistown Area HS; Lewistown, PA; (Y); 29/260; Church Yth Grp; Sec French Clb; Varsity Clb; Nwsp Stf; Stu Cncl; Var Capt Crs Cntry; Var Capt Trk; High Hon Roll; Shippensburg U; Cmmnctns.

BECHTEL, KATHY; Spring Grove SR HS; Hanover, PA; (Y); 61/285; Band; Concert Band; Mrchg Band; Orch; School Musical; Var L Cheerleading; Hon Roll; 100 & 200 Pt Schlstc Achvmnt Awds 84-85.

BECK, BERNARD; Father Judge HS; Philadelphia, PA; (Y); 90/408; Church Yth Grp; Computer Clb; Office Aide; Im Bsktbl; Im Bowling; Hon Roll; Grant Holy Fmly Clg 86; St Champshp Cyo JR SR Bsktbl In Pittsburgh 86; Holy Fmly Clg; Food Mrktng.

BECK, CHERYL L; North Hills HS; Pittsburgh, PA; (Y); 197/524; Church Yth Grp; Cmnty Wkr; VP JA; Key Clb; Library Aide; Thesps; Chorus; School Musical; School Play; Yrbk Phtg; OH ST U; Chrgrphy.

BECK, DAN; Linesville HS; Linesville, PA; (Y); Art Clb; Chess Clb; Church Yth Grp; Ski Clb; SADD; VICA; Band; Concert Band; Jazz Band; Mrchg Band; Cranford Cnty Area Vo-Tech Indstrl Elec 85-86; Indstrl Elec.

BECK, DOUGLAS; Liberty HS; Bethlehem, PA; (S); 145/417; Church Yth Grp; Mgr Nwsp Ed-Chief; Nwsp Rptr; Nwsp Stf; Crs Cntry; Crss Cntry Var Awd 83; John Hochella YMCA Bsktbl Awd 82; Morning Call Yth Run Top 15 Yr Old Frshr 83; Penn ST U; Jrnlsm.

BECK, DOUGLAS E; Fleetwood Area HS; Hamburg, PA; (Y); 1/101; Chess Clb; Church Yth Grp; 4-H; Library Aide; Math Tm; Capt Scholastic Bowl; Hon Roll; NHS; Ntl Merit SF; Aud/Vis; PA Govrs Schl For Sci 85; IU Smmr Enrchmnt Prgm 85; Berks Co Econ Sympsm 85; MIT; Engrng.

BECK, FLOYD; St Marys Area HS; Saint Marys, PA; (Y); Boys Clb Am; JA; Top Slsmn In JR Achvt 84-85.

BECK, JEFFREY F; La Salle College HS; Hatfield, PA; (Y); 14/240; Boy Scts; Jazz Band; School Musical; School Play; NHS; Ntl Merit Schol; Pres Schlr; Ski Clb; Band; Chorus; Tmpl U Outstndng Achvt Schlrshp; Bell Tlphn Dmnd ST Schlrshp; Nrth Penn Area Schlrshp; Allntwn Coll; Temple U; Music.

BECK, JOHN H; Loyalsock Township HS; Williamsport, PA; (Y); 1/122; Boys Clb Am; Latin Clb; Spanish Clb; Yrbk Phtg; Bausch & Lomb Sci Awd; DAR Awd; NHS; Val; Round Table Awds In Sci, Math, Eng, & Span 86; Soroptomist Yth Ctznshp Awd 1st Pl 86; PA ST U; Elect Engineering.

BECK, KAREN; Brandywine Heights HS; Topton, PA; (Y); Girl Scts; Hosp Aide; Band; Concert Band; Jazz Band; Mrchg Band; Pep Band; High Hon Roll; NHS; Physical Therapy.

BECK, KELLY; Mapletown HS; Garards Fort, PA; (Y); 10/75; Aud/Vis; FTA; GAA; Ski Clb; Varsity Clb; Chorus; Var L Bsktbl; Var L Sftbl; Hon Roll; NHS; Distngshd Athlt Awd Marine Corp & Army 86; CA U; Spch Pathology.

BECK, KRISTINE-MARIE; Spring Grove Area HS; Codorus, PA; (Y); 5/220; Sec Drama Clb; School Musical; Pres Soph Cls; Pres Jr Cls; Pres Stu Cncl; Var L Swmmng; DAR Awd; Pres NHS; HOB Foundtn Rep 84-86; Outstndng Stu Awd Schlrshp 86; Most Likely To Succd 86; Bucknell U; Educ.

BECK, LAURA; Belle Vernon Area HS; Belle Vernon, PA; (Y); Pep Clb; Hon Roll; NHS; CA U; Chld Dvlpmnt.

BECK, LORI; Hatboro-Horsham HS; Hatboro, PA; (Y); #2 In Class; Var JV Fld Hcky; Var JV Lcrss; High Hon Roll; Hon Roll; NHS; Sci Awd 84; Spnsh II Awd 85; Algbr II Awd Phase I 86; Nrsg.

BECK, MARTRESE; Cardinal Dougherty HS; Phila, PA; (Y); Girl Scts; Office Aide; Chorus; Drill Tm; Flag Corp; School Play; Gov Hon Prg Awd; Hon Roll; Jr NHS; NHS; Prfcncy Awds Religion, Engl, Trig/Compu 84-86; Acdmc Awds 85-86; Cert Of Athletic Accmpshmnt 83-85; La Salle U; Vet Med.

BECK, MICHELLE; York County Vocational Tech Schl; York, PA; (Y); 20/408; VICA; Hon Roll; AAHPERD Phy Ftnss Awd 85-86; York Coll Of PA; Secndry Educ.

BECK, PATRICIA ANN; Ambridge HS; Sewickley, PA; (Y); Church Yth Grp; German Clb; Girl Scts; Pep Clb; Red Cross Aide; Off Soph Cls; Off Jr Cls; High Hon Roll; Hon Roll; PA Free Entprs Wk 86; CPA.

BECK, SHARON; Harmony Area HS; Westover, PA; (Y); 2/44; Teachers Aide; Band; Concert Band; Mrchg Band; Nwsp Stf; Im Badmtn; Im Bsktbl; Im Bowling; Im Sftbl; Im Vllybl; Pdtrc Nrsng.

BECK, SHERRY LYNN; Harmond HS; La Jose, PA; (Y); 4/45; Band; Chorus; Yrbk Rptr; Sec VP Stu Cncl; Cit Awd; Dnfth Awd; High Hon Roll; Kiwanis Awd; Chrldng 84; Lewie Green Schlrshp 4-H 86; C Metl 1 Top 4 Cls Rankng 86; IN U Of PA; Ed.

BECK, TIM; Hopewell SR HS; Aliquippa, PA; (Y); 32/280; Spanish Clb; Capt L Bsbl; Ftbl; High Hon Roll; Hon Roll; NHS; Ntl Merit Schol; Slippery Rock U; Physcl Educ.

BECK, TRACEY; Ephrata SR HS; Ephrata, PA; (Y); 76/257; Church Yth Grp; Exploring; Girl Scts; Concert Band; Mrchg Band; Orch; Nwsp Rptr; Elem Ed.

BECKAGE, PETER; Bishop Mc Cort HS; Johnstown, PA; (Y); Cmnty Wkr; Spanish Clb; Concert Band; Jazz Band; Mrchg Band; Orch; High Hon Roll; Mu Alp Tht; NHS; Spanish NHS; Cermc Engrg.

BECKER, ANTHONY; Manheim Central SR HS; Manheim, PA; (Y); Am Leg Boys St; Boys Clb Am; Boy Scts; Chess Clb; Cmnty Wkr; Debate Tm; Math Clb; Ski Clb; Spanish Clb; Varsity Clb; Ltr In Bsbl, Ftbl & Bsktbl 85; PA ST Coll.

BECKER, CHERI; Hamburg Area HS; Hamburg, PA; (Y); 3/152; German Clb; Color Guard; School Play; High Hon Roll; Hon Roll; NHS; Acad Ltr Calculus 86; German Awd 86; Acad Ltr Trig Alg 85; PA ST U; Engrng.

BECKER, CLAUDETTE LYNN; Valley HS; New Kensington, PA; (Y); 59/250; AFS; Office Aide; Spanish Clb; Bowling; Sftbl; Montefiore Hosp; Radiography.

BECKER, DANA A; Delone Catholic HS; Hanover, PA; (Y); 56/166; Yrbk Bus Mgr; Yrbk Stf; Rep Sr Cls; JV Var Cheerleading; Rep Jr Cls; Bloomsburg U; Spec Ed.

BECKER, GEORGEANN; Panther Valley HS; Nesquehoning, PA; (Y); Pres Church Yth Grp; Drama Clb; Ski Clb; Sec Chorus; Concert Band; Mrchg Band; Nwsp Stf; Yrbk Stf; Sec Frsh Cls; Hon Roll; Pres Acad Fit Awd 86; Bernard F Boyle Scholar 86; PA ST U; Acctng.

BECKER, GERARD; North Catholic For Boys HS; Philadelphia, PA; (Y); 98/362; Church Yth Grp; Stu Cncl; Var JV Wrstlng; NHS; Acctnt.

BECKER, KIM; Delone Catholic HS; Hanover, PA; (Y); 32/168; Drama Clb; JA; Chorus; School Musical; Yrbk Stf; Hon Roll; NHS; Bus Scholar Farmers Bnk 86; Bus Awd Doubleday 86; Bus Ed Awd Deleone 86; Yorktowne Bus Inst; Bus Adm.

BECKER, LINDA; Dunmore HS; Dunmore, PA; (Y); Church Yth Grp; Computer Clb; Letterman Clb; Spanish Clb; Co-Capt Drill Tm; School Play; Yrbk Stf; Var Tennis; Trk; Hon Roll; Marywood; Bio.

BECKER, LORI; Homer Center JR SR HS; Indiana, PA; (Y); Church Yth Grp; 4-H; French Clb; Girl Scts; Hosp Aide; Varsity Clb; Bsktbl; Sftbl; Vllybl; Hon Roll; DUP; Med Lab Tech.

BECKER, LORI; Pittston Area SR HS; Pittston, PA; (Y); 100/330; Math Clb; Wilkes Coll; Bus Adm.

BECKER, PATRICK; United HS; Armagh, PA; (Y); 20/165; Church Yth Grp; Ski Clb; Varsity Clb; Ftbl; Trk; NHS; Indiana U Of PA; Accounting.

BECKER, RICHARD; Abraham Lincoln HS; Philadelphia, PA; (Y); Boys Clb Am; Church Yth Grp; ROTC; Cit Awd; Sir Thomas Lptn Ctznshp Awd 85; Sp-Sci Acad Stnfrd U CA 86; Psych.

BECKER, SANDRA; Montour HS; Pittsburgh, PA; (Y); Pep Clb; Capt Powder Puff Ftbl; U Pittsburgh.

BECKER, SUSAN; Penn Wood HS; Lansdowne, PA; (Y); 6/349; Church Yth Grp; Intnl Clb; Chorus; Church Choir; School Musical; Yrbk Bus Mgr; Yrbk Ed-Chief; Hon Roll; NHS; Eng.

BECKERLEG, KEIRSTEN; Mt Pleasant Area HS; Mt Pleasant, PA; (Y); 36/249; Cmnty Wkr; GAA; Library Aide; Spanish Clb; Color Guard; Hon Roll; Elem Edu.

BECKLEY, DEBBIE; Penn Wood HS; Darby, PA; (Y); FBLA; Yrbk Phtg; JV Vllybl; Hon Roll; DE County CC; Tchr.

BECKMAN, CHERYL; Reynolds HS; Fredonia, PA; (Y); Latin Clb; Math Clb; Spanish Clb; Varsity Clb; Chorus; Drill Tm; Var Bsktbl; Var Vllybl; Hon Roll; NHS.

BECKNER, KARLA; Carlisle SR HS; Carlisle, PA; (Y); 66/410; Am Leg Aux Girls St; Pres Church Yth Grp; Mrchg Band; Nwsp Stf; Yrbk Stf; Var L Diving; Hon Roll; Bus.

BECKNER, KELLY L; Carlisle SR HS; Carlisle, PA; (Y); Am Leg Aux Girls St; Chess Clb; Church Yth Grp; Debate Tm; Speech Tm; Band; Concert Band; Mrchg Band; Orch; Stage Crew; HOBY Ldrshp Smnr 84; Stu Of Mnth 84; La Salle U; Pltcl Sci.

BECKNER, VICKI; Canon-Mc Millan SR HS; Canonsburg, PA; (Y); Art Clb; Dance Clb; DECA; Library Aide; Y-Teens; Hon Roll; 1st Orange Strp Karate PA Karate Acad 84; Retailing.

BECKWITH, MICHELE; Tyrone Area HS; Pt Matilda, PA; (Y); Church Yth Grp; FBLA; Girl Scts; Library Aide; Pep Clb; Spanish Clb; SADD; Chorus; Color Guard; Powder Puff Ftbl; Accntng.

BECQUET, ANN; Central Cambria HS; Colver, PA; (Y); 35/191; Cmnty Wkr; Trs 4-H; Library Aide; VICA; Capt Twrlr; Hon Roll; Lttrknny Thrftshp Schlrshp 86-87; Carlow Coll; Nrsng.

BECSE, SYLVIA; Canon Mcmillan SR HS; Canonsburg, PA; (Y); 70/371; Ski Clb; Concert Band; Mrchg Band; Yrbk Stf; Hon Roll; Cmnctns.

BEDFORD, KRISTIN; Du Bois Area HS; Reynoldsville, PA; (Y); 18/375; Chorus; School Musical; Pres Stu Cncl; Stat Bsbl; Stat Bsktbl; Capt Twrlr; NHS; Nuclear Engr.

BEDFORD, STACEY; Minersville Area HS; Pottsville, PA; (Y); 12/120; Exploring; French Clb; Girl Scts; Hosp Aide; Ski Clb; SADD; Capt Cheerleading; Hon Roll; NHS; Band; Acad Achvt Awd; Med.

BEDICS, KATHLEEN M; Notre Dame HS; Bethlehem, PA; (Y); 8/78; Chorus; Sec Mrchg Band; Orch; School Musical; School Play; Yrbk Stf; JV Sftbl; Hon Roll; JP Sousa Awd; NHS; Chestnut Hill Acad Scholar 86; Pres Acad Fit Awd 86; 1st Windish Frat Benefit Soc Amer Scholar 86; Chestnut Hill Coll; Mth.

BEDITS, HOPE; Bethel Park SR HS; Bethel Park, PA; (Y); Spanish Clb; Rep Stu Cncl; Hon Roll; Vrsty Rfl Tm MVP Awds 84&86; Vrsty Rfl Tm Capt 86; Lttrd 3 Yrs & Vrsty Lttr Awd Rifle 84-86; CA U Of PA; Elem Educ.

BEDNAR, THOMAS M; Charleroi Area JR-SR HS; North Charleroi, PA; (Y); Science Clb; Ski Clb; Varsity Clb; Var L Trk; Hon Roll; NHS; Med.

BEDNARCZYK, MICHAEL; Ringgold HS; Monongahela, PA; (Y); Boy Scts; Church Yth Grp; Computer Clb; Exploring; JV Trk; Hon Roll; John Hpkns Tlnt Srch Awd 82; Comp Sci.

BEDNER, LORAN; Peters Twp HS; Mc Murray, PA; (S); Pep Clb; Trs Soph Cls; Rep Stu Cncl; JV L Crs Cntry; Var Powder Puff Ftbl; Var L Swmmng; Swmmng WPIALS & PIAA 84-86; Keystone ST Games Chmp; Nrs.

BEDWICK, JOE; E L Meyers HS; Wilkes Barre, PA; (Y); Ski Clb; Chorus; Yrbk Stf; Rep Stu Cncl; JV Bsktbl; Var L Crs Cntry; Var L Trk; Im Vllybl; Jr NHS; NHS.

BEEBY, BRIANNA; Fairview HS; Erie, PA; (Y); Trs French Clb; NFL; Ski Clb; Nwsp Bus Mgr; Nwsp Rptr; Nwsp Stf; Yrbk Stf; Lit Mag; Var L Golf; Hon Roll; Jrnlsm.

BEEGHLY, MOLLY; Mohawk Area HS; Bessemer, PA; (S); 10/129; Church Yth Grp; Band; Concert Band; Mrchg Band; School Musical; School Play; Tennis; Trk; Hon Roll; VP NHS; Westminster Coll.

BEEGLE, JODIE; Northern Bedford County HS; New Enterprise, PA; (Y); Trs FBLA; Yrbk Stf; Hon Roll; Accntng Awd 86.

BEENER, CHRISTY; North Star HS; Boswell, PA; (S); 2/135; Church Yth Grp; FCA; Flag Corp; Stu Cncl; Cit Awd; High Hon Roll; Hon Roll; Eng Awd 84-85.

BEER, CHRISTINA; Greensburg Central Catholic HS; Greensburg, PA; (Y); Church Yth Grp; Ski Clb; Yrbk Stf; Sftbl; Hon Roll; Telecomm.

BEERS, DAWN; Clarion Area HS; Clarion, PA; (Y); Church Yth Grp; Chorus; School Musical; Variety Show; Yrbk Stf; JV Trk; Hon Roll; NHS; Keep PA Beautiful Day Awd, Sfty Town Apprctn Cert Jaycee Women 83; Santas Helper Civic Club 85; U PA Clarian; Sec Math Educ.

BEERS, JEANETTE; Freedom HS; Bethlehem, PA; (Y); 10/445; Chorus; NHS; Ntl Merit Ltr; 4.0 Avrg 2 Yrs 83-85; Gntcs.

BEERS, MARK; Susquenita HS; New Bloomfield, PA; (S); 26/190; Art Clb; Church Yth Grp; Var Crs Cntry; Im Socr; Var L Trk; Hon Roll; PSU & PA Cncl Tchrs Engl Essay Cont 83; Spec Recgntn Awd Dept Transprtn 83; Art.

BEERS, SEAN; Highlands SR HS; Brackenridge, PA; (Y); Church Yth Grp; SADD; Y-Teens; Band; Mrchg Band; JV Bsbl; Im Sftbl; Var Trk; JV Wrstlng; Hon Roll; IN U PA; Crmnlgy.

BEERY, TAMMI; Northwestern SR HS; Albion, PA; (Y); Art Clb; French Clb; Chorus; Hon Roll; Stu Art Awd 84; Art Teacher.

BEGENYI, BARRY; Northern Cambria HS; Barnesboro, PA; (Y); 10/131; Art Clb; Pres Jr Cls; Var Ftbl; Var Trk; Wt Lftg; High Hon Roll; U Of PA Johnstown; Engrg.

BEGONIA, MICHAEL; Norwin SR HS; N Huntingdon, PA; (Y); 2/629; Church Yth Grp; Hon Roll; Straight A Westmoreland Tech 84-85; Straight A & Ranked 2nd In Clss Centrl Westmoreland Voc Tech Schl; USM.

BEHANNA, STACI; Trinity HS; Washington, PA; (Y); 68/374; Hosp Aide; Key Clb; Pep Clb; Drill Tm; Hon Roll.

BEHANNA, VICKI; Ringgold HS; Monongahela, PA; (Y); Church Yth Grp; Ski Clb; Chorus; School Play; Stu Cncl; Cheerleading; Pom Pon; Hon Roll; NHS; Comps.

BEHARY, ANNE; Brownsville Area HS; Brownsville, PA; (S); 14/225; Drama Clb; Band; Chorus; Church Choir; Concert Band; Jazz Band; Mrchg Band; School Play; Swing Chorus; Variety Show; Miss Christmas Seal Pgnt Fnlst & Essy Awd Wnnr 85; Tri-Hi-Y 86; Yth Educ Assoc 85-86; WV U; Music Educ.

BEHERS, LYNDA; Wellsboro Area HS; Wellsboro, PA; (Y); 7/142; Art Clb; Model UN; Pep Clb; Ski Clb; Band; Concert Band; Mrchg Band; Pep Band; School Musical; Yrbk Phtg; Corp Law.

BEHM, CHERYL; Brandywine Heights HS; Mertztwn, PA; (Y); Hosp Aide; Capt Color Guard; Capt Drill Tm; Trs Frsh Cls; Trs Soph Cls; Trs Jr Cls; Trs Stu Cncl; L Fld Hcky; Hon Roll; Art Clb; Med.

BEHM, MIKE; Pine Grove Area HS; Tremont, PA; (Y); Am Leg Boys St; Varsity Clb; Band; Mrchg Band; Nwsp Rptr; Rep Jr Cls; Rep Stu Cncl; JV Var Bsktbl; JV Var Ftbl; Hon Roll; Bio.

BEHREND, ROBT; Chettenham HS; Melrose Pk, PA; (Y); Yrbk Stf; JV Tennis; Bus Mgmt.

BEHRINGER, DAVID; Academy HS; Erie, PA; (S); 4/178; JA; Science Clb; Band; Concert Band; Drm & Bgl; Jazz Band; Mrchg Band; Pep Band; Cit Awd; High Hon Roll; U Of FL; Chmcl Engrng.

BEHRLE, SHARON; Aliquippa HS; Aliquippa, PA; (S); 10/153; DECA; Exploring; French Clb; Pres Library Aide; Rep Jr Cls; Rep Sr Cls; Mgr(s); Hon Roll; Robert Morris Coll; Mktg.

BEHUN, PATRICIA; Norwin HS; N Huntingdon, PA; (Y); 30/550; Spanish Clb; Teachers Aide; Capt Color Guard; Capt Mrchg Band; Hon Roll; Schlrshp To PA ST U 86-87; 3 Yr Hon Stu 83-86; PA ST; Engrng.

BEICHNER, MARSHA; West Forest HS; Tionesta, PA; (Y); Sec Girl Scts; Varsity Clb; Var L Sftbl; JV Vllybl; Hon Roll.

BEICHNER, SHERRY; Keystone JR SR HS; Shippenville, PA; (Y); 15/125; VICA; Chorus; French Hon Soc; High Hon Roll; Hon Roll; Prfct Atten Awd; Cert Apprctn 86; US Skll Olympcs Gld Mdl 1st Plc ST Wnr Csmtlgy Mdl 86; Drctrs Lst 85-86; Csmtlgy.

BEIDELMAN, KAREN; Freedom HS; Bethlehem, PA; (Y); 29/445; Sec Church Yth Grp; VP French Clb; Hosp Aide; Science Clb; Chorus; Church Choir; Hon Roll; NHS; Phys Ed.

BEIDLER, JOHN; Annville Cleona HS; Annville, PA; (Y); 52/105; Boy Scts; Drama Clb; Varsity Clb; Acpl Chr; Chorus; School Musical; Ftbl; Wt Lftg; Jr NHS; NHS; USAF; Air Trfc Cntrlr.

BEIER, TAMMY ANN; Shaler Area SR HS; Pittsburgh, PA; (Y); 168/517; Church Yth Grp; Office Aide; Ski Clb; Nwsp Rptr; Rep Stu Cncl; Var L Bsktbl; Coach Actv; Score Keeper; Var L Vllybl; Hon Roll; Sawyer Bus Inst; Bus.

BEIMEL, KARL; Elk County Christian HS; Kersey, PA; (Y); Model UN; Var Bsbl; Var L Ftbl; Hon Roll; Comp Engrng.

BEIMEL, RICK; St Marys Area HS; Kersey, PA; (Y); Var L Golf; Trk; Hon Roll; NHS.

BEINHOWER, JANETTE; Northeastern SR HS; Manchester, PA; (Y); 3/190; French Clb; Chorus; Color Guard; Rep Stu Cncl; Var Mgr(s); Var Score Keeper; Var L Tennis; High Hon Roll; NHS; Voice Dem Awd; Hnrary Mntn Vc Of Dmcrcy Cntst 84; Cert Svc Prprtn St Jude Dnc Marathn 86; Nmrs Certs Outstndg Frnch.

BEIRNE, MONICA; Mc Keesport Area HS; Mckeesport, PA; (Y); French Clb; Office Aide; Variety Show; Sec Sr Cls; Var L Cheerleading; Var Powder Puff Ftbl; Var L Trk; Var L Vllybl; DAR Awd; Hon Roll; Gannon U; Acc Fam Med Pgm.

BEISEL, CHANIN; Vincentian HS; Pittsburgh, PA; (Y); 21/59; Trs Drama Clb; Hosp Aide; School Musical; School Play; Stage Crew; Stat Bsktbl; Tennis; Hon Roll; NHS; Ntl Merit Schol; Natl Eng Merit Awd 86; Sci Awd 85; Penn ST; Psych.

BEISH, DONNA; Clearfield HS; West Decatur, PA; (Y); Church Yth Grp; Library Aide; Office Aide; Pep Clb; SADD; Teachers Aide; Chorus; Church Choir; Cheerleading; Coach Actv; Typng Awd 83-84; Phy Educ Awd 83-84; Phy Thrpy.

BEISHLINE, NATALIE; Benton Area JR SR HS; Stillwater, PA; (Y); 5/40; Varsity Clb; Band; Concert Band; Mrchg Band; School Musical; School Play; Stu Cncl; Sftbl; High Hon Roll; Hon Roll; York Coll PA.

BELAK, BRETT; Norwin HS; N Huntinbdon, PA; (Y); Church Yth Grp; Letterman Clb; Pep Clb; Ski Clb; SADD; Stu Cncl; Socr; Swmmng.

BELAK, JONATHAN; Penn-Trafford HS; Irwin, PA; (Y); 50/344; FBLA; German Clb; High Hon Roll; Hon Roll.

BELANSKY, PAMELA; North Hills HS; Pittsburgh, PA; (S); JA; Ski Clb; L Tennis; Vllybl; High Hon Roll; NHS; Ecnmcs.

BELCASTRO, LEA; St Maria Goretti HS; Philadelphia, PA; (Y); 87/390; Art Clb; School Musical; Off Frsh Cls; Off Soph Cls; Off Jr Cls; Trs Sr Cls; Stu Cncl; High Hon Roll; NHS; Prfct Atten Awd; Drexel U; Intr Dsgn.

BELCHUNES, MARK; Bethlehem Catholic HS; Bethlehem, PA; (Y); 100/219; Boy Scts; Stage Crew; Var Crs Cntry; Var Wrstlng.

BELFANTI, JOHN; Mount Carmel Area JR SR HS; Mt Carmel, PA; (Y); 13/136; Spanish Clb; Bsbl; Crs Cntry; High Hon Roll; NHS; Deppen Schlrshp 86; Bucknell U; Cvl Engrng.

BELFATTI, JOSEPH W; Hatboro-Horsham SR HS; Hatboro, PA; (Y); 11/275; Drama Clb; Model UN; Chorus; Concert Band; Jazz Band; School Musical; School Play; Hon Roll; NHS; Pres Acad Ftns Awd 86; NY U.

BELFIORE, DAVID; Canon Mc Millan SR HS; Canonsburg, PA; (Y); 30/394; Computer Clb; Latin Clb; Var L Golf; U Pittsburgh; Biomed Engrng.

BELFIORE, JEFFREY; Canon Mc Millan SR HS; Cecil, PA; (Y); 25/390; French Clb; Science Clb; Trs Ski Clb; School Play; VP Sr Cls; Rep Stu Cncl; Golf; Im Ice Hcky; High Hon Roll; VP NHS; Pre-Med.

BELFORD, DAVID; Phil-Mont Christian Acad; Philadlephia, PA; (Y); Church Yth Grp; Stage Crew; Rep Stu Cncl; Capt Crs Cntry; Capt Trk; Rcgnzed Chrstn Chrctr 85-86.

BELGIOVANE, ALEX; Cardinal O Hara HS; Broomall, PA; (Y); Church Yth Grp; Prfct Atten Awd; Schlstc Awd Am Hist 85-86.

BELIN, MARGARET; Clearfield Area HS; Clearfield, PA; (Y); Church Yth Grp; French Clb; School Play; Nwsp Rptr; Yrbk Stf; Off Stu Cncl; Var L Bsktbl; Var L Sftbl; Var L Trk; High Hon Roll; Outstndng Hist, Geom & Bio 85.

BELIN, WENDY; Cedar Crest HS; Lebanon, PA; (Y); 137/295; Church Yth Grp; Drama Clb; FTA; Girl Scts; Office Aide; Church Choir; Variety Show; Hon Roll; 3 Yr Shw/Chrs Awd 85-86; Jimmy Swaggert Bible; Chld Evng.

BELISKY, HARRY; Punxsutawney Area HS; Punxsutawney, PA; (Y); Church Yth Grp; Spanish Clb; Yrbk Phtg; Rep Stu Cncl; Outstndng Undergrad Upward Bound 86; Hnr Stu Upward Bound Summr Pgm 86.

BELKOWSKI, CHELSEA; New Brighton HS; New Brighton, PA; (Y); Air Lines.

BELL, AL H; Mercer JR SR HS; Mercer, PA; (Y); Art Clb; Hosp Aide; Ski Clb; Crs Cntry; 4-H; French Clb; Chorus; Ftbl; Socr; Swmmng; Okinawa Karate 86; Mrcr Cnty Area Agncy Aging Inc 86; Soc Wrkr.

BELL, ANDREW; Montour HS; Coraopolis, PA; (Y); Computer Clb; Acad Excllnc Astronomy 86; Founder & Pres Comp Clb 86; Biomed Engrng.

BELL, ASHLEY; Hempfield HS; Lancaster, PA; (Y); Art Clb; Church Yth Grp; Varsity Clb; Chorus; Church Choir; Stu Cncl; Cheerleading; Tennis; Hon Roll; Spn Art Awd 84-85; Dentl Hyg.

BELL, BRUCE; Unionville HS; Chadds Ford, PA; (Y); 73/300; Boy Scts; Church Yth Grp; FBLA; Intnl Clb; Ftbl; Powder Puff Ftbl; Wt Lftg; High Hon Roll; Hon Roll; Merit Diploma Span IV 84-85; Newpr Carrier Cert Of Achvt 81-82; Penn ST U; Bus.

BELL, COLEEN RYAN; Freeland HS; Freeland, PA; (Y); 4-H; FBLA; Girl Scts; Pep Clb; Spanish Clb; Chorus; School Play; Tennis; Capt Twrlr; 4-H Awd; Penn ST U; Journlsm.

BELL, FRANK; Mid Valley Secondary Ctr; Dickson City, PA; (Y); Chess Clb; Church Yth Grp; Wt Lftg; Wrstlng; Hon Roll; Season Champs Bowling Church Yth Grp 85.

BELL, HARRY; Du Bois Area HS; Dubois, PA; (Y); Church Yth Grp; Var Bsbl; Var Golf; Im Capt Vllybl; Hon Roll; Jrnlsm.

BELL, JAMES; Shenandoah Valley JR-SR HS; Shenandoah, PA; (Y); 16/108; Aud/Vis; Letterman Clb; Yrbk Phtg; Yrbk Rptr; Yrbk Stf; Off Stu Cncl; Var L Bsbl; Hon Roll; Cmnctns.

BELL, JONATHAN; Central Bucks East HS; Warrington, PA; (Y); Temple Yth Grp; Yrbk Ed-Chief; Yrbk Stf; Rep Frsh Cls; Rep Stu Cncl; Bsbl; Ftbl; Hon Roll; Euclidian Math Test Hgst Overall Schl; Cornell Smmr Sessn; Bus.

BELL, JONATHAN D; Cheltenham SR HS; Melrose Park, PA; (Y); 19/375; Math Tm; Chorus; School Musical; School Play; Swing Chorus; Variety Show; Nwsp Ed-Chief; Yrbk Stf; Lit Mag; Stu Cncl; Century Iii Ldrs 85; Lib Arts.

BELL, MADALINE; Cardinal Dougherty HS; Phila, PA; (Y); SADD; Drill Tm; Temple U; Med Rcrd Admin.

BELL, MARK; Portersville Christian HS; Butler, PA; (Y); 3/14; Church Yth Grp; Chorus; Church Choir; Nwsp Phtg; Yrbk Ed-Chief; Yrbk Phtg; High Hon Roll; NHS; Grove City Coll; Ed.

BELL, MICHAEL; Upper Darby HS; Drexel Hl, PA; (Y); JA; JV Bsktbl; Var Im Ftbl; JV Lcrss; Var Trk; Var Capt Wrstlng; Widener U; Bus.

BELL, SANDRA; East Brady/Lenape Vo Tech; Chicora, PA; (Y); SADD; VICA; Chorus; Concert Band; Mrchg Band; Pep Band; Yrbk Stf; Im Vllybl; Im High Hon Roll; Masonic Awd; Duquesne U; Phrmcy.

BELL, SHAWN; Central Bucks E HS; Carversville, PA; (Y); Nwsp Rptr; Nwsp Stf; Socr; High Hon Roll; Hon Roll; Am Leg Boys St Pgm 86; Jrnlsm.

BELL, SHERRI; Saltsburg JR SR HS; Saltsburg, PA; (Y); 11/90; FTA; SADD; Varsity Clb; Flag Corp; Stage Crew; Yrbk Stf; Var L Bsktbl; JV Sftbl; Var Capt Vllybl; Hon Roll; Intl Bus.

BELL, TAMMY; Clearfield Area HS; Woodland, PA; (Y); French Clb; Key Clb; SADD; Chorus; Pres Stu Cncl; Im Vllybl; High Hon Roll; Hon Roll; PA ST U; Bus Adm.

BELL, TOM; Franklin HS; Franklin, PA; (Y); 7/200; Church Yth Grp; Pep Clb; Spanish Clb; Band; Concert Band; Mrchg Band; Orch; Pep Band; High Hon Roll; NHS; Sch Dir Awd 86; Penn ST; Pre-Law.

BELL, TRACEY; Penn Hills SR HS; Pittsburgh, PA; (Y); French Clb; Church Choir; Hon Roll; Boyce CC; Med Secry.

BELLAMY, JACQUELYN; Harrisburg HS; Harrisburg, PA; (Y); 25/450; Dance Clb; Drama Clb; Chorus; School Musical; School Play; Stage Crew; Hon Roll; Hood Coll; Acctng.

BELLANO, CESARE P; Marple-Newtown SR HS; Broomall, PA; (Y); CAP; Exploring; Spanish Clb; SADD; Stage Crew; Nwsp Stf; Stu Cncl; Hon Roll; Prfct Atten Awd; Widener; Htl Mgmt.

BELLAS, MELISSA; Weatherly Area HS; Weatherly, PA; (Y); Rptr 4-H; FBLA; FHA; VP Pep Clb; School Play; Nwsp Rptr; Yrbk Stf; Sec Frsh Cls; Off Jr Cls; Sec Stu Cncl; Keystone JC; Med Tech.

BELLEVILLE, ERIC; Mcguffey HS; Claysville, PA; (S); 30/210; Letterman Clb; Ski Clb; Spanish Clb; Varsity Clb; Band; L Bsbl; L Bsktbl; Coach Actv; Crs Cntry; Co-Capt Ftbl; Bsbl 85 MVP; Bio.

BELLEW JR, WILLIAM F; Archbishop Carroll HS; Berwyn, PA; (Y); Church Yth Grp; Varsity Clb; Nwsp Stf; Im Bsbl; Im Bsktbl; Im Ftbl; Var Socr; Im Sftbl; Im Vllybl; Hon Roll; Bus.

BELLI, RICHARD; Aliquippa HS; Aliquippa, PA; (Y); Boy Scts; Church Yth Grp; French Clb; Mrchg Band; Wrstlng; High Hon Roll; NHS; Prfct Atten Awd; Exploring; Eagle Scout 86; Engrng.

BELLISSIMO, BRIAN; Lincoln HS; Ellwood City, PA; (Y); 8/166; Church Yth Grp; Computer Clb; Exploring; Sec French Clb; High Hon Roll; Lion Awd; NHS; Lions Stu Of Mnth 86; PA ST Beaver Campus Exec Schlrshp 86; Rotry Clb Schlrshp Acad Achvt Awds 86; PA ST U; Sci.

BELLISSIMO, JOSEPH S; Mohawk Area HS; Wampum, PA; (Y); 11/138; FBLA; Latin Clb; Political Wkr; Ski Clb; School Play; Bsktbl; L Ftbl; Socr; Trk; 2nd Pl Pennsylvn Acad Sci Comp Comptn 85; Penn ST U; Govt.

BELLO, FRANK; Hampton HS; Allison Pk, PA; (Y); Am Leg Boys St; Letterman Clb; Varsity Clb; Band; Concert Band; Bsbl; Bsktbl; Ftbl; Wt Lftg; Hon Roll; Business.

BELSEY, MICHELE; Bishop Guilfoyle HS; Altoona, PA; (Y); 10/129; Cmnty Wkr; Speech Tm; Band; Chorus; Cheerleading; Tennis; Hon Roll; Hgh Hnr Roll 83-84; Duquesne U; Phrmcy.

BELTRANTE, MICHELLE; Upper Darby HS; Upr Darby, PA; (Y); VICA; Hon Roll; Philadelphia Coll Art; Art.

BELTZ, CATHERINE M; Hatboro-Horsham SR HS; Horsham, PA; (Y); 24/276; Art Clb; Service Clb; Orch; School Musical; Nwsp Rptr; Cit Awd; High Hon Roll; Hon Roll; Kiwanis Awd; Lion Awd; Siena Schlrshp 86; Ltn, Rssn, & Clthng Awds 86; Acad Schl Ltr 86; Cedar Crest Coll; Fine Arts.

BELTZ, TINA; Northampton Area SR HS; Bath, PA; (Y); Sec Church Yth Grp; Off Drama Clb; Chorus; School Musical; School Play; Var Trk; High Hon Roll; Hon Roll; Church Choir; Schl Ltr Drama Perffmncs 85; Cert Hon Drama Perfmncs 86; Psych.

BELUS, CHRISTINA; Sharon SR HS; Sharon, PA; (Y); Art Clb; Drama Clb; Stage Crew; Mask & Mike Srv 3 Prod 86; Gannon; Cmmnctns.

BELUSKO, BARBARA; West Hazleton HS; Sugarloaf, PA; (Y); Church Yth Grp; Drama Clb; French Clb; FBLA; Pep Clb; SADD; Band; Chorus; Church Choir; Pep Band; PA ST U; Marine Bio.

BELZ, MARK; Penn Hills SR HS; Pittsburgh, PA; (Y); 1/760; AFS; Cmnty Wkr; Computer Clb; Drama Clb; German Clb; Orch; School Musical; School Play; Ed Nwsp Ed-Chief; Bausch & Lomb Sci Awd; Westnghse Fmly & Chancellors Undergrad Merit Schlrshps 86; Mst Outstndng Sci Stdnt 86; U Of Pittsburgh; Biomed Engr.

BEMENT, TIMOTHY; Greater Latrobe SR HS; Latrobe, PA; (Y); 12/409; Church Yth Grp; VP JA; VP Chorus; Church Choir; Jazz Band; Madrigals; Mrchg Band; School Musical; French Hon Soc; High Hon Roll; Arch.

BENAMATI, MARCIA L; Homer-Center JR SR HS; Homer City, PA; (Y); 20/107; FTA; Teachers Aide; Band; Chorus; Capt Flag Corp; Jazz Band; School Musical; Yrbk Stf; Hon Roll; NHS; Dist Band 85; IUP; Elem Ed.

BENAMATI, ROBERT; Bishop Carroll HS; Spangler, PA; (S); #19 In Class; Church Yth Grp; Band; Concert Band; Mrchg Band; Yrbk Sprt Ed; Hon Roll; Aeron.

BENCI, KARLA; Jefferson-Morgan HS; Mather, PA; (Y); Nwsp Stf; Yrbk Stf; Hon Roll; Art Clb; Dance Clb; Office Aide; Varsity Clb; Rep Frsh Cls; Cheerleading; Trk; Amrcn Lgn Awd 83; Nwsppr Stf Awd 86; Chrldng Ltrs 83-86; Penn St Fayette Cmps; Engl Tchr.

BENCO, KELLY; Uniontown HS; Uniontown, PA; (Y); 26/325; VP Church Yth Grp; Spanish Clb; Church Choir; High Hon Roll; NHS; Spanish NHS; Accntnt.

BENDEKOVIC, MICHELE; Center Area HS; Monaca, PA; (Y); 17/184; Church Yth Grp; German Clb; Concert Band; Mrchg Band; Pep Band; School Musical; Variety Show; High Hon Roll; Hon Roll; NHS; Ger High Hnr Awd 85; Beaver Cnty Labr Cncl Schlrshp 86; Parnt Tchr Assoc Schlrshp 86; IN U Of Pa; Hist.

BENDER, DIANE; Blue Ridge HS; New Milford, PA; (Y); 20/120; Pep Clb; Stat Bsbl; Var L Bsktbl; Stat Ftbl; JV Sftbl; L Vllybl; Hon Roll; Studnt Of Month; COMP Sci.

BENDER, GREG; Riverside HS; Beaver Falls, PA; (Y); Rep DECA; Deca ST Awd Cert 85; Dist 2 Food Mkgt Master Emply 1st Plc 86; Fnlst ST Comptn Food Mkgtg 86; Elec.

BENDER, JEANETTE; Ephrata SR HS; Ephrata, PA; (Y); 1/257; Sec Church Yth Grp; Library Aide; Chorus; Nwsp Ed-Chief; High Hon Roll; NHS; Dip Mrt For Hghst Grd Spn II 86; Cert Prmtn Pre-Virtuoso Piano 84; Tch Chld Chrch & Bbl Schl 86; Socl Wrk.

BENDER, JOHN; Cameron County HS; Emporium, PA; (Y); Computer Clb; Yrbk Phtg; Trk; Prfct Atten Awd; ICM Schl Bus; Comp Pgmr.

BENDER, JOHN; Hillidays Burg Area HS; Altoona, PA; (Y); Varsity Clb; VICA; Var Bsbl; Var Mgr(s); L Wrstlng; Hon Roll; Royal Rngrs Gld Mdl Of Achvt 83; FCF Wildrns Frntrsmn 85; PA ST Vica Skl Olmpcs 3rd Pl 86; Penn ST U; Comp Sci.

BENDER, JULIE; Upper Dublin HS; Maple Glen, PA; (Y); 111/334; Nwsp Stf; Rep Frsh Cls; Rep Soph Cls; Rep Jr Cls; Rep Stu Cncl; JV Lcrss; Powder Puff Ftbl; Wt Lftg; Law.

BENDER, KIM; Pottstown SR HS; Pottstown, PA; (S); 10/130; Art Clb; FNA; Spanish Clb; Chorus; Capt Color Guard; Capt Flag Corp; Mrchg Band; Off Jr Cls; Off Sr Cls; JV Fld Hcky; Alvernia; Nrsng.

BENDER, LORETTA; Salisbury-Elk Lick HS; Meyersdale, PA; (Y); FHA; Nwsp Ed-Chief; Nwsp Rptr; Hon Roll; Prfct Atten Awd; Acadmc Al-Amer Schlr Awd 85.

BENDER, LORIE; Canon Mc Millan HS; Canonsburg, PA; (Y); Latin Clb; Office Aide; Pres SADD; Stage Crew; Yrbk Ed-Chief; VP Stu Cncl; Cit Awd; DAR Awd; High Hon Roll; VP NHS; Schl Brd Stu 86; Prvntn Ctr Orgnztn Comm 85-86; Cum Miss Christmas Seals 86; OH ST U; Psychlgy.

BENDER, MARIE; Greater Johnstown HS; Johnstown, PA; (Y); 27/290; Boys Clb Am; Church Yth Grp; French Clb; Y-Teens; Chorus; Church Choir; Color Guard; High Hon Roll; Para Med Careers Clb Schlrshp 86; Lehigh Cnty CC; Physcl Thrpy.

BENDER, NANCY; Octorara Area HS; Parkesburg, PA; (Y); FBLA; FNA; Hosp Aide; Yrbk Stf; Lit Mag; Mat Maids; Hon Roll; Spnsh Merit Awd 85; Earl M Rtnhse Mem Schlrshp 86; St Jsph Hsptl Schl Of Nrsg; Nrs.

BENDER, RENEE; Cambria Heights HS; Carrolltown, PA; (Y); 10/177; Letterman Clb; Varsity Clb; Yrbk Stf; JV Bsktbl; Var L Trk; Elks Awd; Hon Roll; NHS; NEDT Awd; Pres Schlr; Juniata Coll; Pre Med.

BENDER, TAMMY; Williamsport Area HS; Williamsport, PA; (Y); 81/518; Sec VP FHA; Girl Scts; Hosp Aide; Hon Roll; Williamsport Area CC; Exec Sec.

BENDIS, BRIAN; Apollo-Ridge HS; Saltsburg, PA; (Y); 9/164; Sec VP FFA; German Clb; Math Clb; Bsbl; DAR Awd; Hon Roll; Lion Awd; NHS; PA Kystn ST Frmr Degree 86; Dklb Ag Accmplshmnt Awd 86; Jcksnvl U Trste Schlrshp; Louise V Nlsn Mem; Jacksonville U; Mrn Sci.

BENDIXEN, KARLYN; Pocona Mountain HS; Pocono Summit, PA; (Y); 1/320; Exploring; NFL; Pep Clb; Scholastic Bowl; SADD; Nwsp Ed-Chief; Lit Mag; High Hon Roll; NHS; Ntl Merit Ltr; Pre Med.

BENEDETTO, DEBORAH; St Maria Goretti HS; Philadelphia, PA; (Y); #74 In Class; Church Yth Grp; Civic Clb; Cmnty Wkr; GAA; Hosp Aide; Library Aide; Mathletes; Math Clb; Math Tm; Yrbk Stf; Math.

BENEDETTO, MARIA; Clairton HS; Clairton, PA; (Y); 8/107; Trs FBLA; VICA; Color Guard; Drill Tm; Yrbk Sprt Ed; Twrlr; CC Awd; High Hon Roll; Hon Roll; Jr NHS; Vo Tech Awd Schlrshp 86; Penn ST; Bio Med.

BENEDICT, KELLI; Solanco HS; New Providence, PA; (Y); 2/220; Art Clb; Office Aide; Spanish Clb; Teachers Aide; Varsity Clb; Chorus; Drm Mjr(t); Mrchg Band; Yrbk Stf; Stu Cncl; Bloomsburg U; Accntng.

BENEDICT, KEVIN; Greater Latrobe HS; Latrobe, PA; (Y); Exploring; Bsbl; Bsktbl; West VA; Chrprctr.

BENEDICT, TODD; Northeastern SR HS; Mt Wolf, PA; (Y); 4/159; Cmnty Wkr; VP JA; Ski Clb; Chorus; VP Stu Cncl; JV Crs Cntry; JV Golf; JV Trk; High Hon Roll; Hon Roll; Engr.

BENEGASI, BERNADETTE; Mohawk HS; Bessemer, PA; (S); Cmnty Wkr; Latin Clb; Math Tm; Band; Chorus; Concert Band; Mrchg Band; School Musical; Yrbk Stf; Stu Cncl; Acadmc Excllnc Awd Engl 86; JR Miss Contstnt 86.

BENFANTE, LISA; Pittston Area SR HS; Pittston, PA; (Y); Church Yth Grp; Varsity Clb; Var Bsktbl; Trk; Capt Vllybl; Hon Roll; Geisinger Schl Nrsng; Nrsng.

BENFER, MICHELE; Wm Allen HS; Allentown, PA; (Y); 27/567; Pres Band; Pres Concert Band; Pres Mrchg Band; Sec Orch; Stu Cncl; Var L Gym; Hon Roll; NHS; Church Yth Grp; 4-H; SR All Am Hall Of Fame Bnd Hnr 86; Booster Clb Awd Gymnstc 84; Dr Warren E Acker Schrlshp 86; Ursinus Coll; Bio.

BENFER, SHERRI; Shikellamy HS; Sunbury, PA; (Y); 48/312; German Clb; Key Clb; VICA; Hon Roll; Jr NHS; Upward Bound Prjct; Mc Cann Schl Bus; Comp Prgmng.

BENFER, TAMMY; Middleburg HS; Middleburg, PA; (Y); Varsity Clb; Band; Color Guard; Concert Band; Nwsp Stf; Yrbk Bus Mgr; JV Var Sftbl; Hon Roll; Prfct Atten Awd; Bus Mgnt.

BENFORD, BECKY; Rockwood Area HS; Rockwood, PA; (S); 22/98; High Hon Roll; Vllybl; Hon Roll; Church Yth Grp; Socr; Rep Jr Cls; Cheerleading; VICA; Trk; Hme Econ Yr Outstndng Stu 84-85; Vrsty Vllybl Tm Capt 85-86; Bus.

BENINGO, SHIRLEY; Twin Valley JR SR HS; Morgantown, PA; (Y); 18/136; Pres VP JA; Capt Scholastic Bowl; Chorus; School Musical; Nwsp Rptr; Stu Cncl; NHS; Pres Schlr; Comm Clb Pres 85-86; Natl JR Achvrs Cnfrnc Delegate 83-85; Ithaca Coll; Comm.

BENINI, DAVE; Unionville HS; West Chester, PA; (Y); 60/260; Pres Boy Scts; Church Yth Grp; JA; Ski Clb; Variety Show; Nwsp Stf; JV Wrstlng; High Hon Roll; Engrng.

BENINI, KRISTINA; Somerset Area HS; Sipesville, PA; (Y); 42/239; English Clb; Ski Clb; Sec Spanish Clb; Varsity Clb; Yrbk Stf; Rep Stu Cncl; Im Stat Bsktbl; Var L Socr; High Hon Roll; NHS; Pres Physcl Ftns Awd; U Pittsburg; Physcl Thrpy.

BENISH, DOUGLAS; Wyoming Area HS; Pittston, PA; (Y); Chess Clb; Church Yth Grp; Cmnty Wkr; Computer Clb; Radio Clb; JV Bsbl; JV Bsktbl; Var Golf; Hon Roll; Comptr Awd 86; Engrng.

BENJAMIN, CHRIS; South Williamsport Area HS; Williamsport, PA; (Y); 54/140; Yrbk Phtg; JV Var Bsktbl; Im Vllybl; ROTC.

BENJAMIN, KIMBERLY; Warwick HS; Lititz, PA; (Y); 28/237; AFS; Church Yth Grp; Stage Crew; Var Mgr(s); Swmmng; JV Trk; High Hon Roll; Hon Roll; NHS; Pres Schlr; Lancaster Gen; Radiology.

BENJAMIN, LISA ANN; Jules E Mastbaum A V T HS; Philadelphia, PA; (Y); Debate Tm; Drama Clb; FBLA; English Clb; Red Cross Aide; Teachers Aide; Chorus; School Play; Variety Show; Yrbk Stf; Debatng Clb 86; Drama Clb 86; FBA 84; IN U; Econ.

BENJAMIN, RYAN JOSEPH; Danville Area SR HS; Danville, PA; (Y); Letterman Clb; Ski Clb; Concert Band; Mrchg Band; Symp Band; Rep Stu Cncl; Im JV Bsbl; L Ftbl; L Trk; Hon Roll; Gld Mdl Music Awd 83; Kent ST U; Arch.

BENKO, ANGELA S; Ephrata SR HS; Ephrata, PA; (Y); Pep Clb; Yrbk Phtg; Var Cheerleading; Fld Hcky; Powder Puff Ftbl; Hon Roll; Girls Clb Pres 83-87; YEA 83; Hlth Careers Clb 83; Lwyr.

BENKOSKI, RENEE; Hanover Area JR SR HS; Wilkes Barre, PA; (Y); 1/182; Cmnty Wkr; Hosp Aide; Key Clb; Model UN; Yrbk Stf; Var L Cheerleading; High Hon Roll; Pres NHS; Val; Var L Trk; Hgh Avg Dept Awds Math & Scl Stds 86; Chrntski Schlrshp Schlstc Excllnc 86; Coll Prep Hgh Avg Awd 86; U Of Scrntn; Physcl Thrpy.

BENN, CYNTHIA; Hempfield Area SR HS; Irwin, PA; (Y); Art Clb; Pres Church Yth Grp; Pep Clb; Ski Clb; Chorus; Church Choir; School Musical; Yrbk Stf; Off Stu Cncl; Var Cheerleading; Prtl Schlrshp-Pre Coll Art Clss-Carnegie Mellon U 84-85; $50 Svgs Bond-Pstr Cntst; Art Inst PA; Cmrcl Art.

BENN, LISA; Du Bois SR HS; Dubois, PA; (Y); Church Yth Grp; Chorus; Stat Crs Cntry; Mgr(s); Im Sftbl; Stat Trk; Beaver Coll; Physical Therapy.

BENN, MELISSA; Wilson Christian Acad; White Oak, PA; (S); Yrbk Ed-Chief; Var Bsktbl; Score Keeper; Hon Roll; NHS.

BENNARDO, LISA; Mt Alvernia HS; Pittsburgh, PA; (Y); Art Clb; Camera Clb; Cmnty Wkr; Red Cross Aide; Chorus; Yrbk Phtg; Yrbk Stf; Hon Roll; Prfct Atten Awd; Bus Hnr Scty 86; Typng Awd 86; Journlst.

BENNER, BILL; Titusville HS; Centerville, PA; (Y); Math Tm; Concert Band; VP Soph Cls; VP Jr Cls; Bsktbl; Var L Trk; U Of PA; Engrng.

BENNER, BRETT M; Peters Township HS; Bridgeville, PA; (Y); Pres Thesps; Chorus; School Musical; School Play; Stage Crew; Stu Cncl; Hall Fame Awd Theatre 85; Best Actr Awd 85-86; Richard L St Clair Awd Arts 86; Carnegie Mellon U; Drama.

BENNER, CHRISTOPHER; Williamsport Area HS; Williamsport, PA; (S); Key Clb; Chorus; School Musical; Swing Chorus; Rep Sr Cls; Var L Bsbl; All ST Choir 83-84 & 84-85; IN U PA; Bus.

BENNER, CORINA; Gatesville Area SR HS; Coatesville, PA; (Y); 81/536; Aud/Vis; Drama Clb; French Clb; School Play; Rep Sr Cls; Rep Stu Cncl; High Hon Roll; Pep Clb; Ski Clb; SADD; Oscar Awd-Excllnc In Dramtics 86; Excllnc In Study Of Engl 86; WCHS TV Awd 86; PA ST U; Comm.

BENNER, DAN; East Juniata HS; Thompsontown, PA; (Y); Chess Clb; 4-H; Var L Socr; Var L Wrstlng; DE Vly Coll; Farming.

BENNER, DENISE; Shikellamy HS; Sunbury, PA; (Y); 16/321; Church Yth Grp; German Clb; Hon Roll; NHS; Shikellamy Educ Assoc Awd 86; Pres Acdmc Fit Awd 86; Bloomsburg U; Elem Educ.

BENNER, ERINN L; Tidioute HS; Tidioute, PA; (Y); 1/18; Trs SADD; VP Varsity Clb; Trs Jr Cls; Trs Sr Cls; Bsktbl; Sftbl; Capt Vllybl; NHS; Val; Ntl Schlr/Athl Awd 86; Hstry Awd 86; Chem Awd 86; PA ST U; Chem Engrng.

BENNER, GLENDA; East Juniata HS; Mcalistervl, PA; (Y); 2/93; Camera Clb; Chess Clb; School Musical; Yrbk Stf; Trk; High Hon Roll; NHS; Pres Schlr; Sal; Roy Hart Drama Awd 86; Hon Stu 86 Grdtng Clss 86; Penn ST U; Biochem.

BENNER, KAREN; Freedom HS; Bethlehem, PA; (Y); 26/445; German Clb; Mrchg Band; Symp Band; Hon Roll; NHS.

BENNER, KEN; Salisbury HS; Allentown, PA; (Y); 29/130; Rep Soph Cls; Rep Jr Cls; Rep Sr Cls; Rep Stu Cncl; Var L Bsbl; Var L Socr; Hon Roll; Plcd 3rd In St Bsbl 85-86; Chmpnshp Bsbl Team 85-86; Chmpnshp Soccer Team 85-86; 1st Tm Clnl Lge 85-86; Bloomsburg U; Phy Ed Tchr.

BENNER, MATTHEW; Shikellamy HS; Northumberland, PA; (Y); 29/315; Am Leg Boys St; Var L Bsktbl; Hon Roll; James Benner Mem Awd 86; Bloomsburg U; Bus Admin.

BENNER, SUSAN; East Juniata HS; Mcalistervl, PA; (Y); Chess Clb; Church Yth Grp; Drama Clb; Chorus; Camp Fr Inc; Ed Yrbk Stf; Mgr(s); Hon Roll; Beauty Schl; Beautician.

BENNER, TAMMY; Waynesboro Area SR HS; Waynesboro, PA; (Y); Band; Chorus; Yrbk Phtg; Yrbk Stf; Rep Stu Cncl; Var Fld Hcky; JV Trk; Cit Awd; Hon Roll; NHS; Elem Educ.

BENNETT, GREG; Sullivan County HS; Forksville, PA; (Y); 11/86; Ski Clb; Yrbk Ed-Chief; Hon Roll; Bucknell; Dentist.

BENNETT, JORDAN L; Conestoga Senior HS; Paoli, PA; (Y); 23/408; Stu Cncl; Im Bowling; Hon Roll; NHS; Ntl Merit SF; Wrld Affaird Clb 85-86; Acadmc Comptn Tm 85-86; Pre Med.

BENNETT, LEE; Tyrone Area HS; Tyrone, PA; (Y); 16/179; Am Leg Aux Girls St; French Clb; Key Clb; Library Aide; Concert Band; Mrchg Band; Pep Band; High Hon Roll; Hon Roll; Pres Acdmc Fit Awd 86; Wilson Coll; Nrsng.

BENNETT, MARK; Chester HS; Chester, PA; (Y); Boy Scts; Band; Concert Band; Stage Crew; Variety Show; Off Sr Cls; Var Capt Bsbl; Var L Ftbl; Cit Awd; Jr NHS; 1st Tm All Del-Val 86; U Of MD-COLL Park; Comm.

BENNETT, PAMELA; State College Area SR HS; Bellefonte, PA; (Y); 19/480; 4-H; Hosp Aide; Concert Band; Mrchg Band; Var Powder Puff Ftbl; Var Trk; Im Vllybl; Cit Awd; 4-H Awd; High Hon Roll; Playland Schlrshp 86; Fac Schlrs Awd 86; PA ST U; Microbio.

BENNETT, PATRICE; Roxborough HS; Philadelphia, PA; (Y); 79/350; Church Yth Grp; GAA; Hosp Aide; Library Aide; Pep Clb; SADD; Teachers Aide; Church Choir; Yrbk Rptr; Rep Stu Cncl; Committee Coll Schlrshp 86; Rts Of Pssg Hnr Awd Outstndng Ldrshp 86; Chrldg & Pep Stm Awd 86; Pthlgy.

BENNETT, RANDOLPH; Emmaus HS; Macungie, PA; (Y); 10/478; Key Clb; Spanish Clb; SADD; School Musical; School Play; Stage Crew; Yrbk Phtg; Trk; High Hon Roll; Ntl Merit Ltr; Cert Commonwealth PA SAT Scores 86; U DE; Mech Engrng.

BENNETT, ROCHANDA; William Penn HS; Philadelphia, PA; (Y); Church Yth Grp; Computer Clb; Dance Clb; English Clb; FBLA; Model UN; Pep Clb; Chorus; Church Choir; Drill Tm; Comp Prog.

BENNETT, SEAN; Canon Mc Millan HS; Eighty Four, PA; (Y); 11/357; Pres VP Church Yth Grp; Drama Clb; Science Clb; SADD; Thesps; School Musical; School Play; Stu Cncl; L Ftbl; High Hon Roll; Ftbl All Conf, Dist Capt 85-86; WA & Jefferson; Chem.

BENNETT, SHELLEY; Fort Le Boeuf HS; Waterford, PA; (Y); 16/168; Church Yth Grp; Computer Clb; Color Guard; Flag Corp; Stat Trk; High Hon Roll; Elec Engrng.

BENNETT, SUSAN M; Mc Keesport SR HS; Mc Keesport, PA; (Y); 30/350; Color Guard; Mrchg Band; Orch; School Musical; Hon Roll; Jr NHS; NHS; Pres Schlr; Rotary Awd; Kent ST U; Arch.

BENNETT, TRICIA; York Catholic HS; Dallastown, PA; (Y); 4/170; French Clb; Chorus; Flag Corp; Stage Crew; Sec Stu Cncl; Stat Trk; High Hon Roll; NHS; Rotary Awd; Voice Dem Awd; PA ST; Math.

BENNETT, VALERIE KAY; Blairsville SR HS; Blairsville, PA; (Y); VP Church Yth Grp; Drama Clb; Chorus; Concert Band; School Musical; IOJD; Hnrd Queen 84-85; Schrlshp 86; Majorettes 84-86; Schlrshp Musical Dept 86; Point Park Coll; Musicl Theatre.

BENNINGER, APRIL; Northampton SR HS; Bath, PA; (Y); Aud/Vis; Pres Exploring; SADD; Yrbk Stf; Sec Stu Cncl; Tennis; Timer; Trk; High Hon Roll; Hon Roll.

BENNINGER, MARK THOMAS; Catasaqua HS; Catasauqua, PA; (Y); Lit Mag; Var L Ftbl; Hon Roll.

BENNINGER, SANDY; Elk Lake HS; Meshoppen, PA; (Y); 24/104; Church Yth Grp; VICA; Chorus; JV Var Bsktbl; JV Var Sftbl; JV Var Vllybl; 4-H; Library Aide; Williamsport; Acctg.

BENNIS, CHERYL; Upper Darby HS; Drexel Hill, PA; (Y); 38/629; French Clb; Girl Scts; Bowling; Hon Roll; Bio.

BENO, CATHY; Trinity HS; Washington, PA; (Y); French Clb; JA; Key Clb; Office Aide; Pep Clb; Band; Concert Band; Mrchg Band; Pep Band; JV Bsktbl; MBA Regl Sec AA Champs 85; MBA Grnd Natls 85; Grand Champs Norwn And Mc Guffy Comptns 85; Psych.

BENSAVAGE, TODD; Wyalusing Valley HS; Wyalusing, PA; (Y); Spanish Clb; Stat Bsktbl; JV Crs Cntry; Mgr(s); Hon Roll; Prfct Atten Awd; Engrng.

BENSING, GRETA; Ephrata SR HS; Ephrata, PA; (Y); 50/257; FBLA; Chorus; School Musical; Yrbk Stf; High Hon Roll; Gregg Typing Awds 85 & 86; Reading Area CC; Exec Sec.

BENSINGER, KIM; Blue Mountain HS; Sch Haven, PA; (Y); 1/214; Chorus; Nwsp Rptr; Rep Stu Cncl; L Var Cheerleading; Var Diving; Var Swmmng; Var L Trk; Hon Roll; NEDT Awd; Latin Hnr Soc 86; Phys Ther.

BENSON, JULIE; Butler SR HS; Renfrew, PA; (Y); 31/731; VP Sec Church Yth Grp; Band; Drm & Bgl; Mrchg Band; Yrbk Bus Mgr; Im Ftbl; Hon Roll; Pres Acadmc Fitns Awd 86; Juniata Coll; Comp Sci.

BENSON, KIM; Methacton HS; Norristown, PA; (Y); 32/336; Church Yth Grp; Key Clb; Red Cross Aide; Ski Clb; Stu Cncl; Var Chess Clb; Var Lcrss; High Hon Roll; NHS; Messiah Coll; Biolgy.

BENSON, KIMBERLY; Sacred Heart HS; Pittsburgh, PA; (Y); 60/160; Church Yth Grp; Debate Tm; Hosp Aide; Library Aide; VP NFL; Pep Clb; Speech Tm; SADD; Chorus; Stage Crew; Duquesne U; Pre-Law.

BENSON, PATRICK; Butler HS; Butler, PA; (Y); Ftbl; Trk; Hon Roll; Penn ST; Aerospc Engrng.

BENSON, SHELLIE; Middletown Area HS; Middletown, PA; (Y); 5/220; Dance Clb; FCA; Hosp Aide; Radio Clb; Chorus; Church Choir; Swing Chorus; Nwsp Stf; Yrbk Stf; Cheerleading; Wmns Clb Scholar 86; Essay Cont Awd 83-86; Nrsng.

BENSON, SUE; Palmyra Area SR HS; Palmyra, PA; (Y); 19/200; Dance Clb; Drama Clb; Trs French Clb; Library Aide; Teachers Aide; Chorus; Color Guard; Trk; Hon Roll; Ntl Frnch Cntst Cert Of Merit 86; Pre-Med.

BENSON, TRICIA L; Sharon HS; Sharon, PA; (Y); 26/197; Church Yth Grp; Drama Clb; French Clb; VP Pres Service Clb; Flag Corp; Stage Crew; Rep Stu Cncl; Capt Mat Maids; Var Trk; High Hon Roll; Almni Schlrshp 86; Edinboro U; Scndry Educ.

BENT, CINDY; Moon SR HS; Coraopolis, PA; (Y); 30/370; 4-H; JA; L Var Diving; L Trk; Ntl Merit SF; College Plays At Robert Morris College 84-86.

BENTZ, CHRIS; Minersville Area HS; Minersville, PA; (Y); 6/117; Boy Scts; Ski Clb; Spanish Clb; School Play; Trs Frsh Cls; JV Bsbl; JV Bsktbl; JV Ftbl; Hon Roll; NHS.

BENTZ, DEBORAH; Holy Name HS; Wyomissing, PA; (Y); 3/115; Q&S; Band; Chorus; School Musical; Yrbk Ed-Chief; High Hon Roll; Pres NHS; Prsdntl Schlrs Prog & Mitrani Schlrshp Bloomsburg U 86; Prvncl Mdl Of Hnr Oblates Of St Francisde 86; Bloomsburg U; Spch Pthlgy.

BENTZE, JERRY; Cathedral Prep; Erie, PA; (Y); 45/216; Computer Clb; SADD; Im Bsktbl; JV Ftbl; Sftbl; Im Swmmng; Tennis; Im Vllybl; JV Wt Lftg; UCLA; Pre-Vet Med.

BENYO, GERALD; Northwestern JR/Sr HS; New Tripoli, PA; (Y); 36/170; Nwsp Rptr; Nwsp Stf; Var Ftbl; Mgr(s); Var Wt Lftg; JV Wrstlng; Cit Awd; Hon Roll; Pittsburgh U; Pltcl Sci.

BENZ JR, JEROME V; Bishop Hafey HS; Conyngham, PA; (Y); 6/130; Church Yth Grp; Scholastic Bowl; Spanish Clb; Rep Stu Cncl; Var L Tennis; High Hon Roll; Hon Roll; NHS; Spanish NHS; Var L Socr; Ldrshp Awd; Hghst Aver In Alg I; Gym Awd; Med.

BENZ, SHAUNA; Charleroi JR SR HS; N Charleroi, PA; (Y); Aud/Vis; Girl Scts; VICA; Chorus; Im Vllybl; Hon Roll; Waynesburg Coll; Photo.

BENZO, CELESTE A; Pen Hills SR HS; Verona, PA; (Y); VP French Clb; Church Choir; Nwsp Stf; Ed Lit Mag; VP Jr Cls; High Hon Roll; NHS; Camp Fr Inc; Church Yth Grp; Cmnty Wkr; SR Cls Schlrshp Wnnr 86; ST Fnlst Ntl Urban Leag Essy Cntst 86; Advncd Plcmnt Engl Excel Awd 86; La Salle U; Intl Attrny.

BEPPLER, CHERILEE; Scranton Central HS; Scranton, PA; (Y); Church Yth Grp; Dance Clb; German Clb; Ski Clb; Chorus; Church Choir; Var JV Cheerleading; Swmmng; Var JV Trk; Hon Roll; Physcl Thrpy.

BERANEK, JENNIFER; Southmoreland HS; Scottdale, PA; (Y); FTA; JCL; Latin Clb; Varsity Clb; Chorus; Variety Show; Yrbk Ed-Chief; Cheerleading; Gym; Powder Puff Ftbl; IN U Of PA; Elem Ed.

BERARDI, ALAN; Valley View JR SR HS; Peckville, PA; (Y); 39/200; Computer Clb; Spanish Clb; JV Bsbl; Im Ftbl; Im Sftbl; Im Vllybl; Im Wt Lftg; Bsktbl; Bowling; Golf.

BERARDINELLI, JAMES; Altoona Area HS; Altoona, PA; (S); 18/683; Church Yth Grp; Spanish Clb; Stage Crew; Variety Show; Var L Civic Clb; Var L Trk; Jr NHS; NHS; Trck Field Clb Pres 86; Juniata Coll; Lawyer.

BERBACK, KRIS; Liberty HS; Bethlehem, PA; (Y); 29/475; High Hon Roll; Hon Roll; Prfct Atten Awd; Tchng.

BERCAW, KEVIN; Waynesboro Area SR HS; Waynesboro, PA; (Y); 135/353; Exploring; Ski Clb; Socr; Hon Roll; Nuc Engrg.

BERCAW, MIKE; Waynesboro Area SR HS; Waynesboro, PA; (Y); Var JV Socr; Hon Roll; Adrtsng.

BERCHOK, CATHY; Elizabeth Forward HS; Elizabeth, PA; (Y); JV Bsktbl; Var Diving; JV Var Vllybl; High Hon Roll; NHS; Marine Bio.

BERCIK, MONICA; Cambridge Springs HS; Edinboro, PA; (Y); 32/110; Cmnty Wkr; French Clb; Pep Clb; SADD; Concert Band; Drm Mjr(t); Mrchg Band; Pep Band; Nwsp Rptr; Nwsp Stf; Edinboro U PA; Soc Wrkr.

BERDAR, DAVID; Albert Gallatin HS; Masontown, PA; (Y); 11/150; Pres Church Yth Grp; Math Tm; Red Cross Aide; Ski Clb; Varsity Clb; Pres Stu Cncl; Var Bsbl; Var Ftbl; High Hon Roll; NHS; Exchng Club Best Boy Awd 84; U Of Pittsburgh; Comm.

BERDINE, DENISE; Canon-Mc Millan HS; Eighty Four, PA; (Y); Chess Clb; Sec French Clb; Varsity Clb; Band; Var JV Bsktbl; L Sftbl; Twrlr; High Hon Roll; Slippery Rock U; Math.

BERDIS, JOE; Swissvale HS; Pittsburgh, PA; (Y); 18/232; French Clb; JA; Latin Clb; Band; Chorus; Jazz Band; Mrchg Band; Nwsp Rptr; Im Bsktbl; Im Bowling; Aero Engrg.

BERENBAUM, DANIEL; Council Rock HS; Richboro, PA; (Y); 91/845; VP Church Yth Grp; VP Temple Yth Grp; Im Bsktbl; Im Socr; Hon Roll; Rabbi Annonymous Awd Confirm Cls 85; BUS.

BERES, RACHEL E; St Pauls Cathedral HS; Homestead, PA; (S); Drama Clb; Key Clb; VP Spanish Clb; Orch; School Musical; School Play; Nwsp Stf; Lit Mag; High Hon Roll; Spanish NHS; Thespian Soc 85; Prfct Attndnc 85; Intl Rltns.

BERES, STEPHANIE; Fort Le Boeuf HS; Waterford, PA; (Y); 34/180; Off Stu Cncl; Stat Bsktbl; DAR Awd; Hon Roll; Cls Cncl Rep Prom Comm 85; Art Inst Pittsburgh Accptnc; Art Inst Pittsburgh; Fash Merch.

BERES, SUSAN; Shippensburg Area SR HS; Shippensburg, PA; (Y); 19/214; Church Yth Grp; Sec GAA; Trs Girl Scts; Band; Chorus; School Musical; Stu Cncl; Fld Hcky; Trk; Hon Roll; Shippensburg U; Secdry Math.

BERESNYAK, AMY; West Mifflin Area HS; West Mifflin, PA; (Y); Boys Clb Am; Exploring; Teachers Aide; Hon Roll; NHS; W Mifflin Area H S PTSA Fine Art Awd Lit 86; Psych.

BERESNYAK, FRANCINE; Marion Center HS; Home, PA; (Y); FBLA; Latin Clb; SADD; Varsity Clb; Cheerleading; Gregg Typng Awd 86; Lgl Sec.

BERESTECKI, LOUIS J; Yough SR HS; W Newton, PA; (Y); 4/226; Pres Church Yth Grp; Computer Clb; Ski Clb; Spanish Clb; Chorus; High Hon Roll; Lion Awd; NHS; Ntl Merit Ltr; Prfct Atten Awd; PA ST U; Engnrng.

BEREZANSKY, SUSAN; West Allegheny HS; Clinton, PA; (Y); Spanish Clb; Chorus; Nwsp Rptr; Ed Yrbk Phtg; Im Vllybl; Hon Roll.

BERG, BARBARA; Freedom HS; Bethlehem, PA; (Y); 27/392; Church Yth Grp; Cmnty Wkr; Hosp Aide; Science Clb; Band; Chorus; Orch; Fld Hcky; High Hon Roll; NHS; Sr All Star Fld Hockey Tm 85; Northampton Cnty Jr Miss Cntstnt 85; AAUW Schlrshp 86; U Of Scranton; Physcl Thrpy.

BERGAMINO, JACQUELYN; Old Forge JR/Sr HS; Old Forge, PA; (S); Im Coach Actv; Var Sftbl; Cit Awd; Hon Roll; NHS; Anasthslgy.

BERGEMAN, CINDY; Boyertown Area HS; Gilbertsvl, PA; (Y); 49/451; Hosp Aide; Library Aide; Cit Awd; High Hon Roll; Hon Roll.

BERGEN, JOANN; Creative & Performing Arts HS; Philadelphiia, PA; (Y); 59/130; JA; Yrbk Stf; Bsktbl; Sftbl; Vllybl; Penn ST U; Bus.

BERGER, ADAM; Radnor HS; Bryn Mawr, PA; (S); Chess Clb; Sec Debate Tm; NFL; Sec Speech Tm; Chorus; JV Crs Cntry; JV Tennis; High Hon Roll; Hon Roll; Ntl Merit Ltr; Ofcl Mbr Natl Forensics Lg 85.

BERGER, BONNIE; Schuyokill Haven HS; Schuylkill Haven, PA; (Y); Chorus; Yrbk Stf; Trs Frsh Cls; Trs Soph Cls; Hst Jr Cls; Hst Sr Cls; VP Stu Cncl; Var Capt Cheerleading; L Swmmng; Hon Roll; Swmmng Awd 84; SR Cls Stu Forum 86; Prncpls Advsry Comm 85; Penn ST Coll; Compt Sci.

BERGER, COLLEEN; Governor Mifflin HS; Mohnton, PA; (Y); 34/200; Dance Clb; Library Aide; Varsity Clb; Y-Teens; Variety Show; Yrbk Phtg; Yrbk Stf; Var L Cheerleading; Var Trk; Hon Roll; Hewberry; Mgmnt.

BERGER, DAN; Ambridge Area HS; Ambridge, PA; (Y); Am Leg Boys St; Boy Scts; Chess Clb; German Clb; JA; Quiz Bowl; Chorus; Hon Roll; AERNTCL Engr.

BERGER, DIANA; Coudersport JR SR HS; Coudersport, PA; (Y); 6/88; Church Yth Grp; French Clb; Ski Clb; Chorus; Church Choir; Nwsp Stf; Yrbk Stf; Var L Golf; High Hon Roll; NHS; Communications.

BERGER, ERIC; Conrad Weiser HS; Wernersville, PA; (Y); 60/184; Computer Clb; FFA; Spanish Clb; Contntl Math Leag Comp Cntst 85-86; Amer Comp Sci Leag Comp Cntst 4th 85-86; Kutztown U PA; Comp Sci.

BERGER, KELLI; Pennsbury HS; Fairless Hills, PA; (Y); Spanish Clb; Rep Frsh Cls; VP Soph Cls; Rep Jr Cls; Var Bowling; Mgr(s); JV Var Sftbl; Im Vllybl; Mgr Wrstlng; Hon Roll; Elem Educ.

BERGER, LISA; Spring Grove SR HS; Thomasville, PA; (Y); 82/222; Hon Roll.

BERGER, MELISSA; Cheltenham HS; Melrose Pk, PA; (Y); Stu Cncl; JV Cheerleading.

BERGER, PATRICK; Fleetwood Area HS; Fleetwood, PA; (Y); 3/105; Computer Clb; Band; Concert Band; Jazz Band; Mrchg Band; Pep Band; School Musical; Var Golf; Hon Roll; NHS.

BERGER, RENEE; Palisades JR SR HS; Coopersburg, PA; (Y); 27/150; Church Yth Grp; FBLA; Capt Flag Corp; Hon Roll; Jr NHS; NHS; Prfct Atten Awd; 1st Pl Stngrphr II In FBLA 86; Pres Acdmc Ftns Awd For Outstndng Acdmc Achvt 86; Maxwell Inst; Comp Prgmng.

BERGER, ROSALEEN; Eastern HS; E Prospect, PA; (Y); 50/159; Cmnty Wkr; Computer Clb; Library Aide; Red Cross Aide; Hon Roll; Physcl Therapy.

BERGER, RUTH; Greater Johnstown SR HS; Johnstown, PA; (Y); Drama Clb; Pep Clb; Band; Chorus; School Musical; Nwsp Rptr; Sec Stu Cncl; JV L Cheerleading; High Hon Roll; NHS.

BERGER, SCOTT; Greencastle-Antrim HS; Greencastle, PA; (Y); 35/178; Boy Scts; Trs Exploring; Hon Roll; NHS; Var L Swmmng; Swmmng Coaches Awd 86; Water Polo Var Capt 85; Shippensburg U; Crimnl Justc.

BERGERSTOCK, STEVE; Milton SR HS; Milton, PA; (Y); 65/202; Concert Band; Drm Mjr(t); Mrchg Band; Stu Cncl; Var Cheerleading; Socr; Wt Lftg; JV Wrstlng; Church Yth Grp; Chorus.

BERGIN, MELISSA; Gwynedd-Mercy Acad; Warrington, PA; (Y); 21/69; Bsktbl; Fld Hcky; Lcrss; NHS; Rita Preis Almnae Schlrshp 86; La Salle U; OR Nrs.

BERGMAN, KRISTI; Scranton Preparatory Schl; Scranton, PA; (Y); 29/191; PAVAS; Yrbk Stf; Lit Mag; Var L Cheerleading; Var Trk; High Hon Roll; Jr NHS; Hnrbl Mntn Alg, Ltn 84; Hnrbl Mntn Geom, Hstry, Engl 85; Intl Stud.

BERING, CHRISTINE; Cedar Crest HS; Lebanon, PA; (Y); 88/350; Latin Clb; Pep Clb; Spanish Clb; SADD; Band; Concert Band; Pre-Med.

BERISH, DANA; Cambria Heights HS; Patton, PA; (Y); 32/200; Hosp Aide; Band; Chorus; Concert Band; Trs Soph Cls; Var Mat Maids; Var Trk; Hon Roll; Phy Thrpst.

BERK, MARTI; Manheim Township HS; Lancaster, PA; (Y); 57/317; Key Clb; VP Trs Temple Yth Grp; School Play; Yrbk Phtg; Powder Puff Ftbl; Var L Swmmng; Hon Roll; Schlstc Art Cntst Gold Key Awd 84; Lancaster Cnty JR Miss Pgnt 85-86; Dsgnr Yrbk & Schl Clndr Cvrs 86; Cedar Crest Coll; Cmmrcl Art.

BERKEBILE, TRACY; North Star HS; Boswell, PA; (Y); 20/130; Sec Teachers Aide; Nwsp Stf; Yrbk Bus Mgr; Yrbk Stf; Sec Soph Cls; Sec Jr Cls; VP Sr Cls; Var L Bsktbl; Var L Vllybl; Hon Roll; Brdfrd Bus Schl; Lgl Secy.

BERKEY, APRIL R; N Star HS; Boswell, PA; (Y); 12/123; Art Clb; Church Yth Grp; FCA; NHS; Schltc Awd 83-84; 100 Pct Awd 83-85; Hghst PACE Avg Awd 83-85; Cambria-Rowe Bus Coll; Bus Adm.

BERKEY, BRENDA; Johnstown HS; Johnstown, PA; (Y); Pres Key Clb; Library Aide; Pep Clb; SADD; Chorus; Sftbl; Pres Schlr; Rep Stu Cncl; Var Capt Cheerleading.

BERKEY, JONATHAN; Danville SR HS; Danville, PA; (Y); 15/202; Am Leg Boys St; Var Crs Cntry; Var Trk; Am Hist.

BERKEY, KAREN; Somerset Area SR HS; Somerset, PA; (Y); 31/224; Computer Clb; English Clb; French Clb; JA; Q&S; School Play; Variety Show; Yrbk Rptr; Yrbk Stf; High Hon Roll; U Pittsburgh.

BERKHEISER, DAVID; Berwick Area HS; Berwick, PA; (Y); Chorus; Stage Crew; Yrbk Phtg; Yrbk Rptr; Yrbk Stf; L Golf; Penn ST U; Elec Engrng.

BERKLEY, KATHY; Somerset SR HS; Friedens, PA; (Y); 22/211; Pres Church Yth Grp; English Clb; French Clb; JA; Pep Clb; School Play; High Hon Roll; NHS; Pres Schlr; Bradford Schl Bus; Acctng.

BERKOWITZ, ALLISON; Abington SR HS; Roslyn, PA; (Y); 151/540; Key Clb; Band; School Play; Yrbk Stf; Off Sr Cls; Cheerleading; V Ltr 84-86; Temple U; Comm.

BERKSTRESSER, SHAWN; Mc Connellsburg HS; Mcconnellsburg, PA; (Y); 1/67; Church Yth Grp; Spanish Clb; Church Choir; Var Trk; Acadmc All Amer 85-86; Penn ST; Pilot.

BERLIN, ERIC; Manheim Central HS; Manheim, PA; (Y); Boy Scts; Band; Concert Band; Jazz Band; Mrchg Band; Orch; School Musical; Symp Band; Kiwanis Awd; Gov Hon Prg Awd; PA Gov Schl Arts Music 85; Music.

BERLIN, SAMANTHA; Lower Moreland HS; Huntingdon Valley, PA; (S); Church Yth Grp; Exploring; Key Clb; Science Clb; High Hon Roll; Hon Roll; NHS; Stage Crew; Bucks Cnty Dance Co 83-86; NE Regnl Ballet Assoc 83-86; Schlshp Stu Dance Inst 83-85; Stu Forum 86; U Of VA; Med.

BERLINGER, KRISTEN; Upper Moreland HS; Willow Gr, PA; (Y); 56/264; Chorus; School Musical; School Play; Var Bsktbl; Var Fld Hcky; Var L Lcrss; High Hon Roll; Church Yth Grp; Teachers Aide; Church Choir; Dist Chorus 85-86; Rgnl Chorus 86; Beaver Coll; Child Life.

BERLOT, MELISSA; Bishop Hoban HS; Nanticoke, PA; (Y); 3/230; Cmnty Wkr; FBLA; Pres Jr Cls; Rep Stu Cncl; Var Cheerleading; Im Gym; NHS; NEDT Awd; Ski Clb; Miss Swthrt; Pre-Law.

BERMUDEZ, ARMAND; Kennedy Christian HS; Sharpsville, PA; (Y); 19/98; Church Yth Grp; Intnl Clb; JA; Latin Clb; Service Clb; Ski Clb; Spanish Clb; Speech Tm; Stage Crew; Var Bsbl; Actn Clb; Pre-Med.

BERMUDEZ, ISABEL; Little Flower HS; Philadelphia, PA; (Y); 145/437; Hosp Aide; Hon Roll; Cert Drvng Instrctn 86; Incntv Awd Outstndng Emplye 85; Awd Chapel Aide 85; COLL Puerto Rico; Bus Adm.

BERNADOWSKI, BOBBI; California Area SR HS; California, PA; (Y); FBLA; FNA; Mrchg Band; Nwsp Sprt Ed; VP Jr Cls; Var Bsktbl; Var Cheerleading; Var Sftbl; Var Capt Vllybl; Hon Roll; Coal Queen Rep 86; Stu Rep Schl Brd 86-87; IN U PA; Nrsng.

BERNARD, ELISA; Nazareth Acad; Philadelphia, PA; (Y); 49/120; NFL; School Musical; School Play; Nwsp Rptr; Glee Clb83-86; Drma Clb 84-85; Itln Clb 83-86; Harvard U; Law.

BERNARD, JENNY; Central Dauphin HS; Harrisburg, PA; (Y); Church Yth Grp; Teachers Aide; Color Guard; Mrchg Band; Stu Cncl; Capt Twrlr; Im Vllybl; High Hon Roll; Hon Roll; Jr NHS; Intr Dsgn.

BERNARD, PAUL M; Yough SR HS; Madison, PA; (Y); 16/240; Debate Tm; French Clb; Model UN; Band; Chorus; Concert Band; Jazz Band; Mrchg Band; Orch; Pep Band; Named Among Top 5000 SAT Scores PA 585; PA ST U; Bus Admin.

BERNARDO, MARK; Windber Area HS; Windber, PA; (Y); Nwsp Stf; Rep Jr Cls; Hon Roll; Stu Of Month 84-86; Cmmrcl Art.

BERNARDO, NICHOLLE; Moon SR HS; Coraopolis, PA; (Y); 38/304; Dance Clb; Hosp Aide; JA; Key Clb; Office Aide; Band; Symp Band; Rep Frsh Cls; Rep Soph Cls; Rep Jr Cls; Mrt For Dncng 86; Pitt PA ST; Psych.

BERNAT, KARL; Allentown Central Catholic HS; Coopersburg, PA; (Y); 8/210; Pres Church Yth Grp; Lit Mag; Pres Jr Cls; Pres Stu Cncl; L Var Ftbl; High Hon Roll; Trs NHS; Science Clb; JV Bsbl; Var Wt Lftg; Prin Awd Sci 85; Prin Awd Outstndng Svc 86; PA Jr Acad Sci 1st 85; Med.

BERNECKER, DALE A; William Allen HS; Allentown, PA; (Y); Trs Leo Clb; Ski Clb; Hon Roll; Jr NHS; Lion Awd; NHS; Pres Schlr; PA ST U; Elect Engr.

BERNHARD, JEFF; Central Bucks Est HS; Doylestown, PA; (Y); Chorus; Im Badmtn; Im Bsktbl; VP Var Ftbl; Im Gym; Im Socr; Im Sftbl; Im Tennis; JV Trk; Im Vllybl; Med Fld.

BERNHARD, JOHN; Marian HS; Jim Thorpe, PA; (Y); 50/130; Boy Scts; Ski Clb; Ftbl; Wt Lftg.

BERNHART, JOHN; Northwestern HS; New Tripoli, PA; (Y); 5/170; Boy Scts; Debate Tm; Band; School Musical; School Play; Yrbk Ed-Chief; Pres Stu Cncl; Capt Mgr Socr; God Cntry Awd; NHS; Stipend Rsrch Frnkln & Mrshl Coll 85; Hrvrd Smmr Schl Pgm 86; Berkley; Egyptology.

BERNHART, SUSANNAH R; Reading SR HS; Reading, PA; (S); 2/681; Aud/Vis; Debate Tm; Sec Key Clb; Y-Teens; Chorus; Nwsp Rptr; Nwsp Stf; High Hon Roll; NHS; Reading Tutor 85.

BERNICK, STEVE; Norristown HS; Norristown, PA; (Y); 146/478; Boy Scts; Church Yth Grp; Political Wkr; Ski Clb; Chorus; Variety Show; Sec Soph Cls; Stu Cncl; Im Wt Lftg; Hon Roll; Union Leag Awd PA 85; Eagle Sct Natl Eagl Scvt Assoc 83; Order Arrw 83; Naval Acad; Pilot.

BERNINI, MARK; Our Lady Of Lourdes Regional HS; Mt Carmel, PA; (Y); 34/94; Key Clb; Yrbk Stf; Frsh Cls; Soph Cls; Jr Cls; Sr Cls; Bsktbl; Golf.

BERNLOHR, CHRISTOPHER; Central York HS; York, PA; (Y); Church Yth Grp; Band; Concert Band; Jazz Band; Mrchg Band; Symp Band; High Hon Roll; Hon Roll; Pres Schlr; PA Ambssdrs Of Music 84; Grove City Coll; Bus Mngmt.

BERNOSKI, BARBARA; Cambridge Springs HS; Saegertown, PA; (Y); 7/112; Pep Clb; Trs Yrbk Stf; Var L Sftbl; JV L Vllybl; Hon Roll; Prfct Atten Awd; Legal Fld.

BERNOSKI, TRICIA; Wyoming Valley West HS; Larksville, PA; (Y); Church Yth Grp; Key Clb; High Hon Roll; Hon Roll; NHS; NEDT Awd; Phrmcst.

BERNOT, LAWRENCE; Blacklick ValleyJRSR HS; Nanty-Glo, PA; (S); 3/97; Boy Scts; Computer Clb; German Clb; Varsity Clb; VP Trk; High Hon Roll; Hon Roll; Ger Natl Hnr Soc 85; Enrichmnt Pgm; U Pittsburg.

BERNOT, RON; Shaler Area HS; Allison Pk, PA; (Y); 100/550; Im Bsbl; Var Capt Bsktbl; Im Sftbl; Var Vllybl; Im Wt Lftg; Hnr Rll 85-86; Gvrnrs Awd Outstndg SAT 85-86; Drexel U; Elec Engnrng.

BERNOTTI, REMO; Devon Prep; Wayne, PA; (Y); Ski Clb; Stage Crew; Im Ftbl; Var Trk; Hon Roll; Chem Engnrng.

BERNSCHEIN, WILLIAM; Wissahickon HS; Gwynedd, PA; (Y); 47/206; Boy Scts; Key Clb; JV Var Bsbl; JV Var Ftbl; Var Golf; Im Socr; Hon Roll; Rotary Awd; Cert Of Merit Ntl Ltn Exm 86; Loyola Coll; Pre Med.

BERNSTEIN, JASON; High Schl Of Engineering And Science; Philadelphia, PA; (S); 2/229; Science Clb; Hon Roll; NHS; PA Jr Acadmy Sci 1st Awd 83-85; DE Vly Sci Fair 1st Pl 84-85; Schl Dist PA Comm Awd Sci 85; Physics.

BERNSTEIN, RACHEL; Cheltenham HS; Melrose Pk, PA; (Y); School Musical; School Play; Capt Var Gym; Holden Award 86.

BERRESFORD, CHRISTINA; Southmoreland SR HS; Scottdale, PA; (Y); 5/240; French Clb; Math Clb; Lit Mag; French Hon Soc; Sec NHS; Ntl Merit Ltr; St Vincent Coll; Physcs.

BERRETTINI, SUSAN; Wyoming Valley West HS; Forty Fort, PA; (Y); Key Clb; Nwsp Stf; Pres Jr Cls; Pres Sr Cls; L Bsktbl; L Sftbl; Cit Awd; Hon Roll; NHS; NEDT Awd; Wyomng Vally Yth Salute Ldrshp Awd 86; Med.

BERRIER, ANNE; Lewistown Area HS; Lewistown, PA; (Y); Ski Clb; Spanish Clb; Off Frsh Cls; Off Soph Cls; Var Cheerleading; Hon Roll; Orthodontist.

BERRIER, RUSSELL; Juniata HS; East Waterford, PA; (Y); VICA; High Hon Roll; Hon Roll; Jr NHS; NHS; Pres Schlr; Outstndng Prfrmnce Voc Tech Schl Eltrncs 86; Voc Tech Awd 86; Electronic Institutes; Elec.

BERRY, CLARA A; Canon-Mc Millan SR HS; Canonsburg, PA; (Y); 35/340; Latin Clb; Science Clb; Color Guard; Flag Corp; Stage Crew; Im Vllybl; High Hon Roll; Hon Roll; Ntl Merit Ltr; Prfct Atten Awd; Boston U; Astrophysics.

BERRY, ELIZABETH A; Quaker Valley SR HS; Sewickley, PA; (Y); 9/165; Church Yth Grp; Nwsp Rptr; Yrbk Stf; Rep Soph Cls; Rep Jr Cls; Var Bowling; Var L Crs Cntry; Var L Trk; Hon Roll; NCTE Awd; Fin NCTE Awd 84-85; NHS 84-86; Intl Rltns.

BERRY, GEORGIA; Lock Haven SR HS; Lock Haven, PA; (Y); Church Yth Grp; Spanish Clb; Chorus; Church Choir; School Play; Socr; Hon Roll; Mth.

BERRY, JEAN ELLEN MARIE; Bethlehem Center SR HS; Marianna, PA; (Y); 8/156; Church Yth Grp; Pres 4-H; Spanish Clb; Mat Maids; High Hon Roll; Hon Roll; Sec NHS; U S Bus Ed Awds 85; Acad All Amer 85; Natl Ldrshp & Svc Awds 86.

BERRY, LYNDA; John S Fine HS; Nanticoke, PA; (Y); Hosp Aide; Key Clb; Ski Clb; Chorus; Variety Show; Yrbk Stf; VP Soph Cls; VP Jr Cls; VP Sr Cls; Bsktbl; Physcl Thrpy.

BERRY, RICHARD; Waynesburg Central HS; Mt Morris, PA; (Y); 30/190; Letterman Clb; Spanish Clb; Varsity Clb; Ftbl; WV U; Bus.

BERRY, VICTORIA N; Penn Wood HS; Lansdowne, PA; (Y); Mrchg Band; Orch; Yrbk Phtg; Yrbk Stf; Stat Bsbl; Stat Ftbl; JV Tennis; Stat Wrstlng; High Hon Roll; Jr NHS; Received Engl Awds 84 & 86; Bus Admin.

BERTAGNI, DAVID; Father Judge HS; Philadelphia, PA; (Y); 65/358; Computer Clb; German Clb; Comp Sci.

BERTENTHAL, MICHELLE; Chartiers Valley HS; Pittsburgh, PA; (Y); GAA; Ski Clb; Crs Cntry; Trk; High Hon Roll; NHS.

BERTI, LOIS; Wyoming Valley West HS; Swoyersville, PA; (Y); Church Yth Grp; Key Clb; Var Capt Fld Hcky; High Hon Roll; NHS; Phrmcy.

BERTIN, DAVID; Montoursville HS; Montoursville, PA; (Y); 60/194; French Clb; Letterman Clb; Varsity Clb; Bsbl; Var Capt Socr.

BERTINI, LISA V; Dubois Area HS; Dubois, PA; (Y); 60/268; Intnl Clb; L Varsity Clb; Chorus; Pep Band; Swing Chorus; Var L Tennis; Hon Roll; Nice KID Awd 85; MVP Tnns 86; Wilma Boyd Career Schl; Travel.

BERTRAM, CHRISTINA; Sharon HS; Sharon, PA; (Y); Chorus; Church Choir; Orch; School Musical; Crs Cntry; Trk; Bausch & Lomb Sci Awd; Hon Roll; NHS; NEDT Awd.

BERTRAM, JEFFREY; Clearfield Area HS; Clearfield, PA; (Y); 61/296; Key Clb; Ski Clb; JV Bsbl; Im Bsktbl; Im Bowling; Im Ftbl; Im Tennis; Im Vllybl; High Hon Roll; Hon Roll; Mst Spirit Awd Var Golf 84; High Hon Roll 82; Hon Roll 82-86; Juniata Coll; Physcl Thrpy.

BERTRAM, TAMMY; Frazier HS; Perryopolis, PA; (Y); Boys Clb Am; Drama Clb; School Play; Stage Crew; Off Jr Cls; Pres Sr Cls; Stat Bsktbl; Stat Ftbl; High Hon Roll; NHS; Drama Clb Awd 87; Outstng Svc Awd 87; Tutor Awd 87; CMU; Archit.

BERTRES, ANGELA; Marion Center Area HS; Marion Ctr, PA; (Y); 89/170; Church Yth Grp; Intnl Clb; SADD; Varsity Clb; Band; Chorus; Church Choir; Concert Band; Jazz Band; Yrbk Stf; Music.

BERTSCH, DAVE; Kutztown Area HS; Kempton, PA; (Y); 4-H; 4-H Awd; High Hon Roll; Engr.

BERTUCCI, LARA; New Castle SR HS; New Castle, PA; (S); 24/253; Pres Church Yth Grp; NFL; Sec SADD; School Play; Stu Cncl; Var Capt Cheerleading; Coach Actv; Band; Yrbk Stf; Hugh O Biren Yth Ldrshp Awd 85; Dist Stu Cncl Frm Rep 85-86; St Marys Coll; Psychlgy.

BERZINSKY, CLARISSA; Greater Johnstown HS; Johnstown, PA; (Y); Exploring; German Clb; JA; Political Wkr; Chorus; Yrbk Stf; High Hon Roll; Hon Roll; NHS; Rotary Awd; Bsktbl Awd 85-86; Chem Engr.

BERZONSKI, JAMES; Hampton HS; Gibsonia, PA; (Y); 96/255; Exploring; FBLA; Capt Bowling; High Hon Roll; Hon Roll; PA ST U; Acctg.

BESACK, KAREN; Bishop Conwell HS; Bristol, PA; (Y); 16/254; French Clb; Office Aide; Q&S; Ed Lit Mag; Vllybl; Hon Roll; NHS; Holy Family Coll; Tchr.

BESCHEN, ELIZABETH; Saint Basil Acad; Philadelphia, PA; (S); 1/100; Chorus; Madrigals; Yrbk Ed-Chief; Lit Mag; Capt Socr; Hon Roll; Ntl Merit Ltr; Schlrshp St Basil Acad 82-86; Ntl Eng Merit Awd 84; 2nd Pl Sci Fair 84; Eng.

BESECKER, MICHELLE; Waynesboro Area SR HS; Waynesboro, PA; (Y); Sec Church Yth Grp; Stu Cncl; JV Cheerleading; JV Var Fld Hcky; JV Trk; High Hon Roll; Hon Roll; VP NHS; Penn ST; Acctng.

BEST, BARBARA; Chartiers Valley HS; Presto, PA; (Y); 13/308; Church Yth Grp; Cmnty Wkr; Dance Clb; Drill Tm; School Musical; School Play; Pom Pon; NHS; PA ST U; Acctg.

BEST, CHERIE; Keystone HS; Shippenville, PA; (Y); 31/125; Church Yth Grp; Chorus; Sec Concert Band; Sec Jazz Band; Sec Mrchg Band; Sec Orch; Sec Pep Band; Hon Roll; Sec Band; Dist III Band 86; Anderson Coll.

BEST, CONNIE; North East HS; Brookville, PA; (Y); Church Yth Grp; Yrbk Stf; Cheerleading; Vllybl; Dubois Schl Business; Sectrl.

BESTVINA, DIANE M; Penns Manor JR SR HS; Clymer, PA; (Y); 6/75; Band; Chorus; Concert Band; Jazz Band; Mrchg Band; School Musical; High Hon Roll; Hon Roll; NHS; Prfct Atten Awd; IN U Of PA; Med Tech.

BESWICK, JENNIFER; Upper Darby HS; Glenolden, PA; (Y); FBLA; Rep VICA; Rep Jr Cls; Stat Gym; High Hon Roll; Hon Roll; VICA Skills Olympcs 86; Cmmrcl Art.

BETCHER, MICHAEL; Windber Area HS; Windber, PA; (Y); Letterman Clb; Ski Clb; Sec Varsity Clb; Sec Jr Cls; Stu Cncl; Bsbl; Ftbl; Wt Lftg; Hon Roll; Prfct Atten Awd; Stu Of Mnth 85; Pre-Law.

BETHARD, JOHN; Upper Moreland SR HS; Willow Grove, PA; (Y); 85/264; Aud/Vis; Chorus; Church Choir; Lit Mag; Rgt T Dnbrw Media Schlrshp; Penn ST; Film Prdcr.

BETHARD, MARIJANE; Upper Moreland HS; Willowgrove, PA; (Y); 85/253; VP Church Yth Grp; French Clb; Key Clb; Yrbk Stf; Off Soph Cls; Off Jr Cls; Off Sr Cls; Off Stu Cncl; Cheerleading; Hon Roll; Bus.

BETLER, MARIANNE; Mc Guffey HS; Claysville, PA; (Y); French Clb; Pep Clb; Spanish Clb; Chorus; School Musical; School Play; Stage Crew; Yrbk Sprt Ed; Yrbk Stf; Bsktbl; Stu Rcgntn Awd 85 & 86; Natl Hnor Socty; High Hnor Roll; Hnor Roll; Wght Lifting; Score Keeper; Mgr; Westminster Coll.

BETTENISSI, JEFFREY; Penn Hills SR HS; Pittsburgh, PA; (Y); Drama Clb; Nwsp Stf; Stu Cncl; Trk; Hon Roll; Cmmrcl Art.

BETTI, JOSEPH; Roman Catholic HS; Philadelphia, PA; (S); 15/133; Computer Clb; Var Bsbl; Im Bsktbl; Im Coach Actv; Im Tennis; Hon Roll; Ntl Merit Ltr; Acad All Amer; Villanova U; Orthdntst.

BETTLER, DAVID; Northwestern Lehigh HS; Germansville, PA; (Y); 50/143; Aud/Vis; 4-H; Ski Clb; Yrbk Stf; Var Bsbl; JV Bsktbl; Var Ftbl; Im Wt Lftg; 4-H Awd; Hon Roll; Kutztown U; Bus.

BETTOR, LESLIE; Kiski Area HS; New Kensington, PA; (Y); Office Aide; Band; Concert Band; Mrchg Band; Mgr(s); Hon Roll; Nrsng.

BETTS, CRAIG; Christian School Of York; Camp Hill, PA; (S); Band; Chorus; Concert Band; Orch; School Musical; Chrmn Jr Cls; Crs Cntry; Ntl Merit Ltr; Church Yth Grp; Dist Chrs & Bnd; Fine Arts Cmptn; Messiah Coll; Music.

BETTS, DAWN; Punxsutawney Area HS; Walston, PA; (Y); 43/238; FBLA; Hon Roll.

BETTS, DONALD; Delaware County Christian Schl; Radnor, PA; (Y); 25/78; Var JV Bsktbl; High Hon Roll; Hon Roll; Bus.

BETTS, LORRANIE; Warren Area HS; Warren, PA; (Y); Church Yth Grp; Math Tm; VP Spanish Clb; Varsity Clb; Acpl Chr; Madrigals; Stu Cncl; Crs Cntry; Trk; High Hon Roll; Math.

BETTS, TAMMY; Punxsutawney Area HS; Walston, PA; (Y); Hon Roll; Acctng.

BETZ, BRIAN; Berwick Area SR HS; Wapwallopen, PA; (Y); 11/250; Church Yth Grp; Hon Roll; NHS; Penn ST U; Elec Engrng.

BETZ, DAVID; Danville HS; Danville, PA; (Y); Pres Church Yth Grp; Computer Clb; Exploring; Key Clb; Spanish Clb; Var Socr; JV Trk; Law.

BETZ, HEIDI; Donegal HS; Mount Joy, PA; (Y); Trs Church Yth Grp; School Play; Yrbk Ed-Chief; Rep Frsh Cls; Rep Soph Cls; Rep Jr Cls; Rep Stu Cncl; JV Fld Hcky; Var Trk; Hon Roll; Rotary Ldrs Conf Messiah Coll 86; Booster Clb Pres 86-87; Pharm.

BETZER, TOBY; Selinsgrove Area HS; Selingsgrove, PA; (Y); Boy Scts; Spanish Clb; Chorus; Var JV Ftbl; Hon Roll; Game Prtctr.

BETZHOLD, CHERYL; Seton Catholic HS; W Avoca, PA; (Y); Church Yth Grp; Chorus; Im Swmmng; Im Vllybl; Hon Roll; NHS; US Achvt Acad Awd For Spnsh 85; Grtr Pittston Bus & Prof Wmns Clb Schlrshp Awd 86; Marywood Coll; Accntg.

BEUCHER, BETH; Geibel HS; Connellsville, PA; (Y); Dance Clb; Pep Clb; Lit Mag; JV Cheerleading; Vllybl; Hon Roll; PA ST; Bus.

BEUKA, NANCY LYNN; Northwest Area HS; Hunlock Creek, PA; (Y); 20/108; Computer Clb; French Clb; High Hon Roll; NHS; Algbr II & Trig Awd Achvt; Bloomsburg U.

BEURY, KATHRYN; Lancaster Catholic HS; Columbia, PA; (Y); 36/206; Yrbk Sprt Ed; Yrbk Stf; JV Sftbl; Warner Cable Cmmnctns Inc Schlrshp; Millersville U.

BEUTH, DIRK; Ford City HS; Ford City, PA; (Y); 4/150; High Hon Roll; NHS; Provost Schlr 86; Pres Acad Ftns Awd 86; Hnr Stu 86; U Pittsburgh; Microbio.

BEUTTEL, ELIZABETH; Cheltenham HS; Melrose Pk, PA; (Y); Library Aide; Teachers Aide; Cit Awd; Occptnl Therpst.

BEVACQUA, MELISSA; West Mifflin Area HS; W Mifflin, PA; (Y); Band; Jazz Band; Mrchg Band; Yrbk Stf; Hon Roll; Pitt; Spch Thrpy.

BEVAN, JENNA; Pocono Mountain HS; Scotrun, PA; (Y); 27/300; Aud/Vis; Drama Clb; SADD; Chorus; School Musical; Swing Chorus; Rep Frsh Cls; Off Soph Cls; Off Jr Cls; Hon Roll; Music Thtr.

BEVENOUR, MATTHEW T; Archbishop John Carroll HS; Havertown, PA; (Y); 1/166; Church Yth Grp; Cmnty Wkr; Drama Clb; Thesps; School Musical; Nwsp Ed-Chief; Yrbk Stf; Rep Jr Cls; Rep Sr Cls; Stu Cncl; Outstndng Achvt Schlrshp Temple U 86; Temple U; Brdcst.

BEVEVINO, JUDY; Warren Area HS; Warren, PA; (Y); Church Yth Grp; Debate Tm; Varsity Clb; Acpl Chr; Rep Stu Cncl; Trk; High Hon Roll; Jr NHS; NHS; Ntl Merit Ltr; PA ST U; Engrng.

BEVILACQUA, ANN MARIE; West Scranton HS; Scranton, PA; (Y); Ski Clb; Spanish Clb; Mrchg Band; Nwsp Stf; Yrbk Stf; Rep Stu Cncl; Var Pom Pon; Hon Roll; NHS; U Of Scranton; Psych.

BEVLOCK, DANIELLE N; North Pocono HS; Moscow, PA; (Y); 75/246; Church Yth Grp; FBLA; Girl Scts; Ski Clb; Varsity Clb; School Musical; Yrbk Stf; Stu Cncl; Cheerleading; Hon Roll; Ed.

BEY, CAMERON; Schenley Teacher Center; Pittsburgh, PA; (S); Exploring; Wt Lftg; Hon Roll; NHS; Prfct Atten Awd; Mbr Hlth Occptn/Stu Of Amer 84-87; Biolgy.

BEYER, VICKIE; Blue Mountain HS; Orwigsburg, PA; (Y); 69/225; Art Clb; Library Aide; Chorus; Nwsp Rptr; Nwsp Stf; Rep Stu Cncl; Var L Cheerleading; Var Swmmng; Var L Trk; Hon Roll.

BEYERL, LORIE; Shaler Area HS; Allison, PA; (Y); 60/517; Ski Clb; Spanish Clb; Hon Roll; NHS; Spanish NHS; West Palm JR Coll; Nrsng.

BEYNON, BRIDGET; Lackawanna Trail HS; Factoryville, PA; (Y); 10/94; Church Yth Grp; Yrbk Stf; Rep Stu Cncl; Var Bsktbl; Var Sftbl; Hon Roll; NHS; Crimінlgy.

BEZEK, WILLIAM; Central Cambria HS; Johnstown, PA; (S); 3/209; Boy Scts; Computer Clb; Wt Lftg; Hon Roll; Eagle Scout Awds 84.

BHATT, SNEHAL; Bradford Area HS; Bradford, PA; (Y); 3/314; AFS; Debate Tm; Sec Girl Scts; Ski Clb; Chorus; Nwsp Rptr; L Cheerleading; Capt L Tennis; Pres Jr NHS; Rotary Awd; Grl Sct Gld Awd 84-85; MVP Tennis Tm 85-86; Silvr Awd & Gld Awd Ldrshp 83-84; U Of PA; Med.

BHAVANANDAN, SIVAKAMI; Hershey HS; Hershey, PA; (Y); Pres Chess Clb; Dance Clb; German Clb; Math Clb; Model UN; Band; Concert Band; School Musical; School Play; Variety Show; 2nd Pl ST Dance Comp 86; Penn ST; Pre-Med.

BHAVSAR, NEHA; Montour HS; Mckees Rocks, PA; (Y); Exploring; Temple Yth Grp; Band; Concert Band; Mrchg Band; High Hon Roll; Hon Roll; Prfct Atten Awd; Perf Awd Bal Vihar St Fair 86; Awd Essay Statue Of Lib 86; Awd KY Derby Fest 85; Case Western Reserve U; Gen Eng.

BHULLAR, INDERMEET; Bethel Park HS; Bethel Park, PA; (Y); 60/515; Computer Clb; Math Clb; Math Tm; Science Clb; Socr; Tennis; High Hon Roll; 1st Pl PA JR Acad Of Sci 84-86; Pre-Med.

BIAGETTI, LISA; Seton-Lasalle HS; Pittsburgh, PA; (Y); 44/270; Girl Scts; Hosp Aide; Ski Clb; Color Guard; Drill Tm; Nwsp Bus Mgr; Nwsp Rptr; Mgr Sftbl; Hon Roll; Natl Hnr Rll 86; Acad All-Amer 86; Educ.

BIALEK, KIMBERLY; Southmoreland HS; Scottdale, PA; (Y); 17/240; Church Yth Grp; French Clb; Ski Clb; VP Band; Church Choir; VP Concert Band; VP Mrchg Band; Orch; Symp Band; French Hon Soc; Nrsng.

BIALON, DAVID; Greater Latrobe SR HS; Latrobe, PA; (Y); 38/345; VP VICA; Golf; High Hon Roll; Presdntl Acad Fitns Awd 86; W PA Golf Assn Caddie Schlrshp 86; Outstndng Male Voctnl Stu 86; IN U-PA; Mgmt Info Systms.

BIANCHI, DANIELLE; Valley View JR SR HS; Peckville, PA; (Y); Dance Clb; Drama Clb; Latin Clb; Letterman Clb; Varsity Clb; Chorus; School Musical; School Play; Capt Cheerleading; Capt Trk; Acad Excllnc.

BIANCO, CARLA; Center Area HS; Monaca, PA; (Y); Chorus; Jazz Band; School Musical; Variety Show; Nwsp Stf; Yrbk Stf; High Hon Roll; NHS; Latin Clb; Nwsp Rptr; Rprsntd Cntr Beaver Cntys JR Miss PGNT 86; Slctd Hnrs Dstrcts Rgnls ST Chrs 86; 1st Pl Crnvl Crse; Philadelphia Coll; Vce.

BIANCO, JEFFREY; Punxsutawney Area HS; Punxsutawney, PA; (Y); Chess Clb; Spanish Clb; Hon Roll; Stu Mnth Awd 84; Ed.

BIANCO, THOMAS M; Penns Manor HS; Heilwood, PA; (Y); 1/76; French Clb; Pres Jr Cls; Pres Sr Cls; Bsktbl; Golf; Bausch & Lomb Sci Awd; DAR Awd; Pres NHS; Pres Schlr; Val; Amer Leg Awd 83; Actvty Aw, Prsdntl Ftnss Awd 86; IN U PA; Fin.

BIANCULLI, STEVEN J; Seneca Valley HS; Mars, PA; (Y); Boy Scts; Hon Roll; U Of Pittsburgh; Mechncl Engrng.

BIBEL, MICHELLE; Yough SR HS; Smithton, PA; (Y); 32/224; Pres Church Yth Grp; Drama Clb; French Clb; FTA; School Play; Yrbk Rptr; Hon Roll; NHS; Library Aide; Pep Clb; CA U Of PA Faclty Schlrp 86; Yough Educ Assoc Schlrp 86; CA U Of PA; Sec Math Educ.

BIBLEHIMER, HOLLY; Montoursville HS; Montoursville, PA; (Y); Red Cross Aide; Spanish Clb; Chorus; Church Choir; Swmmng; Hon Roll; Spnsh Awd; Erly Chldhd Dvlpmnt.

BIBUS, CHRIS; Hamburg Area HS; Hamburg, PA; (Y); Chess Clb; Church Yth Grp; German Clb; Ski Clb; SADD; Rep Sr Cls; JV Var Bsbl; Var Ftbl; High Hon Roll; Hon Roll; Elect Engrg.

BICER, JEFFREY; St Pius X HS; Pottstown, PA; (S); 51/161; Rep Soph Cls; Rep Jr Cls; Hon Roll; NEDT Awd; Yth Ldrshp Conf; Engrng.

BICKEL, BETH; Altoona Area HS; Altoona, PA; (Y); Pres Key Clb; Ski Clb; Band; Capt Color Guard; Mrchg Band; Orch; Symp Band; Off Sr Cls; Stu Cncl; Var Trk; Penn ST U; Landscape Arch.

BICKEL, PAUL; Parkland SR HS; Allentown, PA; (Y); 52/459; Boy Scts; Church Yth Grp; VP Band; Concert Band; Jazz Band; Mrchg Band; School Musical; God Cntry Awd; High Hon Roll; Hon Roll; Lehigh Cnty Band 86.

BICKER, ALAN D; Knoch JR & SR HS; Cabot, PA; (Y); 1/239; AFS; Am Leg Boys St; Church Yth Grp; SADD; School Play; VP Jr Cls; Off Sr Cls; Trs Stu Cncl; L Trk; Bausch & Lomb Sci Awd; Saxonburg Wmns Clb Schlrshp 86; Biolgy Awd 86; Frnch Awd 85; Bucknell U; Chmstry.

BICKFORD, ROD; Albert Gallatin HS; Masontown, PA; (Y); JA; Varsity Clb; Band; Capt Concert Band; Drill Tm; Drm Mjr(t); Mrchg Band; Stu Cncl; Var Wrstlng; Ntl Merit Schol; Acctng.

BICKHAM, JENNY; Wellsboro Area HS; Wellsboro, PA; (Y); Pres Drama Clb; French Clb; Chorus; School Musical; Nwsp Ed-Chief; Yrbk Stf; High Hon Roll; NHS; Presdntl Acadmc Ftns Awd 86; Friday Clb Engl Awd 86; Oberlin Coll; Lingstcs.

BICKHART, JANET; Ephrata SR HS; Ephrata, PA; (Y); 19/250; Church Yth Grp; Exploring; 4-H; Red Cross Aide; Teachers Aide; Mrchg Band; 4-H Awd; Hon Roll; NHS; Library Aide; Gld Key Art Awd 85; Geisinger Medcl Ctr; Rdtn Thrpy.

BICKSLER, GARY; Tulpehocken HS; Richland, PA; (S); 13/112; VP 4-H; Pres FFA; Var Bsbl; Hon Roll; NHS; FFA Star Grrnhnd Awd 84; FFA Star Chptr Frmr Awd 85; Govrnrs Sch Of Agri 85.

BIDDLE, BRADFORD; Malvern Preparatory Schl; Malvern, PA; (Y); 4/92; Mathletes; Nwsp Stf; Lit Mag; Var Capt Swmmng; Hon Roll; NHS; Ntl Merit SF.

BIDDLE, LISA; Spring Ford HS; Spring City, PA; (Y); 26/237; Church Yth Grp; Church Choir; Bsktbl; Trk; Hon Roll; Awd Shwng Rlgn Cnvctn 86; Bradford Bus Schl; Bus.

BIDDLE, ROBIN; Brownsville Area SR HS; Republic, PA; (Y); VP FBLA; Math Clb; Ski Clb; SADD; Teachers Aide; Band; Stu Cncl; Bsktbl; Hon Roll; Outstndg Shorthand/Wrd Prcssng Stu Awd; Uniontown Beauty Acad; Csmtlgy.

BIDELSPACH, AILEEN; Millville Area HS; Bloomsburg, PA; (S); 2/99; Chess Clb; Pres Church Yth Grp; Drama Clb; Math Tm; Yrbk Stf; God Cntry Awd; High Hon Roll; NHS; Hugh O Brian Schlrshp 85; Pi Mu Alpha Awd-Math 85.

BIDELSPACH, JILL; Southern Columbia Area HS; Elysburg, PA; (Y); Camera Clb; Church Yth Grp; Key Clb; School Play; Pres Frsh Cls; Pres Soph Cls; Pres Stu Cncl; JV Cheerleading; JV Mgr(s); JV Trk; Frgn Lang.

BIDWELL, HOLLY; North Pocono HS; Moscow, PA; (S); 15/250; Ski Clb; Yrbk Stf; Rep Stu Cncl; Var Capt Crs Cntry; Var L Trk; High Hon Roll; Hon Roll; NHS; Cross-Cntry St Meet 85.

BIEBEL, CHRIS; Carlisle HS; Carlisle, PA; (Y); Band; Concert Band; Jazz Band; Mrchg Band; School Musical; Hon Roll; Dist Band 85-86; Sound Of Am 86.

BIEBEL, EDWARD; Holy Ghost Prep Schl; Philadelphia, PA; (Y); 3/82; Pres Aud/Vis; Boy Scts; Library Aide; Mathletes; Ed Nwsp Rptr; Im Bowling; NHS; Ntl Merit Ltr; Holy Ghost Fathers Chrstn Living Awd 86; Germn Awd 85; Rev Andrew A O Rourke Relgn Awd 86; St Josephs U; Lawyer.

BIEBER, BECKY; Burgettstown Area JR SR HS; Burgettstown, PA; (Y); Hosp Aide; Band; Concert Band; Drm Mjr(t); Mrchg Band; Variety Show; Stu Cncl; Hon Roll; NHS; Church Yth Grp; Dist Band; Regnl Band; Pitt Mc Donalds All Star Marching Band; Pre-Med.

BIEBER, KELLY; Brandywine Heights HS; Alburtis, PA; (Y); FNA; Color Guard; JV Cheerleading; Girl Scts; St Josephs Schl Of Nrsng; Nrsng.

BIEBER, RABECCA; Burgettstown Area JR SR HS; Burgettstown, PA; (Y); Hosp Aide; Sec Science Clb; Band; Chorus; Concert Band; Drm Mjr(t); Mrchg Band; Trs Stu Cncl; Hon Roll; NHS; Dist I Bnd; Rgn I Bnd; Pitt-Mc Donalds All Atar Bnd; Music.

BIEBER, SUSAN K; Upper Merion Area HS; King Of Prussia, PA; (S); 28/330; Rep Stu Cncl; Var Bsktbl; Var Fld Hcky; Var Sftbl; Hon Roll; Rotary Awd; Try Intl 4 Way Tst Wnr 85; Sbrbn I 2nd Team Vrsty Bsktbl, Sftbl & Fld Hcky 85; Teacher.

BIEDKA, DIANNE; Central Bucks East HS; Doylestown, PA; (Y); Cmnty Wkr; Hosp Aide; Ski Clb; Yrbk Stf; Fld Hcky; Sftbl; Hon Roll; East Stroudsburg; Educ.

BIEDZINSKI, MARY; Baldwin HS; Pittsburgh, PA; (Y); 217/535; Church Yth Grp; Var L Bsktbl; Mgr(s); Sftbl; Hon Roll; Pittsburgh; Bus Admn.

BIEGA, ROBIN A; Carlisle SR HS; Carlisle, PA; (Y); 68/402; Am Leg Aux Girls St; Church Yth Grp; Dance Clb; Drama Clb; School Musical; School Play; Nwsp Stf; Capt Cheerleading; Hon Roll; Kiwanis Awd; 1st Rnnr Up-Miss Cumberland Vly Pgnt 86; Prfrmng Allenberry Playhouse Theater 86; IN U Of PA; Tv Brdcstng.

BIEHL, CHRISTOPHER; Cedar Grove Christian Acad; Philadelphia, PA; (Y); Boy Scts; Nwsp Stf; Yrbk Stf; Var Bsbl; Var Bsktbl; Var Crs Cntry; Var Socr; Hon Roll; Eagle Sct Boys Sct.

BIEHL, LISA; Hamburg Area HS; Hamburg, PA; (Y); 17/152; Pres German Clb; Band; Chorus; School Musical; Sec Sr Cls; Var Capt Bsktbl; Hon Roll; JP Sousa Awd; NHS; BPW Bk Schlrshp 86; Dstrct Chorus & Dstrct Bnd; Cnty All Star Bsktbl Team 86; Lebanon Vly Coll; Msc.

BIELAWSKI, KIMBERLY; Bishop Kenrick HS; W Norristown, PA; (Y); 13/295; Cmnty Wkr; Math Tm; Science Clb; Ski Clb; Color Guard; Var Cheerleading; Hon Roll; NHS; French Clb; Mathletes; French Awd Best In Class; Math Awd Best In Class; Bio-Med Engr.

BIELEK, AMY; Kiski Area HS; E Vandergrift, PA; (Y); FBLA; Girl Scts; Library Aide; Pep Clb; Band; Concert Band; Mrchg Band; High Hon Roll; Acad Letter 86; Fitness Awd 83-86; Accntng.

BIENIEK, JANET; Bishop Guilfoyle HS; Altoona, PA; (S); 8/130; German Clb; Chorus; Var Vllybl; High Hon Roll; Hon Roll; Achvt 84-85; High Hnr Rll 85-86; Penn ST U; Educ.

BIER, PARICK J; Apollo-Ridge SR HS; Apollo, PA; (Y); German Clb; Band; Concert Band; Mrchg Band; Pep Band; School Play; Lit Mag; Hon Roll; NHS; Chem.

BIERANOSKI, MELISSA; Kiski Area HS; New Kensington, PA; (Y); French Clb; Pep Clb; SADD; Chorus; Color Guard; Drm & Bgl; Yrbk Stf; Rep Stu Cncl; High Hon Roll; Hon Roll; Bus Adm.

BIERI, CYNTHIA; Ambridge Area HS; Freedom, PA; (Y); 54/265; German Clb; Pep Clb; Red Cross Aide; SADD; Band; Concert Band; Mrchg Band; Pep Band; Symp Band; Hon Roll.

BIERLY, M GREGORY; Elizabethtown Area HS; Elizabethtown, PA; (S); Aud/Vis; Jazz Band; Mrchg Band; Orch; Mgr Stage Crew; Symp Band; JV Bsktbl; Ntl Merit Ltr; Rotary Awd; Music Engrng.

BIERNESSER, DARLENE; Fox Chapel Area HS; Pittsburgh, PA; (Y); GAA; Office Aide; Stu Cncl; JV Bsktbl; Coach Actv; Var Capt Socr; Var Vllybl; Hon Roll; WPIAL Coaches Tm Sccr 85; E Regnl Selct Cmp Sccr 84-86; E Regnl Selct Tm Sccr 85; Sprts Med.

BIESER, TINA; Cowanesque Valley HS; Middlebury Ctr, PA; (S); 1/88; Church Yth Grp; Hosp Aide; Ski Clb; Drm & Bgl; Drm Mjr(t); Capt Co-Capt Cheerleading; Twrlr; High Hon Roll; NHS; Pres Ftns Awd; Penn ST; Pre-Med.

BIEVENOUR, MICHAEL G; Dover Area HS; Dover, PA; (Y); Church Yth Grp; JA; Ski Clb; Chorus; Var L Socr; Hon Roll; Millersville U; Ind Arts Ed.

BIGELOW, AILEEN; Twin Valley HS; Morgantown, PA; (Y); 9/127; Church Yth Grp; Pres JA; Quiz Bowl; Spanish Clb; VP SADD; Varsity Clb; School Musical; Trs Soph Cls; Trs Jr Cls; Trs Sr Cls; JA Pres 86; Ntl JA Cong 85-86; JA Schlrshp 86; George Washington U; Intl Rltns.

BIGENHO, AMY ANN; Kiski Area HS; Apollo, PA; (Y); Office Aide; Chorus; Color Guard; Variety Show; Sftbl; Stat Vllybl; DAR Awd; Hon Roll; Rotary Awd; St Vincent Coll; Med Tech/Bio.

BIGGANS, ANDREW; Bellefonte HS; Bellefonte, PA; (Y); 140/243; Boy Scts; Library Aide; Pres Of Oib Clb 86; Comp.

BIGGANS, KAREN; St Huberts HS; Philadelphia, PA; (Y); 35/364; School Play; Hon Roll; Cert Cmndtn Diocesan Bus Ed Comp Acctg I 86; Acctg.

BIGGS, COLLEEN; Allentown Central Catholic HS; Allentown, PA; (Y); 14/210; Church Yth Grp; Exploring; Hosp Aide; Library Aide; Band; Concert Band; Mrchg Band; Pep Band; High Hon Roll; NHS; Diocesan Bnd 85-86; RN.

BIGGS, SCOTT; Moshannon-Valley JR SR HS; Brisbin, PA; (Y); 33/120; Aud/Vis; Church Yth Grp; Spanish Clb; SADD; School Play; Stage Crew; JV Wrstlng; Messiah Coll Grnthm PA; Acctng.

BIGONY, KATHY; Ephrata Area HS; Ephrata, PA; (Y); Church Yth Grp; FBLA; Spanish Clb; Band; Church Choir; Concert Band; Mrchg Band; Orch; School Musical; Symp Band; Cnty Band 84-85; FBLA Rgnl Awd 85-86; Millersville U; Soc Psych.

BIGRIGG, MICHAEL; Quigley HS; Baden, PA; (Y); 13/115; Boy Scts; Camera Clb; VP JA; Math Tm; NFL; Pres SADD; Band; Trk; High Hon Roll; Comp Sci Awd 86; Comp Sci.

BILDER, MATTHEW B; Moravian Acad; Bethlehem, PA; (Y); 3/56; Scholastic Bowl; Chorus; Yrbk Ed-Chief; High Hon Roll; Hon Roll; Ntl Merit SF; Cm Laud Socty 85; W E Doster Lit Awd 85; Bio.

BILEN, SVEN; Avon Grove HS; Landenberg, PA; (Y); 5/170; Church Yth Grp; Exploring; Band; Chorus; School Musical; Nwsp Stf; High Hon Roll; NHS; Mchncl Engr.

BILETNIKOFF II, EPHRIAM; Iroquois HS; Erie, PA; (Y); JV Var Ftbl; Wt Lftg; Hon Roll; FL ST U; Elec Engrng.

BILGER, HYDIE; Mifflinburg Area HS; Mifflinburg, PA; (Y); 25/168; Chorus; School Musical; School Play; High Hon Roll; Hon Roll; NHS; Drama Clb; FBLA; Nwsp Rptr; Dist, Rgnl & St Chorus 85-86; Fac Schlrshp; Am Leg Outstndng Musician Awd; Williamsport Schl Comm; Med Sec.

BILGER, LISA; Solanco HS; Christina, PA; (Y); 4-H; SADD; Color Guard; Flag Corp; School Musical; Yrbk Stf; Prfct Atten Awd; Recvd Cash Awd SADD Pstr 85; Millersville U; Elem Ed.

BILHEIMER, MELISSA; Central Dauphin HS; Harrisburg, PA; (Y); 97/386; German Clb; Chorus; Church Choir; Stat Bsktbl; JV Gym; Im Vllybl; Hstry Tchr.

BILKER, LAWRENCE; Marple Newtown HS; Broomall, PA; (Y); Camera Clb; Pres Computer Clb; Math Clb; Math Tm; PAVAS; Pres Science Clb; Trs Service Clb; Trs Temple Yth Grp; Thesps; Band; Gov Schl Sci Alternate 86; Am Assoc Adv Sci Fnlst 86; Optcl Engr.

BILL, TRICIA; Frazier HS; Grindstone, PA; (Y); FNA; Nwsp Stf; Yrbk Stf; Pres Jr Cls; Rep Stu Cncl; Var Capt Cheerleading; High Hon Roll; Hon Roll; Pres Acad Fit Awd 86; Robert Webster Mem Scholar 86; WA & Jefferson Coll; Psych.

BILLET, CATHERINE; Eastern York HS; Hellam, PA; (Y); 40/159; Yrbk Rptr; Yrbk Stf; Rep Jr Cls; Rep Sr Cls; Rep Stu Cncl; JV Cheerleading; JV Var Vllybl; High Hon Roll; Hon Roll.

BILLET, MICHAEL; Dover Area HS; Dover, PA; (Y); Boys Clb Am; FCA; JA; SADD; Varsity Clb; Var JV Bsktbl; Radford U; Business Mktg.

BILLET, TROY; Eastern York HS; Wrightsville, PA; (Y); Ski Clb; School Musical; School Play; Stage Crew; JV Bsbl; JV Socr; Hon Roll; Prfct Atten Awd; Le High U; Mechncl Engrng.

BILLETS, JERILYN; Abington Hts HS; Clarks Summit, PA; (Y); 6/250; Color Guard; Concert Band; Mrchg Band; Ed Yrbk Stf; Var Bsktbl; Var Vllybl; High Hon Roll; NHS; Pres Schlr; Provost Schlrshp-U Pittsburgh 86; Natl Schlrs Athlt Awd 86; Natl Hnr Soc Schlrshp 86; U Pittsburgh; Pre-Med.

BILLGER, AARON; Newport JR SR HS; Newport, PA; (S); Am Leg Boys St; Aud/Vis; Chorus; School Musical; Swing Chorus; Sec Stu Cncl; Wrstlng; HOBY Ldrshp Awd 85; Soph Of Yr 85.

BILLIA, STEPHANIE; Gwynedd-Mercy Acad; Furlong, PA; (Y); Cmnty Wkr; Girl Scts; SADD; Chorus; Swmmng; Tennis; CC Awd; Cit Awd; PA Good Ctznshp Cit, Fnslt Stdnt Vol Yr, Soroptmst Schlrshp 86; Gettysburg Coll.

BILLIE, MARLO; Burgettstown JR SR HS; Burgettstown, PA; (Y); Art Clb; VP Drama Clb; Ski Clb; Spanish Clb; JV Cheerleading; Fshn Mrchndsng.

BILLIG, KATHY; Columbia-Montour Area Vo-Tech Schl; Catawissa, PA; (Y); 11/186; Red Cross Aide; SADD; Trs VICA; Yrbk Stf; Trs Stu Cncl; Cit Awd; High Hon Roll; Hon Roll; Trs NHS; Prsdntl Acad Ftnss Awd 86.

BILLIG, MICHELLE; Millville Area HS; Millville, PA; (Y); Church Yth Grp; Band; Concert Band; Jazz Band; Mrchg Band; School Musical; School Play; Yrbk Stf; JV Fld Hcky; Hon Roll; Dist Band 85&86; Columbia Co Band 84&85&86; Vol Wrk; Elem Tchr.

BILLINGS, DEANNA; Clearfield Area HS; Shawville, PA; (Y); Church Yth Grp; Office Aide; Band; Concert Band; Flag Corp; Hon Roll; USAF; Med Sec.

BILLITTO JR, CHARLES P; Bishop Kendrick HS; Norristown, PA; (Y); 29/273; Science Clb; Variety Show; Im Bsktbl; Im Ice Hcky; JV Wrstlng; Hon Roll; Villanova U; Cmmrc.

BILLMAN, BETH ANN; Reading HS; Reading, PA; (Y); 320/620; Church Yth Grp; Girl Scts; Library Aide; Office Aide; Rdng Area CC; Bus.

BILLOCK, RHONDA; Brockway Area HS; Brockway, PA; (Y); Trs Art Clb; Girl Scts; Band; Concert Band; Jazz Band; Mrchg Band; Pep Band; Du Bois Bus Coll; Medcl Sec.

BILLOTTE, MELISSA L; Clearfield HS; Frenchville, PA; (S); 9/333; FBLA; Key Clb; Concert Band; Mrchg Band; Orch; Yrbk Stf; Cit Awd; High Hon Roll; Dubois Bus Coll; Med Sec.

BILLOW, SARAH; Upper Dauphin Area HS; Elizabethville, PA; (Y); 15/112; Church Yth Grp; Chorus; Church Choir; School Musical; Soph Cls; Jr Cls; Sftbl; Hon Roll; NHS; Hugh O Brian Yth Ldrshp Sem 84; Vocal Music Awd 85; Liberty U; Engl.

BILLS, MICHELE; Kiski Area HS; E Vandergrift, PA; (Y); FBLA; Pep Clb; SADD; High Hon Roll; Hon Roll; Acdmc Ltr 85; Advsry Cncl 86; 2nd Pl Clrk Typst 85; 5th Pl Ofc Prctc 86; Yth Ftns Awd 85; Monroeville Schl Bus; Exec Sec.

BILLUPS, BERNADETTE; Simon Gratz HS; Philadelphia, PA; (S); Dance Clb; English Clb; Office Aide; ROTC; Teachers Aide; School Play; Variety Show; Hon Roll; Ntl Merit Ltr; Natl Englsh Mrt Awd 85; Temple U; CPA.

BILSKI, ANTOINETTE; Sun Valley HS; Brookhaven, PA; (Y); 10/287; Cmnty Wkr; Intnl Clb; Sec Political Wkr; Spanish Clb; SADD; Teachers Aide; Stu Cncl; Capt Var Trk; Pres Schlr; Spanish NHS; Pres Acad Ftnss Awd 86; St Josephs U; Pre-Med.

BILSKI, ERICA; Central Catholic HS; Reading, PA; (Y); 8/125; German Clb; Pep Clb; Mrchg Band; Stage Crew; Variety Show; NHS; Prfct Atten Awd; Hgst Achvt Awd German I,II,III; Best Wrk Geo Awd; Hahnemann U; Anethslgy.

BILSKI, MICHELLE; James M Coughlin HS; Wilkes Barre, PA; (Y); Band; Concert Band; Mrchg Band; Nwsp Rptr; Yrbk Rptr; Sec Frsh Cls; JV Capt Bsktbl; Var Capt Cheerleading; Sftbl; Natl Schlstc Gold Key Photo 86; Savannah Coll Of Art & Design Schlrshp 86; Penn ST U; Nrsng.

BILTGEN, RENEE; North Allegheny HS; Allison Pk, PA; (Y); 55/650; Church Yth Grp; French Clb; GAA; Ski Clb; Varsity Clb; L Socr; Trk; High Hon Roll; Hon Roll; Jr NHS; Penn ST U; Advrtsng.

BILTZ, LORI; Moon SR HS; Coraopolis, PA; (Y); German Clb; Key Clb; Chorus; Orch; Stu Cncl; Socr; High Hon Roll; Hon Roll; NHS; Duquesne U; Bus.

BIMEAL, KAREN; Central Cambria HS; Johnstown, PA; (S); 4/197; Computer Clb; 4-H; Library Aide; Ski Clb; Mrchg Band; Swmmng; Hon Roll; Coll Misericordia; Occ Thrpy.

BINCK, GEORGE; St John Neumann HS; Philadelphia, PA; (Y); 11/369; Rep Soph Cls; Rep Jr Cls; Rep Sr Cls; Stu Cncl; Im JV Ftbl; High Hon Roll; NHS; Comp Sci.

BINCKLEY JR, THOMAS; Jenkintown HS; Jenkintown, PA; (S); Concert Band; Rep Stu Cncl; Var Bsbl; Var Bsktbl; Var Ftbl; Hon Roll; NHS; Spanish NHS; Sprts Medcn Dr.

BINELLI, KARIN; Boyertown Area SR HS; Boyertown, PA; (Y); 51/451; Church Yth Grp; Dance Clb; Girl Scts; JA; Library Aide; Math Tm; SADD; Teachers Aide; Chorus; Color Guard; Grlsct Slvr Ldrshp Awd 84; Kystn Schl Press Awd 85; U Of DE; Intl Bus.

BINGAMAN, CAROLE; James Buchanan HS; Mercersburg, PA; (Y); 62/228; Church Yth Grp; Ski Clb; Varsity Clb; Co-Capt Var Cheerleading; Var L Fld Hcky; Hon Roll.

BINGMAN, BRIGETTE R; Hyndman HS; Hyndman, PA; (Y); Office Aide; Varsity Clb; Chorus; Yrbk Ed-Chief; Yrbk Stf; Stat Bsktbl; Sftbl; High Hon Roll; Jr NHS; NHS; ACC; Bus Admin.

BINKLEY, CINDY; Pleasant Valley HS; Saylorsburg, PA; (Y); SADD; Yrbk Stf; Rep Jr Cls; Capt Cheerleading; Trk; Bus.

BINKNEY, MERRY; S Allegheny HS; Mckeesport, PA; (Y); French Clb; Pres JA; Y-Teens; Concert Band; Capt Mrchg Band; Ed Yrbk Stf; Sec Stu Cncl; Powder Puff Ftbl; NHS; Dal Carneigie Schlrhsp 86; Cert Pblc Accntn Schlrshp 86; JR Achvt Dist Pres 86; Penn ST U; Science.

BINLEY, CHRISTOPHER R; Monongahela Valley Catholic; Monongahela, PA; (Y); 40/100; Drama Clb; Ski Clb; Rptr Nwsp Rptr; Ftbl; Wt Lftg; WA & Jefferson Coll; Pre-Law.

BINNER, ERIC; Highlands SR HS; Natrona Hts, PA; (Y); DECA; German Clb; Comp.

BIONDI, JOHN; Lincoln HS; Ellwood City, PA; (Y); 37/163; Trs Camera Clb; Pres Church Yth Grp; Drama Clb; Spanish Clb; Yrbk Ed-Chief; Stu Cncl; High Hon Roll; NHS; Pres Schlr; Wolves Clb Schlrshp 86; Gannon U; Pre-Law.

BIONDI, MELISSA; Greensburg Central Catholic HS; Greensburg, PA; (Y); Nwsp Rptr; Nwsp Stf; Hon Roll; Acctng.

BIRCH, KIMBERLY; Conemaughy Township HS; Johnstown, PA; (Y); 29/101; Dance Clb; French Clb; Pep Clb; Stage Crew; Yrbk Stf; Hon Roll; X Ry Tech.

BIRCH, MARIETTE; Homer-Center HS; Homer City, PA; (Y); French Clb; FBLA; SADD; Chorus; Drill Tm; School Musical; Nwsp Stf; Yrbk Stf; Rep Stu Cncl; Cheerleading; U Of Pitt-Johnstown; Psych.

BIRCHARD, CHARLOTTE; Schenley HS; Pittsburgh, PA; (S); 1/163; Sec Church Yth Grp; Exploring; Hosp Aide; Yrbk Bus Mgr; Rep Soph Cls; Rep Jr Cls; Rep Sr Cls; Cit Awd; DAR Awd; High Hon Roll; U Pittsburgh; Nrsng.

BIRCHARD, LISA; Oil City SR HS; Oil City, PA; (Y); 24/241; Hosp Aide; Vllybl; Hon Roll; Pres Schlr; Hnr Grad; Clrn U; Chld Psychlgy.

BIRCHLER, DEBORAH R; Blackhawk HS; Darlington, PA; (Y); 5/280; Church Yth Grp; Chorus; School Play; Var L Cheerleading; Var Gym; Var L Vllybl; High Hon Roll; NHS; Fclty Hnrs Schlrshp 85-86; Schlr Athlt Awd U S Army Rsrve 85-86; Calvin Coll; Comp Sci.

BIRD, BRIAN; Danville Area SR HS; Danville, PA; (Y); Church Yth Grp; Pres FFA; 4-H Awd; Chptr Frmr FFFA 86; DE Valley; Agronomist.

BIRD, CHRISTOPHER; Bishop Kenrick HS; Norristown, PA; (Y); 70/300; Church Yth Grp; Spanish Clb; Socr; Hnr Rll 84 & 85.

BIRD, EVELYN L; Upper Merion Area HS; King Of Prussia, PA; (Y); 32/320; Drama Clb; Stat Fld Hcky; Stat Lcrss; Im Vllybl; Hon Roll; Co Pres Intrct Clb 86; Bus Adm.

BIRD, MELISSA; Bishop Kenrick HS; Norristown, PA; (Y); Cmnty Wkr; Girl Scts; Concert Band; Mrchg Band; School Musical.

BIRDSALL, JAMES; Liberty HS; Bethlehem, PA; (Y); 46/475; Computer Clb; German Clb; Ski Clb; Mrchg Band; Chemcl Engrng.

BIRENBAUM, JOANNE; Robert E Lamberton HS; Philadelphia, PA; (Y); 22/130; Girl Scts; Temple Yth Grp; Bowling; Coach Actv; Capt Tennis; Vllybl; Hon Roll; Trs NHS; 2nd Tm All-Pblc Chmpnshp Awds Tnns 84-86; Rgnl Chmp & Cty Chmp Tnns Trphs 79 & 82; Ntl JR Tnns Lg 85; Temple U; Allied Hlth.

BIRES, MELISSA; Hopewell SR HS; Aliquippa, PA; (Y); Church Yth Grp; Drama Clb; Latin Clb; Chorus; Concert Band; Mrchg Band; Sec Jr Cls; Sec Sr Cls; High Hon Roll; Pres NHS; Cert Merit Drum Maj, Ltr Drama 85-86; Ltr Band 83-86; Ed.

BIRGE, WENDY; Beaver Area JR SR HS; Bridgewater, PA; (Y); 84/177; FBLA; Girl Scts; Office Aide; Chorus; Church Choir; Hon Roll; FBLA Bus Grphcs 2nd Pl Rgnls 86; Cmptrs.

BIRKETT, SUSAN; Central York SR HS; York, PA; (Y); Trs Varsity Clb; School Musical; Nwsp Stf; Yrbk Stf; Rep Stu Cncl; Co-Capt Cheerleading; Hon Roll; Opt Clb Awd; Rotary Awd; Bus.

BIRKHEAD, TUCKER; Archbishop Carroll HS; King Of Prussia, PA; (Y); 27/200; Drama Clb; Stage Crew; Yrbk Stf; Rep Frsh Cls; Rep Soph Cls; High Hon Roll; Hon Roll; Jr NHS; Bio Awd; Ecnmcs Awd; Columbia; Pre-Law.

BIRMINGHAM, BETH; Little Flower HS; Philadelphia, PA; (Y); Church Yth Grp; Cmnty Wkr; Chorus; Hon Roll; Geom Awd 84-85; Hnrbl Mntn Sci Fair 84-85; Temple; Phrmcy.

BIRMINGHAM, STEVEN; Middletown HS; Middletown, PA; (Y); Am Leg Boys St; Model UN; Mgr Radio Clb; Band; Pres Chorus; Orch; Nwsp Phtg; High Hon Roll; Ntl Merit Ltr; Hgh O Brn Yth Fndtn 85; Stu Tour To Frnc 85.

BIRSTER, JOHN E; Mt Caramel Area JR-SR HS; Locust Gap, PA; (Y); 25/136; Pres French Clb; FTA; Q&S; SADD; Chorus; School Play; Nwsp Rptr; Nwsp Stf; Yrbk Rptr; Yrbk Stf; 2nd Pl In Frnch Natl Hnr Tst 86; Air Force; Cmnctns.

BISCOE, MICHELE; Hempfield HS; Columbia, PA; (Y); 41/418; Drama Clb; Chorus; School Musical; Yrbk Bus Mgr; Lit Mag; Hon Roll; 1st Pl Dvsn II Lncstr Cnty Peace Essy Cntst; Cnty Chrs; Engl.

BISEL, LISA; Turkeyfoot Valley Area HS; Confluence, PA; (S); 2/48; Library Aide; Q&S; Nwsp Stf; Yrbk Stf; Trs Frsh Cls; High Hon Roll; Lion Awd; Coll Prep Engl Awd; Shrthnd I Awd; Acctg I Awd; WV Career Coll; Lgl Sec.

BISH, KEITH; Punxutawney Area HS; Punxsutawney, PA; (Y); Church Yth Grp; Varsity Clb; Crs Cntry; Trk; Phrmcy.

BISH, MELANIE; Clarion Area JR SR HS; Shippenville, PA; (Y); Chorus; Mrchg Band; School Musical; Swing Chorus; Variety Show; Stat Bsktbl; Im Gym; Twrlr; Im Vllybl; Hon Roll; Am Lgn Essy Cntst Pl 86; JR Acad Sci 86; Pblc Rltns.

BISH, SANDRA; Redbank Valley HS; Templeton, PA; (Y); French Clb; FHA; Pep Clb; Varsity Clb; Yrbk Phtg; Yrbk Stf; Rep Stu Cncl; Capt Cheerleading; Mat Maids; Hon Roll; Clarion U Of PA; Early Chld De.

BISHOP, ALISON; State College Area SR HS; State College, PA; (Y); 4-H; FBLA; Spanish Clb; Flag Corp; Orch; Nwsp Ed-Chief; Nwsp Rptr; Powder Puff Ftbl; Hon Roll; Math Clb; Priv Pilots Grnd Schl Cert 85; Writng Awd PA Schl Press Assn 85; Glider Pilots Licns 83; Penn ST; Jrnlsm.

BISHOP, BILL; Bethel Park SR HS; Pittsburgh, PA; (Y); DECA; Exploring; FBLA; JA; Ski Clb; Yrbk Stf; Bsktbl; Tennis; Hon Roll; Law.

BISHOP, BRAD; Hershey Senior HS; Hershey, PA; (Y); 55/180; Church Yth Grp; Ski Clb; School Musical; School Play; Tchr Mag; VP Jr Cls; Pres Sr Cls; Hon Roll; Rotary Awd; Schlstc Writing Awds Gold Key 86; Susquehanna U; Mktg.

BISHOP, BRIAN KRAUT O NEAL; Bellefonte Area HS; Lewisburg, PA; (Y); 36/217; Cmnty Wkr; Pres German Clb; Model UN; Stage Crew; Yrbk Stf; Im Fld Hcky; Mgr(s); Im Vllybl; Lincoln Tech Inst; Elec Engr.

BISHOP, DAVID; Seton Lasalle HS; Pittsburgh, PA; (Y); 29/270; Yrbk Rptr; Yrbk Stf; Rep Sr Cls; JV Trk; JV Wrstlng; High Hon Roll; Hon Roll; NHS; Clarion U Of PA; Bus.

BISHOP, GARY; Hazleton SR HS; Drums, PA; (Y); Church Yth Grp; Cmnty Wkr; FFA; Rep Stu Cncl; High Hon Roll.

BISHOP, GREG J; Marple Newtown HS; Newtown Square, PA; (Y); Orch; Variety Show; Stu Cncl; Capt Bsbl; Capt Bsktbl; Crs Cntry; Ftbl; Golf; Cit Awd; Hon Roll; All Cnty 1st Tm Bsktbl MVP Tm 85-86; All Cnty 1st Tm Bsbl 86; Phil Inquirer Plry Of Wk 86; Lafayette Coll; Econmcs.

BISHOP, HOLLY; Marple Newtown HS; Newtown Sq, PA; (Y); 37/380; Teachers Aide; School Play; Stat Coach Actv; Var JV Mgr(s); Stat Score Keeper; Var JV Trk; Hon Roll; Rotary Awd; Art.

BISHOP, KRISTA; Canon-Mc Millan HS; Canonsburg, PA; (Y); 52/390; French Clb; Band; Concert Band; Mrchg Band; Score Keeper; High Hon Roll; Prfct Atten Awd; Outstndng Stu Hm Econmcs 83; Outstndng Stu Indstrl Art 84.

BISHOP, LARRY; Lebanon HS; Lebanon, PA; (Y); 11/300; French Clb; Science Clb; Yrbk Stf; Pres Soph Cls; Pres Jr Cls; Pres Stu Cncl; Var L Bsbl; JV L Bsktbl; Var L Ftbl; VP NHS; Cnty Ftbl 2nd Tm, Hnrbl Leag 85.

BISHOP, MELISSA; Annville-Cleona HS; Cleona, PA; (Y); 40/112; Sec FBLA; Band; Chorus; Concert Band; Drm Mjr(t); Madrigals; Mrchg Band; Stu Cncl; Sftbl; NHS; District Chorus 86; Legal Secy.

BISHOP, PATRICK; Purchase Line JR SR HS; Mahaffey, PA; (Y); 33/140; SADD; Varsity Clb; Chorus; Trs Soph Cls; Stu Cncl; Var L Ftbl; Capt L Trk; Hon Roll; Voice Dem Awd; IN U Of PA; Envrnmntl Sci.

BISIGNANI, LORI; Bishophannan HS; Scranton, PA; (Y); 16/131; Dance Clb; French Clb; JV Var Cheerleading; High Hon Roll; Hon Roll; NHS; U Of Scrntn; Acctg.

BISNEY, LUCINDA; Manheim Central HS; Manheim, PA; (Y); School Musical; School Play; JV Tennis; Hon Roll; Fshn.

BISSAILLON, STEPHANIE; Mt Carmel Area JR SR HS; Mt Carmel, PA; (Y); Church Yth Grp; French Clb; FTA; Hosp Aide; Math Clb; Church Choir; School Musical; French Hon Soc; High Hon Roll; Hon Roll; Fred G Smith Schlrshp 86; Pell Grant 86; Mt Carmel Ed Assc Awd 86; Bloomsburg U; Elem Ed.

BISSAS, NIKI; Northeast HS; Philadelphia, PA; (Y); 13/600; Library Aide; Model UN; Office Aide; Pres Spanish Clb; Yrbk Rptr; Ed Yrbk Stf; Ed Lit Mag; Stu Cncl; Gov Hon Prg Awd; Hon Roll; PA Gov Schl Intl Studs Scholar 85; Senate Awd Outstndng Svc Schl & Cmmnty 86; Wm C Tuttle Awd; Temple U; Pre-Phrmcy.

BISTLINE, MELINDA; Donegal HS; Mount Joy, PA; (Y); 7/164; Sec Church Yth Grp; Var Drama Clb; PAVAS; VP Chorus; School Play; Yrbk Stf; Trk; Hon Roll; NHS; Elem Ed.

BITNER, JOSEPH A; Lock Haven SR HS; Blanchard, PA; (Y); 50/241; Pres Key Clb; Pres Frsh Cls; Pres Soph Cls; Pres Jr Cls; Pres Sr Cls; Capt Var Ftbl; Capt L Wrstlng; JC Awd; Kiwanis Awd; Key Clb Schrlshp Awd 86; Outstndng Ftbl Lineman Awd 86; Rotary Clb Awd 86; Lycoming Coll; Law.

BITNER, SHAUN; Elizabethtown Area HS; Elizabethtown, PA; (Y); German Clb; Var Capt Ftbl; West VA U; Athltc Trng.

BITTLER, SANDI; Mercer HS; Mercer, PA; (Y); 1/125; Chess Clb; Church Yth Grp; GAA; Math Clb; Q&S; Nwsp Ed-Chief; Nwsp Rptr; Yrbk Ed-Chief; Yrbk Rptr; Yrbk Stf; BB MVP ST Slctn; Princeton; Lbrl Arts.

BITTNER, BRAD; St Marys Area HS; Kersey, PA; (Y); 11/290; Camera Clb; JA; Speech Tm; Yrbk Phtg; Var Bsbl; Var Ftbl; Var VP Trk; Wt Lftg; Cit Awd; Elks Awd; Acad Schlrshp $1000/Yr Delaware Vly Coll 86-87; Mst Outstndng Male SR Awd 85-86; Delaware Vly Coll; Landscape.

BITTNER, CHRISTINE; Meyersdale Area HS; Meyersdale, PA; (S); French Clb; Varsity Clb; Concert Band; Mrchg Band; L Sftbl; Pres Phys Fit Awd.

BITTNER, RICHARD; Meyersdale Area HS; Meyersdale, PA; (Y); Church Yth Grp; Drama Clb; French Clb; Quiz Bowl; Scholastic Bowl; Spanish Clb; Band; Chorus; Church Choir; Concert Band.

BITTNER, ROBERT; Burgettstown Area JRSR HS; Burgettstown, PA; (Y); 6/150; Church Yth Grp; Ski Clb; Spanish Clb; SADD; Bsktbl; High Hon Roll; Hon Roll; Jr NHS; NHS; US Air Force Acad; Aerospc.

BITTNER, ROY; Berlin-Brothersvalley HS; Meyersdale, PA; (Y); Chess Clb; Pres 4-H; French Clb; JV Wrstlng; 4-H Awd; Trs NHS; Comp Sci.

BITTNER, SCOTT; Southern Columbia HS; Catawissa, PA; (Y); Art Clb; Church Yth Grp; Letterman Clb; Rep Frsh Cls; Rep Jr Cls; Ftbl; Powder Puff Ftbl; Wt Lftg; Wrstlng; HACC; Bus Mgmt.

BITTNER, TINA; Avella Area HS; Avella, PA; (Y); Art Clb; Church Yth Grp; Drama Clb; Sec Trs Band; Twrlr; Hon Roll; Prfct Atten Awd; Robert Morris; Bus Teach.

BITZ, ROBERT; Canon Mc Millian SR HS; Canonsburg, PA; (Y); Am Leg Boys St; CAP; Letterman Clb; ROTC; Science Clb; Ftbl; Socr; Art Clb; Boys Clb Am; Boy Scts; Spartan Schl Aeronautics.

BIVENS, LISA; Mc Connellsburg HS; Mcconnellsburg, PA; (Y); 10/86; Am Leg Aux Girls St; Debate Tm; English Clb; VP FNA; Red Cross Aide; Chorus; Nwsp Stf; Ed Yrbk Ed-Chief; High Hon Roll; NHS; Pblctns Awd 86; Acdmc All Amer 86; Messiah Coll; Psychlgy.

BIVINS, SHARON L; St Maria Goretti HS; Philadelphia, PA; (Y); 114/427; Church Yth Grp; Spanish Clb; Stage Crew; Nwsp Rptr; Rep Frsh Cls; Rep Soph Cls; Bsktbl; Vllybl; Hon Roll; Prfct Atten Awd; Seton Hill Coll; Cmnctns.

BIXLER, CLARK; Upper Dauphin Area HS; Gratz, PA; (Y); 18/105; Chess Clb; Church Yth Grp; Computer Clb; Yrbk Rptr; Yrbk Stf; Rep Soph Cls; Rep Stu Cncl; Hon Roll; NHS; Thaddeus Stevens Tech; Crpntry.

BIXLER, DIANE; Millersburg HS; Millersburg, PA; (Y); Library Aide; Spanish Clb; Color Guard; Nwsp Sprt Ed; L Bsktbl; Im Powder Puff Ftbl; L Sftbl; Var Trk; Hon Roll; Ntl Merit Ltr; Penn ST; Socl Wrk.

BIXLER, LYNN; Hanover SR HS; Hanover, PA; (Y); 15/141; Aud/Vis; Pres Girl Scts; Varsity Clb; Mrchg Band; Nwsp Ed-Chief; VP Frsh Cls; Capt L Trk; Elks Awd; Hon Roll; Rotary Awd; Semper Fideus-Marines 86; Outstndng Trrack & Field 85-86; S Cntrl PA Sprts Hall Of Fame 86; CA U Of PA; Spec Educ.

BIXLER, MATTHEW; Central Dauphin HS; Harrisburg, PA; (Y); Computer Clb; Chorus; School Musical; School Play; Stage Crew; High Hon Roll; Hon Roll; Jr NHS; NHS; Pres Schlr; Juniata Coll; Comp Sci.

BIXLER, RACHEL; Hamburg Area HS; Shartlesville, PA; (Y); German Clb; Library Aide; Hon Roll; German Hnr Soc; Wilderness Clb.

BIZYAK, JAY; Deer Lakes HS; Tarentum, PA; (Y); 10/170; Chess Clb; Varsity Clb; Nwsp Ed-Chief; Nwsp Rptr; Nwsp Sprt Ed; Var Capt Bsktbl; Var Socr; High Hon Roll; NHS; Awd Of Acadmc Elcelnc 85-86; WPIAL Bsktbl Playoffs 84-86; PA ST Champnship Bsktbl Playoffs 84-85; Pre-Law.

BJORKSTEDT, ERIC; Palymra Area HS; Palmyra, PA; (Y); Boy Scts; French Clb; Chorus; L Bsktbl; Bausch & Lomb Sci Awd; High Hon Roll; Hon Roll; NHS; Ntl Merit Ltr; Mar Biol Sci.

BJORNSON, KRISTEN; Lampeter Strasburg HS; Lancaster, PA; (Y); 5/158; AFS; Church Yth Grp; Band; Concert Band; School Musical; Lit Mag; Mgr(s); NHS; 1st Pl In Chmstry/Sci Fair 86; Peer Cnslng 86-87.

BLACK, BECKY; Avela Area HS; Avella, PA; (Y); 1/73; 4-H; French Clb; FFA; Letterman Clb; Acpl Chr; Band; Chorus; Var L Cheerleading; DAR Awd; High Hon Roll; Penn ST; Chem Engrng.

BLACK, BONITA; Lancaster Catholic HS; Lancaster, PA; (Y); Church Yth Grp; Model UN; Service Clb; Stage Crew; Fld Hcky; Trk; High Hon Roll; Hon Roll; NHS; Blmsbrg U; Bus.

BLACK, BRIAN; Fairchance Georges SR HS; Smithfield, PA; (Y); 14/150; JV Bsktbl; Hon Roll; Chem.

BLACK, BRIAN; Jeannette SR HS; Jeannette, PA; (Y); 1/150; Am Leg Boys St; Pres Church Yth Grp; Pres Ski Clb; Ftbl; Trk; High Hon Roll; Drama Clb; Spanish Clb; Mrchg Band; School Play; Hugh O Brian Yth Fndtn 85; Lions Clb Smnr 86; Bio.

BLACK, DEBBIE; Coudersport JR SR HS; Coudersport, PA; (Y); 14/88; Varsity Clb; Drm Mjr(t); Rep Stu Cncl; JV Var Bsktbl; Var L Trk; Var L Vllybl; Hon Roll; NHS; Trs French Clb; Chorus; Miss Teen PA Scholar & Recgntn Pag 85; Potter-Tioga Maple Sweetheart Cont 1st Rnnr Up 86; Baton Awds; Elem Ed.

BLACK, DENICE; Clarion Area HS; Clarion, PA; (Y); Pres Church Yth Grp; FCA; Band; Chorus; Church Choir; Concert Band; Mrchg Band; Sec Frsh Cls; Stu Cncl; JV Var Cheerleading; Syracuse U; Bus Econmcs.

BLACK, DONNA; Tussey Mountain HS; Saxton, PA; (Y); 1/97; AFS; Drama Clb; Band; School Play; Stu Cncl; Cit Awd; High Hon Roll; Pres NHS; Val; VFW Awd; Natl Ldrshp & Serv & Stu Council Awds 86; Pres Acdmc Fit Awd 86; Penn ST U; Engrng.

BLACK, DOUGLAS; Charleroi Area JR SR HS; Charleroi, PA; (Y); Science Clb; Concert Band; Jazz Band; Mrchg Band; Im Bsktbl; Var Golf; High Hon Roll; Hon Roll; Jr NHS; Optmtry.

BLACK, JANA; York Suburban HS; York, PA; (Y); 30/191; Letterman Clb; Pep Clb; Varsity Clb; Band; Concert Band; Mrchg Band; School Play; Nwsp Rptr; VP Cheerleading; Hon Roll; Temple U; Dntl Hyg.

BLACK, JODI; Big Spring HS; Carlisle, PA; (Y); 36/185; Art Clb; GAA; Office Aide; Pep Clb; Ski Clb; Teachers Aide; JV Crs Cntry; JV Diving; Im Stat Mgr(s); Im Stat Score Keeper; Homecoming Rep 83-84; Stu Advsry Com 84-85; Med.

BLACK, KATHY; Liberty JR SR HS; Liberty, PA; (Y); 11/40; Church Yth Grp; 4-H; FHA; German Clb; Rep Jr Cls; JV Bsktbl; Var Sftbl; JV Var Vllybl; 4-H Awd; Hon Roll; Spch Ther.

BLACK, KIM; Central HS; Roaring Spring, PA; (Y); 33/188; FBLA; Varsity Clb; Yrbk Stf; Var Sftbl; High Hon Roll; Hon Roll; NHS; Ar Trfc Cntrlr.

BLACK, RITA; South Hills HS; Pittsburgh, PA; (Y); 7/168; Exploring; Capt Drill Tm; Yrbk Stf; Hon Roll; Robert Morris Coll; Accntng.

BLACK, ROBERT; Technical HS; Scranton, PA; (Y); Boy Scts; Church Yth Grp; Pep Clb; Var Crs Cntry; JV Trk; Hon Roll; Eagle Sct 84; Electrcn.

BLACK, SHARI; Everett Area HS; Everett, PA; (S); Church Yth Grp; Spanish Clb; Band; Concert Band; Mrchg Band; Pep Band; Hon Roll; Acad Achvt Awd 85; IN U Of PA Hnr Band 84 & 85; IN U; Prfrmng Arts.

BLACK, TORIE; Wilkinsburg JR SR HS; Wilkinsburg, PA; (Y); French Clb; Drm Mjr(t); Mrchg Band; VP Sr Cls; Stu Cncl; Bsktbl; Hon Roll; Jr NHS; Trs Key Clb; Band; 1st Pl Black Hist Cntst Poetry 84; Best Athlte Awd 84-86; Merit Awd Most Spirit Band 85; Pre-Med.

BLACK, TRACIE; Conneaut Lake HS; Conneaut Lake, PA; (Y); Church Yth Grp; Drama Clb; GAA; Spanish Clb; SADD; Chorus; School Musical; School Play; Variety Show; Nwsp Rptr; PA ST U Grv Cty; Accntng.

BLACKBURN, GINA; Hollidaysburg Area SR HS; Hollidaysburg, PA; (Y); 13/351; Sec Trs 4-H; Trs French Clb; JA; Ski Clb; Im Vllybl; High Hon Roll; NHS; Bst Fr I II & III Stu Awd 84-86.

BLACKEDGE, DIANE; Benton Area JR SR HS; Shickshinny, PA; (Y); 1/50; FTA; Keywanettes; School Musical; School Play; VP Jr Cls; Stu Cncl; Fld Hcky; High Hon Roll; Pres NHS; NEDT Awd; Math & Century 21 Typng Awd 85; Penn ST U; Psych.

BLACKHURST, JILL; Washington HS; Washington, PA; (S); French Clb; Band; Concert Band; Mrchg Band; Rep Stu Cncl; JV Vllybl; Hon Roll; Nrsng.

BLACKMAN, ALISSA; Lancaster Country Day HS; Newmanstown, PA; (Y); VP Mgr Drama Clb; School Play; Stage Crew; Ed Lit Mag; Sec Trs Soph Cls; Sec Trs Jr Cls; Var JV Fld Hcky; JV Socr; Var Sftbl; High Hon Roll; Elizabeth Ross Awd; Schlstc Wrtng Awd Hon Mntn/Lncstr; Englsh Lit.

BLACKSTON, MONICA; Harrisburg HS; Harrisburg, PA; (Y); Nwsp Stf; Var Bsktbl; Var Sftbl; Capt Twrlr; Hon Roll; Ntl Schlstc Wrtng Cntst 83; Crmnlgy.

BLACKWELL, DARRYL; Rochester HS; Rochester, PA; (Y); 14/100; Am Leg Boys St; Pep Clb; Stage Crew; VP Jr Cls; Var Bsktbl; L Ftbl; Var Trk; Wt Lftg; VP NHS; Acadmc All-Star Ftbl, Bsktbl 85; Pre-Med.

BLACKWELL, NANCY; Central HS; Philadelphia, PA; (Y); 49/242; Office Aide; Service Clb; Spanish Clb; Teachers Aide; Trs Sr Cls; Var Trk; Prfct Atten Awd; Meritorious 83; Bus.

BLACKWELL, SHARI; H S Of Engineering And Science; Philadelphia, PA; (Y); 15/184; Drama Clb; Chorus; Church Choir; School Musical; School Play; Variety Show; High Hon Roll; NHS; Prfct Atten Awd; Drama Clb Awd; SYNOD Trinity Schlrshp; Oral Roberts U; Comp Sci.

BLADEN, AMY M; Pennsbury HS; Yardley, PA; (Y); 1/800; Drama Clb; PAVAS; Spanish Clb; High Hon Roll; NHS; NEDT Awd; Art Clb; Church Yth Grp; Cmnty Wkr; Dance Clb; Awds In Geo, Bio, Spnsh III, Hist, Art II 84-85.

BLAHOUS, LAURA; Hampton HS; Allison Pk, PA; (Y); Chorus; L Capt Drill Tm; Pep Band; Symp Band; L Capt Pom Pon; High Hon Roll; Hon Roll; NHS; Pittsburgh Yth Symphny Orch 83-87; Tri-M Music Hnr Soc Sec 85-87; PMEA Dist I Band 84-85; Regn Band 85; Comp Sci.

BLAIN, ROBERT; Pine Grove Area HS; Pine Grove, PA; (Y); Pres Trs 4-H; Eltronics Inst; Eltrncs Rpr.

BLAINE, ALYSSA; Greater Latrobe HS; Latrobe, PA; (Y); Pep Clb; Chorus; Nwsp Rptr; Ed Nwsp Stf; Mat Maids; High Hon Roll; Hon Roll; Law.

BLAINE, HOLLYJEAN; Upper Dauphin Arfea HS; Elizabethville, PA; (Y); Church Yth Grp; FBLA; Girl Scts; Hosp Aide; Chorus; Church Choir; Stage Crew; Yrbk Stf; Mgr(s); Score Keeper; Sftbll Trphy 84-86; Awd Chrs, Ensmbl, Accntng & Typng 83-86; Central PA; Scrtry.

BLAINE, RICHELLE; Elmer L Meyers HS; Wilkes-Barre, PA; (S); Church Yth Grp; GAA; Library Aide; Band; Chorus; School Play; Var Sftbl; Var Vllybl; Hon Roll; Med.

BLAIR, DEANNA; Ringgold HS; Donora, PA; (Y); Drama Clb; Nwsp Stf; Yrbk Stf; Hon Roll; Sci-Mth Hnr Soc 85-87; PTSA Cultural Arts Awd 85.

BLAIR, JENNIFER; Frazier JR SR HS; Perryopolis, PA; (S); VP Church Yth Grp; Drama Clb; VP FNA; Library Aide; Ski Clb; Band; Church Choir; Concert Band; Mrchg Band; Pep Band; Seton Hill Coll; Nrs.

BLAIR, LUCAS; Hughesville JR SR HS; Muncy, PA; (Y); Aud/Vis; Boy Scts; Cmnty Wkr; L Bsktbl; Hon Roll; Embry Riddle Aero U; Aviation.

BLAIR, MICHELLE; Fairfield Area HS; Fairfield, PA; (Y); 1/42; Band; School Musical; Ed Nwsp Stf; VP Sr Cls; Pres Stu Cncl; Var L Bsktbl; Var L Vllybl; High Hon Roll; VP NHS; Pres Frsh Cls; Stu Cncl Convtn Rep; Stu Adv Cncl Rep; Cty Band; Dentl Hyg.

BLAIR, REBECCA; Mt Union Area HS; Mt Union, PA; (Y); Sec Church Yth Grp; French Clb; GAA; Band; Concert Band; Jazz Band; Mrchg Band; Dist Cntst Ntl Hstry Day 86; Nrsng.

BLAIR, YVETTE; Freeport HS; Sarver, PA; (S); 18/173; Church Yth Grp; Band; Drm Mjr(t); School Musical; School Play; Var L Trk; Capt Var Vllybl; High Hon Roll; NHS; Air Force Acad; Engrng.

BLAISURE, CHARLENE; Elk Lake HS; Meshoppen, PA; (Y); 10/110; Art Clb; Drama Clb; French Clb; Chorus; School Musical; School Play; High Hon Roll; Hon Roll; Cartoonist.

BLAKE, DINA; Leechburg Area HS; Leechburg, PA; (Y); Drama Clb; School Play; Yrbk Stf; Comm.

BLAKE, ELAINE; Roxborough HS; Philadelphia, PA; (Y); 5/327; Hosp Aide; Nwsp Rptr; Yrbk Ed-Chief; Rep Frsh Cls; Rep Soph Cls; Rep Jr Cls; Mgr(s); High Hon Roll; NHS; Outstndg Frsnmn Of Yr Rnnr Up 84; Hugh O Brien Ldrshp Smnr 85; Jefferson U; Phys Ther.

BLAKE, TAIGE; Liberty HS; Bethlehem, PA; (Y); 61/475; Model UN; Golf; Hon Roll; Schltc Scrimmage Alt 85-86; Physcs Olympcs Capt 85-86; Church Acolyte 83-84; Astrnmy.

BLAKELY, HOPE; Karns City HS; Chicora, PA; (Y); Church Yth Grp; Letterman Clb; Varsity Clb; Chorus; VP Frsh Cls; Var L Bsktbl; Var L Vllybl; Cit Awd; Hon Roll; NHS; Lmp Lrng Awd 86; Jameson Schl Nrsg; Nrsg.

BLAKESLEE, JOHN; Bishop Kenrick HS; Norristown, PA; (Y); 2/300; Mathletes; Science Clb; Nwsp Rptr; Swmmng; Bausch & Lomb Sci Awd; High Hon Roll; NHS; Ntl Merit Ltr; Prfct Atten Awd; Sci Dept, Engl Dept, & Scl Stds Awd; Wslyn U Mdltwn CT; Astrnmy.

BLAKEY, TALAYA; Cecilian Acad; Philadelphia, PA; (S); Trs Church Yth Grp; Drama Clb; Science Clb; Service Clb; Chorus; Sec Church Choir; Nwsp Stf; Rep Jr Cls; Vllybl; NHS; Knights Of Columbus Awd 83; 1st Pl Original Oratory Trnmnt 83; Engrng.

BLALOCK, MARSHALL; Chester HS; Chester, PA; (S); 8/494; Church Yth Grp; French Clb; Band; Church Choir; Concert Band; Mrchg Band; Orch; School Play; High Hon Roll; Hon Roll; Kim Hixon Memrl Awd 85; Comp Sci.

BLAMICK, ELLEN; Norwin HS; N Huntingdon, PA; (Y); AFS; Church Yth Grp; Pres German Clb; Leo Clb; Letterman Clb; Math Clb; SADD; Varsity Clb; Var L Crs Cntry; Var L Trk; CA U PA; Ath Trnng.

BLANAR, BRUCE; William Allen HS; Allentown, PA; (Y); Computer Clb; Math Clb; Nwsp Rptr; Nwsp Stf; Lit Mag; Trk; Hon Roll; Jr NHS; NHS; 1st Pl PLRA Locl Microcomp Prgrmg Comptn & NE Comptn 86; Comp Engrng.

BLANCHARD, ANGELA; Bald Eagle-Nittany HS; Mill Hall, PA; (Y); 10/125; Pres French Clb; Teachers Aide; Pres Chorus; Color Guard; Pres Mrchg Band; Rep Stu Cncl; Cit Awd; High Hon Roll; VP NHS; Sec Drama Clb; SR Hgh Stud Of The Yr 86; PTO Music Awd 86; Lock Haven U; Erly Chldhd Ed.

BLANCHARD, CARI LYNN; Boiling Springs HS; Carlisle, PA; (Y); Girl Scts; Chorus; School Play; Yrbk Phtg; VP Frsh Cls; VP Sr Cls; Score Keeper; Lion Awd; John N Hall Schlrshp & Am Bus Womens Assn Schlrshp 86; Towson ST U; Psych.

BLANCHETTE, JOHN; Notre Dame HS; E Stroudsburg, PA; (Y); 6/42; Cmnty Wkr; Math Tm; Scholastic Bowl; Var Bsbl; Var Bsktbl; Var Socr; Hon Roll; NHS; French Clb; Stage Crew; Geom Awd 83-84; Frnch Awd 83-85; Arch.

BLANCHETTI, DAWN; Forest Hlls HS; Summerhill, PA; (Y); 28/156; Pep Clb; Sec Stu Cncl; Stat Bsktbl; L JV Cheerleading; Var L Trk; Var L Vllybl; High Hon Roll; Hon Roll; Jr NHS; Spanish NHS; Stu Mth 84; CRNA; Nrsng.

BLANCO, TERRY; Central Bucks HS East; Mechanicsville, PA; (Y); 45/468; Jazz Band; Mrchg Band; School Musical; Stage Crew; Nwsp Bus Mgr; Nwsp Ed-Chief; Nwsp Rptr; Nwsp Stf; Hon Roll; Band; Excllnc In Jrnslsm Awd 85-86; Am Music Abroad Tour Of Europe 85; Jrnlsm.

BLAND, DOUGLAS; Martin Luther King HS; Philadelphia, PA; (Y); Church Yth Grp; Teachers Aide; Hon Roll; U Of PA Upwrd Bound Prgrm 86; PA ST U; Soc Psychlgy.

BLANE, CAROLINE; Marion Center Area HS; Home, PA; (Y); FBLA; FNA; Latin Clb; SADD; Band; Chorus; Concert Band; Mrchg Band; Orch; Pep Band; Cty Band,Chorus 85; IUP; Sec.

BLANK, MICHELLE; Bentworth HS; Scenery Hill, PA; (Y); Drama Clb; 4-H; FHA; Girl Scts; Ski Clb; Chorus; Flag Corp; Mrchg Band; School Play; Rep Soph Cls; U Of Ptsburgh.

BLANK, TAMMY; Littlestown SR HS; Littlestown, PA; (Y); 7/120; FBLA; Pep Clb; Varsity Clb; Chorus; School Musical; Yrbk Bus Mgr; Yrbk Phtg; Capt Cheerleading; High Hon Roll; Rotary Awd; Miss Kingsdale Firemns Qn 85-86; Central Penn Bus Schl; Acctg.

BLANKENBILLER, CONNIE; Governor Mifflin HS; Mohnton, PA; (Y); 20/300; VP JA; VICA; Hon Roll; Stu Of Qrtr 86; Law.

BLANKLEY, ANGIE; Everett Area HS; Everett, PA; (S); 1/106; Church Yth Grp; Pres 4-H; Spanish Clb; Band; Concert Band; Pep Band; Twrlr; High Hon Roll; Spanish NHS; Hghst GPA 84-85; Hstry Awd 83-84; PA ST; Vet Med.

BLANNETT JR, ALBERT P; Hanover Area JS SR HS; Ashley, PA; (Y); Pres Church Yth Grp; Ski Clb; Band; Concert Band; Jazz Band; Mrchg Band; Orch; Yrbk Stf; Hon Roll; Outstndng Trumpet Awd 86.

BLASCHAK, NATALIE; Glendale JR SR HS; Irvona, PA; (Y); 9/73; Church Choir; School Play; Capt L Cheerleading; Capt Twrlr; High Hon Roll; NHS; Voice Dem Awd; Drama Clb; Library Aide; Science Clb; Thelma Hall Mem Awd Nrsng Awd 86; Ntl Choral Awd 86; Dstrct Chorus 84-86; Thiel Coll; Nrs.

BLASICK, MATT; Donegal HS; Mt Joy, PA; (Y); 29/164; Band; Jazz Band; Mrchg Band.

BLASINSKY, BRIAN; Carmichaels Area HS; Carmichaels, PA; (S); 1/120; Letterman Clb; Pres Spanish Clb; Varsity Clb; VP Stu Cncl; Var Capt Bsbl; Var Capt Bsktbl; Var Golf; DAR Awd; High Hon Roll; Lion Awd; Law.

BLASIOLE, JENNY; Gbg Central Catholic HS; Greensburg, PA; (Y); Pep Clb; Ski Clb; Varsity Clb; Nwsp Rptr; Ed Nwsp Stf; Capt Cheerleading; Trk; High Hon Roll; NHS; Nwsp Sprt Ed; Sci.

BLASKO, LARRY; Freeland HS; Freeland, PA; (Y); 3/95; Spanish Clb; Pres Frsh Cls; Pres Soph Cls; Pres Jr Cls; Pres Sr Cls; Rep Stu Cncl; Var L Ftbl; Hon Roll; Jr NHS; Church Yth Grp; Hugh O Brian Yth Ldrshp Awd 85; Criminal Justice.

BLASKOWITZ, RICK; Lincoln HS; Ellwood City, PA; (Y); 81/162; Boy Scts; French Clb; Band; Concert Band; Mrchg Band; JV Bsbl; JV Var Ftbl; Var Trk; Hon Roll; Prfct Atten Awd; Phy Ther.

BLATCH, SUE; Southern HS; Philadelphia, PA; (Y).

BLAUCH, BRIAN; Northern Lebanon HS; Jonestown, PA; (Y); 10/179; Concert Band; Mrchg Band; Pep Band; School Musical; School Play; Hon Roll; NHS; Dist Bnd, Reg Bnd 84-86; Lbn Vly Coll Hon Bnd 86; Music.

BLAUER, ELAINE; Wyoming Area SR HS; Exeter, PA; (Y); Art Clb; French Clb; Ski Clb; Yrbk Stf; Educ.

BLAUSER, DEANNA; Annisville Christian Acad; Parker, PA; (Y); Church Yth Grp; Spanish Clb; Church Choir; Color Guard; Score Keeper; High Hon Roll; Hon Roll; Cmpltd Chrstn Yth In Actn Trng Schl 86; Hyles-Andrsn Coll.

BLAUVELT, TAMI LYNN; Delaware Valley HS; Shohola, PA; (Y); 18/130; Ski Clb; Chorus; Church Choir; School Play; Swing Chorus; Yrbk Phtg; High Hon Roll; NHS; Psych.

BLAZER, KEVIN; Greensburg Central Catholic HS; N Huntingdon, PA; (Y); Service Clb; Varsity Clb; Capt L Ftbl; L Trk; Im Vllybl; Wt Lftg; Hon Roll; Crimnlgy.

BLAZER, MICHELLE; West Snyder HS; Beaver Spgs, PA; (Y); Am Leg Aux Girls St; Camera Clb; Sec Trs Church Yth Grp; Drama Clb; Sec Pep Clb; SADD; Varsity Clb; Band; Chorus; Mrchg Band; Awd 2nd Pl 2nd All Str Hcky Team Leag 85; Chld Psych.

BLAZES, DAVID; Scranton Preparatory Schl; Wyoming, PA; (Y); 20/200; Church Yth Grp; Cmnty Wkr; Debate Tm; Political Wkr; Nwsp Rptr; Yrbk Phtg; Yrbk Rptr; Yrbk Sprt Ed; Yrbk Stf; Im Bsktbl; Ntl Greek Awd 85; Med Rsrch.

BLCKSTONE, TRACEY; Harrisburg HS; Harrisburg, PA; (S); #7 In Class; Band; Chorus; Concert Band; Jazz Band; Mrchg Band; Orch; Stu Cncl; Hon Roll; NHS.

BLEAM, BETH; Bensalem HS; Bensalem, PA; (Y); Hosp Aide; Chorus; Concert Band; Rep Frsh Cls; Rep Soph Cls; Rep Jr Cls; Var Crs Cntry; JV Fld Hcky; Mgr Swmmng; JV Tennis; Sierra Aero U; Avatn.

BLECHARZ, KATHLEEN; North Hills HS; Pittsburgh, PA; (Y); Church Yth Grp; Band; Chorus; Flag Corp; Jazz Band; Pres Frsh Cls; Pres Soph Cls; Pres Jr Cls; Pres Sr Cls; Rep Stu Cncl; Ldrshp Awd 86; U Pittsburgh; Cmnctns Brdcstng.

BLEIER, JOSEPH; Bethlehem Catholic HS; Bethlehem, PA; (Y); Aud/Vis; Church Yth Grp; SADD; Accntng Awd Hghst Avg Yr 85-86; 2nd Hnrs 84-85; Accntng.

BLEIL, MARCIA; Harbor Creek HS; Harbor Creek, PA; (Y); 17/211; Off ROTC; SADD; Var L Socr; JV Var Sftbl; Hon Roll; All Cnty Catchr 1st Tm 85 & 86; Amer Red Crs Svc Awd 85; Gannon; Bus Mgmt.

BLEILER, KEITH; Exeter HS; Columbia, MD; (Y); 8/206; Ski Clb; Ice Hcky; Lcrss; Wrstlng; High Hon Roll; Hon Roll; Jr NHS; Gldn Eagle Schlrshp Awd; John Hpkns U; Med.

BLEILER, SUSAN; Northwestern Lehigh HS; New Tripoli, PA; (Y); 11/163; Church Yth Grp; 4-H; Chorus; Nwsp Stf; 4-H Awd; High Hon Roll; Hon Roll; NHS; Middlebury Coll; Pltcl Sci.

BLEVINS, TRICIA; Penn Manor HS; Lancaster, PA; (Y); 20/320; Trs Varsity Clb; Pres Jr Cls; Sr Cls; JV Var Fld Hcky; Im Powder Puff Ftbl; Var L Trk; Hon Roll; Lion Awd; NHS; Rotary Awd; Med.

BLEW, KAREN; Mahanoy Area HS; Barnesville, PA; (Y); Girl Scts; Library Aide; Teachers Aide; Band; Chorus; Church Choir; Concert Band; Mrchg Band; School Play; Anna & Harry Bhrd Awd; Lbry Clb; Bnd; Mc Canns; Exec Secty.

BLEWETT, MARK; Coudersport Area HS; Coudersport, PA; (Y); Church Yth Grp; French Clb; Letterman Clb; Ski Clb; Varsity Clb; Band; Concert Band; Mrchg Band; Stu Cncl; Bsktbl; St Bonaventure U; Bus.

BLICHA, JOHN; Canon-Mc Millan SR HS; Eighty Four, PA; (Y); French Clb; Ski Clb; Varsity Clb; Rep Frsh Cls; Rep Stu Cncl; Var JV Bsbl; Var Bsktbl; Var Golf; High Hon Roll; 1st Pl Awd Frnch Dctn 86; Bus Adm.

BLINER, JERRY; Belle Vernon Area HS; Webster, PA; (Y); Spanish Clb; Ftbl; Hon Roll; Chess Clb; Computer Clb; Spnsh Comp Wheel Of Fortune 2nd Pl 86; PA ST U; Military.

BLISS, BILL; Johnsonburg Area HS; Johnsonburg, PA; (S); 8/90; Varsity Clb; JV Var Bsktbl; Var Trk; Hon Roll; NHS.

BLISS, DEBORAH; Huntingdon Area HS; Hesston, PA; (Y); 13/224; Church Yth Grp; Band; Chorus; Concert Band; Mrchg Band; Hon Roll; NHS; NEDT Awd; Duquesne U.

BLISS, ERIC; Oxford Area HS; Oxford, PA; (Y); Boy Scts; Church Yth Grp; French Clb; Scholastic Bowl; Stage Crew; Yrbk Stf; Hon Roll; NHS; Pres Schlr; Yrbk Asst Edtr Chief 86; Eagle Scout 83; Stu Mnth 86; PA ST U; Aerospc Engrng.

BLISS, LAURIE; S R U HS; Gillett, PA; (Y); Church Yth Grp; Girl Scts; Library Aide; Teachers Aide; Church Choir; Color Guard; Nwsp Rptr; Yrbk Stf; Rep Stu Cncl; Voice Dem Awd; 1st Pl In Ready Wrtng Cntst 86; Cert Of Apprctn Sch Anncmnts 84-86; Hnrb Mntn Poetry Cntst 83; Elnice Bus Inst; Bus Mgmnt.

BLISSMAN, GREGORY C; East Allegheny HS; N Versailles, PA; (Y); Am Leg Boys St; Computer Clb; Exploring; High Hon Roll; NHS.

BLIZZARD, LINDA; Mercer HS; Mercer, PA; (Y); 2/111; Math Tm; NFL; Pres Speech Tm; Symp Band; High Hon Roll; NHS; Sal; Var Cheerleading; Var Capt Vllybl; Speech Svc Awd 86; ST Fin Extemporeaneous Spkng 86; Bowling Green ST U; Pre-Law.

BLOCH, JONATHAN; Parkland HS; Allentown, PA; (Y); 77/459; VP Church Yth Grp; Cmnty Wkr; Computer Clb; Math Clb; Math Tm; Office Aide; Quiz Bowl; Temple Yth Grp; High Hon Roll; Hon Roll; Am Leg Bsbl Tm 86; Bsktbl Tm AZA Champs 85; Mth & Verbal Tlnt Srch 82; Carnegie-Mellon U; Bus.

BLOCH, SCOTT; Highlands HS; Brackenridge, PA; (Y); 44/275; Boy Scts; Jazz Band; Rep Jr Cls; High Hon Roll; NHS; Intnl Clb; Band; Concert Band; Mrchg Band; Off Frsh Cls; Govnrs Sch Of Art 84; Natl Band Assc, Natl Jazz Band 84; Hugh O Brian Ldrshp Semnr 84; N TX ST U; Jazz.

BLOCKER II, WALTER LOUIS; Creative & Performing Arts HS; Philadelphia, PA; (Y); 40/149; Church Yth Grp; Debate Tm; SADD; Chorus; Church Choir; Chrmn Stu Cncl; Cit Awd; Gov Hon Prg Awd; High Hon Roll; NHS; Gov Schrlshp 86; ST Bd Trustees Schrlshp 86; Westminster Choir Coll; Music.

BLODGETT, DIANE; Everett Area HS; Clearville, PA; (Y); 2/109; French Clb; Rep SADD; Chorus; School Musical; Stu Cncl; French Hon Soc; High Hon Roll; Hon Roll; VP NHS; Wdmn Of Wrld Hstry Awd 85.

BLODGETT, STACEY; Canon-Mac Millan SR HS; Canonsburg, PA; (Y); Boy Scts; Cmnty Wkr; Latin Clb; Office Aide; Yrbk Stf; JV Sftbl; Im Vllybl; High Hon Roll; Hon Roll; Molecular Bio.

BLOOM, CYNTHIA; United HS; Blairsville, PA; (S); 12/159; French Clb; GAA; Math Clb; Pep Clb; Ski Clb; Teachers Aide; Chorus; Yrbk Stf; Lit Mag; Pres Stu Cncl; Pol Sci.

BLOOM, DAWN; Harry S Truman HS; Fairless Hills, PA; (Y); Drama Clb; Office Aide; Pep Clb; School Musical; Pres Frsh Cls; Stu Cncl; Var Capt Cheerleading; Hon Roll; Chrldr Of Yr 85-86; PA ST U; Ed.

BLOOM, JILL MEREDITH; Spring-Ford SR HS; Collegeville, PA; (Y); 34/237; Ski Clb; Hon Roll; W Chester U; Bio Chem.

BLOOM, MARC; Central HS; Philadelphia, PA; (Y); Camera Clb; Computer Clb; Library Aide; Varsity Clb; Yrbk Ed-Chief; Yrbk Phtg; Var Tennis; Hon Roll; Drexel U; Bus Adm.

BLOSE, KARINA; Punxsutawney Area HS; Punxsutawney, PA; (Y); 5/238; Church Yth Grp; French Clb; Math Tm; Science Clb; Band; Chorus; JP Sousa Awd; Art Clb; Church Choir; Natl Choral Awd 86; Stu Of Mth Awd 84-86; BPW Girl Of Mnth Awd 86; Clarion U; Foreign Lang.

BLOSE, RHONDA; Elderton JR SR HS; Shelocta, PA; (Y); 20/99; Varsity Clb; Color Guard; Yrbk Stf; Pres Jr Cls; Stu Cncl; Stat Bsbl; Stat Bsktbl; High Hon Roll; Hon Roll; NHS; IN U Of PA; Engl.

BLOSNICK, STEVEN; West Allegheny HS; Imperial, PA; (Y); 23/211; Spanish Clb; Hon Roll; Pres Outstndng Acdmc Achvt 86; PA ST U; Chem Engr.

BLOSS, TAMARA; Liberty HS; Bethlehem, PA; (Y); 159/475; Church Yth Grp; French Clb; Hosp Aide; Red Cross Aide; Chorus; Mgr(s); Hon Roll.

BLOTZER, AMY; Clarion-Limestone HS; Summerville, PA; (Y); 11/83; Chorus; Cheerleading; Hon Roll; NHS; Pres Schlr; Clarion U; Accntng.

BLOUGH, BARBARA; Conemaugh Township HS; Hollsopple, PA; (Y); 19/103; Church Yth Grp; Drama Clb; FHA; Intnl Clb; Spanish Clb; Concert Band; Jazz Band; Mrchg Band; Stage Crew; Hon Roll; Bnd Awd 86; ICM Schl Bus; Med Ofcr Asst.

BLOW, SHANNON; Wyalusing Valley JR SR HS; Wyalusing, PA; (Y); Sec Church Yth Grp; 4-H; Ski Clb; Sec Spanish Clb; SADD; Chorus; School Musical; Cheerleading; Hon Roll; NHS; Air Trnsprtn.

BLOZIK, SCOTT; Brownsville Area HS; Brownsville, PA; (Y); Drama Clb; Pres Band; VP Chorus; Pres Concert Band; Pres Jazz Band; Pres Mrchg Band; Pres Pep Band; L Wrstlng; High Hon Roll; Hon Roll; WVU; Music Ed.

BLOZOUSKY, CHRISTINE; Mahanoy Area HS; Mahanoy City, PA; (Y); 3/125; Drama Clb; FFA; Ski Clb; Band; Chorus; Variety Show; Yrbk Stf; Elks Awd; High Hon Roll; NCTE Awd; Amer Bus Wmns Assoc Schlrshp 86; Franklin&marshall Coll Cmnwlth Schlrshp 86; M D Comerford Schlrshp 86; Franklin & Marshall Coll; Bus.

BLUBAUGH, MELISSA; Turkey Foot Valley HS; Addison, PA; (S); 1/52; Band; Concert Band; Mrchg Band; Yrbk Stf; Sec Frsh Cls; Sec Soph Cls; Sec Jr Cls; Stat Bsktbl; Sftbl; High Hon Roll; Comp Sci.

BLUE, MELISSA; Cheltenham HS; Elkins Pk, PA; (Y); Church Yth Grp; Cmnty Wkr; Varsity Clb; Chorus; Yrbk Stf; Pres Stu Cncl; Capt Cheerleading; Tennis; Trk; Hon Roll; AFNA Schlr 85-86; Hum Rel Comm 83-85; Ballet Prfrmnce Acad Of Music 84-85; Howard U; Intl Bus.

BLUE, REGINALD; Northwestern Lehigh HS; Germansville, PA; (Y); 12/130; Computer Clb; Debate Tm; Math Tm; Quiz Bowl; Band; Concert Band; Jazz Band; Mrchg Band; Pep Band; NEDT Awd; Sci Awd 86; Semper Fidelis Awd 86; Outstndng Physcis Perf 84-86; PA ST U; Pre-Med.

BLUM, MARK; Carson Long Inst; Vestal, NY; (S); 1/36; Chess Clb; Debate Tm; Drama Clb; Mathletes; ROTC; Ski Clb; Var L Bsktbl; JV Ftbl; JV Var Lcrss; Var Socr; Navy ROTC 4 Yr Schlrshp 86; Miguel Tejers Chem Awd 86; Pres Outstndng Acadmc Achvt 86; Boston U; Bus.

BLUM, REBECCA; Penn Hills SR HS; Pittsburgh, PA; (Y); Am Leg Aux Girls St; Library Aide; Office Aide; Spanish Clb; High Hon Roll; Hon Roll; Jr NHS; Art Inst Pittsburgh; Intr Dsgn.

BLUM JR, RONALD; Butler SR HS; Butler, PA; (Y); AFS; Drama Clb; Pres JA; SADD; Thesps; Chorus; Orch; School Play; Swing Chorus; Variety Show; Mercyhurst Coll; Htl Mgmt.

BLUMENTHAL, CONNIE S; Cheltenham HS; Melrose Park, PA; (Y); 1/385; Political Wkr; Service Clb; Temple Yth Grp; Yrbk Stf; French Hon Soc; NHS; Ntl Merit SF; Mgr(s); PA JR Acdmy Of Sci 83-85; Cert Of Merit Frm PA Hghr Ed Astnc Agncy 85; Dstngshd Acdmc Achvt 84; Doctor.

BLUNDO, MARIANNE; Freedom SR HS; Bethlehem, PA; (Y); 135/456; Church Yth Grp; JA; Pep Clb; Spanish Clb; Band; Concert Band; Mrchg Band; Rep Frsh Cls; Rep Stu Cncl; Hon Roll; Mch Imprvd Stu 84; Outstndg Stu 84; Typg Prfcncy Awd 84; NCACC Kutztown; Advrtsng.

BLY, ELLEN; Harbor Creek HS; Erie, PA; (Y); 35/228; Office Aide; Band; Mrchg Band; Rep Stu Cncl; Hon Roll; NHS; Villa Maria Coll; Nrsng.

BLY, KENNETH; Freeport Area HS; Sarver, PA; (Y); 1/173; Varsity Clb; Var L Bsbl; Var L Ftbl; Bausch & Lomb Sci Awd; High Hon Roll; NHS; Opt Clb Awd; Pres Schlr; Val; U S Army Rsrv Natl Schlr Athl 86; Amer H S Athl 86; PA ST U; Elctrcl Engrng.

BLYSTONE, CHERYL; Blairsville SR HS; Blairsville, PA; (Y); Library Aide; Red Cross Aide; Rep Stu Cncl; High Hon Roll; Hon Roll; Pres Phy Fitness Awd 84 & 86; HOSA ST Conf Comptr 86; Dstngshd Hnr Roll Aver 86; Westmoreland Cnty CC; Acctng.

BLYSTONE, JENNIFER; Kiski Area HS; Apollo, PA; (Y); Spanish Clb; Band; Mrchg Band; Symp Band; Rptr Frsh Cls; Crs Cntry; Trk; Hon Roll; Engrg.

BLYSTONE, KRIS; Karns City HS; Chicora, PA; (Y); FNA; Band; Concert Band; Mrchg Band; Pres Jr Cls; Hon Roll; Butler Cnty CC; Nrsng.

BOBACK, LISA; Dallas SR HS; Dallas, PA; (Y); Art Clb; French Clb; Ski Clb; Yrbk Stf; Rep Stu Cncl; High Hon Roll; Hon Roll; Ntl Sci Merit Awd; PA ST; Telecomm.

BOBB, LISA; St Basil Acad; Philadelphia, PA; (S); 8/94; Church Yth Grp; German Clb; Chorus; Church Choir; Madrigals; Orch; Yrbk Stf; Luthern Schlr Awd-Wittenbrg U 85; Wittenberg U; Mnstry.

BOBER, STEPHEN; Mohawk Area JRSR HS; New Castle, PA; (S); Latin Clb; Band; Chorus; Mrchg Band; School Musical; Nwsp Rptr; Yrbk Sprt Ed; Stu Cncl; High Hon Roll; NHS; Phrmcy.

BOBERICK, GARY; Northwest Area HS; Shickshinny, PA; (Y); 20/108; Pres Aud/Vis; VP Chess Clb; VP Computer Clb; 4-H; French Clb; Var Capt Bsbl; JV Bsktbl; Var Capt Ftbl; Im Vllybl; Wt Lftg; Sons Of Italy In Amer 86-87; Penn ST U; Engrng.

BOBICH, CATHERINE; Beaver Area HS; Beaver, PA; (Y); Cmnty Wkr; French Clb; Hosp Aide; Key Clb; Pep Clb; Red Cross Aide; Teachers Aide; Color Guard; School Musical; Stu Cncl; Spec Ed.

BOBIER, KIMBERLY M; Wilson HS; Sinking Spring, PA; (Y); 37/266; Church Yth Grp; French Clb; Color Guard; Var Cheerleading; Powder Puff Ftbl; Var Trk; NHS; Pin Awd-2 Vrsty Lttrs & Top 2/3 Of Cls 86; Word Of Life Bible Inst; Bibl.

BOBIN, GEORGE; Ambridge Area HS; Baden, PA; (Y); Am Leg Boys St; Pep Clb; Spanish Clb; Var L Bsbl; Hon Roll; Robert Morris Coll; Acctng.

BOBINETS, JAMIE; Homer Center; Homer City, PA; (Y); 13/94; French Clb; Varsity Clb; Concert Band; Mrchg Band; Stat Bsktbl; Twrlr; JV Var Vllybl; High Hon Roll; Jr NHS; NHS; Sprts Med.

BOBISH, SUSAN M; Monaca HS; Monaca, PA; (Y); French Clb; Pep Clb; Red Cross Aide; Band; Drill Tm; Pep Band; School Musical; Yrbk Stf; Tennis; NHS; Am Legn Schlrshp; JR Womns Clb Girl Of Mnth 86; Sawyer Bus Schl; Trvl Fld.

BOBKO, JILL; Laurel Valley JR SR HS; New Florence, PA; (Y); FBLA; Library Aide; Chorus; Jazz Band; Variety Show; Wt Lftg; Hon Roll; 2nd Pl Vocal Perform Olympics Of Arts 84; 2nd Pl Span Musical Presentn Humanities Day 86; Dusquene U; Music.

BOBNAK, LAURA; Archbishop Prendergast HS; E Lansdowne, PA; (Y); 41/361; Church Yth Grp; Cmnty Wkr; Hosp Aide; Service Clb; SADD; School Musical; School Play; Hon Roll; Drexel U; Nutrtnl Scntst.

BOBRIN, BRAD; Cheltenham HS; Wyncote, PA; (Y); 75/360; Cmnty Wkr; Scholastic Bowl; Lcrss; 2nd 85, 3rd 86 PJAS; Hon Ment Sci Fair 86; Ltr Rcgntn Hist Soc Phila 85; Cert Recngntn PA Phrmctl Asn; Physics.

BOCCELLA, ERICA AMATA; The Oakland Schl; Pittsburgh, PA; (S); 3/50; Hosp Aide; Latin Clb; Chorus; School Play; Yrbk Stf; Lit Mag; Stu Cncl; DAR Awd; St Lucy Mdln Rdpnt 180 Hrs Vlntr Wrk; :Dntstry.

BOCHAK, PAULA; Scranton Technical HS; Scranton, PA; (Y); Dance Clb; English Clb; French Clb; Band; Pom Pon; Marywood Coll; Nrsng.

BOCHAK, VICTORIA; Ambridge Area HS; Ambridge, PA; (Y); Church Yth Grp; Pep Clb; Red Cross Aide; Concert Band; Mrchg Band; Rep Jr Cls; Gym; High Hon Roll; Hon Roll; Prfct Atten Awd.

BOCHNAK, KATHY; Allentown Central Catholic HS; Allentown, PA; (Y); 48/212; Church Yth Grp; Key Clb; Service Clb; Spanish Clb; Chorus; Church Choir; School Musical; Yrbk Rptr; Twrlr; Hon Roll; PA Jr Acad Of Sci 1st & 2nd Awds Regnl & ST Lvls 83-87; Miss Persnlty 86; Villanova; Foreign Lang.

BOCK, LYNNETTE; Philipsburg-Osceola Area SR HS; Philipsburg, PA; (Y); 3/250; Band; Ed Yrbk Stf; Hon Roll; Jr NHS; Pre Med.

BOCK, WENDY; Bethel Park SR HS; Bethel Park, PA; (Y); Church Yth Grp; French Clb; Band; Sec Mrchg Band; Sec Symp Band; High Hon Roll; Hon Roll.

BOCKELKAMP, RICH; Lackawanna Trail HS; Dalton, PA; (Y); Boy Scts; JA; Wt Lftg; Hon Roll; Keystone JC; Archtctrl Dsgn.

BOCKES, AMANDA; Berlin Brothersvalley HS; Berlin, PA; (Y); 10/87; Sec Church Yth Grp; FBLA; Chorus; Church Choir; School Play; Yrbk Stf; Hon Roll; NHS.

BOCKNACK, BRIAN; Council Rock HS; Holland, PA; (Y); 38/850; JCL; Trs Latin Clb; Spanish Clb; Lit Mag; High Hon Roll; Jr NHS; Ntl Merit Ltr; Chmstry.

BOCSY, ERIN; North Star HS; Boswell, PA; (Y); 8/140; Church Yth Grp; FCA; 4-H; Color Guard; Rep Stu Cncl; JV Var Vllybl; Hon Roll; NHS; Actvts Boosters Stu Of Month 86.

BODAMER, LYNNE; Warren County Christian Schl; Titusville, PA; (S); 3/10; Church Yth Grp; Chorus; Church Choir; Yrbk Stf; Pres Stu Cncl; Var Bsktbl; Cheerleading; Hon Roll.

BODDEN, DIANA; Archbishop Prendergast HS; Darby, PA; (Y); 32/360; Office Aide; Rep Jr Cls; Rep Sr Cls; Rep Stu Cncl; Bowling; Cheerleading; Gym; High Hon Roll; Hon Roll; Pres Schlr; Pres Schlrshp To Wdnr DE Campus 86; Wdnr-DE Campur; Fash Merch.

BODEN, MARIAN; West Perry SR HS; Landisburg, PA; (Y); 11/200; French Clb; Hosp Aide; Pres Varsity Clb; Yrbk Stf; Var L Fld Hcky; Var L Trk; Hon Roll; Sec NHS; Im Vllybl; Coaches Choice Awd Trk 86; All Str Fld Hocky 85-86; Engrng.

BODENSCHATZ, PATRICIA; Forest Hills SR HS; Summerhill, PA; (Y); 19/156; Office Aide; Pep Clb; Spanish Clb; Rep Stu Cncl; Score Keeper; Stat Trk; High Hon Roll; Hon Roll; Jr NHS; Spanish NHS; Elem Educ.

BODENSCHATZ, WENDY; Forest Hills HS; Summerhill, PA; (Y); 17/156; Debate Tm; Pres Drama Clb; Pres NFL; Pres Thesps; Chorus; School Musical; School Play; Nwsp Ed-Chief; Jr NHS; Stu Cncl; Jazz-Rock Concert Choir; Frosh Enlg Awd; JR Miss; Brdcstng.

BODES, JEFF; Salisbury E K Lick HS; Spgs, PA; (Y); 4/35; Pres Church Yth Grp; Band; School Play; Yrbk Stf; Var Bsbl; Hon Roll; U Of Pittsburgh; Cvl Engrng.

BODINE, HEATHER; Unionville HS; Kennett Square, PA; (Y); 33/300; Church Yth Grp; Intnl Clb; Band; Chorus; Church Choir; Flag Corp; Orch; School Musical; Musicnshp Awd 84-85; Hstry.

BODKIN, HEATHER; Cardinal O Hara HS; Springfield, PA; (Y); Camera Clb; Pres Church Yth Grp; Cmnty Wkr; French Clb; Office Aide; Rep Jr Cls.

BODNAR, CHRIS; Bentworth Sr HS; Scenery Hill, PA; (Y); 1/150; Pres Band; Concert Band; Jazz Band; Mrchg Band; Orch; Stage Crew; Symp Band; High Hon Roll; NHS; Louis Armstrong Jazz Awd 86; Acad All Amer 85-86; Ed.

BODNAR, LESLIE; Mt Pleasant HS; Latrobe, PA; (Y); GAA; Latin Clb; Ski Clb; Teachers Aide; Rep Sr Cls; Rep Stu Cncl; Stat Bsktbl; L Tennis; 4-H; Mbr Of The Hmcmng Ct 86; Brooks Coll; Fshn Mrchndsr.

BODNAR, LISA MARIE; Allentown Central Catholic HS; Whitehall, PA; (Y); Church Yth Grp; Computer Clb; Hosp Aide; Key Clb; Spanish Clb; Chorus; School Musical; School Play; Swing Chorus; Rep Soph Cls; PA Jr Acad For Sci 1st Pl Rgn 3rd Pl 85; PJAS 1st Pl Regn 2nd Pl ST 86; Intl Reltns.

BODNAR, RONALD; Carlynton HS; Pittsburgh, PA; (Y); Slippery Rock; Accntnt.

BODNAR, YVONNE; Valley HS; New Kensington, PA; (Y); AFS; Drama Clb; French Clb; Hosp Aide; Pep Clb; Science Clb; Ski Clb; Band; Cheerleading; Swmmng; PTA Hgh Ed Awd 86; U Pittsburgh; Phrmst.

BODVAKE, JOSEPH FRANK; Canon Mc Millan SR HS; Canonsburg, PA; (Y); Chess Clb; Var L Bsbl; JV Ftbl.

BODZIAK, SCOTT; West Allegheny HS; Clinton, PA; (Y); Trk; Hon Roll; Gftd & Tlntd Educ 82-86; IN U Pf PA; Bus Mngmnt.

BODZIUCH, JUSTYNA; Upper Darby HS; Drexel Hill, PA; (Y); 1/580; Pres German Clb; Acpl Chr; Orch; Swing Chorus; Rptr Yrbk Rptr; High Hon Roll; NHS; Ntl Merit Schol; Rotary Awd; Val; Mendenhall-Tyson Schlrshp 86; Soc Women Engrs Hghts Hnrs 85-86; Phi-Beta Kappa Bk Awd 86; MA Inst Of Tech; Chem Engrng.

BOEHM, AMY; Bethel Park HS; Bethel Park, PA; (Y); Art Clb; Mrchg Band; Powder Puff Ftbl; Twrlr; Art.

BOEHM, DEBORAH J; Freedom HS; Easton, PA; (Y); 132/445; Art Clb; Church Yth Grp; German Clb; JV Mgr(s); JV Sftbl; Hon Roll; Northampton Area CC; Drftng.

BOEHM, LYNDA; Hampton HS; Gibsonia, PA; (Y); Band; Concert Band; Mrchg Band; Pep Band; Powder Puff Ftbl; Mgr Socr; Acctng.

BOEHMIG, CINDY; Knoch Jr-Sr HS; Butler, PA; (Y); Concert Band; Mrchg Band; High Hon Roll; NHS; PA ST U; Mech Engrng.

BOEHMKE, SANDRA; Saint Hubert HS; Philadelphia, PA; (Y); 37/365; Church Yth Grp; Office Aide; Bsktbl; Coach Actv; Timer; Prfct Atten Awd; Hotel Mgmt.

BOEHMLER, BRITT; Hazleton HS; Hazleton, PA; (Y); 64/400; Office Aide; Pep Clb; Chorus; Yrbk Stf; Hon Roll; NHS; PA ST U; Nrsng.

BOEHRINGER, C SHAWN; Gov Mifflin SR HS; Reinholds, PA; (Y); 10/310; Nwsp Rptr; Rep Frsh Cls; Rep Soph Cls; VP Jr Cls; Rep Sr Cls; Rep Stu Cncl; Var Bsbl; Var Capt Socr; High Hon Roll; NHS; Russell L Ruble Schlrshp 86; Guy Moser Schlrshp 86; Pres Schlrshp Gettysbrg Coll 86; Gettysburg Coll; Hstry.

BOELL, COLLEEN; Central Bucks East HS; Doylestown, PA; (Y); Church Yth Grp; FBLA; Flag Corp; Stat Mgr(s); JV Vllybl; Hon Roll; Hnr Rl; Elem Ed.

BOESHORE, SHARON; Annville-Cleona HS; Annville, PA; (S); 5/120; Hosp Aide; Band; Chorus; Concert Band; Jazz Band; Madrigals; Mrchg Band; Pep Band; School Musical; Nwsp Rptr; Physical Therapy.

BOETH, JACK; West Scranton SR HS; Scranton, PA; (Y); 6/275; Ski Clb; Spanish Clb; Speech Tm; Thesps; School Musical; School Play; Hon Roll; NHS; Rotary Awd; Philadelphia Coll; Prhmcy.

BOETTCHER, EDWARD JOHN; Abington Hgts HS; Clarks Summit, PA; (Y); 125/275; Ski Clb; Bsbl; Ftbl; Marn Bio.

BOETTNER, BARBIE; Greater Latrobe SR HS; Latrobe, PA; (Y); Church Yth Grp; Varsity Clb; VICA; Yrbk Ed-Chief; Yrbk Phtg; JV Bsktbl; Var Capt Trk; Prfct Atten Awd; CODE; IU Stu Forum; Cmmnctns.

BOFFA, CAROLYN; Nazareth Acad; Philadelphia, PA; (Y); Art Clb; Cmnty Wkr; French Clb; Pep Clb; Lit Mag; Im Fld Hcky; Im Socr; Im Vllybl; La Salle U; Med.

BOFINGER, JENNIFER; Upper Dublin HS; Oreland, PA; (Y); 71/318; FBLA; Intnl Clb; Variety Show; Powder Puff Ftbl; Var L Socr; Trk; 3rd Pl FBLA Regnls Bus Engl 86; Theatre Arts.

BOGACKI, JEFFREY J; Holy Ghost Preparatory Schl; Philadelphia, PA; (Y); Art Clb; Pres Aud/Vis; Cmnty Wkr; English Clb; German Clb; JV Bsktbl; Im Golf; JV Socr; Im Vllybl; Villanoua U; Engrng.

BOGAR, MARK; Central Dauplin East HS; Harrisburg, PA; (Y); 4/271; Ski Clb; Band; Concert Band; Jazz Band; Mrchg Band; School Musical; Rep Stu Cncl; Im Vllybl; Pres Jr NHS; NHS; PA ST U; Engrng.

BOGART, CHRISTINA; Columbia-Montour Area Voc-Tech Schl; Danville, PA; (Y); DECA; High Hon Roll; Hon Roll; DECA Asstnt Hstrn 84-85; DECA Trea 85-86; DECA Pres 86-87; Luzerne CC; Restrnt Mgmt.

BOGDANOVICH, KENNETH C; Scranton Central HS; Scranton, PA; (Y); U Of Scranton; Pre Med.

BOGDEN, EDWARD; Carmichaels Area HS; Riceslanding, PA; (Y); Boy Scts; French Clb; Pep Clb; Ski Clb; SADD; Band; High Hon Roll; CA U; Comptr Sci.

BOGDON, KRISTIN; Cheltenham HS; Glenside, PA; (Y); Church Yth Grp; Chorus; Nwsp Stf; Lcrss; Socr; Sftbl; Trk; Vrsty Sccr & Trk; U Of DE; Bus.

BOGER, JENNIFER; Lebanon Catholic HS; Lebanon, PA; (Y); FHA; Key Clb; Library Aide; Pep Clb; Spanish Clb; SADD; School Play; Stage Crew; Yrbk Stf; Capt Cheerleading; Yth Govt; Peer Cnslr; Duquesne U; Acctg.

BOGGS, DIANNA; German SR HS; Mc Clellandtown, PA; (Y); Spanish Clb; Concert Band; Mrchg Band; Stu Cncl; High Hon Roll; Hon Roll; Jr NHS; 4-H; Band; Chorus; Stud Of The Mnth 83-85; Span I Cert 84; Comp Prgmr.

BOGGS, ERIC; Beaver Area HS; Beaver, PA; (Y); German Clb; Key Clb; Latin Clb; Ski Clb; Im Bsktbl; JV Ftbl; Var L Swmmng; High Hon Roll; Lion Awd; NHS; Acdmc Achvt Awd 84-86; Pres Acdmc Ftns Awd 86; Gnva Schlr Awd 86; CMU; Mech Engr.

BOGLE, AMY; Pennsbury HS; Fallsington, PA; (Y); German Clb; Hosp Aide; Albert Einstein; Nrsg.

BOGNAR, JENNIFER; Columbia Montour AVTS; Berwick, PA; (Y); 3/179; Church Yth Grp; VICA; Chorus; Cheerleading; High Hon Roll; Hon Roll; Kiwanis Awd; NHS; Cosmtlgy Achvt Awd 85-86; Memrl Bonds 85-86; Penn ST; Voctnl Ed.

BOGNAR, SCOTT; Brownsville Area HS; Brownsville, PA; (Y); French Clb; JV Capt Bsktbl; Im Bowling; Hon Roll; Math.

BOGNER, MICHELLE; Lebanon HS; Lebanon, PA; (Y); 50/285; Ski Clb; Teachers Aide; Varsity Clb; Var L Fld Hcky; Var Mgr(s); L Var Sftbl; Hon Roll.

BOGNET, LEWIS; Bishop Hafey HS; Hazleton, PA; (Y); Church Yth Grp; FBLA; Stu Cncl; Bsktbl; Ftbl; Hon Roll; Bio.

BOGO, ROXANNE J; Canon-Mc Millan HS; Eighty Four, PA; (Y); 33/342; Church Yth Grp; Dance Clb; Letterman Clb; SADD; Varsity Clb; Chorus; Stage Crew; Nwsp Stf; Yrbk Stf; Swmmng; Athletic Awd 86; High Hon Roll Awd 85; Westminster Coll.

BOGOCHENKO, MARY; Trinity HS; Washington, PA; (Y); Camera Clb; GAA; Girl Scts; Office Aide; Drm Mjr(t); Orch; Trk; PA Comercial; Scrtry.

BOGOVICH, MARK; Shikellamy HS; Northumberland, PA; (Y); 22/301; Am Leg Boys St; Boy Scts; Cmnty Wkr; VP Jr Cls; Pres Stu Cncl; Var Capt Ftbl; Var Wrstlng; High Hon Roll; Hon Roll; Math.

BOGOZI, LORI; Albert Gallatin SR HS; Masontown, PA; (Y); Church Yth Grp; Band; Concert Band; Drm Mjr(t); Mrchg Band; VP Jr Cls; Var JV Bsktbl; Cit Awd; Hon Roll; Jr NHS; Phy Thrpst.

BOGUSH, CHRISTINE; Mt Carmel Area JR SR HS; Kulpmont, PA; (Y); FNA; FTA; Library Aide; Spanish Clb; Band; Concert Band; Mrchg Band.

BOGUSH, STEPHEN; Southern Columbia Area HS; Elysburg, PA; (Y); 1/89; Exploring; Key Clb; Yrbk Phtg; VP Soph Cls; Var JV Bsbl; JV Bsktbl; High Hon Roll; NCTE Awd; NHS; Pre-Med.

BOHEEN, ERICA; Central Buck High School East; Doylestown, PA; (Y); Drama Clb; Girl Scts; Chorus; School Musical; School Play; Var Swmmng; High Hon Roll; Hon Roll; NHS; Chem.

BOHINSKI, DOREEN ANN; John S Fine SR HS; Nanticoke, PA; (Y); Hosp Aide; Model UN; Chorus; Yrbk Stf; High Hon Roll; Music Awd Unsng Hero Awd & Cert 86; Wilkes Coll; Nrsg.

BOHIZIC, RENEE; Union HS; New Castle, PA; (Y); French Clb; Pep Clb; Band; Concert Band; Co-Capt Drm Mjr(t); Yrbk Stf; Hon Roll; NHS; Psych.

BOHNER, AMY P; Central Bucks West HS; Warrington, PA; (Y); 2/400; Scholastic Bowl; Ski Clb; Rep Stu Cncl; Var L Lcrss; JV Tennis; High Hon Roll; Hon Roll; Pres NHS; Ntl Merit SF; Amer Chmcl Soc Awd-Chem; Ntl Sci Olympd Awd; Ntl Sci Olympd Awd-Bio; Chem.

BOHNER, ANDREW; Emmaus HS; Emmaus, PA; (Y); 40/457; Church Yth Grp; Key Clb; JV Var Socr; Var Trk; Jr NHS; NHS; NROTC Schlrshp 86; Pres Acadmc Ftnss Awd 86; PA ST U; Engrg.

BOHNER, TARA; Bishop Shanahan HS; Boothwyn, PA; (Y); 62/218; Church Yth Grp; Drama Clb; French Clb; Chorus; School Play; VA Weslyan Coll; Cmmnctns.

BOHR, ANDREW C; Northeastern HS; Manchester, PA; (Y); Church Yth Grp; Ski Clb; Band; Chorus; Concert Band; Jazz Band; Mrchg Band; Orch; Pep Band; School Musical; PMEA Dist Band 84-86; Bnkng.

BOHRER, JAMES; Cathedral Prep; Erie, PA; (Y); 199/216; Chess Clb.

BOHUN, KELLY; Northampton SR HS; Bath, PA; (Y); VICA; High Hon Roll; Hon Roll; Allentown Bus; Bus Mgmnt.

BOHUSCH, KATHERINE M; Mc Dowell HS; Erie, PA; (Y); 38/546; Aud/Vis; Pres Chess Clb; Computer Clb; Exploring; German Clb; Library Aide; Math Tm; Science Clb; Church Choir; Rep Sr Cls; Chem.

BOICE, DEBORAH; Tunkhannock Area HS; Tunkhannock, PA; (Y); Hon Roll; Bus Ed Awd 86; Shrthnd Awd 86; Secy.

BOJANOWSKI, CAROL ANN; Philadelphia HS For Girls; Philadelphia, PA; (Y); 30/395; Service Clb; Rep Jr Cls; Rep Stu Cncl; Var Bowling; Var L Crs Cntry; High Hon Roll; Spanish NHS; Coaches Awd For Coaching The St Barnabas Girls Track Tm 85; Physical Therapy.

BOJANOWSKI, STEVE; Neshaminy HS; Feasterville, PA; (Y); 15/752; Yrbk Stf; High Hon Roll; NHS; Engrng.

BOJARSKI, CLARE; Montour HS; Corapolis, PA; (Y); 8/327; Drama Clb; GAA; Girl Scts; Yrbk Ed-Chief; Yrbk Stf; Var Crs Cntry; Var L Trk; High Hon Roll; Hon Roll; Trs NHS.

BOKROS, JIM; Valley SR HS; Arnold, PA; (Y); 5/225; Exploring; JA; Leo Clb; Office Aide; Science Clb; Spanish Clb; Acpl Chr; Yrbk Ed-Chief; Pres Sr Cls; Bsktbl; Pres Acad Fit Awd 86; Acad All Amer 86; Top 10 Hnrs Bnqt; Dickinson Coll; Elec Engrng.

BOLAND, DIANE; North East HS; North East, PA; (Y); 14/151; Q&S; Drill Tm; Var L Bsktbl; Var L Socr; High Hon Roll; Hon Roll; Ntl Merit Ltr; Pres Schlr; Church Yth Grp; Latin Clb; PTA Grant Schlrshp 86; Josephine Scovller Mem Schlrshp 86; Schl Sprt Awd 86; PA ST U; Ath Trng.

BOLAND, PATRICK; Scranton Prep; Scranton, PA; (Y); 81/191; Boys Clb Am; Church Yth Grp; Cmnty Wkr; Political Wkr; Nwsp Rptr; Var L Bsktbl; Im Coach Actv; Var L Golf; Hon Roll; Engrng.

BOLCAROVIC, ROBERT; Tunkhannock Area HS; Tunkhannock, PA; (Y); Band; Concert Band; Mrchg Band.

BOLE, CHRISTINE; Academy Of Notre Dame; Villanova, PA; (Y); 9/72; Computer Clb; FCA; Mathletes; Red Cross Aide; Lit Mag; Pres Frsh Cls; VP Soph Cls; Pres Jr Cls; Rep Sr Cls; Fld Hcky; Ntl Hist Day, Medrti Awd 85; Ntl Sci Olympd 86; Boston Coll; Fin.

BOLENA, CHARLES; Penn Trafford HS; Irwin, PA; (Y); AFS; Chess Clb; JCL; Latin Clb; Chorus; Stage Crew; Var Ftbl; JV Wrstlng.

BOLGAR, MICHELE; Cambria Heights HS; Patton, PA; (Y); Library Aide; Chorus; Church Choir; Yrbk Stf; Cheerleading; Hon Roll; NHS; Seton Hill; Elem Ed.

BOLGER, ANDREW; Juniata HS; Mifflintown, PA; (Y); 9/160; Boy Scts; Varsity Clb; Yrbk Stf; Bsktbl; Socr; Trk; Hon Roll; NHS; Stud Of The Mnth 86; Slctd As Leag MVP In Trk 86; VA Poltch Inst; Engrng.

BOLIG, TANYA; Millersburg Area HS; Millersburg, PA; (S); Church Yth Grp; Ski Clb; Chorus; Concert Band; Mrchg Band; School Musical; Hon Roll; NHS; Temple U; Physcl Thrpy.

BOLINGER, SUSAN; Shenango HS; New Castle, PA; (Y); 15/117; VP Church Yth Grp; Hosp Aide; Office Aide; Concert Band; Flag Corp; School Play; Im Vllybl; Hon Roll; NHS; Edinboro U PA; Nrsg.

BOLINSKY, SUZANNE D; North Schuylkill HS; Frackville, PA; (Y); 3/166; Band; Variety Show; Rep Jr Cls; Rep Sr Cls; JV Var Cheerleading; JV Var Trk; DAR Awd; High Hon Roll; Hon Roll; NHS; Female Schlr Athlete 86; Math & Sci Awd 86; Lebanon Vlly Coll; Chem Engrng.

BOLKOVAC, ALBERT J; Northgate HS; Pittsburgh, PA; (Y); Am Leg Boys St; Camera Clb; Math Tm; Scholastic Bowl; Ftbl; Trk; Hon Roll; Prfct Atten Awd; US Naval Acad; Aerospace Engr.

BOLLAG, JUDY; State College Area HS; State College, PA; (Y); 33/568; Trs Service Clb; Concert Band; Mrchg Band; Soph Cls; Jr Cls; VP Sr Cls; Cit Awd; High Hon Roll; NEDT Awd; Prfct Atten Awd; Penn ST U; Bus.

BOLLES, CHRIS; Chichester SR HS; Boothwyn, PA; (Y); Am Leg Boys St; Art Clb; Computer Clb; Model UN; School Musical; School Play; Stage Crew; Nwsp Stf; Yrbk Stf; Mgr Bsktbl; Amer Lgn Schl Awd 84; 8th Annl PA Lgsltv Art Echbt 85; Annl Mntr Pstr HS Cmptn 86; Tyler; Cmmrcl Art.

BOLLI, CRAIG; Harry S Truman HS; Levittown, PA; (Y); Boy Scts; ROTC; SADD; Color Guard; Drill Tm; Stage Crew; Yrbk Stf; Hon Roll; Rotary Awd; NJROTC Aptitude Awd; World Wars Awd Military Order; NJROTC Acad Tm & Hnr Soc Awd; Oxford U; Corporate Law.

BOLLINGER, ANDREW WARREN; South Western HS; Hanover, PA; (Y); 49/206; Computer Clb; Varsity Clb; School Musical; Trs Sr Cls; Var L Bsbl; Var L Bsktbl; Var L Ftbl; Elks Awd; Hon Roll; All-Cnty Bsbl Tm-Ftbl Tm 86; S W Teen-Of-The-Mnth 86; Made Spch At Graduation; U Of DE; Comp Sci.

BOLLINGER, BECKY; Mechanicsburg SR HS; Mechanicsburg, PA; (Y); 75/311; Band; Concert Band; Mrchg Band; Symp Band; Stat Bsbl; Stat Bsktbl; Hon Roll; Cmnctns.

BOLLINGER, BONNIE; Richland HS; Gibsonia, PA; (Y); 21/190; Sec Church Yth Grp; Hosp Aide; Band; Chorus; School Musical; Swing Chorus; Cheerleading; Trk; High Hon Roll; NHS; 3 Trck Ltrs 84-86; Frnscs Awds 84-86; Chrldng Ltr 86; Capital U; Comm.

BOLLINGER, CRISSY; Bellwood Antis HS; Tyrone, PA; (Y); Chorus; Flag Corp; School Musical; Nwsp Rptr; Hon Roll; Shippensburg U; Psyc.

BOLLINGER JR, JAY; Huntingdon Area HS; Mill Creek, PA; (Y); 4/218; Exploring; Pres VICA; High Hon Roll; Jr NHS; NHS; Rotary Awd; Wlmsprt CC Outstndng Vctnl Stu 85-86.

BOLLINGER, JENNIFER; Shikellamy HS; Northumberland, PA; (Y); 52/364; French Clb; Band; Chorus; Concert Band; Drill Tm; Mrchg Band; Orch; Rep Stu Cncl; High Hon Soc; Hon Roll; St Chmpns Clvcd Bnds 85; Susquehanna Vlly Bnd Flt I 85; 7th Chr 86; 1st Chr 85-86; Dist Bnd Flt Ii 85; Sec Ed.

BOLLINGER, LISA; Jeannette SR HS; Jeannette, PA; (Y); 17/130; French Clb; FBLA; Tennis; High Hon Roll; Hon Roll; St Vincents Coll; Accntng.

BOLLINGER, SUSAN; Philipsburg-Osceola Area SR HS; Philipsburg, PA; (Y); 40/250; Church Yth Grp; Hosp Aide; Pep Clb; SADD; Band; Concert Band; Flag Corp; Stage Crew; Yrbk Stf; IN U Of Pennsylvania; Nrsng.

BOLLINGER, SUSAN M; Highlands SR HS; Natrona Hts, PA; (Y); 26/280; FNA; Hosp Aide; Office Aide; Mrchg Band; Rep Soph Cls; Rep Jr Cls; High Hon Roll; Prfct Atten Awd; Bus.

BOLLMAN, ROBERT; Northern Bedford County HS; Loysburg, PA; (Y); Math Clb; SADD; Varsity Clb; Var Bsbl; Var L Bsktbl; Var L Ftbl; Hon Roll; Mid Penn Conf All Star Ftbl 85; Ftbl Coaches Assoc Defnsv MVP Awd 85; Air Force; Comp.

BOLTON, DIANE; William Allen HS; Allentown, PA; (Y); 11/556; Leo Clb; High Hon Roll; Hon Roll; NHS; Ntl Merit Ltr; Pres Acdmc Fit Awd 86; Shpnsbrg U; Data Proc.

BOLTON, JILL; Norwin HS; N Huntingdon, PA; (Y); Church Yth Grp; Pep Clb; Spanish Clb; SADD; Church Choir; Hon Roll; Pediatrc Nrsng.

BOLTZ, MELISSA; Lebanon Catholic HS; Lebanon, PA; (Y); Hosp Aide; Key Clb; Chorus; Color Guard; School Play; Hon Roll; Diocesan Chrs Fstvl 84 & 85; Psych.

BOLYE, BRENDA; Wilmington Area HS; New Wilmington, PA; (S); 7/123; Church Yth Grp; Drama Clb; Office Aide; Pres Spanish Clb; Hon Roll.

BOLZE, VICTOR; Carlisle SR HS; Carlisle, PA; (Y); Crs Cntry; Tennis; Trk; Hon Roll; NHS; 1st Pl CASAC Awd Chem 85; Engrng.

BOMBERGER, HEATHER; Northern SR HS; Dillsburg, PA; (Y); 14/209; Drama Clb; French Clb; Speech Tm; Band; Chorus; Drm Mjr(t); Jazz Band; Mrchg Band; School Musical; Nwsp Stf; Tri M Hnr Socty; 2nd Pl ST Champ Oral Intrprtn Prose; Pres Frnsc Clb; Pltcl Sci.

BOMBERGER, STEPHEN; Lancaster Catholic HS; Lancaster, PA; (Y); 26/220; Trs Letterman Clb; Service Clb; Trs Varsity Clb; Var L Ftbl; Var L Trk; Im Wt Lftg; Var L Wrstlng; Hon Roll; NHS; Prtl Schlrshp Bucknell U Acad Wrstlng 86; MVP Trk 86; US Math Awd 85; Bucknell U; Civil Engrng.

BOMBOY, BOB; Northwest Area JR SR HS; Shickshinny, PA; (Y); 73/108; Aud/Vis; Cmnty Wkr; Computer Clb; Drama Clb; Sec Band; Chorus; Church Choir; Concert Band; Jazz Band; Mrchg Band; Dist IX Band & Chrs 84 & 86; Regnl IV Chrs 86; Bloomsburg U; Elem Educ.

BONACCI, MARY; Farrell HS; Farrell, PA; (Y); 5/100; Computer Clb; Pres Key Clb; Yrbk Stf; High Hon Roll; Pres Jr NHS; Pres NHS; French Clb; Math Clb; Office Aide; Science Clb; Gld Wtch Grad Hgh Hnrs 86; Slippery Rock U.

BONANO, MATTHEW; Pius X HS; Bangor, PA; (Y); Computer Clb; Speech Tm; Varsity Clb; Var Bsbl; Im Bsktbl; Var Ftbl; JV Wrstlng; Johnson & Wales Coll; Bus Mgt.

BONARRIGO, LIANE; Blairsville SR HS; Blairsville, PA; (Y); 32/141; Church Yth Grp; Ski Clb; Band; Color Guard; Concert Band; School Musical; Yrbk Bus Mgr; Yrbk Ed-Chief; Penn ST; Pdtrc Med.

BONAVITA, NICOLE; Meadville Area SR HS; Meadville, PA; (Y); French Clb; Office Aide; SADD; Y-Teens; Chorus; Var Cheerleading; Trk; Penn ST-BEHREND; Acctng.

BONAWITZ, TAMMY; Central Dauphin HS; Harrisburg, PA; (Y); Hosp Aide; Ski Clb; Chorus; School Musical; Yrbk Stf; Var Fld Hcky; Sftbl; Im Vllybl; Hon Roll; Jr NHS.

BOND, CARRIE; Kutztown Area HS; Kempton, PA; (Y); 33/150; VP Church Yth Grp; Band; Chorus; Concert Band; Mrchg Band; Pep Band; Stu Cncl; JV Var Fld Hcky; Trk; High Hon Roll; Art Schlrshp Baum Schl Art 85-86; Math.

BOND, MICHAEL; Shikellamy HS; Sunbury, PA; (Y); 30/301; Boy Scts; Church Yth Grp; Var Trk; Hon Roll; Outstndng Nwspr Carrier Yr 8k; Geo Washington U; DEA.

BOND, SHARELLE; St Maria Goretti HS; Philadelphia, PA; (Y); Ntl Merit Ltr; Exc Cndct Awd 85-86; Data Prcsng.

BOND, THOMAS; Venango Christian HS; Clarion, PA; (Y); 1/36; Exploring; Intnl Clb; Nwsp Stf; Pres Soph Cls; Rep Stu Cncl; Stat Bsbl; Bsktbl; High Hon Roll; NHS; NEDT Awd; Arch.

BONDE, LISA; Belle Vernon Area HS; Belle Vernon, PA; (Y); Ski Clb; Nwsp Stf; Yrbk Stf; Cit Awd; High Hon Roll; NHS; Pres Soph Cls; VP Jr Cls; VP Sr Cls; Phy Thrpst.

BONDI, JOSEPH; New Castle SR HS; New Castle, PA; (Y); 23/236; Pres Schlr; Penn ST Full-Tm Durng HS 85-86; PA ST U; Comps.

BONE, LINDA JO; Punxsutawney Area HS; Costa Mesa, CA; (Y); 2/243; Sec VP Church Yth Grp; French Clb; Math Tm; Science Clb; Band; Variety Show; High Hon Roll; NHS; Sal; FNA; MajoretteHEAD 82-86; Gifted Program 82-86; Natl Hnr Society Computerized Quin Tm 86; Whittier Coll; Chemistry.

BONELLO, MICHAEL E; Greater Latrobe HS; Latrobe, PA; (Y); Var L Bsbl; Var L Ftbl; Ntl Merit SF; PA ST.

BONENBERGER, ANNE; Palmyra Area HS; Palmyra, PA; (Y); French Clb; Intnl Clb; Pep Clb; Ski Clb; Color Guard; Score Keeper; High Hon Roll; Hon Roll; Bus.

BONENBERGER JR, KENNETH J; Bishop Egan HS; Levittown, PA; (S); 5/276; Exploring; Pres German Clb; Var Crs Cntry; Var Trk; High Hon Roll; NHS; Prfct Atten Awd; PA Cthlc Leag-Al-Cthlc Crs Cntry 85; Bucks Cty Courier Tms Gldn 13 Crs Cntry Tm 85; Relgn Awds 84-85; Pre-Med.

BONENBERGER, REGINA; William Allen HS; Allentown, PA; (Y); 130/604; JCL; Latin Clb; Band; Concert Band; Drm Mjr(t); Mrchg Band; Orch; Yrbk Stf; Hon Roll; NHS; Amer Music Fndtn Band Hnrs 86; JR All Amer Hall Of Fame Band Hnrs 86; Accntng.

BONESSO, LISA; West Allegheny SR HS; Coraopolis, PA; (Y); Sec Church Yth Grp; Spanish Clb; Teachers Aide; Chorus; Church Choir; High Hon Roll; Hon Roll; Pedology.

BONFARDINE, MOLLY; Elk County Christian HS; St Marys, PA; (S); Key Clb; SADD; Chorus; Color Guard; Yrbk Phtg; Yrbk Stf; Stat Bsktbl; High Hon Roll; Clarion; Bus Adm.

BONFIGLIO, JOHN; Hatboro Horsham HS; Horsham, PA; (Y); 33/273; Boy Scts; Church Yth Grp; Computer Clb; FBLA; Var Crs Cntry; JV Trk; Cit Awd; High Hon Roll; Hon Roll; Merit Schlrshp 86-87; Chmpns Of Lrng Gld Mdl Data Prcssng 86; 5th Pl Ntl Indvdl All-Str Cntst 86; Gwynedd Mercy; Comp Sci.

BONFIGLIO, RICHARD; Western Beaver JR SR HS; Industry, PA; (S); Sec Church Yth Grp; Drama Clb; Nwsp Rptr; Pres Frsh Cls; VP Jr Cls; Stu Cncl; Bsbl; Bowling; High Hon Roll; Hon Roll; Hugh O Brian Yth Fndtn Outstndng Soph Awd 85.

BONGHI, TONY; Ridgway Area HS; Ridgway, PA; (S); 10/128; Ski Clb; Spanish Clb; Bsbl; Bsktbl; Capt Ftbl; Wt Lftg; High Hon Roll; Hon Roll; PA ST; Arch.

BONI, DEL; Burgettstown JR-SR HS; Burgettstown, PA; (Y); Boys Clb Am; Sec Trs Spanish Clb; Capt Wrstlng; High Hon Roll; Jr NHS; NHS; Wrstlng MVP; Pre-Dntstry.

BONI, TINA; Burgettstown JR SR HS; Burgettstown, PA; (Y); 33/175; Art Clb; Church Yth Grp; French Clb; Ski Clb; Chorus; Yrbk Stf; Hon Roll; IN U Of PA; Psych.

BONITA, JOHN; James M Coughlin HS; Plains, PA; (Y); 56/350; Band; Var Bsbl; Var Wrstlng; Hon Roll; Jr NHS; NHS.

BONNER, ANNA MARIE; South Phila HS; Philadelphia, PA; (Y); Computer Clb; FFA; JV Badmtn; Var Sftbl; Var Vllybl; Marywood; Cert Pblc Accntnt.

BONNER, DAVE; Johnstown HS; Johnstown, PA; (Y); 61/286; Math Clb; Golf; Hon Roll; Jr NHS; NHS; Prfct Atten Awd; U Pitt Johnstown; Comp Sci.

BONNER, GEORGE; Mercy Vocational HS; Philadelphia, PA; (Y); Rep Soph Cls; Rep Jr Cls; Hon Roll; Ntl Merit Ltr; Acad All Amer Awd 86; Prfct Punctuality 86; JR Olympic Boxing Champ Philadelphia 84; Comp Tech.

BONNER, KIM; Bodine H S For International Affairs; Philadelphia, PA; (Y); 3/95; Dance Clb; Math Tm; Chorus; Var Bsktbl; Cit Awd; High Hon Roll; NHS; Pep Clb; Outstndng Achvt Intl Bus/Mgt, Mayors Schlrshp, Pres Ftns Awd 86; Villanova U; Intl Bus.

BONNEY, CHRISTINE; Liberty HS; Bethlehem, PA; (Y); 80/490; Church Yth Grp; Cmnty Wkr; Drama Clb; Sec French Clb; Hosp Aide; Model UN; School Play; Stu Cncl; Masonic Awd; Chld Psychlgy.

BONNEY, JASON; Boyertown HS; Boyertown, PA; (Y); 99/400; Computer Clb; Var Bsbl; JV Crs Cntry; Var Ftbl; Var Capt Wrstlng; Cit Awd; Hon Roll; Prfct Atten Awd; Outstndg Athlt Of Yr 84; Comp Sci.

BONNEY, LISA; Wilson Area HS; W Easton, PA; (S); 10/160; Drama Clb; Ski Clb; School Musical; School Play; Variety Show; Rep Stu Cncl; Var L Fld Hcky; High Hon Roll; Hon Roll; NHS; Long Island U; Marine Bio.

BONNICI, MARK S; William Allen HS; Allentown, PA; (Y); Boy Scts; Church Yth Grp; Band; Chorus; Concert Band; Mrchg Band; Compu Sci.

BONO, LORI; Kittanning SR HS; Worthington, PA; (Y); Trs Church Yth Grp; Varsity Clb; Trs Chorus; Trs Frsh Cls; Trs Stu Cncl; Capt Cheerleading; Twrlr; High Hon Roll; Hon Roll; NHS; IN U Of PA; Chem.

BONO, RITA ANN; Kiski Area HS; Apollo, PA; (Y); VP Church Yth Grp; Math Clb; Pep Clb; Varsity Clb; Jazz Band; Symp Band; Stu Cncl; Capt Cheerleading; High Hon Roll; NHS; Duquense U.

BONSAVAGE, MARK; Lake-Lehman HS; Dallas, PA; (Y); Camera Clb; Cmnty Wkr; ROTC; Ski Clb; School Play; JV Vllybl; Wt Lftg; JV Wrstlng; Penn ST; Engrng.

BONSER, DOUGLAS; Pleasant Valley HS; Saylorsburg, PA; (Y); Exploring; Math Clb; Band; Concert Band; Jazz Band; Mrchg Band; Pep Band; High Hon Roll; Hon Roll; Prfct Atten Awd; Top 20 Stu 83-85; Comp Sci.

BONSON, BRIAN; Redland HS; Etters, PA; (Y); 30/288; VP Computer Clb; Hon Roll; Comp Sci.

BOOHER, WENDEE; Chief Logan HS; Burnham, PA; (Y); 4-H; German Clb; Key Clb; Pep Clb; Varsity Clb; Stu Cncl; Var Capt Bsktbl; Var Capt Crs Cntry; Var Capt Trk; Hon Roll; Mst Vlbl Plyr Bsktbl Lgu 85-86; All ST Cross Cntry 84-86; All ST Trck 84-86.

BOOK, GRETCHEN; Solanco HS; Quarryville, PA; (Y); 38/238; Varsity Clb; Acpl Chr; Band; Chorus; Concert Band; Mrchg Band; School Musical; Sec Frsh Cls; Sec Soph Cls; Sec Jr Cls; Hmcmng Crt 84; Sr Cls Awd 86; Frm Wmn 17 Awd 86; Widener U.

BOOK, JENNIE; Laurel HS; Portersville, PA; (Y); 10/100; Church Yth Grp; Varsity Clb; Yrbk Ed-Chief; Yrbk Stf; Rep Soph Cls; Rep Jr Cls; Pres Sr Cls; Rep Stu Cncl; Var Capt Bsktbl; Cheerleading; Tom Barnes Schlrshp 86; Robert Morris Clg; Fnce.

BOOK JR, JOSEPH; Mount Union Area HS; Newton Hamilton, PA; (Y); 52/178; Boy Scts; Letterman Clb; Spanish Clb; Trs Soph Cls; Trs Jr Cls; Stu Cncl; Var L Bsbl; Var L Ftbl; Var L Wrstlng; Eagle Scout 86.

BOOK, LISA; Annville-Cleona HS; Annville, PA; (Y); Church Yth Grp; Hosp Aide; Chorus; Church Choir; Mrchg Band; School Musical; Nrsng.

BOOK, SHANNON; Lampeter-Strasburg HS; Lancaster, PA; (Y); AFS; Art Clb; FBLA; FHA; PAVAS; Red Cross Aide; Varsity Clb; Stu Cncl; Fld Hcky; Sftbl; Art.

BOOK, TRACY R; Lampeter Strasburg HS; Lancaster, PA; (Y); 6/150; Art Clb; Trs Church Yth Grp; Thesps; Concert Band; Mrchg Band; School Musical; School Play; Ed Yrbk Stf; NHS; Ntl Merit SF; Bus.

BOOKAMER, DAVID; Scranton Central HS; Scranton, PA; (Y); 21/267; Aud/Vis; Church Yth Grp; Spanish Clb; Band; Concert Band; Mrchg Band; Yrbk Stf; Socr; Trk; Hon Roll; General Motors Inst; Mech Engr.

BOOKER III, ROBERT S; Engineering And Science; Philadelphia, PA; (S); 7/229; Computer Clb; Science Clb; Yrbk Stf; High Hon Roll; NHS; Prfct Atten Awd; Cornell; Chem Engrng.

BOOKER, ZANE A; Arch Bishop Carroll HS For Boys; Philadelphia, PA; (Y); 49/168; Church Yth Grp; SADD; School Play; Variety Show; Frsh Cls; VP Soph Cls; Jr Cls; Stu Cncl; PA Schl Of Dstnct Arts Outstndng Stu Awd 86; NC Schl Of Arts; Dance.

BOOKHAMER, MALISSA; Altoona Area HS; Altoona, PA; (Y); 113/683; Church Yth Grp; FBLA; Chorus; Church Choir; Fld Hcky; Vllybl; Mldrd Brmn Awd 86; IN U Of PA; Acctg.

BOONE, RANDY; Bald Eagle Area HS; Howard, PA; (Y); Am Leg Boys St; Letterman Clb; Varsity Clb; Var L Bsbl; Coach Actv; Var L Ftbl; Powder Puff Ftbl; Wt Lftg; Schlrshp From Woolrich 86; Penn St; Elec Engr.

BOONE, SUSAN; Canon Mc Millan SR HS; Washington, PA; (Y); 4-H; Office Aide; Yrbk Stf; Swmmng; High Hon Roll; Hon Roll; HS Educ.

BOONSWANG, AB; Notre Dame HS; Easton, PA; (Y); 1/100; Scholastic Bowl; Speech Tm; School Musical; Nwsp Sprt Ed; Var Tennis; Opt Clb Awd; Am Leg Boys St; Cmnty Wkr; Debate Tm; NFL; Forensics Rookie Of Yr 84; Highest Gen Avg In Cls 84-86; Hugh O Brien Ldrshp Seminar 85; Harvard; Cardiovsclr Surgeon.

BOONVISUDHI, KITIMA; Monongahela Valley Catholic HS; Monongahela, PA; (S); 2/108; Ski Clb; Boys Clb Am; Nwsp Stf; Yrbk Phtg; Yrbk Stf; Ed Lit Mag; Sec Stu Cncl; Var Capt Vllybl; Spanish NHS; PA Govrnrs Schl For The Arts Poetry 85; U Of Notre Dame; Med.

BOORNAZIAN, MICHELE; Penn Wood HS; Lansdowne, PA; (Y); Band; Concert Band; Mrchg Band; Pep Band; Fld Hcky; Tennis; Hon Roll; NHS; Gntc Engrng.

BOORUJY, JILL; Pocono Mountain HS; Canadensis, PA; (Y); 52/300; Church Yth Grp; SADD; School Play; Yrbk Stf; Hon Roll; Early Admssns Prgrm At East Stroudsburg U; MISSIONARY.

BOOSE, ELIZABETH; Central York SR HS; York, PA; (Y); 45/218; Church Yth Grp; Concert Band; Symp Band; Hon Roll; Book Wrtng.

BOOSE, STUART D; Henderson SR HS; West Chester, PA; (Y); Am Leg Boys St; Boy Scts; Scholastic Bowl; Band; Concert Band; Jazz Band; Mrchg Band; Tennis; NHS; Socr; Essy Cntst 3rd 86.

BOOTERBAUGH, MARY KAY; Penn Cambria HS; Cresson, PA; (Y); Drama Clb; Ski Clb; Spanish Clb; Chorus; Sec Frsh Cls; Cheerleading; Vllybl; High Hon Roll; Hon Roll; Prfct Atten Awd; Engrng.

BOOZ, STEVEN; Oxford Area HS; Nottingham, PA; (Y); 20/160; Ski Clb; Varsity Clb; Yrbk Stf; Stu Cncl; Var Capt Socr; Var Tennis; High Hon Roll; Hon Roll; VP NHS; Rotary Awd; Hght Mth & Algbr Ii Ads 83 & 86; PA ST; Bus Mngmnt.

BOOZE, PATRICIA; Fannett-Metal JR SR HS; Ft Loudon, PA; (S); 4/56; Church Yth Grp; Varsity Clb; Band; Nwsp Ed-Chief; Nwsp Rptr; Var Bsktbl; Timer; Hon Roll; Acad All Amer 85; IN U Pennsylvania; Jrnlsm.

BOOZEL, CHERYL; Mt Union Area HS; Mcveytown, PA; (Y); Trs FBLA; Awrd 2nd Pl Bus Engl FBLA Rgnl Cmptn 86; S Hills Bus Schl; Med Secr.

BOOZER, DEBRA; Brookville Area HS; Brookville, PA; (Y); 8/144; FNA; German Clb; L Band; Chorus; L Jazz Band; School Musical; High Hon Roll; Jr NHS; NHS; Pres Schlr; Adv Plcmnt Engl Awd Excllnce 86; IN U PA; Chem.

BOOZER, KELLIE J; Elizabethtown Area HS; Elizabethtown, PA; (S); 99/247; Church Yth Grp; Varsity Clb; Band; Chorus; Mrchg Band; Orch; Crs Cntry; Swmmng; Trk; Cnty Bnd; 20th Crss Cntry Dist; 3rd Cntys, 5th Dist Crss Cntry; Mst Imprvd, Mst Dedctd Crs Cntry; Lock Haven U; Athltc Trning.

BOPP, LORA; Upper Dauphin Area HS; Lykens, PA; (Y); FBLA; Band; Color Guard; Drill Tm; Yrbk Stf; Trk; FBLA Sec 85-86; Harrisburg Area CC; Human Svcs.

BORCHARDT, CRAIG; Archbishop Carroll HS; King Of Prussia, PA; (Y); 78/162; Boy Scts; Chess Clb; Nwsp Rptr; Yrbk Rptr; Crs Cntry; Prfct Atten Awd; Eagle Sct 86; Art Fair 86; Jrnlsm.

BORD, WENDY; Le Banon HS; Lebanon, PA; (Y); 5/278; Church Yth Grp; German Clb; Pep Clb; Teachers Aide; Chorus; School Musical; Swing Chorus; High Hon Roll; Hon Roll; NHS; Albert D & Esther Boltz Schlrshp 86; Moyer Longacre Schlrshp 86; Cert Of Apprctn Srvng Cmnty At St Mth; Lebanon Vly Coll; Elmntry Ed.

BORDAS, DAWN; West Mifflin Area HS; W Mifflin, PA; (Y); Church Yth Grp; Exploring; Hosp Aide; Band; Concert Band; Jazz Band; Mrchg Band; Nwsp Stf; Yrbk Stf; Off Soph Cls; Braddock Gen Hosp Vol Awd 84; Chrldng Trophy 81; U Pittsburgh; Bio.

BORDAS, TONYA; Connellsville Area SR HS; Dickerson Run, PA; (Y); Camera Clb; FTA; Hosp Aide; Math Clb; Office Aide; Red Cross Aide; Science Clb; SADD; Teachers Aide; VICA; Directors List 86; Mortician.

BORDEN, LISA; West Middlesex HS; W Middlesex, PA; (S); 6/113; Concert Band; Yrbk Stf; Sec Frsh Cls; Sec Soph Cls; Sec Jr Cls; Sec Sr Cls; Pres Stu Cncl; Co-Capt Pom Pon; High Hon Roll; NHS; U Ptsbrg; Phrmcy.

BORDER, HEATH; Millersburg HS; Millersburg, PA; (Y); Church Yth Grp; Cmnty Wkr; SADD; JV Bsbl; Bowling; JV Var Ftbl; Var Swmmng; Var Trk; JV Var Wt Lftg; Hon Roll; Engnrng.

BORDNER, MICHAEL; Upper Daauphin Area HS; Lykens, PA; (Y); 81/101; Varsity Clb; Var Bsktbl; Hon Roll.

BORDNER, SUSAN; Upper Dauphin Area HS; Elizabethville, PA; (Y); 35/110; Band; Chorus; Capt Color Guard; Flag Corp; Sftbl; Hon Roll; VFW Awd; Voice Dem Awd; Cmnty Wkr; Mrchg Band; John Hall Schlrsh, Mary Nestor Schlrshp 86; Harrisburg Area CC; Behvrl Sci.

BORDNER, TRICIA; Palmyra Area SR HS; Palmyra, PA; (Y); 10/200; Drama Clb; Sec French Clb; Chorus; Cheerleading; Diving; Tennis; Trk; High Hon Roll; Hon Roll; NHS; Comp Sci.

BORDO, KAREN; Old Forge HS; Old Forge, PA; (S); 15/70; Drama Clb; Hosp Aide; Political Wkr; School Musical; Yrbk Stf; Hon Roll; NHS.

BORELLI, SEENIE; Northwest Area HS; Benton, PA; (Y); 3/108; Church Yth Grp; Computer Clb; Chorus; Yrbk Phtg; Stu Cncl; High Hon Roll; NHS; Ntl Merit Ltr; Exploring; French Clb; Kean Pllck & Phila Coll Of Phrmcy & Sci Trstee Schlrshps 86; Lynchbrg Coll Hpwood Schlr 85; Phila Coll-Phrmcy/Sci; Phys Thr.

BORENISH, CHRISTINE; Portage Area HS; Portage, PA; (S); 8/113; Drama Clb; Varsity Clb; Chorus; Capt Drill Tm; Nwsp Stf; Yrbk Stf; Score Keeper; Var Trk; High Hon Roll; NHS; Penn ST U; Busnss Admin.

BORETTI, JOHN; Tunkhannock Area HS; Tunkhannock, PA; (S); Spanish Clb; Var L Bsktbl; Var L Golf; Hon Roll; NHS; MIP Golf 84; MIP Bsktbl 84-85.

BORGER, BETH; Bald Eagle Area HS; Snow Shoe, PA; (Y); 84/205; Aud/Vis; Church Yth Grp; 4-H; French Clb; Girl Scts; Library Aide; Pep Clb; SADD; Teachers Aide; Band; Hugh O Brian Yth Fndtn Awd 83-84; SR Music Awd 86; PA Govrnr Schl Arts Awd 84-85.

BORGERSEN, KRISTEN; Mechaniesburg Area SR HS; Mechanicsburg, PA; (Y); 33/311; Girl Scts; NFL; Speech Tm; SADD; Chorus; Mrchg Band; Orch; Yrbk Stf; High Hon Roll; Ntl Merit Ltr; 1st Cls Girl Sct 83; Phrmcy.

BORHAN, ALI; Cathedral Prep; Erie, PA; (Y); 2/249; Chess Clb; German Clb; Socr; Swmmng; Im Vllybl; High Hon Roll; Slippery Rock U Lang Comp Germn I & II 85-86; Pre Med.

BORHANMANESH, ALI; Cathedral Prep; Erie, PA; (Y); 2/241; Chess Clb; German Clb; Socr; Swmmng; Im Vllybl; High Hon Roll; Awd-Slippery Rock U Lang Comp Germn I & II 85-86; Pre Med.

BORICK, MATTHEW; Danville HS; Danville, PA; (Y); Church Yth Grp; Drama Clb; Key Clb; Latin Clb; School Play; Bsktbl; Golf; High Hon Roll; NHS; Sigma Math Awd 84; Natl Lat Exam Magna Cum Laude Awd 86; Law.

BORING, ERIC; Butler HS; Butler, PA; (Y); Church Yth Grp; German Clb; Im Bsktbl.

BORKERT, BARBARA L; Wilson HS; Wernersville, PA; (Y); 3/300; Aud/Vis; Church Yth Grp; French Clb; Model UN; Chorus; Church Choir; Orch; School Musical; Lit Mag; Swmmng; Chem, Socl Stud 83-84; Engl, Socl Stud, Frnch 84-85; Carleton Coll MN; Engl.

BORKOWSKI, NANCY; Norwin SR HS; N Huntingdon, PA; (Y); 17/553; French Clb; FBLA; Letterman Clb; Math Clb; Yrbk Ed-Chief; Yrbk Stf; Rep Stu Cncl; Vllybl; Hon Roll; Sec Jr NHS; Vlybl Schrlshp 86; Schlr Athlete Awd 86; FBLA Regnl Wnnr 86; Eastern KY U; Finance.

BORKOWSKI, STACY; Freeport Area HS; Freeport, PA; (S); 20/173; Trs Church Yth Grp; Girl Scts; Capt Color Guard; Yrbk Stf; Sftbl; High Hon Roll; Hon Roll; NHS; Engrg.

BORLAND, WILLIAM F; Downingtown HS; Downingtown, PA; (Y); Am Leg Boys St; Varsity Clb; Rep Frsh Cls; Rep Soph Cls; Rep Jr Cls; Rep Sr Cls; Rep Stu Cncl; Bsbl; Bsktbl; Ftbl; Shippensburg; Bus.

BORNSTEIN, DORI; Newport JR SR HS; Newport, PA; (Y); GAA; Pep Clb; School Play; Nwsp Rptr; Nwsp Stf; Capt Cheerleading; Gym; Mat Maids; Hon Roll; Frgn Affairs.

BOROS, DONALD; Ambridge Area HS; Baden, PA; (Y); Pep Clb; Spanish Clb; Var Bsbl; Hon Roll; Prfct Atten Awd; Robert Morris Coll; Bus Admin.

BOROSH, OSSIE; Lower Merion HS; Philadelphia, PA; (Y); Sec VP Temple Yth Grp; Chorus; School Musical; Jr NHS; Arts Recgn & Tlnt Srch Fnlst 86; Amer Music Comptn 2nd Pl 84; Tape Audtn Wnnr 17 Mgzn & GM Ntl Compt; Music.

BOROSKY, CAROLYN; Carbondale Area HS; Simpson, PA; (S); 4/132; Pres FBLA; School Play; Yrbk Bus Mgr; Trk; DAR Awd; French Hon Soc; High Hon Roll; NHS; Art Clb; PA Free Enterprise Wk Schlrshp 85; FBLA Regnl Typng II-4TH Pl Awd 85.

BOROSKY, PATRICIA; Carbondale Area HS; Simpson, PA; (S); 1/150; Church Yth Grp; FBLA; Science Clb; Spanish Clb; Rep Jr Cls; Rep Stu Cncl; L Var Bsktbl; L Trk; High Hon Roll; NHS; Sports Med.

BOROTO, SHERRY; Highlands SR HS; Tarentum, PA; (Y); 28/277; Church Yth Grp; Intnl Clb; Church Choir; Color Guard; Off Soph Cls; Off Jr Cls; Off Sr Cls; Hon Roll; Jr NHS; NHS; Schlrshp Bradford Schl Bus 86; Kenneth Howell Mem Schlrshp 86; Schlrshp Achvt Awd 86; Bradford Schl Of Bus; Retailing.

BORRIELLO, SALVATORE; St John Neumann HS; Philadelphia, PA; (Y); Chorus; School Musical; Swing Chorus; Var Socr; Hon Roll; Temple U; Psyclgy.

BORSCH, SANDRA SUSAN; Strath Haven HS; Rutledge, PA; (Y); Art Clb; Boy Scts; Church Yth Grp; Cmnty Wkr; GAA; Yrbk Ed-Chief; Yrbk Stf; Off Jr Cls; Off Sr Cls; JV Var Bsktbl; Tmrrws Ldrs Cnfrnce 86; Grphc Dsgn.

BORST, SCOTT; Norwin SR HS; N Huntingdon, PA; (Y); 102/557; Church Yth Grp; Ski Clb; SADD; Im Bsktbl; Im Vllybl; Hon Roll; Penn ST; Auto Design.

BORST, TRISHA; Lincoln HS; Wampum, PA; (Y); French Clb; Key Clb; Library Aide; Chorus; Drill Tm; Mrchg Band; Hon Roll; Bradford Business Schl; Bus.

BORTNER, LORI; Central SR HS; York, PA; (Y); 7/245; Hosp Aide; Varsity Clb; Var Capt Bsktbl; Var Fld Hcky; Sftbl; Var Trk; High Hon Roll; Hon Roll; NHS; Temple U; Phys Therpy.

BORTREE, BRIAN A; South Hills Christian Schl; Library, PA; (Y); 2/14; Church Yth Grp; Chorus; Church Choir; School Musical; School Play; Nwsp Rptr; Lib Frsh Cls; Pres Soph Cls; Pres Jr Cls; Pres Sr Cls; I Dare You Awd 84; Mr South Hills Christian Schl 85-86; Word Of Life Bible Inst; Tchr.

BORTREE, LISA; North Pocono HS; Moscow, PA; (S); 7/239; Hosp Aide; Ski Clb; Yrbk Stf; Sec Jr Cls; Sec Sr Cls; Rep Stu Cncl; JV Bsktbl; Score Keeper; High Hon Roll; NHS; Kings Coll Moreau Schlrshp 86; Kings Coll; Physcn Asstnt.

BORTZ, DAN; Kiski SR HS; Avonmore, PA; (Y); Chorus; Church Choir; Ftbl; Trk; Wt Lftg; High Hon Roll; Hon Roll; Cnty Chorus Hnrs & Dist Chorus Hnrs 83-86; Sctn Trck Mt 1st & 4th Pl Rbbns 83-84; CA U Of PA; Mech Engnrng.

BORTZFIELD, TRICIA; Lampeter-Strasburg HS; Lancaster, PA; (Y); 38/140; Art Clb; Church Yth Grp; Sec Thesps; Band; Chorus; Concert Band; Madrigals; School Musical; Stage Crew; Bsktbl; Art Awd Wnnr 86; Art.

BORZILLO, KEITH; Owen J Roberts HS; Parkerford, PA; (Y); 51/296; SADD; JV Var Ftbl; Im Vllybl; Im Wt Lftg; Hon Roll; Comp Sci.

BORZILLO, NORMA; Bishop Kenrick HS; Norristown, PA; (Y); 8/294; Cmnty Wkr; Hon Roll; NHS; Eng Awd.

BOSAK, CHRISTOPHER; North East HS; North East, PA; (Y); 39/155; Cmnty Wkr; FCA; German Clb; Latin Clb; Stage Crew; Pres Stu Cncl; L Var Bsbl; L Var Bsktbl; L Var Crs Cntry; Voice Dem Awd; Principals Awd 86; U Pittsburgh; Chem Engrng.

BOSAK, STEPHEN; Punxsutawney Area HS; Delancey, PA; (Y); Varsity Clb; Var JV Ftbl; Elec Engr.

BOSAVAGE, ALICIA; Mahoney Area HS; Mahanoy City, PA; (Y); 1/124; FHA; Spanish Clb; Chorus; Yrbk Stf; L Var Trk; Elks Awd; High Hon Roll; Hon Roll; NHS; Pres Schlr; York Coll Pres Schlrshp 86-90; Helen L Ruth Schlrshp 86-87; Hnbl Ivor D Fenton MD Schlrshp 86-87; York Coll Of PA; Nrsg.

BOSE, MEENEKSHI; Winchester-Thurston HS; Pittsburgh, PA; (Y); 1/40; French Clb; Key Clb; Political Wkr; Service Clb; Stage Crew; Rptr Nwsp Rptr; Lit Mag; Sec Trs Frsh Cls; Sec Trs Jr Cls; Ntl Merit SF; Smith Coll Awd Acad Exc Ldrshp 86; Lit Mag Awd Best Poem 84; Newspaper Awd 86; PA ST U; World Studies.

BOSETTI, HEATHER; Moon SR HS; Coraopolis, PA; (Y); 16/304; Acpl Chr; Chorus; Color Guard; Swing Chorus; Rep Stu Cncl; High Hon Roll; NHS; Bio.

BOSETTI, NORMAN; Yough HS; Smithton, PA; (Y); 73/253; Im Badmtn; Var Ice Hcky; Im Vllybl; Hon Roll; Hsptl Admin.

BOSILOVICH, BARBARA; Immaculate Conception HS; Canonsburg, PA; (Y); 3/51; Hosp Aide; Math Tm; Trs Soph Cls; Sftbl; High Hon Roll; Hon Roll; NHS; Church Yth Grp; Computer Clb; Acdmc All Amer; Engl Awd & French Awd; Pre-Med.

BOSKIE, LYDIA ANA; Franklin Learning Ctr; Philadelphia, PA; (Y); Dance Clb; Library Aide; Teachers Aide; School Musical; School Play; Variety Show; Ntl Merit Ltr; Mayors Smmr Yth Pgm Incntv Awd 85; Temple U; Chld Psych.

BOSLET, HOLLY; Bishop Mc Cort HS; Johnstown, PA; (Y); Band; Concert Band; Mrchg Band; Orch; Var L Crs Cntry; Var L Trk; Crim Jstc.

BOSLET, LEAH; Bishop Guilfoyle HS; Altoona, PA; (S); #12 In Class; Hosp Aide; Science Clb; Ski Clb; SADD; JV Cheerleading; Var Capt Vllybl; High Hon Roll; Hon Roll; Medcl.

BOSS, MICHAEL; Fairfield HS; Fairfield, PA; (Y); Varsity Clb; Band; Chorus; Concert Band; Jazz Band; Nwsp Stf; Rep Stu Cncl; Var L Bsbl; Var L Bsktbl; Var L Socr; Phys Ed.

BOSSERMAN, TRACY; Mechanicsburg Area SR HS; Mechanicsburg, PA; (Y); 40/299; Pep Clb; Rep Stu Cncl; Ftbl; Hon Roll; Bloomsburg U; Psych.

BOSTANY, LISA; Pocono Central Catholic HS; Mt Pocono, PA; (S); 2/29; Church Yth Grp; Chorus; School Musical; Sec Jr Cls; Var L Bsktbl; Var Fld Hcky; Var Sftbl; High Hon Roll; NHS; Spnsh,Sci,Soc Studies Awd 83-86; PA ST U; Bus Mgmt.

BOSTDORF, STEVEN; Elizabethtown Area HS; Elizabethtown, PA; (Y); #10 In Class; Ski Clb; Varsity Clb; Var Bsbl; JV Bsktbl; NHS.

BOSTJANIC, SCOTT; Canon Mcmillan HS; Eighty Four, PA; (Y); Latin Clb; Ski Clb; Band; Concert Band; Jazz Band; Mrchg Band; Pep Band; Stage Crew; JV Golf; JV Var Tennis; Recog Of Achvt Musc 86; PA ST U; Cermc Engrg.

BOTDORF, RHONDA; West Snyder HS; Mcclure, PA; (Y); 4/96; Church Yth Grp; Varsity Clb; Chorus; Color Guard; Drm Mjr(t); Flag Corp; Mrchg Band; School Musical; Swing Chorus; Sec Frsh Cls; Dist Chorus 84-85; Rgnl Chorus 85-86; Penn ST; Elem Ed.

BOTEK, BARBARA; Nativity BVM HS; Port Carbon, PA; (Y); 1/99; Math Clb; VP Spanish Clb; Church Choir; Variety Show; High Hon Roll; Var NHS; Ntl Merit Ltr; Val; Schuylkill Vly Chptr Of Unico Schlrshp 86; Wltn Acad Schlrshp 86; PHEAA Cert Of Merit Outstndg Prf 85; Albright Coll; Acctg.

BOTHELL, MICHELE; Marion Center HS; Creekside, PA; (Y); 34/168; 4-H; FBLA; Trs FHA; Office Aide; Teachers Aide; Color Guard; High Hon Roll; NHS; Acctng.

BOTTERBUSCH, DAVID; Fairfield Area HS; Fairfield, PA; (Y); 6/42; Spanish Clb; Chorus; School Musical; Swing Chorus; Var Bsktbl; Var Crs Cntry; Var Trk; High Hon Roll; Prfrmng Arts.

BOTTI, ADRIENNE; Saint Maria Goretti HS; Philadelphia, PA; (Y); Church Yth Grp.

BOTTI, LOUIS H; Norwin SR HS; N Huntingdon, PA; (Y); Letterman Clb; Ski Clb; SADD; Rep Stu Cncl; Im Bsktbl; Im JV Ftbl; Im Var Trk; Hon Roll; Jr NHS; Ntl Merit Ltr; Arch.

BOTTIGLIERI, DAWNE; St Maria Goretti HS; Philadelphia, PA; (Y); Service Clb; Stage Crew; Nwsp Phtg; Hon Roll; Katharine Gibbs Schl; Wrd Proc.

BOTTORF, ROSS; Lock Haven HS; Lock Haven, PA; (Y); Dance Clb; Key Clb; Spanish Clb; Var L Bsktbl; JV Ftbl; Im Socr; JV Tennis; Hon Roll; NHS; Natl Hstry & Govt Awd 86; Sci.

BOTTS, CRISTINA; Mifflinburg HS; Lewisburg, PA; (Y); Art Clb; VP 4-H; French Clb; Fld Hcky; Trk; 4-H Awd; Bloomsburg U; Elem Ed.

BOTTS, RANDY; Boyertown Area SR HS; Boyertown, PA; (Y); 26/484; Church Yth Grp; Var Golf; JV Tennis; High Hon Roll; Hon Roll; Htl/Rest Mgmt.

BOTYRIUS, TONY; Wyoming Area SR HS; Wyoming, PA; (Y); 1/259; Boy Scts; Computer Clb; Drama Clb; German Clb; Key Clb; Ski Clb; High Hon Roll; NHS; Ad Altare Dei 83; Tp Grmn Stu Awd 83-86; Gftd Prgrm 83-87; Duke U; Surgn.

BOTZER, CINDY; Clarion-Limestone HS; Limestone, PA; (Y); 16/80; Pres Spanish Clb; Teachers Aide; Pres Band; Chorus; Church Choir; Drm Mjr(t); Nwsp Stf; Bsktbl; Capt Var Cheerleading; Var JV Vllybl; Dist Band 85 & 86; Regnl Band 86; Cnty Band 84-86.

BOUCHER, JENNIFER; Brockway Area HS; Brockway, PA; (Y); Band; Capt Color Guard; Pep Band; Commnctns.

BOUCHER, SHERRY; Rockwood Area JR SR HS; Rockwood, PA; (S); 10/95; VP Sec Church Yth Grp; Spanish Clb; Band; Chorus; Concert Band; Mrchg Band; Sec Frsh Cls; Var Sftbl; Var Vllybl; Vet Med.

BOULDIN II, DAVID T; Lincoln HS; Philadelphia, PA; (Y); 3/550; ROTC; Spanish Clb; Color Guard; Yrbk Stf; Swmmng; NHS; SAR Awd; Math Clb; Drill Tm; High Hon Roll; Ntl Sojrnrs Awd 84; Air Force JR Rsrv Outstndg Cadt 83-84; Navy.

BOULTON, KRISTA; Moshannon Valley JR SR HS; Houtzdale, PA; (Y); Hosp Aide; Ski Clb; Varsity Clb; Band; Concert Band; Jazz Band; Mrchg Band; Var L Cheerleading; God Cntry Awd; Hon Roll; Phy Thrpy.

BOURBON, JAY; Abington HS; Jenkintown, PA; (Y); 50/550; Boy Scts; Debate Tm; Spanish Clb; Stu Cncl; Tennis; High Hon Roll; NHS; Pres Acadmc Ftns Awd 86; John R Freed Mem Schlrshp 86; Pres Clsrm-Yng Amer 86; U Of VA.

BOURG, MICHELLE; Canon Mc Millan HS; Muse, PA; (Y); 18/371; Church Yth Grp; French Clb; Office Aide; Band; Color Guard; Concert Band; Mrchg Band; High Hon Roll; NHS; Amer Legion Awd 84.

BOURKE, TIMOTHY; Parkland HS; Fogelsville, PA; (Y); 177/459; Computer Clb; Exploring; Im Bsbl; Im Bsktbl; Hon Roll; Technel Drwng Awd 83-84; PA ST; Elec Engrng.

BOURNE, ROBYN; Troy HS; Columbia Cross Rd, PA; (Y); 16/142; Pres Church Yth Grp; Sec 4-H; Pres Letterman Clb; Band; Chorus; Church Choir; Concert Band; Mrchg Band; Pep Band; Rep Stu Cncl; SF Belwin Organ & Piano Comp; County Band 83-86; Mansfield U; Music Ed.

BOUSUM JR, JOHN V; Downingtown SR HS; Downingtown, PA; (Y); Letterman Clb; Spanish Clb; SADD; Stu Cncl; JV Bsktbl; Var Ftbl; Var Trk; Wt Lftg; Hon Roll; NEDT Awd; Lrbrl Arts.

BOUTON, BRAD; Lewisburg Area HS; Lewisburg, PA; (Y); 8/168; German Clb; JV Crs Cntry; JV Trk; Vllybl; Wt Lftg; Hon Roll; NHS; Hnr Cert Schlrshp 85-86; PA U; Law.

BOVA, KAREN; Mahanoy Area HS; Mahanoy, PA; (Y); 9/122; Spanish Clb; Nwsp Stf; Yrbk Stf; VP Stu Cncl; Var Capt Bsktbl; Var Crs Cntry; Var Trk; Elks Awd; NHS; Mildred Kline Mahanoy Cty Wmns Clb Scholar; Helen L Ruth Scholar; Mahancy Cty Rotary Clb Scholar; E Stroudsburg; Nrsg.

BOVARD, DON; Meadville Area SR HS; Meadville, PA; (Y); 52/280; Aud/Vis; Church Yth Grp; Im Bowling; Var Mgr(s); Hon Roll; Eagan Schrlshp 86; Schlstc Hnr Soc 86; Mercyhurst Coll; Acctng.

BOVE, MICHELLE; Hempfield SR HS; Greensburg, PA; (Y); 37/734; Ski Clb; Rep Frsh Cls; Rep Soph Cls; Sec Jr Cls; Rep Stu Cncl; Var L Cheerleading; Capt L Vllybl; Cit Awd; NHS; Spanish NHS; Pre Vet.

BOWANKO, JOE; James M Coughlin HS; Hudson, PA; (Y); Bsbl; Ftbl; Engnrng.

BOWDEN, ED; Bishop Egan HS; Yaroley, PA; (Y); German Clb; Ski Clb; Yrbk Stf; Bsbl; Ice Hcky; Socr; Loyola Coll.

BOWDERS, JENNIFER; Christian Schl Of York; York, PA; (Y); Capt GAA; Varsity Clb; Yrbk Sprt Ed; Rep Soph Cls; Trs Jr Cls; Capt Bsktbl; Var Fld Hcky; Var Sftbl; Hon Roll; U Of VA Charlottsville; Law.

BOWEN, BETH ANN; Greensburg Central Catholic HS; N Huntingdon, PA; (Y); Art Clb; Drama Clb; Teachers Aide; Acpl Chr; Chorus; School Play; Stage Crew; Lit Mag; High Hon Roll; Hon Roll; Batik Seton Hll Coll Yng Artst Show 85; 3rd Prz Photogrphy WCCC Art Show 86; Hnrbl Mntn Photogrphy 86; IUP; Art Educ.

BOWEN, HEATHER; Kackawanna Trail HS; Dalton, PA; (Y); Camera Clb; Church Yth Grp; Yrbk Stf; Hst Soph Cls; Var Bsktbl; Stat Fld Hcky; Sftbl; Phy Ed.

BOWEN, LESLIE; Juniata HS; Port Royal, PA; (Y); Pres 4-H; VP FFA; Jazz Band; Mrchg Band; Yrbk Stf; Fld Hcky; 4-H Awd; Gov Hon Prg Awd; NHS; Church Yth Grp; PA Dairy Goat Assn Yth Rep 84-85; Miss PA Natl Teen Pagnt 86; Vet.

BOWEN, LYNN; Beaver Area JR-SR HS; Beaver, PA; (Y); 12/179; Cmnty Wkr; VP JA; Pres Key Clb; Pres Stu Cncl; JV Vllybl; High Hon Roll; Hon Roll; Ski Clb; Acad Awd 85; Schlrp Free Enterprs Wk 85; Georgetown Smmr Schl For JRS 86; Corp Law.

BOWEN, ROBERT BYRNE; Susquehannock HS; Shrewsbury, PA; (Y); 2/186; Debate Tm; Speech Tm; School Play; Crs Cntry; NHS; Ntl Merit Schol; Voice Dem Awd; Aud/Vis; Chess Clb; Church Yth Grp; PA ST Exc Awd; PA ST Schlrs Prgm; Ntl Hnr Scty; Englsh Dept Awd For Wrtng Poetry; PA ST U; Envrnmntl Engr.

BOWEN, SHERRI; Wellsboro SR HS; Wellsboro, PA; (Y); Trs FTA; Pep Clb; Band; Yrbk Stf; Trs Jr Cls; Capt L Bsktbl; Var L Trk; Hon Roll; NHS; Var L Vllybl; JR Olympcs 86; Sports Med.

BOWEN, TONYA; West Middlesex HS; Mercer, PA; (S); 7/120; Church Yth Grp; FBLA; Hosp Aide; Spanish Clb; High Hon Roll; Hon Roll; Jr NHS; Spanish NHS; Shenango Vlly Schl Of Bus; Wrd.

BOWER, DONNA; Lockhaven SR HS; Lockhaven, PA; (Y); 175/244; Yrbk Bus Mgr; Sec Soph Cls; Sec Jr Cls; Sec Sr Cls; Var Capt Cheerleading; Art Clb; Spanish Clb; Chorus; Variety Show; Stu Cncl; Busnss Mgmt.

BOWER, HILIARY E; West Perry HS; Blain, PA; (Y); 49/188; Church Yth Grp; VP French Clb; Trs Varsity Clb; Mrchg Band; Var L Bsktbl; Im Crs Cntry; Capt L Trk; Im Vllybl; Lsrshp Awd 86; Trck Awd 86; Hrsbrg Area CC; Bnkng.

BOWER, JULIE; Susquehanna Township HS; Harrisburg, PA; (Y); GAA; Model UN; Teachers Aide; Var Capt Cheerleading; Var Coach Actv; Var JV Mgr(s); Var JV Score Keeper; Var Swmmng; High Hon Roll; Hon Roll; Law Enfrcmnt.

BOWER JR, STANLEY L; Milton Area Joint SR HS; Milton, PA; (Y); 86/214; Boy Scts; Church Yth Grp; Computer Clb; Exploring; Ski Clb; Spanish Clb; Band; Chorus; Concert Band; Mrchg Band; BSA Eagle Scout 85; PA ST U Hazelton; Aerosp Engr.

BOWER, THOMAS; Ford City HS; Ford City, PA; (Y); 14/150; German Clb; SADD; Pres Stu Cncl; L Bsbl; L Bsktbl; L Golf; Elks Awd; NHS; Cit Awd; High Hon Roll; Duquesne U Ldrshp Awd 86; Stwde Yng Lawyrs Mock Trl Comp 86; 2nd Yr Awd 86; Slippery Rock U; Lawyer.

BOWERS, ALICIA; Pennsbury HS; Morrisville, PA; (Y); 180/730; French Clb; SADD; Pres Temple Yth Grp; Band; Concert Band; Mrchg Band; School Musical; School Play; Rep Stu Cncl; Hon Roll; Drmtcs Awd 86; Vldctrn Cnfrmtn Cls 84; Mrchng Band Awds 86; U Delaware; Math.

BOWERS, CAROL; Butler SR HS; Butler, PA; (Y); Church Yth Grp; FBLA; Office Aide; Spanish Clb; Church Choir; Hon Roll; 1st Pl Rgnl Spring Conf FBLA 86; 4th Pl ST Conf FBLA 86; Englsh.

BOWERS, CHARLES; Trinity HS; Washington, PA; (Y); 17/368; Computer Clb; German Clb; Band; Church Choir; Concert Band; Drm Mjr(t); Mrchg Band; High Hon Roll; NHS; NEDT Awd.

BOWERS, CORI; Cheltenham HS; Wyncote, PA; (Y); Temple Yth Grp; Capt Gym.

BOWERS, DOUGLAS; Punxsutawney HS; Punxsutawney, PA; (Y); French Clb; Math Tm; Science Clb; Varsity Clb; Var L Ftbl; Hon Roll; PA ST U; Meterolgy.

BOWERS, HEATHER; Minersville Area HS; Minersville, PA; (Y); 4/120; French Clb; Hosp Aide; Ski Clb; SADD; Nwsp Stf; Yrbk Stf; VP Soph Cls; Jr NHS; NHS; Drama Clb; Acadmc Achvt Awd; Physcl Therpst.

BOWERS, JEFFREY M; Canon Mc Millan HS; Eighty Four, PA; (Y); 47/376; Science Clb; JV Ftbl; JV Wrstlng; U Pittsburgh.

BOWERS, JODI; Punysutawney Area HS; Punxsutawney, PA; (Y); French Clb; FBLA; GAA; SADD; Varsity Clb; Variety Show; Sftbl; Tennis; Trk; Hon Roll; Bradford Schl; Merch.

BOWERS, JULIE; Punxsutawney SR HS; Mayport, PA; (Y); 114/238; Hosp Aide; Office Aide; Variety Show; Stu Of Month 85.

BOWERS, JULIE A; Academy HS; Erie, PA; (Y); 75/213.

BOWERS, MELANIE; Fairchance-Georges HS; Fairchance, PA; (Y); Trs Church Yth Grp; French Clb; FHA; Hosp Aide; Nwsp Stf; Yrbk Ed-Chief; Var Co-Capt Cheerleading; DAR Awd; Sec Jr NHS; Trs NHS; Homecmng Queen 86; Roberts Wesleyan Coll; Nrsng.

BOWERS, RENEE; Mt Alvernia HS; Pittsburgh, PA; (Y); 17/64; Computer Clb; Hosp Aide; VP JA; Sec Red Cross Aide; Chorus; Stage Crew; VP Stu Cncl; Hon Roll; Laura Long Schlrshp 86; Ldrshp Dev Ctr 85-86; Comp Sci.

BOWERS, STACY; Newport HS; Duncannon, PA; (S); Quiz Bowl; High Hon Roll; NHS.

BOWERS, TIM; Cowanesque Valley HS; Westfield, PA; (Y); Letterman Clb; VP Ski Clb; Concert Band; Jazz Band; Bsbl; Var L Bsktbl; Var Capt Ftbl; Wt Lftg; Hon Roll; US Army Rsrv Ntl Schlr Athlt Awd 85-86; Cwnsque Vly Schlr Athlt Awd 85-86; Tri-Cnty Ftbl Lg 85; Sprts Med.

BOWERS, TRACY; Greencastle-Antrim HS; State Line, PA; (Y); Church Yth Grp; Var Capt Crs Cntry; Var Capt Trk; Athltc Schlrshp-AZ ST-CRSS Cntry & Trck 86; AZ ST; Purchsng.

BOWERS, TRACY; Newport HS; Duncannon, PA; (S); Quiz Bowl; High Hon Roll; NHS.

BOWERSOX, DIANNA; Lewistown Area HS; Lewistown, PA; (Y); Spanish Clb; Radlgy.

BOWIE, ANDRE L; Oliver HS; Pittsburgh, PA; (Y); Church Yth Grp; Intnl Clb; Spanish Clb; Nwsp Sprt Ed; Stu Cncl; Bsbl; Bsktbl; Ftbl; Vllybl; Cit Awd; U Of Miami; Dntst.

BOWLEN, LARRY; Fairchance-Georges HS; Smithfield, PA; (Y); Church Yth Grp; Drama Clb; French Clb; Band; Concert Band; Jazz Band; Mrchg Band; Pep Band; School Play; Mgr(s); Comp Pgmmng.

BOWLEN, LISA; Laurel Highlands HS; Hopwood, PA; (Y); Church Yth Grp; 4-H; Library Aide; 4-H Awd; Hon Roll.

BOWLEN, RICHARD; Waynesburg Central HS; Brave, PA; (Y); Pres French Clb; Var Capt Socr; JV Wrstlng; Hon Roll; WV U; Psychlgy.

BOWLER, JANET; Saint Clair Area HS; St Clair, PA; (Y); 1/87; Church Yth Grp; Drama Clb; Exploring; FHA; Quiz Bowl; Ski Clb; SADD; Band; Chorus; Mrchg Band; Schlstc Jrnlst Awd 85-86; Hugh O Brian Outstndg Yth Awd 84-85; Pre Med.

BOWLIN, ERIC; Somerset Area HS; Somerset, PA; (Y); Aud/Vis; English Clb; German Clb; Office Aide; Varsity Clb; Rep Stu Cncl; Socr; Trk; Hon Roll; Engrng Physcs.

BOWMAN, AMY; Seneca Valley SR HS; Callery, PA; (Y); Sec Church Yth Grp; VP Ski Clb; Varsity Clb; Acpl Chr; Chorus; School Musical; L Var Crs Cntry; L Var Trk; High Hon Roll; Hon Roll; Schlstc Awd 85 & 86.

BOWMAN, ANDY; Tamaqua Area HS; Tamaqua, PA; (Y); 13/197; VP Church Yth Grp; Science Clb; JV Var Bsbl; Hon Roll; NHS; Grmn Natl Hnr Soc 86.

BOWMAN, BETH; St Marys Area HS; Benezett, PA; (Y); Drama Clb; Exploring; FCA; Dntl Asst.

BOWMAN, CHRISTINA; Upper Dauphin Area HS; Gratz, PA; (Y); Art Clb; Church Yth Grp; Spanish Clb; Chorus; Stage Crew; Cheerleading; Explrs Grp Polyclnc Hosp 86; Nrs.

BOWMAN, DAVID; Neshaminy HS; Langhorne, PA; (Y); 17/705; Church Yth Grp; Band; Chorus; Church Choir; Concert Band; Jazz Band; Mrchg Band; Orch; Pep Band; School Musical; Boy Yr Philadelphia Boys Choir 84; Stu Achvt Awd 85 & 86; Music.

BOWMAN, DENISE; Halifax Area HS; Halifax, PA; (Y); 11/100; VP FHA; Chorus; Yrbk Stf; Trs Frsh Cls; Pres Soph Cls; VP Jr Cls; Trs Stu Cncl; Prfct Atten Awd; Church Yth Grp; Hgh O Brn Ldrshp Smnr & Awd 86; Hllween Qn Attndnt 86.

BOWMAN, DONALD; Cedar Crest HS; Lebanon, PA; (Y); 9/323; French Clb; FBLA; Pep Clb; High Hon Roll; Hon Roll; Ntl Merit Ltr; Booster Clb Hnr Banq 85-86; Finance.

BOWMAN, HEIDI; Meyersdale Area HS; Meyersdale, PA; (Y); Band; Mrchg Band; Trk; Bst Hrdrssr Awd Vo-Tech Schl 86; Schl Rcrd Lng Jmp 86; Csmtlgst.

BOWMAN, JEFF; Uniontown Area HS; Farmington, PA; (Y); 11/300; Church Yth Grp; Cmnty Wkr; German Clb; Church Choir; High Hon Roll; NHS; Ntl Merit Ltr; Pres Schlr; 1st Pl German Voc Intl Day Cont 86; Penn Tech Inst; Elec.

BOWMAN, JEFFREY; Williams Valley JR SR HS; Tower City, PA; (Y); 7/110; Cmnty Wkr; Church Choir; Var Bsbl; JV Bsktbl; Var Ftbl; Wrstlng; Hon Roll; NHS; Bus Mgmt.

BOWMAN, JOHN D; York Suburban HS; York, PA; (Y); 23/195; Varsity Clb; Band; Var L Bsbl; JV Bsktbl; JV Ftbl; Var L Golf; Hon Roll; Pres Acad Ftnss Awd 86; Mike Gross Mem Awd 86; Lehigh U; Engrng.

BOWMAN, KIMBERLY A; Strath Haven HS; Swarthmore, PA; (Y); Art Clb; Trs German Clb; Ski Clb; Yrbk Stf; JV Tennis; Hon Roll; Ntl Merit SF; Schlrshp Smr Prgrm Moore Coll Art 86; Grmt Clb & Mrdr Mystry Clb; Lbrl Arts.

BOWMAN, LARISSA; Somerset Area SR HS; Somerset, PA; (Y); 10/239; Exploring; VP Pres 4-H; NFL; Acpl Chr; Rep Stu Cncl; 4-H Awd; High Hon Roll; NHS; Ntl Merit SF; Art Clb; Pres Appalachia IU 08 Stu Frm 86-87; Vet.

BOWMAN, LEAH; Cheltenham HS; Cheltenham, PA; (Y); Camp Fr Inc; Church Yth Grp; Cmnty Wkr; Library Aide; Teachers Aide; VICA; Band; Church Choir; Color Guard; Concert Band; Bereau Inst; Csmtlgy.

BOWMAN, LETITIA; Everett Area HS; Everett, PA; (Y); Spanish Clb; Capt Color Guard; Jr Cls; Pres Var Stu Cncl; High Hon Roll; Hon Roll; NHS; VP Spanish NHS; Med Admn.

BOWMAN, LISA; Crestwood HS; Mountaintop, PA; (Y); 4/231; Art Clb; Hosp Aide; Band; Chorus; School Play; Nwsp Stf; Trk; High Hon Roll; NHS; NEDT Awd.

BOWMAN, LORIN; Meadville Area SR HS; Meadville, PA; (Y); 54/267; Church Yth Grp; Dance Clb; French Clb; Nwsp Stf; Yrbk Stf; Stat Vllybl; Hon Roll; Mercyhurst Coll; Mth.

BOWMAN, MARTY; Homer Center HS; Indiana, PA; (Y); Church Yth Grp; Trs 4-H; FBLA; Band; Chorus; Jazz Band; Mrchg Band; School Musical; Yrbk Stf; Futre Bus Ldrs Am Acctng Awd 85; Homer Ctr HS Accntg Awd 85; ICM Schl Bus; Accntng Mgmt.

BOWMAN, MARY; Glendale HS; Coalport, PA; (Y); 17/98; Church Yth Grp; Library Aide; Science Clb; Band; Concert Band; Mrchg Band; Pep Band; Hon Roll; NHS; Cnty And Dist Band Awds 86; Elem Ed.

BOWMAN, MARY A; S Fayette HS; Mc Donald, PA; (S); 6/89; Hosp Aide; Band; Concert Band; Mrchg Band; Pep Band; Nwsp Stf; High Hon Roll; Hon Roll; NHS; Prfct Atten Awd; Awds-Cake Decrtng; Bio.

BOWMAN, MICHELLE; Delaware County Christian HS; Wilmington, DE; (Y); Church Yth Grp; FCA; Chorus; Nwsp Ed-Chief; Nwsp Phtg; Nwsp Rptr; Nwsp Stf; Sec Frsh Cls; L Var Vllybl; Hon Roll; Presdntl Physcl Ftns Awd 85; Mnstry Of Help Accmplshmnt Cert 85; Oral Roberts U.

BOWMAN, SHERRY A; Central Dauphin East HS; Harrisburg, PA; (Y); 15/249; Ski Clb; Pres Varsity Clb; Nwsp Rptr; Rep Sr Cls; Var Fld Hcky; Var Capt Trk; Hon Roll; Jr NHS; NHS; Pres Schlr; Penn ST.

BOWMAN, WILLIAM D; Lewistown Area HS; Lewistown, PA; (Y); 69/262; German Clb; Concert Band; Mrchg Band; Bsbl; Bsktbl; Ftbl; Hon Roll; Indiana U Of PA.

BOWMASTER, MICHAEL; Biglerville HS; Biglerville, PA; (Y); 3/85; Yrbk Stf; Trs Soph Cls; Trs Jr Cls; Var Bsbl; JV Bsktbl; High Hon Roll; Hon Roll; Jr NHS; NHS; Comp Sci.

BOWMASTER, MICHELE; Altoona Area HS; Altoona, PA; (Y); 176/768; FBLA; Political Wkr; Chorus; School Play; Sftbl; Vllybl; Wt Lftg; PA ST U; Lib Arts.

BOWMER, DEREK; Scotland School For Vetrans Children; Philadelphia, PA; (Y); ROTC; Varsity Clb; Band; Concert Band; Jazz Band; Mrchg Band; Symp Band; Var L Bausch & Lomb Sci Awd; JV Bsktbl; JV Var Ftbl; Merit Achvt Awd Music 85-86; Culinary Inst Amer; Chef.

BOWSER, BRIAN; Carmichaels Aera HS; Riceslanding, PA; (Y); 51/101; Aud/Vis; JA; Library Aide; Ski Clb; SADD; Stage Crew; L Var Ftbl; DAR Awd; IN U Of PA; Crmnlgy.

BOWSER, BRIAN; Carmichaels Area HS; Rices Landing, PA; (Y); 51/101; Aud/Vis; JA; Library Aide; Ski Clb; SADD; Stage Crew; JV Var Ftbl; DAR Awd; IN U; Crmnlgy.

BOWSER, CLIFFORD; Uniontown Area HS; Smock, PA; (Y); 26/327; Mathletes; Math Tm; Spanish Clb; Rep Band; Concert Band; Mrchg Band; High Hon Roll; NHS; Spanish NHS; OH ST U; Chem Engr.

BOWSER, LAVERNE; Connellsville Area SR HS; Millrun, PA; (Y); VP Art Clb; Pres Church Yth Grp; Exploring; Sec 4-H; Church Choir; Nwsp Stf; 4-H Awd; Hon Roll; NHS; Retail Merch.

BOWSER, MELISSA; Highlands SR HS; Tarentum, PA; (Y); Spanish Clb; Varsity Clb; Rep Frsh Cls; Rep Soph Cls; Rep Jr Cls; Rep Stu Cncl; Var Capt Gym; High Hon Roll; Hon Roll; NHS; Penn ST; Psych.

BOWSER, MIKE; Chestnut Ridge HS; Alum Bank, PA; (S); 14/142; Nwsp Phtg; Nwsp Rptr; Nwsp Stf; Var Stat Bsktbl; Hon Roll; NHS; Photo Awd-Schl Nwsp 84-85.

BOWSER, PAMELA SUE; Grove City Area HS; Grove City, PA; (Y); 17/143; Church Yth Grp; FBLA; Office Aide; Powder Puff Ftbl; Vllybl; Elks Awd; High Hon Roll; Jr NHS; NHS; Pres Schlr; Butler Cnty CC; Exec Secy.

BOWSER, SCOTT; Kettanning HS; Worthington, PA; (Y); Hon Roll; Sportsmn Clb Comptn Top Gun Awd 86; IN U; Bus Adm.

BOWSER, SHARON; Penn Trafford HS; Trafford, PA; (Y); 52/325; Church Yth Grp; Red Cross Aide; Teachers Aide; Band; Chorus; Church Choir; Concert Band; Mrchg Band; Hon Roll; Lion Awd; Lions Clb Awd 85-86; Flght Attndnt.

BOWSER, SUSAN L; Greater Johnstown HS; Johnstown, PA; (Y); 12/268; German Clb; Math Clb; Concert Band; Mrchg Band; Rep Jr Cls; High Hon Roll; NHS; Rotary Awd; Ger Lang Awd 85-86; Carnegie-Mellon U; Elec Engrng.

BOWSER, THOMAS B; Allegheny-Clarion Valley HS; Parker, PA; (Y); Church Yth Grp; Band; Chorus; Church Choir; Concert Band; Mrchg Band; Pep Band; School Musical; Mgr(s); Trk; Attnded Cnty, Dist & Rgnl Band 84-86; Attnded Dist, Rgnl & All-St Chorus 84-86; Clarion U PA; Music Ed.

BOYANOWSKI, TRACY; Greencastle Antrim HS; Greencastle, PA; (Y); 106/198; Stat Bsktbl; Var Cheerleading; Bus Adm.

BOYCE, LAURIE A; Bishop Sharahan HS; Exton, PA; (Y); 8/211; Debate Tm; Capt Bsktbl; Fld Hcky; Socr; Trk; Hon Roll; NHS; Schlr/Athltc Awd 86; Lehigh U.

BOYD, DENISE; St Marie Goretti HS; Philadelphia, PA; (Y); 127/390; Church Yth Grp; Cmnty Wkr; Dance Clb; GAA; Rep Soph Cls; Rep Jr Cls; Hon Roll; Howard U.

BOYD, DINA; South Phila HS; Philadelphia, PA; (Y); Art Clb; Church Yth Grp; FBLA; Girl Scts; Pep Clb; Nwsp Stf; Law.

BOYD, GREGG; Oxford Area HS; Oxford, PA; (Y); Church Yth Grp; Debate Tm; Drama Clb; FCA; Letterman Clb; Pep Clb; Varsity Clb; Band; School Play; Nwsp Stf; Heidelberg Coll; Sports Med.

BOYD, JENNIFER; Meadville Area SR HS; Meadville, PA; (Y); 19/308; Dance Clb; VP Service Clb; Stu Cncl; JV Cheerleading; JV Var Vllybl; High Hon Roll; Trk; TCAD Hnrbl Mntn Vllybll 86; USSCA 86.

BOYD, KERRI; Oxford Area HS; Oxford, PA; (Y); Latin Clb; Office Aide; Y-Teens; Band; Concert Band; Mrchg Band; JV Bsktbl; JV Fld Hcky; JV Var Sftbl; Twrlr; MVP Hcky & Mst Dedctd Plyr Sftbl 86; Coachs Awd & Chem & Phy Ed 86; Typg Awd & MIP Sftbl 85; Goldey Beacom; Acctg.

BOYD, TRACY; Central SR HS; York, PA; (Y); 8/239; French Clb; Chorus; Flag Corp; School Musical; Nwsp Stf; Yrbk Ed-Chief; Yrbk Stf; High Hon Roll; Trs VP NHS; Pres Schlr; Elmira Key Awd 85; Shippensburg U; Frnch.

BOYDEN, JOHN; Upper Darby HS; Lansdowne, PA; (Y); 225/629; German Clb; Hosp Aide; Hon Roll; St Charles Borromeo Sem.

BOYER, ANDREA; Central Dauphin East HS; Harrisburg, PA; (Y); 43/271; Pres Church Yth Grp; SADD; Acpl Chr; Chorus; Mrchg Band; Orch; School Musical; Rep Stu Cncl; Hon Roll; NHS.

BOYER, BENJAMIN A; Fort Le Boeuf HS; Erie, PA; (Y); 1/180; Trs Church Yth Grp; Computer Clb; Capt Quiz Bowl; SADD; Jazz Band; Var Crs Cntry; Var L Trk; High Hon Roll; Pres NHS; Ntl Merit Ltr; Stu Cncl Scholar 86; Pres Acad Fit Awd 86; Acad Achvt Awd 85; MA Inst Tech; Elec Engrng.

BOYER, BRAD; Hamburg Area HS; Bethel, PA; (Y); Band; VP Chorus; Concert Band; Drm Mjr(t); Jazz Band; Mrchg Band; School Musical; School Play; Rep Stu Cncl; Outstndg Vocal Stu 86; Outstndg Instrmntlst; Lebanon Vly Coll; Music Perf.

BOYER, BRENDA; Boyertown Area SR HS; Bechtelsville, PA; (Y); 28/448; VP Church Yth Grp; SADD; Lib Band; Concert Band; Mrchg Band; Orch; School Musical; High Hon Roll; NHS; Messiah Coll; Chrstn Educ.

BOYER, CHRISTINE; Yough SR HS; Ruffs Dale, PA; (Y); 11/227; French Clb; Girl Scts; Hosp Aide; Concert Band; Mrchg Band; Powder Puff Ftbl; High Hon Roll; NHS; Band; Drill Tm; Hnr Scholar DE Vly Coll Sci & Agri 86; Gold Awd Grl Scouts 86; DE Vly Coll; Animl Husbndry.

BOYER, CLAIRE M; Shamokin Area HS; Gowen City, PA; (Y); 4/251; Sec Science Clb; Varsity Clb; Band; Orch; Nwsp Ed-Chief; Bsktbl; Crs Cntry; Capt Trk; High Hon Roll; NHS; Var Let Winner Track Crs Cntry Bsktbl ; Crs Cntry Course Best Time 85; PA ST U; Bus.

BOYER, CRAIG; Brandywine Heights HS; Mertztwn, PA; (Y); 40/120; Boy Scts; 4-H; JV Var Bsktbl; Var Golf; JV Var Socr; Var L Tennis; Var Capt Vllybl; Hon Roll; Prfct Atten Awd; Vllybll All Str Tm Awd 86; PA ST; Engnrng.

BOYER, HEIDI; Millersburg Area HS; Millersburg, PA; (Y); 9/62; Spanish Clb; Band; Yrbk Stf; Rep Stu Cncl; Sftbl; Hon Roll; MVP Sftbl, Cnsrvtnst Yr, Grl Mnth 86; PA Schl Arts; Cmmrcl Art.

BOYER, JEFFREY; Upper Dauphin HS; Lykens, PA; (Y); Chess Clb; Church Yth Grp; Computer Clb; Letterman Clb; Varsity Clb; Ftbl; Wt Lftg; X Ray Tech.

BOYER, JEFFREY; York Christian HS; York, PA; (Y); Computer Clb; Band; Yrbk Phtg; Rep Stu Cncl; Hon Roll; NHS; Comp Engrg.

BOYER, JULIE; Mohawk HS; Bessemer, PA; (S); VP French Clb; FBLA; Stat Trk; Hon Roll; NHS; Am Legion Awd 84.

BOYER, KATHY; Northern Lebanon HS; Jonestown, PA; (Y); Pep Clb; Band; Concert Band; Mrchg Band; Trk; Wt Lftg; Hon Roll; Fshn Mdsng.

BOYER, KELLY; Waynesboro Area SR HS; Waynesboro, PA; (Y); 52/363; Chorus; School Musical; Swing Chorus; Sec Soph Cls; Sec Jr Cls; Crs Cntry; Var Gym; JV Trk; Cit Awd; High Hon Roll; Var Awd Dist & ST Tm Gymnstcs 85; Mst Consistent Var Awd Mid Penn & Dist Tm Gymnstcs 86; Intl Rltns.

BOYER, KELLY RHONDA; Pine Grove Area HS; Pine Grove, PA; (Y); Am Leg Aux Girls St; Flag Corp; Frsh Cls; Church Yth Grp; Jr Cls; Sr Cls; Stu Cncl; Bsktbl; Vllybl.

BOYER, KRISTINE; Mt Calvary Christian Schl; Elizabethtown, PA; (S); Church Yth Grp; Chorus; School Play; Var Sftbl; Cit Awd; Word Of Life Schlrshps 84-85; Bible.

BOYER, LESLEY; Milton Area SR HS; Milton, PA; (Y); Church Yth Grp; Computer Clb; Pres 4-H; Library Aide; Yrbk Phtg; Yrbk Stf; Var JV Fld Hcky; Var Trk; NHS; Metrlgy.

BOYER, MARIE A; Danville Area HS; Danville, PA; (Y); Church Yth Grp; Drama Clb; Trs French Clb; Latin Clb; Ski Clb; French Hon Soc; High Hon Roll; NHS; Rotary Awd; Bloomsburg ST Coll; Bus Mgmt.

BOYER, MATTHEW; Conrad Weiser JR SR HS; Robesonia, PA; (Y); 57/184; Latin Clb; JV Var Bsbl; JV Var Bsktbl; JV Var Socr; Im Mgr Vllybl; Hon Roll; Bus.

BOYER, MATTHEW; Liberty HS; Bethlehem, PA; (Y); 99/500; Camera Clb; Stage Crew; Penn ST; Elec Engr.

BOYER, MELISSA; North Star HS; Stoystown, PA; (Y); FCA; Nwsp Ed-Chief; Yrbk Stf; Sec Sr Cls; Capt Var Cheerleading; NHS; Pres Church Yth Grp; Hosp Aide; Varsity Clb; Hmcmng Crt 1st Rnnr Up 85; Maple Prncss Pgnt 1st Rnnr Up 85; Semi-Fnlst PA Prfct Teen Pgnt 86; WA & Jeffrsn Coll; Pre Med.

BOYER, MICHELE; West York Area HS; York, PA; (Y); 13/194; Pres Church Yth Grp; Chorus; Church Choir; Jazz Band; Mrchg Band; Sec Symp Band; Rep Stu Cncl; High Hon Roll; Hon Roll; NHS; Fndmntls Of Fire Fghtng Awd 85; Math.

BOYER, RICHELLE; East Pennsboro HS; Enola, PA; (Y); Sec Frsh Cls; Sec Soph Cls; High Hon Roll; Hon Roll; Data Proc.

BOYER, THOMAS; Cumberland Valley HS; Mechanicsburg, PA; (Y); Ski Clb; Band; Mrchg Band; Orch; Symp Band; VP L Bsbl; Wt Lftg; High Hon Roll; Hon Roll; NHS.

BOYES, CHRISTOPHER M; Wyoming Seminary HS; Forty-Fort, PA; (Y); #12 In Class; PAVAS; Chorus; School Musical; School Play; Stage Crew; Nwsp Stf; Hon Roll; Dance Clb; Yrbk Phtg; Yrbk Stf; PA Gov Schl Arts 84; Ntl Gld Mdl Awd Schlstc Art Awds 83-85; Hallmark Hnr Awds $100 Ntl 84-85; Carnegie-Mellon U; Artist.

BOYKIN, TONY; Chester HS; Chester, PA; (Y); Church Yth Grp; JA; Math Clb; Hon Roll; Prfct Atten Awd; Cert Rcgntn Lncln U Pgm 86; MI ST U; Engnrng.

BOYLAN, WILLIAM M; Cambridge Springs HS; Cambridge Springs, PA; (Y); 30/115; Spanish Clb; Trs Jr Cls; Var Bsbl; Var Ftbl; Var Wrstlng; Hon Roll.

BOYLE, BRENDA; Wilmington Area HS; New Wilmington, PA; (Y); 17/122; Drama Clb; Office Aide; Pres Spanish Clb; Hon Roll; NHS.

BOYLE, ELENA J; Panther Valley HS; Lansford, PA; (Y); Nwsp Rptr; Cheerleading; French Hon Soc; Art Clb; Cmnty Wkr; Computer Clb; Dance Clb; Debate Tm; Drama Clb; English Clb; Acadmc All Amer Schlr Benefits 86; PA ST U; Fshn Mrch.

BOYLE, KELLY; Central Catholic HS; Allentown, PA; (Y); Dance Clb; Chorus; Color Guard; High Hon Roll; Hon Roll; Biol.

BOYLE, LISA; Canon-Mc Millan HS; Hendersonville, PA; (Y); 2/346; French Clb; Science Clb; Concert Band; Drm Mjr(t); Nwsp Rptr; Sftbl; High Hon Roll; NHS; Sal; Pres Schltc Ftns Awd 86; Provost Awd Wnr U Of Pgh 85; U Of Pgh; Med.

BOYLE, RICH; Mid Valley Secondary Center; Dickson City, PA; (Y); Rep Soph Cls; Rep Jr Cls; Rep Sr Cls; High Hon Roll; Voice Dem Awd; Acctg.

BOYLE, TARA ANN; Uppermerion Area HS; King Of Prussia, PA; (Y); Band; Mrchg Band; Yrbk Phtg; Powder Puff Ftbl; Capt Tennis; Hon Roll; Jr NHS; NHS; Prfct Atten Awd; Interact Clb-Pres 84-86; Mst Imprvd Stu Awd 85; Penn ST U Univ Pk.

BOYLE, VICKI; Carlynton HS; Carnegie, PA; (Y); French Clb; Color Guard; Hon Roll; Army.

BOZEK, MARIBETH; Uniontown Area HS; Smock, PA; (Y); 2/324; Computer Clb; 4-H; Mathletes; Math Clb; Math Tm; Office Aide; Spanish Clb; Nwsp Bus Mgr; Nwsp Phtg; Nwsp Rptr; Amer Assn U Wmn Scholar 86; Case Western Res U; Engrng.

BOZICK, LYNN; Penn Hills SR HS; Pittsburgh, PA; (Y); AFS; French Clb; Key Clb; Band; Stat Ice Hcky; Hon Roll; Prfct Atten Awd; PA ST U.

BOZZARELLI, ALBERT; Kiski Area SR HS; Avonmore, PA; (Y); Chorus; High Hon Roll; Physcl Ftns Awd 85-86; Pittsburgh Tech Inst; Drftng.

BOZZI, AMELIA; Nazareth Acad; Philadelphia, PA; (S); Drama Clb; Pep Clb; Spanish Clb; Chorus; Church Choir; School Musical; Rep Soph Cls; Stu Cncl; Var Capt Fld Hcky; Pres Glee Clb 85-86; Elem Ed.

BRABAZON, DANIELLE; Central Bucks HS West; Doylestown, PA; (Y); 7/497; Church Yth Grp; Intnl Clb; Concert Band; Jazz Band; Mrchg Band; Var JV Bsktbl; JV Fld Hcky; Var L Trk; Vllybl; NHS; Shared Spnsh Awd 83-84; Latin Awd 85-86; Prfct Atten 84-85; Intl Banking.

BRACCO, JENNIFER; Clearfield HS; Clearfield, PA; (Y); Key Clb; Spanish Clb; Stat Bsktbl; JV Var Cheerleading; Math.

BRACE, PATTIE; E L Meyers HS; Wilkes Bare, PA; (Y); Ski Clb; Band; Chorus; Concert Band; Drill Tm; Mrchg Band; Yrbk Stf; Mgr(s); Mgr Wrstlng; Hon Roll; Essay Cntst Fnlst 82; Nrsng.

BRACHMAN, NOEL; Council Rock HS; Newtown, PA; (Y); Var Gym; High Hon Roll; Bus Adm.

BRACKBILL, KATHY; Altoona Area HS; Altoona, PA; (Y); Church Yth Grp; Computer Clb; Pep Clb; Chorus; Comp.

BRACKEN, SUSAN; Kiski Area HS; Freeport, PA; (Y); Exploring; Math Clb; Mgr Math Tm; Band; Jazz Band; Mrchg Band; Orch; Pep Band; School Musical; Symp Band; Provst Schlr, Schlrshp 86; Acad Letter; PA ST U; Microbio.

BRACY, CHERYL; Parkland HS; Allentown, PA; (Y); 40/462; Leo Clb; Chorus; School Musical; Swing Chorus; High Hon Roll; Hon Roll; NHS; Scl Srvs.

BRADAC, DOUGLAS; North Hills HS; Pittsburgh, PA; (Y); 29/467; Exploring; Key Clb; Var L Bsbl; Var L Bsktbl; High Hon Roll; Pres NHS.

BRADBURY, NOELLE; Mahanoy Area HS; Mahanoy City, PA; (Y); Drama Clb; Hosp Aide; Ski Clb; Spanish Clb; Band; Chorus; Nwsp Stf; Yrbk Phtg; Hon Roll; NHS; Nrsng.

BRADBURY, RUTH; Hoepwell HS; Aliquippa, PA; (Y); 29/260; VP Sec Church Yth Grp; Drama Clb; Spanish Clb; Chorus; Church Choir; Concert Band; Jazz Band; Mrchg Band; School Musical; School Play; Schl Rcrd Grls 3200 M Trk 85; Cnty All Star Jazz Band 86; 1st Pl 3200 M Trk 85; Geneve Coll.

BRADDOCK, LORETTA; Waynesburg Central HS; Carmichaels, PA; (Y); Spanish Clb; JV Bsktbl; Sftbl; JV Vllybl; Spnsh II & III Awds 84-86.

BRADFORD, MARY; ST Huberts HS For Girls; Philadelphia, PA; (Y); Camp Fr Inc; Church Yth Grp; Cmnty Wkr; Chorus; Color Guard; Drill Tm; School Musical; Lit Mag; Rep Jr Cls; Socr; Svc/Ldrshp Awd CSC & Chapel Aid; Nvl Sea Cadet Cert Hnr; Acctg.

BRADFORD, THOMAS S; Friends Select Schl; Philadelphia, PA; (Y); Aud/Vis; School Play; Nwsp Phtg; Ed Yrbk Phtg; Hon Roll; Schltc Art Awds Gold Key & Blue Rbbn 86; Kodak Medlln Exclnce 86; Cmmnctns.

BRADICA, JOHN; Belle Vernon Area HS; Belle Vernon, PA; (Y); Drama Clb; French Clb; Band; Concert Band; Mrchg Band; Pep Band; High Hon Roll; Hon Roll; Church Yth Grp; WA & Jefferson Coll; Intl Law.

BRADISH, RAYMOND; Hazleton HS; Hazleton, PA; (Y); 61/370; Bsktbl; Ftbl; UNICO Awd 86; Mlsrvl U.

BRADLEY, BERNICE; St Huberts HS; Philadelphia, PA; (Y); 247/367; Rep Stu Cncl; Trk; Pre-Law.

BRADLEY, BRIAN; Coudersport Area JR SR HS; Coudersport, PA; (Y); Church Yth Grp; Band; Chorus; Church Choir; Concert Band; Mrchg Band; Pep Band; School Play; Stage Crew; Var Golf; Geolgy.

BRADLEY, CYNTHIA; Lakeland HS; Mayfield, PA; (S); Church Yth Grp; FFA; FHA; Library Aide; Church Choir.

BRADLEY, ELAINE; Bellefonte Area SR HS; Bellefonte, PA; (Y); Ski Clb; Teachers Aide; Yrbk Rptr; Yrbk Stf; Rep Frsh Cls; Rep Soph Cls; Rep Sr Cls; Rep Stu Cncl; JV Cheerleading; Var Trk; PA ST U; Mgmt.

BRADLEY, HELENE; Nazareth Academy HS; Phila, PA; (Y); Dance Clb; Hosp Aide; Orch; School Musical; Lit Mag; VP Frsh Cls; Pres Soph Cls; Capt Var Cheerleading; Tennis; Rosemount; Art.

BRADLEY, JEFF; Dover Area HS; Dover, PA; (Y); Cmnty Wkr; FFA; Letterman Clb; Political Wkr; Teachers Aide; VP Frsh Cls; VP Soph Cls; Bsktbl; Ftbl; Trk; Real Est.

BRADLEY, KATHLEEN; Philipsburg-Osceola HS; Philipsburg, PA; (Y); 37/250; Church Yth Grp; Varsity Clb; Sec Soph Cls; VP Jr Cls; Stu Cncl; Var Bsktbl; Var Cheerleading; Var Golf; Var Sftbl; Wt Lftg; Accntnt.

BRADLEY, LEANNE; Moon SR HS; Maryville, TN; (Y); 76/310; Teachers Aide; Band; Concert Band; Mrchg Band; Pep Band; Symp Band; Variety Show; Hon Roll; Physcl Thrpy.

BRADLEY, ROBERT G; Norwin HS; N Huntingdon, PA; (Y); VICA; Prfct Atten Awd; 3rd Pl Auto Mech Cls VICA Comptn 84-85.

BRADLEY, SHIRLEY; Sayre Area HS; Athens, PA; (Y); 8/116; High Hon Roll; Rotry Clb Awds Steno, Typg 86; Marleah Jordan Cornell Meml Awd 86; Rtry Top 10 Awd 86; Acctg.

BRADLEY, TAMMY; Ringgold HS; New Eagle, PA; (Y); GAA; Hosp Aide; Political Wkr; Ski Clb; Nwsp Rptr; Capt Var Bsktbl; Powder Puff Ftbl; Hon Roll; Mst Promising Plyr Awd Bsktbl 84; Nrsg.

BRADMON, TARA L; Laurel Highlands SR HS; Uniontown, PA; (Y); Church Yth Grp; Dance Clb; FBLA; Var Capt Cheerleading; High Hon Roll; Hon Roll; Penn ST U; Elem Ed.

BRADSHAW, JENNY; Souderton Area HS; Telford, PA; (Y); Church Yth Grp; Dance Clb; Drama Clb; FCA; 4-H; Library Aide; Teachers Aide; Chorus; School Musical; School Play; Outstndng Athlt Awd 85; Ralph Plock Awd-Athlt Ldrshp Patrtsm 84; Al-Buxmont Hcky Awd 84; Mst Imprv Hcky; Sprts Medcn.

BRADY, ADAM C; Slincoln HS; Fombell, PA; (Y); 65/159; Church Yth Grp; Computer Clb; Drama Clb; Church Choir; Concert Band; Jazz Band; Mrchg Band; Orch; Pep Band; Stage Crew; Red Barn Plyrs Schlrshp 86; Timothy Harabosky Band Awd 86; Carnegie Mellon U; Voice Musc.

BRADY, COREEN; Saltsburg JR SR HS; Saltsburg, PA; (Y); Cmnty Wkr; GAA; Trs SADD; Varsity Clb; Flag Corp; School Musical; Yrbk Stf; Var L Bsktbl; Var L Sftbl; Var L Vllybl; IN Cty Lg All Star Sftbl 85 & 86, Vllybl 85; WCCC; Nrsng.

BRADY, KIM; John Harris HS; Harrisburg, PA; (Y); 4-H; PAVAS; Radio Clb; Chorus; Drill Tm; Pep Band; Nwsp Rptr; Nwsp Stf; Bsktbl; Crs Cntry; 2nd Sci Fair 84; Ribbons/Mdls Track 85; Tele-Cmnctns.

BRADY, MARK; Pennsbury HS; Morrisville, PA; (Y); Church Yth Grp; Concert Band; Im Bsktbl; Socr; Im Vllybl; Hon Roll; Chem.

BRADY, MATTHEW; Gov Mifflin HS; Shillington, PA; (Y); Teachers Aide; Var JV Ftbl; JV Swmmng; Var JV Trk; Hon Roll; Hstry.

BRADY, MATTHEW; Lincoln HS; Fombell, PA; (Y); Church Yth Grp; Computer Clb; Drama Clb; German Clb; Band; Concert Band; Jazz Band; Mrchg Band; Orch; Pep Band.

BRADY, STEPHANIE M; Mon Valley Catholic HS; Monongahela, PA; (S); 19/112; French Clb; Pep Clb; Ski Clb; Nwsp Phtg; Nwsp Rptr; Yrbk Phtg; Yrbk Sprt Ed; Rep Jr Cls; Stu Cncl; JV Vllybl; Pre-Med.

BRADY, TEMPLE MAUK; Punxsutawney Area SR HS; Punxsutawney, PA; (Y); FBLA; Hon Roll; Schlrshp Cert 85-86.

BRADY, THOMAS; Nativity B V M HS; St Clair, PA; (Y); 36/100; Chess Clb; Exploring; Hon Roll; Prfct Atten Awd; Hgh Schvt Awd Relgn 84; Accntg.

BRADY, TODD; Danville SR HS; Danville, PA; (Y); 65/202; Exploring; Sec French Clb; Ski Clb; Band; Concert Band; Mrchg Band; Bowling; Golf; Trk; Hon Roll; PA ST U; Med Field.

BRAGG, LISA; Millville Area HS; Millville, PA; (Y); Sec FBLA; Sec Trs Library Aide; Office Aide; High Hon Roll; Hon Roll; NHS; 1st Pl FBLA Reg 7 Bus Engl Awd 86; Schltc Awd 86; Bus.

BRAHENY, DAWN R; Lincoln HS; Ellwood City, PA; (Y); Sec Camera Clb; Drama Clb; Y-Teens; Yrbk Stf; Powder Puff Ftbl; Stat Wrstlng; Hon Roll; Am Bus Womans Asoc Schrlshp 86; Bradford Schl Bus; Sec.

BRAID, LORI; Clearfield Area HS; Clearfield, PA; (Y); 22/301; Pres Church Yth Grp; Key Clb; Pres Spanish Clb; JV Var Cheerleading; L Trk; Cit Awd; High Hon Roll; Hon Roll; NHS; Pres Schlr; Spnsh Schlrshp 86; Church Schlrshp 86; NCA Chrldr 86; IN U Of PA; Spnsh.

BRAIN, PATRICIA; Seneca Valley HS; Harmony, PA; (Y); 12/365; Pres Church Yth Grp; Math Tm; Sec Varsity Clb; Mgr Lit Mag; Capt Var Bsktbl; Capt Var Crs Cntry; Capt Var Trk; NHS; JA; Murray Awd 86; Sherman Awd 86; PA Schlr Educ Awd 86; Grove City Coll; Math.

BRAMANTI, CARMELA; Interboro HS; Prospect Park, PA; (Y); Computer Clb; SADD; Teachers Aide; VICA; High Hon Roll; Hon Roll; NHS; Awds Hnrs Geom & Data Prcssng 85; Data Prcssng.

BRAMBLEY, LYNNE; Everett Christian Acad; Breezewood, PA; (Y); 3/9; Church Yth Grp; 4-H; Band; Church Choir; Concert Band; Bsktbl; Var Vllybl; 4-H Awd; Hon Roll; PA ST; Math.

BRAMER, WILLIAM SCOTT; Perkiomen HS; Glendale, CA; (Y); 18/42; Boy Scts; Church Yth Grp; Cmnty Wkr; Pres Ski Clb; Band; Nwsp Rptr; Pres Stu Cncl; Ftbl; Lcrss; Wrstlng; USC; Dntst.

BRANAGAN, BETH; Montour HS; Corapolis, PA; (Y); Hosp Aide; JA; Band; Mrchg Band; Orch; High Hon Roll; Hon Roll; Chiroprctor.

BRANAM, SUSAN; Shanksville-Stonycreek HS; Friedens, PA; (S); 6/34; Chorus; Church Choir; L Bsktbl; JV Cheerleading; Mgr(s); L Vllybl; Hon Roll; Prfct Atten Awd; Spanish NHS.

BRANCHO, JAMES J; Norwin HS; Pittsburgh, PA; (Y); Drama Clb; German Clb; Mathletes; Math Clb; School Play; Nwsp Rptr; Nwsp Stf; Rep Stu Cncl; JV Crs Cntry; High Hon Roll.

BRAND, CHERI; West Forest HS; Tionesta, PA; (Y); 1/50; Chorus; School Play; JV Cheerleading; JV Vllybl; High Hon Roll; Hon Roll; NHS; Prfct Atten Awd; Cnty, Dist & Reg Chorus 86; High Gate Pgm 86; Sci.

BRANDHORST, KELLY; Warren Area HS; Warren, PA; (S); Church Yth Grp; Debate Tm; Acpl Chr; Madrigals; School Musical; School Play; Rep Soph Cls; Pres Jr NHS; Pres NHS; Ntl Merit SF; Dstrct & Rgnl Choir 85 & 86; Bus Adm.

BRANDON, NICHOLE; Shaler Area HS; Pittsburgh, PA; (Y); Church Yth Grp; Cmnty Wkr; Dance Clb; Concert Band; Mrchg Band; Symp Band; Yrbk Stf; Hon Roll; Spanish NHS; Toddler Chrch Awd 84; Tap Dance Awd 84; Ltr Outstndng Music Work 85; Elem Ed.

BRANDON, VERONICA A; Creative & Performing Arts HS; Philadelphia, PA; (Y); Pres Art Clb; Pres French Clb; VP JA; Q&S; Chorus; School Play; Nwsp Rptr; Ed Nwsp Stf; Yrbk Stf; Rep Jr Cls; Spirit Of Phila Awd Chnnl 10 85-86; Miss Teen Tlnt 85-86; Jr VP Opertn Liftoff 84-86; Boston U; Advrtsng Illstrtn.

BRANDT, ARTHUR; Akiba Hebrew Acad; Philadelphia, PA; (Y); Chess Clb; Computer Clb; Debate Tm; Trs Science Clb; Yrbk Phtg; Rep Jr Cls; Socr; Rep 6th Grade Stu Gov 80-81; Law.

BRANDT, DANIEL; Annville-Cleona HS; Annville, PA; (Y); 34/112; Pres FFA; Ftbl; NHS.

BRANDT, ERIC; Phil Mont Christian Acad; Phialdelphia, PA; (Y); Rep Frsh Cls; Rep Soph Cls; Rep Jr Cls; Rep Stu Cncl; Var JV Crs Cntry; Var JV Trk; JV Wrstlng; Philadelphia Coll; Acctg.

BRANDT, JENIFER; Sharpsville HS; Sharpsville, PA; (Y); Art Clb; Science Clb; Ski Clb; Spanish Clb; Chorus; School Play; Var L Cheerleading; Trk; Wt Lftg; Hon Roll; Acadmc Awd 84-85; Hnrs Bio 85-86; Slippery Rock; Marin Bio.

BRANDT, KENTON D; Swissvale HS; Pittsburgh, PA; (Y); 40/205; Am Leg Boys St; Exploring; Ski Clb; Spanish Clb; Var Capt Socr; Var L Trk; Hon Roll; Case Western RV Summr Sympsm 86; JR Acad Sci Fair 85; 2nd Pl 400 M Dash Keystone ST Games Trk 86; Elec Engrng.

BRANDT, LURENE; Cedar Crest HS; Lebanon, PA; (Y); French Clb; Pep Clb; Spanish Clb; Trs Band; Trs Concert Band; Drill Tm; Trs Mrchg Band; Hon Roll.

BRANDT, MICHELLE; Palmyra HS; Palmyra, PA; (Y); French Clb; Varsity Clb; Chorus; Stu Cncl; Capt Cheerleading; JV Swmmng; Pep Clb; Teachers Aide; Color Guard; Rep Frsh Cls; People To People Stu Ambsdr Prgrm 84-86; Penn ST U; Scl Psychtry.

BRANDT, SUZANNE; Central Dauphin East HS; Harrisburg, PA; (Y); 14/274; Church Yth Grp; Cmnty Wkr; Chorus; Concert Band; Yrbk Stf; Twrlr; High Hon Roll; NHS; Ntl Merit Ltr; Messiah Coll; Bio.

BRANDT, TRACEY; Saint Maria Goretti HS; Philadelphia, PA; (Y); Hon Roll; Penn ST; Bus.

BRANE, CHERI; Bishop Shanahan HS; W Chester, PA; (Y); 15/218; Teachers Aide; Nwsp Ed-Chief; Nwsp Stf; NHS; Prfct Atten Awd; Engl Hnr Awd 84; Acctg.

BRANE, DONNA A; Bishop Shanahan HS; West Chester, PA; (Y); 2/214; Cmnty Wkr; Chorus; School Musical; Nwsp Stf; High Hon Roll; Hon Roll; NHS; Ntl Merit Ltr; Prfct Atten Awd; Cngrssmns Mdl Merit 86; Biol Awd Hghst Avg 86; Relign Awd Hghst Avg 86; Catholic U Amer; Biol.

BRANSCOME, BETH; Villa Maria HS; New Castle, PA; (Y); 5/22; Sec French Clb; Trs GAA; Ski Clb; Yrbk Stf; Pres Stu Cncl; Capt L Tennis; French Hon Soc; NHS; NEDT Awd; Jr Miss Cntstnt 85-86; Jr Acad Sci 1st Rgn & ST 82-83; Miami U; Mrktng.

BRANSTETTER, TERRY; Tyrone Area HS; Tyrone, PA; (Y); 3/183; 4-H; French Clb; Yrbk Phtg; Yrbk Stf; Crs Cntry; Im Vllybl; 4-H Awd; High Hon Roll; Jr NHS; NHS; JR All PA Hlstn Awd 85; Res Grnd Chmpn PA JR 4-H Dry Shw 81 & 82; Engrng.

BRANT, TIM; Shanksville Stonycreek HS; Berlin, PA; (S); 1/32; 4-H; School Play; L Bsbl; Capt L Bsktbl; Dnfth Awd; Hon Roll; NHS; Spanish NHS; Val; U Pittsburgh; Comp Sci.

BRANTNER, WENDY; Altoona Area HS; Altoona, PA; (Y); Sec FBLA; Library Aide; High Hon Roll; Hon Roll; Steno I 4th Pl Rgnls 85; 2nd Pl 86; Bradford Schl; Med Sec.

BRANTON, STEVE; Fairview HS; Fairview, PA; (Y); Church Yth Grp; Varsity Clb; Var L Ice Hcky; Var L Socr; JV Trk; Hon Roll; Cleveland Suburban Hcky Lge T L Barker Awd Good Sprtsmnshp 85.

BRANZ, JACKIE; Freeland HS; Freeland, PA; (Y); 23/90; FBLA; Spanish Clb; School Play; Yrbk Stf; Trs Sr Cls; Rep Stu Cncl; Var Bsktbl; Socr; Hon Roll; Pres NHS; Lock Haven U; Scl Wrk.

BRASCHOSS IV, PETER J; Cheltenham HS; Melrose Pk, PA; (Y); Church Yth Grp; Computer Clb; Political Wkr; Scholastic Bowl; Science Clb; JV Bsbl; Im Bsktbl; Im Socr; Comp Comptn Fnls 85; Bio Hnrs 84-85; Hstry & Math Hnrs 85-86; Drexel; Math Engr.

BRASHER, INETA; Hazleton HS; Milnesville, PA; (Y); Dance Clb; Pep Clb; Drill Tm; Hon Roll; Acctng.

BRASINGTON, MARTY; Warren Area HS; Warren, PA; (Y); Band; Concert Band; Capt Drm & Bgl; Jazz Band; Capt Mrchg Band; Pep Band; School Musical; Spanish Clb; Music Perfrmnce.

BRASWELL, PHILIP; Perry T A HS; Pittsburgh, PA; (Y); 6/137; Orch; Lit Mag; Stu Cncl; High Hon Roll; Hon Roll; Jr NHS; NHS; Camp Fr Inc; Chess Clb; Debate Tm; Pittsburgh U; Psychlgy.

BRATE, CHRISTINE; Central Bucks HS East; Doylestown, PA; (Y); Bsktbl; Var Swmmng; JV Vllybl; Hon Roll; Rotary Awd; Mst Prmsng Frshmn Swmng 83 & 85; Intl Bus.

BRATIS, PERRY; Council Rock HS; Richboro, PA; (Y); 53/845; Mathletes; Temple Yth Grp; Concert Band; Var Tennis; NHS; Ntl Merit Ltr; Engrng.

BRATSPIES, PAMELA; Freedom HS; Bethlehem, PA; (Y); 64/402; French Clb; JA; Model UN; Temple Yth Grp; Acpl Chr; Chorus; School Musical; Nwsp Stf; Hon Roll; Pres Schlr; Emory U; Psych.

BRATTON, DARWIN; Greenwood HS; Millerstown, PA; (S); 2/58; Band; Yrbk Ed-Chief; Pres Jr Cls; Pres Stu Cncl; Var Bsbl; JV Var Bsktbl; JV Var Socr; High Hon Roll; Hon Roll; NHS; PA ST U.

BRAUCHLE, KIMBERLY; Allentown Central Catholic HS; Allentown, PA; (Y); 15/210; Pres Exploring; Key Clb; Math Clb; Chorus; Concert Band; Flag Corp; School Musical; Hon Roll; NHS; PA Jr Acad Sci 3rd Plc 85; Accntng.

BRAUN, AMY; Beaver Area HS; Beaver, PA; (Y); 41/177; Church Yth Grp; FCA; French Clb; Pep Clb; Ski Clb; Band; Mrchg Band; Yrbk Stf; Cheerleading; Powder Puff Ftbl.

BRAUN, ANDREW; Plymouth Whitemarsh HS; Conshohocken, PA; (Y); 16/350; Pres Math Clb; Pres Model UN; School Musical; School Play; Yrbk Stf; Rep Frsh Cls; Rep Soph Cls; VP Jr Cls; VP Sr Cls; JV Socr; Colonial Plyrs Harlequin Awd 86; Mth.

BRAUN, JEFFREY; General Mc Lane HS; Mckean, PA; (Y); 4/236; Chess Clb; French Clb; Band; Concert Band; Mrchg Band; Symp Band; High Hon Roll; Hon Roll; NHS; Pltcl Sci.

BRAUN, MARY LYNN; St Marys Area HS; St Marys, PA; (Y); 19/301; Boys Clb Am; Trs Frsh Cls; Trs Soph Cls; Trs Jr Cls; JV Var Bsktbl; Var L Sftbl; High Hon Roll; NHS; Arch.

BRAUN, MICHAEL; Springfield HS; Oreland, PA; (Y); 21/136; VP Sr Cls; Rep Stu Cncl; Var Ftbl; Var Swmmng; Hon Roll; Swmmng Dist Qual 85-86; James Madison Coll; Sprts Med.

BRAUN, TIMOTHY; Susquehanna Community HS; Susquehanna, PA; (Y); Math Tm; Ski Clb; Nwsp Stf; Hon Roll; Penn ST U; Comp Sci.

BRAVIN, KATHLEEN; Altoona Area HS; Altoona, PA; (S); Drama Clb; PAVAS; Spanish Clb; Chorus; Stage Crew; Off Jr Cls; Off Sr Cls; Var Crs Cntry; Var Trk; Hon Roll; Math Tchr.

BRAWLEY, TONY; Bishop Carroll HS; Carrolltown, PA; (S); Ski Clb; SADD; Chorus; Stage Crew; Hon Roll.

BRAXTON, DARRELL; Northeast HS; Philadelphia, PA; (S); Boy Scts; Church Yth Grp; Computer Clb; FBLA; Office Aide; Ski Clb; Band; Nwsp Ed-Chief; SAR Awd; Eagle Scout 84; Lincoln U; Busnss Admin.

BRAY, JANIS; Hazleton SR HS; Mcadoo, PA; (Y); Church Yth Grp; Drama Clb; French Clb; Office Aide; Pep Clb; Y-Teens; Chorus; Church Choir; Var Bsktbl; Capt Var Swmmng; Swmng Rcds 84-86; Cntr Chrch 85; Ltrmn Vrsty Team Swmng 84-86; Wooster Coll; Physcl Thrpy.

BRAY, LORA; Mc Keesport SR HS; Mckeesport, PA; (Y); 18/339; AFS; Hosp Aide; JA; Drm & Bgl; Capt Drm Mjr(t); VP Orch; Nwsp Stf; Powder Puff Ftbl; Hon Roll; NHS; Otstndng Mjrtt Awd 85; Pre-Med.

BRAZZO, ALLISON; MMI Preparatory Schl; Hazleton, PA; (Y); Church Yth Grp; Science Clb; Ski Clb; SADD; VP Frsh Cls; Pres Sec Stu Cncl; Bowling; Cheerleading; Sftbl; High Hon Roll; Grmn Ntl Hnr Scty; PA JR Of Sci Lcl & ST Wnr.

BREAKEY, MATTHEW; Matthew Breakey HS; Trafford, PA; (S); Rep Stu Cncl; Var Bsktbl; Im Sftbl; High Hon Roll; Hon Roll; Jr NHS; NHS; NEDT Awd; Arch.

BRECHCBIEL, JAY DENNIS; Greencastle-Antrim HS; Greencastle, PA; (Y); 9/186; Boy Scts; JV Bsktbl; Pre-Med.

BRECHT, ERIK M; Coatesville Area SR HS; Coatesville, PA; (Y); 62/502; Boy Scts; Cmnty Wkr; Exploring; Ski Clb; Acpl Chr; School Musical; Stage Crew; Nwsp Rptr; Trk; Hon Roll; Health.

BREDEL, ED; Bethel Park SR HS; Pittsburgh, PA; (Y); 70/515; Science Clb; Variety Show; Rep Frsh Cls; Rep Sr Cls; Hon Roll; Ntl Hnrs Cnvctn Awd 86; Pres Acdmc Ftns Awd 86; U Ptsbrgh; Vtrnry Med.

BREEDING, MARK; Avon Grove HS; West Grove, PA; (Y); 10/172; Church Yth Grp; Stage Crew; JV Bsbl; Im Mgr Bsktbl; Im Mgr Ftbl; JV Socr; High Hon Roll; NHS; Chem Awd 85-86; YMCA Aquatic Cert Lfgrd 85-87; Basic Trng US Army Reserve 86; Crim Just.

BREEN, JENNIFER; East Pennsboro Area HS; Camp Hill, PA; (Y); Church Yth Grp; Spanish Clb; Acadmc Achvt Awd Frnch I, Advncd Chmstry 86; Engrng.

BREEN, JOANNE; Interboro HS; Prospect Park, PA; (Y); Spanish Clb; Hon Roll; Neumann Coll; Nrs.

BREGAR, DEBORAH; Penn Hills HS; Pittsburgh, PA; (S); Exploring; Yrbk Stf; Rep Stu Cncl; Hon Roll; Sec.

BREHM, ROBIN; Windber Area HS; Windber, PA; (Y); Church Yth Grp; Sec 4-H; Hosp Aide; Library Aide; Cit Awd; Hon Roll; Reg Nrs.

BREIDEGAN, RANDY; Northern Lebanon HS; Jonestown, PA; (Y); Varsity Clb; VICA; VP Jr Cls; Wt Lftg; Wrstlng; High Hon Roll; Hon Roll; SR Achvmnt Awd Mchn Shp 85-86; Lebanon Lncstr All-Str Wrstlg Tm 84-85; Mst Pins Fstst Pn MIP Wrstlg; Mchnst.

BREIDIGAM, DARIN; Brandywine Heights Area HS; Mertztown, PA; (Y); 6/147; Boy Scts; Quiz Bowl; Band; Jazz Band; Mrchg Band; Pep Band; L Socr; L Tennis; High Hon Roll; NHS; PA ST U; Aerospace Engrng.

BREIDIGAN, DARIN; Brandywine Heights Area HS; Mertztown, PA; (Y); 4/147; Boy Scts; Scholastic Bowl; Band; Concert Band; Jazz Band; Mrchg Band; Socr; Tennis; High Hon Roll; NHS; PA ST U; Arspc Engrng.

BREIDINGER, PAULETTE; Rocky Grove HS; Cooperstown, PA; (Y); 12/95; Camera Clb; Dance Clb; Library Aide; Chorus; Stat Bsktbl; JV Var Pom Pon; Var L Sftbl; High Hon Roll; Hon Roll; Future Problm Solvng Gftd Prog 83-86; Nrsng.

BREIGHNER, ROBERT; Littlestown HS; Littlestown, PA; (Y); 4/120; Varsity Clb; Yrbk Bus Mgr; Trs Jr Cls; Var L Golf; Var L Tennis; DAR Awd; NHS; Hon Roll; Texas A&M U; Acctg.

BREINICH, TODD; Emmaus HS; Emmaus, PA; (Y); VP Church Yth Grp; Band; Church Choir; Trk; Hon Roll; VFW Awd; Vrsty Letter Stu Trainer 86; Messiah Coll; Hlth.

BREISCH, TRACY; Emmaus HS; Allentown, PA; (Y); Cmnty Wkr; VP Exploring; Girl Scts; Key Clb; Sec Spanish Clb; Band; Concert Band; Mrchg Band; Orch; Ed Nwsp Ed-Chief; Emplymnt Of Handicapped Essay Cntst Wnnr 86; Spelling Bee Fnlst 84.

BREISETH, ABIGAIL; Elmer L Meyers HS; Wilkes-Barre, PA; (S); 26/146; AFS; Church Yth Grp; Cmnty Wkr; French Clb; Chorus; Church Choir; School Musical; Variety Show; High Hon Roll; NHS; Acad All Amer 85-86; Hnr & Mrt Certs 83-85.

BREITENSTEIN, BRETT; Moon SR HS; Coraopolis, PA; (Y); JA; Band; Jazz Band; Mrchg Band; Symp Band; Hon Roll; Ntl Merit SF; Gifted Pgm; Law.

BRELSFORD, DAVID; E L Meyers HS; Wilkes Barre, PA; (Y); 48/140; German Clb; Hon Roll; Comp Sci.

BRELSFORD, PAULA MARIE; Bishop Conwell HS; Morrisville, PA; (Y); 53/255; Church Yth Grp; Q&S; Stage Crew; Yrbk Sprt Ed; Yrbk Stf; Prfct Atten Awd; Marilyn Moyer Schlrshp 86; Temple U; Lib Arts.

BREMBOS, CATHERINE; Pequea Valley HS; Lancaster, PA; (Y); 5/126; Drama Clb; Mrchg Band; School Play; Sec Sr Cls; High Hon Roll; NHS; Pres Schlr; Gym; AFS; Math Tm; Amercn Bus Wmn Assn Schlrshp 86; Geo P Smmrs Schlrshp 86; Armstrng Sci Awd & Ctatn 86; Rutgers U; Pre-Med.

BREMS, BRYAN; Exeter Township HS; Reading, PA; (Y); 20/300; Church Yth Grp; Pres VP Drama Clb; Chorus; Church Choir; School Musical; School Play; Variety Show; JV Ftbl; Golf; Var JV Tennis; Cmpr Yr Lthrn Smmr Music Cmp Schrlshp 85; Asst Dir Btn Rouge Lttl Thtr Wrkshps 86; Outstndng Stu Schlr; Drama.

BRENDLE, JEFFREY SCOTT; Governor Mifflin HS; Mohnton, PA; (Y); 4/292; Church Yth Grp; Model UN; Scholastic Bowl; Band; Concert Band; Jazz Band; Orch; Stage Crew; Bausch & Lomb Sci Awd; Cit Awd; Awd Excllnc 86; PA ST U; Mech Engnrng.

BRENEK, BETH; Avon Grove HS; Avondale, PA; (Y); 23/151; Drama Clb; Color Guard; Cheerleading; NHS; Pres Acad Ftns Awd 86; Art Awd Wtr Clr 86; Hlth Awd; PA ST.

BRENEMAN, JOANNE; Lewistown Area HS; Granville, PA; (Y); 11/263; Sec Trs Church Yth Grp; French Clb; Key Clb; Am Leg Boys St; Varsity Clb; Im Bsktbl; Var L Crs Cntry; Var L Sftbl; Var L Trk; High Hon Roll.

BRENEMAN, LORINE; Faith Mennonite HS; Bainbridge, PA; (Y); Art Clb; Church Yth Grp; Teachers Aide; Acpl Chr; Nwsp Stf; Trs Soph Cls; High Hon Roll; Schl Sci Awd 85-86.

BRENIMAN, KENNETH J; Cameron County HS; Emporium, PA; (Y); 2/91; Intnl Clb; School Play; Nwsp Ed-Chief; Yrbk Ed-Chief; Yrbk Stf; High Hon Roll; Hon Roll; NHS; Prfct Atten Awd; Art Clb; Natl Art Hnr Soc; Psych.

BRENNAN, CAROLYN; Bethlehem Catholic HS; Bethlehem, PA; (Y); Var Cheerleading; High Hon Roll; Hon Roll; Drexel; Fashn Desgn.

BRENNAN, KAREEN; Central Ssr HS; York, PA; (Y); Church Yth Grp; Girl Scts; Chorus; Stage Crew; Yrbk Stf; Im Sftbl; Var L Vllybl; Hon Roll; Opt Clb Awd; Vlybl Dev Pgm 85; Med Tech.

BRENNAN, KERRIE; Owen J Roberts HS; Pottstown, PA; (S); 21/278; Band; Mrchg Band; Symp Band; JV Co-Capt Lcrss; VP NHS; Ntl Merit Ltr.

BRENNAN, KRISTINE MARY; Owen J Roberts HS; Pottstown, PA; (Y); Am Leg Aux Girls St; Letterman Clb; Band; School Musical; School Play; Var L Crs Cntry; Lcrss; Trk; Ntl Merit Ltr; Semifnlst PA Gvrnrs Schl Arts 86; Brwn U Bk Awd 86; Wrtng.

BRENNAN, MARK; Devon Prep Schl; Exton, PA; (Y); Ski Clb; Spanish Clb; Rep Frsh Cls; Bsktbl; Var Socr; High Hon Roll; Hon Roll; NHS; Ntl Merit Ltr; Book Awds Physcs-86, Hstry AP-85 & Alg I-84; Bus.

BRENNAN, MICHELLE; St Basil Acad; Philadelphia, PA; (Y); Cmnty Wkr; GAA; Latin Clb; Math Clb; School Play; Variety Show; Nwsp Phtg; Nwsp Rptr; Yrbk Stf; Fld Hcky; Irish Cmptv Dncng Mdls 84; La Salle; Jrnlsm.

BRENNAN, MICHELLE; Williams Valley HS; Williamstown, PA; (S); 9/100; Ski Clb; Band; Chorus; Mrchg Band; Symp Band; Yrbk Stf; Powder Puff Ftbl; Hon Roll; NEDT Awd; Peer Edctr 85-86; Nrsng.

BRENNAN, PAMELA; Lewisburg Area HS; Lewisburg, PA; (Y); Church Yth Grp; Sec Exploring; German Clb; Girl Scts; Hosp Aide; SADD; Band; Concert Band; Mrchg Band; Pep Band; Dncr Choirs Prod; Jrnlsm.

BRENNAN, TERRI; Williams Valley HS; Tower City, PA; (S); 10/100; Chorus; Mrchg Band; Symp Band; Var L Cheerleading; Powder Puff Ftbl; Wt Lftg; High Hon Roll; Hon Roll; NEDT Awd; Ntl Band Awds 86; Counslrs Aid 84-85; Crmnl Justice.

BRENNAN, TOM; Moon SR HS; Coraopolis, PA; (Y); Church Yth Grp; Exploring; Spanish Clb; Var L Bsbl; Im Bsktbl; Var L Ftbl; Accntng.

BRENNEMAN, DAWN; Frankford & Swenson Skills Center; Philadelphi, PA; (S); Church Yth Grp; Girl Scts; Red Cross Aide; Rep Soph Cls; Var Badmtn; Var Vllybl; Cit Awd; Hon Roll; Samuel S Fels-Schlrshp Awd 84; Natl Yth Phys Ftns Pgm 85; Hlth Occuptns Stu Of Amer-1st Pl 85; Physcns Asstnt.

BRENNEMAN, KATHLEEN; Butler Area SR HS; Butler, PA; (Y); French Clb; JA; SADD; Thesps; School Play; Ed Nwsp Stf; Jr NHS; Wrthy Advsr Btlr Rnbw Assmbly 86; Fml Ld HS Ply; Asst Drctr Tlnt Shw; Cmmnctns.

BRENNEMAN, SHERRY; Greencastle-Antrim HS; State Line, PA; (Y); Band; Pres Hst Concert Band; Drm Mjr(t); Jazz Band; Mrchg Band; Yrbk Stf; NHS; Rotary Clb Schlrshp 86; Musicianshp Awd; Shippensburg U; Bus Info Sys.

BRENNEMAN, TANA; Christian Schl Of York; Glen Rock, PA; (Y); Church Yth Grp; Chorus; Church Choir; Orch; School Musical; Yrbk Stf; Var Bsktbl; Hon Roll; Fine Arts Cert Exc Piano Solo Comptn 85; Med Tech.

BRENNER, DONNA; Roxborough HS; Philadelphia, PA; (Y); 3/364; GAA; Library Aide; Var Bsktbl; Var Bowling; Var Capt Fld Hcky; Var Sftbl; High Hon Roll; Trs NHS; All Pblc Hnr Mntn Sftbl 86; Comp Sci.

BRENNER, ELAINE; Grove City SR HS; Grove City, PA; (Y); 9/193; Girl Scts; Office Aide; Teachers Aide; Concert Band; Mrchg Band; Pep Band; Var JV Bsktbl; Var Mgr(s); Var Capt Trk; Im Capt Vllybl; Spcl Awd Buhl Sci Fair 83; Girl Scout Gold Awd 85; ST Fnlst, Natl Hist Day 81-86, Natl Fnlst 86; Grove City Coll; Pre Med.

BRENNER, ERIC; Mohawk HS; New Castle, PA; (S); French Clb; Nwsp Rptr; Stat Ftbl; Mgr(s); Mgr Trk; NHS; Acdmc All Am Awd 84-86; Frgn Lang Comp 2nd.

BRENNER, MICHAEL Y; Haverford HS; Havertown, PA; (Y); 32/485; Concert Band; Jazz Band; Mrchg Band; Variety Show; Nwsp Rptr; Lit Mag; Wt Lftg; Hon Roll; NHS; Val; Brown U Awd Super Engl Stu 85; Outstndng Solo 86; Rutgers Coll Schlrshp 86; Rutgers Coll.

BRENNER, SARAH; Emmaus HS; Allentown, PA; (Y); French Clb; Girl Scts; Var L Tennis; Hon Roll; NHS; Ntl Merit Ltr.

BRENNER, SUSAN; Roxborough HS; Philadelphia, PA; (Y); GAA; Latin Clb; Nwsp Rptr; Stat Bsktbl; Bowling; Var Mgr(s); Var Vllybl; Hon Roll; Cmnty Coll Philadelphia Schlrshp 86; CC Philadelphia; Early Educ.

BRENNER, TERENCE; Central Catholic HS; Reading, PA; (Y); 32/128; Church Yth Grp; Stage Crew; JV Bsktbl; Var Ftbl; Var Trk; 2nd Hnrs 83-84 86.

BRENNER, WILLIAM; New Castle SR HS; New Castle, PA; (Y); 39/237; Church Yth Grp; Key Clb; Letterman Clb; Pep Clb; Ski Clb; Varsity Clb; Band; Concert Band; Bsbl; Ftbl; Geneva Schrl Ad 86; Bsbl Schlrshp 86; Slippery Rock; Acctng.

BRENSIKE, SCOTT; Emmaus HS; Macungie, PA; (Y); 3/455; Trs Key Clb; Math Tm; Concert Band; Jazz Band; Mrchg Band; Pep Band; Capt Vllybl; High Hon Roll; NHS; Ntl Merit Ltr; Lee Iococca Ledrshp Awd 86; Excllnc In Sci & Social Studies Awds 86; Presdntl Schlr; Perfct Attndc Awd; Penn ST U; Aeronautical Engrng.

BREON, FRANK L; State College Area SR HS; Warriors Mark, PA; (Y); 190/567; Boy Scts; Chess Clb; 4-H; Math Clb; Chorus; Im Socr; Hon Roll; Pwr Of Paws Awd 83-86; Penn ST; Engrng.

BRESLER, JESSICA; Lancaster County Day HS; Lancaster, PA; (Y); 1/30; Model UN; School Play; Yrbk Stf; Rep Stu Cncl; Var L Fld Hcky; High Hon Roll; Amer Hstry Prz; JR Acad Prz; Physcs Prz.

BRESLIN, MARY; Cardinal O Hara HS; Havertown, PA; (Y); 142/772; FNA; Hosp Aide; Chorus; School Play; Off Soph Cls; Hon Roll; Church Yth Grp; Office Aide; Teachers Aide; Im Bsktbl; Nrsng.

BRESLIN, MIKE; Cardinal O Hara HS; Clifton Hts, PA; (Y); 47/740; Var Capt Bowling; 1st Pl Delaware Cnty Sci Fair 84-85; Robert Frankenbergh Schlrshp Awd 82; St Josephs U; Chem.

BRESNAN, DRAKE; Penn-Trafford HS; Claridge, PA; (Y); 127/330; Cmnty Wkr; High Hon Roll; Hon Roll; Bus.

BRESTENSKY, SANDRA; Freeport HS; Sarver, PA; (S); 1/170; Church Yth Grp; GAA; Pres Jr Cls; Var L Bsktbl; Capt L Sftbl; Var L Vllybl; High Hon Roll; NHS; U Pittsburgh; Phys Thrpy.

BRESTENSKY, SANDY; Freeport SR HS; Sarver, PA; (Y); 1/170; Church Yth Grp; GAA; Pres Jr Cls; Var Capt Bsktbl; Var Capt Sftbl; Var Capt Vllybl; High Hon Roll; NHS; Vly Nws Disptch Bsktbl All Str Tm 85-86; Gannon U; Bio.

BRETT, CORINNE; Bethlehem Catholic HS; Bethlehem, PA; (Y); Key Clb; Ski Clb; Yrbk Stf; Im Fld Hcky; Mgr(s); Hon Roll; Bus.

BREUER, KEITH E; Riverise HS; Ellwood City, PA; (Y); Sec Computer Clb; Mrchg Band; School Musical; Symp Band; Ntl Merit Ltr; U Of Pittsburg; Engr.

BREUSTEDT III, SAMUEL K; Bensalem HS; Bensalem, PA; (Y); 98/526; Band; Concert Band; Jazz Band; Mrchg Band; School Musical; Swing Chorus; Rep Frsh Cls; High Hon Roll; Hon Roll; Pres Schlr; Bucks Cnty CC; Comm Music.

BREWER, DANIELLE; Com/Area HS; Spartansburg, PA; (Y); 30/212; Church Yth Grp; SADD; Chorus; Church Choir; Co-Capt Mrchg Band; Sftbl; Hon Roll; Pres Acad Ftns Awd 86; Mc Innes Schrlshp 86; K M Schl Bus; Trvl Mgmt.

BREWER, DAWN MARIE; Pennsbury HS; Yardley, PA; (Y); VP Church Yth Grp; French Clb; Service Clb; Band; Church Choir; Concert Band; Mrchg Band; French Hon Soc; Hon Roll; NHS; Applchn Svc Prjct 84 & 86; Occptnl Thrpy.

BREWER, HOLLY; Albert Gallatin SR HS; Masontown, PA; (Y); Dance Clb; FHA; Varsity Clb; Chorus; Rep Stu Cncl; Stat Bsktbl; Cit Awd; Hon Roll; Stwrdss.

BREWER, KELLEY; Purchase Line HS; Cherry Tree, PA; (Y); FHA; Pep Clb; Spanish Clb; Capt Drill Tm; Sftbl; Twrlr; Hon Roll; Du Bois Bus Coll; Leg Sec.

BREWER, LORI L; Albert Gallatin HS; Pt Marion, PA; (Y); #4 In Class; Am Leg Aux Girls St; Math Tm; Model UN; Spanish Clb; Acpl Chr; Chorus; Church Choir; Yrbk Stf; High Hon Roll; NHS; WV U; Math.

BREWER, MICHAEL; Greensburg Central Catholic HS; Greensburg, PA; (Y); Chess Clb; Letterman Clb; Ski Clb; Varsity Clb; Var Bsktbl; Var L Ftbl; Var Wt Lftg; High Hon Roll; Hon Roll; Bus Mngmnt.

BREWIN, LAURYN K; Hershey SR HS; Hershey, PA; (Y); Art Clb; Church Yth Grp; Hosp Aide; Band; Orch; School Musical; Nwsp Stf; Yrbk Rptr; Rep Soph Cls; VP Capt Fld Hcky; Rotary Intl Ldrshp Conf 86; Int Desgn.

BREWSTER, KAREN; Northwestern HS; East Springfield, PA; (Y); 10/146; Flag Corp; Trs Sr Cls; Rep Stu Cncl; Var Bsktbl; Var Ftbl; Capt Powder Puff Ftbl; Var Sftbl; Hon Roll; NHS; U Of PA Slippry Rck; Sprts Mgt.

BREWSTER, WILLIAM K; Liberty HS; Bethlehem, PA; (Y); 2/453; Capt Math Tm; Model UN; L Scholastic Bowl; Jazz Band; L Bsbl; L Socr; Ntl Merit SF; Church Yth Grp; Debate Tm; Science Clb; Schlrshp-PA Govs Schl For Sci 85; PA All ST Math Tm 85; 1st Pl Sr Hstrcl Paper Rgnl Hstry Day 85; Princeton U; Math.

BREWTON, SAMARIA; Villa Maria Acad; Erie, PA; (Y); 36/132; French Clb; Intnl Clb; JA; Office Aide; Teachers Aide; Color Guard; High Hon Roll; Hon Roll; NHS; Camera Clb; Mcdnlds All Cnty Bnd Stu 82; Ntl Hon Soc 84; Penn ST U.

BREYER, DAVID; Lilncoln HS; Ellwood City, PA; (Y); Drama Clb; Spanish Clb; Bowling; Socr; Tennis; Wrstlng; Hon Roll; Ntl Merit Ltr; NEDT Awd; Marietta Coll; Spts Med.

BREZEALE, CHRISTINA MARIE; Grace Christian Schl; Reading, PA; (S); 1/18; Church Yth Grp; Orch; Pres Soph Cls; High Hon Roll; Hosp Aide; Teachers Aide; Chorus; Church Choir; School Play; Ntl Piano Plyng Guild Audtns 84-85; Intl Piano Recrdng Fetvl 86; Mid Atlantic Christn Schl Assoc 85; Houghton Coll; Music.

BREZNAK, BETH; Hazleton SR HS; Mcadoo, PA; (Y); 55/388; Drama Clb; French Clb; Library Aide; Thesps; Chorus; Church Choir; Stage Crew; Nwsp Rptr; Tennis; Hon Roll; Cert Of Merit-Chorus 84; Cert Of Merit-Mtl Frnch Sco 85-86; Arch.

BRIAN, FERTIG; Saegertown HS; Saegertown, PA; (Y); 4-H; Ski Clb; Varsity Clb; Band; Mrchg Band; Yrbk Phtg; JV Ftbl; Ice Hcky; Var JV Wrstlng; Edinboro U; Photogrphr.

BRIAR, GABRIELLE; Villa Joseph Marie HS; Levittown, PA; (S); Church Yth Grp; Dance Clb; Hosp Aide; Library Aide; Chorus; School Musical; Off Soph Cls; Off Jr Cls; Hon Roll; Prfct Atten Awd; Cert Of Ed Dvlpmnt 84-85; Cert Of Fthfl Vlntr Srv 84-86; Doctor.

BRIAR, JANINE; Carrick HS; Pittsburgh, PA; (S); Church Yth Grp; Q&S; Off Stu Cncl; Hon Roll; Prfct Atten Awd; Busnss.

BRICKELL, SHARON; Purchase Line HS; Clymer, PA; (Y); 5/123; Pres Church Yth Grp; Trs SADD; Varsity Clb; Var L Bsktbl; Var L Sftbl; Var L Vllybl; High Hon Roll; NHS; NEDT Awd; 4-H; 1st Tm All-Cnty Sftbl 86; IN U Of PA.

BRICKER, MICHAEL J; Carlisle SR HS; Carlisle, PA; (Y); 19/400; Am Leg Boys St; Art Clb; Chess Clb; Var Crs Cntry; Var Ftbl; Var Trk; Var Wt Lftg; High Hon Roll; Hon Roll; NHS; Navy ROTC Schrlshp 86; Yth Schrls At Lebanon Vlly Coll 85; 2nd Pl Cptl Area Sci Fair; Villanova U; Chem Engr.

BRICKER, YVONNE; Middletown Area HS; Middletown, PA; (Y); Computer Clb; FBLA; Hosp Aide; Library Aide; Office Aide; Red Cross Aide; Teachers Aide; Color Guard; Flag Corp; Mrchg Band; Plmr Bus Schl; Bus Ownrshp.

BRIDDES, DONNA; Upper Darby SR HS; Upr Darby, PA; (Y); 42/650; Cmnty Wkr; Exploring; Library Aide; Office Aide; SADD; High Hon Roll; Hon Roll; VFW Awd; Lock Haven U; Med Comm.

BRIDEAU, RAYMOND; Henderson B Reed HS; West Chester, PA; (S); 20/348; Church Yth Grp; Computer Clb; Ski Clb; Var JV Socr; French Hon Soc; High Hon Roll; Prfct Atten Awd; Rotary Awd; Chem Engrng.

BRIDGE, KIM; Hampton HS; Allison Pk, PA; (Y); Capt Bsktbl; Var Capt Powder Puff Ftbl; JV Sftbl; Hon Roll; Post Gazette All Star Bsktbl 86; N Hills News Record Top 10 Bsktbl 86; Pitt; Dentl Hyg.

BRIDY, ANDREA; Upper Darby SR HS; Upper Darby, PA; (Y); Camp Fr Inc; Dance Clb; French Clb; Im Mgr Gym; JV Trk; Philadelphia Clg; Phrmcy.

BRIDY, KATIE; Our Lady Of Lourdes; Shamokin, PA; (Y); 31/94; VP AFS; VP Sec French Clb; Library Aide; Pep Clb; Service Clb; Nwsp Rptr; Nwsp Stf; Yrbk Stf; JV Cheerleading; NHS.

BRIEL II, JAMES L; Mahanoy Area HS; Mahanoy City, PA; (Y); Drama Clb; Band; Chorus; Jazz Band; Variety Show; Bsbl; Diving; Swmmng; Wrstlng; NHS.

BRIEM, CHRISTOPHER P; Shady Side Acad; Pittsburgh, PA; (Y); 8/111; Capt Math Tm; Teachers Aide; Capt Color Guard; Ftbl; Trk; DAR Awd; Ntl Merit SF; U S Naval Sea Cadt Corps Leadg Petty Offcr 82-85; Elctd Admssns Cmmttee 84; Navl Offcr.

BRIERCHECK, SCOTT; Quigley HS; Wexford, PA; (S); Mathletes; NFL; Nwsp Rptr; Var Crs Cntry; Var Golf; JV Socr; Var Trk; High Hon Roll; NHS; Debate Tm; Ntl Hnr Ntl Fed Music Clbs 86; Med.

BRIGATI, JACQUELINE; Cardinal Dougherty HS; Philadelphia, PA; (Y); 9/748; Drill Tm; School Musical; School Play; High Hon Roll; NHS; Prfct Atten Awd; Chorus; Mrchg Band; Awds Engl III, Rlgn III 85; Physics In 85 & Prfcncy Awd Compt Sci & Prog 86; Temple U; Ele Engr.

BRIGGS, DAYNA; South Park HS; Library, PA; (S); 2/205; FBLA; Mrchg Band; Orch; Sftbl; High Hon Roll; NHS; Outstndng Achvt Carnegie Inst Sci Activts Awd 86.

BRIGGS, GWEN; John Piersol Mccaskey HS; Lancaster, PA; (Y); 22/551; Church Choir; Cheerleading; Trk; Hon Roll; Spanish NHS; Natl Heritage Awd 84; Shippensburg U; Comp Sci.

BRIGGS, JOHN; Western Wayne HS; Sterling, PA; (Y); Drama Clb; Exploring; Hosp Aide; Red Cross Aide; Scholastic Bowl; School Play; Stage Crew; Rep Frsh Cls; Hon Roll; NHS; Stu Of Ftnght 84-85; Pres Acad Ftns Awd 85-86; Temple U; Poli Sci.

BRIGGS JR, RAYMOND; Bald Eagle Nitnany HS; Beech Creek, PA; (Y); 2/130; Pres Jr Cls; Ftbl; High Hon Roll; NHS; Ntl Merit Ltr; Pres Schlr; Sal; Computer Clb; Debate Tm; Drama Clb; Edward Allen Mem Awd 86; Outstndng Schltc Ath Awd 86; USAF Acad Appt 86; USAF Acad; Aero Engrng.

BRIGGS, SARAH; Yough SR HS; Smithton, PA; (Y); 62/226; Drama Clb; French Clb; Office Aide; Spanish Clb; Band; School Play; Yrbk Stf; High Hon Roll; Hon Roll; Intl Ordr Rnbw Girls 83; U NC Charlotte; Psych.

BRIGHAM, ANTHONY W; Blue Ridge HS; New Milford, PA; (Y); Ski Clb; JV Bsbl; Hon Roll; Prfct Atten Awd; X Ray Tech.

BRIGHAM, DOROTHY; Cardinal Dougherty HS; Phila, PA; (Y); 19/747; Cmnty Wkr; Office Aide; School Play; Stage Crew; Variety Show; Rep Soph Cls; Hon Roll; Pres NHS; Schl Serv Awd 86; Roxborough Sch Nrsg; Nrsg.

BRIGHAM, MICHAEL; William Penn SR HS; York, PA; (Y); Boy Scts; Church Yth Grp; Im Ftbl; Engrng Tech.

BRIGHT, JENNIFER; Shaler SR HS; Allison Pk, PA; (Y); Church Yth Grp; Computer Clb; FBLA; Hosp Aide; School Musical; Cheerleading; BUS Admin.

BRIGHT, JONATHAN; Karns City HS; Chicora, PA; (Y); 1/113; Band; Concert Band; Mrchg Band; Pep Band; Stu Cncl; High Hon Roll; Hon Roll; NHS; Rotary Awd; PA Free Entrpse Wk Schlrshp 86; Grove Cty Coll; Acctg.

BRIGHT, LISA; Steel Valley School District HS; Homestead, PA; (Y); Sec Church Yth Grp; Drama Clb; SADD; Church Choir; L Co-Capt Cheerleading; Gym; Stat L Trk; Varsity Clb; Nwsp Rptr; Nwsp Stf; Acad Achvt Awd Wrtng Skills Upwrd Bnd Pgm 86; Howard U; Pre-Med.

BRIGHT, MICHELLE; Nativity BVM HS; Orwigsburg, PA; (Y); Var L Bsktbl; Var L Sftbl; Var L Vllybl; Hon Roll; Phy Thrpy.

BRIGHT, WILLIAM; St James Catholic HS; Bensalem, PA; (Y); 44/140; Church Yth Grp; Cmnty Wkr; Stage Crew; Im Bsktbl; Var L Bowling; Var L Wrstlng; Hon Roll; Prft Charctr Awd 83-86; Penn ST; Engrng.

BRIGHTBILL, JODI; Palmyra Area HS; Palmyra, PA; (Y); Pep Clb; VP SADD; Teachers Aide; Band; Chorus; Church Choir; Concert Band; Mrchg Band; Trk; Twrlr; Sec.

BRIGHTBILL, KEVIN; Spring-Ford HS; Schwenksville, PA; (Y); 49/237; Church Yth Grp; Sec German Clb; Ursinus Coll Schlrshp 86; Mr-Mrs Warren Francis Grmn Awd 86; Ursinus Coll; Pre-Phrmcy.

BRIGHTBILL, STEF; Northeastern HS; York, PA; (Y); Church Yth Grp; Band; Yrbk Stf; Soph Cls; Jr Cls; Sr Cls; Cheerleading; High Hon Roll; Hon Roll; NHS; Pres Clsrm WA DC 86; Outstndg Acad Awd Accct Hnr Roll 85-86; York Coll; Resp Ther.

BRILES, DAVID; Greater Latrobe HS; Greensburg, PA; (Y); 39/420; Sec Church Yth Grp; French Clb; Letterman Clb; Model UN; Ski Clb; Band; Jazz Band; Var L Socr; French Hon Soc; High Hon Roll; Appalachia Svc 85-86.

BRILL, DANIEL; Elizabethtown Area HS; Elizabethtown, PA; (Y); Boy Scts; Letterman Clb; Varsity Clb; Var Capt Bsbl; JV Bsktbl; Var Crs Cntry; Egl Sct Awd 86; Penn ST U; Engr.

BRILL, ELIZABETH; Nazareth Acad; Philadelphia, PA; (Y); 50/125; Church Yth Grp; Cmnty Wkr; Red Cross Aide; Service Clb; Spanish Clb; Lit Mag; Vllybl; Hon Roll; Christian Brothers Grant La Salle U 86; La Salle U; Elem Spcl Ed.

BRILL, KATHLEEN; Turtle Creek HS; Turtle Creek, PA; (Y); 4/188; Boys Clb Am; Spanish Clb; Nwsp Stf; High Hon Roll; Opt Clb Awd; Spnsh Schlrshp 86; IN U Of PA; Cmmnctn.

BRILL, PATRICK; Our Lady Of The Sacred Heart HS; Aliquippa, PA; (Y); Boy Scts; L Bsbl; Crs Cntry; Med.

BRILLMAN, MARYBETH; New Hope-Solebury JR SR HS; Solebury, PA; (S); 8/87; FBLA; Band; Mrchg Band; Stat Bsktbl; Score Keeper; Sftbl; High Hon Roll; NHS; Art Clb; Church Yth Grp; PA ST U; Bus.

BRIMNER, AMY; Burgettstown JR SR HS; Burgettstown, PA; (Y); Church Yth Grp; Drama Clb; Ski Clb; Sec Trs Band; Sec Trs Concert Band; Sec Trs Mrchg Band; School Play; Variety Show; Stu Cncl; Tennis.

BRINER, HEATHER; West Perry SR HS; New Bloomfield, PA; (Y); 34/183; Spanish Clb; Varsity Clb; Color Guard; Yrbk Stf; Lit Mag; Pres Frsh Cls; Pres Soph Cls; Sec Stu Cncl; Score Keeper; Trk; Elem Ed.

BRININGER, SHAWN; Lewisburg Area HS; Winfield, PA; (Y); 15/143; Chess Clb; Church Yth Grp; Teachers Aide; Capt L Ftbl; Var L Trk; Var L Wrstlng; Hon Roll; NHS; Prfct Atten Awd; Pres Schlr; MVP Defnsv Yr 86; PIAA Regnl Wrstlng Tour 86; Svc Awd; U Pittsburg; Engrng.

BRINK, MELINDA; Dunmore HS; Dunmore, PA; (Y); Church Yth Grp; Exploring; French Clb; Hon Roll; YFU Exchng Stu Dnmrk Schlrshp 85-86; Trnsltr.

BRINK, SHERRI; Laurel Highlands HS; Uniontown, PA; (Y); Cmnty Wkr; 4-H; Nwsp Stf; Swmmng; Vllybl; High Hon Roll; Hon Roll; Bus Awd 84; Pitt U; Psych.

BRINKEL, MICHELE; Hollidaysburg Area SR HS; Hollidaysburg, PA; (Y); 36/370; Chrmn Variety Show; Yrbk Stf; Stu Cncl; Cheerleading; Hon Roll; NHS; PA ST U; Advrtsng.

BRINKER, DIANE; Cardinal Ohara HS; Springfield, PA; (Y); 67/740; Church Yth Grp; Cmnty Wkr; Dance Clb; Office Aide; Service Clb; Spanish Clb; Chorus; Church Choir; School Musical; School Play; Sociology Awd 86; Moravian Coll; Elem Ed.

BRINKLEY, YOLANDA; Simon Gratz HS; Philadelphia, PA; (Y); Aud/Vis; Church Yth Grp; Dance Clb; Debate Tm; Drama Clb; 4-H; Mathletes; Math Clb; Office Aide; Quiz Bowl; Temple U Upward Bnd 84-86; Reprtrs Awd 86; Hon Rl 86; CC Of Phila; TV Brdcstng.

BRINKMAN, PAUL; Arch Bishop Kennedy HS; Norristown, PA; (Y); Boy Scts; Church Yth Grp; Var Socr; Montgomery Cnty CC; Crmnl Jstc.

BRINKMAN, SANDRA; West Allegheny SR HS; Imperial, PA; (Y); 27/211; Sec Computer Clb; FBLA; Office Aide; Chorus; Color Guard; Hon Roll; Pres Acadmc Ftnss Awd 86; Roberts Morris Coll; Econ.

BRINKOS, AMY J; Mc Keesport Area HS; White Oak, PA; (Y); 38/339; AFS; Church Yth Grp; FBLA; NFL; Sec Acpl Chr; School Musical; Nwsp Ed-Chief; Stu Cncl; Exploring; French Clb; PMEA Dist I Hnrs Choir 86; Acad Tlntd Pgm 84-87; Emerson Coll; Jrnlsm.

BRINTON, SUSAN C; Council Rock HS; Wycombe, PA; (Y); Band; Concert Band; Jazz Band; Mrchg Band; Orch; Pep Band; School Musical; Stage Crew; Symp Band; Aud/Vis; Hnr Rll; Bucks Cnty Music Fest Band; Music Ed.

BRION, STEVE; North Penn HS; Blossburg, PA; (Y); 9/72; Ski Clb; Pres Spanish Clb; VP Varsity Clb; Band; Var Bsbl; Var Capt Bsktbl; Var Capt Ftbl; Var Capt Trk; Hon Roll; HS Athlt Of Yr 85-86; 1st Ctzns Ntl Bnk Schlrshp 86; All-Twn Tiers Ftbll Plyr 86; Mansfield U; Bus Admin.

BRISCOE, CHARLES; Simon Gratz HS; Philadelphia, PA; (Y); 12/410; Church Yth Grp; Drama Clb; Office Aide; Nwsp Rptr; Sec Jr Cls; VP Sr Cls; Swmmng; Cit Awd; High Hon Roll; NHS; Prnclpl For A Day 85; Supt Of Dist For A Day 85; Philadlpha Coll-Artsfgrphc Dsn.

BRISCOE, THERESA; Pocono Mountain HS; Cresco, PA; (Y); Band; Chorus; Concert Band; Mrchg Band; Pep Band; School Musical; School Play; Stage Crew; Nwsp Stf; Bus-Profsnl Wmns Clb Schlrshp 86; Millersvl U; Trnsltr.

BRISGONE, ROBERT; Monsignor Bonner HS; Aldan, PA; (Y); Im Ftbl; JV Socr; Hon Roll; Lawyer.

BRISKIN, HOWARD; St John Neumann HS; Philadelphia, PA; (Y); Cmnty Wkr; Mathletes; Nwsp Rptr; Yrbk Stf; Lit Mag; High Hon Roll; NHS; Villanova; Jrnlsm.

BRISTOL, DAVID; Troy HS; Troy, PA; (S); 4-H; FFA; Letterman Clb; SADD; Bsktbl; Bowling; Ftbl; Mgr(s); Wt Lftg; 4-H Awd; Tractor Drvg 83-86; Farmng.

BRITTAIN, CHRISTINA; Benton Area JR-SR HS; Stillwater, PA; (Y); 13/50; Girl Scts; Band; Chorus; Concert Band; Mrchg Band; School Musical; School Play; Stu Cncl; JV Var Fld Hcky; Hon Roll; Pre-Med.

BRITTNER, KELLY; Shaler Area SR HS; Pittsburgh, PA; (Y); 109/517; Pres Church Yth Grp; Church Choir; Rep Jr Cls; Stu Cncl; JV Cheerleading; Var Mgr(s); Var Stat Score Keeper; Var L Sftbl; Var L Vllybl; Chorus; Pre-Med.

BRITTON, MICHELE; Octorara HS; Parkesburg, PA; (Y); Art Clb; Church Yth Grp; Drama Clb; FNA; Hosp Aide; SADD; School Musical; School Play; Var Sftbl; Hon Roll; Brandywine Schl Of Nrsng; RN.

BRITTON, MONIQUE; Phila H S For Girls; Philadelphia, PA; (Y); 74/395; Drama Clb; 4-H; Hon Roll; Prfct Atten Awd; Church Yth Grp; Cmnty Wkr; Exploring; Girl Scts; Library Aide; Office Aide; Pre-Med.

BRLETIC, KENNETH; Plum SR HS; Pittsburgh, PA; (Y); Camera Clb; JA; Hon Roll; Phrmcst.

BRNA, RUTH; Ringgold SR HS; Monongahela, PA; (Y); Drama Clb; Ski Clb; Variety Show; Rep Jr Cls; Mgr(s); Mgr Wrstlng; Arch.

BROADHURST, TIMOTHY; St James HS For Boys; Ridley Park, PA; (Y); 54/140; Cmnty Wkr; Dance Clb; Pep Clb; Pres Service Clb; Chorus; School Musical; VP Jr Cls; VP Stu Cncl; Var JV Crs Cntry; Lion Awd; St Josephs U; Mrktng.

BROADWELL, CATHY; Cardinal O Hara HS; Glenolden, PA; (Y); 90/772; Art Clb; French Clb; School Musical; Chorus; Hon Roll; NHS; O Haras Acdmc Convocation 85-86; Commercial Art.

BROBSON, BOB; Montoursville HS; Montoursville, PA; (Y); 15/164; French Clb; Varsity Clb; Var L Bsbl; Var L Socr; Hon Roll; NHS; Archtctr.

BROBST, JIM; Millville Area HS; Millville, PA; (S); Boy Scts; Exploring; Im Ftbl; Hon Roll; NHS; Bloomsburg U; Optmtry.

BROCHETTI, RICKY; Sun Valley HS; Brookhaven, PA; (Y); 25/308; Intnl Clb; Model UN; Variety Show; Nwsp Rptr; Lit Mag; French Hon Soc; Ntl Merit SF; Drexel U; Itnl Trd.

BROCIOUS, KEVIN; Sharpsville Area Senior HS; Sharpsville, PA; (Y); Camera Clb; Church Yth Grp; Computer Clb; Ski Clb; Spanish Clb; Thesps; Hon Roll; NHS; Elec Engr.

BRODBECK, BETHEL; Dover Area HS; Dover, PA; (Y); 13/237; Pres Sec 4-H; Chorus; Mgr Yrbk Bus Mgr; Yrbk Stf; L Var Bsktbl; L Var Vllybl; 4-H Awd; High Hon Roll; Hon Roll; NHS; Comp Sci.

BRODE, KARRIN; Lebanon HS; Lebanon, PA; (Y); 39/285; Church Yth Grp; Drama Clb; Sec German Clb; Key Clb; Letterman Clb; Pep Clb; SADD; Varsity Clb; Band; Church Choir; Athl Wk WAHT & WVLV 84-86; Psych.

BRODECKI, DAVID; Bensalen HS; Bensalem, PA; (Y); Church Yth Grp; Drama Clb; German Clb; Key Clb; Chorus; Church Choir; School Musical; School Play; Swing Chorus; Bowling; Music Awd 86; Co Crclr Awd 86; Temple; Pre Law.

BRODERICK, ELISSA; Bishop Mc Devitt HS; Glenside, PA; (Y); 50/350; Sec Church Yth Grp; French Clb; Office Aide; Stage Crew; Nwsp Ed-Chief; Capt Crs Cntry; Capt Trk; Hon Roll; All Cath In Cross Cntry & Track 85-86; Athl Awd For Sr Clss 86; Comm.

BRODERICK, ELIZABETH; Pocono Mountain HS; Pocono Summit, PA; (Y); Exploring; Trs Concert Band; Drm Mjr(t); Trs Mrchg Band; School Play; Mgr Stage Crew; Variety Show; Lit Mag; NHS; Prfct Atten Awd; Surg Nrsng.

BRODERICK, TINA ILENE; Conestoga Valley HS; Lancaster, PA; (Y); Art Clb; Dance Clb; Key Clb; Art Awds; Gold Key Awds; 1st Pl Baking Cntst; PA Schl Art; Adv.

BRODOVICZ, STEPHEN; Middletown Area HS; Middletown, PA; (Y); 12/180; Am Leg Boys St; Boy Scts; Church Yth Grp; Latin Clb; Model UN; Concert Band; Mrchg Band; Orch; Acad All-Amer 86; Bio.

BRODSKY, JAY; Shaler Area SR HS; Glenshaw, PA; (Y); 6/517; Drm Mjr(t); Jazz Band; Mrchg Band; School Musical; Ed Yrbk Phtg; Rep Soph Cls; High Hon Roll; NHS; Ntl Merit Ltr; NEDT Awd.

BRODSKY, MATTHEW; Strath Haven HS; Swarthmore, PA; (Y); Ski Clb; Nwsp Phtg; Yrbk Sprt Ed; Var Crs Cntry; JV Trk; Hon Roll; NHS; Ntl Merit SF; Frnch Exch 86; Stu Advsry Cncl 85-87; Grapevine Exec Cmmttee 85-87; Columbia Coll.

BRODY, MICHAEL; Cheltenham HS; Elkins Pk, PA; (Y); 11/365; Yrbk Sprt Ed; Bsbl; Var Ice Hcky; High Hon Roll; Pres Schlr; MVP Vrsty Ice Hockey Tm.

BROFEE, BETH; Octorara HS; Atglen, PA; (Y); 8/200; Church Yth Grp; 4-H; Concert Band; Stage Crew; 4-H Awd; Hon Roll; NHS; Ntl Merit SF; Trk; Aud/Vis; Schlrshp Phila Yrly Meeting Russia 86; Champ Gumtree 4-H Horse Show 86; Res Champ NE MD Horse Shw 86; Vet.

BROGAN, BETH; Cardinal Ohara HS; Swarthmore, PA; (Y); 214/772; Church Yth Grp; Band; Mrchg Band; Orch; School Musical; Stage Crew; Yrbk Stf; Outstndg Achvt Bio 84-85; Science.

BROGAN, MARTI; Meyers HS; Wilkes Barre, PA; (Y); 38/140; Church Yth Grp; Pep Clb; Bsktbl; Sftbl; Swmmng; Trk; Hon Roll; Spanish NHS; Phrmcst.

BROGAN, TINA; Interboro HS; Norwood, PA; (S); 20/250; Ski Clb; Spanish Clb; Capt Flag Corp; Off Frsh Cls; Hon Roll; Jr NHS; NHS; Genetc Engr.

BROGDEN, BONITA; Altoona Area HS; Altoona, PA; (Y); SADD; VICA; Key Clb; Pep Clb; School Play; Variety Show; Hon Roll; Outstndng Voctnl Stu Awd 85-86; 1st Dist VICA Cmptn-Nrs Asstng 85-86; Vo-Tech Cert 85-86.

BROGDEN, DEBRA; Bishop Mc Cort HS; Johnstown, PA; (Y); Math Clb; Pep Clb; Spanish Clb; Chorus; Rep Stu Cncl; JV Capt Cheerleading; High Hon Roll; NHS; Spanish NHS; IN U PA; Bus.

BROGDON, HELENA; Belle Vernon Area HS; Belle Vernon, PA; (Y); 45/270; NHS; Chem.

BROKARS, LAURA; Archbishop Carroll For Girls HS; Narberth, PA; (Y); Church Yth Grp; Cmnty Wkr; Dance Clb; Pep Clb; Service Clb; Spanish Clb; Lit Mag; Hon Roll; Math Awd 83; Tutor 84-85; Villanova U; Bus Admin.

BROKAW JR, WILLIAM; Fox Chapel HS; Pittsbg, PA; (Y); Criminology.

BROMBERG, GENE; Shaler Area HS; Glenshaw, PA; (Y); Chess Clb; Exploring; Nwsp Rptr; Lit Mag; Im Sftbl; Var L Tennis; Hon Roll; Ntl Merit Ltr; John Hopkins Talent Seach 84; Penn ST; Journlsm.

BROMBERG, ROBERT; Lock Haven SR HS; Lock Haven, PA; (Y); Aud/Vis; Boy Scts; Computer Clb; French Clb; Temple Yth Grp; Nwsp Stf; JV Socr; L Trk; Prfct Atten Awd; Comp Prog.

BROMFIELD, PAMELA; Downingtown SR HS; Exton, PA; (Y); 35/560; Church Yth Grp; French Clb; GAA; Orch; Nwsp Ed-Chief; Nwsp Rptr; Tennis; Hon Roll; NHS; NEDT Awd; Pre-Law.

BRONAKOWSKI, LISA; Fort Le Boeuf HS; Erie, PA; (Y); 4/188; Church Yth Grp; Variety Show; Sr Cls; Im Gym; JV Im Vllybl; DAR Awd; High Hon Roll; Hon Roll; Sec Trs NHS; Fclty Choice Spkr Grad 86; Outstndng SR Sci 86; Outstndng SR Socl Stds 86; Behrend Coll; Bio.

BRONDER, LISA ANN; South Side Catholic HS; Pittsburgh, PA; (S); 12/50; Exploring; NFL; Service Clb; School Play; Rep Frsh Cls; Rep Soph Cls; Rep Jr Cls; Var Cheerleading; Hon Roll; Voice Dem Awd; Actg.

BRONISZEWSKI, SHANNON; Our Lady Of The Sacred Heart HS; Mc Kees Rocks, PA; (Y); 18/63; Church Yth Grp; Chorus; Church Choir; School Musical; Nrsng.

BRONOWICZ, SHARON; Shaler Area SR HS; Pittsburgh, PA; (Y); 133/517; Cheerleading; Mgr(s); Trk; High Hon Roll; Hon Roll.

BROOKER, MICHELLE; North Allegheny SR HS; Wexford, PA; (Y); Rep Frsh Cls; Sec Soph Cls; Sec Stu Cncl; Var JV Cheerleading; Hon Roll; Nursing.

BROOKES, WENDY; Unionville HS; Chadds Ford, PA; (Y); 66/300; Yrbk Stf; Rep Stu Cncl; Var Fld Hcky; Var Lcrss; High Hon Roll; Hon Roll; Bio.

BROOKHART, MELISSA; Greenwood HS; Millerstown, PA; (S); 6/62; VP Church Yth Grp; Chorus; Color Guard; School Musical; Swing Chorus; Fld Hcky; Trk; High Hon Roll; Hon Roll; NHS; U Of Pittsburgh; Phy Ther.

BROOKS, CATHY A; Lower Merion HS; Merion, PA; (Y); 25/372; Sec Drama Clb; Spanish Clb; SADD; Thesps; Band; Pres Chorus; Concert Band; Mrchg Band; School Musical; School Play; Dstrct Choir Alto II 84 & 86; Guidance Newsletter Editor 85-86; Northwestern U; Jrnlsm.

BROOKS, DEBRA L; Shaler Area SR HS; Pittsburgh, PA; (Y); Church Yth Grp; Exploring; Girl Scts; Ski Clb; Hon Roll.

BROOKS, HOLLY L; Beaver Falls SR HS; Beaver Falls, PA; (Y); 6/191; VP Art Clb; Pres VP Aud/Vis; L Band; Mrchg Band; Yrbk Stf; High Hon Roll; NHS; Acad All Amercn 84; Ntl Ldrshp Svc Awd 85; Drftng.

BROOKS, JAMIE; Mount Union Area HS; Mt Union, PA; (Y); Church Yth Grp; FCA; JV Bsktbl; Var Socr; Var Sftbl; Hon Roll; Mth Tchr.

BROOKS, JO ELLEN; Chambersburg SR HS; Chambersburg, PA; (Y); 64/593; Sec FTA; Spanish Clb; Chorus; Orch; High Hon Roll; Hon Roll; Dist,Regnl,Cty Chorus 85-86; Elem Ed.

BROOKS, KEN; Greensburg Central Catholic HS; N Huntingdon, PA; (Y); Boy Scts; Exploring; Var Mgr(s); Civil Engrng.

BROOKS, MARK; Solanco HS; Holtwood, PA; (Y); 16/212; Boy Scts; Church Yth Grp; School Musical; Variety Show; Socr; Sftbl; High Hon Roll; Hon Roll; NHS; Pres Acad Phys Fitness Awd 86; Solanco Scholar 83; Ray Long Memorial Award 86; Messiah Coll.

BROOKS, MICHAEL; Boyertown Area SR HS; Boyertown, PA; (Y); SADD; Pres Stu Cncl; Im Bsbl; Var Socr; Var Trk; L Wrstlng; Cit Awd; Hon Roll; Rotary Awd; Aviatn.

BROOKS, MICHELLE; Roxborough HS; Philadelphia, PA; (Y); 3/327; French Clb; Pres JA; Office Aide; Color Guard; Nwsp Rptr; Nwsp Stf; Yrbk Rptr; Yrbk Stf; Pres Jr Cls; Pres Sr Cls; Outstndg Freshmn Awd 83-84; Root Awd 85-86; 2nd Pl Typing Cont 84-85; :Medical Doctor.

BROOKS, STEPHENIE A; Blue Mountain Acad; Ellenville, NY; (Y); Dance Clb; Girl Scts; JA; Spanish Clb; Chorus; Cheerleading; Crs Cntry; Trk; Wt Lftg; Hon Roll.

BROOKS, TINA; J P Mc Caskey HS; Lancaster, PA; (Y); AFS; Church Yth Grp; Dance Clb; Pep Clb; Chorus; Jr Cls; Cheerleading; Powder Puff Ftbl; Trk; Hon Roll; Stu Cncl Clss Rep 85-86; Comp Prgrmng.

BROOKS, TROY; Corry Area HS; Corry, PA; (S); 30/212; JV Bsktbl; Var Golf; Comp Engr.

BROPHY, KAREN; Mohawk JR SR HS; Wampum, PA; (Y); 11/129; French Clb; FBLA; Nwsp Rptr; Nwsp Stf; French Hon Soc; Hon Roll; Bradford Bus Schl; Sec.

BROSCIOUS, KELLIE; Clearfield HS; Clearfield, PA; (Y); Drama Clb; French Clb; SADD; Yrbk Stf; Bsktbl; Cheerleading; Score Keeper; Sftbl; High Hon Roll; NHS; Sci Actvts Cert 85; Trig Achvt Awd 85; Frnch Cert Merit 85; Phrmctcl.

BROSIOUS, SCOTT; Saucon Valley SR HS; Bethlehem, PA; (Y); Im Bowling; Im Vllybl; High Hon Roll; Hon Roll; Hgh Hon Rl 83; Hon Rl 84-85; Bloomsburg; Acctng.

BROSIUS, ANGELA; Nazareth Acad; Feasterville, PA; (Y); Cmnty Wkr; German Clb; Lit Mag; Var Cheerleading; Mktng.

BROSIUS, CATHIE; Millersburg Area HS; Millersburg, PA; (Y); Ski Clb; Spanish Clb; Band; Chorus; Concert Band; Stage Crew; Symp Band; Nwsp Stf; Bsktbl; Powder Puff Ftbl.

BROSIUS, PEGGY; Brookville HS; Sigel, PA; (Y); Church Yth Grp; FHA; Pep Clb; Band; Chorus; Church Choir; Color Guard; Flag Corp; Pom Pon; Hon Roll; Dubois Bus Coll; Acctng.

BROSNAHAN, KELLY E; Bethel Park HS; Bethel Park, PA; (Y); Church Yth Grp; VP FHA; Hosp Aide; Frgn Exch Clb 85-86; A P Amer Hstry Clb 85-86; Homecomg 85-86; Genetcs.

BROSS II, THOMAS; Palmyra Area HS; Pamyra, PA; (Y); 53/186; Var L Swmmng; Church Yth Grp; French Clb; Jazz Band; JV Socr; Hon Roll; Prfct Atten Awd.

BROSSMAN, BRIAN; Neshaminy HS; Langhorne, PA; (Y); 167/752; Art Clb; Nwsp Stf; Yrbk Stf; Lit Mag; Var L Socr; Im Vllybl; Im Wt Lftg; Var Wrstlng; Cit Awd; Hon Roll; Art.

BROSTOSKI, JOHN J; North Pacono HS; Moscow, PA; (Y); 40/250; JV Bsktbl; NHS; U Scranton.

BROSTOSKI, ROBERT; Elk Lake HS; Meshoppen, PA; (Y); 74/101; Church Yth Grp; VICA; Concert Band; Jazz Band; Mrchg Band; School Musical; Stu Cncl; Wt Lftg; Wrstlng; Comptr Repair.

BROTHERS, RETA; Central York SR HS; York, PA; (Y); Church Yth Grp; Yrbk Stf; Hon Roll; Yth For Understndg; Early Chldhd Ed.

BROTON, MICHELE; West Hazleton HS; Sugarloaf, PA; (S); 36/206; Sec Girl Scts; Office Aide; Spanish Clb; SADD; Thesps; Chorus; School Play; Nwsp Stf; Hon Roll; NHS; Literary Awd 83; Wilkes College; Photo Journlsm.

BROUGH, AIMEE; Lincoln HS; Ellwood City, PA; (Y); 13/170; French Clb; Radio Clb; Y-Teens; Stu Cncl; Powder Puff Ftbl; High Hon Roll; Hon Roll; NHS; NEDT Awd; Miami U; Pol Sci.

BROUGHER, JANICE; East Pennsboro Area HS; Enola, PA; (Y); 59/200; Art Clb; Church Yth Grp; Pep Clb; Sec Spanish Clb; SADD; Church Choir; School Musical; Pres Stu Cncl; Twrlr; Hon Roll; Alternate Govnrs Schl Of Art 85; Natl Art Hnr Soc; Pharmacist.

BROUGHTON, GERALD; Liberty HS; Morris, PA; (Y); 2/34; High Hon Roll; NHS; Sal; Penn ST; Engrng.

BROUS, LISA MARIE; Villa Joseph Marie HS; Feasterville, PA; (Y); 16/52; Drama Clb; Spanish Clb; SADD; Chorus; School Musical; Yrbk Stf; Hon Roll; Prfct Atten Awd; DE Vlly Coll Of Sci; Anml Hash.

BROUSE, EDWIN; Milton Area HS; Montandon, PA; (Y); #23 In Class; Boy Scts; Pres Church Yth Grp; Spanish Clb; Chorus; Rep Frsh Cls; Wt Lftg; JV Wrstlng; Hon Roll; NHS; Hilicopter Pilot.

BROVEY, ALEXANDRA P; Easdt Stroudsburg HS; E Stroudsburg, PA; (Y); 3/208; Art Clb; FBLA; Hosp Aide; JA; Math Tm; Model UN; Soroptimist; Teachers Aide; Nwsp Ed-Chief; Nwsp Stf; Army Schlr/Ath Awd 86; Schl Schlr/Ath Awd 86; Natl Hnr Soc Scholar 86; PA ST U; Pre-Law.

BROWDER, KARYN; Meadville Area SR HS; Meadville, PA; (Y); Spanish Clb; SADD; Concert Band; Stage Crew; Yrbk Stf; Trk; Hon Roll; Prfct Atten Awd; Gftd Pgm 83-86; Yth Ftns SR Merit Achvt Awd 85; Intl Bus.

BROWELL, SHERRI; Garden Spot HS; Narvon, PA; (Y); Church Yth Grp; FBLA; German Clb; Office Aide; School Play; Yrbk Phtg; Yrbk Rptr; Yrbk Stf; Powder Puff Ftbl; Mgr Trk; Bus.

BROWER, AMY; Marple-Newtown SR HS; Broomall, PA; (Y); Aud/Vis; Church Yth Grp; Cmnty Wkr; Office Aide; Teachers Aide; Church Choir; Stu Cncl; Mgr Bsbl; Bsktbl; Mgr(s); Dntl Asst.

BROWER, DAWN; Western Beaver JR SR HS; Industry, PA; (Y); 28/80; Trs Girl Scts; SADD; Band; Nwsp Phtg; Yrbk Phtg; Rep Stu Cncl; Stat Bsktbl; Stat Trk; NHS; Girl Scout Gold Awd 86; Thiel Coll; Pol Sci.

BROWER, DONNA; Technical HS; Scranton, PA; (S); 13/270; FBLA; Letterman Clb; School Musical; Yrbk Stf; VP Sr Cls; Co-Capt Cheerleading; Hon Roll; NHS; Co-Op.

BROWER, PATRICIA; Pennridge SR HS; Green Lane, PA; (Y); Rep Jr Cls; Rep Stu Cncl; Cheerleading; High Hon Roll; Hon Roll; Jr NHS; NHS; Dance.

BROWER, SHANE; Bald Eagle Area HS; Howard, PA; (Y); 1/200; Varsity Clb; Var L Ftbl; Var L Trk; High Hon Roll; NHS; Ntl Merit Ltr; Amer Assn Physics Tchrs Outstndng Phys Stu Yr 86; Ntl Sci Olympiad Bio 84; Physics.

BROWN, ANNA; North Penn HS; North Wales, PA; (Y); 43/678; Rep Frsh Cls; Rep Soph Cls; Hst Jr Cls; Rep Stu Cncl; Var Cheerleading; Fld Hcky; Var Lcrss; Powder Puff Ftbl; Hon Roll; NHS; Penn ST; Comms.

BROWN, AUDREY; Halifax Area HS; Halifax, PA; (Y); 4/100; Church Yth Grp; FBLA; Pres FHA; Pep Clb; Varsity Clb; Chorus; Color Guard; Yrbk Stf; Cheerleading; High Hon Roll; Careers In Hlth Clb; Consvtn Clb; Bus Mgmt.

BROWN, BARBARA; William Allen HS; Allentown, PA; (Y); 65/559; Band; Concert Band; Jazz Band; Mrchg Band; Orch; High Hon Roll; Hon Roll; NHS; Band Dir Awd 83-84; Spellng Bee 83-85.

BROWN, BETH; Canton JR SR HS; Canton, PA; (Y); 33/99; Exploring; Letterman Clb; Ski Clb; Chorus; Yrbk Stf; Stu Cncl; Bsktbl; Mgr(s); Vllybl; Williamsport Area CC; Accntng.

BROWN, BETH; Donegal HS; Mount Joy, PA; (Y); 22/120; Capt Color Guard; Sec Frsh Cls; Sec Soph Cls; Sec Jr Cls; Sec Sr Cls; Cheerleading; Crs Cntry; Trk; Hon Roll; Spanish NHS; Brdcstng.

BROWN, CARL; Perry Traditional Acad; Pittsburgh, PA; (Y); #21 In Class; Art Clb; Computer Clb; JA; Math Clb; PAVAS; Varsity Clb; Jr Cls; Bsktbl; Trk; Hon Roll; Bus Mgmt.

BROWN, CATHERINE; Nazareth Acad; Philadelphia, PA; (Y); French Clb; La Salle U; Pre Law.

BROWN, CORNELL; Westinghouse HS; Pittsburgh, PA; (Y); Mrchg Band; Var Ftbl; Var Mgr(s); Var Score Keeper; Trk; Intrschlstc Athltcs Track & Field 86; Cert Natl Schlr/Athlete Awd US Army Awd 86; Army Services-Marines; Compu.

BROWN, COURTNEY; North Penn HS; Lansdale, PA; (Y); 2/639; Key Clb; Off Soph Cls; Off Jr Cls; Stu Cncl; JV Var Cheerleading; High Hon Roll; NHS; Var Fld Hcky; Var Lcrss; Powder Puff Ftbl; Knight Pf Wk 85; Stu Cncl Ldrshp Wrkshps & Cnfrnc 82-86; Duke U; Physcl Thrpy.

BROWN, CYNTHIA; Phila High School For Girls; Philadelphia, PA; (Y); 26/395; 4-H; Pep Clb; Concert Band; Mrchg Band; Orch; Pres Jr Cls; Rep Stu Cncl; Cit Awd; Hon Roll; NHS; Phila Clsscl Soc Cert Merit 84-85; Peds.

BROWN, DALE; Elk Lake HS; Dimock, PA; (Y); Boy Scts; Cmnty Wkr; French Clb; Political Wkr; Band; Trk; Hon Roll; PA ST U; Agri.

BROWN, DARLENE; Sullivan County HS; Forksville, PA; (Y); 11/93; Am Leg Aux Girls St; GAA; Pres Key Clb; SADD; Stu Cncl; JV Var Bsktbl; Var Sftbl; High Hon Roll; NHS; Prfct Atten Awd.

BROWN, DAVID; Bald Eagle Area HS; Julian, PA; (Y); Boy Scts; Exploring; High Hon Roll; Hon Roll; Air Frc; Auto Mchnc.

BROWN, DAVID; Ephrata SR HS; Ephrata, PA; (Y); 32/250; Boy Scts; Chess Clb; Church Yth Grp; Computer Clb; Quiz Bowl; Hon Roll; NHS; Prfct Atten Awd; PA Mthmtcs Lge Awd 86; Physcs.

BROWN, DAVID; Mc Guffey HS; Washington, PA; (Y); 24/216; Pres 4-H; French Clb; Varsity Clb; L Crs Cntry; L Trk; Hon Roll; George Mason U.

BROWN, DAVID; St Marys Area HS; St Marys, PA; (Y); 1/360; High Hon Roll; NHS; Gov Schl Sci 86; Physics.

BROWN, DAVID D; Kiski Area HS; Vandergrift, PA; (Y); Church Yth Grp; Math Clb; Math Tm; Science Clb; High Hon Roll; NHS; Ntl Merit SF; Admc Lttr 83-85; Semi-Fnlst U Of Pittsburgh Math Comp 85; PA ST U; Engr.

BROWN, DAVID P; Liberty HS; Bethlehem, PA; (Y); 58/475; Sec Trs Church Yth Grp; Computer Clb; FCA; FBLA; Acpl Chr; Concert Band; Mrchg Band; VP Orch; Var Golf; Hon Roll; CNIU 20 Microcomp Pgm Contst 85; 1st Pl Data Procssng Reg 21 Ldrshp Confrnc FBLA 85; Comp Engrng.

BROWN, DAVID S; North Penn HS; Lansdale, PA; (Y); Pres Church Yth Grp; Church Choir; School Musical; School Play; Stage Crew; Bsbl; Hon Roll; Comp Prog.

BROWN, DAWN; Penn-Trafford HS; Jeannette, PA; (Y); Drama Clb; Hosp Aide; Sec Spanish Clb; Sftbl; Hon Roll; Bus Mgmt.

BROWN, DAWN; Westinghouse HS; Pittsburgh, PA; (S); 7/180; Capt Sftbl; Capt Tennis; Hon Roll; U Of Pittsburgh; Bus Adm.

BROWN, DONNA; Wyoming Valley West HS; Kingston, PA; (Y); 73/379; Church Yth Grp; Key Clb; Math Clb; Ski Clb; Spanish Clb; Lit Mag; Var Fld Hcky; Var Sftbl; Vllybl; Hon Roll; Prftc Atndnc Awd 86; Wilkes Coll; Accntng.

BROWN, DOUGLAS G; Coudersport Area HS; Coudersport, PA; (S); 15/90; Trs FFA; Speech Tm; Trs Varsity Clb; VP Frsh Cls; Rep Soph Cls; Pres Jr Cls; Rep Stu Cncl; Var L Ftbl; Var L Trk; High Hon Roll; Falcon Achvt Awd Scholar Awd 85; FFA Scholar Awd 85; ST Publc Spkng Awd 85; PA ST U; Ag.

BROWN, ELIZABETH A; William Allen HS; Allentown, PA; (Y); 150/759; Trs Intnl Clb; Political Wkr; Chorus; Flag Corp; Nwsp Rptr; Sec Frsh Cls; Jr NHS; Opt Clb Awd; Church Yth Grp; Drama Clb; Choraliers 85-86; Solo/Duet Intl Dinnr Fr 84-85; Trvl.

BROWN, GAIL J; Mt Lebanon HS; Pittsburgh, PA; (Y); 169/535; Key Clb; JV Var Powder Puff Ftbl; JV Swmmng; Hon Roll; Church Yth Grp; Cmnty Wkr; Pep Clb; Church Choir; Color Guard; Drill Tm; Medallion Awd St Lucys Aux Blind Voluntees Wrk 85; PA ST U; Ed.

BROWN, GLEN; Cambridge Springs HS; Cambridge Springs, PA; (Y); 1/104; French Clb; Sec Pep Clb; Var L Bsbl; Var Capt Bsktbl; Var L Ftbl; Var Capt Vllybl; Var Wt Lftg; Hon Roll; NHS; Prfct Atten Awd; All-Conf 1st Tm Ftbl 85; All Conf 1st Tm Vlybl 86; All-Conf 2nd Tm Bsktbl 85-86; US Military Acad.

BROWN, J TODD; Pequea Valley HS; Gap, PA; (Y); 1/120; Pres AFS; Drama Clb; VP Band; Chorus; Concert Band; Jazz Band; Madrigals; Mrchg Band; School Musical; School Play; ST Bnd Bassoon 86; Rgnl Chors 86; Dstrct Orchstr 86.

BROWN, JACKI; Northeastern HS; Mt Wolf, PA; (Y); Church Yth Grp; Pep Clb; Ski Clb; Chorus; Church Choir; Yrbk Stf; Capt Var Cheerleading; Twrlr; Hon Roll.

BROWN, JANENE; Creative And Performing Arts; Philadelphia, PA; (S); 6/140; Varsity Clb; Orch; School Musical; Var Bsktbl; Var Gym; Im Powder Puff Ftbl; Var Socr; Var Trk; Var Capt Vllybl; High Hon Roll; Math.

BROWN, JEANNETTE; Purchase Line HS; Clymer, PA; (Y); Church Yth Grp; Library Aide; Spanish Clb; Chorus; Hon Roll; Mst Contrib Frgn Lang Clb 85-86; Sec.

BROWN, JENNIFER; Bishop Guilfoyle HS; Altoona, PA; (Y); Church Yth Grp; Dance Clb; French Clb; PAVAS; Science Clb; Church Choir; Mrchg Band; Pom Pon; High Hon Roll; Hon Roll; Hlth Fld.

BROWN, JENNIFER; Unionville HS; Chadds Ford, PA; (Y); 91/287; Chorus; Rep Stu Cncl; Hon Roll; Jr NHS; Acctng.

BROWN, JENNIFER; Western Wayne HS; Lk Ariel, PA; (Y); 3/138; Computer Clb; 4-H; SADD; Yrbk Stf; Pres Sec Stu Cncl; JV Socr; Var Sftbl; Var Tennis; NHS; Sec Ed.

BROWN, JENNY; Mount St Joseph Academy; Oreland, PA; (Y); Art Clb; French Clb; JCL; Hst Latin Clb; Lit Mag; JV Fld Hcky; French Hon Soc; High Hon Roll; VP NHS; Ntl Merit Ltr; Gibbons Schlrshp Cathlc U Amer 86; Catholic U Of Amer; Pltcl Sci.

BROWN, JO ANNE; Quigley HS; Freedom, PA; (Y); 23/103; Hosp Aide; JA; Drill Tm; Yrbk Stf; Bio.

BROWN, JODY; Gonegal HS; Mount Joy, PA; (Y); 14/150; Color Guard; School Play; Yrbk Stf; VP Frsh Cls; VP Soph Cls; VP Jr Cls; Trs Stu Cncl; Cheerleading; Crs Cntry; Trk; Cmmnctns.

BROWN, JUNE; Wyoming Valley West HS; Kingston, PA; (Y); Radio Clb; SADD; Chorus; School Musical; Stage Crew; Im Bsktbl; God Cntry Awd; NEDT Awd; 4-H; Girl Scts; Kings Coll Spnsh Test; William A Passavant Comptv Schrlshp; Girl Scout Silver Awd; Thiel Coll; Elem Ed.

BROWN, KAREN; Dunmore HS; Dunmore, PA; (Y); 5/145; Church Yth Grp; Computer Clb; Ski Clb; Yrbk Stf; Swmmng; High Hon Roll; Jr NHS; NHS; VFW Essy Cntst Wnnr 84.

BROWN, KAREN; Pine Grove Area HS; Pine Grove, PA; (Y); 7/114; Sec SADD; Varsity Clb; Concert Band; Flag Corp; Yrbk Sprt Ed; Stu Cncl; Vllybl; High Hon Roll; Hon Roll; NHS; Central Penn Bus Schl; Off Comm.

BROWN, KEITH; Canon-Mc Millan SR HS; Muse, PA; (Y); Church Yth Grp; Band; Chorus; Concert Band; Jazz Band; Mrchg Band; Pep Band; School Musical; School Play; Stage Crew; Cert Of Rcgntn-CA U Hnrs Jazz Band 86; Cert Of Rcgntn-Cnty Band 85; Chmcl Engrng.

BROWN, KELLI; Greater Works Acad; Irwin, PA; (S); Church Yth Grp; Var Cheerleading; Var Vllybl; Hgh Hnr Roll; Bio Acad Awd Of Hnr; Pres Ftnss Awd; Bio.

BROWN, KELLY; Lake Lehman HS; Dallas, PA; (Y); 35/180; Church Yth Grp; Drama Clb; Hosp Aide; Chorus; School Play; Hon Roll; NHS; Tempk U; Pre-Med.

BROWN, KENNETH; Bald Eagle Area HS; Julian, PA; (Y); 40/204; Math Tm; Model UN; Ski Clb; Concert Band; Jazz Band; Mrchg Band; Stage Crew; Im Fld Hcky; PA ST Slalom Ski Tm 85-86; MIP Rcng Tm 84-85; St Lawrence U; Physcs.

BROWN, KHALID; Olney HS; Philadelphia, PA; (Y); Art Clb; Boy Scts; FNA; Intnl Clb; JA; PAVAS; Red Cross Aide; SADD; Nwsp Phtg; Hon Roll; Gemedco 3-D Awd 86; Schltc Art Awd Cert Of Merit 86; Art.

BROWN, KIM; Wyoming Valley West HS; Larksville, PA; (Y); 13/350; Church Yth Grp; Cmnty Wkr; Key Clb; High Hon Roll; Hon Roll; NHS; Kings Coll; Pre-Law.

BROWN, KIMBERLEY; Archbishop Kennedy HS; Lafayette Hill, PA; (Y); 15/705; Church Yth Grp; 4-H; Girl Scts; Mathletes; Band; Chorus; Color Guard; Mrchg Band; Nwsp Rptr; Nwsp Stf; Vlntr Svc Awd-Miss Amer Coed 86; Cmnty Svc Awd-Archbshp Kennedy 85-86; Penn ST; Aerospc Engrng.

BROWN, KIMBERLY; Lincoln HS; Ellwood City, PA; (Y); 1/162; Art Clb; Pres Drama Clb; Sec French Clb; Hosp Aide; Sec Service Clb; Y-Teens; Stu Cncl; High Hon Roll; NHS; NEDT Awd; Amrcn Chem Soc Cert Merit 87; Acdmc Achvmnt Awd 84-86; U Of Pittsburgh; Psychlgy.

BROWN, LAURA; Waynesburg Central HS; Waynesburg, PA; (Y); 14/190; French Clb; Natl Beta Clb; Band; Concert Band; Drm Mjr(t); Mrchg Band; High Hon Roll; NHS; NEDT Awd; All Cnty Bnd 84-86; Elizabeth Stewart Schlrshp 86fgalpha Tri-Hi-Y 85-86; CA U PA; Scndry Ed.

BROWN III, LEONARD G; Solanco HS; Kirkwood, PA; (Y); Church Yth Grp; 4-H; Varsity Clb; Rep Jr Cls; Pres Stu Cncl; Socr; Trk; 4-H Awd; High Hon Roll; Hon Roll; Vrsty Sprtsmnshp Awd-Sccr 86-87; Poli Sci.

BROWN, LISA; Cumberland Valley Christian HS; Waynesboro, PA; (Y); Art Clb; Church Yth Grp; Drama Clb; Political Wkr; Chorus; Hon Roll; NHS; Ofc Prcdrs Schlrshp 86; Pensacola Christian Coll; Bus.

BROWN, LORA E; Clarion-Limestone JR SR HS; Clarion, PA; (Y); 18/80; French Clb; Intnl Clb; Color Guard; Drill Tm; School Play; Mgr(s); Hon Roll; NEDT Awd; Drama Clb; School Musical; Rifle Clb Pres 82-85; IN U; Pre-Law.

BROWN, LYNNISE VALENCIA; New Castle HS; New Castle, PA; (Y); 51/263; Art Clb; Dance Clb; French Clb; Varsity Clb; Drill Tm; Mrchg Band; Var Trk; Hon Roll; Guid Comm 83-86; Schltc Awd & Pins 83; 2 Yr 400 M Chmp Trk Rnr-Up 800 M 85-86; Soc Degr.

BROWN, MARLENE; Sullivan County HS; Forksville, PA; (Y); 7/90; 4-H; Sec Key Clb; SADD; Yrbk Stf; Mgr(s); Cit Awd; High Hon Roll; Trs NHS; Pres Schlr; Mu Omicron Chptr Awd 86; Wilma Boyd Cr Schl; Arln.

BROWN, MARY; Montoursville HS; Montoursville, PA; (Y); German Clb; Varsity Clb; Band; Concert Band; Var Cheerleading; Mgr(s); Powder Puff Ftbl; Bloomsburg U; Elem Educ.

BROWN, MATTHEW; Greensburg Central Catholic HS; Greensburg, PA; (Y); Chess Clb; Church Yth Grp; AFS; NFL; Speech Tm; Nwsp Bus Mgr; Nwsp Phtg; Nwsp Stf; JV Socr; Cert Merit Natl Frnch Cntst 86.

BROWN, MATTHEW; New Castle SR HS; New Castle, PA; (Y); 37/266; AFS; Aud/Vis; Church Yth Grp; Cmnty Wkr; Pres Spanish Clb; Var Mgr(s); Im Vllybl; Hon Roll; Natl Engl Merit Awd; Acad All-Amer.

BROWN, MELANIE; West York Area HS; York, PA; (Y); Dance Clb; Exploring; French Clb; Chorus; Rep Frsh Cls; Rep Soph Cls; Rep Stu Cncl; JV Fld Hcky; Var Mgr(s); Hon Roll; PSYCH.

BROWN, MELISSA; Connellsville SR HS; Acme, PA; (Y); 77/484; 4-H; Teachers Aide; Band; Drill Tm; Stage Crew; Cheerleading; Vllybl; 4-H Awd; High Hon Roll; NHS; 2nd Pl Readng Comprhnsn Frnch 85-86; Slippery Rock; Paralegal Sec.

BROWN, MICHAEL; Lberty HS; Bethlehem, PA; (Y); 121/475; Church Yth Grp; French Clb; Model UN; Hon Roll; Arln Plt.

BROWN, MICHELE; Franklin HS; Cochranton, PA; (Y); Hosp Aide; Service Clb; Spanish Clb; Band; Concert Band; Mrchg Band; Mgr(s); High Hon Roll; Hon Roll; Prfct Atten Awd; Williams Schlrshp 86-87; Roth Grnt 86; Passavnt Partcptn Awd 86; Thiel Coll; Med Tech.

BROWN, MICHELE; Salisbury HS; Allentown, PA; (Y); Dance Clb; FBLA; Drm Mjr(t); Mrchg Band; School Musical; School Play; Twrlr; Trvl.

BROWN, MICHELLE; Meadville Area SR HS; Meadville, PA; (Y); Debate Tm; German Clb; Speech Tm; SADD; Chorus; School Musical; Nwsp Rptr; Hon Roll; Spch & Debate Trophies 83-84; Engl Tchr.

BROWN, MIKE; Clarion Area HS; New Bethlehem, PA; (Y); Pres 4-H; Chorus; Var L Ftbl; Im Wt Lftg; Hon Roll; Engrng.

BROWN, NATALIE; Wilkinsburg HS; Pittsburgh, PA; (Y); Spanish Clb; Mrchg Band; Pres Stu Cncl; Cheerleading; Dnfth Awd; High Hon Roll; NHS; NFL; Bus.

BROWN, OMAR A; The Hill Schl; Philadelphia, PA; (Y); FBLA; JA; Letterman Clb; Varsity Clb; Nwsp Rptr; Var L Bsktbl; Var L Ftbl; Var L Lcrss; Hon Roll; Business.

BROWN, PAMELA; Simon Gratz HS; Philadelphia, PA; (Y); Computer Clb; Girl Scts; Hosp Aide; Chorus; Drill Tm; Jr Cls; Bowling; Cheerleading; Gym; Trk.

BROWN, RACHEL; Warrior Run HS; Turbotville, PA; (Y); 7/157; AFS; Sec Church Yth Grp; Trs 4-H; Spanish Clb; Nwsp Stf; Yrbk Stf; Trk; Hon Roll; NHS; Cert Schrlshp Hist 85; Physcl Thrpy.

BROWN, RAYMOND; University City HS; Philadelphia, PA; (Y); Boy Scts; Crs Cntry; Hon Roll; NHS; Prfct Atten Awd; Morehouse; Engrng.

BROWN, REBECCA; Lincoln HS; New Castle, PA; (Y); 5/167; Ski Clb; Spanish Clb; Y-Teens; School Musical; Yrbk Ed-Chief; Yrbk Stf; Pres Jr Cls; Pres Sr Cls; Stu Cncl; L Bsktbl; College Club Schlrshp; Carolyn Knox Schlrshp; Hugh O Brian Yth Ldrshp; Carnegie-Mellon U; Ind Mngmnt.

BROWN, RYAN; Belle Vernon Area HS; Belle Vernon, PA; (Y); 124/272; Aud/Vis; Church Yth Grp; Spanish Clb; SADD; Wt Lftg; Hon Roll; Prfct Atten Awd; Medical Clb 84-86; Rifle Clb 83-84; Ind Arts Clb 85-86; E Nazarene Coll; Physcl Thrpy.

BROWN, SEAN; Calvary Baptist Acad; Indiana, PA; (Y); 3/9; Church Yth Grp; Band; Chorus; Church Choir; School Play; Yrbk Phtg; Score Keeper; L Sftbl; Cit Awd; Drama Clb; Outstndng Christian Ldrshp Awd & Schlrshp, ACT Scores Schlrshp 86; Pensacola Christian Coll; Comp.

BROWN, SHANEQUA; Harrisburg HS; Harrisburg, PA; (Y); Debate Tm; Girl Scts; Library Aide; Office Aide; Political Wkr; ROTC; SADD; Teachers Aide; Band; Chorus; Cmptr Tech.

BROWN, SHAWN; Martin Luther King HS; Philadelphia, PA; (Y); Computer Clb; FBLA; SADD; Nwsp Phtg; Yrbk Stf; Var Ftbl; JV Trk; NHS; Track Ltr 86; Bus Adm.

BROWN, SHELLEY; Northeast Bradford JR SR HS; Rome, PA; (Y); Computer Clb; VP Pres 4-H; Sec FHA; Letterman Clb; Rep SADD; Varsity Clb; Nwsp Stf; Mgr Wrstlng; 4-H Awd; Alt Dairy Princss Bradford Cnty 86; Robert Packer Hosp Vlntr Awds 83-85; E Carolina U; Nrsng.

BROWN, SHERI; Brownsville Area HS; Grindstone, PA; (Y); Dance Clb; Hosp Aide; Teachers Aide; High Hon Roll; Hon Roll; RN.

BROWN, SHERRI; Somerset Area SR HS; Somerset, PA; (Y); 48/224; FBLA; JA; Teachers Aide; Yrbk Stf; High Hon Roll; Hon Roll; Prfct Atten Awd; Sec.

BROWN, SHERRI; St Maria Goretti HS; Philadelphia, PA; (Y); Art Clb; Hosp Aide; Pep Clb; Service Clb; Hon Roll; Cert Of Merit Geomtry 85-86; Accntng.

BROWN, STACY; York Catholic HS; York, PA; (Y); 15/169; Library Aide; Pep Clb; Chorus; Nwsp Stf; Yrbk Stf; Stat Bsktbl; JV Vllybl; Hon Roll; NHS; Fash Merch.

BROWN, STACY L; Governor Mifflin SR HS; Mohnton, PA; (Y); 80/310; Cmnty Wkr; Debate Tm; FBLA; Girl Scts; Hosp Aide; SADD; Sftbl; High Hon Roll; Jr NHS; NHS; Bloomesburg U; Bus Adm.

BROWN, STEPHANIE; Central Dauphin HS; Harrisburg, PA; (Y); Band; Concert Band; Drm & Bgl; Mrchg Band; Vllybl; Labanon Vly Coll; Lab Tech.

BROWN, STEVE; Carlynton HS; Carnegie, PA; (Y); 3/190; Band; Bausch & Lomb Sci Awd; Gov Hon Prg Awd; High Hon Roll; NHS; Ntl Merit SF; Pres Schlr; Sal; Boys Clb Am; Natl Socty Profssnl Engrs Schlrshp Carnegie Mellon 86-90; Carnegie Mellon U; Elec Engr.

BROWN, SUSAN; Franklin HS; Franklin, PA; (Y); 62/214; German Clb; Radio Clb; Capt Color Guard; Capt Flag Corp; Variety Show; Yrbk Stf; Off Sr Cls; Stu Cncl; Tennis; Hon Roll; Schl Dir Awd 84-85; Stdnt Cncl Schl Bd 85; Penn ST U; Lib Arts.

BROWN, THOMAS; Line Mountain HS; Leck Kill, PA; (Y); 12/129; Trs Church Yth Grp; Trs Pres 4-H; Band; Concert Band; Jazz Band; Mrchg Band; Pep Band; 4-H Awd; Hon Roll; Band Awd 84-86; Phys Fit Awd 86; Penn ST; Aero Engrng.

BROWN, TINA L; Fannett-Metal HS; Amberson, PA; (Y); Pres Church Yth Grp; Drama Clb; FNA; Teachers Aide; Chorus; Church Choir; High Hon Roll; Hon Roll; Acdmc All Amer Awd 85-86.

BROWN, TRACY; West Catholic High For Boys; Philadelphia, PA; (Y); Bsktbl; Score Keeper; Hon Roll; Prfct Atten Awd; Engrng.

BROWNE, DIANE; Bishop Mc Devitt HS; Philadelphia, PA; (Y); 24/350; Church Yth Grp; Office Aide; Pep Clb; Chorus; Var L Bsktbl; Im Powder Puff Ftbl; Var Capt Sftbl; Im Vllybl; Hon Roll; NEDT Awd; Modrn Miss Schlrshp Fnlst 85; La Salle U; Bus Mgmt.

BROWNE, SCOTT E; Baldwin SR HS; Pittsburgh, PA; (Y); 14/550; CAP; Computer Clb; Exploring; High Hon Roll; NHS; Ntl Merit SF; US Naval Acad Smnr 85; PA JR Acad Sci Lctur 84; Electrcl Engr.

BROWNELL, JOHANNA; Friends Select Schl; Philadelphia, PA; (Y); Cmnty Wkr; Dance Clb; Drama Clb; Intnl Clb; Model UN; School Musical; Variety Show; Yrbk Stf; Mgr Bsktbl; Mgr Mgr(s); Russian Studies.

BROWNING JR, JIM ROBERT; Penn Hills HS; Pittsburgh, PA; (Y); Boy Scts; Orch; L Capt Crs Cntry; L Swmmng; L Trk; Hon Roll; NHS; Schlr Athl Yr Awd 85-86; Kenyon Coll.

BROWNING, MARY KAY; Ringgold HS; Monongahela, PA; (Y); 17/350; Church Yth Grp; Hosp Aide; Ski Clb; Band; Church Choir; Concert Band; Mrchg Band; Rep Stu Cncl; Hon Roll; NHS; Carroll TWP Firemns Awd Acadmc Ablty 86; WV U; Med Tech.

BROWNING, SCOTT; Saint Pius X HS; Stowe, PA; (S); 44/164; JA; Science Clb; Concert Band; School Musical; Im Bowling; JV Ftbl; JV Tennis; Hon Roll; Prfct Atten Awd; Bowling Trophy Lg Champ 85; Drexel; Engrng.

BROWNING, TODD; Shanksville-Stonycreek HS; Stoystown, PA; (S); 4/34; Boy Scts; Church Yth Grp; Band; Concert Band; Mrchg Band; Nwsp Rptr; Hon Roll; Spanish NHS; Pres Phy Ftnss Awd 85; Chem.

BROWNLEE, JONELLE; Kennedy Christian HS; Burghill, OH; (Y); 10/100; Spanish Clb; Stu Cncl; Mat Maids; Score Keeper; Timer; High Hon Roll; NHS; Alpha Beta Omega Soc; Prfct Atten; Youngstown ST U; Pre-Law.

BROWNLEE, SHERRILL; Garden Spot HS; New Holland, PA; (Y); Drama Clb; JV Capt Bsktbl; Mgr(s); Powder Puff Ftbl; Hon Roll; Elem Tchr.

BROZEK, KIM; Waynesboro HS; Waynesboro, PA; (Y); 11/365; Intnl Clb; Library Aide; Math Clb; Concert Band; Mrchg Band; DAR Awd; High Hon Roll; Hon Roll; NHS; Comp Sci.

BROZINO, MELISSA; Jim Thorpe HS; Jim Thorpe, PA; (S); Dance Clb; FHA; German Clb; Library Aide; Ski Clb; Band; Chorus; Church Choir; Flag Corp; School Play; Pt Park Pittsburgh; Dance.

BROZOSKI, DEBORAH; W B Saul HS; Philadelphia, PA; (Y); 12/120; FFA; Nwsp Rptr; Hon Roll; NHS; Prfct Atten Awd; Sales & Svc Awd 84; DE Vly Coll; Anim Husbndry.

BROZOSKI, JOSEPH; Lasalle College HS; Philadelphia, PA; (Y); Art Clb; Church Yth Grp; Crs Cntry; Wrstlng; Hon Roll; NHS; Service Clb; Ski Clb; Trk; Villanova U; Mech Engrg.

BROZOWSKI, MIKE; Dieruff HS; Allentown, PA; (Y); Hon Roll; Tri Cnty Electrcl Awd 85; Tri Cnty Drftng Dsgn Awd 85; Arch.

BRUBACKER, DAVID; Grace Christian Schl; Bethel, PA; (Y); Var Bsbl; Var Mgr Bsktbl; Hon Roll; Ntl Merit Ltr; Dstngshd Chrstn H S Stu 86; Aero Engrng.

BRUBAKER, ALEX S; Manheim Township HS; Lancaster, PA; (Y); 6/330; Church Yth Grp; Var L Socr; High Hon Roll; NHS.

BRUBAKER, AMY; York Country Day Schl; York, PA; (Y); Ski Clb; Varsity Clb; Band; Orch; School Musical; Nwsp Rptr; Nwsp Stf; Cheerleading; Tennis; Hon Roll.

BRUBAKER, BENJAMIN; Homer Center HS; Homer City, PA; (Y); Church Yth Grp; Cmnty Wkr; Exploring; SADD; Hon Roll; NHS; VFW Awd; Counselors Scholarship; Elks Scholarship; Biology Award; IN U; Bio.

BRUBAKER, BONNIE; Williamsburg HS; Williamsburg, PA; (Y); 4/62; Pres Church Yth Grp; Office Aide; Teachers Aide; Nwsp Rptr; Yrbk Stf; Hon Roll; NHS; Pres Schlr; Drama Clb; Band; Hugh O Brian Ldrshp 84; Rotary Intl Exch Stu 84-85; Dickinson Coll; Law.

BRUBAKER, JULIA; Catasavgua HS; Catasauqua, PA; (Y); 12/135; Church Yth Grp; Hosp Aide; Ski Clb; Church Choir; Yrbk Stf; Lit Mag; Rep Frsh Cls; Rep Soph Cls; Rep Jr Cls; Rep Stu Cncl; Chem Engrng.

BRUBAKER, KEVIN A; York Country Day Schl; York, PA; (Y); 1/12; Church Yth Grp; Band; Chorus; Church Choir; Yrbk Stf; Pres Stu Cncl; Capt Bsktbl; High Hon Roll; NHS; Ntl Merit SF; Hghst Grd Avg Faclty Awd 84-85; MVP Bsktbl; Relgn.

BRUBAKER, LISA; Ephrata SR HS; Ephrata, PA; (Y); Sec Church Yth Grp; 4-H; FBLA; Spanish Clb; Chorus; Church Choir; Var Tennis; High Hon Roll; NHS; 4-H Awd; FBLA Reg Typng I Awd 1st Pl 86; Bus.

BRUBAKER JR, RON; Hughesville HS; Muncy, PA; (Y); Hon Roll; NHS; VA Tech; Aerospc Engrng.

BRUBAKER, STEVE; Redlion Area SR HS; Red Lion, PA; (Y); 46/337; Church Yth Grp; Hosp Aide; Science Clb; Hon Roll; Prfct Atten Awd; VFW Awd; Oral Roberts U; Pre-Med.

BRUCE, ANNA; Seneca HS; Wattsburg, PA; (Y); Teachers Aide; Band; Concert Band; Mrchg Band; Pep Band; School Musical; Stage Crew; Hon Roll; Hlth.

BRUCE, TERRY; Farrell HS; Farrell, PA; (Y); Aud/Vis; Computer Clb; French Clb; Key Clb; Pep Clb; Science Clb; Yrbk Stf; Off Frsh Cls; Off Soph Cls; French Hon Soc; U Of South Carolina; Bus.

BRUCK, BETH; Hyndman Middle SR HS; Hyndman, PA; (Y); 3/40; Ski Clb; Spanish Clb; Chorus; Stu Cncl; Cheerleading; Mgr(s); Var Tennis; High Hon Roll; Jr NHS; NHS; IUP; Elem Tchr.

BRUCKER, BETH; Center HS; Monaca, PA; (Y); Pres Church Yth Grp; Exploring; Latin Clb; Rep Stu Cncl; Hon Roll; Med Tech.

BRUCKER, CARON; Churchill HS; Braddock, PA; (Y); 43/224; Art Clb; Library Aide; Pep Clb; Spanish Clb; Nwsp Stf; Capt Cheerleading; Score Keeper; Hon Roll; Schlrshp Awd 86; Acad Awd 85; Math 84; Duquesne U; Pre-Law.

BRUDER, JAMIE; Carlynton HS; Carnegie, PA; (Y); 22/165; French Clb; Capt Color Guard; Yrbk Stf; Rep Jr Cls; Stu Cncl; Mgr(s); Hon Roll; Psych.

BRUECKEN, BARBARA; Shaler Area SR HS; Pittsburgh, PA; (Y); JA; Office Aide; Ski Clb; Spanish Clb; Yrbk Stf; Stu Cncl; Score Keeper; Var Trk; High Hon Roll; Spanish NHS; U Of Pittsburgh; Orthodntst.

BRUMBAUGH, ANNETTE; Central HS; Martinsburg, PA; (Y); FBLA; Office Aide; Band; Color Guard; Altoona Schl Of Cmmrc; Bus Admi.

BRUMBAUGH, KATHI; Bellefonte Area HS; Mingoville, PA; (S); VP Church Yth Grp; Drama Clb; SADD; Band; Chorus; Church Choir; Flag Corp; School Musical; School Play; Nwsp Rptr; Cnty Chorus 83-84; Penn ST U; Prfrmng Arts.

BRUMBAUGH, SUSAN; Meadville Area SR HS; Meadville, PA; (Y); Church Yth Grp; French Clb; Chorus; Crs Cntry; Trk; Hon Roll; Edinboro U; Compu Sci.

BRUMBAUGH, WILLIAM; Tussey Mountain HS; Cassville, PA; (Y); 21/106; Church Yth Grp; Hon Roll; Dresser Fndtn Scholar 86; Penn ST; Engrng.

BRUMLEY, DEBRA; Waynesburg Central HS; Waynesburg, PA; (Y); 5/190; Exploring; French Clb; Rep Stu Cncl; High Hon Roll; NHS; Pres Schlr; Waynesburg Clg Sci Fair Chem Awd 85; Duquesne U Acdmc & Anthony Ames Memrl Schlrshps 86; Duquesne U; Pharm.

BRUNER, DAVID; Connellsville Area SR HS; Champion, PA; (Y); 104/550; VP Church Yth Grp; Chorus; JV Ftbl; JV Tennis; Hon Roll; NHS.

BRUNER, LEANN; Jim Thorpe SR HS; Jim Thorpe, PA; (Y); 19/97; Chorus; Nwsp Stf; Var Cheerleading; Var Pom Pon; Var Vllybl; Hon Roll; Peer Cnslng 84; Hlth.

BRUNETTI, KENNETH; West Catholic HS; Philadelphia, PA; (Y); 40/293; Art Clb; Yrbk Stf; Var Capt Ftbl; Wt Lftg; Hon Roll; NHS; Temple; Acctg.

BRUNGARD, TRACY B; Spring Grove Area SR HS; York, PA; (Y); 55/285; Pres VP Church Yth Grp; Library Aide; Trs SADD; Chorus; Church Choir; Hon Roll; Millersville ST U; Elem Eductn.

BRUNGESS, BARBARA; Owen J Roberts HS; Spring City, PA; (S); 25/300; Church Yth Grp; Church Choir; Hon Roll; NHS; U PA; Vet Med.

BRUNGO, MIKE; Glendale JR SR HS; Coalport, PA; (Y); 23/98; Sec Trs Service Clb; Band; Concert Band; Mrchg Band; JV Var Bsktbl; Im Vllybl; Hon Roll; JV Var Ftbl; Opt Clb Awd; Pres Phy Ftnss Awd; Penn ST U; Htl Mngmnt.

BRUNI, COLETTE; Chichester HS; Boothwyn, PA; (Y); 1/270; Sec Pres Spanish Clb; Stat Bsbl; High Hon Roll; NHS; Val; Hosp Aide; SADD; Rep Stu Cncl; Hon Roll; Jr NHS; Soc Wmn Engrs Cert Merit 86; Alld Chemcl Awd 86; Acadmc Cours Awd 86; Acadmc Excllnc Math Awd 86; Villanova U; Bio.

BRUNI, LISA A; Seton-La Salle HS; Pittsburgh, PA; (Y); 12/260; JA; Ski Clb; Mrchg Band; Yrbk Stf; Capt Pom Pon; High Hon Roll; NHS; Outstndng Acdmc Achvt Acdmc Chem I & Spnsh II 84-85.

BRUNKER, CHRISTINE; Pennsbury HS; Fairless Hills, PA; (Y); 81/712; DECA; Hon Roll; NHS; Tech Schl Gld Pin Awd 85-86; Pres Acad Ftnss Awd 85-86; Bucks Cnty CC; Adv.

BRUNNER, BJOERN; William Allen HS; Allentown, PA; (Y); 63/638; Boy Scts; Band; Concert Band; Mrchg Band; JV Wrstlng; Hon Roll; Jr NHS; NHS; Case Wstrn Resrv U; Mech Engr.

BRUNNER, DOUG; St Marys Area HS; Saint Marys, PA; (Y); Boys Clb Am; Bsbl; Bsktbl; Var L Tennis; Hon Roll; NHS.

BRUNNER, JEFF; Boyertown HS; Gilbertsvl, PA; (Y); 79/471; Hon Roll; RETS; Elecrncs.

BRUNO, BERNARD A; Crestwood HS; Mountaintop, PA; (Y); Art Clb; Band; Concert Band; Mrchg Band; School Musical; Hon Roll; Schlstc Art Achvt Awd 85-86; Full Schlrshp PA Art Wrkshp 86; Semi Fnlst PA Gov Schl Arts 85; Kutztown U; Commnctn Desgn.

BRUNO, BRAD; Norwin HS; N Huntingdon, PA; (Y); Church Yth Grp; Dance Clb; DECA; Pep Clb; SADD; Var L Bsktbl; JV Ftbl; Var L Trk; DECCA Mrktg Awd 85; Three Rvrs Dnc Rcgntn Tp 20 84; Soph Hgh Jmp Schl Rcd 85; Bus Mngmnt.

BRUNO, GINA; General Mc Lane HS; Edinboro, PA; (Y); 16/220; German Clb; Girl Scts; Jazz Band; Mrchg Band; Symp Band; Trs Jr Cls; Rep Stu Cncl; Var JV Sftbl; NHS; SUNY; Envrnmntl Bio.

BRUNO, JOSEPH; Wyoming Area SR HS; Exeter, PA; (Y); Boy Scts; Key Clb; Trs Band; Trs Mrchg Band; Stu Cncl; High Hon Roll; Hon Roll; NHS; Indvdl Edctv Pgm 82-87; Biochmstry.

BRUNO, LORRAINE; St Huberts HS; Philadelphia, PA; (Y); 73/367; Cmnty Wkr; Hosp Aide; Office Aide; Pep Clb; Orch; School Musical; Stage Crew; Variety Show; Yrbk Stf; Gym; Northeastrn Hosp Nrs Schl; Nrs.

BRUNO, MARIA; Bishop Kenrick HS; Norristown, PA; (Y); 5/270; French Clb; Science Clb; Service Clb; Yrbk Ed-Chief; Hon Roll; NHS; Sci Slvr Mdl, Yrbk Gld Mdl 86; Villanova U; Bio.

BRUNO, MARK; Union Area HS; Edinbura, PA; (Y); Art Clb; Church Yth Grp; French Clb; Pep Clb; Var L Bsbl; Var L Ftbl; Hon Roll; Indvdl Ed Prog Gftd Stu 83-85; Slippery Rock U; Bio.

BRUNO, MICHELLE; Bethlehem Center. HS; Brownsville, PA; (Y); 27/150; Church Yth Grp; French Clb; Diving; Hon Roll; Bus.

BRUNO, ROBERT S; Bethel Park SR HS; Pittsburgh, PA; (Y); 82/515; Aud/Vis; Camera Clb; Computer Clb; Exploring; French Clb; Intnl Clb; Model UN; Q&S; Radio Clb; Science Clb; Penn ST.

BRUNSELL, TRACY; Mount Alvernia HS; Pittsburgh, PA; (Y); Church Yth Grp; Drama Clb; Hosp Aide; Pep Clb; Sec Trs Red Cross Aide; Ski Clb; Lit Mag; Sec Jr Cls; Sec Sr Cls; Var Capt Bsktbl; Bus Hnr Soc-Sec; Bus Admin.

BRUSER, AVEN; The Academy Of The New Church; Pineville, LA; (Y); Church Yth Grp; Cmnty Wkr; Pres Stu Cncl; Grntd Schlrshp Trvl Frnc Hmstay Prog 85; Pltcl Sci.

BRUSH, LINDA; Crestwood HS; Mountaintop, PA; (Y); 3/223; Math Clb; Bausch & Lomb Sci Awd; High Hon Roll; NHS; NEDT Awd; Prfct Atten Awd; Philadelphia Coll; Phrmcy.

BRUSSOCK, MARIA; Bishop O Reilly HS; Edwardsville, PA; (Y); 5/106; Pres FBLA; Math Clb; Chorus; Pom Pon; French Hon Soc; Hon Roll; Pres NHS; NEDT Awd; French Clb; Yrbk Stf; PA JR Acad 1st Awd Regnl & ST 82-86; FBLA Regnl Conf 2nd Awd Typng & 5th Pblc Spkng 85-86; E Stroudsburg U; Math.

BRUTOUT, LISA; Beaver Valley Christian Acad; Freedom, PA; (Y); Art Clb; Chess Clb; Debate Tm; Drama Clb; Letterman Clb; Spanish Clb; Chorus; School Play; Nwsp Rptr; Nwsp Stf; Sci & Bio Awd 84.

BRUTTO, LORI ANN; Cardinal Brennan HS; Frackville, PA; (Y); 6/48; German Clb; Sec Trs Science Clb; Chorus; VP Concert Band; VP Mrchg Band; Var L Socr; High Hon Roll; Trs NHS; Schuylkill Cnty Feml Schlr Athl 85-86; Philadelphia Coll Pharm & Sci.

BRYAN, BARRY; Conrad Weiser HS; Robesonia, PA; (Y); 42/182; Boy Scts; Church Yth Grp; JCL; Key Clb; Im Bowling; Cit Awd; Hon Roll; US Navy; Marine Bio.

BRYAN, DANA; Council Rock HS; Richboro, PA; (Y); Key Clb; Flight Attendnt.

BRYAN, DEAN; Ford City HS; Mc Crann, PA; (Y); 40/150; SADD; School Musical; IN U Of PA; Jrnlsm.

BRYAN, FEDDOCK; Crestwood HS; Mountaintop, PA; (Y); #74 In Class; Boy Scts; Cmnty Wkr; Ski Clb; SADD; Band; Concert Band; Mrchg Band; Pep Band; Yrbk Phtg; Yrbk Sprt Ed; Plc Frc.

BRYAN, MICHAEL; Elizabeth Area HS; Elizabethtown, PA; (Y); Ski Clb; FCA; Socr; Wrstlng; &A ST; Engrg.

BRYAN, NICOLLE; James M Coughlin HS; Wilkes Barre, PA; (Y); 20/352; FBLA; VICA; Drill Tm; Orch; JV Var Sftbl; High Hon Roll; Hon Roll; Jr NHS; NHS; Prfct Atten Awd; Outstndg Vo-Tech Stu Awd 86; Dstrct 9 Orchstr 83; Schlstc C Awd 86; L C C C ; Data Entry Oper.

BRYAN, PATRICK; John S Fine HS; Nanticoke, PA; (Y); Key Clb; Letterman Clb; Model UN; Nwsp Stf; Bsbl; Bsktbl; Var L Crs Cntry; Var Trk; Hon Roll; NHS; Sci.

BRYAN, SCOTT; Avonworth HS; Pittsbg, PA; (Y); JCL; Lit Mag; Bsbl; High Hon Roll; Hon Roll; NHS; Avonworth HS Schlr-Athlete Cert 85-86; Vrsty Bsbl Let 85-86; Librl Arts.

BRYAN, TODD; Waynesboro HS; Waynesboro, PA; (Y); Aud/Vis; Ski Clb; Numerous Horse Chmpshps & Mdls 84-86; Hrse Mgt.

BRYANT, LESLEY; Manheim Central SR HS; Lititz, PA; (Y); #87 In Class; Chorus; Rep Soph Cls; Rep Jr Cls; Trs Sr Cls; Rep Stu Cncl; JV Cheerleading; Capt Fld Hcky; Powder Puff Ftbl; Sftbl; Hon Roll; 4-Way Tst Awd 86; Outstndg Dfnsv Plyr Awd Hcky 86; Elizabethtown Coll; Bus Mgt.

BRYANT, RICHANN; Bethel Park HS; Bethel Pk, PA; (Y); Church Yth Grp; Exploring; French Clb; FHA; Intnl Clb; School Musical; Tennis.

BRYCE, TROY; Annville-Cleona HS; Lebanon, PA; (S); 17/121; German Clb; Varsity Clb; Chorus; Trs Soph Cls; Trs Jr Cls; Trs Sr Cls; Stu Cncl; Var Ftbl; Var Wrstlng; Stu Cncl Awd 84; Shippensburg U; Acctg.

BRYER, DONNA; Unionville HS; Kennett Sq, PA; (Y); 135/300; VP Church Yth Grp; Intnl Clb; Chorus; Church Choir; Mrchg Band; School Musical; Twrlr; Girl Scts; Hon Roll; God And Comm; Silvr And Gold Ldrshp; Silvr And Gold Awd; Med.

BRYLA, ERIC; Lakeland HS; Olphant, PA; (S); 10/167; Chess Clb; Science Clb; Golf; NHS; Engrg.

BRYNER, BILL; Beaver Area HS; Beaver, PA; (Y); 2/200; German Clb; JCL; Key Clb; Letterman Clb; L Var Socr; Var L Swmmng; High Hon Roll; Hon Roll; NHS; Sal; Acdmc Achvmnt Awd 83-86; Carnegie-Mellon U; Engrng.

BRYNER, KELLY; Juniata HS; Mifflin, PA; (Y); Drama Clb; French Clb; Chorus; Mrchg Band; School Play; Yrbk Stf; Var JV Cheerleading; Twrlr; Hon Roll; NHS; Schlastc J Awd 85-86; Tri-M 86; Bus Admn.

BRYNER JR, MILT; Bentworth HS; Eightyfour, PA; (Y); Hon Roll; Schlrshp Awd 84 & 86; Military; Electrncs.

BRYNER, SARAH J; Washington HS; Washington, PA; (S); French Clb; Key Clb; Letterman Clb; Library Aide; Pres SADD; Band; Nwsp Phtg; Nwsp Sprt Ed; JV Var Cheerleading; Var Tennis; Psych.

BRYSON, KIRBY; Laurel Valley HS; New Florence, PA; (Y); 4/87; Office Aide; SADD; Varsity Clb; Chorus; Stu Cncl; L Bsbl; L Bsktbl; Stat Ftbl; Hon Roll; NHS; Natl Phys Ed Awd 84-85; Pitt; Phys Thrpy.

BRYSON, PATRICK; Mc Guffey HS; Washington, PA; (Y); 22/219; VP Trs French Clb; Pep Clb; Ski Clb; Varsity Clb; Var L Trk; Hon Roll; Stu Recognition 83-84; Arch.

BRZENCHEK, DAVID; Coughlin HS; Wilkes-Barre, PA; (Y); 3/381; Math Tm; Capt Bsktbl; Capt Ftbl; Wt Lftg; High Hon Roll; NHS; PA ST; Aero Engrg.

BUBASH, CHRIS; Moon SR HS; Coraopolis, PA; (Y); Aud/Vis; Boy Scts; Exploring; Spanish Clb; Band; Mrchg Band; Symp Band; High Hon Roll; Hon Roll; NHS; ROTC; Elec-Comp Engrng.

BUBB, CHARLENE; West Snyder HS; Mcclure, PA; (Y); Am Leg Aux Girls St; Dance Clb; FBLA; Letterman Clb; Varsity Clb; Drill Tm; Nwsp Stf; Yrbk Stf; Stu Cncl; Cheerleading; HOBY Smnr 85.

BUBB, KARI; Lewistown Area HS; Lewistown, PA; (Y); 52/256; Sec Church Yth Grp; 4-H; French Clb; Girl Scts; Chorus; Church Choir; Capt Mrchg Band; Rep Jr Cls; Rep Sr Cls; Hon Roll; Lou Henry Hoover Girl Scout Schlrshp 86; Mim Reynolds Mem Beta Sigma Phi Schlrshp 86; Slvr Awd 85; Temple U; Horticulture.

BUBB, MARCEY; Lincoln HS; Ellwood City, PA; (Y); 31/171; Church Yth Grp; Ski Clb; Spanish Clb; Y-Teens; Chorus; Flag Corp; Mrchg Band; School Musical; Bowling; Coach Actv; Air Force.

BUBB, TOBIN; Chief Logan HS; Lewistown, PA; (Y); Church Yth Grp; Computer Clb; Exploring; FCA; Office Aide; Church Choir; Hon Roll; Electrncs.

BUBE, FRED; Conrad Weiser HS; Robesonia, PA; (Y); 15/184; Computer Clb; Pres 4-H; JCL; Band; Chorus; School Musical; Var Ftbl; Var Wrstlng; Hon Roll; NHS; Engrng.

BUCCI, KAREN; Emmaus HS; Wescosville, PA; (Y); Art Clb; Drama Clb; Key Clb; Chorus; School Musical; School Play; Var L Trk; High Hon Roll; Hon Roll; Jr NHS; Sterring Comm 85-86; PA Gov Schl Theater SF 85-86.

BUCCI, LORI; Blacklick Valley JR SR HS; Belsano, PA; (Y); Trs Church Yth Grp; 4-H; Girl Scts; Ski Clb; Speech Tm; Varsity Clb; School Play; Var Cheerleading; U Of Pitts; Nrsng.

BUCENELL, CAROLYN; Center HS; Monaca, PA; (Y); 22/186; Latin Clb; Band; Chorus; Concert Band; Jazz Band; Pep Band; School Musical; Hon Roll; JP Sousa Awd; NHS; Outstndng Band 83-85; Hnr Bands 83-86; WVU; Music Perfrmnce.

BUCHA, ANNE; Upper Merion HS; Bridgeport, PA; (Y); 38/330; Red Cross Aide; Chorus; Stu Cncl; Socr; Swmmng; Tennis; Hon Roll; Nrsng.

BUCHANAN, BETH; Grove City Area HS; Grove City, PA; (Y); Pres Church Yth Grp; FBLA; Key Clb; Band; Church Choir; Concert Band; Mrchg Band; Pep Band; Bsktbl; Hon Roll; Wrk Couple Nights Wk Jo Ann Fabrics 85; Slippery Rock U; Elem Tchr.

BUCHANAN, CHRISTIE; Coudersport JR SR HS; Coudersport, PA; (Y); 1/87; Varsity Clb; Band; Chorus; School Play; Var L Bsktbl; L Trk; Var L Vllybl; High Hon Roll; NHS; Ntl Merit Ltr; Awd Outstndng Achvt Chem 86; Bskbt Awd Bst Defns & Acadmc Avrg 86; 1st Rnnr Up Hugh Obrien Yth Awd 85.

BUCHANAN, ERIN; Scranton Central HS; Scranton, PA; (Y); 4-H; French Clb; FTA; JA; Office Aide; Red Cross Aide; Chorus; Rep Frsh Cls; Rep Soph Cls; U Scranton; Pre-Law.

BUCHANAN, JENNIFER L; Churchill HS; Pittsburgh, PA; (Y); 6/219; German Clb; Acpl Chr; Madrigals; Orch; School Musical; School Play; Sec Stu Cncl; High Hon Roll; Ntl Merit SF; AFS; PMEA All ST Orch, Wrld Affrs Isnt Pgh 85; Chrch Organ Schlrshp 83; Grove City Coll; Music.

BUCHANAN, SUSAN; Donegal HS; Marietta, PA; (Y); 27/157; VP Church Yth Grp; Pep Clb; Church Choir; Var Tennis; Hon Roll; Acadmc All Amer 86; IN U Of PA; Intr Dsgn.

BUCHANICH, BRIAN; Deer Lakes JR SR HS; Russellton, PA; (Y); 48/210; Varsity Clb; Capt L Bsbl; L Bsktbl; Hon Roll; Kent ST U; Arch.

BUCHANICO, ANGELA; Saint Maria Goretti HS; Philadelphia, PA; (S); 5/445; Art Clb; Mathletes; Model UN; Nwsp Stf; Rptr Yrbk Stf; Rep Soph Cls; High Hon Roll; NHS; 4 Separate Schlrshp To Moore Coll Of Art 85-86; VP Of Wrld Affrs Cncl 85-86; Grphc Dsgn.

BUCHER, ELIZABETH; Lampeter Strasburg HS; Lancaster, PA; (Y); 22/139; Varsity Clb; Chorus; Nwsp Rptr; Mgr Var Ftbl; Var Capt Trk; Var Mgr Wrstlng; Hon Roll; NHS; Schlstc Art Awd 83-84; 4th Pl Cnty Trck Meet In Shot Put 86; PA ST U; Jrnlsm.

BUCHER, GREG; Warwick HS; Lititz, PA; (Y); Browrstown Voc Tech Schl Stu Cncl Pres 85-86; Voc Ind Clbs Of Am 85-86; PA Voc Ind Clbs ST Wnnr; Graphic Communications.

BUCHER, JENNIFER; St Cyril Acad; Milton, PA; (Y); Exploring; Hosp Aide; Teachers Aide; Varsity Clb; Nwsp Stf; Rep Jr Cls; Hst Stu Cncl; Bsktbl; Capt Cheerleading; Hon Roll; Candy Stripg Awd 83; Stu Cncl Awd 84; Piano Guild Fndrs Mdl 86; Nrsg.

BUCHER, LLOYD; Council Rock HS; Richboro, PA; (Y); Hofstra U; Sci.

BUCHER, STEFANIE; Annville Cleona HS; Cleona, PA; (S); 15/110; Aud/Vis; SADD; Chorus; Im JV Bsktbl; JV Var Fld Hcky; Jr NHS; NHS; Prfct Atten Awd.

BUCHHOLZ, MICHELE; Cardinal O Hara HS; Aston, PA; (Y); 209/772; Church Yth Grp; Service Clb; Stage Crew; 1st Pl Celaware Cnty Sci Fair 84; Lehigh U; Math.

BUCHIGNANI, ELIZABETH; Faith Community Christian HS; Pittsburgh, PA; (S); 6/30; Camera Clb; Hosp Aide; Pep Clb; Red Cross Aide; Spanish Clb; Teachers Aide; Y-Teens; High Hon Roll; NHS; Good Condust Awd 85; Bradford Bus Schl; Fash Merch.

BUCHINO, VINCE; Avonworth SR HS; Pittsbg, PA; (Y); Aud/Vis; Chess Clb; Nwsp Rptr; Nwsp Stf; Im Fld Hcky; Im Ftbl; Im Sftbl; Hon Roll; Prfct Atten Awd; Duquesne U Schltc Press Assn 86; PA ST Pittsburgh; Bus Adm.

BUCHKO, MELISSA K; Academy SR HS; Erie, PA; (Y); 2/213; Church Yth Grp; Girl Scts; Chorus; Church Choir; School Play; Nwsp Stf; Yrbk Stf; Var Capt Vllybl; High Hon Roll; NHS; Point Loma Nazarene Coll; Comm.

BUCHLER, ROBERT H; Neshaminy HS; Trevose, PA; (Y); 18/730; Yrbk Stf; JV Var Socr; High Hon Roll; Hon Roll; Chmcl Engrng.

BUCHLMAYER, AMY; Canevin HS; Mckees Rocks, PA; (Y); 45/176; FBLA; Hon Roll; Rbrt Morris Coll; Bus Mngmnt.

BUCHMAN, ANDREW; Westmont Hilltop HS; Johnstown, PA; (Y); 1/130; Art Clb; NFL; Speech Tm; Temple Yth Grp; High Hon Roll; NHS; Ntl Merit Ltr; Pre-Med.

BUCHTA, DAWN; Conrad Weiser HS; Sinking Spg, PA; (Y); Cmnty Wkr; VP FNA; German Clb; Hosp Aide; Red Cross Aide; Tennis; Hon Roll; Nrsng.

BUCHTER, CINDY; Ephrata SR HS; Ephrata, PA; (Y); Camera Clb; Var JV Sftbl; Hon Roll; All Star Conestoga Vly Lg Sftbl 85; Engrng.

BUCHTER, TINA; Governor Mifflin HS; Mohnton, PA; (Y); FBLA; JA; Library Aide; Stage Crew; Hon Roll; FL Inst Of Tech; Bio Ocngrphy.

BUCK, ANGELA; Clfd Area HS; Woodlands, PA; (Y); 17/315; Trs FBLA; Spanish Clb; Mat Maids; High Hon Roll; Hon Roll; NHS; Bus.

BUCK, BARBARA; Grove City Area HS; Grove City, PA; (Y); 10/195; French Clb; Math Clb; Speech Tm; Nwsp Rptr; Var Cheerleading; Powder Puff Ftbl; High Hon Roll; NHS; Ntl Sci Merit Awd 84; Acdmc All Amer 84; Math.

BUCK, JILL; Danville SR HS; Danville, PA; (Y); Exploring; Latin Clb; Rep Frsh Cls; Var L Bsktbl; Var L Sftbl; High Hon Roll; Hon Roll; Dnvl Cls 43 Schlrshp 86; Williamsport; Xry Tech.

BUCK, KELIN; Cocalico HS; Stevens, PA; (Y); Art Clb; Church Yth Grp; GAA; Stu Cncl; Var Cheerleading; Sftbl; Hon Roll.

BUCK, MELANIE; Susquehanna Comm HS; Starrucca, PA; (Y); Ski Clb; Band; Concert Band; Mrchg Band; Powder Puff Ftbl; Sftbl; Vllybl; Math Fld.

BUCK, SHERRY; Curwensville Area HS; Curwensville, PA; (Y); Hst FBLA; Hon Roll; Acad All Amer 84-86; Acctg.

BUCK, TERRI; Central Bucks HS West; New Britain, PA; (Y); 2/483; Hosp Aide; Chorus; Concert Band; Rep Soph Cls; Rep Jr Cls; Rep Stu Cncl; Fld Hcky; Sftbl; NHS; Phy Thrpy.

BUCKALEW, NEILLY ANN; North Allegheny SR HS; Wexford, PA; (Y); Art Clb; Church Yth Grp; Exploring; French Clb; Ski Clb; Chorus; Off Soph Cls; Off Jr Cls; Powder Puff Ftbl; Hon Roll; Pres Ftns Awd 84-85; Pre-Med.

BUCKEL, JEFFREY A; Northgate JR SR HS; Pittsburgh, PA; (Y); 70/135; Aud/Vis; Church Yth Grp; Varsity Clb; Band; Ftbl; Wt Lftg; Hon Roll; Marines; Law Enfrcmnt.

BUCKENMYER, FREDERICK; Saucon Valley HS; Bethlehem, PA; (Y); German Clb; Band; Chorus; Concert Band; Mrchg Band; Stu Cncl; Bsbl; Bsktbl; Ftbl; Wt Lftg; Bus Adm.

BUCKHOLT, DAN; Langley HS; Pittsburgh, PA; (Y); Var L Ftbl; Hon Roll; NHS; Bus.

BUCKINGHAM, CHRISTOPHER; William Penn SR HS; York, PA; (Y); 39/303; JA; Ski Clb; Stage Crew; Yrbk Phtg; Yrbk Stf; Hon Roll; NHS; Prfct Atten Awd; SADD; Nwsp Phtg; Yrk Cnty Educ Assoc Tchr Memrl Awd 86; PTSA Awd 86; Penn ST; Bio.

BUCKINGHAM, ERIC; Bentwood SR HS; Scenery Hill, PA; (Y); 32/103; Chess Clb; 4-H; Band; Concert Band; Jazz Band; Mrchg Band; 4-H Awd; Hon Roll; Penn ST; Ag Mech.

BUCKLES, ANGELLA; Downingtown SR HS; Downingtown, PA; (S); 8/527; VP Pres Church Yth Grp; German Clb; VP Library Aide; Service Clb; Teachers Aide; Chorus; Rep Stu Cncl; High Hon Roll; NHS; NEDT Awd; Excllnt Grmn Awd; 3 Yr Distngshd Hnr Roll; Hofstra U; Intl Bus.

BUCKLEY, JAMES; Danville HS; Danville, PA; (Y); 16/204; Boy Scts; Drama Clb; French Clb; School Musical; School Play; JV Ftbl; Hon Roll; NHS.

BUCKLEY, SARA; Blue Mountain Acad; Fort Salonga, NY; (S); 4/63; Office Aide; Teachers Aide; Chorus; Church Choir; School Play; Yrbk Stf; Trs Sr Cls; High Hon Roll; Prfct Atten Awd; Clmbia Union Coll; Engl.

BUCKLEY, SHERRI; Clearfield Area HS; Clearfield, PA; (Y); 4/298; FBLA; Office Aide; Flag Corp; Mrchg Band; School Musical; Mat Maids; L Var Trk; Cit Awd; High Hon Roll; NHS; Top 10 Grad SR 86; Secyl Awd Hgh Achvt Prsntd By PSI 86; Bkkpng Awd For High Achvt 86; ICM Schl Bus Ptsbrg; Secy Sci.

BUCKLEY, TAMMY; Southern Huntingdon C HS; Cassville, PA; (Y); Computer Clb; Sec FHA; Library Aide; Powder Puff Ftbl; JV Sftbl; Hon Roll; Sectrl Stds.

BUCKNER, ADRIENNE; Wilkinsburg JR SR HS; Pittsburgh, PA; (Y); 2/10; Spanish Clb; Speech Tm; Band; Mrchg Band; Cheerleading; Hon Roll; NHS; Bankng Finance.

BUCYNSKI, KIRK; Huntingdon Area HS; Huntingdon, PA; (Y); 12/224; Var L Bsbl; JV Var Bsktbl; Hon Roll; NHS; Engrng.

BUCZKOWSKI, FRANK; Shaler Area SR HS; Glenshaw, PA; (Y); 140/542; Church Yth Grp; JA; Rep Sr Cls; Im Bsbl; JV Bsktbl; Var Ftbl; Var Trk; Im Vllybl; Im Wt Lftg; Rotary Awd; Volntr Fireman Elfiwild Co 86; Penn ST; Accntng.

BUCZYNSKI, LEON; North East HS; North East, PA; (Y); 45/149; Bowling; Hon Roll; Hnr Grad 86; IN U Of PA; Comm.

BUDACKI, STEPHANIE; New Brighton Area SR HS; New Brighton, PA; (Y); 14/150; Computer Clb; GAA; Concert Band; Yrbk Stf; Sec Soph Cls; Pres Jr Cls; Trs Sr Cls; Rep Stu Cncl; High Hon Roll; Westminster Coll Hnrs Band 84; Stu Wk 84; Stu Forum VP 86; Geneva Coll; Mrktng.

BUDAI, PAM; Union Area Middle HS; New Castle, PA; (Y); Sec Church Yth Grp; Pep Clb; Band; Drill Tm; Yrbk Stf; Trs Sr Cls; Trs Stu Cncl; Capt Cheerleading; Score Keeper; French Clb; Prtcpt Ms TEEN Wstrn PA 86; Bus.

BUDAY, GRETCHEN; Villa Maria HS; Poland, OH; (Y); Spanish Clb; Chorus; Church Choir; School Musical; Rep Stu Cncl; NHS; Nat Fdrtn Music Clbs 84-86; Schl Pnst 84-86; Chrch Orgnst 84-86; YSU Dana Schl Music; Piano.

BUDGE, JERRY; Freeland HS; Freeland, PA; (Y); 24/93; Church Yth Grp; Scholastic Bowl; Spanish Clb; Band; Concert Band; Rep Stu Cncl; L Tennis; Cit Awd; Elks Awd; Ntl Merit Ltr; Westchester U; Frnsc Med.

BUDGE, KELLIE; St Basil Acad; Philadelphia, PA; (S); 1/97; English Clb; Latin Clb; Math Tm; Science Clb; Thesps; Orch; High Hon Roll; Elem Ed.

BUDIHAS, SCOTT; William Allen HS; Allentown, PA; (Y); Exploring; Rep Frsh Cls; Rep Jr Cls; Var Crs Cntry; Var Trk; Hon Roll; Jr NHS; NHS; Johns Hopkins U; Pathlgst.

BUDIN, ERIC M; Lower Merion HS; Wynnewood, PA; (Y); Chess Clb; Debate Tm; Math Tm; Speech Tm; SADD; Nwsp Bus Mgr; Nwsp Ed-Chief; Nwsp Rptr; Stu Cncl; High Hon Roll.

BUDMAN, JEANNIE; Montgomery HS; Allenwood, PA; (Y); 4/28; Yrbk Stf; Cit Awd; Hon Roll; NHS; Svc Awd 86; Mst Outstndng Bus Stu & $50 Awd 86; Shrthn Gregg Awd 60, 70, 80 WPM 85-86.

BUDOSH, DANIEL; Kiski Area HS; Hyde Park, PA; (Y); Cmnty Wkr; Pep Clb; SADD; Band; Nwsp Ed-Chief; Yrbk Stf; Rep Frsh Cls; Rep Soph Cls; Rep Stu Cncl; Hon Roll; Ltr Of Aprctn From Slvtn Army 84; Bus Adm.

BUDWSKY, SHARON; Canon Mc Millan SR HS; Canonsburg, PA; (Y); English Clb; German Clb; Office Aide; Teachers Aide; JV Sftbl; High Hon Roll; Hon Roll; NCTE Awd; Carlow Coll Pittsburgh; Reg Nrs.

BUEHLER, CHRISTINE M; Cedar Crest HS; Lebanon, PA; (Y); SADD; Pres Frsh Cls; Pres Soph Cls; Pres Jr Cls; Pres Sr Cls; French Clb; Key Clb; Letterman Clb; Pep Clb; Cheerleading; Crmnl Law.

BUEHLER, KELLY; New Hope Solebury HS; New Hope, PA; (S); 3/70; Art Clb; FBLA; Mathletes; Drill Tm; Sec Frsh Cls; Sec Soph Cls; Capt Var Bsktbl; Var Crs Cntry; Var Fld Hcky; Socr; Spnsh I, II & III Awds 83-85; Bsktbl Tm MVP & 1st Tm All-Leag 83-84; 1st Tm All Leag Fld Hcky 85; Econ.

BUEK, SUZANNE; Marple Newtown SR HS; Newtown Square, PA; (Y); Ski Clb; Yrbk Sprt Ed; Off Jr Cls; Off Sr Cls; Stu Cncl; Stat Mgr(s); Var Trk; Hon Roll; Prfct Atten Awd; Psyc.

BUELL, MARLIA; Saltsburg JR SR HS; Saltsburg, PA; (Y); Varsity Clb; Nwsp Stf; Yrbk Stf; Stu Cncl; Var Cheerleading; High Hon Roll; Hon Roll; Ski Clb; SADD; Chorus.

BUENTE, LISA; Unionville HS; Chadds Ford, PA; (Y); 176/300; Camera Clb; Cmnty Wkr; GAA; Hosp Aide; Varsity Clb; Bsktbl; Fld Hcky; Lcrss; Hon Roll.

BUERK, DIANE; Sheffield JR SR HS; Sheffield, PA; (Y); FBLA; Letterman Clb; Library Aide; Color Guard; Nwsp Stf; Sftbl; Sec.

BUERKE, BETSY A; Bishop Conwell HS; Yardley, PA; (Y); 9/254; Drama Clb; Trs Science Clb; Spanish Clb; Symp Band; Yrbk Rptr; Yrbk Stf; Vllybl; High Hon Roll; Jr NHS; NEDT Awd; $1000 Alumni Schlrshp-Trntn St Coll 86; Bdnc Rep 86; Trenton ST Coll; Chem.

BUERKLE, JODI; Warren Area HS; Warren, PA; (Y); Spanish Clb; Varsity Clb; Band; Concert Band; Mrchg Band; Yrbk Stf; Bsktbl; Var Capt Sftbl; Hon Roll; Jr NHS; Penn ST Behrend.

BUERMANN, AMY; Council Rock HS; Newtown, PA; (Y); 290/845; Nwsp Rptr; Nwsp Stf; Cmnctns.

BUETIKOFER, ED; Fort Le Boeuf HS; Erie, PA; (Y); 17/184; Chorus; School Musical; Hon Roll; Edinboro U.

BUFALINI, CAROL; Ambridge Area HS; Ambridge, PA; (Y); German Clb; Girl Scts; Pep Clb; Band; Rep Frsh Cls; Rep Soph Cls; Rep Jr Cls; Var L Bsktbl; Var Trk; Var L Vllybl; Medl Vlybl Wnng WPIAL 85; Ltr Vllybl & Bsktbl 83-85; Secdry Tchg.

BUFALINI, DIANE; Hopewell SR HS; Aliquippa, PA; (Y); Church Yth Grp; Spanish Clb; Band; Chorus; Stu Cncl; Cheerleading; Powder Puff Ftbl; Trk; Hon Roll; Bus.

BUFALINI, DIANNE; Ambridge Area HS; Ambridge, PA; (Y); Church Yth Grp; German Clb; Pep Clb; Spanish Clb; Band; Concert Band; Mrchg Band; Symp Band; Rep Stu Cncl; Hon Roll.

BUFFENMYER, JENNIFER; Palmyra HS; Palmyra, PA; (Y); Church Yth Grp; Drama Clb; French Clb; SADD; Tennis; Hon Roll; Htl Mgmt.

BUFFINGTON, TRAVIS; Waynesboro Area SR HS; Waynesboro, PA; (Y); Chess Clb; JCL; Rep Soph Cls; Trs Jr Cls; JV Crs Cntry; Var Wrstlng; Hon Roll; Mst Imprvd Wrstlr 85-86; Engr.

BUGDA, JAMES; Hazleton HS; Hazleton, PA; (Y); 19/388; Church Yth Grp; French Clb; Scholastic Bowl; Stage Crew; Yrbk Stf; VP Sr Cls; Rep Stu Cncl; L Crs Cntry; L Trk; High Hon Roll; Am Legn Awd 83-84; Kline Essy Cntst 85-86; Membrshp Gtfd Prog 85-86.

BUGDONOVITCH, BARBARA ANN; Wyoming Valley West HS; Pringle, PA; (Y); Chess Clb; Church Yth Grp; Computer Clb; French Clb; Girl Scts; Teachers Aide; Chorus; Stu Cncl; Mgr(s); Cit Awd; Luzerne County CC; Nrsng.

BUGGEY, STEVEN; Homner Center HS; Homer City, PA; (Y); 15/94; Chorus; Jazz Band; School Musical; Nwsp Stf; Yrbk Sprt Ed; Pres Jr Cls; VP Stu Cncl; Var L Ftbl; Var L Trk; NHS; 1st Pl Medal Dist Track; 6th Pl ST 86; Acad Math Awd 85; Hnrbl Ment Ftbl 84; Hlth.

BUI, MATTHEW; Lancaster Catholic HS; Lancaster, PA; (Y); 14/212; Chess Clb; Chorus; Church Choir; School Musical; Swing Chorus; Nwsp Rptr; Yrbk Rptr; Tennis; High Hon Roll; NHS; Immclt Coll Crtv Wrtg Awd 1st Pl 86; US Achvt Acad-Natl Awd Sci 84; US Achvt Acad Natl Awd Math 85; Franklin Coll; Engrng Rsrch.

BUI, NGOC-DIEP T; Bristol JR SR HS; New Haven, CT; (Y); 1/102; Trs Church Yth Grp; Science Clb; Service Clb; Chorus; Var Pres Jr Cls; High Hon Roll; Kiwanis Awd; NHS; Pres Schlr; Val; WPVI Bst Of Clss 86; Soc Wmn Engrs Awd 86; Fndtn Of Excptnl Chldrn Schlrshp 86; Yale U; Bio.

BUJNOWSKI, LISA; Villa Maria Acad; Erie, PA; (Y); 24/137; Hosp Aide; PAVAS; Science Clb; Spanish Clb; Chorus; VP L Cheerleading; Trk; High Hon Roll; Hon Roll; Pres Schlr; Outstndng Stu Scholar 86; Diocesan Stu Scholar 86; IN U PA; Ed.

BUKOWSKI, KIRA; Shenandoah Valley HS; Shenandoah, PA; (Y); Pep Clb; Red Cross Aide; Chorus; Flag Corp; Nwsp Stf; Yrbk Stf; JV Cheerleading; Im Vllybl; Hon Roll; Dance Perfmnc.

BULA, JACQUELYN; Villa Maria Acad; Erie, PA; (Y); Office Aide; Y-Teens; Stu Cncl; Hon Roll.

BULAZO, LAURA; Laurel JR SR HS; New Castle, PA; (Y); 1/104; Varsity Clb; Concert Band; Yrbk Bus Mgr; Var Cheerleading; Bausch & Lomb Sci Awd; High Hon Roll; Lion Awd; NHS; Pres Schlr; Val; Outstndng Sci Stu Awd 86; Caroline Knox Savings Bond 86; Stu Cncl Activities Awd 86; PA ST; Pre-Med.

BULEBOSH, BETH; Bethel Park HS; Pittsburgh, PA; (S); 69/530; DECA; FHA; Office Aide; Nwsp Stf; Yrbk Bus Mgr; Lit Mag; Im Wt Lftg; Hon Roll; Prfct Atten Awd; Pres Acadmc Fit Awd 85-86; 3rd Pl DECA ST Conf, 1st Pl Dist Conf 86; Waynesburg Coll; Engl.

BULER, ROBERT; Spring-Ford HS; Royersford, PA; (Y); 24/236; Schl Dist Hnr Awd 86; Vo Tech SR Hghst Acadmc Avg Francis Awd 86; Pres Fit Awd 86; Mnstr Jehovahs Witnss.

BULL, JENNIFER; Linden Hall HS; Lancaster, PA; (S); Cmnty Wkr; Drama Clb; Model UN; Office Aide; Quiz Bowl; Thesps; School Musical; School Play; Stage Crew; Variety Show; Gov Schl For Arts 85; Schlstc Art Awd & Gold Kys 85-86; May Day Queen 86; RI Sch Dsgn; Photo.

BULLA, THEODORE; Perry Traditional Acad; Pittsburgh, PA; (Y); 2/123; High Hon Roll; NHS; U Of Pittsburgh; Elctrcl Engrng.

BULLARD, MICHELLE; St Maria Goretti HS; Philadelphia, PA; (Y); Art Clb; Aud/Vis; GAA; Teachers Aide; Concert Band; Orch; School Musical; Stage Crew; Hon Roll; Hahnemann U; Physcn Asst.

BULLER, CHRISTINE R; Conestoga Valley HS; Lancaster, PA; (Y); 108/243; Dance Clb; Library Aide; Office Aide; Teachers Aide; Variety Show; Yrbk Phtg; Yrbk Stf; Hon Roll; Accntng.

BULLERI, GENA; Council Rock HS; Richboro, PA; (Y); 55/755; Pres Art Clb; Yrbk Stf; High Hon Roll; Awd Spcl Svc Arts & Crfts Clb 86; Prpl Blt Shoto Kan Karate 86; Drexel U; Comp Sci.

BULLICK, SHARON; West Scranton HS; Scranton, PA; (Y); Spanish Clb; Yrbk Stf; Sec Jr Cls; Sec Sr Cls; Hon Roll; NHS; Pre Med.

BULLOCK, JOSEPH; Tunkhannock Area HS; Tunkhannock, PA; (S); 38/280; Boy Scts; Spanish Clb; Varsity Clb; JV Bsbl; Var L Ftbl; Var Trk; Hon Roll; Mansfield U; Phys Educ.

BUMBACO, CANDY; Mercer HS; Mercer, PA; (Y); Library Aide; JV Bsktbl; Capt Cheerleading; Var Mat Maids; JV Trk; Bus.

BUMP, DONNA; Sayre Area HS; Sayre, PA; (Y); Drama Clb; French Clb; Library Aide; Political Wkr; Science Clb; Mrchg Band; School Play; Bowling; Fld Hcky; Rutgers U; Archlgy.

BUNCE, DENISE L; Seneca HS; Union City, PA; (Y); 19/144; Church Yth Grp; FBLA; Hosp Aide; Office Aide; Pep Clb; Yrbk Stf; High Hon Roll; Hon Roll; Library Aide; Rep Jr Cls; 1st Pl In Acctng II FBLA Sprng Comp 86; Cert Of Schlrshp 86; Robert Morris Coll; Admin Mgmt.

BUNDY, MADELYN MARIE; St Maria Goretti HS; Philadelphia, PA; (Y); Camp Fr Inc; Church Yth Grp; Dance Clb; Office Aide; School Play; Hon Roll; Sftbl; Bsktbl; SADD; Drill Tm; Crim Just.

BUNGARD, MICHAEL; Mt Pleasant Area HS; Mt Pleasant, PA; (Y); Band; Concert Band; Mrchg Band; Stage Crew; Bsktbl; Ftbl; Trk; Vllybl; Hon Roll; Army.

BUNN, KAREN; Greater Johnstown HS; Johnstown, PA; (Y); JA; Spanish Clb; SADD; Capt Color Guard; Rep Jr Cls; Rep Sr Cls; Rep Stu Cncl; Var L Trk; High Hon Roll; NHS; FL Inst Of Tech; Mrn Blgy.

BUNNELL, INA; Lancaster Christian Schl; Lititz, PA; (Y); 4/24; Church Yth Grp; Drama Clb; Yrbk Stf; Trs Soph Cls; Sec Jr Cls; Pres Sr Cls; Hon Roll; Natl Sci Merit Awd 86.

BUNNELL, JENNIFER; Delaware County Christian Schl; Wiumington, DE; (Y); 5/78; Church Yth Grp; Cmnty Wkr; Trs Drama Clb; Pres Acpl Chr; Church Choir; Orch; Nwsp Rptr; Ed Nwsp Stf; High Hon Roll; NHS; Lib Arts.

BUNNEY, RENEE S; Lincoln HS; Ellwood City, PA; (Y); 41/168; Spanish Clb; Y-Teens; Chorus; Trs Soph Cls; Powder Puff Ftbl; High Hon Roll; Hon Roll; Ellwood City Jr Womens Schlrshp, Am Bus Womens Schlrshp, Thos Schlrsdhp Alderson Broaddus Coll 86; Alderson Broaddus; Med Assist.

BUNNEY, RICKY; Lincoln HS; Ellwood City, PA; (Y); 41/167; Trs Drama Clb; Spanish Clb; Tennis; Hon Roll; Painter Scholar 86; Wolves Clb Scholar 86; U Pittsburgh; Engrng.

BUNTIN, BARBARA; Cornell HS; Coraopolis, PA; (Y); 18/57; Drm Mjr(t); French Clb; Hosp Aide; Library Aide; Office Aide; Science Clb; Band; Church Choir; Concert Band; Mrchg Band; Samuel Carson Musc And Band Awd 86; Shadyside Hosp; Ped Nrse.

BUNTING, CHRISTOPHER; Lake Lehman HS; Noxen, PA; (Y); Church Yth Grp; German Clb; Church Choir; Nvlst.

BUNTING, KELLY A; Ridley SR HS; Folsom, PA; (Y); 51/399; Flag Corp; Nwsp Phtg; Yrbk Stf; Lit Mag; Cit Awd; Hon Roll; NHS; Pres Schlr; HS Prmnt Schlrshp 86; Coll Of Txtl 3 Sci; Fash Merch.

BUNTING, THOMAS; Arch Bishop Ryan HS For Boys; Philadelphia, PA; (Y); 19/431; Art Clb; Church Yth Grp; Cmnty Wkr; Computer Clb; German Clb; Science Clb; High Hon Roll; Hon Roll; Prfct Atten Awd; Pres Schlr; Presdntl Acadmc Achvt Awd 86; Villanova U; Bus.

BUONADONNA, STEPHANIE; West Catholic HS; Phila, PA; (Y); 70/245; Office Aide; Hon Roll.

BUONOMO, KELLIE; Sacred Heart HS; Carbondale, PA; (Y); Yrbk Sprt Ed; Stu Cncl; Score Keeper; Var Capt Sftbl; High Hon Roll; NHS; Church Yth Grp; Cmnty Wkr; FBLA; Pres Scholar Marywood Coll 86-87; Incentive Awd; Marywood Coll; Med Tech.

BURAKS, KEVIN; Upper Dublin HS; Maple Glen, PA; (Y); Debate Tm; Yrbk Stf; Stu Cncl; Im Bsktbl; JV Bowling; Var Capt Socr; Hon Roll; NHS; Sci Fr 1st Plc Rgnl Awd, 2nd Plc ST 85; 2nd Plc Awd Mntgmry Cnty Sci Fr 85; Pre-Med.

BURANOSKY, JESSICA; Franklin Area HS; Franklin, PA; (Y); 1/220; French Clb; Ski Clb; Varsity Clb; Chorus; Madrigals; School Musical; Variety Show; Rep Stu Cncl; Bsktbl; Pres NHS.

BURANOSKY, RAQUEL; Franklin HS; Franklin, PA; (Y); 1/220; Dance Clb; Drama Clb; Ski Clb; School Musical; Variety Show; Yrbk Ed-Chief; Pres Frsh Cls; Pres Soph Cls; Pres Jr Cls; Pres Sr Cls; Japan US Sen Schlrshp Alt 85; Georgetown U; Pre-Med.

BURBA, CHRISTINE; Purchase Line HS; Arcadia, PA; (Y); Spanish Clb; SADD; Chorus; Church Choir; Concert Band; Mrchg Band; Sftbl; Hon Roll; NHS.

BURCH, KRISTINA; Newport HS; Newport, PA; (Y); 4/99; Concert Band; Mrchg Band; Yrbk Ed-Chief; Yrbk Phtg; Stu Cncl; NHS; Mdrn Music Mstrs; Penn ST U; Lbrl Arts.

BURCH, LISA; Blacklick Valley HS; Nanty Glo, PA; (Y); 26/96; Art Clb; Camera Clb; Church Yth Grp; Pres 4-H; NFL; Pres Ski Clb; Speech Tm; Varsity Clb; Nwsp Stf; Stu Cncl; JR Miss-Semifnlst 86; Conemaugh Vly Mem Hosp; Nrsng.

BURCH, MELISSA; Archbishop Prendergast HS; Prospect Park, PA; (Y); 18/364; Service Clb; JV VP Crs Cntry; Var Mgr(s); High Hon Roll; Hon Roll; Pres Schlr; DE Cnty Tavern Assoc Schlrp 86; Neumann Coll Grant Schlrp 86; Neumann Coll; Comptrs.

BURCH, WILLIAM; Bellwood-Antis HS; Bellwood, PA; (Y); 5/127; Varsity Clb; School Musical; Stage Crew; Yrbk Stf; Chrmn Jr Cls; L Capt Bsktbl; L Ftbl; L Trk; Hon Roll; NHS; Tall Cedars Schlr/Athlete Awd 85; Denny Campbell Mem Blnkt Awd 86; Ken Lantzy Ftblclsc Gme 86; Carnegie Mellon U; Mgmnt.

BURCHER, ELIZABETH; Harrisburg HS; Harrisburg, PA; (S); 56/486; Var Crs Cntry; Var Tennis; Var Trk; Hon Roll; Fshn Board 84-85; Comm Vo-Tech Schl 85-86; Palmer Bus Schl; Bus.

BURCHETT, NICA; Trinity HS; Washington, PA; (Y); 172/274; VP Church Yth Grp; Girl Scts; Hosp Aide; Key Clb; Library Aide; Pep Clb; Color Guard; Mrchg Band; Med.

BURCHETT, RUSSELL; Union Area HS; New Castle, PA; (Y); 25/69; Church Yth Grp; French Clb; FFA; Band; Concert Band; Mrchg Band; Var Trk.

BURCHIANTI, ASHLEE; Geibel HS; Connellsville, PA; (Y); Church Yth Grp; Pep Clb; Yrbk Stf; Var Vllybl; Drama Clb; Ski Clb; JV Bsktbl; Var Sftbl; Vllybll Schlrshp Coll Msrcrda 86; Coll Misericordia; Occptnl Thrp.

BURD, SCOTT; Brownsville Area HS; Brownsville, PA; (Y); Drama Clb; Service Clb; Ski Clb; Trk; High Hon Roll; Hon Roll; NHS; Prfct Atten Awd; Rds Hnda CR 250 Dirt Bk Dist 5-8 Trphys For 1st & 5th Pl 85; Rds Kwski KX 250 & 125 86; CA U Of PA; Mech Engrng.

BURDA, CAROLYN; Minersville Area HS; Branchdale, PA; (Y); German Clb; Ski Clb; SADD; Color Guard; School Musical; Stage Crew; Bsktbl; Vllybl; Hon Roll.

BURDEN, KIM; E L Meyers HS; Wilkes-Barre, PA; (S); Key Clb; Ski Clb; Chorus; Yrbk Stf; Cheerleading; Fld Hcky; Hon Roll; NHS; Hmcmg Qn 86; Westchester U; Bus.

BURDETT, LAURIE; Pittston Area HS; Pittston, PA; (Y); VP Aud/Vis; Sec Band; Chorus; Sec Concert Band; Sec Mrchg Band; Hon Roll; NHS; NEDT Awd; Dist Band 85-86; Prfct Atten Band 84; Band Dir.

BURDGE, SHANNON; W Snyder HS; Mcclure, PA; (Y); 17/100; Varsity Clb; Pres Frsh Cls; JV Bsbl; Var L Bsktbl; JV Socr; Hon Roll; Jr NHS; Air Trffc Cntrllr.

BURDO, TINA; Archbishop John Carroll HS; King Of Prussia, PA; (Y); 111/212; Cmnty Wkr; Girl Scts; Pep Clb; Service Clb; Spanish Clb; SADD; Stage Crew; Sftbl; Widener Coll; Bus Mngmt.

BURDOSH, DANIEL; Kiski HS; Hyde Park, PA; (Y); Cmnty Wkr; Band; Nwsp Bus Mgr; Nwsp Ed-Chief; Yrbk Stf; Rep Frsh Cls; Rep Soph Cls; Trk; Hon Roll; Rotary Awd; Hyde Park Pblc Lbrry Brd 85; Bus Admin.

BURDYN III, WILLIAM E; Bishop O Hara HS; Dickson City, PA; (S); 12/124; Boy Scts; Church Yth Grp; Exploring; French Clb; Latin Clb; JV Bsbl; Var Wrstlng; High Hon Roll; Hon Roll; NHS; Acdmc All Star In Wrstlng 84; Eagle Scout 85; U Scrntn; Dntstry.

BURFEIND, BONNIE; Emmaus HS; Emmaus, PA; (Y); Key Clb; Spanish Clb; SADD; Off Jr Cls; Im Socr; Hon Roll; JV Lttr In Stud Athltc Trning 85-86; Ithaca Coll; Acctg.

BURGAN, TAMMY; Greater Johnstown HS; Johnstown, PA; (Y); JA; Pep Clb; Spanish Clb; SADD; Y-Teens; Var L Bsktbl; Var L Sftbl; Hon Roll; Allied Art JR Cmnty Art Show 2nd 85; Pres Phys Fit Awd 85-86; Blackburn Coll; Bus Admin.

BURGE, LYNNETTE M; Fort Le Boeuf HS; Waterford, PA; (Y); 82/174; Church Yth Grp; Dance Clb; Girl Scts; Chorus; Flag Corp; School Musical; Gym; Stat Wrstlng; Hon Roll; Outstndng Pgm Ms Amer Coed Pgnt 85; Mdl.

BURGER, CAROL; West Hazleton HS; Sugarloaf, PA; (Y); French Clb; Pep Clb; Ski Clb; SADD; Nwsp Stf; Yrbk Stf; Stu Cncl; Var JV Cheerleading; Hon Roll; Ntl Frnch Cntst 1st Pl 84; Med Lab Rsrch.

BURGER, CHRISTINE; Williamsburg SR HS; Williamsburg, PA; (Y); FBLA; Rep Jr Cls; Rep Stu Cncl; JV Var Bsktbl; Powder Puff Ftbl; Sftbl; Stu Of Week In Soc Studies 84-85; Eastern; Nursing.

BURGER, MARGGIE; West Middlesex HS; W Middlesex, PA; (Y); Church Yth Grp; Spanish Clb; Band; Chorus; Church Choir; Concert Band; Co-Capt Drill Tm; Mrchg Band; Variety Show; Stu Cncl; Slippery Rock; Nrsng.

BURGES, DONDA; Somerset Area SR HS; Somerset, PA; (Y); Sec Trs Church Yth Grp; VP JA; English Clb; Library Aide; Q&S; Church Choir; Concert Band; Mrchg Band; Variety Show; Nwsp Stf; Elem Educ.

BURGESS, CHRIS; Bethel Park SR HS; Bethel Pk, PA; (Y); Pres Church Yth Grp; German Clb; Band; Concert Band; Mrchg Band; Wrstlng; Intl Bus.

BURGESS, DEANNA; Shikellamy HS; Sunbury, PA; (Y); Church Yth Grp; French Clb; SADD; Teachers Aide; Slippery Rock U; Bus Adm.

BURGESS, FLOYD; Central Christian HS; Hyde, PA; (Y); Sec Church Yth Grp; FBLA; Ed Nwsp Stf; Hon Roll; 1st Pl Job Intrvw FBLA Reg 14 85-86; Wrd Prcssng.

BURGESS, JEANINE; St Marys Area HS; St Marys, PA; (Y); 5/297; Church Yth Grp; Hosp Aide; Varsity Clb; Var Capt Cheerleading; Stat Crs Cntry; Var Gym; Var Capt Trk; High Hon Roll; Hon Roll; NHS; Stackpl Corp Merit Awd 86; MVP Gymnstcs 83-86; MVP Trck 86; Coll Of Wm & Mary; Intl Bus.

BURGESS, SHAWNA; Canon-Mc Millan SR HS; Eighty Four, PA; (Y); Bsktbl; Hon Roll; Bus Admn.

BURGHARD, JENNIFER; Tyrone Area HS; Tyrone, PA; (Y); Church Yth Grp; FBLA; GAA; SADD; Varsity Clb; Chorus; Stu Cncl; Bsktbl; Bowling; Powder Puff Ftbl.

BURGIS, DAWN; Marple Newtown SR HS; Broomall, PA; (Y); Cmnty Wkr; Hosp Aide; JA; Penn ST; Rec Thrpy.

BURGOS, NAOMI; Little Flower Catholic HS For Girls; Philadelphia, PA; (Y); 20/480; Camera Clb; Spanish Clb; Orch; Hon Roll; NHS; Prfct Atten Awd; Spn Awd 83-84; 1st & 2nd Hnrs 83-86; Temple U.

BURGUM, STACY; Hempfield HS; Lancaster, PA; (Y); 1/450; Camera Clb; Church Yth Grp; Exploring; Service Clb; Church Choir; Nwsp Stf; Im Powder Puff Ftbl; Im Sftbl; Im Vllybl; High Hon Roll; Wm & Mary Coll; Bus.

BURIANEK, MICHELE; Montour SR HS; Coraopolis, PA; (Y); Math Tm; Pep Clb; Concert Band; Mrchg Band; Rep Jr Cls; Stu Cncl; Powder Puff Ftbl; High Hon Roll; Jr NHS; NHS.

BURICH, LISA; Waynesburg Central HS; Waynesburg, PA; (Y); Camera Clb; French Clb; Office Aide; SADD; Yrbk Phtg; Yrbk Stf; Stu Cncl; Vllybl; Hon Roll; Church Yth Grp; Waynesburg Clg; Pltcl Sci.

BURICK, BRIAN; New Castle SR HS; New Castle, PA; (S); 8/236; AFS; Computer Clb; VP Exploring; Spanish Clb; Speech Tm; SADD; Bowling; Tennis; NHS; Ntl Merit Ltr; News Carrier Yr 85.

BURIG, JODY; Mc Guffey HS; Claysville, PA; (S); 1/210; Trs Am Leg Aux Girls St; VP German Clb; Model UN; Pep Clb; Trs Varsity Clb; Yrbk Stf; Var L Bsktbl; Var L Trk; Ntl Merit Ltr; Rotary Intl Acadmc Achvt Awd 85; Jr Marshall 85; Stdnt Recgntn Awd 83-85.

BURKART, CAROL; Council Rock HS; Newtown, PA; (Y); Hon Roll; Chld Dev.

BURKE, COLEEN MARIE; Cardinal O Hara HS; Springfield, PA; (Y); 53/740; Chrmn Church Yth Grp; Cmnty Wkr; French Clb; Intnl Clb; School Musical; Hon Roll; NHS; Service Clb; Prncpls Awd Acdmc Excllnc 84-86; DE Vly Sci Fair Hon Mntn 84-85; DE Cnty Sci Fair Awd Wnnr 83-85; Villanova U; Mech Engrng.

BURKE, DENISE; Southern Huntingdon Co HS; Three Springs, PA; (Y); Camera Clb; GAA; Spanish Clb; Varsity Clb; Stat Trk; NHS; Acad All Amer 84-86; Sci & Chmstry Awds 85-86; Montgomery CC; Acctnt.

BURKE II, JOHN ALLEN; Ligonier Valley SR HS; Ligonier, PA; (Y); 27/164; AFS; Boy Scts; Church Choir; School Musical; Stage Crew; Symp Band; Golf; Trk; Wt Lftg; Prfct Atten Awd; Eagle Sct 86; NS ST U; Mech Engrng.

BURKE, KATIE; Bishop O Hara HS; Dunmore, PA; (Y); Computer Clb; Drama Clb; Pep Clb; Ski Clb; Nwsp Stf; Yrbk Stf; Off Frsh Cls; Off Soph Cls; Off Jr Cls; Off Sr Cls; Coll PA ST.

BURKE, MARK; Tussey Mountain HS; Saxton, PA; (Y); Drama Clb; Band; Chorus; Church Choir; Concert Band; Jazz Band; Mrchg Band; School Musical; Hon Roll; NHS; Hnr Awd 84; All-Amrcn Hll Of Fm Band Hnrs 85; Amrcn Musical Fndtn Band Hnrs 84; Coll Educ.

BURKE, MICHELE; Marian Catholic HS; Mahanoy City, PA; (Y); 53/115; Church Yth Grp; SADD; Band; Church Choir; Concert Band; Jazz Band; Mrchg Band; Pep Band; School Play; Scool Wrk.

BURKE, PAULA; Wyoming Area HS; W Pittston, PA; (Y); French Clb; Girl Scts; Color Guard; Hon Roll; Medical Technology.

BURKE, RICHARD; St Marys Area HS; Weedville, PA; (Y); Telecomm.

BURKE, RON; Penns Manor HS; Heilwood, PA; (Y); 10/99; Camera Clb; Church Yth Grp; Pres SADD; Band; Chorus; Church Choir; Concert Band; Jazz Band; Mrchg Band; Pep Band; IUP Hnrs Band 84 & 85; Rgnl Band 85-86; ST Band 86; IN U Of PA; Music Ed.

BURKE, RONALD; Bethlehem-Center SR HS; Fredericktown, PA; (Y); Church Yth Grp; Yrbk Ed-Chief; Var L Bsktbl; JV Ftbl; Hon Roll; Prfct Atten Awd; Race Horses.

BURKE, SHEILA; Lakeland HS; Clarks Summit, PA; (Y); Cmnty Wkr; FHA; Var Cheerleading; Var Vllybl; Dance Clb; Pep Clb; Chorus; School Musical; PA ST; Adm Justice.

BURKE, WENDY; Ephrata SR HS; Ephrata, PA; (Y); 46/257; Art Clb; Church Yth Grp; German Clb; Girl Scts; Cheerleading; Fld Hcky; Powder Puff Ftbl; Hon Roll; Red Crss Crtfd Swm Instrctr 82-86; Advncd Life Svng Red Crss 86; Schlstc Art Awd Crtfct Of Mrt 86; Kutztown U; Art Educ.

BURKEEN, MICHAEL; Salisbury HS; Allentown, PA; (Y); Trs Church Yth Grp; Debate Tm; Exploring; Key Clb; Orch; Soph Cls; JV Socr; L Swmmng; L Trk; Lion Awd; Hotel Mgmt.

BURKET, BILLIE; Bellwood-Antis HS; Altoona, PA; (Y); 46/127; Drama Clb; French Clb; FBLA; Girl Scts; Key Clb; SADD; Girl Scout Gld Awd 86; Altoona Schl Cmmrc; Accntng.

BURKET, DIANE; Central HS; Roaring Spg, PA; (Y); 45/189; Church Yth Grp; Swmmng; Funrl Dir.

BURKETT, BETH; Central HS; Williamsburg, PA; (Y); 44/176; Church Yth Grp; Drama Clb; FTA; GAA; VP Speech Tm; Pres SADD; School Musical; Nwsp Stf; Stu Cncl; Stat Vllybl; Messiah Coll; Elem Ed.

BURKETT, RICHARD J; Kiski Area HS; Apollo, PA; (Y); Math Tm; Spanish Clb; Rep Stu Cncl; High Hon Roll; NHS; Engineering.

BURKETT, SUSAN; Portage Area HS; Portage, PA; (S); 6/118; Church Yth Grp; Band; Chorus; Concert Band; Mrchg Band; Var Co-Capt Bsktbl; Im Vllybl; High Hon Roll; NHS; Score Keeper; Cnty Chorus Prtcpnt; Med.

BURKEY, DEBORAH; Altoona Area HS; Altoona, PA; (Y); Drama Clb; Spanish Clb; Chorus; Natl JR Hnr Soc 83-84.

BURKEY, TINA; Hamburg Area HS; Shoemakersville, PA; (Y); 34/150; German Clb; Hon Roll; NHS; Delta Epsilon Phi German Honor Society 85.

BURKHARDT, DEBBIE; North Clarion HS; Lucinda, PA; (Y); #23 In Class; Spanish Clb; Chorus; Stat Bsktbl; Hon Roll; Prfct Atten Awd; Secretarial.

BURKHARDT, DIANE; Northwestern Lehigh JRSR HS; Fogelsville, PA; (Y); 1/165; Debate Tm; Drama Clb; Scholastic Bowl; Chorus; School Musical; School Play; Stage Crew; Nwsp Stf; High Hon Roll; NHS; Mth, Physcs, Engl, Wrld Hstry Acad Awds 86; Fnders Scholar & Deans Scholar 86; Messiah Coll; Mth Ed.

BURKHARDT, IRENE; United HS; Vintondale, PA; (Y); 24/157; Ski Clb; SADD; Teachers Aide; JV Var Bsktbl; Var Sftbl; Var Capt Vllybl; Hon Roll; Im Powder Puff Ftbl; Vrsty Lttrs Sftbl & Vllybl 85-86; IUP; Elem Educ.

BURKHART, JEANNE; Corry Area HS; Corry, PA; (S); 21/215; Frsh Cls; Soph Cls; Trs Jr Cls; Sr Cls; Stu Cncl; Gym; Powder Puff Ftbl; Score Keeper; Wt Lftg; Ntl Merit Ltr; Indiana U Of PA; Acctg.

BURKHART, REBECCA MICHELE; Bishop Guilfoyle HS; Duncansville, PA; (Y); Church Yth Grp; Ski Clb; Sec Pres Spanish Clb; Chorus; Jazz Band; Mrchg Band; Pep Band; Yrbk Stf; Pres Sftbl; NHS; PMEA Dist VI & Rgnl Bnd 84-86; ; Ivp Hnrs Bnd 85-86; Alegheny Hrtlnd Rgnl Bnd 83-86; IVP; Music.

BURKHOLDER, KELLY; Montgomery Area JR SR HS; Muncy, PA; (Y); VP Church Yth Grp; Sec 4-H; Thesps; Chorus; Mrchg Band; Ed Yrbk Phtg; Trs Sr Cls; Pres VP Stu Cncl; 4-H Awd; Hon Roll.

BURKHOLDER, KIRSTEN; Strath Haven HS; Wallingford, PA; (Y); Civic Clb; 4-H; Ski Clb; Band; Nwsp Stf; JV Bsktbl; JV Lcrss; JV Mgr(s); Var Trk; JV Vllybl; Fine Arts Svc Awd 86; Syracuse; Grphc Arts.

BURKS, CARMEN; New Brighton HS; New Brighton, PA; (Y); Band; Nwsp Stf; Yrbk Stf; Trk; Hon Roll; All Amer Awd 85; IFLA Awd 85; USNA Awd 84.

BURLEIGH, JIM; Upper Moreland HS; Willow Gr, PA; (Y); Church Yth Grp; Band; Concert Band; Symp Band; Im Bsbl; Im Bsktbl; Im Sftbl; Im Swmmng; Im Vllybl; Comp Sci.

BURLEY, ALICIA; Franklin HS; Franklin, PA; (Y); Spanish Clb; Hon Roll; Intr Dsgn.

BURLEY, CHRISTIAN; Penns Manor HS; Barnesboro, PA; (Y); 10/102; Var Varsity Clb; Band; Pep Band; Var Ftbl; Hon Roll; Chropractr.

BURNETT, LEE F; Germantown Acad; Jenkintown, PA; (Y); Aud/Vis; Lit Mag; Crs Cntry; Cit Awd; NCTE Awd; Ntl Merit SF; Truesdale Memrl Prize Latin 85; Cum Laude Socty; Teacher Classical Lang.

BURNETT, SHEVONNA; Union Are HS; New Castle, PA; (Y); 12/69; Spanish Clb; Chorus; Concert Band; Mrchg Band; Sec Soph Cls; Sec Jr Cls; Sec Sr Cls; Var L Bsktbl; Var L Trk; NHS; Anti-Drunk Drvng Slogan Contst-1st Pl Wnnr 84; Busnss Admin.

BURNETT, TRACEY; Bishop Shanahan HS; West Chester, PA; (Y); 54/218; Church Yth Grp; Cmnty Wkr; Debate Tm; Drama Clb; Pres VP 4-H; Intnl Clb; Quiz Bowl; Chorus; Yrbk Phtg; 4-H Awd; Hrsmn Of Yr Achvt Awd & Hrs Awd; Lawyer.

BURNETT, WENDY; Pottstown HS; Pottstown, PA; (Y); 48/183; Pres Art Clb; Band; Concert Band; Jazz Band; Mrchg Band; Sec Stage Crew; Stu Cncl; Var Sftbl; Lincoln PTA Schlrshp 86; Peoples Pntng Chc Awd 85; De Vry Inst Of Tech; Elctrncs.

BURNEY, NATHANIEL; Valley Forge Military Acad; Fairfax, VA; (Y); 15/200; Debate Tm; Drama Clb; Model UN; Political Wkr; ROTC; L Concert Band; Yrbk Rptr; Im Sftbl; Hon Roll; Chess Clb; USAFA; Engrng.

BURNLEY, JEFFREY L; Upper Moreland HS; Hatboro, PA; (Y); 83/264; Boy Scts; Band; Church Choir; Concert Band; Drm Mjr(t); Jazz Band; Mrchg Band; Symp Band; Yrbk Phtg; Cit Awd; Union League Ctznshp Awd 86; Yth Ldrshp In Amer Awd 84; Johnson & Wales; Food Svc Mgmt.

BURNLEY, JENNIFER; Pottstown HS; Pottstown, PA; (S); 6/200; Key Clb; Ski Clb; Spanish Clb; Pres Sr Cls; Stu Cncl; Bsktbl; Crs Cntry; Fld Hcky; Trk; High Hon Roll; Cmmnctns.

BURNS, AMY; Northwestern HS; Albion, PA; (Y); 15/135; AFS; Flag Corp; Nwsp Stf; Stu Cncl; Mgr Sftbl; Hon Roll; Natl Forgn Lang Awd Spnsh 86; Prom & Banq Comms 85; Acadmc All Amer 86; Bolivar Intl Schl Aviatn; Pilot.

BURNS, BRYAN DOUGLAS; Danville Area HS; Danville, PA; (Y); 32/202; Church Yth Grp; Sec Computer Clb; Key Clb; Ski Clb; Rep Soph Cls; Var Socr; Var Tennis; Var Wrstlng; High Hon Roll; NHS.

BURNS, CHRISTINA; Brookville Area HS; Brookville, PA; (Y); German Clb; Band; Concert Band; Mrchg Band; Pep Band; School Musical; IN U; Comp Sci.

BURNS, ELLEN E; North Allegheny HS; Pittsburgh, PA; (Y); 5/642; Church Yth Grp; Cmnty Wkr; Trs Exploring; Hosp Aide; JV Socr; High Hon Roll; Hon Roll; Jr NHS; NHS; Ntl Merit Ltr; Awd Excel Bio 86, Spnsh 84; Bio.

BURNS, JAMES; Lakeland JR SR HS; Carbondale, PA; (S); 16/168; Art Clb; Library Aide; Hon Roll; Bus Mgmt.

BURNS, KELLY; South Park HS; Library, PA; (Y); Capt Var Cheerleading; Var Diving.

BURNS, KELLY J; Pocono Mountain HS; Stroudsburg, PA; (Y); 3/278; Am Leg Aux Girls St; Pres Service Clb; Pres Chorus; Pres Church Choir; Drm Mjr(t); Jazz Band; Mrchg Band; School Musical; Swing Chorus; Yrbk Ed-Chief; Outstndng Svc Schl & Cmmnty 84-86; PA ST U; Secndry Ed.

BURNS, LEAH; Northern SR HS; Dillsburg, PA; (Y); 44/209; Church Yth Grp; French Clb; Band; Chorus; Drill Tm; Yrbk Rptr; Yrbk Stf; Fld Hcky; Powder Puff Ftbl; Hon Roll; Radio/Tv Communications.

BURNS, LEE ANNE; Albert Gallatin SR HS; Lake Lynn, PA; (Y); 6/150; Pep Clb; Spanish Clb; Band; Concert Band; Jazz Band; Mrchg Band; Nwsp Stf; High Hon Roll; NHS; Pres Schlr; Miriam S Mccln Awd 86; Rbn Clbnk Mccln Awd 86; Soloist Cncrt Band 86; PA ST U.

BURNS, MAXINE; Abington HS; N Hills, PA; (Y); 122/535; Art Clb; Drama Clb; French Clb; Powder Puff Ftbl; Commrcl Art.

BURNS, ROBERT; Cambridge Springs HS; Conneautville, PA; (Y); 3/112; VP Pres Church Yth Grp; Spanish Clb; Church Choir; Stu Cncl; Hon Roll; NHS; Ntl Merit Ltr; 2nd Pl Stu Art GAM-SAC-MAH Festvl Arts-Pen, Pencil, Ink Catigori 86; Producer.

BURNS, SUSAN; Penn Trafford HS; Irwin, PA; (Y); Hosp Aide; JCL; Latin Clb; VICA; High Hon Roll; Hon Roll; Outstndng Perf Natl Latin Exam Cum Laude 84; RN.

BURNS, TOM; Pennsbury HS; Fairless Hls, PA; (Y); JV L Bsbl; Var L Ftbl; JV L Wrstlng; Hon Roll; Ftbl Schlrshp 86; Politacal Sci.

BURNS, TRACEY; James M Coughlin HS; Wilkes Barre, PA; (Y); Aud/Vis; Church Yth Grp; Drama Clb; Ski Clb; Chrmn SADD; Yrbk Ed-Chief; Pres Jr Cls; Hon Roll; Jr NHS; NHS; Ntl Cncl Yth Ldrshp Awd 86; Law.

BURNS, WILLIAM T; Norristown Area HS; E Norritan, PA; (S); Math Clb; Hnr Rll 85; Acctng.

BURNSTAD, DORIAN; Littlestown HS; Gettysburg, PA; (Y); FBLA; Speech Tm; Varsity Clb; Yrbk Stf; Bsktbl; Golf; Tennis; Trk; Loyola U; Pre Law.

BURNWORTH, DAVID; Turkey Foot HS; Confluence, PA; (Y); Church Yth Grp; Drama Clb; Library Aide; School Play; Yrbk Stf; Pres Soph Cls; Hon Roll; Ntl Merit Ltr; Prfct Atten Awd; VFW Awd; Alderson Broaddus; Lib Arts.

BURR, R WILLIAM; Keystone Oaks HS; Castle Shannon, PA; (Y); 47/286; Church Yth Grp; Variety Show; Nwsp Bus Mgr; Ed Nwsp Ed-Chief; Nwsp Rptr; Nwsp Stf; Off Stu Cncl; JV Bowling; Im Vllybl; Hon Roll; Brdcst Comm.

BURRELL, BETH; Hempfield SR HS; Irwin, PA; (Y); FBLA; Pep Clb; Ski Clb; Cheerleading; Hon Roll; Sectrl.

BURRELL, CHRIS; Mt Pleasant Area HS; Acme, PA; (Y); German Clb; Trs VICA; Heatng Air Cond.

BURRIS, CONNIE; Waynesburg Central HS; Waynesburg, PA; (Y); Church Yth Grp; FHA; Office Aide; PAVAS; Hon Roll; Prfct Atten Awd; Vly Forge Christn Coll; Psych.

BURRIS, JANIE; Bellefonte Area HS; Bellefonte, PA; (Y); 25/237; Sec Church Yth Grp; Dance Clb; Spanish Clb; SADD; Chorus; Church Choir; Co-Capt Drill Tm; Rep Frsh Cls; Rep Soph Cls; Rep Jr Cls; PA ST U; Comm.

BURRIS, TAMMY; Freeport SR HS; Freeport, PA; (Y); FBLA; Mrchg Band; Twrlr; Bradford Schl; Mdcl Secy.

BURSKEY, BARBARA L; Cambria Heights HS; Carrolltown, PA; (Y); Ski Clb; Sec Band; Chorus; Concert Band; Mrchg Band; Yrbk Stf; Trk; High Hon Roll; IN U PA; Mrktng.

BURSTYNOWICZ, LINDA; Mount Alvernia HS; Pittsburgh, PA; (S); 1/55; Hosp Aide; Red Cross Aide; VP Frsh Cls; High Hon Roll; VP NHS; Prfct Atten Awd; Amer Red Cross Cncl Secy 84-85; Scty Dist Amer HS Stus 85; PA JR Acad Sci 84; Wshngton & Jffrsn Coll; Pre-Med.

BURTICK, MARIA; Homer Cente JR SR HS; Aultman, PA; (Y); FBLA; SADD; Chorus; Color Guard; Flag Corp; Yrbk Stf; Hon Roll; IN U Of PA; Elem Ed.

BURTON, DARLENE; Curwensville Area HS; Curwensville, PA; (Y); High Hon Roll; Hon Roll; French Clb; Hosp Aide; Im Socr; Im Vllybl; NHS; Natl Engl Merit Awd 86; Phy Thrpst.

BURTON, KELLY; Northern Lebanon HS; Jonestown, PA; (Y); 25/166; Art Clb; Chorus; Stage Crew; Yrbk Stf; Hon Roll; Spnsh Achvt Awd 85; Vet.

BURTON, LORI; Philipsburg Osceola SR HS; Philipsburg, PA; (Y); 32/250; Ski Clb; Yrbk Sprt Ed; Stat Vllybl; Hon Roll; NHS; Prfct Atten Awd; Ntl Sci Merit Awd 84; Beautician.

BURTON, PETER; Fairview HS; Fairview, PA; (Y); Church Yth Grp; Cmnty Wkr; Office Aide; Ski Clb; Yrbk Stf; Trs Rep Frsh Cls; Trs Soph Cls; Pres Trs Stu Cncl; Ftbl; Golf; Mgr Of Erie Limo Serv 85stl Cncl Pres; Vice Pres Of Stu Forum; Westminister Clg; Bus.

BURWELL, PATRICIA; Harrisburg HS; Harrisburg, PA; (S); 34/386; FBLA; Spanish Clb; Trs Jr Cls; Trs Sr Cls; Hon Roll; NHS; HACC; Comp.

BURY, JOHN; Central SR HS; York, PA; (Y); 5/224; Band; Concert Band; Jazz Band; Mrchg Band; Orch; Symp Band; Var Crs Cntry; High Hon Roll; Hon Roll; NHS; Gettysburg Coll; Ed.

BURYCHKA, HEATHER; Boyertown Area SR HS; Perkiomenville, PA; (Y); 10/455; SADD; Chorus; Drill Tm; Nwsp Stf; Rep Soph Cls; Rep Jr Cls; Rep Sr Cls; VP Stu Cncl; High Hon Roll; Pres NHS.

BURZACHECHI, VICTORIA; New Castle SR HS; New Castle, PA; (S); 12/236; AFS; Art Clb; French Clb; Library Aide; Ski Clb; Yrbk Stf; High Hon Roll; Hon Roll; NHS; U Pittsburgh; Art.

BUSCH, ANDREW; Penn Hills HS; Pittsburgh, PA; (Y); VP Church Yth Grp; German Clb; Band; Concert Band; Mrchg Band; Art Clb; JV Vllybl; High Hon Roll; Prfct Atten Awd; Math.

BUSCH, LAURA; Chief Logan HS; Burnham, PA; (Y); Art Clb; Church Yth Grp; Computer Clb; Soroptimist; Spanish Clb; Band; Concert Band; Mrchg Band; Pep Band; Fld Hcky; Ltr Vrsty Marching Band 86; :Medcl.

BUSH, AMY; Homer-Center HS; Homer City, PA; (Y); French Clb; Varsity Clb; VICA; Band; Chorus; Concert Band; Flag Corp; Mrchg Band; Yrbk Stf; Sec Soph Cls; Pittsburgh Beauty Acad; Csmtlgy.

BUSH, GARY; Windber Area HS; Windber, PA; (Y); 45/128; Am Leg Boys St; Boy Scts; Stu Mnth 86.

BUSH, KRISTA; Penn Trafford HS; Jeannette, PA; (Y); Church Yth Grp; Hosp Aide; Ski Clb; Trs Spanish Clb; Mrchg Band; Twrlr; High Hon Roll; Hon Roll; U Pittsburgh; Phys Thrpy.

BUSH, KRISTEN; Kiski Area HS; Apollo, PA; (Y); Library Aide; Pep Clb; Spanish Clb; Pres SADD; Band; Church Choir; Capt Color Guard; Mrchg Band; Pep Band; Symp Band; Hgh Obrn Yth Fndtn Smnr 85; Elem Educ.

BUSH, KRISTEN M; Eastern Lobanon County HS; Myerstown, PA; (Y); SADD; Pres Soph Cls; Pres Jr Cls; Pres Sr Cls; Rep Stu Cncl; Stat Bsbl; Var Fld Hcky; Drexel U; Bus Adm.

BUSH, LORI; Bellwood-Antis HS; Bellwood, PA; (Y); Church Yth Grp; Girl Scts; Letterman Clb; Spanish Clb; Varsity Clb; Chorus; Var L Bsktbl; Hon Roll.

BUSH, LORI JO; Pen Argyl Area HS; Pen Argyl, PA; (Y); Pres Church Yth Grp; Hosp Aide; Pep Clb; Varsity Clb; Nwsp Stf; Yrbk Stf; Fld Hcky; Powder Puff Ftbl; Hon Roll; St Petes Chrch Schlrp 86; E Stroudsburg U; Elem Ed.

BUSH, SCOTT; Bangor Area SR HS; Bangor, PA; (Y); 11/200; Rptr 4-H; Trs Pep Clb; Ski Clb; Vllybl; High Hon Roll; Jr NHS; Pres Schlr; Millersville U; Sci.

BUSHICK, JANET; Mt Carmel Area JR SR HS; Kulpmont, PA; (Y); 49/134; Cmnty Wkr; Key Clb; Pep Clb; Spanish Clb; Acpl Chr; Band; Chorus; Church Choir; Concert Band; Drm Mjr(t); Penn ST; Accntng.

BUSHKO, HOLLY; John S Fine SR HS; Nanticoke, PA; (Y); Church Yth Grp; Hosp Aide; Ski Clb; Chorus; Sec Soph Cls; Sec Jr Cls; Var Crs Cntry; L Trk; High Hon Roll; Psych.

BUSHMIRE, JIM; Hopewell HS; Aliquippa, PA; (Y); 13/295; Math Tm; Spanish Clb; JV Bsbl; Var L Socr; Var L Tennis; High Hon Roll; Lion Awd; Spcl Recgntn Sci-Math Ganon U Erie PA 84; PA ST U; Engrng.

BUSHONG, JUDY; Solanco HS; Quarryville, PA; (Y); 82/235; Church Yth Grp; Ski Clb; Varsity Clb; Band; Concert Band; Jazz Band; Mrchg Band; Pep Band; School Musical; Pres Frsh Cls; Shippensburg U; Physcl Ed.

BUSKEY, JILL; Central Dauphin HS; Harrisburg, PA; (Y); Varsity Clb; Nwsp Ed-Chief; Nwsp Stf; Off Jr Cls; Off Sr Cls; Stu Cncl; Var L Cheerleading; Var L Vllybl; Cntrl Dauphin Highs Athlet Of The Wk 85; IN U Of PA; Comm.

BUSKIRK, MARC; West Middlesex HS; W Middlesex, PA; (S); Bsbl; Wt Lftg; Bus Admin.

BUSKO, NATE; Garden Spot HS; East Earl, PA; (Y); Boys Clb Am; Dance Clb; Varsity Clb; Bsktbl; Crs Cntry; Ftbl; Mgr(s); Socr; Trk; Hon Roll; Pilot.

BUSOCKER, KAREN; Marian Catholic HS; Jim Thorpe, PA; (Y); 16/121; VP Pres 4-H; Pep Clb; Ski Clb; Rep Soph Cls; Stu Cncl; Co-Capt Cheerleading; Sftbl; High Hon Roll; NHS; Blmsbrg U; Bus Admin.

BUSS, CONSTANCE; Liberty HS; Bethlehem, PA; (Y); 19/475; School Musical; Band; Chorus; Church Choir; Concert Band; Jazz Band; Mrchg Band; Orch; Hon Roll; Dist Rgnl & St Orchestra 84-86; Shenandoah Coll-Consrvtry; Musc.

BUSS, DEBORAH; Northwestern Lehigh JR SR HS; Fogelsville, PA; (Y); 33/180; Art Clb; Spanish Clb; Bsktbl; Mgr(s); Hon Roll; Art Awd 84; Fash Merch.

BUSS, DIANA; Lake Lehman HS; Dallas, PA; (Y); Debate Tm; Band; Chorus; Drill Tm; Mrchg Band; JV Socr; Var Trk; JV Bsktbl; Cmmrcl Art.

BUSSE, CLAIRE; Sacred Heart HS; Pittsburgh, PA; (Y); Q&S; Lib Chorus; Mrchg Band; School Musical; School Play; Nwsp Stf; Lit Mag; High Hon Roll; NHS; Engl.

BUSSE, HAGEN; Ridley SR HS; W Germany; (Y); Dance Clb; Nwsp Phtg; Yrbk Phtg; Badmtn; Tennis; Med.

BUSSINGER, KRISTIN; Reading Central Catholic HS; Reading, PA; (Y); Church Yth Grp; Girl Scts; Hosp Aide; Ski Clb; Chorus; Church Choir; Flag Corp; Nwsp Stf; Swmmng; Hon Roll; RN.

BUSSOM, TRACY; Hughesville HS; Picture Rocks, PA; (Y); Church Yth Grp; Ski Clb; Varsity Clb; Chorus; Yrbk Stf; Rep Soph Cls; Rep Stu Cncl; Tennis; Hon Roll; NHS; Green/White Awd 83-84; Athl Ltr Grls Tennis 85; Acctg.

BUSTARD, MELISSA; The Christian Acad; Media, PA; (Y); Chorus; Yrbk Stf; Capt JV Cheerleading; Var JV Fld Hcky; Pep Clb; Red Cross Aide; Church Choir; Rep Frsh Cls; Mgr(s); Mgr Sftbl; Socl Wrkr.

BUSZINSKI, CARRIE; Bentworth SR HS; Bentleyville, PA; (Y); 15/104; Church Yth Grp; Pres FBLA; Office Aide; Concert Band; Mrchg Band; Stu Cncl; Hon Roll; NHS; FBLA 6th Pl PA 86; Robert Morris Coll; Accntnt.

BUTARI, ANGELINA; Bishop Mc Devitt HS; Harrisburg, PA; (Y); 44/120; Art Clb; FBLA; Latin Clb; Spanish Clb; Yrbk Stf; High Hon Roll; Outstndng Perfmnc Bio, Basic Food Prep & Trig/Analytcl Geo 83-86; Wilma Boyd Career Schl; Tvl Agn.

BUTCHER, CAROLYN; Wyoming Valley West HS; Plymouth, PA; (Y); Sec Church Yth Grp; Key Clb; Chorus; Nwsp Stf; Yrbk Ed-Chief; Lit Mag; Cit Awd; NHS; Cmnty Wkr; School Musical; Hugh O Brien Yth Ldrshp Awd 85; Yth Ldrshp Salute 86; Intl Frgn Lang Awd-Spanish 86; Engl.

BUTCHER, DIANNA; Dawningtown HS; Coatesville, PA; (Y); 222/542; Girl Scts; Chorus; Cheerleading; Mgr(s); Trk; Hon Roll; Comptrs.

BUTCHKO, JEAN; Bishop O Reilly HS; Swoyersville, PA; (Y); Debate Tm; Chorus; School Musical; Nwsp Rptr; Yrbk Stf; Var Cheerleading; High Hon Roll; NHS; Acad All-Amer 84; Natl Sci Mrt Awd 85; Commnctns.

BUTCHKO, TINA; Pittston Area HS; Pittston, PA; (Y); 18/365; Computer Clb; Exploring; Key Clb; Math Clb; Swmmng; Vllybl; Hon Roll; NHS; Score Keeper; Wilkes Coll; Mth.

BUTERBAUGH, BETH; Punxsutawney Area HS; Big Run, PA; (Y); Church Yth Grp; Cmnty Wkr; Varsity Clb; Nwsp Stf; Cheerleading; Mgr(s); Hon Roll.

BUTERBAUGH, JEFFERY; Purchase Line HS; Commodore, PA; (Y); 50/120; Pres Letterman Clb; Pres Varsity Clb; Capt Var Ftbl; Capt Var Trk; Appalacian Cnfrc Ftbll & Trk Allstr 85-86; IN U Of PA; Envrnmntl Sci.

BUTIKIS, JOSEPH; North East Catholic HS; Philadelphia, PA; (Y); Art Clb; Computer Clb; Spanish Clb; Bsbl; Bsktbl; Ftbl; Ice Hcky; Wt Lftg; Hon Roll; Penn ST.

BUTINA, BARRY; Bishop Mc Devitt HS; Harrisburg, PA; (Y); Ski Clb; Ftbl; Hon Roll.

BUTINA, BRYAN; Greater Latrobe HS; Latrobe, PA; (Y); L Crs Cntry; L Trk; Hon Roll; Drctrs Crttct Achvmnt Estrn W Moreland Area Voc Tech Schl 86.

BUTLER, ALISSA; Galeton Area Schl; New Hartford, NY; (Y); 1/42; Pres Band; Chorus; Yrbk Ed-Chief; Sec Soph Cls; JV Var Bsktbl; JV L Vllybl; NHS; NEDT Awd; SUNY Cobleskill Schlrshp Incoming Stu 86; Alumni Assoc Schlrshp 86; PA York Chem Awd 85; SUNY; Cldhd Educ.

BUTLER, BETHANY; Keystone JR & SR HS; Knox, PA; (Y); Rep Church Yth Grp; Library Aide; Chorus; School Musical; Nwsp Bus Mgr; Nwsp Phtg; Nwsp Rptr; Nwsp Stf; Hon Roll; Prfct Atten Awd; Jrnlsm Bst Bus Mgr Awd 85-86; U Pittsburgh; Phys Thrpy.

BUTLER, BEVERLY; Central HS; Roaring Sprg, PA; (Y); 31/186; Church Yth Grp; Cmnty Wkr; Band; Chorus; Church Choir; Concert Band; Mrchg Band; JP Sousa Awd; Rose S Byers Music Awd 86; IN U; Crmnlgy.

BUTLER, BRADLEY; Bethel Park SR HS; Bethel Park, PA; (Y); 35/515; Boy Scts; Church Yth Grp; German Clb; Mrchg Band; Symp Band; High Hon Roll; NHS; Eagl Sct & Hnrs Awds; Aerontcl Engrng.

BUTLER, JEFF; Greensburg Central Catholic HS; Greensburg, PA; (Y); Church Yth Grp; Ski Clb; Im Mgr Bsktbl; Im Mgr Sftbl; High Hon Roll; Hon Roll; Dentstry.

BUTLER, JENNIFER; Central HS; Roaring Sprg, PA; (Y); 20/184; Cmnty Wkr; Drama Clb; FNA; GAA; JA; Red Cross Aide; SADD; Church Choir; Yrbk Stf; Im Vllybl; Nurse Awd Sprg Cove Jr Wmns Clb 86; PA ST U; Nrsng.

BUTLER, JULIE; Laurel JR SR HS; New Castle, PA; (Y); 9/103; Letterman Clb; Varsity Clb; Band; Mrchg Band; Nwsp Rptr; Powder Puff Ftbl; Trk; Vllybl; Hon Roll; Prfct Atten Awd; Studnt Activity Awd 86; Air Force; Accntnt.

BUTLER, KIM; Fairview HS; Erie, PA; (Y); 57/157; Drama Clb; French Clb; Ski Clb; Spanish Clb; Nwsp Stf; Crs Cntry; Swmmng; Tennis; Swmmg Ltr 84 & 85; Lib Art.

BUTLER, LORETTA; Bishop Kenrick HS; Norristown, PA; (Y); 36/315; Cmnty Wkr; Intnl Clb; Office Aide; Nwsp Rptr; Rep Frsh Cls; Rep Soph Cls; Rep Jr Cls; Sec Stu Cncl; Hon Roll; Engl.

BUTLER, LORI; Pittston Area SR HS; Pittston, PA; (Y); 56/320; Church Yth Grp; Key Clb; Ski Clb; Chorus; Drill Tm; Bsktbl; Sftbl; Hon Roll; Phys Ther.

BUTLER, MARK; Carlisle HS; W Germany; (Y); 57/460; French Clb; Science Clb; Band; Var Bsbl; Hon Roll; NHS; Physics.

BUTLER, MELODIE; Jefferson-Morgan Jr Sr HS; Waynesburg, PA; (Y); 4/88; Art Clb; French Clb; SADD; Color Guard; DAR Awd; High Hon Roll; NHS; Voice Dem Awd; Govrs Yth Traffic Saftey Cncl 85-87; Interact Club Brd Of Dir 85-86.

BUTLER, NATHANAEL; Cedar Grove Christian Academy; Philadelphia, PA; (Y); Computer Clb; Chorus; Concert Band; Nwsp Stf; Yrbk Stf; Var JV Bsbl; Var JV Socr; Cit Awd; High Hon Roll; NHS; Elec Engrng.

BUTLER, PHIL; Carlynton HS; Pittsburgh, PA; (Y); Computer Clb; Stu Cncl; Var Capt Bsktbl; Var L Ftbl; Var Capt Trk; Im Vllybl; High Hon Roll; Amrcn Lgn Awd 84; MAP Ldrshp Wrkshp U Of Pttsbrgh 84; Cert Of Merit Carlyntn HS Engl Dpt 86; Zoology.

BUTLER, TRACY ANN; Archbishop Ryan HS For Girls; Philadelphia, PA; (Y); 55/475; Pres JA; Service Clb; Rep Frsh Cls; Stu Cncl; Var Cheerleading; Hon Roll; W Chester U; Nrsng.

BUTORAC, ROBERT; German SR HS; Adah, PA; (Y); Art Clb; French Clb; Yrbk Phtg; High Hon Roll; Hon Roll; Jr NHS; NHS; NEDT Awd; Yrbk Stf; Rep Jr Cls; Tribn Rview Yth Of Yr 86; Cltur Clb 84; Sci Olympd-3rd Pl 85; Penn ST U; Archtrcl Engrng.

BUTRIE, MATTHEW; Marian HS; Lansford, PA; (S); 2/114; Chess Clb; Chorus; French Hon Soc; NHS; US Stu Cncl Awd 85; Theolgy.

BUTTERFIELD, CATHERINE; Bald Eagle Area HS; Julian, PA; (Y); 43/208; SADD; Off Frsh Cls; Off Soph Cls; Off Jr Cls; Off Sr Cls; Stu Cncl; Bsktbl; Coach Actv; Mgr(s); Powder Puff Ftbl; Miss Bald Eagle; Prom Decorating Chrmn; Penn ST U; Bus.

BUTTERWORTH, MELANIE; Neshaminy HS; Oakford, PA; (Y); 20/690; Hosp Aide; Key Clb; Drill Tm; Hon Roll; NHS; Stdnt Mnth Rotry 86; Slppry Rock U Schlrshp 86; Slippery Rock U.

BUTTERY, TAMARA; Punxsutawney Area SR HS; Punxsutawney, PA; (Y); French Clb; Var Tennis; Psych.

BUTTILLO, TONY; Salisbury HS; Allentown, PA; (Y); 15/138; Pres Soph Cls; Pres Jr Cls; L Crs Cntry; Var Trk; L Wrstlng; High Hon Roll; Hon Roll; Carbon Cnty Stu Forum 85-86; Qlfd For Sts In Wrestling 83-86; Engr.

BUTTS, CHERYL; Connellsville Area HS; Connellsville, PA; (Y); Chorus; Flag Corp; School Musical; School Play; Nwsp Rptr; Yrbk Bus Mgr; Rep Soph Cls; Rep Jr Cls; Var Capt Trk; Hon Roll; Clarion U PA; Pblc Rel.

BUTTS, DARRON; Mcconnellsburg JR SR HS; Mcconnellsburg, PA; (Y); 9/68; FFA; Var Bsbl; High Hon Roll; Hon Roll; Jr NHS; NHS; FFA Wildlife Mgmt Awd 86; Frnch Awd 85.

BUTTS, DEBORAH; Bishop Mc Devitt HS; Philadelphia, PA; (Y); 6/351; Cmnty Wkr; Pres Debate Tm; Pres French Clb; Hosp Aide; Pres SADD; Yrbk Stf; Im Bsktbl; Cit Awd; High Hon Roll; NHS; Gld Mdl Frnch 82-86; Prnts Assn Gld Mdl Actvties 86; Acad Decath Slvr Mdl Spch 85-86; American U; Intl Stds.

BUTTS, KELLY; Carlynton HS; Carnegie, PA; (Y); French Clb; Pep Clb; Yrbk Stf; Capt Cheerleading; Hon Roll; Cert Merit In Engl 86; Jrnlsm.

BUTTS, MARCIA; Connellsville SR HS; Connellsville, PA; (Y); 20/500; Band; Jazz Band; Mrchg Band; Pep Band; School Musical; Symp Band; High Hon Roll; Spanish NHS; Jazz Imprvstn Clb 84-86; OH Northern; Music Ed.

BUTTS, VALERIE; West Allegheny HS; Oakdale, PA; (Y); Church Yth Grp; Spanish Clb; SADD; Bsktbl; Hon Roll; Robert Morris Coll; Mrktng Mgmt.

BUTZ, STEPHEN D; Mifflinburg HS; Mifflinburg, PA; (Y); 3/170; Key Clb; Spanish Clb; SADD; Trs Sr Cls; Stu Cncl; Var Bsbl; Capt Var Bsktbl; High Hon Roll; NHS; Lebanon Vly Presdntl Schlrshp 86; Lebanon Vly Coll; Hstry.

BUTZER, PAMELA; Ephrata HS; Akron, PA; (Y); 1/250; Church Yth Grp; Cmnty Wkr; Exploring; Library Aide; Teachers Aide; Concert Band; Mrchg Band; Hon Roll; NHS; Diploma Of Merit Hghst Accmltve Percent In Spanish 84; Nrsng.

BUTZLER, THOMAS M; Bethel Park HS; Bethel Park, PA; (Y); 85/515; Boy Scts; French Clb; Concert Band; Jazz Band; Mrchg Band; Symp Band; L Swmmng; PA ST U; Agrcltr.

BUYNAK, SONYA; Philipsburg-Osceola SR HS; Osceola Mills, PA; (Y); #7 In Class; Art Clb; Library Aide; Office Aide; Chorus; Stage Crew; Yrbk Stf; Hon Roll; NHS; NEDT Awd.

BUZANOSKI, AMY; Butler Area SR HS; Butler, PA; (Y); Church Yth Grp; Exploring; JA; Spanish Clb; Chorus; Drill Tm; School Play; Rep Stu Cncl; Pom Pon; Jr NHS; U Of Pittsburgh; Spch Thrpy.

BUZARD, BRENDA; Fort Le Boeuf HS; Waterford, PA; (Y); 16/184; Church Yth Grp; Dance Clb; Hosp Aide; SADD; Drill Tm; Mrchg Band; JV Var Cheerleading; Gym; High Hon Roll; Natl Hstry, Govt Awd 83-84; Crimnlgy.

BUZARD, DENNIS; Lincoln HS; Ellwood City, PA; (Y); 76/163; Computer Clb; JA; Key Clb; Band; Stage Crew; High Hon Roll; Hon Roll; Estrn MI U; Enrgy Mngmnt.

BUZARD, KELLY; Rocky Grove HS; Franklin, PA; (Y); 30/93; Church Yth Grp; 4-H; French Clb; SADD; Var L Bsktbl; Var L Sftbl; Var L Vllybl; 4-H Awd; Hon Roll; Schlrshp For PA ST Cnsrvtn Schl 84; Elem Ed.

BUZBY, MATTHEW; Arch Bishop John Carroll HS; Overbrook Hills, PA; (Y); 7/165; Church Yth Grp; French Clb; Intnl Clb; Model UN; High Hon Roll; Jr NHS; NHS; Pres Schlr; Awd Grad In Top 10 86; American U; Intl Bus.

BUZEK, MELANIE; Mc Keesport Area HS; Mckeesport, PA; (Y); Office Aide; Yrbk Stf; JV Var Cheerleading; Var Gym; Var Powder Puff Ftbl; Hon Roll.

BUZZARD, DEANNA; Linesville Conneaut Summit HS; Linesville, PA; (Y); 18/72; German Clb; Stat Crs Cntry; Mgr(s); Hon Roll; Intl Bus.

BUZZARD, SCOTT; Pen Argyl HS; Windgap, PA; (Y); 8/117; Computer Clb; Ski Clb; Band; Concert Band; Mrchg Band; Orch; Bsbl; Ftbl; High Hon Roll; Hon Roll; Penn ST; Bus.

BUZZARD, TIM; Trinity HS; Washington, PA; (Y); 111/317; Church Yth Grp; Concert Band; Mrchg Band; OH U; Mrtcn.

BUZZELL, DAWN; Waynesboro Area SR HS; Blue Ridge Smt, PA; (Y); 6/381; Church Yth Grp; Chorus; Swing Chorus; Off Soph Cls; Off Jr Cls; Crs Cntry; Swmmng; Cit Awd; High Hon Roll; NHS; Debra A Moore Choral Awd 84; Swm Tm Coaches Awd 84 & 85; Peer Advocate 84-86; James Madison U; Allied Hlth Sc.

BUZZELLA, LYNN; Penn Cambria SR HS; Gallitzin, PA; (Y); 6/224; Camera Clb; Drama Clb; Spanish Clb; Nwsp Stf; Rep Jr Cls; Hon Roll.

BUZZELLI, ANN DEE; Lincoln HS; Ellwood City, PA; (Y); Hosp Aide; Red Cross Aide; Ski Clb; Spanish Clb; Y-Teens; Band; Chorus; Concert Band; Mrchg Band; Stu Cncl; Pt Park Coll; Bus Mgt.

BYBEE, PATRICK; Waynesboro Area SR HS; Waynesboro, PA; (Y); Church Yth Grp; Chorus; Church Choir; School Musical; Swing Chorus; Wrstlng; Lebanon Vly Coll Yth Schlrs Pgm Comm 86; Dist Chrs 84-86; Engrng.

BYERLY, DAVID E; Northgate HS; Pittsburgh, PA; (Y); 29/146; Am Leg Boys St; Church Yth Grp; VP Frsh Cls; JV Bsbl; Var L Ftbl; Var Capt Wrstlng; Hon Roll; Outstndng Wrstlr 84-85; Chrmn Stu Tchrs Equal Prtnrshp 86-87; Resptry Thrphy.

BYERS, ANN; Fairview HS; Erie, PA; (Y); Ski Clb; Varsity Clb; Var L Crs Cntry; Var Socr; Var L Swmmng; Var L Trk; Avtn.

BYERS, BARBARA; Upper Darby HS; Drexel Hill, PA; (Y); Pres Church Yth Grp; French Clb; Hosp Aide; Chorus; Church Choir; JV Bowling; JV Trk; Hon Roll; Prfct Atten Awd; Accounting.

BYERS, DARLENE; Purchase Line HS; Mahaffey, PA; (Y); 22/109; Spanish Clb; JV Sftbl; JV Vllybl; Hon Roll; Vet Asst.

BYERS, JON; Kiski Area HS; Vandergrift, PA; (Y); Boy Scts; Chorus; Custom Auto Body.

BYERS, MISTY; Milton SR HS; Milton, PA; (Y); 60/213; Church Yth Grp; Computer Clb; Key Clb; Teachers Aide; Nwsp Stf; Med Tech.

BYERS, ROBERT; Trinity HS; Amity, PA; (Y); 87/390; Boy Scts; Bsbl; Wldlf Mgmt.

BYERS, TERI; Mc Guffey HS; Avella, PA; (Y); DECA; Pres 4-H; Office Aide; Church Choir; 4-H Awd; Hon Roll.

BYERS, TINA M; Fort Leboeuf HS; Waterford, PA; (Y); 23/184; Church Yth Grp; Chorus; Church Choir; Rep Soph Cls; Sec Sr Cls; Rep Stu Cncl; Cheerleading; High Hon Roll; Hon Roll; Waterford Lnss Clb Schlrshp; Ft Le Boeuf Stu Cncl Schlrshp; Massillon Bptst Coll; Chrstn Ed.

BYKOWSKY, LORI ANN; Shenandoah Valley HS; Shenandoah, PA; (Y); 28/108; Chorus; Flag Corp; JV Bsktbl; JV Sftbl; Var Vllybl; Hon Roll; Acadmc All Amer 84.

BYLER, LARA; Northern Lebanon JR SR HS; Fredericksburg, PA; (Y); 19/179; Church Yth Grp; Concert Band; Mrchg Band; School Musical; Swing Chorus; Var L Crs Cntry; Var L Trk; JP Sousa Awd; NHS; Natl Schl Chrl Awd 86; Stu Of Mnth 85; Messiah Coll; Music.

BYNUM, DIETRA; Rittenhouse Acad; Philadelphia, PA; (Y); Art Clb; Cmnty Wkr; Dance Clb; FNA; Girl Scts; Hosp Aide; Office Aide; SADD; Teachers Aide; Bsktbl; Temple U; Nrsng.

BYRD, FRANK; Devon Preparatory Schl; Exton, PA; (Y); Ski Clb; Trs Soph Cls; Trs Jr Cls; Trs Stu Cncl; Var Bsktbl; JV Var Socr; Var Tennis; High Hon Roll; Hon Roll; NHS; Schlstc Awd Excllnc Amer Hist 86; Boston Coll; Bus Admin.

BYRD JR, JEROME T; West Catholic HS; Philadelphia, PA; (Y); Boy Scts; U Of Bridgeport; Psych.

BYRD, KENNETH; Central H S Of Philadel; Philadelphia, PA; (Y); Church Yth Grp; Cmnty Wkr; Teachers Aide; Jr NHS; NHS; PA ST U; Aerospc Engrng.

BYRNE III, DONALD; Lebanon Catholic HS; Annville, PA; (Y); 1/70; German Clb; Jazz Band; Rep Frsh Cls; Rep Soph Cls; Rep Jr Cls; Rep Sr Cls; Var Bsktbl; Var Ftbl; NHS; Ntl Merit Ltr; HOBY Ldrshp Sem 85; Classcl Lit.

BYRNE, JOHN; Perry Traditional Acad; Millvale, PA; (Y); 9/124; Church Yth Grp; French Clb; Math Tm; Ski Clb; Chorus; Nwsp Rptr; High Hon Roll; NHS; Computer Clb; Nwsp Phtg; Schlrshp Penn ST U 86; 1st Pl Cty Wide Comp Fair 86; Dstngshd Achvt Awd Bd Pblc Educ 86; Penn ST U; Chem.

BYRNE, JOHN; Upper Darby HS; Upper Darby, PA; (Y); 47/627; Service Clb; Rep Jr Cls; Var L Lcrss; JV L Socr; High Hon Roll; Hon Roll; Jr NHS; Prfct Atten Awd; Lit Mag; DAR Awd; Jrnlsm.

BYRNE, JULIE; Bishop Carroll HS; Ebensburg, PA; (S); 22/109; Pep Clb; Spanish Clb; SADD; Rep Soph Cls; Off Jr Cls; Var Bsktbl; L Trk; Hon Roll; Phy Thrpy.

BYRNE, TERRY; Greencastle-Antrim HS; Greencastle, PA; (Y); 30/186; Church Yth Grp; Math Tm; L Ftbl; Trk; Wt Lftg; Hon Roll; VFW Awd; Landis Tool Co Schlrshp Engrng 86; Hon Ment Sci Fair 86; Most Likely Succeed 86; U Of Pittsburgh; Mech Engrng.

BYRNES, HEATHER; Salisbury HS; Allentown, PA; (Y); 10/140; Drama Clb; Hosp Aide; Key Clb; School Musical; School Play; Rep Soph Cls; Rep Stu Cncl; High Hon Roll; Lion Awd; NHS; Lioness Yth Smnr 86; 1st Brnstrmng Session Imprvmnt 86; Nrs.

BYRNES, LISA; Cambria Heights HS; Hastings, PA; (Y); Band; Chorus; Concert Band; Mrchg Band; Pep Band; Yrbk Stf; Bsktbl; Score Keeper; Var L Trk; Hon Roll.

BYRON, KATHLEEN; Bishop O Hara HS; Dunmore, PA; (Y); Pep Clb; Ski Clb; Spanish Clb; Nwsp Stf; Cheerleading; Lackawanna JR Coll; Bus Mgt.

BYSICK, SCOTT; Canon Mc Millon SR HS; Canonsburg, PA; (Y); Ski Clb; Bsktbl; Mgr(s); High Hon Roll; Hon Roll; Navy ROTC; Comp Grphcs.

CABANES JR, FEDERICO R; Central HS; Philadelphia, PA; (Y); 85/217; Computer Clb; Yrbk Stf; Rochester Inst Tech; Comp Tech.

CABILI, MARIA; Penn Hills SR HS; Pittsburgh, PA; (Y); Church Yth Grp; Exploring; Hon Roll; German Clb; Science Clb; Pre Med.

CABLE, LINDA; Somerset Area SR HS; Somerset, PA; (Y); Cmnty Wkr; English Clb; German Clb; Pep Clb; Church Choir; Mrchg Band; Var Socr; Pres Phys Fit Awd 84 & 85; Math.

CABOT, MICHELE; Harriton HS; Bryn Mawr, PA; (Y); Pep Clb; Service Clb; SADD; Nwsp Sprt Ed; Yrbk Stf; Capt Cheerleading; Lcrss; Capt Pom Pon; Capt Tennis; Nwsp Stf; Cert Of Merit PA Hghr Educ Asstnce Agncy Outstndng SAT Prfrmnce 86; Cmmnctns.

CABRAJA, JENNIFER; Center HS; Aliquippa, PA; (Y); 16/190; Hosp Aide; Spanish Clb; School Play; Yrbk Sprt Ed; Stu Cncl; Bsktbl; Crs Cntry; Trk; NHS; Pres Schlr; U PA; Acctng.

CABUNGCAL, CATHERINE; St Basil Acad; Cheltenham, PA; (S); French Clb; GAA; Math Clb; Concert Band; Orch; Variety Show; Socr; Hon Roll.

CACALI, MARILYN; Quaker Valley HS; Sewickley, PA; (Y); Art Clb; Church Yth Grp; Drama Clb; French Clb; Hosp Aide; Chorus; School Play; JV Cheerleading; Var Trk; Hon Roll; Psych.

CACCHIONE, DENNIS; Cathedral Prep; Erie, PA; (Y); Im Bsktbl; Var L Ice Hcky; Im Vllybl; Case Wstrn Rsrv U; Bus.

CACCHIONE, ROBERT N; Mc Dowell HS; Erie, PA; (Y); 2/580; Chrmn Model UN; Quiz Bowl; Rep Stu Cncl; Var L Crs Cntry; Var L Trk; Kiwanis Awd; NHS; Ntl Merit SF; Sal; German Clb; Jets Teams Test 1st Pl Bio 85; Pre-Med.

CACCURO, ANDREA L; St Maria Goretti HS; Philadelphia, PA; (Y); 98/445; Art Clb; Dance Clb; French Clb; Stage Crew; 2nd Pl Drwng Immaculata 85; Schlrshp Moore Coll Art 85-86; Drexel; Fashion Design.

CACHULES, JIM; Bethlehem Catholic HS; Bethlehem, PA; (Y); Drama Clb; Ski Clb; Stage Crew; Trk; Hon Roll; MBA; Bus.

CADE, MICHAEL; Interboro HS; Glenolden, PA; (S); 1/350; Chess Clb; Drama Clb; German Clb; School Play; Stage Crew; Hon Roll; Jr NHS; NHS; Yale; Acctg.

CADWALADER, JASON; Lake-Lehman HS; Dallas, PA; (Y); L Bsbl; L Bsktbl; Capt Ftbl; Hon Roll; Bsbll All Schlstc Sunday Indpndnt 86; Bsbll Times Ldr All Star 1st Tm 86; Physcl Thrpy.

CADY, MICHELE; Fort Le Boeuf HS; Waterford, PA; (Y); 10/188; Art Clb; Stu Cncl; Ftbl; Sftbl; Wrstlng; High Hon Roll; NHS; U Pittsburgh; Phy Ther.

CADY, SHERILYN; Towanda Area HS; Towanda, PA; (Y); 8/135; Sec Trs Church Yth Grp; Girl Scts; Model UN; Concert Band; School Play; Cheerleading; Pom Pon; NHS; Camera Clb; Drama Clb; Rep Ntl Rural Elect Coop Assoc; Grand Confdntl Obsrvr; Order Of Rainbow 86-87; Telecomm.

CAFARO, MARY; North Allegheny HS; Allison Park, PA; (Y); 138/605; FBLA; Chorus; Hon Roll; Jr NHS; Bio Lab Assistant 85-86; FL ST U; Hosp Mgt.

CAFFREY, LAURA; Wyoming Valley West HS; Larksville, PA; (Y); 26/410; Pres Key Clb; Library Aide; Pep Clb; School Musical; High Hon Roll; Hon Roll; NHS; Yth Ldrshp Salute 86; Intl Foreign Lang Awd Frnch 85; Art Disply Schl Art Fair 84-86; Cmmnctns.

CAFFREY, PHAEDRA; Creative & Performing Arts HS; Philadelphia, PA; (S); 17/150; Church Yth Grp; Band; Church Choir; Jazz Band; Orch; School Musical; Symp Band; High Hon Roll; Hon Roll; NHS; Young Artists Comptn Hnr 85; Dist 5 Music & Arts Fest Achvt Awd 86; PA ST U; Music Ed.

CAGAN, SCOTT; Upper Moreland HS; Hatboro, PA; (Y); Key Clb; School Musical; School Play; Lit Mag; High Hon Roll.

CAGLIUSO, ANTHONY J; Center HS; Monaca, PA; (Y); Spanish Clb; High Hon Roll; Hon Roll; Outstndng Spnsh Stu 84-85; PA ST U; Acctg.

CAGNI, BERTHA ANNE; Peters Twp HS; Mc Murray, PA; (Y); 54/300; Church Yth Grp; Key Clb; Thesps; Chorus; School Musical; School Play; Hon Roll; Chld Psychlgst.

CAHALIN, JODY; Central Bucks East HS; Doylestown, PA; (Y); 118/494; Hosp Aide; Pep Clb; Ski Clb; Yrbk Stf; Hon Roll; Church Yth Grp; Cmnty Wkr; Var Cheerleading; Var Mat Maids; Stat Sftbl; Awd Acadmc Excllnc Holicong JR HS 82-84.

CAHILL, COLLEEN; Coatesville SR HS; Thorndale, PA; (Y); 72/535; Spanish Clb; Var Capt Bsktbl; Var Capt Fld Hcky; Var Capt Lcrss; Hon Roll; 1st Tm All Chestmont Fld Hockey, Outstndng Athl, Athl Schlrshp Towson ST 86; Towson ST.

CAHILL, PAULA; Cardinal Brewnan HS; Frackville, PA; (Y); German Clb; Yrbk Bus Mgr; Twrlr; Speech Pthlgy.

CAIAZZO, JUSTINE; Pius X HS; Bangor, PA; (Y); 7/40; Dance Clb; Pep Clb; Church Choir; School Musical; Yrbk Ed-Chief; Yrbk Stf; Rep Jr Cls; Var Cheerleading; Coach Actv; Var Sftbl; Dance Talent Awds 84-86; Allentown Bus Schl; Fash Merch.

CAIAZZO, TONI S; Bangor Area HS; E Bangor, PA; (Y); 1/190; Art Clb; French Clb; Pep Clb; Varsity Clb; Yrbk Ed-Chief; Pres Soph Cls; Pres Crs Cntry; Pres Sr Cls; Trs Stu Cncl; Var Capt Fld Hcky; Bangor Polc Assn Outstndng Awd 86; Stu Cncl All Around Awd 86; David Gingold Mem Scholar 86; Drexel U; Mech Engrng.

CAIMI, RAYMOND; St John Neumann HS; Philadelphia, PA; (Y); 1/321; Science Clb; Lit Mag; DAR Awd; High Hon Roll; NHS; Ntl Merit SF; Val; Phi Bet Kappa Awd 86; Genl Exclnc Eng, Sci, Socl Studies & Regln Mdls 86; Genl Exclnc Germ Hnr Cert; St Josephs U; Natrl Sci.

CAIN, MARTHA; Kiski Area HS; Apollo, PA; (Y); Aud/Vis; Science Clb; SADD; Chorus; Mrchg Band; Stage Crew; High Hon Roll; NHS; Acad Let 85-86; Communications.

CAIN, MELISSA; Kiski Area HS; Apollo, PA; (Y); Mrchg Band; Orch; Pep Band; School Musical; Symp Band; Nwsp Ed-Chief; High Hon Roll; JP Sousa Awd; PA Gov Schl For The Arts 85; Capital U; Elementary Music.

CAIN, RENE; Aliquippa HS; Aliquippa, PA; (Y); 35/135; Drama Clb; VICA; Band; Pep Band; JV Bsktbl; Var L Sftbl; High Hon Roll; Hon Roll.

CAIN, SUSAN A; Bellefonte Area SR HS; Bellefonte, PA; (Y); 3/217; Trs Varsity Clb; Powder Puff Ftbl; Var L Sftbl; High Hon Roll; Hon Roll; NHS; Schlrp Awd 83-86; Bus.

CAIRNS, BRIAN; Ft Le Boeuf HS; Waterford, PA; (Y); 73/200; Spanish Clb; Nwsp Rptr; JV Bsbl; Var L Bsktbl; Var Crs Cntry; Var L Trk; Im Wt Lftg; Hon Roll; Law.

CAIRNS, BRIAN; Mon Valley Catholic HS; Donora, PA; (Y); 1/130; VP JA; Band; Chorus; Church Choir; Yrbk Ed-Chief; Yrbk Sprt Ed; Bausch & Lomb Sci Awd; French Hon Soc; Gov Hon Prg Awd; NHS; Pres Schlrshp St Vincent Coll Challng Prog 85; Engrng.

CAIRNS, LAURA; Boiling Springs HS; Carlisle, PA; (Y); Church Yth Grp; Pres Trs Band; Chorus; Church Choir; Color Guard; Sec Trs Concert Band; Sec Trs Mrchg Band; JV Fld Hcky; JV Powder Puff Ftbl; Var L Swmmng; Harrisberg Area CC; Wrdprcsng.

CAISON, ELMER; Girard College HS; Philadelphia, PA; (Y); 1/28; Ski Clb; Im Badmtn; Var Bsktbl; Var Socr; Im Sftbl; Var Tennis; Trk; High Hon Roll; NHS; Engrng.

CAITO, JENNIFER; St Paul Cathedral HS; Pittsburgh, PA; (S); 2/61; Drama Clb; Trs Chorus; School Musical; Nwsp Ed-Chief; Ed Yrbk Stf; JV Var Vllybl; DAR Awd; VP NHS; NEDT Awd; Cert Of Merit Tp 5000 SAT Tkrs 85; Frnch I, III Awds 82-83 & 84-85; Bio.

CALABOYIAS, DIANNA; Swissvale HS; Pittsburgh, PA; (Y); 13/205; French Clb; Varsity Clb; Y-Teens; School Musical; VP Frsh Cls; Sec Jr Cls; Stu Cncl; Var Co-Capt Cheerleading; High Hon Roll; NHS; Med.

CALABRESE, CHRISTINE; Pittston Area SR HS; Pittston, PA; (Y); 11/368; Computer Clb; Dance Clb; Key Clb; Math Clb; Gym; Var L Trk; High Hon Roll; NHS.

CALABRESE, DANIELLE; West Phila Catholic Girls HS; Philadelphia, PA; (Y); 43/257; VP Exploring; Hosp Aide; Rep Frsh Cls; Rep Soph Cls; Rep Stu Cncl; Capt Var Cheerleading; Hon Roll; NHS; Prfct Atten Awd; La Salle U Chrstn Brthrs Grnt 86; La Salle U; Pre-Med.

CALABRESE, DENISE; West Catholic Girls HS; Philadelphia, PA; (Y); 93/245; Trs French Clb; Office Aide; Rep Stu Cncl; Outstndng Svc & The Schl Awd 86; Prfct Conduct 86; Hnrb Mntn Sci Fair 83; St Josephs U; Crmnl Just.

CALABRESE, JOANNE; Merion Mercy Acad; Phila, PA; (Y); Hosp Aide; Science Clb; Spanish Clb; Im Bsktbl; Var Sftbl; Im Vllybl; High Hon Roll; Prfct Atten Awd; Spanish NHS; 1st Pl Regnl Div Natl Spn Cont 84; Pre-Med.

CALABRESE, MARIA; Pittston Area HS; Pittston, PA; (Y); 7/330; Key Clb; Math Clb; Band; Jazz Band; High Hon Roll; Hon Roll; NHS; Pres Schlr; Gannon U; Pre-Med.

CALABRETTA, MARIO; Bishop Kenrick HS; Norristown, PA; (Y); 4/295; Church Yth Grp; Mathletes; Math Tm; Ftbl; L Socr; Hon Roll; NHS; Ntl Merit Ltr; Exch Clb Norristown Yth Yr 86; Mech Engrng.

CALABRO, DANA; Immaculate Conception HS; Canonsburg, PA; (Y); 25/62; Debate Tm; Drama Clb; FBLA; Political Wkr; SADD; Chorus; Stu Cncl; Cit Awd; High Hon Roll; NHS; Elizabethtwn Coll; Occptnl Thrp.

CALABRO, FRANCINE R; Canon Mc Millan HS; Canonsburg, PA; (Y); Mgr(s); Score Keeper; Hon Roll; Bradford School; Word Procssg.

CALABRO, JOSEPH C; Scranton Prep; Clarks Summit, PA; (Y); 120/200; School Musical; Bsktbl; Mgr(s); PA Poetry Awd 85-86; JR Acad Sci 1st Awds ST 83-84; U Of Scranton; Bio Sciences.

CALAFIORE, AMY; Bishop Mc Cort HS; Johnstown, PA; (Y); Am Leg Aux Girls St; Debate Tm; Hosp Aide; Pep Clb; Speech Tm; Cheerleading; Cit Awd; High Hon Roll; Hon Roll; Jr NHS; Jr Miss Fnlst 86; Corporate Law.

CALAFUT, MARIA; Sacred Heart HS; Carbondale, PA; (Y); 3/45; French Clb; Chorus; School Play; Rep Soph Cls; Sec Stu Cncl; High Hon Roll; NHS; Church Yth Grp; Acdmc All Amer Prgm 85-86; Marywood Coll; Ed.

CALAMAN, GREGORY; Sullivan County HS; Dushore, PA; (Y); 1/86; Rptr 4-H; Key Clb; Pres Band; Mrchg Band; Var Wrstlng; 4-H Awd; NHS; Ntl Merit Ltr; Amer Legn Essy Cntst Awd 17th Dist 84-85; Band Awd 83-86; Rensselaer Poly Inst Schrshp 86; Aerntcl Engrng.

CALAUTTI, CHRISIE; Lakeland HS; Carbondale, PA; (Y); Girl Scts; Drill Tm; Stage Crew; Yrbk Sprt Ed; Yrbk Stf; Pres Stu Cncl; Bsktbl; Capt Cheerleading; Sftbl; Timer; Kystn JC; Physcl Ed.

CALDARELL, KATHLEEN; Ambridge HS; Ambridge, PA; (Y); Off Soph Cls; Off Jr Cls; Off Sr Cls; JV Var Cheerleading; Robert Morris Coll; Accntng.

CALDERON, ALVIN; Westmont Hilltop HS; Johnstown, PA; (Y); 7/140; Drama Clb; Trs French Clb; Key Clb; VP NFL; VP Speech Tm; Yrbk Phtg; VP Jr Cls; Stu Cncl; Capt Tennis; NHS; Glsn Tnns Awd 85-86; Exclnc Englsh Awd 85; Top 10 86; Dickinson; Dctr.

CALDWELL, AMY; Warren Area HS; Warren, PA; (Y); Pres Art Clb; Church Yth Grp; Letterman Clb; Spanish Clb; Varsity Clb; Chorus; Yrbk Stf; High Hon Roll; NHS; Clarion U; Crimnl Justc.

CALDWELL, CRISTAN; Knoch HS; Butler, PA; (Y); Dance Clb; French Clb; German Clb; JA; Chorus; School Musical; School Play; Variety Show; Hon Roll; Duke U; Frgn Lang.

CALDWELL, DEBBIE; Upper Moreland SR HS; Hatboro, PA; (Y); 36/260; Var Bsktbl; Var Sftbl; Var Tennis; High Hon Roll; NHS; Subrbn Sftbl Champ 86; All Record Sftbl Tm 86.

CALDWELL JR, JAMES N; Fort Cherry HS; Westland, PA; (Y); Spanish Clb; Varsity Clb; Bsktbl; Ftbl; Hon Roll; Engineering.

CALDWELL, JOANN; Cambridge Springs HS; Saegertown, PA; (Y); 30/112; Pep Clb; Band; VP Chorus; Capt Color Guard; Mrchg Band; Stage Crew; Hon Roll; Bus.

CALDWELL, LISA; Burgettstown Area JRSR HS; Burgettstown, PA; (Y); 14/176; Church Yth Grp; Ski Clb; Concert Band; Mrchg Band; High Hon Roll; Hon Roll; Edinboro U Of PA; Pre-Law.

CALDWELL, RUSSELL; Waynesburg Central HS; Waynesburg, PA; (Y); Church Yth Grp; Spanish Clb; Band; Orch; High Hon Roll; Hon Roll; Acadmc Achvmnt Under Advrsty 85; Intermediat Unit Prv Flute Lssns At W VA U 86; Past Mstr Cnclr 85-86; Art Inst Pittsburgh; Intr Dsgn.

CALDWELL, SHARON; Bethel Park SR HS; Bethel Park, PA; (Y); Intnl Clb; JA; Ski Clb; Concert Band; Mrchg Band; Yrbk Stf; Spnsh.

CALDWELL, SUSIE; Upper Moreland HS; Hatboro, PA; (Y); 36/273; Key Clb; Chorus; Capt Mrchg Band; School Musical; Off Frsh Cls; Off Soph Cls; Off Jr Cls; Off Sr Cls; Var Cheerleading; JV Trk; ST Chmpns-Mrchng Band 83; Rutztown U; Elem Ed.

CALE, LAURA; Saegertown HS; Meadville, PA; (Y); #8 In Class; 4-H; SADD; Varsity Clb; Chorus; Rep Stu Cncl; Mgr(s); Mgr Sftbl; Vllybl; Hon Roll; Dntl Asst.

CALER, MICAH; North Hills SR HS; Pittsburgh, PA; (Y); Var Golf; JV Var Trk; Hon Roll; Ntl Merit Ltr; Point Park Coll; Comp Sci.

CALEY, GUY; Canon Mc Millen SR HS; Canonsburg, PA; (Y); 60/357; Boy Scts; Trs Church Yth Grp; Sec Exploring; Science Clb; Band; Concert Band; Jazz Band; Mrchg Band; High Hon Roll; Eagl Sct, Eagl Palm Awd 85; U Of Pittsburgh; Math.

CALFO, CHRIS; Gateway HS; Monroeville, PA; (Y); AIM; PA ST; Vet.

CALHOUN, BARRY; Upper Dauphin HS; Lykens, PA; (Y); Art Clb; Church Yth Grp; Cmnty Wkr; Off Soph Cls; Natl Ldrshp & Sci Awd 86; Acad All-Amer Lrg Dvsn 85; Tri-Cnty St, Ntnls Winner 86; Cert Mrt Gold Key 86; Penn St; Psyc.

CALHOUN, CHRISTY; Blairsville SR HS; Blairsville, PA; (Y); French Clb; Hosp Aide; Pep Clb; Ski Clb; Varsity Clb; Band; Chorus; Cheerleading; Pom Pon; Trk; All Cnty Grls Trk Tm 85; Dist Trk 85-86; Duquesne U; Phrmcy.

CALHOUN, DAVID; Uniontown Area HS; Uniontown, PA; (Y); 11/287; Letterman Clb; Spanish Clb; Var Bsbl; JV Bsktbl; Var Ftbl; Var Golf; Var Swmmng; CC Awd; Cit Awd; High Hon Roll; Archlgy.

CALHOUN, JOHN R; Cumberland Valley HS; Mechanicsburg, PA; (Y); JV Wrstlng.

CALIBEO, LISA; Cocalico HS; Denver, PA; (Y); Cmnty Wkr; Var Capt Cheerleading; Var Capt Fld Hcky; Var Capt Sftbl; Hon Roll; Sec NHS; All Amer Chrldr 84-85; Leag All Star Hockey Tm 85; U Of DE; Bus Admin.

CALIBEO, NICOLE; Cocalico SR HS; Denver, PA; (Y); 15/167; FBLA; Hosp Aide; VP Stu Cncl; JV Var Cheerleading; Im Fld Hcky; JV Var Sftbl; Trk; High Hon Roll; Radio Cmmnctns.

CALIVA, DEBORAH; Weatherly Area HS; Weatherly, PA; (Y); 2/62; FBLA; FHA; Nwsp Stf; Cheerleading; Score Keeper; Sftbl; High Hon Roll; NHS; Sal; Salutatorian Awd 86; Schlrshp ULGW.

CALIZZI, MICHAEL D; Kiski Area HS; Apollo, PA; (Y); Church Yth Grp; Key Clb; Symp Band; Pres Soph Cls; VP Jr Cls; Ftbl; Trk; DAR Awd; Lion Awd; NHS; All Star Ftbl; Bucknell U; Engrng.

CALKINS, DENNIS; Cowanesque Valley HS; Westfield, PA; (Y); Boy Scts; Church Yth Grp; French Clb; Chorus; Stat Bsktbl; Hon Roll; Bus Admin.

CALKINS, JIM; Unionville HS; West Chester, PA; (Y); Boy Scts; Church Yth Grp; Computer Clb; Concert Band; Jazz Band; Mrchg Band; Orch; Hon Roll; Jr NHS; Order Arrow 84; Meteorlgy.

CALLA, TERESA C; South.Side Catholic HS; Pittsburgh, PA; (S); Church Yth Grp; School Play; Yrbk Phtg; Yrbk Stf; Sec Sr Cls; High Hon Roll; Hon Roll; Natl HS Exclnc Awd 85; Old Tstmnt & Wrld Cltrs Hghst Grd 83; Chatham; Dance Instrctr.

CALLAGHAN, DENNIS; Archbishop Wood HS For Boys; Southampton, PA; (Y); 15/282; Cmnty Wkr; Political Wkr; Q&S; Nwsp Ed-Chief; Nwsp Rptr; Nwsp Stf; Hon Roll; NHS; Ntl Merit Ltr; Quill & Scroll Gold Key Awd Current Events 84; Fordham U; Journslm.

CALLAGHAN, MARYANNE; Center Area HS; Monaca, PA; (Y); Latin Clb; Letterman Clb; Spanish Clb; Varsity Clb; Nwsp Stf; Yrbk Stf; Var L Trk; Var L Vllybl; Commctn Fld.

CALLAHAN, BILL; Our Lady Of Lourdes Regional HS; Shamokin, PA; (Y); 34/98; Cmnty Wkr; Computer Clb; Key Clb; Letterman Clb; Math Clb; Political Wkr; Varsity Clb; Yrbk Ed-Chief; Rep Frsh Cls; Pres Jr Cls; Hugh Obrien Ldrshp Awd 84-85; Bus Mgmt.

CALLAHAN, EDW; West Catholic For Boys; Philadelphia, PA; (Y); JA; Hon Roll; Ntl Merit Ltr; Temple U; Scndry Ed.

CALLAHAN, JAMES J; Wyoming Area HS; W Pittston, PA; (Y); Art Clb; Boy Scts; Ski Clb; Spanish Clb; Stu Cncl; Bus Mgmt.

CALLAHAN, JOHN; Libety HS; Bethlehem, PA; (Y); #10 In Class; Nwsp Stf; VP Soph Cls; VP Jr Cls; VP Sr Cls; Pres Stu Cncl; Var Crs Cntry; Var Trk; Var L Wrstlng; NHS; Rotary Awd; Med.

CALLAHAN, MARY ELLEN; Kennett HS; Avondale, PA; (Y); 4/155; Band; School Play; Yrbk Ed-Chief; Hst Soph Cls; Hst Jr Cls; Hst Sr Cls; Var Capt Sftbl; VP NHS; Ntl Merit SF; AFS; Rotary Stu Mnth 85; Awd Exc Frnch 83; Intl Pol.

CALLAHAN, MAUREEN; West Middlesex HS; New Wilmington, PA; (S); 11/107; Service Clb; Var Cheerleading; Hon Roll; Spanish NHS; Ntl Sci Merit Awd 84; Med.

CALLAHAN, ROBERT; Bellefonte Area HS; Bellefonte, PA; (Y); JV Ftbl; Im Vllybl; Im Wt Lftg; Hon Roll; Air Force; ST Police Offcr.

CALLAHAN, SUSAN; Spring Grove Area SR HS; Spring Grove, PA; (Y); 5/285; Church Yth Grp; Drama Clb; Chorus; Church Choir; High Hon Roll; Summr Pgm Gifted Mth/Sci 86; Chem Engr.

CALLAHAN, WILLIAM; G A R Memorial HS; Wilkes Barre, PA; (S); 42/177; Var Capt Bsktbl; High Hon Roll; Hon Roll; Jr NHS; NHS.

CALLAN, LISA; West Catholic For Girls; Philadelphia, PA; (Y); Cmnty Wkr; Science Clb; Spanish Clb; Nwsp Rptr; Stu Cncl; High Hon Roll; Hon Roll; Psych.

CALLANDER, MARY; Allegheny-Clarion Valley HS; Parker, PA; (Y); 4/97; Church Yth Grp; Varsity Clb; Sec Stu Cncl; Co-Capt Var Cheerleading; L Var Crs Cntry; L Var Trk; High Hon Roll; NHS; Prfct Atten Awd; Elem Educ.

CALLAS, MARIA; Turtle Creek HS; E Pittsburgh, PA; (Y); 11/180; Computer Clb; Debate Tm; Spanish Clb; High Hon Roll; Prfct Atten Awd.

CALLAWAY, SCOTT; Belle Vernon Area HS; Belle Vernon, PA; (Y).

CALLIHAN, BETH; Karns City Area HS; Chicora, PA; (Y); 8/115; Church Yth Grp; Exploring; Band; Chorus; Church Choir; Concert Band; Pep Band; Hon Roll; NHS; 1st ST Awd Acad Of Sci 86; Grove City Clg; Pre Med.

CALLIHAN, JON; Johnstown Christian HS; Windber, PA; (Y); 3/17; Church Yth Grp; Drama Clb; Chorus; School Play; Yrbk Stf; Pres Sr Cls; Rep Stu Cncl; Var Bsbl; Var Bsktbl; Hon Roll; U Pittsburgh.

CALLIHAN, RICHARD; Greater Johnstown Area Vo-Tech; Johnstown, PA; (Y); 100/320; DECA; Letterman Clb; Ski Clb; VICA; Nwsp Sprt Ed; Nwsp Stf; Stu Cncl; Var Capt Bsktbl; Im Ftbl; Im Vllybl; PA DECA Schlrshp; Thiel Coll; Bus Mngmnt.

CALLIPARE, JAMES; Mt Pleasant Area SR HS; Mount Pleasant, PA; (Y); Boys Clb Am; Exploring; FBLA; SADD; High Hon Roll; NHS; Val; Cmnty Wkr; Library Aide; JV Bsktbl; Indiana U PA; Comp Sci.

CALOMINO, EMIL; Dunmore HS; Dunmore, PA; (Y); 14/155; French Clb; FBLA; Letterman Clb; Capt L Bsbl; Capt L Golf; NHS; FBLA 84 PA ST Bus Math Champ 84; U Scranton Schlrshp 86; SATS ST PA Top 5 Pct 85; U Scranton; Acctg.

CALTER, MARIELLEN F; Upper Morland SR HS; Willow Grove, PA; (Y); 14/276; Camp Fr Inc; Chorus; Concert Band; Mrchg Band; School Musical; School Play; Ed Lit Mag; High Hon Roll; NHS; Ntl Merit SF; Chem.

CALTER, MIMI; Upper Moreland HS; Willow Grove, PA; (Y); 15/280; Camp Fr Inc; Chorus; Mrchg Band; School Musical; School Play; Symp Band; Ed Lit Mag; High Hon Roll; NHS; Ntl Merit Schol; U Of PA; Chem.

CALVIERO, LAURIE A; Bangor Area Joint HS; Roseto, PA; (Y); Pep Clb; Ski Clb; Spanish Clb; Mat Maids; Tennis.

CALVITTI, ALAN; Mc Keesport SR HS; Mckeesport, PA; (Y); 1/350; German Clb; Stage Crew; Acousticl Engrng.

CAMARDA, ANTOINETTE; Shaler Area SR HS; Pittsburgh, PA; (Y); 38/517; Exploring; Hosp Aide; Church Choir; Mrchg Band; Symp Band; Yrbk Stf; Hon Roll; Acad All Amer Schlr 85; U Of Pittsburgh; Socl Wrk.

CAMAROTA, NICOLE; Liberty HS; Bethlehem, PA; (Y); Cmnty Wkr; German Clb; Hosp Aide; Nwsp Stf; Yrbk Sprt Ed; Var Capt Bsktbl; Var L Fld Hcky; Var L Trk; Hon Roll; Outstndng Offnsv Plyr Bsktbl 85; Outstndng Fld Evnts Girls Trk 86.

CAMAROTO, REBECCA A; Williamsburg HS; Williamsburg, PA; (Y); FBLA; Stu Cncl; Prfct Atten Awd; Rtlng.

CAMAS, TIM; Bradford Central Christian HS; Bradford, PA; (Y); Key Clb; Ski Clb; Var JV Bsbl; JV Bsktbl; JV Var Ftbl; Juvenile Justc Crt Awd 86; Bus.

CAMASSE, LAURA; Meyers HS; Wilkes Barre, PA; (Y); FBLA; Girl Scts; Chorus; Mrchg Band; Bus.

CAMBERG, JENNIFER; Altoona Area HS; Altoona, PA; (Y); Computer Clb; Spanish Clb; Jazz Band; Mrchg Band; Orch; Lit Mag; Swmmng; Twrlr; Jr NHS; NEDT Awd; Phys Ftnss Awd 84-85; Engl.

CAMBRUZZI, RITA; Yough SR HS; Ruffsdale, PA; (Y); 6/265; Civic Clb; Computer Clb; Drama Clb; 4-H; Office Aide; Pep Clb; Sec SADD; Thesps; Acpl Chr; Chorus; Hugh O Brian Ldrshp Awd; JR Rep Homecng Ct; Seton Hill Ldrshp Awd; Perfmnc Musical Group Reach Out; Marietta Coll; Communications.

CAMELLIRI, TONY; Marian HS; Mahanoy City, PA; (Y); 52/115; French Clb; SADD; JV Bsbl; Good Ctznshp Awd 83; Comp Sci.

CAMERON, A CHRISTINE; East Juniata HS; Millerstown, PA; (Y); Church Yth Grp; Chorus; Church Choir; School Musical; School Play; Sec Jr Cls; Var Capt Cheerleading; JV Sftbl; Hon Roll; NHS; Worthy Advsr Rainbw 86; Educ.

CAMERON, BETH; Steel Valley HS; W Homestead, PA; (Y); 31/201; Pres Church Yth Grp; Band; Concert Band; Mrchg Band; Rep Jr Cls; Rep Sr Cls; Var JV Score Keeper; Var L Swmmng; Hon Roll; NHS; Bus.

CAMERON, BOB; Montoursville HS; Montoursville, PA; (Y); Church Yth Grp; German Clb; Spanish Clb; Wrstlng; Hon Roll; NHS; Grad Basic Trnng 86; Milligan Coll; Hlth Admin.

CAMERON, CARLA; Milton SR HS; Milton, PA; (Y); 1/216; Spanish Clb; Drm Mjr(t); Yrbk Stf; Fld Hcky; High Hon Roll; NHS; Pres Schlr; Val; Key Clb; Latin Clb; Schlr Awd 86; Alternate PA Gov Schl Intl Studies; Duquesne U; Phrmcy.

CAMERON, CHRISTINE; East Juniata HS; Millerstown, PA; (Y); 10/100; Church Yth Grp; Chorus; Church Choir; School Musical; School Play; Sec Jr Cls; Cheerleading; Sftbl; Hon Roll; NHS; Rnbw Grls Wrthy Advsr 86; Tchr.

CAMERON, JAMIE; Central Cambria HS; Ebensburg, PA; (S); 6/209; French Clb; FBLA; Library Aide; Score Keeper; Sftbl; Hon Roll; Prfct Atten Awd.

CAMERON, KATY; Greenwood HS; Millerstown, PA; (S); 8/70; GAA; Band; Chorus; Lib Chorus; School Musical; Var Bsktbl; Var Fld Hcky; Var Sftbl; High Hon Roll; Hon Roll; Bsktbl Capt 84-85.

CAMERON, ROBERT; East Juniata HS; Millerstown, PA; (Y); 8/92; Varsity Clb; Chorus; School Musical; School Play; Nwsp Stf; Ftbl; Im Wt Lftg; Capt Var Wrstlng; NHS; Ntl Merit SF; Natl Sci Awd 82; WA & Jefferson Coll; Bio.

CAMMACK, STACEY C; Bishop Mc Devitt HS; Harrisburg, PA; (S); Church Yth Grp; Ski Clb; Jr NHS; NHS; Outstndng Stu Cert Achvt Recgntn Acad Exc 86; Alumni Schrlshp Bloomsburg U PA 86; Bloomsburg U-PA; Math.

CAMMERATA, JEFFREY D; Manheim Township HS; Lancaster, PA; (Y); 18/313; Chess Clb; Church Yth Grp; Var L Ftbl; Vllybl; High Hon Roll; NHS; Franklin & Marshall Coll; Phys.

CAMP, JEAN; Leechburg Area HS; Leechburg, PA; (Y); Chorus; NHS; Library Aide; Yrbk Stf; High Hon Roll; Cnty & Dist III Chorus 85-86; Bradford Schl Bus; Acctng.

CAMP, LISA; Saint Benedict Acad; Erie, PA; (Y); 9/63; Cmnty Wkr; Q&S; Quiz Bowl; Variety Show; Yrbk Stf; Lit Mag; Stu Cncl; Bsktbl; Tennis; Hon Roll; HOB Ldrshp Seminar Soph 85; John Carroll; Phl Ther.

CAMPAGNA, KELLY ANNE; Mount Saint Joseph Acad; Huntingdon Vly, PA; (Y); Church Yth Grp; JCL; Latin Clb; Nwsp Stf; Var Cheerleading; High Hon Roll; VP NHS; Latin Hnr Soc 85-86; 1st Pl Awd Acad Sci 84-85.

CAMPALONG, ROBERT; Sto-Rox HS; Mc Kees Rocks, PA; (Y); VP Frsh Cls; Hon Roll; Prfct Atten Awd; Comm Baking.

CAMPANA, ROBBY; St Marys Area HS; Saint Marys, PA; (Y); Varsity Clb; Var L Bsktbl; Var L Ftbl; Var L Trk; Hon Roll; Misericordia; Occptnl Thrpy.

CAMPANELLA, JOANNE; St Maria Goretti HS; Philadelphia, PA; (Y); 146/426; Art Clb; Aud/Vis; Church Yth Grp; Cmnty Wkr; Dance Clb; GAA; Office Aide; Teachers Aide; Hon Roll; Prfct Atten Awd; Comm Coll Of Phila; Med Assist.

CAMPBEL, COREY; Trinity HS; Camp Hill, PA; (Y); Bsktbl; Golf; Bus.

CAMPBELL, ANDREA KARNICE; Pine Forge Acad; Chapel Hill, NC; (S); 6/78; Church Yth Grp; Drill Tm; Rep Jr Cls; Cheerleading; Gym; Vllybl; High Hon Roll; Hon Roll; NHS; Arnolds International; Csmtlgy.

CAMPBELL, ANTOINETTE; Germmantown HS; Philadelphia, PA; (Y); 25/237; Library Aide; Office Aide; Teachers Aide; Varsity Clb; Pres Frsh Cls; Sec Sr Cls; Var Bsktbl; Var Fld Hcky; Mgr(s); Var Sftbl; OK; Accntng.

CAMPBELL, BOB; Albert Gallatin SR HS; Smithfield, PA; (Y); 5/150; Camera Clb; Chess Clb; 4-H; School Play; Rep Frsh Cls; Im Bsktbl; Im Ftbl; Im Mgr(s); Im Socr; Im Vllybl; Johns Hopkins Talent Search Awd 81-82; Colorbearer Natl Jr Hnr Scty 83-84; Natl Res Mgt.

CAMPBELL, BRYAN; Council Rock HS; Holland, PA; (Y); 34/845; Mrchg Band; Orch; Symp Band; NHS; Aerontcl Engrng.

CAMPBELL, DAN; Delaware County Christian Schl; Springfield, PA; (Y); 20/85; Church Yth Grp; Chorus; Pres Frsh Cls; Var L Bsktbl; Var L Socr; Var L Tennis; High Hon Roll; Hon Roll; All Tourn Plyr Bsktbl 85-86; ACSI Ldrshp & Athl Awd Am Christian Schls Intl 85-86.

CAMPBELL, DAWN; Juniata HS; Port Royal, PA; (Y); Computer Clb; Dance Clb; Drama Clb; Hosp Aide; Varsity Clb; Mrchg Band; School Play; Yrbk Stf; Rep Stu Cncl; JV Cheerleading; Phy Thrpy.

CAMPBELL, DAWN; South Allegheny JR-SR HS; Glassport, PA; (S); Church Yth Grp; Exploring; Sec French Clb; JA; Library Aide; Band; Chorus; Concert Band; Mrchg Band; Hon Roll; Med Secry.

CAMPBELL, DAWN; Southern Columbia Area HS; Elysburg, PA; (Y); 19/94; Camera Clb; Drama Clb; 4-H; Pep Clb; Band; Color Guard; Concert Band; Drm Mjr(t); Jazz Band; Mrchg Band; Susquehanna U; Engrg.

CAMPBELL, DEBORAH; Corry Area HS; Corry, PA; (S); 4/215; FTA; Teachers Aide; Concert Band; Mrchg Band; Pep Band; Rep Soph Cls; High Hon Roll; Bus, Prof Wmnr Grl Mnth 85; Edinboro U PA; Sec Educ.

CAMPBELL, DEBORAH; Fairchance Georges SR HS; Smithfield, PA; (Y); 4-H; Girl Scts; Band; Concert Band; Mrchg Band; Yrbk Phtg; Stat Bsktbl; 4-H Awd; Hon Roll; Upward Bnd 84-88.

CAMPBELL, DENNY; Seneca Valley SR HS; Mars, PA; (Y); Art Clb; Letterman Clb; Model UN; Ski Clb; Varsity Clb; Var L Socr; Var L Trk; Hon Roll; Mbr Of The Comm For The Advncmnt Of The Humanties Art Comp 86; Architecture.

CAMPBELL, ELIZABETH; Shikellamy SR HS; Sunbury, PA; (Y); Church Yth Grp; German Clb; NFL; Red Cross Aide; Speech Tm; SADD; Chorus; Concert Band; Mrchg Band; School Musical; Commnctns.

CAMPBELL, ELIZABETH; South Williamsport Area HS; S Williamsport, PA; (Y); 1/140; Hosp Aide; Key Clb; Concert Band; Mrchg Band; Rep Stu Cncl; Var Trk; High Hon Roll; NHS; Computer Clb; French Clb; Amer Lg Aux Awd 85; PA Dist 8 Band & Orch Fest 86.

CAMPBELL, ELIZABETH CAROL; Northern Lebanon HS; Lebanon, PA; (Y); 9/178; Pres Church Yth Grp; Civic Clb; Spanish Clb; Varsity Clb; School Play; Stu Cncl; Stat Bsbl; JV Var Fld Hcky; High Hon Roll; Hon Roll; Penn ST U; Bus Admin.

CAMPBELL, JACQUELINE; Pine Forge Acad; Chapel Hill, NC; (S); 3/60; Teachers Aide; Acpl Chr; Off Sr Cls; Stu Cncl; Var Cheerleading; Sftbl; Swmmng; Cit Awd; High Hon Roll; Natl Hnr Rll 85; Oakwood Coll; Bio.

CAMPBELL, JAY; Emmaus HS; Wescosville, PA; (Y); 95/490; Trs French Clb; Key Clb; Var Capt Bsktbl; Golf; Law.

CAMPBELL, JENNIFER; Ringgold HS; Donora, PA; (Y); 18/342; School Musical; Hon Roll; NHS.

CAMPBELL, JERRY; Wyoming Valley West HS; Kingston, PA; (Y); Im Bsktbl; Var Golf; Var Vllybl; Im Wt Lftg; Hon Roll; NHS; NEDT Awd; Cmmnctns.

CAMPBELL, JIM; Clarion Area HS; Clarion, PA; (Y); Swing Chorus; Capt Ed Yrbk Stf; Sec Frsh Cls; Pres Soph Cls; Var L Ftbl; Var L Trk; Var L Wrstlng; Cit Awd; Hon Roll; Chorus; MVP Track-Ftbl 84 & 86; Gary L Lawrence Schlr Athl Awd 84; US Marine Corps Dstngshd Athl Awd 85.

CAMPBELL, JULIE; Franklin HS; Franklin, PA; (Y); 84/210; Girl Scts; Hosp Aide; Band; Concert Band; Mrchg Band; School Play; Hon Roll; Acctng.

CAMPBELL, KAREN; Shikellamy HS; Sunbury, PA; (Y); 15/315; French Clb; NFL; Speech Tm; School Musical; School Play; Variety Show; Ed Yrbk Stf; Rep Stu Cncl; Hon Roll; NHS; Cathlc Fornsc Leag Natl Qualfr 20th In Nation 85; 2nd Lvl PA Govnr Schl For The Arts 84-85; Towson ST U; Dnc.

CAMPBELL, KELLY; West Greene Middle SR HS; Graysville, PA; (Y); Band; Mrchg Band; Rep Stu Cncl; Stat Bsktbl; Mat Maids; Twrlr; High Hon Roll; NHS; Awd 3 Yrs Mkng Hnr Rll 84-86; Accntng Awd; Accntng.

CAMPBELL, KRISTEN; Altoona Area HS; Altoona, PA; (Y); Key Clb; Spanish Clb; Band; Chorus; Color Guard; Concert Band; Flag Corp; Orch; JV Var Bsktbl; Var Trk; Penn ST; Med.

CAMPBELL, KRISTIN; Central Columbia HS; Berwick, PA; (Y); 29/180; German Clb; Pep Clb; Ski Clb; Stu Cncl; Stat Bsbl; Var Capt Cheerleading; Im Diving; Hon Roll; NEDT Awd; PA ST U; Animl Bio-Sci.

CAMPBELL, MARY ELLEN; Bishop Kenrick HS; Norristown, PA; (Y); 87/295; Cmnty Wkr; Hosp Aide; Spanish Clb; JV Crs Cntry; Hon Roll; Prfct Atten Awd; Nrsng.

CAMPBELL, MEGAN; West Middlesex HS; Pulaski, PA; (S); Chorus; Concert Band; Mrchg Band; Variety Show; Sec Soph Cls; Sec Jr Cls; Sec Stu Cncl; JV Capt Cheerleading; JV Var Vllybl; Jr NHS; Dist Band 85; Pre Law.

CAMPBELL, MICHALE LIN; Bellwood Antis HS; Altoona, PA; (Y); 11/124; Key Clb; VICA; Band; Chorus; Color Guard; Concert Band; Hon Roll; Engl Awd 86; PA ST; Dentl Hyg.

CAMPBELL, MICHELE; Warren Area HS; Warren, PA; (Y); German Clb; Library Aide; Varsity Clb; Yrbk Stf; Var L Sftbl; Jr NHS; Wayne King Scshlrshp Spch 86; Clarion U PA.

CAMPBELL, MICHELLE; Fannett-Metal HS; Doylesburg, PA; (S); 1/53; Trs Church Yth Grp; Drama Clb; Band; Church Choir; Drm Mjr(t); Nwsp Stf; NHS; Ntl Merit Ltr; Mrchg Band; Nwsp Rptr; Acadmc All Amer 84-85; Gftd Clsses; Lit Flm Clb; Shippensburg U; Comp Prgrmg.

CAMPBELL, MIKE; Selinsgrove Area HS; Selinsgrove, PA; (Y); Ski Clb; Spanish Clb; Chorus; Trs Frsh Cls; Trs Sr Cls; Var Socr; Tennis; Wrstlng; High Hon Roll; Hon Roll; Pre Law.

CAMPBELL, RICHARD; Purchase Line HS; Barnesboro, PA; (Y); 40/130; Varsity Clb; Chorus; JV Var Bsktbl; JV Coach Actv; Var Trk; Conf All Star Tm 85-86.

CAMPBELL, ROXANN; Neshaming SR HS; Levittown, PA; (Y); GAA; Ski Clb; SADD; Band; Chorus; Orch; JV Bsktbl; JV Fld Hcky; JV Sftbl; Hon Roll; Poli Sci.

CAMPBELL, STACEY; Wilmington Area HS; New Wilmington, PA; (S); 12/106; Church Yth Grp; Drama Clb; Key Clb; JV Var Bsktbl; Powder Puff Ftbl; Hon Roll; NHS; JV Bsktbl Trophy; Kent ST U; Nrsng.

CAMPBELL, STEPHEN A; Ephrata SR HS; Ephrata, PA; (Y); VP Church Yth Grp; Chorus; Church Choir; Concert Band; Orch; School Musical; Hon Roll; Pres NHS; Pres Schlr; Choral Awd 86; Hibsman Schlrshp; Wold Schlrshp; Thomas Staffuer Mem Schlrshp 86; Eastern Nazarene Coll; Pre-Med.

CAMPBELL, TAMIKA; Chester HS; Chester, PA; (Y); Science Clb; Hon Roll; Var Cheerleading; JV Fld Hcky; Mst Outstndg Math Awd 86; Sci Cert Hghst Grade 84; Pierce JC; Legl Sec.

CAMPBELL, TIMOTHY; Archbishop Wood HS; Churchville, PA; (Y); 61/282; Computer Clb; Hon Roll; Bio.

CAMPBELL, TIMOTHY; Williamsburg HS; Williamsburg, PA; (Y); Church Yth Grp; Nwsp Ed-Chief; Stu Cncl; Var L Bsbl; Var L Bsktbl; Var L Ftbl; Hon Roll; NHS; Prfct Atten Awd; Varsity Clb; Penn ST; Arch.

CAMPBELL, TORRY; Southern Columbia HS; Elysburg, PA; (Y); Chess Clb; Computer Clb; Letterman Clb; Varsity Clb; Band; Concert Band; Mrchg Band; Stu Cncl; Bsktbl; Crs Cntry; Engrng.

CAMPENNI, THOMAS; Wyoming Area SR HS; Exeter, PA; (Y); Church Yth Grp; FBLA; German Clb; Ski Clb; SADD; Rep Stu Cncl; JV Bsbl; JV Bsktbl; JV Ftbl; Tennis; George Mason U; Finance.

CAMPESE, MARK; Quigley HS; Midland, PA; (Y); Boys Clb Am; L Ftbl; Powder Puff Ftbl; Hon Roll; PA Math League 84-85; Elec Engrng.

CAMPOLI, WENDI; New Casle SR HS; New Castle, PA; (Y); 28/263; AFS; Library Aide; Spanish Clb; Westminster Coll; Elem Ed.

CAMPOMIZZI, EDWARD; Greenburg Central Catholic HS; Greensburg, PA; (Y); Chess Clb; Varsity Clb; Var Ftbl; Wt Lftg; Wrstlng; Hon Roll; Bus Mgmt.

CANCEL, SUEJEAN; Delaware Valley HS; Milford, PA; (Y); SADD; VICA; Hon Roll; Amer Alliance For Hlth, Phy Ed, Rcrtn Dnce, Yth Prgrass Awd 84-86; Penn ST; Pre-Med.

CANCELLIERE, LYNN; St Huberts HS; Philsdelphia, PA; (Y); Cmnty Wkr; Office Aide; SADD; Cit Awd; Pierce JC; Bus.

CANCIELLO, RICHARD S; Neshannock HS; New Castle, PA; (Y); 26/102; Drama Clb; School Musical; School Play; Stage Crew; VP Jr Cls; VP Sr Cls; Var L Ftbl; Hon Roll; Prfct Atten Awd; Schl Serv Awds 82-86; 1st Pl Laurence Cnty Bar Assoc Schlrshp 86; U Of Pittsburgh; Lwyr.

CANDIRACCI, LISA; Scranton Preparatory Schl; Avoca, PA; (Y); Dance Clb; Drama Clb; Hosp Aide; PAVAS; Acpl Chr; Chorus; School Musical; School Play; Yrbk Stf; Hon Roll; U Of Scranton; Engrng.

CANE, DAVID; Solebury Schl; New Hope, PA; (S); 5/36; Latin Clb; Nwsp Stf; Yrbk Stf; Stu Cncl; Bsbl; Bsktbl; Lcrss; Socr; High Hon Roll; Hon Roll; Acad All Amer 85-86; Excllnc Shakespeare & Mdrn Amer Fctn 85-86; Sr Grad Awd 85-86; U Of Richmond; Pol Sci.

CANEVARI, JEFFREY; Valley View HS; Blakely, PA; (Y); #53 In Class; Latin Clb; JV Bsbl; JV Ftbl; Golf; Vllybl; Hnbl Mntn Golf All Str Tm 84; Golf All Str Tm 85; Lafayette; Bio.

CANFIELD, JACQUE; Saegertown Area HS; Saegertown, PA; (Y); 3/117; Trs Church Yth Grp; Pres 4-H; Varsity Clb; Trs Chorus; Swing Chorus; Variety Show; Sec Jr Cls; VP Stu Cncl; JV Var Cheerleading; Hon Roll; Bucknell U.

CANNATARO, VINA; St Maria Goretti HS; Philadelphia, PA; (Y); Cmnty Wkr; Soroptimist; Hon Roll; Drexel U; Htl Mgmt.

CANNELLA, JOSEPH; Upper Darby HS; Upper Darby, PA; (Y); 8/632; Cmnty Wkr; Sec Pres French Clb; Capt Quiz Bowl; Rep Soph Cls; Rep Jr Cls; Rep Sr Cls; Stu Cncl; Hon Roll; Boy Scts; Drama Clb; Gen Elec Ldrshp Conf; Free Entrprs Bus Fellwshp; Computtnl Physics.

CANNING, MAUREEN; Archbishop Prendergast HS; Yeadon, PA; (Y); 4/367; Church Yth Grp; French Clb; Latin Clb; Orch; Gym; Im Sftbl; High Hon Roll; Hon Roll; NHS; Pres Schlr; Hghst Gnrl Avrg 84-85; U Scrntn & La Sall U Schlrshps 86; U CRNTN; Bus.

CANNISTRACI, TINA; Tyrone Area HS; Tyrone, PA; (Y); Art Clb; Office Aide; Trs SADD; Chorus; Mrchg Band; Rep Soph Cls; Rep Stu Cncl; Twrlr; Hon Roll; Jr NHS; S Hills Bus Schl; Exec Sec.

CANNITO, CHRISTINE; Upper Darby SR HS; Upper Darby, PA; (Y); Computer Clb; Band; Concert Band; Mrchg Band; Orch; Pep Band; Psychlgy.

CANNON, GRACE; William Allen HS; Allentown, PA; (Y); 7/576; Art Clb; Nwsp Rptr; Nwsp Stf; Lit Mag; High Hon Roll; Jr NHS; NHS; PA Govnrs Schl Art 85; Spec Merit Scholar W W Grainger 86; Pres Acad Fit Awd 86; Bryn Mawr; Fine Art.

CANNON, LINDA; Bishop Hannan HS; Scranton, PA; (Y); 46/130; Spanish Clb; Stage Crew; Hon Roll; NHS; Awds Amer Cultr, Latin & Span 85-86; U Scranton.

CANNON JR, PATRICK J; Butler SR HS; Butler, PA; (Y); 83/777; Exploring; Math Tm; Spanish Clb; Hon Roll; Schltc Awd & Lttr 84; Comp Aided Drftg Clb 85-86; Clemson U; Chem Engrng.

CANNON, ROBERT; Moon SR HS; Coraopolis, PA; (Y); 17/329; Computer Clb; German Clb; Science Clb; Band; Jazz Band; Mrchg Band; Pep Band; Symp Band; Variety Show; High Hon Roll; PA Hghr Ed Asstnce Agency Cert Merit 85; US Navy; Nuclr Engrng.

CANNON, WENDY; Canon Mcmillan SR HS; Canonsburg, PA; (Y); Varsity Clb; Var JV Mgr(s); JV Var Score Keeper; Mgr Var Sftbl; High Hon Roll; Hon Roll; NHS; Pres Schlr; Pres Spanish NHS; Mary Noss Scholar CA U PA 86; CA U PA; Elem Ed.

CANON, KRIS; West Middlesex Area JR SR HS; W Middlesex, PA; (S); 1/120; Pres Trs Church Yth Grp; Sec VP 4-H; Math Tm; Spanish Clb; Band; Chorus; Church Choir; Mrchg Band; Symp Band; Nwsp Ed-Chief; 1st Pl St Sunday Schl Essay Cont 85; WVUFINE Arts Music Camp Schlrshp; Finance.

CANTAFIO, DIANA L; Norristown Area HS; Norristown, PA; (Y); 17/404; Hosp Aide; Concert Band; Orch; Symp Band; Yrbk Stf; Lit Mag; High Hon Roll; Hon Roll; NHS; Ursinus Col6; Pdtrcn.

CANTELLA, KAREN; South Side Catholic HS; Pittsburgh, PA; (S); Camera Clb; Church Yth Grp; Dance Clb; Drama Clb; School Play; Yrbk Phtg; Yrbk Stf; Rep Sr Cls; Rep Stu Cncl; Bowling; Hghst Avg Gnrl Bus Trng 84; New Tstmnt Rlgn 83; Hghst Avg Alg II 84; Pttsbrgh Beauty Acad; Sln Own.

CANTERINO, JOHN; Cardinal O Hara HS; Drexel Hill, PA; (Y); 113/772; Cmnty Wkr; School Play; Im Bsktbl; JV Crs Cntry; Var Ftbl; Im Sftbl; JV Trk; Wt Lftg; York Coll Of PA; Crmnl Justc.

CANTOLINA, PAULA; West Branch JR SR HS; Morrisdale, PA; (Y); Pres Drama Clb; Hosp Aide; Science Clb; Trs Spanish Clb; Chorus; School Play; Stage Crew; Yrbk Stf.

CANTON, ALBERT; Shenango HS; New Castle, PA; (Y); JV Bsbl; Im Bsktbl; JV Crs Cntry; Wt Lftg; NHS; Psych.

CANTONE, AUDRA; Allentown Central Catholic HS; Macungie, PA; (Y); 13/210; Pres Church Yth Grp; French Clb; Pep Clb; High Hon Roll; Jr NHS; NHS; PA Acad Sci 1st Pl Local ST 85; Vet-Med.

CANTOR, SELENA A; Lower Moreland HS; Huntingdon Valley, PA; (S); VP Drama Clb; Red Cross Aide; Jazz Band; Madrigals; School Musical; Hon Roll; Sec NHS; French Clb; Key Clb; Science Clb; 1st Pl Dist & Rgnl Chrs Cmptn 85-86; Mst Mscl Sr 86; Vcl Prfrmr.

CANTWELL, MICHAEL N; La Salle College HS; Furlong, PA; (Y); 3/214; Ed Yrbk Ed-Chief; Var Wrstlng; High Hon Roll; NHS; Ntl Merit Schol; Sal; Wm Connelly Mdl Engl 86; Brother Emilian Latin Mdl 86; James Sullivan Mdl German 86; Brown U.

CANZANO, JOHN C; William Allen HS; Allentown, PA; (Y); 4/576; Boys Clb Am; JCL; Latin Clb; Math Clb; Chorus; Trs Soph Cls; Trs Jr Cls; Trs Sr Cls; JV L Bsktbl; High Hon Roll; Renssir Mdl-Math & Sci Awd 85; Drtmth Book Awd 85; Drxl U Music Awds 85; Duke U; Pre Med.

CAPARONI, DAVID M; Methacton HS; Audubon, PA; (Y); 120/336; Spanish Clb; Yrbk Stf; Stu Cncl; High Hon Roll; Otstndng Stu Cncl Rep 86; PA ST U.

CAPARONI, DENISE; Seton Catholic HS; Exeter, PA; (Y); 29/92; Key Clb; Ski Clb; School Musical; Stage Crew; Yrbk Stf; Var Cheerleading; Im Vllybl; Hon Roll; NHS; Spansh Awd 82-83; Penn ST; Busnss.

CAPASSO, CINDA; Hempfield Area SR HS; Greensburg, PA; (Y); Library Aide; SADD; Capt VICA; Yrbk Ed-Chief; Var Capt Cheerleading; High Hon Roll; Hon Roll; Jr NHS; Letterman Clb; Pep Clb; Pitts Bty Acad; Bty Cltr.

CAPATOSTI, JENNIFER; Brownsville Area SR HS; Brownsville, PA; (Y); 37/222; Drama Clb; Office Aide; Ski Clb; SADD; Band; Concert Band; Mrchg Band; Rep Jr Cls; Stat Trk; Hon Roll; US Achvt Acad 86.

CAPECE, DIANE; John S Fine HS; Nanticoke, PA; (S); 7/242; FTA; Hosp Aide; Key Clb; Chorus; Mrchg Band; Yrbk Rptr; High Hon Roll; NHS; Secondary Educ.

CAPELA, KELLY; Corry Area HS; Spartansburg, PA; (S); 32/215; French Clb; Office Aide; Chorus; Off Sr Cls; Sec Stu Cncl; Stat Vllybl.

CAPELA, TRUDI; Corry Area HS; Corry, PA; (S); 5/212; Model UN; Pres Spanish Clb; Nwsp Ed-Chief; High Hon Roll; CA U Of PA; Sci/Techncl Wrtng.

CAPELLI, ANGELIA; Blacklick Valley HS; Nanty Glo, PA; (Y); 14/91; Art Clb; High Hon Roll; Hon Roll; NHS; Acad All-Amer 86; Accntnt.

CAPELLMAN, JACLYN; Highlands HS; Tarentum, PA; (Y); 6/277; Office Aide; Chorus; Off Stu Cncl; Cheerleading; Trk; High Hon Roll; Jr NHS; Sec NHS; Rotary Awd; Pres Schlrshp 86; Rtry Schlrshp 86; Crlsn Coll Pitsbrg PA; Chem.

CAPEROON, RAY; Central Dauphin HS; Linglestown, PA; (Y); 28/328; Boy Scts; Science Clb; Band; Concert Band; Capt Drm & Bgl; Jazz Band; Mrchg Band; Orch; Hon Roll; Jr NHS; Eagle Scout Awd 82; Carnegie Mellon U; Physcs.

CAPINSKI, WILLIAM; St Pius X HS; Pottstown, PA; (S); 7/161; JA; Latin Clb; Mathletes; Science Clb; Crs Cntry; Trk; Hon Roll; NEDT Awd; Prfct Atten Awd; 2nd Pl JR Acad Sci PA 84; Cvl Engrng.

CAPIROSE, LISA; Pennsbury SR HS; Levittown, PA; (Y); Mathletes; Spanish Clb; Cit Awd; High Hon Roll; NHS; Psychtry.

CAPLAN, TYANA; Winchester Thurston HS; Pittsburgh, PA; (Y); French Clb; Service Clb; Stage Crew; Lit Mag; Almn Schlrshp 82-87; Anthrplgy.

CAPLINGER, JAMES; Tulpehocken HS; Bethel, PA; (Y); Dance Clb; Spanish Clb; Chorus; School Musical; School Play; Swing Chorus; Hon Roll; NHS; Theatr Art.

CAPOBIANCO, DENA; Notre Dame HS; Martins Creek, PA; (Y); 3/88; French Clb; Pep Clb; Teachers Aide; Yrbk Stf; Crs Cntry; Mgr(s); Trk; High Hon Roll; Sec NHS; Med.

CAPOBRES, KIMBERLY; Immaculate Conception HS; Washington, PA; (Y); Rep Stu Cncl; Stat Bsbl; Var L Cheerleading; Hon Roll; Washington/Jefferson; Pre-Med.

CAPONE, CHRIS; Mahanoy Area HS; Mahanoy City, PA; (S); DECA; Var Sftbl; High Hon Roll; Bus Mgmt.

CAPONE, NINA CHRISTINE; Merion Mercy Acad; Drexel Hill, PA; (Y); Cmnty Wkr; French Clb; Mathletes; Stage Crew; Capt Cheerleading; High Hon Roll; Natl Art Hnr Soc 84-86; Moore Coll Of Art Smmr H S Crs Schlrshp 85; Drexel & Fordham U Schlrshps 86-87; Boston U; Pol Sci.

CAPORALI, KRISTEN; Freeport Area HS; Freeport, PA; (S); 25/170; Church Yth Grp; Color Guard; Drill Tm; Var JV Vllybl; High Hon Roll; Hon Roll.

CAPORALI, RENEE; Sacred Heart HS; Carbondale, PA; (Y); Church Yth Grp; Cmnty Wkr; FBLA; GAA; JA; Spanish Clb; Chorus; School Play; Var Capt Bsktbl; Sftbl; U Of Scranton; Accntng.

CAPORUSCIO III, AMERIGO; Altoona Area SR HS; Altoona, PA; (Y); 147/683; Boy Scts; Church Yth Grp; JA; Library Aide; Nwsp Rptr; Nwsp Stf; Spanish NHS; Edinbroro U; Psych.

CAPOUELLEZ, JAMES; Conemaugh Valley HS; Mineral Point, PA; (Y); JV Bowling; Lawrence Inst; Mech Engr.

CAPP, CYNTHIA; Bethel Park SR HS; Bethel Park, PA; (Y); 9/519; Church Yth Grp; Science Clb; JV Var Bsktbl; Var L Sftbl; Var L Vllybl; High Hon Roll; NHS; Prncpl Awd 84; John Leroy Wrtg Awd 84; 2 1st Pl Awds Wstrn PA Indstrl Arts Fair 85; Chem.

CAPP, SANDRA; Bethel Park SR HS; Bethel Park, PA; (Y); 9/519; Church Yth Grp; Science Clb; JV Var Bsktbl; Var L Sftbl; Var L Vllybl; High Hon Roll; NHS; Prncpls Awd 84; John Leroy Wrtg Awd 84; 1st Pl PA Indstrl Arts Fair 85; Chem.

CAPPEL, CHRISTINE; Central Catholic HS; Reading, PA; (Y); Art Clb; Office Aide; Pep Clb; Red Cross Aide; Band; Chorus; Color Guard; Drill Tm; Flag Corp; Mrchg Band; Berks Cnty CYO Art Cntst Hnrbl Mntn 84-86; Typng Awd 86; Penn ST; Music.

CAPPELL, DONNA; Hampton HS; Allison Pk, PA; (Y); Girl Scts; Band; Drill Tm; Mrchg Band; Pom Pon; Flght Atten.

CAPPELLONI, LISA; Scranton Preparatory Schl; Scranton, PA; (Y); 20/192; Chorus; School Musical; School Play; Stage Crew; Yrbk Stf; Lit Mag; High Hon Roll; Jr NHS; NHS; Lang.

CAPPER, REBECCA; Meadville SR HS; Meadville, PA; (S); 87/280; Chorus; Concert Band; Drm Mjr(t); Mrchg Band; Trk; Vllybl; Church Yth Grp; Teachers Aide; Dist Band 86; Regnl Band 86; IN U PA; Elem Ed.

CAPPOLELLA, MARLA; Stroudsburg HS; E Stroudsburg, PA; (Y); Pep Clb; Spanish Clb; Chorus; School Musical; School Play; Yrbk Stf; Stu Cncl; JV Capt Cheerleading; High Hon Roll; Hon Roll; Hm Ec Awd; Locl Rotry Clb Schlrshp; E Stroudsburg U; Cmnctns.

CAPRERI, DEANNA; Upper Dublin HS; Maple Glen, PA; (Y); 96/307; FBLA; Hosp Aide; Teachers Aide; Varsity Clb; Rep Frsh Cls; JV Bsktbl; Var L Fld Hcky; Var L Lcrss; Im Mgr Powder Puff Ftbl; Suburbn I Medl La Crosse & Hcky 85-86; Ithaca; Phy Thrpst.

CAPRINO, LISA; Penn Hills SR HS; Pittsburgh, PA; (Y); French Clb; JA; Ski Clb; Band; Mrchg Band; Orch; School Musical; High Hon Roll; Hon Roll; Pre-Med.

CAPRIOTTI, DEBORA; West Catholic Girls HS; Philadelphia, PA; (Y); 8/240; Drama Clb; Nwsp Stf; Yrbk Stf; High Hon Roll; Hon Roll; Mathletes; Orch; Exmplry Stdnt Awd 84; Acdmc Achvt Bio 85; Engl Acdmc Achvt 85-86; U Of Penn; Nrsg.

CAPRIOTTI, JODI; Merion Mercy Acad; Phila, PA; (Y); 18/86; Mathletes; VP Spanish Clb; Im Bsktbl; Var Sftbl; Im Capt Vllybl; Hon Roll; Spanish NHS; Natl Spnsh Exm Tp 10% 84-86; Tutrng Undrclsmn 85-86; HOPE 84-86; Accntng.

CAPUANO, MEGAN; Cumberland Valley HS; Carlisle, PA; (Y); 150/835; Key Clb; Ski Clb; Band; Var L Fld Hcky; Mgr(s); Trk; Hon Roll; Bus.

CAPUANO, SHEILA; Bethlehem Catholic HS; Bethlehem, PA; (Y); 164/210; Dance Clb; Hosp Aide; Library Aide; Im Fld Hcky; Im Powder Puff Ftbl; Hon Roll; N Hmptn CC; Hotel Mngmnt.

CAPUTO, CRAIG; Mc Keesport Area SR HS; Mckeesport, PA; (Y); 19/331; Quiz Bowl; Coach Actv; Var L Ftbl; Wt Lftg; Var L Wrstlng; High Hon Roll; NHS; Engrng.

CAPUTO, DIANE; St Hubert HS; Philadelphia, PA; (Y); 85/367; Cmnty Wkr; Office Aide; Hon Roll; Philadelphia Coll/Phrmcy; Sci.

CAPUZZI, DAVID M; Harrington HS; Haverford, PA; (Y); Cmnty Wkr; Hosp Aide; Political Wkr; Variety Show; Nwsp Rptr; JV Crs Cntry; Var L Trk; Hon Roll; Jr NHS; Ntl Merit SF; Chem.

CAPUZZI, MARYANN; Saltsburg JR SR HS; Saltsburg, PA; (Y); 10/84; GAA; Letterman Clb; VP SADD; Varsity Clb; Yrbk Sprt Ed; Yrbk Stf; Capt Var Bsktbl; Var L Sftbl; Mgr Vllybl; Elks Awd; Pre-Med.

CARA, CARLA; Hazleton SR HS; Kelayres, PA; (Y); 69/400; FBLA; Office Aide; Chorus; Rep Stu Cncl; Bsktbl; Hon Roll; CPA.

CARABIN, LISA; Central Dauphin HS; Harrisburg, PA; (Y); 107/386; German Clb; Teachers Aide; Chorus; Color Guard; School Musical; Var Crs Cntry; JV Gym; JV Trk; Im Vllybl; Hon Roll; Frgn Lang.

CARACCIOLO, JOHN; Altoona Area HS; Altoona, PA; (S); Spanish Clb; Band; Concert Band; Mrchg Band; Orch; Pep Band; Ed Yrbk Stf; High Hon Roll; Hon Roll; Penn ST; Scndry Educ.

CARACIO, KRISTINE; Pleasant Valley HS; Kunkletown, PA; (Y); 8/233; Letterman Clb; Ski Clb; Varsity Clb; Rep Trs Frsh Cls; Rep Soph Cls; Rep Jr Cls; Rep Stu Cncl; Var L Cheerleading; Var L Sftbl; High Hon Roll; WY Smnry Schlrshp 86; Cnty Spllng Bee Fnlst 86; Advrtsng.

CARANGI, KIM; New Castle SR HS; West Pittsburg, PA; (S); 11/236; Ftbl; Im Vllybl; High Hon Roll; Hon Roll; NHS; Ntl Ldrshp Merit Awd 85; Grove City Coll; Comp Syst.

CARATHERS, CHRISTY; Bentworth HS; Bentleyville, PA; (Y); Art Clb; Varsity Clb; Band; Concert Band; Mrchg Band; Pep Band; Yrbk Sprt Ed; Yrbk Stf; Off Bsktbl; Off Sr Cls; Acdmc Achvmnt Awd 83-86; Art.

CARAVELLA, CHRISTY; New Castle SR HS; New Castle, PA; (Y); 67/253; French Clb; Pep Clb; SADD; Drill Tm; Nwsp Rptr; Ed Nwsp Stf; Hon Roll; Concert Band; Hurricaine Life Nwspaper Awd 86; Fshn Mrchndsng.

CARAVELLA, LISA; Freeland HS; White Haven, PA; (Y); FBLA; Pep Clb; Chorus; Stu Cncl; Capt Cheerleading; Sftbl; Vllybl.

CARBAUGH, DENA; Mc Connellsburg HS; Mcconnellsburg, PA; (Y); FBLA; Trs Varsity Clb; School Play; Yrbk Stf; Trk; Vllybl; Hon Roll; Hagerstown JR Coll; Exec Secty.

CARBAUGH, MICHELLE; Waynesboro Area SR HS; S Mountain, PA; (Y); 13/363; Church Yth Grp; Hosp Aide; Band; Chorus; Church Choir; Concert Band; Mrchg Band; Stage Crew; High Hon Roll.

CARBONARO, DOMENICK; West Catholic H S For Boys; Philadelphia, PA; (Y); 39/268; Teachers Aide; 2nd Hnrs 83-86; Phila Coll; Phrmcst.

CARD, SHAWNA; Northwestern SR HS; Albion, PA; (Y); 7/164; Drama Clb; Red Cross Aide; Thesps; Chorus; Color Guard; Concert Band; School Musical; Hon Roll; Nrsng.

CARDELI, THERESA; Mountain View HS; Nicholson, PA; (Y); Teachers Aide; Chorus; School Musical; School Play; Im Vllybl; Im Wt Lftg; 4-H Awd; Hon Roll; Chess Clb; 4-H; 3rd Pl Essay SFSC 84-85; Penn ST.

CARDENAS, DAVID; Upper Merion Area HS; Kg Of Prussia, PA; (Y); Computer Clb; Variety Show; Vllybl; Bus.

CARDILLO, LISA; Wyoming Valley West HS; Forty Fort, PA; (Y); Key Clb; Flag Corp; Jazz Band; Nwsp Phtg; Yrbk Phtg; Cit Awd; High Hon Roll; NHS; NEDT Awd; Nat Hstry Day St Wnnr 84-85; Bus.

CARDINAL, LYNN; Saint Huberts HS; Philadelphia, PA; (Y); 19/367; Chorus; Orch; Hon Roll; Music.

CARDINALE, JOSEPH; Emmaus HS; Emmaus, PA; (Y); 18/493; Key Clb; Model UN; Concert Band; Mrchg Band; Symp Band; Var Tennis; High Hon Roll; NHS; Ntl Merit Ltr; Boy Scts; Excpt To Yng Peopls Phlhrmnc Co Yth Orch Lehigh Vly 82-87; RIT; Mech Engrng.

CARDONE, KRISTEN; Notre Dame Acad; Bryn Mawr, PA; (Y); Model UN; Service Clb; School Musical; Nwsp Sprt Ed; Nwsp Stf; Yrbk Stf; Lit Mag; Var Capt Fld Hcky; Var Lcrss; Hon Roll; Ovrbrk Glf Clb 1st Rnr Up Sngls & Dbls Tnns 84-87; Hnrb Mntn All Main Lne Fld Hcky 84-85; Bus.

CARDONI, GINA; James M Coughlin HS; Laflin, PA; (Y); 28/342; Church Yth Grp; Math Clb; Concert Band; Var L Fld Hcky; Sftbl; Capt L Swmmng; High Hon Roll; Hon Roll; NHS.

CAREATTI, SUZANNE M; Apollo-Ridge HS; Apollo, PA; (Y); 10/166; Pres Church Yth Grp; FTA; Chorus; Church Choir; Madrigals; Variety Show; High Hon Roll; NHS; Louise V Nelson Memrl Schlrshp 86; SR Grl Mnth 86; Stdnt Mnth Jan Schl Papr 85; Clarion U Of PA; Secdry Ed.

CARENZO, MICHAEL T; Lower Dauphin HS; Hershey, PA; (Y); Am Leg Boys St; Ski Clb; Chorus; School Musical; Rep Jr Cls; Trs Sr Cls; Stu Cncl; Ice Hcky; Tennis; Hon Roll; Bus Admin.

CAREW, DEBORAH; Merion Mercy Acad; Merion, PA; (Y); 1/75; French Clb; Teachers Aide; Chorus; School Play; Nwsp Rptr; French Hon Soc; High Hon Roll; NHS; Ntl Merit Ltr; 7th Pl In Natl Frnch Comp 83-84; 5th Pl In Natl Frnch Comp 84-85; 10th Pl In Natl Frnch Comp 85-86; Ed.

CAREY, ANN; Little Flower HS; Philadelphia, PA; (Y); 27/353; Computer Clb; Drama Clb; GAA; Hosp Aide; Latin Clb; Service Clb; Madrigals; Lit Mag; Bsktbl; Fld Hcky; Harvard Law Schl; Poltics.

CAREY, DANIELLE; Carlynton HS; Carnegie, PA; (Y); 10/176; Church Yth Grp; Drama Clb; Drill Tm; Jr Cls; Stu Cncl; Cheerleading; Vllybl; High Hon Roll; NHS; Carnegie Civic Clb Scholar 86; Pres Acad Fit Awd 86; Penn ST U; Comm.

CAREY, DIANE; Seton Catholic HS; Duryea, PA; (Y); 19/91; Off SADD; Madrigals; School Play; Hon Roll; Magna Cum Laude Awd Latn Exm 85; Grad W/Hons 86; Kings Coll; Engl.

CAREY, JANET; Lakeland JR SR HS; Jermyn, PA; (S); 34/147; Trs Sec Church Yth Grp; FHA; JA; Church Choir; Hon Roll; Phys Ther.

CAREY, JOHN; Bishop Guilfoyle HS; Altoona, PA; (S); 13/150; Science Clb; SADD; Chorus; Var L Bsbl; L Bsktbl; Var Capt Ftbl; High Hon Roll; Hon Roll; Pres NHS; Altoona Mrrs Ftbl Yr Plyr 85; Altoona Mrrs All Strs 1st Tm Offns & Dfns 85; Sci.

CAREY, KIMBERLY; Nativity B V M HS; New Philadelphia, PA; (Y); 29/98; Aud/Vis; Computer Clb; Ski Clb; Flag Corp; Stage Crew; Variety Show; Hon Roll; Hghst Achvt Alg II Awd 86; PA ST U; Indstrl Engrng.

CAREY, KRISTAN; Downingtown SR HS; Exton, PA; (Y); Church Yth Grp; GAA; Pep Clb; Ski Clb; Chorus; School Musical; Swing Chorus; JV Fld Hcky; JV Lcrss; Hon Roll; Ithaca Coll.

CAREY, PAM; North Penn HS; Blossburg, PA; (Y); 11/67; Camera Clb; Sec Trs Church Yth Grp; FBLA; GAA; Library Aide; Red Cross Aide; SADD; Hon Roll; NHS; Central PA Bus Schl; Ofc Cmctn.

CAREY, ROCHELLE; Cambridge Springs HS; Cambridge Springs, PA; (Y); 17/112; French Clb; Hosp Aide; Pep Clb; SADD; Chorus; Nwsp Rptr; Yrbk Ed-Chief; Rep Stu Cncl; Hon Roll; NHS; Gannon U; Pre-Med.

CAREY, SCOTT; Derry Area SR HS; Latrobe, PA; (Y); Sec Computer Clb; Band; Concert Band; Mrchg Band; Pep Band; Symp Band; Im Badmtn; Var Bsbl; Im Ftbl; Im Vllybl; Most Outstndng Mrchng Band 86; U Pittsburgh; Comp Sci.

CAREY, TOM; Scranton Prep Schl; Clarks Summit, PA; (Y); 81/192; Computer Clb; Ski Clb; Hon Roll; Elec Engrng.

CAREY, VALERIE; Seneca HS; Wattsburg, PA; (Y); 12/173; High Hon Roll; Hon Roll; Ntl Merit Ltr; Prfct Atten Awd; Physcl Thrpy.

CARFAGNO, DEBBIE; Bishop Kenrick HS; Norristown, PA; (Y); Nrsng.

CARICHNER, JEANNINE; Moon SR HS; Coraopolis, PA; (Y); Commncmnt Spkr 86; Penn ST U; Bus Admn.

CARINO, LISA; Bishop Mc Cort HS; Johnstown, PA; (Y); Girl Scts; Spanish Clb; Chorus; School Musical; High Hon Roll; Hon Roll; Spanish NHS; Central Bus Schl; Court Reprtng.

CARINO, NOEL; Scranton Preparatory Schl; Peckville, PA; (Y); 38/192; Chorus; School Musical; Stage Crew; Tennis; Trk; High Hon Roll; Hon Roll; Jr NHS; Hihg Hnr Natl JR Clsscl Leag Greek 86; Pre Med.

CARL, DEBRA; Tri-Valley HS; Valley View, PA; (Y); 9/75; Church Yth Grp; Ski Clb; Chorus; Church Choir; Drill Tm; Yrbk Stf; Rep Stu Cncl; Hon Roll; NHS; Wdmn Of Wrld Hstry Awd 84; Schylkll Cnty Mdcl Soc Axlry Schlrshp 86; PA Music Edctrs Assn Dist/Rgn 86; York Coll Of PA; Hlth Rcds Adm.

CARL, GRETA; Tri Valley HS; Spring Glen, PA; (Y); 4/75; Drama Clb; Quiz Bowl; Capt L Band; Chorus; JV Bsktbl; Var Capt Cheerleading; Hon Roll; NHS; Wmns Clb Awd 86; Rtry Stu Mnth 86; U Of CA; Pre-Med.

CARL, JAMES; Beth-Center HS; Fredericktown, PA; (Y); Boy Scts; JA; Ski Clb; Concert Band; Mrchg Band; County Bnd 85-86; Aerontcl Engrg.

CARL, KATHERINE; Central Dauphin HS; Harrisburg, PA; (Y); 14/386; Church Yth Grp; Band; Chorus; Orch; School Musical; School Play; High Hon Roll; Hon Roll; Jr NHS; NHS; Liberal Arts.

CARL, MELVIN; Mc Guffey HS; Washington, PA; (Y).

CARL, RICK; Minersville Area HS; Minersville, PA; (Y); German Clb; Rep Sr Cls; Rep Stu Cncl; Var L Ftbl; Wt Lftg; Hon Roll; Law Enfrcmnt.

CARL, SCOTT; Elizabethtown Area HS; Elizabethtown, PA; (Y); 30/237; Computer Clb; Letterman Clb; Var Wrstlng; Hon Roll; PA ST; Engrng.

CARL, VALERIE; Tri-Valley HS; Valley View, PA; (Y); 4/77; Church Yth Grp; Concert Band; Mrchg Band; Ed Yrbk Ed-Chief; Sftbl; Hon Roll; NHS; NEDT Awd; Miss PA Teen Pgnt 86; PA Gov Schl Intl Studs 86; Fshn Mrch.

CARLANTONIO, JACQUELINE S; Moniteau JR SR HS; Boyers, PA; (Y); 11/128; Sec Art Clb; Pres Church Yth Grp; Chorus; Church Choir; Yrbk Sprt Ed; JV L Badmtn; Var L Vllybl; Hon Roll; NHS; Pres Schlr; Moniteau Schlrshp Fndtn 86; Vrsty Sprts Awd 86; Laroche Coll; Interior Dsgn.

CARLEO, DANA; Norwin HS; Irwin, PA; (Y); 139/546; Leo Clb; Pep Clb; SADD; School Play; Nwsp Rptr; Hon Roll; NHS; Cert Mrt Exclnc Speech 86; Point Park Coll; Comm.

CARLESI, ANDREA; Kittaning SR HS; Kittanning, PA; (Y); 34/274; Church Yth Grp; French Clb; Nwsp Stf; Yrbk Stf; Rep Soph Cls; Rep Jr Cls; Rep Stu Cncl; Var L Tennis; Hon Roll; Smmr Hppng ARIN 86; Intl Law.

CARLETON, JAMES; Wellsboro Area HS; Wellsboro, PA; (Y); Church Yth Grp; Bsbl; Tennis.

CARLIN, EDDIE; Monaca JR SR HS; Monaca, PA; (Y); 2/96; Am Leg Boys St; Var L Bsktbl; High Hon Roll; Hon Roll; NHS; Penn ST; Engrng.

CARLINI, SHARON; Butler Area SR HS; Butler, PA; (Y); AFS; Exploring; PAVAS; Spanish Clb; SADD; Nwsp Rptr; Yrbk Stf; PA ST U; Comm.

CARLISLE, ANTHONY TODD; Ambridge HS; Ambridge, PA; (S); German Clb; Pep Clb; Nwsp Bus Mgr; Nwsp Ed-Chief; Nwsp Rptr; Nwsp Stf; Bsktbl; L Ftbl; Hon Roll; Journlsm.

CARLISLE, ERIC W; Octorara Area HS; Parkesburg, PA; (Y); 57/172; Boy Scts; Pres Church Yth Grp; VP FBLA; Political Wkr; Ed Nwsp Stf; Stu Cncl; Mgr Bsbl; Hon Roll; Lion Awd; Eagl Sct 83; FBLA Acctng II 3rd Pl Rgnls, Tied 2nd ST 86; York Coll PA; Acctng.

CARLSON, ANDREA; Jenkintown HS; Jenkintown, PA; (S); French Clb; Model UN; Varsity Clb; Chorus; School Musical; Nwsp Stf; Var Tennis; French Hon Soc; High Hon Roll; NHS; Poltcl Sci.

CARLSON, CAMME; Blue Mountain Acad; Hatfield, PA; (Y); Chorus; School Musical; School Play; Nwsp Rptr; Sec Jr Cls; VP Sr Cls; Sftbl; Wt Lftg; Hon Roll.

CARLSON, CLARE; General Mc Lane HS; Edinboro, PA; (Y); 19/220; Church Yth Grp; French Clb; Band; Concert Band; Mrchg Band; Pep Band; Hon Roll; ST By-Pss Pgm 86-87; Wthrspn Schlrshp 86-87; Edinboro U Of PA; Med Tchnlgy.

CARLSON, GEOFFREY P; Quakertown Community HS; Quakertown, PA; (Y); Am Leg Boys St; Ski Clb; Rep Stu Cncl; Var Socr; Var Vllybl; High Hon Roll; Hon Roll; NHS.

CARLSON, HEIDI; Franklin Regional HS; Murrysville, PA; (Y); AFS; Band; Yrbk Stf; Bsktbl; Socr; Sftbl; Hon Roll; WPIAL Soccr All Star Tm 85-86; Mst Ath 86; Pittsburgh E All Star Tm Bsktbl 84-86; Wittenberg U.

CARLSON, JOELY; North Allegheny SR HS; Wexford, PA; (Y); 46/642; Church Yth Grp; Cmnty Wkr; Hosp Aide; Band; Chorus; Mrchg Band; Trk; Hon Roll; Jr NHS; NHS.

CARLSON, KATHRYN; Cowanesque Valley HS; Westfield, PA; (S); Sec Church Yth Grp; Trs French Clb; Band; Chorus; Trs Frsh Cls; Trs Soph Cls; Trs Jr Cls; Tennis; Hon Roll; NHS.

CARLSON, RENA; Upper Merion Area HS; King Of Prussia, PA; (Y); 97/308; Hon Roll; Eng Ed.

CARLSON, WENDY; Sheffield JR SR HS; Sheffield, PA; (Y); 4/87; Drama Clb; SADD; Chorus; Color Guard; School Play; Yrbk Ed-Chief; Cit Awd; High Hon Roll; NHS; Prfct Atten Awd; Spec Ed.

CARMEAN, KEVIN; Somerset Area HS; Somerset, PA; (Y); 52/239; English Clb; German Clb; Letterman Clb; Varsity Clb; Var L Bsbl; JV L Bsktbl; Var L Mgr(s); High Hon Roll; NHS; Chem Engr.

CARMICHAEL, JEFFREY; Langley HS; Pittsburgh, PA; (Y); 28/281; Boy Scts; Exploring; Ftbl; Swmmng; Hon Roll; Slippery Rock U; Bio.

CARNACK JR, DANIEL E; Connellsville Area SR HS; Dunbar, PA; (Y); 49/484; Pres FTA; German Clb; Office Aide; Chorus; School Musical; Var Trk; High Hon Roll; Jr NHS; NHS; German Hon Soc 85-86; Salisbury ST Coll; Hstry.

CARNAHAN, ROBERT; Springdale HS; Springdale, PA; (Y); German Clb; Trs Acpl Chr; Pres Jr Cls; Var Bsbl; Var Bsktbl; High Hon Roll; NHS; Ntl Merit Ltr; Prfct Atten Awd; May Ct Stu 85-86; PA ST U; Law.

CARNATHAN, JAMES; Brownsville Area HS; Penn Craft, PA; (Y); Ski Clb; PA ST; Arch Engrng.

CARNER, HEIDI; Fairview HS; Fairview, PA; (Y); Church Yth Grp; Drama Clb; Chorus; Flag Corp; School Musical; Yrbk Stf; Vllybl; Hon Roll; SADD; Thesps; Ft Leboeue Acdmc Achvt Awd 84-85; Smi Fnlst Govr Schl Arts Comptn 85-86; Atnd Dist, Reg, ST Chr 84-85; Psych.

CARNES, ANNE; Punxsutawney Area HS; Punxsutawney, PA; (Y); 28/238; Science Clb; Spanish Clb; Band; Concert Band; Drill Tm; Mrchg Band; Variety Show; Var Vllybl; Hon Roll; VFW Awd; Pres Phys Fit Awd 86; Merit Scholar William Woods Coll 86; Paralegl Scholar William Woods Coll 86; William Woods Coll; Paralgl.

CARNES, DORENDA A; Methacton SR HS; Audubon, PA; (Y); Key Clb; Office Aide; Ski Clb; School Musical; School Play; Swing Chorus; Rep Frsh Cls; Rep Soph Cls; Rep Jr Cls; Rep Sr Cls; Bloomsburg U; Mass Cmmnctns.

CARNES, LAURA; Punxsutawney HS; Punxsutawney, PA; (Y); Spanish Clb; Varsity Clb; Band; Concert Band; Mrchg Band; Rep Soph Cls; Rep Jr Cls; Rep Sr Cls; VP Stu Cncl; Var Capt Cheerleading; Natl Chrldng Achvmnt Awd 86; Pres Physcl Ftns Awd 83-85.

CARNEY, DOYLE; United HS; Seward, PA; (S); 2/157; Camera Clb; Church Yth Grp; Math Clb; Ski Clb; Yrbk Stf; Stat Bsktbl; Hon Roll; Jr NHS; Mu Alp Tht; VP NHS; Penn ST; Comp Sci.

CARNEY, TAMMERA L; Montour HS; Coraopolis, PA; (Y); 13/263; NFL; Mrchg Band; Rep Frsh Cls; Rep Soph Cls; Rep Stu Cncl; Var Capt Gym; High Hon Roll; NHS; GAA; Drill Tm; Schlr Athlt Awd 86; David E Williamd Memrl Schlrshp 86; Allegheny Coll; Pre-Med.

CARNIELLO, SEAN; Waynesboro SR HS; Waynesboro, PA; (Y); 111/400; Church Yth Grp; Cmnty Wkr; Drama Clb; Intnl Clb; Q&S; Ski Clb; Acpl Chr; Chorus; Church Choir; School Musical; Pstrl Muscn 85; Ntl Piano Plyng Audtns Interm Advncd 84-86; Cnty All Dist All Rgnl Chrs 85-86; Music.

CARNOVALE, LAURIE; Cameron County HS; Emporium, PA; (Y); 5/89; Am Leg Aux Girls St; Church Yth Grp; Computer Clb; German Clb; Teachers Aide; Band; Chorus; Church Choir; Concert Band; Mrchg Band; Delta Epsilon Phi 86; Gannon; Pre-Med.

CARNS, DARREN; United HS; Armagh, PA; (S); 3/159; Pres Church Yth Grp; Cmnty Wkr; Math Clb; Chorus; Pres Sr Cls; Var L Bsktbl; Var L Trk; High Hon Roll; Pres Jr NHS; Pres NHS; Arin Iup Semnrs 85-86; Juniata Coll; Chem.

CARON, MICHELLE; Henderson HS; West Chester, PA; (S); 2/343; Church Yth Grp; VP Exploring; Hosp Aide; Intnl Clb; Concert Band; Jazz Band; Mrchg Band; French Hon Soc; High Hon Roll; NHS; TMOT Gen Elect Pgm 84; Bio.

CARONE, LISA; Greencastle HS; Chambersburg, PA; (Y); Drama Clb; Chorus; School Musical; Var Cheerleading; JV Var Tennis; Church Yth Grp; 4-H; Girl Scts; School Play; Hon Roll.

CAROSELLI, JOSEPH; Cardinal O Hara HS; Springfield, PA; (Y); 1/772; Chess Clb; Mathletes; High Hon Roll; NHS; Prfct Atten Awd; Rensselawer Math-Sci Awd, Schlrshp PA Gov Schl Sci 86; Mathlete Yr 84-86; Math.

CARPENETTI, DARREN; Lackawanna Trail HS; Nicholson, PA; (Y); 24/92; Trs Soph Cls; Var L Bsbl; Var L Bsktbl; Hon Roll; PA ST.

CARPENETTI II, DONALD; Lachawanna Trail HS; Nicholson, PA; (Y); Madrigals; School Musical; Trs Jr Cls; Stu Cncl; Var L Bsbl; Var L Crs Cntry; Hon Roll; Lehigh.

CARPENTER, CHARLES; Wyoming Valley W HS; Forty Fort, PA; (Y); 8/410; Church Yth Grp; Coach Actv; Socr; Socr; Trk; High Hon Roll; Hon Roll; NHS; NEDT Awd; Comp Engrng.

CARPENTER, CHRIS; Hyndman Middle SR HS; Buffalo Mls, PA; (Y); Ski Clb; Hon Roll; Prfct Atten Awd; VFW Awd; VP Frsh Cls; VP Soph Cls; Pres VP Stu Cncl; JV Capt Bsktbl.

CARPENTER, KRISTA; Coatesville Area SR HS; Downingtown, PA; (Y); Model UN; Concert Band; Jazz Band; Mrchg Band; Pep Band; School Musical; Symp Band; Off Sr Cls; Drama Clb; German Clb; JR All Americn Musc Hall Of Fm Awd; Prnts Music Club Awd; Indiana U Of PA; Music Educ.

CARPENTER, MATTHEW; Swarthmore Acad; Swarthmore, PA; (S); 1/15; Church Yth Grp; Drama Clb; School Play; Nwsp Stf; Yrbk Stf; Pres Soph Cls; Pres Jr Cls; L Bsktbl; Var L Socr; High Hon Roll; Ovral Acadmc Awd; Math Awd; Sccr Leag Al-Star Tm; U Of PA; Intnatl Bus.

CARPENTER, PAUL; Scranton Central HS; Scranton, PA; (Y); Art Clb; Church Yth Grp; JV Wrstlng; High Hon Roll; Hon Roll; Jr NHS; Boys Clb Am; Art Awd 84-86; PA ST; Physics.

CARPENTER, ROBYN; Susquehanna Community HS; Lanesboro, PA; (Y); Pres Church Yth Grp; Ski Clb; Band; Chorus; Concert Band; Var Cheerleading; Stat Trk; Twrlr; Keystone JC; Bus Admin.

CARPENTER JR, TERRY; Boyertown HS; Boyertown, PA; (Y); Church Yth Grp; Cmnty Wkr; Math Tm; Band; Chorus; Jazz Band; Mrchg Band; School Musical; School Play; Off Soph Cls; US Coast Grd Acad.

CARPENTER, TIMOTHY; Blue Ridge HS; Hallstead, PA; (Y); 4/90; Pep Clb; Scholastic Bowl; Ski Clb; SADD; Yrbk Phtg; Yrbk Sprt Ed; Yrbk Stf; JV Trk; Var Vllybl; High Hon Roll; Giftd Pgm 84-86; PA ST U; Chem Engr.

CARPER, MARK; Somerset SR HS; Somerset, PA; (Y); JA; JV Crs Cntry; Var L Socr; Var L Trk; Hon Roll; Archtctr.

CARPIN, ESPRANZA; St Marys Area HS; Weedville, PA; (Y); 82/301; Church Yth Grp; Yrbk Phtg; Sec Yrbk Stf; Mgr(s); Hon Roll; Bus Admin.

CARPIN, TRACEY; St Marys Area HS; Weedville, PA; (Y); 7/295; Cmnty Wkr; Teachers Aide; Yrbk Stf; Hon Roll; NHS; Physcl Thrpy.

CARR, ANGELA; Danville SR HS; Danville, PA; (Y); Exploring; Spanish Clb; High Hon Roll; NHS.

CARR, BARBARA; Ligonier Valley SR HS; Latrobe, PA; (Y); 33/158; Church Yth Grp; Hosp Aide; Library Aide; Office Aide; Band; Chorus; Church Choir; Concert Band; Drm Mjr(t); Mrchg Band; Wstmrlnd Cnty Bnd 85-86; VP Band 85-86; Indiana U PA; Nrs.

CARR, BARBARA; Little Flower HS; Philadelphia, PA; (Y); 61/413; Cmnty Wkr; Hon Roll; La Salle U; Bus.

CARR, CAROL; Harry S Truman HS; Levittown, PA; (Y); SADD; Hon Roll; NHS; Schlrshp Moore Coll Of Art 86; Schlrshp For Smmr Arts Acad 85; Cmrcl Art.

CARR, CHERYL ANN; Performing Arts HS Of Phila; Somerdale, NJ; (Y); Dance Clb; Yrbk Phtg; Yrbk Stf; Rep Jr Cls; JV Cheerleading; Hon Roll; Prize Schlrshp Perf Arts Schl 86-87; Phila Evening Mag Dancers 85; Lg Dancer Movie Bandstand 86; Dancer.

CARR, DEBORAH; Middletown Area HS; Middletown, PA; (Y); 6/188; FBLA; Latin Clb; Vllybl; Hon Roll; NHS; Acadmc All Am 85-86; Natl Ldrshp And Serv Awd 86.

CARR, DUANE; Punxsutawney Area HS; Punxsu, PA; (Y); 121/244; Church Yth Grp; Teachers Aide; Hon Roll.

CARR, ED; Cardinal O Hara HS; Media, PA; (Y); Chess Clb; Church Yth Grp; JA; Trk; Mnstry.

CARR, LISA G; Brockway Area HS; Brockway, PA; (Y); 9/108; Pres Church Yth Grp; Drama Clb; Thesps; Band; Chorus; Church Choir; Concert Band; Jazz Band; Mrchg Band; JP Sousa Awd; 1 Of 1st Femle Bglrs To Ply For Pst 95 Of Amer Lgn 85; Rcvd Hartley B Dean Schlrshp Frm Mnsfld U 86; Mansfield U; Music.

CARR, ROBERT ALAN; St Marys Area HS; Saint Marys, PA; (Y); Boys Clb Am; Var Bsbl; JV Bsktbl; Var JV Ftbl; Var Trk; Hon Roll; NHS; Prfct Atten Awd; Outstndng Male Phys Ed 85-86.

CARR, SHANNON; Meadville Area SR HS; Meadville, PA; (Y); 75/283; Pep Clb; Varsity Clb; Rep Stu Cncl; Cheerleading; Hon Roll; Achvt Awd 84-85; Clrion U; Comp Sci.

CARR, SHAWN; Northeast Catholic HS; Philadelphia, PA; (S); 1/430; NHS; Cert Of Merit-PA Hghr Ed Asst Agncy 85; Comp Sci.

CARR, SHERVONDA; Germantown HS; Philadelphia, PA; (Y); 18/480; Church Yth Grp; Cmnty Wkr; Drama Clb; Library Aide; Office Aide; Teachers Aide; Chorus; Church Choir; Yrbk Stf; Rep Jr Cls; Temple; Bus.

CARRAGHAN, MELISSA; William Allen HS; Allentown, PA; (Y); 56/604; JA; Latin Clb; Hon Roll; Jr NHS; NHS; Spanish NHS; Med.

CARRAI, GARY; New Kensington-Arnold HS; New Kensington, PA; (Y); 38/205; Chess Clb; French Clb; Key Clb; Bsbl; Bsktbl; Hon Roll; Indiana U PA.

CARRELLO, ANGELA; St Basil Acad; Philadelphia, PA; (Y); French Clb; JA; Variety Show; Capt Cheerleading; Capt Pom Pon; JV Socr; Bus Admin.

CARRICK, GINA MARIE; Norwin HS; N Huntingdon, PA; (Y); 39/557; Spanish Clb; SADD; Nwsp Stf; Sec Jr Cls; VP Sr Cls; Rep Stu Cncl; L Capt Bsktbl; L Capt Crs Cntry; L Trk; Hon Roll; Kass Kovalcheck Mrl Athlt Awd 86; Jdg Charles E Marker Schlr Athl Awd 86; Grad Hnr Stu NHS; Seton Hill Coll; Educ.

CARRICK, LYNNE; Saltsburg HS; Saltsburg, PA; (Y); 3/82; Church Yth Grp; Varsity Clb; Nwsp Stf; Yrbk Ed-Chief; Rep Stu Cncl; Var L Cheerleading; Powder Puff Ftbl; Sftbl; High Hon Roll; NHS; ICM Schl Bus; Med Offc Asst.

CARRIER, JENNY; Ridgway Area HS; Ridgway, PA; (Y); 6/130; Sec Trs Church Yth Grp; Capt Band; Church Choir; Mrchg Band; Yrbk Stf; Vllybl; High Hon Roll; Hon Roll; JP Sousa Awd; NHS; Westminster Coll; Chrstn Ed.

CARRIER, PAUL; Father Judge HS; Philadelphia, PA; (Y); 2/360; Band; Concert Band; Jazz Band; Mrchg Band; Orch; Pep Band; School Musical; Symp Band; High Hon Roll; NHS; Pre-Med.

CARRIGAN, ANDREW STUART; Church Farm Schl; Philadelphia, PA; (Y); 5/25; German Clb; Ski Clb; Church Choir; School Play; Nwsp Rptr; Var Mgr(s); JV Socr; Im Sftbl; Hon Roll; Mst Imprvd Stu Awd 85; Hnr Rll; Poly Sci.

CARRODUS, GWENDOLYN; Brookville Area HS; Summerville, PA; (Y); Art Clb; German Clb; Key Clb; Varsity Clb; Chorus; Nwsp Rptr; Yrbk Sprt Ed; Diving; Swmmng; Hon Roll; Art.

CARROLL, BRIGID; Archbishop Ryan HS For Girls; Philadelphia, PA; (S); 14/484; Dance Clb; JA; Chorus; School Musical; School Play; Rep Frsh Cls; NHS; Italian Awd 83-85; Engl Awd 85; Dance Awds 85; PA ST U; Educ.

CARROLL, DEBBIE; Elizabeth-Forward HS; Greenock, PA; (Y); Art Clb; Church Yth Grp; Computer Clb; GAA; Latin Clb; Ski Clb; Spanish Clb; SADD; Varsity Clb; Bsktbl; W PA Ind Arts Fair 3rd Pl 84; Physcl Fitnss Awds 84-85; Pharmcy.

CARROLL, JOHN; St John Neumann HS; Philadelphia, PA; (Y); 8/338; Mathletes; Math Tm; Science Clb; Spanish Clb; Chorus; Im Bsktbl; Im Score Keeper; High Hon Roll; Hon Roll; NHS; Cardnl Krols 25 Annvrsry 86.

CARROLL, LORIE M; Archbishop Carroll HS; Haverford, PA; (Y); 9/212; Drama Clb; French Clb; Mathletes; SADD; Stage Crew; Rep Stu Cncl; Trk; High Hon Roll; Hon Roll; NHS; Math Awd Hghst Cmltv Avg Trig/Pre Calc 86; Rosemont Coll.

CARROLL, MICHAEL; Shikellamy SR HS; Northumberland, PA; (Y); Concert Band; Mrchg Band; Nwsp Phtg; Var JV Tennis; Bloomsburg U; Sec Ed.

CARROLL, PATRICK W; Father Judge HS; Philadelphia, PA; (Y); 3/403; Mathletes; Nwsp Ed-Chief; JV Ftbl; Var Trk; NHS; Ntl Merit SF; PA Higher Ed Assoc Awd 85; Pres Clsrm 86; Bus.

CARROLL, ROBERT; West Scranton HS; Scranton, PA; (Y); 8/265; Boys Clb Am; Letterman Clb; Pep Clb; Varsity Clb; Crs Cntry; Trk; Wrstlng; Hon Roll; NHS; PA ST U; Engrng.

CARROZZA, JENNIFER; Mount Saint Joseph Acad; Ambler, PA; (Y); JCL; Latin Clb; Chorus; School Musical; Variety Show; Stu Cncl; JV Var Fld Hcky; High Hon Roll; Pres NHS; NEDT Awd; Hon Awd Excllnc Social Stds 86; Hon Awd Sci & Religious Studies 86; U Of PA; Nursing.

CARSON, ALBERT; Rocky Grove JR-SR HS; Franklin, PA; (Y); 25/93; Aud/Vis; Church Yth Grp; 4-H; Band; Concert Band; Jazz Band; Pep Band; Rep Stu Cncl; 4-H Awd; Hon Roll; Nws Herald Awd-Outstndng 4-H Prjct Wrk 85-86; Penn ST U; Poli Sci.

CARSON II, ALBERT PATRICK; Belle Vernon Area HS; Pricedale, PA; (Y); Church Yth Grp; Cmnty Wkr; Letterman Clb; Varsity Clb; Church Choir; Im Bsbl; Var JV Coach Actv; Var Capt Ftbl; Var Capt Wt Lftg; Var Capt Hon Roll; Outstndng Awd In Ftbl 85-86; Ecmnd Art Achvt 85-86; PA ST Coll; Dntst.

CARSON, BOB; Seneca Valley SR HS; Evans City, PA; (Y); Am Leg Boys St; Church Yth Grp; Cmnty Wkr; French Clb; Varsity Clb; Church Choir; Yrbk Phtg; Yrbk Rptr; Yrbk Stf; Socr; Engr.

CARSON, GREGORY; Huntingdon Area HS; Huntingdon, PA; (Y); 17/238; Latin Clb; Teachers Aide; Pres Band; Pres Concert Band; Pres Mrchg Band; High Hon Roll; NEDT Awd; Chem.

CARSON, LARA; Radnor HS; Wayne, PA; (Y); VP Church Yth Grp; Cmnty Wkr; Chorus; Church Choir; School Musical; Yrbk Ed-Chief; Swmmng; Tennis; French Hon Soc; High Hon Roll; Acad Notre Dame De Namur 1/2 Tuitn Schlrshp 83; Williams Coll Bk Awd 86; Pre-Med.

CARSON, LISA; Chestnut Ridge SR HS; Alum Bank, PA; (S); Camera Clb; Chess Clb; Dance Clb; Teachers Aide; Concert Band; Mrchg Band; High Hon Roll; NHS; Prfct Atten Awd; Outstndng Chem I Stu Awd 84-85.

CARSON, RONALD; Middletown Area HS; Middletown, PA; (Y); JV Ftbl; Im Vllybl; Wt Lftg.

CARSON, TAMMY S; Central Dauphin HS; Harrisburg, PA; (Y); 15/328; Ski Clb; Chorus; Color Guard; Concert Band; Jazz Band; Mrchg Band; School Musical; Stat Vllybl; Hon Roll; NHS; Acdmc Stdnt Mnth 86; Schlrshp Amer Bus Womns Assn 86; Pres Acdmc Fit Awd 86; IN U Of PA; Frnch.

CARSON, TED; Bishop Carroll HS; Barnesboro, PA; (S); 26/106; Computer Clb; Rep Stu Cncl; Ftbl; Trk; Hon Roll; NEDT Awd; Cntrl Cambria Cnty All Star Ftbl Team 86; US Naval Acad; Aerosp Engr.

CARSON, WAYNE E; Indiana Wesleyan Schl; Indiana, PA; (Y); 2/9; Rep Soph Cls; High Hon Roll; Hon Roll; NHS; Ntl Merit SF; IN U PA Credits 85; PA ST; Comp Sci.

CARTER, CHRIS; St Josephs Preparatory Schl; Moorestown, NJ; (Y); FCA; Hosp Aide; Latin Clb; Political Wkr; Spanish Clb; SADD; Varsity Clb; Var Ftbl; Var Tennis; 3rd Ntn Crew Tm 86; U Of PA; Ec.

CARTER, DAVID; Curwensville HS; Curwensville, PA; (Y); Art Clb; Boy Scts; Pres Church Yth Grp; Letterman Clb; Varsity Clb; Church Choir; Bsbl; Ftbl; Wt Lftg; Wrstlng; GFWC Wmns Clb Art Awd 1st Pl 86; Pittsburgh Art Inst; Comm Art.

CARTER, ERIC; John Harris HS; Harrisburg, PA; (Y); 156/584; Boy Scts; Chess Clb; 4-H; Pep Clb; ROTC; Band; Concert Band; Jazz Band; Mrchg Band; Orch; Temple U; Psycholagy.

CARTER, GEORGE; Iroquois HS; Erie, PA; (Y); Letterman Clb; Sec Soph Cls; Var JV Bsktbl; Var JV Ftbl; Hon Roll; Prfct Atten Awd; Edinboro; Bus Mgmt.

CARTER, GWENZETTA; Bensalem HS; Trevose, PA; (Y); Pres Church Yth Grp; Chorus; Church Choir; Drill Tm; Mrchg Band; School Musical; Variety Show; Nwsp Stf; VP Frsh Cls; VP Soph Cls; 1st Pl BMCR/Blk Meth Chrch Essay Cont 83; Awd Merit Outstndg Achvt Smmr Yth Pgm 85; DE ST Coll; Psych.

CARTER, JAMES; Pine Forge Acad; Warrensvl Hts, OH; (Y); VP Stu Cncl; Var Capt Bsktbl; Hghst Avg Amer Hstry 85-86; Wnr Blck Hstry Bwl 85-86; John Carrol U; Dntstry.

CARTER, JERRI-LYNN; Central Dauphin East HS; Harrisburg, PA; (Y); French Clb; Flag Corp; Off Jr Cls; Stu Cncl; U Pittsburg; Erly Chldhd Devlp.

CARTER, JULIE; Trinity HS; Washington, PA; (Y); Aud/Vis; Dance Clb; Pep Clb; Drill Tm; Hon Roll; Recrdng Engr.

CARTER, KELLY; Berwick Area HS; Berwick, PA; (Y); Church Yth Grp; Key Clb; SADD; Lib Band; Chorus; Concert Band; Drm & Bgl; Jazz Band; Mrchg Band; Symp Band; Dist Band 85-86; Regn Bnd 85-86; Altrnt Gvrnr Schl Arts 85-86; Temle; Music.

CARTER, KISHA; Simon Gratz HS; Philadelphia, PA; (Y); Drama Clb; Temple Yth Grp; Tennis; Trk; Ntl Merit Schol; Penn ST; Pol Sci.

CARTER, MARY JO; Highlands SR HS; Brackenridge, PA; (Y); 30/277; Church Yth Grp; Intnl Clb; Key Clb; Office Aide; Chorus; Church Choir; Jazz Band; Pres Soph Cls; Pres Jr Cls; Pres Stu Cncl; Hmcmng Qun 85-86; Pres Acdmc Fit Awd 85-86; PPG Fndtn Cmnty Schlrshp 86; Syracuse U; Psych.

CARTER, MICHELLE; Schenley HS Teachers Center; Pittsburgh, PA; (S); French Clb; Varsity Clb; Nwsp Rptr; Trs Stu Cncl; Capt Bsktbl; Cheerleading; Sftbl; Trk; CC Awd; Hon Roll; Pres Physcl Fit; V P Grad Clss; Howard; Pre Law.

CARTER, MIKE; Corry Area HS; Corry, PA; (Y); Aud/Vis; Camera Clb; Cmnty Wkr; Library Aide; Radio Clb; Band; Concert Band; Mrchg Band; Wt Lftg; Cert Svc Volunteer Wrk Corry Sch IMC-AV 85-86; PIA; Avionics Tech.

CARTER, PHOEBE; Bishop Mc Devitt HS; Glenside, PA; (Y); 51/351; Capt Drill Tm; Nwsp Rptr; Yrbk Stf; Bsktbl; Hon Roll; Acad Scholar Immaculata Coll; Smith Partial Scholar Rosemont Coll; Cert Outstndng Achvt Acctng 86; Immaculata Coll; Soclgy.

CARTER, ROBERT; Bishop O Hara HS; Dunmore, PA; (S); 4/124; Scholastic Bowl; VP Science Clb; Ski Clb; Stage Crew; Pres Frsh Cls; L Bsbl; L Ftbl; Capt Wt Lftg; NHS; 1st Tm All Schltc Ftbl 85; All Str Bsktbl 82-83; Army ROTC Schlrshp 86; Engrng.

CARTER, SHAWN; Conrad Weiser J S H S; Wernersville, PA; (Y); 20/137; Drama Clb; JCL; School Musical; Yrbk Stf; Pres Jr Cls; Var Bsbl; Var Ftbl; Var Wrstlng; High Hon Roll; Hon Roll; James Madison U; Cmmnctns.

CARTER, STEPHANIE ANN; Wissahickon HS; Ambler, PA; (Y); Am Leg Aux Girls St; Church Yth Grp; FCA; FBLA; Chorus; Church Choir; Sftbl; Vllybl; Cit Awd; Katharine Gibbs Bus Schl; Bus.

CARTER, TILLARY; Boyertown Area SR HS; Boyertown, PA; (Y); SADD; Teachers Aide; Ed Nwsp Rptr; Yrbk Stf; JV Score Keeper; JV Trk; Cit Awd; Hon Roll; Prfct Atten Awd; Brdcst Jrnlsm.

CARTER, TYRONE; Girard College; Philadelphia, PA; (Y); Quiz Bowl; Ski Clb; Band; VP Soph Cls; JV Socr; JV Tennis; Var Wrstlng; High Hon Roll; NHS; PA Summery Yth Emp Incntv Awd 84-85; Arch.

CARTER, YOLANDA; Pine Forge Acad; Cleveland, OH; (Y); Art Clb; Drama Clb; Girl Scts; JA; Pep Clb; Teachers Aide; Church Choir; Color Guard; Drill Tm; School Play; Social VP 87; Spellman; Law.

CARTIN, JOSEPH W; Archbishop Wood For Boys; Warminster, PA; (Y); Aud/Vis; Computer Clb; Dance Clb; Drama Clb; PAVAS; School Musical; School Play; Variety Show; Cmmnctns.

CARTWRIGHT, CARLISE; William Penn HS; Philadelphia, PA; (Y); Var Badmtn; Var Tennis; Var Vllybl; Prfct Atten Awd; Phys Thrpy.

CARTWRIGHT, CLIFFORD; Westbranch Area JR SR HS; Philipsburg, PA; (Y); 41/120; Church Yth Grp; Var Ftbl; Wt Lftg; Hon Roll; Mtn View Ctr Awd 86; PA ST U; Law.

CARTWRIGHT, DONNA; Calvary Baptist Acad; Norwood, PA; (Y); 2/10; Church Yth Grp; Cmnty Wkr; Teachers Aide; Chorus; Church Choir; School Musical; Variety Show; Rep Jr Cls; Var Capt Bsktbl; Hon Roll; Sportsmnshp Awd Grls Bsktbl 83-85; 2nd Pl Piano Solo ST Comptn 84-85; Pastors Awd 85-86; Liberty U; Elem Ed.

CARTWRIGHT, JOSEPH; Bishop Mc Devitt HS; Philadelphia, PA; (Y); Church Yth Grp; Computer Clb; Crs Cntry; Trk; PA ST; Bus Admin.

CARUSO, ANNA; St Maria Goretti HS; Philadelphia, PA; (Y); 50/390; Aud/Vis; French Clb; Hosp Aide; Math Tm; Teachers Aide; Stage Crew; Rep Soph Cls; Rep Jr Cls; Hon Roll; NHS; Health.

CARUSO, BECCA; Penn Trafford HS; Irwin, PA; (Y); SADD; Stage Crew; Crs Cntry; Trk; Vllybl; NHS; CAP Cmnty Actn Prgm 86.

CARUSO, BETTY JO; Penn Trafford HS; Manor, PA; (Y); 31/329; AFS; Drama Clb; JCL; SADD; Chorus; Swing Chorus; Nwsp Stf; Yrbk Stf; Tennis; Hon Roll; ST VP JR Clscl Lg 85-86; Nwspr Wrtng 85-86; Duquesne U; Pre-Law.

CARUSO, DEAN; Riverview HS; Oakmont, PA; (Y); Key Clb; Ski Clb; Varsity Clb; Var Bsbl; Var Golf; Hon Roll; Accntng.

CARUSO, DIANA; Saint Maria Goretti HS; Philadelphia, PA; (Y); 88/390; Hosp Aide; Chorus; School Musical; Hon Roll; Mcarrie Sch; Med Scrtrl.

CARUSO, DIANE; Little Flower HS; Philadelphia, PA; (Y); 36/446; Church Yth Grp; Hosp Aide; Var Trk; La Salle U; Med.

CARUSO, DOUG; Mt Pleasant Area HS; Mt Pleasant, PA; (Y); Church Yth Grp; Latin Clb; Ski Clb; Var L Bsbl; Var L Ftbl; Var Wt Lftg; Hon Roll; Ftbl All Conf Guard 86; NAMES 86; Educ.

CARUSO, MARIA; Tunkhannock Area HS; Tunkhannock, PA; (Y); Art Clb; Church Yth Grp; Cmnty Wkr; Office Aide; Spanish Clb; VICA; Chorus; Bsbl; JV Var Tennis; Hon Roll; Bsbl Trphy 84; Art Inst Of Philadelphia; Vsl.

CARUSO, ROBERT; Mon Valley Catholic HS; Monessen, PA; (Y); 19/84; Ski Clb; Spanish Clb; Spanish NHS; Acctng.

CARUSO III, SONNY HENRY; Mt Pleasant Area HS; Mt Pleasant, PA; (Y); Church Yth Grp; Latin Clb; Letterman Clb; Ski Clb; Varsity Clb; Off Sr Cls; Rep Stu Cncl; Ftbl; L Trk; Wt Lftg; Mansfield U; Soclgy.

CARVER, CHRIS; Wyoming Area HS; W Pittston, PA; (Y); Computer Clb; Var Bsktbl; JV Golf; High Hon Roll; NHS; Wilkes Coll; Accntg.

CARVER, JOHN; Berwick Area HS; Berwick, PA; (Y); 9/203; Boy Scts; French Clb; Band; Concert Band; Mrchg Band; Nwsp Stf; Yrbk Stf; Var L Swmmng; French Hon Soc; High Hon Roll; Eagle Scout 84; Am Leg Good Citzn Citatn 84; Citatn Hse Rep ST PA Outstndng Merit 84; Pittsburgh U; Pre-Dentstry.

CARVER, LAURA; Lincoln HS; Ellwood City, PA; (Y); Church Yth Grp; Spanish Clb; Y-Teens; Chorus; Chrmn Jr Cls; Powder Puff Ftbl; Hon Roll; Prfct Atten Awd; Cntry 21 Accntng Awd 86; Accntng.

CARVER, REGAN; Villa Maria Acad; Erie, PA; (Y); Model UN; Ski Clb; Stu Cncl; Capt Cheerleading; Im Socr; Var L Trk; Im Vllybl; Hon Roll; John Carroll U; Pre-Law.

CARVIN, AMY; Susquehanna Community HS; Susquehanna, PA; (S); Hon Roll.

CARY, LISA; Middletown Area HS; Middletown, PA; (Y); 8/180; FCA; GAA; Varsity Clb; Band; Chorus; Concert Band; Mrchg Band; Yrbk Stf; Hst Soph Cls; Hst Jr Cls; Phys Thrpy.

CASALANDRA, STACI; Neshannock HS; New Castle, PA; (Y); Office Aide; Pep Clb; Ski Clb; School Play; Yrbk Bus Mgr; Yrbk Stf; Sec Soph Cls; Sec Jr Cls; Stu Cncl; Twrlr; Chld Psych.

CASALE, GEORGE; Pocono Mountain HS; Pocono Pines, PA; (Y); 51/300; Church Yth Grp; JA; Ambassador Clb; Comp Sci.

CASCIANI, MARC; Belle Vernon Area HS; Belle Vernon, PA; (Y); Art Clb; Church Yth Grp; Ski Clb; Yrbk Sprt Ed; Yrbk Stf; VP Stu Cncl; Var L Ftbl; Powder Puff Ftbl; Trk; Wt Lftg; Mech Engrng.

CASCIOLE, CHRISTA; Wilson Area HS; Easton, PA; (S); 3/150; Church Yth Grp; Model UN; Sec Jr Cls; Sec Sr Cls; Mgr(s); Capt Trk; Twrlr; High Hon Roll; Hon Roll; NHS; Easton Exch Clb Stdnt Yr 86; Hmcmg Qn 85; Northampton Cnty JR Miss Pagnt 85; Penn ST U; Actg.

CASCLOTTI, LYNNE; Marple Newtown SR HS; Newtown, PA; (Y); 29/369; Variety Show; Mgr(s); Hon Roll; NHS; Penn ST U; Engrng.

CASE, CHRIS; Millville HS; Millville, PA; (S); Church Yth Grp; Sec Soph Cls; Var Fld Hcky; Var Sftbl; High Hon Roll; NHS.

CASE, LYNN; Northwestern SR HS; Albion, PA; (Y); 4/165; Camera Clb; Library Aide; Chorus; Yrbk Ed-Chief; Yrbk Phtg; Yrbk Rptr; Yrbk Sprt Ed; VP Yrbk Stf; Hon Roll; NHS; Penn ST Behrend; Bus Adm.

CASE, MEGAN; Mount St Joseph Acad; Lansdale, PA; (Y); Art Clb; Church Yth Grp; Cmnty Wkr; French Clb; GAA; Hosp Aide; Im Socr; Moore Coll Art Schlrshp HS Strdy Pgm 85-86; Cls Art Awd 84; Cedar Crest Coll; Art.

CASE, ROBIN; Hamburg Area HS; Hamburg, PA; (Y); 31/152; Art Clb; German Clb; Library Aide; Spanish Clb; Band; School Musical; Yrbk Stf; Tennis; High Hon Roll; Hon Roll; 8th Annual Legislative Sch Art Exhbt 85; Kutztown U Talented Art Stu Summer Prog 84; Kutztown U; Cmmtn Design.

CASELLA, CAMMIE; Pittston Area HS; Duryea, PA; (Y); JA; Key Clb; Math Clb; Capt Drill Tm; Nwsp Stf; Yrbk Stf; VP Soph Cls; Stu Cncl; Mgr Crs Cntry; Mgr Trk; U Pittsburgh; Physcl Thrpy.

CASEY, AMY; Scranton Preparatory Schl; Scranton, PA; (Y); Girl Scts; Hosp Aide; Stage Crew; Var L Swmmng; High Hon Roll; Hon Roll.

CASEY, ANGELA; Butler Area SR HS; Butler, PA; (Y); Church Yth Grp; Exploring; French Clb; JA; Latin Clb; SADD; Church Choir; Nwsp Phtg; Nwsp Rptr; Nwsp Stf.

CASEY, ANGELA; Lake Lehman HS; Shavertown, PA; (Y); Cmnty Wkr; Political Wkr; Ski Clb; Nwsp Rptr; Yrbk Ed-Chief; Var Tennis; Hon Roll; Jr NHS; NHS; Law.

CASEY, COLLEEN; Old Forge HS; Old Forge, PA; (Y); Hosp Aide; Var JV Bsktbl; High Hon Roll; NHS; Acadmc Al-Amer 85; Natl Sci Merit Awd 85; Natl Ldrshp, Svc Awd 86; X-Ray Tech.

CASEY, KERI; Bellefonte SR HS; Bellefonte, PA; (S); French Clb; Girl Scts; Ski Clb; Band; Chorus; Flag Corp; Mrchg Band; Nwsp Stf; Yrbk Stf; Rep Stu Cncl; Pre-Law.

CASEY, KEVIN; Carlisle SR HS; Carlisle, PA; (Y); 21/410; Chess Clb; Model UN; Ski Clb; Sec Soph Cls; JV Socr; High Hon Roll; Hon Roll; NHS; 2nd Pl PA JR Acad Sci 86; Awd Cert Acdmc Excllnc 86; Nuclr Fusn Rsrch.

CASH, EDRA; Scotland HS; Scotland, PA; (Y); 1/36; Am Leg Aux Girls St; GAA; ROTC; Band; School Play; Yrbk Phtg; Stu Cncl; DAR Awd; High Hon Roll; VFW Awd; Acadmc Achvt-ROTC 86; Dickenson; Law.

CASILLI, CHRISTINE; Peters Township HS; Mcmurray, PA; (Y); Mrchg Band; Yrbk Stf; Powder Puff Ftbl; Trk; Acctnt.

CASKIE, STEPHEN; Tulpehocken HS; Myerstown, PA; (Y); 6/106; Spanish Clb; Band; Mrchg Band; Pres Sr Cls; Var L Bsktbl; Var L Golf; Hon Roll; Pres NHS; NEDT Awd; L Var Tennis.

CASLOW, TROY; Philipsburg-Osceola Area HS; Osceola Mills, PA; (Y); Chess Clb; Church Yth Grp; Letterman Clb; Teachers Aide; Bsbl; Crs Cntry; Wt Lftg; Wrstlng; Hon Roll; Ed.

CASNER, LAURA; Lewistown Area HS; Lewistown, PA; (Y); 5/246; Math Tm; Speech Tm; Mrchg Band; Nwsp Rptr; High Hon Roll; NHS; Ntl Merit SF; Pres Schlr; VP Church Yth Grp; Computer Clb; Hugh Carcella Dist Stlwrkrs Union Schlrshp 86; Harry Price Schlrshp 86; PA ST U; Lbrl Arts.

CASNER, SANDRA DENISE; Downington SR HS; Downingtown, PA; (Y); 54/501; Church Yth Grp; GAA; Chorus; Church Choir; Stage Crew; Mgr(s); Var Capt Tennis; High Hon Roll; Hon Roll; Ntl Merit Ltr; Fclty Awd Mst Imprvd Mdrn Dnc 86; U Of Pittsburgh; Physcl Thrpy.

CASO, CHRIS; Notre Dame HS; Stroudsburg, PA; (Y); Thesps; Varsity Clb; School Play; Trs Soph Cls; Trs Jr Cls; JV Bsbl; JV Var Bsktbl; JV Var Socr; U Of NC Charlotte; Arch.

CASPER, BETTYANN; Burgettstown JR/Sr HS; Burgettstown, PA; (Y); Drama Clb; Science Clb; SADD; Chorus; School Play; Hon Roll; Jr NHS; NHS; Voice Dem Awd; Church Yth Grp; 1st Pl Lbry Essy 86; Penn ST; Air Mtrlgy.

CASPER, KELLY; West Hazleton HS; W Hazleton, PA; (Y); Pep Clb; Ski Clb; Thesps; School Play; JV Bsktbl; Var Capt Cheerleading; Var JV Trk; Hon Roll; JC Awd; NHS; Outstndng Chrldr Awd 83-84; Phrmcy.

CASPER, SCOTT; Holy Ghost Preparatory Schl; Bensalem, PA; (S); Chess Clb; Mathletes; Math Clb; Var Crs Cntry; Var Trk; NHS; Art Clb; Camera Clb; Im Bsktbl; Im Socr; Drexel; Elec Engrng.

CASPER, THERESA; Creative And Performing Arts; Philadelphia, PA; (S); 13/145; Church Yth Grp; Chorus; Church Choir; School Musical; Stu Cncl; Hon Roll; Prfct Atten Awd; Harvard; Law.

CASPERO, JOAN E; Baldwin HS; Pittsburgh, PA; (Y); 7/530; Exploring; Math Clb; Nwsp Rptr; Rep Frsh Cls; Rep Soph Cls; Rep Jr Cls; Rep Sr Cls; Var L Diving; High Hon Roll; Hgh SAT Scr In PA 85; PA Govrs Schl Arts Schlrshp 84; High Achvr Awd 83; VA Tech.

CASS, JEAN; Harborcreek HS; Erie, PA; (Y); 22/206; Computer Clb; Exploring; Sec 4-H; Hosp Aide; Spanish Clb; Color Guard; Ed Yrbk Stf; Hon Roll; NHS; Gannon U; Radlgcl Tech.

CASSANO, CHRISTINA; Bishop Kenrick HS; Norrisotwn, PA; (Y); 27/295; Dance Clb; Ski Clb; Soph Cls; Jr Cls; Cheerleading; Prfct Atten Awd; Phys Thrpy.

CASSEDY, KRISTY S; Mc Guffey HS; Washington, PA; (Y); 8/210; German Clb; Concert Band; Jazz Band; Mrchg Band; Pep Band; Nwsp Stf; High Hon Roll; JP Sousa Awd; NHS; Pres Schlr; Eagle Entrepreneurail Schlrshp 86; Washington & Jefferson; Acctg.

CASSEL, BRIDGET; Pequea Valley HS; Gap, PA; (Y); 28/125; Drama Clb; Band; Concert Band; Drm Mjr(t); Jazz Band; Mrchg Band; School Musical; School Play; Cheerleading; Mgr(s); Comp Tech.

CASSEL, CURTIS; Northern Lebanon HS; Myerstown, PA; (Y); 54/167; Varsity Clb; Im JV Ftbl; Var L Trk; JV Var Wt Lftg; Army; Nuclear Med.

CASSEL, REBECCA; Central Dauphin HS; Harrisburg, PA; (Y); 62/386; Church Yth Grp; Pep Clb; Yrbk Stf; Off Stu Cncl; Im Mgr Vllybl; Hon Roll.

CASSEL, SUSAN; Northern York HS; Grantham, PA; (Y); 11/209; French Clb; Band; Color Guard; Concert Band; Mrchg Band; French Hon Soc; High Hon Roll; Hon Roll; Church Yth Grp; Cmnty Wkr; Art Achvmnt Awd 86; Outstndng Achvmnt Math 84; Messiah Coll; Math.

CASSIDY, DEANA; Purchase Line HS; Hillsdale, PA; (Y); Pep Clb; Spanish Clb; Concert Band; Mrchg Band; Sec Jr Cls; Stu Cncl; Var Cheerleading; High Hon Roll; Hon Roll; NHS; Elem Ed.

CASSIDY, DENISE; Villa Maria Acad; Erie, PA; (S); 14/133; Drama Clb; Model UN; Nwsp Rptr; Nwsp Sprt Ed; Stu Cncl; Capt Bowling; Capt Cheerleading; Socr; Sftbl; Hon Roll; Engr Merit Awd 85; Times News Trnmt 85; Gannon U; Phrmcy.

CASSIDY, DONNA; Quigley HS; Ambridge, PA; (S); Capt Drill Tm; Yrbk Bus Mgr; Yrbk Ed-Chief; Stat Bsktbl; High Hon Roll; Hon Roll; NHS; Latin Clb; Math Tm; Pep Clb; PA Jr Acad Sci Awd & Ltn I & II Awds 83-84; Duquesne U Schlrshp 86; Eucharistic Mnstr 85; Duquesne U; Phrmcy.

CASSIDY JR, ROBERT D; St Josephs Prep; Philadelphia, PA; (Y); Office Aide; SADD; Teachers Aide; Varsity Clb; Rep Jr Cls; Rep Sr Cls; Im Bsktbl; Coach Actv; Var L Ftbl; Wt Lftg; Outstndg Lnbckr Joe Nmth Ftbll Cmp 85; Lttle Qkrs Ftbll Ntl Chmpns 85; Bus Admin.

CASSOL, ROBERT H; Franklin Regional HS; Delmont, PA; (Y); Art Clb; VP Church Yth Grp; Science Clb; Capt Crs Cntry; Trk; High Hon Roll; Stu Pilot 85-86; Pittsburgh Marathon 86; Piano Rectls 79-84; US Naval Acad; Engrng.

CASTELLANI, ROBERT; Lake-Lehman HS; Hunlock Crk, PA; (Y); Var L Crs Cntry; Var L Trk; Hon Roll; Vrsty Ltr Awd Crs Cntry 84-86; Temple U; Sci.

CASTELLANO, COLLEEN; York Vo-Tech HS; York, PA; (Y); 4/411; Trs VICA; Rep Stu Cncl; Var Co-Capt Cheerleading; DAR Awd; High Hon Roll; Hon Roll; Pres NHS; VICA Ldrshp Awd 84-86; York Coll; Spcl Educ.

CASTELLENTE, TERRENCE; West Philadelphia Catholic HS For Boys; Philadelphia, PA; (Y); 6/213; Mathletes; Ed Yrbk Stf; Hon Roll; NHS; Nathaniel Hawthorne Coll Presdntl Merit Schlrshp 86; Jacksonvl U Trstees Acadmc Schlrshp 86; FL Inst Tech; Aviatn Mgmt.

CASTELLI, LESLIE; Penn Hills SR HS; Pittsburgh, PA; (Y); Drama Clb; French Clb; JA; Ski Clb; High Hon Roll; Hon Roll; Pre Law.

CASTO, TAMMY; Montour HS; Coraopolis, PA; (Y); Church Yth Grp; Band; Orch; Pep Band; Hon Roll; Hnrs List-Prkwy Wst Tchncl Schl 85; Pttsbrgh Beauty Acad; Elctrlys.

CASTRO, AARON; Abington SR HS; Willow Grove, PA; (Y); Im Bsbl; Im Ftbl; JV Trk; Acctg.

CASTRO, BRIDGET; Mifflinburg Area HS; Lewisburg, PA; (Y); VP French Clb; Key Clb; Im Var Cheerleading; Var Capt Fld Hcky; Stat Trk; High Hon Roll; Hon Roll; Phys Thrpy.

CASTRONOVA, MARGARET LOUISE; Blue Ridge HS; Susquehanna, PA; (Y); Church Yth Grp; Pep Clb; Band; Chorus; Concert Band; Mrchg Band; School Musical; Rep Stu Cncl; Stat Vllybl; Hon Roll; Phrmcy.

CASUCCIO, DIANA; Hopewell SR HS; Aliquippa, PA; (Y); 19/261; German Clb; JA; Band; Concert Band; Mrchg Band; High Hon Roll; Pres Acdmc Fit Awd 86; CC Of Beaver Cnty; Med Sec.

CATALANO, RENEE; Penn Hills SR HS; Pittsburgh, PA; (Y); French Clb; Library Aide; Teachers Aide; Chorus; School Play; Nwsp Stf; Sftbl; Swmmng; Vllybl; Hon Roll; Bus Mgmt.

CATALIOTO, JOSEPH; Everett Area HS; Breezewood, PA; (Y); Hon Roll; Auto Design.

CATANZARITE, JEFFREY; Monaca JR SR HS; Monaca, PA; (Y); 6/90; Trs Jr Cls; Rep Stu Cncl; L Bsbl; Capt Bsktbl; Capt Ftbl; Hon Roll; NHS; Prfct Atten Awd; Engr.

CATANZARO, FRANK; Riverview HS; Oakmont, PA; (Y); L Golf; High Hon Roll; Hon Roll.

CATANZARO, VINCENT MICHAEL; Bishop Kenrick HS; Norristown, PA; (Y); 22/300; Church Yth Grp; Debate Tm; Science Clb; Speech Tm; Band; Concert Band; Jazz Band; Mrchg Band; School Musical; NHS; All Cathlolic Band 85-86.

CATERINA, LORI; Quaker Valley HS; Sewickley, PA; (Y); Sec German Clb; Math Tm; Q&S; Chorus; Nwsp Stf; Yrbk Ed-Chief; Lit Mag; High Hon Roll; School Musical; Yrbk Rptr; Acadmc Awd Excllnc 8 4; Yrbk Awd 84; Awds Excllnc German 84-86; Bio Chem.

CATES, CHRISTINE ANN; Kiski Area HS; New Kensington, PA; (Y); Church Yth Grp; Debate Tm; Pres 4-H; Math Tm; Science Clb; Mrchg Band; School Musical; Var L Swmmng; Hon Roll; Computer Clb; Allegheny-Kiski Vly JR Miss Fnlst 85-86; Penn ST U; Wldlfe Sci.

CATES, DENISE; Kiski Area HS; New Kensington, PA; (Y); Math Clb; Math Tm; Pep Clb; Ski Clb; SADD; Varsity Clb; Band; School Musical; Var L Diving; Hon Roll; Penn ST; Engrng.

CATLIN, KIMBERLY L; Union Area Middle HS; New Castle, PA; (Y); 18/63; Band; Chorus; Concert Band; Jazz Band; Nwsp Rptr; Rep Stu Cncl; Stat Bsktbl; Capt Twrlr; NHS; Church Yth Grp; Bus Admin.

CATON, TAMMY; Freedom HS; Bethlehem, PA; (Y); 127/465; Spanish Clb; Color Guard; Hon Roll; Spanish.

CATONE, GEORGE; Central Catholic HS; Pittsburgh, PA; (Y); 53/273; Art Clb; Church Yth Grp; Lit Mag; Hon Roll; NHS; Arch.

CATTELL, DANIELLE; State College Area SR HS; Pine Grove Mills, PA; (Y); 27/568; Art Clb; Spanish Clb; Thesps; School Musical; School Play; Nwsp Ed-Chief; Hon Roll; Drama Clb; Iberoamerican Cltrl Exch Pgm Scholar 86; Hghst Cumltv Adv Engl Awd 86; Outstndng Nwsp Awd 86; PA ST; Bus Mngmnt.

CAULFIELD, MARIA; Mahanoy Area HS; Mahanoy City, PA; (Y); 11/124; Pres Art Clb; Hosp Aide; Ski Clb; Spanish Clb; Capt Color Guard; School Play; Nwsp Stf; Yrbk Stf; NHS; Amer Legn Schl Awd 86; Helen L Ruth Schlrshp 86; Beaver Coll Schlrshp 86; Beaver Coll; Phy Thrpy.

CAULFIELD, PATRICK; Shenandoah Valley HS; Shenandoah, PA; (Y); 2/108; Nwsp Stf; Yrbk Sprt Ed; VP Frsh Cls; VP Soph Cls; Rep Stu Cncl; JV Var Bsktbl; JV Var Ftbl; JV Var Wt Lftg; High Hon Roll; High Hon Roll; Engrng.

CAUSGROVE, THOMAS; Cathedral Prep; Erie, PA; (Y); 110/216; Church Yth Grp; Library Aide; Im Bsktbl; Im Vllybl; Penn ST.

CAUVEL, MARY; Otto-Eldred HS; Derrick City, PA; (Y); 3/90; Band; Concert Band; Drm Mjr(t); Mrchg Band; Pep Band; Yrbk Stf; High Hon Roll; Hon Roll; NHS; Ntl Merit Ltr; Dist II All ST Bnd Fstvl 86; Regn II All ST Bnd Fstvl 86; Nrsg.

CAVADA, ANTHONY; Jeannette SR HS; Jeannette, PA; (Y); 4/128; Am Leg Boys St; Ski Clb; Spanish Clb; High Hon Roll; Kiwanis Awd; NHS; PA ST U; Engrng.

CAVALCANTE, FRANCEE; Carmichaels Area HS; Carmichaels, PA; (S); 14/120; VP French Clb; SADD; Band; Capt Color Guard; Trs Jr Cls; High Hon Roll; Hon Roll; NHS; Govrns Schl 83-85; WVU; Physcl Thrpy.

CAVALIERI, DANA; St Maria Goretti HS; Philadelphia, PA; (Y); 100/426; Art Clb; Church Yth Grp; Hosp Aide; Office Aide; Science Clb; Spanish Clb; Teachers Aide; School Play; Rep Stu Cncl; Hon Roll; Cert Of Merit For Cndystrpng 83; Meth Hosp Schl Nrs; Nrs.

CAVALIERI, DAVID; Pocono Mountain HS; Tannersville, PA; (Y); Boy Scts; Church Yth Grp; Chorus; Church Choir; Var Ftbl; Var Trk; Hon Roll; Stat Bsbl; Im Bsktbl; JV Crs Cntry; PA ST; Acctng.

CAVALLO, MICHELLE; Wilmington Area HS; Pulaski, PA; (Y); Spanish Clb; School Play; Nwsp Rptr; Powder Puff Ftbl; Hon Roll; Med.

CAVALUCCI, SHERRY; Fort Cherry HS; Mc Donald, PA; (S); 16/131; Church Yth Grp; Computer Clb; Drama Clb; Math Clb; Science Clb; Ski Clb; Spanish Clb; Sec Varsity Clb; Drill Tm; Mrchg Band; NC U Charlotte; Acctg.

CAVANAOUGH, KELLY; Nativity BVM HS; Pottsville, PA; (Y); 22/98; Art Clb; Church Yth Grp; Debate Tm; French Clb; Girl Scts; Science Clb; Ski Clb; Drill Tm; Bowling; Sftbl; Phldlph Coll Phrmcy; Phrmcy.

CAVANAUGH, BRIAN; Troy SR HS; Gillett, PA; (Y); Pres Church Yth Grp; Letterman Clb; VP Ftbl; Trs NHS; Mansfield Hnrs Pgm Schlrshp 86; Mansfield U; Chem.

CAVANAUGH, ERIN; Butler SR HS; Butler, PA; (Y); Math Clb; Office Aide; Chorus; Swing Chorus; Chem Engrng.

CAVANAUGH, MICHELLE; Nativity B V M HS; Pottsville, PA; (Y); 19/98; Art Clb; Church Yth Grp; Cmnty Wkr; Yrbk Stf; Var JV Sftbl; JV Vllybl; Hon Roll; Acctng.

CAVANAUGH, TIMOTHY; Southmoreland HS; Scottdale, PA; (Y); 14/224; Church Yth Grp; German Clb; Latin Clb; Bsktbl; Tennis; Comp Sci.

CAVELL, GEORGE; Bellefonte Area HS; Bellefonte, PA; (Y); Boy Scts; Camera Clb; Church Yth Grp; Ski Clb; VICA; WACC; Cntrctr.

CAWLEY, CYNTHIA; Baldwin HS; Pittsburgh, PA; (Y); 38/535; Math Tm; Office Aide; Stu Cncl; High Hon Roll; NHS; Off Frsh Cls; Off Jr Cls; Var L Tennis; Var Trk; Brnz Good Citznshp Mdl Sons Of Am Revltn 83; Ecnmcs.

CAWLEY, DONNA; Pittston Area Pa; Avoca, PA; (Y); 1/380; Art Clb; Drama Clb; French Clb; Key Clb; Stage Crew; High Hon Roll; NHS; NEDT Awd.

CAYE, SUSAN; Greensburg Central Catholic HS; Murrysville, PA; (Y); 43/250; AFS; Church Yth Grp; Cmnty Wkr; Ski Clb; Stage Crew; Im Powder Puff Ftbl; Var Trk; Im Vllybl; High Hon Roll; NHS; Yth Mnstry 83-87; Art.

CAYS, JOHN MICHAEL; Pocono Mountain HS; Stroudsburg, PA; (Y); PAVAS; Band; Chorus; Jazz Band; Madrigals; Mrchg Band; School Musical; Opt Clb Awd; PA Gvrnrs Arts Schl 85; PCA Pres Schlrshp 86-90; PA Sngng Boys 74-83; Philadelphia Coll/Arts; Art.

CEASE, JASON; John S Fine HS; Nanticoke, PA; (Y); Red Cross Aide; Ski Clb; Teachers Aide; Stage Crew; Nwsp Stf; Trk; Kings Coll; Crmnl Just.

CEBULA, KAREN; Somerset Area SR HS; Friedens, PA; (Y); 4-H; Hosp Aide; Spanish Clb; Band; Color Guard; Concert Band; Mrchg Band; Nwsp Rptr; Im Gym; Var L Sftbl; Occptnl Thrpy.

CEBULAK, MARY; Valley HS; New Kensington, PA; (Y); 16/206; Ski Clb; VP Spanish Clb; Band; Chorus; VP Mrchg Band; Rep Stu Cncl; Var Swmmng; Var Tennis; High Hon Roll; NHS; Pres Acdmc Fit Awd 86; Lou Shammey Schlstc Athletc Awd Rcpnt 86; Acdmc Schlrshp Gannon U 86; Gannon U; Pre Optmtry.

CECCATO, ANGELA; Plum SR HS; Pittsburgh, PA; (Y); 165/378; Service Clb; SADD; Chorus; Yrbk Stf; Mgr(s); Swmmng; AFS; Science Clb; Church Choir; School Musical; Cultural Arts Awd 1st Pl 85; Miss Metro Pgh Pag Top 10 Fin 85; Child Psych.

CECCHETT, DAWN RENE; Yough SR HS; West Newton, PA; (Y); Cmnty Wkr; Red Cross Aide; Ski Clb; Spanish Clb; Band; Chorus; Concert Band; Mrchg Band; School Play; Hon Roll; Gannon U; Bio.

CECCHI, DAVID H; Kiski Area HS; Vandergrift, PA; (Y); Teachers Aide; Chorus; Hon Roll; Prfct Atten Awd; Rotary Awd; Rotary Schlr Awd 85; Bus Mgmt.

CECCHINI, MARYANN; Shenandoah Valley HS; Lost Creek, PA; (Y); Church Yth Grp; Girl Scts; Library Aide; Chorus; Church Choir; Color Guard; Mrchg Band; Var L Crs Cntry; Var Mgr(s); Var Sftbl; Wesley; Paralegal.

CECCOLI, ANGELA; Cambria Heights SR HS; Hastings, PA; (Y); Pres 4-H; Library Aide; Ski Clb; Chorus; Yrbk Ed-Chief; VP Frsh Cls; Var L Vllybl; 4-H Awd; VP NHS; Stu Spkr Grad 86; Vllybll All Star Tm 85-86; Acad All Amer 85-86; Duquesne U; Pharm.

CEGAN, SANDEE; Churchill HS; Pittsburgh, PA; (Y); FBLA; GAA; SADD; Chorus; Nwsp Stf; Rep Frsh Cls; Mgr Bsbl; Var JV Bsktbl; Trk; Hon Roll; Tres Chic Clb 85-86; John Casablancas Mdlng Schl 84-85; Art Awds; Fshn Dsgn.

CEHLAR, ELIZABETH; Pottstown SR HS; Pottstown, PA; (S); 2/200; Church Yth Grp; Trs Key Clb; VP Spanish Clb; Chorus; Church Choir; School Musical; Yrbk Stf; Rep Jr Cls; Tennis; NHS; Hgh Hnr Rll 84-86; Penn ST U; Arch.

CELEBUSKI, CLAUDINE; Liberty HS; Bethlehem, PA; (S); 36/520; Nwsp Rptr; Nwsp Stf; Var Crs Cntry; Var Gym; Var Trk; High Hon Roll; Hon Roll; Nwspr Nws Edtr Liberty Lif 85-86; PA Schlstc Prs Assn 1st Awd Nws Wrtng 85.

CELENTO, AMY; Waynesburg Central HS; Waynesburg, PA; (Y); 10/200; Yrbk Bus Mgr; Yrbk Stf; Pres Frsh Cls; Pres Soph Cls; Pres Jr Cls; Sec Pres Stu Cncl; Trk; DAR Awd; Lion Awd; NHS; Waynesburg Ladies Firemans Aux Schlrshp; Carnegie Mellon U; Indstrl Mgmt.

CELENZA, PAULA; Cardinal Dougherty HS; Phila, PA; (Y); 9/747; Art Clb; Cmnty Wkr; Dance Clb; Drama Clb; Teachers Aide; Chorus; School Musical; School Play; Hon Roll; NHS; St Jsphs U-Prtl Schlrshp 86; Villanova U; Lbrl Arts.

CELESTE, WAYNE; Wyalusing Valley HS; Wyalusing, PA; (Y); 5/152; Ski Clb; Spanish Clb; Off Stu Cncl; Stat Bsktbl; Bausch & Lomb Sci Awd; High Hon Roll; Hon Roll; NHS; Pres Schlr; Penn ST U; Engrng.

CELLA, JEFFREY; Churchill HS; Pittsburgh, PA; (Y); Var Bsbl; Var Capt Ftbl; Hon Roll; Acdmc Achvt Awds 83-86; Gtwy Pblctns All Str Ftbl Team 85; Mst Athltc Male Stu 85-86; Slpry Rock U.

CELLINI, LISA A; Bishop Hafey HS; Nuremberg, PA; (Y); 8/189; Cmnty Wkr; Service Clb; Chorus; School Play; Lit Mag; CC Awd; High Hon Roll; NHS; Pres Schlr; Spanish NHS; Mr & Mrs Marinko Mem Awd 86; Hazleton Standrd Spkr Awd 86; Bloomsburg U Schlrs Pgm & Scholar 86; Bloomsburg U; Engl.

CENCETTI, SONDRA; Pittston Area HS; Pittston, PA; (Y); 1/330; Trs Key Clb; Sec Math Clb; Drill Tm; Yrbk Stf; Hon Roll; VP NHS; Val; Pres Schlrshp 86; U Scranton; Physcl Thrpy.

CENDROSKI, JEANNETTE; South Allegheny HS; Glassport, PA; (Y); French Clb; Chorus; U Of Pittsburgh; Pre-Law.

CENTINI, JACQUELINE; Northern York Co HS; Dillsburg, PA; (Y); 79/200; Spanish Clb; JV Bsktbl; JV Var Powder Puff Ftbl; Hon Roll; Harrisburg Area CC; Bus Mgmt.

CENTIOLE, KATHLEEN; Cardinal Brednan HS; Girardville, PA; (Y); 4/50; Church Yth Grp; Debate Tm; Exploring; Speech Tm; Capt Color Guard; Yrbk Ed-Chief; Stu Cncl; Cheerleading; NHS; VP Spanish NHS; Dio Allntwn Yth Rep 86; Hire The Hndcppd Essy 1st Pl 86; Villa Nova; Cmmnctns.

CENTRE, NICOLE; Northern SR HS; Dillsburg, PA; (Y); 71/209; Cmnty Wkr; Dance Clb; Office Aide; Spanish Clb; Temple Yth Grp; Nwsp Rptr; Nwsp Stf; Yrbk Rptr; Yrbk Stf; Off Soph Cls.

CENTRITTO, MARIA; Archbishop Kennedy HS; Philadelphia, PA; (Y); 10/185; Hosp Aide; Chorus; Nwsp Rptr; Nwsp Stf; Hon Roll; NHS; Prfct Atten Awd; Spnsh Awd 84; Hnrble Mntn Spnsh 86; Acdmc All-Amrcn 85; Temple U; Italian.

CERATO, BRENDA; Scranton Technical HS; Scranton, PA; (Y); 3/236; Nwsp Stf; Stu Cncl; Cheerleading; NHS.

CERBONE, VERONICA; Morrisville JR SR HS; Morrisville, PA; (Y); 3/99; Mrchg Band; School Musical; Nwsp Rptr; High Hon Roll; Hon Roll; NHS; Pres Schlr; Temple U; Bio.

CERCEO, VINCENT; Cardinal O Hara HS; Drexel Hill, PA; (Y); Church Yth Grp; Cmnty Wkr; Pep Clb; JV L Ftbl; Var Capt Trk; Shippensburg U; Hosp Adm.

CERIMELE, GINA; Villa Maria HS; Campbell, OH; (Y); 4/50; Sec Trs Key Clb; Thesps; Chorus; Stage Crew; Yrbk Stf; Lit Mag; Pres Frsh Cls; NHS; NEDT Awd; Spanish NHS.

CERMAK, ELIZABETH MARIE; Ringgold HS; Donora, PA; (Y); Sec Red Cross Aide; Psych.

CERMAK, JOSEPH; Octorara Area HS; Belle-Mead, NJ; (Y); 44/161; Computer Clb; Nwsp Stf; Rep Stu Cncl; Hon Roll; Rutgers U; Metrlgy.

CERNAK, TAMMIE; Greater Johnstown SR HS; Johnstown, PA; (Y); Chorus; School Musical; School Play; JV Var Bsktbl; Var L Sftbl; JV Vllybl; High Hon Roll; Hon Roll; Grls Bsktbl-Vrsty Awd 85-86; Phy Ed Awd-Bsktbl 85-86; IN U Pittsburgh; Radlgy.

CERNICKY, SHAWN; Belle Vernon Area HS; Belle Vernon, PA; (Y); Debate Tm; Wt Lftg; Cit Awd; Hon Roll; Marine Corps Aviatr.

CERONI, BOBBI; Mt Pleasant HS; Mt Pleasant, PA; (Y); Cmnty Wkr; Ski Clb; Color Guard; Nwsp Stf.

CERRA, ELENA; Valley View HS; Archbald, PA; (Y); 62/195; FBLA; Latin Clb; Spanish Clb; Var Trk; Hon Roll; Prfct Atten Awd; 2nd Pl Prlnmtry Prcdrs Rgn 22 FBLA Conf 86; Ntl Ftnss Awd 86; Awd Of Hnr Outstndng Achvmnts PP 86.

CERRA, SUSIE; Lakeland HS; Carbondale, PA; (Y); Cheerleading; Keystone JC; Bio Sci.

CERRITO, KAREN; Hazleton HS; Hazleton, PA; (Y); Drama Clb; FBLA; Pep Clb; Chorus; Ed Nwsp Stf; Ed Yrbk Stf; JV Bsktbl; High Hon Roll; Am Leg Awd, Hnbl Mntn Luzerne Intermdte Unit Comp Cntst 84; Bus Admin.

CERVENAK, DOUGLAS I; Central SR HS; York, PA; (Y); 15/261; Am Leg Boys St; Varsity Clb; L Bsbl; Capt Ftbl; High Hon Roll; Lion Awd; NHS; Ski Clb; Nwsp Stf; Wt Lftg; US Army Rsrv Ntl Schlr-Athl, Pres Acad Ftnss Awds, Acad All Star 86; Carnegie-Mellon U; Mech Engrng.

CERVENAK, JOSEPH C; Moshannon Valley HS; Morann, PA; (Y); 2/133; Spanish Clb; Varsity Clb; Bsktbl; High Hon Roll; Hon Roll; NHS; Sal; Lamont E Close Jr Schlrp 86; Kunkle Schlrp 86; James W Reese Mem Awd & Army Rsrv Awd 86; Penn St Altoona; Bus.

CERVENAK, LORI; Moshannon Valley JSHS; Morann, PA; (Y); 12/133; Spanish Clb; Varsity Clb; Band; Concert Band; Pep Band; Capt L Bsktbl; Var L Sftbl; Hon Roll; Pres Phys Ftns Awd 83-86; US Marine Corps Dstngshd Athl Awd 86; Penn ST U.

CERVONE, MARISSA; Meadville Area SR HS; Meadville, PA; (Y); 109/280; Church Yth Grp; Service Clb; Varsity Clb; Nwsp Stf; Yrbk Stf; JV Var Cheerleading; JV Trk; Hon Roll; NHS; Flyg Chrldr Ftbl 85; Pittsburgh Beauty Acad; Cosmtlg.

CESARE, JOE; Scranton Preparatory Schl; Clarks Green, PA; (Y); 45/192; Service Clb; Ski Clb; JV Bsbl; Im Bsktbl; L Ftbl; Im Vllybl; Im Wt Lftg; High Hon Roll; Hon Roll; Gld Mdl Awd In Bio 85; Gld Mdl Awd In Algbra II & Trgnmtry 86; Brnz Mdl Awd In Intl Afrs 86; Intl Bus.

CESARETTI, KELLY; Deer Lakes HS; Russellton, PA; (Y); 17/189; Nwsp Ed-Chief; Nwsp Phtg; Nwsp Rptr; Nwsp Sprt Ed; Nwsp Stf; High Hon Roll; NHS; Ntl Merit Ltr; NEDT Awd; Pres Schlr; Pres Acadmc Ftns Awd 86; Grd High Hnrs 86; Duquesne U; Bio.

CESARINI, CARRIE; Bishop O Hara HS; Peckville, PA; (S); Church Yth Grp; Dance Clb; Exploring; French Clb; Teachers Aide; Chorus; School Play; High Hon Roll; NHS; Ntl Merit Ltr; U Scranton; Dntstry.

CESSNA, BRIAN; Elderton JR SR HS; Shelocta, PA; (Y); Aud/Vis; Chess Clb; Library Aide; SADD; VICA; Nwsp Rptr; Nwsp Stf; Yrbk Phtg; Yrbk Rptr; Yrbk Stf; Elctrnc.

CESSNA, JULIE; Meyersdale Area HS; Wellersburg, PA; (S); French Clb; Concert Band; Mrchg Band; Bsktbl; Vllybl; Hon Roll; Lock Haven U; Sports Med.

CESSNA, KEITH; Kiski Area HS; Apollo, PA; (Y); VP Church Yth Grp; Pep Clb; JV Bsbl; JV Var Bsktbl; Trk; High Hon Roll; NHS.

CESSNA, ROBIN; Purchase Line JR-SR HS; Glen Campbell, PA; (Y); 18/109; Am Leg Aux Girls St; Church Yth Grp; FBLA; Pep Clb; Chorus; Church Choir; Var L Cheerleading; Var Pom Pon; Hon Roll; Punxy Beauty Schl; Cosmetology.

CESSNA, WENDY; Meyersdale Area HS; Hyndman, PA; (S); French Clb; Library Aide; Chorus; Yrbk Stf; Var L Cheerleading; High Hon Roll; Hon Roll; Csmtlgy.

CHA, SUSAN; Boyertown SR HS; Boyertown, PA; (Y); Church Yth Grp; Library Aide; Chorus; Cit Awd; High Hon Roll; NHS; Prfct Atten Awd; Cert Of Achvt-Schlstc Excllnc Awd 83-84; Cert Of Artstc Achvt 83-84; Music Dept Awd 83-84; Engrng.

CHAAPEL, KITRINA; Canton JR SR HS; Grover, PA; (Y); Girl Scts; Letterman Clb; Pres VICA; Band; Chorus; Concert Band; Mrchg Band; Yrbk Stf; Stu Cncl; JV Var Cheerleading; Yth Fit Achvt Awd 84-86; Intl Teen Miss Scholar Pgnt 86-87; Miss Teen 86; Nrsg.

CHABALA, LINDA; Wyoming Valley West HS; Swoyersville, PA; (Y); Church Yth Grp; FBLA; Rep Stu Cncl; Cheerleading; Cit Awd; Hon Roll; Spnsh Awd 85; Hstry Day Awd 86; Kings Coll; Humn Resrc Mgmt.

CHACON, ANTONIO; William Penn HS; Harrisburg, PA; (S); Church Yth Grp; Rep Jr Cls; Hon Roll; Nov Stu Of Mnth 84; Upwrd Bnd Prog Millersville U 85-86; 2nd Hnrs 85-86; Data Proc.

CHADBOLT, WILLIAM; New Castle HS; New Castle, PA; (Y); 93/263; Boy Scts; Church Yth Grp; Letterman Clb; Pep Clb; Ski Clb; SADD; Varsity Clb; JV Bsktbl; Var JV Ftbl; Var Trk.

CHADWICK, DAVID; Hatboro-Horsham HS; Horsham, PA; (Y); 10/298; Model UN; Jazz Band; School Musical; School Play; Variety Show; Var Trk; NHS; Ntl Merit Schol; U Of PA.

CHADWICK, MELISSA; Mc Guffey SR HS; Washington, PA; (Y); 7/216; Art Clb; Trs French Clb; Yrbk Stf; L Trk; Var L Vllybl; High Hon Roll; Sec NHS; Pep Clb; Varsity Clb; Chorus; Outstndg Stu Rcgntn 86; Outstndg Prfrmnc 86; Acdmc All-Amrcn 86; Nrsng.

CHADY, PETER; Peters Township HS; Mcmurray, PA; (Y); 4/253; Computer Clb; Trs Key Clb; Speech Tm; Thesps; Band; School Musical; School Play; Nwsp Phtg; NHS; Ntl Merit Ltr; Elec Engrg.

CHAFFEE, TAMMIE; Blue Ridge HS; Susquehanna, PA; (Y); Pep Clb; Chorus; Color Guard; JV Var Cheerleading; Psych.

CHALFANT, MICHELE; Charleroi JR SR HS; Charleroi, PA; (Y); VP Trs Church Yth Grp; NFL; Office Aide; Chorus; Nwsp Stf; JV Cheerleading; Hon Roll; Spec Course Gftd Ed REACH; Hlth Careers; Stdnt Tutrs Pblcty Chrprsn; Moore Coll Of Art; Grphc Dsgn.

CHAMBERLAIN, LORI; Lake-Lehman HS; Hunlock Creek, PA; (Y); Church Yth Grp; SADD; Church Choir; JV Fld Hcky; Var Vllybl; Mdld For Ptsbrg Mdlng & Cstng Agncy 84-85; PA ST U; Law.

CHAMBERLAIN, MARK; Huntingdon Area HS; Huntingdon, PA; (Y); 9/223; Am Leg Boys St; Key Clb; Band; Ftbl; Golf; Trk; Wrstlng; High Hon Roll; Trs NHS; Prfct Atten Awd; Chem Engrng.

CHAMBERS, KELLY; Blairsville SR HS; Black Lick, PA; (Y); 9/131; Am Leg Aux Girls St; SADD; Teachers Aide; Concert Band; Mrchg Band; School Musical; VP Frsh Cls; Rep Stu Cncl; High Hon Roll; Prfct Atten Awd; IFLA 85; Smith; Pedtrcn.

CHAMBERS, SHANEE; Mc Keesport HS; Mckeesport, PA; (Y); 186/396; Sec Church Yth Grp; NFL; Y-Teens; Acpl Chr; Mrchg Band; Church Choir; Ed Nwsp Rptr; JV Bsktbl; JV Trk; Hon Roll; Temple U; Lawyer.

CHAMPE, MICHELLE; Hopewell HS; Aliquippa, PA; (S); 41/242; Church Yth Grp; Dance Clb; Spanish Clb; Chorus; Stu Cncl; JV Cheerleading; JV Powder Puff Ftbl; Var Tennis; JV Trk; Hon Roll; IN U Of PA; Nrsng.

CHAN, BETTY; Waynesboro Area SR HS; Waynesboro, PA; (Y); 1/381; Drama Clb; Key Clb; Ski Clb; School Play; Trs Soph Cls; Im Capt Bsktbl; JV Tennis; High Hon Roll; NHS; Spanish Awd 85; Chem Engrng.

CHAN, FRANCES; St Huberts HS Girls; Philadelphia, PA; (Y); 5/367; Church Yth Grp; French Clb; Mathletes; Orch; School Musical; Hon Roll; NHS; Frnch & Music Awd 84-86; Minrty Apprntc Pgm Hahnemann Med Coll 86; Med Resrch.

CHAN, KAI; St Josephs Prep; Philadelphia, PA; (Y); Hosp Aide; Intnl Clb; Library Aide; Mathletes; Science Clb; Spanish Clb; Nwsp Stf; St Francis Xavier Schlrshp 83-87; Svc Awd 86; CSC Svc Awd 86; Swathmore U; Med.

CHANDLER, CASSANDRA L; Towanda HS; Towanda, PA; (Y); 9/164; Am Leg Aux Girls St; Church Yth Grp; Letterman Clb; Science Clb; Swing Chorus; Var L Golf; Var L Sftbl; Var L Swmmng; VP NHS; Bradford Sullivan Counties JR Miss 86; PA JR Miss Kraft Awd Wnnr 86; Most Outstndg Femal Golfer 86; Ithaca Coll; Phys Therapy.

CHANDLER, CINDY; Troy SR HS; Monroeton, PA; (Y); 4-H; FTA; Library Aide; Chorus; 4-H Awd; Prfct Atten Awd; Bus Mgmt.

CHANEY, KIMBERLY; William Allen HS; Allentown, PA; (Y); Camera Clb; Drama Clb; Girl Scts; Hosp Aide; Intnl Clb; Nwsp Phtg; Yrbk Phtg; Yrbk Stf; Sec Stu Cncl; Ortrcl Cntst 1st Rnnr Up & Hon Mntn 85-86.

CHANEY, TYNESE; Brownsville Area SR HS; Hiller, PA; (Y); Drama Clb; FBLA; Chorus; Sftbl; Vllybl; Hon Roll; 1st Pl Trphy Shrthand Ii Compt 86; 4th Pl Trphy Shorthand I Compt 85; Sec.

CHANG, EUGENE J; Shady Side Acad; Greensburg, PA; (Y); 4/115; German Clb; Hosp Aide; Math Tm; NFL; Ski Clb; Chorus; JV Tennis; VP Jr NHS; Ntl Merit SF; Amer Chem Soc Secndry Schl Chem Cont 3rd 84; Sec & Treas Dormtry 85-86; Engrng.

CHANG, FONDA; Charleroi Area HS; Charleroi, PA; (Y); French Clb; Varsity Clb; Nwsp Stf; Yrbk Stf; Sec Soph Cls; Sec Stu Cncl; Var Cheerleading; Hon Roll; NHS; Prfct Atten Awd; Radio/TV Brdcstng.

CHANG, HO CHOONG; Southern Lehigh HS; Coopersburg, PA; (Y); 5/226; Church Yth Grp; Pres JA; Math Clb; Scholastic Bowl; Varsity Clb; Ed Nwsp Stf; Yrbk Stf; Var L Tennis; High Hon Roll; VP NHS; JA Outstndng Stu Yr 85-86, Pres Yr 84-85; Yale U; Biochem.

CHANG, JEANETTE; William Allen HS; Allentown, PA; (Y); 5/604; Ski Clb; Lit Mag; Stu Cncl; Var Tennis; High Hon Roll; Hon Roll; Jr NHS; NHS; Ntl Merit Ltr; Spanish NHS.

CHANG, MAY XUE-MEI; Schenley HS; Pittsburgh, PA; (S); 10/150; Hnr Cert For Excell Achvt In Schlrshp & Citiznshp 85; High Hnr Cert For Achvt In Schlrshp & Ctznshp; Comp Sci.

CHANGCO, ALVIN P; Immaculate Conception HS; Washington, PA; (Y); Am Leg Boys St; Math Tm; Ski Clb; JV Bsktbl; High Hon Roll; Hon Roll; Nicholas C Tucci Chem Awd 85-86; Albright Coll; Astrnmy.

CHANITZ, JEN; Sun Valley HS; Brookhaven, PA; (Y); Band; Mrchg Band; Variety Show; Trk; CC Awd; Hon Roll; Opt Clb Awd; Gregg Typng & Shrthnd Awds 85-86; Goldey Beacon Coll; Exec Sec.

CHAP, CANDACE; Danville Area HS; Riverside, PA; (Y); Drama Clb; French Clb; Ski Clb; Trs Frsh Cls; Var JV Bsktbl; Var JV Cheerleading; Mat Maids; Var L Tennis; Var L Trk; NEDT Awd; Ursinus Coll; Pltcl Sci.

CHAP, JENNIFER; Danville SR HS; Riverside, PA; (Y); Drama Clb; Spanish Clb; Rep Frsh Cls; Im Powder Puff Ftbl; JV L Sftbl; JV L Tennis; Hon Roll; Bus.

CHAPELL, ALLAN; Coulersport Area JR SR HS; Coudersport, PA; (Y); 4-H; French Clb; FFA; Ftbl; Trk; Wrstlng; Hon Roll; Aircraft Mech.

CHAPIN, ALAN; Benton Area HS; Benton, PA; (Y); Boy Scts; Church Yth Grp; Cmnty Wkr; Sr Cls; Wrstlng; Hon Roll; Chef.

CHAPLIK, MARK; Carlynton HS; Pittsburgh, PA; (Y); Band; Concert Band; Mrchg Band; Symp Band; High Hon Roll; Hon Roll; NHS; Engrng.

CHAPLIN, STACEY; Owen J Roberts HS; Pottstown, PA; (S); 7/291; Letterman Clb; Rep Jr Cls; Rep Stu Cncl; Var L Bsktbl; Var L Fld Hcky; Var L Lcrss; Im Vllybl; Hon Roll; NHS; Bus Adm.

CHAPLYNSKY, LIDIA; St Basil Acad; Philadelphia, PA; (S); Dance Clb; French Clb; GAA; Girl Scts; Sec Intnl Clb; Church Choir; Im Vllybl; Hon Roll; Natl Sci Merit Awd 84-85.

CHAPMAN, JESSICA; Oxford Area HS; Lincoln Universit, PA; (Y); 26/162; Hosp Aide; Yrbk Stf; Hon Roll; NHS; Chstr Cnty Assoc Home Ec Schlrshp 86; J W Mc Mullen Schlrshp 86; F J Michaels Schlrshp 86; Albright Coll; Dietcs.

CHAPMAN, KATHARINE; Canon-Mc Millan HS; Canonsburg, PA; (Y); Art Clb; French Clb; Ski Clb; Chorus; Color Guard; Frsh Cls; Hon Roll; WVU; Engl.

CHAPMAN, MELISSA; Seneca HS; Waterford, PA; (Y); VP Trs 4-H; Pres Pep Clb; Band; Concert Band; Mrchg Band; Orch; Yrbk Stf; Rep Trs Stu Cncl; L Trk; Stat Wrstlng; Hugh O Brian Yth Ldrshp Delg 85; PA Free Enterprise Wk Schlrshp 86; Grove City Stu Cncl Ldrshp Wrkshp; Mercyhurst Coll; Rest/Htl Mgmt.

CHAPMAN, NORMAN; South Philadelphia HS; Philadelphia, PA; (Y).

CHAPMAN, WILLIAM; Lincoln HS; Ellwood City, PA; (Y); Spanish Clb; Stu Cncl; L Bsbl; L Ftbl; Hon Roll.

CHAPNELL, DAVID; Lincoln HS; Ellwood City, PA; (Y); 3/163; Church Yth Grp; French Clb; Concert Band; Mrchg Band; Var L Golf; Lion Awd; NHS; NEDT Awd; Cmnty Wkr; Jazz Band; Outstndg SR Mth Awd 86; Dely PA Free Enterprise Wk 85; Gifted Pgm 82-86; Westminster Coll; Math.

CHAPPELL, CYNDI; Richland HS; Gibsonia, PA; (Y); French Clb; Red Cross Aide; School Musical; Nwsp Stf; Rep Stu Cncl; Rep L Cheerleading; Var L Tennis; Var L Trk; High Hon Roll; NHS.

CHAPPELL, NICHOLE; Portage Area HS; Portage, PA; (Y); French Clb; Letterman Clb; Ski Clb; Varsity Clb; Nwsp Stf; Yrbk Stf; L Bsbl; Var L Cheerleading; Score Keeper; Hon Roll; Dntstry.

CHAPPELL, SHAWN; Lincoln HS; Ellwood City, PA; (Y); 66/162; Spanish Clb; VP VICA; Chrmn Y-Teens; Chorus; VP Soph Cls; Stu Cncl; JV Cheerleading; Powder Puff Ftbl; Trk; Hon Roll; Century 21 Acctng I Awd 86; Dentl Asst.

CHAPPELL, TODD R; Lewisburg Area HS; Lewisburg, PA; (Y); Boy Scts; Pres German Clb; School Musical; Trs Sr Cls; Var L Ftbl; Var L Trk; Var L Wrstlng; VP NHS; Science Clb; JV Tennis; Stu Of Mnth 86; U S Cst Grd Acad; Elec Engrng.

CHAPPIE, LEANNA; Greater Johnstown HS; Johnstown, PA; (Y); Hosp Aide; Ski Clb; Spanish Clb; Y-Teens; Nrsg.

CHAPPLE, GAYLE; Warwick HS; Lititz, PA; (Y); 24/237; Hosp Aide; Red Cross Aide; Band; Chorus; Church Choir; Stat Fld Hcky; Var Mgr(s); Var Score Keeper; High Hon Roll; Hon Roll; Free Lnc Photo.

CHAPUT JR, BERNARD R; Father Judge HS; Philadelphia, PA; (Y); Latin Clb; Var Socr; Prfct Atten Awd; Bus.

CHARITON, DEBBIE; E L Meyers HS; Wilkes Barre, PA; (Y); 6/166; Key Clb; Temple Yth Grp; Nwsp Stf; High Hon Roll; Jr NHS; Comm.

CHARLES, JAMES W; Lampeter Strasburg HS; Willow Street, PA; (Y); 22/135; Church Yth Grp; Thesps; Chorus; Concert Band; Jazz Band; Mrchg Band; School Musical; School Play; Hon Roll; NHS; Pres Acad Fit Awd 86; Ctzn & Svc Awd 86; Prfrmg Art Awd 86; Thespian Of Yr 86; Elctrnc Inst Middletown; Elec.

CHARLES, PAULINE; Hughesville HS; Unityville, PA; (Y); Church Yth Grp; Cmnty Wkr; FNA; Hosp Aide; Spanish Clb; SADD; Chorus; School Play; Off Jr Cls; Gym; Robert Packer.

CHARLES, PHILIP B; Warwick HS; Lititz, PA; (Y); 9/237; Church Yth Grp; JA; Orch; Im Vllybl; NHS; Hnr Stu; Electronic Inst; Elctnc.

CHARLSON, JOSHUA; Mt Lebanon HS; Pittsburgh, PA; (Y); 10/550; VP Temple Yth Grp; Sec Stu Cncl; JV Var Socr; High Hon Roll; Ntl Merit Schol; NEDT Awd; Val; Germn Essy Awd 1st Pl 85; U MI Acad Schlrshp 86; U Of MI.

CHARLTON JR, J WILLIAM; Council Rock HS; Newtown, PA; (Y); 88/760; Var L Bsktbl; Var L Golf; Var L Trk; Hon Roll; NHS; Rotary Awd; 2nd Tm All-Sbrbn Glf & Bsktbl Tm; Vllnva U; Chem Engrng.

CHARLTON, JOHN; Chambersburg Area SR HS; Fayettevillie, PA; (Y); 207/572; Church Yth Grp; Drama Clb; JCL; Chorus; Jazz Band; Nwsp Stf; Lit Mag; Bsbl; Ftbl; Stu Sprts Info Dir 85-86; OH U; Cmmnctns Stdy.

CHARNEY, MATT; Wyoming Area HS; W Wyoming, PA; (Y); Aud/Vis; Computer Clb; Var Bsbl; Var Golf; Comp Sci.

CHARNEY, SUSAN; Pittston Area HS; Pittston, PA; (Y); Math Clb; Science Clb; Band; Yrbk Stf; Var Capt Bsktbl; Var Capt Sftbl; Var L Tennis; Wilkes Coll; Comp Info Sys.

CHARRON, JAMES; Moon SR HS; Coraopolis, PA; (Y); JA; Band; Madrigals; Mrchg Band; Orch; Pep Band; Symp Band; High Hon Roll; Hon Roll; NHS.

CHARSKY, BRETT; Wellsboro SR HS; Wellsboro, PA; (Y); Boy Scts; Chess Clb; Church Yth Grp; Pep Clb; SADD; JV Bsktbl; Var Crs Cntry; Var Capt Tennis; God Cntry Awd; Eagle Scout 84; Conservation Essy Wnnr 84; Bradford; Physical Therapy.

CHASE, LORI A; Port Allegany HS; Port Allegany, PA; (Y); Exploring; Trs French Clb; Band; Chorus; Stage Crew; Ed Yrbk Phtg; French Hon Soc; Hon Roll; Ntl Merit SF; Camera Clb; NROTC Fnlst 85-86; PA ST; Pre-Law.

CHASE, RENEE; Pittston Area HS; Pittston, PA; (Y); Key Clb; Math Clb; Ski Clb; JV Sftbl; Var L Swmmng; Acctg.

CHASEN, STEPHEN; Lower Moreland HS; Huntingdon Valley, PA; (Y); 8/211; Debate Tm; French Clb; Key Clb; Mathletes; Science Clb; SADD; Nwsp Ed-Chief; Hon Roll; NHS; Ntl Merit Schol; Stu Of Mnth 86; PA ST U; Pre Med.

CHASKIN, BRENNA; Hazleton SR HS; Hazleton, PA; (Y); 77/388; Drama Clb; Hosp Aide; Office Aide; Pep Clb; Thesps; School Musical; School Play; Variety Show; Yrbk Stf; Hon Roll; Cndy Strpng Badge For Over 200 Hrs Of Srvc 84; Elem Ed.

CHASKO, PATRICIA; Wyoming Valley West HS; Wapwallopen, PA; (Y); 38/350; Key Clb; Concert Band; Jazz Band; VP Mrchg Band; Orch; School Musical; Rep Stu Cncl; Hon Roll; NHS; NEDT Awd; Dist Bandk Reg Band 85-86; WY Vlly W Bnd Parnts Awd 86; Millersville U; Biochem.

CHASTAIN, CURTIS; Pocovo Mountain HS; Swiftwater, PA; (Y); Letterman Clb; SADD; Capt Ftbl; Var Trk; Var Wrstlng; Engr.

CHASTAIN, PATTY; South Fayette JRSR HS; Bridgeville, PA; (S); 10/95; Church Yth Grp; Band; Concert Band; Mrchg Band; Yrbk Stf; Bsktbl; High Hon Roll; Hon Roll; NHS.

CHATFIELD, JEFF; North Hills HS; Pittsburgh, PA; (S); 46/475; Key Clb; Ski Clb; School Play; Rep Jr Cls; Capt Bsktbl; Var L Swmmng; NHS; High Hon Roll; Thesps; Natl Assc Stdnt Cncl Cnvtn 85; Dnc Aprntcshp Allghny Intmdt Unt 85; 17 Mag Teen Brd 86; US Naval Acad; Untl Law.

CHATLEY, ERIN; Henderson HS; West Chester, PA; (Y); 50/349; JCL; Rep Stu Cncl; Fld Hcky; Lcrss; Score Keeper; High Hon Roll; Hon Roll; Jr NHS; NHS; Hood Coll; Bio.

CHATMAN, ANNETTE; Schenley High Schl Teacher Center; Pittsburgh, PA; (S); Y-Teens; School Musical; Nwsp Stf; VP Pres Stu Cncl; Capt Pom Pon; Wt Lftg; High Hon Roll; Hon Roll; NHS; 2 Blck Hstry Essy Cntst Awds 85; Heritage Blck Womn Oratrcl Cntst 86; Pre-Med.

CHAUDHARI, ATUL; Penn Hills HS; Pittsburgh, PA; (S); 1/796; Computer Clb; JA; Math Tm; Spanish Clb; High Hon Roll; NHS; Val; U Of Pittsburgh Engr Schlrshp 86; 2nd Pl Chem Cntst 86; 1st Pl Calcu-Solve Cntst 85; U Of Pittsburgh; Elec Engr.

CHAUDHARY, RAKESH; Gateway SR HS; Torrance, CA; (Y); 2/450; Debate Tm; Math Tm; Model UN; NFL; Concert Band; Rep Sr Cls; High Hon Roll; NHS; Ntl Merit Schol; Sal; Yale U.

CHAUHAN, ALKA; Freedom HS; Bethlehem, PA; (Y); 56/456; Art Clb; Church Yth Grp; French Clb; Pep Clb; Teachers Aide; Temple Yth Grp; Phila Schl Pharmacy; Phrmcy.

CHAUMP, LISA; Wyoming Area HS; W Pittston, PA; (Y); 33/267; Key Clb; Math Tm; Ski Clb; Spanish Clb; Cheerleading; Trk; High Hon Roll; Hon Roll; Acad Schlrshp 86; Kings Coll; Bio.

CHAUVET, DAVID; West Allegheny HS; Oakdale, PA; (Y); #31 In Class; Im Bsktbl; Hon Roll; Jr NHS; PA ST Beaver; Engrng.

CHAWLA, RUMA; Methacton HS; Norristown, PA; (Y); Chess Clb; Debate Tm; Hosp Aide; Intnl Clb; Math Tm; Red Cross Aide; Scholastic Bowl; Chorus; Powder Puff Ftbl; French Clb; Wmn Engrs Of Amer 85-56; Tulane U; Engrng.

CHEAM, THENG; John Harris Campus HS; Harrisburg, PA; (S); 14/386; Science Clb; Tennis; Vllybl; Hon Roll; NHS; VFW Awd; Captl Area Sci & Engrng Fair 85; PA JR Acad Of Sci Rgn Iv 85; PA JR Acad Of Sci ST Meetng 85; Penn ST; Ag Engrng.

CHEARNEY, LAURIE ANN; Connellsville SR HS; Mt Pleasant, PA; (Y); Sec Church Yth Grp; DECA; Office Aide; Chorus; Church Choir; Nwsp Rptr; Nwsp Stf; Yrbk Stf; Sec Jr Cls; Sec Sr Cls; Stdnt Mnth 85; Outstndng NFAVTS 86; Hlth Aid 83-86; Business Careers Inst; Data Cmp.

CHEATLE, MARY J; Elk County Christian HS; St Marys, PA; (Y); 10/98; Cmnty Wkr; Hosp Aide; Library Aide; Church Choir; Color Guard; Mrchg Band; Yrbk Ed-Chief; Stat Bsktbl; Hon Roll; The Natl Hon Roll 84-85; USAF; Sec Police.

CHEATLE, SABINA; St Marys Area HS; Saint Marys, PA; (Y); Boys Clb Am; Church Yth Grp; Cmnty Wkr; Dance Clb; German Clb; Pep Clb; Speech Tm; Church Choir; High Hon Roll; Hon Roll; Fastst Typst 84-85; PA ST; Acctng.

CHEATON, YVONNE; Abraham Lincoln HS; Philadelphia, PA; (Y); Art Clb; Chess Clb; Dance Clb; Girl Scts; Spanish Clb; Varsity Clb; Church Choir; Drill Tm; Jr Cls; Cheerleading; Hnr Rl; Temple U; Lawyer.

CHECHO, PAMELA; West Scranton HS; Scranton, PA; (Y); Sec Trs FNA; Red Cross Aide; Spanish Clb; Nwsp Stf; Yrbk Stf; Stu Cncl; Cheerleading; Hon Roll; NHS; VFW Awd; Reflctn Cntst I Have A Dream 85; Med.

CHECK, BRIAN; Freeport Area SR HS; Freeport, PA; (Y); 30/170; Church Yth Grp; Computer Clb; Stage Crew; Hon Roll; Pre-Med.

CHECK, KELLIE; Carlynton HS; Pittsburgh, PA; (Y); Drama Clb; FBLA; Drill Tm; School Musical; Nwsp Rptr; Rep Stu Cncl; Pom Pon; Ntl Merit Ltr; Rep Frsh Cls; Chem Awd Sci Fair 2nd Pl 85; Ldrshp Awd 85; Robt Morris Coll; Bus.

CHECKET, BETH; Cedar Crest HS; Lebanon, PA; (Y); Latin Clb; Pep Clb; Var L Bsktbl; Var L Sftbl; Tennis; High Hon Roll; VP NHS; Rotary Awd; Vllybl; Hon Roll; Hugh Obrian Ldrshp Conf 85; Med.

CHECKO, CAROLYN M; Old Forge HS; Scranton, PA; (Y); Computer Clb; French Clb; Hosp Aide; Ski Clb; Teachers Aide; Cheerleading; Pom Pon; Tennis; High Hon Roll; Hon Roll; Gregg Typng Awd 85; Natl Gym Awd 84-85; Chrldng Awds 83-84; CMC Schl Of Nursng; RN.

CHEEK, LEE; Waynesburg Central HS; Waynesburg, PA; (Y); French Clb; Band; Concert Band; Drm Mjr(t); Jazz Band; Mrchg Band; High Hon Roll; Hon Roll; Ntl Merit Ltr; Drama Clb; Ntl Educ Dvlpmnt Tst Awd 84-85; Awd Supr Prfrmnc Coll Prep Englsh 85-86; MI ST U; Brdcstng.

CHELEDNIK, TOM; Shade Central City HS; Cairnbrook, PA; (Y); Q&S; Spanish Clb; Varsity Clb; Nwsp Rptr; Nwsp Stf; Bsktbl; Ftbl; Trk; Amer Legion Awd.

CHELGREN, KAREN; Marion Center Area HS; Marion Center, PA; (S); 1/170; Sec Church Yth Grp; Sec Intnl Clb; Library Aide; Chorus; Church Choir; Timer; High Hon Roll; Jr NHS; NHS; Spnsh.

CHEMBARS, REBECCA; Quigley HS; Monaca, PA; (S); 5/112; Cmnty Wkr; Intnl Clb; Math Clb; Nwsp Ed-Chief; Cheerleading; DAR Awd; High Hon Roll; Lion Awd; NHS; Alg, Art, Germn & Svc Awds 82-85; Track Statstcn & Mngr Lettrmn 83-85; Acadmc All Am & Natl Hnr Rll 86; Georgetown; Intl Reltns.

CHEN, ANNA; Lower Moreland HS; Huntingdon Valley, PA; (S); Church Yth Grp; German Clb; Mathletes; Teachers Aide; Orch; Lit Mag; Trk; High Hon Roll; NHS; Rotary Awd; Amer Assoc Grmn Tchrs Mrt Cert 85; Oct Stu Hnr Cert 85; PA Grmn Soc Achvt Cert 85; Pre-Med.

CHEN, CHUN; St Maria Goretti HS; Philadelphia, PA; (Y); 82/390; Mathletes; Spanish Clb; Hon Roll; Prfct Attndc; Hnrbl Mntn Math; Drexel; Math.

CHEN, DOUGLAS; Council Rock HS; Washington Cros, PA; (Y); 53/845; Var Tennis; Im Vllybl; Hon Roll; NHS; Med.

CHEN, EUGENE; Exeter Township HS; Reading, PA; (Y); 10/200; Quiz Bowl; Orch; Yrbk Ed-Chief; NHS; Chess Clb; Drama Clb; School Musical; Variety Show; Gov Hon Prg Awd; High Hon Roll; PA Gvrnrs Schl Art 85; Cnty Dstrct Rgnl Orchstra 81-86.

CHEN, GRACE; Mechanicsburg Area SR HS; Mechanicsburg, PA; (Y); 6/298; Am Leg Aux Girls St; NFL; Speech Tm; Mrchg Band; Symp Band; Nwsp Sprt Ed; Yrbk Stf; Trk; Pres NHS; Ntl Merit SF; Intl Ladies Grament Wrks Un Ntl Schrlshp Awd 86; Alumni Assoc Schrlshp Awd 86; Most Likely Succeed 86; U Chicago; Bus Adm.

CHENEVEY, STEVE; Wilmington Area HS; New Wilmington, PA; (S); 10/123; Drama Clb; Exploring; Radio Clb; Band; Concert Band; Mrchg Band; Pep Band; Stage Crew; Var L Crs Cntry; Var L Trk.

CHENG, CHRISTOPHER; Pennsbury HS; Yardley, PA; (Y); 6/700; VP Debate Tm; Sec Speech Tm; Orch; NHS; Ntl Merit Schol; VP Sec NFL; U Of PA.

CHENG, CYNTHIA; Dieruff HS; Allentown, PA; (Y); 5/327; Quiz Bowl; Acpl Chr; Nwsp Ed-Chief; Rep Stu Cncl; Capt Tennis; Lion Awd; Sec NHS; Ntl Merit SF; Union Carbde Ctznshp Schlrshp; Allentwn Spllng Bee 1st Pl; Medicine.

CHENG, TIMOTHY TIEN-YIN; East SR HS; West Chester, PA; (Y); 18/384; Church Yth Grp; Capt Debate Tm; Capt JCL; Capt Math Tm; Model UN; Capt NFL; Scholastic Bowl; Ed Lit Mag; High Hon Roll; NHS; U Of MI Ann Arbor; Aero Engrg.

CHENGER, JOANNE; Laurel Highlands SR HS; Uniontown, PA; (Y); 34/329; 4-H; FBLA; Hosp Aide; VP JA; Library Aide; Chorus; Flag Corp; Co-Capt Mrchg Band; Stat Crs Cntry; Stat Trk; Ntl JR Achvrs Conf 85; 2nd Rnnr-Up JR Achvt Essy Cont 86; JR Achvt Schlrshp Wnnr 86; Adv Engl Awd 86; IN U Of PA; CPA.

CHENOGA, MICHELE; Punxsutawney Area HS; Punxsutawney, PA; (Y); Band; Mrchg Band; PA ST; Sci.

CHENOT, FREDERICK; Montour HS; Pittsburgh, PA; (Y); 20/306; Chorus; Jazz Band; Mrchg Band; Pep Band; School Musical; Symp Band; High Hon Roll; NHS; Ntl Hnr Soc 86; Jhn Hpkns U; Pre-Med.

CHEPELEVICH, CHRISTOPHER; West Catholic Boy HS; Philadelphia, PA; (Y); 50/275; Chess Clb; Church Yth Grp; Cmnty Wkr; Debate Tm; JA; Library Aide; Teachers Aide; Church Choir; School Musical; School Play; Sec Ed.

CHEPLICK, DENNIS R; Marian Catholic; Nesquehoning, PA; (S); 25/114; Chess Clb; Math Clb; Nwsp Rptr; Nwsp Stf; Ftbl; Trk; Rotary Awd; Sci Awd 82; CYO Art Cont 1st Pl & Hnrary Pl 82.

CHERILLA, KEVIN; Hampton HS; Allison Pk, PA; (Y); 18/280; Boy Scts; Camera Clb; Church Yth Grp; Computer Clb; Drama Clb; 4-H; Intnl Clb; JA; Math Tm; Radio Clb; WV Wesleyn; Elctrcl Engrng.

CHERIPKA, ANGELA; East Allegheny HS; Wilmerding, PA; (Y); Office Aide; Off Sr Cls; Hon Roll.

CHERIS, JON DAVID; Lower Dauphin HS; Hummelstown, PA; (S); Boy Scts; Debate Tm; FFA; Ski Clb; Variety Show; Vet.

CHERKAS, ROD; Pennsburg HS; Yardley, PA; (Y); 1/800; Political Wkr; Nwsp Sprt Ed; Nwsp Stf; Yrbk Stf; JV Bsbl; Hon Roll; NHS; Ntl Merit Ltr; Renssalaer Mdl Outstndng Math & Sci 86; Awd To Attnd Rotarys Ldrshp Camp Neidig 86; Duke U; Math.

CHERNESKI, JUDITH; Hazleton HS; Beaver Meadows, PA; (Y); 29/400; Drama Clb; Drill Tm; Flag Corp; Mrchg Band; Yrbk Stf; Bowling; Stat Trk; French Hon Soc; High Hon Roll; NHS; Penn ST U; Mineral Econ.

CHERNESKY, RITA; Shenandoah Valley HS; Shenandoah, PA; (Y); 15/108; Library Aide; Chorus; Color Guard; Nwsp Stf; Yrbk Sprt Ed; Trk; JV L Vllybl; Hon Roll; Smnr-Upwrd Bnd 85; Bus Mngmt.

CHERNISKY, GEORGE; Jefferson Morgan HS; Rices Landing, PA; (S); 13/98; Boy Scts; Cmnty Wkr; Letterman Clb; Ski Clb; Varsity Clb; Rep Frsh Cls; Rep Jr Cls; Var Bsbl; JV Var Ftbl; JV Var Wt Lftg; Waynesburg Coll; Accntng.

CHERNISKY, MICHELLE; Northern Cambria HS; Barnesboro, PA; (Y); French Clb; Band; Mrchg Band; Stu Cncl; Cheerleading; High Hon Roll; Hon Roll; NHS; Slippery Rock U; Elem Ed.

CHERNITSKY, MARY E; Turkeyfoot Valley HS; Addison, PA; (S); 5/48; Library Aide; Q&S; SADD; Band; Color Guard; Mrchg Band; Yrbk Stf; Sec Frsh Cls; Pres Sr Cls; Sec Stu Cncl; Med Sec.

CHERNOUSKAS, CAROL; Pittston Area SR HS; Pittston, PA; (Y); Key Clb; Science Clb; Sec Jr Cls; Hon Roll; Lion Awd; NHS; Ntl Merit Ltr; U Of Scranton; Med.

CHERNOWSKY, MICHELLE; Bishop O Reilly HS; Forty Fort, PA; (Y); Hosp Aide; Red Cross Aide; Spanish Clb; Chorus; Flag Corp; Nwsp Stf; Yrbk Stf; Prfct Atten Awd; Spanish NHS; Nrsng.

CHERRY, ELIZABETH; Owen J Roberts HS; Glenmoore, PA; (S); Church Yth Grp; Sec Service Clb; SADD; Rep Frsh Cls; Mgr Bsktbl; Lcrss; Hon Roll; NHS; Prfct Atten Awd; Physcl Thrpy.

CHERRY, KEN; Bellwood-Antis HS; Tyrone, PA; (Y); Art Clb; Church Yth Grp; French Clb; JA; Library Aide; Chorus; Church Choir; School Musical; Hon Roll; Amercn Cultr Awd 84-85; Safty Awd 85-86; PA ST U; Elem Educ.

CHERRY, MALLORY ANNE; Mercy Hurst Prep Schl; Erie, PA; (Y); 1/160; Key Clb; Q&S; Pres Spanish Clb; Ed Nwsp Stf; Ed Lit Mag; Var L Vllybl; High Hon Roll; NHS; Pres Schlr; Amer Sterilizer Corp Scholar 86; Tressa Burns Merit Scholar 85; Fin Time Mag Essay Cont 86; U Notre Dame; Acctng.

CHERRY, STEVEN; Lower Moreland HS; Huntingdon Valley, PA; (S); Cmnty Wkr; FBLA; Key Clb; Science Clb; Temple Yth Grp; JV Trk; Hon Roll; NHS.

CHERWONY, BETH; Neshaminy HS; Langhorne, PA; (Y); 35/750; Civic Clb; Key Clb; SADD; Chorus; Nwsp Stf; Stu Cncl; Stat Fld Hcky; Hon Roll; NHS; Bus.

CHESLEY, DENNIS; North East HS; North East, PA; (Y); 16/146; Ski Clb; Ftbl; Golf; Trk; High Hon Roll; NHS; Prfct Atten Awd; Pres Schlr; Latin Clb; Letterman Clb; 3 Yr Prfct Atten Awd 86; Am Leg Svc Awd 86; Behrend Coll; Bus Adm.

CHESNA, WILLIAM J; Crestwood HS; Mountaintop, PA; (Y); Ski Clb; Var Ftbl; Var Trk; Var Wt Lftg; All Schlstc Ftbl Tm Hnbl Mntn 85; Times Ldr All Conf Qtrbck 85; Comp.

CHESS JR, J DUANE; Commodore Perry HS; Hadley, PA; (S); 6/61; Math Clb; Stage Crew; Bsbl; Bsktbl; Hon Roll; NHS; Gannon; Engrng.

CHESTER, KIMBERLY; Ambridge HS; Freedom, PA; (Y); 7/265; Pep Clb; Trs Spanish Clb; Drill Tm; Gym; High Hon Roll; Trs NHS; Fdlty & Depst Co Schlrshp 86; January Grl Of Mnth 86; PA ST U.

CHESTNUT, BETH; Ford City HS; Ford City, PA; (Y); Church Yth Grp; Pep Clb; Spanish Clb; Chorus; School Musical; Rep Frsh Cls; Rep Soph Cls; Rep Jr Cls; Rep Stu Cncl; Cheerleading; Nrsng.

CHESTNUT, JEANETTE; Brookville Area HS; Brookville, PA; (Y); Cmnty Wkr; Debate Tm; 4-H; FNA; Stage Crew; Nwsp Rptr; Nwsp Stf; 4-H Awd; Hon Roll; Jr NHS.

CHESTNUT, KRIS; Hickory SR HS; Hermitage, PA; (S); 18/182; Church Yth Grp; Drama Clb; Service Clb; School Play; Nwsp Stf; Sec Jr Cls; Var Cheerleading; Im Vllybl; NHS; Spanish NHS; Chrldg Acad Awd 85; USCAA 85.

CHEUVRONT, LANCE; Aliquippa HS; Aliquippa, PA; (Y); VP Chess Clb; Band; Mgr(s); Law Enfrcmnt Aerontcs.

CHEW, BERNADETTE; Blairsville SR HS; Blairsville, PA; (Y); Church Yth Grp; Drama Clb; SADD; Stage Crew; Yrbk Phtg; Ed Yrbk Stf; High Hon Roll; Hon Roll; Hnr Rl Awd 86; U Pittsburgh; Acctng.

CHI, JAMES; Cheltenham HS; Philadelphia, PA; (Y); #13 In Class; Boy Scts; Church Yth Grp; Intnl Clb; Math Tm; Church Choir; Pres Frsh Cls; Bowling; Socr; Tennis; Vllybl; Law.

CHIANG, TINA; Hazleton HS; Hazleton, PA; (Y); 3/377; Drama Clb; Trs Leo Clb; Scholastic Bowl; Ski Clb; Concert Band; Drm Mjr(t); Trs Sr Cls; Im Vllybl; NHS; Lehigh U Trustee Scholar 86; Elks Natl Fndtn Mst Valuable Stu Scholar 86; Yth Ctznshp Awd 86; Lehigh U; Engrng.

CHIARAMONTE, GREGORY; Greensburg Central Catholic HS; Scottdale, PA; (Y); 56/223; Chess Clb; French Clb; Latin Clb; Pep Clb; Service Clb; High Hon Roll; Hon Roll; Prfct Atten Awd; WA & Jefferson Coll; Chem.

CHIARAVALLE, JO ANN; Punxsutawney HS; Punxsutawney, PA; (Y); Debate Tm; French Clb; Stat Bsbl; Hon Roll; Tchr.

CHIARELLO, ROSINA; St Huberts HS; Philadelphia, PA; (Y); 177/367; Church Yth Grp; Intnl Clb; Office Aide; Teachers Aide; Chorus; School Musical; Attndce Cert Awd 85; Cert Of Apprctn 86; Junior Coll; Bus.

CHIAVAROLI, DEBORAH; St Maria Goretti HS; Philadelphia, PA; (Y); 53/426; Church Yth Grp; Spanish Clb; Church Choir; Nwsp Rptr; Nwsp Stf; Hon Roll; NHS; Prfct Atten Awd; Gldn Slppr Schlrshp 86; La Salle U; Psych.

CHIAVERINI, MARK; York Catholic HS; York, PA; (Y); Mathletes; Varsity Clb; Rep Stu Cncl; Var Bsbl; JV Ftbl; Im Var Socr; JV Wrstlng; High Hon Roll; Hon Roll; Ntl Merit Ltr; Stu Of Mnth; Indoor Sccr Div Champ; Cornell U; Arch.

CHICCO, PATRICIA; Bishop O Hara HS; Dunmore, PA; (Y); 4/113; Spanish Clb; Yrbk Stf; Rep Frsh Cls; Rep Soph Cls; Rep Jr Cls; Mgr(s); High Hon Roll; NHS; The Ntl Hnr Roll 85.

CHICHESTER, ELIZABETH M; East HS; Erie, PA; (Y); 30/140; French Clb; Hosp Aide; Pep Clb; Y-Teens; Stage Crew; Nwsp Ed-Chief; Nwsp Phtg; Nwsp Rptr; Yrbk Rptr; Lit Mag; Gov Schl Arts Schlrshp 85; Ntl Prsbytrn Schlrshp 86; Temple U; Art.

CHICHY, DAWN; Purchase Line HS; Clymer, PA; (Y); Pres VP 4-H; Spanish Clb; Capt Flag Corp; 4-H Awd; High Hon Roll; Hon Roll.

CHICK, TERESA; Norwin SR HS; Westmoreland City, PA; (Y); 24/550; French Clb; Yrbk Ed-Chief; Hon Roll; Jr NHS; NHS; Prfct Atten Awd; ISDA Dante Alighier #244; 1st Pl Natl Soc Stud Olympaid; Robert Morris; Word Procssng.

CHICKINI, JAMES J; Moon SR HS; Coraopolis, PA; (Y); Intnl Clb; JA; SADD; Y-Teens; Stu Cncl; Bsbl; Mgr(s); Score Keeper; Wrstlng; High Hon Roll; Gntc Engrng.

CHICKIRDA, JENNIFER; Tamaqua Area HS; Tamaqua, PA; (Y); Trs Church Yth Grp; Science Clb; Y-Teens; Chorus; Church Choir; Yrbk Stf; Hon Roll; Pres Schlr; Spanish NHS; Christa Mcauliffe Schlrshp 86; Schlrs Ed Awd 86; Bloomsburg U; Chem Tchr.

CHIDESTER, KELLY; Jefferson Morgan JR & SR HS; Jefferson, PA; (S); 1/95; Pres Intnl Clb; Library Aide; VP Spanish Clb; SADD; Rep Sr Cls; High Hon Roll; Hon Roll; Lion Awd; NHS; Natural Sci Hist Awd 85; Most Outstndng Frgn Lang Stu 85; Intl Frgn Lang Awd 84; Duquesne U; Phrmcy.

CHIEFFALO, DANIEL; Bishop Hannan HS; Scranton, PA; (Y); 10/133; Debate Tm; Var Capt Bsbl; JV Bsktbl; High Hon Roll; Hon Roll; Jr NHS; NHS; Sprtsmnshp Awd 86; Econ.

CHIEN, JENNIFER; Plymouth-Whitemarsh HS; Plymouth Mtg, PA; (Y); 15/286; Hosp Aide; Math Clb; Chorus; Lit Mag; Stu Cncl; Fld Hcky; Lcrss; High Hon Roll; NHS; Prfct Atten Awd; Inv Attnd Yng Mstrs Cnsrtm Arts 85; Med.

CHIESA, LISA; Highlands SR HS; Natrona Heights, PA; (Y); 78/280; Art Clb; Trs FNA; Hosp Aide; NHS; Office Aide; Gym; Sftbl; Jr NHS; ST HOSA Comtpn 1st Pl Extemprns Hlth Display 86; Brown & Gold Schltc Achvt Awds 82-86; Psych.

CHILDRESS JR, RONALD; Elk Lake HS; Meshoppen, PA; (Y); 25/101; Drama Clb; French Clb; Ski Clb; Pres Band; Jazz Band; Orch; Swing Chorus; Stu Cncl; JV Var Socr; Var Capt Trk; Mltry Srv; Tv Wthrmn.

CHILDS, DENISE; Connellsville Area HS; Connellsville, PA; (Y); 67/500; Office Aide; L Sftbl; Cit Awd; High Hon Roll; Hon Roll; Art Clb; Camera Clb; Yrbk Phtg; Bus.

CHILSON, JOHN; Millersburg Area HS; Millersburg, PA; (S); 7/84; Nwsp Rptr; Yrbk Rptr; Off Jr Cls; Pres VP Stu Cncl; Var L Bsbl; Capt L Wrstlng; High Hon Roll; Boy Scts; Schl Patriot & News Corrspndnt 85-86; Yth Forum Rep 85-86; Pres Phys Ftnss Awd 83; Cmmnctns.

CHIMINO, ANGEL; Archbishop Carroll Girls; Narberth, PA; (Y); Church Yth Grp; Drama Clb; French Clb; Girl Scts; Hosp Aide; School Play; Nwsp Rptr; Yrbk Stf; Chorus; Temple U; Math Educ.

CHIN, LILLIAN VERONICA; Cardinal O Hara HS; Springfield, PA; (Y); 57/740; Church Yth Grp; OEA; Service Clb; Yrbk Stf; High Hon Roll; Hon Roll; PA ST; Finance.

CHIN, SONG-OK SUSAN; Plymouth Whitemarsh HS; Conshohocken, PA; (Y); 10/360; Trs Church Yth Grp; Math Clb; VP Science Clb; Mrchg Band; Rep Stu Cncl; Var Trk; Sec Pres NHS; Hello Columbus 1992 Scholar 86; Plymouth Whitemarsh Exch Clb Stu Mnth 86; People To People Schl Ambass; Philadelphia Coll Phrmcy; Phrmc.

CHIORAZZI, CATHERINE; St Hubert For Girls HS; Philadelphia, PA; (Y); 32/367; Orch; Coach Actv; Swmmng; High Hon Roll; NHS; Cert Acdmc Mrt Music 84.

CHIRDON, MICHELE; Penn Cambria HS; Ashville, PA; (Y); Drama Clb; Ski Clb; Spanish Clb; Band; Stage Crew; Nwsp Stf; Pres Frsh Cls; Rep Stu Cncl; Var L Sftbl; Im Vllybl; Pres Physcl Ftns Awd; Educ.

CHIRIELEISON, KELLY; Plum SR HS; Pittsburgh, PA; (Y); Church Yth Grp; Varsity Clb; Symp Band; Nwsp Ed-Chief; Yrbk Stf; Trk; High Hon Roll; NHS; Cultrl Arts Awd Lit, Hgh Achvt Clsrm Awds 86; Pitt Schl Phrmcy; Phrmcy.

CHISHOLM, AVIS V; Harrisburg-Steelton Highspire Vo Tech; Harrisburg, PA; (Y); 110/364; Church Yth Grp; Debate Tm; Chorus; Church Choir; Yrbk Stf; Sci Fr Awd Hnrb Mntn 84-85; Morgan ST U; Accntng.

CHISHOLM, TASHA; Steelton Highspire HS; Steelton, PA; (Y); FBLA; Library Aide; Pep Clb; Spanish Clb; Ed Yrbk Stf; Sec Stu Cncl; Hon Roll; Shippensburg.

CHISTAKOFF, TINA; Minersville Area HS; Branchdale, PA; (Y); 2/117; Church Yth Grp; Cmnty Wkr; Computer Clb; Latin Clb; Office Aide; Spanish Clb; SADD; Chorus; Drill Tm; School Musical; ILGWU Schlrshp Awd, Cass Twnshp Athl Assn Awd, Soroptmst Yuth Ctznshp Awd 86; Wilkes Coll; Bio.

CHIYKA, JEFFREY; Pottsgrove HS; Pottstown, PA; (Y); 37/229; Debate Tm; Math Tm; Science Clb; Spanish Clb; Im JV Trk; JV Wrstlng; Prfct Atten Awd; 3rd Pl Awd Cnty Lvl PA Acad Decathlon 86; Delg To Model Orgnztn Of Amer ST Assbmly WA D C 85; Engrng.

CHIZEK, CHRISTINE; Central Bucks East HS; Doylestown, PA; (Y); Hosp Aide; Band; Concert Band; Mrchg Band; JV Var Fld Hcky; Mgr(s); Score Keeper; Im Socr; Hon Roll; Bst Attitude Awd JV Fld Hcky 84; Pre-Med.

CHIZMAR, DEBORAH; Penn Trafford HS; Jeannette, PA; (Y); 69/364; Church Yth Grp; Drama Clb; Exploring; Hosp Aide; Acpl Chr; Chorus; Swing Chorus; Variety Show; Im Vllybl; Hon Roll; West Penn Schl Of Nrsng; Nrsng.

CHIZMAR, KATRINA; Center HS; Aliquippa, PA; (Y); 10/190; Am Leg Aux Girls St; German Clb; School Musical; Nwsp Stf; Yrbk Stf; Sec Stu Cncl; Var Capt Cheerleading; Coach Actv; High Hon Roll; NHS; Emplye St Frances Cabrini Bingo 83; Prom Commtte; Bus.

CHLEBOWSKI, FELICIA A; Southmoreland HS; Scottdale, PA; (Y); Exploring; French Clb; Office Aide; Pep Clb; Lit Mag; Gym; French Hon Soc; Svc Awd 86; Gannon; Radiolgc Techlgy.

CHMIELEWSKI, LINDA; Bishop Hannan HS; Scranton, PA; (Y); Dance Clb; French Clb; Variety Show; Bowling; French Hon Soc; Hon Roll; Jr NHS; NHS; Algebra II/Trig Awd 86; Amer Cultures Awd 86; Bio Awd 85; U Of Scranton; Phys Thrpy.

CHMIELEWSKI, LORI; West Scranton HS; Scranton, PA; (Y); 15/300; French Clb; Pep Clb; Ski Clb; JV Cheerleading; Coach Actv; Hon Roll; NHS; Penn ST; Acctg.

CHNUPA, KEITH; Clearfield Area HS; Clearfield, PA; (Y); Art Clb; Computer Clb; VICA; Var Ftbl; Var Wt Lftg; Var Wrstlng; High Hon Roll; Hon Roll; Masonic Awd; Pst Master Councelor Awd/Demolay 85; Comp Sci.

CHO, KATHY; Lower Moreland HS; Huntingdon Valley, PA; (S); 9/214; Madrigals; NHS; Church Yth Grp; Drama Clb; French Clb; Key Clb; Science Clb; Acpl Chr; Chorus; Ldrshp Tmmrws Wrld 85; Frnch Awd 83; Vrsty Lttr Music 85; U Of PA; Bio.

CHO, SUSAN; Avon Grove HS; West Grove, PA; (Y); 1/150; Pres SADD; Nwsp Ed-Chief; Trs Soph Cls; Var L Tennis; Bausch & Lomb Sci Awd; NHS; Ntl Merit Ltr; Pres Schlr; Val; U Of MI Ann Arbor; Engr.

CHOBEY, SHANNON; West Scranton HS; Scranton, PA; (Y); Spanish Clb; Pom Pon; Hon Roll; NHS; Lackawanna JC.

CHOBOT, LISA; Chartiers Valley HS; Carnegie, PA; (Y); French Clb; Ski Clb; Varsity Clb; Y-Teens; Rep Frsh Cls; Rep Soph Cls; Rep Stu Cncl; Var Bsktbl; Var Trk; Muskingum Coll; Intl Bus.

CHOCOLAS, DENISE; Hazleton HS; Hazleton, PA; (Y); 78/388; Pres FBLA; Var Cheerleading; Sftbl; Swmmng; Acctg.

CHOFFEL, DENISE; Cochranton JR SR HS; Meadville, PA; (Y); 10/85; French Clb; Ski Clb; SADD; Concert Band; Mrchg Band; Yrbk Stf; Sec Soph Cls; Sec Jr Cls; Sec Sr Cls; Var L Bsktbl; Top 3% Cls-Acadmclly-Chem Trig 85; Top 3% Cls-Pltcl Sci & Engl 86; Cert-Hnr R Ll 4 Or More Times 83-86; U Of Pittsburgh; Psychlgy.

CHOI, NARI; Plymouth Whitemarsh HS; Plymouth Mtg, PA; (Y); Intnl Clb; Model UN; Nwsp Rptr; Nwsp Stf; Lit Mag; Hon Roll; NHS; Church Yth Grp; Chorus; Prfct Atten Awd; 3 Awds Natl Wnnr Intrmed Clss Natl Piano Aud 80-82; Math & Verbl Tlnt Srch Awd Of Partcptn 82; Yale U; Danc Crtc.

CHOI, UN JUNG; Plymouth Whitemarsh HS; Conshohocken, PA; (Y); 5/337; Church Yth Grp; Math Clb; Chorus; Drill Tm; Lit Mag; Sec Stu Cncl; Mgr(s); Trk; Jr NHS; VP NHS; Awd For Acdmc Excllnc 84-86AWD For Prfct Attndnc 84-85; Awd For Distngshd Hon Roll 84-86; Bus Admin.

CHOI, YOUNG; Wissahickon HS; Norristown, PA; (S); 20/377; Math Clb; Band; Concert Band; Jazz Band; Mrchg Band; Orch; JV Ftbl; JV Tennis; Wt Lftg; Pres High Hon Roll; Drexel; Elec Engrng.

CHOKEY JR, JAMES A; Bethel Park SR HS; Bethel Park, PA; (Y); 15/520; French Clb; Science Clb; Trs Jazz Band; Trs Mrchg Band; Orch; School Musical; Trs Flag Corp; High Hon Roll; NHS; Ntl Merit Ltr; Rotary Ingl Ldrshp Cnfrnce 86; CTY Summer Courses 83-84; Engl.

CHOLAK, GREGORY J; Trinity HS; University Park, PA; (Y); 29/384; Aud/Vis; French Clb; Y-Teens; Im JV Bsktbl; Im JV Ftbl; High Hon Roll; Hon Roll; Penn ST U Park; Comp Sci.

CHORBA, BRENDA; Central Columbia HS; Millville, PA; (Y); FHA; Key Clb; Pep Clb; Stu Cncl; Hon Roll; VP Spanish Clb; U Of Pitt; Psych.

CHORGO, PATRICIA; West Mifflin Area HS; W Mifflin, PA; (Y); 2/320; Hosp Aide; Orch; Var Co-Capt Bsktbl; L Crs Cntry; Var L Sftbl; L Trk; Bausch & Lomb Sci Awd; NHS; Pres Schlr; Sal; CMU Schlrshp, Century III Ldrs Wnnr, US Army Rsrve Schlr Athl 86; Carnegie-Mellon U; Bio.

CHOU, GEORGE; Spring-Ford HS; Royersford, PA; (S); 3/250; Art Clb; Library Aide; Var Crs Cntry; Var L Trk; Hon Roll; NHS; Mntgmry Cnty Mcrocmptr Cntst 1st Plc 86; ICPAU Cmptr Cntst 3rd Plc 86; Sprry Cmptr Cntst 1st Plc 86; MIT; Cmptr Engr.

CHOVANEC, MICHAEL; Blairsville SR HS; Blairsville, PA; (Y); 2/129; Band; Chorus; School Musical; Rep Stu Cncl; JP Sousa Awd; Trs NHS; Sal; Concert Band; Jazz Band; Mrchg Band; Kenny Greene Schlrshp 86; Dist Chrs 85 & 86; Rgnl Chrs 85 & 86; Indiana U PA; Phy Ed.

CHOW, MICHELLE; Gateway SR HS; Monroeville, PA; (Y); 32/462; Pres Orch; School Play; Yrbk Stf; Capt Swmmng; Trk; NHS; Full Athltc Schlrshp TX A & M 86-87; TX A & M U; Bus Adm.

CHOWANEC, RICHARD; Mid Valley HS; Dickson City, PA; (Y); Sec Cmnty Wkr; Computer Clb; Band; Concert Band; Mrchg Band; Hon Roll; Phys Thrpst.

CHOWKA, JULIET; Our Lady Of Lourdes HS; Shamokin, PA; (Y); 7/98; Pres Drama Clb; Pres Library Aide; Spanish Clb; Pres SADD; Ed Yrbk Stf; Pres Soph Cls; High Hon Roll; Pres NHS; Spanish NHS; Hugh O Brien Yth Ldrshp Sem 85; Hgst Cumltv Avg 84; Tho Phnr Cls Phys Ed 86; Pol Sci.

CHRIS, KIM; Corry Area HS; Corry, PA; (Y); Church Yth Grp; German Clb; Hon Roll; Grmn Ntl Hnr Soc 84; Prsdntl Acad Ftnss Awd 86; Schlrshp Frm Mc Innes Stl Co 86; Edinboro U; Psych.

CHRIS, MICHELLE; Corry Area HS; Corry, PA; (S); 20/212; Church Yth Grp; SADD; Band; Church Choir; Concert Band; Mrchg Band; Rep Stu Cncl; Delta Epslon Phi 84; Tch Hndcp Chldrn.

CHRISMER, LEVATO; Bermuelian Springs HS; East Berlin, PA; (Y); 28/118; Hosp Aide; Chorus; Nwsp Rptr; Nwsp Stf; Yrbk Rptr; Yrbk Stf; Stu Cncl; Var L Cheerleading; Var Stat Mgr(s); Hon Roll; Outstdg Ribbn Eastern Chrldrs Assn 84; Jrnlsm.

CHRIST, CHERYL; Peters TWP HS; Venetia, PA; (S); 53/256; Hosp Aide; Capt Color Guard; Sec Stu Cncl; Powder Puff Ftbl; Twrlr; Hon Roll; Masonic Awd; Wrld Chmpn Twrlng & Snow Corp 79-86; OH U; Human Rsrc Mgmnt.

CHRIST, MELODY L; Cocalico HS; Denver, PA; (Y); Teachers Aide; Yrbk Bus Mgr; Yrbk Stf; Stat Bsktbl; Var Cheerleading; Stat Fld Hcky; Camera Clb; Timer; Hon Roll; Grls Ldrs 86-87; Yrbk Asst Sprts Edtr 86; Bus Mgmt.

CHRIST, MICHAEL; Morrisville HS; Morrisville, PA; (Y); Red Cross Aide; Concert Band; Bsbl; Bsktbl; Ftbl; High Hon Roll; Hon Roll; NHS; US Army Reserves Natl Schlr/Athlete Awd 86; US Naval Acad.

CHRISTENSEN, ERIC; Roxborough HS; Philadelphia, PA; (Y); 1/250; Cmnty Wkr; Science Clb; Acpl Chr; School Musical; Nwsp Stf; Bsbl; Bausch & Lomb Sci Awd; High Hon Roll; NHS; Ntl Merit SF; Outstndng Achvt Schlr Schlrshp 86-90; Temple U; Actrl Sci.

CHRISTENSEN, PETER N; Central SR HS; York, PA; (Y); 12/239; Varsity Clb; Capt Crs Cntry; Capt Wrstlng; Lion Awd; NHS; Pres Schlr; Church Yth Grp; Chorus; Church Choir; High Hon Roll; Acad All-Star 86; Adam Hamme Mem Music Schlrshp 86; Lester K Loucks Music Awd 86; 1st Pl Wrstlng Tourn; Swarthmore Coll; Engrng.

CHRISTENSON, STACY; Seneca Valley HS; Harmony, PA; (Y); Church Yth Grp; JA; Thesps; School Play; Stage Crew; High Hon Roll; Hon Roll; Intl Bus.

CHRISTIAN, ED; Stroudsburg HS; Stroudsburg, PA; (Y); 18/245; Church Yth Grp; Scholastic Bowl; Spanish Clb; Rep Stu Cncl; JV Bsbl; Im Bowling; JV Ftbl; Var Swmmng; High Hon Roll; NHS; PA ST U; Acctng.

CHRISTIAN, SHANON; St Josephs Acad; Middletown, PA; (Y); 2/19; Girl Scts; Nwsp Rptr; Prfct Atten Awd; Bst Grade & Mst Faithful Religion 84-86; Outstndng Behvr/Hlpng Hand 85-86; Chem, Chld Devlpmnt Achvt; Alvernia Coll; Psych.

CHRISTIAN, THAD; New Brighton HS; New Brighton, PA; (Y); 11/154; Concert Band; Jazz Band; Mrchg Band; School Play; Nwsp Stf; High Hon Roll; Rotary Awd; Computer Clb; Band; Semper Fdls Distngshd Musicn Awd 86; JVEW Brighton JR Wmns Clb Schlrshp 86; Pres Acadmc Ftnss Awd 86; U Pittsbgh; Dntst.

CHRISTIE, CRAIG; Central Bucks West HS; Chalfont, PA; (Y); 47/489; Jazz Band; L Swmmng; Hon Roll; Outstndng Frshmn Swmmr 84; Kngsbry Awd 86.

CHRISTIE, DOUGLAS E; Montgomery Area HS; Montgomery, PA; (Y); 13/63; Trs FBLA; Pres VP Spanish Clb; Thesps; Chorus; Church Choir; School Musical; Yrbk Bus Mgr; Stu Cncl; Mgr(s); NHS; MAEA Clg Schlrshp; Act Awd; PA ST U; Music Ed.

CHRISTINE, KAREN; Freedom HS; Bethlehem, PA; (Y); 79/465; Drama Clb; SADD; Varsity Clb; VP Soph Cls; Pres Rep Jr Cls; Pres Sr Cls; VP Stu Cncl; Var L Bsktbl; Var Sftbl; Hon Roll; Stu Trainr 85-87; Bus Adm.

CHRISTINI, DAVID; Towanda Area HS; Towanda, PA; (Y); 1/160; Am Leg Boys St; Boy Scts; Band; Trs Stu Cncl; Bsktbl; Crs Cntry; Bausch & Lomb Sci Awd; NHS; Ntl Merit Ltr; Rotary Ldrs Camp 85.

CHRISTMAN, DARRYL; Northampton SR HS; Northampton, PA; (Y); Penn ST U; Comm.

CHRISTMAN, JANE; Hershey SR HS; Hummelstown, PA; (Y); 37/200; VP Camera Clb; Church Yth Grp; Ski Clb; Spanish Clb; Teachers Aide; Band; High Hon Roll; Hon Roll; Spanish NHS.

CHRISTMAN, KAREN; Lehighton Area HS; Lehighton, PA; (Y); Church Yth Grp; Girl Scts; Library Aide; Church Choir; Flag Corp; School Play; Nwsp Phtg; Yrbk Stf; Hon Roll; Lion Awd; Ursinus Coll; Psych.

CHRISTMAN, ROBERT; Ringgold HS; Finleyville, PA; (Y); Boy Scts; Chess Clb; JA; Ski Clb; Band; Concert Band; Nwsp Stf; Ftbl; Arch.

CHRISTNER, RANDY; Somerset Area SR HS; Somerset, PA; (Y); 13/250; Church Yth Grp; English Clb; French Clb; Math Tm; Varsity Clb; VP Soph Cls; Pres Jr Cls; Var L Bsbl; Var L Bsktbl; Cit Awd; Frnch,Alg,Bio Awd 85; Engrng.

CHRISTON, EVAN; Rochester Area JR SR HS; Rochester, PA; (Y); Rep Am Leg Boys St; Boy Scts; Church Yth Grp; Ski Clb; Yrbk Phtg; JV Ftbl; Hon Roll; Math Awd 83; Pblc Spkng Awd 81; U Of Pittsburgh; Phrmcst.

CHRISTOPHER, JOY; Northampton SR HS; Bath, PA; (Y); Dance Clb; Drama Clb; Leo Clb; Chorus; School Musical; School Play; Stage Crew; Nwsp Stf; Trk; Hon Roll; 3rd Pl Dance Solo Talent Cmpttn 86; Achvmnt Awd Jazz & Tap Cnvntn 83; Achvmnt Awd Bst Imprvd Dance 86; Dance.

CHRISTY, ANGELA; Meadville Area SR HS; Meadville, PA; (Y); Church Yth Grp; Exploring; FCA; French Clb; JA; Letterman Clb; Pres Pep Clb; Science Clb; Ski Clb; Varsity Clb; Elem Educ.

CHRISTY, MIKE; Grove City SR HS; Grove City, PA; (Y); 29/195; French Clb; Variety Show; Capt Bowling; High Hon Roll; Hon Roll; Prfct Atten Awd; 3rd Pl Dist Hstry Day 85; Penn ST U; Mech Engrng.

CHRISTY, TERESA; Moniteau JR SR HS; Slippery Rock, PA; (Y); 19/133; French Clb; Library Aide; Chorus; Capt Color Guard; Hon Roll; NHS; Law.

CHROMEY, MARY; Mid Valley HS; Dickson City, PA; (Y); Church Yth Grp; Science Clb; Nwsp Rptr; Hon Roll; School Play; Sec Frsh Cls; Sec Soph Cls; Gen Excllnc & Math Excllnc Awds-Upward Bound 84; Marywood Coll; Elemtry Ed.

CHRONISTER, MARTIN; Tyrone Area HS; Tyrone, PA; (Y); Boy Scts; Church Yth Grp; Spanish Clb; Var L Ftbl; Im Wt Lftg; Var L Wrstlng; God Cntry Awd; Hon Roll; Navy; Nuclear Pwr.

CHRONOWSKI, KIMBERLEY; Tunkhannock HS; Factoryville, PA; (S); 23/290; Church Yth Grp; Sec Science Clb; Spanish Clb; JV Var Fld Hcky; Hon Roll; NHS; Phrmcy.

CHU, SIAO MEI; Lock Haven HS; Lock Haven, PA; (Y); French Clb; Chorus; Variety Show; Nwsp Stf; Yrbk Stf; Sec Soph Cls; Off Jr Cls; JV Cheerleading; Socr; High Hon Roll; Bio And Home Ec Awd 84; Top Frnch Stu Levl I And II 84-85; Pre Med.

CHUBA, KELLIE; Valley HS; Arnold, PA; (Y); Drama Clb; Pep Clb; Varsity Clb; Chorus; Color Guard; Yrbk Stf; Rep Stu Cncl; Var Trk; Var Vllybl; High Hon Roll; Nursing.

CHUBIN, ELLEN; Pennsbury HS; Yardley, PA; (Y); 8/712; Off French Clb; Mathletes; Sec NFL; Orch; Nwsp Ed-Chief; Yrbk Ed-Chief; Ntl Merit Ltr; Debate Tm; Drama Clb; Scholastic Bowl; PA ST Champ Girls Spkng 86; Regnl Treas PA Area Fdrtn Temple Yth 84-86; 1st Violin PA Orch Fest 86; Harvard U; Pre Law.

CHUDY, FRANK; Springdale HS; Cheswick, PA; (Y); 50/140; Boy Scts; German Clb; Jazz Band; Mrchg Band; JV L Socr; Var L Tennis; Ad Altare Dei Rel Awd Part I & II 84; Pope Pius XII Regl Awd 85; Aerospace Engr.

CHULVICK, MARY JO; James M Coughlin HS; Wilkes-Barre, PA; (Y); FBLA; Ski Clb; Band; Concert Band; Mrchg Band; L Twrlr; High Hon Roll; Hon Roll; NHS; Pres Acad Ftnss Awd 86; Ctznshp C Awd 86; Typng Awd; Acctng.

CHUN, SUSIE; Hatboro-Hosham HS; Ambler, PA; (Y); 1/255; Church Yth Grp; Model UN; Chorus; Concert Band; Yrbk Stf; Var Trk; Im Vllybl; High Hon Roll; NHS; Val; Outstndng Achvt Schlrshp 86; Sperry Corp Awd Excllnce 86; Phi Beta Kappa 86; Temple U; Pre-Med.

CHUNG, ANDREW; Blue Mountain Acad; Mohnton, PA; (Y); 1/70; Church Yth Grp; Band; Im Ftbl; Im Sftbl; Im Vllybl; High Hon Roll; Ntl Merit Ltr; Val; Sgt-At-Arms Stu Assn 86; Spnch Natl Hnr Soc 85-86; Biochem.

CHUNG, ANTHONY; Interboro HS; Glenolden, PA; (S); Latin Clb; Ski Clb; Rep Soph Cls; Var Trk; Im Vllybl; JV Wrstlng; High Hon Roll; Jr NHS; NHS.

CHUNG, ELIZABETH; Bethlehem Catholic HS; Bethlehem, PA; (S); 1/201; Hosp Aide; Key Clb; Speech Tm; Nwsp Phtg; Nwsp Stf; Var L Crs Cntry; JV Mgr(s); Tennis; NHS; Natl Frnch Contst-Hnrbl Mntn 84; Highest Avg Awds-Frnch II, Hnrs Eng II, Amer Cultrs & Bio 85.

CHUNG, LISA; Neshaminy HS; Penndel, PA; (Y); 10/750; Key Clb; Chorus; Mrchg Band; Orch; Symp Band; Yrbk Stf; Rep Soph Cls; High Hon Roll; NHS; Law.

CHUNG, LIZZ; Bethlehem Catholic HS; Bethlehem, PA; (Y); 1/201; Hosp Aide; Key Clb; Political Wkr; Red Cross Aide; Nwsp Phtg; L Crs Cntry; Im Fld Hcky; Im Socr; Hon Roll; NHS; Dartmouth Bk Awd 86; Awds Hghst Avg Various Subjs 84-86.

CHUNG, WILLIAM; Cathedral Preparatory Schl; Erie, PA; (Y); 21/216; Ski Clb; Var Coach Actv; Var JV Socr; Var L Trk; Hon Roll; Im Bsktbl; Im Vllybl; Latin Honor Soc 84-85; Pre Med.

CHUPAK, LESLIE; West Middlesex HS; W Middlesex, PA; (S); 5/120; Spanish Clb; Chorus; VP Soph Cls; Sec Stu Cncl; JV Var Cheerleading; Stat Trk; Vllybl; Hon Roll; Jr NHS; Spanish NHS; Homecomint Ct; Acad All-Amer Schlr; PA Free Entrprs Wk Lockhaven U 85; Slippery Rock U; Med Tech.

CHUPELA, ANNETTE; Hazleton HS; Hazleton, PA; (S); 151/377; Office Aide; Red Cross Aide; Ski Clb; Chorus; Capt Cheerleading; Sftbl; Elks Awd; Elks Studnt Of Mnth 85-86; Elizabethtown Coll; Nursng.

CHUPKA, PAUL; Ambridge Area HS; Ambridge, PA; (Y); Am Leg Boys St; German Clb; Pep Clb; Jazz Band; Mrchg Band; Orch; Pep Band; Soph Cls; Ftbl; Hon Roll; WA & Jefferson; Chem.

CHUPKO, CYNTHIA; Johnstown Christian Schl; Johnstown, PA; (Y); 1/16; Drama Clb; Chorus; School Play; Trs Jr Cls; Var Socr; Cit Awd; Hon Roll; Advncd Math 86; Engl 86; Amrcn Poltcl Behvr 86.

CHURIK, ALENNA; Plum HS; New Ken, PA; (Y); 101/387; Aud/Vis; Dance Clb; German Clb; SADD; Chorus; Drill Tm; Yrbk Stf; Sec Soph Cls; Sec Jr Cls; Sec Sr Cls; IUP.

CHUSS, TODD; Northampton HS; Northampton, PA; (Y); Cmnty Wkr; Exploring; Red Cross Aide; Dr.

CHVALA, KEITH; Kiso Arco HS; Vandergrift, PA; (Y); Boy Scts; VICA.

CHYTIL, BRIAN; Canon-Mcmillan HS; Canonsburg, PA; (Y); Church Yth Grp; Teachers Aide; Stage Crew; Variety Show; High Hon Roll; ROTC; Military.

CIABATTONI, DAVID; Exeter Township HS; Reading, PA; (Y); 82/238; Boy Scts; Key Clb; Letterman Clb; Varsity Clb; Band; Concert Band; Ftbl; Trk; Hon Roll; Pol Sci.

CIALLELLA, JOHN; New Castle SR HS; New Castle, PA; (S); #23 In Class; AFS; NFL; VP Spanish Clb; Var Golf; Im Vllybl; Hon Roll; NHS; NEDT Awd; Long Island U; Marine Bio.

CIAMACCO, DENEEN; Sto-Rox SR HS; Mc Kees Rocks, PA; (Y); 8/149; Nwsp Stf; Yrbk Stf; Cheerleading; Im Vllybl; Hon Roll; Comm.

CIAN, TODD; Du Bois Area HS; Penfield, PA; (Y); Boy Scts; SADD; Chorus; Hon Roll; Penn ST U; Frnch.

CIANCI, ANGELA; Bishop O Hara HS; Dunmore, PA; (Y); 7/113; French Clb; Ski Clb; Chorus; Rep Stu Cncl; Mgr(s); JV Score Keeper; High Hon Roll; NHS.

CIANCI, STEPHEN; West Catholic HS For Boys; Philadelphia, PA; (Y); 5/300; Pres Cmnty Wkr; Mathletes; Pres Service Clb; Yrbk Rptr; Rep Frsh Cls; Rep Soph Cls; Stu Cncl; Capt Ftbl; JV Ice Hcky; Var Wt Lftg; U DE; Bus.

CIANELLI, ANGELA; Emmaus HS; Emmaus, PA; (Y); French Clb; Latin Clb; Model UN; Rep Frsh Cls; Rep Soph Cls; Rep Jr Cls; Rep Stu Cncl; Cheerleading; Var Sftbl; Var L Swmmng; Hndcpd Essay Fnlst, Prom Court 86; Yth Govt Clerk House 84; Pre-Med.

CIANELLI, LORI; Canon-Mcmillan SR HS; Canonsburg, PA; (Y); 34/342; Library Aide; Office Aide; High Hon Roll; Hon Roll; Futr Stck Brkrs Clb 85-86; Edinboro U Of PA; Math.

CIANELLI, NICK; Canon Mc Millan SR HS; Canonsburg, PA; (Y); Chess Clb; Church Yth Grp; Ftbl; Golf; Trk; Hon Roll.

CIANFICHI, VINCENT P; Scranton Central HS; Scranton, PA; (Y); 180/260; Rep Stu Cncl; Gld Awd In Ftbl & Yrbk Photo 86; Wilkes Coll; Elect Engrng.

CIANFLONE, CINDI; Carbondale Area HS; Carbondale, PA; (S); 8/157; FBLA; Library Aide; Ski Clb; Sec Spanish Clb; Varsity Clb; JV Var Bsktbl; Capt Tennis; High Hon Roll; Hon Roll; NHS; Wilkes Coll; Comp Sci.

CIANFLONE, LISA M; Saint Huberts HS; Philadelphia, PA; (Y); 86/367; Hosp Aide; Red Cross Aide; Teachers Aide; Stage Crew; Hon Roll; Frankford Nrsg Schl; Nrsg.

CIANFLONE, ROSS; Old Forge HS; Old Forge, PA; (Y); 8/67; Ski Clb; School Musical; School Play; High Hon Roll; Hon Roll; NHS; Trea Natl Hnr Soc; U Of Scranton; Accntng.

CIAO, GARY; Central Catholic HS; Pittsburgh, PA; (Y); 40/290; Art Clb; Debate Tm; NFL; Spanish Clb; Teachers Aide; Stat Ftbl; Hon Roll; NHS; Spanish NHS.

CIAO, LISA; Norwin SR HS; N Huntingdon, PA; (Y); Dance Clb; Girl Scts; Hosp Aide; Office Aide; Rep Spanish Clb; SADD; Band; Chorus; Color Guard; Concert Band; Clrgrd Cptn 83-84; JR Cls Crt Repr 85-86; AZ ST; Nrs.

CIARAMELLA, TERRI; Geibel HS; Masontown, PA; (Y); 3/88; Drama Clb; French Clb; Pep Clb; Yrbk Stf; Lit Mag; French Hon Soc; High Hon Roll; NHS; Prfct Atten Awd; 1st PA JR Acad Of Sci 84; Duquesne; Phrmcy.

CIARAMITARO, LEO; Greensburg Central Catholic HS; Murrysville, PA; (Y); Boy Scts; Church Yth Grp; Red Cross Aide; Thesps; Stage Crew; Nwsp Phtg; Nwsp Rptr; Hon Roll; Pre Law.

CIARELLI, MARGARET; Girard Academic Music Program; Philadelphia, PA; (Y); 8/51; Math Clb; Science Clb; Teachers Aide; Chorus; Stage Crew; Nwsp Rptr; Sec Sr Cls; Stu Cncl; Hon Roll; NHS; Cty Of PA Mayrs Schlrshp 86; Dstct 2 Wrtng Awd 85-86; Temple U; Psychlgy.

CIARLARIELLO, HOLLY; Seneca Valley HS; Evans City, PA; (Y); Hosp Aide; Radio Clb; SADD; Thesps; Concert Band; Mrchg Band; School Play; Stage Crew; Prfct Atten Awd; Pre-Law.

CIARROCCHI, CARLA; Abington SR HS; Willow Grove, PA; (Y); 9/563; GAA; Spanish Clb; Stage Crew; Bowling; Var Capt Cheerleading; Var Socr; Sftbl; High Hon Roll; Hon Roll; Jr NHS; Afltn Clb 85-86.

CIBIK, JEANMARIE; West Scranton HS; Scranton, PA; (Y); Church Yth Grp; Pep Clb; Spanish Clb; Speech Tm; Var Cheerleading; Hon Roll; Temple U Phila; Pharm.

CIBIK, MICHELE K; Freeport SR HS; Sarver, PA; (Y); Drill Tm; Trk; Vllybl; Hon Roll; Gannon U; Physcn Asst.

CIBOROSKY, SHELLY; North Pocono HS; Moscow, PA; (Y); Varsity Clb; School Musical; Yrbk Rptr; Yrbk Stf; Rep Stu Cncl; Var Cheerleading; L Gym; Hon Roll.

CIBULAS, CHARLOTTE; GBG Central Catholic HS; Norvelt, PA; (Y); Pep Clb; Vllybl; Hon Roll; U Of Pittsburgh; Math Engr.

CICARONE, ANTHONY; Bishop Kenrick HS; Norristown, PA; (Y); Stu Cncl; Var Bsktbl; Var Tennis; Bus.

CICCARONE, ANTHONY; Bishop Kenrick HS; Norristown, PA; (Y); Rep Frsh Cls; Var Bsktbl; Var Tennis; Bus.

CICCO, CHRIS; Forest City Regional HS; Forest City, PA; (Y); 4/64; Sec Church Yth Grp; Drama Clb; German Clb; Letterman Clb; Scholastic Bowl; Ski Clb; Varsity Clb; Pres Band; Chorus; Concert Band; Pres Acad Fit Awd 85-86; Susquehanna Cnty Repblcn Wmns Clb Scholar 85-86; Natl Sci Awd Chem 84-85; Wilkes Coll; Pre-Med.

CICCO, LYNN; Plum SR HS; Pittsburgh, PA; (Y); 38/378; Church Yth Grp; Service Clb; Varsity Clb; Color Guard; Yrbk Stf; Var Socr; Hon Roll; NHS; Penn ST; Chemcl Engrng.

CICCOCIOPPO, ADALENE; Susquenita HS; Marysville, PA; (S); Am Leg Aux Girls St; Pres Drama Clb; Pres Spanish Clb; Teachers Aide; School Play; VP Jr Cls; Pres Stu Cncl; Capt Fld Hcky; Var Sftbl; VP NHS; Elem Ed.

CICCOCIOPPO, BARRY; Trinity HS; Marysville, PA; (Y); 70/144; Im Bsktbl; Engr.

CICCONE, DONNA; Villa Maria HS; Poland, OH; (Y); Key Clb; Concert Band; Mrchg Band; Pep Band; Var L Bsktbl; JV Cheerleading; Var L Vllybl; High Hon Roll; NHS; Library Aide.

CICERO, KAREN; Notre Dame HS; Easton, PA; (Y); 8/95; Church Yth Grp; Hosp Aide; Nwsp Ed-Chief; Yrbk Stf; High Hon Roll; NHS; Acad Exc Awd Frnch II 85; Stand Up For Life Essay Cntst Awd 84; Pro Life Rep 84-86; Jrnlst.

CICERO, KATHLEEN; Pleasanty Valley HS; Kunkletown, PA; (Y); 39/233; Church Yth Grp; VP German Clb; Ski Clb; Rep SADD; Band; Concert Band; Mrchg Band; Pep Band; Stage Crew; Ed Nwsp Stf; Achiev-O-Gram Dimnsnl Anlysis Chem 85-86; Achiev-O-Gram Media 85-86; Svc Awd Newspaper Ed Wk 85-86; Pre-Med.

CICERO, PATRICIA L; Neshannock HS; New Castle, PA; (Y); 9/102; French Clb; Teachers Aide; Chorus; School Play; Yrbk Ed-Chief; Yrbk Phtg; Yrbk Rptr; Yrbk Stf; NHS; Hnr Awd-Hgh Grd Pt Avg; Kenyon Coll.

CICHONSKI, JANEEN; Saint Hubert HS; Philadelphia, PA; (Y); 50/367; JA; Pep Clb; Sftbl; High Hon Roll; Prfct Atten Awd; Cert Cmndtn Bus Ed Curriculum Cmtee; Cert Achvt Yth & Amer Pol Sys Smnr; Pierce JC; Legal Secy.

CICHONSKI, JAY M; North-East Catholic HS; Philadelphia, PA; (Y); 25/421; JA; School Play; Rep Frsh Cls; Rep Soph Cls; Rep Jr Cls; Rep Stu Cncl; Jr NHS; NHS; Ntl Merit Ltr; Incentv Awd 84-85; Drexel U; Engrg.

CICHOWICZ, JEAN; Our Lady Of The Sacred Heart HS; Pittsburgh, PA; (Y); 2/63; Pep Clb; Church Choir; School Musical; Pres Soph Cls; High Hon Roll; NHS; Hugh Obrien Yth Fndtn Outstndng Soph 85; Hghst Clss Avg 84; U Of Pttsbrgh; Exrcs Physlgy.

CICILIONI, LAURA; Bishop O Hara HS; Dickson City, PA; (S); 12/113; French Clb; Latin Clb; High Hon Roll; NHS; Ntl Merit Ltr; Duquesne; Anesthslgst.

CIECIERSKI, RHONDA; Lewistown Area HS; Lewistown, PA; (Y); 24/262; Girl Scts; Varsity Clb; Var Bsktbl; Var Sftbl; Hon Roll; Var Ltrs Bsktbl & Sftbl 86; Cntrl PA Bus Schl; Bus.

CIERI, FREDERICK; Archbishop Wood For Boys; Southampton, PA; (Y); 3/280; Hon Roll; NHS; Outstndng Achvt Schlrshp 86; Temple U.

CIERO, MARK; Central Columbia HS; Bloomsburg, PA; (Y); 6/178; Pres Key Clb; Varsity Clb; Jazz Band; VP Jr Cls; Pres Sr Cls; Capt Crs Cntry; Capt Swmmng; Trk; Cit Awd; DAR Awd; Aerospc Engrg.

CIESLAK, LISA; Calvary Baptist Christian Schl; Union City, PA; (S); 1/6; Chorus; School Play; Nwsp Ed-Chief; VP Sr Cls; JV Var Cheerleading; Stat Score Keeper; High Hon Roll; Val; Church Yth Grp; Latin Clb; Schlrshp Tlnts Chrst; Awds ST Cmptn Voice; Erie Business Ctr; Medcl Secy.

CIFELLI, CYNTHIA; Perry Traditional Acad; Pittsburgh, PA; (Y); 5/137; Girl Scts; Rep Stu Cncl; High Hon Roll; Jr NHS; NHS; U Ptsbrgh; Archtctrl Engrng.

CIFRULAK, STEPHEN D; Quaker Valley HS; Sewickley, PA; (Y); Am Leg Boys St; Pres Jr Cls; Pres Sr Cls; Rep Stu Cncl; Capt Bsbl; JV Bsktbl; L Ftbl; NHS; Ntl Merit Ltr; Pres Schlr; Dr Harold S Irons Schlrshp 86; Cmmnwlth PA Cert Of Mrt 86; AIU Hstrgrphy Apprentshp 85; West Point; Intl Rel.

CIGARSKI, TRENA; Lake Lehman HS; Wilkes Barre, PA; (Y); Ski Clb; SADD; Band; Concert Band; Jazz Band; Mrchg Band; Orch; Symp Band; Sftbl; Hon Roll; Westchester; Bio.

CILETTI, DORENE; Montour HS; Mc Kees Rocks, PA; (Y); 1/300; Church Yth Grp; Color Guard; Jazz Band; School Musical; Sec Trs Soph Cls; Var Powder Puff Ftbl; L Trk; High Hon Roll; Pres NHS; Acad Achvmnt Awds 86; Loyalty Day Queen 85; Theatre Apprentice 86; Princeton; Cmmnctns.

CIMINO, ELAINE; Cumberland Valley HS; Camp Hill, PA; (Y); 26/522; Key Clb; Ski Clb; Spanish Clb; Band; Mrchg Band; Symp Band; Rep Soph Cls; High Hon Roll; NHS; Spanish NHS; Indstrl Engrng.

CIMINO, PRISCILLA; Scr Central HS; Scranton, PA; (Y); Var Church Yth Grp; Ski Clb; Church Choir; Stage Crew; Yrbk Phtg; Yrbk Rptr; Yrbk Stf; Hon Roll; Jr NHS; Scranton U; CPA.

CIMOCHOWSKI, ANDREW; Neshamwy HS; Levittown, PA; (Y); 37/763; Bsktbl; Im Gym; Var L Socr; Im Vllybl; Im Wt Lftg; High Hon Roll; Hon Roll; NHS.

CINDRICH, DAVE; Beth-Center HS; Marianna, PA; (Y); 6/160; Spanish Clb; Varsity Clb; L Bsbl; Var Bsktbl; High Hon Roll; NHS; Amer Legn Aux Awd 83-84; Offnsv Plyr Yr-Bsbl 86.

CINFICI, WILLIAM; Reading HS; Reading, PA; (S); 22/800; Trs Chess Clb; VP Debate Tm; Model UN; Quiz Bowl; Hon Roll; NHS.

CINICOLA, MARY; Hampton HS; Allison Pk, PA; (Y); French Clb; Pep Clb; Chorus; School Musical; Rep Sr Cls; Var L Bsktbl; Var Score Keeper; JV Sftbl; Var L Vllybl; Sci.

CIOCCO, NICOLE; Greater Latrobe SR HS; Latrobe, PA; (Y); French Clb; Ski Clb; Teachers Aide; Band; Vllybl; High Hon Roll; Hon Roll; U Of Tampa; Marine Bio.

CIOPPA, ROSEMARY; New Castle SR HS; New Castle, PA; (S); 1/253; Exploring; Hosp Aide; SADD; Chorus; Drill Tm; Rep Jr Cls; Rep Stu Cncl; Trk; High Hon Roll; Hon Roll.

CIOTTI, JIM; Minersville Area HS; Minersville, PA; (Y); 11/125; Church Yth Grp; Cmnty Wkr; German Clb; JA; Ski Clb; School Musical; School Play; Stage Crew; Rep Frsh Cls; Rep Soph Cls; PA ST; Comp.

CIPOLLA, MICHELLE; Punxsutawney HS; Punxsutawney, PA; (Y); 40/238; Math Tm; Spanish Clb; SADD; Rep Band; Concert Band; Mrchg Band; Pep Band; Variety Show; Stat Bsbl; High Hon Roll; Margaret C Boles Schlrshp 86; Indiana U Of PA; Pol Sci.

CIPOLLINI JR, DONALD F; Homer-Center JR SR HS; Waterman, PA; (Y); 9/110; Boy Scts; French Clb; Pres Band; Var L Bsktbl; Var L Ftbl; Var L Trk; High Hon Roll; Hon Roll; NHS; Ntl Merit Ltr; IUP Dstngshd Achvr Schlrshp 86; Sns Of Italy Ldg 570 & Grnd Ldg Schlrshps 86; IUP; Bio.

CIPOLLINI, KIMBERLY; Villa Joseph Marie HS; Yardley, PA; (S); 6/74; Trs Stu Cncl; Hon Roll; NHS; Library Aide; Rep Frsh Cls; Var Bsktbl; Var Socr; Var Sftbl; Prfct Atten Awd; 2nd Pl Cnty Poetry Cntst; Johnson & Wales; Hotl Mgmt.

CIPOLLONI, MARK; West Catholic HS; Philadelphia, PA; (Y); Hon Roll; Cert Of Merit 84-86; Drexel U; Elec Engr.

CIPRIANI, JOSEPH; Montgomery Area JR-SR HS; Montgomery, PA; (Y); Boy Scts; Church Yth Grp; Varsity Clb; Var Ftbl; Var Sftbl; Var Wrstlng; Hon Roll; Bloomsburg U.

CIPRIANO, CARRIE; Shaler Area SR HS; Glenshaw, PA; (Y); 152/517; Art Clb; Church Yth Grp; JA; Ski Clb; Vllybl; Hon Roll; Vrsty Ltr-Vllybl 85; Pre-Law.

CIRRA, JOSEPH; Canevin HS; Mcdonald, PA; (Y); Band; Concert Band; Jazz Band; Orch; Camera Clb; School Play; Caneuins High Hnrs In Music 83-84; Teahs Music 85-86; Duyuesne U; Music.

CIRUCCI, COLLEEN M; Downinigtown HS; Exton, PA; (Y); 78/498; Church Yth Grp; Cmnty Wkr; Dance Clb; Pep Clb; Ski Clb; Nwsp Stf; Off Jr Cls; Cheerleading; High Hon Roll; Hon Roll; Daisy Chain; SR Spirit Comm; Bloomsburg U; Creatv Wrtg.

CISKO, KIMBERLY; Penn Trafford HS; Irwin, PA; (Y); Exploring; Library Aide; Math Clb; Science Clb; Kodak-Eastman Schlr 86-89; Alcoa Fndtn Schlr 86-89; 2 U Schlrshps 85-89; U Of Pittsburgh; Elec Engrng.

CISLAK, ROB M; Pennsbury HS; Fairless Hls, PA; (Y); 56/712; Im Bsktbl; Im Vllybl; Hon Roll; NHS; Trenton ST Coll; Elec Engrng.

CISNEROS, ORLINDA; Clearfield Area HS; Bigler, PA; (Y); Art Clb; Church Yth Grp; DECA; Hosp Aide; Acpl Chr; Concert Band; Mrchg Band; Sftbl; Vllybl; Hon Roll; Sectarl.

CISNEY, AMBER; Dover Area HS; Dover, PA; (Y); Band; Concert Band; Jazz Band; Mrchg Band; School Musical; Mgr Trk; High Hon Roll; Hon Roll; NHS; Physcs.

CITARELLI, VINCENT; Upper Darby HS; Upr Darby, PA; (Y); Acpl Chr; Chorus; School Musical; School Play; Swing Chorus; Rep Soph Cls; Pres Jr Cls; JV Bsbl; High Hon Roll; Hon Roll.

CITERONI, KATHLEEN; Blairsville SR HS; Blairsville, PA; (Y); Church Yth Grp; SADD; Band; Chorus; Concert Band; Drm Mjr(t); Mrchg Band; School Musical; Stu Cncl; Hon Roll; Diquesne; Accntng.

CITERONI, TRACY; Blairsville SR HS; Blairsville, PA; (Y); 1/129; Pres Drama Clb; Church Choir; Concert Band; Mrchg Band; Pep Band; School Musical; Sec Sr Cls; NHS; Ntl Merit SF; Val; Acdmc Schlrshp St Vincent Coll 86; St Vincent Coll; Pltcl Sci.

CITINO, CHRISTINA MARIA; St Basil Acad; Philadelphia, PA; (S); 6/97; Science Clb; Spanish Clb; Teachers Aide; High Hon Roll; Hon Roll; Pre-Med.

CITRONE, GREG; St John Neumann HS; Philadelphia, PA; (Y); Im Bsktbl; High Hon Roll; Hon Roll; Jr NHS; JR Engl Chmpn 86; St Nicholas Bsktbl Trnmnt Chmpn 86; Philadelphia Cty Bsbl Chmpns 84; Nclr Physcs.

CITRONE, MICHAEL; York Catholic HS; York, PA; (Y); 35/171; Boy Scts; Latin Clb; Varsity Clb; Nwsp Rptr; Golf; Socr; Wrstlng; Hon Roll; NHS; Letterman Clb; Indr Soccr Plyr Wk 86; Accntg.

CIUCCIO, LAURA; West Scranton HS; Scranton, PA; (Y); Latin Clb; Yrbk Stf; Cheerleading; Hon Roll; NHS; Nrsng.

CIULLO, MARIANNE; Old Forge HS; Old Forge, PA; (Y); 11/71; Church Yth Grp; Hosp Aide; Church Choir; Yrbk Ed-Chief; Yrbk Stf; Cheerleading; High Hon Roll; Hon Roll; NHS; Penn ST Hazleton; Chem Engrng.

CIVELLO, LISA; Palmyra HS; Palmyra, PA; (Y); Church Yth Grp; Ski Clb; Spanish Clb; Yrbk Phtg; Yrbk Stf; Cheerleading; Tennis; Hon Roll; Millersville; Accntng.

CIVERA, LISA; Arch Bishop Prendergast HS; Drexel Hill, PA; (Y); Stage Crew; Yrbk Stf; PA ST U; Sci.

CIVILETTI, PIA; Wyoming Area HS; Pittston, PA; (Y); Dance Clb; German Clb; Chorus; Capt Var Cheerleading; Gymnstcs-2nd & 3rd Rbbns 83-84; Bus.

CIVIS, KELLIE; Bishop Mc Cort HS; Johnstown, PA; (Y); Ski Clb; Hon Roll.

CIZAUSKAS, DENISE; Donegal HS; Maytown, PA; (Y); GAA; JV Capt Bsktbl; Var L Trk; Hon Roll; York Coll PA; Mgmt.

CLAAR, CARMEN; Claysburg-Kimmel HS; Claysburg, PA; (Y); Camera Clb; Church Yth Grp; 4-H; FBLA; Ski Clb; Band; Chorus; Color Guard; Concert Band; Flag Corp; FBLA St Chap Awd 84-85; Fshn Coord.

CLABAUGH, JACQUELINE; Altoona Area HS; Altoona, PA; (Y); Key Clb; Spanish Clb; Rep Jr Cls; Bus Adm.

CLAPPER, HEIDI; Harry S Truman HS; Levittown, PA; (Y); Aud/Vis; Debate Tm; NFL; Chorus; School Musical; Engl Ed.

CLARK, AARON D; State College Area HS; Bedford, PA; (Y); 139/488; Am Leg Boys St; Church Yth Grp; FBLA; Ftbl; Robert Morris Coll; Sprt Mgt.

CLARK, AMY L; St Hubert HS; Philadelphia, PA; (Y); 19/367; Cmnty Wkr; French Clb; Chorus; Stage Crew; Ed Yrbk Stf; Hon Roll; NHS; PA ST U; Nrsng.

CLARK, ANDREA; William Allen HS; Allentown, PA; (Y); 19/604; Church Yth Grp; Drama Clb; Exploring; Hosp Aide; Church Choir; Yrbk Stf; Hon Roll; Jr NHS; NHS; 1st Vocal Solo 86; Bible Quz 10th Pl 85-86; Pediatricn.

CLARK, ANN L; North Allegheny SR HS; Ingomar, PA; (Y); 67/605; Art Clb; Concert Band; Jazz Band; Mrchg Band; School Musical; Symp Band; Hon Roll; Prfct Atten Awd; Grfld Schlrshp 86; Pl H Fll Schlr Dept Of Chem 86; Instrmntlst Mgzn Musicianshp Awd 86; Hiram Coll; Chem.

CLARK, BELINDA; Fairchance Georges HS; Fairchance, PA; (Y); Band; JV Var Bsktbl; Var L Sftbl; Teachers Aide; Chorus; Concert Band; Mrchg Band; Yrbk Stf; Hon Roll; IBM Schl Of Bus.

CLARK, BETH; Manheim Central HS; Manheim, PA; (Y); 71/240; Church Yth Grp; Chorus; Church Choir; Concert Band; Drm Mjr(t); Mrchg Band; School Musical; Var L Fld Hcky; Hon Roll; 4-Way Tst Awd 86; Bhvrl Sci.

CLARK, BILL; Lackawanna Trail HS; Nicholson, PA; (Y); Boy Scts; Chess Clb; Rep Stu Cncl; JV Bsbl; Bsktbl; Wt Lftg; Hon Roll; Accntnt.

CLARK, BRETT; North Allegheny HS; Allison Pk, PA; (Y); 93/642; Aud/Vis; German Clb; Off Jr Cls; Stu Cncl; Var Swmmng; Hon Roll; NHS; 3 Vrsty Lttrs Swwmg 84-86.

CLARK, BRIAN; Tyrone Area HS; Warriors Mark, PA; (Y); 7/196; Pres VP Church Yth Grp; Key Clb; Latin Clb; Stage Crew; High Hon Roll; Hon Roll; Jr NHS; NHS; Prfct Atten Awd; Ftbl; Pres Acdmc Achvt Awd 86; Awd For Exc In Lang Stdy Latin V; Elec Engr.

CLARK, CARDELLE; Carlynton HS; Carnegie, PA; (Y); Mgr Drama Clb; Pres JA; Office Aide; Chorus; Church Choir; Color Guard; Drm & Bgl; Drm Mjr(t); Sec Yrbk Stf; Sec Frsh Cls; Shasda Awd 86; Ldrshp Awd 85; Robert Morris; Paralegal.

CLARK, CARRIE; Belle Vernon Area HS; Belle Vernon, PA; (Y); 24/276; Drama Clb; FBLA; Library Aide; Pep Clb; Chorus; High Hon Roll; Hon Roll; NHS; Prfct Atten Awd; Stu Of The Mnt 86; Bradford Sch Bus; Secr.

CLARK, CHRIS; Perkiomen Valley HS; Schwenksville, PA; (Y); Aud/Vis; Church Yth Grp; Varsity Clb; Chorus; Nwsp Stf; Rep Stu Cncl; Var Cheerleading; JV Lcrss; Hon Roll.

CLARK, CHUCK; Octorara Area HS; Cochranville, PA; (Y); Mrchg Band; Yrbk Phtg; Trk; Outstndng Photogrphy Awd 86; WVU; Aerospce Engr.

CLARK, COREY; Everett Area HS; Everett, PA; (Y); Varsity Clb; Bsbl; Ftbl; Hon Roll.

CLARK, CYNTHIA; Christian School Of York; Mechanicsburg, PA; (Y); Church Yth Grp; Hosp Aide; Band; Chorus; Pep Band; Variety Show; Nwsp Rptr.

CLARK, DANYAEL; Conn Area SR HS; Connellsville, PA; (Y); Church Yth Grp; Cmnty Wkr; Girl Scts; Pep Clb; Teachers Aide; Chorus; Church Choir; School Musical; School Play; Nwsp Rptr; Persnlty Awd 82-83; PA ST U; Comm.

CLARK, DAVID; Fort Cherry HS; Midway, PA; (S); Drama Clb; Math Clb; Science Clb; Ski Clb; Varsity Clb; Chorus; Stage Crew; Bsbl; Ftbl; Wrstlng.

CLARK, DAVID; Hempfield HS; Lancaster, PA; (Y); 117/430; Key Clb; Science Clb; Ftbl; Hon Roll; PA ST; Bus.

CLARK, DAVID; Shamokin Area HS; Shamokin, PA; (Y); 51/251; Chess Clb; Band; Concert Band; Jazz Band; Mrchg Band; Stage Crew; Im Crs Cntry; Im Trk; Hon Roll.

CLARK, DEURWARD W; Martin Luther King HS; Phila, PA; (Y); Teachers Aide; Stage Crew; Crs Cntry; Trk; Elctrncs & Prfct Atten Awds 86; Prfct Atten Awd 85; CC Of Phila; Elctrncs.

CLARK, DIANA; Everett Area HS; Clearville, PA; (S); Church Yth Grp; FHA; GAA; SADD; Band; Church Choir; Concert Band; Mrchg Band; Pep Band; Hon Roll; Csmtlgy.

CLARK, DOUGLAS; Bentworth HS; Scenery Hill, PA; (Y); 3/150; Art Clb; Church Yth Grp; Ski Clb; High Hon Roll; NHS.

CLARK, DOUGLAS; Cornell SR HS; Coraopolis, PA; (Y); Church Yth Grp; Civic Clb; Cmnty Wkr; Key Clb; School Play; Stage Crew; Stu Cncl; Bsktbl; High Hon Roll; Hon Roll; Hugh O Brien Ldrshp Smnr Awd Fnlst; Marine Sci.

CLARK, ELAINE; Faith Mennonite HS; Kinzers, PA; (S); 1/26; VP Church Yth Grp; Pres 4-H; Library Aide; Chorus; Yrbk Stf; 4-H Awd; High Hon Roll; Lancaster Cnty Peace Essay Cntst 85; Nrs.

CLARK, ELIZABETH; Pequea Valley HS; Kinzer, PA; (Y); 1/126; AFS; Chess Clb; Pres Church Yth Grp; Ed Yrbk Stf; Bausch & Lomb Sci Awd; High Hon Roll; NHS; Ntl Merit Ltr; Pres Schlr; Val; Messiah Coll Fndrs Schlrshp 86; Messiah Coll; Math.

CLARK, GLORIA; Clearfield Area HS; Hyde, PA; (Y); French Clb; Var L Bsktbl; Var L Sftbl; JV Stat Vllybl; High Hon Roll; Hon Roll; NHS; Lock Haven U; Secndry Ed.

CLARK, HEATHER; Montour SR HS; Pittsburgh, PA; (Y); Boy Scts; Church Yth Grp; Girl Scts; Hosp Aide; VP JA; Radio Clb; High Hon Roll; Geneva; Commnctns.

CLARK, JERRY; Spring-Ford SR HS; Oaks, PA; (S); 19/261; Boy Scts; Hosp Aide; Im Socr; JV Trk; Cit Awd; Hon Roll; NHS; Allegheny Coll; Pre-Med.

CLARK, JOHN W; Albert Gallatin HS; Smithfield, PA; (Y); Mathletes; Ski Clb; Varsity Clb; Var Bsbl; Var Ftbl; Var Wrstlng; Cit Awd; High Hon Roll; Jr NHS; NHS; Frank Rich Mrl Awd; Wrstlng Captn 83-84; US Armed Forces; Engr.

CLARK, JOYCE; Shenandoah Valley HS; Shenandoah, PA; (Y); Chorus; Yrbk Stf; Hon Roll; NHS; Empire Beauty Schl Schlrshp 86; Rifle Sq Co Captn 85-86; Empire Beauty Schl; Cosmtlgy.

CLARK, KAREN; Central Community HS; Ebensburg, PA; (Y); 50/193; FBLA; Hosp Aide; Office Aide; Mgr(s); Im Powder Puff Ftbl; Score Keeper; Var L Trk; Im Wt Lftg; Hon Roll; 2nd Hnr Stu 86; Mt Aloysius JC; Med Asst.

CLARK, KELLY; Mt Penn HS; Reading, PA; (Y); 19/71; GAA; Ski Clb; Y-Teens; Chorus; Variety Show; Yrbk Stf; Frsh Cls; Soph Cls; Jr Cls; Sr Cls; Judy Yoder Mem Scholar 85-86; Gerald Romich Art Awd 85-86; 2 Schl Svc Awds NHS & Chrldg 85-86; Phila Coll Textiles; Intr Dsgn.

CLARK, LISA; Bishop Hannan HS; Scranton, PA; (Y); French Clb; Hosp Aide; Rep Sec Stu Cncl; JV Var Cheerleading; French I Excellence Awd 84, World Cultures II 85; Marywood Coll; Photo.

CLARK, LORI; Southern Huntingdon HS; Rockhl Furnace, PA; (Y); 12/118; French Clb; Q&S; Speech Tm; School Play; Nwsp Ed-Chief; Nwsp Rptr; Yrbk Stf; Stu Cncl; Hon Roll; NHS; Juniata Coll; Intl Stds.

CLARK, LURA; Cowanesque Valley HS; Westfield, PA; (Y); Sec Camera Clb; Letterman Clb; Concert Band; Mrchg Band; School Musical; Yrbk Bus Mgr; Sec Jr Cls; JV Var Vllybl; Hon Roll; Schlr-Athlete Awd 86; Bus Mgmnt.

CLARK, MARCY; Laurel HS; New Castle, PA; (Y); 20/103; Church Yth Grp; Girl Scts; SADD; Nwsp Rptr; Trk; Vllybl; Hon Roll; Prfct Atten Awd; New Cstl Schl Bty; Csmtlgy.

CLARK, MELISSA; Northern Bedford County HS; Everett, PA; (Y); Art Clb; FBLA; FTA; SADD; Band; Mgr Bsktbl; Hon Roll; Outstndng Achvt Century 21 Acctg 86; Cert Profcncy Century 21 Typwrtg 86; Comp Mgmt.

CLARK, RACHAEL; Hatboro-Horshom HS; Ambler, PA; (Y); Drama Clb; Chorus; School Musical; School Play; Frnch II Awd 85; Show Choir Awd 85 & 86; Temple U; Theatre.

CLARK, RAY; Valley View HS; Jessup, PA; (Y); Pres VICA; Acad Exc 83; Electrncs.

CLARK, RAYMOND; Middletown Area HS; Middletown, PA; (Y); Chess Clb; JV Socr; Military; Fighter Pilot.

CLARK, REBECCA L; Downingtown SR HS; West Chester, PA; (Y); Dance Clb; Trs GAA; Ski Clb; Spanish Clb; Chorus; Rep Stu Cncl; Fld Hcky; Lcrss; Twrlr; Daisy Chain 86; Accntng.

CLARK, RICHARD; Blacklick Valley JR-SR HS; Ebensburg, PA; (S); 7/97; 4-H; German Clb; Varsity Clb; Var Bsbl; High Hon Roll; Hon Roll; Germ NHS 84.

CLARK, ROB; Blairsville HS; Blairsville, PA; (Y); 13/130; Concert Band; Mrchg Band; School Musical; VP Jr Cls; Stu Cncl; JV Bsktbl; L Golf; Trk; High Hon Roll; VP NHS; Engrng.

CLARK, ROBERT; Greater Latrobe SR HS; Greensburg, PA; (Y); 4-H; VICA; Wrstlng; 4-H Awd; High Hon Roll; Hon Roll; 3rd Pl Vo Tech Furn Blg Cntst 86; 2nd Pl 4-H Mrkt Steer Jdg 85; Archlgy.

CLARK, ROBERT; Southern Columbia Area HS; Elysburg, PA; (Y); 6/76; Boy Scts; VP Band; Chorus; JV Bsktbl; High Hon Roll; NHS; Church Yth Grp; Concert Band; Jazz Band; Order Arrow 84; Arian Awd Band 86; PMEA Dist Band & Chorus 85-86; Chem Engrng.

CLARK JR, ROBERT; Blacklick Valley HS; Ebensburg, PA; (S); 14/99; Varsity Clb; VICA; Trs Jr Cls; Var Bsbl; High Hon Roll; NHS; Wllmsprt Area CC; Elec.

CLARK, SHERYL; Lake-Lehman HS; Dallas, PA; (Y); 59/175; Trs Church Yth Grp; Hosp Aide; Church Choir; Sftbl; Swmmng; High Hon Roll; Hon Roll; Haney Fnd Rsng Awd Schlrshp 86; Luzerne Cnty Comm Coll; Gen Std.

CLARK, STEVE; Freedom HS; Bethelehem, PA; (Y); 177/404; Chess Clb; Church Yth Grp; JA; Hon Roll; PA Hghr Educ Asstnc Agncy Crtfct Mrt 85; Bloomsburg U; Blgy.

CLARK, SUSAN; Meadville HS; Meadville, PA; (S); Church Yth Grp; Band; Chorus; Concert Band; Mrchg Band; School Play; Cmnty Wkr; Drama Clb; German Clb; Dist & Rgnl Chrs; Mrchng Bnd Bndfrnt Capt; Music.

CLARK, SUZANNE; South Park HS; Library, PA; (Y); 30/200; VP JA; Color Guard; Yrbk Bus Mgr; High Hon Roll; Hon Roll; Ntl Merit SF; NEDT Awd; Church Yth Grp; Office Aide; Acad Scholar Du Quesne U 86; JA Schoalr 86; VP Admin SW PA JA 86; Du Quesne U; Acctg.

CLARK, TERESA; Northern HS; Dillsburg, PA; (Y); Band; Mrchg Band; Sec Jr Cls; Trs Sr Cls; Rep Stu Cncl; Var Bsktbl; Var Fld Hcky; Var Powder Puff Ftbl; Var Trk; French Hon Soc; Mid Penn Div III All Stars-Bsktbl 85-86; Physcl Educ.

CLARK, TERRY L; B Reed Henderson HS; West Chester, PA; (Y); 139/334; Church Yth Grp; Band; Chorus; Capt Mrchg Band; School Musical; School Play; Hon Roll; Clb Juadims Schlrshp 86; Blck Stu Union Bk Awd 86; PA ST U; Bus Adm.

CLARK, WENDY; Northeast Bradford HS; Rome, PA; (Y); Trs Soph Cls; Trs Jr Cls; Trs Sr Cls; Gym; High Hon Roll; NHS; JR Ms Pgnt 86; Bus Mgt.

CLARKE, BARBARA; Pittston Area HS; Pittston, PA; (Y); Church Yth Grp; Hosp Aide; Variety Show; Yrbk Stf; Trs Soph Cls; Var L Crs Cntry; Var Mgr Trk; Hon Roll; Hnr Rl Cert 82-83; Candystriper Pin 82; Wilkes Coll; Nrsng.

CLARKE, GEORGANN; North Penn HS; Lansdale, PA; (Y); Mathletes; SADD; Rep Soph Cls; Rep Jr Cls; Off Sr Cls; Capt Cheerleading; Powder Puff Ftbl; Jr NHS; NHS; Specl Educ.

CLARKE, ROBERT; Lackawanna Trail HS; Dalton, PA; (Y); 18/84; Church Yth Grp; Ski Clb; Var Crs Cntry; JV Ftbl; NHS; Math Awd-Ntl-Hghst In Schl 86; U Of Scranton; Comp Engrng.

CLARKE, TINA MARIA; West Allegheny HS; Oakdale, PA; (Y); 8/206; French Clb; Chorus; Capt Color Guard; School Musical; Var L Diving; High Hon Roll; NHS; Rotary Awd; Cmnty Wkr; Drill Tm; Pres Acad Ftns Awd 86; PMEA Dist Chorus 83; High Hnr Awd 83; U Pittsburgh; Physcl Thrpy.

CLAUS, DEBBY; Hamton HS; Allison Pk, PA; (Y); 19/255; Boys Clb Am; Church Yth Grp; Exploring; Color Guard; Im Bowling; High Hon Roll; NHS; U Pittsburgh; Acctng.

CLAUSEN, KEN; Strong Vincent HS; Erie, PA; (Y); 4/164; Pres Chess Clb; Sec Debate Tm; Yrbk Ed-Chief; Yrbk Phtg; Yrbk Rptr; Yrbk Stf; Var L Trk; High Hon Roll; NHS; Exploring; Carrier Of Mnth 81; IN U; Cmmnctn Art.

CLAUSIUS, JOHN; Jim Thorpe Area HS; Jim Thorpe, PA; (Y); Stu Cncl; Pres Jr Cls; Pres Sr Cls; JV L Bsktbl; Lincoln Tech Inst; Elec.

CLAUSNER, CARRIE; Mary Fuller Frazier Mem SR HS; Perryopolis, PA; (Y); Drama Clb; Chorus; Capt Color Guard; Pres Mrchg Band; High Hon Roll; Hon Roll; Pres NHS; Peer Tutorng 85-86; Coal Queen Rep 86; Natl Mth Lg Schl Wnnr Geom 85-86; Mngmnt.

CLAWGES, TRACY; Pennsbury HS; Yardley, PA; (Y); French Clb; Acpl Chr; Chorus; School Play; Tennis; Hon Roll; Frnch Hnr Awd 84; Villanova; Bus Mgt.

CLAWSON, DANIEL; North Star HS; Boswell, PA; (S); Trs Church Yth Grp; FCA; Ski Clb; Stu Cncl; Bsktbl; Golf; Hon Roll; Jaycees Stu Of Mnt 85; Ntl Sci Merit Awd 85; Annapolis; Miltry Sci.

CLAWSON, MICHELE; Saltsburg JR SR HS; Saltsburg, PA; (Y); 29/105; Art Clb; Camera Clb; 4-H; GAA; Teachers Aide; Varsity Clb; Chorus; Stage Crew; Nwsp Stf; Yrbk Stf; Penn ST U.

CLAYCOMB, LAURA; Claysburg-Kimmel HS; Claysburg, PA; (Y); 3/58; VP Church Yth Grp; Computer Clb; Sec German Clb; Library Aide; SADD; Band; Chorus; Concert Band; Yrbk Stf; Sec Jr Cls; J P Sousa Dir Awd 83; Phy Thrpy.

CLAYCOMB, RODNEY; Northern Bedford County HS; New Enterprise, PA; (Y); 1/96; Band; Chorus; Jazz Band; Swing Chorus; VP Sr Cls; Stu Cncl; Ftbl; Wrstlng; High Hon Roll; NHS; PA Mth Lg Awd 85; Pres Schlr Athlt 86; All ST Chorus 86; Shippensburg U; Math Ed.

CLAYCOMB, STEVEN; Claysburg-Kimmel HS; Claysburg, PA; (Y); Art Clb; Church Yth Grp; Varsity Clb; Stage Crew; Var L Ftbl.

CLAYPOOL, MANDI; Freeport Area HS; Freeport, PA; (Y); Church Yth Grp; Drill Tm; Yrbk Stf; Stat Sftbl; High Hon Roll; Hon Roll; NHS; Pres Acad Fit Awd.

CLAYPOOL, MELISSA; Allegheny Clarion Valley HS; St Petesburg, PA; (Y); 42/103; Church Yth Grp; FNA; GAA; Chorus; Variety Show; Powder Puff Ftbl; Trk; Air Force.

CLAYPOOL, TAMMY; Freeport SR HS; Freeport, PA; (S); School Musical; Rep Stu Cncl; Im Mgr Cheerleading; Mgr(s); Mgr Trk; High Hon Roll; Hon Roll.

CLAYPOOLE, MELANIE; Harbor Creek HS; Erie, PA; (Y); 21/228; Church Yth Grp; Model UN; Variety Show; Yrbk Stf; Rep Frsh Cls; Rep Soph Cls; VP Pres Stu Cncl; L Pom Pon; NHS; Red Cross 84.

CLAYTON, EARLSHAWNDA; Simon Gratz HS; Philadelphia, PA; (S); Dance Clb; French Clb; Office Aide; ROTC; Teachers Aide; Cheerleading; Gym; Swmmng; High Hon Roll; Hon Roll; Ellis Schlrshp 84-85; Prune Stu 80-86; Nurse.

CLAYTON, JEANNE; Upper Dublin HS; Dresher, PA; (Y); 141/313; Varsity Clb; Rep Frsh Cls; JV Var Cheerleading; Im Fld Hcky; JV Var Lcrss; Im Wt Lftg.

CLAYTON, KIMBERLY ANNE; Jeannette SR HS; Jeannette, PA; (Y); 17/126; Drama Clb; Spanish Clb; Chorus; Concert Band; Drm Mjr(t); Mrchg Band; Stu Cncl; Hon Roll; Val; La Roche Coll; Grphc Dsgn.

CLAYTON, MICHELLE; Shady Side Acad; Pittsburgh, PA; (Y); Drama Clb; French Clb; Library Aide; Acpl Chr; School Play; Yrbk Stf; Lit Mag; Sftbl; Hon Roll; Ntl Merit SF; Natl Achvt Semi-Fnlst 85; Pre Med.

CLAYTON, STEPHANIE; Interboro HS; Prospect Park, PA; (Y); Church Yth Grp; Office Aide; Concert Band; Jazz Band; Mrchg Band; Pep Band; Mgr(s); Hon Roll; Jr NHS; Hon Ment Ldrshp Awd Future Sec Katherine Libbs Schl Rcgntn Of Outstndg Ldrshp Ability 86; Sec.

CLAYTON, WENDY; Milton HS; New Columbia, PA; (Y); Key Clb; Varsity Clb; Chorus; Color Guard; Mrchg Band; Hst Soph Cls; Hst Jr Cls; Rep Stu Cncl; Var Fld Hcky; Powder Puff Ftbl; Geisinger Schl Nursing; Nrs.

CLEARY, CHARLES B; Mckeesport SR HS; White Oak, PA; (Y); Boy Scts; Trs Acpl Chr; Band; Chorus; Church Choir; Concert Band; Jazz Band; Mrchg Band; Pep Band; School Musical; 1st Plc Engr Schl Sci Fr 84; Mid East Msc Fstvl Duquesne U 85-86; Dit Hons Bnd 85; Engr.

CLEARY, JOEY; Clearfield Area HS; Clearfield, PA; (Y); Hosp Aide; Spanish Clb; Hon Roll; Stat Wrstlng; Juniata Coll; Nrsng.

CLEARY, JULIE; Red Lion Area SR HS; Felton, PA; (Y); 14/330; School Play; JV Im Bsktbl; JV Capt Cheerleading; Im JV Sftbl; Im JV High Hon Roll; Var Hon Roll; Hghst Grades Plaques 82-84; Outstndng Achvt Awd 83-84; Bus Mgmt.

CLEMENS, MELISSA; Central Catholic HS; Coopersburg, PA; (Y); Church Yth Grp; Girl Scts; Chorus; Church Choir; Off Frsh Cls; Hon Roll; Kutztown U; Elem Ed.

CLEMENS, NATALIE; Danville Area SR HS; Danville, PA; (Y); Exploring; French Clb; Hosp Aide; Key Clb; Ski Clb; Stu Cncl; Var Trk; High Hon Roll; NHS; Schlrs In Educ Awd PA ST 86; Albright Coll; Math Tchr.

CLEMENT, MARNE; Butler Area SR HS; Butler, PA; (Y); Church Yth Grp; Hosp Aide; Office Aide; SADD; Drill Tm; School Musical; Variety Show; Var Stu Cncl; Hon Roll; Jr NHS; U SC; Psychlgy.

CLEMENTE, KIMBERLY; St Basil Acad; Philadelphia, PA; (S); 6/97; French Clb; JV Capt Cheerleading; Ntl Merit Ltr; Pre-Med.

CLEMMER, P MARTY; Shalom Christian Acad; Marion, PA; (Y); Church Yth Grp; Chorus; Yrbk Ed-Chief; Off Frsh Cls; VP Sr Cls; 4-H Awd; Hon Roll; Dstngshd Chrstn HS Stu ACSI 85-86.

CLEMONS, RICHARD; Henderson HS; West Chester, PA; (Y); 108/358; Ski Clb; Stu Cncl; Capt Ftbl; Capt Lcrss; Wrstlng; Hon Roll; Spanish NHS; Aero Engrng.

CLEVELAND, SANDRA; Canon-Mc Millan HS; Canonsburg, PA; (Y); Cmnty Wkr; Latin Clb; Ski Clb; Pres Sec Band; Concert Band; Mrchg Band; Var L Trk; High Hon Roll; Hon Roll; Prfct Atten Awd; Pre-Phrmcy.

CLEVER, AMY; Chambersburg Area SR HS; Chambersburg, PA; (Y); 23/577; Drama Clb; Hosp Aide; Chorus; School Musical; Variety Show; Rep Stu Cncl; Hon Roll; NHS; PA ST U; Anml Biosci.

CLEVER, MORGAN; General Mc Lane HS; Cambridge Spgs, PA; (Y); 20/250; Aud/Vis; Chess Clb; Church Yth Grp; German Clb; Letterman Clb; Radio Clb; Spanish Clb; Rep Stu Cncl; Stat Bsktbl; Var Ftbl; Med.

CLIFFORD, TAMMY JO; Bangor Area HS; Bangor, PA; (Y); Drama Clb; FHA; Girl Scts; Library Aide; Office Aide; Pep Clb; Yrbk Stf; JV Fld Hcky; High Hon Roll; Hon Roll; Mst Oustndng SR Awd Fd Prep & Srvc 85-86.

CLINE, JULI; Middletown Area HS; Middletown, PA; (Y); 12/180; JV Fld Hcky; Socr; Im Vllybl; Hon Roll; NHS; Acad All-Amer Awd 86; Phys Thrpy.

CLINE, NICOLE; Biglerville HS; Gardners, PA; (Y); Church Yth Grp; Computer Clb; Library Aide; Spanish Clb; Varsity Clb; Yrbk Stf; Rep Frsh Cls; Rep Soph Cls; Rep Jr Cls; Sec Sr Cls; Scl Wrk.

CLINE, TRACI; Kiski Area HS; Apollo, PA; (Y); FBLA; Color Guard; High Hon Roll; Hon Roll; Acdmc Ltr-Acadmc Achvmnt 86; Bus.

CLINE, VICKIE; Boiling Springs HS; Carlisle, PA; (Y); 19/119; Chorus; School Play; Var L Cheerleading; Var Im Diving; Var L Swmmng; Hon Roll; Merit Awd AAA Trafc Safty Postr Desgn 82; Med Tech.

CLINGEMPEEL, CHRISTY; Interboro SR HS; Glenolden, PA; (S); AFS; Cmnty Wkr; Key Clb; Political Wkr; School Play; Rep Stu Cncl; JV Bsktbl; JV Fld Hcky; High Hon Roll; NHS; Psych.

CLINGERMAN, LISA A; Everett Area HS; Artemas, PA; (Y); Church Yth Grp; Computer Clb; GAA; Pep Clb; Varsity Clb; Band; Chorus; Church Choir; Concert Band; Mrchg Band; Allegany CC; Data Prcssng.

CLINK, VICKY; Northeast Bradford HS; Le Raysville, PA; (Y); Church Yth Grp; Pres 4-H; FHA; Chorus; Drill Tm; Mrchg Band; Sec Stu Cncl; Mgr(s); Score Keeper; 4-H Awd; Linda Ballard Hulslander Mem Awd 84; Robert Packer Schl Nrsng; Nrs.

CLINTON, AUTUMN; Sullivan County HS; Dushore, PA; (Y); 4/86; Pres FBLA; Key Clb; Band; Concert Band; Jazz Band; Mrchg Band; Yrbk Stf; Cheerleading; High Hon Roll; NHS.

CLINTON, DAVID; Hazleton SR HS; Hazleton, PA; (Y); 41/388; Church Yth Grp; Pep Clb; Scholastic Bowl; Nwsp Ed-Chief; JV Bsktbl; Var L Crs Cntry; Var L Trk; High Hon Roll; Hon Roll; Luzern Cnty Comp Cntst 2nd Pl 84; Nclr Engrng.

CLIPPINGER, CARYL; Big Spring HS; Newville, PA; (Y); Band; Flag Corp; Mrchg Band; Swmmng; Trk; NHS.

CLISHAM, COLLEEN; Garden Spot HS; New Holland, PA; (Y); 11/186; AFS; Church Yth Grp; Sec 4-H; FBLA; Chorus; Rep Soph Cls; Rep Jr Cls; Rep Sr Cls; JV Var Fld Hcky; Hon Roll; Lancaster Lebanon Sect One All Star Field Hockey Tm 85; SICO Fndtn Schlrshp 86; Homecmng Ct 85; Millersville U; Elem.

CLONEY, KELLEN; Eastern HS; York, PA; (Y); 2/150; Ski Clb; Thesps; Varsity Clb; VP Chorus; Yrbk Stf; Stu Cncl; Capt Cheerleading; Sftbl; High Hon Roll; NHS; Biopyscs.

CLONEY, SHANNON; Eastern York HS; York, PA; (Y); 6/169; Ski Clb; Varsity Clb; Yrbk Stf; VP Frsh Cls; VP Soph Cls; VP Jr Cls; VP Sr Cls; Rep Stu Cncl; L Cheerleading; L Fld Hcky; JR Miss Semi-Fin 86.

CLONTZ, TODD; Punxsutauney Area HS; Stump Creek, PA; (Y); 65/258; Band; Concert Band; Jazz Band; Mrchg Band; Orch; Pep Band; School Musical; Hon Roll.

CLOPPER, ANGIE; Waynesboro Area SR HS; Waynesboro, PA; (Y); 20/125; Pres Church Yth Grp; Church Choir; Capt Bsktbl; Vllybl; High Hon Roll; Hon Roll; Co-MVP Bsktbl 83-84; Chld Psych.

CLOSE, HEATHER; Plum SR HS; Pittsburgh, PA; (Y); Yrbk Stf; Symp Band; Var Bsbl; Var Pom Pon; Im Sftbl; JV Vllybl; Hon Roll; NHS; Prom Ct 86.

CLOSE, LAURE; Dunmore HS; Dunmore, PA; (Y); Art Clb; Camera Clb; Church Yth Grp; Drama Clb; French Clb; Girl Scts; Letterman Clb; Ski Clb; VP Y-Teens; Chorus; Sftbl MVP Awd 85; De Andreas Outstndng Tnns Plyr Awd 86; Arch.

CLOSE, SCOTT; Somerset Area SR HS; Somerset, PA; (Y); 3/233; Trs Stu Cncl; Var L Bsbl; Var L Bsktbl; Bausch & Lomb Sci Awd; High Hon Roll; Pres NHS; Pres Schlr; English Clb; VP German Clb; Pres Math Clb; NHS Scholar 86; Jerry Fisher Mem Bsktbl Awd 86; Sgt Kimmel/Co C Awd 86; U MD; Bus.

CLOSKEY, KATY; Butler SR HS; Butler, PA; (Y); Church Yth Grp; Computer Clb; JA; Spanish Clb; Thesps; Chorus; School Musical; School Play; Swing Chorus; Gym; Elem Ed.

CLOSKY, KRISTINE; Cambridge Springs HS; Venango, PA; (Y); 9/112; Pres VP 4-H; Pep Clb; VP SADD; Yrbk Stf; VP Jr Cls; Pres Stu Cncl; Stat Bsktbl; Var L Sftbl; Hon Roll; NHS; Nrsg.

CLOUD, KARIN L; Norristown Area HS; Norristown, PA; (Y); 26/369; Trs Church Yth Grp; School Play; Rep Frsh Cls; Rep Soph Cls; Rep Jr Cls; Rep Sr Cls; Var L Fld Hcky; Mgr(s); Hon Roll; NHS; U Of Delaware; Physcl Thrpy.

CLOUD, LYNETTE; William Penn HS; Philadelphia, PA; (Y); 6/239; Church Choir; Eastern Coll.

CLOUSE, DAVID; Big Spring HS; Newville, PA; (S); Church Yth Grp; FFA; JV Wrstlng; Hon Roll.

CLOUSE, JEFFREY A; Bethel Park HS; Bethel Park, PA; (Y); Church Yth Grp; JCL; Latin Clb; Quiz Bowl; JV Socr; Trk; Cit Awd; High Hon Roll; Jr NHS; NHS; Outstndng Geomtry Stu 82-83; Penn ST; Elec Engrng.

CLOUSER, BRIAN; Juniata HS; Mifflintown, PA; (Y); Varsity Clb; Stu Cncl; JV Var Bsbl; Im JV Bsktbl; JV Var Cheerleading; JV Var Fld Hcky; Im Var Ftbl; Var Golf; Var Mgr(s); JV Var Socr; Accntng.

CLOUSER, JEFFREY; Boyertown Area SR HS; Bechtelsville, PA; (Y); 43/472; Church Yth Grp; Drama Clb; Speech Tm; SADD; Thesps; Chorus; Church Choir; School Musical; School Play; Swing Chorus; Central CT ST U; Elem Educ.

CLOUSER, MEGAN L; Newport HS; Newport, PA; (Y); Chorus; Concert Band; Jazz Band; School Musical; Stu Cncl; Cheerleading; High Hon Roll; NHS; Opt Clb Awd; School Play; Tri-M Hstrn 85-86; PA ST.

CLOUSER III, RALPH C; Elizabethtown Area HS; Elizabethtown, PA; (Y); 25/237; Varsity Clb; Var L Bsbl; Var L Golf.

CLOUSER, WENDY; Exeter SR HS; Reading, PA; (Y); German Clb; Flag Corp; Fld Hcky; Trk; High Hon Roll; Hon Roll; Jr NHS; NHS; Gntc Engr.

CLOVIS, CHRISTINA; Carmichaels Area HS; Carmichaels, PA; (S); 6/120; Church Yth Grp; Computer Clb; Dance Clb; Rptr 4-H; Ski Clb; Spanish Clb; Mrchg Band; Cheerleading; High Hon Roll; NHS; Rsprtry Thrpy.

CLOWSER, RICHARD; Pottsgrove SR HS; Pottstown, PA; (Y); 21/194; Capt Exploring; Varsity Clb; Rep Sr Cls; Var Capt Ftbl; Var Capt Trk; Var L Wrstlng; Hon Roll; JA; Latin Clb; Im Wt Lftg; Pres Acdmc Fit Awd 86; Cngrsnl Med Of Mrt 86; US Army Schlr Athltc Awd 86; US Army Ft Mc Clellar AL; Mlt.

CLUFF, CYNTHIA; Henderson HS; West Chester, PA; (S); #7 In Class; Hosp Aide; Spanish Clb; Yrbk Ed-Chief; JV Trk; Hon Roll; Spanish NHS.

CLUKEY, JEFF; Mechanicsburg Area SR HS; Mechanicsburg, PA; (Y); 55/311; Chess Clb; Ski Clb; School Play; VP Soph Cls; VP Jr Cls; Rep Stu Cncl; Var Golf; JV Socr; Var Tennis; Hon Roll; Vtrnry Med.

COADY, JENNIFER; Phila HS For Girls; Philadelphia, PA; (Y); 1/395; Church Yth Grp; Teachers Aide; Var Sftbl; JV Vllybl; Ntl Merit SF; Spanish NHS; Bio Chem.

COAKLEY, KELLIE; Bald Eagle Area HS; Bellefonte, PA; (Y); Church Yth Grp; Cmnty Wkr; French Clb; Flag Corp; Mrchg Band; Nwsp Stf; Mat Maids; High Hon Roll; Hon Roll; NHS; IUP; Chldhd Dvlpmnt.

COAST, JENNIFER; Franklin Area HS; Harrisville, PA; (Y); Trs Church Yth Grp; Pres 4-H; French Clb; Radio Clb; Variety Show; Off Soph Cls; Off Jr Cls; Stu Cncl; Var Co-Capt Cheerleading; Stat Crs Cntry; Art.

COAT, CHRIS; Windber Area HS; Windber, PA; (Y); 34/110; Ski Clb; School Play; Var L Ftbl; Var L Trk; Stdnt Of Mnth; U Of Pittsburgh; Phys Thrpy.

COATES, CHARLES; Neshaminy Langhorne HS; Penndel, PA; (Y); 60/720; Hon Roll; NHS; Drexel U; Comp Sci.

COATES, JOSEPH PETER; Belle Vernon Area HS; Fayette City, PA; (Y); 29/272; Drama Clb; NFL; Band; Concert Band; Mrchg Band; Pep Band; School Play; Stage Crew; Hon Roll; U Of Pittsburgh; Bus.

COBB, CHRISTOPHER; Penn Hills SR HS; Pittsburgh, PA; (Y); 1/740; Pres Drama Clb; School Musical; School Play; Ed Nwsp Rptr; Bausch & Lomb Sci Awd; NCTE Awd; Ntl Merit Schol; Pres Schlr; Val; French Clb; Rensselaer Mdl Sci Awd 85; Swarthmore Coll.

COBB, EUGENE; Ambridge Area HS; Ambridge, PA; (Y); Art Clb; Drama Clb; French Clb; Pep Clb; SADD; Chorus; Bsktbl; Ftbl; Score Keeper; Socr; PA Free Entrprse Schlrshp 86; Temple U; Intl Fin.

COBLE, JESSICA; Cedar Crest HS; Lebanon, PA; (Y); 6/347; Drama Clb; French Clb; Pres Latin Clb; Pep Clb; School Musical; School Play; Capt Cheerleading; Capt Trk; NHS; Voice Dem Awd; U Of PA; Biomed Engrng.

COBLE, JULIE; Trinity HS; Washington, PA; (Y); Church Yth Grp; German Clb; Chorus; Swmmng.

COBLE, SCOTT; Elizabethtown Area HS; Elizabethtown, PA; (Y); 2/237; Am Leg Boys St; Aud/Vis; Church Yth Grp; Math Tm; Stage Crew; VP Sr Cls; Tennis; Wt Lftg; NHS; Close-Up Pgm WA Dc 86; Aeronctcl Engrng.

COBLE, TIMOTHY; Faith Christian Schl; East Stroudsburg, PA; (S); 1/11; Church Yth Grp; Off Frsh Cls; Off Soph Cls; Off Jr Cls; Off Sr Cls; Off Stu Cncl; Bsktbl; Sftbl; High Hon Roll; Ntl Merit SF; Taylor U; Pre-Med.

COBLE, TRACEY; Purchase Line HS; Burnside, PA; (Y); 1/130; French Clb; Band; Color Guard; Flag Corp; School Play; High Hon Roll; NHS; Ntl Merit Schol; NEDT Awd; Passauant Schlrshp 86; Stewart Hnrs Schrlshp 86; Thiel Coll; Physics.

COBURN, CORRINE; State College Area HS; State College, PA; (Y); Cmnty Wkr; Ski Clb; Concert Band; Mrchg Band; JV Crs Cntry; JV Var Sftbl; High Hon Roll; Ntl Merit Ltr; PA ST Ski Tm-Alpine 84-86; Pol Sci.

COCCAGNA, CAROL; West Catholic Girls HS; Philadelphia, PA; (Y); 15/240; Cmnty Wkr; French Clb; JA; Library Aide; Mathletes; Nwsp Rptr; Yrbk Rptr; High Hon Roll; Hon Roll; Prfct Atten Awd; 1st Pl HS Sci Fair 84; Math.

COCCARO, MATT; West Mifflin Area HS; W Mifflin, PA; (Y); 59/300; Trs Church Yth Grp; Key Clb; Letterman Clb; Im Bsktbl; Ftbl; L Var Socr; NHS; Duquesne U; Phrmcy.

COCCI, TANIA; Central Catholic HS; Reading, PA; (Y); #32 In Class; Pep Clb; Spanish Clb; Chorus; Color Guard; School Musical; Variety Show; Cheerleading; Central PA; Legal Sec.

COCCO, LOUIS; Archbishop Ryan HS; Philadelphia, PA; (Y); Computer Clb; Rep Frsh Cls; Rep Soph Cls; Stu Cncl; Im Ftbl; Im Ice Hcky; Wt Lftg; Hon Roll; Lwyr.

COCCO, PATRICIA; Upper Darby HS; Drexel Hill, PA; (Y); Girl Scts; Hosp Aide; Office Aide; Church Choir; Swing Chorus; Swmmng; Cit Awd; Hon Roll.

COCHRAN, DAWN R; Du Bois Area HS; Sykesville, PA; (Y); 33/281; German Clb; Band; Concert Band; Mrchg Band; Hon Roll; PA ST U; Engrng.

COCHRAN, LAURA K; Frazier HS; Dawson, PA; (S); 9/121; FNA; Library Aide; Math Clb; Pep Clb; Mrchg Band; Orch; Pep Band; Nwsp Stf; Yrbk Stf; VP Jr Cls; Coal Queen Dely; Prsnnl Mgmt.

COCKRUM, STEPHANY A; Lock Haven HS; Lock Haven, PA; (Y); Spanish Clb; Teachers Aide; JV Bsktbl; JV Socr; Var L Trk; Lock Haven U; Elem Educ.

CODA, DANA; Bethel Park HS; Bethel Park, PA; (Y); Stu Cncl; Powder Puff Ftbl; Trk; IN U Of PA; Crmnlgy.

CODA, KRISTA; Seton-La Salle HS; Bethel Park, PA; (Y); Drama Clb; Ski Clb; Stage Crew; Comm.

CODDINGTON, HOPE; Geibel HS; Uniontown, PA; (Y); 12/100; Church Yth Grp; VP Drama Clb; JA; Library Aide; Pres Pep Clb; School Musical; French Hon Soc; High Hon Roll; NHS; Pres Schlr; Waynesburg Coll Hnr Schlrshp 86; Eagl Crss Awd 86; Waynesburg Coll; Soclgy.

CODELUPPI, JILL; Elizabeth Forward HS; Elizabeth, PA; (Y); Pres Church Yth Grp; Rep Acpl Chr; Band; Pres Chorus; Color Guard; Mrchg Band; Nwsp Rptr; Yrbk Ed-Chief; Stat Swmmng; Hon Roll; Enternatl Plano Rcrdng Competition Bronze 83-85; Rotary Yth Ldrshp Conference; Accntng.

CODER, JASON; Clearfield Area HS; Clearfield, PA; (Y); 15/315; French Clb; Band; Chorus; Mrchg Band; Pep Band; High Hon Roll; NHS; Astronomy.

CODER, JOLENE; Clearfield Area HS; Clearfield, PA; (S); 44/318; Trs Church Yth Grp; Spanish Clb; Band; Chorus; Church Choir; Concert Band; Mrchg Band; Pep Band; Bus Mgmt.

CODISPOT III, LEONARD; Butler SR HS; Butler, PA; (Y); Var Capt Ftbl; VFW Awd; Schlrshp For Ftbl At IN U Of Penn 86; MVP Cubs Hall Awd All Conf Qrtrbck 86; MVP Qlty Inn Awd 86; IN U Pennsylvania; Crmnlgy.

CODISPOT, ROB; Butler SR HS; Butler, PA; (Y); Church Yth Grp; Rep Frsh Cls; Rep Soph Cls; JV Bsktbl; Pre-Dentl.

CODY, LORI; Center HS; Monaca, PA; (Y); 39/188; Varsity Clb; Yrbk Stf; Stat Ftbl; Mgr(s); Powder Puff Ftbl; Var Trk; High Hon Roll; Hon Roll; NHS; Art Clb; Psych.

COE, JULIE; Highlands SR HS; Natrona Hts, PA; (Y); 36/277; Pres Church Yth Grp; Cmnty Wkr; Dance Clb; Hosp Aide; Sec Intnl Clb; Key Clb; Office Aide; Chorus; Church Choir; Drm Mjr(t); Miss Teen PA USA Pag 85; Acad All Amer 85-86; Ldrshp Devlpmnt Comm 85-86; Clarion U; Elem Ed.

COFER, CAMERON G; Franklin Regional SR HS; Murrysville, PA; (Y); 1/327; French Clb; Pres JA; Mathletes; Trs Sr Cls; Socr; Trk; NHS; Ntl Merit SF; Dale Carnegie Schlrshp 84; Ntl Jr Achvmnt Conf 84-85; Hugh O Brian Conf 84; Rice U; Sci Engr.

COFFMAN, DAN; Pennsbury HS; Levittown, PA; (Y); French Clb; Service Clb; Bsbl; Im Bsktbl; Hon Roll; Acctnt.

COFFMAN, DORIS; Shippensburg SR HS; Shippensburg, PA; (Y); 24/220; VP Church Yth Grp; English Clb; Chorus; Nwsp Rptr; Rep Lit Mag; Hon Roll; Stu Mnth GFWC Civic Clb 85; Focus Nwsp Illstrtns 85-86; Acad Hnr Stu Recgntn 85-86; Shippensburg U; Publc Rltns.

COFFMAN, MICHELLE; Mt Pleasant Area HS; Mt Pleasant, PA; (Y); #35 In Class; VP Church Yth Grp; GAA; Ski Clb; Nwsp Rptr; Nwsp Stf; Var Capt Cheerleading; Var Mat Maids; Hon Roll; Prfct Atten Awd; Phys Thrpy.

COFFMAN, SAMARA ROBYN; Lower Moreland HS; Huntingdon Valley, PA; (S); German Clb; Key Clb; Concert Band; Orch; Var Swmmng; JV Trk; Hon Roll; NHS; Awds & Trophies Equestrian Comp 83, 84 & 85; Vet Med.

COGER, FRANCES; West Greene Middle SR HS; Rogersville, PA; (Y); Art Clb; Aud/Vis; Pres Church Yth Grp; Drama Clb; Sec 4-H; Spanish Clb; Chorus; Church Choir; School Play; Nwsp Rptr; Comm.

COGSWELL, CARYN; Forest Hills HS; Elton, PA; (Y); Sec Church Yth Grp; French Clb; Girl Scts; Hosp Aide; Pres JA; Latin Clb; Chorus; Church Choir; Color Guard; CC Awd; Med.

COHEN, ANDREW; Upper Moreland HS; Willow Grove, PA; (Y); 35/260; Cmnty Wkr; Key Clb; JV Bsbl; Var Bowling; High Hon Roll; NHS; Ntl Merit SF; Pltcl Sci.

COHEN, ANDREW W; Germantown Acad; Philadelphia, PA; (Y); Pres Debate Tm; Pres Math Clb; Pres Math Tm; Pres NFL; Nwsp Stf; Lit Mag; Crs Cntry; Cit Awd; Hon Roll; Ntl Merit SF; Fnslt Churcillian Clssc Deb Trmnt 84; Fnlst Roger Reeder Deb Trnmnt 85; 3rd Spkr Vlly Forge Mil Acad; Physics.

COHEN, BETH; Lower Moreland HS; Huntingdon Valley, PA; (S); FBLA; Science Clb; Service Clb; Stage Crew; Stat Bsktbl; Score Keeper; Stat Socr; High Hon Roll; Hon Roll; NHS; Awded 2nd Gup Rank Karate 85; Treas Bnai Brith Grls 85; UVA.

COHEN, DAN; Upper Dublin HS; Dresher, PA; (Y); 69/345; Aud/Vis; FBLA; JA; Political Wkr; Radio Clb; Ski Clb; Stu Cncl; Hagesher Region United Synag Yth Pres 86-87; Wall Street Wrkshp Schlrshp Wnr 85; NYU; Invst Bnkng.

COHEN, JENNIFER; Lower Moreland HS; Huntingdon Valley, PA; (S); Drama Clb; French Clb; Key Clb; Chorus; School Musical; School Play; Ed Lit Mag; Rep Stu Cncl; Kiwanis Awd; NHS; Scholar Gratz Coll 85; Frgn Lang Awd Fr 85; ST Fnlst Miss Teen Scholar & Recog Pagnt 85-86; Frgn Lang.

COHEN, JUDITH D; Cheltenham HS; Elkins Park, PA; (Y); 25/385; Teachers Aide; Chorus; School Musical; Lit Mag; NHS; Ntl Merit SF; NEDT Awd; Cmnty Wkr; French Hon Soc; Hortense & Alvin Greenberg Awd 84; Cheltenham Book Awd 85; PA Hghr Ed Assn Agncy Cert Merit 85.

COHEN, LONNIE; Lower Moreland HS; Huntingdon Valley, PA; (S); 39/214; Sec French Clb; FBLA; Key Clb; Nwsp Rptr; Nwsp Stf; Bsktbl; Var L Crs Cntry; Trk; Hon Roll; Dentistry.

COHEN, MICHAEL E; Harriton HS; Gladwyne, PA; (Y); Computer Clb; Temple Yth Grp; Yrbk Stf; Tennis; NHS; CPA.

COHENOUR, CAROL; Southern Huntingdon HS; Three Spgs, PA; (Y); 22/119; Camera Clb; Church Yth Grp; Computer Clb; FBLA; FHA; Office Aide; Spanish Clb; SADD; Varsity Clb; Band; 40 Et La Societe Schlrshp 86; Juniata-Mifflin; Prctcl Nrsng.

COLA, DONALD; E Bok AVT Schl; Philadelphia, PA; (Y); Boys Clb Am; Cmnty Wkr; Drama Clb; Nwsp Phtg; Nwsp Rptr; High Hon Roll; Hon Roll; NHS; UPS 86; Dbbns Outstndg Vctnl Awd 86; Shp Awd Food Svc 86; Johnson & Wales; Clnry Arts.

COLABERDINO, PATRICIA; Nazareth Acad; Philadelphia, PA; (S); 1/121; Church Yth Grp; Debate Tm; NFL; Pres Speech Tm; Nwsp Stf; Pres Jr Cls; High Hon Roll; NHS; St Speech Comp Qurtr Fnlst 85; City Fnlst Cathlc Forensic League 85-86; Lawyer.

COLABRESE, LISA; Lock Haven HS; Lock Haven, PA; (Y); Art Clb; German Clb; Girl Scts; Hosp Aide; Chorus; School Musical; Mat Maids; Trk; Pittsburg Art Inst; Fshn.

COLADONATO, JOSEPH; Aliquippa HS; Aliquippa, PA; (S); Church Yth Grp; Exploring; French Clb; Math Tm; Band; Concert Band; Mrchg Band; Pep Band; Yrbk Rptr; Yrbk Stf.

COLAGUORI, RONALD J; Swissvale HS; Pittsburgh, PA; (Y); 2/185; Am Leg Boys St; German Clb; Math Tm; Ski Clb; Varsity Clb; Im Bsktbl; Im Ftbl; Capt L Golf; L Tennis; Bausch & Lomb Sci Awd; William A Hoag Memrl Schlrshp 85-86; Harvard Bk Awd 84-85; Woodland Hills Tchg Assn Schlrhsp 85-86; Carnegie Mellon U; Chem.

COLAIVTA, KARNE; Brownsville Area HS; Republic, PA; (Y); Drama Clb; FBLA; Library Aide; Office Aide; SADD; Yrbk Stf; Var Capt Cheerleading; Pom Pon; High Hon Roll; Hon Roll; Med Sec.

COLAIZZI, TRACY; North Hills HS; Pittsburgh, PA; (Y); Key Clb; Var Trk; Hon Roll; Natl Fed JR Fest Piano Solo Superior 85; Natl Fed JR Fest Piano Solo Excllnt 86; Bus.

COLANGELO, DOMENIC; Hopewell HS; Aliquippa, PA; (Y); 25/295; Church Yth Grp; Latin Clb; Jazz Band; School Play; Var L Crs Cntry; Var L Trk; Var L Wrstlng; High Hon Roll; Lion Awd; NHS; Knghts Clmbs Stu Athlt Yr 86; Carnegie Mellon; Engr.

COLARELLI, JOHN A; St John Neumann HS; Philadelphia, PA; (Y); 34/321; Computer Clb; High Hon Roll; Drexel Grant From Drexel U 86; Drexel U; Elec Engrng.

COLAUTTI, ALDO; Keystone Oaks HS; Pittsburgh, PA; (Y); 8/254; Church Yth Grp; Exploring; Mrchg Band; Symp Band; Stu Cncl; DAR Awd; French Hon Soc; High Hon Roll; Hon Roll; NHS; Duquesne U Schlrshp 86; Green Tree Community JR Schlrshp 86; Duquesne U; Intl Bus & Finance.

COLAVITA, ANNAMARIA; St Maria Goretti HS; Philadelphia, PA; (Y); 47/390; Cmnty Wkr; French Clb; GAA; Spanish Clb; Orch; Stage Crew; Prfct Atten Awd; Spanish Awd; French Hnrb Mntn; VP Tri-M Music Hnr Soc; Mktng.

COLBERG, CINDY; Cambria Heights HS; Carrolltown, PA; (Y); Girl Scts; Pep Clb; Chorus; School Musical; Yrbk Stf; Sec Frsh Cls; Mat Maids; U Of Pittsburg; Dent Hygnst.

COLBERT, CHRIS; Council Rock HS; Churchville, PA; (Y); 111/835; Debate Tm; GAA; Intnl Clb; Political Wkr; Im Powder Puff Ftbl; JV Sftbl; Hon Roll; Georgetown; Law.

COLBERT, KRISTIN; Strath Haven HS; Media, PA; (Y); Church Yth Grp; Office Aide; Band; Orch; Yrbk Stf; VP Capt Bsktbl; Var Sftbl; Capt Var Vllybl; Hon Roll; Bus.

COLBERT, SHAWN; Keystone Oaks HS; Pittsburgh, PA; (Y); Band; Mrchg Band; School Play; Symp Band; Bsbl; Wrstlng; Hon Roll; Kent ST U; Aero Tech.

COLBERT, SHELTON; Aliquippa HS; Aliquippa, PA; (Y); 27/200; French Clb; Bsktbl; Ftbl; Let In Ftbl 85; Criminology.

COLBURN, BETH; Bellefonte SR HS; Howard, PA; (S); Church Yth Grp; Library Aide; Model UN; Nwsp Bus Mgr; Nwsp Rptr; Nwsp Stf; Yrbk Stf; High Hon Roll; Hon Roll; NHS; Lock Haven U; Chmstry.

COLDREN, CHRISTINE; Mechanicsburg SR HS; Mechanicsburg, PA; (Y); 8/311; Pep Clb; Mrchg Band; Symp Band; Co-Capt Crs Cntry; Swmmng; Trk; High Hon Roll; NHS.

COLDREN, DANNY L; Schuylkill Haven Area HS; Port Clinton, PA; (S); VP German Clb; Office Aide; Science Clb; Band; Chorus; Concert Band; Mrchg Band; Pep Band; Rep Frsh Cls; Hon Roll; Gvnrs Schl Of Arts 85; Piano Prfrmnc.

COLDREN, MICHAEL; Juniata HS; Mifflintown, PA; (Y); Aud/Vis; Camera Clb; Varsity Clb; Yrbk Phtg; Mgr(s); Tennis; Hon Roll; Elec Tech.

COLDSMITH, ANGEL; Chambersburg Area SR HS; Chambersburg, PA; (Y); 86/640; AFS; JCL; Key Clb; Latin Clb; Chorus; JV Var Fld Hcky; Hon Roll; Shippensburg U; Chld Psychlgy.

COLE, AMY; Butler Area SR HS; Butler, PA; (Y); Trs Pres Church Yth Grp; French Clb; Teachers Aide; Chorus; Church Choir; Hon Roll; Entrpnr.

COLE III, CHARLES C; Emmaus HS; Macungie, PA; (Y); 32/479; Boy Scts; Key Clb; Orch; School Musical; School Play; Hon Roll; Jr NHS; NHS; Ntl Merit SF.

COLE, CHRISTINE; Meadville Area SR HS; Meadville, PA; (Y); 54/365; French Clb; High Hon Roll; Hon Roll; Prfct Atten Awd; PA ST; Lawyer.

COLE JR, DAVID; Emmaus HS; Emmaus, PA; (Y); 69/490; Band; Jazz Band; Jr Cls; Bsbl; Hon Roll; Jr NHS; NHS; Electrical.

COLE II, DONALD J; Tunkhannock Area HS; Tunkhannock, PA; (S); 47/290; Chess Clb; Band; Concert Band; Jazz Band; Golf; Hon Roll; NHS; Marywood Hnrs Bnd 83; Dist Bnd 85 & 86; Qulfd PIAA Indvdl Dist II Chmpnshps 84.

COLE, JAMES; Pennsbury HS; Handley, PA; (Y); 60/729; Boy Scts; NFL; Speech Tm; Yrbk Stf; NHS; Pres Acad Fit Awd 86; IN U PA; Bio.

COLE, JEFFREY; Wyalusing Valley HS; Laceyville, PA; (Y); FBLA; Scholastic Bowl; Ski Clb; Spanish Clb; School Musical; Stu Cncl; JV Bsbl; JV Bsktbl; L Var Crs Cntry; L Var Trk; Bonman Ashe Schlrshp From U Of MAMI 87-90; U Of Miami; Mech Engr.

COLE, JOANNA; Trinity HS; Washington, PA; (Y); 14/374; Church Yth Grp; Hosp Aide; Office Aide; Pep Clb; Band; Chorus; Concert Band; Mrchg Band; High Hon Roll; NHS; ST Chrus 86; Dist, Rgn Chrus 84-86; Solost Cmpus Life 85-86; Spec Ed.

COLE, LISA; Bishop Guilfoyle HS; Altoona, PA; (Y); 20/118; Stu Cncl; JV Var Bsktbl; High Hon Roll; Hon Roll; U IN; Nrsng.

COLE, LORI; Manheim Twp HS; Lancaster, PA; (Y); Church Yth Grp; Color Guard; Mrchg Band; Trk; Hon Roll; Grphc Art.

COLE, MICHELLE; Littlestown SR HS; Littlestown, PA; (Y); Sec Church Yth Grp; DECA; Drama Clb; Teachers Aide; Band; Chorus; Church Choir; Concert Band; Mrchg Band; Pep Band; Math.

COLE, PATTY; Mansfield HS; Mansfield, PA; (S); VP FCA; Trs Key Clb; Library Aide; Ski Clb; VP Soph Cls; Rep Stu Cncl; Var L Bsktbl; Var L Trk; Var Capt Vllybl; Cit Awd.

COLE, SHAHNA; Lincoln HS; Ellwood City, PA; (Y); AFS; Trs VP Exploring; Sec German Clb; Yrbk Stf; Rep Jr Cls; Rep Sr Cls; Stu Cncl; Tennis; Trk; NEDT Awd; U Pittsburgh; Elec Engrng.

COLE, SHARON; Middleton Area HS; Middletown, PA; (Y); Flag Corp; Capt Gym; Hon Roll; Jr NHS; Acad All-Amer 86.

COLEGROVE, STANTON; Elkland Area HS; Nelson, PA; (Y); Drama Clb; SADD; Varsity Clb; School Play; Soph Cls; Jr Cls; Stu Cncl; Var L Bsktbl; Im Coach Actv; L Socr.

COLELLA, CANDACE; New Castle SR HS; New Castle, PA; (S); 10/253; AFS; Rep Church Yth Grp; Exploring; Spanish Clb; Flag Corp; Rep Frsh Cls; Rep Soph Cls; Hon Roll; Jr NHS; Prfct Atten Awd.

COLELLO, JOSEPH; Altoona Area HS; Altoona, PA; (Y); VICA; Ftbl; Trk; Let In Ftbl 85; Comp Sci.

COLEMAN, DANA JOANN MARIE; Lutheran HS; Philadelphia, PA; (Y); Church Yth Grp; Dance Clb; Debate Tm; Drama Clb; Church Choir; Stu Cncl; Cheerleading; Trk; Cit Awd; Hon Roll; Cert Merit Excllnce Span, Latin II & Bio 85; Pre Law.

COLEMAN, DANIELLE; Millersburg Area HS; Millersburg, PA; (Y); Capt Drill Tm; Nwsp Stf; VP Frsh Cls; VP Soph Cls; VP Jr Cls; Var L Bsktbl; Capt Powder Puff Ftbl; Var Sftbl; Var L Trk; Hon Roll; Hmcmng Court 85-86; Prom Prncss 85-86; Westchester; Psychlgy.

COLEMAN, DAVID; Millersburg Area HS; Millersburg, PA; (S); 2/63; French Clb; Red Cross Aide; Soph Cls; JV Bsktbl; Var Trk; High Hon Roll; Ntl Merit SF.

COLEMAN, JOANN; Central York SR HS; York, PA; (Y); Ski Clb; Varsity Clb; Band; Flag Corp; Mrchg Band; Yrbk Stf; Cheerleading; Mgr(s); Hon Roll; NHS.

COLEMAN, JOYCE L; St Pauls Cathedral HS; Pittsburgh, PA; (S); 10/64; Chorus; Nwsp Rptr; Yrbk Stf; VP Jr Cls; VP Sr Cls; Var L Cheerleading; Hon Roll; Shadyside Hosp Med Explrs Clb 84; Achvt Excl Ntl Hist 85; Nrs.

COLEMAN, LAURA; Bishop Guilfoyle HS; Queen, PA; (Y); 34/130; Library Aide; Red Cross Aide; SADD; Flag Corp; Chem Clb; Jr Cls Advsr.

COLEMAN, MATTHEW; Owen J Roberts HS; Pottstown, PA; (S); 11/237; Letterman Clb; Stage Crew; Stu Cncl; JV Socr; Var L Trk; High Hon Roll; Hon Roll; NHS; Engrg.

COLEMAN, MELINDA J; North Allegheny HS; Allison Pk, PA; (Y); 116/605; AFS; Sec JA; Band; Concert Band; Mrchg Band; Pep Band; School Musical; Symp Band; Rep Jr Cls; Jr NHS; Pres Acad Ftnss Awd 86; IN U Bloomington; Bus.

COLEMAN, MELISSA D; Freeport HS; Sarver, PA; (Y); Sec JA; Band; Concert Band; Mrchg Band; Pep Band; Symp Band; Nwsp Rptr; Nwsp Stf; Hon Roll; Slippery Rock U.

COLEMAN, MICHELLE; Technical Memorial HS; Erie, PA; (Y); 21/349; Pres Church Yth Grp; Cmnty Wkr; Pres Church Choir; School Play; Variety Show; Hon Roll; Hgh Achvr Awds Gannon Upwrd Bnd Prog 85-86; Penn ST U; Comp Sci.

COLEMAN, SARAH; Warren County Christian Schl; Warren, PA; (S); 2/10; Church Yth Grp; 4-H; Chorus; Church Choir; School Play; Yrbk Stf; Rep Stu Cncl; Var Cheerleading; Eastern Nazarene Coll; Bus Adm.

COLEMAN, TOM; West Hazleton HS; Drums, PA; (Y); Church Yth Grp; FCA; French Clb; Letterman Clb; Ski Clb; SADD; Crs Cntry; Trk; Hon Roll; Penn ST; Engrng.

COLES, DAWNA; Western Beaver JR SR HS; Midland, PA; (Y); Church Yth Grp; JA; Color Guard; Mrchg Band; Symp Band; Nwsp Phtg; Nwsp Stf; Sec Sr Cls; Stat Bsktbl; Hon Roll; Sec.

COLES, KENNY; Old Forge HS; Old Forge, PA; (Y); Ski Clb; Band; Chorus; Concert Band; Mrchg Band; School Musical; School Play; Stage Crew; Crs Cntry; Ftbl.

COLESON, BRIAN; Ephrata HS; Ephrata, PA; (Y); Church Yth Grp; Concert Band; Mrchg Band; Socr; Hon Roll; Hnrb Mntn Multi-Clr Offst Susqchnna Litho Clb 86; Rochester Inst/Tech; Grphc Arts.

COLEWBRANDER, MARK; Gateway SR HS; Monroeville, PA; (Y); 80/508; JV Bsktbl; Local Cycling Champ Cls B 85; Pittsburgh Mst Imprvd Rider 85; Arch.

COLFLESH, SHERRY; Shanksville-Stonycreek HS; Berlin, PA; (S); 8/35; Church Yth Grp; Spanish Clb; Chorus; Nwsp Rptr; Nwsp Stf; Hon Roll; Spanish NHS; Typing Awd 84; Teen Action Pgm Tap Club 85-86; Intl Frgn Lang Awd 85; UPJ Johnstown; Comp Sci.

COLIA, LISA ANN; Neshannock HS; New Castle, PA; (Y); 28/104; FBLA; Library Aide; Teachers Aide; Chorus; School Musical; Im Tennis; Hon Roll; Duquesne U; Comp Sci.

COLIHAN, JUDITH A; Archbishop John Carroll Hs For Girls; Philadelphia, PA; (Y); 27/214; Drama Clb; French Clb; Nwsp Rptr; Nwsp Stf; Yrbk Rptr; Yrbk Stf; Lit Mag; High Hon Roll; Hon Roll; PA ST U; Pre Law.

COLINEAR, JENNIFER; Norwin HS; N Huntingdon, PA; (Y); 10/560; French Clb; Leo Clb; Letterman Clb; Mathletes; Math Clb; Math Tm; Yrbk Stf; Capt Cheerleading; High Hon Roll; NHS; Nuc Automtn Schlrshp 86; U Pittsburgh; Engrng.

COLL, CHRIS; Weatherly HS; Weatherly, PA; (Y); 8/60; FHA; JV Bsktbl; L Ftbl; CC Awd; NHS; E K Allison Schlrshp 86; Kings Coll; Acctg.

COLL, JIM; Springfield HS; Oreland, PA; (Y); 40/160; Cmnty Wkr; Rep Soph Cls; Bsktbl; Var Golf; Score Keeper; Im Sftbl; Im Tennis; Im Trk; Hon Roll; Rotary Awd.

COLLARINI, LISA; Valleyview HS; Peckville, PA; (Y); Sec French Clb; SADD; Chorus; Rep Stu Cncl; Var Swmmng; Var Trk; Im Vllybl; French Hon Soc; High Hon Roll; Hon Roll; Ldy Lbrty Cnts 1st Pl Hnrs 86; Acad Encllnc Cert 85; Sports Med.

COLLAZO, EDGAR; Cardinal Dougherty HS; Phila, PA; (Y); 7/747; Aud/Vis; French Clb; Library Aide; Mathletes; School Musical; Variety Show; NHS; Ntl Merit Schol; Hld On To Your Drms Schrlshp Awd 86; Harvard Schlrshp Awd; Harvard U; Pre Med.

COLLETTE, NAHNJU C; Riverview HS; Oakmont, PA; (Y); Varsity Clb; Chorus; Flag Corp; Madrigals; Yrbk Phtg; Rep Jr Cls; Rep Stu Cncl; Var L Bsktbl; Var L Tennis; Var L Trk; ST Trck Chmpshp Plcd 4th & 6th 85 & 86; Rtry Ldrshp Conf Reprep 86.

COLLETTI, JACK; Cannon Mc Millan SR HS; Canonsburg, PA; (Y); 1/395; Latin Clb; Ski Clb; Yrbk Phtg; Yrbk Stf; Pres Stu Cncl; Bsbl; Socr; High Hon Roll; NHS; Pittsburgh Piano Tchrs Compstn Wnnr 84; Co-Stu Rep Schl Brd Mtngs 86-87; Naval Acad; Aerospace.

COLLIER, BRIDGETTE; Donegal HS; Mount Joy, PA; (Y); 51/167; FTA; Girl Scts; Pres Trs JA; Chorus; Stage Crew; JV Bsktbl; JV Fld Hcky; Mgr(s); JV Sftbl; Var Stat Trk; Most Imprvd Latin Stu 86; MVP Sftbl 84; Acctng.

COLLIER, KRIS; Karns City HS; Chicora, PA; (Y); 12/124; Church Yth Grp; Dance Clb; Girl Scts; Hosp Aide; Band; Church Choir; Bsktbl; Pom Pon; Score Keeper; Trk; Sawyee Bus Schl; Scrtrl Sci.

COLLINGWOOD, SHAWN M; Canon-Macmillan SR HS; Canonsburg, PA; (Y); 62/342; Varsity Clb; Capt Swmmng; Hon Roll; Prtl Acad Schlrshp-Westminster Coll 86-87; Westminster Coll; Chem.

COLLINS, CHRISTINE; Council Rock HS; Holland, PA; (Y); 217/845; Powder Puff Ftbl; High Hon Roll; Hon Roll; Buck Cnty CC; Bus Sec.

COLLINS JR, DAVID F; Archbishop Ryan H S For Boys; Philadelphia, PA; (Y); 25/430; Boy Scts; Computer Clb; German Clb; JA; Science Clb; Cit Awd; Pres Schlr; 4 Yrs Prfct Condct; Artisns Ordr Mutl Protctn Coll Asstnc Schlrshp; Drexel U; Elec Engr.

COLLINS, HOLLY; Curwensville Area HS; Clearfield, PA; (Y); Nwsp Stf; Hon Roll; Acad All Amer; Du Bois Bus Coll; Sec.

COLLINS, JEANNETTE; Moniteau HS; Chicora, PA; (Y); 31/133; Exploring; Sec 4-H; Library Aide; Spanish Clb; Church Choir; Capt Color Guard; Nwsp Stf; Yrbk Stf; Mgr(s); Hon Roll; Doc.

COLLINS, JESSICA; Fox Chapel HS; Pittsbg, PA; (Y); Key Clb; Ski Clb; Yrbk Stf; Powder Puff Ftbl; Var L Tennis; High Hon Roll; Hon Roll; Key,Cki Clb; Yrbk Staff; Powder Puff Ftbl; Tennis Ltr; High Hnr Rl; Yth Grp.

COLLINS, JO; Central Buck East HS; Warrington, PA; (Y); Boy Scts; Drama Clb; French Clb; Chorus; School Play; Hon Roll; Cert Of Part-Cnty Chorus 83-84; Vrsty Singers 83-85; Temple; Accntng.

COLLINS, KATHERINE A; Wilson SR HS; West Lawn, PA; (Y); 2/286; Debate Tm; Pres French Clb; Quiz Bowl; VP Band; Orch; Lit Mag; Pres NHS; Ntl Merit SF; Church Yth Grp; Math Clb; Region 5 Band; Dist 10 Band & Orch; Yng Musicns Symphy Scholar; Intl Rltns.

COLLINS, KATHY; West Perry SR HS; Loysville, PA; (Y); 1/188; Red Cross Aide; Church Choir; Concert Band; Capt Flag Corp; School Play; Ed Yrbk Stf; VP NHS; Val; Trs Nwsp Stf; Comp Awd 86; Cnty Band & Chorus 83-86; Harrisburg Area CC; Accntng.

COLLINS, KELLY; Mid-Valley HS; Throop, PA; (Y); Thesps; School Play; Stage Crew; Rep Stu Cncl; Pre-Vet.

COLLINS, KEVIN; Curwensville Area HS; Curwensville, PA; (Y); AFS; Computer Clb; Drama Clb; Chorus; Concert Band; Drm Mjr(t); Mrchg Band; Pep Band; Nwsp Rptr; Yrbk Stf; Comp Sci.

COLLINS, LENORA; Belle Vernon Area HS; West Newton, PA; (Y); Hosp Aide; NFL; Band; Nwsp Rptr; Nwsp Stf; High Hon Roll; NHS; Voice Dem Awd; 1st Pl Frnch Cmptn At CA ST U 84; Mth.

COLLINS, LISA; Archbishop Prendergast HS; Upper Darby, PA; (Y); 55/361; Hosp Aide; Service Clb; School Play; Nwsp Rptr; JV Var Gym; Hon Roll; Ntl Bus Hnr Soc 84-86; West Chester U; Bus Mgmt.

COLLINS, MARY E; Bishop Hoban HS; Wilkes Barre, PA; (Y); Church Yth Grp; Hosp Aide; Latin Clb; Math Clb; Ski Clb; Chorus; Cheerleading; Hon Roll; Mu Alp Tht; NHS.

COLLINS, MICHAEL; York Catholic HS; York, PA; (Y); Boy Scts; French Clb; JA; Library Aide.

COLLINS, MICHAEL J; Riverside Beaver County HS; Beaver Falls, PA; (Y); 1/185; Pres Computer Clb; Concert Band; Jazz Band; Capt Mrchg Band; School Musical; Symp Band; High Hon Roll; JETS Awd; NHS; Ntl Merit Ltr; Elect Engr.

COLLINS, MICHELLE; Dover Area HS; East Berlin, PA; (S); Band; Chorus; Concert Band; Mrchg Band; Rep Stu Cncl; Hon Roll; NHS.

COLLINS, MIKE; Muhlenberg SR HS; Laureldale, PA; (Y); Scholastic Bowl; Bsbl; Bsktbl; Bowling; Hon Roll; NHS; Penn ST U; Mech Engrng.

COLLINS, SCOTT A; Clearfield Area HS; Clearfield, PA; (Y); 122/302; Key Clb; Var Bsbl; Var Capt Wrstlng; Cit Awd; Full Athltc Schlrshp 86; WV U; Sprts Stds.

COLLINS, SEAN; St Josephs Prep HS; Philadelphia, PA; (Y); 27/235; Office Aide; Var Bsbl; Var Ftbl; High Hon Roll; Hnrary Schlrshp St Jsphs Prep 83; Georgetown Coll; Bus Mgmt.

COLLINS, STEPHANIE; Everett Area HS; Clearville, PA; (S); 13/105; Church Yth Grp; Spanish Clb; Band; Concert Band; Jazz Band; Mrchg Band; Pep Band; Socr; Hon Roll; Ntl Hstry & Govt Awd 84-85.

COLLINS, TRACELL ALLENDRA; Harrisburg HS; Harrisburg, PA; (Y); Church Yth Grp; Pep Clb; SADD; Thesps; Chorus; School Musical; Sec Frsh Cls; Sec Soph Cls; Sec Jr Cls; Sec Sr Cls; Child Devlpmnt.

COLLINS, WILLIAM; Southern Huntingdon Co HS; Three Springs, PA; (Y); 29/106; JV Ftbl.

COLLISON, JAMES; Bishop Kenrick HS; Norristown, PA; (Y); 47/311; Science Clb; Ski Clb; Nwsp Phtg; Yrbk Phtg; Hon Roll; Phys.

COLLURA, JOSEPH; Palmyra SR HS; Palmyra, PA; (Y); 48/196; Aud/Vis; French Clb; Varsity Clb; JV Var Wrstlng; High Hon Roll; Hon Roll; Cert Merit Frnch 83-84; PA ST U; TV.

COLLWELL, DAVE; New Brighton Area HS; New Brighton, PA; (Y); 31/154; Am Leg Boys St; Varsity Clb; Yrbk Sprt Ed; L Bsbl; Capt L Ftbl; Trk; Wt Lftg; Hon Roll; Lion Awd; Grove City Coll; Chem.

COLOMBO, JIM; Manheim Central HS; Manheim, PA; (Y); High Hon Roll; Hon Roll; Indstrl Tech.

COLOMBO, JON; Council Rock HS; Richboro, PA; (Y); 123/825; Trs Church Yth Grp; Cmnty Wkr; Concert Band; Mrchg Band; Off Jr Cls; Var Socr; Var Tennis; Im Vllybl; Im Wt Lftg; Hon Roll; Archtctrl Engrng.

COLOMBO, MARK; Cardinal O Hara HS; Media, PA; (Y); 21/772; Aud/Vis; Church Yth Grp; School Play; Frsh Cls; Soph Cls; Jr Cls; Sr Cls; Stu Cncl; Socr; High Hon Roll; All Cath Sccr Tm 86; Prinicpals Awd Acadmc Excllnc 85 & 86; Geometry Trigonmetry Awd Excllnce 85; Engineering.

COLON, JOSE; Souderton Area HS; Souderton, PA; (Y); 30/350; Intnl Clb; Ski Clb; School Musical; Rep Soph Cls; Rep Jr Cls; Var L Crs Cntry; Var L Trk; High Hon Roll; Hon Roll; Ntl Merit SF; Biochem.

COLON, MARIA; Little Flower HS; Philadelphia, PA; (Y); 64/395; Hon Roll; Math Achvt 85; Admin.

COLONNA, EDDIE; Aliquippa HS; Aliquippa, PA; (Y); Math Clb; VICA; Band; Concert Band; Mrchg Band; Ftbl; Wt Lftg; Hon Roll; 8th St Comptn Instrl Arts 84.

COLPETZER, CHRISTINA; Lewistown Area HS; Granville, PA; (Y); French Clb; Ski Clb; Band; Chorus; Concert Band; Mrchg Band; Vllybl; High Hon Roll; NHS.

COLTABAUGH, TERRY; Altoona Area HS; Altoona, PA; (S); 9/683; Boy Scts; Church Yth Grp; Math Tm; Science Clb; Nwsp Ed-Chief; Off Sr Cls; God Cntry Awd; NHS; German Clb; Math Clb; Intl Order Of Demolay 85; Union Carbide Spnsrd WA Wrkshp 85; PA ST U; Molecular Bio.

COLUCCI, DINO; Canon Mcmillan SR HS; Mcdonald, PA; (Y); 1/376; Chess Clb; Church Yth Grp; French Clb; Ski Clb; School Play; Trs Jr Cls; Rep Stu Cncl; Socr; Wrstlng; High Hon Roll.

COLURSO, KIM; West Scranton HS; Scranton, PA; (Y); Spanish Clb; Pom Pon; Hon Roll; Elem Ed.

COLVIN, TRICIA; Punxsutawney Area SR HS; Punxsutawney, PA; (Y); Girl Scts; Math Tm; Band; Concert Band; Mrchg Band; Pep Band; Hon Roll; Optmtry.

COLWELL, CAROLE; Red Land HS; York Haven, PA; (Y); 7/287; Church Yth Grp; Cmnty Wkr; VP Trs 4-H; JCL; Hst Latin Clb; Ski Clb; SADD; Band; Concert Band; Drill Tm; 4th Rnnr Up Modern Miss Schlrshp Pgnt; Engrng.

COLYER, JULIE; East Juniata HS; Mc Alisterville, PA; (Y); 10/94; Pres Sec FBLA; Hon Roll; Pres Acadmc Ftnss Awd 86; Top Ten Hnr Stu 86; Secy.

COMELLA, CHRISTINE; Bethel Park HS; Bethel Park, PA; (Y); Pres 4-H; Rep Soph Cls; Rep Jr Cls; JV Bsktbl; JV Vllybl; 4-H Awd; Hi-Point Champ Rider Sddle & Fnce Clb 83; U Of KY; Pre-Vet.

COMISAC, CHRISTOPHER; Hamburg Area HS; Hamburg, PA; (Y); Boy Scts; Spanish Clb; Yrbk Stf; Sec Soph Cls; VP Jr Cls; Var Crs Cntry; Var Ftbl; Var L Trk; High Hon Roll; NHS; Arspc Engr.

COMMO, KIMBERLY; Bishop Kenrick HS; Norristown, PA; (Y); 75/315; Cmnty Wkr; Dance Clb; Hosp Aide; Nrsng.

COMO, ELANA; Bishop Carroll HS; Colver, PA; (S); 14/105; Drama Clb; Girl Scts; Hosp Aide; Pep Clb; Var L Bsktbl; Capt Crs Cntry; Var Trk; Hon Roll; NHS; Pre-Law.

COMPTON, CARESSA; Danville SR HS; Danville, PA; (Y); Cmnty Wkr; 4-H; Sec FFA; Hosp Aide; Rep Frsh Cls; Rep Soph Cls; Rep Jr Cls; Rep Stu Cncl; Bsktbl; 4-H Awd; Star Greenhand 85; Star Chptr Farmer 86; PA ST U; Ornamntl Hortcltr.

COMSTOCK, JEANETTE; Benton Area HS; Stillwater, PA; (Y); FFA; GAA; Ski Clb; Stage Crew; Pres Jr Cls; Var Sftbl; Hon Roll; Greenhand 84; Chptr Farmer 85; Pres Pin 86; Cazenovia Coll; Intr Desgn.

COMSTOCK, MATTHEW; Highlands SR HS; Natrona Hts, PA; (Y); 1/300; AFS; Church Yth Grp; Drama Clb; School Play; Off Jr Cls; Off Stu Cncl; Crs Cntry; Ftbl; Socr; Swmmng; Nclr Physc.

COMSTOCK, VICTORIA; General Mc Lane HS; Edinboro, PA; (Y); Church Yth Grp; Library Aide; Red Cross Aide; Spanish Clb; Teachers Aide; Chorus; Vllybl; Hon Roll; Cazenovia Coll; Trvlng.

COMUNALE, CONSTANCE; East Allegheny HS; Wilmerding, PA; (Y); 30/209; Hosp Aide; Ski Clb; Color Guard; Off Frsh Cls; Off Jr Cls; Off Sr Cls; Stu Cncl; High Hon Roll; Hon Roll; NHS; U Of Pittsburgh; Hlth Rcrds Adm.

CONA, DAVID; Devon Preparatory Schl; Drexel Hill, PA; (Y); Mrchg Band; Nwsp Rptr; Nwsp Stf; Crs Cntry; High Hon Roll; Hon Roll; Mth Awd 84-85; Lbrl Arts.

CONAHAN, JENNIFER; Haverford Township SR HS; Havertown, PA; (Y); 1/482; Am Leg Aux Girls St; Hosp Aide; Spanish Clb; Capt Flag Corp; Mgr Stage Crew; Nwsp Phtg; Swmmng; Hon Roll; NHS; Harvrd Bk Awd 86; Pedtrc Med.

CONAWAY, JOHN; Kittanning Area SR HS; Worthington, PA; (Y); Church Yth Grp; Letterman Clb; Band; JV Bsktbl; JV Var Socr; Hon Roll; Penn ST U; Cmptr Sci.

CONDADINA, ANDREA; Cardinal O Hara HS; Broomall, PA; (Y); French Clb; Service Clb; Yrbk Stf; Rep Stu Cncl; Var Trk; Im Vllybl; Hon Roll; NHS; Prfct Atten Awd; Math.

CONDASH, JUDITH A; West Hazleton HS; Tresckow, PA; (S); Church Yth Grp; VP FNA; Nwsp Stf; Yrbk Stf; Sec Sr Cls; Stu Cncl; Var Capt Cheerleading; Elks Awd; Trs NHS; Penn ST U; Nrsng.

CONDEL, BRIAN; Western Wayne HS; Lake Ariel, PA; (Y); 6/140; Boy Scts; Church Yth Grp; VP Jr Cls; Var Socr; Var Trk; High Hon Roll; NHS; Black Belt Tang Soo Do Karate 83-86; PA ST; Engrng.

CONDI, STEPHEN; Cardinal O Hara HS; Havertown, PA; (Y); 202/800; Church Yth Grp; Bsktbl; JV Ftbl; Var Trk; Vllybl; Hon Roll; Villanova U; Elctrcl Engr.

CONDIT, KATHRYN A; Franklin Regional SR HS; Monroeville, PA; (Y); 9/325; Pres Debate Tm; VP French Clb; VP JA; Thesps; Chorus; Swing Chorus; Nwsp Rptr; High Hon Roll; NHS; Ntl Merit SF; Acad Let & 2nd & 3rd Yr Bars 83-85; JR Achvt Sales & Officer Awds 84; French Awd 85; PA ST U.

CONDON, JOHN; Cumberland Valley HS; Camp Hill, PA; (Y); 100/550; Spanish Clb; Var L Bsbl; Var L Ftbl; Var Wt Lftg; Hon Roll; Engrng.

CONDRACK, PAUL J; Pottsville Area HS; Seltzer, PA; (Y); 13/204; Exploring; Pres Intnl Clb; VP Latin Clb; Capt Swmmng; High Hon Roll; Hon Roll; NHS; Albright Coll; Bio Chem.

CONDRASKY, THOMAS; Cumberland Valley HS; Mechanicsburg, PA; (Y); 56/522; Debate Tm; Key Clb; Math Tm; Ski Clb; Rep Frsh Cls; Rep Soph Cls; NHS; Bus Adm.

CONDRON, MICHAEL; Plum SR HS; Pittsburgh, PA; (Y); Letterman Clb; Varsity Clb; Nwsp Stf; Yrbk Stf; JV Bsktbl; Capt Var Tennis; High Hon Roll; Hon Roll; NHS; NEDT Awd; Westminster Coll; Chem.

CONELIAS, MICHAEL; Freedom HS; Bethlehem, PA; (Y); 111/445; Church Yth Grp; Ski Clb; Off Sr Cls; Rep Stu Cncl; Var L Bsbl; Var L Bsktbl; Score Keeper; Hon Roll; MVP Ptchg 86; EP Conf All Str Bsbl 86; Bethlhm Chptr PIAA Offcls Sprtsmnshp Awd 86; Bus Mgmt.

CONFAIR, DOUGLAS; Benton Area JR SR HS; Benton, PA; (Y); Pres Key Clb; Ski Clb; Var Bsbl; Var Socr; JV Wrstlng; NHS; Coll Penn ST U; Nuclr Engrng.

CONFER, ELLEN; West Branch HS; Pottersdale, PA; (Y); 8/112; Science Clb; Spanish Clb; Yrbk Phtg; VP Soph Cls; Sec Jr Cls; Sec Sr Cls; Pres Stu Cncl; Vllybl; High Hon Roll; Robert Valmont Awd 86; Law Rltd Ed Awd 86; Penn ST U.

CONFER, JOHN; Annville Cleona HS; Annville, PA; (Y); FFA; German Clb; Varsity Clb; Stage Crew; Var Ftbl; Im Ice Hcky; Im Wt Lftg; Var Wrstlng; NHS; Crmnl Jstice.

CONFER, JULIE; Lock Haven HS; Lock Haven, PA; (Y); Concert Band; Mat Maids.

CONFORTI, ED; South Hills HS; Pittsburgh, PA; (Y); Aud/Vis; Boy Scts; Church Yth Grp; Latin Clb; Sec Frsh Cls; Rep Soph Cls; Cit Awd; Hon Roll; Prfct Atten Awd; Cert Achvt Buhl Sci Ctr 82; Connelley Skill Lrng Ct; Elctrn.

CONFORTI, KIP ANTHONY; Scranton Central HS; Moscow, PA; (Y); Art Clb; Pres Boy Scts; Pres Exploring; Ski Clb; Nwsp Phtg; Photo Awd-Art Cntst 86; Ntl Art Hnr Soc-Awd Rcgntn Outstndng Achvt-Photo 86; Psychlgy.

CONGELOSI, CHRISTINE; St Hubert High School For Girls; Philadelphia, PA; (Y); 218/367; Stage Crew; Mgr(s); Vllybl; Hon Roll.

CONGER, PAMELA; United HS; Armagh, PA; (Y); 42/157; Camera Clb; Church Yth Grp; Hosp Aide; Ski Clb; SADD; Chorus; Lit Mag; Trk; Hon Roll; NHS; Rochester Inst Tech; Biomed.

CONGIALDI, JEFFREY; West Catholic HS; Philadelphia, PA; (Y); 10/280; Im Bsktbl; Arch Engrng.

CONIGY, MARY; Bishop Carroll HS; Ebensburg, PA; (S); 12/103; Pep Clb; Ski Clb; Yrbk Sprt Ed; Sec Jr Cls; Sec Sr Cls; Var Cheerleading; Var Trk; Hon Roll; NHS.

CONJELKO, BRIAN J; Richland SR HS; Johnstown, PA; (Y); 1/158; Am Leg Boys St; Math Clb; Rep Stu Cncl; Var Bsktbl; Var Ftbl; Var Trk; Cit Awd; High Hon Roll; NHS; Acadmc All Am Awd 86; Engrng.

CONKLIN, ANISSA; E L Meyers HS; Wilkes-Barre, PA; (S); Church Yth Grp; Hosp Aide; Key Clb; Speech Tm; Band; Jazz Band; Orch; Vllybl; NHS; Dist Band; Dist Orch; Regnl Band; W Chester U; Music Ed.

CONKLIN, CICILY; Lock Haven SR HS; Castanea, PA; (Y); Drill Tm; Hon Roll; NEDT Awd; Wmspt Area Cmnty Coll; Exec Sec.

CONKLIN JR, CLYDE; Riverview SR HS; Oakmont, PA; (Y); 17/93; French Clb; Office Aide; Off Jr Cls; Stu Cncl; High Hon Roll; Hon Roll; Jsph W Kelly Schlrshp 86; PA ST U; Aerospc.

CONKLIN, TIM; Salisbury HS; Allentown, PA; (Y); 23/138; Church Yth Grp; Debate Tm; Drama Clb; Key Clb; School Musical; School Play; Nwsp Rptr; Hon Roll; Ntl Merit SF; Rep Soph Cls; Hopwood Summr Scholar Pgm 86; Engl.

CONLAN, KATHY; Abington HS; Elkins Park, PA; (Y); 217/535; German Clb; Lit Mag; Sftbl; PA ST; Bus Mgmt.

CONLEY, DAVID; West Mifflin Area HS; West Mifflin, PA; (Y); Var Socr; JV Wrstlng; High Hon Roll; Hon Roll; Jr NHS; NHS; Acdmc Curriculum Enrchmnt Gftd Pgm; Mech Engrng.

CONLEY, DIANE; Conneaut Valley HS; Springboro, PA; (Y); 10/70; Pres Pep Clb; Sec Spanish Clb; Band; Pres Stu Cncl; Cheerleading; DAR Awd; NHS; Church Yth Grp; Drama Clb; Exploring; Spnsh Awd 86; Prsdntl Schlrshp 86; Mst Outstndng Stu 86; Mercyhurst Coll; Early Chldhd.

CONLEY, JAMES; Hamburg Area HS; Hamburg, PA; (Y); VP Latin Clb; Spanish Clb; Var L Socr; Var L Tennis; Hon Roll; NHS; Acad Awd In Gmtry 85; Acad Awd In Physcs 86; Engrng.

CONLEY, JULIA D; Coatesville Area HS; Parkesburg, PA; (Y); 65/510; French Clb; Ski Clb; Band; Mrchg Band; High Hon Roll; Hon Roll; Penn ST U; Nrsng.

CONLEY, TIMOTHY J; Mercyhurst Prep; Erie, PA; (Y); 28/168; Q&S; Stage Crew; Ed Nwsp Ed-Chief; Nwsp Rptr; Lit Mag; Hon Roll; NHS; Arts Recog Tlnt Srch 85; Gannon U.

CONN, AMY; Connellsville Area SR HS; Connellsville, PA; (Y); Church Yth Grp; Church Choir; Concert Band; Mrchg Band; School Musical; Symp Band; Yrbk Stf; French Hon Soc; High Hon Roll; NHS; Slippery Rock U; Dpcl Edu.

CONN, GREG; Southmoreland HS; Scottdale, PA; (Y); 15/230; Church Yth Grp; German Clb; Math Clb; Ski Clb; Im JV Bsktbl; Im Score Keeper; JV Var Socr; Im Sftbl; Im Tennis; Im Vllybl; German Natl Hon Soc 85; Penn ST; Elec Engr.

CONNELL, JOEL; Connellsville Area HS; Dunbar, PA; (Y); Chorus; Var L Bsbl; Hon Roll; Physcl Ftnss Awd.

CONNELL, JOHN; North Allegheny SR HS; Wexford, PA; (Y); 110/600; Church Yth Grp; Speech Tm; Teachers Aide; Rep Frsh Cls; Rep Soph Cls; Var Ftbl; Var Wt Lftg; Cert Of Excllnc Amer Govt 86; PA ST; Pre-Law.

CONNELL, LAURA; Villa Maria Acad; Exton, PA; (Y); 15/105; Cmnty Wkr; GAA; Latin Clb; Nwsp Sprt Ed; Lit Mag; Var L Bsktbl; High Hon Roll; Ntl Merit Ltr; Debate Tm; Girl Scts; Pegasus Awd PA Peotry Soc Hrnbl Mntn 86; Latin Awd 85; Cum Laude Awd Natl Latin Exam 86; Duke U; Marine Bio.

CONNELLAN, SIOBHAN; Trinity HS; Mechanicsburg, PA; (Y); Pep Clb; Spanish Clb; Chorus; School Musical; Stage Crew; Nwsp Rptr; Yrbk Stf; Pres Stu Cncl; Bsktbl; Cheerleading; Rifle Line 85; Bus Mgmt.

CONNELLY, SHARON; Penn-Trafford HS; Trafford, PA; (Y); Church Yth Grp; Drama Clb; JCL; Latin Clb; Acpl Chr; Chorus; Church Choir; Jazz Band; School Musical; School Play; Active Lcl Theater Wrk 85-86; Plays & Sings Popular Dance & Show Band 83-86; Music.

CONNELLY, STEPHANIE; Bald Eagle Area HS; Howard, PA; (S); 1/200; Model UN; Chorus; Yrbk Stf; Sec Frsh Cls; Sec Soph Cls; Rep Stu Cncl; Var Bsktbl; Tennis; Capt Twrlr; High Hon Roll.

CONNELLY, SUSAN; Saint Basil Acad; Philadelphia, PA; (Y); Chrmn Church Yth Grp; GAA; Pres Service Clb; Soroptimist; Spanish Clb; Varsity Clb; Nwsp Rptr; Var Fld Hcky; Cit Awd; Egl Crss Awd 86; Terry Mchugh Awd 86; Maria Zielinski Awd 86; Temple U.

CONNELLY, TIMOTHY P; West Mifflin Area HS; W Mifflin, PA; (Y); 32/215; Orch; Hon Roll; NHS; Music.

CONNER, DANIELLE; Archbishop Kennedy HS; Philadelphia, PA; (Y); Camera Clb; Hosp Aide; Teachers Aide; Nwsp Phtg; Yrbk Phtg; US Air Force; Traffic Cntrlr.

CONNER, DAWN; Bellwood-Antis HS; Tyrone, PA; (Y); #75 In Class; Church Yth Grp; JA; Key Clb; VICA; Band; Chorus; Concert Band; Mrchg Band; Ltr Band; Mrchndsng.

CONNER, KATHLEEN J; Morrisville HS; Morrisville, PA; (Y); 2/98; Concert Band; Mrchg Band; Yrbk Ed-Chief; Pres Soph Cls; Var Fld Hcky; Var Sftbl; Pres NHS; Pres Schlr; Rotary Awd; Band Bstrs Awd 86; Outstndng Advncd Bio Stu 86; CO ST U; Vet.

CONNER, KIRSTEN; Fairview HS; Fairview, PA; (Y); French Clb; Ski Clb; Varsity Clb; Nwsp Rptr; Nwsp Stf; Var Crs Cntry; Var Swmmng; Var Trk; Hon Roll; NHS; Winner YMCA Wmns 10k 85; Jr Achvt Awd 85; Advertsng.

CONNER, MICHELLE A; Dallastown Area HS; Dallastown, PA; (Y); 28/334; Church Yth Grp; Band; Chorus; Church Choir; Concert Band; Mrchg Band; School Musical; School Play; Variety Show; High Hon Roll; Elizabethtown Coll; Nrs.

CONNOLLY, COLLEEN; Bethel Park HS; Bethel Pk, PA; (Y); FHA; Hon Roll.

CONNOLLY, CURT; Carrick SR HS; Pittsburgh, PA; (Y); Computer Clb; Exploring; Rep Stu Cncl; Im Bowling; Hon Roll; U Of Pittsburgh; Eng.

CONNOLLY, EILEEN P; Wyoming Valley West HS; Kingston, PA; (Y); 37/440; Sec Key Clb; Chorus; Nwsp Stf; Yrbk Stf; Trs Stu Cncl; L Swmmng; L Trk; Cit Awd; Hon Roll; NHS; ST Qlfr Swmmng 84-86; Acctg.

CONNOLLY, MAUREEN; Bethel Park HS; Bethel Park, PA; (Y); FHA; Powder Puff Ftbl; High Hon Roll; NHS.

CONNOR, BLAINE; Hempfield HS; E Petersburg, PA; (Y); Band; Chorus; Concert Band; Jazz Band; Mrchg Band; School Musical; Vet Med.

CONNOR, CAROL ANN; Susquehanna Township HS; Harrisburg, PA; (Y); AFS; Am Leg Aux Girls St; 4-H; Key Clb; Model UN; Ski Clb; Mrchg Band; VP Frsh Cls; Pres Soph Cls; Pres Jr Cls; Outstndg Acdmc Achvr 86; Supreme Court Judge Keystone Girls ST 86; Bloomsburg Coll Smplr Prg 86; FL A&M; Bus Admin.

CONNOR, CATHERINE M; Tunkhannock Area HS; Tunkhannock, PA; (Y); 28/315; Key Clb; SADD; Yrbk Stf; Off Jr Cls; Off Sr Cls; Cheerleading; Cit Awd; Hon Roll; NHS; Ntl Merit Ltr; Prsdntl Acdmc Ftnss Awd 86; Ntl Merit Prctr & Gmbl Schlrshp Awd 86; Lafayette Coll; Intl Rltns.

CONNOR, DIANE O; E L Meyers HS; Wilkes Barre, PA; (Y); 7/147; Exploring; Pres Key Clb; Chorus; Nwsp Ed-Chief; Yrbk Stf; Stu Cncl; Score Keeper; Kiwanis Awd; NHS; NEDT Awd; Acadmc All Amer 86; Scranton U; Bio.

CONNOR, EILEEN M; Lock Haven SR HS; Lock Haven, PA; (Y); 30/240; VP Service Clb; Sec Spanish Clb; Chorus; Sec Stu Cncl; Var Trs Cheerleading; Trk; Cit Awd; High Hon Roll; NHS; Svc Awd Girls Assoc For Prog & Svc 86; Girl Gvng Mst Svc To Schl 83; Bst FHA Conf Rpt 83; U Of Pitsburgh; Phy Thrpy.

CONNOR, JEFFREY; Montour HS; Coraopolis, PA; (Y); Chorus; Concert Band; Jazz Band; Mrchg Band; School Musical; High Hon Roll; NHS; Music.

CONNOR, KELLY L; Kiski Area HS; Apollo, PA; (Y); Teachers Aide; Color Guard; Yrbk Stf; High Hon Roll; Hon Roll; Mgr Mrchg Band; Acad Ltr 84 & 85; U Pitt Greensburg; Bus Mgmt.

CONNOR, MICHAEL; Sacred Heart HS; Carbondale, PA; (Y); 9/45; Var L Bsbl; Var L Bsktbl; Var Golf; High Hon Roll; Partl Schlrshp 84; Penn ST U; Accntnt.

CONNOR, PHILIP; Devon Prep Schl; Phoenixville, PA; (Y); Dance Clb; Stage Crew; Nwsp Ed-Chief; Var L Bsbl; Camera Clb; Computer Clb; Drama Clb; Mathletes; Math Clb; Newspr Awd 86; Attendance Awd 84; PA ST; Communications.

CONNOR, TRACY; Cedar Crest HS; Myerstown, PA; (Y); Church Yth Grp; Trs FNA; FTA; Pep Clb; Spanish Clb; Capt Swmmng; Hon Roll; NHS; Elem Educ.

CONNORS, JOSEPH PATRICK; Salisbury HS; Allentown, PA; (Y); Computer Clb; VP Exploring; Im Bsbl; Im Bsktbl; High Hon Roll; Hon Roll; Prfct Atten Awd; Bus.

CONNORS, KELLYANNE; St Hubert Cath HS For Girls; Philadelphia, PA; (Y); 125/367; Cmnty Wkr; French Clb; Girl Scts; Hosp Aide; Model UN; Office Aide; SADD; Hon Roll; World Affrs Clb Commmrtv Awd; Criminal Just.

CONNORS, KEN; Cardinal Ohara HS; Havertown, PA; (Y); 92/784; Var L Bsbl; Capt Bsktbl; Vllybl; Hon Roll; Prfct Atten Awd; Drexel U; Cmmrc Engrng.

CONNORS, LISA; Southmoreland SR HS; Scottdale, PA; (Y); 4-H; Office Aide; Pep Clb; Spanish Clb; Band; Concert Band; Mrchg Band; 4-H Awd; Spanish NHS; Mrchng Band-Mst Imprvd 84-85; Prfct Attndnc Awd-Mrchng Band 84-85; Medcl Fld.

CONOSHENTI, JOSEPH; Bishop Kenrick HS; Norristown, PA; (Y); 7/221; Hon Roll; NHS; Prfct Atten Awd; Optimist Oratorical Awd 85.

CONQUER, KAREN; Sheffield Area JR SR HS; Sheffield, PA; (Y); 4/94; FBLA; Office Aide; Pep Clb; SADD; Varsity Clb; Chorus; Stage Crew; Variety Show; Nwsp Ed-Chief; Sec Soph Cls; Hi-Avg Bus Awd 86; Dubois Bus Coll; Exec Sec.

CONRAD, ELIZABETH; Blacklick Valley HS; Nanty-Glo, PA; (S); Art Clb; Church Yth Grp; Hosp Aide; Ski Clb; Varsity Clb; Variety Show; JV Var Cheerleading; Trk; Hon Roll; NHS; Let In Track 85; U Of Pittsburg; Fshn Mrchdsng.

CONRAD, ERIK J; Stroudsburg HS; Stroudsburg, PA; (Y); Spanish Clb; Varsity Clb; Var Capt Bsbl; Var Bsktbl; Var Capt Ftbl; Wt Lftg; High Hon Roll; NHS; U Of PA.

CONRAD, JENNIFER; Cumberland Valley HS; New Kingstown, PA; (Y); 227/551; Camera Clb; Pres Church Yth Grp; Sec German Clb; Girl Scts; Red Cross Aide; Nwsp Phtg; Nwsp Stf; Natl Art Hnr Soc.

CONRAD, SANDRA; Tyrone Area HS; Tyrone, PA; (Y); Church Yth Grp; French Clb; FBLA; Chorus; Hon Roll; Bus Awd 86.

CONRAD, SUSAN; Bishop Carroll HS; Ashville, PA; (S); 25/110; Pep Clb; Drill Tm; Yrbk Phtg; Ed Yrbk Stf; Rep Jr Cls; Stat Bsktbl.

CONRAD, TERRI; Altoona Area HS; Altoona, PA; (Y); Computer Clb; Spanish Clb; Chorus; Penn ST U; Accntng.

CONROY, JENNIFER; Highlands SR HS; Tarentum, PA; (Y); Office Aide; Yrbk Stf; Off Frsh Cls; Off Soph Cls; Off Jr Cls; Cheerleading; Gym; Jr NHS; NHS; Rtry Yth Ldrshp Awd 85-86; Bus Adm.

CONROY, MARY ELLEN; St Hubert HS; Philadelphia, PA; (Y); Cmnty Wkr; Dance Clb; Hosp Aide; Office Aide; Red Cross Aide; Science Clb; Spanish Clb; Orch; School Musical; Lit Mag; Hghst Avg Fds & Clthg 83; Danc Clb Awd 84; Drexel U; Bus Adm.

CONROY, ROBERT; Devon Prep; Malvern, PA; (Y); 4/47; Computer Clb; Math Tm; Var L Crs Cntry; JV Socr; Capt Var Trk; High Hon Roll; NHS; Prfct Atten Awd; Bsktbl; Frnch Bk Awd; Cmmnty Actn Prog; Elec Engrng.

CONSENZA, LORRIE; Wyoming Area SR HS; W Pittston, PA; (Y); French Clb; Chorus; Natl Piano Plyng Audtns 82-84; Pre-Schl Ed.

CONSIDINE, ELLEN; Villa Maria Acad; Erie, PA; (Y); Church Yth Grp; Ski Clb; Golf; NHS; Racquetball Clb VP; Teenage Action Clb; Accntng.

CONSIGLIO, JACKIE; Bishop Guilfoyle HS; Altoona, PA; (S); 20/129; Science Clb; Ski Clb; Yrbk Stf; Vllybl; Hon Roll; Rep Frsh Cls; Rep Soph Cls; Rep Stu Cncl.

CONSIGLIO, KELLIE L; Hollidaysburg Area HS; Hollidaysburg, PA; (Y); Spanish Clb; Varsity Clb; Lit Mag; Pres Frsh Cls; VP Soph Cls; VP Jr Cls; Var L Bsktbl; Sftbl; Hon Roll; NHS; Natl Merit Sci Ltr; Spnsh Awd; Coaches Awd Bsktbl.

CONSIGLIO, LISA; West Mifflin Area HS; Pittsburgh, PA; (Y); Dance Clb; Key Clb; Flag Corp; Nwsp Stf; Yrbk Stf; Stu Cncl; Wt Lftg; Hon Roll; NHS; Girl Scts; Pre Advncd Plcmnt 85-86; U Pittsburgh; Ther.

CONSTABLE, ANNETTE L; Warren Area HS; Warren, PA; (Y); 4/298; Pres French Clb; Office Aide; Varsity Clb; Stu Cncl; L Trk; High Hon Roll; NHS; Pres Schlr; Rotary Awd; Zonta Schlrshp 86; Gannon U; Acctg.

CONSTABLE, FRANCINE M; Bishop O Hara HS; Dunmore, PA; (Y); Ski Clb; Spanish Clb; Chorus; Stage Crew; Yrbk Stf; High Hon Roll; Ntl Merit Ltr; PA ST Sktng Chmpn Dance 83; Estrn Rgnl Dance Chmpn 85.

CONSTANTINE, LISA ANN; Arbp Ryan HS For Girls; Philadelphia, PA; (Y); 87/492; Am Leg Aux Girls St; Cmnty Wkr; JA; Q&S; Service Clb; Spanish Clb; Nwsp Stf; Pres Stu Cncl; Hon Roll; Rep Frsh Cls; Amer Lgn Aux Schlrshp Freedoms Fndtn 85-86; Hotel Mgt.

CONSTANTINI, PAUL; Scranton Central HS; Scranton, PA; (Y); Church Yth Grp; Ski Clb; JV Bsbl; Lackawanna JC.

CONSTANTINO, MICHAEL; Wyoming Area HS; W Pittston, PA; (Y); Art Clb; Church Yth Grp; Nwsp Stf; Im Bowling; JETS Awd; Johnson Tech; Drftng.

CONSTANTINO, TODD; Shady Side Acad; Pittsburgh, PA; (Y); Chess Clb; Varsity Clb; Jazz Band; Orch; Variety Show; Var L Ftbl; Var L Trk; Im Wt Lftg; Hon Roll; Mst Imprvd Offnsv Lnmn Awd 85; GA Washington U; Chem Med.

CONTARDI, JOSEPH; Scranton Techincal HS; Scranton, PA; (Y); Boy Scts; Ski Clb; VICA; Band; Concert Band; Mrchg Band; Orch; Wt Lftg; Cit Awd; Hon Roll; Outstndng Achvt SR Awd 86; Penn ST; Elec Techn.

CONTE, MARIA; Bishop Kenrick HS; Norristown, PA; (Y); 35/292; Civic Clb; Cmnty Wkr; Dance Clb; Ski Clb; Spanish Clb; Hon Roll; Nrsng.

CONTE, MELISSA; Pennsbury HS; Morrisville, PA; (Y); French Clb; Concert Band; Tennis; Hon Roll; U Of Delaware; Jrnlsm.

CONTE, STACY; St Paul Cathedral HS; Pittsburgh, PA; (S); 8/62; Church Yth Grp; FBLA; Ski Clb; Yrbk Bus Mgr; Trs Jr Cls; Pres Stu Cncl; JV Var Bsktbl; Diving; Gym; Sftbl; IN U Of PA; Accntng.

CONTI, EMIDIO; Moniteau JR SR HS; Boyers, PA; (Y); 1/155; Spanish Clb; Band; Concert Band; Jazz Band; Mrchg Band; Pep Band; School Play; VP Soph Cls; Pres Jr Cls; Sec Stu Cncl; Bnd Mst Vlbl Sctn Ldr 86; Good Ctznshp Awd 84; Slippery Rock U; Cmmnctns.

CONVERSE, NOELLE; Williamsport Area HS; Williamsport, PA; (S); 6/600; Church Yth Grp; Key Clb; VP Ski Clb; Chorus; School Musical; Yrbk Rptr; Yrbk Stf; Capt Cheerleading; High Hon Roll; NHS; Bio.

CONWAY, CHARLES; Grove City HS; Grove City, PA; (Y); 46/213; Boy Scts; Pres Church Yth Grp; FBLA; Hosp Aide; Varsity Clb; Band; School Play; Stu Cncl; Crs Cntry; Trk; Floyd Myers Bible Scholar Awd 86; Taccoa Falls; Pastor.

CONWAY, NOEL; Dover Area HS; Dover, PA; (Y); 20/285; Im Bsbl; JV Bsktbl; High Hon Roll; Hon Roll; NHS; Semnr 84-86; Top Sls Rep For Clss Of 87 85; Penn ST; Math Ed.

CONWAY, WILLIAM; Lakeland JR-SR HS; Jermyn, PA; (Y); 1/148; Capt Scholastic Bowl; SADD; Stu Cncl; Ftbl; Capt Trk; Bausch & Lomb Sci Awd; Dnfth Awd; Pres NHS; Val; High Hnr Roll 82-86; Soc Dstngshd Amer H S Stu 84; William Forzier Mem Scholar 86; GMI; Elec Engrng.

COOCH, JANENE; Freedom HS; Bethlehem, PA; (Y); 64/456; Intnl Clb; Spanish Clb; Chorus; School Musical; Coach Actv; Crs Cntry; Var L Swmmng; Hon Roll.

COOK, AMY S; Waynesboro Area SR HS; Waynesboro, PA; (Y); 49/392; Church Yth Grp; Church Choir; Rep Stu Cncl; Cit Awd; Hon Roll; Ctzn Of Mnth 84-85; Phrmcy.

COOK, ANDREA; Annville-Cleona HS; Annville, PA; (S); 1/105; Sec Church Yth Grp; Trs French Clb; Hosp Aide; SADD; Chorus; Concert Band; Mrchg Band; Nwsp Rptr; Lit Mag; NHS; Ntl Ed Dvlpmnt Awd 84; Soc Dstngshd Amer Stds 85; Achvt Acad 85.

COOK, CAROL; Technical HS; Scranton, PA; (S); 30/323; Cmnty Wkr; FBLA; Hosp Aide; Letterman Clb; Q&S; Color Guard; Nwsp Stf; Yrbk Stf; Bsktbl; Cheerleading; Bus.

COOK, CATHERINE; Wyalusing Valley HS; Laceyville, PA; (Y); 38/152; FBLA; Spanish Clb; Band; Chorus; School Musical; Pres Sr Cls; Off Stu Cncl; Capt Cheerleading; Var Vllybl; NHS; 3rd Rnnr Up PA ST Laurel Festvl 86; Creatv & Perfrmng Arts Awd Jr Miss 85; Hmcmng Queen 85; Bloomsburg U; Bus Adm.

COOK, CURT; Deer Lakes JR SR HS; Harwick, PA; (Y); Exploring; Spanish Clb; Elctrcl Engrng.

COOK, DAWNA; Hershey SR HS; Hershey, PA; (Y); Church Yth Grp; English Clb; Library Aide; Office Aide; Hon Roll; Slvr Mdl Mid-MI Bus Cntst 84; Nwspaper Carrier Of Yr 84; Brigham Young U.

COOK, DOEDY; Trinity HS; Washington, PA; (Y); 48/365; Cmnty Wkr; Debate Tm; JA; Pep Clb; Speech Tm; Band; Concert Band; Mrchg Band; Pep Band; High Hon Roll; Chem Engrng.

COOK, ELLEN; Reynolds HS; Greenville, PA; (Y); 26/147; Church Yth Grp; Spanish Clb; Gen Guards 83; Bronz Palm 86; ATES Tech Schl; Med Ofc Asst.

COOK, KATHY; Trinity HS; Camp Hill, PA; (Y); Cmnty Wkr; Pep Clb; Spanish Clb; Chorus; Mrchg Band; Spn.

COOK, KATRINA; Annville-Cleona HS; Annville, PA; (S); 7/125; Church Yth Grp; Pres French Clb; Hosp Aide; Madrigals; Mrchg Band; School Musical; Ed Lit Mag; NHS; Acpl Chr; Rotary Grl Of Mnth 85; Rotary Ldrshp Conf 85; Phy Thrpy.

COOK, KELLY; Carlynton HS; Carnegie, PA; (Y); 14/278; Dance Clb; Band; Drill Tm; Nwsp Stf; Yrbk Stf; Stu Cncl; Pom Pon; High Hon Roll; Hon Roll; Pres Schlr; Washington & Jefferson; Bio.

COOK, KEVIN; East Pennsboro HS; Enola, PA; (Y); 21/201; Church Yth Grp; Computer Clb; German Clb; VICA; Cheerleading; Diving; Socr; High Hon Roll; NHS; Stu Of Qrtr Geomtry & Data Proc 85-86; Data Processing.

COOK, KIMBERLEY C; Lampeter-Strasburg HS; Lancaster, PA; (Y); 5/139; Am Leg Aux Girls St; Varsity Clb; Color Guard; Yrbk Ed-Chief; Var Fld Hcky; Capt Var Trk; High Hon Roll; Hon Roll; NHS; U Of VA; Engrg.

COOK, LAURA; Rocky Grove HS; Oil City, PA; (Y); 4/90; Library Aide; Chorus; Rep Sr Cls; High Hon Roll; Hon Roll; NHS; Venango Cnty Voc Tech Schl Dir Awd 86; Outstndng Achvt Awd Drftng 86; Comp Drftsmn.

COOK, LORI; Montgomery Area HS; Montgomery, PA; (Y); 45/63; Dance Clb; FBLA; FHA; Yrbk Phtg; Yrbk Stf; Stu Cncl; JV Var Cheerleading; Gym; JV Var Trk; Hon Roll; Most Spirit Chrldr Awd 84-85; ; Bus Mgt.

COOK, LORI; W Greene Middle-SR HS; Wind Ridge, PA; (S); Sec Church Yth Grp; Library Aide; Church Choir; High Hon Roll; 3 Hghst In Cls 84-85; 3rd Pl Oratry Cont 83-84; Exec Sec.

COOK, MARISUE; Beaver Area HS; Beaver, PA; (Y); 1/185; Dance Clb; Sec Trs FCA; Ski Clb; Yrbk Ed-Chief; Var L Cheerleading; Powder Puff Ftbl; Stat Trk; Trs NHS; HOBY Ldrshp Awd; Chem I Hgh Exam Awd; Engrng.

COOK, ROSALYN; Bellevernon Area HS; Belle Vernon, PA; (Y); 35/276; Art Clb; Camp Fr Inc; VICA; Chorus; Stage Crew; Trs Frsh Cls; Stu Cncl; High Hon Roll; Hon Roll; Kiwanis Awd; Won VICA Hairstyle Comp 1st Pl 86; VICA Stu Mnth April 86; Advncd Hair Styling Schlrshp 86; Pittsburgh Bty Acad; Hairstylng.

COOK, THERESA M; Northern HS; Dillsburg, PA; (Y); 4/200; Pres Church Yth Grp; VP Band; Church Choir; Concert Band; Mrchg Band; Rep Sr Cls; Var Capt Sftbl; High Hon Roll; Lion Awd; NHS; Pres Acadmc Ftns Awd 85-86; Soc Studies Awd 85-86; West Chester U; RN.

COOK, TOM; G A R HS; Wilkes Barre, PA; (Y); Camera Clb; German Clb; Ski Clb; Chorus; Yrbk Stf; Var L Ftbl; Var L Wrstlng; Hon Roll; Hnr Rll Crtfct; Penn ST; Pre-Law.

COOK, WENDY; Baldwin HS; Pittsburgh, PA; (Y); 5/531; Art Clb; Cmnty Wkr; Exploring; Hosp Aide; Math Clb; Office Aide; Yrbk Stf; Mgr(s); Score Keeper; Stat Sftbl; 100 Hr Candystriper Pin 84; N Amer Phillips Corp Schlrshp 86; Juniata Coll; Math.

COOKE, FRANCINE; Nazareth Acad; Philadelphia, PA; (Y); 9/121; Church Yth Grp; French Clb; Hosp Aide; Pep Clb; Red Cross Aide; Service Clb; Lit Mag; Trs Soph Cls; High Hon Roll; Hon Roll; Villanova; Pre-Med.

COOLBAUGH, CHRISTINE; Wyoming Area HS; Harding, PA; (Y); Art Clb; Church Yth Grp; French Clb; Key Clb; Stat Mgr(s); JV Var Sftbl; Radiographic Tech.

COOLEY, LISA D; Biglerville HS; Aspers, PA; (Y); 7/78; Trs 4-H; Library Aide; Red Cross Aide; Jr NHS; NHS; Pres Schlr; Schl Board Awd 86; Nrsng.

COOLIDGE, KRISTINE; S Williamsport Area SR HS; S Williamsport, PA; (Y); Sec Key Clb; Band; Nwsp Stf; Yrbk Stf; JV Bsktbl; Var L Tennis; Var L Trk; Hon Roll; NHS.

COON, MIKE; Punxsutawney HS; Smicksburg, PA; (Y); Varsity Clb; Var L Bsbl; Var L Golf.

COONEY, KEVIN; Penn Hills SR HS; Pittsburgh, PA; (Y); AFS; Boy Scts; Church Yth Grp; Spanish Clb; Stu Cncl; Bsbl; Vllybl; Hon Roll; Energy Sci.

COOPER, ADAM M; Saint Josephs Preparatory Schl; Philadelphia, PA; (Y); 1/245; Mathletes; Office Aide; Sec Spanish Clb; Band; Sec Concert Band; Pep Band; Nwsp Ed-Chief; Trk; High Hon Roll; Ntl Merit Ltr; Ntl Wnnr-AATF Ntl Frnch Cntst 84-85; Blue Rbbn-Ntl Greek Exam 84-85; Summa Cum Laude-Ntl Latin Exam; Comp Sci.

COOPER, AMANDA L; North Allegheny SR HS; Wexford, PA; (Y); Girl Scts; Quiz Bowl; Scholastic Bowl; VP Acpl Chr; Concert Band; School Musical; School Play; Lit Mag; Vllybl; Bethany Coll Acad Ldrshp Schlrshp Awd 86; Bethany Coll Deans Schlr 86; Bethany Coll; Bio.

COOPER, ARTHUR; Faith Christian Schl; Blairstown, NJ; (Y); 2/4; Chess Clb; Church Yth Grp; Computer Clb; Spanish Clb; Stage Crew; Yrbk Stf; Pres Frsh Cls; Off Soph Cls; Pres Jr Cls; Hon Roll; Physcs Awd 86; Blble Awd 86; Data Proc Awd 86; Comp Scncs.

COOPER, CATHRYN; North Allegheny SR HS; Wexford, PA; (Y); 77/642; Church Yth Grp; Cmnty Wkr; Exploring; Hosp Aide; Band; Mrchg Band; Pep Band; Symp Band; Hon Roll; NHS; Cert Of Merit Outstndng Achvt Spnsh I 83-84; Cert Of Achvt Mrchng Band 84-85; Liberal Arts Coll; Spnsh.

COOPER, CATHY; Harrisburg HS; Harrisburg, PA; (S); 17/397; Dance Clb; Rep Model UN; Pep Clb; Capt Cheerleading; French Hon Soc; High Hon Roll; NHS; Hmcmg Qn 83-85; 2nd Pl Sci Fair Wnnr 84; Black Hstry Achvt Awd Hnrs 83; U Of Pittsburgh; Psych.

COOPER, CONN; Halifax Area HS; Halifax, PA; (Y); Cmnty Wkr; 4-H; FHA; Varsity Clb; Band; Concert Band; Mrchg Band; School Play; Stage Crew; Rep Frsh Cls; Env Law.

COOPER, DAWN; Lewistown Area HS; Lewistown, PA; (Y); AFS; French Clb; Key Clb; Pep Clb; Ski Clb; Yrbk Stf; High Hon Roll; Hon Roll; Law.

COOPER, DEANNA; Elkland Area HS; Elkland, PA; (Y); Church Yth Grp; Drama Clb; Girl Scts; SADD; Band; Chorus; Sec Soph Cls; Im Bsktbl; Im Vllybl; Drama Awd 85-86; Drama Treas 85-86; EYEA 83-85; Mansfield U; Psych.

COOPER, DI ANNA; Southmoreland HS; Scottdale, PA; (Y); 43/240; Hosp Aide; Office Aide; Rep Pep Clb; Ski Clb; Spanish Clb; Chorus; School Musical; JV Powder Puff Ftbl; Im Socr; Spanish NHS; Asst Paino Accompnst 83-84; Eastern Mennonite Coll; Nrsng.

COOPER, GREGORY; Hampton HS; Allison Pk, PA; (Y); Band; Concert Band; Mrchg Band; Symp Band; Hon Roll; Archry 83; Purdue U; Nvl Avtn.

COOPER, HOPE; Upper Dauphin Area HS; Elizabethville, PA; (Y); 51/112; Varsity Clb; Concert Band; Mrchg Band; Rep Frsh Cls; Pres Soph Cls; Pres Jr Cls; Rep Stu Cncl; Var L Bsktbl; Var L Twrlr; Hon Roll; Yth Forum 86-87; Drnk Drvg TV Cmmrcl WGAL Chnnl 8 Nws 86; Southeastern Acad; Arln.

COOPER, JANE; Tunkhannock Area HS; Mehoopany, PA; (S); 5/300; Church Yth Grp; Cmnty Wkr; Pres 4-H; Hosp Aide; VP JA; Key Clb; Band; Church Choir; Cit Awd; NHS; Outstndng Yng Bus Womn Yr 85; 4-H Demonstrtn Blue Rbbn 84; Penn ST; Engrng.

COOPER, KIM; Chambersburg Area SR HS; Chambersburg, PA; (Y); Key Clb; Pep Clb; Ski Clb; Spanish Clb; Rep Frsh Cls; Rep Soph Cls; Rep Jr Cls; Rep Stu Cncl; Cheerleading; Crs Cntry; Hagerstown JC; Bus Mgnt.

COOPER, LAUREN; Freeport Area SR HS; Sarver, PA; (Y); Trs Church Yth Grp; FBLA; Hosp Aide; Yrbk Stf; JV Stat Ftbl; Mgr(s); Score Keeper; Stat Sftbl; Hon Roll; Bus.

COOPER, LINDA; Harborcreek HS; Erie, PA; (Y); 69/228; Trs AFS; Teachers Aide; Yrbk Stf; Var L Trk; Var L Vllybl; Penn ST U.

COOPER, LISA; Ford City HS; Ford City, PA; (Y); 6/155; Chorus; School Musical; Rep Frsh Cls; Rep Soph Cls; Rep Sr Cls; Rep Stu Cncl; Stat Bsktbl; High Hon Roll; Sec NHS; Bus Awd Excllnce Acctng 86; Clarion U; Acctng.

COOPER, MARISSA; Churchill HS; Pittsburgh, PA; (Y); 40/188; AFS; French Clb; Hosp Aide; Key Clb; Sec Temple Yth Grp; Var Tennis; Hon Roll; Cert Achvt Vol Presby U Hosp 84; Pre-Med.

COOPER, MELISSA; Wyoming Valley West HS; Kingston, PA; (Y); Church Yth Grp; French Clb; FHA; Key Clb; Var Capt Fld Hcky; Var Sftbl; Vllybl; Cit Awd; High Hon Roll; Hon Roll; Physical Therapy.

COOPER, MISSI; Twin Valley HS; Honey Brook, PA; (Y); 7/135; Pres Sec 4-H; Spanish Clb; Varsity Clb; Rep Stu Cncl; JV Bsktbl; Im Diving; Var L Fld Hcky; Var L Lcrss; High Hon Roll; Hon Roll; MVP La Crosse 86; Acdmc Achvt Awd 86; Area II JR Traing Champ Eqstrn Evnt 84; Sci.

COOPER, NICOLE; Huntingdon Area HS; Huntingdon, PA; (Y); 20/270; Art Clb; Pres Church Yth Grp; Key Clb; SADD; Concert Band; Rep Soph Cls; Rep Jr Cls; JV Trk; L Capt Vllybl; Hon Roll; Wstmnstr; Chem.

COOPER, RICHARD; Hampton HS; Gibsonia, PA; (Y); 41/234; Political Wkr; SADD; Mrchg Band; Yrbk Phtg; Rep Frsh Cls; VP Soph Cls; Rep Jr Cls; Rep Sr Cls; Rep Stu Cncl; Hon Roll; Prod Assembly Shws 85-86; Pres Acadmc Ftns Awd 86; Merit Cert Voice Of Demcrcy 86; Mary Washington Clg; Polic Sci.

COOPER, ROBYN J; Ferndale Area HS; Johnstown, PA; (Y); 7/57; Church Yth Grp; VP GAA; Leo Clb; NFL; Nwsp Ed-Chief; Co-Capt Cheerleading; NHS; PA Kyston Grls ST 85; JR Miss Fnlst; Frndl Areas Otstndng Speaker Awd; IN U; Speech.

COOPER, SCOTT; Central York SR HS; York, PA; (Y); Church Yth Grp; Band; Chorus; Church Choir; Concert Band; Jazz Band; Mrchg Band; School Musical; Swing Chorus; Symp Band; Elem Educ.

COOPER, STACY; Abington Heights HS; Waverly, PA; (Y); Sec JA; Ski Clb; Chorus; Var Cheerleading; Var Pom Pon; Busnss.

COOPER, STEPHANIE; Hatboro-Horsham HS; Ambler, PA; (Y); 70/289; Key Clb; Model UN; Ski Clb; Color Guard; Stage Crew; Rep Frsh Cls; Rep Soph Cls; Rep Jr Cls.

COOPERMAN, CAMIE; Phila High For Creative & Pref Arts; Philadelphia, PA; (S); 8/140; Dance Clb; Drama Clb; Band; Concert Band; Orch; School Musical; School Play; Variety Show; Off Jr Cls; High Hon Roll; Danc.

COOPIE, JENNIFER; Steel Valley HS; Munhall, PA; (Y); #38 In Class; Cmnty Wkr; Hosp Aide; SADD; Nwsp Rptr; Nwsp Stf; Var Capt Tennis; Hon Roll; NHS; U Pittsburgh; Psych.

COOVER, ROBERT; Northern York HS; Dillsburg, PA; (Y); 3/200; Camera Clb; Im Vllybl; Im Wt Lftg; High Hon Roll; Indstrl Arts Awd SR Awd 86; Penn ST U; Bus Mgmt.

COPE, CARL; Louis E Dieruff HS; Allentown, PA; (Y); 14/327; Capt Scholastic Bowl; Science Clb; Nwsp Rptr; Var Golf; Var L Tennis; Hon Roll; Jr NHS; NHS; Schl Dist Spellng Bee Rnnr Up 83-84; Spellng Bee Champ 85-86; Mock Trial Tm ST SF 85-86; PA ST U; Radio Brdcstng.

COPE, JOHN; Pennsbury HS; Morrisville, PA; (Y); 22/712; French Clb; Yrbk Stf; Lit Mag; Im Vllybl; Hon Roll; NHS; Carnegie-Mellon U; Elec Engrng.

COPE, KAREN; Manheim Central HS; Manheim, PA; (Y); Church Yth Grp; Cheerleading; Powder Puff Ftbl; Trk; Hon Roll; Pres Phys Fit Awd 85-86; Med.

COPE, PAUL; Northern York HS; Dillsburg, PA; (Y); 1/209; Church Yth Grp; French Clb; Bsktbl; Tennis; High Hon Roll; Pres NHS; Ntl Merit SF; Rotary Awd; Comm.

COPE, RICHARD; Connellsville SR HS; Connellsville, PA; (Y); Stage Crew; Var Ftbl; Socr; Wt Lftg; PA ST; Industrl Engr.

COPELAND, MARION; Yough SR HS; W Newton, PA; (Y); 90/265; Band; Chorus; Church Choir; Concert Band; Jazz Band; Mrchg Band; Pep Band; School Play; Symp Band; Girl Scts; Psychlgy.

COPELAND, RICHARD; Pottstown SR HS; Pottstown, PA; (S); JA; Var Bsbl; High Hon Roll; Hon Roll; Prfct Atten Awd; Pennco Tech; Tech.

COPELAND, TRACEY; Rittenhouse Acad; Philadelphia, PA; (Y); Cmnty Wkr; Teachers Aide; Nwsp Rptr; Nwsp Stf; Cit Awd; High Hon Roll; Hon Roll; Ellis Grant 85-86; Majors Lit Pgm 86; PA ST U; Bus Mgmt.

COPENHAVER, DAWN M; Conrad Weiser JS HS; Robesonia, PA; (Y); 12/139; Spanish Clb; Chorus; School Musical; School Play; Sec Soph Cls; Stu Cncl; JV Var Cheerleading; JV Var Fld Hcky; Mgr(s); Hon Roll; Shorthand Awd 85; Accntng Awd 85; Associated Schools Inc; Travel.

COPENHEAVER JR, BLAINE R; Dover Area HS; Dover, PA; (Y); 25/270; Computer Clb; VP JA; Varsity Clb; Chorus; Ftbl; Var L Swmmng; Hon Roll; NHS; Historian Sons Am Legion 85-86; Engrng.

COPPAWAY, CRAIG; Deer Lakes JR SR HS; Russellton, PA; (Y); Church Yth Grp; Drama Clb; Ski Clb; Concert Band; Drm Mjr(t); Jazz Band; Mrchg Band; School Play; Yrbk Ed-Chief; Var Trk; IN U Of PA; Acctg.

COPPENS, SUZAN; Harry S Truman HS; Croydon, PA; (Y); Girl Scts; Chorus; Hon Roll; Med Sec.

COPPER, LEROY; University City HS; Philadelphia, PA; (Y); Church Yth Grp; Cmnty Wkr; Church Choir; Orch; School Play; Var Crs Cntry; Cit Awd; Ntl Merit Ltr; Prfct Atten Awd; Bible Schlrshp 81; Rose K Zukin Fndtn Excllnc Wrtg 85; Cert Of Rank Karate 86; Beaver College; Pre Law.

COPPER, VICKY; Ligonier Valley SR HS; Latrobe, PA; (Y); 27/152; Bradford; Bus.

COPPINGER, JOHN; Saint Josphes Prep; Philadelphia, PA; (Y); Church Yth Grp; Pep Clb; Rep Jr Cls; Off Stu Cncl; Var JV Bsbl; Im Mgr Bsktbl; Im Mgr Ftbl; Im Mgr Score Keeper; Im Mgr Timer; 21st Wrd SR Bsbl Leag Plyr Wk, Leag All Star 86; 21st Wrd SR Bsktbl Leag Hldr Mst Pnts Game 85-86; Acctg.

COPPOLA, DANIEL; Northeast Catholic HS; Philadelphia, PA; (Y); 61/362; Boys Clb Am; Concert Band; Mrchg Band; Hon Roll; Spansh Excelnce Awd; Accntnt.

CORACE, COLLEEN; Gwynedd Mercy Acad; Gwynedd Valley, PA; (Y); GAA; PAVAS; Service Clb; Teachers Aide; Chorus; School Musical; School Play; Variety Show; Nwsp Stf; Var Bsktbl; Am Miss Pgm 85; Gwynedd Meroys MVP 86; Catholic U Am; Perf Arts.

CORAZZI, MELISSA; North Pocono HS; Lake Ariel, PA; (Y); Church Yth Grp; Band; Concert Band; Mrchg Band; Orch; Rep Frsh Cls; Rep Jr Cls; Rep Stu Cncl; Var L Cheerleading; Spch & Debate Club 3rd Pl Dclmtn 84; Mary Wood Hnrs Band 83.

CORBA, MARYANN; St Maria Goretti HS; Philadelphia, PA; (Y); 124/390; Art Clb; Cmnty Wkr; French Clb; GAA; Nwsp Stf; NY Sch Of Inter Dsgn; Intr Dsg.

CORBETT, DAYNA LEIGH; Karns City Area HS; Chicora, PA; (Y); 2/129; Pep Clb; Concert Band; Pres Mrchg Band; JV Stat Bsktbl; High Hon Roll; NHS; Sal; Pres Acdmc Fit 85-86; PTO Schlstc Ltr 84-86; Robert Morris Coll; Rdlgc Tech.

CORBETT, JIM; Quigley HS; Baden, PA; (Y); Church Yth Grp; Math Clb; JV Bsbl; Var Bsktbl; Var Ftbl; Var Golf; Sftbl; Wt Lftg; High Hon Roll; Hon Roll; Pre-Med.

CORBETT, LORI; Steel Valley HS; Munhall, PA; (Y); #28 In Class; French Clb; Varsity Clb; Wt Lftg; Hon Roll; NHS.

CORBETT, MARY PAT; Mount St Joseph Acad; Phila, PA; (Y); Church Yth Grp; French Clb; Intnl Clb; JA; Office Aide; SADD; Bsktbl; Socr; Vllybl; Acad Schlrshp 86; Acad Sci 1st 2nd Plcmnts ST Local 86; Immaculata Coll.

CORBETT, TYRUS; Center HS; Monaca, PA; (Y); Exploring; Pres Latin Clb; Letterman Clb; Varsity Clb; Var Bsbl; Capt Bowling; Var L Ftbl; Var L Trk; Im Wt Lftg; Hon Roll; Ltr Of Cmndtn Frm Cntr Schl Brd For Svng Nghbrs Lf 83; Radio Brdcst On Myslf By Nrmn Vincent 83; Air Trffc Cntrllr.

CORBIN, BRENDA; Franklin Area HS; Franklin, PA; (Y); Office Aide; Var L Swmmng; Hon Roll; Acctg.

CORBIN, JOEL; New Covenant Acad; Wellsboro, PA; (S); Church Yth Grp; Ski Clb; Spanish Clb; School Play; Yrbk Phtg; Yrbk Stf; JV Socr; Houghton Coll.

CORBIN, LESLI; Littlestown SR HS; Littlestown, PA; (Y); 9/143; Speech Tm; Chorus; School Play; Swing Chorus; Yrbk Phtg; Trk; Hon Roll; Pres NHS; Amer Bus Wmns Assoc 86; Brghm Yng U Provo UT; Psych.

CORBIN, MELISSA; Huntingdon Area HS; Huntingdon, PA; (Y); 5/203; Church Yth Grp; French Clb; Key Clb; Pep Clb; SADD; Teachers Aide; Yrbk Stf; French Hon Soc; High Hon Roll; NHS; Presdntl Acad Fitness Awd 86; Frnch Awd 86; WV U.

CORCORAN, KIMBERLY ANN; Our Lady Of Lourdes Regional HS; Elysburg, PA; (Y); Pres AFS; Church Yth Grp; Library Aide; Capt Pep Clb; Spanish Clb; Rep Sr Cls; Hon Roll; Hmcmng Queen 85; U Of Pittsburgh; Pre-Phrmcy.

CORCORAN, MATTHEW; Lancaster Catholic HS; Lancaster, PA; (Y); 23/230; Trs Service Clb; Frsh Cls; Soph Cls; Trs Stu Cncl; JV Bsktbl; Var Capt Ftbl; JV Capt Trk; Boston Coll.

CORCORAN, TAMMY; Bethlehem Catholic HS; Bethlehem, PA; (Y); 46/201; Hosp Aide; Key Clb; Color Guard; Mrchg Band; Var JV Sftbl; Var Twrlr; High Hon Roll; Hon Roll; Med Careers Clb 85-86; Occup Ther.

CORCORAN, THOMAS; The Hill Schl; Salisbury, MD; (Y); 10/105; JA; Ski Clb; Varsity Clb; Nwsp Bus Mgr; Sec Sr Cls; Var Bsktbl; Var Lcrss; Var Socr; High Hon Roll; Model UN; Bst Gen Rcrd 84-85; U VA; Bus Law.

CORCORAN, TINA MARIE; Reynolds JR-SR HS; Transfer, PA; (Y); German Clb; Library Aide; Math Clb; Science Clb; SADD; Stage Crew; Rep Stu Cncl; Capt Cheerleading; L Trk; Amer Bus Wmns Assn Scholar 86; PA ST U; Bus Adm.

CORDARO, WILLIAM; Kiski Area SR HS; Apollo, PA; (Y); High Hon Roll; Hon Roll; PA ST; Med Tech.

CORDAS, DAVID; Pennsbury HS; Yardley, PA; (Y); 81/840; German Clb; Intnl Clb; Varsity Clb; Rep Jr Cls; Rep Stu Cncl; L Diving; Var Swmmng; NHS.

CORDERO, BRENDA; Freedom HS; Bethlehem, PA; (Y); 39/445; High Hon Roll; Hon Roll; NHS; Aerospc Sci.

CORDISCO, IRMA M; Monongahela Valley Catholic HS; Brownsville, PA; (S); 7/112; Hosp Aide; Spanish Clb; Chorus; Yrbk Bus Mgr; VP Jr Cls; VP Sr Cls; Spanish NHS; Hugh O Brian Awd 84.

COREY, KRISTA; Northampton Area SR HS; Danielsville, PA; (S); 6/444; AFS; Girl Scts; Leo Clb; Chorus; Nwsp Rptr; High Hon Roll; Hon Roll; Penn ST; Vet Med.

COREY, WENDY; Harbor Creek HS; Erie, PA; (Y); Cmnty Wkr; Dance Clb; Drill Tm; Variety Show; Pom Pon; Powder Puff Ftbl; Trk; Hon Roll; NHS; Bus Awd 86; Gregg Shrthnd Awd; Sec.

CORINTH, STEVE; Moon Area Prison Camp; Moon, PA; (Y); Aud/Vis; Boy Scts; JA; Band; Mrchg Band; Symp Band; Variety Show; Yrbk Phtg; Ntl Merit SF.

CORKELL, THERESA; John S Fine SR HS; W Nanticoke, PA; (Y); Church Yth Grp; Cmnty Wkr; 4-H; Yrbk Stf; 4-H Awd; Hon Roll; Typng Awd 86; PA ST; Law.

CORKRAN, VICKI L; Southmoreland HS; Scottdale, PA; (Y); Pep Clb; Spanish Clb; Concert Band; Jazz Band; Sec Mrchg Band; Sec Sr Cls; Powder Puff Ftbl; Sec Spanish NHS; Band; Westmoreland Cnty CC Merit Scholar 86-87; WVU Hnrs Bnd, Cnty Bnd 85-86; SR Bnd Hall Fame 86; Westmoreland Cnty CC; Acctg.

CORLE, J TIMOTHY; Upper Darby HS; Drexel Hill, PA; (Y); Boy Scts; Church Yth Grp; Thesps; VICA; Stage Crew; Sftbl; High Hon Roll; High Hon Roll; Prfct Atten Awd; Indust Arts Awd 84-85; Bus.

CORLE, LAURIE J; Chestnut Ridge HS; Imler, PA; (Y); Church Yth Grp; Library Aide; Speech Tm; Chorus; Nwsp Rptr; Trs Soph Cls; Stu Cncl; Var Capt Cheerleading; Homecoming Attndnt; Penn ST U; Elem Educ.

CORMAS, JOHN; Penn Hills SR HS; Pittsburgh, PA; (Y); Exploring; Bsbl; High Hon Roll; AF Acad; Chem.

CORNAGLIA, TINA; St Maria Goretti HS; Philadelphia, PA; (Y); 229/426; French Clb; Hon Roll; Temple U; Spch Path.

CORNALL, KRISTEN; Forest City Regional HS; Vandling, PA; (Y); 11/64; Church Yth Grp; Ski Clb; Spanish Clb; Church Choir; Yrbk Stf; Stu Cncl; Hon Roll; Ntl Merit Ltr; Wilkes Coll; Nrsng.

CORNELISON, ROBERTA; Greenwood HS; Millerstown, PA; (Y); FBLA; Band; Sec Church Choir; Jazz Band; Rep Stu Cncl; Var Trk; JP Sousa Awd; NHS; Office Aide; Chorus; Greenwood Educ Assn Schlrshp 86; Stu Of Month 86; Bloomsbury U; Fincl Mgt.

CORNELIUS, PATRICIA ANN; Kennett HS; Kennett Sq, PA; (Y); Cmnty Wkr; Pres Varsity Clb; Yrbk Sprt Ed; Yrbk Stf; Var L Bsktbl; Var L Sftbl; JV Trk; Var L Vllybl; High Hon Roll; Prfct Atten Awd; Spring Garden Coll; Elctrnc Eng.

CORNELIUS, RANDALL S; Southern Huntingdon County HS; Shade Gap, PA; (Y); 8/120; Camera Clb; Computer Clb; French Clb; Var L Bsktbl; Var L Trk; NHS; Natl Sci Merit Awd 84 & 86; Comp Sci.

CORNELL, KAREN R; Everett Area HS; Everett, PA; (Y); 1/113; VP Drama Clb; SADD; Chorus; Co-Capt Color Guard; School Play; Bausch & Lomb Sci Awd; Hon Roll; NHS; Pres Schlr; Val; Gettysburg Coll; Clncl Psych.

CORNELL, LEWIS; Forest Hills HS; Sidman, PA; (Y); 6/170; Ski Clb; Spanish Clb; Varsity Clb; Var L Bsbl; JV Bsktbl; Var L Ftbl; Wt Lftg; High Hon Roll; Jr NHS; Lion Awd; Engrng.

CORNELL, MICHELE; Everett Christian Acad; Everett, PA; (S); 2/7; Church Yth Grp; Debate Tm; Church Choir; Yrbk Ed-Chief; Pres Sr Cls; Bsktbl; Vllybl; High Hon Roll; Lee Coll; Bus.

CORNELY, CHRISSY; Jenkintown HS; Jenkintown, PA; (S); 4/47; Spanish Clb; Yrbk Bus Mgr; JV Bsktbl; JV Lcrss; Hon Roll; NHS; Spanish NHS; Lasalle U; Optmtry.

CORNELY, DIANE; Bishop Shanahan HS; West Chester, PA; (Y); 17/214; JV Swmmng; Hon Roll; Jr NHS; NHS; Loyola Coll Bltimr MD; Acctng.

CORNER JR, JOHN; Greenville HS; Greenville, PA; (Y); 11/137; Church Yth Grp; Cmnty Wkr; Math Tm; Spanish Clb; Im Ftbl; Wt Lftg; L Wrstlng; High Hon Roll; Hon Roll; Ntl Merit SF; Princeton; Erspc Engrng.

CORNETT, BONNIE; Perry Traditional Acad; Pittsburgh, PA; (Y); 2/120; Church Yth Grp; Debate Tm; FHA; German Clb; Nwsp Rptr; Nwsp Stf; Yrbk Stf; JV Vllybl; High Hon Roll; NHS; Clarion U PA; Early Chldhd Ed.

CORNETT, CYNTHIA L; Delone Catholic HS; Gettysburg, PA; (Y); 6/169; Am Leg Aux Girls St; Church Yth Grp; Teachers Aide; Mrchg Band; Pres Soph Cls; Sec Stu Cncl; Var L Fld Hcky; Hon Roll; VP NHS; Adams Cnty JR MS 85.

CORNITCHER, MONICA; Phila HS For Girls; Philadelphia, PA; (Y); 72/395; Dance Clb; Math Clb; Rep Service Clb; Drill Tm; Pres Frsh Cls; Trs Jr Cls; Off Sr Cls; Rep Stu Cncl; Cheerleading; High Hon Roll; Howard U; Bus Mgmt.

CORNMAN, MICHELLE; Cumberland Valley HS; Newville, PA; (Y); 4-H; German Clb; Band; 4-H Awd; ST Distngshd Jr Stdnt-Holstein Assn 84; Dairy Prodctn.

CORNMAN, THOMAS; Sharon HS; Sharon, PA; (Y); 27/196; Latin Clb; Wrstlng; High Hon Roll; Hon Roll; Degree Hnr Scholar 86; PA ST U; Cmmnctns.

CORNWELL, DAVE; Palmyra Area HS; Mt Gretna, PA; (Y); 40/230; Ski Clb; Chorus; School Musical; Golf; High Hon Roll; Hon Roll; US Air Force Acad; Engrng.

CORPUZ III, MARCELO N; Shady Side Acad; Pittsburgh, PA; (Y); Trs Chess Clb; Dance Clb; VP Spanish Clb; Band; Var L Ftbl; Trk; Wt Lftg; High Hon Roll; Ntl Merit SF; Brown; Med.

CORR, ELIZABETH ANN; Mount Saint Joseph Acad; Doylestown, PA; (Y); Art Clb; Church Yth Grp; Sec Spanish Clb; Yrbk Stf; Im Bsktbl; Im Vllybl; Hon Roll; NHS; NEDT Awd; Spanish NHS; Schlstc Arts Awd/ Hnrb Mntn 85; Cngrtnl Arts Exhbtn 83; Exc In Rlgs Stdys 84; Bstn Coll.

CORR, WARREN V; Wilson Area HS; Easton, PA; (S); 3/140; Boy Scts; Band; Chorus; VP Stu Cncl; JV Crs Cntry; Var Tennis; God Cntry Awd; High Hon Roll; Hon Roll; NHS.

CORRADINO, RANDY; Old Forge HS; Old Forge, PA; (Y); Ski Clb; Var Bsktbl; Ftbl; High Hon Roll.

CORRADO, DANIELLE; St Maria Goretti HS; Philadelphia, PA; (Y); Art Clb; Camera Clb; French Clb; Hosp Aide; Orch; Hon Roll; Moore Clg Of Art; Fshn Dsgn.

CORRADO, JOI; Palmyra Area HS; Palmyra, PA; (Y); Drama Clb; German Clb; Ski Clb; Teachers Aide; Hon Roll.

CORRELL, DARIN; Holy Name HS; Greenfields, PA; (Y); 2/115; VP JA; Color Guard; School Musical; Stage Crew; Yrbk Stf; Im Bowling; High Hon Roll; VP NHS; Sal; Brandeis U; Bio.

CORRELL, JEFFREY A; Western Wayne HS; Waymart, PA; (Y); 6/146; Aud/Vis; Boys Clb Am; Computer Clb; Scholastic Bowl; Yrbk Phtg; High Hon Roll; NHS; Rgnl Comp Prgmng Cont Wnr 83; Rochstr Inst Of Tech; Comp Engr.

CORRIGAN, KELLY; Hazleton HS; Hazleton, PA; (Y); FBLA; Girl Scts; Office Aide.

CORRIGAN, PATRICIA A; Archbishop Carroll HS; Havertown, PA; (Y); 24/240; Bsktbl; Sftbl; Vllybl; Hon Roll.

CORRY, JAMES; Shaler Area HS; Pittsburgh, PA; (Y); 1/519; Computer Clb; Math Tm; Var Im Tennis; High Hon Roll; NHS; Spanish NHS; 1st Pl Graphics Arts Div 85 Buhl Sci Ct Comp Fir 85; Chem Engrng.

CORSALE, FRANK; Cathedral Prep Schl; Erie, PA; (Y); 100/216; Ski Clb; Off Frsh Cls; Off Soph Cls; Bsktbl; Socr; Trk; Dentstry.

CORSETTI, JEFF; New Brighton HS; Rochester, PA; (Y); Computer Clb; L Swmmng; French Hon Soc; High Hon Roll; Rotary Awd; Stu Of Wk 84-85; 1500 Hours Cmmnty Serv 83-86; Chem.

CORSETTI, JOSEPH; West Catholic HS For Boys; Philadelphia, PA; (Y); 21/260; Am Leg Boys St; Cmnty Wkr; Red Cross Aide; Off Frsh Cls; Off Soph Cls; Off Jr Cls; Off Sr Cls; Stu Cncl; Var Bsbl; Var Ftbl.

CORSO, BONITA; Burgettstown HS; Burgettstown, PA; (Y); 17/141; Pres Drama Clb; Exploring; French Clb; Concert Band; Drill Tm; Mrchg Band; Pep Band; Symp Band; Variety Show; Mat Maids; Gannon U; Phys Ther.

CORSO, JILL FOX; Mount Saint Joseph Acad; Blue Bell, PA; (Y); AFS; Art Clb; French Clb; Lit Mag; JV Swmmng; French Hon Soc; High Hon Roll; NHS; Ntl Merit Ltr; NEDT Awd; U VA; Intl Bus.

CORSON, CHERYL; St Huberts HS; Philadelphia, PA; (Y); Cmnty Wkr; Girl Scts; Office Aide; Atten Awd 83-86; Bus.

CORSON, LISA M; Abington Freinds Schl; Blue Bell, PA; (Y); 1/40; Cmnty Wkr; Hosp Aide; Temple Yth Grp; School Musical; Yrbk Stf; Stu Cncl; Mgr(s); High Hon Roll; Ntl Merit SF; Library Aide; Princpls List; Cmmnwlth Of PA Cert Merit Outstndg Perfmnc On SAT; Soc Sci.

CORTAZZO, JENNIFER; East Allegheny HS; East Mc Keesport, PA; (Y); 48/203; Dance Clb; Drama Clb; Girl Scts; Office Aide; Ski Clb; Hon Roll; ICM Schl Of Bus; Wrd Prcssng.

CORTES, LISA E; Meadville Area SR HS; Meadville, PA; (Y); 12/269; Church Yth Grp; French Clb; Trs Ski Clb; Flag Corp; Stu Cncl; Var Trk; High Hon Roll; Hon Roll; NHS; Pres Schlr; Pres Physcl Ftns Awd 84-86; Allegheny Coll; Bio-Med Engr.

CORTEZZO, CONNI; Pen Argyl Area HS; Pen Argyl, PA; (Y); 42/147; Drama Clb; FBLA; Leo Clb; Ski Clb; Teachers Aide; Band; Chorus; Concert Band; Mrchg Band; Orch; Travel.

CORTOLILLO, SUSAN; Bethel Park SR HS; Bethel Park, PA; (Y); Church Yth Grp; Church Choir; Drill Tm; Mrchg Band; Symp Band; Stu Cncl; Hon Roll; NHS; Band; Cnslr Bapt Camp 84 & 86; Bus.

CORUJO, ROBERT; Thomas A Edison HS; Philadelphia, PA; (Y); 6/550; Lit Mag; Var Ftbl; Var Socr; Var Wrstlng; High Hon Roll; Hon Roll; NHS; Prfct Atten Awd; Stewart Rauch Am Philsophcl 84; Free Enterprise Flwshp Hnr 86; Engrng.

CORY, KRISTI; Hampton HS; Allison Pk, PA; (Y); Church Yth Grp; French Clb; GAA; Ski Clb; Ed Nwsp Ed-Chief; Rep Stu Cncl; Powder Puff Ftbl; Sftbl; Vllybl; Hon Roll.

CORY, SUSAN; Wilmington Area HS; New Wilmington, PA; (Y); Band; Church Choir; Concert Band; Mrchg Band; Pep Band; Nwsp Stf; Hon Roll; Slippery Rock U; Bus.

COSGROVE, KATHLEEN; Pittstown Area HS; Pittston, PA; (Y); 11/365; Key Clb; Math Clb; Science Clb; Yrbk Stf; Var L Tennis; Var L Trk; NHS; Ntl Merit SF; Prfct Atten Awd; Atu Athlt Awd 86; PA ST U; Bio.

COSGROVE, KRISTIE LEE; Steel Valley HS; Munhall, PA; (Y); Church Yth Grp; Exploring; FBLA; SADD; Teachers Aide; Varsity Clb; Yrbk Stf; Var Cheerleading; Grt Amer Bnk Intrnshp 86; Bnkng.

COSGROVE, STACEY L; Commodore Perry HS; Hadley, PA; (S); 8/62; Trs Pres Art Clb; Trs VP FBLA; VP Chorus; Sec Jr Cls; VP Sr Cls; Rep Stu Cncl; Var L Cheerleading; Var L Vllybl; Hon Roll; NHS; Comp Sci.

COSLOW, LORI; Ringgold HS; Finleyville, PA; (Y); French Clb; Pep Clb; Ski Clb; SADD; Band; Mrchg Band; Cheerleading; Mgr(s); Timer; Hon Roll.

COSNEK, CARRIE; Avonworth JR SR HS; Pittsburgh, PA; (Y); 1/100; Church Yth Grp; Latin Clb; Band; Mrchg Band; Yrbk Ed-Chief; Lit Mag; Var L Bsktbl; Var L Sftbl; High Hon Roll; NHS; Princeton; Engrng.

COSNER, GAIL; Marple-Newtaon HS; Newtown Square, PA; (Y); 157/367; Church Yth Grp; Off Chorus; Pres Mgr Orch; School Musical; Stu Cncl; Var L Fld Hcky; Var Lcrss; Hon Roll; Dist & Regnl Choir 84 & 86; Grl Mnth 86; Cls Scholar 86; PA ST; Music.

COSSABOON, DAVID; Unionville HS; Chadds Ford, PA; (Y); 54/308; Computer Clb; FBLA; Math Clb; Science Clb; JV Crs Cntry; Var Capt Trk; High Hon Roll; Hon Roll; Jr NHS; Engr.

COSSITOR JR, PETER A; Exeter HS; Reading, PA; (Y); 105/225; JA; Varsity Clb; Var Bsbl; Capt Ftbl; Hon Roll; Berks All Cty Ftbl Tm 85; All Star Bsbl 1st Tm Desgntd Hitter 86; 1st Pl ST Archry Champ 85; Pittsburgh Tech Inst; Comp.

COSSITOR, RICHARD; Exeter SR HS; Reading, PA; (Y); 59/215; Exploring; Trs Key Clb; Trs Spanish Clb; Varsity Clb; Nwsp Rptr; Nwsp Stf; VP Jr Cls; Var L Crs Cntry; Var L Trk; Var Wrstlng; All Cty Hnrbl Ment Cross Cty 85; Ed.

COST, CATHY; Lakeland JR SR HS; Clarks Summit, PA; (S); 10/168; Spanish Clb; Hon Roll; Arch.

COSTA, CHERYL; Central Buck East HS; Danboro, PA; (Y); Chorus; Drill Tm; Madrigals; Mrchg Band; School Musical; Stage Crew; L Twrlr; Hon Roll; Cnty Chrs 83-86; Acad Lttr 86; Nrsng.

COSTA, COSIMO; Lakeland HS; Mayfield, PA; (Y); Church Yth Grp; Spanish Clb; Sec Soph Cls; Sec Jr Cls; Bsbl; Ftbl; Wt Lftg; JV Jr NHS; NHS; Temple U; Pharm.

COSTA, JOHN; Our Lady Of Lourdes Regional HS; Sunbury, PA; (Y); 40/96; AFS; Church Yth Grp; Key Clb; Spanish Clb; Rep Frsh Cls; Rep Sr Cls; Rep Stu Cncl; JV Ftbl.

COSTA, MARIA; Lakeland HS; Mayfield, PA; (S); 39/143; Var Cheerleading; Keystone JC; Med Tech.

COSTA, MICHAEL; Upper Dublin HS; Oreland, PA; (Y); 29/341; Church Yth Grp; Varsity Clb; Sr Cls; Bsbl; Bsktbl; Ftbl; Mgr(s); Swmmng; Wt Lftg; NHS; Jhns Hpkns U; Biomed.

COSTA, TINA; Penn Hills SR HS; Verona, PA; (Y); Drama Clb; French Clb; Spanish Clb; Chorus; Concert Band; Mrchg Band; School Musical; Yrbk Stf; Stu Cncl; High Hon Roll; Nrsng.

COSTABILE, RICHARD; Dover Area HS; Dover, PA; (Y); 67/254; Chess Clb; JA; JV Var Socr; Var L Trk; Hon Roll; York Tech Inst; Elctrncs Tech.

COSTANTINI, EILEEN; Pennsbury HS; Levittown, PA; (Y); Rep Frsh Cls; Rep Soph Cls; Var Fld Hcky; Var JV Sftbl; Hon Roll; Stu Mnth 84; Kent ST; Crmnl Justc.

COSTANZA, ROBERT V; Kiski Area HS; New Kensington, PA; (Y); Pep Clb; Band; Concert Band; Jazz Band; Mrchg Band; Symp Band; Nwsp Stf; Var JV Bsktbl; Hon Roll; Hon Roll; Hmcmng Escort 85; Penn ST; Microcomp Engrng.

COSTANZO, VALARIE; Canon-Mc Millan HS; Canonsburg, PA; (Y); 5/390; Pres French Clb; Office Aide; Ski Clb; Drill Tm; Nwsp Stf; Trs Soph Cls; Trs Sr Cls; Sec Stu Cncl; High Hon Roll; NHS; French Awd Intl Lang Comp Ca St 86.

COSTELLO JR, B PATRICK; Greensburg Central Catholic HS; Greensburg, PA; (Y); 35/243; Computer Clb; JCL; Latin Clb; Ski Clb; Rep Stu Cncl; Im Bsktbl; High Hon Roll; Hon Roll; NHS; Ntl Merit Ltr; U Notre Dame; Bus.

COSTELLO, CHRISTINA; South Park HS; Library, PA; (S); 14/212; Drama Clb; Hosp Aide; Thesps; School Play; Yrbk Ed-Chief; Yrbk Phtg; Yrbk Rptr; Yrbk Sprt Ed; High Hon Roll; NHS; Rotary Intl Yth Ldrshp Conf 86; Bus.

COSTELLO, COLLEEN; Scranton Prep Schl; Dunmore, PA; (Y); 104/192; Cmnty Wkr; Service Clb; Band; Chorus; Concert Band; School Musical; School Play; Lit Mag; Hon Roll; Scranton U; Pblc Rltns.

COSTELLO, JOHN M; Greensburg Central Catholic HS; Greensburg, PA; (Y); 8/240; Church Yth Grp; Ski Clb; Pres Soph Cls; Pres Jr Cls; Im Mgr Sftbl; High Hon Roll; NHS; Ntl Merit SF; JCL; Invitation To Natl Yng Ldrs Conf WA DC 86; Pre-Med.

COSTELLO, JULIE; Bradford Area HS; Bradford, PA; (Y); 76/311; AFS; Pep Clb; Ski Clb; Sec SADD; School Play; Capt Cheerleading; Var Trk; Hon Roll; Jr NHS; NHS; U Of Miami; Bus Mngmnt.

COSTELLO, KATHRYN; Cardnial O Hara HS; Woodlyn, PA; (Y); 35/780; Civic Clb; Hosp Aide; VP JA; Office Aide; Service Clb; Acpl Chr; Chorus; School Musical; School Play; Yrbk Stf; Acadmc Cnvctn 85-86; Widener Pres Schlrshp 86; Pern Grant 86; U Of PA; Nrsng.

COSTELLO, KELLY; Northwestern Lehigh HS; Schnecksvile, PA; (Y); 7/163; Am Leg Aux Girls St; Debate Tm; 4-H; Stu Cncl; Cheerleading; Trk; Dnfth Awd; NHS; AFS; Acad All Am Schlr 86; Acad All Am At Large 86; Ntl Ldrshp Conf I Dare You 86; U MI; Med.

COSTELLO, MICHELE; Connellsville SR HS; Connellsville, PA; (Y); 63/553; Sec Computer Clb; Band; Chorus; Church Choir; Mrchg Band; School Musical; Symp Band; Rep Frsh Cls; JV Cheerleading; Vllybl; Stu Pres Clsrm Yngn Am Sess 7th 86; Music.

COSTELLO, PATRICIA; St Maria Goretti HS; Philadelphia, PA; (Y); Art Clb; Camera Clb; Computer Clb; Dance Clb; Drama Clb; French Clb; German Clb; PAVAS; Variety Show; Nwsp Phtg; Schlrshp Sat Art Clss 85-86; Art Inst Of Phila; Phtgrphr.

COSTELLO, PATRICK; Fairchance Georges SR HS; Fairchance, PA; (Y); 25/160; Pres Soph Cls; Var Ftbl; Hon Roll; Hnr Rl; Comp Field.

COSTELLO, THERESA; Sacred Heart HS; Pittsburgh, PA; (Y); 5/151; Computer Clb; Exploring; Science Clb; Ski Clb; Im Bowling; Im Socr; Var Sftbl; Im Vllybl; High Hon Roll; NHS; U Pittsburgh Schlr Schlrshp 86; Presdntl Acdmc Ftnss Awd 86; Contntl Mathmtcs Leag Awd 86; U Pittsburgh; Biogcl Sci.

COTELLESSE, GERALD; West Catholic Boys HS; Philadelphia, PA; (Y); 29/270; Bsbl; Hon Roll; Jr NHS; NHS; Penn ST U; Bus.

COTLAR, SETH; Central Cambria HS; Ebensburg, PA; (Y); 1/190; School Play; VP Stu Cncl; Var L Crs Cntry; Var L Golf; Var L Trk; Ski Clb; Speech Tm; High Hon Roll; Ntl Merit Schol; Pres Schlr; PA Govs Schl For Sci 85; Brown U.

COTT, SUZANNE; Bethlehem Catholic HS; Bethlehem, PA; (Y); Cmnty Wkr; Hosp Aide; Key Clb; Red Cross Aide; Yrbk Stf; Swmmng; High Hon Roll; Hon Roll; Penn St; Bio.

COTTENDEN, DAVID; Philadelphia Montgomery Chrstn Acad; Hatboro, PA; (Y); Church Yth Grp; Acpl Chr; Yrbk Stf; JV Var Bsbl; JV Var Socr; Ntl Merit SF; Natl Merit Schlrshp Fnlst 86; Calvin Coll; Acctg.

COTTER, MARY JO; St Marys Area HS; St Marys, PA; (Y); 36/200; Am Leg Aux Girls St; Drama Clb; JA; Yrbk Phtg; Yrbk Stf; Coach Actv; Score Keeper; Swmmng; High Hon Roll; NHS; Var Let ST Fnls Swmmng 83-86; Clarion U Of PA; Bio.

COTTERALL, CHRISTINE; Cardinal O Hara HS; Springfield, PA; (Y); 24/772; Church Yth Grp; German Clb; Service Clb; Stage Crew; Hon Roll; NHS; Ntl Merit Ltr; Schlstc Awd Bio 85; Hnrbl Ment Env Sci Fair 86; Engrng.

COTTLE, JOHN; Northern Bedford County HS; Hopewell, PA; (Y); 4/94; Math Clb; SADD; Varsity Clb; L Ftbl; Hon Roll; Sec NHS; Acad All Amer 86; PA ST U; Cvl Engrng.

COTTON, RICHARD D; Elk Lake Schl; Meshoppen, PA; (Y); 2/104; Am Leg Boys St; Spanish Clb; Var JV Socr; Capt Var Vllybl; High Hon Roll; Hon Roll; Prfct Atten Awd; Rotary Ldrs Camp 85; Vllybl All Star Team 86; Elk Lake Gftd Prog 83-86; Comp Info Sytsms.

COUCH, MELISSA; Laurel Highlands HS; Uniontown, PA; (Y); Church Yth Grp; Pres Frsh Cls; VP Soph Cls; VP Jr Cls; Hon Roll.

COUCH, MICHELLE; Southmoreland HS; Scottdale, PA; (Y); 54/240; Church Yth Grp; Cmnty Wkr; Drama Clb; Hosp Aide; Pep Clb; Varsity Clb; Chorus; School Musical; School Play; JV VP Cheerleading; 1st Pl In Vocal Category 85; Oceanography.

COUGHENOUR, SCOTT; Somerset Area HS; Somerset, PA; (Y); 46/239; Am Leg Boys St; Art Clb; English Clb; Math Clb; Red Cross Aide; SADD; School Play; Hon Roll; Prfct Atten Awd; Pres Church Yth Grp; Shippensburg U; Ed.

COUGHENOUR, VALERIE; Elizabeth Forward HS; Elizabeth, PA; (Y); 40/317; Church Yth Grp; Latin Clb; Sec Mrchg Band; Nwsp Stf; Yrbk Ed-Chief; JV Var Swmmng; JV Stat Trk; High Hon Roll; Hon Roll; Pres Schlrshp Carlow 86; Carlow Coll; Scndry Ed.

COUGHENOUR JR, WILLIAM E; Meyersdale Area HS; Salisbury, PA; (S); Letterman Clb; Spanish Clb; Varsity Clb; Yrbk Rptr; Yrbk Sprt Ed; Yrbk Stf; VP Bsktbl; L Ftbl; L Trk; VP Wt Lftg; Pittsburgh-Penn ST; Sci Tchg.

COULSON, CYNTHIA; Pottsville Area HS; Pottsville, PA; (Y); Exploring; FBLA; Chorus; Mrchg Band; Cheerleading; Pom Pon; Hon Roll; John Casablanas U; Mdl.

COULTER, MIKE; Grove City HS; Slippery Rock, PA; (Y); 21/225; Bsbl; Ftbl; Trk; 4-H Awd; High Hon Roll; Hon Roll; NHS; Grove City; Elctrcl Engrng.

COULTER, R CRAIG; Apollo Ridge SR HS; Apollo, PA; (Y); 5/180; Chess Clb; French Clb; Math Clb; Concert Band; Jazz Band; Madrigals; Mrchg Band; Orch; Pep Band; Stu Cncl; PA Gov Schl Sci 85; U Of Pittsburgh Provost Schlrshp 86; Carnegie Mellon Corp Schlr 86; Carnegie Mellon U; Mech Engrng.

COUPER, LEANNE; Quaker Valley HS; Sewickley, PA; (Y); 65/170; Church Yth Grp; Chorus; Stat Bsktbl; Var Sftbl; Var Vllybl; Teen Inst 85-86; Cmmtns.

COURIE, CARLA; Canon Mc Millan HS; Canonsburg, PA; (Y); #70 In Class; Chess Clb; French Clb; Pep Clb; Ski Clb; Varsity Clb; Sec Nwsp Stf; Yrbk Stf; Var JV Cheerleading; High Hon Roll; Hon Roll; Hnr Rll Awd 84.

COURIE, CHARLES; Canon-Mc Millan HS; Canonsburg, PA; (Y); Latin Clb; Hon Roll; CA U; Chiroprctr.

COURSEY, CHRISTOPHER; Spring Ford SR HS; Royersford, PA; (Y); 35/264; French Clb; Ski Clb; Stu Cncl; Trk; Wrstlng; Hon Roll.

COURTRYMAN, MICHAEL; Berlin Brothersvalley HS; Berlin, PA; (Y); 16/90; Church Yth Grp; 4-H; Pres FFA; Speech Tm; Band; 4-H Awd; Hon Roll; NHS; Penn ST; Ag.

COURTWRIGHT, JACOB; West Greene HS; Wind Ridge, PA; (S); FFA; Trk.

COUSINS, DAN; General Mc Lane HS; Girard, PA; (Y); 35/220; Church Yth Grp; Drama Clb; German Clb; Library Aide; Spanish Clb; Church Choir; Nwsp Bus Mgr; Nwsp Rptr; Nwsp Stf; Trs Frsh Cls; SR Advsr Comm 86-87; Bio.

COVAL, ANTHONY; West Branch HS; Hawk Run, PA; (S); 6/112; VP Science Clb; Capt Bsbl; Capt Bsktbl; Crs Cntry; NHS; PA ST Altoona; Engrng.

COVER, SUSAN; Meyersdale Area HS; Meyersdale, PA; (Y); 11/83; Church Yth Grp; Spanish Clb; Chorus; Church Choir; School Musical; School Play; Nwsp Stf; JV Capt Cheerleading; Hon Roll; NHS; Shippensburg U.

COVERT, DENEICE; Southern Huntingdon HS; Shirleyburg, PA; (Y); FHA; GAA; Varsity Clb; School Musical; VP Jr Cls; Var Cheerleading; Var Capt Fld Hcky; Var Sftbl; Hon Roll; NHS; Gen Inf Cntst 86.

COVERT, EDWARD; Neshannock HS; New Castle, PA; (Y); Cit Awd; Ntl Merit Schol; Pres Schlr; Chorus; Bsbl; Bsktbl; Ftbl; Mgr(s); Hon Roll; Hnr Awd; Svc Awd; Med.

COVERT, HEATHER; Butler Area SR HS; Butler, PA; (Y); Church Yth Grp; Exploring; French Clb; Trs FNA; SADD; Band; Church Choir; Concert Band; Mrchg Band; School Musical; Jr Natl Hnr Soc 83-85; Soc Of Distngshd Am H S Stu 85-86; Natl Fed Of Musc Clbs 86; Pre Med.

COWAN, WENDY; Shenango JR SR HS; New Castle, PA; (Y); 17/112; Camera Clb; Church Yth Grp; Cmnty Wkr; Hosp Aide; Red Cross Aide; Service Clb; Yrbk Stf; Hon Roll; NHS; NEDT Awd; Ntl Engl Merit Awd 86; Svc Awds-Intl Ordr Of Rainbow For Girls 85-86; Psych.

COWARD, PAMELA; Middletown HS; Middletown, PA; (Y); Rptr Cmnty Wkr; Model UN; Color Guard; Flag Corp; Mrchg Band; Nwsp Rptr; Nwsp Stf; Hnbl Mtn Essay Cntst Am Leg 86; Model UN, Schl Nswpr, YEA Club; Colorgaurd, Flag Corp, Mrch Band; Elizabethtown Coll; Elem Educ.

COWELL, DANELLE; West Mifflin Area HS; W Mifflin, PA; (Y); 14/339; Church Yth Grp; GAA; Concert Band; Jazz Band; Mrchg Band; Yrbk Stf; Rep Jr Cls; Rep Sr Cls; High Hon Roll; NHS; Pres Acad Ftns Awd 86; Kent ST U; Comptnl Math.

COWELL, KIM; Gateway SR HS; Monroeville, PA; (Y); 70/509; Co-Capt Hosp Aide; Chorus; Variety Show; Yrbk Bus Mgr; Mgr(s); Trk; Yrbk Stf; Econ.

COWELL, WILLIAM; West Mifflin Area HS; West Mifflin, PA; (Y); 13/350; Golf; High Hon Roll; Jr NHS; NHS; Cert Excllnce Physics IN U PA 86; PA ST U; Engrng.

COWHER, DENNY; Claysburg-Kimmel HS; Queen, PA; (Y); 1/55; Varsity Clb; Yrbk Rptr; Yrbk Sprt Ed; Trs Soph Cls; Pres Jr Cls; Bsbl; Bsktbl; Ftbl; NHS; Prfct Atten Awd; Mst Vlbl Plyr On Ftbl Team 86; All ST Catcher In Trnpk Amer Lgn Bsbl League 87.

COWHER, JODY; Tyrone Area HS; Tyrone, PA; (Y); Key Clb; Color Guard; Mrchg Band; Hon Roll; Clr Grd; Hnr Roll; Mrchng Band.

COWIESON, CATHI; Trinity HS; Washington, PA; (Y); 41/374; Church Yth Grp; GAA; Girl Scts; Key Clb; Letterman Clb; Office Aide; Pep Clb; Spanish Clb; Varsity Clb; Bsktbl; Mrn Bio.

COWLEY, AMY; Bethlehem-Center HS; Brownsville, PA; (Y); 25/150; GAA; Ski Clb; Spanish Clb; Acpl Chr; Chorus; Trk; CA U PA; Physcst.

COX, DAWN; Mt Union Area JR SR HS; Mount Union, PA; (Y); 45/160; Trs FHA; GAA; Var Sftbl; Psychtrst.

COX, EDWARD; Father Judge HS; Philadelphia, PA; (Y); 23/358; Latin Clb; Var L Ftbl; Var L Swmmng; Hon Roll; NHS; Law.

COX, JOSEPH; Northeast Catholic HS; Philadelphia, PA; (Y); 59/392; Chess Clb; Rep Jr Cls; Im Bsktbl; JV Var Ftbl; NHS.

COX, KEVIN; Pine Forge Acad; Richmond, VA; (S); Acpl Chr; Yrbk Ed-Chief; Pres Soph Cls; Stat Bsktbl; Score Keeper; Hon Roll; NHS; Biomed Engr.

COX, MICHELLE; Hatboro Horsham SR HS; Horsham, PA; (Y); Concert Band; Mrchg Band; School Musical; Nwsp Rptr; Nwsp Stf; Var Sftbl; JV Tennis; Hon Roll; Drama Awd 84; Hnrbl Ment Germn Soc, Germn Awd 86; Dickinson Coll; Engl.

COX, SHAWN; Pine Forge Acad; Baltimore, MD; (Y); Office Aide; Chorus; Church Choir; Drill Tm; School Musical; Yrbk Stf; Sec Frsh Cls; Cheerleading; Cit Awd; Hon Roll; Oakwood Coll; Bio.

COX, THOMAS; Scranton Central HS; Scranton, PA; (Y); French Clb; JA; Spanish Clb; Bsktbl; Crs Cntry; Comp.

COYLE, DONNA; Nazareth SR HS; Nazareth, PA; (Y); 19/243; Drama Clb; Key Clb; Drill Tm; School Musical; Swing Chorus; Rep Stu Cncl; Capt Twrlr; JV Vllybl; High Hon Roll; Hon Roll; Crimnl Justc.

COYLE, JENNIFER; Canon-Mcmillan SR HS; Canonsburg, PA; (Y); 24/410; Drama Clb; French Clb; Varsity Clb; School Musical; School Play; Var Capt Cheerleading; High Hon Roll; Hon Roll; Trk; Chess Clb; Corp Law.

COYLE, SEAN; Archbishop Ryan HS; Philadelphia, PA; (Y); Camera Clb; Cmnty Wkr; Dance Clb; Cert Of Hnr Outstndng Achvt In Art 86; 2nd Pl SR Cls Art Show 86; Dsgn Tee Shirts Mjr Manufctrs; PA Coll Textiles & Sci; Design.

COYLE, TED; Souderton Area HS; Harleysville, PA; (Y); Ski Clb; Chorus; School Musical; School Play; Stage Crew; Nwsp Stf; Temple; Flm Prdtn.

COYNE, PATRICIA; Archbishop Kennedy HS; Conshohocken, PA; (Y); 16/171; Var Crs Cntry; Var Trk; Hon Roll; Bus Admin.

COYNE, SAMUEL; Conrad Weiser HS; Wernersville, PA; (Y); 37/184; Latin Clb; VICA; High Hon Roll; Hon Roll; Albright Fnancng.

COYNE, SUSAN L; Steel Valley HS; Munhall, PA; (Y); Cmnty Wkr; JA; VP Key Clb; Office Aide; SADD; Yrbk Stf; Hon Roll; Duquesne U; Bus Adm.

COZART, SELENA DIANE; Philadelphia HS For Girls; Philadelphia, PA; (Y); 57/395; VP Church Yth Grp; Band; Church Choir; Concert Band; Mrchg Band; Orch; Pep Band; Trk; Vllybl; Hon Roll; Charles E Ellis Schlrshp 84-87.

COZZA, THERESA; The Lewisburg Area HS; Lewisburg, PA; (Y); 38/151; Church Yth Grp; Pres Latin Clb; Varsity Clb; Var Crs Cntry; Var Fld Hcky; Var Sftbl; High Hon Roll; Hon Roll; Jr NHS; Prfct Atten Awd; Pres Phys Ftnss Awd 83-85; Pres Acadmc Awd 86; Altoona Campus PA ST; Pre-Law.

COZZARELLI, LAURA E; Central Bucks HS West; Chalfont, PA; (Y); Intnl Clb; Model UN; SADD; Yrbk Stf; Fld Hcky; French Hon Soc; High Hon Roll; NHS; Ntl Merit Ltr; Sci Smnr Awd 86; Georgetown U; Med.

CRABLE, JENNIFER; Uniontown Area HS; Uniontown, PA; (Y); 21/287; French Clb; Office Aide; Ski Clb; Mrchg Band; Yrbk Stf; Twrlr; High Hon Roll; NHS; Mjrt Cptn 86-87; Frgn Lng Hnr Scty 85; Indiana U Of PA; Fshn Mrchndsn.

CRABTREE, DARREN S; Altoona Area HS; Altoona, PA; (Y); VICA; Chorus; Nwsp Sprt Ed; Var Ftbl; Capt Wrstlng; PA ST U; Bus Adm.

CRAFT, MARY; Dallas SR HS; Shavertown, PA; (Y); VP Girl Scts; Chorus; Drill Tm; Nwsp Stf; Hon Roll; Grl Scout Gld Awd 85; Misericordia Coll.

CRAFT, MARY KATE; Bishop Kenrick HS; Norristown, PA; (Y); Cmnty Wkr; Hon Roll; NHS; Presdntl Acadmc Fitness Awd 86; Early Childhood Educ.

CRAFT, STEVE; Somerset Area HS; Somerset, PA; (Y); 14/242; English Clb; JA; Ski Clb; Spanish Clb; High Hon Roll; Hon Roll; NHS; Prfct Atten Awd; Mech Engrng.

CRAGO, BRANDON; Carmichaels Area HS; Carmichaels, PA; (Y); 30/101; Boy Scts; Church Yth Grp; French Clb; Letterman Clb; Varsity Clb; Bsktbl; Golf; High Hon Roll; Hon Roll; CA U Of PA; Engr.

CRAHALLA, SHERI C; Crestwood HS; Mountaintop, PA; (Y); 57/223; Ski Clb; School Play; Yrbk Stf; Sec Rep Stu Cncl; Capt Cheerleading; Crs Cntry; Trk; High Hon Roll; Hon Roll; Ntl Ed Dvlpmnt Scr 90 Pct 83-84; Kent ST; Fash Merch.

CRAIG, DEABRA; Punxsutawney Area HS; Punxsutawney, PA; (Y); VP FBLA; Spanish Clb; Bsbl; Bus.

CRAIG, DONNA; West Allegheny HS; Imperial, PA; (Y); 15/200; Sec VP Key Clb; Spanish Clb; Varsity Clb; VICA; VP Soph Cls; Rep Stu Cncl; Var L Cheerleading; Powder Puff Ftbl; Sftbl; High Hon Roll; Csmtlgy.

CRAIG, JACQUELINE; Bishop Hafey HS; Hazleton, PA; (Y); 40/150; Camera Clb; Spanish Clb; Orch; Yrbk Phtg; Yrbk Stf; Spanish NHS.

CRAIG, JENNIFER; Mohawk JR SR HS; New Castle, PA; (Y); Pres Church Yth Grp; Dance Clb; Off FHA; Spanish Clb; Concert Band; Mrchg Band; Hon Roll; Phys Thrpy.

CRAIG, KELLIE; Interboro HS; Prospect Park, PA; (Y); Cmnty Wkr; Hon Roll; Bus.

CRAIG, LYNNE; Freedom HS; Bethlehem, PA; (Y); 22/445; Art Clb; Library Aide; Nwsp Stf; JV Bsktbl; JV Var Sftbl; High Hon Roll; Hon Roll; NHS; Prom Cmmtte 86; Strght A's 85; Lehigh U; Mdcl Engrng.

CRAIG, SHARON; Waynesburg Central HS; Mt Morris, PA; (Y); Cmnty Wkr; 4-H; Natl Beta Clb; Ski Clb; Spanish Clb; Yrbk Stf; 4-H Awd; Hon Roll; W VA U.

CRAIG, TOM; Nes Haming HS; Feasterville, PA; (Y); 100/738; JV Bsbl; Var Ftbl; Hon Roll; Bus.

CRAIGLE, VIRGINIA; West Hazleton HS; W Hazelton, PA; (Y); 84/243; Church Yth Grp; Dance Clb; SADD; Y-Teens; Church Choir; VP Concert Band; VP Mrchg Band; Stu Cncl; Penn ST; Pre-Law.

CRAINE, THOMAS; Penn Cambria HS; Lilly, PA; (Y); Spanish Clb; Varsity Clb; Bsktbl; Mt Aloyisus; RN.

CRALEY, MATTHEW; Northeastern HS; Mt Wolf, PA; (Y); 56/186; Church Yth Grp; Varsity Clb; Band; Chorus; Concert Band; Mrchg Band; Var L Bsktbl; Var L Golf; Var L Trk; Hon Roll; Hlth Ed.

CRAM, MARGARET; St Hubert HS; Philadelphia, PA; (Y); 44/367; Gym; Hon Roll; Hm Ec Achvt Awd; Beaver; Data Entry.

CRAMER, JANETTE; Mt Union Area HS; Shirleysburg, PA; (Y); 56/184; GAA; Spanish Clb; Band; Concert Band; Mrchg Band; Bowling; Twrlr; Nrsg.

CRAMER, JULIA; Hallstead Christian Acad; Great Bend, PA; (S); Hosp Aide; School Play; Yrbk Ed-Chief; Yrbk Phtg; Var L Bsktbl; Capt Var Cheerleading; Vllybl; High Hon Roll; NHS; 1st In ST In Splng 84 & 85; 2nd In ST In Essay 84; Surgeon.

CRAMER, KEITH; Hempfield HS; Mountville, PA; (Y); Ftbl; Schlstc Art Awd 86; PA Schl Of Arts; Fine Art.

CRAMER, KEN; Upper Merion HS; King Of Prussia, PA; (Y); Bsbl; Prfct Attndnce Awd 83-85; U PA Miami; Law.

CRAMER, LAURA; Donegal HS; Marietta, PA; (Y); FBLA; JA; Pep Clb; Chorus; Cheerleading; Sftbl; Trk; Hon Roll; Donegal HS Indian Mascot 85-86; Army; Air Trffc Cntrl.

CRAMER, LISA; Springdale HS; Cheswick, PA; (Y); Church Yth Grp; Spanish Clb; Acpl Chr; Chorus; Swing Chorus; Variety Show; Var L Bsktbl; Var L Cheerleading; Var L Sftbl; High Hon Roll; Bus.

CRAMER, LORI; United HS; Blairsville, PA; (Y); 14/157; Band; Chorus; Nwsp Stf; Yrbk Stf; Lit Mag; L VP Trk; Capt Twrlr; Hon Roll; NHS; Slctd To Attend Summer Happenings At IUP & Wrte A Column In IN Gazette; Attnd Cnty Band; Arch.

CRAMER, SHARI; Laurel Highlands HS; Smock, PA; (Y); 3/340; Pres Hosp Aide; Drm Mjr(t); Flag Corp; Madrigals; CC Awd; High Hon Roll; NHS; Voice Dem Awd; Uniontown Coll Clb Scholar 86; Chem II Awd 85; Anatomy Awd 86; IN U PA; Nrsng.

CRAMER, TERESA; New Brighton SR HS; New Brighton, PA; (Y); Nwsp Rptr; Trk; Hon Roll; Acdmc All Am Awd 86; Intl Frgn Lang Awd 85.

CRAMER, TINA; Greater Latrobe HS; Greensburg, PA; (Y); Color Guard; High Hon Roll; Hon Roll.

CRAMTON, MICHAEL J; Wyoming Seminary HS; Shavertown, PA; (Y); Varsity Clb; Capt Var Bsbl; Capt Var Ftbl; Star Ice Hockey 83-86; Bus.

CRANDALL, MELODY; Blue Mountain Acad; Hamburg, PA; (Y); Camera Clb; Church Yth Grp; Cmnty Wkr; Teachers Aide; Stage Crew; VP Soph Cls; Stat Bsktbl; JV Sftbl; Btty Crckr Awd; Cortez Peters Expert Rhythmic Typng & Typng Proficiency 85; Lgl Sec.

CRANE, CHRISTINE; Lincoln HS; Portersville, PA; (Y); 4-H; Girl Scts; Office Aide; Y-Teens; Band; Concert Band; Mrchg Band; Twrlr; 4-H Awd; ICM Schl Of Bus; Accntng.

CRANGA, MICHAEL; Carlisle SR HS; Carlisle, PA; (Y); Church Yth Grp; Band; Concert Band; Mrchg Band; School Musical; Am Music Abroad Hnr Band 86; Carlisle Indoor Drumline 85-86; Telecomm.

CRANKSHAW, COLLEEN; Archbishop Ryan High Schl For Girls; Philadelphia, PA; (S); 1/483; French Clb; Hosp Aide; Mathletes; Q&S; Ed Yrbk Stf; French Hon Soc; NHS; Prfct Atten Awd; Phil Coll Of Phrmcy/Sci; Phrmct.

CRANNEY, JIEM; Wayneboro SR HS; Waynesboro, PA; (Y); Varsity Clb; Bsbl; Ftbl; Trk; Wt Lftg; High Hon Roll; Hon Roll; Penn ST; Bus Adm.

CRAVEN, KIMBERLY; Little Flower C H G HS; Philadelphia, PA; (Y); 37/419; Drama Clb; German Clb; Q&S; School Musical; School Play; Nwsp Ed-Chief; Nwsp Rptr; High Hon Roll; NHS; Sal; Hghst Avg Vocl Music 82-86; Pres Acdmc Fit Awd 86; Soprno Sectn Ldr Music Dept 85-86; La Salle U; Cmmnctns.

CRAVEN, LISA DAWN; West Mifflin Area HS; W Mifflin, PA; (Y); Co-Capt Flag Corp; Sec Church Yth Grp; Office Aide; Science Clb; Chorus; Church Choir; Orch; School Play; Nwsp Stf; Hon Roll; IN U Of PA.

CRAVER, JOE; Waynesburg Central HS; Mt Morris, PA; (Y); Camera Clb; French Clb; NHS; WV U; Bus Mgt.

CRAWFORD, AMY; Uniontown Area HS; Uniontown, PA; (Y); 32/330; Church Yth Grp; French Clb; Varsity Clb; Band; Concert Band; Drill Tm; Bsktbl; Sftbl; French Hon Soc; High Hon Roll; Acadmc All Em 85.

CRAWFORD, ANDREW; Strath Haven HS; Wallingford, PA; (Y); Aud/Vis; Red Cross Aide; Hon Roll; Penn ST; Med.

CRAWFORD, BARRIE; Chambersburg Area SR HS; Chambersburg, PA; (Y); Pres Church Yth Grp; Latin Clb; Chorus; Orch; Variety Show; Cert Hnr Symphony 86; Cert Hnr Glee Clb 86; Shippensburg U.

CRAWFORD, BETHANNE; Talor Alderdice HS; Pittsburgh, PA; (Y); 73/469; Church Yth Grp; Cmnty Wkr; Exploring; Hosp Aide; Band; Mrchg Band; School Play; High Hon Roll; Hon Roll; Rssn & Prep Clb 82-86; Dusquense U; Phrmcy.

CRAWFORD, CATHY; Lake-Lehman HS; Dallas, PA; (Y); 70/145; Ski Clb; School Play; Stage Crew; Trs Soph Cls; Bsktbl; Westminster; Jrnlsm.

CRAWFORD, DANIEL; Laurel Highlans SR HS; Uniontown, PA; (Y); 98/365; Church Yth Grp; Spanish Clb; Im Bsktbl; Var Ftbl; Var Wt Lftg; Hon Roll; Westminster Coll.

CRAWFORD, JENNIFER; Hampton HS; Allison Park, PA; (Y); French Clb; Hosp Aide; Bus.

CRAWFORD, JULIE L; Redbank Valley HS; New Bethlehem, PA; (Y); VP Church Yth Grp; FHA; Spanish Clb; Varsity Clb; Chorus; Church Choir; Concert Band; School Musical; School Play; Var Cheerleading; Pckd Amer Legn Trip Polc Acad 86; Jrnlsm.

CRAWFORD, KAREN; Highlands HS; Brackenridge, PA; (Y); 41/275; Church Yth Grp; FBLA; Hosp Aide; Trs Intnl Clb; Key Clb; Library Aide; Sec Stu Cncl; Jr NHS; NHS; PA ST U; Acctnt.

CRAWFORD, KATHLEEN; Sacred Heart HS; Pittsburgh, PA; (Y); 34/156; Church Yth Grp; French Clb; Service Clb; Yrbk Stf; Hon Roll; Mission Club Awd 85-86; Bus.

CRAWFORD, KATHLEEN; York County Vo-Tech HS; York, PA; (Y); 8/412; Am Leg Aux Girls St; Girl Scts; Sec VICA; Band; Flag Corp; Cheerleading; Mgr(s); Score Keeper; High Hon Roll; NHS; VICA Open & Clsg Tm Dist Comp 1st & 2nd Pl 85 & 86; USAF; Air Trffc Cntrllr.

CRAWFORD, LAURA; Brookville Area HS; Brockway, PA; (Y); VP FBLA; High Hon Roll; Jr NHS; Pres Acdmc Ftns Awd 86; Bus.

CRAWFORD, LINDA; South Western HS; Hanover, PA; (Y); 4/205; JA; Key Clb; Chorus; Var Capt Cheerleading; JV Vllybl; High Hon Roll; NHS; Ntl Merit Ltr; NEDT Awd; Prfct Atten Awd; SICO Fndtn Scholar 86; Pres Acad Fit Awd 86; Millersville U; Med Tech.

CRAWFORD, MICHAEL; Dittanning SR HS; Worthington, PA; (Y); Pres Church Yth Grp; Var JV Bsktbl; Var JV Ftbl; L Var Tennis; High Hon Roll; 1st Pl ARIN Comp Fair 84; Finc.

CRAWFORD, MICHELLE; Apollo-Ridge HS; Apollo, PA; (Y); Church Yth Grp; Drama Clb; German Clb; Math Clb; Band; Color Guard; Concert Band; Madrigals; Mrchg Band; Pep Band; Soc Dstrgshd Am HS Stu 85; Mrs Max Glaphy Rubin Me Schlrshp 86; Bndsmn Of Yr 86; Edinboro; Elem Ed.

CRAWFORD, MICHELLE; Christian School Of York; York, PA; (Y); Church Yth Grp; Hosp Aide; Library Aide; Band; Chorus; School Musical; School Play; Stu Cncl; Cheerleading; Fld Hcky; US State Achvt Acdmy 84 & 86; Sci.

CRAWFORD, MICHELLE; Slippery Rock Area HS; Slippery Rock, PA; (Y); Intnl Clb; Pep Clb; Teachers Aide; Varsity Clb; Drill Tm; Variety Show; Yrbk Stf; Sec Soph Cls; Sec Jr Cls; Stu Cncl; Cmmnctns.

CRAWFORD, PATRICIA; Chambersburg Area SR HS; Chambersburg, PA; (Y); 11/610; Church Yth Grp; Spanish Clb; Chorus; Church Choir; Orch; High Hon Roll; NHS; VA Polytech Inst; Arch.

CRAWFORD, SHARON; Avon Grove HS; W Grove, PA; (Y); SADD; School Play; Var Capt Cheerleading; High Hon Roll; Hon Roll; NHS; Distngshd Hnr Rll 85-86; Goldey Beacom Coll; Acctg.

CRAWFORD, STACY ALAN; Dover HS; Dover, PA; (S); Pres Church Yth Grp; Chorus; Church Choir; School Musical; School Play; Variety Show; Var Crs Cntry; Tennis; Hon Roll; Dist Chorus 84-86; Renaissance 84-86; Shippensberg U; Pol Sci.

CRAWFORD, TINA; Bradford Central Christian HS; Bradford, PA; (Y); 2/26; SADD; School Musical; VP Soph Cls; Cheerleading; High Hon Roll; Jr NHS; NHS; Ntl Merit Ltr; NEDT Awd; Drama Clb; Mst Val Chrldr Trophy Otto-Eldred Tourn 85; Cmmrcl Art.

CRAWN, THOMAS; Pius X HS; Roseto, PA; (Y); Boy Scts; Rep Soph Cls; Stu Cncl; Var Bsbl; Var Ftbl; Var Wrstlng; Hon Roll; Prfct Atten Awd; Marines; Engrng.

CRAZE, SHERRI; Bethel Park SR HS; Bethel Pk, PA; (Y); Church Yth Grp; Ski Clb; Band; Church Choir; Concert Band; Drill Tm; Mrchg Band; Var Stu Cncl; Var Pom Pon; High Hon Roll; Nrsng.

CREAMER, MICHAEL; Souderton HS; Telford, PA; (Y); FCA; Hosp Aide; SADD; Stage Crew; Rep Frsh Cls; Rep Soph Cls; Pres Jr Cls; Rep Stu Cncl; Im Coach Actv; L Trk; Acdmc Stud Awd Soc Studies 85; Presdntl Phys Fitness Awd 84; Aviation.

CREASY, LESLA; Central Columbia Schl District; Bloomsburg, PA; (Y); 14/178; Hosp Aide; Key Clb; Varsity Clb; Var Capt Swmmng; Var Trk; High Hon Roll; Hon Roll; NHS; Pres Acadmc Achvt Awd 86; Vietnam Vets Mem Achvt Awd 86; Duquesne U Comptv Achvt Schlrshp 86; Duquesne U; Bio.

CREASY, THERESA M; Bloomsburg Area SR HS; Bloomsburg, PA; (Y); 1/111; Scholastic Bowl; Teachers Aide; High Hon Roll; NHS; Pres Schlr; Rotary Awd; Val; 4-H; Rep Stu Cncl; Var Sftbl; Cmncmnt Spkr 86; GM/WBRE 28 Bst Of Cls 86; Blmsbrg U PA; Scndry Ed Math.

CREE, KELLIE; Central Dauphin HS; Harrisburg, PA; (Y); 3/380; Church Yth Grp; Sec PAVAS; Science Clb; Madrigals; Nwsp Ed-Chief; High Hon Roll; Jr NHS; NHS; Aud/Vis; Drama Clb; PTA Awd Socl Stds, Latn, Engl, Sci 84; Acdmc Stdnt Mnth 85; Patriot News Co Engl Awd 84; Spnsh.

CREIGHTON, TOM; Manheim Central HS; Manheim, PA; (Y); Chess Clb; Church Yth Grp; 4-H; School Play; Yrbk Phtg; Rep Sr Cls; Var Ftbl; L Wt Lftg; High Hon Roll; Rotary Awd; Rotary Awd-Outstndng Jr Boy 86; U Of DE; Engrng.

CREMARD, MARYANN; Pittston Area HS; Duryea, PA; (Y); Key Clb; Ski Clb; Sftbl; High Hon Roll; Hon Roll; NHS; Accntng.

CREMO, JULIA; Montoursville Area HS; Montoursville, PA; (Y); Pres Church Yth Grp; Key Clb; Spanish Clb; School Musical; Nwsp Rptr; Nwsp Stf; Stat Socr; Stat Trk; Hon Roll; Crimnl Justc.

CRENETI, JOANNE T; Archbishop Ryan HS For Girls; Philadelphia, PA; (Y); 4/488; Church Yth Grp; JA; Mathletes; Q&S; SADD; Chorus; Nwsp Stf; Yrbk Stf; Bowling; Sftbl; Indiv Clssrm Awds 82-86; All Str Athl 83-84; Var Hnr Sci Italn & Qll & Scrll 84-85; Drexel U; Engrng.

CRESCENZI, MICHAEL; Northern HS; Dillsburg, PA; (Y); 13/200; Quiz Bowl; Church Choir; School Musical; Yrbk Stf; L Crs Cntry; Powder Puff Ftbl; L Trk; Hon Roll; Ntl Merit Ltr; Pres Schlr; PA Sst U.

CRESCENZI, STACIA; Northern HS; Dillsburg, PA; (Y); 20/209; Church Yth Grp; Band; Chorus; Church Choir; Nwsp Stf; Yrbk Stf; JV Var Bsktbl; Powder Puff Ftbl; French Hon Soc; Psychlgy.

CRESKOFF, DANIEL; Cheltenham HS; Elkins Pk, PA; (Y); 171/365; Temple Yth Grp; Stage Crew; Cmnctns.

CRESPO, DEBORAH; Shenango HS; New Castle, PA; (Y); 5/115; Church Yth Grp; Girl Scts; Yrbk Ed-Chief; Yrbk Stf; Stat Gym; High Hon Roll; Hon Roll; Lion Awd; NHS; NEDT Awd; GSA Slvr Awd; Deaf Educ.

CRESSMAN, TIM; Southmoreland HS; Scottdale, PA; (Y); 4/227; Church Yth Grp; French Clb; Letterman Clb; Rep Stu Cncl; Var L Bsktbl; Var L Socr; Var L Trk; French Hon Soc; NHS; Comp Info Systms.

CREW, JESSE R; Owen J Roberts HS; Elverson, PA; (Y); 43/267; Am Leg Boys St; Boy Scts; Letterman Clb; Lit Mag; Var Bsbl; Var Capt Socr; Hon Roll; NEDT Awd; Bloomsburg U Alumni Awd 86; Eagle Scout; Bloomsburg U Of PA; Comp Infor.

CRICHTON, PAIGE; Unionville HS; Kennett Square, PA; (Y); 37/300; Var Crs Cntry; Var Trk; Hon Roll; Eng Awd; All Lg 400m Trck; Blgy.

CRIDER, MATTHEW; Elizabethtown Area HS; Elizabethtown, PA; (Y); 12/280; Church Yth Grp; Model UN; Band; Chorus; Orch; School Musical; School Play; Yrbk Stf; Ftbl; Wrstlng; Pres Human Rltns Clb; Elec Tech; Acad.

CRIDER, ROGER; Seneca Valley HS; Evans City, PA; (Y); 21/370; Church Yth Grp; Letterman Clb; Trs Office Aide; Spanish Clb; Varsity Clb; Capt Bsktbl; L Capt Ftbl; Var L Trk; Hon Roll; Prfct Atten Awd; 2nd Tm Greater Allegheny All Conf Ftbl 86; Post Gazette All Stars Ftbl 86; Engrng.

CRILLEY, JOSEPH PETER; Northwestern SR HS; E Springfield, PA; (Y); 20/165; Boy Scts; Camera Clb; Math Tm; Quiz Bowl; VP Science Clb; Ski Clb; JV L Trk; Hon Roll; PA Fr Entrprs Wk 86; Yng Schlr Smmr Sns U Of CO Boulder 86; PA ST U; Arspc Engrng.

CRIM, APRIL; Liberty HS; Bethlehem, PA; (Y); 100/475; Church Yth Grp; Chorus; Tennis; Bloomsburg U; Spec Educ.

CRIMONE II, JOSEPH; Somerset SR HS; Somerset, PA; (Y); 42/239; Church Yth Grp; English Clb; Letterman Clb; NFL; Jazz Band; Rep Jr Cls; Stu Cncl; Golf; High Hon Roll; NHS; Medical Dr.

CRINITI, ROSA; St Maria Goretti HS; Philadelphia, PA; (Y); 57/390; Church Yth Grp; Pres Exploring; GAA; Office Aide; Spanish Clb; Hon Roll; Prfct Atten Awd; Rep Frsh Cls; Rep Soph Cls; Rep Jr Cls; Amer HS Math Exm; Ntl Math Leag Exms; Bus Mgt.

CRISMAN, TAMMY L; Franklin Area JR SR HS; Franklin, PA; (Y); 30/223; Varsity Clb; Band; Color Guard; Var Capt Sftbl; High Hon Roll; NHS; Church Yth Grp; Concert Band; Schl Brd Dir Awd; Gov Art Exhibit Awd; Westminster Coll; Art.

CRISMAN, TRACY; Allegheny-Clamon Valley HS; Emlenton, PA; (Y); 1/97; Chorus; Mrchg Band; Pep Band; Rep Stu Cncl; Var Cheerleading; Var Trk; Var JV Vllybl; High Hon Roll; NHS; Prfct Atten Awd; 2nd Pl Am Leg Essay Cont 86; U Pittsburgh; Phys Ther.

CRISPELL, CAROL ANNE; Commodore Perry HS; Clarks Mills, PA; (S); 11/64; Drama Clb; Band; Chorus; Concert Band; Mrchg Band; Pep Band; Var Cheerleading; Hon Roll; Church Yth Grp; Office Aide; Band Ltr; JR Yr Bannd Jckt; V Chrldng Jckt; Perf Arts.

CRISPELL, DAVID; Berwick SR HS; Berwick, PA; (Y); Church Yth Grp; Church Choir; Wt Lftg; Wrstlng; High Hon Roll; Hon Roll; NHS; Liberty Bible Coll; Aviation.

CRISSMAN, FRANK; Yough HS; Ruffsdale, PA; (Y); 17/256; Church Yth Grp; Computer Clb; Spanish Clb; Chorus; School Musical; Stage Crew; Bsbl; High Hon Roll; NHS; Comp Sci.

CRIST, BRIAN; Williams Valley HS; Reinerton, PA; (Y); 14/101; Band; Concert Band; Jazz Band; Mrchg Band; Symp Band; Hon Roll; NEDT Awd; 4-H; Pep Clb; Chorus; Cnty Bnd 1st Chair 84-86; SR Twin Valley Band 84-86; Navy; Nuclear Physics.

CRIST, MICHELLE; Halifax Area HS; Halifax, PA; (Y); 24/103; Church Yth Grp; Drama Clb; Band; Chorus; Church Choir; Concert Band; Drm Mjr(t); Mrchg Band; Stage Crew; Hon Roll; Yth Schlrs Inst Awd Lebanon Vly Coll 86; Lebanon Valley Coll; Music Ed.

CRIST, MICHELLE DENISE; Eastern York HS; York, PA; (Y); 6/159; Am Leg Aux Girls St; Church Yth Grp; JV Var Bsktbl; JV Var Vllybl; High Hon Roll; Hon Roll; Jr NHS; NHS; Dist Rep Rtry Ldrs Cnfrnc 86; Amrcn Lgn Schl Awd 83; Prsdntl Physcl Ftnss Awd 83&85; Med.

CRISTOFANO, LEE D; Bethel Park SR HS; Bethel Park, PA; (Y); 49/525; Computer Clb; Math Tm; Science Clb; Golf; Cit Awd; Hon Roll; Pres Schlr; Pres Acad Ftns Awd 86; Outstndng Citznshp Awd 86; Carnegie Mellon U; Physics.

CRITCHFIELD, SHELLEY; Mary Fuller Frazier Memorial HS; Star Junction, PA; (Y); FNA; Yrbk Stf; Off Frsh Cls; Off Soph Cls; Trs Jr Cls; Trs Sr Cls; Stu Cncl; JV Var Cheerleading; Hon Roll; CA U PA; Spch Pthlgy.

CRITCHLEY, MICHAEL J; Carbondale Area HS; Carbondale, PA; (Y); 4/137; FBLA; Trs German Clb; Scholastic Bowl; Yrbk Ed-Chief; Stat Bsbl; Stat Bsktbl; High Hon Roll; NHS; Ntl Merit SF; Jrnlst.

CROCE, CHRISTINA; Lock Haven HS; Lock Haven, PA; (Y); Cmnty Wkr; VP FHA; Spanish Clb; Nwsp Stf; JV Bsktbl; Im Mgr Sftbl; High Hon Roll; NHS; NEDT Awd; Prfct Atten Awd; Mlly Frmm Awd-Excllnc-Bio 85; Tchng.

CROCE, PATRICIA; West Catholic Girls HS; Philadelphia, PA; (Y); 6/240; Drama Clb; French Clb; School Musical; School Play; Nwsp Rptr; Nwsp Stf; Lit Mag; High Hon Roll; Hon Roll; NHS; Kthrn Gibbs Ldrshp Awd 86; Katherine Gibbs School; Scrtrl.

CROCK, TODD; Lackawanna Trail HS; Nicholson, PA; (Y); Bsbl; Bsktbl; Hon Roll; Acctg.

CROCKARD, JAMES; Carmichaels Area SR HS; Carmichaels, PA; (S); 2/101; Boy Scts; Drama Clb; Spanish Clb; SADD; School Play; High Hon Roll; NHS; NEDT Awd; 1st Pl Olympcs Mind 86; Order Arrow 86; Corp Law.

CROCKER, MARIE; Fort Le Boeuf HS; Waterford, PA; (Y); 12/185; Computer Clb; Model UN; Ski Clb; Band; Drill Tm; Rep Sr Cls; Cheerleading; Sftbl; Vllybl; High Hon Roll; Pres Acdmc Fit Awd 86; Mc Donalds All Erie Cnty Hs Bnd 86; Edinboro.

CROFTCHECK, SUZIE; Brownsville HS; Republic, PA; (Y); 27/223; Chess Clb; Church Yth Grp; Drama Clb; Intnl Clb; Office Aide; Ski Clb; SADD; Y-Teens; Band; Drm Mjr(t); U Pittsburgh; Ed.

CROFTON, ANTHONY; Hopewell HS; Aliquippa, PA; (Y); 10/243; Church Yth Grp; Pres Exploring; Spanish Clb; Rep Frsh Cls; Rep Soph Cls; Rep Jr Cls; Var Bsbl; Beaver Cnty Times Nwsp Carrier Yr 83, Fin 84; 2nd Pl PA Nwsp Pblshrs Assn Carrier Yr 83; Pre-Med.

CROLL, HEIDI; West Hazelton HS; Weston, PA; (Y); Church Yth Grp; French Clb; FBLA; Office Aide; Ski Clb; SADD; Teachers Aide; Yrbk Stf; Rep Soph Cls; Mgr(s); Elec Qn Hrts Annl Sprng Frml 84; Fshn Dsgn.

CROLL, MICHELLE L; West Hazleton HS; Zion Grove, PA; (S); 6/192; FBLA; Ski Clb; Color Guard; L Trk; High Hon Roll; NHS; PA ST U; Elec Engrng.

CRONAUER, ANNETTE M; Cambria Hts HS; Carrolltown, PA; (Y); 19/183; Pres FHA; Q&S; Lib Concert Band; Hst Mrchg Band; Ed Nwsp Stf; Elks Awd; High Hon Roll; NHS; Siempre Fidelis Awd Muiscl Excllnce 86; Schltc Prfmnce Awd 86; St Francis Coll; Bio.

CRONCE, DIANE E; Owen J Roberts HS; Elverson, PA; (S); 21/267; Letterman Clb; Jazz Band; Mrchg Band; Symp Band; Var L Lcrss; Var L Sftbl; Var L Tennis; High Hon Roll; Pres NHS; Kutztown U; Spch.

CRONLUND, SARAH L; The Academy Of The New Church; Bryn Athyn, PA; (Y); 1/36; Sec French Clb; Math Tm; Yrbk Bus Mgr; Var Bsktbl; JV Fld Hcky; Im Lcrss; Im Socr; Var L Swmmng; Ntl Merit SF; High Hon Roll; 2nd Cnty Sci Fair 81-82; AM ST Sci Fair; GS Challange & Gld Ldrshp 82-83; HM Cnty Sci Fair; Physcn.

CROOM, ROCHELLE; Wilkinsburg JR SR HS; Wilkinsburg, PA; (Y); French Clb; Y-Teens; Capt Cheerleading; Hon Roll; Mst Schl Spirit Awd 85; Cutest Smile 85; Mst Poplr 85; Secrtrl.

CROPCHO, MARGARET; Burrell HS; Lower Burrell, PA; (Y); JA; Sec VP Spanish Clb; Nwsp Stf; Yrbk Stf; Var L Swmmng; High Hon Roll; Jr NHS; NHS; Ntl Merit Ltr; NEDT Awd.

CROSBY, CATHERINE K; Carlisle SR HS; Erie, PA; (Y); Capt Computer Clb; Dance Clb; Drama Clb; School Play; High Hon Roll; Hon Roll; Jr NHS; NHS; PA Jr Acad Of Sci-St Comptn 1st & 2nd Pl 83-84; Gannon U Comp Prgmng Comptn 3rd Pl 85.

CROSBY, LORI; Pocono Mountain HS; Cresco, PA; (Y); Church Yth Grp; Band; Chorus; Church Choir; School Musical; Rptr Nwsp Rptr; Nwsp Stf; Jrnlstc Cmmntncs.

CROSKEY, PAM; Richland HS; Gibsonia, PA; (Y); AFS; School Musical; Stage Crew; Hon Roll; Bradford Schl; Sec.

CROSKEY, YVETTE M; Mount Saint Joseph Acad; Wyndmoor, PA; (Y); Drama Clb; French Clb; Chorus; Orch; School Musical; School Play; Stage Crew; Lit Mag; Im Socr; Im Vllybl; Free Enterprise Fellowship 86; MSJA Scholarship 83-84; Most Promising Actress 84-85.

CROSS, BRIAN G; Germantown Acad; Wyncote, PA; (Y); Cmnty Wkr; Computer Clb; Math Clb; Teachers Aide; School Play; Ed Lit Mag; French Hon Soc; High Hon Roll; Ntl Merit SF.

CROSS, VALERIE; Brownsville Area HS; Brownsville, PA; (Y); Hosp Aide; Library Aide; Ski Clb; SADD; Band; Drill Tm; Drm Mjr(t); Mrchg Band; Yrbk Bus Mgr; Yrbk Stf; CA U PA; Acctng.

CROSSMAN, CHRISTINE; Owen J Roberts HS; Spring City, PA; (S); 18/291; JCL; Library Aide; Chorus; School Musical; School Play; JV Trk; Im Vllybl; Hon Roll; NHS.

CROSSON, MAYLAND; Westtown Schl; Collegeville, PA; (Y); Computer Clb; German Clb; Mathletes; Service Clb; SADD; Acpl Chr; Chorus; Madrigals; Swmmng; Vllybl; Penn ST U; Bus Mgmt.

CROTEAU, CRAIG; Wyoming Area SR HS; W Pittston, PA; (Y); Chess Clb; French Clb; Kings Coll; Chem.

CROTHERS, RAY; Canon Mc Millan HS; Canonsburg, PA; (Y); 10/350; Ski Clb; Varsity Clb; Ftbl; NHS; Carnegie-Mellon; Ec.

CROUSE, JOANNA; Berwick Area SR HS; Berwick, PA; (Y); Trs Church Yth Grp; Natl Beta Clb; L Band; Concert Band; Jazz Band; Mrchg Band; Mgr(s); Hon Roll; Jr NHS; NHS; Nrsng.

CROUSE, KAREN; Mc Connellsburg HS; Big Cove Tannery, PA; (Y); Cmnty Wkr; FHA; Color Guard; Yrbk Stf; VP Frsh Cls; VP Soph Cls; Trs Jr Cls; RN.

CROUSE, SCHON; Connellsville SR HS; Acme, PA; (Y); Wt Lftg; Penn Tech; Comp Repair.

CROUSHORE, DEANNA; Belle Vernon Area HS; Belle Vernon, PA; (Y); Art Clb; Camera Clb; Pres Library Aide; Pep Clb; Spanish Clb; Chorus; High Hon Roll; Hon Roll; Phchlgy.

CROUSHORE JR, WILLIAM; Southmoreland SR HS; Ruffsdale, PA; (Y); 22/240; Church Yth Grp; German Clb; Latin Clb; Letterman Clb; Ski Clb; Varsity Clb; Stu Cncl; Socr; Trk; Hon Roll; Duquesne U; Pharmacy.

CROW, DAVID; Western Beaver HS; Industry, PA; (Y); Band; Concert Band; Jazz Band; Mrchg Band; Pep Band; Hon Roll; NHS.

CROW, KATHY LYN; Hamburg Area HS; Shoemakersville, PA; (Y); Library Aide; High Hon Roll; Hon Roll; NHS; Intl Frgn Lang Awd Spnsh 85-86; York Coll; Mktg.

CROWE, BRENDA; Waynesboro SR HS; Waynesboro, PA; (Y); Chorus; Capt Fld Hcky; Var Trk; High Hon Roll; Hon Roll; NHS; Achvt Awd Algebra 84; Excellnc Awd Soc Stu 84; Criminology.

CROWE, MARY; Trinity HS; Mechanicsburg, PA; (Y); 37/140; Church Yth Grp; Drama Clb; French Clb; Hosp Aide; Pep Clb; Varsity Clb; Chorus; Church Choir; School Musical; Var L Trk; Med.

CROWLEY, ALISA; Alto-Eldred JR SR HS; Eldred, PA; (Y); Church Yth Grp; Library Aide; Varsity Clb; School Play; Capt Trk; Stat Vllybl; Hon Roll; Lion Awd; Presdntl Acadmc Fitns Awd 86; Hnrs 86; Edinboro U; Comp Sci.

CROWN, STEPHANIE; Northeast Bradford HS; Rome, PA; (Y); Art Clb; Debate Tm; FHA; Red Cross Aide; Chorus; Stage Crew; Nwsp Rptr; Twrlr; Hon Roll; Rotary Awd; Social Wrk.

CROWNER, ROBERT; Cathedral Prep; Erie, PA; (Y); 3/231; Church Yth Grp; Office Aide; L Trk; High Hon Roll; Kiwanis Awd; NHS; Ntl Merit SF; Pres Schlr; Frshmn Exclnc Awd Penn ST; Latin Scty Hnr Summa Cum Laude; Penn ST; Math.

CROWTHER, CURTIS J; Chichester SR HS; Linwood, PA; (Y); Debate Tm; Model UN; Political Wkr; Nwsp Stf; High Hon Roll; Hon Roll; Close-Up Govt Studies Pgm 84 & 85; Frgn Affairs Tele-Conf 86; Neumann Coll; Pol Sci.

CROY, MICHELE; Grove City HS; Grove City, PA; (Y); 20/195; Key Clb; Office Aide; Science Clb; Band; Concert Band; Mrchg Band; JV Var Cheerleading; High Hon Roll; Hon Roll; NHS; Bus.

CROYLE, MARIA; Somerset Area SR HS; Somerset, PA; (Y); 4/239; English Clb; French Clb; Trs Girl Scts; Hosp Aide; Rep Band; Concert Band; Mrchg Band; Yrbk Stf; Trs Jr Cls; Rep Stu Cncl; Millie Mathews Awd Achvt Music 84; Pharmacy.

CROYLE, PAMELA; Conemaugh Twp Area HS; Johnstown, PA; (Y); 12/104; Drama Clb; Girl Scts; NFL; Stage Crew; Yrbk Bus Mgr; Lit Mag; Trk; Dnfth Awd; NHS; Cambria Rowe Schlrshp 86; Cambria Rowe Bus Clg; Exec Sec.

CRULL, TARA; West Perry HS; New Bloomfield, PA; (Y); Spanish Clb; Varsity Clb; Mrchg Band; Yrbk Stf; Stat Sftbl; Twrlr; Hon Roll; Comp Sci.

CRUM, HARRY; Aliquippa HS; Aliquippa, PA; (Y); French Clb; Band; Concert Band; Mrchg Band; Orch; Pep Band; Symp Band; Air Force.

CRUM, JODI; Upper Dauphin Area HS; Halifax, PA; (Y); Church Yth Grp; SADD; Band; Chorus; Concert Band; Mrchg Band; Pep Band; L Capt Trk; 1st Fml All Str Trck Athlt 86; Law.

CRUM, RICHARD; Altoona Area HS; Altoona, PA; (Y); Var Wrstlng; Hon Roll; Sci.

CRUMITY, DOMETA; Aliquippa HS; Aliquippa, PA; (Y); Band; PA ST; Lib Arts.

CRUMLEY, BARBARA; Henderson HS; West Chester, PA; (S); Pres DECA; Art Clb; Chorus; Trs Frsh Cls; Sec Soph Cls; Sec Jr Cls; Rep Stu Cncl; Var JV Fld Hcky; JV Lcrss; NHS; Distr DECA Comp 85-86; Ntl DECA Comp 10fnlst 86; Mngmt.

CRUMLICH, SUSAN; Susquenita JR SR HS; Marysville, PA; (S); 5/153; Am Leg Aux Girls St; French Clb; Quiz Bowl; Drm Mjr(t); Yrbk Ed-Chief; Trs Soph Cls; Trs Jr Cls; VP Sr Cls; Rep Stu Cncl; Pres NHS; Temple U; Physcl Thrpy.

CRUZ, LYNN; East SR HS; West Chester, PA; (Y); DECA; Chorus; Hon Roll; Early Admsn Schlrshp Moore Coll Of Art 86; Moore Coll Of Art; Grphc Dsgn.

CRUZ, ROSE; Little Flower HS; Philadelphia, PA; (Y); 70/416; JA; Latin Clb; Spanish Clb; Orch; School Musical; Symp Band; Hon Roll; Prfct Atten Awd; Pres Schlr; Frankford Nrsng Schl; Nrs.

CRYNOCK, SCOTT; Portage Area HS; Portage, PA; (S); 2/112; Am Leg Boys St; Aud/Vis; SADD; Variety Show; VP Jr Cls; Rep Stu Cncl; Bsktbl; Vllybl; High Hon Roll; Hon Roll; Chem I Awd 84; Calc Awd 86; U Of Pittsburgh-Johnstown; Engr.

CSENSITS, DENNIS; William Allen HS; Allentown, PA; (Y); Varsity Clb; Rep Stu Cncl; Var L Bsktbl; Coach Actv; Var L Crs Cntry; JV Socr; Trk; Hon Roll; Vrsty A Clb Schlrshp 86; Stu Advncmnt Fnd Schlrshp 86; Allntwn Coll; Mth.

CUBA, BARBIE; Punysutawney Area HS; Punxsutawney, PA; (Y); 16/238; French Clb; FBLA; Math Tm; Science Clb; Band; Color Guard; Variety Show; Yrbk Ed-Chief; Hon Roll; NHS; Penn ST U; Math Ed.

CUBBARLEY, JOSEPH; Hughesville JR & SR HS; Hughesville, PA; (Y); Speech Tm; Band; Concert Band; Mrchg Band; Bsktbl; Var Socr; Trk; Ltrd In Trk & Sccr 85-86; Mansfield; Vet-Med.

CUCUZZA, ROBERT J; Bradford Central Christian HS; Bradford, PA; (Y); 1/31; Pres Drama Clb; Key Clb; SADD; School Musical; School Play; Stage Crew; High Hon Roll; NHS; PA Govrs Schl For Arts 85; Exch Clb Stu Of Mnth 85; Ntl Engl Merit Awd 86; Emerson Coll; Threatr.

CUDDINGTON, TODD; Trinity HS; Mechanicsburg, PA; (Y); 12/146; French Clb; Im Bsktbl; Var Socr; Var Trk; Hon Roll; Ntl Merit Ltr; Natl Hnr Roll 85; Engrng.

CUFF, ALICIA; Shenandoah Valley JR/SR HS; Shenandoah, PA; (Y); Pep Clb; Nwsp Stf; Yrbk Stf; JV Cheerleading; Hon Roll; Bus.

CUFF, TOM; Cardinal Brennan HS; Frackville, PA; (Y); 15/51; Letterman Clb; Rep Soph Cls; Rep Sr Cls; Stu Cncl; Var L Bsbl; Var L Ftbl; Im Vllybl; Im Wt Lftg; Hon Roll; Cert Of Hnr Engl III 86; Acdmc All-Amrcn Awd 86; U Of Pittsburgh; Physcl Thrpy.

CULBERTSON, CHRISTOPHER; Oil City HS; Oil City, PA; (Y); Boy Scts; Yrbk Stf; Sec Jr Cls; Sec Sr Cls; Rep Stu Cncl; Var Bsbl; JV Bsktbl; Var Crs Cntry; Im Ftbl; Im Socr; ROTC Schlrshp-Air Force 86; Eagle Scout 84; Gd Ctznshp Awd-PA Hse Of Reps 84; OH ST U; Aerosp Engrng.

CULBERTSON, DEANNE; Youngsville HS; Youngsville, PA; (Y); French Clb; SADD; Band; Chorus; Color Guard; Concert Band; Mrchg Band; School Play; Trk; Vllybl; SOCIAL Working.

CULLEN, ANDREW; Notre Dame HS; E Stroudsubrg, PA; (Y); 2/38; Chess Clb; Cmnty Wkr; French Clb; Math Clb; Math Tm; Quiz Bowl; Scholastic Bowl; Ski Clb; Teachers Aide; Thesps; Mstrs Mates & Plts Schlrshp 86; Pratt Inst Srch Ftr Engrs 86; Conaught Labs 86; Penn ST U; Mech Engr.

CULLEN, DONNY; Donald G Cullen HS; Bentleyville, PA; (Y); FBLA; Letterman Clb; Math Clb; PAVAS; Varsity Clb; Off Sr Cls; JV Bsktbl; Var Ftbl; Wt Lftg; Acctng.

CULLEN, LISA; St Maria Goretti HS; Philadelphia, PA; (Y); Cmnty Wkr; Hosp Aide; Chorus; Hon Roll; CC Of Phila; Resprtry Thrpy.

CULLEN, MARY; Wyalusing HS; New Albany, PA; (Y); German Clb; Band; Concert Band; Mrchg Band; Orch; Trk; Hon Roll.

CULLEN, THERESA; Wyalusing HS; New Albany, PA; (Y); German Clb; Band; Concert Band; Mrchg Band; Orch; Trk; High Hon Roll; Hon Roll; NHS; Prfct Atten Awd; Engrng.

CULLER, BRENT; Mc Connellsburg HS; Mcconnellsburg, PA; (Y); Church Yth Grp; Varsity Clb; School Musical; Var L Socr; Var L Trk; Jr NHS; NHS; Point Park Coll; Poli Sci.

CULLER, CORINNA; Southern Huntingdon County HS; Three Spgs, PA; (Y); 1/118; Sec GAA; SADD; Band; Chorus; Flag Corp; Yrbk Stf; Var Fld Hcky; Powder Puff Ftbl; Bausch & Lomb Sci Awd; NHS; U Pittsburgh.

CULLER, JENNIFER; St Francis Acad; Bethel Park, PA; (S); 6/35; Pres Church Yth Grp; Hosp Aide; Trs Speech Tm; Chorus; Yrbk Stf; Trs Stu Cncl; Twrlr; High Hon Roll; NHS; NEDT Awd; Pa Jr Acad Sci 1st Regnls 2nd ST 83; Furman U; Pre-Med.

CULLEY, LYNN; Slippery Rock Area HS; Slippery Rock, PA; (Y); Church Yth Grp; FBLA; SADD; Chorus; Stat Score Keeper; Hon Roll.

CULLIMORE, JOHN; William Allen HS; Allentown, PA; (Y); Nwsp Rptr; Socr; High Hon Roll; Hon Roll; Jr NHS; NHS; Summ Cum Hnr Schlrshp Awd; Med.

CULP, DAVE; United HS; New Florence, PA; (Y); 12/157; Art Clb; Boy Scts; Church Yth Grp; VP Exploring; Concert Band; Mrchg Band; Trk; High Hon Roll; Hon Roll; NHS; IN U PA; Pltcl Sci.

CULP, DIANE; Columbia Montour AVTS HS; Wapwallopen, PA; (Y); 14/184; Math Tm; VICA; Nwsp Rptr; Nwsp Stf; Hon Roll; Kiwanis Awd; Rotary Awd; Hnrbl Ment Poetry Cntst 86; Pres Acad Ftns Awd 86; Users Grp Schrlshp Awd 86; Luzerne County CC; Bus.

CULP, KIMBERLY; Dallas SR HS; Dallas, PA; (Y); Hosp Aide; Sec Key Clb; Red Cross Aide; Var Crs Cntry; Var Trk; Hon Roll; NHS; Acad Recognition Awd 85; Pres Phys Ftnss Awd 85-86; Obstrn.

CULP, STEVE; Bellwood-Arts HS; Tyrone, PA; (Y); VICA; Var Bsktbl; Im Vllybl; Wt Lftg; JV Wrstlng; Hon Roll; 1st Pl Regional VICA Comp Ind Elec-Placed In St Events 86; PA ST; Elec Engrng.

CULVER, CHRISTINE; Bethlehem Catholic HS; Bethlehem, PA; (Y); 40/201; JV Sftbl; Capt Twrlr; NHS; E Stroudsberg; Elem Ed.

CUMBERLAND, BRENDA; South Allegheny HS; Elizabeth, PA; (Y); VP Sec Exploring; FNA; Girl Scts; Sec JA; Library Aide; Pep Clb; VICA; Y-Teens; Chorus; Capt Powder Puff Ftbl; CA U Of PA; Nrs.

CUMBERLEDGE, BRIAN; Canon Mc Millan HS; Canonsburg, PA; (Y); 45/395; Boy Scts; Church Yth Grp; Latin Clb; Ski Clb; Tennis; Bryant; Accntng.

CUMBERLEDGE, RICK; Seneca Valley HS; Evans City, PA; (Y); 32/380; Ski Clb; Varsity Clb; Rep Frsh Cls; Rep Stu Cncl; Var Ftbl; Hon Roll; Bus.

CUMBERTEDGE, KRISTIE; Waynesburg Central HS; Brave, PA; (Y); FHA; Library Aide; VICA.

CUMMINGS, CRAIG; Sun Valley HS; Brookhaven, PA; (Y); 4/311; Scholastic Bowl; Science Clb; Band; Nwsp Stf; Yrbk Stf; Var Trk; High Hon Roll; Lion Awd; NHS; Ntl Merit Ltr; Cert D Hnr Fr Le Cncrs Ntl De Frncs 84; Brnz Mdlst In PA Sci Olympd 86; Lbn Vly Yth Schlrs Chem 86; Gntcs.

CUMMINGS, ERIN; Mankum Tap HS; York, PA; (Y); 47/365; Key Clb; Stu Cncl; Var Cheerleading; Mgr(s); Powder Puff Ftbl; JV Sftbl; Hon Roll; Lehigh; Bus Invstmnts.

CUMMINGS, JILL; Grove City HS; Grove City, PA; (Y); 15/154; Church Yth Grp; Office Aide; Pep Clb; Science Clb; Ski Clb; Yrbk Stf; Powder Puff Ftbl; Trk; High Hon Roll; Hon Roll; Pres Acad Fit Awd 86; Wmns Clb Home Life Merit Awd 86; Grove CC; Comm Art.

CUMMINGS, KATHERINE D; Kiski Area HS; Vandergrift, PA; (Y); French Clb; Hosp Aide; Office Aide; Y-Teens; Color Guard; Nwsp Stf; High Hon Roll; Hon Roll; NHS; Acad Ltr 83-85; Grad Hnrs 86; Edinboro U; Soc Wrk.

CUMMINGS, MEG; Johnsonburg Area HS; Johnsonburg, PA; (Y); Vllybl; Grls Sftbl Leag All-Star 83-86; Du Bois Bus Coll; Sec.

CUMMINGS, MICHAEL; Scranton Tech; Scranton, PA; (Y); 6/215; VICA; JV Bsbl; Hon Roll; NHS; Pres Acad Ftns Awd 86; Scranton Pres Schlrshp 86; U Scranton; Mgmt.

CUMMINS, LEEANNE; Montour HS; Pittsburgh, PA; (Y); High Hon Roll; Comp Engrng.

CUMPSTON, MICHELE; Burgettstown Area HS; Langeloth, PA; (Y); Drama Clb; French Clb; Chorus; High Hon Roll; Hon Roll; Jr NHS; NHS; Elctrl Engr.

CUNARD, REBECCA; Christian Schl Of York; York, PA; (Y); Church Yth Grp; Hosp Aide; School Play; Yrbk Stf; High Hon Roll; Hon Roll; Chrstn Ldrshp Awd 83; Med.

CUNDEY, MICHELE; Penn Wood HS; Colwyn, PA; (Y); FBLA; Hon Roll; Frank J Keane Schlrshp Fund 86; Penn ST U; Bus Mgt.

CUNKELMAN, BRIAN; Balirsville Sr HS; Blairsville, PA; (Y); 1/137; Pres Church Yth Grp; Ski Clb; SADD; Varsity Clb; Band; School Musical; Rep Stu Cncl; Var Ftbl; Var Trk; High Hon Roll; Brown U; Engrng.

CUNNINGHAM, BARBARA; Punxsutawney Ara HS; Punxsutawney, PA; (Y); FHA; GAA; Nwsp Rptr; Nwsp Stf; Bradford Schl; Fshn Mrchndsng.

CUNNINGHAM, CAROL; Bishop Carroll HS; Ebensburg, PA; (S); 3/109; Pep Clb; SADD; Chorus; Church Choir; JV Stat Bsktbl; Trk; Hon Roll; Med Tech.

CUNNINGHAM, CHRISTINE; Valley View JR SR HS; Blakely, PA; (Y); 6/195; Cmnty Wkr; Sec French Clb; Hosp Aide; Score Keeper; French Hon Soc; High Hon Roll; NHS; 1st Pl-Rgnl Comptn Of Ntl Frnch Cntst 84; 2nd Pl-Rgnl Comptn Of Ntl Frnch Cntst 85.

CUNNINGHAM, JANET; Homer-Center SR HS; Homer City, PA; (Y); VP Pres French Clb; Hosp Aide; Band; Jazz Band; Mrchg Band; Trs Jr Cls; High Hon Roll; Jr NHS; NHS; Pedtrn.

CUNNINGHAM, JOE; Wyoming Area HS; Exeter, PA; (Y); 17/267; Church Yth Grp; Cmnty Wkr; German Clb; Key Clb; Band; JV Bsbl; Im Bsktbl; JV Ftbl; Var Wrstlng; High Hon Roll; Elec Engrng.

CUNNINGHAM, KELLEY; Huntingdon Area HS; Huntingdon, PA; (Y); Church Yth Grp; Key Clb; Chorus; Church Choir; Madrigals; Yrbk Stf; Var Sftbl; Var Tennis; JV Vllybl; NEDT Awd; DE Clg Of Sci & Ag; Bio Chem.

CUNNINGHAM, KELLY; South Phila HS; Philadelphia, PA; (Y); Drama Clb; GAA; Varsity Clb; School Play; Variety Show; Nwsp Stf; JV Bsktbl; JV Vllybl; Cit Awd; High Hon Roll; Schlr Athlt Awd 84-85; Mst Acad Achvmnt 84-85; Penn ST; Acad.

CUNNINGHAM, MICHAEL; Burgettstown JR SR HS; Burgettstown, PA; (Y); 24/150; Ski Clb; Band; Mrchg Band; Pep Band; Yrbk Stf; JV Wrstlng; Hon Roll; Jr NHS; NHS; Engrng.

CUNNINGHAM, NICOLE; Warren Area HS; Warren, PA; (Y); 52/300; Pres Church Yth Grp; French Clb; Varsity Clb; Yrbk Stf; Trs Jr Cls; Crs Cntry; Capt L Diving; Trk; Jr NHS; Rtry Schlrshp 86; Gldn Drgn Awd Cmnty Invlvmt 85 & 86; Coaches Awd Dvng 82-86; U Pittsburgh; Sec Educ.

CUNNINGHAM, RUTH; Coatesville Area SR HS; Coatesville, PA; (Y); Church Yth Grp; Leo Clb; Ski Clb; Spanish Clb; Band; Chorus; Church Choir; Color Guard; Concert Band; Flag Corp; Chstr Cnty Jr Miss 86; Temple U; Bus Admin.

CUNNINGHAM, SHANNA; Huntingdon Area HS; Huntingdon, PA; (Y); 4/223; Church Yth Grp; French Clb; High Hon Roll; NHS; NEDT Awd; Hntgdn Cnty Dairy Prncs 86-87; Physcl Thrpy.

CUNNINGHAM, SHAUNA; Borgettstown Area JR SR HS; Burgettstown, PA; (Y); 9/172; Ski Clb; Spanish Clb; Yrbk Stf; High Hon Roll; Hon Roll; Jr NHS; NHS; IUP; Mngmnt.

CUNNINGHAM, SHELBY; J P Mc Caskey HS; Lancaster, PA; (Y); 75/450; AFS; Chorus; Nsrg.

CUNNINGHAM, STACY; Benton Area JR SR HS; Stillwater, PA; (Y); FTA; Keywanettes; Library Aide; School Play; Nwsp Rptr; Twrlr; Hon Roll; CPR; Accntng I & Typng I Awd; Scndry Educ.

CUOMO, JACQUELINE; Bishop Guilfoyle HS; Altoona, PA; (Y); 12/126; Cmnty Wkr; Ski Clb; Speech Tm; Yrbk Stf; Rep Frsh Cls; Stu Cncl; JV Cheerleading; Hon Roll; PA ST U.

CUPAIUOLO, LISA; Upper Darby HS; Lansdowne, PA; (Y); 13/550; Church Yth Grp; Teachers Aide; Var Capt Bsktbl; Var Sftbl; Var Capt Vllybl; High Hon Roll; Prfct Atten Awd; All Star All Cntrl Sftbl 86; 3rd Tm All Cntrl Vllybl 86; Occ Thrpy.

CUPANI, JULIA; Bishop Hoban HS; White-Haven, PA; (Y); Math Clb; Var L Crs Cntry; Tennis; Hon Roll; Math Awd Medal 86; Silver Cord Awd 86; Pres Phy Ftnss Awd 86; Drexel U; Chem Engr.

CUPEC, JENNIFER; Our Lady Of The Sacred Heart HS; Aliquippa, PA; (Y); Church Yth Grp; Hosp Aide; NFL; Pep Clb; Sec Soph Cls; Sec Trs Jr Cls; Sec Trs Sr Cls; Co-Capt Trk; Hon Roll; NHS; PA ST U; Elem Educ.

CUPILLARI, KRISTIN; Scranton Preparatory Schl; Factoryville, PA; (Y); 18/192; Church Yth Grp; Cmnty Wkr; Drama Clb; Service Clb; Chorus; Stage Crew; Yrbk Stf; High Hon Roll; NHS; Ballt Theater Scranton; Sr Co Soloist And Ballet Mistress.

CUPP, MICHELLE; Center HS; Monaca, PA; (Y); Exploring; Sec Latin Clb; Yrbk Stf; VP Frsh Cls; VP Jr Cls; Im Bowling; Im Sftbl; Hon Roll.

CUPPER, MOLLIE; Mon Valley Catholic HS; Monangahela, PA; (Y); Drama Clb; French Clb; FBLA; JA; Pep Clb; Ski Clb; Chorus; Stage Crew; Variety Show; Nwsp Rptr; Competitive Figure Sktng Cmpttns 80-86; French Natl Hon Soc 84-86; Boca Raton Coll.

CUPPETT, TAMMY; Turkeyfoot Valley Area HS; Addison, PA; (Y); 6/47; Am Leg Aux Girls St; Art Clb; Sec Drama Clb; Office Aide; Q&S; Chorus; School Play; Stage Crew; Nwsp Ed-Chief; Nwsp Phtg; Hnrs Prog Stu; Carlow Coll; BSN.

CUPPLES, JOYCLYN; Ridley HS; Ridley Park, PA; (Y); 48/400; Radio Clb; Thesps; Drill Tm; Hon Roll; NHS; Pres Schlr; Drama Clb; Library Aide; Chorus; Color Guard; Tony Awd Actg 84; Lydia Wade Tn Spch Cntst 85; Outstndng Contrbn ITA 86; Best Thespn 86; West Chester U; Comm.

CURCIO, CARRIE; Cameron County HS; Emporium, PA; (Y); Am Leg Aux Girls St; 4-H; Spanish Clb; Band; Concert Band; Mrchg Band; Pep Band; Yrbk Stf; JV Var Bsktbl; Powder Puff Ftbl; Vet.

CURCIO, LISA; Mary Fullor Frazier Memorial HS; Newell, PA; (Y); Library Aide; VICA; Hon Roll; Drctrs List 86; Pittsburgh Beauty Acad; Elec.

CURCIO, SONYA; Catasauqua HS; Catasauqua, PA; (Y); 7/125; Varsity Clb; Capt Color Guard; Powder Puff Ftbl; Var Capt Trk; Hon Roll; Pres Acad Ftnss Awd 86; Leonard Peckitt Mem Schlrshp 86; Hnr Grad 86; Millersville U; Chem Engrng.

CURCIO, VAUGHN; Kiski Area HS; Avonmore, PA; (Y); Bsbl; Ftbl; Hon Roll; U Ptsbrg.

CURIC, PAULA; Kennedy Christian HS; West Middlesex, PA; (Y); Church Yth Grp; Dance Clb; Library Aide; Science Clb; Yrbk Stf; Hon Roll; Ped.

CURLEY, JOSEPH; Wyoming Area HS; West Pittston, PA; (Y); Church Yth Grp; Computer Clb; French Clb; Ski Clb; Nwsp Rptr; Var Bsktbl; Var Ftbl; Pres Tennis; Var Capt Trk; Hon Roll; Times Leader Schlrshp 86; U Of Pittsburgh; Comptr Sci.

CURRAN, ANTOINETTE; Benton Area SR-SR HS; Benton, PA; (Y); 4/49; Art Clb; Hosp Aide; Keywanettes; Chorus; Co-Capt Drill Tm; School Play; Hst Soph Cls; Hst Jr Cls; Var Cheerleading; Var Fld Hcky; Bloomsburg U; Nrsg.

CURRAN, JENNIFER; Nazareth Acad; Philadelphia, PA; (S); 29/114; French Clb; Hosp Aide; Chorus; Church Choir; Orch; School Musical; Stu Cncl; Sftbl; Tennis; Hon Roll; 3rd Drexel Music Awd Comptn 85; Awd Outstnding Tennis, Sftbl, Sccr Ablty 84; Music.

CURRAN, KRIS; Cedar Crest HS; Lebanon, PA; (Y); Debate Tm; Latin Clb; Pep Clb; Band; Concert Band; Jazz Band; Orch; School Musical; Hon Roll; NHS; Dist Band 83-86; Regnl Band 85 & 86; Dist Orchstra 85; Bio.

CURRAN, MARY KRISTEN; Mc Keesport HS; White Oak, PA; (Y); 26/384; AFS; Trs Exploring; GAA; Office Aide; Teachers Aide; Rep Stu Cncl; Sftbl; High Hon Roll; NHS; Prfct Atten Awd; Rotary Hnr Stu; Coll Clb Schlrshp; Pres Acad Fitnss Awd; Penn ST U; Ele Engrng.

CURRAN, PETER; Blue Mountain Acad; Leesport, PA; (S); 1/64; Trs Latin Clb; Math Clb; Church Choir; JV Var Bsktbl; Var L Socr; Var L Tennis; Cit Awd; NHS; Ntl Merit Ltr; Val; Duke U; Med.

CURRAN, SUSAN M; Blue Mountain Acad; Leesport, PA; (Y); Girl Scts; Chorus; Church Choir; Off Frsh Cls; VP Soph Cls; VP Sr Cls; Stu Cncl; Im Capt Fld Hcky; High Hon Roll; Hon Roll; Andrews U; Psychlgy.

CURRAN, VINCENT; St Josephs Prep; Villanova, PA; (Y); Bsktbl; High Hon Roll; Athlt Of Wk 86; MVP Nrbrth Bsktbl All Stars 86; Ltn Mdl Of Excllnc 84-85; Bus.

CURRENS, KELLY; Gettysburg SR HS; Gettysburg, PA; (Y); 7/253; Pres AFS; Am Leg Aux Girls St; Model UN; Quiz Bowl; Capt Color Guard; Rep Stu Cncl; DAR Awd; High Hon Roll; Drama Clb; VP French Clb; Yth Of The Yr 86; Merit Schlr To The U Of Pittsburgh 86; Independant Rsrch Prj 86; U Of Pittsburgh.

CURRIE, JAMES; St Joes Prep; Drexel Hill, PA; (Y); Trs Church Yth Grp; Pep Clb; Rep Frsh Cls; Rep Jr Cls; Rep Stu Cncl; Wt Lftg; Var Wrstlng; Hon Roll; Schlr/Athltc 83-85; CPA.

CURRY, CATHERINE A; Pennsbury HS; Morrisville, PA; (Y); 8/712; Church Yth Grp; Intnl Clb; Yrbk Stf; Lit Mag; Hon Roll; NHS; Pres Schlr; School Musical; Prfct Atten Awd; Forgn Lang Gld Pin 86; Rider Coll Lang Fornsc Tournmt 86; U Of PA.

CURRY, CHRISTINE M; Greater Johnstown Vo-Tech Schl; Dilltown, PA; (Y); 26/312; Art Clb; Church Yth Grp; Cmnty Wkr; Dance Clb; Hosp Aide; Key Clb; Pep Clb; ROTC; Soroptimist; VICA; Dir Awd 83; Outstndng Young Am 84; Etude Awd 86; Indian U PA; Mus Educ.

CURRY, DENISE; Ambridge Area HS; Baden, PA; (Y); Pres Church Yth Grp; Civic Clb; Cmnty Wkr; GAA; Pep Clb; Sec Spanish Clb; Chorus; Church Choir; School Musical; School Play; Acad All Star 85; Hlth Care.

CURRY, JENNIFER; Nazareth Acad; Philadelphia, PA; (Y); 46/121; Church Yth Grp; Dance Clb; Spanish Clb; Chorus; School Musical; School Play; Variety Show; Lit Mag; Hon Roll; Penn ST; Nrsg.

CURRY, KATHY; Ambridge Area HS; S Heights, PA; (Y); Drill Tm; Hon Roll; Robert Morris Coll; Exec Secy.

CURRY, SHELLEY; Moon SR HS; Corapolis, PA; (Y); 15/329; Key Clb; Concert Band; Mrchg Band; Yrbk Phtg; Yrbk Stf; Rep Stu Cncl; Var L Trk; Var L Vllybl; Hon Roll; NHS.

CURRY, VIRGINIA; Southmoreland HS; Scottdale, PA; (Y); 13/250; Church Yth Grp; French Clb; Pep Clb; Ski Clb; Chorus; Church Choir; Nwsp Stf; Yrbk Stf; Lit Mag; Stu Cncl; Med.

CURTI, CHARLES; Hopewell HS; Aliquippa, PA; (Y); 13/250; Rep Jr Cls; Capt Bowling; Var L Crs Cntry; Score Keeper; High Hon Roll; Cmmnctns.

CURTIS, CHARISSE; Harrisburg HS; Harrisburg, PA; (Y); Church Yth Grp; Pep Clb; Chorus; Nwsp Rptr; Rep Stu Cncl; Twrlr; Hon Roll; NHS; Rotary Awd; Rtry Intrnl Ldrshp Cnfrnc 86; Natl Hnr Scty 86; US Achvmnt Acad 86; Temple U; Cmmnctn.

CURTIS, CHARLES; Forest City Regional HS; Plesant Mt, PA; (Y); 10/63; Yrbk Stf; Hon Roll; Cert Of Cmpltn Of Vo-Tech Auto Mech Prgm 86; Mngmnt Agrcltrl.

CURTIS, DANNA; Kiski Area HS; Leechburg, PA; (Y); Drm Mjr(t); Jazz Band; Mrchg Band; School Musical; Symp Band; Hon Roll; 3 Rvrs Traing Orch 84-85; Partcptd Mid East Symphnc & Cncrt Bands 83-84; BYU.

CURTIS, DOUGLAS; State College Area HS; State College, PA; (Y); Boy Scts; Church Yth Grp; 4-H; Im Bsbl; Im Bowling; JV Crs Cntry; JV Ftbl; Im Vllybl; Var Capt Wrstlng; PA ST U; Pre-Vet Sci.

CURTIS, JENNIFER A; Indiana Area SR HS; Indiana, PA; (Y); 11/297; Red Cross Aide; Mrchg Band; High Hon Roll; Jr NHS; Pres Schlr; Art Clb; Drama Clb; Office Aide; Band; Concert Band; Frshmn Exclnc Awd Schlrshp PA ST U 86; Natl Mrt Spcl Awd G C Mrphy Co 86; PA ST U; Elec Engr.

CURTIS, STEPHEN; Western Wayne HS; Waymart, PA; (Y); 3/140; Church Yth Grp; VP 4-H; JV Var Bsktbl; JV Var Ftbl; JV Socr; Var Trk; 4-H Awd; High Hon Roll; Jr NHS; NHS; Princpls List 82-86; Stu Fortnight Eng 85-86; Gifted Prg 82-86; Biochem.

CURZI, KELLI; Butler SR HS; Butler, PA; (Y); Office Aide; SADD; Var Capt Swmmng; Blmsbrg U; Med Tech.

CUSAT, LINDA; Hazleton HS; Hazleton, PA; (Y); 17/370; Church Yth Grp; FBLA; Pep Clb; Nwsp Stf; Var Capt Bsktbl; Tennis; Hon Roll.

CUSHMA, KATHRYN; Cannon Mcmillan SR HS; Canonsburg, PA; (Y); 66/340; French Clb; Band; Hon Roll; PCBA; Csmtlgy.

CUSHMAN, TAMMY LYNN; Spring Ford HS; Royersford, PA; (Y); 76/237; French Clb; Pep Clb; Ski Clb; Yrbk Stf; Rep Frsh Cls; Rep Soph Cls; Rep Jr Cls; Rep Stu Cncl; Score Keeper; Jr NHS; Cdr Crst Coll; CPA.

CUSIC, LORRAINE; South Park HS; Library, PA; (S); 16/213; Ski Clb; Color Guard; Nwsp Stf; Yrbk Stf; JV Bsktbl; Sftbl; Var Tennis; JV Vllybl; High Hon Roll; NHS; Univ Of Pittsbrgh; Phrmclgy.

CUSIMANO, KIMBERLY; Homer Center HS; Homer City, PA; (Y); Drama Clb; SADD; Varsity Clb; Chorus; School Musical; Nwsp Stf; L Sftbl; Vllybl; High Hon Roll; Hon Roll; Sons Italy Lodge Schrlshp 86; Clothng Fash Desgn Awd 86; Outstndng Achvt Awd Hm Ec 86; IN U; Hm Ec.

CUSSINS, DONNIE; North Clarion HS; Lucinda, PA; (Y); SADD; JV Bsktbl; JV Trk; Hon Roll; Elec.

CUSTER, JEFF; Fannett-Metal HS; Fannettsburg, PA; (Y); Church Yth Grp; Varsity Clb; Pres Frsh Cls; Pres Soph Cls; Pres Jr Cls; Pres Sr Cls; Var Bsbl; Var Bsktbl; Var Socr.

CUSTER, JERRY LYNN; Windber Area HS; Windber, PA; (S); Chess Clb; Church Yth Grp; Exploring; Band; Concert Band; Jazz Band; Mrchg Band; Pep Band; Var Sftbl; JV Vllybl; Ar Frc; Mdcl Technlgy.

CUSTER, MICHELLE; Somerset Area SR HS; Somerset, PA; (Y); 43/233; Pres Church Yth Grp; English Clb; JA; Q&S; Spanish Clb; Band; Chorus; Church Choir; Ed Yrbk Stf; High Hon Roll; Pres Acad Fit Awd; Hnr Rl Awd; St Margarets Hosp Nrsng; Nrsng.

CUSTER, RICHARD D; Palmyra Area HS; Palmyra, PA; (Y); 1/200; French Clb; Science Clb; Ski Clb; Band; Mrchg Band; Stage Crew; Socr; Tennis; High Hon Roll; NHS; Lit Achvt Awd 83-84; Wrld Hstry Awd 83-84; Lang Art Cert & Mdl 83-84; Fr Awd 84-85; 2nd Pl Am Leg Essay; PA ST U; Comp Sci.

CUSTER, ROY; Bentworth HS; Finnleyville, PA; (Y); Varsity Clb; Bsbl; Hon Roll; Comp Tech.

CUSTODIO, MARIBEL; Bethlehem Catholic HS; Bethlehem, PA; (S); 5/214; Hosp Aide; Key Clb; Yrbk Stf; Hon Roll; Natl Lang Arts Olympd Gld Medl 83-84; Spnsh I Awd 83-84; Spnsh II Awd 84-85.

CUTHBERT, ROBERT; Troy HS; Columbia Cross Rd, PA; (Y); 7/145; Computer Clb; Trk; Hon Roll; NHS; Mr-Mrs Lynwood Hough Ntrl Sci Awd 86; Pre-Med.

CUTHBERTSON, JILL; Bradford HS; Bradford, PA; (Y); 12/314; AFS; School Play; Variety Show; JV Tennis; High Hon Roll; Jr NHS; NHS; NEDT Awd; Optmtry.

CUTICH, JENNIFER; Hopewell HS; Aliquippa, PA; (Y); 81/264; Church Yth Grp; German Clb; Color Guard; Rep Soph Cls; Var Bsktbl; Im Powder Puff Ftbl; Var Trk; Capt Twrlr; Hon Roll; 1st Tm All-Sctn Bsktbll 85-86; Hpwll Trny All-Str Tm Bsktbll 85; Ntl Croatian & Srbn Chmpnshp Tms 86; Spcl Educ.

CUTLER, JONATHAN; Lower Moreland HS; Huntingdon Valley, PA; (S); 4/214; Computer Clb; Debate Tm; Drama Clb; French Clb; Math Tm; Science Clb; Temple Yth Grp; Vllybl; Hon Roll; Pres NHS; Mc Gill U; Chem.

CUTLIP, MICHELE KAY; Central SR HS; York, PA; (Y); 24/218; Am Leg Aux Girls St; Church Yth Grp; NFL; Spanish Clb; Concert Band; Mrchg Band; School Musical; Symp Band; Yrbk Stf; Hon Roll; Bank Mgmt.

CUTONE, SUSAN K; Serra Catholic HS; Pgh, PA; (Y); AFS; Cmnty Wkr; French Clb; Math Tm; PAVAS; Chorus; Concert Band; Mrchg Band; Yrbk Phtg; Var Vllybl.

CUTRI, SHERRI; Beaver Area JR SR HS; Beaver, PA; (Y); 24/212; Church Yth Grp; JCL; Ski Clb; Band; School Play; Stu Cncl; Var Sftbl; Twrlr; High Hon Roll; Hosp Aide; Acad Awds Dnnrs 85-86; Gannon; Pre-Med.

CUTRUFELLO, JOSELLE; West Hazleton SR HS; Conyngham, PA; (Y); Ski Clb; Spanish Clb; Color Guard; Hon Roll; Intr Dsgn.

CUTSHALL, CATHERINE E; Grove City HS; Grove City, PA; (Y); Ski Clb; Sec Frsh Cls; Rep Stu Cncl; Cheerleading; Powder Puff Ftbl; Trk; Wt Lftg; High Hon Roll; Hon Roll; Gftd Pgm 85-86.

CUTTER, FRAN; Archbishop Ryan For Boys; Philadelphia, PA; (Y); 73/485; Trk; High Hon Roll; Hon Roll; Art I Awd 84-85; Hstry Awd 85-86; Art II Awd 83-84; Drexel U; Engrng.

CUTTIC, SUZANNE M; Notre Dame HS; Easton, PA; (Y); 10/75; Am Leg Aux Girls St; Nwsp Sprt Ed; Pres Jr Cls; Pres Stu Cncl; Cheerleading; Sftbl; Dnfth Awd; Hon Roll; Trs NHS; Easton Exc Clb Stu Yr 85-96; Awd Schrlshp Ldrshp 86; Pres Ftns Awd 86; PA ST U; Pol Sci.

CUTWRIGHT, VICKI; Laurel Highlands SR HS; Uniontown, PA; (S); 16/383; Cmnty Wkr; Mrchg Band; Rep Jr Cls; Rep Sr Cls; Stu Cncl; Stat Trk; Im Vllybl; High Hon Roll; Jr NHS; NHS; PA ST U; Engrg.

CVETAN, ANGELA; Brownsville Area HS; Brownsville, PA; (S); 11/240; Church Yth Grp; Drama Clb; Key Clb; Ski Clb; SADD; Band; Flag Corp; Stu Cncl; High Hon Roll; Hugh O Brian Outstndg Awd 85; Phy Thrpy.

CWIERTNIE, VICTORIA; Sun Valley HS; Aston, PA; (Y); 30/330; Church Yth Grp; GAA; Intnl Clb; Band; Lit Mag; Rep Sr Cls; Var Tennis; Im Vllybl; Hon Roll; Jr NHS; Penn ST U; Engr.

CWIKLINSKI, FRANCIS J; Bethel Park SR HS; Bethel Park, PA; (Y); Am Leg Boys St; Band; Concert Band; Mrchg Band.

CYCAK, WANDA KAY; Lock Haven HS; Castanea, PA; (Y); 31/241; Sec FHA; Spanish Clb; Teachers Aide; Capt Color Guard; Capt Flag Corp; Mrchg Band; Variety Show; Cit Awd; TIDA Colorgd Schlrshp 86; 3 1st Pl Slk Solo Awds & 3 1st Slk Duet Awds 86; FHA Awd 85; Lock Haven U; Elem Ed.

CYHAN, ADRIAN; Saint Pius X HS; Pottstown, PA; (S); 2/161; Latin Clb; Mathletes; Ski Clb; Rep Soph Cls; Rep Jr Cls; Var Crs Cntry; Var Trk; High Hon Roll; NEDT Awd; Prfct Atten Awd; Med.

CYNAR, ANN MARIE; Greater Johnstown HS; Johnstown, PA; (Y); 91/300; Acpl Chr; Chorus; Church Choir; Color Guard; Orch; Nwsp Ed-Chief; Lion Awd; Tribune Democrt Schltc Jrnlsm Awd 86; Trojan Centralizer Jrnlsm Awd 86; U Of Pittsburgh-Johnstwn; Sclgy.

CYPARSKI, LAURIE; Harbor Creek HS; Erie, PA; (Y); 11/227; Art Clb; Computer Clb; GAA; Office Aide; Hon Roll; Sec.

CYPHER, PAULA; Kittanning HS; Worthington, PA; (Y); Office Aide; Varsity Clb; School Musical; Rep Sr Cls; Rep Stu Cncl; Var Capt Bsktbl; JV Cheerleading; Var L Sftbl; Hon Roll; NHS.

CYPHERS, ALICE; Pocono Mountain SR HS; Henryville, PA; (Y); Pep Clb; Q&S; Nwsp Stf; Lit Mag; Monroe Cnty Law Dy Essy 1st Prz 86; U Of VA; Frgn Crspndnt Paris.

CYPHERT, AMY; Wilmington Area HS; New Wilmington, PA; (S); 8/125; Cmnty Wkr; Drama Clb; Key Clb; Office Aide; Sec Spanish Clb; High Hon Roll; Hon Roll; Mth.

CYPHERT, ESTELLE; Central Christian HS; Penfield, PA; (Y); Pep Clb; Varsity Clb; Yrbk Sprt Ed; Pres Frsh Cls; Trs Jr Cls; Pres Sr Cls; Var L Bsktbl; Var L Sftbl; Var L Vllybl; Hon Roll; Golden Key Ath & Acad 86; St Francis; Bio.

CYR, REBECCA; Kiski Area HS; Saltsburg, PA; (Y); Band; Concert Band; Mrchg Band; Stat Var Tennis; Hon Roll; U Pittsburg; Adm Justice.

CYRON, RON; John S Fine HS; Nanticoke, PA; (Y); 30/255; Ski Clb; Golf; Tennis; Vllybl; High Hon Roll; NHS; NEDT Awd; Med Tech.

CYRUS, ERIC A; West Mifflin Area HS; Pittsburgh, PA; (Y); Cmnty Wkr; Chorus; Bsktbl; Ftbl; Trk; Wt Lftg; High Hon Roll; Hon Roll; HS Mrt Awd 85; Bus.

CYTRYNOWICZ, STEVEN; Upper Moreland SR HS; Willow Grove, PA; (Y); 8/260; Computer Clb; Math Clb; Concert Band; Mrchg Band; Var L Trk; NHS; Rotary Clbs Camp Neidig; Eagle Scout Awd; PA ST; Physicist.

CZAJKOWSKI, DAWN MARIE; St Huberts HS; Philadelphia, PA; (Y); Am Leg Aux Girls St; Aud/Vis; VP Church Yth Grp; Pres Girl Scts; Office Aide; Chorus; Church Choir; School Musical; Gold Awd In Girl Scouts 86; Clthng & Txtls Acadmc Achvmnt 86.

CZAPLINSKI, VALERIE; Spring Ford SR HS; Linfield, PA; (Y); Camera Clb; Cmnty Wkr; Ski Clb; Yrbk Phtg; Yrbk Stf; Jr Cls; Sr Cls; Stu Cncl; Capt Bsktbl; Cheerleading; Mgr Of Yr La Crosse 84&85; Southwestern Coll CA; Toursm.

CZAPRACKI, DAVID; Greater Nanticoke Area HS; Nanticoke, PA; (Y); Art Clb; Red Cross Aide; Rep Jr Cls; Ftbl; Hon Roll.

CZARNECKI, BARBARA; Nazareth Academy HS; Philadelphia, PA; (Y); Cmnty Wkr; Model UN; NFL; Trs Speech Tm; Pres Frsh Cls; Fld Hcky; High Hon Roll; GAA; Hosp Aide; Pep Clb; Cthlc Ntl Trning Inst-Ldrshp & Svc 86; Mssnry Outrch Pgm 86; Sunshn Bibl Cmp Cnslr 86; Scl Wrk.

CZARNECKI, JOHN A; Bishop Mc Devitt HS; Harrisburg, PA; (Y); 10/190; Am Leg Boys St; Jazz Band; Mrchg Band; Nwsp Bus Mgr; Nwsp Ed-Chief; Rep Stu Cncl; Var L Socr; High Hon Roll; NHS; Rep Frsh Cls; Woodmen World Awd Profcncy Am Hist 83; Med.

CZEKAJ, BECKY; Mt Pleasant HS; Mt Pleasant, PA; (Y); 4/250; German Clb; Model UN; Capt Color Guard; Ed Nwsp Stf; High Hon Roll; NHS; Prfct Atten Awd; Chem.

CZEKAJ, GREG; Mount Pleasant Area HS; Mt Pleasant, PA; (Y); 18/230; Latin Clb; Varsity Clb; Var Bsktbl; Var Ftbl; Var Wt Lftg; High Hon Roll; Hon Roll; NHS.

CZEKAJ, LORI; Berlin Brothersvalley HS; Berlin, PA; (Y); 13/90; Ski Clb; Pres SADD; Capt Band; L Bsktbl; Var Cheerleading; L Sftbl; L Vllybl; French Hon Soc; High Hon Roll; NHS; Ldrshp Frnch III 85-86; Ldrshp SADD 86; U Of PA; Law.

CZEPONIS, EVE MARIE; Mt Carmel Area JR SR HS; Mt Carmel, PA; (Y); French Clb; Trs FTA; Spanish Clb; Pres Band; School Musical; Rep Jr Cls; Stu Cncl; High Hon Roll; NHS; Key Clb; Lgsltv Comm Svc Awd 86; Bucknell U; Frgn Lang.

CZERWINSKI, TRACI; Troy HS; Gillett, PA; (Y); 19/162; DECA; GAA; Ski Clb; Hon Roll; NHS.

CZETLI, ROBERT; Octorara HS; Parkesburg, PA; (Y); 17/171; Boy Scts; Chess Clb; Church Yth Grp; Service Clb; Band; Concert Band; Jazz Band; Mrchg Band; Orch; Nwsp Bus Mgr; Dist & Regl Band 86; Svc & Suppt Clb Schlrshp 86; Amer Red Crss Awd Bldmbl & Othr Svcs 86; Penn ST U; Elctrcl Engrng.

CZOLNIK, LUCY; Aliquippa HS; Aliquippa, PA; (S); Sec Chess Clb; Yrbk Stf; Hon Roll; Acctnt.

CZUMBIL, MARIA; Council Rock HS; Washington Crng, PA; (Y); 200/850; Church Yth Grp; Dance Clb; Drama Clb; Hosp Aide; SADD; School Musical; School Play; Lit Mag; Hon Roll; Poetry Awd 85; FIT NYC; Adv.

CZYRNIK, PAMELA; Bishop Mc Cort HS; Johnstown, PA; (Y); 20/125; German Clb; Math Clb; Pep Clb; Chorus; Nwsp Rptr; High Hon Roll; NHS; IN U Of PA; Acctng.

CZZOWITZ, CHRISTINA; Butler Area SR HS; Butler, PA; (Y); Exploring; Hosp Aide; Latin Clb; SADD; Vllybl; Hon Roll; Jr NHS; NHS; Schlstc Ltr Ntl Hnr Soc 85; Sec Law Explrers 86.

D ALESSANDRIS, PAULA; Our Lady Of The Sacred Heart; Aliquippa, PA; (Y); 13/75; Camera Clb; Pep Clb; Radio Clb; School Play; Nwsp Stf; Yrbk Phtg; Lit Mag; Hon Roll; NHS; Acdmc All-Amrcn Awd 85-86; U S Achvmnt Awd 85-86; PA ST; Music.

D ALESSANDRO, ANN; Pequea Valley HS; Paradise, PA; (Y); 36/126; AFS; Church Yth Grp; Drama Clb; Chorus; Church Choir; Concert Band; Flag Corp; School Musical; School Play; Yrbk Stf; Elizabeth College.

D ALESSANDRO, NOELLE; Creative And Performing Arts; Philadelphia, PA; (S); 2/150; Church Yth Grp; Dance Clb; School Play; High Hon Roll; Hon Roll; NHS; Prfct Atten Awd; White Williams Found Schlrshp 84-86; Outstndng Achvt Schlrshp 86-90; Temple U; Acct.

D ALESSANDRO, RALPH; St John Neumann HS; Philadelphia, PA; (Y); 30/356; Church Yth Grp; Spanish Clb; Im Bsktbl; High Hon Roll; Hon Roll; Grant St John Neumann H S 83-84.

D ALESSANDRO, SANDRA; St Maria Goretti HS; Philadelphia, PA; (Y); 108/409; Cmnty Wkr; French Clb; FBLA; Pep Clb; Rep Soph Cls; Crs Cntry; Hon Roll; Ldrshp Awd 86; Cert Commendtn Bus Ed; La Salle U; Hlth.

D AMICO, MELANIE; Scranton Central HS; Scranton, PA; (Y); Exploring; Trk; Hon Roll; Ntl Merit Ltr; Bus Adm.

D AMORE, MARIA; St Maria Goretti HS; Philadelphia, PA; (Y); 151/426; Church Yth Grp; Cmnty Wkr; GAA; Math Clb; Office Aide; Red Cross Aide; Teachers Aide; Rep Sr Cls; Var Stu Cncl; Var Hon Roll; Acdmc All Amer 85-86; U S Stdnt Cncl Awd 85-86.

D AMORE, MELANIE; Elk County Christian HS; St Marys, PA; (S); VP Ed Hosp Aide; JA; Model UN; SADD; Rep Frsh Cls; Rep Soph Cls; Rep Jr Cls; High Hon Roll; NEDT Awd; Spec Ed.

D ANDREA, ANTHONY; Bishop Mc Devitt HS; Oreland, PA; (Y); 4/351; Computer Clb; French Clb; Mathletes; Science Clb; Nwsp Rptr; JV Var Socr; High Hon Roll; NHS; Ntl Merit Ltr; Pres Schlr; Jacksonvl U Trstee Schlrshp 86; Montgmry Cnty & DE Vly Sci Fairs 1st 86; Knghts Pythias Essy Cntst 86; Jacksonville U; Marn Sci.

D ANDREA, MICHELE LEE; Warren Area HS; Warren, PA; (Y); Church Yth Grp; Hosp Aide; Varsity Clb; Band; Orch; Keystone Girls St Shippensburg ST U 86; Crmnl Just.

D ANGELO, FRANCINA; Ambridge Area HS; Ambridge, PA; (Y); 50/265; Rep Church Yth Grp; Pep Clb; Band; Concert Band; Drill Tm; Hon Roll; Fash Merch.

D ANGELO, TRACEY; Hazelton HS; Mcadoo, PA; (Y); 69/335; Drama Clb; French Clb; Var Sftbl; PA ST.

D ANTONIO, CHRISTINE; St Marion Goretti HS; Philadelphia, PA; (S); 3/403; Pres Church Yth Grp; Mathletes; Math Clb; Spanish Clb; Mgr Crs Cntry; High Hon Roll; NHS; Ltn I Hnrbl Ment 83-84; Spnsh I & II Hnrbl Ment 83-85; Bio Hnrbl Ment 84-85; Engrng.

D ARCY JR, WILLIAM F; Archbishop Wood HS; Holland, PA; (Y); 57/282; Computer Clb; Hon Roll; Industrial.

D ARRIGO, ROSITA G; Somerset Area HS; Somerset, PA; (Y); 113/230; English Clb; Varsity Clb; Band; Chorus; Concert Band; Drm Mjr(t); Stu Cncl; Var Cheerleading; JV Vllybl; Hon Roll; Ltr In Bnd 84; U Of Pittsburgh; Psych.

D ORAZIO, LISA; Upper Darby HS; Drexel Hill, PA; (Y); Hosp Aide; Teachers Aide; Rep Frsh Cls; Rep Soph Cls; Rep Jr Cls; Bsktbl; Var Sftbl; High Hon Roll; Hon Roll; Peirre Junior Coll; Comp Pgmr.

DA COSTA, MARIBEL; St Maria Goretti HS; Philadelphia, PA; (Y); 52/390; Spanish Clb; Teachers Aide; Orch; Hon Roll; NHS; Prfct Atten Awd; Modern Music Mstrs Hnr Soc; Music Awd-Prfct Atten Yr.

DA SILVA, THERESA; Freedom HS; Bethlehem, PA; (Y); 24/404; Church Yth Grp; Hosp Aide; Vllybl; High Hon Roll; Hon Roll; NHS; Pres Acad Fit Awd 86; Moravian Coll; Bus.

DABULIS, JEFF; Lourdes Regional HS; Shamokin, PA; (Y); 6/94; Boy Scts; Service Clb; Spanish Clb; Pres Band; Mrchg Band; Pep Band; School Musical; Rep Stu Cncl; High Hon Roll; Spanish NHS; Ordr Arrw Natl Brthhd Sct Hon Cmprs 86; 1st Plc Perfrmng Arts Divisn N Cntrl Dist Pai Fed 84; Elec Engr.

DADO, JOYE; Shenango HS; New Castle, PA; (S); 13/121; 4-H; School Play; Nwsp Stf; Rep Stu Cncl; Bausch & Lomb Sci Awd; Cit Awd; Lion Awd; NHS; Caroline Knox Memrl Schlrshp 86; Hugh O Brian Yth Ldrshp Awd; PA ST U; Bio.

DAGEN, KRISTIN; Pottsgrove HS; Pottstown, PA; (Y); 4/197; Sec French Clb; Math Tm; Pep Clb; Science Clb; Ski Clb; Varsity Clb; School Musical; Yrbk Bus Mgr; Yrbk Sprt Ed; Yrbk Stf; Most Prmsng Modl-Montgmry Cnty 85; Hmcmg Ct 86; Valentine Ct 84; PA ST U; Arch Engrng.

DAGGETT, DONNA; Bishop Kenrick HS; Norristown, PA; (Y); Dance Clb; Girl Scts; Ski Clb; Rep Stu Cncl; Stat Bsktbl; JV Fld Hcky; Im Powder Puff Ftbl; Stat Trk; Mktg.

DAGGETT, MATTHEW; Columbia HS; Manheim, PA; (Y); 12/83; Ski Clb; Varsity Clb; Yrbk Phtg; JV Ftbl; Var L Trk; JV Var Wrstlng; Hon Roll; NHS; Rotary Awd; Mary S Groff Scholar 86; Elizabethtown Coll; Acctng.

DAGIT, HEATHER; Archbishop John Carroll HS; Gladwyne, PA; (Y); 2/217; Church Yth Grp; Cmnty Wkr; Dance Clb; Mathletes; Frsh Cls; Church Yth Grp; Jr Cls; Sr Cls; Fld Hcky; Lcrss; Lafayette Coll; Engr.

DAGOSTINO, TONI; Pine Grove Area HS; Pine Grove, PA; (Y); 4/116; Am Leg Aux Girls St; Varsity Clb; Nwsp Rptr; Ed Yrbk Stf; Rep Soph Cls; Rep Sr Cls; Var L Vllybl; High Hon Roll; NHS; Prfct Atten Awd; Stu Of Mnth 86; Pres Fit Awd 83-86; Intramurals 83-86; Sec.

DAHL, JEFFREY; Warren Area HS; Warren, PA; (Y); French Clb; Ski Clb; Concert Band; School Play; Rep Frsh Cls; L Crs Cntry; Var Trk.

DAHLIN, PHILIP; Bishop Egan HS; Hulmeville, PA; (Y); 4/229; Pres German Clb; Q&S; Yrbk Ed-Chief; Var Co-Capt Socr; Wrstlng; High Hon Roll; Pres NHS; Ntl Merit SF; Rotary Awd; Val; ROTC Army 4 Yr Full Tuitn Schlrshp 86; Syracuse U; Chem Engr.

DAHLKEMPER JR, PAUL; Ft Le Boeuf HS; Erie, PA; (Y); 30/200; Boy Scts; Camera Clb; Varsity Clb; Chorus; Swing Chorus; Im Bsbl; Im Bsktbl; JV Var Ftbl; Im Socr; Im Wrstlng; Eagle Scout 84; Music Awd 86; Athletic Awd 86; USAF; Law Enf.

DAIELLO, DEANA; Freedom HS; Easton, PA; (Y); 82/445; Art Clb; Church Yth Grp; Quiz Bowl; Var Cheerleading; Var Vllybl; Hon Roll; Pres Cmmrcl Art Clss 85-86; Illstrtn.

DAINTY, DANIEL; Belle Vernon Area HS; Belle Vernon, PA; (Y); Boy Scts; Church Yth Grp; Computer Clb; Nwsp Rptr; Var L Bsktbl; Var L Ftbl; Hon Roll; Awd Excel Lang Stdys 85 & 86; Adam Mc Kelvey Mem Outstndng Yth Cnsrvtn Awd 84; PA St U Cnsrvtn Ldrshp; Bio.

DAISLEY, DAWN; Reynolds HS; Greenville, PA; (S); 28/160; Pres DECA; Hosp Aide; Hon Roll; DECA CDC Awds 85 & 86; Outstndng Ldrshp Awd 85-86; Bus Adm.

DAISLEY, RICHARD; Monsignor Bonner HS; Lansdowne, PA; (S); 4/330; Mathletes; Model UN; Political Wkr; Nwsp Rptr; L Socr; High Hon Roll; NHS; Opt Clb Awd; World Affairs Clb Pres; Scots Hi Q; Acctng.

DAIT, MARIANNE; Perkiomen Schl; Lehighton, PA; (Y); 6/72; Varsity Clb; Chorus; Yrbk Ed-Chief; Var Capt Bsktbl; Var Capt Fld Hcky; Var Lcrss; Bausch & Lomb Sci Awd; Kiwanis Awd; NHS; Sal; Hillegass Jrnslm Awd 86; Frank S Riordan Awd 86; VP & Treas JR Cls 84-85; Bryn Mawr Coll; Pre-Med.

DAIT, PIERRE; Perkiomen HS; Lehighton, PA; (Y); 7/43; Ski Clb; Yrbk Stf; Var Bsbl; Var L Bsktbl; Var L Ftbl; Frank C Stefano Awd 85; Accntg.

DALAIMO, JAMES; Father Judge HS; Philadelphia, PA; (Y); 44/358; Latin Clb; Mgr Bsktbl; Mgr Ftbl; JV Var Mgr(s); Score Keeper; Timer; Hon Roll; NHS; Comp Sci.

DALBOW, LAURA; Springdale HS; Springdale, PA; (Y); 7/144; Nwsp Ed-Chief; Rep Jr Cls; Cit Awd; High Hon Roll; NHS; Ntl Merit SF; Pres Schlr; Sr Schlr; Art Clb; Cmnty Wkr; Wilso Pres Schlrshp 86; PPG Fdn Schlrshp 86; Mt Holyoke Coll; Lawyer.

DALE III, CLARK; West Branch Area HS; Morrisdale, PA; (Y); 22/120; Boy Scts; Church Yth Grp; Spanish Clb; Crs Cntry; Socr; God Cntry Awd; Compu Tech.

DALE, DONALD J; Methocton HS; Audubon, PA; (Y); 7/350; Band; Chorus; Jazz Band; Orch; School Play; Rep Sr Cls; Tennis; NHS; Ntl Merit SF; Church Choir; Congrssnl Yth Ldrs Conf; Engrg.

DALESSANDRI, SUSAN; Aliquippa HS; Aliquippa, PA; (S); Church Yth Grp; French Clb; Office Aide; School Play; Yrbk Stf; Hon Roll.

DALEY, GENA; Lackawanna Trl HS; Factoryvle, PA; (Y); 12/85; Yrbk Ed-Chief; Yrbk Rptr; Yrbk Stf; VP Sr Cls; Sec Stu Cncl; Var Cheerleading; Var Capt Fld Hcky; Cit Awd; High Hon Roll; Hon Roll; Military Civilians Wives Clb Schlrshp 86; Stan Coughey Mem Schrlshp 86; Stu Mnth 86; Engl Dept Awd 86; PA ST U; Ed.

DALEY, SAM; Pittston Area SR HS; Pittston, PA; (Y); Pres Aud/Vis; Church Yth Grp; Pres Drama Clb; Teachers Aide; School Musical; School Play; Variety Show; Stu Cncl; Mgr(s); Var L Vllybl; Strctrl Dsgn.

DALEY, SHAWN; Sacred Heart HS; Jermyn, PA; (Y); U Of Scranton; Comm.

DALFO, THOMAS J; Archbishop Wood H S For Boys; Warminster, PA; (Y); 4/280; Church Yth Grp; Nwsp Ed-Chief; Lit Mag; JV Ftbl; High Hon Roll; Kiwanis Awd; Pres NHS; Val; Debate Tm; Chrstn Bros Schlrshp Fr La Salle U 86; Pres Schlrshp To St Jsphs U 86; Anna M Vincent Trst Awd 86; La Salle U; Finance Intl Bnkg.

DALGLISH, GREGORY; Harborcreek HS; Erie, PA; (Y); 3/225; Church Yth Grp; Varsity Clb; Pres Frsh Cls; Var L Bsktbl; JV Socr; Capt L Tennis; High Hon Roll; NHS; 1st Tm Erie Cnty Tnns 85-86.

DALJEV, KIM; Pocono Mountain HS; Stroudsburg, PA; (Y); Pep Clb; Color Guard; Mrchg Band; Bnd Mgr; FSHN Mrchndsng.

DALLAS, LISA; Hazelton HS; Hazleton, PA; (Y); FBLA; 3rd GBT 85-86; FBLA Ofcr 84-86; Penn ST U Hazelton; Bus.

DALLAS, MICHAEL; Wilson HS; West Lawn, PA; (Y); 20/287; Pres Aud/Vis; Spanish Clb; Im Bsktbl; Var L Bowling; Im Wt Lftg; High Hon Roll; NHS; Marvin G Doerrmann Mmrl Schlshp Awd 86; Becks Schlcastrs Awd 86; Pres Acad Ftnss Achvmnt Awd 86; Penn ST U; Bus Mngmnt.

DALLESSANDRO, LONA; Bishop Guilfoyle HS; Altoona, PA; (Y); 7/130; Sec Church Yth Grp; Science Clb; Speech Tm; SADD; Chorus; Capt Color Guard; Hon Roll; NHS; PA ST U; Phrmcy.

DALLMEYER, KELLY; Dallastown HS; York, PA; (Y); Ski Clb; Nwsp Stf; VP Jr Cls; Rep Stu Cncl; Var JV Cheerleading; Powder Puff Ftbl; Var Trk; Hon Roll; Law.

DALON, NANCY; E L Meyers HS; Wilkes-Barre, PA; (S); Ski Clb; Chorus; Concert Band; Drm Mjr(t); Jazz Band; Mrchg Band; Orch; Hon Roll; Jr NHS; Spanish NHS; Dist IX Band 86; Bloomsburg U.

DALPIAZ, HEATHER; Towanda Area HS; Monroeton, PA; (Y); Drama Clb; Girl Scts; Ski Clb; SADD; Concert Band; Mrchg Band; Stu Cncl; Stat Bsktbl; Crs Cntry; Stat Trk; Dir Awd Band-Excptnl Progs In Music 84-85; Ithaca Coll; Phys Ther.

DALSON, BETH; Mon Valley Catholic HS; Brownsville, PA; (Y); 25/82; Ski Clb; Spanish Clb; Soph Cls; Jr Cls; Sr Cls; Stat Bsbl; Capt Vllybl; Spanish NHS; Law.

DALTON, CATHERINE; Pennsbury SR HS; Yardley, PA; (Y); Church Yth Grp; 4-H; Chorus; Stage Crew; Dnfth Awd; 4-H Awd; Delaware Valley Col Sci; Hortcl.

DALTON, KATE; North Allegheny SR HS; Pittsburgh, PA; (Y); 94/642; Cmnty Wkr; Exploring; JA; Ski Clb; Rep Stu Cncl; Powder Puff Ftbl; Var Tennis; Var Trk; High Hon Roll; Outstndng Jr Hme Econ 86; Schlrshp Recpnt PA Free Entrpse Wk 86; Giftd Organ Advnd Lrng 84-86; Bus.

DALTON, MICHELE; St Benedict Acad; Erie, PA; (Y); 20/63; Quiz Bowl; Pres Sr Cls; Rep Stu Cncl; Hon Roll; NHS; Acadmc Schlrshp 83-84; Natl Bus Hnr Socty 85; Teenag Actn Clb 83-86; Spnsh Schlrshp 84-85; Accntnt.

DALUSIO, JEAN; Deer Lakes JR SR HS; Curtisville, PA; (Y); Library Aide; Chorus; Stat Trk; Hon Roll; Law.

DALY, MARGARET ANNE; Chambersburg Area SR HS; Chambersburg, PA; (Y); Science Clb; Concert Band; Drm Mjr(t); Mrchg Band; Orch; School Musical; Stu Cncl; High Hon Roll; JCL; Gannett Nwspr Carrer Schlrshp $4000 86; Franklin Sci Fair 1st Pl 86; Shippensburg U; Med Tech.

DALY, PATRICIA; Peters Township HS; Mc Murray, PA; (Y); 76/275; Dance Clb; Soroptimist; VP Spanish Clb; Drill Tm; School Musical; Stu Cncl; Cheerleading; Powder Puff Ftbl; Sftbl; Hon Roll; Bus.

DAMELIO, MARIO; Father Judge HS; Philadelphia, PA; (Y); 21/403; Chess Clb; FBLA; Latin Clb; SADD; Im Bowling; Im Ftbl; Im Socr; Opt Clb Awd; Drekel U; Finance.

DAMIANO, CHRISTINA MARIE; Dalastown Area HS; Dallastown, PA; (Y); 19/325; Hosp Aide; Ski Clb; Varsity Clb; School Play; Nwsp Stf; Lit Mag; Mgr Crs Cntry; Powder Puff Ftbl; Dgsne U Comptv Schlrshp 86; Dstngshd Hon Roll 82-86; Pares Acdmc Ftns Awd 86; Duquesne U; Pltcl Sci.

DAMIANO, GENA MARIE; Panther Valley HS; Nesquehoning, PA; (Y); 9/129; Drama Clb; Exploring; Ski Clb; Trs Chorus; Mrchg Band; Yrbk Stf; Capt Cheerleading; Trk; High Hon Roll; NHS; Penn ST U; Med Tech.

DAMIANO, KAREN; Old Forge HS; Old Forge, PA; (S); High Hon Roll; NHS; Spnsh & Bio Awds 84-85.

DAMICO, AMY; Villa Maria Acad; Erie, PA; (Y); 55/131; Art Clb; Aud/Vis; Church Yth Grp; Dance Clb; Drama Clb; Model UN; PAVAS; Y-Teens; Church Choir; School Musical; Jo'n Carroll U; Intl Bus.

DAMICO, CHAD; Hempfield SR HS; New Stanton, PA; (Y); Pep Clb; Red Cross Aide; Science Clb; Ski Clb; Stu Cncl; JV Bsktbl; Var Ftbl; Var Socr; Var Trk; Im Wt Lftg; U Pittsburgh.

DAMICO, MICHAEL; Hortheast Catholic HS; Philadelphia, PA; (Y); 100/400; Latin Clb; Var L Ftbl; Var L Trk; Var L Wrstlng; Hon Roll; NHS.

DAMON, MARK; Northeaster SR HS; Manchester, PA; (Y); Boy Scts; VP Dance Clb; Pres Exploring; Rep Stu Cncl; JV Trk; JV Wrstlng; Hon Roll; St Judes Dnce Assmbly Chrmn, Mrthn Chrmn 85-87; Explrng Pres Yrk Adms Area Cncl 85-87; Comp Sci.

DAMON JR, PAUL; Gateway HS; Mornoeville, PA; (Y); Civic Clb; Exploring; Bus Partner Paul & Paul Collectbles 84-86; CC Allegheny Cnty; Bus.

DAMOND, PATRICK; Cathedral Prep; Erie, PA; (Y); 49/216; Exploring; Bsktbl; High Hon Roll; Hon Roll; St Marks Smnry; Thlgy.

DAMORE, CHARLENE; St Marys Area HS; Saint Marys, PA; (Y); 19/296; VP SADD; Yrbk Stf; JV Stat Bsktbl; Timer; Stat Trk; Hon Roll; NHS; Sci.

DAMPF, JULIE; Knoch HS; Butler, PA; (Y); Girl Scts; Mrchg Band; Pep Band; School Musical; Stage Crew; Symp Band; Ed Yrbk Ed-Chief; God Cntry Awd; Hon Roll; NHS; Nrsng.

DANA, DI CAPRIO; Bishop Kenrick HS; Audubon, PA; (Y); 40/310; French Clb; Science Clb; Service Clb; Chorus; Flag Corp; School Play; Yrbk Ed-Chief; Yrbk Stf; NHS; Prfct Atten Awd; Zoolgy.

DANDENEAU, NICOLE; Emmaus HS; Macungie, PA; (Y); French Clb; Latin Clb; Model UN; Chorus; Color Guard; Flag Corp; Mrchg Band; Nwsp Rptr; Nwsp Stf; Hon Roll; 3rd Pl Humane Soc Wrtng Cont; Communications.

DANDO, LISA; Mary Fuller Frazier Me JR SR HS; Fayette City, PA; (Y); Boys Clb Am; Boy Scts; Cmnty Wkr; SADD; Band; Concert Band; Jazz Band; Mrchg Band; School Musical; Ftbl; CA U Of PA; Accntng.

DANEK, TRICIA; Burgettstown JR SR HS; Atlasburg, PA; (Y); French Clb; Concert Band; Variety Show; Yrbk Stf; Cheerleading; High Hon Roll; Commnctns.

DANG, TIEN; Southern HS; Philadelphia, PA; (Y); 12/280; Nwsp Stf; Tennis; Hon Roll; Prfct Atten Awd; Army Rsrv Ntl Essy Cntst 84-85; Clmbs Essy Cntst 85-86; PA ST; Bus Admin.

DANGEL, TRACY; Hollidaysburg Area SR HS; Hollidaysburg, PA; (Y); Church Yth Grp; French Clb; Band; Concert Band; Mrchg Band; Orch; Swmmng; IN U; Pre-Elem.

DANIEL, ALYSSA; Upper Moreland HS; Wheeling, WV; (Y); VICA; Rep Sr Cls; Hon Roll; PSA Awd Ldrshp & Schlstc Ablts At Tech Schl 85; Temple U; Comp Oper.

DANIEL, LORI; Upper Dauphin Area HS; Elizabethville, PA; (Y); 24/112; Pres Church Yth Grp; Band; Chorus; Church Choir; Drm Mjr(t); Jazz Band; Mrchg Band; School Musical; Rep Stu Cncl; Im Sftbl; Acad Achvt Awd Music 86; Phys Ther.

DANIELS, BRIAN J; St Marys Area HS; St Marys, PA; (Y); 1/307; Boy Scts; Math Tm; Chorus; Var L Golf; Tennis; Gov Hon Prg Awd; Hon Roll; NHS; Ntl Merit SF; Govrns Schl For Sci 85; Cornell U; Mech Engr.

DANIELS, BRIDGET; Exeter Township HS; Reading, PA; (Y); 38/232; Sec Leo Clb; Varsity Clb; Color Guard; Rep Stu Cncl; Var L Sftbl; Hon Roll; Extr Wmns Clb Awd Mst Outstndng Sec Stu 86; Slvr Egl Awd Acdmc Achvt 85; Gldn Egl Awd Acdmc Achvt 86; Lansdale Schl Of Bus; Lgl Scrty.

DANIELS, CARLTON; Tunkhannock Area HS; Tunkhannock, PA; (S); 13/280; Church Yth Grp; FCA; JV Var Bsktbl; JV Var Ftbl; Var Trk; NHS.

DANIELS, DEANA; Springfield HS; Oreland, PA; (Y); Cmnty Wkr; Red Cross Aide; Service Clb; Pres Soph Cls; Trs Jr Cls; Rep Stu Cncl; Fld Hcky; Capt Lcrss; Bus.

DANIELS, DEBRA; Millersburg Area HS; Millersburg, PA; (Y); 11/78; French Clb; Spanish Clb; Nwsp Stf; Yrbk Stf; Hon Roll; Ntl Merit Ltr; Top Spnsh Stu Awd 85-86; Susquehanna U; Jrnlsm.

DANIELS, KATHY; Forest Hills SR HS; St Michael, PA; (Y); Library Aide; Office Aide; Pep Clb; VP Y-Teens; Nwsp Stf; Yrbk Stf; Stu Cncl; Var L Cheerleading; Var Trk; Var JV Vllybl; Coaches Awd Chrldng 83; Conemaugh Vly Mem Hosp; Nrsng.

DANIELS, LORI; Conemaugh Township HS; Boswell, PA; (Y); 18/106; Sec Church Yth Grp; Hosp Aide; Key Clb; Pres Chorus; Church Choir; School Musical; Yrbk Stf; Trk; Schl Music Awd 86; Cedarville Col6; Nrsng.

DANIELS, MICHELLE R; Franklin Learning Center HS; Philadelphia, PA; (Y); Church Yth Grp; Dance Clb; FTA; Girl Scts; Rep Stu Cncl; Var Cheerleading; Coach Actv; School Play; JV Trk; Incntv 85 Awds Myrs Yth Prgrm 85; Arts Rcgntn Tlnt Srch 85; NW Rdrs Pgnt 1st Plc Tlnt Awd 84; Columbia Coll; Dnc Educ.

DANIELS, REBECCA; Spring Ford Senior HS; Royersford, PA; (S); Sec French Clb; Pep Clb; Yrbk Phtg; Rep Frsh Cls; Rep Soph Cls; Rep Jr Cls; Var Cheerleading; NHS; Ntl Merit SF; Sec Educ.

DANIELS, STERLING; Martin Luther King HS; Philadelphia, PA; (Y); Dance Clb; Drama Clb; Pep Clb; Band; Mrchg Band; Drama Clb Awd 86; U S Army Coll; Photogrphy.

DANIELS, STEVEN P; Elk County Christian HS; Ridgway, PA; (Y); 18/80; Rep Jr Cls; Rep Stu Cncl; JV Var Bsktbl; High Hon Roll; Hon Roll; Ntl Physcl Educ Awd 85; Duquesne U; Bus Mgmt.

DANIELSON, ERIC; Grove City HS; Grove City, PA; (Y); Boy Scts; Church Yth Grp; Computer Clb; Ski Clb; Im Bsktbl; Hon Roll; Westminster; Bus.

DANIELSON, NANCY L; Mercer Area JR SR HS; Mercer, PA; (Y); 6/121; German Clb; NFL; Q&S; Sec Trs Speech Tm; Band; Concert Band; Jazz Band; Mrchg Band; Orch; Pep Band; Am Legn Schlrshp 86; Lang Arts Stu 86; Hnr Awd Natl Hnr Soc 86; U Of Pittsburgh; Pre Law.

DANIELSON, TROY A; Sheffield Area HS; Warren, PA; (Y); Church Yth Grp; FBLA; SADD; Varsity Clb; Bsktbl; Trk; Hon Roll; Edinboro; Bus Admin.

DANILE, MARC; Shaler Area HS; Pittsburgh, PA; (Y); 99/526; Ski Clb; Grove City Coll; Econ.

DANISAVICH, ALEX; Mahanoy Area HS; Barnesville, PA; (Y); Church Yth Grp; Drama Clb; Ski Clb; Spanish Clb; Varsity Clb; Stage Crew; Variety Show; JV Var Bsbl; JV Var Bsktbl; L Trk.

DANISH, ANNETTE; Mount Union Area HS; Mount Union, PA; (Y); 37/160; French Clb; GAA; Band; Bsktbl; Bowling; Millersville U; Accounting.

DANKO, GARY; West Allegheny SR HS; Imperial, PA; (Y); Church Yth Grp; High Hon Roll; Hon Roll; Air Force; Electn.

DANKO, PATRICIA A; Lansdale Catholic HS; Lansdale, PA; (Y); 15/222; Variety Show; Nwsp Stf; Powder Puff Ftbl; Var L Sftbl; High Hon Roll; NHS; Prfct Atten Awd; Pres Schlr; Nwsp Rptr; JV Crs Cntry; Undrstnd Yth Smmr Switz Exchng Schlrshp 84; Hghst Cls Avg Frnch Awd 83-84; 1st Pl Schl Sci Fair 83; Fshn Dsgn.

DANKO, SANDY; Highlands SR HS; Natrona Hts, PA; (Y); Exploring; Hosp Aide; Varsity Clb; Color Guard; School Play; Stage Crew; Var Swmmng; Hon Roll; NHS; Church Yth Grp; U Of Pittsburgh.

DANKO, SHARON; Hempfield Area SR HS; Greensburg, PA; (Y); French Clb; Pep Clb; Ski Clb; Sec Frsh Cls; Sec Stu Cncl; Stat Ftbl; L Vllybl; Stat Wrstlng; Hon Roll; Sec Jr NHS.

DANKO, TANYA; Belle Vernon Area HS; Belle Vernon, PA; (Y); 20/276; Ski Clb; Yrbk Stf; Gym; Sftbl; Trk; High Hon Roll; NHS; Duquesne U; Pharmacy.

DANN, DEBORAH; B Reed Henderson HS; West Chester, PA; (S); 8/343; Jazz Band; Mrchg Band; French Hon Soc; Hon Roll; NHS; Achvmt Awd 84; Astronomy.

DANNELS, DOUG; Grove City Area HS; Grove City, PA; (Y); 67/195; Var JV Bsktbl; Var L Golf; Var L Tennis; Hon Roll; Math.

DANNER, MARIE; Northampton HS; Bath, PA; (S); Var Sftbl; Hon Roll; Penn ST U; Engrng.

DANOWSKI, DENISE; Villa Maria Acad; Erie, PA; (Y); Exploring; Color Guard; Mrchg Band; Yrbk Stf; Hon Roll; NHS; NEDT Awd; Prfct Atten Awd; COMP Sci.

DANOWSKI, REBECCA; Hatboro-Horsham HS; Hatboro, PA; (Y); Girl Scts; Band; Chorus; Concert Band; Powder Puff Ftbl; Tennis; Trk; Hon Roll; Prfct Atten Awd; Rotary Awd; Hotel & Rest Mgmnt.

DANSER, MARCY; Greater Latrobe SR HS; Greensburg, PA; (Y); 79/337; Hon Roll; ICM Schl Of Bus; Med Off Asst.

DANZI, LISA; Bishop Shanahan HS; Downingtown, PA; (Y); 1/218; Mathletes; Scholastic Bowl; SADD; Nwsp Stf; Yrbk Stf; High Hon Roll; Hon Roll; Jr NHS; NHS; Spnsh Awd 84-86; High Excllnc Geo Awd 85-86; Chem Awd 85; Physcs Awd 86.

DARCANGELO, KELLEY; Grove City HS; Grove City, PA; (Y); AFS; French Clb; Key Clb; Pep Clb; High Hon Roll; Hon Roll; Trs NHS; Opt Clb Awd; Pres Schlr; U Of Central FL.

DARESTA, ANNETTE; Unionville HS; West Chester, PA; (Y); 21/300; Church Yth Grp; FBLA; Mrchg Band; School Musical; Yrbk Stf; Var Cheerleading; JV Var Trk; High Hon Roll; NHS; Cmnty Wkr; Schl On Map Awd 84; Pre-Law.

DARGAY, CHARLES; Hazleton HS; Hazleton, PA; (Y); Im Trk; Im Vllybl; High Hon Roll; Hon Roll; Pres Acad Ftnss Awd 86; PA ST U; Actg.

DARGAY, MICHELE; Hazleton SR HS; Hazleton, PA; (Y); Pep Clb; Band; Chorus; Concert Band; Drm Mjr(t); Mrchg Band; Pep Band; Symp Band; Bowling.

DARIS, SUSAN; Hickory HS; Hermitage, PA; (Y); 15/175; Drama Clb; Latin Clb; Pep Clb; Band; Chorus; Boy Scts; Capt Drill Tm; Jazz Band; School Musical; Nwsp Stf; Statue Of Lbrty Drl Tm; Pres Acad Ftns Awd; Ntl Hstry & Govt Awd; Allgheny Coll; Pre-Med.

DARLING, CHRIS; Elk Lake HS; Meshoppen, PA; (Y); 16/104; VICA; Stat Bsktbl; Tennis; Hon Roll; Prfct Atten Awd; Bio Med.

DARLING, TERRY; Elk Lake HS; Meshoppen, PA; (Y); 20/100; Church Yth Grp; Spanish Clb; Var Capt Bsbl; Var Capt Bsktbl; Tennis; Hon Roll; Mike Rd Wllc Bsktbll Schlrshp 86; Orll Crtr Bsbll Awd 86; U S Army Rsrv Ntl Schlr Athlt Awd 86; PA ST.

DARNELL, BEVERLY; Connellsville Area HS; Dunbar, PA; (Y); 34/500; Nwsp Rptr; French Hon Soc; High Hon Roll; Hon Roll; NHS; Prfct Atten Awd; 1st Pl German Reading Comprhnsn At Inl Day 86; Stero Clb 84-85; Jrnlsm.

DARNELL, KELLY; Bangor Area SR HS; Mt Bethel, PA; (Y); Exploring; Letterman Clb; Pep Clb; Ski Clb; Varsity Clb; Variety Show; Stat Bsktbl; Var L Fld Hcky; Im Powder Puff Ftbl; Var L Trk; Penn St U Money Grants 86; MVP Track 86; Hmcmng Crt 85; Penn ST U; Bus Adm.

DARROHN, MICHAEL; Allentown Central Catholic HS; Allentown, PA; (Y); Boy Scts; Church Yth Grp; JA; Letterman Clb; Varsity Clb; Var L Bsbl; Var L Ftbl; Var L Tennis; Var Wt Lftg; Var L Wrstlng; Bsbl Conf All Str 86; Penn ST; Bus.

DASCANI, CINDY; Catasauqua HS; Catasauqua, PA; (Y); 2/150; Church Yth Grp; Varsity Clb; Trs Soph Cls; Trs Jr Cls; Bsktbl; Fld Hcky; Trk; Dnfth Awd; High Hon Roll; Hon Roll; Pharmacy.

DASCANI, SCOTT; Southmoreland HS; Scottdale, PA; (Y); 96/230; JCL; Latin Clb; Letterman Clb; Ski Clb; Hst Soph Cls; Rep Stu Cncl; Var Bsbl; JV Var Bsktbl; JV Var Ftbl.

DASCOLA, CHRISTINA; St Paul Cathedral HS; Pittsburgh, PA; (S); 6/62; Pep Clb; Stage Crew; Nwsp Bus Mgr; Nwsp Rptr; Yrbk Stf; Rep Jr Cls; Pres Sr Cls; Stu Cncl; Mgr Vllybl; High Hon Roll; Sci Fair Awd 2nd Pl Exprmntl 83; U Pittsburgh; Chem Engrg.

DASCOLI, TERRY C; Midland HS; Midland, PA; (Y); Spanish Clb; Chorus; Yrbk Ed-Chief; Sec Jr Cls; Sec Stu Cncl; Bsktbl; Var Capt Cheerleading; Mgr(s); Var L Sftbl; Duffs Bus Inst; Prof Sec.

DASOVICH, E MARTY; Conneaut Valley HS; Conneautville, PA; (Y); 1/71; VP Spanish Clb; Pres Jr Cls; Pres Sr Cls; Stu Cncl; Elks Awd; Pres NHS; Pres Schlr; St Schlr; Val; Ski Clb; Ruby Marsh Eldres Schl & Estella Van Horne Schl 86; WV U Hnrs Pgm 86; WV U Morgantown; Bus.

DATE, LISA; Moshannon Valley HS; Smoke Run, PA; (Y); Church Yth Grp; Chorus; Im Socr; Altoona Schl Commerce; Acctng.

DATESMAN, DEANA L; Freedom HS; Easton, PA; (Y); 17/404; Trs Church Yth Grp; Cmnty Wkr; Office Aide; Pep Clb; Church Choir; High Hon Roll; Hon Roll; NHS; Pres Schlr; Nrsg Schlrshp 86; Pres Acadmc Fit Awd 86; U Of DE; Nrsg.

DAUBERT, ELIZABETH; Northern Lebanon HS; Fredericksburg, PA; (Y); 6/169; Band; Chorus; School Musical; Stu Cncl; Var Crs Cntry; Var Trk; Dnfth Awd; Hon Roll; NHS; Am Leg Awd Outstndng Grad; Outstndng Stu; Faclty Schlrshp; Gettysburg Coll; Psychlgy.

DAUBERT JR, TOM; Cedar Crest HS; Lebanon, PA; (Y); German Clb; Latin Clb; Pep Clb; Spanish Clb; Millersville U; Comp Sci.

DAUCHESS, DENISE; Marian Catholic HS; Nesquehoning, PA; (Y); 16/115; Church Yth Grp; French Clb; GAA; Office Aide; Scholastic Bowl; Ski Clb; Chorus; Church Choir; School Musical; School Play.

DAUGHERTY, COLLEEN; Upper St Clair & Canonmac HS; Canonsburg, PA; (Y); Aud/Vis; Key Clb; Political Wkr; Service Clb; Mgr Band; Hon Roll; Pre-Law.

DAUGHERTY, DENNIS; Apollo-Ridge HS; Spring Chruch, PA; (Y); Debate Tm; 4-H; FFA; 4-H Awd; Hon Roll; Lion Awd; Many FFA Ofcs 81-86; Cnty Reprtr 1 Term 83; Grnd Champ Lamb Dayton Fair 4-H 81; Slippery Rock U; Mortcn.

DAUGHERTY, DIANE M; Serra Catholic HS; E Mckeesport, PA; (Y); Cmnty Wkr; Exploring; Hosp Aide; Spanish Clb; Nwsp Rptr; Powder Puff Ftbl; Var Sftbl; Hon Roll; NHS; NEDT Awd; Cmnty Svc Awd 85; Paramedic.

DAUGHERTY, FAITH; Clairon-Limestone HS; Strattanville, PA; (S); 30/88; Church Yth Grp; VP Band; Chorus; Concert Band; Mrchg Band; Yrbk Stf; Var Capt Bsktbl; Var Capt Vllybl; Var Capt Trk; MVP Bstkbl 84-85; MVP Bst Sttr Vlybl 85-86; NE Christian JC; Phy Educ.

DAUGHERTY, GINA; Philiposburg-Osceola HS; Philipsburg, PA; (Y); 20/250; Church Yth Grp; Drama Clb; Band; Chorus; Concert Band; Capt Flag Corp; School Musical; Stage Crew; Yrbk Stf; Stu Cncl; Pres Phy Fit Awd; Duquesne U; Phrmcy.

DAUGHERTY, JOHN; Dubois HS; Falls Creek, PA; (Y); Cmnty Wkr; Letterman Clb; Stage Crew; L Ftbl; L Trk; Var Wt Lftg; JV Var Wrstlng; Stu Of Wk 86.

DAUGHERTY, KIMBERLY; Kiski Area HS; Vandergrift, PA; (Y); Church Yth Grp; Library Aide; Swmmng; Hon Roll; Prfct Atten Awd; Yth Ftns Achvt Awd 85; Sci.

DAUGHERTY, LISA; Red Lion SR HS; Red Lion, PA; (Y); 33/337; Girl Scts; Band; Concert Band; Mrchg Band; School Musical; Symp Band; Hon Roll; NHS; Pres Schlr; York Cnty Commuter Merit Schlrshp 86; Earl J & Inez C Frey Mem Schlrshp 86; York Coll Of PA; Med Tech.

DAUGHERTY, MICHELE; Apollo Ridge HS; Apollo, PA; (Y); 4/172; FBLA; FHA; Spanish Clb; SADD; Band; Vllybl; High Hon Roll; Rotary Awd; Johnny Murphy Music Awd; NHS; West Point; Mgmt.

DAUGHERTY, SHARI; Chestnut Ridge SR HS; Bedford, PA; (S); 8/107; Band; Chorus; Concert Band; Jazz Band; School Musical; Variety Show; Nwsp Stf; Twrlr; Hon Roll; NHS; Math Ed.

DAUGHERTY, STEVE; Wellsboro Area HS; Wellsboro, PA; (Y); Art Clb; Pep Clb; Var Swmmng; Wrstlng; Crmnl Jstic.

DAUGHTRY, KAREN M; Meyers HS; Wilkes Barre, PA; (Y); Church Yth Grp; English Clb; FHA; Girl Scts; Ski Clb; Band; Chorus; Church Choir; Concert Band; Jazz Band; IN U; Intl Rltns.

DAUM, CINDY; Penn Hills SR HS; Pittsburgh, PA; (Y); French Clb; Varsity Clb; Yrbk Stf; Wt Lftg; Hon Roll.

DAURA, KEITH; Penn-Trafford HS; Irwin, PA; (Y); Chess Clb; Church Yth Grp; Ski Clb; Spanish Clb; Varsity Clb; Var JV Bsbl; Var L Swmmng; IUP Cul Inst Amer; Chef.

DAUTI, JIM; Bensalem HS; Bensalem, PA; (Y); Bsbl; Socr; Wt Lftg; PA ST U; Lwyr.

DAVELLI, LISA; South Allegheny JR SR HS; Port Vue, PA; (S); 5/185; Trs French Clb; Hosp Aide; Quiz Bowl; Y-Teens; Band; Chorus; Church Choir; Concert Band; Jazz Band; Mrchg Band; Music Schlrshps Organ 83-85; Sci Fair Wnnr 83; Schl Brd Rep 85; U Of Pittsburgh; Phy Therapy.

DAVENPORT, DAWN; Hbg-Steelton Highspire Vo Tech; Harrisburg, PA; (Y); 102/386; Pep Clb; Sec VICA; Hon Roll; Comp Oper.

DAVID, AMY; Laurel Highlands SR HS; Lemont Furnace, PA; (Y); 10/365; Pres FBLA; Spanish Clb; Co-Capt Flag Corp; Ed Nwsp Stf; Yrbk Stf; CC Awd; Pres Jr NHS; NHS; Majorette 84; Scream Team 85; Phrmcy.

DAVIDHEISER, AMBER; Pottstown HS; Pottstown, PA; (S); 5/185; Civic Clb; Spanish Clb; Band; Concert Band; Jazz Band; Mrchg Band; School Musical; Yrbk Stf; Rep Sr Cls; High Hon Roll; Dist Band 84-85; Regnl Band 85; Hstry Day Dist, ST & Natls 85; Cvl Engrng.

DAVIDICK, TIMOTHY; Hazleton SR HS; Milnesville, PA; (Y); Boy Scts; Church Yth Grp; Drama Clb; Ski Clb; SADD; School Play; Variety Show; Hon Roll; Luzerne Co CC; Arch.

DAVIDOCK, JEFFREY; Marian HS; Barnesville, PA; (Y); 92/115; Camera Clb; Church Yth Grp; SADD; Bsbl; Bsktbl; Ftbl; Tennis; Trk; Crmnlgy.

DAVIDSON, DARYL; Sharon HS; Sharon, PA; (Y); 10/196; French Clb; Office Aide; Nwsp Stf; Stu Cncl; High Hon Roll; NHS; Nicholas B Ottaway Fndtn Schlrshp, Pres Acdmc Ftns Awd 86; Schl Nswpr Svc Awd, Outstnndg Frnch Stu 86; PA ST U.

DAVIDSON, DIANA; Steel Valley HS; Munhall, PA; (Y); DECA; Key Clb; Teachers Aide; High Hon Roll; Hon Roll; NHS; DECA Dist Comp 2nd Pl Svc Stat Rtlng Emplyee 86; DECA St Comp 5th Pl 86; Bus.

DAVIDSON, JEFF; Freeport SR HS; Freeport, PA; (Y); Chess Clb; Church Yth Grp; Cmnty Wkr; Computer Clb; Drama Clb; Nwsp Phtg; Yrbk Phtg; Off Jr Cls; Rep Stu Cncl; Trk; Comm.

DAVIDSON, LLOYD; Seneca Valley SR HS; Zelienople, PA; (Y); 45/342; JA; SADD; Varsity Clb; Pres Soph Cls; Off Jr Cls; Pres Stu Cncl; Capt Socr; Capt Swmmng; Trk; NHS; Jennifer Adham Memrl Schlrshp 86; Garman C Murray Outstndng Schlr Athltc Awd 86; Allegheny Coll; Econ.

DAVIDSON, MARIE; Archbishop Prendergast HS; Upper Darby, PA; (Y); 128/361; French Clb; FBLA; VICA; Orch; Im Bsktbl; Im Sftbl; Im Tennis; Im Vllybl; FBLA Schlrshp 86; Creatv Catrg Serv Awd Acadmc Achvt 86; Germ Am Chesf Assoc Saln Awd 86; The Restaurant Sch; Pro Chef.

DAVIDSON, PATRICK; Sheffield Area JR SR HS; Sheffield, PA; (Y); Pres Letterman Clb; SADD; Pres Varsity Clb; Sec Sr Cls; Rep Stu Cncl; Var Capt Bsktbl; Coach Actv; Var Capt Ftbl; Var Capt Trk; Wt Lftg; 1st Tm TCAC All Star Bsktbl, Chrstms Trny 85-86; 2nd Dist Trk Meet 85-86; Edinboro U.

DAVIDSON, SCOTT; Seneca Valley SR HS; Zelienople, PA; (Y); Letterman Clb; SADD; Varsity Clb; Rep Jr Cls; Var Stu Cncl; Var L Socr; Var L Swmmng; JV Trk; High Hon Roll; Hon Roll; Rtry Stu Of Mnth 83; Wils Cooley Awd Swmmng 84; Allegheny; Bio.

DAVIE, WILLIAM; Blacklick Valley JR-SR HS; Vintondale, PA; (S); 1/96; Library Aide; Varsity Clb; Bsktbl; Ftbl; Trk; High Hon Roll; Hon Roll; NHS.

DAVIES, CAROLYN; West Scranton HS; Scranton, PA; (Y); 11/257; Exploring; JA; Latin Clb; Letterman Clb; Red Cross Aide; Nwsp Stf; Yrbk Ed-Chief; Stu Cncl; Sftbl; High Hon Roll; Presdntl Schlrshp-Msrcrdia Coll-Fll Tutn 86; Mst Poplr Grl Awd In Cls 86; Miserocordia Coll; Prelaw.

DAVIES, GWYNN; Owen J Roberts HS; Pottstown, PA; (S); 25/267; Hosp Aide; Band; Chorus; Jazz Band; Mrchg Band; Orch; Pep Band; School Musical; Symp Band; Sftbl; PA Music Edctrs Assoc All ST Band; Dist XII Band; Rgn VI Band; U Of MA; Chem.

DAVIES, RICHARD; Danville Area HS; Danville, PA; (Y); 33/204; Var L Bsbl; NHS; Prfct Atten Awd; Computer Clb; 4-H; Im Bsktbl; Stat Ftbl; 4-H Awd; Hon Roll; Williams Bus Symposium 2nd Pl 86; Chem Engrng.

DAVIS, ALISON; Manheim Township HS; Lancaster, PA; (Y); Chorus; Fld Hcky; Bus.

DAVIS, ANGELA; Line Mountain HS; Dalmatia, PA; (Y); 1/115; Pres Church Yth Grp; Hosp Aide; Mrchg Band; Nwsp Stf; Stu Cncl; Var L Sftbl; High Hon Roll; Kiwanis Awd; NHS; Val; Two Ten Schlrshp 86; Mid Penn Bnk Awd 86; Vldctrn Schlrshp 86; Lebanon Valley Coll; Bio.

DAVIS, BECKY; Seneca Valley HS; Evans City, PA; (Y); Trs Church Yth Grp; Chorus; School Play; Rep Frsh Cls; Rep Soph Cls; Stu Cncl; Var Capt Cheerleading; Var Vllybl; High Hon Roll; Hon Roll; Spch Awd 1st Pl Regnl 84-85; Sci Fair 1st Pl Regnl 85; Vlybl MVP 85; Nrsng.

DAVIS, BLAIR; Tunkhannock Area HS; Tunkhannock, PA; (S); 6/350; Church Yth Grp; French Clb; Hosp Aide; Off Key Clb; School Play; Var Capt Cheerleading; JV Var Tennis; Sec NHS; Ntl Merit Ltr.

DAVIS, BRANDON; West Allegheny HS; Imperial, PA; (Y); 35/207; Spanish Clb; Nwsp Stf; Yrbk Stf; Rep Frsh Cls; Im Bsktbl; Hon Roll; Slippery Rock U; Comm.

DAVIS, BRENDA; Kiski Area HS; Vandergrift, PA; (Y); Band; Chorus; Church Choir; Concert Band; Jazz Band; Mrchg Band; School Musical; Twrlr; Hon Roll; Top Ten Stu 84; Bradford Schl; Acctnt.

DAVIS, BRIAN; Northeast Bradford HS; Le Raysville, PA; (Y); Church Yth Grp; Computer Clb; FFA; Varsity Clb; Capt Bsktbl; Hon Roll; Lycoming Coll; Bus Admnstrtn.

DAVIS, CHANTALE; Waynesboro Area SR HS; Blue Ridge Summit, PA; (Y); 35/376; Ski Clb; Chorus; School Musical; Var Capt Gym; Var Sftbl; JV Trk; High Hon Roll; NHS.

DAVIS, CHRIS; Elizabeth Area HS; Elizabethtown, PA; (Y); 97/237; Boy Scts; Church Yth Grp; Computer Clb; German Clb; Radio Clb; JV Socr; Hon Roll; Prfct Atten Awd; Penn ST U; Poli Sci.

DAVIS, CHRIS; Williamsburg HS; Williamsburg, PA; (Y); Girl Scts; Band; Concert Band; Mrchg Band; Stage Crew; Nwsp Rptr; Yrbk Stf; Rep Jr Cls; Mgr Bsktbl; JV Vllybl.

DAVIS, CHRISTINA M; Ontario Street Baptist Church Schl; Philadelphia, PA; (S); 1/2; Drama Clb; Hosp Aide; Math Clb; Church Choir; Yrbk Stf; VP Socr; High Hon Roll; Prfct Atten Awd; Acad All Amer Schlr Pgm Awd 84; Nrsg.

DAVIS, CLAUDIA; Springside Schl; Plymouth Meeting, PA; (Y); Camera Clb; Drama Clb; Stage Crew; Nwsp Stf; Yrbk Ed-Chief; Yrbk Phtg; Hon Roll; JV Var Bsktbl; JV Var Sftbl; Rebmann Fund 86; Jane Bell Memrl Awd 86.

DAVIS, CLIFTON A; Delaware County Christian Schl; Rosemont, PA; (Y); 2/60; Band; Chorus; Church Choir; School Play; DAR Awd; High Hon Roll; Hon Roll; NHS; Ntl Merit SF; Hnbl Mntn Csehy Smmr Schl Music 84-85; Assn Chrstn Schls Intl Distngshd HS Stdnt 85; Arch.

DAVIS, CRYSTAL JEANNETTE; Chester HS; Chester, PA; (Y); 97/350; Camera Clb; Church Yth Grp; Cmnty Wkr; FBLA; Office Aide; Pep Clb; Bsktbl; Mgr(s); Score Keeper; Hon Roll; Phtgrphy Awd 85; Twnshp Chstr Hon Outstndng Wrk Well Done 85; De Vry Tech Inst; Comp Svc.

DAVIS, DARLA; Seneca Valley HS; Harmony, PA; (Y); 50/380; Trs Church Yth Grp; Ski Clb; Varsity Clb; Chorus; Rep Jr Cls; Var L Crs Cntry; Var L Trk; Beautyshp Quartet; Grove City Coll; Bus Admn.

DAVIS, DARLENE; Mahanoy Area HS; Barnesville, PA; (Y); 15/124; Sec Trs Art Clb; French Clb; FHA; Rep Band; Pres Chorus; Variety Show; Nwsp Stf; Yrbk Stf; L Trk; NHS; Amrcn Bnk Schlrshp 86; Carol Reidler Bottiger Schlrshp 86; Rotory Yth Merit Awd 86; Susquehanna U; Finance.

DAVIS, DEANNA; Faith Christian Schl; Stroudsburg, PA; (S); Church Yth Grp; Spanish Clb; Chorus; School Musical; Yrbk Stf; Trs Soph Cls; Trs Jr Cls; Stat Bsktbl; Sftbl; Hon Roll; Christian Character Awd; Spirit Life Comm; Chapel Committee; Christian Coll; RN.

DAVIS, DIANA; Fairview HS; Fairview, PA; (Y); 24/183; Church Yth Grp; Spanish Clb; Chorus; Drill Tm; High Hon Roll; Ntl Merit Ltr; Coll Of William & Mary; Accntg.

DAVIS, DOUG; Linesville HS; Conneaut Lake, PA; (Y); 22/86; Art Clb; Aud/Vis; SADD; Var Bsbl; JV Ftbl; Wt Lftg; Hon Roll.

DAVIS, DWAYNE; Claysburg Kimmel HS; Imler, PA; (Y); German Clb; Letterman Clb; Varsity Clb; Band; Nwsp Sprt Ed; Yrbk Stf; Var Bsktbl; High Hon Roll; Prfct Atten Awd; Mc Allister Scholar 86; Yth & Govt Sec/Treas 82-86; Penn ST U; Elec Engrng.

DAVIS, ELAINE; Duquesne HS; Duquesne, PA; (Y); 9/85; French Clb; VP Y-Teens; Nwsp Stf; Yrbk Stf; Pres Frsh Cls; Rep Soph Cls; VP Jr Cls; Capt Bsktbl; High Hon Roll; Hon Roll; Merit Awd Mth 85; Acctng.

DAVIS, GARY; Carmichaels Area JR SR HS; Carmichaels, PA; (S); 1/101; Drama Clb; Spanish Clb; SADD; Concert Band; Mrchg Band; School Play; DAR Awd; Gov Hon Prg Awd; NHS; Amer Lgn Awd 81.

DAVIS, GRETCHEN; Lackawanna Trail HS; Dalton, PA; (Y); 8/92; French Clb; Ski Clb; Band; Madrigals; French Hon Soc; Hon Roll; NHS; Phrmcy.

DAVIS, GRETCHEN; Techinical HS; Scranton, PA; (Y); Art Clb; Nwsp Stf; Lit Mag.

DAVIS, JEFF; William Penn SR HS; York, PA; (Y); JV Capt Wrstlng; Hon Roll.

DAVIS, JEFFERY; Pocono Mountain HS; Mount Pocono, PA; (Y); 37/325; JV Bsktbl; Powder Puff Ftbl.

DAVIS, JENNIFER; Hanover SR HS; Hanover, PA; (Y); 11/140; Concert Band; Drm Mjr(t); Orch; School Musical; Swing Chorus; Sec Sr Cls; Rep Stu Cncl; Var Trk; DAR Awd; VP NHS; Stdnt Cncl Schlrshp 86; Jack M Schuler Memrl Awd 86; Pres Acdmc Fit Awd 86; U Of Pittsburgh; Dntstry.

DAVIS, JOAN; Carbondale Area JR SR HS; Carbondale, PA; (Y); FBLA; Ski Clb; Spanish Clb; Chorus; VP Soph Cls; Capt Sftbl; High Hon Roll; NHS.

DAVIS, JOHN; Bald Eagle Area HS; Bellefonte, PA; (Y); Im Bowling; Dstngshed Hnr Roll 85-86; Penn ST U.

DAVIS, JOHN; Boyertown Area SR HS; Boyertown, PA; (Y); 38/465; SADD; Acpl Chr; Church Choir; Pres Concert Band; Pres Mrchg Band; Orch; Pep Band; Swing Chorus; Cit Awd; Hon Roll; Engrng.

DAVIS, JONATHAN LEIGH; New Hope-Solebury HS; New Hope, PA; (S); 10/82; VP FBLA; Sec Soph Cls; Sec Jr Cls; Sec Stu Cncl; JV Var Bsbl; JV Var Bsktbl; High Hon Roll; Hon Roll; NHS; Prfct Atten Awd; Bus Adm.

DAVIS, JUDY; Hanover Arga HS; Wilkes Barre, PA; (Y); Key Clb; Color Guard; Stage Crew; Stu Cncl; Trk; Hon Roll; Wilkes Coll.

DAVIS, KARYN; Abington Hgts HS; Clarks Summit, PA; (Y); 74/278; Dance Clb; JA; Ski Clb; Yrbk Stf; Rep Stu Cncl; Var L Cheerleading; Comm.

DAVIS, KATHLEEN; Palmyra HS; Palmyra, PA; (Y); Church Yth Grp; Pep Clb; Spanish Clb; SADD; Acpl Chr; Chorus; Church Choir; Flag Corp; Hon Roll; Spnsh Clb Awd 86; Elem Ed.

DAVIS, KATHY; Plum SR HS; Pittsburgh, PA; (Y); Church Yth Grp; Spanish Clb; SADD; Socr; Hon Roll; NHS.

DAVIS, KELLEY; Downingtown SR HS; Downingtown, PA; (Y); French Clb; Ski Clb; SADD; Chorus; Var Crs Cntry; JV Trk.

DAVIS, KELLY; Upper Moreland HS; Hatboro, PA; (Y); Church Yth Grp; Band; Chorus; Church Choir; Concert Band; Drm Mjr(t); Mrchg Band; School Musical; School Play; Solo & Ensemble 1st Div Rtngs 83-84.

DAVIS, KIM; Plum SR HS; Pittsburgh, PA; (Y); Library Aide; Ski Clb; Drill Tm; Yrbk Stf; Rep Frsh Cls; Rep Jr Cls; Rep Sr Cls; Stat Bsbl; JV Cheerleading; High Hon Roll; Sec Grls Ldrs Asoc 84-86; U Of PA ST; Engrng.

DAVIS, KIMBERLY; Marion Center HS; Plumville, PA; (Y); 24/140; Pres Church Yth Grp; Pres Q&S; Capt Color Guard; Nwsp Ed-Chief; Pres Sr Cls; DAR Awd; NHS; Intnl Clb; Science Clb; SADD; Hugh O Brien Yth Fndtn Awd 84; Outstndg Sr Greensburg Trib Revw 86; Outstndg Jrnlst Awd Grnsbg Trib 86; Indiana U PA; Jrnlsm.

DAVIS, LINDA; Creative & Performings Arts; Philadelphia, PA; (S); 5/140; Church Yth Grp; Dance Clb; Hosp Aide; Rep Jr Cls; Stu Cncl; High Hon Roll; Hon Roll; Kutztown U; Marine Bio.

DAVIS, LORI; Brookville Area HS; Brookville, PA; (Y); Church Yth Grp; FTA; German Clb; Key Clb; Pep Clb; Varsity Clb; Yrbk Stf; Stat Bsktbl; Stat Ftbl; Mgr(s).

DAVIS, LORI ANN; Western Wayne HS; Lk Ariel, PA; (Y); 13/147; FHA; Sec Leo Clb; Band; Concert Band; Mrchg Band; School Musical; High Hon Roll; Hon Roll; Pa Lions All St Band 85-86; Dist A Band 85; Region IV Bank 85; Bloomsburg U; Nrsng.

DAVIS, MARCIA; Northwest Area HS; Hunlock Creek, PA; (Y); 50/153; Mrchg Band; Trs Jr Cls; Rep Stu Cncl; Cheerleading; Fld Hcky; Gym; Trk; 1st, 2nd & 3rd Pl Awds In Track 84; Elem Ed.

DAVIS, MARY; Brookville Area JR SR HS; Brookville, PA; (Y); Church Yth Grp; FTA; German Clb; Key Clb; Pep Clb; Teachers Aide; Thesps; Varsity Clb; School Play; Yrbk Ed-Chief; Pres Ftns Awd 86; Lttrd Trck-100 Hrdls 84-86; Elem Educ.

DAVIS, MEAGAN; Gateway SR HS; Monroeville, PA; (Y); 106/508; JA; Pep Clb; Chorus; Sr Cls; Stu Cncl; Bsktbl; Swmmng; Trk.

DAVIS, MICHAEL; Clarion-Limestone HS; Strattanville, PA; (Y); 8/66; JV Bsbl; Var Trk; Arch.

DAVIS, MICHAEL JAMES; Warren Area HS; Warren, PA; (Y); Pres Chess Clb; Debate Tm; Trs Exploring; German Clb; Jazz Band; Orch; Var Ftbl; High Hon Roll; NHS; Ntl Merit Ltr; NROTC Marine Option Schlrhsp 86; Penn ST U; Comp Sci.

DAVIS, MINDY; Fairchance-Georges HS; Uniontownd, PA; (Y); Church Yth Grp; Drama Clb; Spanish Clb; Concert Band; Pres Frsh Cls; Sec Soph Cls; Pres Jr Cls; Twrlr; Hon Roll; Sec Jr NHS; Coal Qn Rep Fairchnc Georges 86; Nrsng.

DAVIS, PARIS; Chester HS; Chester, PA; (S); Computer Clb; Concert Band; Nwsp Rptr; Nwsp Stf; High Hon Roll; Rcvd Trphy & Awd For Lncln U Tutorial Prgm 85; Acdmc Achvt Awd 84; Math.

DAVIS, PAUL; West Catholic HS; Philadelphia, PA; (Y); Church Yth Grp; Im Bsktbl; Var Capt Tennis; Hon Roll; Prfct Atten Awd; U Georgetown; Bus Adm.

DAVIS, SALLY; Northern HS; Dillsburg, PA; (Y); Spanish Clb; Band; Concert Band; Rep Soph Cls; Rep Jr Cls; Rep Sr Cls; Sec Stu Cncl; Powder Puff Ftbl; Trk; Hon Roll; Med.

DAVIS, SCOTT; Council Rock HS; New Hope, PA; (Y); 20/850; Church Yth Grp; FCA; French Clb; Stu Cncl; Socr; Trk; Wt Lftg; Hon Roll; NHS; SAR Awd; Yth Understndng Frgn Exchng Stu Schlrshp 86; Engrng.

DAVIS, STEPHANI; Columbia-Montour Area Vo Tech Schl; Catawissa, PA; (Y); Church Yth Grp; 4-H; FHA; Girl Scts; Hosp Aide; Library Aide; 4-H Awd; Hon Roll.

DAVIS, SUSAN; West Hazleton HS; Hazleton, PA; (Y); SADD; Y-Teens; Band; Concert Band; Mrchg Band; Pep Band; Wilks Coll; Bus.

DAVIS, SUSAN; West Scranton SR HS; Scranton, PA; (Y); Church Yth Grp; VP Band; VP Concert Band; Mrchg Band; Orch; Hon Roll; Culinary Arts.

DAVIS, TRENTON; Dubois Area HS; Dubois, PA; (Y); 27/271; Boy Scts; Church Yth Grp; Pres Sr Cls; Rep Stu Cncl; Bsbl; Bsktbl; Golf; Trk; Hon Roll.

DAVIS, W BRADLEY; Clearfield Area HS; Clearfield, PA; (Y); French Clb; Office Aide; VP SADD; Var Bowling; Var Cheerleading; Im Ftbl; Var Trk; Williamsport Area CC; Crpntry.

DAVISON, CHARLES; Seneca Valley HS; Harmony, PA; (Y); Art Clb; Cmnty Wkr; DECA; High Hon Roll; Hon Roll; Schltc Awd Top 12 Cls 86; Poem Publshd Raider Review 86; Bus Mgmt.

DAVISON, HEATHER; Hanover Area HS; Lower Askam, PA; (Y); Color Guard; Drill Tm; Flag Corp; Mrchg Band; Jr Cls; Stu Cncl; Gym; High Hon Roll; Atlantic Coast Champs Winter Color Guard 85; Slvr Mdl Winter Color Guard, Gold Medal Silk Duet 86; Bus.

DAVISON, JODI; Ambridge Area HS; Baden, PA; (Y); 77/265; VP Church Yth Grp; 4-H; Hosp Aide; Rep Jr Cls; Rep Sr Cls; Trk; Twrlr; 4-H Awd; Hon Roll; Fnlst Cnty JR Miss 86; Econ Sftbl Tm 82-85; Clarion U; Spch Pthlgy.

DAVISON, LA TITIA; Wilkinsburg JR SR HS; Pittsburgh, PA; (Y); Drama Clb; Exploring; FBLA; Library Aide; Spanish Clb; Chorus; Hon Roll; NHS; Prfct Atten Awd; Prfct Attndnce Upward Bound 85-86; Penn ST; Med.

DAVISON, PAUL; Brownsville Area HS; Brownsville, PA; (Y); Church Yth Grp; Computer Clb; Letterman Clb; Ski Clb; VICA; Stu Cncl; Bowling; Trk; Wt Lftg; Hon Roll.

DAVISSON, PAUL; Grove City HS; Grove City, PA; (Y); FBLA; JV Bsktbl; Im Bowling; JV Ftbl; Trvl Indstry.

DAVITT, MARLA; Parkland HS; Allentown, PA; (Y); 84/416; Church Yth Grp; Cmnty Wkr; German Clb; Hosp Aide; Leo Clb; Band; Im Fld Hcky; High Hon Roll; Hon Roll; NHS; Dec Stu Of Month 85; Hm Ec Ntl Hnr Soc Awd 86; Misericordia Coll; Ocptnl Thrpy.

DAVY, TEREASA; Lockhaven SR HS; Blanchard, PA; (Y); Cmnty Wkr; VP Sec FHA; Library Aide; Spanish Clb; Color Guard; Variety Show; Hon Roll; FHA Mbr Yr 83-84; FHA Key Scroll & Torch Degrees 85-86; Lock Haven U; Hist Tchr.

DAWSON, ANDREW S; Red Lion Area SR HS; Delta, PA; (Y); 3/341; Pres Sec Church Yth Grp; Pres VP 4-H; Varsity Clb; Yrbk Bus Mgr; Rep Stu Cncl; VP L Crs Cntry; Mgr(s); JV Trk; NHS; Ntl Merit SF; Loyers Phrmcy Chem Awd 85; PA Hghr Edu Asstnc Agcy Cert Of Merit 85; Schl Stu Of Mnth 85; USAF Acad; Aerosp Engr.

DAWSON, HEATHER; Mifflilnburg Area HS; Mifflinburg, PA; (Y); 33/160; French Clb; Key Clb; Cheerleading; Fld Hcky; Trk; Hon Roll.

DAWSON, JEFFREY; Bishop Mc Cort HS; Conemaugh, PA; (Y); Chorus; Hon Roll; Mu Alpha Theta Ntl HS & JR Coll Math Clb 86; PA ST; Comp Pgmr.

DAWSON JR, JOHN F; Mc Keespart SR HS; White Oak, PA; (Y); 113/380; AFS; Church Yth Grp; JA; Acad Games Clb 85-86; 1st Pl Sci Fair 85; PA ST; Engrng.

DAWSON, KATHLEEN; Bishop Shanahan HS; West Chester, PA; (Y); 51/214; Art Clb; Capt Dance Clb; Chorus; School Musical; School Play; Yrbk Stf; JV L Vllybl; Hon Roll; NHS; Schlrshp Awrd 86; W Chester U; Nrsng.

DAWSON, MATTHEW; Saegertown HS; Saegertown, PA; (Y); 25/117; Church Yth Grp; SADD; Chorus; Swing Chorus; Variety Show; Hon Roll; Law Enfrcmnt.

DAWSON, PAM; Coudersport JR SR HS; Coudersport, PA; (Y); Trs Church Yth Grp; French Clb; Band; Chorus; Church Choir; Yrbk Stf; Stat Bsktbl; Var Golf; High Hon Roll; Hon Roll; Psychlgy.

DAWSON, STEVE; Wm Allen HS; Allentown, PA; (Y); Boy Scts; Chess Clb; German Clb; Ski Clb; Ntl Merit Ltr; Muhlenberg Coll; Psychlgy.

DAWSON, TINA; Central Dauphin HS; Harrisburg, PA; (Y); Chorus; Madrigals; School Musical; Nwsp Rptr; Yrbk Stf; Stu Cncl; Stat Trk; Im Capt Vllybl; W Chester U; French.

DAY, BECKY; Lock Haven HS; Howard, PA; (Y); Key Clb; Spanish Clb; Chorus; Sec Frsh Cls; Trs Soph Cls; Sec Jr Cls; Var L Bsktbl; Socr; Var L Tennis; Var L Trk; Dist Trk & Ten; VP GAPS; Bloomsburg U; Spec Ed.

DAY, DIANA; Avon Grove HS; West Grove, PA; (Y); Band; Mrchg Band; Goldey Beacon Coll; Ex Secy.

DAY, DONNA; Karns City JR SR HS; Bruin, PA; (Y); 1/121; Pres Exploring; Sec FCA; Chorus; School Play; DAR Awd; High Hon Roll; Pres NHS; Ntl Merit Ltr; Pres Schlr; Val; John Beck Isabel Beck Johnson Mem Schrlshp 86; Am Leg Aux Awd 82; Rotry Yth Ldrshp Awd 85; Grove City; Engrng.

DAY, SHOREY; Mc Guffey HS; W Alexander, PA; (Y); 9/211; Am Leg Aux Girls St; Pres Church Yth Grp; Pres French Clb; Sec Jr Cls; Trs Stu Cncl; Tennis; Trk; Hon Roll; NHS; Stu Rcgntn Awd 84-85; Bus.

DAY, STEVE; Du Bois Area HS; Reynoldsville, PA; (Y); Chess Clb; Varsity Clb; Var L Bsbl; Hon Roll; NHS; Pres Schlr; Spnsh Awd 86; Penn ST; Bus Admin.

DAYE, PAULA; Hughesville HS; Hughesville, PA; (Y); 22/165; Art Clb; Ski Clb; Chorus; School Play; Yrbk Stf; Trk; 12th Annl Bus Educ Sympsm 4th Pl 86.

DAYOUB, GLADYS; Louise E Dieruff HS; Allentown, PA; (Y); Cmnty Wkr; Capt Debate Tm; JA; Pres Frsh Cls; VP Stu Cncl; Capt Fld Hcky; Capt Trk; Capt Vllybl; Cit Awd; Hon Roll; Muhlenberg Coll; Pre-Law.

DAYTNER, GARY; Union HS; New Castle, PA; (S); 8/66; Church Yth Grp; French Clb; Band; Concert Band; Jazz Band; Mrchg Band; Pep Band; JV Ftbl; Mgr(s); Hon Roll; Math.

DAYTON, DEBORAH K; Pennridge HS; Hilltown, PA; (Y); Trs Church Yth Grp; Drama Clb; Pres Acpl Chr; Church Choir; School Musical; School Play; Lit Mag; Trs Stu Cncl; NHS; Messiah Pres & Dean Schlrshp 86-87; Messiah Coll; Comm.

DAYWALT, DAVID; Cumberland Valley HS; Boiling Springs, PA; (Y); 10/522; Key Clb; Pres Latin Clb; Speech Tm; Jazz Band; Mrchg Band; Nwsp Rptr; Voice Dem Awd; Math Tm; Symp Band; Hon Roll; Dstrct Spch Trnmnt Ust Pl 86; Cptl Area Clscs Fstvl 1st & 2nd Pl 85 & 86; Comp Sci.

DE ANGELIS, BETH; Frazier SR HS; Vanderbilt, PA; (Y); #4 In Class; Trs FNA; Hosp Aide; Ski Clb; Concert Band; Mrchg Band; Pep Band; High Hon Roll; Jr NHS; VP NHS; Prm Comm; Thomas Jefferson; Phy Thrpy.

DE ANGELIS, MICHAEL; Upper Moreland HS; Hatboro, PA; (Y); 18/260; Key Clb; Concert Band; Jazz Band; Mrchg Band; Var Bsbl; Im Bsktbl; High Hon Roll; NHS; Dist Band 85; Cls Cncl 84-86; Penn ST; Bus Adm.

DE ANGELO, LESLIE; North Pocono HS; Moscow, PA; (Y); Church Yth Grp; Varsity Clb; Trs Frsh Cls; Rep Stu Cncl; Var Capt Cheerleading; Var Trk; Hon Roll; Mst Outstdng Chrldr 85; Bloomsburg U; Lbrl Arts.

DE ANTONA, CARMELLE; West Scranton HS; Scranton, PA; (Y); 56/206; Church Yth Grp; Letterman Clb; Drill Tm; Nwsp Stf; Yrbk Stf; Var Diving; Var Swmmng; Hon Roll; Jr NHS; NHS; Hosp Admn.

DE ARMENT, CARMELA; Commodore Perry HS; Greenville, PA; (S); 7/54; Pres FBLA; Library Aide; Math Tm; Office Aide; Chorus; Stage Crew; Var Vllybl; Hon Roll; NHS; 2nd Regnl Lvl Acctg I FBLA 85; Grove City Coll; Acctg.

DE ARMENT, JOHN M; Altoona Area HS; Altoona, PA; (S); 15/700; German Clb; Q&S; Ski Clb; Nwsp Rptr; NHS; Ntl Merit Ltr; NEDT Awd; Cmmnwlth PA Cert Merit 85.

DE BAKER, JODI; Canon Mc Millan HS; Canonsburg, PA; (Y); 27/340; Exploring; Office Aide; Ski Clb; Drill Tm; Yrbk Stf; Stu Cncl; Sftbl; High Hon Roll; Hon Roll; NHS; Amer Lg Awd 83; Slippery Rock U; Mktng.

DE BANDI, YVONNE M; Central York SR HS; York, PA; (Y); 17/252; NFL; Mrchg Band; Orch; School Musical; School Play; Swing Chorus; VP Pres Stu Cncl; Cheerleading; NHS; Optomist Outstndng Youth 84; Rotary Club Ldrshp Camp 85; York Cnty Jr Ms 1st Runner Up,Phycl Ftns 85; FL ST U; Music.

DE BELLIS, JOHN JAY; Northampton Area SR HS; Northampton, PA; (Y); 1/452; Leo Clb; Var L Socr; Var Trk; God Cntry Awd; High Hon Roll; Pres NHS; Computer Clb; Val; Aero Engrng.

DE BERARDINIS, ANDREA; Cardinal O Hara HS; Aston, PA; (Y); 62/772; Cmnty Wkr; Dance Clb; GAA; Variety Show; Rep Stu Cncl; Var L Crs Cntry; Var L Trk; Hon Roll; NHS; Prfct Atten Awd; PA JR Acad Sci 1st & 2nd Awd 85; Acad Hrns Cnvctn 85-86; Educ.

DE BERNARDO, CHRISTINA M; Mercyhurst Prep Schl; Harbor Creek, PA; (Y); 16/150; Girl Scts; Spanish Clb; Yrbk Stf; DAR Awd; High Hon Roll; NHS.

DE BIASE, TONI; East Pennsboro HS; Enola, PA; (Y); VP FBLA; GAA; Office Aide; Teachers Aide; Pres Frsh Cls; Pres Soph Cls; Pres Jr Cls; JV Var Cheerleading; Var Sftbl; Hon Roll.

DE BLASSIO, JEANENE; California Area HS; Coal Ctr, PA; (Y); Church Yth Grp; Drama Clb; JA; Band; Concert Band; Mrchg Band; Coach Actv; Gym.

DE BOLT, MARY BETH; Altoona Area HS; Dysart, PA; (Y); VP Key Clb; Spanish Clb; Chorus; Flag Corp; Stage Crew; Vllybl; Paralegal.

DE BOR, LISA; Butler SR HS; Butler, PA; (Y); Aud/Vis; Library Aide; JV Vllybl; ICM Bus Sch; CPA.

DE BORD, CRIS; Brownsville Area HS; Brownsville, PA; (Y); Am Leg Boys St; Camera Clb; Church Yth Grp; Mathletes; Math Clb; Math Tm; Ski Clb; SADD; Bowling; High Hon Roll; Amer Lgn Schl Awd; Eagle Schlrshp; Washington & Jefferson Coll.

DE CARIA, JAMES; Lincoln HS; Ellwood City, PA; (Y); 60/170; Church Yth Grp; Latin Clb; Spanish Clb; Bsktbl; Ftbl; Wt Lftg; High Hon Roll; Hon Roll.

DE CARLO, KARI; Uniontown HS; Uniontown, PA; (Y); 4/287; Spanish Clb; Concert Band; Mrchg Band; Off Jr Cls; Sec Sr Cls; Cheerleading; DAR Awd; High Hon Roll; NHS; Foreign Lang Hnr Soc 85; Washington & Jefferson; Med.

DE CARLO, NANCY; Mt Pleasant Area SR HS; Mt Pleasant, PA; (Y); FBLA; GAA; Ski Clb; Teachers Aide; Nwsp Rptr; Var L Cheerleading; U Of Pittsburgh; Clncl Pshcy.

DE CARLUCCI, HENRY KEITH; Laurel Highlands HS; Uniontown, PA; (Y); 30/346; Golf; Wt Lftg; High Hon Roll; Jr NHS; USAF Acad; Engrng.

DE CARO, DONALD; Greensbury Central Catholic HS; Greensburg, PA; (Y); 17/212; JCL; Letterman Clb; Rep Stu Cncl; Var L Bsbl; Var L Bsktbl; Var L Ftbl; High Hon Roll; NHS; Pre-Med.

DE CROES, STEPHEN; Dover Area HS; Dover, PA; (Y); Acpl Chr; Chorus; Concert Band; Mrchg Band; Pep Band; Stage Crew; Variety Show; Var Tennis; Comm.

DE FELICE, RHONDA; Neshannock HS; New Castle, PA; (Y); 15/99; Drama Clb; Library Aide; School Play; Nwsp Stf; NHS; Pres Schlr; Stevenson Scholar 86; Millersville U PA; Marine Bio.

DE FILIPPO, JOSEPH M; Keystone Oaks HS; Pittsburgh, PA; (Y); 30/260; Church Yth Grp; Exploring; German Clb; Math Tm; Pep Clb; Ski Clb; Mrchg Band; Pep Band; Var Swmmng; Capt Var Tennis; Pres German Clb 86; VP Marchng Band 86; Carnegie Mellon U; Bio Genetics.

DE FORREST, DEBBIE; Saint Hubert HS; Philadelphia, PA; (Y); Pres Church Yth Grp; JA; SADD; Y-Teens; Chorus; Yrbk Stf; JV Vllybl; Paralegal.

DE FRANCESCO JR, SALVATORE R; Pittston Area HS; Avoca, PA; (Y); 27/348; Boy Scts; Ski Clb; JV Ftbl; Var Swmmng; Hon Roll; Med.

DE FRANK, MATTHEW; Trinity HS; Camp Hill, PA; (Y); Rep Stu Cncl; Var Bsktbl; Ftbl; JV Golf; Im Socr; Im Sftbl; Var Trk; Im Vllybl; Mid Penn Div 2 All Str Tm Bsktbll 86; MVP Atholic Chrstmas Trnmnt 85; Sprts Med.

DE FRANK, STEPHEN; Uniontown Area SR HS; New Salem, PA; (Y); Pres Trs Church Yth Grp; Spanish Clb; Spanish NHS; Histry.

DE FRANTZ, WALTRINA; G A R Memorial HS; Wilkes-Barre, PA; (Y); Church Yth Grp; Dance Clb; Drama Clb; FBLA; Key Clb; Library Aide; Pep Clb; Ski Clb; Chorus; Church Choir; Temple; Pre-Med.

DE FRATE, DIANA L; Bellefonte SR HS; Bellefonte, PA; (Y); 1/217; Yrbk Stf; Off Soph Cls; Off Jr Cls; Off Sr Cls; Capt L Bsktbl; Capt Im Powder Puff Ftbl; Var L Sftbl; DAR Awd; High Hon Roll; NHS; Schlstc Merit Schlrshp-Susquehanna U 86; Natl Hnr Soc 84-86; James H Snyder Awd 86; Susquehanna U; Acctng.

DE FUSCO JR, PASQUALE; West Catholic Boys HS; Philadelphia, PA; (Y); Boy Scts; Cmnty Wkr; Service Clb; Band; Stage Crew; Yrbk Rptr; Yrbk Stf; Govt Service.

DE GENNARO, JAMES; Bellwood-Antis HS; Altoona, PA; (Y); Varsity Clb; Yrbk Ed-Chief; Ftbl.

DE GRAAFF, BECKY; Blue Mountain Acad; Wellsboro, PA; (S); 6/64; Church Yth Grp; Office Aide; Concert Band; Ed Nwsp Stf; Ed Yrbk Stf; Sec Soph Cls; Rep Stu Cncl; High Hon Roll; NHS; Prfct Atten Awd; Outdr Clb Pres 85-86; Paramedic.

DE GROAT, ANDREW; Wissahickon HS; Ambler, PA; (S); 23/276; German Clb; Letterman Clb; Ski Clb; SADD; Varsity Clb; Off Jr Cls; Stu Cncl; Lcrss; Var Capt Swmmng; NHS; Franklin & Marshall Coll; Law.

DE GROAT, RENEE L; Sun Valley HS; Aston, PA; (Y); 9/302; Computer Clb; Hosp Aide; Band; Concert Band; Mrchg Band; Ed Yrbk Ed-Chief; Var Tennis; Var Trk; High Hon Roll; JC Awd; Brookhaven Womens Clb Awd Music 83; SVHS Band Awd Dedctn 86; Bells Adv Commtte Awd 86; Quinnipiac Coll; Sports Med.

DE HECK, BETH; Central Bucks East HS; Jamison, PA; (Y); Church Yth Grp; Drama Clb; Girl Scts; Political Wkr; Chorus; Church Choir; School Musical; School Play; Stage Crew; Pres Schl Concert Choir 86; Bucks County CC; Prmry Educ.

DE HOFF, JENNIFER; Central SR HS; York, PA; (Y); Ski Clb; Varsity Clb; Nwsp Stf; Yrbk Stf; Var L Cheerleading; Hon Roll; Chrldng Co Cptn 83-85, Ltrd 84; Cmnl Jstc.

DE JESUS, LUIS; Roman Catholic HS; Philadelphia, PA; (S); 19/133; Church Yth Grp; Rep Frsh Cls; Rep Stu Cncl; JV Bsbl; Ftbl; Hon Roll; Ntl Merit Ltr; Prfct Atten Awd; Pres Schlr; Faithful Svc Novena 84-85; Hnrs 82-86.

DE JOHN, CHRISTOPHER; Kennedy Christian HS; Sharon, PA; (Y); 17/100; School Play; Pres Stu Cncl; Im Bsktbl; Var Ftbl; Capt Trk; DAR Awd; Hon Roll; NHS; Army, AF, Navy ROTC 86; US Military Acad; Engrng.

DE LEON, LISA; Abington SR HS; Huntingdon Valley, PA; (Y); Pep Clb; Spanish Clb; Varsity Clb; Nwsp Stf; Yrbk Stf; Rep Frsh Cls; Rep Soph Cls; Rep Jr Cls; Rep Sr Cls; Rep Stu Cncl; Mdl Of Amer 85; Ntl Hnr Roll 85; Ms Hmshr 86; Boca Raton Coll; Fash Merch.

DE LESSIO, AMY M; Hazleton HS; Hazleton, PA; (Y); 21/373; Color Guard; High Hon Roll; Ladies Unico Schlrshp Awd 86; Presdntl Acadmc Ftns Awd 86; PA ST U; Engrng.

DE LISIO, ADRIENNE; Hopewell HS; Aliquippa, PA; (Y); Church Yth Grp; Spanish Clb; SADD; Chorus; Yrbk Stf; Sec Soph Cls; Powder Puff Ftbl; Tennis; Hon Roll; Scepter Bearer Hmncmng & May Day Ct 86; Best Dresed 86; Robert Morris Coll; Bus Mgmt.

DE LONG, BETHANI ANN; Ridley HS; Folsom, PA; (Y); 18/412; Church Yth Grp; Drama Clb; French Clb; SADD; Thesps; Chorus; Church Choir; Madrigals; School Musical; School Play; TV Studio Cst, Crew 85-86; Yuth-Yuth 85; Tlntd JRS 84; Sarah Lawrence Coll; Lib Arts.

DE LONG, LISA; Du Bois Area HS; Du Bois, PA; (Y); 10/277; Church Yth Grp; VP Girl Scts; Library Aide; Chorus; High Hon Roll; Hon Roll; Sec NHS; Slvr & Gld Ldrshp Awds Grl Scts 83-84; Fnlst 9th Grd Essay Cntst Penn ST U 84; Indiana U Of PA; Law.

DE LONG, NATANA; Ridley HS; Folsom, PA; (Y); 7/412; Church Yth Grp; Sec Thesps; Chorus; School Musical; Nwsp Rptr; NHS; Pres Schlr; Sec Drama Clb; French Clb; Band; Frgn Lang Tchrs Awd; HS Permnt Schlrshp; Dist, Rgnl Chorus; Middlebury Coll; Frnch.

DE LUCA, DEBORAH LYNN; Center Area HS; Aliquippa, PA; (Y); 19/185; Office Aide; Spanish Clb; Yrbk Stf; Rep Stu Cncl; Im Bowling; Hon Roll; NHS; VFW Awd; Spn Awd 84; Pres Acad Fit Awd 86; Hnr Grad 86; PA ST U; Bus Adm.

DE LUCCA, ANNETTE; Hazleton SR HS; Hazleton, PA; (Y); 89/373; Leo Clb; Bsktbl; Sftbl.

DE MAIOLO, CHRISTINE; Center HS; Aliquippa, PA; (Y); 21/185; Dance Clb; Drama Clb; Pres German Clb; School Musical; Nwsp Rptr; Yrbk Stf; Sec Jr Cls; Sec Sr Cls; Var Cheerleading; VP NHS; Keystone Girls St 85; Chmbr Comm Yth Recgntn Awd 86; Sept Girl Of Mnth 86; PA ST U; Brdcst Jrnlsm.

DE MARCO, LAURIE; Tunkhannock Area HS; Tunkhannock, PA; (S); 1/290; French Clb; Chrmn Key Clb; Latin Clb; PAVAS; School Play; Rep Stu Cncl; Var L Fld Hcky; High Hon Roll; NHS; School Musical; Gold Mdlst Ntl Latin Exm 85; 1st Frnch I 84.

DE MARCO, MARIE; New Brightin Area HS; New Brighton, PA; (Y); 25/152; Am Leg Aux Girls St; Church Yth Grp; Letterman Clb; Yrbk Ed-Chief; VP Jr Cls; L Sftbl; High Hon Roll; Lion Awd; GAA; Cheerleading; Sec Yr Awd 86; Geneva Coll; Bus Adm.

DE MARTZ, GEORGE; Mahonoy Area HS; Barnesville, PA; (Y); 22/122; Spanish Clb; Band; Concert Band; Mrchg Band; Pep Band; Var L Wrstlng; Soc Stu Dept Awd 86; Elctrncs.

DE MASI, CHRISTINE; Archbishop Ryan For Girls; Philadelphia, PA; (Y); 40/475; JA; Office Aide; Q&S; Nwsp Stf; High Hon Roll; Hly Fmly Coll Grnt 86; Bus Studys Hon Mntn 86; Holy Family Coll; Cmmnctns.

DE MAURO, CHRISTINE; Penn Hills SR HS; Pittsburgh, PA; (S); 25/762; French Clb; Varsity Clb; Yrbk Stf; Stu Cncl; Var Trk; High Hon Roll; Jr NHS; NHS; Indiana U PA.

DE MELFI JR, THOMAS M; Central Dauphen HS; Harrisburg, PA; (Y); 56/386; Var L Bsktbl; Im Vllybl; Hon Roll; Jr NHS; Trs NHS; Woodmen Wrld Hstry Awd 83-84; Pin Natl Hnr Socty 83-84; Pre-Med.

DE MORELAND, DONNA; Centeral Bucks East HS; Warrington, PA; (Y); Church Yth Grp; Hosp Aide; Red Cross Aide; SADD; Chorus; Church Choir; Capt Color Guard; Flag Corp; Var JV Sftbl; JV Vllybl; Abington Hosp; X-Ray Tech.

DE MORROW, DENISE; Mid-Valley HS; Dickson City, PA; (Y); Church Yth Grp; Hosp Aide; Yrbk Phtg; Yrbk Stf; Trs Soph Cls; Trs Jr Cls; JV Cheerleading; Hon Roll; Empire Beauty Schl; Cosmetlgst.

DE MUTH, JANET; Penn Wood HS; Aldan, PA; (Y); 25/320; Church Yth Grp; Band; Concert Band; Jazz Band; Mrchg Band; Symp Band; Gym; Sftbl; High Hon Roll; Hon Roll; Wes Chester U; Elmntry Ed.

DE NARDO, ELIZABETH; Bethel Park SR HS; Bethel Park, PA; (Y); 65/515; Spanish Clb; Chorus; Drill Tm; School Musical; Variety Show; Pom Pon; Hon Roll; Pres Schlr; Duquesne U; Acctng.

DE PAOLANTONIO, TERESA; Central Cambria HS; Ebensburg, PA; (Y); 25/192; Drama Clb; Latin Clb; NFL; Red Cross Aide; Teachers Aide; School Play; Sec Trs Stu Cncl; JV Cheerleading; Mgr(s); Powder Puff Ftbl; IN U Of PA; Spcl & Elem Ed.

DE PAOLI, ALAN; Canon Mc Millian SR HS; Eighty Four, PA; (Y); Var Ski Clb; Var Golf; L Var Trk; Hon Roll; Chess Clb; French Clb; SADD; Stage Crew; Chem Engrng.

DE PETRO, LISA; Bradford Area HS; Cyclone, PA; (Y); 19/290; Band; Concert Band; Jazz Band; Mrchg Band; Nwsp Ed-Chief; Nwsp Phtg; Nwsp Rptr; Nwsp Stf; High Hon Roll; Hon Roll; Joe Guido Journalism Awd 85 & 86; Indiana U Of PA; Journalism.

DE PIETRO, ANGELA; Plum SR HS; Pittsburgh, PA; (Y); Aud/Vis; Cmnty Wkr; French Clb; Varsity Clb; Yrbk Stf; Var Capt Socr; Sftbl; L Vllybl; L Stat Wrstlng; Hon Roll; Distrbtv Educ Clb Of Amer 85-87; Mrktng.

DE PIETRO, MARISA; West Scranton HS; Scranton, PA; (Y); Cmnty Wkr; Dance Clb; Ski Clb; Spanish Clb; Rep Jr Cls; JV Var Cheerleading; Hon Roll; Jr NHS; NHS; Oceanogrphy.

DE POFI, KRISTEN; Kennedy Christian HS; Sharpsville, PA; (Y); French Clb; Hosp Aide; Varsity Clb; Yrbk Stf; Sec Frsh Cls; Var Cheerleading; French Hon Soc; Hon Roll; Chtlc Dghts Amer Essy Cntst 85; Soph Hmcmng Attndnt 84; Chld Psychlgy.

DE RISO, DINA MARIE; Greater Works Acad; Pittsburgh, PA; (S); Yrbk Stf; High Hon Roll; JR SR Girls Clb Sec 86; Miss Teen Amer USA Fnlst 85; Acctg.

DE ROBERTIS, DENISE; Union Area HS; New Castle, PA; (Y); 8/66; Library Aide; Office Aide; Chorus; Madrigals; School Musical; Capt Cheerleading; Vllybl; DAR Awd; High Hon Roll; NHS; Slippery Roc U; Elem Ed.

DE ROBERTIS, MEREDITH; Union Area HS; New Castle, PA; (Y); 14/68; Church Yth Grp; French Clb; Library Aide; Office Aide; Chorus; Color Guard; Madrigals; School Musical; Yrbk Stf; VP Stu Cncl; Fshn Merch.

DE ROOS, LISA; Mechanicsburg S HS; Mechanicsburg, PA; (Y); 128/328; Church Yth Grp; Hosp Aide; Trs Key Clb; Band; Church Choir; Mrchg Band; Rep Jr Cls; Rep Stu Cncl; JV Var Bsktbl; Mgr Ftbl; Psychlgy.

DE ROSA, ANN; Central Bucks High School East; Danboro, PA; (Y); 4-H; FBLA; Nwsp Stf; Mgr(s); Score Keeper; 4-H Awd; Hon Roll; Bus Admin.

DE ROSE, LAURA; Ambridge Area HS; Baden, PA; (Y); Church Yth Grp; Cmnty Wkr; German Clb; GAA; Hosp Aide; Pep Clb; Red Cross Aide; Band; Concert Band; Mrchg Band; Phys Therapy.

DE ROSS, DANIEL; Saegertown HS; Saegertown, PA; (Y); 21/124; Stage Crew; Vllybl; Wrstlng; Hon Roll; Jr NHS; NHS; Prfct Atten Awd.

DE SALVO, MARIA ANNETTE; Northern Cambria HS; Nicktown, PA; (Y); Drama Clb; Concert Band; Mrchg Band; Rep Stu Cncl; High Hon Roll; Hon Roll; NHS; W J Taylor Memrl Awd 86; Top 10 Pct Cls 86; PA ST U; Nrsng.

DE SANTIS, JASON; Charleroi Area HS; Charleroi, PA; (Y); 1/170; Ski Clb; Varsity Clb; Stu Cncl; Ftbl; Trk; High Hon Roll; NHS; Ntl Merit Schol; Rensselaer Math Awd 86.

DE SANTIS, MAUREEN; Cntry Day Schl Of The Sacred Heart; Berwyn, PA; (S); Cmnty Wkr; High Hon Roll; NHS; Ntl Merit Ltr; Cntry Day Schl Of Scrd Hrt Effrt Awd.

DE SANTIS JR, THOMAS A; Hazleton SR HS; Hazelton, PA; (Y); 92/400; Quiz Bowl; Band; Concert Band; Jazz Band; Mrchg Band; Symp Band; Stat Bsktbl; Hon Roll; JP Sousa Awd; Pres Schlr; Univ Acad For Music Euro Cncrt Tour 85; L Armstrong Jazz Awd 86; PA ST U; Finnc.

DE SHONG, JILL; Mc Connellsburg HS; Harrisonville, PA; (Y); FHA; High Hon Roll; NHS; Engl Awd 83-85; Bus Awd 85-86; Hlth Awd 86; Hmkg Asst Awd 86; Secy.

DE SHONG, SCOTT; State College Area SR HS; State College, PA; (Y); 38/483; SADD; Band; Lit Mag; Jr Cls; Sr Cls; Stu Cncl; Bsktbl; Cheerleading; Vllybl; High Hon Roll; Donald W Carruthers Jr Mem Scholar Awd 86; Faculty Schlr 86; Judge Richard G Sharp Mem Awd 83; PA ST U; Bus Adm.

DE SIMONE, JOHN; Connellsville Area SR HS; Connellsville, PA; (Y); Bsbl; Ftbl; Wrstlng; High Hon Roll; US Naval Acad Appt 86; Quad A All ST Ftbl 85-86; US Naval Acad; Pilot.

DE SIMONE, LISA; St Maria Goretti HS; Philadelphia, PA; (Y); 92/400; Art Clb; Mathletes; Spanish Clb; Mgr(s); Sftbl; Hon Roll; Temple U; CPA.

DE SOUZA, MICHELE; Dallastown HS; Dallastown, PA; (Y); 75/353; Hosp Aide; Varsity Clb; Var L Crs Cntry; Var Diving; Gym; Trk; High Hon Roll; Rotary Awd; Rtry Intrntnal Exchng Stu Brazil 86-87; Intrntnl Rltns.

DE STEFANO, JAMES; Nativity Bvm HS; Pottsville, PA; (Y); 9/97; Aud/Vis; Chess Clb; Church Yth Grp; Trs Band; Concert Band; Mrchg Band; Var L Crs Cntry; Var L Trk; High Hon Roll; Hon Roll; Nuclr Engrng.

DE STEFANO, MARY ANN; Bishop Hannan HS; Scranton, PA; (Y); Exploring; Hosp Aide; JA; Spanish Clb; Bowling; Hon Roll; NHS; Excel Spnsh I, II 82-84; Excel Wrld Cltrs II 84-85; Excel Sociolgy 85-86; Marywood Coll; Nrsg.

DE TITTA, ANTHONY; Coatesville HS; Coatesville, PA; (Y); 49/490; Debate Tm; ROTC; Spanish Clb; Nwsp Rptr; Rep Stu Cncl; JV Socr; Hon Roll; NHS; NEDT Awd.

DE VICE, FRANK; Cardinal O Hara HS; Glenolden, PA; (Y); 211/772; VP Church Yth Grp; VP Cmnty Wkr; VP Science Clb; VP Service Clb; Im Bsbl; Im Bsktbl; Im Bowling; Im Coach Actv; Var Crs Cntry; Var Trk; La Salle; Comm.

DE VIRGILIS, ALEX THOMAS; Scranton Preparatory Schl; Waverly, PA; (Y); 96/192; Drama Clb; Thesps; Chorus; School Musical; School Play; Lit Mag; Trk; Hon Roll; Gld Mdl Drmtcs 86; Slvr Mdl Chrl 86; Law.

DE WALD, SCOTT; Deer Lakes JR SR HS; Gibsonia, PA; (Y); Church Yth Grp; Var Crs Cntry; Var Trk; High Hon Roll; NHS; Elctrcl Eng.

DE WIRE, TIMOTHY; Mechanicsburg Area SR HS; Mechanicsburg, PA; (Y); 24/300; Boy Scts; SADD; Var L Ftbl; Var L Trk; Hon Roll; Albright Coll Walton Schlr 86-87; Harrisburg Chptr-Intl Soc Ind Engrs Awd 85; I E Herr Fndtn Schlrshp; Albright Coll; Engrng.

DE WITT, DENISE MARIE; Schuylkill Haven Area HS; Schuylkill Haven, PA; (S); 2/87; Computer Clb; German Clb; Science Clb; SADD; Teachers Aide; Nwsp Rptr; JV Var Bsktbl; Var L Trk; Twrlr; Hon Roll; Educ.

DE WOODY, ELIZABETH; Canon Mcmillan HS; Eighty Four, PA; (Y); 145/340; Drama Clb; SADD; Thesps; Varsity Clb; Chorus; School Musical; School Play; Yrbk Stf; Swmmng; Hon Roll; Cnty & Dstrct Chrs Fstvls 84-86; Hornes Dprtmnt Str Tnbrd 85-86; Westminster Coll; Elem Educ.

DEAMER, COLLEEN; Delone Catholic HS; Hanover, PA; (Y); 14/166; Cheerleading; Hon Roll; Top 10% Cls 83-84; Chem.

DEAN, CAROL S; Norristown HS; Norristown, PA; (Y); 35/404; Church Yth Grp; DECA; Fld Hcky; Hon Roll; NHS; FCA; FBLA; Soph Cls; Jr Cls; Sr Cls; Crtsy Awd 86; Sbrbn Phila Bus Ed Assoc Awd 86; Acdmc All Amrcn 86; 3rd Pl DECA Apparl & Accsrs Cmptn; Kutztown U.

DEAN, JILL; Punxsutawney Area SR HS; Du Bois, PA; (Y); Aud/Vis; FBLA; Variety Show; Hon Roll; Jr NHS; NHS; Stu Of Mnth Octbr 85.

DEAN, LAURA; Dallas SR HS; Dallas, PA; (Y); Aud/Vis; Ski Clb; Cheerleading; Hon Roll.

DEAN, LEIGH; Jamestown Area HS; Jamestown, PA; (Y); 8/53; Library Aide; Service Clb; VP Spanish Clb; VP Soph Cls; Stat Bsktbl; Mgr Vllybl; High Hon Roll; Hon Roll; Pres Schlr; Owston Sci Awd 86; Butler County CC; Nrsng.

DEAN, MARGARET; Strath Haven HS; Swarthmore, PA; (Y); French Clb; Girl Scts; Hosp Aide; Acpl Chr; Chorus; Lit Mag; Var Crs Cntry; JV Trk; Hon Roll; Brown U Bk Awd 86; Natl Cncl Frnch Tchrs Concours 84-86; Vrsty Arts Ltr Wrk Lit Magzn 86; Med.

DEAN, MARY KATHRYN; Mercersburg Acad; Bel Air, MD; (Y); 18/123; Camera Clb; Church Yth Grp; French Clb; Key Clb; Library Aide; Science Clb; Var L Sftbl; Var Swmmng; Hon Roll; Bio.

DEAN, VICTOR; Jamestown Area HS; Jamestown, PA; (S); 2/52; Spanish Clb; Varsity Clb; Var Bsktbl; High Hon Roll; Hon Roll; Prfct Atten Awd; Pres Physcl Fit Awd 84-86; Engl & Hist Awd 84; Air Force.

DEANER, ALICIA; Somerset Area SR HS; Somerset, PA; (Y); German Clb; Band; Chorus; Concert Band; Jazz Band; Mrchg Band; Pep Band; Variety Show; Var Trk; Var Wt Lftg; Army; Music.

DEANER, STEPHANIE; Cedar Crest HS; Lebanon, PA; (Y); 18/330; Trs Church Yth Grp; VP FBLA; Symp Band; Capt L Crs Cntry; Capt L Trk; High Hon Roll; NHS; Pep Clb; Spanish Clb; SADD; Alfred U Pres Schlrshp 86; Pres Acad Fitness Awd 86; Amer Music Abroad Tour Europe 84-85; Alfred U; Psychlgy.

DEANGELIS, CARA; Connellsville Area HS; Millrun, PA; (Y); Q&S; SADD; Nwsp Bus Mgr; Nwsp Sprt Ed; Yrbk Sprt Ed; Rep Soph Cls; Rep Jr Cls; High Hon Roll; Hon Roll; NHS; Ldrshp Schlrshp St Vncnt 86; St Vincent Coll; Pltcl Sci.

DEANGELIS, MELISSA; Muhlenberg HS; Laureldale, PA; (Y); Trs Band; Concert Band; Jazz Band; Mrchg Band; Pep Band; School Musical; Hon Roll; Zswtz Outstndg Instrmntlst Awd 86; Millersville U; Comp Sci.

DEANGELIS, MELISSA; Oil City HS; Oil City, PA; (Y); 42/276; German Clb; Varsity Clb; Variety Show; Yrbk Stf; Pres Sr Cls; Rep Stu Cncl; Var L Cheerleading; Var Trk; Var L Vllybl; NHS; Pres Phy Ftnss Awd 84; Vet Med.

DEARDORFF, CRYSTAL; Fairfield Area HS; Fairfield, PA; (Y); 16/42; Spanish Clb; Band; Jazz Band; Hon Roll.

DEARICK JR, KENNETH W; New Oxford HS; New Oxford, PA; (Y); 37/167; Boy Scts; Cmnty Wkr; Exploring; Ftbl; God Cntry Awd; Hon Roll; JR Fire Dept Treas 84-86, Rookie Yr 83, Merit Awd 84-85; Eagle Scout 85; Auto Mech.

DEASY, BRIDGETTE M; Sacred Heart HS; Pittsburgh, PA; (Y); Dance Clb; French Clb; Latin Clb; Pep Clb; Spanish Clb; SADD; Lcrss; Swmmng; Vllybl; High Hon Roll; U Of Pittsburgh; Nrsng.

DEATER, LARISA; Meadville SR HS; Meadville, PA; (Y); 103/344; Rep Frsh Cls; Rep Soph Cls; Rep Jr Cls; Trs Stu Cncl; Var JV Cheerleading; JV Trk; Hon Roll; Reunin Clb; Penn ST; Arch.

DEAVER, WENDY; Northern HS; Dillsburg, PA; (Y); 54/209; Church Yth Grp; Hosp Aide; Stat Bsktbl; Hon Roll; Psych.

DEBARBERIE, MARIE; Archbishop Kennedy HS; Philadelphia, PA; (Y); Lit Mag; Rep Frsh Cls; Rep Soph Cls; Rep Jr Cls; Pres Sr Cls; Pres Stu Cncl; Stat Bsktbl; JV Var Fld Hcky; Stat Ftbl; JV Var Sftbl; All Lg Sftbl 86; Educ.

DEBENEDICT, RAYMOND; Marian HS; Tamaqua, PA; (Y); 32/115; Chess Clb; Concert Band; Jazz Band; Mrchg Band; School Musical; Var L Trk; PA All-ST Lions Band 86; Phrmcy.

DEBO, SHERI; Rochester Area JR SR HS; Rochester, PA; (Y); 7/100; French Clb; JA; SADD; Teachers Aide; Chorus; Sec Stu Cncl; Swmmng; NHS; Sls Clb Awd JR Achvt 85-86; Nrsng.

DEBOE, ANITA; Villa Maria Acad; Northeast, PA; (Y); Church Yth Grp; Hosp Aide; Spanish Clb; Drill Tm; JV Trk; U Maryland; Jrnlsm.

DEBRUTTOLA, AMY; Keystone Oaks HS; Pittsburgh, PA; (Y); Church Yth Grp; Exploring; Pep Clb; Nwsp Rptr; Hon Roll; Acctg.

DEBUIGNE, NICOLE; Northern York County HS; Dillsburg, PA; (Y); 67/210; French Clb; Var Capt Tennis; JV Trk; Im Vllybl; French Hon Soc; Hon Roll; Mark Artist Awd 85; Frgn Lang.

DECAMARA, MATTHEW; St Josephs Prep; Huntingdon Vly, PA; (Y); Church Yth Grp; Cmnty Wkr; Intnl Clb; Nwsp Rptr; Yrbk Rptr; Im Bsktbl; Im Ftbl; Hon Roll; Intrmrl Tm Champ Bsktbll 86; Treas Schls Pro Life Clb 86-87; JR Peer Advsry Prg JPAP 85-86; Bus Mgmt.

DECARLO, DANIELLE; Canon-Mc Millan HS; Mcdonald, PA; (Y); VP FBLA; Ski Clb; Chorus; Stage Crew; Nwsp Stf; Yrbk Stf; Cheerleading; Hon Roll; Robert Morris Col6; Bus Tchr.

DECARLO, MICHELLE; South Phila HS; Philadelphia, PA; (Y); Library Aide; School Musical; Pres Frsh Cls; Hon Roll; Ntl Merit Ltr; Bio.

DECH, BILL; Salisbury SR HS; Bethlehem, PA; (Y); 5/139; Church Yth Grp; Scholastic Bowl; High Hon Roll; Hon Roll; NHS; FL U; Nuc Engrg.

DECH, JONATHAN; Parkland HS; Allentown, PA; (Y); Church Yth Grp; VP JA; Math Clb; Band; Slsmn Yr 84; VP Mktg Yr 85; Outstndng Yng Bssmn 86; Anderson Coll; Pre-Law.

DECHERT, LISA; Grace Christian Schl; Lebanon, PA; (Y); Church Yth Grp; Cmnty Wkr; Chorus; School Play; Yrbk Stf; Mgr(s); Score Keeper; Sftbl; Timer; High Hon Roll.

DECINTI, CAROLYN; G A R HS; Wilkes Barre, PA; (S); 18/187; Library Aide; Chorus; Yrbk Stf; Cheerleading; Score Keeper; Hon Roll; Jr NHS; NHS; Chld Dev.

DECKER, JOHN; Central SR HS; York, PA; (Y); Boy Scts; Church Yth Grp; Computer Clb; JA; Hon Roll; Penn ST York.

DECKER, KELLY M; Moraca HS; Monaca, PA; (Y); Office Aide; Pep Clb; School Musical; Hon Roll.

DECKER, KIMBERLY BETH; Monaca JR SR HS; Monaca, PA; (Y); Pep Clb; School Musical; Albebra II & Math Awd 83; CC Beaver Cnty; Bus.

DECKMAN, DENISE; Northwest Area HS; Shickshinny, PA; (Y); 4/129; Trs Sec Church Yth Grp; Drama Clb; SADD; Chorus; School Musical; Pres Soph Cls; Pres Jr Cls; VP Sr Cls; High Hon Roll; NHS; Most Promising Underclassman Awd In Music 84; Nrsng.

DECKMAN, JOHN; Northern Lebanon HS; Lebanon, PA; (Y); Math Tm; Quiz Bowl; Concert Band; Mrchg Band; Pep Band; School Musical; JV Bsbl; Var Tennis; Hon Roll; Dist Band 85; Widener U; Comp Sci.

DECORT, SUSIEANNE; Portage Area HS; Portage, PA; (Y); 82/123; Chorus; Stage Crew; Nwsp Bus Mgr; Nwsp Rptr; Nwsp Stf; Yrbk Rptr; Yrbk Stf; JV Var Bsktbl; JV Var Vllybl; Hon Roll; Tchr.

DECZKOWSKI, CHRIS; Ambridge Area HS; Ambridge, PA; (Y); 118/265; Boy Scts; Church Yth Grp; German Clb; Pep Clb; Band; Chorus; Orch; Symp Band; Variety Show; Ambridge Wlvs Den III Schlrshp 86; Bdn Lions Clb Schlrshp 86; Eagle Sct Ntl Yth Rep PA Scts Awd 82; Auto Cllsn.

DEDAD, MICHELE; East HS; Erie, PA; (Y); 8/158; Chorus; Variety Show; Cheerleading; High Hon Roll; Jr NHS; Spcl Comm Awd 86; U PA; Pre-Med.

DEDEL, KELLI; Unionville HS; West Chester, PA; (Y); 48/300; Pep Clb; Varsity Clb; Nwsp Stf; Rep Sr Cls; JV Var Cheerleading; Powder Puff Ftbl; Hon Roll; Engl Achvt Awd 86; Engl Cmmndtn; SCCL Chrldng Champs 84; Crim Just.

DEDITCH, JOANN; Bentworth HS; Scenery Hill, PA; (Y); 32/137; FBLA; Ski Clb; Band; Chorus; Hon Roll; Clrk Typst II Trphy 3rd Pl 85-86; Nrsng.

DEEB, MONICA; Salisbury HS; Allentown, PA; (Y); 15/145; Key Clb; SADD; Off Soph Cls; Pres Stu Cncl; Var Bsktbl; Var Sftbl; Var Tennis; Hon Roll; Le High U Ldrshp Awd 85-86; MVP Awd Bsktbll 85-86; Dist Dbls Tennis Champ 84-85.

DEEG, LESLIE; Columbia HS; Columbia, PA; (Y); 21/83; Cmnty Wkr; FNA; Band; Concert Band; Drill Tm; Jazz Band; Fld Hcky; Powder Puff Ftbl; Hon Roll; NHS; St Joseph Schl Nursing; Nrsng.

DEEGAN, GREGORY; Pottstown SR HS; Pottstown, PA; (S); 4/206; VP Key Clb; Spanish Clb; Band; Concert Band; Jazz Band; Mrchg Band; High Hon Roll; NHS; Mth.

DEEGAN, JAMES; Bethlehem Catholic HS; Bethlehem, PA; (Y); Aud/Vis; Church Yth Grp; Key Clb; SADD; School Play; Rep Church Yth Grp; Rep Jr Cls; Phys Thrpy.

DEEGAN, MARY; Geibel HS; Scottdale, PA; (Y); Church Yth Grp; Drama Clb; Girl Scts; Pep Clb; School Musical; Stage Crew; Lit Mag; French Hon Soc; Hon Roll; NHS; Edinboro U; Accntng.

DEEGAN, MICHELLE; Du Bois Area HS; Reynoldsville, PA; (Y); 7/264; Chorus; Im Vllybl; High Hon Roll; NHS; Pres Schlr; Voice Dem Awd; Grad With Hnrs 86; Rlrsktng Awds; Rtry Schlrshp; IN U PA; Psychlgy.

DEELEY, MICHELLE; West Allegheny HS; Coraopolis, PA; (Y); Office Aide; Spanish Clb; Nwsp Rptr; Nwsp Stf; Yrbk Stf; Stu Cncl; Powder Puff Ftbl; Hon Roll; Homecomng Ct 86; Prom Ct 86; Nwsp & Yrbk Advrtsmnt 84-85; Bus.

DEEM JR, JACK C; Riverview HS; Oakmont, PA; (Y); AFS; Boy Scts; Ski Clb; Yrbk Bus Mgr; Trs Jr Cls; Var L Crs Cntry; Var L Trk; High Hon Roll; NHS; NEDT Awd.

DEEMER, KIM; Seneca Valley HS; Evans City, PA; (Y); Church Yth Grp; Cmnty Wkr; Ski Clb; Chorus; Ed Lit Mag; Sftbl; Trk; Hon Roll; Im 3rd Awd-Smmrs Bst 2 Wks 85; 110 Pct Effrt Awd-Smmrs Bst 2 Wks 84; Bus.

DEEMER, TRACI; Lincoln HS; Ellwood City, PA; (Y); 36/163; FBLA; VP Service Clb; Hst Concert Band; Hst Mrchg Band; High Hon Roll; Hon Roll; NHS; Prfct Atten Awd; Scholar Bus & Prof Wmns Clb 86; H S Ushers Clb Scholar 86; Hnr Grad 86; CC Beaver Cnty; Acctg.

DEEP, KELLY; Moon SR HS; Coraopolis, PA; (Y); Church Yth Grp; Spanish Clb; Rep Frsh Cls; Rep Soph Cls; Rep Jr Cls; L Tennis; CC Awd; High Hon Roll; Hon Roll; NHS; PA ST Tnns Dbls Champ 83-85; Wstrn PA Intschtcs Tnns Champ 83-85; Mdwstrn Athltc Conf Sngls 83-85; Pre-Law.

DEERY, ANESSA; Upper Darby HS; Primos, PA; (Y); 45/629; Church Yth Grp; Teachers Aide; Church Choir; Hon Roll; Amer Stds & Bus Ed Awds 86; Exec Secy.

DEETER, JANE; Chestnut Ridge SR HS; Manns Choice, PA; (S); 10/142; Church Yth Grp; SADD; Band; Nwsp Rptr; Stu Cncl; JV Trk; Hon Roll; NHS; Prfct Atten Awd; Hugh O Brian Yth Fndtn Ldrshp Awd 85.

DEFELICE, BILL; Hempfield HS; Youngwood, PA; (Y); French Clb; Nwsp Stf; Penn ST; Engrng.

DEFILIPPI, MATTHEW; Leechburg Area HS; Leechburg, PA; (Y); Chorus; Concert Band; Mrchg Band; Pep Band; Yrbk Stf; Office Aide; Pres Jr Cls; VP Stu Cncl; High Hon Roll; Hon Roll; Medcn.

DEFLITCH, CHRISTOPHER; Mount Pleasant Area HS; Mt Pleasant, PA; (Y); 21/254; Church Yth Grp; Letterman Clb; Ski Clb; JV Var Bsbl; JV Var Ftbl; High Hon Roll; NHS; Pres Schlr; WCCA Schlrshp 86; SR 7 86; Top 10% Awd; Gannon U; Pre Med.

DEFUSO, MICHELE; Weatherly Area HS; Weatherly, PA; (Y); Art Clb; Cmnty Wkr; FHA; Library Aide; Color Guard; School Play; Stage Crew; Hon Roll; Fnlst PA Gvrnrs Schl Arts-Wrtng 84-85; 1st Hnrs-Math 85-86; Cmnty Chst Qun 2nd Rnr-Up 85; Beaver Coll; Theatr Arts.

DEG BRINA, RENEE; Bloomsburg Area SR HS; Bloomsburg, PA; (Y); 38/112; Sec Aud/Vis; 4-H; Chorus; Yrbk Stf; Stat Fld Hcky; Vllybl; Bloomsburg U; Psych.

DEGENHART III, CHARLES; Owen J Roberts HS; Pottstown, PA; (Y); Letterman Clb; Stu Cncl; Bsbl; Ftbl; NHS; Ursinus Coll Freeland & Bombeger Awds 86; Ursinus Coll; Bus.

DEGILIO, MICHAEL; Marian Catholic HS; Lansford, PA; (Y); 52/115; Boy Scts; Church Yth Grp; French Clb; Letterman Clb; Ski Clb; SADD; Capt Bsktbl; Var Ftbl; Trk; Wt Lftg; Ftbl Awds-Unsung Hero 85; MVP Ftbl 86; Crmnl Just.

DEGLAU, ERIC D; Mount Lebanon HS; Pittsburgh, PA; (Y); 100/523; Pres Frsh Cls; Pres Soph Cls; Pres Jr Cls; Pres Sr Cls; Im Sftbl; Var Capt Swmmng; Capt Im Vllybl; Hon Roll; Ntl Merit Ltr; NEDT Awd; ST Swmng Chmpn 84-86; Army Rsrv Schlr Athlt Yr 86; 4-Tm Al-Amercn Swmr 85 & 86; Citatn PA Hous Rep 86; U Of VA; Mchncl Engrng.

DEGLER, DOUGLAS; Muhlenberg HS; Reading, PA; (Y); Boy Scts; Ski Clb; Band; Concert Band; Drill Tm; Jazz Band; Mrchg Band; Pep Band; School Musical; Stu Cncl.

DEGNAN, CATHERINE; St Huberts HS; Philadelphia, PA; (Y); 63/367; JA; Cheerleading; Swmmng; Hon Roll.

DEGRANGE, ROBERT; Belle Vernon Area HS; Belle Vernon, PA; (Y); Cmnty Wkr; Political Wkr; Ski Clb; Variety Show; JV Ftbl; Hon Roll; Rstrnt Mgmt.

DEGRUTTOLA, JASON; Blairsville SR HS; Blairsville, PA; (Y); 36/131; Chess Clb; Church Yth Grp; Computer Clb; FCA; Ski Clb; Stage Crew; Stat Bsktbl; Hon Roll; Ottobein Coll OH; Psychol.

DEHAVEN, MICHELE; Northwestern Lehigh HS; New Tripoli, PA; (Y); Var Bsktbl; Var Capt Crs Cntry; Var Trk; Hon Roll; Fash Merch.

DEHAVEN, PAUL; Marion Center HS; Marion Ctr, PA; (Y); FFA; Varsity Clb; Chorus; Stu Cncl; Var L Bsbl; Im Coach Actv; Var L Ftbl; Im Wt Lftg; Var L Wrstlng; Hon Roll; Mst Imprvd Plyr 85-86; Physcl Educ.

DEHNER, SHARON; North Clarion HS; Tylersburg, PA; (Y); #9 In Class; Drama Clb; French Clb; FBLA; Chorus; Mgr School Musical; School Play; Stage Crew; Bsktbl; Hon Roll; JR Hstrn 85-87; Du Bois; Accntng.

DEHNER, STACY; Bishop Kenrick HS; Norristown, PA; (Y); 13/292; Science Clb; Spanish Clb; Chorus; Color Guard; School Musical; Variety Show; Vllybl; NHS.

DEIBERT, JULIE; Tri-Valley HS; Sacramento, PA; (Y); 15/77; Church Yth Grp; Quiz Bowl; SADD; Band; Mrchg Band; Sec Jr Cls; Var Capt Bsktbl; Var L Sftbl; Var L Vllybl; Hon Roll; D K Schwartz Awd 85-86; Bsktbl MVP 84-86; Vlybl MVP 85-86; Phys Ther.

DEIBERT, KATHY; Warwick HS; Lititz, PA; (Y); 5/237; Math Tm; Quiz Bowl; Stat Fld Hcky; Mgr(s); Score Keeper; Im Swmmng; Stat Trk; Im Vllybl; High Hon Roll; VP NHS; U Pittsburgh-Johnstown Pres Schlrshp, Delta Kappa Gamma Schlrshp, Cmmncmnt Spkr-Top Schlr Awd 86; U Pittsburgh-Johnstown; Math Ed.

DEIBLER, TARA M; Lewistown Area HS; Lewistown, PA; (Y); Church Yth Grp; French Clb; Band; Chorus; Church Choir; Concert Band; Mrchg Band; Nwsp Stf; Mgr(s); Var L Sftbl; Phy Thrpy.

DEIMLER, MARK; Elizabethtown Area HS; Elizabethtown, PA; (Y); 16/227; Trs Church Yth Grp; JV Var Ftbl; Var JV Mgr(s); NHS; Adv Engl Term Paper Awd 86; Kiwanis NHS Pin 86; Pres Acad Fit Awd 86; PA ST; Engrng.

DEININGER, DONNA; Tamaqua Avea HS; Tamaqua, PA; (S); Am Leg Aux Girls St; Girl Scts; Band; Concert Band; Drm Mjr(t); School Musical; Pres Jr Cls; Rep Stu Cncl; NHS; HOBY Fndtn Sem 85; Cnty, Dist, Regnl Chorus 86.

DEISHER, LEANN; Mt Penn HS; Reading, PA; (Y); 2/78; German Clb; Science Clb; Y-Teens; JV Var Fld Hcky; High Hon Roll; Jr NHS; NHS; Sal; Juniata Schlrshp; Juniata Coll; Bio.

DEISLEY, SCOTT; Warwick HS; Lititz, PA; (Y); 38/237; Boy Scts; Model UN; Trs Jr Cls; Trs Sr Cls; JV Crs Cntry; Im Vllybl; JV Wrstlng; High Hon Roll; NHS; Pres Schlr; Yth Ldrshp Of Amer Awd 82; Treas Of Explrer Pst 142 84; Millersville U; Spch Cmnctns.

DEISROTH, ROB; MMI Preparatory Schl; Hazleton, PA; (Y); 25/30; Aud/Vis; Debate Tm; Pres Pep Clb; Pres Ski Clb; Rep Sr Cls; Bowling; Capt Crs Cntry; Tennis; PA ST U; Physcs.

DEITER, MICHELLE; Lampeter-Strasburg HS; Lancaster, PA; (Y); Debate Tm; German Clb; Intnl Clb; Model UN; Political Wkr; School Musical; Stu Cncl; Cheerleading; Thesps; Variety Show; IN U Of PA; Pol Sci.

DEITER, ROSE; Faith Mennonite HS; Lancaster, PA; (Y); Camera Clb; Church Yth Grp; Office Aide; Teachers Aide; Chorus; Bsktbl; Fld Hcky; Ftbl; Socr; Sftbl.

DEITRICH, ANN; Williams Valley JR SR HS; Wiconisco, PA; (S); 1/111; Church Yth Grp; Girl Scts; Office Aide; Quiz Bowl; Chorus; Trs Jr Cls; High Hon Roll; NEDT Awd; Prfct Atten Awd; Hist Awd 84-85.

DEITRICH, DEBRA; Palmyra Area HS; Palmyra, PA; (Y); 3/200; Drama Clb; French Clb; Band; Chorus; Rep Stu Cncl; Var Cheerleading; Var Capt Crs Cntry; Var Trk; High Hon Roll; NHS.

DEITRICH, JEFF; Elizabethtown Area HS; Elizabethtown, PA; (Y); Art Clb; Spanish Clb; Joe Kubert; Animation.

DEITZ, MELINDA; Manheim Central HS; Manheim, PA; (Y); 49/197; Library Aide; Office Aide; Chorus; Fld Hcky; Hon Roll; Cert Sci 83; Cntrl PA Bus Schl; Acctng.

DEIULIIS, NICK; Chartiers Valley HS; Carnegie, PA; (Y); 1/343; Spanish Clb; Socr; Bausch & Lomb Sci Awd; High Hon Roll; NHS; Pres Schlr; Val; Commwlth Merit Awd 86; PA ST U; Chem Engr.

DEL BORGO, ANN; Greater Johnstown HS; Johnstown, PA; (Y); Key Clb; Chorus; Yrbk Ed-Chief; Yrbk Phtg; Yrbk Rptr; Hon Roll; NHS; Vet.

DEL GRECO, CHRISTOPHER; Bethel Park SR HS; Bethel Park, PA; (Y); Trs FBLA; Ski Clb; School Musical; Trs Sr Cls; Rep Stu Cncl; Ftbl; Var Socr; Im Wt Lftg; Capt L Wrstlng; Hon Roll; Kent ST U; Pre Bus.

DEL GRECO, PAULA; Aliquippa SR HS; Aliquippa, PA; (S); VP Art Clb; Exploring; French Clb; Concert Band; Mrchg Band; Yrbk Stf; VP Jr Cls; Twrlr; High Hon Roll; Hon Roll.

DEL VECCHIO, MARK; Downington SR HS; Downingtown, PA; (S); 13/525; Ski Clb; Chorus; Off Stu Cncl; Bsktbl; Trk; High Hon Roll; NHS; Rotry Stu Mnth 85; Aerospc Engr.

DEL VECCHIO, TINA; Kiski Area HS; Hyde Park, PA; (Y); JA; Math Clb; Pep Clb; Spanish Clb; Band; Mrchg Band; Nwsp Stf; Yrbk Stf; Stu Cncl; Cheerleading; Top Ten 83; WV U.

DEL VERME, JODY; Brownsville Area SR HS; Allison, PA; (S); 12/225; Drama Clb; Intnl Clb; Mathletes; Ski Clb; SADD; Band; Drill Tm; Mrchg Band; Sec Frsh Cls; High Hon Roll; Acctg.

DELACH, BETH; Bethel Park HS; Bethel Pk, PA; (Y); DECA; FHA; Band; School Musical; Variety Show; Yrbk Bus Mgr; Rep Frsh Cls; Rep Soph Cls; Var L Cheerleading; Hon Roll; Bus.

DELANEY, ANN; Scranton Central HS; Scranton, PA; (Y); French Clb; VP FTA; Yrbk Stf; Var Cheerleading; Var Trk; Hon Roll; Jr NHS; Intl Bus.

DELANEY, EILEEN; Bishop Carroll HS; Ebensburg, PA; (S); 11/102; SADD; NHS; NEDT Awd; St Francis Coll; Scl Wrk.

DELANEY, NENITA; Jersey Shore SR HS; Jersey Shore, PA; (Y); FBLA; Hosp Aide; Service Clb; Flag Corp; Var Stat Trk; Im Vllybl; Hon Roll; Adeline Jan E Robison Mem Scholar 86; PA Supts & Foremans Assn Scholar 86; Mary Ann Rankin Scholar 86; Bloomsburg U; Nrsg.

DELANEY, SUSAN; Abington HS; Willow Grove, PA; (Y); 45/535; Band; Concert Band; Hon Roll; NHS; Awd Excllnc German 85; Ursinus Coll; Vet.

DELANO, RUTH; Harbor Creek HS; Erie, PA; (Y); 1/205; Capt Scholastic Bowl; Var Pres Concert Band; Mrchg Band; Orch; Pep Band; Variety Show; Yrbk Rptr; NHS; Ntl Merit SF; PA Govrnr Schl Arts 85; Gen Elec STAR Schlrshp 86; Frnch Awd Grad 86; Carnegie Mellon U; Lib Arts.

DELAP, DENNIS; Harry S Truman HS; Levittown, PA; (Y); 18/620; Debate Tm; NFL; Scholastic Bowl; Speech Tm; JV Var Socr; Hon Roll; Chmstry Awd 86; Harry S Truman Bstr Clb Schlrshp 86; PA ST U; Engrng.

DELARCLE, LAURA; Crestwood HS; Mountaintop, PA; (Y); 30/222; Church Yth Grp; Hosp Aide; Band; Concert Band; Mrchg Band; High Hon Roll; Hon Roll.

DELAUTER, ROBIN; Dover Area HS; Dover, PA; (Y); Church Yth Grp; Cmnty Wkr; Girl Scts; Hosp Aide; Hon Roll; Chld Psychlgy.

DELCAMP, MARC; Fleetwood Area HS; Fleetwood, PA; (Y); 4/102; Aud/Vis; Church Yth Grp; Cmnty Wkr; Computer Clb; Drama Clb; Math Tm; Scholastic Bowl; Spanish Clb; School Musical; JV Tennis; Kutztown U; Engl.

DELCONTE, LISA; Cardinal O Hara HS; Broomall, PA; (Y); 82/772; French Clb; Intnl Clb; JA; Latin Clb; Chorus; Flag Corp; Nwsp Rptr; Nwsp Stf; Im Vllybl; Hon Roll; Assist Brownie Ldr 83-84; St Josephs U; Acctnt.

DELEONIBUS, KAREN; Laurel Highlands SR HS; Uniontown, PA; (Y); Vllybl; Cit Awd; Dnfth Awd; High Hon Roll; Hon Roll; Jr NHS; PEMS Hstry Awd 85-86; Nrsg.

DELEWSKI, MARCI; Hamburg Area HS; Hamburg, PA; (Y); 98/152; Trs VP French Clb; Pres Girl Scts; Library Aide; Yrbk Stf; Var Trk; SADD; School Musical; Grl Sct Gold Awd 84; Daisy BB Shooting Tm-Hgh Shooter Awd-Eastern PA 82; Johnson & Wales Coll; Clnry Art.

DELGADO, ABEL; St Josephs Prep; Philadelphia, PA; (Y); 49/230; Cmnty Wkr; Intnl Clb; Library Aide; Model UN; Service Clb; Spanish Clb; Prep Schlr 84-86; St Francis Xavier Schlrshp 83; Spnsh Clb Awd 85; Bst Grde Hist 83; Vet.

DELGADO, WAYNE; Garden Spot HS; East Earl, PA; (Y); 15/168; Rep Sr Cls; Capt Var Socr; Vllybl; High Hon Roll; Jr NHS; NHS; United Chem-Con Awd 86; Shippensburg U; Accntng.

DELGROSSO, PATRICIA; Freedom HS; Bethlehem, PA; (Y); 152/445; Hon Roll; 10 Wk Schlrshp Baum Schl Of Art 83; Art Inst Of Ft Lauderdale; Intr.

DELIO, JENNIFER; Bishop Shanahan HS; Downingtown, PA; (Y); Church Yth Grp; VP 4-H; Office Aide; Pep Clb; Stage Crew; Nwsp Stf; Var Capt Cheerleading; Mgr(s); 4-H Awd; Hon Roll; Millersville U; Elem Educ.

DELISIO, ROBERT F; New Brighton HS; New Brighton, PA; (Y); 5/148; Am Leg Boys St; Varsity Clb; Stage Crew; Yrbk Phtg; Yrbk Sprt Ed; Var Bsbl; Var Capt Ftbl; Var Wt Lftg; High Hon Roll; MAC Hnrb Mntn Ftbl 85; 500 Point Club Offense & Defnse Ftbl 85; Engrng.

DELKER, BETH; St Clair Area HS; Pottsville, PA; (Y); 5/80; Drama Clb; FHA; Nwsp Bus Mgr; Nwsp Stf; Yrbk Stf; Cit Awd; High Hon Roll; Kiwanis Awd; Mu Alp Tht; NHS; Bloomsburg U; Erly Chldhd.

DELL, GWENDOLYNNE; Marple-Newtown HS; Newtown Square, PA; (Y); 50/365; Debate Tm; Sec French Clb; Hosp Aide; JA; Mgr Orch; Nwsp Ed-Chief; Nwsp Rptr; VP Frsh Cls; VP Soph Cls; Swmmng; Frances Nye-Peterson Awd Excllnce Engl 86; Hstry Day Schl Cty & ST 83-85; Hstry Day Natl 84; Villanova; Law.

DELL ARCIPRETE, ANTHONY; West Catholic Boys HS; Philadelphia, PA; (Y); 21/270; Church Yth Grp; Library Aide; Science Clb; Teachers Aide; High Hon Roll; Hon Roll; Sec NHS; Awd For Hghst Mrk Spnsh 84-86; Awd For Chem 85-86; Drexel U; Elect Engrng.

DELLAFIORA, JOHN; Homer-Center HS; Homer City, PA; (Y); Pres Frsh Cls; VP Jr Cls; Stu Cncl; Var Capt Bsktbl; Var Ftbl; Var Capt Trk; Kiwanis Awd; Pres NHS; Sons Of Italy Schlrshp 86; Pres Acad Ftns Awd 86; U Of Notre Dame; Engrng.

DELLAPINA, JENNIFER; Burgettstown Area JR SR HS; Burgettstown, PA; (Y); Church Yth Grp; Drama Clb; French Clb; Rep Stu Cncl; Mat Maids; Var Tennis; High Hon Roll; Hon Roll; Jr NHS; NHS; Cornell U; Htl Adm.

DELLE DONNE II, ROBERT; Kiski Area HS; Vandergrift, PA; (Y); Pep Clb; SADD; Var Golf; High Hon Roll; Hon Roll; Top 10 Frshman 83-84; Clarion; Cmnctns.

DELLEDONNEII, ROBERT; Kiski Area HS; Vandergrift, PA; (Y); Pep Clb; Var Golf; Hon Roll; Top 10 84; Cmmnctns.

DELLERT, CHRISTOPHER; Delaware Valley HS; Milford, PA; (Y); Church Yth Grp; Red Cross Aide; SADD; Lcrss; Trk; High Hon Roll; NHS; NHS & Grad With Hnrs 86; Marine Corp.

DELLEVIONE, ELIZABETH; Bishop Shanahan HS; W Chester, PA; (Y); 3/212; Mathletes; Scholastic Bowl; High Hon Roll; Jr NHS; Ntl Merit SF; Gnrl Acdmc Exc Awd 83-84; Algebra Awd 83-84; Cert Of Hnr In Algebra II Trgnmtry 86; Archtctr.

DELLIBOVI, ANN MARIE; Pocono Mountain HS; Stroudsburg, PA; (Y); 40/289; Var Bsktbl; JV Cheerleading; Var Capt Fld Hcky; JV Sftbl; Var Trk; Hon Roll; Unico Shlrshp 86; Academic Awds 83-85; MVP Offns Hcky 86; Bloomsburg U; Bio.

DELLINGER, LAURA; Conrad Weiser HS; Sinking Spring, PA; (Y); 68/130; Church Yth Grp; Hosp Aide; Spanish Clb; Chorus; School Musical; School Play; JV Trk; Hon Roll; Penn ST U; Police Ofcr.

DELMONACO, NICOLE; Oil City HS; Oil City, PA; (Y); French Clb; Varsity Clb; VP Jr Cls; VP Sr Cls; JV Cheerleading; Trk; Var Vllybl; Hon Roll; VP NHS; Yrbk Stf; Pre-Med.

DELMONICO, JENETTE; Miechanicsburg Area SR HS; Mechanicsburg, PA; (Y); 107/311; Art Clb; Camera Clb; Key Clb; Speech Tm; Trs Stu Cncl; JV Bsktbl; Hon Roll; 4th Pl Anti Drunk Drvng Slogan Cnst Cumberland Cnty 86; Prom/Dance Cmmtte 86; Child Psych.

DELORME, TAMI L; Bangor SR HS; E Bangor, PA; (Y); Sec FBLA; Pep Clb; SADD; Nwsp Stf; Powder Puff Ftbl; FBLA Bus Graphics 5th Pl 86; Travel.

DELP, KATRINA; Souderton HS; Souderton, PA; (Y); Church Yth Grp; Teachers Aide; Chorus; Yrbk Stf; Var L Bsktbl; Var L Lcrss; Stat Wrstlng; Hon Roll; Fshn.

DELP JR, KEITH W; Pleasant Valley HS; Saylorsburg, PA; (Y); Hon Roll; Pell Grant 86-87; Lincoln Tech Inst; Elec.

DELP, MARGARET; Cental Columbia HS; Orangeville, PA; (Y); 5/180; 4-H; German Clb; Math Tm; Scholastic Bowl; Ski Clb; Cheerleading; Hon Roll; NHS; Villanova U; Intl Bus.

DELP, THOMAS; Brookville Area JR SR HS; Brookville, PA; (Y); Trs Church Yth Grp; Drama Clb; Chorus; Stage Crew; Nwsp Rptr; Ed Lit Mag; Trk; High Hon Roll; NHS; Pres Schlr; Clarion U; Sec Ed.

DELP, TRICIA; Archbishop Ryan HS; Philadelphia, PA; (Y); 3/491; Hosp Aide; Q&S; Science Clb; Nwsp Stf; Var L Tennis; French Hon Soc; NHS; Church Yth Grp; Exploring; French Clb; Soc Women Engrs Awd Exc Sci Math 86; Exc Adv Bio 86; Exc Tri 86; Physcl Thrpy.

DELUCA, KEVIN; North Hills HS; Pittsburgh, PA; (Y); Church Yth Grp; Exploring; Concert Band; Mrchg Band; Orch; High Hon Roll; JP Sousa Awd; Allegheny Coll; Optmtry.

DELUCA, SUSAN; North Allegheny SR HS; Wexford, PA; (Y); 152/642; Exploring; Hosp Aide; School Musical; School Play; Sec Soph Cls; Var Tennis; Hon Roll; Mst Imprvd Wrld Cltrs I & II 83-85; Stu Cncl Actvts Awd 84-85; Prtcptn Pttsbrgh Rgnl Schl Sci Fair; Int Dsgn.

DELUCIA, ANNA; Richland HS; Gibsonia, PA; (Y); Letterman Clb; Pep Clb; Varsity Clb; Band; Mrchg Band; Powder Puff Ftbl; Capt Sftbl; Tennis; Hon Roll; Ltr In Sftbl 84-86; Concert Band Ltr 84; Johnson/Wales Coll; Trvl/Toursm.

DELUCIA, THERESA; Cameron County HS; Emporium, PA; (Y); 1/86; Church Yth Grp; Drama Clb; German Clb; Chorus; Yrbk Stf; Rep Stu Cncl; Powder Puff Ftbl; Mu Alp Tht; NHS; Excllnt Frgn Lang 86; Presdntl Acdmc Ftnss Awd 86; PA ST U; Engl.

DELUCY, JAMES; Carbondale Area HS; Carbondale, PA; (Y); 56/144; Spanish Clb; Rep Soph Cls; Bsktbl; Ftbl; Trk; Hon Roll.

DELVECCHIO, LISA; Old Forge HS; Old Forge, PA; (S); Drill Tm; Capt Pom Pon; Hon Roll; NHS.

DELVECCHIO, STACEY; Scranton Central HS; Scranton, PA; (Y); JA; Spanish Clb; Band; Yrbk Phtg; Yrbk Stf; Sftbl; PA ST; Comp Pgm.

DELVISCIO, JULIA; St Maria Goretti HS; Philadelphia, PA; (Y); 19/390; Cmnty Wkr; Mathletes; Math Clb; Lit Mag; Crs Cntry; Hon Roll; NHS; Prfct Atten Awd; Hnrb Mntn Italian II 84-85; Hnrb Mntn Engl 85-86; Jrnlsm.

DEMAGALL, CAROL; Mt Pleasant Area HS; Mt Pleasant, PA; (Y); Drama Clb; Gerndn Clb; Ski Clb; Nwsp Rptr; Mat Maids; Tennis; Hon Roll; U Of Pittsburgh; Physcl Thrpy.

DEMANSKY, BARRY; West Hazleton HS; Nuremberg, PA; (Y); 32/228; Church Yth Grp; Drama Clb; FTA; Scholastic Bowl; Spanish Clb; Thesps; Var Trk; Hon Roll; Intl Thespian Soc 86; PA JR Acad Sci 86; Bio.

DEMARCHI JR, FRANK; William Allen HS; Allentown, PA; (Y); Boys Clb Am; Cmnty Wkr; Drama Clb; Exploring; Key Clb; Leo Clb; Red Cross Aide; Service Clb; Ski Clb; Yrbk Ed-Chief; CPA Altrsm Awd 86; Bttr Cngrssnl Awd 86; Stud Advncmnt Fnd 86; Glassboro ST; Pblc Rltns.

DEMARCO, SANDRA; Dunmore HS; Dunmore, PA; (Y); 12/152; Pres French Clb; Ski Clb; Spanish Clb; Yrbk Phtg; JV Cheerleading; High Hon Roll; Hon Roll; Jr NHS; NHS; Phrmcy.

DEMASKE, CHRISTY ANNE; German SR HS; Mc Clellandtown, PA; (Y); Am Leg Aux Girls St; Ed Nwsp Stf; Yrbk Stf; JV Bsktbl; Var Sftbl; High Hon Roll; NHS; Computer Clb; French Clb; Concert Band; Am Leg JR Aux ST Pres 84-85; Gifted/Tlntd Pgm; 2nd Pl ST Lev Olympcs Mind Comptn 86; Brdcst Jrnlsm.

DEMBOWSKI, DAN; Lake Lahman HS; Noxen, PA; (Y); Church Yth Grp; VICA; Williamsport CC; Grphcs Art.

DEMCHAK, JOE; Philipsburg Osceola SR HS; Osceola Mills, PA; (Y); 60/250; Chess Clb; Band; Mrchg Band; Bsktbl; Elec Engrng.

DEMELLIER, LEAH; E L Meyers HS; Wilkes Barre, PA; (Y); 38/164; Pres Key Clb; Chorus; Nwsp Stf; Yrbk Stf; VP Jr Cls; VP Sr Cls; Bsktbl; Mgr(s); L Trk; Im Vllybl; Radiology.

DEMERJIAN, JEFFREY; Liberty HS; Bethlehem, PA; (Y); 50/475; Boy Scts; Church Yth Grp; Color Guard; Stage Crew; Mech Engrng.

DEMKO, PAMELA; Hazleton HS; Hazleton, PA; (Y); Church Yth Grp; Pep Clb; Im Sftbl; High Hon Roll; Hon Roll; NHS; NEDT Awd; PA ST U; Bio.

DEMKO, SANDY; Moshannon Valley HS; Morann, PA; (Y); 3/150; High Hon Roll; Bus.

DEMKO, TIMOTHY; Mahonoy Area HS; Mahanoy City, PA; (Y); Church Yth Grp; Drama Clb; Chorus; School Musical; Variety Show; Yrbk Phtg; L Bsbl; Im Bsktbl; L Ftbl; Hon Roll; Natl Hon Soc 85; Pre Law.

DEMMITT, TOM; Northeastern HS; York, PA; (Y); Chess Clb; Computer Clb; German Clb; JV Bsbl; JV Bsktbl; JV Var Socr; JV Vllybl; Hon Roll; Sccr Dist II Rnnr Up 85-86; Lttrd In Sccr 85-86; Archtctr.

DEMMY, LISA; Butler Area SR HS; Butler, PA; (Y); Hosp Aide; SADD; Trs Church Yth Grp; Cmnty Wkr; Chorus; Rep Frsh Cls; Rep Soph Cls; Rep Stu Cncl; Hon Roll; Jr NHS.

DEMNYAN, SEAN; Canon Mcmillan SR HS; Canonsburg, PA; (Y); Aud/Vis; Church Yth Grp; Cmnty Wkr; Dance Clb; Band; Church Choir; Concert Band; Orch; School Musical; Pres Buffalo Pittsburgh Diocesan Yth Orgnztn Polish Natl Cath Chrch 85; SR Acalyte 86; Broadcast Inst MD; Rad Brdcstg.

DEMO, PHYLLIS; Johnstown HS; Johnstown, PA; (Y); 17/300; French Clb; Math Clb; Chorus; Rep Jr Cls; Rep Stu Cncl; Capt Cheerleading; Hon Roll; NHS; Pres Ath Awd 83-84; U Pittsburgh.

DEMORA, SAM; Lakeland HS; Jermyn, PA; (Y); 36/195; SADD; Hon Roll; PA ST Coll; Arntcl Engrng.

DEMPKOSKY, CHRISTINE; Wyoming Valley West HS; Larksville, PA; (Y); Church Yth Grp; Hosp Aide; Key Clb; Library Aide; High Hon Roll; Hon Roll; NHS; Prfct Atten Awd; Pre-Med.

DEMPSEY, BILL; Seneca Valley HS; Mars, PA; (Y); 20/347; Ski Clb; Teachers Aide; JV Crs Cntry; Var Tennis; Var Wrstlng; Hon Roll; Schltc Awd; Engrng.

DEMPSEY, DOROTHY; Roxborough HS; Philadelphia, PA; (Y); 19/203; Cmnty Wkr; Library Aide; Office Aide; High Hon Roll; Hon Roll; VFW Awd; Awd Bus Stu 86; Genl Sci Awd 86; CCP; Bus.

DEMPSEY, MICHAEL; Brookville Area HS; Corsica, PA; (Y); 26/145; Band; Concert Band; Jazz Band; Mrchg Band; Pep Band; Ftbl; Hon Roll; Pres Schlr; De Vry; Elctrncs.

DEMPSEY, PATRICIA; Archbishop Kennedy HS; Philadelphia, PA; (Y); 25/180; Capt Church Yth Grp; Sec Intnl Clb; Sec Service Clb; Ed Nwsp Ed-Chief; Lit Mag; Stu Cncl; Var Fld Hcky; VP NHS; Stage Crew; Yrbk Rptr; Svc To Comm Awd 86; Awd Ldrs Of Tommorow Smnr 86; Rec By Phili Inq Revitalizing Schl 85.

DEMSTER, DEBORAH S; Lower Merion HS; Narberth, PA; (Y); Church Yth Grp; Cmnty Wkr; German Clb; Trs Girl Scts; Trs Intnl Clb; Concert Band; Hon Roll; NHS; Ntl Merit SF; Wnnr US Congrs German Bundestag Schlrhsp SR Yr; Med.

DEMYAN, MICHELLE E S; Greater Latrobe SR HS; Latrobe, PA; (Y); 39/327; Cmnty Wkr; Teachers Aide; High Hon Roll; Pres Schlr; Full-Yr Meritrs Schlrshp 86; Westmorelnd Cnty CC; Bus Mgmt.

DENGLER, DEBORAH SUE; Exeter HS; Reading, PA; (Y); 12/200; Leo Clb; Y-Teens; Band; Rep Sr Cls; Rep Stu Cncl; Var L Fld Hcky; Cit Awd; DAR Awd; Lion Awd; NHS; Leo Clb-Marc Simmons Mem 86; Michael Mangiolardo Hstry Awd 6; Exeter Twnshp Wmns Clb Schlrshp 86; U Of DE; Bus.

DENGLER, MICHAEL E; Lancaster Catholic HS; Lancaster, PA; (Y); 40/200; Church Yth Grp; Chorus; Stage Crew; Capt Cheerleading; Ntl JR Clsscl League 86; Nrsng.

DENION, BRYAN; Freeland HS; Freeland, PA; (Y); 9/80; Church Yth Grp; Cmnty Wkr; French Clb; Letterman Clb; SADD; Y-Teens; School Play; Bsbl; Bsktbl; Ftbl; Freeland Hs Athlt Of Yr 86; French Acdmc Awd 84; Shippensburg U; Bio.

DENISH, ADAM; Engineering And Science HS; Philadelphia, PA; (S); 6/176; Math Clb; Math Tm; Stage Crew; Hon Roll; NHS; Green Belt-Karate Clb; AZA Stdnt 83-85; Flr Hockey Capt 84-85; Beaver Coll; Vetrnrn.

DENISON, ERIC; Northeast Bradford HS; Ulster, PA; (Y); Church Yth Grp; Dance Clb; FFA; Letterman Clb; Varsity Clb; Chorus; Bsbl; Crs Cntry; Wrstlng; Stu Cncl; Phys Thrpy.

DENLINGER, MELISSA; Cedar Crest HS; Lebanon, PA; (Y); 41/335; Art Clb; Church Yth Grp; Girl Scts; Pep Clb; Spanish Clb; SADD; Chorus; High Hon Roll; Hon Roll; Hnr Bnqt 85; Pres Acdmc Ftns Awd 86; PA ST U.

DENLINGER, SONJA Y; Manheim Township HS; Lancaster, PA; (Y); Church Yth Grp; Office Aide; Teachers Aide; Varsity Clb; Church Choir; Pres Soph Cls; Pres Jr Cls; Rep Stu Cncl; Var L Cheerleading; Var Capt Fld Hcky; MVP Dfns-Fld Hcky 85-86; Stu Of Mnth 85-86; Altrnt-Jnr Olympcs-Fld Hcky 86-87; Bus.

DENLINGER, VICKI; Galeton Area HS; Galeton, PA; (Y); 4/45; French Clb; Band; School Play; Yrbk Stf; VP Frsh Cls; VP Jr Cls; Rep Stu Cncl; Stat Bsktbl; Var Cheerleading; Mgr(s); Carmen Alby Awd 81; Bus Admin.

DENNE, COLLEEN; South Allegheny JR SR HS; Mckeesport, PA; (Y); 20/184; Trs Church Yth Grp; VP JA; Y-Teens; Pres Chorus; Powder Puff Ftbl; Hon Roll; GATE.

DENNEHY, EILEEN; Abington Heights HS; Dalton, PA; (Y); Church Yth Grp; Cmnty Wkr; SADD; Yrbk Ed-Chief; Pres Soph Cls; Pres Jr Cls; Rep Stu Cncl; Cit Awd; Hon Roll; Chorus; Pat Calvey Ldrshp Awd 86; Stu Cncl Ldrshp Awd 86; Accptnc Gavel-Symbl Ldrshp 85; Mt St Marys Coll; Bus Adm.

DENNETT, SHELLEY; Fairview HS; Fairview, PA; (Y); 49/183; Church Yth Grp; German Clb; Office Aide; Teachers Aide; Varsity Clb; Nwsp Stf; Var Capt Bsktbl; Var Capt Sftbl; Masonic Awd; U Of Pittsburgh.

DENNEY, MINDI; Connellsville SR HS; Connellsville, PA; (Y); Dance Clb; Chorus; School Musical; VP Frsh Cls; Rep Soph Cls; Rep Jr Cls; Off Sr Cls; VP Stu Cncl; JV Capt Cheerleading; Hon Roll; Won Sevrl Bty Pagnts & Tlnt 85; Comptns 85-86; Cmmnctns.

DENNEY, MONICA; Brownsville Area HS; Isabella, PA; (Y); Drama Clb; Ski Clb; Pres SADD; Band; Flag Corp; Mrchg Band; Stage Crew; Sec Jr Cls; Hon Roll; Jr NHS; Embry-Riddle; Aerotntcl Engrng.

DENNIS, BRIAN M; Delaware Valley HS; Milford, PA; (Y); 9/130; Trs Sr Cls; Var Capt Bsktbl; Var Capt Socr; Var Capt Tennis; Hon Roll; NHS; Comp Sci.

DENNIS, LORENA; Valley View JR SR HS; Peckville, PA; (Y); Spanish Clb; School Play; Rep Frsh Cls; Rep Stu Cncl; Var Cheerleading; Trk; Vllybl.

DENNIS, ROBERT SCOTT; Hanover Area JR SR HS; Hanover Green, PA; (Y); Hosp Aide; Leo Clb; SADD; Band; Chorus; Concert Band; Drill Tm; Mrchg Band; School Musical; Nwsp Stf; Awd Leo Clb Pres 86; Bnd Awd 86; Cert Aprctn Wntr Bnd 85; Penn ST; Actng.

DENNISON, KRISTEN; Mechanicsburg SR HS; Mechanicsburg, PA; (Y); 1/311; Art Clb; NFL; Pep Clb; Speech Tm; Chorus; Concert Band; School Play; High Hon Roll; NHS; Prfct Atten Awd; Natl Art Hnr Soc 84-86.

DENNISON, MARQUITA; Bensalem HS; Trevose, PA; (Y); Church Yth Grp; Chorus; Church Choir; School Musical; Gym; Tennis; Trk; High Hon Roll; Hon Roll; Choir Awd 86; Hgh Hnrs Awd 85; Temple U; Comp Sci.

DENNISON, TAMMY; Hyndman Middle- SR HS; Hyndman, PA; (Y); Varsity Clb; Band; Chorus; Church Choir; Yrbk Stf; Sftbl; High Hon Roll; Hon Roll; Jr NHS; NHS; ICM; Data Proc.

DENNISTON, JOHN J; Trinity HS; Mechanicsburg, PA; (Y); Cmnty Wkr; Intnl Clb; Varsity Clb; Chorus; School Play; Bsktbl; Ftbl; Tennis; Vllybl; Wt Lftg.

DENNLER, DENA M; North Catholic HS; Pittsburgh, PA; (Y); 26/255; Church Yth Grp; Ski Clb; Spanish Clb; Yrbk Stf; Capt Bsktbl; Sftbl; Hon Roll; NHS; Miss Pa Amer Coed 86; Acad All-Amer 85; Ntl Ldrshp & Srvce Awd 85; St Vincent Coll; Psych.

DENNY, AMY; Greatr Johnstown HS; Johnstown, PA; (Y); Trs Key Clb; Band; Color Guard; Concert Band; Capt Flag Corp; Nwsp Stf; Yrbk Stf; Rep Jr Cls; Rep Stu Cncl; Hon Roll; Phrmcy.

DENNY, BILL; Uniontown Area HS; Smock, PA; (Y); Boy Scts; FCA; Science Clb; Spanish Clb; Bsbl; Ftbl; Golf; Hon Roll; U Of Pittsburg; Dntstry.

DENNY, MICHAEL; Johnstown HS; Johnstown, PA; (Y); 11/286; Chess Clb; Math Clb; NFL; SADD; High Hon Roll; Trs NHS; Scrub Clb Pres 86; JHS Acdmc Awd 86; PA ST; Chem.

DENT, JEFF; E L Meyers HS; Wilkes Barre, PA; (Y); 10/161; Chorus; Jazz Band; Mrchg Band; Orch; Symp Band; Yrbk Phtg; Var Swmmng; NHS; Ntl Merit Ltr; NEDT Awd.

DENTITH, AMY JO; Pen Argyl HS; Pen Argyl, PA; (Y); 12/117; Church Yth Grp; Red Cross Aide; Ski Clb; Chorus; Trs Stu Cncl; JV Var Cheerleading; Mgr(s); Hon Roll; Bloomsburg Clg; Elem Ed.

DENVER, KAREN; St Hubert For Girls; Philadelphia, PA; (Y); 49/367; Dance Clb; Exploring; French Clb; School Musical; Variety Show; Gym; NHS; Vet.

DEOM, FRANK; Bishop Hafey HS; Drums, PA; (Y); 18/150; Boy Scts; Spanish Clb; Orch; JV Bsbl; JV Bsktbl; Hon Roll; NHS.

DEPALMA, SHELLY; Mt Pleasant Area HS; Mt Pleasant, PA; (Y); GAA; Library Aide; Band; Color Guard; Nrsng.

DEPEW, DAVID; State College Area HS; Boalsburg, PA; (Y); 135/520; Latin Clb; Jr Cls; Sr Cls; Stu Cncl; Im Bsktbl; Coach Actv; VP Socr; Hon Roll; Sccr Tm 4th Pl PIAA ST Chmpnshps 85; Sci Awd 84; Latn Awd 85; PA ST; Pre-Law.

DEPOE, CRAIG; Donegal HS; Mt Joy, PA; (Y); 3/151; Aud/Vis; Computer Clb; Bsbl; Socr; Wrstlng; Cit Awd; DAR Awd; God Cntry Awd; High Hon Roll; NHS; Pres Athltc Trning Clb 84-85; Lcl Awds At Grad 86; Boy Of Mnth Awd 85-86; Elizabetown Coll; Physcl Thrpy.

DEPP, BECKY; Punxsutawney Area HS; Big Run, PA; (Y); Hon Roll; Armed Forces.

DERBIN, GEORGE; North Pocono HS; Moscow, PA; (Y); Church Yth Grp; FBLA; Ski Clb; Nwsp Rptr; Nwsp Stf; Lit Mag; High Hon Roll; NHS; ST Fnlst FBLA Data Proc Concept 86; Phrmcy.

DERBISH, CHRISTINE; North Hills HS; Glenshaw, PA; (Y); Key Clb; Ski Clb; Chorus; School Play; Stage Crew; High Hon Roll; Hon Roll; Robert Morris Coll; Bus Ed Tchr.

DERHAMMER, CHRISTOPHER; G A R Memorial HS; Wilkes Barr, PA; (Y); Chess Clb; Pres Church Yth Grp; Pres 4-H; Math Tm; Nwsp Rptr; Yrbk Rptr; Var L Vllybl; NHS; Ntl Merit SF; JV Bsktbl; Early Entrnc 86; Bard U; Lit.

DERHAMMER, HEIDI; L E Dieruff HS; Allentown, PA; (Y); 24/327; Pres Church Yth Grp; Church Choir; Drm Mjr(t); Mrchg Band; VP Orch; Stu Cncl; Lion Awd; Trs NHS; Band; Chorus; Rgnl Band, Alpha Delta Kappa, Women Tchs Club 86; Lebanon Vly Coll; Mus Educ.

DERHAMMER, HOLLY; Louis E Dieroff HS; Allentown, PA; (Y); 25/327; Trs Church Yth Grp; Scholastic Bowl; VP Science Clb; Mrchg Band; School Play; Nwsp Stf; Yrbk Stf; Stu Cncl; Lion Awd; NHS; Elizabethtwn Acad Schlrshp 86-87; Prsdntl Acad Ftnss Awd 85-86; Hnrs Grad 86; Elizabethtwn Coll; Bio.

DERHAMMER, MIMI; Lake-Lehman HS; Dallas, PA; (Y); Art Clb; Church Yth Grp; Sftbl; Vllybl; Hon Roll; Art Awds 84-85; Vlybl Awds 85; Bus Mgmt.

DERION, KRISTIN; Bethel Park SR HS; Bethel Park, PA; (Y); 53/515; Ski Clb; Drill Tm; Symp Band; Variety Show; Pom Pon; High Hon Roll; NHS; Pres Schlr; Duquesne U; Phrmcy.

DERK, G ERIC; Wilson HS; Wyomissing, PA; (Y); 41/289; German Clb; JA; Ski Clb; Var L Bsbl; Var L Ftbl; Hon Roll; Vn Reed Outstndg Schlr Athlt Awd 86; Rdng Awd Outstndg SR Schlr 86; Gettysburg Coll; Lbrl Arts.

DERNOSHEK, ERIC; Canon Mc Millan SR HS; Canonsburg, PA; (Y); 31/390; Art Clb; Yrbk Ed-Chief; Yrbk Stf; Hon Roll; Art Awd 84; Penn ST U; Arch.

DERO, MARK S; Devon Prep; Bridgeport, PA; (Y); Camera Clb; Computer Clb; Radio Clb; Science Clb; Ski Clb; Stage Crew; Yrbk Ed-Chief; Im Ftbl; JV Socr; JV Trk; Prtl Schlrshp Devon Prep Schl 83-84; Bus.

DEROCHE, CHRISTY; Hampton HS; Allison Pk, PA; (Y); Church Yth Grp; French Clb; Hosp Aide; Ski Clb; Nwsp Rptr; Fld Hcky; Lcrss; Powder Puff Ftbl; Boston Coll; Finc.

DEROMEDI, DONALD; Mt Carmel Area JR SR HS; Kulpmont, PA; (Y); 19/135; Am Leg Boys St; French Clb; Ski Clb; Band; Concert Band; Jazz Band; Mrchg Band; Var Diving; Var Swmmng; Hon Roll; Natl Athl Soc 86; USAF; Morse Syst Oper.

DEROSE, JOSEPH; Bentworth HS; Cokeburg, PA; (Y); Ski Clb; Spanish Clb; Varsity Clb; Rep Soph Cls; Rep Jr Cls; Stu Cncl; Var Ftbl; Var Wt Lftg; Var Wrstlng; High Hon Roll; WA & Jefferson Coll; Lawyer.

DEROSKY, FRANK; West Alleghony SR HS; Imperial, PA; (Y); 16/218; Im Bsbl; High Hon Roll; NHS; Comp Sci.

DEROUIN, JONATHAN; Delaware Valley HS; Milford, PA; (Y); 4/135; Am Leg Boys St; Scholastic Bowl; Stu Cncl; Crs Cntry; Tennis; Trk; High Hon Roll; NHS; Ntl Merit Ltr.

DERR, AMY; Hempfield SR HS; Manheim, PA; (Y); 118/400; Camera Clb; Chorus; Orch; Var Sftbl; Im Vllybl; Hon Roll; Lancstr Cnty Orch 85-86; Grphc Art.

DERR, BETH; Bethlehem Catholic HS; Freemsburg, PA; (Y); Civic Clb; Key Clb; Ski Clb; Yrbk Stf; Hon Roll; Vet Sci.

DERRY, CLIFF; Penn Hills HS; Pittsburgh, PA; (Y); Boy Scts; Church Yth Grp; French Clb; Ski Clb; Capt Tennis; High Hon Roll; Hon Roll; Lmp Of Knwldg; Penn ST U; Arch.

DERSTINE, PATRICIA; Souderton Area HS; Harleysville, PA; (Y); Latin Clb; Yrbk Stf; JV Capt Sftbl; Hon Roll; Sec Ed.

DESANDIS, PEGGY; North Pocono HS; Moscow, PA; (Y); Church Yth Grp; Letterman Clb; Var Bsktbl; Var Crs Cntry; Var Trk; Lackawanna JC; Acctg.

DESANTIS, CAROL; Archbishop Kennedy HS; Conshohocken, PA; (Y); JV Vllybl; Hon Roll; Mrktng Rsrch.

DESANTIS, DAVID; Shapsville Area HS; Sharpsville, PA; (Y); Camera Clb; Church Yth Grp; Cmnty Wkr; Computer Clb; Math Clb; Ski Clb; Spanish Clb; Varsity Clb; Chorus; Yrbk Bus Mgr; Pub Rel.

DESCANO, JAMES; Saint John Neumann HS; Philadelphia, PA; (Y); 24/325; Church Yth Grp; Ftbl; High Hon Roll; Hon Roll; NHS; Temple U; Acctng.

DESKEVICH, DUANE; Somerset Area SR HS; Somerset, PA; (Y); 18/239; Am Leg Boys St; English Clb; German Clb; JA; Letterman Clb; Ski Clb; Nwsp Ed-Chief; Socr; Tennis; High Hon Roll; YMCA Model Legsltr Natl Affairs Conf 86; Poltcl Sci.

DESS, DENNIS; Union Area Middle HS; New Castle, PA; (Y); Spanish Clb; Hon Roll; NHS.

DESS, TOM; Union Middle HS; New Castle, PA; (Y); 29/66; French Clb; Pres Pep Clb; Bsktbl; Var L Ftbl; Var L Trk; Hon Roll; 1st Tm TRI Cnty N Ll Strs Ftbll 85; Slippery Rock U PA; Bus.

DEST, SANDRA; Nazareth Area SR HS; Nazareth, PA; (Y); 5/237; Art Clb; Church Choir; Yrbk Stf; Var L Vllybl; High Hon Roll; NHS; Art.

DESTEFANO, FRANK; St John Neumann HS; Philadelphia, PA; (Y); 35/390; Cmnty Wkr; Computer Clb; Library Aide; Mathletes; Math Clb; Math Tm; Office Aide; Pep Clb; Spanish Clb; SADD; Drexel U; Engrng.

DETER, JAMES; Du Bois Area HS; Sykesville, PA; (Y); 69/300; Varsity Clb; Var Ftbl; Var Trk; Var Wt Lftg; Hon Roll; PA ST.

DETISCH, TIMOTHY; Cathedral Prep; Erie, PA; (Y); 50/216; Pres Church Yth Grp; Bsktbl; Vllybl; Hon Roll; Gannon; Acctg.

DETONE, KIMBERLY; Western Wayne HS; Lk Ariel, PA; (Y); Church Yth Grp; French Clb; Rep Stu Cncl; Bsktbl; Sftbl; Tennis; Hon Roll; NHS; Rotary Awd; Lawyer.

DETRICK, COLIN; Trinity HS; Washington, PA; (Y); Ski Clb; Cmmrcl Pilot.

DETTER, JENNIFER; York Suburban SR HS; York, PA; (Y); 60/191; Pep Clb; Varsity Clb; Color Guard; School Musical; Stat Bsbl; Co-Capt Cheerleading; Hon Roll; Ski Clb; Flag Corp; Mgr(s); Hmcmng Crt 85; Vars Ltrs, Pins & Jckt 83-86; Trip To Mex With Span Cls 84; Univ Of Sc; Pub Rltns.

DETTMER, TAMMY; Northampton SR HS; Northampton, PA; (Y); Church Yth Grp; Library Aide; Church Choir; High Hon Roll; Hon Roll; 3rd Highest Avrg In Algebra I 84; Messiah Clg; Occptnl Therapy.

DETTORE, GLORIA; Abinton Heights HS; Clarks Summit, PA; (Y); 95/280; Drama Clb; Chorus; School Musical; School Play; Stage Crew; Yrbk Phtg; Yrbk Rptr; Yrbk Stf; Mgr(s); Sftbl; Bus Adm.

DETWEILER, DANA; Bedford HS; Bedford, PA; (Y); Spanish Clb; Band; Concert Band; Mrchg Band; Pep Band; JV Var Bowling; JV Var Vllybl; Hon Roll; JR Mss Cntstnt 86; Cnty & Dist Bnd 85&86; US Music Ambssdrs Tour Of HI 86; Music.

DETWEILER, LISA; Pen Argyl Area HS; Pen Argyl, PA; (Y); Church Yth Grp; FBLA; Girl Scts; Pres Leo Clb; Service Clb; Chorus; Church Choir; Mrchg Band; Hon Roll; Dance Clb; Churchman Bus Schl; Acctng.

DETWILER, AMEE; Northern Bedford County HS; Woodbury, PA; (Y); Sec FBLA; Chorus; Yrbk Stf; High Hon Roll; Hon Roll; Acctng I Awd 86; Typng Profcncy Awd 86; Bus Adm.

DETWILER, RHONDA; Bellwood-Antis JR & SR HS; Bellwood, PA; (Y); 10/126; Church Yth Grp; FBLA; FHA; Hosp Aide; VICA; School Play; Yrbk Stf; JV Fld Hcky; Hon Roll; NHS; Outstndng Stu Hlth Assist 86; ICM Schl Bus; Med Sec.

DETZ, CHRISTINA; Warwick HS; Lititz, PA; (Y); Church Yth Grp; Teachers Aide; Sftbl; High Hon Roll; Hon Roll; Opt Clb Awd; Stu Mnth Jan 86; Commnctns.

DEUBLER, KATHY; Tunkhannock Area HS; Mehoopany, PA; (Y); Church Yth Grp; Trs JA; Teachers Aide; Chorus; High Hon Roll; Hon Roll; Comp Sci.

DEUSSING, KARIN; Wallenpaupack Area HS; Greentown, PA; (Y); 1/131; Church Yth Grp; Science Clb; Ski Clb; Band; Concert Band; Capt Cheerleading; Trk; High Hon Roll; NHS; Val; Pike Cnty Bar Assoc Schlrshp 86; Hawley Womens Clb Schlrshp 86; Greene-Dreher Alumni Assoc Schlrshp 86; Wheaton Coll.

DEUTSCH, MARA; Gateway HS; Monroeville, PA; (Y); Hosp Aide; Temple Yth Grp; Sec Ed Yrbk Stf; High Hon Roll; NHS; Ntl Mrt Cmmnded Stu 86; Ntl Mrt Corp Schlrshp Wnr 86; U Of PA; Psych.

DEUTSCH, PAMELA; Seneca Valley SR HS; Mars, PA; (Y); Cmnty Wkr; JA; ROTC; Band; Mrchg Band; Lit Mag; Sftbl; Miss Congenialty Cranberry Twnshp 86-87; Mrksmnshp Awd 84; Bus.

DEVANZO, KAREN; Bishop Hafey HS; Hazleton, PA; (Y); 23/130; Church Yth Grp; Spanish Clb; Chorus; Church Choir; Orch; School Musical; Hon Roll; Jr NHS; NHS; Y-Teens; Awrnss Life Clb Presdnt SR Yr 86-87; RN.

DEVENEY, KELLY; Phoenixville Area HS; Valley Forge, PA; (Y); Church Yth Grp; GAA; Key Clb; Pep Clb; SADD; Varsity Clb; Band; Concert Band; Drm Mjr(t); Jazz Band; Stu Mnth 85; Am Music Abroad Tour Europe 85; Fnlst Local Dogwd Pagnt 86; Marine Bio.

DEVENNEY, PRESTON; Avella JR SR HS; Avella, PA; (Y); Boy Scts; Church Yth Grp; SADD; Band; Jazz Band; Mrchg Band; School Play; Stage Crew; Yrbk Bus Mgr; Rep Soph Cls.

DEVER, DAVID; Cathedral Prep HS; Erie, PA; (Y); 22/215; Exploring; Latin Clb; Church Choir; School Musical; Yrbk Ed-Chief; Yrbk Stf; Hon Roll; Ntl Merit Ltr; Latin Hnr Soc; Electcl Engr.

DEVER, MARY ANN; Nazareth Acad; Philadelphia, PA; (Y); Church Yth Grp; Cmnty Wkr; German Clb; Intnl Clb; Teachers Aide; Variety Show; Lit Mag; Prfct Atten Awd; Engrng.

DEVER, MEGAN; Pottsgrove HS; Pottstown, PA; (Y); 6/229; Church Yth Grp; Pres Science Clb; Ski Clb; Varsity Clb; Rep Stu Cncl; JV Bsktbl; JV Var Fld Hcky; Var Sftbl; Hon Roll; NHS; Temple U; Envir Engrng.

DEVER, THERESA; Mastbaum Vo Tech; Philadelphia, PA; (Y); 18/292; Church Yth Grp; Sftbl; Hon Roll; Peirce JC; Data Prcssng.

DEVILBISS, BEVERLY C; Kennard-Dale HS; Fawn Grove, PA; (Y); 1/121; Church Yth Grp; Varsity Clb; Pres Chorus; School Musical; Yrbk Ed-Chief; Pres Frsh Cls; VP Jr Cls; VP Sr Cls; VP Sec Stu Cncl; Var Capt Bsktbl; MCI Tlcmnctns Schrlshp 86; Arion Awd 86; U Of DE; Mchncl Engr.

DEVINE, AILEEN; Cardinal O Hara HS; Drexel Hill, PA; (Y); 37/772; Church Yth Grp; Cmnty Wkr; 4-H; French Clb; Latin Clb; School Play; 4-H Awd; Hon Roll; NHS; 1st Pl Sci Fair 85; Acad Cnvctn Awd Excllnc 85 & 86; Bus.

DEVINE, JENNIFER; Lebanon Catholic HS; Lebanon, PA; (Y); Church Yth Grp; Girl Scts; Key Clb; Pep Clb; Ski Clb; JV Capt Cheerleading; L Sftbl; Twrlr; Bloomburg U; Med Tech.

DEVINE, MICHELE; Little Flower Catholic HS For Girls; Philadelphia, PA; (Y); 220/420; Rptr Cmnty Wkr; Pres Office Aide; Nwsp Rptr; Ed Yrbk Sprt Ed; Sec Lit Mag; Rep Frsh Cls; Rep Soph Cls; Rep Stu Cncl; Var L Socr; Var L Sftbl; Immaculate Coll; Crimnl Justc.

DEVINE, PATRICK; Northern Le Banon HS; Grantville, PA; (Y); Cmnty Wkr; Varsity Clb; Yrbk Sprt Ed; Capt Bsktbl; Ftbl; Trk; E Stroudsburg U.

DEVINE, THOMAS; St Josephs Preparatory Schl; Havertown, PA; (S); 5/218; Band; Pep Band; Nwsp Ed-Chief; Yrbk Ed-Chief; Im Bsktbl; Im Ftbl; JV Trk; NHS; Concert Band; Jazz Band; Magna Cum Laude Natl Ltn Exm 85; Phldlpha Grmn Soc Cntst Hnrbl Ment 85; Lbrl Arts.

DEVITA, JAMES; Deer Lakes JR/SR HS; Cheswick, PA; (Y); Chess Clb; Debate Tm; French Clb; Ski Clb; Varsity Clb; Var Bsbl; Var Bsktbl; Bowling; Var Golf; Achvt Awd Public Speaking 83-84; U Of Miami; Financng.

DEVLIN, JEFFREY; Montour HS; Coraopolis, PA; (Y); 50/273; Boy Scts; Pres Church Yth Grp; Mrchg Band; Stu Cncl; Var L Socr; Computer Clb; Exploring; Teachers Aide; Band; Chorus; Pipe Pins VI Awd; Eagl Awd 86; Jubilee Awd Outstndng SR 86; St Vincents Clg; Bus Admn.

DEVLIN, JOHN; Cardinal O Hara HS; Springfield, PA; (Y); 100/800; Church Yth Grp; Spanish Clb; Im Bsktbl; Var Golf; Capt Swmmng; Hon Roll; Pres Exc Awd 86; Mid Atlantic Gov Inf Cncl Schrlshp 86; James Maglone Mem Schlrshp 86; Drexel U; Engrng.

DEVLIN, MICHAEL; Cardinal O Hara HS; Havertown, PA; (Y); 353/772; Bsbl; Bsktbl; Crmnl Jstc.

DEVORICK, DENNIS; Greater Johnstown Area Vo-Tech; Johnstown, PA; (Y); 165/300; Pres Church Yth Grp; Ski Clb; VICA; Yrbk Phtg; Yrbk Stf; Parlimentry Proc Tm Dist,ST Wnnr 85-86; Stu Announcing 84-86; U Pitt; Elem Ed.

DEWALD, JODI; Schyulkill Haven HS; Schuylkill Haven, PA; (S); 24/80; Science Clb; SADD; Mrchg Band; Nwsp Rptr; Yrbk Stf; Var Cheerleading; Var Diving; Var Swmmng; JV Trk; Hon Roll; Lwyr.

DEWALT, LEWIS; Catasaugua HS; Catasauqua, PA; (Y); 27/142; Lit Mag; Bsbl; Capt Bsktbl; Hon Roll; Bus.

DEWART, CRISTIN; Mercyhurst Preparatory Schl; Erie, PA; (Y); 16/162; Drama Clb; French Clb; Q&S; Thesps; School Play; Nwsp Ed-Chief; Nwsp Rptr; Ed Lit Mag; Rep Soph Cls; Rep Sr Cls; U Pittsburgh; Pre-Med.

DEWIT, CHRISTOPHER; Moon SR HS; Coraopolis, PA; (Y); 37/327; Computer Clb; Concert Band; Jazz Band; Mrchg Band; Symp Band; Rep Stu Cncl; JV Bsbl; JV Socr; Hon Roll; NHS; IN U PA; Pre-Optmtry.

DEX, DANIEL; Emmaus HS; Allentown, PA; (Y); 3/493; Key Clb; Model UN; Spanish Clb; Pep Band; Stu Cncl; Var L Crs Cntry; Var Tennis; High Hon Roll; NHS; Ntl Merit Ltr; Safe Rides VP 87; Law.

DEXTER, JENNIFER; Wellsboro SR HS; Wellsboro, PA; (Y); VP Drama Clb; French Clb; Model UN; Trs Chorus; School Musical; School Play; Nwsp Stf; High Hon Roll; Hon Roll; Pres NHS; Pres Awd Acad Fit 86; Drama Awd 86; Owlett Mem Scholar 86; Lockhaven U; Humnities.

DEY, LYNNE; Brandywine Heights HS; Fleetwood, PA; (Y); Pep Clb; Chorus; Color Guard; Yrbk Stf; Golf; Hon Roll; NHS; Band Frnt Lttr 86; Kutztwn U; Commrcl Art.

DEYARMIN, HELEN M; United HS; Homer City, PA; (Y); 9/157; Ski Clb; Chorus; School Musical; Nwsp Stf; Yrbk Stf; Lit Mag; Stat Trk; High Hon Roll; Hon Roll; Ntl Merit Ltr.

DEZII, RANDOLPH; St John Neumann HS; Philadelphia, PA; (Y); Exploring; Rep Frsh Cls; Hon Roll; Temple U; Arch.

DHERIT, GREGORY; Northeastern HS; Manchester, PA; (Y); Boy Scts; Computer Clb; Exploring; Band; Concert Band; Mrchg Band; VP L Wrstlng; God Cntry Awd; Hon Roll; Egl Sct Awd Brnz 85; Soc Studys.

DI BLASI, GRACE; Hazleton HS; Hazelton, PA; (Y); 93/388; Drama Clb; French Clb; L Swmmng; Tennis; Hon Roll; 3 Yr Ltrmn In Swmng 83-86; Dntl Hygenist.

DI CAMILLO, LINDA; South Allegheny HS; Port Vue, PA; (S); 5/184; Church Yth Grp; Library Aide; Office Aide; Spanish Clb; Y-Teens; Drm & Bgl; Yrbk Stf; VP Soph Cls; Rep Jr Cls; JV Capt Cheerleading; US Bus Educ Awd 85.

DI CAMILLO, LISA; S Allegheny HS; Port Vue, PA; (S); #5 In Class; Office Aide; Drill Tm; Yrbk Stf; Trs Jr Cls; JV Cheerleading; Powder Puff Ftbl; Co-Capt Twrlr; High Hon Roll; NHS; Bus Ed Awd 85-86; Penn ST; Med.

DI CESARE JR, PATRICK J; Greensburg Central Catholic HS; Jeannette, PA; (Y); Letterman Clb; Im Bsktbl; L Ftbl; Im Sftbl; L Trk; Wt Lftg; High Hon Roll; Bus Adm.

DI CICCO, ANDREA; Nazareth Acad; Philadelphia, PA; (Y); 5/118; German Clb; Church Choir; Lit Mag; Trs Stu Cncl; High Hon Roll; NHS; Pre-Med.

DI CIO, DAN; Canon-Mc Millan SR HS; Canonsburg, PA; (Y); French Clb; Ski Clb; Varsity Clb; Pres Sr Cls; Rep Stu Cncl; Var L Ftbl; Var L Wrstlng; High Hon Roll; Hon Roll; Eagle Schlrshp Entreprnrl Std Washington & Jeffrsn Coll 86; Mst Poplr 86; Duquesne U Pittsburg; Attny.

DI CIO, DAVID; Canon-Mc Millan HS; Canonsburg, PA; (Y); French Clb; Varsity Clb; Yrbk Stf; Rep Frsh Cls; Rep Soph Cls; Rep Jr Cls; Rep Sr Cls; Rep Stu Cncl; Var Ftbl; Var Wrstlng.

DI CLEMENTE, TONI; Sto-Rox SR HS; Mc Kees Rocks, PA; (Y); #28 In Class; Boys Clb Am; Church Yth Grp; FBLA; Girl Scts; Band; Concert Band; Mrchg Band; School Musical; Vllybl; Hon Roll; Sec Of Band 86-87; Bus.

DI DOMENICO, MARGARET; Archbishop Kennedy HS; Ambler, PA; (Y); High Hon Roll; Hon Roll; Acad All Am 86; Math.

DI DONATO, GUY; Huntingdon Area HS; Huntingdon, PA; (Y); 1/244; FCA; Pres Key Clb; Ski Clb; VP Frsh Cls; Pres Soph Cls; VP Pres Jr Cls; Socr; L Tennis; NHS; Govnrs Sch Of Sci 86; Gentc Engrg.

DI ENNO, CHRIS; St Maria Goretti HS; Philadelphia, PA; (Y); 140/390; Cmmrcl Art.

DI FUCCI, AMY; Fairview HS; Fairview, PA; (S); 52/183; Church Yth Grp; French Clb; Band; Church Choir; Mrchg Band; Orch; Rep Frsh Cls; Trk; Hon Roll; VP Cncrt & Jazz Bands 85-86; Pres & VP Holy Crss Teen Cncl 82-84; 1st Chr 2nd Violn Erie Philh 84-85; Psych.

DI GILARMO, BOB; Central Christian HS; Dubois, PA; (Y); SADD; Varsity Clb; Yrbk Ed-Chief; Var Bsktbl; Var Civic Clb6; Var Socr; Hon Roll; Athltc Bsktbl Awd 85 & 86; Penn ST; Mech Engrng.

DI GIOIA, DAVID; Central Catholic HS; Pittsburgh, PA; (Y); Church Yth Grp; Ski Clb; Rep Stu Cncl; Vllybl; Hon Roll; NHS; Spanish NHS; Penn ST; Pilot.

DI IENNO, LISA MARIE; Sacred Heart Acad; Drexel Hill, PA; (S); Drama Clb; School Musical; School Play; VP Soph Cls; Rep Jr Cls; Rep Stu Cncl; Var Bsktbl; Var Lcrss; Hon Roll; NHS; Sprtmnshp Awd Bsktbl 83-84; Sci Merit Awd Bio & Chem 85-86.

DI JOSEPH, PAUL; Upper Darby HS; Primos, PA; (Y); 17/629; Boys Clb Am; Church Yth Grp; JV L Bsbl; Coach Actv; High Hon Roll; Hon Roll; Jr NHS; Chem Engrng.

DI LUCIA, MARY; Mount St Joseph Acad; Norristown, PA; (Y); Art Clb; Church Yth Grp; French Clb; Office Aide; Ed Lit Mag; VP French Hon Soc; Hon Roll; NHS; NEDT Awd; PA Gvnrs Sch Arts 85; Natl Fndtn Advcmnt Arts 86; U Of PA; Lit.

DI MARCELLA, KATHLEEN M; Bishop Kenrick HS; Norristown, PA; (Y); 104/221; Drama Clb; Office Aide; Science Clb; SADD; Chorus; Drill Tm; Drm & Bgl; Mrchg Band; School Musical; Swing Chorus; Grdn Phlps Beauty Schl Schlrshp 86-87; Grdn-Phlps Beauty Schl; Csmtlgy.

DI MARTINO, LYNN; Greensburg Central Catholic HS; Irwin, PA; (Y); VP Church Yth Grp; Hosp Aide; Pep Clb; Ski Clb; Varsity Clb; JV Var Cheerleading; Socr; Im Sftbl; Im Vllybl; Hon Roll; Bus.

DI MARTINO, MARY; Greensburg Central Catholic HS; Irwin, PA; (Y); Church Yth Grp; Hosp Aide; JA; Ski Clb; Yrbk Rptr; Yrbk Stf; JV Var Cheerleading; Im Gym; Im Vllybl; Hon Roll; Penn ST U; Bus Adm.

DI MATTEO, MICHAEL; Canon Mc Millan HS; Canonsburg, PA; (Y); #11 In Class; Aud/Vis; French Clb; Ski Clb; Chorus; Stu Cncl; Var Capt Socr; High Hon Roll; NHS; Bsktbl; Ftbl; U Pittsburgh; Dentist.

DI MATTEO, STEVEN J; Monongahela Valley Catholic HS; Monongahela, PA; (S); 5/106; FBLA; Nwsp Stf; VP Frsh Cls; Pres Soph Cls; Pres Jr Cls; Pres Stu Cncl; JV Var Ftbl; DAR Awd; Ntl Merit Ltr; Spanish NHS; Penn ST U; Engrng.

DI MEZZA, DINA MARIE; Strath Haven HS; Wallingford, PA; (Y); Yrbk Stf; Hon Roll; Make Up Crew Schl Plays; DCCC; Bus.

DI MICELI, CATHY; Panther Valley HS; Nesquehoning, PA; (Y); 38/110; Church Yth Grp; Library Aide; Office Aide; Pep Clb; Ski Clb; Teachers Aide; Band; Mrchg Band; Yrbk Stf; Cheerleading; Bloomsburg U; RN.

DI MUCCI, LUCIA; Archbishop Ryan HS For Girls; Philadelphia, PA; (Y); 31/475; Pres JA; Red Cross Aide; SADD; Off Sr Cls; Hon Roll; NHS; Ntl Merit Schol; Italian Clb-Pres; Italian Hnr Socy; RAP; La Salle U; Comm.

DI MURO, JOHN; The Hill Schl; E Brunswick, NJ; (Y); JA; Teachers Aide; Nwsp Rptr; Yrbk Rptr; Pres Frsh Cls; Pres Soph Cls; Rep Stu Cncl; Var Capt Bsbl; Var Socr; Hon Roll; MVP Bsbl 86; Acad Athltc Schlrshp Hill Schl 83-87; Perfect Stu 86-87; Bus.

DI NARDO, MICHAEL ANTHONY; Hopewell HS; Aliquippa, PA; (Y); 27/254; Church Yth Grp; Office Aide; Band; Chorus; Concert Band; Mrchg Band; Pep Band; Var JV Bsbl; L Var Ftbl; High Hon Roll.

DI PALMA, GIOVANNA; St Maria Goretti HS; Philadelphia, PA; (Y); 62/400; Camera Clb; Church Yth Grp; Hon Roll; NHS; Prfct Atten Awd; Temple U.

DI PAOLO, JOHN P; Holy Ghost Preparatory Schl; Philadelphia, PA; (S); Aud/Vis; JV Socr; NHS; Dir Of Audio-Visl Clb 84; Math.

DI PAOLO, PATRICK; Cathedral Preparatory Schl; Erie, PA; (Y); 106/238; Am Leg Boys St; Art Clb; Church Yth Grp; Letterman Clb; Political Wkr; SADD; Varsity Clb; Y-Teens; Yrbk Stf; Rep Soph Cls; Art Awd 86; Art.

DI PASQUALE, BETH; Central Bucks East HS; Doylestown, PA; (Y); Debate Tm; Spanish Clb; Band; Color Guard; Concert Band; Mrchg Band; Nwsp Ed-Chief; Nwsp Rptr; Coach Actv; Trk; Trk Ltr; Pencl Sktch Publshd Art Textbk 84; Band Ltrs 85-86; Pres Of Bucks Cnty Hrse & Ridrs 85; Law.

DI PEPPE, LEE ANN; Liberty HS; Bethlehem, PA; (Y); 101/475; Dance Clb; Yrbk Stf; Rep Sr Cls; Pom Pon; Vllybl; Hon Roll; West Chester U; Elem Ed.

DI PIANO, JENNIFER; Perkiomen Valley HS; Collegeville, PA; (Y); 14/158; Am Leg Aux Girls St; Stage Crew; Yrbk Rptr; Yrbk Stf; Diving; Hon Roll; NHS; 2nd Prize Schl Art Show 85; 2nd Prize Perkiomen Valley Art Ctr Art Show 86; Commercial Art.

DI PIETRO, MARIA; St Maria Goretta HS; Philadelphia, PA; (Y); 45/402; Church Yth Grp; Cmnty Wkr; FNA; GAA; Math Clb; Science Clb; Service Clb; SADD; Flag Corp; Ed Yrbk Phtg; Algebra Awd 83-84; Nrsng.

DI PIETRO, NINO; Chestnut Hill Acad; Philadelphia, PA; (Y); Stage Crew; Yrbk Stf; Rep Frsh Cls; Rep Soph Cls; Var L Bsbl; Var Capt Socr; High Hon Roll; Glbrt Haven Fall Mem Schlrshp 86; Rnslr Poly Teh Inst Math & Sci Awd 86; 1st Team All Intradmc Soccer; U PA; Bus.

DI PIETRO, STEPHANIE; St Maria Goretti HS; Philadelphia, PA; (Y); 45/426; Dance Clb; Math Clb; Office Aide; Off Frsh Cls; Off Soph Cls; Off Sr Cls; Co-Capt Bowling; High Hon Roll; Hon Roll; NHS; King Schlrshp 86; 2nd Tm All Cathlc Bwlng 86; Phila CC; Fin.

DI PIPPA, TARA; Canon Mc Mill SR HS; Canonsburg, PA; (Y); Exploring; FBLA; FNA; JA; SADD; Cit Awd; High Hon Roll; Sal; Val; Bradford; Lgl Sec.

DI SALVIO, RACHELLE; Council Rock HS; Richboro, PA; (Y); 80/759; Hosp Aide; Spanish Clb; Stu Cncl; Im Powder Puff Ftbl; Hon Roll; NHS; Temple; Physcl Thrpy.

DI SALVO, ROSE; St Maria Goretti HS; Philadelphia, PA; (Y); 131/426; French Clb; Lit Mag; Rep Jr Cls; Var Tennis; Prfct Atten Awd; 2nd Hnrs On Report Card 84-86; Temple U; Comm.

DI SANTE, MARGARET; Freedom SR HS; Bethlehem, PA; (Y); 156/445; Mgr(s); Mat Maids; Score Keeper; Sftbl; Mgr Wrstlng; Hon Roll; Cosmetlgy.

DI SANTO, DENISE; Norristown Area HS; Norristown, PA; (S); 16/503; Church Yth Grp; FCA; FBLA; JA; Teachers Aide; Rep Stu Cncl; Sftbl; Hon Roll; Cert Merit Exclnce Frgn Lang Span 83-84.

DI SILVESTRO, MICHELLE; St Maria Goretti HS; Philadelphia, PA; (Y); #99 In Class; Dance Clb; Girl Scts; Hosp Aide; Church Choir; Variety Show; Sftbl; Hon Roll; T Jefferson U; Rad Tech.

DI SIPIO, ANTHONY; Benton Area HS; Benton, PA; (Y); 2/55; Key Clb; Var Bsbl; Var Bsktbl; High Hon Roll; NHS; Prfct Atten Awd; Math Awd 85; Century 21 Typ Awd 85; A Honor Roll 82-86; Penn ST U; Pre Med.

DI TORE, JOHN; Hatboro Horsham SR HS; Hatboro, PA; (Y); Debate Tm; FBLA; Latin Clb; Varsity Clb; Yrbk Stf; Tennis; Vllybl; High Hon Roll.

DI VECCHIO, LORI; Sto-Rox SR HS; Mc Kees Rocks, PA; (Y); 47/153; Cmnty Wkr; Library Aide; Y-Teens; Nwsp Ed-Chief; Nwsp Sprt Ed; Nwsp Stf; Yrbk Stf; Var JV Bsktbl; Sec Frsh Cls; Trs Var Soph Cls; Beaver Vlly Times 2nd Tm Sftbll 85 & 86; Plyed In 86 Keystone Gaames Sftbll 86; Commun.

DI VITO, VALERIE; Cornell HS; Coraopolis, PA; (Y); Hosp Aide; Sec Key Clb; Concert Band; Mrchg Band; School Play; Ed Nwsp Stf; Var Capt Cheerleading; Twrlr; NHS; Voice Dem Awd; Duquesne U; Radlgy.

DIAKITE, ISMAIL; Carson Long Military Acad; Miami, FL; (Y); 4/52; Drama Clb; Chorus; School Play; Nwsp Ed-Chief; Yrbk Rptr; Lit Mag; Tennis; FL Gvrnrs Pgm Gftd & Tlnted 83; Flwshp Awd; Boston U; Cmnctns.

DIAMOND, ELIZABETH; Upper Dubli HS; Ft Washington, PA; (Y); 71/315; FBLA; Varsity Clb; Sec Frsh Cls; Sec Soph Cls; Rep Jr Cls; Rep Sr Cls; Stu Cncl; Var Fld Hcky; Var Trk; Wnnr Law Cntst 83; Trck Tm Chmps 85; Bus Admn.

DIAMOND, STEPHEN; Conemaugh Twp Area HS; Johnstown, PA; (Y); 3/106; JA; Ski Clb; Cit Awd; Hon Roll; NHS; Pres Schlr; Pittsburgh U Johnstow; Cvl Engr.

DIANDRETH, MARK; Franklin Regional HS; Murrysville, PA; (Y); AFS; Boy Scts; Church Yth Grp; Computer Clb; Crs Cntry; High Hon Roll; Egl Sct 86.

DIAS, ANTONIO; Bethlehem Catholic HS; Bethlehem, PA; (Y); 80/227; Computer Clb; French Clb; Mathletes; Math Clb; Math Tm; JV Capt Socr; High Hon Roll; Hon Roll; Prfct Atten Awd; Bst Conduct & Effort Awd 83; Hghst Geom Avg 85; Rochester Inst Tech; Mech Engr.

DIASCRO, MATTHEW; Perkiomen HS; Red Hill, PA; (Y); 1/6; Thesps; Acpl Chr; School Musical; Yrbk Ed-Chief; Pres Soph Cls; VP Jr Cls; Var Lcrss; Var Socr; Bausch & Lomb Sci Awd; NHS; HOBY Ldrshp Sem 85; Rotary Clb Camp Neidig Ldrshp Camp 86; Dr Anders Awd 85,Dr Carlson Awd 86; Sci.

DIBBLE, MARK; Canton Area HS; Canton, PA; (Y); Church Yth Grp; Bsbl; Bowling; Hon Roll; Williamsport Area CC; Elec.

DIBELER, SONYA; St Maria Goretti HS; Philadelphia, PA; (Y); 12/390; Mathletes; Math Clb; Science Clb; Var L Bowling; Var L Tennis; High Hon Roll; NHS; Ntl Merit Ltr; Prfct Atten Awd; Euclid Div, Contntl Math Leag, 1st Pl 85; Psych.

DIBERT, AUDRA; Penn Cambria HS; Gallitzin, PA; (Y); Camera Clb; Drama Clb; Speech Tm; French Clb; Band; Concert Band; Mrchg Band; Hon Roll; Charles Palmer Davis Awd Outstndng Knowldg Current Affairs 85-86; IN U PA; Jrnlsm.

DIBERT, CREGG; Chestnut Ridge SR HS; Imler, PA; (Y); Chess Clb; Im Bsktbl; Im Ftbl; Military.

DICE, JAMES; Laurel Highlands HS; Uniontown, PA; (Y); 40/365; Church Yth Grp; Ski Clb; Varsity Clb; Acpl Chr; Chorus; Madrigals; Bsbl; Ftbl; Wt Lftg; Wrstlng; Slippery Rock; Phys Thrpy.

DICE, LORI; Fairchance Georges SR HS; Smithfield, PA; (Y); Drama Clb; FHA; Library Aide; School Play; Stage Crew; Sec Frsh Cls; High Hon Roll; Hon Roll; Pastry Chf.

DICE, TINA; Waynesboro Area SR HS; Chambersburg, PA; (Y); Pres Church Yth Grp; Computer Clb; Sec Math Clb; Spanish Clb; Chorus; Church Choir; Stage Crew; Var L Fld Hcky; Score Keeper; High Hon Roll; Shippensburg U.

DICEY, ROSEMARIE; Waynesburg Central HS; Waynesburg, PA; (Y); 94/195; French Clb; Hosp Aide; Spanish Clb; 175 Volenteer Wrk At Greene Cnty Memrl Hosp 85; Lpn.

DICICCO, MARCO; Hopewell SR HS; Aliquippa, PA; (Y); 11/245; Church Yth Grp; Trs Exploring; French Clb; School Play; Variety Show; Rep Soph Cls; Rep Jr Cls; Hst Socr; High Hon Roll; JETS Awd; USAFA; Aero Engrng.

DICK, CATHERINE; Penn Trafford HS; Irwin, PA; (Y); 129/324; VP AFS; FBLA; Hosp Aide; Red Cross Aide; Chorus; Ed Nwsp Stf; Capt Bsktbl; High Hon Roll; Hon Roll; Hnrd 86 Bushops Mdlln Ball Vlntr Wrk 86; Lock Haven U PA; Erly Chldhd.

DICK, SUSAN; Wyoming Area HS; West Wyoming, PA; (Y); Art Clb; Church Yth Grp; German Clb; Girl Scts; Ski Clb; Chorus; Church Choir; Color Guard; Drill Tm; Yrbk Stf; Germn Awd & Girl Scout Slvr Awd 86.

DICKEL, DIANNA; Elizabethtown HS; Elizabethtown, PA; (Y); 28/238; Teachers Aide; Chorus; Cheerleading; Powder Puff Ftbl; Elizabethtown Coll.

DICKER, KYLE; Notre Dame HS; Easton, PA; (Y); 11/75; Flag Corp; Yrbk Stf; Score Keeper; Trk; Twrlr; High Hon Roll; Hon Roll; Pres Acad Ftns Awd 86; Otstndng Achvt Art 84-86; Nat Amer Mth Exm Awd 84; Kutztown U; Cmmnctns Dsgn.

DICKERSON, ARNETTA; Westinghouse HS; Pittsburgh, PA; (Y); Pep Clb; Chorus; Sec Frsh Cls; Trk; High Hon Roll; Hon Roll; Prfct Atten Awd; UCLA; Bus.

DICKERSON, MICHAEL; Exeter Township SR HS; Reading, PA; (Y); 6/215; Exploring; 4-H; Trs Ski Clb; Varsity Clb; VP Band; Concert Band; Mrchg Band; Var JV Socr; Hon Roll; Jr NHS; PA ST; Vet Med.

DICKERSON, STEVEN T; Exeter HS; Reading, PA; (Y); 14/216; Key Clb; Varsity Clb; Bsktbl; Socr; High Hon Roll; Jr NHS; NHS; Ntl Merit SF; Hugh O Brian Ldrshp Rep 83; Bio.

DICKEY, DEBORAH; Jeferson-Morgan HS; Clarksville, PA; (S); 6/96; Library Aide; Office Aide; Spanish Clb; SADD; Yrbk Stf; Rep Sr Cls; Sftbl; High Hon Roll; NHS; Sci Awd 84-85; Mth Awd 84-85; Frgn Lang Awd 84-85; Trvl.

DICKEY, JENNIFER; Butler Area SR HS; Butler, PA; (Y); Church Yth Grp; Girl Scts; Hosp Aide; Service Clb; Spanish Clb; Church Choir; Elem Ed.

DICKEY, MICHAEL; Punxsutawney Area HS; Reynoldsville, PA; (Y); 130/265; Drama Clb; Varsity Clb; Sec Sr Cls; Capt Bsbl; Var L Bsktbl; Coach Actv; L Var Ftbl; Wt Lftg; Rotary Boy Of Mo March 86; Am Lg Bsbl 84-86; 3 Schl Records In HS Bsbl 86; IVP.

DICKEY, REBECCA; Punxsutawney Area HS; Reynoldsville, PA; (Y); Math Tm; Science Clb; Variety Show; Nwsp Ed-Chief; Rep Frsh Cls; Rep Soph Cls; Trs Jr Cls; Pres Sr Cls; Stu Cncl; Bsbl; Rotary Yth Ldrshp Awd 86; Prncpls Awd 86; Grl Mnth 86; U Pittsburg Johnstown; Pre-Med.

DICKINSON, ROBYN; Tunkhannock HS; Lake Winola, PA; (S); 17/290; Church Yth Grp; Science Clb; Spanish Clb; Jazz Band; Off Soph Cls; Off Jr Cls; Fld Hcky; Stat Trk; Hon Roll; NHS; Natl Fratrnty Stdnt Musicn 83; Humn Svcs.

DICKS, MARK; Trinity HS; Washington, PA; (Y); Church Yth Grp; Cmnty Wkr; FCA; Var Bsbl; Mechncl Drwng.

DICKSON, JAMES; Red Lion Area SR HS; Red Lion, PA; (Y); 8/337; Church Yth Grp; Pres Sec Exploring; Yrbk Stf; High Hon Roll; NHS; Schrlshp De Vry Inst Tech; Yrk Idsptch Acad All Stars; Hnr Grad; De Vry Inst Tech; Elec Engr.

DICKSON, SHONA; Seneca Valley HS; Mars, PA; (Y); Cmnty Wkr; GAA; Ski Clb; School Play; Nwsp Stf; Trs Sr Cls; Var L Sftbl; Trk; Hon Roll; Schlstc Achvmnt Rcgntn 85-86; Bus Mngtmnt.

DICKSON, SUE; Conemaugh Township Area HS; Johnstown, PA; (S); 10/101; Art Clb; Drama Clb; Hosp Aide; Pep Clb; Spanish Clb; Ed Nwsp Ed-Chief; Ed Lit Mag; L Bsktbl; L Vllybl; Hon Roll; Spn Excllnce Awd 85; Air Force; Lang.

DICOLA, ROBYN; Butler HS; Butler, PA; (Y); Church Yth Grp; JA; Spanish Clb; SADD; Chorus; Church Choir; School Musical; Nwsp Rptr; Hnrary Lit Awd PA Engl Dep 83; Engl Tchr.

DIDION, ROBERT; North East HS; North East, PA; (Y); Letterman Clb; Speech Tm; Varsity Clb; Band; Crs Cntry; Hon Roll; Penn ST; Elec Engrng.

DIEDERICH, MICHELLE; York Catholic HS; Jacobus, PA; (Y); Drama Clb; Pres JA; Nwsp Rptr; Yrbk Rptr; JV Crs Cntry; JV Trk; High Hon Roll; NHS; Church Yth Grp; Debate Tm; 2nd Low Day Essay Cntst, Merit Awd Jrnlsm 86; Fshn Dsgn.

DIEFENBACHER, ELIZABETH LOUISE; Great Valley HS; Malvern, PA; (Y); 6/273; Am Leg Aux Girls St; Church Yth Grp; Science Clb; Service Clb; Varsity Clb; Yrbk Stf; Pres Soph Cls; Pres Jr Cls; Trk; Dnfth Awd; NASA Spc Shttl Prjct 85-86; Wllsly Bk Awd 86; Hgh O Brn Yth Fndtn Ldrshp Smnr 85; Bio.

DIEFENDERFER, DENISE; West Hazleton HS; West Hazleton, PA; (S); 13/191; Trs FNA; Hosp Aide; Pep Clb; Red Cross Aide; Nwsp Stf; Yrbk Stf; Mgr(s); High Hon Roll; NHS; English Cls Rep 85-86; Bloomsburg U; Phys Ther.

DIEFFENBACH, LESLIE; Tulpehocken HS; Bethel, PA; (Y); Chorus; Yrbk Stf; JV Var Sftbl; Hon Roll; NHS.

DIEFFENBACH, TODD; Carson Long Military Inst; Bethel, PA; (Y); 3/36; Aud/Vis; ROTC; Color Guard; Rep Sr Cls; Trk; Hon Roll; Pres Schlr; Rifle Tm Capt 84-86; Clarion U; Army.

DIEHL, ERIC; Greater Latrobe SR HS; Latrobe, PA; (Y); Letterman Clb; Varsity Clb; Var L Bsbl; Var L Ftbl; Var L Wrstlng; High Hon Roll; Rotary Awd; Spanish NHS.

DIEHL, ERIC; Kutztown Area HS; Kutztown, PA; (Y); Church Yth Grp; Temple Yth Grp; VICA; Band; Concert Band; Bsbl; Ftbl; Trk; Wrstlng; Hon Roll; Honorable Mention Lnmn Wk Ftbl 85-86.

DIEHL, KELLY; Portage Area HS; Portage, PA; (S); 1/120; Chorus; Mrchg Band; Variety Show; Sec Soph Cls; Twrlr; Bausch & Lomb Sci Awd; Hon Roll; NHS; Church Yth Grp; Hgh Achvt Bio I Awd 83-84; Amer Lgn Mdl Awd 83; St Francis Coll; Scndry Educ.

DIEM, VINCENT P; Pequea Valley HS; Kinzers, PA; (Y); Church Yth Grp; Drama Clb; Acpl Chr; Band; Church Choir; Jazz Band; Mrchg Band; School Musical; School Play; God Cntry Awd; Arch.

DIENER, KATHY; Pottsgrove SR HS; Pottstown, PA; (Y); 2/263; Pep Clb; Science Clb; Ski Clb; Sec Spanish Clb; Varsity Clb; Rep Soph Cls; Sec Jr Cls; Var Cheerleading; High Hon Roll; NHS; Model Assmbly 83-85; Bus Admn.

DIERINGER, NOELLE; Du Bois Area HS; Rockton, PA; (Y); German Clb; Band; Concert Band; Orch; Yrbk Stf; Courier Express Essay Wnnr 84; IN U PA Hnrs Band 85; Carnegie Mellon & Bwlng Grn Mus Camps 86; Mus Perf.

DIEROLF, BRIAN; Brandywine Heights HS; Bechtelsville, PA; (Y); JV Var Bsbl; JV Var Bsktbl; High Hon Roll; Hon Roll; Amer Cultures Awd 85; U PA; Acctng.

DIEROLF, BRIAN; Brandywine Hgts HS; Bechtelsvle, PA; (Y); Var JV Bsbl; Var JV Bsktbl; Hon Roll; Amer Culture Top Stu Awd 85; Acctng.

DIEROLF, WILLIAM; Wyoming Valley West HS; Kingston, PA; (Y); Church Yth Grp; High Hon Roll; Hon Roll; NHS; YABA Bwlg Scholar; Penn ST; Aero Engrng.

DIESEL, TRACY; Canon Mc Millan SR HS; Canonsburg, PA; (Y); 14/371; Cmnty Wkr; French Clb; Yrbk Bus Mgr; Yrbk Stf; High Hon Roll; NHS; Hnr Roll Trphy 84; Frnch Cert 84; 2nd Dictation Frnch CA ST 86; Phys Ther.

DIESING, JANET; Linesville HS; Conneaut Lake, PA; (Y); Church Yth Grp; Pep Clb; SADD; Var Cheerleading; Flight Atten.

DIESO, JOHN; James M Caughlin HS; Wilkes Barre, PA; (Y); Boy Scts; Church Yth Grp; Stu Wilkes Barre Vo Tech Schl 3 Yrs; A Stu Desial Mechncs; Autombl Machncs; Desine Wrk.

DIETER, DANIEL; Wilmington Area HS; West Middlesex, PA; (S); 20/124; Radio Clb; Nwsp Sprt Ed; Nwsp Stf; Church Yth Grp; Exploring; Var L Bsktbl; Var Capt Coach Actv; Var L Trk; Wilmington Acad Achvt 83-85; MVP Cross Country Tm, Track Tm 84-85; Engl.

DIETERLE III, NEAL LAURENCE; Northeastern SR HS; Mt Wolf, PA; (Y); 36/153; Aud/Vis; Boy Scts; Band; Jazz Band; Stage Crew; Sec Trs Stu Cncl; Golf; Tennis; St Jude Dance Marathon Co-Chrmn 82-86; Navy; Nculear.

DIETRICH, CHRISTOPHER; Williams Valley HS; Wiconisco, PA; (Y); Art Clb; Chess Clb; High Hon Roll; Hon Roll; Prfct Atten Awd; Arch.

DIETRICH, DANIELLE; Mars Area HS; Valencia, PA; (Y); GAA; Letterman Clb; Office Aide; Pep Clb; Varsity Clb; Chorus; School Musical; Pres Soph Cls; Pres Jr Cls; Rep Sr Cls; RPSC Busnss Schl; Sectrl.

DIETRICH II, DAVID; Norwin HS; N Huntingdon, PA; (Y); Church Yth Grp; Computer Clb; German Clb; Letterman Clb; Math Clb; Pep Clb; Ski Clb; SADD; Varsity Clb; Var L Swmmng; Bus Mgmt.

DIETRICH, DOUG; Pequea Valley HS; Paradise, PA; (S); 42/126; VP Pres Varsity Clb; Capt Bsktbl; Co-Capt Socr; Tennis; Hon Roll; JC Awd; MVP Soccer 86; Lock Heaven U; Mgnt Bus.

DIETRICH, LAURIE; Tamaqua Area HS; Tamaqua, PA; (Y); 3/191; Mrchg Band; Nwsp Stf; Ed Yrbk Stf; Var Cheerleading; Var Pom Pon; High Hon Roll; Hon Roll; NHS; Ntl Merit Ltr; Trs Spanish NHS; Mst Promising Edtrl Staff 85-86; Pre-Med.

DIETRICH, LISA; Kutztown Area Senior HS; Lenhartsville, PA; (Y); 23/150; Band; Chorus; Flag Corp; Mrchg Band; Trk; High Hon Roll; NHS; Schlrshp Baum SCHL Art 85.

DIETRICH, PAMELA; Hamburg Area HS; Hamburg, PA; (Y); 1/152; Rptr FBLA; Ski Clb; Spanish Clb; Rep Stu Cncl; Var Capt Sftbl; Var Capt Tennis; NHS; Val; Library Aide; Bsktbl; Sico Schlrshp Shippensburg U 86; Lutheran Brotherhood Schlrshp 86; NAPUS Schlrshp 86; Shippensburg U; Acctng.

DIETRICH, WADE; Lykens Christian HS; Williamstown, PA; (Y); 1/21; Church Yth Grp; Quiz Bowl; Band; Church Choir; Orch; School Play; Yrbk Ed-Chief; Pres Frsh Cls; Pres Soph Cls; Pres Jr Cls; ACE Intl Stu Conv Comp 86; Penn ST; Comp Engrng.

DIETZ, DEANNA LEIGH; Danville SR HS; Danville, PA; (Y); Church Yth Grp; Ski Clb; Band; Yrbk Stf; Var L Bsktbl; Powder Puff Ftbl; Var L Sftbl; Hon Roll; Prfct Atten Awd; Danville Ed Assc Schlrshp 86; Lock Haven U; Physcl Ed.

DIETZ, HEATHER; Trinity HS; Mechanicsburg, PA; (Y); French Clb; Pep Clb; Ski Clb; Spanish Clb; Yrbk Stf; JV Trk; Hon Roll; Spanish NHS; Cmmnctn.

DIETZ, JAMES J; Bethel Park HS; Pittsburgh, PA; (Y); 73/515; Computer Clb; PAVAS; Science Clb; Orch; School Musical; Hon Roll; Pittsburgh Yth Symph 86; Penn St Hnrs String Quartet Pgm, Penn Mus Educ Assoc Region I Orch 85; Penn ST; Engrng.

DIETZ, JODI; Manheim Central HS; Columbia, PA; (Y); Hosp Aide; Library Aide; Office Aide; Red Cross Aide; Rep Jr Cls; Rep Sr Cls; Var L Cheerleading; Var Powder Puff Ftbl; JV Sftbl; Hon Roll; Four Wy Tst Awd 85; Libr Awd 86; Phys Ftns Awd 86; U Of Pittsburgh; Nrsng.

DIETZ, JULIE; South Western HS; Hanover, PA; (Y); Pres AFS; Key Clb; Teachers Aide; JV Var Bsktbl; JV Var Fld Hcky; High Hon Roll; Hon Roll; Pres Schlr; Hmcmng Rep & Qn 85-86; 1st Rnnr Up Miss PA US Teen Pgnt 86; Mdl.

DIETZ, MELINDA; Lewistown Area HS; Lewistown, PA; (Y); 46/263; French Clb; Hosp Aide; High Hon Roll; Hon Roll; Ntl Merit Ltr; Church Yth Grp; Girl Scts; Pep Clb; Ski Clb; Church Choir; Hnrs Engl 85-86; Frnch 4 Hnrs Crs 86-87; Geisinger; Nrsng.

DIETZ, MICHELLE; West Allegheny HS; Imperial, PA; (Y); Ski Clb; Spanish Clb; Chorus; Concert Band; Mrchg Band; Rep Jr Cls; Twrlr; High Hon Roll; Hon Roll; SHASDA Stu Perf Awd 85; Wilma Boyd; Flght Attndnt.

DIETZ, ROBERT; East HS; Erie, PA; (Y); 5/136; Spanish Clb; Y-Teens; Nwsp Rptr; Nwsp Sprt Ed; Nwsp Stf; Socr; Trk; Hon Roll; NHS; Ntl Cngrss Prnts & Tchrs Schlrshp 86; Behrend Coll; Crmnl Jstc.

DIETZ, STEPHANIE; Saegertown HS; Meadville, PA; (Y); 4-H; Varsity Clb; Variety Show; Rep Jr Cls; JV Var Cheerleading; Hon Roll; Jr NHS; Prfct Atten Awd.

DIFFENDERFER, JENNIE; Manheim Central HS; Manheim, PA; (Y); VP Band; VP Concert Band; VP Jazz Band; VP Mrchg Band; Pep Band; Stage Crew; JV Bsktbl; Var Sftbl; Hon Roll; NHS; 4 Way Tst Awd 86; Sec Ed.

DIFFENDERFER, STEVE; Cumberland Valley HS; Camp Hill, PA; (Y); L Mgr(s); Schlstc Art Gold Key Grphc Dsgn 85; Gold Key Oils 86; Ntl Art Hnr Scty 85-87; Cooper Union; Fine Arts.

DIFRANCESCO, ANDREW; Abraham Lincoln HS; Philadelphia, PA; (Y); Computer Clb; Varsity Clb; Ftbl; Gym; Trk; High Hon Roll; Hon Roll.

DIFRISCHIA, LARA; Laurel HS; Ellwood City, PA; (Y); 31/103; 4-H; Bsktbl; Coach Actv; Powder Puff Ftbl; Sftbl; Trk; Culinary Arts.

DIGGINS, SHELLEY; Plum SR HS; New Kensington, PA; (Y); AFS; FTA; Band; Chorus; Church Choir; Mrchg Band; School Musical; Symp Band; Hon Roll; NHS; Optometry.

DIGGS, REECELLA; Valley HS; New Kensington, PA; (Y); Spanish Clb; Varsity Clb; Chorus; Stat Trk; Var L Vllybl; Hon Roll.

DIGIACOBBE, KIM; North Allegheny SR HS; Gibsonia, PA; (Y); 161/605; Pep Clb; Nwsp Phtg; Yrbk Phtg; Yrbk Stf; Pres Frsh Cls; Rep Soph Cls; Rep Jr Cls; Sr Cls; Cheerleading; Nationwide Algebra Cont; U Of RI; Bus Invstmnts.

DIGNEY, ROSEMARY; Perkimen Schl; Montclair, NJ; (Y); 15/43; Art Clb; Church Yth Grp; Hosp Aide; Model UN; Ski Clb; Teachers Aide; School Play; Stage Crew; Rep Frsh Cls; JV Diving; Srvc Awd, Lab Aide 86; Vet Studies.

DIGREGORIO, JILL; Old Forge HS; Old Forge, PA; (Y); Church Yth Grp; Dance Clb; Ski Clb; School Musical; School Play; Variety Show; Yrbk Stf; High Hon Roll; Hon Roll; NHS; Govs Schl For Prfrmng Arts Schlrshp 86; Asst Teacher At Romar Dance Studio Schlrshp 85; Ballet Thea 85; Dance Perf.

DILAURO, ROBYN; Cardinal Ohara HS; Springfield, PA; (Y); 30/772; Spanish Clb; Rep Soph Cls; Rep Jr Cls; Rep Sr Cls; Rep Stu Cncl; Hon Roll; NHS; US Achvt Acad Awd Stu Cncl 86.

DILIBERTO, ROBERT; Upper Merion HS; King Of Prussia, PA; (Y); Boy Scts; Bsbl; Bus.

DILL, ANTHONY; York Catholic HS; York, PA; (Y); 7/170; French Clb; Rep Frsh Cls; Rep Soph Cls; Rep Jr Cls; L Capt Bsbl; L Bsktbl; JV Ftbl; L Golf; High Hon Roll; NHS; All Cnty Bsbl 85; HOBY Ldrshp Conf 84.

DILL, MICHELLE; United HS; Homer City, PA; (Y); 36/157; Camera Clb; Church Yth Grp; Hosp Aide; Office Aide; Pep Clb; Ski Clb; Stu Cncl; Trk; Hon Roll; Prfct Atten Awd; IUP; Pre-Med.

DILL, THOMAS; Bishop Mc Cort HS; Johnstown, PA; (Y); 24/110; German Clb; Trs Math Clb; Math Tm; Ski Clb; School Play; Ftbl; Capt Var Swmmng; Capt Var Vllybl; High Hon Roll; Ntl Merit SF; Fnlst W PA Alg Cntst 82; IN U Of PA; Cmptr Sci.

DILLALOGUE, JACKIE; Penn Cambria HS; Gallitzin, PA; (Y); 29/200; Art Clb; Drama Clb; FBLA; Hon Roll; Jr NHS; Altoona Schl Of Commerce; Accnt.

DILLAMAN, VALERIE; Grove City HS; Grove City, PA; (Y); 52/154; Chess Clb; French Clb; Key Clb; Yrbk Bus Mgr; Var L Cheerleading; Powder Puff Ftbl; Trk; High Hon Roll; Hon Roll; Hmcmng Ct 85; Slippery Rock U; Bus.

DILLARD, GRACE; Cedar Grove Christian Acad; Philadelphia, PA; (Y); Church Yth Grp; Chorus; Bsktbl; Hon Roll; Dickinson Coll; Engrng.

DILLEN, MELISSA; Northern HS; Mechanicsburg, PA; (Y); 12/200; Nwsp Ed-Chief; Score Keeper; Stat Sftbl; High Hon Roll; Hon Roll; Sec NHS; Rotary Awd; Jrnlsm Achvt Awd Patriot News 86; Womens Club Schlrshp 86; Pres Acdmc Ftns Awd 86; Millersville U; Elem Educ.

DILLER, JEFF; Highlands SR HS; Natrona Hts, PA; (Y); Teachers Aide; School Play; Off Stu Cncl; L Ftbl; L Wrstlng; Hon Roll; Jr NHS; NHS; Mst Valuable Wrstlr 85-86; Criminology.

DILLI, CHRISTINE; Bethlehem Catholic HS; Bethlehem, PA; (Y); Red Cross Aide; Bsktbl; Twrlr; Hon Roll; Englsh Tm 83; FL ST U; Psych.

DILLING, BRENDA; Central HS; Roaring Spring, PA; (Y); Church Yth Grp; Cmnty Wkr; Band; Drm Mjr(t); Cit Awd; Miss U S Tn Pgnt Fnlst 86; Miss Westrn PA US Tn Pgnt Fnlst; Pittsburg Bty Acadmy; Csmtlgy.

DILLING, DEANA; Northern Bedford County HS; Hopewell, PA; (Y); Sec Trs Church Yth Grp; Math Clb; SADD; Chorus; School Musical; Yrbk Bus Mgr; Yrbk Stf; Var JV Bsktbl; Hon Roll; Trs Art Clb; PA Rural Ltr Carriers Jr Pres 85-86; Trvl.

DILLMAN, DENISE; West Perry HS; Loysville, PA; (Y); VP Church Yth Grp; French Clb; Band; Color Guard; Concert Band; Mrchg Band; School Play; Yrbk Stf; JV Var Sftbl; Law.

DILLMAN, TERRI; Exeter HS; Reading, PA; (Y); JA; Band; Trk; Eng Prof.

DILLON, CARLEY; Octorara HS; Cochranville, PA; (Y); 5/161; SADD; Rptr Nwsp Rptr; Lit Mag; Rep Frsh Cls; Rep Soph Cls; Rep Jr Cls; JV Var Cheerleading; JV Var Fld Hcky; Hon Roll; Jr NHS; Olympcs Of Mind; Pa Gov Schl Of The Arts Semi-Flnst Poetry; Sec Of Stu Forum.

DILLON, JOSEPH M; Neshaminy Langhorne HS; Levittown, PA; (Y); Ski Clb; JV Bowling; Hon Roll; NHS.

DILLON, KATHY; Moshannon Valley HS; Houtzdale, PA; (Y); VP Spanish Clb; Chorus; Concert Band; Mrchg Band; School Play; Sec Jr Cls; Var Capt Cheerleading; NHS; Church Yth Grp; Ski Clb; Natl Wnnr/Intermediate Clss/Natl Piano Auditions 84; Schl Rep To Hugh O Brian Ldrshp Sem 85; Bus Admin.

DILLON, KIM; Connellsville Area HS; Scottdale, PA; (Y); Sec Church Yth Grp; Office Aide; Band; Chorus; Church Choir; Mrchg Band; Orch; School Musical; Symp Band; Stat Bsktbl; Pittsburgh Bty Acad.

DILLON, LARRY; York County Vo-Tech; Red Lion, PA; (Y); VICA; Stage Crew; Im Bsbl; JV Ftbl; Hon Roll; Outstndng Stu Of Mnth 82 & 83; Capt Ftbl Tm 82; Mach Oprtr.

DILLON, WILLIAM; Plum SR HS; Verona, PA; (Y); 1/381; Church Yth Grp; Ski Clb; SADD; Varsity Clb; Pres Mrchg Band; Pres Symp Band; Var L Swmmng; Bausch & Lomb Sci Awd; High Hon Roll; Pres NHS; PA JR Acad Sci 1st Plc Reg 2nd Plc ST 86; Outstndng Stu Awd 83-84; Engr.

DILLS, TAMMIE; Spring-Ford HS; Collegeville, PA; (Y); 20/250; Band; Bsktbl; Socr; Sftbl; Hon Roll; Archtr.

DILTS, VIVIAN; Philipsburg-Osceola HS; West Decatur, PA; (Y); Drama Clb; GAA; Hosp Aide; Letterman Clb; Pep Clb; Ski Clb; SADD; Stu Cncl; Bsktbl; Cheerleading; Pschlgy.

DILUCENTE, ANTONIETTA; East Allegheny HS; N Versailles, PA; (Y); 15/209; Library Aide; Hon Roll; NHS; Duquesne U; Bus Ecnmcs.

DILUIGI, PATTY; Highlands SR HS; Natrona Hts, PA; (Y); DECA; Mrchg Band; Symp Band; Highlands Schlstc Achvt Awd 84-86.

DIMARCELLA, DANIEL; Bishop Kenrick HS; Norristown, PA; (Y); Boy Scts; Cmnty Wkr; Computer Clb; Science Clb; Var Bsktbl; Var Ftbl; Compu Sci.

DIMARCO, CHRISTINE; Saint Hubert HS; Philadelphia, PA; (Y); 139/367; Art Clb; Church Yth Grp; Chorus; Cheerleading; American Legion Awd; Interior Dsgn.

DIMEDIO, STACY; West Chester East HS; West Chester, PA; (Y); JA; Gym; Hon Roll; Spanish NHS; Bloomsburg U; Mass Cmmnctns.

DIMENNO, JOSEPH; Anon Mc Millan HS; Canonsburg, PA; (Y); 5/390; VP French Clb; Ski Clb; VP Soph Cls; VP Jr Cls; Pres Sr Cls; VP Stu Cncl; Gym; High Hon Roll; NHS; Amer Lgn Awd 84; HOBY Fndtn Awd 85; PA Gov Schl For Intl Stu Schlrshp 86; Law.

DIMM, LAURIE ANN; Shamokin Area HS; Shamokin, PA; (Y); 10/179; VP Camera Clb; Cmnty Wkr; Ed Yrbk Bus Mgr; High Hon Roll; Hon Roll; Kiwanis Awd; NHS; Church Yth Grp; Drama Clb; Science Clb; Svc Awd, Highest GPA Cler Ofc 86; Stu Mtnh Elks 85; Bus.

DIMMERLING, CHRISTOPHER; Nativity B V M HS; Pottsville, PA; (Y); Church Yth Grp; SADD; Church Choir; Variety Show; Rep Frsh Cls; Var L Bsbl; Var L Bsktbl; L Capt Crs Cntry; Hon Roll; Prfct Atten Awd; Sci Fair 2nd Pl 84; Stu Of Mnth 85; Qlfd ST Comptn X-Cntry 85; Tchng.

DIMMICK, JACK; Mahanoy Area HS; Mahanoy City, PA; (Y); Church Yth Grp; Cmnty Wkr; Letterman Clb; Ski Clb; Varsity Clb; Y-Teens; School Play; Stage Crew; Variety Show; Stu Cncl.

DIMMICK, MATTHEW; Northampton Area SR HS; Northampton, PA; (Y); Church Yth Grp; VICA; Church Choir; Cabinetmkng.

DIMOVSKI, ZORAN; Central Dauphin East HS; Steelton, PA; (Y); Boy Scts; Spanish Clb; Bsbl; Ftbl; Socr; Tennis; Trk; Vllybl; Wt Lftg; Wrstlng; Attndnc Awd 84; Penn ST; Comp Sci.

DINANT, SCOTT; Philipsburg-Osceola HS; Philipsburg, PA; (Y); 12/255; Letterman Clb; Varsity Clb; Yrbk Ed-Chief; Rep Stu Cncl; Im Badmtn; L Var Bsbl; Var Ftbl; Im Vllybl; Im Wt Lftg; Hon Roll; Engrng.

DINAPOLI, DEAN; Penn Trafford HS; Irwin, PA; (Y); Ski Clb; Spanish Clb; Capt Varsity Clb; Bsbl; Bsktbl; Diving; Ftbl; Capt Socr; Swmmng; Trk; Chem Engrng.

DINELLO, RHONDA; New Brighton Area HS; New Brighton, PA; (Y); 39/154; GAA; Varsity Clb; Coach Actv; Capt L Trk; Aud/Vis; Trs Church Yth Grp; Computer Clb; Sec JA; Pep Clb; Spanish Clb; Beaver Cnty Jr Miss Pgnt Finalst 85; May Ct 86; Jr Womns Clb Girl Of Mnth 86; W VA U; Phys Ther.

DINGER, MICHELLE; Schuylkill Haven Area HS; Schuylkill Haven, PA; (S); Am Leg Aux Girls St; Church Yth Grp; FCA; Library Aide; Pep Clb; Science Clb; Spanish Clb; Chorus; School Play; Yrbk Stf.

DINH, SON; Bishop Mc Devitt HS; Highspire, PA; (Y); Art Clb; Cmnty Wkr; Vllybl; Synod Trinity Schlrshp 86; Drexel U; Elec Engr.

DINKINS, LA TANYA; Steelton-Highspire HS; Steelton, PA; (Y); 31/99; Church Yth Grp; Computer Clb; FBLA; Yrbk Stf; VP Sr Cls; Pres Rep Stu Cncl; Var JV Bsktbl; Var Cheerleading; Hon Roll; Library Aide; Accntng.

DINNOCENTI, BRIAN; Spring-Ford HS; Royersford, PA; (S); 12/258; JV Bsbl; Var Ftbl; Var Trk; Im Vllybl; Var Wt Lftg; JV Wrstlng; Hon Roll; NHS; Writer Yr 86; Engr.

DINSE, DANIEL; Northeast Bradford HS; Rome, PA; (Y); Chess Clb; Church Yth Grp; Computer Clb; Capt Quiz Bowl; Band; Chorus; Church Choir; Hst Stu Cncl; Var Wrstlng; High Hon Roll; Houghton Coll; Dntstry.

DINSMORE, DEBRA; Punxsutawney Area HS; Punxsutawney, PA; (Y); Trs Church Yth Grp; Debate Tm; Drama Clb; French Clb; Chorus; Church Choir; School Musical; Hon Roll; Vet.

DIODATO, GINA; York County Area Vo Tech; York, PA; (Y); Chess Clb; VICA; School Musical; Hon Roll; Machinist Engr.

DIOMEDO, ADAM; Notre Dame HS; Easton, PA; (Y); NFL; Scholastic Bowl; School Play; Nwsp Rptr; Nwsp Stf; Trs Stu Cncl; High Hon Roll; Hon Roll; Outstndng Excllnc Art 85-86; Appld Dsgn.

DION, BILL; Council Rock HS; Wash Crsng, PA; (Y); 135/845; Church Yth Grp; Political Wkr; JV Socr; Im Vllybl; Im Wt Lftg; JV Wrstlng; Hon Roll; Pvt Pilots License 86; Newtown Bsbl-Top 8 In US 84; Pol Sci.

DIONNE, EDWARD; Northampton HS; Walnutport, PA; (Y); 9/439; Jazz Band; Var Capt Swmmng; Var L Trk; NHS; Rep Soph Cls; Var Crs Cntry; High Hon Roll; Air Frc ROTC Schlrshp; Exchng Clb Boy Mnth 86; Ovr All Schlr/Athlt 86; Penn ST U; Arch.

DIORIO, CHARLES; Shamokin Area HS; Shamokin, PA; (Y); Camera Clb; Church Yth Grp; Orch.

DIORIO, DENA; Greensburg Central Catholic HS; Mt Pleasant, PA; (Y); Yrbk Stf; High Hon Roll; Hon Roll; Psyclgy.

DIPPOLD, MARCIA; Elk County Christian HS; St Marys, PA; (Y); 10/80; Hosp Aide; Library Aide; JV Cheerleading; Hon Roll; Marine Biology.

DIRIENEO, RICHARD; Cathedral Prep Of Erie; Erie, PA; (Y); 34/216; Trs Frsh Cls; Trs Soph Cls; Trs Jr Cls; Trs Sr Cls; Var L Bsktbl; Var L Golf; Hon Roll; All Trny Tm Jamestown Bsktbl Trnmnt 86; Acctng.

DISABATO, LISA; Altoona Area HS; Altoona, PA; (Y); Cmnty Wkr; Computer Clb; German Clb; Var Stat Bsktbl; Var Capt Tennis; Var Trk; Var Wt Lftg; Hon Roll; Prfct Atten Awd; Sprtsmnshp Awd Tnnis 86; Child Dev.

DISANGRO, MARY; St Hubert HS; Philadelphia, PA; (Y); 8/376; Art Clb; Dance Clb; Lit Mag; Soph Cls; Sr Cls; Stu Cncl; Jr NHS; NHS; HOBY Yth Fndtn Ldrshp Sem Rep 84; Drexel U; Fash Merch.

DISARIO, WILLIAM; Freedom HS; Bethlehem, PA; (Y); 50/450; Church Yth Grp; JA; Science Clb; Yrbk Phtg; Yrbk Stf; Golf; Hon Roll.

DISHAUZI, DAVID A; Center HS; Aliquippa, PA; (Y); Computer Clb; Letterman Clb; Spanish Clb; Varsity Clb; Yrbk Stf; L Socr; Hon Roll; NHS; Outstndng Spnsh Stu Adw 84-85; Gannon U; Chrprctc.

DISQUE, STACI; Union Area JR SR HS; New Castle, PA; (Y); French Clb; VP FHA; Office Aide; Pep Clb; Drill Tm; Var L Bsktbl; Var L Trk; Var Vllybl; Yth Educ Assoc VP 85-86; Behrend Coll; Spec Educ.

DISTEFANO, MARY; Bishop Shanahan HS; W Chester, PA; (Y); 43/218; Cmnty Wkr; Dance Clb; Yrbk Stf; Lit Mag; Stat Bsktbl; Var Tennis; Var Trk; Hon Roll; Bus Adm.

DITRI, ANGELA; St Huberts HS; Philadelphia, PA; (Y); 90/380; Hosp Aide; Office Aide; Orch; Yrbk Stf.

DITRI, PATRICIA; St Huberts HS For Girls; Philadelphia, PA; (Y); 41/371; Hosp Aide; Yrbk Stf.

DITRICH, LAURA; Villa Maria Acad; Erie, PA; (Y); 7/130; Church Yth Grp; Latin Clb; Ski Clb; School Musical; JV Trk; DAR Awd; High Hon Roll; NHS; NEDT Awd; Psych.

DITZ, BEVERLY; North Clarion JRSR HS; Fryburg, PA; (Y); 13/96; French Clb; Varsity Clb; Trs Jr Cls; Rep Stu Cncl; Capt Trk; Var Vllybl; Hon Roll; NEDT Awd; SADD; Bsktbl; PA Fre Entrprs Wk Schlrshp 86; Jr Hstrns; Prm Crt; Mdcl Secy.

DITZ, CAROL; Venango Christian HS; Fryburg, PA; (Y); 2/42; High Hon Roll; NHS; Prfct Atten Awd; Pres Schlr; Rotary Awd; Sal; Immclt Concptn Medal Excllnc Frnch 86; Clarion U PA.

DITZLER, MARCIE ELIZABETH; Lancaster Catholic HS; Conestoga, PA; (Y); 21/196; Am Leg Aux Girls St; JCL; Nwsp Sprt Ed; Frsh Cls; Soph Cls; Jr Cls; Sr Cls; Sftbl; Swmmng; NHS.

DITZLER, ROBERT; Lebanon Catholic HS; Lebanon, PA; (Y); Computer Clb; Ski Clb; Chorus; Im Vllybl; Yth Govt Prg; Comp Opr Cood Lebanon 85-86; Comp Prgmmr.

DIVELY, ANGELA; Claysburg-Kimmel HS; E Freedom, PA; (Y); CAP; VP FTA; Pres SADD; Sec Trs Band; Sec Trs Chorus; School Musical; Yrbk Phtg; VP Sr Cls; JP Sousa Awd; Outstndng Female Cadet Offcr/CAP Grp 1500 86; Amelia Earhart Awd 85; Billy Mitchell Awd 83; Penn ST U; Telecomm.

DIVELY, BRENDA JOANNE; Plymouth-Whitemarsh HS; Norristown, PA; (Y); 9/360; CAP; Library Aide; Mathletes; Math Clb; Office Aide; Service Clb; Band; Chorus; Concert Band; School Musical; Semper Fidelis Awd 86; Sperry Corp Awd 86; IBM Watson Awd 86; Cornell U; Elec Eng.

DIVELY, CHRIS; Shanksville Stoneycreek HS; Central City, PA; (S); 11/31; Chorus; Color Guard; School Play; Bsktbl; Hon Roll; Church Yth Grp; FHA; JV Cheerleading; Ldrshp & Svc Awd 85; Clss VP 82-83; Clss Pres 83-84; RN.

DIVELY, CRAIG; Claysburg Kimmel HS; Claysburg, PA; (Y); 15/70; Drama Clb; FFA; Varsity Clb; Chorus; School Musical; School Play; Stage Crew; Rep Stu Cncl; Var Ftbl; Var Tennis; CACT Awd 86; Claysburg Pblc Lbry Vlntr Awd 86; Mdl Legsltr ST Edtgr In Chf 85; PA ST; Elem Ed.

DIVELY, JODI; Claysburg-Kimmel HS; Claysburg, PA; (Y); 6/72; Camera Clb; Church Yth Grp; SADD; Varsity Clb; School Musical; Nwsp Stf; Yrbk Phtg; Pres Sr Cls; Stu Cncl; Var L Bsktbl; G S Dively Schlrshp, Amer Lgn Awd & Nwspr Art Edtr/Art Dept Awd 86; Temple U PA; Art Thrpy.

DIVINS, DEE; Union HS; Sligo, PA; (Y); 5/60; SADD; Chorus; Flag Corp; Mrchg Band; French Clb; Pep Clb; Stu Cncl; Score Keeper; High Hon Roll; Hon Roll; Mth.

DIXIT, VAISHALI; Laurel Highlands SR HS; Uniontown, PA; (S); 1/365; Math Tm; Temple Yth Grp; Madrigals; School Musical; Stu Cncl; Twrlr; NHS; Ntl Merit Ltr; NEDT Awd; IN Clsscl Dance Grad 83; Drama Awd; Med.

DIXON, DEE DEE; United HS; Vintondale, PA; (Y); 52/159; Library Aide; Ski Clb; Chorus; School Musical; Yrbk Stf; Sec Jr Cls; Sec Sr Cls; Sec Stu Cncl; JV Var Cheerleading; Hon Roll; Penn ST U; Arch.

DIXON, JOHN; Towanda Area HS; Wysox, PA; (Y); Trk; Wt Lftg; Hon Roll; PA ST U; Spnsh.

DIXON JR, KENNETH C; Abington Heights School Dist HS; Clarks Summit, PA; (Y); Boy Scts; Church Yth Grp; Church Choir; Mrchg Band; Htl/Rest Mgmt.

DIXON, LISE; Highlands SR HS; Natrona Hgts, PA; (Y); DECA; Girl Scts; Chorus; Hon Roll; Brwn Awd 82-86; Gld Awd 82; Air Frc; Air Trfc Cntrl.

DIXON, MICHELE; Avon Grove HS; Lincoln Univ, PA; (Y); 23/150; SADD; Nwsp Stf; Var Tennis; High Hon Roll; U Delaware; Psychlgy.

DIXON, RICK; Central Christian HS; Du Bois, PA; (Y); Art Clb; Hon Roll; Amercn Leg & Mst Chrstn Boy Awds 80; Hghst Accntng Awd 86; Penn ST Du Bois Camps; Bus Adm.

DIXON, RODERICK C; Harrisburg HS; Harrisburg, PA; (Y); Church Yth Grp; Office Aide; Ski Clb; Nwsp Stf; Socr; Hon Roll; NHS; Prsdntl Acad Ftns Awd Prncpls Awd 86; Sprntndnts Awd 86; U Of Pittsburgh; Mech Engrng.

DIXON, TAMMIE; Rochester JR & SR HS; Rochester, PA; (Y); 3/100; French Clb; Ski Clb; Hon Roll; Bus.

DLUGOKECKI, BERNADETTE; St Huberton Catholic HS For Girls; Philadelphia, PA; (Y); 8/367; Aud/Vis; Sec Speech Tm; Stage Crew; Nwsp Ed-Chief; Nwsp Rptr; Nwsp Stf; Lit Mag; High Hon Roll; NHS; Prfct Atten Awd; Pres Acadmc Ftnss Awd 86; Audio Visual Club Aide Awd 84-86; Various Speech Team Awds 82-84:Schl Awd 86; Temple U; Bus Adm.

DNEASTER, MICHAEL; Meyersdale Area HS; Garrett, PA; (S); CAP; VP Spanish Clb; Varsity Clb; Trs Band; School Musical; Yrbk Stf; L Ftbl; High Hon Roll; NHS; CAP Hon Cadet 84; CAP Billy Mitchell Awd 84; Pre-Law.

DOAK, ERIC; West Allegheny HS; Oakdale, PA; (Y); 41/208; Computer Clb; FBLA; Ski Clb; Spanish Clb; Lit Mag; JV Bsbl; High Hon Roll; Hon Roll; Prfct Atten Awd; Engrng Schlrshp Frm CCAC 86-87; CCAC; Engrng.

DOBBS, MARC; Ford City JR SR HS; Vandergrift, PA; (Y); 24/163; Church Yth Grp; Pres 4-H; Trs Chorus; School Musical; Var L Ftbl; Var L Trk; 4-H Awd; High Hon Roll; Hon Roll; NHS; Blueform Cnty Wnnr 84; Penn ST.

DOBER, GERRAD; Hampton HS; Gibsonia, PA; (Y); Mrchg Band; Stage Crew; Yrbk Phtg; Coach Actv; JV Ftbl; High Hon Roll; Hon Roll; 1st Pl Blck & White Phtgrphy Westrn PA Indstrl Arts Fair 84; Penn ST; Aerosp Engrng.

DOBERNECK, DIANE; State College Area HS; State College, PA; (Y); 49/560; Rep Church Yth Grp; Library Aide; Mgr Mrchg Band; Rep Soph Cls; Im Socr; Im Vllybl; Hon Roll; Art.

DOBICH, LISA; Aliquippa HS; Aliquippa, PA; (S); 12/160; Exploring; French Clb; Office Aide; Band; Mrchg Band; Yrbk Stf; Hon Roll; NHS; Ntl Phys Educ Awd 86; U Of Pittsburgh; Dntl Hygnst.

DOBIS, ELAINE; Langley HS; Pittsburgh, PA; (Y); Church Yth Grp; Pep Clb; Chorus; School Musical; Yrbk Stf; Var Cheerleading; High Hon Roll; Hon Roll; Jr NHS; NHS.

DOBO, JUDY; West Branch HS; Hawk Run, PA; (S); 3/115; Spanish Clb; Varsity Clb; Stu Cncl; JV Var Cheerleading; Sftbl; Hon Roll.

DOBRANETSKI III, EDWARD B; Gateway HS; Monroeville, PA; (Y); Chess Clb; Computer Clb; Exploring; Ski Clb; Band; Concert Band; Jazz Band; Mrchg Band; Symp Band; Variety Show; Grove City College; Pre Law.

DOBRANSKI, ANN MARIE; John S Fine HS; Nanticoke, PA; (Y); Church Yth Grp; FBLA; Hosp Aide; Ski Clb; Chorus; High Schl Let Chorus 85; Luzerne County CC; Gen Educ.

DOBRANSKI, MICHELLE; Northwestern Lehigh HS; Germansvile, PA; (Y); 34/169; Drama Clb; PAVAS; Chorus; School Musical; School Play; Stage Crew; Swing Chorus; Variety Show; Hon Roll; Stu Mnth 85; Secndry Ed.

DOBRANSKY, JILL I; Brownsville Area HS; W Brownsville, PA; (Y); Cmnty Wkr; Drama Clb; Hosp Aide; Intnl Clb; Math Clb; Office Aide; Ski Clb; SADD; Teachers Aide; Yrbk Bus Mgr; CA U; Tchr.

DOBRICH, MARY; Mohawk JRSR HS; Bessemer, PA; (S); Trs Latin Clb; Band; Concert Band; Mrchg Band; Pres Soph Cls; Pres Jr Cls; Stat Bsbl; High Hon Roll; Hon Roll; NHS; Bus.

DOBSON JR, JON; Lewiston Area HS; Lewistown, PA; (Y); 27/263; AFS; Debate Tm; Key Clb; Var Trk; Im Vllybl; High Hon Roll; 2nd Pl Dist Debate Comptn 86; Acctng.

DOBSON, KATIE; Central Columbia HS; Millville, PA; (Y); 23/180; Key Clb; Pep Clb; Varsity Clb; School Musical; Jr Cls; Swmmng; Trk; Hon Roll; Central Columbia Ed Assn Scholar 86; Prom Queen 86; PA ST U; Bus Adm.

DOBSON, MARK; General Mc Lane HS; Mckean, PA; (Y); Church Yth Grp; Ski Clb; Hon Roll; NHS.

DOBSON, VALERIE; Lower Dauphin HS; Hummelstown, PA; (Y); Chorus; Drill Tm; Mrchg Band; Var Capt Cheerleading; Twrlr; Hon Roll; Dance Instr.

DOCK, CHRISTINE; Crestwood HS; Mountaintop, PA; (Y); 22/243; FBLA; Ski Clb; Sec Soph Cls; VP Stu Cncl; Var JV Cheerleading; L Var Crs Cntry; JV Mgr(s); Var L Trk; Var High Hon Roll; Var NHS; Acctnt.

DOCKERY, JAMES D; Central Dauphin HS; Harrishurg, PA; (Y); Computer Clb; Ski Clb; Rep Stu Cncl; Var Tennis; Im Vllybl; Hon Roll; Pres Acadmc Ftnss Awd 86; PA ST.

DOCKSTADER, JOHN; Dawningtown SR HS; Exton, PA; (Y); 59/563; Boy Scts; Camera Clb; Church Yth Grp; Ski Clb; Spanish Clb; Chorus; Off Stu Cncl; Socr; High Hon Roll; Hon Roll; Eagl Sct 86; Bob Shannn Mem Schlrshp 86; Ynglf & Cmpgnes; Aerontcl Engrng.

DOCTOR, JULIE; Butler SR HS; Butler, PA; (Y); Dance Clb; Hosp Aide; JA; Gym; Sftbl; Hon Roll; Bus.

DODEK, RICHARD; Highlands HS; Brackenridge, PA; (Y); Key Clb; Teachers Aide; Rep Band; Socr; Hon Roll; Jr NHS; NHS; Prfct Atten Awd; Drama Clb; Concert Band; Alle-Kiski Hnrs Bnd 86; Mid-East Msc Fstvl 86; Engr.

DODGE, BRUCE; Sharpsville Area HS; Greenville, PA; (Y); Acdmc All Amer Lrg Div 85-86; Metllrgcl Engrng.

DODSON, AMY; Eastern HS; York, PA; (Y); Church Yth Grp; Chorus; School Musical; Hon Roll; Grace Brthrn Nrth Atlntc Dist Grl Yr 86-87; Pres Physcl Ftns Awd 85-86; Grace Brthrn Lmr Rep Dist 84; Mansfield; Elem Tchr.

DODSON, CHRIS; Girard College HS; Wilmington, DE; (Y); Camera Clb; Letterman Clb; Ski Clb; Yrbk Stf; Var Bsbl; Hon Roll; Yrbk Rptr; Var Wrstlng; Essy Awd; Shrt Stry Awd; Street Hcky Vrsty Lttrmn; U Of DE.

DODSON, DEBBIE; Clysburg-Kimmel HS; E Freedom, PA; (Y); 3/77; Pres FBLA; German Clb; Varsity Clb; Yrbk Stf; Sec Frsh Cls; Rep Stu Cncl; Capt Var Cheerleading; Hon Roll; NHS; Rotary Awd; Natl Bus Hnr Soc Sec 86; D Emmert Brumbaugh Mem Scholar 86; Bus & Prof Wmns Grl Mnth 86; Altoona Schl Commerce; Med Sec.

DODSON, DENA; Everett HS; Clearville, PA; (S); 8/107; Computer Clb; Sec GAA; Letterman Clb; VP Spanish Clb; Band; Var L Bsktbl; Var L Socr; Var L Sftbl; Hon Roll; Spanish NHS; Elem Ed.

DODSON, GAYLE; Claysburg-Kimmel HS; Claysburg, PA; (Y); German Clb; Speech Tm; SADD; Band; Concert Band; School Musical; Sec Soph Cls; Trs Jr Cls; Capt Twrlr; Hon Roll; Bus Adm.

DODSON, GREGORY P; Greensburg Central Catholic HS; Greensburg, PA; (Y); 22/243; Chess Clb; Computer Clb; Pres JA; Trs JCL; Im Vllybl; High Hon Roll; NHS; Latin Clb; Science Clb; Im Bowling; Comptitv Schlrshp-Duquesne U 85-86; Excllnc Accntng 85-86; Prt Time Tchr 85-86; Duquesne U; Bus Adm.

DOEBLER, ANTOINETTE; Meadowbrook Christian Schl; Milton, PA; (S); Church Yth Grp; Office Aide; Teachers Aide; Chorus; Pres Frsh Cls; VP Soph Cls; Cit Awd; Hon Roll; Mst Chrst Like Awd 83-84; Mltn Intrct Clb 85-86; Lbrty Bptst U; Elem Ed.

DOEBLER, CHARLES; Lock Haven HS; Lock Haven, PA; (Y); Chess Clb; German Clb; Model UN; Band; Mrchg Band; NHS; Ecllnc In Chem 85; Mdlyn Shffr Awd Excllnc In Engl 84; Louis L Raff Mem Awd Excllnc In Phycs 86; Boston U; Physcs.

DOEL, PETER; Plum SR HS; Pittsburgh, PA; (Y); AFS; Church Yth Grp; French Clb; Band; Church Choir; School Musical; Symp Band; Hon Roll; Concert Choir.

DOERING, RYAN; Pottsgrave HS; Pottstown, PA; (Y); 17/229; Science Clb; Ski Clb; Spanish Clb; Varsity Clb; Bsbl; High Hon Roll; Hon Roll; NHS; Engrng.

DOHERTY, FRANCIS; Crestwoodd HS; Mountaintop, PA; (Y); 70/265; Math Clb; Ski Clb; Bsbl; Bsktbl; Ftbl; Wt Lftg; Hon Roll; Bus.

DOHERTY, JILL M; Upper Dauphin Area HS; Elizabethville, PA; (Y); 17/105; Am Leg Aux Girls St; School Musical; Yrbk Ed-Chief; Stu Cncl; Cheerleading; Swmmng; Trk; NHS; NEDT Awd; DECA; PA ST U; Frnch.

DOHEY, MICHELLE; Hempfield Area SR HS; Greensburg, PA; (Y); 89/657; Trs French Clb; Pep Clb; Ski Clb; Nwsp Rptr; Yrbk Stf; Stat Trk; High Hon Roll; Hon Roll; Jr NHS; Trs Girl Scts; Frnch Awd 83; Perfct Attndnc 84-85; U Of Pittsburgh; Phy Thrpy.

DOHNER, BRET JONATHAN; Cedar Crest HS; Lebanon, PA; (Y); German Clb; Latin Clb; Pep Clb; Spanish Clb; Varsity Clb; Bowling; Capt Crs Cntry; Capt Trk; Vllybl; Ntl Merit Ltr; U Of Pittsburgh; Chem Engrng.

DOKAS, PATTY; Hanover Area JR SR HS; Wilkes Barre, PA; (Y).

DOLAN, ALICE; Bradford Area HS; Bradford, PA; (Y); AFS; Ski Clb; Yrbk Phtg; Yrbk Stf; Pres Frsh Cls; Rep Stu Cncl; Capt Cheerleading; L Trk; Hon Roll; Bsktbl; U Of Pittsburgh; Cmnctns.

DOLAN, HEATHER; Cameron County HS; Emporium, PA; (Y); Church Yth Grp; Pres Spanish Clb; Band; Concert Band; Mrchg Band; Yrbk Phtg; VP Soph Cls; Capt Cheerleading; Trk; Capt Twrlr.

DOLAN, KELLY; North Hills SR HS; Pittsburgh, PA; (S); 6/505; Church Yth Grp; Keywanettes; Library Aide; Office Aide; Q&S; Ski Clb; Chorus; Nwsp Bus Mgr; High Hon Roll; NHS; U Of Pittsburgh; Comp Sci.

DOLAN, TOM; Sharpsville HS; Sharpsville, PA; (S); #1 In Class; Camera Clb; Church Yth Grp; Drama Clb; German Clb; Science Clb; Thesps; Band; Chorus; Church Choir; Concert Band.

DOLBY, MICHELE L; Brookville HS; Summerville, PA; (Y); Drama Clb; FBLA; FHA; German Clb; Pep Clb; SADD; Acpl Chr; Band; Church Choir; Drm Mjr(t); Summrvl & Jeffrsn Cnty Fire Qn 86.

DOLBY II, ROBERT H; East Brody JR SR HS; Chicora, PA; (Y); 2/84; Church Yth Grp; Cmnty Wkr; SADD; Varsity Clb; VICA; Rep Frsh Cls; Im Bsbl; Var L Bsktbl; L Capt Ftbl; Im Wt Lftg; Engrng.

DOLENCE, PHIL; Johnstown HS; Johnstown, PA; (Y); Aud/Vis; French Clb; Ski Clb; Band; Concert Band; Variety Show; Nwsp Phtg; Yrbk Phtg; U Of Pittsburgh.

DOLEZAL, KARI; New Hope Salebury HS; New Hope, PA; (Y); FBLA; Mgr Socr; High Hon Roll; Hon Roll; NHS; Presdntl Acadmc Ftns Awd 85-86; Villanova U; Chem Engr.

DOLFI, CHRIS; Crestwood HS; Mountaintop, PA; (Y); Ski Clb; JV Bsktbl; Var L Crs Cntry; Var Co-Capt Socr; Var L Trk; High Hon Roll; NHS; Ntl Merit Ltr.

DOLFI, RHONDA; Wyoming Area HS; W Pittston, PA; (Y); French Clb; Vllybl; Long Beach; Hotel/Rest Mgmt.

DOLINGER, STEPHANIE; Kennard-Dale HS; Airville, PA; (Y); #7 In Class; Church Yth Grp; French Clb; Chorus; Church Choir; Stage Crew; JV Bsktbl; Var Crs Cntry; Hon Roll; NHS; Educ.

DOLL, ERIC; Central SR HS; York, PA; (Y); 36/224; Yrbk Stf; Hon Roll; Acad Lttr 86; Juniata; Pre-Med.

DOLL, JAMES; Bishop Kenrick HS; Norristown, PA; (Y); Church Yth Grp; Ftbl; Swmmng; Aerontcs.

DOLL, KAREN; Northeastern HS; Mt Wolf, PA; (Y); Chorus; Erly Chldhd Ed.

DOLL, STACEY; Northeastern HS; Mt Wolf, PA; (Y); AFS; Aud/Vis; Church Yth Grp; Thesps; Acpl Chr; Band; Chorus; Church Choir; Concert Band; Jazz Band; Gld Music Awd 84; Yorks Stdnt Mnth 85; York Cnty JR Miss Fnlst 86; Shippensburg; Europn Hstry.

DOLLENBERG, HEIDI; Springside Schl; Maple Glen, PA; (Y); Orch; Nwsp Stf; Sec Trs Soph Cls; JV Tennis; JV Var Vllybl; High Hon Roll; Mbr Cum Laude Soc 86; U Of ; Va Bk Awd 86; Phila Chmcl Soc Chem Awd 85.

DOLTON, JENNIFER; Hempfield Area SR HS; Greensburg, PA; (Y); FBLA; Spanish Clb; Band; Concert Band; Mrchg Band; High Hon Roll; Hon Roll; Prfct Atten Awd; Bus Mgt.

DOLUISIO, MICHAEL; Freedom HS; Bethlehem, PA; (Y); 19/464; Math Tm; Pres Concert Band; Jazz Band; Pres Mrchg Band; Trs Orch; Mgr School Play; High Hon Roll; NHS; Ntl Merit Ltr; Mgr Drama Clb; Outstndng Musician Awd Wrld Of Music 85; Schrlshp To Berklee Coll Of Music For Outstndng Rhythm 86; Bus Law.

DOMARACKI, CHRISTINE; Connellsville Area SR HS; Connellsville, PA; (Y); Sec Church Yth Grp; Drama Clb; VP Sec 4-H; SADD; Trs Jr Cls; Stat Bsktbl; Stat Ftbl; Mgr(s); 4-H Awd; Hon Roll; High Achvt Eng; Air Force; Aeront Engr.

DOMBROSKY, MICHELLE; Mount Pleasant Area HS; Mt Pleasant, PA; (Y); 50/250; German Clb; Band; Concert Band; Mrchg Band; Pep Band; Nwsp Rptr; Bsktbl; Sftbl; Hon Roll; Chenille Awd 86.

DOMCHEK, SUSAN; Bethlehem Catholic HS; Bethlehem, PA; (Y); 2/219; Key Clb; NFL; Ski Clb; School Musical; School Play; VP Sr Cls; Var Capt Cheerleading; NHS; Ntl Merit Ltr; Girl Scts; Nalt Convntn For Forensics 84; ST Key Club Convntn 2nd Pl In Oratorical Contst 85; Dartmouth; Engrng.

DOMEN, DAVID M; Laurel Highlands SR HS; Uniontown, PA; (Y); Chorus; Bsktbl; Golf; CA U PA; Sec Ed.

DOMENICO, FRANK; Mt Pleasant SR HS; Greensburg, PA; (Y); Ski Clb; JV Wrstlng; High Hon Roll; Hon Roll.

DOMER, CHRISTINA; Red Lion SR HS; York, PA; (Y); 7/337; Church Yth Grp; School Musical; School Play; Nwsp Rptr; Yrbk Stf; High Hon Roll; Hon Roll; NHS; Acad All Str 86; Part Outstdng Young AMS 84; Chrch Swthrt Qn 85; Lancaster Bible Coll; Elem Educ.

DOMHOFF, CONSTANCE; Seneca Valley SR HS; Harmony, PA; (Y); VICA; Var Bsktbl; Im Bowling; L Var Sftbl; Hon Roll; Engrng.

DOMIANO, MICHELE; Old Forge HS; Old Forge, PA; (Y); Ski Clb; Var Bsktbl; Var Sftbl; Hon Roll; Jr NHS; NHS; Secy Of Natl Hnr Socy 86-87; Gregg Typing Awd 86; Hnrb Mntn-Girls Bsktbl 86; Optmtrst.

DOMINGUEZ, DANIEL; Wm Allen HS; Allentown, PA; (Y); Boys Clb Am; Pres Church Yth Grp; VP VICA; Church Choir; Rep Jr Cls; NHS; Exploring; Hon Roll; North Eastern Christian JC.

DOMINICK, LISA MICHELE; Pittston Area HS; Pittston, PA; (Y); Band; Concert Band; Jazz Band; Mrchg Band; Church Yth Grp; Chorus; Church Choir; Hlth Care.

DOMINY, MICHAEL; Parkland HS; Allentown, PA; (Y); 78/407; Varsity Clb; L Trk; Hon Roll; Syracuse U; Bus.

DOMITROVICH, LAURA; Our Lady Of The Sacred Heart HS; Aliquippa, PA; (Y); NFL; Concert Band; School Musical; School Play; Bowling; NHS; Ntl Hist & Govt Awd 86; All Amer Acadmc Awd 86; Phy Therapy.

DOMOGAUER, TAMMY; Wyalusing Valley JR SR HS; Wyalusing, PA; (Y); Church Yth Grp; German Clb; Library Aide; Chorus; Church Choir; Var JV Cheerleading; Stat Mgr(s); Stat Trk; Hon Roll; Socl Wkr.

DOMURAT, MARY JO; Greensburg Central Catholic HS; Greensburg, PA; (Y); 21/248; Teachers Aide; Nwsp Stf; VP Pres Stu Cncl; Capt Bsktbl; L Crs Cntry; Capt Trk; High Hon Roll; Hon Roll; NHS; Letterman Clb; Westmoreland Med Aux Sco Schlrshp 86; Case Western Reserve U; Engr.

DOMYAN, LYNN; Northampton HS; Danielsville, PA; (S); Yrbk Stf; High Hon Roll; Hon Roll; PA ST; Engrng.

DOMYSLAWSKI, KAREN; Shaler SR HS; Allison Pk, PA; (Y); 151/530; Girl Scts; Hosp Aide; Chorus; Flag Corp; School Musical; School Play; Variety Show; Nwsp Stf; Yrbk Phtg; Hon Roll; Ed.

DONAFRIO, CHRISTINE; Shenango HS; New Castle, PA; (Y); JA; Library Aide; Red Cross Aide; Spanish Clb; Nwsp Rptr; Nwsp Stf; Yrbk Rptr; Yrbk Stf; Im Sftbl; Im Vllybl; ST Fnlst In Miss Co-Ed Pgnt 83; Rcvd Schlrshp New Castle Schl Of Bty Clture 86; New Castle Schl; Csmtlgy.

DONAGHY, CHRISTINA; Council Rock HS; Newtown, PA; (Y); Rep Stu Cncl; Var Crs Cntry; Var Socr; Var Trk; Hon Roll; U Of DR; Lib Arts.

DONAHUE, JAMES A; La Salle College HS; Churchvl, PA; (Y); 12/214; Church Yth Grp; Yrbk Bus Mgr; Im Bsktbl; Im Ftbl; NHS; Ntl Merit Ltr; Schlrshps From Navy & Army, La Salle U & Knights Of Columbus 86; U Of PA; Ecnmcs.

DONAHUE, KIMBERLEY; Radnor HS; St Davids, PA; (S); Church Yth Grp; Cmnty Wkr; Drama Clb; Sec Intnl Clb; Hst Speech Tm; Chorus; Church Choir; School Musical; Mgr Stage Crew; Lit Mag.

DONAHUE, LISA M; Council Rock HS; Churchville, PA; (Y); 4/845; Trs Church Yth Grp; Intnl Clb; Variety Show; Var L Cheerleading; High Hon Roll; Hon Roll; Cnty Piano Tchrs Assoc Achvt Awd 85; Vol Piano Concerts.

DONAHUE, MARY; Pittston Area SR HS; Pittston, PA; (Y); Church Yth Grp; Cmnty Wkr; Dance Clb; Key Clb; Ski Clb; Spanish Clb; Yrbk Stf; Psych.

DONAHUE, TAMARA; South Park HS; Library, PA; (S); 18/210; Church Yth Grp; FBLA; Office Aide; Drill Tm; Yrbk Stf; Rep Jr Cls; High Hon Roll; NHS; Ntl Hnr Scty 86; Exc Sec.

DONALD, JAMES; Penn Hills SR HS; Pittsburgh, PA; (Y); Boy Scts; 4-H; Spanish Clb; Band; Hon Roll; Prfct Atten Awd; Duquesne; Pharm.

DONALDSON, ANN; Knoch JR SR HS; Butler, PA; (Y); Am Leg Aux Girls St; Trs German Clb; SADD; School Play; Nwsp Sprt Ed; Sec Jr Cls; VP Rep Stu Cncl; Stat Bsktbl; Var L Trk; NHS.

DONALDSON, BOB; Cambridge Springs HS; Cambridge Springs, PA; (Y); #11 In Class; French Clb; Key Clb; Off Jr Cls; Var Bsbl; Var JV Ftbl; Wt Lftg; High Hon Roll; Crimnl Law.

DONALDSON, DREW; Souderton HS; Souderton, PA; (Y); 65/370; Boy Scts; Camera Clb; Church Yth Grp; Band; Chorus; School Musical; Stage Crew; Socr; Tennis; Vllybl; Sci.

DONALDSON, JERILYNN L; South Philadelphia H S Motivatn; Philadelphia, PA; (Y); Color Guard; Variety Show; Stu Cncl; Crs Cntry; Trk; High Hon Roll; Hon Roll; Prfct Atten Awd; Spec Awd Recgntn Acad Achvt Pgm U PA 85-86; Awd Achvt Shakespeare Cont 86; Ath Awds 84-86; Boston U; Aerospc Engrng.

DONALDSON, MARCI; Gateway SR HS; Monroeville, PA; (Y); 64/509; Church Yth Grp; VP JA; NFL; PAVAS; Pol Sci.

DONALDSON, ROD; Tussey Mountain HS; Saxton, PA; (Y); 1/125; VP Sec Church Yth Grp; Bsbl; Bsktbl; Var L Ftbl; Hon Roll; NHS; Val; Penn ST U; Dntstry.

DONATELLI, SHARON L; Center HS; Aliquippa, PA; (Y); 2/200; Am Leg Aux Girls St; Computer Clb; Exploring; Yrbk Stf; Rep Stu Cncl; Ftbl; JV Var Sftbl; High Hon Roll; NHS; NEDT Awd; Law.

DONATI, DEBBIE; North Pocono HS; Moscow, PA; (Y); Church Yth Grp; Yrbk Stf; L Var Tennis; Hon Roll; NHS; U Scranton; Med Tech.

DONATI, JOANN; Marian HS; Jim Thorpe, PA; (Y); 41/115; Church Yth Grp; French Clb; Office Aide; Ski Clb; SADD; Yrbk Stf; Ftbl; Trk; French Hon Soc; Law.

DONATO, CHRISTINE; Upper Darby HS; Havertown, PA; (Y); Cmnty Wkr; Service Clb; Acpl Chr; Chorus; Yrbk Stf; Sr Cls; Stu Cncl; Sec NHS; Opt Clb Awd; Crtv Wrtg Awd 86; Temple; Telecmnctns.

DONATO, MARK; Penn Hills HS; Pittsburgh, PA; (Y); JA; Ski Clb; Varsity Clb; Stu Cncl; Vllybl; High Hon Roll; Hon Roll; Bus.

DONAWICK, MELINDA J; Unionville HS; West Chester, PA; (Y); 60/283; 4-H; Pep Clb; Yrbk Stf; Rep Frsh Cls; Rep Stu Cncl; Im Sftbl; Im Tennis; High Hon Roll; Hon Roll; Jr NHS; Vet Med.

DONCHES, STEVE; Bethelehem Catholic HS; Bethlehem, PA; (Y); Yrbk Rptr; Pres Sr Cls; Bsktbl; Hon Roll; Pltcs.

DONDERO, CHRISTINE; Stroudsburg HS; Stroudsburg, PA; (Y); #19 In Class; Drama Clb; German Clb; Yrbk Bus Mgr; Lit Mag; High Hon Roll; NHS; JR Acad Sci 85; Top 10 Cls 84-86; Temple U; Phys Thrpy.

DONEL, TIM; Trinity HS; Washington, PA; (Y); 81/374; Aud/Vis; Thesps; Mrchg Band; Stage Crew; Stat Swmmng; OH U; Comm.

DONEY, DE VONNE DANELLE; Waynesburg Central HS; Waynesburg, PA; (Y); Ski Clb; Spanish Clb; Chorus; Jazz Band; L Cheerleading; PMEA JR Dstrct Chrs 84; Cl Qn Rep 86; Beta Alpha; IUP; Arlns.

DONEY, DONNA; Punxsutawney Area HS; Punxsutawney, PA; (Y); Church Yth Grp; FCA; FBLA; SADD; Acpl Chr; Chorus; Church Choir; Hon Roll; Valentine Queen 86; Music Trophey 84; Elem Tchr.

DONGHIA, JAMES; Mohawk JR SR HS; New Castle, PA; (S); Spanish Clb; Trs Varsity Clb; Band; Concert Band; JV Var Ftbl; Var L Trk; Hon Roll; NHS; Bus Adm.

DONIA, SAM; North Star HS; Stoystown, PA; (Y); #30 In Class; Aud/Vis; Church Yth Grp; FCA; Stage Crew; Yrbk Ed-Chief; Yrbk Phtg; Yrbk Stf; JV Ftbl; Var Socr; Hon Roll; FL ST; Psychlgst.

DONIANO, MICHELE; Old Forge HS; Old Forge, PA; (S); Ski Clb; Var Bsktbl; Var Sftbl; Hon Roll; Jr NHS; Gregg Typing Awd 86; Pre Med.

DONKERS, LYNN; Brownsville Area HS; Brownsville, PA; (Y); 50/222; Ski Clb; SADD; JV Bsktbl; Mgr Ftbl; Mgr(s); L Sftbl; Mgr Wrstlng; Hon Roll; Cnty All Stars 86; Comm.

DONLEY, MICHELLE; Meadville Area SR HS; Conneaut Lake, PA; (Y); 88/350; German Clb; Pre-Med.

DONLICK, DEBBIE; Western Wayne HS; S Canaan, PA; (Y); 32/143; Church Yth Grp; SADD; Color Guard; Yrbk Stf; Stu Cncl; Bsktbl; Ftbl; Sftbl; Hon Roll; Prfct Atten Awd; Pat Walsh Schlrshp Awd Bsktbl 86; Natl Sci Olymp Chem 85; Natl Sci Olymp Physcs 86; Lock Haven U; Sports Med.

DONNELLY, BRIAN; Fairview HS; Fairview, PA; (Y); Cmnty Wkr; Debate Tm; Model UN; Var Crs Cntry; JV Socr; JV Trk; Hon Roll; NHS; Latin Natl Hnr Soc; 1st Pl-Lincoln-Douglas Debate Erie Cnty Tourney.

DONNELLY, DIANNE; Cardinal Dougherty HS; Phila, PA; (Y); 10/757; Art Clb; Hosp Aide; Nwsp Rptr; Yrbk Phtg; Yrbk Stf; Stu Cncl; Capt Fld Hcky; High Hon Roll; NHS; St Josephs U; Bus.

DONNELLY, NOREEN C; Cardinal Dougherty HS; Philadelphia, PA; (Y); 16/747; Debate Tm; Latin Clb; Political Wkr; Chorus; Drill Tm; High Hon Roll; Hon Roll; NHS; Holy Name Soc Essay 85; Mock Trial Temple U City Champ 85-6; Prfncy Awd In Morality 85; Widener U; Bus Adm.

DONNELLY, PAM; Altoona Area HS; Altoona, PA; (Y); 49/688; Spanish Clb; Drm Mjr(t); Yrbk Rptr; Sec Frsh Cls; Stu Cncl; Trk; Twrlr; Penn ST; Educ.

DONNELLY, SUSAN; Creative & Performing Arts; Philadelphia, PA; (S); 10/145; Red Cross Aide; Chorus; School Musical; Stage Crew; Variety Show; Hon Roll; Music Perfm.

DONNELLY, THOMAS P; Bethel Park SR HS; Bethel Park, PA; (Y); Chorus; School Musical; School Play; Tennis; High Hon Roll; Hon Roll; NHS; Penn ST U; Blgy.

DONOFRIO, JILL; Greensburg Central Catholic HS; Murrysville, PA; (Y); 90/247; Church Yth Grp; Hosp Aide; JCL; Pep Clb; Science Clb; Ski Clb; Spanish Clb; Varsity Clb; Yrbk Stf; Rep Frsh Cls; WA & Jefferson Coll; Bio.

DONOFRIO, WENDDE; Ville Maria HS; New Castle, PA; (Y); Camera Clb; Church Yth Grp; Cmnty Wkr; Drama Clb; Hosp Aide; Thesps; School Musical; Nwsp Rptr; Rep Frsh Cls; Rep Soph Cls; East Carolina U; Occup Ther.

DONOHUE, ERIN; Louis E Dieruff HS; Allentown, PA; (Y); 29/338; VP Ski Clb; Nwsp Stf; Rep Frsh Cls; VP Soph Cls; Rep Stu Cncl; Co-Capt Cheerleading; Vllybl; Hon Roll; NHS; Jr NHS; Natl Chrldng Assoc All Amer Fnlst 85; Natl Chrldng Assoc Awd Excell 85.

DONOHUE, JANET C; Notre Dame Acad; Upper Darby, PA; (Y); 1/72; Hosp Aide; Mathletes; Red Cross Aide; Chorus; Nwsp Ed-Chief; Stu Cncl; JV Lcrss; High Hon Roll; Ntl Merit Ltr; Pres Schlr; Gen Excllnce Awd For Acad 86; Excllnce In Sci Awd 86; Excllnce In Math Awd 86; St Josephs U; Bio.

DONOHUE, JILL ANN; Bethel Park SR HS; Oakmont, PA; (Y); 120/507; JA; Math Tm; Y-Teens; Sec Mrchg Band; Camera Clb; Sec Symp Band; Powder Puff Ftbl; Score Keeper; Vllybl; Hon Roll; Penn ST-BEHREND; Math.

DONOHUE, KELLIE; Cardinal O Hara HS; Brookhaven, PA; (Y); 174/776; Church Yth Grp; Dance Clb; GAA; Ski Clb; SADD; Y-Teens; Var Cheerleading; Gym; Sftbl; Hon Roll; Psych.

DONOUGHE, KATHLEEN; Bishop Guilfoyle HS; Altoona, PA; (Y); Church Yth Grp; Yrbk Phtg; Yrbk Stf; Rep Jr Cls; Stu Cncl; JV Bsktbl; Var JV Score Keeper; Hon Roll; J Jay Coll Crmnl Justc; Polc Sc.

DONOVAN, DAVID; Moon Area HS; Coraopolis, PA; (Y); Hst German Clb; VP Key Clb; Pres Jr Cls; Pres Sr Cls; JV Var Socr; JV Var Trk; Hon Roll; Prfct Atten Awd; Med.

DONOVAN, GAYANNE; Daniel Boone HS; Douglasville, PA; (Y); 54/186; French Clb; German Clb; JA; SADD; Varsity Clb; Chorus; Mrchg Band; Rep Stu Cncl; JV Var Cheerleading; Mgr(s); Sportsmnshp Awd-Cheerldng 8k; PHYS Thrpst.

DONOVAN, HEATHER; Wilson Area HS; Riegelsville, PA; (S); 2/138; Cmnty Wkr; Drama Clb; Ski Clb; Yrbk Stf; Rep Stu Cncl; Mgr Crs Cntry; Mgr(s); High Hon Roll; NHS; Score Keeper; Mensa 86; Writer.

DONOVAN, KEVIN; West Scranton HS; Scranton, PA; (Y); Varsity Clb; VICA; Crs Cntry; Trk; Bcknl.

DONOVAN, MAUREEN; Archbishop Wood HS For Girls; Churchville, PA; (Y); FBLA; Library Aide; Office Aide; Mgr(s); Score Keeper; Socr; Sftbl; Trk; Vllybl; Bucks CCC; Accntng.

DONOVAN, MIKE; West Mifflin Area HS; West Mifflin, PA; (Y); 40/350; Var L Tennis; Hon Roll; NHS; Pre Ap Engl 85-86; Ap Engl 86-87; PA ST U; Elec Engrng.

DONOVAN, WILLIAM F; Father Judge HS; Philadelphia, PA; (Y); 5/410; Off Church Yth Grp; Cmnty Wkr; Mathletes; Capt Crs Cntry; Var Trk; High Hon Roll; Pres NHS; Ntl Merit SF; Mst Imprvd JR Awd Trck & Fld; Engrng.

DONSKY, JENNIFER; Bensalem HS; Bensalem, PA; (Y); 54/564; Teachers Aide; School Musical; Stu Cncl; Var Cheerleading; Gym; Var Trk; Hon Roll; VP Bnai Brith Yth Orgnztn 82-86; U Of DE.

DONTEN, SUSAN M; Cedar Crest HS; Lebanon, PA; (Y); 10/323; Church Yth Grp; Cmnty Wkr; French Clb; Pep Clb; School Musical; Stat Bsbl; Im Vllybl; High Hon Roll; NHS.

DOOLEY, PATRICK J; Wissahickon HS; Penllyn, PA; (Y); Drm & Bgl; Radio.

DOOLIN, CHRISTINE M; Kennedy Christian HS; W Middlesex, PA; (Y); 2/98; Hosp Aide; Latin Clb; Sec Science Clb; Band; Concert Band; Mrchg Band; Hon Roll; NEDT Awd; St John Newman Schrlsh 83; Good Shephard Parrish Schlrshp 83; Physcl Thrpy.

DOONER, MARY; Cardinal O Hara HS; Broomall, PA; (Y); Church Yth Grp; Chorus; School Musical; School Play; Hon Roll; Crim Just.

DOPKO, MICHELLE; G A R HS; Wilkes Barre, PA; (S); 15/187; Key Clb; Chorus; Nwsp Stf; Rep Stu Cncl; High Hon Roll; Hon Roll; Jr NHS; NHS; Bloomsburg U; Jrnlsm.

DORAL, DINA; Strath Haven HS; Wallingford, PA; (Y); Aud/Vis; Intnl Clb; School Musical; Nwsp Stf; Yrbk Phtg; Yrbk Stf; Var Crs Cntry; JV Fld Hcky; JV Lcrss; Var Capt Swmmng; Temple U Pres Schlrshp 86; Otstndng Acad Achvmnt Awd 83; 4 Yr Vrsty Lttr Awd 86; Temple U; Brdcst.

DORAN, JO ANNE; St Marys Area HS; Kersey, PA; (Y); 23/297; Exploring; Hosp Aide; Band; Concert Band; Jazz Band; Mrchg Band; Vllybl; High Hon Roll; Hon Roll; Jr NHS; SR Band Awd 86; Presdntl Acad Fitns Awd 86; Wm Landes Schlrshp-Susquehanna U 86-87; Susquehanna U; Phys Therpy.

DORAN, SHARON; Danville Area HS; Danville, PA; (Y); Cheerleading; Gym; Capt Trk; Drama Clb; French Clb; Rep Jr Cls; Mat Maids; Powder Puff Ftbl; Lock Haven U; Sprt Med.

DORASKI, LISA; Southern Columbia HS; Catawissa, PA; (Y); FBLA; Key Clb; Mathletes; Bus Admin.

DORAZIO, DEREK; Bishop Shanahan HS; Thorndale, PA; (Y); Im Ftbl; Im Ice Hcky; Im Socr; Hon Roll; NHS; Prfct Atten Awd; Silvr Mdl Mdgt Ftbl Pgm 84-85; Awd Scrng 100 Goals St Hcky Leag 86; Bus.

DORAZIO, LISA; Uniontown HS; Chalk Hill, PA; (Y); 40/380; Sec Church Yth Grp; Sec JA; Letterman Clb; Spanish Clb; Varsity Clb; Stu Cncl; Swmmng; Trk; Jr NHS; Spanish NHS.

DORFNER, DENISE; Seton La Salle HS; Pittsburgh, PA; (Y); 64/247; Church Yth Grp; Ski Clb; Sftbl; Hon Roll.

DORICH, DARLENE ANN; Mercyhurst Prepatory Schl; Erie, PA; (Y); 23/160; Art Clb; Hosp Aide; Yrbk Stf; Trs Bowling; Var L Swmmng; High Hon Roll; NHS; Egan Schlrshp To Mercyhurst Coll 86; Eastside Fed Schlrshp 86; Pres Acadmc Fit Awd 86; Mercyhurst Coll; Cmmrcl Dsgn.

DORISH, MOLLY; Wyoming Valley West HS; Kingston, PA; (Y); Key Clb; Ski Clb; Nwsp Rptr; Nwsp Stf; Yrbk Stf; Lit Mag; Sec Jr Cls; JV Swmmng; Vllybl; Cit Awd.

DORMAN, MICHELE; Bellefonte Area HS; Pleasant Gap, PA; (Y); Church Yth Grp; French Clb; Ski Clb; Varsity Clb; Flag Corp; Rep Soph Cls; Rep Jr Cls; Bsktbl; Powder Puff Ftbl; Trk; Waynesburg Coll; Crmnl Psych.

DORMAN, ROBERT; Freedom SR HS; Bethlehem, PA; (Y); 9/465; Boys Clb Am; Church Yth Grp; German Clb; JA; Math Tm; Im Bsktbl; Hon Roll; NHS; Awd Straight A Stu 85-86; Engr.

DORMAN, TERESA; Bald Eagle Area JR SR HS; Fleming, PA; (Y); Church Yth Grp; Sec French Clb; Hosp Aide; Library Aide; Hon Roll; Ntl Sci Plympd 84; Penn ST; Elem Ed.

DORMAN, TRISHA; Southmoreland HS; Alverton, PA; (Y); Dance Clb; Office Aide; Pep Clb; Spanish Clb; Chorus; Powder Puff Ftbl; Frchld Indstrs Schlrshp 86; Sthmrlnd Hlth Aide Srv Awd 86; ICM Schl Of Bus; Med Assist.

DORMER, TAMMY; Shamokin Area HS; Shamokin, PA; (Y); 7/246; Key Clb; Varsity Clb; Bsktbl; Cheerleading; Crs Cntry; Swmmng; Trk; High Hon Roll; NHS; Band.

DORN, JASON; Owen J Roberts HS; Pottstown, PA; (S); 12/267; Boy Scts; Church Yth Grp; Band; Concert Band; Jazz Band; Mrchg Band; Symp Band; High Hon Roll; Hon Roll; Penn ST U; Elec Engrng.

DORNENBURG, WILLIAM; Carlynton JR SR HS; Carnegie, PA; (Y); French Clb; Band; Concert Band; Drm & Bgl; Mrchg Band; Stage Crew; Symp Band; Mgr(s); High Hon Roll; Penn ST; Elctrncs Engr.

DORNES, ANDREW; Ephrata SR HS; Ephrata, PA; (Y); Aud/Vis; Church Yth Grp; Radio Clb; VICA; Stage Crew; Hon Roll; Elec Tech.

DORNEY, MELODY A; Steel Valley HS; Munhall, PA; (Y); 26/233; Key Clb; Concert Band; Mrchg Band; Yrbk Stf; Hon Roll; NHS; Pres Schlr; Key Clb Scholar 86; Distngshd Pres Awd Key Clb 85; U Pittsburgh; Occ Thrpy.

DORNSTEIN, KEN; Cheltenham HS; Melrose Pk, PA; (Y); 19/360; Variety Show; Nwsp Ed-Chief; Rep Stu Cncl; Bsktbl; French Hon Soc; NCTE Awd; Ntl Merit Ltr; Prfct Atten Awd; Brown U Book Awd 86; PA Gov Schl Arts 86; Exec Comm 86.

DOROZOWSKI, DIANE; Freedom HS; Bethlehem, PA; (Y); 18/392; Church Yth Grp; Band; Concert Band; Mrchg Band; JV Bsktbl; Var Crs Cntry; Var Capt Sftbl; JV Tennis; High Hon Roll; Hon Roll; Amer Assoc Of Univ Wmn Schlrp 86; Messiah Coll; Elem Ed.

DORSCH, LORI; Ringgold HS; Finleyville, PA; (Y); Pres Church Yth Grp; Drama Clb; Teachers Aide; Chorus; Church Choir; School Musical; School Play; Stage Crew; Variety Show; Nwsp Rptr; Chrch Yth Trp Pres/Trea 84; Stage Crew, Stage Mngr 85-86; Drama Clb Tchrs Aide 85-86; Soc Wrk.

DORWARD, LISA; Lehighton Area HS; Lehighton, PA; (Y); 46/225; Pres VP Church Yth Grp; VP 4-H; FHA; Trs Girl Scts; 4-H Awd; Hon Roll; Intl Lds Garment Wrkrs Union Schlrshp 86; Nothampton CC; Dntl Hygn.

DORWART, STEPHEN; Neshaminy HS; Trevose, PA; (Y); VP L Bsbl; L Bsktbl; VP L Ftbl; Im Vllybl; Im Wt Lftg; Jr NHS; NHS; Prfct Atten Awd; Mr Lineman Dfns Ftbl 85-86; Plyr Of Wk 85-86; Gym Night Co Capt 85-86; Bio.

DOSHI, AMOL N; Shadyside Acad; Pittsburgh, PA; (Y); 1/112; VP Spanish Clb; VP SADD; Nwsp Ed-Chief; JV Socr; JV Tennis; Ntl Merit SF; Trs Chess Clb; Church Yth Grp; VP French Clb; JA; Princeton U Alumni Awd 83-85; Rensselaer Polytech Inst Mdl 85; Dickey Mem Awd 84; Banking.

DOTTS, CHRISTINE; Moshannon Valley HS; Glen Hope, PA; (Y); Church Yth Grp; Chorus; Acctng.

DOTTS, TAMMY; Owen J Roberts HS; Pottstown, PA; (Y); Trs Aud/Vis; Debate Tm; Hosp Aide; Library Aide; Q&S; Scholastic Bowl; School Musical; School Play; Lit Mag; Theatr Arts.

DOTY, DEBRA; Bloomsburg HS; Bloomsburg, PA; (Y); Art Clb; FTA; Keywanettes; Pep Clb; Chorus; Var Fld Hcky; Capt Powder Puff Ftbl; Hon Roll; NHS; Navy; Weapnry.

DOUBLE, CHRISTINA; Karns City HS; Karns City, PA; (Y); Chorus; JV Stat Bsktbl; Var L Vllybl; Hon Roll; NHS; Acadmc Ltr 86; Secy Sci.

DOUD, MATT; Mansfield JR SR HS; Mansfield, PA; (S); 1/97; Band; Mrchg Band; VP Soph Cls; VP Jr Cls; Pres Stu Cncl; JV Var Bsktbl; Tennis; Dnfth Awd; High Hon Roll; NHS; Yth Ldr/Tmrrw 86; Mansfield U; Scndry Educ.

DOUD, TINA; Mansfield JR & SR HS; Mansfield, PA; (S); 20/100; FCA; Office Aide; Chorus; Concert Band; Drm Mjr(t); Sec Soph Cls; Sec Jr Cls; Pres Sr Cls; Stat Trk; Im Vllybl; Bus & Pro Wmn Of Mnth 85; Yth Ldrs Of Tomrw 85-86; Mansfield U; Spec Educ.

DOUDRICK, DORTHEY; West Perry SR HS; New Bloomfield, PA; (Y); Church Yth Grp; French Clb; Varsity Clb; Concert Band; Mrchg Band; Yrbk Stf; Stat Sftbl; Hon Roll; NHS; Intrntnl Schlrshp In Arts 86.

DOUDS, MIKE; Bethel Park HS; Bethel Park, PA; (Y); FBLA; Bsbl; Var L Bsktbl; Hon Roll; Rookie Of Yr 85; Bsktbl 86; Gazt S Fabls Five 86; Bsktbl Scorg Ldr 86; Bus.

DOUGALL, PAUL; Shaler Area SR HS; Glenshaw, PA; (Y); 89/517; Church Yth Grp; Hon Roll; Engrng.

DOUGHER, JOE; West Scranton HS; Scranton, PA; (Y); 33/250; Boys Clb Am; Boy Scts; Church Yth Grp; Letterman Clb; Ski Clb; Varsity Clb; Nwsp Stf; Yrbk Stf; Off Jr Cls; Trs Sr Cls; Nuc Med.

DOUGHER, SARA PASSARIELLO; West Scranton HS; Scranton, PA; (Y); 51/250; Dance Clb; Ski Clb; Nwsp Rptr; Nwsp Stf; Yrbk Stf; Var Capt Cheerleading; Hon Roll; Jr NHS; NHS; East Stroudsburg U; Math.

DOUGHERTY, BOB; Emmaus HS; Wescosville, PA; (Y); Band; Concert Band; Mrchg Band; Var Tennis; Hon Roll; Jr NHS; Prfct Atten Awd.

DOUGHERTY, CHRISTINE; Bethlehem Catholic HS; Bethlehem, PA; (Y); Band; Church Choir; Concert Band; Mrchg Band; Orch; School Musical; Variety Show; Hon Roll; Music.

DOUGHERTY, COLLEEN; Bishop Shanahan HS; Exton, PA; (Y); Church Yth Grp; Dance Clb; Intnl Clb; Service Clb; SADD; School Musical; School Play; Lit Mag; Hon Roll; Nrsng.

DOUGHERTY, COLLEEN; Saint Hubert HS; Philadelphia, PA; (Y); 95/367; JA; Var JV Bsktbl; Hon Roll; Prfct Atten Awd; Hlth.

DOUGHERTY, EILEEN M; Cardinal O Hara HS; Glenolden, PA; (Y); 179/749; Service Clb; Speech Tm; Teachers Aide; Chorus; School Play; Nwsp Bus Mgr; Nwsp Stf; Yrbk Stf; DAR Awd; Gwynedd-Mercy Coll; Thrpy.

DOUGHERTY, HELEN; Northwestern HS; Albion, PA; (Y); 13/141; Church Yth Grp; Yrbk Stf; Rep Stu Cncl; High Hon Roll; Hon Roll; Acadmc Schlrshp 86; Gannon U; Acctg.

DOUGHERTY, JUDITH A; West Scranton HS; Scranton, PA; (Y); 1/265; Letterman Clb; Sec Stu Cncl; Var Gym; High Hon Roll; NHS; Ntl Merit SF; Val; Church Yth Grp; Office Aide; Orch; PIAA Intermdte All Around Gym Champ 85; NEIU Schlr Yr 85; Senate Yth Schlrshp 86.

DOUGHERTY, KATHRYN H; Lewistown Area HS; Lewistown, PA; (Y); 7/270; AFS; Church Yth Grp; Dance Clb; Debate Tm; German Clb; Key Clb; Pep Clb; Political Wkr; Science Clb; Service Clb; House Reps Page; Manhattan Coll; Gov.

DOUGHERTY, LAURA ANN; West Perry HS; Loysville, PA; (Y); Church Yth Grp; SADD; Varsity Clb; Var L Fld Hcky; Var L Sftbl; Hon Roll; Prfct Atten Awd; Pride Of W Perry Day Awd 82-84; Fld Hcky Awd Merit 83-84; Lab Tech.

DOUGHERTY, LYNN; Hanover HS; Wilkes Barre, PA; (Y); Sec Key Clb; Ski Clb; Mrchg Band; Yrbk Stf; Var L Trk; L Twrlr; Var Capt Vllybl; Hon Roll; Chld Dvlpmnt.

DOUGHERTY, MICHELLE; Biglerville HS; Aspers, PA; (Y); 28/80; Rptr Trs FFA; Leo Clb; SADD; Band; Chorus; Nwsp Rptr; Yrbk Stf; Stu Cncl; Fld Hcky; Arendtsvl Almni Awd Schlrshp 86; Bnd Outstndng SR Awd 86; FFA Chptr Str Agribus 86; Indiana U PA; Hm Econ.

DOUGHERTY, SHARON; Old Forge HS; Old Forge, PA; (Y); GAA; Sec Jr Cls; Sec Sr Cls; Co-Capt Bsktbl; Hon Roll; Nrsng.

DOUGHERTY, STEPHEN; Penn Wood HS; Darby, PA; (Y); 131/304; Ski Clb; Var Bsbl; JV Ftbl; JV Wrstlng; Hon Roll; Johnson & Wales; Chef.

DOUGHERTY, TOM; Freedom HS; Bethlehem, PA; (Y); 75/465; Church Yth Grp; German Clb; Chorus; Hon Roll; Engrng.

DOUGHERTY, WINFIELD; Malvern Prep Schl; Valley Forge, PA; (Y); 51/85; Church Yth Grp; Band; Concert Band; Mrchg Band; Socr; Tennis; Hon Roll; PA Natl Grd 86; Drexel U; Bus Admn.

DOUGHTERY, MARK; Archbishop Carroll HS; Ardmore, PA; (Y); 10/165; Band; Concert Band; Jazz Band; JV Var Bsktbl; Var Golf; JV Socr; High Hon Roll; Hon Roll; NHS; Acctg.

DOUGHTY, LINDA; Hopewell SR HS; Hookstown, PA; (Y); 15/264; Library Aide; Chorus; High Hon Roll; Lion Awd; Pres Acad Ftnss Awd 86.

DOUGLAS, CHERYL; Milton Area SR HS; Milton, PA; (Y); Art Clb; Pres Church Yth Grp; Library Aide; Yrbk Stf; High Hon Roll; Hon Roll; NHS.

DOUGLAS, KEITH; Kutztown HS; Bowers, PA; (Y); 49/150; Spanish Clb; Teachers Aide; Jr Cls; Sr Cls; Bsktbl; Ftbl; Trk; Wrstlng; High Hon Roll; Hon Roll; Tchng.

DOUGLASS, ANN; Galeton Area JR SR HS; Sabinsville, PA; (S); 4/41; Debate Tm; French Clb; Library Aide; Model UN; Chorus; School Play; JV Stat Vllybl; Hon Roll; NHS; Ntl Merit Ltr; Law.

DOUGLESS, CHRIS; Salisbury SR HS; Birmingham, AL; (Y); 33/138; 4-H; Science Clb; Band; Chorus; Concert Band; Mrchg Band; Hon Roll; U Of AL; Premed.

DOUKAS, CHRIS; Pine Grove Area HS; Pine Grove, PA; (Y); 5/125; ROTC; Rep Varsity Clb; Drill Tm; School Musical; Stage Crew; Nwsp Ed-Chief; Rep Jr Cls; Var Capt Wrstlng; Hon Roll; 2 Tm PA ST Brnz Mdlst Wrstlng 85-86; Ntl Grd Outstndng Cdt Awd ROTC 86; Sup Cdt Awd ROTC 86; Cvl Engnr.

DOURTE, LAURA; Manheim Central HS; Manheim, PA; (Y); Cmnty Wkr; GAA; Pep Clb; Political Wkr; Rep Frsh Cls; Rep Soph Cls; Rep Jr Cls; Rep Sr Cls; Rep Stu Cncl; L Cheerleading; Philadelphia Coll:Fshn Mrchnds.

DOUTRICH, MARK; Tulpehocken HS; Bethel, PA; (Y); #4 In Class; Band; Pep Band; School Musical; School Play; Stage Crew; Hon Roll; NHS; Brdcstng.

DOUTT, CHRISTOPHER; Deer Lakes HS; Cheswick, PA; (Y); Bsktbl; L Capt Socr; L Trk; High Hon Roll; Hon Roll; NHS; NEDT Awd; PA JR Acad Sci Cert 85; Hnr Grad 86; U Pittsburgh; Engrng.

DOUTT, JENNIFER; Sharpsville HS; Clark, PA; (Y); Hosp Aide; Library Aide; Science Clb; Spanish Clb; Thesps; Chorus; Yrbk Stf; U Pittsburgh; Dietitan.

DOUTT, PAULA; Cambridge Springs HS; Saegertown, PA; (Y); 5/112; Church Yth Grp; Pres 4-H; Pep Clb; Yrbk Stf; VP Stu Cncl; Var Capt Bsktbl; Var Capt Sftbl; Var L Vllybl; Hon Roll; NHS.

DOUTY, BRIAN; Sugar Valley HS; Loganton, PA; (S); 1/17; Pres Church Yth Grp; Trs FFA; VP Spanish Clb; Pres Band; Yrbk Ed-Chief; Trs Stu Cncl; High Hon Roll; Rotary Awd; Lion Awd; Hugh O Brien Yth Ldrshp Smnr 84; Dist Band 84-85; Brnz Medal PA ST FFA Frstry Cont 84; Lock Haven U; Elec Engr.

DOWAY, TONYA; Westinghouse HS; Pittsburgh, PA; (Y); JA; Cheerleading; Hon Roll; Duquesne U; Comp Prgmr.

DOWDEN, LESLIE; East Allegheny HS; N Versailles, PA; (Y); Dance Clb; French Clb; PAVAS; Ski Clb; Band; Concert Band; Drill Tm; Drm Mjr(t); Mrchg Band; Orch; Mjrtt Capt 86-87; Cmmnctns.

DOWDY, LISA; Aliquippa HS; Aliquippa, PA; (Y); DECA; French Clb; Off Jr Cls; Hon Roll; ICM Schl Bus; Med Sec.

DOWDY IV, THOMAS C; Archbishop Ryan For Boys; Philadelphia, PA; (Y); 128/458; Spanish Clb; Bowling; Amer Inst Of Drftng; Comp.

DOWER, PATTI; Shenandoah Valley HS; Shenandoah, PA; (S); 36/100; JV Bsktbl; Hon Roll.

DOWEY, KAREN; Harmony Area HS; Cherry Tree, PA; (Y); 9/44; Office Aide; Band; Chorus; Concert Band; Mrchg Band; Trs Jr Cls; Im Badmtn; Stat Bsktbl; Im Bowling; Im Socr; Dntl Hygn.

DOWEY, RON; Harmony Area HS; Cherry Tree, PA; (Y); 11/46; Boy Scts; Church Yth Grp; Band; Mrchg Band; School Play; Yrbk Phtg; Var Score Keeper; Hon Roll; Am Hist Awd 84-85; Pres Acadmc Ftnss Awd 85-86; IN U Of PA; Hist.

DOWLER, MICHAEL H; Greenville HS; Greenville, PA; (Y); 10/150; Church Yth Grp; French Clb; Letterman Clb; Stat Im Bsktbl; JV Ftbl; L Var Golf; JV Socr; Hon Roll; NHS; Voice Dem Awd; Medcl Mission Tm Haiti 85; B Avg Engl 85-86; Awd Winning Shakespeare Fest Cast 86; Engr.

DOWLER, RITA; Fort Cherry HS; Midway, PA; (Y); Church Yth Grp; Computer Clb; Math Clb; Science Clb; Ski Clb; Spanish Clb; Band; Chorus; Yrbk Stf; High Hon Roll.

DOWLING, JANINE; Fairview HS; Fairview, PA; (S); 38/183; Concert Band; Jazz Band; Mrchg Band; Orch; Hon Roll; Church Yth Grp; Drama Clb; Pep Band; School Musical; Var Trk; Dist Orchestra-1st Violin Sectn 85; Music Thrpy.

DOWNES, JENNIFER; California Area HS; Roscoe, PA; (Y); FBLA; FNA; Ski Clb; Nwsp Rptr; Sftbl; Vllybl; Hon Roll; Slippery Rock.

DOWNEY, JOHN; West Branch HS; Morrisdale, PA; (Y); 9/110; Varsity Clb; Bsktbl; Ftbl; Vllybl; Wt Lftg; Hon Roll; Trs NHS; Harrisburg Traffic Club Schlrshp 86; Physics Awd 86; Halden Johnson Mem Awd 86; PA ST U; Elec Engrng.

DOWNIN, AMY; Waynesboro HS; Quincy, PA; (Y); 75/357; Church Yth Grp; Chorus; Church Choir; Rep Soph Cls; Var Fld Hcky; Var Sftbl; Cit Awd; High Hon Roll; Hon Roll; Fld Hcky Coach Awd 84; Chrch Yth Grp VP 85; Chrch Yth Grp Sec 86; Sec.

DOWNING, SAMUEL; Brookville Area HS; Summerville, PA; (Y); Boy Scts; Chess Clb; Church Yth Grp; French Clb; Varsity Clb; Acpl Chr; Band; Chorus; Concert Band; Drm & Bgl; :Elctrncs.

DOWNS, LEVI S; Gateway SR HS; Monroeville, PA; (Y); 46/460; Church Yth Grp; VP JA; Pres Soph Cls; Pres Jr Cls; Pres Sr Cls; Pres Stu Cncl; DAR Awd; NHS; Rotary Awd; Exploring; St Rep To Hugh O Brian Ingl Ldrshp Seminar 84; Duke U; Chem.

DOYLE, ANN MARIE; Upper Moreland HS; Hatboro, PA; (Y); 11/257; Church Yth Grp; Key Clb; Teachers Aide; Nwsp Ed-Chief; Jr Cls; Mgr(s); Score Keeper; High Hon Roll; NHS; Ntl Merit Ltr; Elem Tchr.

DOYLE, CAROLE; Mt St Joseph Acad; Warminster, PA; (Y); Art Clb; Spanish Clb; School Play; Stage Crew; Trk; Im Vllybl; Hon Roll; NEDT Awd; York Coll PA Scholar 86; Hnrs Pgm Trenton ST Coll 86; U Scranton PA; Mktng.

DOYLE, DARLENE; Central Bucks HS East; Furlong, PA; (Y); Chorus; Madrigals; Yrbk Stf; VP Soph Cls; Stu Cncl; Var L Tennis; Hon Roll; Sec Jr NHS; NHS; Rep Frsh Cls; Acad Excllnce Awd.

DOYLE, ERICA; Abington Heights HS; Clarks Summit, PA; (Y); 64/300; Ski Clb; JV Var Cheerleading; JV Trk; High Hon Roll; Med Careers Clb 85-87; Bio Sci.

DOYLE, JAMES; Monsignor Bonner HS; Drexel Hill, PA; (S); 17/320; Sec Church Yth Grp; Mathletes; Nwsp Rptr; Rep Frsh Cls; Rep Soph Cls; Var Crs Cntry; Var Trk; Hon Roll; NHS; Prfct Atten Awd; Math Awd 83-85; Rtry Clb Nov Stu 85; 1st Pl All Delco Two Mile Rly 85; Math.

DOYLE, KATHLEEN; Saint Huberts HS; Philadelphia, PA; (Y); Church Yth Grp; FCA; French Clb; Intnl Clb; Teachers Aide; Crs Cntry; Trk; Hon Roll.

DOYLE, LARA; York Catholic HS; Glen Rock, PA; (Y); Chess Clb; 4-H; French Clb; Girl Scts; Hosp Aide; Intnl Clb; Library Aide; Acpl Chr; Chorus; Church Choir; Acadmc Awd 86; Chestnut Hill Clg; Bio.

DOYLE, MARIA ELENA; Quigley HS; Baden, PA; (S); 1/107; Math Tm; Drill Tm; Nwsp Ed-Chief; Trs Jr Cls; Mgr Powder Puff Ftbl; Var L Trk; High Hon Roll; Lion Awd; Beaver Cnty Jr Miss Pgnt Schltc Achvt Awd 86; PA Jr Sci Acad Rgn 7 2nd Awd 84; Cornell U; Jrnlsm.

DOYLE, MICHAEL; Interboro HS; Lester, PA; (S); Boys Clb Am; Computer Clb; FBLA; VICA; Gov Hon Prg Awd; Hon Roll; NHS; Prfct Atten Awd; Natl Hnr Socty 84-86; Hgh Hnrs 83-86; Comp Anlyst.

DOYLE, MICHELE; Nativity Bum HS; New Phila, PA; (Y); Church Choir; Yrbk Stf; JV Bsktbl; Var Twrlr; Hon Roll; Prfct Atten Awd; Algbr Awd; Majort & Attndnc Awd; Nrs.

DOYLE, PATTY; Gateway HS; Monroeville, PA; (S); 87/508; Church Yth Grp; Dance Clb; NFL; PAVAS; Service Clb; Chorus; Church Choir; Nwsp Rptr; Yrbk Stf; Highland Scottish Dancing Mdls & 1 Trophy 84 & 85; Psych.

DOYLE, SANDY; B Reed Hendersofn SR HS; Exton, PA; (Y); 25/349; Boy Scts; Exploring; French Clb; Drill Tm; Mrchg Band; Yrbk Stf; Rep Stu Cncl; Capt Pom Pon; French Hon Soc; Hon Roll; Penn ST; Vet Med.

DRABINSKY, JENNIFER; Boyertown Area SR HS; Boyertown, PA; (Y); 8/472; Sec Church Yth Grp; Math Tm; Nwsp Rptr; Yrbk Stf; Stat Bsktbl; Stat Crs Cntry; Stat Trk; High Hon Roll; NHS; Girl Scts; Schlstc Awd Excllnc 84; Pre-Medcn.

DRAGO, DOLORES; Bensalem HS; Bensalem, PA; (Y); Cmnty Wkr; Debate Tm; English Clb; JA; Office Aide; Political Wkr; Red Cross Aide; Science Clb; SADD; Teachers Aide; Holy Family Coll; Biochem.

DRAGON, AMY; The Christian Acad; Wallingford, PA; (Y); Church Yth Grp; Pep Clb; Nwsp Stf; Stat Bsktbl; JV Capt Cheerleading; Var L Fld Hcky; Hon Roll; U S Chrldr Achvt Awd.

DRAGON, ANDREW; Danville Area HS; Danville, PA; (Y); 4/170; Church Yth Grp; Drama Clb; VP Key Clb; Spanish Clb; Mrchg Band; Symp Band; NHS; 4-H; Scholastic Bowl; Jazz Band; PA Sci Olympd 85; Amercn Chmcl Soc Comptns 85, 86; Yng Amercns Awd 86; Lehigh U; Chmcl Engrng.

DRAKE, ALLAN; Hopewell SR HS; Aliquippa, PA; (Y); Tennis.

DRAKE, LAURA; Tunkhannock HS; Tunkhannock, PA; (Y); Drama Clb; Library Aide; Ski Clb; Spanish Clb; Acpl Chr; Chorus; Color Guard; School Musical; School Play; Stage Crew; Dstrct IX Chorus Fstvl 85-86; Phy Fitness Awd 82-84; Westchester U; Musical.

DRAKE, MICHAEL ROBERT; Upper Moreland HS; Willow Grove, PA; (Y); 130/270; FCA; Key Clb; Varsity Clb; Var Bsbl; JV Ftbl; Hon Roll; Temple U; Phys Ed.

DRAKE, TRACEY; Chichester SR HS; Boothwyn, PA; (Y); Drama Clb; Chorus; Concert Band; Capt Flag Corp; Mrchg Band; School Musical; Mgr Sftbl; Jr NHS; NEDT Awd; Scotts Hiq; Drama.

DRAKULIC, MILANA; Norwin SR HS; Ardara, PA; (Y); Church Yth Grp; Pep Clb; SADD; Grand Rep To OH Intl Order Of Rainbow Girls 85-86; Worthy Advisor Irwin Assmbly No 42 85; Pediatrician.

DRAN, SHARI; Bethlehem Ctr; Amity, PA; (Y); 8/170; Art Clb; Church Yth Grp; 4-H; Spanish Clb; Chorus; Color Guard; Mrchg Band; High Hon Roll; NHS; Washington & Jefferson; Pre-Med.

DRANCHAK, NANCY; Cambria Heights HS; Hastings, PA; (Y); Library Aide; Yrbk Stf; Hon Roll; PA ST U; Sci.

DRANSITE, JERILYNNE; Peters Township HS; Mcmurray, PA; (Y); Chorus; School Musical; High Hon Roll; Hon Roll.

DRAOVITCH, KATHLEEN M; St Clair Area HS; Pottsville, PA; (Y); 4/82; VP Church Yth Grp; Varsity Clb; Yrbk Sprt Ed; Capt L Cheerleading; Capt L Sftbl; High Hon Roll; Kiwanis Awd; Mu Alp Tht; VP NHS; NEDT Awd; St Clairs Female Schlr Athlete 86; Centurty III Ldrshp Awd 85-86; Hugh O Brien Yth Ldrshp Ambssdr 84; PA ST U; Archtctrl Engrng.

DRAPER, KELLI DANIELLE; Chester HS; Chester, PA; (Y); 19/384; Trs Church Yth Grp; Key Clb; Pep Clb; Chorus; VP Church Choir; Mrchg Band; School Play; Yrbk Stf; Rep Frsh Cls; Rep Church Yth Grp; PA Ind Chem Corp Scholar Awd 86; Clarence H Roberts Scholar Chester Cmnty Assn 86; Brotherhd Brkfst; Millersville U; Bus Adm.

DRASHER, JAMES M; Muhlenberg HS; Reading, PA; (Y); Boy Scts; JV Bsbl; Var Golf; Hon Roll.

DRASHER, ROBIN; Berwick Area SR HS; Berwick, PA; (Y); Color Guard; Nrsng.

DRATHMAN, SARA; Ridgway Area HS; Ridgway, PA; (Y); JV Var Cheerleading; Hon Roll; Bishop Watsn Schlrshp 86; Merryhurst Coll; Educ.

DRAUS, ANTHONY; Pittston Area SR HS; Dupont, PA; (Y); 90/365; Art Clb; Aud/Vis; Boy Scts; Church Yth Grp; Ski Clb; Diving; Swmmng; Trk; Wrstlng; Hon Roll; Wldlf Mgmt.

DRAVAGE, PAUL; Hanover Area JR SR HS; Wilkes Barre, PA; (Y); VICA; Band; Concert Band; Mrchg Band; Hon Roll; Jr NHS; Nwpr Carrier; Comp Maint.

DRAVAGE, TERRY; Hanover Area SJR SR HS; Wilkes Barre, PA; (Y); Band; Concert Band; Mrchg Band; Capt Sftbl; High Hon Roll; Hon Roll; NHS; Toryhanna Army Depot Miltry, Cvlns Wives Clb Schlrshp 86; PMEA Dist, Rgnl Awd-Clarinet 83-86; Luzerne Cty CC; Elem Schl Tchr.

DRAYER, CHRISTINE; Clarion Area JR SR HS; Clarion, PA; (Y); Art Clb; Church Yth Grp; Science Clb; Band; Chorus; Color Guard; Madrigals; Variety Show; Ed Yrbk Stf; Masonic Awd; Smr Acad 85; Prncpls Lst Awd 86; PA ST; Apparel Dsgn.

DRAYER, DARLENE; Du Bois Area HS; Reynoldsville, PA; (Y); Varsity Clb; Yrbk Stf; L Var Swmmng; L Var Tennis; Hon Roll; Mst Imprvd Athlt On Swim Tm 85; Penn ST; Sci.

DRECHSLER, CINDY; South Allegheny JR SR HS; Port Vue, PA; (Y); 15/184; French Clb; Office Aide; Nrs.

DREHER, JONATHAN; Butler SR HS; Butler, PA; (Y); Pres Church Yth Grp; German Clb; Ski Clb; SADD; Band; Church Choir; Jazz Band; Mrchg Band; Orch; Symp Band; Thiathons Marathn Bicylst 85-86; IN U; Lbrl Arts.

DREISTADT, KRISTEN L; William Allen HS; Allentown, PA; (Y); Drama Clb; JCL; Political Wkr; Spanish Clb; Temple Yth Grp; Lit Mag; Rep Stu Cncl; Hon Roll; Spanish NHS; Soroptmst Clb Scholar 86; Pres Scholar U Bridgeport 86; 1st Pl Bnai Brith Yth Orgnztn 84; U Bridgeport; Advrtsng.

DREMSEK, JILL; Canon Mc Millan HS; Bridgeville, PA; (Y); Cmnty Wkr; Ski Clb; Chorus; Drill Tm; School Play; Nwsp Ed-Chief; Nwsp Stf; Frsh Cls; Stu Cncl.

DRENDALL, DALE; James M HS; Wilkes Barre, PA; (Y); 102/355; Var Capt Ftbl; Vllybl; Wrstlng; Hon Roll; Penn ST U; Bus.

DRENNEN, KRISTIN; Butler Area SR HS; Butler, PA; (Y); 6/777; Cmnty Wkr; Exploring; French Clb; Hosp Aide; SADD; Y-Teens; Band; Chorus; Mrchg Band; School Play; Amer Lgn Awd 82; Dedictn Awd Cndystrpng 85; Mst Outstndng Frnch Clb 83; Seton Hill Ldrshp Schlrshp 85; Coll William & Mary; Chem.

DRESCHER, MARIE; Brookville JR SR HS; Brookville, PA; (Y); Trs Church Yth Grp; Cmnty Wkr; FNA; Teachers Aide; Church Choir; Im Vllybl; Hnrd For Hrs Wrkd At Memorial Home 86; Goto Penn ST; Med Sec.

DRESHER, JENNIFER; Upper Dublin SR HS; Ft Washington, PA; (Y); Church Yth Grp; FBLA; JA; Powder Puff Ftbl; Bus.

DRESSEL, KRISTIN E; Norristown Area HS; Norristown, PA; (S); 9/460; Cmnty Wkr; Yrbk Stf; Rep Jr Cls; Rep Sr Cls; Stu Cncl; Capt Swmmng; High Hon Roll; Acdmc All Amer 85; U Of CT; Phy Thrpy.

DRESSEL, RUTH; Steel Valley HS; Homestead, PA; (Y); Drama Clb; JA; Key Clb; SADD; Yrbk Stf; Kiwanis Awd; SOCIOLOGY.

DRESSLER, HEATHER Y; Juniata HS; Mifflin, PA; (Y); Rep Stu Cncl; Var L Sftbl; Hon Roll; NHS; Merit Schrlshp Awd Schlstc Achvt; Shippensburg; Elem Ed.

DRESSLER, KATIE; Du Bois Area HS; Dubois, PA; (Y); Pres Church Yth Grp; SADD; Band; Mrchg Band; Orch; School Musical; Cmnctns.

DRESSLER, THERESA; Dallas SR HS; Dallas, PA; (Y); 62/300; Aud/Vis; Debate Tm; Ski Clb; Yrbk Stf; Stu Cncl; Sftbl; Gifted Pgm 80-87; Flagler; Acctnt.

DREW, JEFFREY; Canon-Mc Millan HS; Mcdonald, PA; (Y); Ski Clb; Socr; Hon Roll; Culinary Inst Amer; Chef.

DREW, PHELICIA; Villa Maria Acad; Erie, PA; (Y); Church Yth Grp; Exploring; Pres 4-H; Church Choir; Var Bowling; JV Sftbl; Var Trk; 4-H Awd; Cert Educ Dev Natl NEDT 85; Erie Metro Bowling Champs Villa Maria Acad 83-84; Times News Bowling 86; Penn Sst Behrend; Engrng.

DREWENCKI, BETH; Knoch JR SR HS; Cabot, PA; (Y); Church Yth Grp; Dance Clb; Exploring; Pep Clb; Church Choir; Drill Tm; JV Var Pom Pon; Hon Roll; Mst Imprvd Stu Awd Alg I 84; Phys Thrpst.

DREY, JESSICA; Schuylkill Haven Area HS; Schuylkill Haven, PA; (S); 13/94; FNA; Pep Clb; SADD; Chorus; Yrbk Stf; Trs Soph Cls; Stu Cncl; Stat Bsbl; Var Capt Cheerleading; Var Pom Pon; Hnr Grd 85; Nrsg.

DRIGGS, ROBERTO L; Cardinal Dougherty HS; Phila, PA; (Y); 96/747; Letterman Clb; Pres Spanish Clb; SADD; Acpl Chr; Chorus; Church Choir; Color Guard; School Musical; School Play; Swing Chorus; Temple U; Intnl Bus Admin.

DRISCOLL, TOBIN; Unionville HS; Chadds Ford, PA; (Y); 1/300; Concert Band; Jazz Band; Orch; School Musical; High Hon Roll; Church Yth Grp; Mrchg Band; NHS; Ntl Merit Ltr; Region VI Band 86; Fnsh Top 10 Pct Statewide Physcs Cmpttn Tst 86.

DRISCOLL, TRACY; Hazleton SR HS; Hazelton, PA; (Y); Dance Clb; FNA; Hosp Aide; Office Aide; Red Cross Aide; Band; Chorus; Color Guard; Mrchg Band; Nwsp Stf; HOSA 84-85; Pres HOSA 85-86; Awd For Hrs Wrkd In Candy-Striping 83-84; Geisinger Schl Nrsng; Nrs.

DROPIK, BARBARA; Mt Pleasant Area HS; Mt Pleasant, PA; (Y); 4/252; Latin Clb; Band; Concert Band; Mrchg Band; Yrbk Stf; Trk; High Hon Roll; NHS; U Ptsbrgh; Engrng.

DROPIK, BETH; Mt Pleasant Area HS; Mt Pleasant, PA; (Y); 33/243; GAA; Latin Clb; Science Clb; Band; Concert Band; Mrchg Band; High Hon Roll; Hon Roll; NHS; U Of Pittsburgh; Nrsng.

DROSS, JENNIFER; Pocono Central Catholic HS; Cresco, PA; (S); 1/29; Scholastic Bowl; Service Clb; SADD; VP Stu Cncl; Var L Bsktbl; Stat Sftbl; Cit Awd; DAR Awd; High Hon Roll; NHS; PA ST Early Admssns 87; PA ST.

DROTT, EDWARD; Strath Haven HS; Swarthmore, PA; (Y); Boy Scts; Church Yth Grp; Ski Clb; Acpl Chr; Chorus; School Musical; School Play; Hon Roll; Ntl Merit Ltr; Rgnl Chours 86; Vlntr Wrk Franklin Inst 86.

DROTT, JEFF; Strath Haven HS; Wallingford, PA; (Y); Chess Clb; FBLA; Letterman Clb; Red Cross Aide; Rep Sr Cls; Rep Stu Cncl; Im Bsktbl; Var Socr; Im Wt Lftg; High Hon Roll; Pres Phys Ftns Awd 83-86; Bus.

DROZ, MICHELLE L; Sylvania Hills Christian Acad; Rochester, PA; (Y); 2/3; Church Yth Grp; Chorus; Church Choir; School Play; Yrbk Bus Mgr; Yrbk Stf; Cheerleading; Variety Show; Vllybl; Hon Roll; Schl,Chrch, & JR Choir Pianest/Organist 83-86; Geneva Coll Acad Schlrshp 86; Schl Music Awd 81-83; Geneva Coll; Music.

DROZDA, JENNIFER; Vincentian HS; Wexford, PA; (Y); 16/64; Camera Clb; Cmnty Wkr; Drama Clb; Hosp Aide; JA; Chorus; Yrbk Stf; Rep Soph Cls; Rep Jr Cls; Sec Stu Cncl; Laroche; Sclgy.

DROZDO, MICHAEL; Oil City SR HS; Seneca, PA; (Y); 4-H; Band; Church Choir; Concert Band; Jazz Band; Mrchg Band; Pep Band; School Musical; Variety Show; Wt Lftg; IN U Of PA; Law Enfrcmt.

DRUASH, NANCY; Monessen HS; Monessen, PA; (Y); 30/100; Pres Church Yth Grp; French Clb; Band; Chorus; Church Choir; Concert Band; Mrchg Band; Rep Soph Cls; Rep Jr Cls; Tennis; Acctng.

DRUCK, CHAD; York County Vo-Tech; Red Lion, PA; (Y); Church Yth Grp; VICA; Elctrncs.

DRUCK, KAREN; Abington Heights HS; Clarks Summit, PA; (Y); 40/260; Ski Clb; Yrbk Stf; Stu Cncl; Capt Var Cheerleading; Trk; Hon Roll.

DRUCTOR, JOSEPH; Northeast Catholic HS; Philadelphia, PA; (Y); 47/362; Chess Clb; Hon Roll; NHS; Busnss.

DRUETTO, JOE; Cowanesque Valley HS; Knoxville, PA; (Y); Boy Scts; Chess Clb; Computer Clb; Letterman Clb; Pres Ski Clb; Varsity Clb; Band; Concert Band; Jazz Band; Bsktbl; Accntng.

DRUFFNER, THOMAS; Scranton Prep; Avoca, PA; (Y); 104/195; Stage Crew; Trk; Wt Lftg; Cmnty Wkr; Drama Clb; Letterman Clb; Hon Roll; Engr.

DRUM, RAY; Columbia Montour Vo-Tech Schl; Wapwallopen, PA; (S); 20/226; Church Yth Grp; Science Clb; High Hon Roll; Hon Roll; Electrnc Engrng.

DRUMMOND, CATHY; North Star HS; Boswell, PA; (Y); 8/124; FCA; Pep Clb; Chorus; Flag Corp; Bsktbl; JV Vllybl; Hon Roll; NHS; American Bus Educ Awd 84; Secretary.

DRUMMOND, LISA ANN; Blairsville SR HS; Blairsville, PA; (Y); 25/129; Trs Girl Scts; Band; Concert Band; Mrchg Band; L Trk; Elks Awd; Hon Roll; NHS; Pres Phys Ftnss Awd 81-86; Schltc Awd 84-85; Slippery Rock U; Phy Ed.

DRUMTRA, NANETTE K; East Stroudsburg HS; E Stroudsburg, PA; (Y); 12/210; Band; Chorus; Concert Band; Jazz Band; Mrchg Band; Pep Band; Swing Chorus; Yrbk Stf; Hon Roll; NHS; Duquesne U; Music Ed.

DRURY, DEBORAH J; Lampeter Stasburg HS; Lancaster, PA; (Y); Church Yth Grp; Cmnty Wkr; FHA; Library Aide; SADD; Thesps; Chorus; Church Choir; School Musical; School Play; Elem Eductn.

DRYDEN, JENNIFER; Upper Darby SR HS; Drexel Hill, PA; (Y); Church Yth Grp; VP French Clb; Band; Concert Band; Drill Tm; Mrchg Band; Comp Sci.

DRYLIE, MARK; Hempfield Area SR HS; Irwin, PA; (Y); Jr NHS; PA ST; Mech Engr.

DRYZAL, JOHN; Central Cambria HS; Johnstown, PA; (S); 16/209; JV Wrstlng; Hon Roll; Vtrnry Med.

DU BOIS, CHRISTINE; Archbishop Carroll HS; King Of Prussia, PA; (Y); 30/216; Dance Clb; Spanish Clb; School Play; Stage Crew; Rep Soph Cls; Rep Jr Cls; Rep Sr Cls; High Hon Roll; Hon Roll; Spanish NHS; Bloomsburg U; Bus Mgmt.

DUBBS, GARRY; Manheim Central HS; Manheim, PA; (Y); Rep Jr Cls; Rep Sr Cls; Stu Cncl; Var L Ftbl; Var L Trk; Wt Lftg; Hon Roll; 4 Way Test Awd-Rotary 85-6; Track MVP Field Awd 85-6; Phys Fitness Awd 85-6.

DUBBS, JIM; Saucon Valley HS; Bethlehem, PA; (Y); Var L Bsktbl.

DUBBS, PAMELA; Shippensburg SR HS; Shippensburg, PA; (Y); 27/221; Church Yth Grp; Sec Girl Scts; Sec Band; Chorus; Jazz Band; School Musical; Var Trk; Hon Roll; Chambersburg Hosp Aux Schrlshp 86; Pres Acad Ftns Awd 86; York Coll; Nrsng.

DUBBS, SCHERI; Williams Valley SR SR HS; Reinerton, PA; (Y); Chorus; Yrbk Bus Mgr; Yrbk Ed-Chief; Yrbk Phtg; Yrbk Stf; Powder Puff Ftbl; Singers 85-86; Elem Tutors 85-86; Sunday Schl Tchr 85-86; Kutztown ST Coll; Bus Mgmt.

DUBE, MIKE; Penn Trafford HS; Irwin, PA; (Y); Chess Clb; Cmnty Wkr; JA; VICA; VICA Awd 85-86; Comp.

DUBERSTEIN, SUSAN; Bethel Park SR HS; Bethel Park, PA; (Y); 3/550; Pres Drama Clb; Thesps; Chorus; Drill Tm; Orch; School Musical; School Play; Variety Show; Rep Frsh Cls; Rep Soph Cls; Provst Day Exm Awd 85; Pres Schlr Semifnlst 86; CMU Vald Schlrshp 86; Carnegie Mellon U; Wrtr.

DUBIN, LANE; George Washington HS; Philadelphia, PA; (Y); 67/769; Var Bsktbl; High Hon Roll; NHS; Prsdntl Ftns Awd 86; Ursinus Coll Schlrshp 86; PAL Schlrshp 86; Ursinus Coll; Chem.

DUBOSKI, STEPHANIE; Riverside JR-SR HS; Moosic, PA; (Y); Ski Clb; Yrbk Stf; Var Capt Cheerleading; Hon Roll; NHS; Bus.

DUBROW, BARRY; Abinton HS; Meadowbrook, PA; (Y); 27/535; Chess Clb; Model UN; Nwsp Ed-Chief; Nwsp Sprt Ed; Nwsp Stf; JV Var Golf; Hon Roll; Jr NHS; NHS; Pres Schlr; U PA.

DUBYAK, MARK; Cambria Heights HS; Patton, PA; (Y); Pres Debate Tm; NFL; Speech Tm; Chorus; School Play; Stage Crew; Ftbl; High Hon Roll; NHS; Acdmc All Amer 86; Penn ST U Altoona; Bus Admn.

DUBYAK, MELISSA; Cambria Heights HS; Patton, PA; (Y); Library Aide; Teachers Aide; Chorus; Church Choir; Color Guard; Flag Corp; School Play; Stage Crew; Elem Educ.

DUCAR, MARY BETH; West Mifflin Area HS; Whitaker, PA; (Y); Church Yth Grp; High Hon Roll; Hon Roll; NHS; Trvl/Trsm.

DUCCESCHI, JOHN; Mechanicsburg Area SR HS; Mechanicsburg, PA; (Y); 117/311; Band; Jazz Band; Mrchg Band; Orch; Symp Band; JV Bsbl; Var L Trk; Chorus; Concert Band; Upper Svn Dist Band 86; Dist Trck 86; Cumberland/Admas Cnty Orch 85-86.

DUCH, DEBORAH; Serra Catholic HS; N Versailles, PA; (Y); 4/128; AFS; Nwsp Stf; Var Capt Bsktbl; Var Mgr(s); Pres French Hon Soc; High Hon Roll; NHS; PA Jr Acad Of Sci 84-86; Brddck Genl Hosp Vlntr 84-86; Yrbk Sctn Edtr 85-86; U Of Notre Dame.

DUCHAN, BARBARA; Schylkill Valley HS; Bernville, PA; (Y); 6/127; FBLA; FTA; JA; Bowling; Fld Hcky; Trk; High Hon Roll; Hon Roll; NHS; Sico Fndtn Schlrshp Awd 86; Outstnding Acad Achvt 85-86; Outstndng Schlstc Achvt 85-86; Kutztown U; Bus Mgmt.

DUCHEK, STEVEN; Connellsville HS; Vanderbilt, PA; (Y); Boy Scts; Camera Clb; Teachers Aide; High Hon Roll; Hon Roll; Acctg.

DUDA, BRIAN; Monsignor Bonner HS; Collingdale, PA; (Y); 71/308; Varsity Clb; Var L Swmmng.

DUDASH, PAM; Hopewell SR HS; Aliquippa, PA; (Y); 60/285; French Clb; Teachers Aide; Yrbk Stf; Hon Roll; Sawyer Bus Schl; Trvl-Toursm.

DUDASH, TAMMY R; Mercer HS; Mercer, PA; (Y); Church Yth Grp; French Clb; School Play; Nwsp Rptr; Yrbk Stf.

DUDASKO, DIANE; Berwick Area SR HS; Berwick, PA; (Y); Church Yth Grp; Computer Clb; Exploring; Hon Roll; NHS; PA ST U; Mcrblgy.

DUDEK, MARK; Purchase Line HS; Arcadia, PA; (Y); 1/115; SADD; Nwsp Stf; JV Bsktbl; Im Ftbl; High Hon Roll; Jr NHS; NHS; Am Legion Awd 85; ROTC; Aeronutcl Engr.

DUDNYK, GABRIELLE J; Central Bucks East HS; Solebury, PA; (Y); 11/492; Am Leg Aux Girls St; Yrbk Stf; Pres Frsh Cls; Rep Jr Cls; VP Sr Cls; Var Cheerleading; Capt Var Trk; Cit Awd; DAR Awd; Ntl Merit SF; Amer Assoc Of U Wmn 86; Boston Coll; Bus Admin.

DUDZIC, MARK; Venango Christian HS; Franklin, PA; (Y); 12/42; Ski Clb; Var L Bsbl; Var L Bsktbl; Var L Golf; Im Vllybl; Edinboro U PA.

DUFALA, JAMIE MARIE; Mercy Hurst Prep Schl; Erie, PA; (Y); Hosp Aide; Key Clb; Ski Clb; Spanish Clb; Chorus; Church Choir; Nwsp Rptr; Yrbk Stf; Hon Roll; PJAS 1st Pl ST Comptn Sci 85, 2nd Pl 86; Nrsng.

DUFFEY, ELIZABETH; Radnor HS; Wayne, PA; (S); Trs Church Yth Grp; Cmnty Wkr; NFL; Sec Speech Tm; Chorus; School Musical; Stage Crew; Rep Soph Cls; High Hon Roll; NHS; Pub Schls Annual Lit Mag 85; Bus Mgmt.

DUFFIELD, AMY; Frankford HS; Philadelphia, PA; (Y); 12/453; Service Clb; DAR Awd; Hon Roll; Lion Awd; Pres NHS; Office Aide; Teachers Aide; Yrbk Stf; Schl Svc Awd 86; Am Leg Awd Citznshp 83; German Engl Awd 83; Temple U; Elem Ed.

DUFFY, JAMES; Upper Moreland SR HS; Willow Grove, PA; (Y); 27/260; Nwsp Stf; Yrbk Stf; Ed Lit Mag; Rep Sr Cls; Rep Stu Cncl; High Hon Roll; Hon Roll; Art Clb; Computer Clb; Key Clb; Kystne Awd-Srious Essy 85-86; Drexel U; Elec Engrng.

DUFFY, JEFFRY; Wyomissing Area HS; Wyomissing, PA; (S); 5/120; Pres Library Aide; Capt Quiz Bowl; Ski Clb; Spanish Clb; Yrbk Stf; Lit Mag; High Hon Roll; NHS; PA Govnrs Schl Sci 85.

DUFFY, TRISHIA; Annville-Cleona HS; Annville, PA; (Y); Church Yth Grp; 4-H; FNA; Chorus; Yrbk Stf; Stu Cncl; Bsktbl; Pres Mat Maids; Hon Roll; NHS; Reading Hosp Schl Of Nrsng; Nrs.

DUGAN, DEBORAH; Crestwood HS; Mountaintop, PA; (Y); 8/168; Girl Scts; Math Clb; Yrbk Stf; Rep Stu Cncl; Var Cheerleading; Crs Cntry; Trk; High Hon Roll; Pres NHS; Duquesne U; Phrmcy.

DUGAN, ELIZABETH; Richland HS; Gibsonia, PA; (Y); 14/183; NFL; Teachers Aide; Chorus; Rep Frsh Cls; Trs Soph Cls; Rep Jr Cls; Trs Sr Cls; L Var Sftbl; High Hon Roll; NHS.

DUGAN, JACQUELINE; Cardinal O Hara HS; Drexel Hill, PA; (Y); 123/740; Church Yth Grp; French Clb; Coach Actv; NHS; Pres Acdmc Ftns Awd 86; Wdnr Merit Schlrshp 86; St Josephs U; Comp Sci.

DUGAN, KATHLEEN; Bristol JR SR HS; Bristol, PA; (Y); Church Yth Grp; School Play; Yrbk Stf; Rep Stu Cncl; Var Bsktbl; Var Capt Cheerleading; Var Fld Hcky; JV Score Keeper; Var Sftbl; Var Trk; All Lg & All Area All Strs In Fld Hcky 85; Cmnctns.

DUGAN, M LAURA; Sharon HS; Sharon, PA; (Y); 29/198; Church Yth Grp; Drama Clb; French Clb; Office Aide; Band; Concert Band; Mrchg Band; Orch; Pep Band; School Musical; PA ST U.

DUGAN, PAUL; Blacklick Valley HS; Nanty Glo, PA; (S); 8/96; Church Yth Grp; German Clb; Ski Clb; Varsity Clb; JV Bsktbl; Var Trk; High Hon Roll; Hon Roll; Jr NHS; NHS; Grmn Ntl Hnr Soc 85; Geneva Coll; Aviation.

DUGAN, SANDRA JANE; North Penn HS; Lansdale, PA; (Y); SADD; Soph Cls; Jr Cls; Stu Cncl; Var Bsktbl; JV Cheerleading; Powder Puff Ftbl; JV Sftbl; High Hon Roll; Hon Roll; Bst Def Awd Sftbl 84; Pres Of Explorer Scouts 85-86.

DUGAN, SEAN; Bald Eagle Area HS; Howard, PA; (Y); 42/210; Varsity Clb; Chorus; Rep Soph Cls; Rep Jr Cls; Rep Sr Cls; Rep Stu Cncl; JV Var Ftbl; Trk; Wt Lftg; JV Var Wrstlng; Pre-Med.

DUGGAL, SUNITA; Strath Haven HS; Swarthmore, PA; (Y); French Clb; VP Intnl Clb; Chorus; School Musical; Ed Nwsp Stf; Var JV Tennis; Hon Roll; NHS; Ntl Merit SF; Williams Coll.

DUGGAN, COLLEEN; West Scranton SR HS; Scranton, PA; (Y); 60/253; Art Clb; Trs VICA; Yrbk Phtg; Yrbk Stf; Hon Roll; NHS; 1st Pl Awd Roth Dist Comm Art 86; Schrlshp Svannah Coll 86; Outstndng Achvt Comm Art; Commcl Artist.

DUGGAN, JEANNE; Pocono Mountain HS; Pocono Lake, PA; (Y); Church Yth Grp; Exploring; NFL; Pep Clb; Nwsp Stf; Stat Bsktbl; JV Var Mgr(s); Hon Roll; NHS; 2nd Pl Awd Jr Acadmy Of Sci Rgnl Comp 86; Bio.

DUGGAN, KATHLEEN; Archbishop Ryan HS For Girls; Philadelphia, PA; (Y); 1/475; Science Clb; High Hon Roll; NHS; Ntl Merit Ltr; Prfct Atten Awd; Spanish NHS; Prtl Chrstn Bros Schlrshp From La Salle U 86; Jewish War Vets Awd 86; La Salle U; Bus.

DUGGER, RUTH; Southmoreland HS; Everson, PA; (Y); Church Yth Grp; FFA; Pep Clb; Chorus; Brnz Pin 1st Yr FFA Flrl & Grnhse 85-86; Bus.

DUGGINS, MICHELE; Pleasant Valley HS; Saylorsburg, PA; (Y); Drama Clb; Math Tm; Band; Chorus; Concert Band; School Musical; Variety Show; Rep Stu Cncl; High Hon Roll; Pres NHS; U Of Scanton; Pre-Med.

DUH, DARIN; Freedom HS; Bethlehem, PA; (Y); 92/456; Boy Scts; JA; Hon Roll; Bus Mngmnt.

DUJUNCO, LOURDES; St Francis Acad; Bethel Park, PA; (S); 1/35; Hosp Aide; Math Clb; Yrbk Bus Mgr; Yrbk Sprt Ed; Sec Frsh Cls; Sec Stu Cncl; High Hon Roll; NHS; NEDT Awd; 1st Pl Crng Mellon U Piano Awd 84; 6th Pl JA Talent Show 83; CMU Carnegie Awds Excell Rtng 83; Wshngtn & Jffrsn Coll; Med.

DUKE, AMY; Allegheny Clarion Valley HS; Emlenton, PA; (Y); 4-H; School Musical; Yrbk Rptr; Yrbk Stf; Stat Crs Cntry; Stat Trk; DAR Awd; NHS; Church Yth Grp; Civic Clb; Cnty Choir; Slct Choir; Htl Mgmt.

DUKE, JOHN; Portage Area HS; Lilly, PA; (S); 5/130; Ski Clb; Gov Hon Prg Awd; High Hon Roll; NHS; Am Legion Essay Awd 84; High Hnrs Trigmetry 86; High Hnrs Math 82; Chem.

DUKOVCIC, JOANNA; Hopewell SR HS; Aliquippa, PA; (Y); 9/256; Church Yth Grp; VP Exploring; German Clb; Band; Chorus; Stu Cncl; Co-Capt Pom Pon; High Hon Roll; NHS; Dist Bnd 85; Engrg.

DUKOVICH, LISA; Moon SR HS; Coraopolis, PA; (Y); German Clb; JA; Key Clb; Band; Mrchg Band; Rep Stu Cncl; Var Trk; JV Vllybl; Hon Roll.

DULANEY, KELLY; Waynesburg Central HS; Waynesburg, PA; (Y); 60/206; Hosp Aide; Library Aide; Chorus; High Hon Roll; Hon Roll.

DUMBAUGH, ERIN; Butler SR HS; West Sunbury, PA; (Y); 150/780; Spanish Clb; Chorus; School Musical; Swing Chorus; Hon Roll; Elem Educ.

DUMBLOSKY, STEPHANIE; Steel Valley HS; Munhall, PA; (Y); 5/207; Pres Church Yth Grp; Co-Capt Flag Corp; L Diving; High Hon Roll; NHS; Psych.

DUMEYER, HEATHER; Hempfield HS; Landisville, PA; (Y); 25/432; Concert Band; Drm Mjr(t); Hst Mrchg Band; Orch; Yrbk Rptr; JV Cheerleading; JV Trk; Im Vllybl; NHS; Ntl Merit Ltr; Cmmnctns.

DUNATHAN, ANDREA L; Westtown Schl; Amherst, MA; (Y); 2/97; Sec Chorus; Madrigals; School Musical; School Play; Stage Crew; JV Fld Hcky; JV Swmmng; Ntl Merit SF; Cmnty Wkr; Mathletes; Brown U JR Engl Awd 85; Rhodes Chem Prz 84; Hghst Schlrp 83-84; Harvard U; Biol Sci.

DUNAWAY, DEBBIE; Connellsville Area HS; Dunbar, PA; (Y); 32/550; Church Yth Grp; French Clb; FTA; Pep Clb; Band; Chorus; Church Choir; Concert Band; Jazz Band; Mrchg Band.

DUNBAR, CHAVOCK; Harrisburg Steelton High Spire Vo-Tech; Harrisburg, PA; (S); 30/440; Church Yth Grp; Rptr DECA; Trs Church Choir; Hon Roll; Stu Month 84-85; Bus Admin.

DUNBAR, HEATHER; Wilson Area HS; Easton, PA; (S); 4/150; Drama Clb; Ski Clb; Capt Fld Hcky; High Hon Roll; Hon Roll; Pres NHS; Bucknell U; Psych.

DUNCAN, DEBBIE; Hopewell SR HS; Aliquippa, PA; (Y); 25/290; Church Yth Grp; Spanish Clb; Chorus; Church Choir; Capt Drm Mjr(t); Twrlr; High Hon Roll; Hlth Crs Clb; Geneva Coll; Spcl Educ.

DUNCAN, DOUGLAS; Valley HS; New Kensington, PA; (Y); Church Yth Grp; Science Clb; Varsity Clb; Stage Crew; Ftbl; Swmmng; Ldrshp & Dedctn Awd Swmmng 85; Libery U.

DUNCAN, ED; Central Catholic HS; Allentown, PA; (Y); JA; Dale Carnegie Inst Schlrshp 86.

DUNCAN, ERIC; Springdale HS; Cheswick, PA; (Y); Trs German Clb; Nwsp Stf; Trs Jr Cls; JV Var Bsbl; Var L Tennis; Hon Roll; Bus Adm.

DUNCAN, JENNA; Slippery Rock Area HS; Portersvlle, PA; (Y); Church Yth Grp; Pep Clb; Teachers Aide; Chorus; Church Choir; Nwsp Rptr; Rep Stu Cncl; High Hon Roll; Hon Roll; Bible Clb Sec Tres; Slpry Rock U; Psych.

DUNCAN II, THOMAS; Mohawk HS; New Castle, PA; (Y); Spanish Clb; Hon Roll; Astro Physcs.

DUNEGAN, M BERNADETTE; Cambria Heights HS; Patton, PA; (Y); Cmnty Wkr; Drama Clb; FHA; Library Aide; Speech Tm; Lit Mag; NEDT Awd; Mngr Ovelty Booth Chrch Festvl; Tchrrs Aide Vol; Art Crafts Clb; Lit Awd; PA ST; Tchr.

DUNHAM, MARCY; New Brighton HS; New Brighton, PA; (Y); Varsity Clb; Chorus; School Play; Yrbk Ed-Chief; Var Cheerleading; Score Keeper; Sftbl; Twrlr; Cit Awd; High Hon Roll; Cmnctns.

DUNHAM, MICHAEL RAY; Albert Gallatin SR HS; Smithfield, PA; (Y); 3/150; Math Tm; Band; Nwsp Ed-Chief; Yrbk Ed-Chief; Stu Cncl; Ftbl; High Hon Roll; Jr NHS; NHS; Vet Med.

DUNHAM, PATRICIA; Cedar Crest HS; Lebanon, PA; (Y); French Clb; FBLA; Pep Clb; SADD; Drill Tm; Mrchg Band; Nwsp Stf; Yrbk Stf; Lit Mag; Twrlr.

DUNHAM, TRACY; Dover Area HS; Dover, PA; (Y); Cmnty Wkr; Dance Clb; German Clb; GAA; Letterman Clb; SADD; Varsity Clb; Color Guard; Drm Mjr(t); Flag Corp; U MD; Psych.

DUNKELBERGER, JIM; Southern Columbia HS; Catawissa, PA; (Y); Sec Boy Scts; Computer Clb; Letterman Clb; Varsity Clb; Var Bsbl; JV Bsktbl; Var L Crs Cntry; Stat Ftbl; Cmptr Prgmng Outstndng Achvt 86; Bloomsburg; Cmptr Sci.

DUNKELBERGER, LAURA; Juniata HS; Mifflintown, PA; (Y); High Hon Roll; Hon Roll; NHS; Computer Clb; Library Aide; Chorus; School Play; Nwsp Stf; Yrbk Stf; Chrch Pianst & Orgnst 83; Schl Orgnst 84-87; Rad Tech.

DUNKERLEY, DOUG; Grove City Area HS; Grove City, PA; (Y); FFA; Diesel Mech.

DUNKLE, FREDERICK; Fannett-Metal HS; Spring Run, PA; (S); Drama Clb; VICA; School Play; Hon Roll; Elec.

DUNKLE, JENNIFER; Northern York County HS; Dillsburg, PA; (Y); 16/209; VP Church Yth Grp; Spanish Clb; Chorus; Concert Band; Mrchg Band; School Musical; Yrbk Stf; Powder Puff Ftbl; Hon Roll; Girl Scts; Sci.

DUNKLE, KRISTI; Bedford HS; Everett, PA; (Y); 5/187; Church Yth Grp; SADD; Chorus; School Musical; Yrbk Ed-Chief; Var L Cheerleading; Crs Cntry; Var L Trk; Hon Roll; Crss Cntry Dist 1st Mdlst 84; Trck Dist 1st Pl Mdl 84-85; Cmmrcl Art.

DUNKLE II, RAY; Everett Area HS; Breezewood, PA; (Y); Pres Church Yth Grp; Computer Clb; Spanish Clb; SADD; Varsity Clb; Stu Cncl; Bsbl; Ftbl; Wrstlng; Hon Roll; Coachs Awd Wrstlg 86; Bedford Cnty Hnbl Mntn Bsbl Adlt Leag 86; Outstndng SR Wrstlg 86; Penn ST Altoona; Comp Sci.

DUNKLE, REBECCA; Sheffield JR SR Area HS; Clarendon, PA; (Y); Drama Clb; Varsity Clb; Mrchg Band; School Musical; School Play; Nwsp Rptr; L Var Bsktbl; L Var Trk; High Hon Roll; Hon Roll; Brbzn Grad Buffalo NY 84; Drama.

DUNKLE, SHARLA; Clarion-Limestone HS; Clarion, PA; (S); French Clb; FFA; Letterman Clb; Chorus; School Musical; Variety Show; JV Cheerleading; Var Mgr(s); Trk; Hon Roll; Miss Congenlgy-Cnty AIF Pgnt 84; Cnty Miss Teen Hemisphere 85; Miss Teen Best Country Instramntlst 85; Busnss.

DUNLAP, TRACY; Marian HS; Delano, PA; (Y); Church Yth Grp; Office Aide; Ski Clb; SADD; Drill Tm; Mrchg Band; School Play; Nwsp Rptr; Nwsp Stf; Yrbk Rptr; Occ Ther.

DUNLAP, WENDY; Middletown Area HS; Middletown, PA; (Y); 7/180; Color Guard; Vllybl; High Hon Roll; Hon Roll; Jr NHS; Acdmc All-Amrcn Awd 86; Engnrng.

DUNLEAVY, JACQUELINE; St Maria Goretti HS; Philadelphia, PA; (S); 5/445; Church Yth Grp; Cmnty Wkr; Co-Capt Mathletes; Math Clb; Math Tm; Spanish Clb; Orch; Hon Roll; NHS; Natl Scl Stds Olympd Cert Merit 85; PA Math Leag Cert Merit 85; Phila Cath Math Cert Merit 85; La Salle U; Accntnt.

DUNLEAVY, KEITH; Devon Prep; Berwyn, PA; (Y); Boy Scts; Mathletes; School Play; Crs Cntry; Trk; High Hon Roll; Hon Roll; NHS; Opt Clb Awd; Computer Clb; Eagle Sct 3 Plms 84; HS Schlrshp 83-87; Sprts.

DUNLOP, KATHLEEN; Strath Haven HS; Swarthmore, PA; (Y); Drama Clb; Intnl Clb; Acpl Chr; Sec Chorus; High Hon Roll; Hon Roll; Ntl Merit SF; Rotary Awd.

DUNN, DAVID; Lewisburg Area HS; Lewisburg, PA; (Y); 20/170; Drama Clb; French Clb; Latin Clb; Concert Band; Jazz Band; Orch; Stage Crew; JV Trk; Jr NHS; NHS; Law.

DUNN, JENNIFER; St Pius X HS; Phoenixville, PA; (S); Cmnty Wkr; Service Clb; Band; Concert Band; Mrchg Band; School Musical; School Play; Hon Roll; NHS; Cert Cum Laude Natl Lat Exam 82; Coll Misericordia; Occ Ther.

DUNN, JOHN; Pennsbury HS; Morrisville, PA; (Y); Computer Clb; German Clb; Hon Roll; Physcs Comptn Cert Of Merit E Stroudsburg U 86; Engrng.

DUNN, MICHAEL FRANCIS; Quigley HS; Sewickley, PA; (S); 4/117; Church Yth Grp; Teachers Aide; Stage Crew; Golf; Socr; Chem Awd 85; Vet.

DUNN, MICHELLE; Yough SR HS; Herminie, PA; (Y); 16/240; Spanish Clb; Band; Mrchg Band; Sec NHS; Duguesne U Schlr Awd 86; Cmmnty Actn Prog Awd 86; IN U Of PA; Nrsg.

DUNN, SHARON I; Strath Haven HS; Wallingford, PA; (Y); Exploring; Intnl Clb; Yrbk Stf; JV Tennis; Var Capt Swmmng; Hon Roll; Ntl Merit Ltr; Cmnty Wkr; Keystone ST Games; Paris Exchng; PA ST Summr Hnrs Acad.

DUNN, SHERRY; Canon Mc Millan HS; Canonsburg, PA; (Y); 29/390; French Clb; Hosp Aide; Capt Drill Tm; High Hon Roll; Phrmcy.

DUNN, STEPHANIE L; Bloomsburg HS; Bloomsburg, PA; (Y); 7/112; Drama Clb; Band; Chorus; Church Choir; Yrbk Ed-Chief; Yrbk Stf; Stu Cncl; DAR Awd; NHS; All-ST Chorus 86; Bucknell U; Bio.

DUNN, THOMAS; Archbishop Carroll HS; Havertown, PA; (Y); 34/189; Rep Frsh Cls; Stu Cncl; Bsbl; Bsktbl; Hon Roll; MVP Bsktbl Sprg Leag Palumbo Rec 86; MVP Bsbl Archbshp Carroll 86; Pre-Law.

DUNNING, KARYN; Bishop Shanahan HS; Wheaton, IL; (Y); 2/218; Debate Tm; School Play; Nwsp Rptr; Yrbk Stf; Var Socr; High Hon Roll; Hon Roll; NHS; Fr III Awd 86; Bus.

DUNSAVAGE, SHARON; Mahanoy Area HS; Barnesville, PA; (Y); Art Clb; Drama Clb; Hosp Aide; Spanish Clb; Chorus; School Play; Nwsp Stf; Yrbk Stf; Trk; Hon Roll; Mc Canns Schl Bus; Exec Sec.

DUNSKI, JONATHAN F; Whitehall HS; Whitehall, PA; (Y); 3/257; Am Leg Boys St; Church Yth Grp; VP Pres German Clb; Scholastic Bowl; Science Clb; Off Jr Cls; Off Sr Cls; VP Rep Stu Cncl; High Hon Roll; Hon Roll; Am Leg Sch Awd 83; Tonsrd Readr 84; Germ Natl Hnr Soc 86; Bio.

DUPAIN, AMIEE; Highlands SR HS; Natrona Hts, PA; (Y); Intnl Clb; Office Aide; Band; Color Guard; Concert Band; Flag Corp; Nwsp Rptr; Yrbk Stf; Jr NHS; NHS; Penn ST; Cmmnctns.

DUPES, ALAN J; Elizabethtown Area HS; Elizabethtown, PA; (S); 78/247; Boy Scts; Concert Band; Jazz Band; Mrchg Band; Pep Band; Variety Show; County Band 85 & 86; Robotics.

DURAND, LORI; Valley HS; New Kensington, PA; (Y); 50/200; Trs AFS; Sec Key Clb; Leo Clb; Office Aide; Pep Clb; SADD; Band; Concert Band; Drill Tm; High Hon Roll.

DURASA, PAULA; Saegertown HS; Conneautville, PA; (Y); 30/124; Church Yth Grp; Girl Scts; Trs Spanish Clb; SADD; Mrchg Band; JV Var Mat Maids; Stat Var Wrstlng; Hon Roll; Jr NHS; Prfct Atten Awd.

DURAZZI, BRUCE J; Easton Area HS; Easton, PA; (Y); 15/505; Band; Chorus; Church Choir; Madrigals; Orch; Lit Mag; NHS; Ntl Merit SF; Natl PTA Reflections Cont Music 3rd Pl 85; Music Tchr.

DURBECK, KATHLEEN M; Cumberland Valley HS; Mechanicsburg, PA; (Y); 2/505; Band; Mrchg Band; Orch; School Musical; Gov Hon Prg Awd; Pres NHS; Rotary Awd; 3rd Pl Harrisbrg Solost Cmptn 85; ST Band 85; ST Orchstra 86; U Of Rchster; Math.

DURBECK, LISA; Cumberland Valley HS; Mechanicsburg, PA; (Y); 9/522; Orch; Symp Band; VP Sr Cls; Stu Cncl; Trs NHS; Church Yth Grp; Sec Latin Clb; Band; Mrchg Band; School Play; Rnnslear Math & Sci Awd 86; Natl Art Hnr Scty 84; PA Gvrnrs Schl Arts 86; Cal Tech; Engr.

DURDAN, LISA; Hughesville HS; Hughesville, PA; (Y); 5/130; FNA; Ski Clb; Band; Color Guard; Concert Band; Mrchg Band; School Musical; Stage Crew; Hon Roll; NHS; Moreau Schlrshp To Kings Coll 86; R N Alumni Awd 86; Rtry Clb 2nd Pl In Sci 86; Kings Coll; Physcns Asstnt.

DURHAM, KYLE; Ringgold HS; Venetia, PA; (Y); 1/319; Sec VP Church Yth Grp; Hosp Aide; High Hon Roll; NHS; Ntl Merit Schol; Val; Yth Rep United Meth Gen Cncl Ministries 84-88; Intl Ordr Oddfllwsx U N Pilgrimage 85; HOBY Ldrshp Sem; U Pittsburgh; Biol.

DURISH, DAVID; Ambridge HS; Ambridge, PA; (Y); Cmnty Wkr; Spanish Clb; JV Bsbl; Var L Bsktbl; Var Capt Ftbl; Var Wt Lftg; Hon Roll; All Sect Ftbl Tm; Poltc Sci.

DURISHIN, LORI; West Hazleton HS; Tresckow, PA; (S); 31/219; Church Yth Grp; FNA; FTA; Thesps; Trk; NHS.

DURITZA, PAULA; Charleroi JR SR HS; Charleroi, PA; (Y); 8/191; Spanish Clb; Varsity Clb; Nwsp Ed-Chief; Capt Var Bsktbl; Var L Socr; Var L Sftbl; Sec NHS; NFL; Science Clb; Service Clb; St Vincent Coll Acdmc/Ldrshp Schlrshp, US Army&steven A Stepanian Schlr/Athl Awd, Frgn Lang Awd 86; St Vincent Coll; Cmmnctns.

DURKIN, BRYAN; Bellefonte Area HS; Bellefonte, PA; (Y); 32/232; Letterman Clb; Pep Clb; Varsity Clb; JV Bsbl; Var L Ftbl; JV Var Wt Lftg; Hon Roll; Sci.

DURKIN, LAWRENCE; Scranton Prep; Dunmore, PA; (Y); 95/192; Band; Concert Band; Jazz Band; Orch; Rep Sr Cls; L Ftbl; Var Trk; L Wrstlng; High Hon Roll; Hon Roll; Scranton Times Paper Boy Yr 82-83; Scranton Dioscn Yth Commssn 82-83; Pres Dunmoreans Agnst Chem Abuse.

DURKIN, NANCY; Abington Heights HS; Clarks Summit, PA; (Y); 2/271; Hosp Aide; Yrbk Stf; Lit Mag; Rep Stu Cncl; Hon Roll; NHS; Ntl Merit SF; PA Govrnrs Schl-Intl Stds; Mxima Cum Laude-Ntl Ltn Exm; Excllnt-Hstry Day Cntst; Bus.

DURNELL, MARNIE; Du Bois Area SR HS; Reynoldsville, PA; (Y); 52/256; Church Yth Grp; Science Clb; SADD; Band; Mrchg Band; Nwsp Stf; Rotry Schlrshp 86; 5th Pl Tm Awd Slppry Rck Bio Olympcs 86; Gannon U; Med.

DURNER, CAROL L; Parkland HS; Allentown, PA; (Y); 40/432; Drama Clb; Teachers Aide; Thesps; Chorus; School Musical; School Play; Swing Chorus; Capt Cheerleading; High Hon Roll; NHS; Hnr Intl Thespn Soc 86; Bucknell U; Elem Ed.

DURNING, KAREN; Bethel Park HS; Bethel Park, PA; (Y); Science Clb; Drill Tm; School Musical; Variety Show; Pom Pon; Swmmng; NHS.

DURNING, STEVE; Council Rock HS; Newtown, PA; (Y); 63/895; Cmnty Wkr; JV Bsbl; Var L Ftbl; Im Vllybl; Im Wt Lftg; High Hon Roll; NHS; NAMES, Acdmc All Am 86.

DURSO, NEIL; Susquehanna Comm HS; Susquehanna, PA; (Y); 1/75; Quiz Bowl; Band; Chorus; Mrchg Band; Orch; Var Bsktbl; Var Capt Ftbl; Bausch & Lomb Sci Awd; Val; U Of Notre Dame; Sci-Math.

DUSHAW, JOSEPH; Bradford Area HS; Derrick City, PA; (Y); 16/329; Boy Scts; Church Yth Grp; Trs FFA; Key Clb; Chorus; High Hon Roll; Hon Roll; NHS; PA Gov Schl Agri 86; Allegheny Mtn Sci Fair 85; PA ST; Hortcltr.

DUSKA, JEFF; Grove City HS; Grove City, PA; (Y); Church Yth Grp; Teachers Aide; School Play; Hon Roll; Grove City Coll; Elec Engrng.

DUSZA, DARREN; Cathedral Prep; Lake City, PA; (Y); 54/215; Letterman Clb; Pep Clb; Varsity Clb; Var L Bsktbl; Coach Actv; Mgr(s); JV Score Keeper; Timer; High Hon Roll; Hon Roll; Bus.

DUSZAK, PETER; Seton Catholic HS; Duryea, PA; (Y); Boy Scts; Exploring; L Golf; Im Vllybl; Hon Roll; Pres Schlr; Presdntl Schlrshp 86; U Of Scranton; Comp Sci.

DUTCHKO, DONNA; Mon-Valley Catholic HS; Elizabeth, PA; (Y); 24/82; FBLA; Office Aide; PAVAS; Powder Puff Ftbl; High Hon Roll; Hon Roll; Decortng Comm Dance Ring Day 86; Soc Fund Raisng Comm 86; Intl Skaters Am Comptn Medals 83-86; Inst Pittsburgh; Fash Desgn.

DUTKIEWICZ, MARGIE; St Hubert HS; Philadelphia, PA; (Y); 100/365; Chorus; Travel.

DUTKO, RUDY; Uniontown Area HS; Uniontown, PA; (Y); 92/320; Debate Tm; Spanish Clb; Pres Band; Concert Band; Jazz Band; Mrchg Band; High Hon Roll; Hon Roll; Prfct Atten Awd; Spanish NHS; Band Pres 85-86; Percssn Sctn Ldr 85-86; Al-Cnty Band 85-86; St Vincent Coll; Bus Finc.

DUTKO, TRACI L; Crestwood HS; Mountaintop, PA; (Y); Rep Stu Cncl; JV Cheerleading; Var Trk; Hon Roll; Pomeroys Teen Brd Rep; Elem Ed; Bloomsburg U.

DUTTON, PETER S; Taylor Allderdice HS; Pittsburgh, PA; (Y); 1/416; Chess Clb; Cmnty Wkr; JCL; Math Tm; Political Wkr; Church Choir; Lit Mag; Var Tennis; High Hon Roll; NHS; Amer Chem Soc Awd 84; Pgh U Provost Day Wnr 85; Wrtng.

DUTTRY, DOLLY JEAN; Central Christian HS; Du Bois, PA; (Y); 4/46; FBLA; Chorus; Sec Sr Cls; DAR Awd; Hon Roll; Sec NHS; Voice Dem Awd; Church Yth Grp; Pres Acadmc Ftnss Awd; Gold Hnr Key Bus 85-86; Rotry Good Citznshp Awd; Rotry Stu Of Mnth 85-86; Gannon U; Acctg.

DUTTRY, JILL; Mechanicsburg Area SR HS; Mechanicsburg, PA; (Y); 21/311; Church Yth Grp; Computer Clb; NFL; Speech Tm; Capt Flag Corp; Yrbk Stf; Stu Cncl; Im L Bsktbl; High Hon Roll; Trs Sec NHS; Spnsh Hrtg Smmr Hmsty Schlrshp 86; Psych.

DUTZIK, ANTHONY; Our Lady Of The Sacred Heart HS; Mc Kees Rocks, PA; (Y); 1/74; NFL; Capt Speech Tm; School Play; Nwsp Stf; Yrbk Stf; Pres Jr Cls; Hon Roll; VP NHS; Ntl Merit SF; Val; PA ST U Excllnce Awd; Natl Cath Forn Lg Natl Trnmnt Fin; PA ST U; Engrng.

DUVALL, LISA; Bethlehem Center HS; Fredericktown, PA; (Y); Cmnty Wkr; Spanish Clb; Color Guard; Concert Band; Mrchg Band; High Hon Roll; NHS.

DUVALL, SEAN; Charleroi Area JR SR HS; Charleroi, PA; (Y); Computer Clb; Exploring; JA; SADD; Band; Concert Band; Jazz Band; Socr; Trk; Hon Roll; CA U PA; Ind Mgt.

DVORCHAK, DARLA; Carrick HS; Pittsburgh, PA; (S); French Clb; Hosp Aide; Q&S; Nwsp Stf; Rep Frsh Cls; High Hon Roll; NHS; Ntl Merit Ltr; Prfct Atten Awd; Recog Awd Candy Strpg 86; Radio Cmmnctns.

DVORSKY, KATHY; Marian HS; Nesquehoning, PA; (Y); 5/115; Band; Concert Band; Mrchg Band; Nwsp Rptr; Yrbk Phtg; Rep Stu Cncl; Trk; High Hon Roll; NHS; Sec Spanish NHS.

DWANE, ANNE; Our Lady Of Lourdes Regional HS; Kulpmont, PA; (Y); French Clb; Pep Clb; Var Cheerleading; Hon Roll; Bloomsburg U; Comp Sci.

DWINAL, MICHAEL; Liberty HS; Bethlehem, PA; (Y); 53/475; Var L Tennis; Hon Roll; Gftd Eductnl Prog 83; Comp Sci.

DWOREK, RICK; Gateway SR HS; Monroeville, PA; (Y); 20/473; Church Yth Grp; Exploring; FBLA; JA; Sr Cls; Bsktbl; Trk; High Hon Roll; NHS; Pres Acad Fitness Awd 86; Cert Of Merit PA Higher Educ Agcy 85; U MI; Medicine.

DWYER, KATHRYN; The Swarthmore Acad; Swarthmore, PA; (S); Church Yth Grp; Drama Clb; Yrbk Stf; Pres Soph Cls; Pres Sr Cls; Bsktbl; L Cheerleading; L Socr; Capt Vllybl; High Hon Roll; Sci Awd Bio 84; U Of PA; Intl Bus.

DY, SYLIM; University City HS; Philadelphia, PA; (Y); 8/198; High Hon Roll; NHS; Synod Trinity Scholar 86-87; Smithkline Beckman Corp Awd 86; Villanova U; Lib Art.

DYCHE, REBECCA; Carlisle SR HS; Carlisle, PA; (Y); Church Yth Grp; Office Aide; Q&S; Spanish Clb; Gold Key 86; Art Schlrshp 86; Engl.

DYDYNSKI, LORI; Wyoming Valley West HS; Plymouth, PA; (Y); Boy Scts; Pres Church Yth Grp; Girl Scts; Hosp Aide; Trs Intnl Clb; Church Choir; Concert Band; Mrchg Band; High Hon Roll; Hon Roll; Grnd Crss Of Color Outstndg Svc Awd 86.

DYER, DANIELLE; Bethel Park SR HS; Bethel Park, PA; (Y); 24/515; FBLA; High Hon Roll; Hon Roll; NHS; Robert Morris Coll; Prlgl.

DYER, DARLENE R; Uniontown Area SR HS; Uniontown, PA; (Y); 102/325; Spanish Clb; Hon Roll; Spanish NHS; Laurel Bus Inst; Acctg.

DYER, DAYNA; Bethel Park HS; Bethel Park, PA; (Y); 24/515; FBLA; NHS; Hgst Hnrs 85-86; Acad Physcl Ftns Awd 85-86; Duffs Bus Inst; Med Assist.

DYER, MICHELE L; North Allegheny SR HS; Allison Pk, PA; (Y); 9/630; Hosp Aide; NFL; Speech Tm; Mrchg Band; Lit Mag; High Hon Roll; Jr NHS; VP NHS; Ntl Merit Ltr; Voice Dem Awd; Pres Acdmc Ftns Awd 86; Dstngshd Achvt Awds 86; U PA; Pdtrcs.

DYKES, HERMAN; Chester HS; Chester, PA; (S); 19/382; L Bsbl; L Ftbl; Var Trk; Wt Lftg; DAR Awd; Hon Roll; Prfct Atten Awd; Church Yth Grp; German Clb; Band; Nov & Dec Stu 85-86; Lockhaven U; Phy Thrpy.

DYLINSKI, MARK; Archbishop Kennedy HS; Conshohocken, PA; (Y); JV Bsktbl; JV Crs Cntry; JV Socr; Prfct Atten Awd; Arch.

DYMKOWSKI, LEA-BUFFY; Gar Memorial HS; Wilkes Barre, PA; (S); 9/177; French Clb; VP Key Clb; Chorus; Capt Drill Tm; Hon Roll; Jr NHS; NHS; NEDT Awd.

DYMOND, CLAYTON; Wyoming Area HS; W Pittston, PA; (Y); 26/253; Church Yth Grp; Computer Clb; German Clb; Key Clb; SADD; JETS Awd; NHS; Ntl Merit SF; Coll Misericordia; Comp Sci.

DYNDA, AMY; St Marys Area HS; St Marys, PA; (Y); 74/290; Cmnty Wkr; Letterman Clb; Red Cross Aide; Service Clb; Varsity Clb; Yrbk Phtg; Pres Frsh Cls; Pres Jr Cls; Sec Stu Cncl; Capt Var Swmmng; Pepperdine U; Psychlgy.

DYSARD, BONNIE; Clearfield Area HS; Clearfield, PA; (Y); Sec Church Yth Grp; Hst SADD; Chorus; High Hon Roll; NHS.

DYSART, KENNETH; Abraham Lincoln HS; Philadelphia, PA; (Y); 12/419; Church Yth Grp; Varsity Clb; Yrbk Sprt Ed; Trs Stu Cncl; Var Capt Bsbl; Var Capt Ftbl; DAR Awd; Hon Roll; Jr NHS; NHS; Outstndng Athlete 86; Schlrshp Character 86; Prof Sci 86; Albright Coll; Bus.

DYSON, JENI; Moon SR HS; Coraopolis, PA; (Y); 102/304; German Clb; Q&S; Yrbk Phtg; Yrbk Rptr; Yrbk Stf; Hon Roll; Photo Apprntcshp W/ Allegheny Intrmdt Unit 85-86; Photo.

DZIAK, JASON; Bentworth HS; Ellsworth, PA; (Y); 5/140; Art Clb; Ski Clb; School Play; Nwsp Rptr; Yrbk Phtg; Yrbk Stf; Wt Lftg; High Hon Roll; NHS; Psychlgy.

DZIEDZICKI, AMY; Southmoreland SR HS; Everson, PA; (Y); Letterman Clb; Pep Clb; Spanish Clb; Pres Band; Church Choir; Pres Concert Band; Jazz Band; Pres Mrchg Band; Pep Band; Pres Spanish NHS; Awd Cntrbtd The Mst Spnsh Ntl Hnr Soc Pres 85-86; Awd Cntrbtd The Mst Mrchng Bnd Cncrt Bnd Pres 85; NCCC; RN.

DZIEKAN JR, RICHARD R; North Penn HS; N Wales, PA; (Y); 41/637; Math Tm; Concert Band; Mrchg Band; Hon Roll; Ntl Merit SF; Cum Laude Natl Latn Exm; Acadmc Achvt Awd; Vrsty Ltr Mrchg Band; Elctrcl Engrng.

DZIKOWSKI, JOHN; Canon-Mc Millan HS; Canonsburg, PA; (Y); Chess Clb; Church Yth Grp; Drama Clb; Exploring; Latin Clb; Science Clb; Chorus; School Play; Hon Roll; Central Intell Agcy 86; CIA Fld Agent.

DZUIBA, SEAN; Hazleton HS; Hazleton, PA; (Y); Computer Clb; Ski Clb; JV Golf; Im Vllybl; Hon Roll; Prfct Atten Awd; Comptr Prgrmng Awd 84; Penn ST; Comptr Sci.

DZURANIN, ANNE; Hazleton HS; Milnesville, PA; (Y); 36/365; Church Yth Grp; French Clb; Office Aide; French Hon Soc; Hon Roll; NHS; Drexel U; Chem Engrng.

EAGLE, STEVEN; Steel Valley HS; Munhall, PA; (Y); 20/207; Chess Clb; Church Yth Grp; Latin Clb; Ftbl; High Hon Roll; Hon Roll; Engrng.

EAKIN, TRACY; Franklin Area HS; Utica, PA; (Y); German Clb; Letterman Clb; Ski Clb; Chorus; Drill Tm; Madrigals; Variety Show; Pom Pon; L Trk; High Hon Roll; Phys Thrpy.

EAKINS, JAMES S; Central Bucks HS West; Chalfont, PA; (Y); 10/421; Mathletes; JV Var Bsbl; High Hon Roll; Hon Roll; Jr NHS; Ntl Merit Schol; NHS; VP Bsbl; Varsity Riffle Team; Physics Olympics; Johns Hopkins; Med.

EALER, JEFF; Henderson SR HS; West Chester, PA; (S); 2/349; Cmnty Wkr; Nwsp Rptr; Trs Soph Cls; VP Jr Cls; Var Socr; Var Tennis; French Hon Soc; High Hon Roll.

EANNACE, VINCENT; Burgettstown Area HS; Burgettstown, PA; (Y); Church Yth Grp; Spanish Clb; Bsbl; Bsktbl; Ftbl; Wt Lftg; High Hon Roll; Jr NHS; NHS; Hnrb Mntn All Dist Bsktbl 86; Engrng.

EARICK, SUZANNE; Fairview HS; Erie, PA; (Y); Cmnty Wkr; Rep French Clb; Hosp Aide; Ski Clb; Varsity Clb; Yrbk Stf; Rep Stu Cncl; Var L Tennis; Hon Roll.

EARL, ELISA; Berwick SR HS; Berwick, PA; (Y); Drama Clb; Key Clb; Keywanettes; Library Aide; Scholastic Bowl; Chorus; Nwsp Rptr; Lit Mag; Fld Hcky; Elks Awd; Womens Civic Clb Stu Rep 85; Physics Awd 2nd Hghst Avg 86; Amer Lgn Schlrshp Awd 86; Lafayette Coll; Pre-Law.

EARLE, CHRISSA JANEL; Pine Forge Acad; S Floral Park, NY; (Y); Church Yth Grp; Drama Clb; Office Aide; Ski Clb; Spanish Clb; Chorus; Pres Frsh Cls; Pres Soph Cls; Pres Jr Cls; VP Stu Cncl; Engl Awd 85-86; All Amer At Large 83-84; Engl Awd 82-83; Oakwood Coll; Bio.

EARLEY, JENNIE; Peters Township HS; Venetia, PA; (S); Rep Frsh Cls; Rep Soph Cls; Rep Jr Cls; Rep Stu Cncl; Var Cheerleading; Mgr Trk; OH U; Spch Ther.

EARLS, MARGARET; Corry Area HS; Corry, PA; (S); Art Clb; Church Yth Grp; French Clb; High Hon Roll; Hon Roll; Top ST SR High Quiz Tm-GARBC Churches 85; Baptist Bible Coll; Bio.

EARNSHAW, SCOTT; Owen J Roberts HS; Spring City, PA; (Y); Bsbl; Bsktbl; Ftbl; Vllybl; Hon Roll; PA ST U; Accounting.

EARWOOD, JOHN SCOTT; Carlisle SR HS; Carlisle, PA; (Y); Boy Scts; Trs Church Yth Grp; Var Socr; Var L Swmmng; Var Trk; Hon Roll; Eagle Sct 85.

EARYES, MICHAEL; Sacred Heart HS; Carbondale, PA; (Y); 10/63; Boy Scts; French Clb; Pres Ski Clb; Chorus; Trs Soph Cls; Var Golf; Var Tennis; Wt Lftg; Elks Awd; High Hon Roll; Frnch Mdl 86; Dstngshd Yng Ldrs US & Wrld 86; PA ST U; Elec Engrng.

EASH, KELLY; Conemaugh Township Area HS; Hooversville, PA; (Y); 16/105; Church Yth Grp; Drama Clb; Hosp Aide; Service Clb; Teachers Aide; Band; Concert Band; Mrchg Band; Stage Crew; Lion Awd; Dwight Krause Mem Bnd Schlrshp 86; Johnstown Vo-Tech; Med Sec.

EASLER, PAUL; Mc Keesport Area SR HS; Mckeesport, PA; (Y); 27/339; AFS; Boy Scts; Church Yth Grp; VP JA; NFL; Science Clb; VP Acpl Chr; School Musical; Var Crs Cntry; Var Trk; Schlstc Awd 85; NEDT Superior Perf Awd 84; Acad Sci 2nd Pl 84; USAF Acad; Intl Affairs.

EASLEY, CHRISTINE; Butler SR HS; Butler, PA; (Y); Computer Clb; French Clb; JA; Pep Clb; SADD; Variety Show; Yrbk Ed-Chief; Yrbk Phtg; Swmmng; Hon Roll; Rochester Inst Tech; Photogrphy.

EAST, M SHANE; Chambersburg Area SR HS; Fayetteville, PA; (Y); Art Clb; Drama Clb; French Clb; Chrmn Ski Clb; Chorus; School Musical; Schltc Art Awd 86; Choristers-Singing Org 85-86.

EASTERDAY, JENNIFER; Downington SR HS; Exton, PA; (Y); GAA; Var Crs Cntry; Mgr(s); Var Trk; Hon Roll; Math.

EASTON, CARRIE; Salisbury Elk Lick HS; Spgs, PA; (Y); 2/22; FFA; Band; Nwsp Phtg; Yrbk Ed-Chief; Pres Frsh Cls; Pres Jr Cls; JV Var Bsktbl; Var Sftbl; High Hon Roll; Jr NHS; Bus.

EASTWOOD, ROBIN; Henderson HS; Westchester, PA; (Y); Art Clb; Church Yth Grp; Westchester U; Law.

EATON, SHERRY; New Brighton HS; New Brighton, PA; (Y); 3/149; Am Leg Aux Girls St; GAA; Varsity Clb; Concert Band; Mrchg Band; L Trk; High Hon Roll; Sci Rsrch.

EAVES, MARGARET; Cardinal Dougherty HS; Phila, PA; (Y); 11/747; Pres Service Clb; Nwsp Rptr; Yrbk Stf; JV Vllybl; Kiwanis Awd; NHS; Sal; Temple U Pres Awd; Raoul Wallenberg Humntrn Awd; Eagl Crss Awd Cmnty Svc Crp; Temple U; Nrsng.

EBBERT, DOLORES; Vincentian HS; Pittsburgh, PA; (Y); Drama Clb; Hosp Aide; JA; Chorus; Church Choir; Yrbk Stf; Rep Soph Cls; Sec Stu Cncl; La Roche.

EBELING, KERRY; Kutztown SR HS; Kutztown, PA; (Y); Church Yth Grp; Exploring; Chorus; Jr Cls; Stu Cncl; Bsbl; High Hon Roll; Jr NHS; NHS; Lycoming CC; Environmtl Resrcs.

EBELING, SHERRI; Bellefonte Area HS; Bellefonte, PA; (Y); 27/250; Cmnty Wkr; 4-H; Red Cross Aide; SADD; Varsity Clb; Chorus; Mrchg Band; Yrbk Stf; Sftbl; Hon Roll; Fres Achvmnt Awd 83-84; PA ST U.

EBERHART, DAWNA; Apollo Ridge HS; Homer City, PA; (Y); 66/177; Ski Clb; Band; Color Guard; Mrchg Band; Sec Yrbk Stf; Trk; Schlrshp Hlth Career Club 86; West Penn Schl; Nrse.

EBERLE, AMY; Penn Manor HS; Lancaster, PA; (Y); Hon Roll; Psych.

EBERLY, CARL; Manheim Central HS; Manheim, PA; (Y); Bsktbl; Ftbl; Wt Lftg; Arch.

EBERLY, DAWN; Cocalico HS; Reinholds, PA; (Y); 45/169; Art Clb; Church Yth Grp; Hosp Aide; Yrbk Stf; Hon Roll; Prfct Atten Awd.

EBERLY, LISA; Ephrata SR HS; Ephrata, PA; (Y); 39/226; FBLA; FNA; Hon Roll; 18th Pl Bus Law ST Comptn 86; Hbshmn Schlrshp 86; Amer Axlry Lgn Awd 86; Chester County Hosptal; Nrsng.

EBERSOLE, JEFF; Scranton Central HS; Scranton, PA; (Y); Wt Lftg; Hon Roll; Johnson Tech; Auto Mech.

EBERSOLE, JOANNE; Donegal HS; Marietta, PA; (Y); Church Yth Grp; Cmnty Wkr; Stage Crew; High Hon Roll; Hon Roll; Millersville Coll; Accntng.

EBERSOLE, MELISSA; Salisbury HS; Allentown, PA; (Y); Debate Tm; SADD; Stat Bsktbl; Var L Fld Hcky; Var L Trk; NHS; Ntl Merit Ltr; Bus.

EBERSOLE, RODNEY; Donegal HS; Mount Joy, PA; (Y); 9/166; Chess Clb; Off AFS; Chorus; Church Choir; Stage Crew; High Hon Roll; Hon Roll; NHS; Penn St U; Pre-Med.

EBERTING, JEFFREY; Emmaus HS; Emmaus, PA; (Y); 24/493; Boy Scts; Drama Clb; Acpl Chr; Church Choir; School Musical; School Play; Var L Crs Cntry; High Hon Roll; NHS; Voice Dem Awd; Dartmouth.

EBLING, ROSEANN; Schuylkill Haven Area HS; Schuylkill Haven, PA; (S); 42/91; Hosp Aide; Science Clb; SADD; Mrchg Band; Yrbk Stf; Rep Stu Cncl; Hon Roll; Hnr Rl 85; Reading Area CC; Nrsng.

EBNER, JOHN; Northampton SR HS; Northampton, PA; (Y); Pres Church Yth Grp; Chorus; Church Choir; Var L Swmmng; Hon Roll; Elem Education.

EBY, ELIZABETH; William Allen HS; Allentown, PA; (Y); 50/530; JCL; Key Clb; Latin Clb; Rep Frsh Cls; Var Trk; Var Twrlr; Hon Roll; NHS; Pres Schlr; Church Yth Grp; Latin NHS 85; Philadelphia Coll; Phrmcy.

EBY, GALEN; Sullivan County HS; Canton, PA; (Y); 11/90; Pres Church Yth Grp; Nwsp Ed-Chief; Lit Mag; NHS; Acctng.

EBY, HEATHER; Carlisle SR HS; Carlisle, PA; (Y); Pres Church Yth Grp; Drama Clb; German Clb; JA; Color Guard; Mrchg Band; Yrbk Stf; Trk; Jr NHS; Shwcse USA Dance Comptn 3rd Pl Solo Tap 84; Bus Admin.

ECCKER, KAREN; Athens Area HS; Sayre, PA; (Y); Hosp Aide; Mrchg Band; Rep Frsh Cls; Rep Soph Cls; Rep Jr Cls; Rep Stu Cncl; JV Var Bsktbl; Var Sftbl; JV Var Vllybl; Med.

ECENRODE, RISHA; Governor Mifflin SR HS; Shillington, PA; (Y); Key Clb; Chorus; Mrchg Band; School Musical; School Play; Swing Chorus; Yrbk Stf; Hon Roll; Jr NHS; FBLA; 9th Grade Major Hon; Poli Sci.

ECHEMENT, SANDY; St Francis Acad; Pittsburgh, PA; (S); 2/37; NFL; Chrmn Service Clb; Ed Yrbk Stf; Rep Jr Cls; High Hon Roll; Prfct Atten Awd; Spnsh Awd 85; Comm.

ECHEVARRIA, DEBORAH; Cedar Grove Christian Acad; Philadelphia, PA; (Y); Church Yth Grp; Drama Clb; Y-Teens; Chorus; Church Choir; Variety Show; Var Crs Cntry; JV Fld Hcky; Var Tennis; Var Trk; Bible Clb Movmnt Awd 85; Light Brigades Spcl Hnr Awd 84; Am Ntl Red Cross Awd 84; Word Life Bible Inst; Physcl Ed.

ECK, BETH; Butler SR HS; Butler, PA; (Y); 150/777; Exploring; FBLA; Drm & Bgl; Clarion U; CPA.

ECK, CAROL; West Forest HS; Tionesta, PA; (Y); 3/44; Sec Church Yth Grp; Yrbk Ed-Chief; Yrbk Phtg; Ed Yrbk Stf; Rep Stu Cncl; Var JV Cheerleading; Var JV Mgr(s); JV Vllybl; Hon Roll; NHS; Crimnl Justc.

ECK, EDWARD; West York SR HS; York, PA; (Y); JA; Penn ST; Comp Prog.

ECKARDT, DIANE; West Scranton HS; Scranton, PA; (Y); French Clb; JA; Ski Clb; Thesps; Pom Pon.

ECKART, KAREN; Berwick HS; Berwick, PA; (Y); Band; Concert Band; Jazz Band; Mrchg Band; Hon Roll; Luzerne Cmmnty Coll; Rstnt Mgr.

ECKBERG, DONNA; Moshannon Valley JR SR HS; Brisbin, PA; (Y); DECA; Varsity Clb; Chorus; Trs Stu Cncl; JV Var Cheerleading; DECA Outstndng Stu Awd 85-86; SE Trvl Acad; Trvl Indstry.

ECKELS, PAMELA; Bishop Guilfoyle HS; Altoona, PA; (Y); 40/130; Cmnty Wkr; German Clb; Church Choir; Stu Cncl; Stat Bsktbl; Mgr(s); Score Keeper; Sftbl; Vllybl; Hon Roll; Ed.

ECKENROD, LAVERNE; Scot Schl For Vet Chld; Cresson, PA; (Y); Am Leg Aux Girls St; Art Clb; Band; Concert Band; Mrchg Band; Pep Band; Symp Band; Yrbk Stf; Var L Bsktbl; Var L Fld Hcky; Bnd Ltr Jckt Arion Awd Mst Career Pts; Am Lgn Schlrshp; IN U; Math.

ECKENROD, ROBERT; Deer Lakes JR SR HS; Tarentum, PA; (Y); Church Yth Grp; Ski Clb; Varsity Clb; Hon Roll; JV Bsbl; Var L Ftbl; Var JV Wt Lftg; Chem.

ECKENRODE, KIMBERLY A; Cambria Heights HS; Patton, PA; (Y); Pres VP Church Yth Grp; Chorus; Church Choir; Nwsp Sprt Ed; Yrbk Stf; Var L Bsktbl; Var Score Keeper; Var L Trk; Var L Vllybl; Slippery Rock U; Elem Ed.

ECKENRODE, SHERRY; Penn Cambria SR HS; Gallitzin, PA; (Y); Camera Clb; FBLA; Band; Concert Band; Mrchg Band; Pep Band; Var L Sftbl; Penn ST U; Accntng.

ECKENRODE, TONYA; Penn Cambria HS; Gallitzin, PA; (Y); 18/200; Camera Clb; FBLA; High Hon Roll; Hon Roll; Jr NHS; 3rd Rgnl Steno Cntst 86; Med Sec.

ECKENROTH, LISA; Central Catholic HS; Reading, PA; (Y); Church Yth Grp; Debate Tm; Drama Clb; Exploring; FNA; Hosp Aide; Latin Clb; Band; Drm & Bgl; Mrchg Band; Offcr Band Drum Majrtt 86; Chem.

ECKER, JANICE; Northgate HS; Pittsburgh, PA; (Y); Chorus; Color Guard; Concert Band; School Musical; Variety Show; Hosp Aide; JA; Library Aide; Band; Church Choir; Awds In Chorus-Triple Trio, Librarian & Concert Choir 84-86; Music.

ECKERT, CAROL; Northern HS; Dillsburg, PA; (Y); Teachers Aide; Band; Concert Band; Mrchg Band; Hon Roll; Laubach Ltrcy Tutor; Sgn Lang Clb; Cptl Clssrm; Bloomsburg U; Pscl Educ.

ECKERT, CHRISTINE; St Basil Acad; Feasterville, PA; (S); 9/94; Drama Clb; Sec German Clb; Yrbk Stf; Var Fld Hcky; NEDT Awd.

ECKERT, JULIE; Lebanon SR HS; Lebanon, PA; (Y); 23/285; VP Church Yth Grp; French Clb; Sec Girl Scts; Hosp Aide; Sec SADD; Teachers Aide; Nwsp Stf; JV Fld Hcky; Hon Roll; Grl Sct Slvr Awd 84; Elem Educ.

ECKERT, MELISSA; Belle Vernon Area HS; Belle Vernon, PA; (Y); 46/276; VP JA; Nwsp Stf; Sec Sr Cls; High Hon Roll; Hon Roll; Full Schlrshp Westmoreland Co CC 86; Achvr Awd At Jr Achvts 84; Westmoreland Co CC; Fin.

ECKERT, SUSAN; Bishop Hoban HS; Hudson, PA; (Y); Sec Church Yth Grp; Rep Computer Clb; Library Aide; Chorus; Church Choir; JV Var Bsktbl; Var L Trk; High Hon Roll; NHS; Gld Hnr Crd 86; Kings Coll; Physcn Asstnt.

ECKERT, TAMARA; Ephrata SR HS; Akron, PA; (Y); VP Church Yth Grp; Band; Chorus; Concert Band; Jazz Band; Mrchg Band; Sec Trs Orch; School Musical; Hon Roll; JP Sousa Awd; NSOA Orchstr Awd 86; IN ST U Gosden; Phylthrpy.

ECKHART, CHARLES; Lehighton Area HS; Lehighton, PA; (Y); Scholastic Bowl; Stage Crew; High Hon Roll; Hon Roll.

ECKHART, KATHLEEN; Crestwood HS; Mountaintop, PA; (Y); French Clb; Pep Clb; Ski Clb; L Swmmng; High Hon Roll; NHS; Psychlgy.

ECKLEY, DEVIN; Newport HS; Newport, PA; (Y); 30/105; FFA; High Hon Roll; Hon Roll; Farming.

ECKMAN, KELLEY; Our Lady Of Lourdes Regional HS; Shamokin, PA; (Y); 6/95; Drama Clb; French Clb; Nwsp Rptr; French Hon Soc; NHS; Sec Frsh Cls; Sec Soph Cls; Sec Jr Cls; Sec Stu Cncl; Var Sftbl; Genetics.

ECKMAN, LINDA; Manheim Township HS; Lancaster, PA; (Y); JA; Off Key Clb; Chorus; Drill Tm; Drm & Bgl; Mrchg Band; School Musical; Stat Bsktbl; Mgr(s); Hon Roll; Schlstc Wrting Awds 83-84; People To People 84-85; U GA; Jrnlsm.

ECKSTINE, REBECCA; Greencastle-Antrim HS; Greencastle, PA; (Y); 4/187; Church Yth Grp; French Clb; Var Fld Hcky; Var Trk; High Hon Roll; NHS; Prfct Atten Awd; Nellie Fox Mem Schlrshp 86; Stu Of Mnth Awd 86; Frnch Awd 86; PA ST Mont Alto.

ECONOMOS, MARIE; Hopewell HS; Aliquippa, PA; (Y); German Clb; Chorus; Swing Chorus; Yrbk Stf; Trs Frsh Cls; Rep Soph Cls; Rep Jr Cls; Rep Stu Cncl; Var Powder Puff Ftbl; L Swmmng; Human Ecology.

EDBERG, DEBORAH L; Sewickley Acad; Pittsburgh, PA; (Y); 3/68; Cmnty Wkr; Ed Lit Mag; Pres Sr Cls; Var Fld Hcky; Var Lcrss; Hon Roll; Ntl Merit SF; Ski Clb; VP Jr Cls; Rep Stu Cncl; Cum Laude; PA Leag All Stars Field Hckey Tm.

EDDINGER, SUE; Montoursville Area HS; Montoursville, PA; (Y); French Clb; Hosp Aide; Red Cross Aide; Stat L Trk; Wlmsprt Schl Cmrc; Med Scrtry.

EDDOWES, ANNETTE; Upper Dublin HS; Ft Washington, PA; (Y); Pres Sec Camera Clb; Sec Church Yth Grp; Girl Scts; Band; Color Guard; Drill Tm; Mrchg Band; Capt Twrlr; Chem.

EDDY, ALLYSON; Archbishop John Carroll Girls HS; Brewster, MA; (Y); 10/214; Church Yth Grp; French Clb; Mathletes; Rep Service Clb; Stu Cncl; High Hon Roll; Hon Roll; NHS; Sal; Sltrn Awd Mdl 85-86; U Of NH; Bio.

EDDY, DAVID; Mercyhurst Prep; Erie, PA; (Y); 17/150; Chess Clb; VP Church Yth Grp; Debate Tm; French Clb; Model UN; Hon Roll; NHS; Engrng.

EDDY, KATHERINE; Marion Center HS; Creekside, PA; (S); 10/200; French Clb; Latin Clb; Spanish Clb; SADD; School Play; Rep Frsh Cls; Rep Soph Cls; Rep Jr Cls; Stat Bsbl; NHS; Ed.

EDDY, ROBIN; Bradford Central Christian HS; Bradford, PA; (Y); 5/28; Yrbk Ed-Chief; Yrbk Stf; Pres Soph Cls; VP Jr Cls; VP Sr Cls; JV Var Bsktbl; Capt Var Cheerleading; High Hon Roll; Jr NHS; NHS; Ntl Engl,Sci Merit Awd 85-86; Acad Allm 85-86; Georgetown; Bus.

EDELMAN, DEANNE; Northampton SR HS; Northampton, PA; (Y); Girl Scts; Leo Clb; Chorus; Var Powder Puff Ftbl; Im Swmmng; Var Tennis; High Hon Roll; Hon Roll; Bloomsburg U; Acctg.

EDELSTEIN, MICHAEL E; Gateway SR HS; Monroeville, PA; (Y); Aud/Vis; Computer Clb; Exploring; Science Clb; Jazz Band; Mrchg Band; Pep Band; Nwsp Rptr; Sftbl; Hon Roll; Schl Ltr Band 85; Band Gld & Wd Plg 86; U Pittsburgh; Pre-Med.

EDER, PAUL; Bethlehem Catholic HS; Bethlehem, PA; (Y); Boy Scts; Trs Church Yth Grp; Hon Roll; Globe Tms Nwspr Carrier Mth 86; Ad Altare Dei-Relgs Awd-Boy Scts 84; Comp Sci.

EDGAR, DJUANA; Pine Forge Acad; Norfolk, VA; (Y); Church Yth Grp; GAA; Church Choir; Rep Stu Cncl; Capt Bsktbl; Hon Roll; Child Psych.

EDGAR, GINGER; North Hills HS; Pittsburgh, PA; (S); 12/485; Church Yth Grp; Drama Clb; NFL; Speech Tm; Chorus; School Play; High Hon Roll; NHS; Prfct Atten Awd; Psych.

EDGE, CHRISTIAN; Freeport Area SR HS; Sarver, PA; (S); 1/180; Chess Clb; Band; Concert Band; Mrchg Band; School Musical; VP Stu Cncl; Trk; High Hon Roll; Biochmstry.

EDGE, DAWN M; Geo Washgtn Carver H S Of Engr & Sci; Philadelphia, PA; (Y); 24/184; Church Yth Grp; Pres Sr Cls; NHS; Am Assoc Of Blcks Enrgy Schlrshp 86; Dr Ruth M Hayre Schlrshp 86; Gen Foods Schlrshp 86; U Of VA Charlottesvl; Pre Med.

EDGELL, LISA; New Brighton HS; New Brighton, PA; (Y); 55/146; 4-H; Chorus; Hon Roll; Bus.

EDGINGTON, SCOTT G; South Allegheny JR SR HS; Mc Keesport, PA; (S); 10/186; German Clb; Pres Science Clb; High Hon Roll; Hon Roll; NHS; Comp Sci.

EDLEMAN, CHRISTINA; Owen J Roberts HS; Pottstown, PA; (Y); Church Yth Grp; Letterman Clb; Im Sftbl; Var L Trk; Im Vllybl; Art Educ.

EDLING, YVONNE; Ambridge Area HS; Freedom, PA; (Y); Pep Clb; Spanish Clb; Color Guard; Mrchg Band; School Play; Stage Crew; Off Frsh Cls; Off Soph Cls; Off Jr Cls; Trk; Acctng.

EDMISTON, HARRY; St John Neumann HS; Philadelphia, PA; (Y); Cmnty Wkr; Hon Roll; Temple; Chrprctr.

EDMUNDSON, GREGORY S; South Park HS; Library, PA; (S); Pres Church Yth Grp; Mrchg Band; Rep Soph Cls; JV Ftbl; Var Golf; Var L Trk; NHS; Var L Wrstlng; High Hon Roll; Hon Roll; PA ST U; Math.

EDRIS, GREGORY; Blue Mountain Acad; Leesport, PA; (S); Ski Clb; Stu Cncl; JV Var Bsktbl; Im Ftbl; Im Gym; Im Sftbl; Im Vllybl; High Hon Roll; Andrews U; Acctg.

EDRIS, SCOTT; Cedar Crest HS; Mt Gretna, PA; (Y); 15/342; Pres Church Yth Grp; VP Pep Clb; Spanish Clb; School Musical; JV Bsktbl; JV Var Socr; Var L Tennis; Im Mgr Vllybl; High Hon Roll; Lion Awd; Army Rsrvs Stu Athlt 86; U Of DE; Chem Engrg.

EDWARDS, AIMEE; North Pocono HS; Lake Ariel, PA; (Y); 5/245; Ski Clb; Variety Show; Rep Stu Cncl; Cheerleading; High Hon Roll; NHS; Ntl Merit Ltr; Bus Adm.

EDWARDS, BRIAN; Central Catholic HS; Reading, PA; (Y); Alvernia; Acctg.

EDWARDS, BRIAN; Plum SR HS; New Kensington, PA; (Y); Varsity Clb; Band; Mrchg Band; Symp Band; L Crs Cntry; Var Trk; U Of Pittsburgh; Mech Engrng.

EDWARDS, CARL A; Wyoming Valley W HS; Kingston, PA; (Y); 42/410; Band; Var L Bsbl; JV Im Bsktbl; Im Bowling; Var L Ftbl; Im Vllybl; Im Wt Lftg; Hon Roll; NHS; NEDT Awd; Chemistry.

EDWARDS, CHERYL; West Perry SR HS; Landisburg, PA; (Y); Cmnty Wkr; VP 4-H; Intnl Clb; Spanish Clb; Varsity Clb; Nwsp Rptr; Yrbk Rptr; Yrbk Sprt Ed; Rep Stu Cncl; Var L Fld Hcky; Cnslng Ctr Aide 84-86; Socl Svcs.

EDWARDS, CHRISTNE A; Mid-Valley HS; Dickson City, PA; (Y); FNA; Pep Clb; Ski Clb; Rep Frsh Cls; Rep Soph Cls; Rep Jr Cls; Rep Sr Cls; Capt Cheerleading; Sftbl; Surg Nrsg.

EDWARDS, DAWN; Churchill HS; Pittsburgh, PA; (Y); 59/188; Church Yth Grp; Library Aide; Office Aide; Teachers Aide; Rep Stu Cncl; Var Stat Bsktbl; Mgr(s); Trk; Vllybl; Hon Roll; Upwrd Bnd Prjct 86; Vrsty Ltrs Vllybll, Trck & Bsktbl 84-86; Law.

EDWARDS, EARL; New Wilmington Area HS; Westmiddlesex, PA; (Y); 62/123; Spanish Clb; Var L Bsbl; Var L Bsktbl; Var L Ftbl; Var Trk; Hon Roll; All-Sctn Hnrs Bsbll 84-85; All-Sctn Hnrs Ftbll 85-86; All-Str Tm Yngstwn Clss B 85; Pre-Med.

EDWARDS, ERIN; Monara JR SR HS; Monaca, PA; (Y); 12/100; Pres Church Yth Grp; Pep Clb; Teachers Aide; Drill Tm; Mrchg Band; Pom Pon; Hon Roll; NHS; Prfct Atten Awd; Leaders Clb 86-87; Accntg.

EDWARDS, GLYNDA; Blairsville SR HS; Blairsville, PA; (Y); Church Yth Grp; SADD; Band; Concert Band; Jazz Band; Mrchg Band; School Musical; High Hon Roll; Hon Roll; Summer Happenings At IUP 86; Music.

EDWARDS, KAREN; Ford Cty HS; Ford City, PA; (Y); 10/149; Chorus; School Musical; School Play; Rep Frsh Cls; Rep Sr Cls; Rep Stu Cncl; Stat Bsktbl; High Hon Roll; NHS; Bus Prof Womens Club Merit Awd 86; U Of Pittsburgh; Soclgy.

EDWARDS, LISA; North Pocono HS; Lake Ariel, PA; (Y); 43/226; FBLA; Ski Clb; Yrbk Stf; High Hon Roll; Hon Roll; NHS; Outstndng Bus Stu Awd 86; Scott Donaghey Memorial Schlrshp; Mary Wood Coll; Fash Rtlng.

EDWARDS, MATTHEW; Freeport Area SR HS; Freeport, PA; (Y); Exploring; School Musical; Stage Crew; Ftbl; Hon Roll; PA ST; Chem Engrg.

EDWARDS, MEL; Hamburg Area HS; Hamburg, PA; (Y); Capt L Bsbl; Capt L Bsktbl; Capt L Socr; Hon Roll; NHS; All-Cnty Bsktbll & Bsbll 85-86; Athlt Of Yr Brks Cnty 86.

EDWARDS, MICHAEL; William Penn HS; Philadelphia, PA; (Y); Boy Scts; Math Clb; Yrbk Sprt Ed; Var Bsbl; Var Ftbl; Hon Roll; Prfct Atten Awd; 4th Annl Essy Cntst Hon Mntn 85; Outstndng Acmplshmnts In Eng 85; Excllnc Wrld Hstry 84; Comm.

EDWARDS, MICHELE; Holy Name HS; Sinking Spring, PA; (Y); 22/115; Camera Clb; Pres French Clb; Pep Clb; Q&S; School Play; Nwsp Bus Mgr; Nwsp Rptr; Ed Nwsp Stf; Vllybl; Hon Roll; U Of DE; Bus.

EDWARDS, MOLLIE; Norwin SR HS; N Huntingdon, PA; (Y); 138/530; French Clb; Pep Clb; Ski Clb; SADD; Var Cheerleading; WA & Jefferson; Optmtry.

EDWARDS, NIKI; William Penn HS; Philadelphia, PA; (Y); Math Clb; Nwsp Bus Mgr; Yrbk Stf; Trs Jr Cls; Pres Stu Cncl; Capt Cheerleading; JV Sftbl; Hon Roll; Prfct Atten Awd; Pres Schlr; Cert Of Awd Hnr Rl 85; Bio Med Sci Prog 85-86; Athltc Awd Chlrdlg 85-86; Temple U; Commtns.

EDWARDS, RENEE; West Scranton SR HS; Scranton, PA; (Y); 8/270; Dance Clb; French Clb; Hosp Aide; Letterman Clb; Var Cheerleading; JV Coach Actv; Var L Crs Cntry; CAP; L Var Trk; High Hon Roll; Nwspaper Artcl Pblshd Scrntn Tms 86; Pre-Med.

EDWARDS, RENEL; Walter Biddle Saul HS; Philadelphia, PA; (Y); 10/120; FFA; VP JA; Pres Sr Cls; Capt Vllybl; Hon Roll; NHS; Debate Tm; Nwsp Stf; VP Frsh Cls; Bsktbl; Maxwell House Blck Schlr Schlrshp 86; PA Ddrtn Tchrs Hmn Rltns Awd 86; Hme & Schl Assoc Ldrshp Awd 86; Tuskegee U; Occptnl Thrpy.

EDWARDS, SHELLEY; Garden Spot HS; Terre Hill, PA; (Y); Pres Church Yth Grp; Cmnty Wkr; Girl Scts; Library Aide; Political Wkr; Teachers Aide; Chorus; JV Var Bsktbl; Tennis; Hon Roll; Bst Ofnsv Awd Bsktbl Scrng Mst Pts 86; 1st Pl Tnns & Crmpts Trnmnts 85; Mnstrs.

EDWARDS, TIM; Gettysburg HS; Gettysburg, PA; (Y); #4 In Class; Computer Clb; Varsity Clb; Band; Concert Band; Jazz Band; Mrchg Band; Pep Band; Symp Band; Var L Socr; Gov Hon Prg Awd; Alt Gov Schl Sci, Presentations PA Sci Tchrs Assoc 85; Alt USAF ROTC Schlrshp 86; Penn ST U; Aeronautical Engrng.

EELLS, PAUL; Mosignor Bonner HS; Glenolden, PA; (S); 2/312; Mathletes; Nwsp Stf; Yrbk Sprt Ed; NHS; Prfct Atten Awd; St Schlr; Church Yth Grp; High Hon Roll; Acdmc All Amer 84; Intl Frgn Lng Awd 84; Engrng.

EGAN, ELIZABETH; Upper Dublin HS; Ft Washington, PA; (Y); 3/310; Intnl Clb; JA; Science Clb; Varsity Clb; Rep Stu Cncl; JV Var Crs Cntry; JV Var Trk; NHS; Ntl Merit SF; Germn Natl Exm Hnbl Mntn 85-86; Bio.

EGAN, ELIZABETH L; Hersget Sr HS; Houston, TX; (Y); 13/188; Pres VP 4-H; Model UN; Sec Spanish Clb; Sec Band; Orch; School Musical; School Play; NHS; Spanish NHS; TX Christian U Deans Schlrshp 86; TCU Schlrsp 86; TX Christian U; Math.

EGAN, JOSEPH; St John Neumann HS; Philadelphia, PA; (Y); 10/338; Science Clb; Coach Actv; High Hon Roll; NHS; La Salle U; Sci.

EGAN, LAURA; Peabody HS; Pittsburgh, PA; (S); Art Clb; Girl Scts; Crs Cntry; Capt Swmmng; Trk; Cit Awd; High Hon Roll; NHS; Creatv Art Schlrshp 82-84; CA ST; Arch.

EGAN, TRACI; Chief Logan HS; Lewistown, PA; (Y); 2/190; Church Yth Grp; Ski Clb; Spanish Clb; Band; Chorus; Concert Band; Mrchg Band; Yrbk Stf; JV Crs Cntry; Var Trk; Music.

EGERCIC, SEAN; Farrell Area HS; Farrell, PA; (Y); French Clb; Stage Crew; Yrbk Stf; Ftbl; Trk.

EGGE, MARY BETH; Central Catholic HS; Northampton, PA; (Y); Church Yth Grp; Yrbk Stf; Rep Frsh Cls; Rep Jr Cls; VP Cheerleading; Crs Cntry; Photo.

EGGER, ERNEST; Lakeview HS; Sandy Lake, PA; (S); 16/120; Drama Clb; Intnl Clb; Letterman Clb; Varsity Clb; Ftbl; Sftbl; 2nd Tm Offensive Tackle For Frnch Crk Vly Conf 85; Hnrd Most Imprvd Lineman-Ftbll 85; Mech Engrng.

EGGLESTON, KIMBERLY; Shippensburg Area SR HS; Shippensburg, PA; (Y); 5/214; Church Yth Grp; Pres French Clb; Var L Crs Cntry; Var Swmmng; Var L Trk; High Hon Roll; NHS; Rotary Awd; JV L Bsktbl; Cert Of Merit From PA Educ Asst Agncy 85; PA Math Lge Cert High Score For Shippensburg 85; IN U Of PA; Art.

EGGLESTON, MICHELE; Interboro HS; Glenolden, PA; (S); Dance Clb; French Clb; Pep Clb; Varsity Clb; Variety Show; Yrbk Stf; Rep Jr Cls; Cheerleading; High Hon Roll; Hnr Classes 84-86; Hnr Soc 84-86; Law.

EGGLESTON, ROBERT BUBBA; Wyoming Seminary; Wilkes Barre, PA; (Y); Varsity Clb; Stu Cncl; Var Ftbl; Var Lcrss; Hon Roll; NEDT Awd; Engrng.

EGOLF, DENNIS; Chambersburg Area HS; Chambersburg, PA; (Y); 70/593; French Clb; German Clb; SADD; Chorus; Rep Jr Cls; Rep Sr Cls; Rep Stu Cncl; Var L Bsbl; Var L Bsktbl; High Hon Roll; Bio.

EGOLF, LEANNE; Purchase Line HS; Mahaffey, PA; (Y); 18/118; FBLA; Spanish Clb; School Play; Stage Crew; Nwsp Stf; Yrbk Stf; Hon Roll; Indiana U Of PA; CPA.

EHMAN, HEATHER; Exeter Twshp SR HS; Reading, PA; (Y); Band; Chorus; Church Choir; Concert Band; Mrchg Band; Pep Band; Soc Psych.

EHMANN, CHRISTOPHER; West Catholic Boys HS; Philadelphia, PA; (Y); Camera Clb; Coach Actv; Crs Cntry.

EHMANN, INGRID; Lower Moreland HS; Huntingdon Valley, PA; (S); French Clb; German Clb; Key Clb; Yrbk Stf; Ed Lit Mag; High Hon Roll; NHS; Ntl German Scty Awds 2nd Pl 84-85; Outstndng Achvmnt 85; Bio Outstndng Achvmnt Best Bio Stu 85; Pre-Law.

EHRENBERGER, JUDY; North Hills HS; Pittsburgh, PA; (Y); Church Yth Grp; Exploring; VP JA; Library Aide; Bsktbl; High Hon Roll; Hon Roll; JC Awd.

EHRENFELD, JOHN; Plum HS; Pittsburgh, PA; (Y); School Play; Crs Cntry; Trk; Hon Roll; NHS; Engrng.

EHRENFRIED, HOLLY; Weatherly Area HS; Weatherly, PA; (Y); 10/62; FBLA; FNA; Hosp Aide; Concert Band; Yrbk Ed-Chief; CC Awd; High Hon Roll; Hon Roll; Pres Schlr; VP Church Yth Grp; Whtwtr Chlngrs Pursuit Of Exc Awd 86; Msrcrd Coll; Ocptnl Thrpy.

EHRHARDT, KATHLEEN; Parkland HS; Allentown, PA; (Y); Boy Scts; Cmnty Wkr; Drama Clb; Intnl Clb; Band; Chorus; Church Choir; School Musical; School Play; Masonic Awd; Schltc Prfrmnc Awd $1000 86; Masonic Awds-Rainbow Grls 84-85; Grand Rep-OR Wrthy Advsr 82 & 85; St Francis Coll; Phys Asst Pgm.

EHRHART, MATTHEW J; Pequea Valley HS; Narvon, PA; (S); 1/150; Pres VP Church Yth Grp; Trs FFA; Stu Cncl; JV Wrstlng; High Hon Roll; NHS; Rotary Awd; 4-H; Im Wt Lftg; Hugh O Brian Yth Ldrshp Smnr 85; 1st Pl Cnty Envrlympcs 85; Star Grnhnd & Wldlf Prfcncy FFA Awds 85; Penn ST; Wldlf Sci.

EHRIG, GRETA; Emmaus HS; Macungie, PA; (Y); French Clb; Key Clb; Teachers Aide; Chorus; Mrchg Band; School Musical; Nwsp Sprt Ed; NHS; German Clb; JCL; Tlnt Shw Awds Orgnl Chrgrphy & Perf 84-85; Schlrhsp To Martha Graham Schl 85.

EIBS, JANET; Keystone Oaks HS; Pittsburgh, PA; (Y); Church Yth Grp; German Clb; Stu Cncl; Hon Roll; Intl Foreign Lang Awd 85-86; Westminster Coll.

EICHELBERGER, EUN HEE; Manheim Central HS; Manheim, PA; (Y); Church Choir.

EICHENLAUB, TIMOTHY; Bald Eagle Nittany HS; Mill Hall, PA; (Y); Wt Lftg; Hon Roll; NHS; Prfct Atten Awd; Lock Haven U PA; Sprts Med.

EICHER, CLYDE; Seneca Valley HS; Ligonier, PA; (Y); Ski Clb; Hon Roll; Gftd Prog 84-87; U Pittsburgh; Engrg.

EICHER, KEITH; Northern Bedford County HS; Roaring Spg, PA; (Y); Aud/Vis; Camera Clb; Computer Clb; Library Aide; Speech Tm; SADD; Band; Chorus; Concert Band; Drill Tm; Dist & Rgnl Chorus 84-86; PA ST U; Sci.

EICHER, KIM; Claysburg Kimmel HS; Queen, PA; (Y); 8/51; Church Yth Grp; FBLA; Library Aide; Band; Chorus; Capt Flag Corp; Twrlr; High Hon Roll; Hon Roll; Ntl Merit Ltr; Math Awd; Altoona; Bus.

EICHER, TRACY; Fairchance-Georges HS; Fairchance, PA; (Y); 4-H; Band; Concert Band; Drm Mjr(t); Mrchg Band; JV Var Bsktbl; High Hon Roll; Hon Roll; Jr NHS; NHS.

EICHEWALD, HELENE; Allen HS; Allentown, PA; (Y); 12/613; Civic Clb; Cmnty Wkr; VP Intnl Clb; Political Wkr; Service Clb; Spanish Clb; Yrbk Stf; Jr NHS; NHS; Spanish NHS; 1st Pl EPA Hstry Dy 85; Intl Fnlst BBYOORTRY Cont 86; Mgg Lvn Mmrl Essy Wnnr 86; Lwyr.

EIDEMILLER, MARSHA; Cocalico SR HS; Ephrata, PA; (Y); 15/174; FBLA; Band; Sec Chorus; Concert Band; Mrchg Band; School Musical; High Hon Roll; Lion Awd; NHS; Spcl Olympcs Chrmn 83-86; Peer Cnslng Grp Ledr 83-86; Lancaster Bus & Prof Wmns S Chlrshp 86; Elizabethtown Coll; Bus Admin.

EIDEN, MELISSA; Northampton Area SR HS; Walnutport, PA; (S); Sec DECA; FBLA; Northampton CC; Bus Adm.

EIFERT, NATHAN; Dover Area HS; Dover, PA; (Y); 30/300; Church Yth Grp; Trs Band; Concert Band; Jazz Band; Mrchg Band; Hon Roll; NHS; Soc Dstngshed Amer HS Stdnts 84-86; Certmerit Amer Assoc Tchrs Grmn 84-85; Wind, Brass Ensmbl; Dntstry.

EIGHME, JAMES; North Hills HS; Pittsburgh, PA; (Y); Church Yth Grp; Exploring; German Clb; Hosp Aide; Ski Clb; High Hon Roll; Pres Schlr; Golf; PHEA Grant 86-87; Volntr Awd 85; PA ST; Med.

EIKOV, LEE; Notre Dame HS; Stroudsburg, PA; (Y); Am Leg Boys St; English Clb; Political Wkr; Temple Yth Grp; Nwsp Ed-Chief; Nwsp Rptr; Nwsp Stf; Lit Mag; Stat Bsktbl; Score Keeper; Pres Bnai Brith 83-86; Ofcs Boys ST; Pol Sci.

EILER, CORY; Hampton HS; Allison Pk, PA; (Y); GAA; Spanish Clb; Chorus; Rep Soph Cls; Sec Jr Cls; Sec Sr Cls; Rep Stu Cncl; Stat Bsktbl; Var L Sftbl; Hon Roll; Smmr Sftbl Allstar 83-86; Acctg.

EILER, TIMOTHY; Philipsburg Osceola HS; Philipsburg, PA; (Y); 60/250; Letterman Clb; Yrbk Stf; JV Var Bsbl; JV Var Bsktbl; Var L Crs Cntry; Tennis.

EINLOTH, THERESA; North Hills HS; Pittsburgh, PA; (Y); 1/505; Keywanettes; Q&S; VP Orch; Nwsp Ed-Chief; High Hon Roll; NHS; Pres Schlr; Val; Cmnty Wkr; Exploring; Dailey Mem Schlrhrp/U Of Notre Dame 86; Dr Rice Mem Schlrshp Awd 86; U Notre Dame; Mtlrgcl Engrng.

EISAMAN, CARL EDWARD; Hempfield Area HS; Greensburg, PA; (Y); 12/647; Chess Clb; High Hon Roll; Hon Roll; Jr NHS; NHS; Pres Schlr; Rotary Awd; Spanish NHS; Acad Awds Bnqts 84 86; Hnr Grad 86; PA ST; Mechanical Engrng.

EISENACHER, RONALD C; Sun Valley HS; Aston, PA; (Y); Am Leg Boys St; Office Aide; SADD; VP Soph Cls; VP Jr Cls; Rep Stu Cncl; Var Socr; Var Wrstlng; Hon Roll; Prncpls Awd Svc; Cmnctns.

EISENBISE, CHRISTINE LOUISE A; Cocalico HS; Reinholds, PA; (Y); 113/172; Church Yth Grp; Stat Bsktbl; Cheerleading; Powder Puff Ftbl; Trk; Cntrl PA Bus Schl; Med Asst.

EISENHAUER, DOROTHY; Cedar Crest HS; Lebanon, PA; (Y); 27/323; Trs Drama Clb; Trs French Clb; Pep Clb; Orch; School Musical; School Play; Socr; Vllybl; Hon Roll; NHS; Hon Bnqt; Theatre.

EISENHOOTH, DAVE; Bald Eagle Area HS; Howard, PA; (Y); Varsity Clb; Var L Ftbl; Var Trk; Var L Wrstlng; High Hon Roll; Hon Roll; NHS.

EISENMAN, BETH; North Clarion HS; Lucinda, PA; (Y); Church Yth Grp; Drama Clb; SADD; Varsity Clb; School Musical; Nwsp Ed-Chief; Pres Jr Cls; Trs Stu Cncl; Stat Bsbl; JV Var Cheerleading; Mrktng.

EISENMAN, LISA; North Clarion HS; Tionesta, PA; (Y); 12/87; French Clb; Chorus; Yrbk Stf; JV Var Bsktbl; Im Socr; JV Trk; Hon Roll.

EISLEY, PATRICIA; Milton SR HS; New Columbia, PA; (Y); 3/201; Sec Church Yth Grp; Computer Clb; Sec FTA; Hosp Aide; Latin Clb; Library Aide; Hon Roll; NHS; Bloomsburg U; Elem Ed.

EISTER, MARK; Shikellamy HS; Northumberland, PA; (Y); Bucknell; Elec Engrng.

EKEY, BARB; North Hills SR HS; Pittsburgh, PA; (Y); Church Yth Grp; Drama Clb; Exploring; Library Aide; NFL; Speech Tm; Yrbk Stf; Var Socr; Var Trk; Hon Roll; IN U; Crmnlgy.

EKIS, CHRISTA; Franklin HS; Polk, PA; (Y); Church Yth Grp; Spanish Clb; Off Frsh Cls; Off Soph Cls; Off Jr Cls; Off Sr Cls; Trk; Vllybl; High Hon Roll; Hon Roll; U Pittsburgh; Occu Ther.

ELBICH, PAULA; Pittston Area HS; Wilkes-Barre, PA; (Y); 10/330; Cmnty Wkr; VP French Clb; Hosp Aide; Key Clb; Yrbk Stf; High Hon Roll; NHS; U MD; Pre-Law.

ELCHIN, SHERRY; Portage Area HS; Portage, PA; (Y); 16/120; Drama Clb; French Clb; Thesps; Varsity Clb; School Play; Bowling; Vllybl; NHS; Penn ST; Pre Med.

ELDER, DAVID; Tussey Mountain HS; Saxton, PA; (Y); Pres Church Yth Grp; Rep Frsh Cls; Rep Soph Cls; Rep Jr Cls; Bsktbl; Ftbl; Hon Roll; NHS; Acctng.

ELDER, LORI L; Commodore Perry HS; Sandy Lake, PA; (S); 5/63; Art Clb; Church Yth Grp; Drama Clb; Trs FBLA; Math Tm; Chorus; Trs Sr Cls; Rep Stu Cncl; L Cheerleading; Hon Roll; 3rd Pl Typing Awd FBLA 83-84; 3rd Pl Prlmntry Procedure Awd FBLA 84-85; Social Wrkr.

ELDER, SANDRA; Cardinal O Hara HS; Chester, PA; (Y); 118/772; Civic Clb; Cmnty Wkr; Drama Clb; Spanish Clb; Hon Roll; W Chester U; Elem Educ.

ELDER, TERRY; Hanover SR HS; Hanover, PA; (Y); 8/104; Aud/Vis; Church Yth Grp; Math Tm; Red Cross Aide; Stage Crew; VP L Bsktbl; Coach Actv; JV Ftbl; VP L Trk; High Hon Roll; Top 10 Prnct Awd Natl NEDT Test 85; Penn ST; Bio-Med Engrng.

ELDER, TRUDY; Wilmington Area HS; New Wilmington, PA; (S); 21/123; Drama Clb; Key Clb; Office Aide; Spanish Clb; Stage Crew; Var JV Bsktbl; Var Powder Puff Ftbl; Hon Roll; Acadmc Achvt List 84-85; Real Est.

ELDRIDGE, CHRISTOPHER; Palisades JR SR HS; Ottsville, PA; (Y); 21/150; VP Church Yth Grp; Chorus; Church Choir; Madrigals; Orch; School Musical; Hon Roll; Jr NHS; NHS; Vocal Music Awd 86; County Dist Regional Chorus 86; Hstry Awd 86; Messiah Coll; Music Edu.

ELEK, KATHLEEN; Fairchance Georges JR SR HS; Fairchance, PA; (Y); FHA; Hon Roll; Travel.

ELEK, KEVIN; Langley HS; Pittsburgh, PA; (Y); 16/275; Dequesne U; Envstmnt Attrny.

ELFAHL, JINAN; Parkland HS; Allentown, PA; (Y); Church Yth Grp; Cmnty Wkr; Debate Tm; Exploring; 4-H; Hosp Aide; JA; Key Clb; Pep Clb; Red Cross Aide; Brdcstg.

ELFAND, SUSAN; Northeast HS; Philadelphia, PA; (Y); 14/690; Yrbk Ed-Chief; Stu Cncl; Var Capt Tennis; Hon Roll; NHS; Prfct Atten Awd; Spanish NHS; Office Aide; Quiz Bowl; Rep Soph Cls; Prsdntl Acadmc Ftns Awd 85; Stu Senate Distgshd Svc Awd 85; Northeast Alumni Assoc Outstndng Svc Awd; Temple U.

ELFONT, HARRY; Lower Moreland SR HS; Huntingdon Valley, PA; (S); 50/214; Pres Drama Clb; Chorus; Jazz Band; Mrchg Band; School Musical; School Play; Nwsp Sprt Ed; Gov Hon Prg Awd; Kiwanis Awd; Rotary Awd; Dirctr.

ELGENBRODE, KRISTINA; Waynesboro SR HS; Waynesboro, PA; (Y); 125/348; Library Aide; Ski Clb; Chorus; Swing Chorus; Hon Roll; Johnson & Wales; Travel.

ELGIN, RACHAEL; Marion Center Area HS; Marion Center, PA; (S); 5/170; Sec Church Yth Grp; Pres Latin Clb; Q&S; Science Clb; SADD; Band; Church Choir; Yrbk Stf; NHS; Scl Wrkr.

ELIAS, MARY; Hempfield SR HS; Forbes Road, PA; (Y); Computer Clb; Exploring; German Clb; Library Aide; Pep Clb; Nwsp Rptr; Wldlf Bio.

ELICK, RAYMOND; Tunkhannock Area HS; Tunkhannock, PA; (S); 23/349; Church Yth Grp; 4-H; Key Clb; Concert Band; Jazz Band; Mrchg Band; Swmmng; Tennis; Trk; Engrng.

ELIZABETH, SCOTT; Churchill HS; Pittsburgh, PA; (Y); 14/188; Ski Clb; Acpl Chr; Color Guard; School Musical; Rep Stu Cncl; Var Sftbl; High Hon Roll; Spanish Clb; Chorus; Concert Band; Resprtry Thrpy.

ELKIN, GLYNN; Penns Manor Area Schl; Penn Run, PA; (Y); Boy Scts; Computer Clb; Varsity Clb; VP VICA; Rep Stu Cncl; Var Capt Bsktbl; Var L Trk; High Hon Roll; Hon Roll; Natl Cmprs & Hkrs Ass PA St Teen Ass VP & Pres 85-87; Penn St U; Elec Engr.

ELKIN, TAMI; Marion Center Area HS; Home, PA; (Y); Church Yth Grp; Hosp Aide; Intnl Clb; SADD; Varsity Clb; Stat Bsbl; Var L Cheerleading; L Sftbl; French Clb; FNA; IUP Gannon; Psych.

ELKINS, DOUG; Cheltenham HS; Melrose Pk, PA; (Y); Drama Clb; Hosp Aide; Acpl Chr; Chorus; School Musical; School Play; Variety Show; VP Soph Cls; Pres Stu Cncl; Theater Arts.

ELKO, STACY; Hazleton HS; Kelayres, PA; (Y); FBLA; Office Aide; OEA; Red Cross Aide; Bsktbl; Swmmng; Trk; 3 Yr Ltr-Swmmng 84-86; Nrsng.

ELL, JENNIFER; Cumberland Valley Christian Schl; Waynesboro, PA; (Y); Art Clb; Church Yth Grp; Office Aide; Political Wkr; Yrbk Stf; Cheerleading; Lbrty U; Bus.

ELLENBERG, JENIFER; Baldwin HS; Pittsburgh, PA; (Y); 53/535; Math Tm; Nwsp Ed-Chief; Nwsp Rptr; Hnr Rll-Achvr 84-86; Jrnlsm.

ELLENBERGER, DEANNA; Cameron County HS; Driftwood, PA; (Y); Yrbk Stf; Powder Puff Ftbl; Hon Roll; NHS; Excllnc Hm Ec Awd 86; RN.

ELLENBERGER, TRACY; Forest Hills SR HS; Elton, PA; (Y); 76/180; Art Clb; Church Yth Grp; Pep Clb; Ski Clb; Y-Teens; Chorus; Im Bsktbl; Im Sftbl; Im Vllybl; U Of Pittsburgh; Wldlf Mngmnt.

ELLINGER, AMY; Lebanon Catholic HS; Quentin, PA; (Y); Church Yth Grp; Debate Tm; Pep Clb.

ELLIOT, AMY; Cumberland Valley HS; Mechanicsburg, PA; (Y); 156/500; Ski Clb; Band; Chorus; Concert Band; Jazz Band; Mrchg Band; Orch; School Musical; Symp Band; Hon Roll; Music.

ELLIOTT, CYNTHIA; Souderton Area HS; Telford, PA; (Y); 24/365; Church Yth Grp; Chorus; Var Bsktbl; Var Crs Cntry; Var Trk; Essay Wnnr, SR High Catgry, Soudertn Area Cmnty Ed, Cncls Essay Contst 85; Sports Med.

ELLIOTT, DENISE; Cumberland Valley HS; Enola, PA; (Y); 48/480; Spanish Clb; Speech Tm; Capt Color Guard; Mrchg Band; Capt Twrlr; Hon Roll; NHS; Shaull Elem Schlrshp 86; Balfour Awd Outstndg Psych Stu 86; Balfour Awd Outstndg Soc Sci Stu 86; U Of Pittsburgh; Journalism.

ELLIOTT, KELLY; Fairview HS; Erie, PA; (Y); Am Leg Aux Girls St; Q&S; Varsity Clb; Nwsp Sprt Ed; Var L Socr; Var Co-Capt Swmmng; Var Co-Capt Trk; NHS; Cmnty Wkr; All-Am Swimming Hnr 86; 2 1st Pl Jrnlsm Awd Sports Writing & Public Svc 86.

ELLIOTT, STEPHANIE; Lincoln HS; Ellwood City, PA; (Y); 23/170; Church Yth Grp; Sec Drama Clb; Hosp Aide; VP Key Clb; Ski Clb; Spanish Clb; Y-Teens; Concert Band; School Play; Tennis; Achvmnt Awd 84-85; ; Ed Ahcvmnt Awd 84-86; Bio Clss Geneva Coll 86; Pitt U.

ELLIOTT, SUE; Annville-Cleona HS; Lebanon, PA; (S); Trs Church Yth Grp; Sec 4-H; FFA; Varsity Clb; Chorus; Madrigals; School Musical; Var Fld Hcky; NHS; Pre-Schl Ed.

ELLIOTT, SUSAN; Jefferson-Morgan HS; Riceslanding, PA; (S); 8/100; Am Leg Aux Girls St; Church Yth Grp; Office Aide; Varsity Clb; Nwsp Ed-Chief; Yrbk Stf; Pres Frsh Cls; Rep Sr Cls; Rep Stu Cncl; Capt Cheerleading; Hmcmng Attndnt; May Day Attndnt; CA U Of PA; Elem Ed.

ELLIS, BERNARD; St John Neumann HS; Philadelphia, PA; (Y); 120/340; Rep Soph Cls; Elec Engrng.

ELLIS, CAROL; Cowanesque HS; Knoxville, PA; (S); 8/100; Drama Clb; Letterman Clb; SADD; Trs Stu Cncl; Stat Bsktbl; Stat Trk; High Hon Roll; Hon Roll; NHS; Med.

ELLIS, CAROLYN; Lower Moreland HS; Huntingdon Valley, PA; (S); 15/214; French Clb; Red Cross Aide; SADD; School Play; Rep Sr Cls; Rep Stu Cncl; Var Fld Hcky; Var Capt Lcrss; NHS; Cmnwlth Of PA Cert Of Merit For Sat Scores 85; Cert Of Merit For Outstndng Frnch Stu 85.

ELLIS, DINA; Central Duphin HS; Harrisburgh, PA; (Y); Teachers Aide; Acpl Chr; Chorus; Madrigals; School Musical; School Play; Swing Chorus; Variety Show; Yrbk Stf; Hon Roll; Sci.

ELLIS, JANENNE; West York Area HS; York, PA; (Y); 14/221; Church Yth Grp; FCA; GAA; Varsity Clb; Church Choir; Var L Bsktbl; Var L Fld Hcky; Var L Trk; Var L Vllybl; High Hon Roll; Crmnl Jstc.

ELLIS, JODI LYNN; Elk Lake HS; Montrose, PA; (Y); 15/100; Drama Clb; French Clb; Library Aide; VICA; Flag Corp; Stage Crew; Nwsp Stf; VP Fld Hcky; Mgr(s); Hon Roll; Cntrl Cty Bus Inst; Lgl Adm.

ELLIS, RONALD; Grove City HS; Grove City, PA; (Y); VICA; Ftbl; Vllybl; High Hon Roll; Hon Roll; Psychtrst.

ELLIS, TINA; Aliquippa SR HS; Aliquippa, PA; (S); 9/154; Church Yth Grp; Cmnty Wkr; Hosp Aide; SADD; Church Choir; Rep Jr Cls; Rep Sr Cls; Cheerleading; Gym; Sftbl; Pro Moderns Pres 85-86; U Pittsburgh; Phrmcy.

ELLIS, VICKI MARIE; Sharpsville HS; Sharpsville, PA; (Y); Camera Clb; Science Clb; Spanish Clb; Thesps; Sec Trs Band; Chorus; Concert Band; Mrchg Band; Pep Band; Nwsp Rptr; Schltc Achvt Ltr 85; Bio.

ELLISON, JAMES PHILIP; Hanover HS; Hanover, PA; (Y); 3/104; Cmnty Wkr; Red Cross Aide; School Play; Nwsp Rptr; Pres Frsh Cls; JV Bsktbl; Var Capt Tennis; Elks Awd; High Hon Roll; NHS.

ELLISON, KATHE; Churchill HS; Pittsburgh, PA; (Y); 16/188; AFS; Church Yth Grp; Cmnty Wkr; Score Keeper; Gov Hon Prg Awd; High Hon Roll; Anthrplgy.

ELLISON, MARK; Grove City HS; Grove City, PA; (Y); 4/179; Boy Scts; Chess Clb; Science Clb; Stage Crew; Var L Bsktbl; Var L Trk; High Hon Roll; NHS; Pres Schlr; VFW Awd; Provost Scholar U Pittsburgh 86-87; Scholar PA Free Entrprse Wk 85; Scholar Wrld Affrs Inst 85; U Pittsburgh; Chem.

ELLSWORTH, KEVIN; Donegal HS; Marietta, PA; (Y); 6/186; Boy Scts; Pres Church Yth Grp; FBLA; Pres Chorus; Var L Trk; Hon Roll; NHS; AME Hgst Math Avrg Frshmn Yr 84; Physics.

ELLSWORTH, LAURA; Carlyton HS; Pittsburgh, PA; (Y); 5/181; Exploring; French Clb; Yrbk Stf; Stu Cncl; Tennis; Trk; High Hon Roll; NHS; Pres Schlr; Sal; Schl Rep HOBY Fndtn Ldrshp Sem 85; Amer Lg Aux Awd 85; PA ST U; Elec Engrng.

ELMALEH, FRANCINE J; Cheltenham HS; Elkins Park, PA; (Y); 1/375; Math Tm; Service Clb; Capt Color Guard; Yrbk Bus Mgr; Lit Mag; Mgr(s); Mgr Swmmng; NHS; Ntl Merit Schol; Teachers Aide; PA JR Acad Of Sci Awds 83-86; Prncpls Advsry Comm Bnd & Orch Advsry Comm 85-86; Comp Fig Sktr 82-86; Med.

ELPHINSTONE, MARK; Freeport SR HS; Sarver, PA; (S); Art Clb; Boy Scts; Church Yth Grp; Stage Crew; High Hon Roll; Hon Roll; Engrng.

ELPHINSTONE, MICHAEL; Freeport Area HS; Sarver, PA; (S); 1/170; Church Yth Grp; Stage Crew; High Hon Roll.

ELSBURY, LORI; Penn Trafford HS; Irwin, PA; (Y); Ski Clb; VICA; Color Guard; Mrchg Band; Nwsp Rptr; Pittsburgh Beauty Acad; Csmtlgy.

ELTMAN, CATHIE; Northern Bedford County HS; Hopewell, PA; (Y); 19/100; SADD; Band; Chorus; Nwsp Rptr; JV Var Bsktbl; Var Trk; High Hon Roll; Hon Roll; Engr.

ELWELL, JO ANN; Conneaut Lake HS; Conneaut Lake, PA; (Y); 6/96; Spanish Clb; SADD; Band; Chorus; Mrchg Band; Pep Band; Nwsp Sprt Ed; Capt Bsktbl; Capt Vllybl; NHS; Rcvd $500 Mem Schlrshp 86; MVP Both Bsktbll & Vllybll 86; PA ST U; Math.

ELWELL, MIKE; Upper Dublin HS; Ft Washington, PA; (Y); 63/310; Intnl Clb; Ski Clb; Varsity Clb; Stage Crew; Nwsp Rptr; Nwsp Stf; Var Bsbl; JV Bsktbl; Var Socr; U Of VA; Business.

ELY, JILL; SheffieldJR Sr HS; Clarendon, PA; (Y); 13/85; Church Yth Grp; SADD; Trs Church Choir; Concert Band; Jazz Band; Mrchg Band; Nwsp Rptr; High Hon Roll; NHS; Drama Clb; Miss Teen PA Schlrshp 86; Communications.

ELY, KATHLEEN; New Hope-Solebury JR-SR HS; New Hope, PA; (S); 8/68; AFS; Church Yth Grp; Cmnty Wkr; Chorus; Var JV Fld Hcky; Var JV Sftbl; High Hon Roll; Hon Roll; NHS; Girl Scts; Psych.

ELY, SUSAN; Eastern York HS; Wrightsville, PA; (Y); 20/159; Pres Church Yth Grp; Exploring; Girl Scts; Chorus; Church Choir; School Musical; Stu Cncl; JV Fld Hcky; JV Trk; Jr NHS.

EMADI, BAQIRALI A; Cumberland Valley HS; Mechanicsburg, PA; (Y); Im Trk; Hon Roll; Engr.

EMANUEL, SYLVIA; Plymouth-Whitemarsh HS; Lafayette Hl, PA; (Y); 131/342; Science Clb; Chorus; School Musical; School Play; Rep Frsh Cls; Rep Soph Cls; Stu Cncl; Lcrss; Swmmng; Tennis; Bio.

EMBICH, JENNY; Cedar Crest HS; Lebanon, PA; (S); 138/343; FFA; Pep Clb; SADD; Vrious Awds With Prjcts FFA 83-86.

EMCH, DANETTE; Seneca HS; Erie, PA; (Y); 5/142; Pep Clb; Ski Clb; School Musical; School Play; Yrbk Stf; Jr Cls; Stu Cncl; Cheerleading; NHS; Pres Schlr; Hugh O Brian Scholar Awd 83-84; Mst Schl Spirit Awd 85-86; PTSU Scholar Awd 85-86; PA ST Behrend; Psych.

EMEL, MELISSA JEAN; Bald Eagle Area HS; Glendale, NY; (Y); 3/203; Church Yth Grp; Office Aide; Variety Show; Off Sr Cls; High Hon Roll; NHS; Hghst Hnrs Awd 86; Outstndng Acctg Awd 86; Boggs Twnshp SR Awd 86.

EMERICH, JANE; Bangor Area SR HS; Bangor, PA; (Y); 4/185; VP 4-H; Pres Band; Concert Band; Jazz Band; Pres Mrchg Band; School Musical; School Play; JP Sousa Awd; Trs NHS; Dist 10 Band 84-86; PMEA Rgn V Band 85-86; Pres Schlr 86; Cornell U; Engrng.

EMERICH, LAURA; Central Cambria HS; Ebensburg, PA; (S); 1/209; Art Clb; Ski Clb; Band; Concert Band; Jazz Band; Mrchg Band; Pep Band; Timer; Trk; High Hon Roll.

EMERICH, SHELLY; Tulpehocken HS; Bethel, PA; (Y); 25/110; Pres 4-H; JA; Band; Chorus; Pres Stu Cncl; Stat Bsktbl; Var Cheerleading; Var Fld Hcky; Var Sftbl; Tulpehocken JR Miss 87; Duquesne; Lawyer.

EMERICK, CURT; Peters Township HS; Mc Murray, PA; (Y); Church Yth Grp; Concert Band; Orch; High Hon Roll; Hon Roll; Acad Achvt Awd For Excllnc 84-85.

EMERUWA, NKECHI I; HS Of Engineering & Sci; Philadelphia, PA; (Y); 18/184; Drama Clb; Math Tm; School Musical; School Play; Yrbk Phtg; VP Pres Stu Cncl; Kiwanis Awd; NHS; Prfct Atten Awd; Rotary Awd; Delt Sig Thet Soror Schlrp 85-89; Alph Delt Kap Gam Chptr Lit Cntst 5th Pl 85; Wolf Mem Fndtn Grant 85; Stanford U; Elec Engrg.

EMERY, LOIS; Eastern York HS; Hellam, PA; (Y); 30/130; Girl Scts; SADD; Teachers Aide; Chorus; Color Guard; Mrchg Band; Powder Puff Ftbl; Hon Roll; Jr NHS; Alvernia Coll; Alchl Cnslr.

EMERY, OLINDA; Freedom HS; Bethlehem, PA; (Y); 14/456; Intnl Clb; Sec Spanish Clb; Yrbk Stf; Off Stu Cncl; Hon Roll; Jr NHS; Pres NHS; JR Miss Rep 86; Moravian Lang Day 1st Pl Spnsh 85; Wake Forest U; Pre-Med.

EMIL, RODNEY; Dallas SR HS; Dallas, PA; (Y); 112/238; Art Clb; Drama Clb; School Play; Stage Crew; Hon Roll; Bus.

EMLER, RICHARD G; South Side HS; Hookstown, PA; (Y); 4/91; Am Leg Boys St; Boy Scts; Church Yth Grp; 4-H; Ski Clb; School Play; VP Soph Cls; VP Jr Cls; VP Sr Cls; Pres Stu Cncl; Eagle Sct 86; Marietta Coll Marietta OH; Law.

EMLING, JOHN; Solanco HS; Nottingham, PA; (Y); 29/235; Sec Varsity Clb; Yrbk Stf; VP Stu Cncl; Var Bsbl; Var Bsktbl; Var Capt Socr; Var Trk; Trs Pres NHS; Socr JV Plyr Of Yr 83; Outstndg VRSTY Undrclssmn Socr 85; Engrng.

EMMERT, CINDY; Elk County Christian HS; St Marys, PA; (Y); Hosp Aide; JA; SADD; Varsity Clb; Band; Mrchg Band; Var L Bsktbl; Var L Tennis; Var L Trk; Edinboro U; Nutrtn.

EMMERT, LAURA; Plum SR HS; Pittsburgh, PA; (Y); 5/438; French Clb; Service Clb; Ski Clb; NHS; NEDT Awd; U Ptsbrgh; Psychlgy.

EMMETT, KELLY; Franklin HS; Harrisville, PA; (Y); Spanish Clb; Chorus; Capt Drill Tm; School Musical; Yrbk Stf; Sec Soph Cls; Sec Jr Cls; Sec Sr Cls; Capt Pom Pon; High Hon Roll.

EMMETT, ROSE; Forest City Regional HS; Forest City, PA; (Y); 10/52; Church Yth Grp; Library Aide; Red Cross Aide; Spanish Clb; Church Choir; VP Stu Cncl; Hon Roll; Asccntng.

EMMINGER, STACY; Donegal HS; Mount Joy, PA; (Y); Church Yth Grp; Drama Clb; Hosp Aide; Pep Clb; PAVAS; Chorus; School Play; Stage Crew; Crs Cntry; Mgr(s); Tchr.

EMMONDS, SUSAN; Ford City JR SR HS; Ford City, PA; (Y); 25/145; Rep Frsh Cls; Rep Jr Cls; Rep Sr Cls; NHS; Chrldr 84-86.

EMORY, NEAL; Tri Valley HS; Hegins, PA; (Y); Boy Scts; Church Yth Grp; Computer Clb; Ski Clb; Band; Jazz Band; School Musical; Bsbl; Bsktbl; Ftbl; 1st Tm Offns Tght End WQIN All Star 85-86; Bys Bsktbl All Star WQIN 85-86; Outstndng Athltc Awd; Engrng.

EMRICH, JEANNETTE; Northern Lebanon HS; Annville, PA; (Y); 25/176; Sec Church Yth Grp; Office Aide; Teachers Aide; Chorus; Church Choir; Rep Flag Corp; Mrchg Band; School Musical; Mgr Stage Crew; Hon Roll; MED Sec.

EMRICH, LISA ANNE; Hershey HS; Hummelstown, PA; (Y); 39/190; Church Yth Grp; Ski Clb; Band; Chorus; Concert Band; Drm Mjr(t); Mrchg Band; School Musical; Swing Chorus; Variety Show; Hershey Ed Assoc Schlrshp 86; Treva Dise Mem Schlrshp 86; Girl Of Mnth Fedrtd Womens Clb 86; Ftns Awd; Messiah Coll PA; Christian Ed.

ENDEAN, MIKE; Northwestern HS; Albion, PA; (Y); Letterman Clb; Pres Ski Clb; Stu Cncl; L Ftbl; Wt Lftg; Hon Roll; Cnsrvtn Schlrshp Awd 86; Albion Area Cvc Clb Schlrshp 86; Behrend-PA ST; Envrmntl Engr.

ENDERS, KRIS; Council Rock HS; Richboro, PA; (Y); 200/759; Church Yth Grp; Capt Var Cheerleading; Hon Roll; WV U; Soc Wrk.

ENDERS, SANDRA; Bethel Park SR HS; Bethel Park, PA; (Y); Church Yth Grp; FBLA; Library Aide; Chorus; Powder Puff Ftbl; Prfct Atten Awd; Awd Otstndng Achvt Hm Econo 85; Airlines.

ENDLER, EDWARD F; Meyers HS; Wilkes Barre, PA; (Y); 33/150; Letterman Clb; Ski Clb; Spanish Clb; Varsity Clb; Chorus; Stu Cncl; Bsbl; Ftbl; Wt Lftg; Jr NHS.

ENDLER, RENEE; Bishop Carroll HS; Nicktown, PA; (S); 7/121; Ski Clb; Band; Mrchg Band; Hon Roll; NEDT Awd; NASA Sci Awd.

ENDLER, RITA; Bishop Carroll HS; Nicktown, PA; (S); 2/105; Church Yth Grp; SADD; Yrbk Bus Mgr; Rep Soph Cls; Trs Jr Cls; Hon Roll; NHS; Ntl Merit Ltr; NEDT Awd; Bus.

ENDY, ROBIN; Pottstown SR HS; Pottstown, PA; (S); 10/238; Church Yth Grp; Key Clb; Rep Jr Cls; High Hon Roll; Hon Roll; NHS; Bus.

ENGART, TIMOTHY R; Upper Moreland HS; Hatboro, PA; (Y); 19/272; Key Clb; Bowling; Trk; High Hon Roll; Hon Roll; NHS; Pres Schlr; Pres Acdmc Ftns Awd 86; Penn ST U; Acctg.

ENGEL, KAREN; Montoursville HS; Montoursville, PA; (Y); Dance Clb; Pres Spanish Clb; Swmmng; Hon Roll; Art Wrk ST Comptn In Schlstcs 83-84; Prom Commtt & Bible Schl Teach 86; Lycoming Cnty Hist Soc 86-87; Forensic Pathlgy.

ENGEL, TRICIA L; Greensburg Central Catholic HS; Export, PA; (Y); PA ST Roller Sktng Cham 85; Eastern Regnl Free Dance Cham 86; Natl Qualifier US Roller Sktng Cham; Fash Design.

ENGELMAN JR, LOWELL; Monaca JR SR HS; Monaca, PA; (Y); Am Leg Boys St; Church Yth Grp; Exploring; FCA; Y-Teens; Stu Cncl; Bsktbl; Hon Roll; Nwsp Carrier Beaver Cnty Times 82-86; PA ST U; Engrng.

ENGELMAN, MARLA; Millville Area HS; Millville, PA; (Y); School Play; Nwsp Stf; Var Cheerleading; Stat Fld Hcky; Gym; Cmmnctn.

ENGLAND, KATHY; Williamsburg HS; Williamsburg, PA; (Y); 4-H; Pres FFA; Varsity Clb; Band; Nwsp Stf; Yrbk Stf; Rep Stu Cncl; Cheerleading; Hon Roll; NHS; Hnry Keystone FFA Dgree 86; PA ST U; Bus Adm.

ENGLE, CHRISTINE; Lebanon Catholic HS; Lebanon, PA; (Y); Cmnty Wkr; FHA; Girl Scts; Hosp Aide; Library Aide; Spanish Clb; SADD; Band; Chorus; Church Choir; Math.

ENGLE, JERE; Lewisburg Area HS; Lewisburg, PA; (Y); Church Yth Grp; VP Frsh Cls; Rep Soph Cls; Rep Jr Cls; JV Var Bsktbl; Trk; Boy Scts; Varsity Clb; JV Bsbl; Var Crs Cntry; Dstrct, League & Coaches Intl Chmpn 86; Jmpr Of Yr Trphy 86; Bus Adm.

ENGLE, KARYN; Pottstown SR HS; Pottstown, PA; (Y); 33/238; Computer Clb; School Play; Nwsp Stf; Rep Frsh Cls; Var Cheerleading; JV Sftbl; High Hon Roll; Hon Roll; Bus.

ENGLE, KIMBERLY; Shikellamy HS; Sunbury, PA; (Y); 3/318; NFL; Quiz Bowl; Spanish Clb; Speech Tm; Concert Band; Mrchg Band; School Musical; Nwsp Rptr; NHS; Sal; Math & Spnsh Awd Hghst Avg 86; Acdmc All Amer 86; Case Western Reserve U; Astrnmy.

ENGLE, MARTA; Freedom HS; Bethlehem, PA; (Y); 39/445; Exploring; Sftbl; Elec Engr.

ENGLE, TAMMY; Southmoreland SR HS; Mt Plsnt, PA; (Y); 24/245; Trs Sec Church Yth Grp; Pep Clb; Ski Clb; Spanish Clb; Nwsp Stf; Yrbk Stf; Lit Mag; Rep Stu Cncl; Powder Puff Ftbl; Spanish NHS; Bus Law.

ENGLE, TERRY A; Upper Dauphin Area HS; Elizabethville, PA; (S); Trs FFA; Var Trk; Hon Roll; NHS; Rotary Awd; Millersville U; Ind Art Ed.

ENGLISH, BRADY; W Branch Area HS; Morrisdale, PA; (Y); Trs Church Yth Grp; 4-H; Varsity Clb; VICA; Crs Cntry; Wrstlng; Triangle Tech; Carpentry.

ENGLISH, CAROL; Pittston Area HS; Pittston, PA; (Y); Art Clb; FBLA; Key Clb; Ski Clb; High Hon Roll; Hon Roll; Jr NHS; NHS.

ENGLISH, JANINE; St Huberts HS For Girls; Philadelphia, PA; (Y); 82/367; Dance Clb; Stu Cncl; Ldrshp Awd Futr Secys Prsntd By Katherine Gibbs 86; Freedms Fndtn Vly Forge Freedm & Ldrshp 86; Pierce JC; Ct Rprtg.

ENGLISH, PAMELA; High Point Baptist Acad; Geigertown, PA; (S); 2/18; Church Yth Grp; Yrbk Ed-Chief; Sec Frsh Cls; VP Sr Cls; Stat Bsktbl; Stat Vllybl; High Hon Roll; NHS; Spanish NHS; Tchg.

ENGLISH, TERRY; Warren Area HS; Warren, PA; (Y); German Clb; Varsity Clb; School Play; Ftbl; Trk; Wt Lftg; Hon Roll; Jr NHS; NHS; U Of Pittsburgh; Elec Engrng.

ENGLS, TOM; Butler Area SR HS; Butler, PA; (Y); 1/36; Church Yth Grp; JA; Band; Swmmng; Bausch & Lomb Sci Awd; Hnr Stu Vo-Tech Drftng 86; Butler Coll; CAD.

ENLOW, JAMES; Sayre HS; Sayre, PA; (Y); 50/116; Boy Scts; Church Yth Grp; Cmnty Wkr; French Clb; Chorus; Church Choir; Swing Chorus; Swmmng; God Cntry Awd; Ruth Frank Choral Mem Awd 86; Most Musical Sr Boy 86; Pittsbrgh U; Poltcl Sci.

ENNIS, JANET; Seneca Valley HS; Harmony, PA; (Y); 10/360; Varsity Clb; Chorus; Symp Band; Pres Yrbk Stf; Rep Jr Cls; Var L Swmmng; Var L Trk; High Hon Roll; NHS; GAA; Acdmc Achvt Awd 85-86.

ENOCH, NICHOLAS JASON; Windber Area HS; Windber, PA; (Y); 35/128; Chess Clb; Political Wkr; Ski Clb; Varsity Clb; Pres Jr Cls; Bsbl; Golf; Hon Roll; Stu Of The Mnth 85; PA Bus Wk At Lock Haven Clg 86.

ENSCOE, YVONNE; South Hills HS; Pittsburgh, PA; (Y); Aud/Vis; Exploring; Spanish Clb; Sftbl; Hon Roll; Prfct Atten Awd; Lttr, Awd, & Trophy S Hills Fast Pitch Sftbll City Champ 86; Inst Security & Tech; Security.

ENSLIN, DEBRA; Western Wayne HS; Lk Ariel, PA; (Y); 47/138; Church Yth Grp; Girl Scts; Hosp Aide; Spanish Clb; Chorus; Church Choir; Lit Mag; Hon Roll; Roberts Wesleyan; Lang.

ENSTROM, KIM; Liberty HS; Bethlehem, PA; (Y); 5/475; Church Yth Grp; French Clb; Model UN; Church Choir; Rep Frsh Cls; Rep Soph Cls; Rep Stu Cncl; JV Var Bsktbl; High Hon Roll; Hon Roll; Med.

EPERESI, CARRIE; Center HS; Monaca, PA; (Y); 30/200; Latin Clb; Varsity Clb; VP Sr Cls; Rep Stu Cncl; Var Capt Cheerleading; Score Keeper; Hon Roll; NHS; Comm Art.

EPPERSON, KIM; Germantown HS; Philadelphia, PA; (Y); 38/327; Girl Scts; Hosp Aide; Office Aide; Teachers Aide; JV Mgr(s); Hon Roll; Spnsh Awd 84-85; Temple U; Nrsg.

EPPERSON, SHARON EMILY; Taylor Allderdice HS; Pittsburgh, PA; (Y); 4/437; Sec Chorus; Nwsp Ed-Chief; Sec Sr Cls; Rep Stu Cncl; Cit Awd; DAR Awd; High Hon Roll; Jr NHS; Kiwanis Awd; NHS; Ntl Achvt Schlr 86; Ntl Tech Assn Schlrshp 86; $1200 Schlrshp Smmr Actnl Pgm Hnr WA DC 85; Hrvard; Jrnlsm.

EPPLEY, HILARY; Middleburg HS; Middleburg, PA; (Y); 1/120; Key Clb; Band; Jazz Band; School Play; Nwsp Ed-Chief; Bausch & Lomb Sci Awd; NHS; Rep Stu Cncl; Var L Fld Hcky; Drama Clb; All ST Band, Rensselaer Math, Sci Awd 86; Woodmn Wrld Amer Hist Awd 85; Physcn.

EPPS, DEXTER; University City HS; Phialdelphia, PA; (Y); Temple Yth Grp; Howard; Med.

EPPS, LISA; St Marin Goretti HS; Philadelphia, PA; (Y); 83/394; Am Leg Aux Girls St; Camp Fr Inc; Pep Clb; SADD; Orch; Pres Symp Orch 86-87; Cert Achvt 86; Penn ST; Psychlgy.

EPSTEIN, AMY; Harritown HS; Gladwyne, PA; (Y); Capt Debate Tm; SADD; VP Band; Jazz Band; VP Mrchg Band; Orch; Nwsp Rptr; Ed Nwsp Stf; Hon Roll; NHS; Psych.

ERACE, RAMONA; W Philadelphia Catholic Girls HS; Philadelphia, PA; (Y); 2/245; Church Yth Grp; Radio Clb; VP Spanish Clb; Ed Nwsp Rptr; Stu Cncl; High Hon Roll; NHS; Prfct Atten Awd; Chrstn Bros Full Tuit Scholar La Salle U 86; Relig Awd 83-86; Spn Awd 83-86; Creat Wrtg Awd 86; La Salle U; Comm.

ERB, JAMES; Boyertown Area SR HS; Boyertown, PA; (Y); Church Yth Grp; Band; Chorus; Church Choir; Jazz Band; Mrchg Band; Orch; Rep Stu Cncl; Var Ftbl; Var Socr; Bus Admin.

ERB, LESTER; Milton Area HS; Milton, PA; (Y); Pres Varsity Clb; Var Bsbl; Var Bsktbl; Var Ftbl; Im Wt Lftg; All Conf Plyr Yr Ftbl 85; Leg All-Star Bsbl 86; Bst Defnsve Plyr Bsktbl 85.

ERB, PHILIP; Manheim Central HS; Manheim, PA; (Y); 26/264; Trs Church Yth Grp; L Crs Cntry; L Trk; Hon Roll; Lion Awd; Prfct Atten Awd.

ERB, SUZANNE; Northern Lebanon HS; Jonestown, PA; (Y); 9/177; Math Tm; Church Choir; School Play; Lit Mag; Var Stat Bowling; High Hon Roll; Hon Roll; Chem.

ERB, TINA; Millersburg Area HS; Millersburg, PA; (Y); Nwsp Bus Mgr; Nwsp Stf; JV Cheerleading; Hon Roll; Stu Mnth 86; Top Bus Stu; Bus.

ERDELY, LISA; Villa Maria Acad; Erie, PA; (Y); 4/134; Church Yth Grp; Pres PAVAS; Mgr Stage Crew; Lit Mag; Kiwanis Awd; Gannon U; Mech Engrng.

ERDELY, MARY BETH; Frazier HS; Perryopolis, PA; (S); Ski Clb; Yrbk Stf; Rep Soph Cls; JV Var Cheerleading; Hon Roll; Leg Sec.

ERDELY, MICHAEL; Charleroi Area JR SR HS; Charleroi, PA; (Y); Church Yth Grp; Band; Concert Band; Jazz Band; Mrchg Band; Stage Crew; Trk; Hon Roll; WV U; Aerospace Engrng.

ERDMAN, DARRON; Northern Lebanon HS; Jonestown, PA; (Y); Church Yth Grp; Computer Clb; Varsity Clb; Band; Church Choir; Concert Band; Mrchg Band; Pep Band; School Musical; Tennis; Harrisburg Area CC; Bus Mngmt.

ERDMAN, KIRSTEN; Cedar Crest HS; Mt Gretna, PA; (Y); 6/325; Art Clb; French Clb; School Musical; Nwsp Rptr; Yrbk Stf; Socr; Hon Roll; NHS; Church Yth Grp; Drama Clb; Schlstc Wrtng Awds 84; Artist Hershey Bears Hocky Offcl Progrm 85-87; Commnctns.

ERDMAN, VIRGINIA; Millersburg Area HS; Millersburg, PA; (Y); 15/74; VP Church Yth Grp; Pres 4-H; Band; Concert Band; Mrchg Band; 4-H Awd; High Hon Roll; Hon Roll; Ntl Merit Schol; JR Bnd Awd; 4-H Cmpn Hrs Awd; Bus.

ERHARD, GRANT; Waynesburg Central HS; Waynesburg, PA; (Y); Aud/Vis; Ski Clb; Spanish Clb; Varsity Clb; Var Bsktbl; Im Fld Hcky; Var Ftbl; Hon Roll; Drug & Alcohol Committee 84-85; Law.

ERHARDT, JOSEPH; Downingtown SR HS; Downingtown, PA; (S); Band; Concert Band; Drm & Bgl; Jazz Band; Off Mrchg Band; School Musical; Symp Band; NHS; Ntl Merit Ltr; Red Cross Aide; NEDT Awd 83; PA Cert Of Merit Coll Bd SAT 85; Amer Music Abrd-Trip To Europe 85.

ERICKSON, KIRSTEN; Unionville HS; West Chester, PA; (Y); 78/269; Church Yth Grp; Variety Show; Nwsp Rptr; Rep Stu Cncl; Var Cheerleading; Var Crs Cntry; Capt Trk; High Hon Roll; Jr NHS; Lit Mag; Amer Red Cross Adv Lfsvg Cert 86; Amer Heart Assn CPR Cert 86; Roanoke Coll VA; Engl.

ERICKSON, KRISTEN; Downingtown SR HS; Chester Springs, PA; (Y); Church Yth Grp; Dance Clb; French Clb; FBLA; Chorus; Jazz Band; School Musical; School Play; Swing Chorus; Church Choir; 2nd Pl Upper Main Line Piano Comp 86; 5th Pl St Wide Future Bus Ldrs Amer; 1100 Hrs Cmmnty Svc 84-85; Intl Bus.

ERICKSON, MARCIE; Central HS; Roaring Spring, PA; (Y); 35/189; FCA; Ski Clb; Varsity Clb; Chorus; School Musical; Rep Jr Cls; Var L Cheerleading; Var L Sftbl; Var Trk; Var L Vllybl; Sec Educ.

ERICSSON, CAROL; Highlands SR HS; Natrona Hts, PA; (Y); Girl Scts; Hosp Aide; Key Clb; Color Guard; Mrchg Band; Rep Stu Cncl; High Hon Roll; Jr NHS; NHS; Nrsng.

ERIKSON, KRISTIN; Mechanicsburg Area SR HS; Mechanicsburg, PA; (Y); 63/311; Debate Tm; NFL; Chorus; Crs Cntry; Trk; Speech Tm; Church Choir; Hon Roll; Psychlgy.

ERLEBACHER, JONAH; Cheltenham HS; Elkins Pk, PA; (Y); 5/300; Computer Clb; Capt Math Clb; Capt Math Tm; Orch; School Musical; Gov Hon Prg Awd; Ntl Merit Ltr; Harvard Bk Awd 86; Physics.

ERMEL, DONALD; Bansalem HS; Bensalem, PA; (Y); Trs Frsh Cls; Capt Swmmng; High Hon Roll; Hon Roll; NHS; Acctg.

ERMI, LISA; Our Lady Of The Sacred Heart HS; Aliquippa, PA; (Y); Pep Clb; Yrbk Stf; JV L Cheerleading; Socr; High Hon Roll; Hon Roll; NHS; Duquesne U; Comm.

ERMIN, DIANA; Altoona Area HS; Altoona, PA; (Y); Var Vllybl; Wt Lftg; High Hon Roll; V Ltr Vlybl 85-86; OH Northern U; Dentistry.

ERMOCIDA, VICKY; Saint Maria Goretti Pa; Philadelphia, PA; (Y); GAA; Mathletes; Math Clb; Hon Roll; NHS; Hnbl Mntn Alg I 83-84; Med.

ERNEST, LEANN; Cambria Heights HS; Hastings, PA; (Y); Trs Church Yth Grp; Ski Clb; Chorus; Church Choir; Hon Roll; NHS; IN U Of PA; Offc Adm.

ERNST, ALECIA; Big Spring HS; Carlisle, PA; (Y); 10/210; Church Yth Grp; Nwsp Ed-Chief; Rptr Nwsp Rptr; Stu Cncl; Mgr Socr; Trk; High Hon Roll; NHS; Engl Excllnce Awd 86; Pres Phys Fit Awd 84-86; Jrnlsm.

ERNST, CARL; Governor Mifflin HS; Shillington, PA; (Y); 68/265; Aud/Vis; Boy Scts; Church Yth Grp; Computer Clb; Exploring; Pres VP FBLA; Intnl Clb; Key Clb; Model UN; Quiz Bowl; Multple Sclerosis Soc Outstndng Yth Awd 85-86; Frgn Svc.

ERNST, ERIC; Parkland HS; Allntwn, PA; (Y); 135/459; Genetics.

ERNST, STEPHEN; Central York SR HS; York, PA; (Y); 65/225; Boy Scts; Varsity Clb; Concert Band; Variety Show; Var L Ftbl; JV Vllybl; Im Wrstlng; Hon Roll; 1st Cls Boy Scout 84; MD U; Marine Bio.

ERNSTHAUSEN, JOHN; Somerset Area SR HS; Somerset, PA; (Y); 36/238; JA; Speech Tm; Chorus; Mrchg Band; Symp Band; High Hon Roll; NHS; IUP Hnrs Band 86; PA ST; Pre-Med.

EROH, BRIAN; Crestwood HS; Wapwallopen, PA; (Y); VICA; JV Bsbl; Elec Tech.

EROH, DAVID; Freedom HS; Easton, PA; (Y); 92/445; JA; Science Clb; Acpl Chr; Chorus; Var Capt Swmmng; Hon Roll; Med.

ERRETT, GWEN; Fort Cherry HS; Mc Donald, PA; (Y); Church Yth Grp; Science Clb; Sec Band; Chorus; Mrchg Band; Yrbk Ed-Chief; Math Clb; Ski Clb; Spanish Clb; Pres Physcl Ftns Awd 85; NRSNG.

ERRICO, JOHN B; Dunmore SR HS; Dunmore, PA; (Y); 10/167; Aud/Vis; Computer Clb; Drama Clb; French Clb; FBLA; Letterman Clb; Chorus; School Musical; Nwsp Sprt Ed; Yrbk Sprt Ed; SR Serv Awd 86; U Of Scranton; Acctg.

ERTEL, STEPHEN; Blue Mountain Acad; Halifax, PA; (S); 11/70; Pres Computer Clb; Off Jr Cls; Capt Ftbl; Sftbl; Vllybl; Hon Roll; Comp Sci.

ERWIN, BETH; Hatboro-Horsham SR HS; Hatboro, PA; (Y); Pres Church Yth Grp; Cmnty Wkr; Key Clb; Concert Band; Mrchg Band; High Hon Roll; Hon Roll; NHS; Prfct Atten Awd; Champ Learng Awd Chem 85-86; Hnbl Mntn Awd Enrgy Ed Assoc 86; Elem Ed.

ESBENSEN, KIM; Sacred Heart HS; Carbondale, PA; (Y); 32/56; Art Clb; DECA; French Clb; Hosp Aide; Library Aide; SADD; School Musical; School Play; Capt Cheerleading; Capt Pom Pon; Rlgn Hgh Hnrs 83; Chrldng Awds 83-86; Keystone JC; Erly Chldhd Ed.

ESCH, MICHAEL; Penn Hills HS; Pittsburgh, PA; (Y); Church Yth Grp; Hon Roll; Pittsbrgh Est Dist Yth Rep 84-87; Mrn Bio.

ESCHENMANN, JULIE; Annville-Cleona HS; Annville, PA; (Y); 18/105; Church Yth Grp; German Clb; Varsity Clb; Sec Jr Cls; Rep Stu Cncl; Mat Maids; Var L Tennis; Var Trk; Stat Wrstlng; Jr NHS; Fach Dsgnr.

ESCHER, TRACY; Penn Hills SR HS; Pittsburgh, PA; (Y); Art Clb; Teachers Aide; Hon Roll; 2 Gregg Shrthnd Awds 86; Cert Of Crdt Typng 86; Sawyer Schl; Sec.

ESCHRICH, WILLIAM; North Star HS; Stoystown, PA; (Y); 14/124; AFS; Math Clb; Ski Clb; Chorus; Concert Band; Mrchg Band; Trs Stu Cncl; Lion Awd; Mu Alp Tht; NHS; Safe Driver Awd 86; Stu Of Mnth 84; Acad Awd Gannon U 86; Gannon U; Physcn Asst.

ESCUETA, LARA K; Chambersburg Area SR HS; Chambersburg, PA; (Y); 67/587; Pep Clb; Varsity Clb; Band; Chorus; Cheerleading; Hon Roll; Chrldng Capt 82-83 & 84-85; Amer Achvt Awd 84-85; IN U Bloomington; Fash Merch.

ESH, RICKY; Pequea Valley HS; Gap, PA; (Y); Church Yth Grp; FFA; Yrbk Phtg; Hon Roll; NHS.

ESHBACH, DEBBIE; Freedom HS; Bethlehem, PA; (Y); 20/465; French Clb; Rep Stu Cncl; Var Gym; Im Powder Puff Ftbl; Capt Twrlr; Hon Roll; NHS; Bucknell U; Scndry Educ.

ESHELMAN, CHRISTINE; Elizabethtown Area HS; Elizabethtown, PA; (Y); 39/221; Yrbk Ed-Chief; Yrbk Stf; Lit Mag; Contengl Press Jrnslm Awd 86; Hood Coll; Optmetry.

ESHELMAN, LISA; Elizabethtown Area HS; Elizabethtown, PA; (Y); Church Yth Grp; Model UN; Teachers Aide; Chorus; Church Choir; Drm Mjr(t); Mrchg Band; Stu Cncl; Trk; Twrlr.

ESHELMAN, NAOMI; Christian School Of York; Carlisle, PA; (S); 2/60; Church Yth Grp; Chorus; Church Choir; Yrbk Phtg; VP Jr Cls; Fld Hcky; Cit Awd; High Hon Roll; Bus Admin.

ESHELMAN, PAIGE LYNN; Ephrata SR HS; Ephrata, PA; (Y); 1/257; Chorus; Drill Tm; Mrchg Band; School Musical; School Play; Yrbk Ed-Chief; Yrbk Stf; High Hon Roll; Sec Trs NHS; Asst Copy Edtr Yrbk 85-86; Jr Clss Cncl Prom Cmmtt 85-86; Lancaster Cnty Jr Miss Cntstnt 86; Schl Anncr; Liberal Arts Coll; Literature.

ESHENOWER, KRISTIN; Cnetral Dauphin HS; Harrisburg, PA; (Y); Church Yth Grp; Chorus; Var L Cheerleading; Vllybl; United Chrch Of Christ Chrch Deacn 84-87; Tchng.

ESHER, CHRISTINA; Pennsbury HS; Yardley, PA; (Y); German Clb; Intnl Clb; Chorus; Yrbk Bus Mgr; Yrbk Stf; Bsktbl; Sftbl; Vllybl; Hon Roll; Rep Frsh Cls; Kutztown U; Educ.

ESHLEMAN, D SCOTT; J P Mc Cuskey HS; Lancaster, PA; (Y); 22/450; Hon Roll; Acctg.

ESHLEMAN, EARL; Donegal HS; Elizabethtown, PA; (Y); 111/154; Pres Church Yth Grp; Pres 4-H; 4-H Awd; Var JV Fld Hcky; Acctng.

ESHLEMAN, QUENTIN; Boyertown Area HS; Bally, PA; (Y); 55/437; Capt Church Yth Grp; Drama Clb; Pres Chorus; Church Choir; School Musical; School Play; Rep Stu Cncl; Hon Roll; Pres Schlr; Cedarville Coll; Music.

ESODA, ERIC; Bishop Hannan HS; Scranton, PA; (Y); 8/126; Debate Tm; NFL; Speech Tm; Bowling; High Hon Roll; NHS; Pres Schlr; VFW Awd; Math Tm; Dist Champion Tm Debate 84-85; Most Likely To Succeed Male SR Cls; Am Govt & Engl IV Exellence Awd; U ScrantonACCNTNG.

ESOLDO, BRYAN; Lincoln HS; Ellwood City, PA; (Y); 64/170; Church Yth Grp; Letterman Clb; Political Wkr; Spanish Clb; Varsity Clb; Var L Bsbl; Var L Bsktbl; Var L Ftbl; Hnrb Mntn MAC 85 Qrtrbck 85.

ESOLEN, MARIANNE; Bishop O Hara HS; Archbald, PA; (S); 3/127; Exploring; French Clb; Latin Clb; Pep Clb; Scholastic Bowl; Stage Crew; Nwsp Rptr; High Hon Roll; NHS; Crmnl Lwyr.

ESPADA, MARIA; St Benedict Acad; Erie, PA; (Y); 10/63; Cmnty Wkr; Exploring; School Play; Stage Crew; Variety Show; Yrbk Stf; High Hon Roll; Hon Roll; NHS; Spnsh Schlrshp, Awd 84-86; Typng Awd 86; Behrend; Med Fld.

ESPEJO, EMMA LYNN; Philadelphia HS For Girls; Philadelphia, PA; (Y); Drama Clb; Chorus; Madrigals; School Musical; Ed Yrbk Stf; JV Fld Hcky; Var Lcrss; Hon Roll; Psych.

ESPENSHADE, GREGG; Garden Spot HS; Narvon, PA; (Y); Art Clb; Church Yth Grp; Chorus; Rep Frsh Cls; Socr; Var Trk; Hon Roll; Prfct Atten Awd.

ESPOSIT, MARY E; Bishop Neumann HS; Williamsport, PA; (Y); 6/45; Pres JA; Trs Frsh Cls; Sec Soph Cls; Pres Jr Cls; Pres Sr Cls; Capt Cheerleading; Mgr Socr; Cit Awd; Hon Roll; NHS; Beaver Coll Schlrshp $4450 86-87; Schl Svc Awd 86-87; Schl Spirit Awd 86-87; Beaver College; Phys Therapy.

ESPOSITO, DOMINIC; Holy Ghost Preparatory Schl; Philadelphia, PA; (S); 5/80; Aud/Vis; Computer Clb; Latin Clb; Math Clb; VP Science Clb; School Play; Variety Show; Yrbk Stf; Jr NHS; NHS; Awd Exclnc Advncd Ltn 86; Physcl Sci.

ESPOSITO, ROSA; Quigley HS; Midland, PA; (S); 10/113; Pres Church Yth Grp; Chorus; High Hon Roll; Med.

ESPOSTO, NUNZIO; Butler Area SR HS; Butler, PA; (Y); 52/780; Var L Diving; Var L Swmmng; Hon Roll; H S All Amer Divg 85-86; ST Champ Divg 85; Hnbl Mntn All Amer Divg 84; U Of TX Austin; Phy Thrpy.

ESSEY, MICHELE L; Mon Valley Catholic HS; Charleroi, PA; (S); 15/104; Church Yth Grp; Girl Scts; JA; Pep Clb; Ski Clb; Chorus; Variety Show; Nwsp Rptr; Pres Frsh Cls; VP Soph Cls; Indiana U Of PA; Nrsng.

ESTEL, SANDRA; Abington HS; Abington, PA; (Y); 59/535; Church Yth Grp; Intnl Clb; Orch; School Musical; Lit Mag; Socr; Jr NHS; NHS; Ntl Merit Ltr; Stanley Whitcanage Awd 86; Lisa Herald Mem Awd 86; Instrmntl Music Awd 86; Engrng.

ESTEP, RICK; Donegal HS; Mt Joy, PA; (Y); Acad All Amer 86; Spartan Schl Aerontcs; Avioncs.

ESTER, MICHAEL; Harbor Creek JR SR HS; Erie, PA; (Y); 11/194; Church Yth Grp; Hon Roll; NHS; Ntl Merit Ltr; Messiah Coll Pres Schlrshp 86; PHEAA Certf Merit SAT Scr 86; Messiah Coll; Tchr.

ESTERLY, BRIAN; Conrad Weiser JR SR HS; Wernersville, PA; (Y); 22/182; Church Yth Grp; Trs Key Clb; Spanish Clb; Ftbl; Wrstlng; Hon Roll; NHS; Cmp Neidig Rtry Intl 86; AIM Coast Grd Acad 86; Villanova; Marn Corps Ofcr.

ESTES, KURT; Father Judge HS; Philadelphia, PA; (Y); Teachers Aide; VP Frsh Cls; VP Soph Cls; Pres Jr Cls; Im JV Bsktbl; Var Ftbl; Var Golf; Hon Roll; Elec Engr.

ESTOCK, DAVID; Meyers HS; Wilkes Barre, PA; (Y); 13/175; Boy Scts; Church Yth Grp; German Clb; Var Swmmng; High Hon Roll; Hon Roll; NHS; Physics.

ESTOCK, KRISTY; Montour HS; Coraopolis, PA; (Y); Art Clb; Church Yth Grp; Girl Scts; Pep Clb; High Hon Roll; Hon Roll; Med Sec.

ESTRIGHT, WILLIAM; Aliquippa HS; Aliquippa, PA; (S); Pres Church Yth Grp; French Clb; Math Tm; Band; Yrbk Phtg; Pres Jr Cls; Wt Lftg; Capt Wrstlng; High Hon Roll; Engrng.

ETALIANO, CRYSTAL; St Marys Area HS; St Marys, PA; (Y); Boys Clb Am; Stat Trk; JV Capt Vllybl; Stat Wrstlng; Hon Roll; NHS; Pres Acad Ftns Awd 86; Vol Spcl Olympics 85-86; PA ST; Ed.

ETHERIDGE, SCOTT; Pennsbury HS; Yardley, PA; (Y); 30/750; Church Yth Grp; German Clb; Political Wkr; Stage Crew; Yrbk Phtg; Stat Ftbl; Var Golf; Hon Roll; NHS; Dsgn Fr Solr Frnc Wn 1st Plc E Stroudsburg U Physcs Olympcs 85; Pre-Med.

ETRISS, DIANE; Cardinal O Hara HS; Brookhaven, PA; (Y); 82/772; Girl Scts; Office Aide; Yrbk Stf; Hon Roll; Schlstc Awd Stengrphy 86; Gregg Typg Awd Achvt 86; 5th Pl Arch Diocese Phila Comptn Stengrphy 86; Temple U; Cmmnctns.

ETTER, STEPHANIE E; Shippensburg SR HS; Shippensburg, PA; (Y); 17/226; Am Leg Aux Girls St; French Clb; Spanish Clb; Sec Trs Chorus; School Musical; Sec Soph Cls; Sec Jr Cls; Sec Sr Cls; VP Stu Cncl; Var L Sftbl; Minstrm Schlrshp 86; Shippensburg U; Bus Inf Sys.

ETZEL, LARA; Wellsboro HS; Wellsboro, PA; (Y); Church Yth Grp; Sec German Clb; Pep Clb; Church Choir; Concert Band; Mrchg Band; Var JV Bsktbl; High Hon Roll; Hon Roll; NHS; Psych.

EUNSON, KAREN L; Clarion-Limestone HS; Apollo, PA; (Y); 2/88; Church Yth Grp; Chorus; School Musical; Yrbk Stf; Pres Stu Cncl; Var L Cheerleading; Var L Trk; NHS; Sal; Pres Acad Fit Awd 86; Hnr Roll 82-86; DAR Awd 85-86; PA ST U; Engrng.

EURY, TROY; Seneca Valley SR HS; Renfrew, PA; (Y); Church Yth Grp; JA; Chorus; Church Choir; Lit Mag; Trk; High Hon Roll; Hon Roll; 1st Pl Keystone Awd 85; U Steubenville; Music.

EUSTON, GREGORY; Moon SR HS; Coraopolis, PA; (Y); Church Yth Grp; Chorus; Drm Mjr(t); Mrchg Band; School Musical; Swing Chorus; Symp Band; Variety Show; Bsbl; Hon Roll; Air Force Acad; Comp.

EUTSEY, AMY; Mary Fuller Frazier Memorial HS; Dawson, PA; (S); FNA; Band; Concert Band; Mrchg Band; Pep Band; Yrbk Stf; High Hon Roll; Jr NHS; Pres NHS; Most Studious, Most Likely To Succeed 85; Carnegie Mellon Chem Olympics 85; Pre-Med.

EUTSEY, LISA; Mt Pleasant Area HS; Mt Pleasant, PA; (Y); GAA; Trs Latin Clb; Ski Clb; Swmmng; Elks Awd; Hon Roll; Am Athlete; Latin Clb Schrlshp; Westmoreland County CC; Nrsng.

EUTSEY, MELISSA; Connellsville Area SR HS; Mt Pleasant, PA; (Y); Church Yth Grp; Teachers Aide; VICA; Chorus; Church Choir; High Hon Roll; Hon Roll; Stu Of Mnth Vctnl Schl; SR Of Yr; Comp Oprtr.

EVACEK, ROBYN; Hazleton HS; Hazleton, PA; (Y); 119/400; Church Yth Grp; FBLA; Hosp Aide; Y-Teens; Color Guard; Hon Roll; Penn ST U; Csmtlgy.

EVACKO, PATRICIA; Forest Hills SR HS; Sidman, PA; (Y); 1/160; Am Leg Aux Girls St; Thesps; Capt Color Guard; School Musical; Nwsp Stf; Yrbk Stf; High Hon Roll; Jr NHS; VP NHS; Spanish NHS; Am Lg Axlry Awd 84; Pharm.

EVAK, SHARON; Hempfield Area SR HS; Adamsburg, PA; (Y); Library Aide; Office Aide; Pep Clb; Ski Clb; Chorus; School Musical; School Play; High Hon Roll; Hon Roll; Ctznshp Hnr Rl; Bus.

EVAN, JOANN; Wymoning Valley Est HS; Plymouth, PA; (Y); Radio Clb; Concert Band; Mrchg Band; Orch; Nwsp Stf; High Hon Roll; NHS; NEDT Awd; Prsdntl Acdmc Ftns Awd 86; WY Vlly W Bnd Mscnshp Awd 86; Dstrct Bnd 85; IN U Of PA; Msc Educ.

EVANCHESKY, JOANNE; Shade-Central City HS; Central City, PA; (Y); Sec Church Yth Grp; FBLA; Library Aide; Trs Spanish Clb; Teachers Aide; Chorus; Var Sftbl; Hon Roll; Messiah Coll; Pre-Vet Med.

EVANCO, MARY BETH; Hazleton SR HS; Haddock, PA; (Y); Ski Clb; VICA; Trk; Hon Roll; Cosmetologist.

EVANGELISTA, ANGELA; St Maria Goretti HS; Philadelphia, PA; (Y); 60/439; JA; Orch; School Musical; School Play; Modern Music Mstrs Hon Soc 86; Hon Mntn Phys Ed 85-86; Temple U; Law.

EVANGELISTA, ANN; East HS; West Chester, PA; (Y); 6/387; SADD; School Musical; Rep Stu Cncl; Stat Ftbl; Var Trk; Co-Capt Vllybl; High Hon Roll; Pres NHS; Rotary Awd; Sec Spanish NHS; U MI; Psych.

EVANGELISTO, TOM; Altoona HS; Altoona, PA; (Y); Ftbl; Trk; Wt Lftg; Electrcn.

EVANISKO, DON; Johnstown HS; Johnstown, PA; (Y); Acpl Chr; Band; Chorus; Concert Band; Mrchg Band; Orch; Pep Band; Variety Show; St Francis; Studio Recrdng.

EVANKOVICH, MICHAEL; Kams City Area HS; Karns City, PA; (Y); 15/123; Drama Clb; Exploring; School Musical; Pres Frsh Cls; Pres Soph Cls; Pres Jr Cls; Sr Cls; Sec Stu Cncl; Crs Cntry; Var L Trk; Pres Schlrshp Wstmnstr Coll 86; Ntl Merit Spec Schlrshp 86; Hoche Mem Schlrshp KCHS 86; Westminster Coll; Med.

EVANOVICH, TANYA; S Fayette JR SR HS; Bridgeville, PA; (S); 16/93; Letterman Clb; Ski Clb; Teachers Aide; Chorus; School Musical; Yrbk Ed-Chief; Cheerleading; Sftbl; High Hon Roll; Hon Roll; Law.

EVANS, ANDREA; Hempfield Area HS; Greensburg, PA; (Y); Library Aide; Office Aide; Orch; High Hon Roll; Hon Roll; Jr NHS; Prfct Atten Awd; Spanish NHS; Governmnt Awd 84; Modeling.

EVANS, BARBARA; Crestwood HS; White Haven, PA; (Y); Church Yth Grp; School Play; High Hon Roll; Hon Roll; NEDT Awd; Bio.

EVANS, CHARLENE; Greensburg Cenorx Catholic HS; Jeannette, PA; (Y); 24/255; Church Yth Grp; Cmnty Wkr; German Clb; Chorus; Color Guard; High Hon Roll; Hon Roll; NHS; VA Wesleyan; Mltry Law.

EVANS IV, CHARLES M; Cocalico HS; Adamstown, PA; (Y); Tennis; Vllybl; Var Wrstlng; Prfct Atten Awd; Underwater Tech.

EVANS, CHERYL; Waynesboro Area SR HS; Waynesboro, PA; (Y); 7/371; Computer Clb; Chorus; Concert Band; Mrchg Band; School Musical; Trs Sr Cls; High Hon Roll; NHS; Cnty Band; U Of PA; Ecnmcs.

EVANS, CHRISTINE; Central York HS; York, PA; (Y); Ski Clb; Concert Band; Mrchg Band; Yrbk Stf.

EVANS, CRYSTAL; Waynesburg Central HS; Brave, PA; (Y); Office Aide; Teachers Aide; Chorus; Nwsp Stf; High Hon Roll; Jr NHS; Top 7 Fresh Cls; Typg I Awd; Eng 11-C Awd; Yorktowne Bus Inst; Sec.

EVANS, DANA; Hickory HS; Hermitage, PA; (S); Drama Clb; SADD; Varsity Clb; Chorus; School Musical; Nwsp Stf; Yrbk Stf; VP Stu Cncl; Capt Cheerleading; Spanish NHS; Hmcmng Queen 84-85; Cmmnctns.

EVANS II, DANIEL E; Mon Valley Catholic HS; Donora, PA; (Y); 17/82; FBLA; Chorus; Var L Bsbl; JV Bsktbl; JV Ftbl; Var L Golf; Duquesne U; Secndry Ed.

EVANS, DAPHNE; Lancaster Christian Schl; Conestoga, PA; (S); 2/30; Church Yth Grp; Chorus; Church Choir; School Play; Sec Jr Cls; Sec Sr Cls; Stat Bsbl; Capt L Fld Hcky; Sal; Fld Hcky Sprtsmnshp Awd 84-85; CA U Of PA; Spch Pthlgy.

EVANS, DENISE; Canton HS; Canton, PA; (Y); 8/96; Church Yth Grp; Letterman Clb; Quiz Bowl; Ski Clb; Band; Concert Band; Mrchg Band; Capt Bsktbl; Capt Sftbl; Capt Vllybl; Guthrie Clinic Allied Hlth Schrlshp 86; Bloomsburg U; Nrsng.

EVANS, DENNIS; Altoona Area HS; Altoona, PA; (S); Church Yth Grp; Computer Clb; Band; Concert Band; Mrchg Band; Orch; Jr NHS; Mid ST Bnk Schlstc Awd Band 83-84; Mnstry.

EVANS, ELIZABETH; Neshaminy HS; Langhorne, PA; (Y); 1/752; Church Yth Grp; Sec Spanish Clb; SADD; Chorus; Orch; School Musical; Nwsp Stf; Fld Hcky; Lcrss; Pres NHS; Hon-Pstv Recog To Neshaminy Schl Dist 86; Law.

EVANS, ERIC; Liberty HS; Bethlehem, PA; (Y); 180/490; School Musical; Nwsp Stf; Var L Wrstlng; Hon Roll; D Lawrence Memrl Sprtsmnshp Awd Lttl Leag Bsbll 84; E Penn Leag All Str Wrstlng 86-87; Aerospace Engr.

EVANS, HEATHER ANN; Elmer L Meyers HS; Wilkes-Barre, PA; (Y); Hosp Aide; Library Aide; Speech Tm; Chorus; Church Choir; JV Fld Hcky; French Hon Soc; High Hon Roll; Hon Roll; Jr NHS; PA Music Ed Assoc Dist & Regnl Chorus 85; Dist Chorus 86; Wilkes-Barre Frgn Lang Comptn 2nd Pl; Lib Arts.

EVANS, HEIDE; Bellefonte Area HS; Bellefonte, PA; (Y); Church Yth Grp; Drama Clb; FHA; German Clb; Pep Clb; SADD; Chorus; School Play; Var Capt Cheerleading; Hon Roll; Phys Therpy.

EVANS, JOSEPH; Bishop Mc Cort HS; Johnstown, PA; (Y); Latin Clb; Ski Clb; Band; Jazz Band; Mrchg Band; School Musical; Stage Crew; Var L Ice Hcky; God Cntry Awd; High Hon Roll; Pre Med.

EVANS, KARIN A; Wyoming Area HS; West Pittston, PA; (Y); Sec Church Yth Grp; German Clb; Key Clb; Color Guard; Var Sftbl; Hon Roll; Coll Dscrvy Prog 85; Barbizon Grad Mdlng Schl 83; Wilkes Coll; Engr.

EVANS, KATHERINE; Tunkhannock Area HS; Tunkhannock, PA; (S); 25/320; Latin Clb; Concert Band; Mrchg Band; Rep Soph Cls; Rep Jr Cls; Rep Sr Cls; Mgr Wrstlng; NHS; Acad All Amer 85-86; Lycoming Coll; Bio.

EVANS, KATHLEEN; Our Lady Of The Sacred Heart HS; Aliquippa, PA; (Y); 5/62; SADD; Trs Frsh Cls; Hon Roll; Acad All Amer; Pittsburgh Tamburitian Philhrmnc Slavjane Folk Ensmble; Bulgarian Natlty Dance Grp; Duquesne U; Cmmnctns.

EVANS, KELLY; Neshaminy SR HS; Feasterville, PA; (Y); 19/752; Sec Church Yth Grp; Girl Scts; Hosp Aide; Red Cross Aide; Service Clb; Church Choir; Hon Roll; NHS; Im Gym; Im Tennis; Med.

EVANS, LINDA ANN; Pottstown SR HS; Pottstown, PA; (Y); Exploring; Key Clb; Spanish Clb; Nwsp Stf; Yrbk Stf; Sec Stu Cncl; Var Capt Cheerleading; JV Var Lcrss; Var Tennis; High Hon Roll; Trvl.

EVANS, MELISSA; Seneca Valley SR HS; Harmony, PA; (Y); 21/370; Cmnty Wkr; SADD; Band; L Mrchg Band; School Play; Nwsp Stf; Lit Mag; High Hon Roll; Hon Roll; NHS; Schlrshp Awd 86; Butler Cnty Schlrshp Lilian L Heck Fnd 86; PA ST Beaver Campus Exec Schlrshp 86; PA ST U Beaver; Physics.

EVANS, MERRY; Owen J Roberts HS; Pottstown, PA; (Y); Church Yth Grp; School Musical; Stage Crew; Rep Soph Cls; Rep Jr Cls; Rep Stu Cncl; Im Vllybl; Intl Stds.

EVANS, RAQUEL; GAR Memorial HS; Wilkes Barre, PA; (S); 3/187; Church Yth Grp; Concert Band; Yrbk Stf; Trs Jr Cls; Var Cheerleading; High Hon Roll; Jr NHS; NHS; Office Aide; Outstndng Sci Stu; Bio Awd 84; Penn ST U; Bus Mgmt.

EVANS, RHONDA; Mary Fuller Frazier HS; Perryopolis, PA; (Y); JV Vllybl; High Hon Roll; Hon Roll; Bus.

EVANS, RICHARD; Westmont Hilltop HS; Johnstown, PA; (Y); Tennis; Wt Lftg; Wrstlng; Var Ltr Ten 85-86; PA ST.

EVANS, SCOTT; Owen J Roberts HS; Pottstown, PA; (Y); 18/291; Boy Scts; FFA; JA; Stu Cncl; Elks Awd; Hon Roll; NHS; Eagle Scout Awd 85; PA ST; Envrnl Engrng.

EVANS, SHARON; Ennaus HS; Zionsville, PA; (Y); Aud/Vis; Girl Scts; Lib Band; Church Choir; Concert Band; Mrchg Band; Pep Band; Fld Hcky; Hon Roll; Silvr Ldrshp Awd 83; Gold Ldrshp Awd 84; Silvr Awd 85; Aero Sci.

EVANS, SHELLEY; Albert Gallatin SR HS; Lake Lynn, PA; (Y); Ski Clb; Band; Concert Band; Mrchg Band; Yrbk Stf; Stu Cncl; Zoology.

EVANS, SIMONE; West Catholic Girls HS; Lansdowne, PA; (Y); 3/240; Mathletes; Spanish Clb; Orch; Nwsp Rptr; Ed Nwsp Stf; NHS; Pre-Med.

EVANS, STEPHEN; Hamburg Area HS; Hamburg, PA; (Y); 21/152; Church Yth Grp; Var Capt Tennis; High Hon Roll; Hon Roll; NHS; Pres Ftns Awd 84-85&85-86; PA ST U; Mech Engrng.

EVANS JR, TERRENCE J; Bishop Neumann HS; Williamsport, PA; (Y); 7/46; Model UN; School Musical; School Play; Trs Sr Cls; JV Var Bsktbl; Var L Crs Cntry; High Hon Roll; Hon Roll; NHS; Trphy Trsty Bsktbll 2 Yrs; Loyola Schlr Schlrshp Loyola Coll MD; Villanova U; Economcs.

EVANS, TOM; Canon Mc Millan SR HS; Canonsburg, PA; (Y); 146/396; Aud/Vis; Computer Clb; Variety Show; Trk; Hon Roll; Awd For Lang Competition 84-85; Architechtural.

EVANS JR, ULYSSES; Center HS; Monaca, PA; (Y); Computer Clb; Exploring; Band; Church Choir; Concert Band; Jazz Band; Mrchg Band; High Hon Roll; Hon Roll; Jr NHS; PA ST U Scholar 86; Outstndng Nwsp Carrier Yr 83; Westminster Hnrs Band, Dist, Cnty 85 & 86; Howard U; Civil Engrng.

EVANS, VALERIE; Hazleton HS; St Johns, PA; (Y); Drama Clb; French Clb; Leo Clb; Pep Clb; Ski Clb; Chorus; Flag Corp; Nwsp Stf; Yrbk Stf; Vllybl; Drexel; Bio Sci.

EVELAND, JOHN; Southern Columbia Area HS; Shamokin, PA; (Y); 13/90; Boy Scts; Chess Clb; Computer Clb; JV Ftbl; Trk; NHS; Outstndng Achvt Comp Math 86; Comp Sci.

EVENS, JAMIE; Port Allegany JR SR HS; Port Allegany, PA; (Y); 19/108; Debate Tm; Spanish Clb; Chorus; Var Bsktbl; JV Ftbl; Var Mgr(s); Var Score Keeper; Var Trk; Im Wt Lftg; Hon Roll; FL Southern; Bus Adm.

EVERETT, DONNA LYNN; Mechanicsburg Area SR HS; Mechanicsburg, PA; (Y); Church Yth Grp; Debate Tm; Girl Scts; Ski Clb; Speech Tm; SADD; Band; Concert Band; Mrchg Band; School Play.

EVERETT, SUSAN; West Hazleton HS; Conyngham, PA; (Y); 11/224; Church Yth Grp; FTA; Pep Clb; Spanish Clb; SADD; Varsity Clb; Var JV Cheerleading; God Cntry Awd; High Hon Roll; Hon Roll; Math.

EVERS, JAMES; Bradford Area HS; Bradford, PA; (Y); 65/273; Key Clb; VICA; Nwsp Bus Mgr; Nwsp Ed-Chief; Nwsp Phtg; Nwsp Rptr; Nwsp Stf; JV Ftbl; Im Vllybl; Hon Roll; Pres Schlrshp Concordia 86; Concordia NY; Tchng.

EVERT, TOM; Bensalem HS; Bensalem, PA; (Y); 75/540; Am Leg Aux Girls St; Band; Chorus; Concert Band; Mrchg Band; Pep Band; School Musical; Diving; Swmmng; Hon Roll; Bucks Cnty Yth Orchstra 82-86; Tri-Cnty Band 82-86; Neshaminy HS Show Band 84; Bucks Coll; Music.

EVES, KEVIN; Palmyra Area SR HS; Palmyra, PA; (Y); 20/196; Cmnty Wkr; Quiz Bowl; Band; Concert Band; Jazz Band; VP Sr Cls; Rep Stu Cncl; Var Swmmng; High Hon Roll; Hon Roll; Music Awd; Lynchbrg Coll Hpwood Smmr Schlrshp Pgm.

EWALD, FREDERIC S; Council Rock HS; Ivyland, PA; (Y); 148/840; Boy Scts; Church Yth Grp; Concert Band; Mrchg Band; Pep Band; Im Socr; Var L Swmmng; Hon Roll; U VT; Comp Sci.

EWALT, JACQUELYN; Our Lady Of The Sacred Heart; Coraopolis, PA; (Y); Teachers Aide; School Play; Stage Crew; Rep Stu Cncl; Im Ftbl; Im Ice Hcky; Hon Roll; Gannon U; Elec Engrng.

EWASKEY, RAE ANN; Chartiers Valley HS; Bridgeville, PA; (Y); Pres Church Yth Grp; Civic Clb; JA; Spanish Clb; SADD; Rep Soph Cls; Rep Jr Cls; Rep Sr Cls; Stu Cncl; Vllybl; D Carnegie Crse, Area, Dst VP Fin JR Achvt 86; Clarion U PA; Bus Mgmnt.

EWING, DAVE; Saegertown HS; Saegertown, PA; (Y); 52/124; Church Yth Grp; French Clb; Ski Clb; SADD; Band; Concert Band; Jazz Band; Mrchg Band; Pep Band; Yrbk Phtg; PA Free Entrprs Wk 86; Mrktng.

EWING, JANET; Moon SR HS; Corapolis, PA; (Y); Church Yth Grp; German Clb; Band; Church Choir; Mrchg Band; Symp Band; Var Swmmng; Im Vllybl; Hon Roll; Med.

EWING, ROBIN; Hempfield SR HS; Greensburg, PA; (Y); Chorus; School Play; Westmoreland CC; Accntng.

EWING, SHAWN; Owen J Roberts HS; Spring City, PA; (Y); 51/350; Trs Church Yth Grp; Girl Scts; Hosp Aide; Letterman Clb; Var L Swmmng; Hon Roll; Physcl Thrpy.

EWONCE, AUDRA; Montour HS; Coraopolis, PA; (Y); Concert Band; School Musical; Capt Twrlr; High Hon Roll; NCTE Awd; NHS; Alegbra Contst 84; Chem Contst 86; Math.

EWT, PAULA; Laurel Valley HS; New Florence, PA; (Y); 1/87; Trs AFS; Band; Mrchg Band; Nwsp Stf; Yrbk Stf; Capt Twrlr; Bausch & Lomb Sci Awd; High Hon Roll; NHS; Ntl Merit Ltr; Biology II Awd 86; Capt Schlstc Quiz Tm 85; Chem.

EYLER, MATT; North Pocono HS; Moscow, PA; (Y); 36/240; Church Yth Grp; Drama Clb; Band; Concert Band; Mrchg Band; School Musical; School Play; Stu Cncl; Bsbl; Trk; Aerntcl Engrng.

EYLER, T BRIAN; Waynesboro SR HS; Waynesboro, PA; (Y); 14/363; Church Yth Grp; Var Golf; High Hon Roll; PA ST; Wildlife.

EYSTER, CHRISTINE E; Spring Grove HS; Seven Valleys, PA; (Y); 4/222; Church Yth Grp; Hosp Aide; Concert Band; Orch; School Musical; Symp Band; Tennis; NHS; Pres Dept Schlrshp York Coll 86-87; MuIC Boosters Schlrshp 86; Academic Fitness Awd 86; York Coll PA; Med Tech.

EYSTER, JANIELLE; Halifax Area HS; Halifax, PA; (Y); 10/104; Sec Church Yth Grp; FBLA; FTA; Band; Chorus; Concert Band; Mrchg Band; Nwsp Rptr; Var JV Cheerleading; Swmmng; Early Childhd Educ.

EYTCHESON, ERIC; York County Area Vo-Tech Schl; York, PA; (Y); VICA; JV Var Ftbl; Var L Trk; Hon Roll; Prfct Atten Awd; Prsdntl Physcl Ftnss Awd 83-84; Arch Engrng.

EZMAN, JENNIFER; Sacred Heart HS; Carbondale, PA; (Y); 16/45; FBLA; Office Aide; Spanish Clb; Teachers Aide; Chorus; Church Choir; School Play; Stage Crew; Rep Frsh Cls; Rep Stu Cncl; Stu Cncl Actvts Awd 84; Awd For Cllctng Mny For Missions 84; U Of Pittsburg; Phy Thrpy.

EZYKOWSKY, PATTI; West Mifflin Area HS; W Mifflin, PA; (Y); 25/327; Hst VP Church Yth Grp; Sec FBLA; Teachers Aide; Rep Jr Cls; Rep Sr Cls; High Hon Roll; Hon Roll; NHS; Pres Schlr; Natl Sci Olympd Awd 83; PA St U; Bus Adm.

FABBRI, LESLIE; Penn Cambria SR HS; Gallitzin, PA; (Y); 20/289; JV Var Bsktbl; Var Trk; Hon Roll; Prfct Atten Awd; Pres Phys Ftns Awd 84, 85&86; Penn ST; Acctg.

FABEY, MARK JOSEPH; Archbishop Ryan HS For Boys; Philadelphia, PA; (Y); 8/431; Boy Scts; Political Wkr; School Play; Yrbk Ed-Chief; Lit Mag; Im Bsktbl; Hon Roll; NHS; Pres Schlr; Bio Awd Western Civ Awd 83; Ger Awd 84; Englsh Awd 85; Villanova U; Bio.

FABIAN, THERESA; Lebanon Catholic HS; Lebanon, PA; (Y); Church Yth Grp; German Clb; Hosp Aide; Chorus; Church Choir; School Play; Nwsp Ed-Chief; High Hon Roll; Pres NHS; Intl Stds.

FABINY, LEE ANN; North Allegheny HS; Pittsburgh, PA; (Y); 75/605; Var JV Vllybl; Hon Roll; Jr NHS; NHS; Penn ST U; Mrktng.

FADALE, SEAN; Warren Area HS; Clarendon, PA; (Y); Boys Clb Am; Church Yth Grp; Letterman Clb; SADD; Varsity Clb; Acpl Chr; Mrchg Band; Stage Crew; Frsh Cls; Soph Cls; Med.

FADDIS, SCOTT; Waynesburg Central HS; Waynesburg, PA; (Y); 39/205; Pres AFS; Rep Chess Clb; French Clb; Political Wkr; Lib Band; Concert Band; Drm Mjr(t); Mrchg Band; High Hon Roll; Voice Dem Awd; Frnch I Awd 84; Anna G Meighen Hist Awd 85; Congrssl Yth Ldrshp Awd 86; Hist.

FAFALIOS, M KRISTINE; Belle Vernon Area HS; Belle Vernon, PA; (Y); Ski Clb; Rep Frsh Cls; Rep Soph Cls; Rep Jr Cls; Cheerleading; Powder Puff Ftbl; Vllybl; High Hon Roll; NHS; Acad All Amer Schlr Pgm 84; Pre-Med.

FAGAN, COLLEEN; Hazleton HS; Hazleton, PA; (Y); 12/380; Leo Clb; Chorus; Yrbk Ed-Chief; Capt L Cheerleading; High Hon Roll; NHS; Presdntl Acad Fitness Awd 86; Penn ST U; Educ.

FAGAN, DANIELLE J; Mc Keesport Area HS; Mc Keesport, PA; (Y); 3/339; Cmnty Wkr; French Clb; Concert Band; Mrchg Band; L Trk; High Hon Roll; NHS.

FAGAN, EARL; South Philly HS; Philadelphia, PA; (Y); Boy Scts; Math Clb; Office Aide; Teachers Aide; Im Bsktbl; JV Ftbl; Im Trk; Cit Awd; Prfct Atten Awd; Bond Awd 81; Sfty Patrl Awd 81; Outstndng Achvt Awd 84; Comptr Engr.

FAGAN, JOHN; Archbishop Wood HS; Warminster, PA; (Y); 50/283; Im Bsktbl; Im Lcrss; JV Socr; Var Swmmng; Hon Roll; Mst Imprvd Swmmr 86; Plt.

FAGAN, JOHN M; Homer-Center JR & SR HS; Homer City, PA; (Y); 10/106; French Clb; Spanish Clb; Band; Concert Band; Nwsp Phtg; Nwsp Sprt Ed; JV Bsktbl; JV Ftbl; Golf; Wt Lftg; St Louis Holy Name Schlrshp 86; SR Of Mnth 86; Penn ST U; Chem.

FAHNESTOCK, DOUGLAS; Manheim Central HS; Manheim, PA; (Y); Church Yth Grp; VICA; Chorus; Bsbl; Hon Roll; Cbnt Mkng.

FAHRINGER, BRUCE; Northampton Area SR HS; Bath, PA; (Y); 27/475; Chess Clb; High Hon Roll; Rotary Awd; Penn ST U; Engrng.

FAHRINGER, STEPHEN; Liberty HS; Bethlehem, PA; (Y); 2/475; French Clb; Model UN; Crs Cntry; Wrstlng; High Hon Roll; NHS; Ntl Merit SF; Biochem.

FAILLACE, PAUL; E L Meyers HS; Wilkes Barre, PA; (Y); Cmnty Wkr; Hosp Aide; High Hon Roll; NHS; Arch.

FAILS, DORINDA; Saltsburg HS; Clarksburg, PA; (Y); 21/88; Sec Trs Church Yth Grp; Library Aide; Chorus; Church Choir; School Musical; Lit Mag; Stat Bsktbl; High Hon Roll; Hon Roll; NHS; Grove City Coll.

FAILS, KAREN; Villa Maria Acad; Erie, PA; (Y); Office Aide; Color Guard; Hon Roll; Gannon U; Acctg.

FAIR III, GEORGE; Bishop Shanahan HS; West Chester, PA; (Y); 68/212; SADD; Var Capt Crs Cntry; Var Capt Trk; Hon Roll; Southern Chester Cnty Leag X-Cntry All-Star Tm 85; MVP Crss Cntry 84; MVP Indoor Trck 84-85.

FAIR, NAOMI; Karns City Area HS; Petrolia, PA; (Y); 21/123; Art Clb; Church Yth Grp; Chorus; Church Choir; Trk; High Hon Roll; Hon Roll; Faclty Schlrshp; Clarion U Of PA; Spec Ed.

FAIR, PATRICIA; St Maria Goretti HS; Philadelphia, PA; (Y); 36/390; Church Yth Grp; Cmnty Wkr; French Clb; Intnl Clb; Math Clb; Pep Clb; Science Clb; Ed Yrbk Stf; Ed Lit Mag; Tennis; Physcl Thrpy.

FAIR, RAYMOND; Knock JR & SR HS; Renfrew, PA; (Y); Church Yth Grp; Debate Tm; German Clb; NFL; ROTC; Science Clb; Speech Tm; Stage Crew; Crs Cntry; Trk; Engrng.

FAIR, TODD; Plum SR HS; Pittsburgh, PA; (Y); Pres Church Yth Grp; Pres JA; Ski Clb; Spanish Clb; Var Golf; Trk; JV Vllybl; Wrstlng; Hon Roll; NHS; Dlae Carnegi Publc Spkng 86.

FAIRLIE, STEVE; Hatboro Horsham HS; Prospectville, PA; (Y); Church Yth Grp; Model UN; Service Clb; Ski Clb; Rep Stu Cncl; JV Ftbl; JV Var Trk; High Hon Roll; Hon Roll; Math Awd.

FAJERSKI, KIMBERLEE; South Side Catholic HS; Pittsburgh, PA; (S); Church Yth Grp; NFL; Service Clb; Yrbk Stf; Rep Soph Cls; Trs Stu Cncl; Sftbl; Hon Roll; NHS; Seton Hill Ldrshp Dev Schlrshp; Awd Excel; Bio Awd Hgst Avg; U Pittsburgh.

FAJT, LYNNETTE; Greater Latrobe HS; Latrobe, PA; (Y); 17/343; French Clb; Concert Band; Jazz Band; Mrchg Band; School Musical; Symp Band; French Hon Soc; High Hon Roll; NHS; Hugh O Brian Outstndg Soph Ldrshp Awd 83-84; Bethany Coll; Intl Bus.

FAL, SHARON; Canon Mc Millan HS; Washington, PA; (Y); French Clb; Band; Concert Band; Trs Pep Band; French Hon Soc; High Hon Roll; NHS; Duquesne; Pharm.

FALBO, NICOLE; Charleroi JR SR HS; Charleroi, PA; (Y); French Clb; Office Aide; Pep Clb; Ski Clb; SADD; Capt Band; Chorus; Capt Mrchg Band; School Musical; Nwsp Stf; Dancing Schl Achvt Tchr 84-85; PA Trck Mt 3rd Pl ST 84; Charleroi YMCA Tnns Leag 1st Pl Sngls 85; Fash Merch.

FALCK, CINDY; Montgomery Area HS; Montgomery, PA; (Y); 2/69; French Clb; Thesps; Chorus; Pres Jr Cls; Pres Sr Cls; Capt Bsktbl; Tennis; Trk; DAR Awd; Sal; MVP Grls Bsktbll, Bill Hall Mem, Otstndng Field Trck 85; MVP Mst Dedicated & Otstsng 86; Susquehanna U; Bus Admin.

FALCONE, KIM; Blairsville SR HS; Blairsville, PA; (Y); VP Church Yth Grp; SADD; Band; Color Guard; Concert Band; School Musical; Yrbk Phtg; Ed Yrbk Stf; Var Vllybl; High Hon Roll; Most Artstc SR Cls Persnlts 86; Art Awd 86; IN U Penn; Art Educ.

FALCONE, YVONNE; Pen Argyl Area SR HS; Pen Argyl, PA; (Y); 7/117; Computer Clb; Drama Clb; Math Clb; Red Cross Aide; Ski Clb; Chorus; School Play; JV Sftbl; High Hon Roll; Jr NHS; Yth Ldrshp Conf Lehigh U 86; Northampton Cnty JR Miss Cntstnt 86; Moravian Coll; Pre Law.

FALENSKI, LISA; Saint Joseph HS; Natrona Hgts, PA; (Y); 3/57; Hosp Aide; School Musical; Yrbk Stf; VP Sr Cls; Rep Stu Cncl; Stat Bsbl; Cheerleading; Tennis; Rotary Awd; U S Army Stdnt Athl Awd 86; Pres Acdmc Fit Awd 86; U Of Pittsburgh.

FALISE, MARLENE; Montour HS; Mc Kees Rocks, PA; (Y); 30/308; Dance Clb; Hosp Aide; Library Aide; Pep Clb; Ski Clb; Swmmng; High Hon Roll; Hon Roll; Mc Donalds Crew Prsn 85-86; Wendys Crew Prsn 86; Shop N Save Cshr 86-87; Pharm.

FALISE, RON; Penn Hills SR HS; Pittsburgh, PA; (Y); Varsity Clb; Swmmng; Hon Roll; Prfct Atten Awd; Marine Bio.

FALISKIE, SHARON; Bishop O Hara HS; Archbald, PA; (S); 5/123; French Clb; GAA; Latin Clb; Pep Clb; Chorus; Stage Crew; Nwsp Rptr; Nwsp Stf; Capt Bsktbl; High Hon Roll; Art Apprctn Awd; U Of Scranton; Pre Law.

FALKENSTEIN, DENISE; Cardinal O Hara HS; Brookhaven, PA; (Y); 225/744; Aud/Vis; School Musical; School Play; Rep Soph Cls; Rep Jr Cls; Var Cheerleading; Kutztown U; Telecommnctns.

FALKOWSKI, ED; Elmer L Meyers HS; Wilkes Barre, PA; (Y); 1/171; Computer Clb; German Clb; Var L Vllybl; Im Wt Lftg; High Hon Roll; Hon Roll; Jr NHS; NHS; NEDT Awd; Engrg.

FALKOWSKI, MARGARET M; E L Meyers HS; Wilkes Barre, PA; (Y); 1/150; FBLA; German Clb; JV Vllybl; High Hon Roll; Jr NHS; NHS; Val; NEDT Awd 82-84; Acadmc All Amer 85-86; Prsdntl Acadmc Ftns Awd 82-86; Elec Engr.

FALLERT, MICHAEL; Thomas Jefferson HS; Pittsburgh, PA; (Y); Pres Spanish Clb; Ntl Merit Cmnd Stu; IN U PA; Psych.

FALLON, STEPHANIE; Coatesville Area SR HS; Coatesville, PA; (Y); 45/500; Ski Clb; Trs Spanish Clb; Chorus; Rep Frsh Cls; Hon Roll; NEDT Awd; Pres Acdmc Achvt Awd 84-85.

FALLONE, JAMIE L; Kiski Area HS; Vandergrift, PA; (Y); FBLA; Varsity Clb; Nwsp Stf; Yrbk Stf; Rep Stu Cncl; VP L Bsktbl; VP L Trk; Hon Roll; JA; Office Aide; Robert Morris Clg; Bus.

FALSETTI, LISA; Fort Cherry HS; Westland, PA; (S); Drama Clb; Math Clb; Science Clb; Ski Clb; Varsity Clb; Chorus; School Play; L Cheerleading; Hon Roll.

FALVO, JAMES; Warren Area HS; Warren, PA; (Y); Church Yth Grp; Latin Clb; Letterman Clb; Varsity Clb; Stage Crew; Rep Stu Cncl; Var Capt Ftbl; Var L Socr; Var Wt Lftg; Hon Roll; Lbrl Arts.

FALVO, ROB; Trinity HS; Washington, PA; (Y); 82/374; Church Yth Grp; Band; Chorus; Concert Band; Jazz Band; Mrchg Band; Orch; Symp Band; Bsktbl; Hon Roll; OH U Nst Outstndng Jazz Mscn Awd 85-86; 1st Chr Schls Bands 85-86; WVU Fine Artsmusic Camp; Music.

FALZETTI, LEANNE; Scranton Central HS; Scranton, PA; (Y); French Clb; Ski Clb; Chorus; Var Cheerleading; Gym; Var Trk; DAR Awd; Hon Roll; Prfct Atten Awd; U Of Scranton; Sprts Med.

FALZONE, REGINA; Tunkhannock Area HS; Harveys Lake, PA; (S); Ski Clb; Spanish Clb; Yrbk Phtg; Yrbk Stf; Hon Roll; Bus.

FAMIANO, COLLEEN M; Norristown HS; Norristown, PA; (S); 26/503; SADD; JV Lcrss; High Hon Roll; Villanova; Crmnl Lwyr.

FANELLI, MARK; Bishop Guilfoyle HS; Altoona, PA; (Y); Chess Clb; Computer Clb; Red Cross Aide; Ski Clb; Chorus; Stage Crew; Ftbl; Law.

FANG, ANDREW; Freedom HS; Bethlehem, PA; (Y); 27/445; Science Clb; Capt Color Guard; Mrchg Band; Pres Orch; Nwsp Stf; Var Crs Cntry; Hon Roll; NHS; Biomed Engrng.

FANNIN, CATHY; St Marys Area HS; Weedville, PA; (Y); Hon Roll; Jr NHS; JR Natl Bus Hon Scty; Bus.

FANNING, LISA; West Hazleton HS; W Hazleton, PA; (Y); FBLA; Color Guard; Sftbl; Hon Roll; NJ Florida; Bus Adm.

FANT, SHELLEY; Elizabeth Forward HS; Elizabeth, PA; (Y); Church Yth Grp; French Clb; Concert Band; Mrchg Band; School Musical; Rep Jr Cls; Cheerleading; Hon Roll; Ski Clb; Var Trk; JR HS Bnd Fstvl 84; E Frwrd-T Jfrsn Dlgt To U N Plgrmg Yth Prgm 86; Howard U DC; Mrktng.

FANTAZIER, ANNE; Hempfeld HS; Mountville, PA; (Y); Church Yth Grp; Girl Scts; Chorus; Orch; Swmmng; Hon Roll; Occ Therapy.

FANTECHI, STEVEN; St Marys Area HS; St Marys, PA; (Y); 68/300; SADD; Bsbl; Ftbl; Wt Lftg; Hon Roll; Penn ST; Mech Engr.

FANTIRI, MARK; Norristown Annex HS; Norristown, PA; (S); Im Trk; Natl Hstry & Govt Awd 86; Acadmc All Amer 86; Air Condtng.

FANTONI, MICHAEL; Chartiers Valley HS; Carnegie, PA; (Y); Exploring; Political Wkr; Band; Jazz Band; Mrchg Band; Var L Bsbl; Im Fld Hcky; Im Ftbl; Im Socr; Im Sftbl; Psych.

FANZO, KATHY K; Penn Hills SR HS; Verona, PA; (Y); 69/762; Science Clb; Spanish Clb; Rep Sr Cls; Var L Sftbl; High Hon Roll; Jr NHS; Kiwanis Awd; NHS; Hon Roll; Juniata Coll; Pre-Med.

FAPORE, JENNIFER; Cameron County HS; Emporium, PA; (Y); 20/89; Church Yth Grp; German Clb; Concert Band; Mrchg Band; Yrbk Phtg; Rep Jr Cls; Var L Bsktbl; Var L Golf; Hon Roll; Phrmcy.

FARA, SANDI; Penn Cambria SR HS; Cresson, PA; (Y); Camera Clb; Drama Clb; Library Aide; Mrchg Band; Twrlr; Hon Roll; PA ST; RN.

FARABAUGH, LAURA; Cambria Heights HS; Patton, PA; (Y); Drama Clb; Ski Clb; School Play; Yrbk Phtg; Var L Cheerleading; Hon Roll; NHS; Ntl Merit Ltr; Pres Schlr; Library Aide; Acad All Amer 86; Juniata Coll; Pre-Med.

FARADAY, KIM; Pittston Area HS; Pittston, PA; (Y); Church Yth Grp; Computer Clb; Band; Concert Band; Drill Tm; Mrchg Band; Crs Cntry; Trk; Luzerne Cnty CC; Nrsng.

FARAH, JANE; Notre Dame HS; Stroudsburg, PA; (Y); Debate Tm; Drama Clb; French Clb; GAA; Ski Clb; Chorus; School Musical; Stage Crew; Var Crs Cntry; Var JV Fld Hcky; Gym MVP Awd 85-86; Yth Debates Energy Awd 4th Pl 84-85; U Toronto; Art.

FARAK, ANITA; Seneca HS; Erie, PA; (Y); 24/163; Church Yth Grp; Computer Clb; School Musical; VP Soph Cls; VP Jr Cls; VP Sr Cls; Rep Stu Cncl; Var Cheerleading; Sftbl; Hon Roll; Mercyhurst Coll; Erly Chldhd.

FARALDO, LYNN; Liberty HS; Bethlehem, PA; (Y); 105/500; German Clb; Hosp Aide; Chorus; Rep Frsh Cls; Mgr(s); Score Keeper; Nrsng.

FARAONE, DENISE; Saint Maria Goretti HS; Philadelphia, PA; (Y); 18/426; Camera Clb; French Clb; Math Clb; Model UN; Nwsp Phtg; Hon Roll; NHS; Prfct Atten Awd; Fr I II & III Hnrb Mntn Awd 83-85; Lit Mag Photo 85-86; Wrld Affrs Cncl; Villanova U; Fr Bus.

FARAONE, TONI; New Castle HS; New Castle, PA; (Y); French Clb; Chorus; Color Guard; Flag Corp; Im Vllybl.

FARBACHER, JENNIFER ANNE; Penn Hills SR HS; Verona, PA; (S); 85/762; Aud/Vis; Spanish Clb; Varsity Clb; Yrbk Sprt Ed; Yrbk Stf; Var Trk; High Hon Roll; Hon Roll; NHS; U Of Pittsburgh; Nrsg.

FARBER, MICHAEL; Pennsbury HS; Yardley, PA; (Y); Cmnty Wkr; Mathletes; Tennis; Hon Roll; NHS; Debate Tm; Hosp Aide; Math Clb; Math Tm; NFL; Placed Distnctn Mth Johns Hopkins Tlnt Srch 82; Straight A 85; Gifted; Mth.

FARBER, MIKE; State College Area HS; State College, PA; (Y); 17/570; Church Yth Grp; Cmnty Wkr; Nwsp Rptr; Rep Soph Cls; Rep Stu Cncl; Im Bsktbl; L Golf; Im Vllybl; Cit Awd; High Hon Roll.

FARDO, AMY; Ambridge Area HS; Ambridge, PA; (Y); German Clb; Letterman Clb; Pep Clb; Thesps; Varsity Clb; Band; Concert Band; Drill Tm; Mrchg Band; School Play; Govs Schl Agri Schlrshp 86; U Of Pittsburgh; Engrng.

FARGO, MIKE; Meadville Area SR HS; Meadville, PA; (Y); Church Yth Grp; Computer Clb; Ski Clb; Spanish Clb; SADD; Mgr Socr; Mgr Vllybl; Comp Sci.

FARIES, MARK; Mechanicsburg Area HS; Mechanicsburg, PA; (Y); 26/311; German Clb; Ski Clb; Chorus; School Play; Tennis; High Hon Roll; NHS; Rotary Awd; Sci.

FARINA, KIMBERLY; Valley View JR SR HS; Archbald, PA; (Y); 28/198; FBLA; VP Ski Clb; Spanish Clb; Cheerleading; Sftbl; Swmmng; High Hon Roll; Hon Roll; NHS; Prfct Atten Awd; Cheerleadng 4th Pl Indiv Awd USCA Summr Camp 84; Swmmng Rec 200 Yd Freestyle Relay Tm 83; FBLA Tm 86; Temple U; Arts & Sci.

FARKASOVSKY, MARY B; Quigley HS; Conway, PA; (S); 7/135; Exploring; Hosp Aide; Math Clb; Band; Mrchg Band; Yrbk Stf; High Hon Roll; NHS; St Vincent Coll; Bio.

FARKOSH, KATHY; Somerset Area SR HS; Somerset, PA; (Y); 75/239; English Clb; German Clb; NFL; Acpl Chr; Chorus; Nwsp Ed-Chief; Nwsp Rptr; Germ.

FARLEIGH, MICHAEL; Bishop Hafey HS; Hazleton, PA; (Y); Exploring; French Clb; Ski Clb; Varsity Clb; Yrbk Stf; Lit Mag; Rep Jr Cls; Rep Stu Cncl; JV Bsbl; Var Capt Ftbl; Foreign Yth Exchng US With France 86; Dickinson Coll; Internatl Bus.

FARLEY, DAVID; St Marys Area HS; Saint Marys, PA; (Y); JA; Var L Trk; NHS; Penn ST U; Mech Engrg.

FARLEY, JENNIFER; Lake-Lehman HS; Shavertown, PA; (Y); 36/158; Girl Scts; Band; Concert Band; Madrigals; Mrchg Band; Symp Band; Hon Roll; Grl Scouts Pres, VP, Treas, Silv Awd 81-86; Band Awd 80-86; 1st Chair Flutist Sectn Ldr 86; PA ST U; Bio.

FARLEY, JOHN; St Josephs Preparatory Schl; Philadelphia, PA; (S); 15/218; VP Band; Concert Band; Jazz Band; Pep Band; Nwsp Ed-Chief; Rep Sr Cls; High Hon Roll; NHS; Ntl Merit Ltr; Drama Clb; JR All Amer Hall Of Fame Bnd Hnrs; All Cthlc Bnd; Natl Grk & Ltn Exam Merit Awds.

FARLEY, STACEY; St Marys Area HS; St Marys, PA; (Y); Pep Clb; Service Clb; Trk; Clarion U Of PA; Bus Admin.

FARLS, BENJAMIN; Quaker Valley HS; Sewickley, PA; (Y); FCA; French Clb; Letterman Clb; Varsity Clb; Chorus; Pres Frsh Cls; Var L Bsbl; Var L Ftbl; Hon Roll; All Section Tm Bsbll 86; Bus.

FARLS, ERIC; Center HS; Matthews, NC; (Y); German Clb; Letterman Clb; Yrbk Stf; Var Bsbl; Var L Ftbl; Hon Roll; NHS; Prfct Atten Awd; Air Force ROTC Schlrshp 86; Pres Acdmc Ftns Awd 86; U NC Chpl Hl; Bus Adm.

FARMAKIS, CHRIS; Sharpsville Area SR HS; Sharpsville, PA; (S); 2/125; Thesps; Acpl Chr; Pres Band; Chorus; Jazz Band; Mrchg Band; School Musical; VP Soph Cls; VP Jr Cls; Trs Stu Cncl; Dist Band 84-86; Hnrs Chrus 83; Dist Chrus 85; Pittsburgh U; Med.

FARMER, ANDREA; Northern Lebanon HS; Fredericksburg, PA; (Y); 56/189; Art Clb; Church Yth Grp; Cmnty Wkr; 4-H; Girl Scts; Model UN; Pep Clb; Band; Chorus; Church Choir; Silver Mdl-Fncng Clb 85; Hall Monitor 86; Cmmrcl Art.

FARMERIE, WENDY; Wilmington Area HS; New Wlmington, PA; (S); 17/123; Church Yth Grp; Spanish Clb; Band; Church Choir; Concert Band; Mrchg Band; Hon Roll; NHS; Pep Band.

FARNEST, STEPHANIE; Philipsburg-Osceola Area HS; Osceola Mills, PA; (Y); 54/250; Church Yth Grp; Band; Chorus; Color Guard; Concert Band; Flag Corp; Mrchg Band; Pep Band; Yrbk Stf; Hon Roll; Nrsng.

FAROLE, ANNETTE MARIE; Panther Valley HS; Nesquehoning, PA; (Y); Camera Clb; Office Aide; Ski Clb; Teachers Aide; Yrbk Stf; Stat Trk; High Hon Roll; Hon Roll; Lehigh Cnty CC; Bus Adm.

FARPOUR, LAURA; Salisbury HS; Allentown, PA; (Y); 2/138; Drama Clb; Exploring; Hosp Aide; Key Clb; Trs Stu Cncl; JV Var Cheerleading; Var Tennis; L Trk; High Hon Roll; NHS; Typing I Awd 84-85; PA Sci Plympid Sci Bowl 86; Sci.

FARQUER, KIMBERLY; Neshaminy HS; Langhorne, PA; (Y); 100/752; Yrbk Stf; Im Vllybl; Hon Roll; NHS; Educ/Tchr.

FARRA, LISA; Upper Moreland HS; Hatboro, PA; (Y); 15/257; Key Clb; Ski Clb; Spanish Clb; Sec Frsh Cls; VP Soph Cls; VP Jr Cls; VP Sr Cls; Pres Stu Cncl; Var Capt Diving; Var Sftbl; Hugh O Brain Ambssdr 85; Elctd All ST Divg 86.

FARRAR, JEFFREY; Ambridge Area HS; Ambridge, PA; (Y); Aud/Vis; Church Yth Grp; Computer Clb; Pep Clb; VICA; Off Soph Cls; Co-Capt Vllybl; Hon Roll; Italian Clb Pres 83-85; Documntry Film Clb-Parlmntrn 85; Drug & Alchl Commtt 84-85; Penn ST U; Engrng.

FARRELL, AMY; Central Cambria HS; Colver, PA; (S); 1/209; Ski Clb; Church Choir; Concert Band; Jazz Band; Mrchg Band; Pep Band; Yrbk Ed-Chief; Sec Frsh Cls; L Sftbl; Hon Roll; Stu Librarian 85; Med.

FARRELL, CHRISTOPHER; Old Forge HS; Old Forge, PA; (S); 2/106; Boy Scts; Ski Clb; Capt Var Crs Cntry; Var Golf; High Hon Roll; NHS; VFW Awd; Voice Dem Awd; Eagle Scout 84; Spnsh Skills Awd 85; US Military Acad; Aerontcl Eng.

FARRELL, COLLEEN C; South Side Catholic HS; Pittsburgh, PA; (S); 2/45; NFL; School Play; VP Frsh Cls; Capt Cheerleading; Sftbl; High Hon Roll; NHS; JC Awd.

FARRELL, CYNTHIA; Harbor Creek HS; Erie, PA; (Y); 9/203; Model UN; School Play; Rep Soph Cls; JV Bsktbl; JV Cheerleading; Powder Puff Ftbl; Var Capt Sftbl; Var Capt Vllybl; High Hon Roll; NHS; Prvst Schlrshp To U Ptsbrgh 86-87; Engrng Schlrshp 86-87; U Ptsbrgh; Engrng.

FARRELL, KATHLEEN; Dallas HS; Dallas, PA; (Y); 12/238; Church Yth Grp; Yrbk Stf; Capt Cheerleading; Hon Roll; NHS; U Of Scranton; Phrmcy.

FARRELL, LINDA; Saint Clair Area HS; Kaska, PA; (Y); 10/85; Drama Clb; FHA; Ski Clb; Variety Show; Sec Jr Cls; Co-Capt Cheerleading; Hon Roll; NHS; Awd Outstndg Prfrmnc NEDT 85; Manor JC; Optmtrc Tech.

FARRELL, PAUL; Bensalem HS; Bensalem, PA; (Y); 91/564; Teachers Aide; Bsbl; Bsktbl; Socr; Sftbl; Wt Lftg; High Hon Roll; Hon Roll; Sccr MVP 86 & 82; U Of Pittsburgh; Civil Engr.

FARRELL, TERRI MARIE; Hempfield Area SR HS; Jeannette, PA; (Y); 138/657; Drama Clb; Library Aide; Pep Clb; Spanish Clb; Chorus; School Musical; Stage Crew; Powder Puff Ftbl; Hon Roll; Spanish NHS; U Of Pittsburgh; Intl Bus.

FARREN, SEAN; Central Catholic HS; Rankin, PA; (Y); Chorus; Bowling; Hon Roll; NHS; Cmmnctns.

FARREN, SEAN; Riverview HS; Oakmont, PA; (Y); 26/122; French Clb; Key Clb; Ski Clb; Varsity Clb; Yrbk Stf; JV Bsbl; Capt Golf; Var Tennis; High Hon Roll; Hon Roll; Natl Hnr Socty; Key Clb; Golf Capt.

FARRIER, MONICA; Carmichael Area JR SR HS; Carmichaels, PA; (S); 12/120; Ski Clb; Spanish Clb; Band; Color Guard; Concert Band; Mrchg Band; Twrlr; High Hon Roll; Hon Roll; NHS; Penn ST; Bus.

FARRIS, RENEE; Center HS; Aliquippa, PA; (Y); Pres Church Yth Grp; Sec Spanish Clb; SADD; Varsity Clb; Nwsp Rptr; Yrbk Stf; Bsktbl; Bowling; Sftbl; Hon Roll; Westminster U; Financ.

FARROW, CHRISTINA; Elizabethtown Area HS; Elizabethtown, PA; (Y); 57/227; Office Aide; Teachers Aide; Mrchg Band; Var Powder Puff Ftbl; Capt Var Twrlr; Bus Stu Of Mnth 86; Elzbthtwn Coll; Bus Adm.

FARULLI JR, CHARLES; Burgettstown Area JR & SR HS; Burgettstown, PA; (Y); Church Yth Grp; Science Clb; Ski Clb; Spanish Clb; Var L Bsbl; Var L Ftbl; Var Sftbl; Wt Lftg; Hon Roll; Jr NHS; Pilot.

FASANO, CAROL; Mifflinburg Area HS; Mifflinburg, PA; (Y); 5/163; Pres VP French Clb; Key Clb; Trs Soph Cls; Sec Stu Cncl; Var L Fld Hcky; JV Sftbl; High Hon Roll; NHS; Ntl Merit Ltr; Cheerleading; Bus Adm.

FASOLD, JENNIFER; Danville SR HS; Danville, PA; (Y); 24/202; French Clb; Hosp Aide; Key Clb; Band; Yrbk Stf; JV Trk; High Hon Roll; Hon Roll; NHS; Chld Life Spec.

FASOLD, MARY; Shikellamy HS; Northumberland, PA; (Y); 13/315; Pres Church Yth Grp; Hst Chorus; Concert Band; School Musical; School Play; Bowling; NHS; Spanish Clb; Nwsp Rptr; Stu Cncl; Dist Band & Orchstra 85-86; ST Chorus 84-86; Rgnl Band & Orchstra 86; IN U Of PA; Music Educ.

FASSANO, LISA; Cardinal O Hara HS; Aston, PA; (Y); 17/740; Aud/Vis; High Hon Roll; Hon Roll; Acdmc Schlrshp Wdnr U 86; Pres Acdmc Ftns Awd 86; Prncpls Awd 86; U Delaware; Comnctns.

FASSNACHT, MATTHEW; Ephrata SR HS; Akron, PA; (Y); 32/270; JA; Spanish Clb; Yrbk Phtg; Rep Frsh Cls; Rep Soph Cls; Bsbl; Bsktbl; Golf; Hon Roll; Arntcl Engr.

FATH JR, DAVID KELLY; Palmyra Area HS; Annville, PA; (Y); 1/195; Am Leg Boys St; Church Yth Grp; Quiz Bowl; Band; Var L Bsbl; Var L Bsktbl; High Hon Roll; NHS; Woodmn Wrld Amer Hstry Awd 86; Law.

FATLA, KATHLEEN; Mount Pleasant Area HS; Mt Pleasant, PA; (Y); 15/245; Drama Clb; French Clb; Library Aide; Church Choir; School Play; Yrbk Stf; High Hon Roll; NHS; Pres Schlr; Rotary Awd; Outstndng Schl Spirit 86; Deno Castelli Chrtbl Schlrshp 86; CA U-Pennsylvania; Comm.

FATTER, LUCY; Strong Vincent HS; Erie, PA; (Y); 2/182; Church Yth Grp; Hosp Aide; Nwsp Rptr; Bsktbl; Trk; Vllybl; High Hon Roll; Hon Roll; NHS; Sal; Schlstc/Athl Awd Army 85; Outstndng Stu 85; Volves Club Schlrshp/Grant 86; Cleveland Inst Art; Cmmrcl Art.

FATTIZZO, DAVID A; Penn Wood SR HS; Yeadon, PA; (Y); 9/313; Civic Clb; VP Cmnty Wkr; Drama Clb; Exploring; VP JA; Political Wkr; Scholastic Bowl; Speech Tm; Teachers Aide; Orch; Amer Lgn Oratorical Chmpn 86; Outstndng Stu Advncd Plcmnt In Englsh 86; Outstndng Stu Wstrn Cvlztns 86; Bcknl U; Pre-Law.

FATTORI, DEANNE; Gribel HS; Connellsville, PA; (Y); Drama Clb; French Clb; School Play; Stage Crew; Yrbk Stf; Mgr(s); Hon Roll; WV U; Clincal Psych.

FATULA, KEITH; Johnstown HS; Johnstown, PA; (Y); Pres Trs Key Clb; Speech Tm; Chorus; Concert Band; Jazz Band; Mrchg Band; School Musical; Nwsp Rptr; Rep Jr Cls; Trs Sr Cls; Clarion U Of PA; Bus Admin.

FATULA, ROBERT; Somerset Area SR HS; Somerset, PA; (Y); 26/249; English Clb; French Clb; JA; Varsity Clb; Var L Bsbl; JV L Bsktbl; High Hon Roll; NHS; Bus.

FATZINGER, AARON; Biglerville HS; Biglerville, PA; (Y); Art Clb; Church Yth Grp; FCA; Spanish Clb; Chorus; Church Choir; Nwsp Rptr; Mgr Bsktbl; Ftbl; Trk; Elemtry Teachng.

FAUDRAY, SUSAN; Baldwin-Whitchal HS; Pittsburgh, PA; (Y); Church Yth Grp; Ski Clb; Orch; JV Tennis; Hon Roll; Duquesne U; Pre-Law.

FAUNCE, DAWN; Little Flower HS For Girls; Philadelphia, PA; (Y); 78/395; Sec Jazz Band; Pres Orch; School Musical; Off Sr Cls; Im JV Bsktbl; Mgr(s); Var L Trk; Hon Roll; Prfct Atten Awd; Sec Dick Crean Strng Band 86-87; Glassboro; Music.

FAUS, JEFFREY; Manheim Central HS; Manheim, PA; (Y); Church Yth Grp; Drama Clb; 4-H; Band; Chorus; Church Choir; Concert Band; Jazz Band; Mrchg Band; School Musical.

FAUSER, PAUL D; Manheim Central HS; Manheim, PA; (Y); 42/254; Boy Scts; Church Yth Grp; God Cntry Awd; Hon Roll; Eagle Scout 83; Shippensburg; Bus Adm.

FAUST, ERIN; Mc Keesport Area HS; Mckeesport, PA; (Y); 13/339; Exploring; French Clb; Hosp Aide; Chorus; Powder Puff Ftbl; Var L Trk; High Hon Roll; NHS; Mss Teen PA Schlrshp & Rcgntn Pgnt 84; Pre-Med.

FAUST, JENNIFER; Lampeter-Strasburg HS; Lancaster, PA; (Y); AFS; Art Clb; Thesps; Chorus; Madrigals; Mrchg Band; School Musical; School Play; Nwsp Rptr; Stat Bsktbl; Cmnctns.

FAUST, JONATHAN; Pen Angyl HS; Nazareth, PA; (Y); Aud/Vis; Church Yth Grp; Bsbl; Bowling; Trk; High Hon Roll; Hon Roll; Cert Of Achvt-Vlntry Actn Ctr Of LV 86; Northampton County CC; Law.

FAUST, LORI; Salisbury HS; Allentown, PA; (Y); Cmnty Wkr; Hosp Aide; Pres Key Clb; Political Wkr; SADD; Rep Soph Cls; Stat JV Swmmng; Drama Clb; Chorus; Yrbk Stf; Outstndg Alg I Wrk; Outstndng Life Skills Wrk; Good Shepherd Rehab Hosp Volnteer; Penn ST U; Pol Sci.

FAUST, RICHARD; Boyertown Area SR HS; Gilbertsville, PA; (Y); Political Wkr; JV Trk; Cit Awd; Hon Roll; PA Mock Trial Cmpltn Regnl Fnlst 86; Pol Sci.

FAUX, GREGORY; Tunkhannock Area HS; Falls, PA; (S); Church Yth Grp; Ski Clb; JV Crs Cntry; Var L Trk; Hon Roll; NHS.

FAUX, NICOLE; Upper Dublin HS; Ft Washington, PA; (Y); #1 In Class; FBLA; Intnl Clb; JA; Political Wkr; Stu Cncl; Lcrss; Tennis; Trk; NHS; Prfct Atten Awd; Intl Bus.

FAUX, ROBERTA; Bishop Shanahan HS; W Chester, PA; (Y); 33/218; Exploring; Girl Scts; Mathletes; Scholastic Bowl; Concert Band; School Musical; Stage Crew; Yrbk Stf; Lit Mag; Hon Roll; Ag Engrng.

FAWCETT, JOHN GAUGHAN; Ambridge Area SR HS; Baden, PA; (Y); 22/349; Am Leg Boys St; Church Yth Grp; Jazz Band; School Musical; Socr; Hon Roll; Prfct Atten Awd; Louis Armstrong Music Awd 86; Eagle Boy Sct 86; Outstndng Yth Of Beaver Cnty 85; U Of Pittsburgh; Elec Engrng.

FAWCETT, TINA; Northwestern HS; Girard, PA; (Y); Pep Clb; Cheerleading; Powder Puff Ftbl; Sftbl; Hon Roll; Ntl Merit Schol; Natl Sci Mrt Awds 86; Physcl-Occptnl Ther.

FAY, TRACY; Corry Area HS; Corry, PA; (S); 47/212; Art Clb; Pres FTA; Spanish Clb; Teachers Aide; Chorus; Tchng Math.

FAYAD, BETTE; Hopewell SR HS; Aliquippa, PA; (S); 4/295; Pres Exploring; Pres German Clb; Chorus; Lion Awd; NHS; School Musical; School Play; Lit Mag; Vllybl; High Hon Roll; Pope Pius XII Awd 84; Fnlst U Of Pittsburgh Provost Day Math Comp 85; Semi-Fnlst Miss P Teen Pgnt 84; U Of Pittsburgh; Nrsng.

FAYTIK, KEN; Shaler Area HS; Allison Pk, PA; (Y); 96/517; Boy Scts; Church Yth Grp; Ski Clb; Hon Roll; Pre-Dentistry.

FAZIO, CHRISTOPHER; General Mclane HS; Edinboro, PA; (Y); Band; Concert Band; Jazz Band; Mrchg Band; Orch; Pep Band; Symp Band; Var L Golf; Var L Trk; Hon Roll; Erie Philharmonic Yth Orchestra 82-86; Pre-Law.

FAZIO, FRANK; Hampton HS; Gibsonia, PA; (Y); Dance Clb; Science Clb; Ski Clb; Yrbk Phtg; Rep Sr Cls; Im Swmmng; Im Tennis; JV Trk; Pre-Med.

FAZIO, MARY-KATHARINE; Bishop Kenrick HS; Norristown, PA; (Y); French Clb; Service Clb; Nwsp Rptr; Early Chldhd Ed.

FEAGLEY, DAWN; Upper Dauphin Area HS; Elizabethville, PA; (Y); 6/105; Pres Church Yth Grp; Capt Drill Tm; Sec Sr Cls; Capt L Trk; NHS; Art Clb; German Clb; Varsity Clb; Band; Chorus; Elizabethvl Rotary Clb Awd 86; Pres Acad Ftnss Awd 86; Irvin E Herr Fndtn Schlrshp 86; Bloomsburg U; Math Tchr.

FEAR, AMY; Littlestown HS; Littlestown, PA; (Y); 6/133; VP Church Yth Grp; Varsity Clb; Chorus; Capt Color Guard; Yrbk Stf; Stu Cncl; Cheerleading; Trk; High Hon Roll; VP NHS; Trvl.

FEASER, JOSEPH K; Eastern Lebanon County HS; Myerstown, PA; (Y); 7/179; Boy Scts; Quiz Bowl; Jazz Band; Mrchg Band; Hon Roll; NHS; Rotary Awd; Chess Clb; Exploring; Scholastic Bowl; YMCA Cnty Govt 86; Eagle Scout 82; Young Rep Awd Outstndng Achvt In Gov; Penn ST; Pub Svc.

FEASTER, JOHN W; Bedford HS; Bedford, PA; (Y); 6/196; Chess Clb; FBLA; Bausch & Lomb Sci Awd; High Hon Roll; NHS; Penn ST; Nuclear Engrng.

FEAY, YVETTE; Warren Area HS; Sheffield, PA; (Y); Church Yth Grp; Hosp Aide; Pep Clb; Concert Band; Mrchg Band; Var Cheerleading; Stat Sftbl; Stat Vllybl; High Hon Roll; NHS; Engr.

FEBBO, LORI; Pen Argyl Area HS; Nazareth, PA; (Y); 53/166; Art Clb; Spanish Clb; Hon Roll; Harrisburg St Art Exhibit Awd 85; $50 Bond Excllnc In Art 86; Nrthmptn Co Area CC; Adv Dsgn.

FECZKO, MARK; Seton La Salle HS; Pittsburgh, PA; (Y); 7/260; Church Yth Grp; Ski Clb; Var L Bsbl; Im Ftbl; Var L Golf; High Hon Roll; NHS; Outstndng Achvt Hist,Religion 83-86; Stu Tutor 84-86.

FEDER, MERYL; Bensalem SR HS; Bensalem, PA; (Y); Debate Tm; Drama Clb; Rep Frsh Cls; Rep Soph Cls; Rep Jr Cls; High Hon Roll; NHS; Ntl Merit SF; Pre Med.

FEDON, MICHAEL; Pius X HS; Bangor, PA; (Y); Exploring; Church Choir; School Musical; JV Bsktbl.

FEDON, MIKE; Pius X HS; Bangor, PA; (Y); Computer Clb; Chorus; Church Choir; School Musical; Bsktbl.

FEDOR, LORY LEIGH; Northwestern HS; W Springfield, PA; (Y); Thesps; Color Guard; Mrchg Band; School Musical; VP Soph Cls; VP Jr Cls; VP Jr Cls; Pres Stu Cncl; Wrstlng; NHS; Lock Haven; Scndry Ed.

FEDOR, PAULA; James M Coughlin HS; Wilkes-Barre, PA; (Y); DECA; Bsktbl; Hon Roll; Lwyr.

FEDORA, MARY; West Allegheny HS; Oakdale, PA; (Y); 4/206; Church Yth Grp; Spanish Clb; Pres VP Band; Sec Chorus; Jazz Band; Mrchg Band; Dnfth Awd; High Hon Roll; Lion Awd; NHS; Eng Dept Awd 86; Penn ST U.

FEDORCHAK, KAREN; Garden Spot HS; East Earl, PA; (Y); 6/201; AFS; Hosp Aide; JA; PAVAS; Red Cross Aide; Chorus; Nwsp Rptr; Rep Frsh Cls; Rep Soph Cls; Sec Jr Cls; Rep Mdl Fshn Shw 85; Stu Of Mnth 85; U Of NC; Intrntinl Bus.

FEDORKO, ANDREW; Portage Area HS; Portage, PA; (Y); 10/118; Church Yth Grp; Ski Clb; Varsity Clb; VP Stu Cncl; L Bsbl; Im Bsktbl; JV Ftbl; Im Vllybl; Hon Roll; NHS; Presdntl Physcl Fitns & Acadmc Awd86; Penn ST U; Elec Engr.

FEDORKO, ERIC; Portage Area HS; Portage, PA; (Y); 30/118; Aud/Vis; Church Yth Grp; Ski Clb; Stage Crew; JV Var Ftbl; Hon Roll; Audio/Vsl Awd Of Serv 86; PA ST; Elect Engrg.

FEDORKO, JOSEPH A; Hazleton HS; Mcadoo, PA; (Y); 19/392; Band; Concert Band; Mrchg Band; Pep Band; Var Tennis; High Hon Roll; Hon Roll; Gifted Prgrm 83, 84, 85, 86; PA ST U; Engrng.

FEDORUK, DANA; Blairsville SR HS; Black Lick, PA; (Y); 32/126; FTA; Chorus; JV Var Sftbl; Hon Roll; IN U; Elem Ed.

FEDYK, NICHOLAS; St Pius X HS; Pottstown, PA; (S); 23/139; Variety Show; Rep Stu Cncl; Bsktbl; Var Ftbl; Var Trk; Wt Lftg; Hon Roll; Jr NHS; VP NHS; Rotary Awd; 1st, 3rd Pl Sci Fair-Catdegry; U Of Pittsbrgh; Arch Engr.

FEE, DAVID CHARLES; Uniontown Area SR HS; Uniontown, PA; (Y); 22/340; Letterman Clb; Var L Ftbl; Var L Golf; Var L Tennis; CC Awd; Dnfth Awd; High Hon Roll; NHS; Prfct Atten Awd; Rotary Awd; HOBY Ldrshp Sem 84; Rotary Wrld Affairs Inst Rep 85; Rotary Clb Boy Awd 86; PA ST U; Ed.

FEE, DOUG; Bradford Area HS; Bradford, PA; (Y); 8/314; Key Clb; Varsity Clb; VP Sr Cls; Rep Stu Cncl; Bsktbl; High Hon Roll; Acdmc Excllnc Soc Stds.

FEE, PATRICIA; Saint Basil Acad; Philadelphia, PA; (Y); French Clb; German Clb; Var Bsktbl; Var Sftbl; Hon Roll; Frnch Achvt Awd 84-85; Mth Achvt Awd 84-85; Mth.

FEE, WILLIAM; Halifax Area HS; Halifax, PA; (Y); 5/100; Drama Clb; Var Bsktbl; Var Trk; High Hon Roll; Hon Roll; Merit Ribbns USNSCC 85-86; St Johns Coll; Pre-Med.

FEEHERY, TERRENCE; Cardinal O Hara HS; Springfield, PA; (Y); 120/790; Rep Frsh Cls; Rep Soph Cls; Rep Jr Cls; Rep Sr Cls; Stu Cncl; Var Capt Swmmng; Cit Awd; Hon Roll; NHS; All-Amer HS Swmng 84; All-Amer YMCA Swmng 85; Union League Phila Good Ctznshp Awd 86; Physcl Thrpy.

FEELEY, MICHAEL; Bishop Egan HS; Croydon, PA; (S); 51/235; Pres Church Yth Grp; Exploring; Latin Clb; Red Cross Aide; Nwsp Sprt Ed; Yrbk Stf; Capt Crs Cntry; Capt Trk; High Hon Roll; NHS; Prfct Atten 82-86; Dstngshd Acad Achvt Wrld Cult & Relgn 84-85; Mst VAL Rnr Egan 85; Cabrini Coll; Comm.

FEEMAN, SCOT; Lebanon Catholic HS; Lebanon, PA; (Y); 37/79; Debate Tm; Drama Clb; Key Clb; Ski Clb; Band; Concert Band; Jazz Band; Mrchg Band; Rep Stu Cncl; Tennis; Poli Sci.

FEENEY, MICHELLE; Nativity BVM HS; St Clair, PA; (Y); 13/100; Art Clb; Church Yth Grp; French Clb; Yrbk Phtg; Yrbk Stf; Rep Frsh Cls; Rep Soph Cls; Rep Jr Cls; Var Vllybl; Hon Roll; Htl Mngmt.

FEENEY, TERRY; Fox Chapel HS; Pittsburgh, PA; (Y); 123/341; Rep Soph Cls; Rep Jr Cls; Rep Stu Cncl; Im Bsktbl; Var Ftbl; Im Powder Puff Ftbl; Var Trk; Var Wt Lftg; Cit Awd; U Of Pittsburgh; Acctg.

FEESE, JOE; Mechanicsburg Area SR HS; Mechanicsburg, PA; (Y); 25/329; German Clb; Band; Chorus; School Play; Yrbk Stf; High Hon Roll; NHS; Comm.

FEESE, PAMELA; Lin Mountain HS; Dornsife, PA; (Y); #9 In Class; Art Clb; Drama Clb; Band; Concert Band; Mrchg Band; School Musical; Nwsp Ed-Chief; Mat Maids; Stat Wrstlng; High Hon Roll; Pres Acad Ftnss Awd 86; Kutztown U; Comm Dsgn.

FEESER, MATTHEW; York Catholic HS; York, PA; (Y); 20/170; VP Church Yth Grp; Var Crs Cntry; JV Trk; High Hon Roll; Hon Roll; NHS; Cross Cty Champ 85; Bus.

FEGGINS, JOEL; St John Neumann HS; Philadelphia, PA; (Y); 88/338; Art Clb; Church Yth Grp; FCA; Q&S; Spanish Clb; Band; Chorus; Concert Band; Jazz Band; School Musical; Cert For Excllnt Attndnc 84-86; Cert For Band 84; Cert For Ftbl 86; U Of PA; Marine Biologist.

FEGLEY, MATT; Greenwood HS; Millerstown, PA; (S); Band; Concert Band; Mrchg Band; Pres Jr Cls; Var Bsbl; Var Socr; Hon Roll; NHS; Modrn Music Mstrs Treas 85; Elizabethtwn Coll; Comp Sci.

FEGLEY, RENEE; Cumberland Valley HS; Camp Hill, PA; (Y); Church Yth Grp; VP Girl Scts; Spanish Clb; Color Guard; Mrchg Band; Orch; Mgr Fld Hcky; Hon Roll; Gettysburg Coll; Envrnmntl Sci.

FEGLEY, SHERRY; Mahonoy Area HS; Barnesville, PA; (Y); Exploring; FHA; Ski Clb; Spanish Clb; Band; Chorus; Flag Corp; Nwsp Stf; Trk; NHS; PA ST; Math.

FEHNEL, DOUGLAS; Nazareth Area SR HS; Nazareth, PA; (S); Ski Clb; Band; Concert Band; Pres Jazz Band; Mrchg Band; Pep Band; Hon Roll; Penn ST; Comp.

FEHNEL, SHARIN; Wilson Area HS; Easton, PA; (S); Model UN; Band; Chorus; Concert Band; Mrchg Band; Nwsp Stf; Yrbk Stf; VP Soph Cls; VP Jr Cls; VP Sr Cls; PA ST U; Hotel Mgmt.

FEHNEL, TAMMY; Bethlehem Catholic HS; Bethlehem, PA; (Y); Dance Clb; Fld Hcky; Lcrss; Mgr(s); Powder Puff Ftbl; Hon Roll; Dntl Hyg.

FEHR, MELANIE; Freedom HS; Bethlehem, PA; (Y); 104/465; Chorus; Nwsp Rptr; Nwsp Stf; Hon Roll; Elem Educ.

FEHR, TRICIA; Pine Grove Area HS; Pine Grove, PA; (Y); 6/122; Yrbk Stf; High Hon Roll; Hon Roll; Cert Of Awrd In Socl Stds, Illstrtn & Bus Ed 86.

FEICHTEL, JOHN; Mechanicsburg SR HS; Mechanicsburg, PA; (Y); 2/311; Am Leg Boys St; Nwsp Bus Mgr; Nwsp Rptr; VP Sr Cls; Var L Bsktbl; Im JV Bsktbl; Var L Ftbl; High Hon Roll; VP NHS; USN Acad; Engrng.

FEICK, JOSEPH H; Brownsville Area HS; Chestnut Ridge, PA; (Y); Drama Clb; Political Wkr; Ski Clb; SADD; Stage Crew; Variety Show; VP Frsh Cls; Pres Jr Cls; Ftbl; Trk; Phy Ed.

FEIGE, KEVIN; Bethel Park SR HS; Bethel Park, PA; (Y); Art Clb; Church Yth Grp; Computer Clb; German Clb; Science Clb; Ftbl; Mgr(s); U Pittsburgh; Comp Sci.

FEIGENBERG, STEVEN; Plymouth-Whitemarsh HS; Lafayette Hill, PA; (Y); 40/400; VP Chess Clb; Math Clb; Math Tm; Teachers Aide; Temple Yth Grp; Band; Crs Cntry; Capt Trk; Hon Roll; Mu Alp Tht; Math Dpt Awd, Pres Acdmc Ftns Awd, Outstndng Acd Achvt 86; Cert Achvt Rec Math Cntst 84; Drexel U; Engr.

FEIGHNER, CHARLES I; Bellefonte SR HS; Bellefonte, PA; (Y); Boy Scts; VICA; Band; Mrchg Band; High Hon Roll; Hon Roll; Oh Diesel Tech; Diesel Mech.

FEILBACH, CAROL; Emmaus HS; East Texas, PA; (Y); Pres Trs German Clb; Key Clb; Latin Clb; Rep Soph Cls; Hon Roll; NHS; Psych.

FEINBERG, KEVIN; Pennsbury HS; Yardley, PA; (Y); Drama Clb; French Clb; NFL; Political Wkr; Speech Tm; Chorus; School Musical; School Play; Hon Roll; NHS; 1st Pl Prsrdng; 3rd Pl Drmtc Intrprtn; 2nd Pl Hmrs Intrprtn.

FEINGOLD, STEPHANIE; Unionville HS; Chadds Ford, PA; (Y); Art Clb; JA; Pep Clb; Ski Clb; SADD; Temple Yth Grp; Hon Roll; NHS; Rep Sr Cls; Rep Stu Cncl; Cmrcl Advrtsng.

FEIST, CAROLYN; Liberty HS; Bethlehem, PA; (Y); 69/475; Dance Clb; Drama Clb; Hosp Aide; Yrbk Stf; High Hon Roll; Hon Roll; Cmptd In A Dnce Cnvntn In NY Cls Rcvd 3rd Pl 84.

FELDBAUER, STEPHEN L; St Marys Area HS; St Marys, PA; (Y); 7/299; JA; Chorus; Var Golf; Var Tennis; High Hon Roll; NHS; Pres Schlr; Merit Schlrshp Awd-Stackpole Carbou 86; Music Awd 86; Carnegie Mellon; Law.

FELDKAMP, JEFF; Souderton Area HS; Telford, PA; (Y); 5/430; Church Yth Grp; Cmnty Wkr; FCA; JV Socr; Var Tennis; High Hon Roll; Hon Roll; Jr NHS; VP NHS; Prfct Atten Awd; Herld Of Christ Chrstn Serv Brigds 86; Lehigh; Mech Engrg.

FELDMAN, ELIZABETH NICOLE; Strath Haven HS; Swarthmore, PA; (Y); Debate Tm; French Clb; Intnl Clb; Ski Clb; School Play; Stage Crew; Lit Mag; Capt Var Fld Hcky; Var Sftbl; NHS; Ltr Arts 86; Wesleyan U; Psychlgy.

FELDMAN, MARK; Brookville Area HS; Brookville, PA; (S); 1/150; Key Clb; Pres Varsity Clb; Nwsp Stf; Pres Frsh Cls; Pres Soph Cls; Pres Jr Cls; Trs Stu Cncl; Var L Bsktbl; Var L Ftbl; Var L Golf; Rnsslr Awd Math & Sci 84-85; Underclssmn Athlt Yr 84-85; Radio Magic 96 Athlt Of Yr For Fall 85; Ed.

FELDMAN, TODD; Abington SR HS; Meadowbrook, PA; (Y); 139/508; Vllybl; Comm.

FELDMANN, LISA; Boyertown Area SR HS; Gilbertsville, PA; (Y); 144/460; Acpl Chr; Band; Chorus; Mrchg Band; School Play; Lit Mag; Off Jr Cls; Off Sr Cls; Var Cheerleading; Cit Awd; York Coll PA; Bus Admn.

FELEGY, TANIA; William Allen HS; Allentown, PA; (Y); Hosp Aide; Leo Clb; Hon Roll; Jr NHS; Cntmpry Affrs 85-86; SGA Stu Govt Assn 85-86.

FELESKY, CAROLINE; North Star HS; Boswell, PA; (Y); Church Yth Grp; Sec 4-H; Math Clb; Chorus; Capt Color Guard; Hon Roll; Lion Awd; NHS; Duquesne U.

FELIX, BRUCE; Central Cambria HS; Ebensburg, PA; (S); 2/198; Art Clb; Church Yth Grp; French Clb; Library Aide; Science Clb; Ski Clb; Var Bsbl; Var Ftbl; Wt Lftg; High Hon Roll; WV U.

FELIX, CHRISTINA; Seneca Valley SR HS; Evans City, PA; (Y); Art Clb; 4-H; Ski Clb; Chorus; School Play; Rep Soph Cls; 4-H Awd; Hon Roll; Stu Of Mnth Oct 83; Butler CC; Lit.

FELIX, MELISSA; Somerset SR HS; Quecreek, PA; (Y); Art Clb; Cmnty Wkr; Pres FFA; JA; Pep Clb; Ski Clb; VICA; Chorus; Mat Maids; Hon Roll; Schlrshp-Vo Tech 86; Ldrshp Awd 86; ST Slvr Drctd Lab Bk 86; Lndscp Arch.

FELKER, JULIE; J P Mc Caskey HS; Lancaster, PA; (Y); 17/555; AFS; Church Yth Grp; Pres JA; Chorus; Trs Soph Cls; Trs Stu Cncl; Var Capt Cheerleading; Var Trk; Hon Roll; Jr NHS; Mary Jane Watt Awd 84; Sci.

FELL, BRAD; Slippery Rock Area HS; Slippery Rock, PA; (Y); #1 In Class; German Clb; JCL; Concert Band; Mrchg Band; Pep Band; Nwsp Stf; High Hon Roll; NHS; Ntl Merit Ltr; Rifle Tm Vrsty Ltr; NRA Yth Advsry Brd 86; Sci.

FELLER, AMY; Conrad Weiser HS; Reinholds, PA; (Y); 1/190; Band; Chorus; Drm Mjr(t); School Musical; School Play; Nwsp Rptr; Yrbk Stf; Var Cheerleading; High Hon Roll; NHS; Bucknell U; Intl Stds.

FELLIN, PATRICK; West Hazleton HS; W Hazleton, PA; (Y); 5/224; Am Leg Boys St; Letterman Clb; Pep Clb; Capt Scholastic Bowl; SADD; Band; Stage Crew; Capt L Bsktbl; Var Trk; High Hon Roll; Penn ST; Engrng.

FELMLEE, LISA; Kishacoquillas HS; Reedsville, PA; (Y); 23/144; French Clb; Hosp Aide; Pres Varsity Clb; Variety Show; Yrbk Stf; Stu Cncl; Capt Cheerleading; Sftbl; Hon Roll; Brookline Nrsng Schlrshp 86-87; Hmcmng Queen Candt 85; Dist Six AA Sftbll Cham 86; Juniats-Miffin Cnty Votech; RN.

FELTENBERG, GERRILYNN; Aliquippa HS; Aliquippa, PA; (Y); Drama Clb; French Clb; Yrbk Stf; Cheerleading; Wt Lftg; Hon Roll.

FELTENBERGER, MICHELLE; Franklin JR SR HS; Polk, PA; (Y); 2/230; Spanish Clb; Drill Tm; School Musical; Rep Frsh Cls; Rep Soph Cls; Rep Jr Cls; Rep Sr Cls; Rep Stu Cncl; Church Yth Grp; Church Choir; TX A&M Galveston; Marine Bio.

FELTER, JOHN; Tunkhannock Area HS; Tunkhannock, PA; (S); 5/297; Letterman Clb; Spanish Clb; Var L Bsktbl; JV Trk; Hon Roll; NHS; Hnrs Banqt 84 & 85; Engrng.

FELTON, DAVID; Johnstown HS; Johnstown, PA; (Y); Art Clb; Boy Scts; JA; Math Tm; Spanish Clb; Ed Yrbk Stf; High Hon Roll; NHS; Engrng.

FELTON, DENISE; Mt Pleasant Area HS; Greensburg, PA; (Y); Church Yth Grp; GAA; SADD; VICA; Var Sftbl; L Trk; Hon Roll; PBA; Csmtlgy.

FELTON, PAT; Williams Valley JR SR HS; Williamstown, PA; (Y); 11/109; Chess Clb; Computer Clb; Chorus; Variety Show; Rep Frsh Cls; Var L Ftbl; Crtfd Pblc Accntnt.

FELTY, COLLEEN; Lake Lehman HS; Shavertown, PA; (Y); 9/140; VP Church Yth Grp; Cmnty Wkr; Hosp Aide; Teachers Aide; Yrbk Ed-Chief; Tennis; High Hon Roll; Jr NHS; NHS; Church Choir; Virtuoso Pianist; Med.

FELTY, HARRY; Hollidaysburg SR HS; Duncansville, PA; (Y); Bsktbl; Vllybl; Penn ST; Pol Sci.

FELTZ, LORIANNE; Villa Maria Acad; Erie, PA; (Y); 7/134; PAVAS; Q&S; Nwsp Ed-Chief; Yrbk Stf; Stu Cncl; Var L Sftbl; Var L Tennis; High Hon Roll; NHS; Sprts Jrnlsm.

FELTZ, THOMAS WILLIAM; Hatboro-Horsham SR HS; Ambler, PA; (Y); 9/296; Church Yth Grp; Band; Chorus; Concert Band; Jazz Band; Capt Mrchg Band; Cit Awd; High Hon Roll; NHS; Home & Sch Assoc Awd Consistent Lvl 86; Pres Acad Fitness Awd 86; Lehigh U; Geophysics.

FENG, WU-CHE; State College Area SR HS; State College, PA; (Y); Band; Im Bsktbl; JV Crs Cntry; Var Trk; Hon Roll; Prfct Atten Awd; PA ST U; Engrng.

FENICCHIA, MARY; Berwick Area SR HS; Berwick, PA; (Y); Church Yth Grp; Chorus; Mrchg Band; Cheerleading; Hon Roll; Athltc Awd Chrldng 85-86; Bloomsburg U; Nrsng.

FENIX, CAROL; Shamokin Area HS; Shamokin, PA; (Y); 30/260; Art Clb; Camera Clb; German Clb; Key Clb; Pep Clb; Science Clb; Varsity Clb; Var Capt Bsktbl; Var Capt Tennis; Var L Vllybl; Slctd To 1st Tm All Lg Sftbl; Archtctr.

FENNELL, GREG; Yough HS; Ruffsdale, PA; (Y); 12/226; Church Yth Grp; Computer Clb; Spanish Clb; Im Badmtn; Im Vllybl; High Hon Roll; NHS; Acdmc Schlrshp Penn ST Mc Keesport 86; PA ST U; Cmptr Sci.

FENNELL, SHERRY; Karns City HS; Chicora, PA; (Y); 5/113; Cmnty Wkr; FCA; SADD; Chorus; Church Choir; Bsktbl; Sftbl; Vllybl; Hon Roll; NHS; West Penn Schl Of Nursing; Nrs.

FENNEN, JOHN; Fannett Metal HS; Ft Loudon, PA; (S); 2/50; Drama Clb; Yrbk Stf; Pres Sr Cls; Socr; NHS.

FENNEY, MICHELLE; Natavity BVM HS; St Clair, PA; (Y); 14/99; Art Clb; Church Yth Grp; French Clb; Yrbk Stf; Rep Frsh Cls; Rep Soph Cls; Rep Jr Cls; Rep Stu Cncl; Var L Vllybl; Hon Roll; Bus.

FENNINGER, ANNETTE; Lancaster Christian HS; Parkesburg, PA; (Y); 14/24; Drama Clb; Chorus; School Play; Yrbk Phtg; Yrbk Stf; Pres Jr Cls; JV Bsktbl; Var Sftbl; Hon Roll; Liberty U; Bus Admin.

FENSTERMACHER, BRIAN; Brandywine Heights HS; Mertztown, PA; (Y); 11/150; Socr; Vllybl; High Hon Roll; NHS; Momp Math Awd 86; Coll Board Prep Awd 86; Geomtry Awd 84; Engrng.

FENSTERMACHER, KAY; Brandywine Heights HS; Mertztown, PA; (Y); Hosp Aide; Sec Band; Chorus; Color Guard; Sec Concert Band; Jazz Band; Sec Mrchg Band; School Play; Swing Chorus; NHS; Bloomsburg U; Soclgy.

FENSTERMACHER, WENDY; Brandywine Heights HS; Mertztown, PA; (Y); 1/98; Am Leg Aux Girls St; Math Tm; Q&S; Quiz Bowl; Yrbk Ed-Chief; Twrlr; VP NHS; Val; Millersville U Alumni Srch For Excllnc Schlrshp 86; Fay Bordner Math Awd 86; Brandywine Hght Ed Schlrs; Millersville U; Ed.

FENSTERMAKER, ELLAN; Millville HS; Millville, PA; (Y); Pres Library Aide; Sec Band; Co-Capt Flag Corp; Hon Roll; Psych.

FENTON, CAROL; Bald Eagle-Nittany HS; Mill Hall, PA; (Y); 6/125; French Clb; Hosp Aide; Model UN; Band; Nwsp Rptr; Pres Sr Cls; Rep Stu Cncl; Var L Bsktbl; NHS; Varsity Clb; PA Free Entrprz Wk Schlrshp 86; Dist Band 85; Phy Thrpy.

FENTON, CHRISTINE; Corry Area HS; Corry, PA; (S); 7/196; Yrbk Ed-Chief; Rep Jr Cls; Rep Sr Cls; VP Stu Cncl; Var L Bsktbl; DAR Awd; High Hon Roll; German Clb; Germ Hnr Soc; Villa Maria Clg; Prof Nrsg.

FENTON, MICHELLE; Abington Heights HS; Clarks Summit, PA; (Y); 49/267; Church Yth Grp; VP Trs 4-H; JA; Chorus; Church Choir; Stage Crew; 4-H Awd; Hon Roll; Equine Studies.

FENTON, TAMMY; Wyalusing Valley JR & SR HS; Sugar Run, PA; (Y); Computer Clb; Spanish Clb; SADD; School Musical; Stage Crew; Trk; Vllybl; High Hon Roll; Hon Roll; Spanish NHS; Tyler Memrl Nrsng Awd 86; Misericordia Dallas; Nrsng.

FENWICK JR, HARRY B; Tunkhannock Area HS; Mehoopany, PA; (Y); Boy Scts; Hon Roll; JV Bsbl; Var Co-Capt Frsh Cls; Var Ftbl; Ctznshp 86; Pres Acdmc Ftns Awd 86; Acdmc All Amer 86; Bloomsburg U PA; Sec Educ.

FEOLA, CHRISTINE; St Pius X HS; Stowe, PA; (Y); 18/137; Drama Clb; JA; Pep Clb; Service Clb; Chorus; School Musical; Var Cheerleading; Twrlr; High Hon Roll; NHS; Millersvl U; Elem Ed.

FERA, JANINE; John S Fine SR HS; Plymouth, PA; (S); 7/242; Hosp Aide; Band; Pres Chorus; Concert Band; Mrchg Band; Yrbk Stf; High Hon Roll; Sec NHS; Presdntl Physcl Ftns Awd 85.

FERENCE, SHANNON; Yough SR HS; Rillton, PA; (Y); FBLA; Office Aide; Color Guard; Drm & Bgl; Mrchg Band; Stage Crew; Powder Puff Ftbl; Ftr Bus Ldrs Amrc Awd 86; Monroevl Schl Of Bus; Stngrphc.

FERENCHICK, STEPHEN J; Wyomissing Area HS; West Reading, PA; (Y); 7/119; Trs Model UN; Scholastic Bowl; Concert Band; Mrchg Band; School Musical; Yrbk Stf; Var Bowling; High Hon Roll; NHS; Ntl Merit SF; Bus Mgt.

FERGUSON, CINDI; Chestnut Ridge SR HS; Schellsburg, PA; (S); 2/142; Pres Church Yth Grp; Pres Spanish Clb; Sftbl; High Hon Roll; Hon Roll.

FERGUSON, JOHN; Sullivan County HS; Laporte, PA; (Y); 12/97; Math Tm; Quiz Bowl; Scholastic Bowl; Stage Crew; Yrbk Stf; Var Bsktbl; Var Capt Socr; Hon Roll; U Of Rochester; Psychologist.

FERGUSON, JONATHAN S; Lehigh Christian Acad; Bethlehem, PA; (Y); Drama Clb; Chorus; School Play; Yrbk Stf; Var Bsktbl; Hon Roll; Ntl Math HS Exam Awd 83-85; Mst Imprvd Plyr Bsktbll 83-84; Hghst Hnrs Engl 85-86; Messiah Coll; Scndry Educ.

FERGUSON, MICHELLE; Corry Area HS; Columbus, PA; (S); 10/212; Church Yth Grp; 4-H; French Clb; SADD; Band; Concert Band; Jazz Band; Mrchg Band; Pep Band; Yrbk Phtg; Duquesne U Of Pitt; Phrmclgy.

FERGUSON, MONICA; Mt St Joseph Acad; Phila, PA; (Y); VP Church Yth Grp; Stage Crew; Nwsp Rptr; High Hon Roll; NHS; Ntl Merit Ltr; Pres Spanish NHS; Drama Clb; JA; JCL; Ntl Achvt Schrlshp 86; Mites Pgm 85; Pa Gov Schl Sci 84; Tufts U; Bio-Chem.

FERGUSON, NOREINE; Apollo-Ridge HS; Kent, PA; (Y); Church Yth Grp; Pep Clb; Ski Clb; Band; Concert Band; Mrchg Band; Trk; Hon Roll; Band & Trk Awds 86; U Of Pittsburgh; Med Tech.

FERGUSON, PAUL; Philipsburg Oscela HS; Philipsburg, PA; (Y); 57/250; Ftbl; Wrstlng; Bus Adm.

FERGUSON, STACY; Bedford HS; Bedford, PA; (Y); Pep Clb; Ski Clb; SADD; Chorus; Frsh Cls; Stu Cncl; Stat Bsktbl; Var Cheerleading; Vllybl; Hon Roll; Nrsg.

FERGUSON, TAMMIE; Bethel Park SR HS; Bethel Park, PA; (Y); 104/520; Rep Frsh Cls; Rep Soph Cls; L Bsktbl; Powder Puff Ftbl; Capt Socr; L Sftbl; Trk; Vllybl; Hon Roll; Bethel Pk Mascot 86; Chem Engr.

FERKETICH, AMY; Upper Perkiomen HS; Green Lane, PA; (Y); 11/250; Church Yth Grp; Debate Tm; Hosp Aide; Chorus; Nwsp Stf; Cheerleading; Tennis; Trk; High Hon Roll; Hon Roll; Nutrition.

FERLITO, BECKY; Clearfield Area HS; Clearfield, PA; (Y); 11/330; Trs Church Yth Grp; Sec French Clb; Concert Band; Mrchg Band; Orch; Yrbk Ed-Chief; Off Stu Cncl; Cit Awd; High Hon Roll; NHS; Acdmc All-Amrcn Schlr 86.

FERN, KIM; Upper Perkiomen HS; E Greenville, PA; (Y); 15/201; Cmnty Wkr; VP Computer Clb; Variety Show; Yrbk Phtg; Powder Puff Ftbl; Var L Socr; High Hon Roll; NHS; U S Army Sci & Engrng Mdlln-DE Vly Sci Fair 84; Millersville U; Math.

FERNALD, JENNIFER; Downingtown HS; Coatesville, PA; (Y); Church Yth Grp; Computer Clb; Band; Church Choir; Jazz Band; Mrchg Band; Stat Socr; High Hon Roll; Hon Roll; Girl Scts; NEDT Test Awd 86; Comp Sci.

FERNANDES, DAVID; Archbishop Kennedy HS; Philadelphia, PA; (Y); 10/170; Church Yth Grp; Cmnty Wkr; Library Aide; Nwsp Rptr; Rep Stu Cncl; JV Trk; High Hon Roll; NHS; Prfct Atten Awd; Acad All-Amer 86; Bus Mgr.

FERNANDES, LISA; West Scranton HS; Scranton, PA; (Y); Art Clb; Letterman Clb; Spanish Clb; Rep Stu Cncl; Crs Cntry; Pom Pon; Trk; Hon Roll; NHS; Sec.

FERNANDEZ, ANGELA; Central Columbia HS; Berwick, PA; (Y); Pres French Clb; Capt Color Guard; Trs Frsh Cls; Pres Stu Cncl; Pres French Hon Soc; Hon Roll; NEDT Awd; Rotary Awd; Army ROTC Schlrshp 86; Dickinson Coll; Intl Rel.

FERNANDEZ, ANTHONY; St Josephs Prep; Philadelphia, PA; (Y); 50/240; Spanish Clb; Yrbk Stf; Im Ftbl; JV Wrstlng; Hon Roll; Prep Schlr 84-86; Bus.

FERNANDEZ, MELISSA; Pennsbury HS; Morrisville, PA; (Y); Spanish Clb; Chorus; School Musical; JV Socr; Var Swmmng; Hon Roll; NHS.

FERRAND, JEFF; Ambridge Area HS; Ambridge, PA; (Y); Am Leg Boys St; Church Yth Grp; Pep Clb; Spanish Clb; Rep Soph Cls; Rep Jr Cls; L Var Gym; Hon Roll; PIAA Still Rings ST Champ Gymnstcs 85 & 86.

FERRANTE, LOUIS; Hampton HS; Allison Pk, PA; (Y); Latin Clb; Science Clb; Ski Clb; Concert Band; Symp Band; Im L Bsbl; Im Wt Lftg; Var L Wrstlng; Hon Roll.

FERRARA, TODD A; Hollidaysburg Area HS; Hollidaysburg, PA; (Y); 50/375; Letterman Clb; SADD; Varsity Clb; Jazz Band; Orch; Bsktbl; Var L Ftbl; Capt L Trk; Wt Lftg; Hon Roll; Ftbl Grant 86-87; Juaniata Coll; Mech Engrg.

FERRARO, JOHN; Scranton Prep; Scranton, PA; (Y); 64/197; Trs Church Yth Grp; Chorus; Church Choir; Orch; Pep Band; God Cntry Awd; Hon Roll; Arch.

FERRARO, JUDITH; West Scranton HS; Scranton, PA; (Y); Church Yth Grp; Drama Clb; Spanish Clb; Thesps; School Play; Stage Crew; Trk; High Hon Roll; Hon Roll; Smmr Schlrshp Mrywood Coll 86; 2nd Plc Dstrct Piano Cmptn 82; Marywood Coll; Frgn Lng.

FERRARO, KIM; Pittston Area SR HS; Hughestown, PA; (Y); 53/348; Art Clb; Pres Aud/Vis; Drama Clb; French Clb; Office Aide; School Play; Nwsp Stf; High Hon Roll; NHS; Schlstc Art Awd Hnr Mntn 85; Cert Compltn Kystn JC Art Wrkshps 85-86; 1st Tele-Comm Prof Nws Cmptn 86; Parsons Schl; Fshn Illstrtn.

FERRARO, MELANIE; Brookville Area HS; Brookville, PA; (Y); 15/144; Sec VP Key Clb; SADD; VP Acpl Chr; School Musical; Pres Swing Chorus; Sec Soph Cls; VP Jr Cls; Rep Sr Cls; Pres Stu Cncl; Capt Cheerleading; Acdmc Schlrshp Elzbthtwn Coll, Ocptnl Thrpy Schlrshp Elzbthtwn Coll, Mst Actv Key Clb Awd 86; Elizabethtown Coll; Occ Thrpy.

FERRARO, TINA; Brockway Area HS; Brockway, PA; (Y); Art Clb; Debate Tm; Varsity Clb; Stu Cncl; Stat Socr; JV Capt Vllybl; Elem Ed.

FERRARO, TRACY; Penn Hills SR HS; Pittsburgh, PA; (Y); Stu Cncl; Gym; Hon Roll; Prfct Atten Awd; USBEA Awd 85-86; Shrthnd Awd Achvt 85-86; Lmp Knwldg Awd 85-86; Spr People Awd 84-85; Exec Secty.

FERREBEE, SHERRY; Hopewell SR HS; Aliquippa, PA; (Y); #22 In Class; French Clb; FNA; Pres JA; Trs Library Aide; Band; High Hon Roll; NHS; Nrsng.

FERREE, CHRISTOPHER; Geibel HS; Uniontown, PA; (Y); Drama Clb; French Clb; School Musical; Yrbk Stf; Lit Mag; French Hon Soc; Hon Roll; 1st Pl Frnch Prse Hmnts Day Comptv 86; Smi Fnlst Thtre PA Gov Schl Arts 85; 1st Pl Frnch Ply Hmnts Dy; Otterbein Coll; Actor.

FERREE, GREGORY; Geibel HS; Uniontown, PA; (Y); 10/101; Drama Clb; Ski Clb; Lit Mag; DAR Awd; Pres French Hon Soc; High Hon Roll; NHS; Pres Schlr; Voice Dem Awd; Elks E Stanley Phillips Hstry Awd 86; Cnty Mrkt Schlrshp 86; Millersville U; French.

FERREE, JESSICA; Spring Grove SR HS; Spring Grove, PA; (Y); 86/285; Church Yth Grp; VP 4-H; French Clb; German Clb; Girl Scts; Varsity Clb; School Play; Nwsp Rptr; Sec Soph Cls; Sec Jr Cls; Fshn Mrchndsng.

FERREE, KANDY; Upper Dauphin Area HS; Berrysburg, PA; (Y); 12/112; Trs Church Yth Grp; Chorus; School Musical; Yrbk Ed-Chief; Var Capt Bsktbl; Var L Sftbl; NHS; Bsktbl Lg All Star Tm 85-86; Lebanon Vly; Psych.

FERREE, LYNN; Eastn York HS; Yorkana, PA; (Y); 65/159; Church Yth Grp; Chorus; Church Choir; School Musical; Hon Roll; Lancaster Bible Coll; Wrld Mssn.

FERREE, RANDY; Cedar Crest HS; Lebanon, PA; (Y); 46/360; Church Yth Grp; French Clb; German Clb; Band; Drm & Bgl; Mrchg Band; School Musical; Stage Crew; Crs Cntry; Trk; Natl Merit Engl Awd; PA ST; Lib Arts.

FERRELL, CHRISTY; Lampeter-Strasburg HS; Strasburg, PA; (Y); Church Yth Grp; VP JA; Band; Chorus; School Musical; Yrbk Bus Mgr; Var L Crs Cntry; Var L Trk; Hon Roll; NHS; VP Persnnl Corp Sec Yr 86; Delg Ntl Achvt Conf 86; Hnrbl Ment Bio Sci Fair 86; Physics.

FERRELL, JIM; Neu Castle SR HS; New Castle, PA; (Y); 25/263; Varsity Clb; Var Ftbl; Var Wt Lftg; Hon Roll; NHS; Carnegie Mellon U; Engrng.

FERRELL, KEVIN; Ridley SR HS; Folsom, PA; (Y); 73/427; Hon Roll; Engnrng.

FERRENCE, BRIAN; Ringgold HS; Finleyville, PA; (Y); Computer Clb; Ski Clb; Varsity Clb; Crs Cntry; Trk; 6 Credits U Pittsburgh Comp Sci 86; Embry-Riddle Aero U; Aviatn.

FERRETTI, CYNTHIA; Lathrobe SR HS; Greensburg, PA; (Y); 46/410; Letterman Clb; Yrbk Sprt Ed; Yrbk Stf; Rep Soph Cls; Rep Stu Cncl; Var Tennis; Var Trk; French Hon Soc; High Hon Roll; Hon Roll; Fashn Merch.

FERRETTI, DANIEL L; Leechburg Area HS; Leechburg, PA; (Y); Nwsp Stf; Yrbk Stf; Pres Frsh Cls; Pres Soph Cls; Pres Jr Cls; Pres Sr Cls; Pres Stu Cncl; Capt Bsbl; Var L Ftbl; Hon Roll; Amer Lgn Awd 81-82; Vrsty Bsbl Sctn All-Tm 85-86; PA ST U.

FERRI, BRENDA; Council Rock HS; Holland, PA; (Y); 290/845; Church Yth Grp; Teachers Aide; Church Choir; Concert Band; Mrchg Band; Nwsp Rptr; Nwsp Stf; Hon Roll; Treas Church Yth Grp 85-86; Jrnlsm.

FERRI, TANYA; Mckeesport HS; White Oak, PA; (Y); JA; Trk; Airln Stwrdss.

FERRIER, MICHAEL; Henderson HS; West Chester, PA; (Y); Band; Concert Band; Jazz Band; Mrchg Band; Pep Band; JV Var Bsbl; Im Ice Hcky.

FERRIGNO, DENISE; West Phila Catholic Girls HS; Philadelphia, PA; (Y); 51/240; Teachers Aide; Hon Roll; Girl Scts; Political Wkr; Pierce Schl Bus; Legal Aid.

FERRILL, LAURA; Hampton HS; Allison Pk, PA; (Y); French Clb; Ski Clb; School Musical; Stage Crew; Cheerleading; Powder Puff Ftbl; High Hon Roll; Hon Roll; La Roche Coll; Attrny.

FERRILLI, CHRISTINA; Saint Maria Goretti HS; Philadelphia, PA; (Y); 250/400; Cmnty Wkr; Y-Teens; Variety Show; Nrsng.

FERRINGER, TINA; Marion Center Area HS; Home, PA; (S); 13/170; Trs Church Yth Grp; VP FBLA; Office Aide; SADD; Varsity Clb; Cheerleading; High Hon Roll; Jr NHS; NHS; IN U Of PA; Bus.

FERRIS, CAROL; Lakeland HS; Whites Crossing, PA; (Y); 42/150; Dance Clb; Hosp Aide; JA; Office Aide; Radio Clb; SADD; Varsity Clb; Color Guard; NHS; FHA; Bloomsburg U; Spch Pathlgy.

FERRONE, LAURETTE; Mid-Valley HS; Throop, PA; (Y); 26/70; Dance Clb; Ski Clb; Trs Jr Cls; Trs Sr Cls; Cheerleading; Wt Lftg; High Hon Roll; Hon Roll; Bloomsburg U.

FERYO, CHRIS; Nativity B V M HS; St Clair, PA; (Y); 21/97; Aud/Vis; Chess Clb; Exploring; High Hon Roll; Hon Roll.

FERYO, CHRISTOPHER; Nativity BVM HS; St Clair, PA; (Y); 24/98; Aud/Vis; Chess Clb; Exploring; High Hon Roll; Hon Roll; Voice Dem Awd; Lebanon Valley Coll Yth Schlrshp 85-86; Acdmc Excllnc Awd 83-84; Fine Arts Awd 83-84.

FESTA, DANIEL; Valley HS; New Kensington, PA; (Y); Science Clb; Spanish Clb; Chorus; Concert Band; Cit Awd; High Hon Roll; Hon Roll; Prfct Atten Awd; PA ST; Mech Engrng.

FESTA, ELISA; Valley HS; New Kensington, PA; (Y); Spanish Clb; Chorus; Lit Mag; Sec Sr Cls; Stu Cncl; Var JV Cheerleading; Var Diving; DECA; NHS; Pres Schlr; U Of S FL; Optometry.

FESTER, SHARON; West Chester East HS; West Chester, PA; (Y); Church Yth Grp; Girl Scts; VICA; JV Gym; Var Vllybl; Hon Roll; Schlrshp Gordan Phillips Beauty Schl 86; Chester Cnty Schl Nrsng; Nrsng.

FETCKO, JODI; Canon Mc Millan SR HS; Strabane, PA; (Y); Church Yth Grp; Hosp Aide; JA; Office Aide; Band; Concert Band; Flag Corp; Nwsp Stf; Yrbk Stf; Hon Roll; Bradford Bus Schl; Ex Sec.

FETHERMAN, JODI; Conrad Weiser JS HS; Robesonia, PA; (Y); 1/184; Hosp Aide; JCL; Pres Key Clb; Teachers Aide; Capt Color Guard; School Musical; Nwsp Rptr; Var Cheerleading; High Hon Roll; NHS.

FETHERMAN, MELINDA; Conrad Weiser HS; Robesonia, PA; (Y); 1/137; Pres Key Clb; Chorus; Nwsp Ed-Chief; Yrbk Stf; Ed Lit Mag; Stat Bsbl; DAR Awd; Sec NHS; Ntl Merit Ltr; Pres Schlr; TAP Altruism Awd Scholar 86; Coll William & Mary; Lib Arts.

FETOCK, MARIA; Brownsville Area HS; Grindstone, PA; (S); 13/255; Computer Clb; Drama Clb; Mathletes; Math Clb; Band; Concert Band; Mrchg Band; Nwsp Stf; Vllybl; High Hon Roll.

FETSKO, CHRISTINE; Portage Area HS; Portage, PA; (Y); Varsity Clb; Chorus; Variety Show; Stu Cncl; Stat Bsktbl; Var Capt Cheerleading; Hon Roll; Spec Olympcs Hugger; Physcl Thrpst.

FETTER, KATHLEEN; Hamburg Area HS; Hamburg, PA; (Y); Sec Spanish Clb; Rep SADD; VP Soph Cls; VP Sr Cls; Rep Stu Cncl; JV Bsktbl; Var L Cheerleading; Var L Fld Hcky; Var L Trk; High Hon Roll.

FETTER, SARAH; Red Land HS; Etters, PA; (Y); 21/275; Trs Church Yth Grp; Spanish Clb; Mrchg Band; Symp Band; Cheerleading; Vllybl; High Hon Roll; Spanish NHS; Band; Concert Band; 7th Pl Spanish Natl Exam 86; Amer Music Abrd European Trng Band 85; Being Dist Band 85.

FETTERMAN, CHRIS; Dallas HS; Dallas, PA; (Y); 82/238; Aud/Vis; Boy Scts; Church Yth Grp; Ski Clb; Var Socr; JETS Awd; Rcvd Eagle Scout Awd 84; Mechanical Engineering.

FETTERMAN, JAY A; Montoursville Area HS; Montoursville, PA; (Y); 2/176; Trs French Clb; Trs Key Clb; Capt Math Tm; Varsity Clb; Yrbk Sprt Ed; L Tennis; Wrstlng; Pres NHS; Letterman Clb; L Ftbl; Gvrnrs Schl For Sci 85; Jacque Weber Schlrshp 85; Natl Schlr-Athlete 85; Le High U; Engrng.

FETTERMAN, MELISSA; Punxsutawney SR HS; Punxsutawney, PA; (Y); Debate Tm; French Clb; Hosp Aide; Science Clb; Spanish Clb; Speech Tm; Hon Roll; Cmnty Wkr; Radio Clb; Rotary Exch Stu Abroad 86; Trvl Spclst.

FETTERMAN, MISSEY; Punxsutawney Area SR HS; Punxsutawney, PA; (Y); Debate Tm; French Clb; Hosp Aide; Science Clb; Spanish Clb; Speech Tm; Hon Roll; Rtry Exchng Stu 86.

FETTEROLF, JODI; Juniata HS; Mifflintown, PA; (Y); Band; Chorus; Church Choir; School Play; Yrbk Ed-Chief; Trs Jr Cls; Var Capt Cheerleading; Var Fld Hcky; JP Sousa Awd; NHS.

FETTEROLF, MICHAEL; Tri-Valley HS; Klingerstown, PA; (Y); 14/77; Pres Church Yth Grp; Pres Computer Clb; Pres FFA; Band; Concert Band; Jazz Band; Mrchg Band; Pep Band; Williamsport Tech; Dsl Eng Mech.

FETTIS, RENEE; Baldwin HS; Pittsburgh, PA; (Y); Math Clb; Band; Jazz Band; Mrchg Band; Orch; School Musical; NHS; 3 Yr Serv Awd Marchng Band; Phys Therpy.

FEUDALE, BARBARA L; Cardinal Brennan HS; Ashland, PA; (Y); 3/48; Chorus; Church Choir; School Musical; School Play; Sec Stu Cncl; Capt Cheerleading; High Hon Roll; NHS; Spanish NHS; Hghst Avg-Eng, Bio, Am Cultrs-1st Rnk 84; Physcs, Socl Studies, Relgn & Eng Awds-3rd Rnk 86; Bucknell U.

FEUERSTEIN, TINA; Freedom SR HS; Bethlehem, PA; (Y); 95/456; Pres Church Yth Grp; Chorus; Church Choir; High Hon Roll; Hon Roll; West Chester U; Elem Ed.

FEYES, AMY; Mckeesport SR HS; Mckeesport, PA; (Y); 67/360; Cmnty Wkr; Acpl Chr; Band; Chorus; Church Choir; Concert Band; Mrchg Band; Orch; School Musical; Variety Show; Penn ST U; Educ.

FIALKOWSKI, KATHLEEN; Abp Prendergast HS; Yeadon, PA; (Y); Church Yth Grp; Girl Scts; NFL; Office Aide; Red Cross Aide; Pres Sec Service Clb; Chorus; Madrigals; School Musical; Hon Roll; Outstndng Svc Cmmnty 86; Outstndng Svc Music 86; Neumann Coll; Med Tech.

FIANDRA, JENNIFER; Nazareth Acad; Philadelphia, PA; (Y); Church Yth Grp; Cmnty Wkr; Dance Clb; French Clb; Library Aide; Rep Soph Cls; Im Bsktbl; Var JV Cheerleading; Var JV Fld Hcky; Hon Roll; Natl Hnr Roll 85-86; St Josephs U.

FIASCKI, CAROLYN; G A R Memorial HS; Wilkes Barre, PA; (S); 10/177; FBLA; Jazz Band; Orch; Nwsp Stf; Pres Sr Cls; Bsktbl; Sftbl; Hon Roll; NHS; Typng I & II Cert.

FICCA, AMY; Southern Columbia Area HS; Elysburg, PA; (Y); 25/93; Art Clb; Chess Clb; Church Yth Grp; Computer Clb; Drama Clb; Exploring; Girl Scts; Key Clb; Library Aide; Band; West Chester U; Commercial Art.

FICCA, JOHN; Mt Carmel Area HS; Mt Carmel, PA; (Y); #32 In Class; Computer Clb; English Clb; Key Clb; Letterman Clb; Spanish Clb; Trs Frsh Cls; Trs Soph Cls; Trs Jr Cls; Trs Sr Cls; Trs Stu Cncl; Dickinson COLL; Pol Sci.

FICCA, ROBERT; Columbia Montour AVTS HS; Elysburg, PA; (S); 4/206; Chess Clb; Math Tm; Science Clb; VICA; Yrbk Stf; High Hon Roll; NHS; Fnlst PA ST Sci Olympcs 86; Penn ST; Comp Engrng.

FICHER, DOUG; Connellsville Area HS; Leisening, PA; (Y); 65/550; School Musical; Stage Crew; Rep Soph Cls; Sec Sr Cls; JV Bsktbl; L Ftbl; Trk; Var Wt Lftg; High Hon Roll; Hon Roll; Dusquesne U; Bus Admin.

FICHTNER, MICHELE; Solanco HS; Quarryville, PA; (Y); Church Yth Grp; Cmnty Wkr; Computer Clb; Trs Girl Scts; Spanish Clb; Trs Band; Trs Chorus; Church Choir; Concert Band; Jazz Band; 3r Pl Lancaster Cty Sci Engrng Fair 84; Awds Solanco Fair; Elizabethtown Coll; Ed.

FICKE, ALANA; Lower Moreland HS; Huntingdon Valley, PA; (S); Drama Clb; German Clb; Acpl Chr; Chorus; Concert Band; Jazz Band; Mrchg Band; Orch; Pep Band; School Musical; I Dare You Natl Ldrshp Awd 86; Pre-Med.

FICKES, F CHRIS; Northern HS; Wellsville, PA; (S); Boy Scts; Church Yth Grp; Rep DECA; JV Bsktbl; JV Socr; West VA Tech; Bus Managmnt.

FICKINGER, KELLY; Canon Mc Millan HS; Eighty Four, PA; (Y); 20/390; Dance Clb; French Clb; Office Aide; Ski Clb; Sec Band; Cheerleading; Crs Cntry; Sftbl; Tennis; High Hon Roll; PA ST U; Bus Mgmt.

FIDALGO, RUI; Olney HS; Philadelphia, PA; (Y); Cmnty Wkr; Dance Clb; Hosp Aide; JV Var Socr; Hon Roll; Nrsg.

FIDLER, STACY; Cumberland Valley HS; Camp Hill, PA; (Y); 47/522; Red Cross Aide; School Musical; Im Vllybl; Hon Roll; NHS; Genetics.

FIDLER, TINA; Norther Lebanon HS; Jonestown, PA; (Y); Church Yth Grp; Quiz Bowl; Band; Church Choir; Pep Band; Nwsp Rptr; Cit Awd; NHS; Pres Acad Fit Awd; Moyer-Longacre Scholar; Stu Mnth; Philadelphia Coll; Elem Ed.

FIDYK, JOHN; Hanover Area JR SR HS; Wilkes Barre, PA; (Y); High Hon Roll; Hon Roll; Jr NHS; Med.

FIEDLINE, JILLYNN; North Star HS; Boswell, PA; (Y); 15/121; Art Clb; FCA; Pres 4-H; Pep Clb; Rep Stu Cncl; Cheerleading; Hon Roll; Lion Awd; NHS; Somerset Cnty Dry Prncss 85; VP Stu Actn Educ 85-86; Hmcmng Crt Miss SR 85-86; Shippensburg U; Intrnl Mgmnt.

FIELD, MARK; Tunkhannock HS; Noxen, PA; (S); 30/330; Computer Clb; Science Clb; Spanish Clb; Wrstlng; Hon Roll; NHS; Engr.

FIELDER, SCOTT A; Carlynton HS; Carnegie, PA; (Y); Am Leg Boys St; Church Yth Grp; Cmnty Wkr; Drama Clb; Exploring; VP German Clb; VP JA; Political Wkr; Trs Spanish Clb; Nwsp Ed-Chief; IUP; Poli Sci.

FIELDING, PRESTON; South Philadelphia HS; Philadelphia, PA; (Y); Boy Scts; Chess Clb; Computer Clb; Rep Stu Cncl; Mgr(s); Var L Tennis; High Hon Roll; Hon Roll; Prfct Atten Awd; Drexel; Chem Engrng.

FIELDING, ROBIN; Seneca HS; Wattsburg, PA; (Y); 2/140; Trs Pres Church Yth Grp; Chorus; Concert Band; Mrchg Band; School Musical; High Hon Roll; Lion Awd; NHS; Sal; Bonnie Winder Musc Schlrshp 86; Kircher Awd 86; Slippery Rock U; Musc Thrpy.

FIELDS, JASON; West Hazleton HS; Conyngham, PA; (S); 21/191; Church Yth Grp; FTA; Scholastic Bowl; Var Ftbl; L Tennis; Hon Roll; NHS; Engrng.

FIELDS, KIM; Pine Forge Acad; Richmond, VA; (S); Church Choir; Drill Tm; School Musical; Cit Awd; Hon Roll; NHS; Treas JR Clss 83-84; Columbia Union Coll; Cmmnctns.

FIELDS, REX; Central Fulton HS; Mcconnellsburg, PA; (Y); Varsity Clb; School Musical; Stu Cncl; Var Bsbl; JV Bsktbl; JV Var Socr; High Hon Roll; Hon Roll; Jr NHS; NHS; Acdmc All Amer 86; Gov & Sociolgy Awd 86; Hon Soc Awds 85-86; Pre Med.

FIELDS, WILLIAM H; Upper Darby HS; Drexel Hill, PA; (Y); 17/534; Pres Service Clb; School Play; Pres Sr Cls; High Hon Roll; Hon Roll; NCTE Awd; NHS; Ntl Merit SF; Drama Clb; Exploring; US Hist AP Awd 84-85; Creatv Wrtng Awd 84-85; Stu Rep-Uppr Darby Schl Brd 85-86; NY U; Brdcst Cmnctns.

FIERRO, DOMENICO; Plymouth Whitemarsh HS; Norristown, PA; (Y); 101/337; Var JV Bsktbl; Var Capt Socr; Hon Roll; Prfct Atten Awd; Acdmc Exclnc 86; Chem.

FIERRO, MARIA; Plymouth-Whitemarsh HS; Norristown, PA; (Y); 31/361; Science Clb; Varsity Clb; Bsktbl; Trk; Jr NHS; Prfct Atten Awd; Pres Schlr; 3rd Co Sci Rsrch Comp, Colnl Ed Assoc Dr Kenneth Wilkinson Mem Schlrshp 86; St Josephs U; Pre-Med.

FIESTA, MELISSA; Moravian Acad; Macungie, PA; (Y); Girl Scts; Variety Show; Nwsp Stf; JV Tennis; High Hon Roll; Hon Roll; New Stu Orientatn Pgm 85-86; Girl Sct 83.

FIFE, BRYAN; Harbor Creek HS; Erie, PA; (Y); 31/288; Am Leg Boys St; Chess Clb; Var L Bsbl; Var L Bsktbl; Ftbl; High Hon Roll; Poli Sci.

FIFE, KAREN S; Lincoln HS; Wampum, PA; (Y); 16/163; Latin Clb; Service Clb; Spanish Clb; Y-Teens; Band; Concert Band; Bowling; Hon Roll; NHS; Prfct Atten Awd; Outstndng Soc Sci Awd 86; Outstndng Latin Stu Awd 85; Duquesne U; Pharm.

FIGAS, CHERIE; Plum SR HS; New Kensington, PA; (Y); Aud/Vis; Cmnty Wkr; Dance Clb; Library Aide; SADD; Chorus; Drm Mjr(t); Yrbk Stf; Mgr(s); Twrlr; Animl Hlth Tech.

FIGLEY, JODI; Hopewell HS; Aliquippa, PA; (S); 7/264; Art Clb; Church Yth Grp; Spanish Clb; Chorus; School Musical; L Golf; Powder Puff Ftbl; CC Awd; High Hon Roll; Sports Illustrated Faces In The Crowd 85.

FIGURA, RACHELLE; Dubois Area HS; Dubois, PA; (Y); 40/270; Diving; Gym; Hon Roll; Presdntl Acad Ftns Awd 86; U Of Pittsbrgh,Paralgl.

FIGURED, BARRY; West Scranton HS; Scranton, PA; (Y); JA; Ski Clb.

FIKE, EUGENE; Somerset Area SR HS; Somerset, PA; (Y); Church Yth Grp; English Clb; Trs French Clb; JA; Ski Clb; L Var Tennis; Hon Roll; Pltcl Sci.

FILBURN, ERIC; Connellsville Area HS; S Connellsville, PA; (Y); Stage Crew; Var Bsktbl; Sftbl; Var L Tennis; Vllybl; Hon Roll.

FILER, DARLA; Freeport SR HS; Freeport, PA; (Y); Band; Chorus; Concert Band; Mrchg Band; Pep Band; Stage Crew; Symp Band; JV Stat Ftbl; Stu Of Mnth 85; Carlow Coll; Nrsng.

FILER, DOREEA; Uppermorland S H HS; Willow Grove, PA; (Y); Mgr(s); Bus.

FILER, JILL; Sharpsville HS; Sharpsville, PA; (Y); Hosp Aide; Math Clb; Science Clb; Sec Spanish Clb; Chorus; Nwsp Stf; Yrbk Stf; JV Bsktbl; Hon Roll; NHS; Acadmc Achvt Awd 85; Med.

FILIAGGI, GINA MARIE; B Reed Henderson HS; W Chester, PA; (Y); 31/340; Cmnty Wkr; Stu Cncl; Cheerleading; Gym; Vllybl; Hon Roll; U Of AZ; Bus.

FILIPOVITS, AMY; Sto-Rox HS; Mc Kees Rocks, PA; (Y); 9/150; Drill Tm; Mrchg Band; Sec Jr Cls; Hon Roll; Penn ST; Engr.

FILIPOWSKI, STEPHANIE; Villa Maria Acad; Erie, PA; (Y); School Play; Trs Frsh Cls; Hon Roll; Trs NHS; Theresa Brns Schlrshp 86; Teeng Actn Clb-4-Roll Sec; Mercyhurst Coll; Htl/Rstrnt Mgt.

FILIPPONE, ERIC; West Philadelphia Catholic HS; Philadelphia, PA; (Y); 15/280; Art Clb; Mathletes; Varsity Clb; Yrbk Stf; JV Var Trk; Hon Roll; Jr NHS; NHS; CSC Mem Outstndng Achvt 84-86; Acad Exclnc Awd Art 86; Cert Of Merit 86; Vilanova U.

FILIPPONI, DIANE; Burgettstown JR SR HS; Slovan, PA; (Y); Church Yth Grp; Exploring; Spanish Clb; Cheerleading; Hon Roll; NHS.

FILLMORE, TRACY L; Dallastown Area HS; Dallastown, PA; (Y); JA; Diving; Var Mgr(s); Var Mgr Swmmng; Var Timer; Im Sftbl; Miss Amer Coed Pgnt Outstndng Pgm 86; Photo.

FILOR, HELEN; Milton Hershey Schl; Milford, NY; (S); 2/109; Art Clb; 4-H; Chorus; Bsktbl; JV Fld Hcky; Var Socr; JV Sftbl; Var Trk; High Hon Roll; Jr NHS; Schlr Of Mnth Awd 85; U Ctr Binghamton; Med.

FILUTZE, JOHN; Fairview HS; Girard, PA; (Y); German Clb; Latin Clb; Model UN; Varsity Clb; Var L Socr; Hon Roll; Pre-Med.

FINA, KERRY; Notre Dame HS; Hope, NJ; (Y); Chorus; Church Choir; Orch; School Musical; School Play; Swing Chorus; Nwsp Ed-Chief; Nwsp Rptr; Yrbk Phtg; Yrbk Rptr; Music.

FINAMORE, JOAN; Creative & Performing Arts; Philadelphia, PA; (S); 5/120; Orch; Camp Fr Inc; Hon Roll; Acad Achvt-Engl 84; Jrnlsm.

FINCH, CARLEEN; Peters Township HS; Mcmurray, PA; (Y); Cmnty Wkr; FBLA; Hosp Aide; Teachers Aide.

FINCH, JULIE; Quaker Valley HS; Sewickley, PA; (Y); 1/179; German Clb; Nwsp Rptr; Yrbk Rptr; Lit Mag; Sec Soph Cls; Stu Cncl; JV Bsktbl; JV Trk; NHS; Ntl Merit SF; 1st Qukr Vlly Frnds Assoc Crtv Wrtg 84&86; VFW Lylty Dy Essy 2nd Cnty-1st Lcl 85; Hugh Obrn Yth Cnfrn.

FINCH, KATHRYN A; Saucon Valley SR HS; Bethlehem, PA; (Y); Am Leg Aux Girls St; Church Yth Grp; Trs French Clb; Hosp Aide; Model UN; School Play; Var L Golf; High Hon Roll; Kiwanis Awd; NHS; Soc Of Wm Engrng Awd 86; Pres Acadmc Ftns Awd 86; PA ST U; Engrng.

FINCH, LORI; Bellwood Antis HS; Altoona, PA; (Y); Church Yth Grp; Key Clb; Band; Chorus; Concert Band; Mrchg Band; Pep Band; Var Trk; Hon Roll; PA ST U; Nrsg.

FINCK, TRICIA; Milton SR HS; Milton, PA; (Y); 31/213; Church Yth Grp; Color Guard; Flag Corp; Mrchg Band; School Musical; School Play; Yrbk Phtg; Yrbk Rptr; Yrbk Stf; NHS; Bus Fld.

FINCKE, AMY M; Sewickley Acad; Pittsburgh, PA; (Y); 7/60; Exploring; Yrbk Stf; Lit Mag; Sec Soph Cls; Lcrss; High Hon Roll; Heinz Memrl Art Awd 83; Skidmore Coll Bk Awd 85; James E Cavalier Schlrshp 85; Amherst Coll; Medcl Schl.

FINDLEY, LISA; Central Cambria HS; Vintondale, PA; (S); 16/209; Computer Clb; French Clb; FBLA; Library Aide; Im Swmmng; High Hon Roll; Hon Roll; Bus Mgmt.

FINE, JULIE; Winchester-Thurston HS; Pittsburgh, PA; (Y); AFS; Key Clb; Political Wkr; Q&S; Quiz Bowl; Radio Clb; Red Cross Aide; ROTC; Scholastic Bowl; Science Clb; Recogntn In Voluntrng 86.

FINE, SANDY; Trinity HS; Mechanicsburg, PA; (Y); Drama Clb; Ski Clb; School Musical; School Play; Nwsp Rptr; Yrbk Stf; Rep Stu Cncl; Hon Roll; Rotary Awd; Spanish NHS; Cmmnctns.

FINE, TODD; Bentworth SR HS; Eighty Four, PA; (Y); Hon Roll; NHS; Physcs.

FINELLE, ANNETTE; Bishop Hannan HS; Scranton, PA; (Y); 2/125; Art Clb; Exploring; Math Clb; Pres Spanish Clb; Orch; School Musical; Stage Crew; High Hon Roll; NHS; 1st Pl Art Awd 85; Marywood; Ed.

FINGER, CAROLINE; Northern SR HS; Dillsburg, PA; (Y); 1/209; Stage Crew; Yrbk Stf; High Hon Roll; Acadmc Excllnce 2nd Mrkng Period Awd; Math.

FINGERET, LAURA; Taylor Allderdice HS; Pittsburgh, PA; (Y); Ski Clb; SADD; Temple Yth Grp; Varsity Clb; School Play; Variety Show; Yrbk Stf; Bowling; Sftbl; Vllybl; Deans Awd Schl Advncd Jewish Stds 85; Legal Advsr.

FINK, ANN MARIE; Peters Twnshp HS; Eighty Four, PA; (Y); 9/245; FBLA; Hosp Aide; Drill Tm; Yrbk Stf; Lit Mag; Gym; High Hon Roll; NHS.

FINK, BRYAN; East Brady JR SR HS; Cowansville, PA; (Y); VICA; Yrbk Stf; Bsktbl; Mgr(s); High Hon Roll; Hon Roll.

FINK, CAMI; South Williamsport Area HS; S Williamsport, PA; (Y); 2/140; Library Aide; VP Spanish Clb; Nwsp Stf; Yrbk Stf; Var Sftbl; High Hon Roll; Hon Roll; Jr NHS.

FINK, CHARLES C; Allentown Central Catholic HS; Macungie, PA; (Y); 9/231; Math Clb; High Hon Roll; NHS; Ntl Merit SF; Engr.

FINK, COLLEEN; Shenango HS; New Casatle, PA; (Y); 41/112; Church Yth Grp; 4-H; Teachers Aide; Band; Concert Band; Mrchg Band; Pep Band; Yrbk Stf; Hon Roll; Jr NHS; Hon Wrkng Hrng Imprd; Tchr.

FINK, JACLYN C; North Allegheny SR HS; Pittsburgh, PA; (Y); Debate Tm; Speech Tm; Lit Mag; Ntl Merit SF; Gftd Pgm 84-86; Pres Yuth Grp 85-86; James Madison U; Comp Info Sys.

FINK, KARIN; Wyalusing Valley JR SR HS; Wyalusing, PA; (Y); 7/150; Band; Chorus; Church Choir; Concert Band; Jazz Band; Mrchg Band; Orch; School Musical; Church Yth Grp; Spanish Clb; Ithaca Coll Schlrshp 86; Zeswitz Awd 86; Ntl Schl Orch Awd 86; Ithaca Coll; Music.

FINK, KELLY; Tyrone Area HS; Tyrone, PA; (Y); Church Yth Grp; Crs Cntry; Powder Puff Ftbl; High Hon Roll; NHS; Cazenovia Coll; Comp Prog.

FINK, MELINDA; Northern Chester County Tech HS; Phoenixville, PA; (Y); Pres Jr Cls; Hon Roll.

FINK, MICHAEL; Venango Christian HS; Titusville, PA; (Y); 24/42; Cmnty Wkr; Yrbk Phtg; Yrbk Stf; Rep Sr Cls; Var Capt Bsbl; Var Capt Ftbl; Var Wrstlng; Hon Roll; NHS; Amer Legion Awd 85-86; Williams Schlrshp 85-86; Bishop Waston Awd 85-86; Mercy Hurst Coll.

FINK, MIKE; Palmyra Area HS; Palmyra, PA; (Y); Ski Clb; Spanish Clb; Ftbl; Hon Roll; Outstanding Artistic Achievement; Temple.

FINK, MITCH; Fleetwood Area HS; Fleetwood, PA; (Y); 47/125; Sec Church Yth Grp; Ski Clb; Band; Mrchg Band; Var L Bsktbl; Var Socr; Var Tennis; Church Cncl Yth Grp 86; Bloomsburg U; Bus Admin.

FINK, PAMELA; Peters Township HS; Eighty-Four, PA; (S); 27/257; Computer Clb; SADD; Yrbk Stf; Ed Lit Mag; VP Stu Cncl; Hon Roll; Prfct Atten Awd; Spanish NHS; Library Aide; Chorus; Stu Cncl Awd 84-86; Bus Ed Awd 85-86; Psychlgy.

FINK, RONDA; Glendale HS; Fallentimber, PA; (Y); 13/96; Trs Church Yth Grp; Band; Chorus; Capt Color Guard; Yrbk Stf; Trs Jr Cls; Hon Roll; JP Sousa Awd; NHS; IUP; Accounting.

FINK, TRACY; Hamburg Area HS; Hamburg, PA; (Y); Pres Sec Church Yth Grp; Library Aide; Trs Spanish Clb; Chorus; High Hon Roll; Hon Roll; NHS.

FINK, VICKIE; Bellefonte Area HS; Bellefonte, PA; (Y); 6/250; SADD; Band; Chorus; Yrbk Stf; Trs Frsh Cls; Trs Soph Cls; Var L Cheerleading; Var L Trk; Hon Roll; NHS; Lock Haven U; Comp Pgmmr.

FINKE, CONNIE; Taylor Allderdice HS; Pittsburgh, PA; (Y); Church Yth Grp; JA; Key Clb; Q&S; Stage Crew; Cheerleading; Var Sftbl; Var Swmmng; Var Trk; High Hon Roll; Ltr In Swmng 84; Ltr In Sftbll 86; Art.

FINKE, GARRETT; Dover Area HS; East Berlin, PA; (Y); Sec 4-H; Nwsp Phtg; Nwsp Rptr; Yrbk Phtg; Yrbk Stf; Crs Cntry; Trk; Hon Roll.

FINKEL, SETH; Plymouth Whitemarsh HS; Norristown, PA; (Y); Aud/Vis; Chess Clb; Computer Clb; Temple Yth Grp; Band; Concert Band; Jazz Band; Mrchg Band; Orch; Nwsp Rptr; Schl Jugllng/Unicycle Clb Tchr 85-86; Cable TV Cameramn Schl; Cmmnctns.

FINKEL, SHANA H; Plymouth-Whitemarsh HS; Norristown, PA; (S); 38/363; Hosp Aide; Science Clb; Temple Yth Grp; Church Choir; Color Guard; School Play; Nwsp Ed-Chief; High Hon Roll; Jr NHS; Prfct Atten Awd; U Of PA; Bio.

FINKELSTEIN, ALANA; William Allen HS; Allentown, PA; (Y); 35/560; Drama Clb; Spanish Clb; School Play; Yrbk Sprt Ed; Rep Stu Cncl; High Hon Roll; NHS; Spanish NHS; JV Gym; Jr NHS; Senderavitz Awd-Outstndng Comm Svc 85-86; Frances Fedgie Shultz Awd For Ldrshp 84-85; Boston U; Psych.

FINN, TERRY; Coughlin HS; Wilkes Barre, PA; (Y); Aud/Vis; Drama Clb; Key Clb; School Play; Hon Roll; Key Clb ST Lieutntn Gov 84-85; Key Clb Sec 85-86; Schl Ldrshp Awd 85-86; PA ST; TV Brdcstng.

FINN, TIM; Lackawanna Trail HS; Dalton, PA; (Y); Madrigals; Rep Frsh Cls; Rep Soph Cls; Hst Jr Cls; VP Pres Stu Cncl; L Bsbl; JV Bsktbl; L Fld Hcky; Wt Lftg; Hon Roll; AZ ST; Elec Engrg.

FINN, WALLY; Clearfield Area HS; Clearfield, PA; (Y); Swmmng; High Hon Roll; Hon Roll; PA ST; Tchng.

FINNEGAN, BEVERLY; West Greene HS; Aleppo, PA; (Y); Library Aide; Rep Frsh Cls; Trs Soph Cls; Stu Cncl; Score Keeper; Vllybl; Hon Roll; Educ.

FINNEGAN, DEBBIE; Bethel Park HS; Bethel Pk, PA; (Y); Pres Church Yth Grp; DECA; FHA; JA; JV Bsktbl; Powder Puff Ftbl; Var L Sftbl; Duquense U; Engr.

FINNEGAN, LESLIE; Chambersburg Area SR HS; Chambersburg, PA; (Y); 40/593; Trs Drama Clb; VP Chorus; Concert Band; Jazz Band; Madrigals; Mrchg Band; School Musical; Stu Cncl; Church Choir; Variety Show; Dstrct & Rgnl Chrs 85-86; Cnty Chrs Accmpnst 86; Nrsng.

FINNERTY, JOHN P; Scranton Central HS; Scranton, PA; (Y); 15/282; Church Yth Grp; Ski Clb; Rep Stu Cncl; High Hon Roll; Jr NHS; NHS; U Of Scranton; Comp Sci.

FINNERTY, MEGAN; Carlynton HS; Pittsburgh, PA; (S); 3/176; VP Drama Clb; Pres French Clb; Girl Scts; Chorus; Church Choir; School Musical; Nwsp Rptr; Nwsp Stf; Pres Sr Cls; Rep Stu Cncl; Allegheny Coll; Lwyr.

FINNIN, JEN; Upper Merion Area HS; Bridgeport, PA; (Y); Cmnty Wkr; Office Aide; Pep Clb; Teachers Aide; Variety Show; Rep Soph Cls; Rep Jr Cls; JV Var Cheerleading; JV Var Coach Actv; JV Var Pom Pon; Penn ST; Acctg.

FINUCAN, JOSEPH; Perry Traditional Acad; Pittsburgh, PA; (Y); 4/312; German Clb; Math Tm; Nwsp Rptr; Yrbk Rptr; Yrbk Stf; Stu Cncl; Bsbl; High Hon Roll; Penn ST; Arch.

FIORE, CATHIE; Bethlehem Catholic HS; Bethlehem, PA; (Y); 91/201; Cmnty Wkr; Key Clb; Science Clb; Nwsp Phtg; Nwsp Stf; Rep Soph Cls; Rep Stu Cncl; George WA U; Pltcl Sci.

FIORE, LISA; Bishop O Hara HS; Scranton, PA; (S); 10/150; Camera Clb; Drama Clb; FNA; Hosp Aide; Latin Clb; Science Clb; Ski Clb; Spanish Clb; Chorus; School Musical; Music, Art Apprctn Awds 82; Candystripe Awd 83, 85; U Scranton; Nrsg.

FIORE, MARY JOAN; Hazleton HS; Hazleton, PA; (Y); 136/400; Drama Clb; FBLA; Hosp Aide; Pep Clb; Chorus; Nwsp Stf; Yrbk Stf; Elem Ed.

FIORITO, DAN; Bethel Park HS; Bethel Park, PA; (Y); 92/519; French Clb; Ski Clb; Var Golf; Var Socr; Var Tennis; Hon Roll; Rutgers Coll; Sci.

FIRCH, MICHAEL; Strong Vincent HS; Erie, PA; (Y); 17/164; Church Yth Grp; Red Cross Aide; Ski Clb; VP Spanish Clb; Yrbk Stf; Pres Sr Cls; Im Bsktbl; JV Var Ftbl; High Hon Roll; NHS; Wtrpolo Vrsty Lttr 85; Engnrng.

FIRELY, MONICA L; Bishop Kenrick HS; Norristown, PA; (Y); 2/270; Church Yth Grp; Cmnty Wkr; Hosp Aide; Concert Band; Nwsp Rptr; Ed Nwsp Stf; Vllybl; Hon Roll; NHS; Ntl Merit Schol; W Norriton Wmns Clb Scholar 86; Brown U Book Awd Engl 85; U PA; Cmmnctns.

FIRESTONE, BLANEY-CAY; Greensburg Central Catholic HS; Irwin, PA; (Y); Sec Church Yth Grp; Dance Clb; Exploring; Hosp Aide; Pres Chorus; School Musical; Rep Stu Cncl; Im Sftbl; Im Vllybl; High Hon Roll; Clsscl Dncr Toe Ballet; Pre-Med.

FIRMENT, KIM; Lenape Vo Tech; Rural Valley, PA; (Y); 1/80; Chrmn SADD; VICA; Band; Concert Band; Mrchg Band; Nwsp Stf; Rep Church Yth Grp; Pres Stu Cncl; JV Sftbl; High Hon Roll; Nursing.

FIRMSTONE, KENNETH; Southmoreland HS; Mt Pleasant, PA; (Y); 7/244; Latin Clb; Letterman Clb; Math Clb; Var L Golf; NHS; Pre-Dentstry.

FIRSTER, ELIZABETH; Grove City SR HS; Grove City, PA; (Y); Thesps; Chorus; Mrchg Band; School Musical; School Play; Swing Chorus; Trk; High Hon Roll; NHS; Church Yth Grp; Stu Mnth Elks Clb 85; Clarion U; Spec Ed.

FIRTH, ROSWITHA M; Sewickley Acad; Thornburg, PA; (Y); 26/61; Church Yth Grp; Chorus; School Musical; School Play; Ed Lit Mag; Hon Roll; Cmnty Wkr; Dance Clb; French Clb; Acpl Chr; Grmn Excllnc Advnd Awd; Natl Mrt Cmmndee; Wstnghse Sci Hnrs Inst; Arch.

FISCH, TRICIA; Bishop Hannan HS; Scranton, PA; (Y); Cmnty Wkr; GAA; Spanish Clb; Teachers Aide; Chorus; School Musical; School Play; JV Capt Bsktbl; Score Keeper; High Hon Roll; Alg, Spn, Engl Excllnce 84; Wrld Cultrs II Excllnce 85; Hnrb Mntn Spn 85; Alg II, Trig Excllnce 86; Acctg.

FISCHER, DANNY; Franklin HS; Franklin, PA; (Y); Concert Band; Mrchg Band; High Hon Roll; Hon Roll; Prfct Atten Awd; Schl Drctrs Awd 86; Slippery Rock U; Accntng.

FISCHER, DAVE; Knoch JR/SR HS; Butler, PA; (Y); Ftbl; High Hon Roll; Hon Roll; NHS; Hnr Cert 84-86.

FISCHER, JANE; Middletown HS; Middletown, PA; (Y); Pres Key Clb; Latin Clb; Cheerleading; NHS; Phrmcy.

FISCHER, JENNIFER; Moon SR HS; Coraopolis, PA; (Y); 71/329; Chorus; High Hon Roll; Hon Roll; Robert Morris; Fshn Mrchndsng.

FISCHER, KIMBERLY A; Upper Moreland HS; Hatboro, PA; (Y); 4/276; Color Guard; Mrchg Band; Sec Frsh Cls; Soph Cls; Jr Cls; Sr Cls; High Hon Roll; NHS; Presdntl Acad Ftns Awd 85-86; Outstndng Stu Awd 85-86; Lehigh U; Bus.

FISCHER, MICHELLE ANN; Lebanon HS; Lebanon, PA; (Y); Trs Latin Clb; Trs Varsity Clb; Yrbk Sprt Ed; Rep Soph Cls; Rep Jr Cls; Var Bsktbl; Var Fld Hcky; Var Trk; High Hon Roll; Hon Roll; Biochem.

FISCHER, STEPH; St Benedict Acad; Erie, PA; (Y); Church Yth Grp; FBLA; GAA; Girl Scts; Office Aide; Pep Clb; Variety Show; Var Cheerleading; Var Sftbl; Scrtrl Legal.

FISH, CHRISTIE; Elkland Area HS; Elkland, PA; (Y); Sec Church Yth Grp; Girl Scts; Band; Cheerleading; Trk; Hon Roll; Med Tech.

FISH, JEREMY B; Coudersport JR SR HS; Coudersport, PA; (Y); 4-H; Pres Ski Clb; Band; Concert Band; Mrchg Band; Pep Band; Nwsp Stf; Yrbk Phtg; JV Var Ftbl; 4-H Awd.

FISHER, AMY; Harry S Truman HS; Levittown, PA; (Y); 48/500; Art Clb; Spanish Clb; SADD; Band; Concert Band; Mrchg Band; Yrbk Stf; Off Stu Cncl; NHS.

FISHER, AMY; St Puis X HS; Douglasville, PA; (Y); 13/140; Art Clb; Latin Clb; Mathletes; Service Clb; Rep Frsh Cls; Var Co-Capt Cheerleading; Hon Roll; NHS; NEDT Awd; Opt Clb Awd; Advstng.

FISHER, AMY L; Emmaus HS; Emmaus, PA; (Y); 10/450; Am Leg Aux Girls St; Church Yth Grp; Hosp Aide; Church Choir; VP Concert Band; Jazz Band; Rep Sr Cls; High Hon Roll; NHS; Pres Schlr; Bnd Drctrs Awd 83; Dstct Bnd Orchstr 86; Tulane U; Blgy.

FISHER, AMY R; Yough SR HS; W Newton, PA; (Y); 33/240; Rep French Clb; Pep Clb; Ski Clb; Spanish Clb; Yrbk Stf; Stat Bsktbl; Powder Puff Ftbl; French Hon Soc; High Hon Roll; Trs NHS; Annie C Mitchell Awd Frnch 85-86; Commnty Actn Prog Treas 85-86; In U PA; French.

FISHER, BECKY; Huntingdon Area HS; Huntingdon, PA; (Y); 26/223; Church Yth Grp; Sec FBLA; Office Aide; Teachers Aide; Band; Church Choir; Concert Band; Mrchg Band; School Musical; High Hon Roll.

FISHER, BRANT; Wilmington Area HS; New Wilmington, PA; (S); Boy Scts; Church Yth Grp; Band; Concert Band; Mrchg Band; Pep Band; Var L Golf; God Cntry Awd; Hon Roll; Hnrs Band 85; Dist Band 85-86.

FISHER, CANDI; Milton Area SR HS; Milton, PA; (Y); 17/250; Art Clb; Computer Clb; Spanish Clb; Varsity Clb; Band; Pres Var Stu Cncl; Cheerleading; Fld Hcky; NHS; Architect.

FISHER, CHERYL; Boyertown SR HS; Gilbertsville, PA; (Y); 5/442; Trs Church Yth Grp; Hosp Aide; VP JA; Math Tm; Scholastic Bowl; Church Choir; Flag Corp; Cit Awd; High Hon Roll; NHS; Cngrsnl Mdl Merit, Cabot Natl Schlrshp, Pres Acdmc Ftns Awd 86; Lycoming Coll; Chem.

FISHER, DANA; Exeter SR HS; Reading, PA; (Y); 27/200; German Clb; Q&S; Y-Teens; Nwsp Rptr; JV Fld Hcky; Hon Roll; Jr NHS; NHS; CPA.

FISHER, DANIEL; Hempfield HS; Lancaster, PA; (Y); 32/470; Chess Clb; Computer Clb; Pres Exploring; Key Clb; Var Socr; Var L Trk; Hon Roll; Chrmn-Lancaster-Lebanon Cncl Explr Ofcr Assn 85 & 86; Law.

FISHER, DEAN; Lehighton SR HS; Lehighton, PA; (Y); Chess Clb; Church Choir; High Hon Roll; Hon Roll; Bio.

FISHER, DEBBIE; Wilmington Area HS; New Wilmington, PA; (S); 13/124; Church Yth Grp; French Clb; Key Clb; Trs Stu Cncl; JV Bsktbl; Var Powder Puff Ftbl; L Trk; Hon Roll; Acdmc Achvmnt Awd 85; Math.

FISHER, DONNA; Blue Mountain Acad; Hamburg, PA; (Y); High Hon Roll; Hon Roll; Prfct Atten Awd; Harris Pine Mls Schlrshp For Good Wrkr 86; Merit Schlrshp 83; Columbia Union Coll; Med.

FISHER, FAITH; Pequea Valley HS; Narvon, PA; (Y); 10/138; AFS; Church Yth Grp; Flag Corp; Stage Crew; Nwsp Rptr; Nwsp Stf; Bsktbl; Sftbl; High Hon Roll; NHS; Cmmnctns.

FISHER, GEORGINA; Lampeter-Straburg HS; Strasburg, PA; (Y); 33/158; Church Yth Grp; Girl Scts; Band; Chorus; Church Choir; Concert Band; Mrchg Band; Pep Band; School Musical; Lit Mag; Bloomsburg; Deaf Educ.

FISHER, HEATH JON; Conrad Weiser HS; Robesonia, PA; (Y); 21/184; Exploring; 4-H; JCL; Band; Chorus; Concert Band; School Musical; Ftbl; Wrstlng; Hon Roll; 4 H Clb Yth Career Awd 85; Chem Engr.

FISHER, HEIDI; Pequa Valley HS; Paradise, PA; (S); Church Yth Grp; Varsity Clb; Band; Chorus; Madrigals; School Musical; Var Fld Hcky; Var Sftbl; Hon Roll; NHS.

FISHER, JEANNETTE; Marion Center Area HS; Marion Ctr, PA; (Y); 4-H; FHA; Intnl Clb; Office Aide; Dubois Bus Coll; Accntng.

FISHER, KEVIN; Carbondale Area HS; Simpson, PA; (Y); Art Clb; Ski Clb; Pittsburgh Art Inst; Comm Art.

FISHER, LARRY; Marion Center Area HS; Home, PA; (Y); Intnl Clb; SADD; Varsity Clb; Band; Jazz Band; Mrchg Band; Pep Band; Var Crs Cntry; Var Trk; Hon Roll; MVR Crs Cntry 85-86; Bus.

FISHER, LINDA C; Pennsbury HS; Yardley, PA; (Y); 1/712; VP Intnl Clb; Concert Band; Mrchg Band; School Musical; Yrbk Stf; High Hon Roll; NHS; Ntl Merit Ltr; Val; Im Gym; A Marlyn Moyer Schlrshp 86; Pennsbury Schlrshp 86; Amherst Coll Schlrshp 86; Amherst Coll; Bio.

FISHER, LISA ANNE; St Hubert HS; Philadelphia, PA; (Y); 6/367; Service Clb; Spanish Clb; Chorus; Stage Crew; Lit Mag; JV Var Bowling; High Hon Roll; Lion Awd; Pres NHS; Prfct Atten Awd; Pres Acdmc Fit Awd 86; Socty Womn Engrs Awd Excllnc Sci & Math 86; Genrl Excllnc Spnsh 85; Penn ST.

FISHER, LORI; Owen J Roberts HS; Pottstown, PA; (S); 10/267; Hosp Aide; SADD; Concert Band; Mrchg Band; School Play; Trk; High Hon Roll; NHS; Ntl Merit Ltr; U DE; Nrsng.

FISHER, LYNETTE; United HS; Armagh, PA; (Y); 30/157; VP Church Yth Grp; Ski Clb; Band; Chorus; Concert Band; Drill Tm; Powder Puff Ftbl; VP Var Trk; Hon Roll; Prfct Atten Awd; Dntl Hygn.

FISHER, MARC; Lewistown Area HS; Lewistown, PA; (Y); 2/263; AFS; Debate Tm; German Clb; Sec Key Clb; Ski Clb; Rep Stu Cncl; Trk; High Hon Roll; NHS; Computer Clb; Grvnrs Schl Intrntl Stdes; Aronutcl Engr.

FISHER, MARK; Central Dauphin HS; Harrisburg, PA; (Y); 31/386; Church Yth Grp; JV Ftbl; Hon Roll; NHS; Drexel U; Engrng.

FISHER, MICHAEL; Northwestern Lehigh HS; Orefield, PA; (Y); Exploring; German Clb; Ski Clb; Pres Soph Cls; Hon Roll; Stdnt Mnth 86; Tri Cnty Indstrl Arts Fair 1st Pl 86; Evng Arts 1st Pl 86; Penn ST U; Bus Adm.

FISHER, PAMELA; Northern York County HS; Dillsburg, PA; (Y); 48/209; Band; Concert Band; Mrchg Band; Stage Crew; JV Powder Puff Ftbl; Hon Roll; Seamstrss.

FISHER, ROBIN; William Allen HS; Allentown, PA; (Y); Church Yth Grp; Cmnty Wkr; Drama Clb; Key Clb; Varsity Clb; Church Choir; Yrbk Stf; Cheerleading; Pom Pon; Miss PA Natl Teen Pagnt Fnlst 85; John Casablanca Model Cont Fnlst 85; Coach Little Lg Chlrdg 85 & 86; Fshn Mrchndsg.

FISHER, RODNEY; Bald Eagle Area HS; Fleming, PA; (Y); 13/204; Pres Church Yth Grp; Varsity Clb; Acpl Chr; Band; Chorus; Church Choir; Rep Soph Cls; Pres Sr Cls; Var Crs Cntry; JV Ftbl; Liberty U Wrstlng Scholar 86; Amer Assn Physics Tchrs Outstndng Stu Yr 85; Cert Merit PA 85; Liberty U.

FISHER JR, RONALD J; Kiski Area HS; Apollo, PA; (Y); Computer Clb; SADD; Chorus; Stage Crew; Nwsp Stf; Yrbk Bus Mgr; Trk; Hon Roll; Rotary Awd; Arch.

FISHER, SHELIA; Lock Haven SR HS; Lock Haven, PA; (Y); Cmnty Wkr; German Clb; Key Clb; JV Var Bsktbl; Mat Maids; Hon Roll; Ntl Merit Ltr; Natl Hstry & Gvrmnt Awd 86; Pre-Law.

FISHER, STACY; Middletown Area HS; Middletown, PA; (Y); #31 In Class; Exploring; 4-H; Latin Clb; Library Aide; Chorus; Hon Roll; Animal Sci.

FISHER, TERESA; Central Cambria HS; Conemaugh, PA; (S); 12/190; Art Clb; NFL; Church Choir; Concert Band; Jazz Band; Mrchg Band; Orch; Pep Band; School Play; Nwsp Phtg; PA ST U; Ed.

FISHER, TIM; Towanda Area HS; Towanda, PA; (Y); Boy Scts; Pres Church Yth Grp; Letterman Clb; Model UN; Band; Chorus; Church Choir; Concert Band; Mrchg Band; Swing Chorus; Biochem.

FISHER, UNEVA; Mc Guffey HS; Washington, PA; (S); 7/216; Art Clb; French Clb; Band; Yrbk Ed-Chief; DAR Awd; High Hon Roll; NHS; 4-H; Concert Band; Drm Mjr(t); All Amer Acad Awd Soc Studs/Govt & Frnch; Comm.

FISHMAN, EILEEN; Cedar Crest HS; Mt Gretna, PA; (Y); 14/326; Latin Clb; Pep Clb; School Musical; Var Capt Bsktbl; L Tennis; Vllybl; Hon Roll; NHS; Julie Pierce Memrl Schlrshp Awd; Pres Acdmc Fit Awd; Hnrs Banqt; Syracuse U; Chem.

FISICHELLA, BERNADETTE; St Maria Goretti HS; Philadelphia, PA; (Y); 26/390; Mathletes; Math Clb; Math Tm; Spanish Clb; Ed Yrbk Stf; Rep Frsh Cls; Rep Jr Cls; Var Tennis; High Hon Roll; NHS; Hon Mntn Spnsh II 85; Awd Math 86; Med Tech.

FISLER, JESSICA; Northern York County HS; Dillsburg, PA; (Y); Sec Church Yth Grp; Cmnty Wkr; French Clb; Sec Chorus; School Musical; Yrbk Stf; French Hon Soc; High Hon Roll; Hon Roll; NHS; Med.

FISTER, DEDE A; Hamburg Area HS; Hamburg, PA; (Y); 15/152; Library Aide; Spanish Clb; Band; Chorus; Concert Band; Mrchg Band; School Musical; School Play; Cheerleading; Tennis; Acadmc Awd-Engl 84; Acadmc Awd-Trig & Alg III 85; Acadmc Awd-Govt 86; U Of NC-CHARLOTTE; Arch.

FITE, ERIC; Millersburg HS; Millerburg, PA; (Y); 32/75; Church Yth Grp; Var Ftbl; Var Trk; Hon Roll; Schlrshp Awd 83-86; Comp Sci.

FITSER, SHERI; Salisbury HS; Allentown, PA; (Y); 21/152; Cmnty Wkr; Drama Clb; Band; Concert Band; Mrchg Band; School Play; High Hon Roll; Hon Roll; Hghst Avg Accntg 86; Yng Vlntrs Action Cert 85; Kutztown U; Crimnl Justc.

FITTRO, KEALY; Bermudian Springs HS; New Oxford, PA; (Y); FHA; Varsity Clb; Var L Cheerleading; JV Vllybl; Fshn Dsgn.

FITZ, VANESSA; Eastern York JR SR HS; York, PA; (Y); 1/123; Pres Church Yth Grp; 4-H; Varsity Clb; Var Capt Vllybl; Elks Awd; Pres NHS; Val; Elizabethtown Pres Schlrshp 86; ABWA Schlrshp 86; Elizabethtown Coll; Bio.

FITZGERALD, CYNTHIA; Ambridge Area HS; Sewickley, PA; (Y); Trs Church Yth Grp; VP JA; Red Cross Aide; Spanish Clb; SADD; Jr Cls; L Golf; Hon Roll; NHS; Pre-Med.

FITZGERALD, DAN; Quigley HS; Insutry, PA; (Y); 45/103; Chorus; Bsktbl; Coach Actv; Ftbl; Trk; Bus.

FITZGERALD, DANIEL; Boyertown Area SR HS; Peckiomenvl, PA; (Y); 20/500; Aud/Vis; Church Yth Grp; Cmnty Wkr; Math Tm; SADD; Stage Crew; Rep Soph Cls; Cit Awd; High Hon Roll; Hon Roll; U Of CA; Chmcl Engr.

FITZGERALD, EDMUND; Father Judge Catholic H S For Boys; Philadelphia, PA; (Y); 17/403; Varsity Clb; Var Crs Cntry; Var Trk; Wt Lftg; High Hon Roll; NHS; Hon Roll; Mst Courageous Athlete Awd Cross Cntry In/Outdoor Track 85-86; Air Force ROTC Schlrshp 85-86; Drexel U; Elec Engrng.

FITZGERALD, HOPE; Sheffield Area JR SR HS; Sheffield, PA; (Y); Church Yth Grp; FHA; Girl Scts; Hosp Aide; Intnl Clb; Library Aide; Pep Clb; Ski Clb; SADD; Chorus.

FITZGERALD IV, JAMES J; William Penn Charter Schl; Philadelphia, PA; (Y); Model UN; Political Wkr; Q&S; Nwsp Rptr; Nwsp Stf; Yrbk Stf; Lit Mag; Var Socr; Capt Tennis; Hon Roll; MVP Awd Tennis 85-86; All-Interac Champ Tennis 84-86; Pltcl Sci.

FITZGERALD, JOSEPH; Ambridge HS; Baden, PA; (Y); Am Leg Boys St; Church Yth Grp; Spanish Clb; Chorus; JV Var Ftbl; Vllybl; Wt Lftg; Hon Roll; Phys Ther.

FITZGERALD, MICHELLE; W B Saul HS; Philadelphia, PA; (Y); FFA; Nwsp Stf; Yrbk Stf; Off Jr Cls; Im Bsktbl; Capt Cheerleading; Im Sftbl; Hon Roll; NHS; Brnz Pl ST FFA Actvts Wk Flrcltr Cntst 85 & 86; 1st Pl JR Flwr Shw 85; Bus.

FITZGERALD, MOIRA; Bishop Mc Devitt HS; Glenside, PA; (Y); 30/352; Hosp Aide; Concert Band; Capt Mrchg Band; School Musical; Nwsp Stf; Ed Yrbk Stf; Im Bsktbl; Powder Puff Ftbl; Hon Roll; NHS; Gold Mdl Music 86; All-Catholic Band 85-86; Pres Schlrshp Allentown Coll; Penn ST; Nrsng.

FITZGERALD, STEPHANIE; Youngsville HS; Irvine, PA; (Y); Camera Clb; Library Aide; Spanish Clb; Teachers Aide; Yrbk Stf; Capt Jr Cls; Var Trk; Libr Aide Awd 85-86.

FITZHENRY, KATHLEEN; Nazareth Acad; Philadelphia, PA; (Y); Pres Church Yth Grp; German Clb; Hosp Aide; Rep Pep Clb; Church Choir; Sec Frsh Cls; Hosp Vlntr 500 Hrs Rcgntn Awd 85-86; Physcl Thrpy.

FITZPATRICK, COLLEEN; Williams Valley HS; Williamstown, PA; (Y); 20/100; Pres Pep Clb; Nwsp Stf; Sec Stu Cncl; Co-Capt Powder Puff Ftbl; NHS; Rotary Awd; Ski Clb; JV Var Cheerleading; HS Schlstc Journlst 86; Bloomsburg U; Accntng.

FITZPATRICK, MARGARET M; Archbishop Wood HS; Warrington, PA; (Y); 18/259; Church Yth Grp; Cmnty Wkr; GAA; Spanish Clb; Rep Jr Cls; VP Sr Cls; VP Stu Cncl; Var Capt Cheerleading; High Hon Roll; Spanish NHS; Hannah Pollack Laura Haddock Awd; Temple U; Phy Thrpy.

FITZPATRICK, SHEILA MARIE; Central Bucks West HS; Doylestown, PA; (Y); 4/483; Am Leg Aux Girls St; Hosp Aide; Concert Band; School Musical; Stu Cncl; NHS; Prfct Atten Awd; Drama Clb; Exploring; Intnl Clb; Bucks Cnty Sci Smnrs 85-86; Prtcpt Pbk Ubtrvw Hanes Michener 85; PA Gov Schl Intl Stds 86.

FITZSIMMONS, KAREN; Harriton HS; Gladwyne, PA; (Y); Church Yth Grp; Intnl Clb; Concert Band; Mrchg Band; Nwsp Rptr; Var Capt Bsktbl; Var Capt Sftbl; Trk; Vllybl; Hon Roll; MVP CYO Bskbll 85; Sprts Med.

FITZSIMMONS, MAUREEN L; Forest City Regional HS; Forest City, PA; (Y); 1/64; Sec Letterman Clb; Scholastic Bowl; Sec Stu Cncl; Var Capt Bsktbl; Bausch & Lomb Sci Awd; Dnfth Awd; High Hon Roll; Pres NHS; Rotary Awd; Val; Renssalaer Awd Sci & Math 84-85; Pres Ftnss Awd 86; Schlr Yr 86; U Scranton; Physcl Therpy.

FITZSIMMONS, THOMAS; Forest City Regional HS; Forest City, PA; (Y); 1/65; Letterman Clb; Spanish Clb; Var Bsktbl; Bausch & Lomb Sci Awd; High Hon Roll; Red Blt Lcl Karate Schl 86; Law.

FIUMARA, THERESA; Catasauqua HS; Allentown, PA; (Y); 36/128; Church Yth Grp; Drama Clb; Teachers Aide; School Musical; School Play; Yrbk Stf; Hon Roll; Elem Ed.

FIVES, JILL; Sacred Heart HS; Carbondale, PA; (Y); Cmnty Wkr; FBLA; Hon Roll; Interior Design.

FLAHERTY, ERIN A; G A R Memorial HS; Wilkes Barre, PA; (S); 18/187; Church Yth Grp; Key Clb; Band; Concert Band; Mrchg Band; Rep Stu Cncl; Var Vllybl; Hon Roll; Jr NHS; NHS; Psych.

FLAHERTY, SUSAN; Vincentian HS; Wexford, PA; (Y); Service Clb; Rep Jr Cls; Var Cheerleading; Hon Roll; NHS; Sec Frsh Cls; Trs Soph Cls; Ntl Merit Schol; Genetic Engr Tech.

FLAHERTY, SUSIE; Mahanoy Area HS; Morea, PA; (Y); Spanish Clb; Chorus; Drm Mjr(t); JV Cheerleading; ASSE Intrntl Exchnge Stu Managing Dir Schlrshp 86.

FLAIL, GREGORY; Governor Mifflin HS; Reading, PA; (Y); Aud/Vis; Computer Clb; Radio Clb; Varsity Clb; Variety Show; Nwsp Phtg; Nwsp Rptr; Yrbk Rptr; Lit Mag; Trk; Qll & Scrll 86; Unfd Achvmnt Awd 86; Ntl Sci Olympd 84; Cmmnctns.

FLAMER, MAURIETTA; Franklin Learning Center HS; Philadelphia, PA; (Y); Church Yth Grp; Teachers Aide; Church Choir; School Musical; School Play; Stu Cncl; Stu Govt Assn Awd 85-86; Extracurricular Choir Awd 85-86; Mock Trial Awd 84-85; Bus Admin.

FLAMINI, ELLEN; Central Daupin East SR HS; Steelton, PA; (Y); 16/274; French Clb; Hosp Aide; Chorus; Concert Band; Mrchg Band; Rep Jr Cls; Hon Roll; Jr NHS; NHS; Penn ST U; Bus Adm.

FLANAGAN, BILL; Cathedral Prep; Erie, PA; (Y); 45/216; French Clb; Office Aide; Ski Clb; Im Bsktbl; Coach Actv; 1st Or 2nd Hnrs Evry Qtr; Cmmnctns.

FLANAGAN, KELLY; West Mifflin Area HS; W Mifflin, PA; (Y); 12/350; Office Aide; Chorus; Variety Show; Yrbk Stf; High Hon Roll; Hon Roll; NHS.

FLANAGAN, SHELLY; Elk County Christian HS; St Marys, PA; (Y); 17/100; Office Aide; Concert Band; Mrchg Band; Ed Yrbk Stf; Trs Bowling; Cheerleading; Tennis; Trk; High Hon Roll; Hon Roll; Bowling High Series, Also High Average 84-85 & 85-86; Miss Bavarian Fest Qn 85; Edinboro U; Bus Admin.

FLANDERS, LORI; Phoenixville Area HS; Valley Forge, PA; (Y); Band; Chorus; Concert Band; Jazz Band; Pres Mrchg Band; Pep Band; School Musical; Rep Soph Cls; Rep Stu Cncl; NHS; Music.

FLANNERY, GERRI; Norwin SR HS; N Huntingdon, PA; (Y); SADD; VICA; Chorus; Hon Roll; Dntl Hygnst.

FLANNERY, KIMBERLY; Scranton Prep; Scranton, PA; (Y); 83/192; High Hon Roll; Hon Roll; Prsh Yth Bsktbl Leag 83-84; Law.

FLANNERY, MICHELE; Scranton Preparatory Schl; Clarks Summit, PA; (Y); Church Yth Grp; Cmnty Wkr; Pep Clb; Stage Crew; VP Soph Cls; VP Jr Cls; JV Capt Bsktbl; Var Sftbl; Vrsty Sftbl All Str 85-86; Cnslg.

FLARTEY, KELLY; Hazleton HS; Hazleton, PA; (Y); 28/388; Church Yth Grp; Pep Clb; Chorus; Nwsp Rptr; Nwsp Stf; Yrbk Stf; Var L Bsktbl; L Trk; Physcl Thrpy.

FLASCO, RACHEL; Quigley HS; Midland, PA; (S); 7/107; Yrbk Stf; Sec Frsh Cls; Sec Soph Cls; Capt Var Cheerleading; Powder Puff Ftbl; L Trk; High Hon Roll; NHS; Hmcmng Ct Queen; Bsktbl Queen; Penn ST U University Pk.

FLASHER, SUZANNE; Mt Union Area HS; Mount Union, PA; (Y); 10/137; Church Yth Grp; GAA; Band; Concert Band; Flag Corp; Mrchg Band; Hon Roll; NHS; Bus.

FLATT, ERIC S; Reading SR HS; Reading, PA; (S); 8/965; Aud/Vis; Boy Scts; VP Chess Clb; Church Yth Grp; Computer Clb; Debate Tm; Model UN; NFL; Quiz Bowl; Church Choir; US Air Force Acad; Chemistry.

FLAUGH, MARK; Central HS; East Freedom, PA; (Y); JV Ftbl; Var Wt Lftg; Engr.

FLAXMAN, MICHELLE LISA; Pocono Mountain HS; Mt Pocono, PA; (Y); 5/320; Hosp Aide; NFL; Scholastic Bowl; Ed Nwsp Ed-Chief; Cheerleading; Hon Roll; NHS; Library Aide; PAVAS; SADD; Cnty Spllng Bee Fnlst, 3rd Cnty Essay Law Day 86; Law.

FLECHER, MARK; Lincoln HS; Ellwood City, PA; (Y); Church Yth Grp; Ski Clb; Spanish Clb; Chorus; Bowling; Socr; Hon Roll; PA ST; Chem Engr.

FLECK, CHRISTOPHER; Huntingdon Area HS; Huntingdon, PA; (Y); Boy Scts; Church Yth Grp; FFA; Church Choir; De Kalb Awd Voctn Ag Stu 86.

FLECK, DALE; Montour HS; Mckees Rocks, PA; (Y); SADD; VP Stu Cncl; Var Ftbl; Var Trk; Hon Roll.

FLECK, JAMES; Tyrone Area HS; Altoona, PA; (Y); 4-H; French Clb; Varsity Clb; Yrbk Stf; Var L Ftbl; Wt Lftg; 4-H Awd; PA ST U.

FLECK, JON; Altoona Area HS; Altoona, PA; (S); German Clb; Ski Clb; Nwsp Rptr; Nwsp Sprt Ed; JV Score Keeper; High Hon Roll; NEDT Awd; Schltc K Pins Awds 82-84; Mth Awd Rnnr Up 84; Jrnlsm.

FLECK, KEELYN; Highlands SR HS; Brackenridge, PA; (Y); Art Clb; Church Yth Grp; Dance Clb; GAA; SADD; Trk; Bio.

FLECKENSTEIN, DAVID; North Allegheny HS; Pittsburgh, PA; (Y); 62/647; Var Capt Vllybl; Hon Roll; NHS; Ntl Merit Ltr; All Amer Vllybl 86.

FLECKENSTEIN, DAWN; Coudersport Area HS; Coudersport, PA; (Y); French Clb; Ski Clb; Band; Chorus; Concert Band; Mrchg Band; Bsktbl; Vllybl; Hon Roll; NHS; Elem Educ.

FLEEGLE, BARBARA; North Star HS; Jennerstown, PA; (S); 9/135; Church Yth Grp; FCA; Pep Clb; Varsity Clb; VP Jr Cls; L Bsktbl; L Vllybl; Pres Frsh Cls; Sec Stu Cncl; Score Keeper; Slpry Rock.

FLEEGLE, LEE ANN; Ferndale Area HS; Johnstown, PA; (S); Church Yth Grp; VP Leo Clb; NFL; SADD; Trs Band; Chorus; Church Choir; School Play; Nwsp Bus Mgr; Yrbk Stf; Mod Miss Volnteer Svc Wnr 84; Bnd Hnrs Musicl Tlnt Dedictn & Svc 85.

FLEEGLE, RHONDA I; North Star HS; Stoystown, PA; (S); 7/130; FCA; FBLA; Hon Roll; Bus.

FLEEK, MELANIE A; Phoenixville HS; Phoenixville, PA; (Y); 1/194; Church Yth Grp; Library Aide; Band; Concert Band; Mrchg Band; Stat Lcrss; Mgr(s); Score Keeper; Timer; Cit Awd; Best Of Cls Acad Exc 86; Lewis A Bicking Awd Sci 86; Frnch IV Hnrs Awd 86; Lebanon Valley Coll; Vet.

FLEET, RENEE; Wyalusing Valley HS; Wyalusing, PA; (Y); Art Clb; Spanish Clb; Chorus; Hon Roll; Elem Ed.

FLEISCHER, LESLIE; Knoch HS; Saxonburg, PA; (Y); Church Yth Grp; Yrbk Stf; Wesley; Fshn Merch.

FLEISHER, ALYSIA; Lewistown Area HS; Granville, PA; (Y); #3 In Class; French Clb; Ski Clb; Var JV Sftbl; High Hon Roll; NHS; Comp Pgmg.

FLEISHER, DANA; West Perry SR HS; New Bloomfld, PA; (Y); 9/188; Sec French Clb; Office Aide; Quiz Bowl; Chorus; Church Choir; Capt Color Guard; Mrchg Band; Ed Nwsp Stf; Hon Roll; NHS; Drvrs Ed Awd 84-85; Ntl Hstry & Govt Awd 85-86; Frd C Noye Hstry Awd 85-86; Bnkng.

FLEMING, CHAD; Spring Grove Area HS; York, PA; (Y); 24/285; Church Yth Grp; Letterman Clb; Varsity Clb; Crs Cntry; Trk; Hon Roll; Physcs.

FLEMING, JOHN; Brockway Area HS; Reynoldsville, PA; (Y); 10/87; Church Yth Grp; Trs 4-H; Pres Trs FFA; PA ST; Ag Engr.

FLEMING, KRISTIN; Emmaus HS; Emmaus, PA; (Y); Art Clb; Ski Clb; Mrchg Band; Cheerleading; Diving; Gym; Church Yth Grp; Hon Roll; Penn ST; Arch Engrng.

FLEMING, LEIGH; Norwin HS; Irwin, PA; (Y); French Clb; Leo Clb; Mathletes; Pep Clb; SADD; Chorus; Color Guard; Nwsp Rptr; Powder Puff Ftbl; Trk; NY U; Drama.

FLEMING, LEISA; Bensalem SR HS; Bensalem, PA; (Y); Aud/Vis; Church Yth Grp; Debate Tm; Drama Clb; ROTC; Chorus; School Musical; School Play; Nwsp Stf; Thomas Jefferson U; Nrsng.

FLEMING, LISA; Knoch JR SR HS; Butler, PA; (Y); Exploring; Band; Mrchg Band; Symp Band; Swmmng; Trk; Hon Roll; NHS.

FLEMING, MARCIA; Brookville Area HS; Sigel, PA; (Y); 15/144; Pres French Clb; Key Clb; Chorus; Concert Band; Mrchg Band; Off Stu Cncl; Var Trk; JV Var Vllybl; Jr NHS; Pep Clb; Siegel Vlntr Fire Co Fire Queen 86; Pres Physcl Ftns Awd 85; IN U; Rsptry Thrpy.

FLEMING, MICHAEL; Jersey Shore Area HS; Jersey Shore, PA; (Y); Hon Roll; Otstndngn Achvt In Welding 85 & 86; Welding.

FLEMING, MICHELE; Glendale JR SR HS; Coalport, PA; (Y); 1/98; Church Yth Grp; Science Clb; Band; Concert Band; Mrchg Band; Yrbk Stf; DAR Awd; Hon Roll; NHS.

FLEMING, PATRICK; Chestnut Ridge HS; Schellsburg, PA; (S); 1/147; Trs 4-H; FFA; Quiz Bowl; Stu Cncl; Var Im Wrstlng; Dnfth Awd; 4-H Awd; High Hon Roll; Hon Roll; NHS; Chemcl Engr.

FLEMING, STEPHANIE L; Moniteau HS; W Sunbury, PA; (Y); 1/130; Church Yth Grp; Chorus; Jazz Band; Mrchg Band; Vllybl; Cit Awd; Sec NHS; Yth Understndng Exch Stu Germny 86; HOBY Ambssdr 85; Misericordia; Music Thrpy.

FLEMING, THERESA; Mc Guffey HS; Washington, PA; (Y); 39/216; Church Yth Grp; Chrmn Hosp Aide; Church Choir; JA; Spanish Clb; Hon Roll; Nrsng.

FLEMINGS, MARTIN S; Thomas A Edison HS; Philadelphia, PA; (Y); 9/300; Boy Scts; School Play; Variety Show; Nwsp Rptr; Nwsp Stf; Cit Awd; Hon Roll; Trs NHS; Prfct Atten Awd; Am Leg Awd 82; Dr Marcus Foster Awd Outstndg Achvt 86; Human Rel 86; Morgan ST U; Polit Sci.

FLESHMAN, KEVIN; Carlisle HS; Carlisle, PA; (Y); Sec Jr Cls; VP Sr Cls; JV Bsktbl; Var Ftbl; NHS; Prfct Atten Awd; Rotary Awd.

FLESNER, ERIKA A; Liberty HS; Bethlehem, PA; (Y); 3/392; Lib Concert Band; Mrchg Band; VP Orch; School Musical; Nwsp Stf; Lit Mag; High Hon Roll; NHS; Ntl Merit Ltr; Jr NHS; Shannon Fnd Schlr 86; Schlrshp Plaque 86; Stage Arts Awd 86; Hvrfrd Coll; Med Rsrch.

FLETCHER, ANGEL; Ambridge Area HS; Baden, PA; (Y); Debate Tm; JV Vllybl; Hon Roll; Crtv Wrtng Awd 84; Cmmnctns.

FLETCHER, CHERYL; Bethel Christian HS; Erie, PA; (S); 2/14; Yrbk Ed-Chief; VP Soph Cls; VP Jr Cls; VP Sr Cls; VP Stu Cncl; Var Capt Bsktbl; Var L Sftbl; Var L Vllybl; Sal; Athl/Yr Awd 84-85; Cedarville Coll.

FLETCHER, DONNA; Charleroi Area SR HS; Charleroi, PA; (Y); Letterman Clb; Office Aide; Spanish Clb; Varsity Clb; Band; Concert Band; Mrchg Band; Nwsp Stf; Bsktbl; Powder Puff Ftbl.

FLETCHER, MARIA; Archbiship Ryan H S For Girls; Philadelphia, PA; (Y); 129/488; Drama Clb; Political Wkr; Im Sftbl; Prfct Atten Awd; 2nd Hnrs; Sftbl Trophy; Immaculata Coll; Psych.

FLETCHER, PAULA; Bishop Conwell HS; Morrisvl, PA; (Y); 24/260; Mathletes; Pres Church Choir; Im Bsktbl; High Hon Roll; Hon Roll; NHS; Ntl Merit Ltr; Church Yth Grp; Drama Clb; Chorus; Gold Tassel 86; Widener Acadmc Schlrshp 86; PA Lttr Of Cmmndtn 85; Widener U; Elec Engr.

FLETCHER, RITA; Southern Fulton HS; Warfordsburg, PA; (Y); Church Yth Grp; Cmnty Wkr; FBLA; FFA; FHA; FNA; Church Choir; Coach Actv; St Schlr; VFW Awd; No 1 Co-Op Cont Out 300 85; No 2 AM Vets Cont 83; IN ST; Law.

FLICK, DARLENE; Annville-Cleona HS; Annville, PA; (Y); Chorus; School Musical; Pres Frsh Cls; Pres Soph Cls; Pres Jr Cls; Pres Sr Cls; Stat Var Bsbl; JV Cheerleading; Sec Swmmng; NHS.

FLICK, HEATHER; Ligonier Valley SR HS; Ligonier, PA; (Y); Yrbk Ed-Chief; Yrbk Stf; Sec Frsh Cls; Sec Soph Cls; Rep Jr Cls; Rep Sr Cls; Rep Stu Cncl; Var Capt Cheerleading; L Trk; High Hon Roll; Homecmng Qne Atten 84; Homecmng Qne Atten 85; Cnty Chrus 83; Bus.

FLICK, JOHN; Seneca Valley HS; Harmony, PA; (Y); 61/359; Boy Scts; Church Yth Grp; Varsity Clb; Jazz Band; Madrigals; Mrchg Band; Symp Band; L Swmmng; Semper Fidelis Awd Musical Excellence, Acdmc Achvt Awd 86; Grove City Coll; Pre-Med.

FLICK, LISA; Gateway SR HS; Pitcairn, PA; (Y); 97/444; Chorus; Color Guard; Mrchg Band; Ptcrn Wmns Clb Schlrshp 86; Advsr Intl Ordr Rnbw Girls 84; Indiana U PA; Chld Psych.

FLICKINGER, DENISE; Central Dauphin HS; Harrisburg, PA; (Y); 4/330; Chorus; School Musical; L Crs Cntry; Im Vllybl; Hon Roll; NHS; Acad Stu Of Mnth 85; Yng Wmn Of Mnth 86; Beneficial Hodsen Schlrshp From Hood Coll $3000 86; Hood Coll; Bio Chem.

FLINCHBAUGH, BRYAN; Venango Christian HS; Oil City, PA; (Y); Boys Clb Am; Camera Clb; Exploring; Math Clb; Math Tm; School Play; Variety Show; Nwsp Stf; Yrbk Stf; Bsbl; Penn ST U; Elec Engr.

FLINN, NANCI; Gettysburg SR HS; Gettysburg, PA; (Y); Church Yth Grp; French Clb; Band; Color Guard; Concert Band; Mrchg Band; School Musical; Mat Maids; Mdcl Fld.

FLOCOS, TIMOTHY JOHN; Shady Side Academy; Pittsburgh, PA; (Y); Church Yth Grp; Model UN; SADD; Nwsp Rptr; Ed Nwsp Stf; Yrbk Rptr; Rep Soph Cls; Pres Sr Cls; Rep Stu Cncl; Lcrss; Franklin; Phlsphy.

FLOOD, DEREK; Susquehanna Twp HS; Harrisburg, PA; (Y); 56/165; Var Capt Ftbl; Var Capt Wrstlng; Hon Roll; Jim Sayers Outstndng Wrstlr Awd 86; All-Star Wrstlng Tm 86; Army.

FLOOK JR, THOMAS; Rochester Area HS; Rochester, PA; (Y); 37/100; Off Band; Concert Band; Jazz Band; Mrchg Band; Orch; Capt Bsbl; Hon Roll; Sports Med.

FLORA, CONNIE; Columbia-Montour Avts HS; Danville, PA; (Y); Letterman Clb; VICA; Capt L Bsktbl; Capt L Sftbl; High Hon Roll; Hon Roll; Pres VP NHS; MVP Bsktbl 85-86; Miss Hustle Bsktbl 84-85; Pres Acdmc Ftns Awd 86; :Data Proc.

FLORA, LISA; York County Area Vo-Tech Schl; Hanover, PA; (Y); VICA; Presdntl Physcl Fitness Awd 100 Pct 83-84; AAHPER Yth Fitness Awd For 50 Pct 85; Psychology.

FLOREK, JENNIFER; Hempfield SR HS; Youngwood, PA; (Y); Art Clb; German Clb; Pep Clb; Mat Maids; Wt Lftg; Hon Roll; IUP; Spch Pthlgy.

FLORENCE, ANTHONY; Central Catholic HS; Pittsburgh, PA; (Y); 6/280; Church Yth Grp; Hosp Aide; Ftbl; Trk; French Hon Soc; High Hon Roll; Rep Hgh O Brn Yth Ldrshp Cntst 85; Acdmc All-Amrcn 86.

FLORES, FLORENCE ELYSSABETH I; St Marys Area HS; Saint Marys, PA; (Y); Church Yth Grp; JA; Pep Clb; Chorus; JV L Bsktbl; Im Capt Bowling; Coach Actv; Var L Vllybl; Hon Roll; Jr NHS; Jr Clss Grls Athletc Awd 85-86; Duquesne U; Pharmacy.

FLORES, MIRNA; Liberty HS; Bethlehem, PA; (Y); 70/407; FFA; VICA; Hon Roll; Sec FFA 85-86; Gordon Phillips; Beautician.

FLORI, LOUIS E; Windber HS; Windber, PA; (Y); 7/135; Math Clb; Yrbk Stf; Rep Stu Cncl; Var Bsktbl; Var Golf; Hon Roll; NHS; Wdmn Of Wrld Hstry Awd 86; Med.

FLORIG, JENNIFER; Pottsgrove HS; Pottstown, PA; (Y); 74/229; Church Yth Grp; French Clb; Trs FBLA; Girl Scts; Library Aide; Science Clb; Color Guard; Stat Ftbl; Stat Sftbl; Lebanon Vly Coll; Mgmt.

FLOWERS JR, ALVIN H; Aliquippa HS; Aliquippa, PA; (Y); Varsity Clb; Nwsp Stf; Bsbl; Bsktbl; Crs Cntry; Ftbl; Gym; Sftbl; Trk; Vllybl; PA ST U; Bus Admin.

FLOWERS, HILARY; Ambridge Area HS; Baden, PA; (Y); Hon Roll; Molecular Physcs.

FLOWERS, THOMAS; Central Dauphin East HS; Harrisburg, PA; (Y); 18/286; AFS; Band; Concert Band; Drm Mjr(t); Pres Soph Cls; Pres Jr Cls; Pres Sr Cls; Var Bsktbl; High Hon Roll; NHS; Hugh O Brien Yth Ldrshp Semnr Rep 85; Pre-Med.

FLOYD, ALBERT; Taylor Allderdice HS; Pittsburgh, PA; (Y); 18/400; Church Yth Grp; JCL; Latin Clb; Math Tm; High Hon Roll; NHS; Ntl Merit SF; Ntl Merit Fnlst 86; Princeton U; Lib Arts.

FLOYD, GENENE; Walter Biddle Saul HS; Philadelphia, PA; (Y); Dance Clb; Drama Clb; FFA; Symp Band; Yrbk Stf; Achvt Awd Outstndng Cont Schl Brd 85; Macro Ecnmcs.

FLOYD, JAMIE; Donegal HS; Marietta, PA; (Y); Varsity Clb; Bsktbl; Fld Hcky; Sftbl.

FLOYD, LISA; Clearfield Area HS; Frenchville, PA; (Y); 14/350; Office Aide; Trs SADD; Chorus; High Hon Roll; Hon Roll; Du Bois Schl Bus; Legal Sec.

FLOYD JR, ROBERT; Northampton Area SR HS; Bath, PA; (Y); Church Yth Grp; Trs 4-H; 4-H Awd; Moravian Coll; Pre Med.

FLUCK, CHRISTOPHER; Upper Perkiomen HS; Pennsburg, PA; (Y); Lib Chorus; Var Bsbl; JV Bsktbl; Var Ftbl; Var Wt Lftg; Hon Roll; Elizabethtown Coll; Cmnctns.

FLUHARTY, CINDY; Hopewell SR HS; Aliquippa, PA; (Y); Church Yth Grp; Drama Clb; German Clb; Hosp Aide; Chorus; Fin.

FLUTY, THERESA; Norhtern Potter HS; Ulysses, PA; (Y); Church Yth Grp; German Clb; Varsity Clb; Band; Chorus; Stat Bsktbl; Var L Crs Cntry; Var L Trk; JV Vllybl; Nrsng.

FLYNN, BETTY; Blue Ridge HS; Great Bend, PA; (Y); Church Yth Grp; SADD; Var Crs Cntry; Var Trk; High Hon Roll; Hon Roll; NHS; Cmnty Wkr; All Conf Slctn Awd Crss Cntry 84; Stu Of Month Awd 84; Var Athltc Awds Trck & Crss Cntry 84-86.

FLYNN, BILL; Father Judge HS; Philadelphia, PA; (Y); 5/360; Golf; Swmmng; High Hon Roll; NHS; Bus.

FLYNN, DAVID; Lakeland JR SR HS; Jermyn, PA; (Y); Pres Boy Scts; SADD; Variety Show; Crs Cntry; Vllybl; High Hon Roll; Hon Roll; Explorer Scouts Pres 85-86; Cross Cntry Ski Clb 85; Pre-Law.

FLYNN, MARY ANN; Union City Area HS; Union City, PA; (Y); 12/103; Church Yth Grp; Computer Clb; Letterman Clb; Pep Clb; Spanish Clb; Chorus; Rep Stu Cncl; Capt Cheerleading; Var Trk; Amer Legion Schlrshp 86; Clarion U; Ed.

FLYNN, MAUREEN; Vinceton HS; Glenshaw, PA; (Y); 2/63; Church Yth Grp; Cmnty Wkr; Service Clb; Yrbk Stf; Rep Soph Cls; NHS; Chorus; Church Choir; High Hon Roll; Crtfct Meritorious Prtcptn Smr Seminar Wrld Affairs 86; Duquesne U; Elem Educ.

FLYNN, PAUL; West Scranton SR HS; Scranton, PA; (Y); 22/253; High Hon Roll; Hon Roll; Jr NHS; NHS; 1st Hnrs German Lange; US Marine Corps.

FLYNN, RUTH A; Old Forge HS; Old Forge, PA; (Y); Trs Church Yth Grp; Exploring; Ski Clb; Church Choir; Var Cheerleading; High Hon Roll; NHS; Pre-Law.

FOBES, TERRI; Sharon HS; Sharon, PA; (Y); Hosp Aide; Spanish Clb; SADD; Teachers Aide; VP Sr Cls; Rep Wrstlng; Hon Roll; Bio Awd 84-85; Ltr Acad Exc 85-86; Surgcl Nrsng.

FOCHLER, NANCY; Altoona Area HS; Altoona, PA; (Y); Church Yth Grp; Key Clb; Pep Clb; Spanish Clb; Drill Tm; School Play; Rep Stu Cncl; Pom Pon; Hon Roll; Kiwanis Awd; Penn ST U; Educ.

FOCHT, SHERRY; Altoona HS; Altoona, PA; (Y); Church Yth Grp; Dance Clb; Drama Clb; German Clb; Key Clb; Ski Clb; Acpl Chr; Band; Chorus; Church Choir; Hnr Roll, 1st Pl Mjrt Awd 83-84; 2nd Pl Mjrt Awd 84-85; Penn ST U; Lib Arts.

FOCHT, TAMARA; Tulpehocken HS; Bernville, PA; (Y); 1/104; Spanish Clb; Band; Chorus; School Musical; School Play; Var L Tennis; High Hon Roll; NHS; Tulpehocken Schlr Awd 85-86; MVP Awd Tnns 85-86; Muhlenburg Coll; Pre-Med.

FOCHTMAN, SUSAN; Chestnut Ridge SR HS; Bedford, PA; (Y); 20/107; Church Yth Grp; School Musical; Variety Show; Nwsp Bus Mgr; Cheerleading; Trk; Hon Roll; NHS; Shepherd Coll; Soc Wrk.

FOCKLER, CRAIG; North Star HS; Boswell, PA; (Y); Church Yth Grp; FCA; Library Aide; Bucknoll U; Chem.

FODOR, TAMMY MARIE; Mt Carmel Area JR SR HS; Mt Carmel, PA; (Y); 29/136; Sec FTA; Key Clb; Sec Q&S; School Musical; Nwsp Rptr; Stu Cncl; Cheerleading; Church Yth Grp; Library Aide.

FOGARTY, ELEANOR; Our Lady Of Lourdes Regional HS; Sunbury, PA; (Y); 11/100; Church Yth Grp; Girl Scts; Spanish Clb; Nwsp Bus Mgr; Yrbk Bus Mgr; Yrbk Ed-Chief; High Hon Roll; Hon Roll; NHS; Spanish NHS; Bus.

FOGARTY, ERIN; Villa Maria HS; Youngstown, OH; (Y); Cmnty Wkr; Drama Clb; 4-H; Spanish Clb; Thesps; Concert Band; School Musical; Nwsp Ed-Chief; Lit Mag; High Hon Roll; Cert From Congrsnl Smnr Washngtn DC 86; Pol Sci.

FOGARTY, THERESA; Central Catholic HS; Allentown, PA; (Y); 10/200; Church Yth Grp; Key Clb; Math Tm; Ski Clb; Y-Teens; Chorus; School Musical; Nwsp Rptr; Ed Nwsp Stf; High Hon Roll; Stand Up Life Essy 2nd Pl Cnty 86; Creat Wrtg.

FOGEL, ANDREA; St Pius X HS; Schwenksville, PA; (S); 8/161; French Clb; VP Service Clb; Teachers Aide; Drill Tm; School Musical; Yrbk Stf; High Hon Roll; NHS; Engl Awd; Yrbk Awd; Psych.

FOGEL, BONNIE; Northampton SR HS; Bath, PA; (Y); Pres Church Yth Grp; Computer Clb; Hosp Aide; Office Aide; Band; Chorus; Color Guard; Capt Mrchg Band; Hon Roll; Pre-Med.

FOGG, DEBORAH; Kittanning SR HS; Worthington, PA; (Y); High Hon Roll; Hon Roll; Butler Co CC; Chld Psych.

FOGLE, JON; Corry Area HS; Corry, PA; (S); 48/225; German Clb; SADD; Capt Bsktbl; Capt Ftbl; Al-ST Hnrbl Mnnyn.

FOGLE, KIM; East Juniata HS; Mcalisterville, PA; (Y); 1/100; Chorus; Church Choir; School Musical; JV Var Cheerleading; JV Var Fld Hcky; Var L Trk; High Hon Roll; NHS.

FOGLE, MICHELLE; Mechanicsburg SR HS; Mechanicsburg, PA; (Y); Concert Band; Symp Band; Rep Frsh Cls; Sec Soph Cls; VP Stu Cncl; Var L Fld Hcky; Var L Sftbl; Var L Swmmng; Hon Roll; All-Star Team Sftbl/F Hockey 85-86; Carlisle Sentnl Athlt Of Yr 85-86; Psych.

FOLEY, CHRISTINA; St Hubert Catholic For Girls HS; Philadelphia, PA; (Y); 7/367; French Clb; Orch; School Musical; School Play; Variety Show; Hon Roll; NHS; Prfct Atten Awd; Cmnty Wkr; Girl Scts; Music Awd; 6 Wk Smmr Course At Temple U 86; Spcl Educ Tchr.

FOLEY, DANIEL; Cheltenham HS; Glenside, PA; (Y); 24/365; Boy Scts; Church Yth Grp; VICA; Church Choir; Variety Show; Yrbk Stf; Im Bowling; Frnch Merit Cert 84-85; CCD Pgm Atten Awd 85-86; Spnsh Merit Cert 85-86; Crmnl Justice.

FOLEY, DAVID; Seneca Valley HS; Mars, PA; (Y); 147/398; Letterman Clb; Varsity Clb; Var Ftbl; Var Trk; Var Wt Lftg; Soph Rck MVP 85; Most Outstndg Trck Athlete 86; Pittsburgh U; Banking.

FOLEY, ERIN; Bethlehem Catholic HS; Bethlehem, PA; (Y); 35/221; Key Clb; Ski Clb; Yrbk Stf; Rep Stu Cncl; Var L Crs Cntry; Im Fld Hcky; Im Socr; Var L Vllybl; NHS; Fairfield U; Bio.

FOLEY, JACQUELINE J; Methacton HS; Trooper, PA; (Y); Art Clb; Chess Clb; Girl Scts; Ski Clb; Yrbk Stf; Rep Stu Cncl; Var Powder Puff Ftbl; Var JV Score Keeper; JV Sftbl; Hon Roll; Arts Natl Fndtn Advncmt Arts 86; Kutztown U; Fine Art.

FOLEY, KEVIN; Canon-Mc Millan SR HS; Canonsburg, PA; (Y); 125/371; Chess Clb; Church Yth Grp; Hon Roll; Jrnlsm.

FOLEY, KEVIN; Lancaster Catholic HS; Millersville, PA; (Y); Boy Scts; Model UN; Band; Chorus; Concert Band; Jazz Band; Mrchg Band; Pep Band; School Musical; Millersville U; Bio.

FOLEY, MARK N; Freedom HS; Bethlehem, PA; (Y); 97/425; Church Yth Grp; Pres Drama Clb; Model UN; Science Clb; Thesps; Acpl Chr; Chorus; School Musical; School Play; Nwsp Ed-Chief; Bst Feature Article HS Paper 84; Educator.

FOLEY, PAIGE L; Lancaster Catholic HS; Leola, PA; (Y); 47/189; Pep Clb; Varsity Clb; School Musical; School Play; Nwsp Phtg; Yrbk Phtg; Off Jr Cls; Var Cheerleading.

FOLLETT, ANGIE; Northern SR HS; Dillsburg, PA; (Y); 22/200; Church Yth Grp; Pres Color Guard; Concert Band; Powder Puff Ftbl; French Hon Soc; High Hon Roll; NHS; Instrmntlst Mgzn Mrt Awd 86; Otstdng Bndfrnt SR 86; IN U Of PA; Cmmnctns.

FOLMAR, JENNIFER L; Montoursville HS; Montoursville, PA; (Y); Church Yth Grp; Dance Clb; German Clb; Church Choir; Stu Cncl; Cheerleading; Pom Pon; Powder Puff Ftbl; Monogram Clb 85-86; Bloomsburg U; Nrs.

FOLMAR, SCOTT; Dubois Area SR HS; Luthersburg, PA; (Y); 180/274; Varsity Clb; Wrstlng; Hon Roll; Vale Tech Inst; Auto Tech.

FOLTZ, ALICIA; Bishop Mc Cort HS; Johnstown, PA; (Y); German Clb; NFL; Pep Clb; Color Guard; Orch; School Play; Nwsp Rptr; High Hon Roll; Mu Alp Tht; NHS; American Legion Oratory Award 86; College Of William & Mary.

FOLTZ, DANA; Johnstown Vo Tech; Johnstown, PA; (Y); Art Clb; Church Yth Grp; German Clb; Teachers Aide; Color Guard; Orch; Var Crs Cntry; Var L Trk; Hon Roll; Piedmont Coll Acadmc Schlrshp Supr SAT Scores 86; Arch Engr.

FOLTZ, JERRY; Shade HS; Cairnbrook, PA; (Y); 1/65; Boy Scts; Church Yth Grp; Varsity Clb; VP Band; VP Frsh Cls; Pres Jr Cls; Rep Stu Cncl; Var L Bsbl; High Hon Roll; Trs NHS; Engrng.

FOLTZ, MICHAEL; East Juniata HS; Mcalisterville, PA; (Y); Sec FFA; Var L Ftbl; JV Socr; JV Trk; Hon Roll; Prfct Atten Awd.

FOLTZ, TRACY; Warwick SR HS; Lititz, PA; (Y); 63/229; Sec Church Yth Grp; Band; Chorus; Church Choir; Concert Band; Mrchg Band; Orch; Hon Roll; Jnr All Amercn Hall Of Fame Band Hnrs 85; Bus.

FONARK, DIANE; Kiski Area HS; Hyde Park, PA; (Y); English Clb; Office Aide; Spanish Clb; Cit Awd; DAR Awd; Hon Roll; Pep Clb; Im Bsktbl; Im Powder Puff Ftbl; Im Score Keeper; Bus Admin.

FONAROW, NICOLE; Hastboro-Horsham SR HS; Horsham, PA; (Y); Key Clb; Color Guard; Drill Tm; Flag Corp; Stage Crew; Rep Jr Cls; JV Swmmng; Hon Roll; Chem.

FONASH, STEVE E; State College Area SR HS; State College, PA; (Y); Im Bsktbl; Im Socr; Im Vllybl; High Hon Roll; Ski Clb; Im Bsbl; Im Golf; Bus.

FONDREN, KELLY; Downingtown HS; Downingtown, PA; (Y); Pep Clb; Ski Clb; Pres SADD; Chorus; Yrbk Stf; Trs Soph Cls; Rep Stu Cncl; JV Lcrss; CC Awd; Ldrshp Awd 85 & 86; Cmmnctns.

FONT, KRIS; Warren Area HS; Warren, PA; (Y); Art Clb; French Clb; Chorus; Yrbk Stf; JV Sftbl; L Swmmng; Var Trk; Hon Roll; Most Impvd Swmmr 85; Clarion; Sprts Med.

FONTANELLA, PATRICK J; Penn Cambria HS; Dysart, PA; (Y); 3/168; SADD; Band; Concert Band; Drm Mjr(t); Jazz Band; Mrchg Band; Stu Cncl; High Hon Roll; Hon Roll; NHS; Outstndng Svc Awd 86; Hgh Schlstc Achvmnt Awd 86; Penn ST U; Chem Engr.

FONTENOY, ROBYN; Clearfield Area HS; Clearfield, PA; (Y).

FOOR, CHARLENE; Chestnut Ridge SR HS; Manns Choice, PA; (S); 3/107; FBLA; Band; Concert Band; Mrchg Band; High Hon Roll; Hon Roll; NHS; Ntl Merit Ltr; Prfct Atten Awd; Med Secy.

FOOR, JEFF; Everett Area HS; Everett, PA; (Y); Church Yth Grp; Varsity Clb; Yrbk Stf; Stu Cncl; Ftbl; Trk; Wrstlng; High Hon Roll; NHS; Acad All Americn 85-86; Engrng.

FOOR, MICHAEL; Everett Area HS; Everett, PA; (S); SADD; Drm Mjr(t); Mrchg Band; Rep Stu Cncl; French Hon Soc; French Clb; Chorus; Concert Band; Jazz Band; Pep Band; Pedtrcn.

FOOR, SONYA; Everett Area HS; Clearville, PA; (Y); Camera Clb; Church Yth Grp; Cmnty Wkr; Computer Clb; English Clb; French Clb; SADD; Chorus; Stu Cncl; Sftbl; Acad Schvt Awds 85-86; Gftd Stud 84-86; Allghny Cmnty Frstbrg; Engl.

FOOSE, CINDY; Pennsburg HS; Yardley, PA; (Y); German Clb; Chorus; Hon Roll; W Chester U; Elem Ed.

FOOSE, STEVEN; Lampeter-Strasburg HS; Strasburg, PA; (Y); 33/160; Church Yth Grp; Varsity Clb; Band; Mrchg Band; Pep Band; School Musical; Stage Crew; Nwsp Rptr; Nwsp Stf; Lit Mag; MVP X-Cntry 85; James Madison U; Comp Sci.

FOOTE, ROBERT; Swissvale HS; Swissvale, PA; (Y); 34/186; Pres Exploring; Radio Clb; Bowling; JV Crs Cntry; Var Trk; High Hon Roll; Ntl Merit Ltr; PA ST U; Engrng.

FORBECK, DANIEL; Shaler Area HS; Pittsburgh, PA; (Y); 116/538; JA; Spanish Clb; Hon Roll; Spanish NHS; Millvale Mem Schlrshp 86; U Of Pitts; Cvl Engrng.

FORBES, CHRISTOPHER; New Hope-Solebury HS; Solebury, PA; (Y); Boy Scts; Ski Clb; Varsity Clb; Stu Cncl; Bsbl; Socr; Med.

FORBES, MARY SUSAN; Central Cambria HS; Colver, PA; (Y); 32/193; Pres VP Art Clb; Church Yth Grp; Debate Tm; Library Aide; Church Choir; Concert Band; Jazz Band; Mrchg Band; Pep Band; School Play; Albert C O Connor Frsc Awd; U Of Pittsburgh; Elmntry Ed.

FORBES, MATTHEW; Hampton HS; Allison Pk, PA; (Y); Ski Clb; Rep Soph Cls; L Bsbl; Var Golf; Hon Roll.

FORBES, MICHELE; Western Wayne HS; Lake Ariel, PA; (Y); 7/147; Debate Tm; Exploring; Pres 4-H; FBLA; Library Aide; Nwsp Rptr; High Hon Roll; Jr NHS; NHS; F Newell Mem Schlrshp, PTA Poster Awds 86; Millersville U; Lib Sci.

FORBES, STACEY; Towanda Area HS; Towanda, PA; (Y); Church Yth Grp; Teachers Aide; Chorus; Church Choir; School Musical; Yrbk Stf; JV Cheerleading; JV Sftbl; JV Vllybl; Hon Roll; Piano Awd 84; Jrnlsm.

FORD, ALISA A; Bishop Mc Devitt HS; Philadelphia, PA; (Y); Church Yth Grp; Computer Clb; Dance Clb; Debate Tm; Exploring; French Clb; FBLA; JA; Office Aide; Political Wkr; Ldrshp Awd 85; Clarion U; Accntnt.

FORD, BETHANY A; Downingtown SR HS; Downingtown, PA; (Y); 7/561; Quiz Bowl; Concert Band; Mrchg Band; Orch; School Musical; Symp Band; Nwsp Stf; High Hon Roll; NHS; NEDT Awd; Dist VII Bnd 85-86; Mth.

FORD, DAPHNE INEZ; Dover HS; Dover, PA; (Y); Art Clb; Dance Clb; Drama Clb; Girl Scts; JA; Ski Clb; Spanish Clb; SADD; Chorus; School Musical; Chrldng Awd 84-86; Easter Seal Chrldng Awd 86; UT U; Art.

FORD, GREGORY; Dover Area HS; East Berlin, PA; (Y); 60/240; Church Yth Grp; Computer Clb; English Clb; Math Clb; Drm & Bgl; Symp Band; Lit Mag; Var Diving; Var Swmmng; Hon Roll; George Parks Drum Major Acad 85; Engrng.

FORD, JUDITH; Ambridge Area HS; Ambridge, PA; (Y); GAA; Rep Pep Clb; VP Spanish Clb; Band; Mrchg Band; Orch; Stu Cncl; Var Capt Cheerleading; L Sftbl; High Hon Roll; Secndry Tchng.

FORD, KATHLEEN T; Archbishop HS For Girls; Philadelphia, PA; (Y); 4/475; German Clb; Nwsp Rptr; Rep Soph Cls; Rep Jr Cls; Var Socr; NHS; Anna Maria Vincent Schlrshp 86; Excllnc In Mathematics 86; German Awd 83-84-85; Drexel U; Arch Engr.

FORD, KELLY L; Wellsboro Area SR HS; Mifflinburg, PA; (Y); Art Clb; Church Yth Grp; Drama Clb; English Clb; Sec Ski Clb; School Play; JV Tennis; Hon Roll; Im Swmmng; Stage Crew; Ntl Poetry Cont Awds 85; Hmcmng Queen 85-86; PSIA 86-87; Bus Adm.

FORD, MARK; North East HS; North East, PA; (Y); 8/149; Am Leg Boys St; VP Soph Cls; VP Jr Cls; Trs Sr Cls; Var Crs Cntry; Var Swmmng; Var Trk; JETS Awd; German Clb; Letterman Clb; US Army Rsrv Schlor-Athltc Awd 86; Outstndg Calculus Awd 86; U Of Pittsburg; Aerosp Engrng.

FORD, MATT; Central Catholic HS; Pittsburgh, PA; (Y); 120/276; Boy Scts; Crs Cntry; Trk; Wrstlng; Hon Roll.

FORE, TRAVIS Q; The Mercersburg Acad; Hagerstown, MD; (Y); 7/130; Boy Scts; Pres Church Yth Grp; Jazz Band; Pep Band; Rep Stu Cncl; Var Bsbl; High Hon Roll; Ntl Merit Ltr; Pres Schlr; Peer Group Leader; NW U; Engrng.

FOREMAN, TIM; Philipsburg Osceola HS; Philipsburg, PA; (Y); 109/250; Sec Letterman Clb; Ski Clb; SADD; Varsity Clb; Yrbk Stf; L Bsbl; L Bsktbl; L Ftbl; Var Wt Lftg; Hon Roll; Detrmntn, Attid Bstbl 85-86; MIP Bsktbl 84-85; Crmnl Just.

FORINGER, DIANE; Ambridge Area HS; Ambridge, PA; (Y); Church Yth Grp; Girl Scts; Pep Clb; Spanish Clb; Off Soph Cls; Off Jr Cls; JV Vllybl; High Hon Roll; Hon Roll; Spec Educ.

FORISH, DEBRA L; Ferndale Area HS; Johnstown, PA; (Y); 9/57; GAA; Leo Clb; Speech Tm; Nwsp Ed-Chief; Yrbk Phtg; Var L Cheerleading; High Hon Roll; Lion Awd; VP NHS; Rotary Awd; PA ST U.

FORKER, SAMUEL; Donegal HS; Marietta, PA; (Y); 42/170; Boy Scts; ROTC; VP Band; Mrchg Band; Yrbk Phtg; Var Ice Hcky; Var Trk; Hon Roll; Var Crs Cntry; Chrmn Prom Committee 85-86; Boston U.

FORMAN, ANDREW; Plymouth Whitemarsh SR HS; Plymouth Mtg, PA; (Y); Boy Scts; Chess Clb; Intnl Clb; Trs Math Clb; Model UN; Nwsp Ed-Chief; Nwsp Rptr; Yrbk Stf; Rep Soph Cls; Rep Jr Cls; Pitt; Pharm.

FORMAN, ROBYN; Bensalem HS; Bensalem, PA; (Y); Aud/Vis; Debate Tm; Drama Clb; School Play; Nwsp Ed-Chief; Nwsp Rptr; Nwsp Stf; Rep Soph Cls; High Hon Roll; NHS; Communctns.

FORMATI, MELISSA; New Castle HS; New Castle, PA; (S); 14/236; Cmnty Wkr; Ski Clb; SADD; Rep Stu Cncl; Im Vllybl; High Hon Roll; Hon Roll; NHS; Ntl Merit Ltr; Slippery Rock U; Comp Sys Anlst.

FORMICA, MICHAEL K; Quakertown SR HS; Quakertown, PA; (Y); Am Leg Boys St; Rep Stu Cncl; Coach Actv; Var Capt Crs Cntry; Var Capt Trk; High Hon Roll; Ntl Merit SF; Church Yth Grp; Computer Clb; Math Tm; ST Sci Cont 86; PA Keystone ST Games ST Champ 3000 M Steeplechase 86; Lehigh; Engrng.

FORNAL, JEFFREY; Mt Pleasant Area SR HS; Mt Pleasant, PA; (Y); SADD; Ftbl; Mr Hustle Hocky Awd WHA 86; PA ST U; Arch.

FORNEY, DENISE; Millersburg Area HS; Millersburg, PA; (Y); 16/58; Ed Yrbk Stf; Pres Soph Cls; Pres Jr Cls; Pres Sr Cls; VP Pres Stu Cncl; Var L Bsktbl; Cit Awd; NHS; Library Aide; Ski Clb; Army Schlstc/Athlt Achvt Awd 86; Babe Ruth Sprtsmnshp Awd 86; Messiah Coll; Physcl Ed.

FORNEY, JAMES; Millersburg Area HS; Millersburg, PA; (Y); 28/75; JV Bsktbl; Var Ftbl; Var Swmmng; Var Trk; Hon Roll; Nuclear Engr.

FORNEY, ROBERT; Kiski Area HS; Apollo, PA; (Y); Computer Clb; Band; Concert Band; Jazz Band; Mrchg Band; Pep Band; Symp Band; Hon Roll; Indiana U Of PA; Crmnlgy.

FORNWALT, DANIELLE; Middletown Area HS; Middletown, PA; (Y); Cmnty Wkr; FNA; GAA; Hosp Aide; Radio Clb; Bsktbl; Powder Puff Ftbl; Trk; Vllybl; Hon Roll; Cont In Miss TEEN Pagent 86; Nursing.

FORREN, ANITA; The Christian Acad; Claymont, DE; (Y); Church Yth Grp; Nwsp Ed-Chief; Nwsp Rptr; Pres Jr Cls; JV Cheerleading; Sftbl; VP Rep Soph Cls; Rep Stu Cncl; Hon Roll; Stu Mnth; Christian Grwth Awd; U DE; Nrsng.

FORREST, JENNIFER LYNN; Punxsutawney Area HS; Punxsutawney, PA; (Y); 7/243; Pres Debate Tm; French Clb; Rptr FBLA; Hosp Aide; Math Tm; Science Clb; Pres Speech Tm; Rep Stu Cncl; Ntl Merit Ltr; Voice Dem Awd; Am Leg Essay Cont ST Wnnr 86; Impromptu Spkg FBLA 2nd ST 86; Mary Ann Irvin Mem Scholar 86; IN U PA; Bus Adm.

FORREST, SCOTT; Strath Haven HS; Wallingford, PA; (Y); Church Yth Grp; Sec Trs Debate Tm; Intnl Clb; Scholastic Bowl; Ski Clb; Concert Band; Mrchg Band; School Musical; Nwsp Stf; Yrbk Ed-Chief; Sons Of Norway Acdmc Schlrshp 86; HS Hnr Roll Letter 85-86; Coll Of William & Mary; Chem.

FORREY, ALLISON; Hempfield HS; Lancaster, PA; (Y); 19/418; Art Clb; Science Clb; Varsity Clb; JV Bsktbl; Var Fld Hcky; Var Sftbl; High Hon Roll; NHS; Penn ST U; Psych.

FORRY, DANIEL L; Hempfield HS; Columbia, PA; (Y); 15/384; Church Yth Grp; Pres 4-H; Math Tm; Science Clb; Var Capt Wrstlng; Hon Roll; Pres NHS; Opt Clb Awd; Pres Schlr; Rotary Awd; PA ST U; Engrg.

FORRY, TAMMIE; Eastern HS; Hallam, PA; (Y); 40/169; English Clb; Band; Chorus; School Musical; Yrbk Stf; JV Var Bsktbl; Var L Fld Hcky; Powder Puff Ftbl; Var Trk; Hon Roll; Unsung Hero Fld Hcky 85-86; Pre-Law.

FORS, BRIAN; Academy Of The New Church; Huntingdon Vly, PA; (Y); Key Clb; Math Clb; Math Tm; Natl Beta Clb; Science Clb; JV Var Bsbl; JV Var Crs Cntry; Hon Roll; NHS; Outstndg Achvmnt Physcs 85-86; Comp Sci.

FORSBURG, BRIAN; South Williamsport Area HS; Williamsport, PA; (Y); JV Trk; JV Wrstlng; Hon Roll; PA ST U; Electrnc Engrng.

FORSEY, MICHELLE; Hanover Area JR SR HS; Wilkes Barre, PA; (Y); 14/169; Hosp Aide; Orch; Band; Chorus; Drill Tm; Drm Mjr(t); Mrchg Band; School Musical; Yrbk Ed-Chief; High Hon Roll; PA JR Acad Sci Rgnl Wnnr, ST Wnnr; Diet.

FORSYTH, LYNN; Coatesville Area SR HS; Coatesville, PA; (Y); 33/600; Drama Clb; French Clb; Ski Clb; SADD; Chorus; School Musical; Stu Cncl; Cheerleading; High Hon Roll; NEDT Awd; PA ST U; Tele Comm.

FORSYTHE, DAWN; Seneca Valley SR HS; Callery, PA; (Y); French Clb; Pep Clb; Teachers Aide; Nwsp Rptr; Yrbk Stf; Pom Pon; Hon Roll; Schlrshp Awd Schlstc Achvt 86; Indiana U Of PA; Crt Stngrphr.

FORSYTHE, KELLY; Gettysburg SR HS; Gettysburg, PA; (Y); Church Yth Grp; Hosp Aide; Office Aide; Chorus; Swing Chorus; Rep Stu Cncl; Hon Roll; Hagerstown Bus Coll; Acctng.

FORSYTHE, KELLY; Marion Center Area HS; Marion Ctr, PA; (Y); 77/169; FBLA; Pres Latin Clb; Pep Clb; Teachers Aide; Varsity Clb; Yrbk Stf; Stu Cncl; Var L Cheerleading; Ntl Scl Stdys Olympd 86; Law.

FORSYTHE, RAYNA; Southmoreland SR HS; Scottdale, PA; (Y); 24/230; Drama Clb; Chorus; Concert Band; Drm Mjr(t); Jazz Band; Mrchg Band; School Musical; School Play; Nwsp Rptr; Lit Mag; Cnty Band 84; Dist Band 86; Spec Educ.

FORTE, JANE; Monongahela Valley Catholic HS; Ellsworth, PA; (Y); 5/80; Dance Clb; Spanish Clb; Band; Church Choir; Concert Band; Mrchg Band; Pep Band; Yrbk Stf; Powder Puff Ftbl; NHS; Pre-Med.

FORTER, MELISSA; Butler Area SR HS; Butler, PA; (Y); Church Yth Grp; French Clb; Ski Clb; SADD; Band; Chorus; Jazz Band; Mrchg Band; Orch; Symp Band; Music.

FORTIER, ANGIE; Loyalsock Township HS; Williamport, PA; (Y); Key Clb; Latin Clb; Spanish Clb; Cmnty Wkr; Ski Clb; Chorus; Gym; Score Keeper; Trk; Wt Lftg; Dntl Hyg.

FORTINO, DAVID; Central HS; Philadelphia, PA; (Y); 50/300; Camera Clb; Yrbk Phtg; Var L Crs Cntry; Var Capt Trk; Cit Awd; Hon Roll; Opt Clb Awd; Barnwell Hnr Rll 84-86; Bachlr Of Arts Deg 86; Serv Awd 86; PA ST U; Telecomm.

FORTINO, DENISE; Saint Huberts HS; Philadelphia, PA; (Y); Debate Tm; JA; Office Aide; Teachers Aide; Gym; Swmmng; Hon Roll; Medical Record Tech.

FORTNER, ALLISON; Neshannock HS; New Castle, PA; (Y); 7/99; Church Yth Grp; Band; Chorus; Concert Band; Jazz Band; Mrchg Band; School Musical; School Play; High Hon Roll; NHS; PA All-ST Chrs 86; JR Miss Schlstc Schachvmnt Schlrshp 85; U Of GA; Lit.

FOSBENNER, GREGORY S; Pennridge HS; Sellersville, PA; (Y); 13/414; Am Leg Boys St; Boy Scts; Church Yth Grp; Yrbk Phtg; Yrbk Stf; Rep Stu Cncl; High Hon Roll; NHS; Prfct Atten Awd; Bucks Cnty I U No 22 Sci Semnr 84-86; PA Free Enterprise Wk 85; PA ST U; Engrng.

FOSKO, LEOCADIA; Wyoming Area HS; Wyoming, PA; (Y); French Clb; Key Clb; Band; Concert Band; Mrchg Band; Pep Band; Kutztown U; Spec Ed.

FOSTER, AMY; Peters Township HS; Venetia, PA; (S); 73/257; Key Clb; Library Aide; Ski Clb; SADD; Ed Nwsp Stf; Yrbk Phtg; Ed Lit Mag; Trs Stu Cncl; High Hon Roll; US Studnt Councl Awd 85; Acadmc Excllnc Awd 85; Acadmc All Amer Schlr; Syracuse U; Advrtsng.

FOSTER, JANETTE; Philipsburg-Osceola Area SR HS; West Decatur, PA; (Y); 6/250; Church Yth Grp; Band; Color Guard; Concert Band; Mrchg Band; Hon Roll; NHS; Pennsylvaina ST U; Vtrnry Med.

FOSTER, JASON; Cornell HS; Coraopolis, PA; (Y); 4/56; Boy Scts; Key Clb; Band; Var L Tennis; DAR Awd; High Hon Roll; Kiwanis Awd; VP NHS; French Clb; Concert Band; Kiwains Schlrshp 86; Math Awd 86; Omega Phi Schlrshp 86; Bucknell U; Chmstry.

FOSTER, KARA; Archbishop Caroll HS; Phoenixville, PA; (Y); Cmnty Wkr; French Clb; Mathletes; Office Aide; Political Wkr; SADD; Trk; Hon Roll; Temple U; Pltcl Sci.

FOSTER, KEITH; Seneca Valley HS; Evans City, PA; (Y); JA; Varsity Clb; Chorus; Rep Frsh Cls; Ftbl; Wrstlng; Hon Roll; Schlrshp Awd Seneca Vly 85-86; Wrstlng Sctn II Chmpns 84-85; JR Achvt 3rd Top Slsmn 84-85; Engnrng.

FOSTER, PATRICIA; Lebanon SR HS; Lebanon, PA; (Y); 23/300; Trs Church Yth Grp; Drama Clb; German Clb; Key Clb; Pep Clb; Teachers Aide; Yrbk Stf; Var Fld Hcky; Var Trk; Opt Clb Awd; 2nd Pl Opt Mst Clb Ortrcl Cntst 84; Comm.

FOSTER, SEAN; Philipsburg-Osceola Area HS; West Decatur, PA; (Y); 25/250; Yrbk Stf; Trs Jr Cls; Stu Cncl; JV Ftbl; Im Wt Lftg; Hon Roll; NEDT Fnlst Awd 84; USC; Music Engrng Tech.

FOSTOCK, TAMRA; Hanover Area JR SR HS; Wilkes Barre, PA; (Y); Church Yth Grp; Key Clb; Library Aide; Nwsp Stf; Yrbk Stf; Sec Stu Cncl; Capt Var Cheerleading; High Hon Roll; VP NHS; Chrldng Ntl World Champ 85-86; Med Tech.

FOTIA, CRISTA; Lincoln HS; Ellwood City, PA; (Y); 21/168; Spanish Clb; Y-Teens; Chorus; Yrbk Stf; Var Capt Cheerleading; Powder Puff Ftbl; Var Trk; High Hon Roll; Hon Roll.

FOTIA, JOE; Lincoln HS; Ellwood City, PA; (Y); 28/169; Latin Clb; Ski Clb; Im JV Bsbl; Im JV Bsktbl; JV Ftbl; High Hon Roll; Hon Roll; Straight A Latin Awd; Pre-Med.

FOTOPOULOS, AFRODITI; Wm Allen HS; Allentown, PA; (Y); Sec Chorus; Off Sr Cls; Twrlr; Hon Roll; NHS; Pres Spanish NHS; Mc Cormick Bk Awd 86; Elem Tchr.

FOTOPOULOS, JAKE; William Allen HS; Allentown, PA; (Y); 9/530; Math Clb; Math Tm; Scholastic Bowl; Nwsp Sprt Ed; Nwsp Stf; Lit Mag; Im Bowling; High Hon Roll; NHS; Co Founder Schls Trivia Clb 86; Lehigh U; Chem Engr.

FOTTA, GINA; Fairchance-Georges SR HS; Smithfield, PA; (Y); 2/146; FHA; Office Aide; Yrbk Stf; Jr NHS; NHS; Val; Prsdntl Acad Ftnss Awd 86.

FOUCHET, LISA; Lampeter-Strasburg HS; Willow St, PA; (Y); 10/168; Thesps; Varsity Clb; School Musical; Sec Soph Cls; Sec Jr Cls; Pres Stu Cncl; Var Cheerleading; Var Sftbl; Hon Roll; NHS; Prds Rtry Stu Mo 86; Bus.

FOUGHT, KEVIN; Millville HS; Millville, PA; (S); 9/74; Yrbk Stf; Var Socr; Hon Roll; NHS; IUP; Comp.

FOUNTAIN, MICHAEL; Delaware Valley HS; Matamoras, PA; (Y); 19/130; Am Leg Boys St; Art Clb; Drama Clb; Stage Crew; Lit Mag; Hon Roll; NHS; Bloomsburg U; Engl.

FOUNTAIN, NANCY; Chester HS; Chester, PA; (S); 2/384; Science Clb; Capt Band; Concert Band; Mrchg Band; Orch; School Play; Nwsp Rptr; Dnfth Awd; DAR Awd; High Hon Roll; Music Schlrshp-Privt Lssns 83-86; Stu Of Mnth 85; LEAD Prgm 85; Industl Engr.

FOUSE, JESSICA; Aliquippa HS; Aliquippa, PA; (Y); Exploring; French Clb; Hosp Aide; Office Aide; Band; Church Choir; Pep Band; Var Sftbl; Hon Roll; Lawyer.

FOUSE, KIMBERLY; Altoona Area HS; Altoona, PA; (Y); Church Yth Grp; German Clb; Key Clb; Ski Clb; Spanish Clb; Stu Cncl; Prfct Atten Awd; PA ST U; Lib Arts.

FOUST, DAVE; United HS; Homer City, PA; (Y); 47/157; Camera Clb; Off Jr Cls; Off Sr Cls; Var Ftbl; Var Wrstlng; JC Awd; All Star Wrstlr, Inter-Co Wrstlng Conf-All Conf Tm 86.

FOUST, JACQUELINE; Central Columbia HS; Bloomsburg, PA; (Y); 14/178; Pres Varsity Clb; Yrbk Ed-Chief; Pres Frsh Cls; Pres Soph Cls; VP Sr Cls; Var Capt Golf; Var Capt Swmmng; French Hon Soc; Hon Roll; HOBY Fndtn Awd 82; Rotary Stu 85; Outstndng Female Ath 86; PA ST U; Librl Arts.

FOUST, KAREN; Danville SR HS; Riverside, PA; (Y); Church Yth Grp; French Clb; Ski Clb; Chorus; Stage Crew; Rep Frsh Cls; Mat Maids; JV L Tennis; High Hon Roll; NHS; Phys Ther.

FOWLER, D THOMAS; Newport JR SR HS; Newport, PA; (Y); Aud/Vis; VP FFA; Nwsp Rptr; Nwsp Stf; Outstndng FFA Stu 86; Svc FFA Reporter 85; Harrisburg Area CC; Bus Mgmt.

FOWLER, JOHN; Waynesburg Central HS; Waynesburg, PA; (Y); 6/206; Church Yth Grp; Spanish Clb; Var L Bsktbl; Var L Crs Cntry; High Hon Roll; Trs NHS; Lions Clb Boy Of Mnth 85; Outstndng Dramatic Lit Stu; Outstndng Engl II-C Stu; PA ST U; Bus Adm.

FOWLER, KATHRYN L; Shaler Area HS; Pittsburgh, PA; (Y); 80/517; Hosp Aide; Mrchg Band; Symp Band; Yrbk Stf; Bus Admin.

FOWLER, REGIS R; Shaler Area HS; Glenshaw, PA; (Y); 6/542; Bowling; Vllybl; High Hon Roll; NHS; Spanish NHS; Purdue U; Engrng.

FOX, DAVID; Northampton HS; Bath, PA; (Y); 19/470; Var Capt Crs Cntry; Var L Trk; Im Vllybl; High Hon Roll; Hon Roll; NHS; Rotary Awd; HS Exchg Clb Boy Of Mnth 85; PA ST U; Mech Engrng.

FOX, HOLLY; Gettysburg SR HS; Gettysburg, PA; (Y); Drama Clb; School Musical; School Play; Stu Cncl; Ski Clb; SADD; Teachers Aide; Chorus; Swing Chorus; Variety Show; Achvt Awd Dance Hildegard Hammer Schl Of Dance 86; Hnrs Choir 86; Philadelphia Coll; Dance.

FOX, JEANNE; West Greene HS; Wind Ridge, PA; (S); 10/70; Chorus; School Play; Hon Roll; Stu 9 Wks 86; Chrstms Attndnt Vo-Tech 85; Csmtlgst.

FOX, JENNIFER L; Western Wayne HS; Waymart, PA; (Y); 24/138; Exploring; FBLA; Yrbk Stf; Mgr(s); Var Trk; Hon Roll; NHS; Membrshp Awd Natl Hnr Socty 85; Wrstlng Tm Mgr Awd 85; Grls Trk Tm Awd 85; Intnatl Studs.

FOX, JIM; Shikellamy Area HS; Northumberland, PA; (Y); 43/315; Boy Scts; Sec Church Yth Grp; Concert Band; Mrchg Band; Crs Cntry; Ftbl; Trk; Wrstlng; Cit Awd; God Cntry Awd; Outstndng Musicn 82-83; Ldrshp Awd Boy Scts 85; Sct Yr MBG Legn Post 84; Penn ST U; Bio.

FOX, KATHLEEN; Lakeland HS; Carbondale, PA; (Y); 46/150; FHA; Ski Clb; Stu Cncl; Hon Roll.

FOX, LORI; Schuylkill Haven HS; Schuylkill Haven, PA; (Y); 30/99; Art Clb; German Clb; Pep Clb; Science Clb; SADD; Teachers Aide; Color Guard; Stat Bsktbl; Var Vllybl; Hon Roll; Bio Sci Fair Awd 82-83; Rittners Schl/Flrstry; Flrcltr.

FOX, LORIANNE; Moon SR HS; Corapolis, PA; (Y); French Clb; Hon Roll; Prfct Atten Awd; Duquesne U; Phrmcy.

FOX, MELISSA ANN; Plymouth Whitemarsh HS; Plymouth Mtg, PA; (Y); Hosp Aide; Intnl Clb; Math Clb; Science Clb; Pres VP Temple Yth Grp; Concert Band; Fld Hcky; Lcrss; Cheerleading; Hon Roll; Med.

FOX, MICHELE; Scranton Preparatory Schl; Scranton, PA; (Y); 57/192; Church Yth Grp; Hosp Aide; Chorus; Yrbk Stf; Lit Mag; Hon Roll; Brnz Mdlst Math 84-85; U Scranton; Pre Law.

FOX, SUSAN; Purchase Line HS; Commodore, PA; (Y); 2/100; VP SADD; Concert Band; Trs Jr Cls; Capt Twrlr; High Hon Roll; Hon Roll; Lion Awd; NHS; Church Yth Grp; Hnrs Clb 83-85; Lcl Nwsp Wrtng Awd 84-85; Acadmc All Amer Awds 83-86; IUP; Spnsh Ed.

FOX, TRISHA; Rocky Grove HS; Oil City, PA; (Y); 23/96; Cmnty Wkr; French Clb; School Musical; Yrbk Stf; Rep Soph Cls; Rep Jr Cls; Rep Stu Cncl; JV Cheerleading; Var L Vllybl; High Hon Roll; MVP Vlybl 85-86; Outstndng Acad Achvt Awd 83-84; Psychlgy.

FOX, YOLANDA L; Overbrook HS; Philadelphia, PA; (Y); 16/500; Hosp Aide; Office Aide; Yrbk Ed-Chief; Pres Jr Cls; Pres Sr Cls; Var Bowling; Var Sftbl; Var Vllybl; Wlsly Bk Awd Wlsly Coll; Hmn Rltns Awd Phila Fed Tchrs; Alpha Kappa Alpha Srrty Athltc Ablty; Villanova U; Cvl Engrng.

FOY, AMY; Rocky Grove HS; Franklin, PA; (Y); Var L Bsktbl; Var L Sftbl; JV L Vllybl; NC Coll.

FOY, CHRISTINE; St Basil Acad; Philadelphia, PA; (Y); Church Yth Grp; Computer Clb; French Clb; Trs Soph Cls; Trs Jr Cls; Trs Sr Cls; JV Var Bsktbl; Im Var Socr; Im Var Sftbl; Prfct Atten Awd; Immaculata Coll Acadmc Schlrshp 86; Immaculata Coll; Bus.

FOY, KAREN; St Maria Goretti HS; Philadelphia, PA; (Y); 19/426; Cmnty Wkr; Math Tm; Teachers Aide; Nwsp Rptr; Nwsp Sprt Ed; Nwsp Stf; High Hon Roll; Hon Roll; NHS; Italian Club; Drexel U; Bus Admin.

FOY, LISA; Venango Christian HS; Oil City, PA; (Y); Cmnty Wkr; SADD; Nwsp Stf; Yrbk Stf; JV Var Bsktbl; Var Capt Cheerleading; Stat Wrstlng; High Hon Roll; Hon Roll; NHS; VMCA Teen Actn Bd 85-86; Spec Olympic Vlntr 86; JR Advncd Theology 85-86; Psych.

FOY, MAUREEN; Archbishop Prendergast HS; Lansdowne, PA; (Y); 11/361; Church Yth Grp; Spanish Clb; Orch; Capt Var Swmmng; Hon Roll; NHS; Opt Clb Awd; Prfct Atten Awd; Spanish NHS; Ntl Bus Hnr Sco; Ntl Spnsh Hnr Soc; Swmmng All Catholic; Pres Acad Ftns Awd; U Scranton; Acctng.

FOY, TINA; Venango Christian HS; Oil City, PA; (Y); 20/36; Cmnty Wkr; French Clb; Yrbk Stf; Golf; Var Sftbl; High Hon Roll; Hon Roll; Erie Bus Schl; Exec Sec.

FRAGOMENI, AMY; Penn Hills HS; Pittsburgh, PA; (Y); Eng.

FRALEY, JAMIE; Ringgold HS; Donora, PA; (Y); 2/349; Church Yth Grp; Computer Clb; Pep Clb; Varsity Clb; Church Choir; Stu Cncl; Bsktbl; ICM; Comp Mgmt.

FRALLEY, MONICA; Pocono Mountain HS; Henryville, PA; (Y); Nwsp Stf; Score Keeper; Var Sftbl; Advertsng.

FRAME, GWYNNE E; North Allegheny HS; Pittsburgh, PA; (Y); 45/628; Spanish Clb; Hon Roll; NHS; Prfct Atten Awd; Grad With Hnr 86; Penn ST U; Bus Admin.

FRAMPTON, DEBORAH; Slippery Rock Area HS; Harrisville, PA; (Y); 8/152; Church Yth Grp; Intnl Clb; Drill Tm; Sec Soph Cls; Trs Jr Cls; Sec Sr Cls; Trs Stu Cncl; JV Cheerleading; Var Capt Crs Cntry; Var Capt Trk; Amer Bus Wmns Assn Wolf Crk Chptr Scholar 86; Grove City Coll; Acctng.

FRAMPTON, KAREN L; West Perry HS; Shermans Dale, PA; (Y); VP Spanish Clb; Varsity Clb; Band; Concert Band; Mrchg Band; Yrbk Rptr; Yrbk Stf; Rep Stu Cncl; Trk; Hon Roll; Harrisburg Artgs Fest Poetry Awd 85; Psych.

FRANCAVILLA, JANE; New Hope-Solebury HS; Lahaska, PA; (S); 2/60; Mathletes; Ski Clb; Drill Tm; Frsh Cls; Soph Cls; Jr Cls; Stu Cncl; Fld Hcky; High Hon Roll; Pres NHS.

FRANCE, MARY LOUISE; Highlands SR HS; Tarentum, PA; (Y); Chorus; Prfct Atten Awd; Schltc Achvt Awd 82-86; IN U PA; Art Ed.

FRANCESKI, AMY; Susquehanna Community HS; Thompson, PA; (Y); Var Cheerleading; Stat Trk; Penn ST U; Bus Mgmt.

FRANCHAK, MICHAEL; Richland HS; Wexford, PA; (S); 1/192; Church Yth Grp; Debate Tm; Exploring; Scholastic Bowl; Nwsp Sprt Ed; Rep Stu Cncl; Var L Bsktbl; Var L Ftbl; Var L Trk; High Hon Roll; AIU Vet Med Apprntcshp I & Ii 85-86; Biomed Engrng.

FRANCIA, MICHELE; Yough School District HS; West Newton, PA; (Y); 27/254; Pep Clb; Ski Clb; Spanish Clb; SADD; Chorus; Capt Cheerleading; Pom Pon; Hon Roll; NHS; Sewickley Vly Hosp Schl; Nrsng.

FRANCIS, BRIAN J; Moon Area HS; Coraopolis, PA; (Y); 5/321; Trs Sr Cls; Var L Crs Cntry; Capt Swmmng; Var L Trk; High Hon Roll; JETS Awd; Lion Awd; NHS; Ntl Merit SF; Spkr Gradtn Crmny 86; Cornell U; Arln Pilot.

FRANCK, LORIE; Warwick HS; Lititz, PA; (Y); 102/230; AFS; Church Yth Grp; SADD; Drm Mjr(t); Flag Corp; JV Cheerleading; Trk; Hon Roll; 1st Pl Wmns Clb Art Awd 86; Artwd Dsplyd PA Cptl Leg Cngrsnl Cntst 86; Gld Key Mxd Media 86; Empire Beauty School; Art.

FRANCUS, MIKE; Keystone Oaks HS; Pittsburgh, PA; (Y); 73/268; Trk; Vllybl; Hon Roll; U Of Pittsburgh; Bus Admin.

FRAND, KARA; Upper Dublin HS; Dresher, PA; (Y); 10/300; NHS; Intnl Clb; Temple Yth Grp; Orch; Lit Mag; Rep Stu Cncl; JV Crs Cntry; JV Socr; JV Tennis; JV Trk; Ecolgy Clb Vp, Outdr Educ Chairprsn 85-87; Intnsv Foreign Lang Study 86; Human Rltns Awd 86; Bates; Anthrplgy.

FRANEK, ANN MARIE; Hazleton HS; Hazleton, PA; (Y); 12/377; Leo Clb; Nwsp Bus Mgr; Yrbk Stf; High Hon Roll; NHS; Summa Cum Laude Awd Ltn 86; Ltn Hnr Soc Awd 86; Pres Acdmc Ftns Awd 86; Temple U; Phrmcy.

FRANEK, MARK; Eastern York HS; York, PA; (Y); 6/170; Drama Clb; Ski Clb; Varsity Clb; Pres Sr Cls; Gym; Capt Socr; L Trk; Hon Roll; NHS; Rotary Awd; Duke U; Engrng.

FRANGIONE, PEGGY; Youngsville HS; Russell, PA; (Y); Math Tm; Spanish Clb; Teachers Aide; JV Vllybl; Hon Roll; Eagle Awd 86; Outstndg Prfmnc In Math Leag 86; FL Inst Of Tech; Marine Bio.

FRANJIONE, LYNNETTE; Chartiers Valley HS; Bridgeville, PA; (Y); 30/336; Ski Clb; Acpl Chr; Chorus; Church Choir; School Musical; High Hon Roll; NHS; U Of Pttsbrgh; Math.

FRANK, ANGELA; Warwick HS; Lititz, PA; (Y); Church Yth Grp; Yrbk Stf; Stat Ftbl; Im Vllybl; High Hon Roll; Blmsbrg U; Nrs.

FRANK, AYAL; Taylor Allderdice HS; Pittsburgh, PA; (Y); 82/475; French Clb; Ski Clb; Temple Yth Grp; Var Capt Socr; Hon Roll; Kiwanis Awd; Acad Letter Mntng High Hnr; $1000 Schlrshp-Jewish Educ; Macalester Coll; Internatl Affr.

FRANK, ELLEN; Plymouth Whitemarsh HS; Norristown, PA; (Y); 42/350; VP DECA; Spanish Clb; Teachers Aide; Capt Flag Corp; Mrchg Band; Nwsp Stf; Rep Soph Cls; Mgr(s); High Hon Roll; Jr NHS; Vrsty Ltr Acdmc Achvt 86; Elem Educ.

FRANK, JENNIFER; Cardinal O Hara HS; Media, PA; (Y); Camera Clb; Church Yth Grp; JA; Latin Clb; Office Aide; School Musical; Trk; Millersville U; Erly Chldhd.

FRANK, JIM; Pottsgrove HS; Pottstown, PA; (Y); 46/225; Math Tm; Spanish Clb; Varsity Clb; Capt Wrstlng; Hon Roll.

FRANK, LISA; Chambersburg Area SR HS; Chambersburg, PA; (Y); 134/612; Pres Church Yth Grp; Hosp Aide; JCL; Church Choir; Hon Roll; Hlth Crs Clb Pres 83-84; Cumm Laude Awd Latin 86; Ricks Coll; Pre-Med.

FRANK, LORI A; Central Dauphin East HS; Harrisburg, PA; (Y); 3/251; Am Leg Aux Girls St; Capt Quiz Bowl; Chorus; Jazz Band; Symp Band; Rep Jr Cls; Var Fld Hcky; Var Sftbl; High Hon Roll; NHS; All ST Bnd 86; Hall Fndtn Schlrshp 86; Pres Acad Ftnss Awd 86; Lafayette; Engrng.

FRANK, MELANIE; Kennedy Christian HS; Farrell, PA; (Y); Pep Clb; Spanish Clb; Nwsp Stf; Hon Roll; Duquesne U; Phrmcy.

FRANK, SHERRI; Central Cambria HS; Ebensburg, PA; (Y); 2/210; Key Clb; Science Clb; Ski Clb; Yrbk Stf; Trs Frsh Cls; Sec Soph Cls; Sec Jr Cls; High Hon Roll; Hon Roll.

FRANK, YVONNE; Central Cambria HS; Ebensburg, PA; (S); 8/209; Pres Key Clb; Yrbk Stf; Var L Bsktbl; Var L Trk; NHS.

FRANKENFIELD, BRENDA; Pottsgrove HS; Pottstown, PA; (Y); 10/229; French Clb; Science Clb; Yrbk Stf; Rep Frsh Cls; Rep Jr Cls; JV Fld Hcky; Stat Sftbl; Hon Roll; French Taught Gftd Elem Cls 84-85; Tutors Clb.

FRANKENFIELD, KERRY; Freedon HS; Bethlehem, PA; (Y); 7/392; Pres Church Yth Grp; Acpl Chr; Chorus; Church Choir; Mrchg Band; Orch; NHS; Ntl Merit Ltr; AAUW Scholar 86; Lamp Knowldge 86; U MD; Phrmcy.

FRANKHOUSER, AMY; Conrad Weiser JR-SR HS; Reinholds, PA; (Y); 6/184; Key Clb; Chorus; Mrchg Band; School Musical; Nwsp Stf; Yrbk Stf; Rep Stu Cncl; Mgr(s); High Hon Roll; Hon Roll; Penn ST U Smmr Hnrs Prog 86; PA ST U; Bus.

FRANKHOUSER, MARK; Philipsburg Osceola Area HS; Philipsburg, PA; (Y); 34/250; Chess Clb; Pres Computer Clb; Rep Stu Cncl; Hon Roll; Prfct Atten Awd; Chess Clb Mem 83-84; Comp Clb Pres 83-84; Soc Of Distgshd Amer HS Stu 84-86; Elec Engrng.

FRANKLIN, ANTHONY; Coatesville Area SR HS; Coatesville, PA; (Y); 107/534; FBLA; Spanish Clb; Nwsp Rptr; Yrbk Stf; Off Soph Cls; Off Sr Cls; Stu Cncl; Trk; Hon Roll; Prfct Atten Awd; Outstdng AFJROTC Cadet 85-86; Outstdng In NAACP 86; Graduated With A Gold Tassel 86; Brandywine Coll; Hotel/Rstrnt.

FRANKLIN, BEN; Northern Cambria HS; Barnesboro, PA; (Y); Church Choir; Rep Jr Cls; Var JV Ftbl; Var Trk; Var Wt Lftg; Hon Roll; Indian U Of Pa; Biology.

FRANKLIN, LISA; Ringgold HS; Finleyville, PA; (Y); Chorus; Nwsp Stf; Resrvtnst.

FRANKO, MICHELLE; Tunkhannock Area HS; Tunkhannock, PA; (S); 14/320; Art Clb; Sec Church Yth Grp; Sec German Clb; VP Library Aide; Rep Jr Cls; Rep Sr Cls; Hon Roll; NHS; Wilkes Coll; Dr Optometry.

FRANKOSKY, MARK; Shad-Central City HS; Central City, PA; (Y); 12/63; Boy Scts; Church Yth Grp; Varsity Clb; Variety Show; Nwsp Sprt Ed; Var Bsbl; Var Bsktbl; Hon Roll; Prfct Atten Awd; PA ST; Bus.

FRANKOVIC, PHILIP; North Hills HS; Pittsburgh, PA; (Y); 25/510; High Hon Roll; Hon Roll; Prfct Atten Awd; Nomntd Natl Hon Scty 84-86; U Pittsburgh; Comp Sci.

FRANKOVICH, LAURI; Shenango HS; New Castle, PA; (Y); 19/106; French Clb; Office Aide; Drill Tm; Sec Frsh Cls; Sec Soph Cls; Sec Jr Cls; Sec Sr Cls; Rep Stu Cncl; Hon Roll; NHS; Phrmcy.

FRANKOWSKI, ALBERTA; Abington Heights HS; Clarks Summit, PA; (Y); Pres Sec Radio Clb; Ski Clb; VP Rep Stu Cncl; JV Socr; Stu Aid Fund Mildred Mumford Scholar 86; Civic Lg Art Dept Awd 86; Schl Brd & Supt Ldrshp Awd 86; Kutztown U; Cmmnctn Desgn.

FRANKS, DIANE; Bellefonte Area HS; Bellefonte, PA; (Y); Varsity Clb; Chorus; Capt Flag Corp; Trs Jr Cls; Pres Stu Cncl; Bsktbl; Hon Roll; Ski Clb; Band; Powder Puff Ftbl; Ms Bellefnte 86-87; Al Star 1st Tm Mntn Leag Bsktbl 85-86; Stu Forum Rep 85-86; Bus.

FRANKS, KEVIN; Kiski Area SR HS; New Kensington, PA; (Y); Computer Clb; Band; Chorus; Concert Band; Jazz Band; Mrchg Band; Nwsp Rptr; Swmmng; S R Ventura Awd 86; Elctrncs Tech.

FRANKS, NANCY LYNN; North Allegheny SR HS; Allison Pk, PA; (Y); 134/630; French Clb; Y-Teens; Orch; Var Gym; Var Trk; Hon Roll; Purdue U; Pre Law.

FRANTY, SUZANNE; Uniontown Area HS; Uniontown, PA; (Y); 9/323; VP Ski Clb; Spanish Clb; SADD; Yrbk Bus Mgr; VP Sr Cls; Stu Cncl; Cheerleading; NHS; Pres Schlr; Spanish NHS; Coal Qn Rep 85; Uniontwn Clg Clb Schlrshp Awd 86; Northeastern U; Intl Bus.

FRANTZ, DEBRA D; East Stroudsburg HS; E Stroudsburg, PA; (Y); 46/215; VP Exploring; Sec Stat Bsbl; Var Capt Cheerleading; Mgr(s); Var Trk; Hon Roll; Prfct Atten Awd; Htl/Rest Mgmt.

FRANTZ, MICHELE; Donegal HS; Mount Joy, PA; (Y); 8/166; Band; Concert Band; Mrchg Band; School Play; Symp Band; Trk; High Hon Roll; Hon Roll; NHS; Math.

FRANTZ, PAM; Elizabethtown Area HS; Elizabethtown, PA; (Y); 64/250; Camera Clb; Church Yth Grp; Mrchg Band; Powder Puff Ftbl; Sftbl; Twrlr; Vllybl; Psych.

FRANTZ, SONIA; Parkland HS; Slatington, PA; (Y); 50/459; Teachers Aide; Im Trk; High Hon Roll; Hon Roll; Prfct Atten Awd; Leukemia Type-A-Thon Cert Of Apprectn 86; Travel Agnt.

FRANZIS, PETER; Dover Greg SR HS; Dover, PA; (Y); Camera Clb; Church Yth Grp; Exploring; Nwsp Phtg; Nwsp Stf; Yrbk Phtg; Yrbk Rptr; Yrbk Stf; Tennis; Hon Roll; Law Explorers VP 85-86; Church Yth Gp Treas 84-85; Marine Res; Bus Law.

FRASCELLA, ANTHONY; Cardinal O Hara HS; Drexel Hill, PA; (Y); 12/772; Pres Computer Clb; French Clb; JA; Mathletes; Capt NFL; Speech Tm; School Play; Var Golf; NHS; Opt Clb Awd; Rcgntn In Ntl Frnch Cntst 86; Serra Clb Altr Boy Awd 83; Dvn Prep Spch Cntst 83; Mth.

FRASE, CHRISTINE; Central York SR HS; York, PA; (Y); Am Leg Aux Girls St; French Clb; Ski Clb; Band; Concert Band; Mrchg Band; Symp Band; Yrbk Stf; Sec Rep Frsh Cls; Sec Rep Soph Cls.

FRASER, BILL; Knoch HS; Butler, PA; (Y); Church Yth Grp; Letterman Clb; Science Clb; Bsktbl; Ftbl; Trk; Hon Roll; 1st Pl Rgnl JR & ST JR Aci Acad 84; Bus Adm.

FRASER, EVAN; Strath Haven HS; Swarthmore, PA; (Y); Chess Clb; Hon Roll.

FRASER, MELISSA; Plum SR HS; New Kensington, PA; (Y); Spanish Clb; School Play; Stage Crew; Yrbk Stf; Lit Mag; Hon Roll; 1st Pl Cltrl Arts Awd Lit 83-84; 2nd Pl Awd Penn ST U Art Cntst 85-86; Art.

FRATANGELI, WILLIAM; Middletown HS; Middletown, PA; (Y); 14/196; VP FCA; Trs Chorus; Concert Band; Mrchg Band; Yrbk Stf; Stu Cncl; Tennis; NHS; Pres Schlr; Rotary Awd; John Hall Schlrshp 86; Rotary Schlrshp 2nd Pl 86; Harrisburg Area CC; Bus Adm.

FRATTAROLE, LISA; Lancaster Catholic HS; Lancaster, PA; (Y); 30/237; Church Yth Grp; Pep Clb; Service Clb; JV Bsktbl; JV Fld Hcky; JV Mgr(s); Score Keeper; Sftbl; Hon Roll; NHS; U DE; Bus.

FRATTINI, NICOLE; Nazareth Acad; Philadelphia, PA; (Y); Varsity Clb; Sec Frsh Cls; Sec Jr Cls; Var Bowling; Hon Roll; Nrsng.

FRATTONE, MICHAEL; St John Neumann HS; Philadelphia, PA; (Y); 3/338; Letterman Clb; Mathletes; Pres Science Clb; Varsity Clb; Nwsp Rptr; Yrbk Stf; Bsktbl; Var L Tennis; High Hon Roll; NHS; Hghst Scr Schlstc Math Assoc Cntst 85-86; U Of PA; Bus Mngmnt.

FRAZEE, DENISE; Burgettstown JR SR HS; Burgettstown, PA; (Y); 20/176; French Clb; Sec FBLA; Chorus; Yrbk Stf; Hon Roll; Jr NHS; NHS; Vp Of Wrestlerettes 85-86; U Of Pittsburgh; Bus.

FRAZER, CHRISTIN; Homer Center HS; Homer City, PA; (Y); 7/96; VP Sec Church Yth Grp; VP Pres Library Aide; VP Soph Cls; VP Jr Cls; High Hon Roll; Jr NHS; NHS; French Clb; Varsity Clb; Yrbk Stf; HOBY Ldrshp Awd 85; Summr Happening Marine Bio 85; PA JR Acad Sci 1st Pl Regnl & ST 83-85.

FRAZIER, LORI; Trinity HS; Washington, PA; (Y); Art Clb; Pep Band; German Clb; Pep Clb; School Play; Nwsp Phtg; Hon Roll.

FRAZIER, MICHELLE; Lakeland HS; Dalton, PA; (S); 20/153; Church Yth Grp; FHA; Girl Scts; Hon Roll; NHS; Prfct Atten Awd; G S Silver Awd 83; Med Asst.

FRAZIER, SUSAN; Mt Pleasant Area SR HS; Mt Pleasant, PA; (Y); 24/247; Church Yth Grp; Drama Clb; GAA; Office Aide; SADD; VP Chorus; Nwsp Rptr; Nwsp Stf; Var JV Var Bsktbl; Mat Maids; Vrsty Schlstc Awd; Cnty Chrus; News Ed; CA U PA; Psych.

FRECH, TIM; Marion Center SR HS; Home, PA; (Y); 38/170; VICA; Band; Hon Roll; Jr NHS; Welding Shop Sctry & V P 85-86; Music.

FREDERICK, JOSEPH B; Owen J Roberts HS; Spring City, PA; (Y); JA; Key Clb; Band; Chorus; Concert Band; Mrchg Band; School Musical; School Play; Crs Cntry; Trk; Millersville U; Comm.

FREDERICK, KIMBERLY M; Kiski Area HS; New Kensington, PA; (Y); Church Yth Grp; Letterman Clb; Math Clb; Rep Frsh Cls; Rep Soph Cls; Rep Jr Cls; Rep Sr Cls; Rep Stu Cncl; L Trk; High Hon Roll; IN U Of PA; Fash Merch.

FREDERICK, KRISTOFER; Central Dauphin East HS; Enhaut Steelton, PA; (Y); 16/286; Church Yth Grp; Debate Tm; Political Wkr; Golf; Trk; High Hon Roll; Jr NHS; NHS; Rotary Awd; Spanish Clb; Acdmc Stu Mnth 86; Hist.

FREDERICK, LISA; Central HS; Martinsburg, PA; (Y); 12/200; Church Yth Grp; FNA; Pres Girl Scts; Pres JA; Nwsp Rptr; Nwsp Stf; Rep Stu Cncl; Im Vllybl; NEDT Awd; 1st Pl PA JR Acad Sci ST 85; PA ST U; Microbio.

FREDERICK, RHONDA; Brockway Area HS; Brockport, PA; (Y); Art Clb; Flag Corp; Mrchg Band; Wt Lftg; Hon Roll; Schlstc Awd 85; Du Bois Bus Coll; Para Legl.

FREDERICKS, JOHN; Nativity Bvm HS; Pottsville, PA; (Y); 1/97; Debate Tm; NFL; Pres Stu Cncl; Stat Bsktbl; Bausch & Lomb Sci Awd; High Hon Roll; NHS; Voice Dem Awd; PA HS Spch Leag ST Radio Nws Chmpn 86; 1st Awd Captl Area Sci Fair-Microbio 86; Chem.

FREDERICKSON JR, CHARLES H; Mt Pleasant Area HS; Latrobe, PA; (Y); 42/248; Pres Church Yth Grp; Latin Clb; Letterman Clb; Varsity Clb; Var Capt Bsktbl; Var L Trk; High Hon Roll; Pres Schlr; Var L Golf; Capt Im Socr; Westmoreland Cnty Coaches Assn Scholar 86; Gld Mdl & Cnty Rcrd 4x100 Relay 86; 1st L Spn Hum Day 86; CA U PA; Bus Adm.

FREDERICKSON, JULIE; Grace Christian Schl; Sinking Spring, PA; (S); 1/18; Hosp Aide; Teachers Aide; Chorus; Orch; School Play; High Hon Roll; Church Yth Grp; Church Choir; Cit Awd; Natl Piano Plyrs Guild 84-85; Envrnmntl Olympcs Dist 85; Mid Atlantic Chrstn Schl Fin Arts Fest 85; Temple U; Law.

FREDERIKSEN, ERIK; Hempfield HS; Lancaster, PA; (Y); 3/400; Key Clb; Teachers Aide; Variety Show; Socr; Hon Roll; Stu Of Mnth-Rotary; UVA; Pre-Med.

FREE, APRIL; Greensburg Central Catholic HS; Penn, PA; (Y); Nwsp Stf; VP Soph Cls; VP Jr Cls; VP Sr Cls; Rep Stu Cncl; Var Capt Cheerleading; Trk; High Hon Roll; Hon Roll; NHS.

FREE, SCOTT; Dover Area HS; Dover, PA; (Y); 23/276; Church Yth Grp; FFA; Socr; Trk; High Hon Roll; Hon Roll; German Certfct 85; Awd Lincoln Intermdt Unit Tutoring 83; Pre-Med.

FREE, SONYA; Fort Cherry HS; Mc Donald, PA; (Y); Ski Clb; Varsity Clb; Nwsp Phtg; Nwsp Stf; Rep Stu Cncl; Mgr Bsktbl; Var L Sftbl; Hon Roll; Phys Fit 84-86; Southeastern Acad; Travlng.

FREEBERRY, JEANNINE; Interboro HS; Norwood, PA; (S); 5/265; Sec Pres AFS; JCL; Sec Key Clb; Hst Latin Clb; Off Jr Cls; Off Sr Cls; Stu Cncl; JV Bsktbl; JV Var Fld Hcky; High Hon Roll; Phila Coll Phrmcy/Sci; Phrmcy.

FREED, DARIN; Salisbury HS; Allentown, PA; (Y); Church Yth Grp; Band; Concert Band; Mrchg Band; Rptr Nwsp Phtg; Yrbk Phtg; Trk; Archtctrl Drwng.

FREED, KAREN; Boyertown SR HS; Gilbertsvl, PA; (Y); FBLA; Library Aide; Flag Corp; Cit Awd; Hon Roll; Prfct Atten Awd; Trvl Consltnt.

FREED, KATHY; Cumberland Valley HS; Carlisle, PA; (Y); 4-H; Band; Color Guard; Mrchg Band; Symp Band; Lockhave U; Jrnlsm.

FREED, MICHAEL; Lincoln HS; Ellwood City, PA; (Y); 61/161; Computer Clb; German Clb; Nwsp Rptr; Bowling.

FREED, MICHELE LYNN; York Catholic HS; York, PA; (Y); 3/169; Cmnty Wkr; Chorus; School Musical; School Play; Nwsp Stf; Yrbk Ed-Chief; Yrbk Stf; Hon Roll; NHS; Opt Clb Awd; Erly Chldhd Educ.

FREEDMAN, KEVIN; Upper Dublin HS; Ft Washington, PA; (Y); 4/310; Varsity Clb; Rep Soph Cls; Rep Jr Cls; Rep Sr Cls; Rep Stu Cncl; Var Capt Crs Cntry; Var Trk; Var Wrstlng; NHS; MD.

FREEH, LISA; Palisades HS; Revere, PA; (Y); 30/150; Pres Church Yth Grp; Pres Chorus; Pres Madrigals; Var Capt Tennis; NHS; Rep Frsh Cls; Rep Soph Cls; Rep Jr Cls; Vcl Music Ldrshp Awd 86; Prsdntl Acad Ftnss Awd 86; Enns Mst Vlble Plyr 84-85; Northampton Cmnty Coll; Den Hyg.

FREELAND, THERESA; Susquenita HS; Duncannon, PA; (S); Leo Clb; Spanish Clb; Yrbk Stf; VP Soph Cls; VP Jr Cls; Stu Cncl; Var L Sftbl; Hon Roll; NEDT Awd; Distinguished Hnrs.

FREEMAN, CHERYL; Mount Pleasant Area HS; Mt Pleasant, PA; (Y); 66/246; DECA; Sec 4-H; French Clb; Ski Clb; Band; Concert Band; Mrchg Band; Mat Maids; Vllybl; Hon Roll; Bus Mgmt.

FREEMAN, DIANNE; Harbor Creek HS; Erie, PA; (Y); 16/289; Church Yth Grp; French Clb; Office Aide; Teachers Aide; Church Choir; Cit Awd; High Hon Roll; Hon Roll; NHS; PA ST U; Ed.

FREEMAN JR, DONALD EARL; Clearfield Area HS; Olanta, PA; (Y); 25/296; Boy Scts; Pres Church Yth Grp; Key Clb; SADD; Church Choir; Rep Stu Cncl; JV Ftbl; Cit Awd; Hon Roll; Pres Adcmdc Ftns Awd 86; U Ptsbrgh; Phrmcy.

FREEMAN, GLORIA; Hickory HS; Hermitage, PA; (Y); Aud/Vis; Camera Clb; Church Yth Grp; Dance Clb; Radio Clb; Teachers Aide; VICA; Nwsp Ed-Chief; Yrbk Stf; Rep Jr Cls; Outstndg Clss Awd 86; IUP; Vo-Tech Instrctr.

FREEMAN, KENNETH; Freedom HS; Bethlehem, PA; (Y); 24/450; Var Science Clb; Band; Chorus; Concert Band; Jazz Band; Mrchg Band; Orch; Symp Band; High Hon Roll; NHS; PA Dist Band 86; U Of MI; Med.

FREEMAN, PEGGY; Greencastle-Antrim HS; Greencastle, PA; (Y); 20/186; Acpl Chr; Band; Chorus; Church Choir; Concert Band; Mrchg Band; School Play; Swing Chorus; Nwsp Stf; High Hon Roll; Legal Stu Schlrshp 86; Musician Awd; Hagerstown Bus Coll; Legal Assi.

FREEMAN, RANDY A; Freedom HS; Bethlehem, PA; (Y); 2/444; Chess Clb; Math Tm; Band; Jazz Band; Orch; NHS; Sal; Model UN; Concert Band; Pep Band; Cngrs/Bundstg Yth Exchng Full Schlrshp 85-86; Top Stu-Estrn PA Rgn/Amercn Math Exm 85; Elctrcl Engrng.

FREEMAN, RUSS; Taylor Allderdice HS; Pittsburgh, PA; (Y); JA; Var JV Bsktbl; Var Ftbl; Bus.

FREEMAN, STEPHANIE; George Washington HS; Philadelphia, PA; (Y); 74/769; Drama Clb; Math Clb; Office Aide; School Play; Stage Crew; Hon Roll; Mu Alp Tht; NHS; Pres Schlr; HOBY Rep; Columbia U; Pol Sci.

FREER, KURT; Northeast Catholic HS; Philadelphia, PA; (Y); 38/409; Boys Clb Am; Boy Scts; Cmnty Wkr; VP Exploring; Latin Clb; Science Clb; High Hon Roll; NHS; Med.

FREESE JR, JOHN H; Pottstown HS; Pottstown, PA; (Y); 17/200; Church Yth Grp; Stu Cncl; Var Bsbl; Var Ftbl; Var Wrstlng; Cit Awd; Hon Roll; NHS; Pres Schlr; Riggs Awd Top Schlr Athl Of PHS 86; Penn ST U; Elec Engr.

FREILICH, MARGARET; Upper Merion Area HS; Wayne, PA; (Y); 16/332; Aud/Vis; Math Tm; JV Fld Hcky; JV Socr; Var Capt Swmmng; High Hon Roll; NHS; Ntl Merit Ltr; Mst Vlbl Swmr 86; Mst Imprvd Swmr 85; Mst Imprvd Sccr Plyr 85; Sci.

FREILING, PATRICIA; Nazareth Acad; Philadelphia, PA; (Y); 23/125; Dance Clb; French Clb; School Musical; VP Jr Cls; Cheerleading; Im Vllybl; High Hon Roll; Hon Roll; Pre-Law.

FRENCH, CARLA; Connellsville Area SR HS; Connellsville, PA; (Y); Church Yth Grp; GAA; Library Aide; VICA; Chorus; JV Var Bsktbl; Sftbl; Var Trk; Var Vllybl; Hon Roll; PBA; Csmtlgy.

FRENCH, JENNIFER SUSAN; Nazareth Acad HS; Philadelphia, PA; (Y); Cmnty Wkr; Drama Clb; GAA; PAVAS; Thesps; Chorus; Church Choir; Drm Mjr(t); School Musical; School Play; C Ellis Schlrshp $4000; Drama Awds 84-86; MVP Sfbl Awd 83-86; Piccoli Allstar Team Comm Team 83-86; Eng/Drama.

FRENCH, JOHN; Trinity HS; New Curberland, PA; (Y); Drama Clb; Spanish Clb; School Play; Rep Frsh Cls; Pres Soph Cls; Im Bsktbl; Var Ftbl; Im Sftbl; JV Trk; Hon Roll; Bus.

FRENCH, ROSEMARIE; Little Flower Catholic HS; Philadelphia, PA; (Y); 104/395; Hosp Aide; Drill Tm; Rep Stu Cncl; Hon Roll; Prfct Atten Awd; PA ST; Comp Pgmr.

FRENCH, SUZANNE; Moon HS; Aliquippa, PA; (Y); 33/304; Church Yth Grp; Exploring; Key Clb; Chorus; Trs Frsh Cls; Rep Soph Cls; Rep Jr Cls; Rep Stu Cncl; Var L Swmmng; Hon Roll; Liberal Arts Coll.

FRENGEL, CHRISTINE L; Butler SR HS; Butler, PA; (Y); 11/731; Church Yth Grp; Cmnty Wkr; Exploring; French Clb; Math Clb; Pep Clb; Chorus; High Hon Roll; NHS; Presdntl Acadmc Ftns Awd 85-86; Grove Cty Coll Schlrshp 86; JR Natl Hnr Socty 83-84; Grove City Coll; Comp Systms.

FRESCH, STACY; Plum SR HS; Pittsburgh, PA; (Y); 12/420; French Clb; Varsity Clb; Var Bsktbl; Var Capt Sftbl; Var Vllybl; High Hon Roll; NHS; Vrsty Ltrs Sftbll 84-86; Vrsty Ltrs Bsktbl 85-86; Dickinson Coll; Bus.

FRESE, WILLIAM G; Abraham Lincoln HS; Philadelphia, PA; (Y); 11/419; Aud/Vis; Debate Tm; Drama Clb; Pres French Clb; Math Tm; School Play; Yrbk Bus Mgr; Yrbk Stf; Capt Crs Cntry; High Hon Roll; Arnld Jurin Memrl Awd-Excellnc-Math 86; Frgn Lang Dept Awd-Excellnc-Frnch 86; PA Math Leag Awd 86; West Chester U; Crmnl Jstc.

FRESHMAN, KARLA; Waynesboro SR HS; Waynesboro, PA; (Y); 45/350; Sec VP Church Yth Grp; Chorus; Boy Scts; Concert Band; Mrchg Band; School Musical; Swing Chorus; High Hon Roll; NHS; Bnd Drctrs Awd 84; Dlgt Natnl Brethren Cnfrnc 86; Cnty Bnd 83-86.

FRETZ, REBECCA; Pen Argyl HS; Nazareth, PA; (Y); 47/129; Pres Church Yth Grp; Band; Concert Band; Mrchg Band; Mgr Stu Cncl; Chorus; SR Rep Pittsburgh Conf Stu Cncl 85; E Strudsburg; Nrsg.

FREUDENBERG, SUSANNE; Greater Latrobe SR HS; Greensburg, PA; (Y); AFS; Exploring; JA; Band; Chorus; High Hon Roll; Hon Roll; NHS; Badreichenhall; Hotel Mgmt.

FREUDERBERGER, JULI; Freedom HS; Bethlehem, PA; (Y); 189/465; Hosp Aide; Intnl Clb; Pep Clb; Band; Concert Band; Mrchg Band; Bio.

FREW, MARY; Minersville Area JR SR HS; Zerbe Tremont, PA; (Y); 28/116; French Clb; FBLA; Red Cross Aide; SADD; Teachers Aide; Acpl Chr; VP Chorus; School Musical; School Play; Yrbk Bus Mgr; Minersville Area Schlrshp Fnd 86; Bloomsburg U; Educ.

FREW, MICHAEL; Minersville Area HS; Newtown, PA; (Y); 26/113; French Clb; FBLA; Pres SADD; School Musical; Nwsp Phtg; Nwsp Rptr; Nwsp Stf; Hon Roll; NEDT Awd; Rep Hugh Obrian Yth Fndtn 85; Rstrnt Mngmnt.

FREY, BRADLEY; Elk County Christian HS; Ridgway, PA; (Y); 19/87; Boy Scts; Library Aide; Ski Clb; Trk; Hon Roll; Dntst.

FREY, COBY; Dover Area HS; Dover, PA; (Y); Sec Intnl Clb; Chorus; Concert Band; Mrchg Band; Nwsp Rptr; Ed Nwsp Stf; Pre-Law.

FREY, JENNIFER; Mmi Preparatory Schl; Sugarloaf, PA; (S); Church Yth Grp; Science Clb; Ski Clb; Church Choir; Nwsp Rptr; Var Crs Cntry; Var Sftbl; Hon Roll; NEDT Awd; Church Yth Grp; PA Acad Sci 1st Pl Regnl ST Comptn 85-86; Poem Publshd Reflctn Mag 86.

FREY, KATHRYN L; Newport JR SR HS; Newport, PA; (S); 2/112; Chorus; School Musical; Gym; High Hon Roll; Sec NHS; Sal; Lebanon Vly Coll Yth Schlr Bio; Tri-M 85-86; Hghst Avg Achvt Bio; Hghst Avg Achvt Engl; IN U PA; Early Childhd Ed.

FREY, MARC; Parkland HS; Allentown, PA; (Y); 156/459; Trk; Wt Lftg; Fitness Team 85-86; Geologist.

FREY, PASCHA; South Williamsport Area HS; S Williamsport, PA; (Y); 12/150; Hosp Aide; Hst Key Clb; Hst Leo Clb; Ski Clb; Spanish Clb; Band; Variety Show; Trk; High Hon Roll; Hon Roll; Penn ST U; Cmmnctns.

FRICK JR, E JAMES; Central Bucks H S East; Doylestown, PA; (Y); 17/473; Am Leg Boys St; Hosp Aide; Pres Frsh Cls; Pres Sr Cls; Off Stu Cncl; JV Trk; Cit Awd; DAR Awd; Hon Roll; Jr NHS; Pres Acadmc Ftns Awd 86; Muhlenberg Coll; Bio.

FRICKANISH, MARK; Lincoln HS; Ellwood City, PA; (Y); Boy Scts; Camera Clb; Exploring; Spanish Clb; Hon Roll; Prfct Atten Awd; Acad Achvt Awd 84.

FRICKERT, TAMI; Northampton Area SR HS; Bath, PA; (S); AFS; Church Yth Grp; DECA; FBLA; Speech Tm; Chorus; High Hon Roll; Hon Roll; PA DECA ST Sec 86; 6th-Apprl & Accssrs DEC Dist Comptn 86; 3rd-Pblc Spkng FBLA Rgn Comptn 86; Fshn Merch.

FRIDAY, EDWARD; Blacklick Valley HS; Nanty Glo, PA; (S); 2/80; Chess Clb; Computer Clb; Pep Clb; Red Cross Aide; VP Band; VP Concert Band; High Hon Roll; NHS; IUP; Mth.

FRIDAY, ERIN; Downingtown SR HS; Exton, PA; (Y); 75/500; Art Clb; Church Yth Grp; French Clb; Library Aide; Office Aide; Chorus; JV Fld Hcky; Mat Maids; Hon Roll; Kutztown U PA; Cmrcl Art.

FRIDAY, PATTI; Central Dauphin HS; Harrisburg, PA; (Y); 61/355; Church Yth Grp; Key Clb; Varsity Clb; Chorus; Off Jr Cls; Var Tennis; Im Vllybl; Hon Roll; Pittsburgh; Phrmcy.

FRIDRICK, KATHY; Western Beaver JR SR HS; Midland, PA; (Y); Church Yth Grp; Drama Clb; FHA; Nwsp Stf; Yrbk Stf; High Hon Roll; NHS.

FRIEDE, SARAH; Bishop Kenrick HS; Norristown, PA; (Y); 14/292; French Clb; Red Cross Aide; Science Clb; Service Clb; Color Guard; School Musical; Nwsp Rptr; Hon Roll; NHS; Ntl Merit Ltr; Soc Studies Awd 84-85; Adv Sci Session Aide 86; Yth Am Pol Sys 86.

FRIEDE, TAMARA; Blue Ridge HS; Great Bend, PA; (Y); Church Yth Grp; French Clb; Pep Clb; Band; Chorus; Concert Band; Mrchg Band; Pep Band; School Play; High Hon Roll; Hnr Roll; Ctznshp Awd.

FRIEDLINE, ERIC; Somerset HS; Somerset, PA; (Y); 6/231; Debate Tm; DECA; French Clb; JA; Letterman Clb; Math Clb; Math Tm; Q&S; Quiz Bowl; Scholastic Bowl; Ftbl & Bsbl Awds Jaycees Awd Stu Councilelks Fndtn Awd JR Achvt Varsity Awd Schltc Quiz Awd; Penn ST; Pre-Med.

FRIEDMAN, ROBERT; Bethel Park SR HS; Bethel Pk, PA; (Y); 50/525; German Clb; Rep Stu Cncl; L Var Ftbl; Var Trk; L Var Wrstlng; High Hon Roll; JETS Awd; US Naval Acad; Elec Engrng.

FRIEDRICH, ANN; Highlands SR HS; Natrona Hts, PA; (Y); Intnl Clb; Library Aide; Office Aide; Nwsp Ed-Chief; Nwsp Rptr; Nwsp Stf; Jr NHS; Prfct Atten Awd; Gld Achvt Awds A Avg 83-86; Point Park Coll; Jrnlsm.

FRIEND, ERIC; Chambersburg Area HS; Chambersburg, PA; (Y); 48/651; Pres Church Yth Grp; Letterman Clb; NFL; Var L Trk; Sports Med.

FRIEND, KELLY; Mapletown HS; Bobtown, PA; (Y); 16/80; Aud/Vis; Cmnty Wkr; FTA; Girl Scts; Library Aide; Band; Chorus; Color Guard; Mrchg Band; Score Keeper; W Virginia U; Speec Pathology.

FRIES, DEBBIE; Mc Guffey HS; Washington, PA; (Y); Art Clb; Math Clb; Band; Concert Band; Mrchg Band; Pep Band; Symp Band; Swmmng; Hon Roll; Typng Awd 86; Art Inst Of Ptsbrgh; Cmrcl Art.

FRISBIE, CAROLYN; East Stroudsburg HS; E Stroudsburg, PA; (Y); 18/190; Band; Var Sftbl; NHS; Church Yth Grp; Concert Band; Mrchg Band; Pep Band; High Hon Roll; Hon Roll; Hnrs Bnqt 84-86; Accntng.

FRISCH, JOHN; Northwestern HS; Germansville, PA; (Y); 24/169; Ski Clb; Rep Stu Cncl; Var Bsbl; Var Ftbl; Hon Roll; NHS; Acdmc All Amer 85-86.

FRISCHAUF, KAREN; Bishop Mc Cort HS; Johnstown, PA; (Y); NFL; Chorus; School Play; High Hon Roll; NHS; Drama Clb; Hosp Aide; Ski Clb; Speech Tm; School Musical; Exchnge Club Yth Month Awd 86; U Pittsburgh; Nrsng.

FRISHKORN, SAM; Seneca Valley HS; Zelienople, PA; (Y); Church Yth Grp; Drama Clb; Ski Clb; School Play; Stage Crew; Variety Show; Nwsp Phtg; Coach Actv; Mgr(s); Score Keeper; Doctor.

FRISINA, ANTHONY; Fort Le Boeuf HS; Waterford, PA; (Y); #43 In Class; French Clb; Stu Cncl; Var L Bsbl; Var Capt Bsktbl; Im Crs Cntry; Im Vllybl; Hon Roll; Sprts Med.

FRISKO, DUSTINE; Hempfield SR HS; Hannastown, PA; (Y); 4-H; French Clb; Ski Clb; Chorus; Mrchg Band; Rep Frsh Cls; High Hon Roll; Hon Roll; Jr NHS; NHS; Data Procsng.

FRITH, JENNIFER; Spring Ford HS; Royersford, PA; (S); 20/242; Trs Church Yth Grp; VP French Clb; Yrbk Stf; Stu Cncl; Hon Roll; Jr NHS; NHS; Frnch Lang Awd 85; Estrn Mennonite Coll; Pre-Med.

FRITZ, BETH; Lampeter-Strasburg HS; Lancaster, PA; (Y); Church Yth Grp; Trs Thesps; Varsity Clb; Chorus; Church Choir; Madrigals; School Musical; Trs Jr Cls; Rep Stu Cncl; Capt Cheerleading; Engl Educ.

FRITZ, CATHLEEN M; Vincentian HS; Pittsburgh, PA; (Y); French Clb; Math Clb; Service Clb; Trs Chorus; School Musical; School Play; Stage Crew; Nwsp Rptr; Var Sftbl; Cit Awd; Louis Caplan Hmntrn Awd 86; Cert Of Apprctn Vlntr Srvcs 84-85; Englsh Effrt Awd 86; Franco Beauty Acad; Csmtlgy.

FRITZ, DAVID; Warwick HS; Lititz, PA; (Y); 59/256; Boy Scts; Pres Exploring; FFA; Stage Crew; Lit Mag; Crs Cntry; Trk; High Hon Roll; Hon Roll; Fairleigh Dickinson U; Bus Admi.

FRITZ, DAWN; Brandyvwine Heights HS; Mertztown, PA; (Y); Camp Fr Inc; Church Yth Grp; Hosp Aide; Band; Chorus; Church Choir; Concert Band; Jazz Band; Mrchg Band; L Bsktbl; Centenary Coll; Elem Tchng.

FRITZ JR, G ROBERT; Cumberland Valley HS; Camp Hill, PA; (Y); 195/550; Boy Scts; Church Yth Grp; Spanish Clb; Chorus; Concert Band; Mrchg Band; Im Badmtn; Im Ftbl; JV Trk; Im Vllybl; Mltry Sci.

FRITZ, J DOUGLAS; Hughesville HS; Benton, PA; (Y); 4/130; Pres Church Yth Grp; 4-H; Ski Clb; Trs Varsity Clb; Rep Stu Cncl; Capt Bsbl; Var L Ftbl; High Hon Roll; Pres NHS; Slvr Medlst Wrld Champ Odessey Of Mind 84; 4-H ST Arch Champ Tm Membr 84; 4-H ST Air Pistl Champ 85.

FRITZ, KELLY E; North Hills HS; Pittsburgh, PA; (Y); JA; Key Clb; Ski Clb; Yrbk Stf; Stu Cncl; Bsktbl; Cheerleading; Trk; Vllybl; Hon Roll; PA ST U; Bus.

FRITZ, LISA; St Hubert HS For Girls; Philadelphia, PA; (Y); Cmnty Wkr; French Clb; Service Clb; Chorus; Orch; School Musical; Variety Show; Yrbk Stf; NHS; Physcl Thrpy.

FRITZ, MARC; North Star HS; Stoystown, PA; (Y); Church Yth Grp; Hon Roll; Lwyr.

FRITZ, TED P; Indiana Area HS; Indiana, PA; (Y); 56/335; Am Leg Boys St; Ski Clb; Spanish Clb; Rep Frsh Cls; VP L Trk; Hon Roll; NEDT Awd; Opt Clb Awd; Pre-Law.

FRITZLEY, JIM; West Allegheny HS; Imperial, PA; (Y); Spanish Clb; High Hon Roll; Hon Roll; Anderson Clg; Bus Admin.

FROCK, SCOTT; South Western HS; Hanover, PA; (Y); 16/255; Church Yth Grp; Computer Clb; Science Clb; Chorus; Mrchg Band; Symp Band; Kiwanis Awd; Lion Awd; NHS; Rotary Awd; De Vry Tech Inst; Comp Sci.

FROCK, TONY; York Area Vo-Tech; Spring Grove, PA; (Y); High Hon Roll; Hon Roll; Auto Mech.

FROEHLICH, ANNETTE; Greater Johnstown HS; Johnstown, PA; (Y); German Clb; Sec Key Clb; Math Clb; Chorus; Yrbk Stf; High Hon Roll; Hon Roll; NHS; Acad All-Amer 86.

FROGGATT, RORY; Moniteau HS; W Sunbury, PA; (Y); 7/140; Ski Clb; Spanish Clb; Stage Crew; Sec Soph Cls; Bsbl; Var Bsktbl; Var Ftbl; Hon Roll; Pres NHS; PA ST U; Bus.

FROLLO, CATHY; Penn Hills SR HS; Verona, PA; (Y); 94/750; Drama Clb; French Clb; School Play; Off Jr Cls; Stu Cncl; Hon Roll; Advrtsng.

FROMM, RICHARD; Marple Newtown SR HS; Broomall, PA; (Y); Math Tm; ROTC; Temple Yth Grp; Nwsp Ed-Chief; Nwsp Stf; High Hon Roll; AHSME Plcd 1st Schl 7th S Eastrn PA Reg; 3rd News Wrtng Catgry DE Cnty Prss; 3rd MAA Cntst; Elec Engr.

FRONZAGLIA, SANDY; Our Lady Of The Sacred Heart HS; Aliquippa, PA; (Y); 14/60; Dance Clb; Pep Clb; School Musical; Yrbk Sprt Ed; Yrbk Stf; VP Jr Cls; Stu Cncl; Var L Bsktbl; Dir Pep Clb 86-87; Stu Gov 86-87; Head Chairprsn Prom Commtte 85-86; Gannon U; Phrmcy.

FROST III, HARRY J; Yough SR HS; Smithton, PA; (Y); 36/253; French Clb; Model UN; Ski Clb; Church Choir; High Hon Roll; NHS; U Pittsburgh; Arch Engrng.

FROWNFELTER, ERIC; Newport JR SR HS; Newport, PA; (Y); Boy Scts; Church Yth Grp; 4-H; Spanish Clb; Ftbl; Wt Lftg; Wrstlng; 4-H Awd; High Hon Roll; Hon Roll; Wildlife Mgmt.

FRUCHTL, KEVIN; Lancaster Catholic HS; Lancaster, PA; (Y); 18/220; Church Yth Grp; Red Cross Aide; Speech Tm; Var L Ftbl; Pres Schlr; Alumni Awd 86; John Wendel Mem Awd 86; Schlstc Schrlshp 86; Allentown Coll; Bus Comm.

FRUIT, KRISTINE; Shenango JR SR HS; New Castle, PA; (S); 4/120; Trs Church Yth Grp; French Clb; Office Aide; Drill Tm; Nwsp Rptr; Rep Stu Cncl; Im Vllybl; Hon Roll; NHS; Jr Miss Pgnt 85; PA ST; Law.

FRUSCO, MELANIE; Nazareth Acad; Philadelphia, PA; (Y); Cmnty Wkr; French Clb; JV Capt Cheerleading; Hnr Many Vlntry Hrs For Crppld Chldrn 85-86; Interior Dsgn.

FRY, HEATH; New Castle SR HS; New Castle, PA; (Y); 98/263; Var Trk; Var Capt Wrstlng; OSU; Chem.

FRY, LAUREN; Hempfield HS; Lancaster, PA; (Y); 23/418; Church Yth Grp; Teachers Aide; Chorus; Orch; School Musical; Nwsp Stf; JV Cheerleading; Powder Puff Ftbl; Hon Roll; NHS.

FRY, LINDA; Connellsville SR HS; Acme, PA; (Y); Church Yth Grp; Pep Clb; Chorus; Church Choir; Rep Soph Cls; Hon Roll; Teen Task Force 83-85; Soc Wrkr.

FRY, MARTHA; Moniteau HS; W Sunbury, PA; (Y); Drama Clb; Spanish Clb; Capt Drill Tm; Stat Trk; NHS.

FRYDRYCH, JOHN; Serra Catholic HS; Wilmerding, PA; (Y); 19/169; Pres Church Yth Grp; Trs French Clb; Teachers Aide; Mgr Band; Mgr Mrchg Band; School Musical; School Play; Stage Crew; French Hon Soc; High Hon Roll; 1st Pl-Fire Prvntn Pstr-PA 78; 3rd Pl-Ntl Hstry Day-Wstrn PA 82; Hnrs 84-86; Cvl Engrng.

FRYE, CHRISTOPHER; Lebanon Catholic HS; Lebanon, PA; (Y); Boy Scts; Church Yth Grp; Library Aide; Pep Clb; PAVAS; Political Wkr; Band; Chorus; Church Choir; Concert Band; Flagler Coll Art Schlrshp 86-87; Flagler Coll; Comrcl Art.

FRYE, MICHELLE; Chief Logan HS; Mcclure, PA; (Y); 4-H; FNA; Soroptimist; Spanish Clb; Varsity Clb; Band; Chorus; Concert Band; Mrchg Band; Var Capt Fld Hcky; Nrsg.

FRYE, RANDY; Central Dauphin HS; Harrisburg, PA; (Y); Math Tm; Chorus; Concert Band; Jazz Band; Mrchg Band; School Musical; Symp Band; NHS; Ntl Merit Ltr; Pres Schlr; NMSC Schlrshp 86; Rotry Clb Colnl Pk Schlrshp 86; Outstndng SR Math Awd 86; PA ST U; Elec Engr.

FRYER, WILLIAM; Punxsutawney Area SR HS; Punxsutawney, PA; (Y); CAP; Band; Mrchg Band; Pep Band; Variety Show; Im Bsktbl; Im Vllybl; Army Ranger.

FRYLING, DEBBIE; Bensalem HS; Bensalem, PA; (Y); Diving; Swmmng.

FSHENBAUGH, AMY; Moniteau JR SR HS; W Sunbury, PA; (Y); Ski Clb; Spanish Clb; Nwsp Stf; Yrbk Stf; Var Bsktbl; Stat Ftbl; Hon Roll; NHS; Bst Free Thrw Pctg Bsktbl 86.

FU, STEPHANIE; Upper Dublin HS; Dresher, PA; (Y); 35/307; FBLA; Hosp Aide; Mrchg Band; School Musical; Yrbk Stf; Lit Mag; Powder Puff Ftbl; Jr NHS; NHS; Upper Dublin Stu Exchng Prog To England 86; NYU; Bus Adm.

FUCHYLO, LISA L; Delaware Valley HS; Milford, PA; (Y); 11/123; Math Clb; Red Cross Aide; Band; School Musical; Bsktbl; Socr; Sftbl; Trs NHS; Pres Schlr; Blmsbrg U; Elem Ed.

FUEGI, STEPHEN; Ambridge Area HS; Ambridge, PA; (Y); Am Leg Boys St; Boy Scts; German Clb; JA; Math Clb; Chorus; Hon Roll; Prfct Atten Awd; PA Govs Schl For Agri 86; Top Indvdl Score High-Q Bowl 86; U Of Pittsburgh; Physics.

FUERMAN, RICHARD; The Hill Schl; Pottstown, PA; (Y); Church Yth Grp; Cmnty Wkr; Hosp Aide; Library Aide; Model UN; Ski Clb; Band; Im Golf; JV Ice Hcky; Im Socr; Soc Distngshd Amer HS Stu 86-87; Schl Scholar 83-87; Pre-Med.

FUGA, MICHAEL; Phoenixville Area HS; Phoenixville, PA; (Y); 40/198; Varsity Clb; Var Capt Bsbl; NHS; All Chestmont Bsbl Tm 86; Anthony J Chiccino Schlrshp Awd 86; Temple U.

FUGEDY, MARY; Cardinal O Hara HS; Springfield, PA; (Y); 33/740; Church Yth Grp; Cmnty Wkr; German Clb; Office Aide; Yrbk Stf; Bowling; Hon Roll; NHS; Hnr Convocation 84-86; German Ntl Hnr Soc 85-86; Drexel U; Intl Bus.

FUGOK, BRIAN; Berwick Area SR HS; Berwick, PA; (Y); 25/285; Boys Clb Am; Exploring; Red Cross Aide; Ftbl; Var L Trk; Hon Roll; Jr NHS; NHS; Prfct Atten Awd; PA ST U; Comp Sci.

FUHR, ERIKA; Emmaus HS; Macungie, PA; (Y); French Clb; Q&S; Ski Clb; Nwsp Stf; Chess Clb; Hon Roll; Boston U; Jrnlsm.

FUHRMAN, DAVE; Palmyra Area HS; Palmyra, PA; (Y); Church Yth Grp; Socr; Trk; Schlrshp Awd SAT Scrs 87-88; Hesston Coll; Agri.

FUHRMAN, JENNIFER; Hanover SR HS; Hanover, PA; (Y); Church Yth Grp; Pep Clb; Varsity Clb; Chorus; Var L Vllybl; High Hon Roll; Hon Roll; NHS; Prfct Atten Awd.

FUHRMAN, RICHARD; Newport JR SR HS; Newport, PA; (S); Church Yth Grp; Quiz Bowl; School Play; Stu Cncl; JV Var Bsktbl; JV Var Ftbl; Wt Lftg; Hon Roll; NHS; Prfct Atten Awd; Australia Exchng Stu 85; Intl Rltns.

FULENO, MELISSA; New Castle SR HS; New Castle, PA; (S); 17/253; Church Yth Grp; French Clb; Hosp Aide; Red Cross Aide; SADD; Rep Frsh Cls; Rep Soph Cls; Hon Roll; Jr NHS.

FULGINITI, ANGELA; Moshannon Valley JR SR HS; Houtzdale, PA; (Y); 4-H; Spanish Clb; Band; Chorus; Concert Band; Mrchg Band; Pep Band; Socr.

FULK, DANA; Central Dauphin HS; Harrisburg, PA; (Y); Sec Church Yth Grp; German Clb; Library Aide; Teachers Aide; Chorus; Concert Band; School Musical; Rep Stu Cncl; Crs Cntry; Jr NHS; Med.

FULLER, BECKY; Beaver Area HS; Beaver, PA; (Y); Aud/Vis; Hosp Aide; Latin Clb; Pep Clb; Ski Clb; Band; Yrbk Stf; Marquette U; Bus Adm.

FULLER, DEANNE LYNN; Aliquippa HS; Aliquippa, PA; (Y); Concert Band; Mrchg Band; Off Jr Cls; Off Sr Cls; Hon Roll; NHS; Wmns Achvmnt Clb Stu Srs 86; Bvr Cnty Hnrs Bnd 86; Quippan Clb Awd 86; IN U Of PA; Accntng.

FULLER, KIM; Conneaut Lake HS; Cochranton, PA; (Y); Sec Church Yth Grp; Drama Clb; JA; Pep Clb; Spanish Clb; Mrchg Band; Nwsp Stf; Yrbk Stf; Hon Roll; Band Cert 86; Band Pin 86; Band Bar 86; Bus.

FULLER, MONICA ANN; Upper Merion SR HS; Wayne, PA; (Y); 78/278; Aud/Vis; Church Yth Grp; Cmnty Wkr; Dance Clb; English Clb; FBLA; GAA; Intnl Clb; PAVAS; SADD; Harcum Grant; Harcum JC; Retl Mrchndsg.

FULLER, TAMARA; Cowanesque Valley HS; Middlebury Center, PA; (S); 5/86; 4-H; Girl Scts; Letterman Clb; Ski Clb; Band; Chorus; Concert Band; Drill Tm; Rep Stu Cncl; Stat Var Bsktbl; Schltc Athl Awd 83-85; PA ST U; Law.

FULLER, TIMOTHY; Jersey Shore Area HS; Jersey Shore, PA; (Y); 4-H; French Clb; Ski Clb; School Musical; Lit Mag; Rep Soph Cls; Rep Jr Cls; Hon Roll; Aud/Vis; Computer Clb; Sec Ed.

FULLERTON, DENISE; Spring Grove HS; York, PA; (Y); 32/223; Hosp Aide; Band; Concert Band; Mrchg Band; Hon Roll; NHS; Banking.

FULMER, CHRISTOPHER E; Upper St Clair HS; Upper St Clair, PA; (Y); 1/392; CAP; NFL; Radio Clb; Pres Thesps; Jazz Band; Yrbk Rptr; Pres Sr Cls; Rep Stu Cncl; Ftbl; Wt Lftg; Westing Hse Sci Hnrs Inst; Inner Circle; CIA Scouts; Stanford U; Astrophysics.

FULMER, DAVID R; Yough SR HS; Herminie, PA; (Y); 5/242; Trs Computer Clb; Math Tm; Drm & Bgl; Bausch & Lomb Sci Awd; NHS; Ntl Merit SF; Chess Clb; Spanish Clb; Teachers Aide; US Mltry Acad Wrkshp 85; SNP Ldg 87, Crcl 52 VP 83; AD Cerne Sci Awd 86; Carnegie Mellon U; Math.

FULMER, ELLEN; Owen J Roberts HS; Pottstown, PA; (Y); 30/300; Chorus; Church Choir; Concert Band; Drm Mjr(t); Mrchg Band; Orch; School Musical; Mgr(s); Score Keeper; Sec NHS; Psych.

FULMER, HEATHER; Saucon Valley HS; Hellertown, PA; (Y); Church Yth Grp; Cmnty Wkr; Spanish Clb; Nwsp Stf; JV Cheerleading; Capt Twrlr; Trphs Awds In Twirl Comp; Modlng Queen 85/Miss Cindys Schl Of Dance; Fash Dsgn.

FULMER, JEREMY; Ephrate HS; Akron, PA; (Y); 84/257; Boy Scts; Trs Church Yth Grp; VICA; Mrchg Band; Var JV Socr; Wrstlng; Hon Roll; 1st Pl Dutchman Holiday Trnmnt 83; Cert Of Schlrshp Bio 86; Hnr Roll Banquet Vo-Tech 86; Air Cond Engr.

FULMER, KATHERINE; J P Mc Caskey HS; Lancaster, PA; (Y); AFS; Pep Clb; Spanish Clb; Band; Chorus; Mrchg Band; School Play; Cheerleading; Fld Hcky; Gym; MVP-FIELD Hockey 84.

FULMER, KRISTIN; Wissahickon HS; Norristown, PA; (S); 47/277; Ski Clb; Varsity Clb; Jr Cls; Var Bsktbl; Capt Var Fld Hcky; Var Lcrss; NHS; Ntl Ldrshp Merit Awds 86; U MD.

FULMER, PAUL D; The Hill Schl; Ephrata, PA; (Y); VP Acpl Chr; Band; VP Chorus; Pres Church Choir; Jazz Band; School Musical; Nwsp Phtg; Yrbk Phtg; Var Diving; Hon Roll; Librl Arts.

FULMER, SHIRLEY; Yough SR HS; West Newton, PA; (S); French Clb; Ski Clb; SADD; Pres VP VICA; Chorus; Nwsp Ed-Chief; Nwsp Rptr; High Hon Roll; Hon Roll; Air Force; Mth.

FULMER, WENDY; Spring-Ford SR HS; Collegeville, PA; (Y); Church Yth Grp; FCA; French Clb; Library Aide; Pep Clb; Chorus; Trk; Hon Roll; 3 Cert Outstndng Perfrmnc 84-86; Ribbns Trk 85; Var Ltr Wnnr Trk 86; Ceder Crest Clg; Socl Wrkr.

FULTON, DOREEN; Carmichaels Area SR HS; Carmichaels, PA; (Y); 42/101; Church Yth Grp; French Clb; JA; Pep Clb; Band; Chorus; Concert Band; High Hon Roll; Hon Roll; Jr NHS; Med Scrtry.

FULTON, LORI; Palmyra Area SR HS; Palmyra, PA; (Y); 1/200; Rep German Clb; Pep Clb; Varsity Clb; Yrbk Stf; Rep Jr Cls; Var Capt Cheerleading; Gym; High Hon Roll; NHS; Shippensburg U; Comp Sci.

FULTON, RICH; Penns Manor Area HS; Penn Run, PA; (Y); Boy Scts; Chorus; Church Choir; School Musical.

FULTON, RODNEY; Plymouth-Whitemarsh SR HS; Lafayette Hl, PA; (Y); Church Yth Grp; DECA; Office Aide; SADD; Church Choir; Trk; Cit Awd; Hon Roll; NHS; WV U; Chem.

FULTON, SUSAN; Saltsburg JR SR HS; Clarksburg, PA; (Y); #3 In Class; Varsity Clb; Variety Show; Yrbk Stf; Off Stu Cncl; Cheerleading; Sftbl; High Hon Roll; Bst All Arnd Chrldr 4; Hnrb Mntn IN Gazette-Sftbl 84; 1st Tm IN Gazette-Sftbl 85.

FULTZ, CHARLES; Portage Area HS; Portage, PA; (S); 17/118; Varsity Clb; L Ftbl; Im Wt Lftg; Hon Roll; NHS.

FUMANTI, MELISSA; Old Forge HS; Old Forge, PA; (Y); Cheerleading; Hon Roll; Typng Awd 84-85.

FUNG, EILEEN CHIA-CHIN; Wilson Area HS; Easton, PA; (S); Drama Clb; School Play; Stage Crew; Lit Mag; Tennis; High Hon Roll; Jr NHS; Art Awd 84-85.

FUNK, APRIL; Swissvale HS; Pittsbuirgh, PA; (Y); 2/205; Pres German Clb; Y-Teens; Acpl Chr; Band; Mrchg Band; School Musical; Ed Yrbk Stf; Score Keeper; Swmmng; NHS; Frgn Lang Awd 84-86; Pre-Law.

FUNK, DAVID; Hempfield HS; Lancaster, PA; (Y); 41/420; Computer Clb; Golf; Socr; Engrng.

FUNK, JACQUELINE; Mt Pleasant Area HS; Mt Pleasant, PA; (Y); Drama Clb; GAA; Hosp Aide; Pep Clb; Science Clb; Yrbk Stf; L Tennis; Trs Sr Cls; Rep Stu Cncl; Stu Of Week 86; Mt Plsnt 5 Mile Rac Wnr 83-86; 1st Pl Sctdl Grt Race 84; IN U Of PA; Pblc Rltns.

FUNK, JEFF; Central Bucks-East HS; Plumsteadville, PA; (Y); 86/468; Boy Scts; FBLA; Political Wkr; Ski Clb; Nwsp Phtg; Nwsp Stf; Yrbk Phtg; Yrbk Stf; JV Var Tennis; Hon Roll; Eagle Scout Awd 86; Princeton U; Intl Reltns.

FUNK, SUSAN; Mars Area HS; Mars, PA; (Y); Pres VP AFS; French Clb; FBLA; Flag Corp; Yrbk Stf; High Hon Roll; NHS; Mrchg Band; Off Jr Cls; Stat Bsktbl; Bus Clb Schlrshp 86; Ralph L Pinkerton Jr Awd Svc AFS 86; Exclnt Bus Sklls Awd 86; Robert Morris Coll; Med Scrtry.

FUNK, VIVIAN GAIL; Lincoln HS; Ellwood City, PA; (Y); Drama Clb; 4-H; Girl Scts; Key Clb; Office Aide; Service Clb; Chorus; Flag Corp; High Hon Roll; Hon Roll; Pro Pilot.

FUNKHOUSER, HEIDI; Riverside HS; Beaver Fls, PA; (Y); Art Clb; Cmnty Wkr; 4-H; FHA; Library Aide; Band; Pres Chorus; Bsktbl; Cheerleading; Crs Cntry; Lbry Awd 84.

FUNKHOUSER, MARK; Hopewell SR HS; Aliquippa, PA; (Y); Chrmn Exploring; French Clb; Pres Band; Chorus; Pres Concert Band; Pres Jazz Band; Pres Mrchg Band; Pep Band; Rep Jr Cls; Vllybl; Abbey Brass 86; Aeron.

FUNYAK, JAWN CHARLES; Seneca Valley HS; Mars, PA; (Y); 50/380; Am Leg Boys St; Church Yth Grp; JA; ROTC; Drill Tm; Jazz Band; Mrchg Band; Symp Band; NHS; Cmnty Wkr; Retired Officers Assoc Awd 86.

FURAR, COLLEEN; Shaler Area SR HS; Glenshaw, PA; (Y); 126/517; Hosp Aide; Red Cross Aide; Variety Show; Pres Frsh Cls; Var Capt Cheerleading; High Hon Roll; U Pittsburgh; Nrsng.

FUREY, GINA; Old Forge HS; Old Forge, PA; (S); Hosp Aide; High Hon Roll; Hon Roll; NHS; PTA Cultrl Arts Awd 86; U Of Scranton; Med Tech.

FURIA, CLAIRE; Archbishop Carroll HS; Haverford, PA; (Y); 1/217; Pres Mathletes; Service Clb; Nwsp Stf; Capt Diving; Capt Swmmng; Var Trk; NHS; Ntl Merit Schol; Opt Clb Awd; Spanish NHS; Mdl Gen Acad Excllnce Awd 86; Mth Assn Amer Awd 86; Archdiocesan Acad Hnrs Convocatn 86; Yale U; Comp Sci.

FURLONG, DAVID; Brownsville Area HS; Brownsville, PA; (S); 20/225; Church Yth Grp; Intnl Clb; Political Wkr; Ski Clb; SADD; Stu Cncl; Var Bsbl; Var Ftbl; High Hon Roll; Hon Roll; Chrprctr.

FURMAN, SUSAN; Coudersport JR SR HS; Coudersport, PA; (Y); 4-H; FHA; 4-H Awd; Accntng.

FURMANEK, LAURA; Montour HS; Pittsburgh, PA; (Y); Pep Clb; Band; Stu Cncl; Cheerleading; Powder Puff Ftbl; Sftbl; High Hon Roll; Hon Roll; Comp Prgmr.

FURMANIAK, DIANNE; Cardinal O Hara HS; Media, PA; (Y); 48/772; Service Clb; Yrbk Stf; Off Jr Cls; Off Sr Cls; Hon Roll; NHS; Hnrs Convoctn 85-86; Media Rotry Clb Stdnt Mnth Feb 86.

FURTKEVIC, KELLY; Portage Area HS; Portage, PA; (Y); 6/119; Band; Pres Chorus; Church Choir; Concert Band; Drm Mjr(t); Mrchg Band; Variety Show; VP Soph Cls; Stat Bsktbl; Twrlr; Pitts U Johnstown; Bus Mgt.

FUSARO, SHARON; Fox Chapel HS; Pittsburgh, PA; (Y); FNA; Hosp Aide; Chorus; Drill Tm; Mrchg Band; JV Cheerleading; Hon Roll; St Francs Schl Pro Nrsng; Nrsng.

FUSCO, CATHERINE; St Maria Goretti HS; Philadelphia, PA; (Y); Office Aide; Stage Crew; Hon Roll.

FUSCO, LEIGH ANN; Bethel Park HS; Bethel Park, PA; (Y); 15/530; Hosp Aide; Drill Tm; Mrchg Band; Symp Band; Rep Frsh Cls; High Hon Roll; NHS; Pres Schlr; Voice Dem Awd; Washngtn & Jffrsn Coll; Pre-Med.

FUSTICH, JENNIFER; Fox Chapel HS; Pittsburgh, PA; (Y); U Pittsburgh; Elem Ed.

FUTCHEL, AMY; John S Fine HS; W Nanticoke, PA; (Y); 8/242; Chorus; Church Choir; High Hon Roll; Kiwanis Awd; NHS; Chorus Awd 86; Wilson Coll; Vet Tech.

FYOCK, CONNIE LYNN; Johnstown HS; Pittsburgh, PA; (Y); 110/275; Sec FBLA; Ski Clb; Spanish Clb; Sec SADD; Band; Rep Jr Cls; Rep Sr Cls; Sftbl; Vllybl; Pep Clb; Pres Wlnt Grv Chrch Brethern Yth Grp 83-86; Bradford Bus; Acctng.

GABEL, DIANNE; Plymouth Whitemarsh HS; Norristown, PA; (Y); Trs 4-H; Cheerleading; Sftbl; Vllybl; Hon Roll; Jr NHS; NHS; Hlth.

GABEL, MARTIN; Bishop O Reilly HS; Swoyersville, PA; (Y); Am Leg Boys St; Spanish Clb; Chorus; Var Bsbl; JV Bsktbl; Var Socr; Spanish NHS; Pres Acadmc Ftnss Awd 85-86.

GABEL, MICHELLE; John S Fine HS; Nanticoke, PA; (Y); Key Clb; Ski Clb; Chorus; Yrbk Stf; Mgr(s); Vllybl; High Hon Roll; NHS; Intl Bus.

GABEL, ROBERT W; Newport HS; Newport, PA; (Y); 11/100; Pres FFA; Var Bsbl; Hon Roll; NHS; Rpres Acad Ftnss Awd 86; Keystone Frmr Deg PA Assn FFA 86; Star Chptr Frmr FFA 86; PA ST U; Dairy Sci.

GABER, MARK; Bethel Park SR HS; Pittsburgh, PA; (Y); 98/500; Band; Bsktbl; Golf; Bus.

GABIG, SARAH; Trinity HS; Camp Hill, PA; (Y); Cmnty Wkr; Debate Tm; Band; Nwsp Rptr; Trk; High Hon Roll; JETS Awd; NHS; CAP; French Clb; Maxima Cum Laude Natl Latin Exam 84-85; Poll Watchr Carlisle Sentnl Newsppr 84-86; Sec Schl Band 86-87; Aerontcl Engr.

GABLE, DEBRA L; Lower Dauphin HS; Hummelstown, PA; (Y); 21/219; Pres Thesps; Chorus; Mrchg Band; Orch; School Musical; School Play; NHS; Trs Church Yth Grp; Pres Drama Clb; Pres Latin Clb; Intl Thespn Awd 86; Outstndng Actg Awd Bucks Cnty Comptn 86; Shenandoah Coll; Music Thrpy.

GABONAY, RENEE; Greensburg Central Catholic HS; West Newton, PA; (Y); 142/243; Pep Clb; Ski Clb; Mat Maids; Powder Puff Ftbl; Indiana U Of PA; Spec Educ.

GABOR, HEATHER; St Basil Acad; Philadelphia, PA; (Y); Church Yth Grp; Latin Clb; Pres Ski Clb; Var Bsktbl; Im Var Sftbl; Im Trk; Im Vllybl; High Hon Roll; Opt Clb Awd; Ntl Hstry & Govt Awd 85-86; Optmst Clbs Yth Apprctn Wk Citation 83-84.

GABOREK, GREG; Westmont Hilltop HS; Johnstown, PA; (Y); 17/169; Pres Art Clb; Camera Clb; Drama Clb; French Clb; Yrbk Ed-Chief; Yrbk Phtg; Yrbk Rptr; Yrbk Sprt Ed; Yrbk Stf; JV Var Bsktbl; Pitt; Pre Med.

GABRIEL, ANN MARIE; St Maria Goretti HS; Philadelphia, PA; (Y); 159/426; Art Clb; Boy Scts; Exploring; Girl Scts; Flag Corp; Hon Roll; Alg II Hghst Avg 85; Gregg Shrthnd Awd Achvt 86; Typng Awd Achvt 86; Fshn Inst Of Phil; Fshn Mrchnds.

GABRIEL, CHERYL; Unionville HS; Kennett Sq, PA; (Y); Church Yth Grp; Hosp Aide; School Musical; Yrbk Stf; JV Fld Hcky; Mgr(s); Hon Roll; Physcl Thrpy.

GABRIEL, VICTORIA; Freedom HS; Bethlehem, PA; (Y); 163/465; Cmnty Wkr; Hosp Aide; Office Aide; Band; Concert Band; Mrchg Band; Polt Sci.

GABRIELSEN, PAMELA; Red Lion Area SR HS; Airville, PA; (Y); Band; Nwsp Rptr; Hon Roll; Navy; Languages.

GABURA, MARK; Gar Memorial HS; Wilkes Barre, PA; (Y); French Clb; Letterman Clb; Chorus; Bsbl; Var Capt Bsktbl; Ftbl; Hon Roll; Wilkes Barre Area Brd Of Ed Cert Of Apprctn 86; Crmnl Jstc.

GABURRI, MICHELE; Chartiers Valley HS; Carnegie, PA; (Y); Church Yth Grp; Cmnty Wkr; Yrbk Stf; Hon Roll; NHS; Nrsng.

GADBOIS, CHRIS; Bethlehem Catholic HS; Bethlehem, PA; (Y); 8/200; Key Clb; Scholastic Bowl; School Musical; School Play; Var L Crs Cntry; High Hon Roll; NHS; Ntl Merit Ltr; Hghst Avrg In Spnsh III Awd 86; Engrng.

GADD, CAROLYN E; Freedom HS; Bethlehem, PA; (Y); Pep Clb; Yrbk Stf; Rep Stu Cncl; JV Cheerleading; JV Tennis; Hon Roll; Elem Educ.

GADE, KRISTEN; Trinity HS; Washington, PA; (Y); 15/387; Art Clb; Key Clb; Math Tm; Ski Clb; Speech Tm; High Hon Roll; Hon Roll; NHS.

GADOLA, ERIK; St John Neumann HS; Philadelphia, PA; (Y); 25/400; SADD; Nwsp Sprt Ed; Im Bsktbl; Var Ftbl; NHS; Ntl Hnr Soc; Nwsp Sprts Edtr; Villanova; Pre-Law.

GADOLA III, GUY P; Sharpsville Area HS; Sharpsville, PA; (Y); Am Leg Boys St; Church Yth Grp; Science Clb; Spanish Clb; School Musical; VP Frsh Cls; Rep Soph Cls; Rep Jr Cls; Pres Stu Cncl; Var L Trk.

GADOLA, PATRICK S; Hickory HS; Hermitage, PA; (Y); Art Clb; Var Bsbl; NHS; Clarion U Of PA; Cvl Engr.

GADOMSKI, LARA; Western Wayne HS; Waymart, PA; (Y); 16/137; Ski Clb; Concert Band; Mrchg Band; Sec Soph Cls; Sec Jr Cls; Im Gym; Hon Roll; NHS; Educ.

GADONAS, MICHELE; St Pius X HS; Phoenixville, PA; (S); 13/161; Hosp Aide; Service Clb; Drill Tm; School Musical; Yrbk Phtg; Rep Soph Cls; High Hon Roll; Jr NHS; NEDT Awd; Med.

GADSBY, ERIN; Karns City Area HS; Bruin, PA; (Y); 15/113; Church Yth Grp; Bsktbl; L Var Crs Cntry; L Trk; Hon Roll; NHS; Acctng.

GADSBY, KAREN; Delaware County Christian HS; Claymont, DE; (Y); Church Yth Grp; Cmnty Wkr; Acpl Chr; Concert Band; Yrbk Stf; JV Var Bsktbl; JV Var Fld Hcky; JV Var Sftbl; High Hon Roll; Band; Knghtns Smll Vcl Ensmbl 85-86; AP Engl; Soc Wrk.

GAETANO, SUSAN; Villa Maria HS; Campbell, OH; (Y); Cmnty Wkr; French Clb; Thesps; Nwsp Stf; Rep Frsh Cls; Pres Jr Cls; Pres Sr Cls; Stu Cncl; NHS; NEDT Awd; Law.

GAFFEY, ERICA; German SR HS; Hibbs, PA; (Y); Concert Band; Yrbk Stf; Pres Frsh Cls; Pres Soph Cls; Pres Jr Cls; Pres Sr Cls; Rep Stu Cncl; Twrlr; Pres Jr NHS; Hst NHS; Yuth Trfc Sfty Cncl 84-86; Hmcmng Qun 85; ST Fnlst Amer Hmcng Qun 86; Carlow Coll; Nrsg.

GAGE, KAREN; Strath Haven HS; Wallingford, PA; (Y); Church Yth Grp; Intnl Clb; Mrchg Band; Nwsp Phtg; Yrbk Ed-Chief; Bsktbl; Fld Hcky; Vllybl; Hon Roll; Ntl Merit Ltr; PA Free Enterprise Wk Scholar 86; Econ.

GAGLIANO, FRANCIS; Mt Lebanon SR HS; Pittsburgh, PA; (Y); 104/500; Ski Clb; School Musical; School Play; Lit Mag; Hon Roll; Prtcpnt Natl Acdmc Games Olympcs GA 85; U Of CA Los Angeles; Flm Mkng.

GAHAGEN, TANYA; Redbank Valley HS; New Bethlehem, PA; (Y); 16/125; Chorus; Capt Drill Tm; School Musical; Yrbk Bus Mgr; Yrbk Ed-Chief; Yrbk Stf; Capt Pom Pon; DAR Awd; Hon Roll; NHS; Pres Acdmc Ftns Awd, Scottish Rite Schlrshp 86; Clarion U PA; Elem Educ.

GAHR, WENDY; Elk County Christian HS; Kersey, PA; (Y); 32/81; Girl Scts; Hosp Aide; Model UN; SADD; Rep Chorus; Rep Mrchg Band; Pep Band; Yrbk Stf; Stat Bsktbl; Hon Roll; Elk Cnty Chrstn H S Sci Fair 84; Sr Div Allghny Mntn Regnl Sci Fair 86; Chem.

GAICHAS, SARAH; North Hills HS; Pittsburgh, PA; (Y); 2/500; Lit Mag; L Crs Cntry; L Trk; High Hon Roll; NHS; Ntl Merit SF; Pres Schlr; St Schlr; Schlr Athltc Awd 86; Ntl Merit Fnlst 86; Swarthmore Coll.

GAIDO, MARY; Trinity HS; Washington, PA; (Y); 28/374; Key Clb; Pep Clb; Spanish Clb; SADD; Chorus; Yrbk Stf; Crs Cntry; Swmmng; Trk; High Hon Roll; NHS.

GAILEY, ANNETTE; Greencastle/Antrim HS; Greencastle, PA; (Y); 70/187; Church Yth Grp; Drama Clb; Chorus; Church Choir; Yrbk Stf; School Musical; School Play; Hon Roll; 2nd Pl Sci Fair 86; GAEA Bk Schlrshp 86; Shpnsbrg U; Elem Tchr.

GAINES, BARRI; William Allen HS; Allentown, PA; (Y); Drama Clb; Temple Yth Grp; Nwsp Stf; Yrbk Stf; 3rd VP Bnai Brith Yth Org 85-86; 2nd VP Bnai Brith Uth Org 86-87; Oratorical Fnlst Sch Dist Cntst 85; Elem Ed.

GAINES, JUDY; Upper Dublin HS; Dresher, PA; (Y); Hosp Aide; Intnl Clb; Yrbk Stf; Lit Mag; Rep Soph Cls; Rep Jr Cls; Rep Stu Cncl; NHS; Ntl Merit Ltr; Cmnty Wkr; Smmr Intnsv Frgn Lang Prog Frnch 85; Free Enterprise Bus Prog 86; Accntng.

GAJDA, DOUG; Wilmington HS; Volant, PA; (Y); Church Yth Grp; Drama Clb; Varsity Clb; Stage Crew; Capt Ftbl; Trk; Wt Lftg; Wrstlng; Hon Roll; Physcl Ed.

GAJDOWSKI, STACI; Saegertown HS; Saegertown, PA; (Y); 7/124; Church Yth Grp; Library Aide; Scholastic Bowl; Varsity Clb; Concert Band; Mrchg Band; Mgr(s); Hon Roll; Jr NHS; NHS; Gannon U; Med.

GAJEWSKA, EWA; Bensalem SR HS; Philadelphia, PA; (Y); Church Yth Grp; Hosp Aide; Latin Clb; Library Aide; Math Clb; Office Aide; Science Clb; Pres Frsh Cls; Tennis; Vllybl; Hygiene Stu Achvt Awd 84; Ultra Sound.

GAJEWSKI, JOSEPH; Cardinal O Hara HS; Glenolden, PA; (Y); 212/776; Hon Roll; Elec.

GAKLE, RENEE; Jersey Shore SR HS; Jersey Shore, PA; (Y); FBLA; Hon Roll; Mst Imprvd Stu-Spnsh 85-86.

GALAIDA, KAREN ANN; Harry S Truman HS; Fairless Hills, PA; (Y); 30/625; NFL; Band; Concert Band; Mrchg Band; Yrbk Stf; Stu Cncl; Swmmng; High Hon Roll; DE Vly Coll Ag/Sci; Vet.

GALAMB, DASHIA; Greater Works Acad; Pittsburgh, PA; (S); Church Yth Grp; Service Clb; Ski Clb; Yrbk Stf; High Hon Roll; Prfct Atten Awd; Snow Queen Awd 84; Pitt; Law.

GALANDA, LAUREL; Trinity HS; Washington, PA; (Y); Camera Clb; Chrmn Hosp Aide; Key Clb; Office Aide; Nwsp Phtg; Yrbk Phtg; Var Capt Swmmng; Stat Vllybl; High Hon Roll; Lib Arts.

GALANTE, ELAINE; Bensalem HS; Bensalem, PA; (Y); Aud/Vis; Church Yth Grp; Acpl Chr; Concert Band; Mrchg Band; Stu Cncl; Mgr(s); Swmmng; High Hon Roll; Sec NHS; Frnch Comptn Rider Coll 86; Cmmcnts.

GALARDI, DAVID; Cardinal O Hara HS; Springfield, PA; (Y); 136/780; Am Leg Boys St; Pep Clb; Variety Show; Lit Mag; JV Var Bsbl; Hon Roll; Neo Natl Spec.

GALASSO JR, JAMES; Hopewell Area HS; Aliquippa, PA; (Y); 10/297; Pres Sec Exploring; Latin Clb; Capt L Vllybl; DAR Awd; NHS; Rep Stu Cncl; High Hon Roll; Lion Awd; Pres Schlr; Chorus; Raccoon PTA Schlrshp 86; Cert Achvt PA Soc Prof Engr 85; PA ST U; Aerosp Engr.

GALBRAITH, BARBIE JEAN; Keystone HS; Knox, PA; (Y); 14/125; Church Yth Grp; Cmnty Wkr; French Clb; Rep FBLA; Hon Roll; Bus Awd 83-84; Art Awd 84-85; Clarion U; Elem Tchr.

GALBRAITH, JODY; Northern Lebanon HS; Lebanon, PA; (Y); 19/105; Dance Clb; English Clb; French Clb; German Clb; Spanish Clb; Hon Roll; Amer Lgn Essay Cntst $40 85-86; Gymnstcs 78-91; Pre-Med.

GALBRAITH, MINDY; Big Spring HS; Carlisle, PA; (Y); Pres Sec 4-H; Var Mgr(s); 4-H Awd; Frd Mtr Car Achvt Awd 84; Amer Qrtr Hrs Awd 83-84; Frm Serv Outstndng Sec Awd 83; Ralston Purina Awd; Bus.

GALBREATH, SHAWN; Brookville Area HS; Sigel, PA; (Y); 12/144; Varsity Clb; Concert Band; Drm Mjr(t); Mrchg Band; Capt Wrstlng; Hon Roll; Jr NHS; NHS; Chess Clb; Letterman Clb; Wrstlng Fed ST Champ 85; PA Free Enterprise Wk 85; Schlrshp Alfred U 85; Engrng.

GALDIERI, SANDRA; West Scranton HS; Scranton, PA; (Y); Cmnty Wkr; Political Wkr; Spanish Clb; Yrbk Stf; Lit Mag; DAR Awd; Hon Roll; NHS; Lackawanna JC; Bus.

GALDONY, PHYLLIS; Center HS; Monaca, PA; (Y); 32/190; Drama Clb; Spanish Clb; Varsity Clb; Drill Tm; Yrbk Stf; Im Bowling; Co-Capt Pom Pon; L Stat Trk; Hon Roll; NHS; Penn ST U; Elem Educ.

GALE, COLLEEN; Central Bucks HS West; Doylestown, PA; (Y); Chorus; Var Trk; Var Vllybl; Hon Roll; Yth Ftnss Achvmnt Awd 84; Nrsng.

GALENTINE, TAMMY; Du Bois Area HS; Luthersburg, PA; (Y); 5/277; Intnl Clb; Chorus; Capt Flag Corp; Capt Mrchg Band; Hon Roll; NHS; PA ST U; Bus.

GALGON, CATHERINE; Allentown Central Catholic HS; Allentown, PA; (Y); 20/275; Hosp Aide; Math Clb; Chorus; School Musical; Yrbk Stf; Stu Cncl; Var Capt Cheerleading; Lion Awd; NHS; Church Yth Grp; Prncpl Awd 85; Amer Music Abrd Europn Tour 86; Boston Coll; Psych.

GALGON, MICHAEL T; Central Catholic HS; Allentown, PA; (Y); 14/231; Exploring; Letterman Clb; Math Clb; Math Tm; Pep Clb; Ski Clb; Lit Mag; VP Sr Cls; Var Bsktbl; Var Tennis; Prncpls Prize 85; Keystone Awd Poetry 84; VP Htl Hnr Soc; Law.

GALGON, NICOLE; Catasavqua HS; Catasauqua, PA; (Y); FBLA; Cheerleading; Trk; Acctg.

GALITSKY, R JOSEPH; East HS; West Chester, PA; (Y); 25/390; Drama Clb; School Musical; School Play; Stage Crew; Nwsp Rptr; Yrbk Stf; Rep Stu Cncl; High Hon Roll; Hon Roll; NHS; Lafayette Coll; Cvl Engrng.

GALL, DANIELE LEE; Seneca Valley SR HS; Harmony, PA; (Y); 6/360; Sec 4-H; ROTC; SADD; 4-H Awd; High Hon Roll; Hon Roll; NHS; Prfct Atten Awd; PA St U Beaver Campus Exec Schlrshp 86; Seneca Vlly HS Schlrshp Awd 84-86; PA ST U; Animal Bio Sci.

GALL, DOREEN MARIE; Big Beaver Falls HS; Beaver Falls, PA; (Y); JA; Radio Clb; Spanish Clb; Chorus; Drill Tm; Madrigals; Yrbk Stf; Pom Pon; High Hon Roll; Hon Roll; 2nd Hghst Sls Bvr Cnty JR Achvt 85; Pdtrcn.

GALL, WALT; Butler HS; Butler, PA; (Y); Church Yth Grp; VICA; Bsbl; Bowling; Golf; Hon Roll.

GALLA, TRACY; Chartiers Valley HS; Bridgeville, PA; (Y); Church Yth Grp; Dance Clb; Drama Clb; Girl Scts; Library Aide; Pep Clb; Prfct Atten Awd; Boyd Schl; Flght Attndnt.

GALLACHER, PATRICIA; Bishop Hannan HS; Scranton, PA; (Y); 3/122; Cmnty Wkr; Computer Clb; French Clb; Scholastic Bowl; Ski Clb; Sec Trs Orch; JV Var Bsktbl; Score Keeper; Hon Roll; NHS; Schlrshp Bishop Hannan High 83; U Scranton; Comp Sci.

GALLAGHER, CAROLYN; Interboro HS; Essington, PA; (Y); Library Aide; VP Spanish Clb; Nwsp Rptr; Nwsp Stf; Rep Jr Cls; Hon Roll; Physical Educ Merit Awd 84; Med Lab Tech.

GALLAGHER, COLLEEN; Central Catholic HS; Allentown, PA; (Y); Sec Frsh Cls; Sec Soph Cls; Sec Jr Cls; Sec Sr Cls; Sec Stu Cncl; JV Var Bsktbl; Var Crs Cntry; Var Capt Sftbl; Hon Roll.

GALLAGHER JR, DONALD; Meyersdale Area HS; Meyersdale, PA; (Y); Church Yth Grp; Trk; Wt Lftg; Wrstlng; Data Proc.

GALLAGHER, JEFF; Fort Leboeuf HS; Waterford, PA; (Y); 11/178; Quiz Bowl; Concert Band; Mrchg Band; Pep Band; Var Trk; Im Vllybl; High Hon Roll; NHS; Ntl Merit Ltr; Engrng.

GALLAGHER, JILL M; Monongahela Valley Catholic HS; Monongahela, PA; (S); 16/105; Drama Clb; Hosp Aide; Pep Clb; Chorus; Church Choir; Stage Crew; Rep Frsh Cls; French Hon Soc; NHS; Nrsg.

GALLAGHER, JOANNE; Minersville Area HS; Minersville, PA; (Y); 23/110; Drama Clb; German Clb; Ski Clb; Church Choir; Drill Tm; School Musical; Stage Crew; Bsktbl; Vllybl; Hon Roll; NHS.

GALLAGHER, JOCELYN; Shenandoah Valley HS; Shenandoah, PA; (Y); 6/108; Pep Clb; Chorus; Nwsp Stf; Yrbk Stf; Sec Soph Cls; Stat Bsbl; Var Co-Capt Cheerleading; High Hon Roll; NHS; Acad All Amer; Comp Sci.

GALLAGHER, JOHN; Cardinal O Hara HS; Broomall, PA; (Y); 120/740; Church Yth Grp; Cmnty Wkr; Hosp Aide; Political Wkr; SADD; Stage Crew; Nwsp Rptr; Hon Roll; PA ST U; Bus.

GALLAGHER, JULIE; Acadamy Of Notre Dame; Wayne, PA; (Y); Art Clb; Cmnty Wkr; Chorus; Stage Crew; Yrbk Stf; VP Soph Cls; VP Sr Cls; Score Keeper; High Hon Roll; Ntl Merit Ltr; Cntry Clb Awd 84; Ed.

GALLAGHER, KAREN; Souderton Area HS; Harleysville, PA; (Y); School Play; Lit Mag; Rep Soph Cls; Rep Jr Cls; Rep Stu Cncl; Var Cheerleading; Var L Gym; Var Vllybl; Hon Roll; E Stroudsberg; Phys Therapy.

GALLAGHER, KATHLEEN; Bethlehem Catholic HS; Bethlehem, PA; (Y); 61/201; French Clb; Key Clb.

GALLAGHER, KATHLEEN; South Park HS; Library, PA; (Y); Rep Jr Cls; Sec Sr Cls; Stat Swmmng; Var L Tennis; Church Yth Grp; Drama Clb; Color Guard; School Play; Nwsp Bus Mgr; Nwsp Rptr; Hnrs Schlrshp Geneva Coll 86; Schlrshp Grove Cty Coll 86; Grove City Coll; Psychlgy.

GALLAGHER, KELLY; William Allen HS; Allentown, PA; (Y); 14/600; Trs GAA; Key Clb; Nwsp Stf; Yrbk Stf; Stu Cncl; Var L Bsktbl; High Hon Roll; Jr NHS; NHS; Villanova; Bus Adm.

GALLAGHER, LISA; South Western HS; Hanover, PA; (Y); Ski Clb; Flag Corp; Nwsp Bus Mgr; Nwsp Stf; W Chester ST U.

GALLAGHER, LYNNE; West Catholic High School For Girls; Philadelphia, PA; (S); 86/241; Pres VP Camp Fr Inc; Church Yth Grp; Debate Tm; JA; Spanish Clb; Nwsp Rptr; Yrbk Stf; Mgr Sftbl; Hon Roll; Exmplry Stu 85; Free Lnce Phtogrphr.

GALLAGHER, MARGARET; Little Flower Catholic HS; Philadelphia, PA; (Y); 8/398; Church Yth Grp; Office Aide; Jazz Band; Orch; School Musical; School Play; Variety Show; High Hon Roll; Hon Roll; NHS; Sci Fair Awd 3rd Pl 83; G W Carver Sci Fair 3rd Pl 83; Sci Fair Awd 2nd Pl 84; Temple U; Bus Adm.

GALLAGHER, MARIE; York Catholic HS; York, PA; (Y); 16/180; Church Yth Grp; 4-H; Pres French Clb; Pep Clb; SADD; School Musical; High Hon Roll; Hon Roll; NHS; Bus.

GALLAGHER, MARY; West Allegheny HS; Coraopolis, PA; (Y); Drama Clb; Spanish Clb; Thesps; Acpl Chr; Chorus; School Play; Stage Crew; Var Cheerleading; Im Vllybl; Hon Roll; Sawer Schl; Travel.

GALLAGHER, MARY C; Central Cambria HS; Ebensburg, PA; (S); 12/193; Debate Tm; 4-H; NFL; Speech Tm; Teachers Aide; School Play; High Hon Roll; Geisinger Med Ctr; Nrsng.

GALLAGHER, MEGAN E; Cardinal O Hara HS; Chester, PA; (Y); 61/789; JA; Office Aide; Spanish Clb; Nwsp Rptr; Yrbk Stf; Rep Jr Cls; High Hon Roll; Hon Roll; NHS; Bus.

GALLAGHER, MELISSA; MMI Preparatory Schl; White Haven, PA; (Y); Trs Frsh Cls; VP Soph Cls; Rep Stu Cncl; Var Crs Cntry; Var Sftbl; High Hon Roll; NHS; Sec Spanish NHS; Art Clb; Aud/Vis; Kings Coll Spnsh Cntst 2nd 84-86; Intl Day 2nd Pl 84; Ntl Spnsh Ex 4th Pl 86.

GALLAGHER, MICHAEL E; Southern Lehigh HS; Coopersburg, PA; (Y); 97/235; Varsity Clb; Var L Bsktbl; Var L Socr; Var L Trk; Kutztown; Hstry.

GALLAGHER, MIRIAM; St Maria Goretti HS; Philadelphia, PA; (Y); 58/390; Boys Clb Am; Church Yth Grp; Im Bsktbl; JV Var Cheerleading; Stat Mgr(s); Hon Roll.

GALLAGHER, PATRICIA; Archbishop Prendergast HS; Collingdale, PA; (Y); 55/356; Trk; Comm.

GALLAGHER, RANDY; Jersey Shore SR HS; Lock Haven, PA; (Y); FBLA; JV Crs Cntry; Wt Lftg; 4th Pl Entreprnrshp II FBLA ST Ldrshp Conf 85-86; 1st Pl Entreprensrshp II Rgn 7 FBLA Conf; Body Guarding.

GALLAGHER, RICHARD; Saint John Newmann HS; Philadelphia, PA; (Y); #50 In Class; Band; Chorus; Concert Band; Jazz Band; Pep Band; Bsktbl; JV Ftbl; Engl.

GALLAGHER, SEAN; Gatewar SR HS; Monroeville, PA; (Y); Science Clb; Ski Clb; Band; Mrchg Band; Orch; Coll Penn ST; Bus Adm.

GALLAGHER, STACIE; Hazleton HS; Mcadoo, PA; (Y); FBLA; Hosp Aide; Office Aide; Red Cross Aide; High Hon Roll; NHS; Outstndg Stu Awd Hlth Asst 84-85; Reading Hosp; RN.

GALLAGHER, STANLEY; South Allegheny HS; Mckeesport, PA; (Y); 20/184; Var L Bsbl; Var L Ftbl; Wt Lftg; Hon Roll; FL ST U; Tele Cmnctns.

GALLAGHER, SUSAN M; Bethlehem Catholic HS; Bethlehem, PA; (Y); 22/220; Girl Scts; Key Clb; Ski Clb; Yrbk Stf; Stu Cncl; JV Cheerleading; Mgr(s); High Hon Roll; NHS.

GALLAGHER, WENDY; Academy Of Notre Dame; Ardmore, PA; (Y); 3/73; Off Service Clb; Ed Nwsp Stf; Yrbk Stf; Sec Trs Sr Cls; High Hon Roll; U Of Scranton Schlrshp 86; St Josephs Pres Schlrshp 86; Awd At Grad For Excellnc In Engl 86; U Of Scranton; Hlth Admin.

GALLAHER, CAREENA; Homer-Center JR SR HS; Lucernemines, PA; (Y); 6/92; FBLA; Girl Scts; Chorus; High Hon Roll; Hon Roll; Jr NHS; NHS; Bst All Arnd Bus Stu 85-86; 4th Pl Clrk Typst Ii, FBLA Regn Iii Ldrshp Conf 86; Frnch Awd 83085; Dubois Bus Coll; Sec.

GALLATIG, CHRISTINE; Bishop Shanahan HS; W Chester, PA; (Y); 21/218; Art Clb; Church Yth Grp; Drama Clb; Office Aide; Lit Mag; Var L Socr; High Hon Roll; Jr NHS; Typg Awd 86.

GALLE, ROBERT; Liberty HS; Bethlehem, PA; (Y); Varsity Clb; Stage Crew; Nwsp Sprt Ed; Nwsp Stf; Bsbl; JV Bsktbl; 1st Pl Awd PA Schl Press Assn Sprts Writng 84-85.

GALLO, JENNIFER; Connellsville Area HS; Connellsville, PA; (Y); Library Aide; Chorus; Rep Frsh Cls; Rep Stu Cncl; High Hon Roll; Hon Roll; PA ST U; Ed.

GALLO, NANCY ANN; Burgettstown Area JR SR HS; Burgettstown, PA; (Y); 4/172; Church Yth Grp; Band; Mrchg Band; Var Capt Bsktbl; NHS; U Pittsburgh; Engrng.

GALLO, ROBIN; Greater Latrobe HS; Latrobe, PA; (Y); 30/337; Trs German Clb; Teachers Aide; Jazz Band; Mrchg Band; Pep Band; School Musical; Symp Band; High Hon Roll; NHS; German Hnr Soc; Mercyhurst Coll; Hotel Mgmt.

GALLOWAY, BOBBI; Blue Ridge HS; Great Bend, PA; (Y); GAA; Letterman Clb; Trs SADD; JV Var Mgr(s); JV Var Vllybl; Cit Awd; High Hon Roll; Hon Roll; Prfct Atten Awd; Bus.

GALLOWAY, DAVID; Fort Cherry HS; Mc Donald, PA; (S); Math Clb; Science Clb; Ski Clb; Spanish Clb; Varsity Clb; Var Wrstlng; High Hon Roll.

GALLOWAY, SHERRY; Frankford HS; Philadelphia, PA; (Y); 3/744; Nwsp Phtg; Nwsp Stf; Var Mat Maids; Var Twrlr; Var Vllybl; Stat Wrstlng; Hon Roll; NHS; VFW Awd; Yth Mnth; Biochem.

GALOSE, ANGELA; Villa Maria HS; Canfield, OH; (Y); Cmnty Wkr; Drama Clb; French Clb; Key Clb; Latin Clb; Ski Clb; Speech Tm; School Musical; Var Tennis; Var Trk; Stnfrd; Csmtc Srgn.

GALSICK, TAMMIE; Johnsonburg Area HS; Wilcox, PA; (Y); 4-H; Girl Scts; Office Aide; Varsity Clb; Yrbk Stf; Stu Cncl; Bsktbl; Vllybl; Natl Physcl Educ Awd 86; Du Bois Bus Coll; Exec Scrtry.

GALT, DANIELLE; Harbor Creek HS; Erie, PA; (Y); 15/222; Sec AFS; SADD; Thesps; Mrchg Band; Variety Show; Yrbk Sprt Ed; Rep Sr Cls; L Pom Pon; Hon Roll; NHS; Schlrshp-PA Free Entrprs Wk 85; Psychlgy.

GALUSKA, AMY; Hampton HS; Allison Pk, PA; (Y); 27/224; SADD; Drill Tm; Pres Stu Cncl; Var Cheerleading; Capt Powder Puff Ftbl; High Hon Roll; NHS; Pres Schlr; French Clb; Ski Clb; Jodi Anderson Meml Schlrshp 86; U Of Pittsburgh; Math.

GALVIN, DANIEL D; William Allen HS; Allentown, PA; (Y); 43/560; Trs Exploring; JCL; Key Clb; Pres Y-Teens; Ed Nwsp Phtg; Off Stu Cncl; Trk; High Hon Roll; JETS Awd; NHS; Edward F Sandow Awd 83; Ldrs Svc Awd 84; Pres Fit Awd 86; Carnegie-Mellon U; Engrng.

GALYA, DIANE; Swissvale HS; Pittsburgh, PA; (Y); Church Yth Grp; French Clb; Ski Clb; Acpl Chr; Mrchg Band; Yrbk Stf; Sec Stu Cncl; Stat Bsbl; French Awd 83.

GAMBACORTA, JOSEPH; Scranton Vo Tech; Scranton, PA; (Y); Ski Clb; VICA; Band; Concert Band; Johnson Tech Inst; CNC Pgmr.

GAMBALE, LYNN; St Maria Goretti HS; Philadelphia, PA; (Y); Cmnty Wkr; Orch; Nwsp Rptr; Lit Mag; Hon Roll; Temple U.

GAMBER, SANDI; Liberty JR SR HS; Roaring Branch, PA; (Y); 5/42; Sec Church Yth Grp; German Clb; Rep Stu Cncl; Var Capt Bsktbl; JV Capt Cheerleading; Var Trk; Var Capt Vllybl; Hon Roll; NHS; JV Bsktbl MVP 84; Var Vllybl MVP 86; German.

GAMBLE, KRISTEN; Cecilian Acad; Philadelphia, PA; (Y); Sec Church Yth Grp; Dance Clb; Office Aide; Pep Clb; Nwsp Stf; Hon Roll; Prfct Atten Awd; French Clb; Latin Clb; Vllybl; Typng Cert 86; CEE Mrthn Cert 86; Cum Laude Ntl Ltn Exm 83.

GAMBLE, LISA; Avella JR SR HS; Washington, PA; (Y); VP 4-H; Sec FFA; JA; Band; Chorus; Church Choir; Drm Mjr(t); Mrchg Band; Twrlr; Hon Roll.

GAMELIER, JILL; North Hills HS; Glenshaw, PA; (Y); 64/467; Sec AFS; Church Yth Grp; Teachers Aide; Band; Concert Band; Flag Corp; Mrchg Band; Orch; Hon Roll; Slippery Rock U; Elem Ed.

GAMMAITONI, LISA M; North Pocono HS; Moscow, PA; (Y); Ski Clb; Variety Show; Trs Frsh Cls; Var L Cheerleading; Var L Ftbl; Var L Trk; PIAA Dist Girls Golf 2nd Pl 85; Spnsh.

GAMMON, JEANEEN; Owen J Roberts HS; Glenmoore, PA; (S); 30/291; Band; Concert Band; Mrchg Band; Yrbk Stf; JV Fld Hcky; JV Lcrss; Hon Roll; NHS; Law.

GAMRAT, FRANK; Central Catholic HS; N Braddock, PA; (Y); 85/267; Art Clb; Boy Scts; Dance Clb; Yrbk Rptr; Yrbk Stf; Mgr(s); Vllybl; Var L Wrstlng; Hon Roll.

GAN, ZAFRIR; Schenley HS; Pittsburgh, PA; (S); Chess Clb; Computer Clb; Exploring; Hosp Aide; Mathletes; Math Tm; Ski Clb; Vllybl; High Hon Roll; NHS; Super Bowl/Problm Slvng; Elec Engr.

GANDZIARSKI, CATHERINE; Deer Lakes HS; Creighton, PA; (Y); Sec VP Church Yth Grp; Library Aide; Varsity Clb; Concert Band; Mrchg Band; School Play; Yrbk Stf; Var L Cheerleading; Hon Roll; NHS; NEDT Cert; Acad Achvt Cert.

GANDZIARSKI, STEPHANIE; Deer Lakes JR SR HS; Creighton, PA; (Y); 8/182; Trs Church Yth Grp; Drama Clb; French Clb; Hosp Aide; Chorus; Flag Corp; Yrbk Stf; High Hon Roll; Hon Roll; NHS; Pres Acad Fit Awd 86; Indiana U Of PA; Frnch.

GANGLOFF, MARY; Franklin Regional HS; Murrysville, PA; (Y); 16/324; Thesps; Church Choir; Concert Band; Mrchg Band; High Hon Roll; NHS; Natl Mrt Cmnd Stu 86; Wstnghs Fmly Schlrshp 86; IN U Penn Hnrs Bnd 86; Purdue U; Foods Ntrtn.

GANIME, ANNE; Archbiship Carroll HS; Gulph Mills, PA; (Y); 54/216; Art Clb; Church Yth Grp; Drama Clb; French Clb; Ski Clb; Teachers Aide; Hon Roll; Art Awd Art II; Schltc Art Awd; Gold Key PCA Art Comptrn; Philadelphia Clg; Arts.

GANNON, STEPHEN; Cardinal Dongherty HS; Melrose Park, PA; (Y); 15/747; Bsktbl; Ftbl; Var Tennis; Wt Lftg; Hon Roll; NHS; Prfct Atten Awd; French & Englsh Profcncy Awd 83; Relgn Profcncy Awd 84; St Josephs U; Math.

GANOE, CRAIG; Seneca HS; Union City, PA; (Y); 1/173; Church Yth Grp; Computer Clb; Pep Clb; Quiz Bowl; Rep Stu Cncl; Stat Bsktbl; Mgr Ftbl; Wt Lftg; NHS.

GANT, LAMONT C; Westinghouse HS; Pittsburgh, PA; (Y); Library Aide; Lit Mag; Wrk On Wall At US Embssy Of Guatemala 85; Dsgn Nationalities Rm Pitt U 85; Acad All Amer Schlr Dir 86; Carnegie Mellon U; Cmmcl Art.

GANTAR, SUSAN; Forest City Regional HS; Forest City, PA; (Y); 3/63; Drama Clb; German Clb; Letterman Clb; Scholastic Bowl; Ski Clb; Varsity Clb; Band; Chorus; Concert Band; Jazz Band; Du Quene U Symph Bnd 85; PA ST U; Chem Engrng.

GANTER, BOB; Bethel Park SR HS; Bethel Park, PA; (Y); French Clb; Var Capt Ice Hcky; Wrstlng; NASC 85; Jr Engrs Clb 85-86; U Of Pittsburgh; Engrng.

GANTER, FRED; Annville-Cleona HS; Cleona, PA; (S); 18/121; Band; Chorus; Jazz Band; Madrigals; Pres Sr Cls; Pres Stu Cncl; Pres Wt Lftg; Dnfth Awd; DAR Awd; NHS; Dstrct Chrs 85; Hnrs Bnd 85; Rtry Boy Of Mnth 85; N TX ST U; Msc Prfrmnc.

GANTERT, BRIAN; Parkland HS; Allntwn, PA; (Y); 45/459; Church Yth Grp; Hon Roll; NHS; PA ST; Bus.

GANTERT, CAROL; Governor Mifflin HS; Reading, PA; (Y); Church Yth Grp; VP FBLA; Office Aide; Chorus; Yrbk Bus Mgr; VP Stu Cncl; JV Bsktbl; Var Sftbl; Var Trk; Var Vllybl; Lgl Sctry.

GANTZ, JOHN; Shenandoah Valley HS; Shenandoah, PA; (Y); 10/108; Computer Clb; English Clb; Exploring; French Clb; Math Clb; Science Clb; Spanish Clb; JV Bsbl; Var L Bsktbl; High Hon Roll.

GANTZ, KARIN; Lewistown Area HS; Lewistown, PA; (Y); AFS; French Clb; Stu Cncl; Cheerleading; Vllybl; High Hon Roll; NHS; Shippensburg; Comp Sci.

GANWARE, TAWNYA; Upper Darby SR HS; Upper Darby, PA; (Y); Civic Clb; Cmnty Wkr; Drama Clb; Teachers Aide; School Musical; School Play; Nwsp Stf; Trk; Hon Roll; Pres Schlr; Prsdntl Athltc Aw 83-85; ESL Aide 86; UN Intrprtr.

GANZELMANN, DARREN; Exeter Township HS; Birdsboro, PA; (Y); Exploring; Band; Concert Band; Crs Cntry; Trk; Bus.

GAPPA, ANISSA; Saint Pius X HS; Phoenixville, PA; (S); 37/139; Civic Clb; Drill Tm; School Play; Stu Cncl; Cheerleading; Sftbl; Tennis; Hon Roll; Sec NHS; Prfct Atten Awd; Bus Adm.

GARAWSKI, MICHAEL; Council Rock HS; Newtown, PA; (Y); 25/845; Political Wkr; Drm Mjr(t); Mrchg Band; Symp Band; Hon Roll; NHS; Prfct Atten Awd; Debate Tm; Band; Jazz Band; ST, All E Band 86; PA Free Entrprs Wk Schlrshp 85.

GARB, RACHEL; Bensalem HS; Bensalem, PA; (Y); Band; School Musical; Nwsp Stf; Yrbk Stf; Tennis; Hon Roll; NHS; Annl Bucks Cnty Music Fest Band 85-86; Math.

GARBACIK, EDWARD J; West Hazleton SR HS; W Hazleton, PA; (S); Scholastic Bowl; SADD; Bsktbl; Ftbl; Trk; Wt Lftg; Hon Roll; NHS; Amer Legion Awd 83; Alchl & Drug Svcs Awd 85; Penn ST U; Pre-Med.

GARBACIK, GARY; Trinity HS; Camp Hill, PA; (Y); Boy Scts; French Clb; Band; Chorus; Church Choir; Concert Band; Jazz Band; Mrchg Band; School Musical; Im Bsktbl; Louis Armstrong Jazz Awd 86; Am Wilderness Ldrshp Schl 86; Eagle Scout Awd 83; Civil Engr.

GARBACIK, JOSEPH; Freeland HS; Freeland, PA; (Y); VP Chess Clb; Sec Computer Clb; Spanish Clb; Yrbk Stf; Stu Cncl; JV L Socr; JV Wrstlng; Hon Roll; NHS; Spanish NHS; Ntl Sci Olympiad 83; Rets Elec Schls; Elec Engr.

GARBER, ALICE; Hempfield Area SR HS; Greensburg, PA; (Y); 16/700; NFL; Pep Clb; Spanish Clb; School Musical; Yrbk Stf; Var Tennis; High Hon Roll; NHS; Spanish NHS; Nuc Engr.

GARBER, DEBBIE; Hempfield HS; Landisville, PA; (Y); Teachers Aide; Chorus; Rep Frsh Cls; Rep Soph Cls; Rep Jr Cls; Rep Sr Cls; Cheerleading; Powder Puff Ftbl; Trk; Hon Roll; Shippensburg U; Bus.

GARBER, DEBBIE; St Huberts HS; Philadelphia, PA; (Y); 212/367; Church Yth Grp; Cmnty Wkr; Exploring; Teachers Aide; PSOT; Acctg.

GARBER, DONOVAN L; Elizabethtown HS; Elizabethtown, PA; (Y); Ski Clb; Pres Band; Concert Band; Jazz Band; Mrchg Band; Orch; School Musical; Symp Band; Hon Roll; NHS; Amercm Music Abroad Tour Europe 85; LLMEA Cnty Band 84-85; Berklee Coll; Music Prod.

GARBER, LYNDA; Pocono Central Catholic HS; Mount Pocono, PA; (S); 5/22; Art Clb; Pep Clb; Service Clb; Ski Clb; Yrbk Stf; Capt Bsktbl; Var Fld Hcky; Var Sftbl; Hon Roll; Penn ST; Engrng.

GARBER, PATRICK; Manheim Township HS; Lititz, PA; (Y); 49/300; Im Bsktbl; Pre-Law.

GARBERA, KIMBERLY; Carbondale Area HS; Simpson, PA; (S); 10/157; Art Clb; Hosp Aide; Library Aide; Ski Clb; Spanish Clb; Chorus; Drill Tm; School Musical; School Play; Hon Roll; Phrmcy.

GARBUTT, BETH; Abington HS; Abington, PA; (Y); 230/528; Church Yth Grp; Cmnty Wkr; Key Clb; Spanish Clb; Varsity Clb; Church Choir; Fld Hcky; Swmmng; Gettysburg Coll; Psychol.

GARCHER, MICHELE; Geibel HS; Masontown, PA; (Y); Art Clb; Science Clb; Spanish Clb; Nwsp Rptr; Nwsp Stf; Yrbk Stf; Lit Mag; JV Crs Cntry; High Hon Roll; Spanish NHS.

GARCIA, ALICIA; Albert Gallatin SR HS; Point Marion, PA; (Y); Library Aide; VICA; High Hon Roll; Hon Roll.

GARCIA, CARMEN; Clarion Area HS; Shippenville, PA; (Y); Church Yth Grp; FCA; FHA; FTA; Library Aide; Pep Clb; Band; Chorus; Church Choir; Flag Corp; Clarion U Of PA; Elem Ed.

GARCIA, CHRIS; Central Dauphin HS; Harrisburg, PA; (Y); Church Yth Grp; German Clb; Soph Cls; JV Bsktbl; Var Sftbl; Hon Roll; NHS; Pres Schlr; Mt San Antonio Coll; Phrmcy.

GARDAS, JENNIFER; Honesdale HS; Honesdale, PA; (Y); Ski Clb; Var Bsktbl; Var Cheerleading; JV Golf; Var L Sftbl; High Hon Roll; Med.

GARDECKI, ROSELLA; MMI Prep; Conyngham, PA; (S); 12/32; Art Clb; Church Yth Grp; Debate Tm; Math Clb; Model UN; Pep Clb; Stat Bsbl; Stat Bsktbl; High Hon Roll; NHS; Bus.

GARDETTO, CHARLES; Kiski Area HS; Vandergrift, PA; (Y); Computer Clb; Exploring; Var Bsktbl.

GARDINA, LEO; Clarin Area HS; Clarion, PA; (Y); Church Yth Grp; Chorus; School Musical; Stage Crew; Swing Chorus; Symp Band; Variety Show; Yrbk Stf; Stu Cncl; Mgr(s); Clarion U Of PA; Cmptr Prgrmng.

GARDINER, DIANE; Palmyra HS; Palmyra, PA; (Y); 8/200; Drama Clb; German Clb; Ski Clb; Chorus; Score Keeper; Sftbl; Twrlr; High Hon Roll; Hon Roll; NHS; Cand People To People 84-85; High Hnrs Awd Germn 84-86; Comp Sci.

GARDINER, LAURA; State College Area SR HS; State College, PA; (Y); Church Yth Grp; Hosp Aide; SADD; Off Sr Cls; Capt Crs Cntry; Capt Trk; Cit Awd; Elks Awd; High Hon Roll; NEDT Awd; PA Relays Champ Of Amer 85; 2 Times PA St Champ 84-86; Fac Schlr 3.75 GPA 86; PA ST U; Librl Arts.

GARDNER, CARRIE; Avon Grove HS; West Grove, PA; (Y); 32/150; Library Aide; SADD; School Musical; School Play; Nwsp Ed-Chief; Yrbk Ed-Chief; Lit Mag; Rep Stu Cncl; Tennis; Hst Frsh Cls; Stu Forum; Millersvl U; Libry Sci.

GARDNER, CINDY; Chestnut Ridge HS; Bedford, PA; (Y); 22/125; Band; Mrchg Band; Nwsp Stf; Var Capt Socr; Sftbl; Stat Trk; Vllybl; Hon Roll; JR Exec Cmmttee 84-85; CPR Cert 84-86; Allegheny CC MD; Acctg.

GARDNER, CORINNE; Hopewell HS; Aliquippa, PA; (S); 1/265; Cmnty Wkr; Latin Clb; VP Library Aide; Band; Concert Band; Mrchg Band; Rep Frsh Cls; Rep Soph Cls; Trs Jr Cls; High Hon Roll; Yngtwn ST U Englsh Awd 85; PMEA Dstrct Bnd 85 & 86.

GARDNER, CYNTHIA; Cumberland Valley HS; Boiling Springs, PA; (Y); 20/522; French Clb; Speech Tm; Teachers Aide; Capt Color Guard; Capt Flag Corp; Lit Mag; Var Swmmng; French Hon Soc; High Hon Roll; Jr NHS.

GARDNER, DARYLIN; Penn Hills HS; Verona, PA; (Y); Spanish Clb; Jr Cls; Cheerleading; Gym; Trk; Hon Roll.

GARDNER, JENNIFER; Mt Pleasant Area R HS; Mt Pleasant, PA; (Y); Church Yth Grp; Cmnty Wkr; French Clb; GAA; Girl Scts; Hosp Aide; Ski Clb; Spanish Clb; Band; Concert Band; CA U; Nrsg.

GARDNER, KIM; Union HS; New Castle, PA; (Y); French Clb; Hosp Aide; JA; Hon Roll; Jr NHS; NHS; Jmsn Schl Nrsng; Nrs.

GARDNER, LESLEY; Elkland Area HS; Elkland, PA; (Y); 2/69; SADD; Varsity Clb; Band; Chorus; Var Bsktbl; Var Trk; Var Vllybl; Cit Awd; High Hon Roll; NHS; Outstndng Feml Athlt 85-86; All Twn Tiers Tm Bsktbl 85-86; Particpd Trk Meet 86; Naval Acad; Pre Med.

GARDNER, LISA; Pocono Central Catholic HS; Pocono Lake, PA; (Y); Am Leg Aux Girls St; Art Clb; Church Yth Grp; Hosp Aide; Pep Clb; Service Clb; Color Guard; School Musical; Stage Crew; JV Stat Bsktbl; Nrsg.

GARDNER, LORRIE; Elmer L Meyers HS; Wilkes Barre, PA; (Y); 16/164; Ski Clb; Crs Cntry; Trk; Vllybl; Hon Roll; Empire Beauty Schl; Cosmtlgy.

GARDNER, MARGY; Portersvill Christian Schl; Ellwood City, PA; (Y); Hosp Aide; Chorus; Nwsp Stf; Yrbk Ed-Chief; Pres Stu Cncl; Var Cheerleading; Var Sftbl; Capt Vllybl; High Hon Roll; NHS; Geneva Coll; Med.

GARDNER, MAYNARD; Newport HS; Newport, PA; (Y); Var Capt Bsbl; Wt Lftg; Hon Roll; Sportsmns Clb Sec 85; Tri Valley Lgu & All Star Tm/Bsbl 86.

GARDNER, MICHELLE; Penn Hills SR HS; Pittsburgh, PA; (Y); JA; Spanish Clb; Hon Roll; PA ST.

GARDNER, MOLLY; Pittston Area HS; Pittston, PA; (Y); 1/363; Computer Clb; Key Clb; Math Clb; JV Bsktbl; Var L Sftbl; High Hon Roll; Trs NHS; NEDT Awd; Psych.

GARDNER, PAUL; St Joesephs Prep; Philadelphia, PA; (Y); Cmnty Wkr; Spanish Clb; Yrbk Stf; Var L Crs Cntry; Var L Trk; Hon Roll; Jrnlsm.

GARDNER, RICHELLE; Sullivan County HS; Dushore, PA; (Y); 16/88; Drama Clb; Trs Key Clb; SADD; VP Band; Nwsp Rptr; Rep Jr Cls; Stu Cncl; Hon Roll; Ntl Merit Ltr; Bi Cnty Band 84-86; Dist Band 86; Master Musicn Awd 86; Cmmnctns.

GARDNER, SUSAN; Pittston Area HS; Hughestown, PA; (Y); 1/330; Drama Clb; FNA; Key Clb; Capt Drill Tm; Nwsp Rptr; Var L Swmmng; NHS; Val; Best Of The Class Awd 86; Pres Acad Ftnss Awd 86; Acad All-Amer-Drill Tm 86; U Of MD; Bio.

GARDNER, TAMI; Frazier HS; Dawson, PA; (Y); FNA; Ski Clb; Vllybl; Nrsng.

GARDNER, TROY D; Hollidaysburg SR HS; Duncansville, PA; (Y); 95/349; Varsity Clb; Ftbl; Wrstlng; Lycoming Coll.

GARDNER, WILLIAM CANNON; Kiski Area HS; Apollo, PA; (Y); Aud/Vis; Church Yth Grp; Debate Tm; JA; Library Aide; Math Clb; Math Tm; Science Clb; Chorus; Nwsp Rptr; VA Polytech Inst; Mech Engrng.

GARDOCKY, DAVID; Union Area HS; New Castle, PA; (Y); 32/68.

GAREY, THERESA; Tunkhannock HS; Falls, PA; (S); 50/310; Church Yth Grp; Church Choir; 4-H Awd; Hon Roll; Kiwanis Awd; NHS; Med.

GARGAN, DONNA; Morrisville HS; Morrisville, PA; (Y); 4/99; Varsity Clb; Church Choir; Yrbk Stf; Sec Sr Cls; JV Var Cheerleading; CC Awd; High Hon Roll; NHS; Pep Clb; Mrsvl Ed Schlrshp 86; Mrlyn Moyer Schlrshp 86; Mt Outstndng Spnsh Stu 85 & 86; La Salle U; Elem Ed.

GARGASZ, JOSEPH; New Wilmington Area HS; Volant, PA; (S); Coach Actv; L Ftbl; Powder Puff Ftbl; Wt Lftg; Hon Roll; Westminster; Bus Admin.

GARGASZ, ROBERTA; Grove City HS; Grove City, PA; (Y); AFS; Yrbk Bus Mgr; Yrbk Stf; Lit Mag; Trs Frsh Cls; Trs Soph Cls; Trs Jr Cls; Trs Sr Cls; Sec Stu Cncl; Powder Puff Ftbl; Retail Mrktng.

GARGIULO, FRANK; Farrell Area HS; Farrell, PA; (Y); 6/100; Aud/Vis; Cmnty Wkr; Computer Clb; French Clb; Science Clb; Lit Mag; Stu Cncl; JV Bsktbl; French Hon Soc; High Hon Roll; 3rd Pl Natl Hlth Cntst 84; Devlpd Cmmnty Redvlpmt Prog Conjctn City Of Farrell 83-85.

GARING, KIM; Karns HS; Chicora, PA; (Y); 23/123; Am Leg Aux Girls St; Pep Clb; Bsktbl; Stu Secretary 86; Butler County CC; Bus Mgt.

GARLESKY, JACKIE; Windber Area HS; Windber, PA; (Y); Art Clb; Pep Clb; Rep Sr Cls; Var JV Bsktbl; JV Trk; Var JV Vllybl; Hon Roll; Stu Of The Mnth; Recgntn For Shown Art Work 85; U Of Pitts; Creative Writing.

GARLINGTON, JEFF; Tech Memorial HS; Erie, PA; (Y); Aud/Vis; VICA; Stage Crew; Nwsp Stf; Lit Mag; Stat Bsktbl; JV Var Ftbl; Artcl Schl Nwspapr Plc ST Comptn 83-84; Edinboro U Of PA; Socl Wrk.

GARMAN, BRYAN; Clearfield Area HS; Clearfield, PA; (Y); 1/314; Key Clb; Spanish Clb; Var Soph Cls; Var Jr Cls; Var Sr Cls; Var Capt Bsbl; Var L Ftbl; DAR Awd; Pres NHS; Val; St Jr Sci & Humanities Symposium; Hugh O Brian Ldrshp Sem; Bucknell U; Chem Engrng.

GARMAN, DAVE; Hershey HS; Hershey, PA; (Y); 34/201; Band; Chorus; School Musical; School Play; Swing Chorus; Variety Show; Yrbk Phtg; Trs Sr Cls; Var L Bsbl; Var L Golf; PA ST U; Radio Cmmnctns.

GARMAN, JULIE; Chestnut Ridge HS; Imler, PA; (S); 16/142; Band; Concert Band; Nwsp Rptr; JV Cheerleading; Var Socr; Var Trk; Hon Roll; NHS; Phys Ther.

GARMEN, BRADLEY; Carlisle SR HS; Carlisle, PA; (Y); Cmnty Wkr; Science Clb; Teachers Aide; Rep Frsh Cls; Var Ftbl; JV Wrstlng; Hon Roll; Prfct Atten Awd; Library Aide; Office Aide; Engrng.

GARMEN, THERESA; Sylvania Hills Christian Acad; Ellwood City, PA; (S); 1/4; Church Yth Grp; Chorus; School Musical; Yrbk Stf; Bsktbl; Hon Roll; Scrptr Memory Awd; Geneva; Accntng.

GARNER, BARBARA; North Penn HS; N Wales, PA; (Y); 118/678; Exploring; VP 4-H; Orch; JV Bowling; JV Trk; 4-H Awd; Hon Roll; Med Research.

GARNER, DEIRDRE RAE; St Marys Area HS; Saint Marys, PA; (Y); French Clb; Hosp Aide; JA.

GARNER, HEIDI; Warwick HS; Lititz, PA; (Y); 27/237; Chorus; Mrchg Band; School Musical; VP Stu Cncl; Trk; Twrlr; High Hon Roll; Millersville; Sec Ed.

GARNER, JENNIFER; Bishop Kenrick HS; Norristown, PA; (Y); 13/295; Science Clb; Ski Clb; Rep Stu Cncl; Cheerleading; Hon Roll; NHS; Cmnty Wkr; Exploring; Office Aide; Drill Tm; Pa Free Entrprse Wk 86; Intl Bus.

GARNER, JUDY; Warwick HS; Lititz, PA; (Y); 33/215; Church Yth Grp; Yrbk Ed-Chief; High Hon Roll; Hon Roll; NHS; Outstndng Achvt Stf Yrbk 86; Acctng.

GARNER, MARLENE MAE; Eastern York HS; E Prospect, PA; (Y); 46/169; Sec Church Yth Grp; Drama Clb; Girl Scts; SADD; Varsity Clb; Trs Chorus; School Musical; School Play; Nwsp Stf; Yrbk Stf.

GARNER, PAMELA; Commodore Perry HS; Hadley, PA; (S); 12/64; Sec Trs Church Yth Grp; VP FBLA; Sec Trs FTA; Chorus; VP Jr Cls; Pres Stu Cncl; Capt Cheerleading; Co-Capt Twrlr; DAR Awd; Hon Roll; Slippery Rock U; Scndry Educ.

GARNER, SANDY; Huntingdon Area HS; James Creek, PA; (Y); 1/223; Trs Church Yth Grp; Sec 4-H; Sec Key Clb; Stu Cncl; Var L Fld Hcky; Var L Sftbl; High Hon Roll; NHS; NEDT Awd; Rotary Awd; PA Farmers Assoc Yth Conf, PA Assoc Farmer Coop 86; 3rd Optimist Essay Cntst 85; Math Educ.

GAROFOLO, MICHAEL A; Norwin SR HS; N Huntingdon, PA; (Y); 235/550; Trs Letterman Clb; Pres Spanish Clb; Nwsp Stf; Var L Crs Cntry; Var Im Tennis; Wt Lftg; Var Wrstlng; High Hon Roll; Hon Roll; N Huntingdon Police Schlrshp 86; Edinboro U Of PA; Crmnl Justc.

GAROMON, WILLIAM; New Hope-Solebury HS; New Hope, PA; (Y); 16/80; Sec FBLA; Ski Clb; Band; Concert Band; Mrchg Band; Bsbl; Socr; Hon Roll; Pennsylvania Free Entrprs Wk Schlrshp 86.

GARR, KATHY; Nazareth Area SR HS; Nazareth, PA; (Y); #9 In Class; Exploring; Pep Clb; Ski Clb; Yrbk Sprt Ed; Yrbk Stf; JV Cheerleading; Var Trk; High Hon Roll; NHS; Prsdntl Physcl Ftnss Awd; Vet.

GARRAHAN, CHRISTINE; Tunkhannock HS; Harveys Lake, PA; (S); Science Clb; Chorus; School Musical; JV Fld Hcky; Dist Chrs 85.

GARRETT, JASON; Peters Township HS; Venetia, PA; (Y); JA; Letterman Clb; Spanish Clb; Varsity Clb; Var L Bsbl; Var L Bsktbl; JV Co-Capt Ftbl; High Hon Roll; Hon Roll; Awd Exc Hnr Rl 84-85; Bus Mgmt.

GARRETT, JOYCE L; Upper Dublin SR HS; North Hills, PA; (Y); 99/337; Am Leg Aux Girls St; Church Yth Grp; Office Aide; Church Choir; Stu Cncl; Bsktbl; Mgr(s); Opt Clb Awd; England-Amer Exchng Prog 85; Black Stu Union BSU Advsr 82-86; PA ST U; Mgmt Info Sys.

GARRETT, KATHLEEN; Bishop Carroll HS; Cresson, PA; (S); 9/109; Spanish Clb; Off Stu Cncl; Capt Cheerleading; High Hon Roll; Hon Roll; NHS; Occptnl Thrpy.

GARRETT, LISA; W Middlesex Area HS; W Middlesex, PA; (S); 7/120; 4-H; Spanish Clb; Band; Chorus; Concert Band; Mrchg Band; High Hon Roll; Jr NHS; Prfct Atten Awd; Spanish NHS; Natl Sci Mrt Awd 84; Brdcst Jrnlsm.

GARRETT, LORI; South Western HS; Hanover, PA; (Y); Key Clb; Rep Keywanettes; Ski Clb; SADD; Band; Mrchg Band; Nwsp Rptr; Yrbk Stf; Stat Bsbl; JV Fld Hcky; Pres Ldrshp Awd; Hood Coll; Pre-Law.

GARRETT, WILLIAM; Penn Center Acad; Philadelphia, PA; (S); 1/29; Nwsp Ed-Chief; Ed Lit Mag; Pres Stu Cncl; Cit Awd; High Hon Roll; Hon Roll; Pres NHS; Natl Achvt Schlrshp Pgm 86; Campbell Soup Co Schlrshp 86; Rgnl Rep PA Assn SC Brd 85-86; U Of PA; Bio.

GARRETY, AMY; Elizabethtown Area HS; Elizabethtown, PA; (Y); 16/236; Rep Frsh Cls; Rep Soph Cls; Cheerleading; NHS; Bus.

GARRICK, TERI; Belle Vernon Area HS; Belle Vernon, PA; (Y); Pep Clb; Ski Clb; Color Guard; Powder Puff Ftbl; High Hon Roll; Hon Roll; Penn ST; Criminology.

GARRIS, RICHARD; Rocky Grove HS; Franklin, PA; (Y); 19/90; Yrbk Stf; Rep Stu Cncl; Tennis; Vllybl; Hon Roll.

GARRIS, VIRGINIA; Raocky Grove HS; Franklin, PA; (Y); 3/92; Church Yth Grp; Library Aide; Variety Show; Yrbk Stf; Jr Cls; VP Sr Cls; Rep Stu Cncl; High Hon Roll; NHS; Pres Schlr; SR Prm Crt 86; Indiana U Of PA; Crmnlgy.

GARRISON, GAIL; Mt Lebanon HS; Pittsburgh, PA; (Y); Camera Clb; VP Church Yth Grp; Exploring; Service Clb; Ski Clb; Spanish Clb; Off Jr Cls; JV Diving; Im Vllybl.

GARRISON, JOSEPH; Crestwood JR Sr HS; Mountaintop, PA; (Y); 6/226; Cmnty Wkr; Math Clb; Ski Clb; School Musical; School Play; VP Capt Socr; VP L Trk; High Hon Roll; Trs NHS; NEDT Awd; PA Comp Coll; TV.

GARRISON, MIKE; Canon-Mc Millan SR HS; Canonsburg, PA; (Y); Church Yth Grp; Exploring; Ski Clb; Pres Jr Cls; Stu Cncl; Var JV Bsbl; JV L Trk; High Hon Roll; Ntl Merit Schol; Duke U; Bio-Med Engrng.

GARRITY, DARA; Donegal HS; Mt Joy, PA; (Y); Church Yth Grp; Cmnty Wkr; Drama Clb; Concert Band; Mrchg Band; Hon Roll; Miss Amer Coed 86; Pres Ftnss Awd 84; Nrsg.

GARRITY, TESS; Sayre Area HS; Sayre, PA; (Y); Church Yth Grp; Cmnty Wkr; French Clb; GAA; Girl Scts; Hosp Aide; Spanish Clb; SADD; Stage Crew; Yrbk Stf; Psychtry.

GARRONE, CARLA; Trinity HS; Washington, PA; (Y); Church Yth Grp; Sec 4-H; VP Hosp Aide; Key Clb; Pep Clb; Ski Clb; Band; Concert Band; Mrchg Band; 4-H Awd; Chem Engr.

GARROWAY, BILL; Lincoln HS; Ellwood City, PA; (Y); Church Yth Grp; Latin Clb; Bsbl; Powder Puff Ftbl; High Hon Roll; Dntstry.

GARTLEY, BILL; Hopewell HS; Aliquippa, PA; (S); 21/243; Office Aide; Spanish Clb; Im JV Bsbl; Stat Im Bsktbl; Im JV Ftbl; Stat Score Keeper; High Hon Roll; Citatn Hse Of Rep & Membr Bsbl 85; Engrng.

GARTMAN, RON; Cheltenham HS; Elkins Pk, PA; (Y); Exploring; Science Clb; SADD; Jazz Band; Badmtn; Swmmng; Hon Roll; Opt Clb Awd.

GARTNER, JUDY; Greater Works Acad; Verona, PA; (S); Service Clb; Ski Clb; Yrbk Stf; Var L Bsktbl; Var Sftbl; High Hon Roll; 1st Plc Sci Fr 84-85; Engnrng.

GARTNER, TABATHA; Central Bucks H S West; Chalfont, PA; (Y); Cmnty Wkr; Band; Color Guard; Drm & Bgl; Jazz Band; Mrchg Band; Orch; School Musical; Nwsp Stf; Rep Frsh Cls; Outstndng Bndsmn Awd 85; Bux-Mont Band 85; Amer Music Abroad 85; Temple; Music.

GARTNER, VIRGINIA A; Moon SR HS; Corapolis, PA; (Y); 30/315; Church Yth Grp; German Clb; JA; Key Clb; Ski Clb; Jazz Band; Pep Band; Symp Band; Capt Var Socr; Hon Roll; Grave City Coll; Bus Admn.

GARUCCIO, JOSEPH; Moon SR HS; Coraopolis, PA; (Y); 10/306; French Clb; School Play; Variety Show; Im Ftbl; Im Swmmng; High Hon Roll; Hon Roll; NHS; Distngshd Hnr Roll Awd 84-85; Chem Engr.

GARVER, STEPHEN JOEL; Phil-Mont Christian Acad; Philadelphia, PA; (Y); 1/37; Church Yth Grp; Cmnty Wkr; Rep Stu Cncl; High Hon Roll; NHS; Superior Awd MACSA JR Arts Fest 86; 1st & 3rd Phil-Mont Christian Acad Art Show 85-86; Engl.

GARVER, TAMMY; New Castle HS; New Castle, PA; (Y); 32/265; Church Yth Grp; French Clb; Medical Explorers Clb 85-86; Yrbk Sales Rep 85-86; Physcl Thrpy.

GARVER, TIMOTHY; Altoona Area HS; Altoona, PA; (S); Math Tm; Spanish Clb; Rptr Stu Cncl; JV Var Bsbl; Im Bsktbl; Jr NHS; NHS; PA ST U; Sci.

GARVIN, MELISSA; Mt Lebanon HS; Mt Lebanon, PA; (Y); 75/507; Chorus; Yrbk Stf; Rep Stu Cncl; Stat Bsktbl; JV Cheerleading; Var Trk; High Hon Roll; Hon Roll.

GARZA, BECKY; Biglerville HS; Bendersville, PA; (Y); #34 In Class; Art Clb; DECA; FBLA; Nwsp Rptr; Nwsp Stf; Hon Roll; Soclgy.

GASBARRO, ALEXANDER SANDY; Upper Darby HS; Secane, PA; (Y); Church Yth Grp; Cmnty Wkr; Band; Nwsp Stf; Frsh Cls; Soph Cls; Bsbl; Crs Cntry; Var L Trk; Page For US House Repsnt 85; Vol Fireman For Upper Darby Twnshp 84; Up With People 87; Annapolis; Naval Air.

GASBARRO, DEBORAH; Kiski Area HS; Vandergrift, PA; (Y); FBLA; Chorus; Hon Roll; Rotary Awd; Bradford Bus Schl; Legal Sec.

GASBARRO, LISA; Kiski Area HS; Hyde Park, PA; (Y); FBLA; Office Aide; Pep Clb; Teachers Aide; Chorus; School Musical; Prfct Atten Awd; New Kensington Cmmrcl Schl; Sec.

GASHEL, ERIC; Mc Guffey HS; Claysville, PA; (S); 35/216; VP 4-H; Spanish Clb; L Ftbl; Trk; Var Wrstlng; 4-H Awd; Hon Roll; Pres Schlr.

GASHEL, PATRICIA JANE; Mc Guffey HS; Claysville, PA; (Y); 13/201; Am Leg Aux Girls St; German Clb; Pep Clb; Varsity Clb; Yrbk Phtg; Sec Soph Cls; Stu Cncl; Var L Trk; Var L Vllybl; NHS.

GASHI, SHIRLEY ANN; Wyalusing Valley HS; Laceyville, PA; (Y); Drama Clb; German Clb; Band; Chorus; Concert Band; Jazz Band; Mrchg Band; Orch; School Musical; NHS.

GASKILL, GENE; Ringgold HS; Monongahela, PA; (Y); High Hon Roll; Hon Roll; NHS; Sci-Math Hnr Soc 84-86; Achvt Awd 84; Stck Mrkt Clb 85; Engrng.

GASKILL, JAN; Ringgold HS; Monongahela, PA; (Y); Art Clb; French Clb; Nwsp Stf; Yrbk Stf; Powder Puff Ftbl; Hon Roll; Art Ed.

GASKIN, RAMONAH; Philadelphia HS For Girls; Philadelphia, PA; (Y); Church Yth Grp; Girl Scts; Spanish Clb; Teachers Aide; Church Choir; PA ST U; Acctg.

GASPARIK, NANCY; Keystone Oaks HS; Pittsburgh, PA; (Y); DECA; Exploring; Spanish Clb; SADD; Teachers Aide; Hon Roll; Data Entry.

GASPER, ROBERT; West Scranton HS; Scranton, PA; (Y); Drama Clb; NFL; Speech Tm; Pres Thesps; School Musical; School Play; Stage Crew; Hon Roll; Penn ST; Thtre.

GASTGER, JAMES; Bethel Park HS; Bethel Park, PA; (Y); Church Yth Grp; Bsbl; Ftbl; Trk; Wt Lftg; Bus.

GASTON, NICK; Marion Center; Rochester Mills, PA; (S); 18/140; Aud/Vis; Chorus; Bsbl; Hon Roll; NHS; Comp Sci.

GATARIC, DRAZENKA; Mt Alvernia HS; Pittsburgh, PA; (Y); Art Clb; Red Cross Aide; Chorus; Stage Crew; Hon Roll; Prfct Atten Awd; Bus Hnrs 86; Type-A-Thon For Leukemia 84; Cllgrphy 85.

GATENS, BARB; Marian Catholic HS; Coaldale, PA; (S); 10/128; Pep Clb; Scholastic Bowl; Yrbk Stf; High Hon Roll; NHS; Spanish NHS; Drexel; Secutries Trdr.

GATES, CAROL; Moon Area HS; Glenwillow, PA; (Y); Church Yth Grp; Intnl Clb; Band; Chorus; Drm Mjr(t); Mrchg Band; Symp Band; Off Jr Cls; Hon Roll; NHS; Phrmcy.

GATES, CHRISTINE EMILY; Hempfield Area HS; Greensburg, PA; (Y); Church Yth Grp; Spanish Clb; Y-Teens; Yrbk Stf; Stu Cncl; Capt Var Cheerleading; High Hon Roll; Hon Roll; NHS; Ntl Merit Ltr; IN U Of PA; Hlth.

GATES, JAMIE; Troy SR HS; Gillett, PA; (Y); Computer Clb; Letterman Clb; Var Bsbl; JV L Ftbl; NHS; Mansfield U; Comp Sci.

GATES, KARMAN M; Bald Eagle Area HS; Howard, PA; (Y); 38/201; Church Yth Grp; French Clb; Hosp Aide; Teachers Aide; Varsity Clb; Acpl Chr; VP Chorus; Nwsp Rptr; Nwsp Stf; Rep Frsh Cls; Miss Bald Eagle 86-87; Missionette Hnr Star 85; Schl Trk Recrd 440 Relay Tm 84; Lawyr.

GATES, LAURA; Troy Area HS; Columbia Crss Rds, PA; (Y); 33/144; 4-H; Letterman Clb; Band; Chorus; Concert Band; Jazz Band; Mrchg Band; Pep Band; School Play; Var L Trk; Bus & Prof Wmns Ed Schlrsp 86; Honorary Band Awd 86; Lock Haven U.

GATES, LYNNE; Tunkhannock Area HS; Tunkhannock, PA; (S); 20/320; Church Yth Grp; FCA; German Clb; Letterman Clb; Vllybl; Hon Roll; NHS; Various Vllybl Awds 85-86; Acad All Amer 85; Bus Adm.

GATES, ROGER; United HS; Seward, PA; (Y); Red Cross Aide; VP Jr Cls; JV Bsktbl; Var L Ftbl; Im Wt Lftg; Hon Roll.

GATES, SHERRI; Forest Hills HS; Mineral Point, PA; (Y); Pep Clb; Y-Teens; High Hon Roll; Hon Roll; Jr NHS; Accntng.

GATON, TIMOTHY; St Marys Area HS; Emporium, PA; (Y); Boys Clb Am; JV Bsktbl; JV Ftbl; Wt Lftg; Hon Roll; NHS; U Ptsbrg Brdfrd; Comp Sci.

GATRELL, GARY; Westgreene HS; Holbrook, PA; (Y); FFA; Letterman Clb; Varsity Clb; School Play; Var Bsbl; Var Ftbl; Var Wrstlng; Hon Roll; WVU; Elec Engrng.

GATSKI, LYNN; Hazleton HS; Hazleton, PA; (Y); 20/380; Office Aide; Pep Clb; Teachers Aide; Chorus; Stage Crew; Nwsp Ed-Chief; High Hon Roll; NHS; Houshld Fin Corp Schlrshp Awd 86; Pres Acad Fitness Awd 86; Kings Coll Span Cont 84; Penn ST U; Pre Med.

GATTA, GRAZIELLA; Saint Maria Goretti HS; Philadelphia, PA; (Y); Cmnty Wkr; VP Exploring; Library Aide; Office Aide; Red Cross Aide; Teachers Aide; School Play; Stage Crew; Variety Show; Rep Soph Cls; Temple U; Bus Adm.

GATTI, MARSY; John S Fine HS; Nanticoke, PA; (Y); Church Yth Grp; Model UN; Chorus; Church Choir; Color Guard; Law.

GATTIKER, ANNE; Chambersburg Area SR HS; Chambersburg, PA; (Y); 1/575; Sec Church Yth Grp; Sec Key Clb; VP Science Clb; Pres Band; Var L Swmmng; Kiwanis Awd; Pres NHS; Letterman Clb; Pres Concert Band; Pres Mrchg Band; Weis Market Schlrshp 86; Wkks Memorial Phys Awd 86; Satter Mem Chmis Awd 86; Dartmouth Coll; Engrng.

GATTO, ANTONINE; Bishop Carroll HS; Ebensburg, PA; (S); 1/108; Pep Clb; Chorus; Yrbk Stf; High Hon Roll; Hon Roll; US Stu Cncl Awds; Engr.

GATTO, JENNIE; Elizabeth Forward HS; Elizabeth, PA; (Y); 33/317; Church Yth Grp; Model UN; Nwsp Rptr; Yrbk Ed-Chief; Rep Sr Cls; Var Trk; Hon Roll; Drama Clb; Q&S; Nwsp Stf; Wrld Affrs Smnr 85; Natl Chmpn Acdmc Gms 85; Dscpln Brd Schl Brd 85; UP; Lwyr.

GAUDET, LENORE; Littlestown HS; Littlestown, PA; (Y); 11/115; Pres Church Yth Grp; Drama Clb; Office Aide; Varsity Clb; Chorus; Yrbk Sprt Ed; Crs Cntry; Mgr(s); Trk; Hon Roll; Phy Thrpy.

GAUDIO, ALYSON C; Villa Maria HS; Youngstown, OH; (Y); Cmnty Wkr; Dance Clb; Spanish Clb; Stage Crew; Nwsp Rptr; NEDT Awd; Spanish NHS; YSU; Bus.

GAUGER, JULIE; Parkland HS; Allentown, PA; (Y); 32/419; VP Church Yth Grp; JCL; Leo Clb; Church Choir; JV Fld Hcky; High Hon Roll; Hon Roll; NHS; Lehigh County CC; Pltcl Sci.

GAUGHAN, JENNIFER; St Huberts HS For Girls; Philadelphia, PA; (Y); Cmnty Wkr; Office Aide; Service Clb; Sea Cadets Mdl 85; Temple; Mth.

GAUGHAN, LAURA; Meadville Area SR HS; Meadville, PA; (Y); Church Yth Grp; Letterman Clb; Varsity Clb; Off Jr Cls; Stu Cncl; L Swmmng; Trk; High Hon Roll; Acdmc All Amer & Ntl Stu Cncl Awd.

GAUGHAN, LIZ; Archbishop Kennedy HS; Philadelphia, PA; (Y); Cmnty Wkr; Girl Scts; Office Aide; Mgr(s); Sftbl.

GAUGLER, MICHELLE; Middleburg HS; Mt Pleasant Mills, PA; (Y); Pres Church Yth Grp; Pres 4-H; FHA; Chorus; Church Choir; High Hon Roll; Hon Roll; Jr NHS; NHS; Prfct Atten Awd; Pres Acad Fit Awd 86; Supr Acad Achvt 86.

GAUL, JAMI; Southern Columbia HS; Catawissa, PA; (Y); Off Key Clb; Chorus; Sec Soph Cls; VP Jr Cls; Stu Cncl; Capt L Bsktbl; L Fld Hcky; L Sftbl; Dnfth Awd; Hon Roll; Acad All Amer 86; Med.

GAULT, LAURA M; Plum SR HS; Pittsburgh, PA; (Y); 1/446; French Clb; FBLA; Math Tm; Pres Science Clb; School Play; Nwsp Rptr; NHS; Ntl Merit SF; NEDT Awd; Acad Sci 1st Pl Awds 85; Gftd & Tlntd Ed Rep 86; Wstnghse Explrs Post 258 Trea 86; Engr.

GAUS JR, FRANK; Tunkhannock Area HS; Tunkhannock, PA; (S); 48/280; Drama Clb; Acpl Chr; Chorus; School Musical; School Play; Stage Crew; L Bsktbl; L Crs Cntry; L Trk; NHS; Astrnmy.

GAUSMAN, NANCY; St Marys Area HS; St Marys, PA; (Y); Art Clb; Computer Clb; German Clb; JA; Pep Clb; Stage Crew; Yrbk Stf; Gym; High Hon Roll; Pres Schlr; Stackpole Merit Awd $250 86; Stackpole Schlrshp $2500 86; Pres Acadmc Ftnss Awd 86; Gannon U; Comp Tech.

GAUTHIER, SCOTT; Sullivan County HS; Dushore, PA; (Y); Boys Clb Am; Ski Clb; Mrchg Band; Socr; Wrstlng; Bus Admin.

GAVITT, LAURIE; West Hazleton HS; Conyngham, PA; (Y); 20/230; Church Yth Grp; Drama Clb; Ski Clb; Spanish Clb; Thesps; Church Choir; School Play; Nwsp Stf; High Hon Roll; Hon Roll; Jrnlsm.

GAVLINSKI, GEORGETTE; Bishop Hannan HS; Clarks Summit, PA; (Y); #11 In Class; Debate Tm; French Clb; Hosp Aide; Speech Tm; Chorus; School Play; Yrbk Stf; High Hon Roll; Hon Roll; NHS.

GAVRAN, LORI; Perry Traditional Acad; Pittsbg, PA; (Y); 25/137; Drama Clb; GAA; School Play; Nwsp Rptr; Yrbk Stf; Sec Trs Stu Cncl; Sftbl; Swmmng; Hon Roll; Soph Cls; Hugh O Brian Ldrshp Awd 85; Elem Educ.

GAWEL, EDWARD; Johnstown Voc Tech; Johnstown, PA; (Y); 91/312; VICA; Var L Crs Cntry; JV Trk; Var L Wrstlng; Ntl Yth Physcl Ftns Pgm Mrne Corps Leag Cert 84-86; Shp Cert Kpng B Avg 86; Computer Tech; Data Proc.

GAWLAS, CAROL; E L Meyers HS; Wilkes-Barre, PA; (S); 7/147; Key Clb; Ski Clb; Chorus; Flag Corp; Yrbk Stf; High Hon Roll; Jr NHS; NHS; NEDT Awd; Spanish NHS; Acad All Amer 86; Bloomsburg U; Nrsng.

GAY, DANIEL; Tunkhannock Area HS; Tunkhannock, PA; (Y); 90/300; Ski Clb; Im Bsbl; Im Bsktbl; French Hon Soc; U Of NV Las Vegas; Bus Mgmt.

GAY, YOLANDA; New Castle SR HS; New Castle, PA; (Y); AFS; Church Yth Grp; Spanish Clb; Band; Church Choir; Concert Band; Jazz Band; Mrchg Band; Rep Soph Cls; Rep Jr Cls; Marching Band Lttr 86; IN U; Fshn Mrch.

GAYDOS, KATHLEEN; James M Coughlin HS; Wilkes Barre, PA; (Y); 16/342; Church Yth Grp; Yrbk Stf; L Var Fld Hcky; L Var Sftbl; High Hon Roll; Jr NHS; NHS.

GAYDOS, KIMBERLY; Fort Le Boeuf HS; Erie, PA; (Y); 6/173; VP Art Clb; Var Capt Bsktbl; Var Capt Sftbl; High Hon Roll; NHS; Wmns Schltc Bsktbl Tm Keystone Games 86; IUP; Graphic Arts.

GAYDOS, MICHELLE; Phoenixville Area HS; Phoenixville, PA; (Y); 13/194; Hosp Aide; Key Clb; SADD; Varsity Clb; School Musical; Rep Jr Cls; Trs Rep Stu Cncl; Var Fld Hcky; Var Capt Sftbl; NHS; Russell E Emrich Mem Schlrshp Awd 86; Anne Longacre Caldwell Awd-Nrsng 86; Evans-Sigmor Nrsng Schlrshp; PA ST U; Nrnsg.

GAYDOS, MICHELLE; Shaler Area SR HS; Glenshaw, PA; (Y); 22/543; Sec Church Yth Grp; Band; Jazz Band; Trs Mrchg Band; School Musical; Variety Show; Mgr(s); Var Swmmng; High Hon Roll; NHS; Nrsng.

GAYDOS, ROBERT; Sch Haven Area HS; Landingville, PA; (Y); 2/99; Aud/Vis; Computer Clb; Science Clb; Spanish Clb; Yrbk Stf; Rep Stu Cncl; Trk; High Hon Roll; Hon Roll; NHS; Lehigh U; Engrng.

GAYLORD, MARK; The Baptist HS; Springville, PA; (S); Chess Clb; Church Yth Grp; Library Aide; Church Choir; Trs Pres Frsh Cls; Pres Soph Cls; Pres Jr Cls; Capt Bsktbl; High Hon Roll; Hon Roll; AACS Hnr Scty 84.

GAYNORD, MIKE F; Mars Area SR HS; Valencia, PA; (Y); 14/157; AFS; Boy Scts; Drama Clb; Thesps; Varsity Clb; Chorus; Madrigals; School Musical; School Play; NHS; Eagle Scout 86; Susquehanna U; Music.

GAYTON, KAREN; James M Coughlin HS; Wilkes-Barre, PA; (Y); VICA; JV Fld Hcky; High Hon Roll; Hon Roll; Jr NHS; NHS; Pres Schlr; ST Ldrshp Conf Hlth Occup Stu 85-86; Ntl Ldrshp Conf Gold Metal 85; Nrsng.

GAZDA, FRANK; Washington HS; Washington, PA; (S); Letterman Clb; Band; Concert Band; Jazz Band; SADD; Symp Band; High Hon Roll; Hon Roll; PMEA Dist 1 Hnrs Bnd; Mid-East All Star Bnd.

GAZI, LEAH MARIE; California Area HS; Roscoe, PA; (Y); 6/110; Drama Clb; FBLA; Flag Corp; School Musical; School Play; Yrbk Stf; CC Awd; Jr NHS; NHS; Church Yth Grp; Coal Queen 85; Ms FBLA Rgn IV 85-86; IN U PA; Fashion Merch.

GBRUOSKI, PAULA J; Mon Valley Catholic HS; Monongahela, PA; (S); 13/105; Spanish Clb; Chorus; Variety Show; Trs Soph Cls; NHS; Spanish NHS; PA ST U; Math.

GDOVIC, WAYNE; South Allegheny HS; Port Vue, PA; (Y); Spanish Clb; Var Bsbl; Var JV Bsktbl; Var Ftbl; Var Wt Lftg; Hon Roll; Amer Lgn Awd 83; Man-Yough Sci Fr Energy Awd 85; Buhl Sci Fr 85; U Of Pittsburgh; Physcl Thrpy.

GEALY, JOE; Lakeview HS; Jackson Center, PA; (S); 14/120; Varsity Clb; VP Bsbl; Ftbl; VP Wrstlng; FCVC Bsbl & Wrstlng Chmps 84-85; FCVC Wrstlng Chmps 83-84; Comp Drftg.

GEANETTE, DAVID; West Perry HS; Blain, PA; (Y); 2/210; Capt Quiz Bowl; Varsity Clb; School Play; Var Capt Wrstlng; High Hon Roll; Hon Roll; Pres NHS; Coaches And Acadmc Awds Wrstlng 85-86; PA ST U; Med.

GEARHART, DAWN; Cumberland Valley HS; Camp Hill, PA; (Y); 55/555; Teachers Aide; Chorus; Church Choir; Color Guard; Drill Tm; Flag Corp; Var L Trk; Im Wt Lftg; High Hon Roll; NHS; Bio.

GEARY, BRIAN; Kisk Area HS; Apollo, PA; (Y); Pep Clb; Ski Clb; Bsbl; Trk; High Hon Roll; Hon Roll; Alleghany Coll; Econ.

GEARY, CHRIS; S Allegheny HS; Glassport, PA; (Y); 10/184; Cmnty Wkr; Computer Clb; Letterman Clb; Science Clb; Varsity Clb; Stage Crew; Im Bsbl; JV Im Bsktbl; Var L Ftbl; Im Golf; Collegiate Sports Am Blue Chip 86; 1st Tm All Conf Ftbl 86; Top Athletes 86; Comp Sci.

GEARY, ERIC TROY; West Allegheny HS; Clinton, PA; (Y); 50/250; Church Yth Grp; German Clb; Crs Cntry; Trk; Bus.

GEARY, KIMBERLEY; Connellsville Area SR HS; Champion, PA; (Y); Camera Clb; FBLA; Office Aide; Hon Roll; Law.

GEARY, MICHELLE; Belle Vernon Area HS; Belle Vernon, PA; (Y); Art Clb; Drama Clb; Library Aide; Sec VICA; Hon Roll; Grphc Arts.

GEARY, SHANA; Pennsbury HS; Levittown, PA; (Y); Intnl Clb; Spanish Clb; Band; Concert Band; Mrchg Band; Bsktbl; NHS; Educ.

GEARY, STACI; Somerset SR HS; Somerset, PA; (Y); 20/240; English Clb; Varsity Clb; Mrchg Band; Off Stu Cncl; Var L Cheerleading; Capt Mat Maids; Var L Socr; Var L Trk; NHS; Physcl Ftns Awd 84-86; Acdmc All Amer Awd 84; Hghst Hon Roll 84-86; Pltcl Sci.

GEASON, EDEE; Mt Lebanon HS; Pittsburgh, PA; (Y); AFS; Church Yth Grp; French Clb; Letterman Clb; Varsity Clb; Crs Cntry; Trk; High Hon Roll; Northeastern U; Bus Adm.

GEBICKI, JENNIFER; Greater Latrobe SR HS; Latrobe, PA; (Y); 35/335; JA; JCL; Latin Clb; Library Aide; Pep Clb; Stu Cncl; Mat Maids; NHS; Pres Schlr; IUP; Mth.

GEBROSKY, LISA; Lincoln HS; Ellwood City, PA; (Y); Church Yth Grp; Library Aide; Service Clb; Spanish Clb; Y-Teens; Powder Puff Ftbl; High Hon Roll; Hon Roll; Prfct Atten Awd; Engrng.

GECKLE, DEAN; Hempfield HS; Greensburg, PA; (Y); VICA; Stage Crew; High Hon Roll; Hon Roll; NHS; Data Prcssng.

GEDMARK, ANN M; Red Land HS; New Cumberland, PA; (Y); 6/268; Am Leg Aux Girls St; Debate Tm; JCL; Latin Clb; Quiz Bowl; SADD; Rep Stu Cncl; Fld Hcky; Trk; VP NHS; Cum Laude Ntl Latn Exm 85; Pre-Law.

GEER, KEVIN; Apollo-Ridge SR HS; Apollo, PA; (Y); 1/164; FFA; JA; Math Clb; Hon Roll; Jr NHS; NHS; Pres Schlr; Val; Lousie V Nelson Schlrshp 86; Penn ST; Elect Engr.

GEESAMAN, KARA; Waynesboro Area SR HS; Waynesboro, PA; (Y); Sec AFS; Church Yth Grp; Nwsp Rptr; Pres Frsh Cls; Rep Chrmn Stu Cncl; Var JV Cheerleading; Cit Awd; Hon Roll; Pittsburgh U; Poltcl Sci.

GEFERT, LEON P; Penn Hills SR HS; Verona, PA; (Y); Cmnty Wkr; Computer Clb; Exploring; Spanish Clb; Carnegie-Mellon U; Engrng.

GEFFEL, MEGAN; Ambridge Area HS; Ambridge, PA; (S); Church Yth Grp; SADD; Nwsp Rptr; Nwsp Stf; Rep Jr Cls; Rep Stu Cncl; Var Bsktbl; Sftbl; Var Vllybl.

GEGNAS, LAURA D; Central Bucks HS East; Furlong, PA; (Y); 3/482; Church Yth Grp; Yrbk Stf; Rep Frsh Cls; Stat L Bsktbl; JV Tennis; High Hon Roll; Trs Jr NHS; NHS; Ntl Merit Ltr; Wlsly Bk Awd 85; Betz Lab Awd For Exc Schlrshp 86; Bucknell U; Chmstry.

GEGUZIS, CATHY; Hazelton HS; Hazleton, PA; (Y); Drama Clb; Leo Clb; Office Aide; Thesps; School Musical; Variety Show; Yrbk Stf; Hon Roll; NHS; Prfct Atten Awd; Fshn Inst Of Phila; Fshn Merch.

GEHMAN, CYNTHIA; Gateway Christian Schl; Bechtelsville, PA; (S); 1/12; Church Yth Grp; Drama Clb; Chorus; School Play; Nwsp Stf; Yrbk Stf; Sec Stu Cncl; Socr; Vllybl; Hon Roll; Christian Character Awd 84-85; Sprtsmnshp Awd 83-84.

GEHO, GLENN; Charleroi SR HS; N Charleroi, PA; (Y); High Hon Roll; Hon Roll; Chem,Physcis Clb; Stu Tutoring; Pre-Law.

GEHOSKY, MICHAEL; United HS; Homer City, PA; (Y); Computer Clb; Exploring; Ski Clb; Sfty Mgmt.

GEHRET, CAROLAN; Fleetwood Area HS; Fleetwood, PA; (Y); Chorus; Drill Tm; Flag Corp; Mrchg Band; Score Keeper; Bus Mgmt.

GEHRING, LYNN; South Park HS; Library, PA; (Y); Spanish Clb; Powder Puff Ftbl; Vllybl; Hon Roll; NHS; Natl Hnr Soc 84-86; U Of Pittsburgh.

GEHRIS, ELIZABETH C; William Allen HS; Allentown, PA; (Y); 39/604; Church Yth Grp; ROTC; Chorus; Drill Tm; Madrigals; School Play; Var L Bsktbl; Var Powder Puff Ftbl; Var L Trk; NHS; NJROTC Acad Tm 1st Nation 86; Mc Cormick Bk Awd 86; Ensign Cadet In Chrge Admi NJROTC 86.

GEHRKE, DENISE; Schuylkill Valley HS; Reading, PA; (S); 10/138; FTA; Chorus; Concert Band; Drm Mjr(t); School Musical; Nwsp Rptr; Yrbk Stf; Rep Stu Cncl; Var Cheerleading; NHS; Hugh O Brian Yth Ldrshp Semnr Rep 85.

GEIB, MELISSA; Elizabethtown Area HS; Fort Payne, AL; (Y); Church Yth Grp; Cmnty Wkr; Library Aide; Speech Tm; Thesps; Church Choir; School Play; Stage Crew; Ed Yrbk Stf; Ed Lit Mag; Law.

GEIBEL, S JEFFREY; Butler SR HS; Butler, PA; (Y); Boy Scts; Science Clb; Spanish Clb; Bsktbl; Butler Bsbl Prep All Star Tm 83-86; Partial Bsktbl Schlrshp-Geneva Coll 86; Geneva Coll; Psych.

GEIBEL, STEPHEN; Butler SR HS; Butler, PA; (Y); Boy Scts; Church Yth Grp; Spanish Clb; Var Capt Bsktbl; Im Ftbl; Prep League All Stars Bsbl 83-86; Prep League Sprtsmnshp Awd 86; Partl Bsktbl Schlrshp 86; Geneva Coll; Psych.

GEICK, LYNN; Ringgold HS; Donora, PA; (Y); 79/342; Drama Clb; Spanish Clb; Teachers Aide; Chorus; Nwsp Rptr; Swmmng; Vllybl; Cit Awd; Hon Roll; Prfct Atten Awd; Duquesne; Psych.

GEIER, ANTHONY; Girard College HS; Philadelphia, PA; (Y); Nwsp Stf; Yrbk Stf; Badmtn; Sftbl; Trk; Wrstlng; Law.

GEIGER, BRIAN; Parkland SR HS; Coplay, PA; (Y); 57/459; Math Tm; Science Clb; High Hon Roll; Hon Roll; Ntl Merit Ltr; IN U PA; Optmtry.

GEIGER, CHARLES; Seneca Valley SR HS; Evans City, PA; (Y); JV Wrstlng; Mdcl.

GEIGER, DEEDEE; Northwestern Lehigh HS; Orefield, PA; (Y); 3/186; Church Yth Grp; 4-H; Fld Hcky; Ftbl; Sftbl; High Hon Roll; NHS; Med Tech.

GEIGER, DOUGLAS; Beaver Area HS; Beaver, PA; (Y); Band; Concert Band; Jazz Band; Mrchg Band; Orch; Yrbk Rptr; Ed Lit Mag; High Hon Roll; Lion Awd; NHS; Gordon Coll; Engl.

GEIGER, JENNIFER; Catasauqua Area HS; N Catasauqua, PA; (Y); 7/148; Debate Tm; Drama Clb; Chorus; Color Guard; Co-Capt Mrchg Band; Ed Lit Mag; Stu Cncl; NHS; Pre Vet.

GEIGER, LINDA; Warwick HS; Lititz, PA; (Y); 22/233; Am Leg Aux Girls St; Church Yth Grp; Chorus; Mrchg Band; Orch; Pres Stu Cncl; Bsktbl; DAR Awd; High Hon Roll; NHS; Teen Wk 86; Houghton Coll; Psych.

GEIGER, MIKE; William Allen HS; Allentown, PA; (Y); 127/604; Exploring; German Clb; Wt Lftg; Hon Roll; Prfct Atten Awd; Penn ST; Crimnlgy.

GEIGER, SCOTT; Hempfield HS; Irwin, PA; (Y); Ski Clb; Stage Crew; Bowling; Ftbl; Wt Lftg; Wrstlng; Hon Roll; Prfct Atten Awd.

GEINZER, BRAD R; Chartiers Valley HS; Pittsburgh, PA; (Y); 29/336; High Hon Roll; Pres Schlr; Penn ST Behrend; Engrng.

GEINZER, RENE; Montour HS; Pittsburgh, PA; (Y); JA; Yrbk Stf; Crs Cntry; Trk; High Hon Roll; Hon Roll; NHS.

GEIS, BARBARA; Cornwell HS; Coraopolis, PA; (Y); 12/88; Yrbk Stf; High Hon Roll; Hon Roll; Jr NHS; NHS; Acctng I Cert 86; Acctng.

GEISEL, DEBORAH; Johnstown HS; Johnstown, PA; (Y); Chorus; Color Guard; Mrchg Band; NHS; High Hon Roll; Hon Roll; Stu Cncl; Church Yth Grp; Drama Clb; French Clb; UPJ; Lwyr.

GEISELMAN, CHRIS; Dover Area HS; Dover, PA; (Y); Art Clb; Church Yth Grp; Dance Clb; Hosp Aide.

GEISLER, ANN; Canon Mc Millan HS; Lawrence, PA; (Y); 72/340; Drama Clb; Ski Clb; Thesps; School Play; Trs Frsh Cls; Stu Cncl; High Hon Roll; Spanish NHS; Am Leg Awd 83; IN U Of PA; Hotel Mgmt.

GEISLER, JOSEPH; Franklin Regional Ssr HS; Murrysville, PA; (Y); Chess Clb; Mathletes; Sec Jr Cls; High Hon Roll; NHS; U Pittsburgh Provosts Day SF 86; U Pittsburgh; Elec Engrng.

GEISLER, KRISTINE ANN; East Pennsboro HS; Camp Hill, PA; (Y); 6/197; FBLA; Trs German Clb; Model UN; Band; Concert Band; Jazz Band; School Play; Hst Frsh Cls; Hst Soph Cls; Hst Jr Cls; Acdmc Schlrshp Immaculata Coll; 3rd Dist Family Svc Essay Cntst; E Pennsboro Acdmc Hnrs; Immaculata Coll; Acctg.

GEISLER, RICHARD W; Bradford Area HS; Bradford, PA; (Y); 8/306; Pres Key Clb; Ski Clb; Concert Band; Mrchg Band; Rep Stu Cncl; Golf; High Hon Roll; Jr NHS; NHS; NEDT Awd; Hnr Grad 86; Gannon U; Optmtry.

GEISLER, RONALD J; Washington HS; Washington, PA; (S); 18/172; Church Yth Grp; French Clb; Spanish Clb; Chorus; Church Choir; Madrigals; School Play; High Hon Roll; Hon Roll; Law.

GEISSINGER, BEATRICE; Spring-Ford SR HS; Royersford, PA; (S); 14/258; Church Yth Grp; FBLA; German Clb; Hon Roll; NHS.

GEISSINGER, MARGARET E; Emmaus HS; Zionsville, PA; (Y); VP Church Yth Grp; Chorus; Church Choir; School Musical; Variety Show; Rep Soph Cls; Rep Jr Cls; Hon Roll; Jr NHS; Prfct Atten Awd; Messiah Coll; Acctng.

GEIST, JAYME; Calvary Baptist Chrisitian Acad; Meadville, PA; (S); 2/7; Church Yth Grp; Hosp Aide; Teachers Aide; Sec Sr Cls; Var Capt Cheerleading; L Vllybl; Sal; Pastor Awd; Top Quizzer Bible; Liberty U; Sec Sci.

GEIST, JERRY; Schuykill Haven HS; Schuykill Haven, PA; (S); 19/88; Church Yth Grp; Science Clb; SADD; Wt Lftg; Wrstlng; Hon Roll; Pres Frsh Cls; Pres Soph Cls; Pres Jr Cls; Sec Stu Cncl; Hugh O Brian Yth Fndtn 84; Schykill Co Cthlc Yth Cncl 85.

GEIST, KERRY; Steelton-Highspire HS; Highspire, PA; (Y); 1/94; Camera Clb; French Clb; Model UN; Yrbk Rptr; Yrbk Stf; Wrstlng; High Hon Roll; Hon Roll; NHS; Val; Drexel U; Chem Engr.

GEIST, PAULA; Line Mountain HS; Leck Kill, PA; (Y); 13/109; Computer Clb; Varsity Clb; Yrbk Rptr; Yrbk Sprt Ed; Yrbk Stf; Mgr Fld Hcky; Sftbl; Hon Roll; Pres Schlr; Germn Stein Awd 86; Amer Legn Awd Germn 86; Natl Physcl Ftns Olympd 86; Bloomsburg; Acctg.

GEIST, SANDRA L; Philipsburg-Osceola Area HS; Philipsburg, PA; (Y); 34/221; Letterman Clb; Pres Pep Clb; Ski Clb; Thesps; School Play; Nwsp Stf; Cheerleading; Sftbl; SADD; Yrbk Stf; Ivy Leaf Awd 86; Centre Cnty JR Miss Cont 85; Penn ST U; Law.

GEITNER, MIKE; Elk County Christian HS; St Marys, PA; (Y); Stu Cncl; Bsktbl; Ftbl; Trk; High Hon Roll; Hon Roll; Gannon U; Elec Engnrng.

GELB, MELISSA; Scranton Prep HS; Scranton, PA; (Y); Pres Temple Yth Grp; Band; VP Tmpl Yth Grp 84-85; Pres Tmpl Yth Grp 85-86; Nrthrn M Chrprsn PAFTY 86-87; Poly Sci.

GELB, STEVE; Council Rock HS; Churchville, PA; (Y); 20/845; Nwsp Phtg; Nwsp Stf; Yrbk Phtg; Yrbk Stf; Im Vllybl; High Hon Roll; Hon Roll; Drexel U; Arch Engr.

GELCHES, KRISTIN; North Pocono HS; Moscow, PA; (Y); Church Yth Grp; Ski Clb; Spanish Clb; Varsity Clb; Chorus; Church Choir; Var Trk; Psych.

GELETEI, KATHY; Charleroi Area JR SR HS; Charleroi, PA; (Y); Church Yth Grp; Exploring; French Clb; Girl Scts; Office Aide; Varsity Clb; Chorus; Color Guard; Drill Tm; Flag Corp; Law.

GELEZINSKY, VINCENT; Pocono Mountain HS; Tobyhanna, PA; (Y); Hon Roll; Acadmc Hnrs 83.

GELLI, JENNIFER; James M Coughlin HS; Plains, PA; (Y); Church Yth Grp; Drama Clb; Ski Clb; Orch; School Play; Cheerleading; JV Var Fld Hcky; Hon Roll; Jr NHS; NHS.

GELOVICH, STEVE; St John Neumann HS; Philadelphia, PA; (Y); 2/350; Civic Clb; Mathletes; Q&S; Science Clb; Nwsp Rptr; Jr NHS; Pres NHS; Sal; Math Tm; Quiz Bowl; 4 Yr 1/2 Schlrshp Fr HS 83; Dungeons & Drgns Clb 83-84; La Salle; Pre-Med.

GELSINGER, ANDREW; Conrad Weiser JSHS; Robesonia, PA; (Y); 10/184; Boy Scts; God Cntry Awd; NHS; Church Yth Grp; Drama Clb; JCL; Latin Clb; Radio Clb; Band; Chorus; Dist 10 Bnd Fstvl 85; Dist 10 Chrs Fstvl 85-86; Psych.

GELSINGER, JACQUELINE; Pine Grove Area HS; Tremont, PA; (Y); 2/117; Chorus; School Musical; Nwsp Stf; Yrbk Ed-Chief; Rep Stu Cncl; High Hon Roll; Sec NHS; Ntl Merit Schol; Prfct Atten Awd; Sal; Grace Coll IN; Elem Educ.

GEMAS, MICHAEL; Connersville Sr HS; Dunbar, PA; (Y); Computer Clb; Trk; Hon Roll; Jr NHS; NHS; ICM Sch Of Bus; Sys Anlst.

GEMEINHART, KEITH; West Mmifflin Area HS; W Mifflin, PA; (Y); 18/320; Boy Scts; Concert Band; Var L Ftbl; Var L Trk; High Hon Roll; Hon Roll; Jr NHS; NHS; Elec Engrng.

GEMEINHART, KEVIN; West Mifflin Area HS; W Mifflin, PA; (Y); Var L Ftbl; High Hon Roll; Hon Roll; NHS; Engr.

GEMELLI, CASSANDRA; Middletown Area HS; Middletown, PA; (Y); FCA; Library Aide; Model UN; Chorus; Color Guard; Nwsp Stf; Yrbk Stf; Fld Hcky; Psych.

GENASEVICH, GARY; West Hazleton HS; W Hazleton, PA; (Y); Aud/Vis; Spanish Clb; Bsbl; Bsktbl; Crs Cntry; Hon Roll.

GENBERG, WENDY; Warren Area HS; Sugar Grove, PA; (Y); Church Yth Grp; French Clb; Office Aide; Varsity Clb; Y-Teens; Yrbk Stf; L Crs Cntry; Stat Trk; Hon Roll; Jr NHS; Gldn Dragon Awd 86; Jamestwn CC.

GENEROSE, MICHAEL; Hazleton HS; Mcadoo Hts, PA; (Y); 60/383; Drama Clb; Quiz Bowl; Ski Clb; Thesps; School Play; VP Stu Cncl; Var Bsktbl; Var Ftbl; Capt Trk; Var Wt Lftg.

GENEROSE, ROSINA; Bishop Hafey HS; Hazleton, PA; (Y); 6/120; Am Leg Aux Girls St; Church Yth Grp; Cmnty Wkr; FNA; Spanish Clb; SADD; Y-Teens; Chorus; Church Choir; Yrbk Stf; Hghst Schlstc Avg Latin 85; Hghst Schlstc Avg Spnsh, Rlgn & Hist 86; Ntl Spnsh Cntst & 84-86; Med Fld.

GENETTI, KATHLEEN; MMI Preparatory Schl; Weatherly, PA; (S); 11/31; Art Clb; Ski Clb; School Play; Stage Crew; Yrbk Stf; Var L Sftbl; High Hon Roll; Hon Roll; Schlstc Art Awd 83-84; Faculty Merit Cert 83-84; Hnrbl Ment Cert Spnsh Cont 82-83; Bus.

GENICOLA, LANCE S; Whitehall HS; Whitehall, PA; (Y); 50/276; Am Leg Boys St; Drm Mjr(t); Jazz Band; Pep Band; Var Trk; Hon Roll; NHS; Prfct Atten Awd; Rep Sr Cls; Rep Stu Cncl; Grmn Ntl Hnr Scty 86; Msc & Engrng Explr Posts 86; Yth Ldrshp Cnfrnc At Lehigh U; USMA; Ncrl Engrng.

GENNARO, MICHELE L; Aliquippa HS; W Aliquippa, PA; (Y); English Clb; French Clb; FBLA; FHA; Hosp Aide; Office Aide; Pep Clb; VICA; Band; Mrchg Band.

GENOVESE, MARYJO; Scranton Technical HS; Scranton, PA; (Y); Art Clb; Cmnty Wkr; FBLA; GAA; Letterman Clb; Q&S; Varsity Clb; Band; Concert Band; Jazz Band; Gold Key Scholastic Art Assoc 85-86; Lackawanna Leg Leadng Scorng Chmp Wm 85-86; Showmoblie Ar 85-86.

GENSEL, BECKY; John S Fine HS; Plymouth, PA; (Y); Church Yth Grp; Girl Scts; Ski Clb; Sec Teachers Aide; Varsity Clb; Church Choir; Yrbk Stf; Rep Frsh Cls; Rep Soph Cls; Rep Jr Cls; Physical Fitness Awd 85-86; Photo.

GENSEL, JULIE; Northwest Area HS; Shickshinny, PA; (Y); 9/108; Band; Chorus; Concert Band; Mrchg Band; School Musical; School Play; Twrlr; High Hon Roll; Hon Roll; NHS; Pres Acad Fit Awd 86; Duquesne U; Phrmcy.

GENSEMER, LORRAINE; Annville-Cleona HS; Annville, PA; (S); 15/105; FBLA; Girl Scts; Library Aide; SADD; Chorus; Mrchg Band; Mat Maids; NHS; Silver Scout Awd 84; Bus.

GENSEMER, MELISSA; Danville HS; Danville, PA; (Y); 4/157; Am Leg Aux Girls St; Sec Church Yth Grp; VP Exploring; Pres Key Clb; Pres Latin Clb; Rep Stu Cncl; Mat Maids; Cit Awd; High Hon Roll; NHS; Yng Amer Awd 86; Aux To Montour Cnty Med Soc Educ Grant 86; Engl Stu Of Mnth 86; Grove City Coll; Psychol.

GENSZLER, ANDREW; Perkiomen HS; Marietta, OH; (Y); 6/40; Church Yth Grp; Jazz Band; Stu Cncl; Bsbl; Bsktbl; Crs Cntry; Socr; Hon Roll; NEDT Awd; VP Stu Body 86-87; Parents Assoc Awd 86.

GENTEEL, COREY; Bangor SR HS; Roseto, PA; (Y); Church Yth Grp; VP Trs Exploring; Chrmn SADD; Church Choir; School Musical; School Play; Jr NHS; Drama Clb; Mrchg Band; Variety Show; Ntl Fed Parents Drug Fee Yth Cert 85; Spcl Guest 1st Annual Roseto Cheftns Show 86.

GENTILCORE, MICHAEL; Bethlehem Catholic HS; Bethlehem, PA; (Y); Variety Show; High Hon Roll; Hon Roll; Jr NHS; NHS; Penn ST Lehigh; Elctrl Engrng.

GENTILE, CECILIA; Highlands HS; Tarentum, PA; (Y); 37/274; Band; Hon Roll; Church Yth Grp; Key Clb; Teachers Aide; Chorus; Concert Band; Mrchg Band; Pep Band; JV Var Sftbl; IN U Of PA; Bus.

GENTILE, DANIELLE; Merion Mercy Acad; Havertown, PA; (Y); Pres Library Aide; Science Clb; Chorus; Church Choir; Im Vllybl; Hon Roll; Vllybl Intl Chmpns 86; Nrsng.

GENTILE, DEANNA; Mt Alvernia HS; Pittsburgh, PA; (Y); 11/68; Sec Exploring; Chorus; Yrbk Stf; Lit Mag; Pres Frsh Cls; Pres Soph Cls; Pres Jr Cls; Sec Stu Cncl; Bsktbl; Socr; Am Leg Ldrshp Awd; Sports Med.

GENTILE, MADELYN; Deer Lakes HS; Gibsonia, PA; (Y); Drama Clb; Hosp Aide; Chorus; School Play; Stage Crew; Pom Pon; Var Vllybl; Hon Roll; Cmmncations.

GENTLESK, PHILIP; St Josephs Prep; Haddonfield, NJ; (Y); 2/244; Rep Frsh Cls; Im Bsktbl; Var Ftbl; Im Wt Lftg; JV Wrstlng; High Hon Roll; Ntl Merit Ltr; Cumm Laude In Latin III Natl Latin Exam 86; Recognized For Ldrshp In JR Peer Advsry Prgrm 86.

GENTZLER, KIMBERLY; Hanover SR HS; Hanover, PA; (Y); #5 In Class; Letterman Clb; Red Cross Aide; Speech Tm; Varsity Clb; School Play; Sec Frsh Cls; Rep Stu Cncl; Var Capt Fld Hcky; Stat Vllybl; Hon Roll; Cmncmnt Spkr; CA U PA; Vet Med.

GENTZYEL, PAULA; Lock Haven SR HS; Lock Haven, PA; (Y); FBLA; Spanish Clb; Yrbk Stf; Mgr(s); Hon Roll; NHS; Medcl Secy.

GENZ, LORI; Wyalusing Valley JR SR HS; New Albany, PA; (Y); 20/130; SADD; Band; School Musical; Pres Rep Jr Cls; VP Rep Stu Cncl; Var Capt Bsktbl; Var Capt Trk; Var Capt Vllybl; High Hon Roll; Hon Roll; Pre Law.

GEORGE, BERNADETTE; Hazelton HS; Hazleton, PA; (Y); 19/367; French Clb; FBLA; Political Wkr; Varsity Clb; Y-Teens; Color Guard; JV Cheerleading; Var Twrlr; French Hon Soc; Hon Roll; Pre-Law.

GEORGE, BETHANY; Purchase Line HS; Commodore, PA; (Y); 8/121; Trs French Clb; FBLA; Trs Spanish Clb; Chorus; Concert Band; Mrchg Band; High Hon Roll; Hon Roll; NHS; Acad All Amer French 85-86; Music Ed.

GEORGE, BRIAN; Avonworth HS; Pittsbg, PA; (Y); Nwsp Phtg; Nwsp Sprt Ed; Yrbk Phtg; Var L Bsbl; Var L Wrstlng; Cit Awd; High Hon Roll; Ntl Merit SF; Church Yth Grp; Letterman Clb; North Boros Yth Awd 86; Top 5 Pct Nationwide Stanford Achvt 83-84, 84-85&85-86; Acctg.

GEORGE, CAROLYN; Homer-Center HS; Homer City, PA; (Y); Dance Clb; Sec French Clb; Band; Color Guard; Concert Band; Flag Corp; Jazz Band; Mrchg Band; Yrbk Stf; JV Sftbl; Penn ST; Arch Engrng.

GEORGE, DOUGLAS; Cumberland Valley HS; Camp Hill, PA; (Y); 35/570; Math Tm; Orch; Stage Crew; Hon Roll; NHS; 6th Ship U Mth Comp 86; Achvt Cert Spn I II & III; Aero Engr.

GEORGE, ERIC; Northwestern Lehigh HS; Germansvile, PA; (Y); Boy Scts; Ski Clb; Yrbk Stf; Socr; Trk; Hon Roll; Arspc Engrng.

GEORGE, ERIC A; Riverside HS; Beaver Falls, PA; (Y); 30/196; Computer Clb; Band; Chorus; Concert Band; Drm & Bgl; Jazz Band; Mrchg Band; Pep Band; School Musical; Symp Band; ST Fstvls In Music 85 & 86; 1st Pl Comp Cmptn 86; OH ST U; Rbtcs.

GEORGE, JEFFREY; St Josephs Prep; Wallingford, PA; (Y); 92/236; French Clb; Spanish Clb; Pres SADD; Nwsp Stf; Yrbk Stf; Rep Stu Cncl; Var L Bsktbl; Im Ftbl; Soc Colnl Dames Essy Cont Semi-Fin 86; Hgplcmnt AP Vergil Exam 86; Mktg.

GEORGE, JOHN; Highlands SR HS; Natrona Hts, PA; (Y); 53/271; Westinghouse Sci Hnrs Inst 85-86; PA Free Enterprise Wk 85; PA ST U; Comp Sci.

GEORGE, KELLEY S; South Western HS; Hanover, PA; (Y); 51/205; Varsity Clb; Pres Chorus; Sec Soph Cls; Trs Jr Cls; VP Sr Cls; VP Stu Cncl; Stat Bsktbl; Var L Tennis; NHS; Ralph E Noble Mem Schlrhsp 86; Ms Hnvr Area Pgnt Cntstnt 85; Mllrsvl U; Spcl Ed.

GEORGE, KIM; Bethel Park SR HS; Bethel Park, PA; (Y); Girl Scts; Hosp Aide; VP JA; Library Aide; Chorus; School Musical; Prfct Atten Awd; Sci.

GEORGE, LISA; Conrad Weiser HS; Robesonia, PA; (Y); 1/185; Computer Clb; Drama Clb; Co-Capt Scholastic Bowl; Chorus; School Musical; School Play; Yrbk Stf; Stat Bsbl; Sftbl; High Hon Roll; Continentl Math Lg Awd For PASCAL 86; Bus Adm.

GEORGE, LISA; Windber Area HS; Windber, PA; (Y); 4/115; VP Drama Clb; Trs French Clb; VP Library Aide; School Play; Yrbk Stf; Rep Jr Cls; Rep Sr Cls; High Hon Roll; Trs NHS; Pres Schlr; Stu Month 5 Tms 83-86.

GEORGE, PAM; Canon-Mc Millan SR HS; Canonsburg, PA; (Y); 78/341; Church Yth Grp; FBLA; Spanish Clb; High Hon Roll; Spanish NHS; 1st & 3rd Pl Bus Englsh 86; Fbla St & Rgnl Ldrshp Cnfrnce 86; 1st Pl Spnch Dictation & Compstn 86.

GEORGE, RANDY; Shenango JR SR HS; New Castle, PA; (Y); Band; Concert Band; Mrchg Band; Pep Band; Hon Roll; Clarion U Of PA; Comp Sci.

GEORGE, RICHARD; Laurel Highlands HS; Uniontown, PA; (Y); Hon Roll.

GEORGE, TAMMY; Greater Johnstown Area Vo-Tech Schl; Salix, PA; (Y); 8/320; Pres 4-H; VP FFA; Girl Scts; Pep Clb; Ski Clb; Y-Teens; Nwsp Stf; 4-H Awd; Hon Roll.

GEORGE, TARA; Archbishop Prendergast HS; Havertown, PA; (Y); 100/360; Church Yth Grp; Rep Frsh Cls; Rep Soph Cls; Rep Jr Cls; Stu Cncl; Silver Mdl-Hm Ec 86; Rosemont Coll; Pre Law.

GEORGE, TERRY; North Clarion HS; Lucinda, PA; (Y); Varsity Clb; Var Socr; Var Trk; Hon Roll; Prfct Atten Awd; Aerospace Engrng.

GEORGE, TOD A; West Middlesex JR SR HS; W Middlesex, PA; (S); 1/135; Pres FBLA; Nwsp Bus Mgr; Yrbk Bus Mgr; VP Stu Cncl; High Hon Roll; Jr NHS; NHS; Ntl Merit Ltr; Spanish NHS; Hugh O Brian Awd 84; Clarion; Bus Adm.

GEORGE, TRACEY; James M Coughlin HS; Wilkes Barre, PA; (Y); 49/372; Yrbk Stf; High Hon Roll; Hon Roll; NHS; Pres Schlr; Kings Coll Acad Awd 86-87; Pres Acad Fit Awd 85-86; Kins Coll; Pre-Med.

GEORGEOU, CLEO; Canon Mc Millan HS; Canonsburg, PA; (Y); Trs Church Yth Grp; Cmnty Wkr; High Hon Roll; Hon Roll; Robert Morris Coll; Accntng.

GEORGETTI, DOM; Central HS; Scranton, PA; (Y); Pres Church Yth Grp; Ski Clb; Band; Rep Jr Cls; Var JV Bsbl; JV Ftbl; Hon Roll; Bsktbl Church; Pol Sci.

GEORGULIS, CHRISTOPHER; Belle Vernon Area; Belle Vernon, PA; (Y); 5/265; Boy Scts; Chess Clb; Church Yth Grp; Computer Clb; JA; Scholastic Bowl; Ski Clb; Band; Concert Band; Mrchg Band; Energy Semnr Penn ST 86; Math Dele CA U PA 86; US Navy; Aero Space Engr.

GEPHART, BARBARA; South Williamsport HS; S Williamsport, PA; (Y); Trk; Hon Roll; Med Sec.

GERACE, JULIE; Bethel Park SR HS; Bethel Park, PA; (Y); Church Yth Grp; Church Choir; Concert Band; Mrchg Band; Yrbk Stf; Mgr(s); Swmmng; Church Yth Grp Pres 85-86; Edinboro U; Elem Ed.

GERAMITA, KIM; South Hills HS; Pittsburgh, PA; (S); 20/191; Pres Latin Clb; Teachers Aide; Yrbk Stf; Trs Frsh Cls; Sec Soph Cls; Capt Cheerleading; Var Powder Puff Ftbl; Cit Awd; High Hon Roll; Hon Roll; U Of Pittsburgh Emrg Ldr Schlrshp 86; Washington Clg; Pre Med.

GERARD, JASON; Charleroi Area HS; Charleroi, PA; (Y); Computer Clb; Science Clb; Bowling; Golf; Hon Roll; NHS; Compu Sci.

GERASIMEK, CAROL; Sharpsville HS; Sharpsville, PA; (Y); 30/129; Art Clb; Camera Clb; Church Yth Grp; Girl Scts; Ski Clb; Pres Thesps; Pres Band; Chorus; Pres Concert Band; Pres Mrchg Band; Acad Achvt Awd 84-85; Grove City Coll; Elem Educ.

GERBA, CRISTINE; Cumberland Valley HS; Mechanicsburg, PA; (Y); 1/500; Debate Tm; Exploring; Key Clb; Var Trk; Bausch & Lomb Sci Awd; Hon Roll; NHS; Ntl Merit SF; Rotary Awd; Val; Awd Exdlnc Merit Fnlst 86; Awd Excllnc JR Acad Of Sci 86; PA ST U; Vet Med.

GERBER, DEAN; Elk County Christian HS; St Marys, PA; (Y); 26/80; Hon Roll.

GERBER, RONNA; Penns Manor HS; Clymer, PA; (Y); 2/99; Girl Scts; SADD; Band; Chorus; Concert Band; Flag Corp; Rep Stu Cncl; Stat Trk; High Hon Roll; NHS; ARIN-IUP Marine Bio Study 85; Physcn.

GERBERICH, WILLIAM; Lebanon Catholic HS; Lebanon, PA; (Y); German Clb; Library Aide; VICA; JV Var Ftbl; Hon Roll; Prfct Atten Awd; Exc In Manual Arts 84-86; Exc In Intro To Econ 85-86; Elec Constrctn.

GERCHMAN, BARBARA; Carbondale Area HS; Simpson, PA; (Y); 28/150; Art Clb; Church Yth Grp; FBLA; Girl Scts; Library Aide; Ski Clb; Spanish Clb; Y-Teens; Drill Tm; Cheerleading; Acctnt.

GERCHUFSKY, MICHAEL B; Tamaqua Area HS; Slatington, PA; (Y); #25 In Class; Art Clb; French Clb; Science Clb; French Hon Soc; Concours Natl De Francais Cert De Merit 84; Stu Recognition Comm Of Tamaqua HS Cert Of Hnr 85.

GERDA, MARY JANE; Mt Pleasant Area HS; Mt Pleasant, PA; (Y); 7/248; Am Leg Aux Girls St; German Clb; GAA; Hosp Aide; Color Guard; Yrbk Stf; High Hon Roll; NHS; Voice Dem Awd; Westmorland Cnty Cmnty Coll Merit Schlrshp 86; Westmorland Cmnty Coll Comp Sc.

GEREGA, DORENE; Ambridge Area HS; Ambridge, PA; (Y); Pep Clb; Spanish Clb; Band; Concert Band; Drill Tm; Mrchg Band; Soph Cls; Trs Jr Cls; Stu Cncl; High Hon Roll; Smmr Smnr Wrld Affrs Duquesne U 86; Optmtry.

GEREGACH, GEORGE; Montour HS; Coraopolis, PA; (Y); Var Bsktbl; Var L Golf; High Hon Roll; Hon Roll.

GEREK, SANDRA; Carbondale Area JR SR HS; Simpson, PA; (Y); 27/150; Church Yth Grp; Ski Clb; Spanish Clb; Band; Concert Band; Mrchg Band; Hon Roll; Acctg.

GERENDA, CURTIS; Bristol JR SR HS; Bristol, PA; (Y); 9/102; Art Clb; Cmnty Wkr; Concert Band; Yrbk Stf; Var JV Ice Hcky; Hon Roll; NHS; Camera Clb; Band; Jazz Band; Juilien Bley Schlrshp 86; Hussian; Commrcl Art.

GERENDA, MICHAEL; Bristol JR SR HS; Bristol, PA; (Y); Aud/Vis; FCA; Intnl Clb; Stage Crew; Yrbk Sprt Ed; Bsbl; Ftbl; Trk; Hon Roll; NHS; PA Free Enterprise Week Lock Haven U 86; Shippensburg U PA; Fin.

GERG, DIANE; Elk County Christian HS; St Marys, PA; (Y); 39/97; Hosp Aide; Model UN; SADD; Varsity Clb; Pres Band; Mrchg Band; Pep Band; Yrbk Ed-Chief; Rep Stu Cncl; Var Tennis; PA Acad Cosmetology; Csmtlgst.

GERGAL, SCOTT A; Cardinal Brennan HS; Frackville, PA; (Y); 5/48; German Clb; Ski Clb; Band; Chorus; Concert Band; Mrchg Band; School Musical; High Hon Roll; NHS; Prfct Atten Awd; Natl Hon Soc Pres 85-86; Smpr Fdls Awd 86; Pres Mrchg/Cncrt Bnd 86; All-ST Lions Bnd & Hon Bnd 84 & 85; Penn ST U; Elec Engrg.

GERHARDS, KIMBERLY A; Northern Lebanon JR SR HS; Annville, PA; (Y); 32/177; Art Clb; Church Yth Grp; French Clb; Red Cross Aide; Teachers Aide; Chorus; School Musical; Hon Roll; Peer Cnslr 85-86; Ped Nrsg.

GERHARDT, AMY; Bensalem HS; Bensalem, PA; (Y); Teachers Aide; Varsity Clb; Var Crs Cntry; Var Trk; Actural Stds.

GERHARDT, DIANE; West Mifflin HS; W Mifflin, PA; (Y); 99/340; Exploring; Hosp Aide; Mrchg Band; Yrbk Stf; Var Twrlr; Candy Strpr 100 Hr Ptch, 250 Hr Cap, 300 Hr Trphy, 500 Hr Chrm Brclt 83.

GERHART, DONNA C; High Point Baptist Acad; Douglassville, PA; (Y); 6/18; Church Yth Grp; Chorus; Yrbk Ed-Chief; Yrbk Stf; Var Bsktbl; Var L Cheerleading; Var Trk; High Hon Roll; Hon Roll; Ntl Merit Ltr; Intl Frgn Lang Awd 83; Kystne Chrstn Ed Assn 2nd Pl Spnsh 85; US Intl Ldrshp Merit Awd 85; Liberty U; Bio.

GERHART, LISA; Cocalico SR HS; Stevens, PA; (Y); 4/166; Teachers Aide; Rep Concert Band; Drm Mjr(t); Mrchg Band; Sec Frsh Cls; Sec Soph Cls; Sec Jr Cls; Sec Sr Cls; Sec Stu Cncl; High Hon Roll; Stu Mnth; Bus.

GERHEIM, REBECCA; Leechburg Area HS; Leechburg, PA; (Y); 5/83; Pres 4-H; Library Aide; Pep Clb; Red Cross Aide; Band; Concert Band; Drm Mjr(t); Mrchg Band; Orch; Pep Band; Rgnl Bnd Rgn II 86; Alle-Kiski Hnrs Bnd 86; Aerspc Engr.

GERIAK, CHRISTINE; Ambridge Area HS; Ambridge, PA; (Y); German Clb; Pep Clb; Band; Drill Tm; Soph Cls; Jr Cls; Hon Roll; U Of Pittsburgh; Physcl Thrpy.

GERKE, CAROL R; Hershey SR HS; Hershey, PA; (Y); AFS; Key Clb; NFL; Q&S; Speech Tm; Band; Mrchg Band; Nwsp Rptr; Stat Var Trk; Hon Roll; Pre-Med.

GERKE, HOLLY; Hempfield HS; Lancaster, PA; (Y); 68/430; Church Yth Grp; Hosp Aide; Office Aide; Band; Chorus; Mrchg Band; Pep Band; School Musical; Nwsp Bus Mgr; Nwsp Sprt Ed.

GERKEN, MICHAEL; Vincentian HS; Gibsonia, PA; (Y); Math Clb; Church Choir; Trs Stu Cncl; Im Badmtn; Im Ftbl; Var Capt Socr; Im Sftbl; Im Vllybl; Hon Roll; NHS; Engrng.

GERLACH, ANDY; Downingtown SR HS; Downingtown, PA; (Y); Ski Clb; Chorus; Lcrss; Tennis; Vrsty Tennis Awds 85-87; Exctv Cncl 86 & 87; PA ST.

GERLACHOVSKY, NICOLE; Frazier HS; Perryopolis, PA; (Y); Cmnty Wkr; French Clb; FNA; Hosp Aide; Color Guard; Mrchg Band; Hon Roll; Spch Path.

GERMAN, BRENDA; Walnut Street Christian Schl; Lebanon, ME; (Y); Church Yth Grp; Cmnty Wkr; Debate Tm; Chorus; Church Choir; School Play; Yrbk Stf; Capt Bsktbl; JV Var Socr; Var Trk; Christian Character Awd 86; All Star Bsktbl Plry Trophy 86; Girls Physcl Ed Awd 84; Baptist Bible Coll; Missns.

GERMAN, SUSAN; Northampton SR HS; Walnutport, PA; (Y); Computer Clb; Hon Roll; Treas Comp Tech Cls 85-86; Acctnt.

GERNERT, AMY; Waynesburg Central HS; Waynesburg, PA; (Y); Church Yth Grp; Spanish Clb; Band; Concert Band; Jazz Band; Mrchg Band; High Hon Roll; NHS; Score Keeper; Timer; All Cnty Band 84-86; Spnsh Awd 84 & 86; Comp Sci Awd 86; Chistmas Ct 84-85; Elem Ed.

GEROFF, ADAM; Lowe Moreland HS; Huntingdon Valley, PA; (S); 5/124; German Clb; Key Clb; Science Clb; SADD; Temple Yth Grp; Ed Yrbk Ed-Chief; Trk; Hon Roll; NHS; Ntl Merit Ltr; AP Amer Hist Achvt Awd; Ger Achvt Awds; Ger Soc Awd; Muhlenberg Coll; Pre-Med.

GEROSKY, JEFF; Pittston Area HS; Pittston, PA; (Y); French Clb; Band; Concert Band; Jazz Band; Mrchg Band; Pep Band; School Musical; Hon Roll; NHS; Music.

GERRITY, LEANNE; West Scranton SR HS; Scranton, PA; (Y); Exploring; French Clb; Girl Scts; Thesps; School Play; Rep Stu Cncl; Pom Pon; Trk; Hon Roll; NHS; U Scranton; Life Sci.

GERSTER, AMY; North Hills HS; Pittsburgh, PA; (S); AFS; Ski Clb; Band; Mrchg Band; High Hon Roll; NHS; Pilot.

GERVIN, POLLY; Mercy Vocational HS; Philadelphia, PA; (Y); Church Choir; Bsktbl; Hon Roll; Church Yth Grp; Rep Frsh Cls; Prfct Pnctlty 85-86; Prfct Atten 84-85; Air Force; Pilot.

GERZINA, CHRISTINE; Corry Area HS; Corry, PA; (S); 29/212; German Clb; Rep Jr Cls; JV Cheerleading; Hon Roll; Grmn Hnr Scty; FL ST U.

GESSNER, JANICE; Shikellamy HS; Paxinos, PA; (Y); 3/315; Hosp Aide; Concert Band; Co-Capt Drill Tm; Mrchg Band; Yrbk Stf; Var Capt Trk; Elks Awd; Hon Roll; NHS; Sal; Woodmen Of Wrld Life Ins Soc Amer Hist Awd 86; Pres Acadmc Fitnss Awd 86; Acadmc All-Amer 85-86; Susquehanna U; Secndry Math Edu.

GESTL, ERIN; Salisbury HS; Bethlehem, PA; (Y); 6/144; Boy Scts; JV Var Socr; High Hon Roll; Hon Roll; NHS; Rifle Tm MVP; Gentc Engrng.

GESUALDI, CHRISTOPHER; St John Neumann HS; Philadelphia, PA; (Y); 50/331; Boys Clb Am; Computer Clb; Mathletes; Office Aide; Hon Roll; Drexel U; CPA.

GETMAN, LAURA; Central Dauphin HS; Harrisburg, PA; (Y); Church Yth Grp; ROTC; Chorus; School Musical; School Play; Yrbk Stf; Stu Cncl; Marine Bio.

GETSY, STEPHEN; Steel Valley Schl; W Homestead, PA; (Y); Boy Scts; Church Yth Grp; Varsity Clb; Band; Drm & Bgl; Jazz Band; Mrchg Band; Bsbl; Bsktbl; Hon Roll.

GETTER, WILL; Delaware Valley HS; Matamoras, PA; (Y); 8/135; Drama Clb; Scholastic Bowl; Concert Band; Jazz Band; School Musical; NHS; Ntl Merit Ltr; School Play; Lit Mag; VP Frsh Cls; WA Wrkshps Cngrssnl Smnr 86; Hugh O Brian Yth Ldrshp Smnr 84; Rtry Ldrs Camp Ophlsphy Clb 84-86; Clark U; Coll Prof.

GETTY, DAWN; Plum SR HS; Pittsburgh, PA; (Y); DECA; Exploring; French Clb; Im Bsktbl; Var Score Keeper; Im Vllybl; Hon Roll; Bus.

GETZ, DENNIS; Forest Hills HS; Salix, PA; (Y); 17/156; Computer Clb; Spanish Clb; Var Bsbl; Im Bsktbl; JV Var Ftbl; Im Sftbl; Im Vllybl; High Hon Roll; Hon Roll; Spanish NHS; Engrng.

GETZ, MICHAEL; Altoona Area HS; Altoona, PA; (Y); 34/700; Drama Clb; Math Tm; Ed Nwsp Stf; Yrbk Phtg; Lit Mag; Rep Jr Cls; Rep Sr Cls; Golf; NEDT Awd; Chess Clb; Henry J Kirshner Yth Svc Awd 86; 3rd Pl Math Tm 86; PA ST U; Chem Engrng.

GETZANDANNER, KATHY; Littlestown SR HS; Littlestown, PA; (Y); #49 In Class; Am Leg Aux Girls St; DECA; French Clb; Office Aide; Teachers Aide; Varsity Clb; Band; Mrchg Band; Mgr Sftbl; York Coll Of PA; Accntng.

GETZEY, DENISE; Greater Johnstown HS; Johnstown, PA; (Y); Art Clb; Cmnty Wkr; Stage Crew; Yrbk Stf; Jr Cls; JA; Hnrbl Mentn Schl Pntng Art Show 83-84; Art Inst Pittsbrgh; Commrcl Art.

GETZOFF, RICHARD; Cheltenham HS; Melrose Pk, PA; (Y); Nwsp Rptr; JV Bsbl; Im Bsktbl; Var Ice Hcky; Hamilton Coll Hcky Schl 85; Cheltenham HS MVP 86; PA Lttl Flyrs Mst Imprvd 85; Med.

GEVAUDAN, RAYMOND; Pittsburgh Central Catholic HS; Pittsburgh, PA; (Y); 92/278; JV Im Bsktbl; Var L Ftbl; Hon Roll; Natl Hstry Day 1st Pl Pittsburgh Rgn 84; Penn Hills Bsbl Assn All Star 84-85; Engrng.

GEWARTOWSKI, KAREN; Central Catholic HS; Allentown, PA; (Y); 39/210; Church Yth Grp; Math Clb; Science Clb; Ski Clb; Rep Soph Cls; Stu Cncl; Sftbl; Tennis; High Hon Roll; Hon Roll; 1st Pl Rgnl Comp Of Pa Jr Acad Of Sci, 2nd Pl St Comp; Penn ST; Bus Mgt.

GEYER, KELLY; Rockwood HS; Markleton, PA; (S); 1/97; Pres NFL; Pres Speech Tm; Chorus; Rep Stu Cncl; High Hon Roll; Hon Roll; NHS; NEDT Awd; Ldrshp Develpmnt Sem Scholar 85; Hghst Cumltv GPA 82-86; Somerset Exch Clb Yth Mnth Awd 85; Sweet Briar; Pol Sci.

GEYER, RANDY; Millersburg Area HS; Millersburg, PA; (Y); Var JV Wrstlng; Hon Roll; Natl Ed Center; Electrncs.

GHANER, HEATHER; Philipsburg-Osceola HS; West Decatur, PA; (Y); 124/250; Church Yth Grp; Ski Clb; Varsity Clb; Church Choir; Drill Tm; School Musical; Nwsp Stf; Yrbk Stf; Trs Frsh Cls; Var JV Bsktbl; Bus.

GHEEN, BECKY; Mc Guffey HS; W Alexander, PA; (Y); 23/220; Am Leg Aux Girls St; Cmnty Wkr; Hosp Aide; JA; Pep Clb; Spanish Clb; Trk; Vllybl; Hon Roll; NHS; Physcl Thrpy.

GHEEN, JENNIFER; Little Flower HS; Philadelphia, PA; (Y); 72/402; Cmnty Wkr; Computer Clb; Hosp Aide; Spanish Clb; Teachers Aide; Rep Frsh Cls; Im Bsktbl; JV Capt Fld Hcky; Hon Roll; PA ST Coll; Mrktng.

GHEORGHIU, CRISTINA; Kennedy Christian HS; Greenville, PA; (Y); 12/98; Drama Clb; French Clb; Ski Clb; School Play; Stage Crew; High Hon Roll; Hon Roll; Schlrshp Psychlgy Prog 86; Schlrshp Kennedy Christ HS 83; Psychology.

GHERGO, LISA; Scranton Central HS; Scranton, PA; (Y); 19/283; Dance Clb; Ski Clb; Spanish Clb; Yrbk Stf; Trs Sr Cls; Stu Cncl; Cheerleading; Twrlr; Hon Roll; NHS; Phys Ther.

GHEZZI, KATHLEEN; Hazelton HS; Hazleton, PA; (Y); 74/400; Sec Church Yth Grp; Drama Clb; Leo Clb; Chorus; Nwsp Rptr; Yrbk Stf; Hon Roll; Spch Pthlgy.

GHILONI, JAMES; Plymouth-Whitemarsh HS; Blue Bell, PA; (Y); 4/337; Trs Math Clb; School Musical; School Play; Nwsp Rptr; Trs Stu Cncl; High Hon Roll; NHS; Ntl Merit SF; Brwn U Bk Awd 86; Acad Awd 84-86.

GHOSH, GREG; Danville SR HS; Danville, PA; (Y); 22/204; Computer Clb; French Clb; Key Clb; Ski Clb; Var Bsbl; Im Bsktbl; Var Socr; Var Tennis; High Hon Roll; NHS; Engrng.

GIACOBBE, FRANK; Mahanoy Area HS; Mahanoy City, PA; (Y); Art Clb; Church Yth Grp; French Clb; Chorus; Mrchg Band; Stage Crew; Variety Show; Nwsp Rptr; Yrbk Phtg; JV Crs Cntry; Drama.

GIACOBELLO, JOS; Garden Spot HS; Blue Ball, PA; (Y); 51/228; JV Var Bsbl; Crimnl Justc.

GIACOMETTI, LISA; Old Forge HS; Old Forge, PA; (Y); 4/71; Hosp Aide; Yrbk Ed-Chief; Capt Cheerleading; High Hon Roll; Hon Roll; Sec NHS; Schlstc Bwl Tm 86; Corprt Lwyr.

GIACOMIN, MELANIE ANN; Penn-Trafford HS; Irwin, PA; (Y); 34/342; Am Leg Aux Girls St; Math Clb; Yrbk Stf; Pres Sr Cls; Var Crs Cntry; Var Sftbl; High Hon Roll; NHS; GAA; Letterman Clb; Stu Forum Rep Westmorland Cnty 85-86; WPIAL Sftbl Allstar Pittsburgh Post 86; Engrng.

GIALLORENZO, EZIO; Aliquippa HS; Aliquippa, PA; (S); 8/140; Church Yth Grp; Drama Clb; Exploring; FCA; French Clb; Math Tm; School Musical; School Play; Stage Crew; Rep Jr Cls; US Army Resrv 86; U Of Pittsburgh; Elec Engr.

GIAMPIETRO, NICHOLAS F; St Pius X HS; Phoenixville, PA; (Y); 48/158; FBLA; School Play; Yrbk Stf; Rep Sr Cls; Var Tennis; Trvl.

GIANCARLO, LEANNA; Scranton Prep; Scranton, PA; (Y); 4/191; Exploring; Orch; School Musical; Yrbk Stf; Lit Mag; High Hon Roll; NHS; Ntl Merit Ltr; VFW Awd; PA JR Acad Sci 1st Pl Regnl, ST 86; Pres III Schlrshp U Scranton; U Scranton; Chem.

GIANELLE, ERIC; Abington SR HS; Roslyn, PA; (Y); 86/535; Church Yth Grp; Varsity Clb; Var Bsbl; Var Ftbl; Var Socr; JV Wrstlng; Hon Roll; Pres Acadmc Fit Awd 86; Indstrl Arts Awd & Prncpls Awd 86; Abington Almn Assoc Schlrshp 86; Syracuse; Arch.

GIANFERANTE, LISA; Danville SR HS; Riverside, PA; (Y); 30/200; Sec Church Yth Grp; Sec Key Clb; Ski Clb; Spanish Clb; JV Cheerleading; JV Var Fld Hcky; Pres Mat Maids; JV Sftbl; Swmmng; Sec NHS; Dietcs.

GIANFRANCESCO, LISA; St Maria Goretti HS; Philadelphia, PA; (Y); 35/405; Church Yth Grp; Cmnty Wkr; Exploring; Math Clb; Sec Spanish Clb; High Hon Roll; Jr NHS; NHS; Bambi Clnrs Schlstc Awd 86; Temple U; Bus.

GIANGIULIO, LOUIS M; Malvern Preparatory Schl; Wayne, PA; (Y); 2/86; Mathletes; Yrbk Ed-Chief; VP Stu Cncl; Capt L Ftbl; Var Capt Wrstlng; Ntl Merit SF; Rep Voice Dem Awd; 1st Pl 185 Lb Phila Area Prep Schl Wrstlng Tourn 85; Hugh O Brien Yth Fndtn Schl Ldrshp Rep 84; Ortho Doc.

GIANNANGELI, DONNA; Penn Hills SR HS; Pittsburgh, PA; (Y); Church Yth Grp; Drama Clb; French Clb; Thesps; School Musical; School Play; Stu Cncl; Hon Roll.

GIANNETTA, CARLA; Saint Huberts HS; Philadelphia, PA; (Y); 41/367; Art Clb; Computer Clb; Intnl Clb; Office Aide; Interior Dsgn.

GIANONI, KARA; North Pocono HS; Moscow, PA; (Y); Church Yth Grp; GAA; Varsity Clb; Yrbk Stf; Sec Sr Cls; Sec Stu Cncl; Var Cheerleading; Trk; High Hon Roll; NHS; Educ.

GIARDINA, LISA; Cardinal O Hara HS; Brookhaven, PA; (Y); Cmnty Wkr; Hosp Aide; Im Vllybl; Villanova; Med.

GIBB, AMY; Hickory HS; Hermitage, PA; (Y); 36/180; Church Yth Grp; Drama Clb; Library Aide; Service Clb; Spanish Clb; Varsity Clb; Band; Chorus; Church Choir; Concert Band; Ntl Govt Awd 85; Stu Tutor 86; Grove City Coll; Elem Ed.

GIBB, JOLYNN; Highlands HS; Natrona Hts, PA; (Y); 3/298; AFS; Church Yth Grp; Intnl Clb; JA; Key Clb; Diving; High Hon Roll; Jr NHS; NHS; Ntl Acad Sci Awd Chem 86; Sci.

GIBBEL, DEAN; Tulpehocken Area HS; Bethel, PA; (Y); 15/106; Church Yth Grp; Spanish Clb; Concert Band; Mrchg Band; Hon Roll; NHS; Tulpehocken Schlr Awd 85-86; Phys Fit Awd 84-86; Lincoln Tech Inst; Elctrncs.

GIBBLE, DAWN; Northern Lebanon HS; Annville, PA; (Y); 24/200; Spanish Clb; Varsity Clb; Color Guard; Mrchg Band; L Bsktbl; L Capt Sftbl; Hon Roll; Grace Pres Awd 86; Northern Lebanon Booster Schlrshp 86; Kiwanis Schlr Athlt Awd 86; Grace Coll; Bus Mngt.

GIBBONS, COLETTE; York Catholic HS; York, PA; (Y); 9/160; French Clb; Hosp Aide; Sec JA; Concert Band; School Play; Nwsp Rptr; Yrbk Bus Mgr; Stat Bsktbl; Var Tennis; High Hon Roll; Alls Ch L Ptry Spch Awd 85; Athlt Mo Tnns 83 & 84; Aerontcl Engrng.

GIBBONS, KIM; Southern Huntingdon HS; Blairs Mills, PA; (Y); Sec FBLA; GAA; Varsity Clb; Yrbk Stf; Sec Stu Cncl; Var L Fld Hcky; Var L Sftbl; All-Str Fld Hcky 85; All-Str Sftbl 86; Physcl Ftnss Awd 85; Physcl Thrpst.

GIBBONS, MOLLY; Hopewell HS; Hookstown, PA; (Y); Church Yth Grp; German Clb; SADD; Color Guard; Concert Band; Mrchg Band; Pep Band; Hon Roll; Robert Morris Coll; Acctg.

GIBBONS, RENEE; Cambria Heights SR HS; Hastings, PA; (Y); Church Yth Grp; Cmnty Wkr; Chorus; School Musical.

GIBBS, MICHAELA; Yough SR HS; Irwin, PA; (Y); 22/250; Girl Scts; Band; Jazz Band; Mrchg Band; Pep Band; School Play; Var Trk; High Hon Roll; NHS; Med.

GIBEL, JEANNINE; Winchester-Thurston HS; Pittsburgh, PA; (Y); AFS; French Clb; GAA; Hosp Aide; School Play; Yrbk Ed-Chief; Mgr(s); U Of PA; Med.

GIBERSON, SCOTT; Wyoming Area HS; W Wyoming, PA; (Y); 4/260; Key Clb; Spanish Clb; Stu Cncl; Bsbl; Bsktbl; High Hon Roll; NHS; Natl Rotary Ledrshp Camp 85; Biologist.

GIBSON, ANGIE; Ligonier Valley SR HS; Ligonier, PA; (Y); 15/147; Church Yth Grp; GAA; Letterman Clb; Office Aide; Varsity Clb; Pres Chorus; Swing Chorus; Pres Soph Cls; Pres Jr Cls; Pres Church Yth Grp; Amer Legn Awd 84; Womns Sprts Foundtn H S All Str Awd 86; PA Free Entrprs Wk Schlrshp 85-86; Villanova; Pre-Med.

GIBSON, AYME; Ambridge HS; Ambridge, PA; (Y); Cmnty Wkr; GAA; JA; Church Choir; JV Capt Bsktbl; Trk; High Hon Roll; Hon Roll; NHS; Prfct Atten Awd; Acad All-Star Bsktbl 83-86; Acad All-Star Trck 83-86; JR Achvt Sls Awd 83-84; Accntnt.

GIBSON, CAROL; Pennsbury HS; Morrisville, PA; (Y); Church Yth Grp; German Clb; Chorus; Pres Soph Cls; Rep Jr Cls; Rep Stu Cncl; Var Cheerleading; Var Gym; Var Sftbl; Hon Roll; Frgn Lang Clb Awd 86.

GIBSON, CHRISTY; Lackawanna Trail HS; Factoryville, PA; (Y); Church Yth Grp; Chorus; Rep Stu Cncl; JV Var Bsktbl; JV Var Fld Hcky; JV Var Sftbl; 1st Tm All-Star Field Hcky 85-86; Gold Medal Wnng ST Fld Scky Championship 85-86; Mst Prmsng Tm Awd; Accntng.

GIBSON, DENISE; Ligonier Valley HS; Ligonier, PA; (Y); 36/154; AFS; Pep Clb; Ski Clb; Chorus; School Play; Yrbk Ed-Chief; Stu Cncl; Cheerleading; Hon Roll; Ntl Merit Ltr; Pre Med.

GIBSON, JAMES; Simon Gratz HS; Philadelphia, PA; (Y); Camera Clb; Church Yth Grp; Cmnty Wkr; Dance Clb; Drama Clb; FBLA; FTA; JA; Library Aide; Mathletes; Treas Frshmn Cls 84; Hugh O Brien Schlrshp 85; Vol Awd/Plaque 2500 Hrs Svc Get Set Day Care; Temple; Acctg.

GIBSON, JOHN; Kiski Area SR HS; Apollo, PA; (Y); Debate Tm; Drama Clb; Exploring; Model UN; Band; Chorus; Swing Chorus; JV Trk; Hon Roll; Prfct Atten Awd.

GIBSON, JOY; S Williamsport Area SR HS; S Williamsport, PA; (Y); 20/149; Key Clb; Spanish Clb; Band; VP Chorus; School Musical; Nwsp Rptr; Yrbk Stf; JV Tennis; Dist Chrs 85-86; Miss Lycmng Cnty 85-86; Lycmng Cnty Plc Camp Cad Cnslr 85-86; Psych.

GIBSON, KELLY; Lewisburg Area HS; Lewisburg, PA; (Y); 22/170; Church Yth Grp; Cmnty Wkr; VP German Clb; Hosp Aide; Chorus; Mrchg Band; School Musical; High Hon Roll; Hon Roll; NHS; Comm.

GIBSON, LOUIS; Kiski Area SR HS; Apollo, PA; (Y); Boy Scts; Exploring; Band; Concert Band; Mrchg Band; Symp Band; Hon Roll.

GIBSON, NATALIE; Williams Valley HS; Orwin, PA; (Y); 21/104; Spanish Clb; Chorus; Mrchg Band; Symp Band; Capt Powder Puff Ftbl; Hon Roll; Bloomsburg; Pre-Med.

GIBSON, REGINA; St Maria Goretti HS; Philadelphia, PA; (Y); 87/390; Church Yth Grp; Cmnty Wkr; GAA; Office Aide; Science Clb; Off Jr Cls; Hon Roll; Widener U; Psychlgy.

GIBSON, SHAWN; Northern Lebanon JR SR HS; Jonestown, PA; (Y); 14/166; Church Yth Grp; Computer Clb; Quiz Bowl; Concert Band; Mrchg Band; Pep Band; Nwsp Rptr; Bausch & Lomb Sci Awd; Hon Roll; Chem Engrng.

GIBSON, SUSAN; Lower Moreland HS; Huntingdon Valley, PA; (S); 18/214; Key Clb; Science Clb; Concert Band; Rep Stu Cncl; Var Bsktbl; Var Capt Crs Cntry; Hon Roll; NHS; 2nd Al-Leag Tm Grls Crs Cntry 85; Socl Stud Achvt Awd 84; U Of VA; Bus.

GIBSON, WAYNE LAWRENCE; Spring Grove Area SR HS; Seven Valleys, PA; (Y); 20/222; VP JA; Band; Concert Band; Drm Mjr(t); Jazz Band; Mrchg Band; School Musical; Trk; Wrstlng; High Hon Roll; Pres Acadmc Ftnss Awd 86; CA ST U; Aero Engrg.

GIEDZINSKI, DAVID; Unionville HS; W Chester, PA; (Y); 125/300; Aud/Vis; Trs Soph Cls; JV Bsktbl; Var Socr; Var Trk; Hon Roll; Jr NHS; Cvl Engrng.

GIERINGER, BRIAN; Fairview HS; Erie, PA; (Y); Speech Tm; Hon Roll; 1st Pl Prlmnry Rounds Engl Spkng Union & Pblc Spkng Cntsts 84; PA ST U; Liberal Arts.

GIES, BARBARA; St Marys Area HS; St Marys, PA; (Y); Boys Clb Am; Sftbl; Managment.

GIEWONT, MARK; Saegertown HS; Saegertown, PA; (Y); 6/119; Ski Clb; Varsity Clb; Band; Jazz Band; Mrchg Band; Var Capt Vllybl; Var Capt Wrstlng; JP Sousa Awd; NHS; Pres Schlr; Semper Fidelis Awd 86; Pres Acdmc Fit Awd Prg 86; Penn ST U; Elec Engrng.

GIFFIN, SUZANNE M; Warren Area HS; Warren, PA; (Y); 3/286; French Clb; Hosp Aide; Library Aide; Band; Concert Band; Mrchg Band; School Musical; School Play; High Hon Roll; NHS; Goldn Dragn Awd 85; AP Hstry Awd 86; Ithaca Coll; Phys Thrpy.

GIFFORD, KATHLEEN; Waynesburg Central HS; Waynesburg, PA; (Y); French Clb; L Trk; High Hon Roll; NHS; Engl & French Schltc Awds 85-86.

GIGANTINO, ADRIENNE; Dunmore HS; Scranton, PA; (Y); 50/149; Ski Clb; Spanish Clb; Capt Flag Corp; Hunter Coll; Spnsh.

GIGER, SHERI L; North Hills HS; Pittsburgh, PA; (Y); 40/507; Pres Thesps; School Musical; School Play; Stage Crew; Drama Clb; NFL; Nwsp Stf; High Hon Roll; Pres Schlr; Carlow Coll; Cmnctns.

GIGLIOTTI, BRAD; Punxsutawney Area HS; Punxsutawney, PA; (Y); Spanish Clb; Bsktbl; Duquesne; Dntstry.

GILBERT, ELIZABETH; Strath Haven HS; Wallingford, PA; (Y); Church Yth Grp; Teachers Aide; Yrbk Stf; Fld Hcky; Sftbl; Hon Roll; Johnson & Wales Acad $1000 Schlrshp 86; Awd Excllnc In Foods/ Nutrition 86; Johnson & Wales Coll; Pstry Art.

GILBERT III, FRANK M; Lower Dauphin HS; Hummelstown, PA; (S); 105/217; CAP; FFA; Var L Bsktbl; Var L Ftbl; Var Capt Trk; Keystone Farmers Degr 86; Brnz Mdl Lng Jmp Keystone ST Games 85; Envrnmntl Stud.

GILBERT, JAMES; Marian Catholic HS; Summit Hill, PA; (S); 10/114; Aud/Vis; Chess Clb; Band; Stage Crew; Trk; High Hon Roll; NHS; Lehigh; Bus Admin.

GILBERT, JAMES M; Kittanning SR HS; Kittanning, PA; (Y); 9/268; Spanish Clb; Concert Band; Mrchg Band; Nwsp Stf; High Hon Roll; Hon Roll; Ntl Merit SF; 3rd Pl PA Jr Acdmy Sci ST Comp 82; US Coast Guard Acad; Comp Sci.

GILBERT, JENNIFER; Oxford Area HS; Oxford, PA; (Y); 1/170; Band; Chorus; Yrbk Stf; Rep Stu Cncl; Var JV Fld Hcky; High Hon Roll; NHS; Ntl Merit Ltr; Val; Cmnty Wkr; Bst All Arnd Grl 86; Cert Of Merit-Soc Of Wmn Engrs 86; Presdntl Acadmc Ftns Awd 86; Northwestern U; Jrnlsm.

GILBERT, MICHAEL; Conrad Weiser HS; Wernersville, PA; (Y); 26/ 186; Church Yth Grp; Computer Clb; JCL; Var Tennis; Hon Roll; NHS; Engnrng.

GILBERT, TRACEY; Pottsgrove HS; Pottstown, PA; (Y); 8/234; Math Tm; Science Clb; Ski Clb; Spanish Clb; School Musical; Rep Stu Cncl; Var Tennis; JV Trk; Hon Roll; NHS.

GILBERT, TRICIA; Eastern York HS; York, PA; (Y); 14/169; VP Varsity Clb; Yrbk Stf; Pres Frsh Cls; Pres Jr Cls; JV Bsktbl; Var L Fld Hcky; Var L Trk; Var L Vllybl; Pres Jr NHS; NHS; Psych.

GILBERTSON, BRYAN; Ford City HS; Manorville, PA; (Y); Spanish Clb; Trs Soph Cls; Rep Jr Cls; Rep Stu Cncl; Var L Bsbl; Var L Ftbl; Ed.

GILBERTSON, JEFFREY E; East HS; West Chester, PA; (Y); 8/384; Pres Chess Clb; German Clb; Nwsp Stf; Hon Roll; NHS; Army ROTC Schlrshp 86; Acad Achvt Awd 85; Acad Exclnce Awd 86; Worcester Polytechnic Inst; Eng.

GILBEY, LISA; Pennsburg HS; Morrisville, PA; (Y); Band; Concert Band; Var Bsktbl; Var Fld Hcky; Im Gym; JV Var Sftbl; Im Vllybl; Im Wt Lftg; Hon Roll; NHS; Phys Thrpy.

GILBOY, ANN; Shenango HS; New Castle, PA; (S); 12/121; Varsity Clb; Band; Concert Band; Jazz Band; Mrchg Band; Pep Band; Nwsp Stf; Var Bsktbl; Score Keeper; L Trk; Accntnt.

GILBRIDE, THOMAS; Scranton Central HS; Scranton, PA; (Y); Church Yth Grp; French Clb; JA; Pep Clb; Political Wkr; Pres Science Clb; Ski Clb; Band; Chorus; Church Choir; U Of Scranton; Pre-Law.

GILCHRIST, CHRISTINE; Emmaus HS; Macungie, PA; (Y); 6/497; Latin Clb; Model UN; Spanish Clb; Var Swmmng; Var Trk; High Hon Roll; Hon Roll; Jr NHS; NHS; Ntl Merit Ltr; Cmmrcl Artst.

GILDENSTON, STACY B; Mercyhurst Preparatory Schl; Erie, PA; (Y); Service Clb; Thesps; Church Choir; School Musical; School Play; Stage Crew; VP Sr Cls; Twrlr; Drama Clb; Drm Mjr(t); Pblctn Drmtc Monologue Telecast 60 Cities 86; Various Thtrcl Schlrshp To U 86; Invlmnt Cmmnty Thtre 86; Musical Theatre.

GILDROY, JOHN; Southmoreland HS; Mt Pleasant, PA; (Y); Art Clb; Exploring; FHA; Latin Clb; Spanish Clb; Rep Frsh Cls; JV Var Ftbl; Sftbl; Vllybl; Wt Lftg; NDSU; Agri.

GILEOT, ANGEL; Moon SR HS; Coraopolis, PA; (Y); Office Aide; Sec Chorus; Variety Show; Rep Soph Cls; Rep Jr Cls; Rep Sr Cls; Rep Stu Cncl; JV Var Sftbl; Stat Vllybl; Hon Roll; St Vincent Coll; Psych.

GILES, ARTHUR; Monaca JR-SR HS; Monaca, PA; (Y); Am Leg Boys St; Band; Concert Band; Mrchg Band; Pep Band; Var Bsbl; JV Bsktbl; Hon Roll; Prfct Atten Awd; Mdcl Lab Techncn.

GILES, ELIZABETH; Canon Mc Millan HS; Canonsburg, PA; (Y); 20/ 340; Library Aide; SADD; Varsity Clb; Var L Crs Cntry; Var L Trk; High Hon Roll; NHS; Prfct Atten Awd; Spanish NHS; Pres Acadmc Fitnss Awd 86; IN U Of Pa; Math.

GILES, ERIC J; Blackhawk HS; Beaver Falls, PA; (Y); 19/270; Boy Scts; Sec Church Yth Grp; Key Clb; Stage Crew; Im Capt Bsktbl; JV Trk; High Hon Roll; Hon Roll; Recgntn Outstndng Pupil Accomp Alg,World Cult 84; Engrng.

GILES, THOMAS; Hempfield Area SR HS; Greensburg, PA; (Y); AFS; Science Clb; Im Bsktbl; High Hon Roll; Hon Roll; Jr NHS; Lion Awd; Penn ST; Gntcs.

GILIBERTI, BRIAN; Warwick HS; Lititz, PA; (Y); 73/500; Boy Scts; Camera Clb; Church Yth Grp; Spanish Clb; SADD; L Crs Cntry; L Trk; High Hon Roll; Hon Roll; North Eastern Boston; Biomed En.

GILIBERTI, DAVID; Warwick HS; Lititz, PA; (Y); 93/500; Boy Scts; Camera Clb; Church Yth Grp; Spanish Clb; SADD; L Crs Cntry; High Hon Roll; Prfct Atten Awd; North Eastern Boston; Ind Engr.

GILL, CRAIG; Tyrone Area HS; Tyrone, PA; (Y); Computer Clb; Ski Clb; Band; Jazz Band; Pep Band; Yrbk Phtg; Var Trk; Hon Roll; Prfct Atten Awd; U Pitt Johnstown HS Comp Prog Cont 1ST Plc 86; Penn ST U; Nuclear Engr.

GILL, KAREN; Tyrone Area HS; Tyrone, PA; (Y); Ski Clb; Chorus; Var JV Cheerleading; Powder Puff Ftbl; Hon Roll; Penn ST; Phys Ther.

GILL, MATT; North Allegheny SR HS; Pittsburgh, PA; (Y); 364/605; Capt Crs Cntry; Var Trk; Clarion U Of PA.

GILL, STEPHANIE; Hollidaysburg Area SR HS; Hollidaysburg, PA; (Y); Church Yth Grp; French Clb; Band; Chorus; Concert Band; Mrchg Band; Orch; School Musical; Hon Roll; IN U PA; Music Ed.

GILL, TAMMY; Neshaminy HS; Langhorne, PA; (Y); 88/685; DECA; Trs 4-H; Yrbk Phtg; 4-H Awd; Hon Roll; Prfct Atten Awd; Langhorne Rotary Stu Of Month 86; Bucks Co CC; Real Est.

GILL, TODD; Hampton HS; Allison Pk, PA; (Y); Ski Clb; Rep Soph Cls; JV Var Bsktbl; Var L Crs Cntry; Var L Trk; NHS.

GILLEN, JENNIFER; Plum HS; Pittsburgh, PA; (Y); AFS; Hst FHA; Ski Clb; Band; Yrbk Stf; L Socr; L Swmmng; Stat Trk; Hon Roll; Bio.

GILLENWATER, ANDREA; Downingtown SR HS; Glenmore, PA; (Y); Church Yth Grp; Spanish Clb; SADD; Chorus; Vllybl; Hon Roll; Bus.

GILLESPIE, KAREN; Unionville HS; West Chester, PA; (Y); 40/300; FBLA; Pep Clb; Yrbk Stf; Rep Soph Cls; Rep Jr Cls; Rep Sr Cls; Chrmn Stu Cncl; Powder Puff Ftbl; High Hon Roll; Hon Roll; Lwyr.

GILLESPIE, RITA; Cardinal O Hara HS; Aston, PA; (Y); 52/778; Church Yth Grp; Hosp Aide; Stu Cncl; Var Crs Cntry; Var Trk; Hon Roll; NHS; Prfct Atten Awd; All Cathlc Crss Cntry 85; Prncpls Awd Acadmc Excllnc 85; Pre-Med.

GILLETTE, CAMMIE; Bishop O Hara HS; Jessup, PA; (S); 16/124; Art Clb; Latin Clb; Science Clb; Spanish Clb; School Musical; Yrbk Stf; Hon Roll; U Of Scranton; Chem.

GILLETTE, DALE; Linesville HS; Linesville, PA; (Y); 7/86; Boy Scts; Church Yth Grp; German Clb; SADD; Chorus; Ftbl; Wt Lftg; Hon Roll; Edinboro U; Crim Just.

GILLETTE, MARGO; Dunmore HS; Dunmore, PA; (Y); 9/150; French Clb; FBLA; Ski Clb; Spanish Clb; Flag Corp; Yrbk Stf; High Hon Roll; Jr NHS; NHS; SOS Stu Instrct Agnst Shplftg 85-86; Explrers 84-86; Hlth Careers Clb & Music Gld 83-86.

GILLIGAN JR, MICHAEL; Northern Potter HS; Harrison Valley, PA; (Y); Boy Scts; Church Yth Grp; Cmnty Wkr; JV Var Trk; High Hon Roll; Hon Roll; Pres Schlr; Natl Merit Sci Awd 86; Russel Wood Accntng Schlrshp 86; Edinboro U Fresh Hnrs Schlrshp 86; Edinboro U; Bus Adm.

GILLILAND, DONALD; Northern Potter JR SR HS; Genesee, PA; (S); 4/90; Debate Tm; Pres French Clb; Trs FFA; Model UN; Ski Clb; Chorus; Concert Band; Pep Band; Yrbk Stf; Sec Soph Cls.

GILLILAND, GEORGE A; Portersville Christian HS; Butler, PA; (Y); Church Yth Grp; Chorus; Nwsp Stf; Yrbk Bus Mgr; Var Cheerleading; Var Socr; Psychology.

GILLILAND, PAMELA A; Tyrone Area HS; Warriors Mark, PA; (S); 9/ 197; Sec Trs French Clb; Key Clb; Ski Clb; Varsity Clb; Chorus; Off Jr Cls; Var JV Cheerleading; High Hon Roll; NHS; PA ST U; Accntng.

GILLIS, FRANK; Trinity HS; Camphill, PA; (Y); Varsity Clb; Ftbl; Trk; Notre Dame; Pre-Law.

GILLMAN, JOY; Crestwood HS; Mountaintop, PA; (Y); Trs Church Yth Grp; Trs FBLA; JV Var Fld Hcky; Mgr(s); Var Vllybl; High Hon Roll; NHS; Prfct Atten Awd; Hnr Awd 86; Amer Leg Axlry Awd 86.

GILLOW, ROMAINE; Pittston Area SR HS; Avoca, PA; (Y); 15/330; Key Clb; Yrbk Ed-Chief; Yrbk Phtg; Rep Stu Cncl; Var L Twrlr; High Hon Roll; Hon Roll; NHS; U Scranton; Pre Med.

GILLS, BRENDA; Grove City Area HS; Mercer, PA; (Y); 27/143; Band; Chorus; Church Choir; Concert Band; Mrchg Band; Capt Powder Puff Ftbl; Co-Capt Trk; High Hon Roll; Hon Roll; NHS.

GILMER, MICHELLE; Canon-Mc Millan SR HS; Canonsburg, PA; (Y); 4-H; Letterman Clb; Var JV Bsktbl; Var JV Sftbl; 4-H Awd; Hon Roll; Church Yth Grp; FFA; Penn ST U; Nrsg.

GILMORE, ANNEMARIE; Nazareth Acad; Philadelphia, PA; (Y); German Clb; Math Clb; Co-Capt Bsktbl; Coach Actv; Var Mgr(s); Im Vllybl; High Hon Roll; Hon Roll; NEDT Awd; Trstee Schlrshp Lehigh U 1986; PHEAA Merit Awd Prfrmnc SATS 85; Lehigh U; Engnrng.

GILMORE, KAREN; Murrell Dobbins AVTS; Philadelphia, PA; (S); #15 In Class; FBLA; Library Aide; Co-Capt Pep Clb; Color Guard; Mgr Gym; Sftbl; Hon Roll; NHS; Prfct Atten Awd; Girl Scts; Westchester U; Acctg.

GILMORE, ROBERT; Penn Hills SR HS; Pittsburgh, PA; (Y); 72/616; German Clb; High Hon Roll; Physics.

GILMORE, SHANE; Penn Wood HS; Yeadon, PA; (Y); 46/349; Aud/Vis; Church Yth Grp; Teachers Aide; Chorus; Church Choir; School Musical; Variety Show; Sec Soph Cls; Pres Jr Cls; Rep Stu Cncl; Cert Specl Rcntn-Svc During Spirit Wk 85; William Penn Schl Dis Svc Awd-Excptnl Svc 84.

GILMORE, TRACIE; Meadville SR HS; Meadville, PA; (Y); 12/422; Church Yth Grp; Dance Clb; SADD; Chorus; JV Var Cheerleading; JV Trk; High Hon Roll; Stu Cncl Natl Awd 85-86; Optometry.

GILOT, BRYANT; Bishop Guilfoyle HS; Altoona, PA; (Y); 27/149; Ski Clb; Chorus; Yrbk Stf; Pres Soph Cls; Pres Jr Cls; Stu Cncl; Mgr(s); Tennis; Acadmc All Amer 85; Ntl Sci Merit Awd 85; Pre Med.

GILPIN, LINDA; Ringgold HS; Monongahela, PA; (Y); 57/342; Sec Church Yth Grp; SADD; Chorus; Pep Band; School Musical; School Play; Nwsp Rptr; Nwsp Stf; Yrbk Rptr; Yrbk Sprt Ed; Piano & Organ Recital 81,83,85; Accntnt.

GILROY, KRISTEN; Lakeland JR-SR HS; Jermyn, PA; (Y); 30/148; French Clb; Yrbk Stf; Capt Cheerleading; Sftbl; Hon Roll; Prfct Atten Awd; U Of Scranton; Psych.

GILROY, ROBERT; Trinity HS; Mechanicsburg, PA; (Y); 20/144; JCL; Ski Clb; Stage Crew; JV L Socr; JV L Trk; Hon Roll; Natl Latn Exm Max Cum Ld 84; Natl Latn Exm Cum Ld 85.

GILSON III, CHARLES A; Moshannon Ralley JS HS; Smithmills, PA; (Y); 15/127; Science Clb; Spanish Clb; Chorus; Swing Chorus; Mgr(s); Var Tennis; Hon Roll; Lock Haven U; Bio.

GILSON, KELLIE; Reynolds HS; Transfer, PA; (Y); Church Yth Grp; Civic Clb; Latin Clb; Math Clb; Science Clb; SADD; Varsity Clb; Band; Mrchg Band; Var L Vllybl; Acdmc All Amer 86; Pres Phy Fit Awd 84-85; Nrsg.

GILVARY, PAULINE C; Seton Catholic HS; Avoca, PA; (Y); 8/93; Drama Clb; Mathletes; NFL; SADD; School Musical; Variety Show; Nwsp Rptr; Cit Awd; High Hon Roll; Acdmc Schlrshp Kings Coll 86; 2 Bnds Coll Bwl Score 84 & 86; Hghst Rnkg Stdnt Frnch 86; Kings Coll; Acctg.

GILYARD, KENA; Franklin Learning Ctr; Philadelphia, PA; (Y); Church Yth Grp; Spanish Clb; Teachers Aide; High Hon Roll; Hon Roll; Nrsng.

GIMBEL, RITA MARY; St Huberts HS; Philadelphia, PA; (Y); 130/364; Sec Office Aide; Nwsp Stf; Lit Mag; Var Capt Crs Cntry; Var Capt Trk; Hon Roll; Prfct Atten Awd; Cmnty Wkr; Hosp Aide; Teachers Aide; Mdls & Rbns Smmr Tck 85-86; Prfct Atndnc Crtfcts 84-86; Holy Family Coll; Nrsng.

GINDER, KAREN; Donegal HS; Mt Joy, PA; (Y); 5/190; Church Yth Grp; Drama Clb; School Play; Stage Crew; Yrbk Stf; High Hon Roll; Hon Roll; NHS; Journlsm.

GINDLESPERGER, KRISTINE; Forest Hills SR HS; Windber, PA; (Y); 8/165; Yrbk Stf; VP Soph Cls; VP Jr Cls; Trs VP Stu Cncl; L Trk; JV Vllybl; High Hon Roll; Jr NHS; Lion Awd; NHS; All Amer Acadmc Awd 85; US Math Awd 85.

GINDLESPERGER, RONALD; Conemaugh Twp Area HS; Johnstown, PA; (S); 13/101; Aud/Vis; Scholastic Bowl; Spanish Clb; Nwsp Rptr; Techng.

GINDVILLE, MARY ANN; St Maria Goretti HS; Philadelphia, PA; (Y); 116/390; Cmnty Wkr; FBLA; JV Capt Bsktbl; GAA; Office Aide; Variety Show; Hon Mntn Bus Kthrn Gibbs Schl; Temple U.

GINGERICH, DENA; Northeastern SR HS; Mt Wolf, PA; (Y); Ski Clb; Teachers Aide; Chorus; Stat Bsktbl; Hon Roll; NHS; Central PA Bus Schl; Acctng.

GINGERY, ANDREW KELLER; Bellefonte Area SR HS; Bellefonte, PA; (Y); Drama Clb; Model UN; School Play; Stage Crew; Yrbk Phtg; Yrbk Rptr; Yrbk Stf; Rep Stu Cncl; Ntl Merit SF; NEDT Awd; Engrng.

GINGRICH, DAVE; Annville-Cleona HS; Annville, PA; (Y); 33/120; Varsity Clb; Chorus; Stu Cncl; Var Bsbl; Var Ftbl; Var Ice Hcky; Var Wrstlng; NHS; Lebanon Cnty All Star Bsbl 85; Ldr Corps 85-86; Amer Boys ST 85-86; Math Tchr.

GINGRICH, ELLEN; East Juniata HS; Mcalistervl, PA; (Y); Church Yth Grp; FHA; Library Aide; Chorus; Concert Band; Mrchg Band; School Play; Yrbk Phtg; Cheerleading; Trk; Comp Sci.

GINGRICH, ERIC; Lampeter-Strasburg HS; Lampeter, PA; (Y); 16/157; Pres Church Yth Grp; Church Choir; Yrbk Stf; Im Bsktbl; Var Socr; Hon Roll; Local Sci Fair; Engrng.

GINGRICH, KRISTIN KAYE; Quakertown Community HS; Quakertown, PA; (Y); Am Leg Aux Girls St; Ski Clb; Varsity Clb; Stage Crew; Off Soph Cls; Off Jr Cls; Off Sr Cls; Bsktbl; Fld Hcky; Trk; West Chester U; Pre-Med.

GINGRICH, PAUL; Dover Area HS; Dover, PA; (Y); Art Clb; Boy Scts; Camera Clb; 4-H; JA; Ski Clb; Crs Cntry; Ftbl; Trk; Wt Lftg.

GINLEY, KATHLEEN; St Hubert HS; Philadelphia, PA; (Y); 134/367; Art Clb; Varsity Clb; Stu Cncl; Fld Hcky; Sftbl; Swmmng; Rep Jr Cls; Psych.

GINTER, MICHAEL S; Littlestown HS; Littlestown, PA; (Y); 21/105; Letterman Clb; Varsity Clb; L Var Ftbl; L Wrstlng; NHS; Prfct Atten Awd; Pys Thrpst.

GINTHER, KAREN L; J P Mc Caskey HS; Lancaster, PA; (Y); 6/486; VP AFS; Math Clb; Q&S; Yrbk Bus Mgr; Lit Mag; Rep Stu Cncl; NHS; Church Yth Grp; Red Cross Aide; Band; Lancaster Exchng Clb Stu Of Mnth 86; Presdntl Acad Ftns Awd 86; Womens Wstrn Golf Fndtn Schlrshp 86; U Of Pittsburgh; Phrmcy.

GIORDANO, BARBARA; St Maria Goretti HS; Philadelphia, PA; (Y); Dance Clb; Pep Clb; Teachers Aide; Chorus; School Musical; JV Cheerleading; Hon Roll; Pierce; Paralgl.

GIORDANO, DOMENIC; Holy Ghost Preparatory HS; Philadelphia, PA; (S); Art Clb; Chess Clb; Cmnty Wkr; Math Clb; Yrbk Stf; NHS; Excllnc Latn,Math And Spnsh; Engrng.

GIORDANO, JOSEPH; Bishop Oreily HS; Kingston, PA; (Y); Spanish Clb; Socr; Wrstlng; Wilkes Coll; Pre-Med.

GIORDANO, MICHAEL; Cardinal O Hara HS; Springfield, PA; (Y); 45/ 740; Computer Clb; Spanish Clb; Yrbk Stf; Acad, Spnsh, Hstry & Chem Awds; Drexel U; Chem.

GIORDANO, STACEY; Little Flower HS; Philadelphia, PA; (Y); Hon Roll; Accntnt.

GIORI JR, MARCELLO; Freeport Area SR HS; Sarver, PA; (Y); Pres Acad Fit Awds Prog 86; Grad Magna Cum Laude 86; Marines.

GIOVANNELLI, PERRY; Valley HS; New Kensington, PA; (Y); 57/230; Exploring; Leo Clb; Pep Clb; Ski Clb; Pres Sr Cls; Stu Cncl; Amer Lgn Awd 83; Physcs Club 86; IN U; Mgmnt Info Sys.

GIPE, DARLA; Fannett-Metal HS; Fannettsburg, PA; (S); 3/55; Camera Clb; Sec Church Yth Grp; Drama Clb; Pres Band; Pres Chorus; School Play; Variety Show; Nwsp Rptr; Hon Roll; JP Sousa Awd; Messiah Coll; Math.

GIRANDA, TONY; Hazleton Area School District; Mcadoo, PA; (Y); Hon Roll; Cbnt Mkng.

GIRARD, ISABELLE; St Paul Cathedral HS; Pittsburgh, PA; (S); 1/65; Drama Clb; French Clb; Nwsp Rptr; VP Frsh Cls; Pres Soph Cls; Var L Vllybl; High Hon Roll; Pres NHS; Ntl Merit SF; Val; Pittsburgh Zoo Intern 85-86; Hist Schlr 84-86; Coll Guest Stu 85-86; Zoology.

GIRARDAT, DENILLE RAE; Cochranton HS; Cochranton, PA; (Y); 8/ 75; Pres Ski Clb; Yrbk Stf; VP Sr Cls; Var Sftbl; Elks Awd; High Hon Roll; Sec NHS; Sec French Clb; Varsity Clb; Band; Muscn Of Yr 85-86; Dist, Regnl Cnty Band 85-86; Acadmc Schlrshp; Johnson & Wales; Fashn Merch.

GIRARDI, GINA; St Maria Goretti HS; Philadelphia, PA; (S); 8/420; Church Yth Grp; Cmnty Wkr; French Clb; GAA; Mathletes; Math Clb; Office Aide; Spanish Clb; Stage Crew; Rep Stu Cncl; Hnr Roll; Natl Hnr Soc; Outstndg Merit Awd Fr; La Salle; Mth.

GIRARDI, PAUL THOMAS; Dubois Central Christian HS; Curwensville, PA; (Y); Art Clb; Church Yth Grp; Cmnty Wkr; Computer Clb; Drama Clb; Exploring; NFL; Ski Clb; SADD; Yrbk Stf; EDU.

GIRDISH, DIANE; Beth-Center HS; Marianna, PA; (Y); 8/157; Drama Clb; Spanish Clb; Band; Concert Band; Mrchg Band; Stage Crew; Yrbk Stf; High Hon Roll; NHS.

GIRDWOOD, DEANA; Ambridge Area HS; Freedom, PA; (Y); Church Yth Grp; Pep Clb; Spanish Clb; Band; Concert Band; Pep Band; Symp Band; Soph Cls; Jr Cls; Hon Roll; Elem Educ.

GIRLING, ANNA; Parkland HS; Allentown, PA; (Y); 71/453; Var Capt Bsktbl; Mgr Socr; Var Trk; Hon Roll; Employee Mnth 86; Bsktbl Wnnr 86; Bsktbl Awd 86; PA ST.

GIRON, APRIL; Millville HS; Benton, PA; (Y); Art Clb; Church Yth Grp; Drama Clb; 4-H; FBLA; Band; Chorus; School Play; Rep Stu Cncl; Hon Roll; Sec Vo Tech Pgm 36 Wks Csmtlgy 85-86; ST Beauty Schl; Csmtlgst.

GIRONE, CHRISTINE; Interboro HS; Prospect Park, PA; (S); 1/265; Pres AFS; Art Clb; Sec Key Clb; Sec Sr Cls; Rep Stu Cncl; Var Capt Fld Hcky; Var Lcrss; High Hon Roll; NHS; Val; Cornell U; Intr Dsgn.

GIRVIN, ERNEST J; Solanco HS; Quarryville, PA; (Y); 28/234; Ski Clb; Varsity Clb; Var Bsbl; Var Ftbl; Hon Roll; Rotary Awd; James Hale Steinman Foundtn Schlrshp 86; Outstndng SR Bsbl Plyr 86; Penn ST; Engrng.

GISE, KEVIN M; Central York HS; York, PA; (Y); 75/248; Church Yth Grp; Varsity Clb; Ftbl; Trk; Hon Roll; Millersville U Of PA.

GISH, MICHAEL; Donegal HS; Mt Joy, PA; (Y); 2/155; Church Yth Grp; Exploring; Band; Mrchg Band; Symp Band; Nwsp Phtg; Nwsp Rptr; Yrbk Sprt Ed; Yrbk Stf; Var Capt Socr; Houghton Clg Presdntl Schlrshp 86; Rensselaer Medal 85; Dist Wnnr Vfw Essay Contst; Houghton Clg; Biochem.

GISH, MICHELE; Southern Columbia Area HS; Catawissa, PA; (Y); Exploring; Girl Scts; Library Aide; Color Guard; Yrbk Bus Mgr; Yrbk Sprt Ed; Yrbk Stf; JV Var Cheerleading; Gym; Var Score Keeper; Bloomsburg U; Elem Ed.

GITTERE, MAGGIE; Villa Maria Acad; Girard, PA; (Y); 4-H; Science Clb; 4-H Awd; Hon Roll; US Pony Clb 84; &A Free Entrprs Wk 86; Cmbnd Trng Comptn 86; Cmnctns.

GIUFFRE, MICHAEL R; Clearfield Area HS; Clearfield, PA; (Y); Church Yth Grp; Church Choir; Socr; Williamsport Tech Coll; Electr.

GIUFFRIDA JR, MICHAEL; St John Newmann HS; Philadelphia, PA; (Y); 17/338; Cmnty Wkr; Science Clb; Teachers Aide; Hon Roll; NHS; Engrng.

GIUNTA, CAROLYN ANN; Bishop Shanahan HS; W Chester, PA; (Y); 53/212; Office Aide; Pep Clb; Service Clb; Rep Frsh Cls; Rep Soph Cls; Rep Jr Cls; Pres Sr Cls; Rep Stu Cncl; Cheerleading; Prfct Atten Awd; Bus Admin.

GIUNTA, LUCIA; Scranton Prep HS; Scranton, PA; (Y); 30/192; VP Church Yth Grp; Debate Tm; Chorus; VP Church Choir; Orch; Pep Band; Trk; High Hon Roll; Hon Roll; NHS; 1st Hnrbl Mntn Pa Poetry Scty Cntst; High Hnr Ntl Greek Exam; Ntl Qlfr Debate; U Of Scranton; Psych.

GIUNTA, MICHAEL; Valley HS; Arnold, PA; (Y); 20/213; Church Yth Grp; Key Clb; Leo Clb; Ski Clb; Spanish Clb; Band; Concert Band; Q&S; Mrchg Band; Cit Awd; H S Schlr Awd St Vincent Coll 86; St Vincent Coll; Bus.

GIUNTOLI, MICHAEL; St Joseph Prep Schl; Haddonfield, NJ; (Y); French Clb; Lit Mag; Var L Crs Cntry; JV Socr; Var L Trk; NHS; Crew JV Awd Vrsty Letter; Linguist.

GIUNTOLI II, ROBERT L; St Josephs Preparatory Schl; Haddonfield, NJ; (Y); 8/218; German Clb; Science Clb; Nwsp Rptr; Yrbk Ed-Chief; Var Crs Cntry; JV Socr; NHS; Ntl Merit SF; Cert Achvt Outstndng Acad Perfrmnce 85; Cert Hnrb Mert Cum Laude 85; Summer Schl Scholar Bio 85; U PA; Pre-Med.

GIURANNA, ANNE; Bishop Shanahan HS; W Chester, PA; (Y); 2/218; Debate Tm; Hosp Aide; Quiz Bowl; Nwsp Stf; High Hon Roll; NHS; Engl.

GJURICH, DANA; Penn Cambria HS; Cresson, PA; (Y); 1/212; Drama Clb; Pres French Clb; SADD; Rep Stu Cncl; High Hon Roll; NHS; Juniata Coll; Pre-Med.

GLACKIN, CHRISTINE; St Hubert Catholic HS; Philadelphia, PA; (Y); 3/367; Hosp Aide; Intnl Clb; Mathletes; Nwsp Phtg; Yrbk Ed-Chief; Yrbk Phtg; Lit Mag; Hon Roll; NHS; Prfct Atten Awd; Cert Acdmc Merit Wrld Cltrs I 84; NHS Phtgrphy Clb Awd 85; NHS Yrbk Awd 86.

GLADFELTER, MICHELLE; Central York HS; York, PA; (Y); 36/257; French Clb; Varsity Clb; Capt Bsktbl; Var Capt Fld Hcky; Var L Trk; All Star Fld Hcky & Bsktbl 85-86; Arm Athl/Acad Hon & Medl 86; Booster & Feml Athl Of Yr 86; York Coll PA; Med Tech.

GLADHILL, PAMELA; Waynesboro Area SR HS; Waynesboro, PA; (Y); AFS; Intnl Clb; Stat Trk; Hon Roll; Lock Haven U; Intl Stu.

GLANCY, PAULA; Montour SR HS; Mckees Rocks, PA; (Y); Hosp Aide; Sec JA; Library Aide; High Hon Roll; NHS; Edinboro; Bus Adm.

GLASBY, STUART; Central Bucks HS East; Lahaska, PA; (Y); 63/468; Var L Crs Cntry; Var L Trk; Ntl Merit Ltr; Rotary Awd; Bus.

GLASER, SALLY; Central Dauphin East HS; Oberlin, PA; (Y); 7/230; Church Yth Grp; French Clb; Color Guard; Drill Tm; Flag Corp; High Hon Roll; Jr NHS; NHS; Elizabethtown Clg; Occpt Thrpy.

GLASGOW, SHERRY; Southern Huntingdon County HS; Mapleton Depot, PA; (Y); Church Yth Grp; 4-H; French Clb; FBLA; FHA; Speech Tm; SADD; Varsity Clb; Band; Chorus; Fut Homemkrs Of Amer St Offcr 85-86.

GLASL, KAREN; Northwestern SR HS; Albion, PA; (Y); Chorus; School Musical; School Play; Var L Trk; Var L Vllybl; Church Yth Grp; Drama Clb; Church Choir; Rep Stu Cncl; Library Aid Awd 82-83; Crmnl Just.

GLASS, BEV; Wilson HS; Bernville, PA; (Y); Exploring; Pep Clb; Ski Clb; Spanish Clb; Soph Cls; Jr Cls; Cheerleading; Pom Pon; Trk; Twrlr; U Of Bridgeport; Elem Educ.

GLASS, CHAD; Chambersburg Area SR HS; Chambersburg, PA; (Y); 101/700; Art Clb; Church Yth Grp; Ski Clb; Spanish Clb; Bsbl; Bsktbl; Coach Actv; Hon Roll; Drexel U PA ST; Engrng.

GLASS, NANCY; Montour HS; Pittsburgh, PA; (Y); Church Yth Grp; Band; Concert Band; Mrchg Band; Pep Band; Yrbk Stf; High Hon Roll; Hon Roll; Geneva Coll; Elem Educ.

GLASS, PAUL; Bishop Shanahan HS; Westchester, PA; (Y); Computer Clb; Varsity Clb; Var Capt Bsktbl; Var Socr; Var Swmmng.

GLASS, SEAN; Greater Johnstown HS; Johnstown, PA; (Y); Boy Scts; VP Church Yth Grp; VP Exploring; JA; Spanish Clb; Engineering.

GLASS, TIFFANY; Muhlenberg HS; Temple, PA; (Y); Church Yth Grp; Science Clb; Chorus; School Musical; Hst Frsh Cls; Hst Soph Cls; Hst Jr Cls; Hst Sr Cls; Rep Stu Cncl; VP Bsktbl; MVP In Track 85; Nrsng.

GLASSER, KIM; North Clarion HS; Lucinda, PA; (Y); Library Aide; Spanish Clb; SADD; School Musical; Socl Wrkr.

GLASSIC, MARY; Lourdes Regional HS; Shamokin, PA; (Y); Church Yth Grp; Pep Clb; PAVAS; Spanish Clb; Mgr(s); Mat Maids; Hon Roll; Bloomsburg U.

GLAUM, ERIC; Trinity HS; Washington, PA; (Y); 101/365; Church Yth Grp; Acpl Chr; Band; Chorus; Church Choir; Mrchg Band; Crs Cntry; Trk; Hon Roll; Messiah Coll; Phys Ther.

GLAVICIC, JOHN; W Catholic Boys HS; Philadelphia, PA; (Y); Letterman Clb; JV Ftbl; Hon Roll; NHS; Engrng.

GLEASON, GREG; Bradford Central Christian HS; Derrick City, PA; (Y); Math Clb; SADD; Trs Jr Cls; Var L Bsbl; Var L Ftbl; Sec Key Clb; School Play; Var Bsktbl.

GLEASON, JUANITA; Elkland Area HS; Tioga, PA; (Y); 1/76; French Clb; Hosp Aide; SADD; Mgr(s); Vllybl; High Hon Roll; Val; Eleanor Donovan Engl Awd 86; US Army Rsrv Natl Schlr Athl Awd 86; Pres Acad Fit Awd 86; Keystone JC; Phys Ther.

GLEASON, LAUREL; Penn Hills SR HS; Pittsburgh, PA; (S); 1/797; French Clb; Office Aide; Science Clb; Cmnty Wkr; High Hon Roll; Jr NHS; NHS; Val; Outstndng Artist Of Mnth 84; Chncllrs Merit Schlrshp U Of Pittsburgh 86; U Of Pittsburgh; English.

GLEASON, STEPHANIE; St Hoberts Catholic H S For Girls; Philadelphia, PA; (Y); Hon Roll; Prfct Attndnc 82-86; Rdlgc Tech.

GLEBA, MICHAEL; Central Catholic HS; Pittsburgh, PA; (Y); 2/286; Boy Scts; Church Yth Grp; Latin Clb; Office Aide; Science Clb; Lit Mag; Bowling; High Hon Roll; NHS; Ntl Merit Ltr.

GLEICH, LISA; Trinity HS; Camp Hill, PA; (Y); 25/141; Drama Clb; Ski Clb; Spanish Clb; Rptr Yrbk Stf; Stat Ftbl; JV Trk; Var Vllybl; Hon Roll; Pres Spanish NHS; Advrtsng.

GLEIM, ROBERT; Hershey HS; Hummelstown, PA; (Y); 12/188; Chess Clb; Computer Clb; Math Clb; Stage Crew; Lit Mag; High Hon Roll; Pres Schlr; Pres Acdmc Ftns Awd, PA Soc Prof Engrs Awd 85-86; PA ST U; Aerospace Engrng.

GLEMSER, KRISTINA; Creative & Performing Arts HS; Philadelphia, PA; (S); 8/120; Hosp Aide; Office Aide; Rep Soph Cls; Trs Jr Cls; Trs Sr Cls; Hon Roll; Jr NHS; NHS; Prfct Atten Awd; Five Star Acad; Cosmetology.

GLENN, DEE ANNE; Interboro HS; Glenolden, PA; (S); Church Yth Grp; Key Clb; Latin Clb; Band; Co-Capt Drill Tm; Mrchg Band; Lcrss; Hon Roll; NHS; Bloomsburg U.

GLENN JR, GREGORY I; Pottstown SR HS; Pottstown, PA; (Y); 59/193; Church Yth Grp; Frsh Cls; Soph Cls; Jr Cls; Sr Cls; JV Bsbl; Var L Bsktbl; Capt Var Ftbl; Wt Lftg; Hon Roll; Outstndng Athlt 86; Martn Luthr Kng Schlrshp 86; Kutztown U; Comp Sci.

GLENN, MARY ANN; Waynesboro Area SR HS; Waynesboro, PA; (Y); 15/371; Library Aide; Yrbk Stf; High Hon Roll; NHS; Silver Spoon Home Ec Awd 84; Alg II OSCAR Awd Rnr-Up 84; Soc Stud Awd 84.

GLENN, PAMELA; George Westinghouse HS; Pittsburgh, PA; (S); 1/211; Library Aide; Science Clb; Band; Nwsp Stf; Yrbk Stf; Off Sr Cls; High Hon Roll; NHS; Semi-Fnlst Achvt Schlrshp Prgm For Outstndng Negro Stu 85; Aerosp.

GLENN, STEPHANIE; North Hills HS; Pittsburgh, PA; (Y); Trs AFS; Church Yth Grp; German Clb; JA; Y-Teens; Stage Crew; Hon Roll; La Roches Coll; Law.

GLENN, TERRANCE; South Vo-Tech HS; Pittsburgh, PA; (Y); 1/50; Boy Scts; Computer Clb; Drama Clb; English Clb; VP JA; Variety Show; Nwsp Rptr; Nwsp Sprt Ed; Nwsp Stf; Yrbk Rptr; Val High Hnr Roll Ntl Hnr Scty 86; Sr Clss Pres Stu Cncl Pres 86; Cptn Of SUT Tennis Team; U Of Pittsburgh; Med Tech.

GLENNON, DAVE; Cathedral Prep; Erie, PA; (Y); 63/216; Am Leg Boys St; Var L Bsbl; Var L Bsktbl; Hon Roll; Ntl Merit Ltr.

GLENNY, DANA; Huntingdon Area HS; Huntingdon, PA; (Y); Church Yth Grp; Drama Clb; Hosp Aide; Key Clb; Library Aide; SADD; Teachers Aide; School Play; Yrbk Stf; High Hon Roll; Juniata Coll Alumni Schlrshp 86; Juniata Coll; Pre Med.

GLENSKY, KEITH; Northern Chester County Tech Schl; Kimberton, PA; (Y); Church Yth Grp; Band; Church Choir; Concert Band; Jazz Band; Mrchg Band; Pep Band; School Musical; Hon Roll; Missnry.

GLESSNER, RUSTIN; Berlin Brothersvalley HS; Berlin, PA; (Y); 4/91; 4-H; Quiz Bowl; Spanish Clb; Speech Tm; School Play; Variety Show; Stat Stu Cncl; Var L Golf; High Hon Roll; NHS; Amer Hstry Awd 85-86; Biothnlgy.

GLICK, CYNTHIA; Lehighton Area HS; Lehighton, PA; (Y); 27/280; Debate Tm; FBLA; Q&S; Scholastic Bowl; School Play; Nwsp Bus Mgr; Nwsp Rptr; Nwsp Stf; Yrbk Stf; Hon Roll; Hugh O Brian Yth Schlrshp Awd 85; Quill & Scroll-Prfrdng Editor 86; Juniata; Med.

GLICK, SARAH; Carlisle HS; Carlisle, PA; (Y); Church Yth Grp; Office Aide; Church Choir; Swmmng; L Var Tennis; Trk; High Hon Roll; Won Carlisle Barracks 86; Tennis Trnmnt 86; Cert Of Ldrshp 87; Cert For Horse & Tennis Clinic Instr 86; Penn ST; Pre-Med.

GLICKMAN, BARBARA; Pennsburg HS; Yardley, PA; (Y); 20/700; Drama Clb; Spanish Clb; VP Temple Yth Grp; Chorus; School Musical; School Play; Yrbk Ed-Chief; Lit Mag; Jr NHS; NHS; Cornell Summer Pgm 86; Psychlgy.

GLICKMAN, DAVID; Parkland HS; Allentown, PA; (Y); 50/462; Hosp Aide; Nwsp Rptr; Hon Roll; NHS; Pres-AZA 86-87; 1st Pl Nwswrtng Mnrng Call Stu Nwsp Advsry Pgm 86.

GLICKSTEIN, LAWRENCE; Parkland HS; Allentown, PA; (Y); 59/460; Scholastic Bowl; Temple Yth Grp; Band; Concert Band; Jazz Band; Mrchg Band; Var Tennis; Hon Roll; Bus.

GLIDDEN, KENNETH; Solanco HS; Quarryville, PA; (Y); Church Yth Grp; Mgr Radio Clb; Teachers Aide; Varsity Clb; Nwsp Sprt Ed; Yrbk Phtg; Lit Mag; Var Golf; High Hon Roll; Hon Roll.

GLINSKY III, JOHN; Mid-Valley HS; Throop, PA; (Y); Spanish Clb; Mrchg Band; JV Var Bsbl; JV Var Bsktbl; Var Vllybl; PA ST U; Bus Admin.

GLISAN, ANGELA; Beaver Area JR SR HS; Farmington, PA; (Y); 5/200; German Clb; JCL; Key Clb; Pep Clb; High Hon Roll; Hon Roll; Kiwanis Awd; Lion Awd; NHS; NEDT Awd; U PA; Biochem.

GLISAN, CARLA; Uniontown HS; Markleysburg, PA; (Y); Sec Trs Church Yth Grp; French Clb; Letterman Clb; Varsity Clb; Yrbk Stf; Var Cheerleading; Stat Trk; French Hon Soc; Hon Roll.

GLISAN, CHARLENE; Northern SR HS; Dover, PA; (Y); 42/200; JV Cheerleading; Hon Roll; Future Sec Assn 84-86; Mrk Artst Awd 82-85; Co-Op Pgm 85-86; SCTRL.

GLISTA, MECHELLE; German Twp HS; Mc Clellandtown, PA; (Y); Art Clb; Teachers Aide; VP Frsh Cls; VP Soph Cls; VP Jr Cls; Stu Cncl; High Hon Roll; Hon Roll; Jr NHS; Germn TWP Rep Albert Galltn Rvr Regtta 85; Homecmng Cand 86; WV Career Clg; Dntl Asst.

GLIVIC, KEITH; Seton La Salle HS; Bethel Park, PA; (Y); 50/280; Var Bsbl; JV Bsktbl; High Hon Roll; Hon Roll; Algebra Award 83; Arch.

GLOSEK, LISA; Line Mountain HS; Trevorton, PA; (Y); Church Yth Grp; Computer Clb; FBLA; Hst Key Clb; SADD; Varsity Clb; Nwsp Stf; Capt Cheerleading; High Hon Roll; Hon Roll; Cert Apprectn Hands Across Am 86; Intl Wk Queen Cntstnt 84.

GLOSS, TINA; Harrisburg HS; Harrisburg, PA; (Y); Drama Clb; Thesps; Chorus; School Play; Stage Crew; 1st Pl Music Pk 84; 1st Pl PA Spch Leag Comptn 85.

GLOVER, GORDON; William Allen HS; Allentown, PA; (Y); Art Clb; JA; Scholastic Bowl; Yrbk Rptr; Lit Mag; NHS; Schltc Art Awd 86; Artist.

GLOVER, KARLENE; Susquehanna Community HS; Starrucca, PA; (S); 1/75; Church Yth Grp; Quiz Bowl; Ski Clb; Church Choir; Yrbk Stf; Powder Puff Ftbl; High Hon Roll; NHS; Messiah Coll; Engrng.

GLOVER, SUE; Susquehanna Community HS; Susquehanna, PA; (Y); Ski Clb; Color Guard; Yrbk Stf; Pres Soph Cls; Pres Jr Cls; Rep Stu Cncl; Cheerleading; Hon Roll.

GLOWA, TOM; Sto-Rox SR HS; Mc Kees Rocks, PA; (Y); 3/142; Church Yth Grp; Hon Roll; Duquesne; Pharm.

GLOWATSKI, TIMOTHY; Mt Carmel Area JR & SR HS; Mt Carmel, PA; (Y); Cmnty Wkr; French Clb; Key Clb; Letterman Clb; Spanish Clb; Var L Bsktbl; Var L Ftbl; Var L Trk; High Hon Roll; Cmmnctn.

GLUNT, DORETTA; Southern Huntingdon County HS; Shade Gap, PA; (Y); 12/118; Trs GAA; SADD; Band; Chorus; Concert Band; Mrchg Band; Yrbk Stf; Powder Puff Ftbl; Cit Awd; NHS; Ntl Sci Merit Awd 83-86; Hork Hosp Schl; Radlgy.

GLUSHKO, LORISSA; Carbondale Area HS; Simpson, PA; (S); 1/137; English Clb; FBLA; Quiz Bowl; Scholastic Bowl; Ski Clb; Spanish Clb; Yrbk Stf; High Hon Roll; NHS; NEDT Awd 82; U Of Pittsburgh; Pharm.

GLYNN, SUSAN; Kennard Dale HS; Stewartstown, PA; (Y); Ski Clb; Varsity Clb; Capt Flag Corp; Yrbk Stf; Stu Cncl; Var Fld Hcky; Fairleigh Dickinson U; Dntl Hyg.

GNAN, MARIA; St Marys Area HS; St Marys, PA; (Y); 4/290; NFL; Ski Clb; Chorus; Concert Band; Jazz Band; Yrbk Phtg; Capt Twrlr; High Hon Roll; NHS; NEDT Awd; Hwrd Jhnsn Schlrshp 86; Mnsfld Schlrs Awd 86; Ftlghtrs Prfrmng Arts Awd 86; Mansfield U; Music Educ.

GNEITING, LISA M; Freeport SR HS; Freeport, PA; (Y); 35/170; FBLA; GAA; Hosp Aide; Band; Concert Band; Mrchg Band; Symp Band; Rep Sr Cls; JV Trk; Hon Roll; Acdmc Achvt Awd 86; 5th FBLA Rgnl Awd 86; 700 Vol Hrs Allegheny Vly Hosp 85; Butler Co CC; Acctg.

GOBBLE, PAUL D; Owen J Roberts HS; Pottstown, PA; (Y); School Musical; School Play; Stage Crew; Yrbk Phtg; Yrbk Stf; JV Golf; JV Trk; JV Wrstlng; Hon Roll; German Amer Exchng Stu 86; Engrng.

GOBRECHT, RENEE; Northern Cambria HS; Barnesboro, PA; (Y); 42/126; Spanish Clb; Drill Tm; Stu Cncl; Twrlr; Vllybl; Spanish NHS; Dietetics.

GOCELLA, JOE; Bradford Central Christian HS; Bradford, PA; (Y); Key Clb; Ski Clb; SADD; Band; JV Bsktbl; JV Var Ftbl; JV Var Mgr(s); Score Keeper; Hon Roll; Jr NHS.

GOCHENAUR, MICHELLE; Lancaster Christian HS; Lancaster, PA; (Y); Church Yth Grp; Yrbk Stf; Fld Hcky; Score Keeper; Hon Roll.

GOCHTOVTT, ANNABEL C; Bishop Shanahan HS; Exton, PA; (Y); 1/218; Drama Clb; Chorus; School Musical; High Hon Roll; Hon Roll; NHS; Debate Tm; Gen Excllnc Awd 86; Princeton U; Theatre Arts.

GODA, STEVE; Mars Area SR HS; Valencia, PA; (Y); Pres Chess Clb; Office Aide; Ski Clb; Pres SADD; Nwsp Phtg; Yrbk Phtg; JV Var Crs Cntry; JV Var Score Keeper; Var Tennis; Var Trk; Grove Cty Coll; Acctng.

GODDING, JOSEPH; Bradford Area HS; Bradford, PA; (Y); 25/276; Boy Scts; Key Clb; Keywanettes; Nwsp Stf; Off Stu Cncl; Ftbl; Hon Roll; Mchnst.

GODFREY, DONALD; Red Land HS; New Cumberland, PA; (Y); 4-H; FFA; Stage Crew; Im Ftbl; Mgr(s); 4-H Awd; Hon Roll; Rookie Shwmn Of Yr 83; Champ Shwmn 4-H Rndup 83; Grnd Champ Resrv 4-H 84; PA ST U; Hrse Trnr.

GODICH, LISA; Hopewell SR HS; Aliquippa, PA; (Y); 71/295; French Clb; Hosp Aide; VP JA; JV Powder Puff Ftbl; Sawyer Schl.

GODISH, DONNA; Penn Cambria SR HS; Lilly, PA; (Y); 34/214; French Clb; Band; Chorus; Concert Band; Mrchg Band; Hon Roll; Tchng.

GODLESKI, BETH; Jamestown HS; Jamestown, PA; (Y); Trs French Clb; Trs Service Clb; Trs Jr Cls; Rep Stu Cncl; Var Cheerleading; DAR Awd; Hon Roll; Trs NHS; Library Aide; Spanish Clb; Prom Queen 86; Fair Queen Atten 82; Duquesne U; Pre-Law.

GODLEWSKI, ROQUEL; Punxsutawney Area HS; Punxsutawney, PA; (Y); Nwsp Stf; Cheerleading; Mgr(s).

GODOMSKI, LARA; Western Wayne HS; Waymart, PA; (Y); 16/130; Ski Clb; Mrchg Band; Sec Soph Cls; Sec Jr Cls; Im Gym; Hon Roll; VP NHS; Elem Ed.

GODWIN, GAIL; Downingtown SR HS; Glenmoore, PA; (Y); 200/563; Church Yth Grp; French Clb; GAA; Ski Clb; Hon Roll; Downingtown Lvng Arts Recog 85.

GODWIN, KENTON R; South Fayette HS; Bridgeville, PA; (S); 6/95; Hosp Aide; Concert Band; Mrchg Band; Yrbk Stf; Rep Stu Cncl; Bsbl; High Hon Roll; NHS; Church Yth Grp; Varsity Clb.

GOEBEL, BETH E; Keystone Oaks HS; Pittsburgh, PA; (Y); Art Clb; Church Yth Grp; German Clb; Pep Clb; Powder Puff Ftbl; L Var Sftbl; High Hon Roll; NHS; Duffs Bus Inst; Ct Rep.

GOEBEL, BRIAN; Lincoln HS; Wampum, PA; (Y).

GOEDEL, RICHARD; Deer Lakes JR SR HS; Cheswick, PA; (Y); Boy Scts; French Clb; Church Choir; Hon Roll; Ntl Egl Sct Awd 86; Vlntr Frmn Comm Serv Awd 85; GATE 82-86; Elec Engnrng.

GOEHRING, EARL; Seneca Valley HS; Harmony, PA; (Y); 22/362; SADD; Rep Soph Cls; Rep Jr Cls; Pres Stu Cncl; Diving; High Hon Roll; NHS; Trs Church Yth Grp; Red Cross Aide; Mrchg Band; Behrend Coll; Bus Adm.

GOEHRS, SUZANNE M; Harry S Touman HS; Fairless Hills, PA; (Y); 253/576; Red Cross Aide; Sec Chorus; School Musical; Swing Chorus; Capt Swmmng; Hon Roll; Bucks County CC; Bio.

GOFF, JEFFREY; Greater Johnstown HS; Johnstown, PA; (Y); Math Clb; Pres Jr Cls; VP Sr Cls; Rep Stu Cncl; Var L Debate Tm; Var L Ftbl; JV Trk; Hon Roll; NHS; U Of Pittsburg; Pharm.

GOGGANS, ANTONIO; Mercy Vocational HS; Philadelphia, PA; (Y); JA; Math Clb; School Play; Stage Crew; Bsktbl; Mgr(s); Trk; Vllybl; High Hon Roll; Prfct Atten Awd; Math A Thn St Jude Chldrn Rsrch Hosp 84; Cert Accmplshmnt Prjct Bus JR 84; Hm Pgm Awd Merit 83; Electrcn.

GOIDA, PAUL E; Panther Valley HS; Lansford, PA; (Y); 15/106; Rep Am Leg Boys St; Church Yth Grp; Mgr Drama Clb; Speech Tm; School Musical; Capt Var Bsktbl; Var L Ftbl; Var L Trk; Hon Roll; Voice Dem Awd; Engrng.

GOIDELL, HILLARY; Wyoming Valley West HS; Wilkes Barre, PA; (Y); 2/378; VP Temple Yth Grp; Nwsp Stf; Lit Mag; Sec Frsh Cls; Var Capt Diving; Var Capt Tennis; Cit Awd; High Hon Roll; NHS; Ntl Merit Ltr; Stu Of Mnth 85-86; Faclty Awd 85-86; Dist MVP Tnns 85-86; Amherst Coll.

GOLACK, KIM; Penn-Trafford HS; Jeannette, PA; (Y); 230/344; Pres AFS; VP Pres FBLA; Office Aide; SADD; Concert Band; Mrchg Band; Bowling; Sftbl; Sal; Church Yth Grp; PBA; Bus.

GOLASA, SHARON; Bishop Kenrick HS; Norristown, PA; (Y); Cmnty Wkr; French Clb; Mgr Bsktbl; Mgr(s); Rosemont Coll; Psychlgy.

GOLD, DANIEL P; State College Area HS; State College, PA; (Y); Band; Nwsp Stf; Lit Mag; JV Crs Cntry; Im Lcrss; Var Trk; High Hon Roll; JETS Awd; Ntl Merit Ltr; Accptd Non Deg Study PSU 86; PA ST U; Arch.

GOLD, JENNIFER LYNN; South Park HS; Library, PA; (Y); 21/198; Church Yth Grp; Drama Clb; Band; Drm & Bgl; Sr Cls; Stu Cncl; Bsktbl; Outstndng Musician Awd 86; Shclrshp Westminster Coll 86; HOBY Outstndng Soph Awd 84; Svc Awd 86; Chatham Coll; Poltcl Sci.

GOLD, MELANIE; Pen Argyl Area HS; Wind Gap, PA; (Y); 23/166; Drama Clb; English Clb; 4-H; Girl Scts; Pep Clb; Spanish Clb; Thesps; Color Guard; Flag Corp; Mrchg Band; Schlrshp To Schl Of Visual Arts NY NY 86; Schl Of Visual Arts; Cmmnctn.

GOLDBERG, BART; Boiling Spring HS; Mt Holly Spgs, PA; (Y); 8/113; Nwsp Ed-Chief; Capt L Bsktbl; Var L Socr; High Hon Roll; Hon Roll; NHS; Lbrl Arts.

GOLDBERG, CHRIS; Pennsbury HS; Morrisville, PA; (Y); Boy Scts; Spanish Clb; Nwsp Rptr; Nwsp Stf; Im Bowling; Hon Roll; NHS; Ntl Merit SF; PA ST U; Elec Engnr.

GOLDBERG, JAMES; Hempfield Area HS; Greensburg, PA; (Y); JV Var Wrstlng; Hon Roll.

GOLDBERG, JULIA; Linden Hall HS; Penn Valley, PA; (S); 2/32; Drama Clb; Q&S; Quiz Bowl; School Musical; Nwsp Rptr; Nwsp Stf; Yrbk Bus Mgr; Yrbk Stf; Rep Jr Cls; Swmmng; Tour Guide 85-86; Pub Intllgnc Jrnls Nwsppr In Ed Cntst 85-86; Jrnslt.

GOLDBERG, LISA A; Archbishop Prendergast HS; Drexel Hill, PA; (Y); 37/361; Political Wkr; Spanish Clb; Stage Crew; Nwsp Rptr; Yrbk Stf; Hon Roll; NHS; Spanish NHS; Ascad Awd Cabrini Coll 86; Cabrini Coll; Psych.

GOLDBLATT, DAVID; Abington SR HS; Huntingdon Valley, PA; (Y); 1/540; Cmnty Wkr; Model UN; Ed Nwsp Stf; Ed Lit Mag; Rep Stu Cncl; High Hon Roll; NHS; Ntl Merit Schol; Amer Chem Socty Awd; Top Engl & Math Stdnt Awds; Engl, Frnch, Sci, Prncpl & Newspr Awds; Brown U; Chem.

GOLDEN, TOM; Middletown Area HS; Middletown, PA; (Y); 5/188; Boys Clb Am; Computer Clb; Im Bsbl; Im Bsktbl; Im Ftbl; Im Socr; JV Var Tennis; Im Wt Lftg; Im Wrstlng; Hon Roll; Trvl.

GOLDEN, TONY; Gettysburg SR HS; Cashtown, PA; (Y); DAR Awd; Hon Roll; Comp Prog.

GOLDFEDER, LYNN; Bethlehem Catholic HS; Bethlehem, PA; (Y); Church Yth Grp; Vllybl; Hon Roll; NHS; Elem Educ.

GOLDIAN, CHRIS; Cambria Heights HS; Hastings, PA; (Y); Chorus; Bsktbl; Trk; Cmrcl Art.

GOLDINGER, BRIAN P; Ford City HS; Freeport, PA; (Y); 4/155; Trs SADD; Ed Nwsp Ed-Chief; Rep Stu Cncl; L Crs Cntry; High Hon Roll; NHS; Ntl Merit SF; Pres Schlr; Rotary Awd; Computer Clb; PA JR Acad Of Sci 81-85; U Of Pittsburgh; Math.

GOLDMAN, AMY; Pennsbury HS; Yardley, PA; (Y); Civic Clb; German Clb; Chorus; Capt Flag Corp; School Musical; Swing Chorus; Off Soph Cls; Rep Stu Cncl; Fld Hcky; Sftbl; Advrtsng.

GOLDMAN, MARC; Taylor Allderdice HS; Pittsburgh, PA; (S); Science Clb; Temple Yth Grp; Nwsp Rptr; Lit Mag; Sec Sr Cls; Bsktbl; Tennis; High Hon Roll; NHS; Tennis Mag Sportsmnshp Awd 85; Jrnlsm.

GOLDMAN, SUZANNE; Harriton HS; Narberth, PA; (Y); Intnl Clb; Model UN; Sec Service Clb; Ed Yrbk Stf; Tennis; Hon Roll; NHS; Volntr At U Of PA Hosp 86.

GOLDSBOROUGH, JENNIFER L; Lower Merion HS; Bala Cynwyd, PA; (Y); Drama Clb; PAVAS; Thesps; Chorus; Church Choir; School Musical; School Play; Stage Crew; Trk; NHS; Blue Rbbn/Gld Ky Fnlst Schlstc Art Awds 86; Dist Rgnl & All-ST Choir 84-86; Thspn Awd 85; Music Educ.

GOLDSTEIN, ELIZABETH; Pennsbury HS; Morrisville, PA; (Y); Drama Clb; Intnl Clb; Political Wkr; Chorus; Stu Cncl; Trk; Gov Hon Prg Awd; Hon Roll; NHS; Law.

GOLDSTEIN, JENNIFER; Pennsbury HS; Morrisville, PA; (Y); 1/712; Spanish Clb; Yrbk Stf; Jr Cls; Sr Cls; Var Tennis; NHS; Bus.

GOLDSTEIN, JOHN; Archbishop Ryan HS For Boys; Philadelphia, PA; (Y); 135/459; Boys Clb Am; Socr; Hon Roll; PA ST U.

GOLDSTEIN, MARTIN; Cumberland Valley HS; Camp Hill, PA; (Y); German Clb; Ski Clb; Temple Yth Grp; Ntl Merit Ltr.

GOLDSTEIN, MICHAEL; Pennsbury HS; Morrisville, PA; (Y); 22/712; SADD; Band; Concert Band; Jazz Band; Mrchg Band; Yrbk Phtg; Trk; Hon Roll; Trs NHS; Pres Schlr; Presdntl Acadmc Ftns Awd; Stu Of Mnth; Franklin/Marshall Coll; Pre-Med.

GOLDSTEIN, NATHAN; Cumberland Valley HS; Camp Hill, PA; (Y); 10/505; Gym; Wt Lftg; High Hon Roll; NHS; Ntl Merit SF; Hall Fndtn Schlrshp 86; PA U; Engr.

GOLDSTEIN, PAUL; Mount Lebanon HS; Pittsburgh, PA; (Y); 215/500; Church Yth Grp; JA; Ski Clb; Spanish Clb; Hon Roll; Penn ST U.

GOLDSWORTHY, JOHN; Mt Pleasant HS; Acme, PA; (Y); Boy Scts; Computer Clb; Ski Clb; Concert Band; Mrchg Band; Hon Roll; PA ST; Arch.

GOLEMBESKY, ANTHONY; Taylor Allderdice HS; Pittsburgh, PA; (Y); Church Yth Grp; Letterman Clb; Library Aide; Office Aide; Pep Clb; Varsity Clb; Band; Concert Band; Mrchg Band; L Bsktbl; Hnr Rl; Bus.

GOLEMBIESKY, JENNIFER; Freeport Area HS; Freeport, PA; (S); 19/170; Church Yth Grp; Mrchg Band; Stage Crew; Yrbk Stf; Mgr(s); Vllybl; High Hon Roll.

GOLIWAS, LYNN; Peters Township HS; Mc Murray, PA; (S); 37/257; Ski Clb; Yrbk Sprt Ed; Lit Mag; Pres Off Stu Cncl; Var Capt Cheerleading; Sftbl; High Hon Roll; Hon Roll; Mercyhurst Coll; Intr Dsgn.

GOLOB, VALERIE; Brockway Area HS; Brockport, PA; (Y); FBLA; Varsity Clb; Nwsp Ed-Chief; Nwsp Rptr; Nwsp Stf; Trs Soph Cls; JV Bsktbl; Var Capt Cheerleading; Wt Lftg; Hon Roll; Lock Haven; Cmptr Sci.

GOLOJUH, DENISE; Knoch HS; Cabot, PA; (Y); Church Yth Grp; Sec FBLA; Band; Concert Band; Mrchg Band; High Hon Roll; Hon Roll; Med Sec.

GOLOVACHA, DEBORAH; Cardinal Dougherty HS; Phila, PA; (Y); 96/748; Civic Clb; German Clb; High Hon Roll; Hon Roll; 1st & 2nd Hnrs 82-86; Hahnemann U; Nrsng.

GOMBEDA, EDWARD; Hazleton HS; Hazleton, PA; (Y); 64/382; Pres Church Yth Grp; Drama Clb; Leo Clb; Stage Crew; Hon Roll; NHS; Pres Schlr; Pres Ftns Awd 86; U Pittsburgh Johnstown; Bio.

GOMBERG, MALISSA; Elk Lake HS; S Montrose, PA; (Y); 19/113; French Clb; Library Aide; Ski Clb; Band; Rptr Yrbk Stf; Var Trk; Var Vllybl; Hon Roll; Kiwanis Awd; Prfct Atten Awd; WY Cnty Medl Soc Schlrshp 86; Susq Cnty Repub Wmns Awd 86; Pres Phys Ftns Awd 85 & 86; Bloomsburg U; Nrsg.

GOMBERT, TRACEY; Hazleton HS; Hazleton, PA; (Y); FBLA; FHA; Pep Clb; Spanish Clb; VICA; Chorus; FL Inst Tech; Engrng.

GOMER, SHAWN; Lower Moreland HS; Huntingdon Valley, PA; (S); 21/214; FBLA; School Musical; Sec Sr Cls; Rep Stu Cncl; Stat Mgr(s); Capt Tennis; High Hon Roll; Jr NHS; NHS; MVP-TENNIS 83-84 & 85-86; Distngshd Honor Rll 84-85; All-Leag Area Team-Tennis 1st Team 82-86; Busnss.

GOMEZ, CHRISTOPHER; Hazleton HS; Drums, PA; (Y); 1/388; Drama Clb; Intnl Clb; Model UN; Scholastic Bowl; L Tennis; French Hon Soc; NHS; Wnnr Kline Essy Cntst 86; 2nd Pl Cntrl Div PA Amer Legn Essy 86; U Of PA.

GOMEZ, ROBERTO; Creative & Performing Arts; Philadelphia, PA; (S); 17/150; Art Clb; Yrbk Ed-Chief; Prfct Atten Awd; Natl Talnt Srch NFAA 86; Loc Schlrshp Awd 86; Tyler Sch Of Art; Comml Art.

GONSAR, JEFF; Halifax HS; Halifax, PA; (Y); FHA; Varsity Clb; Stage Crew; Trs Stu Cncl; Var Bsbl; Var Ftbl; Wt Lftg; Var Wrstlng; Hon Roll; Wqin Big 20 All Star Bsbl Tm 85; Wqin 2nd Tm Defense 85; Wqin All Star Bsbl Tm 86; Central PA Bus Schl; Bus.

GONTA, DARLENE; Hempfield Area SR HS; Greensburg, PA; (Y); Art Clb; Drama Clb; Pep Clb; Trs Spanish Clb; Chorus; Pres Church Choir; School Musical; School Play; Mat Maids; U Of Pittsburgh; Mchncl Engr.

GONZALEZ, DAWN; Villa Maria Acad; Erie, PA; (Y); Sec Dance Clb; Sec Soph Cls; Sec Jr Cls; Stu Cncl; High Hon Roll; Hon Roll; Blck Blt Karate 84; Gannon U; Pre-Med.

GONZALEZ, IRIS; South Philadelphia HS; Philadelphia, PA; (Y); Variety Show; Rep Frsh Cls; Rep Soph Cls; Rep Jr Cls; Var Bsktbl; JV Cheerleading; JV Vllybl; Var Hon Roll; Jr NHS; Teachers Aide; Acad Achvt Awd 85.

GOOD, CHRISTINE; Garden Spot HS; Reinholds, PA; (Y); 28/224; Church Yth Grp; Sec Spanish Clb; High Hon Roll; Hon Roll; Jr NHS; NHS; Data Proc.

GOOD, DENISE; Bishop Mc Devitt HS; Harrisburg, PA; (S); 2/5; Hosp Aide; Service Clb; Spanish Clb; Color Guard; Mrchg Band; Trs Jr Cls; Stu Cncl; Hon Roll; NHS; Chorus; Peer Cnslng 84-85 & 85-86; Mission Rep 84; Fitness Tm 84-85; Villanova U; Nrsng.

GOOD, LEONA; Penns Manor HS; Alverda, PA; (Y); 22/120; SADD; Drill Tm; Co-Capt Flag Corp; Trk; Shadyside Schl Nrsng; Nrsng.

GOOD, LORI; Pequea Valley HS; E Paradise, PA; (Y); Varsity Clb; Band; Chorus; Mrchg Band; Sec Frsh Cls; Sec Soph Cls; Rep Stu Cncl; Var Capt Bsktbl; Var Fld Hcky; Var Sftbl; Gen Hosp Schl Of Nrsng; Nrsng.

GOOD, LORI A; Elizabethtown Area HS; Elizabethtown, PA; (Y); 3/227; Band; Orch; Sec Frsh Cls; Sec Soph Cls; Sec Jr Cls; Sec Sr Cls; NHS; Ntl Merit SF; Rotary Awd; Trs Church Yth Grp; Nov Grl Of Mnth BPW 85; Bucknell U; Mech Engrg.

GOOD, SCOTT; Donegal HS; Mt Joy, PA; (Y); 44/166; Socr; Indstrl Engr.

GOOD, TRUDY; Lancaster Mennonite HS; Lancaster, PA; (Y); 20/144; Church Yth Grp; VP Orch; Stage Crew; Nwsp Ed-Chief; Nwsp Rptr; Nwsp Stf; Cit Awd; Hon Roll; NHS; Rotary Awd; Goshen Coll; Psychlgy.

GOODE, CAMMIE; Dover Area HS; Dover, PA; (Y); Chorus; Capt Var Bsktbl; Hon Roll; NHS; JV Fld Hcky; Elem Ed.

GOODE, JOHN; University City HS; Philadelphia, PA; (Y); Yrbk Stf; Trk; Penco Tech; Electrncs.

GOODE, JOSH; Cheltenham HS; Melrose Pk, PA; (Y); 15/365; Orch; School Musical; Nwsp Ed-Chief; Rep Frsh Cls; Rep Jr Cls; Rep Stu Cncl; Socr; High Hon Roll; Spanish NHS; Montgomery Cnty Frgn Lang Awd 84; PA Bar Assoc Mock Trl Rgnl Fnl 86; Politcs.

GOODFELLOW, PAUL; Yough SR HS; West Newton, PA; (Y); 22/249; French Clb; Ski Clb; Yrbk Phtg; Yrbk Stf; L Co-Capt Trk; High Hon Roll; NHS; W Newton Wmns Clb Bond 86; PA ST U; Engrng.

GOODFORD, CAROLYN; Crestwood HS; Mountaintop, PA; (Y); 36/233; Hosp Aide; Var Twrlr; Hon Roll.

GOODIN, CULLEEN IRENE; Quakertown Comm HS; Trumbauersville, PA; (Y); 16/320; Am Leg Aux Girls St; Church Yth Grp; SADD; Band; Concert Band; Mrchg Band; Mgr(s); Hon Roll; Jr NHS; NHS; Outstndng Schltc Achvt 84-85; Cls Ex Cmmttee 84-87; Pre-Law.

GOODLING, DENISE; Lock Haven HS; Howard, PA; (Y); Church Yth Grp; French Clb; Bowling; Sftbl; Vllybl; :Frnch.

GOODMAN, GREGORY; Elk County Christian HS; St Marys, PA; (Y); 38/80; Model UN; Ski Clb; Hon Roll; U S Army Rsrvs 86; Penn ST U; Chem.

GOODMAN, KELLIE; Wyalusing Valley HS; Wyalusing, PA; (Y); Band; Orch; Trs Jr Cls; Rep Stu Cncl; Capt Cheerleading; Var L Sftbl; High Hon Roll; NHS; Church Choir; School Musical; Dist 8 Band Fest 86; Region 4 Band Fest 86; NTL & All Twin Tiers Sftbl Teams 86; Communctns.

GOODMAN, LYNNE; Line Mt HS; Trevorton, PA; (Y); FBLA; Sec Key Clb; Drill Tm; Stu Cncl; Stat Bsktbl; Cheerleading; Score Keeper; Hon Roll; Mntlly Gftd Prgrm Enrchmnt; Accntng.

GOODREAU, LORI N; Troy SR HS; Troy, PA; (Y); 9/144; Church Yth Grp; Computer Clb; Letterman Clb; Var Sftbl; Var Capt Vllybl; NHS; Grove City Coll; Math.

GOODRICH, CALVIN; Downingtown SR HS; Exton, PA; (Y); 66/563; Ntl Merit Ltr; Aerospc Engrng.

GOODRICH, DEBRA; Hampton HS; Allison Pk, PA; (Y); 45/237; French Clb; SADD; Acpl Chr; Capt Color Guard; School Musical; VP Frsh Cls; Pres Soph Cls; Rep Jr Cls; VP Stu Cncl; High Hon Roll; Allegheny Intrmdiat Unit Stu Frum Pres 86-87; PA Assn Of Stu Cncl Confrc Delg 85; Biochem.

GOODWILL, LORI; Fort Le Boeuf HS; Waterford, PA; (Y); Nwsp Stf; Rep Jr Cls; Rep Stu Cncl; Im Bsktbl; Im Bowling; Score Keeper; Var JV Trk; Var JV Vllybl; Im Wt Lftg; Stat Wrstlng; Phy Thrpy.

GOODWIN JR, JOE; Northeast Catholic HS; Philadelphia, PA; (Y); 20/362; Art Clb; JV Ftbl; Hon Roll; NHS; Prfct Atten Awd; U Of Scranton; Crmnlgy.

GOODWIN, LARRY; Troy SR HS; Troy, PA; (Y); 5/145; Crs Cntry; Trk; Wt Lftg; Hon Roll; NHS; Williamsport Area CC; Elec Tec.

GOODWIN, MICHAEL; Tunkhannock HS; Mehoopany, PA; (S); 20/280; Boy Scts; Church Yth Grp; Letterman Clb; VP Pres Spanish Clb; Var Capt Vllybl; Hon Roll; NHS; PA ST U.

GOODYEAR, SALLY; Penns Manor HS; Clymer, PA; (Y); 11/78; French Clb; SADD; Concert Band; Mrchg Band; Yrbk Ed-Chief; Rep Stu Cncl; Co-Capt Twrlr; Hon Roll; Sec NHS; Mansfield U; Radlgc Tech.

GOODYEAR, VICTORIA ANN; Christ Academy Of Camp Hill; Mechanicsburg, PA; (Y); Church Yth Grp; Hosp Aide; Chorus; Crs Cntry; Trk; High Hon Roll; Hon Roll; NHS; Athletic Ltrs Cert 83-85; Acad Achvt Awd 86.

GOON, CHRISTOPHER; Altoona Area HS; Altoona, PA; (Y); Church Yth Grp; JA; High Hon Roll; Hon Roll; Prfct Atten Awd; Cvl Engrng.

GOOS, LARA; Northampton Area SR HS; Northampton, PA; (Y); 21/454; Church Yth Grp; Chorus; Church Choir; High Hon Roll; Hon Roll; NHS; Hghst Slr Yrbk Ads; Accntng.

GOPEZ, NOREEN; Mechanicsburg Area SR HS; Mechanicsburg, PA; (Y); 7/311; Girl Scts; Ski Clb; Chorus; School Play; Rep Stu Cncl; Fld Hcky; Trk; High Hon Roll; Pres NHS; Ntl Merit Ltr; Dist Trk 85 & 86; Spn Scholar 86; Arch.

GORBY, ROBIN MICHELLE; Trinity HS; Washington, PA; (Y); Camera Clb; Church Yth Grp; Girl Scts; Library Aide; Nwsp Phtg; Yrbk Phtg; High Hon Roll; Hon Roll; Y-Teens; Penn Comm Coll; Bus Admin.

GORDANIER, MICHAEL; Carson Long Military HS; Linden, NJ; (Y); Am Leg Boys St; Boy Scts; ROTC; Varsity Clb; VP Stu Cncl; Capt Bsbl; Coach Actv; JV Ftbl; Var JV Socr; Trk; Columbian Squires 85-86; Ron Freedman Gold Mdl Trck 82-85; Fire Chief Govt Day 84; U Miami; Engrng.

GORDNER, DONNA; Millville Area HS; Millville, PA; (Y); 4-H; Library Aide; Spanish Clb; Band; School Musical; 4-H Awd; Hon Roll.

GORDON, AMY; Connellsville Area HS; Leisenring, PA; (Y); 53/550; Church Yth Grp; FBLA; Office Aide; Church Choir; Rep Jr Cls; Rep Stu Cncl; Var Vllybl; High Hon Roll; Hon Roll; Prfct Atten Awd; Bus Admin.

GORDON, ANGELA; Westinghouse HS; Pittsburgh, PA; (S); 14/211; FHA; Hosp Aide; Church Choir; Flag Corp; Stu Cncl; Cit Awd; Hon Roll; Prfct Atten Awd; Nrsg.

GORDON, BETH; Manheim Township HS; Lancaster, PA; (Y); 19/344; Sec Temple Yth Grp; Nwsp Rptr; Lit Mag; Var Cheerleading; Trk; High Hon Roll; Hon Roll; VP NHS; Accptd-PA ST Smmr Hnrs Acad 86; Lawyr.

GORDON, CAROL; Coatesville Area SR HS; Coatesville, PA; (Y); 10/534; Spanish Clb; Church Choir; High Hon Roll; Hon Roll; Jr NHS; NHS; Soc Wmn Engrs Merit Awd 86; Millersville U.

GORDON, CATHERINE M; Huntingdon HS; Huntingdon, PA; (Y); 67/203; Capt Color Guard; Yrbk Phtg; Ed Yrbk Stf; Var Sftbl; JV Vllybl; Hon Roll; Colorgd Clb; Yrbk Copy Edtr; Eng Ed.

GORDON, DANIEL; Northeast Catholic HS; Philadelphia, PA; (S); 6/435; Var Socr; Hon Roll; NHS; Drexel U; Acctg.

GORDON, DARREN; Chester HS; Chester, PA; (Y); Church Yth Grp; ROTC; Var Crs Cntry; Capt Trk; Hon Roll; Acad Achvt Awd 83-84; Comp Tech.

GORDON, DONNIE; Southern Fulton HS; Needmore, PA; (Y); 4/55; Varsity Clb; Pres Sr Cls; Var Capt Bsktbl; Var Capt Trk; Hon Roll; Lion Awd; NHS; PA ST; Engrng.

GORDON, ELIZABETH; Central HS; Martinsburg, PA; (Y); Drama Clb; JA; SADD; Nwsp Stf; PA ST U; Phych.

GORDON, JEFFREY; Pennsbury HS; Morrisville, PA; (Y); Boy Scts; German Clb; JV Ftbl; USY Bd Stu 85-86; Finance.

GORDON, JOYCE; Montouv HS; Pittsburgh, PA; (Y); Church Yth Grp; Dance Clb; Teachers Aide; Yrbk Stf; High Hon Roll; NHS; Schlstc Achvmnt Awd 86; Trvl Trsm.

GORDON, KAREN ANN; Penn Hills SR HS; Pittsburgh, PA; (Y); German Clb; High Hon Roll; Hon Roll; Lamp Knwldg 83-84; Grmn Lang Olympcs 83-84; Pitt; Med.

GORDON, LESLIE; Frazier HS; Perryopolis, PA; (Y); Church Yth Grp; Intnl Clb; Library Aide; Ski Clb; Church Choir; Nwsp Stf; Score Keeper; Hon Roll; IN U; Accntng.

GORDON, MADELEINE; West Phila Cattholic Girls HS; Phila, PA; (Y); 8/245; Camp Fr Inc; French Clb; Scholastic Bowl; Band; Chorus; Concert Band; Jazz Band; Orch; School Play; Rep Soph Cls; Pres Acad Ftns Awd 86; Distngushd 2nd Hnrs 82-86; Drexel U; Chem Engr.

GORDON, MARK; H S Truman HS; Bristol, PA; (Y); Swmmng; Hon Roll.

GORDON, MATT; Dover Area HS; Dillsburg, PA; (Y); Boy Scts; Church Yth Grp; Drama Clb; Band; Chorus; Church Choir; Concert Band; Jazz Band; Mrchg Band; School Musical; US Army; Mltry Intllnge.

GORDON, ROBERT; Abington SR HS; Jenkintown, PA; (Y); Key Clb; Nwsp Phtg; Yrbk Phtg; Rep Jr Cls; VP Sr Cls; VP Stu Cncl; Bsbl; Lcrss; Hon Roll; Flm Prdcr.

GORE, JENIFER; South Williamsport SR HS; S Williamsport, PA; (Y); FBLA; Band; Chorus; Church Choir; Nwsp Stf; Hon Roll; Color Guard; Guidance Aid 84-85; FBLA 2nd Bus Math 84; FBLA 3rd Gen Bus 85; Williamsport Area CC; Accntnt.

GORE, TODD; Wm Penn Communications Magnet; Philadelphia, PA; (Y); 2/270; Cmnty Wkr; Dance Clb; Debate Tm; Exploring; PAVAS; Political Wkr; Radio Clb; School Play; Variety Show; Nwsp Stf; Howard U; Medicine.

GOREL, LEO; Carbondale Area HS; Carbondale, PA; (S); 3/145; Computer Clb; Letterman Clb; Science Clb; Ski Clb; Spanish Clb; Varsity Clb; Capt Tennis; High Hon Roll; NHS; JR Hstrns 85-86; U Of Scanton; Engrng.

GORGAN, JENNIFER; Bishop Hoban HS; Hunlock Creek, PA; (Y); Church Yth Grp; Cmnty Wkr; FBLA; Yrbk Stf; JV Cheerleading; Fash Mdsg.

GORGAS, STEPHANIE; Lincoln HS; Wampum, PA; (Y); Exploring; FBLA; Girl Scts; Key Clb; Y-Teens; Powder Puff Ftbl; Prfct Atten Awd; Prfct Attdnc Awd; Grl Sct Slvr & Gld Awd 86; ICM Schl Of Bus; Acctng.

GORGONE, PETER; Pittston Area HS; Pittston, PA; (Y); French Clb; Math Clb; Scholastic Bowl; Im Bsktbl; Var L Tennis; High Hon Roll; NHS; NEDT Awd; Rotary Awd; JETS Team 86; MA Inst Of Tech; Physcs.

GORHAM, DANEAN; Penn Hills SR HS; Penn Hills, PA; (Y); Exploring; French Clb; Girl Scts; Acpl Chr; Chorus; Bsktbl; Sftbl; Hon Roll; Law Enfrcmt.

GORI, MICHAEL; Freedom HS; Bethlehem, PA; (Y); Band; Concert Band; Jazz Band; Mrchg Band; Orch; Swing Chorus; JV Wrstlng; Boy Scts; Exploring; Chorus; Egle Sct 83 BSA Ordr Arrw-Vgl Hnr 85; Outstndng Jazz Saxphne 85-86; 195 Distrct Bnd 85; Pennsylvania ST U; Animl Sci.

GORKO, KELLI; Tunkhannock HS; Falls, PA; (S); Church Yth Grp; Ski Clb; Trs Spanish Clb; Concert Band; Mrchg Band; Rep Soph Cls; Rep Jr Cls; Stat Fld Hcky; Hon Roll; NHS; Med Tech.

GORMAN, HILLARY; Cheltenham HS; Stockton, CA; (Y); Drama Clb; 4-H; JCL; Latin Clb; PAVAS; School Musical; Variety Show; Lit Mag; Ntl Merit Ltr; Scholastic Bowl; Acad Decathln Tm 2nd Pl ST 86; Gold Mdl Sci ST Acad Decathln 86; Cum Laude Natl Latin Hnr Soc 84-86; Vet Med.

GORMAN, JAMES; St John Neumann HS; Philadelphia, PA; (Y); 42/348; Band; Concert Band; Pep Band; Ftbl.

GORMAN, JEANNE; Bethlehem Catholic HS; Bethlehem, PA; (Y); 40/225; Cmnty Wkr; Hosp Aide; Key Clb; Varsity Clb; Cheerleading; Mat Maids; High Hon Roll; Hon Roll; Ntl Englsh Olympd Awd 84.

GORMAN-RHODES, MARY LOU; Central HS; Martinsburg, PA; (Y); FBLA; Altoona Schl/Commerce; Mdcl Sec.

GORMLEY, ROBERT; Council Rock HS; Newtown, PA; (Y); 60/750; Boy Scts; Church Yth Grp; Scholastic Bowl; Band; Mrchg Band; Var Crs Cntry; Im Lcrss; Var Trk; JV Wrstlng; Hon Roll; Penn ST; Engr.

GORNICK, SUZANNE; St Hubert HS; Philadelphia, PA; (Y); 2/367; Am Leg Aux Girls St; Church Yth Grp; Cmnty Wkr; Debate Tm; JA; NFL; Speech Tm; Lit Mag; Bowling; NHS; Chem Awd 86; Drexel U; Mech Engrng.

GOROG, BETH; Dover Area HS; Dover, PA; (Y); Church Yth Grp; Cmnty Wkr; Drama Clb; FCA; Chorus; Church Choir; Vllybl; Mgr Hon Roll; Miss YFC Pagnt Crown 85; Messiah Coll; Fmly.

GORONCY, PAULA; Bentworth HS; Scenery Hill, PA; (Y); FHA; Varsity Clb; Band; Chorus; Church Choir; Concert Band; Drm Mjr(t); Mrchg Band; Hon Roll; PMEA Dist 1 Chrs Fstvl Alto 1 86; Reg 1 Chrs Fstvl Alto 1 86; Comp Pgmng.

GORSKI, LORI; John S Fine HS; Nanticoke, PA; (Y); Hosp Aide; Ski Clb; Var L Fld Hcky; Hon Roll; Psych.

GORTON, STACY; Mt Pleasant Area SR HS; Mount Pleasant, PA; (Y); 10/240; 4-H; German Clb; Latin Clb; Band; Mrchg Band; Nwsp Stf; Yrbk Stf; 4-H Awd; Hon Roll; NHS.

GOSCHLER, ROBERTA; Owen J Roberts HS; Phoenixville, PA; (S); 6/276; Varsity Clb; Stu Cncl; Var L Sftbl; Hon Roll; NHS; Juniata Coll; Comp Sci.

GOSHERT, REGGIE; Cedar Crest HS; Lebanon, PA; (Y); 36/320; Pep Clb; Spanish Clb; Jazz Band; School Musical; Var Tennis; Hon Roll; Hnr Banqut 85 & 86; US Nvl Acad; Bus.

GOSHORN, DENISE; Juniata HS; E Waterford, PA; (Y); Church Yth Grp; Drama Clb; School Play; Yrbk Stf; High Hon Roll; Jr NHS; NHS; Cosmtlgy.

GOSHORN, TERRY; Susquenita HS; Duncannon, PA; (Y); Chess Clb; Church Yth Grp; Var Wt Lftg; Var L Wrstlng; High Hon Roll; Hon Roll; Pre-Law.

GOSIEWSKI, LISA; Tunkhannock HS; Harveys Lake, PA; (S); 18/280; Spanish Clb; Var L Vllybl; Hon Roll; Vlybl Trphy MIP 85; ST Vlybl Champs Medal 84-85; FL ST U; Grphc Dsgn.

GOSIN, KAREN; Abraham Lincoln HS; Philadelphia, PA; (Y); 56/430; Sec Sr Cls; Stat Fld Hcky; Stat Sftbl.

GOSNELL, DAVID; Hempfield HS; Columbia, PA; (Y); Trk; Hon Roll; Elec.

GOSNELL, RICHARD; Cambridge Springs HS; Cambridge Springs, PA; (Y); 4/100; Aud/Vis; Pres French Clb; Pep Clb; Ski Clb; Stage Crew; Pres Jr Cls; Trs Stu Cncl; Mgr(s); God Cntry Awd; NHS; Hmcmng Kng 85; Penn ST; Chem.

GOSNELL, TIM; Cumberland Valley HS; Mechanicsburg, PA; (Y); 19/560; Church Yth Grp; FCA; Thesps; Band; Concert Band; Jazz Band; Mrchg Band; Orch; School Play; Symp Band; Acad All Amer 83-84; Ntl Ldrshp Acad 84-85; Engrng.

GOSS, DAVID; West Snyder HS; Mc Clure, PA; (Y); Art Clb; VICA; Stu Cncl; High Hon Roll; Hon Roll; Auto Mech.

GOSS, FRANCIS; Bishop Guilfoyle HS; Altoona, PA; (S); 3/150; Chess Clb; Science Clb; JV Bsktbl; High Hon Roll; Hon Roll; Ntl Merit Ltr; Villanova U; Finance.

GOSS, JAMES; West Snyder HS; Mcclure, PA; (Y); Varsity Clb; Band; Chorus; Concert Band; Jazz Band; Mrchg Band; School Musical; Swing Chorus; Golf; Socr; Jazz Band Awd 84-85.

GOSSERT, DANA A; CarlisleSR HS; Carlisle, PA; (Y); 31/403; JV Wrstlng; Hon Roll; Oper Catapult Rose Hulman Inst Tech 85; Sci Olympics Tm; 2nd Pl CASAC Sci Fair; Rose Hulman Inst Tech; Physics.

GOSSLER, JAMIE LEE; Saucon Valley HS; Bethlehem, PA; (Y); 4/171; Trs German Clb; Science Clb; Nwsp Stf; High Hon Roll; Jr NHS; NHS; Pres Schlr; Soc Wmn Engr Awd 86; Saucon Vlly SR HS Almn Assoc Awd 86; Skidmore Coll; Bio.

GOSTIC, JEFF; Canon Mc Millan SR HS; Canonsburg, PA; (Y); 67/371; Ftbl; Trk; Wt Lftg; High Hon Roll; Hon Roll; Prfct Atten Awd; Crmnlgst.

GOSTON, GRETCHEN; Mount Alvenia HS; Pittsburgh, PA; (Y); Art Clb; Computer Clb; JA; Spanish Clb; Chorus; School Musical; School Play; Nwsp Rptr; Nwsp Stf; Yrbk Rptr; Christ Corps 84; Phys Fit 85; Pitt U; Vet.

GOTLIEB, STEVE; Marple,Newtown HS; Newtown Square, PA; (Y); Science Clb; Service Clb; Ski Clb; Nwsp Bus Mgr; Nwsp Stf; Stu Cncl; Hon Roll; Jr NHS; Bus Adm.

GOTTSCHALK, AMY; Mc Guffey HS; Prosperity, PA; (S); French Clb; Chorus; Yrbk Sprt Ed; Yrbk Stf; Score Keeper; High Hon Roll; Hon Roll; NHS; Nathl Jrnlsm Awd 86.

GOUGLER, ROBERT; Bensalem HS; Trevose, PA; (Y); Computer Clb; Ski Clb; Teachers Aide; Im Badmtn; Im Bsbl; Im Bsktbl; Im Bowling; Im Crs Cntry; Im Golf; Im Swmmng.

GOULD, AMY; Greenville HS; Greenville, PA; (Y); Drama Clb; Thesps; Chorus; Madrigals; School Musical; School Play; Variety Show; Sec Church Yth Grp; Girl Scts; Spanish Clb; Modern Music Masters 85; 1st Rnnr Up Hons Chorus 85; Dist Chrs 84-85; Regnl Chrs 85; Dist Bnd 84; Performing Arts Coll; Prfrm Art.

GOULD, ROBERT A; Shippensburg Area SR HS; Shippensburg, PA; (Y); 46/226; Chess Clb; Band; Chorus; Mrchg Band; Pres Orch; Pep Band; Trs School Musical; Trs School Play; Stu Cncl; Try Ldrshp Cmp Schlrshp Cnty Orchstra 85-86; Cnty Chrs 86; Bloomsburg U; Comp Sci.

GOULD, STEVE; Pleasant Valley HS; Allentown, PA; (Y); Varsity Clb; Var JV Bsbl; Var Golf; Hon Roll; Shippensburg U; Crmnl Jstc.

GOULD, TODD E; Lower Dauphin SR HS; Middletown, PA; (Y); 1/244; Am Leg Boys St; Hst Boy Scts; Church Yth Grp; Cmnty Wkr; French Clb; Band; God Cntry Awd; High Hon Roll; NHS; Val; Eagle Scout-Bronze Palm 83; Brotherhood Of The Order Of Arrow 82; Drumline Capt; Stu Forum; MIT; Comp Sci.

GOULDING, A J; Bradford Area HS; Bradford, PA; (Y); 5/286; French Clb; Key Clb; Ski Clb; School Play; Yrbk Ed-Chief; JV Crs Cntry; L Var Swmmng; Sec NHS; Ntl Merit SF.

GOULDY, LORI; Cedar Cliff HS; New Cumberland, PA; (Y); 38/279; Girl Scts; Spanish Clb; SADD; Chorus; School Musical; Hon Roll; NHS; Spanish NHS; Amercn Bus Womns Assoc Schlrshp 86; Harrisburg Area CC; Bus Admin.

GOURAN, DAVID; State College Area SR HS; State College, PA; (Y); Cmnty Wkr; Jazz Band; Mrchg Band; Symp Band; Nwsp Rptr; Yrbk Stf; High Hon Roll; French Clb; School Play; Teachers Aide; Faculty Schlr Awd 85-86; Dstngshd Prfrmnce Awd 84; Natl Assoc Jazz Eductrs 86; Penn ST U; Admnstrtn.

GOURDIER, LISA; Cardinal O Hara HS; Aston, PA; (Y); 121/772; VP Church Yth Grp; Cmnty Wkr; Office Aide; Hon Roll; NHS; Bus.

GOURLAY, SUSAN; Neshaminy HS; Langhorne, PA; (Y); 1/730; Capt Dance Clb; Intnl Clb; Chorus; Orch; School Musical; Nwsp Ed-Chief; NHS; Ski Clb; Nwsp Rptr; Nwsp Stf; Voice, Piano & Dnc Cls; Won 2 Ntl Chmpnshps-W/Dnc Cls; Vrious Awds As Solost; Comm.

GOURLEY, KIM; Plum SR HS; Pittsburgh, PA; (Y); 27/378; Dance Clb; SADD; Varsity Clb; Chorus; School Play; Nwsp Stf; Yrbk Ed-Chief; Cheerleading; High Hon Roll; NHS; Bus Adm.

GOURLEY, LARRY; Seneca HS; Wattsburg, PA; (Y); 13/170; Boy Scts; Church Yth Grp; Computer Clb; School Musical; Stu Cncl; JV Bsbl; JV Bsktbl; Var Ice Hcky; Var Wt Lftg; Var Hon Roll; Jrnlsm.

GOUVEIA, LYDIA; J P Mc Caskey HS; Lancaster, PA; (Y); 41/468; AFS; Church Yth Grp; Hosp Aide; Band; School Play; Mgr(s); Trk; Vllybl; Hon Roll; NHS; Untd Chem Con Awd 86; IL Institute Tech; Arch.

GOWARTY, MATTHEW E; North Star HS; Boswell, PA; (Y); 15/125; Computer Clb; Math Clb; Capt Quiz Bowl; Capt Scholastic Bowl; Bsbl; Stat Ftbl; Hon Roll; Mu Alp Tht; Robert Morris Coll; Sports Mgmt.

GOWATSKI, JOELLEN; Connellsville Area SR HS; Connellsville, PA; (Y); 4-H; Pres FFA; Hon Roll; Agri.

GOWATSKI, KELLY; Connellsville Area HS; Mt Pleasant, PA; (Y); Church Yth Grp; Band; Color Guard; Mrchg Band; Symp Band; Rep Stu Cncl; French Hon Soc; High Hon Roll; Nwsp Rptr; Nwsp Stf; PA-DE Dstrct Tn Tlnt Fnls Wnd Instrmnt Solo 84 & 85; Physcl Thrpy.

GOWATY, MARGARET; Serra Catholic HS; Mc Keesport, PA; (Y); AFS; Church Yth Grp; Drama Clb; Girl Scts; JA; Science Clb; Speech Tm; Band; Chorus; School Musical; Sls Awd Jr Achvt 85-86; 3rd Pl PA Jr Acad Sci Rgnl Cmptn 84.

GOWER, KELLY; Green Castle Antrim HS; Stateline, PA; (Y); Cmnty Wkr; Exploring; Band; Concert Band; Jazz Band; Mrchg Band; NHS; VFW Awd; Voice Dem Awd; Outstndng Explorer Yr 85; Sci Fair 2nd Pl; U MD; Emergency Hlth Svc.

GOWTON, STEPHANIE; Connellsville SR HS; Mt Pleasant, PA; (Y); 92/600; Office Aide; SADD; Chorus; Pep Band; Variety Show; Yrbk Stf; Rep Stu Cncl; Var Capt Cheerleading; Gym; Hon Roll; Slippery Rock Coll; Phy Ed.

GOYAL, AJAY K; Cedar Cliff HS; Camp Hill, PA; (Y); 7/272; Am Leg Boys St; Boy Scts; Ski Clb; Pres VP Spanish Clb; Trs Frsh Cls; Pres Soph Cls; VP Stu Cncl; DAR Awd; VP NHS; Ntl Merit SF; Hugh O Brian Ldrshp Smnr 83-84; Yth & Govt Govrnr Outstndng Senatr 85-86; Weis Schlr 85-86; U Of MO Kansas City; Lib Arts.

GOYNE, KIM; E L Meyers HS; Wilkes-Barre, PA; (Y); 36/180; Hosp Aide; Ski Clb; Sftbl; Hon Roll; Spanish NHS; Med.

GOZA IV, GRANVILLE; Saegertown HS; Saegertown, PA; (Y); 2/124; Boy Scts; VP Exploring; Math Tm; SADD; VP Band; Concert Band; VP Mrchg Band; JV Wrstlng; Hon Roll.

GRAAF, MICHELE; Weatherly Area HS; Weatherly, PA; (Y); FBLA; FHA; GAA; Hosp Aide; Pep Clb; JV Var Bsktbl; Dist XI Cls A Bsktbl Champ Tm 85-86; Cls A ST Bksltbl Semi-Fin Tm 85-86; Trvl & Toursm.

GRAB, JENNIFER; Saint Francis Acad; Pittsburgh, PA; (S); Hosp Aide; Nwsp Rptr; Yrbk Stf; Stat Bsktbl; JV Gym; Var Vllybl; High Hon Roll; Hon Roll; Ntl Merit Ltr; St Vincent Coll Chllng Prog Awd & Schlrshp 85; Point Park Coll; Jrnlsm.

GRAB, JOSEPH A; Mountain View Bible Church Christn; Middletown, PA; (S); 1/5; Church Yth Grp; Chorus; Church Choir; School Play; Bsktbl; Socr; Sftbl; High Hon Roll; Prfct Atten Awd; Keystone Christian Eductn Assoc-JR High Math 1st Pl 84.

GRABAN, AMY; Villa Maria HS; Lowellville, OH; (Y); 6/57; Cmnty Wkr; Drama Clb; French Clb; Thesps; Band; Drill Tm; School Musical; School Play; Stage Crew; NHS; Pre-Law.

GRABARITS, RICHARD; Northampton SR HS; Northampton, PA; (Y); 22/452; Computer Clb; Leo Clb; Golf; High Hon Roll; Hon Roll.

GRABIAK, JEFF; Mt Pleasant Area SR HS; Mount Pleasant, PA; (Y); Letterman Clb; Trs Ski Clb; L Bsktbl; L Ftbl; Hon Roll; WV U; Pre-Math.

GRABIAK, KAREN; Ambridge Area HS; Baden, PA; (S); 47/365; Pep Clb; Band; Concert Band; Mrchg Band; Nwsp Rptr; Nwsp Stf; Off Jr Cls; Trk; L Vllybl; High Hon Roll; IN U PA.

GRABIEC, LAURI; Meyers HS; Wilkes Barre, PA; (Y); Cmnty Wkr; Ski Clb; Chorus; Flag Corp; Mrchg Band; School Musical; Variety Show; Hon Roll; 2 Gld Mdls In Ice Dance 84; WY Vly Ice Sktng Clb 83-86; ISIA Ice Sktng Inst Of Amer & U S Figure 86; PA ST Blmsbrg; Cmnctns.

GRABIGEL, BRYAN; Highlands HS; Freeport, PA; (Y); Teachers Aide; Concert Band; Jazz Band; Mrchg Band; Pep Band; Hon Roll; Jr NHS; Church Yth Grp; AK Hnrs Band 84; Mideast Musicl Conf 84-85; IN U Of PA; Mgmt Inf Sys.

GRABLE, DEANNA; Hopewell SR HS; Aliquippa, PA; (Y); Spanish Clb; SADD; Drill Tm; VP Frsh Cls; VP Soph Cls; VP Jr Cls; Stu Cncl; Cheerleading; Pom Pon; Hon Roll; Robt Morris Coll; Mgmt.

GRABLE, KEITH; Freedom HS; Rochester, PA; (Y); 4/165; Spanish Clb; Varsity Clb; L Bsbl; L Bsktbl; L Golf; High Hon Roll; Hon Roll; NHS; Monaca Recrtn All Tourney Tm-Bsktbl 85-86; Sec 17-Aa All Stars-1st Tm-Ptchr-Bsbl 86; MAC Plyoff 85-86.

GRABOSKE, SUZANNE; John S Fine SR HS; Nanticoke, PA; (Y); 20/242; SADD; VICA; L Stat Ftbl; High Hon Roll; NHS; Pres Physcl Ftns Awd; PA ST; Bus Adm.

GRABOSKI, ROBERT; Plum SR HS; Monroeville, PA; (Y); 58/400; French Clb; Band; Nwsp Ed-Chief; Yrbk Stf; Crs Cntry; Trk; Hon Roll; U Miami; Arch.

GRABOSKY, KAREN; Central Bucks HS East; Warrington, PA; (Y); Aud/Vis; Chorus; Bsktbl; Sftbl; Hon Roll; Buck Cnty CC; Acctnt.

GRABOWSKI, DAVID A; Bethel Park HS; Bethel Park, PA; (Y); 125/519; Aud/Vis; FBLA; Latin Clb; Hon Roll; Rep Jr Cls; Rep Sr Cls; Rep Stu Cncl; Capt Var Bsktbl; Local Nwspapr All Star Tm Bskbl 85-86; Dapper Dan Roundball Classic 85-86; Washington/Jefferson Coll; Law.

GRABSKI, MARLO; Burgettstown Area JR SR HS; Burgettstown, PA; (Y); 1/175; Am Leg Aux Girls St; Drama Clb; Pres Spanish Clb; Chorus; Concert Band; Drm Mjr(t); School Musical; High Hon Roll; NHS; Voice Dem Awd; Govnrs Sch Arts 85-86; Musc Schlrshp 86; WA Wrkshp Congrssnl Semnr 86.

GRACE, CHRISTINA; Carbondale Area HS; Simpson, PA; (Y); FNA; Ski Clb; Spanish Clb; Chorus; Drill Tm; Hon Roll.

GRACE, KELLY; Moon SR HS; Corapolis, PA; (Y); Cmnty Wkr; Key Clb; Nwsp Rptr; Nwsp Stf; Yrbk Stf; Sec Soph Cls; Sec Sr Cls; Rep Stu Cncl; Mgr(s); Score Keeper; Home Ec.

GRACE, LISA; Tussey Mountain HS; Hopewell, PA; (Y); Drama Clb; Q&S; Varsity Clb; Color Guard; Mrchg Band; Nwsp Bus Mgr; Nwsp Ed-Chief; Nwsp Rptr; Nwsp Stf; Yrbk Stf; FBLA Awd Enterpreneurshp II; Dentstry.

GRACE, MARK; Grove City Area HS; Grove City, PA; (Y); 10/137; 4-H; JV Wrstlng; 4-H Awd; High Hon Roll; NHS; Pres Schlr; Webb Inst Naval Arch; Navl Arch.

GRACZYK, HEATHER G; William Tennent HS; Warminster, PA; (Y); Cmnty Wkr; SADD; School Musical; Yrbk Stf; Sec Stu Cncl; Golf; Var Mgr(s); Hon Roll; Hosp Aide; Chorus; Drums All St Music Awd 83; ST Fnlst Mis Sam Co-Ed Pgnt 86; Criminal Justice.

GRADECK, KRISTY; Carrick HS; Pittsburgh, PA; (S); Church Yth Grp; Cmnty Wkr; French Clb; Q&S; Nwsp Rptr; Nwsp Stf; Yrbk Stf; Powder Puff Ftbl; French Hon Soc; High Hon Roll; Carnegie Mellon U; Creat Wrtg.

GRADEK, LORI; Ambridge Area HS; Ambridge, PA; (Y); Pep Clb; Off Soph Cls; Off Jr Cls; Off Sr Cls; Var Cheerleading; Hon Roll; Roberts Morris Coll; Secy.

GRADOS, ROBERT; Fox Chapel Area HS; Monessen, PA; (Y); Cmnty Wkr; French Clb; JA; Ski Clb; Chorus; Ftbl; Wt Lftg; High Hon Roll; Hon Roll; Georgetown U; Pre-Med.

GRAEFF, CATHY; Hamburg Area HS; Hamburg, PA; (Y); Library Aide; Spanish Clb.

GRAF, ROBERT; Ridley HS; Holmes, PA; (Y); 139/427; Political Wkr; Varsity Clb; Var L Ftbl; Var L Trk; JV L Wrstlng; Hon Roll; Robert W Maxwell Meml Ftbl Clb 85.

GRAFENSTINE, THERESA; Bensalem HS; Bensalem, PA; (Y); Teachers Aide; Nwsp Stf; High Hon Roll; Hon Roll; NHS.

GRAFF, KRISTIN; Laurel Valley HS; New Florence, PA; (Y); FNA; Speech Tm; Band; Church Choir; Concert Band; Mrchg Band; JV Bsktbl; Mgr(s); Var Powder Puff Ftbl; Var Score Keeper; Pitt Coll; Bio.

GRAFFT, TARA L; Center HS; Monaca, PA; (Y); Computer Clb; German Clb; Varsity Clb; Yrbk Stf; Rep Stu Cncl; JV Var Cheerleading; Hon Roll; Marine Bio.

GRAFTON, ANISSA; Leechburg Area HS; Schenley, PA; (Y); 11/71; Church Yth Grp; VP Drama Clb; Office Aide; Sec Jr Cls; Sec Sr Cls; Twrlr; High Hon Roll; Art Clb; VP JA; Chorus; Leechburg Lioness Awd 86; U Pittsburgh; Dentl Hyg.

GRAHAM, ANTONY; Pittston Area HS; Dupont, PA; (Y); Computer Clb; French Clb; Band; Concert Band; Jazz Band; Mrchg Band; Pep Band; US Marine Corps.

GRAHAM, BRADLEY; William Penn Charter HS; Erdenheim, PA; (Y); Nwsp Rptr; Nwsp Stf; Var Bsbl; JV Socr.

GRAHAM, CARLENE; Reading SR HS; Reading, PA; (Y); 51/639; JA; Acpl Chr; Hon Roll; Prfct Atten Awd; Pres Acad Fit Awd 86; Gannon U; RN.

GRAHAM, CHARLES; Ligonier Valley SR HS; Ligonier, PA; (Y); 10/161; Church Yth Grp; Trs French Clb; Stage Crew; Trs Jr Cls; Trs Sr Cls; Rep Stu Cncl; Im Ftbl; Var L Wrstlng; Hon Roll; NHS; Free Enterprise Wk 85; Mech Engr.

GRAHAM, CHERI; Punxsutawney Area HS; Oliverburg, PA; (Y); Pres Hosp Aide; Band; Pep Band; Yrbk Stf; Rep Frsh Cls; Rep Soph Cls; Rep Jr Cls; Rep Sr Cls; Hon Roll; NHS; Med.

GRAHAM JR, DAVID M; Clearfield Area HS; Clearfield, PA; (Y); Boy Scts; JV Ftbl; Var L Trk; U S Nvy; Wldng.

GRAHAM, ELIZABETH; M M I Prep; Mountaintop, PA; (Y); Debate Tm; Model UN; Ski Clb; Lit Mag; Golf; Sftbl; Bowling; Public Spkng Awd 84-85; Pblshd In A Natl Tiserary Magazine 85-86; Penn ST U.

GRAHAM, JAMES; Council Rock HS; Holland, PA; (Y); Mrchg Band; Symp Band; Ntl Merit Schol; Chem.

GRAHAM, JAY; Elkland Area HS; Tioga, PA; (Y); Varsity Clb; Band; Concert Band; Jazz Band; Mrchg Band; Pep Band; Var L Socr; JV Var Trk; Waldo Seamans Music Awd 86; Cnty Chmpn Trck-Shot Put 86; Chmpn Leag-Sccr 85-86; DE Vly; Ag Bus.

GRAHAM, JOANNA FRANCES; Vincentian HS; Pittsburgh, PA; (Y); Drama Clb; JA; Stage Crew; JV Bsktbl; High Hon Roll; Hon Roll; Sec NHS; Outdr Advntrs Clb 84-85; Wrtrs Hnr Soc 84-85; La Roche Clg; Intr Dsgn.

GRAHAM, KIMBERLY; St Hubert Cath HS For Girls; Philadelphia, PA; (Y); 71/367; Library Aide; Office Aide; Nwsp Stf; Lit Mag; Hon Roll; NHS; La Salle U; Psych.

GRAHAM, KRISTEN; Crestwood HS; Wapwallopen, PA; (Y); 19/219; FBLA; Math Clb; Ski Clb; School Play; Stu Cncl; JV Cheerleading; Sftbl; High Hon Roll; NHS; Acctng.

GRAHAM, KRISTEN; Karns City HS; Chicora, PA; (Y); 23/116; Girl Scts; SADD; Chorus; Church Choir; Concert Band; Mrchg Band; Variety Show; Capt Pom Pon; High Hon Roll; Hon Roll; Butler County CC; Bus Mgt.

GRAHAM, MARCAL; Germantown HS; Philadelphia, PA; (Y); Computer Clb; Band; School Play; Sec Frsh Cls; Bsktbl; Tennis; Trk; High Hon Roll; Hon Roll; Martin Lthr King Awd, Schlr Athlt Awd 84; Frnch Awd 85; Temple U; Pre-Med.

GRAHAM, MARYBETH A; Council Rock HS; New Hope, PA; (Y); 8/755; Hosp Aide; Spanish Clb; Nwsp Rptr; Rep Soph Cls; Rep Sr Cls; Rep Stu Cncl; JV Crs Cntry; JV Fld Hcky; Im Powder Puff Ftbl; Var L Socr; U NC; Med.

GRAHAM, SCOTT C; Seneca HS; Union City, PA; (Y); 1/150; French Clb; Scholastic Bowl; Nwsp Rptr; Yrbk Ed-Chief; Stu Cncl; High Hon Roll; NHS; Ntl Merit Ltr; Pres Schlr; Val; Cert Exclnc Jrnlsm 85; Mercyhurst Coll; Poli Sci.

GRAHAM, SHARON; Butler SR HS; Renfrew, PA; (Y); DECA; French Clb; Hosp Aide; Library Aide; Teachers Aide; Drm & Bgl; Rep Stu Cncl; Law.

GRAHAM, SUSAN; Mechanicsburg HS; Mechanicsburg, PA; (Y); 29/311; Latin Clb; Office Aide; SADD; Mrchg Band; High Hon Roll; Hon Roll; NHS; U Of Pittsburgh; Pre Med.

GRAINDA, LORI; Central HS; Martinsburg, PA; (Y); 7/175; GAA; Varsity Clb; Capt Var Vllybl; High Hon Roll; Hon Roll; NHS; PA ST U; Ind Psychlgst.

GRAMLICH, CHRISTINE; Easton Area SR HS; Easton, PA; (Y); 8/511; Debate Tm; Exploring; Ski Clb; Sec Lit Mag; Var Crs Cntry; JV Socr; Var Trk; High Hon Roll; NHS; Ntl Merit SF; Cornell U; Engrng.

GRAMM, ROGER; Palmyra Area HS; Orlando, FL; (Y); 10/200; VP Church Yth Grp; Mgr Band; Concert Band; Mrchg Band; High Hon Roll; Ntl Merit Ltr; Messiah Coll; Arch.

GRANAT III, JOSEPH C; Cambridge Springs HS; Cambridge Springs, PA; (Y); 11/115; French Clb; Key Clb; Hon Roll; Tool/Die Trd Schl; Tool/Die Mac.

GRANATO, SHERRI; St Marra Goretti HS; Philadelphia, PA; (Y); 129/390; Aud/Vis; Church Yth Grp; GAA; Chorus; Orch; Pep Band; School Musical; Prfct Atten Awd; Hnrb Mntn Awd Music 86; Ocn Engrng.

GRANBERY, ANNE MARIE; Seneca Valley HS; Zelienople, PA; (Y); 49/342; Church Yth Grp; Pres 4-H; 4-H Awd; High Hon Roll; Hon Roll; Ntl Merit Ltr; Rotary Awd; PA Polled Hereford Queen 86; PA Hghr Ed Asstnc Agncy Cert Of Merit 85; PA ST U; Agrcltrl Bus.

GRANDAS, FRANK ERIC; North Star HS; Hooversville, PA; (Y); 50/123; FCA; Pres Frsh Cls; Pres Soph Cls; Pres Jr Cls; Var Capt Bsbl; Var Capt Ftbl; Var L Wt Lftg; Letterman Clb; Varsity Clb; JC Awd; US Marine Coprs Distngshd Athlt Awd 86; Big 9 Ftbl Conf Offnsv Plyr 86; Outstndgng Schlr Athlt Awd 86; Lock Haven U; Bus.

GRANDE, CHRISTINE; Sharon HS; Sharon, PA; (Y); French Clb; Speech Tm; High Hon Roll; Hon Roll; Chorus; Rep Stu Cncl; Upwrd Bnd TC Grp Awd 85 & 86; Ltrd Acadmcs 86; Upwrd Bnd Acdmc Achvt Awd 86; Chatham Coll; Law.

GRANDE, ELANA; Marple Newtown HS; Broomall, PA; (Y); Variety Show; Yrbk Stf; JV Cheerleading; JV Mgr(s); Dentl Hygn.

GRANDE, SUSAN; Farrell HS; Farrell, PA; (Y); 14/95; Key Clb; Spanish Clb; Varsity Clb; Concert Band; Mrchg Band; Pep Band; Bsktbl; Trk; Vllybl; NHS.

GRANDINETTI, ROBERT; Chartiers Valley HS; Pittsburgh, PA; (Y); 68/343; Church Yth Grp; Cmnty Wkr; Exploring; Ski Clb; High Hon Roll; Hon Roll; NHS; Poeter Duff Mem Schlrshp 86; Stock Market Clb Interact Clb Coda Clb; Robert Morris Acad Schlrshp; Robert Morris Coll; Acctng.

GRANEY, SUZANNE; Red Land HS; Etters, PA; (Y); 26/275; Chorus; Madrigals; School Musical; School Play; Nwsp Stf; Yrbk Stf; Rep Stu Cncl; French Hon Soc; Hon Roll; Church Yth Grp; Hugh O Brian Yth Ldrshp Awd 85; Publ Rel Spec.

GRANICO, LISA; Shaler Area HS; Allison Pk, PA; (Y); 15/538; Bsktbl; High Hon Roll; Awd Frm Gnnon U 84; U Of Pittsburgh; Pre-Law.

GRANICO, ROSE; Shaler Area HS; Allison Pk, PA; (Y); 129/517; Office Aide; SADD; Variety Show; Rep Jr Cls; High Hon Roll; Hon Roll; WV U; Bus.

GRANISTOSKY, JOY; Conemaugh Twp Area HS; Jerome, PA; (Y); 12/104; Concert Band; Mrchg Band; School Musical; School Play; Nwsp Stf; Yrbk Stf; Lit Mag; Stat Sftbl; NHS; U Pittsburgh; Acctng.

GRANKO, KATHLEEN; Old Forge HS; Old Forge, PA; (S); Ski Clb; Hon Roll; NHS; Ntl Merit Ltr.

GRANNAS, CHRIS; Bellwood-Antis HS; Bellwood, PA; (Y); Church Yth Grp; FHA; Girl Scts; JA; Key Clb; Chorus; Capt Color Guard; Nwsp Rptr; L Bsktbl; Score Keeper; Sfty Rep Awd Altoona Vo Tech 86; ICM Schl Bus; Wrd Proc.

GRANROSE, JONATHAN; Cheltenham HS; Melrose Pk, PA; (Y); 77/365; Computer Clb; JCL; Band; Concert Band; Jazz Band; Orch; Stage Crew; Nwsp Phtg; Yrbk Phtg; Var Lcrss; Cert Hnrb Mntn Merit Cum Laude Natl Latin Exam 86; Instrumntl Magaz Muscn Awd 85; MS Bike Tour Cert; Comp Sci.

GRANT, BARBARA; Little Flower Catholic HS; Philadelphia, PA; (Y); 3/395; Camera Clb; Drama Clb; German Clb; Service Clb; Chorus; School Musical; Nwsp Rptr; Lit Mag; High Hon Roll; NHS; Hghst Music Awd 85-86; 2nd Hghst Music Awd 83-85; 1st Chair Soprano 86-87; Combs Coll Music; Music Thrpy.

GRANT, DAVE; Downingtown HS; Downingtown, PA; (Y); 230/560; Socr; Swmmng; Tennis; Trk; Vllybl; Wt Lftg; Hon Roll; W Chester U; Sprts Med.

GRANT, DAVID; Belle Vernon Area HS; Belle Vernon, PA; (Y); 42/276; CAP; Exploring; Ski Clb; Band; Pep Band; Swmmng; High Hon Roll; Hon Roll; Duquesne U; Phrmcy.

GRANT, HOLLY; Neshaminy HS; Langhorne, PA; (Y); Church Yth Grp; Ski Clb; SADD; Pres Band; Orch; Nwsp Stf; JV Fld Hcky; Var Socr; Hon Roll; NHS; Pol Sci.

GRANT, JENNIFER; Ambridge Area HS; Sewickley, PA; (Y); Girl Scts; Pep Clb; Red Cross Aide; Band; Concert Band; Mrchg Band; Pep Band; Symp Band; Rep Soph Cls; Rep Jr Cls; Drg & Alchl Cmmtee 84-86; Italian Clb 85-86; Robert Morris Coll; Bus Adm.

GRANT, MARK W; Council Rock HS; Churchville, PA; (Y); 350/845; Pres Church Yth Grp; Var Capt Gym; JV Trk; 1st Pl PIAA Advncd All Around Gymnstcs 86.

GRANT, MICHELLE; Mastbaum A V T S; Philadelphia, PA; (Y); Library Aide; Office Aide; Pep Clb; Teachers Aide; Chorus; Church Choir; Capt Var Bsktbl; Prfct Atten Awd; Lincoln U; Mrktng.

GRANT, NICOLE; Pine Forge Acad; Baltimore, MD; (S); 6/54; Sec Church Yth Grp; Hosp Aide; Teachers Aide; Acpl Chr; Chorus; Trs Frsh Cls; VP Stu Cncl; Oakwood COLL; Pre-Law.

GRANTZ, RANDY; Ford City HS; Ford City, PA; (Y); Chess Clb; Exploring; Spanish Clb; VP Jr Cls; High Hon Roll; Hon Roll; PA ST; Elec Engrng.

GRASSIA, ROSEMARY; St Maria Goretti HS; Philadelphia, PA; (Y); 42/426; Church Yth Grp; French Clb; Service Clb; Chorus; Yrbk Stf; High Hon Roll; Hon Roll; Jr NHS; NHS; Prfct Atten Awd; Anna Vncnt Schlrshp; Drexel U; Bus.

GRASSO, MARGARET; Nazareth Acad; Philadelphia, PA; (Y); 23/120; Var Fld Hcky; Var Sftbl; Opt Clb Awd; Bus Mgmt.

GRASSO, MICHELLE; Freedom HS; Bethlehem, PA; (Y); 70/445; Church Yth Grp; French Clb; Hon Roll; Educ.

GRASSO, PHILIP; St Joes Prep; Cherry Hill, NJ; (Y); 10/235; Boy Scts; Camera Clb; Chess Clb; Church Yth Grp; Library Aide; Im Bsktbl; JV Bowling; Im Ftbl; High Hon Roll; Natrl Ldrshp & Svc Awd 85-86; Chem Engr.

GRATZINGER, LISA M; John W HS; Philadelphia, PA; (Y); 15/310; Latin Clb; Cheerleading; High Hon Roll; Hon Roll; Pres Of Activities Reps; Activities Rep; Athletics Rep; Phila Coll Of Text & Sci; Mktg.

GRAU, BARBARA; Susquenita HS; Marysville, PA; (S); 14/185; Church Yth Grp; Quiz Bowl; Teachers Aide; Band; Chorus; Church Choir; Concert Band; Sec Stu Cncl; Fld Hcky; Mat Maids; Schltc Wrtng Awds Cert Of Merit 84; Outstndng Achvt Physcl Ftns Cert Of Merit 85.

GRAVER, KATHRYN RENATE; Upper Merion Area HS; King Prussia, PA; (Y); 79/220; Church Yth Grp; FBLA; Bsktbl; Fld Hcky; Powder Puff Ftbl; Sftbl; Trk; Katherine Gibbs Bus Schl; Sec.

GRAVER, MICHELLE; Panther Valley HS; Summit Hill, PA; (Y); 47/129; French Clb; Ski Clb; Band; Chorus; Yrbk Stf; Sec Jr Cls; Sec Sr Cls; Cheerleading; Twrlr; Penn ST U; Physcl Thrpst Asst.

GRAVES, CLIFFORD S; Northern Potter HS; Ulysses, PA; (Y); 7/75; Math Tm; Stage Crew; Stat Bsktbl; Coach Actv; High Hon Roll; NHS; Prfct Atten Awd; Acad All-Amer 85; Clarkson U; Comp Sci.

GRAVES, KATHLEEN; Otto-Eldred HS; Eldred, PA; (Y); 1/91; Dance Clb; Varsity Clb; Chorus; Nwsp Stf; Var Cheerleading; Var Trk; High Hon Roll; NHS; Val; Alg II Awd 85-86; Geo Awd 84-85; Spnsh II Awd 84-85; Accnt.

GRAVESEN, ALEX A; Phoenixville Area HS; Phoenixville, PA; (Y); 6/192; Church Yth Grp; Quiz Bowl; Stage Crew; Nwsp Stf; Lit Mag; Sr Cls; Im Socr; Jr NHS; Ntl Merit SF; Lehigh U; Engrg.

GRAY, DAVID; Unionville HS; Kennett Sq, PA; (Y); 93/300; Church Yth Grp; Intnl Clb; Ski Clb; Nwsp Rptr; Nwsp Stf; Crs Cntry; Tennis; Hon Roll; Ntl Merit Ltr.

GRAY, DAWN; Christian Acad; Glenolden, PA; (Y); Church Yth Grp; Library Aide; Chorus; Church Choir; Stu Cncl; Hon Roll; Pep Clb; Christian Character Awd Mind Christ 86; Elem Educ.

GRAY, DE LAUN; Kennedy Christian HS; Mercer, PA; (Y); 16/98; French Clb; Band; Concert Band; Mrchg Band; School Musical; Rep Jr Cls; JV Cheerleading; Var Trk; JV Vllybl; High Hon Roll; Track Lttr 86; Law.

GRAY, DIONNE MARIE; Cedar Grove Christian Acad; Abington, PA; (Y); 5/41; Hosp Aide; Band; Chorus; Var Capt Cheerleading; Var Trk; Hon Roll; NHS; Ntl Merit Ltr; Wheaton Coll IL; Chem.

GRAY, DONALD; Belle Vernon Area HS; Belle Vernon, PA; (Y); Church Yth Grp; Debate Tm; VP JA; Nwsp Phtg; Yrbk Phtg; VP Mrktg Of Yr JA 86; Slsmn Of Yr JA 86; Achvr Awd & NAJAC JA 86; Pre-Med.

GRAY, GWENDOLYN LEE; Wilmington Area HS; New Wilmington, PA; (S); 8/106; Band; Concert Band; Jazz Band; Mrchg Band; School Play; Stage Crew; Yrbk Bus Mgr; Sec Soph Cls; Trs Jr Cls; Trs Sr Cls; Pre Med.

GRAY, JAMES; Mercy Vocational HS; Philadelphia, PA; (Y); Plumber.

GRAY, JANET; Huntingdon Area HS; Huntingdon, PA; (Y); 18/203; Office Aide; Chorus; Co-Capt Color Guard; Mrchg Band; Nwsp Bus Mgr; Yrbk Stf; VP Sr Cls; Sec Stu Cncl; Cit Awd; NHS; Pres Acad Fit Awd 86; Schl Achvt & Svc Awd 86; Am Leg Schl Awd 86; Soroptmst Kathryn Oakman Scholar 86; Bradford Bus Schl; Exec Sec.

GRAY, JILL; Juniata HS; Mifflintown, PA; (Y); Varsity Clb; Chorus; Concert Band; Drm Mjr(t); Mrchg Band; School Play; Var Bsktbl; Var Fld Hcky; Var Trk; Hon Roll; Elem Ed.

GRAY, JOHN; Quaker Valley HS; Sewickley, PA; (Y); 32/160; Boy Scts; Church Yth Grp; Debate Tm; French Clb; German Clb; Key Clb; Latin Clb; Q&S; Nwsp Rptr; Yrbk Rptr; Keynate Spkr 85; Gazette H S Edtr 85-86.

GRAY, JOHN JAMES; Butler SR HS; Butler, PA; (Y); Hon Roll; Outstndg Achvmnt Auto Mechncs Vo-Tech 85-86; Law.

GRAY, JOHN RAYMOND; Charleroi Area HS; Monongahela, PA; (Y); 5/187; Sec NFL; Science Clb; Varsity Clb; Trs Stu Cncl; Cit Awd; Gov Hon Prg Awd; High Hon Roll; Lion Awd; NHS; Ntl Merit Ltr; 4 Yr Air Frc ROTC Schlrp; GA Inst Tech; Aerospc Engrg.

GRAY, JOYCELINE; Aliquippa SR HS; Aliquippa, PA; (Y); Chess Clb; Computer Clb; Girl Scts; Key Clb; Math Clb; Pep Clb; SADD; Band; Swmmng; Tennis; PA ST; Lawyer.

GRAY, JULIAN; Center Area HS; Monaca, PA; (Y); Trs Latin Clb; Stage Crew; Im Bsktbl; Im Bowling; JV Ftbl; Hon Roll; NHS; Prfct Atten Awd; Mech Engr.

GRAY, KELLY; Marple Newtown SR HS; Broomall, PA; (Y); Hon Roll.

GRAY, LA RHONDA; St Paul Cathedral HS; Pittsburgh, PA; (Y); Girl Scts; Key Clb; Spanish Clb; Band; Concert Band; Jazz Band; Mrchg Band; School Musical; Stage Crew; Nwsp Stf; Doc.

GRAY, LESLIE; Hazleton HS; Hazleton, PA; (Y); 29/387; Service Clb; Band; Mrchg Band; Rep Stu Cncl; Stat Bsktbl; Hon Roll; Sthrn AR U; Accntng.

GRAY, LESLIE; Hopewell HS; Aliquippa, PA; (Y); Trs Church Yth Grp; German Clb; Hosp Aide; Band; Chorus; Drill Tm; Rep Jr Cls; Rep Stu Cncl; High Hon Roll; NHS; Intl Bus.

GRAY, MARLA; Susquehanna Township HS; Harrisburg, PA; (Y); Drama Clb; Library Aide; Chorus; Color Guard; Capt Cheerleading; Yth Of Yr Awd Yth Urban Svcs Harrisburg YMCA 86.

GRAY, MICHAEL S; Quaker Valley HS; Winter Pk, FL; (Y); 1/156; Trs Key Clb; Math Clb; Spanish Clb; Band; Nwsp Sprt Ed; Socr; Chrmn Tennis; High Hon Roll; Jr NHS; NHS.

GRAY, MONIQUE; Murrell Dobbins AVTS; Philadelphia, PA; (S); 21/450; JA; Varsity Clb; Variety Show; Rep Frsh Cls; Rep Soph Cls; Rep Jr Cls; Rep Sr Cls; Mgr Bsbl; Capt Cheerleading; Mgr Stat Wrstlng; U Of MD; Elec Engrng.

GRAY, THOMAS A; Williamsport Area HS; Williamsport, PA; (Y); Var Wrstlng; Hon Roll; Rotary Awd.

GRAYBILL, BRENT; Dover Area HS; Dover, PA; (Y); 27/227; Church Yth Grp; German Clb; Var Socr; Var Wrstlng; Hon Roll; NHS; Wt Lftg; Pre-Med.

GRAYBILL, LUCINDA; Middleburg HS; Richfield, PA; (Y); 5/130; FNA; Hosp Aide; Nwsp Phtg; Nwsp Rptr; Yrbk Phtg; Yrbk Rptr; Var Sftbl; High Hon Roll; NHS; Acdmc Achvmnt Awd 86; Nrsng.

GRAYBILL, MELINDA; Middleburg HS; Richfield, PA; (Y); 3/130; FNA; Hosp Aide; Nwsp Ed-Chief; Yrbk Ed-Chief; Var Sftbl; High Hon Roll; NHS; Prfct Atten Awd; Acdmc Achvmnt Awd 86; Nrsng.

GRAYBILL, RACHEL; Exeter Township HS; Reading, PA; (Y); Teachers Aide; Varsity Clb; Trs Jr Cls; Trs Sr Cls; Capt Crs Cntry; Gym; Trk; Vllybl; Wt Lftg; Hon Roll; MVP Trk & Field 85 & 86; Berks Cnty Trk & Crs Cntry All Star Tm 84-86; Dentl Hyg.

GRAYBILL, RICHARD; Annville Cleona HS; Annville, PA; (Y); Church Yth Grp; Math Tm; SADD; Band; Madrigals; School Musical; Yrbk Bus Mgr; NHS; NEDT Awd; Bus Adm.

GRAYLIN, RICHARD; Hazleton HS; Hazleton, PA; (Y); 118/374; Ski Clb; Var L Ftbl; High Hon Roll; Hon Roll; U AZ; Physcst.

GRAYSON, MARY BETH; Open Door Christian Acad; Greensburg, PA; (S); 1/9; Church Yth Grp; Capt Quiz Bowl; School Play; Stat Bsktbl; Var Cheerleading; Capt Vllybl; Cit Awd; High Hon Roll; St Schlr; Val; Lbrty U; Scndry Ed.

GRAZIANO, CHRISTINA M; Hatboro-Horsham SR HS; Hatboro, PA; (Y); 8/260; French Clb; Intnl Clb; Key Clb; Chorus; Yrbk Stf; Rep Jr Cls; Var Awd; High Hon Roll; NHS; Pres Schlr; Neighbrs Hatboro Schlrshp 86; Frnch Awd 86; Acdmc Schlrshp Phila Clg Phrmcy-Sci 86; Phila Coll-Phrmcy, Sci; Phrmcy.

GRAZIER, KELLY; Tyrone Area HS; Warriors Mk, PA; (Y); Church Yth Grp; FBLA; Band; Chorus; Color Guard; Mrchg Band; Hon Roll; Prfct Atten Awd; South Hills Bus Schl; Med Secy.

GRAZIO, PAUL; Emmaus HS; Macungie, PA; (Y); Cmnty Wkr; Exploring; Key Clb; Spanish Clb; Off Frsh Cls; Off Soph Cls; Off Jr Cls; Im Vllybl; Engrg.

GRAZIOSI, DAVID A; Susquehannock HS; New Freedom, PA; (Y); 20/228; Church Yth Grp; Cmnty Wkr; Socr; Wt Lftg; Hon Roll; Embry Riddle U; Aerontcl Engr.

GREAR, ANDY; Phoenixville Area HS; Kimberton, PA; (Y); Computer Clb; French Clb; Ski Clb; Varsity Clb; Chorus; School Musical; Var L Bsbl; Var L Socr; Var L Trk; Hon Roll; Soccr Tm Leading Goal Scorer 85; Sports Med.

GREAR, CHRISTINE; Central Bucks East HS; Warrington, PA; (Y); Church Yth Grp; Debate Tm; Drama Clb; French Clb; Ski Clb; Thesps; Chorus; Church Choir; School Musical; School Play; Penn ST; Tchr.

GREAVES, DEBRA; York Catholic HS; Dover, PA; (Y); Pres Church Yth Grp; Debate Tm; Pep Clb; Spanish Clb; Band; Concert Band; Drm Mjr(t); Jazz Band; Mrchg Band; Pep Band; J F Siebenkase Awd; M Flood Awd; Pres Adcmd Ftns Awd; Blmsbrg U; Erly Chldhd Art Ed.

GREBE, JOANN; Lower Moreland HS; Huntingdon Valley, PA; (S); 43/214; Trs Chorus; Orch; School Musical; School Play; Stage Crew; Lit Mag; Hon Roll; NHS; Most Imprvd-Orchestra 83 & 84; Orchestra Svc Awd 85; Beaver Coll; History.

GREBE, LAURA; Western Wayne HS; Lake Ariel, PA; (Y); 32/150; Cmnty Wkr; Computer Clb; Chorus; Nwsp Rptr; Lit Mag; Hon Roll; Rep Jr Cls; Capt Stat Vllybl; Awd Perf Attendnce; PA ST; Comp Sci.

GREBINOSKI, ELIZABETH; Lawrenceville Area Catholic HS; Pittsburgh, PA; (Y); #1 In Class; Pep Clb; Chorus; Drill Tm; School Musical; Yrbk Stf; Rep Frsh Cls; Rep Soph Cls; Rep Jr Cls; Stu Cncl; Var Bsktbl.

GREBINOSKI, MARY; Lawrenceville Area Catholic HS; Pittsburgh, PA; (Y); 1/53; Chorus; Yrbk Ed-Chief; Rep Soph Cls; Rep Jr Cls; VP Stu Cncl; Var Bsktbl; Var Score Keeper; Capt Sftbl; High Hon Roll; NHS; US Army Schlr Athlt Awd 85-86; U Schlr U Of Pittsburgh 86; U Pittsburgh; Engr.

GREBONISKI, MELISSA; Coughlin HS; Plains, PA; (Y); 62/355; Church Yth Grp; Hosp Aide; Ski Clb; Stat Bsbl; Var Capt Bsktbl; Var Cheerleading; Hon Roll; NHS.

GRECK, KRISTI; West Allegheny HS; Oakdale, PA; (Y); Spanish Clb; SADD; Sftbl; Hon Roll; General Business.

GRECO, CARI; Mohawk Area HS; Edinburg, PA; (Y); Church Yth Grp; Pep Clb; VP Spanish Clb; Band; Concert Band; Mrchg Band; School Musical; Rep Stu Cncl; Powder Puff Ftbl; Hon Roll; Penn ST; Educ.

GRECO, CHRISTINE; John S Fine HS; Glen Lyon, PA; (Y); 44/242; Pres Varsity Clb; Yrbk Stf; Rep Jr Cls; Rep Sr Cls; Co-Capt Var Bsktbl; Var Crs Cntry; Var Trk; High Hon Roll; Misericordia Athltc Schlrshp 86; W Side Plygrnd Assoc Awd 86; Linda Motel Awd/Desire For Achvt 85; Misericordia Coll; Radlg Tech.

GREEENSPUN, BRENDA; George Washington HS; Philadelphia, PA; (Y); Library Aide; SADD; Teachers Aide; Temple Yth Grp; School Play; Stage Crew; Pine Manor; Bio-Psych.

GREEN, ANN; Elk Lake HS; Montrose, PA; (Y); 10/98; Church Yth Grp; Drama Clb; 4-H; Library Aide; Spanish Clb; Chorus; School Musical; JV Bsktbl; Var Fld Hcky; Score Keeper; Susquehanna Cnty Democrtc Womns Schlrshp 86; 3200 Run 3rd Pl 85; PIAA Dist 12 Champ Tm Bsktbl 86; Sarah Lawrence; Engl.

GREEN, DAVID; York Catholic HS; York, PA; (Y); Intnl Clb; Church Yth Grp; Debate Tm; Exploring; French Clb; Pep Clb; SADD; Stage Crew; Nwsp Rptr; Nwsp Stf; Philadelphia Coll Phrmcy; Sci.

GREEN, DE LACEY; David Brown Oliver HS; Pittsburgh, PA; (Y); 13/243; Yrbk Stf; Cit Awd; High Hon Roll; Hon Roll; Ntl Merit Ltr; Hnr Grad 86; Financial Mgmt.

GREEN, DIANE M; Bishop Mc Devitt HS; Harrisburg, PA; (Y); 41/200; Computer Clb; Science Clb; Spanish Clb; Church Choir; JV Bsktbl; Cheerleading; Var Sftbl; Tennis; Hon Roll; NHS; Peer Cnslng Pgm 85-86; Phrmcy.

GREEN, DONNA; Carlisle SR HS; Carlisle, PA; (Y); 4/415; Model UN; VP Chorus; School Musical; Swing Chorus; Var Tennis; High Hon Roll; NHS; Cnty Dist & Regnl Chorus 84-86; All-State Chorus 86; Dist Chorus Soloist 86; Northwestern U; Music Educ.

GREEN, JENNIFER; William Allen HS; Allentown, PA; (Y); 24/559; Chrmn Exploring; Hosp Aide; Leo Clb; Political Wkr; Yrbk Stf; Bowling; Hon Roll; Jr NHS; NHS; Sec Spanish NHS; Summo Cum Hnr Schlrshp Awd 86; Merit Awd Physcs Olympcs 86; Sec Of Contp Affrs Clb 86; Phys Thrpy.

GREEN, JODY; Warren Area HS; Warren, PA; (Y); French Clb; Spanish Clb; School Play; Rep Jr Cls; Stu Cncl; High Hon Roll; Hon Roll; Jr NHS; NHS; Latin Clb; Schlstc Awds 85 & 86; Psych.

GREEN, JODYE M; George Washington HS; Philadelphia, PA; (Y); Office Aide; Ski Clb; Spanish Clb; SADD; Teachers Aide; Y-Teens; School Play; Stage Crew; Yrbk Stf; Off Frsh Cls; West Chester U; Elem Ed.

GREEN, JOHN; Karns City HS; Chicora, PA; (Y); 7/111; Exploring; FCA; Spanish Clb; School Play; Variety Show; Rep Stu Cncl; Var Capt Crs Cntry; Var L Trk; High Hon Roll; NHS; Engrng.

GREEN, KAYLEEN; Est Lycoming HS; Hughesville, PA; (Y); Church Yth Grp; Ski Clb; Spanish Clb; Chorus; School Musical; Stu Cncl; JV Bsktbl; Hon Roll; Cntrl PA Bus Schl; Htl Mgmt.

GREEN, KELLY; Girls HS; Philadelphia, PA; (Y); 102/395; Cmnty Wkr; Library Aide; Office Aide; Pep Clb; Rep Service Clb; Teachers Aide; Y-Teens; Rep Frsh Cls; Rep Soph Cls; Rep Jr Cls.

GREEN, MARY S; John A Brashear HS; Pittsburgh, PA; (Y); AFS; Church Yth Grp; JA; Nwsp Stf; Stu Cncl; Var Capt Tennis; High Hon Roll; NHS; Cit Awd; Wt Lftg; AFS Westinghouse Elec Corp Schlrshp 84; Wrld Affrs Cncl Pgh Donald E Farr Awd 86; U Pgh; SE Asian Studies.

GREEN, MICHAEL; Central HS; Philadelphia, PA; (Y); 1/220; Math Clb; Math Tm; Science Clb; Mrchg Band; Orch; Nwsp Phtg; Nwsp Rptr; Nwsp Stf; High Hon Roll; Hon Roll; Phi Beta Kappa Awd 86; Yale U; Physician.

GREEN, MICHAEL; Lower Meron HS; Merion, PA; (Y); Yrbk Stf; Off Soph Cls; Off Jr Cls; Off Stu Cncl; JV Var Bsbl; JV Var Bsktbl; L Socr; Im Wt Lftg; Hon Roll; Pre-Med.

GREEN, RAUBIE; Chester Fe HS; Media, PA; (Y); Math Clb; Variety Show; Pres Soph Cls; Bsktbl; High Hon Roll; Hon Roll; Excllnc Soc Studies & Mst Imprvd Lincoln U Peer Tutoring 86; U Of HI; Com Pgmmg.

GREEN, RHONDA; West Phila Catholic Girls HS; Philadelphia, PA; (Y); Yrbk Stf; NHS; Archdcsn Stngrphy I Comptn 2nd Pl 86; Acctg.

GREEN, STEPHANIE; Harry S Truman HS; Bristol, PA; (Y); Computer Clb; JA; ROTC; SADD; Yrbk Stf; Stu Cncl; Cheerleading; Trk; Vllybl; Hon Roll; Jesse Owens Games Awd Trck & Fld 83; Pres Phys Fit Awd 84-85; Coaches Apprctn Awd Chrldng Capt 85-86; Bucks Cnty CC; Bus Adm.

GREEN, STEVEN KEVIN; Overbrook HS; Philadelphia, PA; (Y); 109/640; Art Clb; Aud/Vis; Church Yth Grp; Computer Clb; Office Aide; Science Clb; Teachers Aide; Varsity Clb; Ftbl; Mgr(s); Philadelphia Coll Art; Sci Ill.

GREEN, TRACEY; Red Land HS; Etters, PA; (Y); 52/285; Band; Concert Band; Jazz Band; Mrchg Band; School Musical; Symp Band; Bowling; Fld Hcky; High Hon Roll; Hon Roll; Elem Ed.

GREENAWALT, BETH; Waynesboro SR HS; Waynesboro, PA; (Y); Drama Clb; Math Clb; Chorus; Sr Cls; Vet.

GREENAWALT, DALE; Sharon HS; Sharon, PA; (Y); 18/175; Aud/Vis; JV Ftbl; High Hon Roll; Hon Roll; Comp Engrng.

GREENAWAY, LISA; Norwin SR HS; N Huntingdon, PA; (Y); 159/557; Letterman Clb; Pep Clb; SADD; Varsity Clb; Stu Cncl; Co-Capt Cheerleading; Powder Puff Ftbl; Hon Roll; ECA Camp Chrldng Champ & Overall Champs 86; Tele Cmmnctgns.

GREENBERG, JUDI; Lincoln HS; Ellwood, PA; (Y); Drama Clb; Ski Clb; Spanish Clb; Y-Teens; Chorus; Yrbk Ed-Chief; Yrbk Stf; JV Cheerleading; Powder Puff Ftbl; IN U Of PA; Fash Merch.

GREENE, CLAYE; Cathedral Prep; Lake City, PA; (Y); JV Var Bsktbl; Trk; Cvl Engr.

GREENE, KAREN; Marple Newtown SR HS; Broomall, PA; (Y); 11/365; Cmnty Wkr; Math Clb; Temple Yth Grp; Variety Show; Ed Nwsp Stf; Yrbk Bus Mgr; NHS; Ntl Merit Ltr; Mrt Awd Frm Soc Of Wmns Engrs 85-86; Schlrshp To Lbanon Vly Coll Yth Schlrs 85; U Of VA; Math.

GREENE, KIMBERLY; Jersey Shore SR HS; Jersey Shore, PA; (Y); Yrbk Stf; Williamsport CC; Hrtcltr.

GREENE, MICHAEL; Bellwood Antis HS; Bellwood, PA; (Y); 3/125; Chess Clb; Pres Church Yth Grp; Trk; Hon Roll; NHS; US Air Frc Acad; Sci.

GREENE, RANDY; Ridley SR HS; Swarthmore, PA; (Y); 153/427; AFS; Church Yth Grp; Cmnty Wkr; Exploring; FFA; Bsbl; Ftbl; Vllybl; Hon Roll; Teachers Aide; Law Enfrcmt.

GREENE, TOM; Iroquois JR SR HS; Erie, PA; (Y); 25/150; Letterman Clb; Var JV Ftbl; Var JV Trk; Im Wt Lftg; Hon Roll; The Behrend Coll; Comp Sci.

GREENER, JILL; Delaware County Christian Schl; Havertown, PA; (Y); 8/78; Church Yth Grp; Bsktbl; Fld Hcky; Sftbl; High Hon Roll; NHS; ACSI 86.

GREENFIELD, BECKY; E I Meyers HS; Wilkes Barre, PA; (Y); German Clb; Key Clb; Ski Clb; Temple Yth Grp; Chorus; Yrbk Stf; Var Swmmng; Old Dominion U; Bus.

GREENFIELD, LAURA; Hillel Acad; Pittsburgh, PA; (S); 2/7; VP Temple Yth Grp; Chorus; Yrbk Phtg; Yrbk Rptr; Yrbk Sprt Ed; VP Stu Cncl; High Hon Roll; NHS; Ntl Merit Schol; Yeshiva U; Bus.

GREENHOLT, SCOTT E; North Allegheny SR HS; Wexford, PA; (Y); 39/605; JA; Var Trk; Hon Roll; NHS; 3rd HS AHSME 86; Carnegie-Mellon U; Bus.

GREENIA, RAYANNE; Saucon Valley SR HS; Hellertown, PA; (Y); Band; Color Guard; Capt Tennis; High Hon Roll; Hon Roll; Northampton County CC; Sec.

GREENIER, JACQUELINE; Seneca Valley HS; Zelienople, PA; (Y); 117/370; School Play; Hotel Mgmt.

GREENJACK, ANDREW S; Unionville Chadds Ford HS; W Chester, PA; (Y); Hst FBLA; Rep Soph Cls; Rep Jr Cls; Var Bsbl; Var Crs Cntry; Var Trk; High Hon Roll; Hon Roll; Jr NHS; Schl Map Awd 84-86; Engrng.

GREENWALD, ANDREW; Bishop Mc Devitt HS; Glenside, PA; (Y); 9/351; Office Aide; Nwsp Rptr; Yrbk Stf; High Hon Roll; Hon Roll; Prfct Atten Awd; Pres Schlr; 3rd Prz Unsns Sci Fair Physics 86; Pres Mntl & Phys Ftns Awd 86; Villanova; Elctrcl Engrng.

GREENWOOD, ANDREA; Harry S Truman HS; Levittown, PA; (Y); Yrbk Stf; Stu Cncl; Crs Cntry; Hon Roll; Bucks County CC.

GREENWOOD, MARY ANN; Wayneburg Centra HS; Waynesburg, PA; (Y); Sec Camera Clb; Church Yth Grp; Computer Clb; Dance Clb; Drama Clb; Office Aide; Spanish Clb; School Play; Stu Cncl; High Hon Roll; Bus Mgmt.

GREENWOOD, TIMOTHY; Yough HS; Ruffs Dale, PA; (Y); 17/243; VP Ski Clb; VP Spanish Clb; Var L Ftbl; Im Wt Lftg; High Hon Roll; Jr NHS; NHS; YALE; PA ST U; Engrng.

GREER, KELLY; South Fayette HS; Cuddy, PA; (S); 2/86; Drama Clb; Key Clb; Pep Clb; Ski Clb; Chorus; Cheerleading; High Hon Roll; Hon Roll; NHS; Prfct Atten Awd; Bio.

GREER, LORI; Deer Lakes JR SR HS; Allison Pk, PA; (Y); 32/193; Church Yth Grp; Drama Clb; SADD; School Musical; School Play; Stage Crew; Variety Show; Hon Roll; Awd Acdmc Excllnc 86; Geneva; Psych.

GREGA, BRIAN; Dunmore HS; Dunmore, PA; (Y); 28/158; JV Ftbl; U Of Scranton; Accntng.

GREGER, DEBORAH; Henderson HS; West Chester, PA; (S); 4/343; Am Leg Aux Girls St; JCL; Var Fld Hcky; Var Trk; Hon Roll; NHS; Spanish NHS; Magna Cum Laude Natl Ltn Exm 85; Engrng.

GREGG, CAROLYN; Avon Grove HS; Landenberg, PA; (Y); Pres Sec Church Yth Grp; Band; Chorus; Concert Band; Mrchg Band; School Musical; School Play; Yrbk Stf; Cheerleading; Tennis; Srv & Ldrshp To Yth Ed Assn Schlrshp 86; Srv To Yth Ed Assn Awd 83; W Boyd Schl Tvl; Trsm.

GREGORI, DINA; Upper Darby HS; Upper Darby, PA; (Y); Cmnty Wkr; Dance Clb; Girl Scts; Office Aide; School Musical; Sftbl; Trk; Hon Roll; Penn ST U; Bus.

GREGOROWICZ, PAULA; John S Fine HS; Namicoke, PA; (S); 3/250; Ski Clb; Nwsp Stf; High Hon Roll; NHS; Ntl Merit Ltr; NEDT Awd.

GREGORY, CHRISTINE; Freeport Sr HS; Sarver, PA; (Y); Church Yth Grp; Band; Church Choir; Concert Band; School Musical; School Play; Stage Crew; Yrbk Stf; Hon Roll; Free Entrprz Wk 86; Nrsng.

GREGORY, DAVID; Quaker Valley HS; Sewickley, PA; (Y); Pres Science Clb; Ski Clb; Spanish Clb; Golf; Var Socr; Tennis; Hon Roll; Westinghouse Sci Awd, PA JR Acad Sci 1st Awd 86; Bio.

GREGORY, JOAN; Elk County Christian HS; St Marys, PA; (S); Model UN; SADD; School Play; Yrbk Rptr; Yrbk Stf; Rep Stu Cncl; High Hon Roll; NHS; NEDT Awd; Penn ST U; Comp Sci.

GREGORY, KEN; Bethel Park SR HS; Bethel Park, PA; (Y); 45/515; Church Yth Grp; Concert Band; Rep Frsh Cls; Rep Jr Cls; Stat Im Bsktbl; Var Capt Socr; Im Vllybl; High Hon Roll; Hon Roll; NHS; Engrng.

GREGORY, PAUL; Benton HS; Stillwater, PA; (Y); Ski Clb; Pres Jr Cls; Wrstlng; Hon Roll; Air Force.

GREINER, CHRISTINE; Muncy HS; Muncy, PA; (Y); 9/72; Drama Clb; Spanish Clb; School Musical; Yrbk Ed-Chief; High Hon Roll; NHS; Spanish NHS; Natl Hnr Socty & Parnt Tchr Assn Schlrshps 86; Grove City Coll.

GREINER III, GEORGE; Altoona Area HS; Altoona, PA; (Y); Sec Boy Scts; Chorus; God Cntry Awd; Hon Roll; Ordr Of Arrow Outstndng Srv Awd 85; De Molay Awd Of Initation 85; PA ST Altoona; Comp Prgmr.

GREINER, GREG; Manheim Central HS; Manheim, PA; (Y); JV Var Ftbl; High Hon Roll; Hon Roll; 4 Way Test Awd 86.

GREINER, MICHELLE; Manheim Central HS; Manheim, PA; (Y); Church Yth Grp; Cmnty Wkr; Hosp Aide; Library Aide; Stu Cncl; Cheerleading; Fld Hcky; Powder Puff Ftbl; Tennis; Hon Roll; 4-Way Test Awd; Lancaster Gen Schl Rad; X-Ray.

GRELA, REBECCA; Rocky Grove HS; Franklin, PA; (Y); 14/83; Church Yth Grp; SADD; School Play; Yrbk Stf; Sec Stu Cncl; High Hon Roll; Kiwanis Awd; NHS; Prfct Atten Awd; 1st Plc Rtry Ortry Cntst 86; Franklin Rgnl Med Ctr; Rdlgy.

GRELLA, DAVIDA; Bishop Mc Devitt HS; Middletown, PA; (S); 14/200; Band; Chorus; Church Choir; Concert Band; Madrigals; Mrchg Band; Pep Band; School Musical; Rep Stu Cncl; NHS.

GRENCAVAGE, LISA; Coughlin HS; Wilkes-Barre Twp, PA; (Y); 12/367; French Clb; Math Clb; Yrbk Stf; Jr NHS; Lion Awd; NHS; Lions Clb Awd 86; U Of Scranton; Psychlgy.

GRENOBLE, ROBERT E; State College Area HS; Penna Furnace, PA; (Y); Church Yth Grp; Band; Mrchg Band; Symp Band; Outstndng Auto Mech 85 & 86; PA ST U.

GRESGOTT, MARK; Slippery Rock Area HS; Slippery Rock, PA; (Y); Boy Scts; Acctng.

GRESH, KAREN L; Norristown Area HS; Norristown, PA; (S); 10/450; Church Yth Grp; Drama Clb; Church Choir; School Musical; School Play; Stage Crew; High Hon Roll; NHS; Opt Clb Awd; Prfct Atten Awd; Allentown Coll; Tech Theatre.

GRESHAM, LAURAJEAN; Pottsgrove HS; Oaks, PA; (Y); 26/229; Church Yth Grp; Library Aide; Math Tm; Science Clb; Service Clb; Spanish Clb; Church Choir; Hon Roll; Psycho-Bio.

GRESKO JR, RONALD J; Saltsburg JR SR HS; Saltsburg, PA; (Y); FFA; VICA; High Hon Roll; Hon Roll; Appliance Repair.

GRESKOVIC, GERARD; Mid-Valley Sec Ctr HS; Olyphant, PA; (Y); 1/121; Scholastic Bowl; Yrbk Stf; High Hon Roll; Hon Roll; Lion Awd; NHS; Ntl Merit Ltr; Pres Schlr; Pres Ntl Hnr Soc 86; Pres Schlrshp PCPS 86; Best Of Cls 86; Phil Coll Of Pharm & Sci; Pharm.

GRESS, KEITH; Allen HS; Allentown, PA; (Y); 52/639; Ski Clb; Band; Concert Band; Mrchg Band; Pep Band; Hon Roll; Jr NHS; NHS; Summo Cum Honore Scholar Awd 86; Biol.

GRESSLY, TAMMY L; Knoch HS; Butler, PA; (Y); Church Yth Grp; Chorus; Yrbk Stf; Var L Vllybl; High Hon Roll; NHS; JV Coach Actv; Var Score Keeper; Ambassador Coll; Acctg.

GRETZ, GEORGE; North Pocono HS; Lake Ariel, PA; (Y); 33/265; Band; Concert Band; Mrchg Band; Orch; Variety Show; Bsbl; Ftbl; Hon Roll; NHS; 2 Ftbl Coach Awds 84-85; Wick Def Plyr Awd 85; Marywood Hnrs Band 83; Penn ST; Pre-Law.

GRETZ, KENDRA; Norwin SR HS; N Huntingdon, PA; (Y); 11/557; Trs Church Yth Grp; Cmnty Wkr; Pres FBLA; Sec Leo Clb; Pep Clb; Powder Puff Ftbl; Score Keeper; Hon Roll; Amer Lgn Awd 83; Bus Stu Of Yr 85 & 86; Bradford Bus Schl; Exec Secy.

GREVE, ALAN E; Norristown Area HS; Norristown, PA; (S); Key Clb; Band; Jazz Band; Orch; School Musical; Symp Band; Bsbl; Socr; Hon Roll; NHS; Schlstc & Athlc Excel Awd 85; Engrng.

GREW, MELODY; Meyersdale Area HS; Meyersdale, PA; (Y); 3/83; Church Yth Grp; Cmnty Wkr; Drama Clb; Letterman Clb; Pep Clb; Varsity Clb; Band; Chorus; Church Choir; Concert Band; Meyersdale Maple Prncss; 2nd Maid Hnr PA Maple Queen Pagnt; IN U PA; Rehab Ed.

GREYBOSH, JOHN; Bishop Hafey HS; Hazleton, PA; (Y); 35/182; Chess Clb; Church Yth Grp; Cmnty Wkr; Hon Roll; NHS; Penn ST U; Engrng.

GREYBUSH, MARY; Freedom HS; Bethlehem, PA; (Y); 20/445; Band; Mrchg Band; Symp Band; Var Capt Bsktbl; High Hon Roll; Hon Roll; NHS; Med Svcs.

GRIEB, KELLY JO; Bald Eagle Area HS; Julian, PA; (Y); Sec Trs Church Yth Grp; Trs Varsity Clb; VP Chorus; Jazz Band; School Musical; Stat Bsktbl; Powder Puff Ftbl; Var L Trk; High Hon Roll; Pres NHS; Centre Daily Times Schlrshp $1000 86; J Snyder Awd 86; Hnr Awd 86; U Of Pittsburgh; Phy Thrpy.

GRIEB, VICKI; Lock Haven SR HS; Flemington, PA; (Y); Church Yth Grp; Computer Clb; Dance Clb; Hosp Aide; Keywanettes; Sec Library Aide; Spanish Clb; Capt Drm Mjr(t); Variety Show; Hon Roll; Free Enterprs Week 85; Awd-Candy Striping 86.

GRIEBEL, MICHELLE; North Clarion HS; Snydersburg, PA; (Y); 32/96; Drama Clb; 4-H; Office Aide; Pep Clb; SADD; Church Choir; School Play; JV Bsktbl; JV Var Cheerleading; Hon Roll; Clarion U; Erly Chldhd Dvlpmnt.

GRIEME, AMY; Pen Argyl Area HS; Pen Argyl, PA; (Y); 31/163; Drama Clb; Leo Clb; Ski Clb; Band; Chorus; Concert Band; Mrchg Band; School Play; Var L Trk; High Hon Roll; PTA Schlrp 86; Bloomsburg U; Mass Commnctns.

GRIER, JENNIFER; Bald Eagle Area JR SR HS; Karthaus, PA; (S); 4/216; Spanish Clb; Acpl Chr; Trs Chorus; School Musical; School Play; Variety Show; Nwsp Ed-Chief; Yrbk Ed-Chief; High Hon Roll; NHS; U Of AZ; Astrnmy.

GRIESEL, EDWARD; Bellwood-Antis HS; Bellwood, PA; (Y); 2/118; SADD; Hon Roll; Stu Of Wk 85-86; PA ST U; Bus Admin.

GRIESER, VICKI; North Hills HS; Pittsburgh, PA; (Y); AFS; Ski Clb; Trk; Hon Roll; U Pittsburgh; Accntng.

GRIESS, ELAINE; Valley Forge Christian Acad; King Of Prussia, PA; (S); 1/7; Pres Church Yth Grp; Office Aide; Yrbk Stf; Sec Soph Cls; Sec Jr Cls; Sec Sr Cls; High Hon Roll; Val; Katharine Gibbs Schl; Exctv Sec.

GRIFFIE, JOHN; New Oxford HS; New Oxford, PA; (Y); 69/200; Am Leg Boys St; Boy Scts; Church Yth Grp; Cmnty Wkr; Computer Clb; English Clb; FCA; JA; Letterman Clb; Spanish Clb; Athletic Awds; Temple U; Cmmnctns.

GRIFFIN, DE WAYNE C; Wilkinsburg SR HS; Wilkinsburg, PA; (Y); 19/145; Art Clb; Computer Clb; Letterman Clb; Spanish Clb; Varsity Clb; Y-Teens; Im Bsktbl; Var Capt Ftbl; Im Tennis; Im Trk; Air Frc; Bus Adm.

GRIFFIN, DEBORAH; Bethel Park SR HS; Bethel Park, PA; (Y); 77/513; Art Clb; Church Yth Grp; Science Clb; Yrbk Stf; High Hon Roll; 1st & 2nd Pl Pa JR Acadmy Sci Regnl & ST Comp 84 & 85; Sci.

GRIFFIN III, JOSEPH; Saint Josephs Preparatory Schl; Flourtown, PA; (Y); 1/240; Cmnty Wkr; Service Clb; Im Bsktbl; Im Fld Hcky; High Hon Roll; Prfct Atten Awd; Bio Chem.

GRIFFIN, ROCHELLE TOY; Norristown Area HS; Norristown, PA; (Y); FCA; FBLA; Key Clb; Nwsp Stf; Stu Cncl; Var Cheerleading; Fld Hcky; Cit Awd; Prfct Atten Awd; Martin Luther King & William A Nowlia Awds 86; Main Line Para Lgl Inst; Law.

GRIFFIN, TIFFANY; Northern Lebanon HS; Jonestown, PA; (Y); 16/166; Model UN; Varsity Clb; Band; Concert Band; Mrchg Band; Swing Chorus; Rep Stu Cncl; Var L Cheerleading; Var Tennis; Hon Roll; U Of Houston; Hotel Mgmnt.

GRIFFIN, TODD; Trinity HS; Washington, PA; (Y); 10/376; Var L Bsktbl; Var L Ftbl; Var L Trk; Im Wt Lftg; High Hon Roll; Hon Roll; NHS; All Conf Hnrb Mntn TE 85-86; Law.

GRIFFIN III, WILLIAM PAUL; Shady Side Acad; Pittsburgh, PA; (Y); 20/102; Swmmng; Tennis; High Hon Roll; U Rochester; Chem Engr.

GRIFFITH, BILLIE SUE; Charleroi Area JR SR HS; Charleroi, PA; (Y); Church Yth Grp; French Clb; Ski Clb; SADD; Chorus; Nwsp Rptr; Nwsp Stf; Yrbk Stf; Rep Frsh Cls; Rep Soph Cls.

GRIFFITH, CHRISTINE; Burgettstown Area SR HS; Bulger, PA; (Y); 39/172; Church Yth Grp; Sec French Clb; Speech Tm; Chorus; Variety Show; Pres Frsh Cls; Rep Soph Cls; Pres Jr Cls; Pres Sr Cls; Hon Roll; Distngshd Svc Awd 86; Stu Cncl Merit Scholar 86; Seton Hill Coll.

GRIFFITH, CYNTHIA; Octorara HS; Parkesburg, PA; (Y); 9/171; Church Yth Grp; Pres FBLA; Yrbk Stf; Rep Stu Cncl; Sftbl; Hon Roll; NHS; Stu Cncl Schlrshp 86; 1st Clerical Awd 86; J P Morgan Schlrshp 86; Goldey Beacom Coll; Exec Sec.

GRIFFITH, DAVID; United HS; Seward, PA; (Y); 29/126; Boy Scts; VP Church Yth Grp; Pres French Clb; Ski Clb; Concert Band; Mrchg Band; Yrbk Phtg; Bsbl; L Var Trk; NHS.

GRIFFITH, ELLEN; Greater Johnstown HS; Johnstown, PA; (Y); Spanish Clb; Y-Teens; High Hon Roll; Hon Roll; Comp Sci.

GRIFFITH, GAIL SHERIDYN; St Hubert HS; Philadelphia, PA; (Y); 165/367; Aud/Vis; Camp Fr Inc; Cheerleading; Hon Roll; Penn ST; Bus Admn.

GRIFFITH, JOHN; United HS; Indiana, PA; (Y); 32/160; JA; Ski Clb; Spanish Clb; Teachers Aide; Band; Stage Crew; Nwsp Stf; Coach Actv; Hon Roll; Prfct Atten Awd; IN U Of PA; Jrnlsm.

GRIFFITH, KELLIE; Pen Argyl HS; Pen Argyl, PA; (Y); Drama Clb; Sec Chorus; School Play; VP Sec Stu Cncl; Var Capt Cheerleading; Sftbl; Kutztown U; Crmnl Jstc.

GRIFFITH, LISA L; Freeport Area SR HS; Sarver, PA; (Y); 11/173; Camera Clb; Church Yth Grp; School Musical; School Play; Stat Bsktbl; Var Cheerleading; L Trk; Wt Lftg; High Hon Roll; Hon Roll; Cls Optimist 86; ICM Schl Bus; Wrd Proc Spclst.

GRIFFITH, WENDY; Burgettstown Area JR SR HS; Langeloth, PA; (Y); VP Church Yth Grp; Exploring; French Clb; Science Clb; Chorus; Yrbk Stf; Voice Dem Awd; WVU; Clincl Psych.

GRIFFITHS, JEFF; Pine Grove Area HS; Tremont, PA; (Y); Varsity Clb; Sec Band; Rep Soph Cls; Rep Jr Cls; Var L Bsktbl; Coach Actv; Im Ftbl; Im Sftbl; Im Vllybl; Hon Roll; Engrng.

GRIFFITHS, KELLY; St Maria Goretti HS; Philadelphia, PA; (Y); Lion Awd; Office Aide; Teachers Aide; Yrbk Phtg; Yrbk Rptr; Yrbk Stf; Cheerleading; Pom Pon; 2nd Hnrs; Temple U.

GRIFFITHS, LYNN; Hazleton SR HS; Hazleton, PA; (Y); 42/388; Church Yth Grp; Drama Clb; Pep Clb; Sec Band; Concert Band; Mrchg Band; School Play; Variety Show; Nwsp Stf; Hon Roll; PA Band Mstrs Awd 84; Elem Educ.

GRIGALONIS, DENICE; Minersville Area HS; Minersville, PA; (Y); 11/123; Spanish Clb; Flag Corp; Jazz Band; Mrchg Band; School Play; Stage Crew; Yrbk Stf; VP Jr Cls; Pres Sr Cls; Capt Twrlr; Penn ST; Engrng.

GRIGG, KAREN; Altoona Area HS; Altoona, PA; (Y); Church Yth Grp; Spanish Clb; SADD; Chorus; Church Choir; School Musical; Stage Crew; NHS; Phys Ther.

GRILLO, LISA; Jefferson-Morgan JR SR HS; Ricelanding, PA; (S); 5/100; Cmnty Wkr; VP French Clb; Sec Yrbk Stf; Rep Jr Cls; Sftbl; High Hon Roll; Hon Roll; VP NHS; Church Yth Grp; Bike Hik Retrd Ctzns Awd 84; Bio.

GRILLO, MARSHA; Charleroi SR HS; Monongahela, PA; (Y); Pep Clb; Science Clb; Ski Clb; Spanish Clb; Varsity Clb; Color Guard; Drill Tm; Nwsp Rptr; Stu Cncl; Hon Roll; Hlth Careers Awd 85-86; Stu Tutrs Awd 85-86; Cgr Courier Art Stf Awd 85-86; Med Tech.

GRIM, BARBARA; Eastern York HS; Wrightsville, PA; (Y); 18/159; Varsity Clb; Var Fld Hcky; Var Mgr(s); Im Powder Puff Ftbl; High Hon Roll; Hon Roll; Jr NHS; Vrsty Clb Treas 86-87; Biochem.

GRIM, CHERI; Boyertown SR HS; Gilbertsville, PA; (Y); Spanish Clb; Mgr Socr; Mgr Trk; High Hon Roll; Hon Roll; Cvl Svc Area.

GRIM, CHRIS; William Allen HS; Allentown, PA; (Y); 22/650; Church Yth Grp; Math Clb; Frsh Cls; Trk; Jr NHS; NHS; Ntl Merit Ltr; Spanish NHS; Trophy Penn-Jersey Chess League Indvidls Tournament 86; Comp Sci.

GRIM, DANIELLE; Bethel Park SR HS; Bethel Park, PA; (Y); 51/515; Church Yth Grp; FHA; Library Aide; Yrbk Stf; Var Timer; Hon Roll; Pres Schlr; Frank Hawthorne Math Schlrshp 86; Edinboro U Of PA; Secdry Ed.

GRIM, EARLEEN; Center HS; Martinsburg, WV; (Y); 8/185; Office Aide; Spanish Clb; SADD; Band; High Hon Roll; Hon Roll; Jr NHS; NHS; Pres Schlr; Shepherd Coll; Bus Adm.

GRIM, KELLY; Emmaus HS; Macungie, PA; (Y); Church Yth Grp; Key Clb; JV Stat Bsbl; Var Stat Bsktbl; High Hon Roll; Hon Roll; Jr NHS; NHS; Archt.

GRIM, REBECCA; Brandywine Heights HS; Alburtis, PA; (Y); Camp Fr Inc; Church Yth Grp; Pep Clb; Band; Church Choir; Concert Band; Mrchg Band; Pep Band; Nwsp Phtg; Nwsp Stf; Bus Adm.

GRIM, SUSAN; Boyertown HS; Barto, PA; (Y); 46/434; Chorus; Ed Yrbk Stf; VP Soph Cls; VP Jr Cls; VP Sr Cls; Var Capt Bsktbl; Var Capt Sftbl; Cit Awd; Scholastic Bowl; NHS; JR Miss Spirit Awd Berks Co 85-86; Wmns Clb Boyertown Scholar 85-86; Booster Clb Scholar 85-86; U DE; Bio Sci.

GRIMALDI, STEVEN V; Penn Hills SR HS; Pittsburgh, PA; (Y); French Clb; Hon Roll; Pt Park Coll; Mech Engrng Tech.

GRIMER, MONICA; York Catholic HS; York, PA; (Y); 37/171; French Clb; Latin Clb; Pep Clb; Var Capt Cheerleading; High Hon Roll; Hon Roll; Physcl Thrpy.

GRIMES, JAMES; Penn Cambria SR HS; Coupon, PA; (Y); French Clb; Band; Mrchg Band; JV Var Bsbl; Var L Ftbl; Var Wt Lftg; Hon Roll; Prfct Atten Awd; Comp.

GRIMES, LEE A; Old Forge HS; Old Forge, PA; (Y); 10/69; Hosp Aide; Ski Clb; Yrbk Ed-Chief; Var Capt Cheerleading; High Hon Roll; Hon Roll; Jr NHS; NHS; PA ST U; Chem Engrng.

GRIMES, MICHELLE; Meadowbrook Christian Schl; New Columbia, PA; (S); 1/8; Church Yth Grp; Yrbk Stf; Trs Frsh Cls; Trs Soph Cls; Trs Jr Cls; Socr; Hon Roll; NHS; Prfct Atten Awd; State Home Ec Awd 84 & 85; Hghst Cls Grd Avr 84 & 85; Bio Awd 85; Nrs.

GRIMES, PATRICK; Towanda Area HS; Wysox, PA; (Y); Boy Scts; Letterman Clb; Concert Band; Var L Crs Cntry; JV Trk; JV Wrstlng; Bus Mgmt.

GRIMM, CAY; Meyersdale Area HS; Meyersdale, PA; (Y); Pres French Clb; Band; Chorus; Church Choir; School Musical; Yrbk Stf; Stat Bsktbl; Wt Lftg; Hon Roll; NHS; 2nd Pl Am Leg Essay Cntst; Fnlst Tri ST Math Comptn; Villanova; Adv.

GRIMM, DANA; Lampeter-Strasburg HS; Lancaster, PA; (Y); 25/158; AFS; FHA; Girl Scts; Lit Mag; Polit Sci.

GRIMM, JEANNETTE; Clarion Area HS; Clarion, PA; (Y); Art Clb; Church Yth Grp; PAVAS; Chorus; Flag Corp; Score Keeper; Hon Roll; PA JR Acad Aci-3rd Pl 85-86; Clarion U; Bus.

GRIMM, MICHAEL; Tyrone Area HS; Tyrone, PA; (Y); Boy Scts; Church Yth Grp; Ski Clb; Varsity Clb; Var Bsktbl; Var Ftbl; Var Mgr(s); Var Trk; Elks Awd; God Cntry Awd; Eagle Scout 84; PA ST U; Mechanical Engrng.

GRIMM, SHAWN; Connellsville HS; Connellsville, PA; (Y); German Clb; Im Ftbl; Im Sftbl; Im Wt Lftg; High Hon Roll; Hon Roll.

GRIMME, TIMOTHY; Conemaugh Township Area HS; Holsapple, PA; (Y); 6/101; French Clb; Quiz Bowl; Ftbl; Trk; Wt Lftg; Hon Roll; NHS; Bst Entry-Silk Scrn Print 84-85; Duquesne; Med.

GRIMONE, BILLIE JO; Cameron County HS; Emporium, PA; (Y); 2/86; VP German Clb; VP Band; Pres Jr Cls; Stu Cncl; Hon Roll; NHS; Dlta Epsln Phi/Grmn Hnr Soc 85-86; Prm Qun 86; Pre-Law.

GRINBERG, MARNI; Taylor Allderdice HS; Pittsburgh, PA; (Y); Dance Clb; Ski Clb; Temple Yth Grp; Rep Stu Cncl; High Hon Roll; Hon Roll.

GRINOLDS, APRIL; St Marys Area HS; St Marys, PA; (Y); Pep Clb; Ski Clb; Yrbk Phtg; Yrbk Stf; Sec Jr Cls; JV Gym; JV Stat Trk; Hon Roll; NHS; Edinboro U; Photo.

GRIPPI, RICHARD F; Bishop Hannan HS; Scranton, PA; (Y); Church Yth Grp; Ski Clb; Speech Tm; JV Bsbl; Var Tennis; High Hon Roll; NHS; Rotary Awd; U Scranton; Crim Jstc.

GRISER, NANCY BETH; Mc Keesport Area SR HS; Mc Keesport, PA; (Y); 54/339; AFS; Exploring; German Clb; Orch; School Musical; Nwsp Stf; Hon Roll; Acad Tlntd Pgm; Med.

GRISWOLD, KATIE; Baldwin HS; Pittsburgh, PA; (Y); 176/535; Art Clb; Camp Fr Inc; Church Yth Grp; Cmnty Wkr; Teachers Aide; Band; Ntl Art Hnr Soc, Tn Inst Fnlst 86; Sec Ed.

GRITZAN, ROBERT W; Bethel Park HS; Bethel Park, PA; (Y); Hon Roll; Church Yth Grp; Computer Clb; JV Ftbl; NHS; Psych.

GROBA, STEVEN R; Elizabeth-Forward HS; Greenock, PA; (Y); Band; Concert Band; Drm & Bgl; Jazz Band; Mrchg Band; School Musical; High Hon Roll; Lion Awd; Mc Keesport Music Clb Schlrshp 86; Duquesne U Comp Awd 86; Duquesne U; Music Educ.

GROBINSKI, ANTHONY; John S Fine HS; Nanticoke, PA; (Y); 35/242; Letterman Clb; Ftbl; Wt Lftg; Capt Wrstlng; High Hon Roll; NHS; Lion Awd; Dr Joseph Gronka MVP Wrstlr 85-86; Dr Edward Baker Acad Achvt 86; Denas Schrlshp; Wilkes Coll; Sec Trch.

GROBLEWSKI, FRANK; Seton Catholic HS; Duryea, PA; (Y); Boy Scts; Mathletes; Ski Clb; Yrbk Phtg; Yrbk Stf; Capt Crs Cntry; High Hon Roll; NHS; Ntl Merit Ltr; U Scranton; Elec Engrng.

GROCHALSKI, RENEE; Seneca Valley SR HS; Mars, PA; (Y); Church Yth Grp; Office Aide; Ski Clb; Off Soph Cls; Off Jr Cls; Off Sr Cls; Off Stu Cncl; Pom Pon; Hon Roll; 2yrs Or More Stu Cncl Awd 85-86; Penn St.

GROCHOT, JULIE; Hempfield SR HS; Greensburg, PA; (Y); GAA; Office Aide; Band; Nwsp Phtg; Nwsp Rptr; JV L Bsktbl; JV L Sftbl; IN U Of PA; Photo Jrnslm.

GRODIN, LESLIE; Taylor Allderdice HS; Pittsburgh, PA; (Y); French Clb; JCL; Latin Clb; Yrbk Ed-Chief; Yrbk Stf; Stu Cncl; High Hon Roll; Hon Roll.

GROEBEL, SHARON; Westmont Hilltop HS; Johnstown, PA; (Y); Art Clb; VP French Clb; Key Clb; Var JV Bsktbl; L Swmmng; Psych.

GROFF, BARBRA; Mc Caskey HS; Bausman, PA; (Y); Chorus; Church Choir; Cheerleading; Mgr(s); Timer; Trk; High Hon Roll; Hon Roll; Jr NHS; St Joes Schl Nrsng; Nrsng.

GROFF, BILL; Manheim Township HS; Lancaster, PA; (Y); 66/325; Boy Scts; Church Yth Grp; Im Bsbl; Im Bowling; JV Socr; High Hon Roll; Hon Roll; JV Hgh Gm Awd 83-85; LYABA Tm Chmpn 84-85; Pre-Vet.

GROFF, JULIE; Lampeter-Strasburg HS; Lancaster, PA; (Y); 13/135; Sec Thesps; Band; VP Chorus; Jazz Band; Madrigals; School Musical; Yrbk Stf; NHS; Opt Clb Awd; Cnty, Dist, Regnl & ST Band 86; West Chester U; Music Educ.

GROFF, KATRINA; Hempfield HS; Mt Joy, PA; (Y); 114/435; Church Yth Grp; Chorus; School Musical; Variety Show; Fld Hcky; Var Powder Puff Ftbl; Hon Roll; Elem Educ.

GROFF, LORI; Blue Mountain HS; Sch Haven, PA; (Y); 57/214; Art Clb; Church Yth Grp; Exploring; Latin Clb; Chorus; Yrbk Phtg; Yrbk Stf; JV Var Cheerleading; Trk; Hon Roll; 3 Vrsty Ltrs 85-86; Penn ST U; Bus Adm.

GROFF, MARCEY; Grace Christian Schl; Ephrata, PA; (Y); Drama Clb; Teachers Aide; Chorus; Yrbk Stf; Var Capt Cheerleading; Var Fld Hcky; Var Sftbl; Var Tennis; Prfct Atten Awd; Coachs Awd Fld Hcky 85-86; Barnabas Awd Fld Hcky 84-86; Joshua Awd Sftbl 84-85; Chld Psych.

GROFF, PAUL; Ephrata SR HS; Ephrata, PA; (Y); 1/230; Trs Church Yth Grp; Math Tm; Nwsp Bus Mgr; VP NHS; Ntl Merit Ltr; Rotary Awd; Val; Computer Clb; Teachers Aide; Church Choir; Elizabeth Shaub Awd Exclnc Eng 86; Sci Fair 3rd Chem 86; Hnrbl Mntn Microcmptr 86; E Mennonite Clg; Comp Info Sys.

GROFF, TINA MARIE; J P Mccaskey HS; Lancaster, PA; (Y); AFS; Am Leg Aux Girls St; Teachers Aide; Chorus; Yrbk Stf; Var Cheerleading; Trk; Hon Roll; 3rd Pl Shot Put All Lg Meet 84; Elem Ed.

GROFF, TRACY A; Hempfield HS; Landisville, PA; (Y); 11/400; Pres Frsh Cls; Pres Soph Cls; Var L Crs Cntry; Var L Trk; NHS; Ntl Merit Ltr; Rotary Awd; Church Yth Grp; Exploring; Quiz Bowl; Michael Lawrence Siepietowski Mem Trk Awd 86; Hempfield Ed Assn Scholar 86; Pres Acad Fit Awd 86; U NH; Spn.

GROHOL, MARK; West Hazleton HS; W Hazleton, PA; (Y); 30/270; Boy Scts; Church Yth Grp; Ski Clb; Golf; Tennis; High Hon Roll; Hon Roll; Optometry.

GROLL, DIANNE; West Mifflin Area HS; W Mifflin, PA; (Y); Teachers Aide; Band; Concert Band; Mrchg Band; Tennis; Trk; Hon Roll; Pa ST U; Acctg.

GROLLER, TRACY; Pen Argyl Area HS; Nazareth, PA; (Y); 9/166; Concert Band; Sec Orch; Pom Pon; Capt Twrlr; High Hon Roll; NHS; Pen Argyl Ed Assoc Schlrshp 86; Pres Acad Ftns Awd 86; Bloomsburg U; Bus.

GROMALSKI, KRISTA; Marian Catholic HS; Mahanoy City, PA; (Y); 39/115; French Clb; SADD; JV Bsktbl; Var L Sftbl; Jrnlsm.

GROMAN, KRISTA; Spring-Ford Area Sr HS; Spring City, PA; (Y); 27/254; Church Yth Grp; French Clb; Girl Scts; Pep Clb; Ski Clb; Rep Frsh Cls; Rep Soph Cls; Rep Jr Cls; Rep Sr Cls; Rep Stu Cncl; All Leag; All Star Tm 85-86; All Area Tm 85-86; Acctg.

GROMAN, MICHAEL J; Marion Center HS; Indiana, PA; (Y); 43/170; Church Yth Grp; Spanish Clb; Varsity Clb; VP Off Frsh Cls; Sec Soph Cls; Off Stu Cncl; Var JV Bsbl; Bowling; Var JV Ftbl; Hon Roll; MIP Bsbl 86; Engrng.

GRONAUER, BOB; G A R HS; Wilkes Barre, PA; (Y); 13/187; Aud/Vis; German Clb; Chorus; Var L Bsbl; JV Bsktbl; Var Capt Ftbl; Var Wt Lftg; Hon Roll; NHS; Law.

GRONAUER, ROBERT; G A R HS; Wilkes Barre, PA; (S); 13/187; Church Yth Grp; Chorus; Var L Bsbl; JV Bsktbl; Var L Ftbl; Wt Lftg; Hon Roll; Jr NHS; NHS; Acctg.

GRONDWALSKI, ANDREA; Highlands SR HS; Natrona Hts, PA; (Y); Hosp Aide; Key Clb; Sftbl; Hon Roll; Dietcs.

GRONSKI JR, JOSEPH G; Pittston Area HS; Pittston, PA; (Y); Trs Math Clb; Science Clb; Ski Clb; Im Sftbl; Var Swmmng; Hon Roll; U Of Scranton; Bio.

GROOM, BRENDA; West Allegheny SR HS; Imperial, PA; (Y); 1/199; Church Yth Grp; Exploring; Office Aide; Spanish Clb; Band; Concert Band; Mrchg Band; Pep Band; High Hon Roll; Pres NHS; Pre-Med.

GROOVER, ANITA L; Canton Area HS; Canton, PA; (Y); 26/124; Trs Church Yth Grp; Letterman Clb; Band; Chorus; Concert Band; Mrchg Band; Rep Stu Cncl; Sftbl; Vllybl; Soc Distngushd Am Stu 83-86.

GROOVER, TAMMY; Cowanesque Valley HS; Westfield, PA; (Y); Church Yth Grp; Computer Clb; 4-H; Chorus; Color Guard; Mrchg Band; Nwsp Stf; Yrbk Stf; JV Cheerleading; JV Pom Pon; Olean Bus Inst; Exec Sec.

GROSCH, LYNN; MMI Prep School; Drums, PA; (S); Art Clb; Pres Debate Tm; Model UN; School Play; Yrbk Stf; Pres Soph Cls; Off Stu Cncl; Hon Roll; NHS; NEDT Awd; Schl Spch Awd; PJAS 2nd Pl; Music Ed.

GROSCH, MICHAEL; Clarion Area HS; Shippenville, PA; (S); Band; Chorus; Church Choir; Jazz Band; Pep Band; School Musical; Swing Chorus; High Hon Roll; Dist & Regnl Band 85; Hnrs Bnd 84; Pharm.

GROSE, WENDY; Hanover Area HS; Wilkes Barre, PA; (Y); 5/169; Model UN; Chorus; Concert Band; Mrchg Band; School Musical; Yrbk Stf; Vllybl; High Hon Roll; Jr NHS; NHS; Cert Of Educ Dev Ntl 84; Outstndng Sci Stu Awd 84; Nrsng.

GROSKO, JOHN; South Park HS; Library, PA; (S); 10/212; Drama Clb; Nwsp Stf; Swmmng; High Hon Roll; NHS; NEDT Awd; Prtcptn Rotary Intl Yth Ldrshp Conf 86; Archtct.

GROSKOPF, NANCY; North Hills HS; Pittsburgh, PA; (S); 28/505; Boy Scts; Church Yth Grp; Exploring; Keywanettes; Nwsp Stf; L Socr; JV Tennis; JV Trk; High Hon Roll; NHS; Natl Fdrtn Msc Clbs Excllnt Rtng 82; Pittsbrgh Piano Tchrs Assoc Supr Rtng 82; PA ST; Finance.

GROSS, ALLEN; Peters Twp HS; Venetia, PA; (Y); Mrchg Band; High Hon Roll; Hon Roll; Prfct Atten Awd; U Of Pittsburgh; Engrg.

GROSS, AMY; Pottsgrove HS; Pottstown, PA; (Y); 40/229; VP JA; Science Clb; Spanish Clb; Teachers Aide; Varsity Clb; Orch; Nwsp Rptr; Var L Fld Hcky; Var Trk; Hon Roll; Elem Educ.

GROSS, BARBARA; Exeter Twp SR HS; Douglassville, PA; (Y); 39/215; Church Yth Grp; Exploring; Q&S; Quiz Bowl; Church Choir; Yrbk Stf; JV Bowling; High Hon Roll; Jr NHS; NHS; Yrbk Achvt Awd 85; Messiah Coll.

GROSS, BILL; Cathedral Prep; Erie, PA; (Y); 1/230; Latin Clb; Model UN; Ski Clb; Var Cheerleading; JV Socr; High Hon Roll; NHS; Ntl Merit Ltr; Val; Im Bsktbl; Prsdntl Acad Ftnss Awd 1986; Rochester Inst Of Tech:Micro.

GROSS, DIANE; Bellfonte Area SR HS; Pleasant Gap, PA; (Y); Ski Clb; SADD; Band; Drm Mjr(t); Rep Jr Cls; Rep Sr Cls; Var L Gym; Im Powder Puff Ftbl; Var L Trk; Im Vllybl; PA ST U; Dietician.

GROSS, JAMES; Quigley HS; Baden, PA; (S); 2/112; Boy Scts; Church Yth Grp; Math Clb; Capt L Crs Cntry; L Trk; High Hon Roll; Lion Awd; NHS; Egl Awd Rcpnt 86; Echrstc Mnstr 85-86; Lehigh U; Cvl Engrng.

GROSS, KIRSTEN; Annville-Cleona HS; Lebanon, PA; (S); 4/110; Church Yth Grp; 4-H; Model UN; Band; Church Choir; Concert Band; Mrchg Band; Coach Actv; Sftbl; 4-H Awd; 4-H ST Chmpn Wrtng Hntr 85; Vrtnry Med.

GROSS, LORI; Northeastern SR HS; Manchester, PA; (Y); SADD; Band; Chorus; Pres Frsh Cls; Rep Soph Cls; Rep Jr Cls; Rep Sr Cls; Rep Stu Cncl; Hon Roll; NHS; Engl.

GROSS, MARIA; Littlestown HS; Littlestown, PA; (Y); VP Band; Chorus; VP Concert Band; Jazz Band; VP Mrchg Band; Pep Band; School Musical; Rep Stu Cncl; Dist Band 85 & 86; Csmtlgy.

GROSS, SHERRI L; Athens HS; Sayre, PA; (Y); 1/125; Drama Clb; Hosp Aide; Library Aide; Chorus; Concert Band; Mrchg Band; Orch; Rep Stu Cncl; Gov Hon Prg Awd; High Hon Roll; Wells Coll; Bio.

GROSS, STACEY; William Allen HS; Allentown, PA; (Y); 111/600; Art Clb; Intnl Clb; JA; Model UN; Pres VP Service Clb; Yrbk Stf; Rep Jr Cls; Rep Sr Cls; Bowling; Sftbl; Ithaca Coll; Sclgy.

GROSS JR, STEVEN H; York County Vo-Tech; Manchester, PA; (Y); 19/391; Church Yth Grp; Cmnty Wkr; 4-H; Ski Clb; VICA; Capt Vllybl; Wt Lftg; 4-H Awd; High Hon Roll; Hon Roll; Shlh Grdn Clb Schlrshp 86; 3rd Pl PA ST VICA Wldng Comptn 86; Yrk Mfg Assn Gld Wtch Awd 86; Cobleskill A&T Coll; Frmr.

GROSS, SUSAN; Bethlehem Catholic HS; Bethlehem, PA; (Y); 1/219; Math Tm; Red Cross Aide; Ski Clb; Band; Yrbk Stf; Frsh Cls; Bsktbl; Fld Hcky; High Hon Roll; NHS; Rnsselaer Poly Tech Inst; Engr.

GROSS, TIMOTHY; Upper Dublin HS; Ambler, PA; (Y); Drama Clb; Intnl Clb; Band; Chorus; Church Choir; Concert Band; Jazz Band; Mrchg Band; Orch; Pep Band; UCLA; Music.

GROSS JR, VINCENT R; West York Area HS; York, PA; (Y); Concert Band; Jazz Band; Symp Band; Hon Roll; Tour Europe W/PA Ambssdrs Of Music 85; Tri-M Ntl Music Hon Soc 85; PA ST U; Acctg.

GROSSEK, PAMELA; Canon-Mc Millan SR HS; Cecil, PA; (Y); Drama Clb; English Clb; Band; Chorus; Concert Band; Flag Corp; Mrchg Band; School Play; Ski Clb; Church Choir; Majrt 83-84; Gftd Prog 83-86; Advtsg.

GROSSER, JAMES; Connellsville Area SR HS; Connellsville, PA; (Y); 22/525; Boy Scts; Camera Clb; Church Yth Grp; Stage Crew; Nwsp Stf; Yrbk Stf; High Hon Roll; Rep Stu Cncl; Mgr(s); Pitts Provost Day Math Comp Semi-Fnlst 85; Provost Schlr Schlrshp 86; Hnrs Engrng Schlrshp 86; U Of Pittsburgh; Elec Engrng.

GROSSGLASS, PAMELA L; Hamburg Area HS; Painted Post, NY; (Y); 11/152; Trs Church Yth Grp; Hst German Clb; Sec Chorus; School Musical; School Play; Rep NHS; Grmn Nat Hnr Scty VP; Acad Awd Trgnmtry & Algbr Iii; Lcl Rtry Clb; Valley Forge Christian Coll; Ed.

GROSSI, KEVIN; West Scranton HS; Scranton, PA; (Y); Letterman Clb; PAVAS; Ski Clb; Band; Concert Band; Drm & Bgl; Jazz Band; Mrchg Band; Orch; Pep Band; 1st Chair Awd-Band 83-86; Dntstry.

GROSSMAN, BETH; Lower Moreland HS; Huntingdon Valley, PA; (S); 40/214; Drama Clb; Sec German Clb; SADD; School Musical; Yrbk Stf; Pres Sr Cls; Var Capt Trk; Hon Roll; PA ST U; Pre-Law.

GROSSMAN, MELISSA; Moniteau JR SR HS; West Sunbury, PA; (Y); Sec Trs FBLA; Library Aide; Spanish Clb; SADD; Chorus; Color Guard; Cheerleading; Hon Roll; Acctg.

GROSSNICKLE, JANET M; Elizabethtown Area HS; Elizabethtown, PA; (Y); 5/221; Church Yth Grp; Computer Clb; Math Tm; Ski Clb; Ed Lit Mag; Powder Puff Ftbl; NHS; Ntl Merit SF; Grl Of Mnth 85-86; Accntg I Awd 84-85; Northwestern U; Ind Engrg.

GROSSO, JANET; Abp Prendergast HS; Upper Darby, PA; (Y); 2/361; SADD; Church Choir; Rep Orch; School Musical; High Hon Roll; NHS; Ntl Merit Ltr; Pres Schlr; Mdrn Music Mstrs 84-86; St Josephs U; Cmptr Sci.

GROSZ, ELIZABETH; Pennsbury HS; Morrisville, PA; (Y); Art Clb; Dance Clb; Intnl Clb; Political Wkr; Church Choir; Var L Diving; Hon Roll; NHS; Ntl Merit Ltr; Rotary Awd; Fshn Dsgn.

GROTE, THERESA; Spring Grove HS; York, PA; (Y); Church Yth Grp; Drama Clb; Key Clb; Acpl Chr; Chorus; Color Guard; School Play; Stage Crew; Var Cheerleading; Jr NHS; Elem Educ.

GROTHEN, CORY; Gettysburg SR HS; Gettysburg, PA; (Y); Chess Clb; Spanish Clb; Pres Sr Cls; Hon Roll; NHS; Arch Drftng.

GROTSTEIN, JODI; Alblerdice HS; Pittsburgh, PA; (Y); French Clb; Ski Clb; Rep Stu Cncl; Bowling; Socr; Hon Roll.

GROUP, CRAIG; Boiling Springs HS; Boiling Spgs, PA; (Y); Band; Jazz Band; Mrchg Band; Stage Crew; Nwsp Rptr; Nwsp Stf; Hon Roll; Pres Acad Fit Awd 86; Sound Of Amer Hnr Band/Chorus 86; PA ST U; Accntng.

GROVE, CHARLES; Hopewell HS; Hookstown, PA; (Y); 37/297; VP Pres Art Clb; VP Pres Spanish Clb; Band; Chorus; Jazz Band; School Play; Variety Show; High Hon Roll; NHS; Pres Schlr; May Crt 86; Slippery Rock U; Spnsh.

GROVE, DAPHNE; Exeter Twp HS; Reading, PA; (Y); Sec Church Yth Grp; Drama Clb; Hosp Aide; Leo Clb; Spanish Clb; Y-Teens; Band; Concert Band; Mrchg Band; Orch; Lafayette; Cmmnctns.

GROVE, DAVID; Beaver Valley Christian Acad; Beaver, PA; (Y); 1/13; Speech Tm; Nwsp Rptr; Nwsp Stf; VP Soph Cls; Pres Jr Cls; Var Bsktbl; Socr; Sftbl; High Hon Roll; Hon Roll; Audio Engnr.

GROVE, JEFFREY A; Big Spring HS; Shippensburg, PA; (Y); Var L Crs Cntry; Var L Swmmng; Var L Trk; Bausch & Lomb Sci Awd; High Hon Roll; Lion Awd; NHS; Ntl Merit Ltr; Air Force ROTC 4 Yr Schlrshp 86; U Deleware; Mechncl.

GROVE, KELLY; West York Area HS; York, PA; (Y); 21/194; Varsity Clb; JV Var Bsktbl; Hon Roll; Prfct Atten Awd; Engnrng.

GROVE, KRISTIE; Middletown Area HS; Middletown, PA; (Y); 3/166; Sec FCA; Band; Chorus; Concert Band; Mrchg Band; Swing Chorus; Yrbk Stf; JV Gym; Hon Roll; NHS; Acad All Amer 85 & 86; Biopsych.

GROVE, LARISA; Mechanicsburg SR HS; Mechanicsburg, PA; (Y); 7/350; Band; Chorus; School Play; Stu Cncl; Socr; High Hon Roll; NHS; Ntl Merit SF; 1st Pl Stu Cmbrlnd Cnty Cnsrvtn Schl 85; 1st Lt NDCC 84&85; Sec Trs Ordr Of Rd Flm 85-86; Bio.

GROVE, LISA; Middletown Area HS; Middletown, PA; (Y); 3/189; Pres FCA; Chorus; Mrchg Band; Symp Band; Nwsp Ed-Chief; Yrbk Ed-Chief; DAR Awd; Kiwanis Awd; NHS; Elks Natl Fndtn Schlrshp 86; Phi Delta Kappa Schlrshp 86; Alumni Assoc Schlrshp 86; Alvernia Coll; Elem Edu.

GROVE, MARK; Cathedral Prep; Mckean, PA; (Y); 71/216; Church Yth Grp; Hon Roll; Prfct Atten Awd; Engrng.

GROVE, PENNY D; Red Lion Area SR HS; Felton, PA; (Y); 21/372; VP Sec Church Yth Grp; Cmnty Wkr; Varsity Clb; Yrbk Rptr; Im Coach Actv; Var L Vllybl; High Hon Roll; Hon Roll; NHS; Church Choir; Volleyball Team Best Attitude Award 84; PENN ST; Vet Med.

GROVE, PETER; Uniontown Area HS; Uniontown, PA; (Y); 15/320; Trs Am Leg Boys St; Ski Clb; Var L Bsbl; Var L Golf; CC Awd; French Hon Soc; High Hon Roll; Jr NHS; NHS; Rotary Awd; WA Coll; Pre-Med.

GROVE, RAFE; Elizabethtown Area HS; Elizabethtown, PA; (Y); 35/237; Chorus; Stu Cncl; Var Capt Cheerleading; Sec Church Yth Grp; Teachers Aide; Church Choir; VP Soph Cls; Trk; All Star Chrldr 85; WA Dc Close Up Prog 86; Polticl Sci.

GROVE, TAMMY; Tyrone Area HS; Altoona, PA; (Y); Key Clb; NFL; Band; Concert Band; Mrchg Band; Nwsp Rptr; Cheerleading; Shippenburg U; Engl.

GROVES, JENNIFER S; Karns City JR SR HS; Petrolia, PA; (Y); 29/122; Band; Chorus; Concert Band; Mrchg Band; Rep Stu Cncl; Hon Roll; VFW Awd; SADD; Jazz Band; Orch; Free Enterprise Wk Schlrshp 86; Hnry K C Band Ad 83-85; Taps Leg Awd 83-86; Butler County CC; Nrsng.

GROVES, TRACY LYNN M; Bradford Central Christian HS; Bradford, PA; (Y); Drama Clb; Pep Clb; Ski Clb; SADD; Yrbk Stf; Hon Roll; Jr NHS; NHS; Ntl Merit Ltr; IN U Of PA; Elem Educ.

GROW, JONATHAN; Conemaugh Township HS; Davidsville, PA; (Y); 11/101; Church Yth Grp; Nwsp Stf; Yrbk Stf; Bsktbl; Golf; Hon Roll; NHS; Penn ST; Arch.

GROW, LISA; Shamokin Area HS; Shamokin, PA; (Y); 20/250; Sec Key Clb; Varsity Clb; Sec Frsh Cls; Sec Soph Cls; Sec Jr Cls; Sec Sr Cls; Sec Stu Cncl; Capt Cheerleading; L Swmmng; NHS; Psych.

GROW, SHANNON; Bellefonte Area SR HS; Bellefonte, PA; (Y); Hosp Aide; SADD; Chorus; Church Choir; Color Guard; Capt Flag Corp; Mrchg Band; School Musical; Yrbk Stf; Stu Cncl; Jnr Miss Cntstnt 85-86; Rgnl & All ST Chrs 86; Penn ST U; Jrnlsm.

GROY, CHRISTINA; Lebanon Catholic HS; Lebanon, PA; (Y); Church Yth Grp; Cmnty Wkr; Dance Clb; Drama Clb; English Clb; FNA; German Clb; GAA; Girl Scts; Hosp Aide; St Josephs Sch Nrsng; Biol.

GROZNIK, TERESA; Montour HS; Mc Kees Rocks, PA; (Y); Church Yth Grp; GAA; JV Var Cheerleading; Var L Swmmng; Var L Tennis; Hon Roll; Phys Thrpy.

GRUBB, CHRIS; Springford HS; Royersford, PA; (Y); 87/256; Church Yth Grp; French Clb; Pep Clb; Yrbk Sprt Ed; Stu Cncl; Cheerleading; Fld Hcky; Lcrss; Sftbl; Hon Roll; Elem Ed.

GRUBB, LINDA; Everett Area HS; Clearville, PA; (Y); 13/100; FHA; GAA; Varsity Clb; L Sftbl; JV Capt Vllybl; Altton Vo-Tech; Culinary Arts.

GRUBB, SUSAN; Middletown Area HS; Middletown, PA; (Y); HACC; Nrsng.

GRUBBS, GRETCHEN; Albert Gallatin HS; Smithfield, PA; (Y); VP 4-H; VP Frsh Cls; Rep Stu Cncl; Stat Bsktbl; God Cntry Awd; Hon Roll; Jr NHS.

GRUBBS, KATE; Avonworth HS; Pittsbg, PA; (Y); AFS; JCL; Latin Clb; Varsity Clb; Band; Nwsp Stf; Pres Frsh Cls; Sec Jr Cls; Trs Sr Cls; Stat Bsktbl; Lib Arts.

GRUBE, HEATHER M; Gettysburg SR HS; Gettysburg, PA; (Y); 1/253; Church Yth Grp; Pep Clb; Varsity Clb; Yrbk Phtg; Yrbk Sprt Ed; Crs Cntry; Trk; DAR Awd; High Hon Roll; Ntl Merit SF; Natl Hnr Soc Treas 85-86; Excllnc Bio 83-84; Medcl Schl.

GRUBE, MICHELLE; Ephrata SR HS; Akron, PA; (Y); 7/235; Rep Church Yth Grp; Nwsp Sprt Ed; Bsktbl; Trk; Hon Roll; NHS; Band; Concert Band; Jazz Band; Orch.

GRUBE, PAMELA; Hamburg HS; Bethel, PA; (Y); 67/150; Rep Frsh Cls; Rep Soph Cls; Rep Jr Cls; Rep Sr Cls; Rep Stu Cncl; Var Capt Fld Hcky; Var Capt Sftbl; Hon Roll; Outstndng Sftbl & Hcky Athltc 86; Alvernia; Phy Thpry.

GRUBE, PETER; New Hope Solebury HS; Solebury, PA; (S); Church Yth Grp; Ski Clb; Yrbk Stf; Rep Stu Cncl; Var Socr; High Hon Roll; NHS; Frnch Awd Merit 84; Engrng.

GRUBE, ROBIN; Liberty HS; Bethlehem, PA; (Y); 40/475; Pres Church Yth Grp; Hon Roll; Var L Fld Hcky; Bus Mgmt.

GRUBE, STEVEN; Clearfield Area HS; Clearfield, PA; (Y); 11/390; Var Ftbl; Natl Hnr Socty; IN U Of PA; Comp Sci.

GRUBE, WENDY; Freedom HS; Bethlehem, PA; (Y); 257/456; Trs Church Yth Grp; Cmnty Wkr; Exploring; French Clb; Trs Hosp Aide; Science Clb; Chorus; Church Choir; School Musical; Nrsng.

GRUBER, MARK; East Pennsboro SR HS; Enola, PA; (Y); 29/180; Art Clb; Boy Scts; VP Church Yth Grp; VP German Clb; Trs Varsity Clb; School Musical; School Play; JV Var Bsbl; JV Var Socr; Swmmng; Presdntl Ftns Awd; Penn ST; Engrng.

GRUBER, TIM; Lower Dauphin HS; Hummelstown, PA; (S); Rptr FFA; JV Var Bsbl; JV L Ftbl; Socr; USNAA U S Natl Ag Awd 85-86; Penn ST; Forst Rngr.

GRUCA, BETH; Bishop Mc Cort HS; Johnstown, PA; (Y); 19/129; Exploring; Girl Scts; Latin Clb; Orch; High Hon Roll; Hon Roll; Boy Scts; Dance Clb; JA; Math Clb; Johnstwn Rotary Foundtn Awd-Schlrshp 86; Natl Schl Orchestra Awd 86; Latin Awd 86; PA ST U-U Pk; Anthroplgy.

GRUCA, TRACY ANNE; Seneca Valley HS; Zelienople, PA; (Y); Sec Church Yth Grp; FTA; Thesps; Chorus; School Musical; School Play; Stage Crew; High Hon Roll; Hon Roll; Spec Ed.

GRUDKOWSKI, DAVID; John S Fine HS; Nanticoke, PA; (S); 9/256; Ski Clb; Golf; High Hon Roll; NHS; U Scranton; Med.

GRUDZINSKI, CINDI; Allentown Central Catholic HS; Allentown, PA; (Y); 18/210; Exploring; Service Clb; Band; Concert Band; Drill Tm; Mrchg Band; Pep Band; High Hon Roll; Hon Roll; NHS; VA Polytech Inst; Archtctr.

GRUENLOH, JENNIE; John S Fine SR HS; Glen Lyon, PA; (S); 2/260; Model UN; Speech Tm; Nwsp Rptr; JV Sftbl; High Hon Roll; NHS; Ntl Merit Ltr; NEDT Awd; Sons Italy Essy Cont Wnr 84; CCD Instrctr 85; Upwrd Bnd Stu Govt 84-85; Med.

GRUNDEN, KYLE; Waynesboro Area SR HS; Blue Ridge Summit, PA; (Y); 24/381; Chorus; Concert Band; Jazz Band; Boy Scts; Rep Jr Cls; Var Ftbl; JV Capt Wrstlng; NHS; Amer Lgn Schl Awd 84; Outstndng Ctznshp Awd 84; Air Force Offcr.

GRUNDY, DAVID; Franklin Regional SR HS; Murrysville, PA; (Y); Art Clb; Wrstlng; High Hon Roll; Hon Roll; Engrng.

GRUSKY, TORI; Punxsutawney Area SR HS; Anita, PA; (Y); Art Clb; FBLA; GAA; Office Aide; Nwsp Rptr; Nwsp Stf; Pres Jr Cls; Rep Stu Cncl; 2nd Pl Bus Grphcs FBLA Reg Conf 85; Sec.

GRUVER, JASON; Governor Mifflin HS; Reading, PA; (Y); 34/274; Rep Stu Cncl; Var JV Socr; Var Trk; JV Wrstlng; Hon Roll; U Of Miami; Intntl Rltns.

GRYCZKO, MARGARET; Scranton Preparatory Schl; Clarks Green, PA; (Y); Church Yth Grp; Dance Clb; Debate Tm; Teachers Aide; Chorus; Trk; PA Jr Acad Of Sci 82-85; Occptnl Thrpy.

GRYZBEK, PETE; Brockway HS; Brockway, PA; (Y); 29/90; Exploring; VP FFA; PA ST; Bus.

GRZECH, HOLLY; Lakeland HS; Carbon Dale, PA; (Y); Scholastic Bowl; Science Clb; Chorus; School Musical; Cheerleading; High Hon Roll; NHS; Ntl Merit Ltr; Pres Schlr; Hstry Awd 86; PA JR Acad Sci Awd 82-84; U Scranton; Med.

GRZYWACZ, LAURA; Scranton Prep; Mayfield, PA; (Y); 114/192; Hosp Aide; Yrbk Stf; Var Trk; Hon Roll; Athltc Trng.

GRZYWINSKI, PATRICIA; Southmoreland SR HS; Scottdale, PA; (Y); Latin Clb; Ski Clb; Spanish Clb; Chorus; Yrbk Phtg; Yrbk Stf; Gym; Powder Puff Ftbl; Spanish NHS; PA Coll Optmtry; Optmtry.

GSELL, DEBBI; Waynesboro Area SR HS; Waynesboro, PA; (Y); Ski Clb; Yrbk Stf; Rep Soph Cls; Rep Sec Stu Cncl; Var Capt Cheerleading; Hon Roll; Prfct Atten Awd; Bio.

GUAETTA, CHAD; Laurel Valley HS; Seward, PA; (Y); 9/87; Church Yth Grp; Varsity Clb; Chorus; JV Var Ftbl; High Hon Roll; Hon Roll; NHS; Hlth.

GUBER, DEBORAH LYNN; Spring-Ford HS; Linfield, PA; (S); 7/230; French Clb; Concert Band; Mrchg Band; High Hon Roll; NHS; Dist XI Band 84-86; Regn XI Band 85-86; Natl Yng Ldrs Conf 86; Smith Coll; Govt.

GUBISH, MICHELE L; Liberty HS; Bethlehem, PA; (Y); 67/475; JV Bsktbl; JV Var Sftbl; Hon Roll; Cert Merit Achvt Typng Olympcs; Cert Merit & Princpls Awd Achvt Typng Olympcs; Aviatn.

GUDAITIS, SUSAN; Gar Memorial HS; Wilkes Barre, PA; (S); Exploring; Key Clb; Chorus; Tennis; Hon Roll; NHS; Luzerne CC; Nrsg.

GUEDES, MATTHEW L; Palmerton Area HS; Palmerton, PA; (Y); 7/149; Am Leg Boys St; Church Yth Grp; Cmnty Wkr; Pres Soph Cls; Var L Bsbl; Bsktbl; Var L Ftbl; Hon Roll; Acadc Awd Sci 83-84; Awd Span 83-84; Awd Am Hist 84; Marine Bio.

GUELCHER, SARA; Villa Maria Acad; Erie, PA; (Y); Ski Clb; Yrbk Rptr; Yrbk Stf; Fshn Mrchndsng.

GUELICH, DENNIS; Clearfield Area HS; Clearfield, PA; (Y); French Clb; Key Clb; Diving; Swmmng; Sierra Acad Aeronautics; Air Pl.

GUERCIO, LESLIE; Kiski Area HS; Leechburg, PA; (Y); French Clb; Pep Clb; Spanish Clb; Y-Teens; Chorus; Nwsp Bus Mgr; Nwsp Rptr; Nwsp Stf; Rep Frsh Cls; Stu Cncl; U Pittsburgh; Publc Rltns.

GUERIN, SHEILA; Canon-Mc Millan HS; Mc Murray, PA; (Y); French Clb; Var Diving; Var JV Gym; Hon Roll; Stdnt Ldrshp Awd 83-84; Arch.

GUERINO, KENNETH; Lower Moreland HS; Huntingdon Valley, PA; (S); Cmnty Wkr; English Clb; French Clb; Band; Concert Band; L Crs Cntry; Ftbl; Trk; Hon Roll; Pres Phys Ftnss Awd 83; Frnch Ctznshp Awd 83.

GUERRA, CHERYL; Phil-Mont Christian Acad; Maple Glen, PA; (Y); Church Yth Grp; Political Wkr; Chorus; Stat Bsktbl; Score Keeper; Hon Roll; Bus.

GUERRANT, DARRYL; Bishop Mc Devitt HS; Philadelphia, PA; (Y); Boy Scts; Morehouse Coll; Comp Sci.

GUERRIERI, AMY; Brownsville Area SR HS; Republic, PA; (S); 1/250; Drama Clb; Ski Clb; Band; Flag Corp; Stat Trk; High Hon Roll; NHS; Mathletes; Math Tm; Sci & Humanities Symposium At Penn ST U 85; Exec Brd Of Interact Clb; Pre-Med.

GUFFEY, TIMOTHY; Milton Area SR HS; New Columbia, PA; (Y); 37/202; Latin Clb; Chorus; JV Ftbl; Im Wt Lftg; JV Wrstlng; Latn Awd Hgh Lvl Stdy Profcncy 85; Stdnt Totl Fit Awd Slvr Levl Of Totl Fitnss 86; Citadel; Elctrcl Engr.

GUFFROUICH, PAUL; John S Fine HS; Nanticoke, PA; (S); 2/260; L Var Bsbl; Capt Var Bsktbl; High Hon Roll; NHS; Undrclsmn Al-ST Bsktbl 83-84; 2-Tm Al-Schlstc Bsktbl 83-85.

GUGLIOTTA, TANYA C; South Fayette JR SR HS; Oakdale, PA; (Y); Drama Clb; Chorus; School Musical; Variety Show; Yrbk Stf; Schlrshp Study MPAC 85-86; Schlrshp To Wk Pittsbrgh Dance Alloy GATE 85; Capa Prfmng Arts 84-85; Dancer.

GUICHETEAU, SUSAN; Bishop Mc Devitt HS; Fort Washington, PA; (Y); 2/356; Art Clb; Church Yth Grp; Science Clb; Ski Clb; Stage Crew; Yrbk Stf; Capt Powder Puff Ftbl; Swmmng; High Hon Roll; Sal; Schlrshp Awd P A Soc Prof Engrns 86; Gold Mdl Acad Exclnc Calculus, Engl 4 86; Villanora U; Engrng.

GUIDASH, LORI BETH; Punxsutawney HS; Punxsutawney, PA; (Y); 56/254; FBLA; Band; Concert Band; Drill Tm; Mrchg Band; Yrbk Stf; Wrstlng; Hon Roll; Ftr Bus Ldrs Am 84-85; Bus Schl.

GUIDASH, MELISSA; Punxsutawney Area HS; Rossiter, PA; (Y); Band; Med.

GUIDO, LISA; Ambridge HS; Ambridge, PA; (S); GAA; Girl Scts; Nwsp Stf; Jr Cls; Sr Cls; JV Bsktbl; Golf; Score Keeper; Var Sftbl; PA ST.

GUIHER, KATHY L; Saltsburg JR SR HS; Saltsburg, PA; (Y); 13/94; Church Yth Grp; Varsity Clb; Band; Concert Band; Mrchg Band; Orch; Pep Band; School Musical; Nwsp Ed-Chief; Sec Frsh Cls; Math.

GUILFOYLE, BRIDGET; Punksutawney Area HS; Punxsutawney, PA; (Y); French Clb; Math Clb; Math Tm; Band; Color Guard; Concert Band; Jazz Band; Mrchg Band; Pep Band; Hon Roll; IN U; Pre Law.

GUILLEUX, FRANCOIS; Upper Dublin HS; Ambler, PA; (Y); 43/320; Boy Scts; Varsity Clb; Rep Frsh Cls; Rep Soph Cls; Chrmn Stu Cncl; Ftbl; L Swmmng; NHS; 1st Pl Spnsh I Cmptn Mntgmry Cnty.

GUILLIAMS, JANET; Nazareth Acad; Philadelphia, PA; (Y); Sec Boy Scts; Pres Sec Exploring; French Clb; Red Cross Aide; Nwsp Stf; Lit Mag; Cert Of Rcgntn Cmpltng SCOP Trnng Prg 85; Trophy 1st Girl Boy Scout Troop 85; Merit Bdg Boy Scouts 85; Thomas Jefferson U; Cyto Tech.

GUIN, MARY; Bensalem HS; Rockaway Township, NJ; (Y); Art Clb; Church Yth Grp; GAA; Key Clb; Latin Clb; Pep Clb; Spanish Clb; Stu Cncl; Var Stat Mgr(s); Var L Tennis; Christiansburg Ten Tm Mst Imprvd 85.

GUINDON, KATHRYN; Lebanon SR HS; Lebanon, PA; (Y); #6 In Class; Pres Church Yth Grp; Pres VP Girl Scts; Band; Chorus; VP Orch; Var Stat Trk; NHS; German Clb; Pep Clb; Science Clb; Natl Orch Awd 86; Pres Envrnmntl Yth Awd 84; Grl Scout Silv Awd 84; Bio.

GUINEE, PATRICK; Bishop Carroll HS; Cresson, PA; (S); 2/107; Ski Clb; Chorus; Rep Stu Cncl; Hon Roll; Jr NHS; NEDT Awd; U S Studnt Councl Awd 85; St Francis Coll Of PA; Med.

GUISE, BRAD; Central York HS; York, PA; (Y); 4-H; JV Ftbl; Im Vllybl; Hon Roll; Envrnmntl Sci.

GUISE, LISA; Owen J Roberts HS; Pottstown, PA; (S); 4/291; Hosp Aide; JA; Concert Band; Mrchg Band; Stu Cncl; Var Swmmng; High Hon Roll; NHS; Ntl Merit SF; Clss Rep To TMOT Spnsrd By GE Space Ctr 85; Med Tech.

GUISE, PATRICK J; Northeast Catholic HS; Philadelphia, PA; (Y); 89/362; Hon Roll; Ntl Merit Ltr.

GUISLER, LISA M; Midland HS; Midland, PA; (Y); 1/42; Band; Chorus; Drm Mjr(t); Jazz Band; Mrchg Band; Yrbk Stf; Trs Jr Cls; Var Bsktbl; Var Cheerleading; Twrlr; Acad All Amrcn 85-86; US Achvt Math & Engl 85-86; U GA; Comp Sci.

GUISTWHITE, JACK B; Mechanicsburg HS; Mechanicsburg, PA; (Y); Band; Jazz Band; Mrchg Band; Pres Orch; Symp Band; Rep Stu Cncl; Var Trk; Church Yth Grp; SADD; Concert Band; Mary C Fox Music Schlrshp 86; 4th Pl Dist III Trck Fld Comptn 86; Cnty Orchstra & Bnd 86; Penn ST U.

GUJDA, MICHAEL J; Holy Ghost Prep Schl; Bristol, PA; (Y); Art Clb; Computer Clb; Math Clb; VP L Crs Cntry; VP L Trk; Hon Roll; NHS; Frnch Schlr Awd-Advncd Lvl; Grmn Schlr Awd-Intrmdt Lvl; Bus.

GULDIN, CHRISTINA; Bishop Conwell HS; Levittown, PA; (Y); 1/254; Church Yth Grp; Mathletes; Scholastic Bowl; Church Choir; Yrbk Stf; High Hon Roll; NHS; Ntl Merit Ltr; Pres Schlr; Loyola Coll Pres & Lehigh U Trstee & Ursinus Coll Brd Of Dir Schlrshps 86; Villanova U; Bus Adm.

GULICK, GREG; Hanover Area HS; Ashley, PA; (Y); Science Clb; Band; Concert Band; Jazz Band; Mrchg Band; Pep Band; School Musical; Variety Show.

GULLO JR, JACK; De Lone Catholic HS; New Windsor, MD; (Y); L Debate Tm; Model UN; Concert Band; Jazz Band; Mrchg Band; Hon Roll; NHS; WA & Jefferson Coll; Bio.

GUM, JOEL; Danville Area HS; Danville, PA; (Y); Trs Key Clb; Band; Rep Stu Cncl; Prfct Atten Awd; Bnd Awd 86; Bnd Axlry Awd 86; Blmsbrg U; Bus Adm.

GUM, SEAN; Governor Mifflin HS; Shillington, PA; (Y); 62/300; Computer Clb; Im JV Socr; Hon Roll; Prfct Atten Awd; Penn ST U; Comp Sci.

GUMBITA, ROBERT J; Mount Pleasant SR HS; Mt Pleasant, PA; (Y); 50/230; Latin Clb; Letterman Clb; Ski Clb; Rep Frsh Cls; Off Sr Cls; Stu Cncl; Bsbl; Bsktbl; Coach Actv; L Ftbl; YEA 86-87; Indiana U Of PA.

GUMBRELL, JEANNE M; Boyertown Area SR HS; Gilbertsville, PA; (Y); 60/448; Drama Clb; Teachers Aide; Sec Trs Chorus; School Musical; School Play; Swing Chorus; Variety Show; High Hon Roll; Soloist Rdng Symphny Orchstr 86; MTNA Regnl & Div Wnnr Vocl Solo 86; U Of Hartford; Vocl Perfmnce.

GUNDAKER, SHEREEN; Roosevelt Annex HS; Richmond, VA; (S); 4-H; SADD; Nwsp Ed-Chief; Nwsp Rptr; Stu Cncl; DAR Awd; High Hon Roll; Hon Roll; Wrld Affrs Cncl 83-86; VA Commonwealth U; Bus Adm.

GUNDERMAN, ERICH; Du Bois Area HS; Dubois, PA; (Y); Boy Scts; Church Yth Grp; Dance Clb; Varsity Clb; Bsktbl; Coach Actv; Ftbl; Golf; Socr; Hon Roll; Penn Free Enterprice Wk Schlrshp Lock Haven U 86; Penn ST U; Athltc Trnr.

GUNDRUM, MICHELLE; Ephrata HS; Ephrata, PA; (Y); Church Yth Grp; VICA; Var JV Fld Hcky; Hon Roll; 3rd Pl Dist Cmptn VICA 86; Barber.

GUNN, WALTER; Cowanesque Valley HS; Knoxville, PA; (Y); VP Church Yth Grp; FFA; Speech Tm; Teachers Aide; Chorus; Wt Lftg; Wrstlng; High Hon Roll; Hon Roll; Tioga Area Frmr Dgr; Vly Frg Coll; Mnstr.

GUNNETT, KATHY; Williamsburg HS; Williamsburg, PA; (Y); Church Yth Grp; FBLA; Office Aide; Cheerleading; Score Keeper; Cit Awd; Hon Roll; Prom & Hmcmng Comm 85-86; Dist Bus Comptn Typng I 84; Bus.

GUNNING, ROBYN; Council Rock HS; Richboro, PA; (Y); 303/845; Stat Powder Puff Ftbl; Lib Arts.

GUNSHORE, JOHN; Bishop O Reilly HS; Luzerne, PA; (Y); Letterman Clb; Chorus; School Musical; Ftbl; Gym; Wt Lftg.

GUNST, SHAWN; Highlands HS; Natrona Heights, PA; (Y); Pep Clb; School Play; Pres Stu Cncl; Var Ftbl; Var Trk; L Vllybl; Wt Lftg; Hon Roll; Hstry.

GUNTRUM, LYNN O; North Clarion JR SR HS; Tionesta, PA; (Y); 28/100; Office Aide; Sec Spanish Clb; Varsity Clb; VP Chorus; School Musical; Nwsp Sprt Ed; Nwsp Stf; Yrbk Stf; Vllybl; Hon Roll; Du Bois Bus Coll; Med.

GUREGHIAN, KIMBERLY KOHARIG; Council Rock HS; Holland, PA; (Y); 32/756; Intnl Clb; Yrbk Phtg; Yrbk Stf; Lit Mag; Vllybl; NHS; Bucks Cnty CC Acadmc Schlrshp 86; Armenian Yth Fedrtn Corr Sec & VP 83-85; Shotokan Karate; Bucks Comm.

GURLEY, DENISE; Archbishop Ryan For Girls; Philadelphia, PA; (Y); 281/491; Camp Fr Inc; Church Yth Grp; Q&S; Nwsp Ed-Chief; Nwsp Stf; JV Bowling; Prfct Atten Awd; Cmnty Svc Hrs 83-85; Cngrssnl Awd Wrkg Toward 86; Acctnt.

GURLEY, KARIN; Mt Lebanon HS; Pittsburgh, PA; (Y); 4/548; Thesps; Jazz Band; School Musical; School Play; Variety Show; VP Stu Cncl; High Hon Roll; Ntl Merit Ltr; Im Vllybl; JV Sftbl; Cum Laude 86; Brown U Bk Awd 85.

GURLEY, WILLIAM; Delaware County Christian HS; Swarthmore, PA; (Y); Church Yth Grp; Chorus; Concert Band; Trs Soph Cls; Trs Stu Cncl; Var L Bsktbl; Var L Crs Cntry; NHS; Band; High Hon Roll; Dstrct, Rgnl & All ST Bnds 85; Dstrct & Rgnl Bnds 86.

GURNARI, JOSEPH; Couglin HS; Wilkes Barre, PA; (Y); 25/385; Math Clb; Math Tm; Hon Roll; NHS; Pres Schlr; PA ST U; Bus Adm.

GURNEY, LIN; Reynolds HS; Transfer, PA; (Y); 23/159; Nwsp Ed-Chief; Yrbk Stf; Ed Lit Mag; Sec Frsh Cls; Sec Soph Cls; Sec Jr Cls; Sec Sr Cls; Trs Stu Cncl; Var JV Bsktbl; NHS; Plcmt YSU Engl Fest 84-86; Jrnlst.

GURNIAK, SANDRA; Hopewell HS; Aliquippa, PA; (Y); 17/265; Band; Concert Band; Mrchg Band; Pep Band; Trk; High Hon Roll; Art Clb; French Clb; Pres Acad Ftnss Awd 86; Beaver Cnty Hnr Band 86; Robert Morris Fclty Recgntn Schlrshp 86; Robert Morris Coll; Bus.

GURZYNSKI, FELICIA; Hanover Area JR SR HS; Wilkes Barre, PA; (Y); 22/156; Exploring; Band; Chorus; Yrbk Stf; Vllybl; Hon Roll; Stu Forum-Wilkes-Barre 86; Hlth Thrphy.

GUSH, CHRISTINE; Lak Lehman HS; Harveys Lake, PA; (Y); Yrbk Stf; NHS; Nrsng.

GUSH, ELIZABETH; Bishop O Reilly HS; Harveys Lk, PA; (Y); Church Yth Grp; Church Choir; High Hon Roll; Hon Roll; Spanish NHS; VFW Awd; Voice Dem Awd; Misericordia Coll; Eng.

GUSIC, ROBB; West Mifflin Area HS; W Mifflin, PA; (Y); Ski Clb; L Crs Cntry; L Trk; Var L Wrstlng; Pole Vltg Recd.

GUSSENHOFEN, EVELYN; Hopewell SR HS; Monaca, PA; (Y); Pres VP Church Yth Grp; Girl Scts; Band; Flag Corp; Var Powder Puff Ftbl; Var Trk; High Hon Roll; NHS; Art Clb; Gold Awd Girl Scotng Highest Awd 85; LF Blaney Conservtn Awd 86; Slvr Awd Girl Sctng 83; Sawyer Bus Schl; Acctng.

GUST, PEGGY; Ringgold HS; Monongahela, PA; (Y); 39/348; Church Yth Grp; Office Aide; Acpl Chr; Chorus; Church Choir; Swing Chorus; Variety Show; Nwsp Stf; Yrbk Stf; Hon Roll; Robert Morris Coll; Busnss Mgmt.

GUSTAFSON, BRYAN; Curwensville HS; Clearfield, PA; (Y); French Clb; JV Bsbl; JV Ftbl; High Hon Roll; Hon Roll.

GUSTAFSON, LESLIE R; Warren Area HS; Warren, PA; (Y); 26/270; Church Yth Grp; Debate Tm; Varsity Clb; Acpl Chr; Concert Band; Jazz Band; Mrchg Band; School Musical; School Play; Var L Vllybl; Warren Cnty Med Aux Scholar 86; NHS 86; Golden Dragon Awd 86; U Pittsburgh; Anesthslgy.

GUSTAFSON, TINA; Saegertown HS; Saegertown, PA; (Y); 8/117; Church Yth Grp; Office Aide; SADD; Chorus; Church Choir; Color Guard; Variety Show; Nwsp Ed-Chief; High Hon Roll; NHS; Bus Awd; Bradford Schl Bus; Rtl Mngmnt.

GUSTAS, GERALD; Wyoming Valley West HS; Plymouth, PA; (Y); 26/374; Chorus; School Musical; Yrbk Stf; L Crs Cntry; Var Trk; Cit Awd; God Cntry Awd; Hon Roll; NHS; NEDT Awd; Dist 9 Chorus Fstvl 85-86; Wilkes Coll; Bio.

GUSTETIC, ADAM; Saint Joseph HS; Brackenridge, PA; (Y); 6/65; Political Wkr; School Musical; School Play; Yrbk Rptr; Var Bsktbl; Var L Tennis; Pres Schlr; Drama Clb; Stage Crew; Nwsp Stf; Duquesne U Intgrtd Hnrs Prog 85; Comp Schlrs 4.0 & Jrnlsm Schlrshp Duquesne U 86; 1s Pl Ntl Hist Day; Duquesne U; Jrnlsm.

GUTH, MICHAEL; Franklin SR HS; Franklin, PA; (Y); 12/250; Church Yth Grp; JV Golf; High Hon Roll; NHS; Schl Directrs Awd 84-86.

GUTHIER, REBECCA; Central Catholic HS; Reading, PA; (Y); Church Yth Grp; Pep Clb; Spanish Clb; School Musical; Variety Show; Var JV Cheerleading.

GUTHRIE, KRISTIN; Dubois Area HS; Dubois, PA; (Y); 93/293; VP Church Yth Grp; French Clb; Girl Scts; SADD; Band; Chorus; Concert Band; Mrchg Band; Rep Stu Cncl; Chem.

GUTHRIE, MELISSA; Pen Argyl Area HS; Pen Argyl, PA; (Y); 46/125; Church Yth Grp; Drama Clb; Ski Clb; Chorus; School Play; Pres Frsh Cls; Pres Soph Cls; Pres Jr Cls; Stu Cncl; Cheerleading; Dntl Hygnst.

GUTHRIE, MICHAEL; Perry Traditional Acad; Pittsburgh, PA; (Y); 1/137; Boy Scts; Math Tm; Nwsp Stf; Var L Crs Cntry; VP L Swmmng; Pres NHS; Ski Clb; Yrbk Stf; Var L Tennis; High Hon Roll; Eagl Sct 85; Bronz Medl City Wm Champ 86; Rep Schl Chem Olympcs Comptn 85; Chem Engrng.

GUTHRIE, RICHARD; Clearfield Area HS; Clearfield, PA; (Y); 70/320; French Clb; SADD; Concert Band; Mrchg Band; Hon Roll; Penn SST U Du Bois; Pre-Dent.

GUTKOWSKI, JOAN; James M Coughlin HS; Wilkes Barre Twp, PA; (Y); 16/386; French Clb; Band; Concert Band; Mrchg Band; Yrbk Stf; High Hon Roll; Hon Roll; Jr NHS; NHS; Pres Schlr; U Of Scranton; Bio.

GUTOSKY, PATTI; Weatherly Area HS; Weatherly, PA; (Y); Art Clb; FBLA; FNA; Library Aide; Red Cross Aide; School Play; VP Sr Cls; Hon Roll; 1st Pl German III Awd 86; Lawyer.

GUTOWSKI, JULIE A; St Marys Area HS; Kersey, PA; (Y); 13/289; Ski Clb; Varsity Clb; Var Swmmng; JV Tennis; JV Trk; Hon Roll; NHS; Coll Wooster; Intl Econ.

GUTOWSKI, KARRIE; Hopewell Area HS; Aliquippa, PA; (Y); Hosp Aide; Latin Clb; Band; Chorus; Sec Drill Tm; Rep Frsh Cls; Rep Soph Cls; Rep Jr Cls; Rep Sr Cls; Rep Stu Cncl; Miss Pennsylvania Teen USA 85; Pre Med.

GUTSHALL, BRENDA; Palmyra Area HS; Campbelltown, PA; (Y); Church Yth Grp; Ski Clb; Spanish Clb; Chorus; Church Choir; Trk; Hon Roll; Phrmcy.

GUTSHALL, TERESA; Cumbeland Valley HS; Carlisle, PA; (Y); Sec Church Yth Grp; Sec Pres 4-H; Church Choir; Orch; Dnfth Awd; 4-H Awd; Nrsng.

GUTTENDORF, RAYMOND; Seton-Lasalle Regional HS; Bethel Park, PA; (Y); 5/234; Church Yth Grp; JA; Math Tm; NFL; Capt Bsktbl; High Hon Roll; NHS; Ntl Merit Ltr; PA ST U; Engrng.

GUTTERMAN, FRANK; Mining And Mechanical Inst; Hazleton, PA; (Y); 1/34; Cmnty Wkr; Computer Clb; Ski Clb; Temple Yth Grp; Rep Frsh Cls; Pres Soph Cls; Pres Jr Cls; Var L Bsbl; Var L Crs Cntry; High Hon Roll; 1st Pl Vly Sctn Amer Chmcl Soc 86; Kings Coll Spnsh Lvl III 2nd Pl 86; PA JR Acad Of Sci Excel Awd; Elec Engrng.

GUTTERMAN, FRANKLIN; M M I HS; Hazelton, PA; (S); 1/32; Computer Clb; Ski Clb; Frsh Cls; Pres Soph Cls; Pres Jr Cls; Var L Bsbl; Var L Crs Cntry; High Hon Roll; Hon Roll; Jr NHS; PA JR Acad Sci Regnl 1st & ST Lvl 1st; Susquehanna Vly Sectn Amer Chem Socty 1st; Intl Chem Olympd; Elec Engrng.

GUY, COLLEEN; Middletown Area HS; Middletown, PA; (Y); 34/180; Nwsp Stf; Cheerleading; Engl.

GUY, GINA; Kiski Area HS; Vandergrift, PA; (Y); Church Yth Grp; SADD; Yrbk Stf; NHS; FBLA; JA; Pep Clb; Stage Crew; Stat Bsktbl; Cheerleading; Clarion U Of PA; Elem Ed.

GUY, MISSY; Lincoln HS; Ellwood City, PA; (Y); Art Clb; Y-Teens; Powder Puff Ftbl; Hon Roll; Cmnty Clg Of Beaver Cnty.

GUYER, KRISTA; Philipsburg-Osceola HS; Philipsburg, PA; (Y); Cmnty Wkr; FCA; SADD; Band; Concert Band; Yrbk Stf; Off Stu Cncl; Sftbl; Stat Vllybl; IUP; Elem Ed.

GUYER, SUELLEN M; Northeastern SR HS; Mt Wolf, PA; (Y); 8/160; Pres Sec Church Yth Grp; Chorus; School Play; Yrbk Stf; JV Bsktbl; Mgr(s); Var JV Vllybl; NHS; Drama Clb; Stu Mnth 86; York Cty Ind Arts Exh 86; Stjude Dance Commtte 85-86; Graphic Arts.

GUYTON, PAT J; Canon-Mc Millan HS; Canonsburg, PA; (Y); 93/357; Spanish Clb; Varsity Clb; Concert Band; Mrchg Band; Capt L Crs Cntry; Mgr(s); L Trk; Hon Roll; Prfct Atten Awd; Spanish NHS; U Pittsburgh; Phrmcy.

GUZA, TRACY; Hazleton HS; Hazelton, PA; (Y); 4/388; Art Clb; Drama Clb; Library Aide; Y-Teens; Stage Crew; High Hon Roll; Ruth M Koch Mem Awd Hazleton Art Lg 86; Kings Coll Spn Cont 1st Pl 84; Fashion Inst Tech; Fash Merch.

GUZIEWICZ, RICHARD S; Archbishop Kennedy HS; Philadelphia, PA; (Y); 1/185; Church Yth Grp; Stu Cncl; Bausch & Lomb Sci Awd; Elks Awd; High Hon Roll; NHS; Prfct Atten Awd; PA City Schlrshp 86; John Mc Kee Schlrshp 86; Am Chem Awd 86; Drexel U; Elect Engr.

GUZMAN, ABIGAIL; Freedom SR HS; Bethlehem, PA; (Y); Church Yth Grp; JA; Band; Chorus; Church Choir; Rep Stu Cncl; Hon Roll; Jr NHS; NHS; Pres Schlr; Spllng Bee Awd 84; Med.

GUZMAN, EVELISE; Freedom HS; Bethlehem, PA; (Y); Pres Church Yth Grp; Office Aide; Band; Chorus; Nwsp Ed-Chief; Hon Roll; Jr NHS; NHS; Med.

GUZOLIK, JERRY; Leechburg Area HS; Leechburg, PA; (Y); 14/90; Stage Crew; Trs Frsh Cls; Stu Cncl; Var Co-Capt Bsbl; Math.

GUZZO, JIM; Our Lady Of Sacred Heart HS; Coraopolis, PA; (Y); Computer Clb; Stage Crew; VP Frsh Cls; Sec Trs Soph Cls; Var L Socr; High Hon Roll; Hon Roll; Amrcn HS Math Exam 1st Pl 83; Engnrng.

GYDOS, MONICA; George Washington HS; Philadelphia, PA; (Y); Church Yth Grp; Cmnty Wkr; Hosp Aide; Teachers Aide; Chorus; Yrbk Stf; JV Co-Capt Cheerleading; High Hon Roll; Pre-Med.

GYERGYO, SUSAN; West Allegheny HS; Oakdale, PA; (Y); 21/206; Pres Trs Church Yth Grp; FBLA; Spanish Clb; Trs Sec Chorus; Nwsp Stf; Yrbk Ed-Chief; Rep Jr Cls; Rep Stu Cncl; High Hon Roll; Hon Roll; Prsdntl Acdmc Ftns Awd 86; 1st Plc Shrthnd II Rgnl FBLA 86; Scrtry Mnth 85; Bradford Bus Schl; Exec Scrtry.

GYURINK, JEFF; Montoursville HS; Montoursville, PA; (Y); 51/174; French Clb; Letterman Clb; Ski Clb; Varsity Clb; Stu Cncl; Var Bsbl; JV Bsktbl; Var Ftbl; Var Powder Puff Ftbl; Outstndng Athlt 86.

GYURKO JR, EDWARD S; Carlisle SR HS; Carlisle, PA; (Y); Am Leg Boys St; Debate Tm; NFL; Speech Tm; School Musical; Stage Crew; Nwsp Rptr; Pre-Law.

HAAF, DEBBIE; Unionville HS; West Chester, PA; (Y); Church Yth Grp; Hosp Aide; Yrbk Stf; Im Crs Cntry; Im Lcrss; Im Powder Puff Ftbl; JV Trk; Im Vllybl; Hon Roll; Ltr Of Cmmndtn 85; JV Trk Cert 85-86; IA ST; Bio-Chem.

HAAG, DANIEL; Central York SR HS; York, PA; (Y); 1/230; German Clb; NFL; School Musical; School Play; Bausch & Lomb Sci Awd; High Hon Roll; NHS; Opt Clb Awd; U DE; Chem Engrng.

HAAG, DAVID E; David B Oliner HS; Pittsburgh, PA; (Y); ROTC; Chorus; Color Guard; Drill Tm; High Hon Roll; Hon Roll; Ntl Soc Of Sons Of Amrcn Rvltn 84; Rsrv Ofcr Assoc Of US 85.

HAAG, JENNIFER; Hamburg Area HS; Shoemakersville, PA; (Y); Sec Camera Clb; Pres Exploring; FBLA; German Clb; Library Aide; SADD; Chorus; Hon Roll; Central PA Bus; Trvl.

HAAK, LORI; Littlestown HS; Littlestown, PA; (Y); 38/143; Church Yth Grp; Pres VP 4-H; FBLA; Speech Tm; Teachers Aide; Chorus; School Play; Yrbk Stf; Crs Cntry; 4-H Awd; Bus Mgt.

HAAS, CORI; Monheim Central HS; Manheim, PA; (Y); Church Yth Grp; Library Aide; Office Aide; Chorus; Stage Crew; Rep Stu Cncl; Var Powder Puff Ftbl; Var Trk; Hon Roll; Comm.

HAAS, FARAH; Owen J Roberts HS; Pottstown, PA; (S); 26/300; Dance Clb; Girl Scts; Intnl Clb; Latin Clb; Letterman Clb; Nwsp Stf; Yrbk Stf; Var JV Bsktbl; Var JV Fld Hcky; Var Gym; Chapel Hill; Comm.

HAAS, GEORGANNE; Pius X HS; Pen Argyl, PA; (Y); 10/40; Dance Clb; Pep Clb; Varsity Clb; Chorus; Church Choir; School Musical; Yrbk Stf; Var Bsktbl; Var Sftbl; Vrsty Lttrs Bsktbll & Sftbl 84-85 & 85-86; Allentown Bus Schl; Fash Merch.

HAAS, GREGORY S; Kutztown Area HS; Kutztown, PA; (Y); Pres Church Yth Grp; Band; Jazz Band; Pep Band; Cit Awd; High Hon Roll; NHS; Engrng.

HAAS, HEATHER; Parkland HS; Schnecksville, PA; (Y); Church Yth Grp; Pres 4-H; JA; Math Tm; Ski Clb; Speech Tm; Rep Soph Cls; Rep Jr Cls; 4-H Awd; Hon Roll; Mrktng.

HAAS, JULIE A; Nazareth HS; Tatamy, PA; (Y); 51/236; Church Yth Grp; Library Aide; Office Aide; Church Choir; Capt Drill Tm; Capt Pom Pon; Var Vllybl; Cit Awd; Hon Roll; E Stroudsburg U; Nrsng.

HAAS, KAREN; Blue Mountain Acad; Emmaus, PA; (Y); Church Yth Grp; Library Aide; Chorus; Church Choir; Orch; Rep Stu Cncl; Hon Roll; Fstr Grndprnts 84-86; Ushrtt 84-86; Prs Ensmbl 85-86.

HAAS, KIMBERLY; Pennsbury HS; Yardley, PA; (Y); French Clb; Library Aide; Office Aide; SADD; Yrbk Stf; VP Jr Cls; Var Tennis; High Hon Roll; Hon Roll; Frnch Poetry & Converstn Cntst 1st 82-83; Ursinus Clg; Chem.

HAAS, SHEILA; Parkland HS; Breinigsville, PA; (Y); 162/415; Sec VP Exploring; Harcum JC; Anml Hlth Tech.

HAASE, DAVID; Strath Haven HS; Swarthmore, PA; (Y); Cmnty Wkr; VP Capt Socr; Cit Awd; Hon Roll; Tennis; Trk; Rep Frsh Cls; Ski Clb; Spanish Clb; Vrsty Soccr Coachs Awd 85-86; Law.

HAASE, JUSTIN; Conestoga Vly HS; Leola, PA; (Y); 50/280; JV Var Bsbl; Bsktbl; JV Var Ftbl; Var Golf; Hon Roll; NHS; Prfct Atten Awd; Cmmnctns.

HAASZ, PAUL; Cedar Grove Christian Acad; Philadelphia, PA; (Y); Church Yth Grp; Chorus; Off Jr Cls; JV Bsbl; Hon Roll; Teengr Yr 85; Soul Wnnr Yr 85-86; Bob Jones U; Bible.

HABAKUS, SCOTT; Governor Mifflin HS; Mohnton, PA; (Y); 57/265; Chess Clb; Var Bsbl; Capt Bsktbl; Im Bowling; Im Vllybl; Hon Roll; Engrng.

HABER, JENNIFER; Freedom HS; Bethlehem, PA; (Y); Drama Clb; French Clb; Pep Clb; Ski Clb; School Play; Nwsp Stf; Trs Jr Cls; Rep Stu Cncl; Capt Var Fld Hcky; Hon Roll; Psychlgy.

HABER, SARAH; Ambridge Area HS; Freedom, PA; (Y); 3/265; Cmnty Wkr; German Clb; Pep Clb; Service Clb; Rep Stu Cncl; Trk; High Hon Roll; NHS; Ntl Merit Ltr; Prfct Atten Awd; Slippery Rock U Acad Schlrshp 86; Slippery Rock U; Spcl Educ.

HABER, SPENCER; Freedom HS; Bethlehem, PA; (Y); 14/404; Pres French Clb; Model UN; Political Wkr; Ski Clb; Nwsp Bus Mgr; Nwsp Stf; Rep Pres Stu Cncl; Tennis; NHS; Ntl Merit Ltr; Meluskey Awd For Govt 86; Cngrsnl Yth Ldrshp Awd 86; U PA; Bus.

HABERBERGER, TAMMY; St Marys Area HS; Saint Marys, PA; (Y); 38/250; Stat Bsktbl; Var Sftbl; Hon Roll; Law.

HABERGERGER, MICHELLE; St Marys Area HS; Saint Marys, PA; (Y); 15/305; Pep Clb; Varsity Clb; VP Stu Cncl; Stat Bsktbl; Stat Crs Cntry; Var L Trk; JV L Vllybl; Hon Roll; NHS.

HABERLEN, JENNIFER; Ligonier Valley SR HS; Ligonier, PA; (Y); 1/154; Sec AFS; Model UN; Trs Frsh Cls; Trs Soph Cls; Rep Stu Cncl; Var Capt Bsktbl; Var L Trk; Gov Hon Prg Awd; High Hon Roll; NHS; AHSME Schl Awd Math 85-86; PA Free Entrprs Wk Schlrshp 85; Engrng.

HABIB, THOMAS K; Bishop O Reilly HS; Kingston, PA; (Y); Church Yth Grp; Red Cross Aide; Band; Pres Frsh Cls; Rep Stu Cncl; Var L Crs Cntry; Var L Socr; Stage Crew; Im Bsktbl; Im Vllybl; Intl Stu Ldrshp Inst 85-86; Rep NE Yth Council ISLI 85; HS Chamber Choir 82-86; Misericordia; Occuptnl Thrphy.

HABLE, KIM; Garden Spot HS; New Holland, PA; (Y); Church Yth Grp; 4-H; Girl Scts; Rep Soph Cls; Rep Jr Cls; Stu Cncl; Var Bsktbl; Var Fld Hcky; Var Trk; Cmnty Wkr; Wrthy Advsr, Cloister Assmbly, Order Of Rainbow Girls 86; Elem Ed.

HABOWSKI, THOMAS; Northern HS; Mechanicsburg, PA; (Y); 35/225; Rep Sr Cls; JV Ftbl; L Golf; L Wrstlng; L Hon Roll; Comp Sci.

HABURSKY, MARY; Villa Maria Acad; Erie, PA; (Y); Latin Clb; Var Capt Swmmng; Hon Roll; NHS; NEDT Awd.

HACH, EDWIN; Otto-Eldred Is HS; Duke Center, PA; (Y); Quiz Bowl; Varsity Clb; Nwsp Rptr; Off Stu Cncl; JV Var Bsktbl; Var Crs Cntry; Trk; Hon Roll; Atten Awd 83-85; Chem Awd 85-86; Its Acad 85-86; St Bonaventure U.

HACK, VIRGINIA A; Burrell HS; Lower Burrell, PA; (Y); 7/197; Spanish Clb; Chorus; Concert Band; Mrchg Band; Variety Show; NHS; Orch; Hon Roll; Jr NHS; Rotary Schlr Awd 85; Schlstc Achvt Awd 85 & 86; Semi Finlst PA Gov Schl Arts 86; ACTRESS On Broadway.

HACKER, BETH; Western Beaver HS; Industry, PA; (S); Chorus; Jazz Band; Mrchg Band; Symp Band; VP Stu Cncl; Capt Twrlr; High Hon Roll; NHS; Church Yth Grp; Exploring; Beaver Cnty JR Miss 2nd Rnnr Up 87; 3 Yr Trck Ltr Wnnr 83-86; U Of Pittsburgh; Phys Thrpy.

HACKER, MONICA; Cheltenham HS; Wyncote, PA; (Y); SADD; Yrbk Phtg; VP Stu Cncl; Fld Hcky; Lcrss; Tulane; Archtct.

HACKETT, LISA; Shaler Area SR HS; Pittsburgh, PA; (Y); 43/517; Ftbl; High Hon Roll; Hon Roll; Spanish NHS.

HACKMAN, JOY; Lackawanna Trail JR SR HS; Factoryville, PA; (Y); 20/86; Church Yth Grp; Trs FHA; Band; Concert Band; Jazz Band; Capt Mrchg Band; French Hon Soc; Hon Roll; NHS; Pres Acadmc Ftnss Awd 86; West Chester U.

HACKWORTH, DAVID; Riverview HS; Oakmont, PA; (Y); AFS; Yrbk Phtg; Var Capt Crs Cntry; Var Capt Trk; Hon Roll; NEDT Awd.

HADDICK, WALTER; Wyoming Valley West HS; Swoyersville, PA; (Y); 51/405; Variety Show; VP Soph Cls; VP Jr Cls; Im Bsktbl; Var L Ftbl; Var L Trk; Im Vllybl; Hon Roll; NHS; PIAA Dist Trck & Fld Medal Wnnr; Physics.

HADDOCK, CRAIG; Belle Vernon Area HS; W Newton, PA; (Y); Var L Socr; Var L Vllybl; Hon Roll; Certfd Sccr Ref-US Sccr Fed 86.

HADIX, CAROLINE; Windber Area HS; Windber, PA; (Y); Math Clb; Ski Clb; Yrbk Stf; Twrlr; High Hon Roll; NHS; Presidntl Phys Fitns Awd 84, 85 & 86; Stu Mnth 84 & 86; Sci.

HADLEY, CATHY; Scranton Central HS; Scranton, PA; (Y); Church Yth Grp; SADD; Band; Sftbl; Swmmng; High Hon Roll; NHS; Athlt Of Wk & Mnth 85-86; Sftbl All-Stars 85-86; Med.

HADUCH, JOANNE; Pittston Area HS; Avoca, PA; (Y); 1/330; Computer Clb; Key Clb; Math Clb; Science Clb; Chorus; High Hon Roll; NHS; Val; Pres Scholar U Scranton 86-87; U Scranton; Phys Thrpy.

HADVANCE, PAULA; GAR Memorial HS; Wilkes Barre, PA; (S); 4/187; Key Clb; Library Aide; Chorus; Yrbk Stf; Var Cheerleading; High Hon Roll; Hon Roll; Jr NHS; NHS; Med.

HAEBERLE, NANCY; St Basil Acad; Philadelphia, PA; (Y); Pep Clb; Science Clb; Spanish Clb; Chorus; School Musical; York Coll PA; Elem Ed.

HAEHN, LISA; Youngsville JR/Sr HS; Grand Valley, PA; (Y); Church Yth Grp; Debate Tm; VP Rptr 4-H; FBLA; Library Aide; Math Tm; Spanish Clb; SADD; Band; Color Guard; Natl Qrtr Hrse Pin 84-86; Outstndng 4-H 85; Ldrshp 86; Phy Thrpst.

HAELIG, MARK; Central Bucks East HS; Doylestown, PA; (Y); Aud/Vis; Computer Clb; Drama Clb; Ski Clb; School Musical; School Play; Stage Crew; Hon Roll; Bus.

HAERTTER, ROCCO; Hempfield HS; Mount Joy, PA; (Y); Chess Clb; Varsity Clb; Crs Cntry; Trk; Wt Lftg; High Hon Roll; York College.

HAERTTER, TIMOTHY; Lancaster Catholic HS; Lancaster, PA; (Y); Church Yth Grp; Band; Concert Band; Mrchg Band; Pep Band; School Musical; Var Cheerleading; JV Ftbl; JV Wrstlng; Hon Roll; Elec Engrng.

HAFEMEISTER, CHRIS; Villa Maria HS; Mantua, OH; (Y); Computer Clb; Drama Clb; Spanish Clb; Thesps; School Musical; Stage Crew; Hon Roll; NHS; Prfct Atten Awd; Spanish NHS; Acadmnc All Amer Awd 84; Dorm Cnclr 86; Natl Ldrshp & Svc Awd 85; U Of Miami; Acctg.

HAGAN, MELISSA; Canon Mc Millan SR HS; Canonsburg, PA; (Y); 57/353; Latin Clb; Sec Varsity Clb; Pres Church Choir; Nwsp Stf; Yrbk Stf; Sec Sr Cls; Trs Rptr Stu Cncl; L Crs Cntry; L Trk; High Hon Roll; Hold Schl Trck Rec 440 Dash 84-86; Econ.

HAGAN, SHELLY; New Hope-Soleburg HS; New Hope, PA; (Y); 21/80; Art Clb; Concert Band; Mrchg Band; JV Fld Hcky; Hon Roll.

HAGEDER, JAMES; Greensburg Salem HS; Greensburg, PA; (Y); 1/320; Pres Church Yth Grp; Mathletes; Model UN; NFL; Rptr Nwsp Stf; Rptr Lit Mag; Pres Jr NHS; Pres NHS; Ntl Merit SF; Val; Greensburg Coll Clb, 1st Cath Lad Assn, Gannon U Acad Schlrshps 86; Gannon U; Philsphy.

HAGEE, MARY; Archbishop Prendergast HS; Drexel Hill, PA; (Y); 2/363; Church Yth Grp; Mathletes; Science Clb; Pres Spanish Clb; Ed Yrbk Stf; Rep Frsh Cls; Gym; High Hon Roll; VP NHS; Spanish NHS; Schrlshp La Salle U 86; Schlrshp Rosemont Coll 86; Rosemont Coll; Comm.

HAGEMANN, AMY; Liberty HS; Bethlehem, PA; (Y); 16/475; Library Aide; Hosp Aide; Office Aide; Band; Chorus; Rep Frsh Cls; Var L Fld Hcky; Var Trk; High Hon Roll; Hon Roll.

HAGEN, ELISABETH; Cumberland Valley HS; Camphill, PA; (Y); 4/600; Key Clb; Pres Latin Clb; Model UN; Spanish Clb; Rep Frsh Cls; Rep Soph Cls; Rep Jr Cls; Rep Sr Cls; Trs Pres Stu Cncl; High Hon Roll; Awd Of Outstndg Achvmnt In Sci USAF,Book Of Month Clb 86; Cmbrlnd Vly Awd Of Exclnce Sci 86; Georgetown U; Med.

HAGEN, HEATHER; William Allen HS; Allentown, PA; (Y); Exploring; Political Wkr; Ski Clb; Nwsp Rptr; Nwsp Stf; Yrbk Rptr; Yrbk Stf; Lit Mag; Rep Frsh Cls; Rep Jr Cls; PA Schl Prss Assn 1st Awd-Shrt Story 84; Lehigh U; Bus.

HAGENBUCH, LISA; Danville SR HS; Milton, PA; (Y); Spanish Clb; VP Sftbl; High Hon Roll; Hon Roll; NHS; Harcum Pres Schlrshp Awd 86; Dorothy Bonawitz Awd 86; Harcum JC; Equine Stds.

HAGENBUCH, STEVE; Danville HS; Milton, PA; (Y); Computer Clb; Spanish Clb; JV Crs Cntry; Var Trk; High Hon Roll; Hon Roll; Parks & Recrtn Mgmt.

HAGER, ERIC; Perry T A HS; Pittsburgh, PA; (Y); Boys Clb Am; Boy Scts; Chess Clb; FCA; French Clb; Hosp Aide; JA; Mathletes; Math Clb; Math Tm; Hlth Ftns Awd 82-83; CMU; Nclr Physcst.

HAGERICH, TRACEY; Central Cambria HS; Mineral Pt, PA; (Y); 31/193; Church Yth Grp; Ski Clb; Color Guard; Hon Roll; WVU; Phrmcy.

HAGERMAN, TRACEY; Kutztown Area HS; Kutztown, PA; (Y); Library Aide; Office Aide; Chorus; School Play; Nwsp Bus Mgr; Nwsp Sprt Ed; Sec Frsh Cls; Sec Soph Cls; Sec Jr Cls; Stat Bsktbl; Juniata Coll; Prsnl Mgmt.

HAGERTY, SUSAN; Little Flower Catholic HS; Philadelphia, PA; (Y); 1/413; Drama Clb; Pres German Clb; School Musical; School Play; Yrbk Stf; High Hon Roll; NHS; Computer Clb; Chorus; Nwsp Stf; Hghst Avrge Grmn 83-86; Hghst Avrge Engl 83-84 & 86; Fll Schlrshp Tmple U & La Salle U 86; La Salle U; Bus.

HAGERTY, TRICIA; Little Flower Catholic HS; Philadelphia, PA; (Y); Church Yth Grp; Cmnty Wkr; French Clb; Science Clb; School Musical; Stage Crew; Lit Mag; Hon Roll; Grphc Dsgn.

HAGETER, KELLIE; Mars Area HS; Butler, PA; (Y); Office Aide; Concert Band; Drill Tm; Mrchg Band; Nwsp Phtg; Yrbk Phtg; Capt Twrlr; High Hon Roll; Hon Roll; Clarion; Tchr.

HAGEY, TANYA; Souderton Area HS; Telford, PA; (Y); 66/375; Church Yth Grp; FCA; Chorus; School Play; Nwsp Stf; Yrbk Stf; Rep Jr Cls; Stu Cncl; JV Stat Fld Hcky; JV Sftbl.

HAGG, CHRISTINE; Tyrone Area HS; Tyrone, PA; (S); 4/197; Cmnty Wkr; Key Clb; Math Clb; Speech Tm; Chorus; Mrchg Band; DAR Awd; High Hon Roll; Chrmn VISTOS Tutor 85-87; Chrch Lector/Cmmntatr 84-87; Temple U; Phys Ther.

HAGGENMILLER, KRISTA; Cardinal Ohara HS; Media, PA; (Y); 26/772; Cmnty Wkr; German Clb; Capt Flag Corp; Stage Crew; Yrbk Stf; Hon Roll; NHS; Rotary Awd; Spanish NHS; 2nd Pl DE Vly Sci Fair 86; Meritrs Prfrmnc Natl Grmn Tst 86; Merit Awd Outstndng Achvt Geom-Trig 85; Engrng.

HAGGERTY, JANET; Strath Haven HS; Wallingford, PA; (Y); Aud/Vis; Church Yth Grp; Cmnty Wkr; Girl Scts; Teachers Aide; School Musical; School Play; Fld Hcky; Cit Awd; High Hon Roll; Grl Scout Gold Awd 84; Home & Schl Assn Awd Excllnce Human Resrcs 86; Pres Acad Fit Awd 86; Miami U OH; Elem Ed.

HAGGERTY, LAURA; Crestwood HS; Mountaintop, PA; (Y); 35/200; Cmnty Wkr; 4-H; Hosp Aide; 4-H Awd; High Hon Roll; Hon Roll; Luzerne Cnty CC; Bus.

HAGGERTY, SEAN; Bishop Hannan HS; Dunmore, PA; (Y); Boy Scts; Computer Clb; Exploring; Ski Clb; Spanish Clb; Stage Crew; JV Bsbl; JV Stat Bsktbl; JV Var Mgr(s); JV Var Score Keeper; Mech Engrng.

HAGMANN, LISA; Villa Maria Acad; Erie, PA; (Y); Rep Sr Cls; Hon Roll; NEDT Awd; Slippery Rock U; Teaching.

HAGSTOTZ, MICHAEL; Northeast Catholic; Philadelphia, PA; (S); CAP; Rptr Nwsp Stf; Rep Frsh Cls; Rep Jr Cls; Rep Stu Cncl; Var Ftbl; JV Trk; High Hon Roll; NHS; Pre-Law.

HAHN, GLENDA; Faith Mennonite HS; East Earl, PA; (S); Sec Library Aide; Office Aide; Teachers Aide; Chorus; Nwsp Rptr; Bsktbl; Powder Puff Ftbl; Socr; Sftbl; Vllybl.

HAHN, HEATHER; Conrad Weiser HS; Robesonia, PA; (Y); 42/184; Church Yth Grp; Cmnty Wkr; Drama Clb; JCL; Quiz Bowl; Chorus; Capt Drm & Bgl; School Musical; Rep Stu Cncl; Hon Roll; Harcum JC; Equine Studies.

HAHN, LUCY; Scranton Preparatory Schl; Jermyn, PA; (Y); 72/192; Letterman Clb; Varsity Clb; Orch; Lit Mag; Tennis; High Hon Roll; Hon Roll; Entrance Exam Schlrshps 83; Natl Piano Auditions Wnnr Awd 77-86.

HAHN, PAM; Warren Area HS; Warren, PA; (Y); 60/300; Pres Church Yth Grp; Spanish Clb; Varsity Clb; VP Mrchg Band; Yrbk Stf; Var L Bsktbl; Var L Crs Cntry; Var L Trk; Hon Roll; Sec Jr NHS; Golden Dragon Awd 85-86; Clarion U; Earl Childhood.

HAHN, PETER JOON; The Haverford Schl; Broomall, PA; (Y); Church Yth Grp; Cmnty Wkr; French Clb; Math Clb; Model UN; Chorus; Orch; Nwsp Rptr; Var Trk; Ntl Merit SF; Robert C Rugg Mem Prize Bio Awd 83; Natl Chem Olympd 2nd Tm 85; Concours Natl De Francazse Cert 85; Bio Resrch.

HAHN, ROBERT; Archbishop Carroll HS; King Of Prussia, PA; (Y); 23/165; High Hon Roll; Hon Roll; NHS; Carroll Hnr Soc 84-85; Villanova Faculty Scholar; Vallanova; Elec Engrng.

HAHN, SUSIE; Chestnut Ridge HS; New Paris, PA; (Y); Church Yth Grp; Dance Clb; Band; Chorus; School Musical; Sec Frsh Cls; Stu Cncl; Var Cheerleading; L Socr; L Trk; Pres Chrus 85-86; JR Exec Comm 84-85; Millersville U; Elem Ed.

HAIBACH, DENISE; Fort Le Boeuf HS; Waterford, PA; (Y); Art Clb; Church Yth Grp; Dance Clb; Yrbk Stf; JV Var Cheerleading; Hon Roll; SOC Srvcs.

HAID, LISA RENE; Altoona Area HS; Altoona, PA; (Y); German Clb; Hosp Aide; JA; Speech Tm; Color Guard; Stage Crew; Nwsp Stf; High Hon Roll; Hon Roll; Church Yth Grp; JA Ms Bsnsprsn 85; Yth Ftns Achvmnt Awd 85.

HAIG, CHARLES; Northeast Catholic HS; Philadelphia, PA; (S); 8/431; JA; Ftbl; High Hon Roll; NHS; Bus Clb; Cmmnty Svc Corps; Jr Prom Comm; Acctg.

HAIGH, CHRISTY; Leechburg Area HS; Leechburg, PA; (Y); Church Yth Grp; Band; Chorus; Church Choir; Concert Band; Jazz Band; Mrchg Band; Pep Band; High Hon Roll; Hon Roll; Monroeville Schl Bus; Med Secry.

HAIGHT, ROBERT; Clearfield Area HS; Clearfield, PA; (Y); Key Clb; Spanish Clb; Chorus; Bsbl; Comp Tech Ptsbrgh; Comp Prgmr.

HAIGLER, DOROTHY; Cheltenham HS; Wyncote, PA; (Y); Church Yth Grp; Girl Scts; Teachers Aide; Chorus; Yrbk Stf; Rep Jr Cls; JV Capt Crs Cntry; JV Fld Hcky; JV Gym; JV Lcrss; Dist Rep Cntntl Yth Cncl 86-87; Dist Sec 85-87.

HAILE, EDWARD; Trinity HS; Camp Hill, PA; (Y); French Clb; Ski Clb; Band; Concert Band; Jazz Band; Mrchg Band; School Musical; School Play; High Hon Roll; Hon Roll; Physics.

HAIN, CHRISTINE; Southern Columbia HS; Elysburg, PA; (Y); 34/91; VP Church Yth Grp; Hosp Aide; Sec Mgr Band; Church Choir; Concert Band; Drm Mjr(t); Jazz Band; Mrchg Band; Pep Band; School Play; Hm Ec Awd 86; Miss TEEN Cntstnt Of PA 85; Pttsvl Hsptl Schl Of Nrsg; RN.

HAIN, RICCI; Spring Ford HS; Royersford, PA; (Y); 4-H; Bsktbl; Crs Cntry; Ftbl; Mgr(s); Socr; Tennis; Trk; Vllybl; 4-H Awd; Bio.

HAINER, LORI; Wilmington Area HS; New Wilmington, PA; (Y); Drama Clb; Key Clb; Spanish Clb; Drill Tm; Mrchg Band; Lit Mag; Cheerleading; Pom Pon; Powder Puff Ftbl; Hon Roll; Intr Dsgn.

HAINES, BARBARA; Lewisburg Area HS; Lewisburg, PA; (Y); Latin Clb; Concert Band; Mrchg Band; Trk; Hon Roll; NHS; Pre-Law.

HAINES, CRAIG; Moshannon Valley HS; Houtzdale, PA; (Y); Church Yth Grp; Band; Concert Band; Jazz Band; Mrchg Band; Pep Band; School Play; God Cntry Awd; Hon Roll; Accntng.

HAINES, DANA; Altoona Area HS; Altoona, PA; (Y); Church Yth Grp; Spanish Clb; Drill Tm; Jr NHS; Psych.

HAINES, DAVID; Mechanicsburg HS; Mechanicsburg, PA; (Y); 130/311; Boy Scts; Var Wrstlng; Hon Roll; Bio.

HAINES, DAVID; Newport HS; Newport, PA; (Y); 29/101; VP Church Yth Grp; Spanish Clb; Band; Chorus; Concert Band; Jazz Band; Mrchg Band; School Musical; School Play; Hon Roll.

HAINES, EDDIE; Moshannon Valley JR SR HS; Houtzdale, PA; (Y); 11/133; Exploring; Varsity Clb; Band; Concert Band; Jazz Band; Mrchg Band; School Play; Var Capt Bsktbl; Hon Roll; PA ST U; Pre-Law.

HAINES, MARGARET; West Catholic Girls HS; Philadelphia, PA; (Y); 1/245; French Clb; JA; Nwsp Sprt Ed; Hon Roll; NHS; Ntl Merit SF; Highest Gnrl Avg In Math & Sci 84-86; Wellesley Book Awd 85-86.

HAINES, RUSSELL; Wyoming Valley West HS; Kingston, PA; (Y); Sec Trs Church Yth Grp; Cmnty Wkr; High Hon Roll; Hon Roll; NHS; Excllnt Atten; Hghst Avg Spn III Cls; Edctn.

HAINES, SEAN P; Ligonier Valley SR HS; Ligonier, PA; (Y); Ski Clb; Chorus; Swing Chorus; Capt L Ftbl; Mgr(s); Wt Lftg; High Hon Roll; Hon Roll; Penn ST U; Bus.

HAINES, STEPHANIE; Moshannon Valley JR SR HS; Houtzdale, PA; (Y); 21/124; Hosp Aide; Pep Clb; Spanish Clb; SADD; Band; Chorus; Concert Band; Flag Corp; Yrbk Ed-Chief; God Cntry Awd; Clarion U; Nrsng.

HAINES, VANESSA; Freedom HS; Bethlehem, PA; (Y); 50/402; Math Clb; Math Tm; Trs Ski Clb; Band; Chorus; Church Choir; Mrchg Band; Hon Roll; Church Yth Grp; Trs Exploring; U Schlrshp-Sthrn Methdst U 86; Pres Acad Ftnss Awd 86; Sthrn Methdst U; Genetics.

HAINES, VICTORIA; Bethel Park HS; Bethel Park, PA; (Y); Art Clb; Church Yth Grp; Office Aide; Rep Stu Cncl; Hon Roll; Stu Rep Natl Assn Stu Cncl 85 & 86; Chrprsn Art Comm NASC 85; Cert Recog Outstndg Svc NASC Natl 85; BYU; Comm Art.

HAINES, WILLIAM G; South Side Catholic HS; Pittsburgh, PA; (S); Science Clb; Service Clb; Stage Crew; Variety Show; Pres Soph Cls; Var Capt Bsktbl; Im Ftbl; High Hon Roll; High Avrg Relgn.

HAINEY, STEVEN; York Catholic HS; York, PA; (Y); Varsity Clb; Chorus; School Musical; School Play; Ftbl; Var Trk; Bus Mgmt.

HAINLEY, AMBER; Garden Spot HS; New Holland, PA; (Y); Church Yth Grp; SADD; Band; Nwsp Stf; Stu Cncl; JV Bsktbl; JV Var Cheerleading; Var Powder Puff Ftbl; Jr NHS; Dental.

HAINS, BRIAN; Lebanon Catholic HS; Lebanon, PA; (Y); German Clb; Key Clb; Letterman Clb; Ski Clb; Varsity Clb; Bsktbl; Ftbl; Hon Roll; Gnrl Bus Awd 84-85; Bus Admn.

HAIRSTON, CAMILLE; Wilkingsburg HS; Pittsburgh, PA; (Y); VP Key Clb; Office Aide; Acpl Chr; Church Choir; Madrigals; School Musical; School Play; Hon Roll; Kiwanis Awd; Prfct Atten Awd; Optmtry.

HAIRSTON, SANTA; Solebury Schl; Lambertville, NJ; (Y); Varsity Clb; Lit Mag; Socr; Latin Awd; Proctor Dormatry.

HAJDUK, CHRISTINE; Mary Fueller Frazier Memorial HS; Star Junction, PA; (Y); Church Yth Grp; Drama Clb; FNA; Chorus; School Play; JV Bsktbl; JV Vllybl; High Hon Roll; Sec Trs NHS; Optmtry.

HAJEC, GLENDA; Corry Area HS; Spartansburg, PA; (S); 12/240; French Clb; Band; Concert Band; Jazz Band; Mrchg Band; Pep Band; Medcl Tech.

HAKE, CARRIE A; Red Land HS; Dover, PA; (Y); 58/285; Band; Concert Band; Mrchg Band; School Musical; Symp Band; Hon Roll; Accntng.

HAKIM, JOHN; Elmer L Meyers HS; Wilkes Barre, PA; (Y); German Clb; VP Ski Clb; Chorus; VP Jr Cls; VP Sr Cls; Rep Stu Cncl; Tennis; Trk; Hon Roll; Jr NHS.

HAKIM, TRACEY; James A Coughlin HS; Plains, PA; (Y); Hosp Aide; Ski Clb; Stat Bsbl; Var Fld Hcky; Stat Score Keeper; Jr NHS; NHS.

HALABURDA, MELISSA; Shenandoah Valley HS; Frackville, PA; (S); Pep Clb; Color Guard; Yrbk Ed-Chief; Trs Frsh Cls; Sec Jr Cls; Sec Hst Stu Cncl; JV Var Mgr(s); JV Var Sftbl; High Hon Roll; Hon Roll; Hnr Grd-Stu Of The Mnth 85; Rep In Miss Christmas Seal Pgnt & Winter Carnival Pgnt 85-86; Marywood Coll; Speech Path.

HALAHAN, LORI; Greensburg Central Catholic HS; Trafford, PA; (Y); Church Yth Grp; Ski Clb; Trk; High Hon Roll.

HALAHURICH, LINNEA J; Hempfield Area HS; Youngwood, PA; (Y); 15/657; VP Church Yth Grp; Sec Concert Band; Drm Mjr(t); Stu Cncl; Pres French Hon Soc; Pres Jr NHS; NHS; Drama Clb; French Clb; Hosp Aide; Presdntl Acadmc Ftns Awd 86; West Penn Memrl Schlrshp 86; Commnwlth PA Cert Of Merit 85; Washngtn & Jffrson Coll; Bio.

HALCOUSSIS, OURANIA SOPHIA; Hampton HS; Allison Pk, PA; (Y); Trs Church Yth Grp; Band; Concert Band; Mrchg Band; Symp Band; Hon Roll; Acctg.

HALDEMAN, DENISE; Manheim Central SR HS; Manheim, PA; (Y); Pres 4-H; Band; Chorus; Church Choir; Concert Band; Mrchg Band; Orch; School Musical; Powder Puff Ftbl; Trk; Estrn Mennonit Coll; Elem Tchr.

HALDEMAN, HEATHER; Pine Grove Area HS; Schuylkill Hvn, PA; (Y); Varsity Clb; Chorus; Yrbk Stf; Rep Soph Cls; Rep Jr Cls; Rep Stu Cncl; Var Cheerleading; Sftbl; Hon Roll; NHS; Physcl Fitnss Awds; Sci Awd 86; Art Awd; Zoology.

HALDEMAN, KEVIN; Lackawanna Trail HS; Dalton, PA; (Y); Band; Concert Band; Mrchg Band; Pep Band; JV Bsbl; Capt Bowling.

HALE, AMY; Tyrone Area HS; Tyrone, PA; (Y); DECA; Spanish Clb; Chorus; Color Guard; Rep Stu Cncl; Powder Puff Ftbl; High Hon Roll; Hon Roll; Fashn Mrchndsng.

HALE, CHRISTOPHER; Montour HS; Mckees Rocks, PA; (Y); Boy Scts; Church Yth Grp; Computer Clb; Math Tm; Var L Vllybl; High Hon Roll; Hon Roll.

HALE, DAYNA; West Branch Area JR R HS; Winburne, PA; (Y); 27/120; Spanish Clb; Varsity Clb; Band; Drill Tm; Mrchg Band; JV Bsktbl; Var Cheerleading; JV Sftbl; Var Twrlr; High Hon Roll; Dubois Campus PA ST.

HALE, KAREN; Nativity B V M HS; St Clair, PA; (Y); French Clb; Drill Tm; 2nd Hnrs 83-84.

HALE, TAMMY; Penns Manor HS; Barnesboro, PA; (Y); 17/78; Pres Church Yth Grp; Pres Varsity Clb; Nwsp Sprt Ed; Nwsp Stf; Var Capt Bsktbl; Var L Cheerleading; Stat Trk; Var Capt Vllybl; High Hon Roll; NHS; IN Cnty Vllybl Al-Stars 86; IUP; Phy Ed.

HALE, WENDY; Northeast Bradford HS; Warren Center, PA; (Y); Church Yth Grp; Sec Soph Cls; Var Cheerleading; Var Crs Cntry; Gym; JV Sftbl; Var Trk; Cit Awd; High Hon Roll; NHS; Outstndg Chrldr 86; Mst Valuable Rnnr Crss Cntry 84-85; Robert Packer Schl; Nrsng.

HALES, TRACEY; Methacton HS; Audubon, PA; (Y); French Clb; Office Aide; Ski Clb; SADD; Trs Rep Frsh Cls; Rep Soph Cls; Rep Jr Cls; Rep Stu Cncl; Var Cheerleading; Var Trk; Nastar Ski Rcng Awds 85; Psychlgy.

HALEY, BRIAN; Sun Valley HS; Aston, PA; (Y); 4/273; Math Clb; Variety Show; Var Bsbl; Var Bsktbl; Var Ftbl; High Hon Roll; Jr NHS; NHS; Pres Schlr; Outstndg Stu/Math 86; All League Hon Mntn Ftbl/Bsbl 86; PA ST U; Engrng.

HALEY, MARK D; South Side Catholic HS; Pittsburgh, PA; (S); 7/48; School Play; Nwsp Rptr; Var Capt Bsktbl; Hon Roll.

HALEY, SCOTT; Blue Ridge HS; Susquehanna, PA; (Y); Computer Clb; 4-H; Ski Clb; Band; Concert Band; Jazz Band; Comp Sci.

HALFAST, LARRY; Corry Area HS; Spartansburg, PA; (S); FFA.

HALFPENNY, JOHN; Scranton Tech; Scranton, PA; (Y); Bsktbl; Hon Roll; Mchnst.

HALL, AMY; Hughesville HS; Montoursville, PA; (Y); 3/132; Art Clb; Church Yth Grp; French Clb; Sec Trs Ski Clb; Varsity Clb; Chorus; School Musical; Yrbk Phtg; Yrbk Stf; Sec Soph Cls; Green & White Achvmnt Awd 85; Stu Council Schlrshp Awd 86; Bus Educ Typing, Accntng & Shorthnd Awd 86; Bloomsburg U; Accntng.

HALL, ANDREW; Bensalem HS; Bensalem, PA; (Y); Var JV Bsbl; Bsktbl; Var JV Ftbl; Hon Roll; Sr Babe Ruth Bsbl 85-86; Kutztown U; Accntnt.

HALL, ANDREW; Red Land SR HS; New Cumberland, PA; (Y); Church Yth Grp; FCA; JV Bsbl; Im Bsktbl; JV Var Socr; Im Sftbl; Im Vllybl; JV Wrstlng; Indstrl Arts Woodwrk 1st 84-85.

HALL, BRIAN; Bethel Park HS; Bethel Park, PA; (Y); Trs Church Yth Grp; Capt Quiz Bowl; Trs Science Clb; Church Choir; High Hon Roll; Comp Engrng.

HALL, BRUCE; Ambridge Area HS; Freedom, PA; (Y); French Clb; VICA; JV Var Mgr(s); JV Var Score Keeper; Hon Roll; Coll; Engnrng.

HALL, CAROL; Linden Hall HS; Houston, TX; (S); Q&S; Quiz Bowl; Chorus; Madrigals; School Musical; Nwsp Sprt Ed; Pres Soph Cls; Pres Jr Cls; Var Capt Bsktbl; Var Fld Hcky; US Army Resrv Natl Schlr-Athlt Awd; Schl Tour Gud; Rice U; Bus Adm.

HALL, CASSONDRA; West Branch Area HS; Kylertown, PA; (S); 7/138; Church Yth Grp; Spanish Clb; SADD; Varsity Clb; Yrbk Phtg; Yrbk Stf; Rep Stu Cncl; Bsktbl; Cheerleading; Crs Cntry; W Point Mltry Acad; Sci.

HALL, CHRISTINE; Fannett-Metal HS; Fannettsburg, PA; (S); 3/43; Trs FBLA; Band; Color Guard; School Play; Trs Stu Cncl; JV Bsktbl; Var Cheerleading; JV Sftbl; NHS; VICA; Hnr Rll Cert 83-85; Comp Opr.

HALL, CYNTHIA; Freedom HS; Bethlehem, PA; (Y); 180/445; Church Yth Grp; Office Aide; Band; Chorus; Church Choir; Concert Band; Mrchg Band; School Musical; Swing Chorus; Symp Band; Miss Amer Coed ST Fin 86; E Stroudsburg U; Elem Ed.

HALL, DAVID; Lincoln HS; Ellwood City, PA; (Y); 62/162; Spanish Clb; Im Mgr Bowling; Var L Ftbl; Var Trk; Wt Lftg; Hon Roll; Go Blue Ftbl Bstr Clb Schlr Athl Awd 86; Bvr Cnty Times Hnrbl Mntn Schlr Athl 86; Physcl Thrpy.

HALL, EDWIN; Connellsville Area HS; Mill Run, PA; (Y); Chess Clb; JV Var Trk; Fish & Game Clb; Tri-Tech Trade Schl; Crpntry.

HALL, EMILY; New Freedom Christian Schl; Shrewsbury, PA; (Y); 2/7; Drama Clb; German Clb; Science Clb; Chorus; Yrbk Phtg; Hon Roll; NHS; Sal; Math Clb; Southern Yrk Cty Rotry Clb Schlrshp 86; Maranatha Baptist; Elem Ed.

HALL, HEATHER; B Reed Henderson HS; West Chester, PA; (Y); 90/357; Civic Clb; Intnl Clb; JCL; SADD; Flag Corp; Yrbk Stf; Stu Cncl; Millersville U; Elem Ed.

HALL, JULIA; Mt Lebanon HS; Pittsburgh, PA; (Y); 65/507; Church Yth Grp; German Clb; Drill Tm; Sec Frsh Cls; Sec Soph Cls; VP Jr Cls; Ice Hcky; High Hon Roll; Church Choir; John Hopkins Tlnt Srch; Usher Music For Mt Lebanon.

HALL, KAREN; State College Area HS; Boalsburg, PA; (Y); 31/580; Church Yth Grp; Hosp Aide; Band; Concert Band; JV Var Fld Hcky; Trk; Hon Roll; Hlth.

HALL, KELLY; Montgomery Area HS; Allenwood, PA; (Y); 4/60; French Clb; Var JV Bsktbl; High Hon Roll; Hon Roll; NHS; U DE; Mech Engrng.

HALL, LESLIE; Northern Bedford HS; New Enterprise, PA; (Y); Pres Church Yth Grp; FBLA; Chorus; Concert Band; Mrchg Band; School Musical; Yrbk Stf; Var Capt Cheerleading; Socr; Hon Roll.

HALL, LINDA; Ephrata SR HS; Ephrata, PA; (Y); 26/226; Cmnty Wkr; Exploring; Concert Band; Nwsp Stf; L Fld Hcky; L Swmmng; Hon Roll; Chess Clb; Pres Acadmc Fitnss Awd 86; Best Time Drop 85 Swmmng 85; Excellnc In Soc Stud Awd 86; Amer U; Intrntl Stud.

HALL, LORI; East Lycoming-Hughesville HS; Montoursville, PA; (Y); 30/156; Church Yth Grp; Varsity Clb; Chorus; School Musical; Yrbk Phtg; Yrbk Stf; Powder Puff Ftbl; Tennis; Trk.

HALL, LYNN; Altoona Area Vo-Tech; Altoona, PA; (Y); #2 In Class; Hosp Aide; VICA; Mgr(s); Vo Tech Merit Ltr 85-86; Stu Mnth 85-86; Intr Dec.

HALL, MICHAEL; Bald Eagle Area HS; Julian, PA; (Y); 4-H; Var L Bsktbl; Var L Crs Cntry; Var L Trk; 4-H Awd; Mem Awd Cross Cntry 86; Hnr Roll Awd 85; Penn ST U; Meteorolgy.

HALL, MICHAEL C; Abraham Lincoln HS; Philadelphia, PA; (Y); 60/400; Computer Clb; Varsity Clb; Yrbk Stf; Stu Cncl; Swmmng; Bloomsburg U; Accntng.

HALL, MICHAEL T; Forbes Road JR SR HS; Hustontown, PA; (Y); 3/48; Varsity Clb; Pres Stu Cncl; Var L Bsbl; Var L Bsktbl; Bausch & Lomb Sci Awd; Cit Awd; High Hon Roll; Pres NHS; Drama Clb; French Clb; Teagle Fndtn Scholar 86; Pres Acad Fit Awd 86; March Dimes Scholar 86; U S Army Res Natl Schlr/Ath Awd; Juniata Coll; Bio.

HALL, RISHA KAYE; Central Columbia HS; Bloomsburg, PA; (Y); 31/177; VP Exploring; French Clb; Key Clb; Pep Clb; School Play; Stu Cncl; Stat L Bsktbl; Var L Tennis; Hon Roll; Frnch Key Awd 86; Dickinson Coll; Frgn Lang.

HALL, THOMAS; Cathedral Prep; Erie, PA; (Y); 28/242; French Clb; Model UN; Im Bsktbl; Ftbl; Im Vllybl; Pre-Law.

HALL, TIM; Shaler Area SR HS; Pittsburgh, PA; (Y); Exploring; Spanish Clb; Hon Roll; Spanish NHS; Elec Engrng.

HALL, TODD; Bethel Park SR HS; Bethel Park, PA; (Y); Sec Trs Church Yth Grp; DECA; Pres Science Clb; Church Choir; Var Trk; Purdue; Bus Mgmt.

HALLAM, ROBERT; Pocono Mountain HS; Cresco, PA; (Y); 30/300; Aud/Vis; Drama Clb; Acpl Chr; Trs VP Band; VP Pres Chorus; Concert Band; Jazz Band; Mrchg Band; Pep Band; School Musical; Outstndng Band Stu 85 & 86; Astrontcs Engrng.

HALLAM, STEVE; Bethel Park SR HS; Bethel Park, PA; (Y); Church Yth Grp; JA; SADD; Rep Stu Cncl; JV Var Ice Hcky; Rep Frsh Cls; Rep Soph Cls; Rep Jr Cls; Rep Sr Cls; JV Ftbl; Cnfrnc Of NASC Awd 85; Slppry Rck; Ed.

HALLAS III, EDWARD S; Ambridge Area HS; Baden, PA; (Y); Am Leg Boys St; German Clb; Pep Clb; SADD; School Musical; JV Var Bsbl; JV Var Ftbl; Hon Roll; USMA Wst Pnt Ny 86; US Mltry Acad.

HALLER, SARA; Monaca HS; Monaca, PA; (Y); 9/85; Office Aide; Sec Pep Clb; Drill Tm; Sec Sr Cls; Stu Cncl; Var L Sftbl; Hon Roll; NHS; Wolves Clv Schlrshp 86; May Queen 86; 1st Rnnr Up Prom & Ftbl Queen 86; Penn ST; Elem Ed.

HALLER, WILLIAM; Cocalico HS; Denver, PA; (Y); 25/250; Art Clb; Science Clb; Varsity Clb; Nwsp Rptr; Rep Stu Cncl; Var Bsktbl; Var Ftbl; Wt Lftg; High Hon Roll; Hon Roll; Air Force Acad; Aero Engrng.

HALLMAN, DREW; Pottsgrove HS; Pottstown, PA; (Y); 68/229; French Clb; Varsity Clb; Stu Cncl; Var L Bsbl; Hon Roll; Comp.

HALLMAN, NATALIE; St Huberts HS; Philadelphia, PA; (Y); Pres JA; Chorus; Church Choir; Jazz Band; Orch; School Musical; Awd-Jazzband-Ntl Hnr Soc 86; 2nd Pl-Song Wrtg Cont-Cath Daug Of Amer 86; Temple U; Music.

HALLOCK, JOHN DAVID; Stroudsburg HS; Stroudsburg, PA; (Y); Varsity Clb; Nwsp Sprt Ed; JV Var Bsbl; JV Capt Bsktbl; JV Var Ftbl; Wt Lftg; E Strdsbrg U; Ecnmcs.

HALLOCK, MICHELE; Coughlin HS; Wilkes Barre, PA; (Y); Church Yth Grp; Hosp Aide; Hon Roll; Comp Sci.

HALLORAN, BRIGITTE; Otto-Eldred HS; Eldred, PA; (Y); Chorus; Nwsp Rptr; Sec Jr Cls; JV Stat Bsktbl; Hon Roll; JR Rep Hmcmng 85; Prom Comm 86; JCC; Mgmt.

HALLORAN, CARRIE; Coudersport JR SR HS; Coudersport, PA; (Y); Church Yth Grp; French Clb; Varsity Clb; Band; Chorus; Flag Corp; Yrbk Stf; JV Var Cheerleading; Pep Clb; Ski Clb; PTA Art Awd 1st Pl Intermdte; 2nd Pl GFWC Fed Womens Clb; Moore Coll Of Art; Art.

HALLORAN, KEVIN; Central Catholic HS; Pittsburgh, PA; (Y); 30/275; Boy Scts; Church Yth Grp; French Clb; School Play; Stage Crew; Swmmng; French Hon Soc; High Hon Roll; Kent ST; Aeronaut Engr.

HALLOWELL, BRENDA; Du Bois Area HS; Dubois, PA; (Y); 52/297; Art Clb; Church Choir; School Musical; Stu Cncl; Score Keeper; Yrbk Stf; Clarton U; Math Ed.

HALLUM, SUSAN; West Allegheny HS; Oakdale, PA; (Y); 14/198; Church Yth Grp; Cmnty Wkr; Hosp Aide; VP Chorus; Church Choir; High Hon Roll; Hon Roll; Dir List Of Hnr Stu Parkway W AVTS 85-86; Wrthy Advsr Intl Order Rainbow For Girls 85-86; Radlgcl Tech.

HALOW, ALEX; Waynesburg Central HS; Waynesburg, PA; (Y); Chess Clb; Exploring; French Clb; Concert Band; Jazz Band; Mrchg Band; Crs Cntry; Trk; NHS; Smmr HS IHP Dqusne U 86; Law.

HALPERN, AMY; Bethel Park SR HS; Bethel Park, PA; (Y); Church Yth Grp; Girl Scts; Hosp Aide; JA; Band; Concert Band; Mrchg Band; Symp Band.

HALSEY, ANDREW; Emmaus HS; Emmaus, PA; (Y); 7/496; German Clb; Key Clb; Letterman Clb; Model UN; Pres Service Clb; SADD; Varsity Clb; Var L Socr; High Hon Roll; NHS; Aero Engr.

HALSTED, DRAYE; Southmoreland HS; Scottdale, PA; (Y); 38/223; French Clb; JCL; Latin Clb; Letterman Clb; Math Clb; Bsktbl; Ftbl; French Hon Soc; Washington & Jefferson; Bus.

HALTERMAN, MICA D; Waynesboro Area SR HS; Waynesboro, PA; (Y); AFS; Concert Band; Mrchg Band; Yrbk Stf; Fld Hcky; Hon Roll; Millersville U; Elem Educ.

HALUKA, LISA; South Park HS; Library, PA; (S); 33/208; FBLA; Spanish Clb; Yrbk Stf; High Hon Roll; Hon Roll; NHS; Bio.

HALUSHAK, AMY; Northampton Area HS; Northampton, PA; (Y); 94/444; Library Aide; Chorus.

HALUSZCZAK, STEPHEN; Carlynton HS; Carnegie, PA; (Y); Trs Church Yth Grp; French Clb; Yrbk Stf; High Hon Roll; Hon Roll; Pres Schlr; U Of Pittsbrgh; French.

HALVERSON, WILLIAM; Interboro HS; Essington, PA; (Y); Var Ftbl; Hon Roll; Bus.

HALVORSEN, KRISTEN; Norristown Area HS; Norristown, PA; (Y); Girl Scts; SADD; Jazz Band; Mrchg Band; School Musical; Yrbk Stf; Lit Mag; Hon Roll; NHS; Cngrs-Bndstg Grmn Exchng Schlrshp 86-87; Intl Rlts.

HAMBLETON, REGINA; Trinity HS; Amity, PA; (Y); 24/376; German Clb; Key Clb; Math Tm; Ski Clb; Chorus; Church Choir; School Musical; High Hon Roll; Medicine.

HAMBLEY, SHERRY; Cambria Heights HS; Hastings, PA; (Y); 70/200; NFL; Hon Roll; Art Inst Pittsburg; Comm Art.

HAMBRIGHT, SANDRA; Cedar Cliff HS; New Cumberland, PA; (Y); Chrmn Pep Clb; SADD; Stu Cncl; JV Capt Cheerleading; Sftbl; Trk; High Hon Roll; Hon Roll; Spanish NHS; Stdnt Trainr 85-86; U Of DE; Phy Thrpy.

HAMEL, JAMES; Oakland Schl; Pittsburgh, PA; (S); 1/60; Dance Clb; Library Aide; Spanish Clb; Stage Crew; Nwsp Rptr; Yrbk Phtg; Yrbk Rptr; Lit Mag; Pres Frsh Cls; Rep Sr Cls; PA ST U; Engrng.

HAMEL, PAUL; Bensalem HS; Bensalem, PA; (Y); Boy Scts; ROTC; Ftbl; High Hon Roll; Prfct Atten Awd.

HAMER, DENNIS; Peters Township HS; Venetia, PA; (Y); JA; SADD; Band; Concert Band; Jazz Band; Pep Band; Symp Band; Hon Roll; VP Stu Cncl; L Diving; Pre Law.

HAMER, WENDIE; Johnstown HS; Johnstown, PA; (Y); Exploring; French Clb; NFL; Band; Chorus; Mrchg Band; Orch; School Musical; Nwsp Rptr; Nwsp Stf; U Of Pittsburgh; Bus.

HAMERLA, DIANE; Upper Merion HS; King Of Prussia, PA; (Y); 57/350; Church Yth Grp; JV Capt Bsktbl; High Hon Roll; Hon Roll; Prfct Atten Awd; Ntl JR Wmns Rwng Cmp 86; Capt & MVP HS Crw Tm 85-86; Brnz & Slvr Mdls Canadian Ntl Rwng Chmpnshps; Physcl Thrpy.

HAMILTON, ANITA; Yough SR HS; W Newton, PA; (Y); Girl Scts; Ski Clb; VP Band; Chorus; VP Concert Band; VP Mrchg Band; Symp Band; Var Sftbl; Var Trk; NHS.

HAMILTON, CHRISTOPHER; Tussey Mountain HS; Saxton, PA; (Y); 5/100; Boy Scts; Church Yth Grp; Ski Clb; Varsity Clb; Nwsp Rptr; Nwsp Stf; Yrbk Stf; VP Frsh Cls; Var L Ftbl; Var L Trk; Eagle Scout Awd 86; Soroptomist Yth Ctznshp; Penn ST; Engrng.

HAMILTON, DAVID B; South Western HS; Hanover, PA; (Y); 67/215; Boy Scts; Chess Clb; JA; Var Trk; Penn ST; Mech Engrng.

HAMILTON, JAMES DOMINICK; Avella Area HS; Washington, PA; (Y); Computer Clb; French Clb; NHS; Outstndng Acad Wrk Bio 84-85, Wrld Cultures II 85-86; 1st Pl Chem Sci Fair 85-86; Sci.

HAMILTON, JIM; West Allegheny HS; Imperial, PA; (Y); 8/205; Science Clb; Varsity Clb; Nwsp Stf; JV Im Bsktbl; Var L Crs Cntry; Var L Trk; Var Wt Lftg; High Hon Roll; NHS; Prfct Atten Awd; French Awds 84-87; Calcls Math Tm 84; Strght A Complmntry Pirate Basbl Tckts 84-87; Chem.

HAMILTON, KELLY; Sharpsville Area HS; Clark, PA; (Y); Camera Clb; Church Yth Grp; Drama Clb; 4-H; French Clb; Hosp Aide; Office Aide; Pep Clb; Science Clb; Ski Clb; Ntl Olympc Awd Bio II 84-85; Penn ST; Sec Educ.

HAMILTON, MATT; Strath Haven HS; Media, PA; (Y); Church Yth Grp; Nwsp Rptr; Nwsp Stf; Ftbl; Trk; Wrstlng; High Hon Roll; Hon Roll; Vrsty Ltr Wrstlng 85-87.

HAMILTON, MIKE; Curwensville HS; Curwensville, PA; (Y); Chess Clb; VICA; Bsbl; OH Diesel Schl; Mech.

HAMILTON, TIMOTHY JOHN; Meadville Area SR HS; Meadville, PA; (Y); 23/267; VP Aud/Vis; Science Clb; Rep VICA; Nwsp Rptr; Yrbk Phtg; Im Bowling; Im Ice Hcky; Hon Roll; Pres Schlr; Western Crawford Cnty Jr Bwlrs Schlrshp Fnd 86; PA ST U; Accntng.

HAMILTON, TRACY; Ambridge Area HS; Baden, PA; (Y); Pep Clb; Nwsp Rptr; Nwsp Stf; Rep Frsh Cls; Rep Soph Cls; Rep Jr Cls; Hon Roll; Sawyer Schl; Travel.

HAMLET, CAROL; Northern York HS; Dillsburg, PA; (Y); 47/209; Chorus; Church Choir; Concert Band; Jazz Band; Mrchg Band; School Musical; Powder Puff Ftbl; Hon Roll; Music Hnr Socty Secy 86; PA All ST Lions Band 86; Fine Arts.

HAMLIN, SYDNEY; Riverview HS; Oakmont, PA; (Y); Band; Concert Band; Drm Mjr(t); Mrchg Band; Trs Jr Cls; Capt Bsktbl; Powder Puff Ftbl; Capt Trk; High Hon Roll; NHS; Rvrvw Ed Assn Schlrshp 86; W VA U; Pharm.

HAMM, DENISE R; Bishop Neuman HS; Williamsport, PA; (Y); 2/46; Church Yth Grp; Cmnty Wkr; Girl Scts; Model UN; NFL; Pres VP Pep Clb; School Musical; School Play; Nwsp Rptr; Sec Soph Cls; Soroptomist Intl Yth Ctznshp Awd 2nd Pl 86; NHS Scholar NASSP NMSC Spec Scholar 86; Stu Of Mnth 854; Loyola Coll; Bus Econ.

HAMM, GILBERT; St James HS; Chester, PA; (Y); 39/141; Boy Scts; Church Yth Grp; Computer Clb; Church Choir; Bsktbl; Crs Cntry; Trk; High Hon Roll; Hon Roll; Amercn Lgn Awd; Drexel U; Bus Adm.

HAMM, GRETCHEN; Taylor Allderdice HS; Pittsburgh, PA; (Y); 98/495; Drama Clb; Model UN; Political Wkr; Nwsp Rptr; Lit Mag; JV Crs Cntry; JV Trk; Wt Lftg; OH U; Cmmnctns.

HAMM, MIKE; Manheim Central HS; Manheim, PA; (Y); 20/240; Var L Ftbl; Wt Lftg; Var L Wrstlng; High Hon Roll; NHS; 4 Way Test Awd 86; Athlete Of The Wk-Ftbl 85; Coaches Awd Ftbl 85.

HAMM, STACEY; Parkland HS; Schnecksville, PA; (Y); 25/459; Exploring; JA; Math Tm; SADD; Pres Trs Stu Cncl; Var L Swmmng; High Hon Roll; NHS; Ntl Merit Ltr; 3rd Pl Dist XI Swmng Chmpnshps.

HAMMACHER, EVERETT; Central Dauplin HS; Harrisburg, PA; (Y); Band; Chorus; Concert Band; Drm & Bgl; Drm Mjr(t); Jazz Band; Mrchg Band; Orch; Pep Band; School Musical; Dist Band 86; Drm Mjr 86-87; PSU; Chem Engrng.

HAMMAD, SOHA; Penn Center Acad; Philadelphia, PA; (Y); 4/30; Yrbk Stf; Stu Cncl; Hon Roll; NHS; Peenn Ctr Acadmy Math Awd 86; The Rose Magil Awd 86; Prnts Assn Awd Acadmc Prgrss 86; Phila Coll Pharm Sci; Bio-Chem.

HAMMAKER JR, KENNETH L; Cumberland Valley HS; Mechanicsburg, PA; (Y); 37/522; Boy Scts; Church Yth Grp; Ski Clb; Band; JV Wrstlng; God Cntry Awd; High Hon Roll; Eagle Scout 83; Villanova; Bus Adm.

HAMMAKER, MICHELE; Susquenita HS; Marysville, PA; (S); 1/184; Church Yth Grp; Leo Clb; Quiz Bowl; Teachers Aide; Chorus; Church Choir; Yrbk Stf; Stu Cncl; Mat Maids; High Hon Roll; Hghst Rnkng In Clss 84 & 85; Duncannon Amer Lgn Aux Essay Wnr 84.

HAMMER, JON; William Allen HS; Allentown, PA; (Y); 114/704; Church Yth Grp; Nwsp Rptr; Lit Mag; Rep Stu Cncl; JV Bsktbl; Hon Roll; Jr NHS.

HAMMER, LISA; St Marys Area HS; St Marys, PA; (Y); 26/290; Cmnty Wkr; Var JV Cheerleading; High Hon Roll; Hon Roll; Jr NHS; NHS; Edinoro U; Crimnl Justc.

HAMMERASH JR, WILLIAM J; Belle Vernon Area HS; Perryopolis, PA; (Y); 3/273; Ski Clb; Bausch & Lomb Sci Awd; High Hon Roll; NHS; Pres Schlr; Mth Awd 86; Sci Awd 86; WA & Jefferson Coll; Chem.

HAMMILL, WENDY; Kiski Area HS; Saltsburg, PA; (Y); Sec Trs Church Yth Grp; Spanish Clb; SADD; Chorus; Church Choir; Concert Band; Mrchg Band; Pep Band; High Hon Roll; Bell Avn Alumni Schlrshp 86; IN U; Ed.

HAMMOND, ARTHUR; New Castle HS; New Castle, PA; (Y); #54 In Class; FCA; Letterman Clb; Spanish Clb; Varsity Clb; Band; Concert Band; Jazz Band; Pep Band; Rep Stu Cncl; Capt L Bsbl.

HAMMOND, MICHAEL; Northern York County HS; Dillsburg, PA; (Y); 46/201; Computer Clb; Spanish Clb; Bsbl; Coach Actv; Ftbl; Powder Puff Ftbl; Wrstlng; Hon Roll; Awds In Ftbl; PA ST Yrk Campus; Elec Engrng.

HAMMOND, PAM; Saint Huberts HS; Philadelphia, PA; (Y); 42/367; French Clb; Pep Clb; Chorus; Drill Tm; Hon Roll; NHS; Prfct Atten Awd; Gwynedd Mercy; Resp Thrpy.

HAMMOND, PAUL; New Hope-Solebury JR-SR HS; New Hope, PA; (S); 6/82; Boy Scts; FBLA; Mathletes; High Hon Roll; Hon Roll; NHS; Prfct Atten Awd; Eagle Scout 86; Glynnis Jaeger Awd In Biolgcl Sci 85; Math Tchr.

HAMMOND, SHEILA; Everett Area HS; Clearville, PA; (Y); Aud/Vis; Computer Clb; Pres FBLA; GAA; Spanish Clb; Nwsp Stf; Yrbk Stf; Hon Roll; NHS; Sec Spanish NHS; Allegany Comm Coll; Med Secr.

HAMPTON, LISA; Exeter HS; Reading, PA; (Y); 14/200; Band; Concert Band; Jazz Band; Mrchg Band; Orch; School Musical; Stu Cncl; NHS; Ntl Merit Ltr; Pres Schlr; APT Schlrshp 86; ETEA Schlrshp 86; West Chester Fresh String Schlrshp 86; West Chester U; Music Educ.

HAMPTON-PIERSON, LENNA; Avon Grove HS; Landenberg, PA; (Y); Sec Trs Church Yth Grp; Pres VP FBLA; SADD; Church Choir; Ed Yrbk Stf; Hon Roll; NHS; Bus Ed Awd 86; Typng III Awd 85; Ldr Awd 86; Sec.

HAMRAHI, DONALD; Moon HS; Coraopolis, PA; (Y); French Clb; JA; Tennis; Penn ST U; Engr.

HAMRIC, MARY; Washington HS; Washington, PA; (Y); 11/149; Letterman Clb; Pep Clb; Spanish Clb; Rep Soph Cls; JV Var Bsktbl; Var Tennis; Var Trk; High Hon Roll; NHS; PA ST U; Engr.

HAMSHER, ANGELA; Northern SR HS; Dillsburg, PA; (Y); Church Yth Grp; Drama Clb; NFL; Spanish Clb; Concert Band; Church Choir; Rep Color Guard; Drill Tm; Mrchg Band; Hon Roll; Spch Path.

HAMSHER, ROBERT; Kutztown Area HS; Lenhartsville, PA; (Y); Science Clb; Band; Concert Band; Jazz Band; Mrchg Band; School Play; Stage Crew; High Hon Roll; Jr NHS; NHS; Ldrshp Traing Camp 86; Drexel; Chem Engrg.

HAN, CLEMENCE; Cheltenham HS; Melrose Pk, PA; (Y); Intnl Clb; Math Tm; Elec Engr.

HANAK, SCOTT; Johnstown HS; Johnstown, PA; (Y); Exploring; Rep Stu Cncl; Hon Roll; Penn ST; Pre-Med.

HANBY, KRIS; Allegheny-Clarion Valley HS; Emlenton, PA; (Y); 1/104; Var L Bsktbl; Var L Trk; Co-Capt L Vllybl; Bausch & Lomb Sci Awd; Cit Awd; High Hon Roll; NHS; Pres Schlr; Val; Army Rsrv Schlr/Athlt Awd 86; U Of Pittsburgh; Phrmcy.

HANCHER, ANDREA; Central Dauphin HS; Harrisburg, PA; (Y); VP Church Yth Grp; VP Exploring; Girl Scts; Chorus; Church Choir; Capt Flag Corp; Hon Roll; GS Slvr Awd 83; GS Slvr Ldrshp Awd 83; Harrisburg Area CC; Acctng.

HANCOCK, KARL; Newport HS; Newport, PA; (S); 15/108; Boy Scts; Varsity Clb; School Play; Var L Bsbl; Var L Bsktbl; Var L Ftbl; Hon Roll; Patriot News Scholar; PA ST U; Mth.

HANCOCK, LAURETTE; Nativity HS; Pottsville, PA; (Y); 2/99; Dance Clb; Hosp Aide; Math Clb; Variety Show; Rep Sr Cls; Var L Crs Cntry; Hon Roll; Pres NHS; Pres Schlr; Sal; Presdntl Physcl Ftns Awd 86; Exellnc Sci Awd-Allied Corp 86; Villanova U; Librl Arts.

HANCOCK, LISA; St Hubert Catholic HS; Philadelphia, PA; (Y); 17/383; French Clb; Girl Scts; Hosp Aide; Pres Pep Clb; Service Clb; Jazz Band; Orch; Stage Crew; NHS; Bus Mgmt.

HANCOVSKY, PAUL; Peters Townshop HS; Mcmurray, PA; (Y); Varsity Clb; L Bsktbl; L Trk.

HAND, KATHY A; Tyrone Area HS; Tyrone, PA; (Y); Church Yth Grp; Cmnty Wkr; FTA; Library Aide; Red Cross Aide; SADD; Hon Roll; Order Of Rainbow; Hero Clb Tres & Secy 84-86; Penn St U; Spec Educ.

HANDERHAN, COLEEN; Carlynton JR SR HS; Carnegie, PA; (Y); Drama Clb; Band; Chorus; Concert Band; Jazz Band; Mrchg Band; School Musical; Symp Band; Hon Roll; Dist & Regn Chorus Festvls 85-86; Mrchng Band Drm Majrtt 86-87; Duquesne U; Music Ed.

HANDY, ERNESTINE; Cheltenham HS; La Mott, PA; (Y); Teachers Aide; Acctg.

HANDZA, EUGENE; Central Catholic HS; N Braddock, PA; (Y); 51/280; Var Tennis; Hon Roll; NHS; Spanish NHS.

HANES, DOUG; St Marys Area HS; St Marys, PA; (Y); 80/297; Boys Clb Am; Office Aide; Hon Roll; Mst Outstndng Drftng Stu 86; Penn ST U; Mech Engrng.

HANES, VICTORIA; Harbor Creek HS; Harbor Creek, PA; (Y); 47/202; Sec Church Yth Grp; Band; Concert Band; Mrchg Band; Orch; Variety Show; Hon Roll; NHS; Cmnty Wkr; SADD; Bible Schl Tch Pre Schl Lvl 85; Ltr Marching Band 85-86; PA ST; Communications.

HANEY, BARBRA; Hopewell HS; Aliquippa, PA; (Y); 1/250; Sec Exploring; French Clb; High Hon Roll; NHS; Ntl Merit SF; Cmnty Wkr; Yrbk Stf; Rep Frsh Cls; Rep Soph Cls; Im Powder Puff Ftbl; Hugh O Brian Yth Found Outstndng Stu 85; Activties Firefighter 83; Emergncy Med Tech 85; Wildlife Vet.

HANEY, MELISSA; Trinity HS; Washington, PA; (Y); 107/342; German Clb; Exec Sec.

HANEY, MICHELE; Hopewell HS; Aliquippa, PA; (Y); 48/297; Church Yth Grp; French Clb; Capt Cheerleading; High Hon Roll; Hon Roll; NHS; Natl Sec Awd 86; Robert Morris; Acctg.

HANEY, MICHELE; Northern Lebanon HS; Jonestown, PA; (Y); 10/175; Church Yth Grp; Varsity Clb; Chorus; Concert Band; Mrchg Band; Stat Bsktbl; JV Var Sftbl; Var Tennis; NHS; Penn ST; Med.

HANFORD, JAMEE; Kiski Area HS; Leechburg, PA; (Y); Pep Clb; Concert Band; Mrchg Band; Symp Band; Rep Jr Cls; Rep Sr Cls; Rep Stu Cncl; Sftbl; Twrlr; Hon Roll; IN U; Med Tech.

HANIFORD, DOUGLAS; Ringgold SR HS; Finleyville, PA; (Y); Boy Scts; Church Yth Grp; Varsity Clb; Stage Crew; Stu Cncl; Bsktbl; Hon Roll; Bsktbl.

HANK, ROBERT; Highlands SR HS; Natrona Hts, PA; (Y); DECA; High Hon Roll; Plz Merch Awd Outstndng D E Stu 86; Dist Educ Stu Of Yr 86; Outstndng Stu Forbes Road E Crpntry 86; Carpentry.

HANKIN, MAXINE; Solebury School; Highland Beach, FL; (S); Dance Clb; Drama Clb; Q&S; Teachers Aide; School Play; Stage Crew; Nwsp Rptr; Nwsp Stf; Var Gym; Hon Roll; Psych.

HANKINSON, BRIAN; Punxsutawney Area HS; Rossiter, PA; (Y); Am Leg Boys St; Math Tm; VP Science Clb; Sec Spanish Clb; Yrbk Stf; Pres Soph Cls; Var Ftbl; Var Trk; Hon Roll; NHS.

HANKS, PAM; Harbor Creek HS; Harbor Creek, PA; (Y); 17/222; Church Yth Grp; Hosp Aide; Ski Clb; Varsity Clb; Variety Show; Var Crs Cntry; Var Capt Trk; Hon Roll; NHS; Most Valuable Plyr 84-86; Allegheny Coll; Bio.

HANKS, VICKI; Somerset Area SR HS; Somerset, PA; (Y); 136/249; GAA; Pep Clb; Varsity Clb; Chorus; JV Capt Bsktbl; JV Vllybl; Hon Roll; Somerset Cmnty Hosp; X-Ray Tech.

HANLE, BARBARA; Pennsburg HS; Yardley, PA; (Y); 27/715; Off Service Clb; Chorus; Rep Stu Cncl; Bsktbl; Capt Cheerleading; Hon Roll; NHS; Pres Schlr; Boston U.

HANLEY, DANIEL; West Scranton HS; Scranton, PA; (Y); Boys Clb Am; Church Yth Grp; Ski Clb; Spanish Clb; Chorus; Yrbk Stf; Bsbl; Sftbl; Hon Roll; NHS; Swathmoore U; Sci.

HANLEY, JENNIFER; Sharpsville HS; Sharpsville, PA; (Y); Spanish Clb; Nwsp Bus Mgr; Nwsp Stf; Yrbk Bus Mgr; Yrbk Stf; Sec Jr Cls; Stu Cncl; Capt Cheerleading; Hon Roll; NHS; Econ.

HANLIN, EDWARD; Big Spring HS; Newville, PA; (Y); Church Yth Grp; Band; Concert Band; Mrchg Band; School Play; Hst Stu Cncl; Diving; Swmmng; Hon Roll; Elem Educ.

HANLIN JR, JOHN D; Riverview HS; Oakmont, PA; (Y); 12/119; AFS; Key Clb; Ski Clb; School Play; Yrbk Phtg; Var Bsbl; JV Ftbl; JV Golf; High Hon Roll; NHS; Attndnc Awd 86; Acad; Math.

HANLIN, KELLY; Avella JR SR HS; Avella, PA; (Y); French Clb; Ski Clb; Yrbk Stf; L Bsktbl; Hon Roll; NHS; Score Keeper; Elem Ed.

HANLON, CARRI; Penn Cambria HS; Loretto, PA; (Y); Drama Clb; 4-H; Trs French Clb; Stage Crew; Sec Frsh Cls; Sec Jr Cls; High Hon Roll; Hon Roll; Prfct Atten Awd; Scndry Math Ed.

HANLON JR, MATTHEW; John S Fine HS; Lower Askam, PA; (Y); Boy Scts; Church Yth Grp; Ski Clb; School Musical; Hon Roll; Rotary Awd; Hugh O Brien Yth Fndtn 85; Upward Bound Stu Govt 85-86; Essay Cntst Wnnr 84.

HANLON, SHERRI; Kiski Area SR HS; Apollo, PA; (Y); Pep Clb; Spanish Clb; Chorus; Swing Chorus; Sec Frsh Cls; Rep Stu Cncl; Hon Roll; Hnr Guard Grad Cls 86; Sec Bldng Commtte 85-86; IN U; Elem Ed.

HANN, CHRISTINE; Cheltenham HS; Elkins Pk, PA; (Y); 44/365; Church Yth Grp; Cmnty Wkr; Hosp Aide; Chorus; Orch; School Musical; Im Vllybl; NEDT Awd; Math Tm; JV Tennis; French 1st Hnrs 84-85; PJAS Sci Fair 1st Pl 85; DE Vly Sci Fair 1st Pl 86; Pre-Med.

HANN, JILL SUZETTE; Connellsville Area SR HS; Connellsville, PA; (Y); Church Yth Grp; 4-H; Service Clb; Band; Jazz Band; Mrchg Band; Symp Band; Pres Soph Cls; 4-H Awd; Hon Roll; California U PA; Spec Educ.

HANN, LEAH; Mt Pleasant Area SR HS; Acme, PA; (Y); 21/246; Exploring; Latin Clb; Band; Concert Band; Mrchg Band; Rep Frsh Cls; Mat Maids; Hon Roll; NHS; Edinboro U; Nrsng.

HANNA, BUSHRA; Allentown Central Catholic HS; Allentown, PA; (Y).

HANNA, JAMES; Franklin HS; Harrisville, PA; (Y); Drama Clb; 4-H; Ski Clb; Chorus; Rep Frsh Cls; Rep Soph Cls; Rep Jr Cls; Rep Sr Cls; 4-H Awd; Hon Roll; Natl Federation Of Music Clbs Awd 84; Pre-Dentistry.

HANNA, MARY; Conneaut Lake Area HS; Atlantic, PA; (Y); 27/97; Spanish Clb; SADD; Band; Color Guard; Concert Band; Mrchg Band; Nwsp Stf; Yrbk Stf; Hon Roll; Art Awd 85-86; Gannon U; Spcl Ed.

HANNA, REEM; Shady Side Acad; Pittsburgh, PA; (Y); 8/120; Church Yth Grp; French Clb; Ski Clb; Teachers Aide; Lcrss; Var Swmmng; Var Tennis; Cum Laude Soc; Leaman/Botti Prize; John Hopkins U; Med.

HANNA, SHAWN; Tyrone Area HS; Warriors Mark, PA; (S); 5/197; Pres Church Yth Grp; Dance Clb; Math Tm; Ski Clb; Chorus; School Musical; Swing Chorus; Golf; High Hon Roll; Hon Roll; Natl Hnr Soc 84-85, 85-86; Most Outstndng Stu 11th Eng 85-86; PA St U; Air Traf Cntrlr.

HANNAH, AMY; Seneca Valley SR HS; Evans City, PA; (Y); JA; Ski Clb; SADD; L Thesps; School Play; Stage Crew; Rep Jr Cls; Ntl Merit Ltr; Scrlt & Gry Schlrshp 86-87; Stdm Schlrshp Drmtry 86-87; OH ST U; Intl Bus.

HANNAH, ROBIN; North East HS; North East, PA; (Y); 50/150; Sec AFS; Letterman Clb; Q&S; School Musical; School Play; Stage Crew; Yrbk Stf; Mgr(s); Swmmng; Hon Roll; Cert Of Achvt For Creative Wrtng 86; Quill & Scroll 86; CA U Of PA; Prof Crtv Wrtng.

HANNAN, KAREN; North Allegheny HS; Pittsburgh, PA; (Y); 68/650; Yrbk Stf; Rep Frsh Cls; Rep Soph Cls; Sec Stu Cncl; Capt L Cheerleading; High Hon Roll; Hon Roll; Jr NHS; Prfct Atten Awd; Church Yth Grp; Distngshd Achvt Awd Sci Fr Bio 85-86; Accntng.

HANNER, DEBORAH; Cumberland Valley HS; Mechanicsburg, PA; (Y); Church Yth Grp; Spanish Clb; DAR 80; Harrisburg Area CC; Real Est.

HANNIGAN, KELLEY; Palmyra HS; Mt Gretna, PA; (Y); Church Yth Grp; Computer Clb; German Clb; Girl Scts; Hosp Aide; Pep Clb; SADD; Band; Chorus; Church Choir; Radiology.

HANNON, CATHIE; Chief Logan HS; Burnham, PA; (Y); 4/198; Math Tm; Yrbk Ed-Chief; VP Frsh Cls; VP Soph Cls; VP Jr Cls; Var Cheerleading; High Hon Roll; NHS; German Clb; Trs Varsity Clb; Dec Stu Of Mnth 84; Grmn Exch Stu July 85.

HANNON, KAREN; James M Coughlin HS; Wilkes-Barre, PA; (Y); 17/350; VICA; Color Guard; Drill Tm; Capt Flag Corp; Mrchg Band; High Hon Roll; Hon Roll; Jr NHS; NHS; Luzerne Cnty CC; Bus Data Proc.

HANNON, KYLE; Harbor Creek HS; Erie, PA; (Y); 14/219; AFS; Model UN; Off ROTC; Scholastic Bowl; Science Clb; Tennis; High Hon Roll; Hon Roll; NHS; VFW Awd; Silv Mdlst Natl Acad Tm Exam NJROTC 85; Distngshd Cadet Awd NJROTC 85; NJROTC Hnr Cadet Awd 86; Hstry Tchr.

HANNON, SEAN; Pittston Area HS; Avoca, PA; (Y); Key Clb; Band; Concert Band; Mrchg Band; Orch; Pep Band; Var Tennis; High Hon Roll; Im Bsbl; Home Hlth Admin.

HANSELL, CHERYL; Plymouth-Whitemarsh HS; Conshohocken, PA; (Y); FBLA; Chorus; JV Lcrss; JV Mgr(s); JV Trk; Hon Roll; Prfct Atten Awd; Bus.

HANSELL, VALERIE; Upper Perkiomen HS; Philadelphia, PA; (Y); Church Yth Grp; Chorus; School Musical; Variety Show; Lit Mag; Socr; Trk; Hon Roll; Hnrs Choirs; Berkeley Coll; Music.

HANSEN, AMY B; Kiski Area HS; Vandergriff, PA; (Y); Drama Clb; French Clb; FBLA; Pep Clb; Spanish Clb; Varsity Clb; Swmmng; Hon Roll; Hood Coll; Psych.

HANSEN, BECKY; Dunmore HS; Dunmore, PA; (Y); French Clb; Ski Clb; Cheerleading; Swmmng; Trk; Twrlr; Hon Roll; Pol Sci.

HANSEN, CHRISTOPHER D; Father Judge HS; Philadelphia, PA; (Y); Art Clb; Camera Clb; Cmnty Wkr; Drama Clb; Stage Crew; Nwsp Phtg; Nwsp Stf; Yrbk Phtg; Yrbk Stf; Bowling; Phtgrphy Art.

HANSEN, DAWN; Northampton Area SR HS; Bath, PA; (S); 209/475; AFS; Dance Clb; Hosp Aide; Band; Mrchg Band; Ed Nwsp Phtg; Ed Yrbk Phtg; Capt Pom Pon; Hon Roll; Yth Ed Assoc VP 85-86; Pom Pon Sqd Cptn 85-86; East Stroudsburg U; Photophy.

HANSEN, HOLLY; Interboro SR HS; Glenolden, PA; (S); Aud/Vis; Quiz Bowl; Band; Chorus; School Play; Nwsp Stf; Yrbk Stf; Stu Cncl; JV L Fld Hcky; NHS; Hnbl Mntn Del-Val Lg Fld Hockey 85-86; Cmmnctns.

HANSEN, JENNIFER; Churchill HS; East Pittsburgh, PA; (Y); 31/224; Library Aide; Ski Clb; Band; Chorus; Stage Crew; Hon Roll; HS Stu Athltc Trainer; Presbyterian U Hosp; Radiology.

HANSEN, KIM; Peters Twp HS; Mc Murray, PA; (S); 20/255; Aud/Vis; Computer Clb; Dance Clb; Hosp Aide; School Musical; Lit Mag; Rep Stu Cncl; High Hon Roll; Hon Roll; Westinghouse Sci Hnrs Inst 85-86; U CA; Physcn.

HANSEN JR, THOMAS G; Beaver Area HS; Beaver, PA; (Y); 31/177; Church Yth Grp; FCA; Ski Clb; Var L Bsbl; Im Coach Actv; Var L Ftbl; Powder Puff Ftbl; Im Wt Lftg; High Hon Roll; Hon Roll; Arch.

HANSON, SUSAN; Cardinal O Hara HS; Ridley Park, PA; (Y); 30/740; Cmnty Wkr; Dance Clb; Yrbk Stf; Vllybl; Hon Roll; NHS; O Hara Acdmc Awds Cnvctn 85-86; 2nd Prz Cnty Sci Fr 85; Hnrbl Mntn DE Valley Sci Fr 85; U Of Scranton; Blgy.

HANUSKA, KARL; Greater Johnstown HS; Johnstown, PA; (Y); FTA; Hosp Aide; NFL; Speech Tm; Chorus; Concert Band; Jazz Band; Mrchg Band; School Musical; JA; Journalism.

HANYO, ANNE; Kiski Area HS; Apollo, PA; (Y); Library Aide; Office Aide; Pep Clb; SADD; Teachers Aide; VICA; Color Guard; Drill Tm; Yrbk Stf; High Hon Roll; Pittsburg Beauty Acad; Teacher.

HANYOK, KIMBERLY; Purchase Line HS; Cherry Tree, PA; (Y); 10/111; 4-H; 4-H Awd; Hon Roll; NHS; Acadmc Al-Amer 84; Natl Ldrshp, Svc Awds 85; Acctng.

HAPP, COLLEEN; Henderson HS; West Chester, PA; (Y); 84/335; Church Yth Grp; DECA; Var JV Cheerleading; Diving; Trk; Hon Roll; NHS; 1st Pl DECA Competition Restrnt Mgmt 86; Hnr For Partcptn In United Cerebral Palsy Holiday Proj 86; Shippensburg; Bus Mgmt.

HAPPY, DENISE; Harbor Creek HS; Erie, PA; (Y); Dance Clb; Exploring; Spanish Clb; Y-Teens; Drill Tm; Mrchg Band; Variety Show; Rep Stu Cncl; Stat Trk; Hon Roll; Ltr Drill Tm 86; Erie Bus Center; Acctng.

HAPS, WANDA; Aliquippa SR HS; Aliquippa, PA; (Y); 2/195; DECA; Drama Clb; French Clb; Library Aide; Office Aide; SADD; Mrchg Band; Nwsp Ed-Chief; Yrbk Stf; Capt Pom Pon.

HAQQ, TOSHALYNN; Simon Gratz HS; Philadelphia, PA; (S); #1 In Class; Computer Clb; ROTC; Sftbl; Hon Roll; NHS.

HARABURDA, JUDY; Mt St Joseph Acad; Phila, PA; (Y); Art Clb; French Clb; JA; Nwsp Rptr; Lit Mag; High Hon Roll; NHS; Ntl Merit Ltr; NEDT Awd; Schlrshp Coll 86-87; Schlrshp HS 82-86; Carnegie-Mellon U; Psych.

HARALDSON, JENNIFER; Harborcreek HS; Erie, PA; (Y); Computer Clb; Girl Scts; Office Aide; Chorus; Acctng.

HARBAUGH, DE WAYNE; Franklin Area HS; Franklin, PA; (Y); 41/234; Cmnty Wkr; Sec French Clb; Political Wkr; School Musical; Yrbk Stf; Off Soph Cls; Off Jr Cls; Off Sr Cls; Stu Cncl; Mktg.

HARBAUGH, WENDY; Hempfield Area HS; Greensburg, PA; (Y); French Clb; Pep Clb; Chorus; High Hon Roll; Hon Roll; Ed.

HARBISON, GLENN; Phil-Mont Acad; Albington, PA; (Y); Art Clb; Computer Clb; Spanish Clb; Speech Tm; Varsity Clb; Band; Var JV Bsktbl; Capt Var Socr; Hon Roll; Spanish NHS.

HARBISON, LORI; Freeport SR HS; Sarver, PA; (S); #75 In Class; Concert Band; Mrchg Band; Pep Band; Off Stu Cncl; L Sftbl; L Vllybl; Hon Roll; Median Schl Of Allied Hlth.

HARDAWAY, CHUCK; Valley HS; New Kensington, PA; (Y); 30/250; Church Yth Grp; Drama Clb; Leo Clb; Science Clb; Ski Clb; Spanish Clb; Varsity Clb; JV Var Bsbl; JV Var Ftbl; Pre Med.

HARDEL, DARCY; Upper Merion SR HS; Wayne, PA; (Y); 6/350; Math Tm; Rep Soph Cls; Sec Jr Cls; Sec Sr Cls; Rep Stu Cncl; JV Fld Hcky; JV Lcrss; Var Swmmng; Hon Roll; Frnch Merit Awd 85-86; Mst Val Swmmr 84 & 86.

HARDEN, JANET L; South Side Catholic HS; Pittsburgh, PA; (S); 3/50; Service Clb; Nwsp Stf; Pres Jr Cls; Pres Stu Cncl; Var Sftbl; NHS; Awd Excllnc 84-85; Math & Engl Awd 84-85; Grgtwn U; Pre Med.

HARDEN, RUTH; Blue Ridge HS; Great Bend, PA; (Y); 22/120; Church Yth Grp; Debate Tm; Pres SADD; Variety Show; Trs Stu Cncl; Sec Bowling; Hon Roll; Lion Awd; Louise Bache Bus & Prof Wmn Amer Grl Yr 86; Air Force; Adm.

HARDING, REGINA; Perkiomen Valley HS; Perkiomenville, PA; (Y); 40/158; Church Yth Grp; Varsity Clb; Yrbk Phtg; Rep Soph Cls; Rep Stu Cncl; Capt L Bsktbl; Var Trk; Hon Roll; Pres NHS; Lcrss; Trck & Fld PIAA ST Champ Hgh Jmp 85-86; Bus.

HARDING, TIM; Lampeter-Strasburg HS; Strasburg, PA; (Y); 8/167; Band; Concert Band; Mrchg Band; VP Jr Cls; Bsbl; Wrstlng; High Hon Roll; NHS; 2nd Pl Local Sci Fair 86, Hnrb Mntn 85; City Cnty Sci Fair Amer Soc Metls Awd 86; PA ST; Engrng.

HARDY, DAMAHN; West Catholic For Boys; Philadelphia, PA; (Y); 21/220; Church Yth Grp; Bsktbl; Coach Actv; Hon Roll; Nat Sci Olympd Bio 85; Hnrs Sci Prjct W Cthlc Bys 85; Bus Mngmnt.

HARDY JR, DAVID E; West Catholic H S For Boys; Philadelphia, PA; (Y); 142/269; VP Church Yth Grp; Cmnty Wkr; Capt Debate Tm; Office Aide; Church Choir; School Play; Rep Stu Cncl; JV Bsktbl; Score Keeper; Prfct Atten Awd; Cert Outstndgn Conduct 85-86; Cert Awd Chorus 86; Cert Triest Colloquim 86; Temple U; Pre-Law.

HARDY, LORI; Harry S Truman HS; Levittown, PA; (Y); 13/573; Band; Concert Band; Mrchg Band; Crs Cntry; Diving; Swmmng; Hon Roll; NHS; Phy Thrpy.

HARDY, RICHARD; John S Fine HS; Glen Lyon, PA; (Y); Bsktbl; Trk; Luzerne Cnty CC; Auto Mech.

HARDY, SHARON JANE; Oxford HS; Oxford, PA; (Y); 17/161; Chorus; Yrbk Bus Mgr; VP Sr Cls; Sec Stu Cncl; Var JV Fld Hcky; Mgr(s); Trs NHS; Beaver Coll; Jourm.

HARE, MICHELLE L; West Perry SR HS; Landisburg, PA; (Y); 11/188; Pres Church Yth Grp; French Clb; Concert Band; Mrchg Band; Stage Crew; Hon Roll; NHS; Pres Schlr; Band; Rep Stu Cncl; Accelerated HS Stu 85; John Hall Merit Awd 85-87; Messiah Coll; Chrstn Psych.

HARES, MICHELLE; Lackawanna Trail JR SR HS; Nicholson, PA; (Y); Ski Clb; Hst Soph Cls; Bsbl; Var Fld Hcky; Score Keeper; Hon Roll; NHS; Physcl Thrpy.

HARGENRADER, KIMBERLY A; Clarion-Limestone HS; Clarion, PA; (Y); 3/81; Spanish Clb; Chorus; School Musical; School Play; High Hon Roll; Hon Roll; NHS; Outstndng SR Awd Scl Stds 86; Pres Acad Ftnss Awd 86; Excpntl Achvt Awd Scl Stds 84; Clarion U.

HARGRAVE, TERRI; New Castle SR HS; New Castle, PA; (Y); 28/243; Library Aide; Color Guard; Rep Frsh Cls; Rep Soph Cls; Rep Jr Cls; JV Var Bsktbl; Trk; Hon Roll; Hampton U; Cvl Engr.

HARGRAVES, JEROME; Chester HS; Chester, PA; (S); Church Yth Grp; High Hon Roll; Band; Concert Band; Mrchg Band; Hon Roll; Spch & Drama Awds 86; Widener U Smmr Hnrs Prog 85; Rotary Clb Chester Awd 85; Drexel U; Elec Engr.

HARGRAVES, MONICA; Valley HS; New Kensington, PA; (Y); Hosp Aide; VP JA; Office Aide; Spanish Clb; Varsity Clb; VICA; Chorus; Church Choir; Color Guard; Mrchg Band; Bd Of Gvrnrs Schlrshp 85-86; Wstmrlnd Cnty Fdrtn Of Wmns Clb 85-86; IN U Of PA; Comp Sci.

HARGREAVES, KELLI; Hatboro-Horsham HS; Hatboro, PA; (Y); 25/269; Pep Clb; SADD; Chorus; Rep Jr Cls; Var Powder Puff Ftbl; JV Socr; JV Tennis; Var Trk; Hon Roll; Prfct Atten Awd; Phy Thrpst.

HARGROVE, JOS; West Catholic Sor Boys; Philadelphia, PA; (Y); 137/215; JA; Saint Josephs U; Med Doctor.

HARHART, JAMES; Northampton SR HS; Walnutport, PA; (Y); 42/475; Model UN; JV Bsktbl; Var L Ftbl; Var L Trk; Im Wt Lftg; Ftbl Schlr Athlete Awd; Play Lehigh Vly All Star Ftbl Classic; US Merchant Marine Acad; Engr.

HARKANSON, DENISE; Little Flower Catholic For Girls; Philadelphia, PA; (Y); 135/415; Computer Clb; Hosp Aide; Office Aide; Teachers Aide; Hon Roll; Sci Awd/Sci Fair Theam 84-85.

HARKCOM, JONI; Somerset Area SR HS; Somerset, PA; (Y); 19/239; German Clb; VP JA; Pep Clb; Band; Concert Band; Mrchg Band; Trs Soph Cls; Pres Jr Cls; High Hon Roll; Hon Roll; Var Band Ltr 85-86; Acadmc Achvt Awd 86; Bus.

HARKER, JODI; Bellwood-Antis HS; Bellwood, PA; (Y); 4/128; Pres VP FBLA; Off Key Clb; Office Aide; School Play; Yrbk Stf; Trs Stu Cncl; Cit Awd; Hon Roll; NHS; Acdmc All Amer 86; IN U PA; Fash Merch.

HARKINS, DIANE; Purchase Line HS; Clymer, PA; (Y); Spanish Clb; Band; Chorus; Concert Band; Mrchg Band; Pep Band; School Play; Hon Roll.

HARKINS, JOHN; Mechanicsburg Ares SR HS; Mechanicsburg, PA; (Y); 18/311; Boy Scts; Church Yth Grp; Cmnty Wkr; Chorus; High Hon Roll; NHS; Eagle Scout 85; Lafayette; Chem Engrng.

HARKINS, JULIANNE; Baldwin HS; Pittsburgh, PA; (Y); Church Yth Grp; Office Aide; SADD; Chorus; Drill Tm; School Musical; Variety Show; Stu Cncl; Prfct Atten Awd; U Pttsburgh; Ped Nrs.

HARKINS, KEITH; Cardinal Brennan HS; Shenandoah, PA; (Y); 1/50; German Clb; Rep Frsh Cls; Rep Soph Cls; Rep Jr Cls; Pres Stu Cncl; Var Bsbl; Bausch & Lomb Sci Awd; Gov Hon Prg Awd; High Hon Roll; NHS; Gvrnrs Schl Intl Stud 85; Sci.

HARKINS, MARIGRACE; Nazareth Acad; Philadelphia, PA; (Y); Church Yth Grp; Hosp Aide; Latin Clb; Chorus; Church Choir; Orch; School Musical; Swing Chorus; Variety Show; Hon Roll; Hartford; Engrng.

HARKLESS, KIM; West Middlesex HS; W Middlesex, PA; (S); 2/114; FNA; Math Tm; Service Clb; Pres Spanish Clb; Yrbk Sprt Ed; Yrbk Stf; Stu Cncl; Bsktbl; Trk; Vllybl; Gannon U; Comp Sci.

HARLACHER, SCOT; West York Area HS; York, PA; (Y); 49/191; Boy Scts; Church Yth Grp; Spanish Clb; Varsity Clb; Var Crs Cntry; Var Trk; Hon Roll; Mltry.

HARLACHER, SELENA; Christian School Of York; East Berlin, PA; (S); Church Yth Grp; Hosp Aide; Library Aide; Chorus; Concert Band; Orch; Sec Jr Cls; Sec Sr Cls; Hon Roll; JA; Miss Yth Christ 84; Lancaster Bible Coll.

HARLACKER, CATHY; Dover Area HS; Dover, PA; (Y); 69/237; Trs Church Yth Grp; VP FFA; Var L Fld Hcky; Ntl Merit SF; VA Tech Ag Yth Forum 86; Penn ST; Anml Sci.

HARLAN, KELLI; Elizabeth Forward HS; Elizabeth, PA; (Y); VP Spanish Clb; Chorus; Flag Corp; Stat Bsktbl; High Hon Roll; NHS; Grove City Coll; Tchr.

HARLEY, BRENDA; Hollidaysburg Area SR HS; Duncansville, PA; (Y); 8/346; French Clb; Science Clb; SADD; Concert Band; Mrchg Band; French Hon Soc; Hon Roll; NHS; Ntl Merit Schol; NEDT Awd; Provost Scholar U Pittsburgh 86; Cnty Band 84-86; U Pittsburgh; Phys Thrpy.

HARLEY, YVONNE; Clearfield Area HS; Clearfield, PA; (Y); 20/301; Church Yth Grp; Key Clb; Coach Actv; Capt Swmmng; Trk; High Hon Roll; NHS; Lycoming Coll; Bus Admin.

HARMAN, DALE RICHARD; Fairview HS; Fairview, PA; (Y); 4/183; Church Yth Grp; Debate Tm; Ski Clb; Varsity Clb; JV Bsktbl; VP NHS; Ntl Merit Ltr; French Clb; NFL; Times Pblshngs Co Schlrshp 86; Allghny Schlrs Awd 86; Allegheny Coll; Med.

HARMAN, JODI; York County Area Vo-Technical Schl; York, PA; (Y); FHA; Bsktbl; Vllybl; Hon Roll; Gallaudet Coll.

HARMAN JR, RONALD R; Freeland HS; Freeland, PA; (Y); 1/95; Chess Clb; Computer Clb; FBLA; Math Tm; Quiz Bowl; Scholastic Bowl; Spanish Clb; Stage Crew; Yrbk Ed-Chief; High Hon Roll; USAF Acad; Astrntcl Engrng.

HARMAN, THERESA; Biglerville HS; Biglerville, PA; (Y); 12/86; Art Clb; FCA; Trs Varsity Clb; Ed Yrbk Stf; Var Bsktbl; Var Capt Fld Hcky; Var Sftbl; High Hon Roll; Jr NHS; Hon Roll; Babe Ruth & Dick Walton Awds 86; US Army Rsrv Ntl Schlr Athl Awd 86; MVP Fld Hocky, Bsktbl, Sftbl 86; Antonellis Inst Of Art; Art.

HARMER, MICHELE; Roxborough HS; Philadelphia, PA; (Y); 4/290; Office Aide; Chorus; School Musical; Nwsp Rptr; Nwsp Stf; Yrbk Ed-Chief; Yrbk Stf; High Hon Roll; Hon Roll; NHS; Temple U; Phy Thrpy.

HARMON, JANEL; Chester HS; Chester, PA; (Y); Chorus; Church Choir; School Play; Variety Show; Hon Roll; Music Thtr Awd 86; Cmptr Pgrmng.

HARMON, MICHAEL; Shanksville Stony Creek Vo Tech; Berlin, PA; (Y); Pres Jr Cls; Williamsport Area CC; Air Cond.

HARMON, NICHOLE; Phila High School For Girls; Philadelphia, PA; (Y); 34/395; Pres Church Yth Grp; Hosp Aide; Service Clb; Nwsp Stf; Stu Cncl; High Hon Roll; Jr NHS; Ntl Merit Ltr; Spanish NHS; Val; 3rt Pl Natl Conf Chrstns & Jews Brthrhd/Sistrhd Wk Essy Cont 86; Pre-Med.

HARMON, RODNEY; John S Fine HS; W Nanticoke, PA; (Y); Cert Of Profcncy-Bkkpng, Accntng, Bus Math & Typwrtng 84-86; Luzerne County CC; Bus.

HARNER, BURNIE; Line Mountain HS; Dornsife, PA; (Y); 25/107; Computer Clb; Drama Clb; FBLA; Chorus; Church Choir; Nwsp Sprt Ed; Stu Cncl; Hon Roll; Lock Haven U; Scndry Educ.

HARNER, PENNY; Tri-Valley HS; Hegins, PA; (Y); 3/75; Pres Church Yth Grp; Band; Yrbk Stf; L Vllybl; DAR Awd; Hon Roll; JP Sousa Awd; NHS; Drama Clb; Concert Band; Hegins Rotary Stu Of Mnth 86; Pres Acad Fit Awd 86; Penn ST; Radlgy.

HARNETT, GEORGE E; Commodore Perry HS; Hadley, PA; (S); 1/65; Math Tm; Ski Clb; Stage Crew; Pres Jr Cls; Var Bsbl; High Hon Roll; NHS; Amer Chem Soc Outstndng Achvt Chem 85; Penn ST U.

HARNEY, CRISSY; Norristown Area HS; Norristown, PA; (Y); Pres VP Church Yth Grp; Exploring; Girl Scts; NFL; VP Sec SADD; Nwsp Rptr; Lit Mag; Hon Roll; Grl Sct Gld Awd 86; Ntl Yth Frst Aid Cmptn 86; Ntl Frnsc Lge 2nd Pl Rgn ST Fnlst 84; Cmmntns.

HARNISH, ERIC; Dover Area HS; Dover, PA; (S); 2/249; Quiz Bowl; Band; Chorus; Concert Band; Var Socr; Var Tennis; NHS; School Musical; School Play; Yrbk Stf; Amer Chemcl Soc Awd 85; Renaissance Chrl Grp Hnrs 84-86; Schlrshp Yth Schlrs Pgm Chem 85; Sci.

HARNISH, JAMES; West Catholic Boys HS; Philadelphia, PA; (Y); 14/268; Mathletes; Variety Show; Yrbk Stf; Im Bsktbl; Im Trk; Hon Roll; NHS; Acdm Exclne Awd Sci 86; Cert Merit Outstndng Cndct 84-86; Outstndng Achvt Intrmrls 86; Drexel U; Engrng.

HARNISH, SARAH; Hempfield HS; Lancaster, PA; (Y); 190/418; Church Yth Grp; Drama Clb; JA; Science Clb; Chorus; Church Choir; Mrchg Band; School Musical; Variety Show; Mdrn Msc Mstrs Hnr Scty 85-87; Lncstr/Lbn Cnty Chorus 84-86; PA Dstrct 7 Chorus 85-86; Elem Ed.

HAROS, NICHOLAS; Salisbury HS; Allentown, PA; (Y); 14/138; Debate Tm; Model UN; SADD; Rep Jr Cls; L Var Bsbl; L Var Ftbl; High Hon Roll; Hon Roll; Rotary Awd; Adv Plcmnt Math,Hist; Law.

HARP, CHADWICK A; Norristown Area HS; Norristown, PA; (S); 20/500; Aud/Vis; Intnl Clb; Ski Clb; Orch; Nwsp Phtg; Yrbk Phtg; Lit Mag; Off Jr Cls; Tennis; NHS; Harvard U; Hstry.

HARPEL, CRIS A; Mars Area HS; Valencia, PA; (Y); Spanish Clb; Rep Soph Cls; Acad Ltr 84-85; Svc Bar Acad 85-86; Art Inst Pittsburgh; Comm Art.

HARPEL, SCOTT; Brandywine Heights HS; Topton, PA; (Y); Var Socr; Var Wrstlng; Frstry.

HARPER, ANGELA; Plymouth Whitemarsh HS; Norristown, PA; (Y); Church Yth Grp; Cmnty Wkr; Computer Clb; Dance Clb; Drama Clb; Drill Tm; Cheerleading; Tennis; Trk; Hon Roll; W Chester U Of PA; Spcl Educ.

HARPER, CRYSTAL; Cecilian Acad; Philadelphia, PA; (S); Girl Scts; Hosp Aide; JA; Pep Clb; Science Clb; Nwsp Stf; Yrbk Stf; NHS; NEDT Awd; Acad Scholar 84-86; NY U; Jrnlsm.

HARPER, CYNDI; Mc Guffey HS; Amity, PA; (Y); Church Yth Grp; French Clb; Trs JA; Pep Clb; Rep Frsh Cls; Rep Soph Cls; Rep Jr Cls; Var Powder Puff Ftbl; Hon Roll; Pre Med.

HARPER, DOROTHY; Schenley Teachers Center HS; Pittsburgh, PA; (S); 20/163; JA; Pep Clb; Church Choir; School Musical; Yrbk Stf; Sftbl; Swmmng; Stu Cncl; Trk; High Hon Roll; Beard Of Govrnr Schlrshp Full 4 Yr Tuitn IN U Of PA 86; IN U Of PA; Bio.

HARPER, PAULA; Uniontown SR HS; Smock, PA; (Y); #10 In Class; JA; Spanish Clb; Band; Concert Band; Mrchg Band; Stu Cncl; Twrlr; High Hon Roll; NHS; Prfct Atten Awd; U Of Pittsburgh; Biochem.

HARPER, RICK; Conrad Weiser SR HS; Robesonia, PA; (Y); 1/184; Computer Clb; Drama Clb; Scholastic Bowl; Chorus; Concert Band; Jazz Band; School Musical; JV Socr; High Hon Roll; NHS.

HARPER, SCOTT; Lewistown HS; Lewistown, PA; (Y); Boy Scts; Debate Tm; German Clb; Letterman Clb; Ski Clb; Speech Tm; Band; Chorus; Concert Band; Mrchg Band; Juniata Coll; Pre Med.

HARPER, SHERRI; Elizabethtown Area HS; Elizabethtown, PA; (Y); Teachers Aide; Band; Yrbk Stf; Var Cheerleading; Powder Puff Ftbl; Big E Booster Clb Mst Improved Chrldng 85-86; Harrisburg Area CC; Erly Chldh.

HARPER, SHERRY; Halifax Area HS; Halifax, PA; (S); #3 In Class; Pres Church Yth Grp; FBLA; Chorus; Flag Corp; Yrbk Stf; Sec Sr Cls; Rep Stu Cncl; Stat Bsktbl; Powder Puff Ftbl; Jr NHS; Indiana U Of PA.

HARPER, TERRI; William Penn HS; Philadelphia, PA; (Y); 3/242; Teachers Aide; Yrbk Stf; Rep Jr Cls; Rep Sr Cls; Rep Stu Cncl; JV Crs Cntry; Capt Im Tennis; JV Trk; Hon Roll; NHS; Bst All Arnd Math-Wright Math Awd 86; Achvt Socl Stds 86; Howard U; Human Dev.

HARPER, TRACI; Meyersdale Area HS; Meyersdale, PA; (S); Pres Church Yth Grp; FBLA; Pep Clb; Spanish Clb; Yrbk Stf; Hon Roll.

HARPER, TROY; Ringgold HS; Donora, PA; (Y); Varsity Clb; Var Ftbl; Wt Lftg; Hon Roll; Ethnic Stud Prog 85-86; Polt Sci.

HARPER, VICKI Y; The Cecilian Acad; Philadelphia, PA; (Y); Office Aide; Pres Pep Clb; Spanish Clb; Yrbk Ed-Chief; Score Keeper; Sftbl; Timer; NHS; Syracuse U; Spnsh.

HARPST, RACHELLE; Reynolds HS; Fredonia, PA; (Y); 4/126; Pres Latin Clb; Q&S; Yrbk Ed-Chief; Trs Stu Cncl; Co-Capt L Bsktbl; Co-Capt L Trk; Capt L Vllybl; DAR Awd; Pres NHS; VFW Awd; Army Schlr/Athltc Awd 86; Schlr Sprt Awd 86; Mercer Cnty Hall Of Fame Awd 86; Grove City Coll; Acctng.

HARPSTER, JOHN; Bellefonte Area SR HS; Bellefonte, PA; (Y); Ski Clb.

HARPSTER, PAMELA; Juniata HS; E Waterford, PA; (Y); Church Yth Grp; FHA; Library Aide; VICA; School Play; High Hon Roll; Hon Roll; NHS; Miss PA Pagnt 86.

HARPSTER, SHERRI; Danville SR HS; Danville, PA; (Y); 22/162; Pres Exploring; Hosp Aide; Ski Clb; Yrbk Stf; Capt Stu Cncl; Bsktbl; Var Sftbl; High Hon Roll; Vastine Bernheimer Mem Fund Scholar 86; Daemen Coll; Phys Thrpy.

HARR, BONNIE; Chestnut Ridge SR HS; New Paris, PA; (S); 5/142; FBLA; Sec Spanish Clb; Chorus; Trs Jr Cls; JV Var Cheerleading; High Hon Roll; Hon Roll; Prfct Atten Awd; Bus.

HARR, KIMBERLY; Hollidaysburg SR HS; Hollidaysburg, PA; (Y); German Clb; GAA; SADD; Y-Teens; Chorus; JV Sftbl; Hon Roll; Prfct Atten Awd; Law.

HARR, LISA; Forest Hills HS; Salix, PA; (Y); 29/168; Hon Roll; Bradford; Accntng.

HARR, TINA M; Hollidaysburg Area SR HS; Hollidaysburg, PA; (Y); Pres Church Yth Grp; JA; SADD; Teachers Aide; Church Choir; Sec Sr Cls; Stu Cncl; Vllybl; Cit Awd; Prfct Atten Awd; Bus Secy.

HARR, YVONNE; Mt Pleasant Area HS; Somerset, PA; (Y); GAA; Pep Clb; Ski Clb; Teachers Aide; Band; Concert Band; Mrchg Band; Pep Band; Vllybl; High Hon Roll; Dstrct Band 85-86; IN U Of PA; Psych.

HARRINGTON, ANITA; South Philadelphia HS; Philadelphia, PA; (Y); Acpl Chr; Hon Roll.

HARRINGTON, MAUREEN; Cardinal Dougherty HS; Pila, PA; (Y); Church Yth Grp; GAA; Hosp Aide; Off Sr Cls; Rep Stu Cncl; Socr; Sftbl; Phy Ed Awd 82-83; Rlgn Awd 82-83; Temple U; Phy Thrpy.

HARRIS, AIMEE; Washington HS; Washington, PA; (S); Church Yth Grp; Library Aide; SADD; Church Choir; Flag Corp; Yrbk Phtg; Bsktbl; Cit Awd; Prfct Atten Awd; Hlth Awd 83-84; Psych.

HARRIS, ANDREA; Manheim Township HS; Lancaster, PA; (Y); 101/325; Church Yth Grp; Rep Jr Cls; Rep Sr Cls; Stu Cncl; JV Cheerleading; Hon Roll; Presb Chrch Sndy Schl Tchr 86.

HARRIS, CAREY; Carlynton HS; Pittsburgh, PA; (Y); Art Clb; Church Yth Grp; Drama Clb; Teachers Aide; Nwsp Rptr; Sec Stu Cncl; Var Cheerleading; Var Swmmng; Hon Roll; NEDT Awd; Sclgy.

HARRIS, DAIVD; Slippery Rock Area HS; Slippery Rock, PA; (Y); Office Aide; Band; Concert Band; Jazz Band; Mrchg Band; Pep Band; School Musical; Var Socr; Ltrmn Rifle Tm 85.

HARRIS, EUNICE; Simon Gratz HS; Philadelphia, PA; (S); 17/300; Pres Church Yth Grp; Pres FBLA; Teachers Aide; Band; Chorus; Church Choir; Concert Band; Orch; School Play; Yrbk Ed-Chief; Distingshd Awd 85; Typng Awd 85; Cmmnctns.

HARRIS, GEORGE; Mifflinburg HS; Mifflinburg, PA; (Y); Drama Clb; 4-H; French Clb; Key Clb; SADD; Stage Crew; Bsktbl; Golf; Socr; Hon Roll; Bus Admin.

HARRIS, JAUNA; Union HS; Rimersburg, PA; (Y); 7/57; Church Yth Grp; Trs French Clb; School Play; Yrbk Ed-Chief; Yrbk Phtg; Rep Stu Cncl; Var JV Bsktbl; Vllybl; Hon Roll; NHS; Engrng.

HARRIS, JILL; Hempfield HS; Lancaster, PA; (Y); 62/450; Varsity Clb; Chorus; Rep Frsh Cls; Trs Soph Cls; Trs Jr Cls; Trs Sr Cls; Var L Diving; Var L Fld Hcky; Var L Trk; Hon Roll; Bus Mgmt.

HARRIS, JIM; E L Meyers HS; Wilkes Barre, PA; (Y); Ski Clb; Chorus; Yrbk Stf; Rep Stu Cncl; Var Crs Cntry; Var Trk; Var Wrstlng.

HARRIS, JOSEPH; St John Neumann HS; Philadelphia, PA; (Y); 67/372; Science Clb; VP Band; Chorus; Concert Band; Pep Band; Rep Soph Cls; Bus.

HARRIS, KIRA; Gateway SR HS; Monroeville, PA; (Y); 94/508; GAA; Keywanettes; Pep Clb; Spanish Clb; Chorus; Variety Show; Nwsp Ed-Chief; Nwsp Rptr; Nwsp Stf; Yrbk Rptr; Howard U; Mass Comm.

HARRIS, LISA; Mc Guffey HS; Taylorstown, PA; (Y); Cmnty Wkr; FHA; Pep Clb; Chorus; School Play; Hon Roll; Washington/Jeffrson Coll; Psych.

HARRIS, LISA; Portage Area HS; Portage, PA; (Y); 39/126; Girl Scts; Ski Clb; Chorus; Stat Bsktbl; JV Cheerleading; Hon Roll; U IN Pittsburgh; Law.

HARRIS, LLOYD; Strath Haven HS; Wallingford, PA; (Y); Art Clb; Boy Scts; Cmnty Wkr; PAVAS; School Musical; School Play; Nwsp Stf; High Hon Roll; Vrsty Arts Awd 86; Musician.

HARRIS, MARK; Brookville Area HS; Brookville, PA; (S); 5/150; Boy Scts; Church Yth Grp; Trs German Clb; Key Clb; Trs Varsity Clb; VP Stu Cncl; Bsbl; Bsktbl; Ftbl; Jr NHS; DAR Good Ctzn Awd 85; Little 12 All-Conf Ftbl Tm 85; Aerospc Engrg.

HARRIS, MATTHEW; North Catholic HS; Pittsburgh, PA; (Y); Cmnty Wkr; German Clb; Off Ski Clb; JV Ftbl; Hon Roll; Duquesne U; Intl Bus.

HARRIS, MELISSA A; Central Columbia HS; Bloomsburg, PA; (Y); 4/187; Drama Clb; Pep Clb; School Play; Stage Crew; Yrbk Ed-Chief; Yrbk Phtg; Yrbk Rptr; High Hon Roll; NHS; Pres Schlr; Mitraine Schrlshp 86; Pres Schlrs 86; Pres Acad Ftns Awd 86; Bloomsburg U; Sec Ed.

HARRIS, ROBERT; Solebury Schl; Philadelphia, PA; (Y); 30/150; Debate Tm; Pres Soph Cls; Swarthmore Coll; Psychtrst.

HARRIS, SALLY; Strong Vincent HS; Erie, PA; (Y); Church Yth Grp; Cmnty Wkr; Trs Spanish Clb; Chorus; Rep Frsh Cls; Rep Soph Cls; Rep Stu Cncl; JV Vllybl.

HARRIS, STEVE; Johnstown HS; Johnstown, PA; (Y); Spanish Clb; JV Var Bsktbl; JV Var Ftbl; Prfct Atten Awd; Chem Engnrng.

HARRIS, THOMAS; Williamsburg Community HS; Williamsburg, PA; (Y); Pres 4-H; Varsity Clb; Var Bsbl; Var Bsktbl; 4-H Awd; IN Inst Of Tech; Comp Sci.

HARRIS, TIM; Upper Darby SR HS; Secane, PA; (Y); Church Yth Grp; Exploring; German Clb; Fld Hcky; Hon Roll; Jr NHS.

HARRIS, WILLIAM; Uniontown Area HS; Uniontown, PA; (Y); Boy Scts; Church Yth Grp; Band; Concert Band; Jazz Band; Mrchg Band; Pep Band; High Hon Roll; Spanish NHS.

HARRISON, CARRIE; Mean Ssr HS; Glenwillard, PA; (Y); Church Yth Grp; Key Clb; Band; Chorus; Church Choir; Concert Band; Mrchg Band; Symp Band; Cit Awd; High Hon Roll; Intrprtng.

HARRISON, CINDI; Harbor Creek HS; Harbor Creek, PA; (Y); Teachers Aide; Yrbk Stf; Vllybl; Hon Roll.

HARRISON, DAVID; Pennsbury HS; Yardley, PA; (Y); 111/729; Rep Frsh Cls; Rep Soph Cls; Rep Stu Cncl; JV Bsbl; Im Bsktbl; Var L Ftbl; Hon Roll; Pres Acad Fitness Awd 86; PA ST U; Bus.

HARRISON, JEFF; Scranton Prep; Archbald, PA; (Y); 100/192; Church Yth Grp; Letterman Clb; Political Wkr; Varsity Clb; Trs Stu Cncl; Var JV Bsktbl; Var Crs Cntry; Var Trk; Hon Roll; Classc Bsktbl Team Five Star 86.

HARRISON, JOHN; York Vo-Tech; York, PA; (Y); Camera Clb; FCA; FHA; Hosp Aide; Office Aide; Red Cross Aide; ROTC; SADD; Y-Teens; School Play; Hnr Roll Cert; Chef.

HARRISON, KAREN; Columbia Montour Area Voc/Tech Schl; Stillwater, PA; (Y); Church Yth Grp; DECA; VICA; Chorus; Rep Frsh Cls; Rep Stu Cncl; Hon Roll; NHS; DECA Dist Competition 4th Pl 85; Finlst DECA ST Competition 85; DECA Dist Competition 3rd Pl 86; Bus Admin.

HARRISON, KELLI; The Swarthmore Acad; Chester, PA; (Y); 1/11; Hosp Aide; Nwsp Stf; Yrbk Stf; VP Socr; High Hon Roll; Ntl Merit SF; Prfct Atten Awd; Cmnty Wkr; JA; Office Aide; Outstndg Overall Acad Prfrmnce 83-85; Outstndg Acad Pfrmnce Mth 83-84; Outstndg Acad Prfrmnc Sci & Mth; Pre-Med.

HARRISON, KELLY; Norwin SR HS; North Huntingdon, PA; (Y); 245/550; FBLA; Office Aide; Pep Clb; Ski Clb; SADD; Capt Color Guard; Hon Roll; Rotary Awd; Wright ST U; Dance.

HARRISON, LISA; Trinity HS; Mechanicsburg, PA; (Y); Pep Clb; Nwsp Rptr; Nwsp Stf; Yrbk Stf; Stu Cncl; Hon Roll; Psychlgy.

HARRISON, LYNDELLE; Farrell HS; Farrell, PA; (Y); French Clb; Bsktbl; Hon Roll; Howard U; Elec Engr.

HARRISON, MARGARET; Saegertown HS; Saegertown, PA; (Y); 9/124; Pres Spanish Clb; Varsity Clb; Mrchg Band; Rep Frsh Cls; VP Jr Cls; Var Capt Cheerleading; High Hon Roll; Hon Roll; Jr NHS; NHS; Proj Enhance 84-87; Miss Cngnlty Saegertown Smmrfest Pagnt 85; Pre-Med.

HARRISON, NIKI; Ringgold HS; Finleyville, PA; (Y); 37/356; Am Leg Aux Girls St; Speech Tm; Varsity Clb; Nwsp Ed-Chief; Var Cheerleading; Var Trk; Voice Dem Awd; Rep Soph Cls; Pres Boys Clb Am; Cmnty Wkr; UN Pilgrmge For Yth 85; Cent III Ldrshp Awd 86; PTSA Literary ST Wnr 84-86; U Pittsburgh; Cmmnctns.

HARRISON, STACEY; Pocono Mountain HS; Mt Pocono, PA; (Y); Church Yth Grp; Dance Clb; Girl Scts; Pep Clb; Ski Clb; Spanish Clb; Band; Chorus; Church Choir; Color Guard; Pres Phys Fit Awd 82; Bloomsburg U; Med Tech.

HARRITY, DANIEL; Bishop Hannan HS; Scranton, PA; (Y); 34/144; French Clb; Orch; School Musical; Nwsp Rptr; Yrbk Stf; Var Crs Cntry; Hon Roll; NHS; Hnrb Mntn-Fnch I, II & III 84-86; Excllnc-Wrld Cltrs I & II 84-85; Hnrb Mntn-Orch I, II & III; Chem.

HARRITY, MARK; Riverview HS; Oakmont, PA; (Y); Boy Scts; Church Yth Grp; ROTC; Scholastic Bowl; Mgr(s); Hon Roll; Outstndng Achvt Voc Hnr 86; OH Northern U; Comp Sci.

HARROLD, DONNA; Hempfield Area SR HS; Greensburg, PA; (Y); FBLA; Pep Clb; High Hon Roll; Hon Roll; Camera Clb; Im Wt Lftg; Kiwanis Awd; Secy.

HARROLD, JENNIE; Marion Center Area HS; Rochester Mls, PA; (Y); Intnl Clb; Office Aide; School Play; Stage Crew; NHS; Pres Of Intl Clb 86; Forgn Exch Stdnt Venezuela 85; Sfty Clb; Penn ST; Intl Bus.

HARROLD, MARK; Northeastern HS; Manchester, PA; (Y); Varsity Clb; Band; Var L Bsbl; Var L Bsktbl; Var L Socr; Var L Vllybl; Hon Roll; NHS; Engr.

HARRY, JOE; MMI Prep Schl; Hazleton, PA; (Y); Pep Clb; Ski Clb; Trs Stu Cncl; Var Bsbl; Bausch & Lomb Sci Awd; High Hon Roll; NHS; Computer Clb; Math Clb; Math Tm; Rensselaer Polythecnic Institute Medal 86; 1st Pl Natl Spnsh Exm; 4 Yr Schlrshp To Wilks Coll 86.

HARRY, JOSEPH; MMI Preparatory Schl; Hazleton, PA; (S); Ski Clb; Trs Stu Cncl; Var Bsbl; Im Vllybl; Bausch & Lomb Sci Awd; High Hon Roll; NHS; Computer Clb; Math Clb; Math Tm; Rensselaer Polytech Inst Mdl 86; 1st Natl Span Exam 84; 4 Yr Full Tiution Schlrshp Wilkes Coll 86.

HARRY, TRACY; Franklin HS; Franklin, PA; (Y); 10/210; French Clb; Radio Clb; Chorus; Capt Color Guard; Madrigals; School Musical; Variety Show; Rep Soph Cls; Rep Jr Cls; High Hon Roll; Schl Dirctrs Awd 84-86; Publc Reltns.

HARSHAW, APRIL; Marple-Newtown HS; Newtown, PA; (Y); Math Clb; Nwsp Rptr; Lit Mag; Stu Cncl; Swmmng; Capt Tennis; High Hon Roll; NHS; Rotary Awd; Wrtng.

HARSHBARGER, AMY; Chief Logan HS; Yeagertown, PA; (Y); 49/195; Sec Church Yth Grp; German Clb; Speech Tm; Yrbk Stf; Mgr Bsktbl; Mgr(s); Score Keeper; Juniata; Engl.

HARSHBARGER, BOBBI; Lewistown Area SR HS; Mc Veytown, PA; (Y); Church Yth Grp; Girl Scts; Spanish Clb; Band; Concert Band; Ed Yrbk Stf; High Hon Roll; Hon Roll; South Hills Bus Schl; Med Sec.

HARSHELL, JIM; Hempfield SR HS; Greensburg, PA; (Y); VICA; Var Ftbl; Wt Lftg; High Hon Roll; Vo Tech Shop VP 85-86; Cabntry.

HARST, TRACY; Exeter SR HS; Reading, PA; (Y); Church Yth Grp; Hosp Aide; Y-Teens; Band; Concert Band; Jazz Band; Mrchg Band; Orch; Stu Cncl; JV Cheerleading; County Bnd; Music.

HART, BLAINE; Bellefonte SR HS; Bellefonte, PA; (Y); Art Clb; Im Ftbl; Hon Roll; Air Force; Mech Engr.

HART, BRIAN; Rocky Grove HS; Franklin, PA; (Y); 6/93; Band; Pep Band; Yrbk Stf; Tennis; High Hon Roll; NHS; PA Govrnr Schl Sci 86; Comp Sci.

HART, DEIDRE; Phil-Mont Christian Acad; Philadelphia, PA; (Y); 6/37; Hosp Aide; Sec Sr Cls; Hon Roll; NHS; Tennis; Messiah; Bio.

HART, JENNIFER; Mercyhurst Prep; Erie, PA; (Y); 42/150; Church Yth Grp; Key Clb; Var JV Bsktbl; Var Socr; Hon Roll; St Schlr; Acadmc All Am 86; Natl Phys Educ Awd.

HART, JOANNE; West Allegheny SR HS; Oakdale, PA; (Y); 17/198; Color Guard; Drill Tm; Mrchg Band; Stu Cncl; Hon Roll; Law.

HART, JODIE; Trinity Area HS; Washington, PA; (Y); Art Clb; Church Yth Grp; 4-H; French Clb; JA; Pep Clb; VICA; Chorus; Bsktbl; 4-H Awd; Gld Mdl VICA Extmprns Spkng 86; Csmtlgy Clss Pres 85-86; West Liberty; Hstry Tchr.

HART, KEVIN; Belle Vernon Area HS; Belle Vernon, PA; (Y); 63/273; Art Clb; Ski Clb; Spanish Clb; Band; Wrstlng; High Hon Roll; U Of Pitt; Mech Engr.

HART, PATRICK; Newport JR SR HS; Newport, PA; (Y); 20/100; Boy Scts; Pres 4-H; Im Gym; 4-H Awd; Hon Roll; Elec.

HART, PETER; Donegal HS; Bridgewater, MA; (Y); Var Bsktbl; Athletic Training Clb 84-85; Bridgewater ST Coll; Lbrl Arts.

HART, REGINA; Hopewell SR HS; Aliquippa, PA; (Y); 8/225; Pres Art Clb; Cmnty Wkr; French Clb; Library Aide; Band; Concert Band; High Hon Roll; Wmns Clb Art Exhbtn Awd 86; IN U Of PA; Psychlgy.

HART, SHAWN; Shenango HS; New Castle, PA; (S); Church Yth Grp; 4-H; Girl Scts; Office Aide; Chorus; Rep Stu Cncl; DAR Awd; High Hon Roll; French Clb; Dist Chrs 84-86; Edinboro.

HART, TODD; Blue Mt Acad; Berwick, PA; (S); Im Ftbl; Gym; Im Sftbl; Im Vllybl; Hon Roll; NHS; Prfct Atten Awd; Solo Flight 85; Wght Lftg 85; Stu Assn 86; Andrews U; Aviatn.

HART, TONY; Interboro HS; Prospect Park, PA; (Y); Computer Clb; Ski Clb; Hon Roll; Drexel U; Comp.

HART, TRACEY; Burgettstown Area JR-SR HS; Bulger, PA; (Y); VP Drama Clb; Band; Chorus; Mrchg Band; School Musical; Symp Band; Pres Stu Cncl; NHS; Church Yth Grp; Cmnty Wkr; Shippensburg Ldrshp Rep Wrkshp; Grove City Stu Cncl Wrkshp; Exp Psych.

HART, VALERIE; Manheim Central HS; Manheim, PA; (Y); Church Yth Grp; 4-H; Chorus; Church Choir; Fld Hcky; Rotary Awd; EMC VA; Math.

HARTE, GLENN; Forest City Regional HS; Forest City, PA; (Y); Boy Scts; Church Yth Grp; Drama Clb; German Clb; Letterman Clb; Ski Clb; Chorus; School Musical; School Play; Stage Crew; Am Leg Awd 83.

HARTER, MICHELLE; Middletown Area HS; Middletown, PA; (Y); Art Clb; Church Yth Grp; FCA; Radio Clb; Color Guard; Retailing.

HARTER, REBEKAH; Benton Area JR SR HS; Stillwater, PA; (Y); 11/52; Church Yth Grp; Teachers Aide; High Hon Roll; NHS; Bus & Karate Clbs; Cert Of Prfcncy Awd; Typng I & II Awds; Williamsport Area CC; Exec Sec.

HARTER, SUZANNA; Bethel Park SR HS; Bethel Park, PA; (Y); Mrchg Band; School Musical; Symp Band; Variety Show; Pom Pon; High Hon Roll; NHS; Math.

HARTFIEL, MELISSA; Conemaugh Township Area HS; Holsopple, PA; (Y); 9/103; Church Yth Grp; Cmnty Wkr; Library Aide; NFL; Q&S; Scholastic Bowl; Yrbk Stf; NHS; Rotry Delg Wrld Affrs Inst 85; Pres Acadmc Ftns Awd 86; WA Wrkshp Congrssnl Semnr 86; U Of Pittsburgh; Am Stud.

HARTFORD, BETHANY; Shippensburg Area SR HS; Shippensburg, PA; (Y); French Clb; Concert Band; Jazz Band; Mrchg Band; VP Orch; School Musical; Trk; High Hon Roll; Sec NHS; SAEA Frnch Awd 86; Drama Awd 86; Kutztown U; Lbrl Arts.

HARTILL, TOM; Kiski Area SR HS; Vandergrift, PA; (Y); VICA; L Trk; Elctrncs.

HARTIN, AMY; Manheim Twp HS; Lancaster, PA; (Y); Church Yth Grp; Hosp Aide; Pep Clb; Spanish Clb; Church Choir; Mrchg Band; School Musical; Hon Roll; Bloomsburg U; Chldhd Educ.

HARTLAND, KELLEY; Sharpsville Area HS; Sharpsville, PA; (Y); Spanish Clb; Chorus; Acctg.

HARTLAUB, CINDY; New Oxford SR HS; Mc Sherrystown, PA; (Y); Cmnty Wkr; FBLA; Hosp Aide; Teachers Aide; High Hon Roll; Hon Roll; Harrisburg Coll; Child Care Mgm.

HARTLE, ANN; Venango Christian HS; Franklin, PA; (Y); 1/42; Yrbk Ed-Chief; Pres Soph Cls; Capt Cheerleading; High Hon Roll; NHS; Ntl Merit Ltr; Pres Schlr; Val; Msgr Antown Mdl Excel Sci 86; Hdmstrs List 4 Qtrs; Washington-Jefferson Coll.

HARTLE, TINA; Moniteau HS; Hilliards, PA; (Y); FBLA; FHA; Hon Roll; Bus.

HARTLEY, AMY; California Area HS; Coal Ctr, PA; (Y); FBLA; FNA; CA Yth Ed Assoc; Bradford Bus Schl; Lgl Sec.

HARTLEY, MELISSA L; S Williamsport Area HS; S Williamsport, PA; (Y); 3/150; Key Clb; Sec Spanish Clb; Flag Corp; Nwsp Ed-Chief; Nwsp Rptr; Yrbk Stf; High Hon Roll; NHS; Pres FBLA; Nwsp Stf; Marching Band Capt 85-87; Semi-Finlst Govrnrs Schl Arts 85; Psych.

HARTLEY, ROBERT; Quaker Valley HS; Sewickley, PA; (Y); Am Leg Boys St; Boy Scts; Debate Tm; Key Clb; Trs Political Wkr; Stage Crew; Nwsp Ed-Chief; Ed Yrbk Phtg; Trs Jr Cls; God Cntry Awd; Cong Awd 86; Law.

HARTLEY, SCOTT; Trinity HS; Washington, PA; (Y); 180/374; Church Yth Grp; Cmnty Wkr; 4-H; FFA; Bsbl; Ftbl.

HARTLINE, HEATHER L; Highlands HS; Tarentum, PA; (Y); Sec JA; Library Aide; Office Aide; SADD; Acpl Chr; Chorus; Church Choir; Time Mgmt Awd 85; Pitt; Psychlgy.

HARTMAN, CHRISTINE; West Mifflin Area HS; W Mifflin, PA; (Y); 31/336; Church Yth Grp; Band; Concert Band; Jazz Band; Mrchg Band; Jr Cls; Var L Vllybl; Hon Roll; NHS; Penn ST U; Psych.

HARTMAN, ERIC; Iroquois HS; Erie, PA; (Y); 40/120; JA; Trk; Wt Lftg; Wrstlng; Hon Roll; Prfct Atten Awd; 1st Pl Wstrn PA Indstrl Arts Fair 86, 2nd Pl 85; Outstndng Wrstlr Awd 84; Draftng.

HARTMAN, JANE; Shamokin Area HS; Shamokin, PA; (Y); Art Clb; FBLA; Science Clb; Spanish Clb; Flag Corp; Hon Roll; Med.

HARTMAN, JOANNE; Freedom HS; Bethlehem, PA; (Y); 81/390; Church Yth Grp; Cmnty Wkr; Drama Clb; French Clb; Girl Scts; Chorus; Church Choir; School Musical; School Play; Hon Roll.

HARTMAN, KATHY; Parkland HS; Allentown, PA; (Y); 110/462; 4-H; Var L Bsktbl; JV Var Sftbl; 4-H Awd.

HARTMAN, LAURIE; Blacklick Valley HS; Twin Rocks, PA; (S); 10/90; VP Church Yth Grp; Sec Exploring; NFL; Ski Clb; Spanish Clb; Speech Tm; Varsity Clb; Flag Corp; School Play; Yrbk Stf; UPJ; Pre-Med.

HARTMAN, RAYMOND; Pennsbury HS; Morrisville, PA; (Y); Drama Clb; German Clb; Band; Concert Band; Jazz Band; Mrchg Band; Orch; School Play; Hon Roll; NHS; Outstndng Musician Awd 83-84 & 84-85; Penn ST U; Vet.

HARTMAN, TOMMY; Charleroi JR SR HS; Stockdale, PA; (Y); Varsity Clb; Rep Soph Cls; Capt Bsbl; L Bsktbl; L Socr; Catonsville CC.

HARTMANN, BEATRICE; Hampton HS; Allison Park, PA; (Y); French Clb; Letterman Clb; Pep Clb; Chorus; Stage Crew; Var L Vllybl; Bus Assn Schlrshp; UNC Charlotte; Bus Adm.

HARTMANN, KRISTEN; Peters Township HS; Mc Murray, PA; (S); Var Cheerleading; Powder Puff Ftbl; Hon Roll; Spanish NHS; Hmcmng Ct 83; Ntl Hist,Gov Awd 85; U Pittsburgh; Occuptnl Thrpy.

HARTNETT, MARK; Central Bucks Hs West; Chalfont, PA; (Y); 39/483; Church Yth Grp; Jazz Band; Trs Frsh Cls; Trs Soph Cls; Sec Jr Cls; JV Var Ftbl; Jr NHS; NHS; Ntl Merit Ltr; Rotary Awd; Hist.

HARTON, TRACY; Venango Christian HS; Franklin, PA; (Y); Nwsp Stf; Yrbk Stf; Rep Soph Cls; Rep Stu Cncl; Var Bsktbl; Vllybl; High Hon Roll; Pres NHS; Rep Stu Cncl Smnr 85; Psych.

HARTRANFT, CATHY; Kutztown Area HS; Kutetown, PA; (Y); VP Church Yth Grp; Chorus; Church Choir; School Play; Var Bsktbl; Var Fld Hcky; Stat Sftbl; Var Trk; High Hon Roll; NHS.

HARTSHORN, KIMBERLY; Mid-Valley Secondary Center HS; Throop, PA; (Y); Girl Scts; JA; Chorus; Church Choir; Off Sr Cls; Bsktbl; Hon Roll; Ctzns Awd Gvn By Throop Hose Co #2 85; Nrsng.

HARTUNG, PETER; West York SR HS; York, PA; (Y); 67/209; Rep Stu Cncl; Bowling; Socr; Prfct Atten Awd; Comp Sci.

HARTY, JENNIFER L; Penn Hills SR HS; Pittsburgh, PA; (Y); 126/797; Church Yth Grp; Dance Clb; Science Clb; Spanish Clb; Drill Tm; Off Sr Cls; Off Stu Cncl; Pom Pon; Hon Roll; Prfct Atten Awd; Penn ST U.

HARTZELL, DAVID L; Cumberland Valley HS; Mechanicsburg, PA; (Y); Church Yth Grp; Hon Roll; Slvr Spgs Amb Assn, S W Paine Schlrshps 86; Houghton Coll; Pre Med.

HARTZELL, JOYCE; Punxsy Area HS; Punxsutawney, PA; (Y); French Clb; Hon Roll; Cultrl Arts Awd Music 81; Cert Chrldng 81; Accntg.

HARTZELL, JULIA; Exeter Twp HS; Reading, PA; (Y); Church Yth Grp; Drama Clb; VP JA; Library Aide; Ski Clb; Teachers Aide; Stat Bsbl; Cheerleading; Hon Roll; 5 Chrstn Cmp Bible Mem Certs, Ldrshp Trng Conf Cert 84; DVCC Bible Memrztn Certs 86; Nestrn Christian JC; Nclr Engr.

HARTZELL, LORRIE; Seneca Valley HS; Renfrew, PA; (Y); Church Yth Grp; FNA; Office Aide; Band; Concert Band; Mrchg Band; Var Trk; Cert For Acad Achvt 84; Butler Cnty Cmnty Coll; Nrsng.

HARTZLER, REGINA A; Belleville Mennonite HS; Belleville, PA; (Y); 2/9; Chorus; School Play; Yrbk Ed-Chief; Yrbk Stf; Pres Soph Cls; VP Sr Cls; Capt Fld Hcky; Dnfth Awd; NHS; Sal; Empire Bty Schl Schlrshp 86; Stu Mnth Awd 84; Alphie Zook Msc Awd 2nd Rnnr Up 86; Empire Bty Schl; Cosmtlgy.

HARVATINE, KRISTINE; Annville-Cleonia HS; Cleona, PA; (S); 3/105; French Clb; Model UN; Trs SADD; Concert Band; Jazz Band; Mrchg Band; Orch; Symp Band; Tennis; NHS; U S Natl Ldrshp Mrt Awd 85; Aerosp Engrng.

HARVEY, DAVID; The Hill Schl; Pottstown, PA; (Y); Off Model UN; Radio Clb; Im Bsktbl; Im Bowling; JV Crs Cntry; Im JV Tennis; High Hon Roll; Psych.

HARVEY, DAWN; Jon S Fine HS; Shickshinny, PA; (Y); Band; Sec Chorus; Concert Band; Mrchg Band; School Musical; High Hon Roll; Hon Roll; Bus Ed Stenogrphy I,II 85-86.

HARVEY, DUANE E; Octorara Area HS; Cochranville, PA; (Y); 30/172; Chorus; School Musical; Capt Wrstlng; Hon Roll; NHS; Pres Schlr; Nwsp Stf; Yrbk Stf; Bsbl; SICO Fndtn Schlrshp To Mlsrvl U 86-90; Team Ldrshp Awd In Wrstlng 85-86; Mlsrvl U.

HARVEY, JAMES; Meadville Area SR HS; Meadville, PA; (Y); Church Yth Grp; Off Frsh Cls; Stu Cncl; Ftbl; Air Frc.

HARVEY, JEFFREY; Fort Le Boeuf HS; Erie, PA; (Y); 14/186; Yrbk Stf; Var Bsbl; Var Bsktbl; JV Ftbl; Im Vllybl; High Hon Roll; All-Cnty Bsbl 86; Jrnlsm.

HARVEY, JOHN; Penn Cambria HS; Cresson, PA; (Y); 24/200; Church Yth Grp; Ski Clb; Spanish Clb; VP Jr Cls; Stu Cncl; Var L Bsbl; Ftbl; Mgr(s); Hon Roll; Ntl Merit Ltr; Pitt; Accntng.

HARVEY, JULIET; Elizabeth Forward SR HS; Elizabeth, PA; (Y); 1/324; Sec Trs Church Yth Grp; Spanish Clb; Church Choir; Yrbk Stf; High Hon Roll; NHS; Intl Piano Recrdng Comptn Slvr Mdls 85-86; Math.

HARVEY, KIMBERLY; Frazier SR HS; Layton, PA; (Y); Am Leg Aux Girls St; Church Yth Grp; Drama Clb; 4-H; Girl Scts; Teachers Aide; Capt Band; Color Guard; Mrchg Band; Pep Band; Band Cmp Bst Rifl Awd & Mdl 85 & 86; California Coll PA; Psychol.

HARVEY, KRIS; Burgettstown JR SR HS; Langeloth, PA; (Y); 12/173; Library Aide; Mat Maids; High Hon Roll; Hon Roll; Bradford Schl; Sec.

HARVEY, LAWRENCE; Cheltenham HS; Philadelphia, PA; (Y); Church Yth Grp; Computer Clb; Library Aide; Bowling; JV Swmmng; Drexel U; Engr.

HARVEY, MARK; Lewisburg Area HS; Lewisburg, PA; (Y); 4-H; German Clb; Letterman Clb; Varsity Clb; L Ftbl; L Socr; L Trk; L Wrstlng; Hon Roll; NHS; Law.

HARVEY, MARY; Liberty HS; Bethlehem, PA; (Y); 48/478; French Clb; Pep Clb; School Musical; School Play; Lit Mag; JV Tennis; JV Trk; Hon Roll; NHS.

HARVEY, MICHAEL A; Pennsbury HS; Yardley, PA; (Y); Temple Yth Grp; Rep Jr Cls; Var Diving; JV Ftbl; Var Swmmng; Im Vllybl; Mth.

HARVEY, TOM; Interboro HS; Essington, PA; (Y); Computer Clb; FBLA; VICA; JV Bsbl; JV Ftbl; Im Vllybl; Hon Roll; Prfct Atten Awd; BP Acad Excllnc Awd 86; A In Vo-Tech 86data Prcssng; Penn ST U; Comp Sci.

HARVEY, WENDY; Downington HS; Downingtown, PA; (Y); French Clb; Intnl Clb; Chorus; Concert Band; Flag Corp; Sec Frsh Cls; Cheerleading; Sec Mat Maids; High Hon Roll; NHS; NEDT Awd 84-85.

HARVIE, DAVID S; William Allen HS; Allentown, PA; (Y); Church Yth Grp; Intnl Clb; JA; Nwsp Rptr; Nwsp Stf; Lit Mag; Im Bsktbl; Im Lcrss; Im Socr; Im Vllybl; Allentown Coll; Comp Sci.

HARWOOD, LESLE; Palmyra SR HS; Palmyra, PA; (Y); Church Yth Grp; Drama Clb; German Clb; Chorus; Church Choir; Stu Cncl; Score Keeper; High Hon Roll; Hon Roll; Mgmt.

HARZINSKI, DEBBIE; Curwensville Area HS; Curwensville, PA; (Y); Drama Clb; Pres French Clb; Letterman Clb; Varsity Clb; Chorus; School Musical; Yrbk Stf; Var Capt Cheerleading; Pom Pon; Hon Roll; Mst Otstndng Chrldr 82-83; Mst Sprtd Chrldr 83-84; JV Cptn Awd 84-85; Anml Tech.

HASENPLUG, KAREN; Sharpsville Area HS; Transfer, PA; (Y); 32/129; Church Yth Grp; FHA; Library Aide; High Hon Roll; NHS; Bus.

HASHEM, LIZA; West Scranton HS; Scranton, PA; (Y); 39/265; Cmnty Wkr; Latin Clb; Ski Clb; Nwsp Stf; Yrbk Stf; Lit Mag; Off Jr Cls; Stu Cncl; Cheerleading; High Hon Roll; Interntl Stds.

HASKINS, JEFF; Coudersport Area HS; Coudersport, PA; (Y); 11/88; Church Yth Grp; FFA; Varsity Clb; Trs Jr Cls; VP Stu Cncl; Var L Ftbl; Var L Trk; High Hon Roll; Hon Roll; PA ST U; Ag.

HASLAM, DAWN; Hazleton HS; Mc Adoo, PA; (Y); 20/384; Chess Clb; Chorus; Sftbl; Swmmng; High Hon Roll; NEDT Awd; Kings Coll Hnr Cert Span 84 & 85; Math Educ.

HASPEL, VICKI; Burgettstown HS; Burgettstown, PA; (Y); Boy Scts; Drama Clb; Exploring; Office Aide; Ski Clb; SADD; Mrchg Band; Pep Band; School Play; Symp Band; Travel Med.

HASSEL, ERIC; West Catholic Boys HS; Philadelphia, PA; (Y); 2/293; Mathletes; JV Var Ftbl; Wt Lftg; High Hon Roll; Hon Roll; Pres NHS; Acad Excllnc Awds In Rssn 84-86; Dstngshd Hnrs Awds 83-85; Acad Excllnc Awds In Mth & Rlgn 83-85; Rssn Intl Rltns.

HASSELMAN, LISA; St Marys Area HS; St Marys, PA; (Y); Engrng.

HASSINGER, DALE; Middleburg HS; Middleburg, PA; (Y); Rptr FFA; Varsity Clb; Var Wrstlng; ST FFA Hon Mntn 85-86; 1st SUN Area Lnd Jdgng Cntst 84-85; Hcky Clb 85-86; WACC; Mchnst.

HASSINGER, LAEL; Millersburg Area HS; Millersburg, PA; (Y); 6/74; Spanish Clb; Band; Concert Band; Jazz Band; Mrchg Band; Nwsp Stf; Yrbk Stf; High Hon Roll; Hon Roll; Band Ltr&pins 84-86; Dickinson Schl Law; Psych.

HASSINGER, TRIXY; Chief Logan HS; Mcclure, PA; (Y); Pres Church Yth Grp; Soroptimist; Var Sftbl; Hon Roll; Prfct Atten Awd.

HASSON, CATHY; Northern Cambria HS; Nicktown, PA; (Y); 12/126; NFL; Spanish Clb; Concert Band; Mrchg Band; Nwsp Stf; Var Trk; JV Vllybl; High Hon Roll; NHS; Spanish NHS; Natl Hstry Day-1st, 2nd ST Cmptn 85 & 86; IN U Of PA.

HASSON, TRACI; Bristol JR SR HS; Bristol, PA; (Y); 15/90; Library Aide; Mrchg Band; Orch; School Play; Yrbk Bus Mgr; Sec Jr Cls; Var Fld Hcky; Stat Sftbl; Trk; Hon Roll; Millersville U; Eled Ed.

HASTINGS, VICTORIA; Upper Darby HS; Drexel Hl, PA; (Y); 151/600; Hosp Aide; Hon Roll; PA ST U; Nrs.

HASTINGS, WILLIAM GUIL; Quaker Valley HS; Sewickley, PA; (Y); Church Yth Grp; Key Clb; VP Service Clb; SADD; School Play; Nwsp Stf; Lit Mag; Pres Soph Cls; Pres Stu Cncl; Socr.

HATAJIK, TODD; Highlands SR HS; Natrona Hts, PA; (Y); 7/301; Letterman Clb; Var L Bsbl; Var L Bsktbl; Var L Ftbl; NHS; Prfct Atten Awd; Rep Stu Cncl; Im Wt Lftg; Jr NHS; Ntl Merit Ltr; Amer Legn Awd 83; 1st Tm All Alle-Kiski Press Ftbl Tm 85; Chmstry.

HATCH, ANDREW; Delaware County Christian Schl; Bryn Mawr, PA; (Y); 12/78; Church Yth Grp; Chorus; High Hon Roll; Hon Roll; Messiah Coll; Comp Sci.

HATCH, KELLY; Altoona Area HS; Altoona, PA; (S); Dance Clb; Drama Clb; Spanish Clb; Nwsp Stf; VP Sr Cls; Rep Stu Cncl; Var Pom Pon; Sec Jr NHS; NEDT Awd; Bio.

HATCH, MARLENE; Corry Area HS; Corry, PA; (S); Church Yth Grp; Drama Clb; German Clb; SADD; Band; Concert Band; Mrchg Band; Pep Band; School Play; Hon Roll.

HATCH, MARY SUE; Peters Township HS; Mc Murray, PA; (S); 9/267; Hosp Aide; Sec Key Clb; Sec SADD; Mrchg Band; Sec Lit Mag; Stu Cncl; DAR Awd; NHS; Spanish NHS; Duquesne U Intgrtd Hnrs Prog Schlrshp; Hugh O Brien Ldrshp Semnr Ambsdr; Med.

HATCH, MELISSA; Bradford Area HS; Rew, PA; (Y); Pres Boy Scts; Pres Church Yth Grp; Cmnty Wkr; Hosp Aide; Flag Corp; Yrbk Stf; Hon Roll; Zonta Clbs Ruth Fisher Schrlshp 86; Mc Kean Cnty Chptr 72 Annual Schlrshp 86; U Pittsburgh; Humn Reltns.

HATCHER, MARYELLEN; Perry Traditional Acad; Pittsburgh, PA; (Y); 3/137; Yrbk Stf; Rep Stu Cncl; High Hon Roll; Hon Roll; NHS; Prfct Atten Awd; Point Park Clg; Pub Rel.

HATFIELD, WILLIAM; Waynesburg Central HS; Mt Morris, PA; (Y); Art Clb; Boy Scts; Chess Clb; French Clb; Ski Clb; Varsity Clb; L Ftbl; L Trk; NEDT Awd; Rsch.

HATHAWAY, PATRICA; Trinity HS; Washington, PA; (Y); 83/374; Dance Clb; Key Clb; Pep Clb; Drill Tm.

HATHHORN, JEFF; Sharpsville Area HS; Sharpsville, PA; (Y); 22/129; Church Yth Grp; Band; Church Choir; Concert Band; School Musical; School Play; Stage Crew; Var Bsbl; Var Bsktbl; L Golf; Elec To Board Of Deacons In 1st Presbtrn Church Of Sharon 85; Jr All-Amer Hall Of Fme Band Hnrs 85-86; Brdcstng.

HATOFF, JACQUELINE; Lower Moreland HS; Huntingdon Valley, PA; (S); 17/213; Drama Clb; FBLA; Hosp Aide; Key Clb; Temple Yth Grp; Mgr(s); Stat Mgr Swmmng; Var Tennis; Hon Roll; NHS; PA Merit SAT Awd 85; Bus.

HAUBER II, WILLIAM R; Manheim Township HS; Lancaster, PA; (Y); Var Ftbl; Var Trk; Hon Roll; James Madison U; Bus Finance.

HAUCK, JESSICA L; Ephrata SR HS; Ephrata, PA; (Y); 80/257; Cmnty Wkr; Rep Soph Cls; Rep Jr Cls; Var L Crs Cntry; JV Fld Hcky; Im Gym; Powder Puff Ftbl; JV Trk; Im Vllybl; Hon Roll.

HAUCK, LINDA D; Sharon SR HS; Sharon, PA; (Y); Aud/Vis; Church Yth Grp; Girl Scts; Hosp Aide; Y-Teens; Band; Concert Band; Mrchg Band; Sharon Schl Of Nrsng; Nrsng.

HAUGER, MARIA; Rockwood Area HS; Rockwood, PA; (S); 26/91; VICA; Band; Chorus; Concert Band; Mrchg Band; Hon Roll; NHS; Amercn Musicl Fndtn 84-85; Schltc Awd 84-85; Comp.

HAUGH, ANNE MARIE; Highlands SR HS; Natrona Hts, PA; (Y); 50/280; Exploring; Girl Scts; Library Aide; Office Aide; Bsktbl; Ftbl; Jr NHS; Gold Awd 84-86; Girl Scout Gold Awd 86; Gilr Scout Slvr Awd 84; Nrsng.

HAUGH, BRIAN; Manheim Central SR HS; Lititz, PA; (Y); JV Bsktbl; Var L Ftbl; Hlth.

HAUGH, MICHELLE; Waynesboro SR HS; Quincy, PA; (Y); Sec Church Yth Grp; Church Choir; Yrbk Ed-Chief; Yrbk Phtg; Yrbk Stf; Rep Jr Cls; Rep Stu Cncl; High Hon Roll; NHS; Hagerstown Bus Coll; Med Sec.

HAUGHEY, JANE; North Allegheny SR HS; Pittsburgh, PA; (Y); 220/642; Teachers Aide; School Musical; Yrbk Stf; JV Bsktbl; Var L Fld Hcky; Socr; Var L Sftbl; Im Vllybl; Hon Roll; Chld Care.

HAUGHTON, KATHRYN; St Hubert HS; Philadelphia, PA; (Y); 41/367; JA; Ed Yrbk Stf; Var Cheerleading; Var Swmmng; NHS; Physcl Thrpy.

HAUGLAND, JOSEPH; Interboro HS; Norwood, PA; (S); 1/230; AFS; Pres Latin Clb; Band; Concert Band; Jazz Band; L Crs Cntry; Var Trk; Hon Roll; NHS; Drexel U; Elec Engrng.

HAUN, JEFF; Keystone JR SR HS; Knox, PA; (Y); 45/125; Varsity Clb; Chorus; School Musical; School Play; Off Sr Cls; Rep Stu Cncl; L Bsbl; L Ftbl; L Golf; Var Trk; IN U Of PA; Acctng.

HAUPT, LENNY; Bellefonte HS; Bellefonte, PA; (Y); 49/217; Spanish Clb; Hon Roll; Art Awd 86; Enrchmnt 77-86.

HAUPT, MELISSA; Nazareth Area SR HS; Nazareth, PA; (Y); 5/240; Church Yth Grp; Yrbk Stf; Rep Frsh Cls; High Hon Roll; NHS; Bus.

HAUS, SHANNON; Milton Area HS; West Milton, PA; (Y); 32/213; Key Clb; Spanish Clb; Varsity Clb; Chorus; Rep Frsh Cls; Rep Soph Cls; JV Bsktbl; Var Crs Cntry; JV Fld Hcky; Var Trk; ST Qlfr Crss Cntry 84-85; Ray Ulrich Meml Awd Runng 85; ST Qlfr Dist Champ Trk 86.

HAUSE, LAURA; Millville Area HS; Millville, PA; (Y); 32/74; Drama Clb; Q&S; Nwsp Rptr; Nwsp Stf; Yrbk Rptr; Yrbk Stf; Lit Mag; Hon Roll; Temple U; Radio.

HAUSER, BRIAN; Penn Hills HS; Pittsburgh, PA; (Y); 1/750; German Clb; Ski Clb; Band; Concert Band; Mrchg Band; Pep Band; High Hon Roll; NHS; Val; Math.

HAUSER, DEAN; Bald Eagle Area HS; Snow Shoe, PA; (Y); 32/192; Boy Scts; Pres Church Yth Grp; Hon Roll; Distngshd Hnr Roll Cert 85-86; Woodworking.

HAUSER, JACKIE; Villa Maria Acad; Erie, PA; (Y); Church Yth Grp; Exploring; GAA; Girl Scts; Hosp Aide; Library Aide; Science Clb; Chorus; School Musical; Bsktbl; Spec Ed.

HAUSER, KIM; New Castle HS; New Castle, PA; (S); 5/237; Computer Clb; JA; Office Aide; Ski Clb; SADD; Teachers Aide; Chorus; High Hon Roll; NHS; NEDT Awd; Scndry Ed-Math.

HAUSHALTER, KURT; State College Area HS; State College, PA; (Y); 60/580; Pres Church Yth Grp; Im Bsktbl; Var JV Ftbl; Im Vllybl; Cit Awd; Hon Roll; Church Choir; Cert Merit Earth, Space Sci 83-84; Cert Merit Wrld Cltrs 84-85; Penn ST U.

HAUSMAN, PAMELA; Northwestern Lehigh HS; New Tripoli, PA; (Y); 6/126; Drama Clb; Intnl Clb; School Musical; School Play; Mgr(s); JV Trk; High Hon Roll; Hon Roll; NHS; Pres Acad Fit Awd Pgm 86; Germn IV Awd 86; PA ST U; Engrng.

HAUSSLER, JEANETTE; St Basil Acad; Philadelphia, PA; (Y); Cmnty Wkr; VP Pres Science Clb; Spanish Clb; Chorus; Madrigals; Hon Roll; NEDT Awd; US Achvt Acad Chem 85; Acdmc All Amrcn 85; Manor JC; Med Lab Tech.

HAUSSMANN, ROBERT; William Allen HS; Allentown, PA; (Y); 7/604; Chrmn German Clb; Math Tm; Model UN; Office Aide; Ski Clb; Nwsp Phtg; Lit Mag; Off Jr Cls; Trs NHS; Church Yth Grp; Rensselaer Polytech Inst Math, Sci Awd 86; Artfcl Intell.

HAUX, CAROL; Archbishop Kennedy HS; Plymouth Mtg, PA; (Y); 1/174; Church Yth Grp; Pres Cmnty Wkr; Mathletes; Nwsp Sprt Ed; Yrbk Stf; Stu Cncl; Var L Crs Cntry; Var L Trk; Hon Roll; NHS; MVP X-Cntry, Trck; Acad All Amer; Schlrshp To Attnd Lock Haven U Free Entrprs Wk; Math.

HAUX, KAREN; Pocono Central Catholic HS; Stroudsburg, PA; (S); 2/22; Pep Clb; Ski Clb; Yrbk Stf; Rep Stu Cncl; Var Bsktbl; Var Fld Hcky; Var Sftbl; Hon Roll; NHS; Moravian Coll; Elem Ed.

HAUX, SUSAN; Archbishop Kennedy HS; Plymouth Meeting, PA; (Y); 4/185; Church Yth Grp; Drama Clb; French Clb; Mathletes; Pep Clb; Service Clb; Chorus; Nwsp Stf; Yrbk Stf; Pres Stu Cncl; Bomberger & Steinberg Schlrshps-Ursinus Coll 86; Acad All Amer Awd 85 & 86; Ntl Schlr-Athl Awd-Army 86; Ursinus Coll; Doc.

HAVENER, STACEY; Henderson HS; Exton, PA; (S); Chorus; School Musical; Variety Show; Hon Roll.

HAVENS, PENNY; Clearfield HS; W Decatur, PA; (Y); Pres Church Yth Grp; Hosp Aide; SADD; Chorus; Church Choir; US Achvt Acad Natl Awd 85; Miss Tean Pgnt-Harrisburg 86; Dubois Bus Schl; Med Sec.

HAVILAND, DOLORES; St Basil Acad; Philadelphia, PA; (S); Boy Scts; Exploring; Science Clb; Service Clb; Spanish Clb; Tennis; Trk; Hon Roll; Ntl Merit Ltr; Schlrshp Basil Acad 83; Pre Med.

HAVLIK, STEPHEN; Freedom HS; Flemington, NJ; (Y); 4-H; VICA; Naval.

HAVRILLA, JENNIFER; Little Flower Catholic HS For Girls; Philadelphia, PA; (Y); 125/395; Pres Church Yth Grp; Science Clb; Mgr Fld Hcky; Var Trk; Accntng.

HAWK, BILL; Punxsy HS; Punxsutawney, PA; (Y); Aud/Vis; Camera Clb; Church Yth Grp; Dance Clb; Math Clb; Office Aide; Science Clb; SADD; Teachers Aide; Bsktbl.

HAWK, JEFFREY; Connellsville HS; Connellsville, PA; (Y).

HAWK, JOSEPH W; Pittston Area HS; Hughestown, PA; (Y); Art Clb; French Clb; Science Clb; Stage Crew; Hon Roll; Schlstc Art Achvmnt Awd 86; Dentstry.

HAWK, LISA; E L Meyers HS; Wilkes Bare, PA; (Y); Cmnty Wkr; 4-H; FBLA; Office Aide; Ski Clb; Sftbl; Hon Roll; Typing Awd 84-85 & 85-86; Shrthnd Awd 85-86; Bus.

HAWK, SCOTT; Hanover HS; Hanover, PA; (Y); 20/105; Varsity Clb; Ftbl; Wt Lftg; Wrstlng; Cit Awd; High Hon Roll; Hon Roll; NEDT Awd.

HAWKES, JANET; George Westinghouse HS; Pittsburgh, PA; (Y); 11/246; Church Yth Grp; Civic Clb; Cmnty Wkr; FHA; JA; Science Clb; Church Choir; Yrbk Ed-Chief; Hon Roll; NHS; Bus Admn.

HAWKINS, BENJAMIN; Kennedy Christian HS; Greenville, PA; (Y); 78/98; Pres Computer Clb; Latin Clb; Library Aide; Varsity Clb; Band; Mrchg Band; Trk; Hon Roll; Wanesburg Coll; Comp Sci.

HAWKINS, JOHN; Aliquippa HS; Aliquippa, PA; (Y); 41/135; JV Trk; High Hon Roll; Hon Roll; Natl PTA Fine Arts Proj Awd 85; PA Congrss Of Parents/Teachrs-Cultrl Arts Awd 84-85; Art Inst Of Pittsburgh; Art.

HAWKINS, KEBRA; Perry Traditional Acad; Pittsburgh, PA; (Y); 42/137; Church Yth Grp; FHA; Office Aide; Teachers Aide; Church Choir; Color Guard; Drill Tm; Nwsp Stf; JV Bsktbl; Mgr(s); Accntng.

HAWKINS, LISA; Delaware Valley HS; Dingmans Ferry, PA; (S); Church Yth Grp; Cmnty Wkr; Band; Var L Crs Cntry; JV L Fld Hcky; High Hon Roll; NHS; Prfct Atten Awd; PA ST U; Med.

HAWKINSON, THERESA; St Basil Acad; Philadelphia, PA; (Y); Boy Scts; German Clb; Yrbk Stf; Sftbl.

HAWLEY, BRYAN; Altoona Area HS; Altoona, PA; (Y); 133/683; Drama Clb; German Clb; Science Clb; Ski Clb; School Play; Im Bsktbl; Var Crs Cntry; Var L Ftbl; Var L Trk; Jr NHS; IN U; Psych.

HAWN, PAM; Biglerville HS; Gettysburg, PA; (Y); 15/87; VP Pres 4-H; Sec Pres Spanish Clb; Rep Soph Cls; Rep Jr Cls; JV Stat Bsktbl; Dnfth Awd; 4-H Awd; Hon Roll; NHS; Cls Sec 85-86; Cls Pres 87; Bus.

HAWRANKO, ALYSSA; M Fuller Franzier Mem JR SR HS; Perryopolis, PA; (Y); 1/126; Drama Clb; FNA; Chorus; Capt Flag Corp; Mrchg Band; School Play; Bausch & Lomb Sci Awd; High Hon Roll; NHS; Church Yth Grp; Hugh O Brian Ldrshp Awd 85; Phrmcy.

HAWTHORNE, JEFFERY; Cornell Education Ctr; Coraopolis, PA; (Y); Boy Scts; Drama Clb; Spanish Clb; Band; School Play; Nwsp Phtg; Yrbk Phtg; Ftbl; Swmmng; Cit Awd; Spartan Schl Of Aerontcs; Pilot.

HAWTHORNE, LORI; Albert Gallatin HS; Lake Lynn, PA; (Y); Acpl Chr; Band; Church Choir; Concert Band; Drm Mjr(t); Jazz Band; Mrchg Band; Hon Roll; Jr NHS; NHS; Ntl Ldrshp Merit Awd 86; WV Career Coll; Med Assist.

HAY, KELLY; Northampton SR HS; Bath, PA; (Y); Drama Clb; Girl Scts; Leo Clb; Chorus; School Play; Stage Crew; Hon Roll; Mgt.

HAY, KIMBERLY; Berlin Brothers Valley HS; Berlin, PA; (Y); 35/87; Church Yth Grp; French Clb; FBLA; Chorus; Color Guard; Drill Tm; VP Soph Cls; Cambria-Rowe Bus Coll; Accntnt.

HAYATH, KARIM; Fairview HS; Thames Ditton; (Y); Cmnty Wkr; French Clb; Hosp Aide; Model UN; Speech Tm; Mrchg Band; Pep Band; Crs Cntry; Trk; Hon Roll; Jets Recog 86; Pre-Med.

HAYDEN, BETH; Moniteau JR SR HS; W Sunbury, PA; (Y); Ski Clb; Varsity Clb; Band; Concert Band; Jazz Band; Mrchg Band; Yrbk Phtg; Bsktbl; Trk; Church Yth Grp; Lost Sheep Mrchng Excllnc Awd 85; FFA Ldrshp Awd 84; IN U PA; Pre-Law.

HAYDEN, DEBORAH; Juniata HS; Mifflintown, PA; (Y); Letterman Clb; Speech Tm; Varsity Clb; Var Fld Hcky; High Hon Roll; Hon Roll; Jr NHS; NHS; Girl Scts; Spanish Clb; Fshn Mrchndsg.

HAYDEN, THOMAS; Moniteau HS; W Sunbury, PA; (Y); Church Yth Grp; French Clb; Ski Clb; Varsity Clb; Stu Cncl; Bsktbl; Ftbl; Wt Lftg; High Hon Roll; Hon Roll; U Pittsburgh; Phrmcy.

HAYDUK, SANDRA; Bethlehem Catholic HS; Freemansburg, PA; (Y); 13/225; Chorus; School Musical; School Play; Variety Show; Yrbk Stf; High Hon Roll; Lion Awd; NHS; Thurrsby Mem Schlrshp 86; Moravian Schlrshp 86; Moravian Coll; Music.

HAYEK, DINA; State College Area HS; State College, PA; (Y); Hosp Aide; Ski Clb; SADD; Band; Mrchg Band; Yrbk Stf; Im Vllybl; Hon Roll; Ntl Merit Ltr; PA ST U; Bus.

HAYES, AMY; Kiski Area HS; Apollo, PA; (Y); Drama Clb; Math Clb; Math Tm; Mrchg Band; School Musical; School Play; High Hon Roll; NHS; 4-H; French Clb; Regnl Orch 86; Govrnr Schl Arts 86; Acdmc Ltr 84-86; Music.

HAYES, BERNADETTE; Archbishop Kennedy HS; Conshohocken, PA; (Y); Chorus; Yrbk Stf; JV Var Cheerleading; JV Trk; Var Vllybl; Hon Roll; Accntng.

HAYES, BEVERLY M; University City HS; Philadelhpia, PA; (Y); Church Yth Grp; Cmnty Wkr; Temple U; Nrsg.

HAYES, CATHERINE L; Warren Area HS; Warren, PA; (Y); Hosp Aide; Acpl Chr; Jazz Band; Madrigals; Orch; School Musical; NHS; School Play; High Hon Roll; Hon Roll; Jr NHS; 85 All-ST Chorus PA 85; All-ST Orchstra PA 86; Allghny Schlr Schlrshp 86; Allegheny Coll; Cmmnctn Arts.

HAYES, CHRIS; Tulpehocken HS; Bernville, PA; (Y); Band; Mrchg Band; School Musical; Trs Soph Cls; Trs Jr Cls; Stu Cncl; Bsktbl; Fld Hcky; Tennis; Trk.

HAYES, CINDY; Calvary Baptist Acad; Clymer, PA; (S); 1/5; Sec VP Church Yth Grp; Quiz Bowl; Band; Chorus; Swing Chorus; Var L Bsktbl; Var L Vllybl; High Hon Roll; Church Choir; Nwsp Rptr; Schl Sci Fair-1st Pl 85; KCEA Regnl Sci Fair-1st Pl 84; KCEA Regnl Essay Comptn-Red Rbbn Awd 86; Bob Jones U.

HAYES, GREGORY; York Central SR HS; York, PA; (Y); VP Drama Clb; NFL; Spanish Clb; School Musical; School Play; Stage Crew; Hon Roll; PA ST.

HAYES, LINETT; Moon HS; Glenwillard, PA; (Y); Drama Clb; Nwsp Rptr; Nwsp Stf; Yrbk Rptr; Yrbk Stf; Sftbl; Vllybl; Duquesne U; Psych.

HAYES, MICHAEL; Crestwood HS; Mountaintop, PA; (Y); 3/223; Math Clb; Ski Clb; Var Ftbl; Wt Lftg; High Hon Roll; NHS; NEDT Awd; Stu Recgntn Nght; Harold Baker Awd; Engrng.

HAYES, ROBERT J; Monongahele Valley Catholic HS; Monessen, PA; (S); 3/110; Spanish Clb; Rep Soph Cls; Pres Stu Cncl; Mgr L Bsktbl; Mgr L Ftbl; Trs NHS; Pres Spanish NHS; Westinghouse Sci Hnrs Inst 85-86; Carnegie-Mellon U; Elec Engrng.

HAYES, RON; Fort Le Boeuf HS; Erie, PA; (Y); 35/167; FCA; Model UN; Concert Band; Var JV Bsktbl; Var Capt Ftbl; Var L Trk; Im Vllybl; Ftbl MVP 85; Defensve Plyr 85; 1st Person Ftbl Hist 100 Tackles 85; Marine Biolgst.

HAYES, SUSAN; Mercyhurst Prep HS; Erie, PA; (Y); French Clb; Hosp Aide; Hon Roll; NHS; NEDT Awd; Pres Schlr; Phi Eta Sigma Hnr Soc 86; Schlrshp Untd Stlwrkrs Amrca 86; Mercyhurst Coll; Acctg.

HAYES, TERRY LEE; Corry HS; Corry, PA; (S); Radio Clb; Ftbl; Vllybl; Wrstlng.

HAYES, TRACY; Ytalpehocken HS; Bernville, PA; (Y); 20/96; Ski Clb; Band; Chorus; Mrchg Band; Pep Band; School Musical; School Play; Stage Crew; Pres Frsh Cls; Pres Stu Cncl; Acad Achvmnt Awd; Mst Sprtd Athlete Hock & Bsktbll; Indiana U Of PA.

HAYES, WANDA; Aliquippa SR HS; Aliquippa, PA; (Y); #2 In Class; Drama Clb; French Clb; Library Aide; Office Aide; Sec SADD; Ed Nwsp Stf; Sec Jr Cls; Sec Sr Cls; Capt Pom Pon; High Hon Roll; S Carolina ST; Bus Admn.

HAYES JR, WILLIAM L; Warren Area HS; Warren, PA; (Y); Art Clb; Boy Scts; Chess Clb; Acpl Chr; Madrigals; Mrchg Band; Orch; Nwsp Stf; God Cntry Awd; Jr NHS; 2nd Awd JR Dvsn Allegheny Mt Sci Fr 84; PA All ST Orcstr 85-86; Chantauqua Yth Orchstr 85-86; Cello Prfrmnc.

HAYKO, TRACY; Spring-Ford HS; Collegeville, PA; (S); 16/258; Pep Clb; Spanish Clb; Yrbk Bus Mgr; Yrbk Phtg; Am Leg Aux Girls St; Off Soph Cls; Off Jr Cls; Stu Cncl; Bsktbl; Cheerleading; Soph & Jr Homecoming Princesses; Educ.

HAYNES, REBECCA; Pocono Mtn HS; Cresco, PA; (Y); Church Yth Grp; Girl Scts; Hosp Aide; Concert Band; Mrchg Band; God Cntry Awd; Band; Nwsp Rptr; Stat Bsktbl; Hon Roll.

HAYNEY, FRANCIS V; St Joseph Prep Schl; Camden, NJ; (Y); Chess Clb; Im Bsktbl; Im Ftbl; Im Ice Hcky; Hon Roll; Ntl Merit Ltr; Prfct Atten Awd; Amer & Natl SR Clsscl Lg Natl Lat Exm Magna Cum Laude 85, Natl Grk Exm Hgh Hnrs 85 & 86, Cum Laude; Clsscs.

HAYWALD, KENNETH; Tunkhannock Area HS; Falls, PA; (Y); 50/270; FCA; Var Ftbl; Var Trk; Var Wt Lftg; Hon Roll; Susquehanna U; Accntng.

HAYWARD, AARON; Creative & Performing Arts; Philadelphia, PA; (S); 10/146; School Play; Stage Crew; Off Soph Cls; Stu Cncl; Hon Roll; NHS; Prfct Atten Awd; U CA Los Angeles; Physhlgy.

HAYWARD, MELINDA; Clearfield HS; Clearfield, PA; (Y); Dance Clb; French Clb; Key Clb; Pep Clb; Ski Clb; Yrbk Stf; Var L Cheerleading; Gym; Score Keeper; Hon Roll; Phy Thrpst.

HAYWARD, MELISSA; Clearfield Area HS; Clearfield, PA; (Y); 16/320; French Clb; Ski Clb; VP VICA; High Hon Roll; Hon Roll; NHS; Bus Adm.

HAYWOOD, JENNA; Pennsbury HS; Washington Crossi, PA; (Y); German Clb; SADD; Chorus; School Musical; Hon Roll.

HAYWOOD JR, ROBERT A; Elizabeth Forward HS; Elizabeth, PA; (Y); Spanish Clb; L Bsbl; Golf; Wt Lftg; Hon Roll; Clarion U Of PA.

HAZELTINE, LANA; Otto-Eldred HS; Eldred, PA; (Y); Church Yth Grp; 4-H; Pep Clb; Varsity Clb; Chorus; Variety Show; Nwsp Rptr; Var Cheerleading; Var Trk; Hon Roll; Roberts Wesylan Coll; Hstry.

HAZLETT, AMY; Highlands SR HS; Natrona Hts, PA; (Y); Sec Church Yth Grp; Key Clb; SADD; Chorus; Hon Roll; Art Inst Of Pittsburgh; Int Dec.

HAZLETT, BONNIE; Freeport SR HS; Sarver, PA; (Y); Hosp Aide; Band; Pep Band; Nwsp Rptr; Rep Stu Cncl; Stat Bsktbl; Sftbl; Swmmng; Hon Roll; Acad All Amer 86; Duquesne; Nrsg.

HAZLETT, JO; Highlands HS; Natrona Hts, PA; (Y); 51/274; FBLA; Office Aide; Chorus; Rep Soph Cls; Rep Jr Cls; Rep Sr Cls; Rep Stu Cncl; Jr NHS; NHS; Prfct Atten Awd; Soph, JR, SR Exec Cmmttes; ICM; Acctg.

HAZLETT, LORI; Highlands SR HS; Tarentum, PA; (Y); 20/275; Intnl Clb; Key Clb; Concert Band; VP Mrchg Band; Nwsp Ed-Chief; Nwsp Rptr; Mgr Swmmng; High Hon Roll; NHS; Pres Acad & Phys Fit Awds 86; Exec Comm 85-86; PSU Minnie Hyman & Hea Mary Louise Sisk Mem Scholars; PA ST U; Jrnlsm.

HAZLETT, TIMOTHY; Warwick HS; Lititz, PA; (Y); 40/240; Math Clb; Varsity Clb; Orch; School Musical; Im Bsktbl; Var Capt Socr; Im Vllybl; Var Wrstlng; High Hon Roll; Rensselaer Schlrshp 86; Rensselaer Poltech Inst; Geophy.

HEACOCK, CANDICE J; Perkiomen Valley HS; Perkiomenville, PA; (Y); 1/191; Church Yth Grp; Pres 4-H; Nwsp Rptr; Var L Lcrss; Co-Capt Var Socr; Dnfth Awd; 4-H Awd; God Cntry Awd; High Hon Roll; NHS; First Cls Sct; ST Farm Shw Awds 84-86; FL Inst Of Tech; Aerontcl Fld.

HEADEN, PAULA; Bishop Mcdevitt HS; Harrisburg, PA; (S); Church Yth Grp; Computer Clb; Drama Clb; Science Clb; Service Clb; Spanish Clb; Band; Chorus; Church Choir; Concert Band; Villanova U; Nrsng.

HEALY, BRIDGET A; Mercyhurst Prep; Erie, PA; (Y); JCL; Latin Clb; Ski Clb; Yrbk Stf; Lit Mag; Hon Roll; NHS; Presdntl Acadmc Ftns Awd 86; Penn ST; Lbrl Arts.

HEALY, MICHELLE; Pennsbury HS; Levittown, PA; (Y); Church Yth Grp; Spanish Clb; Rep Frsh Cls; Bsktbl; Hon Roll; WA & Lee; Child Psych.

HEANEY, DONALD F; North Hills HS; Pittsburgh, PA; (Y); Boy Scts; Chess Clb; Cmnty Wkr; Computer Clb; Exploring; FBLA; Ski Clb; Stage Crew; Swmmng; High Hon Roll; IN U PA Physics Test Comp Wnr 86; Penn ST U; Engrng.

HEARD, PAMELA; Wyoming Area HS; Wyoming, PA; (S); Church Yth Grp; Hosp Aide; Ski Clb; Spanish Clb; SADD; Concert Band; Mrchg Band; Orch; Trk; Hon Roll.

HEARD, WILLIAM; Pius X HS; Roseto, PA; (Y); Varsity Clb; School Musical; Nwsp Stf; Yrbk Stf; Rep Sr Cls; Bsktbl; Mgr(s); KC Awd 86; Lafayette Coll; Economics.

HEARN IV, CHESTER G; Milton Area HS; Potts Grove, PA; (Y); 12/202; Varsity Clb; Yrbk Stf; Rep Stu Cncl; Bsktbl; Var Crs Cntry; Var Trk; Im Wt Lftg; Hon Roll; NHS; Mech.

HEARN, KRISTINA; Warwick HS; Lititz, PA; (Y); #2 In Class; Ski Clb; Rep Frsh Cls; Rep Jr Cls; Var Crs Cntry; High Hon Roll; Jr NHS; NHS; NEDT Awd; Gftd Prog; U DE; Mrn Sci.

HEARN, MICHELLE; Rockwood Area HS; Somerset, PA; (S); 6/95; Spanish Clb; Yrbk Stf; Rep Stu Cncl; Var L Cheerleading; L Stat Vllybl; High Hon Roll; Sci Awd 84.

HEARSEY, STACIE; Annville Cleona HS; Annville, PA; (Y); Varsity Clb; Chorus; School Musical; Yrbk Stf; Trs Jr Cls; Trs Sr Cls; Var Capt Crs Cntry; Var Sftbl; JV Trk; NHS.

HEASLEY, JEFF; Beaver Area JR SR HS; Beaver, PA; (Y); 11/179; Pres FCA; German Clb; JCL; Trs Jr Cls; Trs Sr Cls; Crs Cntry; Powder Puff Ftbl; Trk; High Hon Roll; U MI; Phys Thrpy.

HEATH, KIMBERLY; Philipsburg Osceola Area HS; Osceola Mills, PA; (Y); 1/250; Concert Band; Mrchg Band; Yrbk Stf; Sec Frsh Cls; Stu Cncl; Twrlr; DAR Awd; NHS; NEDT Awd; Pres Church Yth Grp; Pre-Med.

HEATWOLE JR, BILL; Towanda Area HS; Towanda, PA; (Y); Boy Scts; Church Yth Grp; Letterman Clb; Varsity Clb; L Ftbl; L Trk; 2nd JR Olympcs Natl Champnshp 800 M Relay 85; Landscapng.

HEBDING, SONIA; Academy Of Notre Dame HS; Drexel Hill, PA; (Y); 15/72; Mathletes; Math Tm; Model UN; Stage Crew; Nwsp Stf; Yrbk Stf; Socr; JV Tennis; Trk; High Hon Roll; Prtcptn Awd Natl Sci Olm 86; High Hnrs HS 86; Villanova U; Bus Acctg.

HEBERLEIN, JENNIFER; Villa Maria Acad; Erie, PA; (Y); Church Yth Grp; Exploring; Science Clb; Band; Mrchg Band; Rep Frsh Cls; Rep Soph Cls; Twrlr; NHS; Chld Psychlgy.

HEBERT, BRIAN; Chief Logan HS; Mc Clure, PA; (Y); 7/202; Pres Church Yth Grp; Computer Clb; Exploring; French Clb; Math Tm; Pep Clb; Varsity Clb; School Play; Variety Show; Var L Bsbl; Ntl Yng Ldrs Conf-Cngrssnl Yth Ldrshp Cncl 86; Upward Bnd Of PA ST U 85; Comp Sci.

HEBERT, JOHN; Abraham Lincoln HS; Philadelphia, PA; (Y); Art Clb; Political Wkr; Pres Jr Cls; Elec Co Enrgy Art Cntst Awd Phila Sktch Club 86; Phila Yng Artst Cmptn Awd 86; Art.

HEBRANK, JAMES; Hempfield Area SR HS; Greensburg, PA; (Y); AFS; Pres Church Yth Grp; Computer Clb; Drama Clb; JA; Spanish Clb; School Play; Yrbk Phtg; Yrbk Stf; Hon Roll; Bus Adm.

HECHLER, THERESA; Mechanicsburg Area SR HS; Mechanicsburg, PA; (Y); Church Yth Grp; Girl Scts; Hosp Aide; Red Cross Aide; Science Clb; Ski Clb; Chorus; Opt Clb Awd; Env Olympics Assoc Dist Dir 86; Harrisburg Area CC; Bio.

HECK, CHRISTOPHER J; Shady Side Acad; Glenshaw, PA; (Y); 10/121; Trs French Clb; Nwsp Ed-Chief; Yrbk Stf; Bsktbl; Im Wt Lftg; Ntl Merit SF; Engl.

HECK, RENEE; E L Meyers HS; Wilkes Bare, PA; (Y); Church Yth Grp; German Clb; Ski Clb; Flag Corp; Hon Roll; Jr NHS; Nrsng.

HECKATHORN, KIM; West Middlesex Area HS; Mercer, PA; (S); 3/113; Rptr FBLA; Hosp Aide; Yrbk Stf; Stat Trk; Var L Vllybl; Hon Roll; Jr NHS; Spanish NHS; PA Free Entrprs 85; Slippery Rock U; Accntnt.

HECKLER, MICHELLE; Souderton Area HS; Telford, PA; (Y); VP Band; VP Concert Band; VP Mrchg Band; JV Bsktbl; Var Fld Hcky; Var Lcrss; Hon Roll; Shippensburg U Of PA.

HECKMAN, APRIL; Interboro HS; Norwood, PA; (S); 17/264; Church Yth Grp; Drama Clb; Latin Clb; Quiz Bowl; Band; Chorus; Church Choir; Concert Band; Mrchg Band; School Play; Sci.

HECKMAN, CONNIE; Brookville Area HS; Summerville, PA; (Y); 4/143; Pres Church Yth Grp; Nwsp Stf; Yrbk Stf; Lit Mag; Stat Vllybl; High Hon Roll; Jr NHS; NHS; Pennsylvania ST U; Chem Engr.

HECKMAN, J MARK; Punxsutawney SR HS; Punxsutawney, PA; (Y); 230/250; Band; Chorus; Church Choir; Concert Band; Drm Mjr(t); Jazz Band; Mrchg Band; Pep Band; School Musical; School Play; Musc Ed.

HECKMAN, JEFFREY; Lenape AVTS; Vandergrift, PA; (Y); Pres Church Yth Grp; Chrmn SADD; Pres VICA; Band; Mrchg Band; Off Stu Cncl; Var Trk; Hon Roll; Comp Sci.

HECKMAN, JODY; Montoursville Area HS; Montoursville, PA; (Y); Church Yth Grp; French Clb; Hosp Aide; Var Tennis; Hon Roll; NHS; Cert Merit Frnch I 83-84; IVP; Nrsg.

HECKMAN, VICKI; Brookville Area HS; Corsica, PA; (Y); 9/144; Pres VP Church Yth Grp; 4-H; Trs FTA; Key Clb; Pep Clb; Stu Cncl; Hon Roll; NHS; Pres Schlr; Clarion U Of PA; Accntng.

HECTOR JR, THOMAS; Shady Side Acad; Pittsburgh, PA; (Y); Church Yth Grp; Debate Tm; Spanish Clb; SADD; Jazz Band; Nwsp Stf; Rep Frsh Cls; Var L Trk; Var L Wrstlng; Hon Roll; U VT Rsrch Apprntce Pgm 86; Dntstry.

HEDDERICK, DANNY; Hamburg HS; Shoemakersville, PA; (Y); Hon Roll; SR Of Yr Berks East Vo Tech 86; Stu Of Qrtr Cert 85-86; Cash Awd Reading-Berks Gld Crftmn 86; Cabint Mkg.

HEDGLIN, WENDY; Grove City HS; Volant, PA; (Y); 39/150; French Clb; Orch; Trs Frsh Cls; Trs Soph Cls; Trs Jr Cls; Trs Sr Cls; Capt Cheerleading; Powder Puff Ftbl; JV Vllybl; Homecomg Court 85; Winter Fstvl Prncss 85; Hnr Grad 86; Slippery Rock U; Spec Ed.

HEDRICK, ANDY; Everett Area HS; Everett, PA; (Y); 3/110; Church Yth Grp; Spanish Clb; Varsity Clb; Bsbl; Capt Bsktbl; Trk; Cit Awd; High Hon Roll; Hon Roll; Pres NHS; Johnstown Tribune Democrt Schltc Ath 86; Princpls Awd Outstndng Schl Spirit 86; PA ST; Secndry Ed.

HEEBNER, KATRINA; Upper Perkiomen HS; Red Hill, PA; (Y); 22/234; Church Yth Grp; FBLA; Yrbk Sprt Ed; Yrbk Stf; Rep Stu Cncl; Stat Bsktbl; Var Capt Crs Cntry; Var Capt Lcrss; Powder Puff Ftbl; Var Trk; MVP Crss Cntry 85-86; All Bux-Mont Lacrosse 86; Pillsbury Acdmc Achvmnt Schlrshp 86; Lock Haven U; Mgmt Sci.

HEEFNER III, ROBERT E; Shippensburg SR HS; Shippensburg, PA; (Y); 16/226; Pres Varsity Clb; Band; Rep Frsh Cls; Pres Soph Cls; Pres Jr Cls; Rep Sr Cls; Rep Stu Cncl; Var Capt Bsbl; Var Ftbl; High Hon Roll; Lns Clb Stu Of Mnth 86; PA Free Entrprs 85; Shippensburg U; Comp Sci.

HEERY, CHRISTOPHER A; Lehighton Area HS; Lehighton, PA; (Y); Church Yth Grp; Band; Mrchg Band; Orch; School Musical; Nwsp Rptr; Nwsp Stf; Bsktbl; Coach Actv; Hon Roll; Kutztown U; Elem Ed.

HEFFELFINGER, LISA M; Marian HS; Lansford, PA; (Y); 49/121; Art Clb; Library Aide; Office Aide; ROTC; Ski Clb; Yrbk Stf; Trk; Keystone JC; Art.

HEFFELFINGER, LORI; Marian Catholic HS; Lansford, PA; (Y); 30/115; Hosp Aide; Office Aide; Pep Clb; SADD; Mrchg Band; Var L Cheerleading; JV Sftbl; Hon Roll; Secndry Ed.

HEFFELFINGER, RONALD; Neshaminy HS; Penndel, PA; (Y); 24/723; Band; Chorus; Jazz Band; Var Bsktbl; Var Stat Socr; High Hon Roll; Hon Roll; NHS; Bus Admin.

HEFFENTRAGER, TRACY; Berks Christian Schl; Birdsboro, PA; (Y); 1/10; Spanish Clb; Varsity Clb; Chorus; Jazz Band; Pres Sr Cls; L Var Trk; Capt L Vllybl; High Hon Roll; NHS; Val; Math & Sci Awd 86; Prncpls Awd 86; Cnclrs Schlrshp 86; Lbrty U; Bus Adm.

HEFFERNAN, RICH; Bethlehem Catholic HS; Bethlehem, PA; (Y); 77/225; Var Bsbl; Var Capt Ftbl; Wt Lftg; Var Wrstlng; Hon Roll.

HEFFNER, CONNIE L; Hamburg Area HS; Hamburg, PA; (Y); 11/150; SADD; Chorus; Church Choir; Concert Band; Jazz Band; Mrchg Band; Orch; Hon Roll; NHS; Psych.

HEFFNER, RICHELLE; Schuylkill Haven Area HS; Schuylkill Haven, PA; (S); 25/98; Aud/Vis; Computer Clb; German Clb; Pep Clb; SADD; Teachers Aide; Color Guard; Capt Drill Tm; Mrchg Band; Yrbk Stf.

HEFFNER, SHERRY; Coudersport JR SR HS; Coudersport, PA; (Y); Church Yth Grp; French Clb; Ski Clb; Band; Chorus; Concert Band; Mrchg Band; Golf; Hon Roll; Prfct Atten Awd; Comm Art.

HEFFRON, LAURA; Penncrest HS; Media, PA; (Y); Art Clb; Church Yth Grp; Intnl Clb; School Musical; Variety Show; Hon Roll; Southeastern Acad; Trvl Indstry.

HEGARTY, MAUREEN; Allentown Central Catholic HS; Whitehall, PA; (Y); 75/210; Church Yth Grp; Cmnty Wkr; Hosp Aide; Church Choir; Color Guard; Mrchg Band; Ed Nwsp Stf; Hon Roll.

HEGEDIS, CHRISSANDA DAWN; Mapletown JR SR HS; Bobtown, PA; (Y); 10/80; Ed Yrbk Phtg; Yrbk Stf; High Hon Roll; Hon Roll; Yuth Educ Assn; WV U; :X Ray Tech.

HEGGS, RONALD; John Bartram HS; Philadelphia, PA; (S); 24/600; Church Yth Grp; Letterman Clb; Varsity Clb; Stu Cncl; Var Bsktbl; JV Crs Cntry; JV Mgr(s); Trk; High Hon Roll; Chrch Grp; Vrsty Clb; Natl Hnr Soc; Engrng.

HEHN, ELIZABETH D; Bishop Kenrick HS; Audubon, PA; (Y); 9/248; Ski Clb; Nwsp Rptr; Rep Frsh Cls; Rep Soph Cls; Rep Jr Cls; Rep Sr Cls; L Crs Cntry; Jr NHS; NHS; Opt Clb Awd; Engl Awd 86; Art Awd 86; Philadelphia Coll; Fash Desgn.

HEICHEL, DEBBIE; West Branch HS; Morrisdale, PA; (Y); 36/103; Red Cross Aide; Teachers Aide; Chorus; Concert Band; Mrchg Band; Yrbk Stf; Twrlr; Secrtrl.

HEID, CHRISTY; Highlando HS; Natrona Hts, PA; (Y); 12/300; Church Yth Grp; Key Clb; Concert Band; Mrchg Band; Pep Band; Rep Jr Cls; High Hon Roll; Jr NHS; NHS; Ntl Merit Ltr; DMEA Dist I Hnrs Band 86; Alle-Kioki Hnrs Band 84-86; Mus.

HEIDECKER, REGINA A; Wm Allen HS; Allentown, PA; (Y); 58/576; Trs Civic Clb; GAA; Nwsp Rptr; JV Bsktbl; Var L Sftbl; High Hon Roll; NHS; Ntl Merit Ltr; Pres Schlr; EPC All Str Div 2 Sftbll 85-86; Muhlenberg; Lawyer.

HEIDECKER, ROBYN; Harborcreek HS; Erie, PA; (Y); 21/228; AFS; Sec Church Yth Grp; Exploring; Flag Corp; Mrchg Band; Yrbk Stf; Hon Roll; NHS; Spnsh Awd; Bus Admin.

HEIDELBERG, MELANIE A; St Benedict Acad; Erie, PA; (Y); 2/51; Q&S; Yrbk Stf; Trs Frsh Cls; VP Soph Cls; Pres Sr Cls; Pres Stu Cncl; Var Co-Capt Cheerleading; NHS; Ntl Merit Ltr; Dance Clb; Miss Tawny 84-85; Pre-Law.

HEIDENREICH, CAROLE; Butler SR HS; Butler, PA; (Y); 5 Tlr Vo Tch Drftng Otstndng 86; Achvmnt Hnr Awds; Butler CC; Drftng.

HEIDER, SHARON; Forest Hills SR HS; Salix, PA; (Y); 57/156; Church Yth Grp; Drama Clb; Band; Chorus; Mrchg Band; School Musical; School Play; Yrbk Ed-Chief; Hon Roll; Art Clb; Dist Regl Chorus; U Of Pitts; Elem Ed.

HEIDISH, MICHAEL; Shaler Area HS; Glenshaw, PA; (Y); 10/538; Var L Bsbl; High Hon Roll; NHS; Pres Schlr; Spanish NHS; Grove City Coll; Bio.

HEIDORN, DONNA; Windber Area HS; Windber, PA; (Y); Am Leg Aux Girls St; Hosp Aide; Chorus; Color Guard; Flag Corp; Mrchg Band; Hon Roll; PA Acad Of Cosmetology; Cosmet.

HEIDRICH, BRENDEN; Cedar Crest HS; Lebanon, PA; (Y); 30/326; Boy Scts; Pres Church Yth Grp; Drama Clb; Quiz Bowl; School Musical; Im Vllybl; High Hon Roll; Ntl Merit Ltr; German Clb; Pep Clb; U Of PA; Chem Engr.

HEIDRICH, STACY; Cameron County HS; Emporium, PA; (Y); 3/91; German Clb; Chorus; Concert Band; Mrchg Band; Yrbk Sprt Ed; Stat Bsktbl; Var JV Mgr(s); Var JV Vllybl; Hon Roll; NHS; Delta Epsln Phi Germn Hnr Socty; Pre-Law.

HEIDT, SUSAN M; Mercyhurst Prep; Erie, PA; (Y); VP Key Clb; Teachers Aide; Nwsp Rptr; Yrbk Stf; Bowling; Hon Roll; Var L Bsktbl; Var L Socr; Var L Sftbl; Var L Vllybl; St John Fisher.

HEIGLEY, STACI; Marion Center HS; Home, PA; (Y); FNA; Hosp Aide; Latin Clb; Science Clb; Varsity Clb; Band; Mrchg Band; Trs Frsh Cls; JV Var Cheerleading; Var Trk; Gazteland Track Tm 85; IVP; Chld Psychlgy.

HEIKES, LUANNE; Northern HS; Dillsburg, PA; (Y); 85/209; Spanish Clb; Pres Chorus; Church Choir; Color Guard; Drill Tm; Mrchg Band; School Musical; JV Cheerleading; Psychlgst.

HEIL, ANN; Harry S Truman HS; Croydon, PA; (Y); Trk; Hon Roll; Chld Psych.

HEIL, KURT M; North Allegheny SR HS; Pittsburgh, PA; (Y); 6/605; Boy Scts; German Clb; Chorus; Ftbl; Wt Lftg; Wrstlng; High Hon Roll; Jr NHS; NHS; Eagle Scout 84; U Of Notre Dame; Pre-Med.

HEIL, PETER; Shadyside Acad; Pittsburgh, PA; (Y); Aud/Vis; Cmnty Wkr; German Clb; Band; Concert Band; Jazz Band; PHYS Ther.

HEIL, PHOEBE; Mt Alvernia HS; Glenshaw, PA; (Y); French Clb; GAA; Spanish Clb; Chorus; School Musical; School Play; Yrbk Stf; Var L Bsktbl; Var Socr; Hon Roll; Bus Mgmt.

HEILIG, SUSAN M; Emmaus HS; Emmaus, PA; (Y); 51/476; Trs Sec Church Yth Grp; German Clb; JCL; Key Clb; Trs Latin Clb; Band; Stat Bsktbl; Stat Crs Cntry; Im Fld Hcky; Mgr(s); PA ST U.

HEILMAN, BETH; Fairchance Georges HS; Smithfield, PA; (Y); 25/187; Church Yth Grp; Spanish Clb; Band; Concert Band; Mrchg Band; Twrlr; Hon Roll; Dir Awd; Bus.

HEILMAN, SEAN; Ford City HS; Ford City, PA; (Y); 21/151; Computer Clb; L Trk; High Hon Roll; Hon Roll; NHS; U Of Pittsburgh; Comm.

HEIM, DOUGLAS A; Moon SR HS; Corapolis, PA; (Y); 41/365; JA; Acpl Chr; Chorus; School Musical; School Play; Stage Crew; Swing Chorus; Var Tennis; Hon Roll; Ntl Merit SF; Grove Cty Coll; Elec Engnrng.

HEIM, HEATHER; Line Mountain HS; Dalmatia, PA; (Y); Am Leg Aux Girls St; FBLA; Key Clb; Varsity Clb; Rep Stu Cncl; Co-Capt Fld Hcky; Sftbl; High Hon Roll; NHS; Stage Crew; Key Clb Intl Distngshd Svc Awd 86; Pres Phys Fit Awd 85 & 86; Vet Med.

HEIM, LISA; Scranton Central HS; Scranton, PA; (Y); Cmnty Wkr; Computer Clb; Girl Scts; JA; Chorus; Color Guard; Drill Tm; Pep Band; Cheerleading; PA ST; Comp.

HEIM, MARY BETH; Jersey Shore Area HS; Jersey Shore, PA; (Y); Art Clb; VP FBLA; German Clb; Hst Jr Cls; Hst Sr Cls; Trs Stu Cncl; Var Crs Cntry; Var Trk; DAR Awd; NHS; Amer Hstry Awd; Lions Top 10; Earlham Coll; Art Hstry.

HEIMBACH, MARY ANN; Boyertown Area SR HS; Boyertown, PA; (Y); Church Yth Grp; Hosp Aide; SADD; Church Choir; Mrchg Band; Nwsp Stf; Twrlr; Cit Awd; Hon Roll; Wod Life Schlrshp Awd 85; Soc Work.

HEIMBECKER, CHRISTINE; St Basil Acad; Phila, PA; (Y); Aud/Vis; Church Yth Grp; French Clb; Science Clb; Yrbk Stf; Trs Jr Cls; Stu Cncl; JV Var Sftbl; Im Bsktbl; Bus Adm.

HEIMBUCH JR, RICHARD F; Perkinomen Schl; Cliffside Pk, NJ; (Y); Letterman Clb; Ski Clb; Varsity Clb; Var Crs Cntry; Var Capt Lcrss; Var Socr; Hon Roll; 1st Tm NE PA Lacrosse Lg All Stars 86; MVP Lacrosse Awd 86; MIP Crs Cntry Awd 85; Pol Sci.

HEIN, DAVID; West Scranton HS; Scranton, PA; (Y); 20/250; Boy Scts; Pres Church Yth Grp; Ski Clb; Church Choir; VP Orch; God Cntry Awd; Jr NHS; NHS; JR Acad Sci 3rd 84; PA Math Leag 3rd 86; Bloomsburg ST U; Acctng.

HEIN, DIANA; Hamburg Area HS; Hamburg, PA; (Y); 72/152; Color Guard; Stage Crew; Hon Roll; Wildrnss Clb 83-84; Bus.

HEIN, DOUGLAS A; West Scranton HS; Scranton, PA; (Y); 20/250; Church Yth Grp; JA; Ski Clb; JV Trk; NHS; Amer Lgn Aux Mdl Awd 84; Accntg.

HEIN, DWIGHT; Southern Lehigh HS; Coopersburg, PA; (Y); Drama Clb; Trs Key Clb; Chorus; Church Choir; Madrigals; School Musical; School Play; Nwsp Stf; Golf; Hon Roll; Clarion U Of PA; Accntng.

HEIN, WENDY; Northwestern Lehigh HS; Germansville, PA; (Y); 15/130; Debate Tm; Drama Clb; French Clb; Pres Chorus; School Musical; School Play; Cheerleading; High Hon Roll; Hon Roll; Ntl Schl Choral Awd 86; Kutztown U; Pol Sci.

HEINDEL, CRISTI S; Christian School Of York; York, PA; (Y); Church Yth Grp; FCA; JA; Varsity Clb; School Play; Yrbk Stf; Capt Cheerleading; Var Sftbl; High Hon Roll; Hon Roll; World Of Life; Bibl.

HEINDEL, SHERRY; Eastern York HS; Hellam, PA; (Y); 10/169; VP Church Yth Grp; VP Varsity Clb; Drm Mjr(t); Var Stat Bsbl; Im Powder Puff Ftbl; Var Twrlr; High Hon Roll; Hon Roll; Jr NHS; NHS.

HEINEN, TRACY; Burgettstown JR SR HS; Burgettstown, PA; (Y); 33/179; Art Clb; French Clb; Yrbk Stf; Hon Roll; Mary Noss Schlrshp Awd 86; Mst Artstc 86; Fnlst Gvrnr Schl Arts 85; CA U; Art Educ.

HEINEY, JEFFREY; Lampeter Strasburg HS; Lancaster, PA; (Y); 15/181; AFS; Drama Clb; Thesps; Chorus; School Musical; School Play; Nwsp Ed-Chief; Nwsp Rptr; Nwsp Stf; Lit Mag; Cmnctns.

HEINEY, MATT; Hughesville HS; Hughesville, PA; (Y); Camera Clb; Church Yth Grp; Letterman Clb; Ski Clb; Varsity Clb; Chorus; Church Choir; School Musical; School Play; Var L Bsktbl; Tm Ldr Awd Sccr & Tnns 85-86.

HEININGER, ROCHELL; Springdale HS; Springdale, PA; (Y); Art Clb; Yrbk Phtg; Yrbk Stf; Var L Bsktbl; Im Coach Actv; Hon Roll; PA ST; Bus.

HEINLE, ANNE; Beaver Area HS; Beaver, PA; (Y); Trs Church Yth Grp; FCA; VP French Clb; Ski Clb; Ed Yrbk Stf; Im JV Cheerleading; Powder Puff Ftbl; JV Var Trk; High Hon Roll; Jr NHS.

HEINS, JENNIFER; Springside Schl; Dresher, PA; (Y); Pres Jr Cls; Var Capt Tennis; Var Capt Vllybl; Strdy Art Bls Schrlshp Moore Coll Art 85-86; Mdl ST Tnns Assn Rnkng 20th 85-86; Art.

HEINTZELMAN, MICHAEL; Northwestern Lehigh HS; New Tripoli, PA; (Y); 29/158; Exploring; Rptr 4-H; Nwsp Stf; Var L Wrstlng; Hon Roll; Acad Engl Awd 84-85; Engrng.

HEINTZELMAN, TAMMY; Central Dauphin HS; Harrisburg, PA; (Y); Trs German Clb; Teachers Aide; Var Capt Cheerleading; Var Sftbl; Hon Roll; West Chester U; Early Chldhd Ed.

HEISEN, CHRISTOPHER; Pennsbury HS; Yardley, PA; (Y); 1/800; Am Leg Boys St; Drama Clb; French Clb; Intnl Clb; NFL; Political Wkr; Speech Tm; Temple Yth Grp; School Musical; School Play; 7th Pl-Ntl Frnscs Leags Ntl Tourn 86.

HEISEY, ANGIE; Manheim Central HS; Manheim, PA; (Y); Dance Clb; 4-H; Rep Sr Cls; Rep Stu Cncl; JV Var Fld Hcky; Dnfth Awd; Hon Roll; 4-Way Tst Awd 86.

HEISEY, JULIE; Elizabethtown Area HS; Elizabethtown, PA; (S); 14/247; Church Yth Grp; Band; Concert Band; Mrchg Band; Off Frsh Cls; Trs Soph Cls; Powder Puff Ftbl; Tennis; NHS; Pharm.

HEISEY, KELLY; Cedar Crest HS; Lebanon, PA; (Y); 29/344; Church Yth Grp; 4-H; Key Clb; Pep Clb; Spanish Clb; Chorus; Orch; School Musical; Socr; Vllybl; Frm Wmn Soc Schlrshp 86; Mst Outstndng SR Chrs 86; Outstndng SR 4-H Clb 86; Ntl Edu Cntr-Thompson; Med Secr.

HEISEY, LEON; Manheim Central HS; Manheim, PA; (Y); 15/237; Church Yth Grp; FFA; Hon Roll; NHS; Prfct Atten Awd; 4 Way Test Awd 86; Star Grnhnd FFA 84; Star Chptr Frmr FFA 85; PA ST; Engrng.

HEISEY, STEVEN; Elizabethtown Area HS; Elizabethtown, PA; (Y); 28/221; Pres Church Yth Grp; Pres 4-H; Pres FFA; Teachers Aide; Var Capt Ftbl; NHS; Elizabthtwn Rotary Intl Boy Of Mnth 86; Shippensburg U; Math.

HEISEY, SUSAN; Blue Mountain Acad; Newmanstown, PA; (S); 5/60; Computer Clb; FBLA; Office Aide; Sec Stu Cncl; High Hon Roll; Mc Cann Schl Bus; Exec Secrtry.

HEISHMAN, AMY; Waynesboro Area SR HS; Mont Alto, PA; (Y); 18/392; Church Yth Grp; Library Aide; Church Choir; Yrbk Bus Mgr; Yrbk Stf; Stat Trk; High Hon Roll; Trs NHS; Voice Dem Awd; Pinebrook JC; Sec Sci.

HEISHMAN, TODD; Waynesboro Area SR HS; Mont Alto, PA; (Y); 61/381; Am Leg Boys St; Church Yth Grp; JCL; Latin Clb; Library Aide; Church Choir; JV Var Trk; Cit Awd; High Hon Roll; Hon Roll; Keystone St Games Tennis 86; Tchr.

HEISLER, DAWN MARIE; Girard Academic Music Program; Philadelphia, PA; (Y); 2/51; Office Aide; Science Clb; Chorus; Nwsp Ed-Chief; Trs Soph Cls; VP Sr Cls; Rep Stu Cncl; High Hon Roll; NHS; Sal; Outstndng Achvt Scholar Temple U 86; Bst Cls TV Commercl 86; Philadelphia City Scholar 86; Temple U; Acctng.

HEISLER, SHANA; Plymouth-Whitemarsh HS; Lafayette Hill, PA; (Y); Pep Clb; Rep Soph Cls; Rep Jr Cls; Capt Cheerleading; Coach Actv; Fld Hcky; Powder Puff Ftbl; Score Keeper; Hon Roll; Temple; Law.

HEISLER, SUSAN; Canon Mc Millan HS; Bridgeville, PA; (Y); 96/390; Exploring; French Clb; Hosp Aide; Office Aide; Church Choir; Tennis; High Hon Roll; Hon Roll; Prfct Atten Awd; 2nd Pl CA St Coll Intl Day; Frgn Lang.

HEISS, JOHN; Archbishop John Carroll For Boys; Wayne, PA; (Y); 23/162; Band; Concert Band; JV Bsbl; Im Bsktbl; JV Trk; Hon Roll; NHS; Prfct Atten Awd; Im Vllybl; Ntl Hnr Soc Awd; Archbshp John Carrll Hnr Soc; Pltcl Sci.

HEITNER, REESE; Norristown Area HS; Norristown, PA; (S); 3/521; Dance Clb; Debate Tm; Math Clb; NFL; Ski Clb; Concert Band; School Musical; Rep Stu Cncl; Socr; High Hon Roll; Brandeis U; Histry.

HEITZENRATER, CHRIS; Du Bois Area HS; Du Bois, PA; (Y); 24/287; Church Yth Grp; Varsity Clb; Band; Church Choir; Mrchg Band; Sec Stu Cncl; Cheerleading; High Hon Roll; Hon Roll; Spanish NHS.

HEITZENRATER, JULIE; Elkland Area HS; Elkland, PA; (Y); 5/87; Band; Jazz Band; Yrbk Stf; Pres Soph Cls; Sec Jr Cls; JV Var Cheerleading; JV Vllybl; High Hon Roll; Hon Roll; NHS; Williamsport; Beautcn.

HEITZENRATER, MIKE; Punxsutawney Area HS; Punxsutawney, PA; (Y); Varsity Clb; Golf; Trk; Hon Roll; Gifted Pgm 83-87; Geol.

HEITZENRATER, TODD D; Punxsutawney Area HS; Punxsutawney, PA; (Y); Church Yth Grp; 4-H; French Clb; Letterman Clb; Band; Variety Show; Ftbl; Trk; Wt Lftg; 4-H Awd; Gftd Prog; Bio.

HEIZMANN, NOELLE BETH; Central Bucks HS East; Doylestown, PA; (Y); Am Leg Aux Girls St; Debate Tm; Pres Band; Concert Band; Mrchg Band; Orch; Nwsp Stf; Ed Yrbk Stf; Hon Roll; NHS; Bio.

HELENSKI, EDWARD; Upper Merion HS; Swedeland, PA; (Y); 89/320; Var Capt Bsktbl; Var Ftbl; Im Vllybl; Im Wt Lftg; Hon Roll; All Leag Ftbl 85; Finc.

HELFAND, LYNNE M; Plymouth-Whitemarsh HS; Plymouth Meeting, PA; (Y); 50/360; Temple Yth Grp; Nwsp Sprt Ed; Rep Soph Cls; Rep Jr Cls; Rep Sr Cls; Rep Stu Cncl; JV Ntl Merit SF; People-People Stu Ambssdr 85; Psychlgy.

HELFER, LORI; Highlands SR HS; Natrona Hts, PA; (Y); Intnl Clb; Yrbk Stf; Cheerleading; Gym; Jr NHS; Bus.

HELFER, WENDY; Bishop Kenrick HS; Norristown, PA; (Y); 30/320; Cmnty Wkr; High Hon Roll; Hon Roll; NHS; Psych.

HELFRICH, ERIC; Crestwood HS; Mountaintop, PA; (Y); Boy Scts; Math Tm; Band; Chorus; Concert Band; Mrchg Band; Orch; School Musical; High Hon Roll; Hon Roll.

HELFRICH, GARY A; Louis E Dieruff HS; Allentown, PA; (Y); 13/321; Computer Clb; Exploring; JA; Math Tm; Science Clb; Tennis; High Hon Roll; Jr NHS; NHS; Tri-Cnty Arts Bst Show 86; Lincoln Tech Insti Comp Tech Cert 86; PA SR U; Comp Engrng.

HELFRICH, JENIFER; William Penn SR HS; York, PA; (Y); Dance Clb; PAVAS; Teachers Aide; Color Guard; Mrchg Band; School Musical; School Play; Rep Frsh Cls; Rep Soph Cls; Rep Jr Cls; York Cnty Hm Ecnc Stu Of Yr 86; Bys Clb Athltc Assoc Yth Yr 86; YCAACP Ftr Tchr Schlrshp 86; Towson ST U; Elem Educ.

HELFRICH, TODD; Manheim Township HS; Lancaster, PA; (Y); 11/314; German Clb; School Musical; School Play; Yrbk Phtg; JV Socr; Vllybl; Opt Clb Awd; Rotary Awd; Pres Sprts Awd 85-86; Hoop Social Sci Awd 86; Cornell U; Poli Sci.

HELINSKI, MATT; Pocono Mountain HS; Blakeslee, PA; (Y); 70/328; Chorus; Yrbk Stf; Off Jr Cls; Off Sr Cls; Ftbl; Trk; Wt Lftg; Hon Roll; Bus Admin.

HELKOWSKI, DOUGLAS; Greensburg Central Catholic HS; Ruffsdale, PA; (Y); 80/221; Varsity Clb; Chorus; Rep Stu Cncl; Var L Bsbl; Var L Ftbl; High Hon Roll; Variety Show; Rep Jr Cls; Var Wt Lftg; Hon Roll; All Conf Ftbl 85 & 86.

HELLEN, HOPE; Mapletown HS; Greensboro, PA; (Y); Pres VP Church Yth Grp; FTA; GAA; Sec Pres Band; Sec Pres Concert Band; Sec Pres Mrchg Band; Stat Bsktbl; Im Vllybl; High Hon Roll; Hon Roll; Mst Outstdng In Bnd 86; Hnr Stu 86; CA U; Elem Tchr.

HELLER, GLENN J; Geibel HS; Scottdale, PA; (Y); Pres Church Yth Grp; Drama Clb; Chorus; School Musical; School Play; Stage Crew; Yrbk Stf; Lit Mag; Var Ftbl; Wt Lftg; St Vincent Latrobe PA; Acctg.

HELLER, JUDY; Slippery Rock Area HS; Portersville, PA; (Y); Pep Clb; Band; Mrchg Band; Paul Smith Coll; Chef Trainng.

HELLER, RACHEL; George Washington HS; Philadelphia, PA; (Y); 127/800; Dance Clb; School Play; Hon Roll; NHS; Biolgcl Sci.

HELLER, SHARI; Indiana SR HS; Indiana, PA; (Y); 38/320; German Clb; Office Aide; Acpl Chr; School Musical; Trs Stu Cncl; Cheerleading; Hon Roll; Jr NHS; NHS; Pres Y-Teens; Grl Mnth JR Wmns Civic Clb 86; PA ST Remey Scholar 86; Pres Acad Fit Awd 86; PA ST U; Engrng.

HELLER, SUSAN; Jim Thorpe HS; Albrightsville, PA; (S); 3/97; VP FHA; Chorus; Drill Tm; Nwsp Stf; Ed Yrbk Stf; High Hon Roll; NHS; Natl Sci Merit Awd; Flagler Coll; Educ Deaf.

HELLER, VICKY; Frefland HS; Freeland, PA; (Y); 19/91; Church Yth Grp; FBLA; Var L Bsktbl; Var L Sftbl; High Hon Roll; Hon Roll; Mth Ed.

HELLMANN, TODD R; La Salle College HS; Buckingham, PA; (Y); Nwsp Rptr; Yrbk Stf; Stu Cncl; Bsktbl; Var Capt Socr; JV Tennis; Hon Roll; NHS; Ntl Merit SF; Rotary Awd; Econmcs.

HELM, JODI L; Nazareth Area HS; Tatamy, PA; (Y); 22/220; Teachers Aide; Var L Bsktbl; Var L Sftbl; Var L Tennis; Var L Vllybl; High Hon Roll; Hon Roll; Prfct Atten Awd; Pqut Idl Female Athlt 86; SR Awd Sftbl & Vllybl 86; Physcl Educ Awd 83 & 86; Clnl Leag 1st Team; West Chester U; Physcl Educ.

HELMAN, DAVID; Mt Calvary Christian Schl; Palmyra, PA; (S); School Play; Stage Crew; Yrbk Phtg; Rep Frsh Cls; Rep Stu Cncl; Var L Bsbl; Var L Bsktbl; Var L Socr; Cit Awd; Hon Roll; Engrng.

HELMICK, ERIC; Mapletown HS; Greensboro, PA; (Y); Pres Ski Clb; Varsity Clb; Var L Ftbl; Wt Lftg; Wrstlng; Hon Roll; Tri Cnty Ftbl Conf All Star 85; All Dist Ftbl 85; Lifeguard 85-86.

HELMICK, TRACEY; Cedar Crest HS; Lebanon, PA; (Y); Church Yth Grp; Drama Clb; French Clb; Key Clb; Pep Clb; School Musical; Yrbk Ed-Chief; VP Stu Cncl; Sftbl; Hon Roll; Penn ST; Comm.

HELMS, KIMBERLY; Connellsville SR HS; Normalville, PA; (Y); 15/500; Chorus; Church Choir; School Musical; Symp Band; Pres Stu Cncl; Var Capt Swmmng; Var Trk; French Hon Soc; High Hon Roll; NHS; Army Resrv Schlr/Athlt 86; Mst Vlbl Swmr Awd 86; ST Swmng Qualfr PLAA 83-85; Slippery Rock U.

HELSEL, CAROL; Kiski Area HS; Vandergrift, PA; (Y); Church Yth Grp; FBLA; Teachers Aide; Band; Mrchg Band; Prfct Atten Awd; Sec.

HELSEL, MARK; Ambridge Area HS; Baden, PA; (S); Church Yth Grp; German Clb; Nwsp Rptr; JV Var Socr; Comm.

HELSLEY, LORINE; Bellwood-Antis HS; Tyrone, PA; (Y); 30/118; Key Clb; SADD; Chorus; Mrchg Band; School Musical; Variety Show; Nwsp Stf; Yrbk Stf; Twrlr; Hon Roll; Hd Mjrette Sadd Treas Nwspapr Rture Ed; Invstgtr.

HELTERBRAN, TRACEY; Ambridge Area HS; Baden, PA; (Y); Pep Clb; Spanish Clb; Band; Concert Band; Mrchg Band; Pep Band; Symp Band; Soph Cls; Jr Cls; Hon Roll; Bradford Bus Schl; Ex Sec Adm.

HELWIG, CHRISTINE; South Western HS; Hanover, PA; (Y); 24/205; Church Yth Grp; Girl Scts; Band; Concert Band; Mrchg Band; School Musical; Symp Band; JV Var Swmmng; Hon Roll; NHS; IN U PA; Spn.

HEMBURY, LYNN; Sullivan County HS; Dushore, PA; (Y); 9/90; Concert Band; Sec Frsh Cls; Pres Soph Cls; VP Jr Cls; Rep Stu Cncl; Var L Cheerleading; 4-H Awd; High Hon Roll; Church Yth Grp; Sullivan Cnty Dairy Prncss 86-87; Penn ST; Bus Adm.

HEMING, KELLI; United HS; Robinson, PA; (Y); Var Sftbl; Var Vllybl; High Hon Roll; Bio.

HEMMING, HEIDI; Elizabethtown Area HS; Elizabethtown, PA; (Y); 8/250; Art Clb; Computer Clb; Spanish Clb; Chorus; JV Bsktbl; JV Capt Fld Hcky; Im Powder Puff Ftbl; JV Var Sftbl; Im Wt Lftg; NHS; Mst Imprvd Plyr In Fld Hcky 86; PA ST; Bus Mgmt.

HEMPERLY, LAURA; Middletown Area HS; Middletown, PA; (Y); 3/200; French Clb; Trs FBLA; Library Aide; Band; Color Guard; Mrchg Band; Nwsp Bus Mgr; Yrbk Stf; High Hon Roll; Hon Roll; Middletown Area Rtl Com Awd 86; Cental Pa Bus Schl; Ofc Comm.

HENDERSON, AMY; Corry Area HS; Corry, PA; (S); Church Yth Grp; German Clb; Girl Scts; Nwsp Stf; Yrbk Stf; Hon Roll; Cngrss-Bndstg Schlrshp 85-86.

HENDERSON, BOB; Warwick HS; Lititz, PA; (Y); 85/230; Computer Clb; Dance Clb; Im Bsktbl; Im Vllybl; Hon Roll; INSRNCE.

HENDERSON, CARRIE; Hershey HS; Hershey, PA; (Y); Church Yth Grp; Exploring; Model UN; Ski Clb; Spanish Clb; Varsity Clb; Band; Chorus; Church Choir; Color Guard; Scl Wk.

HENDERSON, CATHY P; Hempfield Area SR HS; Greensburg, PA; (Y); 45/657; French Clb; Library Aide; Trs NFL; Ski Clb; Thesps; School Musical; School Play; Yrbk Rptr; French Hon Soc; NHS; PA ST U; Engl.

HENDERSON, CHERYL; Cheltenham HS; Elkins Pk, PA; (Y); Fld Hcky; Lcrss; Swmmng; Pres Ftns Awd 86; Temple U; Art.

HENDERSON, DAWN; Ridley SR HS; Woodlyn, PA; (Y); 76/427; Church Yth Grp; Bsktbl; Var Fld Hcky; Lcrss; Hon Roll; Awd Of Exclnc In Frgn Lang,Math,Hlth & Physcl Ed; Estrn Clg; Occptnl Thrpy.

HENDERSON, DEBRA; Abington HS; Abington, PA; (Y); 82/535; Church Yth Grp; Library Aide; Church Choir; Stage Crew; Bsktbl; Fld Hcky; Powder Puff Ftbl; Trk; Hon Roll; Italian Club-Co Secr 86; Black Stu Union Gospel Choir 85; Nghbrhd Yth Corp Rec Aid Awd 84; U Of Steubenville; Early Child.

HENDERSON, ERIN; Meadville Area SR HS; Meadville, PA; (Y); 124/344; Church Yth Grp; Socr; Wrstlng.

HENDERSON, KRISTI; Trinity HS; Washington, PA; (Y); 18/374; VP Church Yth Grp; Key Clb; Pep Clb; High Hon Roll; Acctng.

HENDERSON, MARLOE; South Phila HS; Philadelphia, PA; (Y); Dance Clb; Drama Clb; 4-H; Model UN; PAVAS; Varsity Clb; Acpl Chr; School Musical; School Play; Stage Crew; Music Awd-Bst Perfmr 84; Drama Outstndg Perfmr 84; TV Brdcstg.

HENDERSON, SCOTT; Indiana Wesleyan Schl; Aultman, PA; (Y); Aud/Vis; Church Yth Grp; Drama Clb; French Clb; Library Aide; Chorus; School Play; High Hon Roll; Hon Roll; Med.

HENDERSON, STACEY; William Penn SR HS; York, PA; (Y); Girl Scts; Drill Tm; Nwsp Stf; Rep Jr Cls; Im Badmtn; Cheerleading; Im Gym; Im Vllybl; Im Wt Lftg; Hon Roll; Yorktowne Business Inst; Acctg.

HENDERSON, STEVEN; Mercy Vicational HS; Philadelphia, PA; (Y); Im Bowling; Elec Engr.

HENDERSON, TAMMY; Grand Army Of The Republic HS; Wilkes Barre, PA; (S); Hosp Aide; Key Clb; Library Aide; Chorus; Orch; Nwsp Stf; Var Bsktbl; Mgr(s); Vllybl; Hon Roll; Kutztown U; RN.

HENDRICKS, LUCILLE F; Martin Luther King HS; Philadelphia, PA; (Y); Church Yth Grp; Cmnty Wkr; English Clb; FTA; Church Choir; Bsktbl; Tennis; Cit Awd; VP Frsh Cls; Rep Soph Cls; Awd For Prtcptng In An 5th Annl Essy Cntst 86; Awd For Prtcptng In The 4th Annl Essy Cntst 85; Bus Mgmt.

HENDRICKS, TRACY; Shikellamy SR HS; Sunbury, PA; (Y); French Clb; Church Choir; Rep Stu Cncl; Var JV Cheerleading; Var Trk.

HENDRIKSMA, HYLDA J E; Cedar Cliff HS; Lemoyne, PA; (Y); 7/272; Pres German Clb; Model UN; High Hon Roll; NHS; Ntl Merit Ltr; Im Bowling; French Hon Soc; Orch; Chorus; Latin Clb; Pres Clsrm Yng Amer Wshngtn DC 85; ACES Grnd Essy Cntst Wnr 86; Stu Of Mnth 86; Frgn Langs.

HENDRY, KELLY; Little Flower HS; Philadelphia, PA; (Y); 54/395; Church Yth Grp; Lit Mag; Hon Roll; School Musical; Creative Writing.

HENERY, K; Towanda Area HS; Towanda, PA; (Y); Cmnty Wkr; Drama Clb; 4-H; French Clb; German Clb; Hosp Aide; Model UN; Spanish Clb; Band; Chorus; PA Governors Sch For The Arts 85; Natl French Cntst Plcmnt 85-86; Model Un Awd 86.

HENES, BRIAN; Father Judge HS; Philadelphia, PA; (S); 10/361; Art Clb; Church Yth Grp; Cmnty Wkr; Debate Tm; Hosp Aide; NFL; JV Bowling; High Hon Roll; NHS; Prfct Atten Awd; Cmmnty Svc Awd 86; Art Instrctn Awd 85; Villanova; Pre-Law.

HENES, TIMOTHY; Father Judge HS; Philadelphia, PA; (S); 70/425; Pres Church Yth Grp; Cmnty Wkr; Pep Clb; Thesps; Yrbk Stf; Var Bsbl; JV Socr; Cit Awd; Hon Roll; NHS; Cert Awd-Faithfl Cmtmnt 85; Awd Merit Outstndng Achvt 85; Cert Yth Mnstry 86; Allentown Coll; Bus Adm.

HENGST, KELLY; Chestnut Ridge SR HS; New Paris, PA; (S); 28/142; Church Yth Grp; Band; Sec Jr Cls; Stu Cncl; Var L Bsktbl; Var L Bsktbl; Var L Sftbl; Var L Vllybl; Hon Roll; NHS; Nrsng.

HENGST, TINA; Greenwood HS; Millerstown, PA; (Y); Sec Chorus; Rep Soph Cls; Rep Jr Cls; Sec Stu Cncl; Capt Cheerleading; Twrlr; Hon Roll; Art.

HENGSTENBERG, NANCY L; Penn-Trafford HS; Level Green, PA; (Y); 76/328; Cmnty Wkr; FBLA; German Clb; Office Aide; Teachers Aide; Hon Roll; 3rd Pl Awd Steno 1 FBLA 85; Cert Of Apprctn Toys For Toys-Marines FBLA 84; Cert Prfcncy Accntng 84; Penn St Un; Bus Adm.

HENICLE, CHRISTINE; Greencastle-Antrim HS; Greencastle, PA; (Y); Exploring; Band; Color Guard; Concert Band; Flag Corp; Mrchg Band; Nwsp Stf; Yrbk Stf; Hon Roll; Shippensburg U; Acctg.

HENKEL, DAVE; Mt Pleasant Area HS; Mt Pleasant, PA; (Y); 92/246; Chess Clb; Band; Concert Band; Mrchg Band; Pep Band; Im Bsktbl; Im Vllybl; Hon Roll; Prfct Atten Awd; PA ST U; Psychlgy.

HENN, BERNARD; Keystone Oaks HS; Pittsburgh, PA; (Y); 5/263; Boy Scts; Church Yth Grp; German Clb; Pep Clb; Ski Clb; Yrbk Stf; Var Swmmng; Trk; High Hon Roll; NHS; Drmnt New Cntry Clb Schlrshp 86; Case Western Rsrv U; Chmcl Engr.

HENNE, DAVID; Garden Spot HS; New Holland, PA; (Y); Var Bsktbl; Var Ftbl; Var Trk; Penn ST; Mechncl Engr.

HENNEBERRY, AMY; Merion Mercy Acad; Phila, PA; (Y); 44/82; Art Clb; Cmnty Wkr; French Clb; Hosp Aide; Office Aide; Service Clb; Teachers Aide; Chorus; Hon Roll; Prfct Atten Awd; Intl Rel.

HENNELLY III, MICHAEL J; Father Judge HS; Philadelphia, PA; (Y); 5/373; Church Yth Grp; Hon Roll; 1st Hnrs.

HENNEMAN, KARL; Laurel JR SR HS; New Castle, PA; (Y); 23/103; Aud/Vis; Church Yth Grp; Varsity Clb; Stage Crew; Yrbk Phtg; Var L Bsbl; Var L Bsktbl; Im Golf; Im Sftbl; Hon Roll; Gannon U; Financ.

HENNEMAN, MICHELLE; Manheim Township HS; Lancaster, PA; (Y); 8/317; Exploring; Jazz Band; Mrchg Band; Ed Lit Mag; High Hon Roll; NHS; Cmnty Wkr; Key Clb; Band; Chorus; Stu Of Mnth 85; Stu Ambsdr Ple To Ple 85; Amer Music Abrd 84; Cornell; Vet.

HENNESSEY, JAMES; St Pius X HS; Pottstown, PA; (S); 5/161; School Musical; Rep Jr Cls; Var Bsktbl; Var Trk; High Hon Roll; 2nd Pl Dist 1 Aa Trk Chmpnshp/Hgh Jmp 84-85.

HENNESSEY, MARY; Bishop Guilfoyle HS; Hollidaysburg, PA; (S); 1/144; Pres Church Yth Grp; Science Clb; Sec Spanish Clb; Church Choir; Rep Stu Cncl; High Hon Roll; Hon Roll; Penn ST U; Elem Ed.

HENNESSY, TIMOTHY; Monsignor Bonner HS; Drexel Hill, PA; (S); 3/330; Church Yth Grp; Library Aide; Mathletes; Scholastic Bowl; Nwsp Stf; Im Bsktbl; Im Ftbl; High Hon Roll; NHS; Prfct Atten Awd; Achvt Awds-Latn I, Wrld Cultrs 83; Achvt Awd Theolgy 84 & 85; Villanova; Sci.

HENNICK, AMY; St Benedict Acad; Erie, PA; (Y); Cmnty Wkr; FBLA; Office Aide; Science Clb; Lit Mag; JV Score Keeper; Var Vllybl; Kerptone Awd 85; Penn JR Acad Sci 84; Ath Awd 85; Clarion U; Bus.

HENNING, LISA; General Mc Lane HS; Edinboro, PA; (Y); Drama Clb; Model UN; Radio Clb; Teachers Aide; Concert Band; Jazz Band; Mrchg Band; Symp Band; Yrbk Stf; Edinboro U; Spec Educ.

HENNINGER, KIMBERLY; Shikellamy HS; Sunbury, PA; (Y); Girl Scts; Hosp Aide; Spanish Clb; Hon Roll; Jr NHS; NHS; Pres Schlr; Shikeilmy Educ Assoc Awd 86; Spnsh Awd 86; Millersville U; Elem Educ.

HENNINGER, MICHELLE E; William Allen HS; Allentown, PA; (Y); Key Clb; Latin Clb; Ski Clb; Stu Cncl; Coach Actv; Var Fld Hcky; Powder Puff Ftbl; Swmmng; Trk; Hon Roll; Villa Nova; Psych.

HENNINGER, SHERI; Upper Dauphin Area HS; Elizabethville, PA; (Y); 2/112; Church Yth Grp; Chorus; Stage Crew; Yrbk Stf; JV Var Bsktbl; Var Capt Sftbl; Hon Roll; NHS; Rotary Stu Of Mth 85-86; Bus Admin.

HENNINGER, THAD E; Huntingdon Area HS; Petersburg, PA; (Y); 11/223; Am Leg Boys St; Boy Scts; Key Clb; Band; Concert Band; JV Var Ftbl; Var Trk; Im Vllybl; NHS; Life Scout 85; Order Of Arrow-Brotherhood 83; Penn ST U; Engrng.

HENNINGER, TIMOTHY; Upper Dauphin Area HS; Elizabethville, PA; (Y); 16/105; Trs Church Yth Grp; Computer Clb; FCA; Chorus; Stage Crew; Rep Stu Cncl; L Bsbl; L Capt Bsktbl; L Capt Ftbl; Hon Roll; Robt C Baker Schrlshp 86; Fndrs Awd 86; Mary Mrgrt Nstr Fndtn 86; Juniata Coll; Bio-Chem.

HENNON, DAVID; Grove City HS; Grove City, PA; (Y); Church Yth Grp; Ski Clb; L Ftbl; L Trk; Hon Roll; Comp Acctng.

HENRY, BOBBI; Clarion-Limestone HS; Strattanville, PA; (Y); Cmnty Wkr; French Clb; Hosp Aide; Pres VICA; Band; Capt Cheerleading; Vllybl; Cit Awd; Hon Roll; Prfct Atten Awd; Rex Wright Cash Schlrshp 86; Am UICA Deg 86; Indvdul Gold Star Awd 84; Dentl Hyg.

HENRY, BRADLEY; Rockwood Area HS; Markleton, PA; (S); 12/97; Church Yth Grp; Trs Frsh Cls; Pres Sr Cls; Pres Stu Cncl; NHS.

HENRY, CHRIS; Glendale HS; Irvona, PA; (Y); Church Yth Grp; Varsity Clb; Yrbk Phtg; Yrbk Stf; Stu Cncl; Ftbl; Powder Puff Ftbl; Wrstlng; MVP-DFNS HS, Sthrn Allegheny Ftbl Coach Assn 85 & 86; K Lantzy Al-Star Ftbl Tm 86; Mid-ST Ftbl 86; Lock Haven U; Educ.

HENRY, CRYSTAL LYNN; West Snyder HS; Beaver Springs, PA; (Y); Am Leg Aux Girls St; VP Church Yth Grp; Drama Clb; Hosp Aide; Red Cross Aide; Chorus; Church Choir; Color Guard; Flag Corp; Mrchg Band.

HENRY, DEBBIE; Tyrone Area HS; Tyrone, PA; (Y); Church Yth Grp; VP SADD; Band; School Musical; Stu Cncl; Twrlr; Atlantc Cst Confnc Majrtt Chmpns 85-86; Penn ST U; Soc Wrk.

HENRY, DIANE; Clarion-Limestone HS; Clarion, PA; (Y); French Clb; Intnl Clb; Chorus; Sec Sr Cls; Rep Stu Cncl; Hon Roll; Indiana U Of PA; Accntg.

HENRY, DOUG; North Star HS; Jennerstown, PA; (Y); Church Yth Grp; Cmnty Wkr; FCA; Trs Sec Math Clb; Varsity Clb; Concert Band; Yrbk Bus Mgr; Var Bsktbl; Var L Ftbl; Acctg.

HENRY, ED; Du Bois Area HS; Luthersburg, PA; (Y); Church Yth Grp; Varsity Clb; Ftbl; Trk; Wt Lftg; Hon Roll; Dist IX AAA Leag All Str Ftbl 85-86; CENPAC All Strs Ftbl 85-86; Duke Burkholder Awd Wghtlftg 84-86; Penn ST; X-Ray Tech.

HENRY, GARY; Connellsville Area SR HS; Connellsville, PA; (Y); VICA; High Hon Roll; Hon Roll; Tech Schl; Elec Engrng.

HENRY, GRACE; Waynesboro Area SR HS; Waynesboro, PA; (Y); 43/379; Church Yth Grp; Intnl Clb; Ski Clb; Band; Chorus; Church Choir; Concert Band; Jazz Band; Mrchg Band; School Musical; Mdcn.

HENRY, JEAN; Chartiers Valley HS; Pittsburgh, PA; (Y); 30/303; Civic Clb; Cmnty Wkr; Dance Clb; Ski Clb; Drill Tm; School Musical; Frsh Cls; Jr Cls; Sftbl; NHS.

HENRY, JENNIFER; Punxsutawney Area SR HS; Big Run, PA; (Y); 21/243; Debate Tm; Drama Clb; Radio Clb; Spanish Clb; Chorus; High Hon Roll; NHS; French Clb; Church Choir; School Musical; Outstndng Writers Awd 86; Spnsh Hnrs Awd 86; Chatham Coll; Pre Law.

HENRY, KARA; Sacred Heart HS; Pgh, PA; (Y); 30/155; Art Clb; Dance Clb; Pep Clb; Chorus; Capt Color Guard; School Musical; Nwsp Stf; Yrbk Stf; Lit Mag; Im Bsktbl; Stu Of Art 81-82; Creative Wrtng Awd 83 & 84; U Of Pittsburgh; Advrtsng.

HENRY, LISA; Newport HS; Newport, PA; (Y); Cmnty Wkr; FBLA; Sec FTA; Intnl Clb; Office Aide; Teachers Aide; Mrchg Band; Yrbk Stf; Hon Roll; Cntrl PA Bus Schl; Bus.

HENRY, MARK; Geibel HS; Mount Pleasant, PA; (Y); 30/103; Boy Scts; Drama Clb; Pep Clb; Political Wkr; School Musical; NEDT Awd; St Vincent Coll Ldrshp Schlrshp 86; Otstndng Parish Sr Awd 86; Bstkbl Anncr 84-86; St Vincent Coll; Bus Admn.

HENRY, MATTHEW; Spring Grove SR HS; Spring Grove, PA; (Y); 41/227; Camera Clb; Nwsp Phtg; Im Socr; Hon Roll; Ntl Merit Ltr; Drexel U; Chmcl Engr.

HENRY, MELINDA; Harmony HS; Cherry Tree, PA; (Y); 5/50; Pres Church Yth Grp; Ski Clb; Teachers Aide; Band; Chorus; Mrchg Band; Sec Stu Cncl; Capt Cheerleading; L Sftbl; High Hon Roll; Pres Phys Fit Awd 86; Dntstry.

HENRY, MICHAEL; Rockwood Area HS; Rockwood, PA; (Y); Band; Chorus; Concert Band; Mrchg Band; School Play; JV Var Bsktbl; Var Golf; Var Trk; Dnfth Awd; Hon Roll; Engrng.

HENRY, PATRICIA; Shenango HS; New Castle, PA; (S); 10/112; French Clb; Drill Tm; Var Co-Capt Cheerleading; Stat Gym; Hon Roll; Biotech.

HENRY, RACHEL; Mon Valley Catholic HS; Monessen, PA; (Y); 22/87; Trk; High Hon Roll; Hon Roll; Phrmcst.

HENRY, SCOTT; Freedom HS; Easton, PA; (Y); 116/404; Boy Scts; Exploring; Math Clb; Band; Concert Band; Jazz Band; Mrchg Band; Pep Band; Hon Roll; Prfct Atten Awd; Egl Sct 84; Mst Imprvd Bwlr 85-86; PA ST U; Bus Admin.

HENRY, SHARON; Juniata HS; Honey Grove, PA; (Y); 1/158; Church Yth Grp; Varsity Clb; Var Bsktbl; Var Fld Hcky; Var Sftbl; DAR Awd; High Hon Roll; NHS; Band; Concert Band; Slctd Tri Valley Leag All Star Sftbll 86; US Naval Acad; Officer.

HENRY, SHELLY; Solanco HS; Peach Bottom, PA; (Y); Office Aide; Pep Clb; Radio Clb; Trs Spanish Clb; Teachers Aide; Varsity Clb; Cheerleading; High Hon Roll; Hon Roll; Sec.

HENRY, STEPHEN; Charleroi JR SR HS; Charleroi, PA; (Y); 8/165; Church Yth Grp; Science Clb; Ski Clb; Varsity Clb; Stu Cncl; JV Var Ftbl; Var L Trk; Hon Roll; NHS; Arch.

HENRY, SUSAN; Central Dauphin HS; Harrisburg, PA; (Y); 10/384; Chorus; Concert Band; Jazz Band; Mrchg Band; Nwsp Rptr; Rep Stu Cncl; Var Bsktbl; Hon Roll; NHS; Ntl Merit Ltr.

HENRY, THERESA; Bethel Park SR HS; Bethel Park, PA; (Y); Powder Puff Ftbl; High Hon Roll; Hon Roll; Prfct Atten Awd.

HENRY, TIMOTHY SEAN; Kiski Area HS; Vandergrift, PA; (Y); Chorus; High Hon Roll; Hon Roll; IN St U Of PA; Pre-Optmtry.

HENSBERGER, MARYBETH; Central Catholic HS; Yukon, PA; (Y); 76/244; Hosp Aide; JCL; Pep Clb; Ski Clb; JV Powder Puff Ftbl; Duquesne U; Pharm.

HENSEL, TAMMY; Connellsville Area SR HS; Mill Run, PA; (Y); 62/500; Art Clb; Dance Clb; Model UN; Band; Concert Band; Nwsp Stf; Hon Roll; Prfct Atten Awd; Dirctrs List N Fayette Vo-Tech Schl 86; HOSA 85-86; RN.

HENSLER, PATRICK; Keystone Oaks HS; Pittsburgh, PA; (Y); 1/257; Church Yth Grp; German Clb; Math Clb; Math Tm; Pep Clb; Mrchg Band; Capt Swmmng; Trk; High Hon Roll; VP NHS; Westnghse Sci Hnrs Inst 85-86; Carnegie-Mellon U; Biochem.

HENSON, ELIZABETH; State College Area SR HS; State College, PA; (Y); 50/502; Nwsp Rptr; Yrbk Rptr; Rep Stu Cncl; JV Var Bsktbl; Im Socr; JV L Trk; High Hon Roll; Ntl Merit SF; Prfct Atten Awd; Ntl Merit Schlrshp-Outstndg Negro Stu Fnlst 86; Acad Excllnc Engl Awd 86; PA ST U Blck Schlrshp Awd; PA ST U; Psych.

HENSON, LAURIE; St Francis Acad; Eighty Four, PA; (S); 5/34; Drama Clb; Hosp Aide; JA; Chorus; Nwsp Stf; Rep Soph Cls; Rep Jr Cls; VP Sr Cls; High Hon Roll; NHS; Volntr Apprentcshp-Vertebrate Paleontalogy 86-87; Acadmc All Amer Awd; Speech & Drama Awd; Bio.

HENSON, NICOLE; Lower Dauphin HS; Harrisburg, PA; (Y); 80/217; Ski Clb; Yrbk Stf; Stat Bsktbl; Var Capt Cheerleading; Im Gym; Hon Roll; Amer Inst-Frgn Study-Spain 84; Millersville U; Acctnt.

HENTZ, SCOTT M; Cedar Crest HS; Myerstown, PA; (Y); Aud/Vis; Drama Clb; Library Aide; Pep Clb; Chorus; Church Choir; School Musical; School Play; Stage Crew; Ftbl; Accntng.

HENZES, MAURE; Valley View JR SR HS; Blakely, PA; (Y); 39/189; Church Yth Grp; French Clb; Latin Clb; Varsity Clb; Rep Stu Cncl; Cheerleading; High Hon Roll; Hon Roll; Acadmc All Amer 85; Kings Coll; Marktng.

HEO, SU-NAM; Liberty HS; Bethlehem, PA; (Y); DECA; Pres Trs French Clb; Model UN; Chorus; Socr; Church Yth Grp; Pres Frsh Cls; Pres Soph Cls; Rep Jr Cls; Rep Sr Cls; 1st Pl Wnnr DECA PA ST 86; Hofstra U; Intl Bus.

HEPBURN, ALAN; Montoursville HS; Mentoursville, PA; (Y); 14/179; Boy Scts; Church Yth Grp; French Clb; Key Clb; High Hon Roll; Hon Roll; Wilkes; Bus.

HEPLER, KATHY; Blue Ridge HS; New Milford, PA; (Y); Pres Pep Clb; Band; Chorus; VP Jr Cls; Var L Cheerleading; Var L Crs Cntry; Var L Trk; Var L Vllybl; High Hon Roll; NHS; Mst Val Crs Cntry 84-86.

HEPLER, SCOTT; Salisbury Elk Lick HS; Springs, PA; (S); 1/37; Church Yth Grp; Concert Band; School Play; Nwsp Ed-Chief; Var L Socr; Ntl Merit SF; Band; Nwsp Stf; Yrbk Stf; Val; Natl HS Math Awd 82-83; Elec Engrng.

HEPNER, MARK; Shikellamy HS; Sunbury, PA; (Y); Band; Concert Band; Jazz Band; Mrchg Band; Orch; Pep Band; School Musical; Stu Cncl; Hon Roll; Jr NHS; JR Acad Sci 2nd Pl Regnl 85; Albright; Biol.

HEPP, BARBARA; Wyalusing Valley JR/SR HS; Wyalusing, PA; (Y); German Clb; Band; Chorus; Concert Band; Mrchg Band; Orch; Pep Band; School Musical; DAR Awd; Hon Roll; Music Educ.

HERB, DAWN; Williams Valley HS; Williamstown, PA; (S); Quiz Bowl; Chorus; Flag Corp; School Musical; Pres Soph Cls; VP Stu Cncl; Var L Bsktbl; Powder Puff Ftbl; Var L Sftbl; JV Vllybl; Pol Sci.

HERBE, SHARI; Shaler Area HS; Pittsburgh, PA; (Y); 84/538; Church Yth Grp; Hosp Aide; Library Aide; Office Aide; Service Clb; Yrbk Stf; CA U Of PA; Elem Ed.

HERBEIN, TARA; Souderton Area HS; Telford, PA; (Y); 14/375; AFS; Drama Clb; Stu Cncl; Var Cheerleading; Var Tennis; Var Trk; Jr NHS; NHS; German Clb; School Play; Frgn Exchng Stu Australia 85-86; Hsptl Adm.

HERBER, BRIAN; Hamburg Area HS; Shoemakersville, PA; (Y); VP Church Yth Grp; 4-H; Rep Jr Cls; Rep Stu Cncl; JV Bsbl; Im Socr; Hon Roll; NHS; Rotary Awd; Intl Suprm Councl Demolayin Awds 85; Acadmc Ltr Awd Wrld Cultrs 85; Acadmc Ltr Awd Plane Geomtry 86; PA ST U; Chem Engrng.

HERBERT, JOHN; Boyertown Area SR HS; Boyertown, PA; (Y); 5/450; Band; Concert Band; Mrchg Band; Orch; School Musical; Nwsp Stf; Cit Awd; High Hon Roll; NHS; Rotary Awd; Navy ROTC Schlrshp; U Of PA; Sci.

HERBERT, KEN; Meadville Area SR HS; Provo, UT; (Y); 50/400; Boy Scts; Church Yth Grp; Computer Clb; Exploring; Spanish Clb; Im Badmtn; JV L Ftbl; Var L Trk; Hon Roll; Brigham Young U; Bus.

HERBERT, ROBERTA; Shenango HS; New Castle, PA; (Y); Church Yth Grp; GAA; Varsity Clb; Trs Frsh Cls; Trs Soph Cls; Trs Jr Cls; Trs Sr Cls; Rep Stu Cncl; Var Gym; Sftbl; Gymnstcs Ltr 84-86.

HERBERT, SHERYL; Little Flower Cath HS For Girls; Philadelphia, PA; (Y); Chrmn Church Yth Grp; Cmnty Wkr; Office Aide; Science Clb; Yrbk Stf; Hon Roll; Black Stu Lgu Awd 86; Garland Yrkbk Awd 86; Sci Lab Aid Awd 85; Spelman U; Crmnlgy.

HERBERT, THOMAS; Lakeland JR SR HS; Olyphant, PA; (Y); 18/134; SADD; Band; Concert Band; L Mrchg Band; Variety Show; L Bsktbl; Capt L Crs Cntry; L Trk; Ntl Sci Mrt Awd 83; Penn ST; Meteorology.

HERBST, ANGELA; Dover Area HS; Dover, PA; (Y); Church Yth Grp; Spanish Clb; Trk; Hon Roll; Comp Tech.

HERBSTER, MATT; Kiski Area HS; Apollo, PA; (Y); Math Tm; Pep Clb; SADD; Rep Frsh Cls; Pres Rep Soph Cls; Pres Capt Jr Cls; Stu Cncl; JV Bsbl; Penn ST; Cmmnctns.

HERBSTRITT, MATTHEW; Elk County Christian HS; St Marys, PA; (S); 10/85; Boy Scts; Red Cross Aide; SADD; Varsity Clb; Band; Concert Band; Jazz Band; Mrchg Band; Pep Band; High Hon Roll; Valdctrn JR Tstmstrs, Slvr, Brnz Mdl Sci Fair 84; Slvr, Brnz Palms; Penn ST; Engrng.

HERCZEG, MELISA; Emmaus HS; Macungie, PA; (Y); Nwsp Rptr; JV Var Cheerleading; High Hon Roll; Hon Roll; NHS; Elem Ed.

HERFORTH, ROBERT C; Bishop Kenrick HS; Norristown, PA; (Y); 1/279; Mathletes; Science Clb; Spanish Clb; Capt Bowling; Bausch & Lomb Sci Awd; Hon Roll; NHS; Compu Awd Gold Medal 86; Math Awd 85; Bowling All Catholic 84-86; Ursinus Coll; Math.

HERILLA, SUSAN; Charleroi Area JR SR HS; Charleroi, PA; (Y); Sec Church Yth Grp; Sec SADD; Varsity Clb; Chorus; Yrbk Ed-Chief; Trs Jr Cls; Sec Stu Cncl; Capt Var Cheerleading; NHS; Hugh O Brian Yth Fndtn Ambsdr; Stu Rep Brd Of Ed.

HERLEMAN, MICHAEL B; Carlynton SR HS; Carnegie, PA; (Y); Var L Ftbl; Var Trk; High Hon Roll; Acad All Amer 86; Engrng.

HERMAN, AMY; Dover Area HS; Dover, PA; (Y); 6/250; Church Yth Grp; Dance Clb; Y-Teens; Band; Chorus; Church Choir; Concert Band; Mrchg Band; Pep Band; School Musical; Hugh O Brian Yth Ldrshp Sem 85; Indstrl Arts Awd 84; Chem.

HERMAN, BRAD; Northeastern HS; Manchester, PA; (Y); Boy Scts; Church Yth Grp; Varsity Clb; Band; Chorus; Concert Band; Var L Crs Cntry; Var L Trk; God Cntry Awd; High Hon Roll; Eagle Sct Awd 86; Arch.

HERMAN, COREY; Shikellamy HS; Northumberland, PA; (Y); 21/304; German Clb; School Musical; School Play; Variety Show; Variety Show; Hon Roll; Cmmnctns.

HERMAN, DANIELLE; Northeastern HS; York Haven, PA; (Y); Pres Chorus; VP Frsh Cls; Off Soph Cls; VP Jr Cls; VP Sr Cls; Rep Stu Cncl; Capt Var Cheerleading; Hon Roll; Stu Of Mnth 84-85; Hugh O Brian Ldrshp Awd 84-85; Stu Of Mnth 85-86; Otstndg Vrsty Sccr Chrldr 85-86; Spnsh Itrprtr.

HERMAN, DAWN; Northampton Area SR HS; Northhampton, PA; (Y); 13/446; Aud/Vis; Leo Clb; SADD; JV Cheerleading; High Hon Roll; Hon Roll; NHS; Med.

HERMAN, HEATHER; Shilkellamy HS; Sunbury, PA; (Y); 70/300; German Clb; Hosp Aide; Teachers Aide; Hst Soph Cls; Stat Crs Cntry; Stat Trk; Hon Roll; Sci.

HERMAN, LEONARD; Pennsbury HS; Yardley, PA; (Y); Church Yth Grp; Hosp Aide; Var Bowling; JV Ftbl; Var Socr; Im Vllybl; Hon Roll; Chrch Yth Pres & Chrch Cncl Yth Rep 84; Swmmng & Life Svng Instrctr 86; Bus Mgmt.

HERMAN, LISA; Plum SR HS; Pittsburgh, PA; (Y); AFS; French Clb; SADD; Varsity Clb; Mrchg Band; Symp Band; Var L Bsktbl; Var L Socr; Var L Trk; NHS; Morning Announcmnt Readr 86; Boston U; Cmmnctns.

HERMAN, PAMELA L; North Hills HS; Glenshaw, PA; (Y); Civic Clb; Temple Yth Grp; Hon Roll; Sec And VP Greatr Pgh Regn Bnai Brith Yth Org 85-86; PA ST U; Bus Adm.

HERMAN, TERESA; Canton Area HS; Roaring Branch, PA; (Y); 17/124; Pres 4-H; Concert Band; Mrchg Band; Rep Stu Cncl; VP Cheerleading; VP Trk; VP Vllybl; Cit Awd; High Hon Roll; Voice Dem Awd; 4-H Keystone Wnnr 85; Soclgy.

HERMANN, JOHN; Holy Ghosp Prep; Yardley, PA; (S); Cmnty Wkr; Library Aide; Math Clb; Pres Science Clb; High Hon Roll; NHS; Cooking Clb 85-86; 1st Prize Sci Fair Wnnr 85-86; 1st Pl Sci Fair Wnnr 84-85; Bio.

HERMANN, MARGARET; Lampeter-Strasburg HS; Lancaster, PA; (Y); 3/165; Sec VP AFS; Trs Concert Band; Trs Mrchg Band; Nwsp Rptr; Lit Mag; Var Trk; High Hon Roll; NHS; Ntl Merit Ltr; Brrws Schlr Awd Frgn Lang 86; Engrng.

HERMIDA, MIGUEL-ANTONIO; Girard College HS; Santa Cruz, CA; (Y); 7/35; Boy Scts; Trs Sr Cls; JV Var Bsbl; JV Var Wrstlng; High Hon Roll; Hon Roll; Mckenzie Math Awd 84; Joseph Campbell Bus Awd 86; Schltc Athltc Awd 84; U C Berkeley; Intl Bus.

HERNANDEZ, SARA N; Little Flower HS; Philadelphia, PA; (Y); 91/395; JA; Spanish Clb; Orch; School Musical; School Play; Variety Show; Hon Roll; Prfct Atten Awd; Attdnc Awd 84-86; Sec Hnrs 84-86; Orch Awd 84-86; Hahnemann U; RN.

HEROLD, SHERRY ANN; Butler Area SR HS; Butler, PA; (Y); Church Yth Grp; Pres Trs 4-H; Library Aide; SADD; 4-H Awd; High Hon Roll; Jr NHS; NHS; Outstndng ST Cmp Cdt PA ST Police 84; Chem.

HERR, DONALD; Lampeter-Strasburg HS; Lancaster, PA; (Y); 1/131; Boy Scts; Band; Concert Band; Jazz Band; Mrchg Band; Bsbl; Bsktbl; Capt Ftbl; High Hon Roll; Lion Awd; Burrows Schlr; PA ST; Chem Engrng.

HERR, SANDY; Northern Lebanon HS; Jonestown, PA; (Y); 3/176; Varsity Clb; Var L Bsktbl; Var L Fld Hcky; Var L Sftbl; High Hon Roll; NHS; Am Athlete 84-85; Physcl Thrpy.

HERR, TONI; Warwick HS; Lititz, PA; (Y); 52/235; Model UN; Yrbk Phtg; VP Frsh Cls; VP Soph Cls; VP Jr Cls; JV Var Cheerleading; JV Fld Hcky; JV Tennis; Hon Roll; Hmcmng, Hallown Qun 86; Schlstc Art Awds-Gld Keys 84-85; Wmns Clb Art Awd 86; VA Cmmnwlth U; Fshn Dsgn.

HERR NECKAR, PHILLIP; G A R HS; Wilkes Barre, PA; (S); Vllybl; Wrstlng; Hon Roll; Comp Sci.

HERRENKOHL, TODD; Freedom HS; Bethlehem, PA; (Y); 103/425; Socr; Co-Capt Wrstlng; Hon Roll; Bus Admin.

HERRERA, ANDRES J; Northeast Catholic HS; Philadelphia, PA; (Y); 27/369; Nwsp Phtg; Nwsp Rptr; Hon Roll; NHS; Ntl Merit Ltr; Excllnce In Spanish 86; Rwng Team In Sprng & Fall 83-87.

HERRING, CHARLES; Wilkinsburg HS; Wilkinsburg, PA; (Y); Boys Clb Am; Spanish Clb; Nwsp Sprt Ed; Pres Sr Cls; Var L Bsktbl; Var L Ftbl; Hon Roll; Rotary Awd; Edinboro U; Comm.

HERRING, DANIEL; Mahonoy Area HS; Barnesville, PA; (Y); Band; Concert Band; Mrchg Band; Stage Crew; Stu Cncl; Im Bsktbl; Var JV Ftbl; Var L Trk; Var L Wrstlng.

HERRING, LISA; Pine Grove Area HS; Pine Grove, PA; (Y); SADD; School Musical; School Play; Stage Crew; Cit Awd; Photo.

HERRING, NADEEN; Harnsburg HS; Harrisburg, PA; (Y); 29/460; Debate Tm; JA; Pep Clb; Speech Tm; Orch; Nwsp Ed-Chief; Nwsp Rptr; Nwsp Stf; Yrbk Stf; Stu Cncl; Schlrshp Dickinson Clg 86; Jrnlsm Achvt Awd 86; Brdcst.

HERRINGTON, TONI LYNN; West Allegheny HS; Imperial, PA; (Y); Teachers Aide; Drill Tm; Var Pom Pon; High Hon Roll; Hon Roll; Robert Morris Coll; Accntnt.

HERRLE, LISA; Dallastown Area HS; York, PA; (Y); Sec Frsh Cls; Rep Sec Soph Cls; Rep Sec Jr Cls; Rep Stu Cncl; Capt Cheerleading; Mgr(s); Powder Puff Ftbl; Trk; Hon Roll; Intl Bus.

HERRLE, SHARI LYNN; Bethel Park SR HS; Bethel Park, PA; (Y); 86/550; Church Yth Grp; Dance Clb; Drama Clb; Key Clb; Chorus; School Musical; High Hon Roll; Hon Roll; Pres Schlr; Duquesne U; Phrmcy.

HERRMAN, KIMBERLY; Northern SR HS; Dillsburg, PA; (Y); 1/201; Church Yth Grp; Color Guard; L Var Crs Cntry; L Var Trk; Bausch & Lomb Sci Awd; VP NHS; Val; Cmnty Wkr; Hosp Aide; Quiz Bowl; Am Leg Aux Unit Awd 86; Eng Awd 86; Woodsmn Wrld Hstry Awd 86; Messiah Coll; Pre-Med.

HERRMANN, DON; Father Judge HS; Philadelphia, PA; (Y); 4/360; Cmnty Wkr; Office Aide; Service Clb; Teachers Aide; Var Golf; High Hon Roll; Hon Roll; Jr NHS; NHS; PA ST; Acctng.

HERRMANN, PEGGY; Chartiers Valley HS; Pittsburgh, PA; (Y); 14/383; Church Yth Grp; Drama Clb; Pep Clb; Ski Clb; Concert Band; Mrchg Band; School Play; Rep Stu Cncl; NHS; Ntl Merit SF; PA ST U; Engrg.

HERRON, JENNIFER; Carrick HS; Pittsburgh, PA; (Y); DECA; Q&S; School Play; Powder Puff Ftbl; Var Sftbl; Hon Roll; U Of Pittsburgh; Law.

HERRON, PAUL; Washington HS; Washington, PA; (Y); 12/150; Boy Scts; Pres Exploring; Spanish Clb; Rep Stu Cncl; High Hon Roll; Hon Roll; Sec NHS; Restrd Liff Awd 84; U Of Pittsburgh; Elec Engrg.

HERSH, LISA; Spring Grove Area HS; Spg Grove, PA; (Y); 41/251; Varsity Clb; Chorus; Mrchg Band; Yrbk Stf; Var L Bsktbl; JV Crs Cntry; JV Var Fld Hcky; Stat Ftbl; Trk; Hon Roll; Unsung Hero Awd Trk & Fld 86; Schlrshp To Empire Bty Schl 86; Empire Bty Schl; Csmtlgy.

HERSHBERGER, ROSS; Northern Bedford County HS; Martinsburg, PA; (Y); Church Yth Grp; FFA; Varsity Clb; Jazz Band; School Musical; Swing Chorus; Yrbk Stf; Tennis; Trk; NHS; Ntl Schl Choral Awd 86; FFA Pub Spkng Cntst 86; Bedford Cty Schrlshp 86; PA ST U; Sci.

HERSHEY, ANNE; Middletown Area HS; Middletown, PA; (Y); 1/163; FCA; Chorus; Orch; Nwsp Stf; Yrbk Stf; Stu Cncl; Crs Cntry; Trk; High Hon Roll; Acad All Amer 85 & 86; Natl Ldrshp & Svc Awd 85-86; Am Leg Essay Cont 3rd Pl 86; Biol.

HERSHEY, DAVID; Manheim Township HS; Lancaster, PA; (Y); Church Yth Grp; Capt Ftbl; Wt Lftg; Lndscpng.

HERSHEY, JILL; Elizabethtown Area HS; Elizabethtown, PA; (Y); Rep Church Yth Grp; Teachers Aide; Rep Stu Cncl; JV Bsktbl; Var Cheerleading; Var Capt Fld Hcky; Var Capt Trk; NHS; HOBY Ldrshp Fndtn Awd 85; Occ Ther.

HERSHEY, JIM; Hanover HS; Hanover, PA; (Y); 20/141; Boy Scts; Band; Chorus; Orch; School Musical; School Play; Var Trk; Var Wrstlng; Eagle Sct 86; Dist Chorus 86; West Chester U; Music.

HERSHEY, LYLE; Pequea Valley HS; Kinzers, PA; (Y); Trs Church Yth Grp; Band; Mrchg Band; Bsbl; Socr; Hon Roll; Prfct Atten Awd; Engr.

HERSHEY, SEAN; Hempfield HS; Landisville, PA; (Y); 100/400; Dance Clb; JV Var Bsktbl; JV Bsbl; James Madison U; Pltcl Sci.

HERSHEY, TINA M; William Penn SR HS; York, PA; (Y); Am Leg Aux Girls St; High Hon Roll; Hon Roll; Prfct Atten Awd; Acadmc Awd 86; Cosmtlgy Cmptn Awd-Stylng 83-84; Empire Bty Schl; Cosmtlgst Tchr.

HERSHKOWITZ, HELAINE; Upper Merion Ara HS; King Of Prussia, PA; (Y); 59/321; Chorus; Hon Roll; Dntl Hygnst.

HERSHMAN, KRISTINE; St Maria Goretti HS; Philadelphia, PA; (Y); Church Yth Grp; Cmnty Wkr; Mathletes; Math Clb; Spanish Clb; Grnt Frm Forhm U 86; Schlrshp Frm Plc Athltc League 86; 1st & Scnd Hnrs 4 Yrs 82-86; Fordham U; Comm.

HERSTER, HEATHER; Kennedy Christian HS; Sharon, PA; (Y); 31/100; Hosp Aide; Capt Drill Tm; Yrbk Stf; JV Bsktbl; Capt Pom Pon; L Trk; Im Vllybl; Hon Roll; NHS; Reading Awd 83; Slippery Rock U.

HERSTINE, CARIE; Canon-Mc Millan HS; Canonsburg, PA; (Y); 45/355; Exploring; Office Aide; Science Clb; VP Ski Clb; Chorus; Yrbk Stf; Sec Frsh Cls; Var L Pom Pon; Var L Trk; High Hon Roll; U Pittsburgh; Chiro.

HERTZBERG, JASON; William Allen HS; Allentown, PA; (Y); Spanish Clb; Pres Temple Yth Grp; Var Swmmng; Var Trk; High Hon Roll; Hon Roll; Jr NHS; NHS; Spanish NHS; Arnold Tannebaum Mem Schlrshp 85; Ntl Cncl Tchrs Eng Achvt Awd 86; Engrng.

HERTZLER, KARYL; Middleburg HS; Middleburg, PA; (Y); Church Yth Grp; Ski Clb; Varsity Clb; Chorus; Var JV Fld Hcky; Var JV Sftbl; Hon Roll; Diving; Yng Amer 86; Vrsty Athlt 86; Mst Vlbl Plyr Awd 86; Bloomsburg U; Elem Ed.

HERTZOG, DEBORAH; Penn Cambria HS; Dysart, PA; (Y); FBLA; Concert Band; Twrlr; Hon Roll; Med Sec.

HERTZOG, DONNA; Grace Christian HS; Newmanstown, PA; (Y); Chorus; Yrbk Stf; High Hon Roll; Hon Roll.

HERTZOG, SCOTT; Exeter Township SR HS; Reading, PA; (Y); Band; Concert Band; Jazz Band; Orch; Lit Mag; Socr; Hon Roll; NHS; American Legion Awd; La Salle U; Pre-Med.

HERVEY, BETHANN; Hampton HS; Allison Pk, PA; (Y); Church Yth Grp; Cmnty Wkr; Church Choir; Concert Band; Mrchg Band; Yrbk Stf; Var Capt Cheerleading; Powder Puff Ftbl; Hon Roll; Erly Chldhd Educ.

HERWIG, MICHELLE LYNN; Hatboro-Horsham SR HS; Horsham, PA; (Y); 64/276; Key Clb; Concert Band; Mrchg Band; School Musical; Hon Roll; Prfct Atten Awd; Offcrs Wives Clb Scholar 86; Horsham Rotary Scholar 86; FF ST U; Nrsng.

HERZ, KIMBERLY; Merion Mercy Acad; Phila, PA; (Y); Art Clb; Cmnty Wkr; Library Aide; Office Aide; Spanish Clb; Teachers Aide; Ntl Art Hnr Scty 86; Moore Coll Of Art Sat Cls Schlrshp 86; Moore Coll Of Art Smr Wrkshp Schlrshp 86; Art Therapy.

HERZING, NANCY; Du Bois Area SR HS; Penfield, PA; (Y); Cmnty Wkr; Chorus; School Musical; High Hon Roll; Hon Roll; Pres NHS; Rotary Awd; Voice Dem Awd; Bio.

HERZOG, KRISTY; Council Rock HS; Richboro, PA; (Y); 148/845; Gym; Hon Roll; Drexel; Bus.

HERZOG, RICHARD; Hickory HS; Hermitage, PA; (Y); 7/190; Church Yth Grp; Drama Clb; Math Clb; NFL; Capt Tennis; NHS; Ntl Merit SF; Debate Tm; Ski Clb; Spanish Clb; Charles H Bonhag Mem Schrlshp Engr 86; Sci Awd 86; Penn ST; Civil Engr.

HESIDENZ, DIANA; Butler SR HS; Butler, PA; (Y); Trs Church Yth Grp; Cmnty Wkr; JA; Library Aide; SADD; Teachers Aide.

HESLIN, HEATHER; Liberty HS; Bethlehem, PA; (Y); 110/475; Church Yth Grp; Hosp Aide; Chorus; Church Choir; Hon Roll; Typg Awd 85; Spec Ed.

HESS, AMY; Susquenita JR SR HS; Marysville, PA; (S); 22/183; Ski Clb; Spanish Clb; Acpl Chr; Band; Chorus; Jazz Band; Mrchg Band; School Musical; School Play; Stat Bsktbl; Cmmctns.

HESS, BARB; Garden Spot HS; New Holland, PA; (Y); 54/173; Church Yth Grp; Drama Clb; School Musical; School Play; Stage Crew; Sec Var Sftbl; Hon Roll; Library Aide; VICA; Bowling; Jane Stauffer Mrl Awd Bckstg Prdctn 86; Grdn Spt Prfrmng Arts Bst Prod Assnt 86; Data Procssng.

HESS, BRENDA; Crestwood HS; Mountaintop, PA; (Y); FBLA; Var Capt Crs Cntry; Var L Trk; Hon Roll; Prfct Atten Awd; Cert Of Achvt In X-Cntry & All Stars 85.

HESS, DARYL; Northern Lebanon HS; Lebanon, PA; (Y); 22/175; Church Yth Grp; Chorus; Church Choir; Var Bsbl; Var Bsktbl; Capt Var Socr; Hon Roll; NHS; Lebanon Vly Coll; Math.

HESS, DAVID P; Easton Area HS; Easton, PA; (Y); Trs Stu Cncl; Var Ftbl; Im Wt Lftg; Hon Roll; JETS Awd; Jr NHS; NHS; James Minotti Schlrshp 86; Exchng Clb Stu Mnth Oct 85; Paul L & Henrietta Mindr Awd 86; Penn ST; Engr.

HESS, DIANE; Shippensburg Area SR HS; Shippensburg, PA; (Y); Trs GAA; Band; Pres Chorus; Concert Band; Mrchg Band; School Musical; Stu Cncl; Sftbl; NHS; Pres Schlr; Bloomsburg U; Mrktng.

HESS, DUANE E; Manheim Central HS; Manheim, PA; (Y); 70/237; Church Yth Grp; School Play; Var L Ftbl; Var Gym; Var Trk; Var Vllybl; Var Wt Lftg; Var L Wrstlng; Hon Roll; Pres Phys Fit 86; Messiah Coll; Accntg.

HESS, ELISABETH; Harrisburg Acad; New Cumberland, PA; (Y); 7/35; VP JA; Teachers Aide; Yrbk Ed-Chief; Yrbk Stf; Rep Stu Cncl; JV Bsktbl; JV Cheerleading; Var L Fld Hcky; JV Trk; Hon Roll; Coaches Awd & Chrldr 83-84; Seiler Awd 86.

HESS, ERIC; Altoona Area HS; Altoona, PA; (Y); Band; Concert Band; Jazz Band; Mrchg Band; Orch; Pep Band; Symp Band; Bowlng Schlrshp Trnmnt 2nd Pl 86; Lehigh U; Acctg.

HESS, HOLLY; Northeastern SR HS; Mt Wolf, PA; (Y); 4/180; GAA; Hosp Aide; Ski Clb; Band; Chorus; Orch; Var Fld Hcky; High Hon Roll; NHS; Lebanan Vly Coll Yth Schlrs Prog For Chem 86; Elizabethtown Coll; Chem/Bio.

HESS, HOWARD; Spring-Ford HS; Spring City, PA; (Y); 10/225; Concert Band; Jazz Band; Mrchg Band; Orch; God Cntry Awd; Hon Roll; JP Sousa Awd; Lion Awd; NHS; Pres Schlr; Penn ST U; Chem Engrng.

HESS, KELLY; Donegal HS; Mount Joy, PA; (Y); 20/167; Church Yth Grp; Drama Clb; PAVAS; Chorus; Church Choir; Stage Crew; Rep Stu Cncl; Stat Trk; Hon Roll; Intr Desgn.

HESS, KEVIN; Fairview HS; Erie, PA; (Y); 19/161; Cmnty Wkr; Teachers Aide; Varsity Clb; VP Stu Cncl; Var Bsbl; Var Bsktbl; Coach Actv; Var Golf; Hon Roll; NHS; BUS.

HESS, KEVIN L; Manheim Central HS; Lititz, PA; (Y); 87/265; Church Yth Grp; 4-H; VICA; Band; Mrchg Band; School Musical; Tennis; 4-H Awd; Hon Roll; 2nd Vo Tech Skls Olympc Dstrcts 85-86; Crpntry.

HESS, LORI; Glendale HS; Blandburg, PA; (Y); Art Clb; Science Clb; Concert Band; Bsktbl; Powder Puff Ftbl; Sftbl; Trk; Hon Roll; Prfct Atten Awd; Pres Physcl Fitnss Awd 85-86; PA ST; Pre Law.

HESS, LORIE; Tussey Mountain HS; Broad Top, PA; (Y); 2/97; Pres Church Yth Grp; Ski Clb; Sec Trs SADD; Varsity Clb; Nwsp Rptr; Nwsp Stf; Yrbk Stf; Stu Cncl; Trk; Vllybl; US Army Rsrve Ntl Schlr/Athltc Awd 86; Prsdntl Acad Ftnss Awd 86; Quill & Scroll Awd 86; PA ST U; Aero Engr.

HESS, MARCY; Faith Mennonite HS; Drumore, PA; (S); 1/26; Church Yth Grp; Library Aide; Acpl Chr; Yrbk Stf; High Hon Roll.

HESS, MARK; Seneca HS; Erie, PA; (Y); 8/173; Pres Church Yth Grp; JV Bsbl; JV Bsktbl; Var Ftbl; High Hon Roll; NHS; JV Lnmn Of Yr 85; Acadmc All-Amer 86; PA ST; Math.

HESS, MATTHEW; West York Area HS; York, PA; (Y); 1/191; Boy Scts; VP Church Yth Grp; Varsity Clb; Var Ftbl; Var Trk; High Hon Roll; Pres NHS; Eagle Scout 86; Engr.

HESS, PATTI; Ephrata SR HS; Akron, PA; (Y); 8/254; Pep Clb; Rep Frsh Cls; JV Bsktbl; Var L Fld Hcky; Var L Sftbl; High Hon Roll; NHS; Comp Sci.

HESS, RENEE; Clearfield Area HS; Clearfield, PA; (Y); VP Art Clb; Pres Church Yth Grp; Drama Clb; German Clb; VP JA; SADD; Yrbk Stf; JV Sftbl; High Hon Roll; NHS; Won Art Cntst Held By Clearfield 86; Brigham Young U; Pre Law.

HESS, RENEE; Gateway Christian HS; Alburtis, PA; (S); Church Yth Grp; Drama Clb; Yrbk Stf; Rep Jr Cls; Stat Vllybl; Bus.

HESS, STACEY; Benton Area HS; Benton, PA; (Y); 1/39; Church Yth Grp; Ski Clb; Chorus; Drm Mjr(t); School Musical; School Play; Var Capt Fld Hcky; DAR Awd; NHS; Val; Rotary Stu; Natl Lang Olympiad Mdl; Penn ST U; Bus Mgt.

HESS, STEVE; Manheim Township HS; Lancaster, PA; (Y); 60/325; VP Church Yth Grp; Computer Clb; VP Science Clb; Yrbk Phtg; Hon Roll; Bio.

HESS, SUZANNE; Eastern JR SR HS; Windsor, PA; (Y); 2/130; Church Yth Grp; Sftbl; Cit Awd; DAR Awd; High Hon Roll; Jr NHS; Lion Awd; VP NHS; Pres Schlr; Sal; Wrghtsvll Almni Assoc Eng Awd 86; Solo Awd Piano, Rosalie Sommers Stdo Msc 86; Wrghtsvll Rtry Schlp; York Coll Of PA; Nrsng.

HESS, TRINA; Keystone HS; Cranberry, PA; (Y); Church Yth Grp; Girl Scts; Letterman Clb; Varsity Clb; Chorus; Church Choir; Variety Show; Crs Cntry; Gym; Trk; ST Crss Cntry Mt 82; Westminster Cnsrvtry Music.

HESSER, AMY; Bishop Guilfoyle HS; Altoona, PA; (S); 34/149; Church Yth Grp; Cmnty Wkr; NFL; Science Clb; Ski Clb; SADD; Varsity Clb; Chorus; Nwsp Rptr; Yrbk Stf; PA Spch Leag Dist Fnlst 85; Cmmnctns.

HESSION, MICHAEL; Roman Catholic HS; Philadelphia, PA; (S); 7/150; Church Yth Grp; JA; Letterman Clb; Red Cross Aide; Varsity Clb; Var Capt Ftbl; High Hon Roll; Hon Roll; NHS; Prfct Atten Awd; Natl Hnr Soc 84-87; Bus.

HESSON, KAREN; Southmoreland HS; Scottdale, PA; (S); Pres Church Yth Grp; DECA; Pep Clb; Church Choir; DECA 4th Pl Trip Dist Comptn & Elgbl ST Comptn Gen Merch Evnt 86; DECA 2nd Pl Apprl & Access 86; Wrk Mktg.

HESTER, JEANNETTE; Cheltenham HS; Philadelphia, PA; (Y); 100/360; Psych.

HESTER, PAUL; Central York SR HS; York, PA; (Y); Ski Clb; Yrbk Sprt Ed; Rep Frsh Cls; Rep Soph Cls; Rep Jr Cls; Pres Stu Cncl; Var Bsbl; High Hon Roll; NHS; Ntl Merit Ltr; Med Dr.

HETRICK, JAMIE; Marion Center HS; Marion Center, PA; (S); 10/170; Drama Clb; Pres FNA; VP Science Clb; SADD; Varsity Clb; JV Bsktbl; Var Trk; Var Vllybl; High Hon Roll; Brkn Trk Recrd-400 Rely 85; IUP; Psychlgy.

HETRICK, JERRY; Father Judge HS; Philadelphia, PA; (Y); 135/360; Teachers Aide; Varsity Clb; Stage Crew; Ftbl; Wt Lftg; Accntnt.

HETRICK, LAVONE; Jefferson-Morgan HS; Clarksville, PA; (Y); Church Yth Grp; Intnl Clb; Red Cross Aide; Church Choir; Yrbk Stf; High Hon Roll; Hon Roll; Waynesburg Coll; Med.

HETRICK, STACEY; Cambridge Springs Joint HS; Cambridge Springs, PA; (Y); Dance Clb; French Clb; Pep Clb; Ski Clb; SADD; Variety Show; Nwsp Ed-Chief; Nwsp Rptr; Trs Var Cheerleading; Capt Pom Pon.

HETRICK, WENDY SUE; Octorara HS; Atglen, PA; (Y); Cmnty Wkr; Library Aide; SADD; Pres Chorus; Church Choir; Stage Crew; Pres Swing Chorus; Hon Roll; Choral Svc Awd 86; Bradford Bus Schl; Lgl Sec.

HETTLER, JESSICA; Penn Trafford HS; Irwin, PA; (Y); 76/360; Church Yth Grp; Pres VP 4-H; Girl Scts; Red Cross Aide; Sec Spanish Clb; Chorus; Yrbk Stf; 4-H Awd; High Hon Roll; Hon Roll; Penn ST U; Comm.

HETZLEIN, ALAINA; Faith Community Christian Schl; Pleasant Hills, PA; (S); 1/33; Computer Clb; Pep Clb; Yrbk Stf; Rep Jr Cls; Rep Stu Cncl; Var Sftbl; High Hon Roll; Ntl Merit SF; NEDT Awd.

HEURING, TOM F; Rochester Area JR SR HS; Rochester, PA; (Y); 20/110; Letterman Clb; Pep Clb; Ski Clb; Teachers Aide; Nwsp Rptr; Nwsp Stf; Bsktbl; Ftbl; Tennis; Hon Roll; Beaver Co Athltc Acadmc Al-Star Tm 85-86; Aviatn.

HEUSCHER, DERRICK; Council Rock HS; Richboro, PA; (Y); 53/845; Boy Scts; VP Computer Clb; Band; High Hon Roll; Hon Roll; NHS; Indstrl Arts Awd-Elec 86; Elec Engrng.

HEVENER, MARCY; Warwick HS; Lititz, PA; (Y); 62/234; Computer Clb; Intnl Clb; Library Aide; Teachers Aide; Band; Concert Band; Mrchg Band; Orch; Symp Band; High Hon Roll.

HEVERLY, BETH; Jersey Shore SR HS; Jersey Shore, PA; (Y); Church Yth Grp; 4-H; French Clb; FBLA; Stage Crew; Bsktbl; Mat Maids; 4-H Awd; Hon Roll; Bus.

HEVERLY, ROBERT; Crestwood JRSR HS; Mountaintop, PA; (Y); 21/225; Boy Scts; Exploring; Library Aide; Math Clb; Stage Crew; NHS; NEDT Awd; Phrmcy.

HEWITT, BERNADETT; Fort Le Boeuf HS; Waterford, PA; (Y); 37/180; Chorus; School Musical; Nwsp Rptr; Rep Soph Cls; VP Sr Cls; Rep Stu Cncl; Bowling; Var L Cheerleading; Hon Roll; Stu Forum 85 & 86; Edinboro U; Soc Wrkr.

HEY, CHRIS; Schuykill Valley HS; Leesport, PA; (S); 30/133; Ski Clb; Rep Frsh Cls; Rep Soph Cls; Rep Jr Cls; Rep Sr Cls; Off Stu Cncl; Var L Swmmng; Var Capt Tennis; Vllybl; Ntl Merit Ltr; Bucknell; Bio.

HEY, TRACEY; Hatboro-Horsham SR HS; Hatboro, PA; (Y); 52/298; Church Choir; School Musical; Capt Cheerleading; JV Lcrss; Im Powder Puff Ftbl; Var Trk; Ntl Merit Ltr; Elem Educ.

HEYDENREICH, MICHELLE; State College Area HS; State College, PA; (Y); 4/510; Jr Cls; Sr Cls; JV Var Cheerleading; Powder Puff Ftbl; JV Im Vllybl; Ntl Merit SF; NEDT Awd; Smith Bk Awd 85; Donald W Carruthers Jr Mem Schlrp Awd 86; Echols Schlr 86; U VA; Med.

HEYER, JERRE P; Seneca HS; Erie, PA; (Y); 23/141; Boy Scts; Pres Church Yth Grp; Computer Clb; Band; Yrbk Bus Mgr; Bsktbl; Hon Roll; NHS; SAR Awd; Soc Studies Contrbutn 86; Eagle Scout 86; MA Inst Tech; Elect Engr.

HEYL, CHRIS; Loyalsock Township HS; Williamsport, PA; (Y); Ski Clb; Spanish Clb; Band; Chorus; Jazz Band; Camera Clb; School Musical; Trk; Concert Band; Pep Band; U Of VT; Engrng.

HEYM, BRIAN; Henderson HS; West Chester, PA; (S); 7/349; JCL; Latin Clb; Ski Clb; Spanish Clb; Rep Soph Cls; Rep Jr Cls; Var L Socr; Var L Tennis; Hon Roll; Rotary Awd; All-Ches-Mont Hnrs Soccer 84; VP Of Interact 85; Bus.

HEYS, GAYLE LYNN; Thomas Jefferson HS; Pittsburgh, PA; (Y); Church Yth Grp; French Clb; Thesps; Church Choir; School Play; Yrbk Stf; Stat Bsktbl; Stat Vllybl; High Hon Roll; NHS; Teen Inst Org 85-86; Grove City Coll; Acctng.

HEYWOOD, KATHLEEN; St Francis Acad; Whitehall, PA; (Y); 6/19; Math Tm; Pep Clb; Spanish Clb; Chorus; School Musical; School Play; Stage Crew; Variety Show; Sec Frsh Cls; Hon Roll; PA JR Acad Sci 86; Cert Hnr Scholar Awd 85; Cert Awd Activities 85; Nrsg.

HEYZ, DONNELL; Norwin SR HS; N Huntingdon, PA; (Y); 297/557; Church Yth Grp; French Clb; Ski Clb; Mgr Band; Concert Band; Jazz Band; Mrchg Band; JV Var Bsktbl; Early Chldhd Devlpmnt.

HICE, MARY JANE; Jefferson Morgan SR HS; Jefferson, PA; (Y); 13/86; Church Yth Grp; Spanish Clb; Teachers Aide; Acpl Chr; Chorus; Madrigals; Swing Chorus; Score Keeper; Stat Sftbl; Hon Roll; Intr Design.

HICKENBOTTOM, BERNADINE; Academy HS; Erie, PA; (Y); 48/213; Church Yth Grp; Computer Clb; French Clb; Chorus; Church Choir; Pom Pon; Hon Roll; Prfct Atten Awd; PA ST Behrend; Psychlgy.

HICKERSON, MURPHY J; Rochester Area HS; Rochester, PA; (Y); 12/98; Church Yth Grp; French Clb; Spanish Clb; SADD; Chorus; Church Choir; Pres Soph Cls; Pres Jr Cls; Pres Sr Cls; Rep Stu Cncl; U Of Pittsburgh; Pedtrcn.

HICKEY, COLLEEN; Wellsboro Area SR HS; Wellsboro, PA; (Y); 2/127; VP Pres French Clb; School Musical; JV Bsktbl; Stat Trk; Capt Var Vllybl; High Hon Roll; NHS; Sal; Model UN; Color Guard; Natl H S Awd Exclince 86; Bus Prof Wmn Girl Of Mnth 85; Westminster Coll; Bio Tech.

HICKEY, DAVID; Seneca Valley HS; Mars, PA; (Y); Boy Scts; Pres Church Yth Grp; Sec Exploring; ROTC; Band; Chorus; Mrchg Band; School Musical; Swmmng; Hon Roll; Eagle Scout Awd 85; Ministr.

HICKEY, LYNNETT ANN; New Brighton Area SR HS; New Brighton, PA; (Y); 50/167; Church Yth Grp; Cmnty Wkr; Y-Teens; Band; Concert Band; Jazz Band; Mrchg Band; Off Jr Cls; Off Sr Cls; Hon Roll; Dstrct Band 85; Wrthy Advsr Rainbow Assmbly 85; Sewickley Vlly Hsp Schl; Nrsng.

HICKMAN, BRETT; Juniata HS; Port Royal, PA; (Y); Varsity Clb; JV Ftbl; Var Trk; JV Wrstlng; Hon Roll; Lincoln Tech Inst; Drafting.

HICKMAN, DIANE; Keystone Oaks HS; Pittsburgh, PA; (Y); 30/260; Pres Pep Clb; Nwsp Phtg; Nwsp Rptr; Yrbk Phtg; Rep Jr Cls; NHS; Penn ST U; Elem Educ.

HICKMAN, LISA; Waynesburg Central HS; Waynesburg, PA; (Y); Ski Clb; Spanish Clb; Hon Roll; Bus Mgmt.

HICKOK, CRAIG; Purchase Line HS; Clymer, PA; (Y); 39/150; Hon Roll; Mnstry.

HICKS, EMMA; Cardinal Dougherty HS; Phila, PA; (Y); 120/735; Civic Clb; Cmnty Wkr; Debate Tm; NFL; Political Wkr; Yrbk Rptr; Var Hon Roll; Exploring; Ed French Clb; Yrbk Stf; Rep Ntl Black Caucus Of St Leg Yth Cngrss 85-86; St Fnlst Miss Amer Coed Pgnt 86; Black Yth 86; Temple U; Pol Sci.

HICKS, JAMES; Central Catholic HS; Verona, PA; (Y); 58/260; Church Yth Grp; Sec Drama Clb; Pep Clb; PAVAS; School Musical; School Play; Stage Crew; Cheerleading; Hon Roll; 2 Hrbl Mntns-1 Blue Rbn-Schlstc Art Awds & Schlrshp For Carnegie-Medlan U 86; Fl Tuitn Schlrshp/Cpr U; Cooper Union; Arch.

HICKS, KELLI A; Lamberton HS; Philadelphia, PA; (Y); 31/130; Camera Clb; Cmnty Wkr; Dance Clb; Girl Scts; Frsh Cls; Soph Cls; Sr Cls; Bowling; Trk; Hon Roll; Acad Exclince Awd 84; Ruth Hayre Scholar 86; Black Incentive Grant 86; PA ST U; Bus.

HICKS, LISA; Moshannon Valley JR SR HS; Houtzdale, PA; (Y); 6/127; Spanish Clb; Varsity Clb; Band; Flag Corp; Mrchg Band; Pep Band; Yrbk Stf; High Hon Roll; Jr NHS; NHS; U Ptsbrg; Nrs.

HICKS, MELISSA; Burgettstown JR SR HS; Burgettstown, PA; (Y); 15/170; Ski Clb; Spanish Clb; Chorus; Drm Mjr(t); Mrchg Band; Hon Roll; Jr NHS; NHS; U Of Pittsburgh; Bus.

HICKS, NICHELLE; Swarthmore Acad; Chester, PA; (Y); 1/12; Concert Band; Orch; Yrbk Stf; Off Soph Cls; Off Sr Cls; Vllybl; High Hon Roll; NHS; Schlrshp To Vassar 86; Outstndng-All Arnd Math, Calculus, Physics 86; Outstndng-Sci & Socl Studies 86; Vassar U; Physics.

HICKS, PAUL; Marion Center Area HS; Marion Ctr, PA; (Y); Varsity Clb; Var Bsbl; Var Ftbl; Var Mgr(s); Var Swmmng; JV Trk; Wt Lftg; High Hon Roll; Hon Roll; Heavy Equip Oper.

HICKS, RANEE; Homer Center HS; Indiana, PA; (Y); 3/98; French Clb; FBLA; SADD; Band; Pres Concert Band; Jazz Band; Mrchg Band; Hon Roll; NHS; Natl Sci Merit Awd 86; IN U Of PA; Psych.

HICKS, STACY; Southern Huntingdon County HS; Todd, PA; (Y); GAA; SADD; Varsity Clb; Chorus; Jazz Band; Var L Fld Hcky; Var L Trk; Hon Roll; NHS; Pres Schlr; Dnstry.

HICKS, TRACY; Catasauqua HS; Catasauqua, PA; (Y); 14/124; Drama Clb; Chorus; Drm Mjr(t); Yrbk Ed-Chief; Yrbk Sprt Ed; Stu Cncl; Mgr(s); Mat Maids; Powder Puff Ftbl; Hon Roll; Pres Acad Ftns Awd 85-86; Juniata Coll; Physlgy.

HICKS, TRESE; Gateway SR HS; Pitcairn, PA; (Y); 39/450; FHA; Office Aide; Teachers Aide; Nwsp Rptr; Nwsp Stf; High Hon Roll; Hon Roll; Prfct Atten Awd; Computer Tech; Wrd Prcssng.

HIDVEGI, JOSEPH E; Berwick Area SR HS; Berwick, PA; (Y); Wilkes-Barre Genrl Hosp; Nuc Md.

HIESTER, EMILY; Hershey HS; Hershey, PA; (Y); 5/208; Teachers Aide; Band; Chorus; Ed Yrbk Stf; Var Fld Hcky; Var Swmmng; High Hon Roll; NHS; Spanish NHS.

HIGDON JR, JAMES M; Wyoming Area HS; Wyoming, PA; (Y); 1/247; Church Yth Grp; Math Clb; Math Tm; Spanish Clb; High Hon Roll; NHS; Val; Suprintndnt Achvt Awd-Hghst Aver 86; DR Paul A Chromey Awd-Hghst Aver 86; Spnsh Awd 83-85; PA ST; Archl Engrng.

HIGGINBOTHAM, SYLVIA LYNN; Burgettstown JR SR HS; Burgettstown, PA; (Y); 23/172; Girl Scts; Ski Clb; Band; Chorus; Concert Band; Mrchg Band; Pep Band; Symp Band; Var L Sftbl; Hon Roll; Dist Band Cert 82-83; Cnty Band Cert 83-86; PA ST; Sci.

HIGGINS, ANITA; Bishop Hafey HS; Hazleton, PA; (Y); Ski Clb; Bloomsburg ST Coll; Nrsng.

HIGGINS, DORIS; Southern Columbia Area HS; Shamokin, PA; (Y); 11/91; Varsity Clb; Chorus; School Play; Stage Crew; Yrbk Ed-Chief; Yrbk Phtg; Yrbk Stf; JV Var Bsktbl; JV Var Fld Hcky; Var L Trk; Hnr Stdnt 86; Rotry Stdnt Mnth & Wk 86; St Josephs U; Chem.

HIGGINS, JANE; Corry Area HS; Corry, PA; (Y); 45/225; Church Yth Grp; Ski Clb; SADD; Band; Concert Band; Mrchg Band; JV Bsktbl; Var L Trk; Mansfield U; Resprtry Thrpy.

HIGGINS, JENNIFER E; Windber Area HS; Saratoga, PA; (Y); 17/114; French Clb; Sec Sr Cls; Stu Cncl; Hon Roll; NHS; Phil Coll Textiles; Int Desgn.

HIGGINS, JOSEPH; Marian HS; Nesquehoning, PA; (Y); 3/116; Am Leg Boys St; Church Yth Grp; Rep Jr Cls; JV Var Ftbl; L Trk; VP NHS; Rotary Awd; Spanish NHS; Aud/Vis; Chess Clb; Hugh O Brian Ldrshp Smnr Ambsdr 85; Lions Clb Ldrshp Smnr 86; US Naval Acad; Elec Engrng.

HIGGINS, LEAH; Dunmore HS; Dunmore, PA; (Y); 4-H; French Clb; FBLA; JA; Spanish Clb; Chorus; Drill Tm; Nwsp Rptr; Yrbk Stf; Bowling.

HIGGINS, MAURA; Marple Newtown HS; Newtown Square, PA; (Y); 52/376; School Play; Yrbk Sprt Ed; Capt Var Crs Cntry; Hon Roll; NHS; MVP Crs Cntry 84; Stu Mth Sci Dept 86; La Salle U; Engrng.

HIGGINS, PATRICK; Dunmore HS; Dunmore, PA; (Y); 30/150; French Clb; Letterman Clb; Ski Clb; Var Ftbl; Var Wt Lftg; Hon Roll; Jr NHS; Villanova U; Bus.

HIGGINS, TARA; Westmont Hilltop HS; Johnstown, PA; (Y); 16/162; Church Yth Grp; Drama Clb; Thesps; Drm Mjr(t); School Musical; School Play; Rep Stu Cncl; High Hon Roll; Hon Roll; Sec NHS; Duke; Pre-Law.

HIGH, ERIC; Pequea Valley HS; Narvon, PA; (S); 29/139; AFS; Varsity Clb; Rep Stu Cncl; JV Var Bsbl; JV Var Socr; Im Wrstlng; Hon Roll; Hnrbl Mntn Bsbl 84-85; Hnrbl Mntn Soccer 85-86; Bus Adm.

HIGH, KEITH; Pequea Valley HS; Paradise, PA; (S); 14/138; Spanish Clb; Wrstlng; High Hon Roll; Hon Roll; Engrng.

HIGHLAND, GIGI DENISE; Grove City HS; Grove City, PA; (Y); 18/200; Sec French Clb; Pres Science Clb; Band; Mrchg Band; Yrbk Stf; Pres Frsh Cls; Pres Soph Cls; Pres Jr Cls; Pres Stu Cncl; Var Cheerleading; Acad All Amer; PA ST.

HIGHLAND, SCOTT; Jim Thorpe HS; Jim Thorpe, PA; (S); Am Leg Boys St; Church Yth Grp; Pres 4-H; Ski Clb; Band; Mrchg Band; Nwsp Stf; High Hon Roll; NHS.

HIGINBOTHAM, MARK; Hempfield Area SR HS; Greensburg, PA; (Y); Church Yth Grp; French Clb; Pep Clb; JV Var Bsktbl; High Hon Roll; Hon Roll; Jr NHS; Prfct Atten Awd; Westmoreland Hosp Medcl Explrs Group 84-86; Double Ltr Wnr Bsktbl & Trk; Bio.

HILBERT, JULIE; Mercyhurst Prep; Erie, PA; (Y); 34/150; Church Choir; Swmmng; Hon Roll; Sprts Med.

HILBERT, SHELLY; Kutztown Area HS; Lyons Sation, PA; (Y); Office Aide; Pep Clb; Band; Chorus; Concert Band; Capt Drill Tm; Stat Bsbl; Var Capt Pom Pon; High Hon Roll.

HILD, DENNIS; West Catholic Boys; Philadelphia, PA; (Y); 8/250; Cmnty Wkr; Rep Frsh Cls; Rep Jr Cls; Sec Stu Cncl; Var L Bsbl; JV Ftbl; High Hon Roll; Hon Roll; NHS; Prfct Cndct 84-86.

HILD, JOANNA; Wilmington Area HS; New Wilmington, PA; (Y); Drama Clb; Key Clb; Office Aide; Spanish Clb; Stage Crew; Powder Puff Ftbl.

HILDEBRAND, AMY; Butler Area SR HS; Butler, PA; (Y); Trs Church Yth Grp; Pres VICA; Chorus; Church Choir; Hon Roll; Cert Exclinc Ntl Fed Music Clbs 86; Singer.

HILDEBRAND, JOAN; Archbishop Kennedy HS; Conshohocken, PA; (Y); Pep Clb; Chorus; Yrbk Stf; Rep Soph Cls; Rep Jr Cls; Rep Sr Cls; VP Stu Cncl; Var Capt Cheerleading; Hon Roll; NHS; Bilingual Exec Asst.

HILDEBRANDT, MATT; Boyertown Area HS; Perkiomenville, PA; (Y); Library Aide; SADD; Nwsp Rptr; Yrbk Rptr; Crs Cntry; Frgn Lang Interprtr.

HILDENBRAND, JENNIFER; Yough HS; Arona, PA; (Y); 14/227; Church Yth Grp; Computer Clb; Girl Scts; Library Aide; Ski Clb; Spanish Clb; Var L Bsktbl; Im Powder Puff Ftbl; Var L Sftbl; Var L Vllybl; US Army Schlr-Athl Awd 86; Spnsh Clb Trip To Spain 85; Spnsh Clb Exclinc Awd 86; U PA; Pre-Law.

HILE, DONALD A; Reynolds HS; Fredonia, PA; (Y); 15/121; Pres Church Yth Grp; German Clb; Math Clb; Science Clb; Chorus; Crs Cntry; Ftbl; Cit Awd; High Hon Roll; Hon Roll; Sr Of Wk Rcrd Args 86; Schlrshp Fr Grv City Coll 86-87; Grove City Coll; Acctg.

HILE, LISA; Reading SR HS; Reading, PA; (Y); 17/638; Acpl Chr; Chorus; Color Guard; Flag Corp; Madrigals; Capt Mrchg Band; School Musical; School Play; Swing Chorus; NHS; T V Brunner Staab Schlrshp 86; Browns Music House Awd 86; Music Dept Awd 86; Millersville U; Comp Sci.

HILEMAN, HOLLY; Central HS; Martinsburg, PA; (Y); Trs FBLA; GAA; Varsity Clb; Chorus; Color Guard; Var Trk; Im Vllybl; Var Hon Roll; NHS; Variety Show; 3rd Pl Bus Engl FBLA Regnls 86; Penn ST Altoona; Bus Adm.

HILER, MATTHEW; Hershey HS; Hershey, PA; (Y); 62/200; Church Yth Grp; Varsity Clb; Band; Chorus; Jazz Band; Orch; School Musical; Crs Cntry; Trk; Dist Band Fest 84-86; PA All St Lions Band 84; Dist & Rgnl Chrs 86; Indiana U PA; Mus Educ.

HILK, BRIAN; Trinity HS; Washington, PA; (Y); L Capt Ftbl; L Wrstlng; High Hon Roll; Hon Roll.

HILL, BRENDA; Philipsburg-Osceola Area HS; Philipsburg, PA; (Y); 28/245; Art Clb; Pres Library Aide; Hotel Mgmnt.

HILL, CHRISTINA; Elkland Area HS; Nelson, PA; (Y); 3/81; Drama Clb; Pres 4-H; FTA; Library Aide; SADD; Teachers Aide; Varsity Clb; School Play; Rep Stu Cncl; Im Gym; Rep Elkland HOBY Ldrshp Sem 84-85; Potter Tioga Maple Sweethrt 86; Mansfield U; Elem Ed.

HILL, CONNIE; Lehighton Area HS; Lehighton, PA; (Y); 64/250; FBLA; FHA; Library Aide; Color Guard; Capt Drill Tm; Acctng.

HILL, CRYSTAL; Olney HS; Philadelphia, PA; (Y); Church Yth Grp; Office Aide; Church Choir; Rep Frsh Cls; Var Crs Cntry; Var Trk; Prfct Atten Awd; FCA; JV Vllybl; CC Schrlshp 86; Negro Coll Fund 86; Temple U; Pre-Med.

HILL, CURTIS L; Southern Fulton HS; Needmore, PA; (Y); Boy Scts; Church Yth Grp; French Clb; Band; Chorus; Trk; God Cntry Awd; High Hon Roll; Pres Schlr; Acdmc Ftns Awd 86; PA ST U; Crmnl Jstc.

HILL, DEANN LACHELLE; Archibishop Carroll HS; Philadelphia, PA; (Y); Church Yth Grp; Cmnty Wkr; School Play; Stage Crew; Gym; Lcrss; Hon Roll; U Of Pittsburgh; Pre-Law.

HILL, HEATHER; Mt Penn HS; Reading, PA; (Y); Hosp Aide; Pres Sec Science Clb; Spanish Clb; Teachers Aide; Y-Teens; Nwsp Rptr; Ed Yrbk Stf; Vllybl; Jr NHS; NHS; Mt St Marys Coll; Psychlgy.

HILL, JEFFREY R; Valley Forge Military Acad; Chatham Twp, NJ; (Y); ROTC; Nwsp Stf; Yrbk Stf; Im Socr; Offcrs Candidate Schl 2nd Lt Compltn 85-86; Hosp Commnder 85-86; Cert CPR Instrctr 84-86; Auburn U; Mech Engr.

HILL, JENNIFER; Bishop Kenrick HS; Norristown, PA; (Y); 116/311; French Clb; Color Guard; School Play; Powder Puff Ftbl; Hon Roll; Pro-Life Rprt 86; Pro-Life Grp 84; Dnstry.

HILL, JENNIFER; Meadville Area SR HS; Meadville, PA; (Y); 100/306; Church Yth Grp; Hosp Aide; Latin Clb; Nwsp Stf; Stu Cncl; Stat Bsktbl; Var L Socr; Hon Roll; Prfct Atten Awd; Pre-Med.

HILL, JENNIFER; West Hazleton HS; Nuremberg, PA; (Y); Drama Clb; Thesps; Chorus; School Musical; School Play; Stage Crew; Hon Roll; 1st Awd JR Acad Of Sci 84-85; Dstrct Chorus 85; Intl Thspn Scty 85-86; Grphc Arts.

HILL, LEONARD; Penn Hills SR HS; Pittsburgh, PA; (S); 143/742; French Clb; Letterman Clb; Ski Clb; Varsity Clb; School Musical; Pres Sr Cls; Ftbl; Wt Lftg; Hon Roll; Prfct Atten Awd; Schl Brd 86; PTSA 85-86; PASC 85; U Pittsburgh; Engr.

HILL, MIKE; Twin Valley HS; Honeybrook, PA; (Y); 36/126; Church Yth Grp; Pep Clb; Nwsp Rptr; Rep Soph Cls; Rep Stu Cncl; Var Ftbl; Var Wt Lftg; Var Capt Wrstlng; High Hon Roll; Hon Roll; Deans Schlrshp 86; PA Coll Of Bible; Bible.

HILL, MONICA; William Penn SR HS; Daytona Beach, FL; (Y); Church Yth Grp; Pep Clb; Y-Teens; Chorus; School Play; Nwsp Rptr; Cheerleading; Swmmng; Bearcats Den Club 85-86; Miss Fine Brown Frame Awd 86; Stetson; Law.

HILL, ROBERTA; Germantown HS; Philadelphia, PA; (Y); 132/327; Latin Clb; Office Aide; Hon Roll; Latin Awd 83; Work Exprnc Awd 85; Work Exprnc Svc Awd 86; Cmnty Coll; Comp.

HILL, STEVE; Linesville HS; Conneautville, PA; (Y); 9/86; Var Capt Crs Cntry; Hon Roll; Bio Engr.

HILL, SUSAN; New Brighton Area HS; New Brighton, PA; (Y); Church Yth Grp; GAA; Varsity Clb; Chorus; Church Choir; Yrbk Stf; JV Bsktbl; JV Var Cheerleading; L Trk; Hon Roll; Physcl Thrpy.

HILL, THOMAS; Northern York HS; Dillsburg, PA; (Y); 21/200; Computer Clb; Quiz Bowl; School Musical; Yrbk Stf; Crs Cntry; Trk; Hon Roll; NHS; Pres Schlr; Chess Clb; Am Lgn Schl Awd 86; Penn ST U; Aero Engr.

HILLANBRAND, PATRICK; Allentown Central Catholic HS; Wescosville, PA; (Y); Exploring; Stage Crew; Wrstlng; Wrstlr Wk 85; Lincoln Tech Inst; Elctrncs.

HILLARD, STEVE; Hollidaysburg Area SR HS; Hollidaysburg, PA; (Y); Ftbl; Wt Lftg; Hon Roll; George Mason U; Aerospc.

HILLBERRY, STACEY; Trinity HS; Amity, PA; (Y); 148/374; Church Yth Grp; Cmnty Wkr; German Clb; Girl Scts; Key Clb; Office Aide; SADD; Sftbl; Hon Roll; Rifle Tm 83-86; Dntl Asst.

HILLEBRAND, JULIE; Elk County Christian HS; St Marys, PA; (Y); 17/80; Letterman Clb; Varsity Clb; Var Crs Cntry; Var Trk; High Hon Roll; Hon Roll; Rotary Awd; Bus.

HILLEGASS, LONNIE; Pottsgrove HS; Pottstown, PA; (Y); 77/229; Ski Clb; Varsity Clb; Bsbl; Hon Roll; Lock Hvn U; Hstry.

HILLER, DAWN; Quaker Valley HS; Leetsdale, PA; (Y); FBLA; Band; Chorus; Flag Corp; Bsktbl; Crs Cntry; Score Keeper; Trk; Vllybl; Hon Roll; Bio.

HILLER, PAUL; Northeast Catholic HS; Philadelphia, PA; (S); 20/390; Hon Roll; NHS; Germn Awd 84; Temple; Math.

HILLIARD, CATHERINE; Big Spring HS; Newville, PA; (Y); 23/189; Church Yth Grp; Pres 4-H; Chorus; Var L Crs Cntry; Var L Trk; High Hon Roll; Hon Roll; NHS; MVP X-Cntry 85-86; Outstndng Sprtsmnshp Awds X-Cntry & Track 85-86; Psych.

HILLIARD, GREGORY A; Olney HS; Philadelphia, PA; (Y); Hon Roll; Illustrn.

HILLIARD, PATTI; Butler SR HS; Renfrew, PA; (Y); Pres Church Yth Grp; French Clb; Teachers Aide; Chorus; Church Choir; School Musical; School Play; Rep Frsh Cls; Vllybl; Hon Roll; Btlr Cnty JR Ms Pgnt 87; Splry Rck U; Spec Ed Tchr.

HILLIAS, STEVEN; Southern Lehigh HS; Coopersburg, PA; (Y); 43/227; Ski Clb; Golf; Wt Lftg; Hon Roll; Aerospace Engrng.

HILLMAN, DARA; Clarion Area HS; Shippenville, PA; (Y); 8/102; VP FTA; Acpl Chr; Chorus; Drm Mjr(t); School Musical; Variety Show; Rep Stu Cncl; JV Vllybl; High Hon Roll; NHS; Gov Schl Intl Studs 86; 2nd Pl ST Lev Sci Comptn 84; Rotary Exch 85; Intl Studs.

HILLMAN, DENISE; Pottstown HS; Pottstown, PA; (S); 7/238; French Clb; Key Clb; Band; Concert Band; Mrchg Band; Yrbk Stf; Off Jr Cls; High Hon Roll; NHS; Poli Sci.

HILLMAN, SHAREASE R; Wilkinsburg SR HS; Wilkinsburg, PA; (Y); Hosp Aide; Math Clb; Math Tm; Scholastic Bowl; Science Clb; Cit Awd; High Hon Roll; Sec French Clb; Y-Teens; Prfct Atten Awd Chathan Coll Upward Bound 86; WVU; Comp Sci.

HILLS, CHRISTOPHER; Northwestern HS; Elizabethville, PA; (Y); 3/160; Church Yth Grp; Computer Clb; Model UN; Chorus; Yrbk Stf; JV Crs Cntry; JETS Awd; NHS; Boy Scts; School Musical; PA Free Enterprise Wk 86; Gannon U Comp Cont 85-86; Utica Coll; Actrl Sci.

HILLS, JULIE; Bradford Central Christian HS; Bradford, PA; (Y); 8/31; Drama Clb; Pep Clb; Chorus; Rep Frsh Cls; Sec Soph Cls; VP Jr Cls; Cheerleading; Hon Roll; Jr NHS; NHS.

HILLY, HOPE; Farrell SR HS; Farrell, PA; (Y); 26/100; Church Yth Grp; French Clb; Hosp Aide; Library Aide; Chorus; Church Choir; Var Cheerleading; Im Vllybl; Paul A Komar Mem Art Awd 86; Shenango Valley 86; Robert Morris Coll; Accntng.

HILSON, MARK; Scranton Central HS; Scranton, PA; (Y); Church Yth Grp; Ski Clb; VP Sr Cls; Hon Roll; VA Militry Inst; Cvl Engr.

HILTON, CAROLYN; Chester HS; Chester, PA; (Y); 7/310; Science Clb; Concert Band; Mrchg Band; Orch; School Play; High Hon Roll; NHS; Ntl Merit SF; Prfct Atten Awd; Rotary Club Chester Acdmc Schlrshp,Widener U Acdmc Schlrshp, PA Indstrl Chem Corp Acdmc Schlrshp 86; Widener U; Psych.

HILTY, CHERYL; Homer-Center HS; Lucerne Mines, PA; (Y); 1/96; Sec French Clb; SADD; Chorus; School Musical; Nwsp Rptr; Sftbl; High Hon Roll; Jr NHS; NHS; IN U Of PA; Psych.

HILTY, NEAL; Kiski Area HS; Vandergrift, PA; (Y); Computer Clb; Key Clb; Pep Clb; Ski Clb; SADD; Varsity Clb; Sec Sr Cls; Rep Stu Cncl; Var L Ftbl; Var L Trk; Hgh Hnr Rl 86; Cavalier Awd 85-86; Mst Imprvd Stu 84-85; IN U PA; Comp Sci.

HILWIG, STUART; Emmaus HS; Macungie, PA; (Y); 45/463; AFS; Cmnty Wkr; Exploring; German Clb; Hosp Aide; Key Clb; Model UN; Ski Clb; SADD; Orch; Schlrshp-Frmn Govt-Smmr Exchng Pgm 84; Hstry.

HIMES, CAMI; Hampton HS; Gibsonia, PA; (Y); Church Yth Grp; Crs Cntry; Powder Puff Ftbl; High Hon Roll; Hon Roll; Pittsburgh Beauty Acad; Csmtlgy.

HIMES, CRYSTAL; Bellwood-Antis HS; Tyrone, PA; (Y); 30/118; Sec Key Clb; Varsity Clb; Capt Bsktbl; Var Trk; Var Wt Lftg; Hon Roll; Hnr Roll 85-86; MVP Girls Bsktbl 85-86; Junita Valley League All Star Team 85-86.

HIMES, DEBORAH; Blairsville SR HS; Blairsville, PA; (Y); 7/131; Rep Church Yth Grp; Drama Clb; Co-Capt Color Guard; Mrchg Band; Nwsp Rptr; High Hon Roll; NHS; Hnrd Queen Jobs Daughters 85-86; Duquesne U; Corp Law.

HIMES, LAURA; Hollidaysburg Area SR HS; Hollidaysburg, PA; (Y); 34/341; Latin Clb; Varsity Clb; JV Bsktbl; Coach Actv; Var L Sftbl; Var L Vllybl; Hon Roll; NHS; Mst Points Awd Vllybl 85-86; U Pittsburgh; Phys Ther.

HIMES, MARY; Clarion-Limestone HS; Summerville, PA; (Y); 6/70; VP Intnl Clb; Varsity Clb; Pres Frsh Cls; Pres Soph Cls; Pres Stu Cncl; Cheerleading; Trk; Vllybl; Hon Roll; Pres NHS; Eng Achvt Awd 85-86; Prom Ct 86; Clarion U; Comm.

HIMES, MELISSA M; Ambridge Area HS; Freedom, PA; (Y); 21/265; Sec Church Yth Grp; Exploring; German Clb; Hosp Aide; Yrbk Stf; Off Soph Cls; Off Jr Cls; Stat Trk; High Hon Roll; NHS; Prfct Attndnce Awd 84-85; Acdmc Schlrshp Gannon U 86; Gannon U; Physician Assist.

HINDERLITER, JULIE; Cumberland Valley HS; Mechanicsburg, PA; (Y); 75/522; Am Leg Aux Girls St; Spanish Clb; JV Bsktbl; Im Bowling; Var Crs Cntry; JV Fld Hcky; Im Sftbl; Var Trk; Hon Roll; Ntl Merit Ltr.

HINDS, BARBIE; Eastern York HS; Wrightsville, PA; (Y); SADD; Varsity Clb; Yrbk Stf; VP Frsh Cls; Var Capt Cheerleading; Powder Puff Ftbl; Twrlr; Vllybl; Hon Roll; PA Acad Theatrical Arts; Theat.

HINE, LORI; Coughlin HS; Wilkes Barre, PA; (Y); Exploring; Band; Mrchg Band; Stage Crew; Stat Bsktbl; Var Fld Hcky; Mgr(s); Score Keeper; JV Vllybl; Hon Roll; Occptnl Thrpy.

HINER, KRISTI; Corry Area HS; Corry, PA; (S); 41/212; Church Yth Grp; Y-Teens; Mrchg Band; Stu Cncl; Stat Scrkpr Bsktbl; L Trk; Capt Twrlr; High Hon Roll; Delta Epsilon Phi Germn Hnr Socty 85; Bus.

HINES, CHARLES E; Bethlehem-Center SR HS; Marianna, PA; (Y); 19/156; Spanish Clb; Nwsp Rptr; Nwsp Stf; Socr; High Hon Roll; Hon Roll; Comp.

HINES, SHEILA; Bishop Carroll HS; Cresson, PA; (S); 14/111; Pep Clb; Spanish Clb; Bsktbl; Trk; Hon Roll; IUP; Bio.

HINES, YOLANDA; Aliquippa HS; Aliquippa, PA; (Y); Church Yth Grp; French Clb; Girl Scts; Band; Chorus; Church Choir; Mrchg Band; Cheerleading; Hon Roll; Duquesne U; Law.

HINISH, MARY; Everett Area HS; Everett, PA; (Y); Computer Clb; Trs GAA; Math Clb; Varsity Clb; Band; Pres Soph Cls; Stu Cncl; Var L Socr; Var L Sftbl; High Hon Roll; Lwyr.

HINKEL, GRETCHEN; Senior HS; Pittsburgh, PA; (Y); Church Yth Grp; Dance Clb; German Clb; Chorus; Stu Cncl; Trk; Psychlgy.

HINKLE, FORREST; Marian HS; Weatherly, PA; (Y); 68/116; Ski Clb; Kurtown U; Bus Mgmt.

HINKLE, JULIE; Northern Lebanon HS; Lebanon, PA; (Y); Church Yth Grp; Teachers Aide; Chorus; Church Choir; Mrchg Band; School Musical; School Play; Stage Crew; Nwsp Stf; Hon Roll; WCTU Essy Cntst 1st Pl Lcl 85-86; WCTU Essy Cntst 2nd Pl Cnty 85-86; Voice Perf.

HINKLE, KIM; Weatherly Area HS; Weatherly, PA; (S); 6/65; FBLA; Rep Stu Cncl; Stat Bsbl; Stat Bsktbl; Score Keeper; Sftbl; Hon Roll; NHS; Natl Eng Merit Awd 85; Comp Sci.

HINKLE, ROBERT; Lehighton Area HS; Lehighton, PA; (Y); Boy Scts; Church Yth Grp; Varsity Clb; Variety Show; Rep Stu Cncl; JV Var Bsbl; JV Var Bsktbl; JV Var Ftbl; Hon Roll; Prfct Atten Awd; All League Defense Ftbl 85, All Valley; Lehigh Vly All Star Ftbl Classic 86; PA ST U; Ag.

HINKLE, TAMMY; Columbia HS; Columbia, PA; (Y); 24/86; Church Yth Grp; Band; Chorus; Church Choir; Color Guard; Concert Band; Mrchg Band; Yrbk Stf; Mgr(s); Powder Puff Ftbl; Yorktown Bus Ins; Accntng.

HINKLER, DAVID; Fort Leboeuf HS; Erie, PA; (Y); 15/187; Spanish Clb; Bowling; Ftbl; Vllybl; Wrstlng; High Hon Roll; NHS; Ntl Ldrshp Svc Awd 85; USAF Acad; Electrcn.

HINNERS, MISSY; Schuylkill Haven Area HS; Schuylkill Haven, PA; (S); 44/87; German Clb; Pep Clb; Science Clb; SADD; Drill Tm; Mrchg Band; Yrbk Stf; Cheerleading; 3rd Pl Bio Sci Fair 84-85; Mst Acad In Grmn II 84-85; Bnd Apprctn Drll Tm 84-85; Flght Attndnt.

HINOJOSA, JOHN; Nestiaminy HS; Langhorne, PA; (Y); 8/732; Computer Clb; Mathletes; JV Bsktbl; JV Socr; Im Tennis; JV Trk; Im Vllybl; High Hon Roll; Prfct Atten Awd; Drexel U; Chem Engr.

HINTON, BRIAN; Red Lion Area SR HS; Red Lion, PA; (Y); 131/330; Church Yth Grp; Varsity Clb; Var L Trk; Var VP Wrstlng; Millersville U.

HINZ, ELLEN; North Pocono HS; Moscow, PA; (S); 23/250; Dance Clb; Band; Concert Band; Mrchg Band; Orch; Yrbk Stf; Var L Trk; High Hon Roll; NHS; Prfct Atten; Band Ltr; Mth.

HIPPLE, BECKY; Montoursville HS; Trout Run, PA; (Y); Church Yth Grp; FBLA; German Clb; Chorus; Church Choir; Hon Roll; Lycoming Cnty Dairy Princess 86; Cntrl PA Bus Schl; Bus Adm.

HIRIAK, KELLY; Upper Perkiomen HS; Barto, PA; (Y); 7/203; FBLA; Yrbk Ed-Chief; Sec Frsh Cls; Pres Soph Cls; Pres Jr Cls; Powder Puff Ftbl; Twrlr; High Hon Roll; NHS; Mgr(s); Acdmc All Amer 86; Cmmnty Schlrshp 86; 3rd Pl ST FBLA Conf 86; Kings Coll; Paraleagle.

HIRIAK, NICHOLAS F; St Pius X HS; Pottstown, PA; (S); Aud/Vis; Science Clb; Stage Crew; JV Trk; Hon Roll; Jr NHS; Accntnt.

HIRKALA, CHRISTINE; Mount Carmel JR SR HS; Natalie, PA; (Y); FTA; Key Clb; Latin Clb; Q&S; Nwsp Stf; Yrbk Stf; Cheerleading; French Clb; Pep Clb; Ski Clb; Masque & Gavel, Amy Vanderbilt Awd Ediuette, I Dare You Awd Ldrshp 86; Bloomsburg U; Cmnctns Disorders.

HIRKO, CHRIS; Pocono Mountain HS; E Stroudsburg, PA; (Y); Library Aide; Teachers Aide; Wrstlng; US Amer Lgn PA ST Plc Yth Wk 86; East Stroudsburg U; Bio.

HIRSCH, JOSEPH; United HS; Seward, PA; (Y); 96/161; French Clb; Ski Clb; Chorus; School Play; Var L Ftbl; Sftbl; Wt Lftg; Wrstlng; Hon Roll; Prfct Atten Awd.

HIRSCH, SCOTT; Upper Dauphin Area HS; Lykens, PA; (Y); 19/105; VP Church Yth Grp; Acpl Chr; Band; Chorus; Concert Band; Mrchg Band; School Musical; Swing Chorus; Var Bsbl; Hon Roll; Cnty, Dist And Regl Chrs 83-86; Schltc Achvt Awd 84-85; Elizbthtwn Hnrs Chr 85-86; U Of Pittsburgh; Aerosp Engrg.

HIRSCH, TRACY; Clearfield Area HS; Clearfield, PA; (Y); Church Yth Grp; VICA; Chorus; Church Choir; Vllybl; High Hon Roll; Hon Roll; Jr NHS; NHS; ICM Schl Of Bus; Comp Mngmt.

HIRSCHFIELD, SUE; David B Oliver HS; Pittsburgh, PA; (Y); 2/243; GAA; Pres VP Math Clb; Ski Clb; Ed Nwsp Stf; Var L Sftbl; High Hon Roll; NHS; Sal; SAR Awd; Dickinson Coll; Pre-Med.

HIRSHFELD, CATHERINE; Strath Haven HS; Swarthmore, PA; (Y); 1/286; Church Yth Grp; Girl Scts; Acpl Chr; Chorus; Orch; Nwsp Ed-Chief; Ntl Merit Schol; Scholastic Bowl; Teachers Aide; Lit Mag; PA Gvnrs Schl/Sci 85; Brookhvn Ntl Lab HS Hnrs Prog 86; All ST Chorus 85-86; Williams Coll; Physics.

HIRSHMAN, PHILIP; Lower Moreland HS; Huntingdon Valley, PA; (S); VP Intnl Clb; SADD; VP Jr Cls; VP Sr Cls; Co-Capt L Trk; DAR Awd; VP NHS; Ntl Merit Ltr; Boys Clb Am; Mensa 84-86; Stu Mth 86; DE Vly Spcl Olympcs Trck-Fld Coch 84-86; Ldrshp Rep-Rotry Ldrshp Camp 85; Lbrl Arts.

HISCOX, CAROL; E L Meyers HS; Wilkes-Barre, PA; (Y); 11/140; Church Yth Grp; Hosp Aide; Key Clb; Pep Clb; Ski Clb; Band; Chorus; Concert Band; Mrchg Band; Orch; Business Management.

HISSONG, BECKY; Windber Area HS; Windber, PA; (S); Ski Clb; Color Guard; Concert Band; Flag Corp; Off Jr Cls; Rep Stu Cncl; Trk; High Hon Roll; NHS; Pres Church Yth Grp; Stu Mnth 83-85; Cmmnctns.

HITCHINGS, JASON; Downingtown SR HS; Downingtown, PA; (Y); 138/544; Boy Scts; Dance Clb; German Clb; Model UN; ROTC; Ski Clb; Diving; Socr; Trk; Hon Roll; Army ROTC 4 Yr Scholar 86; Syracuse U Acad Grant 86; Syracuse U; Mltry Lwyr.

HITCHINGS, LISA ANN; Altoona Area HS; Altoona, PA; (Y); Church Yth Grp; Computer Clb; Drama Clb; Key Clb; Science Clb; Thesps; Acpl Chr; School Play; Off Sr Cls; High Hon Roll; PA ST U; Human Dvlpmnt.

HITE, KIMBERLY; Bishop Carroll HS; Loretto, PA; (S); 29/130; Pep Clb; Spanish Clb; SADD; Yrbk Stf; JV Cheerleading; Hon Roll; 4-H; Ski Clb; Color Guard; Mrchg Band; Penn ST; Phrmcst.

HITE, MARJORIE A; Cambria Heights HS; Patton, PA; (Y); 3/179; Pres VP 4-H; Library Aide; ROTC; Speech Tm; Church Choir; School Play; Yrbk Phtg; Yrbk Stf; NHS; NEDT Awd; Grad Cls Spkr 86; Acadmc Al-Amercn 86; Fornscs Awd 86; PA ST U; Chem.

HITNER, LISA; Upper Dublin HS; Ft Washington, PA; (Y); Cmnty Wkr; JA; Science Clb; JV Fld Hcky; JV Socr; Child Devlpmnt.

HITT, MICHELE; Ambridge Area HS; South Hts, PA; (Y); German Clb; Letterman Clb; Pep Clb; Red Cross Aide; Chorus; Off Jr Cls; Off Sr Cls; Trk; Hon Roll; Lettrmn In Track 84-86; Bronze Mdl In Discus-Beaver Cnty Times Meet 86; WIPIAL Qlfr In Duscus 86; Accntnt.

HITT, TAMMY; Hershey SR HS; Hershey, PA; (Y); 5/200; Math Tm; Chorus; School Musical; School Play; Capt Fld Hcky; Sftbl; High Hon Roll; NHS; Spanish NHS; Hershey Educ Assoc 86; Hershey Bus And Pro Wmns Clb 86; Hershey JR Womns Clb 86; U Of DE; Chem Engrng.

HITTINGER, KYLE; Saucon Valley SR HS; Bethlehem, PA; (Y); Boy Scts; Exploring; Letterman Clb; Library Aide; Band; Concert Band; Mrchg Band; Var Bsbl; JV Bsktbl; Score Keeper; Pre-Med.

HIX, LIESL; Middletown Area HS; Middletown, PA; (Y); Girl Scts; Library Aide; Radio Clb; Band; Chorus; Color Guard; Concert Band; Mrchg Band; Hon Roll; Elem Ed.

HIXENBAUGH, SHARON; Canon-Mc Millan SR HS; Mcdonald, PA; (Y); 141/396; Art Clb; French Clb; FBLA; JV Cheerleading; Hon Roll; Art Inst Of Pgh; Commercl Artst.

HIXON, KATHY; Southern Fulton JR SR HS; Warfordsburg, PA; (Y); Church Yth Grp; Band; Chorus; Church Choir; Madrigals; Mrchg Band; NHS; Ntl Merit Ltr; Amer Muscl Found Band Hnrs 86; Southern Fulton PTSO Fair SR HS Champ 85; PMEA Dist 4 Band Fest 86; Penn ST.

HIXSON, BRAD; Plum HS; Pittsburgh, PA; (Y); Var L Bsktbl; Trk; Var L Vllybl; Hon Roll; NHS; Prfct Atten Awd; Grd Hnrs; Penn ST; Engr.

HIXSON, EMILY; Southmoreland SR HS; Scottdale, PA; (Y); 11/230; Sec Church Yth Grp; German Clb; Pep Clb; Pres Chorus; Church Choir; School Musical; Variety Show; Sec Stu Cncl; Var Powder Puff Ftbl; Var Tennis; Amer Legion Aux Awd 82-83; German Ntl Hnrs Soc 84-87; Uncle Lews Crew-Choir Ensmbl 84-87; Music Thrpy.

HLATKY, GREG; Northern HS; Dillsburg, PA; (Y); 4/209; VP Sr Cls; Rep Stu Cncl; Var L Bsktbl; Var L Ftbl; Powder Puff Ftbl; Var L Trk; High Hon Roll.

HLAVAC, JULIE ANNE; Bishop O Reilly HS; Swoyersville, PA; (Y); Church Yth Grp; Dance Clb; Drama Clb; English Clb; Math Clb; Pep Clb; Political Wkr; Science Clb; Ski Clb; Spanish Clb; Pred-Spnsh Clb & Spnsh Ntl Hnr Soc 84-87; Pres-Ntl Hnr Soc 86-87; Scratnon U; Med.

HLAVATY, ED; Lakeland HS; Jermyn, PA; (S); 17/147; Pres Sr Cls; Rep Stu Cncl; High Hon Roll; Hon Roll; Engr.

HLUSHAK, TRACEY; Bishop Mc Devitt HS; Harrisburg, PA; (Y); 9/190; Service Clb; Rep Stu Cncl; Capt Cheerleading; NHS; Law.

HNOT, REBECCA; Oil City SR HS; Oil City, PA; (Y); AFS; FBLA; Acpl Chr; Chorus; Drill Tm; Mrchg Band; School Musical; Variety Show; Stu Cncl; 2nd Pl Bus Eng Regnl Conf 86; ST Comptn FBLA 86; U Pitt; Comm.

HO, WARREN; Unionville HS; West Chester, PA; (Y); 1/300; Off Church Yth Grp; Scholastic Bowl; Nwsp Sprt Ed; Rep Jr Cls; Rep Trs Sr Cls; Var Tennis; Mu Alp Tht; NHS; Ntl Merit Ltr; PA Govs Schl For The Sci-Semi Fnlst; Engrng.

HO, WILLY W; Unionville HS; West Chester, PA; (Y); 5/269; Chrmn Church Yth Grp; FBLA; Nwsp Rptr; High Hon Roll; Jr NHS; Mu Alp Tht; NHS; Ntl Merit SF; Nwsp Stf; PA Hghr Ed Asst Agncy Cert Merit 85; U DE; Elec Engrng.

HOAGLAND, KIMBERLY; Shenandoah Valley JR SR HS; Shenandoah, PA; (Y); Yrbk Stf; Var Crs Cntry; Var Sftbl; Var Trk; High Hon Roll; Hon Roll; NHS; Bloomsburg U; Chld Psych.

HOAK, DAWN CHRISTINE; Jeannette HS; Jeannette, PA; (Y); 12/145; Am Leg Aux Girls St; French Clb; FBLA; Spanish Clb; High Hon Roll; Accntg.

HOBAN, HELEN; Mid-Valley HS; Olyphant, PA; (Y); Art Clb; Nwsp Stf; VP Jr Cls; VP Sr Cls; Var JV Bsktbl; Var JV Crs Cntry.

HOBBS, GERALDINE; Pittston Area SR HS; Pittston, PA; (Y); 67/365; Science Clb; Yrbk Stf; Var L Sftbl; High Hon Roll; Hon Roll; Bus Adm.

HOBBS, PATRICK; Cornell HS; Neville Isld, PA; (Y); 15/85; Yrbk Stf; Pres Frsh Cls; Pres Soph Cls; Pres Jr Cls; Var L Ftbl; Var L Tennis; Hon Roll; Corporate Lwyr.

HOBDAY, MELISSA; Hempfield HS; Landisvile, PA; (Y); 50/450; Art Clb; Nwsp Ed-Chief; Lit Mag; Fld Hcky; High Hon Roll; Pblc Rltns Staff; Dsgnr Of Schl Clndr & Other Pblctns; Gettysburg U; Pre-Med.

HOBEL, DANIEL; Allentown Central Catholic HS; Coplay, PA; (Y); Varsity Clb; Var Ftbl; Var Ftbl; 3 Adult Ed Elctrncs Courses 85-86; Elec Engr.

HOBEREK, JODIE; Burgettstown Area JR/SR HS; Burgettstown, PA; (Y); 22/147; Drama Clb; French Clb; Science Clb; SADD; Mrchg Band; Symp Band; Yrbk Stf; Tennis; Hon Roll; NHS; Voice Of Democracy 84-85; PA Free Enterprise Wk 85-86; Modern Miss Teen Schlrshp Pgm 85-86; Intl Rltns.

HOBERNEY, ALAN; Portage Area HS; Lilly, PA; (S); 3/111; Aud/Vis; Vllybl; Cit Awd; High Hon Roll; Hon Roll; NHS; Cert Achvt Awd Calculus 86; Sci Awd 85; Natl Hnr Scty Awd 86; U Of Pittsburgh; Comp Pgrmr.

HOBI, CHUCK; Laurel Highlands SR HS; Uniontown, PA; (Y); Aud/Vis; Elec.

HOCHBERG, KATHERINE; Huntingdon Area HS; Huntingdon, PA; (Y); 7/234; Am Leg Aux Girls St; Key Clb; Quiz Bowl; Pres SADD; Teachers Aide; High Hon Roll; VP NHS; NEDT Awd; Tm Capt Sci Bwl Tm Sci Olympd PA 86; Pres Clssrm 86; Psych.

HOCHSTETLER, JOY; Faith Mennonite HS; New Holland, PA; (S); Chorus; Yrbk Ed-Chief; Sec Frsh Cls; Trs Jr Cls; Sec Stu Cncl; High Hon Roll.

HOCK, BRADLEY; Cumberland Valley HS; Boiling Springs, PA; (Y); Church Yth Grp; Acctng.

HOCK, KRISTIE; Bloomsburg HS; Bloomsburg, PA; (Y); 18/143; Church Yth Grp; Drama Clb; Pep Clb; Varsity Clb; Chorus; Church Choir; School Play; Stu Cncl; Cheerleading; Hon Roll.

HOCKENBERRY, BARBARA; Shippensburg Area SR HS; Shippensburg, PA; (Y); 17/225; Camera Clb; Church Yth Grp; Capt Quiz Bowl; Chorus; Church Choir; Concert Band; Mrchg Band; Hon Roll; NHS; Quizzing 86; MVP 86; Comp Sci.

HOCKENBERRY, CARMIE; Fannett-Metal HS; Fannettsburg, PA; (S); Drama Clb; Varsity Clb; VICA; Capt Color Guard; Pres Frsh Cls; VP Soph Cls; VP Jr Cls; Capt Cheerleading; Sftbl; High Hon Roll; Amer Legn Aux Medl Awd 83; Arch.

HOCKENBERRY, CAROL; Fannett-Metal HS; E Waterford, PA; (Y); Drama Clb; Band; Concert Band; Mrchg Band; School Play; Nwsp Ed-Chief; Nwsp Rptr; Nwsp Stf; Sftbl; Hon Roll; RN.

HOCKENBERRY, DENISE; Pen Argyl Area HS; Nazareth, PA; (Y); 17/117; Church Yth Grp; FBLA; Leo Clb; Ski Clb; Chorus; Yrbk Stf; JV Sftbl; High Hon Roll; Hon Roll; 5th Entrprnshp I 84; 3rd Bus Math 85; Leg Sec.

HOCKENBERRY, KELLY; Glendale HS; Flinton, PA; (Y); 5/98; Science Clb; Chorus; Stat Sftbl; Hon Roll; NHS; Drama Clb; Trs FHA; Library Aide; Band; Flag Corp; Bus Admn.

HOCKENSMITH, LENNY; Hanover HS; Hanover, PA; (Y); 20/104; Band; Chorus; Concert Band; Jazz Band; Mrchg Band; Orch; School Musical; School Play; Swing Chorus; JV Bsktbl; NEDT Tst Scrd Top 10% Ntn 85; Bus Admin.

HOCKMAN, LISA; Philipsburg-Osceda Area SR HS; Philipsburg, PA; (Y); 70/250; Church Yth Grp; Ski Clb; Yrbk Stf; Var Bsktbl; JV Vllybl; Prfct Atten Awd; Clarion; Educ.

HODEN, TIM; Sheffield Area HS; Sheffield, PA; (Y); Church Yth Grp; Cmnty Wkr; Drama Clb; Letterman Clb; Science Clb; SADD; Varsity Clb; School Play; Im Bsbl; Bsktbl; Forestry.

HODGIN, MICHELE; Parkland SR HS; Orefield, PA; (Y); Dance Clb; FNA; SADD; Drill Tm; Flag Corp; Mrchg Band; Rep Yrbk Stf; VP Frsh Cls; Rep Stu Cncl; Crs Cntry; Penn ST; Nrsng.

HODGSON, AMY; Punxsutewney Area HS; Punxsutawney, PA; (Y); 75/238; VP Church Yth Grp; FNA; Hosp Aide; Band; Concert Band; Mrchg Band; Variety Show; Wrstlng; Mt Aloysius JC; Crdvasclr Tech.

HODGSON, KELLEY; Ringgold HS; New Eagle, PA; (Y); 10/340; Church Yth Grp; FNA; Pep Clb; Ski Clb; School Musical; School Play; Var Capt Cheerleading; Socr; Sftbl; Hon Roll; Awd Outstndng Schlstc Achvt New Eagle Fire Dept; PA ST U; Aeronutcs Engr.

HODGSON, THERSA; Archbishop Prendergast HS; Havertown, PA; (Y); 39/361; Debate Tm; Drama Clb; NFL; Spanish Clb; SADD; Var L Swmmng; Hon Roll; Spanish NHS; Villanova U; Nrsng.

HODIL, BRYAN; Shaler Area HS; Pittsburgh, PA; (Y); 53/517; Church Yth Grp; Ski Clb; JV Crs Cntry; Var L Trk; High Hon Roll; Hon Roll; Mech Engr.

HOEFLING IV, WILLIAM A; Cedar Crest HS; Cornwall, PA; (Y); 5/295; FBLA; Math Tm; Pep Clb; Quiz Bowl; Var Coach Actv; Var L Socr; Im Vllybl; High Hon Roll; NHS; Ntl Merit SF; Hnr Bnqt Medal Wnnr 84-86; Engrng.

HOEHN, MARK; Central Bucks East HS; Pipersville, PA; (S); 47/474; Boy Scts; Church Yth Grp; German Clb; Acpl Chr; Chorus; School Musical; Nwsp Sprt Ed; Var Vllybl; Hon Roll; Drama Clb; Falcon Fndtn Schlrsp 86; Aerospace Engrng.

HOEKSTRA, ANDREW; Western Wayne HS; Sterling, PA; (Y); 15/150; Pres Church Yth Grp; Band; Concert Band; Jazz Band; Mrchg Band; Im Bsktbl; Hon Roll; NHS; Prfct Atten Awd; US Marine Corps.

HOELTZEL, STEVEN R; Warwick HS; Lititz, PA; (Y); 24/236; Thesps; Acpl Chr; Band; Chorus; Camp Fr Inc; Stage Crew; Variety Show; Hon Roll; NHS; Penn ST U; Math.

HOELZLE, AMY; Nazareth Acad; Fairless Hills, PA; (Y); Girl Scts; Spanish Clb; Chorus; Church Choir; Orch; VP Soph Cls; Hon Roll; Jr NHS; Prfct Atten Awd.

HOERGER, HOLLY; Bethel Park HS; Pgh, PA; (Y); FBLA; Bsktbl; Powder Puff Ftbl; Hgh Hnr 84; Finance.

HOERNER, JOANNE C; Lower Dauphin HS; Hershey, PA; (Y); 4/210; Hosp Aide; Ski Clb; Rep Frsh Cls; Rep Soph Cls; Trs Jr Cls; Rep Sr Cls; Rep Stu Cncl; Hon Roll; NHS; Prsdntl Cdmc Ftnss Awd 86; PA ST U; Cmmnctns Dsrds.

HOETZLEIN, CHRISTINE MARIE; Gateway SR HS; Monroeville, PA; (Y); 78/508; Am Leg Aux Girls St; Church Yth Grp; Cmnty Wkr; Chorus; Off Frsh Cls; Off Soph Cls; Off Jr Cls; Gym; L Tennis; Trk; Chmcl Engrng.

HOETZLEIN, JAMES L; St Joseph HS; Natrona Hts, PA; (Y); 22/55; Drama Clb; JA; Chorus; School Musical; School Play; Im Ftbl; JV Socr; Opt Clb Awd; Schl Sci Fair 3rd Pl Computers 84-85; Natl Hist Day Excllnt Ribbon 84-85; PA ST U; Psychology.

HOEY, ANNE; Hampton HS; Allison Pk, PA; (Y); Church Yth Grp; French Clb; Acpl Chr; Chorus; School Musical; Trk; Hon Roll.

HOFF, JOSH; Upper Moreland HS; Horsham, PA; (Y); 7/263; Computer Clb; Key Clb; Jazz Band; Mrchg Band; High Hon Roll; NHS; Ntl Merit Ltr; Stu Of Month 86; Chem Outstndng Achvt Awd 86; French Outstndng Achvt Awd 84 & 86; Princeton; Comp Sci.

HOFF, PAMELA S; York County Vocational Tech Schl; Dover, PA; (Y); 1/391; Pres VICA; Chorus; Color Guard; Nwsp Stf; JV Capt Cheerleading; Stat Fld Hcky; Stat Vllybl; VP NHS; Rotary Awd; Val; All-Amer Schlr Awd 85-86; Natl Ldrshp-Srvc Awd 86; York Coll Of PA; Med Tech.

HOFF, TYRONE; Spring Grove HS; Spring Grove, PA; (Y); 60/285; Church Yth Grp; Church Choir; Concert Band; Mrchg Band; JV Tennis; Var Trk; Hon Roll.

HOFF, WENDY; Upper Dublin HS; Ft Washington, PA; (Y); VP FBLA; Office Aide; Ski Clb; Varsity Clb; Rep Stu Cncl; JV Lcrss; Var L Swmmng; Im Mgr Wt Lftg; Hon Roll; NHS; All Sbrbn Swmng Free Rly 86; 1st Pl Bus Grphcs Rgnl Comp For FBLA 86; Free Entrprs Exprnc Schlrshp 86; Bus.

HOFFAT, TERESA; Delaware Valley HS; Matamoras, PA; (Y); Band; Mrchg Band; Stat Bsktbl; High Hon Roll; Hon Roll; NHS.

HOFFER, CAROL; Hempfield HS; E Petersburg, PA; (Y); 5/460; Chess Clb; VP Pres Church Yth Grp; Rep Stu Cncl; Im Coach Actv; Im JV Fld Hcky; High Hon Roll; NHS; Hnrbl Mntn Lncstr Cnty Sci Fair 85; Tp 1% Ntl AHSME Math Cmptn 86; 1st Pl Spnsh Hmpflds Frgn Lang Cmp; Elizabethtown Coll; Acctg.

HOFFER, CYNTHIA D; Mt Zion Christian Acad; Acme, PA; (S); 1/8; Church Yth Grp; French Clb; Girl Scts; Chorus; Church Choir; Nwsp Rptr; Ed Yrbk Ed-Chief; Pres Stu Cncl; Co-Capt Vllybl; High Hon Roll; 1st Pl Sci Fair Awd 84-85; PA ST U; Anml Sci.

HOFFER, DAWN; Eastern York HS; Wrightsville, PA; (Y); 17/117; Drama Clb; Chorus; School Musical; School Play; Swing Chorus; Variety Show; Lion Awd; George E Goodling Schlrshp Awd 86; PA ST U; Elem Educ.

HOFFERT, KENNETH D; Springfield HS; Springfield, PA; (Y); 1/260; Church Yth Grp; Scholastic Bowl; Orch; Stu Cncl; Socr; Capt Wrstlng; High Hon Roll; Lion Awd; Pres NHS; Ntl Merit Schol; Harvard Bk Awd; Schlr/Athlete Awd; Voted Wrstlr Or Yr; U Of PA; Engrng.

HOFFERT, SHERRY L; Liberty HS; Bethlehem, PA; (Y); 18/407; Library Aide; Band; Concert Band; Mrchg Band; Pep Band; High Hon Roll; Hon Roll; NHS; Amer Assn U Wmn Scholar 86; Amer Bus Wmns Assn Scholar 86; Wmns Clb Bethlehem Scholar 86; Millersville U; Biol.

HOFFERT, STACEY; Freedom HS; Bethlehem, PA; (Y); 12/404; Computer Clb; Spanish Clb; High Hon Roll; Hon Roll; NHS; Prfct Atten Awd; Moravian Coll Schrlshp 86; Moravian Coll; Comp Sci.

HOFFMAN, AMANDA; Freedom HS; Bethlehem, PA; (Y); 200/445; Hosp Aide; Spanish Clb; JV Bsktbl; Var Crs Cntry; Var Sftbl; Hon Roll; Church Yth Grp; Library Aide; Med.

HOFFMAN, AMY; Frazier HS; Fayette City, PA; (S); Nwsp Stf; Pres Sr Cls; Capt Twrlr; Fairmont ST Coll; Scl Wrk.

HOFFMAN, ANDREA; Bellwood-Antis HS; Altoona, PA; (Y); 20/118; 4-H; Key Clb; Varsity Clb; Band; Chorus; Concert Band; Drm Mjr(t); Mrchg Band; School Musical; Fld Hcky; Sigels Schl Of Dance ST Champ Dance Grp 84-85; PA ST U; Mech Engrng.

HOFFMAN, BETH; Punxsutawney Area HS; Punxsutawney, PA; (Y); 12/238; Math Tm; Science Clb; Spanish Clb; Varsity Clb; Band; Var L Bsktbl; Var L Trk; Hon Roll; NHS; Army Schlr Athl Awd, Mary Anne Irvin Schlrshp 86; U Pittsburgh; Phys Ther.

HOFFMAN, BEVERLY; Brookville Area HS; Brookville, PA; (Y); 33/141; French Clb; FFA; Hosp Aide; Library Aide; Mgr(s); Rotc; Vet Med.

HOFFMAN, CHRISTOPHER; Owen J Roberts HS; Chester Springs, PA; (Y); Boy Scts; Church Yth Grp; JA; Im Vllybl; Var JV Wrstlng; Natl Wnnr Intermdt Cls Natl Piano Audtns86.

HOFFMAN, CHRISTY; Montoursville HS; Montoursville, PA; (Y); German Clb; Key Clb; Letterman Clb; Tennis; Trk; Hon Roll; Church Yth Grp; Dance Clb; Girl Scts; Ski Clb; Trk & Fld Chmpnshps-400m Relay 3rd Pl 85; PA ST; Bus Mktg.

HOFFMAN, DARA; Hazleton SR HS; Mcadoo, PA; (Y); 103/373; FBLA; Hon Roll; Sec.

HOFFMAN, DAVID M; Upper Perkiomen HS; Pennsburg, PA; (Y); 17/198; Am Leg Boys St; VP FBLA; Pres Concert Band; Jazz Band; Pres Mrchg Band; Pres Pep Band; Hon Roll; JP Sousa Awd; Lion Awd; NHS; PA FBLA Schlrshp & All ST Band 86; US Mrn Band Smpr Fdls Awd 86; Allntwn Bus Schl; Mgmt.

HOFFMAN IV, DEAN M; E Pennsboro HS; Summerdale, PA; (Y); French Clb; Science Clb; Spanish Clb; School Musical; School Play; Coach Actv; Ftbl; Wt Lftg; Wrstlng; Hon Roll; Chem Engre.

HOFFMAN, DENISE; Notre Dame HS; Stroudsburg, PA; (Y); Church Yth Grp; Cmnty Wkr; French Clb; Girl Scts; School Musical; School Play; Yrbk Stf; Trs Frsh Cls; Cheerleading; Gym; Gymnastics Coaches Awd 84-85; U Of FL; Psych.

HOFFMAN, DENISE; Warrior Run HS; Turbotville, PA; (Y); Varsity Clb; Drill Tm; Nwsp Stf; Var Cheerleading; Stat Mgr(s); Powder Puff Ftbl; Stat Trk; Williamsport Area CC; Med Sec.

HOFFMAN, DENISE; Willias Valley JR SR HS; Williamstown, PA; (Y); 18/100; Band; Chorus; Church Choir; Concert Band; Jazz Band; Mrchg Band; School Musical; Swing Chorus; Symp Band; Hon Roll; Harrisburg Area CC; Microcomp.

HOFFMAN, DUSTIN; Jersey Shore Area HS; Avis, PA; (Y); Comp Sci.

HOFFMAN, ERIC; Northampton Area SR HS; Northampton, PA; (S); 40/465; Rptr Nwsp Rptr; Ed Yrbk Ed-Chief; Cheerleading; Var L Crs Cntry; Capt L Swmmng; Capt L Trk; High Hon Roll; Hon Roll; NHS; Exchng Clb Boy Mnth Oct 85; Stu Wk 86; Ntl Hnr Scty Schlrshp Fnlst 86; York Coll; Elem Ed.

HOFFMAN, ERIC; Pleasant Valley HS; Brodheadsville, PA; (Y); Church Yth Grp; VICA; Hon Roll; Ind Arts Awd 84; Cert Of Attainmnt PA Emergncy Mgmnt Agncy 86; Williamsport CC; Mach Shp Trng.

HOFFMAN, FRANCIS; Northeast Catholic HS; Philadelphia, PA; (Y); 10/362; Boy Scts; Teachers Aide; Im Bsktbl; NHS; Penn ST; Accntnt.

HOFFMAN, JAMES; Susquenita HS; Duncannon, PA; (S); 10/159; Trs Church Yth Grp; Spanish Clb; Yrbk Bus Mgr; Rep Stu Cncl; High Hon Roll; Hon Roll; NHS; Spanish NHS; De Vry Inst Tech; Elec Engr.

HOFFMAN, JEAN; Bishop Mc Devitt HS; Harrisburg, PA; (Y); Church Yth Grp; Chorus; Madrigals; School Musical; Var L Cheerleading; Stat Mgr(s); JV Sftbl; Jr NHS; NHS; Natl Math Awd 84-85; Cert Of Merit-PA SAT Scores 85; Pre-Dentl.

HOFFMAN, JEANNE; Center Area HS; Monaca, PA; (Y); #9 In Class; German Clb; Pres Sec Girl Scts; Latin Clb; Library Aide; Varsity Clb; Variety Show; Nwsp Stf; Ed Yrbk Stf; Rep Stu Cncl; Powder Puff Ftbl; Penn ST U; Mrktg.

HOFFMAN, JENNY; West Branch Area HS; Karthaus, PA; (S); 1/115; Pres Church Yth Grp; Varsity Clb; VP Jr Cls; Rep Stu Cncl; Var L Bsktbl; Bausch & Lomb Sci Awd; Hon Roll; VP NHS; US Army Schlr/Ath Awd 86; Edinboro U; Nrsng.

HOFFMAN, JILL ANN; James M Coughlin HS; Wilkes-Barre, PA; (Y); 72/385; Trs Church Yth Grp; Ski Clb; Concert Band; Mrchg Band; JV Var Bsktbl; Var JV Fld Hcky; Stat Sftbl; Im Vllybl; Hon Roll; Jr NHS; PA Coll Pharm; Pharm.

HOFFMAN, KIM; Palmyra Area SR HS; Palmyra, PA; (Y); 5/200; Rep Church Yth Grp; Math Tm; Quiz Bowl; Band; Concert Band; Mrchg Band; JV Var Trk; High Hon Roll; NHS; Dist Band 84-86; Math.

HOFFMAN, LEAH; Hillel Acad; Pittsburgh, PA; (Y); Art Clb; Cmnty Wkr; Computer Clb; Dance Clb; Debate Tm; English Clb; Office Aide; Acpl Chr; Lit Mag; Vllybl.

HOFFMAN, LEE; William Allen HS; Allentown, PA; (Y); 1/650; Boy Scts; Trs Church Yth Grp; Pres German Clb; Model UN; Capt Scholastic Bowl; Band; Jazz Band; Rep Stu Cncl; High Hon Roll; NHS; Biol.

HOFFMAN, LESLIE R; Germantown HS; Philadelphia, PA; (Y); Teachers Aide; Rep Frsh Cls; Rep Jr Cls; Hon Roll; Bus Admin.

HOFFMAN, LISA; Franklin HS; Franklin, PA; (Y); 94/234; French Clb; Hosp Aide; Off Soph Cls; Off Jr Cls; Var Sftbl; Hon Roll; Soclgy.

HOFFMAN, LISA; St Marys Area HS; St Marys, PA; (Y); L Trk; Bloomsburg U.

HOFFMAN, MICHAEL; Bethlehem Catholic HS; Bethlehem, PA; (Y); 2/207; JV Var Bsbl; JV Var Ftbl; Im Wt Lftg; High Hon Roll; Pres Jr NHS; Pres NHS; Natl Hnr Soc Pres 86-87; Pre-Med.

HOFFMAN, RANDI; Freeland HS; Freeland, PA; (Y); 8/150; Art Clb; Computer Clb; Spanish Clb; Ftbl; High Hon Roll; Hon Roll; Jr NHS; NHS; MIT; Engrng.

HOFFMAN, ROXANNE CATHERINE; Shippensburg Area SR HS; Newburg, PA; (Y); 13/225; Am Leg Aux Girls St; Varsity Clb; Band; School Musical; Stage Crew; Pres Stu Cncl; Swmmng; NHS; Hon Roll; Smmr Schlrshp Dickenson Coll PA 86; Mech Engrng.

HOFFMAN, SHARON; Montour HS; Coraopolis, PA; (Y); Church Yth Grp; Hosp Aide; Office Aide; Teachers Aide; Church Choir; Concert Band; Mrchg Band; Pep Band; School Musical; High Hon Roll; Robert Morris Coll; Exec Secty.

HOFFMAN, SHERI; Saint Clair Area HS; Pottsville, PA; (Y); Debate Tm; JA; SADD; Nwsp Bus Mgr; Nwsp Ed-Chief; Yrbk Bus Mgr; Yrbk Ed-Chief; Stu Cncl; Swmmng; High Hon Roll; Penn ST; Bus Admin.

HOFFMAN, VONDA; Middleburg HS; Richfield, PA; (Y); Church Yth Grp; 4-H; Hosp Aide; Model UN; Ski Clb; Varsity Clb; Chorus; Gym; Hon Roll; Wmns Clb Schlrshp 86; Rchfld U M Chrch Prl Bsm Fnd Schlrshp 86-87; Lncstr Schl Of Nrsg; RN.

HOFFMAN, YVONNE; Boyertown Area SR HS; Boyertown, PA; (Y); Art Clb; Camera Clb; Drama Clb; Girl Scts; Variety Show; Antonelli Inst Of Art; Comm Art.

HOFFMANN, JEFFREY; Bethel Park SR HS; Bethel Park, PA; (Y); Computer Clb; JA; Science Clb; Ski Clb; Rep Stu Cncl; Hon Roll; U Of Pittsburgh; Pre-Med.

HOFFNER, LARA; Cardinal O Hara HS; Newtown Sq, PA; (Y); 66/772; Trs Church Yth Grp; Cmnty Wkr; Library Aide; Office Aide; Spanish Clb; Teachers Aide; JV Crs Cntry; JV Trk; High Hon Roll; Hon Roll; US Army Sci & Engrng Medallion 85; US Dept Of Energy Awd 86; PA Jr Acad Of Sci 85.

HOFFNER, SUSAN; Bethlehem Catholic HS; Bethlehem, PA; (S); 19/220; NFL; Jazz Band; Mrchg Band; School Musical; School Play; Yrbk Stf; High Hon Roll; Jr NHS; NHS; Ntl Merit SF; IN U Of PA; Cmnctns.

HOFIUS, BECKY; Sharpsville HS; Sharpsville, PA; (Y); Camera Clb; Church Yth Grp; Hosp Aide; Science Clb; Spanish Clb; Nwsp Rptr; Yrbk Phtg; Cheerleading; Vllybl; Hon Roll; Acadmc Achvt Awd; Youngstown.

HOFMANN, JOHANNA; Linden Hall HS; Richland, PA; (Y); Church Yth Grp; Hosp Aide; Model UN; Frsh Cls; Soph Cls; Cit Awd; High Hon Roll; Hon Roll; Jr NHS; NHS; Ntl Hnr Soc 82-86; Bookstore Wrkr Awd 85-86; Spnsh Awd 84-86; Tchr Aide Japanese Exchng Prg 84-86; Spnsh.

HOFMEISTER, LAURA; Valley View JR SR HS; Peckville, PA; (Y); 73/200; FBLA; Latin Clb; Spanish Clb; Varsity Clb; Cheerleading; Vllybl.

HOGAN, BILL; Slippery Rock Area HS; Slippery Rock, PA; (Y); 1/172; Church Yth Grp; Exploring; JCL; Latin Clb; Math Tm; Concert Band; Mrchg Band; High Hon Roll; NHS; Lat Hnr Soc 85-86; Pre Med.

HOGAN, COLLEEN; Bishop O Hara HS; Olyphant, PA; (S); 16/113; Dance Clb; Latin Clb; Spanish Clb; Chorus; School Musical; Var Cheerleading; Score Keeper; High Hon Roll; H S Schlrshp Bishop Ohara & Scranton Prep 83.

HOGAN, EDWARD; Father Judge HS; Philadelphia, PA; (Y); 45/393; JV Trk.

HOGAN, GRACE ANN; Dunmore HS; Dunmore, PA; (Y); Letterman Clb; Ski Clb; Pom Pon; Tennis; High Hon Roll; Hon Roll; Jr NHS; NHS; Church Yth Grp; Drama Clb; Stamp Out Shplftg Stu Edctr 85-86; Title Holdr Miss Buck 86; Elem Ed.

HOGANS, PAM; Altoona Area HS; Altoona, PA; (S); Church Yth Grp; Key Clb; Service Clb; Rep Chorus; Nwsp Stf; Rep Stu Cncl; Twrlr; High Hon Roll; NHS; NEDT Awd; Kystn Wrtng Awd 84; Gnrls Grd 85; Cthrn Bth Awd 86; IUP; Accntng.

HOGE, AMY; Mc Guffey HS; Washington, PA; (S); 16/216; VP Church Yth Grp; Spanish Clb; Concert Band; Mrchg Band; Yrbk Stf; High Hon Roll; Hon Roll; NHS; Stu Recog Awd 83-85; Nrsng.

HOGELAND, PATRICIA; Danville HS; Danville, PA; (Y); 1/157; French Clb; Pres Latin Clb; NFL; Capt Var Fld Hcky; Var Sftbl; Sec NHS; Val; Ntl Schlr Athelte Awd 86; Forensics ST Champ Radio Annuncng 86; Hnr Schrlshp 86; Manhattanville Coll; Pre-Law.

HOGELAND, WESLEY; Neshaminy HS; Langhorne, PA; (Y); Art Clb; Church Yth Grp; Schltc Hnrs Art Awd 83-84.

HOGGA, MICHAEL; Northern Chester County Tech; Phoenixville, PA; (Y); 5/137; Church Yth Grp; Stage Crew; High Hon Roll; Hon Roll; NCCTS Advncd Elec 2nd Pl 86.

HOGLE, KATHY; Bethel Park SR HS; Bethel Park, PA; (Y); Church Yth Grp; French Clb; Band; Drill Tm; Mrchg Band; School Musical; Symp Band; Pom Pon; Powder Puff Ftbl; Timer; Bio.

HOGUE, CHERYL; Moon SR HS; Glenwillard, PA; (Y); 90/327; Band; Concert Band; Mrchg Band; Symp Band; JV Sftbl; Hon Roll; Sewickley Valley Schl; Rdlgy.

HOGUE II, JACK; New Brighton HS; New Brighton, PA; (Y); 55/165; Church Yth Grp; AFS; Computer Clb; Band; Concert Band; Jazz Band; Mrchg Band; Pep Band; Symp Band; Hon Roll; Stu Of Wk 83; 1st Choir Of Amrca 83-86; Lcl Hnrs Soc 86; Clarion U; Elem Educ.

HOGUE, JENNIFER; Cochranton JR SR HS; Cochranton, PA; (Y); 5/85; Trs Church Yth Grp; SADD; Chorus; High Hon Roll; Hon Roll; NHS; Pres Schlr; Acdmc Achvt Awds 85; Acdmc Achvt Awds 86; Slpry Rock U; Bio.

HOGUE, JOSEPH; Kiski HS; Vandergrift, PA; (Y); German Clb; Band; Concert Band; Mrchg Band; Bsktbl; Ftbl; Mgr(s); Hon Roll; Bus Adm.

HOGUE, MICHELLE; Penn Cambria HS; Loretto, PA; (Y); FBLA; Hon Roll; Hnr Roll 85-86; Bradford Schl; Acctnt.

HOGUE, RICHARD; Cochranton JR SR HS; Cochranton, PA; (Y); 24/75; Church Yth Grp; Letterman Clb; Ski Clb; SADD; Crs Cntry; Ftbl; Hon Roll; Penn ST Behrend; Bio.

HOH, LEO; Elk County Christian HS; Johnsonburg, PA; (Y); Aud/Vis; Chess Clb; Bowling.

HOHENBERGER, TRACEY; Shenango JR SR HS; New Castle, PA; (Y); Office Aide; Chorus; Church Choir; Stage Crew; Im Vllybl; Jr NHS; NHS; Sawyer Schl; Med Assist.

HOHL, DAVID; Notre Dame HS; Easton, PA; (Y); 9/90; Pres Stu Cncl; Var Bsktbl; Var Crs Cntry; Var Trk; Hon Roll; NHS; Pres Soph Cls; Rep Jr Cls; Rotary Awd; Bsktbl Mst Imprvd 85 & Mst Vlbl 86.

HOHL, RUTH; Dieruff HS; Allentown, PA; (Y); Aud/Vis; JA; Teachers Aide; Chorus; Yrbk Phtg; Rep Stu Cncl; Hon Roll; Prfct Atten Awd; Baum Schl Art Scholar 83 & 84; Trikia Acad Achvt Awd 86; Outstndng Stu Co-Op Pgm Awd 86; Philadelphia Coll Art; Comm Art.

HOHL, VICKI L; Emmaus HS; Wescosville, PA; (Y); 32/500; Camera Clb; Key Clb; Spanish Clb; Yrbk Stf; High Hon Roll; Hon Roll; Jr NHS; NHS.

HOHMANN, DALE; Deer Lakes JR SR HS; Gibsonia, PA; (Y); Aud/Vis; Library Aide; VICA; Church Choir; Hon Roll; 1 Yr Prfct Atten-HW Beattie AVTS 85-86; Auto Mech.

HOHOWSKI, AMY; Steel Valley HS; Munhall, PA; (Y); GAA; Key Clb; Varsity Clb; Rep Jr Cls; Stu Cncl; Bsktbl; Crs Cntry; Hon Roll; NHS.

HOINKES, PAMELA; Greensburg Central Catholic HS; Irwin, PA; (Y); Pres Church Yth Grp; Hosp Aide; Yrbk Sprt Ed; Trs Soph Cls; Trs Jr Cls; Trs Sr Cls; Stat Bsbl; L Bsktbl; High Hon Roll; Hon Roll; Elect Engrg.

HOJECKI, TINA; Boyertown SR HS; Boyertown, PA; (Y); Dance Clb; Library Aide; Pep Clb; Teachers Aide; Variety Show; Nwsp Stf; Capt Cheerleading; Gym; Kutztown U; Bus.

HOJNOWSKI, LORI; Hamburg Area HS; Hamburg, PA; (Y); 21/162; Chorus; Mrchg Band; Pep Band; School Play; Crs Cntry; Tennis; Trk; High Hon Roll; Hon Roll; NHS; Achvmnt Awd Alg Ii 83; Shippensburg U; Acctng.

HOKE, DAVID; Millersburg Area HS; Millersburg, PA; (S); 1/82; Aud/Vis; Church Yth Grp; Concert Band; Jazz Band; Mrchg Band; Bowling; Golf; Vllybl; Hon Roll.

HOKE, JODY A; Newport HS; Newport, PA; (Y); Pep Clb; Spanish Clb; Varsity Clb; Concert Band; Mrchg Band; Var Cheerleading; Sftbl; Miss Teen Of PA Pgnt 85; Elem Educ.

HOKE, JULIA; Manheim Township HS; Lancaster, PA; (Y); Church Yth Grp; Nwsp Rptr; Lit Mag; Rep Stu Cncl; Var Capt Fld Hcky; Powder Puff Ftbl; Swmmng; Trk; Hon Roll; Prtcpnt People To People Ambsr Pgm 84; Psych.

HOKE, M LARA; Camphill HS; Camp Hill, PA; (Y); 1/75; Model UN; Yrbk Ed-Chief; VP Sr Cls; Pres Stu Cncl; Var L Fld Hcky; Var Capt Sftbl; DAR Awd; NCTE Awd; Ntl Merit Ltr; Val; 4-Yr Nvy ROTC Schlrshp 86; Cornell U; Govt.

HOLBEN, MARK; Brookville Area HS; Brookville, PA; (S); VP Chess Clb; Trs Church Yth Grp; Key Clb; Chorus; Im Bsktbl; Var Trk; High Hon Roll; NHS; Top Accntng I Stu 85; Kent ST U; Air Trfc Contrl.

HOLBEN, MELINDA S; Sharon HS; Sharon, PA; (Y); 57/200; Church Yth Grp; SADD; Mrchg Band; School Musical; Stage Crew; Pres Stu Cncl; Trk; Vllybl; Cit Awd; Hon Roll; Drama Clb 3 Yrs Srv Awd 86; U Of Pittsburgh; Spch/Hrng Thrp.

HOLBERT, SHIRLEY; Waynesburg Central HS; Mt Morris, PA; (Y); Letterman Clb; Natl Beta Clb; Spanish Clb; Varsity Clb; JV Var Cheerleading; Gym; Hon Roll; WV U.

HOLBY, LISA; United HS; Homer City, PA; (Y); 43/155; Church Yth Grp; Library Aide; Math Clb; Pep Clb; Ski Clb; Chorus; Church Choir; Drill Tm; Yrbk Stf; Rep Stu Cncl; Pharm.

HOLCOMB, CHRIS; Liberty JR SR HS; Liberty, PA; (Y); Boy Scts; Exploring; German Clb; Chorus; School Musical; Stage Crew; Var Capt Bsktbl; Var L Crs Cntry; Var L Tennis; NHS; PA ST; Arch Engr.

HOLCOMBE, BONNIE; North Penn HS; North Wales, PA; (Y); Aud/Vis; FCA; Key Clb; Letterman Clb; Science Clb; Ski Clb; Yrbk Stf; Rep Jr Cls; Var Co-Capt Cheerleading; Var Tennis; Eng.

HOLCOMBE, BRADFORD W; Susquehanna Township HS; Harrisburg, PA; (Y); 15/165; Art Clb; Boy Scts; Computer Clb; Math Tm; Quiz Bowl; Teachers Aide; Yrbk Stf; Hon Roll; Lion Awd; Ntl Merit Ltr; Distngshd Schlrs Diplma 86; Presdntl Acadmc Ftns Awd 86; U Of VA; Elec Engrng.

HOLDEN, JEFF; Tunkhannock Area HS; Factoryville, PA; (Y); Chess Clb; Computer Clb; JA; Comp Sci.

HOLDEN, SCOTT; Philipsburg-Osceola Area HS; Philipsburg, PA; (Y); 24/231; Boy Scts; SADD; Band; Concert Band; Mrchg Band; JV Bsktbl; JV Var Crs Cntry; Hon Roll; NHS; PA ST U; Engrng.

HOLDEN, WENDY; Tunkhannock Area HS; Factoryville, PA; (S); 5/330; Church Yth Grp; German Clb; Latin Clb; Letterman Clb; Var Co-Capt Bsktbl; NHS; Natl Latn Exm Slvr Medlst 85; SR Hstrns Sec 85-86; Steerng Cmmttee 82-86; Psych.

HOLDERMAN, KATHY; Bellefonte Area HS; Bellefonte, PA; (Y); 13/240; Ski Clb; Varsity Clb; VP Frsh Cls; VP Soph Cls; Cheerleading; Powder Puff Ftbl; Sftbl; Vllybl; Hon Roll; NHS; Penn ST U; Crmnlgy.

HOLDREDGE, JACQUELINE M; Dallas SR HS; Dallas, PA; (Y); Church Yth Grp; Pres Civic Clb; Cmnty Wkr; Drama Clb; French Clb; Library Aide; Teachers Aide; Chorus; Drill Tm; Stage Crew; Schltc Art Awd; Cls Artist Awd; Nwsp Art Edtr & Stf Wrtr; Yrbk; Stu Cncl; Newbury Coll; Interior Dsgn.

HOLDSWORTH, GENIFFER; William Allen HS; Allentown, PA; (Y); 190/560; Hosp Aide; Ski Clb; Sec Band; Sec Concert Band; Sec Mrchg Band; Pep Band; Powder Puff Ftbl; Hon Roll; Jr NHS; Elem Educ.

HOLECEK, LISA; Abraham Lincoln HS; Philadelphia, PA; (Y); 16/350; Varsity Clb; School Play; Yrbk Stf; VP Frsh Cls; VP Soph Cls; VP Jr Cls; JV Var Cheerleading; Hon Roll; Sec NHS; Prfct Atten Awd; Bachhman Schrlshp; Neumann Coll; Pre-Law.

HOLEFELDER, SUSAN; Chichester SR HS; Aston, PA; (Y); Hosp Aide; SADD; Yrbk Stf; Trs Soph Cls; Trs Jr Cls; Trs Sr Cls; Stu Cncl; Var L Cheerleading; Var L Lcrss; Jr NHS; W Chester Villanova; Comm.

HOLENCIK, LORI; Philipsburg-Osceola Area HS; Philipsburg, PA; (Y); 22/250; Ski Clb; Yrbk Stf; Jr Cls; Hon Roll; NHS; Air Forc.

HOLEVA, DENISE; West Allegheny HS; Mc Donald, PA; (Y); Jr NHS; NHS.

HOLLAN, PATRICK; North Star HS; Hooversville, PA; (Y); AFS; Aud/Vis; Computer Clb; Teachers Aide; Stage Crew; Hon Roll; Harry Horne Scholar 86; U Pittsburgh Johnstwn; Comp Sci.

HOLLAND, JESSE A; Claysburg-Kimmel HS; Portage, PA; (Y); Pep Clb; SADD; Band; Chorus; Concert Band; Mrchg Band; Pep Band; Stage Crew; Rep Stu Cncl; High Hon Roll; Cert Of Recgntn For PA Rural Elec Yth Tour To WA 86; Diploma From Barbizon Model Agency 84; Med.

HOLLAND, MARC C; Penn-Trafford HS; Jeannette, PA; (Y); 75/329; Office Aide; Pep Clb; Varsity Clb; VP Sr Cls; Im Badmtn; Im Bsktbl; Var L Ftbl; Im Sftbl; Im Trk; Im Vllybl; IN U; Food Svc.

HOLLAND, PAM; Towanda Area HS; Towanda, PA; (Y); Church Yth Grp; Drama Clb; SADD; Band; Chorus; Concert Band; Mrchg Band; School Play; Swing Chorus; Yrbk Stf; Drma.

HOLLAND, SHELBY; Warwick HS; Leola, PA; (S); 19/222; Exploring; Nwsp Ed-Chief; Nwsp Phtg; Nwsp Rptr; Yrbk Stf; Var Capt Tennis; Var Trk; High Hon Roll; NHS; VA Tech; Archit.

HOLLAND, VICTORIA L; Norristown Area HS; Jeffersonville, PA; (Y); 38/369; Pres FCA; Intnl Clb; School Play; Yrbk Stf; Lit Mag; Rep Sr Cls; Var Lcrss; Var Swmmng; Hon Roll; NHS; Achvt Acad Awd 86; Ladies Aux Awd 86; Lock Haven U; Bio Chem.

HOLLANDER, DAVID L; Sewickley Acad; Pittsburgh, PA; (Y); 13/61; Drama Clb; Varsity Clb; School Play; Var Socr; Var Wrstlng; Gov Hon Prg Awd; High Hon Roll; School Musical; Variety Show; Acting.

HOLLAWAY, JOHN; Burgettstown SR JR HS; Burgettstown, PA; (Y); 84/180; CA U.

HOLLE, ERIC; Fairview HS; Fairview, PA; (Y); Debate Tm; Speech Tm; Varsity Clb; Var Socr; Var Bsktbl; JV Ftbl; Wt Lftg; Hon Roll.

HOLLEN, GARETH ERIC; Greater Johnstown SR HS; Johnstown, PA; (Y); Pres Church Yth Grp; JA; Concert Band; Jazz Band; Mrchg Band; Orch; Stage Crew; Nwsp Rptr; Rep Stu Cncl; Var L Tennis; Acctng.

HOLLENBACH, DEAN; Shikellamy HS; Sunbury, PA; (Y); Boy Scts; CAP; Wrstlng; Cmptr Elec.

HOLLENBACH, MICHELE L; Mifflinburg Area HS; New Berlin, PA; (Y); 14/169; German Clb; Trs Key Clb; Concert Band; Mrchg Band; Trs Frsh Cls; VP Soph Cls; Stu Cncl; Capt Bsktbl; Var JV Sftbl; NHS; Pennsylvn House Schlrhsp 86-87; Bloomsburg U; Accntng.

HOLLENBAUG, KENNETH; S Middleton HS; Boiling Spgs, PA; (Y); 30/113; Art Clb; Aud/Vis; Boy Scts; Ski Clb; Ftbl; Golf; Hon Roll; NPEA 84; NLSA 85; Shippensburg U; Accntnt.

HOLLENBAUGH, DALE; Milton Area HS; Milton, PA; (Y); 8/200; Church Yth Grp; Computer Clb; Latin Clb; Library Aide; Rep Stu Cncl; Hon Roll; NHS; Latin Awd.

HOLLENBAUGH, DAVID; New Hope-Solebury HS; Solebury, PA; (S); 3/82; Church Yth Grp; FBLA; Mathletes; Ski Clb; Band; Yrbk Stf; Rep Stu Cncl; Var L Socr; High Hon Roll; NHS; Bucks Cnty Advnc Sci Smnrs 84-85; Bus.

HOLLER, BECKY L; Springdale HS; Cheswick, PA; (Y); Church Yth Grp; Concert Band; Mrchg Band; Yrbk Stf; Var L Bsktbl; JV Cheerleading; JV Var Sftbl; High Hon Roll; NHS; Outstndng Achvt Awds-Math, Engl 86.

HOLLIDAY, JEFF; Sharpsville Area HS; Sharpsville, PA; (Y); Math Clb; Science Clb; Spanish Clb; JV Var Bsktbl; Im Wt Lftg; Hon Roll; Schlstc Achvt Awd 85; Bus.

HOLLINGER, BRIAN; Garden Spot HS; New Holland, PA; (Y); Boy Scts; Church Yth Grp; Chorus; Swing Chorus; Rep Frsh Cls; Rep Soph Cls; Rep Jr Cls; Var Capt Bsktbl; JV Var Socr; JV Var Trk; MVP Bsktbl; Sprtn Awd; Engrg.

HOLLINGER, CHRIS; Northern Bedford County HS; Roaring Spgs, PA; (Y); Math Tm; SADD; Chorus; School Musical; Stage Crew; Hon Roll; NHS; Am Math Comptn 86; Oral Roberts U; Elect Engr.

HOLLINGER, GREGORY; The Harrisburg Acad; Hershey, PA; (Y); 12/31; Ski Clb; Var Socr; Silar Awd Mst Imprvd Stu 83-84; Crimnlgy.

HOLLINGER, JANICE; Riverview HS; Verona, PA; (Y); 1/118; Church Yth Grp; Exploring; French Clb; Key Clb; Yrbk Stf; High Hon Roll; NHS; U Pittsburgh; Lang Tchr.

HOLLINGER, PAM; Penn Cambria HS; Lilly, PA; (Y); Drama Clb; Ski Clb; Hon Roll; Prsdntl Phy Ftnss Awd 82-83; PA ST; Law.

HOLLINGSWORTH, BENJAMIN ERIC; York Catholic HS; Dover, PA; (Y); SADD; Varsity Clb; Rep Frsh Cls; Rep Soph Cls; Rep Jr Cls; Rep Sr Cls; Stu Cncl; JV Bsktbl; JV Ftbl; Var Golf; Amer Racquetbl Assn 84; PA ST U; Pediatrician.

HOLLINGSWORTH, G SCOTT; Blacklick Valley JR SR HS; Ebensburg, PA; (S); Ski Clb; Hon Roll; NEDT Awd; Mech Engrng.

HOLLINGSWORTH, SUSAN; Franklin Regional SR HS; Jeannette, PA; (Y); 1/338; French Clb; Girl Scts; Sec Thesps; Band; School Musical; School Play; Stage Crew; NHS; Ntl Merit SF; Acad Ltr 83-85; Slvr Awd Grl Scts 83; Hghst Hon Rl 83-86; Math Tchr.

HOLLINSHEAD, SUSAN; Bethel Park SR HS; Bethel Park, PA; (Y); Pres VP JA; Sec SADD; Chorus; School Musical; Swing Chorus; Var L Swmmng; NHS; Synchronized Swmmng Capt 83-86; Cert Of Achvt From Cnty Commssnrs 86; Congrats On Achvts Senate PA 86.

HOLLIS, CHRISTINA; Leechburg Area HS; Leechburg, PA; (Y); Drama Clb; Chorus; Nwsp Stf; Yrbk Stf; Trs Soph Cls; VP Stu Cncl; Cheerleading; NHS.

HOLLIS, MARK; Bentworth HS; Bentley Ville, PA; (Y); Boy Scts; Church Yth Grp; Ski Clb; God Cntry Awd; Hon Roll; Asst SR Ptrl Ldr Sct Trp 85; Mem Ordr Of Arrow 83; Life Sct Wrkg Eagle Rnk 86.

HOLLIS, SUSAN; Steel Valley SR HS; Homestead, PA; (S); 13/243; Key Clb; Yrbk Sprt Ed; Hon Roll; Hlth Occuptn Stdts Of Amer 84-86; South Eastern Acad; Travl.

HOLLMAN, DEIRDRE; Harrisburg HS; Harrisburg, PA; (S); 2/485; French Clb; VP Science Clb; Chorus; School Play; Rep Stu Cncl; Var Tennis; High Hon Roll; Hon Roll; VP NHS; VFW Awd; PA Govs Schl For Sci Schlrshp 85; Chem.

HOLLOCK, LORI; Crestwood HS; Mountaintop, PA; (Y); Ski Clb; Stat Bsktbl; Var L Fld Hcky; Var L Sftbl; High Hon Roll; Hon Roll; NHS; Bio.

HOLLOWAY, ELAINE; John Harris HS; Harrisburg, PA; (Y); Capt Cheerleading; Swmmng; Hon Roll; NHS; Dance Awds 84-86; Black Hstry Mnth Essay Cont Hnr 86; Synchrnzd Swmmng Awd 84 & 86.

HOLLOWAY, MIKE; Kennett HS; Kennett Sq, PA; (Y); French Clb; Science Clb; JV Wrstlng; Hon Roll; NEDT Awd.

HOLLOWBUSH, KELLY; Brandywine Heights HS; Topton, PA; (Y); 10/126; Band; Chorus; Jazz Band; School Musical; Yrbk Phtg; VP Jr Cls; Sec Stu Cncl; Var Tennis; NHS; Drama Clb; Topton Rotary Clb Hnr Awd; Nrsng.

HOLLOWNICZKY, ROBYN; Blacklick Valley HS; Nanty-Glo, PA; (S); 10/96; Church Yth Grp; Ski Clb; Varsity Clb; VP Jr Cls; Var Bsktbl; Var Sftbl; Var Trk; High Hon Roll; Hon Roll; NHS; BV Ltr 84.

HOLLY, KAREN; Cameron Counmty HS; Emporium, PA; (Y); 12/91; Church Yth Grp; German Clb; Varsity Clb; Band; Chorus; Church Choir; Concert Band; Drm Mjr(t); Mrchg Band; Variety Show; Music.

HOLLY, VALERIE; Hazleton HS; Beaver Meadows, PA; (Y); Art Clb; Drama Clb; Ski Clb; School Musical; Hon Roll.

HOLM, JENNIFER L; Methacton HS; Audubon, PA; (Y); 15/332; Co-Capt Debate Tm; SADD; School Musical; Yrbk Ed-Chief; Pres Stu Cncl; Var Lcrss; Capt Twrlr; Cit Awd; Dnfth Awd; NHS; 2nd Pl Phila Yth Dbts Enrgy 86; Rtry Clb Awd, Lions Clb Awd 86; Dickinson Coll; Pltcl Sci.

HOLMAN, KRISTEN L; Quaker Valley HS; Sewickley, PA; (Y); Math Tm; Band; Drm Mjr(t); Mrchg Band; Pep Band; Symp Band; German Clb; Hon Roll; NHS; Ntl Merit Ltr.

HOLMES, LEE; Hopewell SR HS; Aliquippa, PA; (Y); Pres 4-H; Varsity Clb; Var JV Ftbl; Var Wt Lftg; Var Wrstlng; High Hon Roll; Hon Roll; Navy; Aerontcs Engr.

HOLMES, LEE; Saucon Valley HS; Hellertown, PA; (Y); 6/146; German Clb; Science Clb; Chorus; School Musical; Swing Chorus; Rep Stu Cncl; Var L Cheerleading; Mgr(s); JV Sftbl; NHS.

HOLMES, LESLIE; Moravian Acad; Bethelem, PA; (Y); Church Yth Grp; Hosp Aide; Math Tm; Model UN; Ski Clb; Acpl Chr; Chorus; School Play; Hon Roll; Rotary Awd; Harvard; Med.

HOLMES, MICHAEL; Governor Mifflin HS; Mohnton, PA; (Y); 9/300; Concert Band; Mrchg Band; Stat Bsbl; High Hon Roll; H S Hnr Scty 85-86.

HOLMES, SCOTT; Canton Area JR SR HS; Roaring Branch, PA; (Y); 33/132; Church Yth Grp; Letterman Clb; Chorus; Concert Band; Mrchg Band; Rep Stu Cncl; L Stat Bsbl; Var L Ftbl; JV Var Wrstlng; Messiah Coll; Bio.

HOLMGREN, JAMES; Central York SR HS; York, PA; (Y); Boy Scts; Exploring; German Clb; JA; Varsity Clb; Stage Crew; L Socr; Hon Roll; Penn ST; Elmntry Ed.

HOLOMAN, TRICIA; West Mifflin Area HS; West Mifflin, PA; (Y); Dance Clb; Drama Clb; Hosp Aide; Key Clb; Letterman Clb; Varsity Clb; VICA; Capt Drill Tm; Stu Cncl; Capt Pom Pon; PA Mdrn Ms Pgnt 1st Rnr Up 85; 3rd Pl HOSA Tlnt Show 86; Point Pk Coll; Dance.

HOLOWACH, DEBBIE; Upper Dublin HS; Ambler, PA; (Y); Pep Clb; Yrbk Stf; Cheerleading; JV Tennis.

HOLSCHUH, DOUGLAS; Wyoming Area SR HS; Exeter, PA; (Y); 12/247; French Clb; Rep Stu Cncl; Crs Cntry; Trk; High Hon Roll; Hon Roll; NHS; Ntl Merit Ltr; PA ST U; Aerospc Engrng.

HOLSINGER, MARTHA; Lebanon Catholic HS; Lebanon, PA; (Y); 9/63; Ski Clb; Speech Tm; Band; Chorus; Drm Mjr(t); Jazz Band; School Play; Trs Stu Cncl; JP Sousa Awd; NHS; Dist Band & Orch 82-86; Reg Band 86; PA Gov Schl For The Arts-Music 85; George Washington U.

HOLT, CHRIS; Williamsport HS; Williamsport, PA; (Y); 120/600; Var L Ftbl; Var L Trk; Acctg.

HOLT, LISA; Curwensville Area HS; Curwensville, PA; (Y); 5/114; Drama Clb; French Clb; FNA; Hosp Aide; School Play; Im Capt Socr; Im Vllybl; Hon Roll; NHS; Upwrd Bound 85-86; Presdntl Clsrm Yng Amer 86; Bus Adm.

HOLT, LYNN; Du Bois Area HS; Du Bois, PA; (Y); 48/280; Trs Girl Scts; Trs Intnl Clb; Chorus; Flag Corp; Mrchg Band; Hon Roll; Rdlgc Tech.

HOLT, MELISSA; York Catholic HS; York, PA; (Y); 10/169; German Clb; Girl Scts; VP JA; Chorus; School Play; Nwsp Rptr; High Hon Roll; NHS; Accntng.

HOLTER, MARK; Berwick SR HS; Berwick, PA; (Y); FBLA; Bsktbl; Bloomsburg U; Accounting.

HOLTGRAVER, LESLIE; Shaler Area SR HS; Pittsburgh, PA; (Y); Hosp Aide; JA; Hon Roll; Pittsburgh U; Med.

HOLTHOUSE, KHLAR; Corry Area HS; Corry, PA; (S); 32/215.

HOLTSMASTER, WALTER; Susquehanna Community HS; Thompson, PA; (S); Ski Clb; Yrbk Stf; Trs Sr Cls; Capt Var Ftbl; Capt Var Wrstlng; Hon Roll; NHS; Ntl Merit Ltr; PA ST Moravian Clg; Micrbio.

HOLTZ, BONNIE; Mercyhurst Preparatory Schl; Erie, PA; (Y); 12/150; Key Clb; SADD; High Hon Roll; Hon Roll; NHS; PA Jr Acad Of Sci 1st Rgnls & 2nd St 85; COVE/Volntr Div-United Way Of Erie Cnty 86; IN U Of PA; Phy Ed.

HOLTZ, TARA; Mt Lebanon HS; Pittsburgh, PA; (Y); Church Yth Grp; Cmnty Wkr; Dance Clb; Ski Clb; Spanish Clb; Mrchg Band; Pres Frsh Cls; Pres Soph Cls; Pres Jr Cls; JV Cheerleading; Bus Adm.

HOLTZLEICER, DEBRA; Catasauqua HS; Catasauqua, PA; (Y); Lit Mag; Stu Cncl; Var Cheerleading; JV Fld Hcky; Powder Puff Ftbl; Var Trk; Rotary Awd; Chem Engrng.

HOLTZMAN JR, CHARLES D; Bishop Mc Cort HS; Johnstown, PA; (Y); Aud/Vis; Boy Scts; German Clb; Math Clb; Chorus; Church Choir; High Hon Roll; Lion Awd; Mu Alp Tht; NHS; Acad All Am 86; U Pittsburgh; Bus.

HOLTZMAN, CHERYL; Mc Keesport SR HS; Mc Keesport, PA; (Y); Powder Puff Ftbl; Hon Roll; Pitt U; Psych.

HOLUB, TIMOTHY; Bentworth HS; Bentleyville, PA; (Y); Boy Scts; Exploring; Band; Concert Band; Jazz Band; Mrchg Band; Hon Roll; Prfct Atten Awd; WA County Band 85 & 86; Mc Donalds All Am Band 86.

HOLUPKA, HEIDI; Kiski Area HS; Leechburg, PA; (Y); German Clb; JA; Pep Clb; Spanish Clb; SADD; Color Guard; High Hon Roll; NHS; Chorus; Mrchg Band; Top Ten 83-84.

HOLY, TIM; Upper Dublin HS; Maple Glen, PA; (Y); Am Leg Boys St; Pres Church Yth Grp; VP Debate Tm; Math Tm; Scholastic Bowl; Science Clb; JV Crs Cntry; JV Trk; NHS; Ntl Merit Ltr; 1st Pl Cnty Fair & 4th Pl Chem At Intl Sci & Engrng Fair 8l; Chem.

HOLYFIELD, RICARDO; Peabody HS; Pittsburgh, PA; (S); 19/235; Boys Clb Am; FCA; German Clb; Bsktbl; Crs Cntry; Trk; Cit Awd; High Hon Roll; Hon Roll; NHS; Pitt Univ; Chem Engrng.

HOLZER, STACEY; Churchill HS; Pittsburgh, PA; (Y); GAA; Concert Band; Orch; Pres Frsh Cls; Pres Soph Cls; JV Var Bsktbl; Var L Sftbl; Hon Roll; 4-Yrs Sftbl Ltr 83-86; Hmcmng Crt 86; Snowbl Qun 83; CA ST PA; Tchr-Mntlly Hndcpd.

HOLZINGER, JODY; Liberty HS; Bethlehem, PA; (Y); 45/407; Pres Trs Church Yth Grp; VP DECA; Exploring; FBLA; Var Gym; High Hon Roll; Hon Roll; DECA Troph Gen Mrch 84-86; DECA Medl Humn Rel 84; FBLA 4th Pl Bus Engl 86; Churchmans Bus Schl; Bus.

HOMAN, DOUG; Punxsutawney Area HS; Rochester Mills, PA; (Y); Hon Roll.

HOMAN, GARY; Towanda Area HS; Towanda, PA; (Y); 25/170; Church Yth Grp; Rptr 4-H; Spanish Clb; Prfct Atten Awd.

HOMCHENKO, JULIE; Mercyhurst Prep Schl; Erie, PA; (Y); 73/150; French Clb; Pep Clb; Bio.

HOMER, BETH; Greenwood HS; Millerstown, PA; (S); 11/65; VP Church Yth Grp; Varsity Clb; Trs Band; Trs Chorus; School Musical; Nwsp Stf; Var Bsktbl; Var Fld Hcky; Var Sftbl; Hon Roll; Penn ST U; Chem Tchr.

HOMER, JANELL; Grove City HS; Grove City, PA; (Y); Intnl Clb; Powder Puff Ftbl; Im Var Vllybl; Hon Roll; Vrsty Ltr Vlybl 85-86; Polic Offcr.

HOMICK JR, PAUL S; Highlands SR HS; Brackenridge, PA; (Y); Exploring; Chrmn Intnl Clb; Key Clb; SADD; Band; Rep Jr Cls; Rep Pres Stu Cncl; Jr NHS; NHS; Computer Clb; Auditor Jednota Post 280 86; Christn Yth Ensem 86; Pre-Med.

HOMISON, RENE; Hempfield Area HS; Greensburg, PA; (Y); 72/800; Library Aide; Spanish Clb; Nwsp Stf; Hon Roll; NHS.

HOMMAN, MICHELLE; Clearfield Area HS; Bigler, PA; (Y); DECA; Hosp Aide; Office Aide; Church Choir; Bradford Schl; Retal Mgmnt.

HOMME, JACKIE; Bentworth HS; Ellsworth, PA; (Y); 11/140; Exploring; Varsity Clb; Chorus; Concert Band; Flag Corp; JV Bsktbl; High Hon Roll; Hon Roll; NHS; Prfct Atten Awd; Vet Med.

HOMNACK, PAUL; J S Fine HS; Nanticoke, PA; (Y); Boy Scts; Computer Clb; VICA; L Swmmng; Trk; Hon Roll; Prfct Atten Awd; 1st Comp Sci VICA Cmptn 86; 2nd Comp Sci Penn St JR Acad Sci Cmptn 86; Comp Sci.

HOMOLA, MICHELLE; Cardinal Ohara HS; Chester, PA; (Y); Civic Clb; Cmnty Wkr; German Clb; PA ST; Astronmy.

HOMULKA, GARY J; Mt Pleasant Area SR HS; Mt Pleasant, PA; (Y); 16/256; Latin Clb; Im Vllybl; Cit Awd; Hon Roll; NHS; Humanities Day Awd; Var Schltc Awd; St Vincent Coll; Chem.

HOMZA, SUZANNE; North Hills HS; Pittsburgh, PA; (S); 7/507; Yrbk Bus Mgr; Yrbk Stf; Var Capt Socr; High Hon Roll; NHS; Ntl Merit Ltr; Keywanettes; Nwsp Stf; Trk; PA Hghr Educ Asst Agncy-Cert Merit 85; Eco.

HONEY, CHRISTINE; Strong Vincent HS; Erie, PA; (Y); FBLA; Drill Tm; Erie Bus Ctr; Exec Secretarial.

HONEYWELL, SANDRA D; Lake-Lehman HS; Hunlock Creek, PA; (Y); 13/177; 4-H; Drill Tm; Var L Vllybl; 4-H Awd; Jr NHS; NHS; PA ST; Vet Med.

HONICKER, TRESSA; Hazleton HS; Hazleton, PA; (Y); Drama Clb; FBLA; Pep Clb; Ski Clb; Thesps; School Play; Variety Show; Ed Nwsp Stf; Ed Yrbk Stf; L Crs Cntry; Am Leg Awd 84; Hnbl Mntn Span Lang Cntst 84; Schlrshp Awd To Attend Penn Free Ent Week (Pfew); Acctg.

HONS, DEBRA; Tunkhannock Area HS; Dalton, PA; (S); 21/330; Church Yth Grp; Letterman Clb; Spanish Clb; Band; Concert Band; Mrchg Band; Vllybl; Hon Roll; NHS; JR SR Hstrns; Acadmc All Amer Awd 85; Millersville U; Elem Ed.

HOOD, DIANNA; Hempfield SR HS; Greensburg, PA; (Y).

HOOD, HEATHER; Meadville SR HS; Meadville, PA; (Y); 17/280; Varsity Clb; Nwsp Bus Mgr; JV L Bsktbl; Var L Vllybl; Hon Roll; NHS; Law.

HOOD, JOHN; Cardinal Brennan HS; Ashland, PA; (Y); Boy Scts; Church Yth Grp; Office Aide; Ski Clb; Yrbk Phtg; Yrbk Stf; Rep Stu Cncl; Wrstlng; Bus Mgr.

HOOK, MICHELLE; Hempfield Area SR HS; Greensburg, PA; (Y); AFS; Exploring; Spanish Clb; Orch; High Hon Roll; Jr NHS; NHS; Spanish NHS; Acad Awds Banquet 85-86; 3rd Pl Spn Dramatic Presntatn Humanities Day 86; Spanish.

HOOK, MICHELLE; Solanco SR HS; Peach Bottom, PA; (Y); Drama Clb; Spanish Clb; Thesps; Varsity Clb; School Play; Rep Stu Cncl; Var Tennis; JV Trk; Hon Roll; NHS; Solanco Schlr 84; Schlstc Art Awd Winnr 86; Gftd Prog; Intl Bus.

HOOKS, AMY; Highlands SR HS; Brackenridge, PA; (Y); 12/277; Hosp Aide; Library Aide; Band; Concert Band; Jazz Band; Hst Mrchg Band; Pep Band; High Hon Roll; Jr NHS; NHS; Bus, Profssnl Wmns Clb Grl Yr 86; U Of Pittsburgh; Nrsng.

HOOKS, TAMI; West Greene HS; New Freeport, PA; (S); 1/70; Drama Clb; Letterman Clb; School Play; Var Capt Bsktbl; Var Capt Trk; Var Vllybl; DAR Awd; Pres NHS; Dance Clb; GAA; Lions Clb Stu Of Mnth 85; Voted Mst Lkly To Succeed 86; TX Christian U; Bus.

HOOLEY, PEGGY; Bellefonte SR HS; Bellefonte, PA; (Y); Trs Letterman Clb; Ski Clb; Chorus; Var Capt Cheerleading; Ftbl; Powder Puff Ftbl; Trk; PA ST U.

HOOPER, ANGELA; St Marus Area HS; St Marys, PA; (Y); 9/300; Letterman Clb; Sec Frsh Cls; Sec Soph Cls; Rep Stu Cncl; Var Capt Bsktbl; Var Capt Sftbl; Var Capt Vllybl; High Hon Roll; NHS; Knox Coll Alumni At Large Schlrshp 8690; Stackpole Corp Schlrshp 86-90; Penntech Schrlshp 86; Knox Coll; Elect Engr.

HOOPER, LISA; Bishop Guilfoyle HS; Altoona, PA; (Y); Church Yth Grp; Ski Clb; Pres SADD; Mrchg Band; Yrbk Stf; Capt Twrlr; Hon Roll; NHS; Penn ST U.

HOOSE, BRADLEY D; Troy SR HS; Troy, PA; (Y); FFA; Letterman Clb; Ftbl; Wrstlng; Nclr Engrng.

HOOVER, BRIAN; Bellefonte HS; Bellefonte, PA; (Y); 71/216; Church Yth Grp; Political Wkr; Bsbl; Hon Roll; Drexel U; Hist.

HOOVER, DARYL; Eastern HS; York, PA; (Y); Chess Clb; Church Yth Grp; High Hon Roll; Hon Roll; Erly Admssn Stndt 86-87; Psych.

HOOVER, DAVE; Moniteau HS; W Sunbury, PA; (Y); Trs Spanish Clb; Chorus; Var L Bsktbl; Im Crs Cntry; Var L Trk; Hon Roll.

HOOVER, ELEANOR; Hanover HS; Hanover, PA; (Y); 21/104; Church Yth Grp; Cmnty Wkr; Chorus; Orch; School Play; Variety Show; Trs Jr Cls; Trs Sr Cls; Rep Stu Cncl; Var Bsktbl; Amer Lgn Awd 82-83; USC; Bus.

HOOVER, ELIZABETH; Bishop Guilfoyle HS; Altoona, PA; (S); 9/149; Science Clb; Chorus; Yrbk Stf; Stu Cncl; JV Bsktbl; VP Vllybl; High Hon Roll; Hon Roll; Natl Phys Ed Awd; PA ST U; Music Ed.

HOOVER, JAMES; Sullivan County HS; Forksville, PA; (Y); 21/94; Key Clb; Band; Chorus; Jazz Band; Mrchg Band; Mgr(s); Williamsport Area CC; Comp Sci.

HOOVER, JAMES M; Moon SR HS; Coraopolis, PA; (Y); Church Yth Grp; German Clb; Key Clb; Band; Symp Band; Off Frsh Cls; Off Soph Cls; Off Jr Cls; Off Sr Cls; Trs Stu Cncl; Soc Of Dstngshd Amer Stus 85-86; Sccr WPIAL Chmpns 85; Sccr PIAA ST Fnlst 85; Bus.

HOOVER, JENNIFER; Vincentian HS; Allison Park, PA; (Y); 1/64; Service Clb; Rep Soph Cls; Rep Jr Cls; JV Capt Bsktbl; Var L Fld Hcky; High Hon Roll; NHS; Ntl Merit Ltr; Comp Sci.

HOOVER, JILL; Pequea Valley HS; Gordonville, PA; (Y); 1/126; Church Yth Grp; Pres 4-H; Band; Chorus; Concert Band; Madrigals; School Musical; Lion Awd; VP NHS; Val; G Frtny Mem Schlrshp Awd 86; PA ST; Bus.

HOOVER, JOEL; Hershey SR HS; Hershey, PA; (Y); Ski Clb; Stage Crew; Stu Cncl; Var Bsbl; Var Socr; Hon Roll; St Francis Coll; Engrng.

HOOVER, NANCY; Big Spring HS; Newville, PA; (Y); 8/113; Band; Concert Band; Mrchg Band; Var Powder Puff Ftbl; High Hon Roll; Merit Awd Engl Achvt 86; Frnch Allnc Awd 86; Penn St U; Nrsng.

HOOVER, RICH; Northwestern HS; Albion, PA; (Y); 11/176; Cmnty Wkr; Yrbk Stf; Var Capt Crs Cntry; Var Capt Trk; Hon Roll; NHS; Contng Educ Awd 84 & 86; Cert Of Apprctn 86; Penn ST U; Prks Mngmnt.

HOOVER, RONALEE; Philipsburg Osceola Mills Area HS; Osceola Mills, PA; (Y); Hon Roll; Penn ST U; Art.

HOOVER, SCOTT; Bald Eagle Area HS; Moshannon, PA; (Y); Computer Clb; French Clb; Library Aide; Teachers Aide; Band; Chorus; Im Bowling; Mgr(s); Im Trk; Im Wt Lftg; Home Ec.

HOOVER, STEPHEN; Li Gonier Valley HS; Ligonier, PA; (Y); 11/160; Computer Clb; Debate Tm; Library Aide; Spanish Clb; Band; Chorus; Mrchg Band; School Play; Stu Cncl; Trk; Schlstc Awd 86; Pres Acdmc Ftns Awd 86; U Scranton; Physcl Thrpy.

HOOVER, TABATHA; Punxsutawney Area SR HS; Punxu, PA; (Y); FBLA; Office Aide; Dubois Bus Clg Schlrshp; Mary Ann Irvin Schlrshp Found; Du Bois Bus Clg; Exec Sec.

HOOVER, TERESA; Millersburg Area HS; Millersburg, PA; (Y); Hon Roll; Hm Ec 86; Bus.

HOOVER, THERESA; Southwestern HS; Hanover, PA; (Y); 31/209; Church Yth Grp; JA; Band; Concert Band; Hon Roll; NHS; Rtry Yth Exchng Stu India; Bible Clb SR Rep; U Of Steubenvl; Elmntry Spcl Ed.

HOOVER, VERNA; Bald Eagle Area HS; Karthaus, PA; (Y); 29/209; Pres Church Yth Grp; VP Spanish Clb; SADD; Chorus; School Musical; School Play; Ed Nwsp Stf; Rep Stu Cncl; Powder Puff Ftbl; Hon Roll; Pre-Med.

HOOVLER, MARK; General Mc Lane HS; Mckean, PA; (Y); 19/221; Boy Scts; Spanish Clb; Teachers Aide; Rep Yrbk Stf; Rep Stu Cncl; High Hon Roll; Hon Roll; NHS; Prjct Enhance 84-87; Miss Congeniality Saegertwn Smmrfst Pgnt 85; Pre-Med.

HOPEWELL, VERONICA; Bethlehem Catholic HS; Bethlehem, PA; (Y); Key Clb; Science Clb; Teachers Aide; School Musical; School Play; Yrbk Phtg; Cheerleading; Socr; Hon Roll; PA ST; Mngmnt.

HOPKINS, DAWN; Corry Area HS; Corry, PA; (Y); Trs Church Yth Grp; Dance Clb; Drama Clb; Library Aide; Spanish Clb; SADD; Chorus; Church Choir; School Musical; School Play; Soc Work.

HOPKINS, GARY; West Greene HS; Nineveh, PA; (S); Trs Church Yth Grp; Drama Clb; Ski Clb; Nwsp Rptr; Nwsp Stf; Yrbk Bus Mgr; Pres Frsh Cls; Rep Soph Cls; VP Jr Cls; Rep Stu Cncl; Intl Bus.

HOPKINS, JEFF; William Penn Charter Schl; Oreland, PA; (Y); FCA; Hosp Aide; Intnl Clb; Model UN; Science Clb; Ski Clb; School Play; Stage Crew; Nwsp Stf; Yrbk Stf; Pila Clscl Soc, Amer Clscl League Certs Of Merit Cum Laude 85; All Time Schl Rcrd-Shtl Hrdls Relay 86; Law.

HOPKINS, LISA; Western Beaver JR SR HS; Midland, PA; (Y); Pres Church Yth Grp; Church Choir; Symp Band; Yrbk Ed-Chief; Pres Stu Cncl; Capt Bowling; Capt Cheerleading; Cit Awd; High Hon Roll; NHS; Geneva Schlr Awd 86; Tri-State Area Ctzns Schlrshp Fndtn Awd 86; Geneva Coll.

HOPKINS, MARY CLARE; Bishop Hannan HS; Scranton, PA; (Y); 22/124; Church Yth Grp; Cmnty Wkr; Drama Clb; Chorus; Church Choir; School Musical; Variety Show; Stu Cncl; Hon Roll; NHS; Bishops Awd-Outstndng Achvt Religious Ed 86; Hghst Avg-Theology 86; Bloomsburg U; Elem Ed.

HOPKINS, SETH; Northern Potter HS; Ulysses, PA; (Y); 5/85; Debate Tm; Rptr FFA; Model UN; Varsity Clb; Chorus; Pres Soph Cls; Pres Jr Cls; VP Stu Cncl; Bsktbl; Socr; Bio.

HOPKINS, SHERRY; State College Area SR HS; State College, PA; (Y); Art Clb; Church Yth Grp; 4-H; FHA; Orch; 4-H Awd; Hon Roll; NEDT Awd; Awd Outstndng Sci Stdnt 84-85; Art.

HOPKINS, SUSAN; Bellefonte Area HS; Bellefonte, PA; (Y); 17/217; SADD; Band; Capt Flag Corp; Yrbk Stf; Rep Soph Cls; Rep Stu Cncl; Powder Puff Ftbl; Hon Roll; Sec NHS; PA ST U; Ed.

HOPKINS, SUSAN; Serra Catholic HS; Mckeesport, PA; (Y); AFS; Church Yth Grp; Drama Clb; Chorus; Capt Drill Tm; Mrchg Band; School Musical; School Play; Powder Puff Ftbl; Co-Capt Twrlr; Merit Awd Western Lit; Drill Tm Awd Miss Mon-Youghette 84; ICM Schl; Lgl Sec.

HOPKINS, TRACEY; Wilmington Area HS; New Wilmingtn, PA; (Y); Latin Clb; Pep Clb; Gym; Trk; Hon Roll; Slippery Rock U.

HOPLER, DAVID; Bethlehem Catholic School; Bethlehem, PA; (Y); 66/221; Boys Clb Am; Boy Scts; Key Clb; Ski Clb; Var Bsbl; Var Socr; Hon Roll; Wldlf Mgmt.

HOPPLE, ALLYSON; Annville-Cleona HS; Cleona, PA; (Y); 47/115; VP Church Yth Grp; French Clb; SADD; Band; Concert Band; Mrchg Band; Pep Band; Lit Mag; Fld Hcky; NHS; Lebanon Vally Col Hnrs Bnd 85-86; Messiah Coll; Early Chldhd Educ.

HOPPLE, DALENA; E L Meyers HS; Wilkes Barre, PA; (Y); Art Clb; Church Yth Grp; Computer Clb; Exploring; Pep Clb; Red Cross Aide; Spanish Clb; SADD; Tennis; NHS; Presdntl Acad Fitness Awd; Wilkes Coll; Nrsng.

HOPSON, CHERYL; Seneca HS; Union City, PA; (Y); 11/135; 4-H; Band; Concert Band; Mrchg Band; Hon Roll; Penn ST-BAHREND; Pre-Law.

HOPWOOD, JOHN; Nazareth Area SR HS; Bethlehem, PA; (Y); Camera Clb; Drama Clb; School Musical; School Play; Stage Crew; Var Crs Cntry; Hon Roll; Archlgy.

HORAK, ELLEN; Springdale HS; Springdale, PA; (Y); Church Yth Grp; Exploring; German Clb; Teachers Aide; Band; Color Guard; Concert Band; Mrchg Band; Yrbk Stf; Elem Schl Tchr.

HORAN, SUZANNE; Carbondale JR SR HS; Carbondale, PA; (Y); FBLA; FHA; Ski Clb; Drm Mjr(t); Capt Twrlr; Hon Roll; Bus.

HORANSKY, AMELIA L; Greater Latrobe SR HS; Latrobe, PA; (Y); 28/336; Girl Scts; Am Leg Aux Girls St; Band; Concert Band; Sec Jazz Band; Mrchg Band; Pep Band; School Musical; Symp Band; High Hon Roll; Presdntl Acdmc Fitness Awd 85-86; St Vincent Coll; Med Tech.

HORCHAR, TOM; Homer Center HS; Coral, PA; (Y); 26/98; French Clb; Varsity Clb; School Musical; Stu Cncl; Var Bsktbl; Var L Ftbl; Var L Trk.

HORCHEN, MISSY; Du Bois Area HS; Dubois, PA; (Y); Art Clb; Camera Clb; Cmnty Wkr; Computer Clb; Nwsp Stf; Yrbk Stf; Mat Maids; Vllybl; Hon Roll; Pupil Enrchmt Prgm 77-86; Upwrd Bnd 84-86; Cmnctns.

HORCHLER, MATTHEW; Wilmington Area HS; New Wilmington, PA; (Y); 4-H; Sec Pres FFA; Im Bsktbl; Var L Trk; Exhbtn-Ntl Lvstck Shws 85-86; Penn ST U; Lndscp Arch.

HORCHOLIC, DANA; Swissvale HS; Pittsburg, PA; (Y); 6/206; Church Yth Grp; French Clb; Y-Teens; Acpl Chr; Mrchg Band; School Musical; Stage Crew; Yrbk Stf; High Hon Roll; NHS; Elec Engrng.

HORD, KIMBERLY; Altoona Area HS; Altoona, PA; (Y); Cmnty Wkr; Key Clb; Library Aide; Science Clb; Service Clb; Chorus; Color Guard; Off Jr Cls; Var L Vllybl; High Hon Roll; IN U PA; Bio.

HORECKY, MAGGIE; St Cyril Acad; Danville, PA; (Y); 3/13; Drama Clb; Sec Key Clb; Math Tm; Quiz Bowl; Spanish Clb; Chorus; School Play; Stage Crew; VP Frsh Cls; Pres Soph Cls; Phrmcst.

HORENSKY, SUSAN; Hazleton HS; Drums, PA; (Y); FBLA; Swmmng; High Hon Roll; Lawyer.

HORGAN, COLLEEN; Saint Basil Acad; Philadelphia, PA; (Y); Latin Clb; Science Clb; Orch; Fld Hcky; Socr; Mntgmry Cnty Sci Rsrch Cmptn 84&85; Nuclear Engnrng.

HORINKO, MARIA TERESA; Hazleton HS; Hazleton, PA; (Y); Office Aide; Science Clb; Service Clb; Y-Teens; Color Guard; Flag Corp; Yrbk Stf; High Hon Roll; Hon Roll; NHS; Ntl Hnr Soc 85-86; Bloomsburg U; Spch Pathlgy.

HORN, DEDRA ANN; Huntingdon Area HS; Mill Creek, PA; (Y); 21/234; Am Leg Aux Girls St; Hosp Aide; Key Clb; Service Clb; SADD; Variety Show; Yrbk Stf; Var L Cheerleading; High Hon Roll; NHS; Outstndg Clb Svc Key Clb 85; Psych.

HORN, RICK; West Mifflin Area HS; W Mifflin, PA; (Y); 58/360; JV Bsktbl; Var L Ftbl; Hon Roll; NHS; YABA Trvl Lg Chmpns 86; U Of Ptsbrgh; Elctrcl Engrng.

HORNAK, GENA NICOLE; Boyertown SR HS; Perkiomenville, PA; (Y); 35/485; Hosp Aide; JA; Latin Clb; Math Clb; Spanish Clb; SADD; Drill Tm; Mrchg Band; Cit Awd; High Hon Roll; Pre Med.

HORNAK, LORIE; Pleasant Valley HS; Gilbert, PA; (Y); Drama Clb; Math Clb; Ski Clb; School Play; Ed Yrbk Stf; Rep Jr Cls; Rep Stu Cncl; Trk; Majorette; Tutor; Nrsng.

HORNBERGER, DALE; Millersburg Area HS; Millersburg, PA; (Y); 23/87; Boy Scts; Church Yth Grp; Church Choir; JV Ftbl; Var Wrstlng; Hon Roll.

HORNBERGER, JODIE; Line Mountain HS; Shamokin, PA; (Y); Church Yth Grp; FBLA; VP Key Clb; Church Choir; Co-Capt Drill Tm; School Musical; Stu Cncl; Hon Roll; Jr NHS; NHS; Cert Of Hon-Key Clb Pres 86; 2nd Pl Ldrshp Essy Cont 86; Cert Of Apprctn-Hands Acrs Amer 86; Chld Lf Spclst.

HORNBERGER, KRIS; Manheim Township HS; Lancaster, PA; (Y); 69/344; Church Yth Grp; Chrmn Key Clb; Nwsp Rptr; Nwsp Stf; Lit Mag; Var JV Bsktbl; Var L Fld Hcky; Powder Puff Ftbl; Im Vllybl; Hon Roll; Advrtising.

HORNBERGER, MICHELE; Glendale JR SR HS; Fallen Timber, PA; (Y); 12/73; Drama Clb; Library Aide; Science Clb; Mrchg Band; Nwsp Rptr; Nwsp Stf; Yrbk Phtg; Yrbk Stf; Sftbl; Hon Roll; Majrtt & 1st Co-Capt 83-86; Nike Clb 86; PA ST U; Pre-Law.

HORNBUCKLE, TIMOTHY; Chambersburg Area SR HS; Chambersburg, PA; (Y); 140/640; Church Yth Grp; Civic Clb; Spanish Clb; Speech Tm; Band; Church Choir; Var Bsbl; Stat Ftbl; JV Mgr(s); Var Score Keeper; Scty Dist Amer HS Stu 85-86; TX Tech U; Pre-Med.

HORNCHEK, ERIC; Harry S Truman HS; Fairless Hills, PA; (Y); Aud/Vis; Computer Clb; NFL; Service Clb; Pres Y-Teens; Stage Crew; High Hon Roll; NHS; Prfct Atten Awd; Stu Of Mnth 84; Ldr Of Yr YMCA Ldrs Clb 84-85; Comp Math Awd 85-86; Engrng.

HORNE, GREGORY; Columbia-Montour Vo-Tech; Berwick, PA; (S); 1/206; Letterman Clb; Math Tm; Scholastic Bowl; Science Clb; Spanish Clb; VICA; Yrbk Ed-Chief; Yrbk Stf; Pres Soph Cls; Pres Jr Cls; ST Sci Olympiad Fin Hnr Soc Pres 86; PA ST U; Mech Engrng.

HORNE, HEATHER; Yough HS; W Newton, PA; (Y); Church Yth Grp; Library Aide; Ski Clb; Badmtn; Stat Ftbl; Var Sftbl; Var Trk; Vllybl; Hon Roll; Ntl Merit Ltr; US Air Force Acad; Nuclear Eng.

HORNE, MICHAEL; Cocalico HS; Reinholds, PA; (Y); 11/167; Computer Clb; Spanish Clb; Rep Soph Cls; Off Jr Cls; Rep Sr Cls; Stu Cncl; High Hon Roll; NHS; Spanish NHS; Cert Of Merit For Excell Engl 85.

HORNE, MIKE; Southern Columbia Area HS; Catawissa, PA; (Y); Hon Roll; NHS; Thaddeus Trommeter Awd Outstndng Achvt Ind Arts 85-86; Welder Inst; Welding.

HORNE, RODGER; Spring-Ford HS; Royersford, PA; (Y); 15/237; Pres Church Yth Grp; FBLA; Library Aide; Nwsp Ed-Chief; Capt Socr; Capt Tennis; Hon Roll; NHS; Spring-Ford Rotary Clb Awd 86; Spring-Ford Booster Clb Schlrshp 86; Shippensburg U; Math.

HORNER, CHRISTOPHER; Karns City Area HS; Parker, PA; (Y); 32/120; SADD; Concert Band; Trs Mrchg Band; School Play; Band; Stage Crew; Variety Show; Rep Stu Cncl; All STAR Cncrt Band Awd, Cncl Sprtsmn Clbs Cnsrvtn Awd, PA Fish, Game Commssn Awds 85; IN U PA; Engl.

HORNER, MICHELLE; Punxsutawney Area SR HS; Punxsutawney, PA; (Y); 4/238; Pres Art Clb; VP Spanish Clb; Flag Corp; Variety Show; Yrbk Stf; Bsbl; Twrlr; High Hon Roll; NHS; Spn Hnrs 86; Top Engl Awd 86; Art Clb 86; Art Awds 86; IN U PA; Engl.

HORNER, PATRICIA; Conemaugh Twp Area HS; Boswell, PA; (Y); 15/105; Sec Church Yth Grp; French Clb; Chorus; School Musical; Yrbk Stf; All Cnty Chrs 84-86; Jerome PTO Schlrshp 86; Frnch Awd 86; IN U; Elem Ed.

HORNER, STEVEN; North Allegheny HS; Brentwood, TN; (Y); 46/605; Gov Hon Prg Awd; High Hon Roll; Hon Roll; Jr NHS; NHS; Wrld Yth Symphny Orchstra 85; Pittsbrgh Yth Symphny Orchstra 85-86; IN U Bloomington; Trombn Prfrm.

HORNEY, STEPHANIE; Cedar Crest HS; Lebanon, PA; (Y); Art Clb; Pep Clb; Spanish Clb; Stage Crew; Vllybl; PA Schl Of Arts; Cmmrcl Art.

HORNIK, LISA; Strong Vincent HS; Erie, PA; (Y); Aud/Vis; French Clb; Office Aide; Spanish Clb; Stage Crew; Cmmnctns.

HORNING, NEIL; Ephraton SR HS; Lititz, PA; (Y); 38/233; Chess Clb; Church Yth Grp; Hon Roll; 2nd Prz Wnr Grls Sr Essy 86; Trenton ST Coll; Cmmnctns.

HORNING, TRACY; Conestoga Valley HS; Lancaster, PA; (Y); Church Yth Grp; GAA; Hosp Aide; Red Cross Aide; Stage Crew; Bsktbl; Fld Hcky; Prfct Atten Awd; Schlstc Art Awd 86; Ltr Athltc Trng Vrsty Ltr 85; Physcl Thrpst.

HORNINGER, BETH; Liberty HS; Behtlehem, PA; (Y); 27/535; Cmnty Wkr; Hosp Aide; Var Capt Cheerleading; Im Powder Puff Ftbl; High Hon Roll; NHS; Ntl Chrldrs Assoc Awd Of Excel 85; Interact Clb 83-85; Prncpls Awd 2nd Pl Area Chrldng Comptn 85; Bio Sci.

HORNUNG, DYAN; Peters Township HS; Mcmurray, PA; (Y); Dance Clb; Drama Clb; FBLA; Key Clb; NFL; Ski Clb; SADD; Thesps; Chorus; Church Choir; Wrld Ptry Awd 86; PTA Awd 85; FL Southern Coll; Crmnl Jstc.

HORNUNG, STACEY; St Marys Area HS; Saint Marys, PA; (Y); Camera Clb; FBLA; Radio Clb; Speech Tm; Nwsp Phtg; Yrbk Phtg; Yrbk Stf; Stat Bsktbl; Phtgrphy.

HORNUNG, THOMAS P; Cardinal Brennan HS; Ashland, PA; (Y); 16/48; Church Yth Grp; German Clb; Stage Crew; Var Bsbl; JV Bsktbl; Var Ftbl; Wt Lftg; Hon Roll; NHS; Prfct Atten Awd; Bloomsburag U; Bus Acctg.

HORR, DIANNA; West Greene Middle-SR HS; Pittsburgh, PA; (Y); Dance Clb; Letterman Clb; Ski Clb; Varsity Clb; Nwsp Stf; Yrbk Stf; Trs Jr Cls; Sec Sr Cls; Rep Stu Cncl; Var Capt Cheerleading; Elite Chrldng Sqd WV U 85; Nmd Outstndng Chrldr WVU ICF Cmp 85; Acdmc Awd Exclnc Germn 84; Rdlgy.

HORST, JARED; Annville-Cleona HS; Cleona, PA; (Y); Church Yth Grp; Ski Clb; Chorus; Lit Mag; Var Socr; Var Trk; High Hon Roll; Hon Roll; NHS; 1st Pl HS Art Show 84-85; 1st Pl Fdrtn Wmns Clbs Art 84-85; Shlstc Art Awd 86; HS Art Shw Bst Of Shw; Mech Engnrng.

HORST, SHARON; Ephrata SR HS; Ephrata, PA; (Y); 38/234; Church Yth Grp; Nwsp Stf; Gregg Typng Awd 86; Gregg Shrthnd Awd 86; :Bus Sec.

HORST, STEVE; Lancaster Mennonite HS; Belvidere, NJ; (Y); Hon Roll; Messiah Clg; Mech Engrg.

HORSTMAN, JOSEPH; Moniteau HS; Slippery Rock, PA; (Y); Spanish Clb; Bsktbl.

HORT, KURT; Shikellamy HS; Northumberland, PA; (Y); 10/319; Am Leg Boys St; Varsity Clb; Var Bsbl; Var Bsktbl; Var Ftbl; Hon Roll; NHS; Pthlgst.

HORTER, CRAIG; Mechanicsburg Area HS; Mechanicsburg, PA; (Y); 89/311; Ski Clb; Ftbl; Trk; Hon Roll; Bus.

HORTING, SHANNON; Newport HS; Newport, PA; (Y); Am Leg Aux Girls St; Varsity Clb; Chorus; School Musical; Var L Bsktbl; Var L Fld Hcky; Hon Roll; NHS; Mdrn Music Mstrs.

HORTON, CLYDE; Ringgold HS; Donora, PA; (Y); Computer Clb; Letterman Clb; School Play; Var L Ice Hcky; Hon Roll; Bus.

HORTON, VICKI L; Hamburg Area HS; Hamburg, PA; (Y); 22/150; Sec French Clb; SADD; Pres Soph Cls; Pres Sr Cls; Trs Stu Cncl; L Capt Bowling; Var Trk; High Hon Roll; Hon Roll; NHS; Acad Lttr In Frnch 85; Gmbrg Outstndng Bwlr 86; Elem Schl Tchr.

HORVAT, DAVID J; Valley HS; Arnold, PA; (Y); VP JA; Band; Chorus; Orch; Rep Jr Cls; Capt L Ftbl; Capt L Trk; Outstndng HS Athl Of Amer 85-86; Case Western Rsrv U; Elec Engr.

HORVATH, GINA; Louis E Dieruff HS; Allentown, PA; (Y); Trs DECA; JA; Church Choir; Hon Roll; Prfct Atten Awd; 5th Pl Deca Conf 86; Johnson Wales; Fash Merch.

HORVATH, KAREN; Liberty HS; Bethlehem, PA; (Y); 116/475; Band; Concert Band; Mrchg Band.

HORVATH, LAURA J; Mid-Valley HS; Throop, PA; (Y); Church Yth Grp; Sec Drama Clb; Ski Clb; Band; Concert Band; Mrchg Band; School Play; Stage Crew; Nwsp Rptr; High Hon Roll; PA ST U; Psych.

HORVATH, ROBERT; Bethlehem Catholic HS; Bethlehem, PA; (S); 11/220; Key Clb; Math Tm; Var L Socr; NHS; Pre-Law.

HORVATH, THERESA; Lakeland JR SR HS; Carbondale, PA; (Y); Pep Clb; Spanish Clb; SADD; Flag Corp; Yrbk Stf; Var Capt Cheerleading; Cmnctns.

HORWATH, KIRSTEN; Bethleham Catholic HS; Bethlehem, PA; (Y); Var L Cheerleading; Merch.

HORWATT, CHARLENE; Hopewell SR HS; Aliquippa, PA; (S); 19/295; Hosp Aide; Latin Clb; Library Aide; Sec Spanish Clb; Orch; Var JV Bsktbl; Var L Sftbl; Capt L Vllybl; High Hon Roll; Jr NHS; Beaver County Times Acad All Star Tm 84-85 & 85-86.

HORWATT, CHRISTINA LYNN; Connellsville Area SR HS; Dunbar, PA; (Y); #181 In Class; Library Aide; Office Aide; SADD; Chorus; Color Guard; Mrchg Band; Rep Stu Cncl; Var Cheerleading; Vllybl; Hon Roll; Recvd Schlrshp Pittsburgh Bty Acad 86; Pittsburgh Bty Acad; Cosmtlgy.

HORWATT, DE RICCI; Canon Mcmillan SR HS; Canonsburg, PA; (Y); Church Yth Grp; Drama Clb; Latin Clb; Varsity Clb; Pres Chorus; School Play; Nwsp Rptr; Cheerleading; High Hon Roll; NHS; OH U; Bus Pre-Law.

HOSBACH, THOMAS; New Hope Solebury HS; New Hope, PA; (Y); 34/80; Cmnty Wkr; Ski Clb; Varsity Clb; Band; Concert Band; Mrchg Band; School Musical; Bsbl; Bsktbl; Socr; 1st Tm-Bicentennial Lge-Sccr-Bsbl 85-86; Bucks Cnty All Cnty Band-Trumpet 85-86; Music.

HOSFELD, MATTHEW; Liberty HS; Bethlehem, PA; (Y); 178/475; Boys Clb Am; Ski Clb; Varsity Clb; Band; Concert Band; Jazz Band; Mrchg Band; Var JV Socr; Hon Roll; Medcl.

HOSHOWER, VICTORIA; Manheim Township HS; Lancaster, PA; (Y); Chrmn Key Clb; Capt Color Guard; Drill Tm; Flag Corp; Orch; School Musical; Hon Roll; Outstdng Brd Mbr Key Clb 85-86; Outstdng Silk & Marchng Bands 85; TU 13 Cnty Orch 84-85; Biochem.

HOSKING, CHRISTINE; Benton Area JR SR HS; Benton, PA; (Y); 21/52; Church Yth Grp; Pres 4-H; Band; Chorus; Concert Band; Mrchg Band; School Musical; Nwsp Rptr; Sec Nwsp Stf; NHS; Cert Of Ntl Educ Dvlpmnt 84; 1st Ntl Lang Arts Olympiad 83; Horsebk 4 H Saddleseat St Champ 85; Jrnlsm.

HOSLER, DONALD; Nativity BVM HS; St Clair, PA; (Y); 4/97; Art Clb; Chess Clb; Computer Clb; High Hon Roll; Hon Roll; Prfct Atten Awd; Acad Excel Awd 85; Comp.

HOSP, JENNIFER A; Radnor HS; Wayne, PA; (Y); 13/276; Church Yth Grp; Service Clb; Church Choir; Orch; Yrbk Ed-Chief; JV Trk; Var JV Vllybl; High Hon Roll; NHS; Ntl Merit SF; Natl Cncl Yth Ldrshp 85; Dist Orch 83-84; Most Dedctd JV Vlybl Plyr 84; Med.

HOSTER, ROBERT; Father Judge High Schl For Boys; Philadelphia, PA; (S); 13/403; Church Yth Grp; Cmnty Wkr; Mathletes; Math Tm; Bsktbl; Ftbl; High Hon Roll; Hon Roll; Jr NHS; NHS; Temple U; Acctg.

HOSTETLER, RON; Plum SR HS; Pittsburgh, PA; (Y); 125/378; Church Yth Grp; Band; Var JV Bsbl; Var JV Wrstlng; High Hon Roll; PA ST U; Aerosp Engr.

HOSTETLER, ROY; Somerset Area HS; Somerset, PA; (Y); NFL; Quiz Bowl; School Play; Variety Show; Yrbk Stf; JV Var Bsktbl; Var Trk; Hon Roll; Chess Clb; Church Yth Grp; Yrbk Spcl Svc Awd; Hnrs Prgm; Penn ST; Comm.

HOSTETTER, ROBERTA; Cedar Crest HS; Lebanon, PA; (Y); Art Clb; Debate Tm; Spanish Clb; Band; Mrchg Band; Hon Roll; Pres Acad Fitness Awd 86; Shippensburg U.

HOSTLER, MICHELLE; Northeastern HS; York Haven, PA; (Y); Art Clb; Church Yth Grp; Computer Clb; German Clb; Red Cross Aide; Fld Hcky; Ntl Merit Ltr; Trk; Vllybl; Hon Roll; Amer Red Crss 85-86.

HOSTLER, ROBERT; Dover Area HS; Dover, PA; (Y); Varsity Clb; Var L Bsbl; Var L Ftbl; Var L Trk; Pres Schlr; MVP JV Ftbl 84 & 85; WV U.

HOSU, NICK; Harborcreek HS; Erie, PA; (Y); 44/200; Im Bowling; Var Diving; Var L Ftbl; Var Socr; Var Swmmng; Var L Tennis; Im Vllybl; Im Wt Lftg; Allegheny Coll; Chem.

HOTTENSTEIN, JOHN; Hempfield HS; Lancaster, PA; (Y); Church Yth Grp; Chorus; High Hon Roll; Hon Roll.

HOTTENSTEIN, SHENON; Salisbury HS; Allentown, PA; (Y); 27/130; Cmnty Wkr; Sec SADD; Varsity Clb; Rep Soph Cls; Rep Jr Cls; Var L Bsktbl; Var L Fld Hcky; Var L Sftbl; High Hon Roll; Hon Roll; Fld Hcky-Hon Mntn 85; Bsktbl Hon Mntn 86; Sftbl Hon Mntn 85-86; Pre-Med.

HOUCK, BRENDA; Hempfield HS; Mt Joy, PA; (Y); Dance Clb; Debate Tm; PAVAS; Co-Capt Cheerleading; Co-Capt Gym; Hon Roll; Pre-Law.

HOUCK, CORY; Mohawk HS; Enon Valley, PA; (Y); Camera Clb; Church Yth Grp; Computer Clb; French Clb; Ski Clb; Varsity Clb; Ftbl; Trk; Wt Lftg; Ftbl Ltr 84-85; Trck Ltr 86; Wghtlftng Trphy 85; USAF Acad; Aerntcl Engr.

HOUCK, JANET; Tyrone Area HS; Spruce Creek, PA; (Y); Spanish Clb; Chorus; Rep Stu Cncl; Im Cheerleading; JV Var Powder Puff Ftbl; Hon Roll; SALES Mgr.

HOUCK, PAUL; Southern Huntingdon HS; Cassville, PA; (Y); 4-H; French Clb; SADD; Varsity Clb; Stage Crew; Rep Stu Cncl; Var Bsbl; Var Bsktbl; Var Ftbl; Med.

HOUGH, DONAVAN; Southmoreland HS; Everson, PA; (Y); 15/213; French Clb; Letterman Clb; Math Clb; Ski Clb; Concert Band; Mrchg Band; Stu Cncl; Tennis; French Hon Soc; Hon Roll; Pres Acad Ftns Awd 86; Top 10 Prcnt Awd 86; PA ST U; Lbrl Arts.

HOUGH, MICHAEL SCOTT; Moon HS; Moon Township, PA; (Y); Cmnty Wkr; DECA; VP JA; Var Crs Cntry; JV Var Trk; JV Wrstlng; Hon Roll; High Slsmn JA 85; 1st Pl CC Road Race 86; 2nd Annl Pittsburgh Marthn 86; Accnt.

HOUGH, PAMELA; Northwest Area HS; Stillwater, PA; (Y); 8/108; Computer Clb; SADD; Stu Cncl; Trk; Vllybl; High Hon Roll; NHS; Stu Of Mnth 86; Bloomsburg U; Math.

HOUGH, TIMOTHY; Brownsville Area HS; Hiller, PA; (S); 22/225; Pres Church Yth Grp; Drama Clb; Church Choir; High Hon Roll; Hon Roll; Amer Legion Hist Awd 83; Eckerd Coll.

HOUIS, CURTIS; Franklin HS; Emlenton, PA; (Y); 12/213; Pres Church Yth Grp; German Clb; Letterman Clb; Varsity Clb; Ftbl; Wrstlng; High Hon Roll; NHS; Schl Bd Dir Schlstc Awds 81-82, 83-84 & 85-86; Dickinson Coll; Corp Law.

HOUK, MARY KAYE; Lincoln HS; Ellwood City, PA; (Y); 12/168; AFS; Church Yth Grp; Drama Clb; Girl Scts; JA; Lwyrs & EAEA Schlrshps 86; Grove City Coll PA; Bio.

HOURICAN, MARK; The Swarthmore Acad; Swarthmore, PA; (S); Red Cross Aide; Science Clb; Teachers Aide; Concert Band; Yrbk Phtg; VP Jr Cls; VP Sr Cls; Var L Ice Hcky; Var Capt Socr; Hon Roll; WA Wrkshp Awd 86; Vrsty Bsktbl MVP 85; Pol Sci.

HOUSE, CINDY; Lehighton HS; Lehighton, PA; (Y); 24/246; Church Yth Grp; Girl Scts; Drill Tm; Yrbk Stf; High Hon Roll; Hon Roll; St Lukes Nrsg Schl; Nrsg.

HOUSE, KARI; Fairview HS; Fairview, PA; (Y); Am Leg Aux Girls St; Ski Clb; Varsity Clb; Yrbk Stf; Rep Stu Cncl; Var Cheerleading; Var Crs Cntry; Var Capt Trk; Hon Roll; NHS; Mst Imprvd Track Awd 85; PA ST Track Camp Schlrshp 84.

HOUSE, ROBERT; Upper Dublin SR HS; Ft Washington, PA; (Y); 19/343; Band; Concert Band; Jazz Band; Mrchg Band; School Musical; Symp Band; Yrbk Bus Mgr; High Hon Roll; JP Sousa Awd; NHS; Pres Acad Ftnss Awd 86; Lafayette Coll; Econ.

HOUSEHOLDER, LORI; Penn Trafford HS; Trafford, PA; (Y); #76 In Class; FBLA; Hosp Aide; Office Aide; Yrbk Stf; Hon Roll; Lion Awd; Bradford Bus Schl; Sec.

HOUSEL, SUSAN; Meyersdale HS; Meyersdale, PA; (S); French Clb; Chorus; Yrbk Stf; Off Jr Cls; Var Capt Cheerleading; French Hon Soc; Hon Roll.

HOUSEMAN, KIM; Middletown Area HS; Middletown, PA; (Y); Church Yth Grp; Library Aide; PAVAS; Band; Color Guard; Concert Band; Mrchg Band; School Musical; School Play; Mgr Bsktbl; 2nd Pl Ptry Cnst 83; Crmnllgy.

HOUSENICK, STEPHEN; G A R Memorial HS; Wilkes Barre, PA; (S); 8/178; Debate Tm; Exploring; French Clb; German Clb; Key Clb; Office Aide; Chorus; Stat Bsktbl; Capt Crs Cntry; Score Keeper; Yth Slt Wymng Valley 85; Acdmc All-Amer 85; US Achvmnt Acad Awd 86; Crmnl Jstc.

HOUSER, AMY; West Branch Area JR SR HS; Morrisdale, PA; (Y); Church Yth Grp; Exploring; Library Aide; Science Clb; Teachers Aide; Varsity Clb; Yrbk Stf; Capt Var Sftbl; Im Vllybl; Prfct Atten Awd.

HOUSER, BARBARA; West Hazleton HS; Sybertsville, PA; (S); 26/200; Sec FBLA; Hon Roll; NHS; Luzerne County CC; Acctng.

HOUSER JR, DONALD E; Lock Haven HS; Lock Haven, PA; (Y); Church Yth Grp; Drama Clb; German Clb; Chorus; School Play; Variety Show; Nwsp Stf; Yrbk Phtg; Yrbk Stf; L Trk; Acctnt.

HOUSER, GRETCHEN; Eastern York JR SR HS; E Prospect, PA; (Y); Sec Church Yth Grp; VP Sec 4-H; Chorus; Concert Band; Mrchg Band; Yrbk Rptr; Yrbk Stf; Var JV Bsktbl; Hon Roll; Aud/Vis; Prsdntl Physcl Ftns Awd; Vet.

HOUSER, JENNIFER; Merion Mercy Acad; Springfield, PA; (Y); French Clb; Science Clb; Service Clb; Chorus; Stage Crew; Rep Sr Cls; Off Stu Cncl; Ntl Merit Ltr; Prfct Atten Awd; Acad Schlrshp 83; Ntl Art Hnr Soc 86; Anthropology.

HOUSER, LISA; Cedar Crest HS; Lebanon, PA; (S); Church Yth Grp; Pres FFA; Pep Clb; Church Choir; Hon Roll; Ag.

HOUSER, MARK; New Castle SR HS; New Castle, PA; (S); 12/250; AFS; Church Yth Grp; NFL; Band; Concert Band; Jazz Band; Mrchg Band; School Play; Im Vllybl; High Hon Roll; 3rd Pl Natl Acad Games 84; News Carrier Awd 83; Duquesne U; Comm.

HOUSER, MELISSA; Nazareth SR HS; Bath, PA; (S); 15/231; Color Guard; Drill Tm; Mrchg Band; School Musical; Stu Cncl; Stat Bsktbl; Capt Twrlr; High Hon Roll; Hon Roll; NHS; Moravian Coll; Psych.

HOUSER, TRICIA; Cedar Crest HS; Lebanon, PA; (Y); Drama Clb; French Clb; Pep Clb; School Musical; Yrbk Stf; Cheerleading; Hon Roll; NHS; Psych.

HOUSH, CASSIE V; Unionville HS; West Chester, PA; (Y); 57/300; Pep Clb; Band; Var JV Cheerleading; JV Lcrss; Powder Puff Ftbl; Hon Roll; Acadmc Awd-Eng 85-86; NC ST.

HOUSLER, ANITA L; Cameron County HS; Emporium, PA; (Y); Band; Mrchg Band; Yrbk Ed-Chief; Trs Frsh Cls; Rep Jr Cls; JV Cheerleading; Var Powder Puff Ftbl; Hon Roll; NHS; Prfct Atten Awd; Delta Epsilon Phi-Germn Ntl Hon Soc 83-86; Gannon U; Psych.

HOUSTON, MICHAEL; Pittston Area HS; Avoca, PA; (Y); Computer Clb; Key Clb; Math Clb; Science Clb; Chorus; High Hon Roll; NHS; NEDT Awd; Rotary Awd; Bio.

HOUSTON, NICOLE; Carrick HS; Pittsburgh, PA; (Y); High Hon Roll; Hon Roll.

HOUSTON, SONJA; Harrisburg Steelton Highspire Vo Tech; Harrisburg, PA; (S); 69/400; Church Yth Grp; VP DECA; FHA; Spanish Clb; VICA; Church Choir; Drill Tm; Mst Outstndg Stu 85-86; Stu Of Mnth 85-86; Fshn Mrchndsg.

HOUSTON, TIMOTHY J; North Hills HS; Pittsburgh, PA; (Y); 169/467; AFS; Exploring; Politcl Wkr; Speech Tm; Stu Cncl; Stu Advsry Brd Sec Of Educ 85-86; Schrlshp To PA Free Enterprise Week 85; Stu Page ST House Of Reps; Law.

HOUTZ, JAMES; Montgomery HS; Allenwood, PA; (Y); Hon Roll; Bus Adm.

HOUTZ, LORI; Palmyra Area SR HS; Palmyra, PA; (Y); VP Pres Church Yth Grp; 4-H; Pres SADD; Band; Chorus; Church Choir; Concert Band; Mrchg Band; Stage Crew; Yrbk Stf; Acctng.

HOVAN, MICHELLE; Gateway SR HS; Monroeville, PA; (Y); 139/143; Dance Clb; Hosp Aide; Office Aide; Red Cross Aide; Cheerleading; Trk; Hon Roll; Army; Med Spec.

HOVENSTINE, LAURA; Shikellamy HS; Sunbury, PA; (Y); 98/301; French Clb; Band; Concert Band; Mrchg Band; Twrlr; Hon Roll.

HOVIOUS, JULIE; Fairview HS; Erie, PA; (Y); 1/170; Pres Drama Clb; Varsity Clb; Pres Chorus; Capt Color Guard; School Musical; Var L Bsktbl; Pres NHS; Val; Church Yth Grp; Lit Mag; Natl Schl Choral Awd 85-86; US Army Rsrv Natl Schlr/Ath Awd 85-86; Erie Cnty SR All-Star Bsktbl Team; U VT; Med Tech.

HOWAR, DENNIS; Meyersdale Area HS; Meyersdale, PA; (Y); Boy Scts; Church Yth Grp; Computer Clb; French Clb; Ski Clb; Band; Concert Band; Jazz Band; Mrchg Band; Pep Band; Engrng.

HOWARD, CHERYL LYNN; North East HS; North East, PA; (Y); 1/149; Trs AFS; Church Yth Grp; Debate Tm; Latin Clb; Model UN; Q&S; Science Clb; Band; Concert Band; Mrchg Band; Pres Acad Ftnss Awd 86; Awd Outstndg Schlrshp Ldrshp, Prncpls Awd 86; SR Awd Engl,Advncd Plcmnt 86; Allegheny Coll; Lib Arts.

HOWARD, CHRISTOPHER A; Plum Boro HS; Pittsburgh, PA; (Y); 24/410; AFS; French Clb; JA; Speech Tm; SADD; Chorus; Church Choir; School Musical; School Play; Yrbk Stf; US Army Res 85-86; Boyce CC.

HOWARD, DEBRA; General Mc Lane HS; Girard, PA; (Y); 13/235; German Clb; Band; Mrchg Band; Symp Band; Stat L Vllybl; Hon Roll; NHS; Ntl Merit SF; German Lang Comp Awd 85; Pre-Med.

HOWARD, JEFFREY M; Emmaus HS; Emmaus, PA; (Y); 100/500; Boy Scts; Computer Clb; JA; School Musical; JV Var Socr; Var L Trk; Hon Roll; Ntl Merit Ltr; Aerntcl Engr.

HOWARD, JENNIFER; Cumberland Valley HS; Mechanicsburg, PA; (Y); 119/550; Girl Scts; Key Clb; School Play.

HOWARD, JILL; Shenandoah Valley HS; Shenandoah, PA; (Y); 27/99; Dance Clb; Debate Tm; Pep Clb; Swing Chorus; Variety Show; Yrbk Stf; Cit Awd; High Hon Roll; Hon Roll; NHS; Pltcl.

HOWARD, LISA; Johnsonburg Area HS; Wilcox, PA; (Y); Pres 4-H; Office Aide; Rep Stu Cncl; JV Bsktbl; JV Vllybl; 4-H Awd; Du Bois Bus Schl; Acctg.

HOWARD, MELISSA; Jim Thorpe SR HS; Lake Harmony, PA; (S); 7/108; Camera Clb; Scholastic Bowl; Ski Clb; Nwsp Ed-Chief; Nwsp Phtg; Nwsp Stf; Var L Vllybl; High Hon Roll; NHS; Princeton; Law.

HOWARD, MELISSA; Waynesburg Central HS; Mt Morris, PA; (Y); Natl Beta Clb; Color Guard; Drill Tm; Flag Corp; Madrigals; Twrlr; Hon Roll.

HOWARD, MICHELE L; Trinity HS; Washington, PA; (Y); 83/374; Trs Art Clb; Drama Clb; Pres Key Clb; Pep Clb; School Play; Hon Roll; Natl Art Hnr Scty 86; Edinboro; Nrsng.

HOWARD, RHONDA; Juniata HS; Mifflintown, PA; (Y); 4-H; Spanish Clb; Chorus; School Play; Yrbk Stf; Stat Fld Hcky; 4-H Awd; Hon Roll; Jr NHS; NHS; Adv Math Tchr.

HOWARD, ROBERT; Kutztown Area HS; Kutztown, PA; (Y); VP Church Yth Grp; Chorus; School Play; Rep Stu Cncl; Var L Bsbl; JV Bsktbl; Var L Socr; High Hon Roll; NHS; Med.

HOWARD II, RONALD Y; Grove City HS; Grove City, PA; (Y); Ski Clb; Rep Stu Cncl; JV Bsktbl; Coach Actv; Var L Ftbl; Var L Trk; Wt Lftg; High Hon Roll.

HOWARD, STEVEN; Hanover HS; Hanover, PA; (Y); Church Yth Grp; Varsity Clb; Var L Ftbl; Var L Wrstlng; Hon Roll; Mech Engr.

HOWARD, WAYNE; West Catholic Boys HS; Philadelphia, PA; (Y); 74/281; Letterman Clb; Science Clb; Varsity Clb; Crs Cntry; Score Keeper; Trk; High Hon Roll; Hon Roll; Lincoln U; Pre-Med.

HOWARTH, AIMEE S; Mt Pleasant Area SR-JR HS; Mt Pleasant, PA; (Y); Library Aide; Red Cross Aide; Ski Clb; Spanish Clb; Rep Trs Stu Cncl; Mat Maids; YEA Yth Educ Assoc 85-87; Trvl/Trsm Mgmt.

HOWARTH, DUSTIN; Canon Mc Millan SR HS; Eighty Four, PA; (Y); 1/394; Chess Clb; Rep Latin Clb; Trs Ski Clb; Var Trk; High Hon Roll; Bk Dscssn Grp; Stck Mrkt Game-Tm Capt; Pre-Med.

HOWE, JANE; South Western HS; Hanover, PA; (Y); 12/205; Pres VP Church Yth Grp; Hosp Aide; Chorus; School Musical; Yrbk Stf; Hon Roll; NHS; Ntl Merit Ltr; Rotary Awd; Sorptmst Intl Schlrshp 86; Protstn Nrsg Assoc Schlrshp 86; Pres Acadmc Ftnss Awd 86; Messiah College; Nrsg.

HOWE, MONIKA; Salisbury HS; Bethlehem, PA; (Y); Key Clb; Yrbk Stf; Swmmng; German.

HOWELL, STEPHANIE; State College Area HS; Pa Furnace, PA; (Y); 186/568; Girl Scts; Hosp Aide; Latin Clb; Concert Band; Var L Crs Cntry; Trk; Hon Roll; Intl Bus.

HOWELL, TAMMY; Cowanesque Valley HS; Westfield, PA; (S); 9/87; Drama Clb; Sec French Clb; Letterman Clb; SADD; Chorus; Sec Soph Cls; Rep Stu Cncl; Stat Bsktbl; JV Var Vllybl; NHS; Acadmc Ltr 84-85; Scndry Ed.

HOWELLS, DEBBIE; Marion Center Area HS; Marion Center, PA; (S); 13/170; FBLA; Pep Clb; Varsity Clb; Cheerleading; Pom Pon; Hon Roll; NHS; 2 Typng Awds 85; Model.

HOWELLS, KIMBERLEE A; Upper Moreland HS; Horsham, PA; (Y); 62/276; GAA; Var L Bsktbl; Var Cheerleading; Var L Fld Hcky; Var L Sftbl; Var L Swmmng; High Hon Roll; Hon Roll; Fld Hockey Schlrshp Longwood Coll 86; Outstndng Female Athl 86; Babe Ruth Awd 86; Longwood Coll; Phy Therapy.

HOWER, JONATHAN; Moon SR HS; Coraopolis, PA; (Y); 63/304; Hon Roll; Rep Stu Cncl; L Bsbl; Cvl Engrng.

HOWER, SHERRI; Pleasant Valley HS; Effort, PA; (Y); 25/233; Varsity Clb; VP Jr Cls; Var JV Cheerleading; JV Capt Sftbl; High Hon Roll; Hon Roll; NHS; Most Spirited Vrsty Bsktbl Chrldr 85; Bus.

HOWER, WENDY; Red Lion SR HS; New Freedom, PA; (Y); 22/240; Church Yth Grp; Varsity Clb; Nwsp Stf; Vllybl; Hon Roll; Elem Tchr.

HOWETT, TRACY MICHAEL; Sun Valley HS; Aston, PA; (Y); 10/297; Pres Band; Var L Socr; Capt L Trk; God Cntry Awd; Lion Awd; NHS; Pres Schlr; U S Army Reserv Natl Schlr & Athl Awd 86; St Josephs U; Comp Sci.

HOWLES, VALERIE; Cambridge Springs HS; Saegertown, PA; (Y); Church Yth Grp; Pep Clb; Spanish Clb; Band; Concert Band; Mrchg Band; Pep Band; Stu Cncl; Nrsng.

HOWSARE, BOBBI ANN; Chestnut Ridge HS; Bedford, PA; (Y); Aud/Vis; Church Yth Grp; GAA; School Play; Var L Cheerleading; Var L Trk; Var L Vllybl; SE Coll; Mar Biol.

HOWSARE, CHRIS; Upper Moreland SR HS; Hatboro, PA; (Y); 1/253; Dance Clb; Intnl Clb; Key Clb; Flag Corp; Rptr Nwsp Rptr; Rptr Yrbk Rptr; Yrbk Stf; Lit Mag; Rep Soph Cls; Rep Jr Cls; Acad All Amer 85-86; Mth.

HOWSARE, JACQUELINE; Hatboro Horsham HS; Hatboro, PA; (Y); Concert Band; Mrchg Band; School Musical; School Play; High Hon Roll; Hon Roll; NHS; Girl Scts; Intnl Clb; Key Clb; Musc Awd 83-84; Germ Awd 83-85; Germ Soc Perf Awd 85; SUNY Buffalo; Bio.

HOWSARE, JANIE LINN; Bedford HS; Bedford, PA; (Y); Am Leg Aux Girls St; Church Yth Grp; FCA; Chorus; Church Choir; School Musical; Stu Cncl; Bsktbl; Sftbl; Nrsg.

HOY, BRIAN; Lock Have HS; Lock Haven, PA; (Y); Art Clb; Chorus; School Musical; Variety Show; Ftbl; Socr; Trk; Wt Lftg; Prfct Atten Awd.

HOY, CHERYL; Penns Manor HS; Clymer, PA; (Y); 24/102; VP 4-H; FBLA; Red Cross Aide; SADD; Band; Concert Band; Flag Corp; Mrchg Band; Stu Cncl; 4-H Awd; Res Champ PA ST 4-H Horse Show 84-85.

HOY, KRISTI; Waynesburg Central HS; Waynesburg, PA; (Y); Natl Beta Clb; Ski Clb; Spanish Clb; Hon Roll.

HOY, LAWRENCE; Bald Eagle Area HS; Howard, PA; (Y); Boy Scts; Computer Clb; Spanish Clb; Im JV Bsktbl; Hon Roll; Prfct Atten Awd; Engl Awd 84; Spnsh Awd 85; Penn ST U; Comp Prmgr.

HOY, LISA; Parkland HS; Coplay, PA; (Y); 122/459; Church Yth Grp; Exploring; Hosp Aide; Office Aide; Teachers Aide; Nrsg.

HOY, MARC; Palmyra HS; Coelbrook, PA; (Y); Aud/Vis; Church Yth Grp; SADD; Chorus; Stage Crew; JV Bsbl; Hon Roll; Bus.

HOY, MICHAEL; Montoursville HS; Montoursville, PA; (Y); 48/174; Key Clb; Letterman Clb; Spanish Clb; Ftbl; Trk; Bio-Chem.

HOY, PHIL; Greensburg Salem SR HS; Export, PA; (Y); Pres VP 4-H; German Clb; Chorus; Drill Tm; School Musical; Rep Stu Cncl; 4-H Awd; Hon Roll; 2 High Pt Awds For Day-Horses 85; 1 High Pt End Of Yr Awd-Horses 85.

HOY, ROBERT TODD; Central Greene HS; Waynesburg, PA; (Y); Boy Scts; Church Yth Grp; Sec Ski Clb; Spanish Clb; Stu Cncl; Bsbl; Capt Fld Hcky; JV Var Socr; Hon Roll; Masonic Awd; Order Of De Molay Cnclr 85-87; Concrete Contr.

HOYSAN, BILL; Liberty HS; Bethlehem, PA; (Y); 44/400; JV Bsktbl; Var L Tennis; Hon Roll; Binney-N-Smith Merit Schlrshp 86-87; Northampton Comm Clg; Bus Admin.

HOYT, TAMARA; GAR Memorial HS; Wilkes Barre, PA; (S); 22/187; Key Clb; Chorus; Church Choir; Nwsp Ed-Chief; Yrbk Stf; High Hon Roll; Hon Roll; Jr NHS; NHS; Hugh O Brien Yth Fndtn 85; Kings Coll; Comm.

HRACH, JENNIFER; Mount Alvernia HS; Pittsburgh, PA; (Y); Computer Clb; French Clb; Math Clb; Chorus; JV Var Bsktbl; Var Crs Cntry; Var Trk; Hon Roll; Sports Med.

HREBEN, MATTHEW; Scranton Prep; Moosic, PA; (Y); Cmnty Wkr; Stage Crew; JV Var Ftbl; JV L Trk; JV L Wt Lftg; Penn ST; Bus Law.

HREZIK, KIM; Schuylkill Valley HS; Leesport, PA; (Y); 24/128; Chorus; School Musical; Nwsp Rptr; Nwsp Stf; Yrbk Stf; Var Capt Cheerleading; Trk; Vllybl; Hon Roll; NHS; Sprts Med.

HRIBAR, MONICA; Center Area HS; Aliquippa, PA; (Y); Pres Church Yth Grp; German Clb; Hosp Aide; Spanish Clb; Varsity Clb; Mrchg Band; Pres Frsh Cls; Pres Soph Cls; Capt L Bsktbl; Hon Roll; George Washington U; Intl Affrs.

HRIBAR, SUZANNE L; Fox Chapel Area HS; Pittsburgh, PA; (Y); Church Yth Grp; Key Clb; Var Capt Socr; Var L Swmmng; High Hon Roll; Sec NHS; Ntl Merit SF; Rgnl All Amer 2nd Tm Sccr 85; Engrng.

HRICAK, ANN; Catasauqua HS; Allentown, PA; (Y); FBLA; Hosp Aide; Yrbk Stf; Stu Cncl; Sftbl; Drama Clb; FHA; Band; Flag Corp; Lehigh Cnty CC; Elem Educ.

HRIN, ERIC; Jefferson-Morgan JR SR HS; Jefferson, PA; (Y); 15/92; Civic Clb; Cmnty Wkr; Nwsp Rptr; Nwsp Stf; Yrbk Stf; VP Frsh Cls; Rep Jr Cls; Cit Awd; High Hon Roll; Hon Roll; Fidler-Sadlk AM Lgn Essy Awd 86; Tri-Co Cncl AM Legn Essy Awd 86; Law.

HRITZ, JOHN R; Monogahela Vly Catholic HS; Brownsville, PA; (Y); 5/85; Exploring; Ski Clb; Spanish Clb; Golf; DAR Awd; NHS; Spanish NHS; CMU; Elect Engr.

HRITZ, MICHAEL; Beth-Center HS; Clarksville, PA; (Y); 22/160; Drama Clb; Ski Clb; School Play; Yrbk Phtg; Var Ftbl; Hon Roll; Elect Engr.

HRITZ, TERRY; Union Area HS; New Castle, PA; (S); 7/70; Band; Concert Band; Jazz Band; Pres Mrchg Band; Pep Band; School Musical; Var L Golf; Var L Trk; Hst NHS; Church Yth Grp; Louis Armstrong Jazz Awd 85; U Of Pittsburgh; Engr.

HRIZO, JOHN; Gateway HS; Monroeville, PA; (Y); 189/508; Boy Scts; Church Yth Grp; Band; Concert Band; Mrchg Band; Orch; School Musical; Symp Band; Am Chem Soc Awd Outstndng Chem Wrk 85-86; PA ST U; Forest Ranger.

HROUDA, BOB; N E Catholic HS; Philadelphia, PA; (Y); 111/362; JV Socr; Hon Roll; Mc Carrie Schl; Trvl Agt.

HRUSKA, ANNETTE; Greater Latrobe HS; Latrobe, PA; (Y); Trs Art Clb; Hosp Aide; JCL; Teachers Aide; High Hon Roll; NHS; Pres Schlr; Natl Art Hnr Socty Pres 85-86; Pro Bus Womn Art Awd 86; Seton Hill Coll; Art Thrpy.

HRUSKO, LAURI; Ambridge Area HS; Baden, PA; (Y); Church Yth Grp; Pep Clb; Hon Roll.

HRVOICH, STEVEN J; Ambridge Area HS; Baden, PA; (Y); 41/300; Am Leg Boys St; Aud/Vis; Church Yth Grp; German Clb; Pep Clb; Variety Show; Nwsp Rptr; Hon Roll; PA ST Rep; PA AIASA Conf Publc Spkng 86; PA ST U; Aerospc Engnrng.

HSIEH, FRED; Wyomissing Area HS; Wyomissing, PA; (S); 3/119; Boy Scts; Model UN; Spanish Clb; Mrchg Band; Symp Band; Yrbk Stf; Bausch & Lomb Sci Awd; NHS; Ntl Merit SF; Computer Clb; 3rd Pl A T & T Stu Engrng Fair 85; Medicine.

HSU, GWELLEH; North Hills SR HS; Pittsburgh, PA; (S); 5/485; JA; Radio Clb; VP Trs Orch; Pres Soph Cls; JV Tennis; High Hon Roll; NHS; Church Yth Grp; Computer Clb; 5th Pl Wstrn PA Ntl Frnch Cont 84; Hugh O Brien Yth Smnr 85; Acad Decthln ST Lvl 86; Carnegie-Mellon U; Biomed Engr.

HU, JAMES Y; State College Area SR HS; State College, PA; (Y); 5/568; Math Clb; Model UN; Scholastic Bowl; Im Lcrss; Cit Awd; High Hon Roll; JETS Awd; Ntl Merit Ltr; Rotary Awd; Wrld Affrs Semnr 86; Mechncl Engrng.

HUBAUER, ROBIN; Clarion-Limestone HS; Corsica, PA; (Y); 4/86; Art Clb; VP Varsity Clb; Concert Band; Mrchg Band; Yrbk Sprt Ed; Yrbk Stf; Var L Bsktbl; Capt Trk; Var L Vllybl; Hon Roll; US Army Rsrve Schlr/Athl Awd, Female Athl Yr, Partial Athl Schlrshp U Pittsburgh 86; U Pittsburgh; Bio.

HUBBARD, ALYSIA; Upper Merion Area HS; King Of Prussa, PA; (Y); 22/303; Church Yth Grp; German Clb; Math Tm; Rep Jr Cls; Rep Stu Cncl; Tennis; Trk; Hon Roll; NHS; ST Chmpn In Long Jump 86; Med.

HUBBARD, AMY; Freedom HS; Bethlehem, PA; (Y); 23/445; Church Yth Grp; Pep Clb; Science Clb; Spanish Clb; Chorus; Church Choir; Swmmng; Trk; Hon Roll; NHS; Physcl Thrpy.

HUBER, DEANA; Burgettstown JR SR HS; Burgettstown, PA; (Y); 5/172; Church Yth Grp; Science Clb; Speech Tm; Yrbk Bus Mgr; Yrbk Stf; High Hon Roll; NHS; John L Brunner Mem Scholar 86; Duquesne U; Phrmcy.

HUBER, FLOYD B; Elanco Garden Spot HS; East Earl, PA; (S); 42/200; Church Yth Grp; 4-H; FFA; All Star Deg FFA.

HUBER, LISA; Hershey HS; Hummelstown, PA; (Y); 7/190; Pres Church Yth Grp; Yrbk Ed-Chief; Trs Stu Cncl; Capt L Bsktbl; Capt L Fld Hcky; Capt L Sftbl; Kiwanis Awd; Sec NHS; Trs Spanish NHS; U S Army Rsrv Schlr/Athlt Awd 86; HEA Schlrshp 86; Tri-Athlt Awd 86; Franklin/Marshall Coll; Pre-Med.

HUBER, RICK E; Pine Grove Area HS; Schuylkill Haven, PA; (Y); Am Leg Boys St; Drama Clb; Letterman Clb; Varsity Clb; School Play; Nwsp Phtg; Nwsp Rptr; Var Ftbl; JV Wrstlng; Pres Phys Ftns Awd 86; Outstndng Phys Ed Stu 86.

HUBER, TAMMIE; Solanco SR HS; New Providence, PA; (Y); 52/238; Sec Drama Clb; Office Aide; Thesps; Chorus; School Play; Stage Crew; Nwsp Rptr; Nwsp Stf; Mgr(s); Hon Roll; Harcum JC; Elem Tchg.

HUBERT, DORIS J; North Catholic HS; Pittsburgh, PA; (Y); 47/301; Civic Clb; Cmnty Wkr; Dance Clb; Drama Clb; French Clb; Hosp Aide; JA; Red Cross Aide; Ski Clb; Church Choir; U Of Pittsburgh; Chem Engrng.

HUBLER, CHARLOTTE; Benton Area HS; Benton, PA; (Y); Pres Keywanettes; Yrbk Stf; Rep Sr Cls; Trs Stu Cncl; Var Capt Fld Hcky; Var CAP; Twrlr; Hon Roll; NHS; Columbia-Montour Bar Assn Awd 86; Iva Conner Sports Awd 86; Soda Scholar 86; Ath Wk Fld Hcky 83-85; Bloomsburg U.

HUBLER, KELLY; Curwensville Area HS; Curwensville, PA; (Y); AFS; Camera Clb; VP Sec Church Yth Grp; Drama Clb; Chorus; School Musical; School Play; Yrbk Stf; Hon Roll; NHS; Scl Svcs.

HUBLER, MELISSA; Cedar Cliff HS; Camp Hill, PA; (Y); 2/280; Sec Capt Debate Tm; Pres French Clb; French Hon Soc; High Hon Roll; NHS; Ntl Merit Ltr; Prfct Atten Awd; Pres Schlr; Sal; Church Yth Grp; Rep Keystone Grls ST; Rep W Shr Rtry; Prncpls Schl Svc Awd Cdr Clf; Penn ST; Math.

HUBLEY, KELLY; Eastern York HS; Windsor, PA; (Y); 30/169; Varsity Clb; Concert Band; Mrchg Band; Rep Stu Cncl; Var L Bsktbl; Mgr(s); Stat Socr; JV Var Vllybl; Hon Roll.

HUCHKO, DEBBIE; Hopewell SR HS; Aliquippa, PA; (Y); 50/270; Hosp Aide; Office Aide; Spanish Clb; Yrbk Stf; Hon Roll; Ntl Merit Ltr; Prfct Atten Awd; Beaver Cnty C; Med Lab Tech.

HUCK, ROLAND; Taylor Allderdice HS; Pittsburgh, PA; (Y); 44/437; Camera Clb; Computer Clb; VP JA; Science Clb; Band; Orch; Hon Roll; St Schlr; Outstndng Chem Stu-Amer Chem Soc 86; U Of Pittsburgh; Phrmcy.

HUCKEL, JEFFREY; Bishop Shanahan HS; Coastesville, PA; (Y); 45/218; Church Yth Grp; Political Wkr; Nwsp Rptr; Nwsp Sprt Ed; Crs Cntry; Trk; Hon Roll; Prfct Atten Awd; Comm.

HUCKESTEIN, ANGIE; Seneca Valley SR HS; Evans City, PA; (Y); 70/370; Church Yth Grp; VP FTA; Mrchg Band; School Play; Symp Band; Stat Wrstlng; High Hon Roll; Hon Roll; Mrchng Bnd Ltr 86; Schlrshp Awd Acdmc Achvmnt 85.

HUDAK, MICHAEL A; Blackhawk HS; Beaver Falls, PA; (Y); Boy Scts; Chess Clb; Hon Roll; Comp Sci.

HUDLER, CHRISTINE; Oxford Area HS; Lincoln Univ, PA; (Y); 31/154; Sec FBLA; Hosp Aide; High Hon Roll; Hon Roll; NHS; Bio Awd 84; Shrthnd I Awd 85; Shrthnd II Awd 86; Goldey Beacom CC; Sec.

HUDOCK, BARRY; Punxsutawney Area HS; Punxsutawney, PA; (Y); Art Clb; Math Tm; Science Clb; Spanish Clb; Nwsp Stf; Yrbk Stf; Frsh Cls; Jr Cls; Golf; Hon Roll; Rotary Yth Ldrshp Awd 86; Jrnlsm.

HUDOCK, ROBERT; Geibel HS; Uniontown, PA; (Y); 8/100; Drama Clb; Science Clb; Trs Frsh Cls; Stat Bsktbl; L Var Ftbl; Wt Lftg; High Hon Roll; Hon Roll; NEDT Awd; Spanish NHS; All Conf All Courier Tm Ftbl; Biochem.

HUDSON, BILL; Mechanicsburg Area SR HS; Mechanicsburg, PA; (Y); 151/311; Band; Chorus; Concert Band; Mrchg Band; Symp Band; Hon Roll; Boy Scts; Church Yth Grp; SADD; Rep Stu Cncl; Comp Pgmng.

HUDSON, DIANE M; West Hazleton HS; Hazleton, PA; (S); 23/200; Red Cross Aide; Ski Clb; Nwsp Stf; Yrbk Ed-Chief; Yrbk Stf; VP Sr Cls; Stu Cncl; Tennis; Elks Awd; NHS; Penn ST U; Bus Admin.

HUDSON, SHARON E; William Allen HS; Allentown, PA; (Y); 5/576; Key Clb; Pres Ski Clb; Ed Nwsp Stf; Stu Cncl; Mgr(s); Sec NHS; Dance Clb; Model UN; DAR Awd; High Hon Roll; Schl Soc Stud Awd 86; Claremont Mc Kenna Achvt Awd 86; Georgetown U; Intl Rel.

HUDY, KELLY; Fort Le Boeuf HS; Waterford, PA; (Y); 24/185; French Clb; Capt Cheerleading; Gym; Trk; Vllybl; High Hon Roll; Hon Roll; PA Free Enterprise Wk 86; Acad Achvt Awd 84-85; Bus.

HUDYK, JASON; Carson Long Inst; Westerville, OH; (Y); Drama Clb; Letterman Clb; Speech Tm; Chorus; School Play; Rep Soph Cls; Rep Jr Cls; Var Bsktbl; Var Mgr(s); Var Score Keeper; Blue Ribbon Squad Awd 85; Law Enfrcmnt.

HUDZIK, DANIEL; Lake Lehman HS; Sweet Valley, PA; (Y); Concert Band; Mrchg Band; L Bsktbl; L Trk; Im Wt Lftg; Hon Roll; Engr.

HUDZINA, BETH; Scranton Prep; Scranton, PA; (Y); Church Yth Grp; Cmnty Wkr; Drama Clb; Hosp Aide; Pep Clb; Stage Crew; Nwsp Stf; Yrbk Stf; High Hon Roll; Hstry, Math, Lat & Relgn Hrnb Mntn; Exclnc In Englsh Bronze Mdl; Pre-Med.

HUEGLER, JOSEPH; Muhlenberg SR HS; Reding, PA; (Y); Church Yth Grp; Service Clb; Ski Clb; JV Bsktbl; Var L Ftbl; Var L Trk; High Hon Roll; NHS; Outstndng Soc Studys Stu 84 & 85; Bus.

HUEY, ROMAYNE; Yough SR HS; W Newton, PA; (Y); 1/243; Cmnty Wkr; French Clb; Math Tm; Political Wkr; Spanish Clb; Stat Bsktbl; Var L Vllybl; High Hon Roll; Pres NHS; Val; RTOC Schrlshp 86; Deans Hnr Awd 86; Case Western Reserve U; Engr.

HUEY, VICKIE; Hamburg Area HS; Hamburg, PA; (Y); Cmnty Wkr; Exploring; French Clb; FBLA; JA; Library Aide; Ski Clb; SADD; Lib Chorus; Drill Tm; Acad Ltr Awd Wrld Cultures 85; 3rd Pl Parlmntry Proc FBLA Conf 86; York Coll; Acctng.

HUFF, DAVID; Bellwood-Antis HS; Altoona, PA; (Y); French Clb; Key Clb; VICA; Band; Concert Band; Drm Mjr(t); Mrchg Band; Wrstlng; Hon Roll; Prfct Atten Awd; Natl Hnr Soc 86; Elec.

HUFF, DONNA; Slippery Rock HS; Prospect, PA; (Y); Church Yth Grp; Intnl Clb; Pep Clb; Band; Mrchg Band; Pep Band; Symp Band; Hon Roll; NHS; Pres Acad Fit Awd 86; PA ST U; Engrng.

HUFF, KAREN; West Hazleton HS; Conyngham, PA; (S); 12/206; FTA; Ski Clb; Trs Y-Teens; Nwsp Rptr; Var Bsktbl; Tennis; L Trk; French Hon Soc; High Hon Roll; NHS; Schlrshp-PA Free Enterprs Wk 85; Gftd Prgm-Adv Plcmnt Prgms 82-86; PA JR Acad Sci 1st Pl Biochem 86; PA ST U; Bus Admin.

HUFF, KEITH; Shenango JRSR HS; Wampum, PA; (S); 10/121; Band; Concert Band; Mrchg Band; Pep Band; School Play; Var Bsbl; High Hon Roll; Hon Roll; NHS; NEDT Awd; Natl Eng Merit Awd 86; Natl Sci Merit Awd 86; Allegheny Coll.

HUFF, LAUREL; York County Area Vo-Tech Schl; Abbottstown, PA; (Y); FNA; Chorus; Hon Roll; Psyscl Ftns Awd 85 & 86; Nrsng.

HUFF, MACHELLE; Karns City HS; Chicora, PA; (Y); SADD; Band; Concert Band; Drill Tm; Sec Jr Cls; Stu Cncl; Stat Bsktbl; Co-Capt Pom Pon; Sftbl; Hon Roll; Trophy-Outstndng Stu Kids Klb-Chrch 80; 1st Pl, Al-Star Sftbl Trphy 82-84; Hotel-Restrnt Mgmt.

HUFF, MICHELE; St Marys Area HS; Weedville, PA; (Y); 25/303; Cmnty Wkr; Yrbk Ed-Chief; Yrbk Phtg; Yrbk Rptr; Yrbk Sprt Ed; Yrbk Stf; Stat Coach Actv; Stat Trk; NHS; Prfct Atten Awd; Nrsng.

HUFF, REBECCA; Knoch HS; Butler, PA; (Y); Hosp Aide; JA; Band; Concert Band; Mrchg Band; School Musical; School Play; Trk; High Hon Roll; NHS; Physcl Thrpy.

HUFF, STEPHANIE; Mercyhurst Prep; Erie, PA; (Y); VP Church Yth Grp; Drama Clb; JCL; Sec Latin Clb; Thesps; Chorus; Church Choir; Rep Stu Cncl; Hon Roll; CTE 84; Elem Ed.

HUFF, SUSAN; West Hazleton JR-SR HS; Conyngham, PA; (Y); Cmnty Wkr; Ski Clb; SADD; Stu Cncl; Var Cheerleading; High Hon Roll.

HUFFMAN, BRUCE E; Loyalsock Twp HS; Williamsport, PA; (Y); Church Yth Grp; Drama Clb; Stage Crew; Variety Show; Yrbk Phtg; Rep Stu Cncl; Golf; Hon Roll; Yrbk Photo Awd 86; IN U PA; Comm.

HUFFMAN, CAROLE; Greensburg Central Catholic HS; Mt Pleasant, PA; (Y); Art Clb; 4-H; Service Clb; Sec Trs Band; Concert Band; Jazz Band; Mrchg Band; Pep Band; Stage Crew; Hon Roll.

HUFFMAN, JOYCE; Meyersdale Area HS; Hyndman, PA; (Y); Sec French Clb; FBLA; Library Aide; Chorus; Yrbk Stf; JV Cheerleading; Sftbl; Hon Roll; NHS; Nrsng.

HUFFMAN, KRISTI; Waynesburg Central HS; Waynesburg, PA; (Y); Art Clb; Yrbk Stf; High Hon Roll; Hon Roll; Int Dsgn.

HUFFMAN, MARYANN; Brownsville Area HS; Brownsville, PA; (Y); Church Yth Grp; Yrbk Stf; Hon Roll; Nrsng.

HUFFMAN, PAMELA; Mohawk Area JR SR HS; Edinburg, PA; (Y); 23/141; French Clb; Band; Mrchg Band; Powder Puff Ftbl; Hon Roll; Bio-Chem.

HUFFMAN, TIFFANY; West Allegheny HS; Oakdale, PA; (Y); 38/208; Chorus; Stu Cncl; Var L Cheerleading; Var Powder Puff Ftbl; Var L Sftbl; Var Swmmng; High Hon Roll; Hon Roll; Prom Queen 86; Hmcmng Ct 86; WV U; Dental Hyg.

HUFFORD, CHRISTINE; Central HS; Martinsburg, PA; (Y); 30/188; Hon Roll; Central Honor Soc 85-86; Psychology.

HUFFORD, GWYNETH; Bishop Mcdevitt HS; Hummelstown, PA; (Y); 2/217; Church Yth Grp; School Musical; School Play; DAR Awd; High Hon Roll; NHS; Ntl Merit Ltr; Sal; Drama Clb; French Clb; Natl Achvmnt Schlrshp Wnr 85-86; Lions Clb Yth Exchng Stu 85; Schlstc Wrtng Gld Key 86; Penn ST U; Physics.

HUFFORD, KIMBERLY; Portage Area HS; Portage, PA; (Y); Band; Chorus; Concert Band; Jazz Band; Mrchg Band; Pep Band; Stage Crew; High Hon Roll; Hon Roll; NHS; CA U Of PA; Vet.

HUGAR, LORI; Blacklick Valley HS; Vintondale, PA; (Y); Camera Clb; Church Yth Grp; Office Aide; Varsity Clb; Var Sftbl; Penn ST; CPA.

HUGENDUBLER, KENNETH; Hershey HS; Hershey, PA; (Y); 15/194; Church Yth Grp; Debate Tm; Math Clb; Math Tm; Model UN; Political Wkr; Quiz Bowl; Spanish Clb; Lit Mag; Crs Cntry; Hershey Ed Assn Scholar 86; Susquehanna U Pres Scholar 86; Outstndng Achvt Soc Studs 86; Susquehanna U; Pre-Law.

HUGGINS, KRISTIN; Pennsbury HS; Yardley, PA; (Y); French Clb; Letterman Clb; Varsity Clb; Drill Tm; Mrchg Band; Yrbk Stf; Var Diving; Var L Trk; Hon Roll; NHS; Dist Wide Art Show 84-86; Marchng Band Rose Bowl Parade 86; Natl Phys Fit Awd 85; Bus.

HUGH, STEPHANIE; Knoch HS; Butler, PA; (Y); Sec Exploring; French Clb; Sec German Clb; Hosp Aide; Pep Clb; School Play; Stat Bsktbl; Im Vllybl; Lang.

HUGHES, AARON; Chief Logan HS; Burnham, PA; (Y); Computer Clb; Debate Tm; Pep Clb; Ski Clb; Varsity Clb; Stu Cncl; Var L Bsbl; Stat Bsktbl; Var L Ftbl; Sci.

HUGHES, CHARLES; Hazleton HS; Drums, PA; (Y); Chess Clb; Drama Clb; French Clb; Band; Concert Band; Jazz Band; Mrchg Band; Golf; Tennis; PA ST U; Physclgy.

HUGHES II, CHARLES; Pen Argyl HS; Pen Argyl, PA; (Y); 6/120; VP Church Yth Grp; Computer Clb; Ski Clb; Yrbk Stf; Var L Bsbl; Var Capt Bsktbl; Var L Ftbl; High Hon Roll; Ldrshp Conf Lehigh U 86; ROTC Essay Cont Wnnr 86; Bus Adm.

HUGHES, CHRISTINA M; Elizabethtown Area HS; Elizabethtown, PA; (Y); 2/221; Am Leg Aux Girls St; Church Yth Grp; Girl Scts; Var JV Fld Hcky; Var Capt Sftbl; DAR Awd; NHS; Pres Schlr; Sal; VFW Awd; Hugh O Brien Ldrshp Awd 84; Elizabeth Hughes Awd 86; Bus & Prof Wmns Awd 86; Bryn Mawr Coll.

HUGHES, CHRISTINE; Benton JR SR HS; Stillwater, PA; (Y); 8/39; Chorus; Church Choir; Mrchg Band; Yrbk Stf; Sec Frsh Cls; Sec Stu Cncl; Var Capt Cheerleading; Var Capt Fld Hcky; Kiwanis Awd; VP NHS; Kings Coll Schrlsh Pgm; Bloomsbur U Extnd Pgm Schrlshp; MVP Hockey; Bloomsburg U; Physcl Thrpy.

HUGHES, CINDY; Tunkhannock HS; Falls, PA; (Y); Ski Clb; Spanish Clb; Variety Show; Nwsp Ed-Chief; Nwsp Rptr; Hon Roll; Reporter.

HUGHES, DAN; Chief Logan HS; Lewistown, PA; (Y); Boy Scts; Computer Clb; Scholastic Bowl; Ski Clb; Varsity Clb; Concert Band; Mrchg Band; Var Capt Crs Cntry; Var Capt Trk; Ntl Merit Ltr; Engrng.

HUGHES, DAVID A; Franklin HS; Franklin, PA; (Y); 3/221; German Clb; High Hon Roll; Hon Roll; Kiwanis Awd; NHS; Prfct Atten Awd; Sal; Pres Acad Ftnss Awd 86; Brd Of Schl Dir Awd 83-86; PA ST U; Engrng.

HUGHES, DENNIS; Shaler Area HS; Pittsburgh, PA; (Y); 86/526; Ski Clb; Ftbl; Im Sftbl; Hon Roll.

HUGHES, DOUGLAS; Cedar Crest HS; Cornwall, PA; (Y); 13/333; Drama Clb; FBLA; Spanish Clb; Thesps; Jazz Band; School Musical; Var Swmmng; High Hon Roll; NHS; Ntl Merit Ltr; Hnr Banquet-Bronze & Silver Mdlst 84-86; Elec.

HUGHES, GINGER; West Greene JR SR HS; Aleppo, PA; (S); 2/70; French Clb; VICA; High Hon Roll; Hon Roll; Cosmtlgst.

HUGHES, JANEEN; Avon Grove HS; Landenberg, PA; (Y); 21/148; Church Yth Grp; FNA; Hosp Aide; Band; Concert Band; Mrchg Band; School Play; High Hon Roll; Hon Roll; NHS; Engl, Hstry & Clrcl Awds 84-86; Chester Cnty Hosp; Nrsng.

HUGHES, JEAN; Philipsburg-Osceola HS; Osceola Mills, PA; (Y); 66/244; Church Yth Grp; Band; Color Guard; Concert Band; Mrchg Band; Bsktbl; Vllybl; Hon Roll; Nrsng.

HUGHES, KELLI; South Park HS; Library, PA; (Y); Hosp Aide; ROTC; SADD; Hon Roll; U Pittsburgh; Med.

HUGHES, KRISTA; Thomas Jefferson HS HS; Pittsburgh, PA; (Y); 101/254; Cmnty Wkr; French Clb; Library Aide; Ski Clb; VP Jr Cls; Cheerleading; Ednbrgh PA; Cmmnctns.

HUGHES, MICHAEL; Archbishop John Carroll HS; Wayne, PA; (Y); 11/171; High Hon Roll; Hon Roll; NHS; Pres Schlr; Ski Clb; JV Ftbl; JV Socr; JV Trk; Bio Awd 84; Hlth Ed Awd 84; Fredrick S Fox Jr Schrlshp 86; Clemson U; Comp Engr.

HUGHES, MICHELLE; Central Dauphin HS; Penbrook, PA; (Y); 110/386; Cmnty Wkr; Hosp Aide; Science Clb; Nwsp Sprt Ed; Yrbk Stf; Golf; Thtre Prod Awd 85; Genetcs.

HUGHES, MIKE; Palmyra Area HS; Palmyra, PA; (Y); Church Yth Grp; Concert Band; Mrchg Band; Var Golf; JV Wrstlng; Hon Roll; Math.

HUGHES, POLLY ANN; West Side Area Vo-Tech; Luzerne, PA; (Y); 12/137; Cmnty Wkr; Computer Clb; FBLA; Latin Clb; Chorus; School Musical; High Hon Roll; Hon Roll; Book Scholar 85-86; Sci Awd Craft Advsry Comm 85-86; Scholar Awd Big Bros/Big Sis 85-86; Robert Packes Schl Nrsng; Nrsng.

HUGHES, RETONIA KAY; Philadelphia Schl Of Performng Arts; Camden, NJ; (Y); Church Yth Grp; Cmnty Wkr; Dance Clb; Drama Clb; PAVAS; Church Choir; Drill Tm; School Play; Stage Crew; Variety Show; U PA; Accntnt.

HUGHES, RICHARD J; South Side Catholic HS; Pittsburgh, PA; (S); Chess Clb; Dance Clb; Chorus; Nwsp Rptr; Yrbk Stf; VP Bowling; DAR Awd; High Hon Roll; NHS; Algbra II, Bio II, Frnch & Hstry Awds 85; Geomtry, Chem, West Civ & Hlth Awds 84; Geogrphy Awd 83.

HUGHES, SHAWN; Leechburg HS; Leechburg, PA; (Y); Band; Concert Band; Mrchg Band; Pep Band; Var Bsbl; Law.

HUGHES, STEPHEN R; Hampton HS; Allison Pk, PA; (Y); Chess Clb; Bowling; Slipper Rock U; Mth Tchr.

HUGHES, SUSAN; Du Boise Central Christian HS; Rockton, PA; (Y); Cmnty Wkr; German Clb; Hosp Aide; Math Clb; Band; Concert Band; Trk; Skpd 8th Grd 83; Awds Equestrn Actvts 83-86; Intl Bls.

HUGHES, SUSAN; Lenape Vo-Tech; Spring Church, PA; (S); Church Yth Grp; DECA; FBLA; Library Aide; Pep Clb; Ski Clb; Hon Roll; 1st Pl Gen Mrchndsg Supv Level 85, 2nd Pl 86; Distributive Ed Cls Pres 85-86.

HUGHES, SUZANNE; West Hazleton HS; Sugarloaf, PA; (Y); 8/216; Pep Clb; Capt Scholastic Bowl; Ski Clb; Spanish Clb; SADD; Var L Bsktbl; Var L Sftbl; Var L Trk; High Hon Roll; Gov Schl Sci 86; Awd Sci Talnt Srch 86; Bio.

HUGHES, TAMMY; Mt Alvernia HS; Pittsburgh, PA; (S); Computer Clb; French Clb; Hosp Aide; Lit Mag; Cit Awd; French Hon Soc; High Hon Roll; NHS; Ntl Merit Ltr; Prfct Atten Awd; Pre-Med.

HUGHES, THOMAS; Hampton HS; Allison Pk, PA; (Y); Boy Scts; Jazz Band; Symp Band; Nwsp Phtg; Nwsp Rptr; Nwsp Stf; High Hon Roll; Hon Roll; Pres Schlr; Band; Eagle Sct 86; Clarion U PA; Comm.

HUGHES, TIFFANY; Freedom HS; Bethlehem, PA; (Y); 80/465; Hosp Aide; Chorus; School Musical; Hon Roll.

HUGHES, TRACY; Central Cambria HS; Ebensburg, PA; (Y); French Clb; NFL; Crs Cntry; Trk; Hon Roll; &IAA Dist Corss Cty 6th Pl 86; IN U; Psychlgy.

HUH, ELMER H; Radnor SR HS; Wayne, PA; (Y); FCA; Intnl Clb; Math Clb; Science Clb; Variety Show; Var L Crs Cntry; L Var Trk; High Hon Roll; French Hon Soc; Yrbk Stf; National Council Of Youth Leadership Awd 86; Korean Club Vp; Peace Committee; Engrng.

HUHA, MICHELLE; Norwin SR HS; N Huntingdon, PA; (Y); 57/450; Spanish Clb; Hon Roll; Robert Morris Coll; Acctg.

HULICK, PATRICIA; Souderton Area HS; Schwenksville, PA; (Y); Aud/Vis; Spanish Clb; Rep Stu Cncl; DAR Awd; Hon Roll; NHS; NEDT Awd; Prfct Atten Awd; Soc Acad Achvt Lttr Recp 83-84; NCTE Achvt Awd Wrtng Nominee 85-86; Achvt Awd Top 2% In Class 85-86; Psych.

HULICK, STEVAN; Burgettstown Area JR SR HS; Burgetstown, PA; (Y); 10/145; Spanish Clb; Bsktbl; Ftbl; Score Keeper; Timer; High Hon Roll; Hon Roll; Jr NHS; NHS; Sprts Med.

HULL, ANNMARIE; Pen Argyl HS; Nazareth, PA; (Y); Office Aide; Pep Clb; Scholastic Bowl; Ski Clb; Pres Varsity Clb; Var Capt Cheerleading; Im Gym; High Hon Roll; Hon Roll; NCA All Amer Chrldng Fnlst Awd 84-85; SR Of Mnth 86; Legl Sec.

HULL, CHRISTINE; Lock Haven SR HS; Lock Haven, PA; (Y); Church Yth Grp; Cmnty Wkr; French Clb; SADD; Band; Chorus; Concert Band; Drm Mjr(t); Jazz Band; Mrchg Band; Psychology.

HULL, EDWARD; Bishop Kenrick HS; Norristown, PA; (Y); 1/304; Mathletes; VP Sr Cls; Stu Cncl; Bsbl; Bsktbl; Hon Roll; NHS; 1st Tm All Cthlc Sccr 84 & 85; Hghst Score-Tnl Math Exam 86; Kystn ST Games In Sccr 85 & 86.

HULL, KIMBERLY; Purchase Line HS; Mahaffey, PA; (Y); Hosp Aide; ROTC; Band; Concert Band; Mrchg Band.

HULL, MARK; Greater Latrobe HS; Latrobe, PA; (Y); Letterman Clb; Pep Clb; Teachers Aide; Capt Ftbl; Wt Lftg; Wrstlng; High Hon Roll; Hon Roll; Rotary Awd; Hnrs Phy Ed Class 85-86; PA ST; Engrng.

HULL, SHAWN; Mt Pleasant Area SR HS; Acme, PA; (Y); VICA; Ftbl; Hon Roll; Wrhs Mgmt.

HULL, TRACY; Montgomery HS; Montgomery, PA; (Y); Band; Flag Corp; Yrbk Stf; Var L Bsktbl; Bowling; Var L Cheerleading; Var L Trk; High Hon Roll; Hon Roll; Bsktbl Coaches Awd 86; Chrldng Most Spirited 86.

HULLAK, ANDREA; Canon-Mc Millan SR HS; Canonsburg, PA; (Y); Church Yth Grp; Trs FBLA; Library Aide; Office Aide; Pep Clb; Trk; Hon Roll; Accntng.

HULSEY, AMY; Canon Mc Millan HS; Canonsburg, PA; (Y); 31/371; French Clb; Hosp Aide; Sec Chorus; Drill Tm; Pom Pon; High Hon Roll; Hon Roll; Lttrd 3 Yrs In Drill Tm 85-87; Fstvl Of Music Orlando FL Drill Tm Trphs 86; Drill Tm Camp 85; Phys Thrpy.

HULTMAN, LESLEY; Warren Area HS; Warren, PA; (Y); German Clb; Ski Clb; Var L Bsktbl; Var L Sftbl; NHS; Prsdntl Physcl Ftn Awd 84; Fncne.

HULTZAPPLE, DOREEN; Central Dauphin East HS; Harrisburg, PA; (Y); French Clb; Chorus; Nwsp Rptr; Yrbk Stf; Hon Roll; Jr NHS; NHS; Ntl Merit Ltr; Pres Schlr; PHEAA Cert Of Mrt 84-85; John N Hall Fndtn Schlrshp 86-87; Harrisburg Area CC; Nrsng.

HUMBERGER, DORIS LEE; Hempfield Area SR HS; Grapeville, PA; (Y); FBLA; Library Aide; Pep Clb; Ski Clb; Color Guard; Vllybl; Cit Awd; Hon Roll; Prfct Atten Awd; Bradford Schl; Actg.

HUMBERSON, DAVINA A; West Mifflin Area HS; W Mifflin, PA; (Y); 96/335; VP Exploring; Library Aide; Office Aide; Science Clb; Off Jr Cls; Hon Roll; U Pittsburgh Cert 85; Bio.

HUMBERT, SHERRI; Shade HS; Stoystown, PA; (Y); Hosp Aide; Sec VICA; Yrbk Stf; Hon Roll.

HUMBERT, STEVEN; Somerset Area SR HS; Friedens, PA; (Y); Boy Scts; JA; Chorus; High Hon Roll; Hon Roll; Comp Prgmmg.

HUMENAY, LISA; West Branch HS; Kylertown, PA; (S); 8/147; Science Clb; Ski Clb; Spanish Clb; Varsity Clb; Chorus; Stu Cncl; Sftbl; Hon Roll; NHS; VP,Treas Spanish Clb 84-86; U PA; Lawyer.

HUMENICK, JANICE MARIE; Bishop Hafey HS; Hazleton, PA; (Y); 15/182; Service Clb; Spanish Clb; School Play; Nwsp Rptr; Yrbk Ed-Chief; Ed Lit Mag; High Hon Roll; NHS; Spanish NHS; Kings Coll Acad Schlrshp 86; Pref Atten 85-86; Friendly Sons St Patrick Awd Hgst Avg 86; Kings Coll; Elem Ed.

HUMES, JEFFREY; Seneca Valley SR HS; Mars, PA; (Y); Art Clb; Boy Scts; Band; Mrchg Band; Hon Roll; Eagle Sct, All Eagle Plms; Arch.

HUMMEL, DANETTE; Northampton Area SR HS; Cherryville, PA; (S); Pres Drama Clb; Thesps; Chorus; School Musical; School Play; Stage Crew; Ed Yrbk Stf; Hon Roll; Northhampton Area CC.

HUMMEL, DAVID; Upper Moreland HS; Hatboro, PA; (Y); Key Clb; Rep Frsh Cls; Rep Soph Cls; Pres Jr Cls; Rep Sr Cls; Rep Stu Cncl; Bsbl; Var Capt Ftbl; High Hon Roll; Hon Roll; Acdmc Decthln Slvr Medl Essy 86; SAT; Clss Prnk & 13 Yrs Perf Attndnc 85; Penn ST; Pre-Med.

HUMMEL, DOUG; Shamokin Area HS; Shamokin, PA; (Y); Cmnty Wkr; German Clb; Key Clb; Science Clb; Varsity Clb; Ftbl; Swmmng; Hon Roll; NHS; Engr.

HUMMEL, HARVEY; Bensalem SR HS; Bensalem, PA; (Y); Boy Scts; Church Yth Grp; Stu Cncl; High Hon Roll; Hon Roll; Veterinarian.

HUMMEL, JULIE ANN; Bangor Area SR HS; Bangor, PA; (Y); 23/171; Hosp Aide; Varsity Clb; Band; Chorus; School Musical; School Play; Nwsp Rptr; Bsktbl; Sftbl; High Hon Roll; New Approach Schlrshp In Memry Of Cathy Le Barre 86; ILGWU Schlrshp For Nrsng 86; Josephine Farace Aw; Nrthmptn Cnty Area CC; Radlgy.

HUMMEL, KIMBERLY; Seneca Valley SR HS; Evans City, PA; (Y); 17/355; Sec Thesps; Chorus; Madrigals; Mrchg Band; School Musical; Symp Band; JP Sousa Awd; Sec NHS; SADD; Nwsp Stf; Natl Schl Chrl Awd 86; Dana Schl Music 86; Zelienople Rtry Schlrshp 86; Youngstown ST U Fdn Schlr 86; Youngstown ST U; Flte.

HUMMEL, VIRGINIA; Hopewell HS; Aliquippa, PA; (S); Band; Nwsp Rptr; Capt Var Powder Puff Ftbl; L Var Trk; L Var Vllybl; French Hon Soc; High Hon Roll; NHS; Ntl Merit Ltr; 4th Pl Keystone ST Gms/Javelin 85; Supr Mdl Mrchng FL Assoc 83-84; Silver Mdl Cnty/Javelin 85; Crmnlgy.

HUMMELL, AMY; Washington HS; Washington, PA; (S); 12/170; Pres Church Yth Grp; Hosp Aide; Key Clb; Spanish Clb; Church Choir; Madrigals; Mrchg Band; School Musical; Symp Band; High Hon Roll.

HUMMELL, ANDREW; Hempfield Area SR HS; Manor, PA; (Y); High Hon Roll; Jr NHS; NHS; Pres Acdmc Fit Awd 86; Hnr Stdnt 86.

HUMMER, ALEX; William Allen HS; Allentown, PA; (Y); 11/627; Ski Clb; Var JV Socr; Var Tennis; High Hon Roll; Hon Roll; NHS; Ntl Merit Ltr; Jr NHS; 3rd Pl Medici Bcycl Rcg Leag All Star Chmpnshp 85; Burger King Bcycl Rcg Leag All Star Chmpn 86; Bio Engrng.

HUMMER, LESLIE; Annville-Cleona HS; Lebanon, PA; (S); 5/105; Varsity Clb; Band; Chorus; Orch; Var L Bsktbl; Var L Trk; NHS; Phys Thrpy.

HUMPHREY, KAREN; Penn Wood HS; Darby, PA; (Y); Church Yth Grp; Cmnty Wkr; Drama Clb; FBLA; Girl Scts; Chorus; Church Choir; Drill Tm; Nwsp Stf; Yrbk Stf; Bus Adm.

HUMPHREY, PETER; Penn Hills SR HS; Pittsburgh, PA; (Y); 40/747; Trs Church Yth Grp; German Clb; High Hon Roll; Jr NHS; NHS; Pres Acad Ftns Awd 86; Eng Achvmnt Awd; Penn ST; Archtrl Engr.

HUMPHREY, ROBERTA; Villa Maria Acad; Erie, PA; (Y); Church Yth Grp; Hosp Aide; Chorus; Madrigals; School Play; Stage Crew; Trvl & Tourism.

HUMPHREY, SUSAN; Highlands SR HS; Natrona Hts, PA; (Y); Girl Scts; Concert Band; Mrchg Band; Crs Cntry; Swmmng; Tennis; Jr NHS; NHS; Girl Scout Gold Awd 86; Chem.

HUMPHREYS, DAVID; South Park HS; Pittsburgh, PA; (Y); 1/203; Ski Clb; Var Golf; Mgr(s); CC Awd; High Hon Roll; NHS; Pres Schlr; Val; Pitt Provost Schlrshp 86; Engrng Schlrshp 86; PSEA Schlrshp 86; Bell Tel Of PA Schlrshp 86; U Of Pittsbrgh; Elec Engrng.

HUMPHREYS, DEBRA; South Park HS; Pittsburgh, PA; (S); Church Yth Grp; Drama Clb; Hosp Aide; Ski Clb; Var Socr; Stat Trk; High Hon Roll; NHS; Stage Crew; Yrbk Stf; NEDT Awd 84; Carnegie Museum Of Natural Hstry Sci Awd 86; Schlrshp Awd For Outstdng Acad Achvt 86; Phy Thrpy.

HUMPHREYS, JOHN; Peters Township HS; Mc Murray, PA; (Y); 43/230; Im Badmtn; Var Bsbl; Bsktbl; Var Ftbl; Im Golf; Im Tennis; Im Vllybl; Im Wt Lftg; High Hon Roll; Hon Roll; Intl Bus.

HUMPHRIES, MICHAEL; Frankford HS; Philadelphia, PA; (Y); 24/453; Pep Clb; Red Cross Aide; Varsity Clb; School Play; JV Var Bsbl; Hon Roll; NHS; Vicente De Castro Alumni Assoc Awd 86; Frankford Hgh Hm & Schl Assoc Awd 86; Frankford Histrcl Soc Awd; Drexel UCOMP Sci.

HUNDERTMARK, JAY; Bethlehem Center HS; Fredericktown, PA; (Y); 3/157; Spanish Clb; Band; Concert Band; Jazz Band; Mrchg Band; Pep Band; Bsktbl; High Hon Roll; NHS; Amer Legion Awd 84; Outstndg Musician Awd 84.

HUNKELE, RENEE M; North Allegheny HS; Allison Pk, PA; (Y); 24/605; DECA; Drm Mjr(t); Stu Cncl; N Allegheny Voc Educ Schlrshp 86; U Of Pgh At Johnstown; Pharmcy.

HUNSICKER, DENNIS; Jim Thorpe SR HS; Jim Thorpe, PA; (S); 9/97; Boy Scts; Nwsp Rptr; Yrbk Stf; High Hon Roll; NHS; Egl Sct Awd 85; U Of AL; Aerntcl Engr.

HUNSICKER, LAURA; Parkland SR HS; Neffs, PA; (Y); 8/415; German Clb; Key Clb; Band; Off Stu Cncl; JV Fld Hcky; Hon Roll; Ntl Merit Schol; Rotary Awd; Excllnc Awd Penn ST U 86; AATG Awd Grmn 84-86; PA ST U; Chld Psych.

HUNSICKER, SUSAN; Lehighton Area HS; Lehighton, PA; (Y); Art Clb; Church Yth Grp; FBLA; Girl Scts; Church Choir; Pinebrook JC; Med Secy.

HUNSINGER, STEPHANE; Sullivan County HS; Dushore, PA; (Y); 3/92; Drama Clb; FHA; Key Clb; Scholastic Bowl; Band; Mrchg Band; School Play; Nwsp Rptr; Nwsp Stf; Yrbk Ed-Chief; Case Western Reserve Univ; Bio.

HUNT, CHRIS; Nazareth Area SR HS; Bethlehem, PA; (Y); 16/231; Stu Cncl; Var Capt Bsktbl; Var Capt Ftbl; Var Capt Trk; Cit Awd; Hon Roll; NHS; SAR Awd; Ftbl Schlrshp Villanova U 86; Pequot Socty Ideal Ml Athl Awd 86; Pres Acdmc Fit Awd 86; Villanova U; Cvl Engrng.

HUNT, ELISA; Corry Area HS; Corry, PA; (S); Art Clb; Church Yth Grp; Cmnty Wkr; Library Aide; Hon Roll; Typflsh Awd 85; Mercyhurst Coll; Prmry Educ.

HUNT, LISA D; Mc Guffey HS; W Alexander, PA; (Y); 60/207; French Clb; Pres Pep Clb; Varsity Clb; Chorus; School Musical; Yrbk Stf; VP Soph Cls; Powder Puff Ftbl; Var Capt Vllybl; High Hon Roll; Ldrshp Awd 85-86; Surg Tech.

HUNT, LYNDA; Cedar Crest HS; Lebaon, PA; (Y); 68/352; Exploring; French Clb; Latin Clb; Pep Clb; Science Clb; Varsity Clb; Im Socr; Var Tennis; Im Vllybl; Hon Roll; Ntl Hnr Stu Mdl 85-86.

HUNT, ROBERTA; Seneca HS; Wattsburg, PA; (Y); Exploring; Chorus; Sec Trs Concert Band; Capt Drm Mjr(t); Mrchg Band; Orch; Pep Band; Yrbk Stf; High Hon Roll; NHS; Villa Maria Coll; Nrsng.

HUNT, SEAN; East Pennsboro HS; Enola, PA; (Y); 12/205; Boy Scts; Latin Clb; Spanish Clb; Varsity Clb; Var L Bsbl; JV L Bsktbl; Var L Ftbl; Stat Swmmng; Im Wt Lftg; High Hon Roll; Engrng.

HUNTER, AMY; Apollo-Ridge HS; Homer City, PA; (Y); 10/170; Church Yth Grp; Cmnty Wkr; Office Aide; Nwsp Rptr; NHS; Drama Clb; Teachers Aide; Church Choir; Nwsp Stf; Hon Roll; Arin Adult Learning Center.

HUNTER, BONNIE; Penn Hills SR HS; Verona, PA; (Y); French Clb; Girl Scts; Sec Key Clb; Trs Science Clb; JV Stat Bsbl; Grl Scout Gold Awd 86; Law.

HUNTER, CATHERINE; Delaware County Christian Schl; Drexel Hill, PA; (Y); 13/78; Church Yth Grp; Hosp Aide; Chorus; School Play; Rep Frsh Cls; Var JV Bsktbl; JV Sftbl; High Hon Roll; NHS; Distngshd Chrstn HS Stu 85-86; Phys Thrpy.

HUNTER, DANA MICHELE; Saegertown Area HS; Saegertown, PA; (Y); #14 In Class; Church Yth Grp; French Clb; Ski Clb; SADD; Church Choir; Gov Hon Prg Awd; Hon Roll; Jr NHS; Chld Psych.

HUNTER, DAVE; New Brighton HS; New Brighton, PA; (Y); Aud/Vis; Computer Clb; Letterman Clb; Spanish Clb; Varsity Clb; Chorus; Var Ftbl; Trk; JV Var Wt Lftg; Hon Roll; Electrncs.

HUNTER, STACEY; Coatesville Area SR HS; Coatesville, PA; (Y); 57/480; Church Yth Grp; Civic Clb; FNA; Hosp Aide; Chorus; Nwsp Stf; Rep Stu Cncl; Var JV Fld Hcky; Hon Roll; NHS; Meistersingers Ltr 85-86; Nrsng.

HUNTER, STEVEN J; Butler Area HS; Butler, PA; (Y); 7/786; VP JA; SADD; Band; Concert Band; Mrchg Band; Symp Band; High Hon Roll; Hon Roll; Jr NHS; NHS; Schlstc Ltr Achvt 85; Outstndng VP Mrktg JA 86; Bus Fin.

HUNTER, TAHME; Farrell SR HS; Wheatland, PA; (Y); 12/99; Computer Clb; Key Clb; Math Clb; Band; Mrchg Band; Pep Band; School Play; Hon Roll; NHS; Youngstown ST U; Comp Tech.

HUNTINGTON, GENE; Troy Area HS; Columbia Cross Rd, PA; (Y); Am Leg Boys St; Cmnty Wkr; Letterman Clb; Ski Clb; Trs Jr Cls; Pres Sr Cls; Capt Wrstlng; Dnfth Awd; PA ST U; Lndscp Arch.

HUNTINGTON, TIM; Southwestern HS; Hanover, PA; (Y); Church Yth Grp; Bsbl; Golf; Hon Roll; Miami Of OH U; Bus Law.

HUNTZINGER, DAPHNE; Tri-Valley HS; Spring Glen, PA; (Y); 8/77; Church Yth Grp; Drama Clb; VP 4-H; Band; Chorus; Church Choir; Mrchg Band; Pep Band; 4-H Awd; Hon Roll; VA Western Coll; Accntng.

HUNZER, KATHLEEN; Neshaminy HS; Feasterville, PA; (Y); Girl Scts; Hosp Aide; SADD; Chorus; Concert Band; Mrchg Band; Nwsp Stf; Yrbk Stf; Sec Soph Cls; NHS; Pa ST; Educ.

HURD, WILLIAM; Clearfield Area HS; Clearfield, PA; (Y); Art Clb; Band; Concert Band; Mrchg Band; Automotive Dsgn Engrng.

HURLBURT III, HARRY O; Plymouth-Whitemarsh HS; Ft Washington, PA; (Y); 12/361; Aud/Vis; Nwsp Rptr; Off Soph Cls; Trs Sr Cls; Cit Awd; High Hon Roll; VP NHS; VFW Awd; MI Media Fest Bst Stu Awd 85; Pres Acdmc Ftns Awd 86; Teen Age Mag-1 Most Interesting Teens US 85; Drexel U; Bus.

HURLEY, DEBRA; Danville SR HS; Danville, PA; (Y); VP Church Yth Grp; Exploring; Latin Clb; Chorus; School Musical; Hon Roll; NHS; Comp Sci.

HURLY, STEPHEN; Downingtown HS; Laurel, MD; (S); 25/550; German Clb; Letterman Clb; Ski Clb; VP Soph Cls; VP Jr Cls; Rep Stu Cncl; Var Capt Socr; High Hon Roll; NHS; NEDT Awd; PA Cert Merit 86; Al-Leag 1st Tm Scr 85 & 86; Engrng.

HURSH, JENNIFER; Peters Township HS; Mcmurray, PA; (Y); 65/231; FBLA; Intnl Clb; Key Clb; NFL; Ed Yrbk Bus Mgr; Var Swmmng; Var Trk; Boston U; Bus.

HURST, CAROL; Archbishop Prendergast HS; Collingdale, PA; (Y); Office Aide; Orch; School Play; Mdrn Music Mstrs 85-86; Chldhd Educ.

HURST, JACK; Marian Catholic HS; Barnesville, PA; (Y); 39/124; Aud/Vis; Band; Concert Band; Mrchg Band; Pep Band; Frstry.

HURST, JOHN; Strath Haven HS; Media, PA; (Y); Intnl Clb; Ski Clb; SADD; School Musical; Nwsp Rptr; Nwsp Stf; Lit Mag; Stu Cncl; Lcrss; Socr; Acad Ftns Awd 86; Midd Lebury Coll.

HURST, MICHELE; Upper Darby SR HS; Drexel Hl, PA; (Y); Girl Scts; Library Aide; Science Clb; Acpl Chr; Color Guard; Concert Band; Mrchg Band; Orch; School Musical; Hon Roll; Diexel Hill Grdn Clb Schlrshp 86; Wilson Coll; Vet Med.

HURT, DAVE; South Allegheny HS; Port Vue, PA; (Y); JV Var Bsktbl.

HURTA, TODD; Ambridge HS; Freedom, PA; (Y); Church Yth Grp; Cmnty Wkr; FCA; Pep Clb; SADD; Stage Crew; Bsktbl; Var Capt Ftbl; Wt Lftg; Hon Roll.

HURWITZ, WENDY; Central Bucsk High School East; Doylestown, PA; (Y); Debate Tm; Intnl Clb; Trs Service Clb; Nwsp Rptr; Yrbk Stf; Trs Stu Cncl; JV Swmmng; Var Vllybl; Hon Roll; NHS; Mrktng.

HUSAIN, GAZALA; Villa Maria Acad; Erie, PA; (S); 11/134; Hosp Aide; Model UN; NFL; PAVAS; Science Clb; Madrigals; School Musical; Variety Show; Swmmng; High Hon Roll; 7th Plc Frnscs Trnmnt 86; Hi Hnr Rl Crtfcts 85-86; Natl Hnr Scty Awd 85; Med.

HUSAR, MARIANN; Portage Area HS; Cassandra, PA; (Y); 38/122; Church Yth Grp; French Clb; Band; Chorus; Church Choir; Mrchg Band; Rep Stu Cncl; Med.

HUSBAND, MARY LOU; Connellsville Area SR HS; Connellsville, PA; (Y); 1/550; Church Yth Grp; School Musical; French Hon Soc; High Hon Roll; NHS; Tchr.

HUSTAK, ANNMARIE; Butler Area SR HS; Butler, PA; (Y); Computer Clb; Library Aide; Band; Hon Roll; Comp Pgmng.

HUSTEAD, DELLAS C; Jeannette SR HS; Jeannette, PA; (Y); 9/132; Am Leg Boys St; French Clb; Ski Clb; Bsbl; Wrstlng; High Hon Roll; Hon Roll; Westmoreland Cnty Juvenile Justice Essay Contst Wnnr 86; Engr.

HUSTON, MARGARET PEGGY; Freeport Area HS; Freeport, PA; (S); 13/173; Sec Drama Clb; Hosp Aide; Band; Pep Band; Stage Crew; Yrbk Bus Mgr; Yrbk Stf; Rep Stu Cncl; Stat Trk; NHS; Penn ST U; Nrsg.

HUSTON, SCOTT; Mercy Vo; Philadelphia, PA; (Y); Im Bsktbl; Var Wt Lftg; Var Wrstlng; Hon Roll; Penn ST; Elec Engr.

HUSTWIT, NOEL; Keystone Oaks HS; Pittsburgh, PA; (Y); 84/254; Variety Show; Off Jr Cls; Off Sr Cls; Var L Bsbl; Var L Ftbl; Wt Lftg; 9th Pl Spnsh Lang Comptn Gannon U 85; Allegheny Coll Meadville; Law.

HUTCHESON, DAWN; Susquenita HS; New Buffalo, PA; (S); 21/175; Church Yth Grp; Computer Clb; Nwsp Stf; Rep Stu Cncl; Bsktbl; Fld Hcky; Trk; Hon Roll; Phys Thrpy.

HUTCHINS, ANDREA; Slippery Rock Area HS; Slippery Rock, PA; (Y); Aud/Vis; Church Yth Grp; Chorus; Concert Band; Flag Corp; Mrchg Band; JV Trk; God Cntry Awd; NHS; Girl Scts; Silv Awd Grl Scouts 83-84; Silv Ldrshp Awd Grl Scouts 83-84; Slippery Rock U; Chem.

HUTCHINSON, BARBARA; Juniata HS; Mifflin, PA; (Y); Art Clb; 4-H; FHA; 4-H Awd; High Hon Roll; Hon Roll; NHS; Schlstc J 84-86.

HUTCHINSON, ISAIAH; West Catholic Boys HS; Philadelphia, PA; (Y); 47/300; Church Yth Grp; Cmnty Wkr; Varsity Clb; School Play; Stage Crew; Stu Cncl; Cit Awd; JETS Awd; Ntl Merit Schol; Vrsty Lttr Ftbll, Trk & Jd 86; Prfct Cndct 86; Hnr Rll 86; Temple U; Engrng.

HUTCHINSON, STACIE; Central Dawphin HS; Harrisburg, PA; (Y); Church Yth Grp; Exploring; Pep Clb; Rep Stu Cncl; Var JV Bsktbl; Im Vllybl; Phy Thrpy.

HUTCHISON, AMY; North Catholic HS; Glenshaw, PA; (Y); 3/301; Church Yth Grp; French Clb; Hosp Aide; Pres Service Clb; Ski Clb; Color Guard; Concert Band; Mrchg Band; Sec Sr Cls; Rep Stu Cncl; Frnch Schlr Awd 86; Penn ST U; Pre-Dntl.

HUTCHISON, BILL; Altoona Area HS; Altoona, PA; (S); Church Yth Grp; Mathletes; Ski Clb; Band; Concert Band; Jazz Band; Mrchg Band; School Musical; Var Capt Swmmng; Var L Tennis; Sci.

HUTCHISON, COLLEEN; South Allegheny HS; Mckeesport, PA; (Y); French Clb; Y-Teens; Concert Band; Mrchg Band; Nwsp Stf; Jr Cls; Trs Sr Cls; Rep Stu Cncl; Powder Puff Ftbl; Twrlr; Accntng.

HUTCHISON, ERIC; Nazareth Area SR HS; Stockertown, PA; (Y); Aud/Vis; Computer Clb; VICA; Stage Crew; Elec.

HUTCHISON, TAMMY; Wilmington Area HS; New Wilmington, PA; (Y); 15/123; Sec Church Yth Grp; French Clb; Key Clb; Office Aide; Church Choir; School Play; Trs Jr Cls; Var L Trk; Var Capt Vllybl; High Hon Roll; Scnt Tm Vllybll All-Strs 85; Prtcpt Lawerance Co JR Miss Pgnt 86; Nrsng.

HUTCHISON JR, WILLIAM R; Brownsville Area HS; Grindstone, PA; (Y); VICA; Hon Roll; 3rd Pl VICA Rgnl Cmptn Wldng 86; Triangle Tech; Wldng.

HUTSELL, SCOTT; Bethel Park SR HS; Bethel Park, PA; (Y); Math Clb; Science Clb; Chorus; School Musical; Swing Chorus; Rep Stu Cncl; Cit Awd; Jr NHS; Kiwanis Awd; Opt Clb Awd; Amer Legion Awd 84; Aerospc Engrng.

HUTSKO, CRYSTAL; Hamburg Area HS; Shartlesville, PA; (Y); German Clb; Library Aide; JV Bowling; Stat Trk; Hon Roll; Fshn Mrchndsng.

HUTSON, MIKE; Hughesville HS; Muncy, PA; (Y); Boy Scts; Varsity Clb; Var L Wrstlng; Eagle Scout 85.

HUTTON, HEIDI; Clearfield Area HS; Clearfield, PA; (Y); 90/318; Concert Band; Mrchg Band; Pres Frsh Cls; Pres Soph Cls; JV Var Sftbl; Var Swmmng; Var Trk; Var L Vllybl; Cit Awd; Hon Roll; Nrsng.

HUTTON, JENNIFER; Harmony HS; Mahaffey, PA; (Y); Off Church Yth Grp; Capt Quiz Bowl; Scholastic Bowl; Band; Chorus; Church Choir; Concert Band; Mrchg Band; High Hon Roll; Prfct Atten Awd.

HUTTON, JOSEPH; Monsignor Bonner HS; East Lansdowne, PA; (Y); 63/313; Letterman Clb; Pep Clb; Science Clb; Varsity Clb; Stage Crew; Nwsp Stf; Coach Actv; Ftbl; Mgr(s); Athltc Trnnr.

HUTZ, DIANE; Coughlin HS; Wilkes Barre, PA; (Y); Hon Roll; Jr NHS; Bus.

HUTZEL, DANELLE; Forest Hills HS; Summerhill, PA; (Y); 12/164; Sec FBLA; Band; Chorus; Mrchg Band; Nwsp Stf; Yrbk Stf; Sec Soph Cls; Sec Jr Cls; Sec Sr Cls; High Hon Roll; Stu Mnth 86; Typng Awd 86; ICM Schl Bus; Acctng.

HUTZELL, RODGER; Meyersdale Area HS; Meyersdale, PA; (S); Letterman Clb; Spanish Clb; Varsity Clb; L Ftbl; L Trk; L Wrstlng; Cit Awd; Hon Roll; Prfct Atten Awd.

HUTZLER, KIMBERLY; Fairview HS; Fairview, PA; (Y); 20/183; Debate Tm; Drama Clb; French Clb; Latin Clb; Capt Church Choir; Capt Drill Tm; School Musical; School Play; Rep Frsh Cls; Rep Stu Cncl; Gannon U; Bus.

HUUD, STACY; Moon HS; Corapolis, PA; (Y); Cmnty Wkr; Office Aide; Pres Q&S; Yrbk Bus Mgr; Mgr Yrbk Stf; Hon Roll; Robert Morris Coll; Jrnlsm.

HUWEART, ERIC; Quaker Valley SR HS; Sewickley, PA; (Y); German Clb; Key Clb; Band; Concert Band; Mrchg Band; Pep Band; Symp Band; Socr; High Hon Roll; Med.

HUYNH, KHOA DANG; Harrisburg HS; Harrisburg, PA; (S); 5/442; Socr; Hon Roll; NHS.

HUYNH, LINH; John S Fine HS; Nanticoke, PA; (Y); 17/250; Ski Clb; Crs Cntry; Tennis; Trk; NHS; NEDT Awd.

HUYNH, LONG H; Olney HS; Philadelphia, PA; (S); 8/749; Capt Chess Clb; French Clb; Math Tm.

HUYNH, NGHIA; Harrisburg HS; Harrisburg, PA; (S); 20/397; Office Aide; Service Clb; High Hon Roll; Hon Roll; NHS; Penn ST U; Mech Engrng.

HUYNH, TRUNG; Kensington HS; Philadelphia, PA; (Y); Boy Scts; Temple Yth Grp; Off Sr Cls; Ntl Merit Ltr; City Schrlshp 86; PA ST U; Elect Engr.

HVOZDA, ERIC; Homer Center HS; Homer City, PA; (Y); 18/96; Aud/Vis; Chorus; Stage Crew; Bsktbl; Cheerleading; Ftbl; Vllybl; Hon Roll; VIP Stage Crew 85; Studbull Awd 83; Comp Sci.

HYAMS, MARY; Central Dauphin HS; Harrisburg, PA; (Y); Church Yth Grp; Pep Clb; Band; Church Choir; Yrbk Stf; Off Jr Cls; Swmmng; Mdlng.

HYATT, BETTY; Mc Connellsburg HS; Big Cove Tnry, PA; (Y); Church Yth Grp; FBLA; Teachers Aide; Chorus; Sec Frsh Cls.

HYATT, CREED; Boyertown SR HS; Gilbertsvl, PA; (Y); Church Yth Grp; JV Crs Cntry; JV Socr; Cit Awd; Penn St; Astrnmy.

HYDE, DEBRA; Palmyra Area HS; Palmyra, PA; (Y); Teachers Aide; Flag Corp; Stat Bsktbl; Harrisburg Area CC; Rest Mgmt.

HYDE, JAMES; Warren Area HS; Warren, PA; (Y); Letterman Clb; Spanish Clb; Varsity Clb; Acpl Chr; School Play; Stage Crew; Rep Frsh Cls; Capt L Bsktbl; Ftbl; Hon Roll; Sports Trainer.

HYDE, JANINE; Wyoming Valley West HS; Swoyersville, PA; (Y); Radio Clb; Lit Mag; Hon Roll; Musc Dir; Perfct Attndc; Most Likly Succd; Most Actv Prog; Cert Of Achvt Jrnlsm And Lit Mag; Awd Am Heart; Prnt Media.

HYDE, ROBERT; Hyndman Middle SR HS; Hyndman, PA; (Y); Church Yth Grp; Band; Chorus; School Play; Pres Soph Cls; Pres Jr Cls; Stu Cncl; Bsktbl; High Hon Roll; Hon Roll; Philadelphia Clg; Chem.

HYDO, JOANN; Hazleton SR HS; Beaver Brook, PA; (Y); Cmnty Wkr; Drama Clb; French Clb; Pep Clb; Var Capt Sftbl; French Hon Soc; Hon Roll; Physician Assistant.

HYDOCK, MIKE; Nativity B V M HS; Pottsville, PA; (Y); 5/97; Chess Clb; VP Band; Concert Band; Mrchg Band; Orch; Pep Band; Stage Crew; Symp Band; Variety Show; Prfct Atten Awd; Aerospc Engrng.

HYDUK, STEPHANIE; Norwin SR HS; N Huntingdon, PA; (Y); 53/557; Sec FBLA; Library Aide; Office Aide; Hon Roll; Outstng Soph Bus Stu 84-85; FBLA Typing Awd 3rd Pl 84-85; FBLA Data Proc Awd 4th Pl 85-86; Sawyer Bus Schl; Secretarial.

HYLE, JEFFREY; Warwick HS; Lititz, PA; (Y); 48/240; JV Bsbl; Hon Roll; Shippensburg U; Acctng.

HYLTON, RHONDA; Tri Valley HS; Valleyview, PA; (Y); 13/77; Band; Concert Band; Mrchg Band; Yrbk Stf; Hon Roll.

HYMAN, WAYNE; Emmavs HS; Wescosville, PA; (Y); 15/493; Church Yth Grp; Var JV Bsktbl; High Hon Roll; Jr NHS; NHS; Prfct Atten Awd; William L Graham Plqu/JR Lgn Bsbl Sprtsmnshp Awd 84; Engr.

HYMES, JENNIFER; Altoona Area HS; Altoona, PA; (Y); Drama Clb; Sec French Clb; Speech Tm; Chorus; Concert Band; Mrchg Band; Orch; School Musical; School Play; Hon Roll; Psych.

HYNEMAN, MADELINE J; Exeter Twp SR HS; Birdsboro, PA; (Y); 20/218; Aud/Vis; Drama Clb; Q&S; School Play; Yrbk Stf; Lit Mag; JV Trk; High Hon Roll; Jr NHS; NHS; Brooks Fshn Coll; Fshn Dsgn.

IACONO, REGINA; Saint Maria Goretti HS; Philadelphia, PA; (S); 2/425; Dance Clb; Mathletes; Math Clb; School Musical; Yrbk Ed-Chief; Rep Frsh Cls; High Hon Roll; NHS; Prfct Atten Awd; Hnrbl Mntn In Chem 85; Hnrbl Mntn In Geo 84; Hnrbl Mntn In Latin 83; Mrktng.

IACOVANGELO, LORI; Ringgold HS; Monongahela, PA; (Y); Hosp Aide; Variety Show; Sec Frsh Cls; Capt Pom Pon; High Hon Roll; Hon Roll; Math & Sci Hnr Soc; Acdmc All-Amrcn Awd; Physcl Thrpy.

IADICICCO, JOANNE; Deer Lakes JR SR HS; Gibsonia, PA; (Y); 28/213; French Clb; Varsity Clb; Var Vllybl; Hon Roll; IN U PA; Cmptr Sci.

IADONATO, SHAWN; Punxsutawney Aea HS; Punxsutawney, PA; (Y); French Clb; Math Tm; Science Clb; Band; Concert Band; Jazz Band; Mrchg Band; Pep Band; Yrbk Phtg; Hon Roll; Pre-Med.

IAMS, MELISSA J; Jefferson-Morgan JRSR HS; Jefferson, PA; (Y); Boy Scts; French Clb; Office Aide; Rep Jr Cls; Score Keeper; Stat Sftbl; Hon Roll; PA Game Comm Cnsrvtn Awd 85; Mortitian.

IANARO, JENISE; Clearfield Area HS; Clearfield, PA; (Y); Key Clb; Thesps; Band; Mrchg Band; Trs Jr Cls; Trs Sr Cls; Var Swmmng; High Hon Roll; Hon Roll; Juniata Coll; Pre-Med.

IANNACONE, DAVID; Central Bucks East HS; Furlong, PA; (Y); Im Swmmng; JV Var Trk; Im Wt Lftg; Hon Roll.

IANNACONE, PAUL; South Philadelphia HS; Philadelphia, PA; (Y); High Hon Roll; Hon Roll; Drexel U; Bus Admin.

IANNARELLI, MIKE; Archbishop Wood Boys HS; Southampton, PA; (Y); 59/282; Bsktbl; Hon Roll; Prfct Atten Awd; Acctg.

IANNITTI, THERESA; Chichester SR HS; Boothwyn, PA; (Y); 14/318; Pres French Clb; Band; Nwsp Rptr; Stu Cncl; Co-Capt Fld Hcky; Lcrss; Hon Roll; Jr NHS; Pres NHS; Co-Capt Rotary Awd; All Delco Lacrosse 2nd Tm 85-86; Sptsmnshp Trophy 85-86; Bio.

IANNOZZI, MARIA; Archbishop Kennedy HS; Conshohocken, PA; (Y); 3/180; Aud/Vis; Drama Clb; Mathletes; School Play; Nwsp Bus Mgr; Yrbk Ed-Chief; Lit Mag; Var Fld Hcky; Hon Roll; NHS; Hghst Avg Bio 85, Engl 86; 1st Pl Perfmnc One Act Play Fstvl 85 & 86; Jrnlsm.

IANSON, BERT; Cowanesque Valley HS; Middlebury Ctr, PA; (S); 11/94; Pres Church Yth Grp; Drama Clb; FFA; Letterman Clb; School Play; Stage Crew; VP Ftbl; Hon Roll; NHS; Mansfield; Mth.

IATI, CATHERINE; York Catholic HS; York, PA; (Y); VP NHS; Library Aide; Pep Clb; Spanish Clb; SADD; Yrbk Bus Mgr; Yrbk Stf; High Hon Roll; Mst Outstndng Spkr 84-85; Millersville U; Elem.

IBANEZ, LUCY; Middletown Area HS; Middletown, PA; (Y); Am Leg Aux Girls St; VP FCA; Hosp Aide; JCL; Model UN; Chorus; Sec Mrchg Band; Swing Chorus; Yrbk Stf; NHS; Foxs Mrkt Schlrshp 86; Gettysburg Coll; Pre Law.

ICKES, CAROL; Altoona Area HS; Altoona, PA; (S); Drama Clb; Math Clb; Spanish Clb; School Musical; Twrlr; Var L Vllybl; Kiwanis Awd; NEDT Awd; Coaches Awd Dedctn Vlybl 85; Most Imprvd Awd Weght Traning 85; Susquehanna U; Physcl Thrpy.

ICKES, KANDI; Big Spring HS; Newville, PA; (Y); 35/211; Band; Concert Band; Jazz Band; Mrchg Band; Var L Bsktbl; Powder Puff Ftbl; Var L Sftbl; Hon Roll; Concrt Band Outstndg Muscn Awd 86; Mid PA & Publ Opnion Sftbl All Star 86; Engl Achvt Awd 86; Millersville U; Scndry Math Ed.

IEM, CHANNEARY; Lebanon SR HS; Lebanon, PA; (Y); 1/285; Pres Church Yth Grp; Pres Latin Clb; SADD; School Musical; Yrbk Stf; Rep Soph Cls; High Hon Roll; Hon Roll; NHS; Rotary Awd; Frnch Awd 84-85; Rtry Ldrs Cnfrnc 4 Outstndg Ldrs 85-86; Bio.

IFFT, CURT; Grove City HS; Mercer, PA; (Y); 60/200; Pres Church Yth Grp; VP Ski Clb; Bowling; Crs Cntry; Golf; Trk; Hon Roll; Vrsty Ltr Glfng 85; Vrsty Ltr Trck 86; IN U; Educ.

IGOE, MARK; Father Judge HS; Philadelphia, PA; (Y); 71/369; Cmnty Wkr; Hon Roll; Vrsty Crw Tm; Temple U; Hlth Profssns.

IHRIG, SALLY; Boyertown Area SR HS; Boyertown, PA; (Y); 16/455; Church Yth Grp; FBLA; Teachers Aide; Chorus; Rep Stu Cncl; Var Bsktbl; Var Fld Hcky; Var Lcrss; Cit Awd; High Hon Roll; 2dn Team All Chsmnt Lacrs 86; Hon Mntn Lacrs 85.

IIAMS, LINDA; Avella HS; Avella, PA; (Y); 3/54; Art Clb; Church Yth Grp; Trs French Clb; Church Choir; Drill Tm; School Musical; Variety Show; Yrbk Stf; High Hon Roll; NHS; Am Legion Awd 86; Am Aux Awd 84; Ambassador Coll; Sec.

IKELER, AMY; Danville Area HS; Danville, PA; (Y); Drama Clb; Key Clb; Latin Clb; Spanish Clb; Cmmrcl Art.

ILIK, BOB; Boyertown Area SR HS; Gilbertsville, PA; (Y); 95/484; Band; Concert Band; Jazz Band; Mrchg Band; Pep Band; Var Crs Cntry; Var Swmmng; Var Trk; Hon Roll; Acctng.

IMBER, CHRISTOPHER; Lower Moreland HS; Huntingdon Valley, PA; (S); Cmnty Wkr; Model UN; Science Clb; Y-Teens; Jazz Band; Nwsp Ed-Chief; Yrbk Stf; Cit Awd; High Hon Roll; Prfct Atten Awd; Union Lg Ctznshp Awd 85; Med.

IMLER JR, DALE; Claysburg-Kimmel HS; Imler, PA; (Y); German Clb; Var L Bsbl; Penn ST; Crmc Engr.

IMLER, KIM; Bellwood-Antis HS; Tyrone, PA; (Y); 30/127; DECA; Drama Clb; FBLA; Key Clb; School Play; L Mgr(s); Var Stat Trk; Hon Roll; Civics Spn I 83; Am Culture 84; World Cutlture Cnsmr Math 85; Altoona Schl Commerce; Accntng.

IMMEL, KAREN; Hempfield Area SR HS; Greensburg, PA; (Y); 83/657; Church Yth Grp; French Clb; Pep Clb; Ski Clb; Capt Color Guard; Variety Show; Yrbk Stf; Stat Trk; High Hon Roll; Hon Roll; Kathleen & William Christie Schlrshp 86; Penn ST; Aerosp Engrng.

IMPLAZO, TREVOR; Marple Newtown HS; Newtown Square, PA; (Y); Ftbl; Hon Roll; Prfct Atten Awd; Penn ST; His.

INCH, REBEKAH; Northeastern HS; Manchester, PA; (Y); Sec Church Yth Grp; Dance Clb; Hosp Aide; Office Aide; Chorus; Trk; Hon Roll; Voice Dem Awd; Sign Lang Clb; Psych Clb; Banking.

INDELICATO, RICH; Bethlehem Catholic HS; Bethlehem, PA; (Y); 42/214; Model UN; Stage Crew; Rep Stu Cncl; Crs Cntry; Music Prod.

INDERWISH, DEBBIE; Bethel Park SR HS; Pittsburgh, PA; (Y); Church Yth Grp; FBLA; Science Clb; School Musical; Variety Show; Nwsp Bus Mgr; Ed Yrbk Stf; Sr Cls; Mgr(s); JV Var Powder Puff Ftbl; Syracuse U; Bdrcstng.

INGEL, BARBARA; Bishop Conwell HS; Levittown, PA; (Y); Church Yth Grp; Spanish Clb; Sfty Awd 84; SF Ms Teen All Amrcn 85; Mssns Clb 85; Basic Actng Achvt Awd 86; Villanova U; Lawy.

INGHAM, PAMELA; Greensburg Central Catholic HS; Greensburg, PA; (Y); French Clb; JCL; Latin Clb; Ski Clb; Spanish Clb; Yrbk Stf; Rep Frsh Cls; Var Tennis; High Hon Roll.

INGRAM, CHRISTOPHER; Washington HS; Washington, PA; (S); 7/250; Math Tm; Spanish Clb; Band; Concert Band; Jazz Band; Mrchg Band; Orch; School Musical; High Hon Roll; Mc Donald All Amer Band 85-86; PMEA Hnrs Band 84-86; Astro Physics.

INGRAM, DARA; William Penn HS; Philadelphia, PA; (Y); 3/585; Dance Clb; Math Clb; Yrbk Stf; JV Baktbl; Hon Roll; VP NHS; Pres Schlr; Young Artists Of Am 86; Middlebury U; Fench.

INGRAM, MIKE; St Marys Area HS; Weedville, PA; (Y); 56/295; Am Leg Boys St; Boy Scts; Im Bsbl; Im Bsktbl; Var L Ftbl; Var L Trk; Im Vllybl; Im Wt Lftg; JV L Wrstlng; Hon Roll; Ceramic Engrng.

INGRAM, PAM; Seneca Valley HS; Mars, PA; (Y); 82/356; Art Clb; Ski Clb; Varsity Clb; Sec Trs Stu Cncl; Cheerleading; Trk; Hon Roll; PA ST.

INGRASSIA, DAN; Sayre Area HS; Sayre, PA; (Y); Chess Clb; Crs Cntry; Swmmng; Trk.

INGROS, SHANNON; Punxsutawney Area HS; Punxsutawney, PA; (Y); 20/238; Trs Church Yth Grp; French Clb; Nwsp Phtg; Nwsp Rptr; Nwsp Stf; Lit Mag; Rep Stu Cncl; Hon Roll; NHS; IN U; Engl Educ.

INMAN, JIM; Annville-Cleona HS; Lebanon, PA; (S); 14/107; Varsity Clb; JV Bsbl; L Ftbl; Wt Lftg; Var Wrstlng; NHS; Lebanon Cnty All Stars-Ftbl 85; Mech Engrng.

INNAMORATO, MARY; Saint Huberts HS; Philadelphia, PA; (Y); 60/367; Stu Cncl; Trk; Hon Roll; Prfct Atten Awd; Twn Mtg On Tmrrw TMOT 85-86; Pierce CJ; Exec Secy.

INSTONE, JOHN; Bishop Mc Cort HS; Johnstown, PA; (Y); 50/153; Church Yth Grp; Spanish Clb; Chorus; School Musical; Pres Frsh Cls; VP Soph Cls; Var Bsbl; Var Bsktbl; L Var Ftbl; Var Wt Lftg.

INVERSO, DINA; West Catholic HS; Phila, PA; (Y); 14/257; Art Clb; JA; Office Aide; High Hon Roll; Hosp Aide; Chem Awd; West Chestr; Clncl Microbio.

IOBST, CHRIS; Iroquois HS; Erie, PA; (Y); 5/150; Chess Clb; Quiz Bowl; Varsity Clb; Yrbk Stf; L Capt Bsbl; Var L Bsktbl; L Capt Ftbl; High Hon Roll; NHS; Engl Key Bst Engl Stu 86; Crtty Mem Schlrshp 86; Cornell U; Bio.

ION, PATRICIA; Farrell Area HS; Wheatland, PA; (Y); 5/90; Am Leg Aux Girls St; English Clb; Key Clb; Band; Gov Hon Prg Awd; Trs NHS; Voice Dem Awd; French Clb; Hosp Aide; Concert Band; Amer Legn Aux Essy Cntst 85-86; PA Free Entrprs Wk & Allegheny Coll Smmr Schl Schlrshps 86; Intl Rel.

IONADI, ANDREA; Riverview HS; Verona, PA; (Y); 33/96; Drama Clb; Ski Clb; Varsity Clb; Y-Teens; School Play; Variety Show; Nwsp Rptr; Yrbk Ed-Chief; Rep Frsh Cls; Off Soph Cls; Fnlst Miss Natl Teen Pgnt PA 83; Clarion U; Biol.

IONADI, LISA; Riverview HS; Verona, PA; (Y); 12/120; Drama Clb; French Clb; Ski Clb; Stu Cncl; VP Cheerleading; Powder Puff Ftbl; VP Trk; NHS; NEDT Awd; Arch.

IOPPOLO, NICOLE; Marple Newtown HS; Broomall, PA; (Y); Church Yth Grp; Sec Cmnty Wkr; Hosp Aide; JV Bsktbl; JV Capt Sftbl; Im Tennis; JV Trk; JV Capt Vllybl; Physcl Thrpst.

IRANI, JENNIFER; Central Bucks East HS; Warrington, PA; (Y); Church Yth Grp; Chorus; Lit Mag; JV Fld Hcky; Hon Roll; Jr NHS; Prfct Atten Awd; Ski Clb; Mgr Bsktbl; Mgr Swmmng; Hnrbl Mntn Wrld Poetry 85; Golden Poet Awd Wrld Poetry 85; Bst Musicianship Awd 84.

IRBY, ERIC ODELL LESTER; West Catholic For Boys; Philadelphia, PA; (Y); Cmnty Wkr; Bsktbl; Howard U; Bus Admin.

IRBY, LAVETA; Plymouth-Whitemarsh HS; Conshohocken, PA; (Y); Cmnty Wkr; Computer Clb; JA; Chorus; Rep Jr Cls; Var Bsktbl; JV Fld Hcky; High Hon Roll; Ntl Merit Ltr; NEDT Awd; Prncpls Hon Awd 80-81; CPR Cert 83-84; Hall Of Fame 82-83; Lwyr.

IRELAND, JENNIFER; Lehighton Area HS; Lehighton, PA; (Y); FBLA; High Hon Roll; Accounting.

IRELAND, JENNIFER H; East HS; Erie, PA; (Y); 4/138; Mrchg Band; School Musical; School Play; Powder Puff Ftbl; Vllybl; High Hon Roll; Jr NHS; Kiwanis Awd; NHS; Rotary Awd; Edinboro U; Bus Admn.

IRISH, DIANE; Emmaus HS; Emmaus, PA; (Y); 74/493; Hosp Aide; JCL; Latin Clb; Library Aide; Chorus; School Musical; School Play; Variety Show; Lit Mag; NHS; Psych.

IRONS, JULIE ANNE; Center Area HS; Monaca, PA; (Y); 3/185; Church Yth Grp; German Clb; Letterman Clb; Varsity Clb; Band; Drm Mjr(t); Capt Var Bsktbl; High Hon Roll; NHS; Pres Schlr; 1st Team Bsktbl All Stars Sect II 85 & 86; Pres Acdmc Ftns Awds Prgm 86; Army Rsrv Schlr/Athlt Awd 86; WV U; Aerospace Engr.

IRONS, TRACY; Hopewell SR HS; Aliquippa, PA; (Y); Boys Clb Am; Exploring; SADD; Chorus; Church Choir; School Musical; Stage Crew; Hon Roll; Rep Soph Cls; Rep Jr Cls; Sftbl Cert & Trophies 77-86; Nrs.

IRVINE, CHRISTINE; Marple Newtown SR HS; Newtown Square, PA; (Y); Cmnty Wkr; Ski Clb; Fld Hcky; Lcrss; Lacrosse Ski Club; Sociology.

IRVING, JENNIFER; Lakeland HS; Jermyn, PA; (Y); Cmnty Wkr; 4-H; FHA; JA; Chorus; Off Stu Cncl; Vllybl; Hon Roll; NHS; Ntl Merit Ltr; Pres Phys Ftns Awd 83-86; Pres Acadmc Ftns Awd 86; U Of Scranton; Vet Med.

IRVING, SHARON; Central Dauphin HS; Harrisburg, PA; (Y); Library Aide; Hon Roll; Jr NHS; NHS; Pres Acad Fit Awd 85-86; Harrisburg Area CC; Acctng.

IRWIN, BILL; Deer Lakes HS; Tarentum, PA; (Y); Computer Clb; English Clb; Math Clb; Science Clb; Ski Clb; Spanish Clb; Band; Chorus; High Hon Roll; Hon Roll; Slippery Rock; Bus.

IRWIN, ELAINE; Boyertown HS; Gilbertsville, PA; (Y); Var Crs Cntry; Var Trk; German Clb; GAA; JA; SADD; Stu Cncl; Var JV Bsktbl; Var JV Fld Hcky; Var JV Lcrss; US Fnlst-Mdl Look Of The Yr,Comp Intl Look Of The Yr-Florence Italy 86; Comm.

IRWIN, FLO; Delone Catholic HS; Hanover, PA; (Y); Cmnty Wkr; Varsity Clb; Band; Pres Frsh Cls; Var Cheerleading; Gym; Sftbl; Vllybl; Wt Lftg; Pres Schlr; Peer Cnslr; Cumberland Perry; Dntl Asst.

IRWIN III, FREDERICK H; Conrad Weiser HS; Womelsdorf, PA; (Y); Drama Clb; Chorus; Jazz Band; Mrchg Band; School Musical; Pres Church Yth Grp; JCL; Spanish Clb; Church Choir; Concert Band; Cnty, Dstrct & Rgnl Hnr Chorus 84-86; Lebanon Vly Cbl Awd-Exc In Tv Sprts Brdcstng 86; PA ST U; Msc Ed.

IRWIN, JACQUALYN; Somerset SR HS; Somerset, PA; (Y); Church Yth Grp; CAP; Cmnty Wkr; Debate Tm; English Clb; JA; Library Aide; Chorus; Church Choir; Nwsp Stf; Billy Mitchell Awd Civil Air Patrol 85; Encmpmnt Hnr Cadet Awd Civil Air Patrol 84; Cert Aprctn 84; Frnch.

IRWIN, JAY; Clearfield SR HS; Woodland, PA; (Y); Boy Scts; Church Yth Grp; Civic Clb; Var Swmmng; Hon Roll; Comp Pgmng.

IRWIN JR, JEFFERY; Warren Area HS; Warren, PA; (Y); Church Yth Grp; French Clb; Spanish Clb; Chorus; Im Bsbl; High Hon Roll; Hon Roll; Penn ST Behrend; Erth/Mnrl Sci.

IRWIN, JILL; Palmyra SR HS; Annville, PA; (Y); Church Yth Grp; French Clb; SADD; Chorus; Stat Wrstlng; Hon Roll; Drama Clb; Spanish Clb; Teachers Aide; Stage Crew.

IRWIN, JOSEPH J; La Salle College HS; Philadelphia, PA; (Y); 4/240; Chess Clb; Mathletes; Math Tm; Service Clb; Varsity Clb; Band; Yrbk Ed-Chief; Capt Bowling; Tennis; Hon Roll; Latin, Spnsh, Amer Hstry, Schlstc L Awds; La Salle U; Premed.

IRWIN, TRACI; Steel Valley HS; Munhall, PA; (S); 12/233; Co-Capt Flag Corp; Yrbk Stf; Hon Roll; NHS; Bradford Bus Schl; Sec.

IRWIN, TRACY LINN; Mc Guffey SR HS; Claysville, PA; (Y); 8/210; Am Leg Aux Girls St; English Clb; Spanish Clb; Varsity Clb; Band; Pep Band; Yrbk Stf; Trk; High Hon Roll; Sec NHS; Kystn Grls ST Outstndg Ctzn 85; Rho Chptr Dlta Kappa Gamma Schlrshp 86; PA ST Schlrshp 86; PA ST U; Scndry Englsh Ed.

ISABELLA, GINA ELYSE; Penn-Trafford HS; Irwin, PA; (Y); 17/362; Am Leg Aux Girls St; French Clb; GAA; Ski Clb; Chorus; Yrbk Stf; VP Frsh Cls; VP Soph Cls; Rep Jr Cls; Pres Stu Cncl; Rep & Spkr 86 ALA Cnvtn 86; Ldrshp Dvlpmt Schlrshp At Seton Hl Coll 85.

ISAKOV, CHRISTOPHER M; Scranton Preparatory Schl; Clarks Green, PA; (Y); Dance Clb; Drama Clb; Ski Clb; Concert Band; Jazz Band; Orch; Pep Band; JV Wrstlng; High Hon Roll; Hon Roll; Engrng.

ISAMOYER, SHAWN; Brandywine Heights HS; Topton, PA; (Y); 35/144; Church Yth Grp; Girl Scts; Hosp Aide; Red Cross Aide; Band; Chorus; Concert Band; Mrchg Band; Pep Band; Stu Cncl; Fshn Merch.

ISHMAN, CHRISTINE; Du Bois Area HS; Reynoldsville, PA; (Y); Band; Chorus; Church Choir; Concert Band; Drm Mjr(t); Mrchg Band; School Musical; Swing Chorus; PA ST; Bus.

ISHMAN, MICHAEL; Punxsutawney Area SR HS; Punxsutawney, PA; (Y); Computer Clb; 4-H; FFA; Spanish Clb; Band; Concert Band; Mrchg Band; Pep Band; Bsbl; Var Wt Lftg; IN U Of PA; Comp Sci.

ISLER, JAMIE; Brownsville Area HS; Brownsville, PA; (Y); 42/221; Lcrss; Mathletes; Sec Ski Clb; SADD; School Play; Stage Crew; Stu Cncl; Hon Roll; Tri-Hi-Y Pres 86; CA U Of PA; Scndry Ed.

ITALIANO, JIM; Linocln HS; Ellwood City, PA; (Y); 80/160; Church Yth Grp; Computer Clb; Letterman Clb; Political Wkr; Chorus; Church Choir; School Musical; Pres Frsh Cls; Pres Soph Cls; Pres Stu Cncl; US Air Force; Elec.

ITKIN, LAURIE; Taylor Allderdice HS; Pittsburgh, PA; (Y); 28/410; JA; Math Clb; Model UN; Nwsp Stf; Stu Cncl; High Hon Roll; Hon Roll; NHS; Otstndng Yng Bsnswmn 86; Bst Slsprsn 86; Tp Slsprsn 85; U Of PA; Bus.

ITTERLY, RONALD; Mid-Valley Secondary Center; Scranton, PA; (Y); Pep Clb; Ski Clb; Spanish Clb; VICA; Ftbl; Hon Roll; Coll Oceaneering; Undrwtr Wldng.

ITZEL, ANITA; Canon Mc Millan HS; Canonsburg, PA; (Y); Church Yth Grp; Dance Clb; Office Aide; VP SADD; Varsity Clb; Chorus; Var JV Cheerleading; JV Sftbl; Hon Roll; CA U Of PA; Mdcl Tech.

IVAN, MICHELLE; West Mifflin Area HS; Pittsburgh, PA; (Y); Church Yth Grp; Orch; Off Soph Cls; Rep Stu Cncl; Sftbl; High Hon Roll; Hon Roll; NHS; Chem.

IVANUSIC, WILLIAM; Jefferson-Morgan HS; Clarksville, PA; (Y); Nwsp Rptr; Nwsp Stf; Yrbk Stf; Rep Frsh Cls; Rep Soph Cls; Rep Jr Cls; JV Bsktbl; JV Var Ftbl; L Trk; Hon Roll; Acctng.

IVCIC, JULIE; West Allegheny HS; Oakdale, PA; (Y); 2/198; Color Guard; Yrbk Phtg; Sec Frsh Cls; Pres Jr Cls; Trs Stu Cncl; Pom Pon; Powder Puff Ftbl; High Hon Roll; VP Jr NHS; Trs NHS.

IVERSEN, JOHN; Strath Haven HS; Swarthmore, PA; (Y); Off Frsh Cls; Off Soph Cls; Off Jr Cls; Pres Sr Cls; Var Socr; Var Trk; Rotary Awd; Boy Scts; Cmnty Wkr; Intnl Clb; HSA Svc Awd 86; Rensselaer Sci & Math Mdl 85; Hnrb Mntn PLRA St Comp Cont 85; Harvard; Physics.

IVES, JEFF; Mechanicsburg SR HS; Mechanicsburg, PA; (Y); 2/316; Church Yth Grp; German Clb; Church Choir; Yrbk Stf; Pres Frsh Cls; Pres Soph Cls; Pres Jr Cls; Pres Stu Cncl; Var Capt Socr; High Hon Roll; Stu Advsry Cmmtee; Hd Of Prm Cmmtee.

IVEY JR, JOHN; Punxsutawney Area HS; Punxsutawney, PA; (Y); 1/238; Math Tm; Band; Jazz Band; Nwsp Rptr; Rep Stu Cncl; Bausch & Lomb Sci Awd; NHS; Rotary Awd; Val; Science Clb; IUP Hnrs Band 83-85; PA ST; Indtl Engrg.

IZZO, TRICIA; Ellwood City Lincoln HS; Ellwood City, PA; (Y); French Clb; Spanish Clb; Y-Teens; Chorus; Var L Cheerleading; Gym; JV Var Powder Puff Ftbl; Sftbl; Trk; High Hon Roll.

JABLONSKI, DAVID; Mahandy Area HS; Barnesville, PA; (Y); 1/110; Y-Teens; Nwsp Sprt Ed; Yrbk Phtg; Im Bsktbl; Var Ftbl; Var L Trk; High Hon Roll; Ntl Merit SF; NEDT Awd; Pennsylvania Gvnrs Schl For Sci 86; Nuclear Engr.

JABLONSKI, LINDA; Scranton Vo-Tech; Scranton, PA; (S); Exploring; FBLA; Q&S; Nwsp Ed-Chief; Stu Cncl; Jr NHS; Bus.

JACHIMIAK, RALPH; E L Meyers HS; Wilkes Barre, PA; (Y); 40/160; Trs Art Clb; Camera Clb; Key Clb; Office Aide; Ski Clb; Chorus; Concert Band; Mrchg Band; Yrbk Stf; Rep Stu Cncl; JR Natl Hon Soc 83; Natl Schlstc Photography Awd 86; U Of Scranton; Hlth.

JACHIMOWICZ, DIANE; Lake-Lehman HS; Shavertown, PA; (S); 25/140; Letterman Clb; Lit Mag; Var Bsktbl; Var JV Fld Hcky; Stat Sftbl; Stat Vllybl; Cit Awd; High Hon Roll; Hon Roll; Millersville U; Child Psych.

JACK, NICK; Carmichaels Area HS; Carmichaels, PA; (Y); Church Yth Grp; 4-H; French Clb; Hon Roll; Mchncl Engr.

JACK, RAIKO; Camichaels Area JR SR HS; Carmichaels, PA; (S); 9/118; Exploring; Pres French Clb; Yrbk Ed-Chief; Off Jr Cls; Pres Sr Cls; Stu Cncl; High Hon Roll; Hon Roll; NHS; Bio.

JACK, TODD; Allegheny Clarion Valley HS; Lamartine, PA; (Y); Aud/Vis; Boy Scts; Church Yth Grp; 4-H; Church Choir; Ftbl; Eagle Sct, Ordr Arrw 86; Clarion U PA; Med.

JACK, TROY; Highlands HS; Natrona Hts, PA; (Y); Art Clb; Computer Clb; Intnl Clb; NHS; Brown Awd 84-86; Gold Awd 84-85; PA ST U; Comp Pgmr.

JACKSON, AMBER; Blue Mountain Acad; Coudesport, PA; (Y); Church Yth Grp; Ski Clb; Spanish Clb; Chorus; Bsktbl; Sftbl; Hon Roll; Theta Kappa Gama Trsrr Grls Clb 86; Coudrsprt Chmbr Cmrc Pstr Cmptn 1st Pl 84; Hon Mntn JR Lit 84; Columbia Un Coll; Dntl Hyg.

JACKSON, ANGELA; Philipsburg-Osceola Area SR HS; Philipsburg, PA; (S); 43/240; Church Yth Grp; FCA; SADD; Band; Chorus; Concert Band; Mrchg Band; School Musical; Nwsp Ed-Chief; Yrbk Stf; Liberty U; Telecomm.

JACKSON, EUGENE; William Penn HS; Philadelphia, PA; (Y); 11/234; Boy Scts; Debate Tm; Political Wkr; Nwsp Ed-Chief; Nwsp Rptr; Rep Jr Cls; Var Crs Cntry; Var Trk; Cit Awd; NHS; PA ST U; Fin.

JACKSON, GARY; Penn Trafford HS; Jeannette, PA; (Y); Im Bsktbl; Im Ftbl; Im Sftbl; Im Vllybl; Hon Roll; Slippery Rock; Spychlgy.

JACKSON JR, GEORGE; C B East HS; Doylestown, PA; (Y); Band; Jazz Band; Mrchg Band; Pres Jr Cls; Stu Cncl; L Trk; Hon Roll; Prfct Atten Awd.

JACKSON, HEIDI; Valley View JR SR HS; Blakely, PA; (Y); 30/197; Church Yth Grp; Latin Clb; Spanish Clb; Varsity Clb; Stu Cncl; Capt Cheerleading; Trk; Vllybl; Hon Roll; Trs NHS; Acad All Amer Schlr Dir 85; Kings Coll; Phy Asst.

JACKSON, JACKIE; Little Flower Catholic HS For Girls; Philadelphia, PA; (Y); Color Guard; Drill Tm; Off Soph Cls; Vllybl; Csmtlgst.

JACKSON, JADE; Churchill HS; E Pittsburgh, PA; (Y); Drama Clb; French Clb; Key Clb; Band; Chorus; Score Keeper; Kiwanis Awd; Art Inst Pittsburgh; Intr Dsgn.

JACKSON, JANE; Parkland HS; Allentown, PA; (Y); 144/415; Dance Clb; German Clb; Sec Key Clb; Varsity Clb; Yrbk Stf; Rep Stu Cncl; Var L Cheerleading; Hon Roll; Lehigh Vly Miss Pagnt Fnlst 85; Outstndng Chrldr Awd 86; Outstndng Key Clb Sec Awd 86; Shippensburg U; Elem Ed.

JACKSON, KEITH; High Schl Of Engr & Sci; Philadelphia, PA; (S); 10/220; Boy Scts; Church Yth Grp; Variety Show; Im Ftbl; Hon Roll; NHS; Pittsburg U; Engr.

JACKSON, KEVIN; Strath Haven HS; Swarthmore, PA; (Y); Cmnty Wkr; Ski Clb; SADD; Yrbk Ed-Chief; Yrbk Stf; Off Frsh Cls; Off Soph Cls; Off Jr Cls; Off Sr Cls; JV Var Bsbl; Sociolgy.

JACKSON, KIMBERLY; Downingtown SR HS; Downingtown, PA; (Y); 131/501; Church Yth Grp; GAA; Intnl Clb; Ski Clb; Nwsp Rptr; Yrbk Stf; Rep Stu Cncl; JV Bsktbl; Shippensburg U; Mktg.

JACKSON, MICHAEL; Martin Luther King HS; Philadelphia, PA; (Y); Pres Sr Cls; JV L Socr; JV Mgr Sftbl; Var Tennis; Hon Roll; PRIME 82-86; Upwrd Bnd U Of PA 86; Rtry Clb Spnsrd Tmrrws Ldrshp Conf 86; Law.

JACKSON, PATRICIA; York Catholic HS; Hellam, PA; (Y); 49/171; Art Clb; 4-H; JA; Nwsp Rptr; Sftbl; Hon Roll; NHS; Opt Clb Awd; Spch Cntst 3rd Plc Ovrall 1st Plc Frshmn 83; US Military Acad; Cmptr Mgmt.

JACKSON, PEGGY; Mohawk Area HS; Wampum, PA; (S); 5/130; Sec Spanish Clb; School Musical; School Play; Pres Soph Cls; Pres Jr Cls; Sec Stu Cncl; Capt Cheerleading; Capt Trk; NHS; NEDT Awd; 1 Of 4 Cmmncmnt Spkrs 86; Hmcmng Queen 85-86; Intl Frgn Lng Awd 83; U Of Pittsburgh; Physcl Thrpy.

JACKSON, ROBERT; Cardinal O Hara HS; Media, PA; (Y); 107/800; Aud/Vis; Church Yth Grp; Dance Clb; PAVAS; Spanish Clb; School Musical; Variety Show; Im Bsktbl; JV Ftbl; Hon Roll; Best Dressd, Dncr 86; Villanova; Psych.

JACKSON, SHARON; Mc Keesport Area HS; Dravosburg, PA; (Y); 43/137; Trs JA; Office Aide; Mat Maids; Powder Puff Ftbl; Hon Roll.

JACKSON, SUSAN; Bensalem SR HS; Bensalem, PA; (Y); 1/573; Science Clb; Band; Drm Mjr(t); Stat Swmmng; Gov Hon Prg Awd; High Hon Roll; NHS; Ntl Merit SF; Drama Clb; Key Clb; Westinghouse JR Awd 86; 1st Pl PA JR Acad Sci Regnl Meet, ST 86; Princeton U; Chem.

JACKSON, SUSAN; Tunkhannock HS; Tunkhannock, PA; (S); 34/320; French Clb; Chrmn Key Clb; Letterman Clb; Yrbk Sprt Ed; Swmmng; Mgr Tennis; Mgr Trk; Cit Awd; NHS; All Am Acdmc Awd 85; Jr Bell Choir Church; Pol Sci.

JACKSON, TAMMY; Philadelphia HS For Girls; Philadelphia, PA; (Y); 110/260; Pres Church Yth Grp; Service Clb; Teachers Aide; Pres Church Choir; Rep Stu Cncl; JV Bowling; Hon Roll; Exploring; Catholic Schlrshp Negroes Inc 86; Svc Club Awd Phil H S For Girls 86; Svc Club Awdtutoring Chrpsn 86; U Pittsburgh; Elec Engrng.

JACKSON, TAMMY; Pittston Area HS; Avoca, PA; (Y); Art Clb; FNA; Hosp Aide; Key Clb; Bowling; Var L Sftbl; Var Tennis; Hon Roll; Jr NHS; NHS; E R Nrs.

JACKSON, THERESA; York Catholic; Dover, PA; (Y); Pres Church Yth Grp; Sec Spanish Clb; Rep Frsh Cls; Rep Soph Cls; Rep Jr Cls; Rep Sr Cls; Rep Stu Cncl; Capt Bsktbl; Hon Roll; Sec NHS; Warrington Wmns Clb 86; St Joseph Hosp; Rad Tech.

JACKSON, TRACEY; Northgate HS; Pittsburgh, PA; (S); Trs DECA; Hon Roll; Kiwanis Awd; Prfct Atten Awd; Dist Conf 3rd Pl Apparel & Accssrs 85-86; Mktng.

JACKSON, TRACY; Pennsbury HS; Levittown, PA; (Y); Rep Frsh Cls; Rep Soph Cls; Rep Jr Cls; Intr Design.

JACKSON, YOLANDA D; G W Carver HS Of Engineering- Science; Philadelphia, PA; (Y); 99/184; Church Yth Grp; Cmnty Wkr; JA; Nwsp Stf; Yrbk Stf; Oxford Grant 86; Trvld To Soviet Union Wth Yth Qust 86; Oxford Coll Of Emory U; Bus Adm.

JACOB, DEBRA; Wyoming Valley West HS; Kingston, PA; (Y); Cmnty Wkr; Hosp Aide; Key Clb; Library Aide; Temple Yth Grp; Nwsp Rptr; Nwsp Stf; Yrbk Stf; Lit Mag; Stu Cncl; Jewish Ctr Yth Lit Awd 84; Tufts U; Intl Relations.

JACOB, GAYE P; Akiba Hebrew Acad; Cherry Hill, NJ; (Y); Spanish Clb; Teachers Aide; VP Temple Yth Grp; Chorus; School Musical; Pres Frsh Cls; VP Soph Cls; Trs Jr Cls; Rep Stu Cncl; Mgr(s); Co Chrmn Reg Sci & Humants Confrnc 86; Psychlgy.

JACOB, LARRY; Emmaus HS; Macungie, PA; (Y); 141/493; Key Clb; Ski Clb; Band; Concert Band; Jazz Band; Mrchg Band; Pep Band; JV Bsbl; JV Wrstlng; Engrng.

JACOB, RANDALL; Hempfield Area SR HS; Irwin, PA; (Y); Ski Clb; Band; Concert Band; Jazz Band; Mrchg Band; Pep Band; High Hon Roll; Hon Roll; PA ST U; Bus.

JACOB, RICKEY; Baldwin HS; Pittsburgh, PA; (Y); VICA; High Hon Roll; Hon Roll; Electrnc Engr.

JACOBS, DENISE; Seneca Valley SR HS; Harmony, PA; (Y); Spanish Clb; SADD; Chorus; Color Guard; Pom Pon; Score Keeper; Sftbl; Vllybl; Wt Lftg; Hon Roll.

JACOBS, ERIK; Gateway SR HS; Monroeville, PA; (Y); Im Bsbl; Bowling; JV Var Ftbl; Im Socr; Var Trk; Im JV Vllybl; High Hon Roll; Hon Roll; Chess Clb; Church Yth Grp; German Hon Awd 83-85; Archtctr.

JACOBS, EUSTACE; Germantown HS; Philadelphia, PA; (Y); Boys Clb Am; Socr; High Hon Roll; Hon Roll; NHS; Spnsh Awds; Math Awds; Gym Awd; Comp Sci.

JACOBS, JOHN; Shady Side Acad; Glenshaw, PA; (Y); 67/128; Rep Soph Cls; Im Bsktbl; Var L Ftbl; Im Sftbl; Var Trk; Im Wt Lftg; High Hon Roll; Hon Roll; Partial Schlrshp Shady Side Acad 85-86; Am Leg Awd; Engrng.

JACOBS, KIM; Bethel Park HS; Bethel Pk, PA; (Y); Band; Concert Band; Mrchg Band; Orch; School Play; Stage Crew; Symp Band; Rep Stu Cncl; Powder Puff Ftbl; Engrng.

JACOBS, LAWRENCE; North Hills HS; Pittsburgh, PA; (Y); VP Church Yth Grp; Church Choir; Symp Band; Stu Cncl; High Hon Roll; NHS; PMEA Dstrct Band; Pres Acad Ftns Awd; Allegheny Coll; Econ.

JACOBS, LINDA; Scranton Central HS; Scranton, PA; (Y); 70/281; Temple Yth Grp; Yrbk Stf; Rep Soph Cls; Rep Jr Cls; Rep Sr Cls; Stu Cncl; Trk; Hon Roll; Ithaca Coll; Comm.

JACOBS, PAM; Upper Darby HS; Upr Darby, PA; (Y); Rep Jr Cls; Hon Roll; Prfct Atten Awd; Cmmnty Svc Corps Haverford ST 84-85 & 85-86; Med.

JACOBS, SCOTT; Riverside HS; Beaver Falls, PA; (S); Art Clb; VP DECA; Exploring; Library Aide; Leo Clb; JV Bowling; Natl Educ Develpmnt Test Awd 84; Distrbtv Educ ST, Dist Awd 85-86; Pltcs.

JACOBS, STEPHEN; West Mifflin Area HS; W Mifflin, PA; (Y); Band; Concert Band; Orch; Hon Roll; NHS; U Of Pittsburgh; Engnrng.

JACOBS, WENDY; Mc Dowell HS; Erie, PA; (Y); 42/615; Church Yth Grp; Ski Clb; Var Trk; JV L Vllybl; Hon Roll; YOU Cheerldng Sqd & YOU Vrsty Vllybl Tm 83-86; YOU Cheerldng Sqd Co-Capt 85-86; YOU Track 83-86; Ambassador Coll; Theology.

JACOBSON, STACY; Abington HS; Elkins Park, PA; (Y); 114/563; Key Clb; Spanish Clb; Varsity Clb; Nwsp Stf; Yrbk Stf; Rep Frsh Cls; Rep Soph Cls; Rep Jr Cls; Rep Sr Cls; Rep Stu Cncl.

JACOBY, AMY; Donegal HS; Mt Joy, PA; (Y); NHS; Phys.

JACOBY, BONNIE; Hanover SR HS; Hanover, PA; (Y); JV Var Fld Hcky; Nurse.

JACOBY, CRAIG; Lower Merion HS; Merion, PA; (Y); 7/342; JCL; Math Tm; Spanish Clb; Rep Stu Cncl; Var Capt Bsktbl; JV Socr; Var L Trk; Pres NHS; Ntl Merit SF.

JACOBY, MICHELLE; Freedom HS; Bethlehem, PA; (Y); 253/445; Library Aide; Teachers Aide; Acctg.

JACOBY, MONICA; Northampton SR HS; Northampton, PA; (Y); 74/444; Church Yth Grp; Chorus; Rep Stu Cncl; Var Swmmng; St Lukes Schl Nrsng; Nrsng.

JACOBY, TIFFANY; Palmyra HS; Palmyra, PA; (Y); 40/200; Church Yth Grp; Girl Scts; Hosp Aide; Pep Clb; Spanish Clb; Teachers Aide; Chorus; Im Vllybl; Stat Wrstlng; High Hon Roll.

JACONETTA, PATRICIA; Montour HS; Pittsburgh, PA; (Y); Nwsp Stf; Yrbk Stf; High Hon Roll; NHS; Frnch Awd 84-86; U Of Pittsburgh; Jrnlsm.

JACOWAY, LA VINA DELORES; Farrell SR HS; Farrell, PA; (Y); French Clb; Girl Scts; JV Bsktbl; Im Bowling; JV Trk; Robert Morris Bu; Adm.

JAFKO, LE ANN; Northwestern HS; Albion, PA; (Y); Trs French Clb; Girl Scts; Red Cross Aide; Teachers Aide; Chorus; School Play; Off Soph Cls; Trs Jr Cls; High Hon Roll; Hon Roll.

JAGEMAN, DEANNA; Ford City JR SR HS; Ford City, PA; (Y); 39/164; Band; Chorus; Concert Band; Mrchg Band; Pep Band; Rep Stu Cncl; JP Sousa Awd; Cnty Bnd 83-86; Dist & Rgnl Bnd 86; Cnty Chorus 86; Indiana U Of PA; Music Ed.

JAGEMAN, JAMES; Lenape Vo-Tech Schl; Ford City, PA; (Y); 60/200; Art Clb; Chess Clb; VICA; Chorus; Penn Tech Inst; Machnst.

JAGERSKI, BETH A; Center Area HS; Aliquippa, PA; (Y); Church Yth Grp; Cmnty Wkr; Dance Clb; German Clb; Band; Church Choir; Concert Band; Mrchg Band; School Musical; Im Socr; Swmmng Heat Awds; Med Tech.

JAGTA, TINA; Corry Area HS; Corry, PA; (S); 21/215; Trs French Clb; Hosp Aide; Trs Y-Teens; Hon Roll; U Pittsburgh; RN.

JAHN, CHRISTOPHER; Father Judge HS; Philadelphia, PA; (Y); 6/403; German Clb; School Musical; Yrbk Rptr; Var L Ftbl; Var L Trk; High Hon Roll; NHS; Boy Scts; Church Yth Grp; Latin Clb; US Army Ntl Schlr Athlt Awd 86; Almni Assoc Sr Schlr Awd Outstndng Schlstcs 86; Prsntl Schlrsp 86; La Salle U; Acctg.

JAKOB, CARMELLA; Cowanesque Valley HS; Westfield, PA; (Y); Cmnty Wkr; Library Aide; Red Cross Aide; Band; Concert Band; Mrchg Band; Rep Soph Cls; JV Vllybl; Hon Roll; Mnsfld U; Bus Admin.

JAKUBEC, AMY; Kennedy Christian HS; Fowler, OH; (Y); 5/98; Pres Church Yth Grp; Cmnty Wkr; Hosp Aide; Latin Clb; Library Aide; Pep Clb; Science Clb; Yrbk Stf; Bsktbl; Vllybl; Cthlc Dghtrs Of Amer Essy Wnnr 85; Premed.

JAMANN, FREDERICK; Liberty HS; Bethlehem, PA; (Y); 40/475; Cmnty Wkr; Lit Mag; Hon Roll; Prfct Atten Awd; PA ST U; Comp Engrng.

JAMES, BRYAN; Danville SR HS; Danville, PA; (Y); 15/208; Computer Clb; Key Clb; Spanish Clb; Nwsp Stf; Rep Frsh Cls; Rep Soph Cls; Var Bsbl; Var Capt Bsktbl; Coach Actv; JV Golf; Bloomsburg U; Math Tchr.

JAMES, CLARK; Saucon Valley SR HS; Hellertown, PA; (Y); 20/150; Science Clb; Ski Clb; Spanish Clb; Band; Concert Band; Jazz Band; Mrchg Band; Pep Band; School Musical; School Play; Lehigh U; Bus.

JAMES, DAWN L; Hamburg HS; Shoemakersville, PA; (Y); 19/152; Spanish Clb; Band; Chorus; High Hon Roll; Hon Roll; NHS; Camp Fr Inc; Girl Scts; Mrchg Band; Var Trk; Acdmc Awd Span I & Ii 84; Acdmc Awd Span III 85; Acdmc Awd Span IV 86; Kutztown U.

JAMES, GREG; Otto Eldred JR SR HS; Rixford, PA; (Y); Computer Clb; Chorus; Stage Crew; Yrbk Rptr; Bsktbl; Ftbl; Mgr(s); Swmmng; Wt Lftg; Prfct Atten Awd.

JAMES, HOPE MARIE; Brandywine Heights HS; Topton, PA; (Y); Church Yth Grp; Teachers Aide; Color Guard; Mrchg Band; Yrbk Ed-Chief; Score Keeper; Hon Roll; Outstndng Acadmc Achvt-Am Cltrs 84; Outstndng Acadmc Achvt-Spnsh 85-86; Ed.

JAMES, JASON; Hazleton HS; Drums, PA; (Y); 54/326; Scholastic Bowl; VICA; Var L Ftbl; Wt Lftg; Hon Roll; Bus.

JAMES, JEANNINE; E L Meyers HS; Wilkes-Barre, PA; (S); Church Yth Grp; Hosp Aide; Ski Clb; Band; Concert Band; Jazz Band; Mrchg Band; Trk; High Hon Roll; Jr NHS; Wilkes Coll; Phrmcy.

JAMES, LAURI; Montour HS; Mckees Rocks, PA; (Y); Church Yth Grp; Cmnty Wkr; Debate Tm; NFL; Political Wkr; Teachers Aide; Band; Church Choir; Concert Band; Mrchg Band; U Pittsburgh; Elem Ed.

JAMES, LESLIE; Merion Mercy Acad; Phila, PA; (Y); Art Clb; Hosp Aide; Science Clb; Chorus; Concert Band; Jazz Band; Stage Crew; Hon Roll; Prfct Atten Awd; Crtfct Awd Hsp Of Penn 83; Md Hnr Rll 84; Pre-Vet.

JAMES, LISA; Mid Valley HS; Olyphant, PA; (Y); Church Yth Grp; Frsh Cls; Soph Cls; Jr Cls; Sr Cls; High Hon Roll; Bloomsburg U; Bus Ed.

JAMES, MELISSA; Beaver Area JR-SR HS; Beaver, PA; (Y); 12/180; JCL; Latin Clb; Pep Clb; Ski Clb; Mrchg Band; Powder Puff Ftbl; Twrlr; High Hon Roll; Robert Morris; Med Sec.

JAMES, MICHELLE; Mt St Joseph Acad; Flourtown, PA; (Y); Drama Clb; Pres JA; JCL; Pres Latin Clb; School Play; Mgr Stage Crew; Ed Nwsp Rptr; Var Socr; Hon Roll; NEDT Awd; PA JR Acad Of Sci-1st Pl Rgnl & ST 85; Latn Hnr Soc-Ofcr 84-86; Exlccnc Awds-Engl & Latn IV 86; PA ST U; Avtg.

JAMES, PATRICE; West Hazleton HS; Drums, PA; (Y); 87/214; Ski Clb; Spanish Clb; SADD; Bsktbl; Sftbl; Trk; Hon Roll; Comp Sci.

JAMES, SUZANNE; Saint Basil Acad; Philadelphia, PA; (Y); Exploring; French Clb; Hosp Aide; Variety Show; Nwsp Rptr; Im Sftbl; NEDT Awd; Piano; Rollins Outdoor Advrtsng Acadmc Schlrshp; PA ST U; Nrsng.

JAMES, THERESA; Westmont Hilltop HS; Johnstown, PA; (Y); 17/160; French Clb; Key Clb; Ski Clb; Yrbk Stf; Rep Stu Cncl; Stat Wrstlng; High Hon Roll; Hon Roll; NHS; Exc In Englsh Awd 85; Med.

JAMIESON, NANCY; Warren Area HS; Warren, PA; (Y); Church Yth Grp; Cmnty Wkr; French Clb; Hosp Aide; Office Aide; Chorus; Church Choir; Stage Crew; School Play; Yrbk Stf; Bsktbl; IN U PA; Hstry.

JAMIESON, ROB; Pennsbury HS; Yardley, PA; (Y); 20/730; Church Yth Grp; Cmnty Wkr; Debate Tm; FCA; Intnl Clb; NFL; Political Wkr; Spanish Clb; Speech Tm; SADD; PA Free Enterprise Wk 86; PA Gov Schl Intl Studs 85; Stanford U; Law.

JAMIOLKOWSKI, STEPHANIE; Allentown Central Catholic HS; Allentown, PA; (Y); Band; Concert Band; Mrchg Band; Pep Band; High Hon Roll; Hon Roll; Pharm.

JAMISON, KEITH; Big Spring HS; Carlisle, PA; (Y); 2/218; Boy Scts; Church Yth Grp; Varsity Clb; Rep Sr Cls; Var Capt Crs Cntry; Var Trk; Hon Roll; NHS; Ntl Merit Ltr; DECA; U Of DE; Mchncl Engrng.

JAMISON, MARISA; North Catholic HS; Pittsburgh, PA; (Y); Church Yth Grp; Dance Clb; Chorus; Church Choir; JV Bsktbl; Hon Roll; Prfct Atten Awd; Color Guard; Stage Crew; IN U; Nursing.

JAMISON, MICHELLE; Pottsville Area HS; Pottsville, PA; (Y); 99/242; Trs VICA; Chorus; Mrchg Band; Nwsp Stf; Capt Cheerleading; High Hon Roll; Hon Roll; Prsdntl Phys Ftns Awd 85-86; VICA Ldrshp Awd 84-86; Nwsppr Carrier Mth 85; Empire Beauty Schl; Csmtlgy.

JAN, LOUIS; St Joseph Prep Schl; West Berlin, NJ; (Y); Boy Scts; German Clb; Nwsp Stf; Hon Roll; Ntl Merit Ltr; SAR Awd; VFW Awd; Boy Scts Of Amer Eagle Awd 86; Taiwanese Yth Cncl 84-85; Med.

JANAK, JAMES; Richland Twp HS; Johnstown, PA; (Y); Varsity Clb; Var L Ftbl; Hon Roll; IUP; Comp Sci.

JANCZAK, JAY; Lower Moreland HS; Huntingdon Valley, PA; (S); Rep Jr Cls; Rep Stu Cncl; Var Socr; Hon Roll.

JANDREW, RENEE; Oswayo Valley HS; Shinglehouse, PA; (Y); 3/52; Ski Clb; Varsity Clb; Flag Corp; Pres Frsh Cls; Pres Soph Cls; Sec Stu Cncl; Stat Bsbl; Capt Bsktbl; Capt Cheerleading; Sftbl; Ntl Math,Ldrshp,Achvt Acad 84-86; N C Weselyan; Crmnl Justice.

JANI, KRISTIE; Allentown Central Catholic HS; Allentown, PA; (Y); FBLA; Key Clb; Chorus; Hst Rep Frsh Cls; Var Cheerleading; Hon Roll; Bloomsburg U; Accntng.

JANICKI, CARL; Saint Pius X HS; Collegeville, PA; (S); 19/137; Church Yth Grp; Science Clb; Pres Service Clb; School Musical; Var Capt Bsbl; Var JV Bsktbl; Var L Ftbl; Hon Roll; NHS; Times Herald Nwspapr Carrier Of Yr 83; All Ches-Mont Punter-Kickr 1st Tm Phila Daily News Ftbl 86; U S Military Acad; Biol.

JANIDLO, KAREN; Franklin HS; Franklin, PA; (Y); 5/219; VP Church Yth Grp; German Clb; L Color Guard; Variety Show; Var Coach Actv; JV Var Mgr(s); Var Trk; Var L Vllybl; Hon Roll; Prfct Atten Awd; Radiologic Tech.

JANIK, DIANE; Cumberland Valley HS; Camp Hill, PA; (Y); 3/522; Church Yth Grp; Teachers Aide; Color Guard; Lit Mag; French Hon Soc; High Hon Roll; NHS; Bus Adm.

JANIKOWSKI, JAN; Cathedral Preparatory HS; Erie, PA; (Y); 17/214; Latin Clb; Chorus; Im Bsktbl; Hon Roll; NHS; Ltn Hnr Scty; Acctng.

JANKE, JILL; Slippery Rock HS; Forestville, PA; (Y); Church Yth Grp; Drama Clb; Intnl Clb; Office Aide; Pep Clb; Yrbk Stf; Bsktbl; Cheerleading; Trk; Wt Lftg; Air Force.

JANKOWSKI, WALTER; Northern Chester County Tech Schl; Chester Spgs, PA; (Y); Ski Clb; Im Bsktbl; Im Socr; NHS; Embry Riddle Aerontcl U; Engrng.

JANNENGA, ROY; Souderton Area HS; Harleysville, PA; (Y); Band; Concert Band; Mrchg Band; High Hon Roll; Jr NHS; NHS; Rotary Awd; Richard Arner Sci Awd 84; Best Math Stu 84; Carnegie Mellon U; Robotics.

JANNONE, JOHN; Wyalusing Valley JR SR HS; Camptown, PA; (Y); Drama Clb; German Clb; Ski Clb; Orch; School Musical; Var Crs Cntry; Var Trk; High Hon Roll; Hon Roll; Rural Elec Yth Tour WA D C 86; Natl Merit Schlrshp; Colgate; Lbrl Arts.

JANOFSKY, MAURA E; Bishop Shanahan HS; W Chester, PA; (Y); 42/218; Cmnty Wkr; SADD; Lib Chorus; Church Choir; School Musical; Hon Roll; JR Clss Musc Achvt Awd 86; Musc Serv Cert 86; Elem Ed.

JANORA, LISA; John S Fine HS; Nanticoke, PA; (Y); 20/250; Trs VP Key Clb; Chorus; Yrbk Stf; JV Var Fld Hcky; High Hon Roll; NHS; Physcl Thrpy.

JANOSIK, LESLEY; Laurel Highlands SR HS; Uniontown, PA; (Y); #16 In Class; Capt Math Tm; Sec Band; Concert Band; Mrchg Band; High Hon Roll; Hon Roll; JP Sousa Awd; Jr NHS; Sec NHS; PA Hstry Awd 83; Engl Awd 83; Spn Cert Merit 85; PA ST U; Engrng.

JANOSKI, MICHAEL; Mt Lebanon HS; Pittsburgh, PA; (Y); Chess Clb; Computer Clb; VP Frsh Cls; Im Bsktbl; Im Sftbl; Hon Roll; Duquesne U; Elec Engrng.

JANOV, CHRISTINE SUZANNE; South Side Area HS; Hookstown, PA; (Y); 19/91; Drill Tm; School Play; Nwsp Stf; Yrbk Ed-Chief; Stu Cncl; Powder Puff Ftbl; Trk; Hon Roll; NHS; WV U; Physical Thear.

JANOVICH, LESLIE; Trinity HS; Washington, PA; (Y); Art Clb; Camera Clb; Church Yth Grp; Key Clb; Pep Clb; High Hon Roll; Hon Roll; CA U Of PA; Prsnnl.

JANSEN, JENNIFER; Cumberland Valley HS; Mechanicsburg, PA; (Y); Chorus; Church Choir; Yrbk Stf; Coach Actv; Gym; Hon Roll; Citatn Excllnce House Rep 86; Spec Underclssmn Recgntn Gym 85 & 86; Intl Rltns.

JANSSEN, SUSAN; Dunmore HS; Dunmore, PA; (Y); FNA; Pres Hosp Aide; ROTC; Swing Chorus; Yrbk Rptr; Capt Cheerleading; Mgr(s); High Hon Roll; Hon Roll; NHS; Achvt Awd/Camper Of Wk St Andrew 83 & 85; SOS Course Elmntry Stu Hnr Tchr 86; Nrs.

JANUARY, SHARI; Highlands SR HS; Natrona Heights, PA; (Y); DECA; Key Clb; Sec Soph Cls; Sec Jr Cls; Sec Sr Cls; Rep Stu Cncl; Bsktbl; Tennis; Jr NHS; NHS; Bradford; Secretrl.

JARA, RENEE; Sharpsville Area HS; Sharpsville, PA; (Y); 26/125; Cmnty Wkr; Spanish Clb; Chorus; Nwsp Stf; Yrbk Stf; VP Jr Cls; Rep Stu Cncl; Cheerleading; Hon Roll; NHS.

JARAMILLO, SOPHIA; Bethlehem Catholic HS; Bethlehem, PA; (Y); Mgr Ftbl; High Hon Roll; Hon Roll; NY; Fash Dsgnr.

JARBECK, JULIE; Punxsutawney SR HS; Anita, PA; (Y); Church Yth Grp; Varsity Clb; L Bsktbl; Var Cheerleading; Var Vllybl; IN U PA; Pre-Law.

JAREMKO, SHAWN JEFFREY; The Phelps Schl; Aurora, OH; (Y); Pres Sr Cls; Stu Cncl; Var Capt Bsktbl; Var L Crs Cntry; Var L Socr; Pres Awd, Hdmstrs Awd, Outstndng Prctr Awd, The Stvns Awd 86; Cngrssmns Del Merit 86; Northwood Inst Midland; Bus.

JARRELL, SHARI; Waynesburg Central HS; Spraggs, PA; (Y); AFS; French Clb; Ski Clb; Band; Color Guard; Mrchg Band; Yrbk Stf; Swmmng; Trk; Hon Roll; WVU.

JARRETT, AIMEE; State College Area HS; State College, PA; (Y); 73/567; Church Yth Grp; Rep Frsh Cls; JV Sftbl; Var Vllybl; Mgr Wrstlng; Hon Roll; Nrsg.

JARRETT, JAMES; Bradford Area HS; Bradford, PA; (Y); 3/314; Trs Key Clb; Stu Cncl; Im Vllybl; High Hon Roll; Jr NHS; NHS; Ntl Merit SF; NEDT Awd; Harvey Mudd Coll; Comp Engrng.

JARRETT, SUNNY; Faith Christian HS; Wind Gap, PA; (Y); 5/11; Church Yth Grp; School Musical; School Play; Variety Show; Pres Soph Cls; Sec Jr Cls; Trs Sr Cls; Cheerleading; Hon Roll; Dinsgshd Chrstn HS Stu 85-86; Bookkeepng Awd 86; Schltc Recgntn Awd 86; Messiah Coll.

JARRETT, TINA; Fort Le Boeuf HS; Erie, PA; (Y); 5/182; Nwsp Stf; Pres Jr Cls; High Hon Roll; Hon Roll; Jr NHS; VP NHS; Acad Achvt Awd 84-85 & 85-86; Spec Ed.

JARROW, JOSEPH W; Lakeland JR SR HS; Jermyn, PA; (Y); 72/237; Ski Clb; Stu Cncl; JV Bsbl; JV Bsktbl; JV Crs Cntry; Hon Roll; Penn ST; Mechncl Engrng.

JARROW, MICHELE; Western Wayne HS; Moscow, PA; (Y); 10/148; 4-H; FBLA; Mgr(s); High Hon Roll; NHS; Prfct Atten Awd; Hghst Schlstc Avr In Bus Track 86; Prfct Atndnc For 8 Yrs Awd 86; Lackawanna 4C; Bus Adm.

JARVIS, JOLENE; Laurel Valley JR SR HS; Bolivar, PA; (Y); 41/79; Chorus; JV Var Cheerleading; Var Powder Puff Ftbl; JV Sftbl; Var Pres Wt Lftg; Hlth Crs Clb 86; Wtmoreland Cnty Comm Coll; Nrs.

JARVIS, TODD; Warren Area HS; Warren, PA; (S); Pres French Clb; Varsity Clb; Acpl Chr; School Play; Var L Ftbl; Var L Trk; Hon Roll; Jr NHS; NHS; Grove City Coll; Intl Bus.

JARZINKO, MELISSA; Shenandoah Valley HS; Lost Creek, PA; (S); 15/99; Church Yth Grp; Pep Clb; Flag Corp; Nwsp Stf; Stu Cncl; Sftbl; Hon Roll; Williamsport Area CC; Dietcs.

JASIEWICZ, TERI; Serra Catholic HS; Mc Keesport, PA; (Y); 51/156; Drama Clb; Chorus; Color Guard; Mrchg Band; School Musical; School Play; Nwsp Rptr; Powder Puff Ftbl; Hon Roll; NEDT Awd; Pedtrc Nrsng.

JASKOLA, BILL; Union Area HS; New Castle, PA; (Y); 7/66; Pres Chess Clb; Var L Mgr(s); Var L Trk; High Hon Roll; NHS; Pres Schlr; Hofstra U; Pre-Law.

JASKOWIAK III, WALTER A; Ridley HS; Ridley Park, PA; (Y); 4/412; Am Leg Boys St; Q&S; Jazz Band; Mrchg Band; Yrbk Phtg; DAR Awd; NHS; Pres Schlr; Rotary Awd; Aud/Vis; ROTC Schlrshp 86; Syracuse U; Aerospace Engrg.

JASKULSKI, JODI; West Mifflin Area HS; West Mifflin, PA; (Y); Art Clb; Hosp Aide; Key Clb; Pep Clb; Chorus; Drill Tm; Rep Jr Cls; Rep Stu Cncl; Vllybl; Hon Roll; Ntl Hnr Soc 84; 2nd Pl In Calligrphy Cntst 86; Top 12 Miss PA US Teen Pgnt 85; U Of Pittsburgh; Pharm.

JASLOW, DAVID; Abington SR HS; Abington, PA; (Y); 1/528; Boy Scts; Cmnty Wkr; Hosp Aide; Orch; Nwsp Ed-Chief; Nwsp Stf; Rep Stu Cncl; Var Swmmng; Cit Awd; NHS; Natl Hon Soc Schlrshp 86; Gebbardsbauer Awd Srv & Citzenship 86; Public Rltns Awd 86; Penn ST; Pre Med.

JASTROMB, TRACY; Meadville Area SR HS; Meadville, PA; (Y); Church Yth Grp; Girl Scts; Hosp Aide; Red Cross Aide; SADD; Chorus; School Play; Stu Cncl; Hon Roll; Prfct Atten Awd; Knghts Clmbs Free Thrw Cncl Wnnr 83 & 84; Behrnd Campus Penn ST; CPA.

JASTRZAB, JEFFREY; Greater Johnstown HS; Johnstown, PA; (Y); Sec Intnl Clb; Math Clb; Ski Clb; Trs Spanish Clb; Band; School Musical; Stage Crew; Nwsp Rptr; High Hon Roll; NHS; Penn ST U; Frstry.

JAVORKA, MICHAEL; Liberty HS; Bethlehem, PA; (Y); 92/475; School Play; Rep Frsh Cls; JV Ftbl; Hon Roll; Eastern MI U; Comp.

JAYNE, KEVIN; Sullivan County HS; Dushore, PA; (Y); Am Leg Boys St; Aud/Vis; Church Yth Grp; Key Clb; Concert Band; Jazz Band; Mrchg Band; High Hon Roll; NHS; Cncrt Bnd Drctrs Awd 86; Key Clb 84-86; Audio Visual Awd 86; PA ST U; Aero Sp Engrng.

JAYNE, TAMRA; Wyalusing Valley HS; Laceyville, PA; (Y); German Clb; Varsity Clb; Sec Jr Cls; Var L Cheerleading; Bowling; Var L Sftbl; Var L Vllybl; Hon Roll; NHS; IN U PA; Tchg.

JAYNES, RANDY; Northeast Bradford HS; Stevensville, PA; (Y); 8/79; Computer Clb; Chorus; Concert Band; Drm Mjr(t); Mrchg Band; Yrbk Phtg; Var L Bsktbl; High Hon Roll; Hon Roll; Im Ftbl; Navy; Nuclear Physics.

JEAN, EVANS; Blue Mountain Acad; Brooklyn, NY; (Y); JV Var Bsktbl; Im Mgr Ftbl; Im Mgr Sftbl; Im Mgr Vllybl; Im Mgr Wt Lftg; Bus Admn.

JEANNERETTE, MIKE; Otto-Eldred HS; Duke Center, PA; (Y); 2/95; Varsity Clb; L Var Bsktbl; Bausch & Lomb Sci Awd; High Hon Roll; Hon Roll; NHS; Nwsp Stf; VP Jr Cls; Rep Stu Cncl; L Var Ftbl; U Of VA; Engrng.

JEANTY, MARIE SHEILA; Bishop Mcdevitt HS; Elkins Park, PA; (Y); Church Yth Grp; French Clb; Powder Puff Ftbl; Hon Roll; Frnch Awd; Wrld Culture Awd; Prom Committee Awd; Misericordia Coll; Bio.

JEDDIC, DENISE; Wyoming Area SR HS; West Wyoming, PA; (Y); German Clb; Key Clb; Yrbk Stf; Stu Cncl; Swmmng; Hon Roll; NHS; Marywood Coll; Cmmnctn.

JEDROSKO, MATTHEW; Bradford Area HS; Bradford, PA; (Y); Exploring; Band; Concert Band; Jazz Band; Mrchg Band; Pep Band; Hon Roll; Crmnl Just.

JEFFERS, HEATHER; Trinity HS; Washington, PA; (Y); 125/374; Drama Clb; Pep Clb; Acpl Chr; Chorus; School Musical; School Play; Variety Show; Var JV Crs Cntry; Var JV Trk; Berklee; Music.

JEFFERS, RHONDA; Elkland Area HS; Osceola, PA; (Y); 1/80; Drama Clb; French Clb; Sec SADD; Varsity Clb; Band; Yrbk Stf; L Bsktbl; L Trk; L Vllybl; Pres NHS; Penn ST; Chem Engrng.

JEFFERSON, GEOFFERY; Germantown HS; Philadelphia, PA; (Y); Debate Tm; Library Aide; Office Aide; Teachers Aide; Orch; Var Bsbl; JV L Bowling; Var Swmmng; Hon Roll; Penn St; Bus Mgnt.

JEFFREY, KIMBERLY D; Dover Area HS; York, PA; (Y); 82/247; Drama Clb; Varsity Clb; Var Cheerleading; Trk; Hon Roll.

JEFFREYS, PAMELA; Greater Johnstown SR HS; Johnstown, PA; (Y); Am Leg Aux Girls St; Yrbk Stf; High Hon Roll; Hon Roll; NHS; Nrsng.

JEFFRIES, ROSALIND EVETTA; Chester HS; Chester, PA; (Y); 18/374; Keywanettes; Band; Chorus; Church Choir; Concert Band; Orch; Nwsp Stf; Cit Awd; High Hon Roll; Hon Roll; Essay Cntst Awd; Natl Spch & Drm Awd; PA Indstrl Chem Corp Schlrp; Soc Stds Awd; C-Excel Ltr; Hampton U; Comp Sci.

JEGASOTHY, S MANJULA; Harriton HS; Rosemont, PA; (Y); Hosp Aide; Sec Trs Pep Clb; Nwsp Ed-Chief; Yrbk Stf; JV L Fld Hcky; JV L Lcrss; High Hon Roll; NCTE Awd; Ntl Merit SF; Mst Vlbl Harriton Svc Lge Mbr 83; Mst Imprvd-Lacrosse Tm 84; Hlth Ed Awd 84; Phy.

JEITNER, DAVID; Northeast HS; Philadelphia, PA; (Y); 1/690; VP JA; Math Clb; Science Clb; Ski Clb; Hon Roll; NHS; Ntl Merit Ltr; Cngrssnl Merit Cert Overall Excllnce 86; Pres Acad Fit Awd 86; CA Inst Tech Scholar 86; CA Inst Tech; Aero Engrng.

JEMO, NICK; Weatherly Area HS; Weatherly, PA; (S); 3/63; German Clb; Capt Bsbl; Bsktbl; Capt Golf; Cit Awd; High Hon Roll; Natl Engl Merit Awd 85; Outstndng Germn Stdnt Awd 84; MV Golfr Awd 85; Arch.

JENCKA, LISA; Greensburg Central Catholic HS; Irwin, PA; (Y); French Clb; High Hon Roll; NHS.

JENKINS, AISHA L; Fairview HS; Fairview, PA; (Y); Am Leg Aux Girls St; Model UN; Band; Concert Band; Jazz Band; Mrchg Band; Pep Band; Lit Mag; JV Trk; High Hon Roll; Engrg.

JENKINS, ANNE M; Meyersdale Area HS; Meyersdale, PA; (Y); Band; Chorus; Mrchg Band; School Musical; NHS; Ntl Merit SF; NEDT Awd; Science Clb; Spanish Clb; Hon Roll; IVP Hnr Band 83-85; Dist & Regl Band 84-86; PA All ST Lions Band 85; PA ST; Engrg.

JENKINS, DEBORAH; Upper Darby HS; Drexel Hl, PA; (Y); Pres Art Clb; Cmnty Wkr; JA; Library Aide; Yrbk Stf; Ed Lit Mag; High Hon Roll; Hon Roll; NHS; Pres Schlr; Mhlnbrg Coll; Art Hstry.

JENKINS, ELIZABETH ANN; West Scranton HS; Scranton, PA; (Y); 5/255; Debate Tm; Latin Clb; NFL; Scholastic Bowl; Speech Tm; Thesps; Nwsp Rptr; Nwsp Stf; Yrbk Bus Mgr; Yrbk Stf; Gifted Pgm; Honorary Spch Cert Extmprns Spkng; U Scranton; Secndry Ed.

JENKINS, ERICA B; Abington Heights HS; Waverly, PA; (Y); 9/270; Church Yth Grp; Drama Clb; Pres Girl Scts; Mrchg Band; Stage Crew; Yrbk Stf; JV Var Wrstlng; High Hon Roll; NHS; Library Aide; 1st Pl Kngs Cll Grmn Cntst 84&86; Grl Sct Slvr Awd 84; Dist Band 86; Engnrng.

JENKINS II, GARY D; Bell Vernon Area HS; Belle Vernon, PA; (Y); Pres Church Yth Grp; Ski Clb; Band; Capt Bsktbl; L Ftbl; Wt Lftg; Hon Roll; NHS.

JENKINS, INGEBORG; Freedom HS; Bethlehem, PA; (Y); 122/404; Band; Concert Band; Jazz Band; Mrchg Band; Orch; Pep Band; Symp Band; J F Goodwin Schlrshp 86; Harcum JC; Anml Ctr Mgmt.

JENKINS, JAY W; Owen J Roberts HS; Glenmoore, PA; (S); 16/291; Band; Concert Band; Mrchg Band; Symp Band; Tennis; Hon Roll; NHS; Pol Sci.

JENKINS, JEFF; Mary Fuller Frazier Memorial HS; Perryopolis, PA; (Y); Hon Roll; Prfct Atten Awd; Newspaper Hon Carrier Awd 85 & 86; Carpentry.

JENKINS, KATHLEEN; Deer Lakes JR SR HS; Gibsonia, PA; (Y); Office Aide; High Hon Roll; Hon Roll; NHS.

JENKINS, LYNNIE; West Mifflin Area HS; W Mifflin, PA; (Y); 33/330; Church Yth Grp; JV Bsktbl; JV Ftbl; High Hon Roll; Hon Roll; NHS; Blgy.

JENKINS, MARY KATHERINE; Cambria Heights HS; Patton, PA; (Y); 31/233; Sec Pres Church Yth Grp; FHA; Library Aide; Acpl Chr; Chorus; Church Choir; Yrbk Stf; Sftbl; Hon Roll; OH Nrthrn; Elem Ed.

JENKINS, PAUL R; Western Wayne HS; Lake Ariel, PA; (Y); 25/130; Boy Scts; Church Yth Grp; 1st Pl Cnty Art Cont 83; Roanoke Coll; Pre-Med.

JENKINS, TODD; Yough SR HS; Smithton, PA; (Y); Church Yth Grp; VICA; Hon Roll; Paintr.

JENKINS, TRACY; Milton HS; Milton, PA; (Y); Pres Church Yth Grp; FHA; Office Aide; Variety Show; Var Bsktbl; Powder Puff Ftbl; Var Trk; Wt Lftg; Johnson & Wales; Fshn Mrchndsng.

JENKINS, VICKY LYNN; Lampeter-Strasburg HS; Willow St, PA; (Y); 11/165; Chorus; Madrigals; School Musical; Cheerleading; Sftbl; Hon Roll; Gftd Prog 84-86.

JENNIFER, STANTON; Churchill HS; Pittsburgh, PA; (Y); 52/188; Spanish Clb; Capt Cheerleading; High Hon Roll; Hon Roll; WVU; Bus.

JENNINGS, CARRIE; Plymouth-Whitemarsh HS; Ft Washington, PA; (S); 64/365; Nwsp Sprt Ed; Trs Soph Cls; Trs Jr Cls; Sftbl; Var L Tennis; Var L Trk; Vllybl; Hon Roll; 2 Mi Relay Tm Schl Recd 86; Jrnlsm.

JENNINGS, JEFF; Sharon HS; Sharon, PA; (Y); Teachers Aide; Color Guard; Nwsp Phtg; Nwsp Rptr; Yrbk Phtg; Yrbk Stf; Bsbl; Hon Roll; Law Enfrcmnt.

JENNINGS, KATHLEEN; Blue Mountain Acad; Hamburg, PA; (Y); 2/65; Spanish Clb; Nwsp Bus Mgr; Yrbk Stf; Pres Frsh Cls; Pres Soph Cls; Rep Stu Cncl; Gym; High Hon Roll; NHS; Sal; Andrews U; CPA.

JENNINGS, KELLI; Trinity HS; Washington, PA; (Y); Art Clb; Church Yth Grp; French Clb; Key Clb; Pep Clb; Ski Clb; Hon Roll; Natl Art Hnr Soc 85-8x6; Parsons Schl Arts; Comm Art.

JENNINGS, MELISSA; Pine Grove SR HS; Pine Grove, PA; (Y); Cmnty Wkr; Hosp Aide; Chorus; School Musical; Stage Crew; Nwsp Rptr; Yrbk Stf; Mgr(s); Mgr Wrstlng; Hon Roll; Occptnl Thrpy.

JENNINGS, MICHAEL; Spring-Ford HS; Schwenksville, PA; (Y); 44/237; Aud/Vis; Boy Scts; 4-H; FBLA; Pres Ski Clb; Trk; 4-H Awd; Opt Clb Awd; Abraham L Buckwalter Schlrshp 86; West Chester U; Crmnl Jstc.

JENNINGS, TIMOTHY; Cardinal O Hara HS; Swarthmore, PA; (Y); 54/780; Church Yth Grp; French Clb; JA; Bsktbl; Ftbl; Hon Roll; NHS; Natl Frnch Cont Commendation 85; Bus Law Awd 85-86; Hnrbl Mention Cardinal O Hara Sci Fair 84; Law.

JENSEN, GEORGE; Newport HS; Newport, PA; (Y); 25/93; Church Yth Grp; Cmnty Wkr; Band; Concert Band; Jazz Band; Mrchg Band; Yrbk Stf; JV Wrstlng; High Hon Roll; Hon Roll; Mdrn Music Mstrs; Shippensbrg U; Acctng.

JENSEN, MICHAEL; Altoona Area HS; Altoona, PA; (Y); 219/889; German Clb; Ski Clb; IUP; Natrl Sci.

JENSEN, RAYMOND; East Goshen HS; West Chester, PA; (Y); Band; IN U PA; Biol.

JENSH, SUSAN; Downingtown SR HS; Downingtown, PA; (S); 22/545; Dance Clb; FTA; Pres Intnl Clb; Spanish Clb; SADD; Teachers Aide; Chorus; Color Guard; VP Mrchg Band; School Musical; Peace Corps.

JENTGENS, WILLIAM; Highlands HS; Natrona, PA; (Y); JV Var Bsbl; High Hon Roll; Pres Acadmc Ftnss Awd; PA ST U; Geo.

JERICH, JOE; Springdale HS; Springdale, PA; (Y); Computer Clb; Drama Clb; JA; Spanish Clb; Stage Crew; Hon Roll; IN U; Comp Sci.

JERMACANS, WILLIAM; Phoenixville Area HS; Phoenixville, PA; (Y); Quiz Bowl; Vllybl; High Hon Roll; Hon Roll; NHS; Nclr.

JEROSKY, JEFF; Penn Cambria HS; Gallitzin, PA; (Y); #20 In Class; Hon Roll; Penn ST U; Nuclear Engr.

JERTO, STEPHANIE; Homer Center JR SR HS; Homer City, PA; (Y); 21/86; Natl Sci Merit Awd 86; PYEA; Hlth Career Clb Secy, Pres; Lib Clb Secy 86; IN U Of PA; Bus Adm.

JERVIS, MELISSA; Tunkhannock Area HS; Factoryville, PA; (S); 25/250; Dance Clb; Key Clb; Ski Clb; Band; Concert Band; Stu Cncl; Gym; Tennis; Hon Roll; NHS; Wilkes Coll; Optmtrst.

JESCHKE, DEBORAH NELIDA; Mcdowell HS; Erie, PA; (Y); 15/529; French Clb; GAA; Pep Clb; Rep Stu Cncl; Tennis; Trk; NHS; Pres Schlr; IBEW Lcl Union No 56 Schlrshp $1800 86-87; Rcgntn Math & Sci Ability Gannon U 85; PA ST U; Sci.

JESCHONEK, TONYA; Greater Johnstown HS; Johnstown, PA; (Y); Math Clb; Spanish Clb; Band; Concert Band; Drm Mjr(t); Mrchg Band; Orch; Pep Band; Hon Roll; NHS; PMEA Dist VI Bnd, Rgn III Bnd 85 & 86; Indiana U PA; Comp Pgmr.

JESSE, CHARLES W; Mc Guffey HS; Prosperity, PA; (Y); 34/200; German Clb; Yrbk Stf; Var Stat Bsktbl; High Hon Roll; Hon Roll; NHS; Pres Schlr; Mst Rspctd 86; Comp Pgmg.

JETT, TRACY; North Star HS; Jenners, PA; (Y); FCA; Pres Math Clb; Stu Cncl; Var L Bsktbl; Hon Roll; Lion Awd; Mu Alp Tht; NHS; Pres Schlr; Ivp Physics Tstng Comp 86; Conemaugh Vly; Registered Nrsng.

JEZ, JOSEPH; Pennsbury HS; Yardley, PA; (Y); Boy Scts; German Clb; Intnl Clb; Library Aide; Mathletes; Nwsp Rptr; Yrbk Stf; Hon Roll; NHS; PA Archdiosese Wrtng Schlrshp 84; Biochem.

JEZEWSKI, VICKI; Carmichaels Area HS; Carmichaels, PA; (Y); 44/103; Spanish Clb; Duffs Bus Inst; Accntng.

JIMMIE, DANA; Dunmore HS; Dunmore, PA; (Y); 8/152; Computer Clb; FBLA; Ski Clb; Spanish Clb; Var Cheerleading; Trk; Hon Roll; VP Jr NHS; NHS; Phy Thrpy.

JINDAL, BINU; Central Dauphin East HS; Harrisburg, PA; (Y); 30/274; Debate Tm; French Clb; Chorus; Color Guard; Yrbk Stf; Hon Roll; Jr NHS; NHS; Rotary Awd; Mock Trial Tm 86; Cert Compltn Hindi Lang 84-86; Dickinson Schl Law; Pre-Law.

JING, MAI; B H S Intl Affairs HS; Philadelphia, PA; (Y); #6 In Class; Hon Roll; Penn ST; Eng.

JOBES, SHANE W; Mc Guffey HS; Claysville, PA; (Y); 27/200; German Clb; Band; Mrchg Band; High Hon Roll; Hon Roll; Prfct Atten Awd; Schlstc Achvmnt Awds 84-86; Mbr Joppa Chapter Order Of De Molay 82; WV Inst Of Tech; Mech Engrng.

JOBSON, GARRETT; Western Wayne HS; Moscow, PA; (Y); 38/138; 4-H; Ski Clb; JV Socr; Hon Roll; Rotry Ldrshp Cmp 85; Creatv Wrtg Wrkshp 85; Natl Ski Patrol JR; Keystone JC; Arch.

JOHN IV, FRANK; Abington Heights HS; Dalton, PA; (Y); Church Yth Grp; Chorus; Church Choir; Var L Bsbl; Var Bsktbl; L Capt Crs Cntry; Var L Socr; L Capt Trk; Hon Roll; 2nd Dist Mile 86; Dist Wnnr 2 Mile Relay To ST 86; Undefeated Mile & 2 Mile Relay 85; Baptist Bible Coll; Yth Ministr.

JOHN, MEGAN; Archbishop Kennedy HS; Philadelphia, PA; (Y); Church Yth Grp; Girl Scts; Mgr(s); Score Keeper; Accntng.

JOHNS, ROBERT C; Bishop Kenrick HS; Norristown, PA; (Y); 3/305; Church Yth Grp; Mathletes; Science Clb; Spanish Clb; Rep Stu Cncl; Var Bsbl; Im Bsktbl; High Hon Roll; NHS; Essy Wnnr; Natl Conf Chrstns And Jews 86; Bell Of PA Mgmt Semnr 86; Rotry Ldrshp Camp 86; Bus.

JOHNS, SHELLEY; Keystone HS; Callensburg, PA; (Y); Office Aide; Chorus; Color Guard; VP Frsh Cls; Off Stu Cncl; Hon Roll; Clarion U Of PA.

JOHNSON, AARON D; Wilkinsburg JR SR HS; Pittsburgh, PA; (Y); Art Clb; Chess Clb; Church Yth Grp; Band; Color Guard; Orch; Nwsp Stf; Hon Roll; CAP; Church Choir; Kent St U; Aviatn.

JOHNSON, ADRIENNE RUTH; Camp Hill HS; Camp Hill, PA; (Y); 7/74; Drama Clb; Model UN; Acpl Chr; Chorus; School Musical; School Play; VP Soph Cls; High Hon Roll; NHS; NEDT Awd; Outstndng Potry Awd 85; Summr Schlrshp 85; Rotry Clb Outstndng H S SR 86; Smith College; Psych.

JOHNSON, ALONZO; Strath Haven HS; New York, NY; (Y); JV Ftbl; L Trk; Hon Roll; Hnr Rll; Track Trophies; U Of VA; Bus Mgt.

JOHNSON, AMY; Montour HS; Pittsburgh, PA; (Y); Church Yth Grp; Cmnty Wkr; Dance Clb; French Clb; Pep Clb; Var JV Cheerleading; Coach Actv; Tennis; Trk; Hon Roll; Pittsburgh Beauty Acad; Beautcn.

JOHNSON, APRIL; Mercy Voc HS; Philadelphia, PA; (Y); Cosmetology.

JOHNSON, BAYLEN; Uniontown HS; Uniontown, PA; (Y); Pres 4-H; Letterman Clb; Spanish Clb; JV Bsktbl; Var L Ftbl; Var L Trk; Im Wt Lftg; Upwrd Bnd Prog 83-86; Army Rsrv Ofcrs Traing Schlrshp Applctn 87-88.

JOHNSON, BETSY; Millville Area HS; Millville, PA; (Y); 4-H; FBLA; Spanish Clb; Concert Band; School Musical; Sec Jr Cls; JV Var Sftbl; 4-H Awd; Hon Roll; NHS; Cnty & Dstrct Band 86; Penn ST; Bus Adm.

JOHNSON, BOB; Ferndale Area HS; Johnstown, PA; (S); 8/65; Computer Clb; Band; Concert Band; Jazz Band; Mrchg Band; Var Bsbl; JV Bsktbl; Sec NHS; U Of Pittsburgh-Johnstn; Engrg.

JOHNSON, BRENDA; Wellsboro Area HS; Wellsboro, PA; (Y); SADD; Band; Concert Band; Drm & Bgl; Mrchg Band; School Musical; Cheerleading; Trk; Vllybl; Hon Roll.

JOHNSON, BRYANT; Pine Forge Acad; Philadelphia, PA; (S); 3/76; Sec Church Yth Grp; Drama Clb; Speech Tm; Teachers Aide; Chorus; Pres Frsh Cls; Pres Soph Cls; Pres Stu Cncl; High Hon Roll; NHS; Acad Schlrs Amer Awd 84; Howardd U; Pre-Med.

JOHNSON, CARL; Central Bucks High School East; Doylestown, PA; (Y); Camera Clb; Scholastic Bowl; Acpl Chr; Chorus; Swing Chorus; L Trk; High Hon Roll; Hon Roll; Jr NHS; PMEA Dst, Rgn Chorus 85-86; U PA; Phlsphy.

JOHNSON, CARLA; Ridgway Area HS; Ridgway, PA; (S); 14/131; Drama Clb; Letterman Clb; Ski Clb; Varsity Clb; Chorus; Church Choir; Variety Show; Yrbk Stf; Capt Vllybl; Hon Roll; Dist & Rgnl Chrs 85 & 86; PA Free Entrprs Wk 85; Accntng.

JOHNSON, CHERI; John Harris HS; Harrisburg, PA; (Y); Art Clb; Camera Clb; Ski Clb; Yrbk Stf; Hon Roll; Temple U; Phrmcst.

JOHNSON, CHERRY DENISE; Simon Gratz HS; Philadelphia, PA; (S); ROTC; Teachers Aide; Church Choir; Drill Tm; Orch; Nwsp Bus Mgr; Rep Frsh Cls; Rep Soph Cls; Swmmng; Hon Roll; Cert Of Achvt Fire Patrl 82; Awd Of Merit Blck Hstry 82; Cert Of Awd Hlth Clb 82; Acct Exec.

JOHNSON, CHRISTOPHER; Roman Catholic HS; Philadelphia, PA; (S); 1/155; Church Yth Grp; FBLA; Letterman Clb; Varsity Clb; Rep Soph Cls; Rep Jr Cls; Off Stu Cncl; Var L Ftbl; High Hon Roll; NHS; USAF Naval Acad.

JOHNSON, CHRISTY; Owen J Roberts HS; St Peters, PA; (S); 23/290; Pres Exploring; Service Clb; Teachers Aide; Hon Roll; NHS; Prfct Atten Awd; Arch.

JOHNSON, DARLENE ANDREA; Wallenpaupack Area HS; Hawley, PA; (Y); 4/150; Am Leg Aux Girls St; VP Chorus; Co-Capt Color Guard; School Musical; School Play; Rep Stu Cncl; High Hon Roll; Jr NHS; NHS; Voice Dem Awd; Early Childhood.

JOHNSON, DAVID; Moon Area HS; Coraopolis, PA; (Y); Church Yth Grp; German Clb; Mathletes; Band; Mrchg Band; Orch; Symp Band; High Hon Roll; Hon Roll; NHS; Crngie Mlln U Chem Olympcs 85; Pittsbrgh Yth Symphny 85-86; Ntl Music Cmp Intrlchn 85 & 86.

JOHNSON, DAWN; Tyrone Area HS; Warriors Mark, PA; (Y); Trs Church Yth Grp; Library Aide; Office Aide; Spanish Clb; Trs VICA; Nwsp Stf; Powder Puff Ftbl; Var Sftbl; High Hon Roll; Hon Roll.

JOHNSON, DEBBIE; North Star HS; Boswell, PA; (Y); 53/123; FCA; Pep Clb; Band; Chorus; Color Guard; Nwsp Rptr; Nwsp Stf; Mat Maids; Sec.

JOHNSON, DENISE; Philadelphia HS For Girls; Philadelphia, PA; (Y); 17/395; VP Church Yth Grp; Debate Tm; Spanish Clb; Lib Concert Band; Jazz Band; JV Badmtn; Capt Cheerleading; JV Fld Hcky; JV Trk; Hon Roll; Cert Chrldng & Trophy 85; Ellis Fndtn Girls/U Of Penn 84; Am Fndtn Of Negro Affairs 85; Engl.

JOHNSON, EDWARD; Cedar Cliff HS; New Cumberland, PA; (Y); 100/302; Church Yth Grp; Math Tm; Spanish Clb; Teachers Aide; Im Bowling; JV Trk; Hon Roll; Pres Schlr; Case Wstrn Rsrve U; Elec Engrng.

JOHNSON, EDWARD P; Cardinal Brennan HS; Ashland, PA; (Y); 1/48; Science Clb; Band; Chorus; Var Bowling; Bausch & Lomb Sci Awd; DAR Awd; Hon Roll; NHS; Val; Bucknell U; Elec Engrng.

JOHNSON, ERIC; Palmyra HS; Annville, PA; (Y); 60/200; Pres Church Yth Grp; French Clb; Band; Chorus; Jazz Band; Crs Cntry; Socr; Trk; Wrstlng; Hon Roll.

JOHNSON, ERIC; Penn Trafford HS; Irwin, PA; (Y); 62/362; Boy Scts; German Clb; Chorus; Socr; Hon Roll; MIP PA Trafford Sccr 85; Bio.

JOHNSON, ERICA; Berwick Area SR HS; Berwick, PA; (Y); 20/220; FBLA; Library Aide; Chorus; Color Guard; Flag Corp; Yrbk Stf; Sftbl; Hon Roll; Jr NHS; NHS; 2nd Pl Flg Drl 86; Cmmrcl Art.

JOHNSON, GREGG; Bishop Mc Cort HS; Johnstown, PA; (Y); 3/134; Math Tm; Ski Clb; Yrbk Stf; JV Bsktbl; Var L Crs Cntry; Var Golf; Var L Trk; High Hon Roll; Mu Alp Tht; NHS; Amer Lg Awd Outstndng Boy 84; PA ST U; Arch Engrng.

JOHNSON, JAMES P; Lincoln HS; New Castle, PA; (Y); 51/163; Church Yth Grp; Drama Clb; German Clb; School Musical; Stage Crew; Golf; Hon Roll; NEDT Awd; IN U PA; Chem.

JOHNSON, JANINE; Carmichaels Area HS; Carmichaels, PA; (Y); Art Clb; Library Aide; Office Aide; Ski Clb; Spanish Clb; Stu Cncl; Cheerleading; High Hon Roll; Hon Roll; NHS; Dntl Hygn.

JOHNSON, JANNEL; Center HS; Monaca, PA; (Y); 69/180; German Clb; Drill Tm; Nwsp Stf; Stu Cncl; Pom Pon; Hon Roll; Nursing.

JOHNSON, JEANNE; Meyersdale Area HS; Garrett, PA; (S); Trs Spanish Clb; Band; Mrchg Band; Rep Stu Cncl; Var Bsktbl; Hon Roll; Intl Frgn Lang Awd 85-86.

JOHNSON, JEFF; Bentworth HS; Bentleyville, PA; (Y); 26/141; Varsity Clb; Bsbl; Ftbl; Wrstlng; Hon Roll; West Point; Pre-Med.

JOHNSON, JEFF; Cumberland Valley HS; Mechanicsburg, PA; (Y); Church Yth Grp; Ski Clb; School Play; Im Badmtn; JV Var Ftbl; Im Vllybl; Im Wt Lftg; Bucknell U; Pre-Law.

JOHNSON, JENNIFER; Jamestown Area HS; Greenville, PA; (Y); 9/60; VP Spanish Clb; VP Varsity Clb; Band; School Musical; Rep Frsh Cls; Var Vllybl; Hon Roll; Pres Schlr; Concert Band; Mrchg Band; Spn Awd 86; Outstndng Academic Achvt Awd 86; PA ST U; Accntng.

JOHNSON, JENNIFER; Souderton HS; Telford, PA; (Y); Library Aide; Chorus; Var Fld Hcky; Var Lcrss; Var Tennis; Art.

JOHNSON, JENNIFER; William Tennent SR HS; Southampton, PA; (Y); 97/667; JA; Nwsp Sprt Ed; Rep Stu Cncl; Capt Var Cheerleading; Coach Actv; Powder Puff Ftbl; Vllybl; Hon Roll; Cls Rep-Athletic Council 85-86; U Of DE; Lawyer.

JOHNSON, JENNIFER A; Saegertown Area HS; Meadville, PA; (Y); Exploring; French Clb; Band; Mrchg Band; Pep Band; Nwsp Stf; Stu Cncl; Hon Roll; Edinboro U PA; Accntng.

JOHNSON, JODI; Harbor Creek HS; Erie, PA; (Y); 63/273; Off Stu Cncl; JV Var Vllybl; Hon Roll; U Of Pittsburgh; Sociolgy.

JOHNSON, JOYCE; Duquesne HS; Duquesne, PA; (Y); 5/81; Exploring; Office Aide; Band; Church Choir; Concert Band; Jazz Band; Mrchg Band; Trs Soph Cls; Sec Stu Cncl; Co-Capt Twrlr; U Of Pittsburgh; Acctg.

JOHNSON, KIM; Pennsbury HS; Yardley, PA; (Y); Church Yth Grp; Drama Clb; Capt Drill Tm; Mrchg Band; JV Var Trk; Hon Roll; NHS; French Clb; School Musical; School Play; Rider Coll Frgn Lang Forensic Tourn 86; Marchng Band In Rose Bowl Parade 86.

JOHNSON, KIMBERLY; Chartiers Valley HS; Carnegie, PA; (Y); Dance Clb; English Clb; PAVAS; School Musical; Yrbk Ed-Chief; Off Stu Cncl; Capt Twrlr; Gov Hon Prg Awd; Hon Roll; Church Yth Grp; Rep Chrtrs Vly Gftd & Tlntd Pgm; Rnnrup ; Jr Ms Dance PA 84; Rcrtnl Smmr Pgm 85-86.

JOHNSON, KIMBERLY; Ft Le Boeuf HS; Erie, PA; (Y); 24/184; Art Clb; Dance Clb; Ski Clb; Spanish Clb; School Play; Yrbk Stf; Bowling; High Hon Roll; Hon Roll; Clarion U; Mrktng.

JOHNSON, KRISTIN; Freedom HS; Bethlehem, PA; (Y); 81/402; Art Clb; Exploring; Crs Cntry; Var Capt Swmmng; Hon Roll; ST Grant Ed Assist 86-87; U CT; Sports Med.

JOHNSON, KRISTIN; Greater Latrobe HS; Latrobe, PA; (Y); 95/350; Church Yth Grp; Sec French Clb; Letterman Clb; Pep Clb; Ski Clb; Color Guard; Rep Stu Cncl; Var Crs Cntry; Var Trk; Hon Roll; U Pittsburgh Johnstown; Engrng.

JOHNSON, KRISTINA; Unionville HS; Chadds Ford, PA; (Y); 45/300; Art Clb; Church Yth Grp; Dance Clb; Acpl Chr; Band; Chorus; Church Choir; Concert Band; Orch; School Musical; ST Musc Tchrs Assoc 85-86; Dist Chrs 86; Dist And Regnl Band 86; Musc.

JOHNSON, LANCE; Moon SR HS; Coraopolis, PA; (Y); 60/320; VP Computer Clb; Key Clb; Science Clb; School Play; Nwsp Ed-Chief; Trk; St Champs Odessey Of Mind, 11th Intl 86; AZ ST U; Comp Engrng.

JOHNSON, LESLIE E; Jersey Shore Area SR HS; Jersey Shore, PA; (Y); 86/278; Church Choir; Concert Band; Mrchg Band; Prfct Atten Awd; SR Awd Pin Band 85-86; J Schl Ltr Band 83-84; Mansfield U.

JOHNSON, LISA; Chartiers Valley HS; Pittsburgh, PA; (Y); 18/303; Varsity Clb; Band; Mrchg Band; Rep Stu Cncl; Cheerleading; Powder Puff Ftbl; NHS; Rtry Ldrshp Cnfrnce 86; Bus Admn.

JOHNSON, LISA; Emmaus HS; Macungie, PA; (Y); 27/493; Girl Scts; Band; Concert Band; Mrchg Band; School Musical; High Hon Roll; Hon Roll; Jr NHS; NHS; Arch.

JOHNSON, LISA; West Catholic Girls HS; Philadelphia, PA; (Y); 43/240; Church Yth Grp; JA; Spanish Clb; Church Choir; Yrbk Stf; Hon Roll; Awd Excllnc 79; Sci Olympd Awd 86; Paralegal.

JOHNSON, LORI; Brookville Area HS; Reynoldsville, PA; (Y); Key Clb; Pep Clb; Varsity Clb; Orch; Swmmng; Trk; Jr NHS; Clarion Smmr Acad Sci 86; Nrsng.

JOHNSON, LORI; Villa Maria Acad; Waterford, PA; (Y); Ski Clb; Color Guard; Swmmng; Hon Roll; Prfct Atten Awd.

JOHNSON, LORI; York Catholic HS; York, PA; (Y); French Clb; Hosp Aide; JA; Band; Color Guard; Stage Crew; Sftbl; Ethel M Laws Career Awd 85; Delta Sigma Theata Peppermint Ball Bond 86; UAW Schlrshp Awd 86; Millersville U; Psych.

JOHNSON, MARGARET; Corry Area HS; Spartansburg, PA; (S); 20/215; Cmnty Wkr; Y-Teens; Band; Chorus; Concert Band; Mrchg Band; Stu Cncl; Cheerleading; Sftbl; Dist Choir 86; Fire Dept Teen Aux-VP 85-86; Socl Wrk.

JOHNSON, MARIANNE; New Hope Solebury HS; New Hope, PA; (Y); FBLA; Nwsp Rptr; Nwsp Stf; Yrbk Stf; Edinboro U; Bus Admin.

JOHNSON, MARK; Brownsville Area HS; Brownsville, PA; (Y); Bsbl; Bsktbl; Ftbl; Mgr(s); Score Keeper; Sftbl; Swmmng; Trk; Wt Lftg; Wrstlng.

JOHNSON, MARLENE; Harrisburg HS; Harrisburg, PA; (Y); FBLA; Hon Roll; Prfct Atten Awd; Dt Prcssr.

JOHNSON, MARY; Youngsville JR SR HS; Youngsville, PA; (Y); Trs French Clb; Co-Capt Ski Clb; Band; Chorus; Yrbk Ed-Chief; Yrbk Stf; Sec Jr Cls; Stat Wrstlng; High Hon Roll; NHS; Elem Ed.

JOHNSON, MELANIE F; Shenango HS; New Castle, PA; (Y); 28/117; Church Yth Grp; Pres French Clb; Hosp Aide; Office Aide; Sec VP Chorus; School Play; Im Capt Vllybl; Hon Roll; NHS; Prfct Atten Awd; Westminster Coll Wilminton PA.

JOHNSON, MICHAEL; Hampton HS; Allison Park, PA; (Y); Spanish Clb; Ftbl; Trk; Wrstlng; Hon Roll; U Pittsburgh; Dentl.

JOHNSON, MICHAEL; North Pocono HS; Moscow, PA; (S); 12/245; Church Yth Grp; Ski Clb; Lib Band; Mrchg Band; Orch; High Hon Roll; NHS.

JOHNSON, MICHELE A; Tamaqua Area SR HS; Tamaqua, PA; (Y); 30/160; Am Leg Aux Girls St; VP German Clb; Girl Scts; Pep Clb; Q&S; Ski Clb; Nwsp Ed-Chief; Yrbk Ed-Chief; Isabella M Fisher Essy Awd 86; J H Zerbe Nwspr Awd 86; Juniata Coll; Bus.

JOHNSON, MICHELLE; Corry Area HS; Corry, PA; (Y); Color Guard; Erie Bus Ctr; Bus.

JOHNSON, MOLLY T; Greensburg Central Catholic HS; N Huntington, PA; (Y); 50/250; AFS; German Clb; GAA; Letterman Clb; Office Aide; Pep Clb; Ski Clb; Varsity Clb; Var L Bsktbl; Coach Actv; 2nd Pl Wrtng German Prose 86; Seton Hill Coll; Intrntl Bus.

JOHNSON, PAMELA; W Phila Catholic HS For Girls; Philadelphia, PA; (Y); Church Yth Grp; Dance Clb; French Clb; GAA; Girl Scts; Church Choir; Orch; Cheerleading; Hon Roll; Howard U; Pre Law.

JOHNSON, PAULA; Mastbaum Aut HS; Philadelphia, PA; (Y); Church Yth Grp; Cmnty Wkr; DECA; Band; NHS; Temple U; Law.

JOHNSON, REGINA; Jefferson-Morgan HS; Jefferson, PA; (S); 2/98; French Clb; School Play; Yrbk Stf; High Hon Roll; Pres NHS; NEDT Awd; Acad All Amer 84-86.

JOHNSON, SANDI; Conneaut Lake HS; Conneaut Lake, PA; (Y); Drama Clb; GAA; Hosp Aide; Spanish Clb; VP Stu Cncl; Var L Bsktbl; JV Gym; Var Sftbl; Var L Vllybl; High Hon Roll; Ptsbrgh U; Ocptnl Thrpy.

JOHNSON, SANDY; Mahanoy Area HS; Shenandoah, PA; (Y); GAA; Spanish Clb; Nwsp Stf; Yrbk Stf; L Trk; NHS; Shippensburg U; Med Tech.

JOHNSON, SCOTT; Monessen HS; Monessen, PA; (Y); 2/93; French Clb; Stage Crew; Nwsp Rptr; Var Stat Bsktbl; Var L Golf; Var L Tennis; High Hon Roll; NHS; Amer Legn Rnnr Up 83-84; Gftd Prog; Renselaer Polytech Inst Math & Sci Awd 85-86; Pre Med.

JOHNSON, SELINA; Harry S Truman HS; Levittown, PA; (Y); Church Yth Grp; Latin Clb; Spanish Clb; Y-Teens; Yrbk Rptr; Yrbk Stf; VP Jr Cls; X-Ray Tech.

JOHNSON, SIDNEY; Neshaminy HS; Langhorne, PA; (Y); 121/730; Pres Chorus; School Musical; Pres Frsh Cls; VP Soph Cls; Pres Jr Cls; JV Socr; Var Trk; Concert Band; Jazz Band; Yrbk Stf; Ldrshp Awd; Arch.

JOHNSON, SUSAN; Western Wayne HS; Waymart, PA; (Y); 4-H; Trk; PA ST Coll; Cmptr Sci.

JOHNSON, TINNA; Towanda Area HS; Towanda, PA; (Y); 41/140; Cheerleading; Sftbl; Hon Roll; Typg Awd Outstndng Schltc Achvt 86; Bus.

JOHNSON, WENDY; Scranton Central HS; Scranton, PA; (Y); French Clb; Hosp Aide; Spanish Clb; Chorus; Child Psych.

JOHNSTON, ALYCE C; Central Dauphin East HS; Harrisburg, PA; (Y); 25/287; Am Leg Aux Girls St; Varsity Clb; Band; Chorus; Drm Mjr(t); School Musical; Hst Stu Cncl; JV Capt Fld Hcky; Twrlr; NHS; Latin Awd.

JOHNSTON, BARBARA; Washington HS; Washington, PA; (S); 8/200; Pres French Clb; Hosp Aide; Math Tm; Ski Clb; Band; Chorus; Concert Band; Jazz Band; Mrchg Band; Var Cheerleading.

JOHNSTON, CATHY; Central Daduphin East HS; Dauphin, PA; (Y); Spanish Clb; Chorus; School Musical; School Play; Yrbk Ed-Chief; Yrbk Stf; Rep Jr Cls; Rep Sr Cls; Crs Cntry; Trk; Law.

JOHNSTON, CLARK; Penn Trafford HS; Irwin, PA; (Y); Im Bsbl; Im Bsktbl; Im Ftbl; Im Sftbl; Im Vllybl; Hon Roll; Prfct Atten Awd; Westmoreland County CC; Comp.

JOHNSTON, DAREN; Marion Center HS; Creekside, PA; (Y); 27/170; VP FFA; Chorus; Church Choir; School Play; Stage Crew; Swing Chorus; Hon Roll; FFA Champ Swine Shwmn, Chptr Farmr Awd 85; Star-Green Hnd Awd FFA 84; Penn ST; Ag.

JOHNSTON, DAWN; Yough SR HS; Irwin, PA; (Y); 35/226; Trs Church Yth Grp; Ski Clb; Chorus; School Play; Nwsp Phtg; Nwsp Rptr; Yrbk Ed-Chief; Rep Frsh Cls; Powder Puff Ftbl; NHS; PA ST; Ed.

JOHNSTON, DIANE; Saegertown HS; Saegertown, PA; (Y); 10/127; Varsity Clb; Band; Concert Band; Mrchg Band; Pep Band; Trs Jr Cls; Var JV Sftbl; Var JV Vllybl; Jr NHS; NHS; County Band 83-84 & 84-85; Travel Field.

JOHNSTON, G DANE; Oswayo Valley JR SR HS; Shinglehouse, PA; (Y); 2/51; Ski Clb; Rep Stu Cncl; Var L Bsbl; Var L Bsktbl; Var L Crs Cntry; Im Capt Vllybl; NHS; Prfct Atten Awd; Sal; Amer Legn Aux Schlrshp 86; Gannon U; Elctrcl Engrng.

JOHNSTON, JAMES; Shaler Area HS; Glenshaw, PA; (Y); 8/533; High Hon Roll; NHS; Pres Acdmc Fit Awd 86; Carnegie-Mellon U; Archtctr.

JOHNSTON, JASON E; Kiski Area HS; Avonmore, PA; (Y); Computer Clb; Pep Clb; Science Clb; Band; Concert Band; Jazz Band; Mrchg Band; Pep Band; Crs Cntry; Trk; Penn ST.

JOHNSTON, JENNIFER; Belle Vernon Area HS; Belle Vernon, PA; (Y); Concert Band; Mrchg Band; High Hon Roll; Hon Roll; NHS.

JOHNSTON, JENNIFER; East Pennsboro HS; Enola, PA; (Y); French Clb; Sec Latin Clb; Model UN; Concert Band; Mrchg Band; Trs Stu Cncl; High Hon Roll; NHS; Harrisburg Alumnae Panhllnc Awd 86; PA ST U; Pre-Law.

JOHNSTON, KATRINA; General Mc Lane HS; Edinboro, PA; (Y); 3/220; Church Yth Grp; German Clb; Concert Band; Mrchg Band; JV Bsktbl; JV Var Vllybl; High Hon Roll; NHS; 1st Plc Awd Natl Hstry Day Rgnl Div 86; Med.

JOHNSTON, KIM; Mc Keesport Area HS; Mckeesport, PA; (Y); 25/350; Office Aide; Band; Rep Soph Cls; Stu Cncl; Powder Puff Ftbl; High Hon Roll; Hon Roll; Pres Schlr; Rotary Awd; World Affairs Cncl Rep 86; U Pittsburgh; Bus.

JOHNSTON, MARK R; Belle Vernon Area HS; Belle Vernon, PA; (Y); 88/280; Ski Clb; Var Vllybl; Hon Roll; CA U Of PA; Rbtcs.

JOHNSTON, MATTHEW; North Catholic HS; Pittsburgh, PA; (Y); 16/301; Math Clb; Ski Clb; School Musical; Rep Jr Cls; Stu Cncl; Bsbl; Ftbl; Wt Lftg; High Hon Roll; NHS; Purdue U; Mech Engr.

JOHNSTON, TRACY; Canon Mc Millan HS; Canonsburg, PA; (Y); Church Yth Grp; Drama Clb; FBLA; Ski Clb; Chorus; Church Choir; School Musical; Variety Show; High Hon Roll; Hon Roll; Regnl Sec FBLA 87; Sec FBLA 87; Sec Chorus 86; Robert Morris; Acctng.

JOHNSTON, VICKI; Harmony Area HS; Westover, PA; (Y); 1/44; Trs Church Yth Grp; Library Aide; Band; Chorus; Concert Band; VP Jr Cls; Stat Bsktbl; Score Keeper; DAR Awd; High Hon Roll; Amer Legn Auxlry Cert Of Schl Awd 83; Amer Musical Fndtn Band Hnrs 85.

JOHNSTON, WALTER L; Franklin JR SR HS; Franklin, PA; (Y); Band; Concert Band; Jazz Band; Mrchg Band; Pep Band; School Musical; Stage Crew; Gov Hon Prg Awd; Hon Roll; Ed Wattsjer Music Schlrshp, Margaret Rusk Griffiths Schlrshp 86; PA Governors Arts Schl 84; Baldwin-Wallace Coll; Music Ed.

JOINES, ANGELA; Blue Ridge HS; Susquehanna, PA; (Y); Sec SADD; Band; Trs Jr Cls; JV Var Bsktbl; Stat Score Keeper; JV Var Vllybl; High Hon Roll; Hon Roll; Prfct Atten Awd; Bus Admn.

JOKUBETZ, JO ANNE; Canon Mc Millan SR HS; Canonsburg, PA; (Y); 76/360; French Clb; Capt Drill Tm; Nwsp Stf; High Hon Roll; Hon Roll; U Of Pittsburgh; Phrmcy.

JOLLEY, KENNETH M; East Juniata HS; Thompsontown, PA; (Y); 33/86; Boy Scts; Church Yth Grp; Spanish Clb; JV Bsbl; Stat Socr; Var Trk; High Hon Roll; Hon Roll; Boy Scts Hnr Soc 83; Air Force; Govt Secrty.

JONES, AARON; Cathedral Prep; Erie, PA; (Y); 8/236; Church Yth Grp; French Clb; Im Bsktbl; Var Crs Cntry; Im Socr; Behrend Coll.

JONES, ALBERT; Carlisle SR HS; Carlisle, PA; (Y); Boy Scts; Church Yth Grp; Bsbl; God Cntry Awd; Hon Roll; Eagle Scout 85; Bus Mgmt.

JONES JR, ALLAN; Seneca Valley HS; Zelienople, PA; (Y); 90/378; Am Leg Boys St; Boy Scts; Church Yth Grp; JA; Capt ROTC; Hon Roll; JV Wrstlng; Geneva Schlr Awd 86; Geneva Coll; Engrng.

JONES, ANTOINETTE; Montour HS; Montoursville, PA; (Y); Art Clb; German Clb; Nwsp Stf; Intr Dsgn.

JONES, BILL C; Freeport SR HS; Freeport, PA; (Y); 52/172; Band; Concert Band; Im Stat Ftbl; Var L Mgr(s); High Hon Roll; Hon Roll; Kent ST U; Bio.

JONES, BRENDA; Saegertown HS; Saegertown, PA; (Y); 5/128; 4-H; Letterman Clb; SADD; Varsity Clb; Band; Concert Band; Mrchg Band; Pep Band; JV Var Bsktbl; JV Var Sftbl.

JONES, BRIAN; New Hope Solebury HS; New Hope, PA; (Y); 32/78; Computer Clb; FBLA; Mathletes; Varsity Clb; Band; Var Bsbl; Im Mgr Bsktbl; JV Socr; Im Mgr Sftbl; Im Mgr Vllybl; Elizabethtown Clg; Engrg.

JONES, BRIAN; Newport HS; Newport, PA; (Y); Varsity Clb; Ftbl; Im Wt Lftg; Var Wrstlng; FFA; Bsbl; Im Vllybl; Hon Roll.

JONES, BRIAN; St John Nuemann HS; Philadelphia, PA; (Y); 103/338; Am Leg Boys St; Boy Scts; Church Yth Grp; Spanish Clb; JV Capt Bsktbl; Score Keeper; Trk; Prfct Atten Awd.

JONES, BRIEN; North East HS; North East, PA; (Y); 20/149; AFS; Boy Scts; Camera Clb; Church Yth Grp; Civic Clb; Cmnty Wkr; Debate Tm; German Clb; Latin Clb; Letterman Clb; St Francis Coll; Jrnlsm.

JONES, CARLA; Fairchance-Georges HS; Smithfield, PA; (Y); Drama Clb; French Clb; VP JA; School Play; Stage Crew; High Hon Roll; Hon Roll; Prfct Atten Awd; Natl JA Conf 86; Allegany Dist JA Conf 86; Psych.

JONES, CHRISTINA; Cardinal Brennan HS; Girardville, PA; (Y); 15/65; School Play; Capt Cheerleading; Hon Roll; Spanish NHS; Cardinal Brennan.

JONES, CONNIE; Middletown HS; Middletown, PA; (Y); Nwsp Stf; Yrbk Stf; Im Vllybl; Mt St Marys MD; Bus Admin.

JONES, CRISTY; Oil City SR HS; Cooperstown, PA; (Y); Church Yth Grp; Computer Clb; Band; Mrchg Band; Swmmng; Trk; Hon Roll.

JONES, CRYSTAL; Hollidaysburg Area SR HS; Hollidaysburg, PA; (Y); Church Yth Grp; French Clb; FNA; Science Clb; SADD; Chorus; Church Choir; Nrs.

JONES, DARRIN L; Hopewell SR HS; Aliquippa, PA; (Y); 80/280; Church Yth Grp; Pres 4-H; Band; Wrstlng; Hon Roll; Chrmn-Ntl Rifle Assn 85-86; Army Ntl Guard 86-92; Penn ST U; Elec Engrng.

JONES, DAVE; Elmer L Meyers HS; Wilkes Barre, PA; (Y); Var Bsktbl; Var Capt Ftbl; Hon Roll; NHS; Spanish NHS.

JONES, DAVID; Portage Area HS; Portage, PA; (S); 20/118; Church Yth Grp; Cmnty Wkr; Computer Clb; 4-H; French Clb; Ftbl; Hon Roll; NHS; Engrng.

JONES, DENISE; West Green JR-SR HS; Brave, PA; (S); 8/70; French Clb; VICA; Hon Roll.

JONES, EDWARD; Old Forge HS; Old Forge, PA; (S); Golf; Hon Roll; NHS; PA ST.

JONES, ELAYNE; Philipsburg-Osceola HS; Philipsburg, PA; (Y); 54/240; Drama Clb; School Musical; School Play; Stage Crew; Nwsp Rptr; Nwsp Stf; Comm.

JONES, ERIC; North Catholic HS; Pittsburgh, PA; (Y); 54/260; Church Yth Grp; German Clb; Math Clb; Model UN; Ski Clb; Spanish Clb; Capt Bowling; Hon Roll; Hist Clb Vice Pres; PA ST; Metrlgy.

JONES, GEORGE; Carver HS Of Engineering & Science; Philadelphia, PA; (Y); 81/184; Church Yth Grp; JA; Letterman Clb; Varsity Clb; Rep Frsh Cls; Rep Soph Cls; Rep Jr Cls; Rep Sr Cls; Rep Stu Cncl; Var L Bsktbl; Drexel U; Comp Systms Anlyst.

JONES, GWEN; Cambridge Springs HS; Cambridge Springs, PA; (Y); 9/112; Variety Show; JV VP Bsktbl; Cheerleading; Var L Sftbl; JV L Vllybl; NHS; Church Yth Grp; Sec French Clb; Trs Model UN; Pep Clb; 2nd Tm All Cnty Sftbl, 1st Tm 86; JETS 86; Penn ST; Jrnlsm.

JONES, HAZEL LYNNETTE; Villa Maria HS; Wheatland, PA; (Y); Church Yth Grp; Cmnty Wkr; French Clb; Girl Scts; Hosp Aide; Yrbk Stf; Lit Mag; French Hon Soc; Hon Roll; NHS; RN.

JONES, HEATHER; Blue Mountain HS; New Ringgold, PA; (Y); SADD; Chorus; Church Choir; Rep Stu Cncl; JV Bsktbl; Var Capt Cheerleading; Trk; Hon Roll; Ltn Hnr Soc; Pre-Med.

JONES, HEATHER; Mahanoy Area HS; Mahanoy City, PA; (Y); Sec French Clb; Band; Chorus; Concert Band; Variety Show; High Hon Roll; NHS; FHA; Mrchg Band; Stage Crew; Chem.

JONES, HEATHER; Spring-Ford SR HS; Spring City, PA; (S); #3 In Class; French Clb; Girl Scts; VP Thesps; Sec Chorus; School Musical; School Play; Trk; NHS; Ntl Merit SF; Opt Clb Awd; Allentwn Coll ST Francis; Thtr.

JONES, HERBERT; Ferndale Area HS; Johnstown, PA; (Y); Am Leg Boys St; Church Yth Grp; Computer Clb; Pres Varsity Clb; VP Jr Cls; Pres Sr Cls; Pres Stu Cncl; Bsbl; Ftbl; High Hon Roll; Math.

JONES, JENNIFER; Du Bois Area SR HS; Dubois, PA; (Y); Band; Concert Band; Drm Mjr(t); Jazz Band; Mrchg Band; Pep Band; Yrbk Stf; Hon Roll; Hnred Dist III Bnd 86; Intrior Dcrtng.

JONES, JENNIFER; New Hope Solebury HS; New Hope, PA; (Y); FBLA; Ski Clb; Co-Capt Flag Corp; Rep Stu Cncl; Var Capt Cheerleading; Mst Vlbl Chrldng 85; Mst Dedctd Chrldng 84; Bus.

JONES, JENNIFER; Susquehanna Community HS; Susquehanna, PA; (S); Art Clb; Bowling; Swmmng; Hon Roll; Sec.

JONES, JENNIFER AMI; Schuylkill Valley HS; Leesport, PA; (Y); Am Leg Aux Girls St; Pres FTA; Chorus; Flag Corp; School Musical; Capt Var Cheerleading; Cit Awd; Dnfth Awd; JC Awd; Band; Co, Dist & Rgnl Chorus 85-86; PA ST U; Athltc Trng.

JONES, JILL; Tussey Mountain HS; Robertsdale, PA; (Y); AFS; Church Yth Grp; Band; Concert Band; Mrchg Band; Yrbk Stf; High Hon Roll; NHS; Math.

JONES, JODI; Trinity HS; Mechanicsburg, PA; (Y); Pep Clb; Spanish Clb; Nwsp Stf; Yrbk Stf; Spanish NHS; Johnson & Wales; Foods.

JONES, JOE; Philipsburg HS; Philipsburg, PA; (Y); Church Yth Grp; Im Mgr Badmtn; Var Bsbl; Im Mgr Gym; Im Mgr Tennis; Im Mgr Wt Lftg; JV Var Wrstlng; Hon Roll; PA ST U; Phy Ed.

JONES, JOHN; Hempfield Area SR HS; Adamsburg, PA; (Y); Ski Clb; VICA; Nwsp Rptr; JV Bsktbl; JV Socr; Wstmrlnd Cnty Comm; Elec Engr.

JONES, JOHN C; Portage HS; Portage, PA; (S); 7/120; Aud/Vis; Church Yth Grp; Drama Clb; Ski Clb; School Play; Variety Show; Ftbl; High Hon Roll; Hon Roll; NHS; PA ST U; Orthpdc Srgn.

JONES, JONATHAN; Father Judge HS; Philadelphia, PA; (Y); 34/371; Hosp Aide; JV Trk; Hon Roll; Bus.

JONES, KAREN; Council Rock HS; Richboro, PA; (Y); Var Cheerleading; Hon Roll; Mst Imprvd Chrldr 84; Fash Merch.

JONES, KAREN; Downingtown SR HS; Downingtown, PA; (Y); 68/575; Church Yth Grp; GAA; Teachers Aide; Church Choir; Mrchg Band; Var Capt Bsktbl; High Hon Roll; Hon Roll; NHS; Band; Pres Phy Fit Awd 84; Gregg Typng Awd 85; Spnsh Diplma Of Merit 84; U Of VA; Pre Med.

JONES, KAREN; West Allegheny HS; Oakdale, PA; (Y); Spanish Clb; Varsity Clb; Color Guard; Drill Tm; Nwsp Stf; Yrbk Stf; Pom Pon; Var L Swmmng; High Hon Roll; Flag Corp.

JONES, KARRIE; Washington HS; Washington, PA; (S); 51/159; Debate Tm; VP French Clb; Key Clb; Ski Clb; School Play; Symp Band; Rep Frsh Cls; Twrlr; High Hon Roll; Hon Roll; Pltcl Sci.

JONES, KATHLEEN; Villa Joseph Marie HS; Huntingdon Valley, PA; (S); 3/52; Hosp Aide; Science Clb; Service Clb; Spanish Clb; Trs Chorus; School Musical; Lit Mag; High Hon Roll; Hon Roll; NHS; Nrsg.

JONES, KEVIN; Lincoln HS; Ellwood City, PA; (Y); 23/170; Latin Clb; Spanish Clb; Var Ftbl; Var Trk; Im Wrstlng; High Hon Roll; Hon Roll; 2nd Hgh Pnt Awd Trck 86; Poltcl Sci.

JONES, KIMBERLY; Hempfield SR HS; Greensburg, PA; (Y); 38/657; German Clb; Letterman Clb; Pep Clb; Varsity Clb; Capt Bsktbl; Vllybl; High Hon Roll; Jr NHS; NHS; Sftbl Wrld Series 83; Fem Schlr Athltc 83 & 86; All Star Hon Mntn 86; Marietta; Psych.

JONES, KIMBERLY; West Allegheny HS; Coraopolis, PA; (Y); Church Yth Grp; Concert Band; Mrchg Band; Nwsp Rptr; Nwsp Stf; Yrbk Stf; VP Trs Stu Cncl; Cheerleading; Hon Roll; IN U Of PA; Elem Ed.

JONES, KIMBERLY K; Chartiers-Houston HS; Houston, PA; (Y); #36 In Class; FBLA; Girl Scts; JA; Library Aide; Red Cross Aide; Nwsp Bus Mgr; Nwsp Rptr; Nwsp Stf; Yrbk Stf; Sftbl; 3rd Pl FBLA Typng Cntst 84-85; Bus Clb Awd 85-86.

JONES, KIP; Johnsonburg Area HS; Johnsonburg, PA; (S); Trs Frsh Cls; JV Wrstlng; Hon Roll; NHS; Penn ST; Engrng.

JONES, LARA; Pittston Area SR HS; Pittston, PA; (Y); 121/365; Computer Clb; Drama Clb; Key Clb; Math Clb; Ski Clb; Chorus; Swmmng; Prtcptd PA Keystone STG Games 2 Mdls Brnz Swmmng 85; Pre Law.

JONES, LAURA; Kutztown Area HS; Kutztown, PA; (Y); 5/149; Band; Chorus; Mrchg Band; Pep Band; School Play; Yrbk Stf; Stat Bsktbl; High Hon Roll; NHS; Ntl Merit Ltr.

JONES, LAUREN; Strath Haven HS; Swarthmore, PA; (Y); Church Yth Grp; Cmnty Wkr; French Clb; Teachers Aide; Chorus; L Bsktbl; L Hon Roll; Astrnmy Clb 86; Exchng Stu-France 86; Chrch Bell Chr 85; Physcs.

JONES, LEAH; Central Bucks East HS; Gardenville, PA; (Y); FBLA; Color Guard; Hon Roll; Biol.

JONES, LEONARD; Chichester HS; Twin Oaks Farms, PA; (Y); Cmnty Wkr; Model UN; SADD; School Musical; School Play; Nwsp Ed-Chief; Prfct Atten Awd; Church Yth Grp; Computer Clb; Debate Tm; Temple U Grant 86; Mt Pleasent Schrlshp 86; Stu Cncl 86; Temple U; Intl Bus.

JONES, LISA; Brownsville Area HS; Brownsville, PA; (Y); 31/221; Drama Clb; Library Aide; Ski Clb; Rep Stu Cncl; JV Bsktbl; JV Cheerleading; Hon Roll.

JONES, LISA; Highlands HS; Tarentum, PA; (Y); Exploring; Teachers Aide; Band; Concert Band; Stage Crew; Gym; Mgr(s); VP Swmmng; Hon Roll; NHS; Gold Awds 82-86; IN U PA; Diet.

JONES, LISA; Mid Valley HS; Dicksoncity, PA; (Y); 11/135; Art Clb; Computer Clb; Varsity Clb; Pres Stu Cncl; Bsktbl; Bowling; Score Keeper; Sftbl; High Hon Roll; Hon Roll; PA ST U; Humn Devl.

JONES, MARK; South Williamsport Area HS; S Williamsport, PA; (Y); 5/140; Bsktbl; Vllybl; High Hon Roll; Hon Roll; Wrtng Cntsts 86.

JONES, MAUREEN; Lakeland HS; Jermyn, PA; (S); 10/100; Church Yth Grp; Spanish Clb; Chorus; Var Crs Cntry; JV Sftbl; Var Trk; Hon Roll; Phrmcy.

JONES, MEAGAN; Kiski Area HS; Vanegrift, PA; (Y); French Clb; Office Aide; Drm & Bgl; High Hon Roll; Hon Roll; Top 10 84; Fshn Merch.

JONES, MELISSA S; Northampton Area SR HS; Danielsville, PA; (S); 8/475; AFS; Nwsp Rptr; Nwsp Stf; Var Fld Hcky; Var Sftbl; High Hon Roll; Hon Roll; VP NHS; Mack Trcks Inc Schlrshp Rcpnt 86; Boston U; Biomed Engnr.

JONES, MICHAEL; South Allegheny JR SR HS; Port Vue, PA; (Y); 16/164; Spanish Clb; SADD; Var L Ftbl; Var L Trk; Hon Roll; NHS; CA U Of PA; Bio.

JONES, MICHAEL; West Allegheny SR HS; Oakdale, PA; (Y); Spanish Clb; Chorus; Ed Nwsp Stf; Yrbk Stf; Rep Stu Cncl; JV Bsbl; Var Golf; High Hon Roll; Hon Roll; IN U Of PA; Criminolgy.

JONES, MICHAEL J; Monsignor Bonner HS; Clifton Heights, PA; (Y); 11/310; Church Yth Grp; VP Sr Cls; Var Capt Bsbl; Im Capt Bsktbl; Var L Ftbl; High Hon Roll; NHS; Rotary Awd; James R Hopely Awd 85; Vincent E Trainer Sprtsmnshp Awd Otstndng Sr 86; John R Cappeletti Awd 86; St Joseph U; Accntng.

JONES, MICHELE; Aliquippa HS; Aliquippa, PA; (Y); Cmnty Wkr; Drama Clb; French Clb; Hosp Aide; Office Aide; Spanish Clb; Band; Concert Band; Mrchg Band; Pep Band; John Casablanca; Trvlng.

JONES, MICHELE; Scranton Prep; Scranton, PA; (Y); Cmnty Wkr; Letterman Clb; Pep Clb; Church Choir; Nwsp Rptr; Ed Lit Mag; Capt Cheerleading; Hon Roll; Brnz Mdlst Engl; Cavalier Awd; Excllncy Awd Lit; Marywood Coll; Cmnctns.

JONES, MICHELLE; Norristown Area HS; Norristown, PA; (Y); Dance Clb; Church Choir; Concert Band; Jazz Band; Orch; School Musical; Variety Show; NHS; Girl Scts; Band; Ntl Orchstr Awd 86; Prnts Clb Instrmntl Awd 86; Phildlphia Coll Of Arts; Dnc.

JONES, MICHELLE; Our Lady Or Lourdes Regional HS; Shamokin, PA; (Y); 56/95; VP Art Clb; Sec Library Aide; Mgr Stage Crew; Nwsp Bus Mgr; Ed Yrbk Stf; JV Bsktbl; Penn Svngs Bnk Art Cntst 84-86; Wmns Clb Art Cntst 86; Art Thrpy.

JONES, MORRYA; Purchase Line HS; Commodore, PA; (Y); 25/112; Sec French Clb; Band; Chorus; Concert Band; Drill Tm; Mrchg Band; Twrlr; Hon Roll; US Achvt Acad 84; Acad All-Amer 84; Cosmtlgst.

JONES, PATRICIA; Northeast Bradford HS; Rome, PA; (Y); Church Yth Grp; Pres Sec 4-H; Varsity Clb; Band; Chorus; Var JV Cheerleading; Im Gym; High Hon Roll; NHS; Trk; Stu Of The Month 85; Cnty Chorus 84; Pediatric Nrsng.

JONES, PETE; Liberty HS; Bethlehem, PA; (Y); 37/407; Church Yth Grp; Ski Clb; Church Choir; Var L Crs Cntry; JV Socr; Var Trk; Hon Roll; NHS; Wake Forest; Bus.

JONES, QUENTIN A; Northern Lebanon HS; Jonestown, PA; (Y); 47/177; Church Yth Grp; FCA; Math Clb; Chorus; School Play; Pres Soph Cls; Pres Jr Cls; Pres Sr Cls; Rep Stu Cncl; Var L Ftbl; Amer Legion Essay Cntst 86.

JONES, RACHEL; Harrisburg HS; Harrisburg, PA; (Y); Sec Church Yth Grp; Drama Clb; Library Aide; Office Aide; Pep Clb; SADD; Teachers Aide; Church Choir; School Musical; Nwsp Rptr; Outstndng Ldr Rtry Int 86; Kutztown U; Ed.

JONES, RANDY; Waynesburg Central HS; Spraggs, PA; (Y); Boy Scts; Computer Clb; Teachers Aide; Band; Chorus; Concert Band; Mrchg Band; Mgr(s); Trk; Hon Roll; Comp.

JONES, REBECCA; Pocono Mountain HS; Mt Pocono, PA; (Y); 51/318; 4-H; Pres JA; SADD; Sec Stu Cncl; JR Achvt Dale Crng Crs 85-86; Wlks Coll; Nrsng.

JONES, RICH; Penn Hills HS; Pittsburgh, PA; (Y); Computer Clb; French Clb; Ski Clb; Rep Soph Cls; Rep Jr Cls; JV Bsbl; JV Ftbl; JV Golf; Im Wt Lftg; Hon Roll.

JONES, RICHARD; Manhiem Township HS; Lancaster, PA; (Y); Math Clb; Concert Band; Drm Mjr(t); Mrchg Band; Nwsp Rptr; Rep Jr Cls; CC Awd; Hon Roll; Prfct Atten Awd; Sprtsmnshp Awd 85; Outstndg Bandsmn 84; U Of NC; Mrn Bio.

JONES, RICHARD; Strath Haven HS; Swarthmore, PA; (Y); Church Yth Grp; Cmnty Wkr; Office Aide; Ski Clb; Stu Cncl; JV Bsktbl; Var Ice Hcky; JV Mgr(s); Wt Lftg; Hon Roll; Deans Cncl; Engrng.

JONES, ROBERT; E L Meyers HS; Wilkes Barre, PA; (Y); Ski Clb; Band; Chorus; Concert Band; Jazz Band; Mrchg Band; Orch; Bsktbl; Golf; Tennis; Nrsng.

JONES, ROBERT; Quigley HS; Aliquippa, PA; (Y); 46/110; Exploring; Band; Mrchg Band; Stage Crew; JV Capt Bsktbl; Phys Therapist.

JONES, ROBYN; Unionville HS; Chadds Ford, PA; (Y); Pres 4-H; Girl Scts; Chorus; School Musical; Variety Show; JV Crs Cntry; Var Trk; Im Wt Lftg; 4-H Awd; Hon Roll; Acad Excllnce Engl 86; W Civilzatn Cmmdntn 84; Schl Discus Recd 86; Jrnlsm.

JONES, SANDRA M; St Clair Area HS; St Clair, PA; (Y); 1/83; Yrbk Stf; Var L Cheerleading; High Hon Roll; Kiwanis Awd; Lion Awd; Mu Alp Tht; NHS; NEDT Awd; Pres Schlr; Val; PA ST U; Elem Ed.

JONES, SCOTT; Altoona Area HS; Altoona, PA; (Y); Boy Scts; Church Yth Grp; Var Socr; Var Swmmng; Vet Med.

JONES, STACEY; North Hills SR HS; Pittsburgh, PA; (Y); AFS; Sec Band; Mrchg Band; Symp Band; Rep Frsh Cls; Rep Soph Cls; Rep Jr Cls; Rep Stu Cncl; Hon Roll; Perf Attndnc 81; Ctznshp Awd 81; Thiel Coll; Ed.

JONES, STEPHEN; Cumberland Valley HS; Camp Hill, PA; (Y); 55/560; Church Yth Grp; Cmnty Wkr; Key Clb; SADD; French Hon Soc; High Hon Roll; Hon Roll; Drexel U; Comp Engr.

JONES, SUE; Solanco HS; Nottingham, PA; (Y); Church Yth Grp; Hosp Aide; Office Aide; Band; Concert Band; Mrchg Band; Pep Band; Yrbk Stf; Hon Roll; Prfct Atten Awd; Volunteer Serv Awd 82-84; Goldie Beacon; Accntng.

JONES, SUZANNE; Cumberland Valley HS; Mechanicsburg, PA; (Y); Concert Band; Jazz Band; Mrchg Band; Orch; School Musical; Symp Band; French Hon Soc; Hon Roll; Lion Awd; Music.

JONES, TAMARA; Burgettstown JR SR HS; Burgettstown, PA; (Y); 24/172; Church Yth Grp; Drama Clb; Spanish Clb; Band; Chorus; Church Choir; Concert Band; Co-Capt Drill Tm; Off Mrchg Band; Pep Band; Natl Arion Choral Awd 86; All Star Prfrmr 85-86; IN U; Music.

JONES, TANYA DENISE; Liberty HS; Bethlehem, PA; (Y); Church Yth Grp; Chorus; Journlsm.

JONES, TERI; William HS; Philadelphia, PA; (Y); Aud/Vis; Church Yth Grp; Cmnty Wkr; Nwsp Rptr; Stu Cncl; Var L Badmtn; Var L Cheerleading; Var L Vllybl; DAR Awd; VA Union U; Cmmnctns.

JONES, TODD; West Allegheny HS; Imperial, PA; (Y); 32/201; Scholastic Bowl; Science Clb; Chorus; Lit Mag; Capt Swmmng; Hon Roll; Germn Frgn Lang Essay Comptn 2nd Pl 84-85; Male Quartet Chorus 85-86; Radio Brdcstng.

JONES, TRACEY; Mashannon Valley HS; Ramey, PA; (Y); 2/122; Spanish Clb; Varsity Clb; Bsktbl; DAR Awd; High Hon Roll; NHS; Sal; PA ST U; Bus Adm.

JONES, TRACY; Germantown HS; Philadelphia, PA; (Y); Church Yth Grp; Library Aide; Math Tm; Office Aide; Yrbk Stf; Jr NHS; Hohnemann U; Med Radiolgcl Tech.

JONES, VALERIE; Greater Johnstown HS; Johnstown, PA; (Y); JA; Library Aide; SADD; Hon Roll; NHS; Bus.

JORDAN, ANDREW; Bensalem SR HS; Bensalem, PA; (Y); Debate Tm; Varsity Clb; Var Bsbl; Var Golf; Var Socr; High Hon Roll; Hon Roll; NHS; Bus.

JORDAN, ANNE MARIE; North Pocono HS; Moscow, PA; (Y); Trs VP Church Yth Grp; Teachers Aide; Chorus; Church Choir; Swing Chorus; Variety Show; Yrbk Stf; Drama Clb; Rep Stu Cncl; Yrbk Photo Coordntr 85-86; Stu Of Lcl Volunteer Fire Co 85-86; Rep Of Northeastern Yth Cncl 85-86; Marywood Coll; Scndry Educ.

JORDAN, BRANDI; Saltsburg JR SR HS; Clarksburg, PA; (Y); Varsity Clb; VP Sr Cls; Capt Cheerleading; Sftbl; High Hon Roll; Pres NHS; Hmcmng Queen 85; Tri-Cnty Chrldng Champs 85; IUP; Pre-Engr.

JORDAN, BRENDA; Marple Newtown SR HS; Broomall, PA; (Y); Art Clb; Church Yth Grp; Drama Clb; Chorus; Drm Mjr(t); Mrchg Band; Symp Band; Stu Cncl; NHS; Band; Exc In Dramatic Arts 86; Mrpl Nwtwn Plyrs Schlrshp 86; U DE; Intr Dsgn.

JORDAN, COLLEEN; Bishop Hannan HS; Scranton, PA; (Y); Church Yth Grp; Intnl Clb; Spanish Clb; Concert Band; Orch; School Musical; Rep Stu Cncl; Var Cheerleading; Hon Roll; NHS; Cert Of Excllnc Wrld Cult I, Orch And Hnrbl Mntn Spnsh I 84-86; Phila Clg; Dnce.

JORDAN, DARCY; Brownsville Area HS; New Salem, PA; (Y); Church Yth Grp; Cmnty Wkr; FCA; FHA; Hosp Aide; Red Cross Aide; Spanish Clb; Cit Awd; Hon Roll; Jr NHS; Sec.

JORDAN JR, HILLARY RODGERS; Lasalle College HS; Colmar, PA; (Y); Aud/Vis; Camera Clb; Computer Clb; Ski Clb; Swmmng; Ntl Merit Schol; Stage Crew; Photo Edtr For Yrbk & Nwspr 85-86; Sr Audio-Visual Asst 84-86; GA Inst Of Tech; Info-Comp Sci.

JORDAN, JAMIE; Fox Chapel HS; Pittsburgh, PA; (Y); 132/394; VP JA; Capt Bsktbl; Coach Actv; Capt CAP; Capt Vllybl; Hon Roll; Vllybl & Bsktbl Schlrhsp Carlow Coll 86; YMCA All Sports Banq 86; Post Casette Fabulous 5 H S Bsktbl; Carlow Coll.

JORDAN, JILL; North Hills HS; Pittsburgh, PA; (S); 19/507; NFL; Rep Frsh Cls; Rep Soph Cls; Rep Jr Cls; VP Sr Cls; Rep Stu Cncl; Swmmng; Capt Trk; High Hon Roll; VP NHS; Degree Hnr Natl Frnsc Lg 85; Var Ltr Trk 83-85; 6th Pl WPIAL Finls Trk 85; U MI; Bus.

JORDAN, JOANNE; Cedar Crest HS; Lebanon, PA; (Y); JA; Key Clb; Letterman Clb; Spanish Clb; Varsity Clb; Stu Cncl; Var Sftbl; Var Capt Swmmng; Vllybl; High Hon Roll; PIAA ST Swm Mt 85-86; PIAA All Leag Swm Tm 83-86; U Pittsbrg Jhnstwn; Pre Pharmcy.

JORDAN, JOE; Mc Keesport SR HS; Mckeesport, PA; (Y); Capt Ftbl; Var Wt Lftg; Hon Roll; UNC Chapel Hill; Comp Engrng.

JORDAN, JONATHAN; Delaware City Christian HS; Kennett Sq, PA; (Y); Church Yth Grp; Nwsp Rptr; Rep Soph Cls; Rep Sr Cls; JV Var Bsbl; Tennis.

JORDAN, KAREN; St Marys Area HS; Kersey, PA; (Y); Sec Trs Church Yth Grp; Cmnty Wkr; Spanish Clb; Capt Jazz Band; Mrchg Band; Hon Roll; Ntl Merit Ltr; Prfct Atten Awd; Chem.

JORDAN, KELLEY ANNE; Scranton Preparatory Schl; Scranton, PA; (Y); 20/190; Chorus; Church Choir; Orch; School Musical; School Play; Nwsp Stf; Yrbk Stf; Mgr Wrstlng; High Hon Roll; NHS; Boston Coll; Pre Law.

JORDAN, KELLY; N Schuylkill HS; Frackville, PA; (Y); 2/195; Ski Clb; Var Cheerleading; Trk; High Hon Roll.

JORDAN, MARCI; Punxsutawney Area HS; Punxsutawney, PA; (Y); Color Guard; Mrchg Band; Twrlr; Giftd Pgm 83-87; IN U; Bus Ed.

JORDAN, SUZANNE; Schuylkill Valley HS; Mohrsville, PA; (Y); VP Trs Church Yth Grp; Cmnty Wkr; Chorus; Church Choir; School Musical; Yrbk Bus Mgr; Yrbk Phtg; Pres Soph Cls; Stu Cncl; Var Cheerleading; RI Schl Of Photgrphy.

JORDAN, TERRY; Clearfield Area HS; Woodland, PA; (Y); Church Yth Grp; Key Clb; Church Choir; L Ftbl; L Trk; Im Wt Lftg; Wrstlng; Cit Awd; Hon Roll.

JORDAN, TODD; Plum SR HS; Pittsburgh, PA; (Y); 100/400; VP JA; Band; Concert Band; Mrchg Band; Symp Band; JV Mgr(s); Stat Trk; Hon Roll; Dale Crngie Awd 85; Corp Law.

JORDANO, JAMES; Manheim Township HS; Lancaster, PA; (Y); Boy Scts; Church Yth Grp; Pres Science Clb; Im Bsktbl; L Ftbl; Var Trk; JV Wrstlng; High Hon Roll; Hon Roll; Lion Awd; Lncstr Nwspapers Carrier Of Yr 84-85; J F Mck Sct Cmpr Awd 80-85; Ordr Of Arrw BSA 83; Chem.

JORDEN, HEATHER KAYE; Meadville SR HS; Meadville, PA; (Y); NFL; Speech Tm; Varsity Clb; Jr Cls; Stu Cncl; Bsktbl; Golf; Trk; High Hon Roll; Acad All-Am Awd 86.

JORGENSEN, DAVID W; Pennsbury HS; Yardley, PA; (Y); 6/712; Am Leg Boys St; Boy Scts; Church Yth Grp; NFL; Stu Cncl; JV Socr; Im Vllybl; Hon Roll; NHS; Service Clb; Eagl Sct 85; Pennsbury Stdnt Yr 86; Natl Merit Fnlst 86; Darmouth Coll; Math.

JORIS, LORI; Belle Vernon Area HS; Belle Vernon, PA; (Y); VP Concert Band; VP Mrchg Band; Powder Puff Ftbl; High Hon Roll; NHS; Chem.

JORSTAD, GUY; Knoch JR SR HS; Cabot, PA; (Y); VP Church Yth Grp; Chorus; Madrigals; School Musical; School Play; Stage Crew; High Hon Roll; Hon Roll; NHS.

JOSAR, LAURA; Wm Allen HS; Allentown, PA; (Y); 32/642; Intnl Clb; Leo Clb; Service Clb; Ski Clb; Spanish Clb; Concert Band; Mrchg Band; Pep Band; Yrbk Stf; Hon Roll; Hrbl Mntn-Natl Hstry Day 4th Pl 85; Physics Olympcs-2nd Pl Apparatus Evnt 86; Elem Ed.

JOSEPH, ALLAN; Hanover Area HS; Wilkes Barre, PA; (Y); 5/170; Ski Clb; Variety Show; Var Golf; High Hon Roll; NHS.

JOSEPH, BETH; Kiski Area HS; Export, PA; (Y); Cmnty Wkr; Drama Clb; French Clb; NFL; Chorus; School Play; Rep Frsh Cls; Hon Roll; Ed.

JOSEPH, MATTHEW A; Somerset Area HS; Somerset, PA; (Y); 2/231; Am Leg Boys St; Capt Scholastic Bowl; VP Stu Cncl; Var Bsbl; Capt Var Ftbl; Trs NHS; Sal; Ntl Hnr Soc Schrlsh Pad 86; Tribune Dem Schlr Athlete 86; Soroptmst Intl Citznshp Awd 86; U VA; Engrng.

JOSEPH, PETER; East Stroudsburg HS; E Stroudsburg, PA; (Y); 43/246; Model UN; VP Ftbl; VP Tennis; Cornell; Pre Law.

JOSEPH, THOMAS; Laurel Highlands SR HS; Uniontown, PA; (Y); 12/300; Pres Church Yth Grp; Mathletes; Varsity Clb; Rep Jr Cls; L Ftbl; Var Trk; High Hon Roll; Hon Roll; Jr NHS; NHS; Chmbr Of Cmmrc Stu Of Mnth 86; Engrg.

JOSEY, ALANDA; West Catholic Girls HS; Philadelphia, PA; (Y); 20/240; Cmnty Wkr; Dance Clb; English Clb; Hosp Aide; JA; Latin Clb; Science Clb; Orch; School Play; Yrbk Stf; Philadelphia Classical Soc 84 & 85; Pre-Med.

JOSHI, APARNA; Slippery Rock Area HS; Slippery Rock, PA; (Y); 1/180; Am Leg Aux Girls St; Sec German Clb; JCL; Sec Latin Clb; Math Tm; Pep Clb; Mrchg Band; Nwsp Stf; VP Jr Cls; Pres Sr Cls; Latin Hnr Soc, Rotary Yth Ldrshp Awd Conf 86; Med.

JOSHI, KALPESH; Cedar Crest HS; Lebanon, PA; (Y); 16/306; FBLA; German Clb; Var JV Socr; Var JV Tennis; High Hon Roll; NHS; Sec I Champ Tennis & Soccer; Booster Clb Hnr Awd.

JOURIS, JAIME A; Penn Trafford HS; Export, PA; (Y); 1/328; French Clb; Ski Clb; Teachers Aide; Varsity Clb; Var Capt Tennis; High Hon Roll; NHS; Ntl Merit SF; Im Badmtn; Im Swmmng; Tennis Mag Jr Sprtsmnshp Awd 84; PA Soc Of Prof Engrs Engrng Awd 85; Chem Engr.

JOVER, DOREEN; Valley View HS; Peckville, PA; (Y); 5/205; French Clb; Latin Clb; Vllybl; High Hon Roll; Hon Roll; NHS; Hnrb Mntn Natl Frnch Cont 85 & 86; Acad Excllnce Cert 86; U Scranton; Psych.

JOYCE, JOAN; Bishop O Reilly HS; Wyoming, PA; (Y); French Clb; Chorus; Drill Tm; Var Bsktbl; Var Fld Hcky; Hon Roll; Grad 2nd Hnrs 4 Yrs; PA ST U; Psych.

JOYCE, KATHLEEN; St Basil Acad; Philadelphia, PA; (Y); 13/94; Cmnty Wkr; German Clb; Service Clb; Spanish Clb; Chorus; Hon Roll; Natl Mrt Scty 85; Cert Mrt B Avg Accntng Cntry 21 85; Temple U; Intl Bus.

JOYCE, LEE ANN; Archbishop Ryan HS For Girls; Philadelphia, PA; (Y); 100/480; Church Yth Grp; Computer Clb; VP French Clb; JA; Office Aide; Stage Crew; Im Bsktbl; Im Socr; JV Trk; Cit Awd; Citizens Schlrshp Fndt Amer 86; Burger King Crew Schlrshp 86; St Josephs Food Mktg Schlrshp 86; St Josephs U; Food Mktng.

JOYCE, MAUREEN; Penn Hills SR HS; Pittsburgh, PA; (S); 1/797; AFS; Church Yth Grp; French Clb; Yrbk Stf; Lit Mag; High Hon Roll; Jr NHS; NHS; NEDT Awd; Val; Carnegie Mrt Schlrshp 86; Vry Imprtnt Prsn Awd 85; PA Engl Tchrs Cncl Prtcptn Awd 86; Carnegie-Mellon U; Tech Wrtr.

JOYCE, MICHELLE; Technical HS; Scranton, PA; (Y); 28/241; Art Clb; Church Yth Grp; FFA; Girl Scts; Chorus; Stage Crew; Yrbk Stf; Hon Roll.

JOYCE, PATRICK; Shady Side Acad SR Schl; Pittsburgh, PA; (Y); Cmnty Wkr; German Clb; Letterman Clb; Office Aide; Band; Jazz Band; Yrbk Sprt Ed; Stat Bsktbl; Rep Coach Actv; JV Crs Cntry; 1st Yr Ger Prz 83; John Grey Frgn Lang Prz 84; Vrsty Ltrs Sccr 84-86, Lacrosse 84; Notre Dame; Comm.

JOYCE, PAUL; Taylor Allderdice HS; Pittsburgh, PA; (Y); Aud/Vis; JA; PA ST U; Law.

JOYCE, STEPHEN P; Brentwood JR SR HS; Pittsburgh, PA; (S); 23/130; VP JA; School Play; Nwsp Sprt Ed; Yrbk Ed-Chief; Rep Sr Cls; Rep Stu Cncl; Var Crs Cntry; Score Keeper; Var Trk; NHS; First Rnnr Up Awd Theme Devlpmnt Seven 85; Sprngs Yrbk Semnr 86; Outstndg Ldr Duquesne U 86; Duquesne U; Publc Rltns.

JOYNER, MARC; Ambridge Area HS; Ambridge, PA; (Y); Boy Scts; Spanish Clb; Varsity Clb; Band; Concert Band; Mrchg Band; Im Bsbl; Im Bsktbl; Var Ftbl; Im Sftbl; Bus.

JOZEFCZYK, JOSEPH; Ringgold HS; Statesville, NC; (Y); Am Leg Boys St; Aud/Vis; Church Yth Grp; Ski Clb; Band; Concert Band; Drm & Bgl; Mrchg Band; Stage Crew; Var Bsktbl.

JOZEFIK, DREW; West Branch Area JR SR HS; Kylertown, PA; (S); 1/120; Boy Scts; Church Yth Grp; Drama Clb; Science Clb; Spanish Clb; Varsity Clb; Band; Chorus; Church Choir; Concert Band; Eagle Scout 84; E Nazarene COLL; Us Hist.

JUBA, JENNIFER; Lancaster Catholic HS; Lancaster, PA; (Y); French Clb; Service Clb; Varsity Clb; Rep Soph Cls; Rep Jr Cls; Rep Sr Cls; Stu Cncl; Capt Fld Hcky; Capt Trk; Church Yth Grp; Lancaster Sertoma Schlrshp 86; Lancaster Cthlc Almn Schlrshp 86; Kutztown U; Elem Educ.

JUBARA, BERNADETTE; Portage Area HS; Portage, PA; (S); 4/116; French Clb; Varsity Clb; Chorus; Variety Show; Bowling; Vllybl; High Hon Roll; Hon Roll; Airline Tckt Agnt.

JUBAY, ROBIN; Hazleton SR HS; Hazleton, PA; (Y); 81/430; Pep Clb; Chorus; High Hon Roll; Hon Roll; Penn ST U; Bio.

JUD, LESLIE; Harbor Creek HS; Harbor Creek, PA; (Y); 8/200; Dance Clb; Hosp Aide; Model UN; Political Wkr; Spanish Clb; Teachers Aide; Yrbk Ed-Chief; Powder Puff Ftbl; Hon Roll; NHS; Ball ST U Schlrshp 86; Ball ST U; Arch.

JUDD, LAURA; Kennett HS; Kennett Sq, PA; (Y); 14/155; Pres Church Yth Grp; Varsity Clb; Church Choir; Orch; School Musical; Nwsp Rptr; Var L Crs Cntry; High Hon Roll; Sec NHS; NEDT Awd; Untd Meth Bicentnnl Schlr, Hewlett-Packard Co Employee Schlrshp & Dist Young Layperson Of Yr 86; Lebanon Vly Coll; Sec Math Ed.

JUDGE, DAVID; Lake Lehman HS; Dallas, PA; (Y); 25/177; French Clb; VP Key Clb; Ski Clb; VP Stu Cncl; JV Bsktbl; Var L Crs Cntry; Var L Trk; High Hon Roll; Hon Roll; NHS; Jaycees Book Scholarship 86; Penn ST U; Educ.

JUDGE, LESLIE; G A R Memorial HS; Wilkes Barre, PA; (S); 2/187; Chorus; Church Choir; Mrchg Band; Orch; Rep Stu Cncl; Bsktbl; High Hon Roll; Jr NHS; NHS; Church Yth Grp; Outstndng Sci Stdnt Awd 84.

JUDSON, KEN; North Hills HS; Pittsburgh, PA; (Y); 50/490; Trs Church Yth Grp; Symp Band; Nwsp Stf; Crs Cntry; Trk; Wrstlng; High Hon Roll; Med.

JUDY, DARYL; Bellefone Area HS; Bellefonte, PA; (Y); Pres 4-H; Acpl Chr; Band; Chorus; Capt Color Guard; Jazz Band; Mrchg Band; School Musical; School Play; Yrbk Stf; Drama & Yrbk Awd 86; Bst Musicial 86; PA ST U; Adm.

JUGAN, MICHELE; Duquesne HS; Duquesne, PA; (Y); Art Clb; Church Yth Grp; Exploring; French Clb; FHA; Chorus; Off Frsh Cls; Off Soph Cls; Off Jr Cls; Off Sr Cls; Cert-Acadmc Achvt 86; TCM Schl Of Bus; Comp Mngmt.

JULIAN, JONATHAN N; Mapletown JR SR HS; Greensboro, PA; (Y); 11/72; Varsity Clb; Stu Cncl; Ftbl; Wt Lftg; Wrstlng; High Hon Roll; Hon Roll; Penn ST; Adm Jstc.

JULYE, STACEY; Merion Mercy Acad; Phila, PA; (Y); French Clb; Hosp Aide; Mathletes; Science Clb; Service Clb; Chorus; Cheerleading; Engrng.

JUMPER, JAMES; Hopewell SR HS; Aliquippa, PA; (Y); 39/295; Church Yth Grp; German Clb; Bsbl; L Var Crs Cntry; Ftbl; L Var Swmmng; L Var Trk; Hon Roll; PA ST U; Physics.

JUNAS, PAUL; Hazleton HS; Hazleton, PA; (Y); 65/390; Ski Clb; High Hon Roll; Hon Roll; Gftd Prog; Dggrs; Penn ST; Htl Mgmt.

JUNKIN, JULIE; Fannett-Metal HS; Dry Run, PA; (Y); Drama Clb; Pres 4-H; Band; Pres Chorus; Church Choir; School Play; Mgr(s); Capt Twrlr; Camera Clb; Church Yth Grp; Co Chorus; Toured East Hanbell Choir; Penn ST U; Elem Educ.

JURASINSKI, CHRISTINE; Mount Penn HS; Reading, PA; (Y); 1/78; Sec Science Clb; Pres Y-Teens; Chorus; Yrbk Ed-Chief; Golf; Vllybl; Bausch & Lomb Sci Awd; Ntl Merit Ltr; Pres Schlr; Val; HS JR Miss Cntstnt 86; Pres Schlrshp $4000 Yr 86; Amer Assc U Women Awd 86; Elizabethtown Coll; Med.

JURASKO, DIANE; Hopewell HS; Aliquippa, PA; (S); 23/245; German Clb; Band; Chorus; Drill Tm; Flag Corp; Yrbk Stf; Rep Jr Cls; Stu Cncl; Trk; High Hon Roll.

JURGES, MARCIE; Hopewell HS; Aliquippa, PA; (Y); 100/295; Var L Bsktbl; Var L Socr; Var L Sftbl; German Clb; School Play; Yrbk Stf; Stu Cncl; Powder Puff Ftbl; Hon Roll; Alderson; Sports Med.

JURISTA, BRENT; Tunkhannock Area HS; Tunkhannock, PA; (S); 50/280; Science Clb; Crs Cntry; Trk; Hon Roll; NHS; PA ST; Mech Engrng.

JURY, HILLARY; Abington Heights HS; Waverly, PA; (Y); 65/300; Church Yth Grp; Ski Clb; Yrbk Phtg; Yrbk Rptr; Yrbk Stf; Lit Mag; Ntl Merit SF; NY U; Jrnlsm.

JUSKA, SHARON; Upper Merion Area HS; King Of Prussia, PA; (S); Math Tm; Chorus; Nwsp Rptr; Lit Mag; Hon Roll; NHS; Ntl Merit SF; JV Bsktbl; JV Fld Hcky; Rtry 4-Way Test Awd 84; Pres-Delta Stu Svc Clb 84-85.

JUSTICE, KEVIN; Central Bucks East HS; Doylestown, PA; (Y); 58/385; Church Yth Grp; Ski Clb; JV Var Socr; JV Vllybl; JV Wrstlng; Hon Roll; MVP Woodhaven Sprts Centre Indoor Sccr Tourn Of Champs 85; Pilot.

JUSTICE, WILLIAM; Tunkhannock Area HS; Tunkhannock, PA; (S); 9/280; Boy Scts; Var L Golf; God Cntry Awd; Hon Roll; NHS; Pre-Med.

JUSTIN, KARI; Meadville SR HS; Meadville, PA; (Y); Church Yth Grp; Hosp Aide; Pep Clb; Vllybl; High Hon Roll; Hon Roll.

KABALA, COURTENAY; Mt Lebanon HS; Pittsburgh, PA; (Y); Church Yth Grp; Drama Clb; Thesps; Church Choir; School Play; VP Jr Cls; Ftbl; Mgr(s); Wrstlng; PA Jr Acad Sci 1st Plc Rgnls & 1st Plc ST 83; Buhl Sci Fr Prtcpnt 83; Phys Ther.

KABILKO, SHERI; Pottstown SR HS; Pottstown, PA; (S); Key Clb; Ski Clb; Spanish Clb; Band; Concert Band; Jazz Band; Mrchg Band; Yrbk Rptr; Yrbk Stf; VP Frsh Cls.

KACIK, MELISSA; South Allegheny HS; Port Vue, PA; (S); 18/184; French Clb; FNA; Y-Teens; Concert Band; Mrchg Band; School Musical; Yrbk Phtg; Off Jr Cls; Twrlr; Hon Roll; Photo Apprnctchsp 85-86.

KACINKO, DAVID M; Churchill HS; Pittsburgh, PA; (Y); 73/188; Aud/Vis; Church Yth Grp; Key Clb; Radio Clb; Stage Crew; Var L Crs Cntry; Ftbl; Stat Timer; Var L Trk; Hon Roll; Drftg.

KACZMAREK, MARIA; Mt Carmel Area JR-SR HS; Mt Carmel, PA; (Y); 19/150; Key Clb; Pep Clb; Spanish Clb; Chorus; School Musical; Nwsp Stf; JV Var Cheerleading; Var Trk; High Hon Roll; Hon Roll; Child Psychl.

KACZMARSKI, DEBBIE; Bishop Shanahan HS; W Chester, PA; (Y); 34/218; Drama Clb; VP Chorus; Madrigals; School Musical; Sftbl; Hon Roll; Prfct Atten Awd; Tchng.

KACZMURCZYK, FRANCIS; Conrad Weiser HS; Wernersville, PA; (Y); 29/184; Trs Church Yth Grp; Pres Computer Clb; JV Var Bsktbl; JV Var Crs Cntry; Var Trk; Am Compt Sci Leag Comptn 85-86; Math Leag Comp Sci 85-86; Fnlst Lrng Resrcs Assoc Microcomp Prog 86; Engr.

KACZYNSKI, KRIS; North Hills HS; Pittsburgh, PA; (Y); FBLA; JA; Library Aide; Office Aide; Ski Clb; Stu Cncl; Hon Roll; Robert Morris Coll; Acctng.

KADEL, PAT; Cedar Cliff HS; Mechanicsburg, PA; (Y); Camera Clb; Computer Clb; Key Clb; Ski Clb; Hon Roll; Pres Schlr; Boston U; Elec Engrng.

KADER, CHARLES J; Strong Vincent HS; Erie, PA; (Y); 33/200; Aud/Vis; Church Yth Grp; Cmnty Wkr; Political Wkr; VP Stu Cncl; Ftbl; Swmmng; Wt Lftg; Cit Awd; HI U Manoa; Law Enfrcmnt.

KADLEC, LISA A; Oley Valley HS; Oley, PA; (Y); 2/124; Cmnty Wkr; Quiz Bowl; Concert Band; Mrchg Band; School Play; Nwsp Rptr; Ed Yrbk Stf; High Hon Roll; Ntl Merit SF; Fleetwood Rotary Stu Mnth 86; Cert Merit Outstndng Perf 86; Haverford; Pre-Med.

KADRYNA, KIMBERLY ANN; Selinsgrove Area HS; Selinsgrove, PA; (Y); 14/214; Church Yth Grp; Cmnty Wkr; Girl Scts; Varsity Clb; Chorus; School Play; Mgr(s); Tennis; NHS; Hon Roll; Grl Sct Gld Awd 86; PA ST 1st Pl Pblc Spkng Amer Ind Arts Stud Assn 85-86; Pres ISA 86-87; Aerospc Engr.

KAESS JR, CHRIS; Council Rock HS; Churchville, PA; (Y); 316/850; Boy Scts; Computer Clb; FCA; FBLA; Varsity Clb; Var L Crs Cntry; Var L Gym; Var L Trk; Im Vllybl; Prfct Atten Awd; Mst Imprvd Gym 86; Pres Spts Awd 85; Penn ST; Bus Adm.

KAFLAK, TERESA; St Basil Acad; Philadelphia, PA; (S); 3/95; Drama Clb; French Clb; Yrbk Stf; Pres Soph Cls; Im JV Bsktbl; Mgr(s); High Hon Roll; Hon Roll; Acctng.

KAFRISSEN, DAVID; Randor HS; St Davids, PA; (S); Camera Clb; Debate Tm; Latin Clb; NFL; Red Cross Aide; Speech Tm; Hon Roll; St Finals Extmprns Spkng 84-85; 4th Degree Ntl Frnsc League 86; Sociologist.

KAGARISE, BRIAN; Northern Bedford County HS; Loysburg, PA; (Y); 1/98; FBLA; Math Clb; Varsity Clb; Rep Stu Cncl; Var L Bsbl; Var L Ftbl; Var L Wrstlng; High Hon Roll; NHS; Acdmc All Am Awd 86; USAF Acad.

KAGARISE, ROBBY; Williamsburg HS; Williamsburg, PA; (Y); Rep Soph Cls; Rep Jr Cls; Var L Bsbl; Var L Ftbl; NHS; Cngrssnl Schlr In Ntl Yng Ldrs Cnfrnc 86; Jimmy Swggrt Bible Coll; Mssnry.

KAGEL, PAM; Upper Dublin HS; Ambler, PA; (Y); 84/325; Office Aide; Chorus; Yrbk Stf; JV Bowling; Mgr(s); Score Keeper; Socr; Accntng.

KAGUYUTAN, JANICE VICTORIA; The Mercersburg Acad; Gettysburg, PA; (Y); Church Yth Grp; Intnl Clb; Ski Clb; Spanish Clb; Sec Frsh Cls; Var L Tennis; Hon Roll; Intl Bus.

KAHKONEN, GAY L; Trinity HS; Washington, PA; (Y); 1/374; Am Leg Aux Girls St; German Clb; Math Tm; Orch; Lit Mag; Jr NHS; NHS; Ntl Merit Ltr; Rotary Awd; Val; Carnegie Mellon U; Music Comp.

KAHKONEN, SONJA; Trinity HS; Washington, PA; (Y); Church Yth Grp; French Clb; Math Tm; NFL; Thesps; Concert Band; Mrchg Band; Tae Kwon Do Green Belt.

KAHL, KAREN; Bethlehem Catholic HS; Bethlehem, PA; (S); 8/210; Hosp Aide; Capt Flag Corp; Mrchg Band; Color Guard; NHS; High Hon Roll; Red Crs Lf Svng Badg 85; Cvl Engrng.

KAHLER, ALLAN; Upper Darby HS; Upr Darby, PA; (Y); Church Yth Grp; German Clb; Trk; Hon Roll; Ger II Awd 84-85; Prfct Atten 84-85; Chem Engrng.

KAHLER, KAREN; West Mifflin Area HS; W Mifflin, PA; (Y); 117/350; Drama Clb; Flag Corp; Stu Cncl; Mgr(s); Stat Trk; IN U PA; Cmmnctns.

KAHLEY, SHANI; Chief Logan HS; Lewistown, PA; (Y); Key Clb; Spanish Clb; Mrchg Band; Cheerleading; High Hon Roll; NHS.

KAHN, JESSICA; Cheltonham HS; Wyncote, PA; (Y); Art Clb; Yrbk Phtg; Yrbk Stf; Pres Stu Cncl; JV Gym; Chrctr Awd 83; Intr Dsgn.

KAIDER, SUSY; Conneaut Lake HS; Conneaut Lake, PA; (Y); Drama Clb; Spanish Clb; Band; Concert Band; Mrchg Band; Pep Band; Variety Show; High Hon Roll; Sec NHS; Columbia; Cmnctns.

KAINHOFER, PETRA; Exeter Township SR HS; Reading, PA; (Y); Varsity Clb; Y-Teens; School Play; Variety Show; Nwsp Stf; Stu Cncl; Var Capt Cheerleading; Powder Puff Ftbl; Var Trk; Jr NHS; W Chester U.

KAISER, CHRISTOPHER; Parkland HS; Allentown, PA; (Y); 41/432; JV Wrstlng; Hon Roll; Gld Ky Art Awd 82-83; PA ST U; Arch.

KAISER, CYRSTAL; Connellsville Area HS; Connellsville, PA; (Y); Office Aide; Acpl Chr; Chorus; Swing Chorus; Nwsp Ed-Chief; Nwsp Sprt Ed; Stu Cncl; Var Capt Cheerleading; High Hon Roll; Nwsp Awd; Dist Chrs; Stu Mo; Bus.

KAISER, DEBBIE; Franklin Regional HS; Murrysville, PA; (Y); French Clb; Science Clb; Spanish Clb; Band; Concert Band; Nwsp Stf; High Hon Roll; Hon Roll; Pres Acad Ftns Awd 85-86; Miami U Of OH; Intl Stud.

KAJI, AMY H; Abington SR HS; Philadelphia, PA; (Y); 1/500; VP French Clb; Pres Intnl Clb; Lit Mag; Var Trk; High Hon Roll; NCTE Awd; NHS; Model UN; Orch; Nwsp Rptr; Syracuse Eng Bk Awd 85; Wrld Affrs Clb Awd 85; Philadelphia Area JR Ladies Chmp Fig Sktg 83; Harvard U.

KALAJAINEN, KIM; Shenango JR SR HS; New Castle, PA; (S); #1 In Class; Varsity Clb; Trs Frsh Cls; Trs Soph Cls; Trs Jr Cls; Co-Capt Bsktbl; Trk; Hon Roll; Jr NHS; NHS; Acadmc All Amercn 84-85; Ntl Engl & Sci Merit Awds 85-86; Aerntcl Engrng.

KALAMASZ, ANN; Center HS; Aliquippa, PA; (Y); FHA; Hon Roll; Bus.

KALASINSKI, KRISTINE; Forest City Regional HS; Forest, PA; (Y); 15/63; Church Yth Grp; Library Aide; Spanish Clb; VP SADD; Chorus; Stage Crew; Yrbk Phtg; Yrbk Stf; Crs Cntry; Sftbl; Fed Demo Wmns Clb Schlrshp 86; Gregg Typng Awd 84; Prsntnts Cmnty Prom Cmnty 85-86; Keystone JR Coll; Exec Sec.

KALB, KEVIN; Cedar Crest HS; Lebanon, PA; (Y); 57/365; Church Yth Grp; Pep Clb; Spanish Clb; Varsity Clb; School Musical; JV Var Bsktbl; JV Var Socr; Im Vllybl; Hon Roll; NHS; Pres Acad Ftns Awd 86; Lehigh U; Arch.

KALBACH, KIM; St Maria Goretti HS; Philadelphia, PA; (Y); 124/400; Civic Clb; Dance Clb; French Clb; Hosp Aide; Varsity Clb; Stage Crew; Variety Show; High Hon Roll; Hon Roll; Prfct Atten Awd; Ellis Awd 1st & 2nd Hnrs 83-84; Charles Ellis Schlrshp 84-87; Stock Broker.

KALBAS, TIMOTHY; Cumberland Valley HS; Camp Hill, PA; (Y); Church Yth Grp; French Clb; Key Clb; Trs Spanish Clb; Im Badmtn; JV Bsktbl; Var Golf; Im Lcrss; Im Socr; Var Capt Tennis.

KALEJTA, ROBERT; St Pius X HS; Pottstown, PA; (S); 1/139; Mathletes; Science Clb; Rep Jr Cls; Hon Roll; Pres NHS; Ntl Merit Ltr; NEDT Awd; Prtl Schlrshp U Of Dalles 85-86; Biochmstry.

KALICH, KELLY M; Winchester-Thurston Schl; Mc Keesport, PA; (Y); Dance Clb; Ski Clb; SADD; Sec Trs Orch; School Play; Nwsp Sprt Ed; Yrbk Bus Mgr; Capt Cheerleading; Hon Roll; Bus.

KALICHUK, LISA; Plum SR HS; Pittsburgh, PA; (Y); Service Clb; Ski Clb; Varsity Clb; Var L Cheerleading; L Var Trk; L Vllybl; Hon Roll; Phrmcy.

KALIE, MELISSA; Benton Area HS; Orangeville, PA; (Y); Drama Clb; Library Aide; Band; Chorus; Church Choir; Concert Band; Mrchg Band; School Musical; School Play; Nwsp Rptr; Nrsng.

KALINEY, GEORGE; West Middlesex HS; W Middlesex, PA; (S); 11/114; Spanish Clb; JV Var Bsktbl; Trk; Wt Lftg; High Hon Roll; Hon Roll; Spanish NHS; Electncs.

KALINOWSKI, DAVID; Tunkhannock Area HS; Tunkhannock, PA; (S); 4-H; Swmmng; Tennis; 4-H Awd; Hon Roll; Elctrncl Engrng.

KALINOWSKI, MICHAEL; Greensburg Central Catholic HS; Smithton, PA; (Y); 20/258; Exploring; NFL; Ski Clb; Crs Cntry; Trk; Physician.

KALINOWSKY, MARIA; Cardinal Brennan HS; Frackville, PA; (Y); 2/48; Yrbk Bus Mgr; Hon Roll; NHS; Sal; Spanish NHS; Penn ST U; Pol Sci.

KALISKY, LORI; York Catholic HS; York, PA; (Y); French Clb; FBLA; Pep Clb; Varsity Clb; Rep Frsh Cls; Rep Soph Cls; Rep Stu Cncl; Var Trk; Hon Roll; Trs NHS; Indstrl Engrng.

KALKBRENNER, SHAWNTELLE; Claysburg-Kimmel HS; Claysburg, PA; (Y); French Clb; Trs German Clb; Spanish Clb; Mansfield U; Elmntry Ed.

KALMAN, TRACEY; Liberty HS; Bethlehem, PA; (Y); 55/475; Band; Pres Orch; Lit Mag; Twrlr; Hon Roll; Dist X Orch Exeter 86; Northampton Cty JR Miss Pgnt 86; Crtv Wrtg.

KALMANIR, HEATHER; Windber Area HS; Windber, PA; (Y); Pep Clb; Chorus; Trs Soph Cls; Off Jr Cls; VP Stu Cncl; Var Cheerleading; Vllybl; Hon Roll; Stu Yr 83; Am Legion Awd 84xhughxo Xriax Ldrshp; Rep 85.

KALNA, CHRIS; Bishop O Reilly HS; Swoyersville, PA; (Y); CAP; Math Clb; Science Clb; Spanish Clb; Chorus; Var Bsbl; JV Bsktbl; Var Ftbl; Var Golf; Hon Roll; St Marshal Columbian Squires 84-85; St Notary Columbian Squires 85-86; Ldrshp Awd 86; TX A&M; Engrng.

KALOCHIE, JENNIFER; Minersville Area HS; Minersville, PA; (Y); 1/126; Ski Clb; Trs Spanish Clb; Capt Drill Tm; Var L Bsktbl; Var L Sftbl; Var L Vllybl; High Hon Roll; NHS; Biol.

KALOGERIS, VICKIE; Bethel Park SR HS; Bethel Pk, PA; (Y); Sec Church Yth Grp; Pres FHA; Office Aide; Off Frsh Cls; Off Soph Cls; Hon Roll; IN U; Travel Indust.

KALOWSKY, JAMES; Scranton Prep; Peckville, PA; (Y); 16/194; Boys Clb Am; Letterman Clb; VP Sr Cls; Stu Cncl; Var L Ftbl; Var L Trk; JV L Wrstlng; High Hon Roll; NHS; Rep Frsh Cls; Polc Sci.

KALP, AMY; Mt Pleasant Area HS; Jones Mills, PA; (Y); 18/248; Church Yth Grp; FBLA; GAA; Office Aide; Concert Band; Mrchg Band; Pep Band; Nwsp Ed-Chief; High Hon Roll; NHS; Brdfrd Bus Schl; Rtl Mngmnt.

KALP, JACK; Connellsville SR HS; Melcroft, PA; (Y).

KALP, SUE; Connellsville Area HS; Acme, PA; (Y); Exploring; Library Aide; Office Aide; Sec Science Clb; SADD; Teachers Aide; School Musical; School Play; Stage Crew; High Hon Roll; Spnsh Comptn Awd 83-84; Acadmc Excllnc Pins 82-83 & 85-86; U Of PA; Pre Med.

KALTENBAUGH, DAN; Lakeview HS; Sandy Lake, PA; (S); 7/132; Library Aide; Quiz Bowl; Chorus; Church Choir; Concert Band; Drm Mjr(t); School Play; Crs Cntry; Wrstlng; NHS; Elec Engr.

KALUPANOV, KYRA; Steel Valley HS; Munhall, PA; (Y); Ski Clb; Variety Show; Var Capt Cheerleading; Hon Roll; Prfct Atten Awd; IN U PA; Graphic Desgnr.

KAMDAR, LISA; Sun Valley HS; Aston, PA; (Y); 7/335; Sec Jr Cls; Stu Cncl; Fld Hcky; Lcrss; Score Keeper; DAR Awd; JC Awd; NHS; Grl Mnth 82-83; DE U; Chem.

KAMDAR, MELISSA; St Basil Acad; Rydal, PA; (S); French Clb; Hosp Aide; Science Clb; Rep Frsh Cls; Gym; Swmmng; High Hon Roll; Ntl Merit Ltr; Hugh O Brian Yuth Fdtn Outstndng Soph 85; Sci.

KAMENSKY, ROBIN; Our Lady Of The Sacred Heart HS; Mc Kees Rocks, PA; (Y); Hosp Aide; Pep Clb; School Play; Bsktbl; Bowling; Awd Clss Trndsttr 84-85; Awd Clss Rvltnst 85-86; Syracuse U; Army.

KAMIENIECKI, JOHN; Northeast Catholic HS; Philadelphia, PA; (S); 3/390; Cmnty Wkr; Science Clb; Yrbk Phtg; Crs Cntry; Jr NHS; NHS; Elec Engrng.

KAMINSKI, CHRISTINE; GAR Mem HS; Wilkes Barre, PA; (S); 10/187; Hosp Aide; Key Clb; Office Aide; Chorus; Off Stu Cncl; Sftbl; Trk; Hon Roll; Jr NHS; NHS; Engl Lit.

KAMINSKI, JEFFRI A; Norwin HS; N Huntingdon, PA; (S); 93/590; Exploring; German Clb; Letterman Clb; Math Clb; VP Concert Band; VP Mrchg Band; Var L Socr; Hon Roll; Jr NHS; Presdntl Schlrshp-St Vincent Coll Chllng Pgm 85; Westmorelnd Cty Band 85; Aerntcl Engrng.

KAMINSKI, KAREN; Springdale HS; Cheswick, PA; (Y); Church Yth Grp; German Clb; GAA; Acpl Chr; Band; Var L Sftbl; Var L Vllybl; High Hon Roll; Hon Roll; NHS.

KAMINSKI, KEVIN; Hanover Area JR SR HS; Wilkes Barre, PA; (Y); 23/158; Ski Clb; Capt Golf; Hon Roll; Jr NHS.

KAMINSKI, KRISTINA; Academy HS; Erie, PA; (Y); 50/287; Church Yth Grp; French Clb; Political Wkr; JV Cheerleading; Stewardess.

KAMINSKI III, PETER P; Central Catholic HS; Reading, PA; (Y); Boy Scts; German Clb; VP Band; Concert Band; VP Mrchg Band; VP Orch; School Play; Variety Show; Hon Roll; Prfct Atten Awd; Boy Scouts Pope Puis Awd 86; Fornscs Ptry Coachs Hnr Mntn 84; US Cltrs Soc Stu Top In Clss 85; Chem Engr.

KAMINSKI, SUZANNE; Montour HS; Mckees Rocks, PA; (Y); Church Yth Grp; Exploring; Hosp Aide; High Hon Roll; Cert Of Achvt Frm Vlntr Actn Ctr 84; U Of Pittsburgh; Accntnt.

KAMMERDIENER, JUDITH A; Penns Manor HS; Clymer, PA; (Y); 11/76; Pres Camera Clb; French Clb; Chorus; Yrbk Ed-Chief; Trs Stu Cncl; Cheerleading; NHS; IN U Of PA; Bio.

KAMON, MATTAN; State College Area HS; State College, PA; (Y); 4/570; Computer Clb; Math Clb; Math Tm; VP Science Clb; Pres Temple Yth Grp; Symp Band; JV Vllybl; Gov Hon Prg Awd; Hon Roll; HRB Singer Inc, Smmr Sci Pgm 86; Sci.

KAMOR, PATRICIA ANN; Wyoming Area HS; Exeter, PA; (Y); 2/247; Key Clb; Chorus; Yrbk Ed-Chief; Pres Sr Cls; Var Vllybl; DAR Awd; Elks Awd; High Hon Roll; NHS; Sal; Dr Paul Chromey Awd For Cls Pres & Hghst Schlstc Avg 86; Supts Achvt Awd 86; Natl Yth Cncl Ldrshp 85; U Scranton; Mrktng.

KAMP, LAINE; Wyoming Seminary HS; Wilkes-Barre, PA; (Y); #2 In Class; Church Yth Grp; Hosp Aide; Varsity Clb; Chorus; Ed Nwsp Stf; JV Stat Fld Hcky; Mgr(s); Var L Swmmng; French Hon Soc; High Hon Roll; Cum Laude Soc 85; Curculm, Acad Standrds Comm 84-86; Yale; Bio.

KAMPAS, DENNIS; South Allegheny HS; Glassport, PA; (Y); Bsktbl; Ftbl; Trk; Gftd & Tlntd Enrchmnt Prgrm 86; Penn ST; Psych.

KAMPIAN, LISA; Burgettstown JR SR HS; Bulger, PA; (Y); Church Yth Grp; Ski Clb; Spanish Clb; Chorus; Yrbk Stf; Hon Roll; Wilma Boyd Career Schls; Airlne.

KANA-COLLINS, MICHELLE; Unionville HS; Kennett Sq, PA; (Y); French Clb; Color Guard; Trk; Hon Roll; Penn ST; Bus.

KANAK, DANIEL J; Father Judge HS; Philadelphia, PA; (Y); 27/358; Cmnty Wkr; Hosp Aide; Nwsp Rptr; High Hon Roll; Hon Roll; Temple; Commnctns.

KANDRAC, KAREN; Lower Moreland HS; Huntingdon Valley, PA; (S); 37/214; Church Yth Grp; Cmnty Wkr; German Clb; SADD; JV Bsktbl; Var Fld Hcky; Capt Lcrss; Sftbl; Hon Roll; Kiwanis Awd; Rxbrgh Memrl Hosp Schl; Nrsng.

KANE, ADRIENNE L; Bishop Kenrick HS; Norristown, PA; (Y); 176/274; Cmnty Wkr; Latin Clb; Office Aide; School Musical; School Play; Nwsp Stf; Yrbk Stf; Rep Frsh Cls; Cheerleading; Tobe Cbrn Schl Of Fshn; Fshn.

KANE, ALLEN; Chambersburg Area HS; Marion, PA; (Y); 64/640; Art Clb; Art.

KANE, ANDREA; Ephrata HS; Ephrata, PA; (Y); Church Yth Grp; Intnl Clb; Pep Clb; Hon Roll; J Harry Hibshman Schlrshp 86; PA Sch Of Arts; Intr Dsgn.

KANE, APRYL; Lock Haven SR HS; Lock Haven, PA; (Y); Church Yth Grp; Spanish Clb; Band; Concert Band; Jazz Band; Mrchg Band; Variety Show; Yrbk Stf; VP Mat Maids; Var Trk; Elem Ed.

KANE, BRIAN; Marple Newtown HS; King Of Prussia, PA; (Y); Ski Clb; Variety Show; Rep Stu Cncl; Im Bsktbl; JV Crs Cntry; JV Ftbl; Wt Lftg; Hon Roll; Jr NHS; NEDT Awd; Stu Yth Forum Cncl Rep 86-87; Med.

KANE, JANICE; Wyoming Valley West; Swoyersville, PA; (Y); Church Yth Grp; Key Clb; Rep Soph Cls; Rep Stu Cncl; High Hon Roll; Hon Roll; Temple; Phrmcy.

KANE, JENNINE; St Huberts HS; Philadelphia, PA; (Y); Office Aide; Chorus; Church Choir; Jazz Band; Orch; School Musical; Swing Chorus; Hon Roll; Perf Atten 85-86; Fash Desgn.

KANE, KERRY; Scranton Prep Schl; Olyphant, PA; (Y); 33/192; Debate Tm; Drama Clb; JA; Political Wkr; Service Clb; Orch; Yrbk Stf; Var L Trk; High Hon Roll; Jr NHS; Schlrshp Bishop O Hara H S 83; Brnz Medl Theolgy 85-86; Intl Stds.

KANE, MARK; North Pocono HS; Lake Ariel, PA; (Y); 1/225; Church Yth Grp; Scholastic Bowl; Mrchg Band; Orch; School Musical; Bausch & Lomb Sci Awd; High Hon Roll; NHS; Val; U Of Scranton; Pre Med.

KANE, MATTHEW; Bishop Egan HS; Langhorne, PA; (Y); 38/248; Church Yth Grp; Computer Clb; Office Aide; Im Capt Vllybl; High Hon Roll; Hon Roll; Outstndng Acadmc Perf Geomtry, Chem & Relgn; Lockhaven U Of PA; Elem Educ.

KANE II, RONALD R; Immaculate Conception HS; Amity, PA; (Y); 1/50; Computer Clb; Nwsp Rptr; Nwsp Stf; Yrbk Rptr; Yrbk Stf; High Hon Roll; Hon Roll; Acad Exc Frnch,Hist 86; Brdcstng.

KANE, SEAN; St Josephs Prep; Collingswood, NJ; (Y); Church Yth Grp; SADD; Varsity Clb; Var L Bsbl; Im Bsktbl; Ftbl; Im Ice Hcky; Wt Lftg; High Hon Roll; PA Inquirer Schlrshp 85-86; MVP Bsbl 85.

KANE, STEPHANIE; Shaier Area HS; Pittsburgh, PA; (Y); 148/517; Church Yth Grp; Ski Clb; SADD; Drm Mjr(t); School Musical; Variety Show; Nwsp Phtg; Nwsp Rptr; Yrbk Phtg; NEDT Awd; Capt Flag Tm 86-87; Photogrphy Apprntcshp Pgm 86-87; NYU; Atty.

KANE, TAMI; Yough SR HS; Herminie, PA; (Y); #25 In Class; Computer Clb; Library Aide; Stage Crew; Jr NHS; Child Psychlgst.

KANESKI, STEPHEN; Old Forge HS; Old Forge, PA; (S); Church Yth Grp; Hon Roll; NHS; USAF.

KANEVSKY, MAX; Northeast HS; Philadelphia, PA; (Y); 4/600; VP Computer Clb; Math Clb; Concert Band; Mrchg Band; School Musical; Im Tennis; High Hon Roll; NHS; White-Williams Fndtn Schlrshp 86; Free Sons Of Israel Hebrew Mdl 86; Harvard Coll; Biophyscs.

KANG, HAE EUN; Cheltenham HS; Melrose Park, PA; (Y); 6/368; Church Yth Grp; Chorus; School Musical; School Play; French Hon Soc; High Hon Roll; NHS; Intnl Clb; Science Clb; Church Choir; E Kesilman Music Pgm 86; Ted Gehlmann Memrl Svc Awd 86; 1st Pl PA Jr Acad Sci ST Mtng 84 & 85; U Of PA; Bio.

KANG, HYO-SOK; Cheltenham HS; Elkins Pk, PA; (Y); 33/365; Trs Intnl Clb; Math Tm; Chorus; Church Choir; School Musical; Variety Show.

KANG, SUE-JIN; Lower Moreland HS; Huntingdon Valley, PA; (S); 10/214; Trs Church Yth Grp; Drama Clb; FBLA; Hosp Aide; Key Clb; Yrbk Stf; Stat Trk; High Hon Roll; NHS; Spnsh Awd.

KANG, YOON; Emmaus SR HS; Macungie, PA; (Y); 2/473; Key Clb; School Musical; VP Frsh Cls; VP Soph Cls; Rep Jr Cls; VP Stu Cncl; NHS; Ntl Merit SF; German Clb; Model UN; Sf Rds Prgrm 85-86; Med.

KANISH, KELI; Schuylkill Haven HS; Schuylkill Haven, PA; (S); 7/87; Girl Scts; Science Clb; SADD; Y-Teens; Drill Tm; Mrchg Band; Nwsp Rptr; Cheerleading; Trk; Hon Roll; Ashly Alonge Mem Schlrshp In Ballet 83; Phldlpha Coll Phrmcy; Phrmcy.

KANJORSKI, RUSSELL; John S Fine HS; Nanticoke, PA; (S); #1 In Class; Key Clb; Model UN; Political Wkr; Ski Clb; Ftbl; High Hon Roll; NHS; Ntl Merit Ltr.

KANN, MIKE; Dover HS; Spring Grove, PA; (Y); 69/240; 4-H; FFA; Band; Mrchg Band; Stage Crew; Bsbl; 4-H Awd; Hon Roll; Outstandng 4-H Mbr 85; Ag Bus.

KANON, CAROLYN; Bethel Park HS; Bethel Park, PA; (Y); FBLA; Mrchg Band; Symp Band; Psych.

KANOTZ, ROBERT; Bethel Park HS; Bethel Park, PA; (Y); Boy Scts; Church Yth Grp; FHA; Band; Concert Band; Jazz Band; Mrchg Band; School Musical; Symp Band; Bsbl; U Pittsburgh.

KANOUFF, JERRY; Moshannon Valley JR SR HS; Ginter, PA; (Y); Chess Clb; Varsity Clb; JV Var Ftbl; Comp Tech.

KANOUR, TANYA; Philipsburg-Osceola HS; Sandy Ridge, PA; (Y); 105/250; Ski Clb; Band; Concert Band; Drm Mjr(t); Yrbk Stf; Stat Bsktbl; Capt Twrlr.

KANSJORSKI, RUSSELL; John S Fine HS; Nanticoke, PA; (Y); 1/250; Model UN; Political Wkr; Nwsp Rptr; Var Ftbl; Var Trk; Pres NHS; NEDT Awd; Rep HOBY 85; Rep W Point Wrkshp 86.

KANZELMEYER, TIM; Hopewell HS; Aliquippa, PA; (S); 20/295; Art Clb; Church Yth Grp; Pres Band; Jazz Band; Var Capt Crs Cntry; Var L Swmmng; Var Trk; NHS; Computer Clb; German Clb; Center Area All Star Jazz Band 85-86; Lions Clb Boy Mnth 86; Purdue U; Engrng.

KAPALDO, RICHARD; Montour HS; Coraopolis, PA; (Y); 39/277; Letterman Clb; Spanish Clb; Varsity Clb; Socr; High Hon Roll; Hon Roll; PA ST U; Chem Engrng.

KAPEL, CINDY; Brownsville Area HS; Hiller, PA; (S); 3/240; VP Hosp Aide; Latin Clb; Library Aide; Band; Concert Band; Mrchg Band; Bowling; NHS; Rotary Stu Month 86; U Of Pittsburgh; Accntng.

KAPLEWICZ, DAVE; Cumberland Valley HS; Mechanicsburg, PA; (Y); 29/518; Cmnty Wkr; Key Clb; Latin Clb; Rep Stu Cncl; Im Sftbl; Im Tennis; Var Trk; Im Vllybl; Hon Roll; NHS; Clscs Fstvl Ltn Prjct 2nd Pl 84-85; PA ST U; Nclr Engr.

KAPOURELOS, MARIA; Bishop Shanahan HS; W Chester, PA; (Y); 34/218; Drama Clb; Nwsp Ed-Chief; Nwsp Rptr; Nwsp Stf; Yrbk Stf; Hon Roll; Prfct Atten Awd; Acad All-Amer Schlr Pgm 84; Ltn & Spnsh Awd 86; Intl Bus.

KAPP, JACK; West Scranton HS; Scranton, PA; (Y); 3/270; Church Yth Grp; Letterman Clb; Spanish Clb; Rptr Yrbk Ed-Chief; JV Bsktbl; Capt L Crs Cntry; L Trk; High Hon Roll; Jr NHS; NHS.

KAPPEL, JEFFREY; Canon-Mc Millan SR HS; Mcdonald, PA; (Y); Church Yth Grp; Spanish Clb; Trk; High Hon Roll; Spanish NHS; Elec Engrng.

KAPSHA, ELIZABETH; Serra Catholic HS; Clairton, PA; (Y); 23/127; Hosp Aide; Spanish Clb; Concert Band; Mrchg Band; Yrbk Stf; Powder Puff Ftbl; NHS; Duquesne U; Phrmcy.

KAPUSCHAK, MICHELLE; Riverside JR SR HS; Taylor, PA; (Y); 20/176; Dance Clb; FBLA; Ski Clb; Off Stu Cncl; Cheerleading; Trk; High Hon Roll; Hon Roll.

KAPUSTIN, WENDY; Lower Morelad HS; Huntingdon Valley, PA; (S); Drama Clb; FBLA; Key Clb; Science Clb; Stat Crs Cntry; Sftbl; Swmmng; Tennis; 1st Pl In FBLA Typng Rgnls 85; 3rd Pl FBLA Bus Englsh 86; Intl Rel.

KAPUSTYNSKI, KEVIN; Canon Mc Millan SR HS; Canonsburg, PA; (Y); 74/371; Boy Scts; Church Yth Grp; Pres Exploring; Science Clb; Stage Crew; L Ftbl; Var Trk; Cit Awd; Hon Roll; Ocngrphy.

KARA, HOLLY; Brownsville HS; Brownsville, PA; (Y); Sec Girl Scts; Math Clb; Office Aide; Ski Clb; SADD; Concert Band; Drill Tm; Mrchg Band; Hon Roll; Rotary Awd; Penn ST; Dntl Hygnst.

KARAGEANES, MICHELLE; Bishop Mc Cort HS; Johnstown, PA; (Y); 30/129; Hosp Aide; Library Aide; NFL; Spanish Clb; Concert Band; Jazz Band; Mrchg Band; Orch; High Hon Roll; Spanish NHS; Arion Awd 86; U Of Pittsburg-Johnstown; Bus.

KARALIS, SPIRO; Upper Darby HS; Upr Darby, PA; (Y); 193/650; Church Yth Grp; Capt Ice Hcky; Socr; Wt Lftg; Hon Roll; 9th Grd Prfct Attndnc Awd 83-84; Phrmcsts.

KARCH, MIKE; Kutztown HS; Kutztown, PA; (Y); Band; Jazz Band; Var JA; Var Trk; High Hon Roll; NHS; Opt Clb Awd; Boy Scts; Quiz Bowl; Concert Band; Band Awd 83; Optmst Ortrcl Awd 84; PA ST Cmpsrs Awd 85; Met Ed Sci Awd 86; Pre Med.

KARCHNER, BONNIE; Berwick SR HS; Nescopeck, PA; (Y); Church Yth Grp; Key Clb; Chorus; Church Choir; Hon Roll.

KARCZ, GERMAINE; Hopewell HS; Aliquippa, PA; (Y); Church Yth Grp; Dance Clb; French Clb; Pep Clb; Chorus; Stage Crew; Yrbk Stf; JV Var Cheerleading; Var Powder Puff Ftbl; L Trk; IN U Of PA; Nrsng.

KARCZ JR, JAMES W; Central HS; Martinsburg, PA; (Y); #30 In Class; Boy Scts; Hon Roll; CMPTRS.

KARDELIS, ANTHONY C; Notre Dame HS; Easton, PA; (Y); 12/73; Crs Cntry; Ftbl; Trk; Hon Roll; St Thomas Quinas Merit Schlrshp 86; Pres Acdmc Ftns Awd 86; U St Thomas; Srgn.

KARDELL, JEAN MARIE; Duquesne HS; Duquesne, PA; (Y); 1/82; Sec Concert Band; Jazz Band; VP Sr Cls; VP Stu Cncl; High Hon Roll; Sec NHS; Val; Crawford Schlrshp 86; Hugh O Brien Yth Fndtn Outstndng Soph 84; All Am Hl Fame Band Hnrs 85 & 86; U Pittsburgh; Bio.

KARDOS, DIANNA; Kiski Area HS; Vandergrift, PA; (Y); Trs Church Yth Grp; Math Clb; Office Aide; SADD; Mrchg Band; Symp Band; Yrbk Stf; High Hon Roll; Pres NHS; Vandergrift Bus & Prof Wmns Grl Mnth 85-86; PHEAA Cert Merit 85; Allegheny Coll.

KARDOSH, DEBI; Conneaut Valley HS; Conneautville, PA; (Y); 3/70; Pres Church Yth Grp; Ski Clb; Varsity Clb; VP Band; VP Mrchg Band; Pep Band; JV Var Bsktbl; JV Var Vllybl; High Hon Roll; VP NHS; Presdntl Schlrshp 86; U S Army Rsrv Schlr/Athlt Awd 86; Math Awd 86; Milligan Coll TN; Bus Adm.

KARENBAUER, MARCY ELLEN; Butler SR HS; Butler, PA; (Y); 141/777; Church Yth Grp; Exploring; JA; Office Aide; Band; Concert Band; Var Gym; Im Sftbl; Hon Roll; Pres Acad Ftns Awd 85-86; U Pittsburgh; Phrmcy.

KARGO, RAY; Portage Area HS; Portage, PA; (S); 9/122; Church Yth Grp; Varsity Clb; Var Bsbl; Var Capt Bsktbl; Var Ftbl; Wt Lftg; Hon Roll; NHS; Acad All-Amer 86; Orthodontics.

KARHAN, HEATHER; Coudersport HS; Coudersport, PA; (Y); Drama Clb; French Clb; Band; Concert Band; Mrchg Band; Pep Band; Yrbk Phtg; Yrbk Stf; L Golf; Photogrphy.

KARHOFF, MELINDA; Wissahickon HS; Blue Bell, PA; (S); 20/226; Church Yth Grp; Intnl Clb; SADD; Band; Concert Band; Mrchg Band; Nwsp Rptr; Nwsp Stf; Stat Swmmng; NHS; Psych.

KARKALLA, AMY; Bethel Park HS; Bethel Park, PA; (Y); German Clb; Office Aide; Chorus; School Musical; Swing Chorus; Pom Pon; Powder Puff Ftbl; High Hon Roll; Hon Roll; NHS; Robert Morris Coll; Bus Law.

KARLE, ALANA; Hopewell HS; Aliquippa, PA; (S); 11/265; Drama Clb; French Clb; Pres Latin Clb; Chorus; School Play; High Hon Roll; NHS; Merit Awd PA Prfssnl Engrs 84; U Of Pittsburgh; Frgn Lang.

KARLE, MARY B; Hopewell HS; Aliquippa, PA; (S); 54/245; Church Yth Grp; Drama Clb; French Clb; Hosp Aide; Chorus; School Play; Nwsp Rptr; Ed Nwsp Stf; Yrbk Stf; Crs Cntry; Jrnlsm.

KARLSKI, VALERIE; Belle Vernon Area HS; Belle Vernon, PA; (Y); 27/272; Ski Clb; Band; Concert Band; Mrchg Band; Sec Trs Frsh Cls; Powder Puff Ftbl; High Hon Roll; Pres Acadmc Fitness Awd 86; Schlrshp Hon Awd 86; Best Schlstc Ability 83; Bradford; Acctg.

KARMAZYN, LISA; Hopewell Area HS; Aliquippa, PA; (S); 31/274; Dance Clb; Chorus; Drill Tm; School Musical; Stu Cncl; Trk; High Hon Roll; NHS; Church Yth Grp; Exploring; Hnr Carrier Beaver Valley Times 86; Cert Merit Dnce 84-85; Psych.

KARN, LORINE; Danville Area HS; Danville, PA; (Y); Drama Clb; Intnl Clb; Key Clb; Latin Clb; Yrbk Stf; JV Trk; High Hon Roll; Prfct Atten Awd; Typng Awd 83; PA ST U; Bio.

KARNASH, SAMANTHA L; Hempfield Area SR HS; New Stanton, PA; (Y); 30/657; AFS; Letterman Clb; Office Aide; Pep Clb; Ski Clb; Var Cheerleading; Var L Vllybl; Jr NHS; NHS; U Of NC; Bio.

KARNAVAS, SOPHIA; Ambridge Area HS; Ambridge, PA; (Y); Trs Church Yth Grp; JA; Red Cross Aide; Sec Band; Drm Mjr(t); Stu Cncl; Var L Gym; Var L Tennis; High Hon Roll; Rotary Yth Ldrshp Confrnce 86.

KARNICK, ANDREA; Western Wayne HS; Waymart, PA; (Y); Sec FFA; Ski Clb; Chorus; Co-Capt Flag Corp; School Play; Sec Stu Cncl; Var Cheerleading; Stat Vllybl; Hon Roll; PA ST U; Spnsh.

KARNS, LISA; Penn Cambria HS; Cresson, PA; (Y); 13/164; Drama Clb; Color Guard; School Musical; School Play; Nwsp Rptr; Yrbk Sprt Ed; Yrbk Stf; Rep Stu Cncl; Var L Trk; NHS; Hgh Schlstc Achvt Awd 86; Air Frcfmed Lab Spclst.

KAROL, BRADFORD S; Moon SR HS; Coraopolis, PA; (Y); 71/304; Nwsp Stf; Yrbk Stf; Ftbl; Var L Trk; Im Vllybl; Hon Roll.

KARP, ALYSSA; Bensalem HS; Bensalem, PA; (Y); Debate Tm; Drama Clb; Temple Yth Grp; Rep Frsh Cls; Rep Soph Cls; Rep Jr Cls; Hon Roll; NHS; Psych.

KARPIN, BONNIE; Chichester HS; Boothwyn, PA; (Y); Library Aide; Office Aide; Spanish Clb; Ed Nwsp Sprt Ed; Nwsp Stf; Rptr Yrbk Sprt Ed; Yrbk Stf; Stu Cncl; West Chester U; Soc Work.

KARPUSZKA, DAVID; Gateway SR HS; Mornoeville, PA; (Y); 6/460; Cmnty Wkr; Pres VP Exploring; VP Orch; JV Im Vllybl; Bausch & Lomb Sci Awd; High Hon Roll; VP NHS; Ntl Merit Ltr; Chess Clb; Mathletes; Dayton Schlrshp 86; Math League Tm 1st ST 3rd Induvul 86; U Dayton; Elect Engr.

KARPY, ROYCE; Canon Mc Millan SR HS; Eighty Four, PA; (Y); 20/400; French Clb; Ski Clb; JV Bsktbl; JV Trk; High Hon Roll; NHS; Harvard; Med.

KARSHIN, CHRISTINE; Ferndale Area HS; Johnstown, PA; (Y); Church Yth Grp; Letterman Clb; Varsity Clb; Band; Concert Band; Jazz Band; Mrchg Band; Pep Band; Var Capt Bsktbl; Var Capt Sftbl; Schlr/Athlete Awd U S Army Rsrv 86; Outstndg SR Athlt Awd 86; Applchn Conf Awd All Star B-Bll 85-86; Edinboro U; Health.

KARTESZ, KRISTA; Rockwood Area HS; Rockwood, PA; (S); 9/95; JA; Spanish Clb; Chorus; Stu Cncl; Cheerleading; High Hon Roll; NHS; IN U.

KARUZIE, LISA; Old Forge HS; Old Forge, PA; (Y); Ski Clb; Trs Jr Cls; Trs Sr Cls; Var Cheerleading; Hon Roll; Psych.

KARWASKI, MAUREEN; Bishop Hannan HS; Moosic, PA; (Y); 16/126; Im NHS; Marywood Coll; Accntnt.

KARWOWSKI, ED; Northwestern HS; E Springfield, PA; (Y); 13/101; Boy Scts; Computer Clb; SADD; Chorus; Rep Stu Cncl; Bsbl; Bsktbl; High Hon Roll; Hon Roll; Prfct Atten Awd; Outstndng Choral 84; Edinboro ST Coll; Polc Offcr.

KARYCKI, JOHN; Mt Carmel Area JR SR HS; Mt Carmel, PA; (Y); Letterman Clb; Varsity Clb; Var Bsbl; JV Bsktbl; Var Ftbl; Wt Lftg; Acctg.

KASANICKY, STEPHANIE; Ford City HS; Ford City, PA; (Y); 35/153; Chorus; Pres Frsh Cls; Rep Soph Cls; Rep Jr Cls; VP Sr Cls; Rep Stu Cncl; L Sftbl; JV Var Vllybl; Hon Roll; NHS; Fshn Mrchndsng.

KASARDA, JANENE; Lake Lehman HS; Harveys Lake, PA; (S); 78/142; Art Clb; Key Clb; Ski Clb; Band; Chorus; Jazz Band; School Play; L Bsktbl; L Fld Hcky; Hon Roll; Kings Coll; Art.

KASARDA, STEPHEN; Biship Hafey HS; Hazleton, PA; (Y); 44/141; Aud/Vis; VP Chess Clb; Church Yth Grp; Teachers Aide; Varsity Clb; Concert Band; Orch; Var JV Bsktbl; Var Tennis; Hon Roll; Nrsng.

KASCHALK, LEIGH; Conemaugh Townshp HS; Davidsville, PA; (Y); 14/108; Drama Clb; JA; Pep Clb; Orch; School Musical; School Play; Cheerleading; Hagerstwn Bus Coll; Secrtry.

KASE, TERRI; Shikellamy HS; Northumberland, PA; (Y); Chorus; Color Guard; Mrchg Band; Stu Cncl; Cheerleading; Tennis.

KASECKY, JENNIFER; Kiski Area SR HS; Lower Burrell, PA; (Y); Girl Scts; VP JA; Band; Chorus; Concert Band; Symp Band; Yrbk Stf; Hon Roll.

KASHATUS, LYNNE; John S Fine HS; Glen Lyon, PA; (Y); Cmnty Wkr; Yrbk Stf; Rep Jr Cls; Rep Sr Cls; L Mgr(s); L Trk; Vllybl; Hon Roll; NHS; Unsung Hero Trck Awd 85-86; Phy Thrpy.

KASHNICKI, LOU; John S Fne HS; Nanticoke, PA; (Y); 56/251; Var Swmmng; Hon Roll; Certs Proficncy Bus Math, Bookkpng-Accntg & Typng 85-86.

KASHULA, JACQUELINE; Crestwood HS; Mountaintop, PA; (Y); Pres Key Clb; Red Cross Aide; Yrbk Stf; Rep Stu Cncl; Hon Roll; Gannon U Erie PA; Mech Engrng.

KASIC, ANDREW; Yough SR HS; W Newton, PA; (Y); 19/274; Computer Clb; Nwsp Sprt Ed; Stu Cncl; Bsktbl; High Hon Roll; NHS; Intrmed Stu Forum Rep 85-87; All Dist Bsktbl 85-86.

KASKIN, JENNIFER; Clairton HS; Clairton, PA; (Y); Red Cross Aide; High Hon Roll; Hon Roll; NHS; Hlth Occptns Stu Of Amer 84-86; Wilma Boyd Schl; Trvl.

KASPAREK, ANNETTE; Freeport Area HS; Freeport, PA; (Y); Church Yth Grp; Dance Clb; Drama Clb; Church Choir; Stat Bsktbl; Mgr Cheerleading; Hon Roll; Trs NHS; Stu Mnth 85; Cum Laude 86; U Pittsburgh; Bio.

KASPER, MELANIE; Bald Eagle Area HS; Milesburg, PA; (Y); 4-H; French Clb; Varsity Clb; Band; Chorus; Yrbk Stf; Rep Soph Cls; VP Jr Cls; Rep Stu Cncl; Var Crs Cntry.

KASPICK, KIMBERLY; Philipsburg-Osceola Area HS; Philipsburg, PA; (Y); 19/217; Church Yth Grp; FCA; Thesps; Band; Chorus; School Musical; School Play; Trs Frsh Cls; Rep Stu Cncl; Var Cheerleading; Centre Cntys JR Miss Pagnt 85; Yng Writers Awd 85; U Pittsburgh; Biol.

KASPUTIS, MARY LYNN; Seneca Valley SR HS; Evans City, PA; (Y); 56/369; JA; Drm Mjr(t); Pep Band; Stage Crew; Nwsp Rptr; Nwsp Stf; Yrbk Ed-Chief; Yrbk Rptr; Yrbk Stf; Twrlr; Mst Outstndng Majrtt 85-86; Educ.

KASSEL, KATHY; Phoenixville Area HS; Phoenixville, PA; (Y); Church Yth Grp; Sec SADD; Varsity Clb; Band; Chorus; Pres Soph Cls; Var L Lcrss; Var L Tennis; DAR Awd; NHS; Dist/Reg Choir 84.

KAST, BETHANN; Parkland HS; Allentown, PA; (Y); 125/485; 4-H; Stu Cncl; Var Diving; 4-H Awd; Hon Roll; W Chester U; Pre-Med.

KASUBA, DIANE; Bishop Hannan HS; Scranton, PA; (Y); 1/128; Capt Debate Tm; Capt Scholastic Bowl; Science Clb; Speech Tm; Chorus; Ed Yrbk Ed-Chief; Bausch & Lomb Sci Awd; High Hon Roll; NHS; Val; Cecilia S Cohen Awd 86; ST & Natl Debate Awds 86; Schlr Of Yr Awd 86; U Of Scanton; Chmstry.

KASUMI, TATSUO; Emmaus HS; Allentown, PA; (Y); Model UN; Band; Concert Band; Jazz Band; School Musical; JV Var Socr; Var Tennis; High Hon Roll; Hon Roll; NHS; Cheonkido Martial Arts 83-86; Natl Hstry Day 2nd Pl Dist, 2nd Pl ST 84; Philosphy.

KASUN, PAIGE; Mc Caskey HS; Lancaster, PA; (Y); AFS; Hosp Aide; Band; Nwsp Rptr; Yrbk Stf; Cheerleading; Trk; Hon Roll; Cmnty Wkr; Chorus; Stu Ambsdr 85-86; Amer U; Jrnlsm.

KASZYNSKI, KYRA; Emmaus HS; Macungie, PA; (Y); Church Yth Grp; French Clb; Key Clb; JV Var Bsktbl; JV Var Fld Hcky; NHS; Certfd ASTAN Ski Instrctr 86; Sec Of Safe Rides 86-87; Engrng.

KATEKOVICH, KATHLEEN; Beaver Area HS; Beaver, PA; (Y); Church Yth Grp; French Clb; VP JA; Key Clb; Pep Clb; Ski Clb; Spanish Clb; Nwsp Ed-Chief; Powder Puff Ftbl; Hon Roll; NC ST U; Prsnl Mngmnt.

KATEKOVICH, MICHELLE L; Freedom Area SR HS; Freedom, PA; (Y); Camera Clb; Pres DECA; Pep Clb; Spanish Clb; SADD; Chorus; Yrbk Ed-Chief; Trk; Wt Lftg; High Hon Roll; DECA & Dstrbtve Ed Acadmcs Awd 86; World Cltrs Acadmc Awd 85; Acadmc High Hnrs Awd 84; PA ST U; Engl.

KATHARY, TINA; Center HS; Monaca, PA; (Y); German Clb; Office Aide; SADD; Band; Concert Band; Mrchg Band; Stu Cncl; Im Bowling; Im Trk; Hon Roll; Pittsburgh Schl Of Arts; Merch.

KATSOCK, JOCELYN; Pennsbury HS; Yardley, PA; (Y); Ski Clb; Var Capt Bsktbl; L Cheerleading; Im Gym; Var L Socr; L Sftbl; Var L Trk; Hon Roll; Rotary Awd; All Cty Goldne Twelve Soccer 85-86; Hon Ment Bsktbl 85-86.

KATSULERIS, KELLY; Ringgold HS; Monongahela, PA; (Y); Drama Clb; Pep Clb; Varsity Clb; Chorus; Variety Show; Nwsp Rptr; Nwsp Stf; Yrbk Rptr; Yrbk Stf; Rep Stu Cncl; Hotel Mgmt.

KATZ, DARIN; George Washington HS; Philadelphia, PA; (Y); 3/769; Cmnty Wkr; Drama Clb; Mathletes; Science Clb; Spanish Clb; SADD; Temple Yth Grp; Chorus; School Musical; School Play; Penn ST Teas Schlrshp Awde 86; 3rd Awd Intrntl Sci Fair 85; Prfct Scrs PA JR Acad Sci 81-85; Penn ST; Chem.

KATZ, ERIC; Neshaminy HS; Langhorne, PA; (Y); 39/705; Boy Scts; Teachers Aide; Trk; Hon Roll; NHS; Outstndng Stu 84; Drexel U; Comp Sci.

KATZ, JASON; Mt Lebanon HS; Pittsburgh, PA; (Y); Chess Clb; Latin Clb; Orch; School Musical; JV Ice Hcky; JV Trk; Hon Roll; Orchstr Lttr; Accntng.

KATZENBACH, NICOLE; Pottstown SR HS; Pottstown, PA; (S); 14/237; FNA; Spanish Clb; Concert Band; Mrchg Band; Cheerleading; High Hon Roll; Hon Roll; NHS; Dance Clb; Band; Anchor Clb 85; Cls Cabinet 85; Reading Area CC; Physcns Asst.

KAUCHER, JOSEPH; Central Catholic HS; Reading, PA; (Y); German Clb; Office Aide; Trk; Hon Roll; Prfct Atten Awd.

KAUFFMAN, AMANDA; Lewiston Area HS; Lewistown, PA; (Y); Pres Church Yth Grp; French Clb; Church Choir; Nwsp Rptr; Hon Roll; Ntl Merit Ltr; 4-H; German Clb; Service Clb; Ski Clb; Schlrshp PA Free Entrprs Wk 85; Hnrbl Mntn, Poetry, Cntrl PA Fstvl Of Arts 86; Accntng.

KAUFFMAN, BRENT; Susquentia HS; Duncannon, PA; (Y); Crs Cntry; Ftbl; Sftbl; Trk; Vllybl; Wt Lftg; Wrstlng; Bus Adm.

KAUFFMAN, JOANN; Newport HS; Newport, PA; (Y); GAA; Office Aide; Varsity Clb; JV Var Bsktbl; Stat Fld Hcky; JV Var Sftbl; Hon Roll; Soc Wrk.

KAUFFMAN, LEAH; The Oakland Schl; Pittsburgh, PA; (S); Cmnty Wkr; School Play; Ed Yrbk Ed-Chief; Ed Lit Mag; Rep Sr Cls; Librl Arts.

KAUFFMAN, MELANIE; Wilmington Area HS; Volant, PA; (Y); 27/122; Nwsp Ed-Chief; Stat Bsktbl; Stat Trk; Engl.

KAUFFMAN, MICHAEL W; Octonava Area HS; Parksburg, PA; (Y); 56/170; Church Yth Grp; Drama Clb; SADD; Chorus; School Musical; Nwsp Rptr; Var Golf; Var Socr; Var Tennis; Hon Roll; TN Temple U.

KAUFFMAN, MICHELLE; Christian Schl Of York; York, PA; (Y); Teachers Aide; Chorus; School Play; Capt Cheerleading; Hon Roll; Church Choir; Nyack Coll; Elem Ed.

KAUFFMAN, PAMELA ANN; Red Lion Area SR HS; Red Lion, PA; (Y); 1/330; Am Leg Aux Girls St; Sec Church Yth Grp; Drm Mjr(t); Symp Band; Nwsp Stf; Trs Jr Cls; VP Sr Cls; Rep Stu Cncl; NHS; Concert Band; Modern Music Masters Hnr Soc Pres 86; Amer Chem Soc Cert Of Merit 86.

KAUFFMAN, STEPHANIE; Ephrata SR HS; Ephrata, PA; (Y); 41/259; Pep Clb; JV Var Cheerleading; Powder Puff Ftbl; Hon Roll; Csmtlgy.

KAUFFMAN, SUE; Brandywine Heights HS; Mertztown, PA; (Y); Art Clb; Church Yth Grp; Girl Scts; Color Guard; Mrchg Band; Stu Cncl; Hon Roll; Pep Clb; Band; Art.

KAUFFMAN, TODD; Fort Le Boeuf HS; Waterford, PA; (Y); Computer Clb; 4-H; Ftbl; Comp Sci.

KAUFKI, ALICE ELIZABETH; Roxborough HS; Philadelphia, PA; (Y); GAA; Chorus; School Musical; Nwsp Ed-Chief; Nwsp Stf; Rep Stu Cncl; Var Tennis; Twrlr; Engl.

KAUFMAN, CRYSTAL; Cardinal O Hara HS; Chester, PA; (Y); Office Aide; Chorus; Yrbk Stf; Trk; Cngrssmans Mdl Of Merit Awd 86; Alumni Lylty Awd 86; Poli Sci.

KAUFMAN, MATTHEW; York County Vo-Tech Schl; York, PA; (Y); VICA; Machine Shp.

KAUFMAN, MICHAEL; Conrad Weiser HS; Wernersville, PA; (Y); #25 In Class; Drama Clb; Band; Chorus; Jazz Band; Mrchg Band; School Musical; Socr; Wt Lftg; Hon Roll; Rotary Awd; Juniata Coll; Accntng.

KAUFMAN, TOM; Shenango JR SR HS; New Castle, PA; (Y); Boy Scts; Camera Clb; Church Yth Grp; Computer Clb; Pres 4-H; French Clb; Pep Clb; Band; Mrchg Band; Pep Band; Acctng.

KAUFMANN, PAUL; St John Neumann HS; Philadelphia, PA; (Y); 20/368; Computer Clb; Debate Tm; French Clb; Latin Clb; High Hon Roll; Hon Roll; NHS; Acclrtd-Hnrs Course 83-86; Templ U; Jrnlsm.

KAVALAUSKAS, MARK; St John Neumann HS; Philadelphia, PA; (Y); 20/338; Computer Clb; Letterman Clb; Math Clb; Var Bsbl; JV Var Bsktbl; Hon Roll; NHS; Bus Adm.

KAVANAGH, KATHLEEN; Trinity HS; Mechanicsburg, PA; (Y); Hosp Aide; Pep Clb; Ski Clb; Spanish Clb; Band; Mrchg Band; School Play; Stage Crew; Nwsp Stf; Bus.

KAVCAK, MICHAEL; Nazareth Area SR HS; Nazareth, PA; (Y); 6/231; Chess Clb; Computer Clb; Math Tm; Stage Crew; JV Bsbl; Var Tennis; High Hon Roll; Hon Roll; NHS; Trphy Chss Trnmnt 84; Lttr Tnns 86; Nzrth Wmns Clb Schlrhsp 86; PA ST U; Comp Engnrng.

KAVELINES, PATRICIA; Scranton Technical HS; Scranton, PA; (Y); Computer Clb; JA; Pep Clb; SADD; VICA; Yrbk Stf; Pres Frsh Cls; VP Soph Cls; Rep Jr Cls; Rep Stu Cncl; Food Mngmt Outstndng Achvt Awd 86; Cert Of Cmmndtn-Svc Behlf Of IL 86; Food Mngmt.

KAVULA, KEITH; Pleasant Valley HS; Kunkletown, PA; (Y); Church Yth Grp; Cmnty Wkr; Math Clb; Ski Clb; Church Choir; Jazz Band; Nwsp Rptr; Lit Mag; Rep Jr Cls; Stu Cncl; Altrnt Gvrn Schl 86; Fnlst Cafferata Jackson Mem Comp 86; Suprr Ntl Fed Music Clb Awd 84-86; Prfrmng Arts.

KAWA, CATHY; Bishop Neumann HS; Williamsport, PA; (Y); 13/45; Church Yth Grp; Cmnty Wkr; Chorus; Church Choir; School Musical; Yrbk Stf; Bsktbl; Hon Roll; Pres Schlr; Chrstn Witness Awd 84; Stu Of Mnth 84; Chem Olympd Awd 85; Marywood Coll; Voice.

KAWALEC, ANASTASIA; Notre Dame HS; E Stroudsburg, PA; (Y); School Musical; Yrbk Stf; VP Frsh Cls; VP Soph Cls; VP Sr Cls; French Clb; Nwsp Rptr; Stat Bsbl; Var Cheerleading; Hon Roll; Discpln Bd 85-86; Pocono Mountains JR Miss 85-86; Nov Stu Of Mnth 86; Point Park Coll; Danc.

KAY, SANDRA; Laurel Valley HS; New Florence, PA; (Y); 8/87; AFS; Band; Chorus; Concert Band; Mrchg Band; Trs Frsh Cls; Trs Soph Cls; Trs Jr Cls; Powder Puff Ftbl; Hon Roll; IN U Of PA; Nrsng.

KAYAFAS, KRISTEN; Springdale HS; Harwick, PA; (Y); 20/144; Debate Tm; Sec Trs Drama Clb; VP Spanish Clb; Acpl Chr; Sec Jr Cls; Stat Ftbl; High Hon Roll; Lion Awd; NHS; Church Yth Grp; GATE Prgrm ; Our Ldy Vctry Chrch Schlrshp Awd; Alleghny-Kiski Vly Jr Ms Finlst 86; PA ST U.

KAYLOR, TODD; Grace Christian Schl; Lebanon, PA; (Y); Drama Clb; Spanish Clb; Chorus; School Musical; Bsbl; Bsktbl; Socr; Sftbl; Distngshd Chrstn HS Stu 85-86; Elctrcl Engrng.

KAZEE, BILL; Waynesburg Central HS; Waynesburg, PA; (Y); Boy Scts; Camera Clb; Chess Clb; Exploring; French Clb; Hosp Aide; Am Leg Boys St; Im Fld Hcky; Var Socr; High Hon Roll; WV U; Advrtsng.

KAZMER, DIANE; Ford City HS; Ford City, PA; (Y); 42/149; Chorus; Drm Mjr(t); Rep Jr Cls; Rep Sr Cls; Var L Bsktbl; Var L Sftbl; Var L Vllybl; High Hon Roll; Lion Awd; NHS; Bradfrod Schl Of Bus; Exct Secy.

KAZMERSKI, PATRICIA; Our Lady Of Lourdes Regional HS; Shamokin, PA; (Y); 25/94; VP Civic Clb; Drama Clb; Capt Pep Clb; Spanish Clb; SADD; Chorus; Nwsp Ed-Chief; Nwsp Stf; Hon Roll; Radio Sta Essay Contest 2nd Pl 86; Kings Coll Discovery Pgm Schlrshp 86; Engrng.

KAZMIERCZAK JR, THOMAS E; South Park HS; Library, PA; (Y); 39/219; Ski Clb; Nwsp Ed-Chief; Nwsp Rptr; Nwsp Stf; VP Soph Cls; Pres Jr Cls; Pres Stu Cncl; Yrbk Stf; Hon Roll; Svc Awd 85-86; Prncpls Awd 85-86; Outstndng Stu Yr 84-85.

KCEHOWSKI, TIM; Monaca HS; Monaca, PA; (Y); Am Leg Boys St; Computer Clb; Off Sr Cls; Bsbl; Bsktbl; Golf; Wt Lftg; Hon Roll; Comps Clb 85-86; Comp.

KEAGLE, KRISTAN; North Allegheny HS; Pittsburgh, PA; (Y); Church Yth Grp; Chorus; Church Choir; Stu Cncl; Fld Hcky; Socr; Hon Roll; Position-Western Penn Fld Hockey All Stars & Keystone Fld Hockey Tm 84-85; IN U; Jorunlsm.

KEAGY, KIRSTIN L; Penn Manor HS; Lancaster, PA; (Y); 11/301; Trs Varsity Clb; Co-Capt Bsktbl; Fld Hcky; Co-Capt Trk; DAR Awd; Hon Roll; Lion Awd; Trs NHS; Pres Schlr; Pres Spanish NHS; Educ Assn Schlrhsp 86; U PA; Bio-Chem.

KEAN, MARY BETH; Cardinal O Hara HS; Drexel Hill, PA; (Y); 5/790; Church Yth Grp; Mathletes; Service Clb; Concert Band; Mrchg Band; School Musical; Nwsp Stf; Var Bsktbl; High Hon Roll; NHS; Latn Achvt Awd Philadlph Clsscl Socty 84; 1st Pl Awd DE Cnty Sci Fair 86; Acadmc Convoctn Awd 85-86; Arch Engrng.

KEANE, ANDY; Lincoln HS; Ellwood City, PA; (Y); 36/180; Art Clb; Church Yth Grp; German Clb; Chorus; Church Choir; School Musical; Swing Chorus.

KEANE, KEVIN; Bishop Mc Devitt HS; Harrisburg, PA; (S); 15/203; Q&S; Service Clb; Chorus; School Musical; School Play; Nwsp Phtg; Nwsp Sprt Ed; Yrbk Phtg; Rotary Awd; Cornell U; Vet.

KEANE, THOMAS W; Lincoln HS; Ellwood City, PA; (Y); 4/167; Sec Trs Church Yth Grp; Latin Clb; Chorus; School Musical; Bsktbl; Var Tennis; Bausch & Lomb Sci Awd; High Hon Roll; Lion Awd; NHS; St Agatha Chrch Scl Clb Schlrshp 86; Top 10 Of SR Cls 86; Dstrct & Rgnl Choruses 86; Crng-Mln U; Chem Engrng.

KEAR, KRISTEN; Liberty HS; Bethlehem, PA; (Y); 90/475; Church Yth Grp; Cmnty Wkr; French Clb; Chorus; Church Choir; School Play; Nwsp Rptr; Nwsp Stf; Ed Lit Mag; Trk; Jrnlsm.

KEAR, PATRICIA; St Marys Area HS; Saint Marys, PA; (Y); 13/300; Stat Gym; L JV Vllybl; High Hon Roll; NHS; Yth Ldrshp Ovr Excllnc 86; Phrmcy.

KEAR, TIM; Plum SR HS; Pittsburgh, PA; (Y); Pittsburgh; Comp.

KEARNEY, LISA; Geibel HS; Mount Pleasant, PA; (Y); Drama Clb; Pep Clb; Ski Clb; SADD; School Musical; Stage Crew; Yrbk Ed-Chief; Yrbk Stf; VP Sr Cls; French Hon Soc; Yrbk Awd; Hnr Chord; US Stu Cncl Awd; Boston Coll; Acctng.

KEARNS, CHRISTA; Chief Logan HS; Mcclure, PA; (Y); 46/194; Soroptimist; Spanish Clb; Yrbk Stf; Off Soph Cls; South Hills Bus Schl; Acctg.

KEARNS, GARY; Central SR HS; Emigsville, PA; (Y); 53/261; Pres Church Yth Grp; Band; Mrchg Band; Orch; School Musical; Symp Band; Var Trk; JV Wrstlng; High Hon Roll; Outstndng Bndsmn & Soloist 86; Shippensburg U; Accntng.

KEARNS, JENNIFER; Merion Mercy Acad; Drevel Hill, PA; (Y); 7/75; Church Yth Grp; Science Clb; Service Clb; Spanish Clb; Var Cheerleading; High Hon Roll; NEDT Awd; Spanish NHS; 2nd Pl Ntl Spnsh Cntst AATSP 84; 3rd Pl Ntl Spnsh Cntst AATSP 85.

KEARNS, NATALIE LOUISE; Riverview HS; Oakmont, PA; (Y); 15/99; Drama Clb; Key Clb; Chorus; School Play; High Hon Roll; Hon Roll; NHS; Hnrs Schrlshp Clarion U 86-87; Clarion U; Acctng.

KEATING, ANNMARIE M; Lancaster Catholic HS; Lancaster, PA; (Y); 11/224; Hosp Aide; Pep Clb; Service Clb; Varsity Clb; Nwsp Sprt Ed; Yrbk Stf; Var L Cheerleading; High Hon Roll; NHS; Pres Schlr; 2nd Cnty Hist Day Fair 85; Pres Acadmc Ftns Awd 86; Villanova U; Nrsg.

KEATING, CHRISTINE A; Bishop Shanahan HS; West Chester, PA; (Y); 36/214; Art Clb; Cmnty Wkr; Debate Tm; Nwsp Stf; Hon Roll; NHS; Prfct Atten Awd; Prfct Atten Awd 4 Yrs 82-86; Hon Rl 82-86; West Chester U; Bus.

KEATING, JAMES ALAN; Penn-Trafford HS; Level Green, PA; (Y); 22/362; Chess Clb; JCL; Latin Clb; High Hon Roll; NHS; St Vincent Coll; Bio.

KEAVENEY, KAREN; Lebanon Catholic HS; Hershey, PA; (Y); Library Aide; Ski Clb; Spanish Clb; Chorus; Ed Yrbk Stf; Hon Roll; NHS; Bus Adm.

KEBBERLY, MICHELE L; Uniontown Area SR HS; Chalk Hill, PA; (Y); FNA; Office Aide; Spanish Clb; SADD; Teachers Aide; DAR Awd; High Hon Roll; Jr NHS; Prfct Atten Awd; Spanish NHS; Art & Design.

KECER, TAMMY HUTCHINSON; Corry Area HS; Columbus, PA; (Y); 40/190; Exploring; Color Guard; V E & Betty Phillips Schlrshp 86; U Pittsburgh; Phrmcy.

KECK, CHRISTINE; Columbia HS; Columbia, PA; (Y); 1/82; Cmnty Wkr; Band; Pres Sr Cls; Sec Stu Cncl; Capt Gym; Bausch & Lomb Sci Awd; High Hon Roll; NHS; Ntl Merit Ltr; Val; Tufts U; Mth.

KECK, JANINE; Owen J Roberts HS; Pottstown, PA; (S); 10/267; Church Choir; School Play; High Hon Roll; NHS; Natl Ldrshp Awd; Frnch.

KEEBLER, MARTY; St Marys Area HS; Kersey, PA; (Y); JV L Crs Cntry; JV Wrstlng.

KEEFER, DAVID; Southmoreland HS; Mt Pleasant, PA; (Y); Church Yth Grp; Latin Clb; Letterman Clb; Ski Clb; Spanish Clb; Varsity Clb; Pres Frsh Cls; Rep Stu Cncl; Bsbl; Bsktbl.

KEEFER, JOANNE; Upper Dublin HS; Dresher, PA; (Y); Church Yth Grp; Teachers Aide; Church Choir; JV Cheerleading.

KEEFER, LAUREEN L; North Allegheny HS; Allison Pk, PA; (Y); 28/630; Pres AFS; Hosp Aide; VP Sec JA; Teachers Aide; Yrbk Rptr; High Hon Roll; Jr NHS; NHS; Pres Schlr; Distngshd Achvt Awd Frnch 5 86; U MI; Pol Sci.

KEEFER, LEONA; Dover Area HS; Dover, PA; (Y); Church Yth Grp; Band; Chorus; Church Choir; Var L Mgr(s); Var Score Keeper; Im Socr; Stat Vllybl; High Hon Roll; NHS; Hnr-Awd Teen Tlnt Cntst 86; Vol Hnr Chldrns Aid Soc, Vol Brethren Home 83-86.

KEEFER, SANDRA; Palmyra Area HS; Palmyra, PA; (Y); 11/200; Church Yth Grp; Teachers Aide; High Hon Roll; NHS; Stu Of Mnth 83-84; Lancaster Hops Sch Nrsg; Chld C.

KEEFER, TRACY; Southmoreland HS; Tarrs, PA; (Y); Pep Clb; Spanish Clb; Capt Drill Tm; Yrbk Stf; Var Capt Bsktbl; Powder Puff Ftbl; Sftbl; Capt Twrlr; Trs Spanish NHS; Stu Of Mnth Aprl; Ntl Schlr Athlt Awd; IN U Of PA.

KEEFER, WILLIAM; Connellsville Arew SR HS; S Connellsville, PA; (Y); Var L Bsbl; Var L Wrstlng; Hon Roll; Acctng.

KEELER, SANDY; Owen J Roberts HS; Pottstown, PA; (Y); 103/270; French Clb; Letterman Clb; School Musical; Rep Jr Cls; Stu Cncl; Capt Cheerleading; Vllybl; Physcl Thrpy.

KEEN, AMY; Western Wayne HS; Waymart, PA; (Y); 8/138; Church Yth Grp; Drama Clb; Chorus; Rep Sr Cls; Capt Bsktbl; L Sftbl; Tennis; Vllybl; High Hon Roll; NHS.

KEEN, DENNY; Central Dauphin HS; Harrisburg, PA; (Y); 140/337; Boy Scts; Exploring; Yrbk Stf; Hon Roll; Eagle Sct 83; Kutztown U; Envrnmntl Sci.

KEEN, VANESSA; Lock Haven SR HS; Lock Haven, PA; (Y); Twrlr; Scrtry.

KEENAN, EMMETT; North East Catholic H S For Boys; Philadelphia, PA; (Y); 31/362; Nwsp Rptr; Nwsp Sprt Ed; Nwsp Stf; NHS; Bus Admn.

KEENAN, MAURA; Cardinal Dougherty HS; Phila, PA; (Y); 23/747; Nwsp Stf; Yrbk Stf; Frsh Cls; Soph Cls; Jr Cls; Sr Cls; Stu Cncl; Fld Hcky; Mgr(s); Score Keeper; Drexel U; Persnnl Rel.

KEENAN, NICOLE; Punxsutawney Area HS; Hamilton, PA; (Y); 18/238; Church Yth Grp; French Clb; Math Tm; Band; Concert Band; Mrchg Band; Pep Band; Hon Roll; NHS; Ntl Hnr Soc Schlstc Quz Tm 85-86; IN U PA; Chem.

KEENE, CHRIS; Fort Leboeuf HS; Erie, PA; (Y); 10/180; Model UN; Rep Stu Cncl; Var Capt Wrstlng; High Hon Roll; Crmnl Law.

KEENER, JANELL; Cedar Crest HS; Cornwall, PA; (Y); Art Clb; Pep Clb; Spanish Clb; Hon Roll; Mc Keesport; Chem Engr.

KEENER, KELLY; Elizabethtown Area HS; Elizabethtown, PA; (Y); German Clb; Teachers Aide; VP Jr Cls; Fld Hcky; Trk; Wt Lftg; German Clb; Teachers Aide; Powder Puff Ftbl; Capt Fld Hcky; Mst Imprvd Trck Awd 85-86; Bloomsburg; Occptnl Thrpy.

KEENER, KENNETH; Northeast Catholic HS; Philadelphia, PA; (S); 11/372; Science Clb; Band; Concert Band; Jazz Band; Mrchg Band; Pep Band; NHS; U Of PA; Bio.

KEENER, RICHARD; Chartiers Houston HS; Warren, PA; (Y); Chess Clb; Church Yth Grp; Drama Clb; FTA; Acpl Chr; Band; Chorus; Church Choir; Concert Band; Madrigals; Egan Schlrshp; Mercy Hurst; Eng Tchr.

KEENER, ROBERT; Donegal HS; Mt Joy, PA; (Y); 17/165; Church Yth Grp; Spanish Clb; Trs Chorus; Yrbk Bus Mgr; Rep Frsh Cls; Rep Stu Cncl; JV Bsbl; Hon Roll; Spanish NHS; Pre-Med.

KEENER, SCOTT; Waynesburg Central HS; Waynesburg, PA; (Y); French Clb; Ski Clb; Band; Concert Band; Jazz Band; Mrchg Band; Socr; Trk; Wrstlng; Penn ST; Engrng.

KEENEY, JANYCE LYNN; Chartiers Valley HS; Heidelberg, PA; (Y); 32/343; Pep Clb; Ski Clb; Varsity Clb; Sftbl; Swmmng; NHS; MI ST U; Vtrnry Med.

KEENEY, YVONNE; Central York SR HS; York, PA; (Y); 3/215; VP Church Yth Grp; Hosp Aide; Drill Tm; L Stat Bsktbl; High Hon Roll; NHS; Opt Clb Awd; Sci Olympiad; Acadmc Ltr & Bar; PSYCH.

KEETON, KIMBERLY; Seneca Valley HS; Harmony, PA; (Y); 2/352; Sec Thesps; Jazz Band; Madrigals; Mrchg Band; School Musical; Yrbk Ed-Chief; Rep Stu Cncl; High Hon Roll; NHS; SADD; Westminster Coll Hnrs Band, Chorus 85-86; PMEA Dist V, Rgn I Bands 86; PA Math Leag Cntst Cert Merit; Engr.

KEEVILL, DAWN; Upper Marby HS; Clifton Hts, PA; (Y); Church Yth Grp; Drama Clb; Hosp Aide; School Musical; Yrbk Rptr; Rep Stu Cncl; Var Mgr(s); Vllybl; Hon Roll; Prfct Atten Awd; Ursinus Coll; Secnd Ed.

KEFALOGIANNIS, CHRISTINE; Churchill HS; Pittsburgh, PA; (Y); 50/188; Church Yth Grp; French Clb; Ski Clb; Yrbk Stf; JV Var Bsktbl; Trk; Var Capt Vllybl; High Hon Roll; Hon Roll.

KEFFER, DARLENE; Mary Fuller Frazier HS; Wickhaven, PA; (Y); Trs FHA; VICA; JV Capt Vllybl; 3rd Pl Bronze Mdl Cake Deco Comptn 86; Dir List Food Svc 86; Catering.

KEFFER, KRISTY; Belle Vernon Area HS; Fayette City, PA; (Y); 77/272; Band; Symp Band; Yrbk Rptr; Yrbk Stf; Powder Puff Ftbl; Twrlr; Prfct Atten Awd; Art Clb; Pep Clb; Concert Band; CA U Of PA; Elem Edu.

KEFFER, MARY ANNE; York Catholic HS; York, PA; (Y); FBLA; Pep Clb; Spanish Clb; Teachers Aide; Stu Cncl; Var JV Cheerleading; High Hon Roll; Hon Roll; NHS; Scndry Educ.

KEGARISE, KEVIN; Manheim Central HS; Manheim, PA; (Y); Church Yth Grp; Var L Bsktbl; Var L Ftbl; Var L Trk; Im Wt Lftg; Hon Roll; Ftns Awd 84; Indl Engrng.

KEGERISE, KEVIN; Conrad Weiser HS; Womelsdorf, PA; (Y); Aud/Vis; Church Yth Grp; Drama Clb; JCL; Latin Clb; Band; Chorus; Church Choir; Concert Band; Drm & Bgl; ST Champnshp Trumpet Solo Indpendnce Div 85; Brass Secntl Ldr Band 86; TV Pgm Prod/Edit 86-87; West Chester ST Coll; Arts.

KEHL, DAWN; Brandywine Heights Area HS; Mertztown, PA; (Y); Camp Fr Inc; Church Yth Grp; FBLA; Hosp Aide; Pep Clb; Chorus; Church Choir; Yrbk Bus Mgr; Hon Roll; Prfct Atten Awd; Kutztown U Of PA; Accntng.

KEHLER, DARIN; Tri-Valley HS; Valleyview, PA; (Y); 1/77; Church Yth Grp; Quiz Bowl; Ski Clb; Concert Band; Jazz Band; Pres Jr Cls; L Bsbl; Capt Ftbl; High Hon Roll; NHS; Elec Engrng.

KEHLER, MICHAEL T; Wilson Area HS; Easton, PA; (Y); VICA; Band; Concert Band; Mrchg Band; Pep Band; Wt Lftg; Hon Roll; Moravian Coll Dstrct Bnd 84; HS Dstrct Bnd 85; Zeswits Mscnshp Awd & Elctrncs Tech Achvt Awd 86; PA ST U Hzltn; Elec Engrng.

KEIDERLING, HEATHER; Pittston Area HS; Hughestown, PA; (Y); Drama Clb; Key Clb; Science Clb; Ski Clb; Score Keeper; Tennis; Vllybl; Hon Roll; Psychology.

KEIFER, JENNIFER; Bensalem SR HS; Bensalem, PA; (Y); Key Clb; Color Guard; Mrchg Band; Stu Cncl; Score Keeper; Bus Admin.

KEIFFER, JEFF; Northwestern Lehigh HS; New Tripoli, PA; (Y); 13/160; Boy Scts; Church Yth Grp; German Clb; Nwsp Rptr; Yrbk Phtg; Yrbk Stf; Stu Cncl; Var Bsktbl; Var Ftbl; Im Socr.

KEIL, JENNIFER; Oil City SR HS; Oil City, PA; (Y); 60/252; German Clb; Varsity Clb; Acpl Chr; Chorus; Capt Drill Tm; Mrchg Band; School Musical; Rep Stu Cncl; Trk; Hon Roll; Gannon U; Socl Wrk.

KEIM, BRADLEY; Somerset Area SR HS; Somerset, PA; (Y); Aud/Vis; English Clb; Yrbk Stf; Tennis; Pre-Med.

KEIM, DAVID M; Penn Hills SR HS; Pittsburgh, PA; (Y); 1/797; Church Yth Grp; Church Choir; Orch; School Musical; Nwsp Ed-Chief; Yrbk Stf; NCTE Awd; NHS; Val; Spanish Clb; Ntl Merit Stu 85; OH U; Comm.

KEIM, KATHY; Phoenixville HS; Phoenixville, PA; (Y); Key Clb; Yrbk Stf; High Hon Roll; Hon Roll.

KEIM, LISA MINNICH; Williams Valley JR SR HS; Tower City, PA; (Y); 11/101; Cmnty Wkr; Pep Clb; Chorus; Nwsp Rptr; Nwsp Stf; Cheerleading; Ftbl; High Hon Roll; Hon Roll; Scrtry Clb 86; Stu Scrtry 86; Blmsbrg U; CPA.

KEINER, JENNIFER; John S Fine HS; Nanticoke, PA; (Y); Key Clb; Ski Clb; Chorus; Yrbk Stf; Crs Cntry; Mgr(s); Hon Roll; NHS.

KEIPER, JOSEPH C; William Allen HS; Allentown, PA; (Y); 71/570; FBLA; VP Sr Cls; Var L Golf; Hon Roll; NHS; Hnr Grad 86; Pres Acad Fit Awd 86; PA ST U; Acctng.

KEIPER, STEVE; Hatboro-Horsham HS; Hatboro, PA; (Y); Ftbl; Trk; Comp Sci.

KEIRN, AARON; Clearfield Area HS; Clearfield, PA; (Y); French Clb; Var L Wrstlng; Cit Awd; Hon Roll.

KEISTER, SAMANTHA; Claysburg-Kimmel HS; Claysburg, PA; (Y); 12/51; German Clb; Chorus; Sftbl; Hon Roll; Psych.

KEITER, SANDRA M; Halifax Area HS; Halifax, PA; (Y); 2/100; Church Yth Grp; Rep Band; Mgr Nwsp Stf; Yrbk Stf; Var L Bsktbl; Dnfth Awd; High Hon Roll; NHS; Voice Dem Awd; Engr.

KEITH, AMY; Central HS; Martinsburg, PA; (Y); 18/175; Church Yth Grp; Drama Clb; FCA; Girl Scts; Chorus; Church Choir; Nwsp Ed-Chief; L Trk; JA; Office Aide; Acad All-Amer 85; PHEAA Cert Of Merit 84; W PA PGBC Distrct Chrstn Wrtng Wnnr 86; Grace Coll; Art Ed.

KEITH, LISA; Northern Cambria HS; Barnesboro, PA; (Y); 8/126; Church Yth Grp; Drama Clb; French Clb; Library Aide; Lib Band; Church Choir; Mrchg Band; High Hon Roll; Hon Roll; Jr NHS.

KEITH, THERESA KAY; Hanover HS; Hanover, PA; (Y); 17/138; Band; Chorus; Color Guard; Mrchg Band; School Play; Swing Chorus; Sec Soph Cls; Rep Stu Cncl; Hon Roll; NHS.

KEITT, TESSA MARIE; Coatesville Area SR HS; Coatesville, PA; (Y); Spanish Clb; Rep Jr Cls; Rep Sr Cls; Im Bsktbl; Hon Roll; Cash Hnr Socy 84-86; Socy Of Prgrssrs 84-86; Schl Bank 85-86; Loyola Coll; CPA.

KEKLAK, GREG; Johnstown HS; Johnstown, PA; (Y); German Clb; Speech Tm; School Musical; Yrbk Stf; NHS; Prfct Atten Awd.

KELEMEN, SEAN; Schenley HS; Pittsburgh, PA; (Y); Boys Clb Am; Boy Scts; Camera Clb; Chess Clb; Exploring; German Clb; JCL; Varsity Clb; Var L Golf; Var L Timer; Natl Sci Olympd Biol 2nd Pl 83-84, Chem 3rd Pl 84-85, Physcs 1st Pl 85-86; PA ST U; Engrng.

KELL, DAVID; West Perry HS; New Bloomfield, PA; (Y); 9/188; French Clb; Spanish Clb; Varsity Clb; Var L Bsbl; Var Ftbl; High Hon Roll; Hon Roll; NHS; Aerosp Engrng.

KELLAR, PEG; Cardinal O Hara HS; Havertown, PA; (Y); 101/772; Computer Clb; German Clb; Girl Scts; JCL; Latin Clb; Flag Corp; Mrchg Band; School Musical; Hon Roll; Latin Wk Comptitn Art Magna Cum Laude 84; Acad Exclnc Awd 85; Outstndng Achvt German I Study 86.

KELLEHER, BRIDGET; Lancaster Catholic HS; Leola, PA; (Y); 5/212; NFL; Nwsp Stf; VP Stu Cncl; L Crs Cntry; VP NHS; Ntl Merit Schol; Rotary Awd; Rep Soph Cls; Rep Jr Cls; JV Bsktbl; Villanova U Pres Schlr 86-90; Amer Lg Schl Awd 86; PA Hghr Ed Asst Agency Cert Merit 85; Villanova U; Intl Trade.

KELLER, AMANDA; Annville Cleona HS; Cleona, PA; (Y); 8/124; Madrigals; Mrchg Band; Orch; School Musical; Yrbk Sprt Ed; NHS; NEDT Awd; Most Imprvd Vocal Musician 86; Elra R Worcester Awd 86; Hauck Mfg Awd 85; U Of Hartford; Music Ed.

KELLER, BETH; Council Rock HS; Newtown, PA; (Y); 96/759; Key Clb; Band; Concert Band; Mrchg Band; Symp Band; Rep Soph Cls; Im Powder Puff Ftbl; Hon Roll; Grove City Coll; Bus Adm.

KELLER, DAVID; Chambersburg Area SR HS; Chambersburg, PA; (Y); Rep Am Leg Boys St; Boy Scts; Pres German Clb; Pres Band; Pres Chorus; Orch; Pres Soph Cls; Pres Jr Cls; Var Capt Tennis; Rotary Awd; Pre-Med.

KELLER, KAREN; Abington Heights HS; Clarks Summit, PA; (Y); 6/270; Church Yth Grp; Hosp Aide; Church Choir; Orch; Lit Mag; Var L Trk; Hon Roll; NHS; Ntl Merit Ltr; Ntl Hstry Day 1st Pl 85; 1 Brnz & 2 Gld Ndls For Russian Essay 84, 85 & 86; Physcl Thrpst.

KELLER, KATHY; Palmyra HS; Palmyra, PA; (Y); French Clb; Pep Clb; Chorus; Nwsp Rptr; Nwsp Stf; Yrbk Stf; Var Cheerleading; Capt Crs Cntry; Var Trk; High Hon Roll; Bloomsburg; Bus Mngmnt.

KELLER, KIRK; York Catholic HS; York, PA; (Y); 26/169; Band; Concert Band; Jazz Band; Mrchg Band; Orch; Pep Band; School Musical; Symp Band; Capt Socr; Hon Roll; Comp Sci.

KELLER, LORI; Middletown Area HS; Middletown, PA; (Y); Trs Church Yth Grp; Computer Clb; FBLA; Teachers Aide; JV Var Bsktbl; Hon Roll; FBLA Rgnl Accntng II 1st Pl 84; 3rd Pl Math 83; Harrisburg Area CC; Accntng.

KELLER, PAMELA; Catasauqua HS; Catasauqua, PA; (Y); 11/149; Color Guard; Yrbk Stf; Lit Mag; Rep Stu Cncl; L Fld Hcky; Powder Puff Ftbl; Twrlr; Hon Roll; NHS; Jrnlsm.

KELLER, ROBERT; Emmaus HS; Wescosville, PA; (Y); 168/465; Art Clb; Church Yth Grp; Cmnty Wkr; Pres JA; Quiz Bowl; Capt Scholastic Bowl; Band; Church Choir; Concert Band; Mrchg Band; Displyd Paintng 86; Hosp Svc Merit Awds 83-84; Milersville U; Art.

KELLER, TONIA; Tyrone Area HS; Tyrone, PA; (S); 2/186; Key Clb; Trs Spanish Clb; Yrbk Stf; Stu Cncl; Cheerleading; High Hon Roll; Trs NHS; T Narehood Mst Outstndng Soph Girl Awd 85; Accntng.

KELLERMAN, ANNA; Du Bois Area HS; Reynoldsville, PA; (Y); Mrchg Band; Twrlr; Du Bois Bus Schl; Bus.

KELLERMAN, DARREN; Bald Eagle Area JR-SR HS; Julian, PA; (Y); 9/200; Spanish Clb; Rep Stu Cncl; High Hon Roll; Penn ST; FBI Agent.

KELLERMAN, KIMBERLY A; Penns Valley Area HS; Centre Hall, PA; (Y); 11/144; VP SADD; Varsity Clb; Concert Band; Mrchg Band; Pep Band; Yrbk Rptr; Var L Mgr(s); Var L Sftbl; High Hon Roll; NHS; Outstndng SR Ind Arts; Outstndng SR Athl Girls Sftbl; Mst Schl Spirit; Lock Haven U PA; Spec Ed.

KELLERMAN, SHAWN P; Seneca Valley SR HS; Evans City, PA; (Y); 27/400; Boy Scts; Exploring; SADD; JV Wrstlng; High Hon Roll; Hon Roll; NHS; Vigil Awd 85; U Of Pittsburgh; Engnrng.

KELLEY, DOUGLAS; Delone Catholic HS; Hanover, PA; (Y); 45/168; Wt Lftg; Marine Leag Corp Schlrshp 86; Shippensburg; Mgmt Sci.

KELLEY, EILEEN; Scranton Prep; Pittston, PA; (Y); 49/192; Drama Clb; Church Choir; School Play; Stage Crew; Nwsp Phtg; Yrbk Phtg; Lit Mag; Rep Jr Cls; Bsktbl; Var Trk; Med.

KELLEY, LAURA; Delone Catholic HS; Hanover, PA; (Y); Varsity Clb; Cheerleading; Hon Roll.

KELLEY, LISA; Pine Forge Acad; Baltimore, MD; (Y); Church Yth Grp; Pep Clb; Band; Church Choir; Concert Band; Drill Tm; Mrchg Band; Yrbk Stf; Sec Soph Cls; Hon Roll; Pine Forge Acad; Med.

KELLEY, MELISSA; Waynesburg Central HS; Waynesburg, PA; (Y); Art Clb; Church Yth Grp; Service Clb; Spanish Clb; Jazz Band; Mrchg Band; High Hon Roll; NHS; NEDT Awd; Cmnty Wkr; Spnsh II Awd; Eng Ed.

KELLEY, NANCY BLANCHE; Valley SR HS; New Kensington, PA; (Y); 67/206; AFS; FBLA; Science Clb; Spanish Clb; Chorus; JV Vllybl; Cit Awd; High Hon Roll; Bus Ed Awd Acctng 85-86; IN U; Acctng.

KELLEY, SHARON; Connellsville Area SR HS; Connellsville, PA; (Y); 4/550; Church Yth Grp; Science Clb; School Musical; French Hon Soc; High Hon Roll; NHS; Prfct Atten Awd; Acadmc ExclInc.

KELLEY, TAMMY; Altoona Area HS; Altoona, PA; (Y); Church Yth Grp; VICA; School Play; Pres Soph Cls; Sftbl; Hon Roll; Poster Cntst Pro-Life 86; 1st Stry Wrtng Cntst Pub Lib 84; Art/Stry Pblshd ETC Art/Lit Mag 85 & 86; Sci Fctn Illustrator.

KELLEY, TRACY; Altoona Area HS; Altoona, PA; (Y); Church Yth Grp; VICA; School Play; Sec Frsh Cls; Sec Soph Cls; Sftbl; Hon Roll; 1st Plc Art Pstr Cntst Anti-Smkng 84; 2nd Plc Art Pstr Cntst Pro-Life 86; Art Wrk Accptd ETC Art Mag; Art.

KELLNER, RALPH E; West Allegheny SR HS; Oakdale, PA; (Y); German Clb; Chorus; JV Ftbl; Wt Lftg.

KELLOGG, LAURA V; Loyalsock Township HS; Williamsport, PA; (Y); 3/126; Debate Tm; JCL; Pres Key Clb; Pres SADD; Chorus; Stage Crew; Yrbk Stf; Trs NHS; Ntl Merit Ltr; Bus Prof Wmns Awd, Beta Sigma Phi Awd, Rnd Tbl Awd Frnch 86; U VT; Frgn Lang.

KELLY, ANDREA; Nazareth Acad; Philadelphia, PA; (Y); German Clb; Stu Cncl; Var Fld Hcky; High Hon Roll; VP NHS; Prfct Atten Awd; Bio.

KELLY, ANGELA; Spring-Ford SR HS; Albemarle, NC; (Y); 69/237; French Clb; Hosp Aide; Library Aide; Pep Clb; Sec Ski Clb; Yrbk Stf; NC ST U; Bio.

KELLY, CHRISTOPHER; Norwin SR HS; Ardara, PA; (Y); 19/557; Art Clb; Pep Clb; Spanish Clb; SADD; Pres Sr Cls; Var Ftbl; Var Trk; Hon Roll; Jr NHS; NHS; Outstndng Art Awd 85-86.

KELLY, CHRISTOPHER J; Bethel Park SR HS; Bethel Park, PA; (Y); Art Clb; Boy Scts; Exploring; NFL; Speech Tm; Variety Show; Lit Mag; Socr; US Army.

KELLY, CHRISTOPHER J; North Pocono HS; Moscow, PA; (Y); 60/250; Boy Scts; Church Yth Grp; Var L Bsktbl; JV Ftbl; Var L Tennis; JV Trk; PA ST U; Engrng.

KELLY, DAVID; Pine Forge Acad; Pine Forge, PA; (S); 1/54; Boy Scts; Church Yth Grp; Letterman Clb; Math Clb; Varsity Clb; Color Guard; Drm & Bgl; Pres Frsh Cls; Pres Sr Cls; Mgr Stu Cncl; Alg & Schlrshp Awd 82-83; Hstry Awd 83-84; Oakwood Coll; Elec Engr.

KELLY, DORI; Mt Pleasant HS; Mt Pleasant, PA; (Y); Debate Tm; French Clb; VICA; Nwsp Rptr; Mat Maids; Score Keeper; Trk; High Hon Roll; Hon Roll; Natl Sci Awd 85; Pitt U; Nrsng.

KELLY, JAMES; Canon Mc Millan HS; Eighty Four, PA; (Y); Cmnty Wkr; 4-H; French Clb; Ski Clb; Hon Roll; Res Champn Wstrn PA Ropers Assn 85; Qlfd Natl HS Rodeo Finls 86; Therapeutc Horseback Ride Vlntr; Engrng.

KELLY, JAMES; Cardinal O Hara HS; Springfield, PA; (Y); 56/772; Church Yth Grp; French Clb; Pres Latin Clb; Ed Nwsp Stf; Rep Stu Cncl; JV Crs Cntry; Var Swmmng; High Hon Roll; NHS; Prncpls Awd Acdmc Exclnc 85-86; Sci Prjct Rcgntn Amer Scty Micro-Bio 86; Hnrbl Mntn DE Vlly Sci Fr 86; Sci.

KELLY, JEAN; Oil City Area SR HS; Oil City, PA; (Y); 77/252; AFS; Church Yth Grp; Hosp Aide; Acpl Chr; Concert Band; Drill Tm; Mrchg Band; School Musical; JV Cheerleading; Prfct Atten Awd; Rgnl Bnd 86fwdwnd Qnt 85; Dstrct Bnd 86; Johnson & Wales; Clnry Arts.

KELLY, JENNIFER; Upper Merion Area HS; King Of Prussia, PA; (Y); 46/370; French Clb; Concert Band; Mrchg Band; Fld Hcky; Lcrss; Hon Roll; Prfct Atten Awd.

KELLY, JENNIFER; Yough SR HS; Smithton, PA; (Y); Pres Church Yth Grp; Drama Clb; FBLA; Teachers Aide; School Play; Stage Crew; Yrbk Stf; Rep Stu Cncl; High Hon Roll; NHS; 2nd Pl FBLA Comp Steno 86; Sec.

KELLY, JODY; Saltsburg JR SR HS; Saltsburg, PA; (Y); 1/102; Am Leg Aux Girls St; Church Yth Grp; Ski Clb; Varsity Clb; Band; Yrbk Stf; Rep Stu Cncl; Var Cheerleading; Stat Trk; High Hon Roll; Arin Marn Bio Quest Bahamas 86; Arin IUP Math Metrshp Prog 86; Cheerg Tri Cnty Champs 85; Pre-Med.

KELLY, JONATHAN ALLEN; Cheltenham HS; Lamott, PA; (Y); SADD; JV Bsktbl; Var Ftbl; Mgr(s); Score Keeper; Swmmng; Vllybl; Wt Lftg; Comm Art.

KELLY, KATHLEEN; Dunmore HS; Dunmore, PA; (Y); 7/150; Drama Clb; French Clb; Church Choir; School Musical; Yrbk Stf; Crs Cntry; Trk; High Hon Roll; Jr NHS; NHS; PA ST; Comm.

KELLY, KATHY; Red Land HS; York Haven, PA; (Y); 66/275; Church Yth Grp; Chorus; Church Choir; Color Guard; Jazz Band; Mrchg Band; School Musical; Stage Crew; Twrlr; Hon Roll; Rcrdng Tech.

KELLY, KATIE; Cardinal O Hara HS; Havertown, PA; (Y); 25/758; Church Yth Grp; Hosp Aide; Office Aide; Service Clb; Varsity Clb; JV Bsktbl; Crs Cntry; Trk; Hon Roll; Lion Awd; Villanova U; Sci.

KELLY, KRISTIN; Greensburg Central Catholic HS; Hunker, PA; (Y); AFS; VP Church Yth Grp; Office Aide; JV Bsktbl; Im Sftbl; Var Trk; Im Vllybl; Hon Roll; Deanery IV Yth Cncl Sec 85; Deanery IV Yth Cncl VP 86.

KELLY, MARIE J; Bishop Shanahan HS; West Chester, PA; (Y); Church Yth Grp; Pep Clb; SADD; Rep Jr Cls; Rep Stu Cncl; Cheerleading; Fld Hcky; Sftbl; Nrsg.

KELLY, MARY ELLEN; Cardinal O Hara HS; Holmes, PA; (Y); 227/772; Cmnty Wkr; Spanish Clb; Teachers Aide; Hon Roll; Barry U; Med.

KELLY, MARY JANE; Sto-Rox HS; Mc Kees Rocks, PA; (Y); 30/143; Boys Clb Am; Chess Clb; Y-Teens; VP Concert Band; VP Mrchg Band; Stage Crew; Im Vllybl; Hon Roll; Mc Donalds All Amer Bnd/Piccolo 86; Theater.

KELLY, MATTHEW; Plum Borough SR HS; Pittsburgh, PA; (Y); Boy Scts; Camera Clb; Church Yth Grp; 4-H; JA; Var L Socr; JV Trk; Hon Roll; Bio.

KELLY, PAT D; La Salle College HS; Philadelphia, PA; (Y); 25/240; Cmnty Wkr; Yrbk Rptr; Cheerleading; Golf; High Hon Roll; NHS; Columbia U; Engrng.

KELLY, RICHARD; St John Neumann HS; Philadelphia, PA; (Y); 38/338; High Hon Roll; Hon Roll; 1st Hnrs 84-85; Psych.

KELLY, TAMMY; Altoona Area HS; Altoona, PA; (Y); Church Yth Grp; German Clb; Key Clb; Drill Tm; Flag Corp; Twrlr; Psychlgy.

KELLY, TIMOTHY D; North Catholic HS; Pittsburgh, PA; (Y); 10/301; Chess Clb; Debate Tm; Model UN; NFL; Speech Tm; Nwsp Ed-Chief; Crs Cntry; Socr; High Hon Roll; Hon Roll; U Chicago Scholar 86; NECA Scholar 86; U Chicago; Eng.

KELSEA, CHRISTAL; Karns City JR SR HS; Chicora, PA; (Y); 47/114; Band; JV Cheerleading; Stat Trk; Hon Roll; Masonic Awd; Sawyer Schl Airlines; Stwrdss.

KELSEY, GAIL; Harriton HS; Gladwyne, PA; (Y); Service Clb; Var Fld Hcky; JV Lcrss; JV Swmmng; Vet Med.

KEMBLE, AARON; Council Rock HS; Washington Xing, PA; (Y); 200/850; Church Yth Grp; Ski Clb; Var L Bsbl; Im Ice Hcky; Im Vllybl; Engrng.

KEMBRING, CHARLES; Octorara Area HS; Cochranville, PA; (Y); Boy Scts; VICA; JV Wrstlng; Hon Roll; 2nd Soc Stdies Awd 86; Millersville U.

KEMERER, KIM; Hempfield Area SR HS; Greensburg, PA; (Y); 17/657; AFS; Pep Clb; Spanish Clb; Capt Drm Mjr(t); Yrbk Stf; Trs Jr Cls; Rep Stu Cncl; High Hon Roll; Pres Jr NHS; Trs NHS; Alg Cont Finlst Wstrn PA 83; Westmoreland Hosp Schlrshp 86; WA & Jefferson Coll; Pre Hlth.

KEMLING, SUSAN; Northwestern SR HS; Albion, PA; (Y); Church Yth Grp; Girl Scts; Ski Clb; Spanish Clb; Chorus; Var Bsktbl; Powder Puff Ftbl; Var Sftbl; Var Vllybl; Zoolgy.

KEMMERER, EUGENE; Pleasant Valley HS; Effort, PA; (Y); Ski Clb; Jr Cls; JV Bsbl; Bsktbl; Ftbl; Socr; Trk; Wt Lftg; Hon Roll; Jr NHS.

KEMMERER, KEVIN T; Bangor SR HS; Mt Bethel, PA; (Y); Chess Clb; Ski Clb; Band; Var Crs Cntry; Var L Trk; Im Vllybl; Engrng.

KEMP, BRIAN; Columbia Montour Voc Tech Schl; Berwick, PA; (Y); Boy Scts; Letterman Clb; Var L Bsbl; JV Var Bsktbl; Stat Ftbl; Hon Roll; Crpntry.

KEMP, BRIAN; Corry Area HS; Corry, PA; (S); 36/212; Civic Clb; JV Ftbl; Var Golf; High Hon Roll; Hon Roll; Pittsburgh Inst Aerontcs; Elec.

KEMP, RHONDA; Quigley HS; Industry, PA; (S); 6/106; Math Tm; Chorus; Var L Bsktbl; L Pom Pon; Im Powder Puff Ftbl; Var L Sftbl; High Hon Roll; NHS; Rotary Awd; Tstmstrs Intrntnl; French Awd.

KEMP, TAMARRA; Penn Hills SR HS; Pittsburgh, PA; (Y); Drama Clb; Key Clb; Spanish Clb; Yrbk Stf; Sec Jr Cls; Rep Sr Cls; Pres Stu Cncl; JV Var Cheerleading; Pom Pon; Yth Div PA Hills Black Parent Coalitn 85; Howard; Pre-Law.

KEMP, VINCENT; Youngsville HS; Grand Valley, PA; (Y); 3/97; Boy Scts; Pres French Clb; JV Var Wrstlng; High Hon Roll; NHS; Trs Church Yth Grp; Band; Concert Band; JV Ftbl; Schlrshp Awd-2nd Pl JR Cls 86; Western PA Quizzng-Erie Zone-2nd Pl 86; Penn ST U; Law.

KEMPF III, EDWARD J; Northwestern HS; Cranesville, PA; (Y); 18/164; Band; Chorus; Concert Band; Madrigals; Mrchg Band; School Musical; JV Var Bsktbl; Hon Roll; NHS; Mdrn Music Mstrs; Bnkng.

KEMPF, GWENDOLYN; Towanda Area HS; Towanda, PA; (Y); 11/180; Church Yth Grp; Letterman Clb; Ski Clb; Spanish Clb; Varsity Clb; Var L Crs Cntry; Var L Swmmng; Var L Trk; High Hon Roll; Hon Roll; Dist Cross Cntry Champs 84-85; 4th Pl Dist Track Meet 85-86; Westpoint; Architectur.

KEMPFF, CYNTHIA; Harry S Truman HS; Bensalem, PA; (Y); ROTC; Chorus; Var L Trk; Hon Roll; La Salle; Chmst.

KEMPINSKI, RAYMOND; Northeast Catholic HS; Philadelphia, PA; (Y); 14/362; Art Clb; Lit Mag; Hon Roll; NHS.

KEMPNER, BONNIE; Upper Dublin HS; Dresher, PA; (Y); 3/335; Drama Clb; VP Intnl Clb; Temple Yth Grp; Yrbk Stf; Lit Mag; Rep Stu Cncl; Powder Puff Ftbl; Mgr Socr; NHS; Ntl Merit Ltr; Acad All Amer 84-85.

KEMPTER, JOY; Archbishop Wood HS For Girls; Holland, PA; (Y); 4/248; Church Yth Grp; Dance Clb; French Clb; Service Clb; Teachers Aide; High Hon Roll; Hon Roll; NHS; Hon Mntn-Sci Fair 84 & 86; Awd For Hghst Chem Avg 86; Acad Profcncy-Engl III, Trig, Pre-Calculus 86; Math.

KENAWELL, RALPH; Du Bois Area HS; Dubois, PA; (Y); Boy Scts; Dance Clb; Trs Exploring; SADD; Chorus; School Musical; Rep Frsh Cls; JV Bsktbl; Var Crs Cntry; Var Socr.

KENDALL, JEFFERY T; Shenango JR SR HS; New Castle, PA; (Y); 18/121; Varsity Clb; Var Capt Ftbl; Var Trk; VP NHS; Am Legion Awd 82; Sentae PA ST Citznshp Awd 83; PA ST U; Bio.

KENDALL, LUCIA; Fox Chapel Area HS; Pittsburgh, PA; (S); Church Yth Grp; NFL; Ski Clb; Color Guard; School Play; Nwsp Ed-Chief; Lit Mag; Golf; High Hon Roll; Ntl Merit Ltr.

KENDIG, VICKI; Norhteastern HS; Mt Wolf, PA; (Y); 9/154; Church Yth Grp; Band; Chorus; Concert Band; Orch; School Musical; Nwsp Ed-Chief; Hon Roll; NHS; Dist Band 85-86; Flutist York Little Theater Muscl 84; York Coll; Bus.

KENDRELLA, NANCI; Mt Pleasant HS; Mt Pleasant, PA; (Y); Sec VICA; :Cosmtlgy.

KENGER, AMBER; James M Coughlin HS; Wilkes Barre, PA; (Y); 48/355; Yrbk Stf; Mgr(s); Stat Vllybl; Hon Roll; Jr NHS; NHS; PA ST U; Atty.

KENIA, CHERYL; Tunkhannock Area HS; Dalton, PA; (S); 18/310; Church Yth Grp; Spanish Clb; Stu Cncl; NHS; Acad All Amer 85; Dstngshd Yth Ldrshp Awd 85; Kings Coll; Intl Bus.

KENIA, TOM; Abington Heights HS; Clarks Summit, PA; (Y); 18/271; Hon Roll; Jr NHS; 1st Pl Annual AHSME Mth Exam 86.

KENNA, ED; Archbishop Ryan HS; Philadelphia, PA; (Y); 190/429; Var Ice Hcky; Bus Adm.

KENNEDY, BARB; Knoch JR SR HS; Butler, PA; (Y); Sec Church Yth Grp; Trs FBLA; Band; Concert Band; Mrchg Band; Stage Crew; Acctng.

KENNEDY, CHRISTIE M; Riverside HS; Fombell, PA; (Y); Am Leg Aux Girls St; GAA; Stu Cncl; Mgr(s); Score Keeper; Trk; Hon Roll; Var Ltr Track 85&86; Cmnctns.

KENNEDY, COLLEEN; Shenango JR SR HS; New Castle, PA; (Y); Chorus; Yrbk Stf; Im Vllybl; Hon Roll; NHS; Amer Bus Wmns Assn 86; Clarion U Of PA; Acctg.

KENNEDY, DAWN; Little Flower Catholic HS; Philadelphia, PA; (Y); 1/416; VP GAA; Red Cross Aide; Rep Frsh Cls; Rep Soph Cls; Rep Jr Cls; VP Sr Cls; Stu Cncl; Im Bsktbl; Capt Cheerleading; L Fld Hcky; Schlrshp Tmpl U 86; Hghst Avg Sci Awd 86; Hghst Rnkng HM, Hstry, Acctg Awd 86; Temple U; Psych.

KENNEDY, EDWARD J; West Mifflin Area HS; West Mifflin, PA; (Y); 1/340; Chess Clb; Computer Clb; Math Tm; Mgr(s); High Hon Roll; NHS; Ntl Merit SF.

KENNEDY, EILEEN M; St Huberts HS; Philadelphia, PA; (Y); 36/378; Church Yth Grp; GAA; Office Aide; Yrbk Sprt Ed; JV Capt Bsktbl; Mgr(s); Score Keeper; Cit Awd; Hon Roll; NHS; Outstndng Acad Achvt 86; Philadelphia CC; Bus.

KENNEDY, JAMIE; West Perry SR HS; Loysville, PA; (Y); 2/188; Sec Church Yth Grp; Concert Band; Yrbk Stf; High Hon Roll; Hon Roll; Trs NHS; Ntl Merit Ltr; Sal; Outstndng Math Stdnt 83-85; Natl Hnr Socty & SF Ed Cmmnctns Schlrshps 86; Harrisburg Area CC; Bus Adm.

KENNEDY, JASON B; New Brighton HS; New Brighton, PA; (Y); 10/146; Am Leg Boys St; Band; Concert Band; Jazz Band; Mrchg Band; Var JV Bsktbl; Trk; High Hon Roll; Hon Roll; Engnrng.

KENNEDY, JOHN; Northeastern HS; York, PA; (Y); 8/180; Chess Clb; Ski Clb; Chorus; JV Golf; JV Vllybl; Hon Roll; NHS; Physcs.

KENNEDY, JOSEPH PETER; Cardinal O Hara HS; Broomall, PA; (Y); 24/772; Church Yth Grp; Latin Clb; Var JV Bsbl; Bsktbl; High Hon Roll; Hon Roll; Ntl Merit Ltr; Hnrs Convoctn Top 10 Pct Stu 83-84; All Catholic 1st Tm Bsbl 84-85; All DE Co 1st Tm Bsbl 85-86; Advrtsng.

KENNEDY, KARL; Seneca Valley HS; Evans City, PA; (Y); 8/342; Am Leg Boys St; ROTC; SADD; JV Var Trk; High Hon Roll; NHS; Pres VP Church Yth Grp; Letterman Clb; Church Choir; Drill Tm; Supr Cadet Awd JROTC 85; Am Leg Mltry Exclnce Awd, Natl Guard Assoc PA Mltry Achvt Awd 86; Geneva Coll; Elec Engrng.

KENNEDY, KRISTA; Avon Grove HS; West Grove, PA; (Y); Cmnty Wkr; FBLA; Girl Scts; SADD; JV Bsktbl; Var Sftbl; Hon Roll; Real Est.

KENNEDY, LAURA; Mercyhurst Prep Schl; Erie, PA; (Y); 21/150; School Play; Sec Trs Frsh Cls; VP Soph Cls; Var Cheerleading; Im Ftbl; Hon Roll; Spansh Awd Excelnc 86; IN U; Educ.

KENNEDY JR, LOUIS J; Northeast Catholic HS; Philadelphia, PA; (Y); Boy Scts; JA; Cit Awd; Aud/Vis; CAP; Stage Crew; God Cntry Awd; SAR Awd; VFW Awd; Union Lg Phila Good Ctznshp Awd, Eagle Scout Awd 86; Pittsburgh Inst; Copter Pilot.

KENNEDY, MARIAN; Germantown HS; Philadelphia, PA; (Y); 2/480; Church Yth Grp; Drama Clb; Hosp Aide; Library Aide; Church Choir; High Hon Roll; Hon Roll; COLL Prep Penn ST 83-84; Dscvry Phila COLL Osteopathic Med 85; La Salle; Pyscology.

KENNEDY, MARK; Northeastern HS; Manchester, PA; (Y); Aud/Vis; Camera Clb; Church Yth Grp; Cmnty Wkr; Red Cross Aide; Teachers Aide; Thesps; Stage Crew; Yrbk Phtg; Trk.

KENNEDY, MARY; Shaler Area HS; Allison Pk, PA; (Y); Hosp Aide; Hon Roll; Hosp Aid 83-85; Hnr Roll 83-86; Med.

KENNEDY, MICHAEL; Lincoln HS; Ellwood City, PA; (Y); Latin Clb; Trk; Hon Roll; Am Achvt Awd 83-85; Ed.

KENNEDY, MICHELLE; Tunkhannock HS; Tunkhannock, PA; (S); 15/350; Aud/Vis; Church Yth Grp; Key Clb; Latin Clb; Letterman Clb; Varsity Clb; Rep Jr Cls; Rep Sr Cls; Sec Stu Cncl; Var Capt Crs Cntry; Acad All Amer 84-85; Crss Cntry All Str Awd 84; Qual Crss Cntry ST Champ; Spnsh.

KENNEDY, PATRICIA; St Pius X HS; Pennsburg, PA; (S); 4/160; Pres Church Yth Grp; Cmnty Wkr; French Clb; Nwsp Rptr; Rep Stu Cncl; VP Cheerleading; JV Tennis; High Hon Roll; NHS; NEDT Awd; Schl Sci Fair Awd Montgmry Cnty Sci Fair Awd 84-85; Acad Sci & Theol Awd 85; Dely Twn Mtg On Tmmrrw 85; Med.

KENNEDY, PRISCILLA; Canton HS; Canton, PA; (Y); Trs Church Yth Grp; Yrbk Stf; Var Crs Cntry; Var Trk; 4-H; Library Aide; Chorus; Hon Roll; Bus.

KENNEDY, REBECCA; East Pennsboro HS; Enola, PA; (Y); Art Clb; Drama Clb; French Clb; Drill Tm; Flag Corp; School Musical; School Play; Stage Crew; Hon Roll; Harrisburg Acad CC; Photogrphr.

KENNEDY, SHANNON; Fairview HS; Fairview, PA; (Y); 9/180; Debate Tm; German Clb; Model UN; Nwsp Rptr; Nwsp Stf; Hon Roll; NHS; Odd Fllws United Nat Pilgrimage Yth Delegate 86; Schlrshp PA Free Entrprs Wk 86; Hnrbl Mntn Tri St 86; Journalism.

KENNEDY, SHANNON; Yough HS; Herminie, PA; (Y); 17/256; Model UN; Ski Clb; Spanish Clb; Chorus; High Hon Roll; Jr NHS; NHS; U Of Pittsburgh; Pre Dntstry.

KENNEDY, SUSAN; Bensalem SR HS; Bemsalem, PA; (Y); Teachers Aide; Rep Jr Cls; JV Capt Cheerleading; High Hon Roll; NHS; Mst Vlbl Chrldr 84-85; Vrsty Ltrs In Acdmcs 83-84 & 84-85; Med.

KENNEDY, TIFFANY H; Norwin SR HS; N Huntingdon, PA; (Y); 316/575; DECA; Girl Scts; Pep Clb; VICA; Band; Merit Awd In DECA; Comp Sci.

KENNEDY, TODD; Athens Area HS; Athens, PA; (Y); Var Ftbl; Var Trk; Im Vllybl; Wt Lftg; Bloomsburg U.

KENNELL, TAMMY; Hyndman HS; Hyndman, PA; (Y); Pres Church Yth Grp; SADD; Chorus; Church Choir; Mrchg Band; Yrbk Stf; Rep Stu Cncl; Cheerleading; Twrlr; Hon Roll; Frostburg ST; Music.

KENNELLY, MARIE M; Phoenixville HS; Phoenixville, PA; (Y); Girl Scts; Key Clb; Pep Clb; Flag Corp; Madrigals; School Musical; School Play; DAR Awd; Hon Roll; Prfct Atten Awd; Natl Merit Awd-Foods 86.

KENNEMUTH, RHONDA; Brookville Area HS; Brookville, PA; (Y); 38/143; Church Yth Grp; Sec Drama Clb; Chorus; VP Orch; School Musical; Yrbk Stf; Sec Stu Cncl; Hon Roll; Pres Schlr; German Clb; Natl Schl Orchstr Awd 86; Clarion U; Gen Ed.

KENNEY, KATHY; Moshannon Valley HS; Houtzdale, PA; (Y); 10/120; Ski Clb; Spanish Clb; Teachers Aide; Band; Mrchg Band; Pep Band; Nwsp Stf; Stat Bsktbl; Hon Roll; NHS; Elem Tchr.

KENNEY, KELLI; Ambridge Area HS; Freedom, PA; (Y); Pep Clb; Sec Spanish Clb; Color Guard; Off Soph Cls; Off Jr Cls; Hon Roll; Elem Ed.

KENNEY, MAUREEN; Bishop Conwell HS; Yardley, PA; (Y); 6/253; Church Yth Grp; Mathletes; Office Aide; Nwsp Rptr; Lit Mag; Sec Stu Cncl; Elks Awd; High Hon Roll; Pres NHS; Hugh O Brian Regnl Rep 84; Magna Cum Laude Ltn Awd 84; Villanova U; Lbrl Arts.

KENNEY, RYAN; Geibel HS; Scottdale, PA; (Y); Art Clb; Letterman Clb; Ski Clb; JV Bsktbl; JV L Ftbl; Var Wt Lftg; Var Hon Roll; NEDT Awd; Art Inst Pittsburgh; Grphc Dsgn.

KENNEY, SEAN; Geibel HS; Scottdale, PA; (Y); 7/87; School Play; Stage Crew; Rep Jr Cls; Pres Sr Cls; Stu Cncl; JV Stat Bsktbl; Ftbl; Mgr(s); French Hon Soc; High Hon Roll; Pre-Dentistry.

KENNY, ERIN; B Reed Henderson HS; Westchester, PA; (Y); Intnl Clb; Service Clb; Rep Frsh Cls; Rep Soph Cls; Hon Roll; Lion Awd; NHS; Var Trk; Stat Bsktbl; AFS; Creative Shrt Stry Pblshd In Apprentice Writer Mag 86; ST Off ALA Girls ST 86; Freedom Fndtn 86; Pol Sci.

KENSINGER, KAREN; Central HS; Martinsburg, PA; (Y); 38/184; FCA; Ski Clb; Band; Chorus; Trs Soph Cls; Trs Jr Cls; Trs Sr Cls; Capt L Tennis; Trk; Hon Roll; Dist Regnl Chorus 86; Ntl Schl Choral Awd 86; IN U; Fash Merch.

KENSINGER, NANCY; Palmyra HS; Annville, PA; (Y); Church Yth Grp; Drama Clb; Temple Yth Grp; Band; Stage Crew; Nwsp Stf; Gym; Hon Roll; Chess Clb; Pep Clb; 5yr Camp Achvt Awd 85; Best Chrgrphy Awd 85; Scripture Mastery Awd 86; Brigham Young U; Arts.

KENT, CHRISTOPHER; Punxsutawney Area HS; Punxsutawney, PA; (Y); 12/345; Church Yth Grp; FCA; Math Clb; Varsity Clb; VP Jr Cls; Var Bsktbl; Var L Ftbl; Var Trk; Hon Roll; JC Awd; PA Fre-Enterprs Schlrshp 86; Keystone Games Fnlst-Bsktbl; Bus.

KENT, SEAN; Punxsutawney Area HS; Punxsutawney, PA; (Y); 9/238; Church Yth Grp; FCA; Math Clb; Math Tm; Teachers Aide; Pres Varsity Clb; Trs Soph Cls; VP Jr Cls; Pres Sr Cls; Var Capt Bsktbl; Rotry Boy Mth 86; Outstndng Athlt 86; Dist Chmpn-Javelin 86; US Naval Acad; Engrng.

KENYHERZ, GREGORY E; Central Catholic HS; Pittsburgh, PA; (Y); 4/259; AFS; Dance Clb; Band; Ftbl; Wt Lftg; High Hon Roll; VP NHS; Ntl Merit SF; PA JR Acad Sci 1st Pl Regnl,2nd Pl ST 85.

KENYON, MARGARET; Souderton Area HS; Harleysville, PA; (Y); Drama Clb; Intnl Clb; Nwsp Ed-Chief; Nwsp Rptr; Lit Mag; Hon Roll; Jr NHS; Prfct Atten Awd; Orl Comptn Spnsh Adv 86; Yth Educ Assn Hstrn; Cmmnctns.

KENZAKOSKI, CAROLYN; James M Coughlin SR HS; Wilkes-Barre, PA; (Y); French Clb; Nwsp Stf; Yrbk Stf; Pres Frsh Cls; Capt Cheerleading; Capt Fld Hcky; Capt Sftbl; Wt Lftg; Hon Roll; Jr NHS; Outstndng Englsh Achvt Awd 82-83; Bloomsburg U.

KENZAKOWSKI, MAURA; Bishop Shanahan HS; W Chester, PA; (Y); 29/218; Dance Clb; Drama Clb; Chorus; School Musical; School Play; High Hon Roll; Hon Roll; NHS; Nrsng.

KEOHANE, KELLY; Spring-Ford HS; Schwenksville, PA; (Y); French Clb; Band; Concert Band; Fld Hcky; Lcrss; Mgr(s).

KEPHART, AMY; Moshannon Valley HS; Houtzdale, PA; (Y); 13/121; Trs Church Yth Grp; Girl Scts; Ski Clb; Spanish Clb; Band; Chorus; Concert Band; Flag Corp; Nwsp Stf; Yrbk Ed-Chief; Sprts Medcn.

KEPHART, BRENT; Philipsburg Osceola Area HS; Osceola Mills, PA; (Y); 25/250; Boy Scts; Letterman Clb; Band; Rep Stu Cncl; Var L Ftbl; Im Wt Lftg; Var Wrstlng; Hon Roll; Prfct Atten Awd; Bg 8 Ftbll Cnfrnc All Str 85-86; PA Fr Entrprs Wk 86; PA ST; Engrng.

KEPHART, CORRINE; Clearfield HS; Clearfield, PA; (Y); Acpl Chr; Chorus; Church Choir; School Musical; School Play; Swing Chorus; Variety Show; Church Yth Grp; French Clb; Science Clb; Dist, Rgnl, & All ST Chorus 85 & 86; ST Fnlst Miss Amer Coed Pgnt 86; Piano & Orgn Acmpnst 86; Music.

KEPHART, MICHELLE; Clearfield Area HS; Olanta, PA; (S); 98/318; Band; Concert Band; Mrchg Band; Trs Frsh Cls; Trs Soph Cls; Trs Jr Cls; Capt Bsktbl; Sftbl; Capt Vllybl; Cit Awd; Sftbl-Bttg Chmpn 85; Bsktbl-Bst Foul Shot 84-85; Phy Ed Tchr.

KEPLINGER, CAROLYN; Wyoming Seminary HS; Mtn Top, PA; (Y); 26/87; Dance Clb; Ski Clb; Spanish Clb; Chorus; School Musical; Variety Show; Nwsp Stf; Gov Hon Prg Awd; Jr NHS; NEDT Awd; Ctr For Advncmnt Of Acad Tlntd Yth 82-85; Med.

KEPNER, LORALEE; Susquemta HS; Duncannon, PA; (S); 19/153; French Clb; Leo Clb; Chorus; Flag Corp; Nwsp Sprt Ed; Trk; Hon Roll; NHS; Hotl Mgmt.

KEPPEL, ROBERT; Notre Dame HS; Nazareth, PA; (Y); 1/75; Yrbk Rptr; VP Sr Cls; JV Bsktbl; Var L Crs Cntry; Var L Trk; Im Mgr Vllybl; Hon Roll; VP NHS; Ntl Merit Ltr; Val; Lwr Nzrth Wmns Clb Schlrshp 86; U Of VA; Bus.

KEPPIE, KEN; Franklin Regional HS; Delmont, PA; (Y); Thesps; Sec Trs Chorus; School Musical; School Play; Swing Chorus; Rep Stu Cncl; Var Swmmng; Drama Clb; German Clb; Stage Crew; PMEA Cnty & Dist Chorus 83-84, Cnty Chorus 84-85 & 85-86; Music Ed.

KEPPLER, BECKY; Westmont Hilltop HS; Johnstown, PA; (Y); 42/158; Church Yth Grp; Sec FTA; Speech Tm; Band; Concert Band; Jazz Band; Mrchg Band; Orch; Hon Roll; U Of Pittsburgh-Johnstown.

KEPPLEY, GREGORY A; Eastern Lebanon County HS; Schaefferstown, PA; (Y); 19/172; Trs Church Yth Grp; Church Choir; Var L Bsbl; Var Mgr(s); Var Score Keeper; Var L Socr; Var Timer; Hon Roll; Pres NHS; Juniata Coll; Med Fld Profssn.

KEPPLEY, KIRK; Eastern Lebanon County HS; Schaeffestown, PA; (Y); Church Yth Grp; JV Bsbl; Var Socr; Hon Roll; NHS; Acctng.

KERBER, DONNA; Norwin HS; N Huntingdon, PA; (Y); 27/550; Spanish Clb; NHS; Seton Hill Col6; Home Ec.

KERBER, ED; Norwin SR HS; N Huntingdon, PA; (Y); 18/600; Cmnty Wkr; Computer Clb; Letterman Clb; Spanish Clb; Bsktbl; Tennis; High Hon Roll; Hon Roll; Jr NHS; NHS; Engrng.

KERCH, DANIEL; Portage Area HS; Portage, PA; (S); 19/118; Church Yth Grp; Stu Cncl; Ftbl; Wt Lftg; Wrstlng; 4-H Awd; Hon Roll; NHS; Penn ST; Engrng.

KERENS, KIMBERLY A; Wilmington Area HS; Edinburg, PA; (Y); Sec FBLA; Office Aide; Spanish Clb; Vllybl; Grand Offcr Rainbow Girls 85-86; Bradford Schl Of Bus; Sec.

KERIN, MARY; West Allegheny SR HS; Coraopolis, PA; (Y); 18/201; Computer Clb; FBLA; German Clb; Office Aide; Chorus; Cheerleading; Powder Puff Ftbl; Sftbl; High Hon Roll; Hon Roll; Acad All Amer Schlr 85-86; Bradford Bus Schl; Ex Sec.

KERLIN, KRISTIN A; Bloomsburg HS; Bloomsburg, PA; (Y); Church Yth Grp; GAA; Pep Clb; Varsity Clb; Church Choir; Var Capt Cheerleading; Powder Puff Ftbl; Socr; Bloomsburg U; Sclgy.

KERN, CHARLENE; Mc Guffey HS; Claysville, PA; (Y); 14/210; Sec French Clb; JA; Capt Color Guard; Trs Soph Cls; Trs Rep Jr Cls; High Hon Roll; Trs NHS; Stu Recngtn Awd 84-86; Prom Queen 86; Hmcmng Ct 84-86; Psych.

KERN, JESSE; Garden Spot HS; Denver, PA; (Y); Var Bsbl; Var Ftbl; Var Trk; Var Wt Lftg; Hon Roll; Bio.

KERN, JONATHAN; Freedom HS; Bethlehem, PA; (Y); 56/465; Church Yth Grp; German Clb; Science Clb; Hon Roll; PA ST U; Med.

KERN, MELODY; David B Oliver HS; Pittsburgh, PA; (Y); #6 In Class; Pres Exploring; JA; Rep Stu Cncl; DAR Awd; High Hon Roll; Jr NHS; NHS; Carnegie Mellon; Aerospc Engr.

KERN, PATRICIA E; Villa Maria Acad; Erie, PA; (Y); Church Yth Grp; Cmnty Wkr; FNA; Rep Stu Cncl; Var Cheerleading; Trk; Hon Roll; NHS; Gannon U Erie PA; Phys Ther.

KERNER, ANN; St Benedict Acad; Erie, PA; (Y); 7/63; Am Leg Aux Girls St; Church Yth Grp; Cmnty Wkr; Girl Scts; Model UN; Cheerleading; High Hon Roll; NHS; Elem Educ.

KERNER, SCOTT; Marion Center HS; Creekside, PA; (Y); Church Yth Grp; Intnl Clb; Science Clb; Rep Stu Cncl; Hon Roll; Math.

KERNER, TROY; Hamburg HS; Bernville, PA; (Y); 6/152; Spanish Clb; SADD; JV Bsbl; Var Golf; Im Vllybl; JV Wrstlng; Bausch & Lomb Sci Awd; Cit Awd; NHS; SICO Fndtn Scholar 86; Rotary Clb Scholar 86; U DE; Pre-Med.

KERNS, JEFF; Mc Guffey HS; Prosperity, PA; (S); 9/216; Model UN; Trs Spanish Clb; Golf; L Capt Wrstlng; High Hon Roll; Stu Recgntn Awd 84-85; Med.

KERR, DANIEL; Punxsutawney Area SR HS; Punxsutawney, PA; (Y); Letterman Clb; Varsity Clb; Bsktbl; Ftbl; Timer; Trk; Wt Lftg; Hon Roll; Bus.

KERR, DENISE; St Hubert HS; Phiadelphia, PA; (Y); 46/367; Church Yth Grp; Jazz Band; Orch; School Musical; NHS; Polish Police Awd; Temple U; Spec Ed.

KERR, ERIK; Trinity HS; Washington, PA; (Y); Church Yth Grp; German Clb; Band; Church Choir; Jazz Band; Mrchg Band; Wt Lftg; Cit Awd; Hon Roll; NEDT Awd; Outstndng Solost OH U Jazz Fest 85-86; Hnrs Jazz Band 86; PA All ST Jazz Band Drmr 86; Music.

KERR, KARA; Hopewell SR HS; Aliquippa, PA; (Y); 20/257; Pres Soph Cls; VP Stu Cncl; Var L Bsktbl; Im Powder Puff Ftbl; High Hon Roll; Pres Acad Ftns Awd 86; May Ct 86; Clemson U; Pol Sci.

KERR, KAREN; Shippensburg HS; Shippensburg, PA; (Y); 20/220; Sec Leo Clb; Chorus; Jazz Band; Mrchg Band; Orch; Pep Band; Yrbk Stf; Var Capt Swmmng; Hon Roll; Lion Awd; Deans Schlrshp At Yrk Coll 86; Rsl G & Elnr Gohn Trst Fnd 86; Yrk Coll PA; Mrktng.

KERR, KATHLEEN; Pottstown HS; Pottstown, PA; (S); 1/197; Band; Nwsp Ed-Chief; Lit Mag; Pres Frsh Cls; Pres Soph Cls; Var Capt Cheerleading; Lcrss; High Hon Roll; Varsity Clb; Val; Brown U Bk Awd 85; PA ST U; Lib Arts.

KERR, LAURA BETH; Pennsbury HS; Yardley, PA; (Y); Church Yth Grp; Pres Cmnty Wkr; Dance Clb; French Clb; SADD; School Musical; School Play; Yrbk Stf; Stu Cncl; Hon Roll; Crtcs Awd Exclnc In Actng 86; 3rd Pl ST Of PA Spch Lg Drma Cmptn 85; 1st Pl Estrn Rgn Spch Lg 85; U Of CA Ls Angls; Drama.

KERR, ROBIN; West Greene SR HS; Holbrook, PA; (Y); Band; Concert Band; Jazz Band; Mrchg Band; Nwsp Stf; Rep Stu Cncl; JV Capt Bsktbl; High Hon Roll; NHS; Math.

KERRIGAN, DEANNA; Council Rock HS; Churchville, PA; (Y); 53/845; Spanish Clb; Var Bsktbl; Var Tennis; Hon Roll; NHS; Socr; Sftbl; Alice Southwick Awd For Eng 84; Pre-Law.

KERRIS, DIANE; Lourdes Regional HS; Mt Carmel, PA; (Y); 3/98; AFS; Scholastic Bowl; Var Cheerleading; JV Golf; High Hon Roll; NHS; Spanish NHS; Achvt Acad Chrldng Awd 84; Achvt Acad Math Awd 85; Bio.

KERSKEY, DAVID; Cheltenham HS; Elkins Pk, PA; (Y); 90/360; Nwsp Stf; JV Bsbl; Var Bsktbl; Im Bowling; JV Ftbl; Var Golf; Stu Tckt Co-Chrmn 86-87; Jb Mrkt 85-86; Villanova; Bus.

KERSTETTER, JAMES; Wyoming Valley West HS; Kingston, PA; (Y); Jazz Band; Mrchg Band; Orch; Nwsp Ed-Chief; Lit Mag; Rep Stu Cncl; Var Trk; Cit Awd; NCTE Awd; Stu Liason To Schl Brd 85-87; Stu Cncl Exec Brd; Journalism.

KERSTETTER, JOAN; Susquenita JR SR HS; Marysville, PA; (S); 1/152; Chess Clb; Church Yth Grp; Pres French Clb; Quiz Bowl; Concert Band; Jazz Band; Mrchg Band; Pep Band; School Musical; Nwsp Rptr; Lebanon Vlly Coll Hnrs Band 84-86; Amer Music Abroad-Blue Tour Of Europe 84; Bio.

KERTZ, SUE; Knoch HS; Butler, PA; (Y); Dance Clb; Pep Clb; Drill Tm; Pom Pon; Trk; Im Vllybl; Wt Lftg; Hon Roll; MI Stu Hnr Awd 83-85; Superstar Drill Tm Awd 85; Horse Trl Awds 83-84; Fash Merch.

KERTZEL, AMY; Northeastern SR HS; Dover, PA; (Y); 15/147; Church Yth Grp; SADD; Chorus; Church Choir; Mrchg Band; School Musical; School Play; JV Var Cheerleading; Hon Roll; NHS; Schlrshp; Lebanon Vly Coll; Medcl Tech.

KERWELL, TERRY; Milton Area SR HS; Milton, PA; (Y); JV Wrstlng; Hon Roll; Bus.

KESHISHIAN, AROUSIAG; St Basil Acad; Phila, PA; (Y); Sec Drama Clb; French Clb; Thesps; School Play; Stage Crew; Variety Show; Trs Soph Cls; Trs Sr Cls; Trs Stu Cncl; Law.

KESLAR, CONNIE; Meyersdale Area HS; Meyersdale, PA; (S); Pres Church Yth Grp; VP 4-H; Sec French Clb; Color Guard; Yrbk Stf; Vllybl; Wt Lftg; French Hon Soc; 4-H Awd; Hon Roll; Med Lab Tech.

KESLAR, TAMMY; Mt Pleasant Area SR HS; Acme, PA; (Y); FBLA; GAA; Chorus; Color Guard; Mat Maids; Sawyer Schl; Acctng.

KESSLER, BOB; York Vo-Tech HS; Hanover, PA; (Y); JA; VICA; Chorus; High Hon Roll; Hon Roll; NHS; Comp Tech.

KESSLER, MICHELLE R; Central York SR HS; York, PA; (Y); Am Leg Aux Girls St; Capt Flag Corp; Nwsp Stf; Yrbk Stf; Sec Frsh Cls; Rep Soph Cls; Rep Jr Cls; VP Sr Cls; VP Stu Cncl; Var L Cheerleading; Millersville U; Elem Ed.

KESSLER, SCOT; Brookville Area HS; Brookville, PA; (Y); 18/146; Cmnty Wkr; Varsity Clb; Chorus; Hon Roll; NHS; Pres Schlr; U Pitt; Chem.

KESSLER, SYBIL; Performing Arts School Of Phila; Woodbury Hts, NJ; (Y); PAVAS; School Musical; School Play; Stage Crew; Yrbk Stf; Trs Jr Cls; Hon Roll; Chorus; Madrigals; Nwsp Stf; All South Jersey Choir 83-84; Winter Arts Inst 84-86; Smmr Arts Inst 86; Rutgers U; Theatre.

KESTER, KYRA; Corry Area HS; Spring Creek, PA; (S); 45/212; Church Yth Grp; German Clb; Band; Chorus; Church Choir; Concert Band; Mrchg Band; Orch; Rep Stu Cncl; 1st Pl Wnr JR Div Erie Music Tchrs Assn Scholar Comp 84; Music Tchrs Natl Assn H S Comp 85-86; Music Prfrmnce.

KESTER, MARK C; Pennridge HS; Hilltown, PA; (Y); 20/435; Pres SADD; Rep Sr Cls; Rep Stu Cncl; Var L Bsbl; Var L Bsktbl; Var L Socr; High Hon Roll; VP NHS; Ldrshp Camp Spnsrd Rotary Intl 85-86; Biochem.

KESTER, SHAWN; New Brighton Area HS; New Brighton, PA; (Y); 40/146; Am Leg Aux Girls St; GAA; VP Chorus; School Play; Yrbk Ed-Chief; Yrbk Phtg; Trs Soph Cls; Var Cheerleading; Hon Roll; Dist Rgnl Chorus 84-85&85-86; Rgnl St Chorus 84-85&85-86; Natl Ldrshp Merit Awd 85-86; Slipery Rock U; Educ.

KETCHAM, PAMELA J; Cambridge Springs HS; Cambridge Spgs, PA; (Y); VP 4-H; JA; Sec Spanish Clb; Stu Cncl; 4-H Awd; Hon Roll; NHS; Cert For Cmpltng Dale Crng Course 86; Acdmc Achvt Awd 84-85; Ithica Coll; Accntng.

KETH, PHILIP; Clarion Limestone HS; Clarion, PA; (Y); French Clb; Varsity Clb; Chorus; Off Sr Cls; Ftbl; Trk; Wt Lftg; Clarion U.

KETTER, ANDRE; South Philadelphia HS Motivatn; Philadelphia, PA; (Y); Art Clb; Im Bsktbl; Hon Roll; Prfct Atten Awd; Engrng.

KETTERING, JANINE; Connellsville Area SR HS; Connellsville, PA; (Y); 39/550; Office Aide; Band; Chorus; Jazz Band; Orch; School Musical; Symp Band; Nwsp Stf; Pres Soph Cls; Pres Jr Cls; Hnrs Band 83-85; Gov Schl AIT 86; Region Band 85-86; Dist Band 84-8l; Music Ed.

KETTERING, JOELLE C; Lancaster Christian Schl; Thomson, IL; (Y); 5/28; Church Yth Grp; Drama Clb; Acpl Chr; Chorus; School Play; Sec Stu Cncl; Var L Fld Hcky; Ntl Merit Ltr; Assn Chrstn Schls Intl Dstngshd Christn HS Stu 84-85; Houghton Coll; Englsh.

KETTERMAN, RICHELLE; West York Area HS; York, PA; (Y); 48/208; Varsity Clb; Sec Frsh Cls; Sec Soph Cls; Sec Jr Cls; Sec Sr Cls; Rep Stu Cncl; Var Capt Cheerleading; JV Capt Vllybl; Hon Roll; Nrs.

KEVERLINE, MARGARET; Bradford Central Christian HS; Bradford, PA; (Y); 1/26; Drama Clb; Pep Clb; SADD; Rep Stu Cncl; Cheerleading; Jr NHS; NHS; Penn York Chem Awd 86.

KEW II, WAYNE; Greenwood HS; Liverpool, PA; (S); 12/68; Boy Scts; Church Yth Grp; Quiz Bowl; School Musical; Trk; Gov Hon Prg Awd; Hon Roll; Jr NHS; NHS; Anthrplgy.

KEYBURN, BONNIE LEE; New Hope-Solebury HS; Doylestown, PA; (Y); 32/67; FBLA; Girl Scts; Band; Chorus; Yrbk Stf; JV Cheerleading; Var Mgr(s); Var Socr; Var Sftbl; Hon Roll; Ohos Coho Omong Amer HS Stu 86; Scrtry Ftr Bus Ldrs Amer 85; Martin Luther King Awd 86; Kutytown U; Bus Admin.

KEYES, SEAN; Father Judge HS; Philadelphia, PA; (Y); VP Church Yth Grp; Dance Clb; Var Letterman Clb; Political Wkr; Service Clb; SADD; Rep Frsh Cls; Rep Soph Cls; Rep Jr Cls; Rep Sr Cls; Fresh,Soph & JR Participation Awd 84-86; Temple U.

KEYS, RICHARD D; Beth Center HS; Brownsville, PA; (Y); 14/168; Camera Clb; Church Yth Grp; English Clb; Letterman Clb; Math Clb; Ski Clb; Spanish Clb; Speech Tm; Varsity Clb; Rep Frsh Cls; California U Of PA.

KEYSER, LYNN; Windber Area HS; Windber, PA; (Y); 16/112; Office Aide; Pep Clb; Teachers Aide; Band; Color Guard; Drill Tm; Drm Mjr(t); Flag Corp; Mrchg Band; School Musical.

KHANIN, ALEX; HSES HS; Philadelphia, PA; (S); 1/200; Chess Clb; Computer Clb; Debate Tm; Math Tm; Radio Clb; High Hon Roll; NHS; PJAS 83 & 84; Drexell U; Comp Engrng.

KHANUJA, ASHOO; Villa Maria HS; Warren, OH; (Y); Hosp Aide; Key Clb; Red Cross Aide; Spanish Clb; NHS; Physcn.

KHOA, PHUONG N; Philadelphia High Schl For Girls; Philadelphia, PA; (Y); 20/258; GAA; Teachers Aide; Variety Show; Yrbk Stf; Var Capt Badmtn; High Hon Roll; Hon Roll; NHS; Schlrshp Synod Of The Trinity 86-87; U Of PA; Med.

KIBBE, MIKE; Jersey Shore Area SR HS; Jersey Shore, PA; (Y); Spanish Clb; Acpl Chr; Chorus; Church Choir; School Play; Variety Show; Var Capt Bowling; Hon Roll; High Series 85-86; Mst Imprvd 85-86; Math.

KICINSKI, DEBRA; Seton-La Salle HS; Pittsburgh, PA; (Y); 85/232; Ski Clb; Spanish Clb; Mrchg Band; Yrbk Stf; High Hon Roll; Hon Roll; Tamburitzan Schlrshp 86; Duquesne U; Bus.

KICK, CLARE; Portage Area HS; Portage, PA; (S); 7/118; Aud/Vis; Band; Chorus; Concert Band; Jazz Band; Mrchg Band; Pep Band; Bsktbl; High Hon Roll; NHS; Amuets Amercnsm Essy-2nd Pl Lcl Lvl 84; Premed.

KICK, KEVIN; Richland HS; Gibsonia, PA; (Y); Aud/Vis; Church Yth Grp; Computer Clb; Drama Clb; Letterman Clb; Ski Clb; Band; Concert Band; Jazz Band; Mrchg Band; Cmmnctns.

KIDD, BONNIE; Mt Union Area HS; Mt Union, PA; (Y); 12/160; Church Yth Grp; Cmnty Wkr; French Clb; GAA; SADD; Band; Concert Band; Jazz Band; Mrchg Band; Var Capt Cheerleading; Elem Ed.

KIEF, RANDY; Canon-Mc Millian HS; Canonsburg, PA; (Y); Computer Clb; Library Aide; Acpl Chr; Chorus; Hon Roll; Cert Trnng PA Army Natl Guard 86; PMEA Dist I Chrl Fstvl 84; WVU; Comp Pgmmg.

KIEFER, M CURTIS; West Forest HS; Tionesta, PA; (Y); 2/50; Trs Church Yth Grp; Trs Jr Cls; Rep Stu Cncl; Var Socr; High Hon Roll; Hon Roll; NHS; Accntnt.

KIEFFER, PAM; Central Bucks East HS; Furlong, PA; (Y); FBLA; Pep Clb; Ski Clb; Drill Tm; Mrchg Band; Var Cheerleading; Pom Pon; Sftbl; Vllybl; Hon Roll; Busnss.

KIELY, AYLISSA; Bishop Mc Devitt HS; Harrisburg, PA; (S); 39/196; Pres Sr Cls; Pres Stu Cncl; Capt Cheerleading; Sftbl; Dnfth Awd; Hon Roll; VP NHS; Spanish Clb; Chorus; Mrchg Band; Ftns Tm 82-86; Peer Cnslr 84-86; Stu Of Mnth,Dist Exchng Clb 86; Bio.

KIELY, KITTY; Archbishop John Carroll Girls; Havertown, PA; (Y); 18/212; Church Yth Grp; Spanish Clb; Stage Crew; Nwsp Rptr; Rep Jr Cls; Cheerleading; Crs Cntry; High Hon Roll; Hon Roll; Pope Pius Awd 84; Engr.

KIESLING, MARY E; Brookville Area HS; Brookville, PA; (Y); 9/144; German Clb; Mrchg Band; School Musical; Nwsp Ed-Chief; Nwsp Rptr; Bsktbl; Vllybl; NHS; Ntl Merit Ltr; Duquesne U; Jrnlsm.

KIESSLING, DAWN; Littlestown HS; Littlestown, PA; (Y); Trs FBLA; Girl Scts; Office Aide; Sec Trs Band; Color Guard; Concert Band; Mrchg Band; Capt Bsbl; Hon Roll; Girl Scout Silver Awd 84; Girl Scout Gold Awd 87; Law.

KIGER, TED; Waynesburg Central HS; Mt Morris, PA; (Y); Church Yth Grp; Letterman Clb; Ski Clb; Spanish Clb; Varsity Clb; Pres Band; Pres Concert Band; Pres Jazz Band; Pres Mrchg Band; Trs Stu Cncl; Melivina Haugon Schlrp 85-86; Boy Of Mnth 85-86; WV U; Pre-Pharm.

KIKOLA, DENNIS; Seneca HS; Wattsburg, PA; (Y); 23/172; Exploring; Pep Clb; Quiz Bowl; Nwsp Rptr; Nwsp Stf; Rep Jr Cls; Pres Stu Cncl; Var L Ftbl; Wt Lftg; Hon Roll; Pol Sci.

KIKTA, LISA; Avon Grove HS; Landenberg, PA; (Y); 26/173; Girl Scts; SADD; Chorus; Yrbk Stf; Rep Stu Cncl; Capt Var Cheerleading; High Hon Roll; Hon Roll.

KIKUCHI, ALICIA; Strath Haven HS; Swarthmore, PA; (Y); Girl Scts; Chorus; Church Choir; Stage Crew; Hon Roll; Library Aide; School Musical; School Play; Girl Scout Gold Awd 86; Haverford; Specl Ed.

KILBERT, JENNIFER; West Mifflin Area HS; W Mifflin, PA; (Y); 6/335; Church Yth Grp; Hosp Aide; High Hon Roll; NHS; Pres Schlr; Pres Schlrshp 86; Carlow Coll; Nrsng.

KILCOYNE, KELLY; Mt Alvernia HS; Pittsburgh, PA; (S); Camera Clb; Church Yth Grp; Dance Clb; Hosp Aide; Nwsp Rptr; VP Frsh Cls; High Hon Roll; NHS; Outstndg Achvt Bio 84; Outstndg Ctzn Awd 85.

KILEY, KRISTINA; Bethel Park SR HS; Bethel Park, PA; (Y); Church Yth Grp; Cmnty Wkr; DECA; FBLA; FHA; Hosp Aide; JA; Crs Cntry; Powder Puff Ftbl; Hon Roll; Presdntl Physical Fitness Awd 85-86; Robert Morris Coll; Nursing.

KILGANNON, JOHN; Upper Mooreland HS; Willow Grove, PA; (Y); 113/253; Var Bsktbl; Hon Roll; Prfct Atten Awd.

KILIANY, LISA; Geibel HS; Scottdale, PA; (Y); Cmnty Wkr; Drama Clb; Science Clb; School Musical; Stage Crew; Lit Mag; Mgr(s); High Hon Roll; Hon Roll; Trs NHS; Acctng.

KILKER, ANTHONY; Shenandoah Valley HS; Lost Creek, PA; (S); 12/100; Yrbk Sprt Ed; VP Frsh Cls; VP Soph Cls; Hst Jr Cls; Hst Sr Cls; Stu Cncl; Var Bsbl; Var Capt Bsktbl; Var Ftbl; High Hon Roll; K Of C Bsktbl Trnmnt All Star Tm 85; All-Cnty & All-Anthrct Dfnsv Bck 84 & 85; SR Chrty Bsktbl 85; Engnrng.

KILLEN, DAWN; Nazareth Acad; Philadelphia, PA; (Y); Church Yth Grp; Cmnty Wkr; Debate Tm; French Clb; Math Clb; Sec NFL; Red Cross Aide; Church Choir; NHS; JV Spch Fnlst 85; JV Debate Fnlst 85; Pre-Med.

KILLIAN, NATALIE; Shippensburg HS; Shippensburg, PA; (Y); 20/205; Sec Varsity Clb; JV Var Cheerleading; L Trk; Hon Roll; Lion Awd; Shippensburg U.

KILLINGER, TAMMY; Jersey Shore SR HS; Jersey Shore, PA; (Y); Church Yth Grp; Cmnty Wkr; Drama Clb; Trs VP 4-H; FBLA; Hosp Aide; Library Aide; Ski Clb; Mat Maids; Swmmng; 4-H Awd Best Attndc 84; Yth Grp Outstndng Ldrshp 85; Cazanovia; Chld Care.

KILLINO, MICHELLE; Old Forge HS; Old Forge, PA; (Y); Ski Clb; Var JV Cheerleading; Gregg Typng Awd 85.

KILLION, CLIFFORD; Jersey Shore SR HS; Jersey Shore, PA; (Y); Frstry.

KILLIP, ERIC W; Moon SR HS; Coraopolis, PA; (Y); 114/317; VP Church Yth Grp; Computer Clb; Church Choir; Orch; Hon Roll; Orch Fest Awd Dist 1 83; Spring Gdn Coll; Arch.

KILYANEK, ANNE; Pittston Area HS; Duryea, PA; (Y); 1/365; Church Yth Grp; Computer Clb; Drama Clb; Hosp Aide; Science Clb; Chorus; School Musical; High Hon Roll; NHS; NEDT Awd; U Scrnt; Comp Prgmr.

KIM, BYONG; Cheltenham HS; Elkins Pk, PA; (Y); Church Yth Grp; Intnl Clb; JV Var Socr; Penn ST; Elec Engr.

KIM, HYON; Downingtown SR HS; Downingtown, PA; (Y); 1/563; French Clb; Capt Quiz Bowl; Chorus; Ed Nwsp Bus Mgr; Var Capt Tennis; High Hon Roll; Var NHS; GAA; Acpl Chr; Nwsp Rptr; Brown U Bk Awd 86; Rensselaer Plytchnc Inst Mthmtcs & Sci Awd 86; PA JR Sci & Hmnts Sympsm 85; Law.

KIM, JOHN; Cheltenham HS; Elkins Pk, PA; (Y); 5/365; Church Yth Grp; VP Intnl Clb; Math Tm; Spanish Clb; JV Ftbl; Var Swmmng; JV Trk; High Hon Roll; 1st Pl DE Vly Sci Fair 85; Bk Awd 86; MIT; Elec Engrng.

KIM, JOHN; Lower Moreland HS; Huntingdon Valley, PA; (S); 6/214; Church Yth Grp; Science Clb; Concert Band; Jazz Band; Orch; Nwsp Rptr; Nwsp Stf; Pres Frsh Cls; VP Soph Cls; Pres Jr Cls; Dist Orchstra And Regnl Orchestra 84-86.

KIM, KRISTINE; Butler SR HS; Butler, PA; (Y); Church Yth Grp; French Clb; Hosp Aide; SADD; Orch; Hon Roll; Jr NHS.

KIM, NANCY; Penn Hills SR HS; Pittsburgh, PA; (Y); 1/797; French Clb; Ski Clb; School Musical; Yrbk Ed-Chief; Stu Cncl; High Hon Roll; Sec Jr NHS; Pres NHS; Ntl Merit Schol; Val; Westinghouse Fmly Schlrshp 86; Harvard-Radcliffe U; Pre-Med.

KIM, RICHARD; Central Bucks East HS; Doylestown, PA; (Y); Chess Clb; Debate Tm; Drama Clb; Science Clb; Mrchg Band; Yrbk Stf; Hon Roll; NHS; Tomorrows Ldrs Camp 86; Med.

KIM, ROY H; Shady Side Acad; Uniontown, PA; (Y); 11/111; Pres Camera Clb; VP Church Yth Grp; Ski Clb; Nwsp Phtg; Yrbk Phtg; High Hon Roll; Ntl Merit SF; Golf; Tennis; Wt Lftg; Natl Mrt Fnlst 86; Cum Laude Shdy Sd Acad 86; Brown U; Med.

KIM, SUNKYU; Mechanicsburg Area SR HS; Mechanicsburg, PA; (Y); 6/300; NFL; Speech Tm; Ed Nwsp Rptr; High Hon Roll; Hon Roll; NHS; Jrnlsm Achvt Awd, Cert Part Rotary Ldrs Conf 86; Intl Bus.

KIM, ULANDT U; Pocono Mountain HS; Cresco, PA; (Y); Scholastic Bowl; Var L Crs Cntry; Var L Trk; CC Awd; High Hon Roll; Kiwanis Awd; NHS; Ntl Merit Ltr; Wesleyan U; Bio.

KIMAK, RICHARD; West Mifflin Area HS; W Mifflin, PA; (Y); 38/365; Computer Clb; Band; Concert Band; Jazz Band; VP Mrchg Band; Hon Roll; NHS; U Of Pittsburgh.

KIMBEL, BRIAN; Danville SR HS; Danville, PA; (Y); Rep Church Yth Grp; Key Clb; Latin Clb; Spanish Clb; JV Bowling; Var Socr; High Hon Roll; NHS; Max Cum Laude Cert Ntl Ltn 86; Engrng.

KIMBERLAND, KELLY ANN; Canon Mc Millan HS; Eighty Four, PA; (Y); 68/360; French Clb; Concert Band; Drm Mjr(t); Jazz Band; Mrchg Band; Rep Stu Cncl; Var Sftbl; High Hon Roll; NHS; Piano Achvmnt Awd 84; Hnr Rl Mrt Awd 84; Wshngtn & Jffrsn Coll; Biolgy.

KIMBERLAND, MICHELLE; Bentworth HS; Eighty Four, PA; (Y); 5/103; Office Aide; Ski Clb; High Hon Roll; NHS; Pittsburgh U.

KIMBLE, GLENN; Fleetwood HS; Fleetwood, PA; (Y); Band; Jazz Band; Mrchg Band; Orch; Pep Band; School Musical; School Play; Bsbl; Golf; Socr; Pre-Law.

KIMBLE, SUSAN; Meyersdale Area HS; Meyersdale, PA; (S); Pres Church Yth Grp; Spanish Clb; Band; Concert Band; Mrchg Band; Hon Roll.

KIME, AMY; Harmony HS; Cherry Tree, PA; (Y); 7/43; Chorus; Concert Band; Capt Drill Tm; Drm Mjr(t); Yrbk Stf; Trs Stu Cncl; Dnfth Awd; Mrchg Band; Nwsp Rptr; 3rd Rnnr Up In Mdrn Miss Schlrshp Pgnt Of PA 84; Outstndng Bandfront Mem 85-86; Outstndng Chrldr 86; Phy Thrpy.

KIME, ANDREW M; Ridley SR HS; Woodlyn, PA; (Y); 22/412; Math Clb; Ski Clb; Chorus; Drm & Bgl; Jazz Band; School Musical; School Play; Yrbk Phtg; NHS; Ntl Merit SF; Louis Armstrong Jzz Awd 83; MIT; Aerspc Engrng.

KIMMEL, BRENDA; Hickory HS; Hermitage, PA; (Y); 35/175; Church Yth Grp; Cmnty Wkr; Library Aide; Service Clb; Band; Chorus; Concert Band; Jazz Band; Mrchg Band; Pep Band; Socty Dstngshd Amer H S Stdnts 85; Wrthy Advsr Rainbw Grls Assmbly 84; Cmp Cnslr 85-86; Alderson Broaddus Coll; Nrsg.

KIMMEL, EDWARD ALLEN; Blairsville SR HS; Blairsville, PA; (Y); Mgr(s); Hon Roll.

KIMMEL, JODI; Gateway SR HS; Mornoeville, PA; (Y); Chorus; Pres Acdmc Ftns Awd 86; U Pittsburgh; Pharm.

KIMMEL, KIMBERLY; Tyrone Area HS; Tyrone, PA; (S); 10/197; Church Yth Grp; Science Clb; Spanish Clb; Teachers Aide; Varsity Clb; Var Crs Cntry; Var Trk; High Hon Roll; NHS; Hnr Star Missionettes 85; Cross Cntry Top Ten Lge 85; Esther Awd 86; Ntrlst.

KIMMEL, LEIGH ANN; Marion Center Area HS; Home, PA; (Y); Church Yth Grp; Pres VP 4-H; FBLA; Trs FFA; Office Aide; Quiz Bowl; Teachers Aide; Nwsp Rptr; Yrbk Rptr; 4-H Awd; IN Cnty Dairy Prncss 86-84; ST Pork Prodcrs Awd 86; ST Lvstck Awd Wnnr 86.

KIMMEL, PAMELA; Tri Valley HS; Hegins, PA; (Y); 7/77; Church Yth Grp; Computer Clb; Exploring; 4-H; Hosp Aide; Ski Clb; SADD; Band; Chorus; Concert Band; Pre-Med.

KIMMEN, ANGELA LYN; Bellwood-Antis HS; Bellwood, PA; (Y); 27/115; Key Clb; Varsity Clb; Var L Bsktbl; Var Cheerleading; Hon Roll; Allegany CC; Dntl Hygnst.

KIMMEN, CHARLIE; Altoona Area HS; Altoona, PA; (Y); Drama Clb; Ski Clb; Spanish Clb; Varsity Clb; School Play; Rep Frsh Cls; Stu Cncl; Socr; Swmmng; Hon Roll.

KINARD, BRIAN; Central York HS; York, PA; (Y); 15/220; Trs Church Yth Grp; Varsity Clb; Yrbk Rptr; Yrbk Sprt Ed; Var L Ftbl; High Hon Roll; Hon Roll; Acdmc Lttr Svc Bar; Frgn Lang Clb; Aerospc Engnrng.

KINDELBERGER, MOLLY; Southmoreland SR HS; Scottdale, PA; (Y); Church Yth Grp; Drama Clb; Hosp Aide; Letterman Clb; Pep Clb; Ski Clb; Chorus; Church Choir; Yrbk Stf; Sftbl; Med.

KINDIG, TIFFANI ANN; Central York SR HS; York, PA; (Y); 63/248; Church Yth Grp; Ski Clb; Varsity Clb; Fld Hcky; Hon Roll; York Cnty YCIAA SR All Str Fld Hcky Tm 86; York Dsptchs Hnrbl Mntn Hcky Awd 86; Trvl Tech; Trvl Trsmr.

KINDON, MARK; South Western HS; Hanover, PA; (Y); Church Yth Grp; 4-H; Im Bsbl; JV Ftbl; JV Wrstlng; Hon Roll; Prfct Atten Awd; U S Navy.

KINDT, STEPHANIE; Wilson Area HS; Easton, PA; (S); 16/160; Dance Clb; Model UN; Ski Clb; Chorus; Color Guard; Flag Corp; Nwsp Rptr; Yrbk Rptr; Rep Soph Cls; Rep Jr Cls; Bloomsburg ST U; Nrsng.

KINDZIA, JERRY; Plum SR HS; Plum Boro, PA; (Y); 49/378; Boy Scts; German Clb; Letterman Clb; Tennis; Hon Roll; NHS; Plum Awd Acad Achvmnt 85; Engr.

KING, AARON; Bradford Area HS; Bradford, PA; (Y); 3/271; Cmnty Wkr; Key Clb; Ski Clb; Rep Frsh Cls; Trs Jr Cls; Trs Sr Cls; Rep Stu Cncl; Var L Tennis; Im Vllybl; High Hon Roll; Bus Mgmt.

KING, AMY; Pennsburg HS; Yardley, PA; (Y); Church Yth Grp; French Clb; Political Wkr; JV Var Sftbl; Var Trk; Im Vllybl; Ntl Merit Ltr; Acctg.

KING, AMY; Waynesburg Central HS; Waynesburg, PA; (Y); Camera Clb; Church Yth Grp; Trs French Clb; Office Aide; Ski Clb; Sec Chorus; Church Choir; Jazz Band; Stu Cncl; Trk; WCHS Ensmbl 85-86; Coal Queen Cndidt 1st Rnnr Up 86.

KING, AMY SUE; Southmoreland HS; Scottdale, PA; (Y); Dance Clb; JCL; Latin Clb; Office Aide; School Musical; Nwsp Stf; Lit Mag; Schlstc Dance Awd 86; Carlow Coll Schlrshp 86; Carlow Coll; Ed.

KING, ANDREA; Bishop Kenrick HS; Norristown, PA; (Y); ;Cmnctns.

KING, BILLIE JO; Everett Area HS; Everett, PA; (Y); Church Yth Grp; Computer Clb; French Clb; Library Aide; SADD; Varsity Clb; Band; Chorus; Color Guard; Concert Band; Physcl Thrpy.

KING, BRETT; Moniteau HS; Hilliards, PA; (Y); 1/140; Art Clb; Math Tm; Spanish Clb; SADD; High Hon Roll; Hon Roll; NHS; Ntl Merit SF; Voice Dem Awd; Church Yth Grp; 1st & 2nd Pl Lcl & ST JR Acad Sci 86; Comp Engrng.

KING, CARMEN; Connellsville Area HS; Mill Run, PA; (Y); 49/502; Pres Church Yth Grp; Chorus; School Musical; Swing Chorus; Yrbk Rptr; VP Stu Cncl; Var Cheerleading; L Sftbl; High Hon Roll; NHS; Hmcmng Crt 86; Western PA Schl; Nrsng.

KING, CLARK WILLIAM; Fort Le Boeuf HS; Erie, PA; (Y); 23/180; Band; Mrchg Band; Bsbl; Capt Bsktbl; High Hon Roll; Hon Roll; PSU; Fnc.

KING, COREY; Norther Potter HS; Genesee, PA; (Y); 15/85; Boy Scts; JV Capt Wrstlng; High Hon Roll; Hon Roll; Ntl Merit Ltr; Elec Engr.

KING, DAVID; Apollo-Ridge HS; Vandergrift, PA; (Y); 64/170; Varsity Clb; Jazz Band; Symp Band; Yrbk Stf; Rep Stu Cncl; L Ftbl; L Trk; Wt Lftg; Hon Roll; Rotary Awd; Penn ST; Doctor.

KING, DEBORAH; Dover Area HS; Dover, PA; (S); 5/290; AFS; VP JA; Acpl Chr; Chorus; School Musical; Variety Show; Yrbk Stf; Var Cheerleading; High Hon Roll; NHS; Chem.

KING, DENISE; Scranton Central HS; Scranton, PA; (Y); Drama Clb; French Clb; JA; Latin Clb; Library Aide; Ski Clb; Speech Tm; Nwsp Phtg; Nwsp Rptr; Nwsp Stf.

KING, DONALD; Monessen HS; Monessen, PA; (Y); 4/97; French Clb; Concert Band; Mrchg Band; Nwsp Stf; High Hon Roll; NHS; Bus Admin.

KING, DONNA; Neshaminy HS; Langhorne, PA; (Y); Art Clb; Band; Symp Band; JV Bsktbl; Var Powder Puff Ftbl; JV Socr; Hon Roll; Ntl Merit Schol; Comm Art.

KING, ELIZABETH; West York Area HS; York, PA; (Y); VP Spanish Clb; Rep Stu Cncl; Var Cheerleading; Var Tennis; JV Vllybl; Eng.

KING, GERI; Greencastle-Antrim HS; Greencastle, PA; (Y); 16/200; Church Yth Grp; Sec French Clb; Pep Clb; School Play; Hst Frsh Cls; Hst Soph Cls; Hst Jr Cls; Hst Sr Cls; Stu Cncl; Capt L Cheerleading; Shippensburg U.

KING, HOLLY; Sto-Rox SR HS; Mc Kees Rocks, PA; (Y); 49/134; Boys Clb Am; Church Yth Grp; FBLA; Chorus; Nwsp Stf; Yrbk Stf; VP Frsh Cls; Hon Roll; JA; Teachers Aide; Bys Clb Swm Tm 79-85; Bys Clb Bsktbl Tm 81-84; Wilson Coll; Vet Med Tech.

KING, JAMES; Saucon Valley HS; Bethlehem, PA; (Y); 25/100; Church Yth Grp; Band; Chorus; Concert Band; Jazz Band; Mrchg Band; School Musical; Rep Soph Cls; Hon Roll; Science Clb; Hugh O Brien Awd 85; Bible Coll; Rlgn.

KING, JESSICA; Frazier HS; Grindstone, PA; (S); Pres FNA; Hosp Aide; VP Band; Chorus; Capt Flag Corp; VP Mrchg Band; Hon Roll; NHS; Prfct Atten Awd; Shadyside Hosp Nrsg; Nrsg.

KING, JESSICA; Southmoreland SR HS; Everson, PA; (Y); Exploring; French Clb; VICA; Church Choir; Tennis; Trk; French Hon Soc.

KING, JOHN; Montoursville HS; Clairfield, PA; (Y); Church Yth Grp; JA; Schlstc Art Awds Certf Merit 86; Schlstc Art Awds Achvt Certf 86; Schlstc Art Awds Achvt Certf 85; Archlgy.

KING, KENNETH S; Brookville Area HS; Brookville, PA; (Y); 28/180; French Clb; Pep Clb; Concert Band; Jazz Band; Mrchg Band; Pep Band; School Musical; Variety Show; High Hon Roll; Pres Schlr; Louis Armstrong Jazz Awd 86; Grove City Coll; Intrnl Bus.

KING, KRISTEN; Dover Area HS; Dover, PA; (Y); 21/215; Church Yth Grp; Pres Girl Scts; Intnl Clb; Band; Chorus; Church Choir; Concert Band; Mrchg Band; Hon Roll; NHS; Slvr Ldrshp Awd Grl Scts 84; Chem.

KING, KRISTI; Southmoreland SR HS; Scottdale, PA; (Y); 12/250; Letterman Clb; Ski Clb; Yrbk Ed-Chief; Hst Sr Cls; Cheerleading; Powder Puff Ftbl; Sftbl; Pres Schlr; Spanish NHS; Art Clb; Hnr Grad; IN U Of PA; Nrsng.

KING, MATT; Jim Thorpe HS; Jim Thorpe, PA; (Y); Am Leg Boys St; Boy Scts; Var Crs Cntry; Var Ftbl; Var Gym; Var Wrstlng; Chorus; Swing Chorus; Hon Roll; Peer Cnlsr 85-86; Bruce Pollock Mem Awd 85-86; Elizabethtown; Pre-Law.

KING, MICHAEL; Dover Area HS; Dover, PA; (Y); 19/277; Letterman Clb; Varsity Clb; JV Bsbl; Im Var Bsktbl; Im Ftbl; Golf; Var L Tennis; Hon Roll; Comptr Sci Crse 86; Bus.

KING, PAMELA; Pocono Mountain HS; Long Pond, PA; (Y); 19/328; JA; Variety Show; Off Sr Cls; Var L Cheerleading; Var Trk; Hon Roll; Pres Jr NHS; Excllnc Spllng 84-86; Outstndg Achvmnt Physcs 86; JR Mss Pgnt 86; Intl Rltns.

KING, PETER; Hempfield Area SR HS; Greensburg, PA; (Y); Church Yth Grp; JV Bsktbl; Stat Ftbl; Stat Trk; High Hon Roll; Hon Roll; VP Jr NHS; Spanish NHS; Engrng.

KING, RACHEL A; John Bartram Motivation HS; Philadelphia, PA; (Y); 23/600; Drama Clb; School Musical; Yrbk Stf; Stu Cncl; Bowling; Pres Schlr; Alice Lowengrund Rosenthal Engl Lit Awd; U Of PA Acdmc Achvt; U Of Pittsburgh; Psych.

KING, RENEE N; Leberty HS; Bethlehem, PA; (Y); 25/475; Girl Scts; Band; Chorus; Concert Band; Mrchg Band; Yrbk Rptr; Yrbk Stf; Rep Soph Cls; Hon Roll; NHS; Bio.

KING, RICHARD A; Ringgold HS; Eighty Four, PA; (Y); Boy Scts; Hon Roll; Prfct Atten Awd; Math/Sci Hnr Soc; Penn ST U; Civil Engr.

KING, ROBERT; York Catholic HS; York, PA; (Y); Church Yth Grp; Ski Clb; Spanish Clb; Varsity Clb; Pres Stu Cncl; Var Crs Cntry; Var Trk; Hon Roll; St Champ X-Cntry Tm 85; 1st Soph X-Cntry Invtnl 84; St Rnnr Up X-Cntry Tms 82 & 84; Aerontcl Engrng.

KING, ROSALYN K; Kishacoquillas HS; Allensville, PA; (Y); 12/144; Varsity Clb; Variety Show; Var JV Fld Hcky; Var Trk; Im Vllybl; High Hon Roll; NHS; Church Yth Grp; Chorus; Secty Mo Aprl 86; Kish Bus Clb Secty 85-86; Stu Mo Aprl 85; Sectry.

KING, SAUNDRA; Peabody HS; Pittsburgh, PA; (S); 24/235; Sec JA; Sec Spanish Clb; Band; Concert Band; Mrchg Band; Nwsp Stf; Yrbk Stf; Hon Roll; Prfct Atten Awd; Acctng.

KING, STEVE; Franklin Area Jr SR HS; Franklin, PA; (Y); 45/200; French Clb; Band; Concert Band; Mrchg Band; High Hon Roll; Computer Clb; Letter Band 84-86; AZ ST U; Comp Engr.

KING, SUSAN L; North East HS; North East, PA; (Y); 42/149; Church Yth Grp; VP FHA; Pep Clb; Chorus; Capt Color Guard; Capt Drill Tm; School Musical; Variety Show; JV Vllybl; Hon Roll; Wednesday Musicale Vocal Awd 86; Outstdng SR Chorus Awd 86; Clarion U Of PA.

KING, TANYA; Archbishop John Carroll HS; Havertown, PA; (Y); Capt Cheerleading; High Hon Roll; Spanish NHS; U MD; Spch Cmnctns.

KING, TERICA; Waynesburg Central HS; Waynesburg, PA; (Y); Church Yth Grp; 4-H; French Clb; Girl Scts; Ski Clb; SADD; Chorus; Rep Jr Cls; Hon Roll; IN U; Psych.

KING, TINA; Harbor Creek HS; Erie, PA; (Y); 21/195; AFS; Model UN; Office Aide; School Play; Yrbk Stf; Hon Roll; NHS; Gannon U; Intl Studs.

KING, TRACIE; Otto-Eldred HS; Cuba, NY; (Y); 21/90; Chorus; Yrbk Stf; Cheerleading; Trk; Hon Roll; NHS; Prfct Atten Awd; Amrcn Gvrmnt Econ Awd 86; PHY Ther.

KING, TRACIE; Otto-Eldred HS; Eldred, PA; (Y); 21/93; Chorus; Nwsp Stf; Yrbk Stf; Pres Frsh Cls; Cheerleading; Trk; Hon Roll; NHS; Prfct Atten Awd; Amer Govt & Econ Awd 86; Phys Ther.

KING, TUSHA; North Western SR HS; E Springfield, PA; (Y); Church Yth Grp; GAA; Bsktbl; Trk; Vllybl; Hon Roll; Pres Ftns & Math Awds 85; Vrsty Ltr Awds 85-86; Temple; Comm.

KINGAN, GARY A; Jefferson-Morgan HS; Clarksville, PA; (Y); 27/93; Church Yth Grp; Yrbk Stf; Off Jr Cls; Hon Roll; Ntl Merit Ltr; Miami U; Cmptrs.

KINGSLEY, DANA; Butler SR HS; Butler, PA; (Y); French Clb; FBLA; Spanish Clb; SADD; Chorus; Stage Crew; Rep Frsh Cls; Rep Soph Cls; Im Bsktbl; Gannon U; Comm Arts.

KINGSLEY, JEFFREY; West Scranton HS; Scranton, PA; (Y); Boy Scts; Cmnty Wkr; Ski Clb; High Hon Roll; NHS; Med.

KINGSLEY, ROBYN; Butler Area SR HS; Butler, PA; (Y); Hosp Aide; Service Clb; Spanish Clb; SADD; Hon Roll; Htl Rstrnt Mgmt.

KINGSTON, LAURIE; Mercyhurst Prep Schl; Erie, PA; (Y); 9/150; Art Clb; Spanish Clb; Sec Lit Mag; Im Ftbl; Var Tennis; High Hon Roll; Hon Roll; NHS; Acad All Am 86; Hon Ment Poem,Photo Cntst 84-86.

KINGSTON, MICHELLE; Mansfield JR SR HS; Mansfield, PA; (S); 8/98; Church Yth Grp; FCA; Library Aide; Trs Sr Cls; Capt Bsktbl; Tennis; Co-Capt Vllybl; High Hon Roll; Hon Roll; NHS; Yth Ldr Of Tomrrw 85-86; MYEA Treas 85-86; Bus & Prfssnl Wmn Grl 85; Mansfield U; Frnch.

KINIRY, PATRICIA J; Bishop Mc Cort HS; Johnstown, PA; (Y); Pep Clb; Ski Clb; Nwsp Phtg; Nwsp Rptr; Nwsp Stf; Yrbk Stf; High Hon Roll; Hon Roll; Duquesne U; Fin.

KINKEAD, MATTHEW S; Monaca HS; Monaca, PA; (Y); Am Leg Boys St; Ski Clb; Bus.

KINKELLA, SUSAN; Southmoreland HS; Ruffsdale, PA; (Y); 11/242; Letterman Clb; Capt Color Guard; Concert Band; Mrchg Band; Nwsp Stf; Yrbk Stf; Lit Mag; Off Soph Cls; Stu Cncl; French Hon Soc; Med.

KINNAN, SHERRY; Saltsburg JR SR HS; Clarksburg, PA; (Y); 2/82; Varsity Clb; Concert Band; Yrbk Ed-Chief; Yrbk Stf; Rep Stu Cncl; Var L Cheerleading; Powder Puff Ftbl; High Hon Roll; NHS; Sal; Business Careers Inst; Secy.

KINNEY, NICOLE M; Cambria Heights HS; Elmora, PA; (Y); Cmnty Wkr; Hon Roll; Med Fld.

KINS, ANDREA; Bishop Kenrick HS; Norristown, PA; (Y); Telecmnctns.

KINSEY, BRIAN; Ridgway HS; Ridgway, PA; (S); 4/130; Church Yth Grp; Computer Clb; Mathletes; Science Clb; Ski Clb; Spanish Clb; Varsity Clb; Off Frsh Cls; Off Jr Cls; Off Sr Cls; Amer Chem Soc Cert Outstndg Achvt; Defnsv Cptn Vrsty Ftbl Tm; Chem Engrng.

KINSEY, DAWN; Ligonier Valley SR HS; Ligonier, PA; (Y); 30/160; AFS; Teachers Aide; Chorus; Drm Mjr(t); Swing Chorus; Cheerleading; Stat Ftbl; Var L Vllybl; Pres Schlr; Schlrshp Stanhome Prod Inc $1000 86; Carlow Coll; Bio.

KINSEY, KAREN; Johnstown HS; Johnstown, PA; (Y); 13/286; French Clb; Math Clb; SADD; Flag Corp; Mrchg Band; Stu Cncl; Elks Awd; High Hon Roll; Hon Roll; NHS; Johnstown HS Alumni Schlrshp 86; IN U Of PA; Comp Sci.

KINSKY, CHARLES; Methacton HS; Worcester, PA; (Y); 41/340; VP Exploring; Pres VP 4-H; German Clb; Office Aide; Off Sr Cls; 4-H Awd; High Hon Roll; Hon Roll; NHS; Ntl Merit Ltr; ST Acad Decthln Tm 86; Biomdcl Engrng.

KINTER, MARGOT; Northern Potter HS; Ulysses, PA; (S); French Clb; Nwsp Rptr; Yrbk Stf; French Hon Soc; Hon Roll; FHA; Library Aide; Penn ST; Prelaw.

KINTIGH, LAURA; Peters Township HS; Venetia, PA; (S); 29/265; Key Clb; Spanish Clb; Sec Stu Cncl; Stat Ftbl; Powder Puff Ftbl; Var Capt Swmmng; Spanish NHS; Stu Advsry Commtt Chrprsn/Secy; SHASDA Rep; Penn ST U; Frgn Rltns.

KINZLER, FREDERICK; Frankford HS; Philadelphia, PA; (Y); 1/740; Church Yth Grp; Computer Clb; Math Clb; Math Tm; Jazz Band; Mrchg Band; High Hon Roll; Hon Roll; NHS; Prfct Atten Awd; Comp Sci.

KINZLER, MICHELLE; Quigley HS; Baden, PA; (Y); 4-H; French Clb; NFL; Pep Clb; Science Clb; SADD; Chorus; Nwsp Stf; 4-H Awd; Flight Atten.

KIOSKI, CRAIG; Ligonier Valley HS; Ligonier, PA; (Y); 10/157; French Clb; Letterman Clb; School Play; Sec Jr Cls; Var L Bsktbl; Var L Ftbl; Hon Roll; Lion Awd; NHS; Pre-Dntstry.

KIRBY, BERNICE; Charleroi Area HS; Charleroi, PA; (Y); French Clb; Office Aide; Varsity Clb; VP Soph Cls; VP Jr Cls; Pres Stu Cncl; Var L Swmmng; NHS; Hospitality Clb 84-86; Stu Forum 85-86.

KIRBY, COLLEEN; Archbishop Ryan High Schl For Girls; Philadelphia, PA; (Y); 4/491; Office Aide; Science Clb; Service Clb; Spanish Clb; Rep Jr Cls; Im Bowling; High Hon Roll; NHS; Pres Ntl Hnr Soc 86-87; Awds Art, Bio, Geo 84-85; Acctg.

KIRBY, JOSEPH MICHAEL; St John Neumann HS; Philadelphia, PA; (Y); 97/354; Art Clb; Pres Boy Scts; Church Yth Grp; German Clb; Mrchg Band; Hon Roll; Art Poster Cont Awd 84; Phila Coll Of Art; Comm Art.

KIRBY, MARK; Central York SR HS; York, PA; (Y); Boy Scts; Church Yth Grp; Var Ftbl; Hon Roll; York Coll PA; Sci.

KIRBY, TONI; Brownsville Area HS; Fairbank, PA; (S); 8/225; VP Church Yth Grp; Drama Clb; SADD; Band; Chorus; Church Choir; Mrchg Band; Rep Jr Cls; NHS; Chrstn Educ Awd 85; Engrng.

KIRCH, JEFFREY; Bethel Park HS; Bethel Park, PA; (Y); Church Yth Grp; JA; High Hon Roll; NHS; Engrg.

KIRCHER, KRISTINA; Saegertown HS; Meadville, PA; (Y); 6/117; Am Leg Aux Girls St; Hosp Aide; Concert Band; Mrchg Band; Jr NHS; NHS; Pres Schlr; Church Yth Grp; French Clb; Band; Lang Awd Frnch; Dist Band; Jr Dist Band & Co Band; Cntrl PA Bus Schl; Court Rptr.

KIRCHNER, BETH ANN; Bedford HS; Bedford, PA; (Y); 32/176; Ski Clb; Chorus; JV Bsktbl; Var Cheerleading; Var Sftbl; Var Trk; Var Vllybl; Hon Roll; Tchng.

KIRCHNER, ERIC; Blacklick Valley HS; Vintondale, PA; (S); 12/90; VP German Clb; Varsity Clb; School Play; Stage Crew; Pres Jr Cls; Pres Sr Cls; Var L Bsbl; Hon Roll; US Navy; Sonar Technlgy.

KIRCHNER, KEVIN; Hempfield HS; Greensburg, PA; (Y); Aud/Vis; Camera Clb; Computer Clb; Service Clb; Hon Roll; Math.

KIRK, BARBARA ALLISON; Slippery Rock Area HS; Slippery Rck, PA; (Y); Intnl Clb; Concert Band; Mrchg Band; Pep Band; Stage Crew; Nwsp Rptr; Elks Awd; High Hon Roll; Hon Roll; Pres Schlr; Outstndng Cncrt Bnd Stu Awd 86; Slippery Rock U Of PA; Anthrpl.

KIRK, BRAD; Mechanicsburg SR HS; Harrisburg, PA; (Y); Ski Clb; Var L Bsbl; Mgr Ftbl; Var Capt Golf; Var Swmmng; Im Tennis; Bus Mgmt.

KIRK, COLEEN; Greensburg Cntrl Catholic HS; Greensburg, PA; (Y); Varsity Clb; Var L Tennis; High Hon Roll; NHS; Intl Bus.

KIRK, GEORGE; Moon SR HS; Coraopolis, PA; (Y); 31/325; Church Yth Grp; Computer Clb; Exploring; Key Clb; Red Cross Aide; Sec VICA; Var Socr; Var L Swmmng; Hon Roll; Math.

KIRK, HEATHER; Schuylkill Valley HS; Reading, PA; (S); 2/129; Band; Chorus; School Musical; School Play; Rep Stu Cncl; High Hon Roll; Sec NHS; Pre-Med.

KIRKENDALL, MICHAEL BRIAN; Hempfield Area SR HS; Greensburg, PA; (Y); 57/657; Trs Sr Cls; Rep Stu Cncl; Var L Bsbl; Var Capt Ftbl; Var Capt Trk; NHS; Prfct Atten Awd; Spanish NHS; Garnegie-Mellon U.

KIRKLAND, BELINDA; Blairsville SR HS; Blairsville, PA; (Y); 35/130; Pres Church Yth Grp; SADD; Chorus; NHS; Drama Clb; Trs 4-H; Library Aide; Church Choir; Hon Roll; Englsh.

KIRKLAND JR, CHARLES W; Central HS; Philadelphia, PA; (Y); 56/225; Chess Clb; Math Clb; Nwsp Stf; Ed Yrbk Stf; Hon Roll; Natl Achvt Schlrshp Cmmndtn 85; Philadelphia Inquirers Jrnlsm Career Devlpmt Wrkshp 85; Med.

KIRKLAND, JOHN; Cardinal O Hara HS; Newtown Sq, PA; (Y); Aud/Vis; Chess Clb; Debate Tm; Latin Clb; PAVAS; Political Wkr; Speech Tm; School Play; Stage Crew; Lit Mag; Bus.

KIRKNER, JENNIFER; Danville HS; Danville, PA; (Y); 26/204; Pres Sec Church Yth Grp; Pres VP 4-H; VP SADD; Church Choir; Color Guard; Mrchg Band; 4-H Awd; High Hon Roll; NHS; Prfct Atten Awd; Candystrpg Cert 100 Hrs 85; Psych.

KIRKNER, MATTHEW; Danville Area HS; Danville, PA; (Y); Chess Clb; Church Yth Grp; CAP; Computer Clb; 4-H; Band; Church Choir; Concert Band; Drill Tm; Mrchg Band; PA ST; Aerospc Engrng.

KIRKPATRICK, AMY BETH; Belle Vernon Area HS; Belle Vernon, PA; (Y); Church Yth Grp; Drama Clb; FBLA; Sec FNA; Hosp Aide; Pep Clb; SADD; Chorus; Church Choir; Color Guard; Hosp Vlnteen Awd Cap & Pin For 50 & 100 Hrs Svc 84-85; Med Intrst Clb Plq Ofc JR Coord 86; Secy.

KIRKPATRICK, PATRICIA; Bishop Guilfoyle HS; Altoona, PA; (Y); Church Yth Grp; Cmnty Wkr; Science Clb; Chorus; JV Sftbl; Var L Vllybl; Physcl Thrpy.

KIRKPATRICK, PAULA; Homer Center HS; Lucernermines, PA; (Y); 3/90; Drama Clb; Sec FBLA; Hosp Aide; Office Aide; VP SADD; Pres Band; Pres Chorus; Co-Capt Color Guard; School Musical; High Hon Roll; Rep IN Evening Gazette 85-87; Fnlst :In Cty Miss Pagent 86; Bus.

KIRKWOOD, BONNIE; South Western HS; Hanover, PA; (Y); 1/206; Quiz Bowl; Yrbk Ed-Chief; High Hon Roll; NHS; Ntl Merit Ltr; NEDT Awd; Val; JA; Gldn Glln Awd 86; Pres Acad Ftns Awd 86; PA Twp Lions Cert Of Attnmnt 86; Ursinus Coll; Wrtr.

KIRKWOOD, RENEE; Shenango HS; New Castle, PA; (Y); Dance Clb; Drill Tm; Bsktbl; Cheerleading; Score Keeper; Sftbl; Trk; Vllybl; Hon Roll; Cmptr Pgrmnng.

KIRLIN, CRAIG; Pottsgrove HS; Stowe, PA; (Y); 48/229; Latin Clb; Pres Leo Clb; JV Ftbl; Im Wt Lftg; Var Wrstlng; Hon Roll; Chess Clb; Air Force; Engnrng.

KIRLIN, KERRY; St Maria Goretti HS; Philadelphia, PA; (Y); 168/390; Church Yth Grp; Computer Clb; Hgh Avg Albgra 83; Trvl Agnt.

KIRN, CHRISTINE M; Penn Hills SR HS; Pittsburgh, PA; (Y); 66/789; French Clb; Letterman Clb; Ski Clb; Band; Concert Band; Mrchg Band; Stu Cncl; High Hon Roll; Hon Roll; Jr NHS; PA ST U; Mathmtcs.

KIRSCH, BRENDA; Northern Cambria HS; Wicktown, PA; (Y); 1/120; French Clb; Girl Scts; Chorus; Color Guard; Pres Soph Cls; VP L Bsktbl; L Trk; VP L Vllybl; High Hon Roll; NHS; Fr Awd 83 & 85; IN U PA; Mth Ed.

KIRSCH, DONNA; Nothern Cambra HS; Nicktown, PA; (Y); Girl Scts; Band; Chorus; Concert Band; Jazz Band; Pep Band; Sftbl; High Hon Roll; Hon Roll; Spanish NHS; Indiana U PA; Elem Educ.

KIRSCH, LINDA; Cambria Hgts HS; St Benedict, PA; (Y); 9/200; Concert Band; Mrchg Band; Hon Roll; NEDT Awd; Rdlgc Tech.

KIRSCH, VICKI; Northwestern HS; W Springfield, PA; (Y); Library Aide; Band; Chorus; Color Guard; Mrchg Band; Yrbk Stf; Pom Pon; Var L Trk; Hon Roll; Elem Educ.

KIRSCHNER, WILLIAM; Cardinal O Hara HS; Broomall, PA; (Y); 119/744; Church Yth Grp; Spanish Clb; Var Capt Bsktbl; Var Wt Lftg; Hon Roll; Prfct Atten Awd; Markward Awd 86; MVP Vrsty Bsktbl 86; MVP Ohara Tourn 86; Ursinus Coll; Bus Admin.

KIRTLAND, KELLY; York Catholic HS; York, PA; (Y); Drama Clb; French Clb; Girl Scts; Hosp Aide; Acpl Chr; Chorus; Color Guard; Mrchg Band; School Musical; Variety Show; PA ST; Pathlgst.

KIRWIN, BRIAN; Father Judge HS; Philadelphia, PA; (Y); 12/364; Cmnty Wkr; Nwsp Ed-Chief; Nwsp Rptr; Nwsp Sprt Ed; Nwsp Stf; Brdcst Jrnlsm.

KIS HALAS, KRISZTINA; Upper Merion Area SR HS; King Of Prussia, PA; (Y); 17/330; French Clb; Math Tm; Chorus; Concert Band; Var Trk; Im Vllybl; Hon Roll; Ntl Sci Olympd Prtcpnt 86; Ntl Sci Olympd Prtcpnt 85; Astrnmy.

KISCADDEN, JENNIFER; Cedar Crest HS; Lebanon, PA; (Y); Pep Clb; Band; Color Guard; Lib Concert Band; Drm Mjr(t); Jazz Band; VP Mrchg Band; Pep Band; Hon Roll; Dist Band 86; Cnty Band 85; Amer Music Abroad 85; Social Work.

KISELICA, LYNN; Mt Lebanon HS; Pittsburgh, PA; (Y); Art Clb; Church Yth Grp; Drama Clb; Ski Clb; Spanish Clb; School Play; Frsh Cls; Diving; Trk; Hon Roll; Duquesne U; Psych.

KISER, CHRIS; Avonworth JR SR HS; Pittsbg, PA; (Y); 24/96; Cmnty Wkr; Pres French Clb; Band; School Play; Nwsp Stf; Yrbk Stf; Lit Mag; Rep Frsh Cls; Rep Soph Cls; VP Jr Cls.

KISH, BETH; Palmyra Area HS; Palmyra, PA; (Y); Hosp Aide; JV Var Tennis; High Hon Roll; Outstndng Jr Shrthnd Stu Yr 85-86; Outstndng Jr Typst Yr 85-86; Bus Clb 85-86; Harrisburg Area CC; Psychlgy.

KISH, MONIQUE; Crestwood HS; Mountaintop, PA; (Y); #108 In Class; Ski Clb; Var Trk; Hon Roll.

KISHBACH, AMBER; Central Columbia HS; Berwick, PA; (Y); Drama Clb; FHA; Pep Clb; Govt.

KISHBAUGH, DAWN; Col-Mont Area Vo Tech; Mocanaqua, PA; (Y); FHA; Girl Scts; Off Soph Cls; Off Jr Cls; Fld Hcky; Prmlmntrn-Hero Clb 84-85; Pres Of Hero Clb 85-86; Cook.

KISHBAUGH, WAYNE; Wyalusing Valley HS; Laceyville, PA; (Y); Boy Scts; Church Yth Grp; 4-H; FBLA; Band; Church Choir; Concert Band; Mrchg Band; School Play; 4-H Awd; Eagle Scout 85; Acctng.

KISHLOCK, REGINA; Homer Ctr; Homer City, PA; (Y); FBLA; Q&S; Chorus; Jazz Band; Hon Roll; NHS; IN Cnty Princpls Assn Scholar 86; Bst Acctng Stu 86; IN U PA; Acctng.

KISSEL, MICHAEL; Bethel Park SR HS; Bethel Park, PA; (Y); Church Yth Grp; Latin Clb; Science Clb; PA JR Acad Of Sci 81-86; Sci.

KISSELL, CHRIS; Portage Area HS; Portage, PA; (S); 19/118; Church Yth Grp; Ski Clb; School Play; Im Bsktbl; Hon Roll; NHS; U Of Pittsburgh; Acctg.

KISSINGER, KURT; Mechanisburg Area SR HS; Mechanicsburg, PA; (Y); 7/327; Political Wkr; Concert Band; Mrchg Band; Symp Band; Nwsp Stf; High Hon Roll; NHS; Congress-Bundestag Yth Exch Scholar Pgm 85-86; Intl Rel.

KISSMAN, AMY; Villa Maria Acad; Erie, PA; (Y); Ski Clb; Rep Frsh Cls; Rep Jr Cls; JV Bsktbl; Hon Roll; Mercyhurst Coll; Fshn Merchndsn.

KISTLER, CYNTHIA; Emmaus HS; Macungie, PA; (Y); 47/493; German Clb; Hst Key Clb; Trs Soph Cls; Trs Jr Cls; Off Stu Cncl; L Mgr(s); Var Capt Vllybl; High Hon Roll; Jr NHS; NHS; Howard A Eyer Awd Excllnce 84; Law.

KISTLER, DOUGLAS G; Central York HS; York, PA; (Y); Pres Varsity Clb; Symp Band; Stu Cncl; Var Bsbl; Var Ftbl; Hon Roll; Church Yth Grp; Ski Clb; Church Choir; Concert Band; Pre-Med.

KITABJIAN, PAUL; Marple Newtown HS; Broomall, PA; (Y); 4/350; Chess Clb; Church Yth Grp; Math Clb; Math Tm; Science Clb; Service Clb; Chorus; Church Choir; School Musical; Socr; 2nd Hghst Scr PML Math Cmptn Schls Hstry 85-86; Dist & Rgnl Choruses 84-86; Rnkd 2nd Schl Wd Math 85; Drexel U; Elec Engnrng.

KITCHEN, JANA; Danville SR HS; Danville, PA; (Y); 15/199; Church Yth Grp; 4-H; Spanish Clb; Chorus; Church Choir; Var L Bsktbl; Cit Awd; 4-H Awd; High Hon Roll; NHS; Am Leg Aux Cert Schl Awd 84; Gregg Shorthand Awd 85; Bus.

KITCHEN, STEFANIE; Mercy Vocational HS; Philadelphia, PA; (Y); FBLA; JA; Bsbl; Bsktbl; Bowling; Swmmng; Vllybl; Wrstlng; Prfct Atten Awd; St Schlr; Brandywine Coll; Bus Exc Sec.

KITTA, AMY; Mt Pleasant HS; Mt Pleasant, PA; (Y); Church Yth Grp; Cmnty Wkr; FBLA; GAA; Hosp Aide; Library Aide; Office Aide; Nwsp Stf; Var L Bsktbl; JV Mgr(s); Mc Donalds Emplyee Of The Mnth 86; BCI Inst; Data Prcssr.

KITTELL, KRISTEN; Portage Area HS; Portage, PA; (Y); 25/113; Bowling; Hon Roll; CA U PA; Envrnmntl Consrvtn.

KITTLE, TEREASA MARIE; Troy HS; Troy, PA; (Y); Am Leg Aux Girls St; Pres 4-H; Letterman Clb; Ski Clb; Trs Soph Cls; Trs Jr Cls; Trs Sr Cls; Co-Capt Cheerleading; Sftbl; Cit Awd.

KITZ, JOHN; Mt Pleasant Area HS; Mt Pleasant, PA; (Y); German Clb; Latin Clb.

KITZMILLER, ERVIN; United HS; Blairsville, PA; (S); 1/129; Chess Clb; Lit Mag; Bausch & Lomb Sci Awd; High Hon Roll; Sec Mu Alp Tht; Trs Pres NHS; Val; Penn ST U; Chem Engrng.

KIVADOR, AMY; Sto-Rox HS; Mc Kees Rocks, PA; (Y); Chorus; Nwsp Stf; Yrbk Stf; Trs Stu Cncl; Hon Roll; Miss PA Teen USA Pagnt 84; Comm.

KKRISE, LEO; Clearfield Area HS; Woodland, PA; (Y); 115/298; VICA; Hon Roll; Triangle Tech; Elec Svc Tech.

KLAAS, PAM; Mount Alvernia HS; Pittsburgh, PA; (Y); 16/69; Church Yth Grp; Spanish Clb; Chorus; Yrbk Rptr; Yrbk Stf; High Hon Roll; Hon Roll; NHS; Spanish Awd 83-84; Relgn Awd 83-84; W Penn Nrsng Sch; Nrsng.

KLADNY, KIMBERLY; Freeport Area HS; Sarver, PA; (S); 18/170; Drama Clb; Girl Scts; Chorus; Drill Tm; School Play; Stage Crew; High Hon Roll; Dance Clb; Sftbl; Swmmng; Sci.

KLAHR, AMY; Conrad Weiser HS; Robesonia, PA; (Y); 35/195; VP Spanish Clb; Chorus; School Musical; School Play; Yrbk Stf; VP Jr Cls; Stu Cncl; Cheerleading; Fld Hcky; Hon Roll; Elem Ed.

KLANCHAR, CINDY; Bishop Mc Cort HS; Johnstown, PA; (Y); 20/120; Cmnty Wkr; Exploring; Hosp Aide; Latin Clb; Radio Clb; Spanish Clb; Chorus; School Musical; High Hon Roll; Hon Roll; Cert Of Apprctn Frm Memorial Hosp 86; Inducted Into Span Hnr Soc 86; U Pittsburgh; Pharm.

KLANICA, CHRIS; Kiski Area HS; Freeport, PA; (Y); Aud/Vis; Pep Clb; Band; Chorus; Concert Band; Mrchg Band; Orch; Pep Band; Symp Band; Cit Awd.

KLANICA, DARLA; Freeport Area HS; Sarver, PA; (S); 11/173; Sec Trs Mrchg Band; Sec Trs Symp Band; Nwsp Ed-Chief; Rep Frsh Cls; Rep Jr Cls; Rep Sr Cls; Stu Cncl; High Hon Roll; Pres NHS; Teen Tlnt Comp Instrmntl Solo 83; Grove City Coll; Elec Engr.

KLAPATCH, MARK; Valley View JR SR HS; Peckville, PA; (Y); 15/200; Church Yth Grp; Spanish Clb; Crs Cntry; Trk; High Hon Roll; Hon Roll; NHS; Rotary Awd; PA ST; Hlth And Phys Educ.

KLAPHAKE, JENNIFER; Canon Mc Millan HS; Mc Donald, PA; (Y); 137/349; Aud/Vis; Varsity Clb; Chorus; Diving; Swmmng; Trk; High Hon Roll; Church Yth Grp; FBLA; Library Aide; Hnrbl Mention In Most Contributed To Schl 86; Church Ply 85; Most Athletic Girl 83; Comm Of Alleg; Accounting.

KLAPKOWSKI, KRISTIN; Mc Guffey HS; Claysville, PA; (Y); 2/201; French Clb; Varsity Clb; VP Soph Cls; Stu Cncl; Capt Cheerleading; L Trk; NHS; Rotary Awd; Am Leg Aux Girls St; VP Cnty Stdnt Forum 86-87.

KLAREVAS, LOUIS; James M Coughlin HS; Wilkes-Barre, PA; (Y); 7/382; Math Clb; SADD; School Play; Variety Show; Yrbk Stf; Pres Frsh Cls; Stu Cncl; Ftbl; Trk; JETS Awd; Luzerne Cnty Rep Womens Pol Sci Stu Of The Yr 86; Amer Hellenic Ed Prog Assoc Schlrshp 86; U Of PA; Pol Sci.

KLASE, CHRISTINE E; Liberty HS; Bethlehem, PA; (Y); 26/391; Band; Concert Band; Orch; Bowling; Var Capt Crs Cntry; Var Capt Trk; Hon Roll; NHS; Amer Assn Of U Women 86; PA ST U; Math.

KLASTER, CHRISTINE; Nazareth Acad; Feasterville, PA; (S); 7/125; Girl Scts; NFL; Chorus; School Musical; Rep Soph Cls; Rep Jr Cls; Pres Stu Cncl; Hon Roll; NHS; Opt Clb Awd; Girl Scout Awds 84; 2nd Pl Drexel Mus Awd Voice 85; Hon Mntn Phila Hist Soc Essay Cntst 85; Pol Sci.

KLAYMAN, DEBBIE; Pennsbury HS; Morrisville, PA; (Y); Drama Clb; Intnl Clb; School Play; Yrbk Stf; NHS.

KLAZON, CHARLES; Kiski Area HS; Vandergrift, PA; (Y); Boy Scts; Cmnty Wkr; JA; Spanish Clb; Chorus; High Hon Roll; Hon Roll; IN U Of PA; Comp Sci.

KLEBES, HEIDI; Villa Maria Acad; Erie, PA; (S); 16/140; Pres Church Yth Grp; Spanish Clb; VP Soph Cls; Rep Stu Cncl; Capt L Tennis; Var L Trk; NHS; PIAA Dist X Dbls Chmpn 85; Htl Mgmt.

KLECKNER, JACQUE; Lock Haven SR HS; Lock Haven, PA; (Y); Church Yth Grp; Service Clb; Spanish Clb; Trs Chorus; VP Frsh Cls; Rep Soph Cls; Trs Jr Cls; Var Capt Cheerleading; Cit Awd; NHS; Acad Awds Hme Ec, Engl & Chem 84-85; Hmcmng Crt 84-85; Ctznshp & Acad Achvt Awds 85; Anthrplgy.

KLECKNER, ZOE; Delaware County Christian Schl; Haverton, PA; (Y); 2/77; Math Tm; Chorus; Pres Soph Cls; Pres Jr Cls; Pres Sr Cls; Var Cheerleading; Var Capt Fld Hcky; Var Sftbl; High Hon Roll; NHS; MVP Fld Hcky 85-86; Coaches Awd Sftbl 85-86; MVP Sftbl 84-85; Pre-Med.

KLEIMAN, DAVID; Cheltenham HS; Elkins Pk, PA; (Y); Science Clb; Temple Yth Grp; Lit Mag; Bowling; Socr; NEDT Awd; JR Bk Awd Spnsh 86; PA JR Acad Sci & DE Vly Sci Fair Wnnr 84-86; Temple Bsktbl Leag 84-86.

KLEIN, BETH A; Baldwin HS; Pittsburgh, PA; (Y); 71/531; Church Yth Grp; JA; Trs Key Clb; Chorus; School Musical; Yrbk Stf; Hon Roll; Rosemarie E Cibik Awd 86; Outstdng Treas Key Clb 86; IN U Of PA; Elem Educ.

KLEIN, BRIAN P; George Washington HS; Philadelphia, PA; (Y); 21/737; Yrbk Ed-Chief; Ed Yrbk Phtg; Hon Roll; Trs NHS; Ntl Merit SF; PA JR Acad Sci Awds 81-86; Ofcr YSY 85-86; Ofcr Stu Govt 84-86; Biomed Engrng.

KLEIN, DIANA; Kennard Dale HS; Fawn Grove, PA; (Y); School Musical; Yrbk Phtg; Off Frsh Cls; VP Soph Cls; Off Jr Cls; Off Sr Cls; Pres Stu Cncl; JV Var Vllybl; Hon Roll; NHS; Prtcptd In Hugh O Brien Yth Ldrshp Conf 85; Prtcptd In Stud Cncl Conf 84-85; Grmn Clb 83-86; Culinary Arts.

KLEIN, DONNA; North Hills HS; Pittsburgh, PA; (Y); 20/506; High Hon Roll; Hon Roll; Pres Schlr; La Roche Coll; Acctng.

KLEIN, KAREN; Peters Twp HS; Mc Murray, PA; (Y); 31/230; Church Yth Grp; Key Clb; Science Clb; Drill Tm; Mrchg Band; Orch; School Musical; L Gym; High Hon Roll; Hon Roll; Excllnc Acadmcs 85; Excllnc Lang Stdy Germn 85; Mid East All Str Prgrm 84-85; Engrng.

KLEIN, KIMBERLEY; G A R Memorial HS; Wilkes Barre, PA; (Y); 69/180; Library Aide; Office Aide; Chorus; Drill Tm; Nwsp Rptr; Mgr(s); Mat Maids; Score Keeper; Sftbl; Twrlr; Athltc Schlrshp Coll Msrcrda 86; Coll Misercordia; Elem Educ.

KLEIN, LETHA; East Pennsboro HS; Enola, PA; (Y); 5/200; Cmnty Wkr; German Clb; Latin Clb; Red Cross Aide; School Musical; Stage Crew; Stu Cncl; Stat Mgr Bsktbl; High Hon Roll; NHS; Engrng.

KLEIN, MISSY; Holy Name HS; Wyomsng Hls, PA; (Y); 13/115; Pep Clb; Nwsp Rptr; Var L Bsktbl; Var L Fld Hcky; Var Trk; Vllybl; NHS; Opt Clb Awd; 1st Pl Btny Div Rdng Brks Sci Fair 83; 1st Pl Btny Div PA JR Acad Of Sci 84; Hrld W Schlrshp; PA ST U; Bio.

KLEIN, SHARON; North Hills HS; Pittsburgh, PA; (S); 6/475; VP Church Yth Grp; Keywanettes; Thesps; Capt Drm & Bgl; School Play; Rep Jr Cls; Twrlr; High Hon Roll; NHS; Socty Distngshd Amer H S Stdnts 86.

KLEINFELTER, SCOTT; Palmyra Area HS; Campbelltown, PA; (Y); 99/189; French Clb; Varsity Clb; Capt Ftbl; Trk; Hon Roll; Bus.

KLEINFELTER, TINA; Annville-Cleona HS; Cleona, PA; (S); 20/121; Sec FBLA; Office Aide; Varsity Clb; Band; Chorus; Flag Corp; Yrbk Stf; Var Cheerleading; NHS; Scrtrl.

KLEINHENZ, MARCY LYNN; Penn Hills HS; Pittsburgh, PA; (Y); Cmnty Wkr; Hosp Aide; Office Aide; Teachers Aide; Acpl Chr; Chorus; Swing Chorus; Variety Show; Off Sr Cls; Stu Cncl; Dist Choir 85; Regnl Choir 85; Surgcl Techncn.

KLEIST, STACEY; Meadville Area SR HS; Meadville, PA; (Y); Church Yth Grp; Varsity Clb; Sec Frsh Cls; Sec Stu Cncl; JV Var Cheerleading; Var Gym; Var Trk; Hon Roll.

KLEMM, DEBORAH; Greencastle-Antrim HS; Greencastle, PA; (Y); Sec Trs Church Yth Grp; Hosp Aide; Band; Chorus; Church Choir; Concert Band; Mrchg Band; Yrbk Stf; 3rd Pl-Sci Fair-Chem 85; Allegheny Coll; Psych.

KLEMS, DARLENE E; Chicester SR HS; Boothwyn, PA; (Y); Church Yth Grp; Pres VP FBLA; Model UN; Yrbk Bus Mgr; Im JV Bsktbl; Hon Roll; Jr NHS; 2nd Pl PA FBLA Comp Bus Math 84; Close-Up Govt Studies Pgm 84 & 85; PA Free Enterprise Wk 84; Bradford Schl; Accntng.

KLENOVICH, JANICE; Bethlehem Catholic HS; Bethlehem, PA; (Y); Red Cross Aide; Stat Bsbl; Coach Actv; Mgr(s); Hon Roll; Northampton Area CC; Nrsng.

KLEPPER, PAULA; Hatboro-Horsham SR HS; Hatboro, PA; (Y); Church Yth Grp; FCA; Girl Scts; Natl Beta Clb; Pep Clb; Science Clb; Spanish Clb; SADD; Band; Church Choir; Bio.

KLEVENCE, JENNIFER; Hazleton HS; Hazleton, PA; (Y); Pres Service Clb; Concert Band; Mrchg Band; French Hon Soc; Hon Roll.

KLIAMOVICH, JIM; Lake-Lehman HS; Hunlock Creek, PA; (Y); Radio Clb; Ski Clb; Band; Concert Band; Jazz Band; Mrchg Band; Symp Band; L Golf; JV Vllybl; ROTC; Engrng.

KLICK, ERIC; Lebanon Catholic HS; Lebanon, PA; (Y); 5/86; German Clb; Stage Crew; Nwsp Phtg; Yrbk Phtg; JV Ftbl; High Hon Roll; Ntl Merit SF; Sci Fair Awd-Physics 86; Yth Govt-Asst City Engr 86; Penn ST; Elec Engr.

KLIESCH, JULIE; Downingtown SR HS; Downingtown, PA; (S); 12/544; French Clb; Ski Clb; Concert Band; Mrchg Band; Orch; School Musical; Symp Band; High Hon Roll; Mu Alp Tht; NHS; All-ST Bnd Solo & Ensmbl Awds 83-84; Awd In Wrtng 84-85; Bnd Lttr & Pin 85-86; PA ST U; Premed.

KLIM, PAMELA JO; Chartiers Valley HS; Carnegie, PA; (Y); 18/343; Varsity Clb; Nwsp Sprt Ed; Yrbk Ed-Chief; Capt Cheerleading; Gov Hon Prg Awd; High Hon Roll; NHS; PA Gov Schl Arts SF 84-85; Flagler Coll; Engl.

KLIMEK, BRIAN; Neshaminy HS; Feasterville, PA; (Y); 5/752; Mathletes; Ski Clb; Nwsp Stf; Im Fld Hcky; Im Ftbl; Trk; High Hon Roll; NHS; Prfct Atten Awd; Bus.

KLIMEK, DREW; Crestwood HS; Mountaintop, PA; (Y); 4-H; Math Clb; Stage Crew; 4-H Awd; High Hon Roll; Hon Roll; NEDT Awd; Sci.

KLIMKOWSKI, SANDRA; Sacred Heart HS; Pittsburgh, PA; (Y); 32/160; Debate Tm; French Clb; Hosp Aide; Library Aide; Math Clb; NFL; Speech Tm; Hon Roll; NHS; Dbl Ruby Natl Frnsc Lg 85-86; U Of Pittsburgh; Math.

KLINE, ANGELA; Waynesboro Area SR HS; Waynesboro, PA; (Y); 16/381; Church Yth Grp; Cmnty Wkr; GAA; Yrbk Stf; JV Var Bsktbl; Var L Trk; Im Vllybl; High Hon Roll; NHS; Rookie Yr Bsktbl, Math Awd Rnnr Up 83-84; Chldhd Ed.

KLINE, BARB; St Marys Area HS; Kersey, PA; (Y); Band; Concert Band; Mrchg Band; NHS.

KLINE, BARRY; Central Columbia HS; Bloomsburg, PA; (Y); #12 In Class; Church Yth Grp; German Clb; Letterman Clb; Varsity Clb; Var L Bsktbl; Var L Trk; NHS; Ntl Merit Ltr; Pres Schlr; Anonymous Schlrshp 86; PA ST; Engrng.

KLINE, BETH; Eastern HS; Wrightsville, PA; (Y); Church Yth Grp; Drama Clb; Band; Concert Band; Jazz Band; Mrchg Band; Pep Band; School Musical; School Play; Yrbk Stf; Acctg.

KLINE, CHRIS; Cedar Crest HS; Lebanon, PA; (Y); Latin Clb; Band; Concert Band; Jazz Band; Mrchg Band; Orch; Symp Band; Hon Roll; NHS; German Clb; Hnrs Banq Brnz Mdlln 86; Upper Dist Band 85 & 86; PA ST; Comp Sci.

KLINE, DIANE; Mahanoy Area HS; Mahanoy City, PA; (Y); Art Clb; Hosp Aide; Ski Clb; Spanish Clb; Band; Chorus; Drill Tm; Nwsp Stf; Trk; NHS; Bus Admin.

KLINE, DOUG; Danville Area SR HS; Danville, PA; (Y); Ftbl; Wt Lftg; Hon Roll; Trvl Pursuit Clb 85-86; Penn ST; Athltc Trng.

KLINE, FRANCESCA; Lock Haven SR HS; Lock Haven, PA; (Y); Church Yth Grp; FHA; Spanish Clb; Trs Band; Chorus; Concert Band; Jazz Band; Mrchg Band; Orch; Hon Roll; Miss 4th Of July-Clntn Cnty 85; Kappa Kappa Psi Awd-Band 86; PA Bandmstrs Assn Awd 85; Medcl Tech.

KLINE, JANELLE; Eastern Lebanon County HS; Myerstown, PA; (Y); Church Yth Grp; Band; Concert Band; Jazz Band; Rep Mrchg Band; Pep Band; JV Bsktbl; Var L Sftbl; Sph Cls; Jr Cls; Outstndng JR In Bnd 84-85; Slctd For PA All-ST Lns Bnd 85 & 86; Kutztown U.

KLINE, JENNIFER; Saucon Valley SR HS; Hellertown, PA; (Y); 12/195; Church Yth Grp; 4-H; Science Clb; Spanish Clb; School Play; Fld Hcky; 4-H Awd; High Hon Roll; NHS; Penn ST U; Bio.

KLINE, JOHN; Trinity HS; New Cumberland, PA; (Y); Boy Scts; Ski Clb; Stu Cncl; Bsktbl; Coach Actv; Ftbl; Trk; Ofnsv Plyr Of Week In Ftbl 85; Dfnsv Plyr Of Week In Ftbl 85; Bus Mngmnt.

KLINE, JULIE MARIE; Northern Cambria HS; Nicktown, PA; (Y); 17/126; VP Drama Clb; Chorus; Mrchg Band; School Play; JV Var Bsktbl; Hon Roll; NHS; Jrnlsm.

KLINE, KAREN LYNETTE; Montoursville Area HS; Montoursville, PA; (Y); 26/174; Am Leg Aux Girls St; French Clb; Varsity Clb; Nwsp Ed-Chief; Off Frsh Cls; Off Soph Cls; JV Bsktbl; Var L Sftbl; L Trk; Hon Roll.

KLINE, KELLY; Berwick Area HS; Nescopeck, PA; (Y); Aud/Vis; Chorus; Stage Crew; JV Fld Hcky; Hon Roll.

KLINE, KIM; Mechanicsburg Area HS; Mechanicsburg, PA; (Y); 130/311; Pres Church Yth Grp; Exploring; Key Clb; Pep Clb; Speech Tm; Rep Stu Cncl; Var L Cheerleading; High Hon Roll; Hon Roll; Church Choir; W Chester; Hlth & Phy Ed.

KLINE, LAURA; G A R Memorial HS; Wilkes Barre, PA; (S); 23/177; Key Clb; VP Band; Chorus; VP Concert Band; Jazz Band; VP Mrchg Band; Orch; Stu Cncl; Capt Fld Hcky; Hgh Hnr Rll 84 & 85; Psychlgy.

KLINE, LEANNE; Central Cambria HS; Ebensburg, PA; (Y); FBLA; Science Clb; Yrbk Stf; Bsktbl; Sftbl; Hon Roll; WV U; Physcl Thrpy.

KLINE, LISA M; Cambria Heights HS; Patton, PA; (Y); 1/177; 4-H; Sec FHA; Yrbk Ed-Chief; Hon Roll; Pres NHS; NEDT Awd; Val; Acad All-Amer; Pres Awd For Acad Fitness; Mst Likely To Succeed; PA ST; Chem.

KLINE, MELINDA; Milton SR HS; Milton, PA; (Y); 54/214; FBLA; Sec FHA; Sec Hst Library Aide; Office Aide; Spanish Clb; Yrbk Stf; JV Trk; WACC Bus Symposium-3rd Pl Adv Typng 85; Ofc Mgr.

KLINE, MICHAEL; Susquenita HS; Marysville, PA; (S); 25/185; Sec Church Yth Grp; Spanish Clb; Band; Concert Band; Jazz Band; Mrchg Band; Hon Roll; Awd 3rd Pl Lit,Art Festvl 85; Engrng.

KLINE, MICHELLE; St Marys Area HS; Kersey, PA; (Y); 27/301; Hosp Aide; SADD; Var L Gym; Var L Trk; High Hon Roll; NHS; Girl Scts; Yrbk Stf; Rep Stu Cncl; Schlstc Awd Outstndng JR In Art 86; Fnlst In Gvrnrs Schl For Arts 86.

KLINE, MIKE; Newport HS; Newport, PA; (Y); Var Varsity Clb; Var Capt Ftbl; Var Wt Lftg; Var Wrstlng; Hon Roll; 1st Tm All Lg Wrstlng; Hnbl Mntn Ftbl.

KLINE, PAMELA; Annville-Cleona HS; Annville, PA; (Y); Church Yth Grp; German Clb; Pres SADD; Chorus; Co-Capt Mrchg Band; School Musical; Yrbk Stf; NHS.

KLINE, PAMELA; Everett Area HS; Everett, PA; (Y); FBLA; Spanish Clb; Varsity Clb; Pres Stu Cncl; Socr; Trk; DAR Awd; NHS; Spanish NHS; Mst Outstndg SR Bus 86; Prncpls Awd 86; Med Soc Awd 86; ICM; Med Offc Asst.

KLINE II, RICHARD; Keystone HS; Cranberry, PA; (Y); 4/125; Varsity Clb; Nwsp Ed-Chief; VP Jr Cls; VP Sr Cls; Var Capt Ftbl; Var L Trk; Cit Awd; DAR Awd; High Hon Roll; Hon Roll; Amer Lg Awd 82; Grove City Coll; Chem Engr.

KLINE, SANDI; Hamburg Area HS; Hamburg, PA; (Y); 7/152; German Clb; Chorus; Church Choir; Co-Capt Gym; Co-Capt Twrlr; Hon Roll; Lion Awd; NHS; German Hnr Soc 85; Drexel U; Arch Engr.

KLINE, STEVE; Eastern York HS; Wrightsville, PA; (Y); 81/169; Drama Clb; Varsity Clb; Chorus; School Musical; School Play; Bsbl; Bsktbl; Ftbl; Prfct Atten Awd; Rotary Ldrshp Conf 86; Architectur.

KLINE, STEVE R; North Allegheny HS; Wexford, PA; (Y); 11/628; Church Yth Grp; Math Tm; Jazz Band; Mrchg Band; Bausch & Lomb Sci Awd; Hon Roll; NHS; Ntl Merit SF; Carnegie-Mellon U; Chmcl Engrng.

KLINE, TERRI; St Maria Goretti HS; Philadelphia, PA; (Y); Cmnty Wkr; Teachers Aide; Off Jr Cls; Swmmng; Ellis Awd Scholar 85-87; Court Steno.

KLINE, TINA; Pann Cambria HS; Easton, PA; (Y); Church Yth Grp; NFL; Office Aide; Speech Tm; Chorus; JV Cheerleading; Var L Sftbl; Var L Trk; Hon Roll; Psychol.

KLINEFELTER, DEBBIE; Shaler Area HS; Pittsburgh, PA; (Y); 196/517; Computer Clb; Ski Clb; Concert Band; Symp Band; Var L Socr; Var L Trk; Wstrn PA Coaches All Star Tm 85; Titan Awd Outstndng Indvdl Effort 83-84; Comp Sci.

KLINEPETER, MICHAEL; West Snyder HS; Beaver Spgs, PA; (Y); FFA; Red Cross Aide; VICA; 2nd-Proj Book FFA 86; Greenhand-FFA.

KLINETOB, MICHAEL; Berwick Area SR HS; Berwick, PA; (Y); Aud/Vis; Boy Scts; Church Yth Grp; Exploring; Nwsp Phtg; Nwsp Stf; Rep Jr Cls; JV Var Ftbl; Trk; Hon Roll; Eagle Scout Awd 83; Eagle Scout Awds 86; Coast Guard.

KLING, ALICIA; Southern Hungingdon HS; Burnt Cabins, PA; (Y); 1/100; GAA; Spanish Clb; SADD; Varsity Clb; Rep Stu Cncl; L Cheerleading; Im Gym; High Hon Roll; NHS; Ntl Merit Ltr; Radlgy Tech.

KLING, BENJAMIN; Donegal HS; Mount Joy, PA; (Y); Aud/Vis; Trs Church Yth Grp; Rep Frsh Cls; Rep Soph Cls; Var Capt Ftbl; Var Capt Trk; Var L Wrstlng; Lancaster-Lebanon Off & Def All Star 85-86.

KLING, CRAIG; Altoona Area HS; Altoona, PA; (Y); Key Clb; Math Clb; Band; Concert Band; Drm Mjr(t); Jazz Band; Mrchg Band; Pep Band; Var Bsbl; Prfct Atten Awd; Penn ST U; Acctg.

KLING, DEBORAH; Langley HS; Pittsburgh, PA; (Y); 7/284; Church Yth Grp; Nwsp Rptr; Cheerleading; Trk; Vllybl; High Hon Roll; NHS; Acdmc Schlrshp Carlow Coll 86-87; Carlow Coll; Eng.

KLINGAMAN, RANDY; Parkland SR HS; Trexlertown, PA; (Y); 17/459; L Socr; L Trk; NHS; Ntl Schl Ftns Team 86; Mltry Acad.

KLINGENBERG, ERIC; Seneca Valley HS; Mars, PA; (Y); 26/376; Church Yth Grp; VP JA; ROTC; Varsity Clb; Ftbl; Trk; Hon Roll; Geneva Scholar Awd 86; Ftbl Acadmc Achvt Awd 86; Yth Ldrshp Awd 85; Geneva Coll; Civil Engr.

KLINGENSMITH, BONNIE; Seneca Valley HS; Evans City, PA; (Y); 29/360; Hosp Aide; JA; Mrchg Band; School Musical; Symp Band; Nwsp Stf; Ed Yrbk Stf; Mgr Swmmng; High Hon Roll; NHS.

KLINGER, BARBARA; Southern Columbia Area HS; Catawissa, PA; (Y); Varsity Clb; JV Bsktbl; Var Fld Hcky; Var L Sftbl; High Hon Roll; Hon Roll; NHS; PA ST U; Hortcult.

KLINGER, JOEY E; George Washington HS; Philadelphia, PA; (Y); 46/750; Am Leg Boys St; Yrbk Stf; Var L Crs Cntry; Var L Trk; Cit Awd; Hon Roll; NHS; Pres Acad Ftns Awd 86; NROTC Schrlshp 86; Indoor Track 83-86; Villanova U; Officer.

KLINGER, RITA; Tri-Valley HS; Valley View, PA; (Y); 2/77; Sec Church Yth Grp; SADD; Chorus; School Musical; Sec Stu Cncl; Var L Bsktbl; L Mgr(s); High Hon Roll; NHS; Sal; Med Tech.

KLINGER, SHAWN; Tri-Valley HS; Valley View, PA; (Y); 6/75; Church Yth Grp; Computer Clb; Band; Jazz Band; Mrchg Band; School Musical; Hon Roll; JC Awd; JP Sousa Awd; NHS; PA ST U; Comp Sci.

KLINGER, SUSAN; St Basil Acad; Abington, PA; (S); 10/97; Church Yth Grp; Dance Clb; Drama Clb; Chorus; Variety Show; Nwsp Rptr; Hon Roll.

KLINGLER, KIMBERLY; Marian HS; Summit Hill, PA; (Y); 3/121; French Clb; Math Clb; Church Choir; Nwsp Ed-Chief; French Hon Soc; Gov Hon Prg Awd; High Hon Roll; NHS; Ntl Merit SF; Schltc Jrnlst Awd 86; Ntn Frnch Cntst 1st Pl Awd 86; Prsdntl Acad Ftns Awd 86; Kings Coll; Vet.

KLINZING, ANDREA; Monongahela Valley Catholic HS; Monongahela, PA; (Y); 14/80; Spanish Clb; Band; Mrchg Band; Pep Band; Nwsp Rptr; JV Var Cheerleading; NHS; Spanish NHS; Kent ST U; Audlgst.

KLITUS, THOMAS; Bishop Egan HS; Morrisville, PA; (Y); 3/229; Computer Clb; German Clb; Q&S; Nwsp Stf; Yrbk Ed-Chief; High Hon Roll; NHS; Ntl Merit Schol; Rotary Awd; American U; Sec Math.

KLOCK, BRENDA; Mount Carmel JR SR HS; Kulpmont, PA; (Y); FTA; Key Clb; Spanish Clb; Hon Roll; Cmmnty Serv Awd 86; Educ.

KLOCK, DEBORAH; Boyertown Area SR HS; Gilbertsville, PA; (Y); Drama Clb; Hosp Aide; Library Aide; Q&S; Acpl Chr; Chorus; School Musical; School Play; Yrbk Phtg; Lit Mag; Schuylkill Vlly Rstrnt Assoc Schlrshp 86; Johnson & Wales; Pastry Arts.

KLOCK, JODI; Shikellamy HS; Sunbury, PA; (Y); Trs 4-H; FBLA; Girl Scts; Key Clb; Spanish Clb; Mgr(s); Score Keeper; 4-H Awd; Hon Roll; Elem Ed.

KLOMP, HEIDI; Wilson HS; W Lawn, PA; (Y); Art Clb; French Clb; Pep Clb; Nwsp Stf; Yrbk Phtg; Sec Yrbk Stf; Sec Frsh Cls; Stu Cncl; Powder Puff Ftbl; Wt Lftg; Models Inst; Modeling.

KLOPFER, LAURA M; Iroquois HS; Wesleyville, PA; (Y); 7/156; Am Leg Aux Girls St; Debate Tm; Model UN; Nwsp Rptr; Yrbk Sprt Ed; Trk; Vllybl; NHS; Bsktbl; High Hon Roll; Producer WIHS News, US Bus Educ Awd, Faculty Choice Cmmncmnt Spkr; Allegheny Coll; Cmmnctns.

KLOS, HELENA M; Plum SR HS; Pittsburgh, PA; (Y); Dance Clb; FBLA; Trs FHA; Girl Scts; Library Aide; Office Aide; Color Guard; Flag Corp; Hon Roll; Ski Clb; Robert Morris Coll; Bus Mgmnt.

KLOSS, ALICIA; Central Dauphin HS; Harrisburg, PA; (Y); Dance Clb; French Clb; FBLA; GAA; Girl Scts; Office Aide; Teachers Aide; Chorus; Off Frsh Cls; Off Soph Cls; Ntl Hnr Soc 86; Schlrshp AFSCME 86; Bus Stu Of Yr 86; PA ST; Financng.

KLOSS, TIM; Steel Valley HS; West Homestead, PA; (Y); Trs Church Yth Grp; Swmmng; High Hon Roll; Hon Roll; JA; JCL; Band; Timer; PA ST; Pltcl Sci.

KLOTZ, DARRELL; Somerset Area SR HS; Somerset, PA; (Y); 10/240; Tennis; High Hon Roll; NHS; VFW Awd; Dale Carnegie Spch-Humn Rltns Awd 86; Pre-Med.

KLOTZ, KEVIN; Central Catholic HS; Allentown, PA; (Y); Exploring; FBLA; Stage Crew; Hon Roll; Prfct Atten Awd; Comp Pgmr.

KLOTZ, SHARON; Louis E Dieruff HS; Slatington, PA; (Y); 2/327; Model UN; Concert Band; Orch; Pep Band; School Musical; Gov Hon Prg Awd; NHS; Prfct Atten Awd; Sal; FBLA; Soc Women Engrs Awd 86; Math,Sci Awd 86; Maravian Coll; Psychlgy.

KLUCK, CAROLYN; Carbondale Area HS; Simpson, PA; (Y); 82/144; Art Clb; Church Yth Grp; FNA; GAA; Spanish Clb; Var JV Fld Hcky; Mgr(s); Trk; Hon Roll; Acctg.

KLUCK, JOHN; Venango Christian HS; Rouseville, PA; (Y); 12/36; Church Yth Grp; Nwsp Stf; Yrbk Phtg; Rep Stu Cncl; Hon Roll; NHS; NEDT Awd; Prfct Atten Awd; Gannon U; Comp Sci.

KLUDO, AMY M; Beaver Area JR SR HS; Beaver, PA; (Y); 21/187; FCA; French Clb; Ski Clb; Rptr Yrbk Stf; Var L Cheerleading; Powder Puff Ftbl; Var L Sftbl; NHS; Law.

KLUGH, KELLY; Danville SR HS; Danville, PA; (Y); Church Yth Grp; Key Clb; Spanish Clb; SADD; School Musical; Nwsp Stf; Var Crs Cntry; Var Trk; High Hon Roll; Hon Roll; Med.

KLUGH, SCOTT; Danville SR HS; Danville, PA; (Y); Chess Clb; Computer Clb; Spanish Clb; Ftbl; Score Keeper; Wt Lftg; Hon Roll; Navy ROTC; Mrn Blgy.

KLUGIEWICZ, PATRICIA; Bishop Mc Devitt HS; Harrisburg, PA; (S); 6/200; Drama Clb; Q&S; School Play; Nwsp Ed-Chief; Yrbk Phtg; Rep Frsh Cls; VP Soph Cls; Rep Jr Cls; Rep Sr Cls; NHS; PA JR Acad Sci 1st Plc Rgnl,2nd Plc ST Awd 83; Rtry Intl Ldrs Cnfrnc Top Ldr Awd 85; Biology.

KLUSH, KIM; Pittston Area HS; Pittston, PA; (Y); Church Yth Grp; Dance Clb; Key Clb; Ski Clb; School Musical; Variety Show; Yrbk Stf; Var Trk; Hon Roll; Pharm.

KLYM, AMY; Susquehanna Community HS; Susquehanna, PA; (Y); Girl Scts; Chorus; Stage Crew; Yrbk Stf; JV Var Bsktbl; Powder Puff Ftbl; Stat Var Trk; JV Var Vllybl; Wilkes; Accntng.

KLYNOWSKY, DENISE; Weatherly HS; Weatherly, PA; (S); 1/56; Church Yth Grp; Cmnty Wkr; FBLA; FNA; Library Aide; Political Wkr; Stu Cncl; Mgr(s); High Hon Roll; Hugh Obrian Yth Ldrshp Smnr 85; PA Assn Of Stu Cncls Ldrshp Smnr 85; Natl Englsh Mrt Awd 85; Bloomsburg U; Pre-Med.

KMETZ, KELLY; Jim Thorpe HS; Jim Thorpe, PA; (Y); Am Leg Aux Girls St; Library Aide; Nwsp Stf; Sec Jr Cls; Stu Cncl; Bsktbl; Cheerleading; Sftbl; High Hon Roll; Hon Roll; Amercn Leg Awd 83-84; East Stroudsburg; Pedtrc Nrsng.

KMETZ, MELISSA; John S Fine HS; Nanticoke, PA; (Y); Varsity Clb; Chorus; Capt Color Guard; Rep Frsh Cls; Rep Soph Cls; Rep Jr Cls; Capt Twrlr; High Hon Roll; Hon Roll; NHS; Kings Coll.

KMETZ, PAUL; Westmont Hilltop HS; Johnstown, PA; (Y); Boy Scts; DECA; Drama Clb; Quiz Bowl; Scholastic Bowl; Ski Clb; Band; Chorus; Concert Band; Jazz Band; Med.

KMONK, MICHELLE; Penn Hills SR HS; Pittsburgh, PA; (S); 50/762; FBLA; Spanish Clb; School Musical; Yrbk Stf; Sec Sr Cls; Stu Cncl; Pom Pon; High Hon Roll; Jr NHS; NHS; Mst Outstndng Bus Stu 85.

KNABB, LISA; Kutztown SR HS; Kutztown, PA; (Y); 8/150; Church Yth Grp; Band; Chorus; School Play; Bsktbl; Crs Cntry; Stat Sftbl; Var Trk; High Hon Roll; NHS; 1st Tm Div III Bsktbl 85-86; Optmtry.

KNAPP, CHRIS; Shenandoah Valley HS; Shenandoah, PA; (S); 13/105; Variety Show; Nwsp Stf; Yrbk Stf; Hst Frsh Cls; JV Bsktbl; Var L Ftbl; Var L Trk; JV Var Wrstlng; Hon Roll; NHS; Moravian Coll; Engrng.

KNAPP, DAVE; Beaver Area HS; Beaver, PA; (Y); 1/179; Church Yth Grp; FCA; French Clb; JA; Ski Clb; Var L Crs Cntry; Var L Trk; High Hon Roll; NHS; Im Bsktbl; Schlstc Achvt Awd Exc 85-86.

KNAPP, HEATHER; The Christian Acad; Glenolden, PA; (Y); Church Yth Grp; Hon Roll; Ntl Hnr Scty 85-86.

KNAPP, JEANENE; Curwensville Area HS; Curwensville, PA; (Y); Pres AFS; Debate Tm; Drama Clb; Band; School Musical; Yrbk Ed-Chief; Yrbk Phtg; NHS; PA ST U.

KNAPP, JOHN; Geibel HS; Uniontown, PA; (Y); 2/100; Yrbk Stf; Var L Crs Cntry; Bausch & Lomb Sci Awd; High Hon Roll; Ntl Merit Ltr; NEDT Awd; Sal; Am Leg Boys St; French Hon Soc; Semi Fnlst PA Gov Schl Math & Sci 84-85; J P Foley Mem Schlrshp 86; Marshall Hahn Merit Schlrshp 86; VA Poly Tech Inst; Engrng.

KNAPP, LEO R; Cardinal O Hara HS; Springfield, PA; (Y); 98/800; Ice Hcky; Hon Roll; Drexel; Engr.

KNAPP, TAMI; Rocky Grove HS; Cooperstown, PA; (Y); Church Yth Grp; VICA; Stu Cncl; Var Cheerleading; Hon Roll; Csmtlgst.

KNARR, KATHY ANN; Allentown Central Catholic HS; Northampton, PA; (Y); 22/240; Hosp Aide; Band; Capt Flag Corp; Cit Awd; High Hon Roll; Sec NHS; Prfct Atten Awd; Dance Clb; Drama Clb; PA JR Acad Sci 1st Pl Awd 82-86; Lehigh Cnty Med Axlrys Awd 86; PA ST U; Nrsng.

KNASS, LISA; Seneca Valley HS; Zelienople, PA; (Y); Ski Clb; Psych.

KNAUB, KAREN; Eastern York HS; York, PA; (Y); 34/169; 4-H; Chorus; Color Guard; School Musical; JV Bsktbl; Var JV Vllybl; Hon Roll; Animal Tech.

KNAUB, MICHELE; West York HS; York, PA; (Y); 19/200; Boy Scts; Church Yth Grp; FCA; Girl Scts; JA; Spanish Clb; SADD; L Stat Bsktbl; L Var Crs Cntry; L Var Fld Hcky; Acad Ltr & Svc Bar 85-86; IN U PA; Jrnlsm.

KNAUFF, DAMIAN; Bethel Park SR HS; Bethel Park, PA; (Y); 25/515; Church Yth Grp; JA; Spanish Clb; Band; Var Capt Bsktbl; L Ftbl; High Hon Roll; NHS; Pres Schlr; Concert Band; Princpls Awd 82-83; PA ST U; Bus Adm.

KNAUFF, KYLE; Seneca Valley SR HS; Evans City, PA; (Y); 102/390; Church Yth Grp; SADD; Nwsp Rptr; Nwsp Sprt Ed; Nwsp Stf; Lit Mag; Stat Bsbl; Hon Roll; U Of Pittsburgh; Cmmnctns.

KNEBEL, STEVEN W; Seneca Valley SR HS; Mars, PA; (Y); Art Clb; Church Yth Grp; Cmnty Wkr; Stage Crew; JV Capt Bsktbl; JV Socr; Hon Roll; Penn ST U; Civil Engrng.

KNECHT, ANDREW; Somerset Area HS; Somerset, PA; (Y); VP JA; Chorus; Church Choir; Sec Concert Band; Symp Band; High Hon Roll; Church Yth Grp; English Clb; Ski Clb; Sec Band; VP Of The Yr Mrktng JR Achvt 86; Music Awd Smrst All-Cnty Chrs 85; Mbr Of The YMCA Mdl Yth Gv 85-86; Pre-Med Chrprctr.

KNECHT, MARK; Liberty HS; Bethlehem, PA; (Y); 107/475; Im Wt Lftg; Var Wrstlng; High Hon Roll; Hon Roll; Accntng.

KNEE, CELESTE; Penn Cambria SR HS; Gallitzin, PA; (Y); 7/197; Cmnty Wkr; Drama Clb; Girl Scts; Spanish Clb; Color Guard; High Hon Roll; Prfct Atten Awd; Pres Phys Ftns Awd, Penn Cambria Hnr Soc, Stu Tchr Schl Dance 85-86; St Francis Coll Loretto; Educ.

KNEE, RANDY S; York Suburban SR HS; York, PA; (Y); 2/195; DAR Awd; Elks Awd; High Hon Roll; Lion Awd; NHS; Ntl Merit Ltr; Sal; Hghst GPA Cls; PA Gov Schl Arts Scholar 85; Concrt Soloist York & Harrisburg Symphny 83-86; Cls Awds; U DE; Mth.

KNEFLEY, CHERYL M; Susquehannock HS; New Freedom, PA; (Y); 1/191; Chess Clb; Off Church Yth Grp; Debate Tm; Drama Clb; Chorus; School Musical; School Play; Off Jr Cls; High Hon Roll; NHS; PA Govnrs Schl Sci Accptnce 85; PA Gov Schl Art Fnlst 85; Pre-Med.

KNELL, SUSAN; Kiski Area HS; Vandergift, PA; (Y); French Clb; Chorus; School Musical; Yrbk Stf; High Hon Roll; PA ST U.

KNEPP, CLARISSA L; Chief Logan HS; Mc Clure, PA; (Y); 4-H; Pep Clb; Spanish Clb; Chorus; Flag Corp; Var Trk; Var Twrlr; High Hon Roll; Prfct Atten Awd; Lwyr.

KNEPP, DENISE; Chief Logan HS; Burnham, PA; (Y); 2/180; Library Aide; Pep Clb; Soroptimist; Spanish Clb; Speech Tm; Varsity Clb; Chorus; Fld Hcky; Trk; High Hon Roll.

KNEPP, MICHAEL; Clearfield Area HS; Mineral Springs, PA; (Y); Nwsp Sprt Ed; High Hon Roll; NHS; US Navy.

KNEPSHIELD, TERRY; Leechburg Area HS; Leeburg, PA; (Y); 13/71; Pres JA; Nwsp Rptr; Yrbk Stf; Sec Sr Cls; VP Stu Cncl; St Francis Coll; Med Sci.

KNESS, DAVE; Knoch HS; Cabot, PA; (Y); Boy Scts; Church Yth Grp; Band; Concert Band; Jazz Band; Mrchg Band; Orch; Pep Band; School Musical; School Play; Hons Band 86; Dist Band 86; Rgnl Band 86; Muscn.

KNICKERBOCKER, STEVE; Upper Dublin HS; Oreland, PA; (Y); 70/356; Boy Scts; Band; Concert Band; Jazz Band; Mrchg Band; Symp Band; Hon Roll; NHS; Ntl Merit SF; Drexel U; Elctrcl Engrng.

KNIGHT, BETH; New Brighton Area HS; New Brighton, PA; (S); DECA; Hon Roll; Comp.

KNIGHT, DANIEL; North Penn SR HS; North Wales, PA; (Y); 158/678; Science Clb; Nwsp Stf; Var Golf; JV Socr; Im Sftbl; Im Wt Lftg; Hon Roll; Emory U; Med Exmnr.

KNIGHT, GARY; Lincoln HS; Ellwood City, PA; (Y); #72 In Class; Church Yth Grp; Hon Roll; Agri.

KNIGHT, GREGORY H; United HS; Indiana, PA; (Y); 7/136; Church Yth Grp; Math Clb; Lit Mag; Trk; Hon Roll; Mu Alp Tht; Prfct Atten Awd; Pres Schlr; Ltr Trk; Grove City Coll; Chem Engrng.

KNIGHT, KIMBERLY; Foot Cherry HS; Mcdonald, PA; (Y); Art Clb; Church Yth Grp; Drama Clb; Mathletes; Math Clb; Science Clb; Spanish Clb; Church Choir; Hon Roll; Spanish NHS; Eastern Nazarene Coll; Pre-Med.

KNIGHT, LISA; York Vocational Technical Schl; Hanover, PA; (Y); VICA; Hon Roll.

KNIGHT, MELISSA; Ridgway Area HS; Ridgway, PA; (S); 12/320; Drama Clb; Girl Scts; Chorus; Yrbk Stf; Stu Cncl; Cheerleading; Vllybl; High Hon Roll; Ushrtte 83-86; Marian Awd; Law.

KNIGHT, PHILIP; Aliquippa HS; West Aliquippa, PA; (S); 6/154; Boy Scts; Church Yth Grp; Drama Clb; Letterman Clb; Teachers Aide; Church Choir; School Musical; School Play; Stage Crew; Yrbk Stf; Boy Of Mnth 85; Schlrshp Awd From Geneva Coll 85; Geneva CC; Bus Adm.

KNIGHT, REGINA; St Paul Cathedral HS; Pittsburgh, PA; (S); 5/62; Latin Clb; Pep Clb; Pres Jr Cls; Var Bsktbl; High Hon Roll; Hon Roll; NHS; Outstndng Achvt Ltn Awds 82-86; Natl Hstry Day Cmptn Excllnc 84-85; Sci Fair Excllnc Awd 83-84; TN ST U; Pre-Med.

KNIGHT, RHONDA; Elizabeth Forward HS; Elizabeth, PA; (Y); Pres Spanish Clb; Var Capt Bsktbl; Var Crs Cntry; Var Trk; Bus.

KNIGHTLY, MARK; Bishop Shanahan HS; Kennett Square, PA; (Y); Ski Clb; Villanova U; Engr.

KNIPPLE, DOUGLAS; Geibel HS; Scottdale, PA; (Y); 2/83; Church Yth Grp; Drama Clb; Science Clb; Spanish Clb; Wt Lftg; High Hon Roll; NEDT Awd; Prfct Atten Awd; Spanish NHS; DJAS 2nd Pl; Aerospc Engnr.

KNISEL, LYNNE; Forest Hills HS; Summerhill, PA; (Y); Pep Clb; Band; Chorus; Concert Band; Jazz Band; Mrchg Band; Pep Band; Stu Cncl; High Hon Roll; Hon Roll; Bnd Pres 83-84; Bnd Vp 86-87; Slippery Rock.

KNISELEY, DAVID; Brookville Area HS; Brookville, PA; (Y); 2/143; French Clb; Key Clb; Rep Stu Cncl; Bausch & Lomb Sci Awd; High Hon Roll; Jr NHS; Trs NHS; Sal; Pres Acdmc Fit Awd 86; Brookville Chapter Natl Hon Soc Schlrshp 86; Grove City Coll; Bus Admin.

KNISELY, LORI; Punxstuawney Area HS; Punxsutawney, PA; (Y); Art Clb; French Clb; Varsity Clb; Rep Frsh Cls; Trs Jr Cls; Var Capt Cheerleading; JV Vllybl; Hon Roll.

KNIZNER, KEITH; Immaculate Conception HS; Washington, PA; (Y); 11/51; Boy Scts; Computer Clb; Var L Ftbl; Hon Roll.

KNOLL, CAROLYN; Karns City HS; Chicora, PA; (Y); 32/122; Church Yth Grp; Cmnty Wkr; FBLA; SADD; Variety Show; Yrbk Stf; Soph Cls; Stu Cncl; Cheerleading; Hon Roll; Superior Rtngs Piano Duets & Solo PA Federtn Music Clubs Fest 82-84; Bradford Schl Bus; Sec Sci.

KNOLL, LISA; Karns City HS; Chicora, PA; (Y); 36/126; SADD; Butler Cnty Schlrshp Grnt 86; Butler Cnty Coll; Spcl Ed.

KNOPF, TERI; Northampton Area SR HS; Walnutport, PA; (Y); 4/452; AFS; Computer Clb; Sec Leo Clb; Stu Cncl; JV Var Fld Hcky; High Hon Roll; NHS; Psych.

KNOPP, JAMES; Bethlehem Center SR HS; Vestaburg, PA; (Y); 15/157; Am Leg Boys St; Varsity Clb; Var L Ftbl; Wt Lftg; Hon Roll; Russian Clb 84-86.

KNOPP, KRISTINE J; Louise E Dieruff HS; Allentown, PA; (Y); Drama Clb; Chorus; Mrchg Band; Nwsp Rptr; Yrbk Stf; Capt Twrlr; Hon Roll; Jr NHS; NHS; LEDHS Schlrshp 86; Outstndng News Ed 86; Sempre Fidelis Awd 86; Kutztown U; Speech & Lang.

KNOPSNYDER, HOLLY; Berlin-Brothers Valley HS; Garrett, PA; (Y); 11/87; AFS; GAA; Spanish Clb; Band; Drm Mjr(t); Var Capt Cheerleading; Stat Score Keeper; Var Vllybl; Hon Roll; NHS; FFA Sweetheart 86-87.

KNORR, ADAM; Central Columbia HS; Bloomsburg, PA; (Y); CAP; Exploring; JV Bowling; Hon Roll; NEDT Awd; US Army; Aerosp Engrng.

KNORR, BONNIE; Tri-Valley HS; Hegins, PA; (Y); 20/77; Art Clb; JV Sftbl; Var Vllybl.

KNORR, BRIAN; Berwick Area HS; Berwick, PA; (Y); 30/197; Pres Church Yth Grp; Ski Clb; Nwsp Phtg; Nwsp Rptr; Yrbk Phtg; Yrbk Rptr; L Trk; Capt Wrstlng; Computer Clb; FBLA; Vly Forge Dist Schlrshp 86; Penn-Del Dist Schlrshp 86; Valley Forge Chrstn; Pastrl Stu.

KNORR, ERIC; James M Coughlin HS; Wilkes Barre, PA; (Y); Boy Scts; Civic Clb; Band; Concert Band; Jazz Band; Mrchg Band; School Play; Stage Crew; High Hon Roll; Hon Roll; Engrng.

KNORR, JOANNA; Shikellamy HS; Sunbury, PA; (Y); German Clb; Band; Concert Band; Mrchg Band; Cheerleading; Tennis; Trk; Hon Roll; George E Wertz 9th Grd Grmn Awd 84; Acctng.

KNORR, JODI; Tri-Valley HS; Hegins, PA; (Y); 19/75; Art Clb; Boys Clb Am; Var Sftbl; Var L Vllybl; Hon Roll; Henry Cohen Mem Art Awd 86; Local Rtry Clb Bus Ed Stu With Hghst Avg 86; Secy.

KNOTT, JASON; Cochranton JR SR HS; Canal Fulton, OH; (Y); Drama Clb; Ski Clb; Varsity Clb; Chorus; School Musical; School Play; Stage Crew; JV Bsktbl; Mgr(s); Hon Roll; Archology.

KNOTTS, CODY; Mc Guffey HS; Taylorstown, PA; (Y); Boy Scts; Pres Church Yth Grp; German Clb; Chorus; Church Choir; School Play; Yrbk Stf; Mgr Bsktbl; God Cntry Awd; Bethany Coll; Hist.

KNOTTS, MICHELLE; Altoona Area HS; Altoona, PA; (Y); Key Clb; Ski Clb; Spanish Clb; Chorus; Off Sr Cls; Stu Cncl; Cheerleading; Capt Pom Pon; Sec Jr NHS; NEDT Awd; Psych.

KNOTTS, SHAWN; Danville SR HS; Danville, PA; (Y); 45/202; VP 4-H; Variety Show; Rep Frsh Cls; Var L Ftbl; Wt Lftg; 4-H Awd; Hon Roll; Math Awds 83-84; Bloomsburg U; Math Educ.

KNOUSE III, THERON I; John S Fine HS; Wapwallopen, PA; (Y); 25/242; Boy Scts; Cmnty Wkr; Model UN; Spanish Clb; Capt Vllybl; God Cntry Awd; High Hon Roll; NHS; NEDT Awd; Alumni Schrlshp 86; Rochester Inst Tech; Bio.

KNOWTTON, KELLY; State College Area HS; State College, PA; (Y); 16/586; Cmnty Wkr; Chorus; Rep Frsh Cls; Rep Soph Cls; Rep Jr Cls; Rep Sr Cls; Im JV Vllybl; Cit Awd; High Hon Roll; NEDT Awd; Outstndng Sentr Awd 85; Latn Awd 84; Penn ST U; Arts.

KNOX, ANDREW; Edward Bok Voc Tech; Philadelphia, PA; (Y); FBLA; ROTC; Cit Awd; Accntng.

KNOX, MARK; Punxsutawney Area HS; Rochester Mills, PA; (Y); Church Yth Grp; Band; Mrchg Band; Pep Band; Hon Roll; Prfct Atten Awd; Indiana U Of PA; Bio.

KNUPP JR, GREG; North Star HS; Jennerstown, PA; (Y); 10/130; Varsity Clb; Band; Concert Band; Mrchg Band; Var L Bsktbl; Cit Awd; Hon Roll; NHS; Ntl Merit SF; IBEW-4 Yr Schlrshp 86; U Of PA; Elec Engrng.

KNUPP, TRACI; Rocky Grove HS; Franklin, PA; (S); Church Yth Grp; Library Aide; Chorus; Jazz Band; School Musical; Variety Show; Yrbk Stf; Stu Cncl; Gym; Hon Roll; Wrthy Advsr Franklin Assmbly No 19 85; Schlrshp-Westminster Coll-SAT Scrs 85; Radlgy.

KOBER, TIMOTHY; Hempfield HS; E Petersburg, PA; (Y); 30/432; Church Yth Grp; Science Clb; Teachers Aide; Nwsp Rptr; High Hon Roll; Hon Roll; NHS; Natl Frnch Cont 4th Pl 84; Natl Frnch Cont 3rd Pl 85 & 86; Georgetown U; Foreign Lang.

KOBIERSKI, PAUL; Harborcreek HS; Erie, PA; (Y); 78/212; Boy Scts; Exploring; Ftbl; Swmmng; Hon Roll; Gannon U; Robotics Tech.

KOBILIC, LISA M; Monongahela Valley Catholic HS; Lititz, PA; (S); 14/103; Drama Clb; Hosp Aide; Pep Clb; Chorus; Capt Flag Corp; School Play; Nwsp Stf; Pres French Hon Soc; Sec NHS; Pittsburgh U; Bio Engr.

KOBLE, LYNN M; State College Area HS; State College, PA; (Y); 21/488; Trs Art Clb; Var Trk; Elks Awd; Hon Roll; NEDT Awd; Pres Schlr; Ntl Poster Graphcs Cntst 2nd Pl 85; Hnrbl Mntn Arts Recgntn & Tlnt Srch 86; Half Tutn Schl Art & Dsgn; Alfred U; Art.

KOBUCK, KRISTY; Greensburg Salem HS; Delmont, PA; (Y); 18/296; German Clb; Pep Clb; SADD; Band; Concert Band; School Musical; Nwsp Ed-Chief; Nwsp Rptr; Nwsp Stf; Lit Mag; U Of Pittsburgh.

KOBUCK, LORI; Tyrone Area HS; Warriors Mk, PA; (Y); Art Clb; Church Yth Grp; Key Clb; Office Aide; Spanish Clb; SADD; Varsity Clb; Chorus; Stu Cncl; Var Cheerleading; Paralgl.

KOCH, BILL; North East HS; North East, PA; (Y); 68/149; AFS; FBLA; Trk; Wt Lftg; Penn ST; Bus.

KOCH, HEATHER; Unionville HS; West Chester, PA; (Y); 44/300; Yrbk Phtg; Trs Rep Frsh Cls; Trs Rep Soph Cls; Rep Jr Cls; Sec Rep Sr Cls; Stu Cncl; Capt Fld Hcky; Lcrss; Hon Roll; Bus.

KOCH, KELLY; Pottstown SR HS; Pottstown, PA; (S); 1/238; Pres Latin Clb; Yrbk Bus Mgr; Jr Cls; Cheerleading; Trk; High Hon Roll; NHS; Psychlgy.

KOCH, MICHAEL; Freedom HS; Bethlehem, PA; (Y); 87/406; Nwsp Phtg; Nwsp Stf; Yrbk Phtg; Yrbk Stf; Hon Roll; Moraviah Coll; Pre Med.

KOCH, NOEL; Lehighton HS; Parryville, PA; (Y); 68/269; Pres VICA; Stu Cncl; Ftbl; Wrstlng; High Hon Roll; Hon Roll; Prfct Atten Awd; Prsdntl Physcl Ftnss Awd 85&86; Elctrnc Tchnlgy.

KOCH, SALLY A; West Hazleton HS; W Hazleton, PA; (S); 38/206; FBLA; FTA; Scholastic Bowl; Ski Clb; SADD; Nwsp Rptr; Yrbk Rptr; Yrbk Stf; Hon Roll; NHS.

KOCH, SHANNON; Oil City Area SR HS; Oil City, PA; (Y); 22/231; AFS; French Clb; SADD; Band; Concert Band; Mrchg Band; Pep Band.

KOCH, TERESA; Huntingdon Area HS; Petersburg, PA; (Y); 13/223; Hosp Aide; Key Clb; SADD; Chorus; Tennis; High Hon Roll; Hon Roll; NHS; Prfct Atten Awd; CPA.

KOCH, TODD A; Blue Mountain HS; New Ringgold, PA; (S); 4-H; VP Pres FFA; Hon Roll; Anml Hsbndry.

KOCH, YVONNE; Governor Mifflin HS; Sinking Spring, PA; (Y); 66/300; 4-H; Office Aide; Nwsp Stf; Rep Jr Cls; Rep Stu Cncl; Cheerleading; 4-H Awd; High Hon Roll; Hon Roll; Brandywine Coll; Acctng.

KOCHAN, JON; Schuylkill Valley HS; Leesport, PA; (S); Boy Scts; Band; Concert Band; Mrchg Band; Symp Band; Nwsp Stf; Rep Stu Cncl; L Bsbl; Var L Swmmng; Var L Tennis; Penn ST U; Cmmrcl Art.

KOCHANOWSKI, ROBERT; Pittston Area HS; Duryea, PA; (Y); 63/365; Art Clb; Computer Clb; JA; Stage Crew; Im Bsktbl; Im Socr; JV Trk; JV Var Vllybl; Hon Roll; Comp Anlyst.

KOCHE, DAVID; Abington HS; Longboat Key, FL; (Y); 1/528; Varsity Clb; Orch; Nwsp Sprt Ed; Capt Tennis; DAR Awd; High Hon Roll; Hon Roll; Ntl Merit Schol; Pres Schlr; Ordr Of A 86; Cornell U; Med.

KOCHENBERGER, DIANE L; Liberty HS; Bethelehm, PA; (Y); 108/412; Library Aide; Stage Crew; Hon Roll; Mrktng Dstrbtv Educ Awd 86; Otstndng Cntrbtn Cls Of 86; Mansfield U; Trvl.

KOCHENDERFER, SUE; Pennridge HS; Perkasie, PA; (Y); Church Yth Grp; Rep Frsh Cls; Rep Soph Cls; Rep Jr Cls; Var Capt Cheerleading; Var Powder Puff Ftbl; Var L Sftbl; Hon Roll; Trvl Agnt.

KOCHER, AMY; Upper Dauphin Area HS; Elizabethville, PA; (Y); Church Yth Grp; Pep Clb; Chorus; Church Choir; School Musical; Yrbk Stf; Cheerleading; Hon Roll; Acad Of Med Arts/Bus; Med Asst.

KOCHER, ANNE; Eastern Lebanon County HS; Myerstown, PA; (Y); SADD; Chorus; Yrbk Stf; Stu Cncl; Var L Cheerleading; Var L Fld Hcky; High Hon Roll; Prfct Atten Awd; Church Yth Grp; Band; Cert Alg I 83; Cert English I 83; Estrn Coll; Psyc.

KOCHER, CARL; Mc Keesport Area HS; White Oak, PA; (Y); 75/339; Band; Concert Band; Mrchg Band; Orch; U Pittsburgh; Chem Engr.

KOCHER, JAMI; Susquenita HS; Duncannon, PA; (S); 16/183; Church Yth Grp; Library Aide; Sec Spanish Clb; Yrbk Stf; Rep Stu Cncl; Var L Trk; NEDT Awd; Intl Rltns.

KOCHER, LAURA; Benton Area HS; Benton, PA; (Y); 7/50; Keywanettes; Band; Chorus; School Musical; Sec Frsh Cls; Sec Soph Cls; Sec Jr Cls; JV Var Cheerleading; Hon Roll; NHS; Columbia Cnty Band 83-86; Dist Band 84-85; Regn Band 84-85; Bus Mgmt.

KOCHER, LISA; Upper Dauphin Area HS; Elizabethville, PA; (Y); Trs Church Yth Grp; Varsity Clb; Chorus; Church Choir; Flag Corp; School Musical; Stu Cncl; Var Capt Cheerleading; Hon Roll; NHS; Span Awd 84; Psych.

KOCHIS, KAREN; Bishop Ohara HS; Peckville, PA; (Y); Drama Clb; Latin Clb; Pep Clb; Spanish Clb; Chorus; School Musical; School Play; Nwsp Stf; Mgr Bsktbl; Mgr Ftbl; Marywood Coll; Bus.

KOCINSKI, MICHAEL; N E Catholic HS; Philadelphia, PA; (S); 3/430; Church Yth Grp; NHS; Doctor.

KOCIS, BOB; Ambridge Area HS; Sewickley, PA; (Y); Am Leg Boys St; Art Clb; Spanish Clb; JV Bsktbl; Var L Ftbl; Var L Trk; Im Wt Lftg; Hon Roll; PA Amer Ind Arts Stu Assoc Pub Spkng Awd 86; Military Acad; Aerospc Engrng.

KOCIS, CHRISTINE; Connellsville Area SR HS; Cnlvle, PA; (Y); 52/484; Office Aide; Chorus; Flag Corp; Mrchg Band; School Musical; VP Hst Frsh Cls; Pres Hst Soph Cls; Pres Hst Jr Cls; Stu Cncl; Hon Roll; Tv.

KOCKLER, ANDY; Franklin HS; Franklin, PA; (Y); Am Leg Boys St; Drama Clb; Letterman Clb; Spanish Clb; Varsity Clb; Chorus; Off Jr Cls; Bsbl; Ftbl; Wrstlng; Amer Legion Awd Post 476 82-83; Bus.

KOCON, ROBERT; Central Catholic HS; Allentown, PA; (Y); Exploring; Bsktbl; Im Ice Hcky; Aquatic Bio.

KOCON, WALDEMAR; Bishop Hafey HS; Hazleton, PA; (Y); English Clb; Math Clb; Math Tm; Red Cross Aide; Scholastic Bowl; Science Clb; Capt Ice Hcky; Socr; Swmmng; Tennis; M/M J P Marinko Awd Outstndng Charctr, Crpnter Engl Schlrshp 86; Stdnt Body Salute Awd 85; Penn ST U; Elec Engrng.

KODLICK II, JAMES R; West Snyder HS; Beaver Spgs, PA; (Y); Am Leg Boys St; Boy Scts; Pres 4-H; Im JV Bsbl; Im Vllybl; JV Var Wrstlng; 4-H Awd; High Hon Roll; Hon Roll; Boy Sct Cert Merit 86; Penn ST; Pre-Med.

KODRIC, JUDITH A; Laurel Highlands HS; Uniontown, PA; (Y); Vllybl; High Hon Roll; Hon Roll; Prfct Atten Awd.

KOEGLER, DAVE; Knoch HS; Sarver, PA; (Y); Stu Cncl; Im Bsktbl; Var L Ftbl; Var L Trk; High Hon Roll; Hon Roll; NHS; Am Leg All Star Bsbl 85-86; Most Imprvd Rnnr Track 86.

KOEHLE, BERNARD E; Bellwood-Antis HS; Tyrone, PA; (Y); Boy Scts; VICA; Hon Roll; VICA Comptn Awd 86; Triangle Tech Schl; Air/Refrig.

KOEHLER, BETH ANN; Abington Heights HS; Clarks Green, PA; (Y); 26/289; Ski Clb; Chorus; School Musical; Variety Show; L Cheerleading; High Hon Roll; NHS; Most Spirited Chrldr 85; Franklin & Marshall; Law.

KOEHLER, JASON; Trinity HS; Washington, PA; (Y); 94/374; Boy Scts; Camera Clb; Library Aide; Band; Concert Band; Jazz Band; Mrchg Band; Fld Aviatn.

KOEHLER, MELISSA; Northampton HS; Bath, PA; (Y); FBLA; Chorus; Church Choir; Hon Roll; Nrthamptn Co CC; Data Prcssng.

KOEHN, DAVID A; Bishop Hafey HS; Drums, PA; (Y); Model UN; Scholastic Bowl; Ski Clb; Capt Speech Tm; School Play; Ed Lit Mag; VP Stu Cncl; Var L Trk; NHS; Ntl Merit Ltr; PA Gov Schl For Arts 85; Ntl Frnscs Trnmnt Stu Cngrss Baltimore MD 86; Stu Exch Svc 86; Middlebury VT; Philosophy.

KOENER, CHANTELLE; Greater Johnstown HS; Johnstown, PA; (Y); Church Yth Grp; Sec French Clb; Yrbk Stf; Rep Stu Cncl; Capt Cheerleading; High Hon Roll; NHS; Civic Clb; Cmnty Wkr; Drama Clb; Pres Physcl Ftns Awd 85; Ms Teenage Amer Fnlst & Photo In Teen Magazine 86; Ms PA Teen 85; Law.

KOENIG, ELISSA; Bensalem SR HS; Bensalem, PA; (Y); 1/573; Scholastic Bowl; Science Clb; Band; Concert Band; Mrchg Band; Orch; School Musical; Bausch & Lomb Sci Awd; High Hon Roll; NHS; Smr Schlrshp Crngie-Mllr 86; Tuition Schlrshp Geo Wshngtn U Wshngtn DC 86; Physcs.

KOEPCKE, PAM; Unionville HS; Kennett Sq, PA; (Y); Art Clb; Nwsp Rptr; Stat Ftbl; Var Trk; Im Vllybl; High Hon Roll; Prfct Atten Awd; Archt.

KOEPKE, STEVE; ICS Newport Pacific HS; Eveleth, MN; (Y); High Hon Roll; Hon Roll; VFW Awd; TX A&m; Marine Biolgy.

KOERBER, RONDA; Norwin SR HS; Trafford, PA; (Y); 4-H; FFA; SADD; Chorus; Sec.

KOESTER, ROBIN; Perkiomen Valley HS; Collegeville, PA; (Y); 12/186; Office Aide; Spanish Clb; SADD; JV Fld Hcky; JV Lcrss; High Hon Roll; Hon Roll; Ursinus Coll; Bus Adm.

KOFALT, NANCY ANN; Quigley HS; Beaver, PA; (Y); Cmnty Wkr; French Clb; Girl Scts; Hosp Aide; Math Tm; Chorus; Swing Chorus; Yrbk Stf; JV Cheerleading; JV Mgr(s); Prom Page 85; Stu Ldrshp Awd Seton Hill Coll 84-85; 13 Yrs Dance; Eucharstc Ministr 86; Barrys U; Lib Arts.

KOFFEL, CHRISTINE ROSE; Pennridge SR HS; Perkasie, PA; (Y); 110/433; Am Leg Aux Girls St; VP FBLA; Office Aide; Nwsp Stf; Yrbk Stf; Rep Frsh Cls; Rep Soph Cls; Rep Stu Cncl; Var Lcrss; JV Tennis; Bus.

KOFFLER, LAUREN; Plymouth Whitemarsh HS; Norristown, PA; (Y); 93/335; Service Clb; Temple Yth Grp; School Musical; Nwsp Phtg; Nwsp Rptr; Nwsp Stf; Trs Stu Cncl; JV Tennis; High Hon Roll; Hon Roll; Yng Mstrs Cnsrtm Arts 85-86; Schlrshp Art Cls Moore Coll Art 85; Vrsty Lttr Achvt Hnr Rll 86; Dsgn.

KOFFLER, MIKE; Uniontown Area HS; Uniontown, PA; (Y); 42/324; Letterman Clb; Office Aide; Spanish Clb; Varsity Clb; Stage Crew; Hst VP Soph Cls; Hst VP Jr Cls; Var L Ftbl; CC Awd; High Hon Roll; Chem Engrng.

KOFFMAN, ROBIN; Cheltenham HS; Elkins Pk, PA; (Y); 55/365; Red Cross Aide; Sec Sr Cls; Rep Stu Cncl; Im Bowling; JV Lcrss; Constitn Commtt Chrprsn 85-86; Soc Svcs Commtt Co-Chrprsn 86-87.

KOFLANOVICH, KYRA; Lake-Lehman HS; Shavertown, PA; (S); 28/140; Art Clb; GAA; Letterman Clb; SADD; School Play; Fld Hcky; Hon Roll; Jr NHS; NHS.

KOFLUK, SHAWN; Schuylkill Haven HS; Auburn, PA; (S); 11/120; Boy Scts; Computer Clb; Exploring; Spanish Clb; SADD; Rep Frsh Cls; Rep Soph Cls; VP Ftbl; VP Trk; Wt Lftg; NSMA 84; Natl Ldrshp & Svc Awd 85; Pol Sci.

KOGAN, MARK; Harrisburg Acad; Harrisburg, PA; (Y); Drama Clb; Ski Clb; Temple Yth Grp; Variety Show; Yrbk Phtg; Yrbk Stf; Jr Cls; Socr; Swmmng; Su Derrich Awd 83.

KOGER, FRANK; Our Lady Of The Sacred Heart HS; Mckees Rocks, PA; (Y); 2/63; Chorus; Stage Crew; VP Soph Cls; Hon Roll; NHS; Comp Sci.

KOHAN, DAVE; Blairsville SR HS; Blairsville, PA; (Y); 6/129; Letterman Clb; JV Bsktbl; Var Golf; Var Trk; NHS; Counselors Schlrshp 86; Clark Metals Schlstc Schlrshp 86; Penn ST U; Engr.

KOHANY, PAMELA; Manheim Township HS; Lancaster, PA; (Y); 100/329; Variety Show; Rep Stu Cncl; Var Cheerleading; Im Powder Puff Ftbl; Var Trk; Im Vllybl; Hon Roll; Bus Adm.

KOHAR, ED; Hopewell HS; Aliquippa, PA; (Y); 68/265; Church Yth Grp; Exploring; Pres Latin Clb; Yrbk Stf; Var L Wrstlng; High Hon Roll; Hon Roll; OH Northern U Yrly Grant 86; OH Northern U; Pharm.

KOHL, ANDY; Brandywine Heights HS; Fleetwood, PA; (Y); 24/126; Hon Roll; Catawba; Acctng.

KOHL, RONALD; Bethel Park SR HS; Bethel Park, PA; (Y); 132/530; Boy Scts; Exploring; SADD; Im Bsktbl; Im Ftbl; Im Golf; Wittenberg U; Accounting.

KOHLER, CHRISTOPHER ZANE; Hempfield Area SR HS; Greensburg, PA; (Y); Computer Clb; Pep Clb; VP Jr Cls; Var L Ftbl; Wt Lftg; High Hon Roll; Hon Roll; Jr NHS; NHS; Spanish NHS; Bus Adm.

KOHLER, DANA; Downingtown HS; Glenmoore, PA; (Y); 19/563; French Clb; GAA; Fld Hcky; Lcrss; Socr; High Hon Roll; Sec NHS; NEDT Awd; Teachers Aide; Band; Stu Advsry Brd 85-86; Cert Merit Frnch Hghst Numrcl Avg Cls 83-84; Fnlst JR Miss Pgnt 86-87; Med.

KOHLER, DEBRA; Easton Area HS; Easton, PA; (Y); 30/503; Trs Church Yth Grp; Trs DECA; Pep Clb; Bowling; Stat Fld Hcky; Sftbl; High Hon Roll; NHS; Pres Schlr; Cert Outstndng Achvmnt Mrktng & Dist Educ 86; Vo-Tech Achvmnt Awd 86; Gen Marquis De Lafayette Schlstc.

KOHLER, DREW; Frazier HS; Perrypolis, PA; (Y); Drama Clb; Ski Clb; Stage Crew; Yrbk Ed-Chief; Yrbk Phtg; Rep Soph Cls; Rep Sr Cls; L Bsktbl; JV Var Ftbl; Var Wt Lftg; Pre-Dentistry.

KOHLER, EDANA; Jim Thorpe Area HS; Jim Thorpe, PA; (S); Camera Clb; FHA; Trs Band; Chorus; Ed Nwsp Stf; Ed Yrbk Stf; High Hon Roll; NHS; Bloomsburg U; Mass Comm.

KOHLER, KIMBERLY; Northampton Area SR HS; Walnutport, PA; (Y); 12/476; AFS; Chorus; Swmmng; DAR Awd; High Hon Roll; Hon Roll; NHS; Delta Kappa Gamma Hon Educ Soc Awd 86; Soc Of Women Engrs Cert Of Merit Highest Hon In Sci & Math 86; PA ST U; Education.

KOHLER, SHERRY; Dover HS; Dover, PA; (Y); Dance Clb; Varsity Clb; Chorus; Color Guard; Var Capt Fld Hcky; Nrs.

KOHLI, ERIC; Pennsbury HS; Levittown, PA; (Y); SADD; Rep Stu Cncl; High Hon Roll; NHS; Prfct Atten Awd; Rotry Ldrshp Camp Awd 86; U DE; Math.

KOHN, JOHN; Allentown Central Catholic HS; Allentown, PA; (Y); 23/232; Church Yth Grp; Civic Clb; Math Clb; Lit Mag; Bsktbl; Crs Cntry; High Hon Roll; Hon Roll; Mhlmbrg Coll; Med.

KOHN, KIMBERLEY; Lincoln HS; Philadelphia, PA; (Y); 19/540; Cmnty Wkr; French Clb; Yrbk Stf; Hon Roll; MI Stu In Tae Kwon Do 85; Black Belt Cert 86; Temple; Law.

KOHN, LORA; Bethel Park HS; Bethel Park, PA; (Y); French Clb; JA; Ski Clb; Chorus; Mgr(s); Powder Puff Ftbl; Var L Tennis; Schlstc Achvt 83-84; Frgn Exchng Clb 85-86; Lbrl Arts.

KOHR, DEBORAH; Lower Dauphin HS; Hummelstown, PA; (Y); Church Yth Grp; Chorus; Church Choir; Orch; Swing Chorus; Nwsp Stf; Rep Stu Cncl; Hon Roll.

KOHUT, MARILOU; Technical HS; Scranton, PA; (Y); FBLA; Pep Clb; Lackawanna JC; Bus.

KOIS, JERRY; Mapletown JR SR HS; Dilliner, PA; (Y); 7/85; Art Clb; Computer Clb; English Clb; Ski Clb; Ftbl; Wt Lftg; NHS; Comp.

KOLACKOVSKY, ANN M; Central Dauphin HS East; Harrisburg, PA; (Y); 7/249; Chorus; Nwsp Ed-Chief; Yrbk Stf; Var Capt Bsktbl; Var L Sftbl; Lion Awd; NHS; Pres Schlr; Church Yth Grp; Letterman Clb; US Army Schlr/Athlt Awd 86; Patriot Newsco Jrnlsm Achvt Awd 86; Cntrl Dphn Thms B George Jr Awd 86; Penn Sst U; Bio.

KOLAKOWSKI, MICHAEL; Apollo-Ridge HS; Clarksburg, PA; (Y); 36/170; German Clb; Math Clb; Varsity Clb; Pres Stu Cncl; Capt L Bsbl; Capt L Bsktbl; Hon Roll; Lion Awd; Louise V Nelson Memrl Schlrshp 86; IN Cnty Penn ST Clb Schlrshp 86; US Mrn Corps Dstngshd Awd 86; Penn ST; Engrng.

KOLAR, NIKKI; Forest Hills SR HS; St Michael, PA; (Y); 47/180; Am Leg Aux Girls St; Church Yth Grp; FBLA; Girl Scts; Library Aide; Pep Clb; Y-Teens; Band; Chorus; Church Choir; Sftbl Hnr Awd 85&86; St Francis; Acctg.

KOLATIS, MARY ELLEN; Mid Valley HS; Throop, PA; (Y); 1/117; Quiz Bowl; Scholastic Bowl; Concert Band; Mrchg Band; Nwsp Rptr; Bausch & Lomb Sci Awd; High Hon Roll; NHS; Val; All ST Band 85; Best Of Cls Awd 86; Schlr Of Yr Awd 86; Bloomsburg U; Med Technlgy.

KOLB, CHERI; Owen J Roberts HS; Spring City, PA; (S); 26/270; Pres Church Yth Grp; Letterman Clb; Var Capt Fld Hcky; Var L Trk; Hon Roll; NHS; Trk & Fld MVP 84; 2nd Tm All Chesmont Hcky 84 & 85; Messiah Coll; Spts Med.

KOLBE, KATHRYN L; Pennridge HS; Perkasie, PA; (Y); 44/436; Am Leg Aux Girls St; Ed Yrbk Ed-Chief; Sec Rep Stu Cncl; Var Lcrss; Mgr Wrstlng; High Hon Roll; NHS; Band; Drm Mjr(t); Mrchg Band; Hugh O Brien Yth Ldrshp Schlrshp 84; Class Ldrshp Awd 86; Air Force ROTC Schlrshp 86; Lehigh U; Indstrl Engrng.

KOLBUSH, LISA M; Marian HS; Mc Adoo, PA; (Y); 46/121; Pep Clb; Service Clb; Ski Clb; School Play; Rep Soph Cls; Sec Stu Cncl; Var L Cheerleading; Stat L Sftbl; Mrchg Band; Yrbk Stf; Hmcmng Qn 85-86; Stu Cncl Gvrnmnt Awd 85-86; Allentown Coll; Nrsng.

KOLCUN, KEVIN J; Commodore Perry HS; Hadley, PA; (S); Math Tm; Hon Roll; Gannon U; Engrng.

KOLENDA, LAURA; Carrich HS; Pittsburgh, PA; (S); French Clb; Office Aide; Q&S; Ski Clb; Flag Corp; Mrchg Band; Yrbk Stf; High Hon Roll; Hon Roll; U Pittsburg; Dntl Hygnst.

KOLESAR, AMY L; South Side Catholic HS; Pittsburgh, PA; (S); 14/47; Drama Clb; Service Clb; School Play; Rep Frsh Cls; VP Soph Cls; VP Sr Cls; Cheerleading; Hon Roll; Shadyside Hsp Schl Nrsng; Surgl.

KOLESAR, CHERI; Pittston Area HS; Pittston, PA; (Y); Computer Clb; Drama Clb; French Clb; Science Clb; Ski Clb; Mrchg Band; L Swmmng; High Hon Roll; Hon Roll; Cntrl FL U; Psychlgy.

KOLESSAR, MELISSA; Pottsgrove HS; Pottstown, PA; (Y); 23/229; Girl Scts; Hosp Aide; Library Aide; Spanish Clb; Concert Band; Mrchg Band; Pep Band; Nwsp Rptr; Hon Roll; Ltr Band 86; Kutztown ST U; Elem Ed.

KOLESSAR, MICHAEL; Wyoming Area HS; West Pittston, PA; (Y); 8/268; Boy Scts; Drama Clb; German Clb; Math Clb; Hon Roll; NHS; Math.

KOLICK, KAREN; Jefferson-Morgan HS; Clarksville, PA; (S); 4/97; Dance Clb; School Play; Rep Jr Cls; Stu Cncl; Var JV Cheerleading; High Hon Roll; Trs NHS; French Clb; Varsity Clb; Coal Queen Rep; Homecmg Court; Intl Day Part Awd; Biol.

KOLIVOSKY, CAROL; West Branch JR SR HS; Morrisdale, PA; (Y); 7/113; Church Yth Grp; Spanish Clb; Band; Chorus; Church Choir; Concert Band; Mrchg Band; Vllybl; Hon Roll; NHS; Acctg.

KOLLER, AMY; Canon Mc Millan SR HS; Eighty Four, PA; (Y); 57/371; Church Yth Grp; French Clb; Girl Scts; Hosp Aide; Chorus; Yrbk Stf; Vllybl; High Hon Roll; Hon Roll; Phrmcy.

KOLLER, CHERI; Cedar Crest HS; Lebanon, PA; (Y); French Clb; Pep Clb; SADD; Chorus; Occ Ther.

KOLLER, GINA; Jefferson-Morgan HS; Waynesburg, PA; (Y); 5/88; Art Clb; Church Yth Grp; Computer Clb; 4-H; French Clb; Church Choir; Rep Jr Cls; High Hon Roll; Hon Roll; Amer Lgn Essay Awd 86; Waynesburg Coll; Nrsng.

KOLLER, KIM; Hempfield SR HS; Greensburg, PA; (Y); GAA; Color Guard; Vllybl; Wt Lftg; High Hon Roll; Hon Roll; Prfct Atten Awd; Spanish NHS; Phys Fit Awd 86; Writer.

KOLLER, MICHAEL; Conrad Weiser HS; Sinking Spg, PA; (Y); 71/138; Cmnty Wkr; Drama Clb; Pres German Clb; VP Key Clb; Nwsp Stf; Ed Yrbk Stf; Stu Cncl; JV Socr; Var L Tennis; JV Wrstlng; Key Clb Mth 86; Mst Imprvd Tnns 84; Kent ST U; Bus.

KOLLING, SCOTT R; Montour HS; Coraopolis, PA; (Y); Var Bsbl; Var L Bsktbl; JV Ftbl; JV Vllybl; High Hon Roll; Hon Roll; Pre-Med.

KOLO, MELISSA; South Fayette JR SR HS; Mc Donald, PA; (Y); 4/89; Concert Band; Jazz Band; Mrchg Band; Orch; High Hon Roll; Hon Roll; NHS; Dist & Rgn I Bnd 85; Pittsburgh Zoo Sci Apprntcshps 85-86; Three Rvrs Trnng Orch 83-85; U MI; Zoology.

KOLODYCHAK, MICHAEL; Charleroi Area JR SR HS; N Charleroi, PA; (Y); 12/180; Science Clb; Ski Clb; Spanish Clb; Pres Sr Cls; Pres Stu Cncl; Elks Awd; Lion Awd; NHS; Pres Schlr; Charthene Clb Schlrshp 86; Gannon U; Fmly Mdcn.

KOLOGE, KIM; Pittston Area HS; Avoca, PA; (Y); Drama Clb; Key Clb; Math Clb; Ski Clb; L Swmmng; High Hon Roll; Hon Roll; NHS; Engl.

KOLOJEJCHICK, ANDREW; Wyoming Valley West HS; Swoyersville, PA; (Y); Am Leg Boys St; Concert Band; Jazz Band; Mrchg Band; Orch; School Musical; Cit Awd; Hon Roll; NHS; NEDT Awd; Meyers Stage Bnd Fstvl Outstndg Sax Soloist 86; Music.

KOLONGOWSKI, LAURA; W B Saul HS; Philadelphia, PA; (Y); Girl Scts; JA; Quiz Bowl; Stage Crew; Yrbk Rptr; Sftbl; Tennis; Vllybl; Wt Lftg; Cit Awd; Prfct Attndnc; PA Textile.

KOLOSHINSKY, KAREN R; Greater Latrobe HS; Latrobe, PA; (Y); 77/334; Exploring; 4-H; JCL; Office Aide; French Hon Soc; 4-H Awd; High Hon Roll; NCTE Awd; PA Cnsl Tchrs Eng Wrtng Cntst 85; CO ST U Acadmc Grant 86; Schlrshp U Of WY 86; CO ST U; Pre Vet Med.

KOLP, REBECCA; Council Rock HS; Furlong, PA; (Y); 1/845; Intnl Clb; Orch; School Musical; Lit Mag; Powder Puff Ftbl; High Hon Roll; NHS; Pres Schlr; Pre Med.

KOLSKY, PAM; Bensalem HS; Bensalem, PA; (Y); 24/550; Drama Clb; Office Aide; Nwsp Rptr; Nwsp Stf; Yrbk Rptr; Yrbk Stf; Trk; High Hon Roll; NHS; Pres Acad Achvt Awd 86; Penn ST U; Ind Psych.

KOLSOSKY, BETH; Caron Mc Millan HS; Canonsburg, PA; (Y); Pres Church Yth Grp; Hosp Aide; Chorus; Flag Corp; Jazz Band; School Musical; Nwsp Stf; High Hon Roll; Hon Roll; 1st Pl Englsh Essay/Svngs Bnd 85; IN U; Prfsnl Sngr.

KOLTISKA, KAREN; Marian HS; Mc Adoo, PA; (S); 11/114; Aud/Vis; French Clb; Band; Chorus; Drm Mjr(t); Mrchg Band; Pep Band; School Musical; Hon Roll; NHS; Schuylkill Cnty Band 84-86; Diocesan Band 85-86; PA Dist Bnd 86; Comp Anal.

KOLUS, CHERYL; Mechanicsburg Area SR HS; Mechanicsburg, PA; (Y); 30/299; High Hon Roll; Hon Roll; Hall Foundation Schlrshp 86-87; Harrisburg Area CC; Bus Admin.

KOMAN, KRISTAN G; Trinity HS; Washington, PA; (Y); 52/373; Aud/Vis; Camera Clb; Exploring; Pres Ski Clb; Nwsp Phtg; Ftbl; High Hon Roll; WA Coll; Pre-Med.

KOMARA, PATRICIA; Brownsville Area HS; Republic, PA; (S); 3/225; Computer Clb; Drama Clb; Hosp Aide; Mathletes; SADD; Mrchg Band; Ed Nwsp Ed-Chief; High Hon Roll; NHS; Rotary Awd; Med Tech.

KOMISHOCK JR, PAUL; Bishop Hafey HS; Hazleton, PA; (Y); Scholastic Bowl; School Play; Rep Soph Cls; Pres Jr Cls; Rep Stu Cncl; JV Bsbl; Hon Roll; Jr NHS; Ntl Merit SF; Chess Clb; Amer Lgn Hon Men Schl Awd 83-84; Hgh Cls Avg Englsh 83-84; Intrmrl Awd 83-884.

KOMOREK, KRISTEN; John S Fine HS; Nanticoke, PA; (Y); Library Aide; Yrbk Stf; Hon Roll; Misercordia; Nrsng.

KOMPASS, LYNN; Emmaus HS; Emmaus, PA; (Y); 7/497; German Clb; Math Clb; Model UN; Sec Chorus; Church Choir; Orch; School Musical; Variety Show; High Hon Roll; NHS; U Of Toronto; Math.

KOMULA, MATT; Jefferon-Morgan JR SR HS; Mather, PA; (Y); 20/100; Am Leg Boys St; Church Yth Grp; Spanish Clb; Band; Church Choir; Concert Band; Jazz Band; Mrchg Band; Pep Band; Symp Band; Cnty Band Greene; Dist I Band; Rgnl I Band PMEA; Dusquene U; Music Ed.

KON, JEFF; Ringgold HS; Finleyville, PA; (Y); Varsity Clb; Var L Bsbl; Var L Ftbl; Im Wt Lftg; Hon Roll; NHS; Engrg.

KONARSKI, CHRISTINE; Downingtown SR HS; Pottstown, PA; (Y); 128/550; Church Yth Grp; Hosp Aide; Ski Clb; Spanish Clb; Hon Roll; Bloomsburg U; Elem Ed.

KONCAR, STEVEN M; Middletown HS; Middletown, PA; (Y); 45/190; Boy Scts; VP Frsh Cls; Stu Cncl; Bsbl; Bsktbl; Ftbl; Hon Roll; Mid Penn Divisn II 1st Tm Defnsv Sfty 84-85; Mid Penn Sivisn II 1st Tm Shrtstp 84-86; Shippensburgh U; Bus.

KONDRAS, BRYAN; Elizabethtown Area HS; Mount Joy, PA; (Y); 102/237; Boy Scts; Church Yth Grp; Ski Clb; Acpl Chr; Chorus; Church Choir; Orch; School Musical; Aud/Vis; Cmnty Wkr; Ntl Sci Leag 2nd Chem 85-86; Close Up Pgm 86; Pol Sci.

KONECKE, KELLY; Bishop Hoban HS; Wilkes-Barre, PA; (Y); Dance Clb; FBLA; Math Clb; Spanish Clb; Chorus; Color Guard; Stage Crew; Yrbk Stf; Rep Stu Cncl; High Hon Roll; Kings; Chem.

KONEVITCH, CHRISTOPHER; Cedar Crest HS; Lebanon, PA; (Y); 17/306; Art Clb; Church Yth Grp; Debate Tm; Drama Clb; French Clb; Pep Clb; Hon Roll; NHS; Excllnt Awd Art Natl FCYS Art Fstvl 84; Hnr Banqt Slvr Mdl 86; Drexel U; Archtrl Engrng.

KONG, PEIANN; Upper Darby SR HS; Upper Darby, PA; (Y); 29/629; Cmnty Wkr; Intnl Clb; Office Aide; Teachers Aide; Var Tennis; High Hon Roll; Hon Roll; Prfct Atten Awd; Bio Achvt Awd 84-85; Pre-Med.

KONICK, KRISTEN; California HS; Allenport, PA; (Y); FNA; Ski Clb; Cheerleading; Hon Roll; PTA Cltrl Arts Cont 84; Amer Lgn Hon Awd 85.

KONICKY, COLETTE; Bishop Mc Cort HS; Johnstown, PA; (Y); German Clb; Pep Clb; Ski Clb; Chorus; Yrbk Stf; Vllybl; High Hon Roll; NHS.

KONIECZNY, KRISTIN; Geibel HS; Mt Pleasant, PA; (Y); French Clb; Sec Frsh Cls; VP Soph Cls; Sec Sr Cls; Sec Stu Cncl; L Golf; High Hon Roll; NHS; Prfct Atten Awd; Pope John Paul II Awd 86; Engrng.

KONIOR, ROBERTA; Cambria Heights HS; Hastings, PA; (Y); 15/200; VP Church Yth Grp; Cmnty Wkr; Library Aide; Ski Clb; Yrbk Stf; High Hon Roll; IN U Of PA; Accntnt.

KONOPKE, WALT; Lake Lehman HS; Noxen, PA; (Y); 18/140; Aud/Vis; Var L Bsbl; Var L Bsktbl; High Hon Roll; Hon Roll; Jr NHS; NHS.

KONSTANTINOU, JESSICA; Canon-Mc Millan SR HS; Canonsburg, PA; (Y); Sec Church Yth Grp; Office Aide; Drm Mjr(t); Nwsp Stf; Yrbk Stf; Hon Roll; Fshn Mrchndsng.

KONZEL, STEPHEN; Catherdral Preparatory HS; Erie, PA; (Y); Var Trk; Var L Wrstlng; Pre-Law.

KOOL, LISA; Harriton HS; Pen Vly, PA; (Y); Temple Yth Grp; Nwsp Rptr; JV Swmmng; JV Vllybl; Prfct Atten Awd; CIT; Tght Intstrctnl Swm 85-86; U Of DE; Phys Thrpy.

KOON, DANA; Westing House HS; Pittsburgh, PA; (S); 6/220; Teachers Aide; Color Guard; Pres Soph Cls; Hon Roll; ICM Bus Schl; Wrd Prcsng Splst.

KOONS, JOHN; Pine Grove Area HS; Pine Grove, PA; (Y); Cmnty Wkr; ROTC; VICA; JV Bsbl; Hon Roll; Crpntry.

KOONS, MOLLY; Crestwood HS; Mountaintop, PA; (Y); 1/241; VP Math Clb; Band; Mrchg Band; Var L Fld Hcky; Var L Trk; High Hon Roll; NHS; NEDT Awd; Mu Alp Tht; Prfct Atten Awd; Harold Baker Awd 83-85; CEA Awd 85-86; Sci.

KOONTZ, GEORGE; Mt Pleasant Area SR HS; Mt Pleasant, PA; (Y); Boys Clb Am; Boy Scts; Ski Clb; Nwsp Stf; Off Jr Cls; Bsbl; Ftbl; Trk; High Hon Roll; Hon Roll; Eagle Scout 86; Vigil W Ordr Scts Arrw 86; SAA; Sci Rsrch Clb; King Cym Staf,Outng Clb; Prom Comm; Penn ST; Ag.

KOONTZ, PATRICK; Seton La Salle HS; Pittsburgh, PA; (Y); 75/251; Aud/Vis; Ski Clb; Spanish Clb; Nwsp Stf; High Hon Roll; Hon Roll; Erth Sci Achvt Awd, Cmnctns Achvt Awd 86; Tlcmnctns.

KOONTZ, TINA; Everett HS; Everett, PA; (Y); Pres Church Yth Grp; Pep Clb; SADD; Chorus; Score Keeper; Sftbl; Bus.

KOONTZ, WENDY; North Star HS; Boswell, PA; (Y); 24/120; Church Yth Grp; FCA; Pep Clb; Chorus; Color Guard; JV Vllybl; Hon Roll; NHS; Sec.

KOOSER, LORI; Laurel Highlands HS; Brownfield, PA; (Y); Pres Church Yth Grp; Spanish Clb; Chorus; Madrigals; School Musical; High Hon Roll; Hon Roll; Jr NHS; NEDT Awd; Church Choir; Frnch Awd 86; Penn ST U; Law.

KOOSER, WILLIAM; Central Catholic HS; Pittsburgh, PA; (Y); 1/278; Sec Debate Tm; Sec NFL; Sec Speech Tm; Rep Frsh Cls; JV Socr; French Hon Soc; High Hon Roll; NHS; Ntl Merit Ltr; Val; 1st Pl-Cntrl Cthlc Sci Fair 86; Fnlst-Ntl Cthlc Frnscs Leag Stu Cngrs 86; Bus.

KOPACK, JOHN; Neshaminy HS; Langhorne, PA; (Y); Var Socr; Var Wrstlng.

KOPAS, JULIANNE; Norwin SR HS; Westmoreland City, PA; (S); Trs French Clb; Leo Clb; SADD; Co-Capt Drm Mjr(t); School Play; Nwsp Rptr; Stu Cncl; Twrlr; NHS; Rotary Awd; U Of Pittsburgh; Psychlgy.

KOPEC, MICHAEL; Bishop Kenrick HS; Norristown, PA; (Y); 12/312; FBLA; Off Jr Cls; Off Sr Cls; Off Stu Cncl; Bsbl; Bsktbl; High Hon Roll; Hon Roll; Jr NHS; NHS; Elctrcl Engrng.

KOPELCHECK, KATHLEEN; Danville Area HS; Danville, PA; (Y); Art Clb; Drama Clb; Key Clb; Latin Clb; Tennis; Trk; Semi Finalist For Gov Schl Of Arts 86; Capt Of Tennis Tm 86-87; Graphic Arts.

KOPER, DONALD; Bell Vernon Area HS; Belle Vernon, PA; (Y); Art Clb; Ftbl; Wt Lftg; High Hon Roll; Hon Roll; NHS; Engrng.

KOPERNA, GEORGE; Line Mountain HS; Herndon, PA; (Y); 10/135; Off FBLA; Bsktbl; Crs Cntry; Wt Lftg; Off High Hon Roll; Off Hon Roll; Off NHS; Nuclr Engr.

KOPP, MICHAEL J; Fox Chapel Area HS; Sharpsburg, PA; (Y); Aud/Vis; Computer Clb; Political Wkr; Band; Concert Band; Mrchg Band; School Musical; Stage Crew; Lit Mag; Hon Roll; Natl Sci Olympd 83-84; Carnegie Mellon U; Comp Sci.

KOPPENHAUER, BRAD; Pine Grove Area HS; Ravine, PA; (Y); Varsity Clb; Bsktbl; Hon Roll; Cntrl PA Bus Schl; Comp Tech.

KOPPENHAVER, KELLY; Halifax Area HS; Halifax, PA; (Y); Drama Clb; Band; Chorus; School Musical; Nwsp Rptr; Yrbk Stf; Powder Puff Ftbl; Hon Roll; FHA; FNA; Dauphin Cnty Band & Chrs 84-85; Musc Thrpy.

KOPRIVA, KELLY; Greater Johnstown HS; Johnstown, PA; (Y); Pep Clb; Ski Clb; Chorus; Concert Band; School Musical; Rep Stu Cncl; Var Cheerleading; DAR Awd; High Hon Roll; NHS; Juniata; Bio Sci.

KOPRIVA, LAURA; Bishop Mc Cort HS; Johnstown, PA; (Y); 19/153; Sec Frsh Cls; Var VP Bsktbl; ST Bsktbl Chmpns 85; George Washington U; Bio.

KOPRIVA, MARK A; Ambridge Area HS; Ambridge, PA; (Y); Am Leg Boys St; Church Yth Grp; Pep Clb; Rep Jr Cls; Var L Bsbl; Golf; Var L Wrstlng; Hon Roll; Edinboro U-PA; Spch-Comm.

KOPRIVNAK, LORI; Slippery Rock Area HS; Slippery Rock, PA; (Y); 18/188; Trs Church Yth Grp; Pres FBLA; Intnl Clb; Pep Clb; Mgr School Play; Nwsp Stf; Yrbk Stf; Stat Trk; Hon Roll; Sec NHS; Nrsng.

KOPYSCIANSKI, DENISE; Mount Carmel HS; Mt Carmel, PA; (Y); 83/170; Key Clb; Pep Clb; Spanish Clb; Varsity Clb; JV Var Cheerleading; Phrmcy.

KORB, JOHN; Bethel Park SR HS; Bethel Park, PA; (Y); Spanish Clb; Bsktbl; LAWYER.

KORBAR, MICHELE; Selinsgrove Area HS; Selinsgrove, PA; (Y); 27/215; Church Yth Grp; Spanish Clb; Yrbk Stf; JV Bsktbl; Hon Roll; NHS; Slide Shw Trp Spain 85; Secy/Treas Salem Luthern Chrch 84-85; Wildlife Tech.

KORCHNAK, DEBBIE; Vill Maria HS; Campbell, OH; (Y); Cmnty Wkr; French Clb; Key Clb; Thesps; School Musical; School Play; Stage Crew; Nwsp Rptr; Nwsp Sprt Ed; Nwsp Stf; Stu Cnclr Of Yr 85-86; 2 Stara Thespn Awd Cert 85-86; Achvt Awd Nwspr Pge Edtr 85-86; Med.

KORCZYNSKI, SHERRY; Highlands SR HS; Natrona Hts, PA; (Y); Hosp Aide; Intnl Clb; Trs Key Clb; SADD; Sec Mrchg Band; Rep Stu Cncl; Var Mgr Sftbl; Co-Capt L Tennis; Sec NHS; Ntl Merit Ltr; Alle Kiski Hnrs Bnd 85 & 86; Md Est Hnrs Band 85 & 86; PA Fr Entrprs Wk 86; Bus Admin.

KORDA, SUSAN; Villa Maria HS; Youngstown, OH; (Y); French Clb; Ed Nwsp Ed-Chief; VP Frsh Cls; Rep Soph Cls; Rep Jr Cls; Rep Sr Cls; Stu Cncl; Hon Roll; Jr NHS; NHS; Oberlin; Jrnlst.

KORDEK, MICHAEL; York County Vo-Tech; New Freedom, PA; (Y); AFS; Boy Scts; VICA; School Play; Hon Roll; Ad Altare Del Cthlc Boy Sct Awd 83; Sndy Schl Tchr 85-86; Art Tchr Bible Schl 86; Chapel Hill; Drama.

KORDES, JEFF; Meadville Area SR HS; Meadville, PA; (Y); 39/309; German Clb; Varsity Clb; Var L Diving; Var L Swmmng; Hon Roll; Arch.

KOREA, GERALD; Pittston Area HS; Duryea, PA; (Y); Computer Clb; U Of Scranton; Comp Sci.

KOREN, JOSEPH; Archbishop Ryan HS; Philadelphia, PA; (Y); Chess Clb; CAP; Exploring; Band; Outstndng Achvt In Psychlgy Awd 86; Drxl U; Ecnmcs.

KORIBANIC, STEPHANIE; West Mifflin Area HS; W Mifflin, PA; (Y); 7/336; Church Yth Grp; VP FBLA; Office Aide; Concert Band; Mrchg Band; Stu Cncl; CC Awd; High Hon Roll; Hon Roll; Jr NHS; Sec Stu Yr 86; Pres Acad Fit Awd 86; Schltc Achvt Awd 86; Bradford Schl; Sec.

KORICH, JODI; Allentown Central Catholic HS; Allentown, PA; (Y); Key Clb; Math Clb; Q&S; Ski Clb; Flag Corp; Lit Mag; Hon Roll; PA JR Acad Sci 1st Pl ST Comp 85; Principals Prz Outstndg Wrk Biol 85; PA JR Acad Sci 2nd Pl 86; Biol.

KORMAN, LEIGH; West Scranton SR HS; Scranton, PA; (Y); Ski Clb; Band; Mrchg Band; Nwsp Stf; Yrbk Phtg; Yrbk Stf; Tennis; High Hon Roll; Jr NHS; NHS; Jr Hnrs Band 83; Gftd Pgm 82-86; E Stroudsburg U; Med Tech.

KORMANSKI, JOHN; Tussey Mountain HS; Defiance, PA; (Y); 18/111; Am Leg Boys St; Art Clb; Church Yth Grp; Varsity Clb; Var Capt Bsbl; Var Capt Bsktbl; MVP HS Bsktbll & All Cnty Hnrs 85-86; 1st Tm All Cnty Catcher Bsbll 84-86; Shiensburg U; Ed.

KORMOS, KATHERINE; Bishop O Rielly HS; Luzerne, PA; (Y); Cmnty Wkr; Hosp Aide; Radio Clb; Drm Mjr(t); Var Capt Twrlr; High Hon Roll; Hon Roll; U Scranton; Psych.

KORMOS, WILLIAM A; Upper Moreland HS; Willow Grove, PA; (Y); 2/276; Pres Key Clb; Concert Band; School Musical; Yrbk Stf; Rep Frsh Cls; Rep Soph Cls; Rep Jr Cls; Pres Sr Cls; Stu Cncl; JV L Ftbl; Camp Neidig Rotarys Future Ledrs Camp 85; Pre Med.

KORNEGAY, DANIEL R; Quakertown Community SR HS; Quakertown, PA; (Y); 18/290; Am Leg Boys St; Boy Scts; Pres Chorus; Rep Stu Cncl; Hon Roll; NHS; Opt Clb Awd; VFW Awd; Cmnty Wkr; Drama Clb; Awd Blmsbrg U Mtrn Schlrshp Awd 86-88; Blmsbrg U; Bus.

KORNHAUS, JOHN H; Southmoreland HS; Scottdale, PA; (Y); Drama Clb; French Clb; JCL; Latin Clb; Ski Clb; School Musical; School Play; Variety Show; Lit Mag; PA ST; Elect Engr.

KORNUTIAK, MATT; Mid-Valley Secondary Ctr; Olyphant, PA; (Y); French Clb; Ski Clb; Penn ST U; Real Est.

KOROMAUS, DAVID; Punysutawney Area HS; Delancey, PA; (Y); 66/238; Varsity Clb; Pres VP Stage Crew; VP Sr Cls; Var L Bsbl; Mgr Bsktbl; Var L Ftbl; Rotry Boy Mnth Nov 85; U Of Pittsburgh; Engrng.

KORPANTY, DIANE; Notre Dame HS; E Stroudsburg, PA; (Y); Art Clb; French Clb; Girl Scts; Hosp Aide; Library Aide; Stage Crew; Yrbk Phtg; L Sftbl; Tennis; Charleston Coll.

KORSZNIAK, LISA; Plymouth Whitemarsh HS; Conshohocken, PA; (S); Math Clb; Math Tm; Orch; Rptr Nwsp Bus Mgr; Rep Frsh Cls; Rep Church Yth Grp; Rep Jr Cls; Rep Sr Cls; Rep Stu Cncl; High Hon Roll; Microbiol.

KORTH, CASEY; North Allegheny HS; Pittsburgh, PA; (Y); 250/600; Dance Clb; Chorus; Church Choir; School Musical; School Play; U Of Pittsburgh; Scrptwrtr.

KORVICK, MARK D; North Allegheny HS; Wexford, PA; (Y); 132/686; Chess Clb; Cmnty Wkr; Computer Clb; English Clb; German Clb; Latin Clb; Math Clb; Science Clb; Ski Clb; Band; VA Poly Tech U; Engr.

KORZENIOWSKI, KATRIA; St Basil Acad; Philadelphia, PA; (S); Trs Drama Clb; VP French Clb; Hosp Aide; Variety Show; Nwsp Ed-Chief; Lit Mag; High Hon Roll; NEDT Awd; U Of PA; Intl Bus.

KORZI, MICHAEL; Windber Area HS; Windber, PA; (Y); School Musical; Variety Show; Yrbk Phtg; Yrbk Sprt Ed; Yrbk Stf; Rep Jr Cls; JV Bsktbl; Wt Lftg; High Hon Roll; NHS; UPJ; Engrng.

KOSANOVICH, ELI; Our Lady Of The Sacred Heart HS; Aliquippa, PA; (Y); Boy Scts; NFL; School Play; Pres Schlr; PA ST U; Areo Engrng.

KOSCELNIK, CAROLYN; Villa Maria Acad; Erie, PA; (Y); Computer Clb; Service Clb; Ski Clb; Var Golf; Capt JV Socr; JV Trk; Hon Roll; PA Free Enterprise Wk 86; Accntng.

KOSCHELLA, LISA; Wyoming Valley West HS; Swoyersville, PA; (Y); Chess Clb; Kiwanis Awd; Pres Schlr; Fairleigh Dickenson U; Cmptr Pg.

KOSCO, JENNIFER; Belle Vernon Area HS; Belle Vernon, PA; (Y); Ski Clb; SADD; Band; Color Guard; Stu Cncl; Var Diving; Mgr(s); Powder Puff Ftbl; Swmmng; High Hon Roll; Duguesne U; Nrsg.

KOSER, TINA; Lewiston Area HS; Mc Veytown, PA; (Y); Art Clb; German Clb; Varsity Clb; School Musical; Bsktbl; Fld Hcky; Sftbl; Hon Roll; Regnl Awds Art 86; Art Ed.

KOSIK, KIM; Freedom HS; Bethlehem, PA; (Y); 132/413; Hosp Aide; Library Aide; Ski Clb; Nwsp Stf; Shippensburg U; Educ.

KOSIOR, CONNIE; Lincoln HS; Wampum, PA; (Y); 53/187; Key Clb; Y-Teens; Chorus; Church Choir; Powder Puff Ftbl; Tennis; Hon Roll; Prfct Atten Awd; Intr Dcrtr.

KOSKI, DAVID; New Castle SR HS; New Castle, PA; (Y); Boy Scts; Church Yth Grp; English Clb; Math Clb; Spanish Clb; Nwsp Rptr; Nwsp Sprt Ed; Wt Lftg; Pittsburgh Inst; Aernutcs.

KOSKI, ROBERT; York Vo Tech; York, PA; (Y); ROTC; VICA; Gov Hon Prg Awd; Hon Roll; Rptr NHS; Prfct Atten Awd; Math & Comp Sci Cert Compltn 85; Le High U; Elec Engrng.

KOSKI, SUSAN MARIE; Canon Mc Millan SR HS; Eighty Four, PA; (Y); 5/371; English Clb; French Clb; Band; Mrchg Band; School Musical; Nwsp Rptr; Sec Nwsp Stf; Capt Twrlr; Sec NHS; High Hon Roll; Piano Recitals 83 & 85; Rench Cert High Profcncy 84; Majorettes, Trophy, Lttr, Pin 84-86; U Of Pittsburgh; Engrng.

KOSKO, LISA; Steel Valley HS; Munhall, PA; (Y); Art Clb; Dance Clb; English Clb; Girl Scts; Latin Clb; Speech Tm; SADD; Nwsp Stf; Yrbk Stf; High Hon Roll; Hon Roll; Pitt; Pre-Med.

KOSMOWSKI, JOANN; West Catholic Girls HS; Philadelphia, PA; (Y); Church Yth Grp; JA; Mathletes; Nwsp Rptr; Yrbk Stf; Cheerleading; Sftbl; Hon Roll; NHS; Govt Invstgtns.

KOSMOWSKI, KELLY; Kennedy Christian HS; Greenville, PA; (Y); 14/98; Drama Clb; Ski Clb; Spanish Clb; Band; Chorus; Concert Band; Mrchg Band; School Play; Yrbk Ed-Chief; Yrbk Stf.

KOSOR, KIMBERLY; Yough SR HS; Ruffs Dale, PA; (Y); 59/271; Hosp Aide; Spanish Clb; Yrbk Stf; Rep Frsh Cls; Rep Sr Cls; VP Stu Cncl; Var L Bsktbl; Var Capt Sftbl; Var L Vllybl; Hon Roll; Ldrshp Awd-Chrldng 82-83; Indiana U Of PA; Physical Edu.

KOSSAR, TODD; Belle Vernon Area HS; Belle Vernon, PA; (Y); Church Yth Grp; Ski Clb; JV Powder Puff Ftbl; Var Vllybl; Hon Roll; Zoology.

KOSSEY, JIM; Archbishop Carroll HS; King Of Prussia, PA; (Y); 13/164; Church Yth Grp; Im Bsktbl; JV Ftbl; Golf; Var Tennis; Vllybl; High Hon Roll; Hon Roll; Jr NHS; NHS; Fd Mrktng.

KOSSICK, SHERRY; Springdale HS; Harwick, PA; (Y); Church Yth Grp; Sec German Clb; Band; Mrchg Band; Rep Frsh Cls; L Bsktbl; Sftbl; Twrlr; Hon Roll; Trs NHS.

KOSSMANN, BOBBI; Hazleton HS; Hazleton, PA; (Y); 90/388; Civic Clb; 4-H; FHA; Hosp Aide; Pep Clb; Radio Clb; SADD; Hon Roll; ST Fnlst Mss Pre-Teen PA 82; Prfrmd Cmmnty Thtre 81-83; Jrnlsm.

KOST, BRIAN; Quigley HS; Freedon, PA; (Y); 13/104; English Clb; Math Clb; Stage Crew; JV Bsktbl; Stat Coach Actv; Var L Crs Cntry; Var L Trk; Gov Hon Prg Awd; High Hon Roll; Hon Roll; Euchrstc Min 85-86; Span Awd 84-85; Comp Awd 85-86; USAF; Aerntcs.

KOST, JULIE; Du Bois Area SR HS; Dubois, PA; (Y); Art Clb; Church Yth Grp; GAA; Girl Scts; Hosp Aide; Varsity Clb; JV Bsktbl; Var Cheerleading; Var Gym; Var Mgr(s); Bio.

KOST JR, RICHARD F; Hopewell HS; Aliquippa, PA; (S); 30/295; Pres Drama Clb; Exploring; Latin Clb; School Musical; School Play; Stage Crew; Variety Show; Yrbk Ed-Chief; High Hon Roll; NHS; Youngstown ST U; Creatv Wrtg Cert 84-85; U Of Dayton; Pre-Law.

KOSTANSEK, JIM; Ft Leboevf HS; Waterford, PA; (Y); 3/187; Chess Clb; Cmnty Wkr; Computer Clb; Debate Tm; High Hon Roll; NHS.

KOSTECKY, MIKE; Marian Catholic HS; Tamaqua, PA; (Y); 50/121; Ski Clb; Bsktbl; Ftbl; Wt Lftg.

KOSTELAC, JENNIFER; Montour HS; Pittsburgh, PA; (Y); Hosp Aide; Stat Swmmng; High Hon Roll; Hon Roll; NHS; Vet.

KOSTIAL, JOE; Hopewell Area HS; Aliquippa, PA; (Y); Church Yth Grp; Computer Clb; Spanish Clb; Bsktbl; Engrng.

KOSTIN, BETH; Central Dauphin HS; Harrisburg, PA; (Y); School Musical; Rep Frsh Cls; Rep Soph Cls; Rep Stu Cncl; Var Cheerleading; Var Swmmng; Var Trk; Im Vllybl; High Hon Roll; Hon Roll; Pre-Med.

KOSTLICH, DAWN MARIE; Hopewell HS; Aliquippa, PA; (Y); Church Yth Grp; Dance Clb; Drama Clb; VP German Clb; Chorus; VP Frsh Cls; VP Soph Cls; Pres Sr Cls; Rep Stu Cncl; Capt Cheerleading; JR Miss 1st Rnnr Up 86; Beaver Area Jaycee Schlrshp 86.

KOSUDA, JOSEPH; South Side Catholic HS; Pittsburgh, PA; (S); Chess Clb; Service Clb; Chorus; Rep Frsh Cls; Rep Soph Cls; Rep Jr Cls; Capt Var Bsktbl; Hon Roll; Sci.

KOSYLO, GREGORY; North Catholic HS; Pittsburgh, PA; (Y); JA; Bsbl; Ftbl; Wt Lftg; Pre-Law.

KOT, JOHN; Brockway Area HS; Brockway, PA; (Y); Hon Roll; Air Force; Cbl & Antnna Instltn.

KOTARSKI, ANTHONY; James M Coughlin HS; Laflin, PA; (Y); Chess Clb; Math Clb; Ski Clb; Yrbk Stf; Var L Golf; Var L Vllybl; High Hon Roll; Jr NHS; NHS; Rotary Awd; Wilkes Coll; Chem Engrng.

KOTARY, LISA; State College Area SR HS; State College, PA; (Y); Church Yth Grp; Ski Clb; Band; Chorus; Church Choir; Concert Band; Mrchg Band; Pep Band; Var L Sftbl; Juanita Coll; Intl Bus.

KOTCH, KEVIN; Schuylkill Haven Area HS; Schuylkill Haven, PA; (S); 3/91; German Clb; SADD; Capt Crs Cntry; Var Trk; Bausch & Lomb Sci Awd; Hon Roll; Trs NHS; 3rd Pl Grmn Lang Cntst Bloomsburg U 85; Bloomsburg U; Physcs.

KOTCH, LINDA; Hanover Area HS; Wilkes Barre, PA; (Y); 31/156; Exploring; VP Key Clb; Ski Clb; Color Guard; Rep Stu Cncl; JV Score Keeper; Var Swmmng; Var Trk; Hon Roll; Jr NHS; Medcl.

KOTCH, SANDY; John S Fine SR HS; Nanticoke, PA; (Y); 15/256; Trs Varsity Clb; Yrbk Stf; Var L Bsktbl; L Sftbl; High Hon Roll; NHS; Radlgy.

KOTERSKI, AMY; Unionville HS; Chadds Ford, PA; (Y); 46/300; Church Yth Grp; French Clb; JV Fld Hcky; JV Trk; French Hon Soc; High Hon Roll; Hosp Adm.

KOTLER, LEILA M; Harriton HS; Villanova, PA; (Y); Drama Clb; PAVAS; Thesps; Orch; School Musical; School Play; Variety Show; Yrbk Phtg; Ed Lit Mag; Rep Frsh Cls; Msc Schlrshp Emory U 86; Violnst Phila Yth Orch & Havrfrd Coll 82-85; PA St Dist/Rgnl Orchstr 84-85; Emory; Drama.

KOTOKIS, VASILIKI; St Maria Goretti HS; Philadelphia, PA; (Y); Hon Roll; Hghst Avg Algbr I Awd 83-84; Home Ec Metal 83-84; Fshn Mdse.

KOTSKO, JOHN; John S Fine HS; Nanticoke, PA; (Y); 19/260; Model UN; Im Bsktbl; Var Ftbl; Var Trk; High Hon Roll; Sec NHS; NEDT Awd; Acad All Am 85-86; Villanova U; Bus.

KOTT, BRIAN; Ft Le Boeuf HS; Waterford, PA; (Y); #35 In Class; Rep Stu Cncl; Hon Roll; Gannon; Elec Engrng.

KOTT, TIM; The Church Farm Schl; Panama City, FL; (Y); 2/21; Church Yth Grp; JA; Nwsp Ed-Chief; Nwsp Stf; Var L Crs Cntry; Var L Mgr(s); L Capt Tennis; Hon Roll; Trs NHS; High Acadmc Avrg 86; Marine Trnsptn.

KOTYK, KRISTIN; Canon Mc Millan HS; Canonsburg, PA; (Y); French Clb; Trk; High Hon Roll; Hon Roll.

KOTYK, SUSAN; Hanover Area JR SR HS; Wilkes Barre, PA; (Y); 14/156; Library Aide; Chorus; Mrchg Band; Yrbk Rptr; Yrbk Stf; JV Var Vllybl; High Hon Roll; Jr NHS; NHS; NEDT Awd; Chem Tchr.

KOUKIS, KRISTINE; Kennedy Christian HS; Farrell, PA; (Y); 50/98; Church Choir; Bowling; JV Vllybl; Culinary Inst Of Am; Cooking.

KOURSAROS, HARI; Reading SR HS; Reading, PA; (Y); 6/639; OEA; Stage Crew; Hon Roll; Temple U Pres Awd 86; Pres Acad Fit Awds Pgm 86; Berks Cable Schlcstng Awd 86; Temple U; Filmmkng.

KOUVARAS, GEORGIA MARIE; Seneca Valley SR HS; Zelienople, PA; (Y); Trs Art Clb; Hosp Aide; Office Aide; SADD; Band; Concert Band; School Play; Hon Roll; Bradford-Ptsbrg PA; Graph Dsgn.

KOVAC, CRAIG; Freeport Area HS; Sarver, PA; (S); Band; Concert Band; Mrchg Band; School Musical; Symp Band; High Hon Roll; Elctrcl Engrng.

KOVAC, MATT; Canon-Mc Millian HS; Canonsburg, PA; (Y); Music.

KOVAC, MICHAEL; West Mifflin Area HS; W Mifflin, PA; (Y); Letterman Clb; Bsbl; Ftbl; Trk; Wt Lftg; Hon Roll; Comp Oprtr.

KOVACH, BRETT; Wm Allen HS; Allentown, PA; (Y); 51/559; Key Clb; Ski Clb; Yrbk Stf; Hon Roll; Jr NHS; NHS; Engrng.

KOVACH, GAIL; Central Cambria HS; Revloc, PA; (Y); 30/209; Office Aide; Ski Clb; Teachers Aide; Chorus; High Hon Roll; Hon Roll; Carlow Coll Schlrshp 86; Carlow Coll; Nrsng.

KOVACH, MARK A; Geibel HS; Uniontown, PA; (Y); Church Yth Grp; Stat Bsktbl; Var L Ftbl; High Hon Roll; Hon Roll; Law.

KOVACH, SUE; Pottstown SR HS; Pottstown, PA; (Y); French Clb; FNA; Key Clb; Ski Clb; Mrchg Band; Rep Frsh Cls; Rep Soph Cls; Sec Jr Cls; Sec Sr Cls; Var Capt Cheerleading; Medcl Asst.

KOVACK, VALARIE; Western Beaver HS; Industry, PA; (Y); Dance Clb; Girl Scts; Church Choir; High Hon Roll; ICM; Acctg.

KOVACS, AMY; Nazareth Area SR HS; Nazareth, PA; (Y); 49/200; VP Church Yth Grp; Ski Clb; Color Guard; Mrchg Band; JV Fld Hcky; Stat Mat Maids; Hon Roll; Schlrshp For Wk At PFEW 85; Wk At Washington DC Wrkshp 86.

KOVACS, CHRISTOPHER; Freedom HS; Bethlehem, PA; (Y); 78/456; Ski Clb; Var Ftbl; Hon Roll; Pol Sci.

KOVAL, ANDREW; North Pocono HS; Moscow, PA; (Y); Drama Clb; Exploring; Ski Clb; School Play; Variety Show; Var Ftbl; Var Wt Lftg; U Scranton; Phys Ther.

KOVAL, MARY; Villa Maria HS; Garrettsville, OH; (Y); Sec GAA; Thesps; Chorus; School Musical; Pres Soph Cls; Rep Jr Cls; Var Bsktbl; Var Vllybl; NEDT Awd; Cmnty Wkr; Pres Dorm Cncl 85-86; Cmmnctns.

KOVAL, MICHELLE R; Hazleton HS; Hazleton, PA; (Y); 75/373; Cmnty Wkr; Leo Clb; Letterman Clb; Pep Clb; Ski Clb; Yrbk Stf; Sec Sr Cls; Pres Stu Cncl; Gym; Trk; PA ST U; Apld Ntrtn.

KOVAL, PETER; Ligonier Valley SR HS; Ligonier, PA; (Y); 5/162; Trs AFS; Rep Am Leg Boys St; Boy Scts; Pres Church Yth Grp; Rep Stu Cncl; L Capt Bsktbl; Var Ftbl; Hon Roll; NHS; Pres Schlr; Rotry Schlrshp 86; Savgs And Loan Schlrshp 86; Foundrs Schlrshp 86-87; Juniata Clg.

KOVALCHICK, MICHELLE; Tunkhannock Area HS; Tunkhannock, PA; (S); 3/290; Trs Key Clb; Stat Bsktbl; Var Fld Hcky; High Hon Roll; NHS; Acad All Amer 83-84; Hugh O Brien Ldrshp Awd, Hnrs Banq 84-85; Sci.

KOVALCHIK, KATHLEEN; Mapletown HS; Greensboro, PA; (Y); Church Yth Grp; Library Aide; Yrbk Stf; Var Bsktbl; Score Keeper; Var Sftbl; Var Wt Lftg; High Hon Roll; 1st Pl Sr Div Wstrn PA Essy Cntst/Peopl Cncrnd Unbrn Chld 85; Presdntl Ftns Awd 86; Retl Sales Mgr.

KOVALCHUK, MOSES; Sun Valley HS; Brookhaven, PA; (Y); 36/319; Sec Church Yth Grp; Band; Church Choir; Concert Band; Mrchg Band; Var Socr; JV Trk; Hon Roll; Socr Mst Goals Seasn, MVP 83; Athltc Hnr Rl Mst Goals 1 Game, All Delval 84; 3 Yr Vrsty Awd 85del-Vl; Drexel U; Bus Admin.

KOVALOSKI, JAMES; Glendale JRSR HS; Irvona, PA; (Y); 2/98; Bsbl; Bsktbl; Bausch & Lomb Sci Awd; High Hon Roll; Voice Dem Awd; Chem Engrng.

KOVLER, LYNNE; George Washington HS; Philadelphia, PA; (Y); SADD; Nwsp Phtg; Nwsp Stf; Yrbk Phtg; Hon Roll; Natl Volntry Exam Hebrew Cltr & Knwldg Of Israel 85-86; Hnrbl Mntn Cert Excllnce Hebrew 85-86; Temple; Cmmnctns.

KOWALESWSKI, BETH; Canon Mc Millian HS; Canonsburg, PA; (Y); #73 In Class; Church Yth Grp; Exploring; Hosp Aide; Latin Clb; Office Aide; Ski Clb; Chorus; Stage Crew; Twrlr; Hon Roll; Optmtry.

KOWALEWSKI, CAROLINE; Carmichaels Area HS; Crucible, PA; (Y); 32/110; Spanish Clb; Hon Roll.

KOWALEWSKI, FRANCINE; Tamaqua Area HS; New Ringgold, PA; (Y); Church Yth Grp; Library Aide; Pep Clb; Q&S; Chorus; Nwsp Ed-Chief; Nwsp Stf; Rep Soph Cls; Hon Roll; VFW Awd; 1st Pl ST Comptn Writing 86; Life Savng Cert 84; Wrtng Awds 1st Pl 85; Oral Roberts U; Pre-Med.

KOWALO JR, DAN; Canon Mac Millian HS; Mc Donald, PA; (Y); Chess Clb; Church Yth Grp; Science Clb; Varsity Clb; Chorus; Ftbl; Swmmng; Trk; Wt Lftg; Hon Roll; Penn ST; Wildlf Protctn.

KOWALO, FREDERICK E; Canon-Mcmillan SR HS; Mcdonald, PA; (Y); Drama Clb; French Clb; Thesps; School Musical; School Play; Nwsp Stf; Ftbl; Trk; JV Wrstlng; Hon Roll; Cmnctns.

KOWALSKI, RITA; Bensalem SR HS; Bensalem, PA; (Y); High Hon Roll; Scrtry.

KOWALSKI II, STAN J; Williamsport Area HS; Williamsport, PA; (Y); 96/450; CAP; Key Clb; Band; Chorus; Concert Band; Mrchg Band; Symp Band; Nwsp Phtg; Nwsp Rptr; Ntl Merit Ltr; Pres Acd Ftns Awd 86; Chuck Mc Connell Mem Awd Cmmnty Svc 86; PA ST U; Pol Sci.

KOWASIC JR, WILLIAM CHARLES; Belle Vernon Area HS; Belle Vernon, PA; (Y); 52/261; Drama Clb; Band; Concert Band; Mrchg Band; Pep Band; Variety Show; Hon Roll; JP Sousa Awd; Music.

KOWATCH, LORRAINE; Franklin Regional HS; Murrysville, PA; (Y); 60/325; AFS; Band; Chorus; Swing Chorus; Rep Frsh Cls; Stu Cncl; Capt L Golf; High Hon Roll; NHS; PA ST U; Bus.

KOWKER, MICHAEL; Mahanoy Area HS; Gilberton, PA; (Y); 17/123; Capt L Bsbl; Im Bsktbl; L Ftbl; Prfct Atten Awd; Rotary Awd; Millersville U; Bus Adm.

KOWLSEN, KIM; Waynesburg Central HS; Waynesburg, PA; (Y); 22/190; French Clb; Var Badmtn; French Hon Soc; High Hon Roll; Hon Roll; Natl Trvl Schl; Cruise Ship Dir.

KOYACK, JIM; Shamokin HS; Ranshaw, PA; (Y); #28 In Class; Capt Chess Clb; Orch; Im Bsbl; Im Sftbl; Chess Chmpnshp 84-86; Cmptr Sci.

KOZA, STEPHANIE; Portage Area HS; Portage, PA; (Y); Chorus; Church Choir; Bsktbl; Trk; NHS; Bus Mgmnt.

KOZAK, MICHAEL; Thomas Jefferson HS; Pittsburgh, PA; (Y); Letterman Clb; Ski Clb; Band; Concert Band; Stu Cncl; Bsbl; Ftbl; Pittsburgh U; Bio.

KOZAK, MICHAEL T; Bishop Egan HS; Bensalem, PA; (Y); 88/229; Chess Clb; French Clb; Latin Clb; SADD; Im Badmtn; Var Golf; Im Socr; Im Sftbl; Im Vllybl; Hon Roll; Moravian Coll Grant-In-Aid 86; Hnrs Cnvctn Exclnce Soc Stu 84; Moravian Coll; Pre-Law.

KOZAK, RACHEL ANN; Merion Mercy Acad; Philadelphia, PA; (Y); 3/75; Pres Art Clb; Drama Clb; French Clb; Hosp Aide; Pres Math Tm; Service Clb; Ed Nwsp Stf; Rep Frsh Cls; French Hon Soc; Hon Roll; Carnegie-Mellon U, Drexel U & Lehigh U Schlrshp 86; Carnegie-Mellon U; Ec.

KOZAR, AMY; Blairsville SR HS; Blairsville, PA; (Y); 20/127; VP Church Yth Grp; L Varsity Clb; VP Frsh Cls; Var Capt Cheerleading; Var Trk; Var Vllybl; Hon Roll; NHS; IN U Of PA; Pre-Law.

KOZAR, KAREN S; Southmoreland SR HS; Mt Pleasant, PA; (Y); 6/213; French Clb; Letterman Clb; Office Aide; Ski Clb; Nwsp Phtg; Nwsp Stf; Lit Mag; Var L Tennis; French Hon Soc; High Hon Roll; U Of Pittsburgh; Bus Adm.

KOZEL, JUDITH V; Langley HS; Pittsburgh, PA; (Y); 1/281; Nwsp Stf; Yrbk Ed-Chief; Rep Frsh Cls; Rep Soph Cls; Rep Jr Cls; Sec Sr Cls; Rep Stu Cncl; Var Cheerleading; Cit Awd; High Hon Roll; Supts Salute To Achvt Awd 86; Rotary Stu Of Mnth 86; Harry D Book Mem Schlrp 86; U Pittsburgh; Pharm.

KOZERO, RICHARD; Liberty HS; Bethlehem, PA; (Y); Boy Scts; FBLA; Stage Crew; Hon Roll; Prfct Atten Awd; Wst Chstr U; Bus.

KOZIEL, PAUL; Bishop Hafey HS; Hazleton, PA; (Y); 58/152; Chess Clb; Elec Tech.

KOZIKOWSKI, DENISE; Pequea Valley HS; Paradise, PA; (Y); 50/138; Sec Varsity Clb; Sec Concert Band; Jazz Band; School Musical; Yrbk Stf; Trs Stu Cncl; Var Fld Hcky; Var Gym; Var Sftbl; Hon Roll; Cmmnctns.

KOZLANSKY, GERALD; Central HS; Scranton, PA; (Y); Spanish Clb; Socr; Trk; Ntl Art Hon Soc 86; Gold Awd-Drwg Covr For Yrbk 86; Keystone JC PA; Envrnmntl Sci.

KOZLOFF, SAMUEL; Wyomissing Area HS; Wyomissing, PA; (Y); 13/98; VP JCL; VP Latin Clb; Sec Model UN; Band; Yrbk Sprt Ed; NHS; Rotary Awd; Computer Clb; Drama Clb; French Clb; Natl Lat Hnr Soc 86; Slvr Medal Natl Lat Exam 86; All-Am Yth Hnr Band 85-86.

KOZLOSKI, KARA; Wyoming Area SR HS; Pittston, PA; (Y); 3/247; Church Yth Grp; German Clb; Girl Scts; Key Clb; Yrbk Stf; Rep Frsh Cls; Rep Stu Cncl; Bausch & Lomb Sci Awd; High Hon Roll; Sec NHS; Supt Awd 86; Outstndng Sci Stu 86; U Of Scranton; Pre-Med.

KOZLOSKI, KIM; Lake Lehman HS; Shavertown, PA; (S); 21/150; Drama Clb; Ski Clb; SADD; Yrbk Stf; Sec Frsh Cls; VP Jr Cls; Var Fld Hcky; Var Tennis; Hon Roll; Jr NHS; Yth Ldrshp Awd 86; Boston Coll; Psychlgy.

KOZLOSKI, KIMBERLY; Scranton Prep; Falls, PA; (Y); 44/192; Drama Clb; Service Clb; Chorus; Rep Soph Cls; Rep Jr Cls; Pres Stu Cncl; Var Diving; Im Vllybl; High Hon Roll; NHS; Brnz Medl 2nd Hghst Avg Theolgy 84-85.

KOZLOWSKI, EDMUND; Northampton Area SR HS; Bath, PA; (Y); 28/450; AFS; Exploring; Library Aide; Pres VICA; Chorus; High Hon Roll; Hon Roll; NHS; Air Force; Comp Engr.

KOZLOWSKI, JOSEPH; John S Fine HS; Nanticoke, PA; (Y); Ftbl; Wt Lftg.

KOZLOWSKI, SHARON; Freedom HS; Bethlehem, PA; (Y); 63/445; Sec Church Yth Grp; Cmnty Wkr; Hosp Aide; Sec Intnl Clb; Science Clb; Spanish Clb; Concert Band; Mrchg Band; L Var Sftbl; L Var Swmmng; Humn Rsrcs.

KOZMINSKI, MIKE; Seneca Valley HS; Zelienople, PA; (Y); 80/360; Boy Scts; Church Yth Grp; Service Clb; Ski Clb; Bsbl; Capt Bowling; Ftbl; Socr; Wt Lftg; Hon Roll; Pitt; Phrmcst.

KOZNECKI, TONIA; Washington HS; Washington, PA; (S); French Clb; Nwsp Rptr; Nwsp Stf; Vlntr David Bradford Hs 80-85; Kent ST U; Mag Athr.

KOZO, SANDRA; William Allen HS; Allentown, PA; (Y); 36/556; FBLA; Hosp Aide; Concert Band; Mrchg Band; Orch; Var L Trk; High Hon Roll; NHS; Mitrani Schlrshp 86; Bloomsburg U; Acctng.

KOZOLA, PATRICIA; North Star HS; Boswell, PA; (S); 3/136; Trs 4-H; Math Clb; Band; Chorus; Church Choir; Concert Band; Mrchg Band; Hon Roll; Bio Awd 85; Duquesne; Jrnlsm.

KOZUB, KRISTIN A; Archbishop Ryan HS For Girls; Philadelphia, PA; (Y); 90/484; Art Clb; Cmnty Wkr; JA; Office Aide; Red Cross Aide; Science Clb; Spanish Clb; Hon Roll; Perf Attndnc Awd 82-83; Temple U; Dntl Hygn.

KOZUB, LORI; Gateway SR HS; Monroeville, PA; (Y); 18/426; Church Yth Grp; Exploring; Trs Science Clb; Concert Band; Mrchg Band; Yrbk Sprt Ed; Bsktbl; Vllybl; High Hon Roll; NHS; U Of Pittsburgh; Bio.

KOZUCHOWSKI, THOMAS; Father Judge HS; Philadelphia, PA; (S); 38/413; Hosp Aide; Concert Band; Drm Mjr(t); Jazz Band; Mrchg Band; Yrbk Stf; Im Bsktbl; Hon Roll; NHS; Orch; All Catholic Band Stu 1st Alto Sax 86; Drexel U; Engrng.

KOZY, CHARLENE; Albert Gallatin SR HS; Masontown, PA; (Y); 7/151; Church Yth Grp; VICA; Chorus; Church Choir; High Hon Roll; Hon Roll; Jr NHS; NHS; Pres Schlr; Salutatorian 86; CA U PA; Comp.

KRAEUTER, MATT; West Mifflin Area HS; Pittsburgh, PA; (Y); Boy Scts; Science Clb; L Crs Cntry; Socr; L Trk; Hon Roll; Number 1 Runner Cross Country 86-87; BSA Eagle Scout 86-87; Mech Eng.

KRAFCHICK, CELESTINE; Carbondale Area HS; Carbondale, PA; (S); 2/147; FBLA; Capt Scholastic Bowl; Spanish Clb; Yrbk Ed-Chief; JV Bsktbl; Capt Fld Hcky; L Trk; NHS; Spnsh Awd 85; Dickinson; Law.

KRAFT, MELISSA; Freedom SR HS; Bethlehem, PA; (Y); 60/447; Church Yth Grp; Fld Hcky; Girl Scts; Hosp Aide; Office Aide; Pep Clb; Red Cross Aide; Chorus; Co-Capt Cheerleading; Powder Puff Ftbl; PA US Teen Pag Fin 86; Psych.

KRAFT, MELISSA; Northeastern HS; Manchester, PA; (Y); 3/149; Chorus; Camp Fr Inc; Yrbk Stf; Cheerleading; Twrlr; High Hon Roll; Hon Roll; Lion Awd; NHS; Pres Schlr; Millersville U PA; Socl Wrk.

KRAFT, TINA; Northeastern SR HS; Mt Wolf, PA; (Y); Church Yth Grp; Chorus; Stat Bsktbl; Hon Roll; Yorktown Bus Inst; Secy.

KRAH, WILLIAM; Old Forge HS; Old Forge, PA; (Y); 8/69; Letterman Clb; Ski Clb; Yrbk Sprt Ed; Yrbk Stf; Capt Bsbl; Var Bsktbl; Var Ftbl; Tennis; Wt Lftg; High Hon Roll; U Scranton; Bus.

KRAHE, LISA; North Allegheny HS; Wexford, PA; (Y); 202/642; Pres Church Yth Grp; Cmnty Wkr; Latin Clb; Varsity Clb; School Musical; Yrbk Phtg; Yrbk Stf; Rep Frsh Cls; Pres Soph Cls; Var L Fld Hcky; OH U; Physcl Thrpy.

KRAINAK, MARCIE; Danville SR HS; Danville, PA; (Y); Art Clb; Latin Clb; Color Guard; Mrchg Band; Acctg.

KRAISINGER, REGE; Mt Pleasant Area HS; Mt Pleasant, PA; (Y); 12/250; Boy Scts; German Clb; Ski Clb; Var L Ftbl; Wt Lftg; High Hon Roll; NHS; Acad All Amer Schlr 85-86; Acad All Amer At Large Div 85-86; US Natl Ftbl Awd 85; Engnrng.

KRAJC, ELIZABETH; Greensburg Central Catholic HS; Greensburg, PA; (Y); AFS; Hosp Aide; Band; Chorus; Concert Band; Camera Clb; Rep Stu Cncl; High Hon Roll; Hon Roll; Prmttd To Skip A Grd Frm JR Yr To Coll Frshmn 86; Johns Hopkins U; Astrphscst.

KRAJCI, TRACEY; Central Bucks HS West; New Britain, PA; (Y); 73/495; Sec Church Yth Grp; Cmnty Wkr; Teachers Aide; Church Choir; Var L Cheerleading; Var L Pom Pon; Hon Roll; NHS; Chld Psych.

KRAJEWSKI, LEO; St Joseph HS; Terre Haute, IN; (Y); 19/55; Boy Scts; JA; Latin Clb; Political Wkr; Band; Mrchg Band; Pep Band; School Musical; Yrbk Phtg; Top 500 SAT & ACT Scorer In PA 84-85; Rose-Hulman Inst; Elec Engr.

KRAJNIKOVICH, KIMBERLY; Butler SR HS; Bulter, PA; (Y); Dance Clb; Drama Clb; French Clb; Library Aide; Office Aide; Red Cross Aide; Spanish Clb; Varsity Clb; Band; Drill Tm; Butler Cnty JR Miss 86; Grove City Coll; Bus Mgmt.

KRALIK, CHRIS; Bishop Mc Cort HS; Johnstown, PA; (Y); 6/129; Math Clb; Color Guard; Orch; Capt Twrlr; High Hon Roll; VP NHS; U Of Pittsburg Johnstown.

KRALL, SANDRA; East Stroudsburg Area HS; Ea Stroudsburg, PA; (Y); 20/190; Ski Clb; Capt Drill Tm; Mrchg Band; Rep Frsh Cls; Trs Soph Cls; Trs Jr Cls; Trs Sr Cls; Rep Stu Cncl; Hon Roll; NHS; Yth Of Mnth-Exchng Clb 85-86; Outstndng Sophmr Mrchr-Mrchng Band 83-84; U Of Pitt-Johnstown; Phys Thrpy.

KRALL, STEVE; Eastern Lebanon Co HS; Myerstown, PA; (Y); 12/197; Var L Golf; Var L Tennis; Hon Roll; NHS; Pres Schlr; Hall Fndtn Glf & Acdmc 86; 2nd Pl York Invtnl 84; W R Bolten 2nd Pl & Leban Co JR Glf 85; Millersville U; Math.

KRAMARSKI, ROSANNE; Southmoreland SR HS; Scottdale, PA; (Y); 32/240; Letterman Clb; Spanish Clb; Yrbk Stf; Trs Soph Cls; Trs Jr Cls; Trs Sr Cls; Bsktbl; Sftbl; Tennis; Spanish NHS.

KRAMER, BRIAN; Central Dauphin HS; Harrisburg, PA; (Y); Church Yth Grp; School Play; Var Capt Bsktbl; JV Var Mgr(s); Var Socr; Im Var Vllybl; Hon Roll; NHS; Deans Schlrshp 86; Messiah Coll; Mrktng.

KRAMER, COLLEEN; Shamokin Area HS; Shamokin, PA; (Y); German Clb; Key Clb; Library Aide; Office Aide; Pep Clb; Flag Corp; Nwsp Rptr; Yrbk Stf; Hon Roll; NHS; Bus Mgt.

KRAMER, CURTIS; Louis E Dieruff HS; Allentown, PA; (Y); 33/327; Church Yth Grp; Church Choir; Im Bsktbl; Var Crs Cntry; Var L Trk; Im Wt Lftg; Hon Roll; Jr NHS; NHS; Prfct Atten Awd; Messiah Coll; Comp Inf Systems.

KRAMER JR, GEORGE MICHAEL; Canon-Macmillan SR HS; Canonsburg, PA; (Y); Drama Clb; Math Tm; Spanish Clb; School Play; Trk; High Hon Roll; NHS; Ntl Merit Ltr; Pres Schlr; Canon Mc Millan Sci Awd; U Of Pittsburgh; Elec Engrg.

KRAMER II, JOHN; Moon HS; Corapolis, PA; (Y); Boy Scts; Camera Clb; Chess Clb; Church Yth Grp; Cmnty Wkr; Computer Clb; Band; Church Choir; Mrchg Band; Orch; PA ST; Comp Engnrng.

KRAMER, KIM; Carrick HS; Pittsburgh, PA; (Y); 20/316; Church Yth Grp; Q&S; Capt Flag Corp; Mrchg Band; Nwsp Rptr; Yrbk Stf; High Hon Roll; NHS; Pres Acad Ftns Awd 86; U Pittsburgh; Dentistry.

KRAMER, MEREDITH; Upper Dublin HS; Ambler, PA; (Y); Art Clb; Hosp Aide; Yrbk Stf; Swmmng; Vllybl; Hon Roll; Spanish NHS; Hlth Admin.

KRAMER, MICHAEL; East Pennsboro Area HS; Camp Hill, PA; (Y); 7/196; Varsity Clb; Var L Bsbl; Var L Bsktbl; Var Capt Golf; High Hon Roll; Acadmc All Amer 85; Penn ST U; Engr.

KRAMER, MITCHELL; Solebury HS; Jenkintown, PA; (S); Camera Clb; Cmnty Wkr; Computer Clb; Drama Clb; School Play; Stage Crew; Variety Show; Yrbk Phtg; Yrbk Stf; Rep Frsh Cls; Pres Clssrm 85; Art.

KRAMER, NADINE; Saint Clair Area HS; St Clair, PA; (Y); 7/84; English Clb; VP Ski Clb; Chorus; Capt Drill Tm; Variety Show; Nwsp Stf; Yrbk Stf; Rep Frsh Cls; Rep Soph Cls; Rep Jr Cls.

KRAMER, SCOTT; Pine Grove HS; Pine Grove, PA; (Y); Boy Scts; Drama Clb; Varsity Clb; Band; Concert Band; Mrchg Band; School Musical; Nwsp Stf; Hst Soph Cls; Hst Jr Cls; Arch.

KRAMER, SHERRI; Penn-Trafford HS; Irwin, PA; (Y); Church Yth Grp; Drama Clb; French Clb; FBLA; Office Aide; Teachers Aide; Chorus; Church Choir; High Hon Roll; Hon Roll; Hgh Hnr Stu 85-86; Hnr & High Hnr Rl 85-86; Sawyer Bus Schl; Mdcl Asst.

KRAMER, WILLIAM; Hamburg Area JR-SR HS; Hamburg, PA; (Y); 43/150; Pres Church Yth Grp; JV Var Socr; Hon Roll; Acad Achvt Awd In Physics 86; Penn ST; Arch.

KRAMMES, TRUDY; Schuylkill Haven Area HS; Schuylkill Haven, PA; (Y); 10/99; Pep Clb; SADD; Hon Roll; NHS; Bus.

KRANCE, AMY; Moon SR HS; Corapolis, PA; (Y); Church Yth Grp; Hosp Aide; Key Clb; Chorus; School Musical; Crs Cntry; JR Prom Crt 86; JV Ltr X-Cntry 85.

KRANICH, KARL; Cocalico HS; Denver, PA; (Y); 9/147; Boy Scts; Sec Chess Clb; Computer Clb; Quiz Bowl; Science Clb; School Musical; School Play; Stage Crew; High Hon Roll; Eagle Scout Rank 86; Elec Engrng.

KRANIK, ANNETTE; Northern Cambria HS; Derby, NY; (Y); Art Clb; Drama Clb; FHA; Library Aide; Ski Clb; Band; Concert Band; Mrchg Band; Yrbk Stf; Hon Roll.

KRANKEL, SHARON K; Abington Heights HS; Clarks Summit, PA; (Y); 6/270; Church Yth Grp; Chorus; Yrbk Stf; Trs Frsh Cls; Rep Stu Cncl; Hon Roll; NHS; Ntl Merit Ltr; Ski Clb; School Musical; Stu Rep Schl Brd 86-87; Accmpnst Chorus & Mxd Ensmbl 83-86; Dsgn.

KRANVECZ, FAITH; Freedom HS; Bethlehem, PA; (Y); 63/457; Church Yth Grp; Girl Scts; Nwsp Phtg; Yrbk Phtg; Hon Roll; Psych.

KRANZLER, BOBBIE; Greencastle-Antrim HS; Greencastle, PA; (Y); 16/195; Church Yth Grp; Band; Chorus; Concert Band; Jazz Band; School Musical; Yrbk Phtg; High Hon Roll; NHS; Hnrbl Mntn Sci Fair 83-84; Hagerstown JC; Nrsg.

KRAPF, THERESA; Wm Allen HS; Allentown, PA; (Y); 147/559; Church Yth Grp; Intnl Clb; Ski Clb; Church Choir; JV Var Fld Hcky; Trk; Hon Roll; Jr NHS; Spanish NHS; Bus.

KRAPP JR, DONALD; Northeast Catholic HS; Philadelphia, PA; (S); 7/390; Science Clb; Band; Jazz Band; Mrchg Band; NHS; Sci.

KRASINSKI, CHRISTI; Mcguffey HS; Washington, PA; (Y); 57/216; French Clb; Pep Clb; Chorus; Var Powder Puff Ftbl; Var Tennis; Stat Trk; Stat Wrstlng; Fash Merch.

KRASNANSKY, RONALD K; Bensalem HS; Bensalem, PA; (Y); 62/564; French Clb; Bsbl; Wrstlng; CC Awd; High Hon Roll; NHS; Penn ST U; Bus Mrktg.

KRASNITSKY, SANDY; Minersville Area HS; Pottsville, PA; (Y); 17/115; Off German Clb; Ski Clb; Spanish Clb; Mrchg Band; Stage Crew; Rep Soph Cls; Trs Jr Cls; Var JV Bsktbl; L Sftbl; Hon Roll.

KRASZEWSKI, KELLY; Pennsbury HS; Yardley, PA; (Y); Spanish Clb; Stage Crew; Yrbk Stf; Im Bsktbl; Im Gym; Var Trk; Hon Roll; NHS; Cert Of Merit Eng, Bio II, Spnsh III 84-85; Bus.

KRATOFIL, KRISTEN; Yough HS; Irwin, PA; (Y); Debate Tm; VP 4-H; Ski Clb; Spanish Clb; SADD; Ed Yrbk Ed-Chief; Chorus; Rep Stu Cncl; JV Capt Cheerleading; Tennis; WV U; Communications.

KRATOWICZ, DAWN; Saint Hubert HS; Philadelphia, PA; (Y); 9/367; Chorus; Church Choir; Nwsp Ed-Chief; Nwsp Rptr; Nwsp Stf; Yrbk Stf; Lit Mag; Hon Roll; Jr NHS; NHS.

KRATZ, CHARLENE; Wyoming Valley West HS; Plymouth, PA; (Y); 15/380; Church Yth Grp; Key Clb; Band; Concert Band; Mrchg Band; Yrbk Stf; Lit Mag; Rep Stu Cncl; High Hon Roll; Hon Roll; Brumbaugh-Ellis Schlrshp 86; Bess-Marie Schilling Schlrshp 86; Pres Acdmc Ftns Awd 86; Juniata Coll; Occptnl Thrpy.

KRATZ, KEITH; Plymouth Whitemarsh HS; Plymouth Meeting, PA; (Y); #8 In Class; Bsktbl; Socr; Tennis; High Hon Roll.

KRATZ, MICHELE; Crestwood HS; Nuangola, PA; (Y); Pep Clb; Ski Clb; Hon Roll; Psych.

KRATZER, KIMBERLY; Emmaus HS; Emmaus, PA; (Y); Color Guard; High Hon Roll; Hon Roll; NHS; Trvl.

KRATZER, LIZ; Northampton Area SR HS; Walnutport, PA; (S); AFS; FTA; Yrbk Stf; High Hon Roll; NHS; Muhlenberg Coll; Comm.

KRATZER, RACHEL; Shikellamy HS; Sunbury, PA; (Y); Drama Clb; German Clb; Speech Tm; Teachers Aide; Thesps; Chorus; School Play; Stage Crew; Marine Bio.

KRATZINGER, ERIC; Malvern Preparatory Schl; Malvern, PA; (Y); 22/96; Mgr Drama Clb; School Musical; School Play; Mgr Stage Crew; Var Capt Crs Cntry; JV Capt Ice Hcky; Var Trk; Hon Roll; Prfct Atten Awd; Fathers Club Achvt Awd 86; Bus Fin.

KRAUS, KURT; Fox Chapel HS; Pittsbg, PA; (Y); 191/322; Mrchg Band; Stage Crew; Arch Engrng.

KRAUS, LAURA; Elk County Christian HS; St Marys, PA; (Y); Pres Hosp Aide; Model UN; Concert Band; Drm Mjr(t); Mrchg Band; NHS; Key Clb; Varsity Clb; Sec Band; Model UN Del Schlrshp 85-86; Ms Alleghany Highlnds Schlrshp Pgnt Queen 86; MS PA Schlrshp Pgnt 86; Gannon U; Med Tech.

KRAUS JR, RICH J; Center HS; Aliquippa, PA; (Y); Boys Clb Am; Cmnty Wkr; SADD; Band; Concert Band; Drm & Bgl; Jazz Band; Mrchg Band; School Musical; Ftbl; Outstndng Band Mem 86.

KRAUSE, ANGELA; Northern Lebanon HS; Jonestown, PA; (Y); 41/179; Church Yth Grp; Band; Chorus; Concert Band; Mrchg Band; Pep Band; School Musical; Swing Chorus; Nwsp Stf; Lit Mag; 1st Chair-Clarinet Dist Band 85-86; Rgnl Band 85-86; Cnty Chorus 86; Lebanon Vly Coll; Music Educ.

KRAUSE, DAWN; Carmichaels Area HS; Crucible, PA; (Y); 21/109; Office Aide; Trs Ski Clb; VP Spanish Clb; Band; Mrchg Band; Jr Cls; Stu Cncl; Twrlr; Hon Roll; Jr NHS; Chld Psych.

KRAUSE, JEFF; Carmichaels Area HS; Crucible, PA; (S); 10/120; Letterman Clb; Library Aide; Pep Clb; Spanish Clb; Varsity Clb; Stu Cncl; Ftbl; CA U Of PA; Envrnmntl Resrcs.

KRAUSE, KIMBERLY ANN; Pine Grove Area HS; Pine Grove, PA; (Y); 14/125; Am Leg Aux Girls St; Pres Church Yth Grp; SADD; Chorus; Color Guard; Ed Yrbk Stf; Capt Twrlr; Hon Roll; Sec NHS; JR Strng Cmt 85-86; Bus Ed.

KRAUSE, KRISTIN; Wm Allen HS; Allentown, PA; (Y); 10/610; Girl Scts; Sec Leo Clb; Quiz Bowl; Service Clb; Ski Clb; Nwsp Ed-Chief; Lit Mag; High Hon Roll; Lion Awd; NHS; Phrmcy.

KRAUSE, LORI; Lebanon Catholic HS; Lebanon, PA; (Y); FHA; Ski Clb; Spanish Clb; School Play; Yrbk Stf; Rep Frsh Cls; Rep Soph Cls; Sec Sr Cls; Sec Stu Cncl; Capt Cheerleading; Ldrshp Dvlpmnt Wrkshp 85-86; Spcl Rcgnstn 85; Brdcstng.

KRAUSE, MICHAEL; Seneca Valley HS; Mars, PA; (Y); JA; Ski Clb; Band; Concert Band; Jazz Band; Mrchg Band; Pep Band; Desgng.

KRAUSE, PAMELA N; Delaware Valley HS; Matamoras, PA; (Y); Letterman Clb; Ski Clb; SADD; Varsity Clb; Yrbk Phtg; Yrbk Stf; Var L Tennis; Gov Hon Prg Awd; Hon Roll; AAA Natl Poster Desgn Contst-Hnrb Mntn 85 & 86; Presdntl Physcl Ftnss Awd 84-86; Visual Art.

KRAUSE, TODD; Lower Moreland HS; Huntingdon Valley, PA; (S); Trs FBLA; Hst FFA; Key Clb; Science Clb; Yrbk Stf; JV Bsbl; JV Tennis; High Hon Roll; Hon Roll; 2nd Pl Regnl Bus Math Comp, 10th Pl ST 85; Engl, Am Hist Advncd Plcmnt 85-86; Bus Admin.

KRAUSHAAR, LYNN; Canon-Mc Millan SR HS; Canonsburg, PA; (Y); Church Yth Grp; VP French Clb; Library Aide; Office Aide; Pep Clb; Ski Clb; Drill Tm; Nwsp Phtg; Nwsp Rptr; Nwsp Stf; Penn ST; Engrng.

KRAUSS, CINDY; Brockway Area HS; Brockway, PA; (Y); 1/87; Co-Capt Drill Tm; Yrbk Stf; Pres Church Yth Grp; Rep Stu Cncl; Bausch & Lomb Sci Awd; DAR Awd; Hon Roll; Pres NHS; Psychlgy.

KRAUSS, KAREN; Northwestern Lehigh HS; New Tripoli, PA; (Y); 2/170; Church Yth Grp; Crs Cntry; Fld Hcky; Trk; High Hon Roll; NHS; NEDT Awd; Grmn Awds 85-86; Trignmtry Anlytc Geo 86; Intrntl Rltns.

KRAVETSKY, LAURIE; Kiski Area HS; Avonmore, PA; (Y); Aud/Vis; Church Yth Grp; Library Aide; Pep Clb; SADD; Chorus; School Play; Nwsp Ed-Chief; Yrbk Stf; Stu Cncl; Cthlc Mrthn 1st Pl 85-86; Asst Sec Gov Yth Trffc Sffty Cncl 85-86; Acctng.

KRAVITZ, KYLE; Cheltenham HS; Elkins Pk, PA; (Y); 20/365; Capt Debate Tm; JCL; Model UN; Political Wkr; Ed Nwsp Stf; Stu Cncl; Chorus; School Musical; School Play; NEDT Awd; Magna Cum Laude Awd Ntl Latin Ex 86; Pol Sci.

KRAWCZYK, MIKE; Abraham Lincoln HS; Philadelphia, PA; (Y); 31/480; JV Bsbl; Var Bsktbl; Hon Roll; Opt Clb Awd.

KRAWCZYK, SHARON LYNN; Gateway SR HS; Mornoeville, PA; (Y); 54/474; Church Yth Grp; VP Exploring; FBLA; Off Jr Cls; Off Sr Cls; Stu Cncl; Capt Cheerleading; Hon Roll; Pres Acad Ftns Awd 86; Evergreen Famly Tchr Org Schlrshp 86; Gannon U; Finance.

KRAWIEC, FRANK; Belle Vernon Area HS; Webster, PA; (Y); Hon Roll; NHS.

KRAYNACK, CHRISTOPHER; Tunkhannock Area HS; Tunkhannock, PA; (S); FCA; Ski Clb; Off Jr Cls; JV Bsktbl; Var L Crs Cntry; Var L Trk; Hon Roll; NHS; Carnegie Mellon; Chem.

KRAYNAK, JAMES S; Connellsville Area HS; Connellsville, PA; (Y); 95/550; Band; Concert Band; Var L Ftbl; Var L Wrstlng; Hon Roll; NHS; WPIAL Sectn Wrstlng Champ 85 & 86; Mst Varsty Wrstlng Tm Points Underclssmn 86.

KRAYNAK, JOSEPH; Connellsville Area HS; Connellsville, PA; (Y); 1/438; Mgr L Bsktbl; Mgr L Ftbl; Bausch & Lomb Sci Awd; High Hon Roll; Trs NHS; Ntl Merit Ltr; Prfct Atten Awd; Rotary Awd; Spanish NHS; Val; Chem Awd 86; Acad Achvt 86; U Pittsburgh; Elec Engrng.

KRAYNAK, LARRY; South Allegheny HS; Mckeesport, PA; (Y); Camera Clb; Band; Concert Band; Mrchg Band; Bsktbl; Ftbl; Golf; Hon Roll; Indiana U PA; Bus.

KRCHNAR, CHRISTINA; Maheim Central HS; Manheim, PA; (Y); 6/237; Chorus; Church Choir; Concert Band; Mrchg Band; School Musical; Yrbk Stf; JV Var Cheerleading; Var Trk; High Hon Roll; NHS; Secdry Ed.

KREADY, KIMBERLY; Mt Calvary Christian HS; Elizabethtown, PA; (S); 2/11; Chorus; School Play; Yrbk Phtg; Cheerleading; Fld Hcky; Sftbl; Vllybl; Hon Roll; NHS; Natl Hstry & Govt Awd 85-86; Elem Ed.

KREBS, KENNETH C; Avonworth JR SR HS; Sewickley, PA; (Y); 10/100; Aud/Vis; Boy Scts; Chess Clb; Church Yth Grp; Cmnty Wkr; Spanish Clb; SADD; Band; Concert Band; Drm & Bgl; PMEA Dist Band 84; PMEA Mid-East Conf 82-86; Grove City Clg; Intl Bus.

KREBS, MICHELE; Rockwood Area HS; Rockwood, PA; (S); 5/98; Pres AFS; Quiz Bowl; Chorus; Nwsp Stf; Vllybl; High Hon Roll; Hon Roll; Pres NHS; NEDT Awd; U Of Pttsbrgh-Jhnstwn; Psychlgy.

KREBS, RHONDA; Cedar Cliff HS; Camp Hill, PA; (Y); 46/300; French Clb; Hosp Aide; Church Choir; Flag Corp; French Hon Soc; High Hon Roll; Hon Roll; Prfct Atten Awd; Pres Schlr; PA ST U; Hlth Care Admin.

KREBS, ROBERT; Clearfield Area HS; Clearfield, PA; (Y); Church Yth Grp; Bsktbl; Ftbl; Wt Lftg; Hon Roll.

KRECH, MICHELE; Punxsutawney SR HS; Punxsutawney, PA; (Y); VP Church Yth Grp; French Clb; Hosp Aide; Band; Church Choir; Mrchg Band; Pep Band; Soc Wrk.

KRECHOWSKI, BETH; New Brighton Area HS; New Brighton, PA; (Y); Am Leg Aux Girls St; GAA; Band; Drm Mjr(t); Mrchg Band; Hon Roll.

KRECKEL, BRANDON; Johnsonburg Area HS; Wilcox, PA; (S); Boy Scts; Bsbl; JV Ftbl; Trk; JV Wrstlng; Hon Roll; Ntl Merit Schol.

KREDELL, GREGORY; Pittsburgh Central Catholic HS; Glenshaw, PA; (Y); 19/289; Art Clb; Church Yth Grp; JA; Ski Clb; Var Crs Cntry; Var Socr; Var Trk; High Hon Roll; Hon Roll; NHS; 25th In St Crss Cntry 85; 7th In St Mile Run 86; Bus.

KREDELL, STEPHEN; Pittsburgh Central Catholic HS; Glenshaw, PA; (Y); 13/290; Exploring; Crs Cntry; Socr; Trk; High Hon Roll; NHS; Spanish NHS.

KREELICH, BRIAN; Liberty HS; Bethlehem, PA; (Y); 149/475; Boys Clb Am; JV Var Bsbl; JV Var Socr; Hon Roll; K E Yurchak Mem Awd 85; Cvl Engrng.

KREGER, JOHN C; Seneca Vallley HS; Evans Cty, PA; (Y); 9/356; Art Clb; Church Yth Grp; JA; Ski Clb; Jazz Band; Rep Stu Cncl; Bsbl; Wrstlng; High Hon Roll; NHS; Alumni Clb Schlrshp 86; IN U Physics Testng Comp Wnng Score 85; Ed Agency Cert Merit 85; U MI; Bus Adm.

KREGER, LISA; Villa Maria Acad; Lake City, PA; (S); 1/135; Science Clb; Hon Roll; NHS; NEDT Awd; Phrmclgy.

KREGER, MELANIE; Rockwood Area HS; Markleton, PA; (S); 1/92; Trs Church Yth Grp; Office Aide; Chorus; Church Choir; Yrbk Stf; High Hon Roll; Hon Roll; NHS; Outstndng JR Bus Awd 85; Ntl Hnr Soc Bus Awd 84-85; Shorthand I Awd 85; Robert Morris Coll; Bus Adm.

KREIDER, JODI; Solaris HS; Quarryville, PA; (Y); VP Church Yth Grp; Sec 4-H; Trs Radio Clb; School Musical; Im Powder Puff Ftbl; High Hon Roll; Hon Roll; NHS.

KREIDER, LORI D; Garden Spot HS; E Earl, PA; (Y); 169/218; Drama Clb; 4-H; Spanish Clb; Teachers Aide; Band; Concert Band; Mrchg Band; Stage Crew; Nwsp Rptr; Nwsp Stf; Tchr.

KREIDER, MARY ANN M; Cedar Crest HS; Lebanon, PA; (Y); 6/341; Church Yth Grp; Latin Clb; Pep Clb; Spanish Clb; Var L Fld Hcky; Im Vllybl; Hon Roll; NHS; Ntl Merit Ltr; Ray S Bckslr Mem Schlrshp 86; Lbnn Cnty Soc Pro Engnrs Schlrshp 86; Cdr Crst Bstr Clb Schlrshp 86; PA ST U; Engnrng.

KREIDER, RANDY; Conneaut Valley HS; Conneautville, PA; (Y); 5/70; Computer Clb; Quiz Bowl; Scholastic Bowl; Spanish Clb; SADD; JV Vllybl; High Hon Roll; Hon Roll; Clarion U Of PA; Bus.

KREIDER, ROBERT; Manheim Central HS; Manheim, PA; (Y); 7/256; Church Yth Grp; Church Choir; School Musical; Ed Yrbk Ed-Chief; Yrbk Phtg; Yrbk Stf; Hon Roll; Lion Awd; NHS; Sci Awd 83; 4 Way Tst Awd 86; Millersville; Hstry Tchr.

KREIDER, SUE; Annville Cleona HS; Annville, PA; (Y); 7/112; Church Yth Grp; Cmnty Wkr; 4-H; VP German Clb; Girl Scts; Varsity Clb; Band; Chorus; Mrchg Band; VP Stu Cncl; WAHT Athltc Of The Wk 85-86; Lebanon Lncstr Bsktbl All-Star 85-86; Physcl Ed.

KREIDER, THOMAS; Archbishop Wood HS; Southampton, PA; (Y); 125/282; Boy Scts; Ad, Altare, Dei Awd-By Scts 84; Pope Pius XII Awd-By Scts 85; By Scts Rnk Life 86; Sci.

KREIDER, TIMOTHY MARK; Cedar Crest HS; Lebanon, PA; (Y); French Clb; Key Clb; Latin Clb; Letterman Clb; Pep Clb; School Musical; School Play; VP Sr Cls; Ice Hcky; Socr; MVP Ice Hockey Keystone Games 83&84; MVP Ice Hockey US-RUSSIA & Finland Tour 85; VP Sr Cls 85-86; U CT.

KREIFELS, BRIGITTE; Annville-Cleona HS; Annville, PA; (Y); German Clb; Varsity Clb; Nwsp Stf; Yrbk Stf; Mat Maids; Sftbl; Tennis; NHS; Archit.

KREINER, ANNA S; Cheltenham HS; Wyncote, PA; (Y); 1/385; Hosp Aide; Orch; Nwsp Ed-Chief; NHS; Ntl Merit SF; NEDT Awd; Harvard U Bk Awd.

KREISER, DONNA; Northern Lebanon HS; Jonestown, PA; (Y); FFA; Hon Roll; Kiwanis Awd; Ffa Star Chapter Farmer 85-86; Horticulture.

KREISER, KARLA E; Lower Dauphin HS; Hershey, PA; (Y); Am Leg Aux Girls St; Exploring; Hosp Aide; Stage Crew; Yrbk Stf; Stu Cncl; Var Tennis; Hon Roll; Prfct Atten Awd; VP Med Explrers Post 85-86; Grls Ensmbl Vocal Grp 83-84; Arch.

KREISER, TRAVIS; Palmyra Area HS; Palmyra, PA; (Y); 50/210; Church Yth Grp; Chorus; Hon Roll; Pre Law.

KREISLER, AMY; Elkland Area HS; Elkland, PA; (Y); French Clb; Political Wkr; SADD; Sec Frsh Cls; Stat Bsktbl; Mgr(s); Score Keeper; Swmmng; Trk; High Hon Roll.

KREITZER, DANNY; Hanover Area HS; Wilkes Barre, PA; (Y); VP Key Clb; Off Frsh Cls; Off Soph Cls; Stu Cncl; High Hon Roll; Jr NHS; NHS; PA JR Acad Sci.

KREITZER JR, EUGENE; Northern Lebanon HS; Fredericksburg, PA; (Y); 2/150; Pres Church Yth Grp; Pres FFA; Model UN; Stat Ftbl; Trk; Dnfth Awd; High Hon Roll; Hon Roll; VP NHS; Outstndng Stu Ag 86; Star Greenhand Chptr Farmer 84-86; Woodmen World Prof Am Hist 84-86; Penn ST U; Aeronutcl Engr.

KREJNUS, SUSAN; Cambria Heights SR HS; Elmora, PA; (Y); 25/200; FHA; Library Aide; NFL; Concert Band; Mrchg Band; Yrbk Stf; Hon Roll; NHS; Med.

KRELL, KAY; Pottsville Area HS; Pottsville, PA; (Y); 90/250; Drama Clb; Girl Scts; Latin Clb; Science Clb; Mrchg Band; Hon Roll; Prfct Atten Awd; Color Guard; Teachng.

KRELL, ROY; Tamaqua Area HS; Tamaqua, PA; (Y); Boy Scts; German Clb; Chorus; Bsktbl; Hon Roll; NHS; German Ntl Hnr Scty 86; Engr.

KREMER JR, JOSEPH L; Shikellamy HS; Northumberland, PA; (Y); 11/319; Pres Frsh Cls; Pres Soph Cls; Var Bsbl; Var Ftbl; Var Wrstlng; High Hon Roll; Hon Roll; NHS; West Point; Pre-Med.

KREMITSKE, DONNA; Pittston Area HS; Avoca, PA; (Y); FNA; Science Clb; Ski Clb; Hon Roll; Envrnmntl Awrns Clb 85-86; Penn ST U.

KREMUS, PAM; Northampton SR HS; Northampton, PA; (Y); 36/444; Office Aide; Yrbk Stf; Rep Stu Cncl; Var Capt Swmmng; Trk; High Hon Roll; Hon Roll.

KRENITSKY, MARK P; Knoch JR SR HS; Butler, PA; (Y); 13/226; Pres Science Clb; Orch; High Hon Roll; NHS; Ntl Merit SF; Carnegie Mellon U; Physics.

KRENITSKY, VICTORIA; Old Forge HS; Old Forge, PA; (S); Ski Clb; Nwsp Phtg; Pres Jr Cls; Pres Sr Cls; Capt Sftbl; Hon Roll; NHS.

KREPS, DOUG; North Hills HS; Pittsburgh, PA; (S); 15/470; Chrmn Debate Tm; Drama Clb; NFL; Ski Clb; Thesps; School Play; Lit Mag; High Hon Roll; NHS; Bus.

KRESGE, DANIEL L; Stroudsburg HS; Stroudsburg, PA; (Y); 13/237; German Clb; Scholastic Bowl; Varsity Clb; JV Bsktbl; JV Var Ftbl; Var L Trk; Wt Lftg; High Hon Roll; NHS; Exchng Clb Stu Mnth Feb 86; Hobart Coll.

KRESGE, ROXANE; Pleasant Valley HS; Gilbert, PA; (Y); 30/230; Ski Clb; Teachers Aide; Varsity Clb; Pres Frsh Cls; Pres Soph Cls; Rep Jr Cls; Rep Stu Cncl; Var Cheerleading; Var Sftbl; Hon Roll; Acad All Am 86; Law.

KRESOVICH, JOSEPH; Bellefonte HS; Bellefonte, PA; (Y); Spanish Clb; Sec Varsity Clb; Var L Bsbl; Var L Bsktbl; Var L Ftbl; Im Wt Lftg; Hon Roll; Keystone Games Rep 86; Central PA Leag Bsbl All Star 86; Lbrl Arts.

KRESS, KAREN; Fort Cherry HS; Mcdonald, PA; (Y); 13/128; Drama Clb; Science Clb; Ski Clb; Thesps; Varsity Clb; VP Chorus; Nwsp Stf; Tennis; High Hon Roll; NHS; US Army Rsrv Schlr Athl Awd 85-86; Lttr In Tennis 83-86; Sawyer Schl Of Pittsburgh; Trvl.

KRESS, MELISSA; Northeast HS; Philadelphia, PA; (Y); 25/600; Cmnty Wkr; Hosp Aide; Office Aide; Ski Clb; Teachers Aide; Chorus; JV Fld Hcky; Hon Roll; Jr NHS; NHS; Pres Acadmc Fitness Awd 86; Bowman Ashe Schlrshp U Of Miami 86-87; N E HS Home & Schl Schlrshp 86; U Of Miami; Pre-Med.

KRESSLER, JILL; Saucon Valley SR HS; Hellertown, PA; (Y); 8/146; Church Yth Grp; Hosp Aide; Model UN; Office Aide; Red Cross Aide; Spanish Clb; Mgr(s); Score Keeper; High Hon Roll; NHS; Nrsng.

KRESSLEY, CARSON; Northwestern Lehigh JR SR HS; Orefield, PA; (Y); 14/168; Art Clb; Nwsp Stf; Yrbk Stf; High Hon Roll; Hon Roll; Trs NHS; Outstngn Germ II Stu Awd 84-85; Outstndng Drawg And Paintg Awd 84-85; Outstndng Germ III Stu Awd 85; Arch.

KRETSCHMER, DAWN; Cheltenham HS; Elkins Pk, PA; (Y); Church Yth Grp; JA; Art Clb; JV Fld Hcky; Var Mgr(s); Bus.

KRETZLER, AMY; Moon SR HS; Coraopolis, PA; (Y); 30/325; Church Yth Grp; Hosp Aide; Key Clb; Library Aide; Office Aide; L Crs Cntry; Hon Roll; NHS.

KREY, KAREN; Allentown Central Catholic HS; Allentown, PA; (Y); Church Yth Grp; French Clb.

KRICK, KOREY; Wilson HS; W Lawn, PA; (Y); Yrbk Stf; Var L Bsktbl; Var Capt Fld Hcky; Hon Roll; NHS; Lock Haven U; Soc Wrk.

KRIDLE, ERIK; Albert Gallatin HS; Masontown, PA; (Y); 1/130; Pres Church Yth Grp; Chorus; School Play; Yrbk Stf; Cit Awd; High Hon Roll; NHS; Bible Quz Team Awd Capt; Law.

KRIDLER, BRIAN; Mercyhurst Prep; Erie, PA; (Y); 7/150; Thesps; School Play; Stu Cncl; Bsktbl; Socr; NHS; Art Scholar 85 & 86; Comm Dsgn.

KRIEBEL, DAN; Allegheny Clarion Valley HS; Parker, PA; (Y); Band; Concert Band; Jazz Band; Pres Mrchg Band; Pep Band; Stat Bsktbl; Var L Golf; Trk; Hon Roll; NHS; Grove City Coll; Chem.

KRIEBEL, DEBORAH; Cumberland Valley HS; Mechanicsburg, PA; (Y); Cmnty Wkr; Library Aide; Spanish Clb; NHS; Lib Sci.

KRIEGER, ERIC; Connellsville Area HS; Connellsville, PA; (Y); 27/500; Chess Clb; Church Yth Grp; JV Bsktbl; NHS; Acadmc All Am 85-86; Engrg.

KRIEGISCH, HOLLY; Seneca Valley HS; Zelienople, PA; (Y); 18/374; Church Yth Grp; SADD; Chorus; Color Guard; Mgr(s); High Hon Roll; Hon Roll; NHS; PA ST Beaver Campus Exec Schlrshp; PA ST Beaver Campus Kunkle Schlrshp; PA ST U-Beaver; Bus Admin.

KRILEY, ANDREA; Marian Catholic HS; Jim Thorpe, PA; (Y); 67/122; Library Aide; Ski Clb; SADD; School Play; Cheerleading; Sftbl.

KRILL, MICHAEL; William Allen HS; Allentown, PA; (Y); 108/604; Band; Concert Band; Jazz Band; Mrchg Band; School Play; Mem Of Modrn Music Mstrs VP 85-86; Outstndng Jz Muscn 84-86; Muscns JR Hl Of Fm 85-86; Music Ed.

KRINGER, ANN MARIE; Hazleton HS; Hazleton, PA; (Y); Cmnty Wkr; Drama Clb; Office Aide; Variety Show; Ed Nwsp Stf; Yrbk Stf; JV Bsktbl; L Sftbl; Im Vllybl; Hon Roll; Englsh Merit Awd 84; Pre-Med.

KRISCH, MIKE; Bald Eagle Area HS; Snow Shoe, PA; (Y); JV Bsbl; JV Var Ftbl; Var Trk; Hon Roll.

KRISCH, PAUL; Hanover Area HS; Wilkes Barre, PA; (Y); Church Yth Grp; Wilkes Coll; Chem.

KRISCIUNAS, PATRICK; Father Judge HS; Philadelphia, PA; (Y); 51/403; Boy Scts; Church Yth Grp; Cmnty Wkr; Office Aide; Spanish Clb; Stage Crew; High Hon Roll; Hon Roll; PA ST Ogontz.

KRISE, TINA MARIE; Windber Area HS; Windber, PA; (Y); 72/130; Church Yth Grp; Cmnty Wkr; Hosp Aide; JA; Office Aide; Spanish Clb; Speech Tm; Teachers Aide; Nwsp Rptr; Nwsp Stf; Stu Of Mnth 85; 3200 Mtr Rly Rcrd Brkr Of 86; Pres Phys Ftns Awd 85-86; Sci Ed.

KRISER, ROBYN; Punxsutawney Area HS; Delancey, PA; (Y); Church Yth Grp; French Clb; Rep Stu Cncl; Stat Bsktbl; Var Cheerleading; JV Vllybl; Hon Roll; Elem Ed.

KRISHNA, MOHAN; Emmaus HS; Macungie, PA; (Y); 5/446; German Clb; VP JA; Key Clb; Q&S; Chorus; Orch; School Musical; Yrbk Stf; Var Tennis; High Hon Roll; Wmns Clb-Grmn Awd 86; U Of VA; Arntcl Engrng.

KRISOVITCH, MARYANN; Western Wayne HS; Lake Ariel, PA; (Y); 3/147; School Musical; Yrbk Stf; Sec Jr Cls; Sec Sr Cls; Var Cheerleading; Var Trk; DAR Awd; Rep NHS; Jms Wlf Mem Schlrshp 86; Bette Reed Smsn Awd 86; Stu Of Yr 85-86; PA ST; Spnsh.

KRISPIN, JONATHAN; Phila-Mont Christian Acad; Philadelphia, PA; (Y); Church Yth Grp; Drama Clb; Chorus; School Play; Rep Jr Cls; Var JV Bsbl; Var Stat Bsktbl; JV Bowling; Var Crs Cntry; Hon Roll.

KRISTA, NANCY; Duquesne HS; Duquesne, PA; (Y); 5/80; Rep Frsh Cls; Rep Soph Cls; Trs Jr Cls; Trs Sr Cls; Pres Stu Cncl; Twrlr; CC Awd; DAR Awd; Hon Roll; NHS; CA U; Accntnt.

KRISTEN, SCOT; Elizabeth Forward HS; Mckeesport, PA; (Y); Boy Scts; Chess Clb; Spanish Clb; Band; Concert Band; Jazz Band; Mrchg Band; Stage Crew; Bsbl; Bsktbl; Robt Morris; Bus Admin.

KRISTIN, BURGARD; Churchill HS; E Pittsburgh, PA; (Y); 1/200; Ski Clb; Pres Jr Cls; Pres Sr Cls; Trs Stu Cncl; L Capt Crs Cntry; L Swmmng; L Trk; High Hon Roll; Kiwanis Awd; Rotary Awd; Carnegie Mellon; Bio.

KRISTOFER, COLLEEN; St Basil Acad; Philadelphia, PA; (S); 13/94; Church Yth Grp; Cmnty Wkr; Drama Clb; French Clb; Service Clb; Thesps; Yrbk Phtg; Yrbk Stf; Lit Mag; NEDT Awd; Prncpls List 83-85.

KRISUK, RHONDA; Wilmington HS; New Wilmingtn, PA; (Y); 19/101; Drama Clb; Office Aide; Spanish Clb; Boy Scts; Mrchg Band; Pep Band; Stage Crew; Stu Cncl; High Hon Roll; Hon Roll.

KRITIKOS, KAREN; Waynesboro Area SR HS; Waynesboro, PA; (Y); Art Clb; Chorus; School Musical; Yrbk Stf; Fld Hcky; Mat Maids; Pratt Inst; Archit.

KRIVANEK, MICHELE; Vincentian HS; Allison Park, PA; (Y); GAA; Service Clb; Yrbk Phtg; Trs Sr Cls; Var L Bsktbl; Var Fld Hcky; Var L Sftbl; Var L Tennis; Im Vllybl; All Star Smmn Sftbl 83-86; MVP Bsktbl 86; Bus.

KRIVONICK, DAVID; Marion Center Area HS; Marion Center, PA; (Y); 2/143; Intnl Clb; Service Clb; Varsity Clb; Band; Concert Band; Jazz Band; Mrchg Band; Pep Band; Off Stu Cncl; Var Capt Bsktbl; USAF ROTC 86; Mary Raybuck Schlrhsp 86; Penn ST; Engrng.

KRIZENOSKAS, ANN; Bishop Hoban HS; Plains, PA; (Y); 2/187; FBLA; Math Clb; Chorus; School Musical; Yrbk Ed-Chief; Boy Scts; High Hon Roll; NHS; NEDT Awd; Sal; Outstndng Achvt Sci, Soc Studs, Engl 86; Mt Holyoke Coll.

KRIZMANICH, MARK; Seton La Salle HS; Pittsburgh, PA; (Y); 40/260; Cmnty Wkr; Hosp Aide; Teachers Aide; Bsbl; Bsktbl; Mgr(s); Score Keeper; High Hon Roll; Hon Roll.

KRIZNIK, DAVID; Burgettstown JR SR HS; Burgettstown, PA; (Y); Spanish Clb; Varsity Clb; Var Bsbl; Var Ftbl; Var Sftbl; Var Wt Lftg; Hon Roll; Prfct Atten Awd; Pttsbrgh Inst Aerontcs; Mntnc.

KRNACIK, RON; Valley HS; New Kensington, PA; (Y); 4/202; Leo Clb; Varsity Clb; VP Soph Cls; Rep Stu Cncl; Capt Bsbl; Capt Ftbl; High Hon Roll; NHS; Pres Schlr; Joseph Veltri Schlr/Atlete Schlrshp 86; Davidson; Chem.

KROCK, MICHELLE; Brandywine Heights HS; Alburtis, PA; (Y); Hosp Aide; Spanish Clb; Concert Band; Mrchg Band; Var Trk; Reading Hosp Schl; Rn.

KROH, KRISTA; Bradford Area SR HS; Bradford, PA; (Y); AFS; Service Clb; Ski Clb; Band; Concert Band; Jazz Band; Mrchg Band; Pep Band; Stu Cncl; Hon Roll; Edinboro U; Elem Educ.

KROH, MARK; The Hill Schl; Aaronsburg, PA; (Y); Art Clb; Model UN; Ski Clb; Acpl Chr; Chorus; Church Choir; Diving; Ftbl; Socr; Wt Lftg; Interpreter.

KROH, TAMMY; Cambria Heights HS; Hastings, PA; (Y); 26/195; Yrbk Stf; Mgr(s); Hon Roll; Prfct Atten Awd; Penn ST; Hlth.

KROKOS, JOHN; G A R Memorial HS; Wilkes Barre, PA; (Y); Church Yth Grp; Letterman Clb; Band; Chorus; Church Choir; Concert Band; Drm Mjr(t); Jazz Band; Mrchg Band; Vllybl; Music Educ.

KROKOSKI, SUSAN; G A R Memorial HS; Wilkes Barre, PA; (Y); 65/176; Church Yth Grp; Ski Clb; Teachers Aide; Chorus; Flag Corp; Stage Crew; Nwsp Stf; Stu Cncl; Twrlr; Hon Roll; Ltr Silk Sqd.

KROL, CHRISTINE; Upper Moreland HS; Hatboro, PA; (Y); 34/260; Hosp Aide; Intnl Clb; Key Clb; Drill Tm; Nwsp Rptr; Sec Yrbk Stf; Rep Jr Cls; Rep Stu Cncl; JV Sftbl; JV Trk; PA College; Bio.

KROLICK, CARLA; Purchase Line HS; Dixonville, PA; (Y); 12/123; Church Yth Grp; FBLA; Pep Clb; Spanish Clb; SADD; Varsity Clb; Capt Var Bsktbl; Sftbl; Vllybl; Hon Roll; All Star Conf Bsktbl 86; All Tourny Tm Bsktbl 86; All Gazetteland Tm IN Co Bsktbl, Vllybl 85-86; Indiana U PA; Sec Sci.

KROMASH, AARON M; Pottsgrove HS; Pottstown, PA; (Y); 2/200; German Clb; Hosp Aide; Library Aide; Math Tm; Science Clb; Chorus; School Musical; School Play; Stage Crew; Lit Mag; Outstndng Math Tm Perfrmnc 84-85; Awd & Let In Music 84-85.

KROMIS, JOHN; Hazleton HS; Drums, PA; (Y); Cmnty Wkr; Drama Clb; Pep Clb; Stu Cncl; Var Trk; Susquehanna U; Cmmnctns.

KRONE, AMY; Dover Area HS; Dover, PA; (Y); Church Yth Grp; Spanish Clb; Varsity Clb; Church Choir; Var Swmmng; High Hon Roll; NHS; Shipley Distngshd Ath Awd 85; All Amer 85; All ST Swmmng 85.

KRONE, SUANN; Northeastern HS; Mt Wolf, PA; (Y); 8/156; Service Clb; Bsktbl; Tennis; High Hon Roll; NHS; Ski Clb; Hon Roll; Corp Lawyer.

KRONER, CHARLES; Lewisburg Area HS; Lewisburg, PA; (Y); Chess Clb; Pres Trs Exploring; Sec Chorus; School Musical; JV Ftbl; JV Trk; Hon Roll; Linda Dodd Awd; Bucknell U; Pre Med.

KRONSBERG, CLAUDETTE; Shippensburg Area SR HS; Shippensburg, PA; (Y); Church Yth Grp; Pres Girl Scts; VP Leo Clb; SADD; School Musical; School Play; Nwsp Stf; Lit Mag; Hon Roll; Spanish NHS; Civic Clubs Stu Mnth 86; Shippensburg U; Psych.

KROPIEWNICKI, JOSEPH; John S Fine HS; Nariticoke, PA; (Y); 4/285; Church Yth Grp; Ski Clb; Im JV DECA; Capt L Golf; Var L Vllybl; High Hon Roll; NHS; Merit Awd 85-86; Natl Hnr Scty 85-86; MVP Golf Awds 84-86; Pre Med.

KROPIEWNICKI, JOSEPH; John S Fine SR HS; Nanticoke, PA; (S); 7/250; Ski Clb; JV Bsktbl; VP Golf; VP Vllybl; High Hon Roll; NHS; Ntl Merit Ltr; MVP Golf 85; Pre-Med.

KROPP, RICHARD; Vincentian HS; Wexford, PA; (Y); Chess Clb; Debate Tm; Political Wkr; Speech Tm; Off Frsh Cls; Off Soph Cls; Im Bsktbl; U IL; Bus.

KROUSE, BENITA; Greencastle Antrim HS; Greencastle, PA; (Y); Church Yth Grp; Library Aide; Chorus; Variety Show; Yrbk Stf; Sftbl; Hon Roll; 1st Pl Sci Fair 82-83; Hnrb Mntn At Sci Fair 83-84; Scrtry.

KROUSE, JENNIFER; Red Lion Area SR HS; Airville, PA; (Y); 27/372; Church Yth Grp; Girl Scts; SADD; High Hon Roll; Hon Roll; Acctng.

KROUSE, PAIGE; Chief Logan HS; Lewistown, PA; (Y); 8/180; Church Yth Grp; Cmnty Wkr; FBLA; Math Clb; Pres SADD; Drm Mjr(t); Mrchg Band; School Musical; Lit Mag; NHS; Friends Who Care Founder 86; Cnty Rep Commonwealth VA Against Substance Abuse 85-86; Wingate Scholar; Wingate Coll; Engl Ed.

KROUT, CANDY; Red Lion HS; Windsor, PA; (Y); 194/330; Hon Roll; Army; Police Ofcr.

KROUT, PAULA M; Dallastown Area HS; Dallastown, PA; (Y); 44/319; Ski Clb; Speech Tm; Band; Chorus; Nwsp Stf; Lit Mag; High Hon Roll; Mrchg Band; PA Gov Schl Arts 85; Poetry Publctn 85; Allentown U Cont Poetry Achvt Recgntn 86; PA ST U; Lib Arts.

KROUT, STEPHANIE; Bellefonte Area HS; Pleasant Gap, PA; (Y); Band; Color Guard; Mrchg Band; Capt Twrlr; Hon Roll; Dental Hygienist.

KROUT, WENDY; Cumberland Vally HS; Boiling Springs, PA; (Y); 76/575; German Clb; Orch; School Musical; Var Pom Pon; JV Tennis; Hon Roll; Natl Art Hnr Soc 85; Med.

KROUTCH, ALEXA; Our Lady Of Lourdes Regional HS; Mt Carmel, PA; (Y); 19/94; AFS; Drama Clb; Trs Soph Cls; Trs Jr Cls; Trs Stu Cncl; JV Var Cheerleading; NHS; Spanish NHS; Pep Clb; PAVAS; Outstndng Carrier Patriot Nws 85; Anml Hlth Tech.

KROW, MICHAEL; Lancaster Catholic HS; Lancaster, PA; (Y); Boy Scts; Chess Clb; Var Capt Bsbl; Eagle Scout 84; Millersville U; Math.

KROZNUSKIE, MILLIE; Staint Clair HS; New Philadelphia, PA; (S); 26/85; Computer Clb; DECA; VP Ski Clb; Varsity Clb; Powder Puff Ftbl; Var L Sftbl; Distngshd Hnr Rl NSAVTS 85-86; Outstndng Stu NSAVTS 86; PA ST U; Bio.

KRPATA, JENNIFER; Pocono Mountain HS; Stroudsburg, PA; (Y); Pres Church Yth Grp; 4-H; Chrmn Service Clb; SADD; Stu Cncl; Powder Puff Ftbl; Sftbl; Hon Roll; Office Aide; Q&S; HOBY Found; Intl Stu Ldrshp Inst; St Marys Coll; Nrsng.

KRUCELYAK, KAREN; Punxsutawney Area HS; Punxsutawney, PA; (Y); 36/238; Rep Art Clb; Church Yth Grp; FBLA; GAA; Variety Show; Hon Roll; Bus.

KRUG, ANGELA; Bishop Carroll HS; Nicktown, PA; (Y); Drama Clb; NFL; SADD; Band; Capt Color Guard; School Play; High Hon Roll; NEDT Awd; Voice Dem Awd; Cathlc Dghtrs Of Am Awd 86; IN U; Nrsg.

KRUG, DONNA; Northern Cambria HS; Cherry Tree, PA; (Y); 3/115; French Clb; Color Guard; Concert Band; Vllybl; High Hon Roll; NHS; U Of Pittsburgh Johnstown.

KRUG, JODI; Chartiers Valley HS; Pittsburgh, PA; (Y); Church Yth Grp; Dance Clb; Capt Drill Tm; School Musical; School Play; Pres Frsh Cls; Pres Soph Cls; Pres Jr Cls; Pres Sr Cls; NHS; Chrprctr.

KRUGER, KRISTIN; Pocono Central Catholic HS; Cresco, PA; (S); 7/22; Art Clb; Ski Clb; Soroptimist; Teachers Aide; Yrbk Ed-Chief; Capt Var Bsktbl; Var L Fld Hcky; Var Sftbl; High Hon Roll; Hon Roll; Hist,Spellng Awd 83-84; E Stroudsburg U; Ed.

KRUGER, KRSITIN; Pocano Central Catholic HS; Cresco, PA; (Y); Ski Clb; Teachers Aide; Yrbk Ed-Chief; Var Capt Bsktbl; Fld Hcky; Var Capt Sftbl; High Hon Roll; Hon Roll; VP NHS; E Stroudsburg U; Early Chldhd.

KRUKENBERG, HARRY J; Blackhawk HS; Beaver Falls, PA; (Y); Ski Clb; Trs Jr Cls; Trs Sr Cls; Im Bsktbl; JV Golf; Var Trk; High Hon Roll; Hon Roll; NHS; Im Bsbl; Purdue U; Arch.

KRUL, KEVIN; Penn Hills HS; Verona, PA; (Y); French Clb; Ski Clb; Varsity Clb; Bsbl; Var L Ftbl; Ice Hcky; Wt Lftg; Hon Roll; Bus.

KRULL, TAMARA; Penn Hills SR HS; Pittsburgh, PA; (S); 18/797; Drama Clb; Spanish Clb; Acpl Chr; Chorus; School Musical; School Play; High Hon Roll; Jr NHS; NHS; OH U; Engrng.

KRUMENACKER, GAVIN; Archbishop Wood For Boys; Doylestown, PA; (Y); 75/300; Im Bsktbl; JV Golf; Im Socr; Im Vllybl; Bus.

KRUMM, CHERYL; Wallenpaupock HS; Hawley, PA; (Y); Chorus; Nwsp Rptr; Nwsp Stf; Yrbk Stf; Sec Frsh Cls; Sec Stu Cncl; JV Var Mgr(s); JV Var Score Keeper; JV Sftbl; JV Trk; Acctg.

KRUMRINE, RICHARD H; Octorara Area HS; Parkesburg, PA; (Y); 21/171; Mrchg Band; Rep Stu Cncl; Var L Bsbl; Var L Crs Cntry; Var L Wrstlng; Hon Roll; NHS; Pres Schlr; Color Guard; Yrbk Rptr; U S Marn Corps Distngshd Athl Awd 86; Hghst Schlr Athl Awd 86; PA & Amer Indstrl Arts Stdnts Assn 86; Temple U; Arch.

KRUPA, TODD; Lake Lehman HS; Shavertown, PA; (Y); 11/150; Pres Aud/Vis; School Play; Stage Crew; Var L Bsbl; L Bsktbl; Var Capt Golf; High Hon Roll; Jr NHS; NHS; Rotary Awd; Cmmnctns.

KRUPSKAS, JENNIFER; Mid-Valley Secondary Ctr; Dickson City, PA; (Y); Girl Scts; Var Cheerleading; Var Sftbl; Hon Roll; SF All Amer Chrldr Awd 85; Phys Thrpy.

KRUPSKI, DONNA; North Pocono HS; Lake Ariel, PA; (Y); Varsity Clb; Rep Stu Cncl; Var Cheerleading; Hon Roll; VP Chch Yth Grp 82-83; Nrsg.

KRUSHINSKY, KARA A; Bishop O Hara HS; Moscow, PA; (Y); 24/113; Art Clb; Church Yth Grp; Letterman Clb; Pep Clb; Spanish Clb; School Play; Stage Crew; Swing Chorus; Pres Frsh Cls; Pres Soph Cls; Villanova; Engnrng.

KRUTCH, MICHELE; Conemaugh Valley HS; Park Hill, PA; (Y); Church Yth Grp; French Clb; Hosp Aide; Pep Clb; Scholastic Bowl; Concert Band; Mrchg Band; Nwsp Rptr; Nwsp Stf.

KRUTH, PAUL; Shaler Area HS; Pittsburgh, PA; (Y); 50/520; Computer Clb; Ski Clb; Jazz Band; Symp Band; Rep Jr Cls; Var L Crs Cntry; Var Trk; High Hon Roll; Hon Roll; Spanish NHS; Pre Med.

KRUTZ, MARY; Lakeland HS; Mayfield, PA; (S); 44/149; Dance Clb; FBLA; Co-Capt Drm Mjr(t); Ed Yrbk Stf; Hon Roll; Scty Of Dstngshd Amer HS Stu.

KRYSIAK, BRENDALYN; Cowanesque Valley HS; Westfield, PA; (S); 1/94; Pres Church Yth Grp; Pres French Clb; Girl Scts; Letterman Clb; Band; VP Jr Cls; Var Bsktbl; Var Tennis; NHS; Conservation Essay Awd 84; Acad All-Amer Awd 85; Le Cercle Moderne Prose Awd 84; Hotel & Rstrnt Mgmt.

KRYSIAK, ROBERT; Cathedral Preparatory Schl; Erie, PA; (Y); 60/240; Boy Scts; Chess Clb; Exploring; Im Bsktbl; Var L Golf; Im Vllybl; Hon Roll; Outstndng Carrier Yr Erie Times Publshng Co 84-86; Prep Glf Tm 2nd; Won Tam O Shntr HS Invtnl 85; Pre Med.

KRZYWICKI, JOSEPH; Old Forge HS; Old Forge, PA; (S); Ski Clb; Spanish Clb; JV Bsbl; Var Bsktbl; Var Crs Cntry; Hon Roll; NHS; PA ST; Pre Law.

KRZYWICKI, PAULA; James M Coughlin HS; Plains, PA; (Y); 23/384; Band; Chorus; Concert Band; Jazz Band; Mrchg Band; Orch; Var Sftbl; Var Trk; High Hon Roll; Hon Roll; PA ST U; Vet Med.

KRZYZANOWSKI, LISA M; South Side Catholic HS; Pittsburgh, PA; (S); Church Yth Grp; Service Clb; Teachers Aide; Rep Frsh Cls; Sec Stu Cncl; High Hon Roll; Hon Roll; VFW Awd; Voice Dem Awd; Frnch II Awd; Spch Awd; U Of Pttsbrgh; Psychlgy.

KSIAZKIEWICZ, KEN; Penn Cambria SR HS; Ashville, PA; (Y); Art Clb; Ftbl; NEDT Awd.

KSIENSKY, JACQUELINE; William Allen HS; Allentown, PA; (Y); German Clb; Leo Clb; Hon Roll; Jr NHS; NHS; Pres Acadmc Ftns Awd 86; Kutztown U; Psych.

KUBACKI, DEBRA; St Huberts For Girls; Philadelphia, PA; (Y); Boys Clb Am; Cmnty Wkr; Cmmnctns.

KUBALA, JEFF; Marion Center HS; Creekside, PA; (S); 5/170; Boy Scts; Intnl Clb; Science Clb; Varsity Clb; Band; Pep Band; Rep Stu Cncl; Capt Ftbl; Capt Wrstlng; NHS; Pitt; Engrng.

KUBASKO, JANINE; Pittston Area SR HS; Avoca, PA; (Y); Dance Clb; Drama Clb; Girl Scts; Key Clb; Pep Clb; Ski Clb; Drill Tm; School Play; Yrbk Ed-Chief; Yrbk Stf; E Stroudsburg U; Rehabltn Svs.

KUBEL, JOHN; Notre Dame HS; Easton, PA; (Y); Yrbk Stf; JV Trk; Ntl Merit Ltr; Var Tennis; Law.

KUBIC, JOHN; Ringgold HS; Donora, PA; (Y); Bsktbl; Ftbl; Golf; Mgr(s).

KUBIC, TRICIA; Norwin SR HS; N Huntingdon, PA; (Y); Office Aide; Spanish Clb; Band; Chorus; Concert Band; Drill Tm; Mrchg Band; JV Twrlr; Hon Roll; Jr NHS; X-Ray Tech.

KUBICKI, MICHELE; Greater Latrobe HS; Latrobe, PA; (Y); Church Yth Grp; Letterman Clb; Var JV Bsktbl; Var L Sftbl; Var L Vllybl; High Hon Roll; Hon Roll; Prfct Atten Awd; Bus.

KUBILUS, LORI; North Pocono HS; Lake Ariel, PA; (S); 10/250; Ski Clb; Yrbk Stf; Var L Trk; Var L Vllybl; High Hon Roll; NHS; Phila Coll Phrmcy; Phys Ther.

KUBINA, KIMBERLY; Bensalem HS; Warminster, PA; (Y); Art Clb; Chorus; Stage Crew; Yrbk Stf; Tennis; Hon Roll; Bus Mgmt.

KUBIT, RONALD; Seton-La Salle HS; Pittsburgh, PA; (Y); 22/257; High Hon Roll; Hon Roll; U Of Pittsburgh; Elec Engnrng.

KUCHARSKI, KENNETH; Pennsbury HS; Yardley, PA; (Y); Band; Concert Band; Variety Show; Rep Frsh Cls; Rep Stu Cncl; Im Bsktbl; Im Ftbl; Var Capt Socr; Im Sftbl; Im Tennis.

KUCIK, JOSEPH A; Southmoreland HS; Scottdale, PA; (Y); 1/235; Drama Clb; Math Clb; Ski Clb; Nwsp Rptr; Yrbk Stf; Gym; Swmmng; Pres NHS; Val; Boys Clb Am; Stu Of Mnth 85; Hugh O Brian Ldrshp Awd 84; PA ST U; Elec Engrng.

KUCK, LAURA; Richland HS; Gibsonia, PA; (Y); 4/183; Pres Church Yth Grp; Exploring; NFL; Trs Band; Concert Band; Mrchg Band; Nwsp Ed-Chief; Pep Band; High Hon Roll; NHS; PMEA Dist Hnrs Band 85-86; Natl Forn Lg Degree Hnr 84-85; Allegheny Vly Hnrs Band 84-86; Chem Engrng.

KUCKLA, KELLY; Pittston Area SR HS; Dupont, PA; (Y); French Clb; Key Clb; Ski Clb; Cheerleading; Hon Roll; NHS; Marn Bio.

KUCZLER, SUSAN; East Allegheny HS; N Versailles, PA; (Y); 19/200; Church Yth Grp; Drill Tm; Hon Roll; NHS; Penn ST; Sec Educ.

KUCZYNSKI, GREGORY; Peabody HS; Pittsburgh, PA; (S); 10/290; Chess Clb; Exploring; Yrbk Stf; Sec Frsh Cls; VP Soph Cls; Var L Vllybl; High Hon Roll; Pittsburgh U; Chem Sci.

KUDLIK, CHERYL; Monessen JR SR HS; Monessen, PA; (Y); 33/110; Camp Fr Inc; Church Yth Grp; FBLA; Hosp Aide; Intnl Clb; PAVAS; Teachers Aide; Band; Concert Band; Drm & Bgl; Braddford Schl; Acctng.

KUDRICK, RACHEL; Keystone HS; Knox, PA; (Y); 15/140; Lib Band; Chorus; Mrchg Band; School Musical; VP Trs French Hon Soc; Trs NHS; Ntl Merit Schol; World Affairs Cncl 84-85; Edinboro Smmr Acad 83; Amer Ldrshp Study Groups Eurpn Tour 84; IN U Of PA; Pre-Vet.

KUEHNER, KAREN; Northampton HS; Cherryville, PA; (S); 16/465; AFS; Chorus; Yrbk Stf; Stat Trk; High Hon Roll; Hon Roll; NHS; PA ST U; Crimnl Justice.

KUFFA, BRIAN; Boiling Springs HS; Carlisle, PA; (Y); 4/113; Ski Clb; JV Bsktbl; JV Ftbl; Var Socr; High Hon Roll; Hon Roll; NHS; Ntl Merit Ltr; Prfct Atten Awd.

KUFROVICH, JAMES; Mahonoy Area HS; Mahanoy City, PA; (Y); Band; Chorus; Concert Band; Jazz Band; Mrchg Band; Pep Band; Variety Show; Hon Roll; NHS; Music.

KUGHLER, JANEL; Annville-Cleona HS; Annville, PA; (S); #10 In Class; French Clb; Library Aide; Office Aide; Varsity Clb; Chorus; Madrigals; Var Cheerleading; Mat Maids; Score Keeper; PA ST U; Dentistry.

KUGLER, MICHELE; Saint Huberts HS; Philadelphia, PA; (Y); 51/367; Office Aide; Jazz Band; Mrchg Band; Orch; Hon Roll; Prfct Atten Awd; Cert Of Merit Bus Essntls Hghst Avg 86; Cert Acdmc Merit Amer Soc Hghst Avg 86; Compu Prg.

KUHLEN, LEE; Upper Darby HS; Lansdowne, PA; (Y); Office Aide; High Hon Roll; Hon Roll; Acctng.

KUHLMAN, KAREN; Marple Newtown HS; Media, PA; (Y); Stu Cncl; Var Bsktbl; Capt Sftbl; Hon Roll; Jr NHS.

KUHLTHAU, KIRSTEN; Linden Hall HS; Skillman, NJ; (Y); Drama Clb; Hosp Aide; Model UN; School Musical; Nwsp Ed-Chief; Nwsp Stf; VP Sr Cls; Var L Bsktbl; Var Co-Capt Tennis; Hon Roll; Adv Plcmnt Engl 86; Adv Plcmnt Amer Hstry 86; Mary Baldwin Coll; Cmmnctns.

KUHN, ADRIA; Upper Darby HS; Upper Darby, PA; (Y); Hosp Aide; Office Aide; Thesps; Band; Concert Band; Mrchg Band; Orch; School Musical; Stu Cncl; Nrsng.

KUHN, KARIN; Scranton Prep; Scranton, PA; (Y); 58/192; GAA; Letterman Clb; Pep Clb; PAVAS; Mrchg Band; School Play; Yrbk Stf; L Trk; High Hon Roll; U Of Scranton; Math.

KUHN, LANEY; Cheltenham HS; Elkins Pk, PA; (Y); FTA; SADD; Teachers Aide; Temple Yth Grp; Yrbk Stf; Lit Mag; NEDT Awd; Spnsh Hnrs 83-86; Bryn Mawr Bk Awd 85-86; Lib Arts.

KUHN, STEVE; Richland HS; Gibsonia, PA; (Y); L Ice Hcky; L Socr; L Trk; L Hon Roll.

KUHNI, LORI; Ambridge Area HS; Baden, PA; (Y); Pres Spanish Clb; Lib Band; Concert Band; Mrchg Band; Off Jr Cls; Stu Cncl; Co-Capt Crs Cntry; Trk; High Hon Roll; NHS; Hugh O Brian Awd Mst Outstndng Soph 85; Spirit Jr Miss Awd Co Jaycees, WPIAL Track Champ 1600 M 86; Educ.

KUHNS, DANIELLE N; Saucan Valley SR HS; Hellertown, PA; (Y); Am Leg Aux Girls St; French Clb; Trs Spanish Clb; Sec Sr Cls; Var Capt Fld Hcky; Var L Trk; High Hon Roll; Jr NHS; Sec NHS; Pres Schlr; Amer Assn Of Univ Wmn Schlrshp 86; Montfore E Illick Awd 86; Pres Acad Ftnss Awd 86; Penn ST U; Bus Adm.

KUHNS, KARLA L; Liberty HS; Bethlehem, PA; (Y); 49/407; Band; Concert Band; Mrchg Band; High Hon Roll; Hon Roll; Hmcmng Cmmtt 85; Penn ST U; Spch Pthlgst.

KUHNS, TONIA; Williamsport HS; Williamsport, PA; (Y); Sftbl; Hon Roll; Gym Tchr.

KUHTA, DEBRA; Ford City JR SR HS; Ford City, PA; (Y); Office Aide; Pep Clb; Hon Roll; Sec.

KUJAWA, KIMBERLY; Frazier HS; Dawson, PA; (Y); Drama Clb; Spanish Clb; Yrbk Stf; Soph Cls; Cheerleading; Capt Chrldng 84-85; Homcmng 84-85 & 85-86; Dental Asst.

KUJORSKY, STEPHEN; Lebonon Catholic HS; Lebanon, PA; (Y); Boy Scts; JA; Key Clb; Ftbl; Golf; Sftbl; Wt Lftg; Hon Roll; Fin.

KUKLA, CHERIE; Curwensville Area HS; Curwensville, PA; (Y); Girl Scts; Ski Clb; Band; Chorus; Concert Band; Mrchg Band; Pep Band; School Musical; Im Vllybl; Rcrtnl Thrpy.

KUKLINSKI, REBECCA; St Benedict Acad; Erie, PA; (Y); 20/63; Sec Frsh Cls; Pres Jr Cls; Rep Stu Cncl; High Hon Roll; NHS; Schrlshp Adv Plcmnt Pgm 86; PA ST U Behrend; PA ST U; Psychlgst.

KUKLO, THERESA; North Pocono HS; Moscow, PA; (Y); 7/250; Var Capt Cheerleading; Var Trk; High Hon Roll; NHS; 2nd Pl Dist II PIAA Trk Mt Relay 85; 1st Pl Dist II PIAA Trk Relay 86; N Picono Girls Trk Champs.

KULBA, SUZANNE; Bradford Central Christian HS; Bradford, PA; (Y); Sec Drama Clb; Pep Clb; SADD; Chorus; Rep Frsh Cls; Rep Jr Cls; Stat Bsktbl; JV Var Score Keeper; High Hon Roll; NHS; Rotary Clb Delegate-World Affairs Cncl 85-86; Lions Clb Stu Of Mnth 86; U Of Pittsburgh-Bradford; Bus.

KULCHINSKY, ALISA; Northamption Area SR HS; Walnutport, PA; (S); 32/475; Church Yth Grp; GAA; Yrbk Stf; Var Capt Fld Hcky; Var L Sftbl; High Hon Roll; Hon Roll; NHS; Rcvd Trexler Schlrshp From Cedar Crest Coll 86; Penn ST U; Comp Sci.

KULCZAK, CHERYL; Mt Pleasant Area HS; Mt Pleasant, PA; (Y); Church Yth Grp; Hosp Aide; Nwsp Stf; Yrbk Stf; High Hon Roll; NHS; Prfct Atten Awd; Bus Club Vp & Pres 85-87; Bus Stu Mnth 85; Toys For Tots 85; ICM Schl Bus; Sec.

KULICH, PAM; Saint Benedict Acad; Erie, PA; (Y); 2/63; Office Aide; Ed Q&S; Yrbk Ed-Chief; Yrbk Stf; Stu Cncl; DAR Awd; High Hon Roll; NHS; NEDT Awd; Acad Schlrshp St Benedicts 83-84; 3rdpl Art Schlrshp Comptn 83-84; Acad Exc Soc Studies; PA ST U.

KULICK, LISA; Leechburg Area HS; Leechburg, PA; (Y); 15/82; Drama Clb; Speech Tm; Chorus; Nwsp Sprt Ed; Yrbk Stf; Stu Cncl; Cheerleading; Clarion U; Pltcl Sci.

KULICK, LORI; Mansfield JR SR HS; Mansfield, PA; (S); 3/99; Key Clb; Ski Clb; Band; Rep Stu Cncl; Var L Cheerleading; Var L Tennis; Trk; High Hon Roll; NHS; Ntl Merit SF; Pediatrcn.

KULISH, BETH; Hazleton HS; Hazleton, PA; (Y); Church Yth Grp; Drama Clb; FBLA; Pep Clb; Color Guard; Drill Tm; Flag Corp; Hon Roll; Penn ST U; Acctnt.

KULISH, JANICE; Canon Mc Millan SR HS; Canonsburg, PA; (Y); Latin Clb; Chorus; Hon Roll.

KULISH, KEN; Mt Carmel Area JR SR HS; Mt Carmel, PA; (Y); Pres Church Yth Grp; Band; Church Choir; Concert Band; Mrchg Band; Hon Roll; Prfct Atten Awd; Renatra Fusca Awd 85; Bloomsburg U; Accntng.

KULOUSEK, CHRISTY AIMEE; Baldwin HS; Pittsburgh, PA; (Y); 191/535; Cmnty Wkr; Hosp Aide; SADD; Bsktbl; Ftbl; JV Sftbl; Var Vllybl; Hon Roll; Teen Inst Drug And Alchl Abuse 84; Sprts Med.

KULP, RUTHANNA; Trinity HS; Mechanicsburg, PA; (Y); 3/141; Drama Clb; Hosp Aide; Math Tm; Pep Clb; Quiz Bowl; Stage Crew; Mgr(s); Score Keeper; High Hon Roll; NHS; Harrisburg Acad Summr Enrchmnt Pgm Scholar 85; BMN N Amer Yth Understndng Summr Exch Scholar 86.

KULP, WALTER P; Saint Josephs Prep HS; Philadelphia, PA; (Y); 40/239; Trs VP Church Yth Grp; Pep Clb; Speech Tm; Variety Show; Nwsp Rptr; Rep Jr Cls; Var L Ftbl; Var L Trk; Hon Roll; Var Debate Tm; Loyalty Schl Silver Medlst; Lawyer.

KULTSCHYCKYJ, IWANKA; St Basil Acad; Philadelphia, PA; (Y); VP Drama Clb; French Clb; German Clb; Chorus; School Play; Variety Show; Im Bsktbl; Im Bowling; Im Vllybl; Hon Roll; Sci Fair For St Bsl Acad 3rd Pl 83-84; Duquesne U; Law.

KULYK, JAY; Northwestern SR HS; Albion, PA; (Y); 4/164; Spanish Clb; Var L Bsktbl; JV L Crs Cntry; Vllybl; High Hon Roll; Hon Roll; NHS.

KUMP, LAURA; Southern Fulton HS; Needmore, PA; (Y); FBLA; FFA; Pres Frsh Cls; Sec Soph Cls; VP Jr Cls; Rep Stu Cncl; Var L Sftbl; Hon Roll; Bus.

KUNA, DEBBIE; Pittston Area SR HS; Dupont, PA; (Y); Church Yth Grp; Drama Clb; French Clb; FNA; Chorus; Drill Tm; Swing Chorus; High Hon Roll; Hon Roll; Jr NHS; Bwlg Coca Cola Awd 80-83; Grls Scts USA Relgs Wd; Penn ST U; Technen.

KUNA, MELISSA; Old Forge HS; Old Forge, PA; (Y); Drama Clb; Ski Clb; School Musical; School Play.

KUNCHERIAH, SHYLA; George Washington HS; Philadelphia, PA; (Y); Church Yth Grp; Intnl Clb; Math Clb; Quiz Bowl; Science Clb; Hon Roll; Mu Alp Tht; Quiz Comp India Prz Wnr 83-84; Prz Wnr Makg Hnd Models Indian 83-84; Temple U; Chem.

KUNDICK, SUSAN; Quigley HS; Industry, PA; (S); 14/110; Hosp Aide; Chorus; Cheerleading; Powder Puff Ftbl; Trk; High Hon Roll; Hon Roll; NHS; Dstrct Chrs 86; Miami U Of OH; Pol Sci.

KUNEC, MICHELLE; Bishop Hoban HS; Plains, PA; (Y); 47/230; FBLA; Math Clb; Ski Clb; Rep Stu Cncl; JV Cheerleading; Trk; Hon Roll; Mu Alp Tht; NHS; NEDT Awd; Pre-Med.

KUNES, BRIAN; St Marys Area HS; Weedville, PA; (Y); 19/295; Church Yth Grp; Cmnty Wkr; Computer Clb; Swmmng; High Hon Roll; NHS; Pres Schlr; Tllh Hnly Schlrshp, Mrm Brcrft Blsdl Schlrhshp, Kiwanis Schlsrshp 86; U Pittsburgh; Elec Engrng.

KUNES, LARRY; Lock Haven HS; Blanchard, PA; (Y); 72/241; Key Clb; Band; Ftbl; S Dars Whitey Lawrence Awd Outstndng Ftbl Plyr 86; IN U; Hlth Sci.

KUNES, TISHA; St Marys Area HS; Weedville, PA; (Y); 6/290; Pres Sec Church Yth Grp; FHA; Library Aide; Yrbk Stf; Hon Roll; Lion Awd; NHS; Pres Acad Ftnss Awd 86; IN U PA; Comp Progm.

KUNKEL, MONICA; Brandywine Heights HS; Mertztown, PA; (Y); Color Guard; Mrchg Band; Off Stu Cncl; L Fld Hcky; Mgr(s); JV Sftbl; High Hon Roll; Hon Roll; Band; Temple Yth Grp; Photography Inst; Photo.

KUNKEL, VIRGINIA A; Penn Hills SR HS; Pittsburgh, PA; (Y); 123/762; Church Yth Grp; JA; Office Aide; Teachers Aide; Varsity Clb; Var Vllybl; High Hon Roll; Hon Roll; Oustndng Stu Awd Data Proc 85-86; Vol Specl Olympics 84-86; Clarion U; Bus Admin.

KUNKLE, ERIC; Waynesboro Area HS; Mont Alto, PA; (Y); 50/370; Am Leg Boys St; Church Yth Grp; Letterman Clb; Varsity Clb; Var Bsbl; Var Bsktbl; Var Socr; Cit Awd; High Hon Roll; Bus.

KUNKLE, PAIGE; Emmaus HS; Macungie, PA; (Y); Nwsp Rptr; Ed Nwsp Stf; High Hon Roll; Hon Roll; Jr NHS; NHS; Prfct Atten Awd; Ntl Lang Arts Olympiad Awd 84; Acctng.

KUNOVIC, MONICA; Corry Area HS; Corry, PA; (S); 15/260; Band; Concert Band; Mrchg Band; Pep Band; Var Diving; Var Swmmng; Hon Roll; Ntl Merit SF; Miami; Math.

KUNS, BETH; Nazareth Acad; Philadelphia, PA; (Y); 16/118; Church Yth Grp; Library Aide; Service Clb; Bowling; High Hon Roll; Prfct Atten Awd; Philadelphia Coll; Fshn Merch.

KUNSELMAN, CHRISTOPHER; Beaver Area JR SR HS; Beaver, PA; (Y); Church Yth Grp; VP JCL; Latin Clb; Ski Clb; Mgr Bsktbl; Ftbl; Powder Puff Ftbl; Score Keeper; Trk; Wt Lftg; U Pittsburgh; Comp Sci.

KUNSELMAN, GREGRORY; Punxsutawney Area HS; Punxsu, PA; (Y); 109/238; Trk; IUP; Crmnlgy.

KUNSELMAN, KERRY; Kiska Area HS; Vandergrift, PA; (Y); Dance Clb; German Clb; GAA; Pep Clb; Band; Color Guard; Var Sftbl; Prfct Atten Awd; Church Yth Grp; Letterman Clb; Encore Rgnl Dance Co 1st Pl 86; Encore Natl Dance Co Hnrbl Mntn-5th 86; S Lynns Schl Dance Tchr 86.

KUNTZ, BRIAN; Northwestern HS; Cranesville, PA; (Y); Chess Clb; Computer Clb; Ski Clb; Var Ftbl; Var Trk; Hon Roll.

KUNTZ, DALE; Northwestern HS; Cranesville, PA; (Y); 37/160; Chess Clb; Computer Clb; Var Crs Cntry; Var Trk; Hon Roll; Navy; Nuclear Proplsn.

KUNTZ, SUSAN ANN; Waynesburg Central HS; Waynesburg, PA; (Y); Ski Clb; Spanish Clb; High Hon Roll; Hon Roll; Karate Awds & Trophies 83-86; Top 3 PA Karate ST Champ 84-85; Cmmnctns.

KUNZ, CLAIRE; Sacred Heart HS; Pittsburgh, PA; (Y); Hosp Aide; Pep Clb; Spanish Clb; Pres Frsh Cls; Pres Soph Cls; Pres Jr Cls; Pres Stu Cncl; JV Var Crs Cntry; High Hon Roll; Hon Roll; Pre-Med.

KUNZ, JOANNE; Villa Joseph Marie HS; Philadelphia, PA; (S); 23/56; Library Aide; Varsity Clb; Off Soph Cls; Off Jr Cls; Off Sr Cls; Cheerleading; Tennis; Prfct Atten Awd; Hghst Avg Span II, Am Cults 84-85; La Salle U; Acctg.

KUNZ, MAUREEN; North Hills SR HS; Pittsburgh, PA; (Y); 112/496; Church Yth Grp; Cmnty Wkr; Q&S; Band; Church Choir; Mrchg Band; Symp Band; Nwsp Rptr; Hon Roll; Ntl Hon Roll 85-86; Pitt; Spec Educ.

KUPAS, DAVID; Kiski Area HS; New Kensington, PA; (Y); Concert Band; Jazz Band; Mrchg Band; Pep Band; Symp Band; High Hon Roll; Hon Roll; Prfct Atten Awd; Anthroplogy.

KUPEC, AMY; Kiski Area HS; Lower Burrell, PA; (Y); Pep Clb; Varsity Clb; Band; School Musical; Symp Band; Trs Jr Cls; Rep Stu Cncl; Var Cheerleading; Var Trk; Hon Roll.

KUPFER, DEBORAH A; Taylor Allderdice HS; Pittsburgh, PA; (S); French Clb; Ski Clb; Temple Yth Grp; Nwsp Sprt Ed; Rep Frsh Cls; Trs Soph Cls; Trs Stu Cncl; JV Socr; Capt L Tennis; High Hon Roll; Generations Together 85-86.

KUPFER, JENNIFER E; Meadville Area SR HS; Meadville, PA; (Y); Cmnty Wkr; French Clb; Key Clb; Ski Clb; Spanish Clb; SADD; Rep Stu Cncl; Var Socr; Var Trk; High Hon Roll; Lib Arts.

KUPSKY, JILL; Benton Area JR SR HS; Benton, PA; (Y); VP Art Clb; Pres 4-H; FTA; Chorus; School Musical; School Play; Nwsp Ed-Chief; Hon Roll; NHS; Voice Dem Awd; Pres Acadmc Ftnss Awd 86; Benton Womns Clb Schlrshp 86; Warren L Ketner Schlrshp 86; Bloomsburg U; Elem Educ.

KURASH, JODY; Penn Cambria HS; Cresson, PA; (Y); 15/178; Drama Clb; Intnl Clb; Library Aide; Ski Clb; Spanish Clb; Speech Tm; School Play; PA Cambria SR Spnsh Awd 86; Advrtsng.

KURILKO, MIKE; Mapletown JR SR HS; Dilliner, PA; (Y); 9/74; 4-H; Ski Clb; Spanish Clb; Band; Concert Band; Jazz Band; Mrchg Band; Pres Frsh Cls; Sec Soph Cls; VP Sr Cls; PA ST; Bio.

KURINKO, SHERRI LYNN; Saegertown HS; Saegertown, PA; (Y); 12/124; 4-H; Hosp Aide; Band; Church Choir; VP Stu Cncl; Var L Cheerleading; Stat Vllybl; Hon Roll; Jr NHS; Masonic Awd; Physcl Thrpy.

KURNECK, ROBERT; Hampton HS; Allison Pk, PA; (Y); Var Capt Ftbl; JV Trk; JV Wrstlng; High Hon Roll; Ftbll Schlrshp 86; Clss AAA Gr Allegheny Conf All Star 2nd Linebckr 86; MVP Awd 86; Clarion U; Arts.

KURNIAWAN, HANDANI; S Fayette Twp JR SR HS; Mc Donald, PA; (S); 10/85; Key Clb; Math Tm; High Hon Roll; Hon Roll; NHS; Prfct Atten Awd; Mech Engrng.

KURNIK, AMY; Charleroi Area HS; N Charleroi, PA; (Y); Church Yth Grp; French Clb; FNA; Pep Clb; SADD; Chorus; School Play; Psych.

KURPIEL, KATHY; Southmoreland HS; Mt Pleasant, PA; (Y); 23/270; Hosp Aide; Letterman Clb; Ski Clb; Color Guard; Nwsp Stf; Yrbk Stf; JV Var Bsktbl; JV Sftbl; Prfct Atten Awd; Spanish NHS; Psychology.

KURTA, JAMES A; Elizabeth Forward HS; Mc Keesport, PA; (Y); 54/324; SADD; School Musical; Hon Roll; Church Yth Grp; French Clb; Acpl Chr; Yrbk Stf; Odd Fllws-Rebekahs Awd UN Pilgrmg Yth Recpnt 86; 3rd Pl Tm Ameri-Euro Card-Natl Acadmc Games 86; Air Frc Acad; Intl Rltns.

KURTYKA, KIRK; New Brighton HS; New Brighton, PA; (Y); #14 In Class; Rotary Awd; Air Force; Air Science.

KURTZ, ALICIA; Parkland HS; Allentown, PA; (Y); 23/415; Key Clb; Stu Cncl; High Hon Roll; Hon Roll; NHS; Dance Clb; Hosp Aide; Crs Cntry; U Of Pittsburgh; Physcl Thrpy.

KURTZ, ANDREW N; Rochester JR-SR HS; Rochester, PA; (Y); Am Leg Boys St; Camera Clb; DECA; Letterman Clb; Pep Clb; Red Cross Aide; Ski Clb; SADD; VICA; Stage Crew; 5th Pl Commrcl Photo ST Comptn 86; US Marines; Aveonics.

KURTZ, KAREN; West York SR HS; Myerstown, PA; (Y); 16/194; Church Yth Grp; Exploring; Sec French Clb; Church Choir; Mgr Bsktbl; Bowling; Var Mgr(s); Hon Roll; NHS; Bus Admin.

KURTZ, MELISSA; St Pius X HS; East Greenville, PA; (S); 23/164; Art Clb; Girl Scts; Spanish Clb; Drill Tm; Hon Roll; Sci.

KURTZ, MICHELLE; Carbondale Area JR SR HS; Forest City, PA; (Y); Art Clb; FBLA; Ski Clb; Chorus; Bsktbl; Trk; High Hon Roll; Hon Roll; Bus.

KURTZ, PAULA; Williamsburg HS; Williamsburg, PA; (Y); DECA; School Play; Im Bsbl; Im Bsktbl; Im Gym; Im Sftbl; Im Trk; Im Vllybl; Prfct Atten Awd; Merit Awd 85-86 & 84-86; Accntng.

KURTZ, RACHEL; Schuylkill Haven HS; Schuylkill Haven, PA; (S); 11/84; SADD; Band; Chorus; Concert Band; Mrchg Band; Pep Band; Nwsp Rptr; Nwsp Stf; Yrbk Rptr; Yrbk Stf; County Band 84-85.

KURTZ, STACY; Plymouth Whitemarsh SR HS; Lafayette Hill, PA; (S); Cmnty Wkr; Office Aide; Service Clb; Pres Temple Yth Grp; Ed Nwsp Stf; Yrbk Stf; Rep Soph Cls; Tennis; High Hon Roll; NHS; Ithaca Coll; Phys Ther.

KURTZ, VIRGINIA; Shenandoah Valley HS; Shenandoah, PA; (Y); Chorus; Hst Soph Cls; Stat Bsbl; Bowling; JV Capt Cheerleading; Vllybl; Hon Roll; Cmnty Wkr; Computer Clb; Pep Clb; Notre Dame; Jrnlsm.

KURUC, DAVID; Roman Cathloic HS; Philadelphia, PA; (S); 9/150; Church Yth Grp; Cmnty Wkr; Political Wkr; JV Var Bsbl; Var Bowling; JV Var Ftbl; High Hon Roll; Hon Roll; NHS.

KURZWEIL, DENA; West Scranton HS; Scranton, PA; (Y); 3/280; Aud/Vis; NFL; Speech Tm; Thesps; Orch; School Play; Lit Mag; Pom Pon; High Hon Roll; Jr NHS; Biochem.

KUSER, ALISON; Boyertown Area SR HS; Bechtelsville, PA; (Y); 18/442; Yrbk Bus Mgr; Yrbk Stf; Capt Cheerleading; Mgr(s); Cit Awd; High Hon Roll; NHS; Villanova U; Comm Arts.

KUSHMANICK, ANTOINETTE; Northern-Lebanon JR SR HS; Lebanon, PA; (Y); 54/198; Aud/Vis; German Clb; Band; Chorus; Concert Band; Mrchg Band; School Musical; JV Sftbl; JV Trk; Hon Roll; MI ST; Archlgy.

KUSHMEDER, MICHELE; Hazleton HS; Hazleton, PA; (Y); Church Yth Grp; Pep Clb; Band; Concert Band; Trs Mrchg Band; Nwsp Stf; Hon Roll; Educ.

KUSHNERICK, ED; Dunmore HS; Dunmore, PA; (Y); 32/156; Boy Scts; Computer Clb; French Clb; JA; Hon Roll; Scranton U; Bio.

KUSSMAUL, KIMBERLY; Franklin Regional HS; Murrysville, PA; (Y); AFS; Trs Thesps; Band; Church Choir; Concert Band; Jazz Band; Mrchg Band; School Play; Stage Crew; High Hon Roll; Cngrss-Bundstg Exchng Stu Schlrshp 86-87; PA Msc Ed Assoc Rgnl Bnd 86; IN U Of PA Hnrs Bnd 85; Intl Affrs.

KUTCH, LARA; Lakeland JR SR HS; Jermyn, PA; (Y); Sec Church Yth Grp; Dance Clb; FHA.

KUTSICK, GREGORY; Northern Cambria HS; Barnesboro, PA; (Y); 2/126; Stu Cncl; Ftbl; Wt Lftg; High Hon Roll; NHS; IN U Of PA; Medcl Dr.

KUTTLER, MARCI; Mt St Joseph Acad; Doylestown, PA; (Y); Camera Clb; Pres Church Yth Grp; Office Aide; Service Clb; Spanish Clb; Nwsp Phtg; Var Capt Bsktbl; Capt Vllybl; NHS; Spanish NHS; ROTC Scholar 86; Lehigh U; Envrnmntl Sci.

KUTZ, RENEE; Spring-Ford HS; Collegeville, PA; (Y); Church Yth Grp; Letterman Clb; Ski Clb; Spanish Clb; Var Tennis; Var L Trk; Hon Roll; Span Awd 84-85.

KUTZLER, JENNIFER; Liberty HS; Bethlehem, PA; (Y); 40/400; Sec Church Yth Grp; Hosp Aide; Concert Band; Jazz Band; Mrchg Band; Yrbk Stf; Var L Fld Hcky; High Hon Roll; NHS; Bethlehem Ed Assoc Schlrshp 86; West Chester U; Elem Ed.

KUZMIAK, JUDY; Lakeland JR/SR HS; Olyphant, PA; (S); 37/147; Church Yth Grp; FHA; Ski Clb; Drm Mjr(t); Rep Frsh Cls; Rep Soph Cls; Rep Jr Cls; Rep Sr Cls; Rep Stu Cncl; Stat Bsbl; Marywood Coll; Early Chldhd Ed.

KUZNICKI, NOEL; Lake-Lehman HS; Shavertown, PA; (S); Library Aide; School Play; JV Bsktbl; Var Cheerleading; Var Fld Hcky; Var Sftbl; Hon Roll; NHS; All Star Ldr 1st Tm Sftbl 85; Hon Mntn Fld Hcky 85; Dist Chmps 84 & 85; Penn ST; Math.

KUZUPAS, LISA; Shade HS; Cairnbrook, PA; (Y); Pres Band; Chorus; Color Guard; Concert Band; Mrchg Band; Yrbk Stf; Stu Cncl; Hon Roll; Pres NHS; Psychlgy.

KUZY, DAVID; Immaculate Conception HS; Washington, PA; (Y); 11/51; Nwsp Rptr; Yrbk Stf; High Hon Roll; Hon Roll; Ntl Merit SF; Archeology.

KWATNY, BROOKE; Cheltenham HS; Elkins Pk, PA; (Y); Dance Clb; Drama Clb; Pep Clb; SADD; JV Var Cheerleading; NEDT Awd; Gov Energy Awd 84; Cmmnctns.

KWIATHOWSKI, PATRICK; Central Catholic HS; Pittsburgh, PA; (Y); Boy Scts; Im Bsktbl; L Var Bowling; Im Ftbl; High Hon Roll; Hon Roll; NHS; WPIBL ST Dbls Hndcp Chmpshp 1st Pl Bwlng 86; Bus Mgt.

KWIATKOWSKI, ANN; West Scranton HS; Scranton, PA; (Y); 7/265; Church Yth Grp; Spanish Clb; JV Var Cheerleading; High Hon Roll; Jr NHS; NHS; U Scrntn; Mrktng.

KWITROVICH, MATTHEW; Mount Carmel JR SR HS; Mt Carmel, PA; (Y); Boys Clb Am; Church Yth Grp; Key Clb; Latin Clb; Stage Crew; L Ftbl; Var Trk; Wt Lftg; Hon Roll; Bio.

KYLE, SUSAN; Saucon Valley SR HS; Bethlehem, PA; (Y); Office Aide; Ski Clb; Yrbk Stf; JV L Cheerleading; L Trk; Hmcmg & Prom Qn 85-86; Westchester U; Erly Chldhd Ed.

KYLER, CAROLE; Rocky Grove HS; Cooperstown, PA; (S); 1/87; French Clb; Chorus; School Musical; Mgr Stat Crs Cntry; JV Vllybl; High Hon Roll; NHS; Prfct Atten Awd; Erie Cnty Chptr PA Soc Prfssnl Engrs Mrt Cert 84-85; PA ST U; Elec Engrng.

KYPER, ALEISA; Mechanicsburg SR HS; Grantham, PA; (Y); 4/318; Church Yth Grp; Chorus; Church Choir; Mrchg Band; Yrbk Stf; High Hon Roll; NHS; Ntl Merit Ltr; Ldr Nrsng Hm Essay Cont 1st Pl 86; Messiah Collg; Nrsng.

KYPER, MELODY E; Huntingdon Area HS; Huntingdon, PA; (Y); 4/223; Church Yth Grp; Hosp Aide; Key Clb; Band; Concert Band; Mrchg Band; Yrbk Ed-Chief; Hon Roll; NHS; PMEA Dist IV Band Fstv 86.

KYPER, SHEILA; Mechanicsburg Area HS; Grantham, PA; (Y); 1/315; Church Yth Grp; Speech Tm; Chorus; Church Choir; Color Guard; Yrbk Stf; High Hon Roll; NHS; Ntl Merit SF; Elem Ed.

LA, HANNAH HAISUN; Swissvale HS; Grove City, PA; (Y); 9/225; Church Yth Grp; Computer Clb; Exploring; Latin Clb; Library Aide; Science Clb; Spanish Clb; SADD; Church Choir; Bowling; Shlrshp Frm Cameron/Coca Cola 86; Schlrshp Frm Pilor Clb Of Pittsburgh 86; Merit Awd In Spnsh 84; Grove Cty Coll; Comp Sci.

LA BARRE, LAURIE; Northeast Bradford JR SR HS; Rome, PA; (Y); 10/90; Pres Church Yth Grp; Trs FHA; Girl Scts; Hosp Aide; Varsity Clb; Band; Church Choir; Mrchg Band; Trs VP Stu Cncl; JV Var Cheerleading; Hugh O Brien Yth Fndtn Semnr Delg; Delg UN Intl Schl Confrnc; Natls For Cheerng Squad-Nashville; Bloomsburg & Flagler Coll; Law.

LA BARRE, VIRGINIA; Littlestown SR HS; Littlestown, PA; (Y); Pres 4-H; FFA; Teachers Aide; Band; Color Guard; Mrchg Band; Stat Bsktbl; JV Vllybl; 4-H Awd; Hon Roll; Cobleskill Clg; Anml Husb.

LA BELLA, TINAMARIE; St Maria Goretti HS; Philadelphia, PA; (Y); 65/495; Math Tm; Office Aide; Service Clb; Stage Crew; Im Cheerleading; Im Sftbl; 1st & 2nd Hnrs 82-86; Italian Awd 83-84; Mdl Intramural Sftbl; St Josephs U; Law.

LA BOLD, STEVEN; Upper Dublin HS; Ft Washington, PA; (Y); 40/337; Church Yth Grp; FBLA; Yrbk Ed-Chief; Bsktbl; NHS; Pres Schlr; U Of DE; Bus Admin.

LA CARTE, DAVID; Charleroi JR SR HS; Charleroi, PA; (Y); Ski Clb; Varsity Clb; Off Jr Cls; Rep Stu Cncl; L Bsktbl; Var L Ftbl; Var L Trk; High Hon Roll; Hon Roll; NHS.

LA CIVITA, ANNMARIE; St Maria Goretti HS; Philadelphia, PA; (Y); 232/390; Art Clb; Camera Clb; Latin Clb; PA ST; Inter Dsgn.

LA FAVE, MICHAEL; Pocono Central Catholic HS; Newfoundland, PA; (S); 1/22; Pres Church Yth Grp; Pep Clb; Ski Clb; Yrbk Stf; Rep Soph Cls; Rep Jr Cls; Pres Stu Cncl; L Bsbl; Capt Bsktbl; L Socr; Lehigh U; Engrng.

LA FOLLETTE, JEAN-PAUL; The Mercersburg Acad; Fairmont, WV; (Y); Dance Clb; Concert Band; Jazz Band; Capt Pep Band; Ed Nwsp Phtg; Mgr(s); Hon Roll; Prfct & Proctor Of Dorm Flr 86-87; Spnsh Lang Culture Stu-Costa Rica 85; Trap & Skeet Shtng Capt 86-87; Vet Med.

LA FORCE, RANDY; Newport HS; Newport, PA; (Y); Pres Band; Chorus; Drm & Bgl; Drm Mjr(t); Jazz Band; Mrchg Band; School Musical; School Play; Var Bsbl; Gym; Mdrn Msc Mstrs 86; Elctrncs.

LA FORTE, RENEE M; Quaker Valley HS; Sewickley, PA; (Y); Ski Clb; Spanish Clb; Chorus; Yrbk Stf; Lit Mag; Rep Frsh Cls; Off Soph Cls; Socr; Var Trk; Hon Roll; PA JR Acad Sci 2nd Pl 86; PA ST U; Jrnlsm.

LA GORGA, LINDA ANN; Norwin SR HS; N Huntingdon, PA; (Y); 4/562; Math Tm; Chorus; VP Soph Cls; VP Pres Stu Cncl; Dnfth Awd; NHS; Trs Exploring; French Clb; Mathletes; SADD; Hugh O Brian Ldrshp Awd 84; Century III Ldrshp Awd 85; Outstndg SR Awd 86; U Of PA; Elec Engrng.

LA MONACA, STEPHANIE; St Maria Goretti HS; Philadelphia, PA; (Y); 15/390; Church Yth Grp; Cmnty Wkr; Political Wkr; Teachers Aide; Ed Yrbk Stf; Ed Lit Mag; Rep Soph Cls; Tennis; High Hon Roll; Ntl Merit Ltr; Hnrbl Mntn Awd Engl, Wrld Cultrs, Advncd Plcmt Engl, Frnch III; Georgetown; Educ.

LA MOONEY, DARYL; Grand Army Of The Republic HS; Wilkes Barre, PA; (Y); 31/174; Church Yth Grp; Cmnty Wkr; Exploring; Letterman Clb; Office Aide; PAVAS; Acpl Chr; Band; Chorus; Church Choir; Wilkes Coll; Mus.

LA NUNZIATA, MARISA; Dunmore HS; Dunmore, PA; (Y); 20/149; Computer Clb; French Clb; FBLA; Spanish Clb; School Musical; Nwsp Stf; Ed Yrbk Stf; Var JV Cheerleading; High Hon Roll; Hon Roll; Bus.

LA PLANTE, TREFF; Central Dauphin East HS; Dauphin, PA; (Y); Am Leg Boys St; Boy Scts; Church Yth Grp; Cmnty Wkr; Ftbl; Trk; NHS; Naval Acad Annapolis; Nvl Avtr.

LA POINT, MARK; Cowanesque Valley HS; Middlebury Center, PA; (S); 13/100; Boy Scts; Chess Clb; Bsbl; Cit Awd; High Hon Roll; Hon Roll; Ntl Merit Ltr; Stu Of Mnth 85; Armed Frcs; Navigation.

LA PORTE, MATTHEW; North Hills-Pittsburgh HS; Pittsburgh, PA; (S); 10/500; Ski Clb; Mrchg Band; Orch; JV Bsktbl; JV Ftbl; High Hon Roll; NHS; Chem.

LA ROCCA, JOHN; Sharpsville Area HS; Sharpsville, PA; (Y); Aud/Vis; Chess Clb; Letterman Clb; Stage Crew; Ftbl; Trk; Wt Lftg; Elec Engrng.

LA ROCQUE, MICHAEL; Abington Heights HS; Waverly, PA; (Y); 84/271; Ski Clb; Lit Mag; Im Bsktbl; Im JV Ftbl; Im Golf; Im Sftbl; Im Wt Lftg; Hon Roll; Cert Of Merit Schlstc Art Awds 84; Athltc Awd For Tm Membrshp 84; Traithln 5 Men Tm Chmpns 85; Engrng.

LA ROSA, TAMMY; Carmichaels Area HS; Carmichaels, PA; (Y); French Clb; Library Aide; Office Aide; Ski Clb; Chorus; Golf; High Hon Roll; Hon Roll; Nursing.

LA SALLE, ROBERT; Upper Perkiomen HS; East Greenville, PA; (Y); Chess Clb; FBLA; Band; JV Ftbl; Im Wt Lftg.

LA TULIP, LAUREN; Dowington SR HS; Downingtown, PA; (S); 14/550; Drama Clb; French Clb; SADD; Teachers Aide; School Musical; School Play; Lit Mag; High Hon Roll; NHS; Ntl Merit SF; Telluride Assoc Smmr Schlrshp Cornell 85.

LA VERDE, VICKI; West Allegheny SR HS; Clinton, PA; (Y); 11/211; Pres FBLA; Sec JA; Office Aide; Chorus; Rep Jr Cls; Stu Cncl; High Hon Roll; NHS; Pres Schlr; Future Bus Ldrs Of Amer Schlrshp Rcpnt 86; Duffs Bus Inst; Bus Mngmnt.

LABADIE, TRACEY; Richland HS; Gibsonia, PA; (Y); Church Yth Grp; Speech Tm; Band; Chorus; Color Guard; Drill Tm; Mrchg Band; School Musical; Yrbk Stf; Powder Puff Ftbl; WV U; Psych.

LABADIE, WILLIE; Mt Lebanon HS; Pittsburgh, PA; (Y); Exploring; Band; Concert Band; Mrchg Band; Im Bsktbl; Im Ftbl; Var L Vllybl; Hon Roll; Pres Acdmc Ftns Awd 86; U Dayton; Engrng.

LABB, DONNA; St Maria Goretti HS; Philadelphia, PA; (Y); 22/398; French Clb; Math Clb; School Musical; Yrbk Stf; JV Crs Cntry; JV Tennis; High Hon Roll; NHS; Prfct Atten Awd; Am Leg Awd 83; Religion Awd 83; Engrng.

LABELLA, LARRY; St John Neumann HS; Philadelphia, PA; (Y); #49 In Class; Accntng.

LABENNE, BOB; Iroquois HS; Erie, PA; (Y); 32/142; Church Yth Grp; Letterman Clb; Pres Frsh Cls; Pres Soph Cls; Off Pres Jr Cls; JV Var Ftbl; JV Var Trk; Im Wt Lftg; Var L Wrstlng; Hon Roll.

LABOR, KELLY; Slippery Rock Area HS; Slippery Rock, PA; (Y); Church Yth Grp; Intnl Clb; Pep Clb.

LABRISE, PAUL; Quigley HS; Wexford, PA; (Y); Wrstlng.

LABUDA, KIM; Geibel HS; Connellsville, PA; (Y); Spanish Clb; Hon Roll; Spanish NHS; Spnsh.

LACERDA, CHRISTINA; The Mercersburg Acad; Zanesville, OH; (Y); Intnl Clb; Ski Clb; Nwsp Sprt Ed; Sec Lit Mag; VP Soph Cls; JV Socr; Var Tennis; High Hon Roll; Hon Roll; Awd Otstndng Acmplshmnt Eng Compstn 84; Psych.

LACEY, KELLY; Neshaminy HS; Oakford, PA; (Y); 17/698; German Clb; JA; Political Wkr; Rep Soph Cls; Rep Jr Cls; Stu Cncl; High Hon Roll; Jr NHS; NHS; Ntl Merit SF; Charles E Mc Carthy Schlrshp 86; St Petes; Psychlgy.

LACHAT, LISA; Lock Haven SR HS; Castanea, PA; (Y); Church Yth Grp; FHA; Spanish Clb; Band; Chorus; Church Choir; Concert Band; NEDT Awd; Lockhaven U; Elem Ed.

LACHI, DAVE; Pocono Mountain HS; Henryville, PA; (Y); 102/328; Varsity Clb; Lit Mag; VP Socr; VP Tennis; Prfct Atten Awd; Lehigh U; Mech Engnr.

LACKEY, SHEILA; Franklin HS; Franklin, PA; (Y); Church Yth Grp; Drama Clb; German Clb; Hosp Aide; Library Aide; Radio Clb; Band; Chorus; School Play; Nwsp Stf; Edinboro U; Cmmnctns.

LACKO, JENNIFER; Northampton Area SR HS; Walnutport, PA; (Y); 30/444; Computer Clb; Leo Clb; Office Aide; SADD; Chorus; Stu Cncl; High Hon Roll; Hon Roll; Teen Suicide Intervntn 85-86; Hmrm Pres 84-86; Dist 10 Chorus 85; Fin Northampton Cnty JR Miss Pag 86; PA ST; Sci.

LACOUNT, ROB; Waynesburg Central HS; Waynesburg, PA; (Y); Boy Scts; Church Yth Grp; French Clb; Band; Concert Band; Jazz Band; Mrchg Band; High Hon Roll; Hon Roll; NHS; Order Arrw In Boy Scts 83; Bus & Sci.

LADD, BRIAN A; Sun Valley HS; Brookhaven, PA; (Y); 71/326; Dept PA Marn Corps Leag Schlrshp 86; PA ST U; Bus Mgmt.

LADLEE, KENNETH; E Stroudsburg HS; E Strdbg, PA; (Y); 81/215; Church Yth Grp; Cmnty Wkr; Tennis; Im Wt Lftg; Hon Roll.

LADLEY, STACY; Peters Twp HS; Bridgeville, PA; (Y); Dance Clb; FBLA; Key Clb; Ski Clb; Thesps; Yrbk Phtg; Rep Stu Cncl; Co-Capt Cheerleading; Hon Roll; Chorus; Superstar Drll Tm Grl 85; Engl Hndbell Choir 79-86; OH U.

LAEPPLE, KEITH; Neshaminy HS; Langhorne, PA; (Y); 3/706; Sec Trs Church Yth Grp; Chorus; Mrchg Band; Ed Nwsp Bus Mgr; Rep Stu Cncl; High Hon Roll; NHS; Ntl Merit Ltr; Rotary Awd; Debate Tm; Svc To Schl Outstndg SR Awd 86; A Marlyn Moyer Scholar Fndtn Scholar 86; Rotary Int Scholar 86; VA Polytech Inst; Comp Sci.

LAFFERTY, ERIC; GAR Memorial HS; Nanticoke, PA; (Y); 2/187; Computer Clb; Letterman Clb; Ski Clb; Nwsp Sprt Ed; Yrbk Stf; L Var Wrstlng; High Hon Roll; NHS; Ntl Merit SF; Physcs.

LAFFERTY, RICHARD; Interboro HS; Norwood, PA; (Y); Boys Clb Am; Key Clb; Spanish Clb; Varsity Clb; VICA; Sr Cls; Stu Cncl; Ftbl; Swmmng; Tennis; Nclear Engr.

LAGIOVANE, SHARON; Shaler Area SR HS; Allison Park, PA; (Y); 55/517; Church Yth Grp; Girl Scts; School Musical; Variety Show; Nwsp Stf; Ed Yrbk Stf; Mgr(s); Hon Roll; NEDT Awd; Stu Dir Tlnt Show 86; Comm.

LAGO, MICHELE A; Jeannette SR HS; Jeannette, PA; (Y); 1/129; Cmnty Wkr; French Clb; Hosp Aide; Stu Cncl; Var Bsktbl; Var Cheerleading; High Hon Roll; Kiwanis Awd; VP NHS; Val; Stdnt Forum; 3 Lcl Schlrshps; Washington-Jefferson Coll; Chem.

LAGRUE, LIANE; Wyoming Area SR HS; West Pittston, PA; (Y); 128/247; French Clb; Ski Clb; Stu Cncl; Swmmng; Trk; French Hon Soc; Lackawanna JC; Med Sec.

LAGUNA, NADA; St Clair Area HS; St Clair, PA; (Y); 3/83; Pres Church Yth Grp; Sec FHA; Yrbk Stf; Trs Sr Cls; Stu Cncl; Cheerleading; High Hon Roll; Hon Roll; Kiwanis Awd; Mu Alp Tht; NHS; Pres Acad Fit Awd 86; Am Leg Ctznshp Awd 86; Helen Meikrantz Scholar Awd 86; Penn ST; X-Ray Tech.

LAHART, CHRISTINA; Nazareth Academy HS; Philadelphia, PA; (Y); Church Yth Grp; Hosp Aide; Chorus; Church Choir; School Play; Yrbk Stf; Var Cheerleading; Jr NHS; Penn ST; Genetcs.

LAHEW, TRACY ANN; West Greene HS; Wind Ridge, PA; (Y); 27/79; Art Clb; Camera Clb; Dance Clb; French Clb; Hosp Aide; Ski Clb; Chorus; Yrbk Stf; VP Jr Cls; Trk; Yth Ed Assc 82-83; Waynesburg Coll; Nursing.

LAHIRI, INDRA; Solebury Schl; Chalfont, PA; (S); Mgr Chorus; Church Choir; School Musical; School Play; Lit Mag; Hon Roll; Psych.

LAHR, DONNA; Wilmington Area HS; Edinburg, PA; (Y); 22/101; Church Yth Grp; Cmnty Wkr; Drama Clb; Hosp Aide; Key Clb; Office Aide; Red Cross Aide; Spanish Clb; Hon Roll; Am Nrsng Hm Assoc Apprctn Cert 83-84; St Francis Hosp; Nrsng.

LAHR, TINA; Boyertown Area SR HS; Bally, PA; (Y); Church Yth Grp; SADD; Band; Concert Band; Jazz Band; Mrchg Band; School Musical; Nwsp Stf; Hon Roll; Presdntl Schlrhsp 86; Arlen R Saylor Schlrshp 86; Evelyn K & Henry K Reitnaur Schlrshp 86; Shenandoah Coll & Conserv; Musi.

LAHR, WILLIAM D; Upper Dauphin HS; Lykens, PA; (S); 21/112; FFA; Varsity Clb; Band; Chorus; Concert Band; Mrchg Band; Var Bsbl; Hon Roll; NHS; PA ST FFA Band 83-85; Ag Engnr.

LAI, LEON; Marple Newtown SR HS; Broomall, PA; (Y); Debate Tm; Pres Intnl Clb; Math Clb; Model UN; Pres Service Clb; Rep Jr Cls; High Hon Roll; NHS; Rensselaer Poly Inst Math,Sci Awd 87; Brown Book Awd 87; Bio.

LAICH, CAROL A; Altoona Area HS; Altoona, PA; (Y); 90/684; Trs Church Yth Grp; Science Clb; Band; Chorus; Church Choir; Concert Band; Mrchg Band; Orch; Fld Hcky; Trk; Local 734 Ed Fund Schrlshp 86-90; PA ST U; Microbio.

LAING, MARK; Canon Mc Millan SR HS; Bridgeville, PA; (Y); Aud/Vis; French Clb; Ski Clb; Jazz Band; School Musical; Wt Lftg; U Of Pittsburgh.

LAINO, JOSEPH; St John Neumann HS; Philadelphia, PA; (Y); 57/338; JV Bsktbl; Temple U; Bus Adm.

LAIRD, ERIC; Tyrone Area HS; Tyrone, PA; (Y); 76/196; Pres French Clb; Band; Chorus; Concert Band; Jazz Band; Mrchg Band; Pep Band; Hon Roll; James W Gardner Schlrshp 86; IN U; Econ.

LAIRD, MICHAEL D; Calvary Baptist Schl; Harleysville, PA; (Y); Church Yth Grp; Computer Clb; Chorus; Yrbk Phtg; Yrbk Stf; High Hon Roll; Ntl Merit SF; Hghst Acad Avg 83-85; Lansdale Music Cnsrvtry Grad 85; Comp Sci.

LAIRD, PEGGY; Greensburg Central Catholic HS; Greensburg, PA; (Y); VP French Clb; Ski Clb; Yrbk Sprt Ed; Stat Bsbl; Var L Bsktbl; L Var Vllybl; High Hon Roll; NHS; Fml Schlr Athlt Awd 84.

LAIRD, SONALEE; Glendale JR SR HS; Fallentimber, PA; (Y); 13/74; Art Clb; Band; Chorus; Capt Color Guard; Mrchg Band; Rep Soph Cls; Trs Jr Cls; Sec Sr Cls; Capt Cheerleading; Powder Puff Ftbl; PA ST; Engrng.

LAIRD, STEPHANIE JEAN; Indiana Area SR HS; Indiana, PA; (Y); Acpl Chr; Band; Jazz Band; Madrigals; Orch; School Musical; High Hon Roll; NHS; Pres Schlr; Ind Cnty 86 Jr Ms, 2nd Rnnr Up ST Compt 86; Andrew Johnson Memrl Orchrsta Awd 86; Jr Womns Civc Clb; Indiana U Of PA; Music Educ.

LAIRD, SUSAN; Bensalem HS; Bensalem, PA; (Y); Acpl Chr; Band; Chorus; Concert Band; Jazz Band; Madrigals; Mrchg Band; Pep Band; School Musical; Socr.

LAIRD, TRACY; Iroquois HS; Erie, PA; (Y); 34/150; Church Yth Grp; Drama Clb; FNA; Hosp Aide; Library Aide; Model UN; SADD; Band; Capt Flag Corp; Pep Band; Nrsng.

LAJUDICE, MARY; Archbishop Prinderyast HS; Norwood, PA; (Y); GAA; Spanish Clb; Sftbl; Swmmng; C Chester Mdcl Ctr; Radiolgy.

LAKE, ELIZABETH; Cedar Cliff HS; New Cumberland, PA; (Y); 88/294; Pres Church Yth Grp; Drama Clb; Thesps; Chorus; Church Choir; School Musical; School Play; Hon Roll; Prfct Atten Awd; Schltc Wrtg Awd Orig Song 83; United Fstvl Chrs Tour Aust/New Zealand/HI 86; Millersville U; Elem Ed.

LAKE, JEFFREY; Gateway HS; Monroeville, PA; (Y); 19/440; Socr; Ntl Merit Ltr; Pres Schlr; Purdue U; Engr.

LAKE, JILL A; Northern HS; Wellsville, PA; (Y); 48/200; Rep Frsh Cls; Rep Soph Cls; Rep Jr Cls; Sec Stu Cncl; JV Var Bsktbl; JV Var Powder Puff Ftbl; Var L Trk; Hon Roll; Grace Coll; Psych.

LAKHANI, DEVAL; Villa Maria HS; Boardman, OH; (Y); Hosp Aide; Library Aide; Red Cross Aide; Spanish Clb; Chorus; Ed Yrbk Stf; NHS; Spanish NHS; Hnr Artwrk, Piano 83; Med.

LAKIN, BETH; Mount Pleasant Area SR HS; Mt Pleasant, PA; (Y); GAA; Rep Jr Cls; Rep Sr Cls; Rep Stu Cncl; Mat Maids; Var Swmmng; Hon Roll.

LAKITSKY, MICHELLE; Tamaqua Area HS; Andreas, PA; (Y); Pres Exploring; VP 4-H; Pep Clb; Science Clb; Flag Corp; Yrbk Stf; Rep Jr Cls; Rep Sr Cls; Var Crs Cntry; Var Trk; PA ST; Mth.

LAKO, JAMIE; Monongahela Vly HS; Elizabeth, PA; (Y); 24/85; Library Aide; Ski Clb; Thesps; School Musical; Trk; Pre-Med.

LALA, JACQUELINE M; Central Bucks HS East; New Hope, PA; (Y); 66/487; French Clb; Ski Clb; Acpl Chr; Chorus; Church Choir; Color Guard; Yrbk Bus Mgr; Yrbk Stf; JV Vllybl; Hon Roll; Memorial Schlrshp 86; Chestnut Hill Coll; Frnch.

LALAMA, BRENDA; Aliquippa SR HS; Aliquippa, PA; (S); French Clb; Bsktbl; Cheerleading; Score Keeper; Sftbl; Hon Roll; Phy Educ Awd 85-86.

LALLEY, JOHN; Bishop Ohara HS; Dunmore, PA; (Y); Church Yth Grp; Cmnty Wkr; Letterman Clb; Ski Clb; Varsity Clb; Bsbl; Bsktbl; Wt Lftg; Hon Roll; U Of Scranton; Med.

LALLY III, EDMUND J; Interboro HS; Norwood, PA; (S); 1/275; Art Clb; Aud/Vis; Chess Clb; Church Yth Grp; Computer Clb; Drama Clb; Library Aide; Spanish Clb; Jazz Band; Mrchg Band; Sci.

LALLY, LORA; Sharpsville Area SR HS; Sharpsville, PA; (Y); 36/129; Am Leg Aux Girls St; Rep Church Yth Grp; Spanish Clb; Nwsp Stf; Yrbk Stf; Bsktbl; Crmnlgy.

LALLY, MATTHEW; Archbishop Wood For Boys; Ivyland, PA; (Y); 48/282; Var Ftbl; Wt Lftg; Hon Roll; NHS; Civil Engrng.

LAM, ALLISON; William Allen HS; Allentown, PA; (Y); 1/576; Cmnty Wkr; Acpl Chr; School Musical; Nwsp Stf; Rep Stu Cncl; Var Swmmng; High Hon Roll; Val; Drama Clb; PAVAS; Lehigh Cnty JR Miss 3rd Rnnr Up In PA ST JR Miss 86; Air Prod & Chem Inc Sci Achvt Awd 86; Haverford Coll; Med.

LAM, HUNG; Upper Moreland HS; Willow Grove, PA; (Y); 80/260; Church Yth Grp; Key Clb; Off Stu Cncl; JV Bsktbl; JV Var Ftbl; Var Socr; Var Trk; Hon Roll; UMHS Phys Ftns Awd Outstndng Boy 85-86; Penn ST U; Mchncl.

LAM, MINH; West Catholic HS; Philadelphia, PA; (Y); Penn ST; Elec Engr.

LAMANNA, TAMI; Villa Maria HS; Canfield, OH; (Y); Drama Clb; French Clb; Key Clb; Ski Clb; School Musical; School Play; Nwsp Phtg; Yrbk Phtg; Rep Frsh Cls; Trk.

LAMANQUE, BILL; Hopewell HS; Aliquippa, PA; (Y); VP French Clb; Latin Clb; Rep Jr Cls; L Socr; L Tennis; Hon Roll; Bus.

LAMARI, DANIELE D; Kiski Area HS; Leechburg, PA; (Y); SADD; Varsity Clb; Off Stu Cncl; Sftbl; Vllybl; High Hon Roll; Off Soph Cls; Off Jr Cls; Off Sr Cls; German Clb; MVP Bsktbl, Sftbl 84-86; Schlr Athlt 85-86; Most Athltc Feml 85-86; Slippery Rock U.

LAMB, DANIEL A; Susquehanna Township HS; Harrisburg, PA; (Y); 13/155; Varsity Clb; Var Bsbl; JV Bsktbl; Var Capt Ftbl; Im Golf; Im Wt Lftg; Hon Roll; NHS; Acdmc Athlt All Am 85-86; Mike Giddings Meml Awd Ftbl 85-86; Most Coachabl Ftbl 85-86; Math.

LAMB, DOUG; Greensburg Central Catholic HS; Greensburg, PA; (Y); Boy Scts; Letterman Clb; Pres Spanish Clb; SADD; Varsity Clb; Nwsp Sprt Ed; Capt Ftbl; Capt Tennis; High Hon Roll; NHS; Torontali Awd Econmcs 85; Excllnc Wind Ensmbl Awd 85; Bio.

LAMBERT, AIMEE; Ringgold HS; Monongahela, PA; (Y); Pep Clb; Ski Clb; Mrchg Band; Variety Show; Nwsp Stf; Yrbk Stf; Stu Cncl; Score Keeper; Twrlr; Washington Hosp Schl; Rdlgy.

LAMBERT, BRETT; Upper Moreland HS; Willow Grove, PA; (Y); 73/253; Church Yth Grp; Key Clb; Spanish Clb; Rep Jr Cls; Rep Stu Cncl; JV Socr; High Hon Roll.

LAMBERT, DEBORAH; Cardinal O Hara HS; Chester, PA; (Y); 317/772; Hosp Aide; School Play; Opt Clb Awd; Physcl Thrpy.

LAMBERT, JULIET E; Parkland SR HS; Fogelsville, PA; (Y); 4/459; JCL; Latin Clb; Leo Clb; Math Tm; Chorus; Swing Chorus; Tennis; High Hon Roll; NHS; Ntl Merit Ltr; Lehigh Cnty JR Miss Contestnt 86-87; Sci.

LAMBERT, KIM; Punxsutawney Area HS; Big Run, PA; (Y); 17/238; Pres Church Yth Grp; FBLA; Office Aide; Yrbk Stf; Vllybl; High Hon Roll; NHS; Stu Of The Month Awd 86; Outstndng Bus Stu Awd 86; Du Bois Bus Coll Schlrshp 86; Du Bois Bus Coll Inc; Accntng.

LAMBERT, KIMBERLY; St Francis Acad; Pittsburgh, PA; (S); 1/35; Ed Church Yth Grp; Drama Clb; Pres JA; Math Clb; Red Cross Aide; Chorus; Nwsp Rptr; Yrbk Ed-Chief; High Hon Roll; NHS; Jr Achvt VP Of Finance 1st Pl 85; Acad All-Amer Awd 85; Air Force ROTC 4-Yr Schlrshp Awd 86; Rensselaer Polytech Inst; Physc.

LAMBERT, RENEE; California Area HS; Coal Center, PA; (Y); 17/101; Drama Clb; FNA; Concert Band; Flag Corp; Mrchg Band; Trs Frsh Cls; Trs Soph Cls; Trs Jr Cls; Trs Sr Cls; Stu Cncl; CA U Of PA; Elem Tchr.

LAMBERTI, MATTHEW; Old Forege HS; Old Forge, PA; (Y); Bsktbl.

LAMBERTON, LAURA; Franklin JR-SR HS; Franklin, PA; (Y); Church Yth Grp; Cmnty Wkr; Spanish Clb; Chorus; Church Choir; Color Guard; School Play; Off Soph Cls; Off Jr Cls; Off Sr Cls; Psych.

LAMBING, CHARLENE; Marion Center Area HS; Home, PA; (S); 1/148; Trs Intnl Clb; Science Clb; High Hon Roll; Jr NHS; NHS; Ntl Merit Ltr; Penn ST Jr Sci Sympsm 85; Phil Coll Sci-Phrmcy; Toxclgy.

LAMBRIGHT, ERIC; Upper Dublin HS; Dresher, PA; (Y); 7/312; Pres Church Yth Grp; FBLA; JA; Varsity Clb; JV Bsktbl; Var Golf; JV Trk; NHS; Acdmc All Amrcn 85; Hugh O Brien Ldrshp 85; Sci.

LAMENDOLA, JEAN M; Kiski Area HS; Leechburg, PA; (Y); Letterman Clb; Pep Clb; Science Clb; Varsity Clb; Symp Band; Stat Bsktbl; Cheerleading; Trk; Hon Roll; Drama Clb; Alle Kiski Hnrs Band, Cnty Band 84-86; Dist Ban D 84; IUP Hnrs Band 84 & 86; St Bonaventure; Law.

LAMER, MELANIE; Littlestown HS; Littlestown, PA; (Y); Library Aide; Teachers Aide; Varsity Clb; Color Guard; Mrchg Band; Sftbl; Vllybl; Hon Roll; Cntrl PA Bus Schl.

LAMERAND, SCOTT; Benton HS; Benton, PA; (Y); Exploring; French Clb; Key Clb; Band; Chorus; Mrchg Band; School Musical; School Play; Hon Roll; NHS; Bloomsburg U; Engr.

LAMERAND, WENDY; Benton Area HS; Benton, PA; (Y); Band; Chorus; Concert Band; Jazz Band; Mrchg Band; School Musical; School Play; Var Co-Capt Bsktbl; Stat Fld Hcky; Hon Roll; Psychlgy.

LAMIE, DANIELLE; Saucon Valley SR HS; Bethlehem, PA; (Y); 10/146; French Clb; Girl Scts; Trs Sr Cls; Rep Stu Cncl; Var L Bsktbl; Var L Fld Hcky; Var L Sftbl; High Hon Roll; Hon Roll; Jr NHS; Clnl Leag Lhgh Bcks Nrthmptn All Str Team 1st Team Ofns Fld Hcky 86; Sprts Med.

LAMM, ERIC J; Seneca Valley HS; Harmony, PA; (Y); Art Clb; Church Yth Grp; Ski Clb; Jazz Band; Stage Crew; Hon Roll; NHS; Dirctrs Awd Outstndng Jazz Musicn; Duquesne U; Bus.

LAMONT, MARK; Cambria Hieghts HS; Elmora, PA; (Y); Var L Crs Cntry; L Capt Trk; Hon Roll; 1600 M & 400 M Relay Schl Rcrds 85 & 86; Bus Mgmt.

LAMOONEY, DARYL; GAR Mem HS; Wilkes Barre, PA; (S); 32/164; Acpl Chr; Band; Chorus; Concert Band; Jazz Band; Mrchg Band; Orch; Symp Band; NHS; Richard Ayre Music Awd 85; Dist Regnl ST Band 85-86; Arion Awd Music 84; Wilkes Coll; Music.

LAMOREAU, AMY; Moshannon Valley JR SR HS; Ramey, PA; (Y); 21/133; Hosp Aide; Ski Clb; Spanish Clb; Varsity Clb; Band; Mrchg Band; Pep Band; Yrbk Stf; L Var Bsktbl; Hon Roll; W O Gulbranson Scholar 86; Cntrl PA Schl Nrsng; Nrsng.

LAMOREAUX, PAULA MAE; John S Fine SR HS; Hunlock Creek, PA; (Y); Sec Church Yth Grp; 4-H; Chorus; Church Choir; Nwsp Rptr; Nwsp Stf; Yrbk Stf; 4-H Awd; Hon Roll; Med.

LAMOREUX, LINDA; Bishop Hoban HS; Swoyersville, PA; (Y); Latin Clb; Math Clb; JV Var Bsktbl; Var L Crs Cntry; Var L Trk; NHS; High Hon Roll; Hon Roll; Pres Acdmc Fit Awd 86; Outstndng Sci Stdnt Awd Luzerne Cnty Sci Tchrs Assn 86; U Of ND; Pre-Med.

LAMORTE, LORI; Valley View JR SR HS; Peckville, PA; (Y); FBLA; Var Bsktbl; Var Sftbl; High Hon Roll; Girls Bsktbll Dist 2 Champs & Eastern Champs & ST Runnr Ups 86; Tm Awd MIP 84-85; Bst Dfnsv Plyr 86; Bus.

LAMPKINS, SYBIL; Farrell HS; Farrell, PA; (Y); 26/100; Church Yth Grp; French Clb; Girl Scts; Letterman Clb; Library Aide; Office Aide; Spanish Clb; Varsity Clb; Church Choir; Drill Tm; Hmcmng Qun 85-86; Edinboro U; Socl Wrk.

LAMPRON, COLLEEN; Downingtown HS; Downingtown, PA; (Y); Cmnty Wkr; NFL; Q&S; Spanish Clb; Nwsp Rptr; Ed Lit Mag; Rep Stu Cncl; JV Cheerleading; Var Crs Cntry; Var Trk; Jrnlsm Awd 85; Intl Bus.

LANAGER, DONNA; Clearfield Area HS; Hyde, PA; (Y); 60/300; Drama Clb; French Clb; Chorus; School Musical; JV Sftbl; Var L Vllybl; Hon Roll.

LANAGER, LINDA; Clearfield Area HS; Hyde, PA; (Y); French Clb; Key Clb; Presdntl Acad Fitns Awd 86; Slipper Rock U; Elem Ed.

LANATTO, CHRISTINE; Merion Mercy Acad; Phila, PA; (Y); Church Yth Grp; Dance Clb; Drama Clb; French Clb; Teachers Aide; Hon Roll; NEDT Awd; Secondary Educ.

LANCASTER, MARLO; Roxborough HS; Philadelphia, PA; (Y); Church Yth Grp; Cmnty Wkr; Dance Clb; Hosp Aide; JA; Political Wkr; Red Cross Aide; Spanish Clb; Church Choir; School Play; Temple U; Dntstry.

LANCASTER, MELISSA K; Huntingtdon Area HS; Mill Creek, PA; (Y); 6/208; Sec Trs Chorus; VP Concert Band; VP Mrchg Band; Rep Jr Cls; Rep Sr Cls; Vllybl; High Hon Roll; VP NHS; Church Yth Grp; Key Clb; Ntl Hnr Scty Schlrshp 86; Pres Acdmc Ftns Awd 86; Geneva Schlr Awd 86; Geneva Coll.

LANCASTER, NORMAN; Penn Hills SR HS; Pittsburgh, PA; (Y); French Clb; JV Stat Bsbl; High Hon Roll; Hon Roll; Accntng.

LANCE, BARBARA; Roxborough HS; Philadelphia, PA; (Y); GAA; Hosp Aide; Chorus; Nwsp Rptr; Rep Jr Cls; Var Gym; Var Sftbl; Capt Twrlr; Hon Roll; VP NHS; Phys/Occ Therapy.

LAND, BRIAN; Unionville HS; West Chester, PA; (Y); 24/269; Var Tennis; Var Capt Wrstlng; High Hon Roll; Mu Alp Tht.

LAND, MICHAEL; Bethel Park HS; Bethel Pk, PA; (Y); Boy Scts; Church Yth Grp; Yrbk Stf; Hon Roll; Prfct Atten Awd; EPOCH 85-86; PA ST Consrvtn Schl 83-84; Yth Ldrshp Trng 84-85; Pope Pius XII Awd 85-86.

LAND, PAT; Lancaster Catholic HS; Ephrata, PA; (Y); Boy Scts; Chess Clb; VP JA; Alcoa Schlrshp 86; Kutztown; Scndry Educ.

LANDAU, AUDREY; Wyoming Valley West HS; Kingston, PA; (Y); 13/500; Key Clb; Chorus; Cheerleading; Crs Cntry; Gym; Tennis; Vllybl; High Hon Roll; Hon Roll; NHS; Lehgh U.

LANDAU, BRIAN; Washington HS; Washington, PA; (Y); 2/155; Ski Clb; VP SADD; Pres Frsh Cls; VP Soph Cls; Rep Jr Cls; Var Capt Crs Cntry; Var Tennis; DAR Awd; NHS; Am Lgn Awd 83; Chem Engr.

LANDAU, HELENE; Northern HS; Dillsburg, PA; (Y); 59/224; Computer Clb; Hosp Aide; Letterman Clb; Ski Clb; Yrbk Ed-Chief; Yrbk Sprt Ed; Rep Stu Cncl; L Fld Hcky; High Hon Roll; Hon Roll; Sci.

LANDAU, LESLIE; Northern HS; Dillsburg, PA; (Y); 50/220; Hosp Aide; Yrbk Stf; Rep Frsh Cls; Rep Stu Cncl; Coach Actv; JV Var Fld Hcky; Im Powder Puff Ftbl; High Hon Roll; Hon Roll; NYU; Bus Mgmt.

LANDER, LORI; Upper Dublin HS; Ft Washington, PA; (Y); 27/317; Cmnty Wkr; FBLA; Intnl Clb; Nwsp Rptr; Yrbk Stf; Ed Lit Mag; Rep Frsh Cls; Rep Stu Cncl; JV Sftbl; NHS; Cmmnctns.

LANDERS, JOE; Waynes Burg Central HS; Waynesburg, PA; (Y); Art Clb; Leo Clb; Band; Concert Band; Jazz Band; Mrchg Band; Trk; Hon Roll; Edinboro U; Art Illstrtr.

LANDFRIED, DARRYL; North Allegheny HS; Allison Park, PA; (S); DECA; Wt Lftg; DECA Comptn 1st Pl Dist, 2nd Pl ST, 7th Pl Natl 85-86; IN ST U Bloomington; Bus Adm.

LANDIS, CHRIS; Canton HS; Troy, PA; (Y); 23/105; Church Yth Grp; Letterman Clb; Band; Chorus; Concert Band; Wt Lftg; Var Capt Wrstlng; Pres Schlr; Canton Cvc Clb Awd Mst Vlbl Wrstlr 85-86; PIAA Wrstlng 1st Sec, 2nd Distr, Rgnl,4th ST 86; Lycoming Coll; Bus.

LANDIS, DAWN; Kiski Area SR HS; Leechburg, PA; (Y); Church Yth Grp; French Clb; Chorus; High Hon Roll; Hon Roll; Achvt Awd-Chorus 83-84; Cert Merit Outstndng Achvt Acad Excllnc 84-85; Penn ST U; Comp Sci.

LANDIS, JON; Manhiem Tswp HS; Lancaster, PA; (Y); Pres Frsh Cls; JV Bsktbl; Var Socr; Im Vllybl; Hon Roll; Mayors Yth Ldrshp Conv; Bio Engrng.

LANDIS, KIM; Canton Area JR SR HS; Troy, PA; (Y); 5/125; Pres AFS; Sec Trs Church Yth Grp; Sec Letterman Clb; Co-Capt Pep Clb; Band; Chorus; Concert Band; Drm Mjr(t); Jazz Band; Mrchg Band; Math.

LANDIS, KIMBERLY; Elizabethtown Area HS; Bainbridge, PA; (Y); 60/232; German Clb; Teachers Aide; Varsity Clb; Concert Band; Mrchg Band; Yrbk Sprt Ed; Trs Sr Cls; JV Bsktbl; JV Fld Hcky; Powder Puff Ftbl; Lock Haven; Elem Ed.

LANDIS, LISA; Octorara HS; Lancaster, PA; (Y); Camera Clb; Church Yth Grp; Computer Clb; Math Clb; Red Cross Aide; SADD; Color Guard; Var JV Fld Hcky; 4-H Awd; Hon Roll; O Leary Scholar 86; St Joseph Schl Nrsg; Nrsg.

LANDIS, LYA; Cumberland Valley HS; Carlisle, PA; (Y); GAA; Varsity Clb; Sec Frsh Cls; Stu Cncl; Im Badmtn; JV L Cheerleading; Var L Fld Hcky; Mgr(s); Score Keeper; Im Tennis; Bucknell U; Blgcl Sci.

LANDIS, MARLA; Bellefonte Area HS; Howard, PA; (Y); Church Yth Grp; Cmnty Wkr; VP 4-H; Teachers Aide; Y-Teens; Rep Stu Cncl; Var Cheerleading; JV Sftbl; Hon Roll; Prfct Atten Awd; Early Childhd Educ.

LANDIS, MATT; Bishop Shanahan HS; W Chester, PA; (Y); 128/218; Church Yth Grp; Var Bsbl; JV Bsktbl; Im Ftbl; Im Ice Hcky; Natl Rifle Assoc; Engrng.

LANDIS, MICHAEL; Millersburg Area HS; Millersburg, PA; (Y); 21/75; Church Yth Grp; Spanish Clb; Band; Church Choir; Concert Band; Jazz Band; Mrchg Band; School Musical; Bsbl; Bowling; Pre-Hlth.

LANDIS, MICHAEL; Northern Lebanon HS; Jonestown, PA; (Y); Church Yth Grp; Cmnty Wkr; FCA; 4-H; Var L Ftbl; Im Wt Lftg; Var Capt Wrstlng; 4-H Awd; Hon Roll; Prfct Atten Awd; Aviation.

LANDIS, RAYMOND; Souderton Area HS; Harleysville, PA; (Y); 35/370; Church Yth Grp; Band; Chorus; Church Choir; Concert Band; Jazz Band; Mrchg Band; School Musical; Hon Roll; Bi Cnty Band, Bux MT Band 86; Music.

LANDIS, SCOTT; Berlin-Brothersvalley HS; Berlin, PA; (Y); 12/85; Church Yth Grp; Pres FFA; Church Choir; School Play; Yrbk Stf; NHS; Speech Tm; SADD; Stage Crew; Mgr(s); Conservtn Awd FFA 85; Soil Consrvtn.

LANDIS, SHARON; Souderton Area HS; Telford, PA; (Y); SADD; Chorus; School Musical; School Play; Nwsp Rptr; Yrbk Rptr; JV Fld Hcky; Var Gym; Var Lcrss; Jr NHS; Gymnstc Most Imprvd 85.

LANDMESSER, PATRICIA; Bishop O Reilly HS; Larksville, PA; (Y); Church Yth Grp; Sftbl; Ltn Hnr Scty 83-84; Gnrl Chmstry Hnrs 86; Jrnlsm.

LANDOLINA, MARIA; Shaler Area SR HS; Glenshaw, PA; (Y); 29/517; Cmnty Wkr; Sec Soph Cls; VP Jr Cls; Swmmng; High Hon Roll; NEDT Awd; Spanish NHS; Penn St; Genetcs.

LANDY, JOSEPH; Bethel Park SR HS; Bethel Pk, PA; (Y); Church Yth Grp; FBLA; German Clb; Bsktbl; High Hon Roll; NHS; Ntl Merit SF; Elec Engrng.

LANE, ALYSSA KIM; Coudersport Area JR SR HS; Coudersport, PA; (Y); French Clb; Hosp Aide; Varsity Clb; Band; Chorus; Yrbk Stf; Cheerleading; Vllybl; Hon Roll; NHS; Grad Amer Lgn ST Police Yth Wk 86; JU 9 Bnd Fest 84-86; Dist IX Trck 86; Psych.

LANE, DENISE; Lewistown Area HS; Lewistown, PA; (Y); Spanish Clb; Varsity Clb; VP Frsh Cls; Rep Soph Cls; JV Var Bsktbl; Var Capt Fld Hcky; JV Var Sftbl; High Hon Roll; NHS; Phys Ed.

LANE, JENNIFER; Sharon HS; Sharon, PA; (Y); 85/162; Drama Clb; Office Aide; Concert Band; Mrchg Band; School Musical; School Play; Stu Cncl; Bsktbl; Sftbl; Wt Lftg; Cosmtrlgy.

LANE, KIMBERLY; Sheffield Area HS; Clarendon, PA; (Y); Office Aide; SADD; Varsity Clb; Mrchg Band; Nwsp Stf; Sec Frsh Cls; Stu Cncl; Cheerleading; Score Keeper; Vllybl; Free Enterprise Week Savings Bond 85; Penn ST; Bus.

LANE, SANDRA; Tunkhannock HS; Falls, PA; (S); Church Yth Grp; Intnl Clb; Key Clb; Band; Church Choir; Concert Band; Mrchg Band; Hon Roll; NHS; Nrs.

LANE, SARA M; Central Cambria HS; Ebensburg, PA; (Y); Art Clb; Church Yth Grp; Band; Color Guard; Concert Band; Jazz Band; Mrchg Band; Var Trk; Hon Roll; Prfct Atten Awd; Archt.

LANEY, RENEE; Purchase Line HS; Cherry Tree, PA; (Y); FBLA; Band; Concert Band; Mrchg Band; Pep Band; Hon Roll; Mrchng Band; Cncrt Band; Hnr Rll; Sec.

LANG, BRETT; Kennett HS; Kennett Sq, PA; (Y); 3/160; Radio Clb; Red Cross Aide; VP Science Clb; Chorus; School Musical; Yrbk Stf; Rep Stu Cncl; High Hon Roll; Pres NHS; Computer Clb; Hugh O B Rian Yth Fndtn Ldrshp Awd 85; 2nd Pl Kennett Sq Main St Assc Essay Cntst 86; Bus Admin.

LANG, COLLEEN; Burrell HS; New Kensington, PA; (Y); Library Aide; Spanish Clb; High Hon Roll; Hon Roll; NHS.

LANG, DEBBIE; Shaler HS; Allison Park, PA; (Y); 84/529; Band; Hon Roll; Allegheny Vly Band 85-86.

LANG, DEBORAH ANNE; Calvary Baptist Christian Acad; Meadville, PA; (S); 1/7; Yrbk Ed-Chief; Yrbk Stf; Sec Trs Jr Cls; Trs Sr Cls; Var L Vllybl; Val; VP Church Yth Grp; VP 4-H; Chorus; Sec Trs Nwsp Sprt Ed; Natl Christian Hon Soc 83-85; Amer Hstry Awd 83 & 84; Le Tourneau Chrstn Coll; Mth.

LANG, GAIL; Gateway SR HS; Monroeville, PA; (Y); Church Yth Grp; Chorus; Church Choir; Mrchg Band; Orch; Symp Band; Yrbk Stf; Pres Frsh Cls; Stu Cncl; Hon Roll; Prfct Atten Awd 83; Pres Reagans Acad Fit Awd 86; Slippery Rock U; Comm Radio/TV.

LANG, KIMBERLY; Solanco HS; New Providence, PA; (Y); Spanish Clb; Varsity Clb; Chorus; Color Guard; Mrchg Band; Off Jr Cls; Off Sr Cls; Bsktbl; Fld Hcky; Sftbl; Comp Sci.

LANGAN, DIANE; West Scranton SR HS; Scranton, PA; (Y); JA; Hon Roll; Jr NHS.

LANGAN, MARJORIE; Emmaus HS; Zionsville, PA; (Y); Church Yth Grp; Key Clb; Spanish Clb; Chorus; Color Guard; School Musical; Hon Roll; Jr NHS; NHS; Cnslg.

LANGAN, WILLIAM; Archbishop Carroll HS; Havertown, PA; (Y); 14/162; High Hon Roll; Hon Roll; Jr NHS; NHS; Alg I, Spnsh II And Acctg I Awds 84-86.

LANGDON, DEBRA; Cardinal O Hara HS; Essington, PA; (Y); Church Yth Grp; GAA; Chorus; Church Choir; School Musical; School Play.

LANGDON, ROBERT; Archbishop Carroll HS; Radnor, PA; (Y); 14/165; Nwsp Stf; Im Bsktbl; JV Crs Cntry; High Hon Roll; Hon Roll; Jr NHS; NHS; Spanish NHS; Pres Ftns Awd 86; Penn ST U; Lbrl Arts.

LANGE, ANDREA; Archbishop Ryan HS; Philadelphia, PA; (Y); 4/500; German Clb; JA; Nwsp Stf; Frsh Cls.

LANGE, JAMES; Upper Darby SR HS; Drexel Hl, PA; (Y); Varsity Clb; Var JV Bsktbl; Var JV Lcrss; Hon Roll; Boy Scts; Var JV Socr; Im Vllybl; Prfct Atten Awd; Med Sci.

LANGE, ROBERT; Tunkhannock HS; Tunkhannock, PA; (S); 13/339; Key Clb; Letterman Clb; Math Clb; Science Clb; Spanish Clb; Capt Varsity Clb; JV Bsbl; JV Bsktbl; Capt Golf; High Hon Roll; Schlrshp Bnqt; La Fayette; Chem.

LANGENSIEPEN, LISA; Liberty HS; Bethlehem, PA; (Y); 57/487; Hosp Aide; Band; Mrchg Band; Yrbk Stf; Rep Jr Cls; Rep Sr Cls; Twrlr; Hon Roll; Nrsng.

LANGER, KIM; Beaver Area JRSR HS; Beaver, PA; (Y); 1/179; JCL; Key Clb; Pep Clb; Drill Tm; Stu Cncl; Swmmng; High Hon Roll; NHS; Schlstc Achvt Awd; Math Comptn.

LANGER, KIMBERLY; Quaker Valley HS; Sewickley, PA; (Y); 11/168; German Clb; Math Tm; Band; Concert Band; Mrchg Band; Pep Band; Symp Band; Yrbk Stf; High Hon Roll; JETS Awd; Exc Awd Sci,Math Awd 84; Engrng.

LANGER, TODD; Moon SR HS; Corapolis, PA; (Y); French Clb; Key Clb; Bsktbl; Vllybl; Hon Roll; Edinboro ST Coll; Arch Engrng.

LANGFORD, JENNIFER; Conneaut Lake HS; Conneaut Lake, PA; (Y); 10/90; Drama Clb; GAA; Girl Scts; Spanish Clb; SADD; Band; Chorus; Concert Band; Mrchg Band; JV Cheerleading; Grove City Coll; Rehab.

LANGHORNE, WISTAR A; East HS; West Chester, PA; (Y); 89/365; Red Cross Aide; SADD; Nwsp Stf; Trs Frsh Cls; Rep Soph Cls; Rep Jr Cls; Rep Sr Cls; Rep Stu Cncl; Stat Bsktbl; Stat Ftbl; Pres Ldrshp Schlrshp 86; Book Awds 86; Hood Coll; Stck Brkr.

LANGHURST, MYRNA; Avonworth HS; Sewickley, PA; (Y); 23/105; Church Yth Grp; JA; Band; Chorus; Church Choir; Score Keeper; Socr; Sftbl; Hon Roll; AZ ST U; Math.

LANGLEY, ROBYN; Red Lion Area SR HS; Felton, PA; (Y); 79/372; Church Yth Grp; 4-H; Pep Clb; Teachers Aide; Varsity Clb; JV Bsktbl; JV Var Cheerleading; Powder Puff Ftbl; JV Var Trk; Hon Roll; Empire Beauty Schl; Cosmotlgy.

LANGRAN, IRENE; Archbishop Carroll Girls HS; Rosemont, PA; (Y); 31/216; Pres Cmnty Wkr; French Clb; Pres Political Wkr; Service Clb; School Play; Nwsp Stf; Lcrss; Hon Roll; NHS; Villanova U; Librl Arts.

LANGSTAFF, DAVID; West Greene HS; Wind Ridge, PA; (Y); Church Yth Grp; French Clb; Trk; Hon Roll; Campus Lf Bbl Quzng Tm 2nd Chicgo Trnmt 86; Campus Lf Bbl Quzng Tm 2nd Estrn Rgn Trnmt 86.

LANGSTON, ANTHONY; Northeast Catholic HS; Philadelphia, PA; (Y); Awd Merit Span 85; 2nd Hons 84-85.

LANGSTON, SENATE; Perry Traditional Acad; Pittsburgh, PA; (Y); 12/169; Computer Clb; Debate Tm; JA; Math Clb; Nwsp Rptr; Rep Stu Cncl; L Vllybl; High Hon Roll; Jr NHS; Ntl Merit Schol; Elec Engrng.

LANGTON, ANNETTE; Hopewell Area SR HS; Aliquippa, PA; (Y); 36/245; Church Yth Grp; Exploring; Spanish Clb; Band; Chorus; Concert Band; Mrchg Band; School Musical; JV Var Vllybl; Hon Roll; Nrsng.

LANGTON, DONNA; Saint Clair HS; New Phila, PA; (Y); 2/81; Pres Math Clb; Nwsp Stf; Yrbk Stf; Rep Stu Cncl; Twrlr; Bausch & Lomb Sci Awd; DAR Awd; Kiwanis Awd; Trs NHS; Sal; Schylkll Cnty Acadmc Achvt Awd 86; Blmsbrg U Mtrani Schlrshp 86; Presdntl Acadmc Ftns Awd 86; Bloomsburg U; Comp Sci.

LANGWIG, CYNTHIA; Shaler Area HS; Pittsburgh, PA; (Y); 1/545; Variety Show; Var Capt Crs Cntry; Var Capt Trk; Elks Awd; High Hon Roll; Lion Awd; NHS; Pres Schlr; Val; Lions Schlrshp Wnnr 86; Schlr Athlt Awd 86; Glnshw Cntry Schlrshp Wnnr 86; Grv Cty Coll; Pre Med.

LANHAM, TRACI; Yough HS; West Newton, PA; (Y); 63/224; Church Yth Grp; Drama Clb; FBLA; Math Tm; Teachers Aide; Chorus; Hon Roll; NHS; Hnr Stu 86; FBLA Cmptn 83-86; 6th Pl Bus Engl 86; Wstmrlnd Cnty Cmnty Coll; Bus.

LANICH, TROY; West Branch Area HS; Morrisdale, PA; (S); 2/147; CAP; Drama Clb; Chorus; Concert Band; Mrchg Band; School Play; Yrbk Stf; Rep Stu Cncl; Hon Roll; Ntl Merit Schol; USAF Acad; Aeronaut Engrng.

LANKIEWICZ, PATTY; Plum SR HS; Pittsburgh, PA; (Y); Attnd Forbes Rd E Csmtlgy Pgm 85-87; Pittsburgh Beauty Acad; Hrdrssr.

LANMAN, HENRY A; Mt Lebanon HS; Pittsburgh, PA; (Y); 1/521; Socr; Tennis; High Hon Roll; Ntl Merit SF.

LANNI, AMY; Nazareth Area SR HS; Nazareth, PA; (Y); 30/241; Art Clb; Girl Scts; Sec VP Key Clb; Stu Cncl; Var Stat Bsbl; Var Mgr Ftbl; High Hon Roll; Prfct Atten Awd; Chld Psych.

LANNING, TIMOTHY; Kiski Artea HS; Vandergrift, PA; (Y); Rep Frsh Cls; Rep Soph Cls; JV Ftbl; JV Wrstlng; Clarion U; Frstry.

LANPHIER, TIFFANY; Palmyra Area HS; Palmyra, PA; (Y); 51/207; Drama Clb; French Clb; Hosp Aide; Teachers Aide; Chorus; Drill Tm; Yrbk Stf; Rep Frsh Cls; Rep Stu Cncl; Var Trk; People To People Cndt 85-86; Comp Sci.

LANSBERRY, CINDY; Curwensville Area HS; Curwensville, PA; (Y); Trs FBLA; Nwsp Stf; High Hon Roll; Hon Roll; NHS; Dubois Bus Coll; Acctng.

LANSBERRY, JAMES KEITH; Corry Area HS; Corry, PA; (S); 4/225; Model UN; Chorus; Concert Band; Jazz Band; Mrchg Band; Var L Swmmng; JV Tennis; High Hon Roll; Sys Analys.

LANTEIGNE, LISA; Wyoming Valley West HS; Swoyersville, PA; (Y); Trs FBLA; Key Clb; Radio Clb; Hon Roll; NHS; Wilkes Coll Upward Bound 84-86; Deans Schlrshp 86; Wilkes Coll; Psych.

LANTELME, AMY; Leechburg Area HS; Leechburg, PA; (Y); Drama Clb; Bsktbl; Christmas Trnmnt All Star Tm Awd 86; Computer Programmer.

LANTZ, CHANDRA D; Carlisle SR HS; Carlisle, PA; (Y); 53/348; JA; Key Clb; Ski Clb; Nwsp Rptr; Stu Cncl; JV L Fld Hcky; Var L Sftbl; Hon Roll; Ntl Merit Ltr; Chem.

LANTZ, CHRISTENA; Franklin HS; Franklin, PA; (Y); French Clb; German Clb; Chorus; Concert Band; Hon Roll; PA ST; Engrng.

LANTZ, LISA; Pequea Valley HS; Kinzers, PA; (Y); Concert Band; Mrchg Band; School Play; Rptr Stu Cncl; Powder Puff Ftbl; Bloomsburg U; Accntng.

LANZA JR, ROBERT J; North Allegheny HS; Pittsburgh, PA; (Y); 152/605; JA; Stage Crew; Rep Jr Cls; Capt L Bsktbl; JV Vllybl; Hon Roll; Prfct Atten Awd; CO Schl Mines Mdl Achvt-Math-Sci 85-86; Navy-Marin Corp NROTC Schlrshp 86; Penn ST; Petrlm Engr.

LANZALOTTI, CHARLES; St John Neumann HS; Philadelphia, PA; (Y); 20/350; JA; Science Clb; Band; Concert Band; Jazz Band; Pep Band; Rep Frsh Cls; Rep Soph Cls; Rep Jr Cls; Im Bsktbl; La Salle; Pre-Law.

LANZEL, BONNIE; Elk County Christian HS; St Marys, PA; (Y); 28/80; Hosp Aide; Ski Clb; Var Cheerleading.

LANZELOTTI, MARY ANN; Merion Mercy Acad; Phila, PA; (Y); 9/71; Church Yth Grp; Dance Clb; Service Clb; Pres Spanish Clb; Hon Roll; Prfct Atten Awd; Spanish NHS; Metal Hnr Plcmnt Ntl Spnsh Cntst 86; Sftbl Tm Champ 83; Temple U; Hlth.

LANZENDORFER, LORIE; Central HS; Duncanville, PA; (Y); 16/175; FBLA; JA; High Hon Roll; NHS; Bus Awd 86; Bus Mgmt.

LANZER, BETH; Waynesboro Area SR HS; Waynesboro, PA; (Y); Church Yth Grp; Cmnty Wkr; Intnl Clb; Church Choir; Stage Crew; Mgr(s); Mat Maids; Score Keeper; Hon Roll; Accntng.

LAPE, KAREN; Rockwood Area HS; Somerset, PA; (Y); Church Yth Grp; Office Aide; Band; Chorus; Sec Jr Cls; Sec Sr Cls; Rep Stu Cncl; Cheerleading; Score Keeper; High Hon Roll; Shrthnd Awd 85; Hm Ec Awd 84; Bus.

LAPENNA, ANNETTE; Plymouth-Whitemarsh HS; Conshohocken, PA; (Y); Art Clb; Chorus; Stage Crew; Nwsp Rptr; Nwsp Stf; Lit Mag; High Hon Roll; Hon Roll; Runner Up 2nd Annl Radio Clscs Theatr Comptn 86; Temple U; Journlsm.

LAPIERS, VALERIE; Lakeland HS; Mayfield, PA; (Y); Cmnty Wkr; FHA; Hon Roll; Church Yth Grp; Church Choir; Sftbl; Marywood Coll; Elem Ed.

LAPINA, JOHN J; Jeannette SR HS; Jeannette, PA; (Y); 3/143; Am Leg Boys St; Church Yth Grp; Service Clb; Spanish Clb; Concert Band; Mrchg Band; Rep Stu Cncl; Var L Golf; High Hon Roll; NHS; Engnrng.

LAPINAS, KEITH A; Central Dauphin HS; Harrisburg, PA; (Y); 132/386; Key Clb; Varsity Clb; VP L Bsbl; JV L Bsktbl; Var L Socr; Im Tennis; Im Vllybl; VFW Awd; Engrng.

LAPINSKI, DAVID J; James M Coughlin HS; Wilkes-Barre, PA; (Y); 34/375; Var Ftbl; Var Vllybl; Wt Lftg; Var Capt Wrstlng; Jr NHS; Lion Awd; NHS; NEDT Awd; Pres Schlr; Syracuse U-Full Acadmc & Athltc Schlrshp 86; 1st Tms-Ctzns Voice & Tms Ldr All Stars 86; Syracuse U.

LAPINSKI, PAMELA; Mc Keesport Area HS; Mckeesport, PA; (Y); 17/339; FBLA; Office Aide; Powder Puff Ftbl; Hon Roll; NHS; Prfct Atten Awd; Bus Awd FBLA Acct I 2nd Pl Regnl 86; Bus Adm.

LAPORTE, ANN; Roxborough HS; Philadelphia, PA; (Y); 15/327; Drama Clb; GAA; School Play; Nwsp Sprt Ed; Yrbk Stf; VP Sr Cls; Var Capt Fld Hcky; Var Sftbl; Hon Roll; NHS; All Pblc Fld Hcky Team, Sftbl Team 86; Cmnctns.

LAPOSKY, CRAIG; Greater Latrobe HS; Latrobe, PA; (Y); 43/283; Letterman Clb; Var L Ftbl; Trk; Wt Lftg; High Hon Roll; Hon Roll; St Vincent Clg; Bus.

LAPP, BARBARA JEAN; Ringgold HS; Eighty Four, PA; (Y); 33/347; Dance Clb; VP Library Aide; Acpl Chr; Band; Chorus; Concert Band; Drm & Bgl; Mrchg Band; School Musical; Powder Puff Ftbl; Dist I Band 84-85; Cnty Band 85-86; Mary Noss Scholar 85-86; CA U PA; Spec Ed.

LAPP, DONITA; Octorara HS; Cochranville, PA; (Y); VP Church Yth Grp; FBLA; Band; Concert Band; Mrchg Band; Vllybl; Hon Roll; Goldey Beacom; Accntnt.

LAPP, RENEE; Halifax HS; Halifax, PA; (Y); 5/99; Pres Church Yth Grp; Cmnty Wkr; Pres 4-H; FHA; SADD; Varsity Clb; Chorus; Church Choir; Variety Show; Yrbk Stf; Messiah Clg Music Fstvl Awd Of Excllnt 86; Cnty Chorus Accpnst 84-86; Prfrmnc Piano.

LAPRAIRIE, DANIELE; Christian School Of York; Dover, PA; (Y); Hosp Aide; Library Aide; Teachers Aide; School Play; Yrbk Stf; Hon Roll; Lancaster Bibl Coll; Elem Ed.

LARCK, KELLY; Riverview HS; Oakmont, PA; (Y); French Clb; Color Guard; Capt Flag Corp; Yrbk Stf; Stu Cncl; High Hon Roll; Hon Roll; Navy Acad; Psych.

LARIMER, SCOTT; Bellefonte HS; Bellefonte, PA; (Y); 7/224; Trs German Clb; Model UN; School Musical; Yrbk Ed-Chief; Rep Frsh Cls; Rep Jr Cls; Trs Stu Cncl; Var L Cheerleading; Trk; NHS; Bruce E Knox Yth Srv Awd 85; Acad All-Amer 84-86; HRB-SNGR Phys Sci Awd 86; PA ST U; Engrng.

LARIMER, WILLIAM J; Bethel Park SR HS; Bethel Park, PA; (Y); Capt Debate Tm; Pres JA; Pres NFL; Science Clb; High Hon Roll; NHS; Ntl Merit SF; Bioengrng.

LARIVIERE, CHIP; Church Farm Schl; Paoli, PA; (Y); Art Clb; Boy Scts; Church Yth Grp; Spanish Clb; Nwsp Stf; Im Crs Cntry; Var Mgr(s); Score Keeper; Johnson & Wales; Culinary Arts.

LARKO, SUSAN; Mt Pleasant Area HS; Mount Pleasant, PA; (Y); Art Clb; 4-H; German Clb; Band; Concert Band; Mrchg Band; 4-H Awd; Art.

LARME, MELISSA; Warren Area HS; Warren, PA; (Y); Church Yth Grp; Rep Soph Cls; Pres Jr Cls; Pres Sr Cls; Stu Cncl; Var Capt Bsktbl; Var Trk; Var Capt Vllybl; High Hon Roll; Hon Roll.

LARNERD, NANCY; Pittston Area HS; Dupont, PA; (Y); FNA; Hosp Aide; Science Clb; Rep Stu Cncl; Var L Vllybl; Hon Roll; NEDT Awd; Mentally Gftd Clb Treas 85-86; Mntlly Gftd Cls 83-86.

LAROSE, SUSAN; Christian School Of York; Hellan, PA; (Y); 26/62; Church Yth Grp; Cmnty Wkr; Girl Scts; Cheerleading; Hon Roll; Comp Sci.

LAROSSE, MARLE C; Greenwood HS; Newport, PA; (Y); Sec Church Yth Grp; Red Cross Aide; Band; Chorus; Nwsp Stf; Yrbk Stf; Var L Trk; Hon Roll; Emrgncy Med Tech 84-86; Pthfndr Hnr Awds 83-84; Hrrsbrg Area Comm Coll; Prmdc.

LAROUERE, EDWARD R; Greensburg Central Catholic HS; Manor, PA; (Y); 34/243; Boy Scts; Chess Clb; Church Yth Grp; Exploring; ROTC; Varsity Clb; Var L Wrstlng; High Hon Roll; NHS; Army Rsrve Ntl Schlr Athltc Awd 86; Purdue U; Elect Engrng.

LARSEN, ERIK ALLAN; Moniteau HS; Slippery Rock, PA; (Y); 1/126; Computer Clb; Math Tm; Spanish Clb; Mrchg Band; Bausch & Lomb Sci Awd; NHS; Val; Boy Scts; Chess Clb; Church Yth Grp; PA Govr Schl For Sci/Math 85; PA Govr Schl For Intl Stud 84; Jr Acadmy Of Sci 83-86; VA U; Aerospc Engrng.

LARSEN, FRANK; Susquehanna Community HS; Susquehanna, PA; (Y); Var JV Ftbl; Var Trk; Mth.

LARSON, CHRISTINE; Dunmore HS; Dunmore, PA; (Y); 62/149; FBLA; Key Clb; Letterman Clb; Band; Chorus; Concert Band; Mrchg Band; Hon Roll; Drama Clb; Ntl JR Hall Of Fm For Band Hnrs 86; Scl Wrk.

LARSON, KRISTIN; Greater Latrobe SR HS; Latrobe, PA; (Y); Hosp Aide; Ski Clb; Teachers Aide; Off Chorus; Concert Band; Mrchg Band; School Musical; Variety Show; High Hon Roll; NHS; Penn ST; Elem Educ.

LARSON, PAULA; Clarion-Limestone HS; Strattanville, PA; (Y); 4/66; Am Leg Aux Girls St; French Clb; Hosp Aide; Band; Concert Band; Mrchg Band; Pep Band; Trk; Hon Roll; NHS; Clarion Lmstn Area; Fbry Achvmnt Awd Advncd Math 86; Clarion Lmstn Area; March Achvmnt Awd 86; Pre-Med.

LARSSON-AYER, LINDA; Lancaster Country Day Schl; St Croix, VI; (Y); Church Yth Grp; 4-H; Intnl Clb; Key Clb; Model UN; School Play; Yrbk Rptr; Yrbk Stf; Lit Mag; Var Bowling; Natl Drssg Fnls 85-86; Vrs Hgh Scr & Hgh Jr Rdr Rdng Hrsbck 85-86; Franklen Coll; Psych.

LASCH, LORI; Nazareth Acad; Philadelphia, PA; (Y); Var Church Yth Grp; Cmnty Wkr; Hosp Aide; Pres Soph Cls; Pres Jr Cls; Stu Cncl; Socr; Hon Roll; GAA; Sec Latin Clb; Magna Cum Laude Awd Latin Natl Exam 85; Peer Counslng 86-87; Med.

LASCO, CORI B; Towando Area HS; Towanda, PA; (Y); Boy Scts; Church Yth Grp; Ski Clb; Bsktbl; Crs Cntry; Trk; Wt Lftg; God Cntry Awd; Bio.

LASCUOLA, GINA; Butler Area SR HS; Butler, PA; (Y); AFS; Cmnty Wkr; Exploring; Office Aide; Pep Clb; SADD; Jr NHS; NHS; Physcl Thrpy.

LASECKI, JOSEPH; Hanover Area HS; Wilkes Barre, PA; (Y); Church Yth Grp; Key Clb; Yrbk Stf; Stu Cncl; Trk; Wt Lftg; High Hon Roll; Hon Roll; NHS; Prfct Atten Awd; Scranton U; Pre Law.

LASEK, RICHARD; Meadville Area SR HS; Meadville, PA; (Y); Science Clb; Chorus; Concert Band; Pres Mrchg Band; Pep Band; Nwsp Phtg; PPG Cmnty Schlrshp 86; Allegheny Coll; Econmcs.

LASH, DINA; Curwensville Area HS; Grampian, PA; (Y); French Clb; Sec VICA; VP Band; Chorus; Concert Band; Drill Tm; Flag Corp; Mrchg Band; Twrlr; PA Acad Costmtlgy; Cosmtlgy.

LASHAY, JACQUELYN; Our Lady Of Lourdes Regional HS; Shamokin, PA; (Y); 37/100; AFS; Camera Clb; Church Yth Grp; Pep Clb; Spanish Clb; Nwsp Stf; Trs Sr Cls; Off Stu Cncl; Cheerleading; Hon Roll; Bus Mgmt.

LASHER, MARY; Warren Area HS; Warren, PA; (Y); French Clb; Acpl Chr; Band; Concert Band; Mrchg Band; Orch; School Musical; Hon Roll; Mercyhurst Coll; Elem Educ.

LASHER, SCOTT; Kittanning SR HS; Adrian, PA; (Y); Church Yth Grp; Cmnty Wkr; JV Ftbl; Wt Lftg; Hon Roll.

LASHER, SUSAN; Ford City JR SR HS; Ford City, PA; (Y); 16/157; AFS; Trs Drama Clb; Chorus; School Musical; Sec Frsh Cls; Rep Soph Cls; Rep Sr Cls; Rep Stu Cncl; L Tennis; NHS; Spcl Actvts Awd 84-86; Hgh Hnr Rl 84-85; Indiana U.

LASITIS, BONNIE; Penn Trafford HS; Irwin, PA; (Y); French Clb; FBLA; Library Aide; Hon Roll; Prfct Atten Awd; Cert Profcncy-Cntry 21 Acctng 85; Jmp Rope Hrt 83-85; Tp Money Raiser Penn Trafford Msclr Dystrphy Asn; Acctng.

LASKAS, KARL M; East Allegheny HS; North Versailles, PA; (Y); 1/209; Chess Clb; Mathletes; Math Clb; Math Tm; Model UN; Political Wkr; Scholastic Bowl; Science Clb; Orch; High Hon Roll; Blk Blt Karate 82; Sci Proj Schl & Mon-Yough Area Wnr 83; Cultrl Art Reflctn Awd Lit 84; Carnegie-Mellon U; Physcs.

LASKEY, CARRIE; Archbishop Prendergast HS; Collingdale, PA; (Y); 32/361; French Clb; Latin Clb; Office Aide; Swmmng; High Hon Roll; Hon Roll; NHS; Prfct Atten Awd; Drexel U Schlrshp 86; U DE Schlrshp 86; U Of DE; Mdcl Tech.

LASKEY, JAYNI; Butler SR HS; Butler, PA; (Y); Church Yth Grp; Trs Exploring; French Clb; Hosp Aide; Library Aide; SADD; Teachers Aide; Hon Roll; Jr NHS; Schlstc Ltr 85; Physcl Thrpy.

LASLO, GREGORY; Annville Cleona HS; Annville, PA; (Y); Camera Clb; Math Tm; SADD; School Musical; Yrbk Phtg; JV Ftbl; Socr; Im Vllybl; Im Wt Lftg; Jr NHS; Bus.

LASPINA, LAZAE; Penn-Trafford HS; Irwin, PA; (Y); 23/328; Pres Drama Clb; Acpl Chr; Chorus; School Musical; School Play; Ed Yrbk Stf; Cheerleading; High Hon Roll; Lion Awd; NHS; PA Gov Schl Arts Schlrshp 85; Westmoreland Co CC Art Show 1st 85 & 3rd 86; Producing.

LASSIGE, DAVID; West Mifflin Area HS; Whitaker, PA; (Y); Boy Scts; Mgr Ftbl; High Hon Roll; Hon Roll; NHS; Altr Boy St Ritas Chrch 83-87; Carnegie Mellon U; Airln Plt.

LASSITER, DEBBIE; Owen J Roberts HS; Pottstown, PA; (Y); 87/270; Yrbk Stf; Hon Roll; Bus Mgmt.

LASSITER, PAMELA; The Perfrming Arts Schl; Willingboro, NJ; (Y); Dance Clb; Drama Clb; Chorus; Variety Show; Pres Frsh Cls; Pres Soph Cls; Pres Jr Cls; High Hon Roll; Hon Roll; Mdrn Dance Awd Excel; U Pittsburgh; Psych.

LASSITER, TRACEY; Creative & Performing Arts HS; Philadelphia, PA; (S); 4/146; Band; Concert Band; Jazz Band; Pres Orch; School Musical; Symp Band; Off Stu Cncl; Gov Hon Prg Awd; High Hon Roll; NHS; Dist 2 Essay Cntst 1st Pl Wnnr 84; Music Prfrmnc.

LASWELL, HEATHER; Gar Memorial HS; Wilkes Barre, PA; (S); 10/187; Chorus; Mgr Bsktbl; L Tennis; Hon Roll; Jr NHS; NHS; Geolgy.

LATIMORE, KAREN; Moniteau HS; W Sunbury, PA; (Y); 13/132; French Clb; Library Aide; Color Guard.

LATSHA, MELISSA; Shikellamy HS; Sunbury, PA; (Y); Chorus; Rep Stu Cncl; NHS; Pres Schlr; Drexel U; Bus Adm.

LATSHA, TIM; Line Mountain HS; Herndon, PA; (S); Church Yth Grp; Computer Clb; FBLA; Trs Chorus; Concert Band; Mrchg Band; School Musical; School Play; Rep Stu Cncl; Stat Bsktbl; Elem Tchr.

LATSHAW, SHANON L; Shamokin Area HS; Shamokin, PA; (Y); 21/251; German Clb; Key Clb; Science Clb; Varsity Clb; Rep Stu Cncl; Var Swmmng; Var Trk; Hon Roll; NHS; Art Clb; Yth Schlrs Bio 86; Psychlgy.

LATSHAW, SHERRY; Pottstown SR HS; Pottstown, PA; (Y); Church Yth Grp; Key Clb; Spanish Clb; Nwsp Stf; Var Tennis; Dist Wnr Natl Hist Day 1st Pl 86; ST Wnr Natl Hist Day 1st Pl 86; Natl Wnr Natl Hist Day 1st Pl 86; Psych.

LATTANZIO, KATHRYN; Danville Area SR HS; Danville, PA; (Y); Cmnty Wkr; Drama Clb; French Clb; Hosp Aide; Ski Clb; School Musical; School Play; Nwsp Ed-Chief; Yrbk Rptr; Rep Jr Cls; Outstndng Wrk Awd Nwspr Staff, Cert Outstndng Wrk SGA 86; Highest GPA Awd Choral Mus 84; Penn ST; Jrnlsm.

LATTANZIO, LORI; Kennett HS; Avondale, PA; (Y); 13/157; Latin Clb; Pres Science Clb; Chorus; Stage Crew; Stu Cncl; Var Trk; High Hon Roll; NHS; Pres Phys Ftnss 83-84; Pres Acadmc Awd 86; PA ST U; Frgn Serv.

LATUSICK, LISA; Our Lady Of The Sacred Heart HS; Mckees Rocks, PA; (Y); Church Yth Grp; Girl Scts; School Musical.

LAU, ELLEN; Cardinal Dougherty HS; Phila, PA; (Y); 22/747; Cmnty Wkr; French Clb; Nwsp Stf; Yrbk Stf; JV Trk; NHS; Drexel U; Bus.

LAUBACH, RACHELLE; Danville SR HS; Riverside, PA; (Y); JV Var Bsktbl; JV Fld Hcky; JV Var Sftbl.

LAUBACH, WENDY; Benton Area JR SR HS; Benton, PA; (Y); 6/54; Sec Church Yth Grp; VP FTA; Keywanettes; Ski Clb; Trs Band; Concert Band; Mrchg Band; Orch; School Musical; School Play; Bloomsburg U; Elem Ed.

LAUBER, KELLYANNE; St Basil Acad; Philadelphia, PA; (S); 20/95; Church Yth Grp; French Clb; German Clb; Hon Roll; Prfct Atten Awd.

LAUDER, ALAN; Unionville HS; Kennett Square, PA; (Y); 1/269; Concert Band; School Play; Stage Crew; Ntl Merit Schol; Val; JA; Band; Mrchg Band; Orch; Pep Band; Amer Chem Scty 86; PA ST U; Engr.

LAUDERBAUGH, LAUREN; Wyoming Valley West HS; Courtdale, PA; (Y); 22/364; Cmnty Wkr; Key Clb; Red Cross Aide; Yrbk Bus Mgr; Lit Mag; Stu Cncl; High Hon Roll; Jr NHS; Pres Schlr; Key Clb Dist Conventn 1st Pl Impromptu Essay Contst 84-86; Moravian Coll Comenius Schlrshp 85-86; Moravian Coll; Jrnlsm.

LAUDERBAUGH, LORI; South Park HS; Library, PA; (S); 12/202; Ski Clb; Sec Sr Cls; JV Capt Vllybl; High Hon Roll; NHS; Med.

LAUDO, LEIGH; West Middlesex HS; W Middlesex, PA; (S); 1/140; Office Aide; Spanish Clb; Chorus; Stu Cncl; High Hon Roll; Jr NHS; NHS; Spanish NHS; Pres Acad Ftns Awd 84-85; Point Park Coll-Pittsbg; Acctg.

LAUER, CONNIE; North Clarion HS; Shippenville, PA; (Y); Camera Clb; Computer Clb; DECA; FHA; Library Aide; Office Aide; Radio Clb; SADD; Y-Teens; Nwsp Stf; Home Ed Clb; Cosmotology.

LAUER, DANAE S; Christian Schl Of York; York, PA; (Y); 15/59; Church Yth Grp; Chorus; School Play; Yrbk Bus Mgr; Rep Stu Cncl; Cheerleading; Hon Roll; Psychlgy.

LAUER, DAVE; Shanksville-Stonycreek HS; Shanksville, PA; (S); 6/31; Aud/Vis; Stage Crew; Nwsp Stf; Stu Cncl; Var JV Bsktbl; Hon Roll; U Of Pittsburgh; Elec Engrng.

LAUER, JULIE; Central York SR HS; York, PA; (Y); Drill Tm; Yrbk Stf; Hon Roll; Allied Hlth.

LAUER, KARLA; East Stroudsburg Area HS; E Stroudsburg, PA; (Y); 3/230; AFS; Intnl Clb; Key Clb; Model UN; Political Wkr; SADD; Yrbk Phtg; High Hon Roll; NHS; Aud/Vis; Johns Hopkins U; Med.

LAUER, KIMBERLY; Northern Lebanon HS; Jonestown, PA; (Y); Church Yth Grp; FBLA; Math Clb; Office Aide; Chorus; JV Var Trk; Hon Roll; Secy.

LAUER, RACHEL; Eastern York HS; York, PA; (Y); Art Clb; Varsity Clb; Band; Concert Band; Mrchg Band; Yrbk Stf; Hst Sr Cls; Var Bsbl; Var Powder Puff Ftbl; Hon Roll; Elem Educ.

LAUFER, WILLIAM; Archbishop Wood HS; Richboro, PA; (Y); 80/342; Church Yth Grp; Computer Clb; Mathletes; Stat Crs Cntry; L Var Mgr(s); Trk; Prfct Atten Awd; Engrng.

LAUFFENBURGER, MICHAEL; General Mclane HS; Edinboro, PA; (Y); 1/240; Church Yth Grp; Computer Clb; German Clb; Office Aide; Quiz Bowl; High Hon Roll; Hon Roll; 2 1st Pl & 1 2nd Pl Slippery Rock U Lang Comp 85 & 86; U NC Chapel Hill; Med.

LAUGHLIN, CATHERINE; Beaver Area JR-SR HS; Beaver, PA; (Y); 3/191; French Clb; FTA; Key Clb; Color Guard; Concert Band; Jazz Band; Lit Mag; DAR Awd; High Hon Roll; Pres NHS; Schlstc Achvt Awd 84-86; Prncpls Awd Excllnc 86; Pres Acad Ftnss Awd 86; Shippensburg U; Math.

LAUGHLIN, JAMES B; South Side HS; Hookstown, PA; (Y); 18/132; Am Leg Boys St; Boy Scts; Band; Pep Band; School Play; Yrbk Bus Mgr; Pres Jr Cls; Hon Roll; NHS; Schl Chrmn Operation Prom Grad; Schl Prog Teen Drinkng & Drvng; Gannon U; Med.

LAUGHMAN, JULIE; West York HS; York, PA; (Y); Church Yth Grp; Cmnty Wkr; JA; Spanish Clb; SADD; Rep Frsh Cls; Rep Soph Cls; Rep Jr Cls; JV Cheerleading; Var Mgr(s); Bst Spnsh Spkr 84-86; York Coll; Lwyr.

LAUGHREY, MICHAEL S; Blackhawk HS; Beaver Falls, PA; (Y); 2/272; Math Tm; Political Wkr; School Play; Yrbk Stf; Pres Stu Cncl; Var Ftbl; L Wrstlng; NHS; Sal; PA Gvrnrs Schl Sci 85; PA Gvrnrs Schl Intl Stud 85; Air Force Acad; Aviatn.

LAUNTZ, MICHELE; Westmont Hilltop HS; Johnstown, PA; (Y); #40 In Class; Key Clb; Pep Clb; Chorus; Color Guard; Variety Show; Cheerleading; Capt Twrlr; Hon Roll; Bus Admn.

LAURENSON, LORI; Upper Dublin HS; Willow Grove, PA; (Y); 26/318; Pres FBLA; Trs Intnl Clb; Varsity Clb; Band; Mrchg Band; Rep Jr Cls; Rep Sr Cls; Mgr(s); Powder Puff Ftbl; Sftbl; Free Entrprs Fllwshp 86; Wall St Smnr 86; Twn Mtng Tmrrw 85; Bus.

LAURENT, DANIEL; Carrick HS; Pittsburgh, PA; (S); French Clb; Q&S; Nwsp Sprt Ed; Yrbk Sprt Ed; Off Jr Cls; Stu Cncl; Trk; High Hon Roll; Hon Roll; Kent ST; Jrnlsm.

LAURIA, JUDI; St Maria Goretti HS; Philadelphia, PA; (Y); Hon Roll; Prfct Atten Awd; Sci.

LAURITO, KIMBERLY; Aliquippa HS; Aliquippa, PA; (Y); French Clb; VICA; Band; Pep Band; Bsktbl; Sftbl.

LAUSCHUS, KIM; Riverview HS; Oakmont, PA; (Y); 15/119; AFS; Pres Drama Clb; French Clb; Chorus; Yrbk Stf; Powder Puff Ftbl; Mgr Vllybl; High Hon Roll; NHS; Intl Frgn Lang Awd 86; Acad All Am 86; Comp Sci.

LAUSO, ROSEANN; West Mifflin Area HS; Pittsburgh, PA; (Y); 14/331; Church Yth Grp; Exploring; Chorus; Yrbk Stf; Off Sr Cls; High Hon Roll; Hon Roll; Jr NHS; NHS; Pres Schlr; PA ST U Mc Keesport Schlrshp 86; Pa ST U.

LAUTENSCHLAGER, ERIC; Carlynton HS; Pittsburgh, PA; (Y).

LAUVER, DANE A; Juniata HS; Thompsontown, PA; (Y); Aud/Vis; Church Yth Grp; Letterman Clb; Varsity Clb; Band; Concert Band; Jazz Band; Mrchg Band; Stage Crew; Rep Jr Cls; Hortcltr.

LAVELLE, DAVID J; Bethel Park HS; Bethel Park, PA; (Y); 70/515; JA; Concert Band; Jazz Band; Mrchg Band; Symp Band; Variety Show; Rep Frsh Cls; French Hon Soc; Hon Roll; Prfct Atten Awd; Percussnst Am Yth Symp Band European Cncrt Tour 85; PA ST U; Intl Affairs.

LAVELLE, KEVIN; North Hills HS; Pittsburgh, PA; (Y); Exploring; Key Clb; ROTC; Ski Clb; JV Var Bsktbl; Miami; Bus.

LAVELLE, TOM; Scranton Prep; Scranton, PA; (Y); 135/192; Var Ftbl; L Trk; Var Wt Lftg; Elctrcl Engr.

LAVER, JULIE; Central SR HS; York, PA; (Y); Color Guard; Yrbk Stf; Hon Roll.

LAVERTY, MICHELLE; Cardinal O Hara HS; Folsom, PA; (Y); 101/772; Church Yth Grp; Yrbk Stf; Im Vllybl; Med.

LAVERY, DENA; Pennsbury HS; Yardley, PA; (Y); Church Yth Grp; Intnl Clb; Service Clb; Chorus; Yrbk Stf; Trk; Hon Roll; Nrsng.

LAVERY, KRISTEN; Lakeland JR SR HS; Carbondale, PA; (S); 16/160; Ski Clb; Teachers Aide; Variety Show; VP Frsh Cls; VP Soph Cls; VP Jr Cls; Stu Cncl; Ftbl; Hon Roll; Prfct Atten Awd; Villanova; Med.

LAVERY, MARK; Notre Dame HS; Palmer, PA; (Y); 6/74; Capt Quiz Bowl; Capt Scholastic Bowl; VP Speech Tm; Rep Sr Cls; Var L Bsbl; Var L Tennis; High Hon Roll; Lion Awd; NHS; Ntl Merit Ltr; Plmr Lions Clb Schlrshp 86; Mst Imprvd-Vrsty Tnns Tm 86; Cert-Outstndng Achvt-SAT 86; U Of Notre Dame; Law.

LAVIN, MEREDITH; Harriton HS; Narberth, PA; (Y); VP Pep Clb; Service Clb; SADD; Sec Temple Yth Grp; Varsity Clb; Nwsp Bus Mgr; VP Stu Cncl; Var Cheerleading; Vrsty Crew 82-86; Rnr-Up Miss PA Pagnt 85; SR Rep Human Concrns Comm 86; Tulane; Lang.

LAVIN, PATRICK; Bishop Shanahan HS; Westchester, PA; (Y); 120/218; Off Stu Cncl; JV Bsbl; JV Ftbl; Rep Jr Cls; Rep Frsh Cls; Psych.

LAVOIE, RACHEL; Cedar Cliff HS; Camp Hill, PA; (Y); 76/272; French Clb; Spanish Clb; Stage Crew; French Hon Soc; High Hon Roll; Johnson & Wales Acad Schlrshp 86; Pres Acad Fit Awd 86; Johnson & Wales Coll; Pstry Art.

LAVRICH, JOANN; Shaler Area SR HS; Pittsburgh, PA; (Y); Acpl Chr; Chorus; Madrigals; School Musical; Swing Chorus; Yrbk Stf; Hon Roll; Spanish NHS; Aerontcl Engrng.

LAW, CHARLES; Blacklick Valley HS; Nanty Glo, PA; (Y); Drama Clb; NFL; Ski Clb; Yrbk Sprt Ed; Var Bsktbl; Capt Crs Cntry; Capt Trk; God Cntry Awd; High Hon Roll; Art Clb; Eagle Scout; Law.

LAW, L KIMBERLY; Hatboro-Horsham SR HS; Horsham, PA; (Y); 4/276; French Clb; Key Clb; Chorus; Mrchg Band; School Musical; Vllybl; Cit Awd; High Hon Roll; NHS; Pres Acadmc Ftns Awd 86; Hm & Schl Assn Awd 86; Champ Of Lrng Awds-Band, Psych, Math, Econ, Etc 86; Lafayette Coll.

LAW III, LA MAR DAVID; Cumberland Valley HS; Mechanicsburg, PA; (Y); Key Clb; Ski Clb; Var L Ftbl; Im Vllybl; Im Wt Lftg.

LAW, WILLIAM; Red Land HS; Etters, PA; (Y); 17/285; Boy Scts; JV Ftbl; Var L Swmmng; Var Trk; Im Wt Lftg; God Cntry Awd; High Hon Roll; Prfct Atten Awd; Shppnsbrg Forgn Lang Comptn 1st Pl Grmn Comptn 84-85; Mech Engrng.

LAWBAUGH, JOHN J; Carson Long Military Inst; Dickerson, MD; (Y); 9/50; Boy Scts; ROTC; Varsity Clb; Nwsp Phtg; Yrbk Phtg; VP Frsh Cls; Rep Jr Cls; Var L Socr; High Hon Roll; Pres Schlr; Awd Mbrshp Schls Hs Rprsntvs 85-86; Awd Bng Appntd Cmndr Drll Tm 83-86; Mltry.

LAWER, JON; Shikellamy HS; Sunbury, PA; (Y); Church Yth Grp; Varsity Clb; Stu Cncl; Bsktbl; Ftbl; Tennis; Trk; High Hon Roll; Hon Roll; PA ST; Aerospc Engnrng.

LAWLEY, LORIANN; Villa Joseph Marie HS; Churchville, PA; (S); Art Clb; Church Yth Grp; Drama Clb; Library Aide; Off Chorus; School Musical; School Play; Stage Crew; Art Enrgyy Awd 84; Stg Mgr Awd-Glee Clb 85; Glee Clb Awd 84; Marine Bio.

LAWLOR, ERINNE; Greenwood HS; Millerstown, PA; (S); 2/65; GAA; Varsity Clb; Trs Soph Cls; Trs Jr Cls; Var Bsktbl; Var Fld Hcky; Var Sftbl; Hon Roll; Trs NHS.

LAWLOR, KELLY E; Little Flower HS; Philadelphia, PA; (Y); 20/313; German Clb; Library Aide; Office Aide; Teachers Aide; Chorus; Church Choir; School Musical; Variety Show; Off Sr Cls; Hon Roll; Coll Perf Arts; Dance.

LAWRENCE, AMY; Manheim Townshiop HS; Lancaster, PA; (Y); 18/365; Nwsp Phtg; Rep Jr Cls; Rep Sr Cls; Stu Cncl; Var L Diving; Var Trk; High Hon Roll; Hon Roll; NHS; Nwsp Rptr; Schlstc Gld Key Wnr Photgrphy 86; Chem Engrg.

LAWRENCE, BROOKS; Hampton HS; Allison Pk, PA; (Y); Ski Clb; Spanish Clb; Concert Band; Mrchg Band; Var Socr; PA ST U; Arch.

LAWRENCE, CAROL; Villa Maria HS; Youngstown, OH; (Y); 7/24; Drama Clb; Sec French Clb; Hosp Aide; Red Cross Aide; Thesps; School Musical; School Play; Stage Crew; VP Sr Cls; Mgr Tennis; Sr Yr 86; 2-Str Thespn 86; John Carroll U; Educ.

LAWRENCE, CHRISTOPHER S; Troy Area HS; Columbia C R, PA; (Y); Hon Roll; NHS; Ntl Merit Ltr; Am Lgn Axlry Esy Awd 86; Prsdntl Acad Ftns Awd; Pennsylvania ST U.

LAWRENCE, DAVID; Hempfield HS; Lancaster, PA; (Y); 3/450; Church Yth Grp; Science Clb; Stu Cncl; JV Socr; High Hon Roll; NHS; Ppl To Ppl Ambssdr To Erp 86; Sx Awds Sci Fr 85; Premed.

LAWRENCE, ERIC W; Gateway SR HS; Monroeville, PA; (Y); 7/432; Boy Scts; Chess Clb; Computer Clb; Exploring; Math Clb; Science Clb; Concert Band; Mrchg Band; Orch; Im Sftbl; Physics Cntt Awd 85; Penn ST U; Chem Engr.

LAWRENCE, KATHRYN; Hanover HS; Hanover, PA; (Y); Mrchg Band; School Play; VP Soph Cls; Pres Jr Cls; Pres Sr Cls; Bausch & Lomb Sci Awd; High Hon Roll; NHS; Ntl Merit Ltr; NEDT Awd; Bst Drctr Awd 85-86; Engr.

LAWRENCE, KIMBOL; Gateway SR HS; Houston, TX; (Y); 16/431; Girl Scts; Acpl Chr; Madrigals; Orch; Ed Lit Mag; Var L Swmmng; High Hon Roll; NHS; Ntl Merit Schol; Model UN; Girl Scout Gold Awd 86; Regnl Chorus 86; WPIAL Qualifr Swmng 85-86; Rice U; English.

LAWRENCE, LEIGH A; Wyoming Seminary; Kingston, PA; (Y); 16/98; Church Yth Grp; Cmnty Wkr; Hosp Aide; Varsity Clb; Nwsp Rptr; Capt Var Fld Hcky; Cit Awd; Hon Roll; NHS; NEDT Awd; MVP Hocky Game 85; Feml Athlt Of Yr 85-86; Schlrshp Awd Grad 86; Bucknell U; Chem.

LAWRENCE, SALLY; Wilmington Area HS; Pulaski, PA; (S); French Clb; Trs Jr Cls; JV Cheerleading; High Hon Roll; Hon Roll; Youngstown ST U; Comp Tech.

LAWRENCE, THOMAS; Delone Catholic HS; New Oxford, PA; (Y); 18/168; Bsktbl; Ftbl; Hon Roll; Trs NHS; George A Goodling Scholar 86; Outstndng Scholar Sthestrn PA Sectn Chem Soc 85; Pres Acad Fit Awd 86; PA ST; Engrng.

LAWRENZI, LISA; Yough HS; Lowber, PA; (Y); 23/253; Debate Tm; Drama Clb; 4-H; French Clb; Concert Band; Mrchg Band; Symp Band; Var Capt Bsktbl; Powder Puff Ftbl; Var L Sftbl; Nrsg.

LAWSON, BETH; Middletown Area HS; Middletown, PA; (Y); VP Key Clb; Chorus; Color Guard; Nwsp Stf; Yrbk Stf; Var JV Gym; Var JV Trk; Outstndng Literary Awd 86; JV Lettr Gymnastics 84; Modern Miss Schlrshp Pgnt 85; Duquesne U; Jrnlsm.

LAWSON, ERIC; Hanover Area JR SR HS; Ashley, PA; (Y); 18/156; Cmnty Wkr; Sec Key Clb; Trs Jr Cls; Var L Bsbl; Var L Bsktbl; Ftbl; High Hon Roll; Jr NHS; NHS; WY Vly All Schlstc Bsktbl 1st Tm 85-86; Pace Setters Bsktbl Tm; Bus.

LAWSON, JEANNE; Liverty JR SR HS; Liberty, PA; (Y); Rep FHA; German Clb; Stu Cncl; Bsktbl; Capt Cheerleading; Sftbl; Trk; Vllybl; Hon Roll; Bus Mgmt.

LAWSON, LISA; Charleroi Area HS; Charleroi, PA; (Y); Ski Clb; Spanish Clb; SADD; Capt Color Guard; Nwsp Stf; Yrbk Stf; Off Soph Cls; Off Jr Cls; Off Sr Cls; Hon Roll; Spnsh Trnsltn.

LAWSON, ROBYN; Archbishop Carroll For Girls; Philadelphia, PA; (Y); Rep French Clb; Office Aide; Band; Chorus; Concert Band; Cit Awd; Prfct Atten Awd; Close Up VP; PA ST U; Bus Adm.

LAWSON, ROSE; Northern Lebanon HS; Fredericksburg, PA; (Y); #44 In Class; French Clb; German Clb; Spanish Clb; Chorus; School Musical; School Play; Stage Crew; Yrbk Phtg; Yrbk Rptr; Yrbk Stf.

LAWTON, DENNIS; Fort Le Boeuf HS; Waterford, PA; (Y); 37/180; Camera Clb; Chess Clb; Church Yth Grp; Computer Clb; Yrbk Phtg; Trk; Hon Roll; Prfct Atten Awd; Woodwrkng Awd 86; Moody Bible Inst; Intl Ministrs.

LAWTON, DENNIS; South Moreland HS; Scottdale, PA; (Y); JCL; Latin Clb; Letterman Clb; Math Clb; Im Ftbl; Var L Socr; Var L Trk.

LAWTON, MICAH; William Penn HS; Philadelphia, PA; (Y); 9/239; Aud/Vis; Capt Stage Crew; Rep Stu Cncl; JV Bsktbl; Tennis; Ntl Freedom Day Mtchg Schlrshp 86; Albert J D Nuncio Meml Awd 86; Samuel Malkin Almni Awd 86; Villanova U; Sprtscstg.

LAWVER, WAYNE; Littlestown SR HS; Littlestown, PA; (Y); 7/142; Math Tm; Varsity Clb; Drm & Bgl; Mrchg Band; School Musical; School Play; Capt Var Bsbl; Capt Var Wrstlng; Hon Roll; NHS; Pres Acad Ftns Awd 86; Pres Physcl Ftns Awd 86.

LAY, JOYCE; Abiquippa HS; Aliquippa, PA; (Y); DECA; Drama Clb; Pom Pon; Hon Roll; Quipprhrs Sec & Co Capt 86-87; Bradford; Bus.

LAY, KEVIN; Big Spring HS; Newville, PA; (Y); 19/213; Church Yth Grp; Civic Clb; Ski Clb; Band; Concert Band; Mrchg Band; Pep Band; Var Wrstlng; Hon Roll; NHS; Richard Loy Cmmnty & Svc Awd 86; Harrisburg Area CC; Bus Mgmt.

LAY, LISA; Carlynton JR SR HS; Carnegie, PA; (Y); 40/172; French Clb; Girl Scts; Drill Tm; Rep Stu Cncl; Psych.

LAY, SHEILA; Aliquippa HS; Aliquippa, PA; (S); 7/155; DECA; Pres French Clb; SADD; Off Jr Cls; Off Sr Cls; Bsktbl; Hon Roll; Jr NHS; Lion Awd; NHS; NAACP Awd Outstndg Achvmnts 85; Wilber Force U; Accntng.

LAYAOU, MARY JANE; Tunkhannock HS; Tunkhannock, PA; (Y); 56/315; Key Clb; Soph Cls; Sr Cls; Score Keeper; Var Vllybl; Hon Roll; NHS; Wilkes Coll; Math.

LAYTON, CHRISTINA LYNN; Everett Area HS; Everett, PA; (Y); Spanish Clb; Band; Chorus; Concert Band; Drm Mjr(t); Mrchg Band; Pep Band; Stat Mgr(s); Trk; Hon Roll; Cnty Band; Co-Capt Of Mjrtt Squad; Allgny Comm Coll; Med Secy.

LAYTON, JOY; Garden Spot HS; New Holland, PA; (Y); 51/218; Church Yth Grp; Trs 4-H; Girl Scts; Chorus; 4-H Awd; Hon Roll; Jr NHS; Grange Actvty Offcr; Hm Ecnmcs.

LAZAR, MATTHEW G; Bishop Hafey HS; Beaver Meadows, PA; (Y); 22/182; Church Yth Grp; Capt Debate Tm; Drama Clb; Math Clb; Model UN; Spanish Clb; Speech Tm; SADD; Thesps; Chorus; Am Leg Awd 82; Temple; Orthdntst.

LAZARCHICK, LORI; Minersville Area HS; Pottsville, PA; (Y); #5 In Class; Dance Clb; Sec French Clb; JCL; School Musical; Rep Stu Cncl; Var Capt Cheerleading; JV Vllybl; French Hon Soc; Hon Roll; NHS; Am Leg Awd 83; Fr Awd 84-86; FBLA Reg Typg Awd; Law.

LAZARUS, JENN; Marple Newtown SR HS; Broomall, PA; (Y); ROTC; Chorus; Variety Show; Stu Cncl; High Hon Roll; Hon Roll; Jr NHS; Tutonal Clb 85-86; Tennis Mgr.

LAZARUS, LAURA; Harriton HS; Rosemont, PA; (Y); Off Yrbk Bus Mgr; Yrbk Stf; Rep Frsh Cls; Rep Soph Cls; Rep Jr Cls; Rep Sr Cls; Tennis; Jr NHS; Intl Bus.

LAZICKI, TAMMY; Our Lady Of Lourdes HS; Ranshaw, PA; (Y); 1/98; Cmnty Wkr; Pep Clb; Spanish Clb; Nwsp Ed-Chief; Rep Soph Cls; High Hon Roll; VP NHS; Spanish NHS; Acad All Amer 85-86; Duquesne; Law.

LAZOR, AMY L; Greensburg Central Catholic HS; Greensburg, PA; (Y); 34/244; Chess Clb; Church Yth Grp; Computer Clb; Hosp Aide; JCL; Yrbk Ed-Chief; Im Bsktbl; High Hon Roll; NHS; Dept Awd For Jrnlsm 86; U Ptsbrg; Engrng.

LAZOR, JENNIFER; Geibel HS; Connellsville, PA; (Y); French Clb; Yrbk Stf; Cheerleading; JV Vllybl; French Hon Soc; Hon Roll; St Francis Clg.

LAZOR, LISETTE M; Parkland HS; Allentown, PA; (Y); Hosp Aide; JCL; Key Clb; Library Aide; Ed Lit Mag; Opt Clb Awd; Kutztown ST U; Librarian.

LAZOR, NICK; Vincentian HS; Pittsburgh, PA; (Y); NFL; Band; Church Choir; Im Ftbl; Bio.

LAZOR, SUSAN; Biship Carroll HS; Ebensburg, PA; (S); 13/102; Drama Clb; NFL; Science Clb; Ski Clb; SADD; High Hon Roll; NHS; Dance Clb; Red Cross Aide; Spch Awd 85; Sci Awd 85; Lab Inst Merchnds; Fshn Mrchnds.

LAZUR, TARA; Elizabeth Forward HS; Elizabeth, PA; (Y); Office Aide; Ski Clb; Color Guard; Yrbk Stf; Var Swmmng; Hon Roll; Teach.

LAZZARETTI, JUDY; Our Lady Of The Sacred Heart HS; Ambridge, PA; (Y); 11/58; Capt NFL; Chorus; School Play; Yrbk Rptr; VP Sr Cls; NHS; Voice Dem Awd; Var Bsktbl; Bowling; Acad Engl Awd 85-86; Acad All-Amer 85-86; Vet.

LE, HUONG; St Benedict Acad; Erie, PA; (Y); Model UN; Trs Sr Cls; Stu Cncl; Cheerleading; Tennis; Hon Roll; NHS; Prfct Atten Awd; Math Awd 85-86; Ganon; Phrmcst.

LE, LY; Philadelphia H S For Girls; Philadelphia, PA; (Y); Art Clb; Church Yth Grp; Dance Clb; French Clb; Girl Scts; JA; Math Clb; Gym; French Hon Soc; High Hon Roll; Music Awd Hnr Roll 83-85.

LE, THANG; Upper Darby HS; Drexel Hill, PA; (Y); 6/600; Chess Clb; Computer Clb; JA; Science Clb; JV Var Tennis; High Hon Roll; Hon Roll; NHS; Ntl Merit Ltr; Awds Physcs II & Calculus II 86; Aronimink Hm & Schl Schlrshp 86; Calculus I Awd 85; U Of PA; Engnrng.

LE, TRANG; Somerset Area SR HS; Somerset, PA; (Y); 9/230; French Clb; Math Clb; Q&S; Soroptimist; Yrbk Stf; Var L Tennis; High Hon Roll; Mu Alp Tht; NHS; Library Aide; Pres Acad Ftns Awd 85-86; Franklin/Marshall Coll; Pre-Med.

LE CALSEY, CHRISTOPHER; Manheim Township HS; Lancaster, PA; (Y); Boy Scts; Letterman Clb; Varsity Clb; High Hon Roll; Hon Roll; People To People 85; Rifle Tm 83-86; Enrchmnt Pgm 83-86.

LE FEBURE, JEROME; Western Beaver JR SR HS; Industry, PA; (Y); Band; Concert Band; Jazz Band; Mrchg Band; Stage Crew; Mgr(s); Var Wt Lftg; High Hon Roll; NHS; Prfct Atten Awd.

LE FEBVRE, MARIE T; Hatboro-Horsham SR HS; Horsham, PA; (Y); 53/273; Art Clb; Teachers Aide; School Musical; Mgr(s); Var Sftbl; Cit Awd; Hon Roll.

LE FEVRE, DAWN; Wm Allen HS; Allentown, PA; (Y); 29/560; Drama Clb; Exploring; Intnl Clb; Sec Concert Band; Jazz Band; Sec Mrchg Band; Hon Roll; Jr NHS; NHS; U Of Bridgeport CT.

LE GENDRE, DANIELLE; Upper Merion Area HS; King Of Prussia, PA; (Y); #89 In Class; Church Yth Grp; Cmnty Wkr; Var Socr; Var Capt Swmmng; Spcl Educ.

LE VAN, TANYA; Jersey Shore SR HS; Jersey Shore, PA; (Y); FBLA; Letterman Clb; Model UN; Rep Frsh Cls; Rep Soph Cls; Rep Jr Cls; Rep Stu Cncl; Crs Cntry; Mat Maids; Var Capt Trk; Psychlgy.

LEA, CATHERINE; Cecilian Acad; Philadelphia, PA; (S); 1/51; FBLA; VP Service Clb; Yrbk Stf; Im Vllybl; Hon Roll; Pres NHS; NEDT Awd; Prfct Atten Awd; Gnrl Excllnc 82-85; Math Hghst Stu Awd 82-85; La Salle U; Bus Mgmt.

LEACH, JAMES A; Slippery Rock HS; Portersville, PA; (Y); Am Leg Boys St; Aud/Vis; Exploring; Stage Crew; Nwsp Stf; JV Wrstlng; Hon Roll; Syracuse U; Aerospace Engrng.

LEADBITTER, PATRICK J; Canon Mcmillan HS; Mc Donald, PA; (Y); Science Clb; Varsity Clb; School Play; Var L Ftbl; L Var Trk; High Hon Roll; NHS; NEDT Awd; Allegheny Coll; Pre-Med.

LEAHY, ELIZABETH; York Catholic HS; York, PA; (Y); 15/160; Church Yth Grp; Debate Tm; French Clb; Girl Scts; Hosp Aide; Pep Clb; Varsity Clb; Chorus; School Musical; Nwsp Stf; Hon Mntn Relgn & Biol Scis 86; Temple U; Phys Ther.

LEAKEY, LESTIE; Garden Spot HS; Blue Ball, PA; (Y); Cmnty Wkr; Rep Off Drama Clb; Teachers Aide; Chorus; School Musical; School Play; Variety Show; Nwsp Stf; Yrbk Stf; Stat Mgr(s); Sign Lng Clb 83; Ktztwn ST U; Spec Ed Tchr.

LEAMAN, SHERRI; Halifax HS; Halifax, PA; (Y); 14/99; FTA; Pep Clb; Spanish Clb; Chorus; Capt Flag Corp; Rptr Yrbk Stf; Powder Puff Ftbl; Im Tennis; Hon Roll; Ltr Bndfrnt 86; Ldrshp Awd Bndfrnt 86; Clncl Phrmcst.

LEAMER, KIM; Northern Cambria HS; Barnesboro, PA; (Y); Pres Church Yth Grp; Drama Clb; French Clb; Hosp Aide; NFL; Band; Mrchg Band; Symp Band; Yrbk Stf; Rep Stu Cncl; ST Hstry Day 84; Conemaugh Vly Memrl Hosp; Nrsng.

LEANCH, DEAN; William Allen HS; Allentown, PA; (Y); Intnl Clb; JCL; Church Choir; JV Ftbl; Hon Roll; ORU; Thlgy.

LEANDRO, PAULO; Cambridge Springs HS; Cambridge Springs, PA; (Y); 2/101; French Clb; Pep Clb; Var Capt Bsktbl; Var Vllybl; Hon Roll; NHS; Prfct Atten Awd.

LEAP, KATHLEEN; Greater Johnstown HS; Johnstown, PA; (Y); 5/286; Sec Church Yth Grp; German Clb; Math Clb; Orch; Stu Cncl; Mgr Bsktbl; Mgr Sftbl; Var L Tennis; NHS; Ntl Merit Schol; Highest Hnr Rll; Alumni Schlrshp; U Of Pittsburgh; Math.

LEAP, TINA; Tyrone Area JR-SR HS; Tyrone, PA; (Y); Key Clb; Speech Tm; Band; Chorus; Concert Band; Mrchg Band; School Musical; Hon Roll; JP Sousa Awd; US Marine Corps Smpr Fdls Music Awd 86; Dist Bnd 85-86; Rgnl Bnd 85-86; W Chester U; Music Ed.

LEAR, HEATHER; Crestwood HS; Mountaintop, PA; (Y); Trs Church Yth Grp; Pres Key Clb; Band; Chorus; Church Choir; Color Guard; Concert Band; Mrchg Band; School Musical; School Play; Meterology.

LEAR, MICHAEL; Meyersdale Area HS; Garrett, PA; (S); Church Yth Grp; French Clb; Band; Concert Band; Mrchg Band; Pep Band; Bsktbl; Cit Awd; Hon Roll; WV U; Hist.

LEARD, HOLLY; Freeport Area SR HS; Worthington, PA; (Y); 13/170; Pres Church Yth Grp; Hosp Aide; Church Choir; Nwsp Ed-Chief; Nwsp Rptr; Yrbk Stf; High Hon Roll; Hon Roll; Jr NHS; NHS; Stu Mnth 85; Grove City Coll; Elem Ed.

LEARDI, KATHLEEN; Cardinal O Hara HS; Springfield, PA; (Y); 6/772; JA; Band; School Musical; Pres Frsh Cls; Pres Soph Cls; Pres Jr Cls; Pres Sr Cls; Pres Stu Cncl; Swmmng; High Hon Roll; Hi-Q Tm 85-86; Chnnl 6 Whiz Kid 86; Pre-Med.

LEARN, JENNIFER; Weatherly HS; Weatherly, PA; (S); 2/73; FBLA; FHA; Concert Band; Yrbk Stf; Rep Frsh Cls; Var Mgr(s); Twrlr; High Hon Roll; NCTE Awd; NHS; Comm Concert Assn Mbrshp Awd 85; PA ST U; Engrng.

LEARN, JERRY; Purchase Line HS; Commodore, PA; (Y); 4-H; Scholastic Bowl; Spanish Clb; Band; Concert Band; Mrchg Band; Nwsp Rptr; Var Trk; Hon Roll; NHS; Penn ST U; Arch.

LEARN, KENNETH; Curwensville Area HS; Curwensville, PA; (Y); 7/110; Computer Clb; French Clb; Var L Bsktbl; High Hon Roll; NHS; Bus.

LEARN, PAM; Weatherly HS; Weatherly, PA; (S); 8/58; FBLA; FNA; Church Choir; Pres Frsh Cls; VP Soph Cls; VP Jr Cls; Stu Cncl; Crs Cntry; Hon Roll; Hlth Fields.

LEARN, PENNY; Punxsutawney Area HS; Punxsutawney, PA; (Y); French Clb; Math Tm; Science Clb; Band; Concert Band; Mrchg Band; Pep Band; Stat Wrstlng; Hon Roll; NHS; IN U PA Hnrs Band; Dist Band; Regnl II & III Band; Bio.

LEARY, MAUREEN; Lampeter-Strasburg HS; Lancaster, PA; (Y); 4/158; Ed Yrbk Rptr; Ed Lit Mag; Tennis; Hon Roll; Natl Merit Cmmnded Stu, Hnbl Mntn Sr Short Story-Loc Schlstc Wrtng Awd.

LEARY, PAUL; United HS; Blairsville, PA; (Y); 14/129; Letterman Clb; Library Aide; JV Var Ftbl; L Var Trk; Wt Lftg; High Hon Roll; Hon Roll; Pres Schlr; Ken Lantzey All Star Ftbll Tm 85; All Conf 1st Tm 85; Washington & Jefferson; Accntng.

LEAS, NOEL; Lackawana Trail JR SR HS; Dalton, PA; (Y); 1/95; Art Clb; French Clb; Library Aide; Band; Mrchg Band; French Hon Soc; High Hon Roll; Hon Roll; NHS; Acad All-Amer Awd 86; U Of Ptsbrgh; Phrmctcls.

LEASE, MINDY; Freedom HS; Bethlehem, PA; (Y); 106/445; Church Yth Grp; Band; Concert Band; Jazz Band; Mrchg Band; Pep Band; Hon Roll; Northeastern U; Med Tech.

LEASGANG, LISA; St Marys Area HS; Kersey, PA; (Y); Trs Sec Church Yth Grp; Var Cheerleading; Cit Awd; Hon Roll; Wrd Prcsr.

LEASURE, MICHAEL; North Star HS; Boswell, PA; (Y); 17/180; FCA; Spanish Clb; Ftbl; Cit Awd; Hon Roll; PTI; Drftg.

LEASURE, SONJA; Sheffield Area JR-SR HS; Sheffield, PA; (Y); Church Yth Grp; FHA; Hosp Aide; Pep Clb; SADD; Acpl Chr; Band; Color Guard; Mrchg Band; Yrbk Stf; Nrsng.

LEATHERMAN, GERRY S; Lancaster Mennonite HS; Coatesville, PA; (Y); Church Yth Grp; Acpl Chr; Orch; School Play; Chess Clb; Chorus; High Hon Roll; Hon Roll; NHS; Ntl Merit SF; Hans Herr Schlrshp 83; Merit Awd 83; Goshen Coll; Elec Engr.

LEATHERMAN, NEAL; Word Of Life Christian Acad; Tamaqua, PA; (S); Church Yth Grp; Spanish Clb; Yrbk Stf; Hon Roll.

LEATHERS, JOY; High Point Baptist Acad HS; Birdsboro, PA; (S); 2/32; Church Yth Grp; Chorus; Church Choir; Yrbk Stf; VP Frsh Cls; Sec Jr Cls; Var Capt Cheerleading; High Hon Roll; Amer Christian Hon Soc 85; Bob Jones U; Music.

LEAVENWORTH, TAMMY; Bald Eagle-Nittany HS; Beech Creek, PA; (Y); 4-H; Band; Concert Band; Drm Mjr(t); Mrchg Band; Pep Band; School Play; Stage Crew; Twrlr; Shippensburg U.

LEBBON, LEE T; Bethel Park SR HS; Pittsburgh, PA; (Y); 54/515; Spanish Clb; Bsktbl; Trk; DAR Awd; High Hon Roll; NHS; U Of CO; Bio Sci.

LEBDA, ROBYN; Moshannon Valley JR-SR HS; Smoke Run, PA; (Y); 15/133; SADD; Varsity Clb; VICA; Band; Capt Co-Capt Color Guard; Concert Band; Nwsp Stf; Stat Bsktbl; High Hon Roll; Hon Roll; Altoona Schl/Commerce; Sec.

LEBDER, STEPHEN; Plum SR HS; Pittsburgh, PA; (Y); 9/388; VP JA; VP Science Clb; Band; Mrchg Band; Symp Band; Var Trk; NHS; NEDT Awd; All Amer Band Awd 86; Rifle Tm 86.

LEBEC, MIKE; Canon Mc Millan HS; Canonsburg, PA; (Y); Drama Clb; SADD; Varsity Clb; School Play; Var Bsktbl; High Hon Roll; Grove City Coll; Bio.

LEBEDDA, JEFF; Steel Valley HS; Munhall, PA; (Y); 36/220; Tennis; Vllybl; Hnr Mntn Hmstd Hist Soc Essay 8; U Of Pittsburgh; Media Arts.

LEBER, BRAD; Eastern York JR SR HS; Hellam, PA; (Y); 11/126; JV Bsbl; Pres Jr NHS; Hnr Grad 86; Pres Acad Fit Awd 86; Millersville U; Biol.

LEBER, JILL; South Park HS; Library, PA; (S); 30/210; Ski Clb; Color Guard; Nwsp Stf; Yrbk Stf; Tennis; Hon Roll; NHS; Sec Frsh Cls; Trs Jr Cls; Sec Stu Cncl; Law.

LEBO, GARRISON; Halifax Area HS; Halifax, PA; (Y); Boy Scts; Drama Clb; French Clb; FHA; Varsity Clb; Concert Band; Ftbl; Wt Lftg; Wrstlng; All Conf Ftbll 1st Tm 85; Bus Adm.

LEBO, NICOLE; Tulphhocken HS; Fredericksburg, PA; (Y); Church Yth Grp; Girl Scts; Band; Fld Hcky; Sftbl; Hon Roll; Cild Care Center.

LEBO, SHARON; Millersburg Area HS; Millersburg, PA; (S); 2/80; Sec Church Yth Grp; NFL; Trs Spanish Clb; Band; Concert Band; Jazz Band; Mrchg Band; Stage Crew; Stu Cncl; Capt Trk; Amer Legn Awd; Psychlgy.

LEBRON, JOSE; Parkway Program Unit Zeta HS; Philadelphia, PA; (Y); Math Clb; U Of Penn; Acctng.

LECHEL, DANIELLE; Greensburg Central Cath HS; Levelgreen, PA; (Y); VP Pres AFS; Pres Church Yth Grp; Cmnty Wkr; Pres JCL; Latin Clb; SADD; Rep Frsh Cls; Rep Jr Cls; Trs Sec Stu Cncl; Trk.

LECHLEITNER, KAREN; North Pocono HS; Moscow, PA; (Y); 23/250; Varsity Clb; Pres Soph Cls; Pres Jr Cls; Rep Stu Cncl; Var Capt Cheerleading; Hon Roll; NHS; Voice Dem Awd; Mst Outstndng Chrldr Awd 84; Mst Cngnl Chrldr Awd 83; Rep PA Schl Brds Assoc 84; Bloomsburg U; Acctng.

LECHMAN, ERIC R; Center HS; Aliquippa, PA; (Y); Am Leg Boys St; German Clb; School Musical; Im Bsktbl; Im Bowling; Hon Roll; NHS; Med Field.

LECHNER, AMY; Shenango JR SR HS; Wampum, PA; (Y); Church Yth Grp; Sec VP 4-H; Office Aide; Teachers Aide; Chorus; Church Choir; Yrbk Stf; 4-H Awd; Hon Roll; EARLY Chld Dvlpmnt.

LECHNER, BRIAN; Bradford Area HS; Bradford, PA; (Y); Key Clb; Im Vllybl; Letter-Rfle Team 85; Drftng.

LECHNER, LYNN; Saucon Valley SR HS; Hellertown, PA; (Y); 13/146; Hosp Aide; Spanish Clb; Nwsp Stf; Mgr(s); Stat Mgr Wrstlng; High Hon Roll; Hon Roll; Jr NHS; NHS; Elem Ed.

LECKER, MELISSA; Elk County Chrisitan HS; St Marys, PA; (Y); Dance Clb; 4-H; JA; Key Clb; Library Aide; SADD; Yrbk Stf; 4-H Awd; Hon Roll; Pres Schlr; Dr Howard Mem Schlrshp 86; Grad Cum Laude 86; IN U; Med Tech.

LECKEY, RONALD; Portage Area HS; Portage, PA; (S); 10/127; Trs Church Yth Grp; Cmnty Wkr; French Clb; Varsity Clb; L Ftbl; Im Socr; L Wrstlng; Hon Roll; NHS; Acad All Amer Schlr Pgm 85-86; Bio.

LECKY, JOHN H; Harrtion HS; Gladwyne, PA; (Y); Socr; Wrstlng; Hon Roll; NHS; Ntl Merit SF; Engnrng.

LECOMPTE, MEMOREE; Punxsutawney Area HS; Punxsutawney, PA; (Y); Spanish Clb; Band; Color Guard; Mrchg Band; Trk; Twrlr; Art Inst In Pittsbrugh; Int Dsg.

LEDBETTER, WILLIAM; Cambridge Springs HS; Saegertown, PA; (Y); Pep Clb; Spanish Clb; SADD; School Play; JV Ftbl; JV Wrstlng; Hon Roll; Comp Prgrmg.

LEDFORD, NANCY MELINDA; Owen J Roberts HS; Pottstown, PA; (Y); 55/264; Library Aide; Concert Band; Mrchg Band; Symp Band; Im Vllybl; Hon Roll; Anchr Clb & Sfty Comm; Nrsg Awd From Norchester Opti Mrs; Reading Hosp Schl Nrsg; Nrsg.

LEDNOVICH, MELISSA; Valley View JR SR HS; Peckville, PA; (Y); 7/201; Dance Clb; FBLA; Spanish Clb; Yrbk Stf; High Hon Roll; NHS; Pres Schlr; Blakely Borough Schlrshp 86; U Scranton; Psychrst.

LEDONNE, GINA; Hampton HS; Allison Pk, PA; (Y); Pep Clb; Ski Clb; Varsity Clb; Yrbk Stf; Var Capt Cheerleading; Gym; Capt Powder Puff Ftbl; Trk; High Hon Roll; Hon Roll.

LEE, BILL; Palmyra HS; Palmyra, PA; (Y); 43/220; German Clb; Chorus; Var L Bsktbl; Var Ftbl; Var L Trk; Hon Roll; Pre-Law.

LEE, BRUCE; Upper Dublin SR HS; Ft Washington, PA; (Y); Church Yth Grp; FBLA; Ski Clb; Rep Jr Cls; Bsbl; Socr; Trk; Vllybl; Natl Sci Mrt Awd; Hlth Phy Ed Awd; IN U; Bus Admn.

LEE, CHARLES P; La Salle HS; Southampton, PA; (Y); 7/214; Cmnty Wkr; Nwsp Stf; Yrbk Stf; Var L Swmmng; High Hon Roll; NHS; Union Leag PA Good Ctznshp Awd 85; U S Air Frc Acad 86; Ntl Merit Schlrshp Fnlst 86; U S Air Force Acad; Intl Affrs.

LEE, CHESTER; Moon SR HS; Corapolis, PA; (Y); 1/350; Computer Clb; JA; Orch; Yrbk Phtg; High Hon Roll; NHS; Ntl Merit SF; Val; Westinghse Sci Hnrs Inst 86.

LEE, CHI; Central HS; Philadelphia, PA; (Y); Chess Clb; Latin Clb; Library Aide; Math Clb; Math Tm; Science Clb; Teachers Aide; Lit Mag; Hon Roll; Phila City Schlrshps 86-90; Cert Of Traing Smmr Sci Acad CC Phila 85; U Of PA; Elctrcl Engrng.

LEE, CRAIG C; State College SR HS; State College, PA; (Y); 137/580; Boy Scts; Math Clb; Ski Clb; Band; Concert Band; Mrchg Band; Yrbk Stf; Hon Roll; NEDT Awd; Dist Supr Ntl Fratnty Of Muscns 85; PA ST; Acctg.

LEE, DAVID; Exeter Township SR HS; Reading, PA; (Y); 7/210; Trs Key Clb; Chorus; Orch; Var Golf; Var Capt Tennis; NHS; Ntl Merit SF; Hosp Aide; Math Tm; Quiz Bowl; All ST Orchstr 12 Regn Iv Orch 10,11,12 Dist; Berks Cnty Dbls Cham Tnns 85; Keyclb PA Dist 1st Pl 85; U PA; Bio.

LEE, DEANNA; William Allen HS; Allentown, PA; (Y); Church Yth Grp; Exploring; FBLA; Leo Clb; Chorus; Church Choir; Madrigals; School Musical; School Play; Swing Chorus; Secr.

LEE, DENNIS; Monaca JR SR HS; Monaca, PA; (Y); Band; Concert Band; Mrchg Band; Orch; Pep Band; Stage Crew; Symp Band; Hon Roll; Pittsburgh Tech Inst; Engrng.

LEE, DIANE; Portage Area HS; Portage, PA; (Y); French Clb; Chorus; Hon Roll.

LEE, DON; Conestoga Valley HS; Lancaster, PA; (Y); 69/240; Computer Clb; Quiz Bowl; Science Clb; Hon Roll; Prfct Atten Awd; PA ST AIASA Toothpick Brdg Chmp 84 & 86; 2nd Pl Extmp Spkg 86; Bus Mgmt.

LEE, EUNHEE; Wissahickon Sr HS; Norristown, PA; (S); 1/277; Pres AFS; Pres Trs Intnl Clb; SADD; Rep Stu Cncl; Var Lcrss; JV Tennis; JV Trk; Hon Roll; NHS; Opt Clb Awd; Mtgmry Cnty Smr Intnsv Frgn Lng Schlrshp 85; PA Free Entrprs Week Schlrshp 85; Intl Bus.

LEE, GERALD; Harbor Creek HS; Erie, PA; (Y); Chess Clb; Exploring; Model UN; Science Clb; Ed Yrbk Stf; JV Var Ftbl; Mgr(s); Var Socr; Var Trk; Schlrshp PA Free Entrprs Wk 85; Pltcl Sci.

LEE, J DANCER; Germantown HS; Philadelphia, PA; (Y); 1/327; Chess Clb; DAR Awd; Val; Debate Tm; Math Clb; Tennis; High Hon Roll; Hon Roll; NHS; Gen Mtrs & Chnnl 6 Bst Of Cls 86; 1st Math Awd, Bio, Chem, Physcs Awd 86; Prncpls Schlrshp 86; Drexel U; Mech Engrng.

LEE II, JAMES A; Academy HS; Erie, PA; (S); 55/176; Concert Band; Jazz Band; Mrchg Band; Orch; VP French Clb; Pres Stu Cncl; Var Crs Cntry; Var Socr; Var Trk; USAF; Bus Admin.

LEE, JANE; Salisbury HS; Allentown, PA; (Y); 8/138; Rep Jr Cls; Rep Stu Cncl; Stat Bsktbl; JV Cheerleading; JV Sftbl; Capt L Swmmng; Im Tennis; Var Trk; Im Vllybl; Im Wt Lftg; Lafayette; Chem Engrng.

LEE, JEFFREY; Sayre Area HS; Sayre, PA; (Y); Varsity Clb; Var Capt Crs Cntry; JV Ftbl; Var Capt Swmmng; Var Capt Trk; High Hon Roll; Elctd NEPSL All-Str Tm Perf 100 Yd Pckstrk 84-86; NEPSL All-Str Tm Perf 400 Freestyl Rly 85-86; Lycoming Coll; Pre-Med.

LEE, JOHN; Bishop Kenrick HS; E Norristown, PA; (Y); 14/306; Science Clb; Ski Clb; NHS; Opt Clb Awd.

LEE, JOHN; Hershey SR HS; Hershey, PA; (Y); 34/192; Boy Scts; Trs Computer Clb; Math Tm; Band; Concert Band; Mrchg Band; JV Socr; Stat Swmmng; Var Trk; Ntl Merit Ltr; Elec Engnrng.

LEE, JOHN; M M I Preparatory Schl; Hazleton, PA; (Y); Computer Clb; Ski Clb; Var Bsbl; Var Crs Cntry; Var Golf; Im Vllybl; High Hon Roll; Hon Roll; Hst NHS; VP Frsh Cls; Grmn Ntl Hon Soc 86.

LEE, KATHY; Carmichaels Area SR HS; Carmichaels, PA; (Y); Church Yth Grp; Drama Clb; Library Aide; Office Aide; Ski Clb; Spanish Clb; Stage Crew; Off Jr Cls; Hon Roll; CA U PA; Intrntnl Stds.

LEE, KEE; Hatboro-Horsham SR HS; Horsham, PA; (Y); 6/270; Var JV Socr; JV Trk; High Hon Roll; Hon Roll; NHS; Prfct Atten Awd.

LEE, KELLY; Northwest Area HS; Shickshinny, PA; (Y); Chorus; Orch; Var Cheerleading; Var JV Fld Hcky; Hon Roll; Voice Dem Awd.

LEE, KELLY; Quaker Valley HS; Sewickley, PA; (Y); Church Yth Grp; Band; Pres Church Choir; Concert Band; Mrchg Band; Pep Band; Var Capt Bsktbl; Var Sftbl; Var Vllybl; Hon Roll; Chemistry.

LEE, KIM; Sullivan County HS; Eaglesmere, PA; (Y); 17/91; Church Yth Grp; FHA; SADD; Hon Roll; Lycoming Coll; Sclgy.

LEE, LARRY; Bethel Park SR HS; Bethel Park, PA; (Y); 17/504; VP Computer Clb; Capt Math Clb; Orch; School Musical; Nwsp Rptr; Nwsp Stf; Yrbk Stf; High Hon Roll; NHS; Prfct Atten Awd; Wimmer Schlrshp 85; Westinghouse Fmly, Bio, Acad Ldrshp Schlrshps 86; St Vincent Coll; Pre Med.

LEE, LEROY; Walter Biddle Saul HS; Philadelphia, PA; (Y); Computer Clb; Debate Tm; English Clb; FFA; JA; Church Choir; Nwsp Rptr; Sec Frsh Cls; Rep Soph Cls; Pres Sr Cls; Myr Cty PA Awds 83-86; Myrs Yth Advsry Cmmtee 85-86; U Of PA; Law.

LEE, LESLIE; Laurel Highalnds SR HS; Uniontown, PA; (Y); 5/360; Cmnty Wkr; Math Clb; Math Tm; Pep Clb; Yrbk Phtg; Yrbk Stf; Rep Jr Cls; Im Vllybl; CC Awd; High Hon Roll; Law.

LEE, LISA; Governor Mifflin HS; Reading Flying Hi, PA; (Y); 12/300; FBLA; Key Clb; Orch; High Hon Roll; Hon Roll; Prfct Atten Awd; Math Awd 86; Hnr Socty 86; U Of PA; Bus.

LEE, MARK; Bethel Park HS; Bethel Park, PA; (Y); Church Yth Grp; Capt Math Tm; L Var Sftbl; L Var Tennis; High Hon Roll; NHS; Math Comptn Fnlst 86; JR Engrs Clb Pres 86; Engrg.

LEE, MEGAN; Pottsgrove HS; Pottstown, PA; (Y); 1/229; Hosp Aide; Math Tm; Flag Corp; Orch; Yrbk Ed-Chief; Yrbk Stf; Stu Cncl; Stat Bsktbl; High Hon Roll; Pres NHS; Acad Decathalon 86; Phys Therpy.

LEE, MICHELE; Charleori Area JR SR HS; Charleroi, PA; (Y); Church Yth Grp; Exploring; Office Aide; Ski Clb; SADD; Varsity Clb; Yrbk Stf; Stu Cncl; Capt Cheerleading.

LEE, MICHELLE; Archbishop Rayn HS For Girls; Philadelphia, PA; (Y); JA; Office Aide; High Hon Roll; Sec NHS; Tmpl U Grnt 86; Certs Of Prfcncy Alg I&II-GEOM-REL I&II-PHYSCL Ftnss 82-86; Hnrbl Mtn Grmn I 82-86; Tmpl U; Elec Engnrng.

LEE, MICHELLE; Emmaus HS; Macungie, PA; (Y); 50/500; Rep Key Clb; Spanish Clb; Acpl Chr; Yrbk Stf; Sec Frsh Cls; Sec Soph Cls; Rep Stu Cncl; Capt Var Cheerleading; High Hon Roll; NHS; Dist Fnlst Engl Cmpttn; Natl Fnlst NEDT Tstng 95 Pct; U Of FL; Advrtsng.

LEE, MING; Upper Darby HS; Upr Darby, PA; (Y); Computer Clb; 4-H; Intnl Clb; Math Clb; Math Tm; Science Clb; Varsity Clb; Socr; Trk; Bausch & Lomb Sci Awd; Algebra II & Geometry Awds 83; Comp Sci Awd 84; Physcs II, Clcls II & Chmstry Awds 85; CA Inst Of Tech; Engrng.

LEE III, ROBERT E; Councl Rock HS; Churchville, PA; (Y); 10/755; Science Clb; Capt Swmmng; Cit Awd; High Hon Roll; Hon Roll; Kiwanis Awd; Pres NHS; Ntl Merit SF; Prfct Atten Awd; Cornell U; Pre-Med.

LEE, RONALD; Central Catholic HS; Pittsburgh, PA; (Y); Lit Mag; High Hon Roll; JV Trk; Hon Roll; Jr NHS.

LEE, STEPHANIE; Springside Schl; Huntingdon Valley, PA; (Y); Church Yth Grp; Variety Show; Nwsp Rptr; Nwsp Stf; Lit Mag; Capt Cheerleading; Var Sftbl; Hon Roll; Honors In Mathematics 84.

LEE, SUNG; Cedar Crest HS; Lebanon, PA; (Y); 1/323; French Clb; FBLA; Math Tm; Pep Clb; Quiz Bowl; Orch; Pres Soph Cls; Var Tennis; High Hon Roll; NHS; AIME 86.

LEE, SUNG; Central HS; Philadelphia, PA; (Y); 42/360; Camera Clb; Chess Clb; Church Yth Grp; Cmnty Wkr; FCA; Math Clb; Science Clb; Teachers Aide; Nwsp Phtg; Yrbk Phtg; Won Bridge Bldng Cntst ST Wide Entrd Ntn Wide 86; U Of PA; Bus.

LEE, SUNMIN; Johnstown HS; Johnstown, PA; (Y); 25/320; French Clb; Math Clb; Band; Mrchg Band; NHS; Prfct Atten Awd; Dentstry.

LEE, SUSAN ANN; South Fayette HS; Oakdale, PA; (Y); 12/92; Key Clb; Yrbk Stf; Hon Roll; Kiwanis Awd; NHS; U Pittsburgh; Engrng.

LEE, TIM; Highlands SR HS; Natrona Hts, PA; (Y); 3/286; High Hon Roll; Hon Roll; Chem Olympcs 86; Nclr Fld US Navy.

LEE, TOM; Central Catholic HS; Pittsburgh, PA; (Y); 24/268; Church Yth Grp; Dance Clb; Rep Soph Cls; Rep Jr Cls; JV Bsktbl; Im Crs Cntry; JV Im Ftbl; Var Trk; High Hon Roll; Hon Roll; X-Cntry Chmpn 84-85.

LEE JR, TYRONE T; Taylor Allderice HS; Pittsburgh, PA; (Y); French Clb; JA; Rep Stu Cncl; Im Bsktbl; JV Var Vllybl; High Hon Roll; Hon Roll; Bst Slsprsn 1st Runner-Up 86; Vllybl 86; Urban Jrnlst Certificate 86; Howard U; Elec Engrng.

LEECH, BETH; Albet Gallatin SR HS; Smithfield, PA; (Y); #10 In Class; Church Yth Grp; Ski Clb; Acpl Chr; Band; Mrchg Band; Cheerleading; Hon Roll; Jr NHS; NHS; Physcl Thrpy.

LEECH, JILL; Swissvale HS; Pittsburgh, PA; (Y); 16/205; German Clb; Acpl Chr; Chorus; Bowling; High Hon Roll; Comp Sci.

LEECH, KAREN; Butler SR HS; E Butler, PA; (Y); Church Yth Grp; Exploring; FBLA; Office Aide; Drill Tm; Mrchg Band; Var Gym; JV Twrlr; Hon Roll; 4th Pl Regnl Math Comptn 85; Med.

LEEDSTROM, JOYCE; Carlynton HS; Pittsburgh, PA; (Y); #13 In Class; Office Aide; Sec Jr Cls; Sec Sr Cls; Mgr(s); Vllybl; High Hon Roll; NHS; Sec Rotary Awd; Robt Morris Coll; Accntng.

LEES, BARB; Mechanicsburg Area SR HS; Mechanicsburg, PA; (Y); 76/311; Art Clb; Church Yth Grp; JV L Bsktbl; Var Sftbl; JV L Vllybl; High Hon Roll; Hon Roll; NHS; VP Natl Art Hnr Soc 85-86; Art.

LEES, CORIE; Ridley SR HS; Secane, PA; (Y); 17/413; Hosp Aide; Q&S; Nwsp Rptr; Ed Yrbk Rptr; Stu Cncl; Vllybl; High Hon Roll; NHS; Sntr Bells Cmmtt; Elizabethtown Coll; Occ Ther.

LEES, GARY; Delaware Valley HS; Milford, PA; (Y); 5/140; Am Leg Boys St; Church Yth Grp; Drama Clb; Chorus; School Musical; School Play; Yrbk Stf; Var Socr; Var Tennis; Var Capt Wrstlng; Hugh Obrian Youth Foundation Leadership Seminar 85; Engrng.

LEESE, MELANIE; Littlestown HS; Littlestown, PA; (Y); 11/143; Varsity Clb; VP Band; Chorus; School Musical; Trs Stu Cncl; L Cheerleading; L Crs Cntry; Trk; Capt L Vllybl; NHS; IN U Of PA; Tchr Deaf.

LEESE, TAMMY; Red Lion Area SR HS; Windsor, PA; (Y); 40/372; Girl Scts; Stage Crew; Cheerleading; Aero Engrng.

LEESER, MIKE; Emmaus HS; Macungie, PA; (Y); 24/497; Church Yth Grp; Var Swmmng; High Hon Roll; Hon Roll; Jr NHS; NHS; Mdl Atlntc Intl Age Grp Swm Team 85; All Amer Hnrb Mntn Mdly Rly 86.

LEFCHAK, NICOLE; Tunkhannock Area HS; Tunkhannock, PA; (Y); 42/330; Aud/Vis; FCA; Key Clb; Latin Clb; Letterman Clb; Spanish Clb; Yrbk Sprt Ed; Yrbk Stf; Stat Ftbl; VP Capt Sftbl; Ambrose Dutch Keller Awd; Stu Cncl Awd; SR Athlc Awd; Susquehann U.

LEFCHIK, DEANNA; Ford City HS; Ford City, PA; (Y); Hosp Aide; Spanish Clb; SADD; Chorus; NHS; BUS Mngmnt.

LEFEVER, PAMELA; Elizabethtown Area HS; Mt Joy, PA; (Y); 23/247; Sec Trs Church Yth Grp; Drama Clb; Library Aide; Chorus; Church Choir; School Musical; Powder Puff Ftbl; High Hon Roll; Hon Roll; NHS; Nrsng.

LEFFERTS JR, RONALD; Council Rock HS; Holland, PA; (Y); 112/850; Church Yth Grp; Tennis; Vllybl.

LEFFLER, BOB; Our Lady Of Lourdes HS; Shamokin, PA; (Y); 5/94; Rep Frsh Cls; VP Jr Cls; Var Bsbl; JV Bsktbl; Var Ftbl; French Hon Soc.

LEGARHT JR, DALE L; Pine Grove Area HS; Pine Grove, PA; (Y); 30/125; Off ROTC; Yrbk Stf; Rep Soph Cls; Rep Jr Cls; Trs Stu Cncl; JV Bsbl; Hon Roll; Elec Engr.

LEGG, DAVID; Old Forge HS; Old Forge, PA; (Y); JA; Outstndng Stu Karate 84; Blck Blt Karate 84; Wilkes Coll; Orthpdc Srgn.

LEGG, KAREN SUE; Chartiers Valley HS; Carnegie, PA; (Y); 91/346; Dance Clb; Drama Clb; French Clb; JA; Thesps; Band; Chorus; Concert Band; Mrchg Band; School Musical; Robert Morris Coll; Accntng.

LEGGETT, JEANNIE; Pennsbury HS; Yardley, PA; (Y); Church Yth Grp; Cmnty Wkr; French Clb; GAA; Intnl Clb; Political Wkr; Bowling; Sftbl; Hon Roll; Engrng.

LEGTERS, STEVE; Jamestown Area HS; Jamestown, PA; (S); 1/55; Church Yth Grp; Band; Chorus; School Musical; Pres Jr Cls; VP Stu Cncl; Var L Bsktbl; High Hon Roll; NHS.

LEGUTKO, KAREN; Littlestown HS; Littlestown, PA; (Y); 3/140; Varsity Clb; Yrbk Ed-Chief; Rep Stu Cncl; Var Crs Cntry; Var Trk; Bausch & Lomb Sci Awd; NHS; Adams Cntyh JR Miss Acad Awd 86; Engr.

LEGUTKO, ROBERT; Mahanoy Area HS; Mahanoy City, PA; (Y); Band; Chorus; Orch; Variety Show; Nwsp Ed-Chief; Var L Bsbl; Var Bsktbl; Var L Crs Cntry; NHS; Concert Band; Pottsville Schuylkill Cnty Orch 85; Shenandoah Lgn Bsbl Tm 86.

LEHERR, MICHAEL; North Hills HS; Pittsburgh, PA; (Y); 41/635; Church Yth Grp; Exploring; Letterman Clb; Var Bsbl; Capt Ice Hcky; Hon Roll; NHS; 3rd Pl AAPT/Metrolgc Physcs Cntsts 85; Al-City Al-Star Hcky 85-86; Notre Dame; Engrng.

LEHET, MICHAEL; Benton Area JR SR HS; Benton, PA; (Y); Key Clb; Chorus; Concert Band; School Musical; School Play; Nwsp Rptr; Hon Roll; NHS; Art Clb; Library Aide; Dstrct Chrs; Rgnl Chrs; Mansfield Rdy Wrtng Cntst; Elec Engrng.

LEHETT, AMY; West Middlesex HS; W Middlesex, PA; (S); 19/107; French Clb; Sec Library Aide; Service Clb; Twrlr; High Hon Roll; Hon Roll; Jr NHS; Ed.

LEHMAN, CARY; Hershey HS; Hershey, PA; (Y); 14/192; Debate Tm; Math Tm; Pres Band; Mrchg Band; School Musical; Capt Diving; High Hon Roll; Hon Roll; Var Pres NHS; Voice Dem Awd; Sico Foundtn & Beck & Irvin E Herr Foundtn Schlrshps 86; Kutztown U; Pre Dntstry.

LEHMAN, CHRISTINE; Central York SR HS; Emigsville, PA; (Y); Art Clb; Hon Roll; Natl Art Hnr Society 85; SECRETARIAL.

LEHMAN, CINDY; Shikellamy HS; Sunbury, PA; (Y); 15/301; German Clb; Var Fld Hcky; JV Sftbl; Hon Roll; Jr NHS; Cert Of High Achvt In Grmn 84-86; Recgntn Of Achvt In Chmstry 85; Rtgrs Coll Phrmcy; Phrmcy.

LEHMAN, DAVID; Cheltenham HS; Cheltenham, PA; (Y); Boy Scts; Church Yth Grp; Dance Clb; Nwsp Rptr; Yrbk Phtg; Stu Cncl; Theatrical Arts.

LEHMAN, DEBORAH J; Southwestern HS; Hanover, PA; (Y); 4/205; Church Yth Grp; Chorus; Church Choir; Concert Band; Jazz Band; Mrchg Band; School Musical; Symp Band; High Hon Roll; JC Awd; Otstndng Muscn & Typt 85 & 86; Elizabethtown Coll; Music Thrp.

LEHMAN, JESSICA; Palmyra Area HS; Lebanon, PA; (Y); Church Yth Grp; Hosp Aide; Teachers Aide; Chorus; Stat Diving; Stat Swmmng; Trk; Hon Roll; E Stroudsburg U; Motel Mngmnt.

LEHMAN, JOSEPH; Avella HS; Burgettstown, PA; (Y); Church Yth Grp; Computer Clb; 4-H; French Clb; Nwsp Stf; JV Bsktbl; Var Ftbl; DAR Awd; Hon Roll; NHS; Bus.

LEHMAN, LORETTA; Mt Pleasant Area HS; Mt Pleasant, PA; (Y); 24/245; GAA; Concert Band; Mrchg Band; Yrbk Stf; Var L Trk; High Hon Roll; NHS; Prfct Atten Awd; JR Clss Cndy Rep 85-86; Prom Comm 86.

LEHMAN, MELANIE; Nativity B V M HS; Ravine, PA; (Y); 6/98; Art Clb; French Clb; ROTC; Flag Corp; Yrbk Stf; Stu Cncl; Bsktbl; French Hon Soc; High Hon Roll; Hon Roll; Schl Sci Fair-2nd Pl Microbio 85; Dickenson Coll Sci Fair-Hnrbl Mntn 85; Sci Fair-2nd Pl Physiolgy 86; Lehigh U; Bio.

LEHMAN, ROSALIE D; Elkland Area HS; Elkland, PA; (Y); 12/78; French Clb; Rep Frsh Cls; Rep Soph Cls; Rep Jr Cls; Trs Sr Cls; Stat Bsktbl; Mgr(s); Sec Vllybl; Hon Roll; Horace Packer Fndtn Schlrp 86-87; Mansfield U; Math Ed.

LEHMAN, SANDY; Shikellamy HS; Sunbury, PA; (Y); 22/340; German Clb; JV Capt Fld Hcky; JV Sftbl; Hon Roll; Jr NHS; Outstndng Achvt Grmn-Awd 84-86; Bloomsburg; Med Tech.

LEHMAN, SCOTT; Northern Potter HS; Ulysses, PA; (Y); Boy Scts; Church Yth Grp; Varsity Clb; Trk; Wrstlng; High Hon Roll; All Amer Acad 86; Nclr Med.

LEHMAN, SHELLY; Cumberland Valley HS; Camp Hill, PA; (Y); Ath Trnr JV & Vrsty Lttrs 83-85; Intr Dsgn.

LEHMAN, TROY; Beaver Area HS; Beaver, PA; (Y); Exploring; VP JA; Sec JCL; Sec Latin Clb; Ski Clb; Yrbk Phtg; Yrbk Stf; Ftbl; Swmmng; Wt Lftg; Bus Adm.

LEHMANN, KATRINA; Pottstown SR HS; Pottstown, PA; (Y); 30/191; Key Clb; Sec Spanish Clb; Nwsp Stf; Lit Mag; L Tennis; NHS; 1st Pl Wnnr Dist Comp Natl Hstry Day Temple U, Wnnr ST Comp PA ST U, 1st Pl Natl Comp U MD 86; Hampshire Coll; Biol.

LEHN, KRISTEN E; Cedar Crest HS; Lebanon, PA; (Y); 4-H; JA; Pep Clb; SADD; Nwsp Sprt Ed; JV Bsktbl; Var Sftbl; Var Tennis; Vllybl; 4-H Awd; Bio.

LEHR, KENNETH W; La Salle HS; Southampton, PA; (Y); VP Debate Tm; VP Speech Tm; Nwsp Rptr; Nwsp Stf; Yrbk Phtg; Yrbk Rptr; Yrbk Stf; NHS; Ntl Merit Ltr; NEDT Awd; Bruno E Jacob Frnsc Awd 86; St Josephs U Pres Schlrshp 86; St Josephs U; Psych.

LEHTO, CHRIS; West Middlesex HS; New Wilmington, PA; (S); 10/113; Band; Chorus; Rep Stu Cncl; 4-H Awd; Ntl Merit Schol; Spanish NHS; Dist Band 85; Kent ST; Fshn Merch.

LEIB, KELLY M; West York Area SR HS; York, PA; (Y); Pres Church Yth Grp; Varsity Clb; Hst Frsh Cls; Hst Soph Cls; Hst Jr Cls; Rep Stu Cncl; L JV Cheerleading; L Var Fld Hcky; Stu Canal Person Of Yr 86; St Jude Chldrns Hosp Dstngshd Svc Awd 85.

LEIBENSPERGER, AMY; Hamburg Area HS; Shoemakersville, PA; (Y); Library Aide; Sec Ski Clb; SADD; Trs Jr Cls; Trs Sr Cls; Rep Stu Cncl; JV VP Cheerleading; VP L Trk; Hon Roll; NHS; Engrg.

LEIBMAN, KAREN; James M Couglin HS; Wilkes Barre, PA; (Y); 1/342; Church Yth Grp; Nwsp Ed-Chief; Nwsp Stf; VP L Bsktbl; VP L Vllybl; High Hon Roll; Jr NHS; NHS.

LEIBY, KRAIG; Kutztown Area HS; Kutztown, PA; (Y); Boy Scts; Band; Chorus; Drm Mjr(t); Jazz Band; Var Socr; God Cntry Awd; High Hon Roll; Eagle Sct 85; Hlt Fld.

LEIBY, WENDY; Tamaqua Area SR HS; Tamaqua, PA; (Y); Exploring; Pres Trs 4-H; Pep Clb; Ski Clb; Acpl Chr; Band; Chorus; Mrchg Band; Swing Chorus; Yrbk Stf; Schuylkill Cnty Chrs 85-86; Co-Capt EMT 1st Aid Tm 85-86; Nrsg.

LEICHLITER, MICHAEL G; William Penn SR HS; York, PA; (S); Church Yth Grp; Drama Clb; Jazz Band; Mrchg Band; Orch; School Musical; Off Jr Cls; Hon Roll; Jr NHS; NHS; Studnt Of Mnth 84-86; Counslng.

LEICHT, DOUGLAS; Northwestern HS; Albion, PA; (Y); 13/162; Varsity Clb; JV Bsbl; Var L Bsktbl; Var Capt Ftbl; Hon Roll; Penn ST U; Engrng.

LEIDEN, ANITA; Bishop Carroll HS; Patton, PA; (S); 3/103; Pres 4-H; Speech Tm; Band; Church Choir; L Trk; NHS; Ntl Merit Ltr; NEDT Awd; Spanish Clb; Dist Band 85-86; PA ST U; Engrng.

LEIDIG, BARBARA; Greencastle-Antrim HS; Greencastle, PA; (Y); Science Clb; Church Choir; Yrbk Stf; Stu Cncl; $600 Schlrshp From Head Hntrs Acad Of Csmtlgy 86; Head Hunters Acad; Csmtlgst.

LEIDY, PAMELA; Mount Union Area HS; Shirleysburg, PA; (Y); Church Yth Grp; FBLA; GAA; Band; Concert Band; Mrchg Band; Sftbl; Typing I & II Awds 85-86; Med Sec.

LEIGH, SPENCER; Shikellamy HS; Northumberland, PA; (Y); 32/285; Boy Scts; Church Yth Grp; Library Aide; Chorus; Church Choir; Hon Roll; BYU; Chem Engr.

LEIGHLITER, BRENDA LEA; Connellsville SR HS; Connellsville, PA; (Y); 10/500; Pep Clb; Y-Teens; Chorus; Flag Corp; Pep Band; School Play; Stage Crew; Symp Band; Yrbk Stf; Frsh Cls; Most Likely Succeed 81-82; 2nd Rnnr Up Cinderella Ct 85-86; Temple U; Arch.

LEIGHTHARDT, JOSEPH; Archbishop Ryan For Boys; Philadelphia, PA; (Y); 90/429; Boys Clb Am; Pres Cmnty Wkr; Pres Exploring; Hosp Aide; Political Wkr; Nwsp Stf; Cit Awd; God Cntry Awd; Chapel Of 4 Chaplains Awd 86; Socl Justice Awd 86; Excllnc Englsh 86; Law Enfrcmnt.

LEIKER, NICOLE; Philadelphia High School For Girls; Philadelphia, PA; (Y); Letterman Clb; Spanish Clb; Teachers Aide; Varsity Clb; Var L Gym; Hon Roll; Jr NHS; Spanish NHS; Bailey Williams Mem Hnr Key Awd 85; Acptd To AFNA New Access Rts To Lgl Careers 84.

LEINHAUSER, KAREN M; Archbishop Predergast HS; Sharon Hill, PA; (Y); 118/361; Service Clb; Band; Church Choir; Concert Band; Mrchg Band; Orch; School Musical; School Play; Duquesne U; Spch Pthlgy.

LEINHEISER, MICHAEL; Roman Catholic HS; Philadelphia, PA; (S); 3/140; Rep Sr Cls; Rep Stu Cncl; Var L Bsktbl; Hon Roll; NHS; Drexel U; Civil Engr.

LEINHEISER, PATRICE; Harry S Truman HS; Edgely, PA; (Y); 52/620; Latin Clb; Band; JV Capt Cheerleading; High Hon Roll; Penn ST Co-Op Schlrshp 86; Pennco Tech; Comp Pgmmng.

LEININGER, BRAD; Shikellamy HS; Northumberland, PA; (Y); 62/300; Rep Frsh Cls; Rep Soph Cls; Trs Stu Cncl; JV Var Bsbl; JV Var Bsktbl; JV Var Golf; Amer Lgn ST Plc Yth Wk 86; Crmnl Jstc.

LEIS, SEBASTIAN; Bishop Mc Cort HS; Johnstown, PA; (Y); Rep Latin Clb; Chorus; Var Bsbl; Bsktbl; Var L Ftbl; Var L Trk; High Hon Roll; Hon Roll; Mu Alp Tht; NHS; PA ST U; Sci.

LEISNER, DENISE; St Hoberts HS; Philadelphia, PA; (Y); 68/367; Church Yth Grp; Exploring; French Clb; Spanish Clb; Teachers Aide; Orch; Sr Cls; Bowling; Hon Roll; Temple U; Lang.

LEISTER, BRIAN; Chief Logan HS; Lewistown, PA; (Y); 33/200; German Clb; Trs Pep Clb; Varsity Clb; Nwsp Phtg; Ed Yrbk Phtg; Pres Stu Cncl; Var L Bsbl; Var L Ftbl; Var L Trk; Var L Wrstlng; Ftbll Awd 85; Bus Admin.

LEITHOLF, SUSAN; Chartiers Valley HS; Pittsburgh, PA; (Y); 17/340; Varsity Clb; Acpl Chr; Orch; Crs Cntry; Sftbl; L Swmmng; Trk; NHS; Pres Acad Ftnss Awd 86; Natl Presbyterian Schlrshp 86; Coll Of Wooster; Math.

LEITZEL, BRIAN; Shikellamy HS; Sunbury, PA; (Y); 8/316; French Clb; High Hon Roll; Hon Roll; Jr NHS; NHS; Pres Schlr; Penn ST.

LEITZEL, STACEY K; Line Mountain HS; Catawissa, PA; (Y); Key Clb; Ski Clb; Varsity Clb; Drm Mjr(t); School Musical; Nwsp Stf; Off Stu Cncl; Bsktbl; Hon Roll; Bloomsburg U; Elem Educ.

LEITZEL, TONIA; Millersburg Area HS; Millersburg, PA; (Y); Ski Clb; Spanish Clb; Church Choir; Yrbk Rptr; Yrbk Stf; Var L Cheerleading; Mgr(s); Powder Puff Ftbl; High Hon Roll; Hon Roll; Cnsrvtn Clb 85-86; Enrchmnt Pgm 83-85; Outstndg Acdmc Achvmnt Awd 83-84; Bus Admin.

LELLOCK, DAVID E; Punxsutawney Area SR HS; Punxsutawney, PA; (Y); 23/245; Math Tm; Band; Concert Band; Jazz Band; Mrchg Band; Pep Band; Im Bsktbl; Hon Roll; NHS; Stu Month 84; Engrng.

LEMKE, MARY; Seneca HS; Erie, PA; (Y); Exploring; Color Guard; School Musical; VP Stage Crew; Yrbk Stf; JV Cheerleading; Var Trk; Edinboro U; Anthrplgy.

LEMLEY, HEATH; Waynesburg Central HS; Mt Morris, PA; (Y); #2 In Class; VP Camera Clb; Chess Clb; Mrchg Band; Yrbk Stf; Trk; Bausch & Lomb Sci Awd; High Hon Roll; NHS; Sal; Melvina Haugen Schlrshp 86; Waynesburg Coll Sci Comptn 84-85; 1st Pl PA ST Fayette Cmps Sntst; WV U; Pre-Chmstry.

LEMMERT, MICHILLE; Southern Fulton HS; Wardfordsburg, PA; (Y); Church Yth Grp; FBLA; Band; Jazz Band; Mrchg Band; School Play; JV Bsktbl; Var Capt Vllybl; Hon Roll; Messiah Chrstn Coll; Acctng.

LEMMON, DOUG; Marion Center Area HS; Marion Center, PA; (S); 14/148; Pres VICA; Concert Band; Mrchg Band; Pep Band; High Hon Roll; Jr NHS; NHS; Gld Mdl PA ST VICA Cabinet Mkng Comp 85; Slvr Mdl Natl VICA Cabinet Making Comp 85; Genl Cntrctr.

LEMMON, KELLY E; Germantown Acad; Lansdale, PA; (Y); Trs Debate Tm; Drama Clb; French Clb; Girl Scts; Intnl Clb; NFL; Orch; Stage Crew; Lit Mag; Rep Sr Cls; Cum Laude Soc 85; Carey Excllnc Non Tyspn Thtre Trphy 85.

LEMMON, MATTHEW S; Big Spring HS; Newburg, PA; (S); 3/189; Pres FFA; Band; Concert Band; Jazz Band; Mrchg Band; Hon Roll; NHS; Penn ST U; Agribusnss.

LEMON, CINDY LYNN; Rochester Area HS; Rochester, PA; (Y); Church Yth Grp; Dance Clb; Pep Clb; Ski Clb; Nwsp Rptr; Nwsp Stf; Yrbk Stf; JV Var Cheerleading; Var Trk; NHS; Chrldr Capt 84-85; Duquesne U; Sprts Medcn.

LENA, KARYN; Latrobe SR HS; Latrobe, PA; (Y); 58/344; Teachers Aide; Capt Color Guard; Nwsp Rptr; Ed Nwsp Stf; Spanish NHS; Pep Clb; Mat Maids; High Hon Roll; Latrobe Wntr Guard-Rfl-Co Capt 83-86; Sarah Mccomb Acadmc Schlrshp 86; St Vincent Acadmc Schlrshp 86; St Vincent; Cmnctns.

LENARD, ALEXANDER N; The Shipley Schl; King Of Prussia, PA; (Y); Rep Frsh Cls; Pres Soph Cls; Rep Jr Cls; JV Bsbl; Var Lcrss; Var Wrstlng; Ntl Merit SF; Amer Chem Soc Outstndng Achvt 84; PA Achvt Awd 85.

LENARD, LISA; Bethel Park SR HS; Bethel Park, PA; (Y); French Clb; Hgh Hnr Awd 83-84; PA ST; Finance.

LENCER JR, HENRY; North Clarion JR SR HS; Leeper, PA; (Y); Church Yth Grp; Drama Clb; School Musical; School Play; Stage Crew; Im Bsktbl; JV Trk; Hon Roll.

LENETSKY, MARA; Neshaminy HS; Langhorne, PA; (Y); 118/750; Nwsp Stf; Yrbk Sprt Ed; Yrbk Stf; Rep Frsh Cls; Capt Cheerleading; Powder Puff Ftbl; Hon Roll; Miss Redskin Outstndng Chrldr Awd 85; U Pittsburgh; Med.

LENG, DAVID; Seton-La Salle HS; Pittsburgh, PA; (Y); Computer Clb; Math Tm; High Hon Roll; NHS; Church Yth Grp; Exploring; Ski Clb; Spanish Clb; Stage Crew; Acad Achvt Awd Geo 84.

LENGEL, GARTH; Susquehanna Twp HS; Harrisburg, PA; (Y); 19/155; Church Yth Grp; Model UN; Chorus; Church Choir; Orch; Var Capt Socr; JV Wrstlng; Hon Roll; VP NHS; Rnnr Up Hoby Ldrshp Awd 84-85.

LENGEL, THOMAS; Lackawanna Trail HS; Nicholson, PA; (Y); VP Jr Cls; Var Ftbl; Wt Lftg; Var Wrstlng; Hon Roll; Pres Physcl Ftns Awd 83 & 84; Schl Rcrd Pullups 84; Sec Educ.

LENGEL, TINA; Pine Grove Area HS; Pine Grove, PA; (Y); Varsity Clb; Chorus; Bsktbl; Mgr(s); Score Keeper; Sftbl; Hon Roll; Sec.

LENGEN, DESIREE; Bishop Hafey HS; New Coxeville, PA; (Y); 48/140; Church Yth Grp; French Clb; Library Aide; Hon Roll; Prfct Atten Awd; Anml Sci Tech.

LENGLE, GINA; Cedar Crest HS; Lebanon, PA; (Y); FBLA; Pep Clb; Spanish Clb; Bowling; L Stat Fld Hcky; Mgr(s); Trk; Hon Roll; York Coll Of PA; Hlth Rcrd Adm.

LENGLE, KARLA; Cedar Crest HS; Lebanon, PA; (Y); 90/323; Church Yth Grp; French Clb; FTA; Pep Clb; SADD; Bowling; Hon Roll; Scndry Math Tchr.

LENGYEL, JEFF; Bethel Park HS; Bethel Park, PA; (Y); Speed Skating Roller 82-86; Stage Crew; Acad Awd; Engrng.

LENGYEL, TERESSA LYNN; Panther Valley HS; Nesquehoning, PA; (Y); 1/131; French Clb; Teachers Aide; Trs Sr Cls; Co-Capt Cheerleading; Bausch & Lomb Sci Awd; NHS; NEDT Awd; Pres Schlr; Val; Lehigh U; Engrng.

LENGYEL, VALERIE; Hopewell HS; Aliquippa, PA; (Y); VP Exploring; Latin Clb; Sec Pres Science Clb; Chorus; Yrbk Stf; Powder Puff Ftbl; Hon Roll; NHS; Rep Beaver Cnty Enviro-Lympics 85; Vet Med.

LENHART, HEATHER; Millville HS; Millville, PA; (Y); Band; Chorus; School Play; Cheerleading; Hon Roll; NHS; NEDT Awd; Envrnmntl Sci.

LENHART, TAMARA; Clearfield Area HS; Clearfield, PA; (Y); 74/272; French Clb; FBLA; Key Clb; Chorus; Color Guard; Orch; Rep Stu Cncl; Stat Score Keeper; High Hon Roll; Hon Roll; Northeastern Christian JC; Bus.

LENHART, TAMMY; Meyersdale Area HS; Meyersdale, PA; (Y); FNA; SADD; Hon Roll; Prfct Atten Awd; Conemaugh Vlly Schl; Nrsng.

LENKER, DAVID; Upper Merion Area HS; King Of Prussa, PA; (Y); 16/310; Math Tm; Hon Roll; Bio.

LENNON, MELISSA K; Villa Maria Acad; Exton, PA; (Y); School Musical; School Play; Yrbk Ed-Chief; Ed Lit Mag; French Hon Soc; Ntl Merit SF; Church Yth Grp; Drama Clb; English Clb; French Clb; Eng.

LENT, BETH; Central Dauphin HS; Harrisburg, PA; (Y); German Clb; Band; Chorus; Drm Mjr(t); Orch; Off Soph Cls; Off Jr Cls; NHS; Concert Band; Jazz Band; Witman Gingrich Awd 86; Penn ST U; Anim Biosci.

LENTINI, FRANK; Allentown Central Catholic HS; Whitehall, PA; (Y); 90/250; Drama Clb; Band; Chorus; Concert Band; Drm Mjr(t); Jazz Band; Mrchg Band; Pep Band; School Musical; School Play; Music.

LENTINI, ROBERT; Holy Ghost Preparatory Schl; Philadelphia, PA; (S); Exploring; Mathletes; Var Trk; NHS; Ntl Merit Ltr; SR Math Soc.

LENTOWSKI, ANDREW; Pittston Area HS; Duryea, PA; (Y); Aud/Vis; Camera Clb; Chess Clb; Computer Clb; JA; Math Clb; Science Clb; Spanish Clb; Bsbl; Bowling.

LENTZ, ADAM; East HS; Glen Mills, PA; (Y); Aud/Vis; Boy Scts; Cmnty Wkr; Yrbk Phtg; Yrbk Sprt Ed; West Chester Area Schl Dist Cert Achvmnt 86; Rochester Inst; Compu Engr Tech.

LENTZ, BARRY; Shamokin Area HS; Gowen City, PA; (Y); 40/250; German Clb; Science Clb; L Wrstlng; Comm.

LENTZ, EDWARD T; Wyomissing Area HS; Wyomissing, PA; (Y); 8/119; VP JA; Pres Model UN; Scholastic Bowl; Trs Soph Cls; Rep Stu Cncl; Var Golf; NHS; Ntl Merit SF; German Clb; Ski Clb; Gld Medl PA Sci Olympd Comp Prgrmmg 85; Bus Adm.

LENTZ, LISA; Curwensville Area HS; Grampain, PA; (Y); Am Leg Aux Girls St; Church Yth Grp; French Clb; Pres FBLA; FNA; Office Aide; JV Diving; JV Trk; Im Vllybl; Hon Roll; U Of CA; Accntnt.

LENTZ, SCOTT; Moon SR HS; Coraopolis, PA; (Y); 7/327; Church Yth Grp; JA; Band; Church Choir; Drm Mjr(t); Mrchg Band; Pep Band; School Musical; School Play; Symp Band; Abrasive Engrng Soc Scholar 86; NROTC Scholar 86; Bucknell U; Bio.

LENZ, HOLLY; Upper Dublin HS; Dresher, PA; (Y); 32/320; Church Yth Grp; FBLA; Varsity Clb; Frsh Cls; Soph Cls; Jr Cls; Sr Cls; Stu Cncl; Bsktbl; Fld Hcky; 1st Tm All Lg Field Hcky & La Crosse 85-86; 1st Pl Bus Graphics Rgn FBLA 86.

LEO JR, CHARLES; Meyers HS; Wilkes Barre, PA; (Y); 30/160; Church Yth Grp; Letterman Clb; Ski Clb; SADD; Chorus; Yrbk Phtg; Stu Cncl; Var Capt Bsbl; Var Golf; Var Wrstlng; Ltr Wrstlng 84-85; Jr Natl Hnr Socty 83-84; Spnsh Natl Hnr Socty 84-85; Penn ST; Bio.

LEONARD, CARRIE; Canton Area HS; Grover, PA; (Y); Church Yth Grp; Church Choir; Yrbk Stf; High Hon Roll; Erie Bus Ctr; Exec Secy.

LEONARD, CHRIS; Blairsville SR HS; Blairsville, PA; (Y); 30/117; Chess Clb; Varsity Clb; JV Bsktbl; Var Trk; Hon Roll; NHS; Physcl Thrpst.

LEONARD, DEBORAH; Dubois Area HS; Grampian, PA; (Y); Church Yth Grp; Chorus; Im Swmmng; Hon Roll; NHS; Nice Kid Awd 86; Medcl Dr.

LEONARD, EDITH; Uniontown Area HS; Ohiopyle, PA; (Y); 35/346; 4-H; Latin Clb; Library Aide; SADD; 4-H Awd; High Hon Roll; NHS; Penn ST; Criminology.

LEONARD, JAMIE; Brownsville Area HS; Brownsville, PA; (S); 7/225; VP Church Yth Grp; Drama Clb; Math Clb; SADD; Church Choir; High Hon Roll; Hon Roll; Jr NHS; NHS; Spch Thrpst.

LEONARD, JODY; Upper Merion Area HS; King Of Prussia, PA; (Y); Church Yth Grp; Cmnty Wkr; German Clb; Fld Hcky; Lcrss; Swmmng; Trk; Hon Roll; German Lang.

LEONARD, KATHLEEN; Seton Catholic HS; Pittston, PA; (Y); 24/93; Church Yth Grp; Key Clb; Chorus; Madrigals; School Play; Stage Crew; Yrbk Stf; Bsktbl; Crs Cntry; Tennis; Latn Awd 84; Frnch Awd 86; St Marys College; Elem Ed.

LEONARD, KRISTEN; Warren Area HS; Warren, PA; (Y); Camera Clb; Drama Clb; French Clb; Chorus; School Play; Stage Crew; Yrbk Stf; Stu Cncl; High Hon Roll; NHS; Point Park Col6; TV Brdcstng.

LEONARD, LARISSA; Connellsville HS; Dawson, PA; (Y); 3/550; Pres Frsh Cls; VP Soph Cls; Pres Jr Cls; Rep VP Stu Cncl; Var L Trk; Var L Vllybl; High Hon Roll; Spanish NHS; Pres Jr NHS; NHS; Hgst Grade Pt Afg 83-84; Achvt Exc Awd Math,Sci,Spnsh 83-86; MVP Vlybl 85-86; Med.

LEONARD, LEANN; Hempfield Area HS; Irwin, PA; (Y); Pep Clb; Nwsp Rptr; Ed Nwsp Stf; Yrbk Phtg; Yrbk Stf; French Clb; Sftbl; Wt Lftg; Cit Awd; Jrnlsm.

LEONARD, MALINDA; Uniontown Area HS; Markleysburg, PA; (Y); 25/320; Trs Church Yth Grp; French Clb; French Hon Soc; High Hon Roll; Jr NHS; NHS; H Brice Schlrshp 86; Pres Acdmc Ftnss Awd 86; CA U Of PA; Elem Ed.

LEONARD, MARIA; Blacklick Valley JR SR HS; Nanty-Glo, PA; (S); 9/96; Camera Clb; Ski Clb; Varsity Clb; Concert Band; Pres Jr Cls; Sec Stu Cncl; Cheerleading; Trk; Hon Roll; NHS.

LEONARD, MELISSA; Minersville Area HS; Minersville, PA; (Y); 14/116; Teachers Aide; Pres Chorus; School Musical; Swing Chorus; Yrbk Stf; Pres Stu Cncl; Stat Crs Cntry; DAR Awd; NHS; Pres Schlr; Kutztown U; Elem Music Ed.

LEONARD, RICKY; Rockwood Area HS; Markleton, PA; (S); Socr; Hon Roll; U Of Pittsburgh; Engrng.

LEONARD, ROGER; Huntingdon Area HS; Huntingdon, PA; (Y); 18/250; Boys Clb Am; Church Yth Grp; Cmnty Wkr; Computer Clb; Teachers Aide; Cit Awd; High Hon Roll; Pensacola Chrstn Coll; Polc Ofc.

LEONARD, RONALD; Uniontown Area HS; Ohiopyle, PA; (Y); Pres Church Yth Grp; Letterman Clb; Var L Bsbl; NHS; Spanish NHS; PA ST U; Engrng.

LEONE, EDWARD; Bishop Hannan HS; Chinchilla, PA; (Y); 55/131; Trs Church Yth Grp; NFL; PAVAS; Speech Tm; Pres Orch; Hon Roll; NHS; 3rd Pl Ex-Temp Spkng 85; Outstndng Nwspr Carrier Awd 85fcarrier Of Yr 86; Intl Rltns.

LEONE, JOE; Tonkhannock Area HS; Montros, PA; (Y); 38/320; Ski Clb; Concert Band; Drm Mjr(t); Jazz Band; Mrchg Band; School Musical; Hon Roll; NHS; IN U Of PA Awd For Physc 86; Susquehanna U; Biochem.

LEONE, MARYLYNNE; Ringgold HS; Donora, PA; (Y); Drama Clb; Rep Spanish Clb; Hon Roll; Spanish NHS; Vet Med.

LEONE, MONICA M; Archbishop Wood For Girls; Feasterville, PA; (Y); Art Clb; Cmnty Wkr; French Clb; Nwsp Phtg; Hon Roll; Temple U; Tchng.

LEONG, KEVIN; Lower Moreland HS; Huntingdon Valley, PA; (S); VP Key Clb; Science Clb; Teachers Aide; Chorus; Concert Band; Orch; Nwsp Stf; Yrbk Stf; High Hon Roll; NHS; Full Schlrshps Jenkintown Music Schl 85; Chem Engr.

LEONHARDT, CHERYL; St Pius X HS; Pottstown, PA; (Y); Art Clb; Church Yth Grp; Cmnty Wkr; GAA; Hosp Aide; Office Aide; Service Clb; Ski Clb; SADD; Variety Show; PJAS 81-85; Theology Awd 83; Phys Thrpy.

LEONOVICH, KAREN; Southern Columbia Area HS; Elysburg, PA; (Y); Band; Trs Concert Band; Jazz Band; Trs Mrchg Band; Orch; Pep Band; Symp Band; High Hon Roll; Hon Roll; NHS; Bloomsburg U; Psych.

LEOPARDO, SHANA; Mohawk Area JR SR HS; Wampum, PA; (Y); 8/127; French Clb; FBLA; Band; Mrchg Band; VP Sr Cls; Var JV Bsktbl; Powder Puff Ftbl; Stat Trk; French Hon Soc; Hon Roll; 2nd Tm All Star Choice Bsktbl 84-85 & 85-86; Hmcmng Ct 85-86; Slippery Rock U; Bus Adm.

LEOPOLD, KATHY; Ambridge HS; Ambridge, PA; (Y); Church Yth Grp; Girl Scts; Band; Concert Band; Mrchg Band; Symp Band; Rep Jr Cls; Prfct Atten Awd; Pittsburg Beatucy Acad; Csmtlgy.

LEPEY, MARK; North Star HS; Boswell, PA; (Y); FFA; VICA; Wrstlng; Hon Roll.

LEPICH, JEANINE; Fairview HS; Fairview, PA; (Y); Church Yth Grp; Cmnty Wkr; Red Cross Aide; Teachers Aide; Varsity Clb; Orch; JV Cheerleading; Var L Crs Cntry; JV Sftbl; Var L Swmmng.

LEPKOSKI, CHRISTOPHER; Bishop Hannon HS; Moosic, PA; (Y); Computer Clb; Exploring; Ski Clb; Trgnmtry & Crp Walk Awd 86; PA ST; Comp Sci.

LEPLEY, MARK; North Star HS; Boswell, PA; (S); VICA; Machinist.

LEPLEY, MICHAEL; West Snyder HS; Beaver Spgs, PA; (Y); Church Yth Grp; Computer Clb; Varsity Clb; Var Bsbl; JV Var Socr; Im Vllybl; JV Var Wrstlng; Hon Roll; NHS; PA JR Acad Sci 2nd Pl ST Comptn 86 & 2nd Pl Rgnl Comptn 85; 2nd Tm Tri Vly Lgu Soccer All Star 85; PA ST U; Astronomy.

LEPORE, ANDREA; Upper Dublin HS; Ambler, PA; (Y); Yrbk Stf; Var Capt Cheerleading; JV Lcrss; Spec Ed.

LEPORE, JEFFREY; Wyoming Valley West HS; Kingston, PA; (Y); Ski Clb; Nwsp Stf; Yrbk Stf; Var L Bsbl; JV Bsktbl; Var Wrstlng; High Hon Roll; Hon Roll; Im Vllybl; Im Wt Lftg; PA ST U; Engrng.

LEPOSKY, STEPHANIE; Trinity HS; Washington, PA; (Y); 71/374; Math Tm; Var Bsktbl; Var Crs Cntry; Var Sftbl; Var Tennis; Var Trk; High Hon Roll; Hon Roll; Slow Pitch Sftbl ASAPA ST Champ 85; Keystone ST Games 2nd Pl Trk 85; Girls Bsktbl All Star Hon Men; Biomed Engrng.

LEPPERT, TAMMY; Trinity HS; Washington, PA; (Y); 27/439; Debate Tm; German Clb; Hosp Aide; Ski Clb; Speech Tm; Chorus; Swmmng; High Hon Roll; 2nd Pl Ntl Qulfrrs Debate 86; West Liberty ST Coll; Math.

LEPSIC, ROBERT; Venango Christian HS; Oil City, PA; (Y); 16/42; Latin Clb; Pep Clb; Rep Frsh Cls; Rep Stu Cncl; Var Capt Bsktbl; Hon Roll; Clarion U Of PA; Scndry Educ.

LERCH, CHRIS; Gov Mifflin SR HS; Reading, PA; (Y); #41 In Class; Stu Of Qtr-Machnst-Toolmaker-Vo-Tech Berks Co 85 & 86.

LERCH, JENNIFER; Pen Argyl HS; Nazareth, PA; (Y); 17/129; Ski Clb; Band; Chorus; Concert Band; Jazz Band; Mrchg Band; Orch; Rep Stu Cncl; Church Yth Grp; Computer Clb; Sqd Of Yr 85; Sctnl Ldr Of Wndwds 86; Elite Sng Grp 85-87; Comp Sci.

LERCH, SUZANNE; Middletown Area HS; Middletown, PA; (Y); 1/167; Cmnty Wkr; FCA; Varsity Clb; Band; Chorus; Nwsp Stf; Yrbk Stf; Trs Frsh Cls; Trs Soph Cls; Trs Jr Cls; 1st Pl Amer Lgn Essy Nclr Engry 86; Acadmc All Amer 85-86; Mid Penn Conf All Star In Fld Hockey 85-86; Bio.

LERDA, ELIZABETH; Peters Township HS; Mc Murray, PA; (Y); 56/257; Church Yth Grp; Dance Clb; Thesps; Band; Concert Band; Drill Tm; Orch; School Musical; Hon Roll; Ntl Hist, Govt Awd 85; Ntl Ldrshp, Svc Awd 86; Librl Arts.

LERNER, HENRY; Susquehanna Township HS; Harrisburg, PA; (Y); 33/155; Library Aide; Band; Chorus; Jazz Band; Mrchg Band; School Musical; Hon Roll; Cmnty Wkr; Teachers Aide; Temple Yth Grp; Amer Music Abroad Europn Tour 86; 1st Pl Schl, Locl, Cnty Amer Legn Essy Cntst.

LEROSE, ANTONIO; St John Newmann HS; Philadelphia, PA; (Y); 33/338; Mathletes; High Hon Roll; Hon Roll; NHS; Acctg.

LERSCH, DAWN; California Area HS; Coal Center, PA; (Y); 12/101; Church Yth Grp; Drama Clb; Pres 4-H; FNA; Science Clb; Chorus; Church Choir; Nwsp Stf; 4-H Awd; Hon Roll; CA U; Lib Arts.

LERSCH, SHARI; Shaler Area HS; Pittsburgh, PA; (Y); 75/545; Church Yth Grp; Library Aide; Teachers Aide; Rep Frsh Cls; Rep Soph Cls; Rep Jr Cls; Rep Sr Cls; Rep Stu Cncl; Outstndng Prfrmnc & Excptnl Achvt Typg 85-86; Sawyer Bus Schl; Secy.

LERWICK, TANYA; Wissahickon S HS; Ambler, PA; (S); 15/277; CAP; Drama Clb; Chorus; Church Choir; School Musical; School Play; Variety Show; High Hon Roll; Hon Roll; NHS; Crtcs Awd-Excllnc Actng-Anul Scndry Schl Drma Festvl 85; St Olaf Coll; Intl Rltns.

LESAK, LYNDA; Carbondale Are HS; Simpson, PA; (Y); 17/140; Pres French Clb; FBLA; Ski Clb; Leo Clb; Letterman Clb; Church Yth Grp; School Play; French Hon Soc; High Hon Roll; Jr NHS; U Scranton; Biol.

LESCHEK, LISA; Gateway SR HS; Monroeville, PA; (Y); Exploring; Sec Science Clb; Band; Chorus; Concert Band; Jazz Band; JV L Trk; Hon Roll; 1st Pl Buhl Sci Fair 83; 1st Monroeville Sci Fair 83; Duquesne U; Pre-Med.

LESCOTT, BETH; Peters Twp HS; Bridgeville, PA; (Y); Church Yth Grp; Ski Clb; Capt Drill Tm; Yrbk Stf; JV Cheerleading; Powder Puff Ftbl; Trk; Hon Roll; Acadmc Ltr Excllnc 84-85; Hmcmng Ct Rep 84 & 85; Hmcmng Ct; Penn ST U.

LESE, VICKIE; Bentworth HS; Bentleyville, PA; (Y); Dance Clb; Boy Scts; Drill Tm; Rep Stu Cncl; JV Var Bsktbl; JV Var Sftbl; Var Vllybl; W Liberty; Dental Hygentist.

LESH, JULIE KAY; Bedford HS; Bedford, PA; (Y); 27/187; VP Sec Church Yth Grp; Chorus; Rep Stu Cncl; Var L Bsktbl; Score Keeper; Var L Vllybl; Hon Roll; FBLA Typng I Awd 85; Micro-Comp Tech I Awd 86; Juniata; Medcn.

LESHEN, SHANNON; West Mifflin Area HS; West Mifflin, PA; (Y); 95/340; Key Clb; Varsity Clb; Co-Capt Color Guard; Stu Cncl; Var L Bsktbl; Powder Puff Ftbl; Var L Sftbl; Hon Roll; NHS; Crmnl Jstc.

LESHER JR, JAMES M; Upper Dauphin Area HS; Gratz, PA; (S); 25/100; 4-H; FFA; Bsbl; L Wrstlng; 4-H Awd; Alferd ST Coll.

LESHER, JULIE; Kutztown Area SR HS; Lenhartsville, PA; (Y); 4/150; VP Church Yth Grp; Band; Chorus; Church Choir; Concert Band; Capt Drill Tm; Mrchg Band; Swing Chorus; NHS; Quiz Bowl; HOBY Fndtn Awd 84-85; Fmly Prac Med.

LESHER, KERRY; Archbishop Kennedy HS; La Fayette Hill, PA; (Y); Church Yth Grp; Cmnty Wkr; Drama Clb; Office Aide; Pep Clb; Chorus; School Play; Rep Stu Cncl; JV VP Score Keeper; Vllybl; Anne Gleba Awd 86; Grtst Effort Achive Diploma; PA St Grant 86; PA Textile & Science; Fash Des.

LESHINSKY, ANN MARGARET; Villa Maria HS; New Castle, PA; (Y); 8/24; Drama Clb; French Clb; Teachers Aide; Thesps; School Play; Stage Crew; Stu Cncl; Mgr Tennis; John Carroll U; Psychlgy.

LESHKO, ROBERT; Hazleton HS; Mcadoo, PA; (Y); Church Yth Grp; Cmnty Wkr; Red Cross Aide; VICA; Elks Awd; Hon Roll; Mansfield U; Thrpy.

LESIK, TAMMY; Fort Le Boeuf HS; Waterford, PA; (Y); Dance Clb; Chorus; JV Sftbl; Var Trk; JV Var Vllybl; Hon Roll; Physcl Ftns Awd 84-87; Mst Imprvd Plyr Awd Vllybl 85-86; Dist Qulfr Trck 86; Bus.

LESKEY, TRACY; Rockwood Area HS; Rockwood, PA; (S); AFS; NFL; Quiz Bowl; Speech Tm; Chorus; School Musical; Nwsp Stf; Yrbk Stf; Rep Stu Cncl; High Hon Roll; Hon Roll; All Cnty Chorus 84-86; Wilson Coll; Pre-Med.

LESKO, MERLE; Canon Mc Millan SR HS; Mcdonald, PA; (Y); 22/376; Crs Cntry; Trk; U Of Pittsburgh; Elec Engrng.

LESKO, TAMMY; Carmichaels Area; Crucible, PA; (S); 8/127; VP Art Clb; Yrbk Bus Mgr; Yrbk Ed-Chief; Off Jr Cls; Sftbl; High Hon Roll; NHS; Full Tuition Schlrshp At Uniontown Beauty Acad 84; CA U Of PA; Comp Sci.

LESKOVANSKY, SUSAN; Moshannon Valley JRSR HS; Morann, PA; (Y); Accntng.

LESKOWYAK, BETH; Western Beaver HS; Beaver, PA; (Y); Sec Exploring; Pres 4-H; Chorus; Mrchg Band; Bowling; Twrlr; High Hon Roll; Hon Roll; Equestrian Mgmt.

LESKUSKY, VINCENT; St Pius X HS; Pottstown, PA; (S); 2/137; Capt Crs Cntry; L Trk; Capt Wrstlng; High Hon Roll; NHS; Ntl Merit Ltr; NEDT Awd; Latin Clb; Science Clb; Amer Chemcl Soc Awd 84; Al-Area Crss-Cntry-Wrstlng 85 & 86; Pre-Med.

LESLIE, HEATHER; Wilson Area HS; W Easton, PA; (S); 5/129; Ski Clb; Mrchg Band; School Play; Trk; Twrlr; Hon Roll; Pres Jr NHS; NHS; Bloomsburg U; Elem Educ.

LESLIE, KAREN; Mohawk HS; Enon Valley, PA; (S); 9/141; Pres Church Yth Grp; French Clb; Sec FFA; FHA; Nwsp Rptr; Var Powder Puff Ftbl; L Var Trk; NHS; Yth Page Corrspndnt Newspaper 85-86; Math Tchr.

LESLIE, KRISTIE; Bishop Shanahan HS; Coatesville, PA; (Y); Church Yth Grp; Cmnty Wkr; Debate Tm; Hosp Aide; Pep Clb; Cheerleading; Coach Actv; Mgr(s); Hon Roll; NHS; Pre-Law.

LESNAK, LYNETTE; Marion Center Area HS; Indiana, PA; (S); 6/170; Church Yth Grp; Girl Scts; Latin Clb; Q&S; Band; Concert Band; Mrchg Band; School Play; Variety Show; Yrbk Bus Mgr; Math-Vrbl Tlnt Srch/J Hopkins U; Natl Socl Stud Olympd Dstnctn 84; Psychlgy.

LESNIEWSKI, MARIA; Sacred Heart HS; Simpson, PA; (Y); 16/56; Drama Clb; French Clb; FBLA; Ski Clb; Chorus; School Play; Stage Crew; Yrbk Stf; High Hon Roll; NHS; Pro Life Clb; Penn ST; Acctg.

LESZCZYNSKI, THERESA; Hampton HS; Allison Pk, PA; (Y); 24/255; Jazz Band; Mrchg Band; Pep Band; School Musical; Symp Band; High Hon Roll; NHS; Dist Hnrs Band 83-85; Regn Band 84; Allegheny Vly Hnrs Band 84-86; Music.

LETCHER JR, ROBERT; Hazleton Senior HS; Hazleton, PA; (Y); 90/360; Pres Chess Clb; French Clb; Pep Clb; Band; Concert Band; Drill Tm; Mrchg Band; Drama Clb; Tennis; High Hon Roll; Outstndng Achvt Comp Sci 86; Jr Ltr Bowling 85; Penn ST U; Comp Pgmr.

LETCHER, TAMMY; Hazleton HS; Hazleton, PA; (Y); VICA; Hon Roll; Ptsbrgh Art Inst; Photo.

LETCHFORD, ARDEAN; Tyrone HS; Tyrone, PA; (Y); Varsity Clb; Pres Frsh Cls; Pres Soph Cls; Pres Jr Cls; Pres Stu Cncl; Im Bsktbl; Var Ftbl; L Trk; Capt Wt Lftg; Var Wrstlng; Lock Haven U; Pblc Rltns.

LETHAM, KRISTIN; Elizabeth Forward HS; Mckeesport, PA; (Y); 40/315; Pres JA; Acpl Chr; Concert Band; Jazz Band; Mrchg Band; Cheerleading; High Hon Roll; NHS; Pres Schlr; School Musical; Mon-Yough Dist Banker 86; Penn ST U; Nrsng.

LETTIERI, MARIA L; Bishop Hannan HS; Old Forge, PA; (Y); Church Yth Grp; French Clb; Latin Clb; Chorus; Pres Sr Cls; Sec Rep Stu Cncl; JV Var Cheerleading; Var Tennis; Bishop Hannan Schlrshp 82-86; Scranton U; Bio Chem.

LETTO, DORI; Villa Maria Acad; Erie, PA; (Y); Cmnty Wkr; Model UN; Ski Clb; Stage Crew; Yrbk Stf; Swmmng; Hon Roll; Bus.

LEUBUSCHER, LYNN A; State College Area SR HS; State College, PA; (Y); Church Yth Grp; French Clb; Acpl Chr; Church Choir; JV Crs Cntry; Var Trk; Frnch Tst Grnd Cncrs 85-86.

LEUNG, LILY; The Mercersburg Acad; New York, NY; (Y); French Clb; Hosp Aide; Intnl Clb; Library Aide; PAVAS; Chorus; Fld Hcky; Tennis; High Hon Roll; Lion Awd; E P Manley Schlrshp Awd; Intl Frgn Lang Awd; Bio.

LEUNG, LISA; Council Rock HS; Holland, PA; (Y); 5/755; Church Yth Grp; Intnl Clb; Key Clb; High Hon Roll; Hon Roll; Jr NHS; NHS; Ntl Merit Schol; Pres Clsrm Schlr 85; Grmn Awd 86; Rlng Hls Elem Schlrshp 86; PA ST U; Hstry.

LEUTZE, STACY L; Schuylkill Valley HS; Leesport, PA; (Y); Rptr FBLA; Yrbk Stf; Kutztown U; Bus.

LEVAN, KIM; Hamburg Area HS; Hamburg, PA; (Y); 15/152; Hon Roll; NHS; Nrsng Schlrshp 86; Physic Achvt Awd 85; D O E Clb Awd 86; Reading Schl Of Nrsng; Nrsng.

LEVAN, KIMBERLY; Bishop Shanahan HS; West Chester, PA; (Y); 4/214; Cmnty Wkr; Exploring; Library Aide; Mathletes; Yrbk Stf; High Hon Roll; NHS; Prfct Atten Awd; Hghst Avrg Englsh, Spnsh, SR Soc Stds 85-86; New Cntry Clb Awd 85-86; 4 Yr Prfct Attndnce 85-86; Albright Coll.

LEVAN, PAMELA; Pine Grove Area HS; Pine Grove, PA; (Y); Church Yth Grp; Teachers Aide; Varsity Clb; Rep Sr Cls; Rep Stu Cncl; Var L Bsktbl; Var L Sftbl; Dlgt UN Sponsrd Odd Fellows 86; Prsdntl Ftns Awd 84-86; Soc Stds High Avg 86; History Tchr.

LEVATO, TERRI; Ambridge Area HS; Ambridge, PA; (Y); Pep Clb; Pres Jr Cls; Capt Cheerleading; Bradford Bus Schl; Scrtry.

LEVENSON, SCOTT; Freedom Area HS; Conway, PA; (Y); 27/160; Chess Clb; Intnl Clb; JA; Pep Clb; Spanish Clb; Orch; High Hon Roll; Hon Roll; Prfct Atten Awd; Pres Schlr; U S Nvy ROTC Schlrshp 86; Old Dominion U; Engr.

LEVENTHAL, MARK; Upper Dublin HS; Dresher, PA; (Y); 16/307; Am Leg Boys St; FBLA; Math Clb; Lit Mag; Rep Frsh Cls; Sec Jr Cls; Sec Sr Cls; Im Bsktbl; CC Awd; NHS; Acctng.

LEVERS, REBECCA; Pleasant Valley HS; Brodheadsville, PA; (Y); L Band; Chorus; Concert Band; Mrchg Band; Pep Band; School Musical; Nwsp Rptr; Hon Roll; Jr NHS; Coll Of New Rochelle NY; Wrtr.

LEVI, DANIEL; Canon Mcmillan SR HS; Eighty Four, PA; (Y); Drama Clb; Exploring; Latin Clb; School Play; Bsbl; Hon Roll; Pre Med.

LEVIN, JENNIFER; Upper Dublin HS; Dresher, PA; (Y); 20/307; Trs FBLA; Intnl Clb; Temple Yth Grp; Chorus; Yrbk Stf; Lit Mag; Stu Cncl; JV Socr; NHS; 1st Pl FBLA Rgnl Cmpttn Imprmpt Spkng 86; U Of PA; Intl Bus Rltns.

LEVIN, WENDY; Clearfield Area HS; Clearfield, PA; (Y); 7/320; Cmnty Wkr; French Clb; SADD; Church Choir; Im Bowling; High Hon Roll; NHS; Pre-Med.

LEVINE, LORI; Peabody HS; Pittsburgh, PA; (S); 14/235; Art Clb; Nwsp Stf; JV Crs Cntry; Mgr(s); Var L Trk; High Hon Roll; NHS; Half Schlrshp Art Pgm.

LEVIS, BILL; Bishop Kenrick HS; Eagleville, PA; (Y); Acctng.

LEVIS JR, JAMES W; Bethel Park SR HS; Bethel Park, PA; (Y); 208/535; Boy Scts; Robert Morris Coll; Mktg.

LEVIS, NICOLE; Brockway Area HS; Brockway, PA; (Y); Drama Clb; Band; Color Guard; Drill Tm; Variety Show; Yrbk Stf; Stu Cncl; Pom Pon; Sftbl; Hon Roll; 4th July Queen 86; Penn ST; Librl Arts.

LEVITSKY, JANET; Northwestern Lehigh HS; Breinigsvile, PA; (Y); French Clb; Y-Teens; Chorus; Yrbk Stf; Trk; Hon Roll; Cnsrvtn Clb; Interact; Kutztown U; Crmnl Justice.

LEVKULICH, TRACY; Canon Mc Millan HS; Lawrence, PA; (Y); Chorus; Nwsp Rptr; Wilma Boyd; Airline Res.

LEVY, ERIK; Emmaus HS; Emmaus, PA; (Y); 1/500; Computer Clb; French Clb; Scholastic Bowl; School Musical; School Play; High Hon Roll; NHS; Voice Dem Awd; Key Clb; Variety Show; Govs Schl For Intl Studies 85; Govs Schl For Scis 86; Harvard; Intl Studies.

LEVY, JONATHAN; Central HS; Philadelphia, PA; (Y); Ski Clb; Band; Jazz Band; Mrchg Band; School Play; Ftbl; Lcrss; Swmmng; Hon Roll; Ntl Merit SF; Naval Pilot.

LEVY, MARK; Freedom HS; Bethlehem, PA; (Y); 57/450; Yrbk Stf; Im Bsktbl; Var L Ftbl; Im Wt Lftg; JV Wrstlng; Hon Roll; Engrng.

LEVY, MARY; Mercy Vocational HS; Philadelphia, PA; (Y); Library Aide; Teachers Aide; School Play; Stu Cncl; Bowling; Sftbl; Hon Roll; Scl Stdys Awd 82; Chld Care & Chld Psychlgy Awd 82-83; Dntl Asstnt.

LEVY, SUSAN; Philadelphi HS For Girls; Philadelphia, PA; (Y); 92/395; Hosp Aide; Service Clb; Off Frsh Cls; Pres Sr Cls; Tennis; High Hon Roll; Fld Hcky; Lcrss; Hugh O Brian Yth Fndtn Amb 85; Oprtn Undrstndg 86; Blck Hist Mnth Ortrcl Cntst Awd 86; PR Ed-In-Chf 86; Bus/Corp Law.

LEWANDOSKI, BETH; Western Wayne HS; Lk Ariel, PA; (Y); 27/138; Pres 4-H; FBLA; Girl Scts; Office Aide.

LEWANDOWSKI, ANDREW; Father Geibel HS; Mt Pleasant, PA; (Y); Drama Clb; SADD; School Musical; Yrbk Stf; Lit Mag; High Hon Roll; NHS; Spanish NHS; PA Jr Acadmy Of Sci 1st Pl Reg/2nd Awd ST 84-85; Spnsh Merit Awd 84-86; Translator.

LEWANDOWSKI, GREG; Geibel HS; Mount Pleasant, PA; (Y); Ski Clb; Var Capt Ftbl; French Hon Soc; High Hon Roll; NHS; Athltc Grnt Frm Prnctn U-Ftbl 86; Henry J Oppermann Schlr Athlt Awd 86; All-Cnty Ftbl Plyr 86; Princeton U; Cvl Engrng.

LEWANDOWSKI, HELEN; Academy HS; Erie, PA; (Y); Church Yth Grp; Drama Clb; French Clb; Trs Model UN; Chorus; Variety Show; Yrbk Stf; Rep Frsh Cls; L Var Vllybl.

LEWANDOWSKI, PATRICIA; Academy HS; Erie, PA; (Y); 8/190; Chess Clb; Church Yth Grp; French Clb; Hosp Aide; Library Aide; Pres Model UN; Orch; Yrbk Ed-Chief; NHS; Eagan Schlr Awd 86; Mercyhurst Coll; Elem.

LEWARS, KATHY; Exeter HS; Reading, PA; (Y); 76/200; Church Yth Grp; Drama Clb; Leo Clb; Chorus; School Musical; Lit Mag; Hon Roll; Outstdng In Art-Exeter Wmns Clb 86.

LEWELLEN, JOHN; Holy Ghost Prep; Southampton, PA; (S); Mathletes; VP Pres Science Clb; Nwsp Stf; NHS; PA Gvnrs Schl Of Sci 85; Nvrl Acad Sci Smnr 86; Engrng.

LEWERT, SHARON; Pittston Area SR HS; Pittston, PA; (Y); Church Yth Grp; Dance Clb; Drama Clb; French Clb; Hosp Aide; Key Clb; Science Clb; Ski Clb; Nwsp Stf; Hon Roll; Nrsng.

LEWINGER, WILLIAM; Bangor Area SR HS; Bangor, PA; (Y); Camera Clb; Computer Clb; Red Cross Aide; Stage Crew; Nwsp Phtg; Nwsp Rptr; Nwsp Stf; Trk; High Hon Roll; Jr NHS; U Of Michigan; Psych.

LEWIS, AARON; Danville Area HS; Danville, PA; (Y); Computer Clb; Pres Drama Clb; German Clb; Key Clb; NFL; Ski Clb; Spanish Clb; Speech Tm; School Musical; School Play; Theatre.

LEWIS, ANDREA; Lincoln HS; Ellwood City, PA; (Y); Drama Clb; Hosp Aide; Y-Teens; Concert Band; Drm Mjr(t); Mrchg Band; School Musical; High Hon Roll; Hon Roll; NEDT Awd; Geneva Coll; Psych.

LEWIS, ARLEY; Punxsutawney Area SR HS; Punxsutawney, PA; (Y); #4 In Class; Rep Art Clb; French Clb; Math Tm; Science Clb; Yrbk Phtg; Rep Stu Cncl; High Hon Roll; Hon Roll; Rotary Awd; Hugh O Brien Awd 85.

LEWIS, BARBARA; Sheffield Area JR-SR HS; Sheffield, PA; (Y); Church Yth Grp; FBLA; Office Aide; Red Cross Aide; Teachers Aide; VP Chorus; Church Choir; Color Guard; Nwsp Stf; Achvt Awd-Driving 85; Jamestown Bus Coll; Lgl Secy.

LEWIS, BRIAN; Hanover Area JRSR HS; Warrior Run, PA; (Y); Church Yth Grp; High Hon Roll; NHS.

LEWIS, CHRISTOPHER; Curwensville Area HS; Curwensville, PA; (Y); Chess Clb; Church Yth Grp; Letterman Clb; VICA; Stage Crew; Bsbl; Ftbl; Wt Lftg; Wrstlng; Drftng.

LEWIS, CYNTHIA D; Mount Union Area JR SR HS; Mount Union, PA; (Y); Church Yth Grp; GAA; Library Aide; Spanish Clb; Band; Mrchg Band; JV Im Bsktbl; Mgr(s); Var Sftbl; Var Trk; PA ST U; Compu.

LEWIS, DARLENE; Bishop Hannan HS; Scranton, PA; (Y); 21/125; French Clb; Girl Scts; Hosp Aide; JA; Ski Clb; Stage Crew; Bowling; High Hon Roll; NHS; Lawyer.

LEWIS, DAVID; Emmaus HS; Emmaus, PA; (Y); 80/500; Trs Church Yth Grp; Exploring; German Clb; Key Clb; High Hon Roll; Hon Roll; Jr NHS; Ntl Merit Ltr; Syracuse; Engrng.

LEWIS, DAVID; Hanover Area JR SR HS; Wilkes Barre, PA; (Y); Trs Church Yth Grp; Model UN; Band; Chorus; Concert Band; Mrchg Band; School Play; VP Stu Cncl; Trk; Hon Roll; Acad Sci 82-86; Regnl Dist Chorus 84-85; Dist Regnl Band 85.

LEWIS, DEAN; Nazareth HS; Nazareth, PA; (Y); JV Bsbl; Var L Ftbl; Im Wt Lftg; Wrstlng.

LEWIS, DENISE; Bishop Hafey HS; W Hazleton, PA; (Y); 15/129; Trs German Clb; Hosp Aide; Stu Cncl; High Hon Roll; Hon Roll; NHS; PA Acad Sci Awd 84; Med Tech.

LEWIS, GARY; Fort Leboeuf HS; Waterford, PA; (Y); Church Yth Grp; Band; Concert Band; Mrchg Band; Pep Band; Var L Bsbl; Im Ftbl; High Hon Roll; Hon Roll; Edinboro ST; Farming.

LEWIS, GREG; Council Rock HS; Newtown, PA; (Y); Bsktbl; Bentley Coll; Bus.

LEWIS, JANNET; Meadville HS; Meadville, PA; (Y); Drama Clb; French Clb; Y-Teens; Chorus; Color Guard; Mrchg Band; Trk; Cazenovia; Arch Dsgn.

LEWIS, JENNIFER; Shikellamy HS; Sunbury, PA; (Y); Rep French Clb; Varsity Clb; Acpl Chr; Concert Band; Mrchg Band; School Musical; School Play; Rep Frsh Cls; Rep Soph Cls; Pres Jr Cls; Shippensburg U; Accntnt.

LEWIS, JENNIFER; Towanda HS; Towanda, PA; (Y); Rep Church Yth Grp; Drama Clb; French Clb; Girl Scts; Hosp Aide; Ski Clb; Concert Band; Var L Bsktbl; NHS; JR Mss 86; Pre-Dntstry.

LEWIS, LANCE; Spring-Ford SR HS; Collegeville, PA; (S); French Clb; FBLA; Ski Clb; SADD; Var Trk; Im Vllybl; Var Wrstlng; Cit Awd; Hon Roll; NHS; Intl Bus.

LEWIS, LESA; Hopewell SR HS; Aliquippa, PA; (Y); 42/295; Pres Church Yth Grp; Exploring; Trs Spanish Clb; Chorus; Church Choir; High Hon Roll; Hon Roll; NHS; PA ST U; Pre Med.

LEWIS, MARC; Germantown HS; Philadelphia, PA; (Y); Church Yth Grp; ROTC; Bsbl; Bsktbl; Crs Cntry; Ftbl; Swmmng; Trk; Wt Lftg; Hon Roll; Naval Acad; Navy.

LEWIS, MARK E; Cameron County HS; Emporium, PA; (Y); Boy Scts; Chess Clb; Band; Mrchg Band; Pep Band; JV Var Bsktbl; Var L Trk; Cit Awd; Hon Roll; JP Sousa Awd; PA ST U; Frstry.

LEWIS, MARK K; Pocono Mountain HS; Cresco, PA; (Y); 6/300; Drama Clb; Drm Mjr(t); School Musical; School Play; Lit Mag; Gov Hon Prg Awd; High Hon Roll; Ntl Merit Ltr; Rotary Awd; Church Yth Grp; Penna Dist Chorus Schlrshp 86; Carnegie Mellon U; Music.

LEWIS, MARY EDITH; Ambridge Area HS; Baden, PA; (Y); 10/265; Pres French Clb; Band; Jazz Band; VP Stu Cncl; L Trk; VP NHS; Ntl Merit Ltr; High Hon Roll; Hon Roll; PA All ST Band 86; Instrmntlst Mag Awd 86; All Amer Hall Fame Band Hnrs 86; Grove City Coll; Cmmnctn Arts.

LEWIS, MICHELLE; Garden Spot HS; New Holland, PA; (Y); 18/228; Church Yth Grp; Spanish Clb; Band; Orch; Stu Cncl; Cheerleading; Sftbl; Hon Roll; Jr NHS; Sec NHS.

LEWIS, PATRICIA; St Basil Acad; Philadelphia, PA; (Y); 2/97; Drama Clb; French Clb; Latin Clb; Lit Mag; Var Bsktbl; Var Fld Hcky; Var Sftbl; High Hon Roll; Hon Roll.

LEWIS, PAUL; Pocono Mountain HS; Mt Home, PA; (Y); 88/300; Pep Clb; SADD; Rep Sr Cls; Im Golf; Var Powder Puff Ftbl; Var Socr; Im Trk; Wrstlng; Bloomsburg U; Bus Mgmt.

LEWIS JR, RICHARD O; East SR HS; West Chester, PA; (Y); 14/376; Church Yth Grp; Cmnty Wkr; JA; Capt Var Trk; Elks Awd; French Hon Soc; NHS; Spanish NHS; Teachers Aide; Cit Awd; West Chester Area Hnrs Assmbly 85 & 86; Penn ST U; Sec Ed.

LEWIS, SCOTT; Oil City SR HS; Oil City, PA; (Y); Cmnty Wkr; Y-Teens; Rep Stu Cncl; JV Ftbl; JV Trk; Wt Lftg; Wrstlng; Hon Roll; Prfct Atten Awd; Arch.

LEWIS, SHELBY; Clarion Area HS; Sligo, PA; (Y); Trs Art Clb; Church Yth Grp; FCA; Trs FTA; Ed Yrbk Stf; Stat Ftbl; Capt Trk; Hon Roll; Trck Ltrmn; Chld Psychlgy.

LEWIS, STEVEN; Wyalusing Valley JR SR HS; Wyalusing, PA; (Y); 15/150; Am Leg Boys St; Var L Bsbl; Var L Bsktbl; Var L Ftbl; NHS; Letterman Clb; Spanish Clb; Varsity Clb; High Hon Roll; Hon Roll.

LEWIS, SUSAN; Pottsgrove HS; Stowe, PA; (Y); 2/195; Science Clb; Chorus; School Musical; Nwsp Ed-Chief; Rep Soph Cls; Rep Sr Cls; Elks Awd; High Hon Roll; VP NHS; SAR Awd; Century Club Schlrshp 86; Villanova U; Comm Arts.

LEWIS, TAMMY; Northern SR HS; Dillsburg, PA; (Y); 14/200; Church Yth Grp; Girl Scts; JV Fld Hcky; Powder Puff Ftbl; Hon Roll; NHS; Junzata Coll; Doctor.

LEWIS, TINA; Cedar Cliff HS; Camp Hill, PA; (Y); 14/287; Math Tm; Pres Spanish Clb; Capt Flag Corp; Mrchg Band; Stage Crew; Yrbk Stf; Rep Stu Cncl; High Hon Roll; Trs NHS; Pres Schlr; Wmns Clb Schlrp 86; 3 Gld Keys & 1 Blue Rbbn Schlstc Art Awds 85-86; 19th Cngrssnl Dist Art Awd 86; Kutztown U; Elem Ed.

LEWIS, TODD; Tyrone Area HS; Tyrone, PA; (S); 8/190; Church Yth Grp; 4-H; FFA; Speech Tm; Band; Chrmn Soph Cls; Chrmn Jr Cls; Wrstlng; High Hon Roll; NHS; Star Chptr Farmer Awd 86; Penn ST U; Animal Sci.

LEWIS, WALLY; West Scranton HS; Scranton, PA; (Y); 97/267; Boys Clb Am; Church Yth Grp; Letterman Clb; Ski Clb; Varsity Clb; Var Capt Bsbl; Var Capt Bsktbl; Im Wt Lftg; VFW Awd; Vtd To Schlstc Var Bsbl All Strs 86; Bus Mgmt.

LEWIS, WENDY; Mercuyhurst Preparatory Schl; Erie, PA; (Y); 50/150; Dance Clb; Exploring; French Clb; Thesps; School Musical; School Play; Ftbl; 3rd Pl Awd Poetry Schl Mag 85-86; Hon Drwng Schl Yrbk 85-86; Archtctr.

LEWULLIS, KAREN; Central Catholic HS; Allentown, PA; (Y); 11/220; Church Yth Grp; Pres Exploring; Math Clb; Service Clb; Ski Clb; Var Tennis; High Hon Roll; Hon Roll; Jr NHS; NHS; PA ST U; Pre-Dntstry.

LEYO, MARIANNE; Glendale JR/Sr HS; Coalport, PA; (Y); 2/73; Science Clb; Chorus; Yrbk Ed-Chief; Yrbk Stf; Var L Sftbl; NHS; Sal; Duquesna U; Phrmcy.

LEYSHON, DAWN; Sharpsville Area HS; Sharpsville, PA; (Y); Camera Clb; FBLA; Hosp Aide; Spanish Clb; Thesps; Church Choir; Nwsp Rptr; Yrbk Bus Mgr; Hon Roll; Yrbk Stf; Elem Ed.

LEYSOCK, CHRISTINE; Homer Center HS; Homer City, PA; (Y); 7/99; Chorus; Jazz Band; School Musical; Yrbk Ed-Chief; Sec Frsh Cls; Trs Soph Cls; Trs Jr Cls; Stu Cncl; Vllybl; Bausch & Lomb Sci Awd; Acad Achvt Awd 86; JR Acad Sci Awds 83-86.

LEYSOCK, SHERRI; Homer Center HS; Lucerne Mines, PA; (Y); 17/96; French Clb; Varsity Clb; Rep Stu Cncl; Var Capt Bsktbl; Var Capt Sftbl; Var Capt Vllybl; High Hon Roll; Hon Roll; NHS; Prfct Atten Awd; Appalachian Conf Plyr Of Yr 85 & 86; All Gazetteland 1st Tm Bsktbl Vllybl & Sftbl 84-86; Bus Mgmt.

LHEUREAU, THOMAS; Fort Cherry HS; Mc Donald, PA; (S); Computer Clb; Drama Clb; Math Clb; Science Clb; Ski Clb; VP Varsity Clb; VP Stu Cncl; L Bsbl; Mgr(s); NHS; Sports Med.

LIBENGOOD, CARLA; Charleroi JR SR HS; Charleroi, PA; (Y); Trs Church Yth Grp; FNA; Office Aide; Science Clb; Varsity Clb; Mrchg Band; Stu Cncl; Diving; Sftbl; Hon Roll; U Pittsburgh; Nrsng.

LIBERATI, NICK; Springdale HS; Cheswick, PA; (Y); Rep Stu Cncl; Var Capt Socr; Sccr WPIAL All-Str; Pittsburgh Pst Gztte Sccr Drm Tm.

LIBERATO, LYNNE; Blue Mountain HS; Auburn, PA; (Y); 16/249; Art Clb; Drama Clb; French Clb; SADD; School Musical; Yrbk Stf; Cheerleading; Swmmng; Trk; High Hon Roll; Trvl.

LIBERATO, REGINA; Chichester SR HS; Marcus Hook, PA; (Y); 46/270; Intnl Clb; Model UN; SADD; School Play; Yrbk Stf; Stu Cncl; Hon Roll; Widener U; Acctng.

LIBERATORE, KENNETH; St Josephs Preparatory Schl; Yeadon, PA; (Y); Im Bsktbl; Im Ftbl; St Josephs Prep Schlr Awd 83-86; Engrng.

LIBERI, CYNTHIA; West Chester East HS; West Chester, PA; (Y); 8/385; Hosp Aide; Chorus; Nwsp Sprt Ed; Var Capt Fld Hcky; Var Gym; French Hon Soc; High Hon Roll; VP NHS; French Clb; GAA; Stu Forum Rep & Stu 84-86; James E Deaver Memrl Schlrshp 86; James Madison U; Phy Thrpy.

LIBERTO, MURIEL; Central Catholic HS; Allentown, PA; (Y); 12/200; Intnl Clb; Math Tm; Ski Clb; Yrbk Ed-Chief; Lit Mag; NCTE Awd; NHS; Ntl Merit Ltr; PA Gov Schl Sci 86; 5-Day Chem Yth Schlrs Prg 86; Bio.

LIBERTZ, CATHERINE; Merion Mercy Acad; Phila, PA; (Y); 17/86; Cmnty Wkr; Office Aide; Spanish Clb; High Hon Roll; Hon Roll; Spanish NHS; Top 10 AATSP Spnsh Cmpttn 84-85; Top 20 Pct AATSP Spnsh Cmpttn 86; Cmmnctns.

LIBONATI, GENENE; Hazleton HS; Hazleton, PA; (Y); 7/343; French Clb; Scholastic Bowl; Service Clb; Color Guard; Stu Cncl; French Hon Soc; High Hon Roll; Jr NHS; NHS; Amer Lgn Aux Dpt Of PA Schl Awd 84; Wellesley Bk Awd 86; PA ST U; Engl.

LIBONATI, MICHAEL; Central HS; Philadelphia, PA; (Y); Intnl Clb; Science Clb; Im Vllybl; High Hon Roll; Hon Roll; Prsdntl Clssrm For Yng Amrcns 86.

LIBRANDI, DEBRA; New Castle HS; New Castle, PA; (S); 1/256; Church Yth Grp; Library Aide; Yrbk Stf; High Hon Roll; NHS; Prfct Atten Awd; Val; Youngstown ST U; Psychlgy.

LICHIENFELS, KERI; United HS; Robinson, PA; (Y); 31/157; Band; Mrchg Band; Yrbk Stf; Lit Mag; Var L Bsktbl; JV Powder Puff Ftbl; Var L Trk; Capt Twrlr; Hon Roll; NHS; All Cntry Trck Tm 85-86; Mst Valble Fld Athlete IN Cnty Trck Mt 86; Tchng.

LICHTENFELS, RAYMOND; Norwin HS; N Huntingdon, PA; (Y); 95/557; Church Yth Grp; Computer Clb; SADD; Chorus; Drill Tm; Hon Roll; Comptr Engrg.

LICHTENSTEIN, SETH H; Mt Lebanon HS; Pittsburgh, PA; (Y); 12/521; NFL; VP Speech Tm; Temple Yth Grp; Ntl Merit SF; NEDT Awd; Med.

LICHTENWALNER, CHARLES; Freedom HS; Bethlehem, PA; (Y); Church Yth Grp; French Clb; Band; Chorus; Church Choir; Concert Band; Drm Mjr(t); Jazz Band; Mrchg Band; Orch; Music.

LICHTENWALNER, MICHAEL; Emmaus HS; Emmaus, PA; (Y); 43/493; Church Yth Grp; Band; Concert Band; Jazz Band; Mrchg Band; School Musical; Bsbl; High Hon Roll; Jr NHS; NHS; Music Engr.

LICHTENWALNER, PRISCILLA; Emmaus HS; Macungie, PA; (Y); 164/475; Church Yth Grp; Pres FHA; Key Clb; Church Choir; Nwsp Rptr; Hon Roll; Erly Chldhd Ed.

LICHTINGER, JULIE; Fort Le Boeuf HS; Waterford, PA; (Y); 40/200; Chorus; School Musical; School Play; Rep Soph Cls; Rep Jr Cls; Stu Cncl; Stat Bsbl; Cheerleading; Ice Hcky; High Hon Roll; Hmcmng 86; Edinboro; Elem Ed.

LICHTY, LARRY; Emmaus HS; Wescosville, PA; (Y); 14/493; Boy Scts; Chess Clb; VP Computer Clb; German Clb; Math Tm; Scholastic Bowl; Church Choir; Lib Trs Mrchg Band; Rep Stu Cncl; High Hon Roll.

LICKER, LORANE; Lebanon SR HS; Lebanon, PA; (Y); 21/285; Camera Clb; Rep Church Yth Grp; French Clb; SADD; Chorus; Church Choir; School Musical; Nwsp Phtg; Yrbk Phtg; Hon Roll; Lebanon Vly Coll Ldrshp Smnr 85; Psych.

LICKMANN, DEBBI; Cedargrove Christian Acad; Philadelphia, PA; (Y); Church Yth Grp; Chorus; Church Choir; High Hon Roll; Hon Roll; Summer Missnry Traing Schl 85-86; Word Of Bible Inst; Psych.

LICWINKO, JOSEPH; Bishop Kenrick HS; Norristown, PA; (Y); 40/310; Band; Concert Band; Jazz Band; Mrchg Band; Orch; School Musical; School Play; Hon Roll; CPA.

LIDDICK, HOLLY; Susquenita HS; Duncannon, PA; (S); 19/183; FBLA; Leo Clb; Chorus; Hon Roll; Scrtry.

LIEB, DAVE; Hanover HS; Hanover, PA; (Y); Chess Clb; Cmnty Wkr; Rep Jr Cls; Im Badmtn; JV Bsbl; Var Bsktbl; Var Ftbl; Im Sftbl; Im Tennis; JV Trk; Sci.

LIEB, PAMELA M; Northampton SR HS; Bath, PA; (S); 58/465; AFS; Ed Yrbk Phtg; Yrbk Stf; Trs Stu Cncl; Var Capt Cheerleading; Capt Powder Puff Ftbl; Hon Roll; NHS; Stu Of Month 86; PA ST U; Pre Med.

LIEB, RONALD; Seneca Valley SR HS; Harmony, PA; (Y); Boy Scts; Church Yth Grp; Clarion U PA.

LIEBEL, CHERYL; Villa Maria Acad; Erie, PA; (Y); 42/133; Ski Clb; Cheerleading; NHS.

LIEBERMAN IV, JOHN B; Nativity BVM HS; Pottsville, PA; (Y); Ski Clb; Rep Frsh Cls; Stu Cncl; Capt L Ftbl; L Trk; Wt Lftg; Bus.

LIEBERMANN, LAURA; Sececa Valley HS; Mc Kees Rocks, PA; (Y); VP Sec Church Yth Grp; Drama Clb; VP Exploring; Girl Scts; Hosp Aide; Chorus; Ed Yrbk Stf; Tennis; Hon Roll; Pre-Med.

LIEBETRAU, EMILIE; Carlisle SR HS; Carlisle, PA; (Y); Cmnty Wkr; JV Var Fld Hcky; Hon Roll; Metropolitan Harrisbrg Outstndng Stu 86; Annl Schlstc Hnrs Bnquet 86; U In India; Lab Rsrch-Equine.

LIEBLER, CHRISTINE; Karns City HS; Chicora, PA; (Y); 18/116; Church Yth Grp; Chorus; Church Choir; School Play; Variety Show; Pom Pon; Grove City Coll; Cmmnctn Arts.

LIEBLER, CINDY; Mt Lebanon HS; Pittsburgh, PA; (Y); 2/524; Dance Clb; Hosp Aide; Office Aide; Pep Clb; PAVAS; Drill Tm; Mrchg Band; School Play; Variety Show; Sec Frsh Cls; Pre-Med.

LIEBLING, WILLIAM; Gateway SR HS; Monroeville, PA; (Y); Math Clb; Ski Clb; Ed Yrbk Stf; High Hon Roll; Hon Roll; NHS; Pres Acad Ftnss Awd 86; U Of Pittsburg.

LIEBMAN, LIONEL; North Hills HS; Pittsburgh, PA; (S); 27/475; Church Yth Grp; VP JA; Key Clb; Ski Clb; Im Bsktbl; Var Ftbl; JV Trk; Im Wt Lftg; High Hon Roll; Trs NHS; Aerospace.

LIED, STACEY L; Cocalico HS; Stevens, PA; (Y); 26/169; Exploring; Off Soph Cls; Pres Sr Cls; VP Stu Cncl; Capt JV Fld Hcky; Powder Puff Ftbl; JV Sftbl; Var Trk; High Hon Roll; Hon Roll.

LIED, TRACY; Ephrata HS; Ephrata, PA; (Y); 13/285; Church Yth Grp; Cmnty Wkr; Church Choir; Stage Crew; JV Fld Hcky; Im Powder Puff Ftbl; Stat Score Keeper; JV Trk; Im Vllybl; Hon Roll; MESSIAH; Psych.

LIEDTKA, STEPHEN; Bishop Egan HS; Morrisville, PA; (S); 1/257; Spanish Clb; Nwsp Rptr; JV Bsktbl; Var Tennis; High Hon Roll; Chess Clb; Latin Clb; Varsity Clb; Pres Frsh Cls; NHS; Ntl Hnr Scty 85-86; Cmnty Srv Corps 85-86; Jrnlst.

LIEN, MARCUS; Gateway SR HS; Monroeville, PA; (S); 1/508; Pres Chess Clb; Math Tm; Pres NFL; Sec Nwsp Stf; Lit Mag; Var Tennis; Gov Hon Prg Awd; High Hon Roll; NHS; Val; Scrng Higher Than 100 AHSME 86; Wstnghs Hs Sci Schlrshp 85; Engr.

LIESCHE, DARRIN; Abington SR HS; Phila, PA; (Y); 147/508; Intnl Clb; Tennis; Abington SR HS; Engrng.

LIETO, SUZANNE; Wallenpaupack HS; Hawley, PA; (Y); 14/153; 4-H; Band; Pres Concert Band; Pres Mrchg Band; Pres Stu Cncl; Var Bsktbl; Var Trk; High Hon Roll; Hon Roll; Sec NHS.

LIEU, THANH TU; Mount Penn HS; Reading, PA; (Y); Church Yth Grp; VP FBLA; Trs FTA; VP JA; Library Aide; VP Science Clb; SADD; Chorus; Nwsp Stf; Yrbk Rptr; Ray Kroc Yourth Achvt Awd 86; Sci Merit Schlrshp Awd 84-85; Intnl Teen Miss Rep 86; Drexel U; Bus.

LIGAMBI, PHILIP; St John Neumann HS; Philadelphia, PA; (Y); 74/338; Boys Clb Am; Temple; Law.

LIGENZA, ANGELA M; Marian Catholic HS; Nesquehoning, PA; (Y); 37/121; Art Clb; Cmnty Wkr; Ski Clb; School Play; Yrbk Stf; Annette Kielbasa Mem Awd 86; PA ST U.

LIGGITT, JEANNINA; Canon-Mcmillan SR HS; Southview, PA; (Y); 155/396; French Clb; FBLA; Chorus; Mgr(s); Score Keeper; Hon Roll; X-Ray Tech.

LIGHT, CHRISTINA D; Wallenpaupack Area HS; White Mills, PA; (Y); 5/129; Sec Church Yth Grp; Band; Church Choir; Jazz Band; Trs Sr Cls; High Hon Roll; Jr NHS; NHS; Sec Computer Clb; Scholastic Bowl; Pres Scholar 86-90; Bridgewater Gen Scholar 86-87; Bridgewater Coll; Bus Adm.

LIGHT, DOREE; Grace Christian Schl; Lebanon, PA; (Y); 6/20; Church Yth Grp; Drama Clb; PAVAS; Chorus; Church Choir; School Musical; School Play; Off Stu Cncl; Hon Roll; Dstngshd Chrstn HS Stu 85-86; 1st Pl Fne Arts Comptn 85-86; 2nd Pl Ntl Chrstn Comptn 83-85; Liberty U; Music.

LIGHT, MATT; Annville-Cleono HS; Annville, PA; (Y); 12/126; Math Tm; Quiz Bowl; Var Golf; Var Wrstlng; Pres Acad Ftns Awd 86; Rtry Boy Of Mnth 86; Air Force; Aerosp Engrng.

LIGHTNER, TINA; Bishop Guilfoyle HS; Altoona, PA; (Y); 44/144; Cmnty Wkr; Trs Frsh Cls; Rep Soph Cls; Rep Jr Cls; Trs Sr Cls; Rep Stu Cncl; JV Bsktbl; Var Vllybl; Hon Roll; Ntl Physcl Ftnss Awd 86; PA ST U.

LIGUS, PAULA; Montour HS; Coraopolis, PA; (Y); Pep Clb; High Hon Roll; Hon Roll; NHS; Pittsburgh U; Dietcn.

LIJEWSKI, MICHELLE M; West Mifflin Area HS; West Mifflin, PA; (Y); Exploring; FBLA; Pep Clb; Ski Clb; Concert Band; Orch; L Socr; L Trk; Bethany Coll; Acctng.

LILJA, JACQUELINE; Coudersport Area JR SR HS; Coudersport, PA; (Y); Church Yth Grp; VP Varsity Clb; Chorus; Concert Band; Mrchg Band; Var JV Bsktbl; Var Trk; High Hon Roll; NHS; Computer Clb; Conservation Ldrshp Schl Outstndg Stu 84.

LILLER, NICOLETTE A; Our Lady Of The Sacred Heart Acad; Coraopolis, PA; (Y); Band; Chorus; Orch; School Musical; Vllybl; Hon Roll; NHS; Hghst Achvt Frnch 85-86; Hghst Achvt Instrmntl Instrctn 84-85; Hgh Achvt Studio Art 84-85; U Of Pittsburgh; Intl Bus.

LILLEY, CHANDRA; Manheim Township HS; Lancaster, PA; (Y); 73/325; VP Church Yth Grp; Nwsp Phtg; Nwsp Rptr; Hon Roll; JV Cheerleading; JV Trk; Awds Ballet & Tap Dancng 85; Awds Jazz & Tap Dancng 84; Psych.

LILLEY, RENEE; Southmoreland SR HS; Mt Pleasant, PA; (Y); French Clb; Hosp Aide; Letterman Clb; Pep Clb; Chorus; Cheerleading; Powder Puff Ftbl; Hon Roll; IN U Of PA; Nrsng.

LILLEY, TODD; Mount Pleasant Area HS; Donegal, PA; (Y); Church Yth Grp; VP 4-H; Ski Clb; Band; Concert Band; Jazz Band; Mrchg Band; Pep Band; Yrbk Stf; Trk.

LILYQUIST, MICHELLE; Bald Eagle Area HS; Howad, PA; (Y); Church Yth Grp; SADD; Chorus; Church Choir; Rep Jr Cls; Off Sr Cls; Rep Stu Cncl; Var L Cheerleading; High Hon Roll; Hon Roll; Bio Achvt Awd 83-84; Jump Rp Hrt Merit 8384; Cert Of Crdt Typng 85-86; PA ST U; Cmmnctn.

LIM, HUY; Upper Darby SR HS; Upr Darby, PA; (Y); Intnl Clb; Spanish Clb; SADD; Orch; School Play; Nwsp Phtg; Yrbk Phtg; High Hon Roll; Hon Roll; Tennis; Pharmacy Coll Of Sci; Pharm.

LIM, JAMES; Pennsbury HS; Princeton, NJ; (Y); Computer Clb; French Clb; Orch; School Play; Bsbl; Socr; Wrstlng; Hon Roll; NHS; Prfct Atten Awd; Purdau Music Schlrshp 86.

LIMBACHER, JOHN E; Knoch HS; Saxonburg, PA; (Y); Am Leg Boys St; Church Yth Grp; VP FBLA; Mrchg Band; Pep Band; School Play; Stage Crew; High Hon Roll; NHS; Voice Dem Awd; Accntng.

LIMCUANDO, JANE; Somerset SR HS; Somerset, PA; (Y); Cmnty Wkr; English Clb; JA; Q&S; Spanish Clb; Varsity Clb; Ed Yrbk Stf; Chrmn Stu Cncl; NHS; Pres Schlr; Dcknsn Coll.

LIMONGELLI, JOHN; Archbishop John Carroll HS For Boys; Norristown, PA; (Y); 2/169; Mathletes; Quiz Bowl; Nwsp Rptr; Nwsp Stf; Yrbk Stf; JV L Tennis; High Hon Roll; NHS; Sec Schl Hnr Soc 85-86; Econ.

LIN, ANGELA; Ephrata SR HS; Ephrata, PA; (Y); 26/259; Trs Church Yth Grp; Chorus; Church Choir; Jazz Band; Lib Orch; School Musical; Nwsp Rptr; Gov Hon Prg Awd; NHS; Hon Roll; German Awd 85; Music.

LIN, CHARRISSA Y; Freedom HS; Bethlehem, PA; (Y); 4/424; Debate Tm; German Clb; Math Tm; Science Clb; Orch; Yrbk Rptr; NHS; Ntl Merit SF; Hosp Aide; JA; Dist Orch; PA Govr Schl For Sci; Genetcs.

LIND, LAURA; Taylor Allderdice HS; Pittsburgh, PA; (S); 57/376; Drama Clb; School Play; Nwsp Ed-Chief; Yrbk Ed-Chief; JV Bsktbl; Cit Awd; High Hon Roll; Crngie Mrt Schlrshp Awd 86; Wrtng Pblshd In Kngsly Assocns "creative Conspiracy" 83-84; Carnegie-Mellon U.

LINDAHL, KAREN; Strath Haven HS; Swarthmore, PA; (Y); French Clb; German Clb; Intnl Clb; Mrchg Band; Yrbk Stf; Stu Cncl; JV Capt Fld Hcky; Lcrss; Wt Lftg; Hon Roll; Pre-Law.

LINDAUER, KERRI; Norwin HS; Irwin, PA; (Y); 150/550; AFS; Debate Tm; French Clb; Leo Clb; NFL; Political Wkr; Speech Tm; SADD; High Hon Roll; Hon Roll; Delegate Wrld Affairs Cncl 85; Spec Olymnpcs Buddy 85-86; Alt Delegate World Affairs Conf Japan 85; Duquesne U; Accntng.

LINDEMANN, KRISTA; Harbor Creek HS; Erie, PA; (Y); AFS; Church Yth Grp; 4-H; French Clb; Girl Scts; Pep Clb; SADD; Band; Concert Band; Mrchg Band; Penn ST; Journalism.

LINDENAU, LISA; York Catholic HS; York, PA; (Y); 1/160; French Clb; Acpl Chr; Chorus; School Musical; Nwsp Stf; JV Vllybl; High Hon Roll; NHS; Bus Admn.

LINDENBERG, SARA; Northern Lebanon SR HS; Jonestown, PA; (Y); 1/170; Chorus; Concert Band; Mrchg Band; Orch; School Musical; School Play; NHS; Band; Church Choir; Arion Awd, JR Chem Awd 86; Frgn Lang.

LINDERMAN, J RUSSELL; Belle Vernon Area HS; Belle Vernon, PA; (Y); Church Yth Grp; Debate Tm; Ski Clb; Band; Crs Cntry; Socr; Vllybl; Wrstlng; High Hon Roll; NHS; Neurolgy.

LINDERMAN, TAMI; Southern Columbia Area HS; Elysburg, PA; (Y); 72/91; Hst Band; Chorus; Concert Band; Mrchg Band; Pep Band; School Play; Nwsp Rptr; JV Fld Hcky; Var JV Mgr(s); Var Trk; County Band; Actng.

LINDROSE, VALARIE; Blacklick Valley JR SR HS; Nanty Glo, PA; (S); 4/90; Camera Clb; Library Aide; Office Aide; Varsity Clb; Ed Yrbk Stf; Sec Jr Cls; Cheerleading; Vllybl; Hon Roll; VP NHS; Cambria-Rowe Business Coll.

LINDSAY, ANNE; New Hope-Solebury HS; New Hope, PA; (Y); Girl Scts; Concert Band; Trs Sr Cls; Rep Stu Cncl; Var Capt Bsktbl; JV Var Fld Hcky; JV Var Sftbl; Hon Roll; Bucks Cnty All-Cnty Band 83-84; Boston U.

LINDSAY, LAURA D; Mc Guffey HS; Claysville, PA; (Y); 7/200; Am Leg Aux Girls St; Sec German Clb; Varsity Clb; Chorus; School Musical; Yrbk Stf; JV Var Bsktbl; Var L Trk; High Hon Roll; NHS; Pres Acdmc Schlr Awd 86; Outstndng Stu Rcgntn Awd 83-86; Outstndng Ac Dmc Perf Awd 86; Penn ST U; Nrsng.

LINDSAY, ROBERTA; Benton Area HS; Benton, PA; (Y); DECA; FBLA; FHA; Letterman Clb; Library Aide; Chorus; School Play; Stage Crew; Sftbl; Twrlr; Acctnt.

LINDSEY, AVILDA; Harrisburg High John Harris Campus; Harrisburg, PA; (S); Pep Clb; Band; Concert Band; Mrchg Band; Trs Frsh Cls; Trs Soph Cls; Trs Jr Cls; Trs Sr Cls; Stu Cncl; Cheerleading; HACC; Bus.

LINDSEY, BRENDA; Corry Area HS; Corry, PA; (S); 37/215; French Clb; Chorus; Church Choir; Color Guard; Mrchg Band; School Musical; Rep Frsh Cls; Powder Puff Ftbl; High Hon Roll; Hmcmng Crt 83-85; Edinboro U; Spch & Hrng Thrpst.

LINDSEY, CAROL; Downingtown SR HS; Downingtown, PA; (Y); 140/519; Chorus; Rep Stu Cncl; Stat Mgr(s); Brd Ov Gvnrs Schlrshp Mlrsvl U 86-87; Shrthnd Awd; Mlrsvl; Bus Adm.

LINDSEY, CYD; Aliquippa SR HS; Aliquippa, PA; (Y); Church Yth Grp; Band; Church Choir; Concert Band; Mrchg Band; Rep Jr Cls; Stu Cncl; JV Trk; Hon Roll; Prfct Atten Awd; Robert Morris Coll; Legal Sec.

LINDSEY, DEBBIE; Northwestern HS; Lantana, FL; (Y); 43/150; French Clb; Girl Scts; Pep Clb; Chorus; School Musical; Hon Roll; Prfct Atten Awd; Assoc Schls Inc; Airlines.

LINDSEY, JOYCE; Bethel Park SR HS; Pittsburgh, PA; (Y); FBLA; FHA; Chorus; Sec Stage Crew; JV Vllybl; High Hon Roll; Hon Roll; Bus.

LINDSEY II, KIRBY C; Sheffield Area JR SR HS; Sheffield, PA; (S); 19/85; SADD; Sec Varsity Clb; Var L Wrstlng; High Hon Roll; Hon Roll; PA ST U; Engrng.

LINDSEY, SHERRY; Northampton Area SR HS; Northampton, PA; (S); 49/444; DECA; Exploring; Girl Scts; Library Aide; Mrchg Band; Hon Roll; 6th Pl PA DECA Dist Cmptn-Fin & Credt 86; 2nd VP Schl Chptr PA DECA 85-86; ST Cmptn PA DECA 86; Acctg.

LINDSEY, THERESA; Ambridte HS; Aliquippa, PA; (Y); Art Clb; Church Yth Grp; Dance Clb; Office Aide; SADD; Church Choir; Sec Trs Drill Tm; Nwsp Rptr; Sec Stu Cncl; Pom Pon; Accntnt.

LINDSTROM, LYNN; Clearfield SR HS; Clearfield, PA; (Y); 1/312; French Clb; SADD; Chorus; NHS; Acad All Amer 86; Bio.

LINEHAN, JEANINE; Cardinal O Hara HS; Clifton Hts, PA; (Y); 90/772; Church Yth Grp; Service Clb; Var Cheerleading; Coach Actv; Hon Roll; Intl Law.

LINEMAN, EDWARD; Landsdale Catholic HS; Lansdale, PA; (Y); 4-H; Var Ftbl; Var Ice Hcky; High Hon Roll; NHS; Exc In Accntng II 84-85; W Chstr U; Bio-Chmstry.

LINEMAN, KIM; West Forest HS; Oil City, PA; (Y); AFS; Chorus; School Musical; School Play; Stage Crew; Sftbl; Hon Roll; Erie Bus Schl; Bus Adm.

LINER, RON; Norwin SR HS; N Huntingdon, PA; (Y); 23/557; Ski Clb; JV Var Trk; Hon Roll; Prfct Atten Awd; Mchn Trd.

LINEY, BRENDA; Unionville-Chadd Ford HS; Coateville, PA; (Y); 123/300; Hon Roll; Goldey Beacom; Comp Opr.

LINGAFELT, GARY; Penn Cambria HS; Lilly, PA; (Y); Var Trk; Hon Roll; Mechanical Engr.

LINGENFELTER, BRIAN; Bellwood-Antis HS; Bellwood, PA; (Y); 7/123; Nwsp Phtg; Yrbk Phtg; Yrbk Stf; High Hon Roll; Sr Key Awd 85-86; Acad All-Amer 85-86; PA ST; Pre-Law.

LINK, DAWN; Carrick HS; Pittsburgh, PA; (S); Q&S; School Musical; Stage Crew; Nwsp Stf; Rep Frsh Cls; Rep Soph Cls; Capt Twrlr; Hon Roll; Pt Park Coll PA; Dance Educ.

LINK, JOANNE; Notre Dame Green Pond HS; Easton, PA; (Y); Church Choir; Yrbk Stf; JV Sftbl; High Hon Roll; Hon Roll; Easton Exchange Club 2nd Pl Freedom Shrine Test; Excllnc In Sec Studies; Dancer.

LINK, THOMAS; Central Catholic HS; Pittsburgh, PA; (Y); Aud/Vis; Boy Scts; Church Yth Grp; Computer Clb; Drama Clb; Band; Stage Crew; Lit Mag; Stat Socr; Hon Roll; U Of Pittsburgh.

LINNEMAN, DOUG; Unionville HS; West Chester, PA; (Y); 63/300; Boy Scts; Church Yth Grp; Intnl Clb; Band; Stage Crew; Variety Show; JV Trk; God Cntry Awd; Hon Roll; Egl Sct; Arch.

LINSENBIGLER, MARK; Clearfield Area HS; Clearfield, PA; (Y); French Clb; Var Bsbl; High Hon Roll; Hon Roll.

LINSEY, JASON; Northern HS; Wellsville, PA; (Y); 26/209; Var L Bsbl; Var L Ftbl; Var L Wrstlng; Hon Roll; NHS.

LINT, RICHARD; Connellsville Area HS; Connellsville, PA; (Y); Boy Scts; Ski Clb; VICA; Ftbl; Trk; Wrstlng; Vo-Tech Hnrbl 85-86; Crpntry.

LINT, TAMMY; Frazier HS; Dawson, PA; (Y); Church Yth Grp; Library Aide; Chorus; Hon Roll; Penn ST; Photogrphr.

LINTON, DAVID; Donegal HS; Mount Joy, PA; (Y); 6/150; Church Yth Grp; Computer Clb; L Bsbl; Var Socr; High Hon Roll; NHS; Ntl Merit Ltr; Rotary Awd; Spanish NHS; Dngl Sccr Bstr Clb Schlrshp 86; E Stroudsburg U; Comp Sci.

LINTON, TAMMY; Shamokin Area HS; Shamokin, PA; (Y); 35/236; Art Clb; Camera Clb; Drama Clb; Key Clb; Office Aide; Pep Clb; Science Clb; Spanish Clb; Varsity Clb; Band; SCLGY.

LINTZ, BRIAN; Reading SR HS; Reading, PA; (Y); 8/600; Band; Concert Band; Jazz Band; Mrchg Band; Pep Band; School Musical; Hon Roll; NHS; Ruth C Jones Schlrshp 86; Gldn R Serv 86; Pres Acad Ftnss Awd 86; Millersville U; Comp Sci.

LIO, DOMINIC; Riverview HS; Oakmont, PA; (Y); 22/125; AFS; Am Leg Boys St; Varsity Clb; Yrbk Sprt Ed; Rep Stu Cncl; Capt Ftbl; Capt Tennis; Hon Roll; NHS; Prfct Atten Awd; U Of Pittsburgh; Phrmcy.

LIOTT, NATALIE; Hazleton SR HS; Hazleton, PA; (Y); 109/400; Church Yth Grp; French Clb; Service Clb; Yrbk Stf.

LIPINSKI, DOREEN; Bishop O Reilly HS; Swoyersville, PA; (Y); Hosp Aide; Ski Clb; Spanish Clb; School Play; Stu Cncl; Cheerleading; High Hon Roll; NHS; Spanish NHS; Dist Chorus 85; 3rd Pl Natl Hstry Day Cntst 84; Indvdl Outstndng Achvt Chrldng 84 & 85; Kings Coll; Cmmnctn Brdcstng.

LIPINSKI, JOSPEH; Scranton Central HS; Scranton, PA; (Y); JA; Letterman Clb; Spanish Clb; Varsity Clb; Chorus; Bsbl; Ftbl; Trk; Hon Roll; Pre-Med.

LIPINSKI, MICHELLE; St Huberts HS; Philadelphia, PA; (Y); 40/367; Rep Cmnty Wkr; French Clb; Rep Soph Cls; Rep Jr Cls; Trs Sr Cls; Rep Stu Cncl; Cheerleading; Hon Roll; NHS; Prfct Atten Awd; Bio-Chem.

LIPKA, JILL; Central Cambria HS; Revloc, PA; (S); 1/195; Band; Church Choir; Concert Band; Jazz Band; Mrchg Band; Pep Band; Prfct Atten Awd; Val; Natl Hnr Roll 85; PA ST U; Arch.

LIPP, THERESA; St Hubert HS; Philadelphia, PA; (Y); 33/368; Church Yth Grp; Jazz Band; Orch; Hon Roll; NHS; Prfct Atndnc Awd.

LIPPE, CRAIG; Shady Side Acad; Pittsburgh, PA; (Y); Hosp Aide; Letterman Clb; Ski Clb; Nwsp Stf; Var L Ftbl; Capt L Ice Hcky; Wt Lftg; Hon Roll; U Of VT; Bio.

LIPPERT, BRIAN; Quigley HS; Baden, PA; (S); 10/110; Math Clb; Var L Bsbl; Var L Bsktbl; Var L Ftbl; Im Wt Lftg; High Hon Roll; Lion Awd.

LIPPERT, KELLEY; Mechanicsburg HS; Mechanicsburg, PA; (Y); 52/299; Trs Frsh Cls; Var Capt Bsktbl; Var Capt Fld Hcky; Var Trk; Var High Hon Roll; HS High Hon Sprts Awd 86; US Army Reserve Schlr/Athlete Awd 86; Fink Steiner Athlete & Schlr Awd 86; Shippensburg U.

LIPPY, KELIE; Northeastern HS; Manchester, PA; (Y); Office Aide; Hon Roll; NHS; Cosm.

LIPSETT, ANDREW; Minersville Area HS; Minersville, PA; (Y); 8/114; Boy Scts; Exploring; Ski Clb; Spanish Clb; JV Ftbl; Var Wrstlng; High Hon Roll; Hon Roll; NHS; Engrng.

LIPSKY, ROBERT; Minersville Area HS; Minersville, PA; (Y); 2/112; French Clb; Ski Clb; Yrbk Stf; Var JV Bsbl; Var L Wrstlng; High Hon Roll; NHS; NEDT Awd; VFW Awd; Arspc Engrng.

LIPTAK, BARBIE; South Allegheny HS; Port Vue, PA; (Y); 39/165; French Clb; Office Aide; Y-Teens; Nwsp Rptr; Yrbk Stf; VP Stu Cncl; Cheerleading; Hon Roll; NHS; Comm Schlrshp Wmns Clb 86; Pittsburgh U; Hlth Rcrds Adm.

LISAC, MICHELE; Kennedy Christian HS; Sharpsville, PA; (Y); Drama Clb; JA; Spanish Clb; School Play; Nwsp Stf; Yrbk Bus Mgr; Capt L Crs Cntry; L Trk; High Hon Roll; NHS.

LISCHNER, DENISE; West Mifflin Area HS; Pittsburgh, PA; (Y); Var L Powder Puff Ftbl; High Hon Roll; Hon Roll.

LISELLA, GUY; Towanda Area HS; Towanda, PA; (Y); Drama Clb; Ski Clb; Spanish Clb; Band; Concert Band; Drm Mjr(t); Mrchg Band; School Play; Trs Frsh Cls; VP Pres Stu Cncl; Aviatn.

LISHER, SANDRA; Abraham Lincoln HS; Philadelphia, PA; (Y); 101/400; Church Yth Grp; Hosp Aide; Pres Soph Cls; JV Vllybl; Hon Roll; Comp Sci.

LISHINSKY, DAVID; Punxsutawney Area HS; Punxsutawney, PA; (Y); 10/250; Exploring; Math Tm; Science Clb; Varsity Clb; Sec Soph Cls; Var L Bsbl; Var L Bsktbl; Var L Golf; High Hon Roll; NHS; Gftd Prgm; Physcl Thrpy.

LISHMAN, JENNIFER; Brandywine Heights Area HS; Topton, PA; (Y); 27/144; Pres Church Yth Grp; FNA; Band; Church Choir; Concert Band; Mrchg Band; Pep Band; School Play; Yrbk Stf; Hon Roll; Kutztown U; Elem Ed.

LISIEWSKI, LISA MARIE; St Huberts Catholic HS For Girls; Philadelphia, PA; (Y); 70/367; Church Yth Grp; Cmnty Wkr; Office Aide; Drill Tm; School Play; Stage Crew; Yrbk Stf; Hon Roll; NHS; Prfct Atten Awd; Temple U Grnt; Semi Fnlst Phila Cty Schlrshp; Temple U; Phrmcy.

LISJAK JR, LEONARD T; Central Catholic HS; Pittsburgh, PA; (Y); Dance Clb; VP JA; Ski Clb; Ice Hcky; Wt Lftg; Hon Roll; St Bonaventure U; Bus Adm.

LISOTTO, MICHAEL; Fox Chapel HS; Pittsburgh, PA; (Y); Church Yth Grp; Var Crs Cntry; Var L Trk; High Hon Roll; Hon Roll; Prfct Atten Awd; Ntl Sci Olympd 83; IN U PA; Bus Mgmt.

LISS, JENNIFER; Neshaminy HS; Langhorne, PA; (Y); Chorus; School Musical; Stu Cncl; Stat Bsktbl; Mgr(s); Score Keeper; Hon Roll; Comm.

LISS, KIMBERLY; Gateway SR HS; Monroeville, PA; (Y); Girl Scts; Science Clb; Temple Yth Grp; Concert Band; Mrchg Band; School Play; Nwsp Rptr; Rep Frsh Cls; Rep Soph Cls; Rep Sr Cls; Dickinson COLL; Intl Studies.

LISS, MICHAEL; Southhills HS; Pittsburgh, PA; (Y); 3/118; Letterman Clb; Ski Clb; Spanish Clb; Varsity Clb; Stage Crew; Pres Jr Cls; Stu Cncl; Var Capt Crs Cntry; JV Trk; Hon Roll; 1st Crss Cntry 84; 1st Frgn Lang Poster Cntst 84; 2nd Frng Lang Poster Cntst 85; Sprts Med.

LISTON, JOHN; Frazier HS; Grindstone, PA; (Y); Library Aide; Rep Frsh Cls; Var L Ftbl; Im Wt Lftg; Hon Roll; Acad All Am 86; Achvt Acad Sci 83.

LITAK, JOSEPH; Bethlehem Catholic HS; Bethlehem, PA; (Y); 8/215; High Hon Roll; PA ST.

LITCHKO, JOHN; Chichester HS; Boothwyn, PA; (Y); 13/318; Drm Mjr(t); JV Bsbl; JV Bsktbl; Jr NHS; Sec NHS; Rotary Awd; Pres Spanish NHS; Church Yth Grp; Political Wkr; Spanish Clb; Acad All Amer 86; Rotary Interact Schlrshp 86; Sprtsmnshp Awd 84; Neuman Coll; Accntng.

LITCHKOWSKI, JODY; John S Fine HS; Nanticoke, PA; (Y); FBLA; Hosp Aide; Letterman Clb; Varsity Clb; Variety Show; Nwsp Stf; Yrbk Stf; Cheerleading; Diving; Swmmng; Medcl Secy.

LITTELL, KIRK; Richland HS; Gibsonia, PA; (Y); Exploring; Nwsp Sprt Ed; Stat Ice Hcky; L Socr; Trk; Hon Roll; HS Art Shw 2nd & 3rd Pl 86; Pttsbrgh Hrns Art Shw Hnrbl Mntn 86.

LITTELL, TINA; Northwestern SR HS; E Springfield, PA; (Y); Model UN; Political Wkr; Spanish Clb; Yrbk Ed-Chief; Powder Puff Ftbl; Trk; Outstndng Stu Soc Studies 86; Schlrshp To PA Free Entrprz 85; Vol Fire Fghtr Sprngfld 86; Edinboro U; Pre-Law.

LITTLE, BRIAN; Belle Vernon Area HS; Belle Vernon, PA; (Y); Art Clb; Ski Clb; Var L Golf; High Hon Roll; NHS; Finance.

LITTLE, CHRISTINE; Lewisburg Area HS; Lewisburg, PA; (Y); 17/155; Chorus; Ed Yrbk Stf; Pres Frsh Cls; Stu Cncl; Bsktbl; Fld Hcky; Sftbl; Tennis; Hon Roll; Pres NHS; Joseph J Roy Schlrshp 86; PA House Awd/Schlrshp 86; U Of FL; Actg.

LITTLE, CRAIG; Altoona Area HS; Altoona, PA; (S); 2/683; Chess Clb; German Clb; Math Clb; Math Tm; Trs Science Clb; NHS; Ntl Merit Ltr; Sal; Carnegie-Mellon; Comp Sci.

LITTLE, CRYSTAL; Mc Keesport HS; Mckeesport, PA; (Y); GAA; Girl Scts; Varsity Clb; Band; Church Choir; Concert Band; Mrchg Band; Symp Band; Bsktbl; Cheerleading; Acctng.

LITTLE, HEATHER; Richland HS; Gibsonia, PA; (Y); 7/183; French Clb; Concert Band; Mrchg Band; Orch; School Musical; High Hon Roll; Hon Roll; NHS; Psych.

LITTLE, JEFF; South Western HS; Hanover, PA; (Y); Computer Clb; Ski Clb; Im Sftbl; Im Vllybl; Reloadng Clb 83-86; Penn ST U; Bus.

LITTLE, KARI; Central Dauphin HS; Harrisburg, PA; (Y); Ski Clb; Band; Mrchg Band; Orch; School Musical; Crs Cntry; Trk; High Hon Roll; Jr NHS; NHS.

LITTLE, LANCE; Hughesville HS; Hughesville, PA; (Y); Chess Clb; Hon Roll; Compu.

LITTLE, MELISSA; Kennard Dale HS; Stewartstown, PA; (Y); 12/130; Church Yth Grp; French Clb; Hosp Aide; Band; Chorus; School Musical; Yrbk Stf; Stu Cncl; Co-Capt Var Cheerleading; JV Vllybl; Dist Chrs 85-86; Pol Sci.

LITTLE, SANDY; Frazier HS; Perryopolis, PA; (Y); Church Yth Grp; Band; Concert Band; Mrchg Band; Pep Band; Sftbl; California U PA; Psych.

LITTLE, SHAWN; Newport HS; Newport, PA; (Y); Varsity Clb; Sec Jr Cls; Bsktbl; Fld Hcky; Sftbl; Hon Roll.

LITTLEFIELD, DEBORAH; Eisenhower HS; Russell, PA; (Y); #1 In Class; Church Yth Grp; Thesps; Chorus; Mrchg Band; School Musical; School Play; Swing Chorus; VP Frsh Cls; Sec Sr Cls; Var Cheerleading; Birgham Young U.

LITTLEFIELD, GEOFF; Council Rock HS; Holland, PA; (Y); 63/895; Band; Concert Band; Mrchg Band; Pep Band; Symp Band; High Hon Roll; Hon Roll; Vrsty Lttr Mrchng Bnd 84-85; Laser Technlgs.

LITTLETON, DAN; Governor Mifflin HS; Mohnton, PA; (Y); 80/300; Bsktbl; Crs Cntry; Trk; Bus Admn.

LITWHILER, CATHERINE; Benton Area JR SR HS; Benton, PA; (Y); Pres Church Yth Grp; Drama Clb; Pres Chorus; Lib Concert Band; Mrchg Band; School Musical; School Play; Stu Cncl; Var Cheerleading; NHS; Bloomsburg U; Math.

LITZ, JENNIFER LYNN; Butler Area SR HS; Butler, PA; (Y); 67/777; Science Clb; Thesps; Mrchg Band; School Play; Stage Crew; Jr NHS; Ntl Merit Ltr; 4-H; Library Aide; Spanish Clb; Pres Acad Ftns Awd 86; PA Higher Ed Assist Cert Merit 86; Partial Merit Schlrshp 86; Grove City Coll; Bio.

LITZELMAN, SUZANNE; Sullivan County HS; Dushore, PA; (Y); Church Yth Grp; Key Clb; Drm Mjr(t); Mrchg Band; Nwsp Bus Mgr; Nwsp Rptr; Nwsp Stf; Var Cheerleading; Var Pom Pon; Hon Roll; Awd Cert Newspaper Bus Mgr & Reporter 86.

LITZENBERGER, CHARLENE; Cocalico HS; Stevens, PA; (Y); Library Aide; Band; Concert Band; Mrchg Band; Yrbk Ed-Chief; Yrbk Stf; JV Sftbl; High Hon Roll; Hon Roll; Intr Dsgn.

LITZENBERGER, DINA; Boyertown Area SR HS; Boyertown, PA; (Y); Church Yth Grp; Girl Scts; SADD; Chorus; Orch; School Musical; High Hon Roll; NHS; Prfct Atten Awd; Library Aide; Girl Sct Gold Awd 86; Med Tech.

LITZENBERGER, SARA; Bethlehem Catholic HS; Riegelsville, PA; (Y); 20/215; Church Yth Grp; Key Clb; Church Choir; Var Bsktbl; Coach Actv; Mgr(s); Var Sftbl; High Hon Roll; NHS; Latin Awd 86.

LIU, SAM; Penn Hills HS; Pittsburgh, PA; (Y); 70/796; Church Yth Grp; German Clb; Science Clb; Varsity Clb; Church Choir; JV Var Bsktbl; Var L Trk; Jr NHS; NHS; Pres Schlr; Carnegie Mellon U; Elctrcl Engr.

LIVERMORE, CHARLA; Altoona Area HS; Altoona, PA; (Y); 33/750; Concert Band; Drm Mjr(t); Jazz Band; Mrchg Band; Crs Cntry; Trk; NHS; Pres Schlr; High Hon Roll; Sftbl; Instrmntl Music Stu Of Yr 86; Howard Pop Lindaman Musical Achvt Awd 83; IN U OfPA; Acctng.

LIVINGOOD, JOHN; La Salle College HS; Glenside, PA; (Y); 28/240; Pep Clb; Nwsp Rptr; Nwsp Stf; Yrbk Rptr; Lit Mag; Var Capt Crs Cntry; Var Trk; Hon Roll; NHS; Ntl Merit Ltr; J Wood Platt Caddie Schlrshp 86; Bucknell U Schlrshp Grant 86; Bucknell U; Pre-Law.

LIVINGSTON, DOUG; Mckeesport Area HS; Mckeesport, PA; (Y); 99/399; Off Jr Cls; Rep Stu Cncl; Var Capt Bsbl; Var Capt Ftbl; Var Wrstlng; All Sctn Tm Bsbll 85&86; All Cnfrnc Tm Bsbll 86; All Sctn Tm Ftbll 86; Bus.

LIVINGSTON, GWEN; Eastern York HS; York, PA; (Y); 2/170; Ski Clb; Nwsp Stf; High Hon Roll; Jr NHS; NHS; Erly Admssn To Clg 86.

LIVINGSTON, KELLEY; Fairchance-Georges HS; Smithfield, PA; (Y); Pres Church Yth Grp; Cmnty Wkr; Drama Clb; Trs FHA; Library Aide; Quiz Bowl; SADD; VICA; Chorus; Church Choir; Choir Stu Yr Awd 83; Creat Wrtng Short Stories Awd 84 & 86; Nrsng.

LIVINGSTON, TIMOTHY; Elizabethtown Area HS; Elizabethtown, PA; (Y); 27/237; Church Yth Grp; Trs Varsity Clb; Var Bsbl; Capt Var Ftbl; Var Wrstlng; Ftbl Plyr Of Wk 84-85; Rotry Boy Of Mnth 86; All Star Bsbl Tm 86.

LIVOLSI, JOE; Canon Mc Millan HS; Canonsburg, PA; (Y); 96/371; Cmnty Wkr; Latin Clb; Bsbl; Ftbl; Trk; Wt Lftg; High Hon Roll; Hon Roll; Ftbl Ltrmn 85-86; Wg'tlftng Trphs 86; Crmnlgy.

LIZAK, KIMBERLY; Pittston Area HS; Dupont, PA; (Y); 34/330; Computer Clb; French Clb; FNA; Ski Clb; JV L Sftbl; Var L Tennis; Var Trk; High Hon Roll; Hon Roll; Jr NHS; Luzerne Cnty Cmmnty Coll; Nrsng.

LIZIK JR, LAWRENCE; Kiski Area HS; Apollo, PA; (Y); Boy Scts; Exploring; Math Clb; Ski Clb; Varsity Clb; Chorus; Var L Bsbl; Var L Bsktbl; Var L Swmmng; High Hon Roll; W VA U.

LIZZUL, KATHLEEN; Shamokin Area HS; Shamokin, PA; (Y); VP Key Clb; Pep Clb; Varsity Clb; Orch; Yrbk Stf; Stu Cncl; Var L Bsktbl; Var L Crs Cntry; Var L Trk; High Hon Roll.

LLADOC, SARAH M; Notre Dame HS; Stroudsburg, PA; (Y); 9/49; Church Yth Grp; JA; Chorus; School Musical; School Play; Yrbk Stf; Sec Stu Cncl; JV Var Bsbl; JV Var Bsktbl; JV Var Cheerleading; Geo,Spnsh Awd Hgst Avg 85-86; Intl Studies.

LLEWELLYN, JOAN; Danville SR HS; Danville, PA; (Y); Church Yth Grp; Sec FHA; Office Aide; Chorus; Church Choir; School Musical; Nwsp Stf; High Hon Roll; Hon Roll.

LLEWELLYN, RICHARD; Blackic Valley JR SR HS; Nanty Glo, PA; (Y); 20/90; Camera Clb; Church Yth Grp; 4-H; German Clb; Varsity Clb; JV Bsktbl; Var JV Ftbl; Im Vllybl; Hon Roll.

LLOYD, BETHANN; Greater Latrobe SR HS; Latrobe, PA; (Y); 62/450; Church Yth Grp; Hosp Aide; Band; Concert Band; Mrchg Band; Pep Band; Symp Band; Var Sftbl; High Hon Roll; 4-H; Cnty Band 85; Medcl Explrs 84; Elec Engrng.

LLOYD, CHRISTINE; Glendale JR SR HS; Glasgow, PA; (Y); 6/76; Drama Clb; Science Clb; Band; Yrbk Phtg; Ed Yrbk Stf; Var Cheerleading; JV Var Powder Puff Ftbl; Var Sftbl; Hon Roll; NHS; B P W Woman Yr 86; PA ST; Bus Mgmt.

LLOYD, DAWN; Hazleton HS; Hazleton, PA; (Y); FBLA; Stu Cncl; Cheerleading; Bus Grphics Reg Ldrshp Cnfrnc 5th Pl 85; Cert Of Aprctn FBLA 85.

LLOYD, DIANE; Exeter SR HS; Reading, PA; (Y); 29/217; High Hon Roll; Hon Roll; Alvernia Coll; Accntng.

LLOYD, GWEN; Emmaus HS; Emmaus, PA; (Y); French Clb; Key Clb; Orch; Stage Crew; Nwsp Rptr; Lit Mag; Rep Soph Cls; Var L Tennis; Var Trk; Hon Roll; PA Govnrs Schl Arts Buchnell U 85; Pres Ottee Emplymnt Handcppd Essay Cont 86; All ST Band 86.

LLOYD, JEFFREY; Greater Latrobe SR HS; Latrobe, PA; (Y); 25/330; High Hon Roll; Hon Roll; NHS; Prfct Atten Awd; Prsdntl Acdmc Ftnss Awd 86; St Vncnt Coll Acdmc Schlrshp 86; St Vincent Coll; Acctg.

LLOYD, KATHY A; Belle Vernon Area HS; Perryopolis, PA; (Y); 64/276; Trs FBLA; Pep Clb; Ski Clb; Rfl Clb 84-85; CA U; Accntng.

LLOYD, LORILEI; United HS; Vintondale, PA; (Y); FBLA; Ski Clb; Band; Chorus; Concert Band; Capt Drill Tm; Mrchg Band; Trk; Hon Roll; Rifle Squad Capt 85-86; Cambria Rowe Bus Coll; Exec Sec.

LLOYD, MARK; Burgettstown HS; Burgettstown, PA; (Y); NHS; PA ST U.

LLOYD, MARK W; Susquehanna Township HS; Harrisburg, PA; (Y); 5/200; Am Leg Boys St; Model UN; Varsity Clb; Yrbk Rptr; Yrbk Stf; Rep Frsh Cls; Rep Soph Cls; Rep Jr Cls; Rep Stu Cncl; Var JV Bsktbl; Outstndng Frnch I Stu 84-85; Outstndng Frnch II Stu 85-86; Hghst Avg Advncd Math 85-86.

LOANE, ROBERT; Delaware County Christian Schl; West Chester, PA; (Y); 20/80; Church Yth Grp; Varsity Clb; Chorus; Rep Frsh Cls; Sec Soph Cls; Rep Sr Cls; Rep Stu Cncl; Var Capt Bsktbl; JV Socr; High Hon Roll; Pre-Law.

LOAR, MICHELLE; Mt Pleasant Area HS; Donegal, PA; (Y); 1/243; FTA; Concert Band; Jazz Band; Mrchg Band; Yrbk Stf; Tennis; CC Awd; High Hon Roll; Pres NHS; U Of Pittsburgh; Elec Engrg.

LOAR, TRACI; Waynesburg Central HS; Waynesburg, PA; (Y); VP Church Yth Grp; Camera Clb; Church Yth Grp; French Clb; Letterman Clb; Rep Stu Cncl; Var L Bsktbl; L Capt Trk; High Hon Roll; Hon Roll; Girl Month; Geom Awd & Alg II Awd; Sunfest Engry Fair 1st Pl; IN U; Math.

LOBAUGH, FAY; Biglerville HS; Aspers, PA; (Y); 4/78; Church Yth Grp; Pres FFA; Varsity Clb; Yrbk Stf; Var L Sftbl; NHS; Var L Fld Hcky; High Hon Roll; Cecil R Snyder Outstndng FFA Stu 86; Scott Ebbert Trostel Awd 86; Pres Acad Fit Awd 86; DE Vly Coll; Agribus.

LOBAUGH, KAY E; Biglerville HS; Aspers, PA; (Y); 6/78; Church Yth Grp; VP FFA; Varsity Clb; Yrbk Stf; Var L Sftbl; NHS; JV Tennis; High Hon Roll; Pres Acad Fit Awd 86; Cecil Snyder Outstndng FFA Stu 86; Schl Brd Schlr 86; DE Vly Coll; Agribus.

LOBEL, SUSAN; New Hope-Solebury HS; Doylestown, PA; (Y); 10/66; FBLA; Mgr(s); Score Keeper; Stat Socr; High Hon Roll; Hon Roll; Pres Acad Fit Awd 85-86; PA ST U; Bus.

LOBER, WALT; Mc Guffey SR HS; Washington, PA; (S); 30/216; Church Yth Grp; German Clb; Letterman Clb; Varsity Clb; Rep Soph Cls; Rep Jr Cls; VP L Bsbl; VP L Bsktbl; VP L Ftbl; VP L Trk; All-Conf Ftbl 85.

LOBLEY, JENNIFER; New Hope Solebury JR SR HS; New Hope, PA; (Y); 22/79; Drama Clb; Band; Chorus; Mrchg Band; School Musical; VP Jr Cls; Pres Sr Cls; Stu Cncl; JV Tennis; Hon Roll; Poltc Sci.

LOBOS, SUSAN; Lewisburg Area HS; Lewisburg, PA; (Y); 12/147; Red Cross Aide; Spanish Clb; Varsity Clb; Var Capt Crs Cntry; JV Fld Hcky; Var Capt Trk; Hon Roll; NHS; Pres Schlr; Spanish NHS; PA ST U; Lbrl Arts.

LOBOZZO, MICHAEL; Canon Mc Millon HS; Canonsburg, PA; (Y); Thiel; Mecncl Engr.

LOBRON, NEIL; Saint Josephs Preparatory HS; Philadelphia, PA; (Y); Pres Chess Clb; Cmnty Wkr; German Clb; Office Aide; Stage Crew; Yrbk Stf; Socr; Stat Mgr(s); Sprtsmnshp Awd-City Chmpn Olney Sccr Clb 83; Certfd Amer Red Crs Adv Lfgrd 84; Germn Exch Prgm 86; Aero Engrng.

LOBUS, KELLY; St Francis Acad; Coopersburg, PA; (Y); Chorus; School Musical; Nwsp Rptr; Nwsp Stf; Lit Mag; PA Jnr Acad Of Sci 2nd Pl-ST Comptn 86; Mdcl Technlgy Awd 86; PA Jnr Acad/Sci-2nd Pl Rgnl Comptn 85.

LOCH, MICHAEL; North Catholic HS; Pittsburgh, PA; (Y); Boy Scts; Drama Clb; Hosp Aide; Ski Clb; Concert Band; Mrchg Band; School Musical; Yrbk Phtg; Eagle Scout 85; Hugh O Brien Ldrshp Awd 84; Du Quesne U; Bus.

LOCH, NANCY; North Catholic HS; Pittsburgh, PA; (Y); 8/301; Church Yth Grp; Pres Red Cross Aide; Ski Clb; Concert Band; Capt Mrchg Band; Nwsp Sprt Ed; High Hon Roll; JP Sousa Awd; NHS; Otstndng Grad In Music 86; Dequesne U.

LOCH, SANDRA; Pennsbury HS; Yardley, PA; (Y); Band; Concert Band; Mrchg Band; Im Bsktbl; Im Gym; Im Vllybl; Engrng.

LOCHRIE, JAQUENETTE; Homer Center HS; Homer City, PA; (Y); French Clb; Girl Scts; Band; Concert Band; Jazz Band; Mrchg Band; Orch; Pep Band; School Play; Jr NHS; Band Member Of Month 86; Thiel Col6; Pre Pharmcy.

LOCK, RICHARD R; Devon Preparatory Schl; Paoli, PA; (Y); 3/48; Hosp Aide; Math Tm; Ed Nwsp Stf; Pres Jr Cls; Pres Stu Cncl; Var Socr; Capt Var Trk; High Hon Roll; Trs NHS; Harvard Book Awd; AP Bio Awd; Devon Prep Spirit & Loyalty Awd; Pre Med.

LOCKARD, JENNIFER; Immaculate Conception HS; Washington, PA; (Y); 7/51; Yrbk Stf; Sftbl; Vllybl; High Hon Roll; Hon Roll; NHS; Acad All Amer 86; Acctg.

LOCKARD, SHELLY; Chestnut Ridge SR HS; Imler, PA; (S); 5/107; Church Yth Grp; FBLA; Teachers Aide; Church Choir; Nwsp Rptr; Nwsp Stf; High Hon Roll; Hon Roll; NHS; Ldrshp Awd Ntl Hnr Soc 85.

LOCKAWICH, LISA A; Williamsburg Community HS; Williamsburg, PA; (Y); Trs Church Yth Grp; Nwsp Rptr; Nwsp Sprt Ed; Yrbk Ed-Chief; Yrbk Stf; Trs Jr Cls; Var L Bsktbl; JV Vllybl; Hon Roll; NHS; Careers Hlth Clb Treas 86-87; Rep SR Hgh Senate 85-86; Engrng.

LOCKBAUM, STEFANIE; Waynesboro SR HS; Mt Alto, PA; (Y); Pres Church Yth Grp; Intnl Clb; Ski Clb; Color Guard; School Musical; Gym; Cit Awd; Hon Roll.

LOCKCUFF, LORI; South Williamsport HS; S Williamsport, PA; (Y); 22/140; Pres French Clb; Sec Leo Clb; Band; Chorus; Church Choir; Var Trk; Hon Roll; Marine Bio.

LOCKE, MARY; Country Day Schl Of The Sacred Heart; Villanova, PA; (S); 1/16; Drama Clb; Nwsp Bus Mgr; Yrbk Bus Mgr; Off Frsh Cls; Off Soph Cls; Off Jr Cls; Off Sr Cls; Stu Cncl; Bsktbl; Fld Hcky; Manhattenville Coll Eng Awd 85.

LOCKE, MICHELLE; Brownsville Area HS; Chestnut Ridge, PA; (Y); Math Clb; Office Aide; Teachers Aide; Band; Hon Roll; U Of Pittsburgh; Crmnlgy.

LOCKE, SUSAN; Country Day Schl Of The Sacred Heart; Villanova, PA; (S); 6/40; Art Clb; GAA; Stage Crew; Yrbk Stf; Rep Soph Cls; Rep Jr Cls; Stu Cncl; Bsktbl; Fld Hcky; Lcrss; Moore Coll Of Art-Saturday Schlrshp 86; Art.

LOCKERMAN, LAURIE; Vincentian HS; Pittsburgh, PA; (Y); VP Church Yth Grp; Drama Clb; School Play; Stage Crew; Nwsp Stf; Yrbk Stf; Pres Frsh Cls; VP Stu Cncl; Var Capt Bsktbl; Var Coach Actv; Phys Thrpy.

LOCKETT, MONICA; Valley HS; New Kensington, PA; (Y); 22/227; JA; Spanish Clb; Varsity Clb; Chorus; Church Choir; Stu Cncl; Mgr Trk; High Hon Roll; NHS; Cnty, Dist Chorus Rep 83-84; Howard U; Cmnctns-Brdcst.

LOCKOVER, DOROTHY; Pocono Mountain HS; Pocono Summit, PA; (Y); Cmnty Wkr; JA; Library Aide; SADD; Nwsp Stf; Stat Fld Hcky; Wt Lftg; Hon Roll; JC Awd; Med.

LOCKWOOD, DEBORAH A; Kutztown Area HS; Kutztown, PA; (Y); 7/122; Band; Chorus; School Musical; Variety Show; Stu Cncl; Var JV Fld Hcky; High Hon Roll; JC Awd; NHS; Pres Church Yth Grp; Grimley Trust Schlrshp 86; Millersville U; Socl Wrk.

LODER JR, JOSEPH H; Valley Forge Military Acad; Wayne, PA; (Y); Boy Scts; ROTC; Drm & Bgl; L Golf; Jr NHS; GA Tech; Engrng.

LOEB, DANIEL; Hamburg Area HS; Lenhartsville, PA; (Y); Yrbk Ed-Chief; Var Bsbl; Var Bsktbl; Var Trk; Hon Roll; NHS; Kutztown; Acctg.

LOERCHER, LAUREN; Warwick HS; Lititz, PA; (Y); 100/259; Drama Clb; Thesps; Chorus; School Musical; School Play; Nwsp Rptr; Lit Mag; Var L Cheerleading; Hon Roll; Jr Actvty Clb 85-86; Drmtc Arts.

LOFFREDO, BOB; Mechanicsburg Area HS; Mechanicsburg, PA; (Y); 166/299; Spanish Clb; Band; Concert Band; Mrchg Band; Symp Band; Hon Roll; Messiah Coll.

LOFINK, RENEE; Hampton HS; Gibsonia, PA; (Y); Yrbk Stf; Powder Puff Ftbl; Vllybl.

LOFINK, RENEE; Moon SR HS; Coraopolis, PA; (Y); 27/330; Church Yth Grp; Key Clb; Color Guard; Capt Drill Tm; Mrchg Band; Symp Band; Rep Soph Cls; VP Stu Cncl; Hon Roll; NHS; Amercn U; Politcs.

LOFTUS, CAROL; Villa Joseph Marie HS; Warminster, PA; (S); 35/74; Cmnty Wkr; VP Service Clb; SADD; Chorus; School Musical; School Play; Coach Actv; Trk; Commnctns.

LOFURNO, AMY; St Huberts HS; Philadelphia, PA; (Y); Stage Crew; Nwsp Rptr; Fld Hcky; Trk; NHS.

LOGAN, CHRISTINA A; Manheim Township HS; Lancaster, PA; (Y); Church Yth Grp; Exploring; Pep Clb; Varsity Clb; Stage Crew; Rep Frsh Cls; VP Soph Cls; Sec Jr Cls; Rep Sr Cls; Sec Stu Cncl; Lncstr/Cntrl Penn Tnns Fmly Of Yr 86; Physcl Thrpy.

LOGAN, DOUG; Moon Area SR HS; Coraopolis, PA; (Y); German Clb; Var L Crs Cntry; Var L Socr; Var L Tennis; Var Capt Wrstlng; Hon Roll; NHS; Dist Champ In Wrestling 86; Schlr Athlet Awd WPIAL 86; U Of Chicago; Bus.

LOGAN, KAY M; Youngsville HS; Youngsville, PA; (Y); FBLA; Spanish Clb; High Hon Roll; NHS; Prfct Atten Awd; 3rd Pl Schlrshp Hnr Awd 85-86; Spnsh III,Chem Awd 86.

LOGAN III, SAMUEL TALBOT; Cheltenham HS; Glenside, PA; (Y); 10/365; Chorus; School Musical; School Play; Ntl Merit Ltr; NEDT Awd; Supt Awd Annual PA Schl Brd Assn Conv 86; Stck Brkr.

LOGAN, TIMOTHY; Norristown Area HS; Norristown, PA; (S); 152/396; VP DECA; JV Bsbl; JV Ftbl; Im Vllybl; JV Wrstlng; Hon Roll.

LOGUE, ELISSA; Bethlehem Catholic HS; Bethlehem, PA; (Y); 50/250; Key Clb; Model UN; Cheerleading; U MD; Fshn Merch.

LOGUE, KEIREN ANNE; Venango Christian HS; Cooperstown, PA; (Y); Cmnty Wkr; Dance Clb; Rep Debate Tm; Rep Model UN; Rep Spanish Clb; SADD; Variety Show; Nwsp Stf; Yrbk Stf; Trs Frsh Cls; Dstrbute Splys-Americare Found 85-86.

LOGUE, MARYANN; St Maria Goretti HS; Philadelphia, PA; (Y); 100/400; Camera Clb; Hosp Aide; Mathletes; Math Clb; Spanish Clb; Stage Crew; Nwsp Phtg; Yrbk Stf; Tennis; Hon Roll; Nrsng.

LOHR, CHRISTINA; Bensalem HS; Bensalem, PA; (Y); 3/538; Band; Chorus; Concert Band; Jazz Band; Madrigals; Mrchg Band; Orch; School Musical; Stu Cncl; JV Bowling; Regnl Band,Chorus 86; Dist Orch 86; Millersville U; Comp Sci.

LOHR, GREGORY A; Richland SR HS; Johnstown, PA; (Y); 3/128; Am Leg Boys St; Pres Key Clb; Math Clb; Ski Clb; Jazz Band; Mrchg Band; Orch; VP Jr Cls; Vllybl; NHS; IUP Hnrs Band 86; Natl Elks Fndtn Scholar 86; Pres Scholar UPJ 86; Rotary Scholar 86; U Pittsburgh Johnstown; Pre-Med.

LOHR, MARCI; Westmont Hilltop HS; Johnstown, PA; (Y); 75/163; Art Clb; Church Yth Grp; Drama Clb; JA; Thesps; Stage Crew; Yrbk Rptr; Yrbk Sprt Ed; Yrbk Stf; Psych.

LOHR, TINA MARIE; Shade HS; Stoystown, PA; (Y); 1/74; Church Yth Grp; DECA; FBLA; Hosp Aide; Chorus; Lit Mag; Rep Stu Cncl; Hon Roll; Val; Schrlshp Acad Of Cosmtlgy; Arts & Sci 86; Penn; Bty.

LOHT, BELINDA; Chief Logan HS; Mcclure, PA; (Y); French Clb; Band; Chorus; Church Choir; Concert Band; Mrchg Band; JV Fld Hcky; Hon Roll; Med Asst.

LOJAS, MARLENE; Hempfield Area HS; Irwin, PA; (Y); #84 In Class; Pep Clb; Color Guard; Vllybl; Hon Roll; Jr NHS; Penn ST; Bus.

LOLLA, RAYNA; Cheltenham HS; Maple Glen, PA; (Y); Art Clb; Aud/Vis; Church Yth Grp; Science Clb; Rep Stu Cncl; Tennis; Hon Roll; PA JR Acad Sci 1st, 2nd ST 85; Temple; Sci.

LOMBARDI, JOSEPH; St John Meumann HS; Philadelphia, PA; (Y); 30/330; Computer Clb; Science Clb; Spanish Clb; Yrbk Phtg; Yrbk Stf; Rep Frsh Cls; Rep Soph Cls; Rep Jr Cls; Stu Cncl; High Hon Roll; La Salle; Pre-Med.

LOMBARDI, PAULA; Faith Community HS; Washington, PA; (S); 2/28; Spanish Clb; SADD; Church Choir; Rep Frsh Cls; Sec Pres Stu Cncl; Capt Cheerleading; High Hon Roll; Awd Outstndng Achvt Engl 85; U Of MI; Music.

LOMBARDI, SILVANO; Archbishop Ryan HS; Philadelphia, PA; (Y); 98/429; Hon Roll; Temple; Arch.

LOMBARDO, ANGELA; Bishop Kenrick HS; Norristown, PA; (Y); 72/300; Drama Clb; Band; Church Choir; Concert Band; Mrchg Band; Orch; Pep Band; School Musical; School Play; Nwsp Stf; Brdcstng.

LOMBARDO, DANIELLE; St Maria Goretti HS; Philadelphia, PA; (Y); 51/300; French Clb; Hosp Aide; Teachers Aide; Variety Show; High Hon Roll; NHS; Ellis Grnt Scholar 86-87; NHS 85-87; 1st Hnrs 83-85; Jefferson Med Coll; Nrsg.

LOMBARDO, DIANA; Mohawk JR SR HS; New Castle, PA; (Y); Pres Latin Clb; Chorus; Flag Corp; School Musical; Stat Bsktbl; Stat Crs Cntry; Stat Trk; Hon Roll; PA JR Acad Sci Comp Sci 85.

LOMBARDO, LISA; Bishop Kenrick HS; Norristown, PA; (Y); 17/300; Band; Church Choir; Concert Band; Mrchg Band; Orch; Pep Band; School Musical; School Play; Nwsp Rptr; Nwsp Stf; All Catholic Bnd 86; Journalism.

LOMBRA, SHERRI; State College Area SR HS; State College, PA; (Y); 28/502; Rep Jr Cls; Rep Sr Cls; Var Capt Cheerleading; Im Sftbl; Im Vllybl; High Hon Roll; Kiwanis Awd; NEDT Awd; Prfct Atten Awd; PA ST U; Bus.

LOMMAN, KIMBERLY; West York Area HS; York, PA; (Y); 10/200; Band; Concert Band; Mrchg Band; Symp Band; High Hon Roll; Hon Roll; NHS; Mdrn Msc Mstrs Hnr Scty 84; JR Miss Fnlst 85; Rnld Young Schlrshp 86; York College Of PA; Mrn Blgy.

LONDON, NANCY; Punxsutawney Area HS; Big Run, PA; (Y); 11/247; Trs Church Yth Grp; Sec Science Clb; Sec Varsity Clb; Variety Show; Bsktbl; Ftbl; Var Trk; Var Vllybl; Hon Roll; NHS; Mary Ann Irvin Schlrshp 86; BPW Girl Of Mnth 86; MVP Vllybl 85-86; WV U; Phys Therpy.

LONDON, SHELLI; Coatesville Area SR HS; Malvern, PA; (Y); Library Aide; Office Aide; Flag Corp; Mrchg Band; Rep Stu Cncl; Hon Roll; Kathern Gibbs Bus Schl; Execsec.

LONDON, SUSAN; Upper Merion Area HS; King Of Prussa, PA; (Y); 15/320; Pres Intnl Clb; Math Tm; Model UN; Temple Yth Grp; Chorus; High Hon Roll; Ntl Merit Ltr; Hosp Aide; Red Cross Aide; Service Clb; Interact Pres 86; Acad Awd 84-85; Frnch Awd 84; Psychlgy.

LONG, ANDY; Cedar Cliff HS; Camp Hill, PA; (Y); 96/270; Nwsp Rptr; Nwsp Sprt Ed; Nwsp Stf; Rep Stu Cncl; Bsbl; Bsktbl; Hon Roll; Pres Schlr; IN U; Bus.

LONG, CHRIS; Laurel Valley HS; Bolivar, PA; (Y); 27/87; Boys Clb Am; Science Clb; Band; Mrchg Band; Golf.

LONG, DAYNA; Central Bucks HS West; Chalfont, PA; (Y); Cmnty Wkr; Acpl Chr; Drm Mjr(t); Jazz Band; Madrigals; Mrchg Band; Nwsp Stf; Hon Roll; NHS; Drama Clb; Amercn Musicl Fndtn Band Hnrs 85; JR Al-Amer Hall Fame Band Hnrs 85; Presdntl Acadmc Ftns Awd 86; W Chester U.

LONG, DIANE; Bishop Carroll HS; Ebensburg, PA; (S); 8/103; Sec Spanish Clb; Yrbk Stf; Rep Stu Cncl; L Cheerleading; Trk; Hon Roll; NHS; NEDT Awd; PA ST U; Med Technlgy.

LONG, ERICK; Hatboro-Horsham SR HS; Hatboro, PA; (Y); 43/286; Pres Church Yth Grp; Drama Clb; Pres Intnl Clb; Pres Service Clb; Acpl Chr; Pres Church Choir; Mrchg Band; School Play; Pres Stu Cncl; Boy Scts; Frgn Langs.

LONG, JANET; Bishop Carroll HS; Ebensburg, PA; (S); 5/102; Drama Clb; JA; NFL; Spanish Clb; Speech Tm; School Play; Rep Soph Cls; Rep Jr Cls; Rep Sr Cls; Var Capt Vllybl.

LONG, JENNIFER; Elisabethtown Area HS; Elizabethtown, PA; (Y); Color Guard; Flag Corp; Mrchg Band; Powder Puff Ftbl; Bus Adm.

LONG, JULIE; Columbia-Montour Area Voc-Tech Schl; Catawissa, PA; (Y); VP FHA; Hosp Aide; Nwsp Rptr; High Hon Roll; Hon Roll; Sec NHS; Bloomsburg Fair Assoc Schlrshp $1000 Awd 86; Rrotary Club Stu Of Wk 86; Outstndg Achvmnt Awd 86; Mansfield U; Home Ecnmcs.

LONG, JULIE A; Solanco HS; Peach Botton, PA; (Y); 30/238; Church Yth Grp; Dance Clb; Drama Clb; Office Aide; Radio Clb; Spanish Clb; Teachers Aide; Yrbk Stf; Capt Cheerleading; Mgr(s); Solanco Ed Sec Awd 86; Cert Awd Engl IV Hghst GPA 86; Elizabethtown Coll; Bus Adm.

LONG, KARYN; Trinity HS; New Bloomfield, PA; (Y); Church Yth Grp; French Clb; Hosp Aide; Pep Clb; High Hon Roll; Hon Roll; Radlgst.

LONG, KATHRYN; William Allen HS; Allentown, PA; (Y); 76/603; VP Key Clb; Letterman Clb; Ski Clb; Varsity Clb; Yrbk Stf; Sec Stu Cncl; Capt Tennis; Trk; Hon Roll; NHS; Cmptv Fgr Sktr 76-83; Bus.

LONG, LORRAINE; Harrisburg HS; Harrisburg, PA; (S); 20/443; Band; Chorus; Concert Band; Jazz Band; Mrchg Band; Orch; Pep Band; Symp Band; Rep Stu Cncl; Hon Roll; Mst Musicl Stu Of Yr 82; LSU; Music Ed.

LONG, MARK; Line Mountain HS; Dalmatia, PA; (Y); 17/109; Church Yth Grp; FBLA; Varsity Clb; Ftbl; Wt Lftg; Elks Awd; High Hon Roll; Hon Roll; NHS; Pres Schlr; Woodman Of World Hist Awd 85; Hghst Male Engl, Hist & Foreign Lang Awds 85; Schlr/Athlete Awd 86; Millersville U; Bus Admin.

LONG, MARY BETH; Greensburg Central Catholic HS; Greensburg, PA; (Y); AFS; Spanish Clb; Teachers Aide; Rep Soph Cls; Rep Stu Cncl; Swmmng; High Hon Roll; Hon Roll; Hnr Roll 83-86; Prmry Educ.

LONG, MELISSA; Seneca Valley SR HS; Zelienople, PA; (Y); 10/369; Thesps; Chorus; Color Guard; Mrchg Band; Pep Band; School Play; Symp Band; Var Trk; High Hon Roll; Hon Roll; Schlrshp Awd Recog & Schlstc Achvt 85-86; Gftd Prog; Bio.

LONG, MICHELLE; Karns City JR SR HS; Karns City, PA; (Y); 41/116; Am Leg Aux Girls St; Chorus; Hon Roll; 1st Pl Locl Write & Illus Own Bk Cntst Locl Libry 85.

LONG, MICHELLE; Mt Pleasant SR HS; Latrobe, PA; (Y); GAA; Spanish Clb; Color Guard; Mat Maids; Timer; Hon Roll; Spanish NHS; Business Career Inst; Acctg.

LONG, MICHELLE; Palmyra HS; Palmyra, PA; (Y); Drama Clb; Spanish Clb; Chorus; Cheerleading; Trk; Hon Roll; HACC; Bus.

LONG, PAM; Ringgold HS; Donora, PA; (Y); Camp Fr Inc; Church Yth Grp; French Clb; GAA; SADD; Band; Church Choir; Concert Band; Mrchg Band; Nwsp Ed-Chief; Nrsry Schl Tchr.

LONG, PAMELA; Altoona Area HS; Altoona, PA; (S); 7/683; French Clb; Key Clb; Math Tm; PAVAS; Science Clb; School Play; Rep Jr Cls; Jr NHS; NHS; NEDT Awd; PA ST U; Chmcl Engr.

LONG, PAUL; Northeast Catholic Schl; Philadelphia, PA; (Y); 14/362; High Hon Roll; NHS; Acctg.

LONG, PENNY; Pine Grove Area HS; Tremont, PA; (Y); 1/126; School Musical; Yrbk Ed-Chief; Yrbk Rptr; Rep Jr Cls; Rep Stu Cncl; High Hon Roll; NHS; Drama Clb; Girl Scts; Chorus; Hugh O Brian Yth Found Ldrshp Semnr 85; PA Free Entrpse Wk 86; Lang Range Planng Comm 86.

LONG, SANDY; Downingtown HS; Downingtown, PA; (Y); Exploring; Hosp Aide; Ski Clb; SADD; Chorus; Flag Corp; Yrbk Stf; Sftbl; Mgr Wrstlng; Cit Awd; Lvng Arts Awd 2nd Plc 86; Cardvsclr Tech.

LONG, SHERRI; Northern Lebanon HS; Annville, PA; (Y); Art Clb; German Clb; Chorus; School Musical; Swmmng; Vllybl; Hon Roll; NHS; Yth For Undrstndg Exch Stu To Austrlia 86; Form Capt Doveron Hgh Austrlia 86; 3rd Pl Pub Spkg Cntst 86; Flight Attndnt.

LONG, TAMMY; Hempfield HS; Lancaster, PA; (Y); Art Clb; Pres 4-H; Pres Library Aide; Quiz Bowl; Chorus; Church Choir; Drill Tm; Var Powder Puff Ftbl; JV Sftbl; Var Trk; Millersville U; Psychol.

LONG, TODD; Trinity HS; Carlisle, PA; (Y); 16/140; Cmnty Wkr; Dance Clb; Political Wkr; Ski Clb; Spanish Clb; Stage Crew; Variety Show; Rep Soph Cls; Rep Jr Cls; VP Stu Cncl; Crss-Cntry MVP 85-86; PA Math Leag Cert Of Merit 85-86.

LONG, TRACI A; Commodore Perry HS; Greenville, PA; (S); 8/65; Cmnty Wkr; Office Aide; Chorus; Church Choir; Yrbk Ed-Chief; Hon Roll; NHS; Thiel Coll; Bus Adm.

LONG, VANNA SON; Kensington HS; Philadelphia, PA; (Y).

LONG JR, WILLIAM A; Lock Haven SR HS; Blanchard, PA; (Y); 1/255; Pres Church Yth Grp; Sec Key Clb; Jazz Band; JV Var Bsktbl; High Hon Roll; NHS; French Clb; Band; Concert Band; Hghst Oveall Cls Avg Awd 84; Delg HOBY Ldrshp Sem 85; Excllnce Physcs Awd 86.

LONGACRE, TAMMY; East Juniata HS; Richfield, PA; (Y); 12/87; Camera Clb; Chess Clb; Rep Stu Cncl; Stat Bsktbl; Var L Fld Hcky; Stat Ftbl; Stat Trk; Hon Roll.

LONGACRE, TOBY; Hamburg Area HS; Hamburg, PA; (Y); 26/152; German Clb; Ski Clb; SADD; Yrbk Stf; Im Bsbl; Im Bsktbl; Var L Golf; Im Socr; Im Sftbl; Var L Tennis; Joseph Bruno Mem Schlrshp 86; Bloomsburg; Bus.

LONGDON, GAIL; Washington HS; Washington, PA; (S); Church Yth Grp; SADD; Acpl Chr; Band; Chorus; Concert Band; Madrigals; Pres Bowling; Hon Roll; PA ST; Mrktg.

LONGENBACH, LYNN; Allentown Central Catholic HS; Allentwn, PA; (Y); Church Yth Grp; Political Wkr; School Musical; Nwsp Stf; Yrbk Stf; Rep Stu Cncl; Hon Roll; Prfct Atten Awd; Crmnl Lawyer.

LONGENECKER, AMY; Lebanon SR HS; Lebanon, PA; (Y); 27/266; Church Yth Grp; Sec Latin Clb; SADD; Chorus; Church Choir; School Musical; JV Cheerleading; Hon Roll; Awd ESOL Tutor Peer Cnslr 83-86; Giftd Pgm 83; Svc Proj Vol 83-86; U DE; Bio.

LONGENECKER, BETH; Cedar Crest HS; Minot, ND; (Y); Church Yth Grp; 4-H; French Clb; Key Clb; Pep Clb; Color Guard; Mrchg Band; School Musical; Vllybl; Hon Roll; Nrsng.

LONGENECKER, JILL MARIE; Lampeter-Strasburg HS; Strasburg, PA; (Y); 11/158; AFS; Drama Clb; Sec FHA; Thesps; Chorus; School Musical; School Play; Stage Crew; JV Sftbl; Reg Nrs.

LONGLEY, KIM; Northampton SR HS; Bath, PA; (Y); FBLA; Fld Hcky; Hon Roll; Med Sec.

LONGMAN, ABBE M; Radnor HS; Villanova, PA; (Y); 56/378; Debate Tm; Drama Clb; Exploring; NFL; Speech Tm; Chorus; Madrigals; School Musical; High Hon Roll; Ntl Merit Ltr; ST Fnlst In Miss PA Co-Ed Pgnt 85; PA ST U; Pre-Med.

LONGNECKER, MARK; Red Lion Area SR HS; Red Lion, PA; (Y); 90/327; Varsity Clb; Band; Concert Band; Jazz Band; Mrchg Band; Pep Band; School Musical; Symp Band; Var L Tennis; JP Sousa Awd; Outstndng Concrt Band Awd 86; Stu Yr Awd 86; PAIS Scholar 86; Millersville U; Mth Ed.

LONGO, CARMELA; St Maria Goretti HS; Philadelphia, PA; (Y); Art Clb; GAA; Stage Crew; Tennis; High Hon Roll; Hon Roll; 1st,2nd Hnrs; Immaculate Coll; Pre-Med.

LONGO, DEBORAH; North Hills SR HS; Pittsburgh, PA; (Y); Office Aide; Var Bsktbl; JV Var Socr; Hon Roll.

LONGO, PETER; Girard Academic Music Program; Philadelphia, PA; (Y); 3/51; School Musical; Nwsp Stf; Yrbk Ed-Chief; Trs Soph Cls; High Hon Roll; NHS; Computer Clb; Science Clb; Chorus; Color Guard; Medl Hnr 84; Hghst Avg Mth, Chem, Italian, Music 82-85; Girard Home & Schl Acad Scholar 86; Drexel U; Htl/Rest Mgmt.

LONTZ, PAM; Millersburg Area HS; Millersburg, PA; (Y); Church Yth Grp; Band; Capt Color Guard; Concert Band; Mrchg Band; Nwsp Phtg; Yrbk Phtg; Stat Bsktbl; Sftbl; Hon Roll; Accntnt.

LOOMIS, BRETT; New Freedom Christian HS; Seven Valleys, PA; (S); Church Yth Grp; Chorus; School Play; Bsbl; Bsktbl; Hon Roll; Prfct Atten Awd; Hyles-Anderson Coll; Scndry Ed.

LOOS, WILLIAM L; Wilson HS; West Lawn, PA; (Y); 20/286; Aud/Vis; Church Yth Grp; FBLA; JA; Spanish Clb; L Bowling; Cit Awd; High Hon Roll; NHS; Pres Schlr; Elizabethtown Coll; Bus.

LOOSE, ERIN; Williamsburg HS; Williamsburg, PA; (Y); Am Leg Aux Girls St; JA; Nwsp Stf; Yrbk Stf; L Vllybl; Hon Roll; NHS; Intl Studies.

LOPATA, ANDREA; Aliquippa HS; Aliquippa, PA; (S); French Clb; Office Aide; Band; Concert Band; Yrbk Stf; High Hon Roll; Hon Roll; PA ST U; Pre-Law.

LOPAZ, PATRICIA; St Maria Goretti HS; Philadelphia, PA; (Y); 24/426; Mathletes; Math Clb; Soroptimist; Spanish Clb; Yrbk Stf; Rep Jr Cls; Rep Sr Cls; Cheerleading; NHS; Prfct Atten Awd; Villanova U; Chem Engrng.

LOPER, JILL; North Allegheny HS; Pittsburgh, PA; (Y); JA; Yrbk Bus Mgr; Mgr Yrbk Stf; JV Fld Hcky.

LOPEZ, DONATO; Pennsbury HS; Fairless Hills, PA; (Y); French Clb; SADD; Rep Frsh Cls; Rep Soph Cls; Rep Jr Cls; JV Ftbl; JV Swmmng; JV Trk; JV Wrstlng; Hon Roll; CA U Davis; Aerntcl Engr.

LOPEZ, ESTHER; Avon Grove HS; Avondale, PA; (Y); 59/150; Church Yth Grp; FBLA; SADD; School Play; Bsktbl; Vllybl; Hon Roll; Prfct Atten Awd; Immaculata Coll; Psych.

LOPEZ, EVELYN; Little Flower Catholic HS; Philadelphia, PA; (Y); Trs Spanish Clb; Orch; Rep Frsh Cls; High Hon Roll; Prfct Atten Awd; Palmer Methd Good Wrtrs Awd 80; Pierce JC; Bus Adm.

LOPEZ, FLOR; Jules E Mastbaum Voc Tech; Philadelphia, PA; (Y); Church Yth Grp; Spanish Clb; Acpl Chr; Band; Chorus; Mrchg Band; Bsbl; Vllybl; High Hon Roll; Hon Roll; Temple U; Elect Tech.

LOPEZ, MARIA; Thomas Edison HS; Philadelphia, PA; (Y); High Hon Roll; Hon Roll; Cmmnty Coll Schlrshp 86; Math Achvt Awd 84; Coll Of Philadelphia.

LOPINSKI, JULIE; Northern SR HS; Dillsburg, PA; (Y); 38/209; Church Yth Grp; Girl Scts; Band; Chorus; Concert Band; School Musical; Stage Crew; French Hon Soc; Hon Roll; NHS; Peer Cnslr; Bloomsburg U; Spch Path.

LOPINSKI, THERESA; A C Valley HS; Parker, PA; (Y); Sec Church Yth Grp; French Clb; Capt Drill Tm; Sec Jr Cls; Capt Cheerleading; Var Trk; High Hon Roll; NHS; Prfct Atten Awd; DAR Awd; Clarion U; Secndry Ed.

LORAH, AUDRA; W Hazleton HS; Ringtown, PA; (Y); FTA; Ski Clb; SADD; Thesps; Mrchg Band; Ed Yrbk Ed-Chief; Pres Stu Cncl; Cheerleading; Var Trk; Capt Twrlr; Walter Hagelagans Post Aux Awd 86; Most Outstndg Sut Cncl 86; Bloomsburg U; Education.

LORAH, HEATHER; Moon SR HS; Corapolis, PA; (S); DECA; French Clb; Teachers Aide; L Var Mgr(s); Var Score Keeper; L Var Wrstlng; DECA Cmptn Plcd ST Apparel Accessories 85-86; DECA Cmptntn 1st In ST 85-86; DECA Cmptntn 85-86; Bus Coll.

LORAH, MELISSA; Mahanoy Area HS; Delano, PA; (Y); Church Yth Grp; Drama Clb; Trs French Clb; Chorus; Variety Show; Trk; High Hon Roll; Hon Roll; NHS; NEDT Awd; Penn ST Hazleton; Elec Engrng.

LORCHAK, JOHN J; Panther Valley HS; Nesquehoning, PA; (Y); 24/133; Church Yth Grp; Trs Jr Cls; Bsbl; Co-Capt Ftbl; Trk; Hon Roll; Lycoming Coll; Bio.

LORD, CATHY; Mt Alvernia HS; Pittsburgh, PA; (S); 2/70; Computer Clb; Drama Clb; French Clb; Chorus; Stage Crew; JV Cheerleading; High Hon Roll; NHS; Ntl Merit Ltr; Prfct Atten Awd; Psych.

LORD, CHRISTOPHER FRANK; Stroudsburg HS; Stroudsburg, PA; (Y); 14/250; Church Yth Grp; German Clb; Scholastic Bowl; Spanish Clb; Varsity Clb; Stage Crew; Capt Bowling; JV Socr; High Hon Roll; NHS; PA Jr Acad Sci 3rd & 2nd Plc 84-85; The Coll Of Insurance; Actrl Sc.

LORD, LISA; Creative & Performing Arts; Philadelphia, PA; (S); 5/148; Church Yth Grp; Cmnty Wkr; Debate Tm; Chorus; School Musical; Variety Show; Yrbk Stf; VP Pres Stu Cncl; High Hon Roll; NHS; U Hartford Scholar 86; Wagner Coll Scholar 86; Music Mgmnt.

LORD, LOUISE; Purchase Line HS; Cherry Tree, PA; (Y); 41/127; Hst FBLA; Color Guard; Stat Trk; Bus Math 3rd Pl 85; Outstndg Stu Awd 85; Outstndg Bus Stu 86; Clarion U; Acctg.

LORD, RICHARD; South Park HS; Pittsburgh, PA; (S); 2/200; Boys Clb Am; Church Yth Grp; Nwsp Rptr; Mgr Swmmng; High Hon Roll; NHS; Ntl Merit SF; Natl Sci Celebrtn Guest 86; Schl Recrd Sit-Ups 85-86; U Pittsburgh Provosts Day Hnrb Mntn 86; Pol Sci.

LORD, STEFANIE; Conrad Weiser HS; Robesonia, PA; (Y); 1/184; Drama Clb; JCL; Key Clb; Chorus; School Musical; Capt Cheerleading; NHS; Sec Soph Cls; L Fld Hcky; L Trk; Cnty Dstrct Rgn Chrs 86; Conrad Weiser Sprt Awd 85; Ust Pl Ovrl Tlnt ST Ky Clb Cnvntn 86; Allentown Coll; Thtr Arts.

LORDI, TONI; Lincoln HS; Ellwood City, PA; (Y); 55/163; Service Clb; Spanish Clb; Y-Teens; Chorus; Yrbk Stf; Powder Puff Ftbl; Tennis; High Hon Roll; Hon Roll; Acad Awd; Spn Clb Awd; Slippery Rock U; Med Tech.

LORELLI, DAWN; Punxsy Area HS; Anita, PA; (Y); French Clb; Varsity Clb; Variety Show; JV Var Vllybl; Hon Roll; IUP; Elem Ed.

LORIA, JOSEPHINE; Central Bucks East HS; Warrington, PA; (Y); Cmnty Wkr; Chorus; Yrbk Stf; Hon Roll; NHS; Social Wk.

LORINC, KIMBERLY SUE; Gateway SR HS; Pitcairn, PA; (Y); 61/520; Church Yth Grp; Cmnty Wkr; Band; Church Choir; Concert Band; Mrchg Band; Symp Band; Psychlgy.

LORINCE, DONNA; Hazleton HS; Kelayres, PA; (Y); #51 In Class; French Clb; Teachers Aide; Chorus; Color Guard; Drill Tm; Twrlr; French Hon Soc; Hon Roll; Phys Thrpy.

LORINCZ, TERRY S; Southern Lehigh HS; Coopersburg, PA; (Y); VP Pres Exploring; VP JA; Scholastic Bowl; High Hon Roll; Hon Roll; Hnr Grad 86; Cngrssnl Mdl Hnr Recip Records 85; Messiah Coll; Elec Engr.

LORISO, ROBERT; South Park HS; Library, PA; (Y); Art Clb; Swmmng; Church Yth Grp; Hon Roll; Painting Go To 3 Rivers Art Fstvl 86; Navy; Pilot.

LOSAK, DIANE; Sun Valley HS; Brookhaven, PA; (Y); 47/349; Cmnty Wkr; VP FNA; Trs Political Wkr; SADD; Teachers Aide; Variety Show; Lit Mag; Cit Awd; Hon Roll; Jr NHS; Distngushd Stu 86; Stu Mnth 86; Awd Wrtng Comptn 85; Millersville U; Lib Arts.

LOSE, KELLY; Jersey Shore SR HS; Jersey Shore, PA; (Y); French Clb; FBLA; Band; Chorus; Concert Band; Mrchg Band; School Musical; Hon Roll; Bloomsburg U; Accntng.

LOSER, ANTHONY; Lebanon Catholic HS; Lebanon, PA; (Y); Letterman Clb; Var Bsbl; Var L Bsktbl; Var Golf; DE Valley Coll; Food Mgmt.

LOSS, EMMA; Villa Maria Acad; Erie, PA; (Y); Model UN; NFL; Science Clb; Band; Orch; Stu Cncl; JV Trk; Hon Roll; NHS; NEDT Awd; Merit Awd Stuart Hall Schlstc Awds Essy Comptn 85.

LOTZ, MARY; Mechanicsburg HS; Mechanicsburg, PA; (Y); Church Yth Grp; Cmnty Wkr; Chorus; Church Choir; Orch; Var Sftbl; Var L Swmmng; Var L Trk; High Hon Roll; Hon Roll; Cnty Orchstr 84-86.

LOUCKS, JEFF; Elkland Area HS; Osceola, PA; (Y); 4/87; Am Leg Boys St; SADD; Varsity Clb; Yrbk Sprt Ed; Rep Stu Cncl; Var Bsktbl; Var Socr; Var Trk; Hon Roll; NHS; Amer Legn Bsbl & All Star 85-86; Chmcl Engrng.

LOUCKS, THADDEUS JAMES; Altoona Area HS; Altoona, PA; (S); French Clb; Crs Cntry; Trk; Bio.

LOUDER, DANA; Clarion Area HS; Clarion, PA; (Y); Church Yth Grp; Band; Chorus; Concert Band; Jazz Band; Pep Band; School Musical; Swing Chorus; Variety Show; L Bsktbl; Prsdntl Physcl Ftnss Awd 84-86; Schlrshp Frd Wrngs HS Chorus 86; Music.

LOUDERBACK, DAVID; Council Rock HS; Wycombe, PA; (Y); Teachers Aide; Stage Crew; Trk; Vllybl; Hon Roll; Bucks Co CC.

LOUEY, MICHELLE; Littlestown HS; Littlestown, PA; (Y); 17/120; Band; Chorus; School Musical; Swing Chorus; Symp Band; Nwsp Stf; Yrbk Stf; High Hon Roll; Hon Roll; Med.

LOUGHERY, ROB; Central Bucks East HS; Warrington, PA; (Y); Boy Scts; Church Yth Grp; FCA; Chorus; Church Choir; Yrbk Sprt Ed; Var Bsbl; Var Bsktbl; Var L Ftbl; God Cntry Awd; Duke; Law.

LOUGHIN, MICHELE; Upper Meron HS; Norristown, PA; (Y); Girl Scts; Chorus; Church Choir; School Musical; High Hon Roll; Stu Exchng Prog YTU 86; Fashn Mdse.

LOUGHMAN, LAURIE M; Rochester Area HS; Rochester, PA; (Y); 5/100; Dance Clb; DECA; Teachers Aide; Drill Tm; Trs Frsh Cls; Trs Soph Cls; Trs Jr Cls; JV Cheerleading; Hon Roll; Trs NHS; Phys Ther.

LOUGHNER, DEBORAH S; Blackhawk HS; Beaver Falls, PA; (Y); 8/272; Chorus; School Musical; School Play; Yrbk Stf; Sec Stu Cncl; Powder Puff Ftbl; NHS; Mc Dermott Schlrshp; Locl 1082 Steelwrkrs Union; Grove City Coll; Tech Wrtg.

LOUGHNEY, CAROL; Pittston Area HS; Pittston, PA; (Y); 1/365; French Clb; Key Clb; Math Clb; Ski Clb; Var Trk; L Var Vllybl; Hon Roll; NHS; Para-Legal.

LOUGHRY, KEN; Karns City HS; Chicora, PA; (Y); 11/126; Spanish Clb; Var Capt Bsktbl; Var L Ftbl; Var Capt Trk; Hon Roll; NHS; Pres Schlr; Pres Acad Fit Awd 86; US Mrn Corps Dstngshd Athl Awd 86; Grove City Coll; Mech Engr.

LOUTZENHISER, TIMOTHY PAUL; East Pennsporo HS; Enola, PA; (Y); Camera Clb; Dance Clb; Trs German Clb; PAVAS; Ski Clb; Band; Concert Band; Mrchg Band; Pep Band; Stage Crew; Amer Musicns Abrd 85; Yrbk Achvt Awd 86; Gannon U; Fin.

LOVE, CARRIE; Mt Pleasant Area SR HS; Mt Pleasant, PA; (Y); 10/253; Latin Clb; Ed Nwsp Stf; Ed Yrbk Stf; Im Vllybl; High Hon Roll; NHS; Finance.

LOVE, DIANE; Lake-Lehman HS; Sweet Valley, PA; (Y); Band; Concert Band; Mrchg Band; Coll Miseracordia; Nrs.

LOVE, KEVIN; Derry SR HS; Derry, PA; (Y); Church Yth Grp; Drama Clb; French Clb; PAVAS; Chorus; School Musical; School Play; Nwsp Rptr; Yrbk Stf; Hon Roll; St Vincent; Theatre.

LOVE, KIMBERLY; Cornell HS; Coraopolis, PA; (Y); 1/87; Church Yth Grp; Key Clb; Science Clb; Sec Band; Nwsp Stf; JV Var Cheerleading; High Hon Roll; Jr NHS; NHS; Voice Dem Awd; Sci.

LOVE, LETTY; Brookville Area HS; Corsica, PA; (Y); German Clb; Key Clb; Pep Clb; Band; Chorus; Church Choir; Concert Band; Drill Tm; Sec Stu Cncl; Im Cheerleading; PA ST; Med Secy.

LOVE, LISA M; West Perry HS; Shermans Dale, PA; (Y); 27/190; Library Aide; Band; Color Guard; Concert Band; Flag Corp; Jazz Band; Mrchg Band; Pep Band; Hon Roll; JP Sousa Awd; PA All ST Lns Band 86; Cnty Band 84-86; Ldrshp Clb 86; Btcn.

LOVE, MATTHEW S; Emmaus HS; Macungie, PA; (Y); 37/498; Church Yth Grp; German Clb; Church Choir; Jazz Band; Orch; School Musical; Off Soph Cls; Off Jr Cls; Off Sr Cls; High Hon Roll; U Of DE; Chem Engrng.

LOVE, TOD; York Area Vo-Tech; York, PA; (Y); JA; VICA; Bsbl; Wt Lftg; Wrstlng; Hon Roll; PA ST U; Elec Tech.

LOVELACE, MAURI; Hanover HS; Hanover, PA; (Y); Concert Band; Mrchg Band; High Hon Roll; Hon Roll; NHS; Ntl Merit SF; NEDT Awd; Acturial Sci.

LOVELESS, KIMBERLY; Sayre Area HS; Sayre, PA; (Y); Drama Clb; French Clb; Office Aide; Ski Clb; Yrbk Stf; Lit Mag; Rep Jr Cls; Var Mat Maids; Hon Roll; U Of GA; Jrnlsm.

LOVERANES, MARIO; Corry Area HS; Corry, PA; (S); 10/215; Sec French Clb; Model UN; Rep Soph Cls; Rep Jr Cls; VP Stu Cncl; Var L Crs Cntry; Var L Trk; High Hon Roll; Case Western Reserve U; Pre-Med.

LOVETT, JILL; Charlenoi Area HS; Charleroi, PA; (Y); 7/185; French Clb; Science Clb; Service Clb; Ski Clb; Varsity Clb; Trs Soph Cls; Trs Sr Cls; Stu Cncl; Capt Cheerleading; Trs NHS; Charthene Jan Girl Of The Mnth 86; Natl Sci Merit Awd 86; Prom Queen 86; PA ST U; Bus Admin.

LOVING, DEBBIE; Bethlehem Catholic HS; Hellertown, PA; (Y); Church Yth Grp; Color Guard; Mrchg Band; Hon Roll; Exec Sec.

LOVRINIC, CHRISTINE; Tunkhannock Area HS; Tunkhannock, PA; (S); 4-H; French Clb; JA; Color Guard; Flag Corp; Hon Roll; NHS.

LOWDEN, AMY; Uniontown Area Sr HS; Ohiopyle, PA; (Y); 73/308; French Clb; German Clb; Teachers Aide; Chorus; Church Choir; School Play; French Hon Soc; High Hon Roll; Hon Roll.

LOWDEN, MELISSA; Shaler Area HS; Glenshaw, PA; (Y); 79/543; Church Yth Grp; GAA; Hosp Aide; Office Aide; Ski Clb; Yrbk Stf; Socr; Hon Roll; Rotary Awd; Spanish NHS; U Of Pittsburgh; Cmmnctns.

LOWE, DIANE; Millersburg Area HS; Millersburg, PA; (S); 3/82; French Clb; Key Clb; Spanish Clb; Var Powder Puff Ftbl; French Hon Soc; High Hon Roll; Hon Roll; Lang.

LOWE, ERIC; Manheim Central SR HS; Manheim, PA; (Y); 33/237; Church Yth Grp; Cmnty Wkr; Debate Tm; 4-H; Rptr FFA; Vllybl; 4-H Awd; High Hon Roll; FFA Awd Pblc Spkng 85-86; FFA Awd Lvstck Jdgng 84-85; Frm Show Awd 85-86; PA ST U; Ag Engrng.

LOWE, JAMES P; Muncy JR SR HS; Muncy, PA; (Y); 2/70; VP French Clb; Red Cross Aide; Varsity Clb; Pres Stu Cncl; Ftbl; Score Keeper; Timer; High Hon Roll; NHS; Sal; US Military Acad; Engrng.

LOWE, KAREN; Franklin Regional HS; Murrysville, PA; (Y); Varsity Clb; Var Bsktbl; Var L Sftbl; Clarion U; Spch Pathlgy.

LOWE, ROD; Great Valley SR HS; Malvern, PA; (Y); 20/258; Am Leg Boys St; FBLA; Science Clb; Spanish Clb; Varsity Clb; Bsktbl; Ftbl; Trk; High Hon Roll; NHS; Georgetown U; Acctg.

LOWENSCHUSS, ALAN; Harriton HS; Gladwyne, PA; (Y); Concert Band; Jazz Band; Mrchg Band; Orch; Bsbl; Crs Cntry; Trk; Hon Roll; NHS; Prfct Atten Awd; Bio.

LOWENSCHUSS, EDWARD; Harriton HS; Gladwyne, PA; (Y); Chess Clb; Math Tm; Band; Concert Band; Mrchg Band; Orch; JV Bsbl; JV Ftbl; JV Tennis; Var Trk; 2 Mile Relay 5th Pl Mdl Novice Meet 85-86; Law.

LOWER, DAVID A; Richland HS; Gibsonia, PA; (Y); Boy Scts; Church Yth Grp; Debate Tm; Speech Tm; Band; Jazz Band; Mrchg Band; Orch; Pep Band; Ftbl; Eagle Awd Sctng 86; Cornell; Archtctr.

LOWERY, ENJAY; Wilkinsburg JRSR HS; Pittsburgh, PA; (Y); Latin Clb; L Y-Teens; Drill Tm; High Hon Roll; Hon Roll; Spanish NHS; Bus Adm.

LOWERY, LEANN; Northwestern HS; Albion, PA; (Y); 12/162; French Clb; Library Aide; Chorus; Sec Yrbk Stf; Hon Roll; Edinboro U; Corp Lawyer.

LOWRANCE, ANDREA; Upattinas HS; Phoenixville, PA; (Y); Key Clb; Pep Clb; Scholastic Bowl; JV Lcrss; High Hon Roll; Hon Roll; Brd Natl Coalitn Altrnt Cmmnty Schls 86-87; Stdnt Rep Brd 86-87.

LOWRY, MARDI A; State College Area HS; State College, PA; (Y); 21/568; Hosp Aide; Ski Clb; SADD; Acpl Chr; Pres Band; Sec Chorus; Church Choir; Pres Concert Band; Drm Mjr(t); Mrchg Band; Fred Waring US Chorus Scholar 86; 1st Chair Dist Chorus 86; Outstndng Engl Awd 86; PA ST U; Mth Ed.

LOWSON, ALAN; Waynesboro SR HS; Mont Alto, PA; (Y); 15/353; Boy Scts; VP Church Yth Grp; Jazz Band; Var L Ftbl; Var L Trk; Capt Wt Lftg; Cit Awd; God Cntry Awd; High Hon Roll; Pres NHS; Eagle Scout 83; Biochem.

LOYA, SUSAN; Springdale HS; Cheswick, PA; (Y); 11/114; Art Clb; Spanish Clb; Yrbk Stf; Bsktbl; Coach Actv; High Hon Roll; Hon Roll; Art.

LOYACK, SHERRY; Towanda Area HS; Wysox, PA; (Y); 10/135; Drama Clb; French Clb; Model UN; Red Cross Aide; Spanish Clb; Sec Sr Cls; Hon Roll; NHS; 2nd Pl Natl Frnch Contest 83-84; 1st Pl Natl Frnch Contest 84-85; Lang Inst CA; Modern Lang.

LOZIER, GILLIAN; Sharpsville Area HS; Sharpsville, PA; (Y); Camera Clb; Cmnty Wkr; Math Clb; Science Clb; Spanish Clb; Thesps; Nwsp Stf; Yrbk Stf; JV Bsktbl; NHS; Early Admssn Opprtnty PA ST 86; PA ST U; Philosphy.

LOZINAK, LISA; Forest City Regional HS; Forest City, PA; (Y); Library Aide; Spanish Clb; SADD; Nwsp Stf; Hon Roll; NHS.

LU, THAT VAN; Unionville HS; Embreeville, PA; (Y); FBLA; Socr; Vllybl; Wrstlng; Cit Awd; Hon Roll; Jr NHS; Law.

LUBBERT, HARRY W; North Hills HS; Pittsburgh, PA; (Y); Var L Ftbl; Var JV Trk; Hon Roll.

LUBERT, AMY; Northern Cambria HS; Spangler, PA; (Y); Church Yth Grp; Drama Clb; NFL; Chorus; Color Guard; Yrbk Stf; Rep Stu Cncl; High Hon Roll; NHS; IN U Of PA.

LUBERT, MICHELLE; Monaca HS; Monaca, PA; (Y); 10/95; Library Aide; Pep Clb; Red Cross Aide; Spanish Clb; High Hon Roll; Hon Roll; NHS; Pre Med.

LUBINSKI, LYNN; Tunkhannock Area HS; Tunkhannock, PA; (Y); Computer Clb; Drama Clb; Chorus; Mrchg Band; School Musical; Capt Twrlr; Chrl Dir Awd 86; WTA Ms Mjrtt Mo 86; Twrlng Instrctr.

LUBINSKI, SUSAN; Pittston Area HS; Pittston, PA; (Y); 22/330; FNA; Drill Tm; High Hon Roll; Hon Roll; Trs Jr NHS; NHS; Prfct Atten Awd; Luzerne Cnty CC; Nrsg.

LUBY, DAVE; Bensalem SR HS; Bensalem, PA; (Y); Bsktbl; Ftbl; Wt Lftg; High Hon Roll; Hon Roll; Outstndng Athletes Amer 85-86; Proud Clb; Pol Sci.

LUCA, SHERRY; Lincoln HS; Ellwood City, PA; (Y); 48/162; French Clb; Key Clb; Band; Concert Band; Bowling; Powder Puff Ftbl; High Hon Roll; Hon Roll; Prfct Atten Awd; Acadmc Achvt Awds.

LUCABAUGH, MELISSA; Northeastern SR HS; Manchester, PA; (Y); Chorus; High Hon Roll; Hon Roll; NHS; Bus.

LUCARELLI, ANGELA; Hempfield Area HS; Irwin, PA; (Y); Computer Clb; Pep Clb; Service Clb; Soroptimist; Color Guard; Cit Awd; Gov Hon Prg Awd; High Hon Roll; Jr NHS; Spanish NHS.

LUCARELLI, MICHELLE; Mohawk HS; Edinburg, PA; (Y); 16/141; Church Yth Grp; Pres Spanish Clb; Mrchg Band; VP Soph Cls; Rep Stu Cncl; Var Bsktbl; Mgr(s); Powder Puff Ftbl; Sftbl; Hon Roll; Natl Right Life Poster Cntst Hon Ment 86; Compu Sci.

LUCARELLI, NICOLE; Mohawk HS; Edinburg, PA; (S); French Clb; Band; Concert Band; Mrchg Band; Score Keeper; Tennis; High Hon Roll; Hon Roll; NHS; Natl Essay Cont Hnrb Mntn 85; Gifted Pgm 83-86; Acctng.

LUCAS, CHRISTINE; Shaler Area HS; Pittsburgh, PA; (Y); 10/517; Yrbk Bus Mgr; Stu Cncl; JV Vllybl; High Hon Roll; Outstndng Schlr Ath 84-85; Acad All Amer Schlr 85; JV Awd 84-85; Duquesne U; Acctng.

LUCAS, DANA; North Star HS; Boswell, PA; (S); 11/135; Church Yth Grp; FCA; Stu Cncl; Mat Maids; Score Keeper; JV Vllybl; Stat Wrstlng; Hon Roll; North Star Actvty Boostes Stu Of Mnth 83-84; Bus.

LUCAS, KATHLEEN; Steel Valley HS; Munhall, PA; (Y); 39/201; JCL; Latin Clb; SADD; Varsity Clb; Rep Frsh Cls; Var L Swmmng; Var L Vllybl; Wt Lftg; High Hon Roll; Hon Roll; Stu Mo 85; Gftd & Tlntd Pgm 83-86; S V Try Bike A Thn Mst Miles 84; Envrnmntl Sci.

LUCAS, KELLY; North Allegheny HS; Pittsburgh, PA; (Y); 44/642; Exploring; German Clb; Ski Clb; Rep Frsh Cls; Stu Cncl; Sftbl; High Hon Roll; Hon Roll; Jr NHS; NHS; Physcl Thrpy.

LUCAS, KRIS; Dover Area Schl; Dover, PA; (Y); 9/239; Church Yth Grp; Pres Girl Scts; Library Aide; Sec Nwsp Stf; Stat Var Bsbl; High Hon Roll; Hon Roll; NHS; Woodmen Wrld Outstndng Hist Stu 86; Gld & Slvr Ldrshp Awds GSA 84 & 85; Stu In France 86; Hist.

LUCAS, LISA; Chambersburg Area SR HS; Chambersburg, PA; (Y); 100/641; Drama Clb; Chorus; School Musical; School Play; Lit Mag; JV Crs Cntry; Hon Roll; Art Clb; Church Yth Grp; English Clb; Phys Fit Awd 84; Outstndg Spn Stu 84; Cullinary U Amer; Cul Art.

LUCAS, MARK; Windber Area HS; Windber, PA; (S); 7/115; Chess Clb; Pres Band; Concert Band; Mrchg Band; High Hon Roll; Hon Roll; NHS; Stu Of Mnth 83-85; Dist Band 85; U Of Pittsburgh; Engrng.

LUCAS, MONICA; Cameron County HS; Emporium, PA; (Y); #7 In Class; Church Yth Grp; Spanish Clb; Teachers Aide; Band; Concert Band; Mrchg Band; Pep Band; Yrbk Stf; Trs Jr Cls; Stu Cncl; Intl Frgn Lng Awds 86.

LUCAS, PAMELA; Bald Eagle Area JR SR HS; Howard, PA; (S); Spanish Clb; SADD; Teachers Aide; Nwsp Rptr; Nwsp Stf; Yrbk Stf; Hon Roll; Color Guard; Mrchg Band; Mat Maids; Faculty Edtr Yrbk Stf 85-86; Lock Hvn U PA; Comp Sci.

LUCAS, STEVE; West Catholic HS For Boys; Philadelphia, PA; (Y); Boys Clb Am; Boy Scts; Church Yth Grp; Computer Clb; French Clb; Chorus; Off Frsh Cls; Off Soph Cls; Bsktbl; Crs Cntry; Serv & Merit Awds 82; Hamon Rltns & Yth Ftnss Awds 83; Temple U; Comp Sci.

LUCAS, TIMOTHY; Freeport SR HS; Freeport, PA; (Y); 1/173; School Musical; God Cntry Awd; Gov Hon Prg Awd; VP NHS; Pres Schlr; Val; Boy Scts; Pres Church Yth Grp; Chorus; Presby Schlrshp 86; Yng Presby Singer European Concert Tour 84; Freeport By Yr 85-86; Westminster Coll; Bio.

LUCAS, TRACY L; Freeport SR HS; Freeport, PA; (Y); Church Yth Grp; Dance Clb; Hosp Aide; Drill Tm; Yrbk Stf; Hon Roll; NHS; Carlow Coll; Nrsng.

LUCCHETTI, LOUIS; Central Catholic HS; Allentown, PA; (Y); Church Yth Grp; Drama Clb; Political Wkr; Rep Band; Chorus; Concert Band; Jazz Band; Mrchg Band; Orch; Pep Band; Distr X Band 86; Keystone Literary Awd 85; Finance.

LUCCI, JOSEPH; Center HS; Aliquippa, PA; (Y); Boy Scts; Chess Clb; Church Yth Grp; Civic Clb; Exploring; Pep Clb; Ski Clb; Spanish Clb; Band; Concert Band; Valley Forge Music Schlrshp Awd 86; 4 Yr Letterman HS Band 82-86; Valley Forge Military Acad; Sci.

LUCCI, ROBERT; Chartiers Valley HS; Pittsburgh, PA; (Y); NHS; Pres Schlr; Natl Hnr Soc 85; Presdntl Acadmc Ftns Awd 86; PHEA Cert Merit 85; Penn ST U; Engrng.

LUCCI IV, SAM J; Center Area School Dist; Monaca, PA; (Y); Church Yth Grp; German Clb; Political Wkr; Im Bsktbl; Hon Roll; Bus Adm.

LUCE, EMILY; Ft Le Boeuf HS; Waterford, PA; (Y); Church Yth Grp; PAVAS; Yrbk Stf; VP Soph Cls; Stu Cncl; Capt Cheerleading; Hon Roll; Comm.

LUCENTE, RICHARD; Ambridge Area SR HS; Baden, PA; (Y); 9/265; Am Leg Boys St; Chess Clb; Church Yth Grp; German Clb; Pep Clb; High Hon Roll; Lion Awd; Navy ROTC Schlrshp; PA ST Kunkle Schlrshp 86-87; PA ST U; Aerospace Engrng.

LUCERA, NICOLE; Hatboro-Horsham HS; Hatboro, PA; (Y); Pep Clb; Ski Clb; School Musical; School Play; Rep Soph Cls; Rep Stu Cncl; Cheerleading; Fld Hcky; Hon Roll; Psych.

LUCHETA, SUSAN; Franklin Regional HS; Murrysville, PA; (Y); 1/338; Mathletes; Math Tm; Spanish Clb; High Hon Roll; NHS; Chrch Lay Rdr; Tutor; Elem Span Instrctr; PA JR Acad Sci Many Awds 84; U Pittsbg Mth Comp Hghst Scr 86; Span.

LUCHETTI, KIM; James M Couglin HS; Plains, PA; (Y); Hosp Aide; Red Cross Aide; Band; Concert Band; Mrchg Band; Orch; Symp Band; Yrbk Phtg; Yrbk Stf; JV Fld Hcky; Kystn JC; Physcl Thrpy.

LUCHETTI, MARY KAY; Seton Catholic HS; Pittston, PA; (Y); 2/92; Mathletes; School Musical; Ed Nwsp Stf; Trs Jr Cls; VP Sr Cls; Var L Cheerleading; High Hon Roll; NHS; Ntl Merit Ltr; Accntg Awd Hghst Avg 85; US Chrldr Achvt Awd 86; Cert Distnctn & Trphy Frm Diocesan Cncl Mth Tchrs 84; Marywood Coll; Dietetics.

LUCHETTI, PATRICIA; Wyoming Area HS; W Wyoming, PA; (Y); Church Yth Grp; Cmnty Wkr; French Clb; Key Clb; Comptr Sci.

LUCHKO, ROBIN; Dunmore HS; Dunmore, PA; (Y); 32/148; Exploring; French Clb; Spanish Clb; Twrlr; Hon Roll; Art Edtr Yrbk & Nwsp 86-87; Comp.

LUCIA, ANISA; West Scranton HS; Scranton, PA; (Y); Spanish Clb; Nwsp Rptr; Nwsp Stf; Yrbk Rptr; Yrbk Stf; Rep Jr Cls; Var Cheerleading; JV Var Trk; Hon Roll; Jr NHS; Crmnl Justice.

LUCID, HENRY; North Hills HS; Pittsburgh, PA; (Y); Camera Clb; NFL; Ski Clb; Yrbk Phtg; Trk; High Hon Roll; Hon Roll; NHS; Engrng.

LUCIFERO, DENINE; Southern HS; Philadelphia, PA; (Y); Math Clb; Political Wkr; Service Clb; Off Sr Cls; Swmmng; Trk; Cit Awd; High Hon Roll; NHS; Prfct Atten Awd; Silver Metal Good Grades 86; Music Awd 86; Bus Awd 86; CC; Bus.

LUCIUS, ANN; Red Lion SR HS; Red Lion, PA; (Y); 71/337; Varsity Clb; School Musical; School Play; Yrbk Sprt Ed; Off Frsh Cls; Off Soph Cls; Off Jr Cls; Sec Sr Cls; JV Bsktbl; Var L Tennis; Millersville U; Cmnctns.

LUCKENBAUGH, DANIEL; Central York SR HS; York, PA; (Y); 24/224; Church Yth Grp; Varsity Clb; Ftbl; Wt Lftg; Co-Capt Wrstlng; Hon Roll; NHS; Outstndng Wrestler Coaches Awd 84; Sci Plympaid 86; Arch.

LUCKENBILL, KATHY; Tulpehocken HS; Bernville, PA; (Y); 4/105; Pres Church Yth Grp; Chorus; Church Choir; School Musical; JV Var Sftbl; Hon Roll; NHS; Comp Sci.

LUCKEY, JUDITH; Elizabeth Forward HS; Elizabeth, PA; (Y); AFS; Church Yth Grp; Library Aide; Acpl Chr; Concert Band; Drm Mjr(t); Mrchg Band; School Musical; Hon Roll; Mass Media.

LUCKOCK, DAVID R; Conneaut Lake HS; Conneaut Lake, PA; (Y); Trs Church Yth Grp; JV Bsktbl; Bowling; Var L Crs Cntry; Im Vllybl; Hon Roll; NHS; Frshmn Awd-Bsktbl 84; Bus Mngt.

LUCKOWSKI, STEPHEN; B Reed Henderson HS; Downingtown, PA; (S); 3/336; Capt Debate Tm; Hon Roll; NHS; German Scty PA Awd 84; Elec Engrng.

LUCOVITZ, BILL; Ringgold SR HS; Monongahela, PA; (Y); Boy Scts; High Hon Roll; Hon Roll; Construction.

LUCY, CHUCK; Bentworth HS; Bentleyville, PA; (Y); Art Clb; Ski Clb; Varsity Clb; Ftbl; Hon Roll; IUP; Engrng.

LUDOVICI, AMY; Ambridge Area HS; Ambridge, PA; (Y); Office Aide; Pep Clb; Red Cross Aide; Spanish Clb; Drill Tm; Off Jr Cls; Hon Roll; Comm.

LUDT, SHARI; Big Spring HS; Carlisle, PA; (Y); 2/187; Church Yth Grp; Nwsp Rptr; Yrbk Rptr; Jr Cls; Cheerleading; Powder Puff Ftbl; Trk; High Hon Roll; NHS; Newville Wmns Clb JR Mnth 86; Summr Cls Scholar Dickinson Coll 86; Spanish.

LUDWIG, DAVID; Waynesboro Area SR HS; Waynesboro, PA; (Y); Church Yth Grp; Band; Concert Band; Jazz Band; Mrchg Band; School Musical; Ftbl; Hon Roll; Accntng.

LUDWIG, STEPHANIE; Harborcreek JR SR HS; Erie, PA; (Y); 66/238; Art Clb; Church Yth Grp; Girl Scts; Letterman Clb; SADD; Acpl Chr; Chorus; Color Guard; Variety Show; Hon Roll; Scty Dist Amer HS Stu 86; Penn ST U; Pre-Vet.

LUDY, ERIC; Somerset Area SR HS; Somerset, PA; (Y); English Clb; Q&S; SADD; Varsity Clb; Stage Crew; Yrbk Phtg; Ftbl; High Hon Roll; Mu Alp Tht; NHS; PA ST U; Bus Admin.

LUFFEY, WILLIAM; Moon SR HS; Coraopolis, PA; (Y); Key Clb; SADD; Chorus; Variety Show; JV Bsktbl; Im Coach Actv; Var L Ftbl; Var Trk; Im Vllybl; PA ST Gld Mdl Kystn ST Gms 86; Fld Athlt Mt Seneca Vlly Invtnl 85; All Cnfrnc Hnrbl Mtn Dfnsv 85; Math.

LUFFY, ELIZABETH; Moon SR HS; Coraopolis, PA; (Y); 42/327; Nwsp Ed-Chief; Yrbk Bus Mgr; Pres Frsh Cls; Im Gym; JV Var Mgr(s); High Hon Roll; Hon Roll; Prfct Atten Awd; 1st Pl Creatv Wrtng 83-84; UCLA; Acting.

LUFT, DONNA; Exeter SR HS; Reading, PA; (Y); 8/217; Pres Church Yth Grp; VP Leo Clb; Pres Y-Teens; Band; Nwsp Stf; Bsktbl; Fld Hcky; Sftbl; Jr NHS; NHS; St Ignatius Jr Olympic Bsktbll Team 86; Stu Rcgntn In NAMES 86; All Star In 3 Sports Plyd 84-86; Math.

LUGIN, LEANDRA; Moon SR HS; Coraopolis, PA; (Y); Church Yth Grp; Chorus; Bus.

LUISI, KIMBERLY P; Kiski Area HS; Apollo, PA; (Y); Church Yth Grp; Pep Clb; SADD; Color Guard; Concert Band; Nwsp Rptr; Yrbk Ed-Chief; Hon Roll; Rotary Awd; Office Aide; Top 10 Cls 84; Rotary Schlr 85; Bus.

LUISI, KRISTIN; Canon Mc Millan HS; Canonsburg, PA; (Y); 11/394; French Clb; Hosp Aide; Trs Concert Band; Trs Mrchg Band; Var Sftbl; French Hon Soc; High Hon Roll; NHS; Chem Engrng.

LUKAN, JEFF; Fort Cherry HS; Midway, PA; (S); Church Yth Grp; Computer Clb; Drama Clb; JA; Math Clb; Science Clb; Ski Clb; Thesps; Varsity Clb; School Play; Phy Ftnss Hnrs 83-85; All Str Ftbl Cnfrnce Tm Wshngt-Greene Co 85.

LUKAS, GIGI; Belle Vernon Area HS; Belle Vernon, PA; (Y); Art Clb; Church Yth Grp; Ski Clb; Nwsp Ed-Chief; Stu Cncl; Powder Puff Ftbl; JV VP Sftbl; 4 Natl Art Awds 82-85; Elem Educ.

LUKE, LISA; Penn Cambria HS; Gallitzin, PA; (Y); 20/215; Drama Clb; French Clb; Girl Scts; Hon Roll; Prfct Atten Awd; Bus Admin.

LUKETIC, KIM; South Allegheny JR SR HS; Glassport, PA; (Y); Church Yth Grp; French Clb; Office Aide; Y-Teens; Rep Sr Cls; Powder Puff Ftbl; Hon Roll; Bus.

LUKITSCH, JANET; St Paul Cathedral HS; Pittsburgh, PA; (Y); Church Yth Grp; Dance Clb; FNA; Pep Clb; Pres Spanish Clb; Stage Crew; Yrbk Stf; VP Frsh Cls; Capt Cheerleading; Sftbl; Nrsng.

LUKITSCH, KRISTEN L; Franklin Regional HS; Murrysville, PA; (Y); 1/360; AFS; Church Yth Grp; French Clb; VP Key Clb; Mathletes; Band; Chorus; Church Choir; Concert Band; School Musical; Hugh O Brien Ldrshp Awd 85; Chem.

LUKO JR, DANIEL E; Bentworth SR HS; Bentleyville, PA; (Y); 39/149; Varsity Clb; VP Sr Cls; Var L Bsbl; Var L Ftbl; Wt Lftg; Hon Roll.

LUKOS, KIMBERLEE; Moon Area HS; Coraopolis, PA; (Y); Var L Crs Cntry; Var L Swmmng; Var L Trk; Med.

LUKOWSKY, ANN; Ford City JR SR HS; Ford City, PA; (Y); 45/154; Church Yth Grp; German Clb; Spanish Clb; JV Bsktbl; Im Cheerleading; High Hon Roll; Hon Roll; NHS; Jrnlsm.

LUMADUE, BRIAN; Bishop Guilfoyle HS; Altoona, PA; (S); 14/149; Pres Science Clb; Ski Clb; Acpl Chr; Variety Show; Yrbk Stf; Stu Cncl; High Hon Roll; Hon Roll; Cnty Chorus 84-86; PA ST U; Elec Engr.

LUNCHER, MARK; Penn Hills SR HS; Pittsburgh, PA; (S); 102/779; Drama Clb; Pres French Clb; Varsity Clb; School Musical; School Play; Yrbk Stf; Co-Capt Swmmng; Hon Roll; VP Jr NHS; NHS; Gamon U.

LUND, ERIK; B Reed Henderson HS; West Chester, PA; (Y); 102/349; Var L Ftbl; Var L Lcrss; Var L Wrstlng; 2nd Tm All Chesmont/Wrstlng 86; Aerontcl Engrng.

LUND, JOHN; Upper Moreland HS; Hatboro, PA; (Y); 76/253; FCA; Var Bsbl; Var Bsktbl; Var Ftbl; Hon Roll; Acctng.

LUND, KAREN; Archbishop Carroll HS; Wayne, PA; (Y); 17/216; Camera Clb; Girl Scts; Mathletes; Spanish Clb; Chorus; Socr; Sftbl; High Hon Roll; Hon Roll; Cmnty Schlrshp Ursns Coll 86-87; Emrsn Elec Co Schlrshp 86-87; Ursinus Coll; Bio.

LUNDVALL, LORI; Avon Grove HS; West Grove, PA; (Y); SADD; Sec Sr Cls; Tennis; High Hon Roll; NHS; Parent Adv Cncl Schrlshp 86; PA ST; Elem Ed.

LUNGER, STACY; Punxsutawney SR HS; Punxsutawney, PA; (Y); French Clb; Hon Roll; X-Ray Tech.

LUNIFELD, AMY; Penn Hills HS; Pittsburgh, PA; (Y); Exploring; Girl Scts; Hosp Aide; Concert Band; Mrchg Band; Orch; High Hon Roll; NHS; All ST Band PA 86; Red Crss Ldrshp Devlpmt Ctr Grove Cty Delg & Coll Stff 84 & 85-86; Math.

LUNOE, RICHARD; Central Bucks East HS; New Hope, PA; (Y); Aud/Vis; Camera Clb; Church Yth Grp; Intnl Clb; Ski Clb; Chorus; Stage Crew; JV Var Socr; JV Var Vllybl; Hon Roll; Cntntl Lg Math Awd 84; Schlstc Achvmnt Awd 86; Engr.

LUONCO, PATRICK; Dunmore HS; Dunmore, PA; (Y); Church Yth Grp; Cmnty Wkr; Computer Clb; French Clb; Quiz Bowl; Ski Clb; Varsity Clb; Stu Cncl; Var Ftbl; Var Trk; Engrng.

LUONG, MINH; Central Dauphin HS; Harrisburg, PA; (Y); 10/380; Hon Roll; Jr NHS; NHS; PA ST U; Engrng.

LUONGO, PAT; Dunmore HS; Dunmore, PA; (Y); 30/150; Church Yth Grp; Computer Clb; French Clb; Quiz Bowl; Ski Clb; Stage Crew; JV Ftbl; Var Trk; Var Wt Lftg; Hon Roll; U Scranton; Engrng.

LUPINACCI, MARY; Saint Paul Cathedral HS; Pittsburgh, PA; (Y); Dance Clb; Hosp Aide; Red Cross Aide; Chorus; High Hon Roll; Rotary Awd; Cathedral Sci Fair 85; Carnegie-Mellon U Hstry Day 86.

LUPINETTI, ANDREA; Penn Cambria HS; Gallitzin, PA; (Y); #2 In Class; Drama Clb; French Clb; SADD; Stage Crew; Rep Frsh Cls; Rep Soph Cls; Rep Jr Cls; Stu Cncl; High Hon Roll; Hon Roll; Pre-Med.

LUPOLD, LINDA; Solanco HS; New Providence, PA; (Y); 21/212; Sec Trs Church Yth Grp; Band; Concert Band; Drm Mjr(t); Mrchg Band; Orch; Yrbk Ed-Chief; Rep Frsh Cls; JV Fld Hcky; JV Trk; Amer Bus Wmns Assoc Schlrshp 86; Slnco Msc Bstrs Schlrshp 86; Amer Msc Abrd 86; Messiah Coll; Nrsng.

LUPREK, KATHY; Forest Hills SR HS; Windber, PA; (Y); 71/156; Art Clb; VP Church Yth Grp; Library Aide; Pep Clb; Y-Teens; Church Choir; Sftbl; Hon Roll; Cambria-Rowe Bus Coll; Sec.

LUPTAK, LISA; Union Area HS; New Castle, PA; (Y); Art Clb; French Clb; FHA; High Hon Roll; Hon Roll; NHS.

LUPTAK, SHERYL; Wilmington Area HS; New Bedford, PA; (Y); 51/122; Rep Church Yth Grp; Rptr VP FBLA; Library Aide; Office Aide; Nwsp Stf; Key Clb; Cmps Lf Stu Ldr 85-86; Cmps Lf Chr The Lstng Imprssns 83-86; Bethel Coll St Paul MN; Bus Ed.

LUQUE, ERIC; Conestoga Valley HS; Leola, PA; (Y); 70/247; Church Yth Grp; Cmnty Wkr; JV L Bsbl; JV L Bsktbl; Var L Ftbl; Wt Lftg; Hon Roll; Bus.

LUSCKAY, DORI; West Mifflin Area HS; W Mifflin, PA; (Y); 17/325; Exploring; FBLA; Ski Clb; Stu Cncl; Powder Puff Ftbl; High Hon Roll; Hon Roll; Jr NHS; NHS; FBLA Sprng Ldrshp Conf Steno I 4th Pl 86; Gregg Typg Awd 72 WPM 86; Gregg Typg Awd Prod Test 86; Duffs Bus Schl; Court Rptr.

LUSHER, TAMMY; Trinity HS; Washington, PA; (Y); Office Aide; ICM; MOA.

LUSHKO, SCOTT; Ferndale Area HS; Johnstown, PA; (Y); Church Yth Grp; Ski Clb; Stage Crew; Bsktbl; Hon Roll; All Stars-Bsktbl-Applchn Conf 86; Sthrn Cmbria Leag-A S 86; Jhn Rly Clssc Shp Awd 86; Liberty U-Lynchburg VA.

LUSK, BILL; Chapel Christian Schl; Bentleyville, PA; (S); 1/3; VP Church Yth Grp; Church Choir; School Play; Yrbk Stf; Var Capt Bsktbl; Var Capt Ftbl; Var Sftbl; High Hon Roll; Extraordnry Christian Stu Of Amer 86; U Of Pittsburgh.

LUTER, MELISSA; Norristown Area HS; E Norriton, PA; (Y); Cmnty Wkr; School Play; Nwsp Rptr; Nwsp Stf; Lit Mag; Prfct Atten Awd; Stu Of Yr Exchng Clb 86; Leighton M Matthews Mrl Awd 86; John G Grantham Mrl Awd 86; Temple U; Radio.

LUTERMAN, KIM; Northeast HS; Philadelphia, PA; (Y); Im Bowling; Var Sftbl; High Hon Roll; Engl Awd For Exclnc 84; Cert De Competencia In Span 84; Jwsh War Vets Of The US Sci 84; Elem Educ.

LUTHER, DANIEL J; Mt Pleasant Area HS; Donegal, PA; (Y); 47/243; Boy Scts; Pres Library Aide; Church Choir; Ed Nwsp Stf; CC Awd; Hon Roll; Bus Stu & Stu Of Month 86; Thiel Coll; Accntng.

LUTHER, JONATHON D; Mc Keesport Area HS; White Oak, PA; (Y); 28/339; Office Aide; High Hon Roll; Hon Roll; Prfct Atten Awd; GMI Engr & Mgt Inst; Mech Engr.

LUTHER, KEVIN; Altoona HS; Altoona, PA; (Y); VICA; Band; Off Sr Cls; Penn ST; Comp Prog.

LUTHER, MATTHEW; Cambria Heights HS; Carrolltown, PA; (Y); 11/200; SADD; Pres Soph Cls; Pres Jr Cls; VP Stu Cncl; Var L Bsbl; Var L Ftbl; Wt Lftg; Wrstlng; Hon Roll; NHS; Schl Recrd Mst Runs Scrd Bsbl 86; Acctng.

LUTJENS, THERESA; Stroudsburg HS; Stroudsburg, PA; (Y); 37/240; Pep Clb; Spanish Clb; Varsity Clb; School Musical; Yrbk Stf; JV Var Cheerleading; JV Trk; High Hon Roll; Hon Roll; Bloomsburg U; Nrsng.

LUTTERSCHMIDT, TIMOTHY; Allen HS; Allentown, PA; (Y); 31/630; German Clb; ROTC; Pres Ski Clb; Chorus; JV Var Ftbl; Capt L Vllybl; Hon Roll; Jr NHS; VP NHS; Opt Clb Awd; Pre Law.

LUTTON, ALAN; Sun Valley HS; Aston, PA; (Y); 32/302; Pres Computer Clb; VP Drama Clb; Chorus; Concert Band; Mrchg Band; School Musical; Ed Yrbk Phtg; JP Sousa Awd; Ntl Merit SF; Scholastic Bowl; PMEA Dist & Rgnl Chorus 84-86; Chorus Soloist Awd 86; Drexel U; Compu Engrng.

LUTTY, DARLENE; Deer Lakes JR SR HS; Cheswick, PA; (Y); Church Yth Grp; Varsity Clb; Capt Flag Corp; School Play; Nwsp Stf; Yrbk Stf; Crs Cntry; Mgr(s); Capt Trk; Hon Roll; Dstsngshed Achvt Intl Undrstndg 86; Cert Supr Achvt Pub Spkng, Slvr Ldrshp Awd 84; Counclr.

LUTZ, CARLA; Kutztown Area HS; Lenhartsville, PA; (Y); 3/135; Pres Church Yth Grp; Hosp Aide; Band; Chorus; Concert Band; Drill Tm; Pep Band; School Musical; Yrbk Stf; JV Var Fld Hcky; Cnty Band 83-85; Dist Band 84-85; Nrsng.

LUTZ, CHRISTINE; Portage Area HS; Portage, PA; (S); 23/118; Ski Clb; Band; Chorus; Concert Band; Jazz Band; Pep Band; Var Trk; Im Vllybl; Hon Roll; NHS; Pre-Med.

LUTZ, GEORGE; Columbia Montour Vo-Tech; Danville, PA; (Y); Teachers Aide; Rep Jr Cls; Crs Cntry; Trk; Wt Lftg; Wrstlng; Hon Roll; NHS.

LUTZ, HEIDI; Kiski Area HS; Avonmore, PA; (Y); GAA; JA; OEA; Pep Clb; Teachers Aide; Chorus; Drill Tm; Yrbk Stf; Off Frsh Cls; Stu Cncl; Bradford Schl Of Bus; Acctng.

LUTZ, HEIDI; Wissahickon SR HS; Ambler, PA; (S); Art Clb; Pres Church Yth Grp; Lit Mag; High Hon Roll; Hon Roll; NHS; Opt Clb Awd; Bio.

LUTZ, JUDY; Nazareth Area SR HS; Nazareth, PA; (Y); 29/231; Girl Scts; Band; Color Guard; Concert Band; Drill Tm; Mrchg Band; High Hon Roll; Hon Roll; Outstndng Prof Stu; Band Librarian; Accntng.

LUTZ, KENNETH; West Side Vo Tech; Courtdale, PA; (Y); 20/153; Church Yth Grp; Computer Clb; FBLA; Var Capt Bsbl; Var Capt Bsktbl; High Hon Roll; Hon Roll; Luzerne County CC; Hotel & Res.

LUTZ, KEVIN; Portage Area HS; Portage, PA; (S); 8/118; Letterman Clb; Varsity Clb; Var L Ftbl; Im Socr; Var L Wrstlng; High Hon Roll; NHS; Elec Engrng.

LUTZ, MARIA; John S Fine HS; Glen Lyon, PA; (S); #2 In Class; Ski Clb; Yrbk Stf; JV Bsktbl; Im Ftbl; Var L Sftbl; High Hon Roll; NHS; NEDT Awd; Home Stdy Art Schlrshp 83; Engrng.

LUTZ, MICHAEL; Danville SR HS; Danville, PA; (Y); JV Bsbl; JV Ftbl; Var Golf; High Hon Roll; Hon Roll; Alg I Hgh Avg Awd 84; STATISTICS.

LUTZ, PATRICK; Warwick HS; Lititz, PA; (Y); 23/235; JV Var Wrstlng; High Hon Roll; NHS; Millersville U; Comp Sci.

LUTZ, REGINA; Northern Lebanon HS; Fredericksburg, PA; (Y); Varsity Clb; Color Guard; Mrchg Band; School Play; Trs Soph Cls; Trs Jr Cls; Bsktbl; Cheerleading; Fld Hcky; Sftbl; Ntl Hnr Soc Pres 86-87.

LUTZ, RENEE; Jefferson-Morgan HS; Rices Landing, PA; (Y); 13/88; Spanish Clb; School Play; Yrbk Stf; Hon Roll; St Vincents Clg; Comp.

LUTZ, ROCHELLE; Ambridge Area SR HS; Freedom, PA; (Y); 33/265; Exploring; Trs French Clb; Pep Clb; Band; Mrchg Band; Symp Band; Off Jr Cls; Off Sr Cls; Twrlr; Hon Roll; Penn ST; Bus Adm.

LUTZ, RON; Baldwin Whitehall HS; Pittsburgh, PA; (Y); Boy Scts; Church Yth Grp; Bsktbl; Bus.

LUTZ, SUSAN L; Conrad Weiser HS; Womelsdorf, PA; (Y); 37/185; Drama Clb; Hst JCL; Chorus; Yrbk Stf; Pres Jr Cls; Stu Cncl; Var L Cheerleading; Var L Fld Hcky; Var L Trk; Hon Roll.

LUTZ, TERRI; Our Lady Of The Sacred Heart HS; Aliquippa, PA; (Y); 17/75; Cmnty Wkr; Pep Clb; SADD; Chorus; School Musical; Stage Crew; Yrbk Stf; Score Keeper; Hon Roll; NHS; Acad All Amer Awd 84-85 & 85-86; Hghst Aver Philosophy 86; CA U Of PA; Indus Psych.

LUTZ, TIMOTHY; Lakeland HS; Clarks Summit, PA; (Y); Bsbl; Bsktbl; Ftbl; Penn ST; Engrang.

LUTZ, VIKKI L; Hempfield Area SR HS; Jeannette, PA; (Y); 10/657; Cmnty Wkr; Hosp Aide; Political Wkr; Ski Clb; Spanish Clb; Yrbk Stf; High Hon Roll; NHS; Sec Spanish NHS; Intl Frgn Lang Awd Spnsh 86; Acadmc All-Amer Awd 86; PA ST U; Vet Med.

LUTZ, WENDY JO; Eastern Lebanon Co HS; Robesonia, PA; (Y); Color Guard; Rep Jr Cls; Rep Stu Cncl; Var JV Bsktbl; Stat Trk; Hon Roll; Rotary Awd; Church Choir; Physical Fitness Tm 82-84; Regional Lvr Natl Level Art Awds 82-84; Cedar Crst Coll Onyx Schlrshp 86-87; Cedar Crest Coll; Genetic Engrn.

LUTZI, DAWN; Wilson Area HS; Easton, PA; (S); 11/160; Ski Clb; Drm Mjr(t); Nwsp Rptr; Nwsp Stf; Sec Soph Cls; Stu Cncl; Var Capt Bsktbl; Cheerleading; Var Capt Sftbl; Trk; Stu Month 85-86; Hmcmng Ct 85-86; Muhlenburg Coll; Elem Educ.

LUTZKANIN, SHARI; St Clair Area HS; St Clair, PA; (Y); 7/83; Church Yth Grp; FHA; Ski Clb; Co-Capt Drm Mjr(t); Nwsp Stf; Yrbk Stf; High Hon Roll; Hon Roll; Trs Mu Alp Tht; NHS; Bloomsburg U; Bus Fin.

LUX, GRACIE; Bishop Mc Cort HS; Johnstown, PA; (Y); French Clb; GAA; Pep Clb; Chorus; School Musical; VP Frsh Cls; Sec Soph Cls; L Bsktbl; Var Socr; Im Sftbl.

LUXON, DYAN L; Penn Hills HS; Verona, PA; (Y); Spanish Clb; Band; Nwsp Stf; Stu Cncl; Hon Roll; Clarion U Of PA; Cmmnctns.

LUZAR, JUSTIN; Salisbury HS; Allentown, PA; (Y); 10/140; Boy Scts; Exploring; Y-Teens; Im Bsktbl; Var L Golf; High Hon Roll; Hon Roll; Rotary Awd; Eagle Sct 86.

LUZAR, LORI; Yough HS; Hutchinson, PA; (Y); 65/226; Pres Church Yth Grp; French Clb; Chorus; Yrbk Stf; Powder Puff Ftbl; Hon Roll; NHS; IN U Of PA; Nrsng.

LUZIER, CATHY; Clearfield Area HS; Clearfield, PA; (Y); 177/315; DECA; Hon Roll; Guidnc Aide 85-86; Comp Data.

LUZIER, JEFF; Clearfield Area HS; Clearfield, PA; (Y); 3/350; French Clb; SADD; Wrstlng; High Hon Roll; Bucknell; Engrng.

LY, PAULINE; Upper Darby HS; Upper Darby, PA; (Y); Cmnty Wkr; Spanish Clb; Yrbk Stf; Crs Cntry; Trk; Chem.

LY, PHENG; Schenley HS; Pittsburgh, PA; (S); Art Clb; FBLA; Intnl Clb; Math Clb; Ski Clb; Gym; Socr; Vllybl; High Hon Roll; Prfct Atten Awd; Aeronatical Engrng Schl.

LYDICK, TERRI L; Blairsville SR HS; Blairsville, PA; (Y); 29/129; Chess Clb; High Hon Roll; Hon Roll; Jr NHS; NHS.

LYLE, DEAN; East Allegheny HS; N Versailles, PA; (Y); Letterman Clb; Ski Clb; Ftbl; Wt Lftg; Hon Ment All Conf Guard 85; Washington & Jefferson; Bus Adm.

LYLE, JOANN; Baldwin HS; Pittsburgh, PA; (Y); 54/531; JA; High Hon Roll; Grove City Coll; Econ.

LYLE, KIMBERLY; Columbia HS; Lancaster, PA; (Y); 8/82; VP Sr Cls; Pres Stu Cncl; Capt Bsktbl; DAR Awd; Hon Roll; NHS; Mary S Groff Schlrshp 86; Hmcmng Queen 85-86; U DE; Physcl Thrpy.

LYMAN, JENNIFER; Downingtown SR HS; Downingtown, PA; (S); 16/544; Church Yth Grp; German Clb; Intnl Clb; Spanish Clb; Chorus; Flag Corp; DAR Awd; Hon Roll; NHS; Rotary Awd; Frgn Lang Stu Week; Law.

LYMAN, SHANNON; Coudersport JR SR HS; Coudersport, PA; (Y); Varsity Clb; Band; Chorus; Concert Band; Yrbk Stf; Bsktbl; Trk; High Hon Roll; Hon Roll; NHS; SR IU 9 Dist Band 85.

LYMAN, STEVE; Greater Latrobe HS; Greensburg, PA; (Y); 26/374; German Clb; JA; School Musical; Variety Show; Mgr(s); Co-Capt Tennis; NHS; Pres Schlr; Kiwanian Mnth 86; PA ST U; Bus Adm.

LYMAN, VERONICA; West Hazleton HS; Conyngham, PA; (Y); 41/250; Church Yth Grp; Spanish Clb; SADD; Nwsp Rptr; Yrbk Stf; JV Var Bsktbl; Var Cheerleading; Var L Sftbl; Hon Roll; Physical Education.

LYNCH, BOB; Shaler Area HS; Glenshaw, PA; (Y); Rep Church Yth Grp; Ski Clb; Rep Sr Cls; Bsbl; JV Var Ftbl; Sftbl; Var Trk; JV Var Wt Lftg; Wrstlng; High Hon Roll; SR Altar Boy St Sebastns Chch 86; Citadel; Comp Sci.

LYNCH, CHERIE; Penn Cambria HS; Gallitzin, PA; (Y); Achvt Hm Ec 84; Outstndng Readng Awd 84; Perf Atten Hnr 84; PA ST; Acctng.

LYNCH, DAVE; Moon SR HS; Coraopolis, PA; (Y); 8/330; German Clb; Key Clb; Var Crs Cntry; Var L Trk; High Hon Roll; NHS; JV Socr; Im Vllybl; Hon Roll; PA ST U.

LYNCH, EARL; Quigley HS; Sewickley, PA; (S); 14/107; Stage Crew; Hon Roll; VFW Awd; Phy Sci Acad Achvt Awd 83-84; Ltn I & II Acad Achvt Awds 83-85; Carnegie-Mellon U; Chem Engrng.

LYNCH, JEANINE; Abington Heights HS; Clarks Summit, PA; (Y); 17/256; Pres Church Yth Grp; VP Sec JA; Chorus; Church Choir; Mrchg Band; Rep Stu Cncl; Hon Roll; NHS; IN U Of PA M Flagel Harte Mem Schlrp 86-87; Knghts Clmbs J E Ryan Mem Awd 86; Pres Acad Fit Awd 86; Indiana U Of PA; Biol.

LYNCH, KATHLEEN; Lackawanna Trail HS; Nicholson, PA; (Y); 4/90; Church Yth Grp; Ski Clb; VP Stu Cncl; Mgr(s); French Hon Soc; Hon Roll; NHS; Ntl Merit Ltr; Soc Wrkr.

LYNCH, KATHLEEN V; Cardinal Dougherty HS; Cheltenham, PA; (Y); 30/704; Am Leg Aux Girls St; German Clb; Band; Concert Band; Jazz Band; Capt Mrchg Band; Orch; Pep Band; School Musical; Nwsp Rptr; 3rd Pl ST Essy Cntst & Yth Wk Cadet PA Amer Lgn 84&86; Music Schlrshp Awd 86; Temple U; Music.

LYNCH, KEN; Upper Moreland HS; Hatboro, PA; (Y); Church Yth Grp; Computer Clb; FCA; French Clb; Key Clb; Math Clb; Ski Clb; High Hon Roll; NHS; 1st Montgomery Co Sci Fair 86; 8th Comp Bowl Competition 85; Lehigh; Elec Engrng.

LYNCH, KENDALL; Southern Fulton HS; Warfordsburg, PA; (Y); 1/51; VP FBLA; Pres FHA; Chorus; School Play; Yrbk Ed-Chief; Rep Frsh Cls; DAR Awd; Trs NHS; Val; Outstndng Choral Stu Awd 84; 1st In FBLA ST Comp, Bus Engl 86; Natl Choral Awd 86; Shippensburg U; Crim Just.

LYNCH, KRIS; Archbishop Wood HS For Boys; Warminster, PA; (Y); 93/282; Computer Clb; Band; Sec Concert Band; Jazz Band; Mrchg Band; Pep Band; School Musical; Stage Crew; Lit Mag; Histry.

LYNCH, MICHAEL; Central HS; Philadelphia, PA; (Y); French Clb; Intnl Clb; Model UN; Political Wkr; Teachers Aide; Vllybl; Intl Bus.

LYNCH, PATRICIA; Clearfield Area HS; Clearfield, PA; (Y); 77/350; Debate Tm; 4-H; VICA; Mat Maids; Tennis; Acctng.

LYNCH, RICH; Shaler Area HS; Pittsburgh, PA; (Y); 85/542; Chorus; Hon Roll; Wendy Lynch Awd For Courage 85; Pgh Sprts Ablty Wintr Games Brk 2 Swm Rcrds 86; Edinboro U; Cmmnctns.

LYNCH, SANDY; Interboro HS; Prospect Park, PA; (Y); Church Yth Grp; Spanish Clb; School Play; Rep Frsh Cls; Gym; Mgr(s); Vllybl; High Hon Roll; Hon Roll; Kiwanis Awd; Schlrshp Phila Coll Prfrmng Arts 85; Pd 2 Mo Trip Italy-Wrk Prfssnl Model 86; Prfssnl Model.

LYNCH, SHERRY; Owen J Roberts HS; Spring City, PA; (S); Letterman Clb; Tennis; Hon Roll; NHS; Opt Clb Awd; Mst Vlbl Tnns Plyr 84-85; 1st Tm Tnns 84-85; 1st Tm All Area Tnns 84; Bucknell Coll; Elec Engr.

LYNCH, THEODORE D; Honesdale HS; Honesdale, PA; (Y); 6/250; Drama Clb; School Musical; Yrbk Stf; Stu Cncl; Var L Bsbl; L Co-Capt Bsktbl; L Co-Capt Ftbl; High Hon Roll; NHS; Hon Roll; Enrchmnt Pgm 84-87; DAR Essay Awd Wnnr 85; Aerontcl Engrng.

LYNCH, TOM; Meadville HS; Meadville, PA; (S); 30/330; Band; Chorus; Concert Band; Jazz Band; Mrchg Band; Pep Band; Trk; High Hon Roll; Hon Roll; Jr NHS.

LYND, ANDREW; Knoch HS; Saxonburg, PA; (Y); German Clb; Band; Concert Band; Mrchg Band; Pep Band; Symp Band; Mgr Bsktbl; Hon Roll; Clarion U; Cmnctns.

LYNN, DAVID; Uniontown SR HS; Smock, PA; (Y); Exploring; 4-H; FFA; Spanish Clb; Band; Swmmng; 4-H Awd; High Hon Roll; Hon Roll; Aero Engr.

LYNN, KRISTEN; Ford City HS; Ford City, PA; (Y); Rep Chorus; School Musical; School Play; Variety Show; Off Soph Cls; Off Jr Cls; Off Sr Cls; Sec Stu Cncl; Capt Cheerleading; Sftbl; Drma Awd 86; Stu Actvty Awd 86; Slippery Rock U; Engl.

LYNN, LISA; Brownsville Area HS; New Salem, PA; (Y); FBLA; SADD; Dentl Asst.

LYNN, SANDY; Ford City HS; Ford City, PA; (Y); 19/155; Church Yth Grp; Pep Clb; Chorus; School Musical; Soph Cls; Jr Cls; Stu Cncl; Var Capt Cheerleading; Hon Roll; Stu Actvts Awd 86; Math.

LYNN, STACEY; Harry S Truman HS; Bristol, PA; (Y); Aud/Vis; Church Yth Grp; PAVAS; Spanish Clb; Church Choir; Stu Cncl; Crs Cntry; Trk; Hon Roll; Brstl Twnshp Art Show Cert 84-85; Nuclr Med.

LYNN, STEPHEN; Central HS; Philadelphia, PA; (Y); 2/341; Var Tennis; High Hon Roll; Brown U Bk Awd 86; John Seely Hart Engl Awd 86; Albert H Smyth Lit Prz 86; Engrng.

LYNOTT, JOHN; Scranton Preparatorh HS; Olyphant, PA; (Y); 6/192; Var Bsktbl; High Hon Roll; Amer Chem Soc Test 2nd Pl 86; Med.

LYON, DEBBIE; Butler Area HS; Butler, PA; (Y); Church Yth Grp; Exploring; Hosp Aide; Office Aide; Band; Mrchg Band; Rep Stu Cncl; Var Tennis; Hon Roll; Tnns Hstl Awd; BCCC; Med.

LYON, MARGARET; Cameron County HS; Emporium, PA; (Y); 10/86; Pres 4-H; Yrbk Bus Mgr; JV Var Bsktbl; Powder Puff Ftbl; High Hon Roll; Hon Roll; NHS; Cameron Mc Kean All Star Bsktbl Tm 86; Edinboro U.

LYON, PATRICIA; East HS; West Chester, PA; (Y); 97/387; Latin Clb; JV Fld Hcky; JV Lcrss; JV Trk; CCD Awd 86; Fld Hcky Chmps 82; Shpnsbrg U; Elem Ed.

LYON, RICHARD D; Washington HS; Washington, PA; (Y); 8/150; French Clb; Key Clb; Ski Clb; SADD; Jazz Band; Mrchg Band; Stage Crew; High Hon Roll; NHS; Letterman Clb; Amer Math Cmptns AHSME Schl Wnr 86; Msclr Dystrphy Assoc Smmr Cmp & Tlthn Vlntr 84-86; PA ST U; Pre-Med.

LYONS, ABBY; Annville-Cleona HS; Annville, PA; (Y); French Clb; Stu Cncl; Trk; Jr NHS; NHS; Nrsng.

LYONS, DENISE; St Marys Area HS; Saint Marys, PA; (Y); JV Var Bsktbl; High Hon Roll; Hon Roll; NHS; Allegany CC; Dntl Hygnst.

LYONS, EILEEN; Upper Dublin SR HS; Ambler, PA; (Y); 51/307; Color Guard; Mrchg Band; Yrbk Rptr; Yrbk Stf; NHS; Psych.

LYONS, KIM; Ringgold HS; New Eagle, PA; (Y); 49/283; Art Clb; Drama Clb; JA; Library Aide; Ski Clb; Chorus; Color Guard; Drill Tm; Nwsp Stf; Hon Roll; IN U PA; Indstrl Safety Sci.

LYONS, LINDA; Butler Area SR HS; Connoquenessing, PA; (Y); Exploring; FBLA; GAA; Political Wkr; Ski Clb; Socr; Trk; Hon Roll; Outstndg Stu Athlt Awd Sccr 85; 1st Pl Entrprnrshp II Rgnls FBLA 86; 1st Pl Gnrl Bus Bus Olympcs 86; IN U Of PA; Crmnlgy.

LYONS, MICHAEL; Millville HS; Orangeville, PA; (S); 3/74; Church Yth Grp; Scholastic Bowl; VP Band; Chorus; Pep Band; Nwsp Stf; Yrbk Bus Mgr; VP Sr Cls; DAR Awd; High Hon Roll; Johnson Bible Clg; Yth Mnstry.

LYONS, MICHELLE; Sheffield Area JR SR HS; Tiona, PA; (Y); 45/98; Church Yth Grp; Sec FHA; Pep Clb; SADD; Varsity Clb; Chorus; Color Guard; Concert Band; Trk; Vllybl; U Pittsburgh Bradford.

LYONS, THOMAS; St Josephs Prep; Merion, PA; (Y); Boy Scts; JCL; Spanish Clb; Rep Soph Cls; Golf; High Hon Roll; Hon Roll; Opt Clb Awd; Mrktg.

LYSAGHT, JAMES; Cardinal O Hara HS; Warrenton, VA; (Y); 209/780; Boy Scts; Capt Color Guard; Capt Drill Tm; Mrchg Band; School Musical; School Play; SAR Awd; Good Ctznshp Awd Union Lg Philadelphia 85; Good Ctznshp Awd Am Lgn 84; Hnrs Bys Scts Dvsn Wrld Clss 84; Pysics.

LYSAK, JENNIFER; State College Area HS; State College, PA; (Y); 6/483; Church Yth Grp; Mrchg Band; Orch; Symp Band; Yrbk Stf; Ntl Merit Schol; Math Tm; Church Choir; Concert Band; Nwsp Stf; PA Dist & Regnl Bands 86; Faculty Schlr 86; Assemblies God Dist Teen Tlnt Wnnr 85 & 86; PA ST U.

LYSCIK, CHARMANE; West Allegheny HS; Oakdale, PA; (Y); Art Clb; Pres FBLA; Var Cheerleading; Var Crs Cntry; Var Diving; Var Swmmng; Hon Roll; Sawyer Bus Sch; Travel Agent.

LYSEK, SPENCER M; Saucon Valley HS; Bethlehem, PA; (Y); Church Yth Grp; Band; Concert Band; Jazz Band; Mrchg Band; Var Bsktbl; Var Ftbl; Trk; Yth Board Chrmn-PA NE Conf Untd Chrch Christ 86; Chrch Yth Grp Pres 85-86; Band, Ftbll, Bsktbll 83-6; Lockhaven U; Intl Studies.

LYSKO, SCOTT; Avonworth JR SR HS; Pittsbg, PA; (Y); 25/96; Aud/Vis; Church Yth Grp; Computer Clb; Spanish Clb; Band; Nwsp Rptr; Ftbl; Golf; Tennis; Wt Lftg; Villanova U; Engrng.

LYTLE, CHRISTIAN ROSS; Franklin Area HS; Franklin, PA; (Y); Band; Concert Band; Jazz Band; Mrchg Band; Pep Band; School Musical; Yrbk Phtg; Yrbk Sprt Ed; Yrbk Stf; Govnrs Schl Art Semi-Fin Photo 86.

LYTLE, ROBERT; Chambersburg Area SR HS; Chambersburg, PA; (Y); 8/600; Am Leg Boys St; Boy Scts; Drama Clb; Ski Clb; School Play; Crs Cntry; Trk; U Of PA; Undrgrad Bus.

LYTTLETON, COLLEEN; Germantown HS; Philadelphia, PA; (Y); 2/327; Debate Tm; Library Aide; Leo Clb; Band; Yrbk Stf; High Hon Roll; NHS; Cngrss Bndstg Yth Exch Schlrshp 85; Ntl Hnr Soc 85; Grmntwn Acadm Excel Awd 86; U PA; Lib Arts.

MAADDI, SHADI; St John Neumann HS; Philadelphia, PA; (Y); 1/338; Capt Mathletes; Science Clb; Yrbk Stf; NHS; Math Tm; High Hon Roll; St John Neumann Full 4 Yr Schlrshp 83-87.

MAAS, KAREN; North East HS; North East, PA; (Y); 25/150; Church Yth Grp; Letterman Clb; Pep Clb; Chrmn Q&S; School Play; Yrbk Phtg; Ed Yrbk Stf; Chrmn Sr Cls; Hon Roll; Pres NHS; Bowling Green ST U; Ocptl Thrp.

MABEN, PAUL; Wissahickon HS; Springhouse, PA; (S); 44/279; Ski Clb; Varsity Clb; Golf; Var Tennis; Hon Roll; NHS; All Conf Tennis 85; 2nd St Mixed Doubles 85; U Pittsburgh.

MABIUS, BRYAN J; East Pennsboro HS; Summerdale, PA; (Y); Church Yth Grp; Cmnty Wkr; Var Wrstlng; Hon Roll; Masonry Constrctn.

MAC, MOTRYA; Bethlehem Catholic HS; Bethlehem, PA; (Y); 4/201; Drama Clb; French Clb; Chorus; Deg Excel Ukranian Stds; Columbia U; Kremlinlgst.

MAC CLUSKIE, JULIE; Northern York County HS; Dillsburg, PA; (Y); 32/200; Band; Chorus; Concert Band; Mrchg Band; VP Jr Cls; Pres Sr Cls; Var Crs Cntry; Var Powder Puff Ftbl; Var L Trk; Hon Roll; Bst Prsnlty Awd 85-86; Prom Queen 85-86; Messiah Coll; CPA.

MAC DONALD, ALAN; Bradford Central Christian HS; Bradford, PA; (Y); 6/32; Key Clb; Nwsp Sprt Ed; Pres Jr Cls; Pres Sr Cls; L Bsbl; Capt Bsktbl; Hon Roll; NHS; 3rd Pl Tm Starter 84; MVP Otto Eldred X Mas Tourn 85; Stu Athlete Awd Sports 86; Wofford Coll.

MAC DONALD, BRIAN J; Scranton Prep; Scranton, PA; (Y); 37/192; Boy Scts; Letterman Clb; Pep Band; Var Crs Cntry; Var Trk; High Hon Roll; NHS; Engr.

MAC DONALD, DONALD J; Butler Area SR HS; Butler, PA; (Y); 13/754; Church Yth Grp; Exploring; Pres German Clb; SADD; Thesps; School Musical; School Play; Swing Chorus; Variety Show; Var L Swmmng; Carnegie-Mellon U; Archtctr.

MAC DONALD, EILEEN; North Hill SR HS; Pittsburgh, PA; (Y); 57/507; Exploring; Trs Keywanettes; Letterman Clb; Symp Band; Rep Frsh Cls; Rep Soph Cls; Capt Var Swmmng; Var L Trk; High Hon Roll; Pres Schlr; Swmmng ST Qlfr 84-86; Rgnl Swmmg Fnlst Westrn PA 84-86; Lafayette Coll; Engr.

MAC DONALD, KRISTIN; Greensburg Central Catholic HS; Murrysvilla, PA; (Y); 20/222; Hosp Aide; NFL; Service Clb; VP Chorus; School Musical; Rptr Yrbk Stf; High Hon Roll; NHS; Math.

MAC DONOUGH, TED; Western Wayne HS; Lk Ariel, PA; (Y); 32/140; Church Yth Grp; Computer Clb; French Clb; Latin Clb; Red Cross Aide; Ski Clb; SADD; Off Frsh Cls; Crs Cntry; Ftbl; Natl Ski Patrol 84-86; Local Fire Dept 86; Penn ST U; Forestry.

MAC FARLAND, MIKE; Carlynton HS; Carnegie, PA; (Y); Boys Clb Am; Var L Bsbl; L Ftbl; Hon Roll.

MAC GOWAN, TRACI; Wyoming Valley West HS; Forty Fort, PA; (Y); 11/375; Sec Church Yth Grp; VP Cmnty Wkr; Library Aide; Science Clb; Orch; Lit Mag; Var L Crs Cntry; Var L Fld Hcky; Var L Trk; Vllybl; Stu Of Mnth 85; Frty Frt Busnssmn & Prffssnls Schlrshp Awd 86; James Madison U; Psych.

MAC KRELL, GARRY; Karns City Area HS; Chicora, PA; (Y); 9/119; Church Yth Grp; Concert Band; Trs Mrchg Band; Pep Band; Hon Roll; NHS; 1st Schltc Achvt Ltr 85; Natl Rifle Assn Marksmnshp Awd 85; Butler Cnty CC; Aquaculture.

MAC MURDO, RICHARD; Lincoln HS; Ellwood City, PA; (Y); 19/162; German Clb; Chorus; High Hon Roll; Hon Roll; NHS; Engrng.

MAC NABB, SHERRY; East HS; Erie, PA; (Y); 21/135; French Clb; Y-Teens; Ed Nwsp Ed-Chief; Nwsp Stf; Stu Cncl; NHS; Air Force; Admin.

MAC PHERSON, HEATHER; Hempfield HS; Landisvile, PA; (Y); Church Yth Grp; Drama Clb; Band; JV Trk.

MACARCHICK, ELLEN; West Scranton HS; Scranton, PA; (Y); Aud/Vis; French Clb; Drill Tm; Hon Roll; NHS.

MACAULEY, KAREN M; Abington HS; Huntingdon Valley, PA; (Y); 1/528; Sec Key Clb; Service Clb; Drm Mjr(t); Mrchg Band; Masonic Awd; NHS; Ntl Merit SF; Voice Dem Awd; Wellesley Coll Awd 85; Am Music Abroad-Hnrs Bnd 84; Achvt Awds-Band & French 84; Belmont Coll Nashville; Mus Bus.

MACCALLUM, BILL; Mid-Valley HS; Dickson City, PA; (Y); Cmnty Wkr; Political Wkr; Mrchg Band; JV Var Bsbl; JV Var Bsktbl; Im Vllybl.

MACCARELLI, LISA MARIE; Gateway SR HS; Monroeville, PA; (Y); Am Leg Aux Girls St; Band; VP Chorus; Sec Frsh Cls; Sec Soph Cls; Sec Jr Cls; Stu Cncl; Var Cheerleading; Var Sftbl; Hon Roll; U Of Pittsburgh; Psychlgy.

MACE, ANN; West Hazleton HS; W Hazelton, PA; (Y); Church Yth Grp; FBLA; Girl Scts; VICA; Band; Concert Band; Jazz Band; Mrchg Band; Orch; Pep Band; U S Army Resrv; Bloomsburg U; Tchg Spec Ed.

MACE, ELAINE; Pottstown SR HS; Pottstown, PA; (Y); 24/238; Sec Trs Art Clb; Church Yth Grp; Stage Crew; Nwsp Stf; Rep Stu Cncl; Var Lcrss; Stat Mgr(s); High Hon Roll; Hon Roll; NHS; 2nd Pl Awd For Art 86; Lansdale Schl Bus; Sec.

MACE, PATRICIA; Hazleton HS; Hazleton, PA; (Y); 64/388; French Clb; FBLA; Intnl Clb; Color Guard; Yrbk Stf; JV Bsktbl; Hon Roll; Psych.

MACEIKO, MICHELLE; Lake-Lehman HS; Harveys Lk, PA; (Y); 14/140; Sftbl; High Hon Roll; Hon Roll; Jr NHS; NHS; Math.

MACENCZAK, STEVEN; North Star HS; Jenners, PA; (Y); Aud/Vis; Letterman Clb; Varsity Clb; Band; Concert Band; Orch; Bsbl; Ftbl; Trk; Lion Awd; U Pittsburgh; Sci.

MACEVOY, ERICA; Penn Trofford HS; Trafford, PA; (Y); JCL; High Hon Roll; NHS; Prfct Atten Awd; Bkng.

MACEYAK, BRIAN; Southmoreland HS; Scottdale, PA; (Y); 41/204; German Clb; JA; JCL; Latin Clb; Letterman Clb; Ski Clb; Stu Cncl; Var Ftbl; Var Trk; Var Wt Lftg; All Bay-West Ftbl Tm 86.

MACEYKO, RUDY; Greater Johnstown HS; Johnstown, PA; (Y); German Clb; NFL; School Musical; Hon Roll; Prfct Atten Awd; Comp Engrng.

MACHAK, MICHELE; Burgettstown JR SR HS; Langeloth, PA; (Y); 39/175; French Clb; Teachers Aide; Band; Chorus; Concert Band; Drill Tm; Mrchg Band; Pep Band; Symp Band; Off Stu Cncl; Fnlst Clmx Schlrshp 86; Robert Morris; Bus Adm.

MACHAMER, MICHELE; Northwest Area HS; Hunlock Creek, PA; (Y); 16/110; SADD; Pres Chorus; School Musical; Stu Cncl; High Hon Roll; NHS; NEDT Awd; Church Yth Grp; Computer Clb; Drama Clb; Dist Chrs 84-86; Reg Chrs 84-86; NEAE Schlrshp; Bloomsburg U; Spec Educ.

MACHCOVIAK, JUDY; Johnsonburg Area HS; Johnsonburg, PA; (Y); 13/87; Sec Church Yth Grp; Cmnty Wkr; VP Stu Cncl; Bsktbl; Mgr(s); Score Keeper; Vllybl; Rep NHS; Villa Maria Coll; Bio.

MACHER, SCOTT; West Allegheny SR HS; Coraopolis, PA; (Y); Spanish Clb; JV Var Bsbl; Bsktbl; Var L Golf; Hon Roll; Bus Admin.

MACHI, JEFFREY; Deer Lakes JR SR HS; Allison Pk, PA; (Y); SADD; Band; Church Choir; Concert Band; Mrchg Band; Pep Band; School Play; Yrbk Stf; Hon Roll; Allegheny-Kiski Vly Hnrs Bnd Cncrt 85-86; PMEA Dist I HS Bnd Fstvl 86; Pgh Dicesan Yng People 84-85; Bus.

MACHOVIAK, JUDY; Johnsonburg Area HS; Johnsonburg, PA; (S); 15/96; Sec Church Yth Grp; Cmnty Wkr; Girl Scts; Varsity Clb; Church Choir; Rep Stu Cncl; JV Stat Bsktbl; Stat Ftbl; JV Vllybl; Stat Wrstlng; Chrmn St Jude Bike-A-Thn Lif 85; Villa Maria Coll; Bio.

MACIOGE, DANIELLE; Pennsbury HS; Yardley, PA; (Y); SADD; Rep Jr Cls; Rep Stu Cncl; Cheerleading; Im Gym; Hon Roll; NHS; Visl Comm.

MACK, CHRISTINE; Central Dauphin HS; Harrisburg, PA; (Y); 4-H; Ski Clb; Chorus; Color Guard; Im Vllybl; Hon Roll; Quaified For States In 4-H 86; Sci.

MACK, DEBRA; Northern Lebanon HS; Jonestown, PA; (Y); Church Yth Grp; DECA; Library Aide; Church Choir; Mgr(s); Trk.

MACK, EDWARD L; H S For Perform & Creative Arts; Philadelphia, PA; (S); Boys Clb Am; Band; Concert Band; Drm & Bgl; Jazz Band; Mrchg Band; Orch; School Musical; Symp Band; Hon Roll; PA Golden Gloves Champ 85-86; USA-ABF Regnl Champ Amat Bxg 85-86; MAABF Champ Amat Bxg 86; Temple U; Engrng Tech.

MACK, JENNIFER; Conemaugh Township HS; Hollsopple, PA; (Y); 3/101; Spanish Clb; Nwsp Phtg; Lit Mag; Sec Trs Stu Cncl; Trk; Hon Roll; NHS; I Dare You Awd 86; Span Awd 85-86; Stu Citzn Awd 84; U Pittsburgh; Engrng.

MACK, JENNY; Conemaugh Township Area HS; Hollsopple, PA; (S); 3/101; Spanish Clb; Nwsp Phtg; Lit Mag; Trs Stu Cncl; Var L Trk; Hon Roll; NHS; Stage Crew; Outstndng Achvt Spn 85; Pres Phys Fit Awd 84; Stu Ctzn Mnth 84; U Pittsburgh.

MACK, LISA; Pen Argyl Area HS; Pen Argyl, PA; (Y); #2 In Class; Pres Sec Church Yth Grp; Drama Clb; Scholastic Bowl; Ski Clb; Concert Band; Mrchg Band; Orch; Yrbk Stf; High Hon Roll; NHS; The Kings Coll; Physcl Thrpy.

MACK, MICHELLE; United HS; Homer City, PA; (Y); #49 In Class; Church Yth Grp; Hosp Aide; Library Aide; Office Aide; Ski Clb; Mgr Jr Cls; Trs Stu Cncl; JV Var Cheerleading; JV Var Trk; Hon Roll; Chrldng,Track Awd 86; Cls Mgr Awd 86; IN U; Phrmcy.

MACKAY, CHRIS; Minersville Area HS; Pottsville, PA; (Y); 3/117; Hosp Aide; Color Guard; Nwsp Phtg; Yrbk Stf; High Hon Roll; NHS; Bloomsburg U; Bus Adm.

MACKCOVIAK, APRIL; St Marys Area HS; Weedville, PA; (Y); Camera Clb; Yrbk Phtg; Yrbk Stf; Var L Cheerleading; Para-Legal.

MACKERETH, KARA; Dover Area HS; Dover, PA; (Y); Drama Clb; Band; Chorus; Concert Band; Mrchg Band; School Musical; Nwsp Stf; Rep Frsh Cls; Rep Soph Cls; Hon Roll; Bus.

MACKEWICZ, DAVID; Pottstown HS; Pottstown, PA; (S); 12/273; Key Clb; Yrbk Stf; JV Bsbl; Var L Ftbl; Var Trk; High Hon Roll; Hon Roll; NHS; Prfct Atten Awd.

MACKEY, SALLYANN; Faith Christian Schl; Windgap, PA; (Y); 4/11; Church Yth Grp; Teachers Aide; Chorus; School Musical; School Play; Yrbk Stf; Off Jr Cls; Off Sr Cls; Hon Roll; Christn Charctr Awd 84-85; ACSI Distngshd Chrstn Stu 86; Christn Hnr Soc 86; Northampton Cnty; Acctg.

MACKEY, SUZANNE; Abington Heights HS; Clarks Summit, PA; (Y); 46/273; Drama Clb; School Play; Stage Crew; Sec Stu Cncl; Hon Roll; NHS; Presdntl Clssrm Washington DC 86; Cedarville Coll; Poltcl Sci.

MACKIE, CECELIA; Bishop Hannan HS; Scranton, PA; (Y); Art Clb; Awd Excellnc Sociolgy 86; Awds Honrbl Mentn Theolgy III & Art II 86; Sociolgy.

MACKIN, BRUCE; Philipsburg-Osceola SR HS; Philipsburg, PA; (Y); 7/250; Church Yth Grp; Pres Drama Clb; French Clb; Pres Thesps; Ed Yrbk Ed-Chief; Trs Soph Cls; Stu Cncl; Im Badmtn; JV Ftbl; Var Socr; Thespian Awd Best Actor 86; Gannon U Outstndng Stu Awd 86; Outstndng Achvts Sci 84; Notre Dame U; Chem Engr.

MACKIW, PAULA; Dunmore HS; Dunmore, PA; (Y); 33/155; Computer Clb; French Clb; Quiz Bowl; Ski Clb; Stage Crew; Yrbk Phtg; Cheerleading; Mgr(s); High Hon Roll; Hon Roll; CMC Hospital; Xry Tech.

MACKO, CATHY A; G A R Memorial HS; Wilkes Barre, PA; (S); Library Aide; Chorus; Yrbk Ed-Chief; Trs Jr Cls; Cheerleading; Sftbl; Bus.

MACKOR, KIM; Bethlehem Center HS; Beallsville, PA; (Y); Art Clb; JA; Pep Clb; Ski Clb; Varsity Clb; Nwsp Stf; Soph Cls; Bsbl; Bsktbl; Cheerleading; MIP Vrsty Bsktbl 85-86; Russian Clb 83-86; Trvl.

MACKOVJAK, KATHLYN; Harbor Creek HS; North East, PA; (Y); 7/228; Model UN; Mrchg Band; Pep Band; Variety Show; Var L Cheerleading; Var Crs Cntry; Var Trk; JV Vllybl; High Hon Roll; NHS; Engrng.

MACKRELL, CINDY; Valley View HS; Archbald, PA; (Y); French Clb; High Hon Roll; NHS; U Scranton; Pol Sci.

MACKY, CAMERON; Wilminton Area HS; New Wilmington, PA; (S); 1/125; Drama Clb; Concert Band; Mrchg Band; School Play; Stage Crew; Rep Stu Cncl; Var Capt Bsktbl; Var Capt Crs Cntry; Var L Trk; NHS.

MACLAY, HEATHER; Northern HS; Lewisburg, PA; (Y); Library Aide; Ski Clb; Band; Chorus; Concert Band; Mrchg Band; Stage Crew; Yrbk Stf; Stu Cncl; Var Capt Cheerleading; Bear Singers An Elite Grp Slctd Sngrs 83-86; Ed.

MACMURDO, JIM; Westmont Hilltop SR HS; Johnstown, PA; (Y); 63/140; Church Yth Grp; Juniata Coll; Bus.

MACOM, JAMIE; Lincoln HS; Wampum, PA; (Y); Computer Clb; Exploring; German Clb; Ski Clb; Chorus; Church Choir; School Musical; Bowling; Hon Roll; Engrg.

MACOMBER, MARY; Claysburg-Kimmel HS; Portage, PA; (Y); Ski Clb; SADD; Hon Roll; Bus Mngmnt.

MACON, ALIAUNDA A; Franklin Learning Ctr; Philadelphia, PA; (Y); Dance Clb; Exploring; French Clb; Library Aide; Teachers Aide; School Musical; Variety Show; Sftbl; Hon Roll; Prfct Atten Awd; ARTS 85-86; Fellwshp Farm Hmn Rltns Pgm 86; W Chester U; Librl Arts.

MACRI, CARRIE; Crestwood HS; Mountaintop, PA; (Y); Intnl Clb; Key Clb; Library Aide; Chorus; Mgr(s); Trk; Hon Roll; NEDT Awd; Pre-Med.

MACRI, DEAN; Wilmington Area HS; Pulaski, PA; (S); Latin Clb; Band; Concert Band; Mrchg Band; Pep Band; Crs Cntry; Trk; High Hon Roll; NHS.

MACWILLIAMS, LAURA LYNN; Harborcreek JR/SR HS; Erie, PA; (Y); AFS; Church Yth Grp; Hosp Aide; Model UN; School Play; Yrbk Bus Mgr; Miss PA Teen USA Pagnt 85; Cncl Volunteers Erie Cnty 84; Mod U N Assmbly 86; U Pittsburgh; Phrmcy.

MADAYA, KEVIN; Northampton Area HS; Northampton, PA; (Y); 45/458; Leo Clb; Var Bsbl; Var Diving; JV Var Ftbl; Hon Roll.

MADDALENA, MICHELLE; Glendale JR SR HS; Coalport, PA; (Y); 18/72; Church Yth Grp; Drama Clb; Library Aide; Science Clb; Sec Band; Trs Chorus; Church Choir; Concert Band; Mrchg Band; Pep Band; Ntl Hnr Soc 85-86; Stu Rep Schl Brd 85-86; Dist Band & Dist Chorus 85-86; St Francis Coll; Elem Educ.

MADDAS, MARDI; Connellsville SR HS; Dunbar, PA; (Y); Church Yth Grp; FBLA; Office Aide; Pep Clb; Band; Chorus; Sec Soph Cls; Var Jr Cls; Mgr(s); Score Keeper; Marine Bio.

MADDEN, KAREN; Lebanon Catholic HS; Hershey, PA; (Y); FHA; Library Aide; SADD; Stage Crew; High Hon Roll; Foods/Nutr Awd 86; Greatest Acad Imprvt Over 4 Yrs 86; Gordon Phillips Bty Sch; Cosmet.

MADDEN, MARTIN; Ambridge Area HS; Baden, PA; (Y); Church Yth Grp; Pep Clb; Spanish Clb; Off Jr Cls; Off Sr Cls; Rep Stu Cncl; Coach Actv; JV Ftbl; Socr; Hon Roll; PA ST U; Conservation.

MADDEN, PAMELA; Knoch JR SR HS; Butler, PA; (Y); 5/225; AFS; Spanish Clb; SADD; Varsity Clb; Rep Stu Cncl; L Var Cheerleading; High Hon Roll; NHS; Pres Schlr; Butler Countys JR Miss 86; S Butler Fed Of Tchrs Schlrhp 86; Gertrude De Sellem Mem Schlrshp 86; PA ST U; Nursing.

MADDEN, SANDRA A; Gwynedd-Mercy Acad HS; Churchville, PA; (Y); 17/69; Service Clb; Var L Crs Cntry; Fld Hcky; Capt Var Swmmng; High Hon Roll; Hon Roll; NHS; Hnrb Mntn Hghst Mth Avg; Commendable Achvt Hstry & Calculus; La Salle U; Comp Sci.

MADDEN, SEAN; Mt Carmel HS; Atlas, PA; (Y); 33/163; Cmnty Wkr; Drama Clb; FCA; Key Clb; Letterman Clb; Political Wkr; Spanish Clb; Varsity Clb; School Musical; Variety Show; Law.

MADDEN, TAMMY; Owen J Roberts HS; Pottstown, PA; (Y); Church Yth Grp; Exploring; Letterman Clb; Var L Diving; Var Mgr(s); Score Keeper; JV Sftbl; Stat Swmmng; Var Timer; Im Vllybl; Pre-Med.

MADDEN, TONYA; Titusville SR HS; Titusville, PA; (Y); 40/203; SADD; Y-Teens; Yrbk Ed-Chief; Yrbk Phtg; Yrbk Stf; High Hon Roll; Hon Roll; Sec.

MADDONNA, ANTHONY S; Bishop Kenrick HS; Norristown, PA; (Y); Band; Chorus; Concert Band; Jazz Band; Mrchg Band; Pep Band; School Musical; School Play; Excllnce Awd Music Hgh Acad 85-86; All Cath Bnd 85-86; FL U; Music.

MADDY, MISSY; Shade-Central City HS; Central City, PA; (Y); Pres Spanish Clb; Chorus; Nwsp Stf; Yrbk Stf; Sec Frsh Cls; Hon Roll; NHS; Dntl Hygn.

MADEIRA, BRIAN; Governor Mifflin HS; Shillington, PA; (Y); 71/325; Boy Scts; Church Yth Grp; JA; Band; Concert Band; Mrchg Band; Bus.

MADEIRA, SHARON; Governor Mifflin HS; Shillington, PA; (Y); 86/275; Church Yth Grp; FBLA; Girl Scts; Color Guard; Flag Corp; Mrchg Band; Prfct Atten Awd; Acctnt.

MADEJ, JEANNE; Saint Francis Acad; Bethlehem, PA; (Y); 1/20; Science Clb; Chorus; School Musical; Stage Crew; Pres Frsh Cls; Capt Cheerleading; Btty Crckr Awd; High Hon Roll; NHS; Soc Wmn Engrs Cert Merit Hgh Hons 86; JR Sci & Humnts Sympsm 85; Reg 1st Pl Awd PA Acdad Of Sci 86.

MADER, LORI; Burgettstown Jr Sr HS; Langeloth, PA; (Y); Ski Clb; Sec Spanish Clb; Var Capt Cheerleading; High Hon Roll; Hon Roll; NHS.

MADER, TAMMY; Wyalusing Valley HS; Wyalusing, PA; (Y); German Clb; SADD; Band; Color Guard; School Play; Yrbk Stf; Stat Ftbl; Var Mgr(s); Stat Trk; High Hon Roll; Arch.

MADEY, KIM; Apolio-Ridge HS; Clune, PA; (Y); 26/186; Ski Clb; Band; Capt Color Guard; Madrigals; Mrchg Band; School Musical; Yrbk Stf; Trk; Hon Roll; Trs NHS; Hlth Prof Schlrshp 86; Western PA; Nrsng.

MADIANOS, GREG; St Josephs Prep; Jenkintown, PA; (Y); #3 In Class; Rep Jazz Band; School Musical; Nwsp Rptr; Nwsp Stf; Lit Mag; Rep Soph Cls; Rep Jr Cls; Var Socr; Capt Tennis; Var Wrstlng; Sprts Med.

MADISON, MARC A; La Salle College HS; Philadelphia, PA; (Y); Church Yth Grp; Ski Clb; Im Bsktbl; Im Ftbl; JV Socr; Im Tennis; JV Var Trk; Im Vllybl; French Hon Soc; Ntl Merit SF.

MADJERICK, MICHELLE; Gateway SR HS; Monroeville, PA; (Y); Ed Yrbk Stf; Off Jr Cls; Off Sr Cls; High Hon Roll; Prsdntl Acdmc Ftnss Awd 86; Eqstrn.

MADL JR, THOMAS; Freedom HS; Bethlehem, PA; (Y); 110/445; Band; Mrchg Band; Orch; Pep Band; Symp Band; Dntstry.

MADLER, STACEY; Bethel Park SR HS; Bethel Park, PA; (Y); Am Leg Aux Girls St; French Clb; Drill Tm; Mrchg Band; Orch; Symp Band; Pom Pon; Powder Puff Ftbl; Hon Roll; Wstrn Dist Jnr H S Bnd Fstvl 84; Mid-East Instrmntl Music Fstvl 85; Flutist.

MADONNA, NAN; Ambridge HS; Alquippa, PA; (Y); Church Yth Grp; Cmnty Wkr; French Clb; Intnl Clb; Pep Clb; Band; Frsh Cls; Soph Cls; Jr Cls; L Cheerleading; Cont Teen Miss USA 86; Rutgers; Nursing.

MADONNA, SANDRA A; Penn Cambria HS; Gallitzin, PA; (Y); 7/167; Drama Clb; Hosp Aide; SADD; VP Frsh Cls; Stat Bsktbl; Stat Trk; Hon Roll; Trs NHS; Hgh Schltc Achvt Awd 86; Frnch, Engl, Home Ec, Alg Awds 83; St Francis Coll; Physcn Asst.

MADORE, ERIC; Connellsville Area HS; Cnlvle, PA; (Y); 76/500; Concert Band; Mrchg Band; Symp Band; L Var Diving; JV Golf; L Var Swmmng; JV Var Trk; High Hon Roll; Hon Roll; Prfct Atten Awd; CPIAL Qlfyr In Diving 85-86; Duquesne U; Bus.

MADURA, MELISSA; Penn Hills SR HS; Pittsburgh, PA; (S); 20/797; Concert Band; Mrchg Band; Yrbk Sprt Ed; Yrbk Stf; Sr Cls; Stu Cncl; High Hon Roll; Jr NHS; NHS; Prfct Atten Awd; Eagle Schlrshp-WA & Jefferson Coll 86; Eng Wrtng Awd 86; WA & Jefferson; Bus.

MAGARO, AMY; Shippensburg Area SR HS; Shippensburg, PA; (Y); 16/221; Girl Scts; Pres Leo Clb; SADD; Concert Band; Mrchg Band; Nwsp Bus Mgr; NHS; Spanish NHS; U Pittsburgh; Physcl Thrpy.

MAGARO, LORI A; Lower Dauphin SR HS; Middletown, PA; (Y); 2/217; Model UN; Chorus; Capt Color Guard; School Musical; School Play; Lit Mag; High Hon Roll; NHS; Sal; Drama Clb; John Hall Fndtn Schlrshp 86; Publshd Poetry In Accolades 86; Media Mag Awd 86; Syracuse U; Jrnlsm.

MAGARO, STEPHANIE; Northern HS; Wellsville, PA; (Y); 5/205; Chorus; Church Choir; School Musical; Nwsp Stf; High Hon Roll; NHS; Debate Tm; Speech Tm; School Play; &HSSL Forensic League Sec,Treas,Pres 85-87; Comptv Drama Chairman 86-87; Bio.

MAGDA, FRANK ALAN; Bethlehem-Center HS; Millsboro, PA; (Y); Spanish Clb; Varsity Clb; Band; VP Jr Cls; Stu Cncl; Capt Bsktbl; Var Ftbl; L Trk; Hon Roll; Stu VFW Natl Band Post 47 83-86; Crmnlgy.

MAGDA, MICHELLE; G A R HS; Wilkes Barre, PA; (S); 6/187; FBLA; Stage Crew; Hon Roll; NHS; Capt Varsty YABA Bwlng Assn 82-83; Lgl Or Med Sec.

MAGDELINSKAS, WILLIAM; Neshaminy HS; Langhorne, PA; (Y); Letterman Clb; Varsity Clb; Chorus; Var L Ftbl; Var L Wrstlng; Hon Roll; Math.

MAGDICH, MARY ANNE; Canon Mc Millan SR HS; Canonsburg, PA; (Y); 81/371; Church Yth Grp; Latin Clb; Band; Concert Band; Mrchg Band; Yrbk Stf; Tennis; Hon Roll; Math.

MAGEE, BYRON; Shippensburg Area SR HS; Shippensburg, PA; (Y); Varsity Clb; Var Capt Bsbl; Var Capt Ftbl; Hon Roll; NHS; Spanish NHS; Spirit Victory Natl Schlr Ath Awd 86; PA ST; Bio.

MAGEN, BARRY; George Washington HS; Philadelphia, PA; (Y); 15/737; Math Clb; Science Clb; Crs Cntry; Trk; High Hon Roll; Hon Roll; Ntl Merit Ltr; Free Sons Of Israel Hebrew Awd 86; Crss Cntry Dedctn Awd 86; Amoco Chem Awd 85; Penn ST; Pre-Med.

MAGERA, GEORGE; Bentworth SR HS; Cokeburg, PA; (Y); 2/138; Varsity Clb; Stu Cncl; Bsktbl; Ftbl; High Hon Roll; NHS; Pre-Law.

MAGGI, C PATRICK; State College Area SR HS; State College, PA; (Y); Aud/Vis; Boy Scts; Computer Clb; Teachers Aide; Stage Crew; Cit Awd; Eagle Scout Awd 86; Am Ind Arts Stu Assoc 86; CAD Drawng Comptn 2nd Pl Ntls; PA ST U; Engrng.

MAGGS, MICHELE; Henderson HS; West Chester, PA; (Y); 31/336; Church Yth Grp; Exploring; Hosp Aide; Pres Intnl Clb; Office Aide; Var Cheerleading; Trk; Hon Roll; NHS; Sec Spanish NHS; Millersvl U; Spnsh.

MAGILL, MIKE; Philipsburg Osceola SR HS; Sandy Ridge, PA; (Y); Boy Scts; Chess Clb; Im Ftbl; Im Wrstlng; God Cntry Awd.

MAGISO, PETER; Marple Newtown HS; Newtown Square, PA; (Y); Ski Clb; Variety Show; Rep Stu Cncl; Im Bsktbl; Var Crs Cntry; JV Ftbl; Im Swmmng; Var Trk; Hon Roll; Stu Cncl Convntns Atten Awd 85-86; Chairmn Cannd Food Dr 85-86; Yth Forum Mem; UCLA; Law.

MAGLICCO, BRUCE; Norwin HS; N Huntingdon, PA; (Y); Computer Clb; DECA; SADD; DECA Awd 86; Bus Adm.

MAGLIDT, TAMMY; St Marys Area HS; Kersey, PA; (Y); 24/290; JA; Band; Capt Color Guard; Concert Band; Flag Corp; Stat Trk; High Hon Roll; Jr NHS; NHS; Outstndng JR Hlth; IN U PA; Med Tech.

MAGNESS, PATRICIA; Mars Area SR HS; Mars, PA; (Y); 20/157; Varsity Clb; School Musical; Stage Crew; Nwsp Stf; Sec Frsh Cls; Rep Soph Cls; Rep Jr Cls; Rep Sr Cls; High Hon Roll; Hon Roll; Educ Assns Wllm Imler Schlrshp 86; Bus Awd 86; Clarion U-PA.

MAGNI, KIM; Lebanon Catholic HS; Lebanon, PA; (Y); FCA; French Clb; FHA; German Clb; Key Clb; Pep Clb; Ski Clb; SADD; Thesps; Drill Tm; Smmr Yuth, Bio Schlrshps, 3rd Schl Sci Fair 86; OK ST U; Pre Vet.

MAGNOTTA, JOE H; Center HS; Monaca, PA; (Y); 1/183; Am Leg Boys St; Computer Clb; German Clb; Var Bsbl; Bsktbl; High Hon Roll; NHS; Cntr Gifted & Talntd Pgm 83-87; Cntr High Q Tm 86; Cntr Am Lg Bsbl Tm 86-87; Engineering.

MAGNOTTA, MARC C; North Pocono HS; Moscow, PA; (Y); Church Yth Grp; Var Bsktbl; Var Golf; Hon Roll; NHS; Prfct Atten Awd; Golf Vrsty MVP 83-86; Vrsty Bsktbll 84-87; Ntl Hnr Soc 84-86; Engr.

MAGOR, ERIKA; Old Forge HS; Old Forge, PA; (S); Church Yth Grp; French Clb; Thesps; Color Guard; Drill Tm; School Musical; School Play; Yrbk Stf; Twrlr; High Hon Roll; Featr Dancr 84-86; Miss Deviltt Marchg Unts 86-87; Colr Grd Capt 82-84; Erly Chldhd.

MAGUIRE, COLLEEN; East Allegheny HS; N Versailles, PA; (Y); 43/209; Church Yth Grp; Pep Clb; Ski Clb; SADD; School Musical; Yrbk Stf; Rep Frsh Cls; Rep Soph Cls; Capt Cheerleading; Hon Roll; Sawyer Business Schl; Busnss.

MAGUIRE, SEAN ABRAHAM; Central HS; Philadelphia, PA; (Y); Science Clb; Temple Yth Grp; JV Crs Cntry; Var L Golf; Mgr(s); Im Vllybl; Im Wt Lftg; Ntl Merit SF; Barnwell Hnr Rl 84-86; West Point.

MAGYOR, KIM; Mt Pleasant Area SR HS; Mount Pleasant, PA; (Y); FBLA; FHA; GAA; Color Guard; Rep Frsh Cls; Mat Maids; Hon Roll; Pre Schl Tchr, Guide, Wrk Slw Chlrn, Olympd Wrk Gr Schl Sprts; Phtgrphy.

MAGYOR, TAMMY; Mt Pleasant SR HS; Mt Pleasant, PA; (Y); Color Guard; Nwsp Stf; Yrbk Stf; Mat Maids.

MAH, LESLEY; Upper Merion SR HS; Kg Of Prussia, PA; (Y); 28/308; Mrchg Band; Orch; School Musical; Var Cheerleading; Fld Hcky; Lcrss; Twrlr; Hon Roll; Supr Ratg Musc Tchrs Fest Fnls 83; Intl Piano Recd Comptn Hnrbl Mntn 86.

MAHAFFEY, RACHEL; Warren Area HS; Warren, PA; (Y); Cmnty Wkr; French Clb; Pres Soroptimist; School Play; Yrbk Stf; Hon Roll; U Buffalo.

MAHAFKEY, JEREMY M; Seneca Valley SR HS; Mars, PA; (Y); Boy Scts; Church Yth Grp; Computer Clb; Ski Clb; Band; Chorus; Bsktbl; Tennis; Hon Roll; Rifle Tm Capt 81-86; Pittsburgh Penn ST; Math.

MAHAJAN, SANJOY; Fox Chapel HS; Pittsburgh, PA; (Y); 14/350; Pres Chess Clb; Pres Math Clb; Math Tm; Quiz Bowl; Ski Clb; JV Socr; JV Tennis; High Hon Roll; NHS; Ntl Merit SF; 2nd Pl Shippensborg PA Math Cntst 85; 1st Pl Area Chss Trnmnt 84; 2nd Pl Calcu-Slv Bwl 85; Stanford U; Comp Sci.

MAHAN, AMY; Trinity HS; Washington, PA; (Y); Cmnty Wkr; Pep Clb; SADD; Bsbl; Crs Cntry; Ftbl; Sftbl; Swmmng; Trk; High Hon Roll; Nrsng.

MAHAR, TRICIA; Upper Merion HS; King Of Prussa, PA; (Y); 15/350; Church Yth Grp; Capt Math Tm; Var Capt Bsktbl; Var Capt Socr; Hon Roll; Pres NHS; Pre-Med.

MAHARTY, DAVID; G A R Memorial HS; Wilkes Barre, PA; (S); 13/187; Aud/Vis; French Clb; Ski Clb; Acpl Chr; Chorus; Capt L Ftbl; Wt Lftg; Wrstlng; Hon Roll; NHS; Coaches Awd Wrstlg 83; Scranton U; Dntstry.

MAHELTZ, LINDA; John S Fine HS; Sheatown, PA; (Y); Church Yth Grp; VP FBLA; Hosp Aide; Key Clb; Band; Chorus; Color Guard; Drm & Bgl; Nwsp Stf; Bus Mgmt.

MAHLMEISTER, MARYANN; Knoch JR SR HS; Saxonburg, PA; (Y); Band; Co-Capt Color Guard; Mrchg Band; Butler Cnty CC; RN.

MAHLON, BARBARA J; Curwensville Area HS; Grampion, PA; (Y); Camera Clb; Sec Church Yth Grp; Cmnty Wkr; French Clb; Church Choir; Nursing.

MAHLON, COBY; Clearfield HS; Clearfield, PA; (Y); 29/315; Church Yth Grp; Concert Band; Mrchg Band; Orch; JV Var Bsktbl; JV Vllybl; High Hon Roll; Educ.

MAHLON, DEBRA; Freedom HS; Bethlehem, PA; (Y); 198/456; French Clb; Chorus; Score Keeper; Nuclear Med Tech.

MAHOLIC, JULIE; Council Rock HS; Richboro, PA; (Y); 256/755; Church Yth Grp; Band; Chorus; Church Choir; Jazz Band; Mrchg Band; Orch; School Musical; Symp Band; Hon Roll; Lttr From Band 84; Section Ldr In Band For Trombones 85; Mansfield U.

MAHOLTZ, AMY; St Marys Area HS; Saint Marys, PA; (Y); Color Guard; Var L Cheerleading.

MAHOLTZ, WENDY; Du Bois Area SR HS; Penfield, PA; (Y); 18/256; Letterman Clb; Varsity Clb; Chorus; Church Choir; School Musical; Score Keeper; Sftbl; Vllybl; High Hon Roll; VP NHS; Huston Twp Alumni Scholar 86; IN U PA; Finance.

MAHON, ADRIAN; Kennedy Christian HS; Sharpsville, PA; (Y); 4/98; Cmnty Wkr; Latin Clb; Ski Clb; Yrbk Stf; Kennedy Chrstn HS Schlrshp 83; Librl Arts.

MAHON, MICHELE; Weatherly Area HS; Weatherly, PA; (Y); Cmnty Wkr; FBLA; FHA; Girl Scts; Office Aide; Pep Clb; Hst Frsh Cls; Trs Stu Cncl; Mgr Bsbl; 1st Pl Pub Spkng FBLA Comptn 86; Psychlgy.

MAHONEY, ALICE; Albert Gallatin SR HS; New Geneva, PA; (Y); 4-H; FHA; Sec Library Aide; 4-H Awd; High Hon Roll; Hon Roll; Army Rsrv; Comp Anlys.

MAHONEY, ALICE; St Pius X HS; Trappe, PA; (S); 31/137; Var Bsktbl; Var Crs Cntry; Var Trk; High Hon Roll; NHS; Cabrini Coll; Acctg.

MAHONEY, DAWN; ST Basil Acad; Philadelphia, PA; (S); 5/94; Church Yth Grp; Hosp Aide; Pres Spanish Clb; Chorus; NEDT Awd; Ntl Engl Merit Awd 86; Ntl Lang Merit Awd 85; Abingtom Mem Hosp Schl; Nrsng.

MAHONEY, DEBBIE; Saegertown HS; Saegertown, PA; (Y); Church Yth Grp; 4-H; Girl Scts; Ski Clb; Band; Concert Band; Mrchg Band; Yrbk Stf; Hon Roll; Rsprtry Thrpsy.

MAHONEY, KELLY; Laurel Highlands SR HS; Uniontown, PA; (Y); 34/340; Cmnty Wkr; Band; Concert Band; Mrchg Band; Vllybl; High Hon Roll; Hon Roll; Jr NHS; Acadmc Schlrshp-Jhnsn & Wls Coll 86; Dplma Of Merit-Advncd Spnsh III 85; Johnson/Wales Coll; Fshn Rtlng.

MAHONEY, MATTHEW; Freedom HS; Bethlehem, PA; (Y); 101/450; Exploring; Stage Crew; Yrbk Phtg; Hon Roll; Morning Call Carrier Of Wk 85; Aerntcs.

MAHONEY, SHANE; Ambridge Area HS; Ambridge, PA; (Y); Boy Scts; German Clb; Cit Awd; Hon Roll; Germ Clb Awd 84-86.

MAHONEY, YVONNE; Mc Keesport SR HS; Mckeesport, PA; (Y); 72/380; French Clb; Hosp Aide; Band; Powder Puff Ftbl; Hon Roll; Cazenovia; Day Care Svcs.

MAHOOD, JULIE; Moniteau JR SR HS; Hilliards, PA; (Y); 12/103; Chorus; Drill Tm; Jazz Band; Var L Bsktbl; Var L Trk; Var L Vllybl; Hon Roll; NHS; Church Yth Grp; Spanish Clb; Bio.

MAHOVLICH, SUSAN; Western Beaver HS; Industry, PA; (Y); Church Yth Grp; FHA; High Hon Roll; Hon Roll; NHS.

MAIDA, ANDREA; Geibel HS; Acme, PA; (Y); Art Clb; Drama Clb; English Clb; French Clb; Pep Clb; Ski Clb; Church Choir; School Musical; School Play; Yrbk Stf; Mscl Theatre.

MAIDA, SUSAN; Strath Haven HS; Wallingford, PA; (Y); Hosp Aide; Library Aide; Teachers Aide; Concert Band; Drill Tm; Mrchg Band; Lit Mag; Hon Roll; Villanova U; Psych.

MAIDEN, HOPE; Millersburg HS; Millersburg, PA; (Y); 23/84; Yrbk Stf; Pres Frsh Cls; Pres Soph Cls; Pres Jr Cls; Cheerleading; High Hon Roll; Hon Roll; NHS; Pep Clb; Pom Pon; Intr Dsgnr.

MAIDENFORD, CINDY; Pine Grove Area HS; Pine Grove, PA; (Y); Am Leg Aux Girls St; Teachers Aide; Varsity Clb; Rep Frsh Cls; Rep Jr Cls; Var Bsktbl; Stat Ftbl; Var Mgr(s); Var Sftbl; Kutztown; Elem Educ.

MAIER, CHRISTINE; Greater Works Acad; Pittsburgh, PA; (S); Hosp Aide; Concert Band; Yrbk Phtg; Var Cheerleading; Var Mgr(s); Var Mgr Trk; High Hon Roll; Physcl Thrpy.

MAIER, NANCY; Eastern York HS; Hellam, PA; (Y); Varsity Clb; Band; Concert Band; Mrchg Band; Nwsp Stf; Yrbk Stf; Rep Stu Cncl; JV Cheerleading; Var Fld Hcky; JV Trk; Phy Ftns 83-85; Hnrbl Mntn Hcky 84; Psych.

MAIER, SUSANNE; Beaver Area SR HS; Beaver, PA; (Y); Girl Scts; JCL; Key Clb; Latin Clb; Teachers Aide; Chorus; Color Guard; Stage Crew; Tennis; High Hon Roll; Acad Awd 84; Pres Acad Ftnss 86; PA ST U; Biochem.

MAIETTA, JAYNE M; Lincoln HS; Ellwood City, PA; (Y); 60/163; French Clb; Chrmn Y-Teens; Chorus; School Musical; Capt Bsktbl; Cheerleading; Coach Actv; Powder Puff Ftbl; Trk; Beavr County Comm Coll; Accntng.

MAIETTA JR, RONALD; Montoursville HS; Montoursville, PA; (Y); #36 In Class; Aud/Vis; Boy Scts; Cmnty Wkr; Debate Tm; Exploring; German Clb; Radio Clb; Ski Clb; Bloomsburg U; Bus.

MAIN, GEORGE; Trinity HS; Washington, PA; (Y); Letterman Clb; Varsity Clb; Pres Frsh Cls; Pres Soph Cls; Pres Jr Cls; Pres Sr Cls; Capt Var Socr; Var L Wrstlng; George M Main JC; Engineering.

MAIN, KEVIN; West Greene Middle SR HS; Waynesburg, PA; (S); Trs Science Clb; Chorus; School Musical; Nwsp Stf; Pre Coll Oceanogrphc Pgm 85; Regnls & ST PA JR Acad Sci 85-86; Acad Achvt Awd 2nd Pl 85.

MAINE, ROBERT; Franklin Regional SR HS; Rochester Mills, PA; (Y); Spanish Clb; Im Ftbl; Socr; Embry-Riddle Aerntcl U; Aerntc.

MAINOLFI, DONNA; G A R Memorial HS; Wilkes Barre, PA; (S); 22/177; Drama Clb; Pres FBLA; Key Clb; Color Guard; School Play; Nwsp Stf; Hon Roll; NHS; Shthnd I Profcncy Cert 84-85; Typng II Profcncy Cert 84-85.

MAINS, CHRISTINE; South Allegheny HS; Port Vue, PA; (S); 13/184; French Clb; Hosp Aide; Office Aide; Y-Teens; Concert Band; Mrchg Band; Off Jr Cls; Powder Puff Ftbl; High Hon Roll; NHS; Sci Fair Hnrbl Mntn 84-85.

MAINS, DIANA; South Allegheny HS; Glassport, PA; (Y); Office Aide; Y-Teens; School Play; Trs Soph Cls; Im Rptr Jr Cls; Rep Stu Cncl; Var Bsktbl; JV Capt Cheerleading; Powder Puff Ftbl.

MAINS, KAREN; Susquenita HS; Duncannon, PA; (S); 8/158; Church Yth Grp; 4-H; Office Aide; Quiz Bowl; Band; Chorus; Mrchg Band; School Play; Rep Stu Cncl; L Capt Crs Cntry; Penn ST; Nrs.

MAIO, WENDI; Freedom HS; Bethlehem, PA; (Y); 58/456; Dance Clb; Pep Clb; Band; Mrchg Band; Hon Roll; NBTA Twrlng Awds 84-85; Pre Law.

MAIONE, STACIE; Mon Valley Catholic HS; Monessen, PA; (S); 9/104; Church Yth Grp; Hosp Aide; Pep Clb; Spanish Clb; Chorus; Nwsp Rptr; Sec Soph Cls; Sec Jr Cls; Pres Sr Cls; NHS; Span Natl Hnr Soc 85-86; Natl Hnr Soc 85-86; U Pittsburgh; Occ Ther.

MAIORANO, ROSANNE; St Maria Goretti HS; Philadelphia, PA; (Y); 69/390; Church Yth Grp; Cmnty Wkr; Sec Exploring; GAA; Hosp Aide; Yrbk Sprt Ed; Var Capt Bowling; Var Tennis; Prfct Atten Awd; Yth & The Pltcl Systm-Smnr-La Slle U-Phila 86; Toursm.

MAISANO, ANITA; St Maria Goretti HS; Philadelphia, PA; (Y); 24/390; Church Yth Grp; GAA; Orch; School Musical; School Play; Rep Sr Cls; Hon Roll; NHS; Tri-M Music Hnr Soc Treas 86; Acadmc All-Amer Awd 84; PA Coll; Pharmcy.

MAISH III, GEORGE O; Saucon Valley HS; Bethlehem, PA; (Y); 2/174; Boy Scts; German Clb; Science Clb; Socr; Capt L Swmmng; High Hon Roll; NHS; Ntl Merit Ltr; Sal; Congressman Ctznshp Awd 86; PA ST U; Pre-Med.

MAIZE, JENNIFER; Greenwood HS; Liverpool, PA; (S); 1/64; Pres Camera Clb; 4-H; Sec Concert Band; Flag Corp; School Musical; Nwsp Phtg; Var L Bsktbl; Var L Trk; NHS; Ntl Merit Ltr; Air Force Acad Smmr Scntfc Smnr 85; Hugh O Brien Yth Ldrshp Smnr 84; Stu Forum Rep 84-86.

MAJCHRZAK, CHARLES; Ridgway Area HS; Ridgway, PA; (Y); 1/130; Boy Scts; Spanish Clb; Nwsp Rptr; Var Tennis; High Hon Roll; NHS; Ntl Merit Schol; Pres Schlr; Val; Boy Scouts Am Eagle Scout 85; Gannon U; Med.

MAJESKI, CARL; Coughlin HS; Hudson, PA; (Y); Computer Clb; Var Bsbl; Var Bsktbl; Var Golf; Hon Roll; Times Ldr Bsbl All Str Tm 1st Tm Ptchr 86.

MAJETIC, ANTHONY; Moon SR HS; Coraopolis, PA; (Y); 21/327; Exploring; Nwsp Stf; Hon Roll; NHS; Exec Ofcrs Scholar Penn ST 86; Beaver Campus Scholar Penn ST 86; 2nd Pl Poster Wnnr 85; PA ST U; Engrng.

MAJHAN, SUSAN; Ligonier Valley SR HS; Laughlintown, PA; (Y); AFS; Ski Clb; Spanish Clb; Nwsp Stf; Rep Stu Cncl; JV Stat Bsktbl; L Trk; JV Vllybl; Old Dominion U; Rcrtn.

MAJKOWSKI, JACKIE; Little Flower Catholic HS; Philadelphia, PA; (Y); 85/402; German Clb; Hosp Aide; Letterman Clb; Red Cross Aide; Service Clb; Varsity Clb; Lit Mag; Rep Stu Cncl; Var Fld Hcky; Var Mgr(s); Northwd Civic Assn Cmnty Svc Awd 83; Hahnemann Med Coll; Nrsng.

MAJOR, DOUG; Northwestern Lehigh HS; New Tripoli, PA; (Y); Aud/Vis; Boy Scts; Computer Clb; German Clb; Stage Crew; Cit Awd; Comp Sci.

MAJOR, MELISSA; Nazareth Acad; Quantico, VA; (Y); Sec FCA; Sec Trs Chorus; Madrigals; School Musical; School Play; Yrbk Stf; Off Soph Cls; Hon Roll; Sec NHS; Spanish Clb; Music.

MAJOR, THOMAS; West Hazleton HS; Sugarloaf, PA; (S); 37/198; Church Yth Grp; French Clb; FNA; Scholastic Bowl; Band; L Bsbl; L Bsktbl; L Capt Ftbl; Wt Lftg; God Cntry Awd; Bloomsburg U; Pre Med.

MAJUMDAR, JOEY; Quigley HS; Monaca, PA; (S); 3/112; Cmnty Wkr; Math Tm; Quiz Bowl; Chorus; Gov Hon Prg Awd; High Hon Roll; Lion Awd; NHS; Rotary Intl Schlrp To Japns Symposm 84; Intl Relatns.

MAKARAVAGE, DONNA; G A R Memorial HS; Wilkes-Barre, PA; (S); 25/187; Hosp Aide; Key Clb; Chorus; Stage Crew; Stat Bsktbl; Var Trk; Var JV Vllybl; Hon Roll; Score Keeper; Med.

MAKAREVITZ, MICHELLE; Pottstown HS; Pottstown, PA; (S); VP FNA; Service Clb; Color Guard; Rep Soph Cls; Rep Jr Cls; Rep Sr Cls; Co-Capt Cheerleading; Var Lcrss; NHS; Villanova.

MAKAREWICZ JR, EDWARD P; Hazleton HS; Hazelton, PA; (Y); Capt Chess Clb; FBLA; Bsbl; Swmmng; Penn ST; Accounting.

MAKOSEY, BETH; Hempfield HS; Irwin, PA; (Y); French Clb; Nwsp Stf; Yrbk Bus Mgr; Yrbk Ed-Chief; Yrbk Phtg; Yrbk Stf; Tennis; High Hon Roll; Hon Roll; Camera Clb; Pitt Johnstown; Eng.

MAKOWER, SHARON H; Cheltenham HS; Elkins Park, PA; (Y); 1/385; Church Yth Grp; Math Tm; Model UN; Chorus; Orch; Stage Crew; Yrbk Stf; Gov Hon Prg Awd; NHS; Ntl Merit SF; Pol Sci.

MAKUTA, DENISE M; West Hazelton HS; W Hazleton, PA; (S); 32/192; Sec VICA; Stu Cncl; Cheerleading; Trk; High Hon Roll; Hon Roll; NHS; Intl Crrspndnc Schls; Cld Care.

MAKUTA, MARY ANN; Bishop Hafey HS; Hazleton, PA; (Y); Church Yth Grp; FNA; Hosp Aide; Spanish Clb; Orch; Hon Roll; St Francis De Sales; Nrsg.

MALACHIAS, CHRISTINA; Baldwin HS; Pittsburgh, PA; (Y); 111/535; Math Clb; Stat Trk; Hon Roll.

MALAMISURO, CHRISTOPHER; Greater Works Acad; N Huntingdon, PA; (Y); 2/36; Church Yth Grp; Nwsp Stf; Yrbk Stf; Var Jr Cls; Pres Sr Cls; Bsktbl; Ftbl; Wt Lftg; High Hon Roll; Sal; Schlrshp Oral Rbrts U 86-87; Oral Roberts U; Law.

MALARKEY, JOHN; Bishop O Reilly HS; Swoyersville, PA; (Y); Computer Clb; Latin Clb; Math Tm; Band; Im Badmtn; Im Mgr(s); Stat Score Keeper; Var Socr; Var Trk; Im Vllybl; Paul Smith Schlrshp Awd; Big Brthrs & Sisrs 86; PA ST U; Acctng.

MALARKEY, MARIANNE; Abington SR HS; Roslyn, PA; (Y); 21/508; Flag Corp; Nwsp Rptr; Fld Hcky; Swmmng; High Hon Roll; Hon Roll; NHS.

MALARNEY, KATIE; Cumberland Valley HS; Mechanicsburg, PA; (Y); Key Clb; Ski Clb; Nwsp Rptr; Yrbk Rptr; Yrbk Stf; Stu Cncl; Cheerleading; Educ.

MALASAVAGE, ADELE; Marian Catholic HS; Mahanoy City, PA; (S); 33/114; Church Yth Grp; Band; Chorus; Church Choir; Concert Band; JV Capt Cheerleading; Trk; High Hon Roll; Hon Roll; Spanish NHS; Theology II Awd 84-85; Lycoming Coll; Nrsng.

MALATESTA, LAURIE; Sharpsville Area HS; Sharpsville, PA; (Y); Camera Clb; FHA; Hosp Aide; Science Clb; Teachers Aide; Chorus; Nwsp Rptr; Var Cheerleading; Hon Roll; NHS; Sharpsville Hgh Acad Achvt Awd 85; Mem Of Gifted Prog 83-86; Pre Law.

MALCOLM, PHILIP; Valley Forge Christian Acad; Phoenixville, PA; (S); Art Clb; Aud/Vis; Computer Clb; Yrbk Phtg; Rep Stu Cncl; Capt Bsktbl; Var Socr; Trk; High Hon Roll; Hon Roll; Temple U; Grphc Dsgn.

MALDONADO, MIKE; Berlin Brothersvalley HS; Berlin, PA; (Y); Sec VICA; PITT U; Mltry.

MALEK, BETH; Corry Area HS; Columbus, PA; (Y); 19/250; Office Aide; Teachers Aide; Band; Concert Band; Jazz Band; Mrchg Band; High Hon Roll; Hon Roll; Pres Ftnss Awd, Prfssnl Bus Wmn 86.

MALENCIA, DALE; South Park HS; Library, PA; (Y); Aud/Vis; Computer Clb; High Hon Roll; Comp Engr.

MALEY, CRAIG; Waynesburg Central HS; Waynesburg, PA; (Y); Ski Clb; Spanish Clb; Bsbl; Fld Hcky; Ftbl; Hon Roll; Voice Dem Awd; Edinboro U PA; Bus Admin.

MALEY, DENISE; Hollidaysburg SR HS; Duncansville, PA; (Y); Library Aide; VP Spanish Clb; Band; Chorus; Mrchg Band; School Musical; Variety Show; Nwsp Rptr; Nwsp Stf; Yrbk Stf; PA ST U; Lawyer.

MALEY, JAMES J; Northwestern-Lehigh HS; Germansville, PA; (Y); 16/158; Ski Clb; Yrbk Stf; JV Ftbl; JV Trk; High Hon Roll; NHS; 2nd Pl Art Show; Outstndng Wrk Art Awd; Engl Awd; PA ST U.

MALEY, REBECCA; Trinity HS; Amity, PA; (Y); 37/374; Church Yth Grp; 4-H; Band; Mrchg Band; Hon Roll; Nrsng.

MALFARA, TIMOTHY; St Josephs Prep Schl; Philadelphia, PA; (Y); Boy Scts; Church Yth Grp; Im Stat Bsktbl; Im Ftbl; Mgr(s); Var Trk; Ntl Merit Ltr; Acadmc Schlrshp St Jo Prep 83; Cum Laude Nalt Latn Exm 84; Med.

MALICK JR, EARL J; Shikellamy HS; Sunbury, PA; (Y); 35/301; Church Yth Grp; German Clb; SADD; Chorus; Var L Ftbl; JV Wrstlng; High Hon Roll; Hon Roll; Elec.

MALICK, THERESA; Cardinal O Hara HS; Upland, PA; (Y); 174/772; Church Yth Grp; Cmnty Wkr; Spanish Clb; Hon Roll; SPEC Educ.

MALICKI, MARK; Philipsburg Osceola Area HS; Philipsburg, PA; (Y); 1/245; Church Yth Grp; French Clb; Letterman Clb; Red Cross Aide; Ski Clb; Trs Stu Cncl; Golf; High Hon Roll; NHS; Phys Ftnss Awd 85; Pre Med.

MALIK, ADAM G; Holy Ghost Prep; Richboro, PA; (Y); Boy Scts; Exploring; Mathletes; Nwsp Rptr; Capt Var Crs Cntry; JV Socr; Var L Trk; High Hon Roll; NHS; Ntl Merit SF; Physcs.

MALIKOWSKI, LISA; Crestwood HS; Mounatintop, PA; (Y); FBLA; Girl Scts; Key Clb; Chorus; Flag Corp; School Musical; School Play; Yrbk Stf; Mgr(s); High Hon Roll; 1st Rgnl & 5th St Ldrshp Conf FLBA Typing I 86; Art Dsgn.

MALIN, MATT; Central Bucks West HS; Chalfont, PA; (Y); 77/495; Boy Scts; Band; Mrchg Band; JV Socr; JV Swmmng; JV Vllybl; Hon Roll; Jr NHS; Geolgy.

MALINA, KIMBERLY ANN; Notre Dame HS; Easton, PA; (Y); VICA; Hon Roll; Prfct Atten Awd; Outstndng Achvmnt Awd In Csmtlgy 86; Outstndng Achvmnt Vo-Tech & Notre Dame 86; Allentown Schl Csmtlgy; Teach.

MALINCHAK, CHRISTINA; Mc Keesport HS; Mckeesport, PA; (Y); Exploring; Band; Chorus; Concert Band; Mrchg Band; JV Vllybl; High Hon Roll; PA ST; Engrg.

MALINGOWSKI, CHRIS; Behtel Park HS; Bethel Pk, PA; (Y); #180 In Class; Am Leg Aux Girls St; Church Yth Grp; FHA; NFL; Science Clb; SADD; Y-Teens; Stu Cncl; Crs Cntry; Powder Puff Ftbl; 2 First Pl In Pennsylvania Jr Academy Sci 83; Broadcasting.

MALINISH, SHAWN A; Windber HS; Windber, PA; (Y); 35/112; FBLA; Political Wkr; Ski Clb; Varsity Clb; Stage Crew; Yrbk Stf; VP Frsh Cls; Pres Sr Cls; Trs Stu Cncl; JV Bsktbl; Stu Of The Month 85-86; U Of Pittsburgh; Bus.

MALINOFF, JOSH; George Washington HS; Philadelphia, PA; (Y); Computer Clb; French Clb; Math Clb; Teachers Aide; French Hon Soc; Hon Roll; Mu Alp Tht; 1st Pl Drexel U Comp Cntst 84; Engr.

MALINS, DANETTE; Ambridge Area HS; Baden, PA; (Y); 18/264; Off Frsh Cls; Off Soph Cls; Off Jr Cls; Off Sr Cls; Stu Cncl; Bsktbl; Sftbl; Trk; Vllybl; High Hon Roll; Atheletic All-Stars; Girl Of Mnth/Ambridge Bus & Profssnl Women; Athletic/Acad Schlrshp-Waynesbrg Coll; Waynesburg Coll; Math Educ.

MALINSKI, MARY ANN; Bishop Hannan HS; Scranton, PA; (Y); 4/126; Computer Clb; Scholastic Bowl; High Hon Roll; NHS; Maxima Cum Laude Awd Natl Latn Exm 85; St John Neumann Awd Teachg Relgs Ed 86; U Of Scranton; Acctg.

MALINSKY, LISA D; State College Area SR HS; State College, PA; (Y); 18/567; Pres Art Clb; Church Yth Grp; Spanish Clb; Ed Nwsp Ed-Chief; Yrbk Stf; Frsh Cls; Soph Cls; Var Golf; JV Sftbl; High Hon Roll; Gold Merit Schlstc Art Awd-ST Lvl 85; Intl Rltns.

MALINSKY, MICHAEL; Albert Gallatin SR HS; Masontown, PA; (Y); Church Yth Grp; Varsity Clb; Chorus; School Musical; Bsktbl; Hon Roll; Exchng Club Stu Of Yr 85; Acadmc Top 10 84-85; Pre-Dentistry.

MALISH, JEDD; Cheltenham HS; Cheltenham, PA; (Y); 118/365; JCL; Latin Clb; Nwsp Stf; Yrbk Stf; Im Bsktbl.

MALITS, CHRISTINE; Plum SR HS; Pittsburgh, PA; (Y); Church Yth Grp; Pres 4-H; Girl Scts; Spanish Clb; Yrbk Stf; 4-H Awd; High Hon Roll; NHS; Prfct Atten Awd; Penn ST; Animal Sci.

MALITSKY, KRISTIN; Tunkhannockm Area HS; Tunkhannock, PA; (S); 1/300; Computer Clb; Exploring; Spanish Clb; Rep Frsh Cls; Rep Soph Cls; Rep Jr Cls; Tennis; Cit Awd; High Hon Roll; Debate Tm; Acad All Amer 83-84; Sci.

MALITZKI, WARREN; Freedom HS; Bethlehem, PA; (Y); 147/445; Church Yth Grp; Cmnty Wkr; FCA; VICA; Bsbl; Hon Roll; Penn ST U; Aerontcs.

MALIZIA, CHERYL; Bishop Mc Devitt HS; Harrisburg, PA; (Y); Church Yth Grp; French Clb; Ski Clb; Yrbk Stf; Var Cheerleading; High Hon Roll; Hon Roll; 2nd Pl Sci Fair 84; Natl Hstry Day Exclint Awd 84; 2nd Pl Art Shw 84; Med.

MALJAK, KEVIN M; North Allegheny SR HS; Allison Park, PA; (Y); 211/629; Church Yth Grp; Computer Clb; Off Jr Cls; Acad Grant Duquesne U 86; Distngushd Achvt Awd Physcl Ed 86; Duquesne U; Phrmcy.

MALKOWIAK, BILL; Lincoln HS; Ellwood City, PA; (Y); 6/170; Latin Clb; Ski Clb; Yrbk Stf; High Hon Roll; NHS; VP Soph Cls; VP Jr Cls; VP Sr Cls; Amer Lgn Acdmc Awd 83; Engrng.

MALKOWSKI, ROBERT; Northeast Catholic HS; Philadelphia, PA; (Y); 195/362; Church Yth Grp; VICA; Im Capt Bowling; Hon Roll; Elec Engr.

MALLIK, STEPHANIE; Moon SR HS; Coraopolis, PA; (Y); Sec Church Yth Grp; Exploring; Teachers Aide; Chorus; School Musical; Rep Stu Cncl; Var L Cheerleading; JV Var Sftbl; JV Var Vllybl; Child Care.

MALLINGER, TARA; St Pauls Cathedral HS; Pittsburgh, PA; (S); 5/55; Red Cross Aide; Spanish Clb; Nwsp Rptr; High Hon Roll; NHS; Sci Fair Awd-Specl Hnr 84 & 85; Outstndng Achvt-Western Civlztn 85; Outstndng Achvt-Spansh II 85; Vetrnry Med.

MALLORY, CARRI LYNN; Fort Le Beouf HS; Waterford, PA; (Y); 64/184; School Play; Rep Frsh Cls; Rep Soph Cls; Rep Jr Cls; Trs Sr Cls; Var JV Cheerleading; Sftbl; Stat Wrstlng; Hon Roll; Erie Bus Ctr; Acctng.

MALLOY, BERNADETTE; Christian School Of York HS; York, PA; (Y); 21/59; Church Yth Grp; Cmnty Wkr; School Play; Yrbk Stf; Chrmn Stu Cncl; Var Cheerleading; Var Sftbl; Dnfth Awd; Hon Roll; Fnlst Miss PA Ntl Teen Ager Pagnt 86; Delg Assoc Christn Schls Interntl Ldrshp Conf 84-85; Comp Pgmr.

MALLOY, DENISE; Sheffield Area HS; Sheffield, PA; (Y); 12/98; Trs Church Yth Grp; Trs VP FHA; Pres SADD; Varsity Clb; Pres Trs Stu Cncl; Vllybl; High Hon Roll; NHS; VFW Awd; Shfld Schlrshp Fnd Recpnt 86; Awd Excllnc Soc Stds 86; Du Bois Business Coll; Acctg.

MALLOY, KATHY; Hopewell SR HS; Aliquippa, PA; (S); 13/295; Cmnty Wkr; Sec German Clb; Latin Clb; Band; Concert Band; Mrchg Band; Powder Puff Ftbl; Var Trk; High Hon Roll; NHS; Paralegl.

MALLOY, MICHELLE; Freeport Area HS; Sarver, PA; (Y); 1/172; GAA; Mrchg Band; Symp Band; Capt L Bsktbl; Trk; High Hon Roll; NHS; Pres Schlr; Stu Of Mnth 85; Acad Schlrshp Gannon U 86; Acad All Amer 83; Gannon U; Fmly Med Pgm.

MALLOY, TAMMY A; Bethel Park HS; Bethel Park, PA; (Y); 18/520; Church Yth Grp; NFL; Science Clb; Spanish Clb; Nwsp Ed-Chief; Off Soph Cls; NHS; Nwsp Rptr; High Hon Roll; Prfct Atten Awd; PJAS US Army Sci Awd 86; PA JR Acad Of Sci Regnls 1st Pl ST 2nd Pl 86; Grove City Coll; Psych.

MALMROSE, ELIZABETH; Sheffield Area JR & SR HS; Clarendon, PA; (Y); 72/98; Drama Clb; Girl Scts; Library Aide; Pep Clb; Chorus; Color Guard; School Musical; School Play; Stage Crew; Yrbk Stf; Ralphael Schl Of Beauty; Stylst.

MALONE, MARLA; Pius X HS; Bangor, PA; (Y); 7/33; 4-H; Pep Clb; Varsity Clb; Church Choir; Stage Crew; Var Bsktbl; 4-H Awd; Hon Roll; NHS; Vet.

MALONE, SANDRA; State College Area SR HS; Boalsburg, PA; (Y); Exploring; Girl Scts; Concert Band; Jazz Band; Mrchg Band; Hon Roll; Gold Awd 85; Penn ST; Bio-Chem.

MALONEY, KELLY; Harborcreek HS; Erie, PA; (Y); Pep Clb; Pres Jr Cls; Pres Sr Cls; Stu Cncl; JV Var Bsktbl; L Cheerleading; Var L Sftbl; Tennis; Vllybl; Wt Lftg; All Co Sftbl Hnbl Mntn Short Stop 86.

MALONEY, KRISTEN; Gettysburg SR HS; Gettysburg, PA; (Y); 6/248; Model UN; Pres Soph Cls; Pres Jr Cls; Pres Sr Cls; Sec Stu Cncl; High Hon Roll; NHS; Opt Clb Awd; Church Yth Grp; Cmnty Wkr; Exch Clb Yuth Mnth; Stdnt Mnth; Cnty Sorptmst Awd; Hamilton Coll; Psych.

MALONEY, LANCE P; Moon SR HS; Coraopolis, PA; (Y); 53/317; Aud/Vis; Boy Scts; Trs Church Yth Grp; Jazz Band; Mrchg Band; Rep Sr Cls; Hon Roll; Voice Dem Awd; Band; Church Choir; Ord Arrw Boy Scts 84; Trnng Orch, 84-85; Clarion U Clarion; Comm.

MALOY, KELLI; Greensburg Central Catholic HS; Greensburg, PA; (Y); 14/240; Church Yth Grp; Cmnty Wkr; English Clb; Math Clb; Spanish Clb; Teachers Aide; Nwsp Ed-Chief; Im Vllybl; High Hon Roll; NHS; Psych.

MALSKY, DIANE; Wyoming Area HS; Exeter, PA; (Y); Art Clb; French Clb; JV Trk.

MALTA, DEAN; G A R Memorial HS; Wilkes Barre, PA; (Y); Letterman Clb; Chorus; Var L Ftbl; Var Vllybl; Var Capt Wrstlng; High Hon Roll; Hon Roll; Intl Frgn Lang Awd Grmn 85; Wltr S Crpntr Schlrshp Engnrng 86; Wilkes Coll; Elec Engnrng.

MALTMAN, MICHAEL L; Abington SR HS; Glenside, PA; (Y); 295/535; Service Clb; Montgomery Cnty CC; Art.

MALUTIC, SALENA; Villa Maria HS; Campell, OH; (Y); 10/60; Hosp Aide; Library Aide; Ski Clb; Spanish Clb; Yrbk Ed-Chief; Sftbl; Tennis; High Hon Roll; NHS; Spanish NHS; Sec Grk Cathlc Union JR Bwlrs 84-86; Brown U; Med.

MALVESTUTO, MICHAEL; Montour SR HS; Mckees Rocks, PA; (Y); 40/307; Drama Clb; Math Tm; Trs Stu Cncl; Var Trk; Im Ftbl; High Hon Roll; Hon Roll; US Naval Acad; Aerospc Engrng.

MALVET, MARK; Ferndale Area HS; Johnstown, PA; (S); 1/60; Church Yth Grp; Computer Clb; NFL; VP Band; Concert Band; Jazz Band; Mrchg Band; Yrbk Stf; DAR Awd; Lion Awd; Coaches Awd 85; John Phillip Sousa Band Awd 85; PA ST; Pre-Med.

MALYS, ANN; Venango Christian HS; Rouseville, PA; (Y); 2/42; Rep Frsh Cls; Rep Soph Cls; Rep Stu Cncl; Var Bsktbl; Stat Sftbl; Var Vllybl; NHS; NEDT Awd; Prfct Atten Awd; Marine Bio.

MAMARY, CHRISTINE MICHELE; Central York SR HS; York, PA; (Y); 40/220; Sec Art Clb; Rep Church Yth Grp; Dance Clb; Sec French Clb; Intnl Clb; Stage Crew; Nwsp Ed-Chief; Yrbk Stf; Im Stat Bsktbl; High Hon Roll; Journlsm Awd 86; Art Srv Awd 86; Millersville U; Elem Ed.

MAMINSKI, KENNETH; Central HS; Philadelphia, PA; (Y); Chess Clb; Library Aide; Math Clb; Science Clb; Teachers Aide; Band; Mgr(s); Barnwell Hon; Naval.

MAMMARELLA, TERRE; Brownsville Area HS; Hiller, PA; (S); 1/225; Church Yth Grp; French Clb; Mathletes; Math Clb; Ski Clb; SADD; Band; Flag Corp; Mrchg Band; Yrbk Stf; Stu Month 86; U Of Pittsburgh Schlr 86; Hnrs Prgrm 86; U Of Pittsburgh; Math.

MAMMARELLI, VINCENT; St Josephs Prep; Collingswood, NJ; (Y); Church Yth Grp; Cmnty Wkr; Computer Clb; Exploring; Intnl Clb; Science Clb; Nwsp Rptr; High Hon Roll; Prep Schlr Awd 83-86; Outstndng Acadmc Perfmnc Awd 85; Comp.

MANARCHUCK, NELLIE; Carbondale Area JR SR HS; Carbondale, PA; (Y); 5/157; Math Clb; AFS; Ski Clb; Chorus; Variety Show; Cheerleading; Trk; High Hon Roll; NHS; Prfct Atten Awd; Schlstc Art Awds 85-86; Med Field.

MANARCZYK, ANITA; Geibel HS; Everson, PA; (Y); Spanish Clb; SADD; Yrbk Stf; Lit Mag; JV Bsktbl; Mgr(s); Im Sftbl; High Hon Roll; Spanish NHS; CA U Of PA; Chldhd Educ.

MANAS, ERIC; Central HS; Philadelphia, PA; (Y); Art Clb; Camera Clb; Computer Clb; French Clb; Library Aide; Teachers Aide; Ed Yrbk Stf; Mgr(s); Var Tennis; Hon Roll; Barnwell Hnr Key 84-86; Temple U; Psych.

MANASSERI, MICHELLE; Pen Argyl Area HS; Pen Argyl, PA; (Y); #2 In Class; Am Leg Aux Girls St; Cmnty Wkr; GAA; Ski Clb; Concert Band; Capt Mrchg Band; Yrbk Stf; Trs Jr Cls; JV Var Sftbl; NHS; Ldrshp Pgm Le High U 86; Pre-Med.

MANBECK, WENDY; Tulpehocken HS; Bethel, PA; (Y); 9/115; Church Yth Grp; School Musical; Yrbk Ed-Chief; Trs Stu Cncl; Var Cheerleading; Var Fld Hcky; Var Capt Trk; Hon Roll; NHS; Shipensburg U; Bus Ed.

MANCABELLI, JEFFREY; Bishop Hannan HS; Moosic, PA; (Y); 50/133; Church Yth Grp; Computer Clb; Debate Tm; Drama Clb; JA; Jazz Band; School Play; Variety Show; Rep Stu Cncl; Hon Roll; U Scranton; Acctng.

MANCINI, DARA LYNN; Aliquippa HS; Aliquippa, PA; (S); #1 In Class; Church Yth Grp; Drama Clb; Exploring; French Clb; Band; Concert Band; Mrchg Band; School Play; Yrbk Stf; Rep Jr Cls.

MANCINI, DAVID J; Valley View JR SR HS; Peckville, PA; (Y); 1/194; Computer Clb; Spanish Clb; Chorus; Concert Band; Mrchg Band; High Hon Roll; NHS; Prfct Atten Awd; VFW Awd; Aahperd Yth Ftns Achvt Awd 86; Hnrbl Ment Kings Coll Spnsh Comp 85; 3rd Pl Kings Coll Spnsh Comptn; Bio.

MANCINO, BARB; Corry Area HS; Corry, PA; (S); 16/212; Civic Clb; Drama Clb; French Clb; Teachers Aide; Flag Corp; Rep Jr Cls; High Hon Roll; Ntl Merit Ltr; Frnch.

MANCOS, MICHAEL; Pittston Area HS; Pittston, PA; (Y); Church Yth Grp; Concert Band; Jazz Band; Mrchg Band; Var L Tennis; NHS; Pres Schlr; Rotary Awd; Hnr With Dstnctn Magna Cum Laude 86; Penn ST U; Aerospc Engrng.

MANCUSO, DALE; Washington HS; Washington, PA; (S); 40/160; FBLA; Key Clb; Ski Clb; Spanish Clb; Sec Jr Cls; Stu Cncl; Crs Cntry; Socr; Wt Lftg; Hon Roll; IUP; Acctg.

MANCUSO, GREG; Sacred Heart HS; Carbondale, PA; (Y); French Clb; Varsity Clb; Bsktbl; Golf; Tennis; Bus.

MANCUSO, SEAN; Valley View HS; Archbald, PA; (Y); 14/205; Computer Clb; Latin Clb; Var Ftbl; Var Vllybl; Wt Lftg; Physicl Ftns Merit Awd 86; Chem.

MANCUSO, SUSAN; Valley View HS; Archbald, PA; (Y); 29/200; Trs French Clb; Hosp Aide; Latin Clb; SADD; Drill Tm; Cert De Marite En Frns Au Cours 84 & 86; Cert Of Prfcncy 86; Jrnlsm.

MANCZUA JR, MICHAEL D; Cathedral Prep; Erie, PA; (Y); 18/236; Bsbl; Bsktbl; Cheerleading; Coach Actv; Hon Roll; JC Awd; NHS; Cathedral Prep Gold Medallion Awd Athltcs 86; Wiwohl Memrl Awd Athltcs 86; Gross Memrl Awd Bsktbl Awd; Allegheny Coll; Pre-Med.

MANDALAKAS, ANNA; Norwin SR HS; N Huntingdon, PA; (S); 6/650; Sec Dance Clb; Leo Clb; SADD; Band; Trs Jr Cls; Trs Sr Cls; Chrmn Stu Cncl; Var L Crs Cntry; Var L Trk; NHS; Med.

MANDES, ROBERT; Bishop Carroll HS; Ebersburg, PA; (S); 10/103; Ski Clb; Rep Frsh Cls; Pres Soph Cls; Co-Capt Ftbl; Capt Trk; High Hon Roll; Pep Clb; SADD; Hon Roll; PA Higher Educ Asstnc Agncy Cert Of Merit 85; Ntl Sci Merit Awd 85; Acad All-Amer 84; Mech Engrng.

MANEVAL, CHRISTINE; West Snyder HS; Beavertown, PA; (Y); Art Clb; Pres Trs Church Yth Grp; Sec Trs Computer Clb; Drama Clb; 4-H; Science Clb; Chorus; School Musical; School Play; Prfct Atten Awd; W Chester; Psychology.

MANEY, DOUGLAS; Bald Eagle Area HS; Karthaus, PA; (Y); Church Yth Grp; Cmnty Wkr; Engr.

MANFRE, GREGORY; Monsignor Bonner HS; Upper Darby, PA; (Y); 114/308; Office Aide; Im Bsbl; Var Bsktbl; Im Ftbl; Im Golf; Hon Roll; Acad Excllnc Engl; Phys Ther.

MANFREDI, MICHAEL; Bishop Hafey HS; Hazleton, PA; (Y); Chess Clb; Prfct Atten Awd; Spanish NHS; Kings Coll Spnsh Awd 85-86; Cert Merit Spnsh 85-86; Spnsh Cntst Awd 85-86; PA ST; Sci.

MANGAN, DAWN; Lakeland JR SR HS; Olyphant, PA; (S); 40/149; FBLA; Yrbk Rptr; Yrbk Stf; Hon Roll; Soc Of Dstngshd Amer HS Stu 85; Bus Admin.

MANGAN JR, JOSEPH R; G A R Memorial HS; Wilkes Barre, PA; (Y); Chorus; Bsbl; Mgr(s); Score Keeper; Hon Roll; Metrglst.

MANGAN, MEREDITH; Bethlehem Catholic HS; Bethlehem, PA; (S); 10/219; French Clb; Key Clb; Model UN; Ski Clb; Key Clb 1st Intrntlly 85; Comp Sci.

MANGAN, MOLLY; Abington Heights HS; Clarks Summit, PA; (Y); Ski Clb; Variety Show; Rep Stu Cncl; Var L Cheerleading; Im Socr; Im Sftbl; Var Trk; Congenial Awd 85.

MANGES, BOBBI J; Chestnut Ridge HS; New Paris, PA; (S); 15/142; Library Aide; Spanish Clb; Nwsp Rptr; Ed Nwsp Stf; Lit Mag; Stat Bsbl; Stat Bsktbl; JV Var Score Keeper; Hon Roll; Prfct Atten Awd; Pub Rltns.

MANGES, BRIAN; Shippensburg Area SR HS; Newburg, PA; (Y); Church Yth Grp; Trk; High Hon Roll; Lion Awd; NHS; Spanish NHS; Penn ST Mont Alto Campus Schlrshp 86; Penn ST; Nuclr Engrng.

MANGES, RICHELE; Bishop Mc Cort HS; Hooversville, PA; (Y); 3/129; 4-H; Band; Orch; Sec VP Stu Cncl; Score Keeper; Vllybl; High Hon Roll; Sec NHS; Ntl Merit Ltr; Physics Awd 86; AFROTC Scholar 86; JR Miss Fin 85-86; U VA; Aerospc Engrng.

MANGIATERRA, RUTH; Solanco HS; Quarryville, PA; (Y); Exploring; Intnl Clb; Office Aide; Radio Clb; Teachers Aide; Hon Roll; Seton Hill U; Pol Sci.

MANGINE, DANIEL; Our Lady Of The Sacred Heart HS; Coraopolis, PA; (Y); 12/60; Pres Frsh Cls; JV Bsbl; Stat Bsktbl; L Socr; U Pittsburgh; Law.

MANGINE, STEVE; Wm Penn Charter Schl; Philadelphia, PA; (Y); Aud/Vis; Drama Clb; Intnl Clb; Stage Crew; Var L Bsbl; JV Socr; Ntl Merit SF; Chem.

MANGINI, MELISSA; Greater Latrobe SR HS; Crabtree, PA; (Y); 110/327; Church Yth Grp; French Clb; Teachers Aide; Nwsp Bus Mgr; Nwsp Phtg; Nwsp Rptr; Yrbk Bus Mgr; Hon Roll; SES Exchng Stu Fo Frnc 84; SES Exchng To Englnd 86; Mercyhurst Coll; Htl Rstrnt Mgm.

MANGLE, GERI; Cumberland Valley HS; Mechanicsburg, PA; (Y); 9/600; Pres Church Yth Grp; Church Choir; Color Guard; Mrchg Band; French Hon Soc; NHS; Ntl Merit Ltr; Amercn Lgn Awd 83; Bloomsburg; Comp Sci.

MANGOL, PAM; Cumberland Valley HS; Mechanicsburg, PA; (Y); Spanish Clb; Band; Chorus; Concert Band; Drill Tm; Mrchg Band; Symp Band; Ntl Merit Ltr; Mrchng Bnd Awd Of Exc 84-85 & 85-86; Army ROTC; Cmrcl Art.

MANGOLD, DOUGLAS; Mount Lebanon HS; Pittsburgh, PA; (Y); 120/500; Church Yth Grp; JV Bsbl; Im Bsktbl; Im Sftbl; Hon Roll.

MANGUS, TINA; Bradford Area HS; Bradford, PA; (Y); Exploring; Library Aide; Chorus; JV Crs Cntry; Im Gym; JV Var Trk; Hon Roll; Prfct Atten Awd; IN U PA; RN.

MANIERI, EVIE; Upper Darby HS; Drexel Hill, PA; (Y); 5/600; Pres Drama Clb; Thesps; Chorus; Orch; School Musical; School Play; Swing Chorus; Nwsp Rptr; Ed Nwsp Stf; JV Vllybl; Smith Coll Book Awd 86; Feofndtn Youth Ldrshp Conf 86; Jrnlsm.

MANIET JR, EDWARD R; Chartiers Valley HS; Pittsburgh, PA; (Y); 16/334; Model UN; Band; Concert Band; Jazz Band; Mrchg Band; School Musical; Stage Crew; NHS; Bucknell U; Elec Engrng.

MANION, KELLY; Peters Twp HS; Mcmurray, PA; (Y); Church Yth Grp; Dance Clb; Drama Clb; FBLA; SADD; Band; Church Choir; Mrchg Band; School Play; Sec Sr Cls; Bus Mngmnt.

MANK, CHRISTINE; Northern HS; Dillsburg, PA; (Y); 76/209; French Clb; FBLA; Nwsp Stf; Var L Cheerleading; French Hon Soc; Intrntl Stud.

MANKER, GORDON; David B Oliver HS; Pittsburgh, PA; (Y); 36/243; Boys Clb Am; Church Yth Grp; Computer Clb; JA; ROTC; Spanish Clb; Church Choir; Tennis; Vllybl; Hon Roll; Electrncs.

MANKEVICH, MARILYN SHARYL; Seneca Valley SR HS; Mars, PA; (Y); Drama Clb; VP Thesps; Chorus; Madrigals; School Musical; School Play; Stage Crew; Beautyshop Quartes 85-86; Music.

MANKEY, KIM; Waynesburg Central HS; Waynesburg, PA; (Y); Aud/Vis; Ski Clb; Spanish Clb; Band; JV Bsktbl; Capt Bowling; Wt Lftg; Hon Roll; Chmstry.

MANKO, GERARD; Our Lady Of The Sacred Heart HS; Ambridge, PA; (Y); 5/60; Boy Scts; Church Yth Grp; Computer Clb; Exploring; Chorus; School Play; Bowling; High Hon Roll; All Am Schlr Awd 85-86; Comp Sci.

MANLEY, BARBARA ANN; Mid-Valley HS; Throop, PA; (Y); 12/160; Boys Clb Am; Computer Clb; Pres JA; Pep Clb; Spanish Clb; High Hon Roll; Hon Roll; U Of Scranton; Nrsng.

MANLEY, ED; Scranton Prep; Clarks Summit, PA; (Y); Boy Scts; Varsity Clb; JV Ftbl; Trk; Bus.

MANLEY, LAURA CELESTE; Country Day School Of The Sacred; Haverford, PA; (S); 2/16; Drama Clb; Stage Crew; Yrbk Phtg; Var Fld Hcky; Lcrss; Hon Roll; NHS; Chestnut Hill Coll Regnl Frnch Cntst 83; CDSSH Awd Effort & Achvt 84; Nrsg.

MANLEY, LORI; Northampton Area SR HS; Bath, PA; (S); 1/458; Trs AFS; Trs Leo Clb; Ski Clb; Nwsp Rptr; Var JV Fld Hcky; High Hon Roll; Voice Dem Awd; Schl Art Awd 85; Pre-Law.

MANMILLER, TERRY; Muhlenberg HS; Laureldale, PA; (Y); Boy Scts; Church Yth Grp; Computer Clb; Ski Clb; Chorus; Church Choir; Bsktbl; Ftbl; Tennis; Hon Roll; 3rd Pl Trphy Bshy Rhds Mem Brbrshp Quartet Cntst 85; PA ST; Acctng.

MANN, CORY; Palmyra Area HS; Palmyra, PA; (S); VP DECA; VP Sr Cls; Score Keeper; Trk; Hon Roll; Slippery Rock ST Coll; Law Enf.

MANN, JAIMIE MARIE; Bishop Kenrick HS; Norristown, PA; (Y); 4/262; Church Yth Grp; Mathletes; Science Clb; School Play; NHS; Ntl Merit Schol; Calculus Awd; Accntng Awd; Ursinus Coll; Accntng.

MANN, JAMES S; York Suburban SR HS; York, PA; (Y); Boy Scts; Ski Clb; Varsity Clb; Band; Off Soph Cls; Off Jr Cls; VP Sr Cls; Var L Crs Cntry; Var L Trk; Ntl Merit Ltr.

MANN, JENNIFER; Wm Allen HS; Allentown, PA; (Y); 80/604; Church Yth Grp; Cmnty Wkr; Debate Tm; Key Clb; Political Wkr; Pres Sr Cls; Rep Stu Cncl; Hon Roll; Jr NHS; NHS; American U; Pol Sci.

MANN, JOHN; Perry Traditional Acad; Pittsburgh, PA; (Y); 13/125; Cmnty Wkr; VP JA; Nwsp Stf; Yrbk Rptr; High Hon Roll; Engrng.

MANN, JOSEPH; Pen Argyl Area HS; Pen Argyl, PA; (Y); 69/129; Art Clb; Church Yth Grp; CAP; Ski Clb; Spanish Clb; Chorus; JV Bsbl; JV Trk; JV Wrstlng; Hon Roll; US Army; Arntcl Engr.

MANN, KELLY; South Park JR SR HS; Library, PA; (Y); 25/230; French Clb; Teachers Aide; Y-Teens; High Hon Roll; NHS; Duquesne; Phrmcy.

MANN, MELISSA; West Branch HS; Kylertown, PA; (Y); 40/114; AFS; Teachers Aide; Chorus; Church Choir; Concert Band; Yrbk Bus Mgr; Yrbk Ed-Chief; Capt Twrlr; Bus.

MANN, MIKE; Philipsburg-Osceola HS; Philipsburg, PA; (Y); #80 In Class; French Clb; Ski Clb; Varsity Clb; Yrbk Stf; VP Stu Cncl; Var Ftbl; Wt Lftg; Var Wrstlng; Hon Roll; Accntng.

MANN, PATRICIA; Altoona Area HS; Altoona, PA; (S); Chess Clb; Trs Church Yth Grp; Drama Clb; VP French Clb; Math Tm; Science Clb; Nwsp Rptr; Rep Jr Cls; Ntl Merit SF; NEDT Awd; Phrmcy.

MANN, SUSAN; Beaver Area HS; Beaver, PA; (Y); Church Yth Grp; Exploring; JCL; Key Clb; Ski Clb; Chorus; Capt Color Guard; High Hon Roll; Hon Roll; NHS; Indiana U Of Pa; Resprtry Thrpy.

MANN, TABITHA R; David B Oliver HS; Pittsburgh, PA; (Y); 9/245; Pres Church Yth Grp; Cmnty Wkr; Nwsp Rptr; Yrbk Rptr; Pres Frsh Cls; Pres Sr Cls; Cheerleading; High Hon Roll; 4-H; Chorus; Carnegie Mellon U Schlrshp 86; Natl Achvt Schlrshp Cmmnd Stu 86; Comm.

MANNELLA, JULIANN; Mt Pleasant Area SR HS; Mt Pleasant, PA; (Y); Latin Clb; Ski Clb; Teachers Aide; Concert Band; Mrchg Band; Sec Jr Cls; Sec Sr Cls; Stu Cncl; Mat Maids; Cnty Bnd 82-83; Hmcmng Crt 85-86; U Of Pittsburgh; Dntl Hygn.

MANNELLI, GENE; Neshaminy HS; Feasterville, PA; (Y); Church Yth Grp; Drama Clb; Pres Science Clb; School Play; Trk; Hon Roll; 1st Pl Env-Olympcs Cnty Chmpn 86; E Stroudsburg; Env Sci.

MANNHARDT, JIM; George Washington HS; Philadelphia, PA; (Y); Band; Stage Crew; Wt Lftg; Hon Roll; Elctrncs.

MANNING, JAMI; Trinity HS; Washington, PA; (Y); 4-H; Penn Commerical; Beautcn.

MANNING, JEFFREY S; Hempfield HS; Lancaster, PA; (Y); Pres Exploring; Chorus; School Musical; Var L Gym; L JV Socr; Jeffeson Awds Hnrb Mntn Outstndng Comm Svc 86; ST Cert EMTS; Eurpn Socr Tour 85; EMS Admin.

MANNING, JOHN; Upper Perkiomen HS; Pennsburg, PA; (Y); 6/200; Cmnty Wkr; Computer Clb; Rep Stu Cncl; Socr; High Hon Roll; Hon Roll; Lion Awd; Pres Schlr; Temple U Outstndng Achvt Schlrshp 86; Temple U Pres Schlrshp 86; Temple U; Math.

MANNING, JON; Connellsville Area HS; Connellsville, PA; (Y); Aud/Vis; Chess Clb; SADD; High Hon Roll; Psych.

MANNING, KELLY; Elk County Christian HS; St Marys, PA; (Y); 36/80; Office Aide; Yrbk Stf; Bus.

MANNINO, TINA; Carlisle HS; Carlisle, PA; (Y); Church Yth Grp; Cmnty Wkr; Dance Clb; Spanish Clb; Teachers Aide; Varsity Clb; Off Frsh Cls; Off Soph Cls; Off Jr Cls; Rep Sr Cls; Leag, Dist Chmpns Gymstcs, ST Fnlst Vault Gymstcs 86; U MD; Pre Med.

MANNO, JAMES; Elk County Christian HS; Ridgway, PA; (Y); 21/80; Ski Clb; Trk; High Hon Roll; Hon Roll; NHS; NEDT Awd; US Natl Ldrshp Mrt Awd 85; Penn ST; Bus Admin.

MANNS, SCOTT; Yough SR HS; Ruffs Dale, PA; (Y); 7/240; Spanish Clb; Stage Crew; Im Badmtn; JV Var Ftbl; Var Trk; Im Wt Lftg; High Hon Roll; Hon Roll; NHS; U Miami; Mech Engrng.

MANSBERGER, JAMES; Mount Union Area HS; Calvin, PA; (Y); 6/160; Boy Scts; Model UN; Spanish Clb; Band; Chorus; School Musical; Nwsp Stf; Bowling; Hon Roll; NHS; Vet.

MANSBERGER, JUNE; Middletown Area HS; Middletown, PA; (Y); 25/181; Am Leg Aux Girls St; Girl Scts; Chorus; Sec Concert Band; Jazz Band; Sec Mrchg Band; Orch; Hon Roll; VP NHS.

MANSELL, EDWARD; Wilmington Area HS; New Wilmington, PA; (S); 1/122; Chess Clb; Latin Clb; Concert Band; Mrchg Band; Pep Band; Nwsp Stf; High Hon Roll; Bio-Chem.

MANSFIELD, BRIAN; West York Area HS; York, PA; (Y); 10/191; Boy Scts; Exploring; Pres Sec Spanish Clb; Stat Bsktbl; Stat Ftbl; God Cntry Awd; High Hon Roll; NHS; Eagle Scout 85; Rotary Intl Dist 739 Ldrs Conf 86.

MANSFIELD, DAVE; Northern Chester County Tech Schl; Phoenixville, PA; (Y); Church Yth Grp; Band; Im Vllybl; Hon Roll; 1st Pl VICA Awd Elec 86; NHS 86; Eastern Baptist; Yth Ministry.

MANSFIELD III, FREDERICK; Suszuehanna Township HS; Harrisburg, PA; (Y); 37/155; Varsity Clb; Rep Frsh Cls; Rep Stu Cncl; JV Var Bsktbl; JV Var Ftbl; Hon Roll; Rotary Awd; Acadmc All Am 85-86; Temple; Law.

MANSKE, CARLA; Wyomissing Area HS; Wyomissing, PA; (S); 2/121; Pres French Clb; VP German Clb; Yrbk Ed-Chief; High Hon Roll; Jr NHS; NHS.

MANSKI, KELLIE J; Vincentian HS; Glenshaw, PA; (Y); 2/55; JA; Service Clb; School Play; Yrbk Stf; Pres Jr Cls; Trs Stu Cncl; High Hon Roll; NCTE Awd; NHS; Sal; Duquesne U; Math.

MANSMANN, DENISE; Ringghold HS; Eighty Four, PA; (Y); Church Yth Grp; 4-H; Ski Clb; Band; Mgr(s); Hon Roll; NCTE Awd.

MANSOUR, SORAIA; Nazareth Acad; Fairless Phills, PA; (Y); Cmnty Wkr; French Clb; Chorus; Drm & Bgl; Orch; School Musical; Nwsp Rptr; Hon Roll; Hnr Cert Merit 85-86; Mgmt.

MANSUR, ANDREW K; Downingtown HS; Downingtown, PA; (Y); 38/520; Church Yth Grp; Ski Clb; Church Choir; Mrchg Band; Symp Band; Yrbk Stf; Var Trk; Hon Roll; Ntl Merit SF; Quiz Bowl; Amer Music Abroad Tour Of Europe 85; Millersville U; Math.

MANTEL, BRIAN K; Liberty HS; Bethlehem, PA; (Y); 80/417; Trs FBLA; Var Bsbl; Var Bsktbl; High Hon Roll; Hon Roll; French Awd 85-86; Millersville U PA; Accntng.

MANTELLA, ROSE; Mount Alvernia HS; Pittsburgh, PA; (S); 5/68; Spanish Clb; Yrbk Ed-Chief; Pres Soph Cls; Pres Jr Cls; High Hon Roll; Hon Roll; Sec NHS; Ntl Merit Ltr; Prfct Atten Awd; Laura Long Memorial Schlrshp 85; Duquesne; Forgn Lang.

MANTZ, LEE; Panther Valley Jointure HS; Summit Hill, PA; (Y); 30/131; Penn ST U; Astronomy.

MANTZ, SHELLEY; Brandywine Heights HS; Macungie, PA; (Y); 19/126; Band; Concert Band; Mrchg Band; Pep Band; Hon Roll; Outstndg Acdmc Achvmnt Amr Cultures II 85-86; Pre-Med.

MANUEL, KIM; Moniteau HS; W Sunbury, PA; (Y); 25/133; FBLA; Spanish Clb; Yrbk Rptr; Bsktbl; Fld Goal Awd Grls Bsktbl Tm 85-86; Med Sec.

MANZANO, MICHAEL; Dunmore HS; Dunmore, PA; (Y); Pres Drama Clb; Letterman Clb; Off Band; School Musical; Ed Yrbk Stf; High Hon Roll; NHS; VFW Awd; Pres Scholar 86; Drama Clb Awd 86; U Scranton; Hstry.

MANZANO, SUSIE; Dunmore HS; Dunmore, PA; (Y); 25/140; Pres Band; Chorus; Swing Chorus; High Hon Roll; NHS; Drama Clb; Concert Band; Mrchg Band; PA Music Ed Assn Dist 9 Band 85 & 86; PMEA Regn 4 Band 85 & 86; PMEA All ST Band 86; Music Ed.

MANZINI, TRACY; Yough HS; West Newton, PA; (Y); 38/228; Spanish Clb; Yrbk Stf; Rep Frsh Cls; Sec Soph Cls; Sec Jr Cls; Sec Sr Cls; JV Var Cheerleading; Hon Roll; NHS; Spanish NHS; Cnty Mkt Acad Schlrshp 86; WV Weslyan; Nrsg.

MANZO, NATALIE A; Bishop Kenrick HS; Norristown, PA; (Y); 1/280; Cmnty Wkr; French Clb; Office Aide; Science Clb; Yrbk Ed-Chief; Cit Awd; DAR Awd; High Hon Roll; NHS; Schlrshp To La Salle U 85-86; Genl Excllnc Awd 85-86; Montgomery County CC; Acctg.

MAO, KELVIN; Emmaus HS; Emmaus, PA; (Y); Off Computer Clb; Exploring; JV Ftbl; Hon Roll; NHS; Comp Pgmmng.

MAPES, LINDA; Wyalusing Valley HS; Wyalusing, PA; (Y); Spanish Clb; Var L Mat Maids; Twrlr; Hon Roll; Psych.

MAPP, MONICA; St Maria Goretti HS; Philadelphia, PA; (Y); 161/390; Camera Clb; Exploring; Lit Mag; Hon Roll; Psych.

MARAFKA, LYNETTE; Apollo-Ridge HS; Saltsburg, PA; (Y); German Clb; JA; Band; Concert Band; Mrchg Band; Pep Band; Hon Roll; Louise V Nelson Mem Schlrshp, Custom Mgt Voc Awd US Svngs Bond 86; Indiana U PA; Fd Svc Mgt.

MARANEY, LISA; S Hills Christian HS; Library, PA; (S); 1/14; Church Yth Grp; Church Choir; Nwsp Stf; Var Bsktbl; Var Cheerleading; Var Sftbl; Var Vllybl; High Hon Roll; Val; Liberty U; Home Ec.

MARANKI, JOANN; Bishop Hafey HS; Freeland, PA; (Y); French Clb; FNA; VP Chorus; Church Choir; Yrbk Stf; French Hon Soc; High Hon Roll; Hon Roll; VP NHS; Prfct Atten Awd; Pediatrcn.

MARASA, FRANK J; Central HS; Philadelphia, PA; (Y); 40/383; Boys Clb Am; Church Yth Grp; Teachers Aide; High Hon Roll; Hon Roll; P N I Schrlshp Assist Awd 86; Temple U.

MARASCO, MELISSA; Ambridge Area HS; Baden, PA; (Y); French Clb; VP Sec JA; Pep Clb; Hon Roll; PA Free Entrps Wk Schlrshp 86; Northeastern U; Intl Bus.

MARASCO, MICHAEL; Farrell SR HS; Farrell, PA; (Y); 1/100; Computer Clb; Key Clb; Science Clb; Bausch & Lomb Sci Awd; Elks Awd; High Hon Roll; NHS; Pres Schlr; Val; English Clb; Slippery Rock U.

MARATTA, MEGAN; Cornell HS; Coraopolis, PA; (Y); Dance Clb; Hosp Aide; Trs Key Clb; Concert Band; Mrchg Band; Sec Jr Cls; Cheerleading; High Hon Roll; Hon Roll; Jr NHS.

MARBURGER, GREGORY E; Seneca Valley HS; Harmony, PA; (Y); Church Yth Grp; JV Bsbl; JV Var Ftbl; Trk; Wt Lftg; Hon Roll; Wghtlftng & Bwlng Trphys 85; Bus Mngmnt.

MARCELIS, DANIEL; Harry S Truman HS; Levittown, PA; (Y); 14/600; Drama Clb; Bsbl; Ice Hcky; Hon Roll; NHS; Drexel U; Engrg.

MARCELLA, ROBERT; Wyoming Valley West HS; Plymouth, PA; (Y); 18/400; Church Yth Grp; Var Trk; Cit Awd; Hon Roll; NHS; PA ST U; Engrng.

MARCELLINI, JULIE; Pittston Area SR HS; Pittston, PA; (Y); #22 In Class; French Clb; Science Clb; Chorus; High Hon Roll; Hon Roll; U Of Scranton.

MARCH, BARBARA; Brandywine Heights HS; Fleetwood, PA; (Y); Hosp Aide; Chorus; Color Guard; Mrchg Band; Hon Roll; Prfct Atten Awd; Nrsng.

MARCH, CHRIS; South Allegheny HS; Glassport, PA; (Y); Computer Clb; Exploring; JV Mgr(s); Mon-Ygh & Buhl Sci Fair 3rd Pl 86; PA ST; Comp Sci.

MARCH, KAREN; Coatesville Area SR HS; Glenmoore, PA; (Y); 82/510; VP Drama Clb; French Clb; Ski Clb; Concert Band; Drm Mjr(t); Mrchg Band; Orch; Pep Band; Rep Jr Cls; Rep Sr Cls; Outstndng Sr Band Mbr, Eng Dept Awd 85-86; Lancaster Genl Hosp; Nrsng.

MARCHESE, JAMES; Dunmore HS; Dunmore, PA; (Y); 14/154; Drama Clb; Letterman Clb; Ski Clb; Frsh Cls; Soph Cls; Stu Cncl; Ftbl; Trk; Wt Lftg; Hon Roll; Owen Dougherty Trck Awd 86; Ruters Coll Of Pharmacy; Pharm.

MARCHESINI, CLAUDETTE; Bethlehem Center HS; Millsboro, PA; (Y); 28/160; Pep Clb; Spanish Clb; Varsity Clb; Band; Jazz Band; Mrchg Band; Yrbk Stf; Cheerleading; Amer Legn Aux Awd; Elem Ed.

MARCHESKI, JENNIFER A; Danville HS; Danville, PA; (Y); 35/202; Aud/Vis; Computer Clb; French Clb; Rep Stu Cncl; L Bowling; L Tennis; Cit Awd; High Hon Roll; NHS; Accntng.

MARCHETTI JR, ANTHONY; St Josephs Prep Schl; Philadelphia, PA; (Y); French Clb; SADD; Nwsp Stf; Yrbk Stf; Im Bsktbl; Im Ftbl; High Hon Roll; Ntl Merit SF; Spec Honorary Scholar 83; Prep Schlr 83-86; Bus.

MARCHETTI, DANIELLE; Bishop Hafey HS; Hazleton, PA; (Y); 12/129; Ski Clb; Spanish Clb; Y-Teens; Capt Var Bsktbl; Capt Var Trk; High Hon Roll; Hon Roll; NHS; Spanish NHS; Bio.

MARCHETTI, SAM; Hazleton HS; Hazleton, PA; (Y); German Clb; Hon Roll; Certf Merit German Clb 84-85; Architctr.

MARCHEWKA, JAMES; Canon Mc Millan SR HS; Cecil, PA; (Y); 12/360; VP Church Yth Grp; Exploring; School Play; Pres Frsh Cls; Rep Soph Cls; Rep Stu Cncl; JV Ftbl; JV Swmmng; Im Wt Lftg; French Hon Soc; Ftbl Schlrshp 86; Dvdsn Coll; Dntstry.

MARCIN, SCOTT; Marian HS; Tamaqua, PA; (S); 8/114; Chess Clb; Math Clb; Band; Chorus; Concert Band; Jazz Band; Mrchg Band; Orch; Pep Band; School Musical; Allentown Diocesan Band Mbr 85-86; Villanova U; Engrng.

MARCINEK, GWENDOLYN; Archbishop Kennedy HS; Philadephia, PA; (Y); Art Clb; Hosp Aide; Band; Concert Band; Lit Mag; Art.

MARCINKEVICH, FRANK; Mid-Valley HS; Dickson City, PA; (Y); Boy Scts; Trs Drama Clb; School Play; Nwsp Ed-Chief; VP Frsh Cls; Pres Stu Cncl; Hon Roll; Jr NHS; Egl Sct 84; Attrny.

MARCINKUS, BRIAN; Neshaminy SR HS; Levittown, PA; (Y); 83/723; Political Wkr; SADD; Var Bowling; Var Golf; High Hon Roll; Hon Roll; VA Poly Tech; Chem Engr.

MARCINOWSKI, JEFFREY; St Josephs Prep; Philadelphia, PA; (Y); Camera Clb; Chess Clb; Ntl Merit SF; Hnrb Mntn Natl Latin Exam 85; Top 3rd Natl Germn Exam 85; Prep Schlr; MI U; Aerospc Engr.

MARCO, CHRIS; Leechburg Area HS; Leechburg, PA; (Y); VP Frsh Cls; VP Soph Cls; Rep Stu Cncl; Var Bsbl; Notre Dame; Bio.

MARCON, LARA; William Allen HS; Allentown, PA; (Y); 8/559; Am Leg Aux Girls St; Key Clb; Varsity Clb; Yrbk Stf; VP Stu Cncl; Var L Diving; Hon Roll; NHS; PA Dist Dvng Champ.

MARCUS, KAREN; Riverview HS; Oakmont, PA; (Y); 33/100; Girl Scts; Hosp Aide; Pres VP Key Clb; Hon Roll; Kiwanis Awd; Hnr Schlrshp 86; Davis & Elkins Coll; Fash Merch.

MARCUS, SARA; Central Dauphin HS; Harrisburg, PA; (Y); French Clb; Ski Clb; Stu Cncl; Im Socr; Im Sftbl; L Swmmng; Im Vllybl; Hon Roll; Villanova; Intl Rel.

MARCUS, STEVEN; Northeast HS; Philadelphia, PA; (Y); 65/742; CAP; Trs Soph Cls; Hon Roll; PA ST U; Engl.

MARCY, FREDERICK; Greater Latrobe SR HS; Latrobe, PA; (Y); Boy Scts; Church Yth Grp; French Clb; Letterman Clb; Ski Clb; Band; Stage Crew; Symp Band; JV Bsktbl; Var Trk; Indstrl Design.

MARDIS, PAMELA A; United HS; Vintondale, PA; (Y); 32/159; Cmnty Wkr; Pres FNA; Hosp Aide; Chorus; Hon Roll; Hosp Volunteer Awd 85-86; Nursing.

MAREK, TAMMY; Uniontown Joint SR HS; Uniontown, PA; (Y); JA; Spanish Clb; Sec Soph Cls; High Hon Roll; Hon Roll; Carlow Coll; Ther.

MARELL, TONJA; Harry S Truman HS; Levittown, PA; (Y); 15/580; Yrbk Sprt Ed; Yrbk Stf; Stu Cncl; Socr; Hon Roll; NHS; U Of MD; Pre Engrng.

MARESCO, RITA; St Maria Goretti HS; Philadelphia, PA; (Y); 49/390; Cmnty Wkr; GAA; Math Clb; Math Tm; Model UN; School Musical; Lit Mag; Rep Soph Cls; Rep Jr Cls; Rep Sr Cls; Talent Am Awd 84; Villanova U; Child Psych.

MARFINETZ, JOHN; Brownsville Area HS; Allison, PA; (S); 15/225; Drama Clb; Key Clb; Ski Clb; Trs SADD; School Play; VP Jr Cls; High Hon Roll; Hon Roll; Crmnlgy.

MARFLAK, EDWARD; Bethel Park SR HS; Bethel Pk, PA; (Y); Church Yth Grp; Computer Clb; Latin Clb; Political Wkr; Science Clb; SADD; Hon Roll; Trs Sr Cls; Trs Stu Cncl.

MARGETAN, JOHN; Johnstown SR HS; Johnstown, PA; (Y); Chorus; Concert Band; Mrchg Band; Orch; Hon Roll.

MARGHELLA, GINA; Brownsville Area HS; Brownsville, PA; (S); 5/230; Church Yth Grp; Trs FBLA; JA; Office Aide; SADD; NHS; Ntl Merit Ltr; Rotary Awd; 1st Pl Offc Prcdrs-FBLA Rgnl 86; 4th Pl Bus Math-FBLA Rgnl 84; I Dare You Awd 86.

MARGOLIS, FRANKLIN; Pennsbury HS; Levittown, PA; (Y); 27/712; Var Bsbl; Var Crs Cntry; Capt Trk; Hon Roll; NHS; Ntl Merit Ltr; Pres Schlr; Rotary Awd; Pennsbury Schlrshp Fndtn Schlrshp; All Leag 1st Tm Trk; UCLA; Bio.

MARGONERI, KIMBERLY; Yough SR HS; W Newton, PA; (Y); Cmnty Wkr; French Clb; FBLA; Library Aide; High Hon Roll; Hon Roll; NHS; Westmoreland County CC Meritorious Schlrshp 86; Hon Stu 85-86; Westmorfeland Cnty CC; Accntng.

MARHANKA, CURTIS; Greensburg Salem HS; Delmont, PA; (S); VICA; Hon Roll; 3rd Vo-Tech Comp Pgm Comp 85; Pittsburgh U; Comp Sci.

MARHEFKA, KRISTINE; Geibel HS; Uniontown, PA; (Y); Hosp Aide; Pep Clb; High Hon Roll; Hon Roll; Ldrshp Schlrshp-Seton Hill Coll 85; Med.

MARHEFKA, ROBERT; Shanksville Stonycreek HS; Central City, PA; (S); 7/31; Boy Scts; Chrmn Ski Clb; Mgr Band; School Play; Nwsp Bus Mgr; Yrbk Bus Mgr; Frsh Cls; Soph Cls; Jr Cls; Sr Cls; Catholic Rlgs Sctng Awds 84-85; W Point Mltry Acad; Elec Engrng.

MARHEFKA, ROBIN; Shanksville-Stonycreek HS; Central City, PA; (S); Drm Mjr(t); Pres Soph Cls; Pres Jr Cls; Stu Cncl; Stat Bsbl; Var Capt Cheerleading; Hon Roll; NHS; Spanish NHS; Outstdng Home Ec Awd; Math.

MARHEFKA, SUSAN; Upper Dublin HS; Maple Glen, PA; (Y); 6/307; Pres Aud/Vis; Pres Radio Clb; NHS; Ntl Merit Ltr; Cmnty Wkr; Lit Mag; Lat Hon Sco 86; Various HS Telecommunications Awds 85 & 86.

MARIANO, DARREN; Canevin HS; Pittsburgh, PA; (Y); Var Tennis; Pre-Dntstry.

MARIANO, PAUL; Mechanicsburg SR HS; Mechanicsburg, PA; (Y); 113/315; Art Clb; Ski Clb; Chorus; Church Choir; Hon Roll; Ntl Art Hnr Soc 85-87; De Molay; Show Choir Cnty Chorus 84-87; Tyler Art Schl; Art.

MARIETTA, KARA; Franklin Regional SR HS; Delmont, PA; (Y); 105/338; AFS; Church Yth Grp; JV Swmmng; Wt Lftg; Hon Roll; Mt Aloysious JC; Occ Ther.

MARIETTA, MARTIN; Cumberland Valley HS; Camp Hill, PA; (Y); Camera Clb; Computer Clb; Latin Clb; Badmtn; Swmmng; Trk; Vllybl; Hon Roll; Ntl Merit Ltr; Frst Pl Awd Cptl Ara Sci 86; 1st Pl Rgnls 2nd Pl ST JR Acad Sci 86; Awd Of Exclnc Cmbrlnd Vly HS 86; Sci Rsrch.

MARINARI, JILL; Gwynedd Mercy Acad; Collegeville, PA; (Y); 19/69; Art Clb; Computer Clb; Service Clb; Stage Crew; Variety Show; Lcrss; Mgr(s); Swmmng; Co Jr Miss Fnlst; Fairfield U; Bio.

MARINARO, SEAN; Interboro HS; Norwood, PA; (Y); French Clb; Var JV Ftbl; Acad All Am 85-86.

MARINE, KATHLEEN; St Puis X HS; Pottstown, PA; (S); 35/161; Art Clb; Cmnty Wkr; Office Aide; Spanish Clb; Var Crs Cntry; Var Swmmng; Var Trk; Hon Roll; NHS; NEDT Awd; Acctg.

MARINE, NATALIE J; Burrell HS; Lower Burrell, PA; (Y); 1/197; Sec French Clb; School Play; Stage Crew; Pres Stu Cncl; DAR Awd; Pres NHS; Ntl Merit SF; Service Clb; Ski Clb; Drill Tm; Cntry III Ldrs ST Fnlst; Alle-Kiski JR Miss Pgnt 1st Rnnr Up; Thtre Mjr Gvrnrs Arts Schl; American U; Hmnts.

MARINELLI, KATHY; Scranton Tech; Scranton, PA; (S); Letterman Clb; Concert Band; Nwsp Stf; Cheerleading; Sftbl; Elem Tchr.

MARINKOVICH, ALAN; Bethlehem Center SR HS; Beallsville, PA; (Y); Pres Church Yth Grp; Drama Clb; Spanish Clb; School Play; Variety Show; Nwsp Rptr; Nwsp Stf; Hon Roll; CA U; Elem Tchng.

MARINO, ANGELA; Pleasant Valley HS; Wind Gap, PA; (Y); Service Clb; Ski Clb; Rep Jr Cls; Rep Sr Cls; Rep Stu Cncl; Jr NHS; Svc Awd Tutoring 85-86; Bus Mgt.

MARINO III, ARTHUR J; Central Catholic HS; Pittsburgh, PA; (Y); Rep Jr Cls; Rep Stu Cncl; Var Bowling; Hon Roll; U Of Pittsburgh; Film Indstry.

MARINO, DANA; Plum SR HS; Pittsburgh, PA; (Y); Dance Clb; French Clb; Ski Clb; School Musical; Stage Crew; Variety Show; Nwsp Stf; Hon Roll; NEDT Awd; PTSA Essy Cntst-Hnrbl Mntn; Cmnctns.

MARINO, SUZANNA; Northern Cambria HS; Barnesboro, PA; (Y); #1 In Class; Band; Concert Band; Mrchg Band; High Hon Roll; NHS; Acad All Amer 86; Biol.

MARINOS, STACY; Lewistown Area SR HS; Lewistown, PA; (Y); 47/259; Church Choir; Mrchg Band; Nwsp Sprt Ed; VP Frsh Cls; Off Soph Cls; Off Jr Cls; Off Sr Cls; Off Stu Cncl; Var Capt Bsktbl; Hon Roll; Beneficial Finance Schlrshp 86; Penn ST U; Envir Sci.

MARINUCCI, CAROLINE; Bishop Kenrick HS; Norristown, PA; (Y); 29/296; Art Clb; Cmnty Wkr; Science Clb; Ski Clb; Lit Mag; Var JV Fld Hcky; Hon Roll; Opt Clb Awd; School Play; Nwsp Stf; Career Cnslr; Frnch Mrt Awd; Fash Dsgnr.

MARION, KATHY; Manheim Township HS; Lancaster, PA; (Y).

MARIOTTI, KATHLEEN; Scranton Prep Schl; Old Forge, PA; (Y); 169/200; Drama Clb; Pep Clb; PAVAS; Chorus; School Musical; School Play; Sec Sr Cls; Stu Cncl; Cheerleading; Early Chldhd Dev.

MARK, ALLISON; Lakeland JR SR HS; Carbondale, PA; (Y); 67/169; FHA; Chrmn Drill Tm; School Musical; Cheerleading; ST Fin PA Miss Co-Ed Pgnt 85; Grad From Barbizon Schl Of Modeling 84; Bus Adm.

MARK, HEATHER; Tulpehocken HS; Myerstown, PA; (Y); 15/105; Hon Roll; Tulpehocken Schlr Awd 85-86; Med Scrtry.

MARK, JULIE; Bellefonte Area HS; Howard, PA; (Y); 23/246; Rptr 4-H; Hosp Aide; Spanish Clb; Band; Chorus; Church Choir; Concert Band; Mrchg Band; Rep Soph Cls; Hon Roll; Ms Chrstms Seal 1st Rnnr Up 85; Fnlst JR Ms Cntre Co 86; Dist Bnd 86; Lock Haven U; Rec Thrpy.

MARK, TODD; Annville-Cleona HS; Annville, PA; (S); 11/105; Varsity Clb; VP Frsh Cls; VP Soph Cls; VP Jr Cls; Trs Stu Cncl; Socr; Wrstlng; VP NHS; Amer Lgn Awd 83-84.

MARK, WAYNE; Central HS; Philadelphia, PA; (Y); Church Yth Grp; Im Bsktbl; Hon Roll; Ophthlmlgst.

MARKEE, KATHLEEN; West Philadelphia Catholic Girls; Philadelphia, PA; (S); 9/245; Camp Fr Inc; Church Yth Grp; Pep Clb; Spanish Clb; School Play; Nwsp Bus Mgr; Nwsp Rptr; Yrbk Stf; NCTE Awd; NHS; Wo He Lo Medallion 85; Congressional Awd 86; La Salle U; Spec Educ Tchr.

MARKEL, ANITA; Halifax Area HS; Halifax, PA; (S); 3/100; Church Yth Grp; Pres Band; Pres Chorus; Drm Mjr(t); School Musical; Cheerleading; DAR Awd; NHS; Drama Clb; Zeswitz Music Awd 83-84; Lancaster Bible Coll; Elem Ed.

MARKET, PATRICK; Mohawk Area HS; New Castle, PA; (Y); 25/141; Intl Frgn Lang Frnch Awd 84-86; Millersville U; Mtrlgy.

MARKEY, KAREN; Christian School Of York HS; York, PA; (S); Teachers Aide; Band; Chorus; School Play; Bsktbl; Fld Hcky; Sftbl; Vllybl; Hon Roll; Cedarville Coll; Hist.

MARKIEWICH, CARLA; Carmichaels Area JR SR HS; Carmichaels, PA; (S); 4/101; French Clb; Ski Clb; High Hon Roll; NHS.

MARKIEWICZ, NOREEN; Mt Pleasant Area SR HS; Mt Pleasant, PA; (Y); 96/243; GAA; Teachers Aide; Chorus; Color Guard; Mrchg Band; School Musical; JV Var Bsktbl; High Hon Roll; Hon Roll; Bus Careers Inst; Sectrl Ofc.

MARKINSON, KAREN; Fairview HS; Fairview, PA; (S); Drama Clb; Teachers Aide; Varsity Clb; VP Chorus; Mrchg Band; School Musical; School Play; Lit Mag; Var L Cheerleading; L Trk; Athltc Training.

MARKLE, JEFF; Hanover HS; Hanover, PA; (Y); Varsity Clb; Var Bsbl; JV Var Ftbl; Amrcn Lgn Bsbl; Sprts Apprctn Clb; Phy Ed.

MARKLE, MELISSA A; West Hazleton HS; Jeanesville, PA; (S); 50/192; Sec FNA; Hosp Aide; Office Aide; Red Cross Aide; Thesps; School Musical; JV Var Mat Maids; Capt Twrlr; NHS; Luzerne Cnty CC; Dntl Hygnst.

MARKLE, SHERRI; Columbia Montour AVTS; Berwick, PA; (Y); FNA; Hosp Aide; Key Clb; Keywanettes; Library Aide; Red Cross Aide; Hon Roll; Cuzenovia Coll; Nrs.

MARKLEY, SHANAN; West Mifflin Area HS; W Mifflin, PA; (Y); 35/350; Exploring; Key Clb; Ski Clb; Speech Tm; Yrbk Stf; Off Jr Cls; Off Sr Cls; Stu Cncl; Var Capt Cheerleading; Powder Puff Ftbl; IN U Of PA; Bus Admin.

MARKOVIC, BRIAN; S Allegheny HS; Port Vue, PA; (Y); 63/180; Computer Clb; 4-H; VP JA; Stage Crew; Rep Stu Cncl; Im Bsktbl; Var L Golf; Var Trk; JA Sales Club 84-85; JA VP Completion Course 85-86; JA Achvr Awd 85-86; Penn ST; Mktg.

MARKOVICH, ED; E L Meyers HS; Wilkes Bare, PA; (Y); Cmnty Wkr; FNA; Hosp Aide; Bsbl; Bsktbl; Ftbl; Hon Roll; LCC; Nrsng.

MARKOWITZ, RACHEL; Taylor Allderdice HS; Pittsburgh, PA; (S); Cmnty Wkr; Ski Clb; Nwsp Rptr; Stu Cncl; Tennis; High Hon Roll; NHS; Cmmnty Svc Awd 83; Wrtng.

MARKOWSKI, ANNETTE; Conrad Wriser J S H S; Womelsdorf, PA; (Y); Key Clb; SADD; Chorus; Drama Clb; GAA; JCL; Latin Clb; Teachers Aide; School Musical; School Play; Key Clubber Mnth 85; Genetic Rsrch.

MARKOWSKI, CHRISTINE; John S Fine SR HS; Nanticoke, PA; (S); 11/256; Science Clb; Var Swmmng; High Hon Roll; NHS; Bloomsbury U; Marn Bio.

MARKOWSKI, LYNN; Seneca Valley SR HS; Zelienople, PA; (Y); 8/352; Aud/Vis; SADD; Thesps; Chorus; Mrchg Band; Symp Band; High Hon Roll; NHS; Muscn Of Mnth 86; Comm.

MARKS, BRIAN; Plum SR HS; Pittsburgh, PA; (Y); Band; Stage Crew; Variety Show; JV Bsbl; Im Bsktbl; Im Fld Hcky; Im Socr; Im Sftbl; Im Vllybl; Hon Roll; Frnch Clss Awd Hghst Grd Avg Yr 84; 4 Clssrm Awds Bio, Wrld Cltrs, Frnch, Plane Geom 85; Music.

MARKS, DOUGLAS; Cedar Crest HS; Lebanon, PA; (Y); 20/295; Pep Clb; Science Clb; Spanish Clb; Bausch & Lomb Sci Awd; High Hon Roll; NHS; Hon Bnqt 84-86; Lehigh U; Elec Engrng.

MARKS, FRED; Nativity BVM; Minersville, PA; (Y); 43/99; Computer Clb; Bsktbl; Med.

MARKS, JEFF; William Penn Charter Schl; Penn Vly, PA; (Y); 4/75; Pres Computer Clb; Library Aide; Math Clb; Model UN; Pres Spanish Clb; Teachers Aide; Yrbk Bus Mgr; Im Socr; Im Trk; High Hon Roll; Econ.

MARKS, JOLCENE; Milton SR HS; New Columbia, PA; (Y); Computer Clb; Latin Clb; Varsity Clb; JV Var Fld Hcky; Powder Puff Ftbl; JV Var Sftbl; Wt Lftg; High Hon Roll; Hon Roll; NHS; Offnsv Plyr Of Yr Awd Fld Hcky 86; Hgh Achvt Awd Latin 84-86.

MARKS, LORI; Tunkahnnock Area HS; Tunkhannock, PA; (S); 15/280; Drama Clb; French Clb; Key Clb; Latin Clb; Trs Science Clb; School Musical; School Play; Var Cheerleading; Hon Roll; NHS; U Of VA; Med.

MARKS, SEAN; Downingtown SR HS; West Chester, PA; (S); 1/550; German Clb; Letterman Clb; Capt Scholastic Bowl; Rep Stu Cncl; Var Capt Wrstlng; High Hon Roll; NHS; Rotary Awd; Natl Yth Ldrshp Conf 85; US Navl Acad; Mech Engrng.

MARKS, VANESSA; William Allen HS; Allentown, PA; (Y); Cmnty Wkr; ROTC; Drill Tm; Hon Roll; NHS; NJROTC Awds 86; Villanova U; Offcr Marine Corps.

MARKS, WENDY; Bloomsburg SR HS; Bloomsburg, PA; (Y); 60/143; Church Yth Grp; Teachers Aide; Varsity Clb; Chorus; Stu Cncl; Cheerleading; Powder Puff Ftbl; Acad Hair Design; Csmtlgy.

MARKUS, JOHN JOSEPH; Father Judge HS; Philadelphia, PA; (S); 38/381; German Clb; Yrbk Stf; JV Bsktbl; Hon Roll; NHS.

MARLATT, DAVID; West Allegheny SR HS; Clinton, PA; (Y); Spanish Clb; High Hon Roll; Hon Roll; Chem Engr.

MARLEY, TODD A; Canon Mc Millan HS; Mc Murray, PA; (Y); 38/390; Boy Scts; Varsity Clb; Var Capt Ftbl; Golf; Sftbl; Var Capt Trk; Wt Lftg; Wrstlng; High Hon Roll; Aerontcl Engr.

MARLOWE, DALE; Laurel JR SR HS; New Castle, PA; (Y); Aud/Vis; Church Yth Grp; Cmnty Wkr; Computer Clb; Church Choir; Cit Awd; Hon Roll; Lion Awd; Prfct Atten Awd; Air Force; Comp.

MARMAGIN, JOELLE; Ambridge Area HS; Baden, PA; (Y); Church Yth Grp; French Clb; VP JA; Office Aide; Rep Jr Cls; Rep Stu Cncl; Capt Cheerleading; Pom Pon; Trk; Hon Roll; The Wilma Boyd Crr Schl; Ex.

MARNELL, MARY; Greensburg Central Catholic HS; Greensburg, PA; (Y); French Clb; Ski Clb; Chorus; Var Tennis; Duquesne U; Pre-Law.

MARODY, SHARON; Yough SR HS; Sutersville, PA; (Y); Library Aide; VICA; Color Guard; Mrchg Band; Yrbk Stf; Data Prcsng.

MAROFSKY, BRIAN; Mercyhurst Prep; Erie, PA; (Y); 38/150; Var L Socr; Lndscp Arch.

MARONE, MIKE; Saint Josephs Prep; Cherry Hill, NJ; (Y); Church Yth Grp; Service Clb; Var L Socr; Var L Tennis; High Hon Roll; Ntl Merit Ltr; Cum Laude Awd Ntl Ltn Exm 85-86; Maxima Cum Laude Ntl Ltn Exm 84-85; Engl Olympd 83-84.

MARONE, TINA; Windber Area HS; Windber, PA; (Y); 1/130; Office Aide; Color Guard; Mrchg Band; Yrbk Bus Mgr; Yrbk Stf; Rep Stu Cncl; Twrlr; High Hon Roll; Jr NHS; NHS; Stu Of Mnth Awd Physcs & Mcrblgy 86; Acad Achvt Awd 82-86; Mercyhurst; Chmstry.

MARONIC, DARYL; Central Dauphin HS; Harrisburg, PA; (Y); 50/386; School Musical; Rep Stu Cncl; Var Bsbl; JV Bsktbl; Var JV Ftbl; Hon Roll.

MAROTTA, EDDIE; Waynesburg Central HS; Waynesburg, PA; (Y); AFS; Boy Scts; French Clb; Nwsp Rptr; Nwsp Sprt Ed; Nwsp Stf; Golf; Trk; Hon Roll; WA & Jefferson Coll; Med Rsrch.

MAROTTA, PAUL; Notre Dame HS; E Stroudsburg, PA; (Y); Aud/Vis; Scholastic Bowl; Stage Crew; Nwsp Stf; Yrbk Stf; Sec Jr Cls; JV Bsbl; Im Var Bsktbl; Hon Roll; Cmnty Wkr; Comp Sci.

MAROUCHOC, JIM; Freedom HS; Allentown, PA; (Y); 49/445; Var L Bsbl; Var L Ftbl; Im Wt Lftg; Hon Roll; John W Butler Awd Mst Outstndng Lnmn 85; Bus.

MAROVIC, DONNA; Albert Gallatin SR HS; Masontown, PA; (Y); Dance Clb; Jr NHS; NHS; Computer Clb; Chorus; Yrbk Stf; JR Acad Sci 82; Dancer.

MARPLE, DAN; Troy SR HS; Troy, PA; (Y); 13/143; Pres Church Yth Grp; Letterman Clb; Red Cross Aide; Chorus; Church Choir; Var L Bsktbl; Hon Roll; NHS; Dean Hrtly Awd 86; Mnsfld Schlrs Awd 86; Mnsfld U; Med Lab Tech.

MARPLE, KATHLEEN; Brookville Area HS; Brookville, PA; (Y); 3/144; Drama Clb; Band; Chorus; Concert Band; Jazz Band; Hon Roll; Ntl Merit SF; French Clb; Library Aide; Mrchg Band; Provasts Schlrshp 86; Silvr Mdl ST Hist Day 85; U Pittsburgh; Comm.

MARQUARDT, DONNA; Council Rock HS; Newtown, PA; (Y); 5/847; Sec Church Yth Grp; Hosp Aide; Mrchg Band; Symp Band; High Hon Roll; NHS; Ntl Merit Ltr; Philadephia Coll Bible; Elem Ed.

MARQUARDT, MARK; North Hills HS; Pittsburgh, PA; (Y); Church Yth Grp; Ski Clb; Bsktbl; Golf; High Hon Roll; NHS; Pres Schlr; U FL; Pre-Med.

MARQUET, JOHN; Moon SR HS; Corapolis, PA; (Y); Boy Scts; Sec Exploring; German Clb; JV Socr; Moon Twp Vol Fireman 85; Emergncy Med Tech 86; Order Arrow 84.

MARRA, BRIAN; Valley View JR SR HS; Eynon, PA; (Y); 4/200; Church Yth Grp; Computer Clb; Math Tm; Spanish Clb; Var Crs Cntry; Var Trk; Capt Vllybl; High Hon Roll; NHS; Ntl Merit Ltr; Engrng.

MARRA, CATHY; St Maria Goretti HS; Philadelphia, PA; (Y); 57/440; Cmnty Wkr; GAA; Spanish Clb; Teachers Aide; Off Frsh Cls; High Hon Roll; 1st & 2nd Hnrs.

MARRA, LISA MARIE; Chartiers Valley HS; Heidelberg, PA; (Y); 6/340; Church Yth Grp; Hosp Aide; Pep Clb; Ski Clb; Spanish Clb; Church Choir; Yrbk Stf; NHS; Prfct Atten Awd; JR Acad Sci Wrkshp 84; PA ST; Lib Arts.

MARRA, ROBERT; Upper Dauphin Area HS; Elizabethville, PA; (Y); 2/105; Art Clb; Red Cross Aide; Chorus; Nwsp Rptr; Nwsp Sprt Ed; Nwsp Stf; Yrbk Stf; Rep Soph Cls; Trs Sr Cls; Var L Bsbl; Spnsh Awd-Top Stu 85-86; Eng Awd-Top Stu 84; Ftbl All Stars 85-86; John Hopkins U; Wrtng Smnrs.

MARRACCINI, MARK; Elizabeth Forward HS; Elizabeth, PA; (Y); Acpl Chr; School Musical; Nwsp Stf; Yrbk Stf; Rep Jr Cls; JV Crs Cntry; JV Diving; Var L Swmmng; JV Stat Trk; Hon Roll; Scndry Engl Educ.

MARRAPODI, DAWN; Seton Catholic HS; Pittston, PA; (Y); Church Yth Grp; Cmnty Wkr; Dance Clb; Girl Scts; Hosp Aide; Chorus; School Musical; Variety Show; Var Cheerleading; Phys Thrpy.

MARRONE, ANDREW; Lebanon Catholic HS; Palmyra, PA; (Y); Church Yth Grp; Science Clb; Chorus; Concert Band; Jazz Band; Mrchg Band; Variety Show; Hon Roll; Exc In Cmptr Prgmng; Hnrs Chorus; Diocesan Chorus; Cmptrs.

MARRONE, VINCENT; Dunmore HS; Dunmore, PA; (Y); 15/153; High Hon Roll; Hon Roll; NHS; Philadelphia Schl; Med Tchnlgy.

MARSDEN, DAVID; Susquenita HS; Marysville, PA; (Y); 15/175; German Clb; Ski Clb; L Band; Chorus; Jazz Band; School Musical; Crs Cntry; L Trk; High Hon Roll; NHS; Sci Fair 86; Hnr Chrs 86; Penn ST; Air Force.

MARSDEN, JENNIFER; Hatboro Horsham HS; Hatboro, PA; (Y); 10/289; SADD; Varsity Clb; Chorus; Off Jr Cls; Socr; Swmmng; Trk; High Hon Roll; Hon Roll; NHS; Frnch Awd For Yr 85-86; Scl Stud Awd 85-86; Anml Sci.

MARSH, COLLENE; Sharpsville Area HS; Sharpsville, PA; (Y); 31/129; German Clb; Pep Clb; Chorus; Drill Tm; Nwsp Ed-Chief; Yrbk Stf; Hon Roll; NHS; Camera Clb; Ski Clb; Hnrs Bio; Acdmc Achvmnt Awd; Stu Agnst Trtmnt Of Anmls; OH ST; Mrktng.

MARSH, DANA; State College Area HS; State College, PA; (Y); 126/537; Red Cross Aide; SADD; Rep Stu Cncl; Powder Puff Ftbl; JV L Vllybl; Hon Roll; 2 Pwr Fo The Paws Awds Prde Achvt Wrk Sprt 84.

MARSH, JAMES E; Greater Latrobe HS; Latrobe, PA; (Y); 63/300; Letterman Clb; Ice Hcky; Hon Roll; Lion Awd; Frnk Andrws Mem Schlrshp 86; Penn Technical Inst; Electncs.

MARSH, KELLY; Fairview HS; Fairview, PA; (Y); 1/150; Q&S; Off Varsity Clb; Rep Sr Cls; Var Capt Crs Cntry; Var L Swmmng; Var Capt Trk; NHS; Val; Dance Clb; French Clb; All ST PIAA Champnshps Crs Cntry 85; Publc Svc Awd Gannon Jrnlsm 86; PIAA ST Qlfr Crs Cntry 84-85; Pre-Law.

MARSH, KELLY A; Trinty HS; Washington, PA; (Y); 8/383; Pres Church Yth Grp; Chorus; Yrbk Ed-Chief; Ed Lit Mag; High Hon Roll; NCTE Awd; VP NHS; Ntl Merit Ltr; James E Casey Schlrhp 86; Amer Lgn Essay Cntst Wnnr 85.

MARSH, LORI; Ambridge Area HS; Baden, PA; (Y); Sec Church Yth Grp; Pep Clb; Red Cross Aide; Spanish Clb; Band; Church Choir; Soph Cls; Jr Cls; Hon Roll; WV U; Physcl Thrpy.

MARSH, MARIANNE; Steel Valley HS; Munhall, PA; (Y); 32/219; Pres Church Yth Grp; Key Clb; Band; Church Choir; Concert Band; Jazz Band; Pep Band; Var Mat Maids; Hon Roll; NHS; Edinboro U PA; Psych.

MARSH, ROBERT M; Shady Side Acad; Pittsburgh, PA; (Y); German Clb; Math Tm; Rep Stu Cncl; Var Lcrss; Hon Roll; Ntl Merit SF; Treas Flm Clb; Williams Coll; Ec.

MARSH, VICKI; East Pennsboro HS; Enola, PA; (Y); Hosp Aide; VICA; Stu 3rd Qrtr Med Asst 86; Acad Achvt Cert Typng 86; Med Asst.

MARSHALEK, ANN; Montoursville Area HS; Montoursville, PA; (Y); German Clb; Key Clb; Rep Sr Cls; Stat Socr; Var L Sftbl; Var L Trk; Hon Roll; NHS; PA ST U; Bus Adm.

MARSHALEK, JOANNE M; Old Forge HS; Old Forge, PA; (Y); 7/70; Yrbk Stf; Var Cheerleading; Hon Roll; NHS; U Ptsbrg; Med Tech.

MARSHALICK, LUBOW; Our Lady Of Lourdes Regional HS; Shamokin, PA; (Y); 4/94; VP Library Aide; Yrbk Ed-Chief; L Stat Bsktbl; High Hon Roll; NHS; Spanish NHS; Hghst Avg Spnsh 85-86; 2nd Hghst Avg Spnsh 83-84; Bloomsburg U; Medcl Technlgy.

MARSHALL, DARLA; Shenango JR SR HS; New Castle, PA; (Y); 14/112; Hosp Aide; Library Aide; Math Tm; Office Aide; Flag Corp; Yrbk Stf; Stat Trk; JV Vllybl; Hon Roll; NHS; 2nd Pl Ligguishtiks 86; 2nd Pl Propaganda 85; 1st Pl Poetry Cntst 86; Bio Med Engrng.

MARSHALL, DAVID; Penn-Trafford HS; Jeannette, PA; (Y); 122/362; Pres Church Yth Grp; Computer Clb; JCL; Latin Clb; Varsity Clb; Stat L Bsktbl; JV Var Mgr(s); JV Var Score Keeper; Hon Roll.

MARSHALL JR, GARY R; New Brighton Area HS; New Brighton, PA; (Y); 8/165; Computer Clb; Math Tm; Chorus; Nwsp Rptr; Var Ftbl; Var Trk; French Hon Soc; High Hon Roll; NEDT Awd; Temple U; Arch.

MARSHALL, HEATHER; West Scranton HS; Scranton, PA; (Y); French Clb; Hosp Aide; Speech Tm; Hon Roll; Jr NHS; NHS; Mrktng.

MARSHALL, HEIDI; Sharpsville Area HS; Clark, PA; (Y); Acpl Chr; Chorus; School Musical; Yrbk Phtg; Trs Jr Cls; Stu Cncl; Stat JV Bsktbl; JV Golf; Score Keeper; Hon Roll; Summr Ldrshp Wrkshp Grove City Coll 86; Grove City Coll; Advrtsng.

MARSHALL, JAMES; East Pennsboro HS; Enola, PA; (Y); Boy Scts; Latin Clb; Spanish Clb; Band; School Musical; School Play; Var Bsktbl; Var Socr; Var Trk; Hon Roll; Outstndg Carrier Harrisburg Patriot News 86; Chemistry.

MARSHALL, KAREN; Connellsville Area SR HS; Dunbar, PA; (Y); Q&S; Chorus; Stage Crew; Nwsp Rptr; Nwsp Stf; Yrbk Ed-Chief; Yrbk Rptr; Yrbk Stf; Hon Roll; NHS; CA U PA.

MARSHALL, KAREN; St Basil Acad; Philadelphia, PA; (Y); Boys Clb Am; GAA; Latin Clb; Im JV Cheerleading; Phil Coll Txtl & Sci; Intr Dsgn.

MARSHALL, KERRY; Trinity HS; Camp Hill, PA; (Y); Drama Clb; Pep Clb; VP Band; School Musical; School Play; Nwsp Rptr; Rep Stu Cncl; Im Sftbl; Spanish NHS; Political Wkr; Harrisburg Patriot Nws Schlrsp Wrtng Awd 85; Harrisburg Diocesan Bnd 84-85; Harrisburg Diocesan Chrs; Cmmnctns.

MARSHALL, LEE H; Stroudsburg HS; Stroudsburg, PA; (Y); 13/265; Aud/Vis; Pep Clb; SADD; Varsity Clb; School Play; Nwsp Phtg; Pres Frsh Cls; Pres Soph Cls; Pres Jr Cls; Pres Sr Cls; PA JR Acad Sci 1st Regnl 1st ST Outstndg ST Physcs 1st Alt; Rotary Intl Ldrshp Cmp 1st Pl Sec; Penn ST; Elec Engrng.

MARSHALL, MELISSA R; Lincoln HS; Ellwood City, PA; (Y); 31/163; VP Sec AFS; Drama Clb; VP French Clb; German Clb; Hosp Aide; Office Aide; Y-Teens; Chorus; Tennis; High Hon Roll; Italy Exch Stu Summr 85; Gannon U; Intl Bus.

MARSHALL, NICOLE; Hershey HS; Hershey, PA; (Y); #3 In Class; Ski Clb; Chrmn School Musical; Yrbk Bus Mgr; Sec Sr Cls; Capt Cheerleading; Tennis; High Hon Roll; NHS; Pres Schlr; Spanish NHS; SR Awd Cntrbtd Masrt To Actvts; Penn ST; Optmtrst.

MARSHALL, REBECCA D; Peters Township HS; Mc Murray, PA; (Y); 21/231; Sec Varsity Clb; Yrbk Stf; Sec Jr Cls; Var Capt Trk; High Hon Roll; Hon Roll; Phys Therapy.

MARSHALL, RICHARD; Chambersburg Area SR HS; Chambersburg, PA; (Y); 46/647; Boy Scts; German Clb; Teachers Aide; Chorus; Var L Trk; Var L Wrstlng; Hon Roll; PA ST U; Pre-Med.

MARSHALL, RICHARD; Moniteau HS; W Sunbury, PA; (Y); 20/133; Church Yth Grp; FCA; Letterman Clb; Varsity Clb; Bsbl; Var L Ftbl; Var L Trk; JV Var Wt Lftg; Hon Roll; NHS; Ftbl Recrd Fld Goals, Pl Kickng 83-85; Al-Star Bsbl Tm 83; Qulfd ST PIAA Trck-Fld/Pole Vlt 86; Elem Engr.

MARSHALL, WILLIAM J; Sayre Area HS; Sayre, PA; (Y); French Clb; SADD; Varsity Clb; Crs Cntry; Trk; Wrstlng; Hon Roll; Phy Therapy.

MARSICANO, SUZANNE; Pottsville Area HS; Pottsville, PA; (Y); Aud/Vis; Library Aide; Spanish Clb; Chorus; Mrchg Band; VP Frsh Cls; VP Soph Cls; VP Jr Cls; Off Stu Cncl; Cheerleading; Penn ST U; Arch.

MARSICO, PETER; Fox Chapel HS; Pittsburgh, PA; (Y); 144/322; Church Yth Grp; Pres Exploring; Crs Cntry; Hon Roll; Prfct Atten Awd; Italian Clb 84-86; Aspinwall Vol Fireman 86; Mgmt.

MARSLAND, SCOTT; Owen J Roberts HS; Parkerford, PA; (S); 1/291; Pres JA; Chorus; School Musical; VP Jr Cls; Rep Stu Cncl; Ftbl; High Hon Roll; NHS; Dstrct Chrs 85; Schl Brd JR Clss Rep 85-86; Georgetown; Intl Rltns.

MARSTELLAR, MICHAEL; Freedom HS; Bethlehem, PA; (Y); 136/456; Church Yth Grp; JA; VICA; Hon Roll.

MARSTELLER, GARY; Lakeview HS; Sandy Lake, PA; (S); 1/134; Chorus; Jazz Band; Mrchg Band; School Play; Nwsp Rptr; L Trk; Elks Awd; Val; Intnl Clb; Library Aide; Penn ST U; Elec Engrng.

MARSTON, CHUCK; Gateway HS; Pitcairn, PA; (Y); 181/507; Accntg.

MARSTON, LAURA; Berwick Area SR HS; Berwick, PA; (Y); 111/220; Church Yth Grp; Chorus; Church Choir; Color Guard; Mrchg Band; Twrlr; Bloomsburg U; Primary Educ.

MARTE, KRIS; Carlisle SR HS; Carlisle, PA; (Y); 85/400; Art Clb; Chess Clb; Ski Clb; Band; Color Guard; Drill Tm; Mrchg Band; JV Cheerleading; Im Vllybl; Hon Roll; Schlstc Art Awd Gld Key Art 83; Moore Coll; Art.

MARTELL, KATHLEEN J; Bedford HS; Bedford, PA; (Y); 1/196; Am Leg Aux Girls St; Church Yth Grp; Chorus; School Musical; Var L Tennis; Var L Trk; Cit Awd; Hon Roll; VP NHS; Val; Schlrs Educ Awd 86; Acad Schlrshp-Elizabethtown Coll 86; Elizabethtown Coll; Math.

MARTELL, SUE; Saint Hubert HS; Philadelphia, PA; (Y); 60/367; Church Yth Grp; Office Aide; Spanish Clb; Yrbk Stf; Fshn.

MARTELLA, MICHAEL; Abington SR HS; Glenside, PA; (Y); 122/535; Latin Clb; Stage Crew; Nwsp Stf; JV Socr; NHS; $250 Schlrshp From Abington Chptr NJHS 86; Slvr Mdl Hist Exam Of Acadmc Dcthln Cnty Lvl 86; RI Schl Of Dsgn; Arch.

MARTENS, JOHN; Freedom HS; Bethlehem, PA; (Y); 85/456; Church Yth Grp; Cmnty Wkr; JA; Science Clb; Ski Clb; JV Socr; Var Swmmng; Hon Roll; Engnrng.

MARTI, STEPHEN; Warren Area HS; Warren, PA; (Y); Ski Clb; Spanish Clb; Varsity Clb; Acpl Chr; Concert Band; Var Bsbl; Var Ftbl; Wt Lftg; High Hon Roll; Trs Jr NHS; Clarkson U; Chem Engrng.

MARTIN, ALIZA; Greater Works Acad; Pittsburgh, PA; (S); Service Clb; Ski Clb; Band; Yrbk Stf; Vllybl; High Hon Roll; Merit Band Awd 84; Spch Achvt & Blue Rbbn Prjct Educ Div Flwr Shw 84; Sci.

MARTIN, AMY; Moniteau JR SR HS; Karns City, PA; (Y); Church Yth Grp; Drama Clb; FBLA; Girl Scts; Spanish Clb; SADD; Color Guard; Yrbk Phtg; Mgr Vllybl; Hon Roll; God & Church Awd 84; Acctng.

MARTIN, ANDY; Manheim Central HS; Mt Joy, PA; (Y); 71/250; Church Yth Grp; Var Ftbl; Im Wt Lftg; Hon Roll; Engr.

MARTIN, ANNETTE; Steel Valley HS; W Homestead, PA; (Y); 4/207; Sec Church Yth Grp; Cmnty Wkr; Dance Clb; Varsity Clb; Variety Show; Vllybl; Wt Lftg; High Hon Roll; NHS; Bio.

MARTIN, BERNARD G; Lancaster Catholic HS; Columbia, PA; (Y); 36/218; Service Clb; Varsity Clb; School Play; Ftbl; Villanova U; Bio.

MARTIN, BRIAN; Laurel Highlands HS; Uniontown, PA; (Y); Boy Scts; Cmnty Wkr; Mrchg Band; Crs Cntry; Trk; Hon Roll; Upward Bound Olympiad 83; S Union Yth Volunteer Wrkrs 83; Law Enfrcmnt.

MARTIN, CHERYL; Blue Mountain Acad; Natick, MA; (S); Church Yth Grp; Exploring; Church Choir; Pres Soph Cls; Trs Stu Cncl; Stat Bsktbl; Stat Gym; Stat Sftbl; Stat Vllybl; Hon Roll; Andrews U; Busnss.

MARTIN, COLLEEN; Northern Lebanon HS; Jonestown, PA; (Y); 8/179; Exploring; German Clb; Varsity Clb; School Play; Tennis; Hon Roll; Outstndng Grmn Stu 86; Vrsty Ltr 84-86; Hnr Pin 84-85; York Coll; Med.

MARTIN, CURTIS; Cocalico HS; Denver, PA; (Y); 39/169; Church Yth Grp; Var Capt Bsbl; Var L Ftbl; High Hon Roll; Hon Roll; Math.

MARTIN, DANIEL; Warwick HS; Lititz, PA; (S); 85/200; Church Yth Grp; FFA; Im Bsktbl; Ftbl; Im Vllybl; Hon Roll; Chptr Star Farmer FFA 84; Red Rose Star Agri-Bus Cnty FFA 85; Keystone Degree ST FFA 86; Williamsport & Area CC; Dairy.

MARTIN, DAVID; Canon Mc Millan SR HS; Eighty Four, PA; (Y); Trk; Wrstlng; High Hon Roll; Awd Hnr Rl; High Hnr Rl; Stock Mrkt Game; Psychlgy.

MARTIN, DAVID; Danville SR HS; Danville, PA; (Y); Church Yth Grp; Key Clb; Ski Clb; Rep Spanish Clb; Varsity Clb; VP Jr Cls; Socr; High Hon Roll; Hon Roll.

MARTIN, DAVID; Millville HS; Millville, PA; (Y); Chess Clb; School Play; Var Bsbl; Var Bsktbl; Var Socr; Elks Awd; Hon Roll; NEDT Awd; AAA Achvt Awd 86; 2nd Tm All Leag Scr 86; Engrng.

MARTIN, DEBORAH; North Allegheny HS; Pittsburgh, PA; (Y); 68/642; Girl Scts; Drill Tm; School Musical; Lit Mag; Rep Jr Cls; Hon Roll; Jr NHS; NHS; Mt Holyoke; Law.

MARTIN, DENISE; Tunkhannock Area HS; Falls, PA; (S); Art Clb; Church Yth Grp; Key Clb; Spanish Clb; NHS; Bus.

MARTIN, DIANE; Keystone Oaks HS; Pittsburgh, PA; (Y); Church Yth Grp; Pep Clb; Variety Show; Nwsp Sprt Ed; Rep Jr Cls; Rep Sr Cls; Var L Bsktbl; Var Powder Puff Ftbl; Var L Tennis; Var Capt Trk; MVP Tnns & Trck 86; Duquese U News Wrtng Awd DUSPA 86; Clarion U; Brdcstng.

MARTIN, DINA; Deer Lake HS; Bairdford, PA; (Y); 3/210; Ski Clb; Varsity Clb; VP Frsh Cls; Trs Jr Cls; Trs Sr Cls; Stu Cncl; Capt Cheerleading; High Hon Roll; Trs NHS; Pres Schlr; Acadmc Excllnc Awd 86; Robert Krauland Schlrshp 86; J Laurent-P L Laurent Schlrshp 86; Penn ST U; Pre Med.

MARTIN, ELDRED CHAD; Charleroi Area HS; Stockdale, PA; (Y); Boy Scts; Church Yth Grp; Hosp Aide; Ski Clb; Spanish Clb; Varsity Clb; Ftbl; Trk; Wt Lftg; NAMES 86; Chem Club; WV U; Engrng.

MARTIN, ERIC; Uniontown Area HS; Chalkhill, PA; (Y); 48/287; Boy Scts; Letterman Clb; Yrbk Phtg; Pres Soph Cls; Pres Jr Cls; Pres Sr Cls; L Capt Crs Cntry; Var L Swmmng; Var L Trk; French Clb; Schl Msct 86-87; Mns JR Whtwtr Kayak In US 1st Pl Wrld Chmpnshp In Spittal Austria 86; Engrng.

MARTIN, GREG; Upper Dublin HS; Dresher, PA; (Y); 11/307; Church Yth Grp; Math Tm; Ski Clb; Im Bsktbl; Wt Lftg; Cit Awd; NHS; Prfct Atten Awd; Math Clb; Schlrshp Wall St Sem New York City 86; De Molay-Jr Cnclr & Dist Chpln-Ritual Awd 84-86; Cricket Clb 85; Elec Engrng.

MARTIN, GREGORY; Shgalom Christian Acad; Marion, PA; (Y); Trs Church Yth Grp; Bsktbl; Ftbl; Socr; Sftbl; Vllybl; Hon Roll; Fireman.

MARTIN, HEATHER; United HS; Seward, PA; (Y); 20/160; Drama Clb; French Clb; Girl Scts; SADD; Concert Band; Drm Mjr(t); School Musical; School Play; Hon Roll; NHS; Slvr Awd Grl Sctng 84; ST Fnlst Miss Amer Cd Pgnt 86; Hstry.

MARTIN, JACQUELINE; Lower Moreland HS; Huntington Valley, PA; (S); German Clb; Ski Clb; Rep Stu Cncl; L Lcrss; L Swmmng; Hon Roll; High Pt Swimmer 84-85; Georgetown U; Bio.

MARTIN, JAMES R; Bethel Park SR HS; Bethel Park, PA; (Y); 200/525; Bsbl; High Hon Roll; NHS; Street Hockey 82-86; Penn ST; Bus.

MARTIN, JEFF; Iroquois HS; Erie, PA; (Y); 26/159; Pres Church Yth Grp; Letterman Clb; Varsity Clb; Band; Yrbk Phtg; Yrbk Rptr; Yrbk Stf; Im L Bsktbl; Im Bowling; Im Ftbl; Triangle Tech; Arch.

MARTIN, JEFFREY J; Center HS; Aliquippa, PA; (Y); 6/183; Am Leg Boys St; Camera Clb; Exploring; Latin Clb; School Musical; Nwsp Ed-Chief; Nwsp Phtg; Nwsp Rptr; Yrbk Stf; High Hon Roll; Jrnlsm.

MARTIN, JENNIFER L; Pocono Mountain HS; Scotrun, PA; (Y); 11/296; Library Aide; Pep Clb; Rep Stu Cncl; Bowling; Hon Roll; Amrcn Assoc U Wmn 86; Knghts Clmbs 86; Natl Cncl Sprvsrs Math 86; U Of DE; Bus Admnstrtn.

MARTIN, JILL DIANNE; Pequea Valley HS; Narvon, PA; (Y); AFS; Church Yth Grp; Drama Clb; German Clb; Chorus; Church Choir; School Musical; School Play; Stage Crew; Yrbk Phtg; Home Ec Awd 2nd Pl 86; Widener U; Htl Mgmt.

MARTIN, JILLIAN S; Lower Dauphin HS; Hummelstown, PA; (Y); Church Yth Grp; Pres Debate Tm; Hosp Aide; Library Aide; Model UN; Office Aide; Spanish Clb; Thesps; Chorus; Church Choir; Dist Debate Vrsty 84-85; Grls Vcl Ensmbl 82-83; SR Hgh Vcl Ensmbl 85-86; BYU; Pol Sci.

MARTIN, JODI; Chambersburg Area SR HS; Chambersburg, PA; (Y); JCL; Latin Clb; Chorus; Rep Frsh Cls; Rep Soph Cls; Rep Jr Cls; Rep Sr Cls; Rep Stu Cncl; L Mgr(s); L Stat Trk; Cmptr Info Sys.

MARTIN, JODI; Waynesboro Area SR HS; Waynesboro, PA; (Y); Pres Sec Church Yth Grp; Chorus; Yrbk Phtg; Yrbk Stf; Rep Stu Cncl; High Hon Roll; Hon Roll; NHS; Intl Frgn Lng Awds Spnsh 86; Bus Clb 85-86.

MARTIN, JOHN; Getysburg HS; Gettysburg, PA; (Y); Vllybl; Shpnsbrg U; Accntng.

MARTIN, JOSEPH; Ambridge Area HS; Ambridge, PA; (Y); Ski Clb; Spanish Clb; VICA; Chorus; School Musical; School Play; Stage Crew; Hon Roll; Schlrshp-Pittsburgh Bty Acad 87; Pittsburgh Bty Acad; Csmtlgy.

MARTIN, JOSEPH; Christian School Of York; York, PA; (Y); Church Yth Grp; JA; Band; Chorus; Church Choir; Concert Band; Pep Band; School Musical; School Play; Trs Frsh Cls; Olympd Soc Studys Awd 85; Band & Chrs Fine Arts 1st Pl 84-86; Oral Roberts U; Pol Sci.

MARTIN, JULIE; Meadville Area SR HS; Meadville, PA; (Y); 48/306; Art Clb; Church Yth Grp; French Clb; Hosp Aide; Orch; Stage Crew; Yrbk Stf; Rep Jr Cls; Hon Roll; Yth Ftns Achvt Awd Merit 86-87; Elem Ed.

MARTIN, KAREN; Carbondale Area JR SR HS; Carbondale, PA; (S); FBLA; FFA; Chorus; Church Choir; Area Dgree 86; Gld Mdl PA ST Rcrd Kpng 86; Pblc Spkng 1st Plc 86.

MARTIN, KAREN; Manheim Central HS; Mount Joy, PA; (Y); 6/193; Church Yth Grp; Rep Sr Cls; Rep Stu Cncl; Capt Cheerleading; Powder Puff Ftbl; High Hon Roll; Sec NHS; Ntl Merit Ltr; Pres Schlr; Clothng Textiles Awd 86; Deans Schlrshp 86; Messiah Coll.

MARTIN, KATHLEEN; Scranton Prep; Scranton, PA; (Y); 52/192; Drama Clb; School Musical; School Play; Stage Crew; Nwsp Stf; Yrbk Stf; JV Var Cheerleading; Trk; High Hon Roll; Hon Roll; Bus.

MARTIN, KIMBERLY; Steel Valley HS; Munhall, PA; (S); 17/232; Office Aide; Yrbk Ed-Chief; Trs Jr Cls; Trs Sr Cls; Wt Lftg; Hon Roll; NHS; Ntl Merit Ltr; Rotary Awd; Teachers Aide; 2nd Pl Essy-Wrld Peace/ Rotary Intl 86; U Of Pittsburgh; Crmnl Psych.

MARTIN, KRIS; Warren Area HS; Warren, PA; (Y); Pres Sec Church Yth Grp; Spanish Clb; Varsity Clb; Concert Band; Mrchg Band; School Play; Nwsp Rptr; Stat Bsktbl; Hon Roll; Jr NHS; Silver B Awd 83-84; Int Design.

MARTIN, LAINIE; Academy Of Notre Dame; Villanova, PA; (Y); Cmnty Wkr; Dance Clb; Yrbk Ed-Chief; Swmmng; High Hon Roll; Ntl Merit SF; Thomas J Watson Mem Scholar Awd 86; U PA.

MARTIN, LISA; Gateway HS; Pitcairn, PA; (Y); Church Yth Grp; FBLA; Office Aide; Chorus; Nwsp Ed-Chief; Off Frsh Cls; Off Jr Cls; Off Sr Cls; Stu Cncl; Var Capt Cheerleading; Pittsburgh Bty Acad; Cosmtlgy.

MARTIN, LISA; West Perry HS; Shermans Dale, PA; (Y); Pres Church Yth Grp; French Clb; Rep Stu Cncl; JV Fld Hcky; Im Gym; JV Trk; Im Wt Lftg; Mary E Almoney Awd 84; 2nd Pl In Civic Clb Art Cntst 85; Drwng Pblshd In A Perry Cnty Sktchbk 86; Photo.

MARTIN, LISA ANN; Garden Spot HS; New Holland, PA; (S); 56/186; Sec Church Yth Grp; FFA; Hon Roll; Vol Wrk Camp-Handicap & Spcl Kids 82-85; PA Assn Farmer Coop Inst 85; Natl FFA Conv 85.

MARTIN, LORI J; Ephrata SR HS; Ephrata, PA; (Y); Rep Soph Cls; Rep Jr Cls; Var JV Bsktbl; Im Fld Hcky; Var Sftbl; Hon Roll; Elem Educ.

MARTIN, MELISSA; Palmyra SR HS; Palmyra, PA; (Y); 30/186; French Clb; Yrbk Stf; Stat Swmmng; JV Var Tennis; Trk; Hon Roll; PA ST Callgrphy Champ 86; Schltc Art Awd 86; Legsltv Art Awds 85; Comm Art.

MARTIN, MICHAEL J; Mt Pleasant Area SR HS; Mt Pleasant, PA; (Y); Ski Clb; Spanish Clb; Bsktbl; Bausch & Lomb Sci Awd; High Hon Roll; NHS; NEDT Awd; Spanish NHS; Notre Dame; Sci.

MARTIN, MICHELE N; Penn Hills SR HS; Pittsburgh, PA; (Y); 123/ 762; Pres Church Yth Grp; Drama Clb; Sec German Clb; Sec JA; Band; Concert Band; Drm Mjr(t); Mrchg Band; Orch; School Musical; SR Cls Schlrshp, Outstndng Instr Awd, Employee Mnth 86; Penn ST U; Bus Admin.

MARTIN, MICHELLE; Conestoga Valley HS; Leola, PA; (Y); FCA; German Clb; Var Capt Fld Hcky; Var Capt Sftbl; Dntl Hygnst.

MARTIN, MICHELLE; Manheim Central HS; Elm, PA; (Y); Yrbk Ed-Chief; Yrbk Stf; Hon Roll; Yrbk Awd 85; Bnk Bus Awd 85; 4-Way Test Awd 86; Cls '67 Yrbk Awd 86; Sec.

MARTIN, MICHELLE R; Williamsburg HS; Williamsburg, PA; (Y); Varsity Clb; Chorus; Concert Band; Mrchg Band; Nwsp Rptr; Im Bsktbl; JV Cheerleading; Bausch & Lomb Sci Awd; Vllybl; Bus Mgmt.

MARTIN, PAULINE M; Ephrata SR HS; Akron, PA; (Y); 2/216; Trs Church Yth Grp; Library Aide; Teachers Aide; Chorus; Nwsp Ed-Chief; Nwsp Rptr; Ed Nwsp Stf; Hon Roll; NHS; Ntl Merit Ltr; Estrn Mennonite Coll; Engl Ed.

MARTIN, REBECCA ANN; Hollidaysburg SR HS; Duncansville, PA; (Y); Library Aide; Varsity Clb; Variety Show; Yrbk Stf; Stu Cncl; Var Capt Cheerleading; Timer; Vllybl; Hon Roll; VFW Awd; MV Chrldr 85-86; PA ST; Adv.

MARTIN, RENITA; Garden Spot HS; E Earl, PA; (Y); French Clb; Trs Concert Band; Drm Mjr(t); Orch; Mgr Trk; Hon Roll; Lion Awd; NHS; Ntl Merit Ltr; Pres Schlr; Teen Wk 86; Stu Mnth 86; Green Circle Clb 82-86; Grove City Coll; Chem.

MARTIN, ROBYN; Lampeter Strasburg HS; Lancaster, PA; (Y); 30/150; Church Yth Grp; Drama Clb; PAVAS; Thesps; Varsity Clb; Band; Chorus; Church Choir; Concert Band; Jazz Band; Cnty, Dist, Rgnl Chorus/Band 86; Cnty, Dist, ST Trck 86.

MARTIN, RONALD; Downingtown SR HS; West Chester, PA; (Y); Boy Scts; 4-H; Spanish Clb; 4-H Awd; God Cntry Awd; Hon Roll; W Chester U.

MARTIN, SCOTT; Owen J Roberts HS; Pottstown, PA; (S); 13/291; Boy Scts; Drama Clb; JA; Quiz Bowl; Scholastic Bowl; NHS; NY Inst Of Technlgy; Mech Engr.

MARTIN, SHERRI; Charleroi Area JR SR HS; Stockdale, PA; (Y); French Clb; Ski Clb; SADD; Chorus; Yrbk Stf; Trs Soph Cls; Rep Jr Cls; Stu Cncl; Capt Cheerleading; NHS.

MARTIN, SHERRY; Warwick HS; Lititz, PA; (Y); FBLA; Band; Concert Band; Mrchg Band; Nwsp Stf; Tennis; Hon Roll; JV Let-Band; Medcl Sec.

MARTIN, STEPHEN; Riverview HS; Oakmont, PA; (Y); 4/118; VP AFS; Ski Clb; Band; Jazz Band; Ed Yrbk Phtg; Stu Cncl; Var Crs Cntry; Var Trk; NHS; NEDT Awd; Ed All Amer 86.

MARTIN, TERESA; Conrad Weiser HS; Robesonia, PA; (Y); 78/184; Church Yth Grp; JCL; Library Aide; Chorus; Church Choir; School Musical; Yrbk Stf; Var L Trk; Hon Roll; Temple U; Dntl Hygn.

MARTIN, TIMOTHY D; Norwin SR HS; N Versailles, PA; (Y); 1/580; Debate Tm; French Clb; Mathletes; Math Clb; Math Tm; NFL; NHS; Ntl Merit SF; Rotary Awd; Val; Amer Chem Soc Annl Tst-Hnrb Mntn 85; U Of PA-PRVST Day Wnr 85; Westmnstr U-5th Pl Math Comptn 85.

MARTIN, TODD; Wilmingtonn Area HS; Volant, PA; (S); 13/123; Church Yth Grp; Drama Clb; Spanish Clb; Band; Mrchg Band; Pep Band; Stage Crew; L Golf; Hon Roll; NHS; Aerospc Engr.

MARTINA, JOHN; Selinsgrove Area HS; Selinsgrove, PA; (Y); VP Spanish Clb; School Musical; Nwsp Rptr; Rep Frsh Cls; Rep Soph Cls; VP Sr Cls; Rep Stu Cncl; Var L Bsktbl; Capt L Golf; MVP Golf 84-86; Golf.

MARTINAK, LORI; Belle Vernnon Area HS; Fayette, PA; (Y); Ski Clb; Band; Concert Band; Drm Mjr(t); Mrchg Band; Yrbk Stf; L Bsktbl; Powder Puff Ftbl; L Sftbl; Pep Clb; Presdntl Phys Ftns Awd; Hgh Hnr Awd; Pre-Med.

MARTINAZZI II, ROBERT; Bishop Carroll HS; Nanty Glo, PA; (S); 14/ 103; Aud/Vis; Computer Clb; SADD; Varsity Clb; Im Bowling; Var Ftbl; High Hon Roll; NHS; NEDT Awd; US Naval Acad; Aerosp Engr.

MARTINELLI, BERNARD; Waynesburg Central HS; Waynesburg, PA; (Y); Chess Clb; French Clb; JV Bsktbl; Var Socr; Hon Roll; NEDT Awd; IN U Of PA.

MARTINELLI, NICOLETTE; Archbishop Kennedy HS; Conshohocken, PA; (Y); 5/187; Drama Clb; Mathletes; Office Aide; Chorus; School Play; Off Stu Cncl; High Hon Roll; NHS; Prfct Atten Awd; St Jsphs U Schlrshp Qukr Chem Anl 86; Chem Awd Anthny De Pallo Schlrshp Awd 86; 3rd Pl Actng Awd 85-86; St Jsphs U; Fnc.

MARTINEZ, ALAN; Hanover Area HS; Wilkes Barre, PA; (Y); 7/169; Var Ftbl; High Hon Roll; NHS; Bus Mngmnt.

MARTINI, CHRIS; Emmaus HS; Wescosville, PA; (Y); 90/493; Band; Concert Band; Jazz Band; Pres Frsh Cls; Var L Bsktbl; Var L Ftbl; Wt Lftg; Bus Mgmt.

MARTINI, DAVID; Cedar Cliff HS; Wormleysburg, PA; (Y); 70/300; Varsity Clb; Rep Stu Cncl; Var L Ftbl; Hon Roll; Lycoming Coll; Acctg.

MARTINI, ILEEN; Cardinal O Hara HS; Havertown, PA; (Y); 290/740; Cmnty Wkr; French Clb; Office Aide; Yrbk Stf; Duquesne U; Phrmcy.

MARTINI, LISA; Brownsvill HS; Grindstone, PA; (Y); Chess Clb; Dance Clb; Drama Clb; Ski Clb; SADD; Stage Crew; Cheerleading; Gym; Sftbl; Gus Giordanio Dance Schlrshp 83; Lab Tech.

MARTINI, RENA MICHELLE; Homer-Center School Dist; Homer City, PA; (Y); 3/90; Library Aide; Chorus; School Musical; Yrbk Ed-Chief; Sec Stu Cncl; L Vllybl; High Hon Roll; NHS; Summr Happenings IUP 85; Natl Sci Merit Awd Chem 85; Cnty Chorus 84-85; Mktng.

MARTINIE, JOHN; Devon Preparatory Schl; Exton, PA; (Y); School Play; Stage Crew; Sec Frsh Cls; Sec Stu Cncl; Var Capt Bsktbl; Im Capt Ftbl; Im Ice Hcky; Var Capt Socr; JV Trk; Im Vllybl; Schl Geom Awd 84-85; Schl Trig Awd 85-86; Duke U; Pre-Med.

MARTINIS, TRACY; South Allegheny HS; Port Vue, PA; (Y); JA; Office Aide; Pep Clb; Spanish Clb; Y-Teens; Chorus; Yrbk Stf; Stu Cncl; Bsktbl; Trk; Arline Rsrvtnst.

MARTINO, FRED; Ridley HS; Morton, PA; (Y); 26/453; Pres JA; Q&S; Radio Clb; Service Clb; Nwsp Ed-Chief; Nwsp Rptr; Stu Cncl; Hon Roll; NHS; Voice Dem Awd; Ray A Kroc Yth Achvt Awd; Outstndng Svc Schl Newspaper; Exc Awd TV Prod; Ithaca Coll; Brdcst Jrnlsm.

MARTINO, JEANNE; Downingtown SR HS; Exton, PA; (Y); 59/501; Spanish Clb; Twrlr; High Hon Roll; NHS; U Of Scranton; Chem.

MARTINO, JOSEPH; Moniteau HS; Boyers, PA; (Y); Recog Outstndng Effrt Achvt 81-82; Vet.

MARTINO, PAUL; Upper Moreland SR HS; Hatboro, PA; (Y); 30/273; Concert Band; Jazz Band; Mrchg Band; School Musical; Symp Band; Stu Cncl; Im Bsbl; Im Bsktbl; Var L Trk; Cit Awd; Uppr Mrlnd Music Ptrns Band Schlrshp 86; All-ST Jzz Band 86; Music Hnr Awd 86; Villanova U; Mech Engnrng.

MARTINSEN, DANA; Bensalem HS; Bensalem, PA; (Y); Band; Concert Band; Mrchg Band; Pep Band; Mgr(s); Stat Swmmng; High Hon Roll; Hon Roll; Music Schlrshp-Settlement Music Schl/Flute 84-86; Swm Cls Tchr 85-86; West Chester U; Scndry Ed-Math.

MARTOCCI, JOSEPH; Pius X HS; Roseto, PA; (Y); 10/35; School Musical; Ftbl; Dnfth Awd; Hon Roll; Prfct Atten Awd; Embry Riddle Aerontcl U; Aeront.

MARTOCCI, ROBERT; Archbishop John Carroll HS; Bala Cynwyd, PA; (Y); 2/165; Computer Clb; Drama Clb; Intnl Clb; Mathletes; Quiz Bowl; SADD; School Play; Yrbk Stf; High Hon Roll; VP NHS; Drexil U; Comp Engrng.

MARTON, CHRISTINE D; St Marys Area HS; St Marys, PA; (Y); 2/300; Var L Tennis; NHS; Ntl Merit SF; Bus Adm.

MARTYAK, CHRISTINE; MMI Prep HS; Hazleton, PA; (S); 10/32; Art Clb; Pep Clb; Ski Clb; School Play; Rep Frsh Cls; Trs Stu Cncl; Bowling; Hon Roll; Parsons; Fshn Merch.

MARTYNUSKA, MARTIN; Penn Cambria HS; Lilly, PA; (Y); 36/167; Spanish Clb; SADD; Varsity Clb; Rep Stu Cncl; Var Capt Crs Cntry; Score Keeper; Var L Trk; PIAA Hnrbl Mtn All ST Cls 2 A Crss Cntry 85; Jhnstwn Trbn Dmcrt Schlr Athlt Awd 86; W Landes Schlrsp; Susquehanna U; Elem Ed.

MARTYNUSKA, MATT; Penn Cambria HS; Lilly, PA; (Y); Letterman Clb; Soph Cls; Var Bsbl; Var Bsktbl; Var Ftbl; Var Trk; Acctnt.

MARTZ, BOB; Mt Pleasant Area SR HS; Mt Pleasant, PA; (Y); Boy Scts; Church Yth Grp; Latin Clb; Var Mgr(s); Var Wt Lftg; Var Wrstlng; Hon Roll; Schl Tchr.

MARTZ, DANA; Punxsutawney Area HS; Mayport, PA; (Y); 4-H; FBLA; Hon Roll; French Clb; Trk; 4-H Awd; IUP; Trvl.

MARTZ, DANA LEE; Line Mountain HS; Dalmatia, PA; (Y); Am Leg Aux Girls St; Rep Pres FBLA; Mrchg Band; Sec Jr Cls; Rep Sec Stu Cncl; Co-Capt Cheerleading; Sftbl; Cit Awd; Hon Roll; Physical Ftns Awd 84-86; 1st Pl Rgnl Bus Graphics 5th St 86; 4th Pl Rgnl Entrprnurshp I 85; Athltc Trng.

MARTZ, KYLE LESTER; Bedford And Hyndmon HS; Hyndman, PA; (Y); Band; Trs Soph Cls; Trs Jr Cls; Rep Stu Cncl; Bsbl; Co-Capt Bsktbl; Socr; High Hon Roll; Hon Roll; Jr NHS; Schlstc Mdl Of Hon; Ltrs 3 Vars Sprts 3 Yrs; Natl Hon Soc; Garrett CC.

MARTZ, MELISSA; Danville Area HS; Danville, PA; (Y); 14/202; Exploring; French Clb; Latin Clb; NFL; Var Capt Fld Hcky; Im Powder Puff Ftbl; Var Trk; High Hon Roll; NHS; Cathlc Frnsc Lg Natl Qlfr 86; 2nd Tm Var Field Hcky All Star 85; Pre-Med.

MARTZ, MICHELLE; Highlands SR HS; Tarentum, PA; (Y); Intnl Clb; Key Clb; Band; Sec Chorus; Color Guard; Jazz Band; Swing Chorus; Natl Frat Stu Musicians 85, Local 84; Music.

MARUCCI, LISA; Archbishop Kennedy HS; Philadelphia, PA; (Y); 34/ 174; Drama Clb; Hosp Aide; School Play; JV Cheerleading; Hon Roll; Comp.

MARUHNICH, PAM; Hopewell HS; Aliquippa, PA; (Y); #25 In Class; Band; Trs Drill Tm; Soph Cls; Jr Cls; Powder Puff Ftbl; High Hon Roll; Hon Roll; Chem.

MARUSKIN, LYNN; Ringgold HS; Monongahela, PA; (Y); Sec Church Yth Grp; Hosp Aide; JA; Service Clb; Ski Clb; Concert Band; Mrchg Band; High Hon Roll; NHS; Elem Ed.

MARVIN, KERRI; Susquehanna Community HS; Susquehanna, PA; (Y); Art Clb; Pep Clb; Ski Clb; Band; Chorus; Concert Band; Yrbk Stf; Cheerleading; Trvl.

MARVIN, MICHAEL; Center HS; Aliquippa, PA; (Y); 30/200; Spanish Clb; Bsbl; Hon Roll; PA ST; Elec Engrng.

MARZOLA, TARA; Salisbury HS; Allentown, PA; (Y); Drama Clb; Key Clb; School Play; Stu Cncl; Var JV Cheerleading; Hon Roll; Prfct Atten Awd; E Stroudsburg.

MARZZACCO, ANTHONY; South Williamsport HS; S Williamsport, PA; (Y); 13/150; Pep Clb; Science Clb; Varsity Clb; VP Soph Cls; VP Jr Cls; VP Capt Bsktbl; L Ftbl; Hon Roll; NHS; PA ST; Secndry Ed.

MASCARO JR, ROBERT; Scranton Prep; Dunmore, PA; (Y); 150/195; Pep Clb; Ski Clb; Y-Teens; Lit Mag; Jr Cls; Bsktbl; U Of Scranton; Engrg.

MASCELLINO, SEAN; Carlynton HS; Carnegie, PA; (Y); Bsktbl; Ftbl; Wt Lftg; U Pittsburgh; Acctng.

MASCHI, ROBERT; Neshaminy HS; Langhorne, PA; (Y); 33/705; Ski Clb; Chorus; Rep Jr Cls; Var Socr; Var Trk; High Hon Roll; NHS; Ldrshp Awd 85-86; Phys Thrpy.

MASCI, MARY BETH; Sheffield Area JR SR HS; Clarendon, PA; (Y); 3/ 75; Drama Clb; Pep Clb; SADD; Band; Concert Band; Mrchg Band; Pep Band; School Musical; School Play; Symp Band; Physclgy Tech.

MASCI, ROBERT; Valley View JR SR HS; Jessup, PA; (Y); Church Yth Grp; Scholastic Bowl; Vllybl; High Hon Roll; Hon Roll; Awd Acdmc Excllnc 84&86; U Of Scranton; Bio.

MASCI, VALERIE; St Maria Goretti HS; Philadelphia, PA; (Y); 159/390; Hosp Aide; Library Aide; Office Aide; Hon Roll; Ntl Merit Ltr; White Williams Schlrshp 84-86; Nrsg.

MASCIA, MICHELE; Seneca Valley HS; Harmony, PA; (Y); Science Clb; Varsity Clb; Chorus; Rep Frsh Cls; Rep Soph Cls; Sec Rep Jr Cls; Sec Rep Sr Cls; Sec Rep Stu Cncl; Capt L Crs Cntry; Capt L Swmmng; MVP X-Cntry 83; Rotary Stu Mnth 86; Carlow Coll Pittsburgh; Med.

MASCIARELLI, TAMMY; Waynesburg Central HS; Spraggs, PA; (Y); French Clb; Yrbk Stf; Hon Roll; Outstndng Stu Qrtr Greene Cnty Vo-Tech 85-86; Sec Of AM Hosa Greene Cnty Vo-Tech 85-86; Pres 86-87; Greene Cnty Vo-Tech; Nrsng.

MASCILLI, SCOTT; Valley HS; Arnold, PA; (Y); 48/245; Chess Clb; Drama Clb; FBLA; VP JA; Key Clb; Spanish Clb; Bsktbl; Hon Roll; IUP; Acctnt.

MASCIOCCHI, CORRADO; Everett Area HS; Everett, PA; (Y); Church Yth Grp; Computer Clb; French Clb; Band; Concert Band; Jazz Band; Pep Band; Stu Cncl; JV Var Bsktbl; Coach Actv.

MASCUS, ANN; Elk Lake JR SR HS; Montrose, PA; (Y); 26/105; Computer Clb; Band; Chorus; Concert Band; Hon Roll; ASVAB Test Scrd Upper 14 Pct 86; Compu Rltd.

MASEYKO, MONA; North Pocono HS; Lake Ariel, PA; (Y); Chorus; Concert Band; Mrchg Band; Orch; School Play; Tennis; Hon Roll; Band; Yrbk Stf; Natl Faternity Of Stu Musicians; Stu Div Of Amercn Coll Of Musicians; Stu Of Piano Hobbyst Of Wrld.

MASGAI, JOSEPH; Northeast Catholic Hs For Boys; Philadelphia, PA; (S); 9/416; Nwsp Ed-Chief; High Hon Roll; Pres NHS; Science Clb; Nwsp Rptr; Nwsp Stf; Yrbk Rptr; Yrbk Stf; Im Bowling; Hon Roll; Sci Dept Achvt Cert 83; Lang Dept Diploma De Merito 85; Smmr Emplymnt Incntv Awd 84; Pre-Med.

MASH, JEFFREY; Jeannette SR HS; Jeannette, PA; (Y); 29/140; Am Leg Boys St; Hosp Aide; Ski Clb; Spanish Clb; Stage Crew; Pres Stu Cncl; Trk; Wt Lftg; Hon Roll; Kiwanis Awd; Deno Castelli Schlrshp Awd 86; Jr Rotarian Of Mnth 85; Lions Clb-Cub Of Mnth 85; U Of Pittsburgh; Phys Thrpy.

MASI, SONIA RENE; Punxsutawney Area HS; Punxsutawney, PA; (Y); Spanish Clb; Capt Cheerleading; Trk; IN U Of PA; Psych.

MASKREY, KRIS; Plum SR HS; Pittsburgh, PA; (Y); 48/378; Stage Crew; French Clb; FHA; Scholastic Bowl; Band; Lit Mag; Sftbl; L Trk; Hon Roll; Ntl JOAD Champ; AZ ST U; Comm.

MASLOWSKI, SCOTT; State College Area HS; State College, PA; (Y); Cmnty Wkr; VP Key Clb; SADD; Trs Frsh Cls; Rep Stu Cncl; JV Bsktbl; Var Ftbl; Powder Puff Ftbl; Swmmng; Im Vllybl; Engineering.

MASNEY JR, RICHARD; Mon Valley Catholic HS; Merrittstown, PA; (Y); French Clb; Ski Clb; Yrbk Phtg; PA JR Acad Sci 83; Culinary Inst Amer; Culinary.

MASON, DAVID; Waynesburg Central HS; Morgantown, WV; (Y); Boy Scts; Church Yth Grp; Hosp Aide; Science Clb; Spanish Clb; Band; Chorus; Church Choir; Concert Band; Jazz Band; WV U; Music.

MASON, DAWN; Strath Haven HS; Media, PA; (Y); French Clb; Stage Crew; Stat Bsbl; Stat Bsktbl.

MASON, JANEE; Manheim Central HS; Lititz, PA; (Y); Church Yth Grp; Drama Clb; Hosp Aide; Library Aide; Red Cross Aide; Church Choir; School Musical; School Play; Yrbk Phtg; Yrbk Stf; Blngul Awd Spnsh & Grmn 86; Deans Schlrshp Mssh Coll 86; Erly Coll Entrnce 86; Messiah Coll; Med.

MASON, JOHN; Pennsbury HS; Morrisville, PA; (Y); Stage Crew; Var L Socr; Trk; Im Vllybl; Hon Roll; Prfct Atten Awd; Physcl Ftnss Awd 84&85; Rcd Engnrng.

MASON, KELLI; Schenley HS; Pittsburgh, PA; (S); School Play; Stage Crew; Pres Sr Cls; Sec Stu Cncl; Swmmng; Cit Awd; High Hon Roll; Hon Roll; Jr NHS; NHS.

MASON, LAURA; Kiski Area HS; Leechburg, PA; (Y); Church Yth Grp; Hosp Aide; VP JA; Math Clb; Science Clb; Spanish Clb; Mrchg Band; High Hon Roll; Hon Roll; Library Aide; 3rd Pl-Chem Olympcs 84-85; Phrmcy.

MASON, MARTIN; Aliquippa HS; Aliquippa, PA; (S); 27/154; DECA; Band; Pep Band; Off Jr Cls; Off Sr Cls; Var L Ftbl; Trk; Full Athltc Schlrshp-Wake Forest 86; Wake Forest U; Crimnlgy.

MASON, MICHELLE; Manheim Central HS; Lititz, PA; (Y); 49/298; Pres Church Yth Grp; Pres Drama Clb; German Clb; Library Aide; Spanish Clb; Chorus; Church Choir; Cit Awd; Hon Roll; Ldrshp Awd 86; Vly Forge Chrstn Coll; Ministry.

MASON, PAMELA; Cardinal O Hara HS; Glenolden, PA; (Y); Cmnty Wkr; Service Clb; High Hon Roll; NCTE Awd; NHS; Cert Of Merit Amer Assoc Tchrs Of Frnch 85-86; Top 20 Pct Stu O Hara Enrlld Lang Course 84-85; Engl.

MASON, PERRY; Purchase Line HS; Commodore, PA; (Y); Boy Scts; Pep Clb; Varsity Clb; Chorus; Church Choir; School Play; JV Bsktbl; Var Ftbl; Var Trk; Hon Roll; US Army Rsrve.

MASON, RICHARD T; Du Bois Area HS; Du Bois, PA; (Y); Ski Clb; Varsity Clb; Concert Band; Mrchg Band; Var Golf; JV Tennis; Hon Roll; NHS; Nice Kid Awd 86; PA ST U; Elect Engr.

MASON, RONALD; St John Neumann HS; Philadelphia, PA; (Y); 50/321; CAP; Computer Clb; Chorus; Yrbk Stf; Bsktbl; Drexel U; Elec Engrng.

MASON, SHERYL; Phoenixville HS; Phoenixville, PA; (Y); VP Church Yth Grp; SADD; Rep Band; Concert Band; Drm Mjr(t); Mrchg Band; Stat Trk; Im Vllybl; High Hon Roll; Hon Roll; Music Educ.

MASON, SUSAN; Maplewood HS; Guys Mills, PA; (Y); Hosp Aide; Sec Key Clb; Pep Clb; VICA; Color Guard; Mrchg Band; Yrbk Stf; Hon Roll; Edinboro U Of PA; Social Wrk.

MASON, TIMOTHY J; Elizabethtown Area HS; Elizabethtown, PA; (Y); Church Yth Grp; Cmnty Wkr.

MASQUELIER, LISA; Ft Cherry HS; Mc Donald, PA; (S); 11/121; Church Yth Grp; Drama Clb; FBLA; Math Clb; Science Clb; Ski Clb; Thesps; Chorus; School Play; Sec Jr Cls.

MASSACK, TROY; Riverview HS; Oakmont, PA; (Y); Varsity Clb; Bsbl; Bsktbl; Ftbl; Jr Cls Comm; Comp Sci.

MASSAKOWSKI, CAROLYN; Seton Catholic HS; Avoca, PA; (Y); 3/93; Hosp Aide; Mathletes; Nwsp Rptr; High Hon Roll; JETS Awd; NHS; Ntl Merit Schol; AMOA Wayne E Hesch Mem Schlrshp 86-87; Presdntl III Schlrshp Scranton U 86-87; Scranton U; Pre-Med.

MASSARO, PAUL; New Castle SR HS; New Castle, PA; (S); 3/243; Church Yth Grp; Cmnty Wkr; SADD; Jazz Band; Mrchg Band; School Play; Sec NHS; Computer Clb; French Clb; Concert Band; Westminster Coll Hnrs Bnd 84-86; PA JR Acad Sci 1st Pl Wnr 84-85; U Notre Dame; Engrng.

MASSEY, AUDREY MARIE; Methacton SR HS; Collegeville, PA; (Y); 23/336; Library Aide; Off Soph Cls; Off Jr Cls; Off Sr Cls; Powder Puff Ftbl; JV Swmmng; Var Trk; High Hon Roll; NHS; Ralston Schlrshp 86; Methacton Edu Assoc Schlrshp Awd 86; Millersville U PA; Elem Edu.

MASSEY, CYNTHIA; Greater Latrobe HS; Greensburg, PA; (Y); 8/423; Am Leg Aux Girls St; Church Yth Grp; FCA; Letterman Clb; Pep Clb; Ski Clb; Mgr Cheerleading; Mgr Socr; High Hon Roll; Hon Roll; Bus Adm.

MASSEY, ELIZABETH; Villa Maria HS; New Castle, PA; (Y); 14/52; Drama Clb; Thesps; Madrigals; School Musical; School Play; Rep Sr Cls; French Hon Soc; NHS; NEDT Awd; Computer Clb; Dist Chorus 86; Rgnl Chorus 86.

MASSEY, PAULA; Abraham Lincoln HS; Philadelphia, PA; (Y); Var Mgr(s); Score Keeper; West Chester; Law.

MASSIH, SALLY; Beaver SR HS; Beaver, PA; (Y); Church Yth Grp; Pep Clb; Spanish Clb; High Hon Roll; Bus Adm.

MASSON, LYNN ANN; New Brighton JR SR HS; New Brighton, PA; (Y); 7/154; Computer Clb; Exploring; GAA; Concert Band; Mrchg Band; Rep Stu Cncl; Trk; Btty Crckr Awd; High Hon Roll; Geneva Hon Schlrshp 86; Chem Awd 86; High Hon Awd 85-86; Geneva Coll; Chem.

MASSON, TRACY; New Castle SR HS; New Castle, PA; (S); 2/253; Church Yth Grp; Math Tm; Concert Band; Mrchg Band; Yrbk Stf; Rep Soph Cls; Rep Jr Cls; Stu Cncl; High Hon Roll; Band; 3rd Pl Ntl Acad Games Overall Lang Arts Awd 85.

MAST, BRIAN; Tunkhannock Area HS; Tunkhannock, PA; (S); Church Yth Grp; Computer Clb; Letterman Clb; Ski Clb; Var L Ftbl; Var L Trk; Hon Roll; NHS.

MAST, KAREN; Hamburg HS; Shoemakersville, PA; (Y); 51/152; Sec Pres Church Yth Grp; Library Aide; Spanish Clb; Sec SADD; Chorus; Hon Roll; Trs Jr Cls; Rep Stu Cncl; Messiah Coll.

MASTELLER, CHERYL; Bald Eagle HS; Bellefonte, PA; (Y); Church Yth Grp; Girl Scts; Valley Forge Chrstn Coll.

MASTER, TIM; East Juniata HS; Mc Alisterville, PA; (Y); Var Bsbl; Socr; Chess Clb; Band; Stage Crew; Var Bsktbl; Cncrt.

MASTERMONICO, MARIA; Seneca Valey HS; Mars, PA; (Y); Art Clb; Hosp Aide; JA; Varsity Clb; Var L Cheerleading; Stat Diving; Stat Swmmng; JV Trk; Hon Roll; Gannon U; Bus.

MASTERS, ANDREA; Penncrest HS; Media, PA; (Y); 45/290; Church Yth Grp; Intnl Clb; Ski Clb; Yrbk Stf; JV Fld Hcky; Var Trk; NHS; Frnch Awd 1st Plc French V 86; Gettysburg Coll; Bus.

MASTERS, REGINA; Ligonier Valley HS; Ligonier, PA; (Y); AFS; VP Church Yth Grp; French Clb; Library Aide; Trs Chorus; Church Choir; Color Guard; Stu Cncl; Hon Roll; Frnch Achvt Awd 85-86; Library Asst Awd 83-86; Westmoreland Coll; Soc Wrkr.

MASTERS, THOMAS; Parkland HS; Breinigsville, PA; (Y); 148/459; JA; Ski Clb; Band; Bus Admin.

MASTERSON, JOHN; Ephrata SR HS; Akron, PA; (Y); Boy Scts; Church Yth Grp; JA; Mrchg Band; Socr; Arch.

MASTERSON, TAMMY; Elizabethtown Area HS; Elizabethtown, PA; (Y); French Hon Soc; Slctd Out Top 60 ESCP Sci 83-84; Chsn Pre Coll Bio 84-85; Chsn Pre Coll Chem 85-86; Penn ST; Fshn Mrchndsng.

MASTERSON, YUKA; Crestwood HS; Mountaintop, PA; (Y); 3/226; Math Clb; Socr; Trk; Cit Awd; High Hon Roll; NHS; NEDT Awd; Nwsp Stf; PTSA Cult Art Cntst 83-85; PTSA Outstndng Achvt Awd 84-86; Schlrshp Sec Schl Stud 86; Pre Law.

MASTRANGELO, CHRISTINE; Canon-Mc Millan SR HS; Muse, PA; (Y); Church Yth Grp; French Clb; Mrchg Band; Capt Twrlr; Hon Roll.

MASTRANGELO, LISA; Interboro HS; Prospect Park, PA; (S); 2/265; Sec Trs AFS; VP Frsh Cls; Sec Soph Cls; VP Jr Cls; Off Sr Cls; Pres Sec Stu Cncl; Var Capt Cheerleading; High Hon Roll; NHS; French Clb; Rotary Yth Merit Awd 85; Bus Admin.

MASTRICOLO, MICHAEL; Central Bucks HS West; Chalfont, PA; (Y); 4/495; Bsktbl; High Hon Roll; Hon Roll; Jr NHS; Prfct Atten Awd.

MASTRIPOLITO, EDWARD; St John Neumann HS; Philadelphia, PA; (Y); 24/338; Church Yth Grp; Science Clb; Chorus; Church Choir; Im Bsktbl; Im Vllybl; High Hon Roll; Hon Roll; Acctng.

MASTRIPPOLITO, JEANNE; Unionville HS; Coatesville, PA; (Y); Church Yth Grp; Rep Frsh Cls; Rep Soph Cls; Rep Jr Cls; Rep Sr Cls; Rep Stu Cncl; Fld Hcky; Mgr(s); Tennis; High Hon Roll; Spanish Awd 82; Penn ST; Bus.

MASTROBERTI, KELLY; Dubois Area HS; Dubois, PA; (Y); Intnl Clb; Chorus; Bus Admin.

MASTROGIUSEPPE, BONNIE; Lincoln HS; Ellwood, PA; (Y); 11/162; Chrmn Church Yth Grp; Chrmn French Clb; Pres Trs Key Clb; Y-Teens; Powder Puff Ftbl; High Hon Roll; Hon Roll; NHS; Cntry 21 Accntng I Awd 86; Grove City Coll; Math.

MASTROIANNI, ANGELA; Bishop Hannan HS; Scranton, PA; (Y); 19/133; VP Church Yth Grp; Speech Tm; Orch; Rep Frsh Cls; Rep Soph Cls; Off Jr Cls; Off Sr Cls; Stu Cncl; Hon Roll; NHS; Career Awareness Explorer 84-85 & 85-86.

MASULLO, JEFF; Bellefonte Area HS; Bellefonte, PA; (Y); 43/250; Church Yth Grp; Letterman Clb; Varsity Clb; Stage Crew; Wt Lftg; Wrstlng; Hon Roll; Williamsport CC; Crpntry.

MATARAZZI, JENNY; Lebanon County AVTS HS; Lebanon, PA; (S); Trs DECA; Pep Clb; Chorus; Mgr(s); Score Keeper; Trk; 3rd Pl Gen Merch Deca 86.

MATCHULAT, KATHY; North Pocono HS; Moscow, PA; (Y); 16/255; 4-H; Girl Scts; JA; Ski Clb; Rep Jr Cls; Rep Stu Cncl; JV Bsktbl; Var Trk; High Hon Roll; NHS; U Of Scranton; Phy Ther.

MATEER IV, JOHN C; Upper Dauphin Area HS; Elizabethville, PA; (Y); 1/105; VP Church Yth Grp; Chorus; School Musical; Capt L Bsbl; Capt L Bsktbl; Capt L Ftbl; Bausch & Lomb Sci Awd; VP NHS; Val; Am Leg Boys St; USAF Acad; Pilot.

MATEER, ROGER; Middleburg Joint HS; Middleburg, PA; (Y); 41/132; Art Clb; School Play; Stage Crew; JV Bsbl; JV Stu Cncl; Hon Roll; Cert Of Schltc Achvt 85-86; Athl Awd 84-85; West Chester U; Pre-Med.

MATEFF, CATHY; Saucon Valley SR HS; Hellertown, PA; (Y); 11/171; Model UN; Office Aide; Sftbl; Tennis; High Hon Roll; Jr NHS; Trs NHS; Allentown Coll; Spnsh.

MATEJKA, CHRISTOPHER; Hopewell HS; Aliquippa, PA; (Y); Robert Morris; Mngmnt.

MATELAN, MICHELLE; Hampton HS; Allison Pk, PA; (Y); Ski Clb; Nwsp Rptr; Nwsp Stf; JV Bsktbl; Mgr(s); Powder Puff Ftbl; Hon Roll; Scrtrl.

MATERIA, LOUIS; Holy Name HS; Reading, PA; (Y); 39/116; Aud/Vis; Boy Scts; Band.

MATHAI, LEENA; Cedar Grove Acad; Philadelphia, PA; (Y); Church Yth Grp; Chorus; High Hon Roll; NHS; Prfct Atten Awd; Frnch Awd 86; Med.

MATHER, MARK; Palmyra HS; Mt Gretna, PA; (Y); 12/250; Church Yth Grp; French Clb; Band; Chorus; Concert Band; Jazz Band; Mrchg Band; Crs Cntry; Trk; High Hon Roll; Penn ST; Earth Sci.

MATHES, CYNTHIA; Marple Newton SR HS; Newtown Square, PA; (Y); Var Bsktbl; Var Fld Hcky; Var Lcrss; Hon Roll; Jr NHS; NHS; Mst Val Plyr La Crosse 85; Schl Rcrd Pts Lacrss 85; Sprts Med.

MATHIAS, DENISE; Spring Grove SR HS; Spring Grove, PA; (Y); 81/283; Chorus; Drill Tm; Mrchg Band; Jr Cls; Soph Cls; Stu Cncl; Bsktbl; Cheerleading; Coach Actv; High Hon Roll; X-Ray Tech.

MATHIAS, PATRICK; Hershey HS; Hummelstown, PA; (Y); 50/200; Ski Clb; Stage Crew; Yrbk Stf; Rep Stu Cncl; Im Bsktbl; Var L Socr; Im Sftbl; Hon Roll; Pre-Med.

MATHIS, KEITH; Simon Gratz HS; Philadelphia, PA; (Y); Cmnty Wkr; Stage Crew; Gym; Swmmng; Cit Awd; Temple U; Comp Pgm.

MATHNA, PAM; Shippensburg Area SR HS; Newburg, PA; (Y); Camera Clb; Spanish Clb; High Hon Roll; Hon Roll; NHS; GFWC Cvc Clb Shppnsbrg Stu Of Mnth Awd 85; George Mason U; Elec Engnrng.

MATIA, ROBERT; Moshanon Valley HS; Houtzdale, PA; (Y); VICA; Hon Roll; Crmnlgy.

MATIANSKI, JACKIE; Charleroi Area HS; Monongahela, PA; (Y); French Clb; Library Aide; Varsity Clb; Sftbl; Swmmng; Vllybl; Hon Roll; NHS.

MATICH, JEFFREY; Aliquippa HS; Aliquippa, PA; (Y); DECA; Band; Concert Band; Mrchg Band; Pep Band; Hon Roll; Bus.

MATICIC, STEPHANIE; Forest Hills HS; Windber, PA; (Y); Library Aide; Pep Clb; Y-Teens; Hon Roll; Conemaugh Vly Mem Hosp Schl.

MATLACK, RICK; S Williamsport Area HS; S Williamsport, PA; (Y); 35/140; Teachers Aide; Stage Crew; Var Capt Bsbl; Im Bsktbl; JV Ftbl; Var Golf; Im Vllybl; Hon Roll; Dist Chmpns Bsbl 85; Elctrcl Engrng.

MATLOCK, KELLEE; Pius X HS; Nazareth, PA; (Y); Letterman Clb; Pep Clb; Varsity Clb; Stage Crew; Yrbk Stf; Rep Stu Cncl; Var Bsktbl; Var Powder Puff Ftbl; Var JV Sftbl; Vllybl; Med.

MATOS, ANTONIO G; Souderton Area HS; Souderton, PA; (Y); Aud/Vis; Spanish Clb; Rep Jr Cls; Law.

MATOS, STACEY E; Freedom HS; Bethlehem, PA; (Y); 157/475; Sec Trs Church Yth Grp; Hon Roll; Prncpls Awd/Acdmc Rsrc Prgm For Hspnc Stu 86; Cert Of Merit For Math 85; Nrthmptn Cnty CC; Bus Mngmnt.

MATOSKY, JODY; Wyoming Valley West HS; Swoyersville, PA; (Y); French Clb; Orch; Lit Mag; High Hon Roll; NHS; NEDT Awd; Excllnt Atten Awd; Pres Acad Ftns Awd; Hghst Avg Spnsh I; Bloomsburg U PA; Engl.

MATOUS, GREGORY M; Penns Manor HS; Penn Run, PA; (Y); Camera Clb; Chess Clb; French Clb; L Trk; Mrn Bio 84; IN U Of PA; Edgrng.

MATOUSHEK, KATHY; Western Wayne HS; Waymart, PA; (Y); 4-H; FBLA; Co-Capt Cheerleading; Trk; High Hon Roll; Hon Roll; NHS; MVP Grls Trck 85; MVP Chrldng 86; Prsdntl Acdmc Ftnss Awd 86; Bloomsbrg U; Math.

MATOUSHEK, SUSAN; Western Wayne HS; Waymart, PA; (Y); 32/135; Church Yth Grp; Var JV Bsktbl; Var Cheerleading; High Hon Roll; Hon Roll; NHS.

MATRAGAS, DEBRA; Bethel Park SR HS; Bethel Pk, PA; (Y); Bus.

MATSINGER, LISA; John Bartram HS; Philadelphia, PA; (S); 8/600; Office Aide; Yrbk Rptr; Rep Jr Cls; Stu Cncl; Var Badmtn; Var Fld Hcky; Hon Roll; Jr NHS; Achvt Engl, Wrld Hist Cert 82; Badminton Div Chmpshp Trphy 85; Bus.

MATSKO, CAROL; Mt Pleasant Area SR HS; Mt Pleasant, PA; (Y); GAA; Ski Clb; Band; Mrchg Band; Mat Maids; Hon Roll; Bus.

MATSON, CHRISTOPHER; Monsignor Bonner HS; Drexel Hill, PA; (S); 6/310; Pres Sec Church Yth Grp; Mathletes; School Play; Stage Crew; Nwsp Ed-Chief; Yrbk Stf; NHS; Ntl Merit SF; 1st Pl 2nd Lvl Natl Spnsh Exm 85; U Of PA; Spnsh.

MATSON, PHIL; Conemaugh Twp HS; Davidsville, PA; (Y); 25/101; Ski Clb; Spanish Clb; Bsbl; Ftbl; Trk; Hon Roll; Law.

MATTA, MICHAEL; Northern Chester County Tech Schl; Phoenixville, PA; (Y); 20/150; Letterman Clb; Math Clb; Var Bsktbl; Var Trk; Hon Roll; JC Awd.

MATTEI, ANTHONY; Central HS; Philadelphia, PA; (Y); Yrbk Sprt Ed; Hon Roll.

MATTEI, MARTIN; Old Forge HS; Old Forge, PA; (S); Ski Clb; Spanish Clb; VP Jr Cls; Var Ftbl; Im Wt Lftg; Hon Roll; NHS; Phrmcy.

MATTEI, RENEE; Lakeland JR SR HS; Olyphant, PA; (S); 4/157; Church Yth Grp; VP Girl Scts; VP JA; Ski Clb; Spanish Clb; Band; Flag Corp; Var Sftbl; High Hon Roll; Ntl Sci Merit Awd Bio & Adv Chmstry 84-85; Grl Scts Ldrshp Awds 84; Engrng.

MATTEO, JIM; Hazleton HS; Hazleton, PA; (Y); Var Bsktbl; High Hon Roll; Ed.

MATTEO, KRISTEN; Kiski Area SR HS; Apollo, PA; (Y); JA; Chorus; Hon Roll.

MATTEO, MARNIE; Hazleton SR HS; Hazleton, PA; (S); 18/377; Drama Clb; Sec Leo Clb; Ski Clb; Chorus; Nwsp Ed-Chief; Var Cheerleading; Var L Trk; High Hon Roll; NHS; Luzerne Cnty Jr Ms Fnlst 85; Casette Clb Cbnt Mbr 85-86; Hmcmng Ct 85-86; Intr Design.

MATTER, HEATHER; Sacred Heart HS; Pittsburgh, PA; (Y); Exploring; French Clb; Ski Clb; Rep Sr Cls; Hon Roll; Allegheny Coll.

MATTER, LEANN; Bald Eagle-Nittany HS; Mill Hall, PA; (Y); 4/125; Pres Drama Clb; French Clb; Band; Chorus; Mrchg Band; Orch; School Musical; Elks Awd; Sec NHS; NEDT Awd; Lee & Bessie Graham Schlrshp 86; Lck Hvn Music Clb Awd 86; Med Auxlry Schlrshp 86; U Of Ptsbrg; Nrsg.

MATTER, MINDY; Millersburg HS; Millersburg, PA; (S); 3/62; VP French Clb; VP Spanish Clb; Nwsp Ed-Chief; Ed Yrbk Stf; Stu Cncl; Capt Cheerleading; High Hon Roll; NEDT Awd; Schl Awds 85; Lock Haven U; Intl Stds.

MATTER, STEVE; Cedar Cliff HS; Camp Hill, PA; (Y); 31/296; Latin Clb; Model UN; Ski Clb; Spanish Clb; Var Swmmng; Var Trk; Jr NHS; NHS; Pres Schlr; Spanish NHS; U Of Miami; Marine Sci.

MATTERN, ANGELA; Upper Dauphin Area HS; Elizabethville, PA; (Y); 25/105; Pres Church Yth Grp; Varsity Clb; Band; Chorus; Concert Band; Mrchg Band; School Musical; School Play; Stage Crew; Yrbk Rptr; Pres Acdmc Fit Awd 86; Bloomsburg U Of PA; Bus Mgmt.

MATTES, SUSAN M; Notre Dame HS; Easton, PA; (Y); 10/74; Band; Chorus; School Musical; School Play; Stage Crew; Yrbk Rptr; Yrbk Stf; Hon Roll; NHS; Otstndng Achvmnt Ltrgcl Music Awd 86; Anthony Minotti Schlrshp 86; Pres Acad Fitness Awd 86; Moravian Coll; Music.

MATTHEWS, BRIAN K; Lutheran HS; Philadelphia, PA; (Y); Church Yth Grp; Debate Tm; Acpl Chr; Church Choir; Variety Show; JV Bsktbl; JV Crs Cntry; Var Hon Roll; Yth Achvt Awd 85; Ntl Achvt Schlrshp 85; 1st Hnrs; Eastern U; Comms.

MATTHEWS, COURTNEY; Hempfield HS; Lancaster, PA; (Y); 4/340; Church Yth Grp; Exploring; Q&S; School Play; Nwsp Ed-Chief; Bsktbl; Mgr Fld Hcky; Mgr(s); Powder Puff Ftbl; High Hon Roll; Stu Aide Clb; Engl.

MATTHEWS, DAWN; Germantown HS; Philadelphia, PA; (Y); Library Aide; Yrbk Stf; High Hon Roll; Hon Roll; Prfct Atten Awd; Brown U Bk Awd 86; Hm Schl Assoc Awd 83; PA ST; Pol Sci.

MATTHEWS, DENISE; North Star HS; Stoystown, PA; (S); Church Yth Grp; FCA; Math Clb; Hon Roll; Mu Alp Tht; Boosters Stdnt Mnth 86.

MATTHEWS, DINA; Center HS; Aliquippa, PA; (Y); Office Aide; Spanish Clb; Hon Roll; Cert Profcncy Filing; Penn ST; Bus Adm.

MATTHEWS, DOMINIC A; Peabody/CAPA HS; Pittsburg, PA; (Y); Art Clb; Aud/Vis; Cmnty Wkr; JA; Library Aide; SADD; Chorus; Stage Crew; Gov Hon Prg Awd; Hon Roll; Chatham; Fshn Dsgn.

MATTHEWS, JODY; Connellsville SR HS; Connellsville, PA; (Y); 12/600; French Clb; FTA; Stat Ftbl; French Hon Soc; High Hon Roll; Acdmc Exc; Ed.

MATTHEWS, MICHELE; Northeastern HS; Mt Wolf, PA; (Y); 18/150; Ski Clb; Chorus; Gym; Hon Roll; NHS.

MATTHEWS, SUSAN; E L Meyers HS; Wilkes-Barre, PA; (S); 1/160; Chorus; Orch; Stu Cncl; Bausch & Lomb Sci Awd; God Cntry Awd; High Hon Roll; NHS; Ntl Merit Ltr; NEDT Awd; PA Govnrs Schl For Art 85; Dist & Regnl Band & Chrs 84-86; Bio.

MATTHEWS, WENDY; Downingtown SR HS; Downingtown, PA; (Y); 90/550; French Clb; Intnl Clb; Ski Clb; SADD; Concert Band; Mrchg Band; Mat Maids; Im Trk; Twrlr; Hon Roll; Psychlgy.

MATTHEWS, WILLIAM W; La Salle HS; Glenside, PA; (Y); 7/240; Pres Church Yth Grp; Nwsp Sprt Ed; Rep Stu Cncl; Var Bsbl; DAR Awd; High Hon Roll; Kiwanis Awd; Pres NHS; Rotary Awd; Val; U Of PA Schlrshp, La Salle U Schlrshp & Lafayette U Schlrshp 86; La Salle U; Econ.

MATTICOLA, GINA; Bishop Mc Devitt HS; Philadelphia, PA; (Y); 18/352; Cmnty Wkr; Dance Clb; Hosp Aide; Spanish Clb; SADD; Band; Mrchg Band; Yrbk Stf; Powder Puff Ftbl; Cit Awd; St Josephs U.

MATTIFORD, SCOTT; Chichester SR HS; Boothwyn, PA; (Y); Church Yth Grp; Spanish Clb; Nwsp Rptr; Hon Roll; Jr NHS; Rotary Awd; Spanish NHS; Penn ST; Comp Sci.

MATTIONI, ELIZABETH S; Plymouth Whitemarsh HS; Ft Washington, PA; (Y); 8/370; Math Clb; Yrbk Stf; Off Soph Cls; Off Jr Cls; Stu Cncl; JV Fld Hcky; JV Lcrss; High Hon Roll; Ntl Merit SF; Chorus; Acad Awd 84-86; Law.

MATTIS, JOSEPH G; Windber Area HS; Windber, PA; (S); 10/115; Drama Clb; Speech Tm; Band; NHS; French Clb; JA; Mrchg Band; Orch; School Play; Hugh O Brien Outstndng Soph 84; Penn ST U.

MATTISE, CHRIS; Lakeland HS; Jermyn, PA; (S); 28/149; Boy Scts; JV Bsbl; Var Bsktbl; Capt Golf; Hon Roll; Ursinue Coll; Athl.

MATTISON, MARK; Northampton Area SR HS; Northampton, PA; (Y); Aud/Vis; JV Bsbl; Var L Bsktbl; Ftbl; Swmmng; Hon Roll; Bus.

MATTOCKS, DAVID; Tunkhannock Area HS; Tunkhannock, PA; (S); 11/310; Church Yth Grp; Pres 4-H; Pres FFA; Church Choir; Bsbl; 4-H Awd; Hon Roll; Kiwanis Awd; NHS; PA ST U; Ag.

MATTOCKS, LUKE; Laurel JR SR HS; New Castle, PA; (Y); 5/105; Boy Scts; Band; Concert Band; Jazz Band; Mrchg Band; Pep Band; Trk; Hon Roll; Sec NHS; Pres Schlr; Caroline Knox Mem Schl Fund Band; Sci Symp; Music Clb; GMI; Engrng.

MATTOCKS, STEPHEN; Troy SR HS; Troy, PA; (S); 4-H; FFA; JV Ftbl; 4-H Awd; FFA Keystone Frmg Deg 86; Cnty FFA VP 85; Chptr FFA VP 85; Dairy Frmr.

MATTOX, DAVID D; Trinity Christian HS; Pittsburgh, PA; (S); 1/16; Chorus; Nwsp Rptr; Pres Jr Cls; Vllybl; High Hon Roll; Jr NHS; NHS; U Of PA; Acctng.

MATTSON, AMY; Unionville HS; Coatesville, PA; (Y); 50/300; Church Yth Grp; Pep Clb; Teachers Aide; JV Powder Puff Ftbl; High Hon Roll; Hon Roll; Jr NHS; Cert Profcncy Century 21 Acctng 86; Diploma Merit Spn I 84; Nrsng.

MATTSON, JOHN; Coatesville Area SR HS; Coatesville, PA; (Y); VICA; JV Var Ftbl; Wt Lftg; Hon Roll; Schroon Lk Bible Coll; Plmbng.

MATTY, DEAN; Belle Vernon Area HS; Belle Vernon, PA; (Y); Boy Scts; Debate Tm; Ski Clb; Band; Var Socr; Var Vllybl; Var Wrstlng; High Hon Roll; Hon Roll; Prfct Atten Awd; Elec Engr.

MATUSKEVICH, CINDY; Bishop O Hara HS; Archbald, PA; (S); 3/113; Boy Scts; Latin Clb; Pep Clb; Spanish Clb; Chorus; High Hon Roll; NHS; VFW Awd.

MATVEY, DAVID; Central Catholic HS; Pittsburgh, PA; (Y); 7/255; Church Yth Grp; Letterman Clb; Acpl Chr; Chorus; Var Cheerleading; Var Capt Vllybl; French Hon Soc; High Hon Roll; NHS; Penn Sst U; Aerospace Engrng.

MATVEY, MARK; Penn Hills SR HS; Verona, PA; (Y); Boy Scts; Key Clb; Science Clb; Ski Clb; Spanish Clb; Off Frsh Cls; Off Soph Cls; Off Jr Cls; Golf; Tennis; Bsbl Trphy 80; Rain Guttr Regata Awd 78; IN U; Acctnt.

MATVEY, MICHAEL; Central Catholic HS; Pittsburgh, PA; (Y); 37/260; Church Yth Grp; Dance Clb; Chorus; Var L Vllybl; Hon Roll; NHS; PA ST; Pltcl Sci.

MATVEY, TERRY; West Middlesex HS; Mercer, PA; (S); 7/107; Office Aide; Spanish Clb; Drm & Bgl; Drm Mjr(t); Mrchg Band; Twrlr; High Hon Roll; Jr NHS; NHS; Spanish NHS; Miss Western PA Majrtt Captn 83-84; Acctnt.

MATVEY, TRACEY; West Middlesex HS; Mercer, PA; (S); Church Yth Grp; JA; Office Aide; Drm Mjr(t); Off Jr Cls; Twrlr; High Hon Roll; Hon Roll; Jr NHS; NHS; Acctng.

MATWAY, CATHY; Mary Fuller Frazier HS; Perryopolis, PA; (Y); Library Aide; Band; Color Guard; Flag Corp; Nwsp Stf; Yrbk Stf; Bsktbl; Sftbl.

MATYJEVICH, PETE; West Scranton HS; Scranton, PA; (Y); Boys Clb Am; Ski Clb; Spanish Clb; Var Crs Cntry; Var Trk; High Hon Roll; NHS; U Scranton; Math.

MATYS, MAUREEN; Wyoming Area HS; Falls, PA; (Y); French Clb; FHA; Ski Clb; Band; Concert Band; Jazz Band; Pep Band; Sftbl; Vllybl; Marywood Coll; Phtgrphy.

MATZ, JOHN E; North Allegheny SR HS; Pittsburgh, PA; (Y); 135/628; Boy Scts; Computer Clb; Off ROTC; Hon Roll; Ntl Merit SF; Giftd Pgm; Ntl Sci Olympiad Cntst; Cert Merit Acad Bio; Bucknell; Chem Engr.

MATZ, TERRIE; Governor Mifflin SR HS; Mohnton, PA; (Y); 12/266; Church Yth Grp; VICA; Capt Vllybl; Hon Roll; NHS; 1st Pl Dist ST Comptn Dentl Assist 85-86.

MATZONI, JEFFREY; John S Fine SR HS; Nanticoke, PA; (S); 6/242; Chess Clb; Ski Clb; SADD; Varsity Clb; Variety Show; Var L Bsbl; Im Bsktbl; Im Ftbl; Im Vllybl; High Hon Roll; Unsung Hero Bsbl Awd 85; Scranton U; Pre-Med.

MAUERY, ANDREA; Chief Logan HS; Lewistown, PA; (Y); 6/200; Art Clb; French Clb; Pep Clb; Ski Clb; Chorus; Var Capt Crs Cntry; Var Trk; High Hon Roll; NHS.

MAUGER, JANET L; Methacton HS; Audubon, PA; (Y); 1/330; Hosp Aide; Math Tm; VP Bsktbl; VP Crs Cntry; VP Sftbl; VP Trk; NHS; Ntl Merit SF; Girl Scts; Library Aide; Harvard Clb Phil Prz Bk Awd 85; GS Silver Awd 84; U DE; Nrsg.

MAUGER, JOHN; Shade HS; Central City, PA; (Y); 8/74; Chorus; Im Bsbl; Im Var Bsktbl; Var JV Trk; Hon Roll; U Pittsburg; Comp Sci.

MAUGER, KATHLEEN; Elizabeth-Forward HS; Monongahela, PA; (Y); French Clb; Chorus; Yrbk Stf; Hon Roll; Library Aide; School Musical; Physcl Thrpy.

MAULDIN, SHANNON; John Harris HS; Harrisburg, PA; (S); 26/386; Band; Chorus; Church Choir; Concert Band; Jazz Band; Mrchg Band; School Musical; Stu Cncl; Im Crs Cntry; Hon Roll; PA Coll Of Txtls & Sci.

MAURER III, CHARLES V; Nativity B V M HS; Pottsville, PA; (Y); 6/99; Boy Scts; Church Yth Grp; Sr Cls; High Hon Roll; Kiwanis Awd; Pres Schlr; SAR Awd; PA State U; Eng.

MAURER, LYNNETTE; Cedar Crest HS; Lebanon, PA; (Y); 18/346; Church Yth Grp; Pres Sec Drama Clb; FBLA; Key Clb; Pep Clb; VP Spanish Clb; Chorus; Church Choir; School Musical; School Play; Penn ST; Radiology.

MAUS, SHELLEY; Central Dauphin HS; Harrisburg, PA; (Y); 19/386; Band; Concert Band; Mrchg Band; Hon Roll; NHS; Ntl Merit Ltr; Assn For Gftd & Tlntd Ed Medal 83-84; French.

MAUSER, MARISA L; Canon-Mc Millian SR HS; Canonsburg, PA; (Y); 91/365; FBLA; Ski Clb; Band; High Hon Roll; Comp Tech.

MAUSER, RACHEL; Upper Dauphin Area HS; Elizabethville, PA; (Y); Sec Church Yth Grp; Computer Clb; FBLA; Chorus; School Play; Stage Crew; Hon Roll; Nstr Fndtn Schlrshp 86; Harrisburg Area CC; Acctg.

MAUTINO, SALLY; Springdale HS; Cheswick, PA; (Y); 11/138; Church Yth Grp; Computer Clb; Acpl Chr; Church Choir; Nwsp Stf; Capt Var Cheerleading; High Hon Roll; VP Pres NHS; E Stewart Hnr Schlrshp-Thiel Coll 86; Dist, Rgnl ST Choir Rep 86; Presdntl Acadmc Ftns Awd 86; Thiel Coll; Bus Adm.

MAVRICH, ANGIE; Hopewell HS; Aliquippa, PA; (S); 6/265; Sec Church Yth Grp; Sec Computer Clb; French Clb; Church Choir; Pres Frsh Cls; Pres Soph Cls; Pres Jr Cls; Var L Bsktbl; JV Cheerleading; Var Capt Crs Cntry; Penn ST U; Dietcn.

MAWBY, ANDREA BRITT; Villa Maria HS; New Castle, PA; (Y); 24/52; Drama Clb; French Clb; Key Clb; Ski Clb; Thesps; Chorus; School Musical; Nwsp Rptr; Stu Cncl; NHS; 1 Str Thespn 86; VISA Clb & Admssns 84-86; Northwestern U; Cmmnctns.

MAWHINNEY, MICHELE; Rocky Grove HS; Franklin, PA; (Y); 8/86; Pres Sec 4-H; Hosp Aide; Band; Pep Band; Yrbk Stf; 4-H Awd; High Hon Roll; Hon Roll; NHS; Yng Wmns 4-H Ldrshp Awd 85; Cert Awd Outstndng Achvt Schlrshp 86; Edinboro U Of PA; Frgn Lang.

MAXIMO, LISA; Cardinal O Hara HS; Berwyn, PA; (Y); 53/772; German Clb; Swmmng; Hon Roll; NHS; MVP Swmmng 84-86; Athletc Hnr Rl 86; Most Outstndng Swmmr 86.

MAXTON, DAVID; Edison HS; Philadelphia, PA; (Y); Pep Clb; SADD; Pep Band; Im Score Keeper; Var Trk; High Hon Roll; Hon Roll; Cook.

MAXWELL, BRIAN; Wilmington Area HS; Volant, PA; (Y); 57/121; Yrbk Ed-Chief; VP Soph Cls; VP Jr Cls; Art Ed.

MAXWELL, JESSE; Swissvale HS; Pittsburgh, PA; (Y); 38/175; Aud/Vis; Stage Crew; IN U PA; Cmptr Sci.

MAXWELL, KIM; Shenango HS; New Castle, PA; (Y); 52/112; Var Cheerleading; PA ST Col6; Comp Sci.

MAXWELL, SCOTT L; Seneca Valley HS; Evans City, PA; (Y); 36/342; Pres Church Yth Grp; Varsity Clb; Jazz Band; Capt Mrchg Band; Symp Band; L Capt Diving; Hon Roll; NHS; Aud/Vis; Letterman Clb; Ntl Frtrnty Of Stu Musicians 83-85; Cert Of Merit Erie Ct Chptr Of Prffssnl Engrs 84; Vanderbild U; Bio-Med.

MAY, CINDY; East Lycoming School Dist; Hughesville, PA; (Y); 4-H; Ski Clb; Soroptimist; Varsity Clb; Sftbl; Trk; Hon Roll; Williamsport Area CC; Acctg.

MAY, CONNIE; Northern York HS; Dillsburg, PA; (Y); Sec Church Yth Grp; Chorus; Church Choir; School Musical; Stage Crew; Variety Show; Natl Music Hnr Socty 86; Bloomsburg; Deaf Ed.

MAY, HEATHER; Lock Haven SR HS; Lock Haven, PA; (Y); Church Yth Grp; French Clb; Model UN; Service Clb; Spanish Clb; Pres Band; Chorus; Jazz Band; Mrchg Band; Variety Show; Dist & Regl Bands; Dist Chorus; Chiroprctc.

MAY, LINDA; Nazareth Acad; Philadelphia, PA; (Y); Church Yth Grp; Girl Scts; Spanish Clb; Chorus; School Musical; Im Vllybl; Acctg.

MAY, MELINDA; West York Area HS; York, PA; (Y); 16/209; Sec Pres Church Yth Grp; High Hon Roll; Hon Roll; Shippensburg; Elem Educ.

MAY, RENEE M; Palmyra Area HS; Palmyra, PA; (Y); 17/200; Drama Clb; Spanish Clb; Chorus; High Hon Roll; Hon Roll.

MAY JR, RONALD; John S Vine HS; Nanticoke, PA; (Y); 2/242; SADD; High Hon Roll; NHS; Wilkes Coll; Elect Engr.

MAY, SHIRLEY; Connellsville SR HS; Mill Run, PA; (Y); Pres Camera Clb; Church Yth Grp; Office Aide; School Play; Nwsp Phtg; Nwsp Stf; Yrbk Phtg; Yrbk Stf; Sec Soph Cls; High Hon Roll; German Hnr Soc 86; U Pittsburgh; Physcl Thrpy.

MAY, SHONDA; Center HS; Monaca, PA; (Y); 28/180; Office Aide; Teachers Aide; Chorus; Yrbk Stf; Stu Cncl; Hon Roll; Pres Schlr; Profsnl Sec Intl Awd 86; Bus Ed Dept Awd 86; Bradford Schl; Lgl Sec.

MAY, TERRY; Connellsville Area SR HS; Mill Run, PA; (Y); Cmnty Wkr; High Hon Roll; Prfct Atten Awd.

MAY, TODD; Trinity HS; Camp Hill, PA; (Y); 46/144; Drama Clb; School Play; Im Bsktbl; JV Socr; Im Sftbl; Var Tennis; High Hon Roll; NEDT Awd; SADD; Belmont Abbey; Sec Ed.

MAY, TYRONE; Benjamin Franklin HS; Phila, PA; (Y); 5/32; SADD; Cit Awd; Prfct Atten Awd; 4-H; Church Choir; Yrbk Stf; Pres Frsh Cls; Rep Sr Cls; JV Socr; Electrcn.

MAY, WENDY; Scranton Preparatory Schl; Scranton, PA; (Y); Sec Band; Chorus; Church Choir; Jazz Band; Orch; Pep Band; Stage Crew; L Trk; Hon Roll; Bio.

MAYBERRY, LAURA; Pottsgrove HS; Pottstown, PA; (Y); 165/229; French Clb; Band; Chorus; Concert Band; Mrchg Band; Orch; Trk; Vrsty Awd Mrchng Band 86; Spcl Educ.

MAYER, FRANK; Shaler Area HS; Allison Pk, PA; (Y); 30/517; Jazz Band; Pres Mrchg Band; Camera Clb; School Musical; School Play; Mgr Stage Crew; Symp Band; Variety Show; Yrbk Phtg; High Hon Roll; Engnrng.

MAYER, JENNIFER; Northwestern HS; Albion, PA; (Y); Am Leg Aux Girls St; Church Yth Grp; French Clb; Library Aide; Red Cross Aide; Spanish Clb; Trs Yrbk Stf; High Hon Roll; Hon Roll; NHS; Bilingl Tchr.

MAYER, JENNIFER; Pennsbury HS; Morrisville, PA; (Y); Church Yth Grp; Girl Scts; Spanish Clb; Chorus; Yrbk Stf; Var Trk; Hon Roll; Silver Awd Gilr Scouts 84; U WY; Spch.

MAYER, KEITH; Central Cambria HS; Johnstown, PA; (S); 5/182; Chess Clb; Computer Clb; Var Ftbl; Wrstlng; Hon Roll; Ntl Merit Ltr; PA ST; Chem Engrng.

MAYER, ROBERT; Marple Newtown HS; Broomall, PA; (Y); 6/365; Boy Scts; Debate Tm; Band; Mrchg Band; Symp Band; Hon Roll; NEDT Awd; Optmst Stdnt Qrtr 86; Penn ST; Aerosp Engrng.

MAYES, JOEL; Warren County Christian Schl; Warren, PA; (S); 1/10; Church Yth Grp; Band; School Musical; School Play; Variety Show; Yrbk Stf; Pres Stu Cncl; Var Bsktbl; Var Socr; High Hon Roll; Messiah; Ed.

MAYFIELD, DAWN; St Maria Goretti HS; Philadelphia, PA; (Y); Office Aide; Teachers Aide; Hon Roll; Bus.

MAYKOVICH, DAWN; Cambria Hts HS; Patton, PA; (Y); Band; Concert Band; Drm Mjr(t); Mrchg Band; Yrbk Rptr; Yrbk Stf; Twrlr; Hon Roll; NHS; NEDT Awd; Altoona Schl Of Commerce; Bus.

MAYLATH, MARK; West Hazelton HS; Sugarloaf, PA; (Y); Spanish Clb; Concert Band; Mrchg Band; Law Enfrcmnt.

MAYLISH, DAVID; Upper Darby HS; Secane, PA; (Y); 37/360; Cmnty Wkr; Drama Clb; German Clb; Band; Concert Band; Jazz Band; Mrchg Band; Orch; Ice Hcky; Hon Roll; PMEA Distr & Regnl Band 86; Instrumntlst Magzn Awd 86; PA ST U; Cmmnctns.

MAYNARD, INGER MARLO; Cheltenham HS; Elkins Pk, PA; (Y); 150/365; Cmnty Wkr; Library Aide; Band; Color Guard; Concert Band; Flag Corp; High Hon Roll; Hon Roll; Prfct Atten Awd; Hands Acrss Amer 86; March Of Dimes Wlk-A-Thon 84-86; Miss Calendr Girl-Alpha Kappa Alpha Srrty Inc 86; Soc Wrk.

MAYO, JENNIFER A; Kennett HS; Kennett Square, PA; (Y); 26/156; French Clb; Color Guard; School Musical; Yrbk Stf; Lit Mag; Fld Hcky; Score Keeper; Trk; High Hon Roll; Hon Roll; PA ST U; Fine Art.

MAYR, KARIN; Allentown Central Catholic HS; Allentown, PA; (Y); 1/200; Am Leg Aux Girls St; Church Yth Grp; Capt Math Tm; Capt Scholastic Bowl; Lit Mag; High Hon Roll; NHS; Carnegie Mellons Summper Prgm For Arch 86; PA Jr Acad Of Sci-1st In Sts For Experiment; Arch.

MAYS, LENA; Montour HS; Coraopolis, PA; (Y); 46/277; Drama Clb; Library Aide; Mrchg Band; Stu Cncl; Bsktbl; Crs Cntry; Powder Puff Ftbl; Trk; Ntl Spch Drma Awd 86; Acdmc Achvmnt Awd Drma 86; Bthny Coll; Tlvsn Brdcstng.

MAYS, TYMEKA; University City HS; Phialdelphoa, PA; (Y); Prfct Atten Awd; Nrsng.

MAYSE, KELLY; Uniontown Area HS; Markleysburg, PA; (Y); 45/325; Spanish Clb; High Hon Roll; Hon Roll; Jr NHS; Spanish NHS; Hmrm VP Pres 84-85.

MAZESKI, MATTHEW; St Puis X HS; Sanatoga, PA; (S); 1/161; Latin Clb; Rep Frsh Cls; Rep Soph Cls; Rep Jr Cls; High Hon Roll; NEDT Awd; Prfct Atten Awd; 2nd Pl Sci Fair Awd 84; 1st Pl Latin Story Contst Awd 84; Studnt Councl Regnl Conf Rep 85; Villanova U; Journlsm.

MAZIARZ, CHRISTOPHER; Meadville Area SR HS; Meadville, PA; (Y); VP Key Clb; Science Clb; SADD; Varsity Clb; Rep Soph Cls; L Bsktbl; L Swmmng; High Hon Roll; Engrng.

MAZONIS, DIANE; Pittston Area HS; Inkerman, PA; (Y); Drama Clb; Key Clb; Ski Clb; Chorus; Yrbk Stf; Hon Roll; Wilkes Coll; Cmnctngs.

MAZUMDAR, MAITREYI; Taylor Allderdice HS; Pittsburgh, PA; (S); Debate Tm; VP Trs French Clb; Math Clb; Math Tm; Q&S; Nwsp Ed-Chief; Nwsp Stf; Im Swmmng; Var Tennis; Cit Awd; Amer Chmcl Soc 85; Amer Music Schlrshp Assoc 84 & 86; Physcs.

MAZUR, MICHELLE; Ambridge Area HS; Baden, PA; (Y); Sec VP Church Yth Grp; Girl Scts; Band; Concert Band; Mrchg Band; Pep Band; School Musical; Symp Band; Off Jr Cls; Hon Roll; Grl Scout Silv Awd 85; Beaver-Castle Grl Scouts Brd Dirctrs 86-87; Publc Rltns.

MAZUR, TRINETTE; Bishop Carroll HS; Portage, PA; (S); 23/110; Pep Clb; Ski Clb; Chorus; Var Bsktbl; Var Trk; Var Vllybl; Hon Roll; NEDT Awd; Intl Law.

MAZURKEVICH, KRISTA; Mt Carmel Area JR SR HS; Mt Carmel, PA; (Y); 19/180; Key Clb; Pep Clb; Ski Clb; Spanish Clb; Nwsp Stf; Rep Stu Cncl; Im Cheerleading; JV Sftbl; Cit Awd; High Hon Roll; Bucknell; Pre-Med.

MAZZA, AMY L; South Side Catholic HS; Pittsburgh, PA; (S); 6/45; VP Church Yth Grp; NFL; School Play; Nwsp Rptr; Pres Frsh Cls; Cheerleading; Sftbl; Hon Roll; Algebra Awd; Acctg.

MAZZA, CHRISTINA; Marple Newtown HS; Broomall, PA; (Y); Trs Band; Drm Mjr(t); School Play; VP Sec Stu Cncl; JV Sftbl; Hon Roll; Jr NHS; NHS; Ntl Merit Ltr; NEDT Awd; Hugh O Brien Ldrshp Awd 85; Natl Assoc St Cncls Conf 86; Natl PA Assoc Stu Cncls ST Conf 85.

MAZZACCARO, LAURIE A; Old Forge HS; Old Forge, PA; (Y); 5/70; Hosp Aide; Yrbk Ed-Chief; JV Bsktbl; Var Cheerleading; High Hon Roll; NHS; Penn ST U; Pre Med.

MAZZAFERRI, PAULA; Kutztown Area HS; Kutztown, PA; (Y); 11/150; Band; Concert Band; Flag Corp; Mrchg Band; School Play; Yrbk Stf; Bsktbl; Tennis; High Hon Roll; NHS; Boston Coll; Comm.

MAZZARELLA, JOSEPH; Wyoming Area HS; Exeter, PA; (Y); 6/250; French Clb; Key Clb; Rep Stu Cncl; Bsktbl; Trk; High Hon Roll; NHS; Natl Cncl Yth Ldrshp 85; Penn ST U; Aerosp Engrng.

MAZZATESTA, JENNIFER; Susquehanna Township HS; Harrisburg, PA; (Y); Church Yth Grp; Girl Scts; Key Clb; Model UN; Chorus; Mrchg Band; Cheerleading; Hon Roll; Dentstry.

MAZZATOSTA, SEAN; Wyoming Valley West HS; Kingston, PA; (Y); Band; Chorus; School Musical; Stage Crew; Vllybl; Hon Roll; NEDT Awd; Talnt Show 85-86; Comp Sci.

MAZZATTA, KEVIN; Scranton Central HS; Scranton, PA; (Y); Art Clb; Wrstlng; Hon Roll; Engrng.

MAZZEI, DAMIAN; New Brighton Area HS; New Brighton, PA; (Y); Computer Clb; Red Cross Aide; Spanish Clb; Chorus; School Play; High Hon Roll; Stu Wk 83; Pres Yth Vlntrs Red Cross 84; Ldr Explores Beaver Cnty Med Ctr 84; Pre-Med.

MAZZOCCO, ANDREA; Uniontown Area HS; Uniontown, PA; (Y); Cmnty Wkr; Debate Tm; Drama Clb; NFL; School Play; Off Sr Cls; Var Bsktbl; CC Awd; High Hon Roll; NHS; Ntl Qlfr Ntl Frnsc Lg Trnmnt 86; Poly Sci.

MAZZONI, CARLA M; Carbondale Area HS; Carbondale, PA; (Y); Drama Clb; FBLA; FHA; FNA; GAA; Ski Clb; Chorus; School Musical; School Play; Variety Show; Grdt Brbzn Schl Mdlng 84; Smifnlst Ms Teen USA Schlrshp Pgnt 86; Bloomsburg U; Bus.

MAZZUCA, DAVID; Millville HS; Benton, PA; (Y); Chess Clb; Band; Mrchg Band; JV Bsbl; JV Im Bsktbl; Var L Socr; Elks Awd; Hon Roll; Safe Driver Awd 85-86; Pres Fit Awd 85-86; Engrng.

MBONU, CHIMDI; Church Farm Schl; Philadelphia, PA; (Y); #3 In Class; Letterman Clb; Acpl Chr; Rep Stu Cncl; Var Bsktbl; Var Ftbl; Var Trk; Hon Roll; NHS; Union League Of Philadelphia Ctznshp Awd 85; Library Aide 84-85; Bus.

MC ADOO, JAMES; Punxsutawney SR HS; Glen Campbell, PA; (Y); Math Tm; Science Clb; Trs Spanish Clb; Band; Mrchg Band; Symp Band; Yrbk Stf; High Hon Roll; NHS; Gannon U; Physcn.

MC AFEE, HEATHER; West Hazleton HS; Zion Grove, PA; (S); 56/191; FTA; VP Spanish Clb; Trs Thesps; Mrchg Band; School Musical; School Play; Stage Crew; NHS; Band; Concert Band; Penn ST U; Scndry Educ.

MC ALANIS, VICKI; Schuykill Haven HS; Auburn, PA; (Y); FNA; SADD; Lit Mag; Cmnty Wkr; English Clb; Girl Scts; Hosp Aide; Library Aide; Psychlgy.

MC ALEER, LORI; Freedom HS; Bethlehem, PA; (Y); 112/445; Pres Art Clb; French Clb; Hon Roll; Moravian Coll; Art Educ.

MC ALILEY, LAUREN; Bishop Kenrick HS; Norristown, PA; (Y); Church Yth Grp; Dance Clb; Spanish Clb; Drill Tm; School Musical; Mgr(s); Powder Puff Ftbl; Sftbl; Hon Roll; FL Inst Tech; Chld Psychol.

MC ALLISTER, ALEXANDER; Conrad Weiser HS; Womelsdorf, PA; (Y); 85/185; Art Clb; Computer Clb; Spanish Clb; Chorus; Socr; Tennis; Hon Roll; Tutor Awd 84; Bus Adm.

MC ALLISTER, CHARLES; Father Judge HS; Philadelphia, PA; (Y); 48/403; Church Yth Grp; Cmnty Wkr; Im Bsktbl; Socr; High Hon Roll; Fd Mrktng Grnt St Joseph U 86-87; Fd Mrktng Schlrshp 86-87; PHEAA Grnt 86-87; St Josephs U; Fd Mrktng.

MC ALLISTR, JEROME; Dunmore HS; Dunmore, PA; (Y); Boys Clb Am; Computer Clb; French Clb; FBLA; Spanish Clb; JV Bsktbl; Var Golf; Hon Roll; U Scranton.

MC ALONIS, MICHELE; Christian Schl Of York; Wrightsville, PA; (Y); Am Leg Aux Girls St; Church Yth Grp; Office Aide; Chorus; Var JV Trk; Hon Roll; Radlgy.

MC ANALLEN, STACEY; Lincoln HS; Ellwood City, PA; (Y); 30/163; Church Yth Grp; French Clb; Pres Y-Teens; Yrbk Rptr; Sec Trs Jr Cls; Stu Cncl; Pom Pon; Hon Roll; NHS; NEDT Awd; Gannon U Acad Scholar 86; Gannon U; Chem Engrng.

MC ANDREW, LISA; Moniteau HS; Butler, PA; (Y); Var Cheerleading; Gannon Coll; Med Tech.

MC ANDREW, SHARON; Bishop O Hara HS; Archbald, PA; (S); 9/113; Church Yth Grp; French Clb; Latin Clb; Chorus; Stage Crew; Nwsp Stf; Sec Frsh Cls; High Hon Roll; NHS; Ntl Merit SF; Fnlst PA Govrnr Schl Arts Creatv Wrtg 85; U Of Scranton; Cmmnctns.

MC ANDREW, WENDY; Susquehanna Community HS; Thompson, PA; (S); Cmnty Wkr; Scholastic Bowl; Var Cheerleading; Hon Roll; NHS; Natl Sci Merit Awd 86; Natl Ldrshp Merit Awd 85; Penn ST; Nrsng.

MC ANINCH, AMY; Franklin Area HS; Franklin, PA; (Y); Church Yth Grp; German Clb; Letterman Clb; Varsity Clb; Color Guard; Drill Tm; School Musical; Off Jr Cls; Trk; Vllybl; Occ Ther.

MC ANINCH, CHERYL; Redbank Valley HS; Mayport, PA; (Y); 10/120; Sec French Clb; Varsity Clb; Stat Mat Maids; Var L Trk; Var L Vllybl; Hon Roll; Library Aide; Yrbk Phtg; Rdban Vly Acad Hnr Soc; Grad With Hghst Hnrs; Presdntl Acad Fttnss Awd; Penn ST U At Du Bois; Engrng.

MC ANLIS, COLLEEN; Mohjawk Area JR HS HS; Enon Valley, PA; (S); 4/140; Girl Scts; Concert Band; Jazz Band; Mrchg Band; School Musical; Nwsp Rptr; Yrbk Stf; Stu Cncl; NHS; Ntl Merit Ltr; Gld Awd Grl Scts; Bio-Chmstry.

MC ANN, JOSEPH; Carmichaels Area JR SR HS; Carmichaels, PA; (S); 10/129; Church Yth Grp; Spanish Clb; Sr Cls; Var Bsbl; Hon Roll; Lion Awd; NHS; Palmer Coll; Chiroprctr.

MC ANULTY, COLLEEN; St Hubert HS For Girls; Philadelphia, PA; (Y); 76/367; Var L Cheerleading; Hon Roll; Mst Vlbl Plyr Chrldng St Timothys 83; Temple U; Accntng.

MC ANULTY, ERIN K; Homer Ctr; Homer City, PA; (Y); 47/128; FNA; Hosp Aide; Band; Color Guard; Jazz Band; School Play; Sftbl; High Hon Roll; Prfct Atten Awd; Band Mbr Of Month 86; Armstrong Cnty Schl; Rdlgst.

MC ARTHUR, TIFFANY; Harrisburg Acad; Lemoyne, PA; (Y); 5/31; Library Aide; Off Stu Cncl; Var L Fld Hcky; Mgr(s); Hon Roll; Ntl Rollersktng Champ 3rd Pl 83-84; Regnl Skater Yr 85-84; Sports Med.

MC AUVIC, ROSEMARY; Wyoming Valley West HS; Forty Fort, PA; (Y); Chorus; Jazz Band; School Musical; Swing Chorus; Rep Soph Cls; Rep Jr Cls; L Twrlr; Hon Roll; Prfct Atten Awd; Church Yth Grp; Frnch Achvt Awd; Luzerne County CC; Elem Educ.

MC AVOY, TIMOTHY; Hanover Area HS; Wilkes Barre, PA; (Y); Boy Scts; Key Clb; Ski Clb; Teachers Aide; Stage Crew; Bsktbl; Crs Cntry; Trk; Vllybl; Capt Jvln.

MC BRIDE, AMY; Mechanicsburg SR HS; Shiremanstown, PA; (Y); 38/311; Ski Clb; Cheerleading; Ftbl; High Hon Roll; NHS; Comp.

MC BRIDE, KARON; Seneca Valley SR HS; Evans City, PA; (Y); 116/342; Ski Clb; SADD; Pres Varsity Clb; Band; Symp Band; Sec Sr Cls; L Bsktbl; L Crs Cntry; L Trk; Prfct Atten Awd; Doc O Shea Awd 86; Top Athlete Track 86; Seneca Vly Holiday Tourn 85; WV U; Fash Degnr.

MC BRIDE, LYNNETTE; Seneca Valley SR HS; Evans City, PA; (Y); JA; Ski Clb; SADD; Varsity Clb; Var L Bsktbl; Var Crs Cntry; Var L Trk; High Hon Roll; Hon Roll; NHS; MVP Trck Senca Vly 86; Top Slsprsn JR Achvt 85; Lnd Yr Acdmc Awd 86; Bus Admn.

MC BRIDE, MARGARET; Marian HS; Jim Thorpe, PA; (S); 20/114; Church Yth Grp; Cmnty Wkr; Ski Clb; Spanish Clb; Stat Ftbl; JV Var Sftbl; Hon Roll; Spanish NHS; Teacher.

MC BRIDE, NANCY; St Maria Goretti HS; Philadelphia, PA; (Y); 230/426; Art Clb; French Clb; Church Choir; Orch; Bsktbl; Sftbl; St Agnes Nrsng Sch; Nrsng.

MC BRIDE, PAULA; Gateway SR HS; Monroeville, PA; (Y); 19/431; Intnl Clb; Band; Mrchg Band; Lit Mag; High Hon Roll; NHS; Prfct Atten Awd; Pres Schlr; Grove City Col; Bio.

MC BURNEY, DALE; Peabody HS; Pittsburgh, PA; (Y); DECA; Drama Clb; French Clb; Key Clb; Varsity Clb; Chorus; School Play; Yrbk Phtg; Var Tennis; Vllybl; Hnr Roll & High Hnr Roll 85-86; DECA Merit Awd.

MC BURNEY, JANE; Millersburg Area HS; Millersburg, PA; (Y); Trs Church Yth Grp; Chorus; Church Choir; Nwsp Bus Mgr; Powder Puff Ftbl; Trk; Restrnt.

MC CABE, CHRISTINA; Spring-Ford SR HS; Royersford, PA; (Y); 64/264; German Clb; Pep Clb; Ski Clb; Spanish Clb; Bsktbl; Cheerleading; Mgr(s); Score Keeper.

MC CABE, KRISTINA M; Bishop Shanahan HS; West Chester, PA; (Y); Girl Scts; Band; Chorus; School Musical; Camp Fr Inc; Nwsp Stf; Vllybl; Math.

MC CABE, MICHELLE; Lake Lehman HS; Harveys Lake, PA; (Y); Sec Church Yth Grp; Bowling; High Hon Roll; Hon Roll; Penn ST; Accntng.

MC CABE, PAM; Schuylkill Haven Area HS; Sch Haven, PA; (Y); 22/85; Art Clb; Pep Clb; SADD; Church Choir; Mat Maids; Var L Trk; Var L Vllybl; Hon Roll; NHS; Cntrl Penn Bus Schl; Fshn Merch.

MC CABE, TRACEY JOHN; Connellsville Area SR HS; Mt Pleasant, PA; (Y); 145/484; Boy Scts; FBLA; Office Aide; School Musical; School Play; High Hon Roll; Hon Roll; Prfct Atten Awd; ICM Schl Of Bus; Comp Pgmmng.

MC CAFFERTY, MALINDA; Interboro HS; Essington, PA; (S); JCL; Flag Corp; Yrbk Stf; Rep Frsh Cls; Rep Jr Cls; Rep Stu Cncl; Jr NHS; NHS; Computer Clb; Latin Clb; US House Of Rep Page 85-86; Culture Vulture Pops 85-86; Dngns & Drgns Clb 84-85; Crmnl Sci Invstgtn.

MC CAFFERTY, MEGAN; Shaler Area SR HS; Allison Park, PA; (Y); 24/517; Church Yth Grp; Library Aide; Office Aide; Ski Clb; Spanish Clb; School Musical; High Hon Roll; Hon Roll; Spanish NHS; Law.

MC CAFFERY, ANDY; Danville SR HS; Danville, PA; (Y); 44/204; Aud/Vis; Chess Clb; Exploring; Latin Clb; Red Cross Aide; JV Wrstlng; High Hon Roll; Hon Roll; Prfct Atten Awd; Attndc PA ST Plc Acad 86; PA ST U; Mtrlgy.

MC CAFFREY, LEE ANN; Seton La Salle HS; Behtel Park, PA; (Y); 50/250; Church Yth Grp; Dance Clb; Spanish Clb; Variety Show; JV Crs Cntry; Var Mgr(s); High Hon Roll; Hon Roll; Music Awd 84; Med.

MC CAGUE, MARK; Riverview HS; Oakmont, PA; (Y); 6/118; Trs Drama Clb; School Play; Yrbk Sprt Ed; Rep Stu Cncl; Capt Crs Cntry; Capt Trk; High Hon Roll; NHS; Ntl Merit Ltr; NEDT Awd; Acad All-Amer 86; Outstdng Perf Of Clss Play 86.

MC CAIN, JAMES; Meadville Area SR HS; Meadville, PA; (Y); JV Ftbl; JV Wt Lftg; Hon Roll; Arch.

MC CAIN, JENNIFER; Tunkhannock HS; Tunkhannock, PA; (S); Aud/Vis; German Clb; Var Capt Bsktbl; Var L Trk; Hon Roll; NHS; Acctng.

MC CAIN, MELANIE SUE; Warwick HS; Lititz, PA; (Y); 85/232; Girl Scts; Varsity Clb; VICA; Lit Mag; Var Cheerleading; Hon Roll; FORCE Drug & Alcohol Action Grp; JR Activites Clb; Prom Committee; Early Childhood Educ.

MC CALL, BRUCE; Karns City JR SR HS; Chicora, PA; (Y); 13/113; Church Yth Grp; Exploring; Crs Cntry; Trk; Hon Roll; NHS; PA Free Entrprs Wk Schlrshp 86; Grove City Coll; Engrng.

MC CALLION, GEORGE; St John Neumann HS; Philadelphia, PA; (Y); Boy Scts; Exploring; Capt Ski Clb; Off Spanish Clb; JV Ice Hcky; Mayors Smmr Yth Prgrm Incentive Awd 85; UCLA; Med.

MC CALMONT, DEBBIE; Appollo Ridge HS; Apollo, PA; (Y); 15/170; Art Clb; Drama Clb; French Clb; JA; Letterman Clb; Math Clb; Ski Clb; Cheerleading; Mgr(s); Trk; Ldrshp Sem; UPJ; Elem Ed.

MC CAMANT, STACY; Lebanon HS; Lebanon, PA; (Y); German Clb; Pep Clb; JV Bsktbl; Hon Roll; Shippensburg U; Accntng.

MC CAMEY, KAREN; Perry Traditional Acad; Pittsburgh, PA; (Y); Church Yth Grp; Dance Clb; German Clb; Library Aide; Office Aide; Chorus; Nwsp Rptr; Nwsp Stf; Mgr Swmmng; High Hon Roll; Cert Of Compltn Of A Basic Rprtng Wrkshp At Point Park Coll 85; CCAC Pont Park; Jrnlsm.

MC CAMMON, ELIZABETH; General Mc Lane HS; Mckean, PA; (Y); Exploring; 4-H; German Clb; Hosp Aide; Band; Mrchg Band; Rep Stu Cncl; High Hon Roll; Hon Roll; NHS; Ovr 300 Hrs Vlntrd Cndystrpr 86.

MC CANCE, RICHARD A; East Juniata HS; Liverpool, PA; (Y); Computer Clb; Stu Cncl; Var Capt Bsktbl; Var Socr; Var Trk; High Hon Roll; Hon Roll; PA Schlrstc Art Awd-Cert Mrt & Gold Key 86; Arch.

MC CANDLESS, DAVID M; James Buchanan HS; Mercersburg, PA; (Y); 1/189; Pres Church Yth Grp; Band; Chorus; Jazz Band; Swing Chorus; NHS; Ntl Merit SF; Val; Dstrct Bnd 84-85; Dstrct & Rgnl Chrs 86; Lafayette; Math.

MC CANDLESS, RACHEL; Slippery Rock Area HS; Prospect, PA; (Y); 28/131; Camera Clb; Pep Clb; Capt Color Guard; Drm & Bgl; Capt Flag Corp; Mrchg Band; Hon Roll; Gifted Prog 83-87; Psych.

MC CANN, CHRIS; Lancaster Catholic HS; E Petersburg, PA; (Y); 53/207; Concert Band; Mrchg Band; Var Trk; Drexel U; Engrng.

MC CANN, ELLEN; St Hubert Catholic HS; Philadelphia, PA; (Y); 4/367; Cmnty Wkr; French Clb; Science Clb; Teachers Aide; Var Swmmng; High Hon Roll; Opt Clb Awd; Latin Awd; Amer Culture Awd.

MC CANN, JIM; Butler Area SR HS; Butler, PA; (Y); Exploring; 4-H; Hon Roll; U Of Pittsburgh; Chem Engrng.

MC CANN, KAREN B; Academy Of Notre Dame; King Of Prussia, PA; (Y); Hosp Aide; Chorus; School Musical; Hon Roll; Sunday Schl Tchr 84-86; Chrch Lctr 84-86; Psych.

MC CANN, MICHAEL; Canon Mcmillan HS; Canonsburg, PA; (Y); Chess Clb; Latin Clb; Letterman Clb; Ski Clb; Nwsp Sprt Ed; L Bsktbl; Capt L Crs Cntry; Capt L Trk; Hon Roll; WV U; Pre-Psych.

MC CANN, SCOTT; Freedom HS; Bethlehem, PA; (Y); 38/445; Drama Clb; French Clb; Thesps; School Play; Stage Crew; Yrbk Phtg; Yrbk Rptr; Var Ice Hcky; Var Tennis; Hon Roll; Arntcl Engrng.

MC CANN, STACIE; Bradford Central Christian HS; Bradford, PA; (Y); Math Clb; Pep Clb; SADD; Ed Yrbk Ed-Chief; Sec Sr Cls; Bsktbl; High Hon Roll; NHS; Ntl Merit Ltr; U Pittsburgh Bradford; Bus Mgt.

MC CANNEY, MARSHA A; Central HS; Philadelphia, PA; (Y); 99/250; Art Clb; Church Yth Grp; Cmnty Wkr; Chorus; Church Choir; Color Guard; Variety Show; Yrbk Stf; JV Badmtn; Hon Roll; Energy Contst Awd-Moore Coll Of Art 86; Sketch Clb Awd 86; RI Schl Of Design; Fash Dsgn.

MC CARDLE, JENNIFER; Chief Logan HS; Yeagertown, PA; (Y); 1/200; Church Yth Grp; Band; Chorus; Concert Band; Mrchg Band; Fld Hcky; High Hon Roll; NHS; Shippersburg U; Elem Ed.

MC CARRAHER, JAMES; Cedar Grove Christian Acad; Philadelphia, PA; (Y); Church Yth Grp; Drama Clb; School Play; Nwsp Rptr.

MC CARTHY, BRENDA; Neshaminy HS; Hulmeville, PA; (Y); 4-H; GAA; Bsktbl; Stat Fld Hcky; Mgr(s); Var Capt Socr; High Hon Roll; Hon Roll; U Of PA; Vet Med.

MC CARTHY JR, JACK; Du Bois Area HS; Dubois, PA; (Y); 7/256; Im Vllybl; High Hon Roll; Hon Roll; NHS; Recgntn Maintaining A Avg 86; Pres Acad Fit Awd 86; Scholar Hnrs Cert 90 Pct Acad 86; PA ST U; Bus Adm.

MC CARTHY, MICHELE M; Archbishop Kennedy HS; Lafayette Hill, PA; (Y); 11/180; Cmnty Wkr; Girl Scts; Political Wkr; JV Var Fld Hcky; Stat Score Keeper; JV Var Vllybl; Hon Roll; NHS; Villanova U; Accntng.

MC CARTHY, PATRICIA; Liberty HS; Bethlehem, PA; (Y); 111/475; Chorus; Rep Stu Cncl; Var L Fld Hcky; Im Powder Puff Ftbl; Hon Roll; HOOP Grls 85-86; Bus.

MC CARTHY, SUZANNE; Liberty HS; Bethlehem, PA; (Y); 112/407; Mgr Nwsp Stf; Score Keeper; Hon Roll; Var Mgr(s); Awd Outstndg Advrtsng Sls Schl Nwspaper 85; Millersville U; Psychlgy.

MC CARTHY, TARA; Shaler SR HS; Pgh, PA; (Y); 45/541; Dance Clb; Office Aide; Rep Soph Cls; Pres Jr Cls; Swmmng; High Hon Roll; Rotary Awd; Spanish NHS; Float Queen 85; Carnegie Mellon U; Art.

MC CARTNEY, ERIN; Marian HS; Mahanoy City, PA; (S); 32/114; Church Yth Grp; Drill Tm; Yrbk Stf; Bsktbl; Mgr(s); Hon Roll; Cnslng.

MC CARTNEY, JENNIFER; Lewistown Area HS; Lewistown, PA; (Y); AFS; Sec Art Clb; French Clb; Key Clb; Ski Clb; Chorus; Cheerleading; High Hon Roll; Hon Roll; NHS.

MC CARTNEY, NANCY; Bald Eagle Area HS; Howard, PA; (Y); GAA; Letterman Clb; SADD; Varsity Clb; Variety Show; Nwsp Rptr; Rep Frsh Cls; Rep Soph Cls; Rep Jr Cls; Rep Sr Cls; Lock Haven U; Mgmt Sci.

MC CARTNEY, PAUL; Quigley HS; Evans City, PA; (S); 10/113; JA; Math Clb; Teachers Aide; Trk; High Hon Roll; Toastmaster Speech Awd 85; Alg I Awd 83-84; Acad All Amer 86; Carnegie Mellon; Life Sci.

MC CARTNEY, SHELLEY L; Trinity HS; Washington, PA; (Y); 16/374; Key Clb; Ski Clb; Drm Mjr(t); Mrchg Band; Twrlr; High Hon Roll; Hon Roll; Chmcl Engrng.

MC CARTY, TRUDY L; Charleroi Area JR SR HS; Van Voorhis, PA; (Y); Library Aide; Nwsp Stf; Yrbk Stf; Vllybl; Hon Roll; Duffs Bus Schl; Crt Rprtng.

MC CASLIN, SUSAN L; Muncy HS; Muncy, PA; (Y); Pres Church Yth Grp; Pres VP 4-H; Sec VP Spanish Clb; SADD; Rep Stu Cncl; Cit Awd; Hon Roll; NHS; Spanish NHS; PA Intl Forgn Yth Trvl Schlrshp & 4-H Japns Delg 86; Outstndng 4-H Lycoming Cnty PA 85; Ag.

MC CAUGHAN, MICHAEL W; Central Bucks High School East; Doylestown, PA; (Y); 1/474; Capt Debate Tm; Scholastic Bowl; High Hon Roll; Ntl Merit SF; Math Tm; Band; Socr; Jr NHS; Prfct Atten Awd; Awd Acad Exclince.

MC CAULLEY, ERRIN; Bellwood-Antis HS; Bellwood, PA; (Y); Church Yth Grp; Key Clb; Letterman Clb; Varsity Clb; Chorus; Stu Cncl; Bsktbl; Ftbl; Trk; Wt Lftg; Williamson Trad Schl; Schl Tchr.

MC CAUSLAND, NANCY; Jamestown Area JR SR HS; Jamestown, PA; (S); 3/60; Varsity Clb; Band; Chorus; Sec Frsh Cls; JV Bsktbl; Var Mgr(s); Var Vllybl; High Hon Roll; Hon Roll; VP NHS; HOBY Conf Rep; PA Free Entrprs Rep; Stu Forum Rep; Gannon U Of Erie PA; Bio.

MC CAUSLAND, TRISH; Upper Darby HS; Upr Darby, PA; (Y); 4/629; Service Clb; Chorus; School Musical; Yrbk Stf; Rep Stu Cncl; JV Vllybl; High Hon Roll; Office Aide; Spanish Clb; Mgr Bsbl; Alg II Awd 83-84; Spnsh II Awd 84-85; Amer Lit Awd 85-86; Law.

MC CAW, KATHLEEN; Marple Newtown HS; Newtown Square, PA; (Y); 40/360; Spanish Clb; Varsity Clb; Rep Stu Cncl; Var L Bsktbl; JV Fld Hcky; Var L Sftbl; Var Vllybl; Hon Roll; U DE; Phys Ther.

MC CHESNEY, BRETT; Huntingdon Area HS; Huntingdon, PA; (Y); 83/241; Church Yth Grp; French Clb; Ski Clb; 4-H Awd; Hon Roll; NEDT Awd; Juniata; Chem.

MC CLAIN, BECKY; Belle Vernon Area HS; Belle Vernon, PA; (Y); Trs Church Yth Grp; Library Aide; Pep Clb; Ski Clb; SADD; Color Guard; Hon Roll; Elem Ed.

MC CLAIN, JAMES; South Moreland HS; Scottdale, PA; (Y); Computer Clb; VICA; Pittsburg U.

MC CLAIN, KEITH; H S Of Engineering & Science; Philadelphia, PA; (Y); Church Yth Grp; Drama Clb; Leo Clb; Mathletes; Math Tm; Model UN; Office Aide; Science Clb; Ski Clb; Teachers Aide; Penn St; Presbyterian Minister.

MC CLAIN, LORIANNE; Tunkhannock Area HS; Tunkhannock, PA; (Y); 37/320; Aud/Vis; Pres FCA; Key Clb; Letterman Clb; Rep Frsh Cls; Rep Soph Cls; Rep Jr Cls; Rep Sr Cls; Rep Stu Cncl; Var L Swmmng; Grove Cty Coll; Blgy.

MC CLAIN, ROCHELLE; St Maria Goretti HS; Philadelphia, PA; (Y); 184/459; Cmnty Wkr; Lit Mag; Hahnemann U; Rdlgc Tech.

MC CLAIN, STACY; Burgettstown JR SR HS; Burgettstown, PA; (Y); Ski Clb; Spanish Clb; Varsity Clb; Chorus; Stu Cncl; Cheerleading; Sftbl; Hon Roll; NHS; Pharm.

MC CLAINE, TONI; Punxsutawney Area HS; Punxsutawney, PA; (Y); 85/238; FNA; Spanish Clb; Variety Show; Nwsp Rptr; Nwsp Stf; VP Trk; Var Wrstlng; Hon Roll; Story Pblshd In Punxsys Litry Mag 86.

MC CLAY II, RALPH; Saegertown HS; Meadville, PA; (Y); VICA; Ice Hcky; Hon Roll; Refree Yth Hckey; Mbr Of Saegertown Vlnteer Firemn; Mbr Of Saegertwn Sprtsmn Clb; Elec.

MC CLAY, TODD A; Neshannock HS; New Castle, PA; (Y); 19/99; Sec Church Yth Grp; Library Aide; Pres Band; Concert Band; Jazz Band; Mrchg Band; Pep Band; School Musical; School Play; Hon Roll; Semper Fidelis Music Awd 86; Svc Awd 86; New Castle Music Clb Awd 86; Bowling Green ST U; Phys Ther.

MC CLEARY, HEATHER; Grove City HS; Grove City, PA; (Y); Key Clb; Office Aide; Chorus; Drill Tm; Var L Cheerleading; High Hon Roll; Hon Roll; Smmr Acad At Slippery Rock U 86; Accntng.

MC CLELLAN, CARRIE; Sheffield Area JR-SR HS; Tiona, PA; (Y); VP Church Yth Grp; Pres FHA; SADD; Varsity Clb; Band; Color Guard; Mrchg Band; Stu Cncl; Stat Var Bsktbl; High Hon Roll; Ntl Hnr Soc Schlrshp 86; U Of Pittsburgh; Phy Thrpy.

MC CLELLAN, CINDY; West Greene HS; Sycamore, PA; (S); DECA; Trs VICA; Chorus; Color Guard; Stage Crew; High Hon Roll; Hon Roll; St Rep DECA 86-87; Retail Mgt.

MC CLELLAN, DEBBIE; Glendale JR SR HS; Blandburg, PA; (Y); 25/98; Art Clb; Church Yth Grp; Drama Clb; Library Aide; Band; Concert Band; Mrchg Band; Yrbk Stf; JV Cheerleading; Capt Twrlr; Pres Phys Ftns Awd 85; Comp Sci.

MC CLELLAN, JONATHAN C; Gateway SR HS; Morneoville, PA; (Y); 33/444; Pres Band; Pres Concert Band; Pres Jazz Band; Pres Mrchg Band; Orch; Pres Pep Band; School Musical; High Hon Roll; NHS; Comptv Scholar Duquesne U 86-90; Dist & Regnl Band Awds 85-86; Duquesne U.

MC CLELLAND, CRAIG; Clarion HS; Shippenville, PA; (Y); JV Var Ftbl; Var Wt Lftg; Edinborough U; Criminolgy.

MC CLELLAND, DANIEL; Brockway Area HS; Reynoldsvl, PA; (Y); 26/86; 4-H; FFA; L Capt Wrstlng; Agri.

MC CLELLAND, MICHAEL; Pocono Mountain HS; Bartonsville, PA; (Y); Boy Scts; Debate Tm; Drama Clb; Key Clb; Model UN; Pep Clb; Political Wkr; Q&S; Radio Clb; Ski Clb; Jrnlsm.

MC CLELLAND, MICHELE; Brownsville Area HS; New Salem, PA; (Y); Drama Clb; Library Aide; Math Clb; SADD; Variety Show; Nwsp Rptr; Rep Jr Cls; Vllybl; High Hon Roll; Hon Roll; Wilma Boyd; Arln Stwrdss.

MC CLELLAND, SCOTT; Masnonnon Valley HS; Madera, PA; (Y); 39/132; Church Yth Grp; Varsity Clb; Band; Chorus; Church Choir; Concert Band; Mrchg Band; Pep Band; School Musical; Swing Chorus; Phys Ftns Awd 84-86.

MC CLENDON, DESIREE; William Penn HS; Philadelphia, PA; (Y); Hon Roll; NHS; Hon Stu Lamda Kappa Mu Schlstc Achvt 83-84; Temple; Acctnt.

MC CLENNEN, DAWN; Interboro HS; Norwood, PA; (S); AFS; French Clb; VP Key Clb; Hst Latin Clb; Drill Tm; Ed School Play; Trs Stu Cncl; Sftbl; Hon Roll; Rep NHS; Widener U; Accntnt.

MC CLIMANS, TRACI; Jamestown JR SR HS; Hartstown, PA; (Y); Church Yth Grp; Drama Clb; Service Clb; VICA; Drill Tm; School Play; Stage Crew; Yrbk Stf; Co-Capt Pom Pon; Prfct Atten Awd; Penn ST U; Hstry.

MC CLINTIC, DENISE; East HS; Erie, PA; (Y); Spanish Clb; Y-Teens; Bsktbl; JV Var Cheerleading; JV Tennis; Fmly & Bus.

MC CLINTIC, MICHAEL; Center Area HS; Aliquippa, PA; (Y); 3/190; Am Leg Boys St; Boy Scts; Spanish Clb; Band; Jazz Band; School Musical; Var L Socr; Hon Roll; NHS; Ntl Merit SF; L Armstrong Jazz Awd 84-85.

MC CLINTOCK, JOHN; United HS; Seward, PA; (Y); 25/157; Chess Clb; Church Yth Grp; Ftbl; Trk; Wrstlng; Liberty U; Engrng.

MC CLINTOCK, ROB; Yough SR HS; Ruffs Dale, PA; (Y); Chess Clb; Drama Clb; Spanish Clb; Band; Concert Band; Jazz Band; Mrchg Band; School Play; Stage Crew; Symp Band; U Of Pittsburgh; Engnrng.

MC CLINTOCK, TAMY; Mifflinburg Area HS; Mifflinburg, PA; (Y); 13/170; Church Yth Grp; French Clb; JV Mgr Sftbl; High Hon Roll; NHS; Prfct Atten Awd; Bloomsburg U; Elem Ed.

MC CLOSKEY, ANTHONY; Central Dauphin HS; Harrisburg, PA; (Y); 6/390; Church Yth Grp; Science Clb; Band; Vllybl; Cit Awd; High Hon Roll; Hon Roll; Pres Jr NHS; Pres NHS; Concert Band; Am Legn Awd 84; Engineering.

MC CLOSKEY, EDWARD TED; Bishop Gwlfoyle HS; Duncansville, PA; (Y); Science Clb; Service Clb; Chorus; Jazz Band; Pep Band; Yrbk Rptr; Stu Cncl; Golf; Hon Roll; PA ST U; Musician.

MC CLOSKEY, JAMES; Bristol JR SR HS; Bristol, PA; (Y); 4/86; FBLA; Political Wkr; Science Clb; VP Service Clb; School Play; Stage Crew; Lib Yrbk Stf; Rep Trs Stu Cncl; L Capt Crs Cntry; L Trk; Rotary Schlrshp 85-86; Free Enterprise Week Lock Haven U PA Schlrshp 86; US Milit Acad; Intl Reltns.

MC CLOSKEY, JODI; Norht Clarion HS; Tylersburg, PA; (Y); French Clb; Sec SADD; Band; Church Choir; School Musical; Sec Soph Cls; Sec Jr Cls; Rep Stu Cncl; JV Bsktbl; Hon Roll; Jr Historian 84-86; Elmntry Tchr.

MC CLOSKEY, JOEL; Millersburg Area HS; Millersburg, PA; (Y); 17/75; Church Yth Grp; Spanish Clb; Band; Church Choir; Concert Band; Jazz Band; Mrchg Band; Var Bsbl; Var Golf; Hon Roll; Hnr Awd 84-85; Middletown Elec Inst; Comp Tech.

MC CLOSKEY, MELANNE; Jamestown HS; Jamestown, PA; (Y); Church Yth Grp; FBLA; Band; Chorus; Church Choir; Mrchg Band; Pep Band; School Musical; Var Cheerleading; Drama Clb; Dist Chorus 86; Regnl Chorus 86; Bnkng.

MC CLOSKEY, SAMANTHA; Bellefonte Area HS; Bellefonte, PA; (Y); Church Yth Grp; Chorus; Rep Frsh Cls; Rep Stu Cncl; Hon Roll; Bus Adm.

MC CLOSKEY, SCOTT; Bellwood Antis HS; Bellwood, PA; (Y); Cmnty Wkr; Varsity Clb; VICA; Chorus; School Musical; Stage Crew; Im Bsbl; Im JV Bsktbl; JV Ftbl; Var Mgr(s); Williamson Trade Schl; Pwr Plnt.

MC CLOSKEY, SHANNON; West Hazleton HS; Hazleton, PA; (Y); 18/280; Y-Teens; Band; Concert Band; Mrchg Band; School Musical; Hon Roll; PA ST.

MC CLOSKEY, SUSAN; Central HS; Martinsburg, PA; (Y); 30/179; Drama Clb; FBLA; GAA; VP JA; JV Bsktbl; Im Vllybl; Hon Roll; Penn ST U; Bus Adm.

MC CLOY, KELLY; Mt Pleasant Area SR HS; Mt Pleasant, PA; (Y); 40/246; Chess Clb; Church Yth Grp; German Clb; Latin Clb; Science Clb; High Hon Roll.

MC CLUCAS, TONYA; Chestnut Ridge HS; New Paris, PA; (S); 11/107; Office Aide; Band; Sec Soph Cls; Sec Jr Cls; Sec Sr Cls; Pres Stu Cncl; Capt Twrlr; Capt L Vllybl; DAR Awd; NHS; Ms Constncy Vllybl Awd 84; Hd Mjrett 83-85; Hmcmng Qun 85; Juniata Coll; Elem Ed Tchr.

MC CLUNG, LISA; Langley HS; Pittsburgh, PA; (Y); 36/278; Sec JA; VP Jr Cls; Pres Sr Cls; Stu Cncl; High Hon Roll; Hon Roll; Prfct Atten Awd; Duffs Bus Inst; Exec Sec.

MC CLUNG, SANDRA; Downingtown SR HS; Glenmoore, PA; (S); 4/545; Sec Pres Church Yth Grp; Nwsp Rptr; Rep Stu Cncl; Bsktbl; Sftbl; Trk; High Hon Roll; NHS; NEDT Awd; Dance Clb; PA Free Enterprise Wk Schlrshp 85; U Pitts Sunr Mnth 85; Intl Bus.

MC CLURE, BRIAN D; Central HS; Martinsburg, PA; (Y); 65/175; Boy Scts; Speech Tm; Nwsp Rptr; Var Trk; Outstndng Srvc Awd Roarng Sprng Amblnc 86; Emrgncy Med Tech MAST 85; Egl Sct 86; U Pitts; Pre Med.

MC CLURE, DARREN; Laurel Valley HS; Bolivar, PA; (Y); 2/86; AFS; Varsity Clb; Trs Stu Cncl; Var Bsbl; Var Bsktbl; Var Ftbl; High Hon Roll; NHS; Applchn Cnfrnc All-Strs Bsktbll 85-86; Applchn Cnfrnc All-Strs Hnrbl Mntn Ftbll 85-86; Engnrng.

MC CLURE, DAVE; Curwensville Area HS; Curwensville, PA; (Y); French Clb; Letterman Clb; Var JV Bsbl; JV Ftbl; Var L Wrstlng; Carpentry.

MC CLURE, RICHARD W; Hamburg Area HS; Hamburg, PA; (Y); 75/152; VP Art Clb; Rep Camera Clb; Stu Cncl; Var L Crs Cntry; Var L Ftbl; Var L Trk; Hon Roll; Shippensburg U.

MC CLUSKEY, JODI; St Marys Area HS; Benezett, PA; (Y); 47/290; Gov Schl Ag 86; Penn ST.

MC CLUSKEY, KARYN; St Francis Acad; Pittsburgh, PA; (S); JA; Chorus; Drm Mjr(t); School Play; Yrbk Stf; VP Frsh Cls; Rep Soph Cls; Pres Jr Cls; Sftbl; NHS.

MC CLUSKEY, SANDRA; West Mifflin Area HS; W Mifflin, PA; (Y); FBLA; FTA; Teachers Aide; Band; Concert Band; Mrchg Band; Hon Roll; Pres Schlr; Penn ST U; Econ.

MC CLYMONDS, ANN; Grove City Area SR HS; Grove City, PA; (Y); 52/199; Pres Church Yth Grp; 4-H; Key Clb; Band; Church Choir; Concert Band; Jazz Band; Mrchg Band; Pep Band; Powder Puff Ftbl; Intl Soc Christian Endeavor Albert H Diebold Awd Rnnr Up 83; PA Hist Day 2nd Pl Dist 84; Equestrian Studies.

MC CLYMONDS, KIM; Ford City JR-SR HS; Ford City, PA; (Y); 35/356; Hosp Aide; Pep Clb; Chorus; Off Soph Cls; Off Jr Cls; Off Sr Cls; Stu Cncl; Var Cheerleading; Vllybl; Hon Roll.

MC CLYMONT, CYNTHIA; Gettysburg SR HS; Gettysburg, PA; (Y); 67/253; AFS; FCA; French Clb; Variety Show; Yrbk Bus Mgr; Yrbk Stf; Rep Stu Cncl; L Bsktbl; L Fld Hcky; Capt Sftbl; Schltc Wrtng Awds Cert Merit 86; Bus Ed Scholar Awd 86; Andrews U; Mktng.

MC CLYMONT, K J; Tunkhannock Area HS; Tunkhannock, PA; (Y); 1/350; Hosp Aide; Scholastic Bowl; School Play; Var Capt Swmmng; Dnfth Awd; Pres NHS; Val; Aud/Vis; Church Yth Grp; Ntl Cncl On Yth Ldrshp; Ntl Yth Ldr Of Yr 86; Jostens Fndtn Ntl Schlrshp 86; Bucknell U; Bio.

MC COLGAN, JENNIFER; Central Bucks East HS; Warrington, PA; (Y); Church Yth Grp; FBLA; GAA; Chorus; Rep Stu Cncl; Var Capt Bsktbl; Var Capt Sftbl; Var Tennis; Hon Roll; Jr NHS; MVP & Bst Dfnsv Plyr Bsktbll 85-86; Bar Wnnr Sftbll 86; Hnr Rll 84-86; Pre-Law.

MC COLLIM, JOHN; Valley HS; New Kensington, PA; (Y); Chess Clb; Computer Clb; JA; Science Clb; Spanish Clb; Varsity Clb; JV Bsbl; JV Ftbl; Hon Roll; Oceanography.

MC COLLOUGH, LESLEY; Manheim Township HS; Lancaster, PA; (Y); 19/325; VP JA; Nwsp Stf; Yrbk Stf; Lit Mag; Rep Stu Cncl; L Fld Hcky; High Hon Roll; Pres NHS; HOBY Ldrshp Sem 85; Mayors Yth Ldrshp Conf 85; Natl JA Conv 86; Pol Sci.

MC COLLUM, LORIE; Central HS; Philadelphia, PA; (Y); Church Yth Grp; Girl Scts; Spanish Clb; Band; Chorus; Madrigals; Bsktbl; Bowling; Sftbl; Ntl Merit SF; Med.

MC COMBS, BRIAN; Bald Eagle Nittany HS; Mill Hall, PA; (Y); 6/125; Am Leg Boys St; Church Yth Grp; German Clb; Key Clb; Model UN; Trs Jr Cls; Ftbl; NHS; Trs Sr Cls; Appt USAF Acad 86; US Air Frc Acad; Engrng.

MC COMSEY, SUSAN; Octorara HS; Atglen, PA; (Y); 20/161; Trs Sec Church Yth Grp; Cmnty Wkr; Teachers Aide; Band; Mrchg Band; Nwsp Stf; Yrbk Stf; Fld Hcky; Trk; Hon Roll; Sec Ed.

MC CONAHY, KATHY; Central HS; Martinsburg, PA; (Y); Camera Clb; Sec Church Yth Grp; FBLA; SADD; Yrbk Stf; Hon Roll; 2nd Pl Bus Math FBLA Rgnl Cmptn 85; Bus Schl; Med Sec.

MC CONELLE, DAVID; York Catholic HS; York, PA; (Y); Church Yth Grp; French Clb; Latin Clb; Pep Clb; Varsity Clb; Nwsp Stf; Rep Sr Cls; Stu Cncl; JV Var Bsbl; JV Var Crs Cntry.

MC CONNELL, ART; Upper Dublin HS; Ft Washington, PA; (Y); Boy Scts; Socr; PA ST.

MC CONNELL, BRADLEY; Hampton HS; Allison Pk, PA; (Y); 3/260; Exploring; Pep Clb; Spanish Clb; Varsity Clb; Stu Cncl; Crs Cntry; Tennis; Trk; High Hon Roll; NHS; Biochem.

MC CONNELL, CHRISTIE; Fairview HS; Erie, PA; (Y); French Clb; Varsity Clb; Yrbk Stf; Rep Stu Cncl; Var Cheerleading; Var Socr; JV Sftbl; Hon Roll; Free Enterprs Week Schlrshp 86; Elem Ed.

MC CONNELL, CRAIG; United HS; New Florence, PA; (Y); 7/129; Camera Clb; Chess Clb; Computer Clb; Math Clb; JV Wrstlng; Hon Roll; Jr NHS; Trs NHS; FL Inst Of Tech; Comp Engrng.

MC CONNELL, JILL; Sayre Area HS; S Waverly, PA; (Y); 4-H; Girl Scts; Band; Chorus; Concert Band; Mrchg Band; Pep Band; JP Sousa Awd; Moose Music Awd 86; Ruth Frank Music Awd 86; Army Band.

MC CONNELL, KELLY; Jersey Shore Area SR HS; Jersey Shore, PA; (Y); German Clb; Girl Scts; Ski Clb; Varsity Clb; Acpl Chr; Chorus; Church Choir; School Musical; School Play; Variety Show; Jersey Shore Hosp Schlrshp 86; Behrend Coll; Pre Med.

MC CONNELL, LESLIE; Punxsatawney Area HS; Punxsutawney, PA; (Y); Church Yth Grp; Pep Clb; Varsity Clb; Variety Show; Cheerleading; Pom Pon; Trk; IN U PA; Elem Ed.

MC CONNELL, MATTHEW; Hickory HS; Hermitage, PA; (Y); 13/175; Computer Clb; Math Clb; Spanish Clb; Pres Stu Cncl; Capt Ftbl; Capt Wrstlng; Cit Awd; Pres NHS; Pres Schlr; Rotary Awd; Marsden Mc Bride Mem Awd, Phi Delta Kappa, KDKA-TV 2 Extra Effort Awd 86; Davidson Coll NC; Econ/Govt.

MC CONNELL, MATTHEW W; Bethel Park HS; Bethel Park, PA; (Y); 18/531; FBLA; Math Clb; Rep Frsh Cls; Rep Soph Cls; Rep Jr Cls; Rep Sr Cls; Bsktbl; Golf; Trk; High Hon Roll; Hmcmg Kng 86; Mst Lkly Sccd 86; Boston Coll; Ecnmcs.

MC CONNELL, SUSANNA; Bentworth SR HS; Bentleyville, PA; (Y); 17/144; FBLA; FHA; Ski Clb; Band; Concert Band; Mrchg Band; Stu Cncl; High Hon Roll; Hon Roll; NHS; Elem Educ.

MC CONNELL, TAMMY; Bishop Guilfoyle HS; Altoona, PA; (Y); 9/125; Church Yth Grp; Library Aide; Ski Clb; Chorus; Yrbk Stf; Rep Frsh Cls; Rep Soph Cls; Trs Sr Cls; Var Capt Cheerleading; High Hon Roll; Phrmcy.

MC CONNELL, TERESA; Northern Cambria HS; Spangler, PA; (Y); Drama Clb; French Clb; Band; Chorus; Concert Band; Cheerleading; French Hon Soc; High Hon Roll; Hon Roll.

MC CONVILLE, DAN; Mary Fuller Frazier SR HS; Perryopolis, PA; (Y); Boy Scts; Yrbk Phtg; Yrbk Stf; Ftbl; Penn ST; Tchng.

MC CONVILLE, KELLY; Plum SR HS; Pittsburgh, PA; (Y); Dance Clb; Spanish Clb; SADD; Teachers Aide; Twrlr; High Hon Roll; NHS; Grls Ldrs Assn 86; OH ST; Jrnlstc Cmnctns.

MC CONVILLE, MELISSA; Freeport SR HS; Sarver, PA; (S); 1/170; Drill Tm; School Play; Yrbk Stf; Rep Frsh Cls; Sec Soph Cls; Off Jr Cls; Stu Cncl; Sftbl; Vllybl; High Hon Roll; St Marys Coll; Soclgy.

MC COOL, DENISE; St Basil Acad; Philadelphia, PA; (S); Cmnty Wkr; Sec French Clb; GAA; Ed Nwsp Stf; Hon Roll; Ntl Merit Ltr; NEDT Awd; Opt Clb Awd; Pre-Law.

MC CORD, REGINA; Gateway SR HS; Monroeville, PA; (Y); Church Yth Grp; Debate Tm; Drama Clb; NFL; Pres PAVAS; Chorus; Church Choir; School Musical; School Play; JA; Martin Luther King Jr Oratrcl Contst 86; Howard U; Mgmt Informtn Systms.

MC CORKLE, PETER; Harrisburg Acad; New Cumberland, PA; (Y); Drama Clb; Math Tm; Ski Clb; School Play; Yrbk Stf; Var Lcrss; Var Socr; Var Tennis; Bus.

MC CORMIC, DEBORAH; Brownsville Area HS; Grindstone, PA; (S); 30/225; Church Yth Grp; FBLA; Office Aide; SADD; Church Choir; High Hon Roll; Hon Roll.

MC CORMICK, ANDY; Pennridge HS; Sellersville, PA; (Y); 40/400; Soroptimist; Band; Jazz Band; Crs Cntry; Socr; Trk; Wt Lftg; High Hon Roll; Hon Roll; Frgn Bus.

MC CORMICK, BRIAN; Devon Prepartory Schl; Audubon, PA; (Y); Cmnty Wkr; Ski Clb; School Play; Nwsp Rptr; VP Stu Cncl; VP Bsbl; JV Socr; Hon Roll; NHS; NEDT Awd; HS Acad Schlrshp 83-87; Jrnslst.

MC CORMICK, DIANA L; Mc Guffey HS; Washington, PA; (S); 20/216; Pres 4-H; German Clb; Church Choir; Concert Band; Jazz Band; Mrchg Band; Yrbk Stf; High Hon Roll; Hon Roll; NHS.

MC CORMICK, JAMES; Columbia-Montour Area Vo-Tech HS; Bloomsburg, PA; (Y); High Hon Roll; NHS; US Marines; Gunsmith.

MC CORMICK, MARY CATHRINE; New Castle SR HS; New Castle, PA; (S); 23/236; Exploring; Band; Concert Band; Drill Tm; Mrchg Band; Stu Cncl; Im Vllybl; Hon Roll; NHS; Hmcmng Ct 84 & 85; Nrsng.

MC CORMICK, MICHAEL; Wyanesboro Area SR HS; Waynesboro, PA; (Y); Spanish Clb; Hon Roll; NHS; Prfct Atten Awd; Chef.

MC CORMICK, RANDALL; Danville SR HS; Danville, PA; (Y); 42/202; Boy Scts; Pres Church Yth Grp; Key Clb; Latin Clb; NFL; Spanish Clb; Speech Tm; Ed Lit Mag; JV Crs Cntry; JV Socr; 6th ST Spch Leag Poetry 86; Jrnlsm.

MC CORMICK, RHONDA L; Knoch JR SR HS; Renfrew, PA; (Y); 12/226; Am Leg Aux Girls St; Church Yth Grp; Exploring; German Clb; Science Clb; Drill Tm; School Musical; School Play; Pom Pon; High Hon Roll; Butler Cnty JR Miss Schlrshp 85; Wrld Affrs Inst Schlrshp 85; Keystone Girls ST Awd 85; Georgetown U; Intl Affairs.

MC CORMICK, SUSAN; Archbishop Ryan For Girls HS; Philadelphia, PA; (Y); 18/475; Church Yth Grp; JA; Science Clb; Service Clb; Lit Mag; High Hon Roll; NHS; Penn ST U; Food Sci.

MC COSKEY, DENISE E; Norristown Area HS; Norristown, PA; (S); 1/450; VP Trs Intnl Clb; Band; School Play; Ed Lit Mag; JV Fld Hcky; Kiwanis Awd; NHS; Ntl Merit SF; Val; Clssrm For Yng Amer Wash DC 86; 3yrs Math In 2 Yrs 82-83; Social Studies.

MC COSKEY, SUZANNE; Norristown Area HS; Norristown, PA; (S); 2/450; FCA; VP Intnl Clb; Orch; Yrbk Stf; Var Fld Hcky; Sftbl; NHS; Ntl Merit Ltr; Schlrshp Exch Stu Germany 85-86; GE Town Mtng Of Tomorrow 85; Frgn Svc.

MC COURT, CHRISTINE; Archbishop Ryan For Girls; Philadelphia, PA; (Y); 10/475; Office Aide; OEA; High Hon Roll; Cmltv Frst Hnrs 86; Excllnc Rlgn III 85; Excllnc Frnch I & II 83-84; Scrtrl Wrk.

MC COURY, MISSY; Spring Grove Area SR HS; Thomasville, PA; (Y); #36 In Class; Church Yth Grp; Varsity Clb; Orch; School Musical; Stu Cncl; Cheerleading; High Hon Roll; NHS; Captain Of Majorette Swngflg Sqd 85; 14 Yrs Of Dance Instruc 72-86; PA ST U; Comp Sci.

MC COWAN, DEBBIE; Warwick HS; Lititz, PA; (Y); Nwsp Stf; Lit Mag; Var JV Tennis; Hon Roll; NHS; Schlstc Art Awd Gold Key 86; Engrng.

MC COWAN, FULLER STUART; Canon-Mc Millian HS; Eighty Four, PA; (Y); Pres Aud/Vis; Chess Clb; Latin Clb; Pres Stage Crew; Med.

MC COY, AMY JO; Ambridge Area HS; Ambridge, PA; (Y); Church Yth Grp; Cmnty Wkr; Pep Clb; Red Cross Aide; Spanish Clb; VICA; Church Choir; Off Jr Cls; High Hon Roll; Hon Roll; PA ST U; Elem Educ.

MC COY, EILEEN; Greenwood HS; Thompsontown, PA; (S); 14/62; Aud/Vis; Sec Church Yth Grp; 4-H; FTA; GAA; Varsity Clb; Color Guard; Mrchg Band; Nwsp Stf; Bsktbl; Lock Heaven; Tchng.

MC COY, HELEN LE ANN; Hopewell HS; Aliquippa, PA; (Y); 61/295; Drama Clb; French Clb; Band; School Play; Ed Nwsp Ed-Chief; Ed Yrbk Ed-Chief; High Hon Roll; Voice Dem Awd; Church Yth Grp; Eugene Morris Memrl Schlrshp 86; IN U Of PA; Jrnlsm.

MC COY, KEVIN; Frankford HS; Philadelphia, PA; (Y); Boys Clb Am; Varsity Clb; Var Bsktbl; Var Capt Ftbl; Var Trk; Var Wt Lftg; All Pblc Ftbl All Prpos Bck 85-86; Lead Cty Tchdwns & Pnts Scrd 85-86.

MC COY, KIMBERLEE; St Marys Area HS; Kersey, PA; (Y); 38/296; Sec Church Yth Grp; Library Aide; Concert Band; Jazz Band; Mrchg Band; Orch; Pep Band; Stage Crew; Hon Roll; NHS; JR IU No 9 Band 84; SR IU No 9 Band 86; Comp Sci.

MC COY, LISA; Strong Vincent HS; Erie, PA; (Y); 25/164; French Clb; Spanish Clb; Chorus; IN U Bloomington; Engrng.

MC COY, LORI; Greenwood HS; Thompsontown, PA; (S); 10/62; Trs Church Yth Grp; Varsity Clb; Color Guard; Nwsp Rptr; Rep Frsh Cls; Stu Cncl; Bsktbl; Fld Hcky; Sftbl; Hon Roll; Lock Haven; Socl Wrk.

MC COY, MARGO; Oil City HS; Franklin, PA; (Y); 21/231; Cmnty Wkr; Office Aide; Teachers Aide; Yrbk Phtg; Stu Cncl; Hon Roll; NHS; Hosp Aide; Wrstlng; Prncpls List 85-86; Edinboro U Smmr Acad 83-84; Vol For Spec Olympcs & Easter Seal Soc Prog 85-86; Fur Dsgnr.

MC COY, MARY; Grove City Area SR HS; Slippery Rock, PA; (Y); 42/154; Church Yth Grp; Key Clb; Concert Band; Mrchg Band; Var Powder Puff Ftbl; Stat Vllybl; High Hon Roll; Kiwanis Awd; AFS; FBLA; Nicholas B Ottaway Schlrshp; Slippery Rock U; Socl Wk.

MC COY, RHONDA; Highesville HS; Hughesville, PA; (Y); 14/130; Drama Clb; Key Clb; Library Aide; Teachers Aide; Mrchg Band; High Hon Roll; Hon Roll; 5th Pl Hon Mntn Wacc Symposium For Bus Law 86; Millersville; Early Chldhd Ed.

MC COY, ROB; Kiski Area HS; Leechburg, PA; (Y); Key Clb; Keywanettes; VP Frsh Cls; Capt Golf; Hon Roll; Slippery Rock U; Econ.

MC COY, TINA; Greencastle-Antrim HS; Greencastle, PA; (Y); 12/187; Sec Trs Church Yth Grp; Pres Acpl Chr; Chorus; School Musical; Pres Soph Cls; Elks Awd; High Hon Roll; NHS; Drama Clb; JR Womens Club Schlrshp 86; Shippensburg U; Bus Mngmnt.

MC COY, WALTER; Tunkhanock HS; Tunkhannock, PA; (S); Letterman Clb; Spanish Clb; Bsbl; Ftbl; Wt Lftg; Hon Roll; Comp.

MC CRABB, KELLY; Muhlenberg HS; Laureldale, PA; (Y); Science Clb; School Play; Cheerleading; Mgr(s); Trk; NHS; Vet.

MC CRACKEN, ALEX; Bishop Kenrick HS; Pottstown, PA; (Y); 52/313; Computer Clb; Mathletes; Hon Roll; Archt Lndscpng.

MC CRACKEN, ANDREA; Commodore Perry HS; Hadley, PA; (Y); FTA; Office Aide; Chorus; School Play; Stu Cncl; Stat Bsbl; Var Capt Cheerleading; Capt Twrlr; Hon Roll; NCA All Amer Chrldr 85; Slippery Rock; Music.

MC CRACKEN, CINDY; Curwensville Area HS; Mahaffey, PA; (Y); 72/107; DECA; Chorus.

MC CRACKEN, LYNN; Knoch HS; Sarver, PA; (Y); Drama Clb; Band; Drill Tm; Mrchg Band; Orch; Pep Band; School Musical; Stage Crew; High Hon Roll; NHS; Psych.

MC CRACKEN, PATRICK; Greensburg Salem SR HS; Greensburg, PA; (Y); 17/302; French Clb; Math Tm; Var L Crs Cntry; Var L Trk; French Hon Soc; High Hon Roll; NHS; Pres Schlr; Tutoring Cert 85-86; MVP Underclsmn Awd 84-85; Natl Athl Schlrshp Soc Cert 86; IN U; Comp Sci.

MC CRACKEN, TIMOTHY; West Chester East HS; West Chester, PA; (Y); 70/384; Cmnty Wkr; JA; SADD; Acpl Chr; Church Choir; School Musical; School Play; Off Sr Cls; Hon Roll; Boy Scts; St Josephs U; Comp Sci.

MC CRAY, CURTIS; Coatesville Area HS; Coatesville, PA; (Y); 138/542; FBLA; Varsity Clb; Capt Var Crs Cntry; Capt Var Trk; Cit Awd; Hon Roll; Rotary Awd; St Josephs U Athltc Grant Schlrshp 86-87; St Josephs U; Bus Admin.

MC CRAY, DARREN; Corry Area HS; Corry, PA; (S); VP 4-H; Pres Ski Clb; VICA; Outstndng Stu Awd Auto Mech 84-85 & 85-86; Dist VICA Comptn 3rd Pl 85; OH Diesel Tech Inst; Auto Mech.

MC CRAY, DENISE; Corry Area HS; Corry, PA; (S); Art Clb; Civic Clb; Drama Clb; Flag Corp.

MC CRAY, LAURA; Corry Area HS; Elgin, PA; (Y); Concert Band; Mrchg Band; High Hon Roll; Gannon U; Math.

MC CRAY, MICHAEL L; Central HS; Philadelphia, PA; (Y); 65/238; Pres Church Yth Grp; Math Tm; Chorus; Pres Church Choir; Nwsp Rptr; Lit Mag; Var Crs Cntry; Var Trk; Ntl Merit SF; Rep Frsh Cls; Natl Achvt Semi Fin 85-86; Comp Sci.

MC CREA, BRIDGET; Valley View HS; Peckville, PA; (Y); 23/200; French Clb; Library Aide; Chorus; Yrbk Stf; JV Swmmng; Im Vllybl; Hon Roll; Hnrble Mntn Natl Frnch Cntst 85 & 86; Commun.

MC CREA, MICHAEL; North Hills HS; Pittsburgh, PA; (S); Church Yth Grp; Key Clb; Var Bsbl; Var Bsktbl; High Hon Roll; Hon Roll; NHS; Bus.

MC CREADIE, THOMAS; Clearfield Area SR HS; Clearfield, PA; (Y); French Clb; Key Clb; Rep Stu Cncl; High Hon Roll; Hon Roll; Presdntl Acadmc Ftns Awd 86; Penn ST U; Comp Sci.

MC CREADY, JAMES T P; Panther Valley HS; Summit Hill, PA; (Y); Am Leg Boys St; Boy Scts; Church Yth Grp; Drama Clb; Ski Clb; Band; Concert Band; Mrchg Band; Eagl Sct 85; Bus Adm.

MC CREARY, JOE; Windber Area HS; Windber, PA; (S); 51/113; Pres VP Band; Chorus; Concert Band; Jazz Band; Mrchg Band; Pep Band; School Play; Directors Awd 82; IN U Of PA; Music Ed.

MC CREESH, SHAWN; Archbishop Ryan High School For Boys; Phiadelphia, PA; (Y); 125/429; Ftbl; Hon Roll; Awd Prsnl Typg 86; Mech Engnr.

MC CRORY, DAWN; Blairsville SR HS; Blairsville, PA; (Y); 7/137; Band; Concert Band; Mrchg Band; School Musical; Var Cheerleading; High Hon Roll; NHS; Sec Educ.

MC CUCH, THOMAS A; Devon Prep; Gulph Mills, PA; (Y); 7/35; Boy Scts; Math Tm; Yrbk Ed-Chief; Var Socr; Hon Roll; NHS; Egl Sct 85; PA ST; Engrng.

MC CUE, TERRY; Penn Hills SR HS; Pittsburgh, PA; (Y); 44/616; Church Yth Grp; Computer Clb; German Clb; Letterman Clb; Varsity Clb; L Var Wrstlng; High Hon Roll; Vrsty Athltc Awds 86; Grove City Coll; Chem Engrng.

MC CUEN, SCOTT; Mc Guffey HS; Avella, PA; (S); 11/212; French Clb; Varsity Clb; Pres Soph Cls; Pres Jr Cls; Rep Stu Cncl; Var L Ftbl; Var L Trk; Var Wt Lftg; High Hon Roll; NHS.

MC CULLEN, MAUREEN; Huntingdon Area HS; Huntingdon, PA; (Y); 31/242; Am Leg Aux Girls St; Trs Church Yth Grp; Key Clb; SADD; Yrbk Stf; Sec Soph Cls; Var L Fld Hcky; Var L Trk; Hon Roll; Juniata; Math.

MC CULLOUGH, BETH; Trinity HS; Washington, PA; (Y); 4/370; Am Leg Aux Girls St; Key Clb; Math Tm; Pep Clb; High Hon Roll; NHS; Ntl Merit Ltr; Ntl Merit Ltr; Intl Rltns.

MC CULLOUGH, BOBBIE; Milton SR HS; Milton, PA; (Y); 76/202; Central Penn Bus Schl; Lgl Sec.

MC CULLOUGH, DAVID; Mercer Area HS; Mercer, PA; (Y); 32/120; Pres 4-H; Trs FFA; VICA; Capt Wrstlng; Str Grnhnd 83; Mst Imprvd Wrstlr 85; Agrcltr.

MC CULLOUGH, DOUGLAS; Belle Vernon Area HS; Belle Vernon, PA; (Y); SADD; Band; Concert Band; Mrchg Band; Var L Bsbl; Var L Bsktbl; Im L Ftbl; High Hon Roll; Hon Roll; NHS; Pres Mdcl Interest Club 86-87; 1st Pl Family Life Esy Contst 83; Pres Phy Fitness Awd 83; Pharmacy.

MC CULLOUGH, KELLY; Bishop Shanahan HS; W Chester, PA; (Y); 22/218; Dance Clb; Service Clb; Ski Clb; School Musical; Variety Show; JV Var Cheerleading; Vllybl; Hon Roll; Drexel U; Fshn Mrchndsg.

MC CULLOUGH, LORI; Deer Lakes JR SR HS; Gibsonia, PA; (Y); 1/170; Church Yth Grp; Hosp Aide; Band; Flag Corp; School Musical; Nwsp Stf; Yrbk Stf; High Hon Roll; Pres NHS; U Pittsburgh; Prelaw.

MC CULLOUGH, MARK; Union Area HS; New Castle, PA; (Y); Church Yth Grp; French Clb; Office Aide; Var L Ftbl; Var L Trk; High Hon Roll; Hon Roll; Engrg.

MC CULLOUGH, ROBERT W; Northeast Catholic HS; Philadelphia, PA; (Y); 15/369; Stage Crew; High Hon Roll; NHS; Aerosp Engrng.

MC CULLOUGH, TOM; Lanape AVTS; Worthington, PA; (Y); Boy Scts; VICA; Band; Concert Band; Mrchg Band; Socr; Hon Roll; Comp Prgrmg.

MC CULLOUGH, TRISHA; Christian School Of York; York, PA; (S); Church Yth Grp; Chorus; Bsktbl; Sftbl; Hon Roll; NHS; Ntl Merit Schol; Vrsty Bsktbl & Sftbl Achvt Awds 83-85; Accntng.

MC CULLUM, CHRIS; Elizabeth Forward HS; Elizabeth, PA; (Y); Church Yth Grp; Spanish Clb; Teachers Aide; Rep Jr Cls; Rep Sr Cls; Var Cheerleading; Var Swmmng; High Hon Roll; Hon Roll; NHS; PA ST; Nutrition.

MC CUNE, JAMES; Peters Township HS; Venetia, PA; (Y); Nwsp Stf; Lit Mag; USMC; Spec Forces.

MC CURDY, KATHY; Penn Hills SR HS; Verona, PA; (Y); Debate Tm; French Clb; Library Aide; Political Wkr; Ski Clb; High Hon Roll; Hon Roll; Ntl Merit SF; Rotary Awd; Best Spkr Debt Tm 84.

MC CUTCHEON, AMY; Cornell Education Center; Coraopolis, PA; (Y); 12/70; Computer Clb; French Clb; Science Clb; Concert Band; Mrchg Band; Yrbk Bus Mgr; Jr Cls; High Hon Roll; Hon Roll; NHS; Bond Essay Hist 86; 2nd Pl Patricia Cullen Memorl Spllng Bee 83-84; Bus.

MC CUTCHEON, LINDA; Riverview HS; Oakmont, PA; (Y); 20/95; Drama Clb; Trs Key Clb; Concert Band; Mrchg Band; School Play; High Hon Roll; Hon Roll; NHS; Prfct Atten Awd; Alleghny Vly Hnrs Band 84-87; PMEA Dist I Hnrs Band 83-86; PMEA Rgn I Hnrs Band Fest 86-87; Penn ST; Soclgy.

MC DADE, CRAIG WILLIAM; Elk County Christian HS; Johnsonburg, PA; (Y); 18/96; Var L Ftbl; High Hon Roll; NHS; NEDT Awd; Pres Schlr; Chess Clb; JA; Library Aide; JV Bsktbl; JV Var Timer; Fr Thomas Curley Achvt Awd 82; A C Kriegael Schlr Awd 82; Am Leg Essay Awd 82; U Pittsburgh; Phrmcy.

MC DADE, EILEEN; Scranton Prep; Clarks Summit, PA; (Y); Church Yth Grp; Drama Clb; Exploring; School Musical; School Play; Cheerleading; Polit Sci.

MC DADE, KAREN; Penn Hills SR HS; Verona, PA; (Y); German Clb; Acpl Chr; Swing Chorus; Yrbk Stf; Stat Ice Hcky; High Hon Roll; Gannon U; Comm.

MC DAID, PATRICK; Archbishop Wood Boys HS; Warminster, PA; (Y); 7/282; Yrbk Stf; Rep Jr Cls; Bsbl; Socr; Hon Roll; Physcl Thrpy.

MC DANIEL, JULIE; Germantown HS; Philadelphia, PA; (Y); Computer Clb; Office Aide; Hon Roll; NHS; Awd-City Wide Typng Cntst-3rd Pl 86; Bus Adm.

MC DANIEL, MARGARET; Upper Dublin HS; Ambler, PA; (Y); VICA; Church Choir; Bsktbl; Sftbl; High Hon Roll; UICA Dist II Ldrshp Comptns 2nd Pl 85; Wmn In Hstry Postr Cntst Fnlst 86; Stu Of Wk 86; Commrcl Art.

MC DEAVITT, STACY; Slippery Rock Area HS; Slippery Rock, PA; (Y); Pres 4-H; Pep Clb; SADD; Chorus; High Hon Roll; Hon Roll; NHS; Teachers Aide; Butler CC.

MC DERMOTT, BRIGID E; Churchill HS; Pittsburgh, PA; (Y); 1/219; Q&S; Mrchg Band; Mgr Stage Crew; Yrbk Ed-Chief; Pres Sec Stu Cncl; Var L Swmmng; High Hon Roll; Ntl Merit SF; Math Tm; Ski Clb; Rensselaer Mth & Sci Awd; Westinghouse Sci Hnrs Inst.

MC DERMOTT, KATHRYN A; Freedom HS; Bethlehem, PA; (Y); 1/416; Model UN; Red Cross Aide; Science Clb; Chorus; Orch; Var JV Fld Hcky; NHS; Ntl Merit SF; Val; Church Yth Grp; Oboist Yng Peoples Phlhrmnc Of Lehigh Vly 85-86; Lehigh U; Engl.

MC DERMOTT, MARIANN; Technical HS; Scranton, PA; (S); 3/270; FBLA; Q&S; Pres Chorus; Nwsp Ed-Chief; Sec Sr Cls; Hon Roll; NHS; Bus Adm.

MC DERMOTT, NICOLE; Marple Newtown HS; Newtown Square, PA; (Y); Dance Clb; Drama Clb; Ski Clb; School Musical; Variety Show; Yrbk Stf; Var Cheerleading; Var Swmmng; High Hon Roll; Jr NHS; Theater.

MC DERMOTT, STEPHANIE; St Maria Goretti HS; Philadelphia, PA; (Y); 36/426; Church Yth Grp; Math Clb; Spanish Clb; High Hon Roll; Prfct Atten Awd; Pres Schlr; Teamsters Local 830 Schlrshp $8000 86; Emple U; Comm.

MC DEVITT, AMY; Bishop Kenrick HS; Norristown, PA; (Y); #7 In Class; Cmnty Wkr; Ski Clb; Hon Roll; NHS; Mathletes; Science Clb; Spanish Clb; School Musical.

MC DEVITT, KARA; St Basil Acad; Philadelphia, PA; (Y); 7/96; German Clb; Orch; Nwsp Sprt Ed; Var Bsktbl; Hon Roll; NEDT Awd; Opt Clb Awd; VFW Awd; Artisans Coll Scholar Awd 86; U DE; Physics.

MC DEVITT, TODD; Lincoln HS; Ellwood City, PA; (Y); 9/162; Pres Computer Clb; Band; Concert Band; Jazz Band; Mrchg Band; Nwsp Ed-Chief; Stu Cncl; Hon Roll; Prfct Atten Awd; NHS; PA Free Enterprise Wk 86.

MC DIVITT, MONA; Punxsutawney Area HS; Punxsutawney, PA; (Y); #78 In Class; Church Yth Grp; FBLA; GAA; Variety Show; Pres Soph Cls; Sec Jr Cls; Cheerleading; Mary Ann Irving Schlrshp 86; Vrty Shw Co Dir 86; Ftbl Prncs 86; IN U PA; Elem Educ.

MC DONALD, ANGELA; Laurel Valley HS; Seward, PA; (Y); 22/87; Varsity Clb; Drill Tm; Bsktbl; Sftbl; Hon Roll; IN U Of PA; Law.

MC DONALD III, CHARLY; Strath Haven HS; Wallingford, PA; (Y); Camera Clb; PAVAS; Spanish Clb; Stage Crew; Nwsp Rptr; Yrbk Sprt Ed; Rep Stu Cncl; Var Bsbl; Var Capt Socr; Hon Roll; Eastern PA Yth Sccr Assoc Select Tm 85; Keystone ST Sccr Select Tm 85 & 86; Communications.

MC DONALD, COLLEEN; Lancaster Catholic HS; Lancaster, PA; (Y); Yrbk Stf; Sec Frsh Cls; Sec Soph Cls; Pres Jr Cls; Rep Sr Cls; Stu Cncl; JV Capt Bsktbl; Var Capt Fld Hcky; Cmmnctns.

MC DONALD, HEATHER; New Brighton HS; New Brighton, PA; (Y); 16/165; Band; Concert Band; Jazz Band; Mrchg Band; School Play; Nwsp Rptr; Hon Roll; Nwsp Stf; Air Frce ROTC Schlrshp 86; Westmnstr Hnrs Band 84-86; Distrct V & Regn I Band 84-86; U Of Pittsbrgh; Comp Sci.

MC DONALD, JEROME; Conneaut Lake HS; Conneaut Lake, PA; (Y); 1/85; Rep Stu Cncl; Var Capt Bsktbl; Var Ftbl; NHS; Ntl Merit SF; Val; VFW Awd; SADD; L Trk; Im Vllybl; Gannon U Engrng Awd 86; Acad Chllng 1st Pl 85-86; JR Engrng Tech Soc 1st Pl Chmstry 86; Ansthslgy.

MC DONALD, JOANNE; Cardinal Brennan HS; Girardville, PA; (Y); 5/54; Off Sr Cls; NHS; Spanish Clb; School Play; Var Capt Bsktbl; Stat Ftbl; Im Vllybl; Hon Roll; Spanish NHS.

MC DONALD, KAY ANNE; Cardinal Brennan HS; Girardville, PA; (Y); 7/48; Church Yth Grp; Trs Sr Cls; Capt Bsktbl; High Hon Roll; NHS; Opt Clb Awd; Spanish NHS; Hosp Aide; Spanish Clb; Off Frsh Cls; Knights Columbus Al-Star Tm Bsktbl 84; Stu Mth 86; Hghst Avg Bio Awd 86; Beaver Coll; Phys Thrpy.

MC DONALD, KIMBERLY ANN; Interboro SR HS; Prospect Park, PA; (Y); JCL; Latin Clb; SADD; VICA; Antonelli; Photo.

MC DONALD, LES; Highlands HS; Tarentum, PA; (Y); Boys Clb Am; Church Yth Grp; Church Choir; JV Bsbl; JV Var Ftbl; Var Trk; JV Var Wt Lftg; JV Wrstlng; Prfct Atten Awd; WPIAL All Star Team 85; -Spial All Conference Team 85; Chld Psych.

MC DONALD, MARIA; Purchase Line HS; Cherry Tree, PA; (Y); 15/109; Pres Sec 4-H; Sec Spanish Clb; SADD; Chorus; Color Guard; Concert Band; 4-H Awd; Hon Roll; Acadm All Am Awd 84-86; Natl Ldrshp & Svc Awd 85; IUP; Education.

MC DONALD, RICHARD; Perry Traditional Acad; Pittsburgh, PA; (Y); 17/148; Debate Tm; Drama Clb; Red Cross Aide; School Play; Rep Stu Cncl; Hon Roll; Rotary Awd; U Of Pittsburgh; Med.

MC DONALD, TAMMY; Belle Vernon Area HS; Belle Vernon, PA; (Y); Art Clb; Dance Clb; Pep Clb; Band; Pep Band; Stage Crew; Yrbk Ed-Chief; Yrbk Phtg; Powder Puff Ftbl; Hon Roll; Semi-Fin Govrnrs Hnr Prog 85-86; U Of Pittsburgh; Pharm.

MC DONALD, TISA; Danville SR HS; Danville, PA; (Y); 54/202; Church Yth Grp; Computer Clb; Drama Clb; Exploring; French Clb; Hosp Aide; SADD; Chorus; School Musical; School Play.

MC DONALD, WILLIAM; Cardinal Brennan HS; Girardville, PA; (Y); 10/50; Science Clb; Rep Frsh Cls; Var Bsbl; JV Bsktbl; Coach Actv; Hon Roll; Hnr Roll; Cert Of Rcgntn Alg II With Trig 85-8; Awd Of Excllnc Penta Thalon Enrgy Cntst 85-86.

MC DONNELL, ERIN; Moravian Acad; Allentown, PA; (Y); Church Yth Grp; Ski Clb; Acpl Chr; Chorus; School Play; Variety Show; Rep Stu Cncl; JV Fld Hcky; Hon Roll; Opt Clb Awd; Fld Hcky Coach Awd 85; Intl Fin.

MC DONNELL, KELLY; St Basil Acad; Philadelphia, PA; (S); Sec Church Yth Grp; VP GAA; Spanish Clb; Var Fld Hcky; Service Clb; Lit Mag; Im Vllybl; Hon Roll; Ntl Schlstc Wrtng Awd 84; Drama.

MC DONNELL, PATRICK J; State College Area SR HS; State College, PA; (Y); 11/550; Debate Tm; Pres Model UN; NFL; Band; Jazz Band; Rep Soph Cls; Im Socr; Hon Roll; Rotary Awd; Math Clb; Engrng.

MC DONNELL, STEPHEN; Eastern Montgomery Co Vo-Tech; Cheltenham, PA; (Y); Carpntr.

MC DONNELL, WILLIAM; St Josephs Prep Schl; Drexel Hill, PA; (Y); 24/236; Im Bsktbl; Im Ftbl; Capt Swmmng; All Catholic Swmmr,Rower 86; Prep Schlr; Engrng.

MC DONOUGH, ANDREA; Bishop Hannan HS; Scranton, PA; (Y); 11/121; Orch; Yrbk Stf; JV Bsktbl; JV Var Crs Cntry; High Hon Roll; NHS; Slvr Mdl Ntl Ltn Exam 10; Law.

MC DONOUGH, COLLEEN; Upper Darby HS; Aldan, PA; (Y); 2/620; Yrbk Stf; Var Bsktbl; Var Fld Hcky; Var Lcrss; High Hon Roll; NHS; Ntl Merit Ltr; Soc Wmn Engrs Cert Merit 86; Math.

MC DONOUGH, LINDA; Cardinal O Hara HS; Broomall, PA; (Y); Church Yth Grp; JA; Pres Latin Clb; Flag Corp; Nwsp Stf; Yrbk Stf; Lit Mag; Stu Cncl; Hon Roll; Office Aide; Cert Of Apprctn Natl Assn Of Stu Cncls 84; Cert Of Achvt Yth & Amer Pol Systm Semnr 86; Intl Law.

MC DONOUGH, SANDRA; Jenkintown HS; Jenkintown, PA; (S); Library Aide; Acpl Chr; Stage Crew; Yrbk Stf; VP Soph Cls; Pres Jr Cls; Capt Tennis; Hon Roll; NHS; Spanish NHS; Schlrshp Art Cls Moore Coll Art 85; Schlrshp Comp Trip Japan 85; Phila Coll Art; Cmmrcl Art.

MC DOWELL, ARLEEN; St Maria Goretti HS; Philadelphia, PA; (Y); Sec Church Yth Grp; Spanish Clb; Orch; School Musical; Stage Crew; Rep Stu Cncl; Bsktbl; Sftbl; Westchester U; Cmmnctns.

MC DUFFIE, SONYA A; Bristol JR SR HS; Bristol, PA; (Y); Drama Clb; ROTC; Spanish Clb; Capt Varsity Clb; Sec Soph Cls; Capt Cheerleading; :Med Tchnlgy.

MC DYRE, CULLEN; Central Bucks High School East; Furlong, PA; (Y); Letterman Clb; Var Capt Bsbl; Hon Roll; Church Yth Grp; Ski Clb; Spanish Clb; Nwsp Phtg; VP Frsh Cls; Var Ftbl; Var Golf; Bux-Mnt Lg Bsbl Tm 86; Am Lgn Bdy Mly Cp Bsbl All Str Tm 86; Nclr Engr.

MC ELHANEY, CHERYL; Connellsville Area SR HS; S Connellsville, PA; (Y); Hosp Aide; Drm Mjr(t); Flag Corp; Symp Band; French Hon Soc; High Hon Roll; NHS; Library Aide; Science Clb; Band; Duquesne U Schlrs Awd 86-87; Lynchburg Smmr Schlr 85; Tri Hi Y Schlrshp Awd 86; Duquesne U; Phrmcy.

MC ELHANEY, MELANIE; Connellsville SR HS; So Connellsville, PA; (Y); Hosp Aide; Science Clb; Capt Flag Corp; School Play; Symp Band; French Hon Soc; High Hon Roll; NHS; BPW Girl Of Yr Awd 86; PMEA Hnrs Bnd 83; Lynchburg Smmr Schlrs Prog 85; U Pittsburgh; Engrng.

MC ELHATTAN, TAMMY; Quigley HS; Beaver, PA; (Y); 48/100; Spanish Clb; JV Sftbl; High Hon Roll; Hon Roll; Personal Exc Svc SOS 85-86; Cartez W Peters Jr Typng,Profcncy Cert 85-86; Theolgy.

MC ELROY, ERIC; Wilson Area HS; Easton, PA; (S); 5/150; Drama Clb; Model UN; Ski Clb; School Play; Crs Cntry; Trk; High Hon Roll; Hon Roll; Jr NHS; NHS; Juniata; Chem.

MC ELROY, JASON; Strath Haven HS; Woodlyn, PA; (Y); Boy Scts; French Clb; JA; Ski Clb; Trk; Bausch & Lomb Sci Awd; Hon Roll; Ntl Merit Ltr; Bio-Engr.

MC ELWAIN, DEAN; Lincoln HS; Fombell, PA; (Y); #40 In Class; Church Yth Grp; VP Computer Clb; German Clb; Band; Stage Crew; Nwsp Bus Mgr; Engrng.

MC ELWAIN, PATRICIA; Sugar Valley HS; Loganton, PA; (S); 2/17; Model UN; Pres Spanish Clb; Trs Band; Sec Sr Cls; Pres Stu Cncl; Co-Capt L Cheerleading; Var Capt Gym; High Hon Roll; Lions Club Stu Of Mnth 85; Miss Christmas Seal Rep 85; Woodmans Hstry Awd 82; Sci-Marine Bio.

MC ELWEE, WENDY; Northern SR HS; Dillsburg, PA; (Y); 30/240; Drama Clb; French Clb; FBLA; NFL; Speech Tm; Thesps; School Play; Hon Roll; Sally Grdrss Mem Schlrshp 86; 4th Pl ST Job Dscrptn Mnl FBLA 86; Trvl.

MC EVILLY, CHRISTOPHER; Pennsbury HS; Yardley, PA; (Y); 147/729; Ski Clb; Spanish Clb; SADD; Tennis; Hon Roll; Achvt Ecnmcs & Amer Govt & Major Authrs 84-86; PA ST U; Pre-Law.

MC EWEN, HEIDI; Canon-Mc Millan HS; Eighty Four, PA; (Y); 64/371; French Clb; Office Aide; Varsity Clb; Nwsp Stf; Cheerleading; High Hon Roll; CA U Of PA; Secdry Bio Tchr.

MC FADDEN, CHAS; Waynesboro SR HS; Waynesboro, PA; (Y); Chorus; Church Choir; School Play; Stage Crew; Swing Chorus; Stat Bsktbl; Var Golf; Hon Roll; Penn ST U; Elec Engrng.

MC FADDEN, JAMES A; Penns Valley Area HS; Spring Mills, PA; (Y); Boy Scts; Chess Clb; Church Yth Grp; Computer Clb; Nwsp Rptr; Hon Roll; NHS; Early Enrllmnt Penn ST U 85; HRB Sngr Smmr Intrn 85; Penn ST U; Elec/Comp Engrng.

MC FADDEN, JOHN; Archbishop John Carroll HS; Ardmore, PA; (Y); 29/162; Computer Clb; Var Bsbl; Var Socr; Cit Awd; Hon Roll; Am Leg Boys St; Varsity Clb; High Hon Roll; NHS; Drexel; Engrng.

MC FADDEN, JULIE; Bishop Shanahan HS; West Chester, PA; (Y); 33/275; Debate Tm; GAA; Hosp Aide; Teachers Aide; Bsktbl; Crs Cntry; Trk; Hon Roll; NHS; PA ST U; Hlth.

MC FADDEN, KENNETH J; Northeast Catholic HS; Philadelphia, PA; (S); 10/400; Aud/Vis; Radio Clb; Teachers Aide; Thesps; Nwsp Rptr; Yrbk Bus Mgr; Var Stu Cncl; Crs Cntry; Trk; Hon Roll; Drexel U; Chem Engrng.

MC FADDEN, MICHELE; Bethel Park HS; Bethel Park, PA; (Y); Girl Scts; JA; Band; Mrchg Band; Symp Band; Yrbk Stf; JV Vllybl; NHS; Pres Schlr; U SC; Intl Bus.

MC FADDEN, ROBERT; Meyers HS; Wilkes Barre, PA; (Y); 17/160; Church Yth Grp; Letterman Clb; Chorus; Var L Crs Cntry; Var L Trk; L Wrstlng; Jr NHS; NHS; Spanish NHS; Wrstlng 1st Dist, 1st Rgnls, 3rd ST 86.

MC FADDEN, SCOTT; Grove City HS; Grove City, PA; (Y); 62/195; Drama Clb; Ski Clb; Band; Chorus; School Musical; School Play; Stage Crew; Swing Chorus; Ftbl; Trk; Hnrs Chorus 85; Clarion U; Radio-Tv Brdcstng.

MC FADDIN, JILL; Charleroi Area JR SR HS; Charleroi, PA; (Y); Ski Clb; Pres SADD; Stu Cncl; Vllybl; High Hon Roll; Hon Roll.

MC FALL, CHERYL; Canton Area JR SR HS; Grover, PA; (Y); 9/127; AFS; French Clb; Chorus; Nwsp Rptr; Nwsp Sprt Ed; Nwsp Stf; Yrbk Phtg; Yrbk Stf; Stat DECA; Hon Roll; Williamsport Schl Of Commerce.

MC FARLAND, AMY; Hempfield Area SR HS; Greensburg, PA; (Y); 15/715; AFS; Spanish Clb; Orch; Hon Roll; Jr NHS; NHS; Ntl Merit Ltr; Spanish NHS; 3rd Pl Spn Dramatc Presntatn U Pittsburgh 86; Pre-Med.

MC FARLAND, ANN MARIE; Marian Catholic HS; Mahanoy City, PA; (Y); 28/123; Church Yth Grp; Dance Clb; Pep Clb; Ski Clb; SADD; Band; School Play; Stage Crew; Yrbk Stf; Rep Stu Cncl; Acctg Awd Hghst Ovrll Avg 84-85; Bus Adm.

MC FARLAND, CHERYL; Waynesburg Central HS; Mt Morris, PA; (Y); Church Yth Grp; Natl Beta Clb; Office Aide; Ski Clb; Pres Spanish Clb; Church Choir; VP Soph Cls; Pres Stu Cncl; Stat Bsbl; Var Bsktbl; Penn ST U; Bus Admn.

MC FARLAND, JOHN; Swissvale HS; Pittsburgh, PA; (Y); 32/205; Boy Scts; Computer Clb; German Clb; Math Tm; Band; Mrchg Band; School Musical; School Play; Stage Crew; Pres Sr Cls; Acctng.

MC FARLAND, SEAN; Bishop Hannan HS; Old Forge, PA; (Y); 31/128; Boy Scts; Pres Computer Clb; Nwsp Stf; Hon Roll; NHS; Ntl Merit Ltr; Pres Schlr; Top Stu Comp Sci Awd 86; Pres Phys Ftnss Awd 86; U Of Scranton; Comp Sci.

MC FARLAND, WENDY; Downingtown SR HS; Downingtown, PA; (Y); French Clb; DAR Awd; High Hon Roll; Hon Roll; Ntl Merit Ltr; NEDT Awd; Sclgy.

MC FARLANE, CHRISTINE; Deleware Valley HS; Dingmans Ferry, PA; (Y); Church Yth Grp; Cmnty Wkr; Hosp Aide; VP Spanish Clb; Hon Roll; Engl/Spnsh.

MC FEATERS, SCOTT; Northern Lebanon HS; Annville, PA; (Y); 11/179; Church Yth Grp; Cmnty Wkr; Var Bsbl; Var Golf; Bausch & Lomb Sci Awd; Hon Roll; NHS; Ki-Wanis Clb Schlrshp 86; SICO Schlrhsp 86; Millersville U; Earth Sci.

MC FEELY, EMILIE; Grove City HS; Grove City, PA; (Y); 7/195; Pres Girl Scts; Library Aide; Band; Concert Band; Mrchg Band; Yrbk Sprt Ed; Cheerleading; Powder Puff Ftbl; High Hon Roll; NHS; Hugh O Brian Yuth Fdtn Sem 85; Gannon U; Pre Med.

MC FEELY, JULIA; Shippensburg Area SR HS; Shippensburg, PA; (Y); 7/221; Pres Leo Clb; Band; Chorus; Concert Band; Mrchg Band; School Musical; NHS; Rep Rotary Clb Ldrshp Conf 85; Dickerson Coll Summr Scholar 85; U Pittsburgh; Indstrl Engr.

MC FILLIN, KATHY; Bishop Conwell HS; Bensalem, PA; (Y); 19/254; FNA; Office Aide; Stage Crew; Yrbk Rptr; Yrbk Stf; Rep Frsh Cls; Swmmng; French Hon Soc; Hon Roll; NHS; Prtl Tuitn Holy Fmly Coll Nrsng Prog 85-86; Louise M Kutney RN Schlrshp 85-86; Holy Family Coll; Nrsng.

MC GARRIGLE, ALICE; St Maria Goretti HS; Philadelphia, PA; (Y); 90/390; JV Bsktbl; Hon Roll; Nrsng.

MC GARRY, DANIEL; Hazleton SR HS; Hazleton, PA; (Y); Exploring; Pep Clb; Rptr Stu Cncl; Var Bsbl; Var L Cheerleading; Var Ftbl; Var L Trk; PA ST; Bio.

MC GARRY, EUGENE; Seranton Prep; Moosic, PA; (Y); 7/192; Spanish Clb; Lit Mag; High Hon Roll; Ntl Greek Examntn Hghst Hnr & Amer Clscl Lgu 86; Pre-Med.

MC GARRY, KATHLEEN; Pittston Area SR HS; Inkerman, PA; (Y); 32/350; Drama Clb; French Clb; Key Clb; Math Clb; Church Choir; Drill Tm; High Hon Roll; Hon Roll; Spch & Cmmnctn Disorders.

MC GARVEY, DOUGLAS; Punxsutawney Area SR HS; Punxsutawney, PA; (Y); Varsity Clb; Ftbl; Wt Lftg; Var Wrstlng; Edinboro U; Comp Sci.

MC GARVEY, TIMOTHY; Donegal HS; Mt Joy, PA; (Y); Ftbl; Bausch & Lomb Sci Awd; Hon Roll; NHS; Comp.

MC GARY, COLLEEN; Northern Cambria HS; Barnesboro, PA; (Y); Pres French Clb; Chorus; Church Choir; Stu Cncl; Cheerleading; French Hon Soc; High Hon Roll; Hon Roll; Pres NHS; Indiana U Of PA; Comp Sci.

MC GAUGHEY, ERIK; Freedom SR HS; Bethlehem, PA; (Y); 52/445; Church Yth Grp; Nwsp Rptr; Nwsp Stf; Cit Awd; High Hon Roll; Hon Roll; Jr NHS; Ecnmcs.

MC GEE, COLLEEN M; Bishop Kennick HS; Norristown, PA; (Y); 5/269; French Clb; Capt Crs Cntry; Capt Trk; High Hon Roll; Hon Roll; NHS; Cmnty Wkr; Bsktbl; YWCA Assoc Cntrl Montgomery Co Ralston Schlrshp Awd, Mt St Marys Coll & St Francis Trck Schlrshp 86; Mt St Marys Coll; Intl Rel.

MC GEE, DEIDRA L; Overbrook HS; Philadelphia, PA; (Y); 42/589; JA; Office Aide; Teachers Aide; Yrbk Stf; JV Var Badmtn; Prfct Atten Awd; Dr Ruth W Hayre Schrlshp Awd; U Pitts; Lbrl Arts.

MC GEE, KIM; Mc Keesport SR HS; Mckeesport, PA; (Y); 114/339; Church Yth Grp; Exploring; French Clb; Chorus; Powder Puff Ftbl; Trk; Acad.

MC GEE, KRISTY; Leechburg Area HS; Leechburg, PA; (Y); Chorus; Yrbk Stf; Var JV Bsktbl; Var JV Cheerleading; Im Vllybl; PA ST; Med Lab Tech.

MC GEE III, TIM F; Marian Catholic HS; Lehighton, PA; (Y); Cmnty Wkr; Stage Crew; Ftbl; Wt Lftg; IN Inst Tech; Comp Sci.

MC GEE, TODD; Punxsutawney Area HS; Punxsutawney, PA; (Y); 127/238; Church Yth Grp; Science Clb; Varsity Clb; Church Choir; Variety Show; Rep Soph Cls; Var Bsktbl; Var Cheerleading; Var Tennis; Stu Mnth 83; Messiah Coll; Bus Adm.

MC GEEHAN, KIM; Bishop Havey HS; Hazleton, PA; (Y); English Clb; French Clb; Intnl Clb; Ski Clb; Y-Teens; Bsktbl; Score Keeper; Sftbl; French Hon Soc; Hon Roll; Hghst GPA English II 85; Exchng Stu To France 86; Lbrl Arts.

MC GEEHAN, MICHAEL; West Hazelton HS; Hazleton, PA; (Y); 35/224; Church Yth Grp; Cmnty Wkr; Letterman Clb; Spanish Clb; SADD; Varsity Clb; Var L Bsktbl; Coach Actv; Trk; Hon Roll; Mountain Dew Plyr Of Game Awd Bsktbl 85-86; Amer Cancer Soc Cert 85-86; Vet Med.

MC GEHRIN, KELLY A; St Maria Goretti HS; Philadelphia, PA; (S); 7/402; Church Yth Grp; Cmnty Wkr; French Clb; GAA; Mathletes; Math Clb; Math Tm; JV Crs Cntry; Hon Roll; NHS; Villanova; Elec Engrng.

MC GEORGE, RANDY; West Allegheny HS; Coraopolis, PA; (Y); Nwsp Rptr; Ed Yrbk Stf; Trs Frsh Cls; Stu Cncl; JV Bsbl; Var L Golf; Hon Roll; Rtry Yth Ldrshp Awd 85-86; Westminster; Bus Admin.

MC GETTIGAN, DAVID; Council Rock HS; Holland, PA; (Y); 91/865; Church Yth Grp; Hon Roll; Prfct Atten Awd; Emply Of Mnth Awd 85; Excdg Perfrmnc Expctns Awd 86; Engrg.

MC GETTIGAN, EDWARD; Archbishop Ryan Boys HS; Philadelphia, PA; (Y); 100/429; Boy Scts.

MC GHEE, SCOTT H; Upper Moreland HS; Hatboro, PA; (Y); 133/272; Key Clb; Rep Frsh Cls; Rep Soph Cls; Rep Jr Cls; Rep Stu Cncl; JV Bsktbl; JV Socr; Hon Roll; Hstry.

MC GHEE, SHERRI; Tussey Mountain HS; Saxton, PA; (Y); AFS; Camera Clb; Pres Church Yth Grp; Ski Clb; SADD; Band; Concert Band; Mrchg Band; Rep Stu Cncl; Powder Puff Ftbl; Acdmc All Amer 86; Penn ST Altoona; Law.

MC GILL, DANIELLE; Acad Of Notre Dame De Namur; Springfield, PA; (Y); Debate Tm; Mathletes; Service Clb; Nwsp Stf; Var Socr; Var Trk; Hon Roll; Dance Clb; Fnlst Mis PA Teen Pagnt; Schlrshp Comm Svc Awds; Acad Schlrshp; Pre-Law.

MC GILL, JENNIFER; Harry S Truman HS; Levittown, PA; (Y); Off Stu Cncl; Hon Roll.

MC GILL, MARC; Rocky Grove HS; Franklin, PA; (Y); 34/92; Pres Church Yth Grp; Band; Concert Band; JV L Bsktbl; Sftbl; Hon Roll; Elctrnc Engnrng.

MC GILL, MATT; North Pocono HS; Moscow, PA; (Y); Church Yth Grp; Ski Clb; Var L Bsbl; Var Golf; High Hon Roll; Hon Roll; NHS; Amer Hrt Assn Cert Apprctn 85; Mrktng.

MC GILL, PAUL; Girard College; Philadelphia, PA; (Y); Chess Clb; Ski Clb; Cit Awd; Hon Roll; Im Badmtn; Var Bsbl; Var Crs Cntry; Im Sftbl; Var Swmmng; JV Tennis.

MC GILLIVRAY, JANICE; Hampton HS; Allison Pk, PA; (Y); Letterman Clb; Red Cross Aide; Ski Clb; Varsity Clb; Nwsp Stf; JV Sftbl; Capt Var Swmmng; High Hon Roll; Pres Schlr; IN U; Pre-Med.

MC GINLEY, JOHN; Bensalem HS; Bensalem, PA; (Y); Varsity Clb; Var Capt Ftbl; Vllybl; Wt Lftg; Hon Roll; Engrng.

MC GINLEY, JOSEPH; Cardinal O Hara HS; Broomall, PA; (Y); 17/750; Church Yth Grp; Computer Clb; Latin Clb; Spanish Clb; Im Bsktbl; High Hon Roll; Hon Roll; NHS; Prfct Atten Awd.

MC GINLEY, MELISSA; Butler HS; Renfrew, PA; (Y); Church Yth Grp; Cmnty Wkr; Pres VICA; Hon Roll; Rstrnt Mngmnt.

MC GINN, LETITIA A; Pocono Central Catholic HS; Tannersville, PA; (Y); 11/22; Pres Girl Scts; Pres JA; Pres NFL; Ed Nwsp Ed-Chief; Ed Yrbk Ed-Chief; Sec Stu Cncl; Trs Art Clb; Church Yth Grp; Pres Debate Tm; MVP Vrsty Sftbl Plyr 85 & 86; Pres Stu Forum 85-86; Living Lovg & Lrng Scholar 86; La Salle U; Comm.

MC GINN, PATRICIA E; Pocono Central Catholic HS; Tannersville, PA; (S); 10/29; Scholastic Bowl; Speech Tm; Trs Stu Cncl; Var Bsktbl; Var Fld Hcky; Var Sftbl; Hon Roll; Art Clb; VP Church Yth Grp; Intlxstu Ldrshp@inst 84-86; IU Ctu Forum; Stu Adv Bd Rep 84-86; Dale Carnegie Crse Spkng 85-86; Ed.

MC GINN, SHERRI; Shamokin Area HS; Shamokin, PA; (Y); 38/192; Varsity Clb; Var L Sftbl; Var L Vllybl; High Hon Roll; Hon Roll; Mc Cann Schl Bus Highest Secretarial Av 86; Ldrshp Awd PTA 86; Sev Shorthand Awds Princ 85-86; Mc Cann Schl Bus; Bus.

MC GINNES, KIM; Wellsboro SR HS; Honolulu, HI; (Y); Pres Art Clb; Church Yth Grp; German Clb; Pep Clb; Var L Cheerleading; Capt L Tennis; Var L Vllybl; High Hon Roll; Hon Roll; NHS; U Of CA-DAVIS; Vet Med.

MC GINNIS, LINDA; Sharon HS; Sharon, PA; (Y); 7/205; Church Yth Grp; Chorus; Church Choir; Rep Stu Cncl; Swmmng; High Hon Roll; Hon Roll; Opt Clb Awd; Legal Secys Assoc 86; Pres Acad Fit Awd 85-86; Youngstown ST U; Wrd Procssng.

MC GINNIS, MARK; Keystone Oaks HS; Carnegie, PA; (Y); 52/260; Church Yth Grp; Variety Show; Var Capt Ftbl; Var L Wrstlng; Hon Roll; KDKA Extra Effrt Awd 85-86; Elzbth Stewart Schlrshp-Thiel Coll 86; Thiel Coll.

MC GINNIS, MARLO; Ligonier Valley SR HS; Ligonier, PA; (Y); Church Yth Grp; Library Aide; Chorus; Church Choir; Concert Band; Var L Twrlr; Stat Wrstlng; Hon Roll; Majorette Capt 86-87; Miss Ligonier Pagnt Fnlst 86; Law.

MC GINNIS, MICHELLE; Central Buck East HS; Doylestown, PA; (Y); Church Yth Grp; Hosp Aide; Flag Corp; Achvt Ovrcmg Handcp Deaf 85; Doylestwn Hosp Vlntr Awd 86.

MC GINTY, MARK; Meadville Area SR HS; Meadville, PA; (Y); 110/344; Church Yth Grp; French Clb; Nwsp Phtg; Nwsp Stf; Im Badmtn; JV Bsktbl; Im Bowling; JV Socr; Var Tennis; Hon Roll; Navy; Elem Ed.

MC GINTY, VICKI; Plum SR HS; Pittsburgh, PA; (Y); 61/378; French Clb; SADD; Drill Tm; Nwsp Stf; Yrbk Stf; Rep Sr Cls; Pom Pon; Trk; Hon Roll; Hnr Rl Awd; Ltr Track; Indiana U Of PA; Nrsng.

MC GIVERN, PAT; Hopewell SR HS; Aliquippa, PA; (S); 8/295; Spanish Clb; High Hon Roll; Penn ST U; Aero Engrng.

MC GLADE, KATHLEEN; Cardinal O Hara HS; Glenolden, PA; (Y); Math Clb; Cmnty Wkr; Girl Scts; Red Cross Aide; Flag Corp; Nwsp Phtg; Grl Scouts Slvr Ldrshp Awd; Grl Scouts Slvr Awd; Educ.

MC GLONE, MARY; Pennsbury HS; Levittown, PA; (Y); JV L Trk; Hon Roll; Physcl Fnts Awd 84; Intrct Rtry Clb 85-86; Trenton ST; Psych.

MC GLYNN, JOHN; St Josephs Preparatory Schl; Philadelphia, PA; (Y); 12/200; French Clb; Nwsp Rptr; JV Crs Cntry; Var Trk; High Hon Roll; Brown U Bk Awd Ltrtr 86; Hnrb Mntn Awd Crw PA Cthlc Lg 86.

MC GLYNN, JUSTIN; St Josephs Prep; N Wales, PA; (Y); Nwsp Stf; Yrbk Ed-Chief; Lit Mag; L Diving; Var Trk; Voice Dem Awd; Schl Nwsp Awd Of Merit 86; Jrnlsm.

MC GLYNN, KELLI; Neshaminy HS; Trevose, PA; (Y); 128/735; JV Bsktbl; Var Fld Hcky; Var Sftbl; Hon Roll; 2nd Tm Subrbn I All Lg 86; Hon Mntn Fld Hcky Sbrbn 1 All Lg 85; Bloomsburg; Med Tech.

MC GLYNN, MICHELE; Blacklick Valley JR SR HS; Twin Rocks, PA; (S); 6/96; Pres Church Yth Grp; German Clb; School Play; Yrbk Stf; Hon Roll; NHS; Germn Natl Hnr Soc 85; Notre Dame; Bus Adm.

MC GOLDRICK, PATRICIA; Archbishop John Carroll For Girls; Havertown, PA; (Y); 63/216; Dance Clb; Hosp Aide; Pep Clb; Service Clb; School Play; Nwsp Sprt Ed; Cheerleading; Lcrss; Socr; Hon Roll; Salutatorian Fnlst; Mdl Winner In Irish Dncng; Villanova U; Bus.

MC GONAGLE, DENISE; Council Rock HS; Churchville, PA; (Y); 99/745; Cmnty Wkr; Powder Puff Ftbl; Socr; Hon Roll.

MC GONAGLE, ROBERT; Devon Preparatory Schl; West Chester, PA; (Y); Cmnty Wkr; Drama Clb; Spanish Clb; School Play; Stage Crew; Rep Frsh Cls; Rep Soph Cls; Pres Jr Cls; Var L Bsktbl; Var Capt Socr; Cmnctns.

MC GONIGAL, GREG; Marion Center Area HS; Home, PA; (S); Ftbl; NHS; Coach Elem Flag Ftbl; Chrch Chrstn Yth Grp; Automtv Mechncs.

MC GONIGLE, DAN; Central Catholic HS; Whitehall, PA; (Y); 52/217; Boy Scts; JA; Ftbl; Wt Lftg; Hon Roll; Comp Sci.

MC GOUGH, ERIN MARIE; Bishop Hannan HS; Scranton, PA; (Y); 13/120; Computer Clb; Sec Trs Exploring; Pres Ski Clb; Band; School Musical; Nwsp Rptr; Sec Stu Cncl; High Hon Roll; NHS; Pres Schlr; Gradtn Cord 86; Pres Phys Fitness Awds 83 & 84; Awds Fr Hgh Grds-Hstry, Math, Sci, Lang 82-86; Millersville U; Physics.

MC GOUGH, KEVIN; Central Catholic HS; Pittsburgh, PA; (Y); 40/260; Dance Clb; Office Aide; Chorus; School Musical; Stage Crew; Trk; Hon Roll; NHS; Pres Church Yth Grp; Drama Clb; Cert Achvt US Army 86; PA JR Acad Sci 1st Awd 86; Ithaca Coll; Marine Bio.

MC GOVERN, JEFF; Crestwood HS; Mountaintop, PA; (Y); 38/230; Cmnty Wkr; Math Clb; Political Wkr; Ski Clb; Var Bsbl; JV Bsktbl; Coach Actv; Capt Var Ftbl; Wt Lftg; Hon Roll; Engrng.

MC GOVERN, SHAUN; Cardinal O Hara HS; Drexel Hill, PA; (Y); 12/740; Latin Clb; Spanish Clb; School Play; Yrbk Stf; Lit Mag; High Hon Roll; Hon Roll; Sec NHS; Cardinal Gibbons Schlrshp 86; Catholic U; Biomed Engrg.

MC GOWAN, ANN; Valley View Jr - SR HS; Archbald, PA; (Y); 28/205; Var Bsktbl; Var Sftbl; Hon Roll; Computer Clb; Latin Clb; Im Vllybl; Pre-Med.

MC GOWAN, BRIAN; Fort Le Boeuf HS; Erie, PA; (Y); #2 In Class; Church Yth Grp; Rep Jr Cls; Var L Bsktbl; Var L Ftbl; Var L Trk; High Hon Roll; VP NHS; Fst Tm All-Cnty Trck; Hld Cnty Rcd 100m Dsh; Pol Sci.

MC GOWAN, CATHY; Cardinal O Hara HS; Havertown, PA; (Y); 365/772; Ski Clb; Coach Actv; Cardinal O Harn Schlstc Awd 86.

MC GOWAN, EROL; Moniteau JR SR HS; Karns City, PA; (Y); 5/151; Pres Church Yth Grp; Varsity Clb; Band; Concert Band; Mrchg Band; Trs Jr Cls; Stu Cncl; Bsktbl; Trk; Wt Lftg; Arch Engrng.

MC GOWAN, JOYCELYN; Technical HS; Scranton, PA; (Y); 35/215; Letterman Clb; Red Cross Aide; Pres Band; Trs Chorus; Mrchg Band; Orch; Yrbk Stf; Stu Cncl; JV Bsktbl; U Pittsburgh; Psych.

MC GOWAN, KELLIE; Chichester SR HS; Boothwyn, PA; (Y); Cmnty Wkr; Sec Spanish Clb; Band; Concert Band; Stat Bsktbl; Var Fld Hcky; Var JV Lcrss; Hon Roll; Jr NHS; Prfct Atten Awd; 1st Pl Mrns Tstng Pgm Chichester 85; Psychlgy.

MC GOWAN, KIMBERLY L; The Christian Acad; Media, PA; (Y); Hosp Aide; Library Aide; Chorus; School Play; Sec Frsh Cls; Sec Soph Cls; Stu Cncl; Capt Cheerleading; Var Fld Hcky; Hon Roll; Chrldng Coaches Awd 85; Nrsng.

MC GOWAN, MARK; Upper Moreland HS; Hatboro, PA; (Y); 48/270; Var Capt Bowling; Hon Roll; JV Socr; Bwlng MVP Awd 86.

MC GOWAN, MATHIEU L; Cardinal O Hara HS; Newtown Square, PA; (Y); 53/744; Letterman Clb; Office Aide; Varsity Clb; School Musical; Nwsp Rptr; Ftbl; Score Keeper; Trk; Wt Lftg; Wrstlng; PA ST U; Acctg.

MC GOWAN III, NICHOLAS; Saucon Valley SR HS; Bethlehem, PA; (Y); 29/146; Var Bsbl; Var Bsktbl; Var Golf; Colnl Lgue All-Lgue Outfld 85-86; Appted Schl Brd Task Frc Male Ath Rep 86-87; Coll; Law.

MC GOWAN, STEVE; Dawningtown HS; Glenmoore, PA; (S); 32/524; Letterman Clb; Pep Clb; JV Var Bsbl; JV Var Bsktbl; NHS; Engr.

MC GRADY, BRIAN; Carrick HS; Pittsburgh, PA; (Y); Church Yth Grp; Q&S; Ski Clb; Stage Crew; Nwsp Sprt Ed; Sec Jr Cls; Trs Sr Cls; L Tennis; Hon Roll; NHS; Cmnctns.

MC GRADY, GEORGE; Trinity HS; Washington, PA; (Y); Boy Scts; Chorus; Bsbl; High Hon Roll; Hon Roll.

MC GRANAHAN, DEVIN; Warren Area HS; Warren, PA; (Y); Art Clb; Debate Tm; Math Tm; Pres Spanish Clb; Nwsp Phtg; Yrbk Phtg; Stu Cncl; Crs Cntry; Trk; NHS; Tri Cty Debate Awd 86; Am Chem Soc Awd 86; Engrng.

MC GRATH, DENNIS; Mars Area HS; Mars, PA; (Y); 35/157; Church Yth Grp; SADD; Varsity Clb; Nwsp Sprt Ed; Ftbl; Trk; DAR Awd; High Hon Roll; Letterman Clb; Off Frsh Cls; Mbr Schl Bd 85; Superintendants Advsry Comm 85-86; Eyth-Williams Awd/Outstndng Stu Athl 86; Marietta Coll; Sprts Med.

MC GRATH, DOTTIE; Riverview HS; Oakmont, PA; (Y); 10/100; AFS; Drama Clb; Exploring; French Clb; Key Clb; Capt Drill Tm; Nwsp Stf; Yrbk Stf; French Hon Soc; NHS; Kiwanis Unselfish Svc Awd 86; L Caplan Hmn Rltns Awd 86; Stu Cncl Schlrshp 86; Muskingum Coll; French.

MC GRATH, KELLY; Freedom HS; Easton, PA; (Y); 62/405; Computer Clb; Pres Exploring; Hon Roll; Pres Ftns Awd 86; Millersville U; Comp Sci.

MC GRATH, MICHAEL J; Frankford HS; Philadelphia, PA; (Y); 4/510; Var Bsbl; Var Crs Cntry; High Hon Roll; Lion Awd; NHS; Coca-Cola Schlrshp, 13 Club Awd, Athl Awd 13 Club 86; Temple U; Bus Mgt.

MC GRATH, SARA; Interboro HS; Glenolden, PA; (Y); French Clb; Key Clb; Off Soph Cls; Off Jr Cls; Off Sr Cls; Var Bsktbl; Var Fld Hcky; Var Lcrss; U Of Westchester; Phys Ed.

MC GRAW III, JAMES P; Scranton Central HS; Scranton, PA; (Y); 12/273; Church Yth Grp; VP JA; Band; Yrbk Stf; High Hon Roll; NHS; Prfct Atten Awd; Pres Schlr; Germn Hgh Hons Awd 86; Math 2nd Hgh Hons Awd 86; U Of Scranton; Pre-Med.

MC GRAW, ROBERT; West Scranton HS; Scranton, PA; (Y); 1/250; Boys Clb Am; Boy Scts; Letterman Clb; Ski Clb; Jazz Band; Orch; Var L Golf; Var L Tennis; High Hon Roll; Hon Roll; Hnrbl Ment Ntly PTA Reflctn Lit 85; PA Acad Sci Exc Bio 85; Gov Schl For Sci 86; Princeton; Physics.

MC GREADY, JOHN; Wissahickon HS; Ambler, PA; (S); 20/280; Drama Clb; School Play; JV Trk; High Hon Roll; Hon Roll; NHS; Math.

MC GREGOR, KAE; Dover HS; East Berlin, PA; (Y); 81/289; Church Yth Grp; JA; Chorus; Church Choir; Yrbk Stf; Rep Jr Cls; Rep Stu Cncl; Var L Vllybl; CA U PA; Early Chldhd.

MC GREW, MELANIE; Charleroi Area HS; Charleroi, PA; (Y); Library Aide; Ski Clb; Nwsp Stf; Hon Roll; CA U PA; Psych.

MC GROARTY, COLLEEN; Little Flower HS; Philadelphia, PA; (Y); 14/395; Chorus; School Musical; School Play; Variety Show; Nwsp Rptr; Hon Roll; Jr NHS; NHS; Philadelphia Coll; Pharmcst.

MC GROGAN, DANIEL; Langley HS; Pittsburgh, PA; (Y); Boy Scts; Church Yth Grp; Exploring; Band; Drm & Bgl; Mrchg Band; Swmmng; VFW Awd; School Musical; VP Frsh Cls; Eagle Scout Awd 86; Musically Tlntd 84; Career Shdwng With Rotary 86; Bio.

MC GROGAN, RITA; Yough SR HS; W Newton, PA; (Y); Library Aide; Office Aide; Var L Bsktbl; Im Powder Puff Ftbl; Var L Trk; Im Vllybl; High Hon Roll; NHS; Bus Adm.

MC GROSKY, MARK; Bethel Park HS; Bethel Pk, PA; (Y); 77/519; FBLA; Letterman Clb; Ski Clb; Im Coach Actv; Var L Wrstlng; High Hon Roll; Hon Roll; Psych.

MC GROTTY, KYLE; Upper Moreland HS; Huntingdon Vly, PA; (Y); 26/260; Pres Key Clb; Pres Frsh Cls; Pres Soph Cls; Pres Jr Cls; Pres Sr Cls; Rep Stu Cncl; Var L Bsktbl; Cit Awd; High Hon Roll; NHS; Rtry Stu Of Mnth 86; Kiwanis Awd For Key Clb 86.

MC GUANE, JOHN; Susquehanna Comm HS; Susquehanna, PA; (Y); Church Yth Grp; Pres Frsh Cls; Var Bsktbl; Var Ftbl; Var Trk; Saber Trck Tm 1st Pl 86; Meteorolgst.

MC GUCKIN, TRACEY; St Maria Goretti HS; Philadelphia, PA; (Y); 34/390; Cmnty Wkr; Mathletes; Office Aide; Orch; Rep Soph Cls; Rep Jr Cls; Hon Roll; All Amer Acdmc Achvmnt Awd 84-85; U Of PA; Pre-Med.

MC GUIGAN, JOHN D; Norristown Area HS; Norristown, PA; (S); 15/580; Cmnty Wkr; Debate Tm; FBLA; Band; Concert Band; Drm Mjr(t); Mrchg Band; High Hon Roll; Prfct Atten Awd; Social Studies Awd 84; Band Awd 85; Johns Hopkins Awd 82; Bus.

MC GUIGAN, PATRICK J; Clarion Area JR SR HS; Clarion, PA; (S); Trs Frsh Cls; Sec Soph Cls; Pres Jr Cls; Stu Cncl; Bsbl; Var Capt Bsktbl; JV Var Ftbl; Wt Lftg; Hon Roll; Engrng.

MC GUINN, ELLEN; Cardinal Dougherty HS; Phila, PA; (Y); 3/749; Var Capt Crs Cntry; Var Capt Trk; NHS; Rep Soph Cls; Stu Cncl; Stat Wrstlng; Cit Awd; DAR Awd; High Hon Roll; Hon Roll; Bstn Coll Schlsrhp, La Salle U Schlrshp 86; U Scrntn Pres Schlrshp 86; Boston Coll; Law.

MC GUIRE, ERIN; Archbishop John Carroll HS For Grls; Wayne, PA; (Y); 12/216; Church Yth Grp; Cmnty Wkr; Teachers Aide; Yrbk Sprt Ed; Var Lcrss; Bausch & Lomb Sci Awd; Hon Roll; NHS; Ntl Merit Schol; Quiz Bowl; Pres Acad Ftns Awd 86; Bucknell U; Elec Engrng.

MC GUIRE, JAMES; Bishop O Reilly HS; Dallas, PA; (Y); Acpl Chr; Chorus; School Musical; Swing Chorus; Pres Sr Cls; Rep Stu Cncl; Ntl Merit Ltr; Var L Golf; Latin Clb; Ldrshp Awd 86; Drama Awd 85-86; Cls Ldr 86; Wilkes Coll; Bio.

MC GUIRE, JILL; Meyers HS; Wilkes Barre, PA; (Y); Nwsp Sprt Ed; Nwsp Stf; Pres Stu Cncl; Bsktbl; Crs Cntry; Sftbl; Cit Awd; Hon Roll; Spanish NHS; Ltr Bsktbl & Sftbl; Schl Nwspr Cert; Wilkes Coll; Chld Care.

MC GUIRE, MARGARET; Monn SR HS; Coraopolis, PA; (Y); 9/304; Sec Exploring; Key Clb; Rep Jr Cls; Var Trk; Hon Roll; NHS; Aud/Vis; Im Bsktbl; JV Sftbl; Im Vllybl; Schlrshp Summer Seminar Wrld Affrs 86; Olympics Of Mind SW Pa Reg Trnmnt 86; Carnegie Mellon U; Elec Engrng.

MC GUIRE, MAUREEN; Bishop Hannan HS; Scranton, PA; (Y); French Clb; Chorus; School Play; Rep Stu Cncl; JV Var Cheerleading; High Hon Roll; Sec NHS; Excllnc-Engl, Phys Sci, Fr & Algb 84; Excllnc-Fr, Wrld Cultrs, Geom & Bio 85; Drexel; Engrng.

MC GUIRE, SCOTT; Northern Cambria HS; Nicktown, PA; (Y); 12/130; Pres 4-H; VP Sr Cls; Rep Stu Cncl; Capt Bsktbl; Capt Ftbl; Trk; Wt Lftg; 4-H Awd; High Hon Roll; VP NHS; D R Lovette & John B Mccombie Awd $25 86; Indiana U Of PA; Pre-Dentistry.

MC GUIRE, WENDI KAY; Smethport Area JR SR HS; Smethport, PA; (Y); 4/99; French Clb; Varsity Clb; VP Swing Chorus; Var Capt Cheerleading; Mgr(s); High Hon Roll; Sec NHS; Cmnty Wkr; Library Aide; Chorus; Amer Chem Socty Awd 86; Big 30 All Str Chrldr & MVP Chrldr 86; JR-SR Proms & SR Hmcmg Attdnt 85-86; IN U Of PA; Elem Ed.

MC GUIRK, NOREEN; Pocono Mountain HS; Pocono Lake, PA; (Y); 42/320; Church Yth Grp; Acpl Chr; Band; Chorus; Church Choir; Concert Band; Mrchg Band; School Musical; School Play; Hon Roll; Penn ST U; Law.

MC GURRIN, PATRICK; Technical HS; Scranton, PA; (Y); FBLA; Trs Sr Cls; Rep Stu Cncl; JV Crs Cntry; Var Wrstlng; Hon Roll; Lackawanna JR Coll; Law Enfrcm.

MC HALE, AMIE; Scranton Prep; Scranton, PA; (Y); 153/192; Service Clb; Ski Clb; Stage Crew; Nwsp Stf; Yrbk Stf; Trk.

MC HALE, DENISE; Little Flower HS; Philadelphia, PA; (Y); 130/450; Cmnty Wkr; Hosp Aide; Library Aide; Office Aide; Teachers Aide; Stage Crew; Trk; Hon Roll; Holy Family Coll; Nursng.

MC HALE, SCOTT; Tunkhannock Area HS; Falls, PA; (S); 12/350; Letterman Clb; Ski Clb; Varsity Clb; Var L Swmmng; Var L Trk; Hon Roll; NHS; Arntcl Engr.

MC HENRY, BRIDGET; Ambridge Area HS; Baden, PA; (Y); JA; Pep Clb; Red Cross Aide; Band; Mrchg Band; Pep Band; Yrbk Stf; Off Frsh Cls; Off Soph Cls; Off Jr Cls; Sawyer Schl Of Bus; Trvl.

MC HENRY, LINDA; General Mclane HS; Edinboro, PA; (Y); 55/250; German Clb; Girl Scts; Band; Concert Band; Mrchg Band; Symp Band; Nwsp Stf; Powder Puff Ftbl; Sftbl; Hon Roll; Edinboro U; Comm.

MC HENRY, PATRICK; Archbishop Wood HS; Hatboro, PA; (Y); 64/297; JV Ftbl; Math.

MC HUGH, CRISTIN; Bishop Hafey HS; Hazleton, PA; (Y); Cmnty Wkr; French Clb; Latin Clb; Y-Teens; Orch; Sftbl; Commnctn.

MC HUGH, JENNIFER; Hazleton SR HS; Hazleton, PA; (Y); Church Yth Grp; Drama Clb; Library Aide; Office Aide; Ski Clb; Spanish Clb; Thesps; Y-Teens; Var Bsktbl; Mgr(s); Temple U; Econ.

MC HUGH, KATHLEEN; Scranton Prepartory Schl; Scranton, PA; (Y); 5/192; Service Clb; Chorus; School Musical; School Play; Stage Crew; Yrbk Stf; Lit Mag; Trk; High Hon Roll; Jr NHS; Corp Law.

MC HUGH, LISA; Cardinal O Hara HS; Broomall, PA; (Y); 162/772; Church Yth Grp; Cmnty Wkr; Hon Roll; Prfct Atten Awd.

MC ILNAY, JODI; Mt Pleasant Area HS; Stahlstown, PA; (Y); Church Yth Grp; GAA; Chorus; Cheerleading; Mat Maids; Sftbl; Vllybl; Hon Roll; Yth Educ Assoc; Bus Clb 85-86; Jr Cls Candy Sale Rep 85-86; Bus.

MC ILVAIN, JOHN; Butler SR HS; Butler, PA; (Y); Church Yth Grp; Spanish Clb; Stage Crew; Im Bsktbl; Var Ftbl; Hon Roll; Jr NHS; Kent ST U; Bus Adm.

MC ILVAIN, TRACY; Hopewell SR HS; Aliquippa, PA; (Y); 35/295; Pres Church Yth Grp; German Clb; Chorus; Church Choir; Capt Drill Tm; Capt Pom Pon; Cit Awd; High Hon Roll; NHS; SR Ctzn Awd Eckerd Coll Scholar 86-89; 4th Rnr-Up Miss Metro Pittsburgh Natl Teen 85; Miss Photo 84; Sewickley Vly Hosp.

MC ILVAINE, EDWARD; Archbishop Kennedy HS; Philadelphia, PA; (Y); #21 In Class; Cmnty Wkr; Hon Roll; Hghst Avg Geomtry, Blgy, Chmstry & Algbra II 84-86.

MC INDOE, ALISON; Danville SR HS; Danville, PA; (Y); Drama Clb; French Clb; Hosp Aide; Ski Clb; School Play; Nwsp Ed-Chief; Sec Frsh Cls; JV L Tennis; Hon Roll; Chorus Awd 84; Govt Pin & Awd 84; Musical/Drama Awd 84; Intr Dsgn.

MC INTIRE, CHRISTINE; Kittanning SR HS; Worthington, PA; (Y); Church Yth Grp; Library Aide; Band; Trs Nwsp Stf; Yrbk Stf; High Hon Roll; Hon Roll; NHS; Comp Sci.

MC INTIRE, DAVE; Gateway SR HS; Monroeville, PA; (Y); Var Capt Swmmng; Athltc Schlrshp Swmmng 86; NISCA ST Top 10 Awd 86; Mel Nash Awd 86; Northeastern U; Phys Thrpy.

MC INTIRE, TAMMY; Bellwood-Antis HS; Tipton, PA; (Y); Dance Clb; FHA; Girl Scts; JA; Library Aide; Chorus; Color Guard; Concert Band; School Play; Nwsp Rptr; Military.

MC INTIRE, TAMMY; Waynesburg Central HS; Mt Morris, PA; (Y); Camera Clb; VP Letterman Clb; Trs Spanish Clb; Nwsp Sprt Ed; Yrbk Phtg; Sec Soph Cls; Var Capt Bsktbl; Coach Actv; Sftbl; Vllybl; Schlrshp To CA U Of PA 86; Hld Wshngtn -Grn Cnty Scrng Rcrd Bsktbl 86; Rcrd Mst Pnts Scrd 1 Gm 85; CA U Of PA; Sprts Med.

MC INTOSH, ANGEL; Upper Darby HS; Lansdowne, PA; (Y); Hosp Aide; Acpl Chr; Chorus; Color Guard; Capt Flag Corp; Mrchg Band; School Musical; Rep Jr Cls; Rep Stu Cncl; Hon Roll; Penn St; Pre-Med.

MC INTOSH, CHRISTINA; Mercy Vocational HS; Philadelphia, PA; (Y); Church Yth Grp; Church Choir; Prfct Atten Awd; Medical Records Clerk.

MC INTYRE, BRADLEY; Dmanheim Township HS; Lancaster, PA; (Y); Boy Scts; Mrchg Band; Var Gym; Hon Roll; Chem.

MC INTYRE, FRANK; Elk Lake HS; Meshoppen, PA; (Y); 34/104; Art Clb; Computer Clb; VICA; Trs Frsh Cls; VP Jr Cls; Stu Cncl; Wt Lftg; Wrstlng; Hon Roll; Trk; Cert Awd Wrtslng,Track,Stu Cncl 84-86; Comp Anlyst.

MC INTYRE, TAMMY; Northern Chester County Vo-Tech; Phoenixville, PA; (Y); 33/150; Pres FNA; VP Pres Jr Cls; Pres Sr Cls; Off Stu Cncl; Ftbl; Kiwanis Awd; Dogwood Pgnt Ct 85; Miss Chester Cnty Intl Teen Miss PA 86; Psych.

MC ISSAC, JEFFREY; Downingtown SR HS; Exton, PA; (S); 1/540; Church Yth Grp; French Clb; Red Cross Aide; Drm Mjr(t); Im Vllybl; High Hon Roll; NHS; Ntl Merit Ltr; Acad Cmptn Tm 85-8; Carnegie-Mellon U; Elec/Comp En.

MC JETT, RECHELLE; Creative & Performing Arts HS; Philadelphia, PA; (S); 11/150; Variety Show; Hon Roll; NHS; Blck Achvt Awd 86; PA ST U.

MC KAHAN, TAMMY; German SR HS; Uniontown, PA; (Y); Model UN; SADD; VICA; Chorus; Church Choir; Yrbk Stf; Pres Soph Cls; Pres Jr Cls; Rep Stu Cncl; JV Cheerleading; Perfct Atten, Straight A Awd 81; Stu Mnth 83; Stu Of Mnth 84; Photo.

MC KAIN, GREGORY; St John Neumann HS; Philadelphis, PA; (Y); 64/338; Var Tennis; Hon Roll.

MC KAIN, KELLI; Donegal HS; Marietta, PA; (Y); 3/159; Church Yth Grp; Band; Concert Band; Mrchg Band; Rep Frsh Cls; Rep Stu Cncl; Var Capt Cheerleading; High Hon Roll; Hon Roll; NHS; Rensselaer Mdl.

MC KAIN, NOREEN; St Pauls Cathedral HS; Pittsburgh, PA; (S); 7/55; Camera Clb; French Clb; Library Aide; Science Clb; Chorus; Yrbk Stf; Sec Soph Cls; JV Vllybl; French Hon Soc; High Hon Roll; Pitt; Pre-Med.

MC KAY, MAUREEN; West Mifflin Area HS; West Mifflin, PA; (Y); FBLA; Office Aide; Yrbk Ed-Chief; Frsh Cls; Soph Cls; Jr Cls; Sr Cls; Hon Roll; Jr NHS; NHS.

MC KAY, MICHAEL; Monaca HS; Monaca, PA; (Y); 2/89; VP Jr Cls; Stu Cncl; Bsbl; Bsktbl; Ftbl; Engrng.

MC KAY, PATRICK; Brockway Area HS; Brockway, PA; (Y); FCA; Letterman Clb; Pep Clb; Varsity Clb; Stage Crew; Variety Show; Rep Sr Cls; L Bsbl; L Ftbl; Im Wt Lftg; Hnr Stndg; Lttrs Ftbll & Bsbll; Marine Corps.

MC KEAGUE, CARRIE; Lock Haven SR HS; Castanea, PA; (Y); 9/243; German Clb; Concert Band; Bsktbl; Tennis; Hon Roll; NHS; Prfct Atten Awd; PA ST U Park; Lib Arts.

MC KEAN, GINA E; Bald Eagle-Nittany HS; Beech Creek, PA; (Y); 11/125; French Clb; Key Clb; Model UN; School Musical; Nwsp Phtg; Pres Stu Cncl; JC Awd; NHS; Drama Clb; JV Cheerleading; Hugh O Brian Yth Ldrshp Semnr 84; PA Free Entrprs Wk 85; Assn Of Clinton Cnty Eductrs Schlrsp 86; IN U Of PA.

MC KEANEY, DAWN; Council Rock HS; Churchville, PA; (Y); 63/845; Church Yth Grp; Cmnty Wkr; FCA; Office Aide; SADD; Varsity Clb; Rep Frsh Cls; Rep Soph Cls; Rep Jr Cls; Rep Sr Cls; Svc Awd Stu Cncl 86; Comms.

MC KEE, ALICIA; Hollidaysburg SR HS; Hollidaysburg, PA; (Y); Church Yth Grp; French Clb; Hosp Aide; Library Aide; Hon Roll; NHS; Prfct Atten Awd; Poems Pub Bks 85-86; Psych.

MC KEE, BETH; Ford City HS; Ford City, PA; (Y); Chorus; Color Guard; Drill Tm; School Play; Yrbk Stf; Rep Sr Cls; Rep Stu Cncl; Hon Roll; NHS; Bradford Bus Schl; Scrtrl.

MC KEE, BONNIE; Leechburg Area HS; Leechburg, PA; (Y); 9/82; Church Yth Grp; Drama Clb; Hosp Aide; Band; Concert Band; Mrchg Band; School Play; Nwsp Rptr; Var L Sftbl; Var Twrlr; Duquesne U; Poltcl Sci.

MC KEE, KELLY; Milton SR HS; New Columbia, PA; (Y); 2/202; Sec Church Yth Grp; Computer Clb; German Clb; Varsity Clb; Band; Fld Hcky; Powder Puff Ftbl; Sftbl; High Hon Roll; Hon Roll.

MC KEE, LISA; Marion Center HS; Clymer, PA; (S); 25/170; FBLA; Intnl Clb; Q&S; Science Clb; SADD; Nwsp Rptr; Hon Roll; Film/Dir.

MC KEE, SAMUEL; Trinity HS; Duncannon, PA; (Y); Band; Jazz Band; Mrchg Band; School Play; Engl.

MC KEE, TODD; Waynesboro Area SR HS; Zullinger, PA; (Y); 27/363; Pres Church Yth Grp; Nwsp Ed-Chief; Rep Soph Cls; Pres Jr Cls; Rep Stu Cncl; JV Crs Cntry; Stat Trk; Cit Awd; Hon Roll; NHS; HOBY Found ST Amb 85; Messiah Coll; Ed.

MC KEE, VERONICA; Upper Darby SR HS; Primos, PA; (Y); 53/600; Rep Soph Cls; Rep Jr Cls; Stu Cncl; JV Cheerleading; Hon Roll; Opt Clb Awd; Hugh O Brian Yth Fndtn Schl Rep 85; PA ASCC Stu Cncls Conf Rep 85; Sthestrn Stu Cncl Regnl Conf 84; Drexel; Intr Dsgn.

MC KEEHEN, JOHN D; State College Area HS; State College, PA; (Y); Church Yth Grp; Rep Jr Cls; Rep Stu Cncl; Lcrss; Socr; Swmmng; Tennis; Vllybl; Hon Roll; PA ST U; Aerosp Engr.

MC KEEL, CRYSTAL; Beaver Area JR-SR HS; Beaver, PA; (Y); Church Yth Grp; French Clb; Hosp Aide; Pep Clb; Ski Clb; Spanish Clb; Chorus; Church Choir; Yrbk Bus Mgr; Hon Roll; Bus Mgmt.

MC KEEVER, JOE; New Hope Solebury HS; Doylestown, PA; (Y); 18/65; Nwsp Stf; Capt Crs Cntry; JV Socr; Capt Wrstlng; Hon Roll; Dist Chmpn Wrstlng 86; Mst Vlbl Wrstler 85-86; Mst Imprvd Acadmc 86; Penn ST; Engrng.

MC KEEVER, SCOTT; Saltsburg JR SR HS; Clarksburg, PA; (Y); DECA; Chorus; Church Choir; High Hon Roll; Hon Roll; PA ST; Bus Adm.

MC KEEVER, THOMAS; Father Judge HS; Philadelphia, PA; (Y); 7/371; Church Yth Grp; Mathletes; Math Clb; Math Tm; JV Bsktbl; High Hon Roll.

MC KENDRY, CHRISTINE; Archbishop Ryan HS For Girls; Philadelphia, PA; (Y); 27/485; Cmnty Wkr; VP French Clb; JA; School Play; Rep Stu Cncl; Var Bsktbl; Var Socr; Var Capt Tennis; Hon Roll; NHS; PA Free Entrprs Wk Lock Hvn Coll 85; 1st Hnr Stu 83-86; All-Cath Tns 84-85; Drexel U; Cmmnctns.

MC KENNA, JOHN R; Father Judge HS; Philadelphia, PA; (Y); 47/403; Church Yth Grp; Im Bowling; Coach Actv; JV Socr; Hon Roll; Allentown Coll; Bus.

MC KENNA, MARY; Sacred Heart HS; Pittsburgh, PA; (Y); 41/150; Exploring; FBLA; GAA; Hosp Aide; Pres Ski Clb; Yrbk Bus Mgr; Yrbk Stf; Bsktbl; Var JV Score Keeper; Capt Tennis; Louis Cpln Hmn Rltns Awd 86; Svc Awd 86; Mercyhurst Coll; CPA.

MC KENNA, MELISSA; Springdale HS; Springdale, PA; (Y); Spanish Clb; Acpl Chr; Church Choir; Yrbk Ed-Chief; Im Vllybl; Hon Roll; Sci.

MC KENRICK, DONNA; Curwensville HS; Curwensville, PA; (Y); French Clb; Hosp Aide; Pep Clb; Ski Clb; Chorus; Nwsp Stf; Hon Roll; Nrsg.

MC KENZIE, JANICE; Clearfield Area HS; Clearfield, PA; (Y); Church Yth Grp; Drama Clb; Spanish Clb; Stage Crew; Mat Maids; Score Keeper; Capt Twrlr; Hon Roll; Trs Mrchg Band.

MC KENZIE, ROBBY; Berlin Borthers Valley HS; Myersdale, PA; (Y); Church Yth Grp; French Clb; Chorus; JV Var Vllybl; French Hon Soc; Hon Roll; Prfct Atten Awd; Cert For French 86; U Of Pittsburgh; Accntnt.

MC KENZIE, TIMOTHY; Waynesboro Area SR HS; Waynesboro, PA; (Y); 56/381; Church Yth Grp; Chorus; Concert Band; Drm Mjr(t); Jazz Band; Mrchg Band; JV Crs Cntry; High Hon Roll; NHS; Prfct Atten Awd; Phrmcy.

MC KEOWN, SHANNON; Manheim Township HS; Leola, PA; (Y); 99/317; Chess Clb; JA; Nwsp Bus Mgr; Nwsp Rptr; Sftbl; Trk; Hon Roll; Elizabeth U; Bio.

MC KIM, LA MONT; B Reed Henderson HS; West Chester, PA; (Y); 12/336; Pres Frsh Cls; Var Bsktbl; Var Lcrss; Var Capt Socr; Var Trk; High Hon Roll; NHS; Ntl Merit Ltr; VP Spanish NHS; Upward Bnd Pgm; MVP Sccr; Blck Stu Union Pres, Pblc Rltns Offcr; U Of VA; Pre-Med.

MC KIM, LAMONT; B Reed Henderson HS; W Chester, PA; (S); 12/336; Pres Frsh Cls; Var Bsktbl; Var Lcrss; Var Capt Socr; Var Trk; Hon Roll; NHS; Spanish NHS; Natl Merit Schlrshp Outstndng Negro Stdnts 85-86; Lincoln U Mr Upward Bound Awd 84-86; U Of VA; Pre-Med.

MC KIMM JR, RALPH; Cameron County HS; Emporium, PA; (Y); 13/83; German Clb; Var JV Bsbl; Var JV Bsktbl; Powder Puff Ftbl; JV Trk; High Hon Roll; Hon Roll; Mu Alp Tht; NHS; German Hnr Scty 84-86; Acadmc All Amer 86; Barclay Schlrshp & Mc Allister Schlrshp 86; Penn ST; Comp Sci.

MC KINLEY, KIM; Chief Logan HS; Lewistown, PA; (Y); Church Yth Grp; Key Clb; Sec Spanish Clb; Varsity Clb; Capt Flag Corp; Mrchg Band; Yrbk Stf; Hst Soph Cls; Hst Jr Cls; Mgr Bsbl; Radlgc Tech.

MC KINLEY, KRISTEN; Valley HS; Arnold, PA; (Y); 6/225; Church Yth Grp; Girl Scts; VP JA; Spanish Clb; SADD; Band; Church Choir; Rep Stu Cncl; Var Trk; NHS; Girl Sct Silver Awd 86; JR Achvr Awd NAJAC Scholar 85; JR Exec Awd ADJAC & NAJAC Schoalr 86; Elem Ed.

MC KINLEY, VICKI; Somerset Area HS; Somerset, PA; (Y); 17/211; Q&S; Soroptimist; Concert Band; Sec Mrchg Band; School Play; Yrbk Ed-Chief; High Hon Roll; Mu Alp Tht; NHS; English Clb; GTE Schlrshp 86; All Cnty Bnd 83-86; PA ST U; Bus Adm.

MC KINNEY, COLLEEN RENEE; Ringgold HS; Finleyville, PA; (Y); Church Yth Grp; Office Aide; Chorus; Drill Tm; Variety Show; Cheerleading; Pom Pon; High Hon Roll; Hon Roll; NHS; Union Finley Ath Assn 1st Pl Sftbl 80-83; Bus.

MC KINNEY, DIANNE; United HS; Robinson, PA; (Y); 5/129; Math Clb; Ski Clb; Band; Concert Band; Jazz Band; Mrchg Band; Powder Puff Ftbl; Var L Trk; Pres Schlr; Mst Schlr Athltc Grl 86; CVMH; Nrsng.

MC KINNEY, JANICE; Pine Forge Acad; Albuquerque, NM; (Y); Church Yth Grp; Computer Clb; Spanish Clb; Chorus; Church Choir; Nwsp Rptr; Bausch & Lomb Sci Awd; Hon Roll; Bible Awd 84-86; Engl Awd 85-86; Mikey Awd Engl 84-85; U NM; Pedtrcn.

MC KINNEY, KIMBERLY; Meyersdale Area HS; Meyersdale, PA; (Y); Pres Church Yth Grp; Cmnty Wkr; Spanish Clb; Band; Mrchg Band; Nwsp Stf; Yrbk Stf; Hon Roll; NHS; Natl Ldrshp Awd 86; Indian U; Psych.

MC KINNEY, MICHAEL S; Bishop Shanahan HS; West Chester, PA; (Y); 15/225; Boy Scts; Mathletes; Stu Cncl; Bsbl; Socr; Trk; God Cntry Awd; NHS; SAR Awd; Egl Sct Awd 84; Sct Of Yr 84; Slvr Bckl Awd 83; U CO; Engrng.

MC KINNEY, REBECCA; Seneca Valley SR HS; Evans City, PA; (Y); GAA; VP JA; Ski Clb; Church Choir; Pres Frsh Cls; Trs Soph Cls; Pres Jr Cls; Sec Stu Cncl; Hon Roll; Natl Jr Achvt Conf 86; Allegheny Coll; Ecnmcs.

MC KINNEY, TERRI; Knoch JR & SR HS; Cabot, PA; (Y); Church Yth Grp; Chorus; Drill Tm; Cmnty Wkr; Mgr(s); Pom Pon; Trk; Wt Lftg; High Hon Roll; NHS; Stu Month 81-82; Certf Merit Mst Outstndng Hlth Cls 85; Nrsng.

MC KINNEY, THERESA; Susquehanna Community HS; Susquehanna, PA; (Y); Am Leg Aux Girls St; Dance Clb; Ski Clb; Stu Cncl; Var L Bsktbl; Var Capt Cheerleading; Sftbl; Var Trk; Var Capt Vllybl; Hon Roll; Trck Dist Mdls 83-86; Am Lg Awd 82; Am Co-Ed Pgnt Miss Photogenic & Fnslt 86; Fashion Merchandising.

MC KINNON, ROBERT; Eastern York Jr/Sr HS; Wrightsville, PA; (Y); 13/123; Church Yth Grp; Nwsp Rptr; Yrbk Ed-Chief; Yrbk Sprt Ed; Var L Bsbl; High Hon Roll; Hon Roll; JC Awd; Jr NHS; NHS; Jaycees Schlrshp 86; PA ST U; Brdcstng Jrnlsm.

MC KINSTRY, TARA; William Penn HS; York, PA; (Y); Art Clb; Aud/Vis; Church Yth Grp; Dance Clb; Science Clb; Spanish Clb; SADD; Band; Chorus; Church Choir; Acadmc All Stars 86; Penn ST U; Pre-Med.

MC KISSOCK, MATT; Youngsville HS; Youngsville, PA; (Y); 3/120; Boy Scts; Math Tm; Political Wkr; Yrbk Phtg; Elks Awd; High Hon Roll; JETS Awd; NHS; ROTC; School Play; 1st Pl Natl Math Exam 85; 1st Pl PA Mth Lg 86.

MC KITO, JOE; Ringgold HS; Donora, PA; (Y); Ski Clb; Stu Cncl; NHS; Sci Math Hnr Soc 85-86.

MC KITTEN, CARLA; Villa Maria HS; Chicora, PA; (Y); Drama Clb; Key Clb; Library Aide; Science Clb; Service Clb; Ski Clb; Spanish Clb; Thesps; School Musical; School Play; PA JR Acad Sci 1st & 2nd Pl 85-86; Visa Clb Awd 86; Case Western Reserve; Med.

MC KIVISION, VEDA; Bald Eagle-Nittany HS; Beech Creek, PA; (Y); 12/128; Church Yth Grp; Key Clb; Pres Spanish Clb; Band; Mrchg Band; Stu Cncl; Capt Twrlr; High Hon Roll; Hon Roll; Prfct Atten Awd; R Winters Awd Outstndng Band 86; 85 Alantic Coast Chmpn Band 85; Lock Haven U; Mgmt Sci Prog.

MC KNIGHT, HEATHER; Council Rock HS; Richboro, PA; (Y); Schlrshp Newtown Arts Co 86; Thomas Wood Mem Schlrshp 86; Shop N Save Schlrshp 86; Dance.

MC KOWN, MICHAEL T; Sheffield Area JR SR HS; Sheffield, PA; (S); Letterman Clb; Varsity Clb; Trs Frsh Cls; Trs Soph Cls; VP Jr Cls; VP Sr Cls; Var L Ftbl; Var L Wrstlng; High Hon Roll; NHS; Iron Man Cont Wnnr Wrstlng 84-85 & 85-86; Wrstlng Dedicated Dozen 85-86.

MC KRUIT, CHRISTINE; Valley SR HS; New Kensington, PA; (Y); Drama Clb; Key Clb; Spanish Clb; Varsity Clb; Chorus; Stage Crew; Mgr(s); Var Vllybl; Hon Roll; Rotary Awd; Flght Attndnt.

MC LACHLAN, RON; General Mc Lane HS; Edinboro, PA; (Y); Aud/Vis; Teachers Aide; Concert Band; Variety Show; Mrchg Band; Pep Band; Stage Crew; Rep Stu Cncl; Hon Roll; Comp.

MC LAIN, LORI; North Pocono HS; Moscow, PA; (Y); Pep Clb; Ski Clb; Rptr Pres VICA; Chorus; Orch; Hon Roll; NHS; 4th Pl LCAVTS S Ladies Hairstlng Comptn 85 & 86; Prom Queen 86; Beautcn.

MC LAIN, PHYLLIS ANAICE; West Phila Catholic Girls HS; Richmond, VA; (Y); 60/245; Church Yth Grp; Exploring; Spanish Clb; Band; Concert Band; Orch; Hon Roll; Spnsh Awd 84; 1st Pl Intermedt Div Sci Fair 85; Awd Merit Natl Poetry Essay Press 85; VA Union U; Math.

MC LAINE, JAMES; Pennsbury HS; Morrisville, PA; (Y); Church Yth Grp; German Clb; Acpl Chr; Chorus; Church Choir; School Musical; Rep Jr Cls; Rep Sr Cls; JV Trk; Hon Roll; Adv Mgmt.

MC LAINE, TAMI; Clarion Area JR SR HS; Clarion, PA; (Y); Hosp Aide; Band; Chorus; Color Guard; Concert Band; Drill Tm; Jazz Band; Mrchg Band; Pep Band; School Musical; Clarion U; Acctg.

MC LAUGHLIN, BECKY; United HS; Seward, PA; (Y); Ski Clb; Var L Sftbl; Var L Vllybl; Pep Clb; Spanish Clb; SADD; Varsity Clb; JV Bsktbl; Hon Roll; Prfct Atten Awd; IUP; Phy Ed.

MC LAUGHLIN II, CHARLES W; Ringgold HS; Donora, PA; (Y); Boy Scts; Band; Jazz Band; Hon Roll.

MC LAUGHLIN, DAVID; Freedom HS; Bethlehem, PA; (Y); 81/445; Church Yth Grp; Var Bsbl; Var Bsktbl; JV Socr; High Hon Roll; Bus.

MC LAUGHLIN, GRANT R; North Hills HS; Pittsburgh, PA; (Y); Sec Pres AFS; Exploring; VP JA; Key Clb; Ski Clb; Band; Nwsp Stf; Yrbk Stf; Rep Stu Cncl; Hon Roll; Cmmnctns.

MC LAUGHLIN, JOHN D; West Greene JR SR HS; Wind Ridge, PA; (S); 2/70; Drama Clb; Band; Concert Band; Drm Mjr(t); Mrchg Band; School Musical; School Play; Nwsp Stf; Yrbk Ed-Chief; Stu Cncl; Outstndng Ger Awd 82-86; Top 3rd Cls 83-86; Hist Awd 85; IN U Pennsylvania; Intl Stud.

MC LAUGHLIN, LAURA; Wilmington Area HS; New Wilmington, PA; (S); Church Yth Grp; Sec Trs Drama Clb; Key Clb; Band; Nwsp Rptr; Stu Cncl; Var Capt Crs Cntry; Var L Trk; Cit Awd; High Hon Roll; Dir Awd Band 83; Outstndg Perf Chrctr Role 84; Sch Recrd 800 Mtr Run 84; Pre-Med.

MC LAUGHLIN, MARGY; Kennard-Dale HS; Stewartstown, PA; (Y); Church Yth Grp; Varsity Clb; Chorus; Concert Band; Orch; School Musical; Yrbk Stf; JV Var Bsktbl; JV Var Vllybl; NHS; Dist Band, Adams Elec Yth Tour WA 86; Stu Mnth 85-86; Rec Mngmnt.

MC LAUGHLIN, MATTHEW; Emmaus HS; Macungie, PA; (Y); 120/500; Im Bsbl; JV L Wrstlng; Hon Roll; NHS; Trivia Clb 83; PA ST U; Chem Engrng.

MC LAUGHLIN, MICHELLE; New Hope-Solebury HS; New Hope, PA; (S); Cmnty Wkr; FBLA; Pep Clb; Pres Frsh Cls; Cheerleading; Powder Puff Ftbl; Sftbl; High Hon Roll; Hon Roll; NHS; Ntl Pop Wnnr Schlr Chrldr 83; Law.

MC LAUGHLIN, PATRICK; Emmaus HS; Macungie, PA; (Y); Camera Clb; Computer Clb; Quiz Bowl.

MC LAUGHLIN, SHARON; Deer Lakes HS; Creighton, PA; (Y); Church Yth Grp; Drama Clb; French Clb; Office Aide; Soroptimist; Varsity Clb; Var Capt Trk; Var L Vllybl; Hon Roll; Med Sec.

MC LAUGHLIN, SHEILEEN; Trinity HS; Mechanicsburg, PA; (Y); French Clb; Pep Clb; Ski Clb; Spanish Clb; Thesps; School Play; Im Tennis; JV Vllybl; Spanish NHS; Theatre.

MC LAUGHLIN, SUSAN; Bishop Kenrick HS; Norristown, PA; (Y); Art Clb; Aud/Vis; Church Yth Grp; Var Score Keeper; Var Trk; JV Vllybl; PA ST; Arch.

MC LAUGHLIN, TIM; South Philadelphia HS; Philadelphia, PA; (Y); JV Crs Cntry; Arch.

MC LAUGHLIN, TRACY; Tamaqua Area SR HS; Tamaqua, PA; (Y); Drama Clb; Service Clb; Color Guard; Flag Corp; School Musical; Ed Yrbk Stf; Var Capt Cheerleading; Var Crs Cntry; Phys Thrpy.

MC LAUGHLIN IV, WILLIAM; Springfield HS; Wyndmoor, PA; (Y); Rep Jr Cls; Var Bsbl; JV Bsktbl; Var Ftbl; Var Golf; Bus.

MC LEAN, ALYSON; Archbishop Carrool HS; Gladwyne, PA; (Y); 78/220; Mgr Cmnty Wkr; Mgr French Clb; Mgr Office Aide; Mgr SADD; Mgr Hon Roll; Jrnlsm.

MC LEAN, COLLEEN; Elkland Area HS; Elkland, PA; (Y); 22/80; Drama Clb; Library Aide; School Play; Yrbk Ed-Chief; Yrbk Stf; Rep Stu Cncl; Var JV Vllybl; Hon Roll; NHS; Prfct Atten Awd; Mansfield U; Spec Ed.

MC LEAN, PATRICIA; Archbishop John Carroll HS; King Of Prussia, PA; (Y); Cmnty Wkr; School Play; Ed Nwsp Rptr; High Hon Roll; NHS; Spanish NHS; Val; Creativ Art Awd 86; Schlrshp Rsmnt Coll 86; Pres Acadmc Fitnss Awd 86; Acdmc Schlrshp Cabrine Coll; Rosemont Coll; Fine Arts.

MC LEOD, KAREN; Du Bois Area SR HS; Reynoldsville, PA; (Y); 42/253; Art Clb; Pep Clb; Chorus; School Musical; Trs Jr Cls; Trs Sr Cls; Capt Twrlr; Hon Roll; Pres Acdmc Fit Awd 86; Wmns Clb Art Shw 1st Pl Cllgrphy Lcl Cnty & Rgnl, 3rd Pl ST Lvl 86; IN U PA; Art Cmrcl Illstrtn.

MC LINDEN, ROBERT J; State College Area SR HS; Port Matilda, PA; (Y); Im Bsktbl; Im Bowling; Var L Ftbl; Var L Trk; High Hon Roll; Fac Schlr Awd, Coachs Awd Ftbl 86; Penn ST; Aerosp Engrng.

MC LINTOLK, TAMY; Mifflinburg Area HS; Mifflinburg, PA; (Y); 13/169; Church Yth Grp; French Clb; Mgr(s); Sftbl; High Hon Roll; Hon Roll; NHS; Bloomsburg U; Elem Ed.

MC LOUGLIN, TIMOTHY; South Phila HS; Philadelphia, PA; (Y); Church Yth Grp; Crs Cntry; Hon Roll; Prfct Atten Awd; Arch Engr.

MC LOVICH, DANA; Freeland HS; Freeland, PA; (Y); 14/95; FBLA; Spanish Clb; Band; Chorus; Concert Band; JV Var Bowling; Twrlr; FLBA High Aver & Typg Awd 85-86; Grls High Gm Bwlng 85-86; Grls JV Chmpnshp 85-86; Harcum JC; Vet Assist.

MC MAHAN, KAREN; Baldwin HS; Pittsburgh, PA; (Y); 55/535; Church Yth Grp; Girl Scts; Key Clb; Concert Band; Mrchg Band; Bsktbl; High Hon Roll; NHS; School Musical; Symp Band; Physcl Thrpy.

MC MAHON, AMY; Bradford Area HS; Bradford, PA; (Y); 77/307; AFS; Church Yth Grp; Ski Clb; Band; Mrchg Band; Rep Stu Cncl; Var Cheerleading; Hon Roll; Jr NHS; NHS; Schlrshp PA Free Enterprise Week 85; Prom Committee 85; U Pittsburgh; Bus Admin.

MC MAHON, JOAN; Sullivan County HS; Dushore, PA; (Y); Sec Church Yth Grp; VP 4-H; FBLA; Band; Chorus; Color Guard; Concert Band; Mrchg Band; Nwsp Stf; Trs Frsh Cls; Brdcst Jrnlsm.

MC MAHON, KEITH; Spring-Ford SR HS; Collegeville, PA; (Y); 40/268; Pres Ski Clb; Capt Ftbl; Capt Trk; German Clb; Yrbk Phtg; Wt Lftg; Hon Roll.

MC MAHON, KELLI; Bensalem HS; Bensalem, PA; (Y); Trs Sr Cls; Stu Cncl; NHS; Wrstlr 85-86; JR Actvty Commitee 85-86; Ed.

MC MAHON, KEVIN; Mohawk Area HS; Enon Valley, PA; (Y); Latin Clb; Thesps; Band; Chorus; Concert Band; Mrchg Band; School Musical; Yrbk Phtg; Yrbk Stf; Hon Roll; Comp Sci Awd 2nd Pl 84-85; Penn ST U; Psych.

MC MAHON, MARY; West Greene HS; Waynesburg, PA; (Y); Art Clb; Church Yth Grp; DECA; Hosp Aide; Library Aide; SADD; VICA; Chorus.

MC MAHON, PATRICIA; Boyertown SR HS; Green Lane, PA; (Y); Pres 4-H; French Clb; Spanish Clb; Chorus; School Musical; Cit Awd; 4-H Awd; Socl Work.

MC MAHON, ROCHELLE; Du Bois Area HS; Du Bois, PA; (Y); Exploring; Intnl Clb; Library Aide; SADD; Chorus; Color Guard; Hon Roll; Pres Schlr; WA & Jefferson Coll; Psych.

MC MAHON, WENDY; Albert Gallatin SR HS; Ronco, PA; (Y); #13 In Class; Ski Clb; Stu Cncl; High Hon Roll; Hon Roll; Jr NHS; NHS; Pre-Med.

MC MANAMA, MAUREEN; Montour HS; Mckees Rocks, PA; (Y); Church Yth Grp; Hosp Aide; Pep Clb; Teachers Aide; Var Crs Cntry; Sftbl; Var L Swmmng; Var L Trk; Hon Roll; Nrsng.

MC MANAMON, CAREN; West Scranton HS; Scranton, PA; (Y); 24/367; Dance Clb; FNA; Sec Latin Clb; Letterman Clb; Pep Clb; Red Cross Aide; Ski Clb; SADD; Varsity Clb; Nwsp Phtg; E Stroudsburg U; Nrsng.

MC MANAMON, CHERYL; West Scranton HS; Scranton, PA; (Y); Dance Clb; Drama Clb; Latin Clb; Speech Tm; School Play; Nwsp Rptr; Yrbk Rptr; Hon Roll; Jr NHS; NHS; Syracuse U; Jrnlsm.

MC MANIGLE, ELIZABETH; Brookville Area HS; Brookville, PA; (Y); 18/141; Key Clb; Chorus; JV Cheerleading; Hon Roll; Jr NHS; NHS; IN U Of PA; Nrsg.

MC MANN, SAMANTHA; Harbor Creek HS; Erie, PA; (Y); Yrbk Phtg; Rep Jr Cls; Stu Cncl; Coach Actv; Trk; Hon Roll; Law Enfrcmnt.

MC MANUS, JENNIFER; G A R HS; Wilkes Barre, PA; (S); 17/178; Hosp Aide; Key Clb; Orch; Rep Stu Cncl; Golf; Swmmng; Jr NHS; NHS; Bloomsburg U; Med Tech.

MC MANUS, SHERRY; Bethlehem Center SR HS; Clarksville, PA; (Y); Art Clb; VP Church Yth Grp; Dance Clb; Girl Scts; Spanish Clb; Sftbl; Hon Roll; CA U; Psychlgst.

MC MARTIN, LEIANNE; Northern Lebanon HS; Jonestown, PA; (Y); Church Yth Grp; Model UN; Spanish Clb; Chorus; School Musical; School Play; Var L Fld Hcky; JV Trk; High Hon Roll; Ntl Tchng Cntst 2nd Pl Schlrshp 85; Math.

MC MASTER, GARY; Somerset HS; Somerset, PA; (Y); 15/236; English Clb; French Clb; Rep Stu Cncl; L Var Bsbl; High Hon Roll; Rep NHS; Varsity Clb; Chorus; JV Bsktbl.

MC MILLEN, JESSICA; New Brighton HS; New Brighton, PA; (Y); 4/157; Computer Clb; GAA; Varsity Clb; Var L Bsktbl; Var L Vllybl; High Hon Roll; Ethel Seavy Simpson Schlrshp IUP 86-87; IN U Of PA; Forgn Lang.

MC MILLEN, MELANIE; Sheffield Area JR SR HS; Sheffield, PA; (Y); 15/97; Church Yth Grp; Color Guard; School Musical; Yrbk Ed-Chief; Yrbk Phtg; Stu Cncl; Stat Bsktbl; Stat Vllybl; DAR Awd; NHS; Varsity Clb 85-86; U Of Pittsburgh; Englsh Educ.

MC MINN, LONNIE; Carmichaels Area HS; Carmichaels, PA; (Y); Church Yth Grp; French Clb; Ski Clb; Varsity Clb; L Bsbl; L Golf; High Hon Roll; Hon Roll; NHS; Earth & Sp Sci.

MC MONAGLE, MIKE; Bishop Mc Cort HS; Johnstown, PA; (Y); 83/153; German Clb; Chorus; Var L Ftbl; Hon Roll; Hist.

MC MORRIS, WILLIAM; Chanbersburg Area SR HS; Chambersburg, PA; (Y); AFS; Art Clb; Drama Clb; JCL; Key Clb; Latin Clb; Ntl Merit SF; RI Schl Of Desgn; Indstrl Dsgn.

MC MULLEN, ANTHONY; Oil City SR HS; Oil City, PA; (Y); 32/256; German Clb; Band; Im Bsktbl; Im Fld Hcky; Im Socr; Im Vllybl; Hon Roll; Prfct Atten Awd; PA Free Enterprise Wk 86; Hstry.

MC MULLEN, MARK; Blacklick Valley HS; Nanty Glo, PA; (Y); 19/120; Letterman Clb; Ski Clb; Spanish Clb; Varsity Clb; VP Bsbl; Var L Bsktbl; Im Ftbl; Hon Roll; Acadmc All Amer 84.

MC MULLEN, MARY PAT; Pittston Area HS; Avoca, PA; (Y); Church Yth Grp; Computer Clb; GAA; Math Clb; Ski Clb; Bsktbl; Tennis; Trk; NHS; PA ST U.

MC MURRAY, JAMES; Rocky Grove HS; Franklin, PA; (Y); 16/88; Church Yth Grp; Cmnty Wkr; SADD; Yrbk Stf; Hon Roll.

MC MURRAY, RENEE; Bald Eagle Area HS; Bellefonte, PA; (Y); 73/205; GAA; SADD; Jr Cls; Sr Cls; Var L Crs Cntry; Var Trk.

MC MURRAY, WENDY; Clearfield HS; Clearfield, PA; (Y); Drama Clb; Key Clb; Spanish Clb; Concert Band; Mrchg Band; School Musical; Variety Show; Pres Stu Cncl; Diving; High Hon Roll; Pre-Med.

MC MURTRIE, SUSAN; J P Mc Caskey HS; Lancaster, PA; (Y); 30/550; Band; Chorus; School Play; Nwsp Stf; Yrbk Stf; Var Cheerleading; Var Fld Hcky; Var Trk; Hon Roll; Jr NHS; 1st French Cntst Bloomsburg U 85; MVP Track 84; Faculty Appreciation Awd 84; Art.

MC NALLY, AMY M; South Side Catholic HS; Pittsburgh, PA; (S); VP Exploring; Church Choir; Stage Crew; Nwsp Stf; Yrbk Stf; Sec Frsh Cls; High Hon Roll; Sec Trs NHS; Pres VP Rotary Awd; Red Cross Ldrshp Devlp Ctr Co-Dir 86; HS Cncl Pres 84-86; Diocese Stu Advsry Bd 83-86; Cmmnctns.

MC NALLY, ANDREA; Phoenixville Area HS; Phoenixville, PA; (Y); 5/202; Church Yth Grp; Chorus; Concert Band; Mrchg Band; School Musical; Stat Bsktbl; Var L Lcrss; Jr NHS; NHS; Ntl Merit Ltr; Med.

MC NALLY, COLLEEN; Seneca Valley SR HS; Mars, PA; (Y); Church Yth Grp; SADD; Chorus; Bus.

MC NALLY, JEANNE; Upper Merion SR HS; King Of Prussia, PA; (Y); 27/320; German Clb; Band; Concert Band; Sec Frsh Cls; Sec Soph Cls; Pres Jr Cls; JV Var Cheerleading; Coach Actv; JV Lcrss; Hon Roll; Outstndng Overal Chrldr 85; Intnatl Bus.

MC NALLY, KAREN; Franklin HS; Franklin, PA; (Y); French Clb; Radio Clb; Color Guard; Flag Corp; Variety Show; Yrbk Stf; Off Frsh Cls; Off Soph Cls; Off Jr Cls; Stu Cncl; Ntl Hon Soc 85-86; Schl Dirctrs Awd 83-86; PA ST.

MC NALLY, KEVIN; Shaler Area HS; Pittsburgh, PA; (Y); 183/518; Office Aide; Rep Jr Cls; Bsbl; Ftbl; Sftbl; Wt Lftg; Hon Roll.

MC NAMARA, CHRISTINE; Cornell HS; Coraoplis, PA; (Y); Nwsp Rptr; Nwsp Stf; Yrbk Stf; Var Sftbl; Hon Roll; Law Enforcement Ofcr.

MC NAMARA, JOHN; Church Farm Schl; Philadelphia, PA; (Y); School Play; Nwsp Rptr; Nwsp Sprt Ed; Sec Stu Cncl; Mgr Bsktbl; JV Mgr Socr; Var Mgr Tennis; Var Mgr Trk; Cit Awd; Hon Roll; Archtr.

MC NAVISH, LORI; Chartiers-Houston HS; Houston, PA; (Y); 4/138; JA; Mathletes; Science Clb; Varsity Clb; Pres Frsh Cls; Pres Soph Cls; JV Var Cheerleading; Mu Alp Tht; VP NHS; Pres Schlr; Hmcmng Queen 85; PA ST U; Bus Adm.

MC NEAL, CAROLINE; Sayre Area HS; Sayre, PA; (Y); French Clb; Hosp Aide; Spanish Clb; Yrbk Stf; High Hon Roll; Hon Roll; Var L Swmmng; Var L Trk; Temple U; Bio Chem.

MC NEAL, GREG; Sheffield HS; Sheffield, PA; (Y); Church Yth Grp; Ski Clb; Varsity Clb; L Bsktbl; L Ftbl; L Trk; Vllybl; Wt Lftg; High Hon Roll; Hon Roll.

MC NEFF, JACKIE; Upper Moreland HS; Hatboro, PA; (Y); 59/260; Key Clb; School Musical; Rep Frsh Cls; Rep Soph Cls; Rep Jr Cls; JV Var Lcrss; High Hon Roll; Hon Roll; Nrsng.

MC NEIL, JAMES; Brookville Area HS; Brookville, PA; (Y); French Clb; Letterman Clb; Pep Clb; Ski Clb; Varsity Clb; Chorus; L Ftbl; L Trk; Hon Roll; Bus Admin.

MC NEIL, TOWANDA R; Little Flower Catholic HS; Philadelphia, PA; (Y); Cmnty Wkr; Office Aide; Speech Tm; Color Guard; Rep Frsh Cls; Trk; Hon Roll; Temple Clg; Law.

MC NELIS, MONICA MARIE; Altoona Area HS; Altoona, PA; (Y); Drama Clb; German Clb; Ski Clb; Pres Jr Cls; Rep Sr Cls; Sec Stu Cncl; Capt Pom Pon; Dance Clb; PAVAS; Drm Mjr(t); IN U Of Pa; Psych.

MC NELLIE, JENNIFER ANNE; Venango Christian HS; Oil City, PA; (Y); Girl Scts; Rep Soph Cls; Bsktbl; Cheerleading; Vllybl; Hon Roll; NHS; Prfct Atten Awd; Nwsp Stf; Bus.

MC NELLIE, JODI; Venago Christian HS; Oil City, PA; (Y); 7/36; Cmnty Wkr; JA; Rep Frsh Cls; Rep Soph Cls; Rep Stu Cncl; JV Capt Cheerleading; Vllybl; CC Awd; High Hon Roll; NHS; Physcl Educ.

MC NICHOLAS, MEGAN A; Archbishop Ryan HS For Girls; Philadelphia, PA; (Y); 10/483; VP JA; Spanish Clb; Rep Soph Cls; Off Jr Cls; Sec Sr Cls; Sec Stu Cncl; Im Bsktbl; Var Cheerleading; Dnfth Awd; High Hon Roll; Anna M Vincent Schlrshp 86; Most Prmsng Exc Woman Awd 86; City Phil Incntv Awd 85; Temple U; Bus Adm.

MC NITT, CAROL; Kishacoquillas HS; Reedsville, PA; (Y); 10/150; Drama Clb; French Clb; Library Aide; Varsity Clb; Nwsp Stf; Im Bowling; Var Fld Hcky; Mgr(s); Var Trk; Im Vllybl; Army Schlr Athl Awd; Penn ST.

MC NULTY, BETH; Strath Haven HS; Rose Valley, PA; (Y); Church Yth Grp; Intnl Clb; Ski Clb; School Musical; Yrbk Phtg; Rep Stu Cncl; JV Var Cheerleading; High Hon Roll; Hon Roll.

MC NULTY, JENNIFER; West Perry SR HS; Green Park, PA; (Y); 10/211; Sec Computer Clb; Spanish Clb; Varsity Clb; Nwsp Stf; Yrbk Stf; Pres Jr Cls; JV L Cheerleading; Var L Trk; High Hon Roll; NHS; Dept Hon Hghst Grd Comp Sci 86; MVP Trphy Vars Trck 86; U Of Pitt; Phys Ther.

MC NULTY, KAREN; Cambria Heights HS; Carrolltown, PA; (Y); FHA; Library Aide; Chorus; Church Choir; Yrbk Stf; Trk; PA ST U.

MC NULTY, KELLY; Lower Dauphin SR HS; Middletown, PA; (Y); Hosp Aide; Ski Clb; SADD; Rep Frsh Cls; Pres Soph Cls; Rep Jr Cls; Rep Sr Cls; Rep Stu Cncl; Cheerleading; Rosemont Clg; Bus/Acctg.

MC NULTY, MONICA; Bishop Guilfoyle HS; Altoona, PA; (Y); 3/130; Drama Clb; NFL; Ski Clb; Speech Tm; Band; Chorus; Drm Mjr(t); Yrbk Stf; High Hon Roll; NHS; Prtcptd 1st PA Stwd Mck Trl Comp 86; 1st Plc Cathlc Dghtrs Amrc Essy Comp & 3rd Plc ST 86; Law.

MC NULTY, PAUL; St Clair HS; St Clair, PA; (Y); Boy Scts; Hon Roll; NHS; Arch.

MC NULTY, ROBERT J; Cambria Heights HS; Chest Springs, PA; (Y); 22/200; Sec 4-H; NFL; ROTC; Hon Roll; Outstndng Cadet 86; Cadet Semester 85; Army Natl Guard Awd 83.

MC NUTT, CARLA; Franklin HS; Franklin, PA; (Y); Church Yth Grp; Cheerleading; Hon Roll; Slippery Rck Grive Cty; Elem Ed.

MC NUTT, SHERRIE; Dover Area HS; Dover, PA; (Y); 8/210; Drama Clb; Pep Clb; SADD; Varsity Clb; Chorus; Pres Jr Cls; Off Stu Cncl; Cheerleading; Coach Actv; High Hon Roll; Trvl & Toursm.

MC NUTT, STACY; Beaver JR SR HS; Beaver, PA; (Y); Church Yth Grp; JCL; Latin Clb; Band; Concert Band; Jazz Band; Mrchg Band; Symp Band; Powder Puff Ftbl; Embry Riddle Aero U; Cmmrcl Pil.

MC OWEN, KATHLEEN; Villa Joseph Marie HS; Churchville, PA; (S); Trs GAA; Library Aide; JV Bsktbl; Var Crs Cntry; Var Capt Socr; Var Capt Trk; Hon Roll; NHS; Prfct Atten Awd; Bucks Cty Courier Tms Nwsp Gldn 12 Al-Area Sccr Tm, Al-Area Trk Tm 83-85 & 85; Spnsh Awd Hghst Avg 85; Beaver Coll; Erly Chldhd.

MC PHELIM, BARBARA; Archbishop John Carroll HS; Audubon, PA; (Y); 32/212; Church Yth Grp; Cmnty Wkr; Red Cross Aide; Service Clb; SADD; Chorus; High Hon Roll; Hon Roll; Jr NHS; NHS; Adv Lfsvg & Wtr Sfty Bdg 85; CPR Bdg 85; Villanova U; Bus Adm.

MC PHERSON, CHRIS; East Pennsboro HS; Enola, PA; (Y); Camera Clb; Church Yth Grp; JV Bsktbl; Hon Roll; Cumberland Perry Area Vo-Tech.

MC PHERSON, HEATHER; Seneca Valley SR HS; Evans City, PA; (Y); Church Yth Grp; Thesps; Chorus; Madrigals; School Musical; School Play; Stage Crew; Alt PA Gov Schl Arts Theatr 85 & 86; Musicl Theatr.

MC PHERSON, SUSAN; Avonworth HS; Pittsbg, PA; (Y); AFS; Trs French Clb; JA; Band; Capt Drill Tm; Mrchg Band; School Musical; School Play; Yrbk Stf; Rep Stu Cncl; CA U Of PA; Acctg.

MC PHILLIPS, NEIL; Arch Bishop Ryan Boys HS; Philadelphia, PA; (Y); French Clb; Political Wkr; Im Bsktbl; Hon Roll; Fshn Mktg.

MC QUADE, LISA; Highlands SR HS; Tarentum, PA; (Y); Church Yth Grp; Cmnty Wkr; Hosp Aide; Intnl Clb; Key Clb; Library Aide; Hon Roll; NHS; Prfct Atten Awd; Duquesne U; Pre-Law.

MC QUADE, TAMMY; Mc Connellsburg HS; Mc Connellsburg, PA; (Y); VP FBLA; Bsktbl; High Hon Roll; Hon Roll; Bus Awd 82-83; Bus/Actg Awd 85-86.

MC QUATE, CINDY; Northern Lebanon JR SR HS; Lebanon, PA; (Y); Art Clb; Varsity Clb; Var L Cheerleading; Trk.

MC QUEEN, JULIE; Chambersburg Area SR HS; Fayetteville, PA; (Y); AFS; Church Yth Grp; German Clb; Church Choir; Socr; High Hon Roll; Hon Roll; Chem Awd 86; Engl Awd 86; Acctg Awd 86; Slippery Rock U; Acctg.

MC QUEEN, TODD; Coatesville Area SR HS; Coatesville, PA; (Y); 2/480; Ski Clb; Spanish Clb; Concert Band; Mrchg Band; Yrbk Stf; Stu Cncl; Hon Roll; NHS; NEDT Awd; Bus.

MC QUILLAN, BRYAN; Plymouth Whitemarsh HS; Norristown, PA; (Y); Chess Clb; Computer Clb; Service Clb; VICA; Hon Roll; Distngshd Honors 86; Machnst.

MC QUILLEN, JEFFREY; Clearfield Area HS; Mineral Spgs, PA; (Y); Drama Clb; French Clb; Yrbk Stf; Im Bowling; Im Ftbl; Im Trk; Im Wrstlng; Hon Roll; Cmptr Sci.

MC QUISTON, APRIL; Franklin Area SR HS; Harrisville, PA; (Y); Church Yth Grp; Sec 4-H; Spanish Clb; 4-H Awd; High Hon Roll; Hon Roll; NHS; Prfct Atten Awd.

MC QUISTON, JULEE; Corry Area HS; Corry, PA; (S); 17/212; Yrbk Ed-Chief; Rep Jr Cls; Rep Stu Cncl; High Hon Roll; French Clb; Office Aide; Sec Trs Y-Teens.

MC QUISTON, SUZANNE; Lincoln HS; Ellwood City, PA; (Y); 21/167; Pres AFS; Pres Church Yth Grp; Pres German Clb; Trs Spanish Clb; High Hon Roll; NHS; French Clb; Y-Teens; Chorus; Powder Puff Ftbl; Spnsh IV Awd 86; German II Awd/Wnr Of DANK Essay Contst 86; Kalon Ldrshp Awd 86; Bethany Coll; German/Spnsh.

MC QUOWN, TAMMY; Punxsutawney Area HS; Punxsutawney, PA; (Y); 90/249; Church Yth Grp; Cmnty Wkr; Teachers Aide; Church Choir; Stu Of Yr 84-85; Tchr.

MC RAE, SHARON; Peters Twp HS; Planoray, TX; (Y); 80/230; Church Yth Grp; FBLA; Q&S; SADD; Nwsp Bus Mgr; Ed Nwsp Rptr; Nwsp Stf; Yrbk Stf; Lit Mag; L Socr; Socr MIP 85; Fnlst WVU Wrtg Cont 86.

MC ROBERTS, COLLEEN; Beaver Area JR SR HS; Beaver, PA; (Y); Church Yth Grp; Exploring; JCL; Pep Clb; Concert Band; Mrchg Band; Yrbk Stf; Powder Puff Ftbl; Hon Roll; Nrsng.

MC ROBERTS, LINDA S; Bethel Park SR HS; Bethel Park, PA; (Y); 5/520; JA; Latin Clb; Drill Tm; Mrchg Band; School Musical; Symp Band; JV Vllybl; High Hon Roll; Sec NHS; Pres Schlr; Alcoa Fndtn Schlrshp 86; Virginia Tech; Engrng.

MC SHANE, COLLEEN; Cornell HS; Coraopolis, PA; (Y); 2/57; French Clb; Trs Key Clb; VP Band; Church Choir; Yrbk Ed-Chief; Sec Sr Cls; Swmmng; Cit Awd; DAR Awd; Pres NHS; Sci Hnrs Inst 86; ROTC Schlrshp 86; U Of Notre Dame; Aerosp Engrg.

MC SHANE, SEAN; Cornell HS; Coraopolis, PA; (Y); French Clb; Key Clb; Mgr Mrchg Band; JV Var Bsktbl; Ftbl; Mgr(s); Hon Roll; NHS; Engr.

MC SHEFFERY, ROXANNE; Fairchance Gerorges HS; Uniontown, PA; (Y); Band; Concert Band; Mrchg Band; Sec Jr Cls; Var Twrlr; Hon Roll; Jr NHS; NHS; Dntl Hygntst.

MC SORLEY, DANIELLE; Arch Bishop Ryan HS; Philadelphia, PA; (Y); Camp Fr Inc; Church Choir; VP Jr Cls; Stu Cncl; Cheerleading; Gym; Pom Pon; Socr; Sftbl; Swmmng; Med.

MC SORLEY, WM; Roman Catholic HS; Philadelphia, PA; (S); 5/150; Church Yth Grp; JA; Mathletes; Office Aide; Quiz Bowl; Stat Score Keeper; Cit Awd; High Hon Roll; Hon Roll; NHS; Comm.

MC SPARRAN, VICKI; Elizabethtown Area HS; Elizabethtown, PA; (Y); Church Yth Grp; Y-Teens; Church Choir; Var Powder Puff Ftbl; Var Score Keeper; Var Trk; Elizabethtown Aguatic Clb; W Shore Swm Tm 84-85; Mid Atlntc All-Star Cmptn 1st Pl 85.

MC SWAIN, WILLIAM; West Chester Henderson HS; West Chester, PA; (S); 1/348; JCL; Quiz Bowl; Ski Clb; Nwsp Rptr; Lit Mag; VP Tennis; VP Wrstlng; French Hon Soc; High Hon Roll; Ntl Merit SF.

MC TAVISH, LORI; Clearfield HS; W Decatur, PA; (Y); Pres Church Yth Grp; Hosp Aide; Pres SADD; Chorus; Church Choir; Variety Show; Hon Roll; Prfct Atten Awd; Pres SADD 86, VP 87; Elem Ed.

MC TEAR, GERALDINE; Downingtown SR HS; Exton, PA; (S); 10/553; GAA; Ski Clb; Spanish Clb; Teachers Aide; Im Bowling; Var Fld Hcky; Im Vllybl; High Hon Roll; NHS; Opt Clb Awd; 1st Tm All Chestmont Fld Hcky.

MC TIERNAN, KELLY; Norwin SR HS; N Huntingdon, PA; (Y); 11/563; Hosp Aide; Spanish Clb; SADD; Nwsp Rptr; High Hon Roll; NHS; St Vincent Coll; Englsh.

MC TIGHE, KAREN; S Park HS; Library, PA; (Y); Rep Jr Cls; Var L Bsktbl; Var L Sftbl; Var L Vllybl; High Hon Roll; NHS; Prfct Atten Awd; Scholar Awd 86.

MC TIGUE, MICHAEL; Kennedy Christian HS; Sharon, PA; (Y); Boy Scts; Church Yth Grp; Civic Clb; Letterman Clb; Ftbl; Trk; Wt Lftg; Wrstlng; Hon Roll; Gannon U Erie PA; Mech Engrg.

MC TIGUE, MICHAEL W; Central Bucks West HS; Chalfont, PA; (Y); 23/386; Drama Clb; Mathletes; Political Wkr; School Play; Nwsp Stf; VP Frsh Cls; VP Soph Cls; Pres Sr Cls; Hon Roll; Lion Awd; Parsdntl Acad Ftnss Awd 86; U Pa.

MC VAY, DUNCAN; WM Penn Charter Schl; Philadelphia, PA; (Y); Art Clb; Pres Chess Clb; Dance Clb; Stage Crew; Yrbk Stf; Var L Crs Cntry; Var L Trk; Hon Roll; NHS; Penn ST; Bus Adm.

MC VERRY, ERIN; Mt Lebanon HS; Pittsburgh, PA; (Y); 18/500; SADD; Pres Soph Cls; Pres Jr Cls; Rep Stu Cncl; JV Var Vllybl; High Hon Roll; Hon Roll; Church Yth Grp; French Clb; GAA; Outstndng Svc Awd 86; Pre-Law.

MC VETTA, LEE R; Carlisle SR HS; Carlisle, PA; (Y); Am Leg Boys St; JV Bsbl; JV Bsktbl; Var Trk; High Hon Roll; Hon Roll; NHS; Stu Mnth 85; Commrcl Art.

MC VEY, WAYNE; Henderson HS; Exton, PA; (Y); 38/349; Bsbl; Hon Roll; NHS; W Chester Area Schl Dist Ed Assn Achvt Awd 86; Med.

MC VICKER, JENNIFER; Ft Cherry HS; Mcdonald, PA; (Y); 30/119; Church Yth Grp; FNA; Math Clb; Science Clb; Ski Clb; Spanish Clb; Varsity Clb; Chorus; Church Choir; Capt Var Bsktbl; Sci Of Exrcs.

MC WILLIAMS, DANIEL; Blue Mountain Acad; Milton, PA; (S); School Play; Yrbk Bus Mgr; Yrbk Ed-Chief; Off Frsh Cls; VP Soph Cls; Rep Stu Cncl; JV Bsktbl; Capt Sftbl; High Hon Roll; Prfct Atten Awd; Andrews U; Bus Mgmnt.

MC WILLIAMS, LAURIE; North Allegheny HS; Pittsburgh, PA; (Y); Church Yth Grp; Concert Band; Mrchg Band; School Musical; Symp Band; Yrbk Stf; Rep Stu Cncl; Hon Roll; Gftd Orgnztn N Allegheny 82-86; N Allegheny Schlrhsp; Kent ST U; Nrs.

MC WILLIAMS, SEAN; Norristown Area HS; Norristown, PA; (S); DECA; Exploring; FBLA; JA; Im Socr; JV Var Tennis; Hon Roll; Schlrshp For Pa Free Entrprse Wk 86; 2nd Pl St For FBLA 86; 1st Pl St Gold Mdlln For DECA 86; Villanova U; Mktng.

MEACHAM III, ROGER H; Henderson HS; Exton, PA; (Y); Church Yth Grp; Red Cross Aide; JV Var Lcrss; JV Var Socr; Coll For Commrcl Art; Advrtsng.

MEADE, CHRIS; Hatboro-Horsham HS; Hatboro, PA; (Y); Boy Scts; Church Yth Grp; Key Clb; Yrbk Stf; Mgr(s); Stat Socr; Rifle Tm Var, Capt, Ltr 84-86; BSA Scout Yr 82; Westminster Coll; Comp.

MEADE, DANIELLE; Wilkinsburg JR SR HS; Wilkinsburg, PA; (Y); Dance Clb; French Clb; Key Clb; Concert Band; Mrchg Band; School Play; Stage Crew; Sec Sr Cls; Mgr(s); Hon Roll; Cert Of Accmplshmnt 83-84; IUP; Med Tech.

MEADE, DONNA; Lake-Lehman HS; Noxen, PA; (Y); 80/186; Church Yth Grp; Red Cross Aide; Ski Clb; Church Choir; School Play; Stat Crs Cntry; JV Fld Hcky; Stat Trk; LCCC; Rsptry Ther.

MEADE, JAMES; Cameron County HS; Emporium, PA; (Y); Aud/Vis; Chess Clb; Computer Clb; Debate Tm; Spanish Clb; School Play; Yrbk Phtg; Yrbk Stf; JV Bsktbl; Hon Roll.

MEADE, LEONARD; Aliquippa HS; Aliquippa, PA; (S); 5/159; Church Yth Grp; French Clb; Hon Roll; Engrng.

MEADOW, SHARI; Central Bucks West HS; Chalfont, PA; (Y); Art Clb; Cmnty Wkr; Natl Beta Clb; Service Clb; Spanish Clb; Teachers Aide; Temple Yth Grp; JV Trk; High Hon Roll; Spanish NHS; Mst Outstndng Art Clb Stdnt 84-85; Mst Outstndng GPA 84-85; Blu Rbbn Awd Dist Comptn Art 84-85; Greensboro Coll; Spec Ed.

MEADOWS, CHERYL; New Hope-Solebury JR SR HS; New Hope, PA; (Y); Church Yth Grp; Drama Clb; FBLA; Pep Clb; Band; Concert Band; Drm Mjr(t); Mrchg Band; Orch; Pep Band; Bllt; Chrgrphy 83 & 85; Chld Psyclgy.

MEADOWS, DAN; Cathedral Prep; Erie, PA; (Y); 164/216; Im Bsktbl; JV Var Ftbl; Var Wt Lftg; FL A & M; Bus.

MEAGHER, GREG; Greater Johnstown HS; Johnstown, PA; (Y); Boy Scts; Church Yth Grp; Spanish Clb; Band; Mrchg Band; Orch; Nwsp Ed-Chief; Nwsp Rptr; Nwsp Stf; Bowling; U Of Pittsburgh; Psych.

MEALS, MELINDA; Ridgway Area HS; Ridgway, PA; (Y); 3/127; Nwsp Ed-Chief; Yrbk Ed-Chief; VP Soph Cls; Var L Cheerleading; Trk; High Hon Roll; NHS; Laura Arnold Engl Awd, Daniel E Rouse Jrnlsm Awd 86; Stackpole Corp Schlrshp 86; Pres Fit Awd 86; Syracuse U; Brdcastng.

MEALS, TIMOTHY; Mt Calvary Christian Schl; Elizabethtown, PA; (S); Chess Clb; School Play; Nwsp Stf; Pres Stu Cncl; Var Capt Bsktbl; Var Capt Socr; Hon Roll.

MEANS, PAUL; Connellsville Area HS; Connellsville, PA; (Y); Office Aide; High Hon Roll; NHS; Washington/Jefferson Coll:Med.

MEANS, RHONDA; Punxsutawney Area HS; Valier, PA; (Y); 74/238; FBLA; Pst Wrthy Advsr Intl Ordr Rnbw Glrs 84; Ust Pl Bus Englsh Rgnl Cmptn 86; Punxsy Beauty Schl; Csmtlgy.

MEARKLE, LAURIE; Everett Area HS; Everett, PA; (Y); French Clb; GAA; Pep Clb; SADD; VICA; Band; Pres Frsh Cls; Stu Cncl; Capt Cheerleading; Trk; Scndry Educ.

MEARKLE, SHERI DEE; Shippensburg HS; Shippensburg, PA; (Y); Trs Leo Clb; Color Guard; Nwsp Sprt Ed; Lit Mag; Var Sftbl; Hon Roll; Jrnlsm.

MEASEL, ELLAINA; Grove City SR HS; Volant, PA; (Y); Key Clb; Library Aide; Band; Concert Band; Mrchg Band; Score Keeper; Hon Roll; Cosmtlgy.

MEBANE, DEBORAH; Wyoming Valley West HS; Larksville, PA; (Y); Trs Church Yth Grp; Hosp Aide; Library Aide; Ski Clb; Chorus; Church Choir; Rep Stu Cncl; High Hon Roll; Hon Roll; Wilkes Coll; Nrsng.

MECH, BARBARA ANN; Hanover Area JR-SR HS; Ashley, PA; (Y); 25/181; Key Clb; Ski Clb; Trs Sr Cls; Rep Stu Cncl; Hon Roll; Sec Jr NHS; NHS; Mbr Swthrt Court; Hon Mntn Peotry Cntst; Lock Haven U; Compu Sci.

MECK, BONNIE JEAN; Tussey Mountain HS; Saxton, PA; (Y); 3/97; Sec Church Yth Grp; Drama Clb; Mgr Band; Chorus; Church Choir; Concert Band; Jazz Band; School Play; Yrbk Stf; Stu Cncl; Srarcia Sci Awd 86; Amrcn Lgn Awd 86; Hlth Prfssn Schlrshps 86; Milton S Hershey Med Ctr; Radlg.

MECK, JULIE; Hanover Area HS; Warrior Run, PA; (Y); Cmnty Wkr; Hosp Aide; Nwsp Stf; Hon Roll; Jr NHS; NHS; Luzurne Cnty CC; Legal Sec.

MECK, SUSAN; Brandywine Heights HS; Mertztown, PA; (Y); 4/122; Hosp Aide; Math Clb; Band; Concert Band; Jazz Band; Mrchg Band; Pep Band; High Hon Roll; Hon Roll; NHS; County Bnad 84-85 & 85-86; Penn ST; Nursing.

MECKLEM, ROBIN; Lakeview HS; Fredonia, PA; (S); 9/125; Trs Intnl Clb; Library Aide; Chorus; Concert Band; Mrchg Band; Mgr School Play; Yrbk Stf; Stu Cncl; JV Var Cheerleading; Dist Chors, Hnrs Chors 85.

MECKLEY, ANN MARGARET; Chambersburg Area SR HS; Chambersburg, PA; (Y); 15/606; Am Leg Aux Girls St; Trs Debate Tm; NFL; Spanish Clb; Yrbk Stf; Stu Cncl; High Hon Roll; Hon Roll; Ambssdr Hgh O Brn Yth Ldrshp Smnr 85; Rochester Inst Of Tech.

MECKLEY, DIANA; Punxsutawney Area SR HS; Punxsutawney, PA; (Y); 115/238; VP Church Yth Grp; Pres Hosp Aide; Teachers Aide; Variety Show; Trk; Wrstlng; Slippery Rock U; Athl Trng.

MECKLEY, JENI; Warwick HS; Lititz, PA; (Y); Church Yth Grp; Band; Mrchg Band; JV Cheerleading; Hon Roll; Med.

MECKLEY, JOEL; Selinsgrove Area HS; Selinsgrove, PA; (Y); Church Yth Grp; Spanish Clb; Nwsp Bus Mgr; JV Ftbl; Hon Roll; NHS; Engrng.

MECKLEY, JULIE; Liberty HS; Bethlehem, PA; (Y); 70/500; Church Yth Grp; Drama Clb; Chorus; School Play; Chrmn Lit Mag; JV Cheerleading; High Hon Roll; Hon Roll; Microbiol.

MECKLEY, SUZANNE; Cocalico HS; Stevens, PA; (Y); 12/169; Camera Clb; Church Yth Grp; Yrbk Sprt Ed; Im Badmtn; Im Powder Puff Ftbl; Var Capt Tennis; Im Vllybl; Im Wt Lftg; High Hon Roll; Hon Roll; Radiology.

MEDIC, SHAUN; Moon HS; Coraopolis, PA; (Y); 70/320; Church Yth Grp; Key Clb; Pres Chorus; Pres Sr Cls; Var L Bsbl; Var Capt Ftbl; Kiwanis Awd; Acpl Chr; School Musical; Rep Stu Cncl; Grnd Prz Dnt Drnk & Drv Cntst Orgnl Sng 86; Rgnl Chrs 86; Dstct Chrs Solo 82; Grove City Coll; Pltcl Sci.

MEDINA, EDWIN; Bristol JR SR HS; Bristol, PA; (Y); Boy Scts; Church Yth Grp; Stage Crew; Off Frsh Cls; JV Bsktbl; Var JV Ftbl; Capt Mgr(s); Hon Roll; ARM.

MEDINA, MABEL; Central Catholic HS; Walnutport, PA; (Y); Intnl Clb; Math Clb; Q&S; Scholastic Bowl; School Musical; Ed Lit Mag; Trs Stu Cncl; High Hon Roll; Hon Roll; Pres NHS; Engrng.

MEDINA, PATRICIA; Bentworth SR HS; Bentleyville, PA; (Y); Church Yth Grp; FFA; Hon Roll; Prfct Atten Awd; Acctg.

MEDLINSKY, PAM; Shenandoah Valley HS; Lost Creek, PA; (S); 7/98; Hosp Aide; Drm Mjr(t); Yrbk Ed-Chief; Rep Frsh Cls; Rep Jr Cls; Var Capt Bsktbl; Var Capt Vllybl; Hon Roll; NHS; Female Schlr Athl 86; Acad All Am 86; PA Coll; Physcl Thrpy.

MEDRICK, LINDA; Meadville Area HS; Meadville, PA; (Y); 26/324; Key Clb; Spanish Clb; SADD; Y-Teens; Hon Roll; Bus.

MEDVETZ, AUDREY; Pottstown HS; Pottstown, PA; (S); 2/197; Key Clb; Spanish Clb; Concert Band; Drm Mjr(t); Jazz Band; Mrchg Band; School Musical; Ed Yrbk Stf; High Hon Roll; NHS; Penn ST U; Engrng.

MEDVIT, JAMES S; Union Area HS; New Castle, PA; (Y); 6/66; French Clb; Pep Clb; Varsity Clb; Bsktbl; Ftbl; Trk; Wt Lftg; High Hon Roll; Hon Roll; Sec NHS; Schlr Athlete Awd 85-86; FL ST U; Bus Admin.

MEECH, MICHELLE M; Meadville Area SR HS; Meadville, PA; (S); 21/287; Art Clb; Chorus; Concert Band; Drm & Bgl; Drm Mjr(t); Mrchg Band; Pep Band; School Play; Yrbk Ed-Chief; French Clb; IN U Pennsylvania; Music Ed.

MEEHAN, JENNIFER; Central Dauphin HS; Harrisburg, PA; (Y); Exploring; Red Cross Aide; Chorus; Concert Band; Jazz Band; Mrchg Band; School Musical; Hon Roll; NHS; Pre-Law.

MEEHAN, MICHELLE; Nazareth Acad; Philadelphia, PA; (Y); Drama Clb; Spanish Clb; Chorus; School Play; Sftbl; Vllybl; Theatrical Arts.

MEEHAN, REBECCA; Villa Maria HS; Lowellville, OH; (Y); Drama Clb; Hosp Aide; Ski Clb; Spanish Clb; Thesps; Acpl Chr; Chorus; School Musical; School Play; Lit Mag; Biopsych.

MEEKER, KAREN; Northwest HS; Shickshinny, PA; (Y); 6/108; Pres Church Yth Grp; Chess Clb; Computer Clb; Latin Clb; Var Capt Crs Cntry; Var Capt Trk; High Hon Roll; NHS; Mst Valuable Runner 84; Bucknell U; Engl.

MEENAN, MICHAEL B; Cardinal O Hara HS; Springfield, PA; (Y); 18/750; Church Yth Grp; School Play; Im Bsktbl; JV Crs Cntry; JV Socr; High Hon Roll; Hon Roll; NHS; Ntl Merit SF; Prfct Atten Awd; Prncpls Awd 85; U Of PA; Bus.

MEERTZ, HEIDI; Academy Of Notre Dame; Rosemont, PA; (Y); FCA; Mathletes; Red Cross Aide; Variety Show; Var Fld Hcky; Var Capt Lcrss; Hon Roll; Wake Forest U.

MEFFORD, JUDY; Waynesburg Central HS; Waynesburg, PA; (Y); Sec Trs FHA; Chorus; Hon Roll; Cook.

MEGARGEL, BRET; Central Dauphin HS; Harrisburg, PA; (Y); 7/386; Key Clb; Var Bsbl; Var Ftbl; Var Wt Lftg; High Hon Roll; Hon Roll; NHS; West Point; Engr.

MEGOSH, CYNTHIA; Our Lady Of Lourdes HS; Mt Carmel, PA; (Y); 11/97; Capt Pep Clb; Ed Nwsp Stf; Yrbk Stf; Sec Stu Cncl; Stat Bsktbl; Sftbl; Hon Roll; Sec NHS; Fred Smith Schlrshp 86; Lourdes Alumni Assoc Schlrshp 86; Bloomsburg U; Acctg.

MEHALIK JR, JOHN T; Beaver Area HS; Beaver, PA; (Y); Aud/Vis; Church Yth Grp; Exploring; FCA; Trs French Clb; Ski Clb; Teachers Aide; Bsktbl; Var Ftbl; JV Trk; Comp.

MEHALLO, CHRISTOPHER; West Hazleton HS; Harwood, PA; (Y); 48/225; Library Aide; Ski Clb; VICA; Off Soph Cls; VP Sr Cls; Hon Roll; Mech Engr.

MEHOLICK, DAVE; Du Bois Area HS; Sykesville, PA; (Y); 56/288; Boy Scts; Varsity Clb; Bowling; Var Capt Ftbl; DAR Awd; Rotary Awd; Stu Of Yr 85-86; Otstndng Schlr Ag Rsrcs 84-86; Otstndng Englsh Stu 85-86; Edinboro U Of PA; Poli Sci.

MEHRER, KATIE; Jenkintown HS; Jenkintown, PA; (S); Model UN; NFL; Q&S; School Play; Nwsp Rptr; Yrbk Rptr; Mgr Crs Cntry; JV Fld Hcky; JV Lcrss; Hon Roll; Smmr Intnsv Frgn Lang Prog 85.

MEHTA, SANJAY; Columbia HS; Columbia, PA; (Y); 7/86; Quiz Bowl; Ski Clb; Varsity Clb; Ftbl; Socr; Trk; High Hon Roll; Hon Roll; Trs NHS; Prfct Atten Awd; Grinnell Schlrshp, Tchrs Educ Awd, Harry S Smoker Schlrshp 86; Penn ST U; Bus Admin.

MEIER, GWEN; Mc Guffey HS; W Alexander, PA; (Y); 2/218; Church Yth Grp; German Clb; Church Choir; VP Jr Cls; Rep Stu Cncl; High Hon Roll; NHS; Congress Bundestag Yth Exch 86-87; PA Gov Schl Intl Studies 86; Macalester Coll; Intl Studies.

MEIER, KARYN; Pequea Valley HS; Paradise, PA; (Y); AFS; Church Yth Grp; FBLA; Color Guard; Drill Tm; Stage Crew; Yrbk Stf; Mgr Gym; High Hon Roll; NHS; Temple U; Phrmcy.

MEIER, ROBERT; G A R Memorial HS; Wilkes Barre, PA; (S); 24/187; Aud/Vis; Camera Clb; Computer Clb; Drama Clb; German Clb; Chorus; School Play; Bowling; Golf; Hon Roll; Comp Sci.

MEIER, SHANA; Tunkhannock Area HS; Tunkhannock, PA; (S); Art Clb; French Clb; Color Guard; Flag Corp; Mrchg Band; Hon Roll; NHS; Fash Merch.

MEIKLEJOHN, CHERYL; Owen J Roberts HS; Phoenixville, PA; (S); 21/273; GAA; Hosp Aide; Letterman Clb; SADD; Varsity Clb; Var Bsktbl; Var Fld Hcky; Var Capt Lcrss; High Hon Roll; Hon Roll; U S Fld Hcky Assoc; MVP La Crosse; La Crosse 1st Tm All Area 2nd Tm All Chesmont; U Of VA; Psych.

MEINERT, LINDA; Quigley HS; Ambridge, PA; (S); Yrbk Stf; Stat Bsktbl; Powder Puff Ftbl; L Tennis; High Hon Roll; Hon Roll; Cortez Peter JRS Typg Cert 85-86; Mktg.

MEINHART, KELLY; Pleesant Valley HS; Kunkeltown, PA; (Y); Camp Fr Inc; Church Yth Grp; Drama Clb; Ski Clb; Stage Crew; Lit Mag; Trs Soph Cls; Trs Jr Cls; Stu Cncl; Trk; Comm.

MEISENBACH, MICHELLE; Bishop Conwell HS; Melbourne, FL; (Y); 26/254; Church Yth Grp; French Clb; Intnl Clb; Political Wkr; Service Clb; Variety Show; Yrbk Rptr; Yrbk Stf; Im Bsktbl; Hon Roll; French Achvt Awd 84; FL Inst; Comm Airline Pilot.

MEISLIK, MICHELLE; Seneca Valley HS; Mars, PA; (Y); JA; Ski Clb; Drill Tm; School Play; Nwsp Stf; Rep Frsh Cls; Rep Jr Cls; Rep Sr Cls; Capt L Pom Pon; U Pittsburgh; Phrmcst.

MEISTER, CHRISTOPHER R; Cathedral Prep; Erie, PA; (Y); 5/231; Quiz Bowl; Yrbk Stf; Im Bsktbl; JV Socr; Im Vllybl; High Hon Roll; NHS; Gld Mdln Exclnce Christian Doctrine, Copy Wrtng Awds Wk Yrbk, US Educ Physical Ftns Awd 86; John Carroll U; Acctg.

MEKO, BILL; Punxsutawney Area SR HS; Punxsutawney, PA; (Y); Camera Clb; Church Yth Grp; Letterman Clb; Teachers Aide; Varsity Clb; Nwsp Phtg; Nwsp Rptr; Nwsp Stf; Wt Lftg; Var L Wrstlng; 3rd Pl Dist In Wrstlng 86; Lock Haven U; Gym Tchr.

MEKO, DOUGLAS; Punxsutawney Area HS; Punxsutawney, PA; (Y); 44/270; Math Tm; Variety Show; Ftbl; Capt Wrstlng; High Hon Roll; Hon Roll; Stu Of Mnth 82.

MEKULSKI, LORI; Mechanicsburg Area SR HS; Mechanicsburg, PA; (Y); Am Leg Aux Girls St; Church Yth Grp; Nwsp Rptr; Yrbk Stf; Capt Var Bsktbl; Var L Sftbl; Var L Trk; Wt Lftg; Hon Roll; Diocesan Yth Council 85; Engl.

MEKUTA, NOELLE; Pocono Mountain HS; Mt Pocono, PA; (Y); Church Yth Grp; SADD; Var Powder Puff Ftbl; Hon Roll; Excllnc In Splling Awd 83-84; Fshn Merch.

MELARAGNO, KATHRYN; Villa Maria Acad; Erie, PA; (S); 14/139; NFL; PAVAS; Orch; Nwsp Ed-Chief; Hon Roll; NHS; NEDT Awd; Hopwood Summr Scholar 85; Gannon U; Pre-Law.

MELBY, LEIGH ANN; Conneaut Lake HS; Conneaut Lake, PA; (Y); 4/90; Church Yth Grp; Spanish Clb; SADD; Band; VP Sec Mrchg Band; Pep Band; School Musical; Nwsp Ed-Chief; Stu Cncl; Var L Sftbl; Dist And Regnl Band 86; Greenvl Symphny Orch 86; U Of Notre Dame; Aerosp Engrg.

MELCHIONDO, ELANA; New Hope-Solebury JR SR HS; New Hope, PA; (S); 6/82; FBLA; Mathletes; Pep Clb; Trs Rep Stu Cncl; Var JV Cheerleading; JV Var Fld Hcky; High Hon Roll; NHS; Ski Clb; Yrbk Stf; PA Free Entrprse Wk Schlrshp 85; FBLA Rgn Cmptn 1st Prz Stnogrphy I 85; Engrng.

MELEGO, LARRY; Mt Pleasant Area HS; Mt Pleasant, PA; (Y); 50/250; Boy Scts; Church Yth Grp; Exploring; Latin Clb; JV Ftbl; Hon Roll; Eagle Sct, Ldrshp Corps 85; Indian Dance Tm Chrmn 84-86; Pgm Vice Chf, Awd Excel Ind Fncy Dance 86; Penn ST.

MELENYZER, LISA; Riverview HS; Oakmont, PA; (Y); 1/118; VP Key Clb; Trs SADD; Concert Band; Mrchg Band; Yrbk Ed-Chief; Var Trk; Stat Vllybl; High Hon Roll; NHS; NEDT Awd.

MELESKY, SCOTT J; Riverside JR-SR HS; Moosic, PA; (Y); 38/140; Pres Ski Clb; Nwsp Stf; Ftbl; Trk; Hon Roll; PA ST U; Bus.

MELEY, CHAD; North Allegheny HS; Allison Park, PA; (Y); Boy Scts; Debate Tm; Drama Clb; Speech Tm; Thesps; School Musical; School Play; Rep Jr Cls; Var Tennis; Hon Roll; Bus.

MELHORN, CHRISTY; Spring Grove SR HS; Thomasville, PA; (Y); 32/220; German Clb; JA; Variety Show; Ed Yrbk Stf; High Hon Roll; Hon Roll; Millersville U; Grmn.

MELLARKEY, SHERI; North Pocono HS; Moscow, PA; (Y); Church Yth Grp; Dance Clb; Exploring; FBLA; Chorus; Church Choir; High Hon Roll; Hon Roll; NHS; Wrtg.

MELLATT, TAMELA JOEENE; Mc Cannellsburg HS; Mc Connellsburg, PA; (Y); Am Leg Aux Girls St; Varsity Clb; Chorus; School Musical; Stu Cncl; L Trk; Var L Vllybl; High Hon Roll; VP Jr NHS; NHS; Advncd Biol Awd 86; Geom Awd 85; Co-Edtr Yrbk 86-87; Pre-Law.

MELLE, MELISSA; Bishop Kenrick HS; Norristown, PA; (Y); Dance Clb; Office Aide; Service Clb; Off Stu Cncl; Var Bsktbl; Var Fld Hcky; Im Mgr Powder Puff Ftbl; Var Sftbl; Bus.

MELLIN, STEPHEN; Wm Allen HS; Allentown, PA; (Y); 30/530; Civic Clb; Leo Clb; Math Clb; Math Tm; Hon Roll; NHS; Pres Schlr; Wnnr In U Of Pa Physics Tstng Comp 85; Le High U; Elec Engr.

MELLINGER, ANDREW; Somerset Area SR HS; Somerset, PA; (Y); French Clb; Band; Orch; Hon Roll; NHS; Charles Suibner Mem Art Awd 84; Coll Of Wooster; Aerosapce Engr.

MELLINGER, CHRISTINA; Hempfield HS; Landisville, PA; (Y); Cmnty Wkr; Chorus; Orch; School Musical; Variety Show; Var L Crs Cntry; Var L Trk; Dnfth Awd; NHS; Bible Clb.

MELLINGER, HEATHER; Eastern York HS; Wrightsville, PA; (Y); 32/159; Hosp Aide; Chorus; Church Choir; Flag Corp; School Musical; Variety Show; Nwsp Rptr; Yrbk Stf; Bsktbl; Hon Roll; Schlrshp Awd Cert 85-86; IN U PA; Elem Ed.

MELLISH, MARGARET RENEE; Knoch JR SR HS; Saxonburg, PA; (Y); 1/223; Girl Scts; NFL; Band; Concert Band; Mrchg Band; Pep Band; School Musical; High Hon Roll; NHS; Val; Catholic Marian Awd 83; Saxonburg Dist Wmns Clb Schlrshp 86; Gertrude Desellem Mem Schlrshp 86; WV U; Music Educ.

MELLIX, DONNIELLE; Penn Wood HS; Yeadon, PA; (Y); 14/336; Church Yth Grp; Pres FBLA; Red Cross Aide; Yrbk Stf; Stu Cncl; Stat Bsktbl; Stat Trk; Hon Roll; NHS; Natl Achvt For Negro Stu 85-6; Penn ST U; Bio.

MELLON, MARLENE; Greater Johnstown HS; Johnstown, PA; (Y); 2/286; Church Yth Grp; Key Clb; Office Aide; Ski Clb; Mrchg Band; Sr Cls; NHS; Sal; Heffley Scholar U Pittsburgh Johnstown 86; SR Schltc Scholar 86; U Pittsburgh Johnstown; Engrng.

MELLOR, JENNIFER; Little Flower Catholic H S For Girls; Philadelphia, PA; (Y); 1/398; Aud/Vis; Pres French Clb; Sec Science Clb; Ed Lit Mag; Bausch & Lomb Sci Awd; Hon Roll; NCTE Awd; NHS; Ntl Merit Ltr; Prfct Atten Awd; PA Gvrnrs Schl Of Agrcltr & Intl Stds Schlrshp 86; Amer Chmcl Soc Cert 85; Vet Med.

MELLOTT, AMY K; Central Dauphin East HS; Steelton, PA; (Y); Pres Church Yth Grp; Quiz Bowl; Concert Band; Jazz Band; Mrchg Band; Hon Roll; Jr NHS; NHS; Ntl Merit SF; St Schlr; Schl Acadmc Stu Of Mth 85; PA ST U; Comp Sci.

MELNICHUK, THERESA; St Hubert HS For Girls; Philadelphia, PA; (Y); 155/367; Cmnty Wkr; Dance Clb; Office Aide; Chorus; Prfct Atten Awd.

MELNICK, ALEXANDER; GAR HS; Wilkes-Barre, PA; (Y); French Clb; Letterman Clb; Varsity Clb; Nwsp Stf; Yrbk Stf; Var Bsbl; Var Bsktbl; Hon Roll; Jr NHS; Wilkes Coll; Phys Thrpy.

MELNICK, TAMMY; Seton Catholic HS; Dupont, PA; (Y); Art Clb; Key Clb; Mathletes; Chorus; School Musical; School Play; Yrbk Stf; Hon Roll; Marywood Coll; Elem Educ.

MELNYK, KATHY; Hopewell HS; Aliquippa, PA; (Y); Computer Clb; Exploring; Latin Clb; Chorus; School Play; Yrbk Stf; Pres Stu Cncl; Bowling; Powder Puff Ftbl; NHS; WV U; Phrmcy.

MELOCCHI, LORI; Steel Valley HS; Munhall, PA; (Y); 43/201; VP Sec Key Clb; Mat Maids; Hon Roll; NHS; Accntng.

MELOVICH, SUZANNE; Pennsburg HS; Levittown, PA; (Y); Cmnty Wkr; Rep Spanish Clb; Rep SADD; Varsity Clb; Pres Frsh Cls; Rep Soph Cls; Rep Jr Cls; Rep Sr Cls; Rep Stu Cncl; Capt Swmmng; Miss TEEN Pgnt Cont 86; Olympc Trls Comp 84; JR Olympc Natl 86; PA ST Behrend; Cmmnctns.

MELOY, MIKE; Cumberland Valley HS; Mechanicsburg, PA; (Y); Bsbl; NHS; Air Force; Elec.

MELTON, MELISSA M; Pottsgrove SR HS; Pottstown, PA; (Y); 12/234; Math Clb; Varsity Clb; Chorus; Concert Band; Jazz Band; Mrchg Band; Rep Stu Cncl; Var Capt Bsktbl; Hon Roll; NHS; Intrcnty Cncrt Bnd & Jazz Bnd 84; Tutrng Elem Stu Frnch 85; Engrng.

MELTON, WILLIAM C; Hollidaysburg Area HS; Hollidaysburg, PA; (Y); Spanish Clb; Var L Bsktbl; JV Ftbl; Var L Tennis; PA ST.

MELUCCI, CHRISTINA; Bethel Park HS; Pittsburgh, PA; (Y); Church Yth Grp; Orch; Hon Roll; Pittsburgh Yth Symph Prncpl Violnst 83-86; Tanglewood Yng Art 84; Troy Qrtet Pgm 85-86; Eastman Schl Music; Prof Violns.

MELUSKY, AMY; Nativity BVM HS; Mar-Lin, PA; (Y); Art Clb; Spanish Clb; Variety Show; Rep Frsh Cls; Rep Soph Cls; Off Jr Cls; Var L Bsktbl; Gym; Hon Roll; Hghst Achvt Bio, Spnsh II 84-85; Bus.

MELVIN, ELIZABETH; Pittston Area SR HS; Pittston, PA; (Y); High Hon Roll; Hon Roll; NHS; Stenogrphr.

MENAND, STEVE; Beaver Area JR SR HS; Beaver, PA; (Y); JCL; Ski Clb; Concert Band; Jazz Band; Mrchg Band; School Musical; High Hon Roll; NHS; Atnd Wrld Afrs Cncl Ptsbrgh Rtry Schlrshp 85; SR Math Awd; Lehigh U; Math.

MENAPACE, SHARON; Mt Carmel Area JR & SR HS; Atlas, PA; (Y); Key Clb; Pep Clb; Ski Clb; Spanish Clb; School Musical; Nwsp Rptr; Stu Cncl; Cheerleading; Sftbl; Hon Roll; Spch Path.

MENCER, MICHELE; Marion Center Area HS; Indiana, PA; (S); 9/170; Church Yth Grp; SADD; VP Jr Cls; Sec Stu Cncl; L Cheerleading; Var Trk; Hon Roll; NHS; Intnl Clb; Q&S; Qualified Dist In Trk 85; 1st Tri-Cnty Cheering Cmptn 84; Chrmn Hmcmng 85; Psych.

MENDICINO, CARMINE; Sacred Heart HS; Carbondale, PA; (Y); 7/49; Cmnty Wkr; Pres Spanish Clb; SADD; Nwsp Rptr; VP Jr Cls; Pres Stu Cncl; Var L Bsktbl; NHS; Stu Cncl Ldrshp Awd 85; Bus.

MENDICINO, MARK; Waynesburg Central HS; Waynesburg, PA; (Y); Spanish Clb; Capt Band; Capt Concert Band; Jazz Band; Capt Mrchg Band; High Hon Roll; PA All-State Lions Band 86; Mcdonalds All-American High Sch Band 86; WV U; Music.

MENDICINO, MISSY; Perkiomen Schl; Brookhaven, PA; (Y); Ski Clb; Varsity Clb; Chorus; Nwsp Ed-Chief; Yrbk Phtg; Var Bsktbl; Var Fld Hcky; Var Sftbl; High Hon Roll; NHS; Gld Acdmc Ky 85; MVP Fld Hcky 84; MVP Sftbll 86; Pre-Med.

MENDOFIK, MICHELLE J; West Hazleton HS; W Hazleton, PA; (S); 59/192; FNA; Hosp Aide; Office Aide; Red Cross Aide; School Musical; Var Mgr(s); JV Var Mat Maids; NHS; Luzerne County CC; Dentl Hyg.

MENDOLA, EDWARD; Charleroi Area HS; Charleroi, PA; (Y); Church Yth Grp; Varsity Clb; Off Soph Cls; Off Jr Cls; Stu Cncl; Im Bsktbl; Var L Ftbl; High Hon Roll; Hon Roll; NHS; Bus.

MENDOLA, JANINE; Parkland HS; Fogelsville, PA; (Y); 4/431; Cmnty Wkr; VP German Clb; Hosp Aide; Trs Key Clb; School Play; DAR Awd; Pres NHS; Voice Dem Awd; Political Wkr; Nwsp Stf; Pres Clsrm Yng Amers 85; Karate Wht, Yllw, Orng & Grn Blts 83-86; PA ST U; Pre-Med.

MENES, LINDA; Vincentian HS; Pittsburgh, PA; (Y); 5/56; Rep Church Yth Grp; Hosp Aide; Service Clb; Chorus; Yrbk Ed-Chief; VP Soph Cls; Var Capt Fld Hcky; Var Capt Sftbl; High Hon Roll; Trs NHS; Century III Ldr 86; OH Wesleyan U; Psych.

MENGEL, TIM; Hamburg Area HS; Hamburg, PA; (Y); 29/152; Church Yth Grp; Pres SADD; Chorus; Church Choir; Concert Band; Jazz Band; L Mrchg Band; Pep Band; NHS; Cnty Bnd Orch & Chrs 86; Dist Bnd & Orch 86; Rgnl Bnd & Orch; W Chester U; Music Ed.

MENGLE, TERRY; Middleburg HS; Mt Pleasant Mls, PA; (Y); Key Clb; Band; Chorus; Nwsp Stf; Yrbk Stf; VP Sr Cls; Var JV Fld Hcky; High Hon Roll; Hon Roll.

MENHORN, ALLEN; Moniteau HS; W Sunbury, PA; (Y); VP Church Yth Grp; Spanish Clb; Band; Church Choir; Concert Band; Mrchg Band; Hon Roll; NHS; Thiel Coll; Sci.

MENICHETTI, AMY; Valley View HS; Peckville, PA; (Y); Church Yth Grp; FBLA; Vllybl; High Hon Roll; Hon Roll; Bus Englsh Awd 85; Bus Mngmnt.

MENKEL, LINDA SHERRI ARLENE; John A Brashear HS; Pittsburgh, PA; (Y); 27/372; Art Clb; Chess Clb; Cmnty Wkr; FBLA; Math Tm; Office Aide; Spanish Clb; Teachers Aide; Band; Chorus; Plaque Hnrs Grad 86; Cert Best Typst 86; Bradford Bus Schl; Exec Sec.

MENNOW, RON; Deer Lakes JR SR HS; Gibsonia, PA; (Y); Band; Concert Band; Jazz Band; Mrchg Band; Pep Band; School Musical; School Play; Yrbk Stf; Ftbl; Trk; Alle-Kiski Hon Bnd 84 & 85; PMEA Dist Bnd 86; Dqusn U Cncrt Bnd 84 & 85; Music.

MENON, VIKAS; Fairview HS; Erie, PA; (Y); Debate Tm; Model UN; NFL; Q&S; Nwsp Stf; German Clb; Nwsp Rptr; Lit Mag; Hon Roll; 1st Pl Features Awd Gannon U, Tri-ST Schlstc Jrnlsm Cont 85-86; Commnctns.

MENSINGER, RACQUEL; Hazleton HS; Hazleton, PA; (Y); 88/383; Art Clb; Drama Clb; Office Aide; Pep Clb; Spanish Clb; Chorus; School Musical; School Play; High Hon Roll; Penn ST U; Elm Ed.

MENTO, DAWN; Penn Cambria HS; Loretto, PA; (Y); French Clb; Band; Concert Band; Mrchg Band.

MENTZER, JEFF; Biglerville HS; Arendtsville, PA; (Y); Boy Scts; Computer Clb; FCA; Bsbl; Ftbl; Mgr(s); Wrstlng; Comptr Prgrmng.

MENTZER, TODD; Waynesboro Area SR HS; Waynesboro, PA; (Y); 42/392; Church Yth Grp; Church Choir; Concert Band; Drm Mjr(t); Jazz Band; Mrchg Band; Swing Chorus; Crs Cntry; Trk; High Hon Roll; Acctng.

MENTZER, TRACEY; Claysburg-Kimmel HS; Claysburg, PA; (Y); Camera Clb; Church Yth Grp; German Clb; Ski Clb; Speech Tm; SADD; Band; Mrchg Band; Sftbl; Penn ST U; Psych.

MENYO, MELISSA; Marple Newtown SR HS; Broomall, PA; (Y); Hosp Aide; Lit Mag; Trk; Var L Vllybl; Hon Roll; Prfct Atten Awd.

MENZ, BETH; Penn Trafford HS; Trafford, PA; (Y); 156/362; FBLA; JCL; IN U; Acctng.

MENZEL, KARIN; Mercy Hurst Prep; Erie, PA; (Y); 52/150; Spanish Clb; JV Sftbl; Var Swmmng; PA ST.

MEOLA, JOLYNDA; West Allegheny HS; Imperial, PA; (Y); Church Yth Grp; High Hon Roll; VP Wst Alghny Chrstn Clb 85-86; Csmtlgy.

MERCADANTE, FELICE; Norwin HS; N Huntingdon, PA; (Y); DECA; Accntng.

MERCADANTE, LISA ANN; Hopewell HS; Aliquippa, PA; (Y); 65/285; Yrbk Stf; Stu Cncl; High Hon Roll; Hon Roll; PA ST; Bus.

MERCALDO, VITTORIA MARIA; Bishop Neumann HS; Williamsport, PA; (Y); Quiz Bowl; Chorus; School Play; Yrbk Phtg; Yrbk Stf; Trs Frsh Cls; Trs Soph Cls; JV Var Bsktbl; Var L Sftbl; Stdnt Mnth, IHM, Fr Castello Schlrshps 86; Marywood Coll; Cmptr Sci.

MERCANTI, CHRISTOPHER; St Josephs Prep; Philadelphia, PA; (Y); Spanish Clb; Yrbk Stf; Var Bsbl; JV Bsktbl.

MERCER, ANGELA; Butler Area SR HS; Renfrew, PA; (Y); 29/740; AFS; VP 4-H; JA; Ski Clb; 4-H Awd; High Hon Roll; Hon Roll; Ntl Merit SF; Pres Schlr; Pittsburgh U; Nrsng.

MERCHANT, TONI; Geibel HS; Connellsville, PA; (Y); 20/120; Drama Clb; Hosp Aide; School Play; Yrbk Stf; Co-Capt Var Cheerleading; High Hon Roll; Pres Schlr; Dance Mstrs Am Schlrshp 85-86; Humanities Awd Spnsh 86; Vail Schlrsh Denison U 86; Denison U; Pre-Law.

MERCHLINSKY, GREG; Mahanoy Area HS; Gilberton, PA; (Y); Aud/Vis; Pep Clb; PAVAS; Band; Pep Band; School Play; Variety Show; Sec Frsh Cls; Var L Ftbl; JV Swmmng; Millersville Coll; Music.

MEREAR, JAMEY; Mapletown JR SR HS; Bobtown, PA; (Y); Aud/Vis; Library Aide; Pep Clb; Ski Clb; Mrchg Band; Yrbk Stf; Jr Cls; Twrlr; Vllybl; Hon Roll; Air Force.

MEREDITH, AMY; Mechanicsburg Area SR HS; Mechanicsburg, PA; (Y); 6/313; VP Girl Scts; NFL; Ski Clb; Drm Mjr(t); Trs Mrchg Band; Symp Band; Yrbk Stf; NHS; Ntl Merit Ltr; Im Cheerleading; Spn Heritage Scholar Awd 85; Bus.

MEREDITH, DENNIS; Northeast Catholic HS; Philadelphia, PA; (Y); 30/370; Band; Jazz Band; Orch; NHS; Med.

MEREDITH, SANDRA; John Harris HS; Harrisburg, PA; (Y); Church Yth Grp; Debate Tm; ROTC; Speech Tm; Band; Chorus; Drill Tm; Fld Hcky; Trk; High Hon Roll; Amercn Leg Mltry Excllnc 85-86; U Of CA-SAN Diego; Bus Mngmt.

MERES, ROSEMARY; Swissvale HS; N Braddock, PA; (Y); 15/182; French Clb; Pep Clb; Y-Teens; Chorus; Nwsp Stf; Yrbk Stf; JV Var Cheerleading; Hon Roll; NHS; U Of Pittsburgh; Comm.

MERGEL, KAREN; Bethlehem Catholic HS; Bethlehem, PA; (S); VP Soph Cls; Pres Jr Cls; JV Cheerleading; Hon Roll; Elem Ed.

MERICLE, MELISSA A; Warrior Run HS; Muncy, PA; (Y); AFS; Church Yth Grp; French Clb; Hosp Aide; Varsity Clb; Jr Cls; Cheerleading; Powder Puff Ftbl; Trk; Im Vllybl; Penn ST U; Accntng.

MERISKO, JILL; Steel Valley HS; Munhall, PA; (Y); 20/234; Pres Key Clb; VP Latin Clb; Office Aide; Pres Band; Concert Band; Ed Yrbk Stf; Stu Cncl; High Hon Roll; NHS; Dir Awd 86; Gldn SV Awd 86; Penn ST U; Elem Educ.

MERKEL, DONNA; Governor Mifflin HS; Shillington, PA; (Y); 25/300; Varsity Clb; Rep Jr Cls; Rep Stu Cncl; Cheerleading; Fld Hcky; Swmmng; Hon Roll; Phys Ther.

MERKEL, STEPHANIE; William Allen HS; Allentown, PA; (Y); 50/604; Art Clb; Leo Clb; Yrbk Stf; Off Stu Cncl; Jr NHS; NHS; PA ST U; Adv.

MERKEL, STEVE; Hamburg Area HS; Hamburg, PA; (Y); 24/150; Church Yth Grp; Var L Wrstlng; Hon Roll; Ntl Merit Ltr; Acad Ltr Awd Hstry 85-86; Acctng.

MERLI, DEAN; Highlands HS; Natrona Hts, PA; (Y); Am Leg Boys St; Boy Scts; Church Yth Grp; Computer Clb; Drama Clb; Intnl Clb; Pres Key Clb; SADD; Band; Concert Band; Eagle Scout-Trp 186 85; Psych.

MERLINO, JOANN; Creative And Performing Arts; Philadelphia, PA; (S); 1/150; Dance Clb; Girl Scts; Hosp Aide; Yrbk Stf; High Hon Roll; Hon Roll; NHS; Ithaca Coll; Psych.

MERLO, JODY; Charleroi Area HS; Charleroi, PA; (Y); 29/185; Trs French Clb; FNA; Office Aide; Science Clb; Yrbk Ed-Chief; Off Jr Cls; Off Sr Cls; Stu Cncl; Powder Puff Ftbl; Hon Roll; WV U; Ansthslgy.

MERLOT, TRACY; Riverview HS; Oakmont, PA; (Y); Band; Concert Band; School Play; Off Jr Cls; Off Sr Cls; Stu Cncl; Var Capt Cheerleading; Pom Pon; Powder Puff Ftbl; Stat Score Keeper; IN U Bloomington.

MEROLA, JILL AMY; Freedom HS; Bethlehem, PA; (Y); 95/445; Science Clb; Ski Clb; Orch; Capt L Cheerleading; Powder Puff Ftbl; Hlth Sci.

MERRIFIELD, DOUG; Palmyra HS; Campbelltown, PA; (Y); Band; Concert Band; Jazz Band; Mrchg Band; Orch; Pep Band; Hon Roll; Acctg.

MERRILL, CHRISTINE D; Sayre Area HS; Athens, PA; (Y); Chorus; Nwsp Stf; Yrbk Stf; Lit Mag; Gym; Hon Roll; Ptry Awd 86; Elmira Business Inst; Data Proc.

MERRILLS, ROBERT; Huntington Area HS; Huntingdon, PA; (Y); 72/209; Am Leg Boys St; Church Yth Grp; Chorus; Trs Soph Cls; Trs Jr Cls; VP Stu Cncl; JV Capt Bsktbl; JV Var Ftbl; Trk; Ntl Merit Ltr.

MERRITT, BETTY; West Branch Area HS; Winburne, PA; (S); #3 In Class; VP Drama Clb; Spanish Clb; Band; Concert Band; Mrchg Band; School Play; Stage Crew; Stat Bsktbl; Hon Roll; NHS; Butterworth Awd Music 86; Sci.

MERRITT, SCOTT; Northwestern HS; Albion, PA; (Y); 14/150; JV Var Bsbl; Var Ftbl; Var Wrstlng; Hon Roll; Penn ST.

MERRITT, TRACEY; Northeastern HS; Mt Wolf, PA; (Y); Church Yth Grp; Chorus; Concert Band; Mrchg Band; School Musical; Nwsp Ed-Chief; Yrbk Stf; Off Jr Cls; Off Sr Cls; Hon Roll; Phrmcy.

MERRITT, TRISHA; Laurel Valley JR SR HS; Bolivar, PA; (Y); AFS; Chorus; School Play; Variety Show; Nwsp Rptr; Cheerleading; Powder Puff Ftbl; Trk; Hon Roll; County Chorus 84-86; Geneva Coll; Elem Educ.

MERRITTS, STEFANY; Bellwood-Antis HS; Tyrone, PA; (Y); FHA; Chorus; School Musical; Capt Twrlr; Hon Roll; Most Enthsiastc Mjrtt 86; Hardwrkng Awd-Majortt Camp 86; Twrlng Unlmtd 1st Pl Trophy 86; Math.

MERRYMAN, AUDRA; Northwestern SR HS; Albion, PA; (Y); 16/164; Church Yth Grp; Model UN; Pep Clb; Science Clb; Flag Corp; Stage Crew; Trs Stu Cncl; Var Capt Cheerleading; Powder Puff Ftbl; JV Sftbl; Phys Thrpy.

MERSCHAT, JOHN; Turkeyfoot Valley Area HS; Markleysburg, PA; (S); 1/49; Church Yth Grp; Ski Clb; Varsity Clb; Var Bsbl; Var Capt Ftbl; High Hon Roll; NHS; Stu Of Mnth 85; Carnegie-Mellon; Mech Engrng.

MERSHON II, CHARLES; Blue Ride HS; New Milford, PA; (Y); 19/107; Scholastic Bowl; Stu Cncl; Im Bsktbl; Var L Ftbl; Var L Trk; Var L Vllybl; Wrstlng; Hon Roll; Blue Ridge Schlstc Bowl Champs Schlrshp Awd 85-86; Penn ST U; Law.

MERSHON, JILL; Blue Ridge HS; New Milford, PA; (Y); 12/107; High Hon Roll; NHS; Worthington Scranton Campus Scholar 86; Worthington Scranton Campus Hnrs Pgm 86; PA ST U; Early Chldhd Ed.

MERTZ, AMY; Dayton JR SR HS; Smicksburg, PA; (Y); 4/40; Concert Band; Mrchg Band; Pep Band; School Musical; Nwsp Ed-Chief; Nwsp Phtg; Nwsp Sprt Ed; Stat Socr; Gov Hon Prg Awd; NHS; Estrn Nazarene Coll; Med.

MERTZ, DANIEL; Northampton HS; Danielsville, PA; (Y); Boy Scts; VICA; Tennis; Hon Roll; Engrng.

MERTZ, HEATHER; Beaver Area JR-SR HS; Beaver, PA; (Y); 10/179; Church Yth Grp; French Clb; JCL; Key Clb; Band; Drill Tm; Var L Swmmng; High Hon Roll; NHS; Natl Latin Exam Awd; Lawyer.

MERTZ, KIM; Lehighton Area HS; Lehighton, PA; (Y); Sec Art Clb; Dance Clb; Capt Drm Mjr(t); Capt L Twrlr; Church Yth Grp; Drama Clb; PAVAS; Pep Band; Variety Show; Prfct Atten Awd; Decath Mdl Talent Olympcs 86; Scholar Awd Philadelphia Acad Theatr Art 85; Dnce.

MERTZ, MATT; Northampton HS; Walnutport, PA; (Y); Im JV Bsbl; Im Bsktbl; Im Bowling; Im Ftbl; Im Tennis; Amer Leg Aux Awd 81; Mayors Awd Bwlng Achvt 86; Ntl Tp 10 Bwlng Awds, 3rd JR Mxd Div; PA Coll; Optmtry.

MERTZ, SANDY; Villa Maria Acad; Fairview, PA; (Y); Ski Clb; Off Frsh Cls; Hon Roll; U Of Dayton; Mktng.

MERVINE, KATHERINE; Warren Area HS; Warren, PA; (Y); Trs Art Clb; Camera Clb; French Clb; Ski Clb; Chorus; Nwsp Stf; Hon Roll; Estrn Lk Erie Reg Sc'lstc Art Awd 86; Pepperdine Malibu; Cmrcl Art.

MERWEDE, COREY; Gettysburg SR HS; Gettysburg, PA; (Y); Church Yth Grp; Rep Frsh Cls; VP Soph Cls; Var Ftbl; Var Mgr(s); Var Tennis; Phrmcy.

MERZ, LISA; Jamestown Area HS; Jamestown, PA; (Y); 4/56; FBLA; Library Aide; VICA; Chorus; School Play; Yrbk Phtg; Yrbk Stf; Rep Frsh Cls; Rep Soph Cls; Rep Sr Cls; Voc Indus Clbs Of Amer VP 86.

MESA, INGRID; Sacred Heart HS; Pittsburgh, PA; (Y); 15/150; Computer Clb; Ski Clb; School Play; Yrbk Stf; Sftbl; Hon Roll; Pres Schlr; Westinghouse Science Honors Institute 86; U Of Pittsburgh; Comp Sci.

MESAROS, JODY; William Allen HS; Allentown, PA; (Y); Church Yth Grp; Hosp Aide; Scholastic Bowl; Yrbk Stf; Hon Roll; Bio Olympics Gntcs Exprt For HS 86; Burger King Bcycl Rcng Legue All-Star Grls Chmpnshps 2nd Pl 86; Temple U; Chem.

MESEROLE, STEPHEN; Otto-Eldred JR SR HS; Duke Center, PA; (Y); Nwsp Rptr; Stat Bsktbl; High Hon Roll; Hon Roll; World Hstry Awd 85; Dwng & Dsgn Awd 85; Sci Awd 84; Chem.

MESHEY, TAMMY; Conestoga Valley HS; Ronks, PA; (Y); 70/247; VP Art Clb; Trs Girl Scts; Band; Mrchg Band; Stage Crew; Yrbk Stf; Hon Roll; Accntnt.

MESHYOCK, LACRISHA; Huntingdoin Area HS; Mill Creek, PA; (Y); FBLA; Hosp Aide; Red Cross Aide; Soroptimist; Chorus; Tennis; Hon Roll; Drama Clb; French Clb; Key Clb; Pres Of Soroptomists 86-87; Phys Ther.

MESICH, BETH ANN; Albert Gallatin SR HS; Masontown, PA; (Y); Church Yth Grp; Dance Clb; Ski Clb; Varsity Clb; Chorus; VP Soph Cls; Pres Jr Cls; Off Stu Cncl; Var Cheerleading; Gym.

MESKE, GENA; Berwick Area SR HS; Berwick, PA; (Y); Church Yth Grp; Drama Clb; Key Clb; Library Aide; Ski Clb; Chorus; Stage Crew; Ed Yrbk Phtg; Sec Soph Cls; Sec Jr Cls; Pres Acad Ftns Awd 86; Grl Of Mnth Wmns Cvc Clb 86; Bsc Phys Ftns Awd 85 & 86; Pres 84; E Strdsbrg U; Phys Ed.

MESNAR, GINGER; Highlands SR HS; Tarentum, PA; (Y); 83/280; Girl Scts; Office Aide; Drill Tm; Mrchg Band; Stu Cncl; Mgr(s); Swmmng; Twrlr; Jr NHS; NHS; St Fnlst Miss Natl Teenager 85&86; St Fnlst Miss Teen All Am 85; Pitt U; Sprts Med.

MESORACA, CARMELA; St Mariagoretti HS; Philadelphia, PA; (Y); Cmnty Wkr; Exploring; Teachers Aide; Stage Crew; Crs Cntry; Hon Roll; Perf Attndnc; Ed.

MESSENGER, MICHAEL; Fort Le Boeuf HS; Waterford, PA; (Y); Mrchg Band; Nwsp Stf; VP Jr Cls; Im Cheerleading; JV Crs Cntry; Im Tennis; Var Trk; Im Vllybl; High Hon Roll; Hon Roll; Chess Champ 84; Psych.

MESSENGER, SHELLY A; Corry Area HS; Columbus, PA; (S); 8/210; Pres Art Clb; Church Yth Grp; Pres 4-H; French Clb; Library Aide; Yrbk Stf; Sec Sr Cls; Stu Cncl; Cit Awd; 4-H Awd; Three Rivers Art Fstvl Art Awd 83; Comm Art.

MESSENLEHNER, MARY LOUISE; Nazareth Area SR HS; Nazareth, PA; (Y); 1/250; Dance Clb; Ski Clb; Yrbk Stf; JV Cheerleading; JV Var Mat Maids; High Hon Roll; NHS; Top Ten In AAHPER Yth Phys Ftnss Test 85.

MESSER, AMY; Carlynton HS; Crafton, PA; (Y); VP Sec Church Yth Grp; Drama Clb; Sec German Clb; Drill Tm; Nwsp Stf; Rep Soph Cls; Rep Jr Cls; Rep Sr Cls; Pom Pon; High Hon Roll; Slippery Rock; Psych.

MESSICK, CHERRY; Downingtown SR HS; Downingtown, PA; (Y); Drama Clb; 4-H; German Clb; Concert Band; Mrchg Band; School Musical; School Play; Nwsp Rptr; Tennis; 4-H Awd; Erth Sci Awd 84; Jrnlsm.

MESSINA, JAMES; Kennedy Christian HS; Burtonsville, MD; (Y); 29/98; Ski Clb; Spanish Clb; Var Bsbl; JV Bsktbl; Im Ftbl; Im Swmmng; MD U.

MESSINA, JAMES; Kennedy Christian HS; Farrell, PA; (Y); 33/100; Science Clb; Spanish Clb; Var Bsbl; JV Im Bsktbl; Im Ftbl; Im Swmmng; Im Wt Lftg; Hon Roll; MD U.

MESSINGER, ANGELA; Greater Works Acad; Pittsburgh, PA; (S); 2/41; Pres Jazz Band; Nwsp Ed-Chief; Yrbk Stf; VP Stu Cncl; Var Bsktbl; Swmmng; Var Trk; Var Vllybl; High Hon Roll; Jr NHS; Pres Physcl Ftns 84-86; Carnegie Mellon U; Engrng.

MESSINGER, GARY; Northern Lebanon HS; Fredericksburg, PA; (Y); 18/177; VP Church Yth Grp; Quiz Bowl; Varsity Clb; Band; Chorus; School Play; Nwsp Stf; Var Bsbl; Var Bsktbl; Var Ftbl; Bsbl Am Legall Star All E Tm PA 86; Mth Tchr.

MESSNER, DIANA; Hampton HS; Allison Pk, PA; (Y); Pres Church Yth Grp; French Clb; Girl Scts; Band; Church Choir; Concert Band; Mrchg Band; Symp Band; Powder Puff Ftbl; Sftbl; IN U Of PA; Elem Educ.

MESSNER, STERLING; Harrisburg HS; Harrisburg, PA; (S); 18/442; Church Yth Grp; Church Choir; Stat Bsbl; Hon Roll; Brdcstg.

METALIK, TAWNYA; Fort Cherry HS; Bulger, PA; (S); Computer Clb; Drama Clb; VP FNA; Math Clb; Science Clb; Chorus; Drill Tm; Mrchg Band; School Play; High Hon Roll; Sewickley Vly Hosp Schl; RN.

METALONIS, CHERYL; Philipsburg Osceola Area HS; Philipsburg, PA; (Y); Church Yth Grp; Pep Clb; SADD; Sec Lib Chorus; Stage Crew; Stu Cncl; Hon Roll; Prfct Atten Awd.

METAXAS, NICOLE; William Allen HS; Allentown, PA; (Y); Key Clb; Letterman Clb; Yrbk Stf; Var Bsktbl; Hon Roll; Jr NHS; NHS; Soclgy.

METCALF, FRED; Northern Potter HS; Westfield, PA; (Y); Art Clb; 4-H; Ntl Merit Ltr.

METCALF, KIM; Unioville HS; Chadds Ford, PA; (Y); 6/269; Concert Band; Jazz Band; Orch; Rep Frsh Cls; Pres Soph Cls; Pres Jr Cls; Pres Sr Cls; JV Var Fld Hcky; Var Sftbl; NHS; Hugh O Brian Ldrshp Smnr; Gene Davis Southern Chstr Cnty Lg Athltc Awd; Schl Key; Northwestern U; Bus.

METCALFE, LYNDA; Seneca Valley HS; Harmony, PA; (Y); 69/352; Church Yth Grp; SADD; Elem Tchr.

METCALFE, SONYA; Charleroi HS; Charleroi, PA; (Y); Dance Clb; Drama Clb; SADD; Varsity Clb; Chorus; School Play; Swing Chorus; Var JV Cheerleading; Elks Awd; Prfct Atten Awd; Outstndng Mus Awd 84; Pa Anncrs Awd 86; Tech Crew Awd 86; West Lib Coll; Erly Chldhd Devl.

METCALFE, SUSAN; Hempfield HS; Lancaster, PA; (Y); 14/500; Boy Scts; Cmnty Wkr; Dance Clb; Drama Clb; Exploring; Library Aide; Office Aide; PAVAS; Political Wkr; Spanish Clb; Amer Lgn-Outstndng Ctzn 83; Hstry Awd-Hghst Grd 83; Pres Schlrshp-Elizabethtwn Coll 86; Elizabethtown Coll; Eng.

METELO, DINA; St Maria Goretti HS; Philadelphia, PA; (Y); Cmnty Wkr; Hosp Aide; Office Aide; Stage Crew; Variety Show; Off Jr Cls; Stu Cncl; High Hon Roll; Hon Roll; Prfct Atten Awd; Ellis HS Grant 83-87; Pierce JC; Exec Scrtry.

METELSKY, GEORGE; Ambridge Area HS; Ambridge, PA; (Y); Am Leg Boys St; Church Yth Grp; German Clb; Pep Clb; VICA; L Golf; High Hon Roll; NHS; Prfct Atten Awd; Comp Sci.

METHENEY JR, WILLIAM D; Grove City HS; Grove City, PA; (Y); Church Yth Grp; Crs Cntry; Ftbl; Trk; Wrstlng; Hon Roll; Cert Achvt Awd Prfct Attndnc 84-86.

METHENY, DANA K; Trinity HS; Washington, PA; (Y); 36/385; Pres 4-H; Speech Tm; Sec Trs Band; Concert Band; Jazz Band; Mrchg Band; High Hon Roll; Church Yth Grp; Debate Tm; Chorus; WVU Creative Arts Schlrshp 86; Cmmnty Wind Ensemble 85-86; PMEA Dist I Hnrs Band 85; WV U; Mus Educ.

METRO, DAVID; Chartiers Valley HS; Pittsburgh, PA; (Y); 1/350; Civic Clb; Letterman Clb; Ski Clb; Off Stu Cncl; Tennis; High Hon Roll; NHS; Mert Schlr 86; U Pittsburgh; Pre Med.

METRO, MICHAEL; Marian Catholic HS; Lansford, PA; (Y); 32/115; Band; Chorus; Concert Band; Mrchg Band; Pep Band; School Musical; School Play.

METROKA, JANELLE RAE; Hanover Area HS; Ashley, PA; (Y); Exploring; Pres Key Clb; Library Aide; Ski Clb; School Musical; Off Stu Cncl; Socr; Twrlr; High Hon Roll; Pres NHS; Elem Ed.

METZ, BILL; Bensalem HS; Bensalem, PA; (Y); 50/535; Varsity Clb; Bsbl; Ftbl; Ice Hcky; High Hon Roll; High Hon Roll 82-86; Temple U; Law.

METZ, DAVID; West Middlesex HS; W Middlesex, PA; (Y); Chorus; Hon Roll; Carpenter.

METZ, DEBI; Norwin SR HS; N Huntingdon, PA; (Y); DECA; Chorus; Rep Frsh Cls; Rep Stu Cncl; DECA Voting Delg St Conf 85-86; Bradford Schl; Mrktng.

METZ, DONNA; Greater Latrobe SR HS; Latrobe, PA; (Y); 35/337; Yrbk Ed-Chief; Trs Sr Cls; Rep Stu Cncl; High Hon Roll; Prfct Atten Awd; Mark Funk Jr Jrnlsm Awd 86; Mst Outstndg Bus & Jrnlsm Stu 86; Harold E Stover Bus Awd 85; Westmoreland Cnty CC; Bus Mgmt.

METZ, GAIL; Exeter Township SR HS; Reading, PA; (Y); 38/206; Varsity Clb; Band; Jazz Band; Rep Stu Cncl; Fld Hcky; Capt Swmmng; Capt Trk; Hon Roll; Jr NHS; NHS; Outstndng Athlc 86; St Lawrence Wmns Clb Schlrshp 86; US Army Res Ntl Schlr/Athlc Awd 86; NC ST U; Lbrl Arts.

METZ, JULIE; Freedom HS; Bethlehem, PA; (Y); Pep Clb; Science Clb; Color Guard; Drill Tm; Yrbk Stf; Nrsng.

METZ, KATHY; Bensalem HS; Bensalem, PA; (Y); Color Guard; Var Socr; High Hon Roll; NHS; 1st Rnr-Up Miss PA Coed Pgnt 86; Schl Evltn Committee 86-87; Acctng.

METZ, LISA; Hamburg Area HS; Hamburg, PA; (Y); 29/150; French Clb; Library Aide; Spanish Clb; SADD; Band; Church Choir; Concert Band; Mrchg Band; Rep Stu Cncl; Jr NHS; NHS; Soclgy.

METZ, MELISSA; Waynesboro SR HS; South Mtn, PA; (Y); Band; Yrbk Stf; Bsktbl; Fld Hcky; Trk; Hon Roll; Hagerstown JC; Bus Sec.

METZGAR, JANICE; Pocono Mountain HS; Cresco, PA; (Y); Band; Flag Corp; Hon Roll; Bus.

METZGER, ANNISSA; Canton Area HS; Canton, PA; (Y); 2/127; AFS; Ski Clb; Chorus; Church Choir; Hon Roll; Church Yth Grp; Letterman Clb; Var Trk; Pre-Med.

METZGER, EARL S; Bishop Kenrick HS; Norristown, PA; (Y); JV Bowling; Intrmrl Flr Hcky Chmps; Chmcl Engrng.

METZGER, EVA; Blaver Area HS; Beaver, PA; (Y); Church Yth Grp; German Clb; JCL; Latin Clb; Chorus; Powder Puff Ftbl; Socr; Var Capt Sftbl; Vllybl; High Hon Roll; All Star Tm 85-86; Acctng.

METZGER, NEAL; Spring Grove HS; Spg Grove, PA; (Y); 17/289; Church Yth Grp; German Clb; Letterman Clb; JV Golf; Var L Wrstlng; High Hon Roll; NHS; MVP Wrstlr 85 & 86; Sctnl, Dist Chmp, 6th Pl ST 86; Engrng.

METZLER, GREG; Elizabethtown Area HS; Elizabethtown, PA; (Y); 18/237; Var Socr; NHS; Amer Comp Sci Lge Team 85-86; Math.

METZLER, PAULA; Solanco HS; Quarryville, PA; (Y); Office Aide; Teachers Aide; Vllybl; High Hon Roll; Hon Roll; Millersville U; Bio.

METZLER, ROSS; Manheim Central HS; Manheim, PA; (Y); 67/237; VICA; Graphic Arts.

METZLER, SARAH; Solanco SR HS; New Providence, PA; (Y); Art Clb; Girl Scts; Ski Clb; Spanish Clb; Band; Concert Band; Mrchg Band; Orch; School Musical; Symp Band; Solanco Schlr, Co Wind Ensemble, Schlstc Art Awd Hmbl Mntn 83-4; Symph Band Co 83, 84, 85&86; Millersville U; Mus.

MEYER, CECILIA; Wyoming Area SR HS; W Pittston, PA; (Y); 13/230; Art Clb; French Clb; Key Clb; Red Cross Aide; Stu Cncl; Var Cheerleading; Var Trk; High Hon Roll; Hon Roll; NHS; Gymnstcs Awds; Physcl Thrpy.

MEYER, CHRISTINE; St Basil Acad; Philadelphia, PA; (S); Church Yth Grp; Cmnty Wkr; Exploring; GAA; Latin Clb; Service Clb; Lit Mag; Im Cheerleading; Im Trk; Pol Sci.

MEYER, DAVID; The Baptist HS; Clarks Summit, PA; (Y); 1/14; Church Yth Grp; Acpl Chr; Chorus; Bsktbl; L Socr; Cit Awd; High Hon Roll; 1st Pl Ntl Assoc 85-86; Schlrshp US Snt Japan Undrstndng Yth 85-86; 1st Pl Mns Pblc Spkg 85-86; Baptist Bible Coll; Intl Stds.

MEYER, JAMIE; Annville-Cleona HS; Lebanon, PA; (Y); 37/106; Dance Clb; FBLA; Mrchg Band; Cheerleading; Hon Roll; Jr NHS; NHS.

MEYER, JANICE; The Oakland Schl; Monroeville, PA; (S); Art Clb; Cmnty Wkr; Exploring; German Clb; Madrigals; Orch; Nwsp Stf; Yrbk Bus Mgr; Yrbk Stf; Lit Mag; Math Cncl Western PA Alg Cntst 82; Arts Rcgntn & Tlnt Search Part 85; Cmmrcl Art.

MEYER, KRISTEN M; Canon Mc Millan HS; Canonsburg, PA; (Y); Church Yth Grp; French Clb; Letterman Clb; Ski Clb; Varsity Clb; Var Swmmng; L Trk; Hon Roll; Secndry Tchng.

MEYER, MARK; Wyoming Seminary College Prep Schl; Kingston, PA; (Y); 2/84; Cmnty Wkr; Quiz Bowl; Nwsp Rptr; Yrbk Rptr; Yrbk Stf; Sec Frsh Cls; Trs Soph Cls; Trs Jr Cls; Pres Sr Cls; Pres Stu Cncl; Brown Bk Awd 85; Pres Prz Outstndng Serv To Schl 86; Irving Robin Ldrshp Prz 86; Haverford Clg.

MEYER, REBECCA; Lewisburg Area HS; Lewisburg, PA; (Y); Band; Chorus; Church Choir; Concert Band; Drm Mjr(t); Jazz Band; Mrchg Band; Orch; School Musical; School Play; Arion Music Awd 86; Mst Imprvd Musicn Awd 85; Dist Band 85-86; Music Ed.

MEYER, SUZANNE R; Gateway SR HS; Monroeville, PA; (Y); Exploring; Model UN; Political Wkr; Ski Clb; Band; Chorus; Color Guard; Mrchg Band; Orch; Lit Mag; U Pittsburgh; Intl Rltns.

MEYER, VICKI; Burrell HS; Lower Burrell, PA; (Y); Spanish Clb; Chorus; Stage Crew; Stat Bsktbl; High Hon Roll; Hon Roll; Rotary Club Schlr 85; Elem Educ.

MEYERS, ALISA; Somerset Area HS; Somerset, PA; (Y); Art Clb; French Clb; Pep Clb; Ski Clb; Band; Chorus; Var Cheerleading; French Hon Soc; Hon Roll; Church Yth Grp; Art Achvmnt Awd; Cmmrcl Art.

MEYERS, DAVID; HS Of Engineering And Sci; Philadelphia, PA; (Y); 9/160; Capt Chess Clb; Math Tm; Quiz Bowl; High Hon Roll; Trs NHS; PA JR Acad Of Sci ST And Regl 85; PA ST U; Bus Adm.

MEYERS, GEORGE; Northeast Catholic HS; Philadelphia, PA; (Y); 24/398; Socr; High Hon Roll; Hon Roll; Jr NHS; NHS; Drexal; Elec Engr.

MEYERS, KELLIE; Seneca HS; Union City, PA; (Y); Pres VP Church Yth Grp; Pep Clb; Chorus; Church Choir; Color Guard; School Musical; Pres Sec Stage Crew; Yrbk Stf; Var Trk; Hon Roll; Edinboro U; Socl Wrkr.

MEYERS, LISA; Bishop Mc Cort HS; Stoystown, PA; (Y); FCA; Hosp Aide; Pep Clb; Band; Chorus; Concert Band; Mrchg Band; Orch; Stu Cncl; Hon Roll; Socl Wrkr.

MEYERS, MICHELLE; G A R Memorial HS; Wilkes Barre, PA; (S); 16/177; Exploring; French Clb; Hosp Aide; Key Clb; Band; Chorus; Orch; Nwsp Stf; Capt L Trk; Hon Roll; U Scrntn; Pre Med.

MEYERS, STEPHANIE; James Buchanan HS; St Thomas, PA; (Y); 20/220; VP Sec AFS; Church Yth Grp; Pres VP 4-H; French Clb; Ski Clb; Pres Trs SADD; Band; Sec Stu Cncl; Hon Roll; NHS; Alternte Gov Schl Ag 86; Ntl 4 H Awd Wnnr 86; Pub Rel.

MEYERS, TOM; Carrick HS; Pittsburgh, PA; (S); Stage Crew; Var Capt Bsbl; JV Ftbl; Var L Golf; High Hon Roll; Hon Roll; Pittsburgh U; Schl Tchr.

MEZAN, KELLY; Jefferson-Morgan HS; Rices Landing, PA; (S); 15/100; Trs Intnl Clb; Spanish Clb; VP Sec Band; Ed Yrbk Stf; Pres Jr Cls; Rep Sr Cls; Sec Trs Stu Cncl; Twrlr; Hon Roll; Waynesburg Coll; Anesthst.

MICELI, STEVE; Mechanicsburg Area SR HS; Mechanicsburg, PA; (Y); 114/309; Am Leg Boys St; Jazz Band; Mrchg Band; School Play; Symp Band; Pres Jr Cls; Pres Sr Cls; Rep Stu Cncl; Band; Concert Band; Michael Lingenfelter Meml Schlrshp 86; Most Outstndg Stu Awd-Upr Allen Ladies Aux 86; Edinboro U Of PA.

MICHAEL, ELIZABETH; Riverview HS; Oakmont, PA; (Y); Church Yth Grp; Drama Clb; French Clb; Key Clb; Band; Church Choir; Concert Band; Mrchg Band; Var Pom Pon; JV Sftbl; Teen Inst 84-85; Westminster; Theater.

MICHAEL, KEN; Butler Area HS; Butler, PA; (Y); Boy Scts; Church Yth Grp; Exploring; Hon Roll; Elec Engnrng.

MICHAEL, MARK; Freedom HS; Allentown, PA; (Y); 95/404; Var L Ftbl; Im Wt Lftg; Hon Roll; J F Mc Lernon Mem Awd Mst Imprvd Plyr 84.

MICHAEL, TARA; Northern Lebanon HS; Fredericksburg, PA; (Y); Band; Color Guard; Rep Stu Cncl; Var Tennis; Hon Roll; Psych.

MICHAEL, TIM; Warwick HS; Lititz, PA; (Y); 32/230; Varsity Clb; Off Frsh Cls; Off Soph Cls; VP Sr Cls; Bsbl; Ftbl; Swmmng; Vllybl; Wt Lftg; Hon Roll; PA ST U; Arch Engr.

MICHAEL, VICKI; Northern Lebanon HS; Jonestown, PA; (Y); 3/173; Sec Church Yth Grp; Chorus; Church Choir; Concert Band; Mrchg Band; School Musical; Dnfth Awd; High Hon Roll; NHS; Ntl Merit Ltr; Bible.

MICHAELS, LISA; Butler Area HS; Butler, PA; (Y); Drama Clb; JA; Science Clb; Spanish Clb; Thesps; Rep Stu Cncl; Hon Roll; Penn ST; Englsh.

MICHAELS, ROBERT; Marple Newton SR HS; Broomall, PA; (Y); Library Aide; Band; Concert Band; Mrchg Band; Orch; Symp Band; Bowling; Tennis; Hon Roll; Penn ST U; Hotel Restrnt Mgmt.

MICHAELS, SCOTT; Penns Manor HS; Heilwood, PA; (Y); 2/107; Varsity Clb; Capt Stage Crew; Var L Trk; High Hon Roll; NHS; NEDT Awd; Prfct Atten Awd; Pitt; Dntstry.

MICHAELS, SHANA; North Hills HS; Pittsburgh, PA; (Y); AFS; Church Yth Grp; Girl Scts; Keywanettes; Library Aide; Speech Tm; Lit Mag; Crs Cntry; Trk; High Hon Roll; Kalamazoo Coll; English.

MICHALKA, DENISE; Canon-Mc Millan SR HS; Mc Donald, PA; (Y); Art Clb; French Clb; Ski Clb; Band; Concert Band; Twrlr; High Hon Roll; Hon Roll; Nwsp Rptr; Crn Pres Schlrshp 86; Chthm Merit Schlrshp Tstng 86; Gftd & Tlntd Ed Pgm 78-86; Chthm Coll; Art.

MICHALSKI, JEFF; Abington Heights HS; Clarks Summit, PA; (Y); Letterman Clb; Ski Clb; Varsity Clb; Var L Ftbl; Var L Trk; Hon Roll; Ntl Merit Ltr; Psych.

MICHEL, HEATHER; South Park HS; Library, PA; (Y); 15/203; French Clb; Ski Clb; Color Guard; Mrchg Band; Yrbk Stf; Rep Frsh Cls; Rep Soph Cls; Rep Jr Cls; Powder Puff Ftbl; High Hon Roll; Acdmc Achvmnt Awd 86; U Of Pittsburgh; Engnrng.

MICHEL, MELISSA; Seneca HS; Erie, PA; (Y); 10/167; Sec Church Yth Grp; Computer Clb; FBLA; School Musical; Yrbk Stf; JV Var Cheerleading; Stat Ftbl; Stat Trk; Hon Roll; Trs NHS; Typng Awd; Cadtts; Sci.

MICHEL, RICARDO; West Catholic Boys HS; Phila, PA; (Y); 6/217; Pres Church Yth Grp; Sec Debate Tm; Nwsp Sprt Ed; Yrbk Sprt Ed; Crs Cntry; High Hon Roll; VP NHS; Art Clb; Cmnty Wkr; Speech Tm; 4 Yr Schlrshp Tmpl U 86; Dr Chrls Drw Cmmnty Svc Awd 86; Concerned Blck Mn Awd Cmmnty Svc 86; Temple U; Acctg.

MICHELANGELO, NANETTE; Keystone Oaks HS; Pittsburgh, PA; (Y); 4/250; Math Tm; Pep Clb; Im Var Crs Cntry; Im Capt Swmmng; Var Im Trk; High Hon Roll; NHS; Dormont Coll Clb Schlrshp 86; Feml Schlr Athlt Of The Schl 86; U Of Pittsburgh; Phy Thrpy.

MICHELETTI, CORINNE; James M Coughlin HS; Plains, PA; (Y); Ski Clb; Yrbk Stf; Stu Cncl; Var Cheerleading; Sftbl; High Hon Roll; Hon Roll; Jr NHS; NHS; NEDT Awd; Med.

MICHELINI, MICHELLE; Freeport SR HS; Freeport, PA; (S); 14/173; FBLA; SADD; Twrlr; Hon Roll; NHS; Butler CC; Exec Scrtry.

MICHELL, BRIAN; Archbishop Jon Carroll HS; W Conshohocken, PA; (S); 1/376; Mathletes; Scholastic Bowl; Nwsp Rptr; Yrbk Stf; Trk; High Hon Roll; Hon Roll; Pres Jr NHS; Pres NHS; French Clb; Hghst Avg Awd Mth, Sci, Relign, Latin 83-84, Wrld Cultures, Engl, Mth 84-85; Med Sci.

MICHELONE, JEFF; Homer Center HS; Homer City, PA; (Y); 17/96; Varsity Clb; Sec Frsh Cls; Stu Cncl; Bsbl; Bsktbl; Golf; High Hon Roll; Hon Roll; NHS.

MICHNIAK, DANNY; Mapletown HS; Bobtown, PA; (Y); 2/28; Church Yth Grp; Spanish Clb; Varsity Clb; Bsbl; Ftbl; Sftbl; Wt Lftg; High Hon Roll; Hon Roll; Bus Mgmt.

MICHUCK, RONNA; Brockway Area HS; Brockway, PA; (Y); #12 In Class; Debate Tm; Drama Clb; Thesps; Concert Band; Jazz Band; Mrchg Band; Pep Band; Stage Crew; Rep Stu Cncl; Hon Roll; Vet Med.

MICKEL, CHRISTINE; William Allen HS; Allentown, PA; (Y); VP JA; Library Aide; Model UN; Ed Yrbk Stf; Hon Roll; PA ST Allentwn; Bus Adm.

MICKELONIS, KATHY; Shenandoah Valley HS; Shenandoah, PA; (Y); Hosp Aide; Pep Clb; Ed Yrbk Stf; Sec Stu Cncl; Cheerleading; Gym; Capt Vllybl; DAR Awd; High Hon Roll; Sec NHS; Stu Of The Month; Gifted Prgm; Penn ST U; Bus.

MICKENS III, LEON D; Westinghouse HS; Pittsburgh, PA; (S); 15/211; Science Clb; Off Jr Cls; Trs Stu Cncl; Swmmng; Trk; Vllybl; High Hon Roll; NHS; Prfct Atten Awd; Homewood Bruston Cmmnty Imprvmt Assoc Awd 85; Pittsburgh Regnl Engrng Prog PREP 82-86; Penn ST; Engrng.

MICKEY, SCOTT; Penn Trafford HS; Trafford, PA; (Y); Chess Clb; FBLA; JCL; Latin Clb; Ski Clb; PA ST Roller Sktng Champ 84-86; Eastrn Regnl Roller Sktng Champ 85-86; U Pittsburgh; Mktng.

MICKLESAVAGE, ROSS; Holy Name HS; Reading, PA; (Y); 43/115; Pep Clb; JV Bsbl; JV Var Ftbl; Hon Roll; Kutztown U; Comp Sci.

MICOCCI, NANCY; John S Fine SR HS; Nanticoke, PA; (Y); Aud/Vis; Church Yth Grp; Hosp Aide; Key Clb; Model UN; Red Cross Aide; Nwsp Stf; Hon Roll; Psych.

MICSKY, RUSSELL JAMES; Reynolds HS; Greenville, PA; (Y); 1/122; German Clb; Math Clb; Q&S; Science Clb; Nwsp Sprt Ed; Var L Bsktbl; VP NHS; NEDT Awd; Pres Schlr; Val; PA ST U Shenango Vly; Engrng.

MIDDEKAUFF, RONDA; Lackawanna Trail HS; Dalton, PA; (Y); Church Yth Grp; Band; Chorus; Cheerleading; Hon Roll; Penn ST; Arch.

MIDDLEMAN, KARLA; St Maria Goretti HS; Philadelphia, PA; (Y); 135/390; Cmnty Wkr; Hon Roll; Hanahmen; Radlgy.

MIDDLESWORTH, AUTUMN SAGE; Montoursville Area HS; Montgomery, PA; (Y); 11/177; German Clb; Hosp Aide; Key Clb; Varsity Clb; School Musical; Off Frsh Cls; Off Soph Cls; Off Jr Cls; Im Powder Puff Ftbl; Stat Wrstlng; Cls 1983 Jeanine M Kline Scholar Awd 86; Rutgers ST U; Phrmcy.

MIDDLETON, BRETT; Pleasant Valley HS; Sciota, PA; (Y); 9/176; Math Tm; Varsity Clb; VP Frsh Cls; VP Soph Cls; VP Jr Cls; VP Sr Cls; Rep Stu Cncl; Var Capt Ftbl; Var Trk; NHS; Schlr Athl Awd; Monroe Cnty Prof Wmns Club; Big 33 Checklist Ftbl; Shippensburg U; Bio.

MIDWAY, DEBRA; Blue Mountain Acad; Beach Haven, PA; (S); School Play; Stage Crew; Nwsp Ed-Chief; Nwsp Rptr; VP Jr Cls; Capt Sftbl; Im Vllybl; Hon Roll; Prfct Atten Awd; Natl Hstry & Govt Awd 85-86; Natl Ldrshp Awd 85-86; Acctng.

MIELE, MICHELLE; Nazareth Acad; Philadelphia, PA; (Y); Church Yth Grp; French Clb; GAA; Hosp Aide; Service Clb; Yrbk Stf; Hon Roll; Prfct Atten Awd; JV Scrkpr Bowling; Im Mgr Fld Hcky; Nrsg.

MIELKE, ROBERT; Cumberland Valley HS; Mechanicsburg, PA; (Y); 15/518; German Clb; JV Socr; Hon Roll; NHS.

MIERNICKI, JOHN; Nazereth HS; Nazareth, PA; (Y); 19/241; Var JV Bsbl; JV Var Ftbl; Im Wt Lftg; High Hon Roll; Hon Roll; Bus Admin.

MIERZEJEWSKI, LYNN; St Basil Acad; Philadelphia, PA; (S); Art Clb; Cmnty Wkr; French Clb; FBLA; Chorus; Madrigals; High Hon Roll; Hon Roll; Sci Fair Prjct Hnrbl Ment 85.

MIETHE, LORI; Central Bucks East HS; Pipersville, PA; (Y); 22/474; Drama Clb; Pres VP 4-H; Hosp Aide; Ski Clb; Mgr(s); Capt Twrlr; 4-H Awd; Hon Roll; NHS; Engr.

MIFKA, SYLVIA; Bishop Hannan HS; Scranton, PA; (Y); 12/128; VP French Clb; Latin Clb; Color Guard; Nwsp Rptr; Nwsp Stf; Rep Frsh Cls; Rep Soph Cls; Rep Jr Cls; Rep Sr Cls; JV Var Cheerleading; US Army Rsrv Outstndng Stu/Athlt Awd 86; All Star 3rd Bsmn 83-84 & 86; Outstndng Stu/Athl Bshp H 86; Villanova U; Nrsng.

MIGLIARINO, SONIA; Merion Mercy Acad; Phila, PA; (Y); 12/70; Church Yth Grp; Computer Clb; French Clb; Intnl Clb; Library Aide; Scholastic Bowl; Science Clb; Service Clb; Varsity Clb; Vllybl; Good Sportsmnshp Awd 84-86; Vllybl Champs 85-86; Comp Bowl Awd 85-86; Sci Clb 85-86; Tutoring Clb 85-86; Med.

MIGLIORI, DAVID; Tunkhannock Area HS; Dalton, PA; (Y); Church Yth Grp; Computer Clb; Acpl Chr; Chorus; Madrigals; Mgr Stage Crew; Im Sftbl; Im Vllybl; God Cntry Awd; Hon Roll; Chrl Dir Awd 86; Dist A Chrs PMEA 86; PA ST U; Mtrlgy.

MIGLIOSI, ROBERT; Wyoming Area SR HS; Exeter, PA; (Y); 19/268; Computer Clb; French Clb; Math Clb; Ski Clb; Bsktbl; Bowling; Crs Cntry; Golf; Trk; Vllybl; Drexel U; Psych.

MIHALCIN, AMI; Kennedy Christian HS; Greenville, PA; (Y); 37/99; Sec Church Yth Grp; Civic Clb; Pep Clb; Spanish Clb; Stage Crew; Im Bsktbl; Im Vllybl; Hon Roll; Psych.

MIHALCZO, HEIDI; Western Beaver HS; Industry, PA; (Y); GAA; Chorus; Nwsp Rptr; Yrbk Rptr; Trs Frsh Cls; Trs Soph Cls; Pres Jr Cls; L Cheerleading; Sftbl; Capt Twrlr; Dec Stdnt Mnth 85; Dist Chorus 86; Sftbl Awd Excllnc 86; Slippery Rock U.

MIHOCI, MIKE; Conneaut Lake HS; Conneault Lake, PA; (Y); VP Jr Cls; Ftbl; Hon Roll; Ltrmn Ftbll Vrsty & Capt 86; Meadville Tribunes Vrsty Ftbl Dream Tm Selec Offnsve Tm 85; IN U; Math.

MIHOLOVICH, STEVE; Penn-Trafford HS; Trafford, PA; (Y); 42/363; Latin Clb; Im Bsktbl; Var JV Ftbl; High Hon Roll; Hon Roll; Prfct Atten Awd; Optmtry.

MIKA, MOLLY; James M Coughlin HS; Wilkes Barre, PA; (Y); Church Yth Grp; Drama Clb; Hosp Aide; Chorus; Church Choir; Variety Show; Nwsp Stf; Yrbk Stf; High Hon Roll; Hon Roll; Small Select Chrs 84-87; Hnrary Music Awd 84; Occ Ther.

MIKA, PAMELA; Burgettstown Area JRSR HS; Burgettstown, PA; (Y); 14/178; Ski Clb; Concert Band; Drm Mjr(t); Sr Cls; Stu Cncl; High Hon Roll; Hon Roll; JP Sousa Awd; Jr NHS; NHS; Mrchg Aux Grnd Champ Drum Major 85; Mrchg Aux Hnr Roll 85; Climax Scholar Fnlst 85; PA ST U; Comm.

MIKALONIS, AMY C; Bishop Kenrick HS; Norris, PA; (Y); 112/315; Cmnty Wkr; Dance Clb; Service Clb; Prfct Atten Awd; Chld Psych.

MIKAN, SUSAN; Shaler Area HS; Glenshaw, PA; (Y); 84/517; Camp Fr Inc; Spanish Clb; Spanish NHS.

MIKESELL, NICOLE; Punxsutawney HS; Rossiter, PA; (Y); Girl Scts; Varsity Clb; Cheerleading; Sftbl; Bus.

MIKHAEL, JULIET DINKHA; Waynesboro SR HS; Odessa, TX; (Y); 36/349; Church Yth Grp; Intnl Clb; Church Choir; Color Guard; Mrchg Band; School Play; Stage Crew; Yrbk Stf; Hon Roll; Coll Clb Schlrshp 86; ABWA, WAEA Schlrshp 85-86; Odessa Coll; Psych.

MIKITA, KELLY; North Schuylkill HS; Ringtown, PA; (Y); Nwsp Stf; Yrbk Stf; Stat Var Bsbl; Var Capt Cheerleading; Hon Roll; Bloomsburg U; Elem Ed.

MIKITA, STEVE; Shenandoah Valley JR SR HS; Shenandoah, PA; (S); Stage Crew; Yrbk Stf; Rep Frsh Cls; Var L Bsktbl; Var L Ftbl; High Hon Roll; NHS.

MIKLAVIC, JEFF; S Fayette HS; Bridgeville, PA; (S); 5/80; French Clb; Band; Concert Band; Jazz Band; Mrchg Band; High Hon Roll; Hon Roll; NHS; Psychlgy.

MIKLUS, BETH; Plum SR HS; Pittsburgh, PA; (Y); Church Yth Grp; FHA; GAA; Ski Clb; Spanish Clb; SADD; Teachers Aide; Varsity Clb; Band; Color Guard; Indiana U Of PA; Psychol.

MIKOVCH, ERIC J; Northwestern HS; Cranesville, PA; (Y); 8/164; Chess Clb; French Clb; Nwsp Ed-Chief; Rep Stu Cncl; Var L Bsbl; Var L Bsktbl; Var L Ftbl; Im Vllybl; High Hon Roll; Rotary Awd; Acad All-Amer Schlr Prgm 84-85; Ivy-League U; Pre-Law.

MIKSA, LORRI; Saint Hubert H S For Girls; Philadelphia, PA; (Y); 145/364; Church Yth Grp; Cmnty Wkr; Drama Clb; JA; Office Aide; Spanish Clb; School Musical; Play Spr; Messiah Coll; Biol.

MIKULA, ERIC; Altoona Area HS; Altoona, PA; (Y); Church Yth Grp; German Clb; Nwsp Phtg; Yrbk Phtg; Yrbk Stf; Rep Frsh Cls; Crs Cntry; Ftbl; Trk; High Hon Roll; Pre-Med.

MIKULA, JEFFREY; Nonessen HS; Monessen, PA; (Y); 7/87; Aud/Vis; Boy Scts; Quiz Bowl; Chorus; Yrbk Ed-Chief; Var L Wt Lftg; Bausch & Lomb Sci Awd; Ntl Merit Schol; U Of Pittsburgh; Engrg.

MIKULA, LINDA; Shade-Central City HS; Central City, PA; (Y); 9/74; FBLA; Nwsp Rptr; Nwsp Stf; Yrbk Stf; Trs Sr Cls; Rep Stu Cncl; Hon Roll; Amer Legn Awd 86; Schlstc Quiz Team 85-86; U Pittsburgh; Soc Work.

MIKULCA, DONNA; Hazelton HS; Beavermeadows, PA; (Y); Pres FBLA; Teachers Aide; High Hon Roll; NHS; FBLA Tp Secy Awd, Intl Lad Grmnt Wrks U Oustndng Bus Stdnt Awd, Pres Acad Achvt Awd 86; Med Secy.

MIKUS, ELEANOR ANN; Archbishop Wood HS For Girls; Holland, PA; (Y); Church Yth Grp; Cmnty Wkr; Hosp Aide; Red Cross Aide; Hon Roll; Prfct Atten Awd; Pres Schlr; Pres Acad Ftnss Awd 86; Grad With Hnrs 86; Sentr Of Incntv Tutrng 86; Millersville U.

MIKUS, LISA; Deer Lakes JR SR HS; Gibsonia, PA; (Y); Church Yth Grp; Exploring; Library Aide; Chorus; Church Choir; Drill Tm; Yrbk Stf; Pom Pon; Score Keeper; Hon Roll; JR Dist Chorus 83-84; Duquene; Phrmcy.

MIKUS, NEIL; Carlynton JR-SR HS; Carne0e, PA; (Y); JV Var Bsktbl; Im L Ftbl; Robert Morris Coll; Sprt Mgmt.

MIKUS, RICHARD; Cardinal Dougherty HS; Phila, PA; (Y); VP Church Yth Grp; Exploring; School Musical; School Play; Im Vllybl; Hon Roll; Prfct Atten Awd; St Josephs U; Chem.

MILAVEC, TRACY; Shaler HS; Glenshaw, PA; (Y); Capt Flag Corp; Mrchg Band; Symp Band; Variety Show; Yrbk Stf; Hon Roll; U Pittsburgh; Engl.

MILBOWER, STEFANIE; Canon Mc Millan SR HS; Cannonsburg, PA; (Y); Church Yth Grp; French Clb; Yrbk Rptr; Yrbk Stf; High Hon Roll; Hon Roll; Trvl.

MILBURN, DALE; West Phila Catholic HS For Boys; Phila, PA; (Y); 13/206; VP Debate Tm; Church Choir; Drm & Bgl; Ed Yrbk Stf; Hon Roll; NHS; Ntl Merit Schol; Church Yth Grp; Cmnty Wkr; Yrbk Rptr; Black Men Inc Hon 85-86; Drexelu Acad Grant 86; Am Found Negro Affirs 83-86; Drexel U; Elect Engr.

MILCHUCK, JOHN; Ridgway Area HS; Ridgway, PA; (S); 2/130; Church Yth Grp; Ski Clb; Off Sr Cls; Rep Stu Cncl; Var L Tennis; High Hon Roll; NHS; Ntl Merit Ltr; Sal; Air Frc ROTC Schlrshp; PA ST U; Aerontcl Engrng.

MILES, DAVE; Otto-Eldred JR SR HS; Eldred, PA; (Y); 25/90; Varsity Clb; Var Bsktbl; Var Ftbl; Var Trk; Hon Roll; IN U; History Educ.

MILES, HEATHER; Canon Mc Millian HS; Canonsburg, PA; (Y); Church Yth Grp; Hosp Aide; VP Thesps; Pres VP Chorus; School Musical; Nwsp Ed-Chief; Rep Stu Cncl; Hon Roll; Drama Clb; Exploring; Atnd Dist Chrs 83-84; Cnty Chrs 85-86; Smll Ensmbl 84-86; Awd Bst Mscn 83-84; Elem Educ.

MILES, PENNY; Bald Eagle Area JR SR HS; Julian, PA; (Y); SADD; Chorus; Nwsp Stf; Rep Soph Cls; Rep Jr Cls; Sec Stu Cncl; JV Cheerleading; Stat Ftbl; Hon Roll; NHS; Med.

MILES, SHANNON; Upper Darby HS; Upr Darby, PA; (Y); 92/629; Cmnty Wkr; Political Wkr; Red Cross Aide; SADD; Varsity Clb; Lit Mag; Off Jr Cls; Swmmng; Cit Awd; Church Yth Grp; Amer Leag Auxlry Cert Of Part 86; Intrior Dcrtr.

MILES, TABITHA; Meadville Area SR HS; Meadville, PA; (Y); 42/356; Church Yth Grp; VP Hosp Aide; Science Clb; Spanish Clb; Speech Tm; Concert Band; Nwsp Rptr; Yrbk Stf; High Hon Roll; Band; Dplma Acad Biblcl Insghts; Acdmc Achvmnt Awd Frm Upwrd Bnd Prog & HS 85-86; Gvrnmnt.

MILETO, SUZANNE; West Scranton HS; Scranton, PA; (Y); 24/250; Letterman Clb; Pep Clb; Spanish Clb; Orch; Bsktbl; Sftbl; Tennis; Hon Roll; Jr NHS; NHS; PA ST; Sci.

MILEWSKI, STEVE; Harbor Creek HS; Erie, PA; (Y); Boys Clb Am; Cmnty Wkr; Im Bsktbl; Penn ST U; Accntng.

MILEY, ARTHUR; Carbondale Area JR-SR HS; Carbondale, PA; (Y); 37/160; FBLA; Ski Clb; Band; Chorus; Mrchg Band; Trs Soph Cls; Pres Jr Cls; Hon Roll; Boy Scts; Office Aide; PA Free Enterprize Schlrsp 86; MD Coll Hnr Band 85; PTA 1st Pl Cultural Arts Photo 85; BUS Adm.

MILHEIM, KIM; Central Columbia HS; Mifflinville, PA; (S); FBLA; Sec FHA; Girl Scts; Key Clb; Trs Library Aide; Sec DECA Emplyd Cntrl Schl Store 82-85; Won Cmptitns Fshn ST Comps 84-85; Frnc Cmptitns 85; Art Inst Of Phila; Fshn Merch.

MILIOS, HELEN; Upper Darby SR HS; Upper Darby, PA; (Y); Church Yth Grp; Teachers Aide; Soph Cls; Hon Roll; Acctg.

MILIOTO, TRACY; Canon Mc Millan SR HS; Canonsburg, PA; (Y); 58/360; French Clb; Concert Band; Drm Mjr(t); Mrchg Band; JV Bsktbl; L Twrlr; High Hon Roll; Hon Roll; Marine Bio.

MILITO, DAVID; Mc Caskey HS; Lancaster, PA; (Y); Drama Clb; Thesps; School Play; Stage Crew; Nwsp Stf; Bst Male Actr 85-86; Millersville U; Comm.

MILJENOVICH, MELISSA; Greater Johnstown HS; Johnstown, PA; (Y); Chorus; Color Guard; Rep Jr Cls; Var L Tennis; Hon Roll; NHS; Psychlgy.

MILKE, DANA; Cumberland Valley HS; Mechanicsburg, PA; (Y); Key Clb; Ski Clb; Band; Ed Nwsp Ed-Chief; Nwsp Stf; Ed Lit Mag; Sec Soph Cls; Rep Stu Cncl; Var Cheerleading; Sftbl; Hlth Adm.

MILKENT, HEATHER; Belle Vernon Area HS; Belle Vernon, PA; (Y); Ski Clb; Band; Yrbk Stf; L Swmmng; Hon Roll; WV U; Pre Law.

MILKO, ELAINE; Seton Catholic HS; Pittston, PA; (Y); 19/93; Trs SADD; Pres Chorus; Jazz Band; VP Madrigals; School Musical; School Play; Variety Show; Hon Roll; NHS; Music Theory II Awd 85-86; Sec Sci Awd 85-86; Mc Cann Schl Of Bus; Mrktng.

MILKOVICH, AMY; Westmon Hilltop HS; Johnstown, PA; (Y); 13/161; Sec Y-Teens; Band; Capt Color Guard; Concert Band; Jazz Band; Mrchg Band; Orch; Symp Band; High Hon Roll; NHS; IN U; Psychlgy.

MILKOVITZ, CHRISTINE; Bethlehem Catholic HS; Bethlehem, PA; (Y); 22/219; Hosp Aide; Band; Color Guard; Mrchg Band; Twrlr; High Hon Roll; NHS; Outstndng Achvt Intro Calculus, Fountain Hill Exch Club Schlrshp; Outstndng Achvt Chem; PA ST U; Nrsng.

MILLAN, DONNA M; Whitehall HS; Whitehall, PA; (Y); 31/295; Am Leg Aux Girls St; German Clb; Scholastic Bowl; Nwsp Ed-Chief; Nwsp Stf; Yrbk Ed-Chief; Yrbk Phtg; NHS; Pres Schlr; German Natl Hnr Soc; Ithaca Coll Ithaca NY; German.

MILLARD, STEPHEN; St Pius X HS; Schwenksville, PA; (S); 8/135; FBLA; Pres JA; Pres Ski Clb; School Musical; Variety Show; Var L Ftbl; JV Wrstlng; High Hon Roll; NHS; NEDT Awd; Jr Achvt Outstndng Yng Busmn 84; Syracuse U; Corprt Law.

MILLER, ALAN; Middletown Area HS; Middletown, PA; (Y); 21/186; Concert Band; Mrchg Band; Var Ftbl; Var Socr; Im Vllybl; High Hon Roll; NHS; Boy Scts; Church Yth Grp; Band; Pres Acdmc Ftnss Awd 86; Amer Lgn Schl Awd 86; H K Alwine Schlrshp 86; U Of Pittsburg Johnstown; Bio.

MILLER, ALICIA; Cumberland Valley HS; Mechanicsburg, PA; (Y); 50/600; Model UN; Pres Soph Cls; Var Bsktbl; Var Fld Hcky; Keystone ST Gms Schlstc Grls Sccr Tm Stu 84-86; Hist.

MILLER, AMY E; Conemaugh Township Area HS; Hollsopple, PA; (Y); 2/105; Church Yth Grp; Drama Clb; Concert Band; Mrchg Band; School Play; Yrbk Stf; Lit Mag; NHS; Pres Schlr; Sec Soph Cls; U Pittsburgh; Pre Phrmcy.

MILLER, ANDREW; Elizabethtown Area HS; Elizabethtown, PA; (Y); Rep Stu Cncl; Bsbl; Ftbl; Powder Puff Ftbl; Wt Lftg; Capts Awd Ftbl 86; Var Ltr Ftbl 86; Cntrl PA; Phys Thrpy.

MILLER, ANDREW; Lincoln HS; Ellwood City, PA; (Y); 41/162; Sec Church Yth Grp; Computer Clb; Drama Clb; Trs Key Clb; School Play; Stu Cncl; Hon Roll.

MILLER, ANN; Pine Grove Area HS; Schuylkill Haven, PA; (Y); Cmnty Wkr; Office Aide; Chorus; Hon Roll; Prfct Atten Awd; Hme Eco Awd-Hghst Avg 85-86; Sec.

MILLER, ANN MARIE; Williams Valley HS; Lykens, PA; (Y); 16/100; Church Yth Grp; Chorus; Yrbk Ed-Chief; Yrbk Phtg; Yrbk Stf; Var Capt Cheerleading; Capt Ftbl; High Hon Roll; Hon Roll; Outstndng Chorus; Peer Educ Grp; Singers; Bus Adm.

MILLER, ANNE MEREDITH; Harriton HS; Bryn Mawr, PA; (Y); Church Yth Grp; SADD; Var Sftbl; Var Swmmng; Stat Vllybl; Commrcl Art.

MILLER, ANNETTE; Somerset Area SR HS; Friedens, PA; (Y); English Clb; VP JA; Letterman Clb; Spanish Clb; Varsity Clb; Nwsp Rptr; Nwsp Stf; Stu Cncl; Var Trk; Hon Roll; 2nd Pl Spnsh Orytry Intrntl Awrns Day 86; Rcrd Hldr 3200m Rly Tm 85 & 86; Schlrshp Brdfrd Coll 86; Educ.

MILLER, AUDREY L; Quakertown Community SR HS; Quakertown, PA; (Y); 13/290; Chorus; Concert Band; School Musical; School Play; Rep Stu Cncl; Bsktbl; High Hon Roll; Hon Roll; NHS; Amer Lg Awd 83; Elizabethtown Coll; Bus Adm.

MILLER, AUDREY M; Twin Valley HS; Honey Brook, PA; (Y); 29/127; Am Leg Aux Girls St; Pres Church Yth Grp; Pres FBLA; Girl Scts; Pep Clb; Spanish Clb; Concert Band; Mrchg Band; School Musical; Lcrss; PA Free Entrprs Wk Schlrshp 85; Ms FBLA 86; PA ST; Pre Law.

MILLER, BARB; Bethel Christian Schl; Waterford, PA; (S); Church Yth Grp; Drama Clb; Chorus; School Musical; School Play; Variety Show; Pres Jr Cls; Var Bsktbl; Cit Awd; High Hon Roll; Msc.

MILLER, BART; Dover Area HS; Dover, PA; (Y); 69/240; Pres Trs Church Yth Grp; Im L Bsktbl; Var L Crs Cntry; Im L Ftbl; Var L Trk; Hon Roll; Bus Adm.

MILLER, BETH A; South Side Catholic HS; Pittsburgh, PA; (S); English Clb; Service Clb; Nwsp Rptr; Nwsp Stf; Frsh Cls; Soph Cls; Jr Cls; Stu Cncl; Hon Roll; Dntl Hygn.

MILLER, BETTY; Cambridge Springs HS; Saegertown, PA; (Y); 4/94; Sec Church Yth Grp; Pres VP 4-H; Sec Spanish Clb; Teachers Aide; Chorus; Yrbk Ed-Chief; Stu Cncl; Hon Roll; Kiwanis Awd; NHS; Phi Delta Kappa Schlrshp 86; Schl Fclty Schlrshp 86; Slippery Rock U; Elem Educ.

MILLER, BILL; South Allegheny HS; Port Vue, PA; (Y); French Clb; Chorus; Hon Roll; Prfct Atten Awd; Bus Mgmt.

MILLER, BRAD; Du Bois Area HS; Sykesville, PA; (Y); Aud/Vis; Boy Scts; Stage Crew; Penn St.

MILLER, BRAD; Seneca Valley SR HS; Harmony, PA; (Y); Radio Clb; ROTC; Var L Bsbl; Var Tennis; Slippery Rock U; Accntng.

MILLER, BRANDY; Wilson Area HS; Easton, PA; (Y); Model UN; Office Aide; School Play; Nwsp Stf; Yrbk Stf; Rep Stu Cncl; Mgr Bsbl; Mgr Bsktbl; Cheerleading; Crs Cntry.

MILLER, BRENDA; North Star HS; Boswell, PA; (Y); FCA; Varsity Clb; Band; Trs Soph Cls; Stu Cncl; L Bsktbl; L Sftbl; Computer Clb; Letterman Clb; Ski Clb; Bswl Jaycees SR Bsktbl Athlt 86; Vrsty Clb SR Athlt Bsktbl-Sftbl 86; Stnly Dvs Schlr Athlt 86; U Ptsbrgh Jnstwn; Pre-Phys Thpy.

MILLER, BRETT; Liberty HS; Bethlehem, PA; (Y); 101/392; Pres Church Yth Grp; DECA; FBLA; Red Cross Aide; VP Ski Clb; CAP; Exploring; Hosp Aide; JA; Political Wkr; 4th Pl Ad & Dsply Svcs 86; 2nd Pl Role Ply 86; 2nd Pl Role Ply 85; Northwood Inst; Adv.

MILLER, BRIAN; St Marys Area HS; Saint Marys, PA; (Y); JV L Bsktbl; JV Crs Cntry; Hon Roll; Acctg.

MILLER, CAMELA; Central Dauphin East HS; Dauphin, PA; (Y); 32/274; Band; L Crs Cntry; Capt L Trk; Hon Roll; Jr NHS; NHS; Red Cross Aide; Ski Clb; Varsity Clb; Chorus; People To People Stu Ambsdr Smmr 86; Outstndng Rnnr Cross Cnty 83-85; Cross Cnty Tm Schlstc Awd 84-85; Comm.

MILLER, CAROL; Cedar Grove Christian Acad; Philadelphia, PA; (Y); Church Yth Grp; Chorus; High Hon Roll; NHS; Prfct Atten Awd; City Comptn Acctng I Awd 86; Exec Sec.

MILLER, CHAD; Palmyra HS; Palmyra, PA; (Y); Boy Scts; Camera Clb; Church Yth Grp; Chorus; Church Choir; School Musical; Bsktbl; Socr; Hon Roll; Prfct Atten Awd; 1st Pl Sci Fair; Harrisburg Area CC; Comp Tech.

MILLER, CHRIS; Greater Latrobe HS; Greensburg, PA; (Y); 202/409; Sec VP Church Yth Grp; Letterman Clb; Var L Ftbl; JV Wrstlng; Rotary Awd; Accntng.

MILLER, CHRISTINA; Nazareth Acad; Philadelphia, PA; (Y); Church Yth Grp; Spanish Clb; Teachers Aide; Sec Soph Cls; VP Jr Cls; Var Bsktbl; Im Bowling; Im Coach Actv; Var Fld Hcky; Var Sftbl; Hugh O Brien Yth Orgnztn Esy Cntst 85; Pre Med.

MILLER, CHRISTINE; Altoona Area HS; Altoona, PA; (S); VP Sec Chess Clb; Pres Church Yth Grp; Math Clb; Math Tm; Pres Science Clb; Spanish Clb; Var L Swmmng; Gov Hon Prg Awd; Jr NHS; NHS; Rensselaer Medl Excllnc Math & Sci 86; Bio.

MILLER, CHRISTOPHER; William Penn SR HS; York, PA; (Y); 10/320; Pres JA; JV Bsbl; Var Capt Socr; High Hon Roll; Jr NHS; NHS; Prfct Atten Awd; Hnr Grad 85-86; Presdntl Acad Ftns Awd 85-86; Navy; Nuclear Elec.

MILLER, CHRISTOPHER ALLAN; West Mifflin Area HS; West Mifflin, PA; (Y); Church Yth Grp; Key Clb; Letterman Clb; Ski Clb; Varsity Clb; Coach Actv; Var Ftbl; Var Capt Socr; Var Wrstlng; Hon Roll.

MILLER, CHRISTY; Peters Township HS; Mcmurray, PA; (Y); Church Yth Grp; Cmnty Wkr; Nwsp Bus Mgr; Nwsp Rptr; Nwsp Stf; Yrbk Phtg; Rep Stu Cncl; Stat Bsktbl; Var Powder Puff Ftbl; Stat Var Socr; Fin WV U Jrnlsm Cont 86; Elem Ed.

MILLER, CINDY; Charleroi HS; Charleroi, PA; (Y); Debate Tm; French Clb; Hosp Aide; JA; NFL; Science Clb; Band; Concert Band; Mrchg Band; Nwsp Stf; J A 500 Dollar Sls Clb & Merit JR Achvt 85; CHAMPS PTA Mst Helpfl Cls 84; Nrs.

MILLER, COREY D; Bellefonte SR HS; Bellefonte, PA; (Y); 6/265; Band; Concert Band; Jazz Band; Mrchg Band; Hon Roll; NHS; Prfct Atten Awd; Dist,Regnl And All State Band 85-86; Natl Assoc Of Jazz Eductrs Outstndg Muscnshp Awd 85-86; PA ST U; Vet Sci.

MILLER, CYNTHIA; Purchase Line HS; Mahaffey, PA; (Y); Church Yth Grp; Spanish Clb; Varsity Clb; Band; Concert Band; Drm Mjr(t); Mrchg Band; Var L Trk; DAR Awd; Hon Roll; Dist, Regnl Band 85 & 86; Music Educ.

MILLER, DALE; Aliquippa HS; Aliquippa, PA; (Y); VICA; Hon Roll; Outstndng Stu Awd Wldng Voc Tech Schl 86; Rbtcs.

MILLER, DANA; Liberty JR SR HS; Liberty, PA; (Y); 6/40; Pres Sec 4-H; Pres FHA; German Clb; Chorus; School Musical; Yrbk Ed-Chief; Stat Bsktbl; JV Var Cheerleading; Hon Roll; NHS; Penn ST U; Fshn Merch.

MILLER, DANE R; Mc Connellsburg HS; Big Cove Tannery, PA; (Y); Boy Scts; Church Yth Grp; 4-H; FFA; Band; 4-H Awd.

MILLER, DANIELLE; Hazleton HS; Hazleton, PA; (Y); 56/388; Drama Clb; Office Aide; Pep Clb; Chorus; School Play; Rptr Yrbk Stf; Var L Cheerleading; Hon Roll; Law.

MILLER, DARREN; Sharpesville HS; Shaprsville, PA; (Y); Math Clb; Science Clb; Spanish Clb; Thesps; Chorus; School Musical; Im Bsktbl; Acad Achvt Awd 84-85; Psyclgy.

MILLER, DAVID; Canton JR SR HS; Canton, PA; (Y); Art Clb; Church Yth Grp; Cmnty Wkr; 4-H; FHA; Letterman Clb; Library Aide; Chorus; School Play; Nwsp Phtg; Pres Phys Fit 82-86; Camp Cadet Polc Camp 84; Grphc Art.

MILLER, DAVID; Lompeter Strasburg HS; Strasburg, PA; (Y); JV Socr; Hon Roll; Bus Mgmt.

MILLER, DEANNE LYNN; Brookville Area HS; Knox Dale, PA; (Y); 24/143; VP Church Yth Grp; Sec FTA; Concert Band; Mrchg Band; Lit Mag; Rep Stu Cncl; High Hon Roll; Jr NHS; NHS; Pres Schlr; Clarion U PA; Educ.

MILLER, DEBRA; Lock Haren SR HS; Castanea, PA; (Y); FHA; Trk; FHA Chptr Pres 85-86; FHA Chptr Stu Yr 85-86; Lock Haven U; Elem Ed.

MILLER, DENISE; Chestnut Ridge HS; New Paris, PA; (S); 11/142; Church Yth Grp; Band; Concert Band; Sec Frsh Cls; Sec Soph Cls; Rep Stu Cncl; Var Sftbl; Var Vllybl; Hon Roll; NHS.

MILLER, DENNIS; Central Catholic HS; Wilkinsburg, PA; (Y); 62/278; Church Yth Grp; Math Clb; Var Bowling; Hon Roll; Intrmrl Ftbl Chmps, Intrmrl Bsktbl Chmps 85-86; CMU; Mech Engrng.

MILLER, DIANA; Grove City SR HS; Slippery Rock, PA; (Y); 1/137; French Clb; Mrchg Band; Elks Awd; VP Pres NHS; Opt Clb Awd; Pres Schlr; Val; AFS; Hosp Aide; Key Clb; Wmns Clb Yth Mnth 86; Jamesway Awd & Scholar 86; E S & Sylvia Hassler Awd 86; Mt Union Coll; Mth.

MILLER, DIANE; Berwick Area SR HS; Berwick, PA; (Y); Sec Keywanettes; Office Aide; Red Cross Aide; Chorus; Color Guard; JV Var Bsktbl; Northampton County CC; Lgl Sec.

MILLER, DINA; Central Dauphin HS; Hattiesburg, PA; (Y); 2/386; High Hon Roll; Hon Roll; Jr NHS; NHS; Acad Stu Mnth Awd 85.

MILLER, DONNA; Cambridge Springs HS; Saegertown, PA; (Y); 14/112; Trs Church Yth Grp; Sec VP 4-H; Chorus; Mrchg Band; Yrbk Stf; Sec Jr Cls; Stu Cncl; Pom Pon; 4-H Awd; Hon Roll; Sec.

MILLER, ELIZABETH; Benton Area HS; Orangeville, PA; (Y); Library Aide; Hon Roll; NHS; Elem Ed.

MILLER, ELLEN J; Parkland SR HS; Laurys Sta, PA; (Y); Chess Clb; Church Yth Grp; Girl Scts; Flag Corp; Hon Roll; NHS; Kutztown U Of PA; Psychlgy.

MILLER, ERIK R; Emmaus HS; Allentown, PA; (Y); 26/479; Boy Scts; Exploring; Hst Key Clb; Jazz Band; Mrchg Band; Nwsp Phtg; High Hon Roll; NHS; Ntl Merit Ltr; Top 10 Pct Natl Jets Engrng Tst 85; High Statewide Scorer SAT Test 85 & 86; U DE; Chem Engrng.

MILLER, ERIKA; Abington SR HS; Rydal, PA; (Y); 14/535; Pres French Clb; Intnl Clb; Pres Latin Clb; Model UN; Orch; Ed Yrbk Stf; Lit Mag; Var Cheerleading; JV Socr; Hon Roll; Latin Clb Awd 86; U Of PA; Intrnl Law.

MILLER JR, GARY A; Williamsburg HS; Williamsburg, PA; (Y); 3/66; Boy Scts; Church Yth Grp; Nwsp Stf; Yrbk Stf; Stat Bsktbl; High Hon Roll; Prfct Atten Awd; Eagl Sct 84; Hnr Awd 83-84; Aerntcl Engrng.

MILLER, GREGORY; Lewisburg Area HS; Lewisburg, PA; (Y); Drama Clb; Science Clb; Rep Stu Cncl; JV Bsktbl; Var Bowling; Var Socr; Var Tennis; Im Vllybl; Hon Roll.

MILLER, GREGORY; Palmyra Area HS; Palmyra, PA; (Y); 63/196; Trs German Clb; VP Frsh Cls; L Var Bsbl; L Var Bsktbl; L Var Ftbl; Wt Lftg; Hon Roll.

MILLER, HEATHER; Central HS; Martinsburg, PA; (Y); 34/188; Church Yth Grp; Ski Clb; Varsity Clb; Chorus; School Play; Trs Jr Cls; Stu Cncl; Capt Cheerleading; Wt Lftg; Hon Roll; Am Acad Achvt Awd Stu Cncl 83; Acad Achvt Awd Spnsh 86; Radlgy.

MILLER, HEATHER; Cocalico HS; Reamstown, PA; (Y); 50/169; Art Clb; Church Yth Grp; Cmnty Wkr; 4-H; GAA; Girl Scts; JV Bsktbl; Hon Roll; Equine Stud.

MILLER, HEATHER; Scranton Technical HS; Scranton, PA; (Y); 7/220; Cmnty Wkr; Lit Mag; Hon Roll; Jr NHS; NHS.

MILLER, HEIDI; Bangor Area SR HS; E Bangor, PA; (Y); 10/175; Art Clb; Computer Clb; Pep Clb; Scholastic Bowl; Yrbk Stf; Bsktbl; Score Keeper; Im Vllybl; High Hon Roll; Hon Roll; VP NHS 85-86; Merit Awd Brandywine Coll 86; Brandywine Coll; Travel/Trsm.

MILLER, HOLLY; Tulpehocken HS; Bethel, PA; (Y); Sec Church Yth Grp; Hon Roll; Tlphckn Schlr Awd 85-86.

MILLER, JACQUELYN; Lancaster Catholic HS; Lancaster, PA; (Y); 11/207; Pep Clb; Varsity Clb; Stage Crew; JV Var Cheerleading; Hon Roll; NHS; Ntl Merit Ltr; U Schlrshp Frm St Josephs U 86; Pres Acad Ftnss Awd 86; St Josephs U; Major.

MILLER, JAMES; Central Catholic HS; Pittsburgh, PA; (Y); Aud/Vis; VP JA; Im Ftbl; Im Ice Hcky; Hon Roll; Bus.

MILLER, JAMES; Pine Grove Area HS; Pine Grove, PA; (Y); 12/119; Church Yth Grp; Cmnty Wkr; ROTC; Teachers Aide; Nwsp Rptr; Rep Stu Cncl; JV Bsbl; Hon Roll; Trs NHS; Rotary Awd; Red Arrow Svc Awd 86; Stu Mnth 86; Prsdntlacad Ftnss Awd 86; PA Pwr & Lght.

MILLER, JAMES; Portersville Christian Schl; Portersville, PA; (Y); Church Yth Grp; Teachers Aide; Chorus; Yrbk Phtg; Yrbk Sprt Ed; Yrbk Stf; Var Capt Bsktbl; Var Capt Socr; Var Sftbl; High Hon Roll; Advsry Cmmttee Elec Occptns 85-86; Elec Occptns.

MILLER, JASON; Mechanicsburg HS; Mechanicsburg, PA; (Y); Stage Crew; Im Bowling; High Hon Roll; Hon Roll; NHS.

MILLER, JASON; Mount Penn HS; Reading, PA; (Y); 7/78; Sec Model UN; Concert Band; Pres NHS; Quiz Bowl; Trs Science Clb; Band; Jazz Band; Mrchg Band; High Hon Roll; Hon Roll; Homigan Amer Schlrshp 86; Lehigh U; Mech Engr.

MILLER, JAY; Abington Heights HS; Clarks Summit, PA; (Y); 100/285; Cmnty Wkr; Band; Concert Band; Mrchg Band; Rifle-MVP 86; Bstr Clb Achvt Awd-Rifl 85-86; 3rd Pl NE PA Rifl Leag 86; Misericordia Coll; Radiatn Tech.

MILLER, JEFF; Ford City JR SR HS; Mcgrann, PA; (Y); 48/154; Chorus; School Musical; Golf; Trk; Hon Roll; Soc Wrk.

MILLER, JEFF; Harmony Area HS; Cherry Tree, PA; (Y); 10/44; Boy Scts; Camera Clb; Ski Clb; Band; Pres Frsh Cls; VP Soph Cls; Pres Jr Cls; Var L Bsbl; Var L Bsktbl; High Hon Roll; Am Leg Schl Awd Hnrb Mntn 84; Am Musical Fndtn 84; Stu Of Month 86.

MILLER, JEFFREY; Cedar Crest HS; Lebanon, PA; (Y); 32/328; Crs Cntry; Ftbl; Trk; Hon Roll; Comp Pgmr.

MILLER, JENNIFER; Conneaut Lake Area Joint HS; Conneaut Lake, PA; (Y); Spanish Clb; Band; Mrchg Band; Stat Ftbl; JV Var Mgr(s); Hon Roll.

MILLER, JENNIFER; Cumberland Valley HS; Mechanicsburg, PA; (Y); 31/545; French Clb; Office Aide; Pep Clb; SADD; Color Guard; School Play; Var Cheerleading; Var Gym; Hon Roll; NHS; Foreign Law.

MILLER, JENNIFER L; Central Bucks HS West; Chalfont, PA; (Y); 18/421; Model UN; Nwsp Rptr; Rep Stu Cncl; VP Fld Hcky; Capt Var Swmmng; Hon Roll; Dance Clb; NHS; Ntl Merit SF; JV Lcrss; Mst Imprvd Swimmer 85; Russian Achvt Awd 85; Librl Arts.

MILLER, JILL; Clearfield Area HS; Clearfield, PA; (Y); 19/300; Hst Frsh Cls; Mat Maids; JV Var Sftbl; High Hon Roll; Hon Roll; NHS.

MILLER, JIMMY; Greater Johnstown HS; Johnstown, PA; (Y); Math Clb; Spanish Clb; High Hon Roll; Hon Roll; NHS; Med Fld.

MILLER, JODI; Kishacoquillas HS; Belleville, PA; (Y); 76/142; DECA; Variety Show; Mgr(s); Mgr Sftbl; Hon Roll; SR Awd Voc Tech Schl 86.

MILLER, JOHN; Conrad Weiser HS; Robesonia, PA; (Y); 15/137; Church Yth Grp; JCL; Key Clb; Band; Chorus; Concert Band; Jazz Band; Mrchg Band; Pep Band; School Musical; By Scts-Egl Sct-JASM 85; NEED Cmp Stff 86; PA ST U; Hrtcltur.

MILLER, JOHN; Shaler Area SR HS; Allison Pk, PA; (Y); 45/517; Exploring; Concert Band; Mrchg Band; JV Bsbl; Var Trk; Hon Roll; Aerontcl Engr.

MILLER, JON; Northampton Area SR HS; Bath, PA; (Y); 7/462; Model UN; High Hon Roll; Ntl Merit Ltr; Rotary Awd; Cornell U; Elec Engrng.

MILLER, KARA; Ringgold HS; Eighty Four, PA; (Y); 10/349; Office Aide; Varsity Clb; Band; Chorus; Drill Tm; School Musical; Variety Show; Cheerleading; High Hon Roll; NHS; Sci Math Hnr Soc 84-86; 1st Pl Dist Lit Div Cltrl Arts Cntst 85; Bio Olympcs 85; Pre-Med.

MILLER, KARA; Shenango HS; New Castle, PA; (Y); 24/117; French Clb; Letterman Clb; Varsity Clb; Yrbk Stf; Var Bsktbl; Var Cheerleading; Var Trk; Stat Vllybl; Hon Roll; NHS; Westminster College.

MILLER, KAREN; Canemauh Valley JRSR HS; Johnstown, PA; (Y); Pep Clb; Sftbl; Hon Roll; NHS; Prfct Atten Awd; Penn ST U; Chem Engrng.

MILLER, KAREN; Mechanicsburg SR HS; Mechanicsburg, PA; (Y); Chorus; Mrchg Band; Orch; Symp Band; Yrbk Stf; High Hon Roll; Cnty Band 84-86; Psych.

MILLER, KAREN; Neshaminy HS; Penndel, PA; (Y); 38/723; Trs Church Yth Grp; Girl Scts; Sec Service Clb; Concert Band; Mrchg Band; Orch; Ed Nwsp Rptr; Hon Roll; NHS; Prfct Atten Awd.

MILLER, KATHLEEN; Quigley HS; Baden, PA; (Y); Girl Scts; Pep Clb; SADD; Chorus; JV Var Cheerleading; Mgr(s); Score Keeper; Var L Sftbl; JV Var Vllybl; Hon Roll; Bus Adm.

MILLER, KATHY; Seneca Valley HS; Zelienople, PA; (Y); #14 In Class; Dance Clb; Letterman Clb; SADD; Varsity Clb; Chorus; Var L Sftbl; Capt Var Swmmng; JV Tennis; Hon Roll; Acctng.

MILLER, KEITH; Technical Memorial HS; Erie, PA; (Y); 27/345; Art Clb; Boy Scts; Yrbk Stf; Columbus Schl Of Art; Comm Art.

MILLER, KELLEY; Bishop Kenrick HS; Norristown, PA; (Y); 142/292; Cmnty Wkr; Drama Clb; Office Aide; Spanish Clb; School Musical; School Play; Yrbk Stf; Jr Cls; Stu Cncl; Bsktbl; Cmmnctns.

MILLER, KELLY; Hanover HS; Hanover, PA; (Y); Church Yth Grp; Cmnty Wkr; Band; Chorus; Church Choir; Concert Band; Jazz Band; Mrchg Band; School Play; Stage Crew; Disc Jcky.

MILLER, KELLY; Solanco HS; Christiana, PA; (S); Debate Tm; Sec Pres FFA; Office Aide; Pep Clb; Ski Clb; Speech Tm; Teachers Aide; Nwsp Stf; High Hon Roll; Hon Roll; Prdctn Credit Rcrdkpng Awd; Schlrshp Pin; Solanco Schlr In Ag; Secy.

MILLER, KENNETH; Clearfield Area HS; Shawville, PA; (Y); Church Yth Grp; VICA; Var Trk; Hon Roll; Elctrncs-Voc Tech Schl Of Clrfld 85-86; Air Force Acad; Plt.

MILLER, KENNETH; Conemaugh Township Area HS; Holsapple, PA; (Y); 4/101; Boy Scts; Pres Church Yth Grp; Drama Clb; Spanish Clb; Band; Concert Band; Mrchg Band; School Musical; Hon Roll; NHS.

MILLER, KENNETH; Lewistown Area HS; Lewistown, PA; (Y); VP Church Yth Grp; Key Clb; Spanish Clb; Varsity Clb; Ftbl; Capt Trk; Wt Lftg; Wrstlng; High Hon Roll; Hon Roll; Aerosp Engrng.

MILLER, KERRI; New Brighton Area SR HS; New Brighton, PA; (Y); 3/154; Am Leg Aux Girls St; Pres Computer Clb; VP Girl Scts; Library Aide; VP Chorus; Church Choir; Score Keeper; High Hon Roll; NEDT Awd; PA ST; Acctg.

MILLER, KERRI; Scranton Technical HS; Scranton, PA; (Y); FBLA; Letterman Clb; Pep Clb; Ski Clb; Nwsp Stf; Yrbk Stf; Stu Cncl; Capt Cheerleading; Jr NHS; Coop Wrk Exp Prgm 86-87.

MILLER, KERRY; Newport HS; Newport, PA; (Y); German Clb; Math Clb; Science Clb; Wt Lftg; Wrstlng; Hon Roll.

MILLER, KIM; Pottsgrove SR HS; Pottstown, PA; (Y); GAA; Library Aide; Pep Clb; Ski Clb; Spanish Clb; Varsity Clb; Stu Cncl; Bsktbl; Trk; Montgomery Cnty CC.

MILLER, KIMBERLY S; North Hills SR HS; Pittsburgh, PA; (Y); 1/505; Church Yth Grp; NFL; Q&S; Pres Orch; Nwsp Stf; Elks Awd; NHS; Ntl Merit Ltr; Pres Schlr; Val; PA JR Acad Sci 1st Pl Regnl Awd, 1st Pl ST Awd, Dirs Awd Ecolgy 86; Guideposts Yth Wrtg Schlrshp; U Notre Dame; Chem Engrng.

MILLER, KRISTINE; Bellwood-Antis HS; Bellwood, PA; (Y); 1/118; Var Capt Bsktbl; Var L Trk; High Hon Roll; Pres NHS; Ntl Merit SF; Prfct Atten Awd; Bsktbl-Juniata Vly Lg All-Star 86.

MILLER, LARRY; Kishacoquillas HS; Reedsville, PA; (Y); 74/144; Boy Scts; Church Yth Grp; Band; Concert Band; L Mrchg Band; Stage Crew; Variety Show; L Trk; Hon Roll; Acad Ltr 85-86; Egl Sct 85; Otstndng Mchnst Awd 86; Williamsport Area CC; Mchnst.

MILLER, LAURIE; Franklin Regional HS; Jeannette, PA; (Y); Dance Clb; Hosp Aide; Pep Clb; Spanish Clb; Color Guard; Yrbk Stf; Gym; Stat Score Keeper; Tennis; Auburn U.

MILLER, LAWRENCE; Somerset Area SR HS; Somerset, PA; (Y); 71/239; Drama Clb; Varsity Clb; Wt Lftg; Var Wrstlng; Hon Roll.

MILLER, LEANA V; Bedford Area SR HS; Bedford, PA; (Y); Church Yth Grp; Science Clb; Chorus; Pres Jr Cls; Pres Stu Cncl; Cheerleading; Gym; Trk; DAR Awd; NHS; Hugh Obrian Awd 84; Outstndng Grl 83-85; Elizabethtown Coll.

MILLER, LESLEY; Tyrone Area HS; Tyrone, PA; (Y); Varsity Clb; Y-Teens; Chorus; Bsktbl; Powder Puff Ftbl; Sftbl; Hon Roll; Pharmcy.

MILLER, LISA; Cambridge Springs HS; Cambridge Springs, PA; (Y); 26/101; Church Yth Grp; French Clb; Pep Clb; SADD; Yrbk Stf; Stu Cncl; Var L Bsktbl; Var L Sftbl; Var L Vllybl; Hon Roll; Pres Physcl Ftns Awd 83-85; Prom Aide 84; Med.

MILLER, LISA; East Allegheny HS; N Versailles, PA; (Y); Girl Scts; Hosp Aide; Band; School Musical; Nwsp Ed-Chief; Rep Sr Cls; Swmmng; CC Awd; Hon Roll; Sawyer Bus Schl; Sec Sci.

MILLER, LISA; Mc Connellsburg HS; Mcconnellsburg, PA; (Y); Church Yth Grp; French Clb; Teachers Aide; Chorus; Drm Mjr(t); Stage Crew; Rep Soph Cls; Trk; Jr NHS; Hon Roll.

MILLER, LISA; Philadelphia HS For Girls; Philadelphia, PA; (Y); Church Yth Grp; Teachers Aide; Chorus; Church Choir; Drill Tm; Jrnlsm.

MILLER, LISA; Shamokin Area HS; Paxinos, PA; (Y); 13/251; Church Yth Grp; Drama Clb; German Clb; Pres Science Clb; School Musical; Capt Twrlr; High Hon Roll; NHS; Chorus; Church Choir; Sci Olympcs Tm 86; Elem Educ.

MILLER, LORI; South Williamsport Area SR HS; Duboistown, PA; (Y); 50/140; Camera Clb; Drama Clb; FBLA; Hosp Aide; VP JA; Library Aide; Chorus; Nwsp Stf; Yrbk Stf; Dale Carnegie Awd-Hmn Relatns 86; Comp.

MILLER, MARK; Leechburg Area HS; Leechburg, PA; (Y); Exploring; Band; Mrchg Band; Pep Band; Stage Crew; Yrbk Phtg; Yrbk Stf; VP Jr Cls; Hon Roll; Mech Engrng.

MILLER, MARK; Northeastern HS; Manchester, PA; (Y); Pres VP Church Yth Grp; Varsity Clb; Band; Var Capt Bsktbl; Manchstr PTO Schlrshp 86; Penn ST; Bus Adm.

MILLER, MARSHA; Western Beaver JR SR HS; Industry, PA; (Y); Chorus; Capt Drill Tm; Jazz Band; Yrbk Stf; Trs Stu Cncl; Capt Pom Pon; Hon Roll; NHS; CC Beaver County; Secty.

MILLER, MARY; Central Cambria HS; Mineral Pt, PA; (Y); 55/191; FBLA; Teachers Aide; Band; Concert Band; Mrchg Band; Pep Band; High Hon Roll; Hon Roll; Prfct Atten Awd; Accntng & Stngrphc Bus Awds 86; Msc Awd 86; Clarion U; Accntng.

MILLER, MARY; Merion Mercy Acad; Phila, PA; (Y); Cmnty Wkr; Drama Clb; PAVAS; Service Clb; Teachers Aide; Acpl Chr; Chorus; School Musical; School Play; Variety Show; Natl Music Hnr Soc 85-86; Pres Lit Clb 85-86; Music.

MILLER, MATTHEW D; Red Lion Area SR HS; Red Lion, PA; (Y); 100/375; Am Leg Boys St; JCL; Varsity Clb; Sec Soph Cls; Ftbl; Powder Puff Ftbl; Tennis; Wrstlng; Hon Roll.

MILLER, MELISSA; Charleroi JR-SR HS; Charleroi, PA; (Y); Science Clb; Band; Mrchg Band; Spch Pathlgy.

MILLER, MELISSA; Clearfield Area HS; Clearfield, PA; (S); 79/318; Church Yth Grp; Pres French Clb; VP Pres Band; Pres Chorus; Orch; School Musical; Swing Chorus; Hon Roll; Music Ther.

MILLER, MELISSA; Northeastern HS; Mt Wolf, PA; (Y); 1/179; Concert Band; Mrchg Band; Nwsp Ed-Chief; Sec Jr Cls; Rep Sr Cls; Rep Stu Cncl; High Hon Roll; NHS; Hon Roll; Rtry Stu Of Mnth 86; Engr.

MILLER, MICHAEL; Annville-Cleona HS; Annville, PA; (Y); FBLA; Model UN; Nwsp Ed-Chief; Yrbk Rptr; Lit Mag; NEDT Awd; Optmst Clb Awd; Newspaper Layout Editor; Am Pub Assoc Found Awd; CA U; Jrnlsm.

MILLER, MICHAEL; Bensalem HS; Bensalem, PA; (Y); Band; Var Trk; JV Wrstlng; High Hon Roll; Jr NHS; NHS; Distingshd Acvht John Hopkins U Tlnt Srch 82; Invstmnt Bnkr.

MILLER, MICHAEL; Lewisburg Area HS; Lewisburg, PA; (Y); 30/168; Am Leg Boys St; Spanish Clb; Pres Frsh Cls; Pres Soph Cls; Rep Jr Cls; Stu Cncl; Hon Roll; Jr NHS; NHS; Spanish NHS; Union Count Internshp Prog 85-86; Arch.

MILLER, MICHAEL; Marple Newtown SR HS; Newtown Square, PA; (Y); Civic Clb; Cmnty Wkr; JV Bsbl; JV Bsktbl; JV Socr; JV Tennis; JV Trk; High Hon Roll; Hon Roll; Jr NHS; Interact Clb Rotary Clb Newtown 85-86; Med.

MILLER, MICHELLE; Charleroi Area HS; Monongahela, PA; (Y); 21/180; Office Aide; Spanish Clb; Varsity Clb; Lit Mag; Var Capt Swmmng; Hon Roll; NHS; Natl Merit Sci Awd 86; Acad Schlrshp-SVC 86; Girl Of The Mnth-Chanthene Clb 86; St Vincent Coll; Bus Adm.

MILLER, MICHELLE; Mt Carmel JR SR HS; Mt Carmel, PA; (Y); 29/171; Key Clb; Q&S; Ski Clb; Speech Tm; Drm Mjr(t); Nwsp Rptr; Rep Jr Cls; Stu Cncl; Capt Cheerleading; Hon Roll; 1st Rnr-Up Mt Carmel Homecomg Queen Cont 86; Legis Cmnty Svc Awd 86; Pre-Med.

MILLER, MICHELLE; Seneca Valley HS; Evans City, PA; (Y); Pres VP Church Yth Grp; Drama Clb; Sec 4-H; Ski Clb; SADD; Thesps; Chorus; School Musical; School Play; Rep Stu Cncl; 4-H Jdgng Cmptn 1st Pl 84; 4-H Shwmnshp Awd 85; Liberal Arts.

MILLER, MIKE; Spring-Ford HS; Phoenixville, PA; (Y); 67/256; Ski Clb; Spanish Clb; Variety Show.

MILLER, MIRIAM; South Philadelphia HS; Philadelphia, PA; (Y); Exploring; VP Frsh Cls; Rep Soph Cls; Rep Stu Cncl; Cit Awd; Hon Roll; Ntl Merit Ltr; Bus.

MILLER, MONICA; Central Bucks HS East; Warrington, PA; (Y); Church Yth Grp; Drama Clb; Chorus; Church Choir; School Musical; School Play; Capt Cheerleading; Mgr(s); High Hon Roll; Hon Roll; Psych.

MILLER, MYRA JONAI; Harrisburg HS; Harrisburg, PA; (Y); 42/442; Church Yth Grp; Cmnty Wkr; French Clb; Girl Scts; Hosp Aide; Latin Clb; Science Clb; Color Guard; Rep Jr Cls; Hon Roll; Ntl Awd Wnnr USAA Ntl Hnr Rll 86; Howard U; Nrs Anshtst.

MILLER, NANCY; Grove City HS; Grove City, PA; (Y); 25/137; Church Yth Grp; Pres Key Clb; Band; Stat Bsktbl; Im Powder Puff Ftbl; Var L Trk; L Stat Vllybl; Hon Roll; NHS; Walt Pretko Mem Awd 86; Jiggs Wolford Awd 86; Grove City Coll; Acctng.

MILLER, PAMELA; Valley HS; New Kensington, PA; (Y); 12/210; Pres Drama Clb; Ski Clb; Spanish Clb; Chorus; School Play; Nwsp Ed-Chief; Ed Yrbk Stf; Stu Cncl; NHS; AFS; Svc Above Self Awd; IN U Of PA.

MILLER, PAMELLA SUE; Pennsbury HS; Fairless Hills, PA; (Y); Drama Clb; Band; Chorus; Concert Band; Mrchg Band; School Musical; School Play; Swmmng; Hon Roll; Prfct Atten Awd; Exclice Actng Awd Bucks Cnty Playhouse 85; Outstndng Swmmr Awd 85; Theater Arts.

MILLER, PATTI; Forest Hills SR HS; South Fork, PA; (Y); 15/156; Pep Clb; Spanish Clb; Y-Teens; Cheerleading; Hon Roll; Jr NHS; Spanish NHS; Jaycettes 85.

MILLER, PATTY; Chambersburg Area SR HS; Chambersburg, PA; (Y); Church Yth Grp; JCL; Latin Clb; NFL; Spanish Clb; Spanish Clb; Band; Chorus; Church Choir; School Play; Amercn Bus Wmn Schlrshp 86; Bus Prfssnl Wmn Schlrshp 86; Bloomsburg U; Elem Ed.

MILLER, PAUL; J N Coughlin HS; Wilkes Barre, PA; (Y); Boy Scts; Church Yth Grp; Ski Clb; Band; Golf; The Citadel; Electrical Engrng.

MILLER, PAULA; Fannett-Metal HS; Spring Run, PA; (S); 2/53; Trs Church Yth Grp; Concert Band; Mrchg Band; Nwsp Phtg; Stat Bsktbl; JV Sftbl; High Hon Roll; Hon Roll; NHS; Amer Lgn Essy Cntst 2nd Pl 84-85; Reach Amer Proj Mbr 85-86; Penn ST U; Hist.

MILLER, PAULA; Trinity HS; Washington, PA; (Y); Key Clb; Office Aide; Pep Clb; Color Guard; Mrchg Band; Cmmndr Of Aux 85-86.

MILLER, PENNY; Avonworth HS; Pittsbg, PA; (Y); AFS; Varsity Clb; Yrbk Stf; Trs Soph Cls; Socr; Sftbl; High Hon Roll; Hon Roll; Score Keeper; Southern Meth U; Real Est.

MILLER, QUENTIN; Lancaster Mennonite HS; Mt Joy, PA; (Y); Church Yth Grp; FFA; Stu Cncl; Ftbl; Wt Lftg.

MILLER, RACHEL; Aliba Hebrew Acad; Wynnewood, PA; (Y); Hosp Aide; Science Clb; Varsity Clb; VP Frsh Cls; VP Soph Cls; Pres Jr Cls; Var Capt Bsktbl; Var Mgr(s); Var Capt Socr; MVP Bsktbl 86-87; MVP Socr 86; All Arnd Athlt 86; Rehab Med.

MILLER, RHONDA; Yough HS; Herminie, PA; (Y); Library Aide; Ski Clb; Band; Concert Band; Mrchg Band; Stage Crew.

MILLER, RICH; Tri-Valley HS; Valley View, PA; (Y); 8/75; VP Ski Clb; Varsity Clb; Var Bsbl; Capt Var Ftbl; Wt Lftg; Cit Awd; High Hon Roll; Hon Roll; NHS; NEDT Awd; Schlrs Athlt 86fWQIN Schlr Athlt In Bsbl 86; Pres Acdmc Ftns Awd 86; Shpnsbrg U; Lbrl Arts.

MILLER, RICHARD; Beaver Area HS; Beaver, PA; (Y); Boy Scts; Church Yth Grp; German Clb; Ski Clb; Band; Bsbl; Trk; PA ST; Engrng.

MILLER, RICHARD; Waynesboro SR HS; Waynesboro, PA; (Y); Ski Clb; Bsbl; Ftbl; Wrstlng; High Hon Roll; Hon Roll; Army.

MILLER, ROBERTA F; St Puis X HS; Pottstown, PA; (S); 20/161; French Clb; Hosp Aide; Tennis; Hon Roll; Prfct Atten Awd; Med.

MILLER, ROXANNE; Lock Haven SR HS; Castanea, PA; (Y); Keywanettes; Band; Chorus; Concert Band; Jazz Band; Mrchg Band; Orch; Variety Show; Bsktbl; Hon Roll; Earth Space Sci Awd 84; Band Awd 84; Lock Haven U; Bio.

MILLER, RUSSELL; Cambria Heights HS; Patton, PA; (Y); 22/177; NFL; Pres Band; Pres Chorus; Drm Mjr(t); Mrchg Band; School Play; Stage Crew; Yrbk Ed-Chief; Hon Roll; Pres Acadmc Fit Awd 86; Fclty Awd Apprctn Svc 86; Juniata Coll; Pre-Med.

MILLER, SANDRA; Ford City HS; Mcgrann, PA; (Y); AFS; Cmnty Wkr; Hosp Aide; Political Wkr; Spanish Clb; Band; Concert Band; Drm Mjr(t); Mrchg Band; Pep Band; IN U Of PA; Elem Ed.

MILLER, SANDY; Bald Eagle Area HS; Julian, PA; (Y); Soph Cls; Jr Cls; Cheerleading; Gym; Powder Puff Ftbl; Accntng.

MILLER, SCOTT; N Penn HS; Covington, PA; (Y); Camera Clb; 4-H; Letterman Clb; Ski Clb; Varsity Clb; L Ftbl; L Trk; Hon Roll; Outstndng HS Athlts In Amer 86; Offensive Plyr Of Yr 84-85; Lycoming Clg; Liberal Arts.

MILLER, SCOTT A; Mechanicsburg HS; Mechanicsburg, PA; (Y); Band; Concert Band; Jazz Band; Mrchg Band; Symp Band; JV L Bsktbl; Hon Roll; Penn ST; Lwyr.

MILLER, SHANE; Greater Lafrobe SR HS; Youngstown, PA; (Y); Band; Pres Chorus; Church Choir; Mrchg Band; School Musical; Symp Band; High Hon Roll; Kiwanis Awd; NHS; Latrobe Music Assoc Awd 86; Grove City Coll; Math.

MILLER, SHANNON; Hollidaysburg Area SR HS; Hollidaysburg, PA; (Y); 63/351; Drama Clb; German Clb; Varsity Clb; Band; Capt Drill Tm; Yrbk Stf; Rep Frsh Cls; Rep Stu Cncl; Mgr(s); Swmmng; Fash Inst Tech; Fshn Mrchndsg.

MILLER, SHARI; Kiski Area HS; Vandergrift, PA; (Y); Church Yth Grp; Spanish Clb; Chorus; Church Choir; Swing Chorus; Nwsp Rptr; Im Sftbl; Var Trk; High Hon Roll; Hon Roll; Wesminster Coll; Cmmnctns.

MILLER, SHARON; Elk County Christian HS; St Marys, PA; (Y); 18/80; Library Aide; Office Aide; Stat Bsktbl; Stat Ftbl; Mgr(s); Tennis; Hon Roll; Crmnlgy.

MILLER, SHAWN; Millville HS; Millville, PA; (Y); Chess Clb; Trs Church Yth Grp; FBLA; Varsity Clb; School Play; Yrbk Stf; JV Bsbl; Var JV Bsktbl; Var JV Socr; Wt Lftg; Math.

MILLER, SHERI; Berwick Area SR HS; Nescopeck, PA; (Y); Sec Church Yth Grp; Pres Key Clb; Chorus; Nwsp Rptr; JV Fld Hcky; Var L Sftbl; Merch.

MILLER, SHERRY LYNN; Central Bucks HS West; Doylestown, PA; (Y); VP Drama Clb; Acpl Chr; Pres Chorus; Madrigals; School Musical; School Play; Stage Crew; Variety Show; Hon Roll; Tlnt & Svc Awds-Chr 86; Bst Costume Dsgn/Mkr-For Harlequin Clb 86; Temple U; Vcl Prfmnc.

MILLER, STACEY; Warwick HS; Lititz, PA; (Y); Hosp Aide; Teachers Aide; Rep Jr Cls; Trs Sr Cls; Var Trk; Hon Roll; NHS; Opt Clb Awd; Lititz Womans Clb Schrlshp 86; U DE; Physcl Thrpy.

MILLER, STEPHANIE; Laurel Valley HS; Lewistown, PA; (Y); 3/78; AFS; Church Yth Grp; Library Aide; Chorus; School Play; Yrbk Stf; Stu Cncl; High Hon Roll; NHS; Sal; Gannon U; Elem Ed.

MILLER, STEPHEN; Holy Name HS; Wyomissing, PA; (Y); 10/115; Church Yth Grp; French Clb; Science Clb; Nwsp Rptr; Im Bsktbl; Var Crs Cntry; Var Trk; High Hon Roll; NHS; Ntl Merit Ltr; U Of Notre Dame; Med.

MILLER, SUSAN; Cambria Heights HS; Hastings, PA; (Y); 2/183; Chorus; Yrbk Stf; Var Capt Bsktbl; Var Capt Trk; Bausch & Lomb Sci Awd; NHS; Pres Schlr; Rensselaer Mdl 85; Acadmc All Am 86; Natl Schlr And Athlt Awd 86; U Of Pittsburgh; Phys Thrpy.

MILLER, SUSAN; Ford City JR SR HS; Ford City, PA; (Y); 9/145; Sec Church Yth Grp; Cmnty Wkr; Spanish Clb; SADD; Drill Tm; Rep Frsh Cls; High Hon Roll; Lion Awd; NHS; IN U Of PA; Comp Sci.

MILLER, SUZANNE; Waynesboro Area SR HS; Waynesboro, PA; (Y); 6/331; Ski Clb; Chorus; Capt Var Crs Cntry; Capt Var Trk; Cit Awd; High Hon Roll; NHS; Ntl Merit Ltr.

MILLER, SUZANNE ELIZABETH; Hempfield HS; Lancaster, PA; (Y); 16/418; Am Leg Aux Girls St; Church Yth Grp; Varsity Clb; Chorus; Var L Swmmng; High Hon Roll; NHS; Pol Sci.

MILLER, SUZY; Berlin Brothers Valley HS; Berlin, PA; (Y); 10/87; Am Leg Aux Girls St; 4-H; GAA; NFL; Red Cross Aide; Spanish Clb; Band; Concert Band; Drm Mjr(t); Mrchg Band; Pius Springs Women Club Outstndng Band Mbr, Fnlst Co Jr Miss Pgm 86; VP IUO8 Stu Forum 86-87; Indiana U PA; Intl Bus.

MILLER, TABBI; North Pocono SR HS; Moscow, PA; (S); 19/250; Ski Clb; Concert Band; Mrchg Band; Orch; Yrbk Stf; High Hon Roll; Hon Roll; NHS; U Scranton; Pre-Med.

MILLER, TAMMY; Catasauqua HS; Catasauqua, PA; (Y); 3/130; Yrbk Stf; Lit Mag; Hst Soph Cls; Hst Jr Cls; Rep Stu Cncl; Var L Bsktbl; Var L Fld Hcky; Powder Puff Ftbl; Var L Sftbl; Hon Roll; Ntl Sci Awd 85; Engr.

MILLER, TAMMY; Frazier HS; Wick Haven, PA; (Y); Drama Clb; French Clb; Chorus; Color Guard; Flag Corp; Sec Mrchg Band; School Play; Sec Jr Cls; Twrlr; Hon Roll; Cazenovia Coll; Fshn Mdse.

MILLER, TAMMY; Lakeview HS; Sandy Lake, PA; (S); 12/119; Church Yth Grp; Trs FHA; Girl Scts; School Play; Capt Cheerleading; SECRTRL.

MILLER, TAMMY; Rentworth SR HS; Finleyville, PA; (Y); 7/150; Church Yth Grp; FHA; Hosp Aide; Ski Clb; Yrbk Stf; Frsh Cls; Soph Cls; High Hon Roll; Ntl Merit Schol; Chorus; Pharmacy.

MILLER, TANA L; Red Lion Area SR HS; Brogue, PA; (Y); 19/327; Church Yth Grp; Hosp Aide; JCL; Latin Clb; High Hon Roll; Hon Roll; Jr NHS; NHS; J Herbert Beard Schlrshp 86; Lancaster General Hosp Of Nrsg.

MILLER, TERI; Mt Pleasant Area HS; Mt Pleasant, PA; (Y); SADD; Color Guard; Nwsp Ed-Chief; Rep Frsh Cls; Rep Jr Cls; Rep Stu Cncl; Capt Bsktbl; Cit Awd; High Hon Roll; Hon Roll; Psych.

MILLER, THOMAS; Elizabethtown Area HS; Elizabethtown, PA; (Y); 5/266; Spanish Clb; Teachers Aide; Pres Frsh Cls; Stu Cncl; Var Crs Cntry; Var Ftbl; Capt Var Wrstlng; NHS; Pre-Med.

MILLER, TODD; Ferndale Area HS; Johnstown, PA; (S); 1/58; JA; Leo Clb; NFL; Band; Concert Band; Jazz Band; Mrchg Band; Pep Band; Nwsp Sprt Ed; Yrbk Ed-Chief; Amercn Legn Awd 82; Lions Clb Stu Of Mnth 85-86; Juniata Coll; Med.

MILLER, TONIA; Bellefonte Area HS; Howard, PA; (Y); PA ST U; Bus Mgmt.

MILLER, TRACY; Rocky Grove JR SR HS; Franklin, PA; (Y); 9/93; Camera Clb; French Clb; Sec SADD; Chorus; Yrbk Stf; Rep Jr Cls; Rep Stu Cncl; Stat Sftbl; High Hon Roll; Hon Roll; Erly Chldhd Educ.

MILLER, TRENNI; Lakeview HS; Sandy Lake, PA; (S); 10/124; Intnl Clb; Office Aide; School Play; Nwsp Rptr; Cit Awd; High Hon Roll; Hon Roll; Frnch Achvt Awd 84; Behrend-Penn ST; Telecomm.

MILLER, WENDY; Conemaugh Township HS; Jerome, PA; (Y); 24/101; Drama Clb; Hosp Aide; JA; Band; Concert Band; Mrchg Band; Stu Cncl; Hon Roll; Nrsng.

MILLER, WENDY; Williams Valley HS; Tower City, PA; (S); 9/101; Church Yth Grp; Girl Scts; Chorus; Church Choir; JV Var Bsktbl; Var L Sftbl; High Hon Roll; Hon Roll.

MILLER, WILLIAM; Northern Bedford HS; Loysburg, PA; (Y); FFA; Teachers Aide; Var Bsbl; Var Bsktbl; Var Ftbl; Hon Roll; FFA Ag Mechncs Awd 86; Consrvtn.

MILLER, WILLIAM P; Berwick Area HS; Berwick, PA; (Y); Boy Scts; Letterman Clb; Varsity Clb; Var Capt Ftbl; Var Wt Lftg; Var L Wrstlng; U S Navy; Nuclear.

MILLER-DORWART, JULIE; Jersey Shore Area HS; Jersey Shore, PA; (Y); 45/290; Church Yth Grp; Computer Clb; French Clb; FBLA; Hosp Aide; Yrbk Stf; Lit Mag; Rep Frsh Cls; Rep Soph Cls; Hon Roll; Bus.

MILLETT, JOY ANNE; Cardinal O Hara HS; Clifton Hgts, PA; (Y); 98/772; Church Yth Grp; French Clb; Science Clb; Nwsp Ed-Chief; Ed Nwsp Stf; Yrbk Stf; Hon Roll; NHS; HS Hon Cnvctn 85; Schl Sci Fair 85; DE Cnty Sci Rall 85; Nrsng.

MILLETTE, DONNA; Oxford Area HS; Lincoln Univ, PA; (Y); #4 In Class; Church Yth Grp; Computer Clb; FBLA; Science Clb; Spanish Clb; Nwsp Stf; Var Bsktbl; Var Trk; Var Vllybl; High Hon Roll; Jack & Jill Scholar 86; Oxford Rotary Clb Stu Mnth 86; Natl Achvt Scholar Pgm Outstndng Negro Stu 86; Spelman Coll; Comp Sci.

MILLETTI, CHRISTINA; Nazareth Acad; Langhorne, PA; (Y); 25/125; Church Yth Grp; Spanish Clb; Nwsp Rptr; Nwsp Sprt Ed; Rep Soph Cls; JV Var Fld Hcky; Var Socr; Var Sftbl.

MILLHEIM, ROCHELLE; Nazareth SR HS; Tatamy, PA; (S); 2/215; Church Yth Grp; Band; Church Choir; Concert Band; Mrchg Band; School Musical; DAR Awd; High Hon Roll; NHS; Frnch.

MILLHEIM, STEVEN M; Pen Argyl Area HS; Nazareth, PA; (Y); 7/159; Church Yth Grp; Exploring; Band; Chorus; Concert Band; Mrchg Band; Orch; School Play; Yrbk Stf; Stu Cncl; Albright Coll; Pre-Med.

MILLHOUSE, BRIAN S; Solanco HS; Drumore, PA; (Y); Boy Scts; Church Yth Grp; Ski Clb; God Cntry Awd; Hon Roll; Grn Blt Moo Duk Kwan Karate 85; Gftd Stdnt Prog 75-86; Bnkg.

MILLHOUSE, CHARLES; West York Area SR HS; York, PA; (Y); 14/200; Exploring; Pres Spanish Clb; Nwsp Stf; Bsbl; Bsktbl; Ftbl; Socr; Trk; Wt Lftg; High Hon Roll.

MILLICH, RICHARD; Franklin Area SR HS; Polk, PA; (Y); Letterman Clb; Spanish Clb; High Hon Roll; Hon Roll; Ntl Merit Ltr; Slippery Rock Frgn Lang Comptn Spnsh 85-86; Carnegie-Mellon U; Comp Prog.

MILLIGAN, BRENDA L; Pine Grove Area HS; Pine Grove, PA; (Y); 10/114; Am Leg Aux Girls St; Yrbk Stf; Sec Soph Cls; Sec Jr Cls; Sec Sr Cls; Stu Cncl; Hon Roll; NHS; US Ldrshp Merit Awd; Cntrl Penn Bus Sch; Chldcr Mgmt.

MILLIGAN, CATHY; Beaver Area HS; Beaver, PA; (Y); Exploring; 4-H; French Clb; Girl Scts; JCL; Band; Drm & Bgl; Jazz Band; Orch; School Play; Worthy Advsr-Beaver Rainbw Assmbly 86; Erly Coll Pgm Accptnc 86; Tp 10 Pct Cls 85 & 86; Boston U; Biomdcl Engrng.

MILLIGAN, GAIL; Punxsutauney Area SR HS; Punxsutawney, PA; (Y); Math Tm; Band; Flag Corp; Mrchg Band; Yrbk Stf; Pres Stu Cncl; Score Keeper; Stat Wrstlng; Hon Roll.

MILLIGAN, SHAUNE; Saucon Valley HS; Hellertown, PA; (Y); 9/147; Church Yth Grp; Science Clb; Spanish Clb; Chorus; Church Choir; School Musical; High Hon Roll; Hon Roll; NHS; Bio.

MILLIKEN, ALLISON; Moniteau JR SR HS; Eau Claire, PA; (Y); 28/152; Spanish Clb; Nwsp Stf; Yrbk Stf; Bsktbl; Capt Cheerleading; Hon Roll; Theil; Nrsng.

MILLIKEN, CHRISTINE; Central Dauphin HS; Linglestown, PA; (Y); Church Yth Grp; Trs Girl Scts; Off Stu Cncl; JV Fld Hcky; Accntnt.

MILLIKEN, JENNIFER; North Hills HS; Pittsburgh, PA; (Y); Sec Church Yth Grp; Cmnty Wkr; Political Wkr; Chorus; Rep Frsh Cls; Sec Soph Cls; VP Rep Stu Cncl; Mgr(s); Tennis; High Hon Roll; St Joon Medallion Vlntr Serv Hosp 85; Otstndng Female Serv Awd 86; Stu Govnt Conf 85; William & Mry Coll.

MILLIKEN, SUSAN; Knoch HS; Butler, PA; (Y); Church Yth Grp; L Chorus; Drill Tm; Madrigals; School Musical; Nwsp Rptr; Trs Frsh Cls; Sec Soph Cls; Stat Bsktbl; L Pom Pon; Penn ST; Stckbrkr.

MILLIN, ROBYN; Everett HS; Everett, PA; (Y); Art Clb; Church Yth Grp; Exploring; Pres 4-H; French Clb; VP FBLA; FHA; Chorus; School Musical; Nwsp Rptr; Cntrl Penn Bus Schl; Htl/Rest.

MILLINER, KAREN; Wyoming Valley West HS; Edwardsville, PA; (Y); Cmnty Wkr; Girl Scts; Radio Clb; Chorus; Hon Roll; Luzerne Cnty Cmnty Coll; Pharm.

MILLION, RANDY; Hempfield SR HS; Greensburg, PA; (Y); Church Yth Grp; JA; VICA; Prfct Atten Awd; Comp.

MILLIRON, JEANNE K; Clearfield Area HS; Carlisle, PA; (Y); 49/301; Trs Church Yth Grp; Band; Church Choir; Drm Mjr(t); Mrchg Band; Yrbk Ed-Chief; Yrbk Phtg; Yrbk Stf; Cit Awd; High Hon Roll; PA ST U; Accntng.

MILLS, ALISA M; Forest Hills HS; Salix, PA; (Y); 12/159; Am Leg Aux Girls St; Art Clb; Drama Clb; Pep Clb; School Musical; Stu Cncl; Score Keeper; Hon Roll; Jr NHS; Spanish NHS; PA ST; Comp Sci.

MILLS, ANNE; Commodore Perry Schl; Greenville, PA; (Y); FBLA; Office Aide; Hon Roll; YEA Yth Edctrs Assoc 84-86; Accntng.

MILLS, GLENDA; Belle Vernon Area HS; Belle Vernon, PA; (Y); Drama Clb; NFL; Band; Concert Band; Mrchg Band; Powder Puff Ftbl; Trk; High Hon Roll; NHS; Ntl Merit Art Awd 84; OH U; Tele Comm.

MILLS, JEFFREY; Highlands SR HS; Brackenridge, PA; (Y); 5/301; Church Yth Grp; Cmnty Wkr; Computer Clb; Exploring; Letterman Clb; Varsity Clb; Stu Cncl; Bsktbl; Capt Tennis; High Hon Roll; Pre-Med.

MILLS, JENNIFER; Pennsbury HS; Yardley, PA; (Y); French Clb; Orch; Hon Roll; NHS.

MILLS, JULIE; Shanksville Stonycreek HS; Friedens, PA; (S); Church Yth Grp; CAP; Pres Spanish Clb; Band; Chorus; Concert Band; Yrbk Stf; Stu Cncl; Var Cheerleading; Hon Roll; FL Inst Of Tech; Pilot.

MILLS, KRIS; Unionville HS; Coatesville, PA; (Y); Variety Show; Lit Mag; Rep Frsh Cls; Rep Soph Cls; Rep Jr Cls; Rep Sr Cls; Im Powder Puff Ftbl; JV Trk; High Hon Roll; Hon Roll; Hollins Coll; Lawyer.

MILLS, MARLENE; Greater Latrobe HS; Latrobe, PA; (Y); Pres Am Leg Aux Girls St; Girl Scts; Hosp Aide; Library Aide; Pep Clb; Bsktbl; Hon Roll; U Pitt-Johnstown; Psychlgy.

MILLS, MICHELE; Bellwood Antis HS; Bellwood, PA; (Y); 17/118; FHA; Varsity Clb; Chorus; School Musical; JV Var Cheerleading; NHS; Chrldng, Jv Bsktbl Capt, V Bsktbl Capt 2v Ltrs; Mt Atoysius Jc; Med Secr.

MILLS, MICHELE; Bishop Shanahan HS; W Chester, PA; (Y); 18/218; Cmnty Wkr; Dance Clb; School Musical; JV Var Fld Hcky; Var Swmmng; High Hon Roll; Hon Roll; NHS.

MILLS, RICHARD; Altoona Area HS; Altoona, PA; (S); 15/683; Church Yth Grp; German Clb; Science Clb; Band; Mrchg Band; Golf; NHS; Ntl Merit SF; Chmcl Engrng.

MILLS, RICHARD; Lewistown Area HS; Lewistown, PA; (Y); French Clb; Key Clb; Pep Clb; Chorus; Var L Bsktbl; Hon Roll; Tchng.

MILLS, STACY; Chambersburg Area SR HS; Marion, PA; (Y); 174/641; Sec Church Yth Grp; Spanish Clb; Band; Chorus; Church Choir; Concert Band; Mrchg Band; Ed Nwsp Stf; Hon Roll.

MILO, STACY C; Pleasant Valley HS; Gilbert, PA; (Y); 6/200; Math Clb; Office Aide; Scholastic Bowl; Stu Cncl; Var JV Cheerleading; High Hon Roll; Hon Roll; Tp 20 Cls Awd 84 & 85.

MILON, DEIRDRE; Fox Chapel HS; Pittsburgh, PA; (Y); 21/377; Ski Clb; Chorus; Powder Puff Ftbl; Tennis; Elks Awd; High Hon Roll; Pres Schlr; St Marys Coll; Acctg.

MILOS, TINA; Susquehanna Comm HS; Thompson, PA; (Y); Ski Clb; Band; Concert Band; Jazz Band; Mrchg Band; Yrbk Stf; Trk; Vllybl; Hon Roll; Cnty Band 84; Envrnmntl Hlth Engr.

MILOSER, MICHAEL; Lincoln HS; Wampum, PA; (Y); 48/163; Boy Scts; Church Yth Grp; Sec Computer Clb; French Clb; Band; Church Choir; Concert Band; Jazz Band; Mrchg Band; Orch; PA ST; Aero Engl.

MILOSH, KATHY; Meadville Area SR HS; Conneaut Lake, PA; (Y); 110/344; French Clb; Ski Clb; Spanish Clb; JV Bsktbl; Var Sftbl; Accntng.

MILSOM, JOHN ANDREW; Kiski Area HS; Apollo, PA; (Y); 2/388; Computer Clb; Math Clb; Math Tm; Science Clb; Nwsp Rptr; L Tennis; NHS; PA ST U; Engrng.

MILTENBERGER, SHARON; Emmaus HS; Macungie, PA; (Y); 13/467; German Clb; Model UN; Yrbk Phtg; Yrbk Stf; Stu Cncl; Var L Swmmng; Var L Tennis; High Hon Roll; VP NHS; Ntl Merit Ltr; U VA Dartmouth; Law.

MILTON, CAROLE; Punxsutowney Area HS; Punxsutawney, PA; (Y); Spanish Clb; Varsity Clb; Off Soph Cls; Off Jr Cls; Trs Sr Cls; Cheerleading; Trk; Vllybl; Hon Roll; Stdy Psych.

MILTZ, DON; Bentworth HS; Bentleyville, PA; (Y); Church Yth Grp; Engr.

MILZ, STEVEN; Hanover Area HS; Ashley, PA; (Y); 14/220; Key Clb; Var Trk; NHS; NEDT Tst Cert 84; Air Force; Comp Sci.

MINARDI, NICOLE; Conestoga Valley SR HS; Leola, PA; (Y); 80/245; Church Yth Grp; Dance Clb; Library Aide; Cheerleading; Mgr(s); Hon Roll; Engl.

MINARIK, AMY; Bethlehem Catholic HS; Bethlehem, PA; (S); 14/219; Chorus; School Musical; Var Capt Cheerleading; Crs Cntry; Gym; JV Var Sftbl; High Hon Roll; Sec NHS; Ntl Merit SF; Hgh GPA Algbr II; Hgh Perfrmnc Englsh Olympd Rcgntn; Public Svc.

MINARIK, DOUG; Mercer HS; Mercer, PA; (Y); Band.

MINCEMOYER, JODI ANN; Warrior Run HS; Milton, PA; (Y); Am Leg Aux Girls St; Trs Art Clb; Debate Tm; Sec French Clb; Varsity Clb; Nwsp Ed-Chief; Yrbk Stf; Var L Fld Hcky; Trk; French Hon Soc; PA Schlstc Press Assoc 2 1st Pl Awds 85; 3rd Pl Essay PA Right To Wrk Dfns & Educ Fndtn 86.

MINCER, CHRISTY; Butler Area SR HS; Butler, PA; (Y); 234/740; Sec Church Yth Grp; Concert Band; Drm & Bgl; Mrchg Band; Symp Band; Powder Puff Ftbl; Hon Roll; Butler County CC; Comp Sci.

MINCH, JAY; Mc Guffey HS; W Alexander, PA; (Y); 32/250; Pres Sec FBLA; High Hon Roll; Hon Roll.

MINCIN JR, DANTE; Trinity HS; Washington, PA; (Y); 6/379; Am Leg Boys St; Debate Tm; Math Tm; NFL; Acpl Chr; Var Tennis; High Hon Roll; NHS; SR Hgh Dist Chorus & Regn Chorus 86; Chem Engrng.

MINDA, LISA; Avella HS; Avella, PA; (S); 8/74; VP Trs DECA; Library Aide; Chorus; School Play; Yrbk Ed-Chief; Sec Stu Cncl; Score Keeper; High Hon Roll; Hon Roll; NHS; Sawyer Schl; Trvl.

MINDER, MARTIN; Bishop Kenrick HS; Norristown, PA; (Y); 23/305; Ski Clb; JV Var Ftbl; Hon Roll; Elec Engrng.

MINECH, LAURA; Moon Area SR HS; Coraopolis, PA; (Y); 8/304; Church Yth Grp; Capt Drill Tm; School Play; Stage Crew; JV Var Trk; High Hon Roll; NHS; Engl.

MINELLA, MARIA; North Pocono HS; Moscow, PA; (Y); 30/250; Dance Clb; 4-H; Yrbk Stf; High Hon Roll; Hon Roll; NHS; Nrsg.

MINELLA, PAUL; Olds Forge HS; Old Forge, PA; (S); Bsktbl; Crs Cntry; High Hon Roll; Hon Roll; NHS; Phila Coll Phrmcy & Sci; Phrmcy.

MINEO, ANDREA M; Mt Pleasant Area HS; Mt Pleasant, PA; (Y); GAA; JA; Science Clb; Ski Clb; Bsktbl; Sftbl; Trk; Vllybl; NHS; Prfct Atten Awd; Sftbl Ltr & Pin 85; Prfct Atten Cert 84; Spts Cert Life 84; FSC; Hum Svc.

MINER, BRENDA; Tunkhannock Area HS; Mehoopany, PA; (S); 50/290; Church Yth Grp; VP Soph Cls; VP Jr Cls; Var L Fld Hcky; Var L Swmmng; Var L Trk; NHS; Spanish Clb; VP Frsh Cls; Hon Roll; Mst Dedctd Wmmr Awd 84; Offnsv Plyr Awd Fld Hcky 85; 1st Pl Age Grp Run For The Torch 84.

MINERD, DAVID; Freedom HS; Conway, PA; (Y); 3/160; FCA; Letterman Clb; Math Tm; Spanish Clb; Stu Cncl; Capt Bsktbl; Ftbl; High Hon Roll; NHS; Sal; Penn ST U; Chem Engrng.

MINERD, DONNA; Carmichaels Area HS; Carmichaels, PA; (Y); #13 In Class; Trs French Clb; Office Aide; Ski Clb; SADD; Off Jr Cls; Hon Roll; NHS; Cmnctns.

MINERD, MICHAEL; Connellsville SR HS; Connellsville, PA; (Y); 14/342; Drama Clb.

MINEWEASER, JOSEPH; Bethel Park SR HS; Pittsburgh, PA; (Y); 102/515; Hi Hnr Awd 86; U Of Pittsburgh; Engrng.

MINEWEASER, PATRICIA J; Brookville Area HS; Brookville, PA; (Y); 24/184; French Clb; Key Clb; Varsity Clb; Yrbk Stf; Sec Frsh Cls; Rep Soph Cls; Rep Jr Cls; JV Var Bsktbl; Hon Roll; Jr NHS; Pine Creek Twnshp Fire Queen 86; Slippery Rock U; Spec Educ.

MINGIONI, JOSEPH; Bishop Shanahan HS; W Chester, PA; (Y); 51/223; Church Yth Grp; Cmnty Wkr; Dance Clb; Pep Clb; Pres SADD; Teachers Aide; Lit Mag; Rep Frsh Cls; Pres Soph Cls; Rep Jr Cls; Phys Sci Awd 83-84.

MINGLE, MICHELLE; Bensalem HS; Bensalem, PA; (Y); Art Clb; Office Aide; Teachers Aide; Capt Color Guard; Var Trk; Im Vllybl; High Hon Roll; Hon Roll; Prfct Atten Awd; FL Inst Of Tech; Chemist.

MINICK, AMY; North Star HS; Somerset, PA; (Y); FCA; FHA; Church Choir; School Play; Yrbk Stf; Mat Maids; Pep Clb; Chorus; Nwsp Stf; Stu Mnth 85; Home Ec Currclm Awd 86; 2nd Rnnr Up Hmcmng Cont 86.

MINJOCK, JAYLYNN; Elizabeth Forward HS; Mc Keesport, PA; (Y); 37/327; Rep Frsh Cls; Rep Soph Cls; Rep Jr Cls; Rep Sr Cls; Capt Cheerleading; L Trk; Hon Roll; NHS; Pres Schlr; Carlow Coll; Nrsng.

MINK, AILEEN; Pocono Mountain HS; Cresco, PA; (Y); 14/273; SADD; Sec Band; Sec Concert Band; Sec Mrchg Band; Sec Pep Band; School Musical; Hon Roll; NHS; Drama Clb; Pres Girl Scts; Hgh O Brn Yth Ldrshp Fndtn Rep 84; Wmn Mrns Assn Schlrshp 86; Pocono Mtn Educ Assn Schlrshp 86; PA ST U; Frgn Lang.

MINK, RONDA; Hampton HS; Allison Pk, PA; (Y); French Clb; Ski Clb; Cheerleading; Im Crs Cntry; Im Powder Puff Ftbl; Im Trk; High Hon Roll; Hon Roll; Educ.

MINK, TAMMY; Central Catholic HS; Allentown, PA; (Y); 9/231; Math Clb; Math Tm; Q&S; Yrbk Ed-Chief; Lit Mag; High Hon Roll; NHS; Natl Sci Merit Awd 84; 2nd Pl PJAS 84; Penn ST U; Secondry Educ.

MINK, THERESE L; Greater Works Acad; Pittsburgh, PA; (Y); 13/36; Trs Sec Church Yth Grp; Band; Concert Band; Yrbk Stf; Capt Cheerleading; Vllybl; Hon Roll; Oral Roberts U; Bus.

MINNICH, ANN; Nazareth HS; Nazareth, PA; (S); Key Clb; Mrchg Band; Stat Bsktbl; Vllybl; Rifle Squad Capt 84-86; Winterguard 83-86; Med Sec.

MINNICH, KEVIN; Parkland HS; Slatington, PA; (Y); 129/431; Exploring; VP Sec 4-H; Letterman Clb; Library Aide; Var L Trk; Cit Awd; 4-H Awd; Prfct Atten Awd; Voice Dem Awd; 1st Lehigh U Stock Mkt Game 86; 1st PhyICS Olympics ESU 82; Lehigh County CC; Mech Engrng.

MINNICH, SHARON; Schuylkill Valley HS; Mohrsville, PA; (Y); 2/128; School Musical; Nwsp Rptr; Yrbk Stf; VP Soph Cls; VP Stu Cncl; Var Cheerleading; Var Swmmng; Var Trk; High Hon Roll; NHS; Poltcl Sci.

MINNICK, SHERI; St Pius X HS; Pottstown, PA; (S); 16/139; Art Clb; Cmnty Wkr; Latin Clb; Mathletes; Math Tm; Pep Clb; Science Clb; Var Capt Cheerleading; Pom Pon; NHS; Scndry Ed.

MINNOCCI, MELISSA; Lincoln HS; Ellwood City, PA; (Y); 23/163; Sec Trs Church Yth Grp; Y-Teens; Chorus; Yrbk Stf; Powder Puff Ftbl; Math.

MINNOCK, BRENDAN; Taylor Allderdice HS; Pittsburgh, PA; (Y); 151/400; Ski Clb; Spanish Clb; Teachers Aide; Chorus; School Play; Crs Cntry; Trk; Cit Awd; Hon Roll; Edinboro; Engr.

MINTEER, MINDI; Lincoln HS; Ellwood City, PA; (Y); 56/163; Church Yth Grp; Drama Clb; Spanish Clb; Y-Teens; School Musical; L Var Crs Cntry; L Var Gym; Powder Puff Ftbl; Capt Var Trk; Hon Roll; Gannon U; Ind Engr.

MINTLER, CATHERINE R; Villa Maria HS; Youngstown, OH; (Y); Cmnty Wkr; Drama Clb; French Clb; Chorus; Church Choir; School Play; Yrbk Stf; Lit Mag; NHS; NEDT Awd; OH Tchrs Music Assn 83-84; Northwestern U; Pub Comm.

MINTO, BETH; Lincoln HS; Ellwood City, PA; (Y); 5/180; Ski Clb; Trs Spanish Clb; VP Y-Teens; Sec Chorus; Sec Jr Cls; Powder Puff Ftbl; VP NHS; Church Yth Grp; Sec Trs Soph Cls; Hugh O Brian Yth Ldrshp Awd 84-85; JR & Soph Cls Ldrshp Awds 84-86; Med.

MIRABELLA, MIKE; Bellwood-Antis HS; Tyrone, PA; (Y); Im Mgr Badmtn; JV Bsbl; Im Mgr Vllybl; Hon Roll; Elctrncs.

MIRANDA, BRIGITTA; Hempfield Area SR HS; Greensburg, PA; (Y); Am Leg Aux Girls St; NFL; Spanish Clb; Yrbk Phtg; High Hon Roll; Jr NHS; NHS; Spanish NHS; Acad Achvt Awd 86; 1st Pl Spnsh Reci Provos Day U PA 86; Internl Pol.

MIRANDA, MELISSA; Saucon Valley SR HS; Bethlehem, PA; (Y); 20/170; Church Yth Grp; Dance Clb; Exploring; FNA; Hosp Aide; Spanish Clb; Color Guard; Mrchg Band; Rep Stu Cncl; Cheerleading; Pittsburgh U; Nrs.

MIRASOLA, LISA; York Catholic HS; York, PA; (Y); Church Yth Grp; Pres Civic Clb; Cmnty Wkr; Debate Tm; Drama Clb; Library Aide; Sec Pep Clb; Rep Spanish Clb; Speech Tm; Acpl Chr; 22nd Pl ST Of PA Chorus 85-86; 1st Pl Tamaha Electne Orgn Festvl 84; Stu Mnth Mrch 86; U Of Pennsylvania; Bus.

MISAVAGE, BRADLEY; Norwin HS; N Huntingdon, PA; (Y); German Clb; JV Ftbl; Hon Roll; Jr NHS; NHS; Mech Engrng.

MISCHEN, PAMELA; Deer Lakes JR SR HS; Gibsonia, PA; (Y); 1/160; Drama Clb; Ski Clb; SADD; School Play; Stage Crew; Yrbk Ed-Chief; Yrbk Stf; High Hon Roll; NHS; Allegheny Intermediate Units Rgnl Smmr Schl Of Excllnc In Sci 86; Bio-Chem.

MISCHLER, MICHAEL; Cathedral Preparatory Schl; Erie, PA; (Y); 40/215; Chess Clb; Civic Clb; Cmnty Wkr; French Clb; Pep Clb; Nwsp Ed-Chief; Nwsp Phtg; Nwsp Rptr; Nwsp Sprt Ed; Bsktbl; All-Cty Ftbll Tckl 86; All-Cty Dscs Thrwr 86; Pres Teen Actn Clb 86-87; Pre-Law.

MISCIAGNA, CAROLINE; Altoona Area HS; Altoona, PA; (S); 16/684; Science Clb; Spanish Clb; Sec Trs Speech Tm; Capt Color Guard; Ed Nwsp Stf; Yrbk Ed-Chief; Lit Mag; Capt Trk; Jr NHS; NHS; Cornell U; Bus Admin.

MISERA, JOSEPH; Bishop Mc Cort HS; Johnstown, PA; (Y); Spanish Clb; Chorus; Hon Roll; Spanish NHS.

MISH, LORI; Conemaugh Twp Area HS; Davidsville, PA; (S); 9/101; VP Church Yth Grp; Drama Clb; VP 4-H; Sec French Clb; VP JA; Speech Tm; Ed Nwsp Stf; Ed Lit Mag; Pres Trs Stu Cncl; Var L Cheerleading; Vet Med.

MISHRELL, SHERRIE; Fort Le Boeuf HS; Waterford, PA; (Y); Art Clb; Church Yth Grp; 4-H; Band; Mrchg Band; Var L Bsktbl; Var L Sftbl; 4-H Awd; Hon Roll; MVP Vrsty Sftbl 86; Mdcl.

MISKEVICH, FRANK; Baldwin HS; Pittsburgh, PA; (Y); 6/535; Exploring; Key Clb; Math Tm; Science Clb; SADD; Hon Roll; NHS; Ntl Merit SF; NEDT Awd; Westnghse Lctr Series 85-86.

MISKEVICH, SHARON; Baldwin HS; Pittsburgh, PA; (Y); 143/535; Art Clb; Cmnty Wkr; Key Clb; Mrchg Band; High Hon Roll; Ntl Art Hnr Soc; Elem Ed.

MISKIMMIN, RENEE; South Allegheny HS; Mckeesport, PA; (S); 4/163; Sec German Clb; Pres Girl Scts; Hosp Aide; Chorus; Concert Band; Capt Mrchg Band; Stage Crew; Rep Stu Cncl; God Cntry Awd; NHS; Safari Clb Wldrnss Ldrshp Schl Schlrshp 84; PA Music Edctrs Assn All-St Chorus 85; Johns Hopkins; Pre-Med.

MISKIV, DOUGLAS A; Bethel Park SR HS; Bethel Park, PA; (Y); Boy Scts; JA; Yrbk Phtg; Yrbk Stf; Rep Soph Cls; Rep Sr Cls; Ftbl; IN U Of PA; Crmnlgy.

MISKOLCZE, ROBIN; Lincoln HS; Ellwood City, PA; (Y); 10/180; French Clb; Ski Clb; Y-Teens; Trs Jr Cls; Trs Sr Cls; Capt Powder Puff Ftbl; High Hon Roll; Hon Roll; NHS.

MISLEVY, KIMBERLY A; Tunkhannock Area HS; Factoryville, PA; (S); 33/310; Latin Clb; Spanish Clb; Hon Roll; NHS; SR Hstrns 85-86; SR Steerg Cmmttee 85-86; Pre-Law.

MISSIEN, IAN; Jersey Shore SR HS; Jersey Shore, PA; (Y); 4/256; Computer Clb; Var L Bsktbl; Var L Crs Cntry; Var L Trk; Hon Roll; NHS; US Army Reserve Natl Schlr-Athlete Awd 86; Knights Of Columbus All Svc Awd 86; Ramsey Schlrshp 86; PA ST U; Engrng.

MISTRANO, SAM; Lower Moreland HS; Huntingdon Valley, PA; (S); 16/215; VP SADD; Nwsp Rptr; Rep Soph Cls; Stu Cncl; Capt Crs Cntry; Capt Trk; Gov Hon Prg Awd; NHS; Key Clb; Socl Stud Merit Awd 84; Mst Sprtd 86; Al-Leag Crss Cntry 84 & 85; Stanford; Gynclgst.

MISTYSYN, VINCE; Nativity B V M HS; Pottsville, PA; (Y); 12/100; Computer Clb; Var Capt Bsbl; Var L Bsktbl; Hon Roll; NHS; Hilton Awd Tp Ml In Cls 86; 3rd Pl Sci Fr 83; U Of Scranton; Acctng.

MITCHELL, ANDREA; Central Dauphin HS; Harrisburg, PA; (Y); Church Yth Grp; Girl Scts; Band; Chorus; Stu Cncl; Fld Hcky; JV Vllybl; Masonic Awd; NHS; Citatn Sen Shumaker 85; Law.

MITCHELL, CINDY; Marion Center HS; Indiana, PA; (S); 23/170; Intnl Clb; Latin Clb; Spanish Clb; Co-Capt Flag Corp; Nwsp Bus Mgr; Rep Stu Cncl; Var Stat Bsktbl; VP NHS; Pep Clb; PSPA Awd For Jrnlsm-2 2nd Pl, 3 3rd Pl & 1 4th Pl.

MITCHELL, COREY; Hempfield HS; Landisville, PA; (Y); 29/452; High Hon Roll; Ntl Merit Ltr; Top 1 Pct In Nation On The Amer HS Math Exam 85-86; Bus Admin.

MITCHELL, CYNTHIA JEAN; Peters Twp HS; Mc Murray, PA; (Y); Church Yth Grp; FBLA; Intnl Clb; Church Choir; Mrchg Band; Yrbk Stf; Mgr Lit Mag; Var L Sftbl; Hon Roll; Sght & Snds Cmptn Cmptrs 86; Waynesburg Coll; Accntng.

MITCHELL, DAVID; Cathedrial Prep Schl; Erie, PA; (Y); 71/216; Chess Clb; Hon Roll; Gannon; Law.

MITCHELL, DEAN A; Smethport Area JR SR HS; Smethport, PA; (Y); Library Aide; Band; Chorus; Color Guard; Jazz Band; Mrchg Band; Pep Band; School Play; Nwsp Sprt Ed; Trk; Cmmnctns Ed.

MITCHELL, DIANE; Clearfield Area HS; Clearfield, PA; (S); 4/337; Debate Tm; French Clb; Band; Chorus; Drm Mjr(t); Orch; Nwsp Stf; Yrbk Stf; High Hon Roll; Kiwanis Awd; PA ST U; Pre-Med.

MITCHELL, DONALD; Council Rock HS; Churchville, PA; (Y); 37/865; Boy Scts; Im Ice Hcky; Im Socr; Hon Roll; NHS; Prfct Atten Awd; Engrng.

MITCHELL, GARY D; Westtown Schl; Glenolden, PA; (Y); Boy Scts; Var Capt Bsktbl; Hon Roll; Cmmnded Stdnt Ntl Negro Merit Schlrshp 84-85; Marine Bio.

MITCHELL, JAMES; Cathedral Prep; Erie, PA; (Y); Wt Lftg; COMMRCL Arcrft.

MITCHELL, JILL; Waynesboro Area SR HS; Mont Alto, PA; (Y); Chorus; School Play; Swing Chorus; Rep Soph Cls; Rep Jr Cls; Rep Stu Cncl; Var Gym; Var Trk; High Hon Roll; NHS; Dist Chmpn Advncd Gymnstcs 84-85; MVP Gymnastcs Awd 84-86.

MITCHELL, JODI; Montrose HS; Montrose, PA; (Y); 26/170; Church Yth Grp; Sec FBLA; Band; Concert Band; Mrchg Band; Crs Cntry; All Stars Crs Cntry Awd 85; Dmcrtc Wmns Clb Schlrshp 86; Bob Jones U; Intr Dcrtng.

MITCHELL, KAREN; Central HS; Philadelphia, PA; (Y); Aud/Vis; Office Aide; Sec Stu Cncl; Mgr Stat Bsktbl; Hon Roll; HS Rep Variety Clb Telethon 86; Convetion Stu Govt Of Ares HS Of Philadelphia 86; Pennsylvania ST U.

MITCHELL, KAREN; Reynolds HS; Fredonia, PA; (Y); VICA; Var Mat Maids; JV Vllybl; Ptsbrg Bty Acad; Csmtlgy.

MITCHELL, KATHLEEN; Little Flower HS; Philadelphia, PA; (Y); 141/433; Camera Clb; Cmnty Wkr; French Clb; Rep GAA; Office Aide; Church Choir; Stu Cncl; Hon Roll; St Josephs U; Business Mgmt.

MITCHELL, KIM; Mapletown JR SR HS; Waynesburg, PA; (Y); 5/75; GAA; Hosp Aide; Concert Band; Drm Mjr(t); Mrchg Band; Yrbk Stf; Pres Soph Cls; Rep Stu Cncl; NHS; Band; Pres Acdmc Ftns Awd 86; U Of Pittsburgh.

MITCHELL, KIM DENISE; Washington HS; Washington, PA; (Y); 20/160; Cmnty Wkr; Trs Drama Clb; Pres Hosp Aide; Key Clb; Pres Ski Clb; Spanish Clb; Concert Band; Trs Soph Cls; Off Jr Cls; Trs Stu Cncl; Jaycees Ldrshp Awd 86; WA & Jefferson Coll; Pre-Dntl.

MITCHELL, LANCE; Ephrata SR HS; Ephrata, PA; (Y); 59/246; Boy Scts; Church Yth Grp; Math Clb; Science Clb; Var L Bsbl; Var L Ftbl; Cit Awd; Elks Awd; Hon Roll; Lion Awd; Penn ST U; Engrng.

MITCHELL, LAURIE; Burrell SR HS; Lower Burrell, PA; (Y); 5/197; JA; Spanish Clb; Nwsp Phtg; Yrbk Phtg; Yrbk Sprt Ed; Var Capt Bsktbl; High Hon Roll; Jr NHS; NHS; Rotary Awd.

MITCHELL, LETHA; Frazier HS; Grindstone, PA; (S); Library Aide; Band; Concert Band; Jazz Band; Mrchg Band; Pep Band; Nwsp Stf; Hon Roll; Prfct Atten Awd; CA ST U; Acctng.

MITCHELL, LINDA; Marion Center Area HS; Indiana, PA; (Y); 10/140; Pres Intnl Clb; Model UN; Trs Q&S; SADD; Co-Capt Band; Nwsp Stf; High Hon Roll; Pres NHS; Ntl Merit SF; Seton Hill; Psych.

MITCHELL, LORI; Surgettstown JRSR HS; Eldersville, PA; (Y); Church Yth Grp; Ski Clb; Pres Mrchg Band; Rep Pep Band; Symp Band; High Hon Roll; Jr NHS; NHS; Nrsng.

MITCHELL, MELLISSA DIANNE; Exeter Township HS; Reiffton, PA; (Y); 89/216; Library Aide; Varsity Clb; Band; Chorus; Mrchg Band; Pep Band; Cheerleading; Diving; Fld Hcky; Sftbl; Penn ST; Chld Psych.

MITCHELL, MITCH; Washington HS; Washington, PA; (Y); Church Yth Grp; Spanish Clb; Band; Concert Band; Jazz Band; Mrchg Band; Pep Band; Bsbl; NC ST U; Comp.

MITCHELL, REBECCA L; Freedom HS; Bethlehem, PA; (Y); 3/423; Church Yth Grp; French Clb; Math Tm; Model UN; Mgr Chorus; Church Choir; Rep Stu Cncl; Hon Roll; VP NHS; Ntl Merit SF; Var Schlr 83-85; Hugh O Brien Ldrshp Semnr Part 84; PA Msc Tchrs Assn Awd 83 & 85; Psych.

MITCHELL, ROBERT; Archbishop Carroll HS; Bryn Mawr, PA; (Y); 8/167; Cmnty Wkr; Nwsp Rptr; Rep Jr Cls; Stu Cncl; Im Bsktbl; Var Mgr(s); Var Score Keeper; High Hon Roll; NHS; Dance Clb; Stu Cncl & Social Stds Achvt Awds 84-86; High Avg Awd 86; Law.

MITCHELL, ROBERT; Cambria Heights HS; Hastings, PA; (Y); 24/200; Church Yth Grp; Hon Roll; Teacher.

MITCHELL, STEPHANIE; Solanco HS; Quarryville, PA; (Y); Church Yth Grp; Hon Roll; Prfct Atten Awd.

MITCHELL, SUSAN; South Williamsport HS; S Williamsport, PA; (Y); 9/140; French Clb; Key Clb; Band; Concert Band; Mrchg Band; Tennis; NHS; Sgn & Frgn Lng Clb; Gntc Rsrch Sci.

MITCHELL, TIMOTHY; Jefferson Morgan HS; Waynesburg, PA; (S); 7/101; Letterman Clb; Pres Varsity Clb; Var L Bsbl; Var L Ftbl; High Hon Roll; NHS; Golf; Sftbl; Wt Lftg.

MITCHELL, TODD; Greater Johnstown HS; Johnstown, PA; (Y); Ski Clb; Spanish Clb; SADD; Jr Cls; Sr Cls; Stu Cncl; Var L Bsbl; Var Capt Ice Hcky; High Hon Roll; NHS.

MITCHELL, TOM; Hampton HS; Gibsonia, PA; (Y); 65/223; Band; Jazz Band; Mrchg Band; Symp Band; Var Bsbl; Var Wrstlng; Hon Roll; Accntng.

MITCHELL, TRACEY; Middleburg HS; Mt Pleasant Mls, PA; (Y); Pres Church Yth Grp; Hosp Aide; Key Clb; Band; Chorus; School Musical; Cheerleading; Fld Hcky; Hon Roll; NHS; Nrsg.

MITCHELTREE, ERIC; Muncy HS; Muncy, PA; (Y); Letterman Clb; Varsity Clb; School Musical; School Play; Capt Ftbl; Capt Wrstlng; Hon Roll; Lock Hoven U PA; Pre Med.

MITCHEM, YVONNE; Kiski Area HS; Apollo, PA; (Y); Hosp Aide; Office Aide; Pep Clb; Varsity Clb; Nwsp Bus Mgr; Nwsp Rptr; Sec Jr Cls; Stu Cncl; Var Cheerleading; High Hon Roll; IN U PA; Psych.

MITCHESON, LARY; Apollo-Ridge HS; N Apollo, PA; (Y); Art Clb; Drama Clb; FBLA; Pep Clb; Ski Clb; Band; Color Guard; Drill Tm; Drm & Bgl; Flag Corp; WCCC; Fash Merch.

MITHANI, NAUSHINA; Pocono Mourtair HS; Mtn Home, PA; (Y); 14/288; Nwsp Rptr; Rep Frsh Cls; Trk; Hon Roll; NHS; PA ST U; Sci.

MITMAN, MARK; Freedom HS; Bethlehem, PA; (Y); 51/445; Church Yth Grp; Debate Tm; German Clb; Intnl Clb; Political Wkr; Hon Roll; 2nd Pl ST Sci Fair 83-84; Cyclng Clb 86-87; Yng Rpblcns 86; Law.

MITRA, PUSHPITA; Plum SR HS; Pittsburgh, PA; (Y); 4/435; AFS; Sec French Clb; Hosp Aide; Math Tm; Chorus; Stage Crew; Im Bsktbl; Var Trk; DAR Awd; High Hon Roll; AAUW Schlrshp 86; Prvsts Day Semi-Fnlst 85; Boston U; Med.

MITROUICH, NED; Aliquippa HS; Aliquippa, PA; (Y); Church Yth Grp; French Clb; VICA; Off Jr Cls; Wt Lftg; Wrstlng; Hon Roll; NHS; U Of Pitts; Med.

MITROVICH, NED; Aliquippa HS; Aliquippa, PA; (S); Church Yth Grp; Science Clb; Off Jr Cls; Wt Lftg; Wrstlng; Hon Roll; U Pittsburgh; Phy Thrpy.

MITSCH, WILLIAM; Montour HS; Pittsburgh, PA; (Y); Var Ftbl; Var Trk; Wt Lftg; High Hon Roll; NHS; Mech Engrng.

MITTEN, BARB; North Schuylkill JR SR HS; Ashland, PA; (Y); 18/198; Rep Jr Cls; JV Var Cheerleading; Hon Roll; NHS; Bloomsburg U; Bus Adm.

MITTMAN, BRIAN; Upper Dublin SR HS; Maple Glen, PA; (Y); 30/315; Computer Clb; Ski Clb; Temple Yth Grp; Rep Stu Cncl; Crs Cntry; Trk; Vllybl; Wt Lftg; High Hon Roll; Hon Roll; Abraham Joshua Heschel Hon Soc 86-87; Mechanical Engineering.

MITURA, JOSEPH; St Josephs Prep; Philadelphia, PA; (Y); Boy Scts; Cmnty Wkr; Yrbk Stf; Im Bsktbl; Im Ftbl; Hon Roll; SAR Awd; Eagl Sct Awd 85; Engrng.

MIZIKAR, ANITA; Greensburg Central Catholic HS; Mt Pleasant, PA; (Y); 15/235; AFS; Pep Clb; Church Choir; Cit Awd; High Hon Roll; NHS; Nutrition.

MLECIK, RONA; Homer Center; Graceton, PA; (Y); 12/106; French Clb; FBLA; Varsity Clb; Chorus; School Play; JV Var Sftbl; High Hon Roll; NHS; Pres Acdmc Fit Awd 86; Hm Ecnmcs Awd 86; Trig Awd 85; IN U Of PA; Chld Dvlpmt.

MLECIK, SHERI; Homer Center JR SR HS; Graceton, PA; (Y); 36/96; French Clb; Library Aide; Varsity Clb; Bsktbl; Sftbl; Med Tech.

MLINAR, LAURA; Sacred Heart HS; Carbondale, PA; (Y); 2/50; FBLA; Latin Clb; Spanish Clb; School Musical; High Hon Roll; NHS; Ntl Merit SF; Hosp Aide; Library Aide; Schlrshp HS 83-87; USMA Invtnl Acdmc & Engrng Wrkshp 86; US Military Acad; Med.

MLYNAR, KATHY; Wilson HS; Sinking Springs, PA; (Y); FBLA; Teachers Aide; Qstr Awd Offc Prctc I 86; Physcl Achvmnt Awd 86; Hnrbl Mntn Outstndg Achvmnt Guidnc Clss 84; PA ST Bus Schl; Bus.

MOATS, BRIAN; Sharpsville Area HS; Clark, PA; (Y); 12/125; Math Clb; Science Clb; Ski Clb; Spanish Clb; Hon Roll; NHS.

MOCK, CHRISTY; Connellsville Area HS; Indiana, PA; (Y); 27/550; Sec Church Yth Grp; Pres Chorus; Church Choir; School Musical; Stat Diving; Mgr(s); Score Keeper; Stat Swmmng; High Hon Roll; NHS; Acadmc Excllnc 86; IN U Of PA; Dntl Hygnst.

MOCK, JODI L; Altoona Area SR HS; Altoona, PA; (Y); 96/683; Church Yth Grp; Drama Clb; Chorus; Capt Flag Corp; Jazz Band; Orch; School Musical; Variety Show; Sec Sr Cls; Fine Arts Schlrshp 86; Louis S Walton JR Meml Schlrshp 86; Juniata Clg Alumni Schlrshp 86; Juniata Clg; Bio.

MOCK, SCOTT; Reynolds HS; Greenville, PA; (Y); Church Yth Grp; VICA; Church Choir; Clnry Arts.

MOCK, SHARON; Penn Cambria HS; Cresson, PA; (Y); Drama Clb; Spanish Clb; Stage Crew; JV Cheerleading; Var JV Trk; Pep Clb; Mt Aloysius JC; Mdcl Asst.

MOCK, VINCE; Conemaugh Township HS; Johnstown, PA; (Y); 26/101; Boy Scts; Stage Crew; Trk; U Of Pittsburgh Johnstown.

MOCNIAK, JUDI; Mapletown JR SR HS; Garards Fort, PA; (Y); 23/74; GAA; Ski Clb; Varsity Clb; Yrbk Phtg; Yrbk Stf; Sec Soph Cls; JV Var Bsktbl; Im Vllybl; Hon Roll; Nrsng.

MODESITT, KEITH; Center HS; Aliquippa, PA; (Y); German Clb; Bowling; L Trk; Hon Roll; Yth Legue Bsbl All Star Tm 85-86; Slippery Rock U Frgn Lang Comptn Hnrbl Ment 86; Forestry.

MODICA, FRANK; St Clair Area HS; New Phila, PA; (Y); French Clb; Varsity Clb; Yrbk Bus Mgr; Yrbk Stf; Rep Jr Cls; Rep Sr Cls; Var L Bsbl; Var L Bsktbl; JV Ftbl; Wt Lftg; William Wolff Mem Awd 86; Mansfield U; Pub Rel.

MODY, BHAVANA G; Frankford HS; Philadelphia, PA; (Y); Hosp Aide; JA; Library Aide; Office Aide; School Play; Nwsp Bus Mgr; Yrbk Rptr; Badmtn; Vllybl; Hon Roll; Cmmdntn 2(d Hnrs , Certs; Vol Pin 100 Hrs.

MOEBUS, JONATHAN; Ringgold HS; Monongahela, PA; (Y); Computer Clb; Ski Clb; Rep Stu Cncl; Golf; Cmptr Sci.

MOEGEN, TIM; Penn Ridge HS; Perkasie, PA; (Y); Var L Socr; Wrstlng; High Hon Roll; Hon Roll; Drexel; Accntng.

MOEHLER, MICHELLE; Windber Area HS; Windber, PA; (Y); Art Clb; Library Aide; OEA; Ski Clb; Color Guard; Yrbk Stf; High Hon Roll; NHS; Stu Of Mnth Awds 84-86; Acadmc Achvt Awd Art 86; Grphc Dsgn.

MOELLER, MARIA; Mt St Joseph Acad; Glenside, PA; (Y); Cmnty Wkr; Drama Clb; JCL; Latin Clb; School Musical; School Play; Stage Crew; Lit Mag; Ntl Merit Ltr; Art Clb; Ntl Ltn Magna Cum Laude, NJCL Crtv Wrtng 83; Deans; U VA; Drama.

MOESLEIN, FRED M; Cumberland Valley HS; Boiling Springs, PA; (Y); 11/471; Speech Tm; Hon Roll; Kiwanis Awd; VP NHS; Ntl Merit Ltr; Quiz Bwl SF, Balfour Achvt Ad Sci 86; Case Western Reserve U; Bio Med.

MOFFA, ANTHONY; Hatboro Horsham HS; Horsham, PA; (Y); Ice Hcky; Hon Roll.

MOFFAT, EVELYN; Tossey Mountain HS; Saxton, PA; (Y); VP Sec Drama Clb; Band; Concert Band; Mrchg Band; School Play; Yrbk Phtg; Rep Stu Cncl; Var L Trk; Hon Roll; PMEA Rgnl III Bnd 86; Pres Acdmc Ftns Awd 86; PA ST U; Cmnctns.

MOFFITT, CHRISTOPHER; Notre Dame Of Green Pond HS; Bethlehem, PA; (Y); 17/72; Cmnty Wkr; Yrbk Stf; Var Bsbl; Var Co-Capt Bsktbl; Hon Roll; Bsbl-MVP Awd 86; St Josephs U Phil PA; Psych.

MOFFITT, LEANNE; Our Lady Of Lourdes Regional HS; Mt Carmel, PA; (Y); AFS; Am Leg Aux Girls St; Cmnty Wkr; Library Aide; Pep Clb; Spanish Clb; Stat Bsktbl; Score Keeper; Spch Ther.

MOHALLATEE, MICHAEL; William Allen HS; Allentown, PA; (Y); Chess Clb; Yrbk Phtg; Yrbk Stf; Hon Roll; Jr NHS; NHS; Chem.

MOHLE, MICHAEL; West York HS; York, PA; (Y); 34/210; French Clb; Color Guard; Vllybl.

MOHLER, KATE; Ridgway HS; Ridgway, PA; (S); 19/130; Chorus; Mrchg Band; School Musical; School Play; Ed Yrbk Phtg; Yrbk Rptr; Yrbk Stf; Rep Stu Cncl; Trk; Hon Roll; Jrnlsm.

MOHN, CYNTHIA; Pine Grove Area HS; Donaldson, PA; (Y); Am Leg Aux Girls St; Intnl Clb; Varsity Clb; Band; Chorus; Concert Band; Mrchg Band; School Play; Var Bsktbl; Stat Sftbl.

MOHN, KAREN; Lincoln HS; Philadelphia, PA; (Y); Var Mgr(s); JV Sftbl; JV Vllybl; Hon Roll; Teacher Math.

MOHNEY, BRIAN; California Area HS; California, PA; (Y); Church Yth Grp; Computer Clb; Science Clb; NHS; Eastern Nazarene Coll; Bio.

MOHNEY, KEN; Mt Pleasant Area SR HS; Mount Pleasant, PA; (Y); Church Yth Grp; Latin Clb; High Hon Roll; Hon Roll; Private Secrty.

MOHNEY JR, LARRY E; Lake View HS; Stoneboro, PA; (Y); Intnl Clb; Letterman Clb; VICA; Mgr(s); Wrstlng; Prfct Atten Awd.

MOHR, BECKY; Northern Bedford County HS; Bakers Summit, PA; (Y); Church Yth Grp; Trs 4-H; Band; Chorus; Jazz Band; School Musical; High Hon Roll; VP NHS; Band-Chorus Ltr 86; Jazz Band Awd 85-86; Choral Accompyst Awd 85-86; West Chester U; Music Educ.

MOHR, RHONDA; Bayertown Area HS; New Berlinvl, PA; (Y); 14/484; Pres VP Church Yth Grp; Girl Scts; Chorus; Church Choir; Concert Band; Mrchg Band; High Hon Roll; VP NHS; Outstndng Choral Achvt Awd 84; Schlstc Awd Exc 84; Psychlgy.

MOHR, THOMAS; Emmaus HS; Macungie, PA; (Y); 58/458; Rep Sr Cls; Rep Stu Cncl; JV L Bsbl; Var L Crs Cntry; Var L Socr; Jr NHS; NHS; Girl Scts; Latin Clb; Ski Clb; Falcon Fndtn Schlrshp 86; Valley Forge Military JC Schlrshp 86; Valley Forge Military JC.

MOIST, KEVIN; Chief Logan HS; Lewistown, PA; (Y); 17/165; Acpl Chr; Band; Chorus; Concert Band; Jazz Band; Mrchg Band; Pep Band.

MOLCANY, EILEEN; Greensburg Central Catholic HS; N Huntingdon, PA; (Y); Pres Girl Scts; Pep Clb; Ski Clb; Teachers Aide; Hon Roll; Marion Awd 83; Silver Ldrshp Silver Awd 84; Gold Ldrshp 86; Intl Bus.

MOLINARI, ANITA; Saint Maria Goretti HS; Philadelphia, PA; (Y); 105/390; Exploring; Hosp Aide; SADD; Chorus; Church Choir; School Musical; Italian Clb 84-85; Bus.

MOLINARI, BEATRICE; St Maria Gofetti HS; Philadelphia, PA; (Y); 20/400; Church Yth Grp; Cmnty Wkr; Library Aide; Math Clb; Office Aide; Teachers Aide; Tennis; High Hon Roll; NHS; Prfct Atten Awd; Hnrble Mntn Math 85; Pres Acad Ftns Awd 86; Temple U; Bnkng.

MOLINARI, GLORIA; St Maria Goretti HS; Philadelphia, PA; (S); 2/402; Church Yth Grp; Cmnty Wkr; Teachers Aide; Yrbk Stf; High Hon Roll; NHS; Prfct Atten Awd; Italian II, Latin II, Relgn II Awds 85; Italian I & Latin I Awds 84.

MOLINARI, MILISSA; Quakertown SR HS; Ottsville, PA; (Y); 19/313; Nwsp Rptr; Nwsp Stf; Yrbk Stf; Rep Soph Cls; Rep Jr Cls; Stu Cncl; Lcrss; L JV Vllybl; High Hon Roll; NHS.

MOLINARO, MARJORIE; Bishop Ohara HS; Dickson City, PA; (Y); Art Clb; Drama Clb; Ski Clb; Chorus; Yrbk Ed-Chief; Yrbk Stf; Miss Ntl Teen Pgnt Fnlst 85; Mgmt.

MOLINO, CHRISTOPHER; South Williamsport Area HS; S Wmspt, PA; (Y); Leo Clb; Pres Stu Cncl; Var L Ftbl; Var L Trk; Var L Wrstlng; Hon Roll; All Lg Tm Ftbl 84-85; Dist Qlfr Trk & Field 84 & 85.

MOLINO, MIKE; S Williamsport Area HS; S Williamsport, PA; (Y); Var L Golf; Im Vllybl; Var L Wrstlng; Dist IV Golf Champ 85; Ath Of Wk 85.

MOLISON, MATTHEW; Spring Green SR HS; Hanover, PA; (Y); 53/223; Church Yth Grp; Letterman Clb; Crs Cntry; Trk; NHS; Millersville U; Bio.

MOLITORIS, KAREN; Coughlin HS; Wilkes-Barre Twp, PA; (Y); Pres French Clb; Capt Color Guard; School Play; Nwsp Stf; Yrbk Ed-Chief; Yrbk Rptr; Yrbk Stf; Mgr Bsktbl; Mgr Fld Hcky; Mgr(s); Pres Acad Awd 86; Ldrshp Ltr Awd 86; Kings Coll; Frnch.

MOLL, LORI; Wm Allen HS; Allentown, PA; (Y); 14/578; Color Guard; Yrbk Stf; High Hon Roll; Jr NHS; NHS; Spanish NHS; Muhlenberg Coll; Mrktng.

MOLL, THOMAS R; Quakertown Comm SR HS; Quakertown, PA; (Y); 10/273; Church Yth Grp; Debate Tm; Model UN; Political Wkr; Scholastic Bowl; Madrigals; School Musical; School Play; High Hon Roll; Jr NHS; Pres Schlrshp 86; GA Pcfc Fdn 86; Am U; Erpn Itgrtn.

MOLLO, BENJAMIN; Blairsville SR HS; Blairsville, PA; (Y); Varsity Clb; Var Ftbl; Var Trk; Var Wrstlng; Hon Roll; Kiwanis Awd; PA Germny Exch Wrstlng Tm 84; PA HI Wrstlng Tm Ldr 86.

MOLLO, JEANNE; State College Area HS; State College, PA; (Y); 8/523; Girl Scts; Yrbk Ed-Chief; Var Tennis; High Hon Roll; Ntl Merit Ltr; Vrsty Let 84-85; Silver Awd In Girl Scouts 82; PA ST; Engrng Sci.

MOLLO, JULIE; Homer Center HS; Homer City, PA; (Y); Pres Church Yth Grp; Trs French Clb; Pres FNA; Hosp Aide; SADD; Chorus; Church Choir; Color Guard; Pres Concert Band; Jazz Band; Hlth Careers Clb Schlrshp 86; SR Of Mnth 86; Sec Runnr Up Homecmng Ct 86; Mt Alaysius JC; Surg Tech.

MOLLURA, DANELLE; Clearfield Area HS; Clearfield, PA; (Y); Art Clb; French Clb; Speech Tm; Band; Chorus; Flag Corp; Nwsp Bus Mgr; Crs Cntry; Var L Trk; Hon Roll; Track Dist Champ 83-85; Art Awd 85-86; Jrnlsm.

MOLNAR, CHRISTINE; Cheltenham HS; Wyncote, PA; (Y); Chorus; School Play; Hon Roll; Lbrl Arts.

MOLNAR JR, GEORGE M; Frazier HS; Perryopolis, PA; (Y); Chess Clb; Computer Clb; Ski Clb; Spanish Clb; Speech Tm; Nwsp Stf; Soph Cls; Hon Roll; Moto Crss Natl Chmpnshps 85; CA U Of PA; Comp Systms Mgmt.

MOLNAR, LINDA; Shaler Area HS; Pittsburgh, PA; (Y); 6/540; Yrbk Rptr; Capt Tennis; Var Trk; High Hon Roll; NHS; Ntl Merit Ltr; NEDT Awd; U Of Pittsbrgh Provst Schlrshp 86; Etna Elks Schlrshp 86; Westinghouse Sci Hnrs Inst 86; U Of Pittsburgh; Phrmcy.

MOLNAR, MARK; Bishop Carroll HS; Johnstown, PA; (S); 20/102; Aud/Vis; Ski Clb; Trs Spanish Clb; Im Capt Bowling; Var Golf; Hon Roll; U Of Pitt Johnstown; Comp Sci.

MOLNAR, MELISSA; Northampton SR HS; Northampton, PA; (Y); 12/444; AFS; Computer Clb; Leo Clb; Var Powder Puff Ftbl; Var JV Sftbl; High Hon Roll; Hon Roll; NHS; Temple U; Med.

MOLONEY, COLLEEN; Bishop Guilfoyle HS; Altoona, PA; (S); 5/129; Cmnty Wkr; Sec German Clb; Hosp Aide; Red Cross Aide; Service Clb; Chorus; Sec Jr Cls; JV Var Cheerleading; High Hon Roll; Hon Roll; Duquesne U; Phrmcy.

MOLTZ, MARIANNE; Venango Christian HS; Oil City, PA; (Y); 12/36; Var Bsktbl; JV Cheerleading; Var Sftbl; Hon Roll; NHS; Prfct Atten Awd; Hugh O Brien Ldrshp Awd; Commnctns.

MOLZ, MARIA; Kutztown HS; Kutztown, PA; (Y); Church Yth Grp; Girl Scts; Hosp Aide; Pep Clb; Red Cross Aide; Band; Chorus; Church Choir; Color Guard; Concert Band; Penn ST; Nrsng.

MONACO, DANIELLE; Bishop Kenrick HS; Norristown, PA; (Y); Cmnty Wkr; Dance Clb; Varsity Clb; Rep Soph Cls; JV Var Fld Hcky; Powder Puff Ftbl; Var Sftbl; Var Trk; Wt Lftg; Hon Roll; Bus.

MONACO, STEVEN; Peters Township HS; Mc Murray, PA; (Y); 8/230; Pres Computer Clb; Science Clb; Var Ftbl; High Hon Roll; NHS; PA Gov Schl For Sci Schlrshp 86; Amer Comp Sci Leag-Top Scorer PA Div Of SR Div 86; Engrng.

MONAGHAN, DIANE J; Archbishop Wood Girls HS; Huntingdon Vly, PA; (Y); 12/259; Church Yth Grp; FBLA; Rep GAA; Hosp Aide; Nwsp Rptr; Nwsp Stf; Capt Cheerleading; CC Awd; French Hon Soc; Lion Awd; Chesapeake Corp Fndtn Schlrshp 86; Pres Acad Ftnss Awd 86; KC Fr Gallen Cncl Awd 86; U Of DE; Brdcst Jrnlsm.

MONAGHAN, JAMES; Bensalem HS; Bensalem, PA; (Y); 117/700; Var L Ftbl; Var L Trk; Var L Wrstlng; Hon Roll; Prfct Atten Awd; Pride Awd Ftbl 85-87; Lower Bucks Cnty Courier Times Golden 31 Trk Awd 86; Bus.

MONAHAN, TERI; West Scranton HS; Scranton, PA; (Y); Speech Tm; Thesps; VP Orch; School Musical; School Play; Church Yth Grp; Debate Tm; Drama Clb; Stage Crew; Pom Pon; Govnrs Schl For The Arts 86; Spch Awds-Fnlsts In St & Natls 84-86; Forensic Lge Comptn 86; Theater.

MONCAVAGE, SANDY; Mt Carmel Area JR SR HS; Mt Carmel, PA; (Y); 21/141; Debate Tm; French Clb; Key Clb; Pep Clb; Band; Concert Band; Mrchg Band; School Musical; Stat Bsktbl; Hon Roll; Masque & Gavel Soc Indctns 86; Schlrshp Bloomsburg U 86; Varsty Ltr-Swimmng, Bsktbl & Trck 84-86; Bloomsburg U; Soc Welfr.

MONCRIEF, MATTHEW; Bishop Shanahan HS; W Chester, PA; (Y); 33/223; Drama Clb; Band; Chorus; Jazz Band; Madrigals; School Musical; School Play; Lit Mag; Archdiocesan Hnrs Band 85 & 86.

MONDELLO, JULIE; Hampton HS; Allison Pk, PA; (Y); 10/234; Chorus; School Musical; Stage Crew; Rep Soph Cls; Rep Jr Cls; Rep Sr Cls; Rep Stu Cncl; Bsktbl; Hon Roll; NHS; Arion Awd Chorus; U Pittsburgh Johnston; Comp Sci.

MONGIELLEE, LISA; North Pocono HS; Moscow, PA; (S); 5/226; Church Yth Grp; Yrbk Stf; High Hon Roll; U Of Scranton; Pre-Med.

MONIODES, SYLVIA; Shenango Area HS; New Castle, PA; (Y); 30/112; Church Yth Grp; 4-H; Office Aide; Drill Tm; Yrbk Stf; Sec Stu Cncl; Sftbl; Swmmng; Capt Im Vllybl; 4-H Awd; Teachng.

MONIOT, MARGOT; North Hills SR HS; Glenshaw, PA; (Y); VP Church Yth Grp; Girl Scts; Rep Political Wkr; Mrchg Band; Lit Mag; VP Frsh Cls; Sec Soph Cls; Rep Jr Cls; Twrlr; DAR Awd; Yng Frnch Hnr Stu; U Pittsburgh; Advrtsng.

MONK, SUSAN S; Kennett HS; Mendenhall, PA; (Y); 6/156; Church Yth Grp; Sec Chorus; Church Choir; Madrigals; School Musical; Nwsp Rptr; Rep Stu Cncl; High Hon Roll; NHS; Ntl Merit SF; Soc Wmn Engrs Mth & Sci Hnrs 85; Spn Awd 83 & 85; Fleet Reserve Assn Essay Cont 3rd Pl 85; UNC; Bio.

MONKEMEYER, ANDREW; Marple Newtown SR HS; Newtown Square, PA; (Y); Camera Clb; Chess Clb; Church Yth Grp; CAP; Var Debate Tm; Band; Concert Band; Mrchg Band; Orch; Band Awd 86; IN U Of Penn; Accntng.

MONKO, KAREN; E L Meyers HS; Wilkes Barre, PA; (Y); FBLA; VP Key Clb; Ski Clb; Varsity Clb; Band; Chorus; Mrchg Band; Yrbk Stf; Stu Cncl; Capt Bsktbl; Ltr Wnr & All-Schlstc Sftbl & Bskbl 84-86; 3rd Pl Spch Cntst FBLA 86; Central Penn Bus Sch; Trvl/Trsm.

MONKS, ROBYN L; Jersey Shore Area HS; Jersey Shore, PA; (Y); German Clb; Hosp Aide; Ski Clb; Band; Chorus; Church Choir; Concert Band; Mrchg Band; School Musical; School Play; Dist Chorus 85-86; Regnl Chorus 85-86; PA ST; Theater Arts.

MONNIN, BETTY; Sharon HS; Sharon, PA; (Y); Church Yth Grp; French Clb; Hon Roll; Acad Lttr 86; Elem Educ.

MONOSKI, SEAN; Williamsport Area HS; Williamsport, PA; (Y); Var L Crs Cntry; Var Trk; 300 & 298 Bwlng Awd Scrs 84-85; 300 Bwlng Awd Scr 85-86; Drftng.

MONOVICH, JOE; Brownsville Area HS; Allison, PA; (Y); Drama Clb; Ski Clb; SADD; Teachers Aide; Stage Crew; Variety Show; Yrbk Stf; Stu Cncl; JV Bsbl; Var Ftbl; Air Force CC; Contrctng.

MONREAN, REGINA; Keystone JR SR HS; Knox, PA; (Y); 39/125; VP Pres Church Yth Grp; French Clb; FBLA; Girl Scts; Trs Yrbk Bus Mgr; Rptr Yrbk Ed-Chief; Yrbk Stf; Prfct Atten Awd; Hosp Axlry For Wmn Schlrshp 86; Dstngshd HS Stu Of Amer 85 & 86; Outstndng Alto In Cncrt Choir 86; Erie Bus Cntr; Med Scrtry.

MONROE, ANDREA LA SHAWN; Mt Pleasant SR HS; Mt Pleasant, PA; (Y); 113/253; VP Church Yth Grp; French Clb; FBLA; Chorus; Church Choir; Color Guard; Mrchg Band; Variety Show; Trk; High Hon Roll; PA Free Enterprise Scholar 86; U Pittsburgh; Bus Adm.

MONROE, JULIE; Upper Merion HS; King Of Prussia, PA; (Y); 43/330; Rep Stu Cncl; Bsktbl; Trk; Gifted Pgm; Bloomsburg U Ldrshp Smnrs; Pre Med.

MONTAGNA, GREGORY; Brownsville Area HS; Cardale, PA; (Y); Drama Clb; Capt Mathletes; Ski Clb; Mrchg Band; Wrstlng; High Hon Roll; Jr NHS; NHS; Prfct Atten Awd.

MONTAGNA, PATRICK; Pittston Area SR HS; Pt Griffith, PA; (Y); JV Ftbl.

MONTANARO, FREDERICK F; Northern Cambria HS; Barnesboro, PA; (Y); 50/115; Band; Concert Band; Jazz Band; Mrchg Band; Symp Band; Var L Trk; JP Sousa Awd; Spanish NHS; Clarion U PA; Mus Educ.

MONTANTE, STEVEN; Scranton Prep Schl; West Pittston, PA; (Y); 21/192; School Musical; School Play; Nwsp Rptr; Nwsp Stf; Yrbk Stf; Swmmng; High Hon Roll; NHS; Amer Clscl League Ntl Greek Exam Merit Ad 86; High Hnrs 84-86; Doctor.

MONTEIRO, MELODY; Midland HS; Midland, PA; (Y); 3/39; Church Yth Grp; Latin Clb; Church Choir; Yrbk Stf; Sec Frsh Cls; Sec Soph Cls; Rep Jr Cls; Rep Stu Cncl; Hon Roll; Psych.

MONTELEONE, JASON; Bishop Mc Cort HS; Johnstown, PA; (Y); 2/144; Church Yth Grp; French Clb; Latin Clb; Library Aide; Math Clb; Math Tm; NFL; Science Clb; Speech Tm; VP Stu Cncl; Attrny.

MONTELEONE, LISA; Saegertown HS; Saegertown, PA; (Y); 24/130; Ski Clb; Spanish Clb; Varsity Clb; Pres Soph Cls; Rep Stu Cncl; Var Capt Bsktbl; Stat Ftbl; Jr NHS.

MONTGOMERY, BRIAN; Highlands SR HS; Natrona Hts, PA; (Y); Intnl Clb; Brwn & Gld Awd-Acadmc Achvt.

MONTGOMERY, BRIDGETTE; Mc Keesport SR HS; Mckeesport, PA; (Y); Var L Bsktbl; Powder Puff Ftbl; Trk; Cit Awd; Elks Awd; Hon Roll; IUP; Acctg.

MONTGOMERY, DAWN; Norwin SR HS; N Huntingdon, PA; (Y); Art Clb; Church Yth Grp; Cmnty Wkr; Hosp Aide; Library Aide; Chorus; Stage Crew; Yrbk Stf; Sftbl; Trk; Art Hnrbl Mntn 86; Laroche; Fash Merch.

MONTGOMERY, DONNA; Clarion Area HS; Sligo, PA; (Y); Chorus; Color Guard; School Musical; Variety Show; Yrbk Stf; Stat Crs Cntry; High Hon Roll; Hon Roll; Drama.

MONTGOMERY, EDWIN; Penn Hills SR HS; Verona, PA; (Y); 140/797; Pres Computer Clb; French Clb; Science Clb; Rep Sr Cls; Rep Stu Cncl; Cit Awd; High Hon Roll; Hon Roll; 1st Pl Allegheny Cnty Comptr Fair 86; Carnegie-Mellon U; Elec Engrg.

MONTGOMERY, LORA; Towanda HS; Wysox, PA; (Y); VP Trs Church Yth Grp; Drama Clb; FTA; Band; Church Choir; Concert Band; Mrchg Band; Elmntry Ed.

MONTGOMERY, PATTIE; Fairview HS; Erie, PA; (Y); 67/183; Office Aide; Varsity Clb; Chorus; School Musical; Var L Swmmng; Var L Tennis; Var L Trk; Hon Roll; Athltc Yrbk 82-84; Bowling Green ST U.

MONTROSS, JEFFREY H; Tunkhannock HS; Centermoreland, PA; (Y); 88/315; Boy Scts; Church Yth Grp; Spanish Clb; JV Bsbl; JV Ftbl; JV Wt Lftg; Hon Roll; Crimnl Justc.

MOODY, JOHN; Shamokin Area HS; Paxinos, PA; (Y); 2/252; Am Leg Boys St; Boy Scts; Orch; Golf; High Hon Roll; NHS; Sal; Val; JV Trk; Wrstlng; Eagle Scout Awd 85; Chem.

MOODY, MELISSA; Farrell Area HS; Farrell, PA; (Y); 3/96; French Clb; Hosp Aide; Teachers Aide; Varsity Clb; Chorus; Sec Frsh Cls; Rep Jr Cls; Capt L Diving; Capt L Swmmng; Sec NHS; Diving Record 85-86; Giftd Pgm; 1st Pl Diving Champ 86; Frgn Lang.

MOOKERJEE, SRIKANTA; Carlynton HS; Carnegie, PA; (Y); Chess Clb; Debate Tm; Intnl Clb; Math Clb; Science Clb; Spanish Clb; Teachers Aide; School Play; Variety Show; High Hon Roll; U Of Ptsbrgh; Med.

MOON, CARRIE M; Rocky Grove JR SR HS; Cooperstown, PA; (Y); 32/92; Hosp Aide; Office Aide; Chorus; Rep Stu Cncl; Var Mgr(s); JV Vllybl; Hon Roll; Slippery Rock U; Psych.

MOON, HYUNG; Abington SR HS; Huntingdon Valley, PA; (Y); Church Yth Grp; Intnl Clb; Latin Clb; Nwsp Rptr; Rep Jr Cls; Var Ftbl; Var Lcrss; JV Wrstlng; Hon Roll; Jr NHS; Bausch & Lomb Sci Awd 86; U PA; Surgeon.

MOON, KIMBERLY; Quigley HS; Ambridge, PA; (S); 20/109; Math Clb; Pep Clb; High Hon Roll; Hon Roll; NHS; Natl Hnr Rll; IN U Of PA; Spch Pathlgy.

MOONEY, ANDREA; Upper Dublin HS; Ambler, PA; (Y); 41/307; Sec JA; JV Socr; JV Sftbl; JV Tennis; NHS; Phy Thrpst.

MOONEY JR, MARTIN C; Bishop Egan HS; Burlington, NJ; (S); German Clb; Var Ice Hcky; High Hon Roll; NHS; Acad Awd Alg I,Geomtry,Scrptur,Eng,Bio,Latin,German 84-85.

MOONEY, SHEILA; Neshannock HS; New Castle, PA; (Y); 9/99; Church Yth Grp; Teachers Aide; Church Choir; School Play; Nwsp Rptr; JV Vllybl; Hon Roll; NHS; Pres Schlr; Acad All Amer 84-85; 1st Pl Hoyt Tlnt Shwcse Piano Solo 86; Bethel Coll MN; Intrior Dsgn.

MOONEY, TRACI L; Big Spring HS; Carlisle, PA; (Y); Sec Church Yth Grp; Pep Clb; Y-Teens; Rep Stu Cncl; Var Cheerleading; Var Powder Puff Ftbl; JV Vllybl; Hon Roll; Chrldng Awd 86; Nrsng.

MOONIS, JULI; South Allegheny HS; Mc Keesport, PA; (S); French Clb; Band; Chorus; Jazz Band; Capt Mrchg Band; School Musical; Yrbk Sprt Ed; Frsh Cls; Church Yth Grp; Jr Cls; Optmst Clb Spch Awd 81; U Of SC; Pblc Reltns.

MOORE, ALLISON; Lampeter-Strasburg HS; Lancaster, PA; (Y); 11/158; AFS; Church Yth Grp; Pres FHA; Girl Scts; Thesps; Varsity Clb; Chorus; Church Choir; School Musical; Stage Crew; Millersville U; Nclr Med Tech.

MOORE, ANDREW C; Bensalem HS; Bensalem, PA; (Y); 44/562; Ski Clb; Band; Chorus; Concert Band; Jazz Band; Mgr Stage Crew; Im Vllybl; NHS; Ntl Merit Ltr; Pres Schlr; County Band 84-85; County Choir 83; Rensselaer Polytech Inst; Physc.

MOORE, CHRISTIAN S; Cedar Cliff HS; Camp Hill, PA; (Y); 14/250; Am Leg Boys St; Boy Scts; Model UN; Speech Tm; Orch; High Hon Roll; Trs NHS; Voice Dem Awd; Church Yth Grp; Exploring; Hugh O Brian Yth Ldrshp Sem 85; YMCA Yth Conf On Natl Affairs 86; Presdntl Clsrm For Young Amer 86; Polit Sci.

MOORE, CHRISTINA; Northern Chester County Tech Schl; Phoenixville, PA; (Y); 2/120; Girl Scts; Pep Clb; High Hon Roll; Hon Roll; Masonic Awd; NHS; Rotary Awd; Sal; Stu Mnth 86; Embry Riddle; Comp Sci.

MOORE, COLLEEN; Archbishop Kennedy HS; Conshohocken, PA; (Y); Library Aide; Office Aide; Pep Clb; Rep Stu Cncl; Crs Cntry; Hon Roll; Hnr Roll 82-85; Hmcmng Queen 85-86; Amer Hmcmng Queen 85-86; Hghst Avrg In Englsh, Wrld Cltr & Rltn 83; Harcum JC; Hlth Si.

MOORE, DARLENE; South Park HS; Library, PA; (Y); 22/203; Dance Clb; Drill Tm; Rep Soph Cls; Rep Jr Cls; L Cheerleading; High Hon Roll; NHS; Pittsburgh U; Nrs.

MOORE, DENICE; Danville SR HS; Danville, PA; (Y); French Clb; Red Cross Aide; Chorus; Rep Jr Cls; JV Bsktbl; L Trk; Bus.

MOORE, DENNIS; Middletown Area HS; Middletown, PA; (Y); 29/166; Varsity Clb; Var Bsktbl; Var Ftbl; Var Trk; Wt Lftg; Hon Roll; Lion Awd; NHS; W Harold Gerberich Memrl Awd; Bio.

MOORE, HEIDI L; Bethel Park SR HS; Bethel Park, PA; (Y); 14/515; Cmnty Wkr; Sec German Clb; Mrchg Band; School Musical; Symp Band; NHS; ST Orch & ST Band Fest 85-86; U Of VT; Phy Thrpy.

MOORE, JAMES; Fort Cherry HS; Bulger, PA; (S); 2/140; Am Leg Boys St; Church Yth Grp; Math Clb; Pres Science Clb; Varsity Clb; Chorus; Stu Cncl; Wrstlng; Bausch & Lomb Sci Awd; Grove City Coll; Engr.

MOORE, JEFFREY; George Washington HS; Philadelphia, PA; (Y); 333/710; Chess Clb; Church Yth Grp; Exploring; Stat Bsktbl; Var Score Keeper; Cit Awd; DAR Awd; Var Timer; Participant Of Operation Understanding 85; Human Rltn Cncl 85-86; Penn ST U; Bus Admin.

MOORE, KERRY; Carmichaels Area HS; Carmichaels, PA; (S); 10/102; Ski Clb; Spanish Clb; SADD; Color Guard; Cit Awd; DAR Awd; High Hon Roll; NHS; Prfct Atten Awd; Spnsh Awd 86; Engl.

MOORE, KEVIN D; Henderson SR HS; West Chester, PA; (Y); 38/336; Intnl Clb; Nwsp Rptr; Rep Soph Cls; Rep Stu Cncl; Var JV Lcrss; High Hon Roll; Hon Roll; NHS; Spanish NHS; Church Yth Grp; Charles Edison Free Enterprise Video Fest 85-86; Penn ST; Aerospace Engr.

MOORE, KIMBERLEA; Harbor Creek HS; Harbor Creek, PA; (Y); ROTC; Teachers Aide; Band; Concert Band; Mrchg Band; Sec Pep Band; JV Trk; Hon Roll; Edinboro U; Psychlgy.

MOORE, KRISTINA L; High Schl Of Engineering And Science; Philadelphia, PA; (Y); 75/197; Church Yth Grp; Civic Clb; Science Clb; Speech Tm; Church Choir; Nwsp Stf; Lit Mag; Rep Stu Cncl; Ntl Merit Ltr; Ind Engrg.

MOORE, LANI; Waynesburg Central HS; Spraggs, PA; (Y); Church Yth Grp; Natl Beta Clb; Spanish Clb; Flag Corp; Yrbk Stf; Stu Cncl; Trk; Hon Roll; Wash Dist Cncl Yth Mstrs Pres 85-86; CA U Of PA; Elem Educ.

MOORE, LISA; Yough SR HS; Herminite, PA; (Y); Drama Clb; Ski Clb; VICA; Band; Chorus; Church Choir; Concert Band; Jazz Band; Stage Crew; Symp Band; Cnty Band 84-85; IUP; Resp Thrpy.

MOORE, LORI; Bethlehem Ctr; Clarksville, PA; (Y); 21/145; JV Bsktbl; 4-H; Spanish Clb; Drvrs Ed Sfty Comptn 86; Comptr.

MOORE, LUCINDA; North Hills HS; Pittsburgh, PA; (S); 49/476; Ski Clb; Band; Mrchg Band; Orch; Symp Band; NHS; Bus.

MOORE, MELISSA; Bellwood-Antis HS; Tyrone, PA; (Y); 15/110; FBLA; Hon Roll; Altoona Schl Commerce; Sec.

MOORE, MELISSA; Monessen HS; Monessen, PA; (Y); Office Aide; Band; Chorus; Color Guard; Variety Show; Nwsp Phtg; Yrbk Stf; VP Frsh Cls; Trs Soph Cls; Trs Sr Cls; MD U Morehouse; Elmntry Ed.

MOORE, MICHAEL T; Elderton JR-SR HS; Ford City, PA; (Y); German Clb; Varsity Clb; Yrbk Phtg; Yrbk Stf; Pres Sr Cls; Stu Cncl; Vllybl; High Hon Roll; Ntl Merit SF; Boston U; Aerspc Engrng.

MOORE, MICHELE; Washington HS; Washington, PA; (S); Hosp Aide; Ski Clb; Spanish Clb; Band; Concert Band; Jazz Band; Mrchg Band; School Musical; Symp Band; Twrlr.

MOORE, MIKE; Meyers HS; Wilkes Barre, PA; (Y); Boy Scts; Church Yth Grp; Stage Crew; Variety Show; JV Var Wrstlng; Hon Roll; Jr NHS; Spanish NHS; Comm.

MOORE, NATHAN; Moniteau HS; Slippery Rock, PA; (Y); Drama Clb; Pres French Clb; Spanish Clb; Sec Jr Cls; Butler Cnty Cmnty Coll 1st, 2nd & 3rd Pl Poetry 86; Clarion U 4th Pl Poetry 86; Slippery Rock U; Crtve Exprssn.

MOORE, NELLITA; Center HS; Monaca, PA; (Y); 17/180; Church Yth Grp; German Clb; Latin Clb; Band; Church Choir; Yrbk Rptr; High Hon Roll; Hon Roll; NHS; Pres Schlr; Northwestern U; Pre-Med.

MOORE, PAULA; Central York SR HS; York, PA; (Y); Varsity Clb; Concert Band; Jazz Band; Mrchg Band; Orch; School Musical; Symp Band; Yrbk Stf; Tennis; Hon Roll; 1l Fnlst York Cnty JR Miss Pgnt 86; Dstrct Band & Orchstr 84-86; Temple U; Advrtsng.

MOORE, PETE; Mt Pleasant Area HS; Mt Pleasant, PA; (Y); 75/253; French Clb; JV Var Bsktbl; JV Var Ftbl; JV Trk; Wt Lftg; Hon Roll; Engrng.

MOORE, SHARON L; Sacred Heart HS; Pittsburgh, PA; (Y); 35/165; Art Clb; Camera Clb; Dance Clb; VP Debate Tm; Drama Clb; VP French Clb; VP NFL; VP PAVAS; Radio Clb; Speech Tm; 2nd Pl PHSSL ST Trnmnt Radio Anncng 86; 2nd Pl Hmrs Intrp Frnscs 86; 1st Pl Drmtc Intrp Frnscs 86; Clarion U PA; Spch Cmnctns.

MOORE, SHERRI; Hempfield HS; E Petersburg, PA; (Y); Red Cross Aide; SADD; Bowling; Powder Puff Ftbl; Cit Awd; Gov Hon Prg Awd; NCTE Awd; NHS; Val; Awd State Ldrshp Conf 86; Trophy LYABA Dbl Champ 2nd Pl 86; Sec & Treas Salem UCC Columbia 86; Pittsburgh Beauty Acad; Csmtlgs.

MOORE, STACEY; Belle Vernon Area HS; Belle Vernon, PA; (Y); 1/287; Pres Art Clb; Band; Concert Band; Mrchg Band; Ed Yrbk Stf; Rep Jr Cls; Rep Stu Cncl; High Hon Roll; NHS; CA U Frnch Compt 1st Frnch Vocab II 85; 2nd Pl Frnch Vocab III & IV 86; Prom Comm 86; Pre-Law.

MOORE, STEPHEN; Montoursville HS; Montoursville, PA; (Y); 31/174; Spanish Clb; Varsity Clb; Stu Cncl; Coach Actv; Ftbl; Socr; Trk; Hon Roll; PA St U; Comp Prgng.

MOORE, SUSAN; Du Bois Area HS; Dubois, PA; (Y); 2/255; Chorus; School Musical; Swing Chorus; Bsktbl; Capt Crs Cntry; Var Trk; NHS; Ntl Merit Ltr; Rotary Awd; Sal; PA ST U.

MOORE, TERRI L; Coudersport Area JR-SR HS; Coudersport, PA; (Y); Drama Clb; French Clb; Varsity Clb; School Play; Yrbk Stf; Cheerleading; Trk; High Hon Roll; NHS; Ntl Merit Ltr; 1st Pl ST Cmptn PTSA Reflctns Cntst-Lit 86; 1st Pl Dist IX AA Trck Mt 3200 Meter Rn 86; Frnch Awd; Genetc Engrng.

MOORE, TIM; Bald Eagle-Nittany HS; Mill Hall, PA; (Y); VP 4-H; Key Clb; Model UN; Spanish Clb; Varsity Clb; Mrchg Band; Stage Crew; Nwsp Stf; Var Stu Cncl; Var Mgr(s).

MOORE, TODD; Fairfield HS; Fairfield, PA; (Y); 2/42; Spanish Clb; VP Band; Pres Chorus; School Musical; School Play; Trs Stu Cncl; High Hon Roll; Pres NHS; Rotary Awd; 3rd Amrcn HS Math Exm 86; Engrng.

MOORE, VIRGINIA; Lewisburg Area HS; Lewisburg, PA; (Y); 7/155; Church Yth Grp; Trs Spanish Clb; Chorus; School Musical; School Play; Rep Stu Cncl; DAR Awd; Hon Roll; NHS; Spanish NHS; Pres Acad Fit Awd; Furman U; Bus.

MOORE, WENDY; Du Bois Area HS; Reynoldsville, PA; (Y); Church Yth Grp; Science Clb; SADD; Nwsp Stf; Stu Cncl; Hon Roll; NHS; Ntl Merit SF; Publctn Clarion Spring Fest Arts 85; 1st Pl Stu Div Brockway Old Fash 4th Art Show 86; Bio.

MOORE, WILLIAM; Ft Cherry HS; Mc Donald, PA; (Y); Pres Church Yth Grp; Science Clb; Ski Clb; Concert Band; Mrchg Band; Yrbk Phtg; Yrbk Stf; Bi-Cntnnl Schlrshp Untd Mthdst Chrch 86; WV Wesleyan Coll; Chrstn Educ.

MOORHATCH, STEVE; Delaware County Christian Schl; Paoli, PA; (Y); 12/88; Church Yth Grp; Drama Clb; Math Clb; Acpl Chr; Chorus; School Play; Var L Socr; Var L Trk; High Hon Roll; Ntl Merit Ltr; ACSI Distngshd Stu 86; Mech Engr.

MOORHEAD, WENDY; Penn Hills HS; Pittsburgh, PA; (S); 276/762; Church Yth Grp; Band; Church Choir; Concert Band; Jazz Band; Mrchg Band; Hon Roll; US Bus Educ Awd 86; Bus Mstr Cmnctn Awd 86; Prof Awd Spllng 86; Boyce Campus; Med Secry.

MOORMAN, ROGER; Our Lady Of The Sacred Heart HS; Coraopolis, PA; (Y); Pep Clb; Varsity Clb; JV Bsktbl; Stat Crs Cntry; Phy Ed 85-86; Most Popular 85-86; MVP Of Bsktbl JV Tm 84-85; Restaurant Mgmt.

MOOSE, TRAVIS; Emmaus HS; Emmaus, PA; (Y); Boy Scts; Church Yth Grp; JA; Library Aide; Red Cross Aide; Stat Crs Cntry; Mgr(s); Stat Trk; Seat Blt Sfty Awd; Cmmrcl Art.

MORAN, DESIREE; Counciul Rock HS; Southampton, PA; (Y); 227/788; Girl Scts; Var L Fld Hcky; Var Capt Socr; Schlrshp U Of Hartford Womns Soccr 86; U Of Hartford; Psych.

MORAN, JILL; MMI Preparatory Schl; Hazleton, PA; (S); 7/32; Art Clb; Aud/Vis; Trs Debate Tm; Drama Clb; Model UN; Ski Clb; Speech Tm; SADD; School Play; Nwsp Stf; Best Spkr Awd Dale Cargenie Crse 85; Spnsh Awd 84; Excell Awd Engl 85; Law.

MORAN, KIM; Haverford SR HS; Havertown, PA; (Y); 50/450; Church Yth Grp; Political Wkr; Service Clb; Var Swmmng; Hon Roll; Econ Awd 85-86; Comptv Swmmng Lower Merion Aquatic Clb 84-85; Gettysburg Coll; Law.

MORAN, MARY; West Scranton SR HS; Scranton, PA; (Y); Hon Roll; NHS; U Of Scranton; Plcwmn.

MORANDUZZO, LISA; Conemaugh Township Area HS; Davidsville, PA; (Y); 1/101; Trs Spanish Clb; Lit Mag; Stu Cncl; Cheerleading; Sftbl; Hon Roll; NHS; Natl Engl Merit Awd 85-86; Acad All Amer 85-86.

MORASCO, NADINE; Lebanon Catholic HS; Cleona, PA; (Y); FHA; Key Clb; Science Clb; Ski Clb; SADD; Band; Chorus; Mrchg Band; Nwsp Stf; Yrbk Stf; All Cathlc Chorus 83-86; Fut Homemkrs Of Amer 86; Essay Awd 86; Reg Dieticn.

MORATELLI, BECKY; Williams Valley HS; Wiconisco, PA; (Y); Cmnty Wkr; Chorus; Rep Stu Cncl; Stat Bsbl; Var Capt Cheerleading; Acad Schlrshp 86; Musicl Awds 86; Coll Misericordia; Occptn Thrpy.

MORAVEK, GEORGINE; Panther Valley HS; Lansford, PA; (Y); 15/131; Church Yth Grp; Library Aide; Ski Clb; VP Band; Chorus; VP Concert Band; VP Mrchg Band; Yrbk Stf; Co-Capt Trk; Hon Roll; Slovok Cathlc Sokol Schlrshp 86; Onyx Schlrshp-Cedar Crst Coll 86; Cedar Crest Coll; Nrsng.

MORCOM, JENNIFER; Lakeland JR SR HS; Jermyn, PA; (Y); Girl Scts; Spanish Clb; SADD; Drill Tm; Rep Stu Cncl; JV Crs Cntry; Var Pom Pon; Var Sftbl; High Hon Roll; Hon Roll; U Of Scranton; Exec Scrtry.

MORCOS, PETER G; Dallas SR HS; Dallas, PA; (Y); 5/198; Computer Clb; Yrbk Phtg; Yrbk Stf; Sec Jr Cls; Stu Cncl; High Hon Roll; JETS Awd; Trs NHS; Ntl Merit SF; Aud/Vis; PA Govnrs Schl Sci 85; Physcs.

MORDAN, BOB; Danville Area SR HS; Danville, PA; (Y); 29/202; Church Yth Grp; Cmnty Wkr; Key Clb; Im JV Bsbl; Im JV Bsktbl; Im JV Ftbl; Im Gym; Hon Roll; NHS; Prfct Atten Awd.

MOREHEAD, WILLIAM J; Waynesburg Central HS; Mt Morris, PA; (Y); Ftbl.

MOREIRA, SHERRIS; Wilmington Area HS; New Wilmington, PA; (S); 10/101; Drama Clb; Church Choir; Concert Band; Mrchg Band; School Play; Variety Show; Nwsp Rptr; Crs Cntry; Trk; NHS; Lancaster Bible Coll; Christ Ed.

MORELLI, JOE; Center HS; Aliquippa, PA; (Y); Letterman Clb; Spanish Clb; SADD; Varsity Clb; Im Bsktbl; Im Bowling; Var L Ftbl; Im Wt Lftg; Hon Roll; NHS.

MORELLO, GREGORY L; Carlisle HS; Carlisle, PA; (Y); 19/420; Nwsp Rptr; Lit Mag; VP Stu Cncl; Var L Socr; Var Tennis; Hon Roll; Masonic Awd; NCTE Awd; NHS; Rep De Molzy Awd 84; Jrnlsm.

MORELLO, SALVATORE; Upper Merion SR HS; King Of Prussia, PA; (Y); Var Tennis; Im Vllybl.

MORGAN, AMY; Canton Area JR SR HS; Canton, PA; (Y); 11/124; Letterman Clb; Spanish Clb; Band; Chorus; Concert Band; Mrchg Band; JV Var Mgr(s); JV Var Vllybl; High Hon Roll; Hon Roll; Ltr Acadmc Achvt 85-86; Acctng.

MORGAN, AMY; Union Area HS; New Castle, PA; (Y); 2/63; Art Clb; Pep Clb; Y-Teens; Sec Trs Band; Mrchg Band; Pep Band; School Musical; Yrbk Stf; Var L Bsktbl; Var L Vllybl; Top Decile 85 & 86.

MORGAN, BARBARA; Apollo-Ridge SR HS; Mcintyre, PA; (Y); Sec Debate Tm; Pep Clb; Ski Clb; Nwsp Stf; Yrbk Stf; Trk; Hon Roll; NHS; Acad Achvt Awd 83; Monterey Peninsula Coll; Bio.

MORGAN, BRIAN; Clearfield Area HS; Clearfield, PA; (Y); Church Yth Grp; Bsktbl; JV Wt Lftg; Comp Sci.

MORGAN, CHRIS; Newport HS; Newport, PA; (S); 4/90; Capt Bsbl; Capt Bsktbl; Golf; High Hon Roll; Hon Roll; NHS; Prfct Atten Awd; Var Bsktbl Ltr 85-86; Var Bsbl Ltr 84-86; Mth.

MORGAN, DAVID; Hanover Area HS; Wilkes Barre, PA; (Y); Key Clb; Ski Clb; Var Trk; Im Vllybl; High Hon Roll; Hon Roll; Jr NHS; NHS; NEDT Awd; Penn ST U; Ecnmcs.

MORGAN, JAMES; Scranton Technical HS; Scranton, PA; (Y); Hon Roll; Hnr Soc 86; U Of Scranton; Zoolgy.

MORGAN, JAMES; Seneca Valley HS; Zelienople, PA; (Y); 4/370; Chess Clb; Math Tm; ROTC; Varsity Clb; Var Swmmng; Var L Tennis; Bausch & Lomb Sci Awd; High Hon Roll; Hon Roll; Pres NHS; Superior Cadet Awd; IN U Hons Schlrshp; Schlstc Excllnc Awd Am Lg; IN U Bloomington; Pre-Med.

MORGAN, JAMIE; Laurel Highlands SR HS; Uniontown, PA; (S); 1/365; Pres Hosp Aide; Math Tm; Trs Band; VP Madrigals; School Musical; Swing Chorus; Sec Sr Cls; Rep Stu Cncl; Jr NHS; NHS; 2nd Rnr-Up Bitumns Cool Qun Pgnt 85; Rotry Wrld Affrs Cncl 85; Amer Lgn Cnty Essy Wnr 85; U Of Pittsburgh; :Nrsng.

MORGAN, JOHN; Wm Allen HS; Allentown, PA; (Y); 65/605; Church Yth Grp; Letterman Clb; Varsity Clb; Bsbl; Bsktbl; Ftbl; Wt Lftg; Hon Roll; NHS; Ltrmn Ftbl 84-85; E PA Conf All Star Tight End 85; Phrmcy.

MORGAN, KIMBERLY; Scranton Central HS; Scranton, PA; (Y); 91/273; Sec Church Yth Grp; French Clb; Sec JA; Chorus; Church Choir; Color Guard; Nwsp Rptr; Yrbk Stf; Powder Puff Ftbl; Jr NHS; Pres Acadmc Ftns Awd 86; Marywood Coll; Hlth Svc Adm.

MORGAN, LARRAINE; Central Dauphin HS; Harrisburg, PA; (Y); Key Clb; Color Guard; Flag Corp; Nwsp Stf; Twrlr; Var L Vllybl; Hon Roll; Jr NHS; Hnr Mntn Showat Ldr Nrsng Hm 86; Gldn Key Cert Ntl Schstc Art 86; Htl Mngmnt.

MORGAN, MARCY; Waynesburg Central HS; Waynesburg, PA; (Y); 32/207; Church Yth Grp; FCA; 4-H; French Clb; Natl Beta Clb; Dnfth Awd; 4-H Awd; Lion Awd; Voice Dem Awd; Voice Of Dem; Girl Of Mnth; WV U; Elem Ed.

MORGAN, MATTHEW; Hopewel JR HS; Aliquippa, PA; (Y); 7/261; Church Yth Grp; French Clb; Math Clb; Math Tm; Var Bsbl; L Bsktbl; Capt Socr; High Hon Roll; Pres NHS; Pres Schlr; Air Force ROTC 4 Yr Schlrshp 86; Naval ROTC 4 Yr Schlrshp 86; PMMA Of Pittsburg Schlrshp 86; Air Force Acad; Engr.

MORGAN, MICHAEL; Bishop Hoban HS; Kingston, PA; (Y); 18/187; FBLA; Latin Clb; Math Clb; Nwsp Sprt Ed; Co-Capt Var Bsbl; Capt Swmmng; High Hon Roll; NHS; NEDT Awd; All-Amer 4 Tms Swmng 84-86; Schlr/Athlt Schl 86; Pres Acdmc Ftns Awd 86; U Of PA; Bus.

MORGAN, MICHELLE; Fort Le Boeuf HS; Waterford, PA; (Y); Lib 4-H; VP FFA; Trk; FFA Lvstck Jdgng Awd 1st Lcl Cntst 85-86; Hnr Roll Cert Bng On Hnr Roll 83-84; Str Grnhnd FFA 83-85.

MORGAN, MIREILLE; Annville-Cleona HS; Annville, PA; (S); 4/121; Girl Scts; Hosp Aide; Varsity Clb; Acpl Chr; Band; VP Chorus; Concert Band; Mrchg Band; Pep Band; School Musical; Hugh O Brian Yth Fndtn Smnr 84; Slvr Scout Awd 84; Outstndng Undrclsmn Mscn 84 & 85; Shpnsbrg; Crmnlgy.

MORGAN, PAMELA; Saint Huberts HS; Philadelphia, PA; (Y); Camera Clb; JA; Office Aide; Gym; Psych.

MORGAN, RANDY; Annville Cldona HS; Annville, PA; (Y); 30/140; Math Tm; SADD; School Musical; JV Bsbl; JV Bsktbl; Im Ftbl; Var Socr; Jr NHS; NHS; NEDT Awd; Comp Pgmg.

MORGAN, RHONDA; Rockwood Area HS; Rockwood, PA; (S); 11/97; VP Frsh Cls; Pres Soph Cls; Pres Jr Cls; VP Sr Cls; Trs Stu Cncl; Capt Bsktbl; Capt Sftbl; Capt Vllybl; High Hon Roll; NHS; Seton Hill Coll; Marn Bio.

MORGAN, SALLIE; Pennsbury HS; Yardley, PA; (Y); 33/744; Pres Church Yth Grp; French Clb; Service Clb; SADD; Chorus; School Musical; Var Swmmng; Cit Awd; NHS; Cmnty Wkr; PA Free Enterprise Wk Schlrshp 86; Int Bus.

MORGAN, SCOTT; Jamestown HS; Jamestown, PA; (Y); VP Frsh Cls; High Hon Roll; Hon Roll; Prfct Atten Awd; Thiel Coll; Bus Adm.

MORGAN, SUSAN; William Allen HS; Allentown, PA; (Y); 52/529; Drama Clb; Leo Clb; Math Tm; Ski Clb; Off Sr Cls; High Hon Roll; Jr NHS; NHS; Law.

MORGAN, TINA; Line Mountain HS; Trevorton, PA; (Y); Church Yth Grp; 4-H; Key Clb; Band; Concert Band; Mrchg Band; Stage Crew; Stat Bsktbl; Score Keeper; Prfct Atten Awd; Hnds Acrs Amer Cert Apprctn 86; Band Vrsty Ltr, Pin 85-86; Euchrstc Minstr St Patrcks Chrch 86; Bloomsbrg U; X-Ray Technlgy.

MORGANO, VIOLA; Sacred Heart HS; Pittsburgh, PA; (Y); 7/151; Drama Clb; Math Clb; Trs Spanish Clb; Chorus; School Musical; Variety Show; High Hon Roll; Elec Engrng.

MORIDA, DEERA; Lincoln HS; Ellwood City, PA; (Y); Drama Clb; French Clb; VP Trs Key Clb; JV Var Bsktbl; Powder Puff Ftbl; Sftbl; Tennis; High Hon Roll; Hon Roll; Kiwanis Awd; Bradford; Bus.

MORINI, PAULA; Lincoln HS; Ellwood City, PA; (Y); 29/163; VP Y-Teens; School Musical; Yrbk Stf; VP Soph Cls; VP Jr Cls; VP Sr Cls; Var Gym; NHS; Pres Schlr; Spanish Clb; Y Teens Schlrshp 86; Carnegie-Mellon U; Info Sys.

MORLEY, KAREN; Sayre HS; Sayre, PA; (Y); 6/116; Church Yth Grp; French Clb; Hosp Aide; Letterman Clb; Varsity Clb; Sftbl; Swmmng; Tennis; L Vllybl; High Hon Roll; Brigham Young U; Frnch.

MORLEY, KRISTIN E; Methacton SR HS; Audubon, PA; (Y); 112/394; Art Clb; Church Yth Grp; Drama Clb; Hosp Aide; Chorus; School Musical; School Play; Off Jr Cls; Cheerleading; Trk; Art.

MORNINGSTAR, BARBIE; Sayre Area HS; Sayre, PA; (Y); Pres SADD; Chorus; L Var Bsktbl; Sftbl; Trk; Var L Vllybl; Hon Roll; All-Star Tm Of Christmas Tourn 85-86; Sec.

MORO, NADINE; Hazleton HS; Beaver Mdws, PA; (Y); Church Yth Grp; Drama Clb; JV Bsktbl; Var Crs Cntry; PA Accrdn Tchrs Assn Piano Evltn Awd 84-85.

MOROCCO, MARY ANN; Penn-Trafford SR HS; Irwin, PA; (Y); 98/367; Church Yth Grp; Acpl Chr; Band; Chorus; Concert Band; Jazz Band; Mrchg Band; Pep Band; School Musical; Variety Show; Hnrs Choir 84-85; Dist I Chorus 85-86; Rgnl I St Chorus 8586; Berklee Schl Mus; Mus Prod.

MOROZIN, JOHN; Archbishop Ryan HS; Philadelphia, PA; (Y); 198/429; Varsity Clb; Var Ice Hcky; Hon Roll; Acadmc Achvt Awd Social Studies 83-84; History.

MORRAL, TIM; Wellswboro SR HS; Wellsboro, PA; (Y); Boy Scts; Church Yth Grp; German Clb; Band; Capt Bowling; Golf; High Hon Roll; Hon Roll; NHS; Dickinson; Law.

MORRALL, CHRISTOPHER; Cardinal O Hara HS; Rutledge, PA; (Y); 201/797; Church Yth Grp; Crs Cntry; Ftbl; Trk; Wt Lftg; Hon Roll; Prfct Atten Awd; Bus.

MORREALE, DAWN; Coughlin HS; Plains, PA; (Y); Ski Clb; SADD; VICA; Capt Var Vllybl; High Hon Roll; Mst Otstndng Stu Csmtlgy WBAVTS 86; Empire Beauty Schl; Tchr.

MORRELL, KRISTIN; North Hills HS; Pittsburgh, PA; (Y); Pres VP Keywanettes; Chorus; Sec Rep Sr Cls; Tennis; Trk; High Hon Roll; VA Tech; Mth Ed.

MORRELL, LEE; Wyoming Valley West HS; Kingston, PA; (Y); Computer Clb; Radio Clb; Ski Clb; Temple Yth Grp; Nwsp Phtg; Nwsp Rptr; Nwsp Stf; Yrbk Phtg; Yrbk Rptr; Yrbk Stf; Bn Brth Yth Orgnztn Shld Dvd Awd 86; Wilkes Coll; Engl.

MORRELL, MARC J; Pennridge HS; Sellersville, PA; (Y); 22/415; Church Yth Grp; SADD; VP Frsh Cls; Pres Soph Cls; Var L Bsbl; Var Capt Crs Cntry; Cit Awd; High Hon Roll; NHS; Prfct Atten Awd; PA Free Entpr Wk 84; Zimmerman Schlrshp 86; Penn ST U; Aerosp Engrng.

MORRET, TRACI; Mechanicsburg Area SR HS; Mechanicsburg, PA; (Y); 10/311; Nwsp Rptr; Var L Crs Cntry; Var Sftbl; Var L Swmmng; High Hon Roll; NHS.

MORRET, VICKI; Newport HS; Newport, PA; (Y); Service Clb; Sec Varsity Clb; Chorus; School Play; Variety Show; Yrbk Stf; JV Var Cheerleading; Fld Hcky; Gym; Vllybl; Secy.

MORRETT, JILL; Red Lion Area SR HS; Red Lion, PA; (Y); 12/327; Varsity Clb; School Play; Yrbk Stf; Stu Cncl; Var Mgr(s); Vllybl; High Hon Roll; Hon Roll; Lion Awd; NHS; Lebanon Vly Coll; Acturl Sci.

MORRIS, ALICIA; Millville Area HS; Millville, PA; (Y); Rep Drama Clb; Trs VP 4-H; Trs Band; Chorus; Concert Band; Jazz Band; Mrchg Band; School Musical; School Play; 4-H Awd; Eqstrn Mgmt.

MORRIS, CHARLES; Waynesburg Central HS; Mt Morris, PA; (Y); 18/200; Camera Clb; Church Yth Grp; Spanish Clb; Band; Concert Band; Jazz Band; Mrchg Band; Var Trk; Hon Roll; NHS; Penn ST; Engrg.

MORRIS, CHERYL; Scranton Central HS; Scranton, PA; (Y); Church Yth Grp; French Clb; Pep Clb; Ski Clb; Band; Chorus; Church Choir; Yrbk Stf; Twrlr; Hon Roll; Penn ST; Fshn Merch.

MORRIS, CHRIS; Kennedy Christian HS; Brookfield, OH; (Y); 52/98; Aud/Vis; French Clb; Library Aide; Hon Roll; Kent ST U; Engl Ed.

MORRIS, DANIEL; West Greene HS; Waynesburg, PA; (Y); Computer Clb; Drama Clb; VP Science Clb; Church Choir; School Musical; Nwsp Ed-Chief; Nwsp Rptr; Nwsp Stf; JV Bsktbl; Prfct Atten Awd; 1st Awds-Rgnl & ST Comptn-PA Jnr Acad Of Sci 85-86; Hnrb Mntn-Comp Grphcs Cntst 86; Waynesburg Coll; Pre-Med.

MORRIS III, HARRIS L; Penncrest HS; Media, PA; (Y); 55/329; Intnl Clb; Trs Ski Clb; SADD; Variety Show; Off Sr Cls; Var Gym; Var Socr; Var Trk; High Hon Roll; Hon Roll; Soccr All Leag, Cnty, MVP 85.

MORRIS, JENNIFER; Upper Merion Area HS; King Of Prussia, PA; (Y); 13/364; Hosp Aide; Math Tm; Nwsp Stf; Crs Cntry; Hon Roll; Bus.

MORRIS, JO ANNE R; Upper Dublin SR HS; Maple Glen, PA; (Y); Dance Clb; FTA; Teachers Aide; Nwsp Stf; Yrbk Stf; Stu Cncl; Cheerleading; Mat Maids; Pom Pon; Sftbl; Millersville; Elem Ed.

MORRIS, JOEL; Millville Area HS; Millville, PA; (Y); 7/80; Boy Scts; Chess Clb; Church Yth Grp; Math Tm; Trs Soph Cls; Trs Jr Cls; Var JV Socr; High Hon Roll; Hon Roll; NHS; Math.

MORRIS, JOHN K; Palisades HS; Coopersburg, PA; (Y); Art Clb; Computer Clb; Lit Mag; Ftbl; Var Capt Socr; Trk; Hon Roll; NHS; Acpt Bucks Cnty Schls Smmr Arts Acad 85; Cmmrcl Art Awd 86; PZ Math League Cntst Wnnr 86; CA Coll-Arts/Crfts; Film Anmtn.

MORRIS, KATHY; Martin Luther King HS; Philadelphia, PA; (Y); Drama Clb; OEA; Color Guard; Off Frsh Cls; Off Soph Cls; Sec Jr Cls; Sec Sr Cls; Hon Roll; Prfct Atten Awd; Outstndng Summr Yth Wrkr 83; Prm Qn 86; Outstndng Bus Stu Of Yr 86; Philadelphia Sch; Exec Sec.

MORRIS, MARK; Northwestern HS; Cranesville, PA; (Y); JV L Ftbl; Triangle Tech; Wldng.

MORRIS, ROBERT S; Troy HS; Troy, PA; (Y); 11/160; Am Leg Boys St; Church Yth Grp; Cmnty Wkr; Computer Clb; Letterman Clb; Service Clb; Ski Clb; Spanish Clb; Chorus; Church Choir; Penn ST U; Engrng.

MORRIS, RUSSELL A; Neshannock HS; New Castle, PA; (Y); 3/104; Church Yth Grp; Math Clb; Math Tm; Science Clb; Im Bsktbl; Var L Tennis; Im Vllybl; Bausch & Lomb Sci Awd; High Hon Roll; NHS; PA ST U; Engrng.

MORRIS, SHARON; Pittston Area SR HS; Pittston, PA; (Y); 32/356; Church Yth Grp; French Clb; Hosp Aide; Key Clb; Church Choir; Rep Stu Cncl; Var L Swmmng; High Hon Roll; Hon Roll; Pres NHS.

MORRIS, SONJA; Central Dauphin East HS; Harrisburg, PA; (Y); 42/271; Art Clb; Church Yth Grp; Girl Scts; Color Guard; Flag Corp; Hon Roll; NHS; SEC Math.

MORRIS, THOMAS; St John Neumann HS; Philadelphia, PA; (Y); 38/338; Library Aide; Science Clb; Hon Roll; Bio.

MORRIS, TODD; Exeter Township HS; Reading, PA; (Y); 24/207; Exploring; Varsity Clb; Bowling; Hon Roll; 4th Pl Berks Cnty HS Athlt Assc Bwlng Trnmnt 85; VP Explr Pst 85-86; Bus.

MORRISON, CHARLES; Leechburg Area HS; Vandergrift, PA; (Y); 10/71; De Vry Inst Tech; Elec Engr.

MORRISON, COLETTE; Warrne Area HS; Warren, PA; (Y); Church Yth Grp; French Clb; Cheerleading; Trk; Jr NHS.

MORRISON, DAVID; Hempfield HS; Landisville, PA; (Y); 2/440; Boy Scts; Math Tm; Quiz Bowl; Chorus; Concert Band; Jazz Band; Mgr Mrchg Band; Pep Band; School Musical; Stage Crew; Millersville U ISC Knwldg Cmptn 2nd Pl 85; IN U Of PA Physcs Tstng Cmptn For Stu 86; Math Exm 85-86; Engnrng.

MORRISON, HEATHER; Uniontown HS; Uniontown, PA; (Y); 61/359; Church Yth Grp; Debate Tm; French Clb; Letterman Clb; Spanish Clb; Speech Tm; Thesps; Band; Color Guard; Mrchg Band; U Of Pittsburgh; Pre-Med.

MORRISON, JERRY; Clearfield Area HS; Clearfield, PA; (S); 4/318; Pres Church Yth Grp; Debate Tm; Speech Tm; Pres Band; Chorus; Concert Band; Mrchg Band; Orch; School Musical; JV Bsktbl; Eastern Coll; Ecnmcs.

MORRISON, LYNNE; South Western HS; Hanover, PA; (Y); 42/205; Church Yth Grp; Key Clb; Band; Concert Band; Mrchg Band; Pep Band; Symp Band; Hon Roll; York Coll PA; Nrsng.

MORRISON, MELISSA A; Mt Pleasant SR HS; Mt Pleasant, PA; (Y); Art Clb; GAA; Intnl Clb; Latin Clb; Library Aide; Ski Clb; Church Choir; Church Choir; Mrchg Band; Hon Roll; Art Comp 1st Pl Humanities Days U Of Pittsburgh 86; Comp Sci.

MORRISSEY, JUDY; Cardinal Dougherty HS; Phila, PA; (Y); 119/758; Cmnty Wkr; German Clb; Rep Frsh Cls; Var Bsktbl; Capt Fld Hcky; L Var Sftbl; Cit Awd; Prfct Atten Awd; Athletic Schlrshp Fld Hcky 86; 1st Tm All Catholic & Tm MVP & Co-Capt 85-86; Saint Josephs U; Bus.

MORRISSEY, MAUREEN; Cedar Crest HS; Lebanon, PA; (Y); 10/341; Key Clb; Pep Clb; Pres Spanish Clb; Im Vllybl; Hon Roll; Lion Awd; NHS; Ntl Merit Ltr; Opt Clb Awd; Voice Dem Awd; U Of Pittsburgh Merit Schlrshp 86; U Of Pittsburgh; Cmmnctns.

MORROW, JEFF; Pennsbury HS; Yardley, PA; (Y); Spanish Clb; Im Bsktbl; Im Ftbl; Im Sftbl; Var Tennis; Im Vllybl; JV Wrstlng; Cit Awd; High Hon Roll; Hon Roll; Forgn Lang Clb 85-86; Outstndg Crftsmn Awd 83-85.

MORROW, JENNIFER A; Deer Lakes HS; Tarentum, PA; (Y); Teachers Aide; Chorus; School Play; Yrbk Stf; Hon Roll; Chorus Secty; Pennsylvania U; Elem Educ.

MORROW, JULIE; Upper Darby HS; Upper Darby, PA; (Y); Church Yth Grp; Church Choir; Sec Frsh Cls; Sec Soph Cls; JV Bsktbl; Var Lcrss; Var Tennis; Outstndng Stu Of Marking Prd 85-86; Psych.

MORROW, MEGAN; Freeport Area HS; Freeport, PA; (S); Concert Band; Jazz Band; Mrchg Band; Pep Band; Stage Crew; Symp Band; Trs Frsh Cls; Rep Jr Cls; High Hon Roll; PA ST U; Biotech.

MORROW, PHILIP; Montour HS; Pittsburgh, PA; (Y); Boy Scts; Ski Clb; Concert Band; Jazz Band; Pep Band; School Musical; Stu Cncl; High Hon Roll; FL Inst Of Tech; Marine Bio.

MORROW, SUSAN; Plum SR HS; Pitts, PA; (Y); 69/489; Cmnty Wkr; Dance Clb; Pres DECA; SADD; Varsity Clb; School Musical; VP Soph Cls; VP Jr Cls; VP Sr Cls; Capt Cheerleading; PA DECA Scholar 86; Prom Court 85; 1st Pl Dist & ST Lvl DECA 84-86; Natl DECA Fnlst 86; Robert Morris; Mktg Engr.

MORROW, TODD; West Perry SR HS; New Bloomfield, PA; (Y); 6/216; Pres Church Yth Grp; French Clb; Spanish Clb; Yrbk Stf; Trk; High Hon Roll; Hon Roll; NHS; RIT Allegheny; Medcl Tech.

MORSE, DIANNE; Hempfield HS; Landisville, PA; (Y); 16/400; Science Clb; Varsity Clb; Orch; JV Sftbl; Capt Var Swmmng; Hon Roll; NHS; Pres Schlr; Stu Mth 84; Columbia U; Lbrl Arts.

MORSE, KARIN; Northwestern HS; E Springfield, PA; (Y); 19/148; Sec VP Drama Clb; Thesps; Sec VP Chorus; VP Madrigals; JV Var Cheerleading; Sec Church Yth Grp; Church Choir; Mrchg Band; Pep Band; 1st Pl Fml Vclst NE Rgn 85; 4th Pl Fml Vclst Ntlnls 85; All Am Acadm Schlr Ntl Yth Ldrshp Awd 85; Oral Rbrts U; Voice.

MORSEY, MARLO; South Allegheny HS; Mc Keesport, PA; (S); 10/162; French Clb; Office Aide; Science Clb; SADD; Y-Teens; Off Jr Cls; Off Sr Cls; Powder Puff Ftbl; Stat Trk; Hon Roll; U Ptsbrg; Bus Adm.

MORT, MARK; United HS; Seward, PA; (Y); 16/157; Math Clb; Ski Clb; Trs Jr Cls; Trs Sr Cls; High Hon Roll; Hon Roll; Mu Alp Tht; NHS; Ntl Merit Schol; Church Choir; Pre-Med.

MORT, TAMMY; United HS; Armagh, PA; (Y); 57/157; Church Yth Grp; VP FNA; Girl Scts; Hosp Aide; Hon Roll; Awd Fr Vlntrng Mrcy Hosp & Memorial Hosp 84-85; Memorial School Of Nursing; RN.

MORTIMER, CYNTHIA; Ambridge Area HS; Freedom, PA; (Y); Trs French Clb; Off Frsh Cls; Off Soph Cls; Hon Roll; Drug/Alcohol Comm Beaver Co Drug/Alcohol Cncl 85-86; 1st Co, 5th Natl MADD Essay 84-85; Achvt Awd 86; U Pittsburgh; Nrsng.

MORTIMER III, LEO F; Ambridge Area HS; Freedom, PA; (Y); French Clb; Pep Clb; High Hon Roll; Hon Roll; Drg & Alchl Cmt 85-86; U Ptsbrgh; Chem Engr.

MORTIMER, SUSAN; Plymouth-Whitemarsh HS; Norristown, PA; (Y); Aud/Vis; Church Yth Grp; Rep Frsh Cls; Rep Soph Cls; Rep Jr Cls; Mat Maids; Twrlr; Hon Roll; Telecomm.

MORTON, DARREN; Grove City Area HS; Jackson Center, PA; (Y); 65/225; Band; Concert Band; Jazz Band; Mrchg Band; Pep Band; Slippery Rock Coll; Brdcstg.

MORTON, JAMES; Simon Gratz HS; Philadelphia, PA; (Y).

MORTON, MOLLY; Corry Area HS; Spartansburg, PA; (S); 4/204; Church Yth Grp; Band; Chorus; Drm Mjr(t); Jazz Band; Mrchg Band; Cheerleading; High Hon Roll; U Rochester NY; Genetics.

MOSACK, LYNN; Kiski Area HS; Apollo, PA; (Y); Pep Clb; Spanish Clb; Varsity Clb; Chorus; Nwsp Stf; Rep Frsh Cls; Rep Stu Cncl; Stat Bsbl; JV Var Cheerleading; High Hon Roll.

MOSBACHER, KEVIN; Meadville Area SR HS; Meadville, PA; (Y); Church Yth Grp; Spanish Clb; Varsity Clb; Var Bsktbl; Var Socr; Capt Vllybl; Hon Roll.

MOSENG, EDWIN; Phil-Mont Christian Acad; Hatboro, PA; (Y); 1/50; Church Yth Grp; Teachers Aide; Stat Bsbl; Score Keeper; High Hon Roll; NHS; Messiah Coll; Math Tchr.

MOSER, CHARLES; Highlands SR HS; Tarentum, PA; (Y); Church Yth Grp; Cmnty Wkr; Math Clb; ROTC; SADD; Nwsp Rptr; Rep Stu Cncl; Var L Bsktbl; Var Capt Tennis; High Hon Roll.

MOSER, SHEILA; Weatherly HS; Weatherly, PA; (S); #4 In Class; Am Leg Aux Girls St; FBLA; JA; Yrbk Stf; Bsktbl; Score Keeper; Sftbl; Hon Roll; Engl Cert 84-85.

MOSER, STEVE; Hamburg Area HS; Bernville, PA; (Y); Spanish Clb; Ftbl; Trk; Wrstlng; Hon Roll; All Cnty 1st Tm Ftbl, Schlstc Tm 85; Drftsmn.

MOSER, SUZANNE M; Archbishop Wood HS For Girls; Langhorne, PA; (Y); 2/259; Drama Clb; School Musical; Nwsp Ed-Chief; Nwsp Stf; High Hon Roll; NCTE Awd; NHS; Spanish NHS; Outstndng Achvmnt Schlrshp Temple U 86; Temple U; Theatre.

MOSES, TRACY; Pine Forge Acad; Baltimore, MD; (S); Teachers Aide; Church Choir; Nwsp Sprt Ed; Trs Sr Cls; Hon Roll; NHS; Kickbl Trnmnt Awd 83-84; Columbia Union Coll; Accntnt.

MOSESSO, LINDA; Carrick HS; Pittsburgh, PA; (S); 2/321; Church Yth Grp; Hosp Aide; Math Tm; Ski Clb; Yrbk Ed-Chief; Yrbk Stf; Frsh Cls; Capt Cheerleading; Stat Trk; Pres NHS; U Schlr-Full Schlrshp-Duquesne U; Duquesne U; Phrmcy.

MOSHOLDER, SHAWN; Rockwood Area HS; Rockwood, PA; (S); 19/95; VP Pres Church Yth Grp; Cmnty Wkr; Spanish Clb; Chorus; Variety Show; Var Trk; High Hon Roll; Hon Roll; Psych.

MOSIER, BARBARA; St Marys Area HS; Kersey, PA; (Y); Camera Clb; Church Yth Grp; Cmnty Wkr; Girl Scts; Hosp Aide; Hon Roll; NHS; GSA Gold Awd 85; Soc Wrkr.

MOSIER JR, FRANK A; Manheim Township HS; Lancaster, PA; (Y); 28/325; Political Wkr; Nwsp Bus Mgr; Nwsp Rptr; Rep Stu Cncl; Socr; Swmmng; High Hon Roll; Ntl Merit Ltr; Stu Ambsdr 85; Intrntl Rltns.

MOSIER, JOY DAWN; Belle Vernon Area HS; Belle Vernon, PA; (Y); Drama Clb; Sec NFL; SADD; School Play; Stage Crew; Nwsp Phtg; Nwsp Rptr; Nwsp Stf; Stat Bsktbl; Voice Dem Awd; PA Govs Schl For Arts ST Finlst Creat Wrtng 85-86; IN U Of PA Smmr Happening Creat Wrtng 85-86; Secondary Educ.

MOSIER, KATHY; North East HS; North East, PA; (Y); 5/149; Trs AFS; Trs Church Yth Grp; Q&S; Band; School Musical; Yrbk Stf; Swmmng; Hon Roll; NHS; NE Wmns Clb Art Cntst 1st 85; Hiram Coll.

MOSIER, LOUIS; St Marys Area HS; Kersey, PA; (Y); 59/290; Boy Scts; Church Yth Grp; Cmnty Wkr; Hon Roll; NHS; Boy Sct Eagle Awd 84; California U Of PA; Ind Arts.

MOSKYOK, DEBRA JEAN; Gateway SR HS; Monroeville, PA; (S); 173/508; Church Yth Grp; Exploring; NFL; VP PAVAS; Chorus; Nwsp Ed-Chief; Lit Mag; Hon Roll; Acting.

MOSLEY, SUE JUAN; Susqushanna SR HS; Harrisburg, PA; (Y); Church Yth Grp; Computer Clb; Drama Clb; Model UN; Red Cross Aide; Church Choir; Nwsp Rptr; Swmmng; Tennis; Trk; Vrsty Ltrs In Trk & Fld Hcky; PA ST U; Med Dr.

MOSLOCK, BRENDA; Danville Senior HS; Danville, PA; (Y); 2/202; Am Leg Aux Girls St; Exploring; Pres VP 4-H; Key Clb; Powder Puff Ftbl; JV Var Sftbl; High Hon Roll; NHS; Latin Clb; Red Cross Aide; PA Gov Schl Ag 86; Hugh O Brien Ldrshp Sem 85; Vet Med.

MOSORJAK, SUZANNE; Johnstown SR HS; Johnstown, PA; (Y); Chess Clb; German Clb; Girl Scts; Pep Clb; Ski Clb; Speech Tm; SADD; Color Guard; Hon Roll; Deaf Ed.

MOSS, BILL; West Middlesex Area HS; W Middlesex, PA; (S); 7/100; Bsbl; Ftbl; Wt Lftg; Hon Roll; Spanish NHS; West VA U.

MOSS, ELLEN; Bethel Park SR HS; Bethel Park, PA; (Y); Concert Band; Drill Tm; Mrchg Band; Orch; School Musical; Symp Band; High Hon Roll; NHS; Hghst Hnr Spnsh 83-84; Ed.

MOSS, JOHN; Central Catholic HS; Munhall, PA; (Y); Exploring; Swmmng; Hon Roll; NHS; 50 Yd Freestyl Swmmg Chmpn WPIAL 86; 4th-50 Yd Freestyl PA ST Chmpnshps 86.

MOSS, KENNETH; North Pocono HS; Moscow, PA; (Y); 29/245; Rep Am Leg Boys St; Rep Church Yth Grp; Computer Clb; VP FBLA; Ski Clb; Variety Show; Nwsp Stf; Vllybl; High Hon Roll; NHS; Med.

MOSS, LISA; William Penn HS; Philadelphia, PA; (Y); 17/236; Var Bsktbl; Var Capt Sftbl; Var Capt Vllybl; Hon Roll; US Air Frc; Mchncl Engr.

MOSS, MALINDA; Sharon HS; Sharon, PA; (Y); 36/190; Yrbk Stf; Capt Cheerleading; Pom Pon; Aud/Vis; Cmnty Wkr; Hosp Aide; Office Aide; Pep Clb; Service Clb; Spanish Clb.

MOSS, NATALEE; Nazareth Area SR HS; Nazareth, PA; (Y); 31/241; Camera Clb; Red Cross Aide; Ski Clb; Yrbk Phtg; Yrbk Rptr; Pres Soph Cls; Pres Jr Cls; Trs Stu Cncl; Var JV Cheerleading; Hon Roll; Art 1st Pl 84.

MOSS, PAM; West Scranton HS; Scranton, PA; (Y); 10/300; Pep Clb; Service Clb; Ski Clb; Spanish Clb; JV Cheerleading; Hon Roll; NHS; Penn ST; Acctng.

MOSS, RICHARD; West Catholic Boys HS; Phila, PA; (Y); Var L Bsbl; Cit Awd; Hon Roll; NHS; Miller High Lefe Youth Awd 85; Citizenship Awd Union Leag PA 86; Accntng.

MOSS, THOMAS; Bentworth HS; Eighty Four, PA; (Y); 14/103; Art Clb; High Hon Roll; Jr NHS; Pres NHS; Ntl Merit Ltr; Prfct Atten Awd; Vale Tech; Auto Tech.

MOSSEL, LISA; Unionville HS; Chadds Ford, PA; (Y); 34/300; Church Yth Grp; French Clb; Chorus; School Musical; Yrbk Stf; JV Vllybl; High Hon Roll; Jr NHS; NHS; Stu Adv Ldrshp Trng Hghtn Coll 86; Pltcl Sci.

MOSTELLER, LORI; Meyersdale Area HS; Garrett, PA; (Y); 5/135; French Clb; VP VICA; Chorus; Church Choir; Hon Roll; NHS.

MOSTOLLER, LORI; Meyersdale Area HS; Garrett, PA; (S); Church Yth Grp; French Clb; VP VICA; Chorus; Church Choir; Hon Roll.

MOTEN, ROBYN; Harrisburg HS; Harrisburg, PA; (S); 1/442; Intnl Clb; Trs Science Clb; Chorus; Stu Cncl; Hon Roll; Sec NHS; VFW Awd; Intl Frgn Lang Assoc Awd 83; Chmcl Engrng.

MOTISKO, CHRISTINE; John S Fine HS; Nanticoke, PA; (Y); 26/242; Church Yth Grp; Drama Clb; Speech Tm; VP Chorus; Yrbk Stf; Mgr(s); High Hon Roll; NHS; NEDT Awd; Prtl Acad Schlrshp Coll Misericordia 86; Coll Misericordia; Occuptnl Thr.

MOTTER, CATHY; Lock Haven SR HS; Lock Haven, PA; (Y); Church Yth Grp; Keywanettes; Spanish Clb; Band; Concert Band; Mrchg Band; Stu Cncl; Trk; Hon Roll; NHS; Pre-Med.

MOTTER, KAREN; Brookville Area HS; Clarington, PA; (Y); 75/141; GAA; Hosp Aide; Intnl Clb; Key Clb; Sec Trs Ski Clb; Varsity Clb; Trs Lit Mag; L Var Trk; Color Guard; Yrbk Rptr; Prsdntl Physcl Ftnss Awd 85-86; Indn Ink Awd Lit Arts Mag 85-86; Stff Achvmnt Awd 84-85; Scl Wrk.

MOTTO, ANNE-MARIE; Lourdes Regional HS; Excelsior, PA; (Y); 8/94; Pres Library Aide; Pep Clb; Sec PAVAS; Rep Spanish Clb; Thesps; School Play; Hon Roll; NHS; Spanish NHS; Polit Sci.

MOTUK, LONNIE; Minersville Area HS; Pottsville, PA; (Y); German Clb; Yrbk Stf; JV Var Bsktbl; Hon Roll; Prfct Atten Awd; Mechanics.

MOTYCKI, GARY; Charleroi Area JR SR HS; Charleroi, PA; (Y); Bsktbl; Law.

MOUL, BRIAN; Spring Grove HS; E Berlin, PA; (Y); 43/285; JA; Band; Concert Band; Drm Mjr(t); Jazz Band; Mrchg Band; Hon Roll; Rotary Awd; Mech Engr.

MOUL, ROBERT; Hanover SR HS; Hanover, PA; (Y); VICA; Im Ftbl; High Hon Roll; Hon Roll; Comp Prgrmg.

MOULD, DANIEL; Lackawauig Trail HS; Factoryville, PA; (Y); Church Yth Grp; Pres JA; Ski Clb; Band; Concert Band; Jazz Band; Madrigals; Mrchg Band; School Musical; Hon Roll; Prom Comm 85-86; Auto Tech.

MOUNT, KATIE; Lincoln HS; Ellwood City, PA; (Y); Drama Clb; Key Clb; Chorus; Concert Band; Jazz Band; Mrchg Band; School Musical; School Play; Gov Hon Prg Awd; Church Yth Grp; Acad Achvt Awd; Recog Awd Govnrs Schl Art; Drama.

MOUNTAIN, MARYJANE B; Baldwin SR HS; Pittsburgh, PA; (S); 370/535; DECA; JA; Rep Jr Cls; Rep Stu Cncl; Im Bsktbl; High Hon Roll; 3 Trophies In DECA In My Rookie Yr 86; Rep For Hs Clss 86; Hnr Roll 3.0 Avg 86; Temple; Ed.

MOUNTAN, DEBBIE; Everett Area HS; Everett, PA; (S); Church Yth Grp; Computer Clb; Hst French Clb; GAA; SADD; Band; Concert Band; Jazz Band; Mrchg Band; Pep Band; Bedford Cnty Bnd 86; US Air Force; Nrsng.

MOUNTS, RHONDA; New Castle SR HS; New Castle, PA; (Y); AFS; Pres Church Yth Grp; Spanish Clb; Teachers Aide; Chorus; Church Choir; Yrbk Stf; Rep Frsh Cls; Trk; Vllybl; Miss PA Yth Cmpr 86.

MOUNTZ, TAMMY; Conrad Weiser HS; Robesonia, PA; (Y); 1/149; Sec Key Clb; VP Band; Sec Lib Chorus; Ed Yrbk Stf; Sec Sr Cls; Capt Var Trk; Pres NHS; Val; Church Yth Grp; Debate Tm; Hugh O Brien Ldrshp Sem 84; Soc Women Engnrs Awd, Am Assoc U Women Awd, Outstndng Hist Awd 86; Penn ST U; Elem Educ.

MOURER, JAMI; West Hazleton HS; Onieda, PA; (Y); Art Clb; Church Yth Grp; 4-H; VICA; 4-H Awd; Art.

MOVINSKY, JAMES; Purchase Line HS; Barnesboro, PA; (Y); Church Yth Grp; VICA; Hon Roll; Williamsport Coll; Diesl Mech.

MOWAD JR, THOMAS; Aliquippa HS; Aliquippa, PA; (S); 8/135; Aud/Vis; Drama Clb; Trs French Clb; Band; L Bsbl; L Capt Ftbl; Wt Lftg; Jr NHS; Lion Awd; Gftd Prgrm Math.

MOWCHAN, ANNE MARIE; Seton-La Salle HS; Mc Murray, PA; (Y); 11/236; Math Tm; Ski Clb; Rep Frsh Cls; Sr Cls; Capt Socr; VP Trk; VP Vllybl; High Hon Roll; NHS; Rotary Awd; U Notre Dame.

MOWERY, DANNA; Freeport HS; Sarver, PA; (Y); FHA; Color Guard; Trk; Hon Roll; NHS; Art Inst Of Pittsburgh; Fashn.

MOWERY, DAVID C; Greensburg Central Catholic HS; Greensburg, PA; (Y); 8/243; Chess Clb; Debate Tm; JCL; NFL; Speech Tm; High Hon Roll; NHS; U Pittsburg; Pre-Med.

MOWERY, JIM; United HS; Robinson, PA; (Y); 7/157; Church Yth Grp; High Hon Roll; Hon Roll; NHS; Prfct Atten Awd; Archry Clb Sec 84-85; Guidnc Ofc Aide 85-86; Arch Engrng.

MOWERY, MARY L; Big Spring HS; Newville, PA; (Y); Dance Clb; Drama Clb; Office Aide; Pep Clb; Off Stu Cncl; Cheerleading; Powder Puff Ftbl; Sftbl; Wt Lftg; Hon Roll; Chrldng Schlrshp 84-85; Hagerstown Bus Coll; Paralegal.

MOWERY III, ROBERT H; United HS; Robinson, PA; (Y); 22/129; Boy Scts; Lit Mag; Var L Bsktbl; Var L Trk; Hon Roll; Hst NHS; Prfct Atten Awd; Pres Schlr; Voice Dem Awd; 2nd Pl Dist 6 & 9th Pl PIAA ST Trk 86; WA & Jefferson; Comp Sci.

MOWRER, KATHLEEN; Hanover SR HS; Hanover, PA; (Y); Chorus; Hon Roll; Prfct Atten Awd; Early Chldhd Educ.

MOWRER, MARY; Delone Catholic HS; Hanover, PA; (Y); 1/169; Sec Church Yth Grp; Hosp Aide; Model UN; Chorus; Concert Band; Mrchg Band; School Musical; NHS; Ntl Merit Ltr; Val; Drew U; Comp Sci.

MOWREY, DENNIS; Du Bois Area HS; Dubois, PA; (Y); 95/250; Church Yth Grp; Intnl Clb; Library Aide; Varsity Clb; Rep Stu Cncl; Im Tennis; Penn ST; Educ.

MOWREY, KELLY; Yough SR HS; Herminie, PA; (Y); 16/250; Ski Clb; Spanish Clb; Chorus; Drm Mjr(t); Yrbk Bus Mgr; Yrbk Ed-Chief; Cheerleading; Stat Trk; Twrlr; High Hon Roll; Elem Educ.

MOWRY, MICHELE; Chestnut Ridge SR HS; Schellsburg, PA; (S); 7/107; FBLA; Red Cross Aide; Teachers Aide; Chorus; School Musical; JV Cheerleading; Score Keeper; High Hon Roll; Hon Roll; NHS; Bedford Cty Fire Queen 85-86; Shawnee Vly Fire Queen 85-86; Jr Miss Contstnt 85; Ferrum Coll; Merchdsng.

MOWRY, WALLY; Hyndman Middle SR HS; Hyndman, PA; (Y); Pep Clb; Ski Clb; Varsity Clb; Ed Nwsp Stf; Rep Stu Cncl; Var L Bsbl; Golf; Var L Socr; JV Wrstlng; Hon Roll; AR ST; Prof Bsbl.

MOXIE, KARA; Highland SR HS; Natrona Hts, PA; (Y); 58/280; Hosp Aide; Intnl Clb; SADD; Varsity Clb; Yrbk Stf; Sec Frsh Cls; Pres Soph Cls; Pres Jr Cls; Rep Stu Cncl; JV Var Cheerleading; Suptndnt Advsry Comm 85; Handbk Comm 86; Med.

MOXLEY, STEPHANIE; Western Beaver HS; Midland, PA; (Y); Drama Clb; Stat Bsbl; Score Keeper; Var JV Sftbl; Hon Roll; NHS; Crmnl Psych.

MOY, PAM; Cardinal O Hara HS; Broomall, PA; (Y); 43/772; 4-H; Hosp Aide; Service Clb; Spanish Clb; Var Trk; Im Vllybl; NHS; Prfct Atten Awd.

MOYAR, GINA; Canon Mc Millan SR HS; Canonsburg, PA; (Y); 56/390; FHA; Hosp Aide; Library Aide; Band; Concert Band; Mrchg Band; Hon Roll; Bnd Librarn 85-86; Bnd Vp 86-87; Chatham; Pre-Med.

MOYE, MONIQUE; St Benedict Acad; Erie, PA; (Y); 12/80; Q&S; Nwsp Ed-Chief; Yrbk Stf; VP Soph Cls; Rep Stu Cncl; Var Capt Cheerleading; High Hon Roll; NHS; Church Yth Grp; Computer Clb; Acdmc All Amer 86; Yrbk Cpy Edtr 86-87; Crmnl Law.

MOYE, NICOLE; Aliquippa SR HS; Aliquippa, PA; (Y); Band; Concert Band; Drm Mjr(t); Mrchg Band; Pep Band; School Play; Capt Trk; Hon Roll; Trck 4 Troph & 13 Medls 85; Band Drm Majr 86-87; Millersville; Law.

MOYER, BETH; Berwick SR HS; Berwick, PA; (Y); 50/250; Church Yth Grp; Chorus; Color Guard; Mrchg Band; High Hon Roll; Hon Roll; Jr NHS; NHS; Ntl Merit Ltr; Prfct Atten Awd; Brwck Entrprs Hnr Carr Of The Mnth 83; JR Div Wnnr 83; Prss-Entrprs Carr Of The Yr 83; Nrsng.

MOYER, BOB; Lincoln HS; Ellwood City, PA; (Y); Church Yth Grp; Computer Clb; Band; Mrchg Band; Stage Crew; Nwsp Rptr; Nwsp Stf; Hon Roll; Enrchmnt Pgm 80-86; Clarion U; Cmnctns.

MOYER, BRUCE; Liberty HS; Bethlehem, PA; (Y); 13/450; Computer Clb; Math Tm; Model UN; Scholastic Bowl; Band; Concert Band; Mrchg Band; Orch; Bowling; JV Golf; Vrsty Rfl Tm 85-86; Brnz Medl Lou Erb Invtnl Bwlg Tourn 85-86; MIT; Physcst.

MOYER, CHRISTOPHER A; Elkland Area HS; Osceola, PA; (Y); 22/74; Drama Clb; French Clb; Varsity Clb; School Musical; Yrbk Stf; Rep Jr Cls; Rep Stu Cncl; Var L Socr; Var L Tennis; Hon Roll; Chem Sci.

MOYER, COLLEEN DIANE; Shikellamy HS; Northumberland, PA; (Y); 20/300; German Clb; Sec Key Clb; Nwsp Rptr; Ed Lit Mag; Sec Frsh Cls; Stu Cncl; JV Var Cheerleading; Wt Lftg; Cit Awd; Hon Roll; Hmcmng Rep 83; PA Gvrnrs Schl For Arts 85-86; Beaver Coll; Med Ilstrtn.

MOYER, DANIEL; Central HS; Duncansville, PA; (Y); 15/175; Yrbk Stf; Rep Stu Cncl; NHS; PA ST U.

MOYER, DANIELLE; Exeter Townshiop SR HS; Reading, PA; (Y); 13/215; Church Yth Grp; Drama Clb; German Clb; Hosp Aide; Leo Clb; Y-Teens; Band; Orch; School Musical; NHS; Gldn Egl Hgh Hons 85 & 86.

MOYER, DEBORAH E; Daniel Boone HS; Douglassville, PA; (Y); 12/148; Church Yth Grp; German Clb; Varsity Clb; Concert Band; Mrchg Band; Ed Yrbk Stf; Bsktbl; Crs Cntry; Trk; NHS; Optmst Club, DB Sprts Boosters Schlrshps; Prsdentl Acad Ftnss Awd 86; U Scranton; Phy Thrpy.

MOYER, ERIC; Altoona Area HS; Altoona, PA; (Y); German Clb; Ski Clb; Band; Concert Band; Mrchg Band; Var Crs Cntry; Var Trk; Prfct Atten Awd; Penn ST; Engrng.

MOYER, HOLLY; Emmaus HS; Emmaus, PA; (Y); Church Yth Grp; Girl Scts; Hosp Aide; Latin Clb; Spanish Clb; Chorus; Flag Corp; Stu Cncl; Hon Roll; Jr NHS; SCLGY.

MOYER, JACLYN L; Ephrata HS; Ephrata, PA; (Y); Church Yth Grp; Exploring; JA; Service Clb; Off Jr Cls; Var Capt Cheerleading; Powder Puff Ftbl; Swmmng; Tennis; Hon Roll; YMCA Swmmng Ntls FL 85; Coaches Awd Grls Swm Tm 85; Brdcstng.

MOYER, JENNIFER; Cardinal O Hara HS; Drexel Hill, PA; (Y); Church Yth Grp; Cmnty Wkr; Mgr(s); Psych.

MOYER, JILL; Mount Penn HS; Reading, PA; (Y); Chess Clb; Drama Clb; Pres Exploring; German Clb; GAA; Quiz Bowl; Science Clb; High Hon Roll; Jr NHS; NHS; Albright Coll; Biol.

MOYER, JILL; Northern SR HS; Dillsburg, PA; (Y); 66/200; Drama Clb; VP Speech Tm; Chorus; School Musical; ST Compttv Drama 4th Pl 83-84; Mst Outstndg Forensic Prtcpnt Of Clss 86; Clarion U; Educ.

MOYER, KAREN; Spring-Ford SR HS; Royersford, PA; (S); 15/258; French Clb; Radio Clb; Band; Chorus; Jazz Band; Mrchg Band; Nwsp Ed-Chief; Yrbk Stf; NHS.

MOYER, MATT; Bishop Mc Cort HS; Johnstown, PA; (Y); Church Yth Grp; Cmnty Wkr; Computer Clb; Off Sr Cls.

MOYER, MELISSA; Kutztown Area HS; Lenhartsville, PA; (Y); Pres Church Yth Grp; Teachers Aide; Band; Chorus; Church Choir; Swing Chorus; Variety Show; High Hon Roll; Hon Roll; NHS; Hm Ec Awd 86; Rnnr Up Time Mag Essay Cntst 86; Kutztown U; Elem Ed.

MOYER, MELISSA; Wilson Area HS; Easton, PA; (S); 16/149; Drama Clb; Band; Chorus; Concert Band; Mrchg Band; Var JV Bsktbl; Juniata College.

MOYER, MIKE; William Allen HS; Allentown, PA; (Y); Spanish Clb; Mechanical Engineering.

MOYER, REBECCA; Pocono Mt HS; Tannersville, PA; (Y); 46/280; Rep Jr Cls; Var L Fld Hcky; Var Capt Sftbl; Hon Roll; Elem Educ.

MOYER, RHONDA; Derry Area SR HS; Loyalhanna, PA; (Y); 7/260; AFS; Math Clb; Yrbk Ed-Chief; Yrbk Stf; Im Vllybl; High Hon Roll; Hon Roll; NHS; Penn ST Renaissance Schlrshp 86; Natl Sci Olympd Awd 84 & 86; PA ST U; Premed.

MOYER, SEAN; West Perry SR HS; Landisburg, PA; (Y); Varsity Clb; Nwsp Stf; Yrbk Stf; Bsbl; Bsktbl; Socr; Law.

MOYER, SHANNON; E L Meyers HS; Wilkes Barre, PA; (Y); Art Clb; FBLA; Chorus; Hon Roll; Cert Typing Ii 86; Cert Shrthnd I 86; LCCC; Med Secy.

MOYER, SHARON; Hazleton HS; Hazleton, PA; (Y); Office Aide; Pep Clb; Chorus; Yrbk Stf; Capt Cheerleading; Hon Roll; Bloomsburg; Sec.

MOYER, STEVEN; Valley Forge Military Acad; Denver, PA; (Y); German Clb; ROTC; Band; JV Swmmng; High Hon Roll; Hon Roll; NHS; Jazz Band; Mrchg Band; VWF, ROTC Medal, Am Chem Soc Awd, PA All St Band 86; Physic.

MOYER, THOMAS A; William Allen HS; Allentown, PA; (Y); JCL; Latin Clb; Chorus; Yrbk Stf; Lit Mag; Hon Roll; Ntl Merit Ltr; Church Choir; School Play; Comenius Scholar 86; Summa Cum Laude Cert Natl Latin Exam 86; IN U PA Physcs Tstng Comptn Wnnr 85; Moravian Coll; Med Tech.

MOYER, TINA; Hughesville HS; Muncy, PA; (Y); Church Yth Grp; Hosp Aide; Library Aide; SADD; Church Choir; Swmmng; Tennis; Vllybl; Cit Awd; Prfct Atten Awd; Nrsng.

MOYER, TRACEY; Sch Haven HS; Auburn, PA; (S); 31/85; Girl Scts; Spanish Clb; Teachers Aide; Church Choir; Off Soph Cls; Stu Cncl; Lang Arts Awd 85; MT ST U; Lab Tech.

MOYER, VALERIE; Berwick Area SR HS; Wapwallopen, PA; (Y); 13/218; FBLA; Spanish Clb; Chorus; Stu Cncl; High Hon Roll; Jr NHS; Voice Dem Awd; Fnlst In Luzerne Cnty Jr Miss 86; 1st Pl In Pblc Spkng In FBLA Comp 85; 1st Pl Cncr Scty Tlnt Shw 85; Scranton U; Med Doctor.

MOZDY, PATRICIA; Meadville Area SR HS; Meadville, PA; (Y); Church Yth Grp; Dance Clb; French Clb; Varsity Clb; Rep Stu Cncl; Var Capt Socr; High Hon Roll; NHS; Pres Schlr; Trk; Yth Ftns Achvt Awd 3 Yrs 83-84; Egan Schlrshp Mrcyhrst Coll 86-87; Mercyhurst Coll; Bio.

MOZEKO, GARY; Bethlehem Catholic HS; Bethlehem, PA; (Y); 100/230; Church Yth Grp; Band; Concert Band; Jazz Band; Mrchg Band; Phila Schl Of Phrmcy; Phrmcy.

MOZELEWSKI, LORI; Highland HS; Natrona, PA; (Y); Art Clb; Church Yth Grp; SADD; Visual Arts.

MOZES, RAYMOND P; Commodore Perry HS; Greenville, PA; (S); 4/61; Pres 4-H; Math Tm; Stu Cncl; Wrstlng; NHS; PA ST; Engrng.

MOZINA, SAMANTHA; Cambria Heights HS; Patton, PA; (Y); 2/200; ROTC; Speech Tm; Concert Band; Mrchg Band; Ed Yrbk Stf; Var L Cheerleading; Mat Maids; L Trk; Twrlr; Hon Roll; Cnty Band 83-84; 6th Pl Fin Dist Frnsc Comptn 83-84; SF Cambria-Somerset JR Miss Pag 85-86; Sci.

MOZZOCCIO, CATHYRN; New Castle HS; West Pittsburg, PA; (S); 5/253; French Clb; Ski Clb; Var Cheerleading; Sftbl; High Hon Roll; NHS; Guidnc Rep 84-85; Phrmcy.

MOZZOCIO, CATHY; New Castle SR HS; W Pittsburgh, PA; (Y); 5/253; French Clb; Rep Stu Cncl; Cheerleading; High Hon Roll; NHS; Ntl Merit Ltr; Phrmcy.

MRAZ, JOSEPH M; Exeter Township SR HS; Reading, PA; (Y); Am Leg Boys St; Key Clb; Pres Varsity Clb; Orch; JV Capt Bsktbl; Golf; Tennis; Hon Roll; Jr NHS; Trs NHS; U Of DE; Bus Admin.

MRAZ, KIM; New Castle SR HS; New Castle, PA; (S); 20/253; Church Yth Grp; Office Aide; Im Vllybl; Cit Awd; Hon Roll; Slippery Rock U; Elem Ed.

MRAZ, MIKE; Ford City HS; Ford City, PA; (Y); 33/160; SADD; Rep Soph Cls; Rep Stu Cncl; Var L Ftbl; Hon Roll; NHS; Indiana U PA; Bnkng.

MRAZIK, SALLY; Swissvale HS; Swissvale, PA; (Y); 16/182; Computer Clb; German Clb; Ski Clb; Varsity Clb; Stage Crew; Off Stu Cncl; Capt Var Bsktbl; Var Capt Sftbl; High Hon Roll; NHS; Stu Ath Awd US Army 86; IN U PA; Mgmt Info Systms.

MROCZKA, MATT; Carbondale Area JR SR HS; Carbondale, PA; (S); 25/140; Drama Clb; FBLA; Pres Spanish Clb; Chorus; School Musical; School Play; Yrbk Stf; High Hon Roll; Hon Roll; NHS; Itln Clb Pres 85-86; Art Awd 82-83; Tlnt Show 1st Pl 84-86; PA ST; Acting.

MROSKO, DENISE; Laurel Highlands SR HS; Uniontown, PA; (Y); 106/336; FBLA; Chorus; Concert Band; Drm Mjr(t); Mrchg Band; Nwsp Stf; Rep Soph Cls; Sec Jr Cls; Hon Roll; NHS; Frnch Intrprtr.

MROZ, JOY; Bishop Hannan HS; Scranton, PA; (Y); Latin Clb; Spanish Clb; Chorus; School Play; Rep Stu Cncl; Capt Bowling; High Hon Roll; Hon Roll; NHS; Amer Athl Awd 84; Amer Achvt Awd 84; Schl Awds; U Of Scranton; Med Tech.

MROZEK, CONNIE; Portage Area HS; Portage, PA; (Y); French Clb; Sec Band; Chorus; Concert Band; Mrchg Band; Pep Band; Variety Show; Sec Jr Cls; Trk; Hon Roll; Med Rcptnst.

MROZEK, ERIC; New Castle HS; New Castle, PA; (S); 7/256; Church Yth Grp; Band; Concert Band; Mrchg Band; High Hon Roll.

MRUK, DAVID; Plum SR HS; Pittsburgh, PA; (Y); 43/378; Church Yth Grp; FTA; Library Aide; Band; Chorus; Jazz Band; Mrchg Band; School Musical; Hon Roll; Rifle Tm 85-86; Grove City Coll; Comp Sci.

MRVOS, MARC; Mc Keesport SR HS; Mckeesport, PA; (Y); 90/340; Boys Clb Am; Church Yth Grp; Teachers Aide; School Musical; Stage Crew; Rep Frsh Cls; Rep Soph Cls; Rep Stu Cncl; Bsbl; Ftbl; SPCH Comm.

MUADDI, EVELYN A; Ridley SR HS; Holmes, PA; (Y); 82/427; Office Aide; Drill Tm; Mrchg Band; Capt Twrlr; FBLA; Library Aide; Spanish Clb; Mgr(s); Score Keeper; High Hon Roll; Trvl Agnt.

MUCCIOLO, NATALIE; Old Forge HS; Old Forge, PA; (S); Drill Tm; Yrbk Bus Mgr; Pres Jr Cls; Pres Sr Cls; Capt Sftbl; High Hon Roll; Hon Roll; NHS; U Of Pittsburgh; Math.

MUCHA, STANLEY; Central Bucks HS East; Doylestown, PA; (Y); Aud/Vis; Computer Clb; Chorus; High Hon Roll; Hon Roll; Jr NHS; Vet Med.

MUCHA, STEPHEN; Cathedral Prep HS; Erie, PA; (Y); Spanish Clb; PA ST.

MUCHICKA, LORI; Bethel Park HS; Bethel Park, PA; (Y); Church Yth Grp; French Clb; Drill Tm; Mrchg Band; School Musical; Swing Chorus; Variety Show; Stu Cncl; Pom Pon; High Hon Roll.

MUCKEL, KAREN; Williamsport Area HS; Cogan Station, PA; (Y); 40/458; Trs Church Yth Grp; Office Aide; Band; Church Choir; Mrchg Band; Rep Soph Cls; Trk; Hon Roll; NHS; Ntl Merit SF; Natl Merit Fnlst 86; Nyack Coll; Psych.

MUDD, MICHELE; Downingtown SR HS; Exton, PA; (S); 33/527; Church Yth Grp; French Clb; Hosp Aide; Trs Intnl Clb; Ski Clb; Chorus; School Musical; Yrbk Stf; Off Stu Cncl; High Hon Roll; Intl Bus.

MUDLOCK, LYNN; Pittston Area HS; Inkerman, PA; (Y); 16/365; Church Yth Grp; Hosp Aide; Sftbl; High Hon Roll; Hon Roll; Jr NHS; NHS.

MUDRICK, STACEY; West Allegheny HS; Coraopolis, PA; (Y); 93/205; Sec JA; Office Aide; Spanish Clb; Chorus; Rep Stu Cncl; Var Capt Cheerleading; High Hon Roll; Chrldng Ltr 85; Clarissa Schl Fash; Fash Desgnr.

MUDRICK, SUSAN; Villa Joseph Marie HS; Fairless Hills, PA; (S); 5/52; Church Yth Grp; Cmnty Wkr; Math Clb; Pres Science Clb; Chorus; School Musical; Yrbk Stf; Lit Mag; Rep Frsh Cls; Rep Soph Cls; Ambsdr Hugh O Brien Ldrshp Sem 84.

MUELLER, DAVID; Penn Hills SR HS; Pittsburgh, PA; (Y); Church Yth Grp; German Clb; JA; Ski Clb; Church Choir; Variety Show; Trs Sr Cls; Rep Stu Cncl; Hon Roll; JR Achvt Sales Awd 84-85; Wstrn PA Race Clb Ski Rcng; US Ski Assn Ski Cmptn 84; Eckerd Clg; Bus.

MUELLER, LISA; North Hills HS; Pittsburgh, PA; (Y); 66/525; Cmnty Wkr; Drama Clb; Library Aide; Teachers Aide; Thesps; Chorus; School Play; Stage Crew; Lit Mag; High Hon Roll; Gldn Poet Awd 85; Slvr Poet Awd 86; Drama.

MUFF, JENNIFER; Upper Darby HS; Upr Darby, PA; (Y); 66/689; Church Yth Grp; Cmnty Wkr; JV Fld Hcky; Hon Roll; Toxicology.

MUGFORD, LORI; Pittston Area HS; Pittston, PA; (Y); Drama Clb; JA; Key Clb; Science Clb; Ski Clb; Spanish Clb; Mgr(s); Score Keeper; Trk; High Hon Roll; Chld Care.

MUHA, TERESA; West Mifflin Area HS; W Mifflin, PA; (Y); 7/360; Key Clb; Office Aide; Chorus; Mgr Color Guard; Ed Yrbk Stf; Off Frsh Cls; Off Soph Cls; Off Jr Cls; Var L Trk; Jr NHS; Engr.

MUHLENKAMP, LISA M; North Allegheny HS; Bradfordwoods, PA; (Y); 88/605; Mrchg Band; Yrbk Phtg; Sec Sr Cls; Vllybl; Hon Roll; Ntl Merit Ltr; Emory U.

MUIR, NANCY; Connellsville Area HS; S Connellsville, PA; (Y); AFS; Church Yth Grp; Girl Scts; Ski Clb; SADD; Chorus; Church Choir; Stage Crew; Mgr(s); Vllybl; Int Design.

MUIR, RITA; United JR SR HS; Blairsville, PA; (Y); 69/157; Pep Clb; Ski Clb; Chorus; JV Bsktbl; Powder Puff Ftbl; Var L Sftbl; Hon Roll.

MULAC, MICHELE; Connellsville SR HS; Connellville, PA; (Y); 50/485; Library Aide; Chorus; Sec Stu Cncl; Mat Maids; Score Keeper; High Hon Roll; Hon Roll; NHS; Hgh GPA Awd 86; Uniontown Hosp Schl; Nrsg.

MULCAHY, CHRISTINE; Wyoming Valley West HS; Forty Fort, PA; (Y); 6/385; Orch; School Musical; Rep Soph Cls; High Hon Roll; Hon Roll; NHS; NEDT Awd; Pres Schlr; 3rd Hghst Acdmc Avg 84; Charles N Mary Memrgl Awd 86; Regnl Orch 85; Kings Coll.

MULCAHY, CYNTHIA; G A R Memorial HS; Wilkes Barre, PA; (S); 15/177; Chorus; Orch; Nwsp Stf; Trs Sr Cls; High Hon Roll; Jr NHS; NHS; Hon Roll; Dist Orch 82-85; Regnl Orch 84-86; Mech Engr.

MULHAIR, KEVIN; Bethel Park SR HS; Bethel Park, PA; (Y); 30/512; Cmnty Wkr; JA; Latin Clb; Varsity Clb; Var L Ftbl; Wt Lftg; JV Wrstlng; High Hon Roll; JETS Awd; NHS.

MULHOLLAN, BRIAN; Dubois Area HS; Reynoldsville, PA; (Y); Boy Scts; Im Bowling; Im Socr; Hon Roll; Accntng.

MULHOLLAND, JOSEPH; Holy Ghost Prep; Philadelphia, PA; (S); Latin Clb; Science Clb; Teachers Aide; Concert Band; High Hon Roll; NHS; Wnnr Social Studies Awd; Pre Med.

MULHOLLAND, KATHLEEN; Waynesburg Central HS; Waynesburg, PA; (Y); Church Yth Grp; Cmnty Wkr; Dance Clb; Exploring; Spanish Clb; Chorus; JV Capt Vllybl; Hon Roll; Office Aide; Band; NEDT Hgh Scoring Top 10 84; Mth Tchr.

MULHOLLAND, MARTIN; Scranton Prep; Clarks Green, PA; (Y); Drama Clb; School Play; Ftbl; Var Swmmng; U Of Scranton; Law.

MULITS, LINDA; Allentown Central Catholic HS; Whitehall, PA; (Y); 90/217; VP Church Yth Grp; FBLA; German Clb; Pep Clb; Lib Chorus; Flag Corp; L Twrlr; Hon Roll; Acctg.

MULL, HEATHER; Somerset SR HS; Somerset, PA; (Y); 37/239; English Clb; Varsity Clb; Concert Band; Jazz Band; Mrchg Band; Var L Socr; Var L Trk; Im Wt Lftg; High Hon Roll; NHS; Grphc Arts.

MULLANEY, MATT; Seton-La Salle HS; Pittsburgh, PA; (Y); 30/256; Church Yth Grp; Math Clb; High Hon Roll; NHS; SAR Awd; Spn Achvt 85; Poetry & Compstn Achvt 84; U Pittsburgh; Chem.

MULLEN, ANNE; Bishop O Hara HS; Jessup, PA; (S); 4/114; Spanish Clb; Chorus; Nwsp Stf; Yrbk Ed-Chief; Rep Stu Cncl; High Hon Roll; NHS; Art Awds 84 & 85; Elem Deaf Tchr.

MULLEN, DEIRDRE; Wellsboro Area HS; Wellsboro, PA; (Y); Art Clb; Trs Drama Clb; VP English Clb; Library Aide; Chorus; School Musical; Yrbk Stf; Trk; Hon Roll; Fnlst Gvrns Schl Of Arts Crtv Wrtng 86; Antthrplgy.

MULLEN, GLENN; Susquenita HS; New Bloomfield, PA; (Y); 28/175; Quiz Bowl; Var Bsbl; Var Bsktbl; Var Capt Ftbl; Hon Roll; Mid-St Offnsv Plyr Of Wk 85; All Conf QB 85; Top 100 Plyrs Mid-St Area 85-86; Bus Adm.

MULLEN, JODIE; Rocky Grove HS; Franklin, PA; (Y); Pres 4-H; Office Aide; Chorus; L JV Bsktbl; L JV Vllybl; 4-H Awd; High Hon Roll; Hon Roll; Acad Exc Awd 84-85; Bwlng Dist 1 SR Grl Hgh Game 85-86; Phys Ther.

MULLEN, JULIE; Le Banon SR HS; Lebnaon, PA; (S); Trs DECA; JA; SADD; Teachers Aide; DECA Dist Career Conf 1st Pl Gen Merch 86; Comptncy Awd Wrttn & Oral Gen Merch 86.

MULLEN, KELLY; Valley View HS; Eynon, PA; (Y); French Clb; Drill Tm; Vllybl; French Hon Soc; Hon Roll; Educ.

MULLEN, KELLY; West Scranton HS; Scranton, PA; (Y); Pres FNA; Latin Clb; Letterman Clb; Red Cross Aide; Nwsp Stf; Yrbk Stf; Stu Cncl; Cheerleading; Hon Roll; NHS; U Of Scranton; Comp Engr.

MULLEN, MARY; Bishop Hannon HS; Scranton, PA; (Y); High Hon Roll; Hon Roll; NHS; Hnr Crd At Grad 86.

MULLER, DANA L; Abington HS; Abington, PA; (Y); 29/528; Church Yth Grp; Cmnty Wkr; Key Clb; Spanish Clb; High Hon Roll; Hon Roll; Ntl Merit SF; PA Hghr Ed Asstnc Agncy Cert Of Merit 85; WA U St Louis; Psycholgy.

MULLER, KIRK; Council Rock HS; Churchville, PA; (Y); 389/850; Aud/Vis; Boy Scts; Camera Clb; Church Yth Grp; Cmnty Wkr; Radio Clb; Stage Crew; Nwsp Phtg; Yrbk Phtg; Yrbk Sprt Ed; TV Prog 85-86; Sports Video 85-86; Audio Engr 83-86; Temple U; TV Prod.

MULLER, MICHELLE; Saint Basil Acad; Philadelphia, PA; (Y); Spanish Clb; Yrbk Bus Mgr; Yrbk Phtg; Yrbk Rptr; Yrbk Stf; Bsktbl; Socr; Sftbl; Vllybl; Hon Roll; Temple U; Phrmcy.

MULLICAN, MICHAEL; Wyalusing Valley HS; Wyalusing, PA; (Y); Pres Church Yth Grp; Computer Clb; Spanish Clb; Band; Concert Band; Mrchg Band; Bsktbl; Ftbl; Mgr(s); Trk; Computers.

MULLIG, ROBERT; Canon-Mc Millan SR HS; Canonsburg, PA; (Y); 52/357; Church Yth Grp; Spanish Clb; Varsity Clb; Swmmng; High Hon Roll; Hon Roll; Spanish NHS; Duquesne U Grant 86; Duquesne U; Phrmcy.

MULLIGAN, SARAH; Wyomissing Area HS; Wyomissing, PA; (S); 3/125; Church Yth Grp; Drama Clb; Exploring; Trs Sec French Clb; Girl Scts; Intnl Clb; Latin Clb; Sec Trs Library Aide; Model UN; Quiz Bowl.

MULLINS, DENISE; Williamsburg HS; Williamsburg, PA; (Y); 11/63; Sec Trs Church Yth Grp; DECA; FTA; Teachers Aide; Pres Chorus; Yrbk Stf; Sec Stu Cncl; Vllybl; Hon Roll; NHS; David Gutshall Mem Hnr Ctznshp Awd 86; Prft Attend Awd Grds 7-12 86; Hnr Awd Schlr Awd 86; PA ST U; Elem Educ.

MULLINS, SHELLY; Curwensville Area HS; Curwensville, PA; (Y); Sec FBLA; Teachers Aide; Pres Band; Chorus; Concert Band; Mrchg Band; Stage Crew; Trs Stu Cncl; Twrlr; Stat Wrstlng; Sectrl.

MULLISKY, JOHN; Sacred Heart HS; Carbondale, PA; (Y); Art Clb; French Clb; FBLA; Ski Clb; High Hon Roll; Hon Roll; Engr.

MULRANEY, DEANNA; Northern Cambria HS; Spangler, PA; (Y); Camera Clb; French Clb; Chorus; Mgr Mrchg Band; Mgr(s); Var L Trk; Var Vllybl; High Hon Roll; Hon Roll; Frnch Lang.

MULRONEY, KELLY; Mount St Joseph Acad; Meadowbrook, PA; (Y); Pres French Clb; JV Var Bsktbl; Var L Socr; French Hon Soc; High Hon Roll; NHS; Ntl Merit Schol; Church Yth Grp; Cmnty Wkr; JCL; Hoby Outstndng 84; Army Res Ntl Schlr Athlete 86; Latin Hnr Soc 84-85; U PA; Political Sci.

MULROY, JEAN; St Pius X HS; Collegeville, PA; (Y); 52/139; Cmnty Wkr; Pep Clb; Church Choir; School Musical; Rep Soph Cls; Rep Jr Cls; Rep Sr Cls; Stu Cncl; Cheerleading; Crs Cntry.

MULVANEY, TIM; Hampton HS; Allison Pk, PA; (Y); 4/255; Boy Scts; Capt Bsbl; Capt Socr; Wrstlng; High Hon Roll; NHS; Ntl Merit Ltr; NEDT Awd.

MULVIN, JENNIFER; Harbor Creek HS; Erie, PA; (Y); 12/219; VP Church Yth Grp; Model UN; Yrbk Bus Mgr; Var Bsktbl; Capt L Crs Cntry; L Trk; Hon Roll; NHS; Rotary Awd; Cmnty Wkr; Yth Triennium Spnsr Prsbtrn Chrch USA 86; Ed.

MUMAW, KIMBERLY; Council Rock HS; Newtown, PA; (Y); Church Yth Grp; Pres Trs Girl Scts; Band; Concert Band; Mrchg Band; Symp Band; Girl Scout Silver Awd 84; Bus.

MUMBY, TRACY; Carlisle HS; Carlisle, PA; (Y); 9/485; Am Leg Aux Girls St; FCA; Hst Keywanettes; Pres Jr Cls; Stu Cncl; L Bsktbl; L Golf; Im Trk; Cit Awd; NHS; Lng Bch ST; Physcl Thrpy.

MUMFORD, MARSHA; Cameron County HS; Emporium, PA; (Y); 7/91; Band; Chorus; Color Guard; Concert Band; Mrchg Band; Cheerleading; Trk; Twrlr; Hon Roll; NHS; JR & SR IU 9 Band 84-85; Dist Orchestra 85; Rdlgc Tech.

MUMMA, JOYCE; Waynesboro Area HS; Waynesboro, PA; (Y); 71/365; Girl Scts; Ski Clb; Band; Chorus; Concert Band; Mrchg Band; Bsktbl; Fld Hcky; Trk; High Hon Roll; IN U Bloomington; Bus Law.

MUMMA, KAREN; State College Area HS; State College, PA; (Y); Church Yth Grp; Hosp Aide; Band; Mrchg Band; Symp Band; Nwsp Ed-Chief; Nwsp Stf; Yrbk Sprt Ed; Yrbk Stf; High Hon Roll; Penn ST U.

MUMMA, RENEE; Manheim Central HS; Manheim, PA; (Y); 12/241; Yrbk Stf; Powder Puff Ftbl; JV Var Sftbl; High Hon Roll; NHS; Engl Awd 84; 3rd Rotary Wrtng Cmptn 86; Bi-Lingual Awd Spanish & German 86; Millersville U; Scndry Engl Edu.

MUMMERT, MARK; Unionville HS; Chadds Ford, PA; (Y); 116/300; Art Clb; Crs Cntry; Ftbl; Wrstlng; Hon Roll; Jr NHS; Lion Awd; Frstry.

MUNDELL, MICHAEL; Carmichaels Area HS; Rices Landing, PA; (Y); 25/103; Spanish Clb; Bsbl; Bowling; Ftbl; High Hon Roll; NHS.

MUNDIS, DAVID; Christian School Of York; York, PA; (Y); 39/59; Church Yth Grp; Office Aide; Chorus; Church Choir; School Play; Nwsp Phtg; Nwsp Stf; Hon Roll; Yorktown Bus Inst; Bus.

MUNDKOWSKY, BRENDA; Northwestern SR HS; W Springfield, PA; (Y); Sec Drama Clb; French Clb; School Musical; School Play; Stage Crew; Swing Chorus; Rep Jr Cls; JV Bsktbl; JV Var Sftbl; Var Vllybl; Behrend Coll; Socl Sci.

MUNDY, PAUL; Scranton Technical HS; Scranton, PA; (Y); 4/225; Ski Clb; Wt Lftg; High Hon Roll; Hon Roll; Jr NHS; Gftd Prog 84-86; Outstdng Nwspr Carrier 85; Penn ST; Elec Engrng.

MUNION, CHRISTINE; Norristown Area HS; Norristown, PA; (S); 2/519; Trs Church Yth Grp; Symp Band; Yrbk Stf; Var Bsktbl; Var Sftbl; Var Tennis; High Hon Roll; Hon Roll; NHS; Prfct Atten Awd; Lamp Learning Awd 84; Bio Awd 85; ST Selctr Socr Plyr PA 85; NC Chapel Hill.

MUNION, JEAN M; Norristown Area HS; Norristown, PA; (S); 1/519; VP Church Yth Grp; Church Choir; Orch; Symp Band; Yrbk Stf; Diving; JV Fld Hcky; Var Lcrss; High Hon Roll; NHS.

MUNIZ, CHRISSY; Ringgold HS; Donora, PA; (Y); 30/349; FNA; Cheerleading; High Hon Roll; NHS; Office Aide; Ski Clb; Varsity Clb; Off Soph Cls; Off Jr Cls; Off Sr Cls; Hmcmng Crt 95; Mercy Hosp; Nrsg.

MUNLEY, CHRISTINE; Tunkhannock HS; Tunkhannock, PA; (S); 8/320; Art Clb; Church Yth Grp; Pres Girl Scts; Sec Key Clb; Flag Corp; School Play; High Hon Roll; NHS; Rosseti Memrl Art Cntst 4th Pl 84; E Stroudsburg U.

MUNLEY, JANICE; Valley View HS; Archbald, PA; (Y); Latin Clb; Hon Roll; Health Occp Stu America 85-87; Hlth & Human Serv.

MUNNELL, MICHELLE; Mc Guffey HS; Claysville, PA; (Y); 1/210; Pres VP JA; Model UN; Spanish Clb; Rep Stu Cncl; 4-H Awd; Gov Hon Prg Awd; Pres NHS; Rotary Awd; Sec Trs Church Yth Grp; Office Aide; Pres WA Dstrct Cncl Yth Mnstrs 86-87; Dstrct Rep W PA Cnfrnc Cncl Yth Mnstrs 85-86; Pre-Med.

MUNRO, JOYCE L; John Piersol Mccaskey HS; Lancaster, PA; (Y); 11/460; Trs AFS; Pres Church Yth Grp; VP Service Clb; Band; Jazz Band; Hon Roll; Jr NHS; Exploring; Red Cross Aide; Chorus; Outstndng Yth Vlntr Of Yr Awd-Jnr Leag 86; Latin Hnr Soc 86; Lncstr Cnty Red Crss Brd Of Dir 86; Intl Law.

MUNSON, TRACY; W V W HS; Plymouth, PA; (Y); Church Yth Grp; Key Clb; Rep Stu Cncl; French Hon Soc; High Hon Roll; Hon Roll; Physcns Asst.

MUNSTER, MICHELE; Cardinal O Hara HS; Chester, PA; (Y); 184/740; VP Church Yth Grp; Pres FBLA; Girl Scts; VICA; School Musical; School Play; Hon Roll; B P Oil Acadmc Excllnce Awd Top 2%; De Cnty Voc Tech Schl; Acadmc Achvmnt Awd; Comp Sci.

MUNUKUTLA, SARAT; Freedom HS; Bethlehem, PA; (Y); 9/404; Concert Band; Variety Show; High Hon Roll; Hon Roll; NHS; L Pres Schlr; Gifted Stu Prgrm 84 86; TTU; Dr.

MUNUKUTLA, USHA; Freedom HS; Bethlehem, PA; (Y); 12/450; JA; Math Tm; Office Aide; Yrbk Rptr; Mgr(s); JV Tennis; High Hon Roll; NHS; Gifted Student83-86; TN Tech U; Elect Engrng.

MURANO, MICHELE; Carlynton HS; Carnegie, PA; (Y); Drama Clb; Sec Band; Concert Band; Jazz Band; Sec Mrchg Band; Pep Band; Symp Band; Hon Roll.

MURCH, CLAYTON; Susquehanna Community HS; Susquehanna, PA; (S); 7/72; Scholastic Bowl; Var L Bsbl; Var L Ftbl; Var L Vllybl; Hon Roll; NHS; Comp Sci.

MURCKO, CINDY; Farrell SR HS; Farrell, PA; (Y); Drama Clb; Office Aide; Spanish Clb; Var L Cheerleading; NHS.

MURDAH, KIMBERLY; Springside Schl; Philadelphia, PA; (Y); GAA; Nwsp Stf; Var L Lcrss; Var L Socr; Var L Vllybl; Tri Vrsty Awd 86; Psych.

MURDOCCA, ROBERT; Mechanicsburg Area SR HS; Shiremanstown, PA; (Y); 3/321; Church Yth Grp; Rep SADD; Yrbk Stf; Rep Stu Cncl; JV L Bsktbl; Var L Socr; High Hon Roll; NHS; Opt Clb Awd; Prfct Atten Awd; Dickinson Coll Schlrshp, Navy ROTC Fnlst 86; U VA; Bus Admn.

MURDOCK, CATHERINE; Crestwood HS; Mountaintop, PA; (Y); FBLA; High Hon Roll; Bus.

MURDOCK, TAMI; Conneaut Lake HS; Conneaut Lake, PA; (Y); Church Yth Grp; Rptr Pres 4-H; Spanish Clb; VICA; Nwsp Rptr; Yrbk Rptr; Yrbk Stf; L Stat Ftbl; 4-H Awd; High Hon Roll; Gannon; Radlgy.

MURGAS, SANDRA; State College Area SR HS; State College, PA; (Y); Church Yth Grp; Cmnty Wkr; Hosp Aide; SADD; Acpl Chr; Band; Yrbk Stf; Rep Stu Cncl; High Hon Roll; Chorus; Faculty Schlr 86; Cert Merit 86; U Pittsburgh; Bio Sci.

MURIN, TRACY L; Washington HS; Washington, PA; (Y); Key Clb; Pep Clb; Spanish Clb; Nwsp Stf; Yrbk Ed-Chief; Yrbk Stf; Stu Cncl; High Hon Roll; Hon Roll; NHS; Johnson & Wales Coll; Fshn Merc.

MURNAGHAN, JACQUELINE; Academy Of Notre Dame; Yeadon, PA; (Y); Girl Scts; Service Clb; School Play; Nwsp Stf; Yrbk Stf; High Hon Roll; Math Awd 86; St Joseph U; Bus.

MURNYACK, MELISSA; Bald Eagle Area HS; Clarence, PA; (Y); 17/200; Chorus; Nwsp Sprt Ed; Sec Stu Cncl; Capt Cheerleading; Capt Twrlr; Hon Roll; NHS; School Play; Nwsp Stf; Sec Frsh Cls; Svc To Humnty Awd 86; Band Bostr Clb Awd Majrt 86; Miss Flaming Foilage & Miss Blad Eagle 85.

MURNYACK, TAMMY; Bald Eagle Area HS; Clarence, PA; (Y); Hosp Aide; Chorus; Yrbk Sprt Ed; Yrbk Stf; Trs Jr Cls; Trs Sr Cls; Var JV Bsktbl; Var Capt Cheerleading; Hon Roll; Cmnty Wkr; Centre Cnty JR Miss Contstnt 86; Dist & Regnl Chorus 86; Grls Ldrs Clb 85-87.

MUROSKI, DONNA; Johnsonburg Area HS; Johnsonburg, PA; (S); 10/85; Yrbk Stf; Pres Sr Cls; JV Capt Cheerleading; Edinboro ST U; Pre-Schl Ed.

MURPHEY, MELISSA; North Star HS; Boswell, PA; (S); FCA; Math Clb; Band; Chorus; Concert Band; Drm & Bgl; Mrchg Band; Pep Band; Stage Crew; Hon Roll; Cty Band 84-86; Dist VI Band Reg 3 Band 86; Allegny Hrtland Reg Band 84-86; Psychtrst.

MURPHY, AMY; Central York HS; York, PA; (Y); French Clb; Intnl Clb; Ski Clb; Boy Scts; Flag Corp; Jr Cls; Sr Cls; Stu Cncl; Chrmn St Jude Marathon Dance 86; Lib Arts.

MURPHY, BARBARA A; Elk County Christian HS; Ridgway, PA; (S); Letterman Clb; Model UN; Yrbk Stf; VP Soph Cls; VP Jr Cls; Stat Bsktbl; Cheerleading; Var L Crs Cntry; Var Trk; High Hon Roll; Psychlgy.

MURPHY, CHANDRA; St Paul Cathedral HS; Pittsburgh, PA; (Y); Pep Clb; Red Cross Aide; Service Clb; Ski Clb; Yrbk Stf; Badmtn; Swmmng; Tennis; Wt Lftg; Boys Clb Am; Psych.

MURPHY, CHRIS; Mt Pleasant Area HS; Greensburg, PA; (Y); Church Yth Grp; Nwsp Rptr; Nwsp Stf; Yrbk Ed-Chief; Yrbk Stf.

MURPHY, CHRISTINA; Penn Hills SR HS; Verona, PA; (S); 1/797; Aud/Vis; Library Aide; Spanish Clb; Yrbk Stf; Lit Mag; JV Bsktbl; Stat Mgr(s); High Hon Roll; Jr NHS; NHS; Carnegie-Mellon U; Engl.

MURPHY, CHRISTINE; Lancaster Country Day HS; Lancaster, PA; (Y); Drama Clb; Key Clb; Political Wkr; Chorus; Yrbk Stf; Lit Mag; Fld Hcky; Maude M Bates Meml Schlrshp-Merit In Acad 83-87; Polit Sci.

MURPHY, CHRISTINE; Seton-La Salle HS; Pittsburgh, PA; (Y); 12/263; Exploring; Hosp Aide; Cheerleading; High Hon Roll; Hon Roll; Jr NHS; NHS; Htl Mgmt.

MURPHY, CHRISTOPHER; Penn Hills SR HS; Pittsburgh, PA; (Y); German Clb; Spanish Clb; Varsity Clb; Var L Ftbl; Var L Ice Hcky; Wt Lftg; Hon Roll; Prfct Atten Awd; 3 Yr Lttr Wnnr Hcky 84-87; Cmnctns.

MURPHY, CINDY; Central Cambria HS; Colver, PA; (S); 14/209; Art Clb; Church Yth Grp; Hosp Aide; Ski Clb; JV Bsktbl; JV Crs Cntry; JV Trk; Hon Roll.

MURPHY, DEBRA SUSAN; Ridley HS; Morton, PA; (Y); 47/411; Church Yth Grp; Cmnty Wkr; Q&S; Pres Service Clb; Stage Crew; Lit Mag; Hon Roll; NHS; Pres Schlr; Stu Of Mnth 85; US Natl Merit Ldrshp Awd 86; Ridley Educ Assoc Schlrshp 86; PA ST U; Spcl Educ.

MURPHY, DEE; Burgettstown JR SR HS; Burgettstown, PA; (Y); Girl Scts; Chorus; Concert Band; Mrchg Band; Sftbl; Hon Roll; Scrtry.

MURPHY, DIANE; Gateway HS; Monroeville, PA; (Y); 76/443; Church Yth Grp; Exploring; French Clb; Teachers Aide; Chorus; Color Guard; Mrchg Band; Yrbk Stf; Hon Roll; Ntl Band Awd 86; Pres Acad Achvt Awd 86; PA ST U; Engrng.

MURPHY, DONNA; Johnstown Area Voc Tech Schl; South Fork, PA; (Y); 11/250; Art Clb; Speech Tm; SADD; Flag Corp; School Musical; High Hon Roll; Jr NHS; NHS; Vo-Tech Achvt Awd Of Emplblty; Clncl Psych.

MURPHY, FRANCIS; Archbishop Kennedy HS; Ambler, PA; (Y); 18/190; Varsity Clb; Rep Frsh Cls; Rep Soph Cls; Rep Jr Cls; Sec Sr Cls; Sec Stu Cncl; Var L Ftbl; Var L Trk; Var L Wt Lftg; High Hon Roll; Dedicatn, Determntn, Desire Awd Ftbl; Schlr Ath US Army; Montgomery Cnty Schlr Ath Hnr; Villanova; Bus Adm.

MURPHY, KELLY; Minersville Area HS; Pottsville, PA; (Y); 7/124; Trs Exploring; Girl Scts; Pres Ski Clb; Mrchg Band; School Play; Stage Crew; Yrbk Stf; Sec Soph Cls; Sec Jr Cls; Stu Cncl; SR Girl Sct Awd 86; Schltc Achvt Awd 86; Stu Of Mnth, Yth Fitness Achvt Awd 83-86; PA ST U; Hotl Mgmt.

MURPHY, KEVIN; Bishop Hoban HS; Plymouth, PA; (Y); Pres Church Yth Grp; Cmnty Wkr; Rep Jr Cls; Stu Cncl; Scl Wrk.

MURPHY, KRISTIN; Riverview HS; Oakmont, PA; (Y); 18/120; Pres Trs AFS; Girl Scts; Band; Color Guard; Yrbk Stf; Stu Cncl; Sftbl; Vllybl; High Hon Roll; NHS; Rtry Yth Ldrshp Cnfrnce Awd 86; Amer Fld Svc Exchnge Pgm Ireland 86; Elem Educ.

MURPHY, LAUREEN; Hazleton HS; Drums, PA; (Y); 19/377; Girl Scts; Jazz Band; Trs Mrchg Band; French Hon Soc; God Cntry Awd; High Hon Roll; NHS; Mala Tack Grant 86; Drctrs Awd For Bnd 86; Pres Acdmc Ftns Awd 86; Temple U; Phrmcst.

MURPHY, LINDA; Highlands HS; Natrona Hts, PA; (Y); FBLA; Hosp Aide; Key Clb; Office Aide; Church Choir; Stage Crew; Var Twrlr; Cit Awd; Jr NHS; Penn ST; Bus Admin.

MURPHY, LISA; Abington Sr HS; Roslyn, PA; (Y); 66/508; Jr Cls; Fld Hcky; Lcrss; NHS; Sci.

MURPHY, MARK L; Northampton Area SR HS; Middletown, NY; (Y); 2/475; AFS; Math Clb; Capt Scholastic Bowl; Concert Band; Mrchg Band; School Musical; High Hon Roll; Ntl Merit SF; Voice Dem Awd; Chess Clb; PA Govnrs Schl Sci 85; Rotarys Cmp Neidig 85; Engrng Physcs.

MURPHY, MAUREEN; Brandywine Heights HS; Fleetwood, PA; (Y); 15/144; FBLA; Hosp Aide; Library Aide; Fld Hcky; Trk; High Hon Roll; NHS.

MURPHY, MEGAN; Pittston Area HS; Pittston, PA; (Y); 11/330; Art Clb; Church Yth Grp; Drama Clb; FNA; JA; Key Clb; Ski Clb; Spanish Clb; School Play; Diving; Prsdntl Acad Ftnss Awd 86; US Ldrshp Merit Awd 85-86; IN U Of PA; Crmnlgy.

MURPHY, MEGHAN; Downingtown SR HS; Exton, PA; (Y); French Clb; Office Aide; Ski Clb; Rep Stu Cncl; Hon Roll.

MURPHY, MICHAEL; Northeastern HS; Mt Wolf, PA; (Y); 23/154; Aud/Vis; Jazz Band; Stage Crew; Yrbk Phtg; Yrbk Stf; Im Bsktbl; JV Im Vllybl; High Hon Roll; Hon Roll; NHS; Elec Engr.

MURPHY, PATRICK; Scranton Prep; Dunmore, PA; (Y); 21/191; Boys Clb Am; Service Clb; Nwsp Stf; Yrbk Stf; L Bsktbl; Im Wt Lftg; High Hon Roll; Hon Mntn All Star Bsktbl 86; Brnze Mdlst Math 86.

MURPHY, RICHARD T; Waynesboro Area SR HS; Waynesboro, PA; (Y); Am Leg Boys St; Pres Church Yth Grp; Cmnty Wkr; Exploring; Political Wkr; Varsity Clb; VP Stu Cncl; Var Capt Bsktbl; Var Capt Socr; Cit Awd; Schlrshp Drxl U Bsktbl; Drexel U; Finance.

MURPHY, ROBERT M; West Scranton HS; Scranton, PA; (Y); 40/270; Letterman Clb; Spanish Clb; Sec Band; Concert Band; Drm Mjr(t); Mrchg Band; Orch; Stage Crew; NHS; U Of Scranton; Scl Sci Educ.

MURPHY, SANDRA; York Vo Tech; Emigsvtlle, PA; (Y); Church Yth Grp; Office Aide; Church Choir; Hon Roll; Health Occuptns Stu Of Amer 83-86; Organztn For Rehbltn Training Awd 86; Hlth Occuptns/Treas VP 85-86; Yorktowne Bus Inst; Leg Secrtry.

MURPHY, SEAN; St James HS; Chester, PA; (Y); 17/140; Aud/Vis; Pep Clb; Service Clb; School Play; Variety Show; Hon Roll; NHS; Opt Clb Awd; Outstndng Achvt Pblc Spkng Awd 86; Presdntl Acadmc Ftns Awd 86; Cngrssmns Medl Merit 86; Temple U; Radio-TV-FILM.

MURPHY, SEAN MICHAEL; Elizabeth-Forward HS; Elizabeth, PA; (Y); 24/312; Var Ftbl; Var Capt Trk; CC Awd; Hon Roll; NHS; Pres Schlr; Big 10 Dfnsv Plyr 85; Elizabeth Forward Schlr Athl 86; 4 Yr Lttr Trck, 3 Yr Lttr Ftbl; USCG Acad; Govt.

MURPHY, SHARON; Downingtown SR HS; Downingtown, PA; (Y); 81/563; French Clb; Service Clb; Ski Clb; Color Guard; Mrchg Band; Mgr(s); Hon Roll; U Of CA; Marine Sci.

MURPHY, STEVEN; Red Land HS; Mechanicsburg, PA; (Y); 23/275; Aud/Vis; Spanish Clb; Pres Stage Crew; Tennis; High Hon Roll; Hon Roll; Spanish NHS; Pilot.

MURPHY, SUE; St Huberts HS; Philadelphia, PA; (Y); 119/367; Office Aide; Off Stu Cncl; Hon Roll.

MURPHY, TROY; Exeter SR HS; Reading, PA; (Y); 4-H; Key Clb; Pres Band; Concert Band; Jazz Band; Mrchg Band; Orch; Pep Band; Off Stu Cncl; JV Bsktbl; Kutztown U; Educ.

MURPHY, WILLIAM; M L King HS; Phila, PA; (Y); Var Bsbl; Cert Hnr Electrncs 86; Drexel U; Elec Engr.

MURRAY, ANNEMARIE; St Maria Goretti HS; Philadelphia, PA; (Y); 30/400; Trs Church Yth Grp; French Clb; GAA; Hosp Aide; Math Clb; Nwsp Phtg; Yrbk Stf; Hon Roll; NHS; Catholic Yth Orgnz Awd Of Merit 85.

MURRAY, DEBRA; Greenwood HS; Liverpool, PA; (S); 3/50; Pres FBLA; Trs GAA; Band; Yrbk Stf; Trs Sr Cls; JV Var Cheerleading; Twrlr; Hon Roll; Sec NHS; Girl Scts; Mst Outstndng Bus Stdnt Yr Awds 83-85; Hmcmg Qn 85-86; Oct Grl Mnth 85-86; Flght Attndt.

MURRAY, EDWARD; Deer Lakes JR SR HS; Tarentum, PA; (Y); AFS; Church Yth Grp; Drama Clb; Pres Varsity Clb; School Play; JV Var Bsktbl; JV Var Socr; Hon Roll; Sec NHS; NEDT Awd; Engr.

MURRAY, GREG; Deer Lakes HS; Gibsonia, PA; (Y); French Clb; High Hon Roll; NHS; NEDT Awd; Prfct Atten Awd; PA Jr Acad Of Sci Hnr Cert 85; Awd Of Acdmc Excllnc Deer Lks HS 85-86; Alleghny Coll; Pre-Med.

MURRAY, JANET L; Central Cambria HS; Ebensburg, PA; (S); 12/189; JA; VICA; Y-Teens; Yrbk Ed-Chief; JV Sftbl; High Hon Roll; Jr NHS; PA ST U; Genetcs.

MURRAY, JENNIFER; Punxsutawney Area HS; Punxsutawney, PA; (Y); French Clb; Math Tm; Science Clb; Spanish Clb; High Hon Roll; NHS; Frgn Lang Comptn Slippery Rock U 3rd Pl Spnsh III & 2nd Pl Frnch III 86; Physcs.

MURRAY IV, JOHN J; Norristown Area HS; Norristown, PA; (Y); 70/420; Church Yth Grp; FCA; Key Clb; Var Capt Swmmng; Hon Roll; Boy Scts; Yrbk Stf; Mst Imprvd-Swmmng Awd 84; Coachs Awd-Swmmng 86; Watr Polo Tm-Capt 86; Shippensburg U; Bus Mngmt.

MURRAY, KATIE; Our Lady Of The Sacred Heart HS; Mckees Rocks, PA; (Y); 17/58; Sec Trs Sr Cls; Voice Dem Awd; Pep Clb; Chorus; School Musical; Nwsp Stf; Psych.

MURRAY, KEITH; West Perry HS; New Bloomfield, PA; (Y); Boy Scts; Church Yth Grp; Band; Concert Band; Jazz Band; Mrchg Band; School Play; Var Trk; French Clb; Egl Sct 85; Sct Of Yr Awd 85; Fld Cpt To Ast Drm Mjrs Mrchng Bnd 86; ROTC; Cmmnctns.

MURRAY, KEVIN; Sun Valley HS; Aston, PA; (Y); 1/318; Yrbk Stf; Var Socr; Wt Lftg; Bausch & Lomb Sci Awd; High Hon Roll; NHS; Ntl Merit Ltr; Pres Schlr; Val; Amer Legn Awd 86; Ofc Aid 85-86; Johns Hopkins U; Biomed Engrng.

MURRAY, KIMBERLEY; Mechanicsburg SR HS; Mechanicsburg, PA; (Y); 2/321; Pres Girl Scts; Band; Chorus; Drm Mjr(t); Jazz Band; Mrchg Band; Orch; Symp Band; High Hon Roll; NHS; 1st Pl Dist PA Hstry Day 86; Grl Sct Gld Awd 86.

MURRAY, MATT; Plum SR HS; Pittsburgh, PA; (S); Aud/Vis; DECA; School Musical; Yrbk Stf; Office Aide; Varsity Clb; Im Bsktbl; JV Ftbl; Im Sftbl; Var L Tennis; Penn ST; Mrktng.

MURRAY, MAUREEN; Blairsville SR HS; Blairsville, PA; (Y); 10/134; SADD; High Hon Roll; NHS; Prfct Atten Awd; IUP Summer Happening Act 86; BUS.

MURRAY, MICHAEL W; Spring Grove SR HS; York, PA; (Y); 31/289; Am Leg Boys St; Band; Concert Band; Jazz Band; Mrchg Band; High Hon Roll; Hon Roll; NHS; Best Trumpet Solost Awd William Penn Jazz Fest 8l; Gannon U; Med.

MURRAY, MICHELE; Deer Lakes JR SR HS; Tarentum, PA; (Y); Church Yth Grp; Hosp Aide; Varsity Clb; Band; Ed Yrbk Stf; JV Var Bsktbl; Ftbl; Trk; Hon Roll; Sec NHS; Chatham Coll; Bio.

MURRAY, NANCY; Gateway SR HS; Monroeville, PA; (Y); 13/472; Dance Clb; Chorus; Drm Mjr(t); Mrchg Band; School Musical; Variety Show; Cheerleading; High Hon Roll; NHS; Pres Schlr; WAMO Hot Trcks Dancer 86; Monroeville Mall Tn Brd 86; Miss Indpndnc Day Monroeville 85; PA ST U; Engr.

MURRAY, ROBERT; Carlisle SR HS; Carlisle, PA; (Y); Chess Clb; Church Yth Grp; Drama Clb; Spanish Clb; Y-Teens; Crs Cntry; Socr; Trk; Wt Lftg; Hon Roll; Engrng.

MURRAY, SEAN; South Park HS; Library, PA; (Y); 25/230; Aud/Vis; Camera Clb; Drama Clb; English Clb; Exploring; Spanish Clb; Thesps; School Play; Stage Crew; Variety Show; Actg Awd 86; Film Dir.

MURRAY, SHAWN; Norristown Area HS; Norristown, PA; (Y); Boy Scts; Church Yth Grp; FCA; Key Clb; Var Capt Swmmng; Hon Roll; Yrbk Stf; Most Mprvd Swmmng 84; Coaches Awd 86; Ltr Swmmng 83; Shippensburg U; Bus.

MURRAY, SHERRY; Peters Township HS; Venetia, PA; (Y); Cmnty Wkr; Drama Clb; Girl Scts; Thesps; School Musical; School Play; Variety Show; Nwsp Stf; Yrbk Stf; Trs Frsh Cls; CA ST U; Bus Adm.

MURRY, SHANE; Hempfield HS; Columbia, PA; (Y); Boy Scts; Church Yth Grp; Sec Exploring; VICA; JV Wrstlng; Cit Awd; Hon Roll; Merit Awd 86; Eagle Scout 86; Mech Engr.

MUSCH, SCOTT; Bradford Area HS; Bradford, PA; (Y); 1/300; Debate Tm; French Clb; Key Clb; Ski Clb; School Play; Trs Frsh Cls; Rep Stu Cncl; Var L Swmmng; High Hon Roll; Jr NHS; Current Events Clb Hstry Awd 86; 3rd Pl Sci Fair Awd SR Div 85; PA Free Enterprise Wk Schlrshp 86; Bus.

MUSGROVE, KRIS; Hempfield SR HS; Greensburg, PA; (Y); 29/657; Hosp Aide; Spanish Clb; High Hon Roll; Hon Roll; Jr NHS; NHS; Spanish NHS; All Dist Hnr Awd 83; IN U Of PA; Mdcl.

MUSHINSKY, CHRIS; Mt Alvernia HS; Pittsburgh, PA; (Y); Exploring; Chorus; Hon Roll; Bus Hon Soc 86.

MUSHNOK, MARY ANN; Western Beaver HS; Midland, PA; (Y); Trs Church Yth Grp; Exploring; FHA; High Hon Roll; Hon Roll; NHS; Prfct Atten Awd; Bradford Bus Schl; Exec Secy.

MUSHRUSH, CHRISTOPHER D; Highlands SR HS; Natrona Heights, PA; (Y); 43/282; Exploring; Key Clb; Trs Soph Cls; Trs Jr Cls; Trs Sr Cls; Stu Cncl; Crs Cntry; Var L Trk; High Hon Roll; NHS; NROTC.

MUSIAL, PAMELA; St Basil Acad; Philadelphia, PA; (Y); Sec Trs Church Yth Grp; GAA; VP Spanish Clb; Chorus; Var Bsktbl; Fld Hcky; Var Sftbl; Im Vllybl.

MUSIAL, THOMAS; Central Catholic HS; Pittsburgh, PA; (Y); 6/260; Boy Scts; Drama Clb; Concert Band; School Musical; Var Swmmng; High Hon Roll; VP NHS; JA; PAVAS; Band; 1450 PSAT Score 85; 1540 SAT Score 86; 800 Prfct Score PSAT Math; Ivy League Coll.

MUSIKE, SHAWN; Freedom HS; Easton, PA; (Y); Elec.

MUSKEY, ANNEMARIE; Hempfield HS; E Petersburg, PA; (Y); 78/400; Camera Clb; Pres Science Clb; Chorus; Var L Gym; DAR Awd; Hon Roll; Bio Clb Schlrshp 86; Millersville U; Bio.

MUSONE, JOHN; Meadville SR HS; Meadville, PA; (Y); Var L Ftbl; Wt Lftg; Hon Roll; Penn ST; Electrncs.

MUSSELMAN, DEBRA; Claysburg-Kimmel HS; Claysburg, PA; (Y); 2/53; Sec Trs Girl Scts; Sec Trs SADD; Concert Band; Mrchg Band; Stat Bsbl; Stat Bsktbl; High Hon Roll; Hon Roll; NHS; Slvr Awd Grl Scts Amer 84; Libry Vlntr Awd 85; Perf Attndnc Awd 85; Lock Haven U At PA; Elem Ed.

MUSSELMAN, JESSICA; Northern York SR HS; Dillsburg, PA; (Y); Church Yth Grp; Civic Clb; FBLA; Hon Roll; Home Ec Best All Around 85-86.

MUSSER, COURTNEY; Kiski Area HS; Murrysville, PA; (Y); Math Clb; Math Tm; Spanish Clb; Chorus; Yrbk Stf; Stat JV Bsbl; JV Var Cheerleading; Vllybl; High Hon Roll; NHS.

MUSSER, DARYL; Garden Spot HS; East Earl, PA; (Y); Church Yth Grp; FBLA; High Hon Roll; Hon Roll; 4th Pl Bus Math Bus Ldrs Of Amer 85; Engr.

MUSSER, DONNA J; Blue Mountain Acad; Elizabethtown, PA; (Y); Church Yth Grp; Hosp Aide; Chorus; Church Choir; Cmnty Wkr; Gym; Score Keeper; Socr; Sftbl; Vllybl; Reading Hospital; Rn.

MUSSER, JOHN EVANS; Mt Pleasant Area HS; Somerset, PA; (Y); German Clb; Ski Clb; Band; Tennis; Hon Roll; Yth Educ Assoc 85&86; Pre-Med.

MUSSER, SHERISSA; Dover Area HS; Dover, PA; (Y); Varsity Clb; Color Guard; Jazz Band; Mrchg Band; Fld Hcky; German,Athletic Awd 84-85; Lock Haven U; Physcl Thrpy.

MUSSER, STEPHEN J; Solanco SR HS; New Prvidence, PA; (Y); 1/209; Chess Clb; Pres VP Church Yth Grp; Exploring; Rep Sr Cls; High Hon Roll; NHS; Prfct Atten Awd; Schlr 84-86; Acctng.

MUSSER, TRICIA; Elizabethtown Area HS; Elizabethtown, PA; (Y); Sec Church Yth Grp; Pres 4-H; FFA; Office Aide; Chorus; School Musical; Im Fld Hcky; Var Tennis; JV Trk; 4-H Awd; Lancaster Cnty 4-H Shprd Of Yr 84; Bus.

MUSSO, MARTY; Scranton Central HS; Scranton, PA; (Y); CAP; Cmnty Wkr; Exploring; JA; Math Clb; Math Tm; OEA; Political Wkr; Ski Clb; Varsity Clb.

MUSSO, MICHELLE; Scranton Central HS; Scranton, PA; (Y); Church Yth Grp; Dance Clb; Hon Roll.

MUSSOLINE, BETHANN; Hazleton SR HS; Hazleton, PA; (Y); Drama Clb; French Clb; Hosp Aide; Chorus; Color Guard; School Musical; Nwsp Stf; Phys Thrpy.

MUSTA, LAURIE; Carlynton HS; Pittsburgh, PA; (Y); Church Yth Grp; Drama Clb; French Clb; VP JA; Chorus; Church Choir; Color Guard; Flag Corp; Nwsp Stf; Yrbk Stf; PA ST; Zoolgy.

MUSTO, DENISE; Northampton Area SR HS; Bethlehem, PA; (Y); AFS; Drama Clb; FTA; Leo Clb; SADD; Chorus; Mrchg Band; School Play; Nwsp Sprt Ed; Pom Pon; Bus Adm.

MUSTO, PAMELA; Old Forge HS; Old Forge, PA; (Y); Stage Crew; Var Cheerleading; Hon Roll.

MUTCH, MICHAEL; West Mifflin Area HS; W Mifflin, PA; (Y); 23/350; Ski Clb; Socr; High Hon Roll; Hon Roll; NHS; U Of Pittsburgh; Engrng.

MUTH, LORI; Du Bois Area HS; Luthersburg, PA; (Y); Sec Church Yth Grp; Cmnty Wkr; Girl Scts; Hosp Aide; Chorus; Hon Roll; St Frncs Coll; Physcns Assist.

MUTHLER, ANNA M; Bald Eagle-Nittany HS; Mill Hall, PA; (Y); French Clb; Hosp Aide; Model UN; Color Guard; Concert Band; Mrchg Band; Pep Band; High Hon Roll; Hon Roll; NHS.

MUTKUS, JUDY; Hjopewell HS; Aliquippa, PA; (Y); 67/247; Trs Latin Clb; Band; Chorus; Concert Band; Jazz Band; Mrchg Band; Rep Frsh Cls; Rep Soph Cls; Rep Jr Cls; Var L Sftbl; All Star Jazz Band 85-86; Musc Ed.

MUTONE, ENRICO; Seton La-Salle HS; Pittsburgh, PA; (Y); 20/256; Computer Clb; Intnl Clb; Math Tm; Spanish Clb; Band; Pep Band; Gov Hon Prg Awd; High Hon Roll; Kiwanis Awd; NHS; Gvnrs Schl Intl Stds 86; Intl Law.

MUTZ, ROBIN; Ambridge Area HS; Sewickley, PA; (Y); 7/256; Am Leg Aux Girls St; Pres Hst German Clb; Capt Crs Cntry; L Trk; High Hon Roll; NHS; Voice Dem Awd; Church Yth Grp; 4-H; Office Aide; Schlrshp Awds-Vin Vncnt Psno Memrl, Ampco-Pttsbrgh Fndtn Coll & Eco Wmns Clb Annl 86; William Woods Coll; Eqstrn Sci.

MUZYKA JR, JOSEPH F; Archbishop Ryan For Boys; Philadelphia, PA; (Y); 145/429; Church Yth Grp; Dance Clb; Office Aide; Rnk #2 In Mech Drwng 86; Amern Inst; Mech Drwng II.

MYCHAK, PAM; Mt Carmel JR-SR HS; Mt Carmel, PA; (Y); Computer Clb; FHA; FTA; Hosp Aide; Pep Clb; Ski Clb; Spanish Clb; Chorus; Nwsp Rptr; Cheerleading; 6th Pl Wnnr Miss Keystone ST Modelng 85; 2nd Pl Keystone ST Nutrtn Cntst 85; Ed.

MYER, DEANNE; Manheim Central HS; Manheim, PA; (Y); VP Band; Jazz Band; Mrchg Band; Orch; Rep Jr Cls; Rep Sr Cls; DAR Awd; JP Sousa Awd; Hon Roll; Robert Morris Hstry Awd 86; Wmns Symph Assn Of Lancaster Awd 86; Co, Dist & Rgnl Band Co Orch 86; Houghton Coll NY; Music Educ.

MYER, RONALD; Solanco SR HS; Quarryville, PA; (Y); 12/235; Church Yth Grp; Varsity Clb; Stage Crew; Var Bsbl; Var Bsktbl; Var Crs Cntry; Var Golf; High Hon Roll; Outstndg Awd Bsc Comp Prgmg 86; Outstndg Awd Bio 84; MVP Bsktbl Cmp 86; Bus Adm.

MYERS, AMY; Bellwood-Antis HS; Tyrone, PA; (Y); 9/100; Church Yth Grp; GAA; JA; Key Clb; Varsity Clb; Chorus; Church Choir; School Musical; Swing Chorus; Variety Show; Spnsh II Awd 86; Amer Cultures Awd 85; Spnsh I Awd 85; Sec.

MYERS, AMY; Seneca Valley SR HS; Mars, PA; (Y); 67/374; Church Yth Grp; JA; Ski Clb; Hon Roll.

MYERS, AMY; West Branch HS; Hawk Run, PA; (Y); 12/114; Sec Drama Clb; Band; Chorus; Yrbk Stf; Sec Stu Cncl; Twrlr; JP Sousa Awd; Sec NHS; Rchrd Btrwrth Awd 85; Co-Chrprsn Prom Comm 85-86; Grdtd Hons 86; South Hills School; Med Scrtry.

MYERS, AMY SUE; Bald Eagle Area HS; Port Matilda, PA; (Y); 8/203; Pres Church Yth Grp; Off Jr Cls; Off Sr Cls; Rep Stu Cncl; Stat Crs Cntry; Im Powder Puff Ftbl; Stat Trk; Cit Awd; High Hon Roll; NHS; Distinguished Hon Roll Awd; Bus Dept Awd; Highest Hons Awd; Sec.

MYERS, ANDREW; M M I Prep; Mountaintop, PA; (Y); Cmnty Wkr; Science Clb; Var Capt Socr; Var Tennis; Hon Roll; NEDT Awd; R L Bloom Schlrshp 86; Bio Med Engrng.

MYERS, ANN; Kennard-Dale HS; Stewartstown, PA; (Y); 11/119; Church Yth Grp; Chorus; Flag Corp; School Musical; School Play; Yrbk Stf; Var Capt Cheerleading; Hon Roll; NHS; Rotary Awd; Clnl Yrk Chptr ABWA Schlrshp 86; Sthrn Yrk Cnty Rtry Clb Schlrshp 86; Stwrtstwn Pro Bus Wmns Assn; Messiah Coll; Chldhd Educ.

MYERS, BARRY; Northern York County HS; Dillsburg, PA; (Y); 5/220; Church Yth Grp; Computer Clb; Yrbk Stf; High Hon Roll; Hon Roll; NHS; Ntl Merit SF; Pres Schlr; Rotary Awd; Penn ST; Engrng.

MYERS, BARRY E; Northeastern HS; York Haven, PA; (Y); Art Clb; Lit Mag; Computer Clb; Cmrcl Art.

MYERS, BETHANN; Lock Haven SR HS; Lock Haven, PA; (Y); Spanish Clb; Chorus; Stu Cncl; Trk; Stu Of Mnth.

MYERS, BETTY; Union HS; Rimersburg, PA; (Y); 4/64; Pep Clb; SADD; VICA; Hon Roll; Dir List 85-86.

MYERS, BILL; Central Dauphin East HS; Harrisburg, PA; (Y); 18/250; Stage Crew; Var Trk; NHS; Penn ST; Microbio.

MYERS, BRENDA LEE; Crestwood HS; Wapwallopen, PA; (Y); VICA; High Hon Roll; NHS; Brd Ed Awd 86; Data Proc.

MYERS, BRIAN; York Vo-Tech HS; Dover, PA; (Y); VICA; High Hon Roll; Hon Roll; NHS; Rotary Awd; Penn ST York; Mech Engr.

MYERS, BRIDGET; Bishop Guilfoyle HS; Altoona, PA; (Y); NHS; Monsignr Harkins Awd Soc Studs; Natl Phys Ed Awd; PA ST U; Lib Arts.

MYERS, CHERYL; Tech Memorial HS; Erie, PA; (Y); 45/380; Yrbk Stf; Gannon U; Radiolgcl Tech.

MYERS, CHRISTINA L; Red Lion Area SR HS; Red Lion, PA; (Y); 75/341; Varsity Clb; VP Chorus; School Musical; Pres Jr Cls; Stu Cncl; Cheerleading; Powder Puff Ftbl; High Hon Roll; Modrn Mus Mstrs 86; Wm Penn Art Inst 85-86; Prof Actrss.

MYERS, CHRISTINE; Lebanon SR HS; Lebanon, PA; (Y); 31/285; French Clb; Teachers Aide; Varsity Clb; Off Jr Cls; Var Capt Bsktbl; Coach Actv; Var Capt Crs Cntry; Var Trk; Hon Roll; Lebanon Cnty Trck 83-86; Dist Crss-Cnty Meets 83-86; Kutztown U; Comp Info.

MYERS, CHRISTINE; Mt Pleasant Area HS; Greensburg, PA; (Y); 10/254; FTA; GAA; Concert Band; Mrchg Band; Ed Yrbk Bus Mgr; Tennis; High Hon Roll; Trs NHS; Pres Schlr; PSEA Schlrshp 86; Rotary Schltc Awd 86; Grove City Coll; Elem Educ.

MYERS, CHRISTOPHER; Somerset SR HS; Somerset, PA; (Y); German Clb; Letterman Clb; Math Clb; Q&S; Varsity Clb; Yrbk Rptr; Yrbk Sprt Ed; Yrbk Stf; Rep Stu Cncl; Var Bsbl; Hmrm Treas, German Club Sec, Mu Alpha Theta Treas 85-86; Penn ST U; Bus.

MYERS, DEBBIE; Grove City HS; Grove City, PA; (Y); 43/195; Drama Clb; Trs Science Clb; Stage Crew; Hon Roll; Grove City Coll; Comp Sci.

MYERS, DENISE; Henderson HS; West Chester, PA; (S); 5/349; Ski Clb; Band; Mrchg Band; Sftbl; Vllybl; French Hon Soc; Hon Roll.

MYERS, DENISE; West York Area HS; York, PA; (Y); 28/194; JA; Sec Spanish Clb; Teachers Aide; Varsity Clb; Nwsp Sprt Ed; Nwsp Stf; Bsbl; Vllybl; High Hon Roll; Hon Roll; Elem Ed.

MYERS, DONNA; Phoenixville Area SR HS; Phoenixville, PA; (Y); 26/200; Key Clb; Pep Clb; Spanish Clb; School Musical; Stat Trk; Im Vllybl; Hon Roll; NHS; Foods I Awd 86; Cabrini Coll Radnor PA; Biol.

MYERS, DOUG; Newport HS; Newport, PA; (Y); 22/103; Spanish Clb; Varsity Clb; School Play; Trs Frsh Cls; Trs Soph Cls; Trs Jr Cls; Trs Sr Cls; Var Bsktbl; Var L Ftbl; Im Vllybl; Coaches Awd Ftbll 85; MIP Awd Ftbll 85; Engr.

MYERS, ERIC; Dallastown Area HS; York, PA; (Y); Band; Chorus; Concert Band; Jazz Band; Mrchg Band; Pep Band; School Musical; Symp Band; JV Wrstlng; Hon Roll; Bus Adm.

MYERS, GAVIN; Biglerville HS; Biglerville, PA; (Y); 16/85; Boy Scts; Band; Concert Band; Mrchg Band; Pep Band; PA ST; Metrlgy.

MYERS, GLENN; Taylor Allderdice HS; Pittsburgh, PA; (Y); Boys Clb Am; Varsity Clb; Stat Bsktbl; Var L Ftbl; Score Keeper; Var L Trk; Im Wt Lftg; DAR Awd; High Hon Roll; NHS; Howard Smmr Acturial Pgm Schlrshp 86; Engrng.

MYERS, GREGORY; Northeastern HS; Mt Wolf, PA; (Y); 4/126; Aud/Vis; Church Yth Grp; Teachers Aide; Bsktbl; Score Keeper; Timer; L Var Vllybl; High Hon Roll; Hon Roll; NHS; Sci.

MYERS, GRETCHEN; Southmoreland SR HS; Scottdale, PA; (Y); French Clb; Band; Concert Band; Jazz Band; Mrchg Band; Pep Band; French Hon Soc.

MYERS, JANET; Bethel Park SR HS; Bethel Park, PA; (Y); 83/530; Art Clb; Church Yth Grp; German Clb; Science Clb; Acpl Chr; Chorus; Church Choir; School Musical; School Play; Swing Chorus; Geneva Coll Schlr Awd 86; 1st Pl PA JR Acad Sci ST Lev 83; Pres Acad Fit Awd 86; Geneva Coll; Elem Ed.

MYERS, JASON; Scranton Prep; Peckville, PA; (Y); 13/103; Concert Band; Jazz Band; Im Bsktbl; Var Swmmng; Var Vllybl; NHS; Ntl Merit SF; Rotary Awd; Faculty Schlrsh P86; Carnegie Mellon U; Chem.

MYERS, JEFFREY L; Mt Zion Christian Acad; Mt Pleasant, PA; (S); Boy Scts; Church Yth Grp; French Clb; Band; Rep Stu Cncl; High Hon Roll; Hon Roll; Highest Bio, Alg, & Geo Grade In Schl 83-84; Elec Engnrng.

MYERS, JENNIFER; Warriore Run HS; Allenwood, PA; (Y); 12/160; Spanish Clb; VP Chorus; School Musical; Swing Chorus; Yrbk Stf; Rep Stu Cncl; Var Co-Capt Cheerleading; Var Trk; High Hon Roll; Hon Roll; Ed.

MYERS, JODI; Clarion-Limestone HS; Clarion, PA; (Y); French Clb; Chorus; Yrbk Phtg; Socr; Trk; Photographer.

MYERS, KAREN; Leechburg Area HS; Leechburg, PA; (Y); 2/82; Band; Chorus; Concert Band; Mrchg Band; Pep Band; Yrbk Stf; Sec Jr Cls; High Hon Roll; Hon Roll; NHS; Outstndng Band 83-84; Penn ST; Med.

MYERS, KATHIE; Chestnut Ridge HS; New Paris, PA; (Y); Church Yth Grp; Dance Clb; Band; Chorus; Concert Band; Mrchg Band; Variety Show; Stu Cncl; Cheerleading; Prfct Atten Awd; Hmcmg Attndt 84; Altoona Beauty Schl; Csmtlgst.

MYERS, KELLIE; Littlestown HS; Littlestown, PA; (Y); 34/105; DECA; FBLA; Letterman Clb; Pep Clb; Teachers Aide; Varsity Clb; Band; Color Guard; Mrchg Band; Cheerleading; NE U; Trvl Cmmnctns.

MYERS, KELLY; Crestwood HS; Mountaintop, PA; (Y); Art Clb; FBLA; School Play; Yrbk Stf.

MYERS, LAUREL A; Harbor Creek HS; Erie, PA; (Y); 18/206; Church Yth Grp; Exploring; Hosp Aide; Office Aide; Sec Pres Chorus; Mrchg Band; Variety Show; Ed Yrbk Stf; High Hon Roll; NHS; Kent ST U Pres Scholar & Hnrs 86; Camphausen Music Scholar Wmns Clb Erie 86; Hopwood Scholar 85; Kent ST U; Music.

MYERS, LORA; Dover Area HS; Dover, PA; (Y); Band; Chorus; Concert Band; Jazz Band; Mrchg Band; Soclgy.

MYERS, MATT; Youngsville HS; Garland, PA; (Y); VP SADD; JV Var Ftbl; Var L Trk; Var Wt Lftg; Hon Roll; Prfct Atten Awd; Bst Newcmr Trck 85; Elctrncs.

MYERS, MELISSA; Elizabethtown Area HS; Manheim, PA; (S); 7/221; Chorus; Drm Mjr(t); Jazz Band; Mrchg Band; Orch; School Musical; School Play; Twrlr; NHS; Millersville U; Elem Ed.

MYERS, MICHAEL T; Dover Area HS; Dover, PA; (Y); 40/204; Boy Scts; Ski Clb; Teachers Aide; Band; Concert Band; Jazz Band; Mrchg Band; Pep Band; Hon Roll; Semper Fidelis Awd 86; Stu Of Mnth 86; U Pittsburgh; Mech Engrng.

MYERS, MICHELLE; Northern Cambria HS; Barnesboro, PA; (Y); 39/126; Chorus; Hon Roll; Typng,Steno Awd 86; Sec.

MYERS, NATHAN; Philipsburg-Osceola Area HS; Osceola Mills, PA; (Y); 8/265; Chess Clb; Band; Concert Band; Mrchg Band; High Hon Roll; Hon Roll; NHS; Prfct Atten Awd; Alsop Music Awd 84; NEDT Achvt Awd 84; U Pittsburgh; Phrmcy.

MYERS, PERRY; Engineering & Science; Philadelphia, PA; (S); 7/184; Chess Clb; Math Clb; Math Tm; Pres Temple Yth Grp; Rep Soph Cls; Rep Stu Cncl; High Hon Roll; NHS; Smith Klein Bckmn Math Leag Cty Wnnr 83; Hebrew Ntl Hnr Soc 83; Temple U; Actrl Sci.

MYERS, RICHARD; Northwestern HS; W Springfield, PA; (Y); Chess Clb; Computer Clb; Exploring; Model UN; Quiz Bowl; Ftbl; Gym; Trk; Wt Lftg; Comptr Prgmmg.

MYERS, RONALD; Roman Catholic HS; Philadelphia, PA; (S); Y-Teens; Hon Roll; NHS; Englsh Awd Upward Bnd 85; 2nd Hnrs Wrld Cuttures 84; MIT; Comp Engr.

MYERS, RUSSELL A; The Christian Acad; Upper Darby, PA; (Y); Computer Clb; Drama Clb; Thesps; Acpl Chr; Chorus; School Musical; School Play; Stage Crew; Variety Show; Ntl Merit SF; PA Hght Ed Asstn Agcy Cert Merit 85; Physics.

MYERS, SEAN; Fairchance Georges JR SR HS; Hopwood, PA; (Y); Library Aide; Im Ftbl; High Hon Roll; Hon Roll; Jr NHS; Physcl Thrpst.

MYERS, SHARON; Solanco HS; Peach Btm, PA; (Y); Art Clb; Church Yth Grp; Exploring; 4-H; Quiz Bowl; Spanish Clb; Nwsp Stf; JV Sftbl; JV Tennis; 4-H Awd; Art.

MYERS, SILAS; Penn Hills SR HS; Verona, PA; (S); 1/797; VP JA; Trs Sr Cls; Var Capt Ftbl; High Hon Roll; Pres Jr NHS; NHS; Val; French Clb; Science Clb; Varsity Clb; 2 Yr Vrsty Awd 85; Black Achvmnt Awd 86; VIP Awd 86; Harvard U; Pre-Med.

MYERS, STEVEN R; Mount Union Area HS; Mt Union, PA; (Y); 19/164; Trs Church Yth Grp; Cmnty Wkr; Spanish Clb; Varsity Clb; Var Bsktbl; Score Keeper; Var Trk; Im Wt Lftg; Joseph T Rothrock Chptr Ordr De Molay Offcr 86; SR Prom Commt 86; Math Tchr.

MYERS, TAMARA; Ford City HS; Ford City, PA; (Y); 22/175; Key Clb; Yrbk Stf; VP Frsh Cls; Rep Sr Cls; Sec Rep Stu Cncl; Tennis; High Hon Roll; Hon Roll; NHS; Trs Church Yth Grp; MVP-VRSTY Tnns 86; MVP-VRSTY Sftbl 85.

MYERS, THOMAS; Sharon SR HS; Sharon, PA; (Y); Art Clb; Church Yth Grp; Drama Clb; Varsity Clb; Band; Concert Band; Mrchg Band; School Musical; School Play; Var Crs Cntry; 1st Sectn 2-AA Wrstlg Champ 86; 3 Yr Ltrmn 3 Dif Sprts 83-86; Mst Vlbl Rnnr Awd Crss Cntry 85; Art.

MYERS, TINA; York County Vocational Tech Schl; East Berlin, PA; (Y); 41/410; Church Yth Grp; English Clb; 4-H; FHA; VICA; Nwsp Rptr; Nwsp Stf; Yrbk Ed-Chief; Yrbk Phtg; Yrbk Rptr; Awd Yrk Intrst Fair 84-85; Awd FHA 2nd Pl Altrtn ST 85-86; Awd FHA Chrmn Ldy Fndrasr 85-86; Cntrl Penn Bus Schl; Fshm Mrdsn.

MYERS, TRACY; Greencastle-Antrim HS; Greencastle, PA; (Y); 3/189; Drama Clb; Pres Chorus; School Musical; School Play; Nwsp Ed-Chief; Pres Sr Cls; Sec Rptr Stu Cncl; Var L Trk; VP NHS; Jessie Spielman Omwake Awd 86; Le Ona L Held Rcrtmnt Grnt 86; James Madison U; Spch Pthlgy.

MYERS, TRICIA; Eastern York HS; York, PA; (Y); 11/269; Camera Clb; Hosp Aide; Varsity Clb; JV Var Bsktbl; JV Var Vllybl; Hon Roll; Jr NHS; NHS; Schlrshp Awd 83-86; Trvl.

MYFORD, DONNA; Grove City HS; Grove City, PA; (Y); 20/200; Key Clb; Sec Jr Cls; Var L Bsktbl; Var L Tennis; Hon Roll; Acad All Amer Schlr Pgm 84-86; Bus.

MYIRSKI, LYNDA; Freedom HS; Bethlehem, PA; (Y); Cmnty Wkr; Girl Scts; Hosp Aide; Science Clb; Service Clb; Teachers Aide; JV Sftbl; Hon Roll; Cert Appreciation 82-83; 1st Cls G S Be Prepared Pin 83; NCACC; Bus Adm.

MYLER, WENDY; Penn Hills SR HS; Pittsburgh, PA; (Y); French Clb; Hosp Aide; JA; Library Aide; Hon Roll; St Vincent Coll; Psych.

MYRGA, JILL; Frazier HS; Newell, PA; (Y); Library Aide; Ski Clb; Rep Soph Cls; Rep Sr Cls; Rep Stu Cncl; Cheerleading; Gym; Sftbl; Hon Roll; CA U; Sec.

MYSZA, FRANK; Mc Guffey Area HS; Washington, PA; (S); 28/250; German Clb; Red Cross Aide; Varsity Clb; Var L Bsbl; Var L Ftbl; Wt Lftg; Var L Wrstlng; Hon Roll; Ntl Merit Schol; Penn ST; Engr.

NACCARATO, DIANA; Shaler Area HS; Glenshaw, PA; (Y); 172/521; Ski Clb; SADD; Band; Color Guard; Concert Band; Flag Corp; Mrchg Band; School Musical; Nwsp Stf; Im Bowling; 3rd Yr Lttrmn-Mrchg Band/Flg Tm 86; Outstndg Perfm Pgh Vets Day Parade 85; 1st Pl Flg Tm Cmptn 86; Inter Dsgn.

NACCARATO, VICKI; Elizabeth Forward HS; Mc Keesport, PA; (Y); French Clb; Mrchg Band; Nwsp Stf; Rep Frsh Cls; Rep Soph Cls; Twrlr; High Hon Roll; NHS; Bus Mgmt.

NACE, KIM; Mt Pleasant Area HS; Latrobe, PA; (Y); GAA; Ski Clb; Nwsp Phtg; Nwsp Stf; Yrbk Stf; Var Tennis; Var Twrlr; High Hon Roll; Hon Roll; Chorus; Humnts Day Awd 1st Plc Dramtc Perf Latin & German 84-85; Archtctr.

NACE, KIRK; Susquenita HS; Duncannon, PA; (S); 7/250; Quiz Bowl; Teachers Aide; Rep Frsh Cls; Sec Soph Cls; Rep Jr Cls; Stu Cncl; Var L Bsktbl; Var L Ftbl; Var Capt Trk; High Hon Roll; Engrng.

NACE, MISSY; Dover Area HS; Dover, PA; (Y); Pep Clb; SADD; Varsity Clb; Mrchg Band; Nwsp Stf; Hst Sr Cls; Rep Stu Cncl; Var Capt Cheerleading; Hon Roll; NHS; Outstndng Typst Awd; Central Penn Bus; Med Sec.

NADOLNY, MICHELLE; Corry Area HS; Corry, PA; (S); Church Yth Grp; Cmnty Wkr; Chorus; School Musical; Var L Bsktbl; Var Capt Vllybl; MVP Vllybl 85-86; All Star Sftbl 83 & 84; Mth Tchr.

NADOLSKY, MARIE; Penn Cambria SR HS; Lilly, PA; (Y); 16/214; Drama Clb; Spanish Clb; High Hon Roll; Hon Roll; Erly Chldhd Ed.

NADOLSKY, SAN DEE; Penn Cambria HS; Lilly, PA; (Y); Engrng.

NADONLEY, CHRISTINE; Windber Area HS; Windber, PA; (Y); Pres Church Yth Grp; Math Clb; Church Choir; Hon Roll; IN U PA; Nrsng.

NAESSIG, CHERYL; E L Meyers HS; Wilkes Barre, PA; (Y); AFS; Key Clb; Concert Band; Jazz Band; Mrchg Band; Trs Sr Cls; Stu Cncl; Capt Var Bsktbl; Capt Var Sftbl; NHS; Beatice Rosenthal Mem Awd 86; Natl Yth Salute 85; Pres Acadmc Ftnss Awd 86; U Of Scranton.

NAGEL, DAVE; Vincentian HS; Valencia, PA; (Y); Math Tm; School Musical; Im Badmtn; Im Ftbl; Var L Socr; Im Sftbl; Im Vllybl.

NAGG, KRISTIN; Upper Daughin Area HS; Elizabethville, PA; (Y); Art Clb; VP Church Yth Grp; Math Clb; Varsity Clb; Band; Chorus; Church Choir; Concert Band; Mrchg Band; School Musical; Stu Cncl Awd 86; Span Awd 84; US Stu Cncl Achvt Awd 86; La Salle U; Pre-Med.

NAGLE, BETSY; Meyers HS; Wilkes Barre, PA; (Y); 10/160; 4-H; Girl Scts; Key Clb; Pep Clb; Chorus; Swmmng; Trk; Vllybl; High Hon Roll; Hon Roll; PA ST U.

NAGLE, CLAUDINE; Northern Cambria HS; Barnesboro, PA; (Y); 27/126; Chorus; Yrbk Stf; JV Bsktbl; Mgr(s); L Sftbl; Hon Roll; NHS; Centre; Travel.

NAGLE, DAWN B; Dover Area HS; Dover, PA; (Y); 6/200; VP JA; Concert Band; Jazz Band; Mrchg Band; Mgr(s); High Hon Roll; NHS; Ntl Merit SF; SADD; Variety Show; Hugh O Brian Yth Ldrshp Awd 84; Harvard Secndry Smmr Schl 85; Intl Reltns.

NAGLE, DEANNA; William Allen HS; Allentown, PA; (Y); 58/604; Cmnty Wkr; Sec Intnl Clb; Leo Clb; School Play; Nwsp Stf; Lit Mag; Hon Roll; Jr NHS; NHS; Mc Crmick Bk Awd For Illstrtn 86; Muhlenberg; Psych.

NAGLE, JOSEPH; York Catholic HS; York, PA; (Y); JV Ftbl; Business.

NAGY, EDWARD W; New Brighton HS; New Brighton, PA; (Y); 12/156; Aud/Vis; Boy Scts; Computer Clb; Spanish Clb; Stage Crew; Nwsp Sprt Ed; Trs Frsh Cls; Bsbl; Hon Roll; Rotary Awd; Pres Acad Ftnss Awd 86; Edinboro U PA; Med Tech.

NAGY, LAURA; Freedom HS; Bethlehem, PA; (Y); 66/404; JA; Pep Clb; Science Clb; Var L Fld Hcky; Hon Roll; Fieldhockey Trophy Most Imprvd 83; Pres Acad Ftns Awd 86; Shippensburg U; Comp Sci.

NAGY JR, MICHAEL S; Fort Cherry HS; Mc Donald, PA; (S); Drama Clb; French Clb; Science Clb; Ski Clb; Thesps; Chorus; School Play; Mrtry Sci.

NAGY, ROBERT G; Downingtown SR HS; Downingtown, PA; (Y); Cmnty Wkr; Ski Clb; Spanish Clb; Bsktbl; Socr; High Hon Roll; Hon Roll; Bk Awd For Rlgn 84; Engr.

NAGY, THOMAS C; Malvern Prepartory Schl; Malvern, PA; (Y); 35/106; Boy Scts; Nwsp Rptr; Yrbk Stf; Stu Cncl; Bsbl; Ftbl; Jr NHS; Economics.

NAGY, TODD; Manheim Township HS; Lancaster, PA; (Y); 8/345; Exploring; JV Socr; Var Wrstlng; High Hon Roll.

NAHAS, CYNTHIA A; Monongahela Valley Catholic HS; Monongahela, PA; (S); Hosp Aide; Pep Clb; Spanish Clb; Chorus; Variety Show; Nwsp Ed-Chief; Yrbk Ed-Chief; Yrbk Stf; NHS; Sec Spanish NHS; Amer Legion Awd; Penn ST U; Htl-Rstrnt Mgmt.

NAHOLNIK, MELISSA; Western Wayne HS; Waymart, PA; (Y); 30/138; FBLA; Yrbk Stf; Rep Sr Cls; Var Bsktbl; Var Cheerleading; Var Sftbl; Hon Roll; Jr NHS.

NAIR, BRENDAN; Redbank Valley HS; New Bethlehem, PA; (Y); 13/150; Pres French Clb; Pres Varsity Clb; Trs Soph Cls; Pres Jr Cls; VP Sr Cls; Var L Bsbl; Var Capt Bsktbl; Var Capt Ftbl; Var L Trk; Var Wt Lftg; Ftbl Schlrshp Clarion U 86-87; All Conf 85; Clb Awd 86; Clarion U.

NAJDA, SUSAN; Shenandoah Valley HS; Shenandoah, PA; (Y); 4/107; Pep Clb; Yrbk Ed-Chief; Stu Cncl; Stat Bsktbl; Capt Cheerleading; Capt Pom Pon; High Hon Roll; NHS; Pres Schlr; CPA.

NAJERA, CLAUDIA P; Central Catholic HS; Reading, PA; (Y); Dance Clb; German Clb; Office Aide; Church Choir; Hon Roll; Pol Sci.

NALEPPA, HEIDI; Chartiers Valley HS; Carnegie, PA; (Y); 15/343; Dance Clb; German Clb; Drill Tm; School Musical; School Play; Rep Stu Cncl; Pom Pon; Trk; Hon Roll; NHS; IEP Higher Achvt Pgm 82-86; Acdmc Schlrshp Washington&jefferson 86; Washington & Jefferson; Bio.

NALESNIK JR, BERNARD J; Palmerton Area HS; Palmerton, PA; (Y); 1/150; Am Leg Boys St; Debate Tm; JV Var Bsbl; JV Var Bsktbl; Var Capt Ftbl; Var Wrstlng; Bausch & Lomb Sci Awd; High Hon Roll; NHS; Ntl Merit Ltr; Wrstlg Ldrshp Awd 86; Ftbl Outstndng Lnmn 85; Bsktbl JV MVP 85; Pre-Med.

NALL, JENNIFER; Brookville Area HS; Brookville, PA; (Y); 28/152; Drama Clb; Varsity Clb; Chorus; Madrigals; Orch; School Musical; Stu Cncl; Cheerleading; Hon Roll; Indiana U Of PA; Piano.

NALLY, COLLETTE; Archbishop Kennedy HS; Lafayette Hill, PA; (Y); Nwsp Stf; Rep Soph Cls; Rep Jr Cls; Sec Sr Cls; Sec Stu Cncl; Capt Cheerleading; Vllybl.

NANCE, REGGIE; Monongahela Valley Catholic HS; Brownsville, PA; (Y); Ski Clb; Variety Show; Wt Lftg; Embry-Riddle U; Engrng.

NANIEWICZ, BERNIE; Lakeland HS; Olyphant, PA; (S); 22/152; Ski Clb; Ftbl; Trk; Wt Lftg; High Hon Roll; Hon Roll; Prfct Atten Awd.

NANNA, CRAIG; Central Cambria HS; Ebensburg, PA; (S); 4/192; Church Yth Grp; Band; Stu Cncl; High Hon Roll; Prfct Atten Awd; Music Awd 85-86; Cnty, Dist & Rgnl Band 84-86; Acad All Amer 85-86; Oral Roberts U; Theolgy.

NANNI, MARY BETH; Marion Center Area HS; Creekside, PA; (S); 24/170; Sec Church Yth Grp; VP Intnl Clb; Q&S; Capt Flag Corp; Trs Soph Cls; Trs Jr Cls; Rep Stu Cncl; NHS; Teachers Aide; Rep To Hugh O Brian Western PA Ldrshp Semnr 84-85.

NAPE, LEAH; Bishop Hannan HS; Scranton, PA; (Y); 8/128; Chorus; School Musical; Trs Jr Cls; Rep Stu Cncl; JV Var Cheerleading; Var Sftbl; High Hon Roll; Hon Roll; Sec NHS; Ann Hilson Mem Scholar 82-86; Bishop Hannan Scholar 82-86; Biochem.

NAPE, MARNA; Bishop Hannan HS; Scranton, PA; (Y); 14/133; VP Jr Cls; Stu Cncl; Capt Cheerleading; Golf; Sftbl; High Hon Roll; NHS; Ann Hilson Mem Scholar; Engrng.

NAPIERALSKI, JAY; Lake Lehman HS; Shavertown, PA; (Y); Church Yth Grp; Var L Tennis; Hon Roll; Kings Coll; Math.

NAPLES, TONY; Meadville Area SR HS; Meadville, PA; (Y); 68/200; Church Yth Grp; French Clb; Letterman Clb; Varsity Clb; Stu Cncl; Var L Ftbl; Im Wt Lftg; JV Wrstlng; High Hon Roll; Hon Roll; Physcl Ftnss Achvt Awd Phys Ed Hnr SR Merit 83-86; Cert Of Prof Speed In Typng Awd 84-85; Bus Adm.

NAPOLETANO, MARIO; Downingtown SR HS; Downingtown, PA; (Y); Intnl Clb; Ski Clb; Teachers Aide; Concert Band; Jazz Band; Bowling; Lcrss; Var Trk; Hon Roll; NHS.

NAPOLI, MARIO; St John Neumann HS; Philadelphia, PA; (Y); 49/338; Radio Clb; Red Cross Aide; ROTC; SADD; Bsbl; Ftbl; Good Ctznshp Awd 85; Penn ST; Sales.

NAPOVANIC, NOELLE A; Monongohela Valley Catholic HS; Donora, PA; (Y); 15/86; French Clb; Ski Clb; Band; Chorus; Drm Mjr(t); Flag Corp; School Musical; Yrbk Bus Mgr; Yrbk Ed-Chief; Powder Puff Ftbl; U Pittsburgh; Chem Engr.

NARA, LARRY; Laurel Highlands HS; Uniontown, PA; (Y); 58/360; French Clb; French Hon Soc; Hon Roll; Air Force Cmnty Coll; Law Enfor.

NARDELLA, LOUIS; West Scranton HS; Scranton, PA; (Y); 5/253; Pres Church Yth Grp; Letterman Clb; Scholastic Bowl; Spanish Clb; Trs Sr Cls; Off Stu Cncl; Var L Bsbl; JV Bsktbl; Var Capt Golf; Hon Roll; U Scranton; Physcs.

NARDIS, STACEY; West Greene HS; Wind Ridge, PA; (Y); Dance Clb; Drama Clb; Library Aide; Science Clb; Varsity Clb; Capt Cheerleading; High Hon Roll; Trs NHS; Yrbk Stf; Stat Bsktbl; 15th Intrntnl Opn Chrldng Chmp 85; Pres Yth Educ Assoc 86; U Of SC; Chrprctr.

NARDONE, DOMINQUE; Wyoming Area HS; West Pittston, PA; (Y); Art Clb; Key Clb; Ski Clb; Spanish Clb; Stage Crew; Sec Frsh Cls; Sec Soph Cls; JV Bsktbl; Bloomsburg.

NARDONE, JAMES; Pittston Area SR HS; Pittston, PA; (Y); French Clb; Chorus; Hon Roll; NHS.

NARDOZZA, JOLEEN; Clearfield Area HS; Clearfield, PA; (Y); 101/313; Church Yth Grp; Key Clb; Spanish Clb; Band; Chorus; Church Choir; Color Guard; Mrchg Band; Stat Bsktbl; Hon Roll; Alvernia Coll; Phys Thrpy.

NARDUCCI, RENEE; North Penn HS; Lansdale, PA; (Y); 43/678; Ski Clb; Off Frsh Cls; Off Soph Cls; Off Jr Cls; Off Stu Cncl; Var Cheerleading; Powder Puff Ftbl; Sftbl; Tennis; High Hon Roll; Outstndng HOBY Fndtn Stu 85; Hnr Rl Awds; Pol Sci.

NAREHOOD, WILLIAM; Quigley HS; Conway, PA; (S); 4/112; Chess Clb; Math Tm; Service Clb; VP Frsh Cls; VP Soph Cls; Var L Bsbl; Capt L Ftbl; High Hon Roll; Lion Awd; NHS; Knghts Clmbs Stu/Athlt Yr 86; Acdmc All Amrcn 86; PA ST U; Engnrng.

NARROW, JODI; Hazelton SR HS; Hazleton, PA; (Y); 35/388; Cmnty Wkr; Drama Clb; FBLA; Hosp Aide; Quiz Bowl; School Play; Nwsp Ed-Chief; Ed Yrbk Stf; Hon Roll; NHS; Easter Seals Top Seller 85; Cancer Soc Top Seller 84; Nrsg.

NARSAVAGE, PETER; Scranton Prep Schl; Moscow, PA; (Y); 42/192; Band; Chorus; Concert Band; Orch; Pep Band; School Musical; High Hon Roll; NHS; 1st Pl Amer Chemcl Soc HS Cmpttn 86.

NARTATEZ, AMY; Philipsburg Osceola Area HS; Philipsburg, PA; (Y); 11/250; Church Yth Grp; Letterman Clb; Ski Clb; Varsity Clb; Pres Jr Cls; VP Stu Cncl; JV Var Bsktbl; JV Var Vllybl; Im Wt Lftg; NHS; Bus Admn.

NARVAEZ, MARK; Freedom HS; Bethlehem, PA; (Y); 28/445; Mathletes; Pep Clb; Band; Concert Band; Mrchg Band; Pep Band; Symp Band; JV Var Socr; Hon Roll; NHS; Med.

NASADOS, CHRISTOPHER; Fleetwood Area HS; Fleetwood, PA; (Y); 42/109; Boy Scts; Quiz Bowl; Scholastic Bowl; Band; Jazz Band; Mrchg Band; Orch; School Musical; Var Bsktbl; Cit Awd; Eagle Scout 86; Chemistry.

NASE, PAMELA; Souderton Area HS; Souderton, PA; (Y); 30/400; Church Yth Grp; Sec FCA; SADD; Chorus; School Musical; Rep Stu Cncl; Capt Cheerleading; Cit Awd; High Hon Roll; Trs NHS; Hmcmng Queen 85-86; Bloomsburg U; Nrs.

NASH, YOLANDA; Lutheran HS; Philadelphia, PA; (Y); Capt Debate Tm; Teachers Aide; Church Choir; Mst Imprvd-Latin 83-84; Psychlgy.

NASPINSKI, ED; Wyalusing Valley HS; New Albany, PA; (Y); 1/140; Am Leg Boys St; Chorus; Jazz Band; Orch; Rep VP Stu Cncl; Var Capt Crs Cntry; Var Capt Trk; Bausch & Lomb Sci Awd; High Hon Roll; NHS; Elec Engrng.

NASRANI, PAUL; Hazleton HS; Hazleton, PA; (Y); 3/389; Boy Scts; Pres Church Yth Grp; FBLA; Scholastic Bowl; Nwsp Ed-Chief; Pres Sr Cls; JV Capt Bsktbl; Var Trk; High Hon Roll; Am Leg Awd 84; Penn ST; Acctg.

NASSAR, DAVID; Bishop Kenrick HS; Audubon, PA; (Y); 20/297; Cmnty Wkr; Capt Debate Tm; Model UN; NFL; ROTC; Speech Tm; Nwsp Rptr; Cit Awd; NHS; Opt Clb Awd; PA Statewide Mock Trial Comptn 86; Law.

NASSAR, MARK; Valley Forge Military Acad; Fairfax Sta, VA; (Y); ROTC; Varsity Clb; Var Bsbl; Acad Cadet Of Mnth 86; Naval Aviatn.

NATALE, BETH; New Castle SR HS; New Castle, PA; (S); 8/253; Varsity Clb; Var Bsktbl; Var Capt Tennis; Elem Educ.

NATALE, GREG; Carlynton HS; Pittsburgh, PA; (Y); Drama Clb; Chmcl Engrng.

NATH, KRISTIN; Hempfield Area SR HS; Greensburg, PA; (Y); 124/649; German Clb; NFL; Pep Clb; Band; Color Guard; Flag Corp; Mrchg Band; Pep Band; Yrbk Stf; Hon Roll; Westmoreland Cnty Med Soc Aux Schlrp 86; U Pittsburgh; Hearing Impaird.

NATHAN, DAVID; Lower Moreland HS; Huntingdon Valley, PA; (S); 1/214; Debate Tm; Mathletes; NFL; Science Clb; Stage Crew; Lit Mag; JV Crs Cntry; NHS; Val; US Senate Schlrshp Pgm-Japan 85.

NAUGHTON, LEANNE; Bethel Park HS; Bethel Pk, PA; (Y); Drama Clb; JA; Chorus; Drill Tm; Mrchg Band; School Musical; Swing Chorus; Variety Show; Var Pom Pon; Hon Roll.

NAUGHTON, SUE; West Scranton HS; Scranton, PA; (Y); Exploring; French Clb; Pom Pon; Law.

NAUGLE, BARBRA ALYSON; New Castle SR HS; New Castle, PA; (S); 1/253; AFS; Pres Church Yth Grp; Pres French Clb; Hosp Aide; Band; Rep Stu Cncl; Stat Gym; Var L Trk; High Hon Roll; Perfect Attndnce 82-84; Acdm Games Part Ntl, ST, Regnl, Local 84; Ithaca Coll; Phy Therapy.

NAUGLE, CHRISTY; Conemaugh Township HS; Hollsopple, PA; (Y); Am Leg Aux Girls St; Church Yth Grp; FHA; Q&S; Ski Clb; Chorus; Mrchg Band; Yrbk Stf; Twrlr; Drama Clb; Americanism Awd 86; U Pittsburgh; Child Care.

NAUGLE, MARK; New Castle SR HS; New Castle, PA; (S); 1/236; Church Yth Grp; Computer Clb; French Clb; NFL; Ski Clb; Var Capt Ftbl; Var L Trk; High Hon Roll; NHS; Grmmr Awd 83; Acadmc Game Prtcptn Natl Rgnl ST, Locl 83 & 84; Harvard U; Sci.

NAULTY, DANA; Canon Mc Millan HS; Canonsburg, PA; (Y); Camera Clb; Latin Clb; Ski Clb; Spanish Clb; SADD; Yrbk Phtg; Stu Cncl; Var Fld Hcky; Var Powder Puff Ftbl; Hon Roll; Pol Sci.

NAUMAN, KAROLYN; Manheim Cental HS; Manheim, PA; (Y); 11/193; Pep Clb; Band; Concert Band; Mrchg Band; Stu Cncl; Cheerleading; Powder Puff Ftbl; High Hon Roll; Rotary 4 Way Tst Awd 86; Bus Awd 85; Southeastern Acad FL; Comp.

NAUS, KIMBERLY; Berrwick Area SR HS; Berwick, PA; (Y); Rep Church Yth Grp; FBLA; Scholastic Bowl; Nwsp Stf; Yrbk Rptr; Hon Roll; Jr NHS; NHS; Pres Schlr; Library Aide; Accptd U Schlrs Prog 86; Bloomsburg U; Med Tech.

NAUSE, KEITH; Cedar Cliff HS; Camp Hill, PA; (Y); 53/272; Spanish Clb; Wrstlng; High Hon Roll; Spanish NHS; Old Timers Atltc Assn Outstndg Wrstlr 86; Prsdntl Acdmc Fitness Awd 86; PIAA Wrstlg ST Trnmnt 86; Penn ST U; Business.

NAUSE, LORI; Brookville Area HS; Brookville, PA; (Y); Sec Church Yth Grp; Pres FBLA; NHS; Pres Acadmc Fitns Awd 86; Outstndg Bus Educ Awd 86; Advncd Typewrtng Awd 85; Secy.

NAUSE, REBECCA; Hatboro-Horsham SR HS; Hatboro, PA; (Y); 32/286; French Clb; Key Clb; Chorus; Stu Cncl; JV Bsktbl; Var L Bowling; Var L Fld Hcky; Var L Lcrss; Sftbl; Swmmng; Nrsng.

NAVARRO, ALBERT; Blue Mountain Acad; Pipersville, PA; (S); 3/70; Quiz Bowl; Ski Clb; Nwsp Phtg; Nwsp Rptr; Yrbk Phtg; Pres Soph Cls; JV Bsktbl; Im Sftbl; Capt Vllybl; Prfct Atten Awd; A-Leag All-Star Sftbl Capt; Hgh Hnrs Schlrshp; Columbia Union Coll; Chem.

NAVARRO, EFREN; Central York SR HS; York, PA; (Y); Band; Concert Band; Mrchg Band; Orch; School Musical; Symp Band; Im Socr; High Hon Roll; Hon Roll; NHS; Engrng.

NAVAZIO, MICHELLE; Saint Maria Goretti HS; Philadelphia, PA; (Y); 41/390; Church Yth Grp; Lit Mag; Rep Frsh Cls; Rep Soph Cls; Hon Roll; Philadelphia Collp; Phrmcy.

NAVONEY, CATHERINE; Quigley HS; Mars, PA; (Y); Church Yth Grp; Dance Clb; Band; Concert Band; Drill Tm; Mrchg Band; Stat Bsbl; Stat Bsktbl; Coach Actv; Diving; Euchrstc Mnstr; Prom & Hmcmg Comm; Ms Cranberry 1st Rnnr Up Beauty Cntst; Slippery Rock; Acctg.

NAWROCKI, LAURA; Susquehanna Township HS; Harrisburg, PA; (Y); 2/155; Am Leg Aux Girls St; Drama Clb; Math Tm; Chorus; School Musical; Nwsp Rptr; Capt L Fld Hcky; High Hon Roll; NHS; Art Clb; Outstndg Spnsh III Stu 85-86.

NAYLOR, FRANCINE; Wm Penn SR HS; York, PA; (Y); 47/321; Church Yth Grp; Office Aide; Church Choir; Hon Roll; Delores Brym Schlrshp 86; Delta Sigma Theta Schlrshp 86; Vincent B Stankus Awd 86; Lincoln U; Bus Adm.

NAYLOR, HOLLY; West Perry HS; Landisburg, PA; (Y); 16/216; VP Computer Clb; Pep Clb; Spanish Clb; Varsity Clb; Yrbk Stf; Yrbk Rptr; Yrbk Sprt Ed; Yrbk Stf; Hon Roll; NHS; Compu Sci.

NAYLOR, JILL; Gwynedd-Mercy Acad; Meadowbrook, PA; (Y); 31/70; Cmnty Wkr; Varsity Clb; Yrbk Stf; Diving; Var Lcrss; Var Socr; JV Sftbl; JV Tennis; JV Vllybl; Purdue U; Lbrl Arts.

NAYLOR, LAURA; Belle Vernon Area HS; Belle Vernon, PA; (Y); FBLA; Color Guard; Yrbk Stf; Powder Puff Ftbl; Hon Roll; Sawyer Schl; Med Asst.

NAYLOR, LISA C; Mechanicsburg Area SR HS; Shiremanstown, PA; (Y); 49/299; Church Yth Grp; Girl Scts; Hosp Aide; Red Cross Aide; Ski Clb; SADD; Drill Tm; Nwsp Stf; Yrbk Stf; Mgr Fld Hcky; Hstd Exchng Stu Frm Spain 85; Vstd Spain 1 Mnth Lvd Wth Fmly; Millersville U; Scndry Educ.

NAYLOR, RICHARD; Harry S Truman HS; Croydon, PA; (Y); 31/620; Rep Frsh Cls; Var JV Bsbl; Var JV Bowling; Hon Roll; Rider Coll; Bus Admin.

NEAL, BARBARA; Central York SR HS; York, PA; (Y); 16/224; Sec Church Yth Grp; Chorus; Mrchg Band; School Musical; Symp Band; Yrbk Ed-Chief; High Hon Roll; NHS; Rotary Awd; Band; Pres Clsrm Young Am 86; Penn ST; Lib Arts.

NEAL, CHARLES; Butler SR HS; Butler, PA; (Y); 90/786; Latin Clb; Math Tm; ROTC; Spanish Clb; Rep Soph Cls; JV Var Crs Cntry; JV Socr; Jr NHS; Acad Excllnce Awd JROTC 85; Acad Excllnce Awd Am Leg 85; Supr JR Cadet Awd Dept Army 86.

NEAL, DAWN; Tussey Mountain HS; Saxton, PA; (Y); Church Yth Grp; Drama Clb; Intnl Clb; Band; Chorus; Church Choir; Stat Bsbl; Hon Roll; Spanish Clb; Concert Band; Messiah Coll; Nrsng.

NEAL, DONALD E; Punxsutawney Area SR HS; Punxsutawney, PA; (Y); 137/238; Varsity Clb; Variety Show; Var L Bsbl; Var L Bsktbl; MVP Bsbl 86; Methodist Coll.

NEAL, ERIC J; Blairsville SR HS; Blairsville, PA; (Y); Pres Church Yth Grp; Band; Church Choir; Concert Band; Mrchg Band; VP Swmmng; VP L Trk; Im Wrstlng; Hon Roll; VICA; YMCA St & Dist Swim 86; Grove City Coll; Elec Engrng.

NEAL, LARRY; Nativity BVM HS; Tremont, PA; (Y); 40/97; French Clb; ROTC; Chorus; Hon Roll; Ntvty Sci Fair 3rd Pl In Chem 86; Philadelphia Coll; Bio.

NEAL, LISA; Kiski Area HS; Leechburg, PA; (Y); Pres Church Yth Grp; Chorus; Yrbk Stf; Var Trk; Hon Roll.

NEAL, MINDI; Brookville Area HS; Brookville, PA; (Y); 14/141; Key Clb; Pep Clb; Varsity Clb; Yrbk Stf; JV Bsktbl; Var Diving; Var Swmmng; JV Var Vllybl; High Hon Roll; Jr NHS; Lndscp Archtct.

NEAL, ROBIN; Franklin HS; Polk, PA; (Y); 20/200; French Clb; Library Aide; JV Vllybl; High Hon Roll; Hon Roll; NHS; Schl Dirctrs Awd 84-85 & 85-86; Gannon U; Family Med.

NEAL, SHELLEY; Northern York HS; Dillsburg, PA; (Y); Computer Clb; Debate Tm; NFL; Speech Tm; Nwsp Stf; Stat Bsbl; Powder Puff Ftbl; Hon Roll; Harrisburg Cmnty Coll.

NEAL, TARA; Punxsutawney Area HS; Punxsutawney, PA; (Y); Spanish Clb; Varsity Clb; Cheerleading; Vllybl; Hon Roll; Pres Phys Ftns Awd 84-86; PIAA St Gymnastics Comp 85; USGF St Gymnastics Comp 84-85; Phys Ther.

NEALON, JOSEPH; Scranton Preparatory Schl; Scranton, PA; (Y); Church Yth Grp; Cmnty Wkr; Ski Clb; Stage Crew; VFW Awd; Bus.

NEALON, KAREN DIANE; West Scranton HS; Scranton, PA; (Y); Aud/Vis; Cmnty Wkr; JA; Spanish Clb; Speech Tm; Thesps; Orch; School Play; Stu Cncl; Hon Roll; PA ST U; Theatr.

NEARHOOF, SHARON; Tyrone Area HS; Warriors Mark, PA; (Y); Key Clb; SADD; Capt Color Guard; Flag Corp; Yrbk Rptr; Score Keeper; Hon Roll; Church Yth Grp; Latin Clb; Office Aide; Astrnmy.

NEASE, MATTHEW; Blairsville SR HS; Blairsville, PA; (Y); Varsity Clb; Ftbl; JV Trk; Wt Lftg; High Hon Roll.

NEBGEN, ELLEN; Tyrone Area HS; Altoona, PA; (Y); Drama Clb; Sec VP 4-H; Key Clb; Thesps; Band; Chorus; Church Choir; Concert Band; Mrchg Band; Pep Band; Pharm.

NECCIAI, WILLIAM; Ringgold HS; Donora, PA; (Y); Boy Scts; Varsity Clb; Var L Bsbl; JV Bsktbl; Bowling; Var Ftbl.

NED, JEMAL; Connellsville SR HS; Connellsville, PA; (Y); Science Clb; Hon Roll.

NEDDOFF, JOHN; G A R Memorial HS; Wilkes Barre, PA; (S); 20/187; Church Yth Grp; Drama Clb; Trs Key Clb; Chorus; Ed Yrbk Stf; Rep Stu Cncl; Capt Swmmng; Jr NHS; Computer Clb; Ski Clb; Sr Natl Hnr Socty 84-85; Swmng Awds Mst Imprvd, Mst Dedctd 84; Wilkes Coll; Engrng.

NEDEROSTEK, BETH; Parkland HS; Allentown, PA; (Y); 168/416; Pres Church Yth Grp; Cmnty Wkr; Red Cross Aide; Var L Sftbl; JV Trk; Immaculata Coll Acad Schlrshp 86; Immaculata Coll; Pre-Med.

NEDEROSTEK, JENNIFER; Marian HS; Jim Thorpe, PA; (S); 30/114; Church Yth Grp; French Clb; Pep Clb; Teachers Aide; Yrbk Stf; Hon Roll; Speech Therapy.

NEDROW, DAVID E; Elizabethtown Area HS; Elizabethtown, PA; (Y); 1/221; Am Leg Boys St; Boy Scts; VP Sr Cls; Rep Stu Cncl; Var L Socr; Var Swmmng; Var L Trk; NHS; Ntl Merit SF; Church Yth Grp; Century III Ldr 85; Amer Comp Sci Leag Top Scr PA Div 84-85; Outstdng JR Sci Stu 84-85; Lwyr.

NEDROW, KIMBERLY; Mt Pleasant Area HS; Stalhstown, PA; (Y); GAA; Band; Nwsp Stf; Mat Maids; Hon Roll; Bus Stu Of Mnth 86; Bus Clb Treas 87; WCCC; Sec.

NEDROW, RICHELLE; Hempfield Area SR HS; New Stanton, PA; (Y); 54/700; Pep Clb; Ski Clb; Spanish Clb; Rep Stu Cncl; Cheerleading; Vllybl; High Hon Roll; Hon Roll; Jr NHS; NHS; U Of Pittsburgh; Pharm.

NEE, DAWN; Upper Darby HS; Upr Darby, PA; (Y); 25/630; Yrbk Stf; Var Bsktbl; Var Lcrss; Var Vllybl; High Hon Roll; Hon Roll; Ntl Merit Ltr; Gentc Engrng.

NEEL, HEATHER; Jefferson-Morgan HS; Jefferson, PA; (Y); 1/86; Pres Service Clb; Spanish Clb; SADD; School Play; Rep Stu Cncl; Var Sftbl; Cit Awd; NHS.

NEEL, JOHN; Norwin HS; N Irwin, PA; (Y); Golf; WV U.

NEELY, DONALD; Trinity HS; Washington, PA; (Y); 19/370; Church Yth Grp; Church Choir; Var Crs Cntry; JV Ftbl; Var Trk; Hon Roll; Rcvd Pres Awd Phy Fit; Rcvd Outstndg Nwscrr Of Yr; Law.

NEELY, DOUGLAS; Grove City SR HS; Charlotte, NC; (Y); Ski Clb; School Play; Yrbk Phtg; Pres Sr Cls; Stu Cncl; Bsktbl; Ftbl; Tennis; Elks Awd; NHS; Wake Forest U; Pltcl Sci.

NEESEN, JAMES; Pennsbury HS; Yardley, PA; (Y); Spanish Clb; Ed Nwsp Stf; Yrbk Stf; Rep Frsh Cls; Rep Soph Cls; Rep Jr Cls; Trs Sr Cls; Im Bsktbl; JV Golf; Im Vllybl; Vlntr Wrk Congrssnmn Awd 85; Johns Hopkins Tlnt Srch Awd 81; Stanford; Engrng.

NEFF, BRIAN; Bishop Kenrick HS; Blue Bell, PA; (Y); Boy Scts; Church Yth Grp; Band; Concert Band; Mrchg Band; School Musical; Rep Sr Cls; JV Bsktbl; St Josephs.

NEFF, CYNTHIA; Butler Area SR HS; Chicora, PA; (Y); 32/780; Church Yth Grp; SADD; Teachers Aide; Color Guard; Hon Roll; Jr NHS; NHS; Optmtry.

NEFF, GWENDOLYN; Mt Lebanon HS; Pittsburgh, PA; (Y); 10/493; Church Yth Grp; Chorus; Mrchg Band; School Musical; Symp Band; Chrmn Yrbk Ed-Chief; Pom Pon; High Hon Roll; Ntl Merit Ltr; Cum Laude Soc; Oberlin COLL; Biopsychlgy.

NEFF, MATT; Hollidysburg SR HS; Hollidaysburg, PA; (Y); Band; Chorus; Church Choir; Concert Band; Jazz Band; Mrchg Band; Orch; Swing Chorus; All ST Orchestra 86; Music Educ.

NEGAHBAN, DARYUSH JCP; Lower Merien HS; Ardmore, PA; (Y); Pres VP Model UN; Spanish Clb; School Musical; Mgr School Play; Stage Crew; Hon Roll; 1st Pl Hwfrd Coll Mdl UN Nvc Scrty Cncl 83; 8th Pl IN U PA Physcs Achvt 85; Cmnwlth PA PHEAA Cert; Temple U; Math.

NEGLEY, KELLY; Knoch SR HS; Butler, PA; (Y); Aud/Vis; Sec Trs 4-H; Orch; School Musical; Stage Crew; 4-H Awd; NHS; Cert Profcncy Acctng 86; Orch Ltrmn 86; Grove City Coll; Acctg.

NEGRON, RAYMOND; Olney HS; Philadelphia, PA; (Y); Cmnty Wkr; Nwsp Rptr; Rep Frsh Cls; Rep Soph Cls; Rep Jr Cls; Var JV Bsbl; Hon Roll; Prfct Atten Awd; NHS; Advncd Coll Exprnc Pgm; Comp Pgmr.

NEHRER, DANIEL B; North Allegheny SR HS; Sewickley, PA; (Y); 178/642; Am Leg Boys St; Aud/Vis; Debate Tm; German Clb; ROTC; Rep Frsh Cls; Rep Soph Cls; Rep Jr Cls; Rep Stu Cncl; JV Bsktbl; U S Nvl Acad; Nvl Avtr.

NEHRIG, SUSAN; Homer Center HS; Homer City, PA; (Y); 4/106; Pres Sec Church Yth Grp; French Clb; Hosp Aide; Library Aide; Concert Band; School Play; Twrlr; Elks Awd; 4-H Awd; NHS; M Supinka JR Schlrshp 86; IN U Of PA; Nrsng.

NEHRING, ELIZABETH; Bishop O Reilly HS; Kingston, PA; (Y); Church Yth Grp; Band; Jazz Band; Orch; Pep Band; School Musical; Wright ST U; Math.

NEIBERGER, DAVID; Cardinal Brennan HS; Frackville, PA; (Y); 13/47; German Clb; Band; Chorus; Concert Band; Mrchg Band; School Play; Yrbk Phtg; Hon Roll; NHS; West Chester U; Chmst.

NEIDERER, KELLY; Delone Catholic HS; Hanover, PA; (Y); 9/168; VP Girl Scts; Model UN; Varsity Clb; Stage Crew; Ed Yrbk Stf; Rep Stu Cncl; Var Mgr Vllybl; Hon Roll; JC Awd; Kiwanis Awd; Moreau Schlrshp Kings Coll 86; Chas Boyd-Appleton Papers Schlrshp, Grad Hnrs 86; Kings/Wilkes-Barre; Crim Law.

NEIDIGH, DUANE; Palmyra HS; Annville, PA; (Y); 43/210; Band; Var Bsbl; Var Golf; Hon Roll; Biolgy.

NEIDLINGER, LORA; Schuylkill Haven HS; Schuylkill Haven, PA; (S); 8/85; German Clb; Band; Chorus; Concert Band; Mrchg Band; Pep Band; Rep Stu Cncl; Sftbl; Hon Roll; Crmnl Justc.

NEIDLINGER JR, RONALD; Tulpehocken HS; Myerstown, PA; (Y); Computer Clb; Stage Crew; Hon Roll; Vo-Tech Schl Stu Of Qurt Data Prcsng 86; Comp Prog.

NEIFERT, STACEY; Tamaqua Area HS; Tamaqua, PA; (Y); Girl Scts; Q&S; Chorus; Nwsp Rptr; Ed Nwsp Stf; Germn Ntl Hnr Scty; Tamaqua Area Stu Career Orgnztn; Bible Clb Pres; X-Ray Tech.

NEILL, JAMES; West Allegheny HS; Oakdale, PA; (Y); Boy Scts; VP Computer Clb; Bsbl; Hon Roll; Army.

NEILSEN, ROBERTA; Penn Wood HS; Clifton Heights, PA; (Y); 12/313; Drama Clb; Girl Scts; Band; Concert Band; Mrchg Band; Stu Cncl; Gym; Lcrss; Capt Vllybl; Hon Roll; N Grubb Ed Awd 86; Stu Cncl Awd 86; After-Glo Comm Awd 86; Neumann Coll; Bio.

NEIMEYER, SHEILA; Brandywine Heights HS; Mertztown, PA; (Y); 4/144; Am Leg Aux Girls St; Church Yth Grp; Yrbk Ed-Chief; Pres Frsh Cls; Pres Soph Cls; Pres Jr Cls; Var Sftbl; Var Tennis; High Hon Roll; NHS; Bus.

NEIN, RHONDA; Tyrone Area HS; Tyrone, PA; (Y); 97/198; French Clb; Office Aide; Sec SADD; Chorus; Church Choir; School Play; Capt Powder Puff Ftbl; Capt Sftbl; Hon Roll; Penn ST U; Elem Ed.

NEISWORTH, HEATHER; Quighley HS; Ambridge, PA; (Y); 34/103; Art Clb; Church Yth Grp; Drama Clb; French Clb; Girl Scts; Hosp Aide; Political Wkr; Ski Clb; SADD; Teachers Aide; Duquesne U; Law.

NEJMAN, PAUL; Technical Memorial HS; Erie, PA; (Y); 82/349; Band; Jazz Band; Wrstlng; Berklee Coll; Muisc.

NELABOVIGE, MARY; Reading Central Catholic HS; Hamburg, PA; (Y); Church Yth Grp; Debate Tm; Drama Clb; NFL; Office Aide; Chorus; Variety Show; Hon Roll; 3 1st Pl Extmprneous Spkng 85-86; Chem.

NELKO, MATTHEW J; Ambridge Area HS; Baden, PA; (Y); Trs Church Yth Grp; French Clb; Pep Clb; Mrchg Band; Symp Band; Hon Roll; U Pittsburgh; Bus Adm.

NELLES, JAMES; Garnet Valley HS; Glen Mills, PA; (Y); 16/160; Church Yth Grp; German Clb; Letterman Clb; Varsity Clb; L Socr; L Trk; L Wrstlng; Hon Roll; Named Most Outstndg Wrstlr 85-86; Dist 1 Wrsltng Champ 86; Aerodynamic Engineering.

NELSON, AIMEE; Coudersport JR SR HS; Coudersport, PA; (Y); 21/84; French Clb; Ski Clb; Band; Chorus; Concert Band; Mrchg Band; Yrbk Stf; Rep Stu Cncl; JV Var Score Keeper; Hon Roll; Marching & Concert Band 83-87; Chorus 83-87; Hon Roll 83-86; Soc Worker.

NELSON, ANTHONY; St John Neumann HS; Philadelphia, PA; (Y); 101/321; JA; Library Aide; Spanish Clb; Sr Cls; Stu Cncl.

NELSON, CARLA; Bellwood-Antis HS; Bellwood, PA; (Y); VP Church Yth Grp; SADD; Varsity Clb; JV Fld Hcky; Var L Trk; Im Vllybl; Hon Roll; NHS; Acad All Amer 86; Messiah Coll; Sprts Med.

NELSON, CAROL; Harborcreek HS; Erie, PA; (Y); 25/228; Sec Church Yth Grp; Model UN; Concert Band; Mrchg Band; Pep Band; Variety Show; Hon Roll; PA Free Entrprse Week At Lockhaven U Schlrshp 86; Grove City Coll; Bus Mgmt.

NELSON, CINDY; Northern Potter HS; Mills, PA; (Y); Varsity Clb; Band; Chorus; Bsktbl; Trk; Vllybl; High Hon Roll; Hon Roll; Sec NHS; IN U PA; Bus Mgmt.

NELSON, ELIZABETH; Montour HS; Pittsburgh, PA; (Y); Drama Clb; French Clb; Band; Chorus; Church Choir; Lib Concert Band; Lib Mrchg Band; School Musical; School Play; Ntl Merit Ltr; Music.

NELSON, JULIE; Central HS; Duncansville, PA; (Y); 57/189; Ski Clb; Varsity Clb; Var Trk; Hon Roll; Bus.

NELSON, KAMILLE; Clairton HS; Clairton, PA; (Y); JV Var Bsktbl; Hon Roll; Natl Hon Rl 86; Point Park COLL; Cmmnctns.

NELSON, KEVIN; Annville-Cleona HS; Annville, PA; (Y); 25/129; Church Yth Grp; VP French Clb; Math Clb; Math Tm; School Musical; School Play; Nwsp Rptr; Yrbk Phtg; Jr NHS; NHS; Rochester Inst Of Tech; Prntng.

NELSON, KRISTY; Greenville Sr HS; Greenville, PA; (Y); 6/132; Church Yth Grp; Pres 4-H; Band; Chorus; Sec Mrchg Band; School Musical; Variety Show; Var Cheerleading; 4-H Awd; NHS; Soph Otrch Cnslr Drg & Alchl Prgrms 86; Cmmnctns.

NELSON, MIKE; Annville-Cleona HS; Cleona, PA; (Y); 30/115; Varsity Clb; Band; JV Bsbl; Var Capt Ftbl; JV Trk; Wt Lftg; Var JV Wrstlng; Jr NHS; NHS; Prfct Atten Awd.

NELSON, SANDY; Calvary Baptist Christian Acad; Meadville, PA; (S); 1/5; Church Yth Grp; Chorus; Pep Band; Yrbk Stf; JV Var Cheerleading; L Sftbl; L Vllybl; High Hon Roll; NHS; KCEA ST Com JR Comprhnsv Engl 1st Pl 84; MVP Grls Vlybl 84; All A Hnr Rl 83-85; Phys Ther.

NELSON, TRACI; Dover Area HS; Dillsburg, PA; (Y); 40/241; Spanish Clb; Color Guard; Drill Tm; Mrchg Band; Hon Roll; Elem Ed.

NEMCOFF, MARK; Strathhaven HS; Wallingford, PA; (Y); Variety Show; Bsbl; Bsktbl; Socr; Tennis; High Hon Roll; Hon Roll; Pres Schlr; 1st Pl Battle Of The Bands 86; Berklee Coll Of Music.

NEMEC, JOEL; Charleroi JR SR HS; Monongahela, PA; (Y); Ski Clb; Spanish Clb; Varsity Clb; Band; Im Bsktbl; JV Var Ftbl; Hon Roll; CA U Of PA.

NEMEC, LAURI; Yough SR HS; W Newton, PA; (Y); 50/250; Library Aide; Ski Clb; Spanish Clb; Chorus; Drm Mjr(t); Mrchg Band; Mgr(s); Powder Puff Ftbl; Twrlr; Hon Roll; Pitt; Nrsg.

NEMETH, JAMES; Northampton SR HS; Northampton, PA; (S); 28/475; Aud/Vis; Computer Clb; DECA; VP FBLA; Letterman Clb; Varsity Clb; Yrbk Phtg; Pres VP Stu Cncl; JV Bsbl; Var Bsktbl; PA ST Bd-Stu Cncl 85-86; Stu Of Mnth, Exch Clb 85; Pres Of Stu Cncl 85-86; Villanova U.

NEMETH, MIKE; Northampton Area HS; Northampton, PA; (Y); Trs Frsh Cls; Var Crs Cntry; Var L Swmmng; Var Trk; Hon Roll; Dist Champ Swmmng; Conf All Star Tm Swmng.

NEMETZ, ALLISON; Phoenixville Area HS; Phoenixville, PA; (Y); Church Yth Grp; Key Clb; Library Aide; Pep Clb; Quiz Bowl; SADD; Chorus; Stage Crew; Nwsp Stf; Yrbk Stf; Cmntctns.

NEPA, FRANK; Laurel Highlands SR HS; Uniontown, PA; (Y); 1/350; Church Yth Grp; Math Tm; Band; Mgr(s); CC Awd; High Hon Roll; Jr NHS; NHS; Ntl Merit Ltr; NEDT Awd; Stu Yr 84; Exch Clb Stu Semester 84; Elec Engrng.

NEPOMUCENO, RANDY RAY; St Josephs Preparatory Schl; Jenkintown, PA; (Y); French Clb; Mathletes; Im Bsktbl; Im Ftbl; JV Wrstlng; High Hon Roll; Ntl Merit Ltr; Camera Clb; Intnl Clb; Library Aide; Fnlst Spllng Bee 83-84; Hnry Schlrshp Prep Sch 83-84; 1st Pl Trphy Wrstlng 84-85; U Of PA; Pre Med.

NEPPACH, BECKY; Quigley HS; Baden, PA; (Y); Pep Clb; Sec Frsh Cls; Hon Roll; Elem Educ.

NERO, PAM; New Castle HS; New Castle, PA; (S); 14/253; Chorus; Hon Roll.

NERONE, BECKY; South Park HS; Library, PA; (Y); Ski Clb; Band; Drill Tm; Mrchg Band; High Hon Roll; NHS; Duquesne U; Bus.

NESBIT, CHRIS; Weatherly Area HS; Blakeslee, PA; (Y); FBLA; Pep Clb; VICA; Hon Roll; FBLA Regnl Data Prcssng Cncpts 3rd Plc 86; Hghst Engl Avg 92% 86; Comp Prgrmmng.

NESBIT, JOELLE; Villa Maria Acad; Erie, PA; (Y); 25/145; Church Yth Grp; Model UN; Science Clb; Color Guard; Nwsp Stf; Yrbk Stf; Stu Cncl; Hon Roll; Pre-Law.

NESBITT, JULIA; Marple Newtown HS; Broomall, PA; (Y); Band; Var Sftbl; Var Capt Vllybl; Bausch & Lomb Sci Awd; Hon Roll; NHS; Prfct Atten Awd; Church Yth Grp; Concert Band; Mrchg Band; 2 Vllybl Var Ltrs 84-85; Am Chem Soc Awd 85; 2 Sftbl Var Ltrs 85-86.

NESBITT, STEPHANIE; Avon Grove HS; Lincoln Univ, PA; (Y); 3/179; SADD; Concert Band; School Musical; VP Frsh Cls; Rep Jr Cls; Rep Sr Cls; Var L Fld Hcky; Var L Gym; Var L Trk; Pres NHS; Physics Awd 85-86; Ec Awd 85-86; Hon Stu 85-86.

NESFEDER JR, DAVID G; William Allen HS; Allentown, PA; (Y); Computer Clb; Hon Roll; Jr NHS; NHS; Presdntl Awd Grade Point Avrg 86; PA ST U; Comp Sci.

NESGODA, DENISE M; Marian Catholic HS; Hazleton, PA; (Y); 53/119; Church Yth Grp; Cmnty Wkr; Dance Clb; SADD; Yrbk Stf; Lbrl Arts.

NESMITH, EMMILYN L; J R Masterman HS; Philadelphia, PA; (Y); Church Yth Grp; Hosp Aide; School Musical; Mgr Stage Crew; Yrbk Stf; Var Bowling; Score Keeper; Var Vllybl; Ntl Merit Schol; Ntl Achvt Fnls Schlrshp 86; GA Inst Tech; Bus Adm.

NESS, LISA; Red Lion Area SR HS; Red Lion, PA; (Y); 75/330; Library Aide; SADD; Hon Roll.

NESTLER, CAROLE; Baldwin HS; Pittsburgh, PA; (Y); 33/546; Cheerleading; High Hon Roll; Hon Roll; Jr NHS; NHS; Accntng.

NESTOR, GREG; Fox Chapel Area HS; Pittsburgh, PA; (Y); Cmnty Wkr; Var L Crs Cntry; Var L Trk; Hon Roll.

NETHING, TRACEY L; Mars Area SR HS; Valencia, PA; (Y); Church Yth Grp; German Clb; Library Aide; SADD; High Hon Roll; Hon Roll; Day Care.

NETTLES, JAMES; Minersville Area HS; Pottsville, PA; (Y); 15/115; Ski Clb; Spanish Clb; Stage Crew; JV L Bsbl; JV L Bsktbl; Im Ftbl; Im Sftbl; Im Vllybl; Im Wrstlng; High Hon Roll; PA ST U; Archtctrl Engr.

NETTROUR, ELIZABETH; North Allegheny HS; Alison Park, PA; (Y); Drama Clb; Pep Clb; PAVAS; Ski Clb; Thesps; School Musical; School Play; Variety Show; Off Jr Cls; Rep Stu Cncl; Girl Mo 86; Nrth Allghny Drma Achvt, Drma Awd 86; Westminster Coll; Thtr.

NEU, ANDREW; Hatboro Horsham SR HS; Hatboro, PA; (Y); 28/276; Key Clb; Service Clb; Chorus; Concert Band; Jazz Band; Mrchg Band; Stage Crew; Variety Show; Trk; Hon Roll; French; Hnr Soc; Band; Aerospace Engrng.

NEUBERGER, CHERYL; Our Lady Of The Sacred Heart HS; Aliquippa, PA; (Y); 4-H; Girl Scts; Library Aide; Service Clb; Yrbk Stf; Trs Frsh Cls; Bowling; Var L Vllybl; Hon Roll; GS Slvr Ldrshp Awds 84; GS Gld Ldrshpa Wd, Gld Awd 86; Duquesne U; Law.

NEUBERT, DEBRA; St Marys Area HS; Saint Marys, PA; (Y); Yrbk Stf; Crs Cntry.

NEUIN, LISA MARIE; Schuylkill Haven Area HS; Schuylkill Haven, PA; (Y); #26 In Class; Am Leg Aux Girls St; SADD; Teachers Aide; Band; Chorus; Concert Band; Mrchg Band; Pep Band; School Musical; Stage Crew; Schuylkill Cnty Chorus Fstvl 84; Hon Banquet & Guard 86; Blind Ed.

NEULIGHT, JOSEPH; Parkland SR HS; Allentown, PA; (Y); Q&S; Ski Clb; Var Trk; High Hon Roll; NHS; Nwsp Sprt Ed; Ng Calls Stu Nwsp Advsry Pgm-SNAP 86.

NEUMAN, ERIN; Allentown Central Catholic HS; Whitehall, PA; (Y); 51/217; Church Yth Grp; German Clb; Nwsp Rptr; Nwsp Stf; Var Capt Cheerleading; High Hon Roll; Hon Roll; 2nd Pl PA JR Acad Sci 84-85; Engl.

NEUMANN, ANN M; Owen J Roberts HS; Pottstown, PA; (S); 7/291; JA; Scholastic Bowl; JV Sftbl; DAR Awd; High Hon Roll.

NEUMANN, KEN; Hatboro-Horsham HS; Hatboro, PA; (Y); Boy Scts; Band; Chorus; Concert Band; Jazz Band; Mrchg Band; God Cntry Awd; Hon Roll; Prfct Atten Awd; Bst Wkshp Soph 85; Woodwrkr.

NEUMEISTER, SUZANNE; Southern Columbia Area HS; Shamokin, PA; (Y); 4/75; Church Yth Grp; Varsity Clb; Pres Soph Cls; Sec Jr Cls; JV Bsktbl; Var L Fld Hcky; Stat Sftbl; High Hon Roll; NHS; Engrng.

NEUMYER, TODD M; Central Dauphin East HS; Harrisburg, PA; (Y); 33/274; Boy Scts; Church Yth Grp; VP Exploring; Letterman Clb; Chorus; L Socr; Im Vllybl; L Wrstlng; Hon Roll; NHS; Wrstlng Capt, Bst Tkdwn Awd, 5 1st Pls, PA Big 12 Hon Ment 86; PA ST U; Pre Med.

NEUPAUER, KAREN L; South Williamsport SR HS; S Williamsport, PA; (Y); Pep Clb; Gym; Trk; Med Sec.

NEUPAUER, MICHAEL; Lincoln HS; Ellwood City, PA; (Y); 40/190; Var Pres Latin Clb; Ski Clb; Yrbk Stf; Stu Cncl; Ftbl; High Hon Roll; Hon Roll; Engl.

NEVEL, MICHAEL; Berwick Area SR HS; Berwick, PA; (Y); Math Clb; Rep Stu Cncl; Hon Roll; NHS; Prfct Atten Awd.

NEVILLE, AMY; Redbank Valley HS; New Bethlehem, PA; (Y); 2/120; French Clb; Church Choir; Concert Band; Mrchg Band; Pep Band; School Musical; Hon Roll; NHS; Sal; PDACA Schrlshp 86; PA ST U; Arch.

NEVILLE, JONATHAN C; East Pennsboro Area HS; Camp Hill, PA; (Y); 5/190; Drama Clb; Office Aide; School Play; Yrbk Ed-Chief; Yrbk Stf; High Hon Roll; Ntl Merit SF; French Clb; Stu Cncl; PA Gvrnrs Schl For Arts 85; Acclds Wrtng Awd 85; Schltc Wrtng Awds-Hnrbl Mntn 85; Northwestern U; Actor.

NEVINS, MARYBETH; Central Bucks East HS; Doylestown, PA; (Y); Church Yth Grp; Chorus; Flag Corp; Mrchg Band; Twrlr; Hon Roll; Bnd Front 84-86; Ltr Swing Flgs 85-86; Partcptn Awd Choir; Span.

NEVISON, SCOTT; Harry S Truman HS; Fairless Hills, PA; (Y); 1/576; Spanish Clb; Wt Lftg; High Hon Roll; Hon Roll; Spanish NHS; Distngshd Achvt Awd For Spnsh Excllnc 85; Physcs.

NEWBALL, ALBERT; Blue Mountain Acad; Bellport, NY; (Y); Computer Clb; Chorus; Trs Jr Cls; Off Stu Cncl; Im Bsktbl; Im Vllybl; Archtrl Engr.

NEWCASTER, JAYANNE; Butler Area SR HS; Butler, PA; (Y); Exploring; Hosp Aide; VP Spanish Clb; SADD; Drill Tm; Rep Stu Cncl; NHS; PA YMCA Yth & Govt Scrtry Of House Of Rep 86; Engrng.

NEWCOMB, JEANNINE; St Maria Goretti HS; Philadelphia, PA; (Y); 200/370; Dance Clb; Drama Clb; FBLA; PAVAS; School Musical; School Play; Variety Show; Cheerleading; Gym; Tchrs Cert In Dance In NY 85-86; Cert Of Merit For 1st Prize In A Tap Cntst 85-86; Coll Of Perf Arts; Dance.

NEWCOME, JENNIFER; Brookville Area HS; Brookville, PA; (S); 4/147; Pres 4-H; German Clb; Varsity Clb; Stu Cncl; Var L Sftbl; Var L Vllybl; 4-H Awd; High Hon Roll; Jr NHS; NHS; PA 4-H Horse Shw ST Mstrshwmn 85; IN U PA; Elem Spec Ed.

NEWCOMER, DAVIN L; Freedom HS; Easton, PA; (Y); 40/402; Church Yth Grp; Im Bsbl; Im Wrstlng; High Hon Roll; Hon Roll; NHS; Pres Acadmc Awd 86; Cls Spkr-Cmmncmnt 86; Lehigh U; Elec Engrng.

NEWCOMER, TODD; Manheim Central HS; Mt Joy, PA; (Y); Boy Scts; Church Yth Grp; 4-H; VICA; Band; Concert Band; Mrchg Band; CC Awd; 4-H Awd; Hon Roll; Mnt Joy Vo-Tech A H Weidman Awd 86; Martina Roettger Mem Awd 86; VICA Dist Electrl Occuptn 2nd Pl 86; De Vry Tech Inst; Electrnc Tech.

NEWELL, KIM; St Marys Area HS; Saint Marys, PA; (Y); #11 In Class; VP Church Yth Grp; VP JA; Acpl Chr; Band; Chorus; Church Choir; Color Guard; Concert Band; Drill Tm; Drm & Bgl; Band 84-86; IUP Hnrs Band,Outstndng JR In Music 85-86; Gvnrs Schl For Arts In Music 86; Music.

NEWHARD, CHRISTOPHER A; Whitehall HS; Whitehall, PA; (Y); Am Leg Boys St; CAP; Leo Clb; Ski Clb; Band; Concert Band; Mrchg Band; School Musical; NHS; Ntl Merit Ltr.

NEWHART, BRIAN; Elk Lake HS; Meshoppen, PA; (Y); 27/98; Art Clb; Spanish Clb; Varsity Clb; Off Sr Cls; Bsktbl; Hon Roll; USAF; Elec.

NEWHART, GLEN; Blue Mountain Acad; Harrisburg, PA; (Y); Church Yth Grp; Library Aide; Quiz Bowl; Jr Cls; Capt Bsktbl; Capt Ftbl; Capt Sftbl; Var Vllybl; Hon Roll; Ntl Merit Schol; Natl Merit Schlrshp 85-86; Jr Cls Srgnt Arms 85-86; Vrsty Lvl Vlybl 84-86; Brigham Young HI; Trvl Mngmnt.

NEWHART, NANCY; Benton Area HS; Benton, PA; (Y); Mrchg Band; Var Sftbl; Capt Twrlr; Hon Roll; NHS.

NEWHART, SANDEE; North Pocono HS; Lake Ariel, PA; (S); 16/240; Letterman Clb; Varsity Clb; L Crs Cntry; Capt L Trk; High Hon Roll; NHS; Cross Cntry All Str Team; Rfl Team; Mst Vrstl Athlt Awd; Penn ST; Engrng.

NEWHOUSE, ALICE; Hempfield Area SR HS; Greensburg, PA; (Y); Art Clb; Church Yth Grp; Drama Clb; Pep Clb; Ski Clb; Band; Yrbk Stf; Cartogrphy.

NEWILL, DONALD E; Mt Pleasant Area HS; Mt Pleasant, PA; (Y); Boy Scts; FFA; VICA; High Hon Roll; Hon Roll; Newspaper Carrier Yr 86; Penn ST; Ag.

NEWLIN, JENNIFER; Downington HS; Downington, PA; (Y); Church Yth Grp; Dance Clb; German Clb; Ski Clb; Chorus; Church Choir; Drm Mjr(t); Mrchg Band; Orch; School Musical; Dist 12 Chorus PMEA 86; Duquesne U; Music Therapy.

NEWLIN, MATTHEW; Tyrone Area HS; Tyrone, PA; (S); 3/197; Varsity Clb; Ed Yrbk Ed-Chief; VP Jr Cls; Var L Bsktbl; Var L Tennis; High Hon Roll; NHS; Mst Outstndng Boy C 85; Law.

NEWLIN III, PAUL F; Spring-Ford SR HS; Schwenksville, PA; (Y); 55/261; VP Ski Clb; Trs Frsh Cls; Trs Soph Cls; Trs Jr Cls; Var Bsbl; Var Ftbl; Wt Lftg; Archtctr.

NEWLIN, SHELLEY K; North Allegheny HS; Sewickley, PA; (Y); 58/605; Off Sr Cls; Pres Stu Cncl; Capt Golf; Hon Roll; NHS; Colgate U.

NEWMAN, AMY; Pennsbury HS; Yardley, PA; (Y); Hosp Aide; Chorus; Yrbk Stf; Rep Stu Cncl; Tennis; Hon Roll; Accounting.

NEWMAN, MICHAEL E; West Greene HS; Rogersville, PA; (S); French Clb; High Hon Roll; Hon Roll; Aerosp Engrng.

NEWMAN, MICHELE; Cedar Crest HS; Lebanon, PA; (Y); Drama Clb; Key Clb; Spanish Clb; Var L Bsktbl; JV Sftbl; JV Trk; Im Vllybl; Hon Roll; NHS; Hnr Banquet 85-86; Pre-Med.

NEWMAN, MYRNA; Hopewell SR HS; Clinton, PA; (S); 5/295; Church Yth Grp; German Clb; Band; Chorus; Church Choir; School Play; L Crs Cntry; Trk; Sec NHS; Hpwl Twnshp Lions Clb Grl Of Mnth 85; Tchr.

NEWMAN, SUZANNE; Elk County Christian HS; St Marys, PA; (S); SADD; High Hon Roll; NHS; 1st Pl Awd Allegheny Mtn Sci Fair Jr Div 83; Acctng.

NEWMAN, TASHA A; Council Rock HS; Newtown, PA; (Y); Drama Clb; Intnl Clb; Key Clb; Office Aide; SADD; Stage Crew; Yrbk Stf; Swmmng; Trk; High Hon Roll; Bucks Cnty Cmnty Clg; Spch Path.

NEWPORT, EMILY; Canevin HS; Mc Kees Rocks, PA; (Y); 18/189; Church Yth Grp; Band; Concert Band; Jazz Band; Mrchg Band; Orch; Rep Frsh Cls; Rep Soph Cls; Rep Jr Cls; Rep Sr Cls; D Newell Schlrshp 86; Chatham Coll; Psych.

NEWTON, STACEY; Selinsgrove Area HS; Selinsgrove, PA; (Y); 39/221; Drama Clb; German Clb; Varsity Clb; Nwsp Stf; Bsktbl; Var Capt Cheerleading; Sftbl; Hon Roll; U Of Richmond; Mrktng.

NEY, JOHN KEVIN; Seton-La Salle Regional HS; Pittsburgh, PA; (Y); Aud/Vis; Exploring; German Clb; Office Aide; Political Wkr; Radio Clb; Teachers Aide; High Hon Roll; Hon Roll; Earned 3 Univ Credits-4.0 Grd-Slippery Rock Univ Of PA 86; Med.

NEY, JOSEPH STEPHEN; West Hazleton JR SR HS; Oneida, PA; (Y); 78/200; Political Wkr; Scholastic Bowl; Teachers Aide; Pres Clsrm 86; Dist Ldr; PA ST U; Forensic Pathlgy.

NEYER, JOHN; Schuykill Haven Area HS; Schuylkill Haven, PA; (Y); 9/99; German Clb; Band; Concert Band; School Musical; School Play; Crs Cntry; Swmmng; Trk; NHS; PA ST U Schuylkill; Elect Eng.

NEYHARD, LAUREL; Bloomsburg HS; Bloomsburg, PA; (Y); 34/143; Drama Clb; Thesps; Chorus; Church Choir; School Musical; Cheerleading; Socr; Vlntr Alvina Kraus Theatre 85-86; PA ST U; The Arts.

NEZNESKI, PATRICE; Portage Area HS; Portage, PA; (S); Cmnty Wkr; Ski Clb; Concert Band; Jazz Band; Pep Band; School Musical; Capt Twrlr; NHS; Prfct Atten Awd; Aud/Vis; Dist Chrs & Band 84-86; Rgnl Chrs 86; Phrmcy.

NG, YVONNE; South Park HS; Pittsburgh, PA; (Y); 1/212; Trk; High Hon Roll; NHS; PA Govrnrs Schl For Scis 85; Founded Stu Tutoring Stu Prog Schl Founder 85.

NGO, MONG DIEP; Little Flower HS; Philadelphia, PA; (Y); #3 In Class; Sec Aud/Vis; Science Clb; Lit Mag; NHS; Prfct Atten Awd; Latin I & II 85 & 84; Accntng.

NGO, THANH; John Harris HS; Harrisburg, PA; (S); 18/386; High Hon Roll; Hon Roll; NHS; Cert Of Awd Outstndng Acdmc Achvt 84; Chmcl Engrng.

NGUYEN, CAN; Central HS; Philadelphia, PA; (Y); 45/257; French Clb; Var Mathletes; Var Math Clb; Capt Math Tm; Chorus; School Musical; Capt Vllybl; Wt Lftg; High Hon Roll; Hon Roll; Barnwell Awd 84-86; Frnkel Ctznshp Awd 85-86; Villa Nova U; Pre-Dntl.

NGUYEN, DUNG H; Souderton Area HS; Telford, PA; (Y); Hon Roll; Temple U; Elec Engr.

NGUYEN, GIANG; Mt Alvernia HS; Pittsburgh, PA; (S); 3/60; Computer Clb; Exploring; Hosp Aide; Library Aide; Red Cross Aide; Science Clb; Chorus; Yrbk Stf; Hon Roll; NHS; Algbr, Physcs, Comp Awds 86; Georgetown; Med.

NGUYEN, HA; St Josephs Prep; Philadelphia, PA; (Y); Church Yth Grp; Band; Concert Band; Drm Mjr(t); Im Bsktbl; Im Ftbl.

NGUYEN, HIEU; Marple Newton SR HS; Broomall, PA; (Y); Math Clb; Capt Math Tm; Science Clb; JV Socr; High Hon Roll; Hon Roll; Prfct Atten Awd; Amer Invttnl Math Exmntn 86; Elec Engrng.

NGUYEN, HOANG; Harrisburg HS; Harrisburg, PA; (S); 4/386; Chess Clb; Stu Cncl; 4-H Awd; Hon Roll; NHS; PA ST U; Engr.

NGUYEN, HOANG; Souderton Area HS; Souderton, PA; (Y); Trk; Vllybl; Lincoln:Elec Commnctns.

NGUYEN, HUONG; John Bartram HS; Philadelphia, PA; (Y); 15/600; GAA; Office Aide; Var Badmtn; Hon Roll; Sec NHS; Hnr Sci & Math Soc Women Engrs 86; Gold Key Math 86; Herbert Reisgen Mem Awd 86; Temple U; Elec Engrng.

NGUYEN, LINH; Central Dauphin HS; Harrisburg, PA; (Y); Chorus; Color Guard; Flag Corp; Score Keeper; High Hon Roll; VP Jr NHS; NHS; Schltc Stu Of Mnth Awd 85; Chem.

NGUYEN, MAC-PHUONG; United HS; Robinson, PA; (S); 5/159; Aud/Vis; Camera Clb; Church Yth Grp; Drama Clb; Ski Clb; Yrbk Stf; High Hon Roll; Hon Roll; NHS; Voice Dem Awd; Temple U; Bio.

NGUYEN, NHAN; Annville-Cleona HS; Annville, PA; (S); French Clb; FNA; Mathletes; Math Tm; Speech Tm; Chorus; Yrbk Stf; Fld Hcky; Hon Roll; Penn ST; Pre Med.

NGUYEN, THAO; Archbishop John Carroll-Girls HS; Malvern, PA; (Y); 89/212; Rep Frsh Cls; Hon Roll; Math Awd 86; Villanova; Acctng.

NGUYEN, TRINH; St Benedict Acad; Erie, PA; (Y); 25/63; Art Clb; Chorus; Stage Crew; Hon Roll; Edinboro U PA Arts Comp 85; Arts/Crafts Awd 85&86; Penn ST Behrend; Comp Pgmr.

NGYUEN, TRANG; Upper Darby SR HS; Upper Darby, PA; (Y); Hosp Aide; Library Aide; Nwsp Rptr; Ed Nwsp Stf; Rep Jr Cls; JV Crs Cntry; JV Tennis; High Hon Roll; Prfct Atten Awd; Alge I 83-84; Bryn Mawr; Sci.

NIBERT, MARCIA; United HS; Indiana, PA; (Y); 17/157; Ski Clb; Chorus; Yrbk Sprt Ed; Lit Mag; Stu Cncl; Stat Wrstlng; Hon Roll; Sherman Coll; Chrprctr.

NIBERT, MICHEL; United HS; Indiana, PA; (Y); 15/157; Pres Math Clb; Ski Clb; Chorus; Drill Tm; Yrbk Stf; Lit Mag; Rep Stu Cncl; Powder Puff Ftbl; Stat Wrstlng; Hon Roll; Rep For Hugh O Brien Yth Ldrshp Seminar 85; Shrmn Coll; Chrprctr.

NICASTRO, WILLIAM; Hopewell HS; Aliquippa, PA; (Y); 75/295; Church Yth Grp; French Clb; Bsbl; Socr; Hon Roll; IN U PA; Sfty Sci.

NICHOL, CHRISTINE; Purchase Line HS; Cherrytree, PA; (Y); FBLA; Spanish Clb; SADD; School Play; Hon Roll; Cntry 21 Spd Typng Awd 85; PA Acad Of Csmtlgy; Csmtlgst.

NICHOL, DALE; Saegertown HS; Saegertown, PA; (Y); 30/114; Sec Aud/Vis; Boy Scts; Pres Exploring; SADD; Hon Roll.

NICHOL, TRACY; Taylor Allderdice HS; Pittsburgh, PA; (Y); 245/437; Hosp Aide; Nwsp Rptr; Nwsp Stf; Hon Roll; Pt Park College; Jrnlsm.

NICHOLAS, JEFFREY; Mil,Ton HS; Milton, PA; (Y); Key Clb; Varsity Clb; Im Vllybl; Var Wrstlng; High Hon Roll; Hon Roll; NHS; Pres Schlr; Boy Scts; VP Computer Clb; Northumbrlnd Cnty Peer Jury; Comp Sci Awd; PA ST U; Aerosp Engrng.

NICHOLAS, ORISHA; Chester HS; Chester, PA; (S); 1/494; Art Clb; Spanish Clb; Chorus; Nwsp Ed-Chief; Cit Awd; High Hon Roll; Spnsh Awd 84-85; Natl Honor Soc 84-85; Art Awd 84-85; Advrtsng.

NICHOLAS, STACEY D; Norristown Area HS; Norristown, PA; (S); 21/503; Drama Clb; Chorus; School Musical; Stu Cncl; Var Fld Hcky; High Hon Roll; Hon Roll; NHS; Girl Scts; Diving; Lmp Learng Acadmc Excllnc Awd 84; Slvr Awd Grl Scts 84.

NICHOLLS, KEVIN; Washington HS; Washington, PA; (Y); JA; Ski Clb; Band; Concert Band; Mrchg Band; School Musical; School Play; Stage Crew; JV Bsbl; JV Var Ftbl; Order Of The Arrow 82.

NICHOLLS, SUSAN; Marple Newtown SR HS; Broomall, PA; (Y); 12/367; Hosp Aide; Yrbk Ed-Chief; Cit Awd; DAR Awd; God Cntry Awd; High Hon Roll; NHS; Sal; Art Clb; Church Yth Grp; Brown U Bk Awd Excllnce Eng 85; Womens Club Schlrshp, Soroptimist Intl Yth Ctznshp Awd 86; U DE; Bus Admin.

NICHOLS, DEAN; Fox Chapel SR HS; Pittsbg, PA; (Y); 16/322; Church Yth Grp; Exploring; Band; Mrchg Band; High Hon Roll; NHS; Chem Olympics Awd 86; Elec Engr.

NICHOLS, DWAYNE; Millville HS; Bloomsburg, PA; (S); 2/75; Boy Scts; Church Yth Grp; Q&S; Chorus; School Musical; School Play; Nwsp Stf; High Hon Roll; NHS; JV Bsbl; Eagle Scout; Minister.

NICHOLS, JOHN G; Slippery Rock Area HS; Slippery Rock, PA; (Y); 1/172; Am Leg Boys St; Trs Drama Clb; JCL; Thesps; School Play; Nwsp Ed-Chief; Stu Cncl; High Hon Roll; NHS; School Musical; Natl Sci Merit Awd,Biogrphy US Achvt 84; 1st Pl JR Compsrs Cont Challener Awd 85; PA Govn Schl Arts; Lbrl Arts.

NICHOLS, LISA; Panther Valley HS; Summit Hill, PA; (Y); 19/129; Church Yth Grp; Var Ski Clb; Hon Roll; Pres Schlr; Hm Ec Awd 86; Emrsn & Drthy Stvns Mem Awd 86; E Stroudsburg U; Htl Rest Mgmt.

NICHOLS, MARK; Purchase Line HS; Barnesboro, PA; (Y); Ftbl; Hon Roll; Reflection Cntst Litature 85; Welding.

NICHOLS, MIKE; Marple Newtown HS; Newtown Sq, PA; (Y); Variety Show; Stu Cncl; Im Bsktbl; Crs Cntry; L Ftbl; Trk; Wt Lftg; High Hon Roll; Hon Roll; Jr NHS; Amer Lgn Awd 81; Ind Arts Awd 83; Inter-Act Clb 86; Law.

NICHOLS, RICK; Lakeland HS; Jermyn, PA; (Y); Wt Lftg; Penn ST; Elec Engr.

NICHOLS, SHARON; Wmsport Area HS; Williamsport, PA; (S); 15/560; Key Clb; Chorus; Church Choir; School Musical; Var L Cheerleading; Var L Sftbl; Hon Roll; Coaches Awd 85; 1st Prize Tlnt Show Dance 86; Lib Arts.

NICHOLSON, ADAM; Curwensville Area HS; Curwensville, PA; (S); 40/112; VP DECA; JV Bsktbl; Cit Awd; NHS; 1st Pl & 3rd Pl Mini Awd St DECA Comptn 85-86; Finance.

NICHOLSON, BARBARA; Somerset Area HS; Somerset, PA; (Y); 50/216; Church Yth Grp; Dance Clb; Band; VP Chorus; Concert Band; Mrchg Band; School Play; High Hon Roll; Pres Schlr; Dr C B Krns Prsnl Ftnss Awd 86; Shippensburg U.

NICHOLSON, BRIAN; Carmichaels Area HS; Carmichaels, PA; (Y); 52/101; Spanish Clb.

NICHOLSON, DANA; Turkeyfoot Valley Area HS; Confluence, PA; (Y); 4/46; Q&S; Color Guard; Nwsp Ed-Chief; Yrbk Stf; Hst Jr Cls; Stu Cncl; High Hon Roll; NHS; Lioness Mnth Lions Clb 86; Buyer.

NICHOLSON, JODI; Connellsville SR HS; Normalville, PA; (Y); High Hon Roll; Dir List Vo Tech; Bty Acad Schlrshp; Pittsburgh Beauty Acad; Csmtlgy.

NICHOLSON, LORI; Connellsville HS; Normalville, PA; (Y); Church Yth Grp; FFA; GAA; Hosp Aide; VICA; Trk; Hon Roll; Jr NHS; NHS; NFAVTS Dirctrs Lst 85 & 86; Pittsburgh Beauty Acad; Csmtlgy.

NICHOLSON, MARYLOU; Carmichaels JR SR HS; Carmichaels, PA; (Y); 28/115; Boys Clb Am; DECA; VICA; Color Guard; Mrchg Band; Hon Roll; Won 4 Plc Gen Merchnds Dist Lvl 85; Bardford; Mgmt Retail.

NICHOLSON, ROBERT; Wilmington Area HS; New Wilmington, PA; (S); 2/101; Cmnty Wkr; Key Clb; Pres Spanish Clb; Nwsp Sprt Ed; L Bsktbl; Capt L Ftbl; L Trk; Wt Lftg; High Hon Roll; NHS; Fnlst-Thom Mc An Schlr-Athlt Of Yr 85; Hnrbl Mntn-Tri Cnty Qrtrbck 84-85; Ftbl Boosters Schlr/Athlt 85; Law.

NICHOLSON, SHELLY; Turkeyfoot Valley Area HS; Fort Hill, PA; (S); 3/48; Q&S; Band; Chorus; Nwsp Stf; Yrbk Stf; JV L Bsktbl; L Sftbl; Capt Twrlr; Lion Awd; NHS; All-Cnty Band, Sftbl & Chorus; US Air Force.

NICHOLSON, TRACY; Connellsville Area HS; Normalville, PA; (Y); 42/500; High Hon Roll; NHS; Actors Clb 85-86; Presdntl Badge-Gym 82-83; PAJS 82-83; IN U Of PA.

NICJOLAS, CARISSA; Ambridge Area HS; Baden, PA; (Y); Girl Scts; Spanish Clb; Band; Pep Band; Off Soph Cls; Stu Cncl; Capt Golf; JV Vllybl; NHS; Pep Clb; PA Free Entrprs Wk Schlrshp 86; Pre-Law.

NICKELSON, RAYMOND E; Milton Area SR HS; New Columbia, PA; (Y); 9/206; Computer Clb; Key Clb; Hon Roll; NHS.

NICKEY, CONSTANCE; Chichester SR HS; Boothwyn, PA; (Y); Sec Spanish Clb; Band; Chorus; Drm Mjr(t); School Musical; Yrbk Ed-Chief; Cit Awd; NHS; Spanish NHS; Church Yth Grp; Louis Armstrong Jazz Awd 84; Yth Trnnm Dlgt 86; Acad Engl Oral Intrprtn Cntst Awd 1st Pl 85; Intl People.

NICKEY, RONDA; Big Spring HS; Walnut Bottom, PA; (Y); GAA; Hosp Aide; Letterman Clb; Fld Hcky; Powder Puff Ftbl; Trk; Med Aid.

NICKLAS, KYLE; Warren Area HS; Warren, PA; (Y); French Clb; Ski Clb; High Hon Roll; Jr NHS; Schlstc Lttr 85-86; Alfred U; Mech Engr.

NICKLAS, MARY E; Little Flower HS; Philadelphia, PA; (Y); 90/395; Cmnty Wkr; Girl Scts; Hosp Aide; Office Aide; Hon Roll; Hosp Assn Pin 84; CSC Tutoring 86; Temple U; RN.

NICKLE, DAMON; Unionville HS; Kennett Square, PA; (Y); 24/250; Church Yth Grp; Computer Clb; Band; Jazz Band; Mrchg Band; Orch; Pep Band; School Musical; School Play; Symp Band; Villanova U; Stock Brkr.

NICKLE, HEATHER; Uniontown Area HS; Ohiopyle, PA; (Y); Church Yth Grp; VP 4-H; French Clb; Office Aide; Sec Soph Cls; Var Swmmng; DAR Awd; French Hon Soc; 4-H Awd.

NICKLE, JOHN; South Middleton HS; Boiling Spgs, PA; (Y); Boy Scts; Church Yth Grp; Ski Clb; Band; Chorus; Concert Band; Drm Mjr(t); Mrchg Band; Bsbl; Socr.

NICKLEACH, TRACI; Lempe Vocational-Technical Schl; Worthington, PA; (Y); Church Yth Grp; Library Aide; SADD; VICA; Yrbk Stf; VP Stu Cncl; JV Var Bsktbl; Var L Sftbl; Hon Roll; NHS.

NICKLOS, RICHARD; Penn Hills SR HS; Verona, PA; (S); 28/767; Pres French Clb; VP Soph Cls; NHS; Ntl Merit Schol; FTA; Office Aide; Pres Rep Stu Cncl; Im Vllybl; Im Wrstlng; High Hon Roll; Chancellors Undrgrad Mrt Schlrshp 86; Engrng Hnrs Schlrshp 86; PHEAA Cert Of Mrt 86; U Of Pittsburgh; Elec Engrng.

NICKLOW, MARIANNE; Berlin Brothersvalley HS; Berlin, PA; (Y); 7/67; 4-H; Ski Clb; Pres Spanish Clb; SADD; Band; Mrchg Band; School Play; Yrbk Stf; Stat Bsktbl; NHS; Penn ST; Educ.

NICKOLAS, CARISSA; Ambridge Area HS; Baden, PA; (Y); 40/265; Girl Scts; Pep Clb; Spanish Clb; Band; Pep Band; Stu Cncl; Capt Golf; JV Vllybl; NHS; Hon Roll; Schlrshp Pennsylvna Free Entrprse Week 86; Pre-Law.

NICKS JR, GERALD; Iroquios HS; Erie, PA; (Y); 19/110; Boy Scts; Exploring; Concert Band; Mrchg Band; Hon Roll; NHS; Engrng Explr Proj 1st Pl 86; Eagl Sct 86; Rensselaer Polytechnic Inst.

NICKUM, BEV; William Allen HS; Allentown, PA; (Y); 104/530; Civic Clb; FBLA; German Clb; High Hon Roll; Hon Roll; Acctg.

NICODEMUS, KENNETH; Richland SR HS; Johnstown, PA; (Y); 15/137; Computer Clb; Math Clb; High Hon Roll; Mu Alp Tht; NHS; U Of Pittsburgh; Pre-Med.

NICOLELLA, DANA; St Maria Goretti HS; Philadelphia, PA; (Y); 23/390; Library Aide; Office Aide; Lit Mag; High Hon Roll; NHS; Ntl Merit Ltr; U CA; Frnch.

NICOLETTE JR, LAWRENCE J; Penn-Trafford HS; Harrison City, PA; (Y); 70/300; Trs Drama Clb; Pres Band; Pres Concert Band; School Musical; Symp Band; Var Trk; Hon Roll.

NICOTERA, SALLY; Mt Pleasant Area HS; Mt Pleasant, PA; (Y); French Clb; FTA; GAA; Girl Scts; Hosp Aide; Ski Clb; Band; Concert Band; Mrchg Band; Nwsp Stf.

NIEBAUER, MARIE; Fairview HS; Fairview, PA; (S); Pres Church Yth Grp; Drama Clb; Exploring; Spanish Clb; Teachers Aide; Band; Chorus; Church Choir; Color Guard; Concert Band; Knghts Columbus Scholar Fnlst 86; Edinboro U PA; Chem Ed.

NIEBISCH, STEFANIE; Hatboro-Horsham SR HS; Hatboro, PA; (Y); 1/270; Cmnty Wkr; Model UN; Service Clb; Tennis; High Hon Roll; NHS; Ntl Merit Ltr; PA Govnrs Schl For Intl Studys 85; Rensselaer Mdl Math & Sci 86; Intl Studys.

NIEDECKER, STACY; Shaler Area HS; Glenshaw, PA; (Y); 61/517; Cmnty Wkr; Chorus; School Play; Ed Yrbk Rptr; Var Hon Roll; Ntl Merit Ltr; NEDT Awd; Spanish NHS; Church Yth Grp; Computer Clb; NIE Cntst Wnnr 86; Natl Sci Olympd Bio Cntst Awd 84; Engl.

NIEDZIELKA, AMY; Seton-La Salle HS; Pittsburgh, PA; (Y); 1/260; Math Tm; Nwsp Sprt Ed; Var Bsktbl; Powder Puff Ftbl; Var Sftbl; Var Vllybl; High Hon Roll; NHS; Ntl Merit SF; U Of Pittsburgh Prvst Day Math Comp Final & Schlrshp Wnnr 85-86; Part Invtnl Acad Wrkshp W Pnt NY 86; Engrng.

NIEDZIELKA, MINDY; Seton-La Salle HS; Pittsburgh, PA; (Y); 2/260; Math Tm; Variety Show; Nwsp Ed-Chief; High Hon Roll; NHS; Ntl Merit Ltr; Provost Day Math Comp Final & Schlr Wnnr 85-86; PA Gvrnrs Schl Arts Bucknell U Schlr Ballet 85; Engrng.

NIEDZIELSKI, KAREN; St Benedict Acad; Erie, PA; (Y); 23/63; Hosp Aide; SADD; Mrchg Band; Hon Roll; Social Wrkr.

NIEDZIELSKI, STEVEN C; Bishop Kenrick HS; Bridgeport, PA; (Y); 96/278; Church Yth Grp; Hon Roll; Prfct Atten Awd; Villanova U; Accntng.

NIEFER, DOLORES; Marple Newtown HS; Broomall, PA; (Y); Cmnty Wkr; Hosp Aide; Yrbk Ed-Chief; Stat Sftbl; Var Swmmng; Hon Roll; Soc Wrk.

NIEHAUS, WILLIAM J; Wyomissing Area SR HS; Wyomissing, PA; (S); 6/125; French Clb; Math Tm; Scholastic Bowl; Yrbk Stf; High Hon Roll; NHS; Ntl Merit Ltr; Church Yth Grp; Computer Clb; Drama Clb; PA Govr Schl Sci-Carnegie Mellon U Smmr 85; PCT Math Awd 84-85; Berks Cnty Ten Chmpn Sngls 85; Engrng.

NIELSEN, LESLIE; Villa Maria Acad; Erie, PA; (Y); Ski Clb; JV Socr; Hon Roll; Nrsg.

NIELSEN, PAUL; Valley View JR-SR HS; Archbald, PA; (Y); Aud/Vis; Spanish Clb; Varsity Clb; Bowling; Golf; Vllybl; Spanish NHS; Hnrbl Mntn Ntl Span Tst 85-86; Schl Art Awd 86; Math.

NIEMEYER, DARLENE; Fort Le Boeuf HS; Waterford, PA; (Y); Art Clb; Cmnty Wkr; Bsktbl; Bowling; Vllybl; Hon Roll; U AL; Socl Wrk.

NIEMOND, NIKKI; Lewistown Area HS; Lewistown, PA; (Y); 3/255; AFS; Camera Clb; Cmnty Wkr; German Clb; Hosp Aide; Key Clb; Pep Clb; Red Cross Aide; Science Clb; Ski Clb; Stu Of Mnth 85; Hugh O Brian Ldrshp Conv 84; Temple U; Phy Thrpy.

NIEMRITZ, TRACEY; Johnstown HS; Johnstown, PA; (Y); French Clb; FNA; Key Clb; Office Aide; Ski Clb; Sec Jr Cls; L Var Swmmng; Nrsg.

NIEVES, MICHELLE; Olney HS; Philadelphia, PA; (Y); 18/1025; Church Yth Grp; Cmnty Wkr; Red Cross Aide; Spanish Clb; School Play; Sec Frsh Cls; Trk; Vllybl; High Hon Roll; Jr NHS; Cty Philadelphia Incntv Awds 85; Temple; Bus Adm.

NIEWINSKI, BRIAN; Scranton Prep; Forty Fort, PA; (Y); 124/198; Var Bsbl; Var Bsktbl; Schlrshp-Bskbl Cmp-MVP Of Cnty 83; MVP-CNTY Bsbl Game 85; Villanova; Math.

NIEWIRSKI, BRIAN; Scranton Prep; Forty Fort, PA; (Y); 125/198; Church Yth Grp; Exploring; Var Bsbl; Var Bsktbl; JV Ftbl; Hon Roll; MVP Bsktbl Cmp Schrlshp 83; Gldn Glve Cnty All Str Game 85; 1000 Pts Bsktbl 83; Villanova; Math.

NIGGEL, DAVID; Hempfield HS; E Petersburg, PA; (Y); 120/450; High Hon Roll; U Of CA Long Bch; Intl Bus.

NIGRO, AMY M; Parkland HS; Allentown, PA; (Y); 24/450; Pres Drama Clb; German Clb; Thesps; Band; Mrchg Band; School Play; Trk; High Hon Roll; Hon Roll; NHS; PA Govr Schl For Arts Smmr 85; Theatr Arts Schlrshps-WV U, Syracuse U, Allentown Coll 86; U Of NC Chapel Hill; Thtr Arts.

NIHEN, CAROLYN; Marian Catholic HS; Lansford, PA; (Y); Cmnty Wkr; Library Aide; Service Clb; Ski Clb; SADD; Capt Drill Tm; Awd For Hghst Acad Achvt Stngrphy 86; Lehigh Cnty CC; Med Asst.

NIKLAUS, NEAL; Shaler Area HS; Glenshaw, PA; (Y); 81/565; Spanish Clb; Pres Sr Cls; High Hon Roll; NHS; Prfct Atten Awd; AAA Awd For Auto Maint & Repair 86; Prfct Atndnc Plaque 86; Mech.

NIKOLISHEN, KATE; Central Cambria HS; Ebensburg, PA; (S); 6/202; Art Clb; French Clb; Girl Scts; Speech Tm; Var Trk; Var L Vllybl; Hon Roll; Lib Arts.

NIKOLISHEN, LORI; Villa Maria Acad; Erie, PA; (Y); 12/132; Science Clb; Service Clb; Ski Clb; Hon Roll; NHS; Ntl Merit Ltr; NEDT Awd; Church Yth Grp; Cmnty Wkr; Model UN; Mdl UN Schlrshp 85-86; Mission Clb-Secy 84-86; Penn ST U; Phys Thrpy.

NILES, LAURENCE; East HS; Reston, VA; (Y); Model UN; Quiz Bowl; VP Soph Cls; L Tennis; Trk; DAR Awd; High Hon Roll; Pres NHS; Rotary Awd; Sal; Phelps Scholar Awd 86; George Mason U; Elec Engrng.

NILSON, SONJA; Rocky Grove HS; Franklin, PA; (Y); Church Yth Grp; Science Clb; Band; Chorus; Pep Band; Vllybl; Hon Roll; Sec NHS; Dist III Bnd 86; Rgnl II Bnd 86.

NIMMO, HEATHER; Tioga Central HS; Sayre, PA; (S); 3/125; Church Yth Grp; Hosp Aide; School Musical; Variety Show; Nwsp Stf; JV Fld Hcky; High Hon Roll; NHS; Dance Prfrmncs 83-86; Lang.

NINO, STEPHANIE; Strathaven HS; Swarthmore, PA; (Y); U Of PA; Hstry.

NISHIK, SUSAN; Quigley HS; Zelienople, PA; (Y); 18/103; Pep Clb; High Hon Roll; Hon Roll; Persnl Excllnce Religion Awd 86; Distnctn 85-86; La Roche Coll; Hstry.

NISHNICK, RHONDA; West Allegheny HS; Manhattan Bch, CA; (Y); Spanish Clb; Rep Frsh Cls; Var L Swmmng; High Hon Roll; Hon Roll; Spanish NHS; All Acad Amer 85; Cert Of Training-USAIR 86; Mt San Antonio; Aviation Svcs.

NISSEL, TOBY; St Marys Area HS; St Marys, PA; (Y); 43/290; Chess Clb; Computer Clb; Capt Bsktbl; Im Mgr Ftbl; Im Mgr Wt Lftg; U Of Pittsburgh; Comp Sci.

NISSLEY, GIL; Souderton Area HS; Telford, PA; (Y); Boy Scts; VICA; High Hon Roll; NHS; Air Frc; Elctrnc Tech.

NISSLEY, GWENDOLYN; Lewisburg Area HS; Lewisburg, PA; (Y); 1/140; Pres Church Yth Grp; Math Tm; Spanish Clb; Yrbk Stf; VP Sr Cls; Stu Cncl; Tennis; Trk; High Hon Roll; Jr NHS; Rensselaer Medl-Excllnc In Math & Sci; Woodmen Of Wrld Awd Amer Hstry; Amer Chem Soc Awd; Eastern Mennonite Coll; Pre-Med.

NISSLEY, MARK; Annville-Cleona HS; Annville, PA; (Y); 27/105; FBLA; Yrbk Stf; Rep Stu Cncl; NHS; PA ST U; Vet Med.

NISSLY, SHARON L; Donegal HS; Mt Joy, PA; (Y); 52/169; Girl Scts; Hosp Aide; JV Fld Hcky; Ftbl; Hon Roll; Grl Scts-Slvr Awd 85; Grl Scts-Gld Awd 86; Estmn Kdak Co Rgnl Sci & Engrng Fair Awd 86; Nrsng.

NITCHMAN, TINA; West York Area HS; York, PA; (Y); 36/210; Church Yth Grp; Girl Scts; Hosp Aide; Spanish Clb; Yrbk Stf; Mgr(s); Hon Roll; Temple; Nrsng.

NITTERHOUSE, JODI; Chambersburg Area SR HS; Chambersburg, PA; (Y); French Clb; Chorus; Soph Cls; Jr Cls; Stu Cncl; Hon Roll; Bus.

NIXON, DEBBIE; Cedar Crest HS; Myerstown, PA; (Y); Church Yth Grp; FNA; Pep Clb; Spanish Clb; Trk; Hon Roll; Nrsng.

NIXON, MICHAEL; Pittsburgh Central Catholic HS; Pittsburgh, PA; (Y); 50/268; Exploring; Band; Concert Band; Mrchg Band; Pep Band; Lit Mag; Crs Cntry; Trk; Cit Awd; High Hon Roll; 1st Pl CA U Of PA Invtatnl JV Cls 85; U Of Pittsburgh; Med.

NIZICH, RENEE; Wyoming Area SR HS; West Pittston, PA; (Y); Church Yth Grp; German Clb; SADD; Chld Psychlgst.

NO, MINDY; Philadelphia High School For Girls; Philadelphia, PA; (Y); 15/259; Chess Clb; Sec Church Yth Grp; Sec Girl Scts; Teachers Aide; Acpl Chr; Band; Concert Band; Mrchg Band; Orch; Stage Crew; Phila City Schlrshp 86; U Of PA; Econ.

NOAH, DAWN; Western Beaver HS; Industry, PA; (Y); Computer Clb; Ed Yrbk Stf; Stu Cncl; Bowling; Pom Pon; Hon Roll; NHS; Radiology.

NOAKER, DENISHA; Susquenita HS; Duncannon, PA; (S); Girl Scts; Leo Clb; Ski Clb; Spanish Clb; Chorus; Stage Crew; Hon Roll; Var Fld Hcky; JV Score Keeper; Var Trk; Psych.

NOBLE, DELISA; Southwark Motivation HS; Philadelphia, PA; (Y); Church Yth Grp; Computer Clb; Church Choir; Nwsp Rptr; Yrbk Stf; High Hon Roll; Hon Roll; Prfct Atten Awd; Supr Achvt & Excel Prfrmnc Shkspr Cntst 86; Charles E Ellis Grnt & Schlrshp Fnd 84-87; Temple U; Nrsng.

NOBLE, HOLLY; Ft Le Boeuf HS; Waterford, PA; (Y); 11/200; Art Clb; Church Yth Grp; Band; Mrchg Band; Trs Soph Cls; Capt Cheerleading; Score Keeper; Sftbl; High Hon Roll; NHS; Ntl Ldrshp & Svc Awd 85; Ntl Hist & Gov Awd 84; Free Entrse Wk Schlrshp 86; Edinboro U; Bus.

NOBLE, SEAN P; Methacton HS; Audubon, PA; (Y); 5/361; Computer Clb; Var Debate Tm; VP Jr Cls; Crs Cntry; JETS Awd; NHS; Ntl Merit SF; Rotary Awd; U S Acad Decathlon PA Tm Co-Capt 85-86; Elec Engrng.

NOBLE, TIFFANY; Littlestown HS; Littlestown, PA; (Y); 12/120; Sec Trs Church Yth Grp; Cmnty Wkr; Dance Clb; Hosp Aide; Varsity Clb; School Musical; Pres Frsh Cls; Pres Soph Cls; Pres Jr Cls; Pres Sr Cls; Psychlgy.

NOBLE, WILLIAM; Penn Trafford HS; Harrison Cty, PA; (Y); Church Yth Grp; JCL; Latin Clb; Pep Clb; Ski Clb; Im Bsktbl; Var JV Ftbl; Im Sftbl; Var Trk; 2nd Pl Awds Proj Mdl 86; 3rd & 1st Pl Lat 84; Edin Coll; Crmnlgy.

NOCCHI, MARK; MMI Prep Schl; Freeland, PA; (Y); Chess Clb; Church Yth Grp; Computer Clb; Ski Clb; PA Jr Acad Sci Awd 86; Kngs Coll Grmn Awd 85; Tutrng Prog Awd 86; Pre-Law.

NOCCO, RITA; Nazareth Acad; Philadelphia, PA; (Y); Cmnty Wkr; Exploring; Pep Clb; Political Wkr; Service Clb; Spanish Clb; Cheerleading; Coach Actv; Gym; Pom Pon; Bus.

NOCK, BOB; Avonworth JR SR HS; Pittsbg, PA; (Y); Varsity Clb; Band; Mrchg Band; Nwsp Stf; VP Frsh Cls; Pres Soph Cls; Pres Jr Cls; VP Sr Cls; Var L Bsbl; Var L Bsktbl; Allghny Cnty Lwyrs Axlry Essy 1st Rnnrup 86; N Borghs Intl Yth Awd 85; Schlr Athlt Awd 84-86.

NODERER, KEITH; Sharpsville Area SR HS; Sharpsville, PA; (S); 5/110; Science Clb; Band; Chorus; School Musical; Sec NHS; Ntl Merit Ltr; Century III Ldrshp Cmptn Wnnr 85; Hugh O Brian Yth Ldrshp Awd 84; PA ST U; Engrng.

NOECHEL, CHRISTINE; Riverview HS; Oakmont, PA; (Y); Capt Color Guard; Mrchg Band; Ed Yrbk Phtg; Powder Puff Ftbl; JV Sftbl; Stat Trk; High Hon Roll; Hon Roll; Bus Career Devlpmt Prog 85; Robert Morris Coll; Bus Adm.

NOEL, CHRISTINA; Chestnut Ridge SR HS; Schellsburg, PA; (S); 13/104; Church Yth Grp; Chorus; School Musical; Nwsp Sprt Ed; Stu Cncl; Var Capt Cheerleading; Trk; Dnfth Awd; Hon Roll; Sec NHS; Medien Schl Of Alleid Health.

NOEL, KELLEY; Danville SR HS; Danville, PA; (Y); 50/202; Church Yth Grp; FBLA; FHA; SADD; Chorus; Color Guard; JV Bsktbl; JV Bowling; Trk; Hon Roll; Shorthand Therory, Transcription, & Speed 85-86; Typing Awd Top Of Clss 84; Secretarial.

NOEL, MICHELLE; Bellwood-Antis HS; Bellwood, PA; (Y); 23/118; French Clb; Pres SADD; Chorus; Yrbk Stf; Rep Soph Cls; Rep Jr Cls; Pres Stu Cncl; JV Var Bsktbl; Hon Roll; Trs NHS; Cosmtlgy.

NOFSINGER, CINDY; West Allegheny HS; Oakdale, PA; (Y); Church Yth Grp; Drama Clb; Off PAVAS; Spanish Clb; Off Band; Off Chorus; Concert Band; Mrchg Band; Hon Roll; Music.

NOGA, ANITA; Burgettstown JR SR HS; Burgettstown, PA; (Y); Church Yth Grp; Hosp Aide; Library Aide; SADD; Chorus; Yrbk Stf; Hon Roll; NHS; ICM; Med Asst.

NOGA, MARY; York Catholic HS; York, PA; (Y); Church Yth Grp; FBLA; Hosp Aide; Library Aide; Acpl Chr; Chorus; Hon Roll; Yrk Hosp Pn 300 Hrs Svc 85-86; Music Awd Pn Outstndg Achvmnt 85-86; U Of Pittsburgh; Physcl Thrpy.

NOGA, SUZANNE; St Maria Goretti HS; Philadelphia, PA; (Y); 32/390; Cmnty Wkr; Dance Clb; GAA; Rep Sr Cls; High Hon Roll; VP NHS; Prfct Atten Awd; Natl Sci Leag 85-86; Natl Math Leag 85-86; VP Natl Hnr Soc 86-87; Gen Bus.

NOGGLE, SUSAN M; Hazleton HS; Hazleton, PA; (Y); Hosp Aide; Leo Clb; Office Aide; Spanish Clb; Band; Chorus; Concert Band; Mrchg Band; Orch; Pep Band; PA ST U; Phys Thrpy.

NOGOWSKI, JOANNE; Little Flower Catholic HS; Philadelphia, PA; (Y); Church Yth Grp; Drama Clb; 4-H; Varsity Clb; Chorus; Church Choir; School Musical; School Play; Nwsp Rptr; Rep Stu Cncl; Chldhd Ed.

NOHAILE, MICHAEL; Altoona Area HS; Altoona, PA; (S); 1/683; Chess Clb; Computer Clb; French Clb; Math Tm; Model UN; Speech Tm; Var Swmmng; High Hon Roll; NHS; Ntl Merit SF; Pres Ntl Hnr Soc 85; Pres Chess Clb; Pres Jr Acad Of Sci; Physics.

NOLAN, JOHN P; St Josephs Prepartory Schl; Cheltenham, PA; (Y); 2/180; Nwsp Rptr; Yrbk Stf; Sec Stu Cncl; Crs Cntry; Trk; NHS; Ntl Merit SF; Awd Excllence Schlrshp & Stu Ldrshp 85; High Hnr ACL/NJCL Ntl Greek Exam Level II 85; Classics.

NOLAN, KELLY; Bishop Mc Devitt HS; Glenside, PA; (Y); Church Yth Grp; French Clb; School Play; Nwsp Rptr; Fld Hcky; Mgr(s); Score Keeper; NHS; Shrthnd Cert-60 & 80 WPM 85-86; Jack Jns Memrl Schlr Awd 85; 50 Hrs Svc-Abngtn Hosp 85; Manor JC; Bus.

NOLDER, DOUGLAS; Mckeesport HS; White Oak, PA; (Y); Church Yth Grp; Debate Tm; Sec Exploring; French Clb; NFL; SADD; Band; Mrchg Band; School Musical; School Play; Penn ST; Bus.

NOLDY, MARK; Sayre Area HS; Sayre, PA; (Y); 25/116; Chess Clb; Spanish Clb; Varsity Clb; Var Bsbl; Var L Crs Cntry; Var Capt Swmmng; Var Trk; Hon Roll; Jr Rtrn 86; IN U Of PA.

NOLE, KIM; Dunmore HS; Dunmore, PA; (Y); 21/155; French Clb; Yrbk Phtg; Var L Bsktbl; Var L Sftbl; High Hon Roll; Hon Roll; PA ST; Elem Ed.

NOLE, MARIANNE; Dunmore HS; Dunmore, PA; (Y); 24/150; Spanish Clb; Yrbk Sprt Ed; Var Capt Bsktbl; Var L Sftbl; Var Tennis; Rep Frsh Cls; VP Soph Cls; VP Jr Cls; VP Sr Cls; VP Stu Cncl.

NOLF, LAURIE; Freeport HS; Sarver, PA; (Y); School Musical; Rep Frsh Cls; Pres Soph Cls; Sec Jr Cls; Cheerleading; Hon Roll.

NOLF, MARY ANN; Leechburg Area HS; Leechburg, PA; (Y); 7/71; Pres Church Yth Grp; Chorus; Church Choir; Ed Yrbk Stf; Hon Roll; Soc Distngshd Amercn HS Stu 83-86; Chorus-Ensmbl Accmpnst; Rssn Clb; Grove City Coll; Math.

NOLKER, KURT; Deer Lakes HS; Tarentum, PA; (Y); Spanish Clb; High Hon Roll; Acad Excllnce Awd; GATE; Outstndg Achvt & Bst Of Shop Mech Drwg; Grove City Coll; Engrng.

NOLL, BRETT; Dover Area HS; Dover, PA; (Y); 49/241; Nwsp Rptr; Millersville U; Law.

NOLL, DIANE LOUISE; Muhlenberg HS; Laureldale, PA; (Y); 28/172; Church Yth Grp; Exploring; Nwsp Stf; Rep Frsh Cls; Crs Cntry; Trk; Cartech Rifle Clb Outstndng Female 84-85; Outstndng Home Ec 86; 1st Pl Berks Cnty Fed Of Wmns Clb 86; Allentown Bus Schl; Acctng.

NOLL, JAMES; West Miflin HS; W Mifflin, PA; (Y); 3/300; Boy Scts; Church Yth Grp; High Hon Roll; NHS; Chem Engr.

NOLL, MICHELLE; Reynolds HS; Greenville, PA; (Y); German Clb; Intnl Clb; Math Clb; Science Clb; Varsity Clb; Yrbk Stf; Stu Cncl; JV Var Bsktbl; Score Keeper; NHS.

NOLL, THOMAS; Scranton Technical HS; Scranton, PA; (Y); #5 In Class; Boys Clb Am; Boy Scts; VICA; Band; Concert Band; Jazz Band; Mrchg Band; Bsktbl; Hon Roll; NHS; Diesel Mech.

NOLL, TIFFANY; Freedom HS; Easton, PA; (Y); 49/425; Debate Tm; Drama Clb; French Clb; Intnl Clb; JA; Pep Clb; Political Wkr; Red Cross Aide; Chorus; School Play; Temple U Pres Awd Schlrshp 86; U S Stu Ambssdr To France 84-85; Temple U; Intl Law & Bus.

NOLT, TIMOTHY; Hempfield HS; Lancaster, PA; (Y); Trs Church Yth Grp; Computer Clb; Ski Clb; Off Frsh Cls; Rep Jr Cls; Rep Sr Cls; Stu Cncl; JV Var Socr; JV Var Tennis; JV Var Trk; Harrisburg Area CC Regnl Comp Cntst Partcpnt; Lancaster Cnty Sci Fair Awd Microbio Assn Amer; Duke; Comp Sci.

NOLTE, BRADLEY; Cornell HS; Coraopolis, PA; (Y); 60/89; Church Yth Grp; Band; Comp Auto Repair.

NONEMAKER, JOAN; Downingtown SR HS; Exton, PA; (S); 25/527; Cmnty Wkr; Intnl Clb; Spanish Clb; Im Bowling; Im Vllybl; High Hon Roll; Bus.

NONEVSKI, CHRIS; Lincoln JR SR HS; Ellwood, PA; (Y); 27/170; Boy Scts; Camera Clb; Chess Clb; Computer Clb; Key Clb; Library Aide; Ski Clb; Spanish Clb; Ftbl; Tennis; Washngtn & Jefferson Coll; Bio.

NONNENBERG, SHARON; Penn Hills SR HS; Verona, PA; (Y); Church Yth Grp; Office Aide; JV Var Vllybl; High Hon Roll; Hon Roll; Bus Educ Awd-Typg II 86; Exec Sec.

NOON, MELISSA; Chestnut Ridge HS; Imler, PA; (S); 8/144; Spanish Clb; Band; VP Chorus; Mrchg Band; School Musical; Nwsp Rptr; Nwsp Stf; Stu Cncl; High Hon Roll; Hon Roll; Dist Regnl ST Choruses 85; Music Ed.

NOONE, KELLEY; New Hope-Solebury HS; New Hope, PA; (Y); 10/84; Art Clb; Exploring; Ski Clb; Chorus; Rep Stu Cncl; Bsktbl; Hon Roll; VFW Awd; U VA; Lawyer.

NORDSTROM, ERIC; The Hill Schl; Leola, PA; (Y); Church Yth Grp; Chorus; Jazz Band; Orch; School Musical; Nwsp Phtg; Pres Frsh Cls; Var Ftbl; JV Lcrss; Var Socr; JR Golfr Of Yr Awd Lancaster Cntry Clb 85; Bus Admin.

NORMAN, CAROLYN; Liberty JR SR HS; Liberty, PA; (Y); 6/35; Pres 4-H; Pres FFA; Rep Band; Ed Yrbk Stf; VP Sr Cls; Off Stu Cncl; Co-Capt Cheerleading; Vllybl; DAR Awd; NHS; FFA Keystone Frmr Dgr 86; 4-H Cnty Outstndng SR Girl Awd 85; Maple Sugar Swthrt 85; Penn ST U; Dairy Prod.

NORMAN, KIMBERLY; West Snyder HS; Beavertown, PA; (Y); Church Yth Grp; Cmnty Wkr; 4-H; FNA; Hosp Aide; Pep Clb; Red Cross Aide; Science Clb; Varsity Clb; Band; Sci, Comm Achvt, Hlth Careers, S E Good Music Awds 86; 11 Hnrs Bands 84-86; Lycoming Coll; Nrsg.

NORMAN, THOMAS; Northern Chester County Tech Schl; Phoenixville, PA; (Y); Boy Scts; Church Yth Grp; Spanish Clb; Im Ftbl; Im Mgr(s); JV Tennis; Hon Roll; Penn ST; Elec Engr.

NORMAN, TRACY; Owen J Roberts HS; Chestersprings, PA; (S); Trs 4-H; School Play; Swmmng; Hon Roll; NHS; Pre Med.

NORQUEST, LAURIE; Millville HS; Millville, PA; (Y); Cmnty Wkr; FBLA; Chorus; Hon Roll; 4th Pl Bus Engl At Fbla Reg 7 Comp 86; Bus.

NORRIS, CRAIG; Huntingdon Area HS; Hesston, PA; (Y); 10/235; Church Yth Grp; Teachers Aide; Concert Band; Yrbk Stf; Var Bsbl; Var Wrstlng; High Hon Roll; NHS; Prsdntl Phys Ftns Awd 85-86.

NORRIS, GARY; Elizabethtown Area HS; Elizabethtown, PA; (S); Band; Chorus; Concert Band; Drm & Bgl; Jazz Band; Mrchg Band; Orch; School Musical; School Play; Swing Chorus; Vrsty Ltr & Sweater Trk 84-85; Westchester U; Music Ed.

NORRIS, THOMAS P; Wilmington Area HS; New Wilmington, PA; (Y); FFA; Var L Bsbl; Im Bsktbl; Coach Actv; JV Var Ftbl; Im Wt Lftg; Im Wrstlng; Kent ST; Bus Admin.

NORRIS, TRACY; Moon SR HS; Coraopolis, PA; (Y); Key Clb; School Musical; Rep Jr Cls; Rep Stu Cncl; Var Capt Cheerleading; Hon Roll; JA; Acpl Chr; Chorus; Swing Chorus; Pre Med.

NORTH, KRISTY; Hampton HS; Allison Pk, PA; (Y); French Clb; Pep Clb; Ski Clb; Nwsp Rptr; Rep Frsh Cls; Rep Soph Cls; Rep Jr Cls; Rep Sr Cls; Im Powder Puff Ftbl; JV Sftbl; Vlybl Sec Al-Star Tm; Keystn ST Games Vllybl; MVP Westminster Vllybl Trnmnt.

NORTH, SUSAN; Purchase Line HS; Mahaffey, PA; (Y); Pres FFA; Spanish Clb; SADD; Chorus; School Play; Hon Roll; NEDT Awd; Keystone Farmer Dgree 86; ST Pub Spkg Awd 3rd Pl 86; FFA Cnty Rptr 85-86; USMC.

NORTHIME, TIMOTHY; Karns City HS; Chicora, PA; (Y); Band; Hon Roll.

NORTON, ALISA; Avon Grove HS; West Grove, PA; (Y); SADD; Band; Concert Band; Mrchg Band; School Play; Stu Cncl; Var Cheerleading; Var Pom Pon; High Hon Roll; Hon Roll; Med Tech.

NORTON, BARB; Scranton Central HS; Scranton, PA; (Y); Dance Clb; Drama Clb; French Clb; Hosp Aide; Ski Clb; Spanish Clb; Yrbk Phtg; Yrbk Stf; Rep Stu Cncl; Hon Roll; Psychlgy.

NORTON, DANA; Schuylkill Valley HS; Mohrsville, PA; (Y); 13/129; FBLA; JA; Quiz Bowl; Capt Bowling; Co-Capt Fld Hcky; Sftbl; Co-Capt Vllybl; VP NHS; Ntl Merit Schol; Most Ideal Stu 86; Flechner Awd 86; TX A & MAERO Engrg.

NORTON, DONNA; Muncy HS; Muncy, PA; (Y); Church Yth Grp; Spanish Clb; Varsity Clb; Band; Mrchg Band; School Play; Yrbk Phtg; Yrbk Stf; Concert Band; Janet Englehart Awd Creative Wrtng 86; Muncy Ed Assoc Awd 86; PTSA Stu Of 6 Wks 86; Lock Haven U; Chem.

NORTON, EDWARD; Northeast Catholic HS; Philadelphia, PA; (Y); 84/362; Band; Concert Band; Jazz Band; Mrchg Band; School Musical; JV Trk; Hon Roll; NHS; All Catholic Concert Band 86; VP Of Cmnty Svc Corps 86-87.

NORTON, JEANNIE; South Williamsport SR HS; S Williamsport, PA; (Y); Leo Clb; Spanish Clb; Chorus; Occptnl Thrpy.

NORWOOD, RUTH; Freedom HS; Bethlehem, PA; (Y); 47/445; Sec French Clb; Science Clb; Band; Concert Band; Mrchg Band; Hon Roll; Dntstry.

NOTARIANNI, LISA; West Scranton HS; Scranton, PA; (Y); 2/253; Church Yth Grp; Scholastic Bowl; Spanish Clb; Yrbk Stf; Stu Cncl; Capt Pom Pon; NHS; Sal; Girl Yr Scranton Bus & Prof Womens Clb 86; Diocese Scranton Bishops Awd 86; U Of Scranton; Phys Ther.

NOTZOLD, KIRSTEN; W C East HS; West Chester, PA; (Y); Ski Clb; Lit Mag; Mgr(s); Exchng Stu In Norway 84-85; Boston U; Intl Rltns.

NOULLET, MICHELLE; Bethel Park SR HS; Pittsburgh, PA; (Y); FBLA; FHA; Chld Psych.

NOVABILSKI, BERNARD; Old Forge HS; Old Forge, PA; (Y); Spanish Clb; Yrbk Stf; High Hon Roll; Hon Roll; NHS; Spanish NHS; Gregg Typng Awd 84-85; Spnsh Awd-Medal 85-86; U Of Scranton; Med Tech.

NOVACK, MARK; Weatherly Area HS; Weatherly, PA; (S); FBLA; FHA; Stu Cncl; Var Bsbl; Var L Bsktbl; Var L Golf; Tennis; Hon Roll; Intl Frgn Lang Awd 84; Bus Adm.

NOVAK, CHRISTINA; Bishop O Hara HS; Dickson City, PA; (Y); Cmnty Wkr; French Clb; Chorus; Sec Soph Cls; Trs Sr Cls; Rep Stu Cncl; High Hon Roll; NHS; Paderewski Mdl 10 Yrs Nat Piano Adtvrs 86; Dstrct 9 Chrs Fstvl Alto Ii 86; Cndt Gvrnrs Schl Arts Music; Music.

NOVAK, CHRISTINE; Ringgold SR HS; Finleyville, PA; (Y); JA; Band; Concert Band; Drill Tm; Mrchg Band; Pom Pon; Hon Roll; School Musical; Math Sci Hnr Soc Hi Hnr; Amer Legn Aux Awd Outstndng Stu; Pharmacy.

NOVAK, DAVID; Salisbury SR HS; Bethlehem, PA; (Y); Debate Tm; Model UN; Rep Soph Cls; Rep Jr Cls; Rep Stu Cncl; JV Bsktbl; JV Var Socr; Var Trk; High Hon Roll; NHS; US Military Acad Invttnl Acdmc Workshp Awd 86; Bio.

NOVAK, FRANCES; G A R Memorial HS; Wilkes Barre, PA; (S); 7/176; French Clb; Key Clb; Office Aide; Ski Clb; Chorus; Nwsp Rptr; High Hon Roll; Jr NHS; NHS; Bloomsburg U; Med Tech.

NOVAK, KAREN; Marian HS; Mc Adoo, PA; (S); 7/114; Hosp Aide; Chorus; Drill Tm; Rep Soph Cls; Rep Jr Cls; High Hon Roll; NHS; Spanish NHS; Chld Cnslng.

NOVAK, MONICA; Windber Area HS; Windber, PA; (Y); 5/128; VP French Clb; Yrbk Stf; Rep Stu Cncl; Cheerleading; High Hon Roll; Hon Roll; NHS; Acdmc Achvt Awd Adv Plcmt Engl 85-86; U S Stdnt Cncl Awd Wnnr 84; Psych.

NOVAK, WENDY; Trinity HS; Washington, PA; (Y); Chorus; Hon Roll; Soc Wrk.

NOVATNACK, HEATHER; Lehighton Area HS; Lehighton, PA; (Y); Rep Stu Cncl; Var L Bsktbl; Var L Fld Hcky; Var L Trk; Church Yth Grp; FBLA; Ski Clb; Pres Phys Ftns Awd 84-86; All Leag 2nd Tm Fld Hcky 84-85; All Leag Hon Mntn Fld Hcky 85-86; Sprts Med.

NOVISKI, EDWARD; Trinity HS; Washington, PA; (Y); 184/374; Var L Bsbl; Var L Ftbl; Hnrbl Mntn Pkwy Conf AAA Tckl 85; NC Tarheels; Bus.

NOVOBILSKI, THERESA M; Carbondale Area HS; Simpson, PA; (Y); 21/150; Pres Church Yth Grp; FBLA; Girl Scts; Spanish Clb; Chorus; Trs Jr Cls; Rep Stu Cncl; Var JV Cheerleading; High Hon Roll; Hon Roll; Pres & Secy Of Church Orgnztn Sodality 84-86; Elem Educ.

NOVOSEL, EDDIE; Plum Borough SR HS; Pittsburgh, PA; (Y); High Hon Roll; NHS; Ntl Merit SF; NEDT Awd; Prfct Atten Awd.

NOVOTNY, JESSICA; St Piux X HS; Pennsburg, PA; (S); 20/161; VP FBLA; Office Aide; High Hon Roll; Hon Roll; NEDT Awd; Social Wrk.

NOVOTSKY, JOYCE; Mid-Valley HS; Dickson City, PA; (Y); Ski Clb; Band; Drill Tm; Off Frsh Cls; Crs Cntry; High Hon Roll; Hon Roll; Zool.

NOWACKI, MARIA; Nazareth Acad; Philadelphia, PA; (Y); Spanish Clb; Orch; School Musical; Sec Jr Cls; JV Capt Cheerleading; Nrsng.

NOWAKOWSKI, SCOTT; John S Fine SR HS; Nanticoke, PA; (Y); 1/242; Var L Bsbl; Var L Bsktbl; Var L Ftbl; Elks Awd; Kiwanis Awd; Lion Awd; NHS; Val; Church Yth Grp; Ski Clb; Ntl Piano Plyg Adtn Cert 83; Amer Lgn Cert Of Schl Awd 86; Outstndg Sci Stu Awd 86; Kings Coll; Pre-Med.

NOWARK, MARIA; Fairview HS; Fairview, PA; (Y); Library Aide; Varsity Clb; JV Crs Cntry; Var L Sftbl; Var L Swmmng; Hon Roll; Acctng.

NOWLAND, JEFF; Avon Grove HS; Landenberg, PA; (Y); 18/168; VP Band; School Musical; Stage Crew; Yrbk Bus Mgr; Pres Sr Cls; Var Bsktbl; NHS; Ntl Merit Ltr; Aud/Vis; Concert Band; VP, Pres Yuth Ed Assn; Cnty Stdnt Forum; Cnst Engrng.

NOWLIN, AMY; Tyrone HS; Tyrone, PA; (Y); Church Yth Grp; DECA; Library Aide; Office Aide; Church Choir; Color Guard; Mrchg Band; Hon Roll; Comm.

NOWOTARSKI, SUSAN; Exeter SR HS; Reading, PA; (Y); Pep Clb; Varsity Clb; Y-Teens; Band; Cheerleading; Twrlr; Hon Roll.

NOYER, CAROL; Iroquois HS; Erie, PA; (Y); 5/148; Am Leg Aux Girls St; Drama Clb; Model UN; Chorus; Pep Band; Yrbk Stf; Jr Cls; Cheerleading; High Hon Roll; NHS; Hnrb Mntn Painting Lawrence Park Art Show 86; Best Squad 1st Pl DCA Chrldng Camp 86.

NOYES JR, DAVID; Governor Mifflin HS; Shillington, PA; (Y); 6/274; Boy Scts; Chess Clb; Computer Clb; Pres Model UN; Var Bsbl; Var Swmmng; Hon Roll; NHS; Ntl Merit Ltr; Unified Achvt Awd 86; Drexel U; Secndry Ed.

NOZZI, MICHAEL; Dunmore HS; Dunmore, PA; (Y); 10/150; Cmnty Wkr; Yrbk Stf; Bsbl; Bsktbl; Hon Roll; NHS; Ath Of Week 86; Le High U; Engrng.

NUDO, DANIEL R; E L Meyers HS; Wilkes Barre, PA; (Y); Church Yth Grp; French Clb; Key Clb; Chorus; Nwsp Rptr; VP Jr Cls; Stu Cncl; Hon Roll; Jr NHS; NHS; Pres Ldrshp Schrlshp Awd 86-91; Pres Acad Ftns Awd 86; Ntl Schl Choral Awd 86; Lebanon Valley Coll; Comp Sci.

NUGENT, KELLY; Boyertown Area SR HS; Perkiomenvl, PA; (Y); School Play; Trs Frsh Cls; Rep Jr Cls; Capt L Cheerleading; L Lcrss; L Tennis; L Trk; Hon Roll; Pres Clsrm Schlshp 86; Outstndg Amer H S Athlt 86; Educ Fndtn For Frgn Stdy In Austria 86; Hood Coll; Intl Rel.

NULL, CHRIS; Cumberland Valley Christian Schl; Chambersburg, PA; (Y); Church Yth Grp; Office Aide; Band; Yrbk Rptr; Bsktbl; Capt Cheerleading; Var Sftbl; High Hon Roll; NHS; Blazer Awd Chrldng, Yrbk Pin, Bsktbl All Str Tm 86; Hagerstown Bus Coll; Legal Asst.

NULL, JODIE; Charleroi JR SR HS; Charleroi, PA; (Y); Hosp Aide; Pep Clb; Nwsp Ed-Chief; Nwsp Stf; Cheerleading; Sftbl; NHS; Mercy Hosp; Nrsng Tech.

NULL, MICHAEL; Charleroi Area HS; Charleroi, PA; (Y); Debate Tm; NFL; Varsity Clb; Nwsp Sprt Ed; Yrbk Sprt Ed; Rep Frsh Cls; Rep Soph Cls; Rep Jr Cls; Rep Sr Cls; Stu Cncl; St Vincent Coll; Pre-Med.

NULPH, RANDALL LEE; Grove City Area SR HS; Jackson Center, PA; (Y); 30/179; Boy Scts; Var Crs Cntry; Var L Trk; Var Wrstlng; High Hon Roll; Pres Acad Ftnss Awd 85-86; Crtfd Pblc Accnt.

NULTY, AMY; Mazareth Academy; Philadelphia, PA; (Y); 11/118; VP German Clb; Library Aide; Model UN; NFL; Speech Tm; Yrbk Ed-Chief; Bsktbl; Hon Roll; NHS; Pre-Dntstry.

NULTY, LESLIE; Nazareth Acad; Philadelphia, PA; (Y); 23/118; Library Aide; Model UN; NFL; Spanish Clb; Speech Tm; Yrbk Ed-Chief; Rep Sr Cls; Rep Stu Cncl; Bsktbl; NHS; Pre-Med.

NUNEMAKER, MELISSA A; Commodore Perry HS; Hadley, PA; (S); 10/65; Math Tm; Office Aide; Chorus; Yrbk Stf; Hon Roll.

NURICK, TODD; Plymouth-Whtemarsh HS; Lafayette Hill, PA; (Y); Math Clb; Band; Jazz Band; Capt Mrchg Band; Tennis; High Hon Roll; Mu Alp Tht; Ntl Merit SF; USAF Acad; Elec Engrng.

NURMINEN, KRISTIN; Connellsville Area SR HS; Acme, PA; (Y); 21/525; Exploring; 4-H; FTA; Girl Scts; Pep Clb; Science Clb; Band; Mrchg Band; Symp Band; JV Trk; Natl Hstry Day Awd Carnegie Mellon 86; PA JR Acadmy Sci 84; PA ST U; Micro-Bio.

NURNEY, SARAH M; Upper Moreland HS; Hatboro, PA; (Y); 24/273; Key Clb; Ski Clb; Nwsp Rptr; Lit Mag; Cheerleading; Sftbl; Tennis; Vllybl; High Hon Roll; NHS; Carnegie Mellon U; Bio.

NUSS, GRETCHEN; Cambria Heights HS; Patton, PA; (Y); Q&S; Band; Concert Band; Mrchg Band; Orch; School Play; Nwsp Stf; VP Stu Cncl; Hon Roll; NHS; Cnty Bnd Fstvl, Dist Bnd Fstvl 86; Yth Educ Assn Tutor 84-85; Pennsylvania ST U; Math.

NUSS, HEATHER; Pocono Mountain HS; Pocono Lk, PA; (Y); Art Clb; Model UN; Pep Clb; Ski Clb; JC Awd; Art Shw Awds; JR Miss Pgnt; Tlnt Awd For JR Mss; Syracuse U; Comm Art.

NUSS, MELISSA; Eastern Lebanon HS; Newmanstown, PA; (S); 4-H; FHA; Chorus; Nwsp Rptr; 4-H Awd; Hon Roll.

NUSSBAUM, JULIE; Elk County Christian HS; St Marys, PA; (Y); Cmnty Wkr; Hosp Aide; JV Capt Cheerleading; RN.

NUSSBAUM, KATHY; Ephrata SR HS; Akron, PA; (Y); 32/250; Pres VP Church Yth Grp; Acpl Chr; Trs Chorus; Concert Band; Orch; School Musical; VP Soph Cls; VP Jr Cls; VP Stu Cncl; Var JV Fld Hcky; Outstndng Germ Stu 83; Akron Womns Cvc Clb Schlrshp 86; Goshen Clg Achvt Awd 86; Goshen College; Elem Educ.

NUSSBAUM, SHARON; St Marys Area HS; Saint Marys, PA; (Y); Yrbk Stf; JV Cheerleading; High Hon Roll; Hon Roll.

NUTTALL, MICHELLE A; Hampton HS; Allison Pk, PA; (Y); Church Yth Grp; French Clb; Capt Drill Tm; School Musical; Rep Frsh Cls; Sec Church Yth Grp; Rep Jr Cls; Rep Sr Cls; Powder Puff Ftbl; U Of Pittsburgh.

NUTTER, AMY; Hempfield Area HS; Hunker, PA; (Y); 100/630; Church Yth Grp; French Clb; Pep Clb; Ski Clb; Chorus; Yrbk Stf; Cheerleading; Vllybl; Feml Voc Quart Regls; Lwyr.

NUTTER, SCOTT; Christian School Of York HS; Wrightsville, PA; (Y); Church Yth Grp; Band; Concert Band; School Play; Bsbl; Bsktbl; Socr; Chorus; Church Choir; Pep Band; Oper Barnabas Denom Smmr Mssnry Tm 86; MVP Vrsty Bsbl 85; All Conf Brsty Bsktbl 85-86.

NUZZO, JODY; Corry Area HS; Corry, PA; (S); Church Yth Grp; Cmnty Wkr; Political Wkr; Band; Concert Band; Jazz Band; Mrchg Band; JV Bsktbl; Stat Ftbl; Var Trk; Washgtn Wrkshps-Congrssnl Smnr 86; Pre Cndidt U S Nvl Acad, Appntd B V Rep Thoms Ridge 85; Doc.

NYBERG, KRISTEN; Cumberland Valley HS; Carlisle, PA; (Y); 35/510; Church Yth Grp; Trs Pres Latin Clb; Band; Gym; Hon Roll; Kiwanis Awd; NHS; Sci Dept Achvt Awd Bio; John Hall Schlrshp & Patriot Nws Schlrshp; Harrisburg Area CC.

NYE, LES; Eastern York HS; York, PA; (Y); 3/159; Church Yth Grp; Cit Awd; High Hon Roll; Hon Roll; Jr NHS; NHS; Amer Lgn Schl Awd 84; PA ST; Comp Sci.

NYE, ROBYN; Dowingtown SR HS; Downingtown, PA; (Y); 76/563; French Clb; GAA; Ski Clb; Chorus; Var Bsktbl; Var Fld Hcky; Var Lcrss; NHS; PASLA Tournmnt Chesmont & PA Team 85-86; All Chestmont 1st Team Lacrosse 86; Ed.

NYE, RONALD; Schuykill Valley HS; Leesport, PA; (Y); 11/130; Boy Scts; Church Yth Grp; FBLA; Var L Bsbl; Var L Ftbl; High Hon Roll; NHS; Mickey Silverman Awd Athlt 86; Physcl Educ Awd 86; Pres Shyscl Ftns Awd 86; PA STBERKS Campus; Elec Engrn.

NYESTE, BROOKE ANN; Spring Grove Area SR HS; Seven Valleys, PA; (Y); 52/223; Pres VP SADD; Acpl Chr; School Play; Swing Chorus; Nwsp Ed-Chief; Hst Soph Cls; Hst Jr Cls; Rep Stu Cncl; Hon Roll; Library Aide; Music Boosters Schlrshp 86; Penn ST; Cmrcl Advrtsng.

NYGA, BETH; Highlands HS; Natrona Hts, PA; (Y); 46/280; Exploring; JA; Nwsp Rptr; Rep Soph Cls; Rep Jr Cls; Var Tennis; High Hon Roll; Hon Roll; Jr NHS; NHS; Cmmnctns.

NYGA, KENNETH C; South Park HS; Library, PA; (Y); Var Socr; High Hon Roll; NHS; Engrng.

NYKAZA, LISA; Riverside JR SR HS; Taylor, PA; (Y); 4/200; Church Yth Grp; German Clb; Ski Clb; Variety Show; Nwsp Stf; Stu Cncl; High Hon Roll; NHS; Govnrs Sch Perfrmng Arts 86; U Of Scranton; Med.

NYKIEL, SHERRY; Nazareth Acad; Philadelphia, PA; (Y); Debate Tm; French Clb; NFL; Trs Speech Tm; Jazz Band; Orch; School Musical; Variety Show; Trs NHS.

NYPAVER, PATTY; Springdale HS; Harwick, PA; (Y); Band; Yrbk Ed-Chief; Yrbk Stf; Var JV Vllybl; High Hon Roll; Hon Roll; NHS; Psych.

NYQUIST, KURT; St Marys Area HS; Kersey, PA; (Y); 35/295; Am Leg Boys St; Var L Bsktbl; Wt Lftg; High Hon Roll; NHS.

NYQUIST, POLLY; Unionville HS; Chadds Ford, PA; (Y); 4/300; Church Yth Grp; Chorus; Church Choir; School Musical; Nwsp Bus Mgr; Rep Stu Cncl; Mgr(s); NHS; Ntl Merit Ltr; Intnl Clb.

NYSSE, JOHN D; Pennsbury HS; Levittown, PA; (Y); Bsktbl; Hon Roll; Prfct Atten Awd.

O BARTO, WENDY; South Allegheny HS; Glassport, PA; (S); 3/184; Pres Church Yth Grp; FBLA; VP JA; Office Aide; VP Y-Teens; Nwsp Stf; Yrbk Stf; Off Jr Cls; Powder Puff Ftbl; High Hon Roll; Acctng.

O BLACK, MISSY; Plum HS; Pittsburgh, PA; (Y); 9/378; AFS; FTA; Hosp Aide; Nwsp Bus Mgr; Capt Tennis; NHS.

O BOYLE, JAMES; Meyers HS; Wilkes Bare, PA; (Y); German Clb; Ski Clb; Band; Chorus; Yrbk Stf; Stu Cncl; L Ftbl; L Trk; Wrstlng; NEDT Awd; Htl Mang.

O BOYLE, STEVEN M; Pittston Area HS; Avoca, PA; (Y); Key Clb; Math Clb; Chorus; Var L Bsktbl; L Trk; High Hon Roll; NHS; V-Pres Natl Hnr Scty.

O BRIEN, DANIEL; Pocono Central Catholic HS; Mt Pocono, PA; (Y); Service Clb; Ski Clb; Nwsp Sprt Ed; Bsbl; Bsktbl; Capt Socr; NHS; Pep Clb; Quiz Bowl; Amer Lgn Awd; Hugh O Brien Yth Ldrshp Smnr; U Spnsrd Prblm Slvng Smnr Dscssn Ldr; Boston Coll; Cmmrc & Fnc.

O BRIEN, ERIN; Northwestern HS; Albion, PA; (Y); 26/160; Am Leg Aux Girls St; Drama Clb; Thesps; Concert Band; Drm Mjr(t); Madrigals; School Musical; Rep Stu Cncl; JV Var Cheerleading; JV Sftbl.

O BRIEN, ERIN; William Allen HS; Allentown, PA; (Y); Pres Exploring; Intnl Clb; Leo Clb; Political Wkr; Service Clb; Ski Clb; Yrbk Stf; Hon Roll; Jr NHS; NHS; 1st Pl Estrn PA Hstry Day 85; Fnlst Spllng Bee 84.

O BRIEN, PATRICK; Tyrone Area HS; Tyrone, PA; (Y); 17/196; Boy Scts; Pres Key Clb; Varsity Clb; Band; Yrbk Bus Mgr; L Var Ftbl; L Var Trk; L Var Wrstlng; High Hon Roll; NHS; Engrng.

O BRIEN, RENEE; Aliquippa HS; Aliquippa, PA; (S); Aud/Vis; French Clb; Math Clb; Band; Mrchg Band; Pep Band; Yrbk Stf; Hon Roll; Gftd & Tlntd Pgm; Bus Admin.

O BRIEN, SEAN ROBERT; Bethlehem Catholic HS; Allentown, PA; (S); 19/202; Church Yth Grp; Model UN; NFL; Church Choir; School Play; Capt Crs Cntry; Hon Roll; NHS; Prfct Atten Awd; Pre-Law.

O BRIEN, THOMAS J; Archbishop Wood For Boys HS; Warminster, PA; (Y); 63/282; Chess Clb; Speech Tm; Band; Concert Band; Mrchg Band; School Musical; School Play; Hon Roll; Prfct Atten Awd; Archbishop Wood Sci Fair Gld Mdl Bst In Fair 84; Delaware Vly Sci Fair 2nd Pl 84 & 1st Pl 85; Drexel U; Comp Engrg.

O BRUBA, CHRISTINE; Central Columbia HS; Bloomsburg, PA; (Y); 13/178; Key Clb; NFL; School Musical; Yrbk Stf; Var Capt Cheerleading; Var Capt Trk; French Hon Soc; Hon Roll; Lang Art S Key Awdf 85-86; Social Stds Key Awd 85-86; Pres Awd Acdmc Fit 85-86; PA ST; Law.

O CONNELL, JAMES; Roman Catholic HS; Philadelphia, PA; (S); 9/155; VP Church Yth Grp; Cmnty Wkr; Letterman Clb; Rep Soph Cls; JV Var Ftbl; Capt Var Golf; Capt Socr; High Hon Roll; Hon Roll; NHS; Bus Law.

O CONNELL, JAYNE; Williamsport Area HS; Williamsport, PA; (S); Teachers Aide; Chorus; Comp.

O DONNELL, ANNETTE; Scranton Preparatory Schl; Dunmore, PA; (Y); 28/200; Dance Clb; Latin Clb; Off Frsh Cls; Off Soph Cls; Stu Cncl; Capt JV Cheerleading; High Hon Roll; Jr NHS; French Hon Soc; Fll Schlrshp PA Govrs Schl Arts-Danc Mjr 85; Poli Sci.

O DONNELL, CHRISTINE; Lancaster Catholic HS; Lancaster, PA; (Y); 61/218; Political Wkr; VP Service Clb; Pres Varsity Clb; Nwsp Bus Mgr; Rep Stu Cncl; VP Capt Crs Cntry; Capt Trk; Mayors Yth Cncl Gov 85-86; Sunday Schl Tchr 85-86; Procter Gamble Co Womens Sports Awd 84; U VA; Comm.

O DONNELL, EDD; Brookville Area HS; Sigel, PA; (Y); Boy Scts; Chess Clb; Pres Key Clb; Varsity Clb; Var L Ftbl; Eagle Sct Awd BSA 85; Natl Eagle Sct Assn BSA 85; Ordr Of Arrow BSA 85; Lock Haven; Athltc Trnr.

O DONNELL, EVANGELINE; Pennsbury HS; Yardley, PA; (Y); French Clb; Chorus; Nwsp Stf; Hon Roll; NHS; DR.

O DONNELL, KARREN; Solanco HS; Nottingham, PA; (Y); 110/235; Art Clb; Spanish Clb; SADD; Teachers Aide; Schlstc Art Awd Cert Of Merit 86; Cert Engl Awd 86; Annl Spnsh Comptn 1st Pl 84 & 86; Psych.

O DONNELL, MARK; Archbishop Ryan HS; Philadelphia, PA; (Y); 127/429; Bsbl; Bsktbl; Ftbl; Golf; Vllybl; Wt Lftg; Hon Roll.

O DONNELL, MICHAEL; Archbishop Wood For Boys; Southampton, PA; (Y); 23/289; VP Church Yth Grp; Mathletes; Spanish Clb; SADD; Nwsp Stf; JV Bsbl; Im Bsktbl; JV Crs Cntry; Im Ftbl; JV Trk; PA ST U; Engrng.

O DONNELL, THOMAS; St Josephs Prep; Philadelphia, PA; (Y); Spanish Clb; Lit Mag; Wrstlng; Bio.

O DONNELL, THOMAS J; Parkland SR HS; Orefield, PA; (Y); 118/459; Church Yth Grp; Bsktbl; L Var Ftbl; Wt Lftg; Pre-Dntstry.

O FLAHERTY, COLLEEN; Pequea Valley HS; Kinzers, PA; (Y); AFS; French Clb; JA; Library Aide; Spanish Clb; Chorus; School Musical; Ed Yrbk Stf; Hon Roll; Millersville U; Lbrry Sci.

O GARA, TAMMY; Clearfield HS; Clearfield, PA; (Y); DECA; Band; Gym; 4th Dist Level Of Dist Ed Comp 86; Bus.

O HARA, KARA ANN; Hollidaysburg Area HS; Jupiter, FL; (Y); Church Yth Grp; Trs French Clb; Rep Key Clb; Science Clb; SADD; JV Swmmng; JV Vllybl; Hon Roll; Ntl Merit SF; Anat & Physlgy Hnrs Awd 86; Excllnce Cls Part Awd 86; Georgetown U; Frgn Svc.

O HARA, NANNETTE; Marple Newtown HS; Broomall, PA; (Y); 32/362; Office Aide; Service Clb; Rep Jr Cls; Rep Sr Cls; Fld Hcky; Mgr(s); High Hon Roll; Hon Roll; Sec NHS; Marple Newtowro Cls Schrshp 86; PA ST U; Bus.

O HARA, PATRICIA; North Pocono HS; Moscow, PA; (Y); Girl Scts; Hosp Aide; Chorus; Capt Flag Corp; Lit Mag; Hon Roll; NHS; East Strousberg U; Bio.

O HARA, RENEE; Homer Center HS; Homer City, PA; (Y); 8/106; French Clb; Hosp Aide; Library Aide; Chorus; Drm Mjr(t); School Play; Sftbl; High Hon Roll; Kiwanis Awd; NHS; Kiwanis Clb Schlrshp 86; Wmns Clb Schlrshp 86; U Of Pittsbrgh; Phy Thrpy.

O HARA, TIMOTHY F; Scranton Prep; Dunmore, PA; (Y); 5/190; Boy Scts; Exploring; Letterman Clb; Quiz Bowl; Yrbk Sprt Ed; Capt Crs Cntry; Var L Trk; High Hon Roll; NHS; Ntl Merit Schol; U Of PA.

O HARAH, DANIELLE; Harborcreek HS; Harbor Creek, PA; (Y); 52/230; Church Yth Grp; Dance Clb; Band; Variety Show; Var L Pom Pon; Var Trk; Hon Roll; NHS.

O HORA, STEPHANIE; Chief Logan HS; Lewistown, PA; (Y); 62/202; French Clb; Hosp Aide; Ski Clb; Color Guard; Mrchg Band; Ed Yrbk Stf; Trk; Hon Roll; Prfct Atten Awd; Dental Hygiene.

O KRESIK, STEPHEN; Hickory SR HS; W Middlesex, PA; (Y); 51/189; Drama Clb; Letterman Clb; NFL; Speech Tm; Varsity Clb; Acpl Chr; Chorus; Church Choir; School Musical; Bsktbl; IN U Of PA; Pre-Med.

O LEARY, ANNE; Villa Maria Acad; Erie, PA; (Y); 71/146; Model UN; Science Clb; Color Guard; Yrbk Stf; Rep Stu Cncl; Hon Roll; NHS; Socl Wrk.

O MALLEY, JULIANNE; Scranton Prep; Scranton, PA; (Y); 43/192; Nwsp Rptr; Nwsp Stf; Var L Gym; High Hon Roll; Hon Roll; Ntl Merit Ltr.

O MALLEY, LUCY; Scranton Prep HS; Moscow, PA; (Y); 13/192; Rep Church Yth Grp; Dance Clb; Drama Clb; School Play; Var L Cheerleading; Var Trk; High Hon Roll; NHS; Ntl Merit Ltr; ISLI 84; Cmmnctns.

O MARA, ELIZABETH D; West Catholic Girls; Philadelphia, PA; (Y); 4/241; FBLA; GAA; Mathletes; Pep Clb; Science Clb; Band; Orch; Yrbk Ed-Chief; Yrbk Stf; Cheerleading; Villanova; Jrnlsm.

O MATZ, MARK; Bethel Park SR HS; Bethel Park, PA; (Y); Art Clb; Church Yth Grp; French Clb; Stu Cncl; JV Bsktbl; Var Ftbl; Im Wt Lftg; Hon Roll; Off Soph Cls; Penn ST U.

O NEAL, BRIDGET; Mercyhurst Prep HS; Erie, PA; (Y); Church Yth Grp; French Clb; Girl Scts; Key Clb; Chorus; Church Choir; Hon Roll; Girl Scouts Ldrshp Pin 86; 10 Yr Pin Girl Scouts 86; Physcl Thrpy.

O NEIL, MICHELLE; Allegheny-Clarion Valley HS; Parker, PA; (Y); 4/103; Concert Band; School Musical; Sec Jr Cls; Sec Sr Cls; JV VP Bsktbl; Co-Capt Cheerleading; NHS; Office Aide; Varsity Clb; Yrbk Stf; Prsdntl Acdmc Ftnss Awd 86; Prm Qn 86; Hmcmt Ct 85; Sec.

O NEILL, BRIAN JAMES; Strath Haven HS; Gwynedd, PA; (Y); Boy Scts; Church Yth Grp; Hosp Aide; Band; Variety Show; Rep Frsh Cls; JV Bsbl; Hon Roll; Faculty Schlrshp-Villanova U 86; Newsboy Of The Month Delaware Co Daily Times 81; Villanova U; Commerce.

O NEILL, COLLEEN; Sharon HS; Sharon, PA; (Y); Aud/Vis; Latin Clb; Office Aide; Service Clb; Spanish Clb; Nwsp Stf; VP Soph Cls; Twrlr; Hon Roll; NHS; Jrnlsm.

O NEILL, DIANNE; Little Flower HS; Philadelphia, PA; (Y); Hosp Aide; Hon Roll; Algebra 2 Merit Awd 85-86; Stu Personnel 86-87; Accntng.

O NEILL, JOHN; Bishop Mc Devitt HS; Elkins Park, PA; (Y); Aud/Vis; Computer Clb; Science Clb; Nwsp Rptr; Rotary Awd; St Josephs U; Ecnmcs.

O NEILL, KELLY A; Hopewell SR HS; Aliquippa, PA; (Y); 62/280; Church Yth Grp; Debate Tm; Exploring; German Clb; Chorus; School Musical; School Play; Sec Stu Cncl; Stu Forum 84-86; Penn ST; Nutrition.

O NEILL, LISA M; Ambridge Area HS; Ambridge, PA; (Y); Pep Clb; Red Cross Aide; Off Frsh Cls; Off Soph Cls; Off Jr Cls; Hon Roll; Accntng.

O NEILL, MARY M; Merion Mercy Acad; Ardmore, PA; (Y); Cmnty Wkr; Drama Clb; Service Clb; Spanish Clb; Church Choir; School Musical; Rep Jr Cls; Pres Stu Cncl; Cheerleading; Hon Roll; Latin Clscl Soc Cum Laude Awd 82; Natl Assn Stu Cncls Mbrshp 84; Acad Svc Awd 86; Villanova U; Pub Rel.

O NEILL, MICHELE; St Maria Gorehi HS; Philadelphia, PA; (S); 5/401; VP Church Yth Grp; Orch; Ed Lit Mag; Rep Jr Cls; JV Crs Cntry; High Hon Roll; NHS; Acad All Amer 83-84; Dist 12 Orch 85-86; Town Meet Tomorrow GE 85-86.

O NEILL, PATRICK; Bishop Hafey HS; White Haven, PA; (Y); Sec Chess Clb; Church Yth Grp; Computer Clb; Teachers Aide; Im Bsktbl; Im Var Socr; Hon Roll; Acctg.

O NEILL, PATTI; Norwin SR HS; North Huntingdon, PA; (Y); SADD; Crs Cntry; Trk; Clarion U Of PA; Bus.

O NEILL, PETER D; Red Land HS; New Cumberland, PA; (Y); 13/290; Latin Clb; Var L Ftbl; Var L Socr; Var L Swmmng; Var L Trk; High Hon Roll; Hon Roll; JETS Awd; NHS; Mid-Pen All-Star Sccr 84 & 86; Mid-Pen All-Star Ftbll Kicker 86; Princeton; Engrng.

O NEILL, TIM; Sharon HS; Sharon, PA; (Y); 1/196; Latin Clb; Y-Teens; Rep Stu Cncl; JV Tennis; Elks Awd; Kiwanis Awd; Pres Schlr; Val; Amer Chem Scty Awd 85; Rnsslr Medal 85; Mercyhurst Coll.

O REILLY, AMY; Saint Basil Acad; Philadelphia, PA; (Y); 23/90; Art Clb; Church Yth Grp; Civic Clb; Cmnty Wkr; Drama Clb; GAA; Hosp Aide; Latin Clb; Thesps; Bsbl; Cthlc Ntl Traing Inst Ldrshp Svc 85; Ntl Cthlc Yth Conf Phldlpha Delgt 85; Comm Svc Corp Merit Awd; Scranton U; Hlth Svc.

O RORKE, BARRY J; Shaler Area HS; Glenshaw, PA; (Y); Church Yth Grp; Ski Clb; SADD; Rep Frsh Cls; Rep Soph Cls; Rep Jr Cls; Pres Sr Cls; Pres Stu Cncl; Var L Socr; Var Tennis; Rtry Intl Lttrs Peace 1st Pl Dist; Bshps Egl Of Crss Awd; Rtry Yth Ldrshp Awd Rtry Cnfrnc; Carnegie-Melon U; Indstrl Mngmt.

O ROURKE, COLLEEN; Spring-Ford SR HS; Collegeville, PA; (Y); 39/237; Band; Concert Band; Jazz Band; Mrchg Band; Pep Band; Yrbk Stf; Off Sr Cls; Stu Cncl; Capt Var Lcrss; Hon Roll; Barbara Ann Karwoski Music Awd 86; Indiana U PA.

O SHEA, AMY; Carlynton HS; Pittsburgh, PA; (Y); Letterman Clb; Spanish Clb; Trs Jr Cls; Score Keeper; Swmmng; High Hon Roll; NHS; Amer Legion Awd 85.

O SHEA, PATRICK; Churchill HS; Braddock, PA; (Y); 41/188; Spanish Clb; Rptr Nwsp Rptr; Nwsp Stf; High Hon Roll; Hon Roll; Church Yth Grp; Drama Clb; Jrnlsm.

O SHELL, TODD; Harmony HS; Cherry Tree, PA; (Y); 15/44; Church Yth Grp; Ski Clb; VP Concert Band; Mrchg Band; Yrbk Phtg; Rep Stu Cncl; Var L Bsbl; JV Var Bsktbl; Dnfth Awd; Slippery Rock U; Hist.

O SULLIVAN, AMY; Bethel Park HS; Bethel Park, PA; (Y); Ski Clb; Band; Mrchg Band; Orch; School Play; Symp Band; Powder Puff Ftbl; High Hon Roll; NHS; Bnkg.

O TOOLE, MARGARET; Sacred Heart HS; Pittsburgh, PA; (Y); 5/150; Dance Clb; Hosp Aide; Latin Clb; Math Clb; Pep Clb; Ski Clb; Spanish Clb; Var Crs Cntry; Capt Gym; Capt Sftbl; Hghst Hnr.

OAKES, KIM; Northampton Area SR HS; Bath, PA; (S); AFS; Drama Clb; Model UN; Political Wkr; Band; School Musical; School Play; Nwsp Stf; JV Trk; Hon Roll; Ntl Merit Lttr Rec 85; Penn ST; Pol Sci.

OAKES, MICHAEL; Bishop Shanahan HS; W Chester, PA; (Y); 31/218; High Hon Roll; Hon Roll; Prfct Atten Awd; Washington & Jefferson U; Med.

OAKLEY, ANEIDA JEAN; Penn Hills SR HS; Pittsburgh, PA; (S); 71/797; Drama Clb; Exploring; Office Aide; Spanish Clb; Yrbk Stf; Stu Cncl; Cit Awd; Hon Roll; Jr NHS; NHS; Miss Black Teenage Pgnt SF 85; Carneigie Mellon U; Econ.

OAKLEY, DEANNE; Chester HS; Chester, PA; (Y); 35/365; Band; Concert Band; Capt Drm Mjr(t); Mrchg Band; Orch; VP Jr Cls; Cit Awd; Elks Awd; Jr NHS; Prfct Atten 82-86; Morgan ST U; Bus Adm.

OBELDOBEL, JUDY; Carrick HS; Pittsburgh, PA; (S); 9/311; Library Aide; School Musical; Yrbk Stf; Rep Stu Cncl; High Hon Roll; NHS; U Of Pittsburgh; Bio.

OBENOUR, CAITIE L; Fort Cherry HS; Hickory, PA; (Y); Church Yth Grp; Drama Clb; 4-H; Thesps; Chorus; Church Choir; School Play; Nwsp Rptr; Stu Cncl; NFAA Arts Recgntn & Talnt Search Awd-Hnrbl Mentn 86; PA Govnrs Schl For Arts 85; Pittsburg Ballet Theatre Co.

OBENREDER, CHRISTINE; Harbor Creek HS; Erie, PA; (Y); Political Wkr; Nwsp Ed-Chief; Nwsp Rptr; Nwsp Sprt Ed; Nwsp Stf; Yrbk Phtg; Stu Cncl; Pom Pon; JV Tennis; Hon Roll; Cmmnctns.

OBER, DANETTE M; Elizabeth Area HS; Elizabethtown, PA; (Y); 90/227; Church Yth Grp; Teachers Aide; Chorus; Church Choir; School Musical; Variety Show; Mgr Bsktbl; Mgr Ftbl; Mgr Wrstlng; Elizabethtown Coll Scholar 85-86; Millersville U; Intr Decrtng.

OBERDICK, MARK; Cornell HS; Coraopolis, PA; (Y); Boy Scts; Key Clb; Science Clb; School Play; Var L Bsktbl; Var Ftbl; Var L Tennis; Hon Roll; Jr NHS; NHS.

OBERG, ANDREW; Rochester Area HS; Rochester, PA; (Y); Am Leg Boys St; Civic Clb; French Clb; Pep Clb; Nwsp Stf; Sec Sr Cls; Var L Ftbl; Var L Trk; Im Wt Lftg; Boy Scts; Ftbl Plyrs Regn Natl H S Ftbl Magzn 86; Bus.

OBERKIRCHER, AMY; Danville SR HS; Danville, PA; (Y); 8/202; Drama Clb; Key Clb; Latin Clb; Ski Clb; School Play; Rep Stu Cncl; JV Tennis; JV Trk; High Hon Roll; NHS; Amer Classcl Leagues Natl Latin Exam 86; Med.

OBERLE, KEN; North Hills HS; Pittsburgh, PA; (Y); 20/500; Church Yth Grp; Ski Clb; Var Capt Ftbl; Var Trk; Hon Roll; NHS; YMCA Schlr Athlt 85-86; Presdntl Acadmc Ftns Awd 86; MD U; Engr.

OBERRATH, KRISTIN; Maplewood HS; Guys Mills, PA; (Y); 7/124; Sec 4-H; Pep Clb; Spanish Clb; Sec SADD; Yrbk Stf; Pres Stu Cncl; JV Vllybl; NHS; Office Aide; 4-H Awd; Grad Asst Dale Carnegie Course 86; Mst Likely To Succeed 86; Robert Morris Coll; Adm Spec.

OBERST, KYLE; West Hazleton SR HS; Conyngham, PA; (Y); Boy Scts; VICA; PFC US Army Rsrve Early Enlstmnt Pgm 86; Us Army.

OBIDINSKI, JILL; Scranton Prep; Scranton, PA; (Y); Church Yth Grp; Cmnty Wkr; Stage Crew; Im Bsktbl; JV Var Cheerleading; Im Coach Actv; Im Score Keeper; Hon Roll; U Scrntn; Bio.

OBLINGER, JOHN; Aliquippa SR HS; Aliquippa, PA; (Y); Boy Scts; French Clb; Yrbk Stf; Var Ftbl; Mgr Wrstlng; Cit Awd; God Cntry Awd; Hon Roll; SAR Awd; Boy Sct Eagle Sct 85; Crimnlgy; Gov Investgtns.

OBORSKI, JOSEPH; Cathedral Prep Schl; Erie, PA; (Y); 59/216; Church Yth Grp; Library Aide; Model UN; Spanish Clb; Var Trk; Im Vllybl; Prfct Atten Awd; Penn ST; Earth Space Sci.

OBOYLE, EILEEN M; Scranton Preparatory Schl; Clarks Summit, PA; (Y); 19/192; Church Yth Grp; Girl Scts; Orch; Yrbk Stf; Tennis; Trk; High Hon Roll; NHS; Med.

OBRINGER, CHRISTINE A; Mon Valley HS; Eighty-Four, PA; (S); 23/102; Band; Concert Band; Capt Twrlr; Var Pres French Hon Soc; CA U PA; Sprts Med.

OBRYON, SCOTT; Trinity HS; Washington, PA; (Y); 130/374; Ski Clb; JV Var Bsbl; Var Golf; Hon Roll; U NV; Crmnl Jstice.

OBRZUT, ANNETTE; Mahonoy Area HS; Mahanoy City, PA; (Y); Am Leg Aux Girls St; FFA; Hosp Aide; Band; Twrlr; Amer Leg Aux Educ & Schlrshp Awd 86; Mc Canns Schl/Bus; Med Sec.

OBUCHOWSKI, JODI; Mt Lebanon HS; Mt Lebanon, PA; (Y); Cmnty Wkr; German Clb; Hosp Aide; Ski Clb; Variety Show; Pres Frsh Cls; Pres VP Soph Cls; Pres Jr Cls; Stu Cncl; Var Bowling.

OCASIO, MARIA M; Pottstown SR HS; Pottstown, PA; (Y); Art Clb; JA; Key Clb; Library Aide; Nwsp Stf; JV Fld Hcky; Var Lcrss; Prfct Atten Awd; Sec.

OCASIO, SARA; Liberty HS; Bethlehem, PA; (Y); 196/475; Church Yth Grp; VICA; Church Choir; Hon Roll; Secy Of Data Prcssng Cls Vo-Tech 84-86; Data Prcssng.

OCCHIPINTI, MICHELE; Riverside HS; Taylor, PA; (Y); Art Clb; Drama Clb; Ski Clb; Chorus; School Musical; School Play; Variety Show; Rep Jr Cls; Stu Cncl; Cheerleading; Bloomsburg U; Physcl Thrpy.

OCHESTER, BETSY; Elderton HS; Shelocta, PA; (Y); 3/91; Pres Church Yth Grp; Trs German Clb; Y-Teens; Band; Concert Band; Mrchg Band; Pep Band; Yrbk Stf; VP Sr Cls; Stu Cncl; 1st Prz IN Comp Fair 84; Wake Forest U; Psychlgy.

OCHOTORENA, CHRIS; Berwick SR HS; Berwick, PA; (Y); Key Clb; Chorus; Tennis; Trk.

OCHWAT, KAREN; St Paul Cathedral HS; Cheswick, PA; (Y); 15/60; Computer Clb; French Clb; Girl Scts; Intnl Clb; Red Cross Aide; Science Clb; SADD; Yrbk Stf; JV Vllybl; High Hon Roll; Gannon U; Med.

OCKER, BRAD; Shippenburg Area SR HS; Shippensburg, PA; (Y); 40/260; Am Leg Boys St; Church Yth Grp; Band; School Musical; VP Soph Cls; VP Jr Cls; Pres Sr Cls; Rep Stu Cncl; Var Crs Cntry; Var Trk; Shippensburg U; Psych.

OCKUN, LYNNE; Unionville HS; Kennett Square, PA; (Y); 84/265; SADD; Rep Frsh Cls; Rep Frsh Cls; Jr Cls; Rep Sr Cls; Stu Cncl; Fld Hcky; Lcrss; Powder Puff Ftbl; High Hon Roll; Fld Hcky Schlrshp-U Of VA 86; All-Amer & All-League Lacrosse 86; All-League Fld Hcky 84 & 85; U Of VA; Arch.

OCONNELL, CHRISTOPHER; Strath Haven HS; Wallingford, PA; (Y); Spanish Clb; Rep Frsh Cls; Rep Soph Cls; Rep Stu Cncl; Var Ice Hcky; JV Socr; Brdcstng.

OCONNOR, DOUGLAS; Hughesville HS; Hughesville, PA; (Y); 1/156; French Clb; JA; Letterman Clb; Ski Clb; Varsity Clb; Stage Crew; VP Soph Cls; Pres Jr Cls; Stu Cncl; Var L Bsbl; Grn Wht Awd 85-86; Penn ST U; Aerontcl Engrng.

ODDO, TANA JEAN; Serra Catholic HS; Jefferson Boro, PA; (Y); Red Cross Aide; Spanish Clb; Chorus; Church Choir; Sec Trs Jr Cls; Bowling; Cheerleading; Sftbl; Trk; Vllybl; Merit Awd For Modern Amer Cultures 86; Ambassador Clg; Lang Trnsltr.

ODELL, BRIAN; Kennedy Christian HS; Brookfield, OH; (Y); Church Yth Grp; Letterman Clb; Science Clb; Ski Clb; Spanish Clb; Varsity Clb; Var L Bsbl; JV Bsktbl; Im Wt Lftg; Hon Roll; OH Northern U; Pharm.

ODELLI, TERRY; Yough HS; Smithton, PA; (Y); French Clb; Letterman Clb; Spanish Clb; Var L Bsbl; Var L Ftbl; Hon Roll; NHS; Washington & Jefferson; Engr.

ODEN, LORA; Yough SR HS; Ruffsdale, PA; (Y); FBLA; Office Aide; Vllybl; Steno Awd 86; Sec.

ODONNELL, THOMAS; Scranton Prep; Dunmore, PA; (Y); 108/191; Church Yth Grp; Letterman Clb; Varsity Clb; Var L Ftbl; Var L Trk; Schl Rcrd Hldr Jvln Dst Trck Cnfrnc Gld Mdl 86; 8th ST Trck Mt 86; Hnrbl Mntn Mdls 85-86.

OEHLER, DUSTIN; Otto-Eldred HS; Eldred, PA; (Y); Computer Clb; Pres Trs 4-H; German Clb; Library Aide; Quiz Bowl; 4-H Awd; Rotary Awd; Outstndng By 86; Mst Cngnl 86; Bus Mgmt.

OELER, ROLF; William Allen HS; Allentown, PA; (Y); 192/559; Boy Scts; Church Yth Grp; Letterman Clb; Political Wkr; Nwsp Rptr; Nwsp Sprt Ed; Nwsp Stf; VP Soph Cls; Var L Diving; Var L Socr; Columbia Schltc Press Awd 85; Morning Call Stu Nwspaper Pgm Spts Wrtg 86; Jrnlsm.

OESTERLING, DANA; Butler SR HS; Bulter, PA; (Y); Church Yth Grp; Exploring; French Clb; SADD; Thesps; Concert Band; Mrchg Band; Orch; Symp Band; L Jr NHS; Let And Pin In JR Natl Hnr Soc 85; Grove City Clg; Accntng.

OESTERLING, DIANNE; Butler SR HS; Butler, PA; (Y); Chorus; Hon Roll; Butler Cnty Area Vctnl Tech Schl Hnr Awds 85-86.

OFFIE, JAMES; Sharpsville High Area Schl; Transfer, PA; (Y); Church Yth Grp; Thiel Coll; Chem.

OGBURN, TRICIA; Trinity HS; Washingon, PA; (Y); 4-H; German Clb; Science Clb; Ski Clb; Yrbk Stf; Cheerleading; Crs Cntry; Socr; Trk; 4-H Awd; Horse Trnr-Won Top PQHA Yr 84; Long Filly Awd 85; Phys Ftns Awd 83; PA Top Female 4-H; OH ST; Engrng.

OGDEN, MARTHA; Carlynton HS; Pittsbugh, PA; (Y); Spanish Clb; Stage Crew; Vllybl; High Hon Roll; Hon Roll; Villa Maria Coll; Chem.

OGDEN, VALERIE; West York HS; York, PA; (Y); 1/210; Church Yth Grp; School Play; Trs Sr Cls; Rep Stu Cncl; Bsktbl; Var Co-Capt Fld Hcky; High Hon Roll; VP NHS; Opt Clb Awd; Val; David E Beckmyer Schlrshp, Eliz M Young Mem Schlrshp, Engrng Soc York Schlrshp 86; U Pittsburgh; Genetic Engrng.

OGIN, CHERYL; Wyoming Valley West HS; Kingston, PA; (Y); Church Yth Grp; Girl Scts; Hosp Aide; Key Clb; Chorus; Church Choir; School Musical; Swing Chorus; Hon Roll; Wilkes Coll Upwrd Bnd 84-86; Upwrd Bnd Outstndg Day Stu & Cert Acvht 84; Upwrd Bnd Ctznshp Awd 86; Wilkes Coll; RN.

OGLINE, TIMOTHY E; Montrose Area HS; Hallstead, PA; (Y); 58/176; Art Clb; Boy Scts; Latin Clb; Yrbk Ed-Chief; Wt Lftg; NEDT Awd; English Clb; 4-H; Nwsp Rptr; Yrbk Stf; PA Govnrs Schl-Arts At Bucknell U-Cert Of Attndnc 85; PA Higher Educ Ass Agncy Cert Mrt 85; Temple U; Fine Art.

OGOZALY, WALTER; Lakeland HS; Carbondale, PA; (Y); Chess Clb.

OGROSKY, JASON; W Mifflin Area HS; W Mifflin, PA; (Y); Aud/Vis; Church Yth Grp; FCA; Ski Clb; L JV Ftbl; High Hon Roll; Hon Roll; Jr NHS; NHS.

OGURCHAK, ANDREW; Greensburg Central Cath HS; Greensburg, PA; (Y); Art Clb; Cmnty Wkr; Trs VP 4-H; 4-H Awd; High Hon Roll; Hon Roll; Engnrng.

OHARA, JOE; Archbishop Wood For Boys; Warminster, PA; (Y); 70/300; FCA; Varsity Clb; Var L Bsbl; Var L Socr; U Of Temple; Arch.

OHLER, KEVIN M; South Side Catholic HS; Pittsburgh, PA; (S); Chess Clb; Nwsp Stf; Spnsh Awd 84; Westrn Cvlztn Awd 85; Acctg.

OHLER, MELISSA; Rockwood Area HS; Rockwood, PA; (S); 13/95; Hosp Aide; Spanish Clb; Chorus; Yrbk Stf; Stu Cncl; Stat Bsbl; Stat Bsktbl; JV Vllybl; Hon Roll; Pres Ftnss Awd 84-85.

OHLER, TAMMY; Forest Hills HS; Windber, PA; (Y); 36/156; Hon Roll; Hmntrm Clb 85-86; Trv Prs Clb 84-85; Math.

OHLMANN, JANINE; Archbishop Wood For Girls; Warminster, PA; (Y); 9/259; Church Yth Grp; Cmnty Wkr; German Clb; Library Aide; Yrbk Phtg; Yrbk Stf; Rep Frsh Cls; Rep Soph Cls; Rep Jr Cls; Var Mgr Swmmng; German Hnr Soc-Delta Epsilon Phi; Hnbl Mntn Amm Assoc Tchrs Grmn Cntst, Adolf Klarmann Schlrshp 86; La Salle U; Psych.

OHLRICH, TINA; Tech Memorial HS; Erie, PA; (Y); 54/349; VICA; Chorus; Stu Cncl; Trk; Nrsng.

OHLS, ARDEN; Wilmington Area HS; Pulaski, PA; (Y); French Clb; Spanish Clb; Yrbk Stf.

OKABAYASHI, SUSAN; Abington SR HS; Roslyn, PA; (Y); 39/535; French Clb; Latin Clb; Varsity Clb; Rep Stu Cncl; Var Socr; Var Capt Tennis; JC Awd; NHS; Pres Schlr; MVP Tnns 85-86; U CT; Bus.

OKAMOTO, NEIL; Council Rock HS; Holland, PA; (Y); 1/845; Computer Clb; Jazz Band; Capt Mrchg Band; Symp Band; High Hon Roll; Pres NHS; Ntl Merit SF; PA Dist 11 Band 85; German Soc PA Hon Ment 86; Bucks Cnty Music Fstvl 83-85; Engrng.

OKRASINSKI, LORI; Elmer L Meyers HS; Wilkes-Barre, PA; (S); German Clb; Chorus; Concert Band; Jazz Band; Mrchg Band; Orch; L Bsktbl; Sftbl; Hon Roll; PA ST U; Spec Ed.

OLAH, ERIC; Kiski Area HS; Salina, PA; (Y); Boy Scts; French Clb; Chorus; Rep Frsh Cls; Hon Roll; De Vry Inst Of Tech; Compu Sci.

OLBRICH, ERIC P; Lewiston Area HS; Lewistown, PA; (Y); 55/265; AFS; Boy Scts; Church Yth Grp; Ski Clb; Band; Chorus; Concert Band; Mrchg Band; School Musical; Stu Cncl; Egl Sct 86; U S Music Ambssdrs Hawiian Tour 86.

OLCZAK, JENNIFER; Highlands HS; Natrona Heights, PA; (Y); Church Yth Grp; DECA; JA; Library Aide; Office Aide; Band; Color Guard; Concert Band; Mrchg Band; Symp Band; Brown & Gold Awd 84-86; St Francis; Physcns Asst.

OLCZAK, TED; Council Rock HS; New Hope, PA; (Y); 207/845; Chess Clb; Church Yth Grp; Cmnty Wkr; 4-H; Spanish Clb; Variety Show; JV Wrstlng; Hon Roll; Bus Intrl.

OLDFIELD, HEATHER; St Pius X HS; Phoenixville, PA; (S); 27/162; Cmnty Wkr; Dance Clb; High Hon Roll; Hon Roll; NHS; Intl Comm.

OLDRATI, BRIAN E; St John Neumann HS; Philadelphia, PA; (Y); 16/338; Spanish Clb; High Hon Roll; NHS; Usher Crps 84-87; Elctrncs.

OLEARY, CHRIS; St Marys Area HS; St Marys, PA; (Y); Var L Bsktbl; Army; Cmmnctns.

OLEARY, SHAWN; Upper Moreland HS; Hatboro, PA; (Y); 50/275; Rep Key Clb; VP Soph Cls; VP Jr Cls; Var L Bsbl; Bsktbl; Var Capt Socr; MVP Sccr 86; Suburban 1st Tm All-League Bsbl, 1st Tm All-League Sccr 86; Gettysburg Coll; Bio.

OLEJARCZYK, PAUL; Fairview HS; Fairview, PA; (Y); 13/186; Church Yth Grp; Cmnty Wkr; Ski Clb; Teachers Aide; JV Bsktbl; JV Golf; Im Vllybl; Hon Roll; NHS; PA ST U; Bus.

OLENCHAK III, EDWARD; North Pocono HS; Lake Airel, PA; (Y); 55/236; Model UN; Off Frsh Cls; Rep Stu Cncl; Im Bsktbl; Var L Vllybl; Penn ST U; Mnrl Sci.

OLENCHICK, PAULA; Northern Cambria HS; Spangler, PA; (Y); Spanish Clb; Chorus; Pres Frsh Cls; VP Stu Cncl; Var Capt Cheerleading; Hon Roll; U Of Charleston; Pre-Law.

OLENCHOCK, MICHAEL; Greensburg Central Catholic HS; Latrobe, PA; (Y); Library Aide; Chorus; High Hon Roll; Hon Roll; Im Sftbl; Comp Sci.

OLENIK, BRYAN; South Allegheny JR & SR HS; Glassport, PA; (S); 2/184; Church Yth Grp; French Clb; Teachers Aide; Yrbk Phtg; Stu Cncl; High Hon Roll; NHS; Pitt; Comp Pgmng.

OLESKO, ANDREA; Brownsville Area HS; Republic, PA; (Y); High Hon Roll; ICM Schl Of Bus; Med Ofc Asst.

OLESON, CARRIE; St Benedict Acad; Erie, PA; (Y); 25/63; Stage Crew; Variety Show; Yrbk Ed-Chief; Yrbk Stf; Var Sftbl.

OLEXY, LAURA; Riverside HS; Taylor, PA; (Y); 33/160; Church Yth Grp; Drama Clb; Hosp Aide; Ski Clb; Chorus; School Musical; School Play; Yrbk Stf; JV Var Cheerleading; Hon Roll; Natl Cncl Yth Ldrshp Achvt Fnlst 85; Duquesne U; Phrmcst.

OLIPHANT, SCOTT J; Yough SR HS; West Newton, PA; (Y); Office Aide; Red Cross Aide; Ski Clb; Spanish Clb; Acpl Chr; Chorus; Stu Rep Schl Brd 85-86; Pres Westmoreland Cnty Comm Action Pro 85-86; SR Awd Voice Yough 86; Penn ST U; Advertsng.

OLIVA, CATHY; Pius X HS; Pen Argyl, PA; (Y); 16/30; Letterman Clb; Pep Clb; Varsity Clb; Band; Chorus; School Musical; Yrbk Stf; Var Capt Bsktbl; Var Powder Puff Ftbl; Var Capt Sftbl; 4 Yr Ltr Sftbl & 3 Yr Ltr Bsktbl & Musicns Protctv Awd 86; Allentown Coll; Crmnl Jstc.

OLIVER, A JAMES; M M I Prep Schl; Bear Creek, PA; (Y); 15/32; Art Clb; Aud/Vis; Church Yth Grp; Civic Clb; Cmnty Wkr; Pep Clb; Service Clb; Ski Clb; Speech Tm; Pep Band; U Pittsburgh; Bus Adm.

OLIVER, CHARLES; Carlisle SR HS; Carlisle, PA; (Y); Art Clb; Spanish Clb; Bsktbl; Crs Cntry; Trk; Hon Roll; Antnlli Schl Of Art; Cmrcl Art.

OLIVER, JENNIFER; Nanticoke Area HS; Nanticoke, PA; (Y); 29/251; Key Clb; Ski Clb; Chorus; Nwsp Stf; Yrbk Stf; Mgr(s); High Hon Roll; NHS; NEDT Awd; Harvard U; Bus.

OLIVER, JILL; Pittston Area SR HS; Pittston, PA; (Y); 1/356; Church Yth Grp; Cmnty Wkr; Drama Clb; Key Clb; Library Aide; Math Clb; Chorus; High Hon Roll; NHS; Math.

OLIVER, KARIN; Strong Vincent HS; Erie, PA; (Y); 25/164; Church Yth Grp; Library Aide; Church Choir; Pensacola Christ Coll; Bible.

OLIVER, LISA; West Middlesex HS; W Middlesex, PA; (S); 19/107; 4-H; Spanish Clb; Concert Band; Mrchg Band; Pep Band; Var L Bsktbl; Var Sftbl; Hon Roll; Prfct Atten Awd; 3rd Cls Bnd Awd 85; Educ.

OLIVER, SAMANTHA; Center HS; Aliquippa, PA; (Y); 14/184; Spanish Clb; Varsity Clb; Stu Cncl; Capt Cheerleading; High Hon Roll; Hon Roll; NHS; Hmcmng & Prom Corts 85-86; PA Sst U; Accntng.

OLIVERI, MICHELLE; Pittston Area HS; Pittston, PA; (Y); 38/325; High Hon Roll; Luzerne Cnty CC.

OLIVERIO, JOHN S; South Park HS; Pittsburgh, PA; (Y); 6/203; Exploring; Teachers Aide; Yrbk Stf; Trs Off Stu Cncl; High Hon Roll; NHS; Prfct Atten Awd; Prt-Tm Job 85-87; Altr By 83-85.

OLKUS, TRACEY; Philadelphia HS For Girls; Philadelphia, PA; (Y); Art Clb; Civic Clb; Political Wkr; Teachers Aide; Variety Show; Nwsp Stf; High Hon Roll; Hon Roll; Spanish NHS; Hnry Mntn Phila Schl Dist Art Dept 86; Communctns.

OLMSTEAD, ELLIOT; Hershey HS; Hershey, PA; (Y); 20/206; Chess Clb; Computer Clb; Spanish Clb; Mrchg Band; Lit Mag; Crs Cntry; High Hon Roll; Hon Roll; NHS; Spanish NHS; Chess Champ 83; PA ST U; Aerontcl Engrng.

OLMSTEAD, KRISTA KAY; Carlisle SR HS; Carlisle, PA; (Y); 21/450; Church Yth Grp; German Clb; Intnl Clb; Model UN; Ski Clb; Var Capt Sftbl; Var Tennis; High Hon Roll; Hon Roll; Intl Bus.

OLNEY, MARY BETH; Saint Francis Acad; Bethlehem, PA; (Y); 4/20; Chorus; School Musical; Sec Stu Cncl; Hon Roll; PA JR Acad Of Sci 1st Pl Regnls & 2nd Pl STS 86; Erly Educ.

OLSEN, LISA; Interboro HS; Norwood, PA; (S); AFS; Spanish Clb; Hon Roll; Jr NHS; NHS; Penn ST U; Math.

OLSEN, ROBERT; New Hope-Solebury HS; Lahaska, PA; (S); 8/82; Cmnty Wkr; Band; Mrchg Band; Pep Band; School Musical; JV Var Bsktbl; JV Var Socr; High Hon Roll; Hon Roll; NHS; MIP Bsktbl & Sccr 84-85; Bicntnl Athl Leag, All-Leag 2nd Team Sccr 85; Capt JR Cls Blue/Gold Comp 85; Engr.

OLSHEFSKI, SANDRA; Northwest Area HS; Shickshinny, PA; (Y); 18/108; Computer Clb; NHS; Hon Roll 86; Bloomsburg U; Math.

OLSHEVSKI, ERIC; Wellsboro SR HS; Wellsboro, PA; (Y); 10/140; Art Clb; Computer Clb; VP Frsh Cls; Sec Soph Cls; Var L Bsbl; Var Capt Bsktbl; Var L Ftbl; Var L Trk; Hon Roll; Jr NHS; Ntl Hnr Scty 86; U Ptsbrgh; Bus Adm.

OLSON, BETH; Lakeview HS; Stoneboro, PA; (Y); 24/119; Church Yth Grp; Band; Concert Band; Jazz Band; Mrchg Band; Pep Band; Nwsp Stf; JP Sousa Awd; NHS; Monday Music Clb Band 86; Anderson Coll; Elem Ed.

OLSON, CYNTHIA L; Montrose Area JR/SR HS; Friendsville, PA; (Y); 5/169; Pres Church Yth Grp; Co-Capt Scholastic Bowl; Chorus; School Musical; NHS; Ntl Merit Ltr; NEDT Awd; Art Clb; French Clb; Quiz Bowl; Sharp & Hnrs Prog Schlrshps U Of DE 86; Pres Acdmc Ftnss Awd 86; Engl Awd 86; U Of DE; Engl.

OLSON, DAN; Iroquois HS; Erie, PA; (Y); 4/156; Letterman Clb; Varsity Clb; Var Bsbl; Var Golf; High Hon Roll; NHS; Robert Johnstone Mem Schlrshp 86; Penn ST.

OLSON, DAWN; Henderson HS; Westchester, PA; (Y); 85/348; Ski Clb; Mrchg Band; Pom Pon; Hon Roll; Frnch.

OLSON, ERIC; Elk County Christian HS; St Marys, PA; (Y); Library Aide; Natl Beta Clb; Ski Clb; Bowling; Ftbl; Wrstlng; Opt Clb Awd; Engl.

OLSON, JODY; Vincentian HS; Glenshaw, PA; (Y); 4/56; JA; Service Clb; Chorus; Yrbk Stf; Rep Stu Cncl; Im Sftbl; Var Tennis; Im Vllybl; High Hon Roll; NHS; PA ST U; Psych.

OLSON, KRISTEN; Council Rock HS; Holland, PA; (Y); 250/755; Cmnty Wkr; German Clb; Intnl Clb; Key Clb; L Var Bowling; Powder Puff Ftbl; Hon Roll; U DE; Cnsmr Ecnmcs.

OLSON, MARY-ALICE; Blairsville SR HS; Blairsville, PA; (Y); 3/130; Capt Color Guard; Concert Band; School Musical; Nwsp Stf; High Hon Roll; NHS; Prfct Atten Awd; Pres Schlr; Mrchg Band; Variety Show; PA JR Acad Of Sci 84-86; Schls And Scrbs 84-86; JR Miss 3rd Runnr Up 85; U Of Pittsburgh; Psych.

OLSON, MICHELLE S; Allentown Central Catholic HS; Allentown, PA; (Y); 4/234; Art Clb; Math Clb; Chorus; Yrbk Stf; NHS; Ntl Merit SF; PA ST U Frosh Schlrp 86; Italo Rossoli Mem Awd 86; PA ST U; Aerospc Engrg.

OLSON, SIRI ANNE; Gateway SR HS; Monroeville, PA; (Y); Dance Clb; Hosp Aide; Science Clb; High Hon Roll; Pres Schlr; U Of Pittsburgh; Intl Affrs.

OLSZANSKI, DOUGLAS; Fairview HS; Erie, PA; (Y); 2/156; Church Yth Grp; Debate Tm; Model UN; Ski Clb; Varsity Clb; JV Bsktbl; Var L Socr; Var L Trk; High Hon Roll; NHS; Math/Sci Rensselaer Mdl 86; Med.

OLSZEWSKI, CORINE; John S Fine HS; Nanticoke, PA; (Y); Yrbk Stf; Hon Roll; Kutztown; Commnctns.

OLSZEWSKI, LINDA; Salisbury HS; Allentown, PA; (Y); 16/130; Exploring; Key Clb; Stu Cncl; Stat Bsbl; Trk; Mgr(s); Comp Sci.

OLSZEWSKI, MARY; E L Meyers HS; Wilkes-Barre, PA; (S); Key Clb; Ski Clb; Yrbk Stf; Bsktbl; Var L Fld Hcky; Var L Sftbl; Hon Roll; Jr NHS; NEDT Awd; Spanish NHS.

OLUJICH, ANITA; Ambridge Area HS; Ambridge, PA; (Y); German Clb; Band; Concert Band; Mrchg Band; Pep Band; School Musical; Symp Band; Crs Cntry; Trk; Hon Roll.

OLWEILER, LAURA; Elizabethtown Area HS; Elizabethtown, PA; (Y); 42/237; Ski Clb; Mrchg Band; Trs Frsh Cls; Trs Jr Cls; Trs Sr Cls; Stu Cncl; Var JV Fld Hcky; Powder Puff Ftbl; Hon Roll; Am Leg Aux Girls St; Close Up Washington Dc, Wall Street Seminar Ny 86; Penn ST U.

OMALLEY, PATRICK; North Allegheney HS; Pittsburgh, PA; (Y); 169/642; Var JV Ftbl; Hon Roll.

OMARZAI, NAJIBULLAH; Roxborough HS; Philadelphia, PA; (Y); 1/327; Science Clb; Nwsp Rptr; Rep Stu Cncl; Bowling; Var Socr; Pres NHS; Rotary Awd; Office Aide; Yrbk Stf; Phila Inquirer-Daily Nws Schlrshp Asstnc Awd 85; City Of Phila Incntv Awd 84; Outstndng Nws Carrier 85; Pre-Med.

OMLOR, STEPHEN; Millville HS; Millville, PA; (S); Trs 4-H; JV Bsbl; Var Capt Wrstlng; 4-H Awd; 2nd Pl Sci Proj Bloomsburg Fair 84; Natural Sci.

OMSTEAD, MICHAEL; Seneca Valley SR HS; Zelienople, PA; (Y); VP JA; Band; Var Bsbl; Capt Ftbl; JV Trk; JV Wt Lftg; Im Wrstlng; Law Enfrcmnt.

ONDANGSY, SOMXAY; Harrisburg High John Harris Campus; Harrisburg, PA; (S); Socr; Swmmng; Vllybl; Hon Roll.

ONDECK, MICHAEL W; Central Dauphin HS; Harrisburg, PA; (Y); Var L Socr; L Trk; Cvl Eng.

ONDER, SHARON; Portage Area HS; Portage, PA; (S); 6/118; Aud/Vis; Band; Chorus; Rep Frsh Cls; Stat Bsktbl; JV Var Vllybl; High Hon Roll; NHS; Concert Band; Jazz Band; Amvets Amrcnsm Essy 1st Plc Lcl & ST 84; Hugh Obrien Yth Fndtn Otstndng Sphmr Awd 85; Vetrnrn.

ONDISH, MIKE; Norwin HS; N Huntingdon, PA; (Y); 91/561; Computer Clb; German Clb; Var Socr; Hon Roll; Hustlr Soccr 84; MVP Soccr 85; Carnegie Mellon; Elect Engrg.

ONDO, DIANA; Reynolds HS; Greenville, PA; (Y); German Clb; Hosp Aide; Math Clb; Science Clb; Band; Trs Concert Band; Trs Mrchg Band; Pep Band; Yrbk Stf; Grnd Ushrtt Intl Order Of Rainbow For Girls 85-86.

ONDO, LISA; Philipsburg-Osceola Area SR HS; Philipsburg, PA; (S); 32/214; Drama Clb; SADD; Sec Thesps; Band; Chorus; Drm Mjr(t); Nwsp Rptr; Yrbk Stf; Rep Stu Cncl; Var Cheerleading; PA ST U; Surgcl Tech.

ONDOVCHIK, MARGARET; Aliquippa HS; West Aliquippa, PA; (S); 2/148; Church Yth Grp; Exploring; French Clb; Hosp Aide; Concert Band; Mrchg Band; Yrbk Stf; High Hon Roll; Lion Awd; NHS; Med Tech.

ONDREJKO, SHELLY; Belle Vernon Area HS; Belle Vernon, PA; (Y); 18/272; FBLA; Ski Clb; Powder Puff Ftbl; NHS; IN U PA; Resp Thrpy.

ONDRUSEK, KELLIE; Ford City HS; Ford City, PA; (Y); 71/154; Church Yth Grp; VP FBLA; Office Aide; Chorus; Drill Tm; Rep Stu Cncl; Cheerleading; Vllybl; Hon Roll; ICM Bus Schl; Acctg Mgt.

ONEILL, CHARLES; Clarion Area HS; Clarion, PA; (Y); Camera Clb; Yrbk Stf; Var Golf; Var Wt Lftg; IN U PA; Engrng.

ONEILL, TALMADGE; Church Farm Schl; Groveland, CA; (Y); 3/19; Yrbk Rptr; Var Crs Cntry; Var Trk; Capt Wrstlng; VP NHS; Art Clb; Debate Tm; Library Aide; Teachers Aide; Hon Roll; Unon Leag Phldlph Awd 85; Nwsppr Ftrs Edtr, Nwsppr Stu Actvts Edtr 85-86; Hon Plque 80-85; Claremnt Mckenna Coll; Intl Afr.

ONGIRI, AMY A; St Francis Acad; Bethlehem, PA; (Y); Q&S; Stage Crew; Nwsp Stf; Yrbk Stf; Lit Mag; VP Jr Cls; VP Sr Cls; Var Capt Bsktbl; Socr; Hon Roll; Hnrbl Ment Arts 85; Gov Schl For Arts 84; Bryan Mawr Coll; Eng.

ONSTEAD, DAVID; Somerset Area SR HS; Boswell, PA; (Y); English Clb; German Clb; JA; Band; Church Choir; Concert Band; Jazz Band; Mrchg Band; Pep Band; VFW Awd.

ONUSCHECK, MARK; Peters Township HS; Mcmurray, PA; (Y); 60/230; Key Clb; VP Thesps; Chorus; School Musical; School Play; Swing Chorus; Hon Roll; Prfct Atten Awd; Church Yth Grp; NFL; Thespn Hl Of Fame 86; Thespn Spcl Awd 85; Thespn Lttr.

ONUSCONICH, ANNE; Northampton SR HS; Danielsville, PA; (Y); AFS; Leo Clb; Yrbk Stf; Occupational Thrpy.

OPACIC, ELIZABETH; Greater Johnstown HS; Johnstown, PA; (Y); 16/268; German Clb; Math Clb; Pep Clb; Orch; High Hon Roll; NHS; Alumni Schlrshp 86; U Pittsburgh; Engrng.

OPALACH, DIANA; The Christian Acad; Wilmington, DE; (Y); Church Yth Grp; Chorus; Stu Cncl; Hon Roll; Girl Scts; Library Aide; Prfct Atten Awd.

OPALISKY, KIM; St Hubert HS; Philadelphia, PA; (Y); 23/387; Camera Clb; French Clb; Service Clb; Nwsp Rptr; Sftbl; Hon Roll; NHS; Lasalle U; Comm.

OPANEL, CHERYL; Shenandoah Valley JR SR HS; Frackville, PA; (Y); 48/108; Pep Clb; Nwsp Stf; Yrbk Stf; Var Cheerleading; Library Aide; Chorus; Mrchg Band; Crs Cntry; Gym; Hon Roll; Secy.

OPFER, VAUGHANA; Mapletown JR SR HS; Garards Fort, PA; (Y); 11/87; Aud/Vis; Church Yth Grp; Pres GAA; Band; Concert Band; Mrchg Band; Rep Jr Cls; Rep Stu Cncl; DAR Awd; Hon Roll; Waynesburg Coll; Nrsng.

OPHER, DORIT R; Akiba Hebrew Acad; Havertown, PA; (Y); Science Clb; Nwsp Stf; Rep Stu Cncl; Var Bsktbl; L Mgr(s); Physcl Thrpy.

OPIELA, JOHN BARTLEY; Coughlin HS; Wilkes-Barre, PA; (Y); 13/359; Math Clb; Band; Capt Tennis; High Hon Roll; Hon Roll; Jr NHS; NHS; Ntl Merit Ltr; Rotary Awd; Penn ST U; Elec Engrng.

OPPERMAN, KATHY; Interboro HS; Glenolden, PA; (Y); Church Yth Grp; Teachers Aide; Acpl Chr; Chorus; Swing Chorus; Rep Frsh Cls; Rep Soph Cls; J R Powers; Model.

OPPERMANN, JOANNE; Geibel HS; Connellsville, PA; (Y); 6/100; Ski Clb; Spanish Clb; Trs Stu Cncl; Var Capt Cheerleading; Stat Vllybl; High Hon Roll; Sec NHS; NEDT Awd; Spanish NHS; Cnnllsvl Bus & Prfsnl Wmns Girl Yr 86; Penn ST U; Acctg.

OPSITNIK, LEAH; General Mc Lane HS; Edinboo, PA; (Y); 10/221; French Clb; Model UN; Radio Clb; Band; Chorus; Concert Band; Mrchg Band; Pep Band; Symp Band; High Hon Roll; Westminster Coll; Bio Tech.

OQUENDO, MILDRED; Little Flower Catholic HS; Philadelphia, PA; (Y); 69/413; Cmnty Wkr; Computer Clb; JA; Latin Clb; Concert Band; Jazz Band; Orch; School Musical; School Play; Hon Roll; Mann JC; Mental Hlth.

ORANGE, ADAM; Punxsutawney SR HS; Rossiter, PA; (Y); 83/238; Science Clb; Nwsp Rptr; Nwsp Stf; Hon Roll; Hnr Cert 86; Mary A Erving Schlrshp 86; Clarion U; Comp Sci.

ORANGE, KELLIE; Penn Trafford HS; Jeannette, PA; (Y); 99/363; Church Yth Grp; FBLA; Spanish Clb; Yrbk Stf; Hon Roll.

ORAVECZ, PAMELA; Portage Area HS; Portage, PA; (Y); Computer Clb; French Clb; Pep Clb; Varsity Clb; Rep Stu Cncl; Cheerleading; Trk.

ORAVITZ, AMY; West Allegheny SR HS; Oakdale, PA; (Y); FBLA; Office Aide; Teachers Aide; Flag Corp; Powder Puff Ftbl; High Hon Roll; Hon Roll; Exec Sec.

ORAVITZ, AMY SUSAN; Abraham Lincoln HS; Philadelphia, PA; (Y); 6/419; French Clb; Varsity Clb; Yrbk Stf; Lit Mag; Pres Stu Cncl; Var Capt Cheerleading; Pom Pon; Cit Awd; High Hon Roll; NHS; Alum Railspltr III Schlrshp Awd 86; Acadmc Al-Amer 86; Cngrssnl Merit Cert; Muhlenberg Coll; Cmnmctns.

ORAZZI, MICHAEL J; Lakeland HS; Carbondale, PA; (S); 42/152; Science Clb; VP Sr Cls; JV Var Bsbl; Var Capt Golf; Hon Roll; Penn ST U.

ORBAN, GERALD; Hampton HS; Gibsonia, PA; (Y); 86/255; Church Yth Grp; Exploring; French Clb; Var L Ftbl; Im Powder Puff Ftbl; Var Socr; Im Wt Lftg; Hon Roll.

ORBIN, PAUL; Waynesburg Central HS; Waynesburg, PA; (Y); Boy Scts; Spanish Clb; Trs Band; Trs Concert Band; Trs Jazz Band; Trs Mrchg Band; JV Bsktbl; Hon Roll; County Band 84-86; Arch.

ORCUTT, CHRISTOPHER; Pennsbury HS; Farmington Hills, MI; (Y); 88/712; German Clb; Nwsp Rptr; Nwsp Stf; Yrbk Rptr; Yrbk Stf; Im Socr; High Hon Roll; Hon Roll; NHS; Pres Schlr; MI ST U; Engr.

OREHEK, ALLEN; Forest City Regional HS; Vandling Pa, PA; (Y); Golf; Socr; Vllybl; Hon Roll; NHS; Natl Sci Merit Awd 85; Gregg Typg Awd 86; Math & Vrbl Tlnt Srch John Hopkins 82; Moleclr Biol.

OREWILER, KIRBY; Hanover HS; Hanover, PA; (Y); Aud/Vis; Church Yth Grp; Computer Clb; Spanish Clb; SADD; Varsity Clb; L Var Bsbl; Capt L Bsktbl; L Var Golf; Hon Roll; MVP Boys Vrsty Bsktbl 86; Bus.

ORLANDI, LISA; Sharon HS; Sharon, PA; (Y); 9/175; Exploring; Spanish Clb; Y-Teens; Hon Roll; NHS; U Of Pittsburgh; Physcl Thrpy.

ORLANDO, ANNETTE; GAR Mem HS; Wilkes Barre, PA; (S); 28/187; German Clb; Orch; Nwsp Stf; Gym; Hon Roll; NHS; Med.

ORLOSKI, JAN; Crestwood HS; Mountaintop, PA; (Y); Trs Art Clb; Church Yth Grp; Ski Clb; Y-Teens; L Crs Cntry; L Trk; Hon Roll; Nrsng.

ORLOW, MARC STEWART; Northeast HS; Philadelphia, PA; (Y); 46/661; Civic Clb; Cmnty Wkr; German Clb; School Play; Lit Mag; Trs Jr Cls; Capt Wrstlng; High Hon Roll; Lion Awd; NHS; German Am Police Assoc Awd, Cannstatter Volksfest-Verein Awd, B F Fndtn Awd 86; Beaver Coll; Psych.

ORMOND, LOUIS; Cedar Crest HS; Lebanon, PA; (Y); 41/323; Pep Clb; Varsity Clb; Nwsp Bus Mgr; Swmmng; Trk; Hon Roll; Barnegat Bay Yacht Rcg Assn M-Scor Chmpn 85; PA ST; Fin.

ORMOND, VALDAMIR; Father Judge HS; Philadelphia, PA; (S); 10/365; Im Bsktbl; Var L Ftbl; Hon Roll; NHS; Cert Of Hnr Outstndng Achvt Acads 86; Bus Admin.

ORNDORFF, HOLLY; Gettysburg SR HS; Gettysburg, PA; (Y); 24/235; Varsity Clb; Rep Frsh Cls; Rep Soph Cls; VP Jr Cls; Rep Stu Cncl; Var Capt Fld Hcky; Im Sftbl; High Hon Roll; Hon Roll; VP NHS; PA ST U; Sci.

ORNDORFF, JUDY; New Oxford HS; Gettysburg, PA; (Y); FBLA; Chorus; Hon Roll; Sec.

ORNDORFF, KAREN; Littlestown SR HS; Gettysburg, PA; (Y); 20/150; Church Yth Grp; Pres Rptr 4-H; SADD; Band; Chorus; Concert Band; Mrchg Band; Pep Band; Yrbk Stf; Var Vllybl; Dntl Hygn.

ORNDORFF, ROBBIE; Connellsville Area SR HS; Mill Run, PA; (Y); 65/500; Pres Church Yth Grp; Var L Bsbl; French Hon Soc; High Hon Roll; Hon Roll; NHS; 1T Tm All-Sctn Bsbll 86; Acdmc Excllnc Slvr Pin 84; Outstndg Art Achvmnt Awd 84.

ORNER, DEBRA; Bishop Mc Cort HS; Johnstown, PA; (Y); Pep Clb; Spanish Clb; Chorus; Nwsp Rptr; Nwsp Stf; Yrbk Stf; Bsktbl; High Hon Roll; Hon Roll; Spanish NHS; Hnrs Course; Law.

ORNER, JIM; Mechanicsburg SR HS; Shiremanstown, PA; (Y); Wrstlng; High Hon Roll; Marine Bio.

ORNER, KIMBERLY; Meyersdale Area HS; Meyersdale, PA; (Y); Sec Church Yth Grp; Pres VP Spanish Clb; Band; Concert Band; Mrchg Band; Ed Nwsp Stf; Yrbk Stf; Var L Bsktbl; L Sftbl; DAR Awd; CA U; Educ.

OROSZ, SCOTT; Mc Keesport Area HS; Mc Keesport, PA; (Y); 35/370; Church Yth Grp; JA; Library Aide; Church Choir; Concert Band; Jazz Band; Mrchg Band; Orch; School Musical; Symp Band; PA St U; Aerospc Engrg.

OROURKE, TAMMY; Sharon HS; Sharon, PA; (Y); 75/196; Art Clb; Aud/Vis; Church Yth Grp; Drama Clb; Office Aide; Spanish Clb; School Musical; School Play; VP Cheerleading; Hon Roll; Fash Merch.

OROZCO, MISSIE; Emmaus HS; Trexlertown, PA; (Y); #7 In Class; Sec Church Yth Grp; Exploring; Var Cheerleading; Wt Lftg; Hon Roll; Prfct Atten Awd; Spnsh.

ORR, BILL; Blairsville HS; Blairsville, PA; (Y); VP Church Yth Grp; Ski Clb; Varsity Clb; Trs Sr Cls; Stu Cncl; Ftbl; L Trk; Wrstlng; High Hon Roll; Hon Roll; Elect Engr.

ORR, DEANNE; Charleori JR SR HS; Charleroi, PA; (Y); Church Yth Grp; SADD; Sec Chorus; Church Choir; Color Guard; Drill Tm; Flag Corp; Mrchg Band; Stage Crew; Hon Roll; Schl For Arts; Music.

ORR, ELIZABETH; Saltsburg JRSR HS; Clarksburg, PA; (Y); 4/94; Pres Church Yth Grp; Trs Band; Trs Jr Cls; Var L Bsktbl; Var L Vllybl; High Hon Roll; Hon Roll; NHS; Trs Drama Clb; Sec Ski Clb; Dist III Bnd 85-86; Reg II Bnd 85-86.

ORR, MARK; Bishop Egan HS; Croydon, PA; (Y); 34/229; Church Yth Grp; Church Choir; Var Trk; High Hon Roll; Hon Roll; NHS; Prfct Atten Awd; Temple U; Bus.

ORR, RHONDA; Linesville HS; Linesville, PA; (Y); 11/86; Yrbk Ed-Chief; VP Soph Cls; VP Jr Cls; Sec Pres Stu Cncl; Var L Bsktbl; Var L Sftbl; Hon Roll; German Clb; Band; Yrbk Stf; ST Chmp Girls Bsktbl 85-86; 1st Tm All Cnty Sftbl Ptchr 84; 2nd Tm All Cnty Sftbl Ptchr 85; Frgn Lang.

ORR, ROSALYNN; Pine Forge Acad; Cleveland, OH; (Y); 10/81; Church Choir; Rep Trs Frsh Cls; Trs Soph Cls; Trs Jr Cls; Stu Cncl; Co-Capt Cheerleading; Cit Awd; High Hon Roll; VP Pres Of Grls Dorm 85-86; Cleveland ST U; Med.

ORR, ROSALYNN; Pine Forge Acad; Pine Forge, PA; (S); 8/81; Pep Clb; Acpl Chr; Chorus; Trs Frsh Cls; Trs Soph Cls; Trs Jr Cls; Chrmn Stu Cncl; Cheerleading; Cit Awd; Hon Roll; VP Of Dorm 85-86; Cleveland ST U; Med.

ORR, SHARON; Williamsport Area HS; Williamsport, PA; (Y); Church Yth Grp; Key Clb; Chorus; Church Choir; Flag Corp; Rep Soph Cls; Rep Jr Cls; JV Bsktbl; Hon Roll; Prfct Atten Awd; Soc Stud Tchr.

ORR, STEVEN; Millersburg Area HS; Millersburg, PA; (Y); Am Leg Boys St; Boy Scts; Church Yth Grp; Variety Show; Trk; Wrstlng; WQIN Stu Ath Wrstlg 86; All Star Wrstlg 84-86; Lock Haven U PA; Chem.

ORR, VALERIE; Parkstown Christian Acad; New Castle, PA; (Y); Church Yth Grp; Pres Exploring; FCA; Stu Of Wk 85-86; Rainbow Girl Elected Line Ofcr 85-87; Fashion Merchandising.

ORRIS, JULIE; Boiling Springs HS; Carlisle, PA; (Y); Art Clb; Pres Church Yth Grp; Hosp Aide; Chorus; Flag Corp; Hon Roll; NHS; Central PA Bus Schl; Phy Thrpy.

ORSBORN, JEFFREY M; Butler SR HS; Renfrew, PA; (Y); Pres Church Yth Grp; SADD; Band; Mrchg Band; Symp Band; Stu Cncl; High Hon Roll; Jr NHS; Masonic Awd; Comp Sci.

ORSENO, LISA; St Huberts HS; Philadelphia, PA; (Y); 196/367; Office Aide; Teachers Aide; Lit Mag; 2nd Hnrs JR; Awd Hnr Bnqt; Bus.

ORSINI, CAROL; Hempfield Area SR HS; Greensburg, PA; (Y); AFS; French Clb; Hosp Aide; Spanish Clb; Band; Concert Band; Mrchg Band; Nwsp Rptr; Hon Roll; Jr NHS; Intl Bus.

ORSINO, TINA M; Cranberry Area HS; Franklin, PA; (Y); 6/122; Cmnty Wkr; FBLA; Girl Scts; Science Clb; Spanish Clb; Teachers Aide; Chorus; Co-Capt Drill Tm; Orch; Hon Roll; Physcl Thrpy.

ORSINO, TOM; Norwin SR HS; N Huntingdon, PA; (Y); Band; Concert Band; Jazz Band; Mrchg Band; Westmoreland Cnty CC; Law Enfr.

ORT, SHAWN; Northeastern HS; Dover, PA; (Y); Hon Roll; Comp Prgrmng.

ORTH, LISA; Wyomissing Area HS; Wyomissing, PA; (Y); 18/97; Church Yth Grp; French Clb; JA; Chorus; Capt Flag Corp; Capt Mrchg Band; Var Bowling; Im Sftbl; Im Vllybl; High Hon Roll; Mth.

ORTIZ, MYRA; Little Flower HS; Philadelphia, PA; (Y); 85/400; Camera Clb; Exploring; Spanish Clb; Orch; School Musical; School Play; Hon Roll; Prfct Atten Awd; Bus Clb 85-86; Chpl Aide 85-86; Bus Adm.

ORTMAN, TINA; Manheim Central HS; Manheim, PA; (Y); Hon Roll; Bus.

ORTZ, BETH; Clarion Area HS; Clarion, PA; (Y); Csmtlgy.

OSBORN, BRIAN; Fort Le Boeuf HS; Waterford, PA; (Y); 28/168; Trs Church Yth Grp; Model UN; JV Var Bsktbl; Var L Ftbl; Vllybl; Wt Lftg; Hon Roll; Milty Hist.

OSBORN, MICHAEL; West Allegheny HS; Coraopolis, PA; (Y); Science Clb; Chorus; JV Var Bsbl; JV Var Bsktbl; Var Crs Cntry; JV Ftbl; High Hon Roll; NHS; Acad All Amer Awd 85; Natl Ldrshp & Svc Awd 86.

OSBORNE, COREY; Trinity HS; Mechanicsburg, PA; (Y); 15/144; Varsity Clb; Var L Bsktbl; Var L Ftbl; Var L Trk; High Hon Roll; Engrng.

OSBORNE, DAVID; Sharpsville Area HS; Sharpsville, PA; (Y); Aud/Vis; Church Yth Grp; Band; Chorus; Church Choir; Concert Band; Jazz Band; Mrchg Band; Pep Band; JV Stat Bsktbl; Hnrs Sci & Math; Bio.

OSBORNE, DEBBIE; Reynolds HS; Fredonia, PA; (Y); 1/160; Church Yth Grp; Latin Clb; Chorus; Concert Band; JV Var Cheerleading; Var L Trk; JV Vllybl; Hon Roll; NHS; NEDT Awd; Acad All Amer 85-86; Grove City Coll; Pre Med.

OSBORNE, HEIDI; Sharon SR HS; Sharon, PA; (Y); Art Clb; Spanish Clb; Trk; Hon Roll; NHS; Pittsburgh Inst CMRCL Artst.

OSBORNE, JEFF; Trinity HS; Washington, PA; (Y); Var L Bsbl; Var Bsktbl; Var Ftbl; High Hon Roll; Hon Roll; Prfct Atten Awd.

OSBORNE, MATT; Spring Grove HS; Codorus, PA; (Y); 50/279; Pres Church Yth Grp; Orch; Off Stu Cncl; Var Bsbl; Var Ftbl; Wt Lftg; JV Wrstlng; Hon Roll; Rsrc Mngmt.

OSBORNE, SHARON; Saegertown HS; Meadville, PA; (Y); 14/130; Hosp Aide; Sec Spanish Clb; SADD; Varsity Clb; Band; Concert Band; Mrchg Band; Stat Bsktbl; JV Sftbl; Stat Vllybl; High Hnr Rll 83-86; Med.

OSBURN, SHELLY; Slippery Rock Area HS; Forestville, PA; (Y); 43/156; Dance Clb; Pep Clb; Varsity Clb; Variety Show; Nwsp Phtg; Yrbk Phtg; Stu Cncl; Capt Cheerleading; Hon Roll; Trs Soph Cls; Intl Chrldng Fndtn 1st Pl 84-86; 2nd Pl ST Regnl Chrldng Comptn 84-85; Clarion U Of PA; Engl.

OSGOOD, BARBARA; Marion Center HS; Manassas, VA; (Y); Trs Intnl Clb; ROTC; Sec Science Clb; Band; Pep Band; Ed Nwsp Stf; Var Cheerleading; JV Crs Cntry; Mgr Swmmng; Stat Trk; Tri Cnty Chmpn Vrsty Chrldrs 85; Ntl Scl Stdy Olympiad In Amer Hstry 86.

OSHALL JR, WILLIAM H; Glendale HS; Fallentimber, PA; (Y); 3/98; Church Yth Grp; Science Clb; Church Choir; Yrbk Stf; Wrstlng; Hon Roll; NHS; Law.

OSHMAN, ANGELA; Shikellamy HS; Sunbury, PA; (Y); 10/310; French Clb; Nwsp Rptr; Ed Lit Mag; Socr; Hon Roll; NHS; 1st Packwood House Art Exhib 86; Wrtng.

OSINKOSKY, ERIN; Christian Schl Of York; Mt Wolf, PA; (Y); Church Yth Grp; Band; Chorus; Nwsp Rptr; Fld Hcky; Var Trk; High Hon Roll.

OSINKOSKY, TONYA M; Christian School Of York; Mount Wolf, PA; (Y); 3/39; Church Yth Grp; Speech Tm; Chorus; School Play; Nwsp Rptr; VP Stu Cncl; Var Fld Hcky; Var Trk; Cit Awd; Teachers Aide; Ntl Hnr Roll 83-84; ACSI Dstngshd Chrst HS Stu 85-86; Acdmc All Amer 85-86; Messiah Coll; Chrst Ed.

OSINSKI, JOSEPH; Steel Valley HS; Munhall, PA; (Y); 66/240; Aud/Vis; Stage Crew; Nwsp Phtg; Yrbk Phtg; Prfct Atten Awd; IUP; Crmnlgy.

OSKIN, DONNA; Mc Keesport SR HS; Dravosburg, PA; (Y); 19/387; Yrbk Stf; Powder Puff Ftbl; Hon Roll; Wmns Clb Hnr Stu 86; $300 Awd From PA ST 86; PA ST; Bus.

OSKOWSKI, JONATHAN; Hopewell SR HS; Aliquippa, PA; (Y); Church Yth Grp; Exploring; JA; Spanish Clb; Band; Concert Band; Jazz Band; Mrchg Band; Hon Roll.

OSLICK, LYNN; Montour SR HS; Mc Kees Rocks, PA; (Y); Church Yth Grp; Cmnty Wkr; Band; Concert Band; Mrchg Band; Var L Diving; Gym; Swmmng; High Hon Roll; NHS; Mst Imprvd H S Divr Troph 86; WPIAL Divg Qualfr 86; 6th Pl Fnsh MAC Divg Tourn Medl 86; Psych.

OSMAN, JENNIFER; Monaca JR-SR HS; Monaca, PA; (Y); 17/91; Pep Clb; Sec Red Cross Aide; Pres Spanish Clb; Band; Nwsp Rptr; Yrbk Stf; VP Frsh Cls; Capt Pom Pon; Hon Roll; NHS; Acctg.

OSMAN, TODD; Montour HS; Coraopolis, PA; (Y); 1/310; Band; Concert Band; Jazz Band; Mrchg Band; Socr; Trk; High Hon Roll; NHS; Chem Olympics 85; Superior Perf Awd Sci 86; Chem Engr.

OSMOND, HEATHER; Swissvale HS; Pittsburgh, PA; (Y); 38/205; Church Yth Grp; French Clb; Ski Clb; Y-Teens; School Musical; School Play; Yrbk Stf; Sec Stu Cncl; Cheerleading; Tennis.

OSOVICH, TIMOTHY R; Hazleton SR HS; Dyer, NV; (Y); 1/383; Church Yth Grp; French Clb; Leo Clb; French Hon Soc; High Hon Roll; NHS; Ntl Merit SF; Pres Schlr; Rotary Awd; Val; Deep Springs Coll; Lbrl Arts.

OSSELBURN, KRISTIN; Somerset Aria HS; Somerset, PA; (Y); 6/235; English Clb; French Clb; Chorus; Gym; Mat Maids; Var Sftbl; High Hon Roll; NHS; X-Ray Tech.

OSTERBLOOM III, THOMAS A; North Hills HS; Pittsburgh, PA; (Y); Quiz Bowl; Lit Mag; High Hon Roll; Ntl Merit SF; Med.

OSTERGARD, KERRY; Warren Area HS; Warren, PA; (Y); French Clb; Acpl Chr; School Play; Hon Roll; Jr NHS; NHS; Elem Educ.

OSTOPICK, STACY LEORA; John S Fine HS; W Nanticoke, PA; (Y); Ski Clb; Chorus; Yrbk Stf; Mgr(s); Mgr Trk; JV Var Wrstlng; High Hon Roll; Hon Roll; Art Awd HS Dist & Council Levels 86; LCCC; Nursing.

OSTRANDER JR, JOSEPH L; Lebanon Catholic HS; Lebanon, PA; (Y); Science Clb; Ski Clb; Chorus; Church Choir; School Play; Vetenary Medicine.

OSTROSKY, JOHN J; Windber Area HS; Windber, PA; (Y); Am Leg Boys St; Chess Clb; French Clb; JA; Church Choir; Jazz Band; Variety Show; High Hon Roll; NHS; Hon Roll; Frnch 3 Acad Achvt Awd 85-86; Juilliard Schl; Music.

OSTROWSKI, KIMBERLY; Baldwin HS; Pittsburgh, PA; (Y); 191/535; Church Yth Grp; Band; Mrchg Band; Rep Frsh Cls; Rep Soph Cls; Sec Jr Cls; Rep Stu Cncl; Cheerleading; Hon Roll; Psychlgy.

OSTROWSKI, LORI; Pittston Area HS; Pittston, PA; (Y); Art Clb; Church Yth Grp; Drama Clb; French Clb; Chorus; Trs Soph Cls; Engl.

OSTROWSKY, KEVIN M; Tunkhannock Area HS; Tunkhannock, PA; (Y); Boy Scts; Church Yth Grp; Computer Clb; Hosp Aide; Ski Clb; Church Choir; Ftbl; Hon Roll; NHS; Albrght; Pre-Med.

OSTRUM, TAMMY; Bradford Area HS; Bradford, PA; (Y); 21/276; AFS; French Clb; Concert Band; Mrchg Band; Rep Sr Cls; Rep Stu Cncl; JV Var Bsktbl; Var Swmmng; Var Tennis; Hon Roll; Hd Cnslr Cnsrvtn Camp 83-84; HS Magazine 1st Poetry, 2nd Shrt Stry 83-84; Med.

OSWALD, FRANK; Cardinal Brennan HS; Ashland, PA; (Y); 4/48; Chess Clb; Rep Frsh Cls; Rep Soph Cls; Rep Jr Cls; Stu Cncl; Bsbl; Bsktbl; Ftbl; High Hon Roll; NHS; Pres Scholar III 86; Pres Acad Fit Awd 86; U Scranton; Phys Thrpy.

OSWALD, JAMES; Brandywine Heights HS; Mertztown, PA; (Y); 12/144; FBLA; Trk; Vllybl; Hon Roll; NHS.

OSWALD, JAMIE; Westmont Hilltop HS; Johnstown, PA; (Y); 21/159; Key Clb; School Musical; High Hon Roll; NHS; Hosp Aide; Chorus; Hghst Hnr Rl 83-84; IN U Pennsylvania; NRSNG.

OSWALD, JOHN; Nativity BVM HS; Port Carbon, PA; (Y); 23/99; Church Yth Grp; Computer Clb; High Hon Roll; Hon Roll; Prfct Atten Awd; Rotary Awd; Pres Acadmc Ftnss Awd 86; Mc Cann Schl Of Bus Awd For Hghst Achvmnt In Bus 86; Bloomsburg U; Accntng.

OSWALD, KYLE D; Kutztown Area HS; Kutztown, PA; (Y); 29/149; JV Bsktbl; Var Golf; JV Socr; Var Tennis; High Hon Roll; NHS; Military Acad; Law.

OSWALD, WILLIAM; Coughlin HS; Plains, PA; (Y); 1/384; Am Leg Boys St; Math Clb; Ftbl; High Hon Roll; Jr NHS; NHS; NEDT Awd; Val; Mst Outstndng Stdnt Athl Ftbl 85; Plains Lions Clb Achvt Awd 86; Bst Of Clss 86; U Of PA; Elctrcl Engrng.

OSWALT, WENDY; Forest Hills HS; Salix, PA; (Y); Church Yth Grp; Pep Clb; Y-Teens; Chorus; Church Choir; Hon Roll; IN U P A; Elem Ed.

OTIS, RHONDA; Pennsbury HS; Yardley, PA; (Y); Church Yth Grp; French Clb; Cheerleading; Sftbl; Swmmng; Hon Roll; Smmr Schl Abrd France 85; Art.

OTT, DAN; Punxsutowney Area SR HS; Big Run, PA; (Y); Ftbl; Trk; Wt Lftg; Wrstlng; Arch.

OTT, JAMES DANIEL; Easton Area HS; Riegelsville, PA; (Y); 16/503; Boy Scts; Church Yth Grp; Ski Clb; God Cntry Awd; High Hon Roll; Hon Roll; Masonic Awd; NHS; Pres Schlr; U Of MD; Astronatcl Engnrng.

OTTAVIANI, SIMONE; Mansfield JR SR HS; Mansfield, PA; (S); Church Yth Grp; Ski Clb; Pres Jr Cls; VP Stu Cncl; Var L Bsktbl; L Trk; High Hon Roll; Kiwanis Awd; NHS.

OTTERBEIN, CHRISTINE; Jersey Shore SR HS; Jersey Shore, PA; (Y); 4-H; Girl Scts; Spanish Clb; Band; Concert Band; Drill Tm; Mrchg Band; Nwsp Stf; Lit Mag; 4-H Awd; Wmspt Area Cmnty Coll; Comm.

OTTO, BONNY; Lackawanna Trail HS; Factoryville, PA; (Y); 25/95; Chess Clb; Church Yth Grp; JA; Trs Band; Chorus; Concert Band; Drill Tm; Mrchg Band; JV Sftbl; Hon Roll; Jrnlsm.

OTTO, CAROL; Penn Trafford HS; Jeannette, PA; (Y); 117/365; Drama Clb; Ski Clb; Varsity Clb; Yrbk Ed-Chief; Yrbk Stf; Sftbl; Trk; Vllybl; Hon Roll; Crmnlgy.

OTTO, ELLEN; North East HS; North East, PA; (Y); 19/151; AFS; Pres FHA; VP Trs Pep Clb; School Musical; Nwsp Bus Mgr; Rep Stu Cncl; Var JV Vllybl; High Hon Roll; FBLA; Latin Clb; FBLA 1st Regnl Acctng I 86; PSPA Stu ST Bd 84-85; Outstndng Achvt Chorus,Hm Ec,Latin,Acctng 86; Gannon U; Acctng.

OTTO, GENE; Lebanon Catholic HS; Lebanon, PA; (Y); 3/80; German Clb; Nwsp Rptr; Rep Frsh Cls; Rep Soph Cls; Rep Jr Cls; VP Sr Cls; VP Stu Cncl; JV Bsktbl; L Ftbl; Trs NHS.

OTTO, KELLY; Salisbury-Elk Lick HS; Springs, PA; (S); 2/35; Church Yth Grp; Band; Concert Band; Mrchg Band; School Play; Nwsp Rptr; Yrbk Stf; VP Sr Cls; VP Co-Capt Cheerleading; Hon Roll; Accntng.

OTTO, ROSEANNE; Scotland Schl For Veterans Children; Aldan, PA; (Y); 4/45; Art Clb; Hosp Aide; ROTC; Flag Corp; Ed Nwsp Stf; Yrbk Stf; DAR Awd; Hon Roll; VFW Awd; Voice Dem Awd; Vlly Forge Frdm Found Essey Awd 86; Ladies Aux Chamberburg Post Essay Awd 86; U Of Pittsburgh; Phsy Therapy.

OUSEY, JOEL; Harry S Truman HS; Croydon, PA; (Y); Art Clb; Hon Roll; Cert Of Art Apprctn 85 & 86; Cmmrcl Art.

OUTLAR, KENDRA; Lancaster Christian HS; Lititz, PA; (S); 3/31; Chorus; School Play; Yrbk Stf; Pres Stu Cncl; Var L Fld Hcky; Var Capt Sftbl; NHS; NEDT Awd; Hmecmng Queen 86; Acad All Amer 86; Houghton Coll; Pre-Med.

OUTT, BENJAMIN; Danville Area HS; Danville, PA; (Y); 45/202; Pres Church Yth Grp; Computer Clb; Drama Clb; School Play; Var Socr; JV Trk; Wrstlng; Hon Roll.

OVERBAUGH, LYNN; Delone Catholic HS; Hanover, PA; (Y); 3/168; JA; Library Aide; Nwsp Rptr; Yrbk Sprt Ed; Trs Stu Cncl; Capt Vllybl; High Hon Roll; Sec NHS; VA Polytech Inst; Bus.

OVERFIELD, CLAIRE; Corry Area HS; Corry, PA; (S); 20/216; Church Yth Grp; Band; Concert Band; Drm Mjr(t); Jazz Band; Mrchg Band; Pep Band; Powder Puff Ftbl; High Hon Roll; Sound Of Amer Hnr Band 84; Penn ST.

OVERFIELD, DANE; Cathedral Prep; Erie, PA; (Y); 8/240; Art Clb; Computer Clb; Exploring; Library Aide; Yrbk Stf; Im Bsktbl; Hon Roll; NHS; Mc Donalds Art Cntst; Rochester Inst Of Tech; Engrg.

OVERFIELD, MARY; Corry Area HS; Corry, PA; (S); 25/216; Spanish Clb; High Hon Roll; Ntl Merit Ltr; Mc Donalds Employee Mnth 85; Yon Kyu Purple Belt Karate 84; Gannon U; Sci.

OVERHOLSER, DEBORAH; Du Bois Area HS; Dubois, PA; (Y); #64 In Class; Church Yth Grp; Varsity Clb; Chorus; School Musical; Off Frsh Cls; VP Soph Cls; VP Jr Cls; VP Sr Cls; Rep Stu Cncl; Var Gym; Work With Deaf.

OVERLY, PATTI; Punxsutawney Area HS; Punxsutawney, PA; (Y); FNA; Chorus; School Musical; School Play; Yrbk Phtg; Yrbk Stf; Stat Cheerleading; High Hon Roll; Hon Roll; NHS; Psych.

OVERLY, SCOTT; Mt Pleasant Area HS; Mt Pleasant, PA; (Y); 26/255; German Clb; Letterman Clb; Pres Spanish Clb; L Trk; High Hon Roll; Hon Roll; NHS; Ntl Merit Schol; Pres Schlr; Westmoreland Cnty CC; Cmpu Sci.

OVERMAN, CAROL; Unionville HS; W Chester, PA; (Y); 18/300; Chorus; Concert Band; Co-Capt Flag Corp; Orch; School Musical; JV Crs Cntry; L Var Trk; High Hon Roll; NHS; Brnz Dance Fig Sktg 85; Vet Med.

OVERSON, KELLY; Lebanon Catholic HS; Lebanon, PA; (Y); Church Yth Grp; Library Aide; Spanish Clb; Church Choir; NHS; Ntl Merit Schol; Prfct Atten Awd.

OVERTON, KIRK; Upper Dublin HS; Ft Washington, PA; (Y); 82/335; Church Yth Grp; Math Tm; Drm Mjr(t); Jazz Band; Mrchg Band; School Musical; Symp Band; JP Sousa Awd; Drama Clb; Intnl Clb; ST Mrchng Band Chmpnshps 83 & 84; 2nd Pl ST Indr Clr Grd Chmpnshps 84-86; PA ST U; Engrng.

OVERWISE, KIM; Frankford HS; Philadelphia, PA; (Y); Library Aide; Lit Mag; Im Bsktbl; Im Fld Hcky; JV Sftbl; Im Vllybl; Cit Awd; High Hon Roll; Hon Roll; NHS; Court Rprtng.

OVITSKY, ERIC; Hempfield HS; Greensburg, PA; (Y); Art Clb; Church Yth Grp; Debate Tm; NFL; Pep Clb; Ski Clb; Spanish Clb; Orch; Nwsp Ed-Chief; Nwsp Rptr; Lehigh; Arch.

OWCZARZAK, JOHN; Church Farm HS; Philadelphia, PA; (Y); Aud/Vis; Red Cross Aide; Yrbk Stf; Var Crs Cntry; JV Socr; Var Tennis; Var Trk; JV Wrstlng; Schlrshp Church Fram Schl 84-87; Marine Bio.

OWEN, DAWN; Clearfield Area HS; Shawville, PA; (Y); Art Clb; Church Yth Grp; Computer Clb; Drama Clb; French Clb; Pep Clb; SADD; Chorus; Church Choir; School Play; Outstnndg Wrk Comp Pgmng 84-85; Le Contes Hills Fire Queen 86.

OWEN, JODI; Susquenita HS; Marysville, PA; (S); 5/152; VP Church Yth Grp; Pres 4-H; Drill Tm; Nwsp Stf; 4-H Awd; High Hon Roll; Hon Roll; NHS; Penn ST; Vet.

OWENS, BRIAN; Clearfield HS; Clearfield, PA; (Y); Key Clb; Crs Cntry; Var Wrstlng; Hon Roll; Heart Awd Wrstlng 85-86; Comp Sci.

OWENS, ELLIE; Gettysburg Area Schl; Orrtanna, PA; (Y); Girl Scts; Chorus; Church Choir; High Hon Roll; NHS; Bus-Profsnl Wmns Schlrshp 86; Mont Alto; Horticltr.

OWENS, JOSEPH A; South Side Catholic HS; Pittsburgh, PA; (S); Boy Scts; Chess Clb; Exploring; School Play; Nwsp Stf; Yrbk Stf; Rep Soph Cls; Sec Jr Cls; Rep Sr Cls; Stu Cncl; U Of Pittsburgh; Biochem.

OWENS, MELANIE; Clearfield Area HS; Clearfield, PA; (Y); Cmnty Wkr; FBLA; Key Clb; Office Aide; Ski Clb; Chorus; Yrbk Stf; Bowling; Cheerleading; Mat Maids; Good Citznshp Phys Fitns; Stu Coun Pres; DAR; Dubois; Elem Educ.

OWENS, MICHELLE Y; York Suburban HS; York, PA; (Y); Pres FBLA; Sec JA; Chorus; Cheerleading; Mgr(s); Trk; Pierce JC; Legal Sec.

OWENS, SANDY; Avonworth HS; Pittsbg, PA; (Y); Var Capt Cheerleading.

OWENS, SARA; Clearfield Area HS; Frenchville, PA; (Y); Rep DECA; French Clb; Trs SADD; Hon Roll; Prfct Atten Awd; Fire Queen 2nd Pl 85-86; Prncple Stu Fin & Advsry Bd 83-86; Tchr.

OXENREIDER, JOLYN; Conrad Weiser JR & SR HS; Wernersville, PA; (Y); 35/182; Drama Clb; JCL; JV Bsktbl; Var L Fld Hcky; Var L Trk; Im Vllybl; Hon Roll; Sports Med.

OYEFESO, OLANIKE; Villa Maria HS; Berea, OH; (Y); Cmnty Wkr; French Clb; Nwsp Stf; Yrbk Ed-Chief; Yrbk Stf; Im Stat Mgr(s); Stat Trk; JV Vllybl; Dorm Cncl Pres 86-87.

OYLER, JOHN; Mt Lebanon HS; Pittsburgh, PA; (Y); 22/570; Am Leg Boys St; Science Clb; Ski Clb; Var L Socr; Var L Swmmng; Ntl Merit Ltr; Pres Schlr; German Clb; Latin Clb; Letterman Clb; 2nd Engrng Intl Sci/Engrng Fair, Bst Show Pitts Sci/Engrn Fair, 1st Astrntcl Soc Intl Sci/Engrng 86; MIT; Laser Tech.

OZANICH, BERNADETTE; Fairchance Georges SR JR HS; Uniontownd, PA; (Y); Drama Clb; French Clb; Band; Concert Band; Flag Corp; Mrchg Band; School Play; Stage Crew; Phtgrphy.

OZEGOVICH, DAWN R; Yough SR HS; Smithtown, PA; (Y); 92/241; French Clb; Ski Clb; Hon Roll; Accntng.

OZIMEK, GREGORY; Hopewell HS; Aliquippa, PA; (Y); Spanish Clb; Chorus; School Musical; School Play; JV Bsbl; Var Bowling; L Golf; Cmmnctns.

PABIS, DENNIS; Bishop O Hara HS; Blakely, PA; (Y); 14/124; Camera Clb; Drama Clb; Red Cross Aide; Ski Clb; School Musical; Stage Crew; Yrbk Phtg; High Hon Roll; High Hon Roll; NHS; Phila Coll/Phrmcy & Sci; Phrmcy.

PABST, BILL; Scranton Central HS; Scranton, PA; (Y); 50/286; Church Yth Grp; French Clb; JA; Var L Bsktbl; Im Wt Lftg; Hon Roll; NHS; Penn ST U; Electrical Engrng.

PACAK, ROBERT S; Monessen SR HS; Monessen, PA; (Y); 7/93; Library Aide; Pres Stage Crew; Yrbk Stf; Pres Soph Cls; Rep Jr Cls; Stu Cncl; Var JV Bsktbl; Ftbl; Co-Capt Golf; High Hon Roll; Pride Prog.

PACE, CORINNE MARIE; Wyoming Area SR HS; Wyoming, PA; (Y); Pres FBLA; FHA; Hosp Aide; Key Clb; Ski Clb; Sftbl; Coll Misericordia; Pre-Law.

PACEK, KAREN LYNN; St Joseph HS; Natrona Heights, PA; (Y); Art Clb; Band; Sec Stu Cncl; Score Keeper; Var Sftbl; L Tennis; Mrchg Band; School Play; Stage Crew; Yrbk Stf; Hmcmng Queen 85; Prom Queen 86; Carnegie Mellon Hstry Day 2nd Plc 83; PA ST U Altoona; Hlth Educ.

PACK, MICHAEL; Mc Connellsburg HS; Harrisonville, PA; (Y); Chess Clb; Church Yth Grp; Spanish Clb; Concert Band; Mrchg Band; School Musical; School Play; Stage Crew; Symp Band; Hon Roll; Ntl Sci Olympd Awd 85-86; Estrn Nazarene Coll; Pre-Med.

PACKAGE, ANNE; Trinity HS; Washington, PA; (Y); 3/370; German Clb; Pres Math Tm; NFL; Pres Concert Band; Pres Mrchg Band; NCTE Awd; VP NHS; Ntl Merit Ltr; NEDT Awd; Rotary Awd; Law.

PACKARD, JAMIE; Millersburg Area HS; Millersburg, PA; (Y); Library Aide; Spanish Clb; Varsity Clb; Color Guard; Capt Drill Tm; Stu Cncl; Var Bsktbl; Var Powder Puff Ftbl; Var Sftbl; Hon Roll; Bus Admin.

PACKARD, RICHARD; Canton Area JR SR HS; Canton, PA; (Y); AFS; Aud/Vis; Boy Scts; Camera Clb; Drama Clb; French Clb; Letterman Clb; VP Bsktbl; Cit Awd; Rotary Awd; Electronic Inst; Elec.

PACKER, CARL J; Tunkhannock Area HS; Dalton, PA; (Y); Am Leg Boys St; Boy Scts; Church Yth Grp; ROTC; Band; Jazz Band; Mrchg Band; Rep Sr Cls; Swmmng; Hon Roll; Egl Sct 86; Amrcn Lgn ST Police Wk 85; Bysct Jmbree 85; U Of Scranton; Crmnl Jstc.

PACKER, MARY BETH; Tunkhannock HS; Dalton, PA; (S); Church Yth Grp; Drama Clb; Spanish Clb; Teachers Aide; Concert Band; Jazz Band; School Play; Rep Jr Cls; Fld Hcky; Hon Roll; Educ.

PACKI, KIMBERLY; Pequea Valley HS; Kinzers, PA; (Y); High Hon Roll; Cum Laude 86; Outstndg Stu Awd 86; Bus.

PACZEK, STEPHEN; Windber Area HS; Windber, PA; (Y); Boy Scts; Church Yth Grp; Stu Cncl; Ftbl; Trk; Hon Roll; Am Legion Good Citznshp Citatn 84; Eagle Scout 84; Stu Mnth 84-85; U Pittsburgh; Pre-Med.

PADAMONSKY, GEORGE P; Northwestern Lehigh HS; Schnecksville, PA; (Y); 23/128; Am Leg Boys St; Teachers Aide; Bsbl; Var Capt Ftbl; Trk; Var Wrstlng; Hon Roll; Schlr Ath Ftbl 86; Outstndng Male Ath 86; Rotary Exchng Clb Mexico 86; Hofstra U; Mech Engrng.

PADEZANIN, SUSAN; Ambridge HS; Freedom, PA; (Y); 81/292; French Clb; Pep Clb; Red Cross Aide; Drm Mjr(t); Variety Show; Rep Frsh Cls; Rep Soph Cls; Rep Jr Cls; Rep Sr Cls; Twrlr; Edinboro U; Spch Comm.

PADILLA, ANTHONY; Bethlehem Catholic HS; Bethlehem, PA; (Y); Exploring; Key Clb; Yrbk Stf; Rep Soph Cls; Rep Jr Cls; Var Crs Cntry; Wrstlng.

PADILLA, DEL; Bristol JRSR HS; Bristol, PA; (Y); Computer Clb; Debate Tm; Scholastic Bowl; Acpl Chr; Ed Lit Mag; Rep Frsh Cls; Gov Hon Prg Awd; Amer Legn Essay Awd 85-86; St Joseph U; Bus Admin.

PADINSKE, JENNY; Pottsville Area HS; Pottsville, PA; (Y); 20/294; Art Clb; German Clb; Latin Clb; Ski Clb; Spanish Clb; Mrchg Band; Sec Stu Cncl; Var L Cheerleading; Var L Swmmng; Hon Roll; U DE; Crmnl Jstc.

PADULA, RICH; Scranton Prep Schl; Dunmore, PA; (Y); Cmnty Wkr; Letterman Clb; Political Wkr; Bsbl; Bsktbl; Coach Actv; Wt Lftg; Hon Roll; NHS; U Of Scranton.

PAE, CINDY; Clarion Area JR SR HS; Shippenville, PA; (Y); Chorus; Swing Chorus; Yrbk Stf; JV Cheerleading; L Trk; Var L Vllybl; Stat Wrstlng; High Hon Roll; Hon Roll; NHS; PA Free Entrprs Wk Schlrshp 85; Rtry Yth Ldrshp Schlrshp 86; PA ST U; Bus.

PAFF, KRISTINE; Wyoming Area HS; Harding, PA; (Y); Art Clb; Computer Clb; Drama Clb; German Clb; Vllybl; U Of Scranton; Bio.

PAGAC, CHRISTY; Bethlehem Center HS; Brownsville, PA; (Y); 5/147; Art Clb; VP Pep Clb; VP Varsity Clb; Sec Trs Chorus; School Play; Yrbk Stf; Var Capt Cheerleading; High Hon Roll; Hon Roll; Trs NHS; U Of Pittsburgh; Neo-Natl Nrsg.

PAGAC, EDWARD; Bethlehem-Center HS; Richeyville, PA; (Y); 1/168; Church Yth Grp; Drama Clb; Varsity Clb; School Play; Var Bsktbl; Var Golf; Bausch & Lomb Sci Awd; High Hon Roll; NHS; Engrng.

PAGANO, ANGELA; Saint Maria Goretti HS; Philadelphia, PA; (Y); 73/390; Boy Scts; Church Yth Grp; Exploring; GAA; Mathletes; Math Clb; Math Tm; Office Aide; Hon Roll; 2nd Pl Natl Math Leag; Phldlpha Cthlc Math Leag; Svc Awd; Htl Rstrnt Mgt.

PAGE, GARY; Allegheny Clarion Valley HS; Parker, PA; (Y); 3/105; Varsity Clb; Var L Bsktbl; Var L Ftbl; Var L Trk; Gov Hon Prg Awd; High Hon Roll; NHS; Pres Schlr; Computer Clb; 4-H; Penn St Sci & Hmnties Symposium 85; Pres Acadmc Ftns Awd 86; Al-Valleys Outstndng Acadmc Athlt Awd 86; Westminster Coll; Cnslng.

PAGE, JANEEN; A C Valley HS; Parker, PA; (Y); 4-H; Spanish Clb; Nwsp Rptr; Nwsp Stf; VP Frsh Cls; Pres Soph Cls; VP Jr Cls; Stu Cncl; Bsktbl; Bowling; Rtry Intl Ldrshp Camp 86; Rtry Achvt Awd 86; Educ.

PAGE, JOHN M; Central HS; Philadelphia, PA; (Y); Nwsp Stf; Yrbk Stf; Lit Mag; Hon Roll; Jr NHS; Ntl Merit SF; M/M Leon Buskin Awd Drawing 85; Bl Rbbn & Gld Key Schlstc Art Awds 84; Natl Merit Schlrp Sm-Fnlst 85; Vis Arts.

PAGE, MICHELLE; Mckeesport Area HS; Dravosburg, PA; (Y); 58/350; Hosp Aide; School Musical; Nwsp Stf; Sec Stu Cncl; Var L Cheerleading; Var Powder Puff Ftbl; Capt L Trk; Lion Awd; MVP Trck 86; WPIAL Rcrds Trck 86; Gold Mdl Baldwin Relays Long Jump 86; U Of Pittsburgh; Pre Dnstry.

PAGLIA, JOHN; Meadville Area SR HS; Meadville, PA; (Y); JA; Letterman Clb; Science Clb; Spanish Clb; Varsity Clb; Rep Frsh Cls; Rep Soph Cls; Rep Jr Cls; Rep Sr Cls; Rep Stu Cncl; 2nd Tm All Star In Sccr 85-86; Cannon U; Business Mgmt.

PAGLIA, LU ANN; Union Area SR HS; New Castle, PA; (Y); 1/62; French Clb; Teachers Aide; Y-Teens; Chorus; Drill Tm; Nwsp Rptr; Yrbk Sprt Ed; Rep Stu Cncl; Stat Bsktbl; High Hon Roll; Ntl Sci Merit Awd Wnnr 85; Pre-Med.

PAGLIO, KIMBERLY; Mt Pleasant Area SR HS; Mt Pleasant, PA; (Y); 20/243; Office Aide; Teachers Aide; Nwsp Stf; Yrbk Phtg; High Hon Roll; Hon Roll; NHS; Cmnty Wkr; GAA; Girl Scts.

PAHLS, LOIS E; William Allen HS; Allentown, PA; (Y); 35/556; Church Yth Grp; Band; Church Choir; Concert Band; Mrchg Band; Orch; Yrbk Ed-Chief; Trk; Hon Roll; Pres Acad Ftnss Awd 86; Summa Cum Laude Awd 85; Pres Clssrm For Young Amer 86; Susquehanna U; Bus.

PAIDA, DOUGLAS; Bishop Shanahan HS; W Chester, PA; (Y); 19/218; Church Yth Grp; Mathletes; Nwsp Stf; High Hon Roll; NHS; Outstndng Achvt Geom 85; Outstndng Achvt Alg II 86; Prfct Score Math Tm 86; Engrng.

PAINE, GAIL; Calvary Baptist Christian HS; Wilkes-Barre, PA; (S); Church Yth Grp; Hosp Aide; Church Choir; School Play; Yrbk Ed-Chief; Sftbl; Vllybl; High Hon Roll; Hon Roll; Sal; Maranadia Bptst Bibl Coll; Educ.

PAINE, STEPHANIE; Mechanicsburg Area SR HS; Mechanicsburg, PA; (Y); 82/311; Debate Tm; Band; Chorus; Concert Band; Jazz Band; Mrchg Band; Orch; Pep Band; Symp Band; Var Capt Vllybl; PA All ST Bnd 85-86; Deystone Gms Vllyb 84, Sccr 85-86; Music Ed.

PAINELY, JENNIFER; Fairchance Georges SR HS; Uniontown, PA; (Y); 1/170; Drama Clb; Band; Mrchg Band; School Play; Hst Soph Cls; Twrlr; Bausch & Lomb Sci Awd; High Hon Roll; Jr NHS; NHS; Engrng.

PAINTER, AARON F; Kiski Area HS; Leechburg, PA; (Y); Pres Debate Tm; German Clb; Band; Jazz Band; Mrchg Band; Orch; Pep Band; School Musical; Symp Band; Stu Cncl; Johnny Murphy Music Awd 83-84; U FL; Phrmcy.

PAINTER, COURTNEY; Warren Area HS; Warren, PA; (Y); Church Yth Grp; Drama Clb; French Clb; Office Aide; Acpl Chr; Chorus; Church Choir; School Play; Nwsp Rptr; Nwsp Stf; Corp Lwyr.

PAINTER, DAWNE; Manheim Central HS; Manheim, PA; (Y); Church Yth Grp; FHA; Office Aide; Church Choir; Hon Roll; Med Sec.

PAINTER, DIANE; Brookville Area HS; Summerville, PA; (S); 2/140; Cmnty Wkr; FTA; German Clb; Hosp Aide; Teachers Aide; Nwsp Stf; High Hon Roll; Jr NHS; Chess Clb; Orch; Occptnl Thrpy.

PAINTER, GERALD; Wyoming Valley West HS; Larksville, PA; (Y); Trk; High Hon Roll; Hon Roll; NHS; Prfct Atten Awd; Scranton U; Bio.

PAINTER, JACQUELINE; Yough SR HS; Smithton, PA; (Y); 65/250; FBLA; Spanish Clb; Vllybl; Sawyer Schl; Med Asst.

PAINTER, KRISTIE; Red Linn Area SR HS; Felton, PA; (Y); 39/327; Varsity Clb; Var Capt Crs Cntry; Var Capt Trk; Hon Roll; 1st Capitl Amer Bus Wmns Assn Scholar 86; Amer Lg Post 543 Scholar 86; Unsung Hero Awd 86; Lebanon Valley Coll; Bio.

PAINTER, TIFFANY; Seneca Valley HS; Evans City, PA; (Y); Art Clb; GAA; Mgr(s); Var Sftbl; High Hon Roll; Hon Roll; Sftbl All Star 82-86; Hist.

PAJAK, JOAN; Saint Basil Acad; Philadelphia, PA; (Y); Church Yth Grp; French Clb; Girl Scts; Math Clb; Chorus; Variety Show; High Hon Roll; Hon Roll; Prfct Atten Awd; Art Clb; Golden Poet Awd & Silver Poet Awd From World Of Poetry 85 & 86; Educ.

PAK, HUI KYU; Harrisburg HS John Harris; Harrisburg, PA; (S); 3/397; Chess Clb; ROTC; Drill Tm; Tennis; Hon Roll; NHS; Rotary Awd; Resrv Offcrs Assn Awd 85; Cmmndr Navl Ed Trn Awd ROTC 84; Engrng.

PAKOLA, STEVE; Cedar Crest HS; Lebanon, PA; (Y); 27/326; Pep Clb; Spanish Clb; School Musical; Capt Var Socr; JV Tennis; Im Vllybl; NHS; Lebanon Lancaster 1st Tm All Star Soccer 84-85; MVP Soccer 85; Pres Acad Ftns Awd 86; U Villanova.

PALACH, STEVE; Saegertown HS; Saegertown, PA; (Y); 33/124; Spanish Clb; SADD; Band; Concert Band; Mrchg Band; Var Bsbl; Var Golf; Var JV Wrstlng; Edinboro U PA; Chiroprctr.

PALADINO, CATHERINE; Sto-Rox HS; Mc Kees Rocks, PA; (Y); Church Yth Grp; Hosp Aide; Office Aide; Chorus; Stu Cncl; JV Var Cheerleading; Hon Roll; Drama.

PALADINO, DAWN; Milton Secondary HS; Lewisburg, PA; (Y); 47/202; Church Yth Grp; Chorus; Color Guard; School Musical; School Play; Rep Stu Cncl; Trk; Hon Roll; Hosp Aide; Band; Central PA; Law.

PALADINO, JUDITH; Owen J Roberts HS; Spring City, PA; (Y); Church Yth Grp; Exploring; Red Cross Aide; Band; Concert Band; Pep Band; School Play; Var Capt Bsktbl; JV Capt Socr; Im Vllybl; Bus Adm.

PALAISA, ANDREA; Laurel Highlands SR HS; Uniontown, PA; (Y); 12/340; JA; Mathletes; Swmmng; NHS; NEDT Awd; U Pittsburgh.

PALAISA, LISA DAWN; Uniontown Area SR HS; Fairbanks, PA; (Y); Office Aide; Pep Clb; Spanish Clb; SADD; School Play; Score Keeper; Timer; High Hon Roll; Hon Roll; Photo.

PALAKOVICH JR, FRANK E; Rochester Area School District; E Rochester, PA; (Y); 4/110; Am Leg Boys St; Exploring; SADD; Band; Church Choir; Concert Band; Drm & Bgl; Mrchg Band; Orch; Pep Band; High Achvt In Spnsh 84 & 86; Mst Musical Of Sr Class 86; Stu Of The Mnth 86; IN U Of PA; Rsprtry Thrpy.

PALANGE, DEBRA; Governor Mifflin HS; Reading, PA; (Y); 53/350; JA; Band; Chorus; Concert Band; Mrchg Band; Stage Crew; Var Bsktbl; Var Fld Hcky; Var Sftbl; Hon Roll; Bus.

PALANSKY, LISA MARIE; Allentown Central Catholic HS; Allentown, PA; (Y); 27/210; Civic Clb; Girl Scts; Key Clb; Spanish Clb; Stu Cncl; Var L Crs Cntry; Hon Roll; Crmnl Justice.

PALEOS, JOHN; Ambridge Area HS; Ambridge, PA; (Y); Church Yth Grp; Dance Clb; SADD; Variety Show; Stat Ftbl; CC Of Beaver County; Elec Engr.

PALERINO, JODI; Pottsville Area HS; Pottsville, PA; (Y); 17/260; Drama Clb; Latin Clb; Ski Clb; Speech Tm; Stu Cncl; Cheerleading; Swmmng.

PALERMINI JR, JOHN J; Shade Central City HS; Hooversville, PA; (Y); VICA; School Musical; Stage Crew; Variety Show; Rep Jr Cls; Stu Cncl; Score Keeper; Trk; Prfct Atten Awd; Elec Tech.

PALERMO, PAMELA; Bishop Hafey HS; Hazleton, PA; (Y); Drama Clb; Service Clb; Ski Clb; Spanish Clb; Y-Teens; Orch; Hon Roll; Bus Admin.

PALICHAT, PATRICIA; Ambridge Area HS; Ambridge, PA; (Y); German Clb; Pep Clb; Red Cross Aide; Band; Concert Band; Drm Mjr(t); Off Frsh Cls; Off Soph Cls; Off Jr Cls; Hon Roll; Engrng.

PALLADINI, KELLY; Ambridge Area HS; Freedom, PA; (Y); Pep Clb; Spanish Clb; Band; Concert Band; Mrchg Band; Off Frsh Cls; Off Soph Cls; Off Jr Cls; Hon Roll; Nrsng.

PALLADINO, DONALD; Penn-Trafford HS; Irwin, PA; (Y); German Clb; Math Clb; Varsity Clb; Var Bsbl; Im Bsktbl; NHS.

PALLAN, THOMAS; Quaker Valley HS; Sewickley, PA; (Y); 17/150; Church Yth Grp; German Clb; Key Clb; Golf; Socr; L Trk; High Hon Roll.

PALLONE, ARTHUR K; Southmoreland HS; Scottdale, PA; (Y); 1/240; Boy Scts; Drama Clb; Latin Clb; Math Clb; Band; Drm Mjr(t); Stu Cncl; NHS; Pep Clb; Spanish Clb; HOBY Fndtn Sem 85; Natl Knowldge Master Open 85-86; Aerospc Engrng.

PALLONE, NICK; Westside Tech Schl; Courtdale, PA; (Y); 15/153; Boy Scts; FBLA; Wrstlng; High Hon Roll; Comp Sci.

PALM, JEFF; Carlisle SR HS; Carlisle, PA; (Y); Band; Concert Band; Jazz Band; Mrchg Band; Hon Roll; Prfct Atten Awd; Math.

PALMER, JACQUELINE; Penns Manor Area HS; Pittsburgh, PA; (Y); 2/76; French Clb; Varsity Clb; Band; Concert Band; Jazz Band; Mrchg Band; Var L Bsktbl; High Hon Roll; NHS; Sal; Co Conselors Schlrshp, Pres Acdmc Ftns Awd, US Army Rsrve Natl Schlr Athl Awd 85-86; U Pittsburgh; Chem Engrng.

PALMER, JENNIFER L; Slippery Rock Area HS; Harrisville, PA; (Y); 6/147; Am Leg Aux Girls St; Church Yth Grp; Chorus; School Musical; Variety Show; Trk; Vllybl; Elks Awd; NHS; Pres Schlr; Grove City Clg; Math Tchr.

PALMER, KIM; Waynesburg Central HS; Waynesburg, PA; (Y); Trs VP 4-H; Sec French Clb; Ski Clb; Pres Frsh Cls; Pres Jr Cls; Sec Stu Cncl; Cheerleading; Trk; AFS; Church Yth Grp; JR Prom Ct Attndnt 86; JR Saddleseat Eqitation ST Champ 83; Miss Tri-ST Talent Qn 86; WA & Jefferson Coll; Pre Law.

PALMER, LISA; Ambridge HS; Baden, PA; (Y); Pep Clb; Spanish Clb; Yrbk Stf; Off Jr Cls; Vllybl; Cmmnctns.

PALMER, MARK; Deer Lakes JR/SR HS; Gibsonia, PA; (Y); Church Yth Grp; Varsity Clb; Variety Show; Nwsp Ed-Chief; Nwsp Sprt Ed; Bsktbl; Coach Actv; Ftbl; High Hon Roll; Hon Roll; JR Var Capt Letter Bsktbll 85-86; JR Var Letter Ftbll 85-86; Pre Med.

PALMER, MARY; Salisbury HS; Allentown, PA; (Y); 15/138; Church Yth Grp; Drama Clb; Hosp Aide; Key Clb; SADD; School Musical; JV Fld Hcky; High Hon Roll; Hon Roll; Nrsng.

PALMER, STEPHANIE; Bishop Shanahan HS; Dowingtown, PA; (Y); Dance Clb; Pep Clb; Trs SADD; Off Soph Cls; Rep Jr Cls; Var JV Cheerleading; DAR Awd; Bus.

PALMIERI, FRANK; Turtle Creek HS; Forest Hills, PA; (Y); 21/180; Exploring; Band; Concert Band; Drm & Bgl; Jazz Band; Mrchg Band; Pep Band; School Musical; School Play; Stage Crew; Boy Mnth 86; PA ST; Bus Mngmnt.

PALMIERI, JAMES; East Allegheny HS; E Mckeesport, PA; (Y); Am Leg Boys St; Bsbl; Socr; Hon Roll; NHS; PA ST; Engrg.

PALMIERI, LORI; Gateway SR HS; Monroeville, PA; (Y); 35/501; Church Yth Grp; FHA; Office Aide; Chorus; Ed Yrbk Stf; Var Swmmng; High Hon Roll; Trs NHS; 4th Rnnr Up Monroevl Miss Indpndnc Day Qns Cntst 86; Bus Adm.

PALMIERI, VIRGINIA; Neshaminy HS; Langhorne, PA; (Y); 68/702; Red Cross Aide; Lit Mag; JV Var Fld Hcky; Var JV Sftbl; Vllybl; Wt Lftg; Hon Roll; NHS; JV Gym; JV Trk; Acdmc/Athl Schlr Awd; Hugh O Brien Ldrshp Sem; Suburban I Tm Fld Hcky; Temple U; Pre-Law.

PALMISCNO, RANDALL; Kiski Area HS; Salina, PA; (Y); Math Clb; Math Tm; Pep Clb; Chorus; School Musical; Frsh Cls; Soph Cls; Stu Cncl; High Hon Roll; NHS; Pro Vost Schlr 86; Bell Avon Alumni Assoc Schlrshp 86; U Pittsburgh; Pre-Med.

PALMO, MARK; Marion Center HS; Creekside, PA; (Y); Boy Scts; Cmnty Wkr; Teachers Aide; JV Trk; Wt Lftg; Elks Awd; Hon Roll; Natl Soc Stds Olympd 83-84; Yllw Blt Karate 85; 15 Merit Bdgs 83; Indiana U Of PA; Bus.

PALOCHAK, DENNIS; Aliquippa HS; Aliquippa, PA; (Y); Aud/Vis; French Clb; SADD; Im Bsbl; Var Ftbl; Im Golf; Var Wt Lftg; Var Capt Wrstlng; PA Tp 100 AA Wrstlng 85-86; Athlt Wk Pckd Bvr Cnty Tms 86; Bus Admin.

PALOMBI, SUE; Carlynton HS; Carnegie, PA; (Y); French Clb; Band; Chorus; Drill Tm; Drm & Bgl; Flag Corp; Mrchg Band; Twrlr; 1st Pl Wrld Chmpn Mjrette Solo 85; 3rd Pl Mjrette Trio Ntl Cmption 84; Hnr Roll 84; Pittsburgh; Psych.

PALOMBO, MARIANN; Aliquippa SR HS; Aliquippa, PA; (S); 1/141; Church Yth Grp; Drama Clb; French Clb; Hosp Aide; Band; Church Choir; Mrchg Band; Pep Band; School Musical; School Play; Prfrmng Artist.

PALOMBO, MICHAEL; Canevin HS; Pittsburgh, PA; (Y); Ski Clb; JV Var Ftbl; Elks Awd; Hon Roll; Acad Excllnce Supr Achvt PSAT 85 & 86; Duquesne U; Law.

PALOMERA, MICHELLE; Gateway HS; Monroeville, PA; (Y); Church Yth Grp; Pres FBLA; Yrbk Stf; Off Frsh Cls; Off Soph Cls; Off Jr Cls; Off Sr Cls; Stu Cncl; Pres Schlr; Dance Clb; Pres Acad Fit Merit Awd 86; Hmcmng Queen 85-86; Boston Coll; Bus.

PALOMERA, MIHELLE; Gateway HS; Monroeville, PA; (Y); Church Yth Grp; Pres FBLA; Yrbk Stf; Rep Frsh Cls; Rep Soph Cls; Rep Jr Cls; Rep Sr Cls; Rep Stu Cncl; Im Vllybl; Pres Schlr; Boston Coll; Bus Pre Law.

PALONDER, BRYON; Belle Vernon HS; Belle Vernon, PA; (Y); Ski Clb; Band; Concert Band; Mrchg Band; Pep Band; L Golf; Hon Roll; Penn ST.

PALOVICK, JOSEPH; Mt Carmel Area JR SR HS; Mt Carmel, PA; (Y); 1/136; Pres Key Clb; Math Clb; Pres Soph Cls; Rep Stu Cncl; Capt Ftbl; Cit Awd; High Hon Roll; Pres NHS; Ntl Merit Ltr; Val; Swarthmore Coll; Engnrng.

PALSON, JAMES; Northern SR HS; Dillsburg, PA; (Y); 57/209; JV Ftbl; Grphc Printing.

PALUMBO, ANTHONY J; Springfield Twp HS; Philadelphia, PA; (Y); 21/150; Intnl Clb; Trs Thesps; School Musical; School Play; Nwsp Rptr; Nwsp Stf; Lit Mag; Ntl Merit SF; Pres Schlr; William H Fricke Memrl Awd 86; Drmtcs Awd 86; John Hopkins; Wrtr.

PALUMBO, KELLY; Neshannock HS; New Castle, PA; (Y); 1/120; FBLA; Math Tm; Ski Clb; Drill Tm; Stage Crew; Nwsp Bus Mgr; Nwsp Ed-Chief; Nwsp Stf; NHS; Ntl Merit Ltr; Acdmc All Amer 85; Med.

PALYO, JOHN; South Allegheny HS; Mckeesport, PA; (Y); School Play; JV Var Bsktbl.

PAMBIANCO, AMY; Valley View HS; Peckville, PA; (Y); 26/200; Church Yth Grp; French Clb; Hosp Aide; Chorus; School Play; Rep Stu Cncl; Cheerleading; Vllybl; French Hon Soc; Hon Roll; Dist Chorus Stu 85.

PAMBIANCO, MARIA; Bishop Hoban HS; Plains, PA; (Y); 32/190; Church Yth Grp; FBLA; Color Guard; Yrbk Sprt Ed; Yrbk Stf; Capt Twrlr; High Hon Roll; NHS; Acad All-Amer Awd 85-86; Natl Yth Salute Awd 85-86; Natl Ldrshp & Svc Awd 85-86; Geisinger Med Ctr; Radiology.

PAMPE, BRENDA; Marion Center Area HS; Marion Center, PA; (S); 21/148; FBLA; FNA; SADD; Hon Roll; 5th Pl Grnl Comp Typing II 84; IN U Pennsylvania; Acctng.

PAMPENA, MARIE ANNETTE JEAN; Sacred Heart HS; Pittsburgh, PA; (Y); Drama Clb; Pres FBLA; Office Aide; Spanish Clb; SADD; Chorus; School Musical; School Play; Yrbk Stf; Pres Stu Cncl; Proficncy Typg Spd & Accrcy Awd 86; Euquesne U; Psychol.

PAMPENO, SHERYL; Ford City HS; Ford City, PA; (Y); Rep AFS; Rep SADD; Band; Chorus; Concert Band; Nwsp Rptr; Nwsp Stf; High Hon Roll; Hon Roll; Acctng.

PAMULA, CHRISTINE; St Benedict Acad; Erie, PA; (Y); 28/63; Girl Scts; Pres Band; Pres Chorus; Color Guard; Mrchg Band; Variety Show; Var L Socr; Hon Roll; Music Exc Awd 85-86; Fut Secys 85-87; Grls Ensmbl 84-87; Villa Maria Coll; Med Secy.

PAN, DOROTHY; Blue Mountain Acad; Limekiln, PA; (Y); VP Girl Scts; Church Choir; Yrbk Stf; VP Stu Cncl; Stat Gym; Capt Sftbl; Capt Vllybl; Hon Roll; Andrws U; Bus.

PANASCI, KATHY; Johnstown SR HS; Johnstown, PA; (Y); Pep Clb; SADD; School Musical; Nwsp Phtg; Nwsp Rptr; Rep Jr Cls; Rep Stu Cncl; Var Cheerleading; U Pittsburgh Johnstown.

PANASE, JIM; Gov Mifflin SR HS; Shillington, PA; (Y); 80/250; Varsity Clb; VICA; Socr; Wrstlng; Bus Mgmt.

PANCHOLI, MEETA; Bethel Park SR HS; Pittsburgh, PA; (Y); Drama Clb; JA; Band; Concert Band; Mrchg Band; School Musical; School Play; Yrbk Stf; High Hon Roll; Hon Roll; Pre-Med.

PANCOE, DONALD C; Kiski Area HS; Leechburg, PA; (Y); Science Clb; Jazz Band; Mrchg Band; Orch; Pep Band; Symp Band; High Hon Roll; Hst NHS; Semper Fidelis-Awd Musicl Excellnc 86; PA ST U; Elec Engrng.

PANCU, DIANA; Philadelphia HS For Girls; Philadelphia, PA; (Y); 2/392; GAA; Hosp Aide; JA; Varsity Clb; Stage Crew; Nwsp Sprt Ed; Fld Hcky; Mgr(s); Tennis; High Hon Roll; Awd Spnsh Ntl Cntst; U VA Bk Awd 86; Med.

PANDICH, JENNIFER; Susquehanna Community HS; Susquehanna, PA; (S); 6/94; Quiz Bowl; Ski Clb; School Play; Stage Crew; Nwsp Rptr; Hon Roll; Laurel Street Thtre Crl Soc Brd 85-86; Theatre.

PANE, THERESA; Ambridge Area HS; Baden, PA; (Y); 2/265; Am Leg Aux Girls St; 4-H; Pep Clb; Chorus; Rep Soph Cls; Stu Cncl; Crs Cntry; Trk; Elks Awd; High Hon Roll; Ntl Schlr/Athltc Army Res 86; Carnegie Mellon U; Math.

PANEBIANCO, ANNETTE MARIE; Canevin Catholic HS; Pittsburgh, PA; (Y); FBLA; NFL; Chorus; Church Choir; Hon Roll; Psych.

PANEBIANCO, PATRICK; Greensburg Central Catholic HS; Greensburg, PA; (Y); 70/277; Pep Clb; Ski Clb; Yrbk Phtg; Yrbk Stf; Trk; Vllybl; Hon Roll; Clarion U; Comm.

PANEK, HEATHER; North Pocono HS; Moscow, PA; (S); 8/247; Chorus; Orch; Tennis; High Hon Roll; Natl Sci Merit Awd 84 & 85.

PANETTA, ANGELA; Center HS; Aliquippa, PA; (Y); 23/180; Am Leg Aux Girls St; Trs German Clb; Girl Scts; Co-Capt Drill Tm; Yrbk Ed-Chief; Trk; Pres NHS; Girl Scout Gold Awd 85; Center Civics Girl Mnth 85; Congsnl Art Comptn 3rd Pl 85; U Pittsburgh; Engrng.

PANETTIERI, ANTOINETTE; Valley View HS; Eynon, PA; (Y); 107/250; Drama Clb; Ski Clb; Spanish Clb; SADD; Chorus; School Play; Stu Cncl; Tchr.

PANGALLO, DIANE; Brookville Area HS; Clarington, PA; (Y); 6/146; Sec French Clb; Sec Band; Jazz Band; Pep Band; School Musical; Hon Roll; Jr NHS; NHS; Acctng I Awd 86; Marines Band Awd 86.

PANGELINAN, SHANNON L; Rittenhouse Acad; Philadelphia, PA; (Y); Drama Clb; School Play; Variety Show; Nwsp Stf; Trs Sr Cls; U CA Los Angeles; Drama.

PANGONIS, KAREN J; Marian HS; New Boston, PA; (Y); 7/124; Church Yth Grp; SADD; Mrchg Band; School Play; Capt Twrlr; Cit Awd; High Hon Roll; NHS; Pres Schlr; Spanish NHS; Insttnl Schlrshp 86; Phil Coll Pharm/Sci; Phrmcy.

PANIAN, JODY; Harrisburg HS; Harrisburg, PA; (S); 11/442; Exploring; NHS; Bus.

PANICHELLI, ANDREA; St Maria Goretti HS; Philadelphia, PA; (Y); 40/402; Cmnty Wkr; Spanish Clb; Hon Roll; Med Lab Tech.

PANICO, ANGELA M; Lansdale Catholic HS; Lansdale, PA; (Y); 54/220; Cmnty Wkr; Drama Clb; SADD; Yrbk Stf; Pres Sr Cls; Pres Stu Cncl; Var Cheerleading; Hon Roll; Opt Clb Awd; Prfct Atten Awd; Chsn-Ntl Ldsrhp Wk; Villanova U; Pltcl Sci.

PANKEY, KIMBERLY; West Phila Catholic Girls HS; Phila, PA; (Y); JA; Service Clb; Band; Concert Band; Jazz Band; Orch; School Musical; Hon Roll; Prfct Atten Awd; W Chester ST U PA; Crmnl Jstc.

PANKEY, MARK; Laurel Highlands SR HS; Uniontown, PA; (Y); 50/340; Boy Scts; Church Yth Grp; Cmnty Wkr; Exploring; Ski Clb; Band; Var L Golf; Stat Swmmng; High Hon Roll; Hon Roll; Outstndng Nwsp Carrier 83; James Madison U; Bus.

PANKUCH, JENNIFER R; Bloomsburg HS; New Holland, PA; (Y); 8/111; Am Leg Aux Girls St; Drama Clb; Thesps; Varsity Clb; Yrbk Ed-Chief; Yrbk Sprt Ed; Var Cheerleading; Var Socr; High Hon Roll; NHS; Penn ST U; Sprts Med.

PANNAMAN, MICHELLE; Hempfield Area SR HS; New Stanton, PA; (Y); 27/657; German Clb; Spanish Clb; Rep Stu Cncl; Var L Bsktbl; Var Golf; Var Trk; Vllybl; High Hon Roll; NHS; Ntl Merit Ltr; Henry King Stanford Schlrshp 85; Spcl Natl Merit Schlrshp 86; U Of Miami; Pre-Law.

PANNAPACKER, WILLIAM A; Father Judge HS; Philadelphia, PA; (Y); 12/425; Boy Scts; Cmnty Wkr; Pres Speech Tm; Nwsp Ed-Chief; High Hon Roll; NHS; Ntl Merit SF; Publ Spkng Awds 82-86; Eagle Sct, Commnty Svc Awds Merit 85; Med.

PANNEBAKER, JAY; Clearfield Area HS; Woodland, PA; (Y); Church Yth Grp; VICA; Church Choir; Im Wrstlng; High Hon Roll; Hon Roll; Comp Sci.

PANNEPACKER, SCOT D; Council Rock HS; Newtown, PA; (Y); 21/769; Nwsp Rptr; Hon Roll; Ntl Merit SF; Cert Merit Outstndng SAT Scrs PA 85; Bus Adm.

PANOUSIS, PAMELA; West Mifflin Area HS; West Mifflin, PA; (Y); Exploring; FHA; JA; Hon Roll; Sls Clb Awd Jr Achvmnt 85-86; Nrsng.

PANTALEO, KIM; Hopewell HS; Aliquippa, PA; (Y); Church Yth Grp; Dance Clb; Sec Exploring; Girl Scts; Spanish Clb; Teachers Aide; Capt Drill Tm; Stu Cncl; High Hon Roll; Hon Roll.

PANTAS, LEE J; Council Rock HS; Washington Crssng, PA; (Y); 3/755; Var L Bsbl; High Hon Roll; Lion Awd; NHS; Ntl Merit SF; U S Naval Acad Summr Sci Sem 85; Bucks County Sci Sem 84; Aerospc Engrng.

PANTLE, LORI; Lake Lehman HS; Sweet Valley, PA; (Y); Sec Jr Cls; Var Cheerleading; Var L Fld Hcky; Var L Sftbl; Crmnl Jstc.

PANYI, LYNN; Shaler Area HS; Glenshaw, PA; (Y); 15/517; Office Aide; Ski Clb; Nwsp Stf; Yrbk Stf; Var Trk; Hon Acdmc Achvt.

PANZA, JANICE; Penn Hills HS; Verona, PA; (Y); French Clb; Varsity Clb; Sr Cls; Stu Cncl; Capt Swmmng; High Hon Roll; Jr NHS; NHS; PA ST U; Biochem.

PAOLINO, STEPHANIE; Archbishop Carroll HS; Malvern, PA; (Y); 20/212; Spanish Clb; SADD; Yrbk Stf; Im Fld Hcky; JV Sftbl; Hon Roll; Bus.

PAONE, ANTHONY; St John Neumann HS; Philadelphia, PA; (Y); 83/338; Spanish Clb; JV Var Ftbl; Im Vllybl; Wt Lftg; Temple U; Comp Prog.

PAPALE, ANDREA; St Benedict Acad; Erie, PA; (Y); 18/63; Model UN; Variety Show; Yrbk Stf; Trs Jr Cls; Var Socr; Var Sftbl; High Hon Roll; Hon Roll; NHS; Slippery Rock U; Psych.

PAPANIA, AMY L; Mars Area SR HS; Mars, PA; (Y); 1/160; VP French Clb; GAA; Letterman Clb; Varsity Clb; Sec Soph Cls; Pres Stu Cncl; Stat Ftbl; L Trk; High Hon Roll; NHS; Maude Neithercoat Awd Outstndng Stu Athlt 85-86; Hmcmng Crt 85-86; Mst Lkly Sccd & Mst Rlbl 85-86; Grove City Coll; Intl Bus.

PAPAPONE, FRANK; Wissahickon HS; Ambler, PA; (S); Civic Clb; Key Clb; Letterman Clb; Varsity Clb; JV Var Bsbl; Var JV Ftbl; Var Trk; NHS.

PAPOUTSIS, JOHN; Waynsboro Area SR HS; Waynesboro, PA; (Y); 14/370; Boy Scts; Church Yth Grp; JCL; Ski Clb; Ftbl; Golf; High Hon Roll; NHS; Franklin & Marshall Coll; Med.

PAPP, KATHY; West Middlesex HS; W Middlesex, PA; (Y); Church Yth Grp; English Clb; Girl Scts; Office Aide; Spanish Clb; Temple Yth Grp; Chorus; Sftbl; Hon Roll; Engl.

PAPP, SUSAN; Spring Ford HS; Limerick, PA; (S); 12/263; Church Yth Grp; Trs 4-H; French Clb; Band; JV Bsktbl; L Fld Hcky; JV Lcrss; L Trk; Wrstlng; 4-H Awd; Old Dominion; Pol Sci.

PAPP, SUZANNE; Cardinal O Hara HS; Morton, PA; (Y); 26/772; German Clb; Office Aide; High Hon Roll; Hon Roll; Prfct Atten Awd; Grmn Hnr Soc 85-86; Schlstc Awd 85-86; Prncpls Awd Acadmc Excllnc 85-86; Drexel U; Mdcl Technlgy.

PAPPAS, IDA; Avonworth JR SR HS; Pittsbg, PA; (Y); 12/88; French Clb; JA; Speech Tm; Chorus; Church Choir; Drill Tm; School Musical; School Play; Variety Show; Yrbk Rptr; Dist I Chorus 86&87; Rgnl Chorus 86; Mus Awd Piano/Voice 86; Carnegie Mellon U; Cmmnctns.

PAPPAS, SUSAN L; Freedom HS; Bethlehem, PA; (Y); 62/445; Art Clb; Library Aide; Jazz Band; Nwsp Bus Mgr; Nwsp Stf; Im Bsktbl; High Hon Roll; Nwspr Crcltn Ed 84-85; Riot Sqd Schl Sprt 85-86; Prm Comm 85-86.

PAQUET, KAREN; Interboro HS; Prospect Park, PA; (S); French Clb; Rep Jr Cls; Stu Cncl; Mgr Bsktbl; Cheerleading; Mgr Sftbl; High Hon Roll; Hon Roll; Jr NHS; NHS; Bus Admin.

PAQUET, LAURIE; Interboro SR HS; Prospect Park, PA; (S); Hosp Aide; Key Clb; Yrbk Stf; Rep Jr Cls; Rep Sr Cls; Bsktbl; Sftbl; High Hon Roll; Hon Roll; VP NHS; Beaver Coll; Phy Thrpy.

PARA, AMY; Valley View JR SR HS; Peckville, PA; (Y); 23/200; Chrmn French Clb; SADD; Sec Jr Cls; Sec Stu Cncl; Co-Capt Cheerleading; Tennis; French Hon Soc; Hon Roll; NHS; Acctg.

PARADISO, FERN; Exeter SR HS; Reading, PA; (Y); Drama Clb; German Clb; Hosp Aide; Band; Chorus; Concert Band; Mrchg Band; Pep Band; School Musical; Jr NHS; PCP & S; Pharmcy.

PARANICK, KRISTI; Yough SR HS; W Newton, PA; (Y); 69/224; Trs Church Yth Grp; French Clb; Pep Clb; Ski Clb; SADD; Nwsp Stf; Yrbk Ed-Chief; Mgr(s); Powder Puff Ftbl; Cmnty Action Pgm Awd 86; Humnties Day 86; WV U; Lbrl Arts.

PARASCENZO, PAULA; Canon Mc Millan SR HS; Canonsburg, PA; (Y); 21/340; Church Yth Grp; Latin Clb; SADD; Chorus; L Diving; Capt Swmmng; NHS; PA ST U; Comp Sci.

PARELLA, JONATHAN; Upper Merion HS; Wayne, PA; (Y); French Clb; Math Tm; Hon Roll; Prfct Atten Awd; U Of PA; Bnkng.

PARENTE, BETTY; Liberty HS; Bethlehem, PA; (Y); 15/475; Hosp Aide; Hon Roll; Prfct Atten Awd; Medcl.

PARENTE, DINA; Bishop Kenrick HS; Norristown, PA; (Y); 7/310; VP Cmnty Wkr; Mathletes; Science Clb; Spanish Clb; Nwsp Rptr; Yrbk Rptr; Yrbk Stf; JV Var Cheerleading; NHS; Sci.

PARETTI, JENNIFER; Chambersburg Area SR HS; Chambersburg, PA; (Y); 4/593; Letterman Clb; Varsity Clb; Band; Mrchg Band; Var L Crs Cntry; Var L Trk; High Hon Roll; Spnsh Awd 85-86; Shippensburg ST U; Engrng.

PARFITT, ANTHONY; Hempfield Area HS; Bovard, PA; (Y); 138/676; Letterman Clb; Pep Clb; School Musical; Var L Bsktbl; Var L Ftbl; Im Wt Lftg; Hon Roll; St Vincent Acad Scholar 86; St Vincent Coll; Lib Art.

PARINISI, ANDREA; West Scranton SR HS; Scranton, PA; (Y); 13/260; Ski Clb; Spanish Clb; Crs Cntry; Trk; Hon Roll; Jr NHS; NHS; Med Field.

PARIS, NICOLE; Scranton Central HS; Scranton, PA; (Y); French Clb; Ski Clb; Yrbk Phtg; Yrbk Stf; Hon Roll; Med Field.

PARISE, JEWELL; Brmudian Springs HS; York Springs, PA; (Y); 18/80; Drama Clb; Chorus; Madrigals; School Musical; Swing Chorus; Off Stu Cncl; Var Capt Cheerleading; Var Mgr(s); Var L Vllybl; Hon Roll; Susquehanna U; Cmnctns.

PARISE, RALPH; Washington HS; Washington, PA; (S); 21/150; French Clb; Letterman Clb; Math Tm; Var L Crs Cntry; Var Trk; Var L Wrstlng; Hon Roll; Dntstry.

PARISELLA, JILL; Bradford Area HS; Bradford, PA; (Y); 60/300; AFS; Church Yth Grp; Acpl Chr; Church Choir; Variety Show; Yrbk Stf; VP Stu Cncl; Capt Cheerleading; Var Trk; Jr NHS; Miss Bradford Area HS 86; PA Dist & Regional Chorus 85-86; PA Dist Trk Meet 84-86.

PARK, JUDY; North Penn HS; North Wales, PA; (Y); 24/678; Pres Church Yth Grp; Intnl Clb; Jazz Band; Madrigals; JV Trk; 4-H Awd; High Hon Roll; NHS; 4-H; Girl Scts; SF Ntn Amer Home Swng Assn 84; Ltr Rcgntn Rep R Godshall, Wnnr ST 4-H Fash Rvu 85; U PA Leigh; Engrng.

PARK, LORI; State College Area SR HS; State College, PA; (Y); Church Yth Grp; Im Vllybl; Hon Roll; Jazz Awd Annual Altoona Area Dance Wrkshp 84; Jazz Dance Schlrshp 84-85; 3rd Pl Dane Fest World Comptn; Biology.

PARK, MARVEL; Marple-Newtown SR HS; Broomall, PA; (Y); Chess Clb; Church Yth Grp; Math Clb; Science Clb; JV Socr; Hon Roll; Biochem.

PARK, MICHELLE; Ridgway Area HS; Ridgway, PA; (S); Penn ST; Art Dsgnr.

PARK, OHN; Cheltenham HS; Elkins Pk, PA; (Y); 4/365; Math Tm; Rptr Model UN; Orch; Ed Nwsp Stf; Trs Stu Cncl; Capt Bowling; NHS; Ntl Merit Schol; Rotary Awd; French Awd 84-86.

PARK, SANG; Harry S Truman HS; Fairless Hills, PA; (Y); Drama Clb; SADD; Varsity Clb; School Play; Yrbk Phtg; Off Sr Cls; Hst Stu Cncl; Var Wrstlng; Hon Roll; U Of PA; Bus Admn.

PARK, SANG J; Plymouth Whitemarsh HS; Philadelphia, PA; (Y); 15/320; Chess Clb; Church Yth Grp; German Clb; Math Clb; Science Clb; Teachers Aide; Varsity Clb; Chorus; Symp Band; Off Stu Cncl; Lehigh U; Aerospace Engrng.

PARK, SCOTT; Brookville Areas HS; Sigel, PA; (Y); Chess Clb; Key Clb; Varsity Clb; Band; Var L Bsbl; Var L Ftbl; Var L Wrstlng; Hon Roll.

PARK, STEVE; Northeast HS; Philadelphia, PA; (Y); Art Clb; Church Yth Grp; Intnl Clb; Jazz Band; Bsbl; Bowling; Socr; U DE; Law.

PARK, THOMAS; Wyoming Area HS; Exeter, PA; (Y); Boy Scts; German Clb; Quiz Bowl; Ski Clb; Band; PA ST; Engr.

PARK, TRICIA; St Hubert HS; Philadelphia, PA; (Y); 15/367; Computer Clb; Orch; School Musical; Hon Roll; Drexel U; Comp Prgmmng.

PARKE, AMY; Kiski Area HS; Apollo, PA; (Y); French Clb; Pres German Clb; Math Tm; Spanish Clb; Sec SADD; Mrchg Band; Var L Swmmng; High Hon Roll; NHS; Church Yth Grp; Schlrshp Govs Schl Intl Study 86; Intl Rltns.

PARKER, DEBORAH; Lewistown Area HS; Lewistown, PA; (Y); 22/252; AFS; Church Yth Grp; Key Clb; Pep Clb; Service Clb; Spanish Clb; Chorus; Rep Jr Cls; Rep Sr Cls; Rep Stu Cncl; Stu Of Mnth 86; PA ST U; Bus.

PARKER, EDWARD THOMAS; Freeport HS; Sarver, PA; (Y); JV Bsktbl; Hon Roll; Karate 84-86; Bsbl 78-85; Edinboro; Chem.

PARKER, GEORGE; Yough HS; W Newton, PA; (Y); Boy Scts; Hon Roll.

PARKER, JACKIE; Ridgway Area HS; Ridgway, PA; (Y); 16/123; Capt Gym; Im Vllybl; Hon Roll; Pres Schlr; Army Rsrv Schlr Athlt Awd 86; IN U Of PA; Educ Excptnl Stu.

PARKER, JULIA; Trinity SR HS; Washington, PA; (Y); Art Clb; Camera Clb; Drama Clb; Math Tm; NFL; Ski Clb; Speech Tm; School Play; Trk; High Hon Roll; Pre-Vet Med.

PARKER, SCOTT; Karns City HS; Petrolia, PA; (Y); Pres FCA; Library Aide; Varsity Clb; Ftbl; Hon Roll; Ftbl Ltrmn 83-85; Kent ST U; Sprts Med.

PARKER, SHERRY; Fairchance Georges JR SR HS; Union Town, PA; (Y); Church Yth Grp; French Clb; Girl Scts; Band; Church Choir; Concert Band; Mrchg Band; Score Keeper; Hon Roll; Prfct Atten Awd; Doctor.

PARKER, WENDY; Strath Haven HS; Swarthmore, PA; (Y); Girl Scts; Ski Clb; Flag Corp; Mrchg Band; Nwsp Stf; Yrbk Stf; Var JV Lcrss; Var Trk; High Hon Roll; NHS; Instrmntl Music Awd 86; Mst Imprvd Grls La Crosse 86; Vrsty Ltr Awd 86; IN U Of PA; Chem.

PARKES, DOUGLAS; West Chester East HS; W Chester, PA; (Y); Ski Clb; JV Socr; Var Tennis; Tnns All-Lg Plyr 86; Ymaha Kybd Prfrmnc Awd 83.

PARKES, STEVE; Archbishop Ryan HS; Philadelphia, PA; (Y); Ice Hcky; Excllnce In Engl Awd 86.

PARKIN JR, RONALD L; Highlands SR HS; Natrona, PA; (Y); JA; Bus Mgt.

PARKINSON, SCOTT T; Parkland HS; Fogelsville, PA; (Y); 291/434; Chess Clb; Exploring; Library Aide; Office Aide; Teachers Aide; Ntl Merit SF.

PARKS, ERIC; Kittanning SR HS; Worthington, PA; (Y); 7/224; Church Yth Grp; Computer Clb; French Clb; High Hon Roll; NHS; Rotary Awd; PA Jr Acad Sci-Comp 8 1sts 84-86; Outstndng Stu Math, Comp Sci 85; Indiana U P A Bio/Chem Awds 85-86; Comp Sci.

PARKS, JARED; Kennedy Christian HS; Farrell, PA; (Y); 4/98; VP Church Yth Grp; Computer Clb; Library Aide; Spanish Clb; Rep Frsh Cls; Rep Soph Cls; Pres Jr Cls; Pres Stu Cncl; Bsktbl; High Hon Roll; Cmmrcl Pilot.

PARKS, KATHLEEN DAWN; Lincoln HS; Ellwood City, PA; (Y); 89/167; Cmnty Wkr; FBLA; Hosp Aide; Y-Teens; Bsktbl; Tennis; Hon Roll; Slippery Rock U; Thrpy.

PARKS, STACY; Lewistown Area HS; Lewistown, PA; (Y); French Clb; Drill Tm; Mrchg Band; JV Cheerleading; JV Twrlr; Im Vllybl; Im Wt Lftg; Penn ST; Psychiatry.

PARKS, THOMAS; Kennard-Dale HS; Stewartstown, PA; (Y); 3/111; Pres VP 4-H; Pres Sec FFA; Acpl Chr; Pres Band; Trs Chorus; Pres Concert Band; Pres Mrchg Band; Orch; School Musical; School Play; Sthestrn Educ Assn Schlrshp 86; Amer Lgn Citznshp Awd 82; Kennard-Dale Band Arion Awd 86; VA Polytech; Biochem.

PARNAY, LISA; Shenango JR-SR HS; New Castle, PA; (Y); 20/110; Church Yth Grp; French Clb; School Play; Yrbk Stf; Im Vllybl; Hon Roll; Gannon U; Physcl Thrpy.

PARNELL, BRIAN; Kiski Area HS; Vandergrift, PA; (Y); Cmnty Wkr; JA; Yrbk Phtg; Yrbk Rptr; Yrbk Stf; Rep Frsh Cls; Ftbl; Trk; High Hon Roll; Hon Roll; Hstry.

PARONISH, SUELLEN L; Altoona Area HS; Altoona, PA; (Y); 75/683; Church Yth Grp; Drama Clb; Girl Scts; Spanish Clb; SADD; Orch; Rep Jr Cls; Rep Sr Cls; Hon Roll; NEDT Awd; Marian Medal 83; IN U.

PAROSKY, LEAH; Bishop Hafey HS; Hazleton, PA; (Y); Church Yth Grp; French Clb; Orch; Photo.

PARRISH, CAROL; Ephrata SR HS; Ephrata, PA; (Y); Sec Church Yth Grp; Chorus; Church Choir; Concert Band; Jazz Band; VP Orch; School Musical; School Play; Rep Stu Cncl; Sr Cls; Drama.

PARRISH, KIRK; Brownsville Area HS; Grindstone, PA; (S); 18/225; Ski Clb; Var Ftbl; Var Trk; Hon Roll; Engr.

PARRISH, MICHAEL; Penn Cambria HS; Cresson, PA; (Y); Church Yth Grp; Ski Clb; Spanish Clb; Jr Cls; Bsbl; Bsktbl; Ftbl; High Hon Roll; Hon Roll; NHS.

PARRY, BRYAN; Canon-Mc Millan SR HS; Mc Donald, PA; (Y); Art Clb; Chess Clb; French Clb; School Play; Yrbk Phtg; Yrbk Stf; JV Socr; High Hon Roll; Hon Roll.

PARSHALL, TAMMI SUE; Shenango HS; New Castle, PA; (Y); Church Yth Grp; Cmnty Wkr; French Clb; Office Aide; Church Choir; Mrchg Band; Nwsp Stf; Hon Roll; Jr NHS; NHS; Am Bus Wmns Assn Scholar 86; Youngstown ST U Gold Mdl 86; Robert Morris Coll; Bus Adm.

PARSON, LISA; West Greene HS; Graysville, PA; (Y); VP Church Yth Grp; Sec Trs Ski Clb; School Musical; School Play; Nwsp Stf; Yrbk Bus Mgr; Rep Stu Cncl; Vllybl; Hon Roll; Sec NHS; Mip Softbl 84-85; Bus Mgmnt & Admin.

PARSON, LORNA; West Allegheny HS; Imperial, PA; (Y); 22/216; Church Yth Grp; Band; Chorus; Drm Mjr(t); Jazz Band; Bsktbl; Trk; Hon Roll; Jr NHS; Educ.

PARSONS, BRENDA; Wellsboro Area SR HS; Wellsboro, PA; (Y); Art Clb; French Clb; Pep Clb; Cheerleading; Mgr(s); Hon Roll.

PARSONS, BRIAN; Juniata HS; Port Royal, PA; (Y); Computer Clb; Scholastic Bowl; Spanish Clb; School Play; Yrbk Stf; High Hon Roll; Hon Roll; NHS; Schltc J 84-86; Distngshd Hnr Stu 83-86; Engrng.

PARSONS, KEVIN; Saeger Town Area HS; Saegertown, PA; (Y); Boy Scts; Church Yth Grp; Exploring; SADD; Band; Concert Band; Mrchg Band; Pep Band; Stage Crew; Variety Show; Amer Lgn Schl Awd 86; Intl Coll Fine Arts; Comm Art.

PARSONS, STEPHANIE; Hazleton HS; Drums, PA; (Y); 17/388; Drama Clb; French Clb; Leo Clb; Pep Clb; Ski Clb; Color Guard; Yrbk Stf; French Hon Soc; Hon Roll; Med.

PARTINGTON, STATIA; Portersville Christian Schl; Ellwood City, PA; (Y); 1/7; Church Yth Grp; Teachers Aide; Nwsp Stf; Yrbk Stf; Rep Stu Cncl; Capt Cheerleading; High Hon Roll; NHS; Val; Dstngshd Christian HS Stu 86; Grove City Coll; Pre-Med.

PARTRIDGE, BRIAN; Hempfield Area SR HS; Greensburg, PA; (Y); Church Yth Grp; Drama Clb; Hosp Aide; Latin Clb; NFL; Ski Clb; School Musical; School Play; Im Bsktbl; Im Vllybl; Bio.

PARTYKA, PAUL; Scranton Prep Schl; Eynon, PA; (Y); 2/190; Church Yth Grp; Science Clb; Tennis; High Hon Roll.

PARULO, DEBBIE; Meadville Area SR HS; Meadville, PA; (Y); 26/348; Church Yth Grp; Key Clb; Yrbk Rptr; Yrbk Stf; High Hon Roll; Hon Roll; NHS; Prfct Atten Awd; Typng Awds-Speed & Accrcy 84-86; Elem Ed.

PARZANESE, MARIA; St Maria Goretti HS; Philadelphia, PA; (S); 4/402; Church Yth Grp; French Clb; Mathletes; Math Clb; Orch; School Musical; Nwsp Rptr; Rep Jr Cls; Hon Roll; NHS; Acadmc All Amer Schlr 84; Hnrbl Mentn-IPS, Music, Rel & Alg 84; Hnrbl Mentn-Geomtry & CML Distctn 85; Math.

PARZYNSKI, MICHAEL J; Mon Valley Catholic HS; Belle Vernon, PA; (Y); 31/102; Boy Scts; French Clb; Pres FBLA; Variety Show; Nwsp Stf; Stu Cncl; Ftbl; Wt Lftg; French Hon Soc; Secy Raquettebl 86; St Vincent Coll Latrobe; Biol.

PASCOE, PAMELA; Hanover Area JR SR HS; Sugar Notch, PA; (Y); Hon Roll; Accounting.

PASCOE, VICKIE; New Castle SR HS; New Castle, PA; (Y); 63/260; Exploring; Girl Scts; Hosp Aide; Library Aide; Spanish Clb; SADD; Chorus; Church Choir; Hon Roll; Relgn.

PASCUZZI, JOSEPH; Muhlenberg HS; Reading, PA; (Y); Aud/Vis; Science Clb; Pep Clb; Band; Concert Band; Jazz Band; Mrchg Band; Pep Band; School Musical; School Play; Sci.

PASCUZZO, LINDA; Carmichaels Area HS; Carmichaels, PA; (S); #11 In Class; Office Aide; Ski Clb; Spanish Clb; SADD; Off Jr Cls; High Hon Roll; NHS; Cosmtlgy.

PASLES, PAUL; Council Rock HS; Holland, PA; (Y); Church Yth Grp; Mathletes; Chorus; Hon Roll; NHS; Ntl Merit Ltr; PA Schlrs In Ed Awd 86; Choir Achvt Awd 86; Pres Clssrm 85; U Of PA; Mth.

PASQUALE, BRIAN P; Girard Clg; Philadelphia, PA; (Y); 6/28; Boy Scts; Exploring; Ski Clb; Varsity Clb; Rep Stu Cncl; Var L Bsbl; Var L Crs Cntry; Var L Socr; Var L Tennis; Var Wrstlng; Distngshd Chem Awd 85; Distngshd Drftg Awd 86; Good Sprtsmnshp Awd 85; FL Inst Of Tech; Aviatn Mgmt.

PASQUALE, LINDA; New Brighton HS; New Brighton, PA; (Y); 9/154; GAA; Varsity Clb; Chorus; Jazz Band; Yrbk Ed-Chief; Cheerleading; Hon Roll; Rotry Ldrshp Awd 85; Grove City Coll; Actg.

PASQUALIN, KRISSY; Hopewell HS; Aliquippa, PA; (Y); Latin Clb; Band; Chorus; Rep Jr Cls; Rep Stu Cncl; High Hon Roll; NHS; Concert Band; Mrchg Band.

PASQUALINI, CHRISTINA; Arch Bishop Kennedy HS; Conshohocken, PA; (Y); 30/197; Cmnty Wkr; Vllybl; Hon Roll; Schlrshp To Attnd Arch Bishop Kennedy 84.

PASQUARELLA, JACQUELINE; Merion Mercy Acad; Drexel Hill, PA; (Y); Intnl Clb; Pep Clb; Service Clb; Ed Yrbk Stf; Off Sr Cls; Stu Cncl; Im Bsktbl; Im Vllybl; Hon Roll; Pres Spanish Clb; Hstry.

PASQUARELLO, CONCETTA; Harry S Truman HS; Levittown, PA; (Y); 166/562; French Clb; Ski Clb; Stu Cncl; Bsktbl; Fld Hcky; Var Socr; Sftbl; Wt Lftg; High Hon Roll; Hon Roll; Dist Art Shw; Girls Var Sccr; Stu Cncl; Hmrm Rep; Temple; Elem Educ.

PASQUINELLI, PAULA; St Marys Area HS; Saint Marys, PA; (Y); 59/300; Dance Clb; Spanish Clb; Speech Tm; Variety Show; Hon Roll; Vldctrn Yth Ldrshp Pgm 86; 2nd Pl Spkr Yth Pgm 86; Snca Hghlnds Enrchmnt Pgm UPB 86; Penn ST U; Mktg.

PASQUINO, JENNIFER; Altoona Area HS; Altoona, PA; (Y); Dance Clb; Drama Clb; Hosp Aide; Key Clb; Spanish Clb; Drill Tm; School Musical; School Play; Stu Cncl; Pom Pon; Pres Phy Ftnss 84; Mount AL; Nrsng.

PASS, MELISSA; Moon SR HS; Corapolis, PA; (Y); Art Clb; French Clb; Key Clb; Socr; Sftbl; Swmmng; Vllybl; Hon Roll.

PASSERI, ANGIE; Canton HS; Canton, PA; (Y); Letterman Clb; Mrchg Band; Trs Soph Cls; Trs Jr Cls; Cheerleading; Coach Actv; Twrlr; Hon Roll; NHS.

PASSERINI, GABRIELLA; Sun Vally HS; Brookhaven, PA; (Y); 8/287; Sec Band; Sec Mrchg Band; Variety Show; Yrbk Stf; High Hon Roll; Hon Roll; Jr NHS; NHS; Prfct Atten Awd; Sons Italy Schlrshp 86; Christoher Columbus Mem Assoc Schlrshp Awd 86; Phyllis Jeanne Sach Meml Awd 86; Widener U; Acctg.

PASSIO, LORI; St Maria Goretti HS; Philadelphia, PA; (Y); 25/390; Church Yth Grp; French Clb; GAA; JA; Math Clb; Hon Roll; Jr NHS; Trs NHS; Ntl Soc Stu Olympd Awd 86; Achvmnt In Yth & The Amer Pol System Smnr 86; Philadelphia Coll Of Pharm.

PASSMORE, HOWARD JOSEPH; Neshaminy SR HS; Feasterville, PA; (Y); 301/702; Church Yth Grp; Computer Clb; Library Aide; ROTC; Church Choir; Drill Tm; Prfct Atten Awd; Amer Lgn Aux Awd & Mdl Schlstc Excllnc 86; Dept Army ROTC Awds & Mdl 10% Cls Outstndng Apprce & Prof; St Davids Coll; Cmptr Sci.

PASSMORE, WENDI; Moshannon Valley HS; Curwensville, PA; (Y); Spanish Clb; Varsity Clb; Band; Concert Band; Mrchg Band; JV Var Cheerleading; Hon Roll; Clrldg Spirit Awd 86; IN U Of PA; Phys Ther.

PASTERICK, GENE; Belle Vernon Area HS; Belle Vernon, PA; (Y); Church Yth Grp; Var L Ftbl; Wt Lftg; Hon Roll; NHS.

PASTERICK, MICHELLE; Mon Valley Catholic HS; Monessen, PA; (Y); 29/82; Band; Chorus; Drm Mjr(t).

PASTERNAK, KIMBERLY; South Allegheny HS; Elizabeth, PA; (S); 1/162; French Clb; Office Aide; Science Clb; Nwsp Stf; Yrbk Stf; Rep Stu Cncl; Powder Puff Ftbl; DAR Awd; High Hon Roll; Pres NHS; PA ST U.

PASTIERIK, JENNIFER; Valley HS; New Kensington, PA; (Y); 19/199; Concert Band; Rep Stu Cncl; Im Capt Cheerleading; Var Capt Sftbl; Var Tennis; Var Capt Twrlr; High Hon Roll; Hon Roll; Kiwanis Awd; NHS.

PASTOR JR, FRANK; Nroth Hills HS; Pittsburgh, PA; (S); 21/475; Church Yth Grp; Nwsp Sprt Ed; Ftbl; Var JV Socr; High Hon Roll; Hon Roll; NHS.

PASTOR III, MICHAEL J; Penn Hills HS; Pittsburgh, PA; (Y); 177/616; Computer Clb; Letterman Clb; Pres Library Aide; Ski Clb; Ed Lit Mag; Mgr L Diving; L Socr; Mgr L Swmmng; Ntl Merit SF; Stu Cncl; VIP Awd Excllnc Mangng Free Sprt Ltrylrt Magzne 86; OH-WESLEYAN U; Engl.

PASTORE, JOSEPH; Seneca Valley HS; Wexford, PA; (Y); Science Clb; Varsity Clb; School Play; Lit Mag; Var Badmtn; Var L Socr; Var L Trk; Hon Roll; Prfct Atten Awd; Penn ST U; Indstrl Engrng.

PASTORE, THERESA; Lower Moreland HS; Huntingdon Valley, PA; (S); 76/214; Library Aide; Office Aide; Teachers Aide; VICA; Stage Crew; Stu Advsnrs VICA 85-86; Hnr Roll 83-85; VICA Rep 84-85; IN U PA; Hear Impair.

PASTOREK, JOSEPH; Highlands HS; Brackenridge, PA; (Y); 43/274; Band; Jazz Band; L Golf; Hon Roll; Prfct Atten Awd; 10 Gold Awds 2 Brown Awds 81-86; Medal In WPIAL Golf Sect Witn An 81 86.

PASTORELLA, MICHELLE; Hazleton HS; Milnersville, PA; (Y); 135/400; Band; Concert Band; Mrchg Band; Lincoln Tech Inst; Elect Tech.

PASTUSZAK, ANDREW M; Father Judge HS; Philadelphia, PA; (S); 51/417; Boy Scts; Church Yth Grp; Cmnty Wkr; Computer Clb; German Clb; Yrbk Stf; Hon Roll; NHS; Cert Hnr Acadmcs 86; Biogst.

PASTUSZEK, PAM; North Pocono HS; Lake Ariel, PA; (Y); Drama Clb; Ski Clb; Chorus; School Musical; School Play; Sec Frsh Cls; Sec Frsh Cls; Pres Jr Cls; Rep Sr Cls; Capt Twrlr; 1st Plc Vcl Tlnt Shw; 2nd Plc Miss Mjrtt Mnth; Lang.

PASTUSZEK, TARA; Cardinal Ohara HS; Media, PA; (Y); 149/772; Aud/Vis; Lit Mag; Im Bsktbl; Im Vllybl; Cmnctns.

PATACKAS, LISA; John S Fine SR HS; Nanticoke, PA; (S); 4/242; Hosp Aide; Key Clb; Model UN; Speech Tm; Yrbk Stf; NHS; NEDT Awd; Scranton U; Pre Med.

PATASKI, HOLLY; Beth-Center HS; Vestaburg, PA; (Y); Art Clb; Drama Clb; GAA; Ski Clb; SADD; Varsity Clb; School Musical; School Play; Cheerleading; Sftbl; CA U; Crmnlgy.

PATEL, HITESH; Neshaminy HS; Levittown, PA; (Y); 4/748; Trs Computer Clb; Mathletes; High Hon Roll; Hon Roll; NHS; Ntl Merit SF; Rotary Awd; Presdntl Clsrm-Yng Amercns 86; 4th Pl-Regnl Comp Cntst 85; Med.

PATEL, JYOTIN; Upper Darby HS; Clifton Heights, PA; (Y); Boys Clb Am; Boy Scts; Cmnty Wkr; Yrbk Stf; Hon Roll; Perf Attndnce 83-86; Comm Svc Corps Awd Recgntn 84; Drexel U; Elect Engr.

PATEL, KIREN; Bishop O Hara HS; Dunmore, PA; (Y); 39/113; Boy Scts; Debate Tm; JA; NFL; Yrbk Phtg; Yrbk Stf; Bsbl; Bowling.

PATEL, SHAILESH M; La Salle College HS; Huntingdon Vly, PA; (Y); 1/240; Mathletes; Math Tm; Ed Yrbk Stf; Im Bsktbl; Var Ice Hcky; Im Socr; High Hon Roll; VP NHS; Ntl Merit Ltr; Val; Natl Soc Prof Engrs 86; Princpls Mdl Acad Excllnce 86; Stu Mnth 86; MIT; Engrng.

PATERNOSTER, CHRISTINA MARIE; James M Coughlin HS; Hudson, PA; (Y); 87/385; FBLA; Spanish Clb; Capt Pom Pon; Swmmng; Hon Roll; NHS; Mansfield U; Soc Wrk.

PATERRA, SCOTT A; South Park HS; Pittsburgh, PA; (Y); 25/195; Church Yth Grp; Computer Clb; Trk; High Hon Roll; Hon Roll; Schlrshp Awd 86; Svc Awd 86; U Of S FL; Engr.

PATRENE, DANA; Peters Township HS; Mc Murray, PA; (S); Ski Clb; Rep Stu Cncl; Var JV Bsktbl; Var Cheerleading; Swmmng; Var Trk; Hon Roll; Penn ST; Accntng.

PATRESS, MICHELE; Trinity HS; Washington, PA; (Y); Art Clb; High Hon Roll; Hon Roll; Band; Mrchg Band; Symp Band; Nwsp Phtg; CA U; Art Thrpy.

PATRICIO, BOBBY; Wyoming Valley West HS; Swoyersville, PA; (Y); Im Bsktbl; JV Ftbl; Var Trk; Im Vllybl; PA St; Vet-Med.

PATRICK, ANN; Seneca Valley HS; Evans City, PA; (Y); VP Chrmn Church Yth Grp; Math Tm; Trs Thesps; School Musical; School Play; Stage Crew; High Hon Roll; Hon Roll; NHS; Bst Prop Prsn Awd 84-85; Bst Snd Prsn Awd 85-86; Bst Femle Cameo Awd 85-86; Hlth.

PATRICK, KENNETH G; Greensburg-Salem HS; Greensburg, PA; (Y); 1/325; VP French Clb; JV Var Ftbl; Var L Trk; Wt Lftg; Cit Awd; DAR Awd; French Hon Soc; High Hon Roll; VP NHS; Ntl Merit SF; KDKA Tv Extra Effort Awd 85; All Conf Offnsve & Defnsve Tackle 85; Cmmnwalth PA Cert Merit 85; Arch.

PATRICK, KRISHNI; St Francis Acad; Bethlehem, PA; (Y); 4/21; Office Aide; Pres Service Clb; Chorus; School Musical; Nwsp Rptr; Pres Soph Cls; Pres Jr Cls; Hon Roll; Church Yth Grp; Pep Clb; 2nd Pl Frnch Rectn Comptn 84-85; Diocescan Choir 85-86; 4th Pl Frnch Perf Comptn 84-85.

PATRICK, LYNN; Chapel Christian Schl; Belle Vernon, PA; (S); 1/6; FCA; Band; Nwsp Stf; Yrbk Ed-Chief; Rep Frsh Cls; Sec Soph Cls; Stu Cncl; JV Capt Cheerleading; High Hon Roll; Princeton U; Atty.

PATRICK, PAM; Moshannon Valley HS; Smithmill, PA; (Y); Church Yth Grp; Central PA Bus Schl; Ct Rep.

PATRONE, MICHELE; Saint Maria Goretti HS; Philadelphia, PA; (Y); Camera Clb; Cmnty Wkr; Chorus; Church Choir; School Musical; Nwsp Phtg; High Hon Roll; Hon Roll; Prfct Atten Awd; Temple; Pre-Law.

PATRONIE, KIMBERLY; Canon Mc Millan HS; Canonsburg, PA; (Y); Latin Clb; Chorus; Hon Roll; Bus Mgmt.

PATSIGA, LYNN; Freedom Area HS; New Brighton, PA; (Y); 6/165; 4-H; Math Tm; Ski Clb; Spanish Clb; Yrbk Sprt Ed; Var Cheerleading; 4-H Awd; High Hon Roll; NHS; Top Stu Hnrs Engl 84-85; Engl Awd 85-86; Spn III & IV Awd 85-86; Chatham Coll; Biochem.

PATSY, JOHN E; New Brighton Area HS; New Brighton, PA; (Y); 1/154; Am Leg Boys St; Computer Clb; Varsity Clb; Nwsp Rptr; Stu Cncl; L Golf; Cit Awd; High Hon Roll; Pres Schlr; Val; Rotry Boy Mth 86; U Of Pittsburgh; Phrmcy.

PATTERSON, CARLA; Purchase Line HS; Clymer, PA; (Y); Church Yth Grp; Spanish Clb; Chorus; High Hon Roll; Amer Lgn Auxlry Awd 84; Bus Adm.

PATTERSON, CINDY; Cowanesque Valley HS; Westfield, PA; (Y); FFA; Vllybl; Hon Roll.

PATTERSON, DAWN; Penn Trafford HS; Irwin, PA; (Y); Church Yth Grp; Chorus; Church Choir; SPRTS Dir.

PATTERSON, ERIC; Wellsboro SR HS; Wellsboro, PA; (Y); 1/141; Chess Clb; Model UN; Var Bsktbl; Var Ftbl; JV Trk; High Hon Roll; NHS; Ntl Merit SF; Rotary Awd; Church Yth Grp; Ntl Mth Exm 86; Wst Pt USMA; Prfsnl Army Ofcr.

PATTERSON, GINA; Elizabeth-Forward HS; Monongahela, PA; (Y); Chorus; School Musical; NHS; Spanish Clb; High Hon Roll; 1st Pl Wnnr Natl Soc Arts & Ltrs Ballet 85; Gov Schl Arts Scholar 84-85; Briansky Ballet Scholar 85.

PATTERSON, JOAN; Richland HS; Gibsonia, PA; (Y); 5/190; Church Yth Grp; French Clb; NFL; Pres Speech Tm; Sec Band; Jazz Band; Mrchg Band; School Musical; Yrbk Phtg; High Hon Roll; Allegheny Vly Dist Band 84 & 86; PA Speech Finlst 85 & 86; PMEA Dist Band 84; Eng.

PATTERSON VI, JOHN J; West Perry SR HS; New Bloomfield, PA; (Y); 1/220; Quiz Bowl; Mrchg Band; Yrbk Ed-Chief; Socr; High Hon Roll; NHS; Ntl Merit SF; Amer Lg Schl Awd 83; Rep HOBY Ldrshp Sem 85; US Naval Acad Summr Sci Sem 86; USAF; Aviatn.

PATTERSON, JOHN W; Laurel HS; New Castle, PA; (Y); 12/104; Boy Scts; 4-H; FFA; Band; Concert Band; Jazz Band; L Mrchg Band; Pep Band; Hon Roll; Pres Schlr; Helen Engl Memrl Schlrshp 86; Grove Cty Coll Fnancl Aid 86; Pa ST Grant Frsh Appalachian Schlrshp 86; Grove Cty Coll; Mech Engrng.

PATTERSON, KELLY; Kiski Area SR HS; Leechburg, PA; (Y); Pres VICA; Chorus; Stu Cncl; High Hon Roll; Hon Roll; Hnr Roll Hgh Hnrs 84-86; 2nd & 3rd Pl VICA Elctrcty Plqs 85-86; Yngstwn ST U; Elctrcl Engrng.

PATTERSON, KELLY; Mechanicsburg Area SR HS; Mechanicsburg, PA; (Y); 72/299; Debate Tm; NFL; Speech Tm; School Play; Rep Stu Cncl; Hon Roll; Vrln Corp Schlrshp 86; Drexel U; Chmcl Engrng.

PATTERSON, KENNETH; Marion Center Area HS; Indiana, PA; (Y); Letterman Clb; Varsity Clb; VICA; Wrstlng; High Hon Roll; Prfct Atten Awd; Pres Of Applnc Repr 85-86; 2nd Pl PA ST Vica Comptn 85-86.

PATTERSON, KIM; Reynolds HS; Greenville, PA; (Y); 54/160; German Clb; Latin Clb; Math Clb; Office Aide; Science Clb; Flag Corp; Yrbk Stf; U Pittsburgh; Phys Thrpy.

PATTERSON, LINDALE; Belle Vernon Area HS; Belle Vernon, PA; (Y); VP Church Yth Grp; Hosp Aide; Capt Color Guard; Pres Jr Cls; Pres Sr Cls; Pres Stu Cncl; L Mgr(s); Powder Puff Ftbl; High Hon Roll; NHS; Frnch Stu Of Mnth 86; Chrmn Of Stu Forum 86-87; Pre Law.

PATTERSON, LORI; Northwest Area HS; Hunlock Creek, PA; (Y); 29/108; Drama Clb; Hosp Aide; SADD; Chorus; School Musical; Variety Show; Hon Roll; PA ST U.

PATTERSON, MELISSA; Western Beaver HS; Industry, PA; (Y); Computer Clb; Office Aide; Chorus; Stu Cncl; Bowling; Cheerleading; Robert Norris Clg; Ad Bus Spclt.

PATTERSON, MICHELLE; Fort Le Boeuf HS; Erie, PA; (Y); 39/169; Sec Church Yth Grp; Pres Girl Scts; Model UN; Chorus; Church Choir; Nwsp Stf; Sec Stu Cncl; God Cntry Awd; Hon Roll; Stu Cncl Achvt Awd 85-86; Gannon; Socl Wrk.

PATTERSON, RONAE; Washington HS; Washington, PA; (S); French Clb; Key Clb; Letterman Clb; Library Aide; Varsity Clb; Rep Frsh Cls; Trs Soph Cls; Pres Jr Cls; Stu Cncl; Var Capt Cheerleading; Corp Law.

PATTERSON, SHARON; St Maria Goretti HS; Philadelphia, PA; (Y); Church Yth Grp; Dance Clb; Church Choir; Color Guard; Drill Tm; Stage Crew.

PATTERSON, TAMARA; South Williamsport HS; S Williamsport, PA; (Y); 10/140; Library Aide; Spanish Clb; Chorus; Nwsp Rptr; Yrbk Rptr; Yrbk Stf; L Var Tennis; Im Vllybl; NHS; Trck 82; Acclrtd Math, Sci 82; Marine Bio.

PATTERSON, VALERIE; Coatesville Area SR HS; Coatesville, PA; (Y); Girl Scts; Hon Roll; Prfct Atten Awd; Phys Thrpst.

PATTON, ANDREW; Center Area HS; Aliquippa, PA; (Y); OH Valle Coll.

PATTON, BILL; Tunkhannock Area HS; Noxen, PA; (Y); Cmnty Wkr; FFA; Bsbl; Bsktbl; Hon Roll; Gftd Stu Pgm 84-86; Pilot.

PATTON, BRADLEY; Wyoming Valley West HS; Luzerne, PA; (Y); French Clb; Radio Clb; Stage Crew; Im Vllybl; High Hon Roll; Hon Roll; NHS; Pre-Law.

PATTON, CARA; Lakeview HS; Sandy Lake, PA; (S); 8/118; Sec Intnl Clb; Library Aide; Band; Chorus; Concert Band; Mrchg Band; Pep Band; School Play; Yrbk Stf; NHS; U Of PA.

PATTON, CHRIS; Wyoming Valley West HS; Kingston, PA; (S); 50/320; Letterman Clb; Ski Clb; Nwsp Stf; Trs Soph Cls; Bsbl; Diving; Golf; Swmmng; High Hon Roll; Hon Roll.

PATTON, HEATHER; Tyrone Area HS; Tyrone, PA; (Y); 14/182; FBLA; Key Clb; Latin Clb; Chorus; Secy.

PATTON, ROBYN; Nazareth Acad; Philadelphia, PA; (Y); Rep French Clb; Pep Clb; Var Bowling; Coach Actv; La Salle U; Bus Adm.

PATTON, TERA; Lakeview HS; Sandy Lake, PA; (S); Sec Intnl Clb; Library Aide; Band; Chorus; Concert Band; Mrchg Band; Pep Band; School Play; Nwsp Ed-Chief; NHS.

PATTON, TYRONE; Girard College HS; Philadelphia, PA; (Y); 15/30; Drama Clb; Letterman Clb; Teachers Aide; Band; Church Choir; Nwsp Stf; Yrbk Stf; Sec Sr Cls; Mgr(s); Hon Roll; Almni Stu Awd 86; Voc Essy Awd 86; Westchester U; Elem Educ.

PATTON, VAUGHN; Ford City JR SR HS; Ford City, PA; (Y); 34/152; Church Yth Grp; Hosp Aide; Spanish Clb; SADD; Chorus; Nwsp Stf; Rep Jr Cls; Vllybl; High Hon Roll; Hon Roll; Air Force; Physcl Thrpst.

PATYNSKI, WALTER M; Milton Area SR HS; Milton, PA; (Y); 2/226; Varsity Clb; Rep Stu Cncl; Bsbl; Bsktbl; Var Ftbl; Cit Awd; Hon Roll; NHS; Opt Clb Awd; All ST Hon Ment Bsktbll 84-86; All Leag Ue 1st Tm Ftbll 84-86; Pres Acdmc Fit Awd 86; PA ST U; Sci.

PAUCHNIK, TOM; Burgettstown Area JR SR HS; Atlasburg, PA; (Y); Ski Clb; Spanish Clb; Hon Roll; PA ST U; Elec Engrng.

PAUCKE, JON; Williamsport Area HS; Williamsport, PA; (Y); Letterman Clb; Varsity Clb; Var L Bsbl; Im Bsktbl; JV Golf; JV Swmmng; Im Vllybl; Im Wt Lftg; Hon Roll; Engrng.

PAUL, DIANNA; St Hubert HS; Philadelphia, PA; (Y); 79/367; Hon Roll; Prfct Atten Awd.

PAUL, FREDERICK; Northeast Catholic HS; Philadelphia, PA; (Y); 119/362; Band; Concert Band; Mrchg Band; Bowling; Penn ST U; Astro Physcs.

PAUL, LISA; Berlin Brothersvalley HS; Garrett, PA; (Y); 10/87; Sec FBLA; Band; Church Choir; Color Guard; Concert Band; Twrlr; Hon Roll; NHS; Ldrshp Clrgrd 86; Secy.

PAUL, MIKE; Bethleham Center SR HS; Marianna, PA; (Y); 57/158; 4-H; Ski Clb; VICA; Spartan Aviation; Pilot.

PAUL, MITCHELL; Lower Moreland HS; Huntingdon Valley, PA; (S); Boy Scts; Cmnty Wkr; FBLA; Key Clb; Rep Stu Cncl; JV Bsbl; JV Bsktbl; Im Diving; JV Ftbl; Hon Roll; Asian Cult Sem 86; Stu Forum 85-87; Doctor.

PAUL, RAYMOND; Shickshinny HS; Shickshinny, PA; (Y); 12/108; Computer Clb; Nwsp Phtg; Yrbk Phtg; Yrbk Stf; High Hon Roll; NHS; Kodak Medallion Of Excllnc-Photo 86; Gold Achvt Key 86; Luzerne Cnty CC; Telecomm.

PAUL, STEPHANIE; Upper Dauphin Area HS; Lykens, PA; (Y); 8/126; JA; Varsity Clb; Band; Jazz Band; Mrchg Band; Rep Stu Cncl; Var Sftbl; High Hon Roll; Hon Roll; NHS; Cert Achvt Sci 85-86; S E PA Sect Am Chem Soc Cert Merit 86; Cert Achvt Lebanon Vly Coll-Chem 86; Penn ST U; Chem Engrng.

PAUL, TAMMY ANN; Mt Carmel Area JR SR HS; Mt Carmel, PA; (Y); Pres FNA; Hosp Aide; Key Clb; Latin Clb; Library Aide; Pep Clb; Q&S; Nwsp Stf; Stu Cncl; Stat Bsktbl; Geisinger Schl/Nrsng; RN.

PAUL, TINA; Mt Carmel Area JR SR HS; Mt Carmel, PA; (Y); FTA; Key Clb; Latin Clb; Concert Band; Mrchg Band; Stu Cncl; JV Bsktbl; Var L Swmmng; Var L Trk; Hon Roll; Legisltv Communty Svc Awd 86; Speech Pathlgy.

PAUL, TRACEY L; Hatboro Harsham HS; Horsham, PA; (Y); 7/300; Church Yth Grp; Sec Trs Model UN; Sec Frsh Cls; VP Soph Cls; Sec Jr Cls; Sec Sr Cls; Rep Stu Cncl; Var Fld Hcky; Var Lcrss; Cit Awd; Daniel Boone Fndtn Awd 86; Lehigh U; Comp Sci.

PAULAT, ROD; Plum SR HS; Pittsburgh, PA; (Y); 7/439; JA; Ski Clb; Varsity Clb; Symp Band; Var L Bsbl; High Hon Roll; NHS; Ntl Merit Schol; PHEAA Cert Of Merit 86; U Of Pittsburgh Prvsts Schlrshp; U Of Pittsburgh; Biochem.

PAULES, JONATHAN W; Central York SR HS; York, PA; (Y); Boys Clb Am; Church Yth Grp; Hosp Aide; Political Wkr; Chorus; Church Choir; School Musical; Var Ftbl; Trk; Poli Sci.

PAULIN, JAMIE LYNN; Hopewell HS; Aliquippa, PA; (S); 16/290; AFS; Exploring; Sec French Clb; Chorus; Drill Tm; Stu Cncl; Var Pom Pon; Var L Trk; High Hon Roll; NHS; Chem.

PAULINE, KENNETH; Elk G Christian HS; St Marys, PA; (Y); 29/97; Trs Band; Concert Band; Jazz Band; Mrchg Band; Pep Band; Bowling; High Hon Roll; Hon Roll; Pres Acdmc Ftns Awd, Semper Fidelis Awd US Marine Corps Mus Exclnce 86; Art Awd-Ceramics; Triangle Tech-Du Bois; Drftng.

PAULING, DIANE; Selinsgrove Area HS; Selingsgrove, PA; (Y); Drama Clb; Spanish Clb; Thesps; Chorus; Flag Corp; School Musical; School Play; Cheerleading; Hon Roll; Church Yth Grp; Dstct Chrs 86; Cmmnctns.

PAULOVICH, DANIELLE; Western Beaver HS; Midland, PA; (Y); JA; Red Cross Aide; Band; Chorus; Concert Band; Mrchg Band; Symp Band; Stat Bsktbl; JV Cheerleading; Hon Roll; Psychlgy.

PAULSHOCK, JOAN; Weatherly HS; Weatherly, PA; (Y); Art Clb; Church Yth Grp; FBLA; FHA; Library Aide; Cheerleading; Hon Roll; Allentown Business Schl; Fshn.

PAULSON, DENISE; Cardinal O Hara HS; Glen Mills, PA; (Y); Office Aide; PAVAS; Spanish Clb; Chorus; School Musical; School Play; Yrbk Stf; Rep Jr Cls; Hon Roll; NHS; Music.

PAULSON, DREW; Delaware County Christian HS; Berwyn, PA; (Y); Church Yth Grp; Civic Clb; Cmnty Wkr; Chorus; Var L Bsbl; Var L Bsktbl; Var L Socr; Tennis; Dstngshd Christn HS Stu 86; Natl Hnr Roll 86; U Of VA; Engrng.

PAULSON, TIMOTHY; Tunkhannock Area HS; Tunkhannock, PA; (S); 10/280; Church Yth Grp; Spanish Clb; JV Bsktbl; Golf; JV Trk; Hon Roll; NHS.

PAUTZ, DONALD; Cowanesque Valley HS; Westfield, PA; (S); 11/94; Boy Scts; Church Yth Grp; Drama Clb; Letterman Clb; Band; Mrchg Band; Var Bsktbl; Var Ftbl; Var Trk; High Hon Roll; Eagle Scout 85; Natl Merit Sci Awd 84-85; Engnr.

PAVALONE, JOE; Carbondale Area JR SR HS; Carbondale, PA; (S); 8/140; English Clb; FBLA; Letterman Clb; Ski Clb; Spanish Clb; Varsity Clb; Yrbk Stf; Pres Stu Cncl; Var Bsbl; L Var Bsktbl; Trk Gld & Diamnd Clb 83-86; Wm Mc Donnough Awd; Athl, Acad, & Cmmnty Ldrshp Awd 85-86; Crmnl Jstce.

PAVAO, TRACY; Chief Logan HS; Lewistown, PA; (Y); 2/175; Church Yth Grp; Trs Pep Clb; Spanish Clb; Sec Varsity Clb; Pres Soph Cls; Pres Jr Cls; Var Cheerleading; Var Score Keeper; High Hon Roll; NHS.

PAVE, MARK; Catasauqua HS; N Catasauqua, PA; (Y); 37/142; Lit Mag; Stu Cncl; Var Bsktbl; Bus Mngmnt.

PAVELEK III, MICHAEL; Hershey HS; Hershey, PA; (Y); Band; Church Choir; Concert Band; Jazz Band; Mrchg Band; Orch; School Musical; Trk; Cit Awd; Penn ST U; Bus.

PAVELEK, TRACY; Beaver HS; Beaver, PA; (Y); 15/177; Sec Key Clb; Band; Concert Band; Drm Mjr(t); Mrchg Band; School Musical; Rep Stu Cncl; JV Bsktbl; L Sftbl; Hon Roll; Acad Awd Brinquet Top 10 Pct Of Class 85; Bus Mngt.

PAVELKO, LISA; Northern Cambria HS; Barnesboro, PA; (Y); Church Yth Grp; Drama Clb; Band; Hst Concert Band; Mrchg Band; Trk; High Hon Roll; Hon Roll; NHS; Schlrshp Elizabeth Stewart 86; Typng Awd 84; 1st Pl Wnd Pntng Cntst 84; Blgy Tchr.

PAVELL, SUZANNE; West Hazelton JR SR HS; W Hazleton, PA; (Y); Sec FBLA; Hon Roll; Comp.

PAVIA, DEBRA; New Castle SR HS; New Castle, PA; (S); 25/253; Computer Clb; SADD; Hon Roll; Psychlgy.

PAVICK, CATHY; Waynesburg Central HS; Waynesburg, PA; (Y); 55/209; Chess Clb; Cmnty Wkr; French Clb; Hosp Aide; Hon Roll; Rotary Awd; Yllw Blt Krate 85-86; Waynesburg Coll; Intl Stds.

PAVIDUS, GINA; West Catholic Girls HS; Philadelphia, PA; (Y); 4/245; Hosp Aide; Orch; School Play; Soph Cls; Jr Cls; High Hon Roll; NHS; Cntnnl Schlrshp 86; Bus & Engl Awds 84-86; Pierce JC; Med Sec.

PAVLICK, ALICIA; Freeland HS; Freeland, PA; (Y); FBLA; Hosp Aide; Spanish Clb; Chorus; Color Guard; Drill Tm; Flag Corp; School Play; Yrbk Stf; Hon Roll; Geisinger Med Ctr; Nrsng.

PAVLICK, JEFF; Keystone Oaks HS; Pittsburgh, PA; (Y); 67/321; VA Polytech; Ag Engrng.

PAVLICK, ROBERT; West Hazleton HS; W Hazleton, PA; (Y); Church Yth Grp; JV Var Bsbl; JV Bsktbl; Hon Roll.

PAVLIK, ANDREA; Norwin SR HS; N Huntingdon, PA; (Y); German Clb; Math Clb; SADD; Band; Chorus; Church Choir; Concert Band; Mrchg Band; Hon Roll; Jr NHS; Dickinson Coll; Physcs.

PAVLIK, BETH; Spring-Ford SR HS; Mont Clare, PA; (S); 20/258; French Clb; Radio Clb; Off Frsh Cls; Off Soph Cls; Off Jr Cls; Stu Cncl; Var Sftbl; Var Tennis; Hon Roll; NHS; MVP Tennis 85.

PAVLIK, HOLLY; Bethel Park SR HS; Bethel Park, PA; (Y); Church Yth Grp; DECA; Pres NFL; School Musical; Wheeling Coll; Bus Mgmt.

PAVLIN, TERRENCE; Sharpsville Area HS; Sharpsville, PA; (Y); Church Yth Grp; FCA; Spanish Clb; Nwsp Rptr; JV Var Bsktbl; Im Crs Cntry; Var L Trk; Hon Roll; Elect Engr.

PAVLOCAK, JEFF; Mt Pleasant SR HS; Mt Pleasant, PA; (Y); 4-H; German Clb; Ski Clb; Band; Concert Band; Mrchg Band; Pep Band; Yrbk Stf; Wrstlng; Music.

PAVLOVCAK, DONNA; Council Rock HS; Churchville, PA; (Y); Girl Scts; East Straudsberg; Educ.

PAVLOWSKI, THERESA; Bishop O Hara HS; Dickson, PA; (Y); Drama Clb; French Clb; Latin Clb; Science Clb; School Musical; School Play; Var Capt Sftbl; Hon Roll; Prfct Atten Awd; Perfct Attndnc Awd 85-86; Sftbll All Str Southrn Divisn 86; Marywood Coll; Speech Ther.

PAVOLIC, CASSANDRA J; Coatesville Area SR HS; Coatesville, PA; (Y); Drama Clb; Chorus; Nwsp Phtg; Stu Cncl; Capt Cheerleading; Coach Actv; Gym; Hon Roll; Mrchg Band; Nwsp Stf; Psych Club-Treas 85-86; Homecmng Qn 85-86; Dance.

PAVTIS, LAURIE; Belle Vernon Area HS; Belle Vernon, PA; (Y); Church Yth Grp; Girl Scts; Pep Clb; Ski Clb; Drm & Bgl; Mrchg Band; Variety Show; VP Soph Cls; Sec Jr Cls; JV Powder Puff Ftbl; Miss Majorette Of East 82; Phys Ther.

PAVUCHAK, ANN; West Mifflin Area HS; West Mifflin, PA; (Y); FBLA; Key Clb; SADD; Concert Band; Soph Cls; Jr Cls; Stu Cncl; Cheerleading; Co-Capt Pom Pon; ACE-PGM Advncd Stu 83-86; Bus.

PAVUK, LYNN; Mt Pleasant Area HS; Mt Pleasant, PA; (Y); German Clb; Red Cross Aide; Spanish Clb; SADD; Chorus; Rep Frsh Cls; Sec Soph Cls; Sec Jr Cls; Sec Sr Cls; Sec Stu Cncl; Stdnt Cncl Awd, Viking Rcgntn Awd 84; Penn ST U; Nrsg.

PAWK, LAURA; Knoch HS; Renfrew, PA; (Y); Pep Clb; Chorus; Madrigals; School Musical; Swing Chorus; Sec Frsh Cls; Sec VP Stu Cncl; Var Cheerleading; Var Golf; Outstndng Stu Govt Awd 87; Chrldng Ltr 87; Chorus Ltr 87.

PAWLAK, CAROL; Shaler Area HS; Pittsburgh, PA; (Y); 37/532; Ski Clb; Variety Show; Yrbk Stf; Score Keeper; Hon Roll; NHS; Penn ST; Ag Bus Mgmt.

PAWLIK, MAGDALENA; Saucon Valley SR HS; Hellertown, PA; (Y); French Clb; Library Aide; Spanish Clb; SADD; Band; Church Choir; Concert Band; Mrchg Band; Rep Stu Cncl; Jr NHS; Cert Achvmnt 84-85; Princeton U; Arch.

PAWLING, MARK; Warwick SR HS; Lititz, PA; (S); 92/250; Var Crs Cntry; Star Grnhnd Awd FFA 83-84; Star Elctrcn FFA 84-85.

PAWLOSKY, MICHAEL; Canon-Mc Millan SR Schl; Canonsburg, PA; (Y); Cmnty Wkr; Letterman Clb; Ski Clb; Varsity Clb; Bsbl; Ftbl; Golf; Swmmng; Wrstlng; Hon Roll; U TN; Mech Engrng.

PAWLOWSKI, KATHERINE; John S Fine HS; Nanticoke, PA; (Y); 30/300; Church Yth Grp; Band; Chorus; Concert Band; Mrchg Band; Nwsp Rptr; Yrbk Stf; High Hon Roll; NHS; Dist Chorus 85-86; PA ST U; CPA.

PAXSON, PATRICIA; Morrisville HS; Morrisville, PA; (Y); Church Yth Grp; FBLA; GAA; Church Choir; Var Bowling; Var L Sftbl; Hon Roll; NHS; Outstndng Achvt Awd Engl 86; Shippensburg U; Bus.

PAYNE, BRADLEY; Laurel Valley JR SR HS; Bolivar, PA; (Y); Science Clb; Varsity Clb; Mgr Bsbl; Stat Bsktbl; Ftbl; Hon Roll; Ntl Merit SF.

PAYNE, CELESTE; Central Dauphin E HS; Harrisburg, PA; (Y); 6/271; Am Leg Aux Girls St; Band; Chorus; Orch; Trs Stu Cncl; High Hon Roll; NHS; Acad Stu Of Mnth 84 & 86; Smmr Schlrs Pre-Med Curric Washington & Lee U 86; Pre-Med.

PAYNE, CHRISTINE; The Christan Acad; Chester, PA; (Y); Church Yth Grp; Drama Clb; Office Aide; PAVAS; School Play; Bsktbl; Outstndg Stu Awd 81-85; Pfct Attndnc Awd 81-85; PA ST U; Accounting.

PAYNE, DAVID; Danville Area HS; Danville, PA; (Y); 4/208; Church Yth Grp; Debate Tm; Key Clb; Latin Clb; NFL; Speech Tm; Yrbk Stf; JV Bsktbl; L Trk; High Hon Roll.

PAYNE JR, JAMES L; Christian School Of York; Dover, PA; (S); Church Yth Grp; Chorus; Concert Band; School Play; Pres Sr Cls; Rep Stu Cncl; Trk; Hon Roll; Ntl Band Awd 85; Christian Lib Arts Coll; Bus Ad.

PAYNE, JOHN; Father Judge HS; Philadelphia, PA; (S); 2/361; Cmnty Wkr; Hosp Aide; Mathletes; Hon Roll; NHS; Ntl Merit Ltr; Finance.

PAYNE, JOSEPH R; Everett Area HS; Breezewood, PA; (Y); Aud/Vis; Cmnty Wkr; Computer Clb; Trs Spanish Clb; SADD; Varsity Clb; Trs Stu Cncl; L Bsktbl; L Golf; L Tennis; Mst Imprvd Tennis Plyr 85; Outstndg Tennis Plyr 85-86; Delg ST & Ntl Stdnt Cncl Mtngs 85-86; Penn ST; Telecommunications.

PAYNE, KIMBERLY; Rochester JR SR HS; Rochester, PA; (Y); Church Yth Grp; French Clb; Ski Clb; Chorus; Variety Show; Trk; NHS; Pres Schlr; Jr NHS; Outstndng Achvt Frnch 83-85; U Pittsburgh; Gud Cncslr.

PAYNE, SANDRA K; Hempfield Area SR HS; Greensburg, PA; (Y); 1/657; Drama Clb; Red Cross Aide; Chorus; School Play; Yrbk Bus Mgr; Stat Wrstlng; French Hon Soc; NHS; Rotary Awd; Val; Consldtd Gas Trnsmsn Corp Schlrsp 86-90; Greensburg Fndtn 86; Carnegie-Mellon U Mrt Schlrsp 86; Carnegie-Mellon U; Chem Engrng.

PAYNE, URSULA; Union Area JR SR HS; New Castle, PA; (Y); 3/66; Church Yth Grp; Spanish Clb; Church Choir; Concert Band; Drill Tm; School Musical; Rep Stu Cncl; Bsktbl; Trk; NHS; PA Gvnrs Schl Of Arts 86; 1st Trck Trpl Jmpr 86; 2nd Pl Trpl Jmp PA PIAA ST Mt 86; Math.

PAZDERSKI, HOLLY; Warren Area HS; Warren, PA; (Y); Church Yth Grp; Cmnty Wkr; French Clb; Hosp Aide; Office Aide; Chorus; Timer; High Hon Roll; Hon Roll; Jr NHS; Psych.

PCHOLINSKY, LYNN; Sacred Heart HS; Pittsburgh, PA; (Y); Church Yth Grp; Spanish Clb; Yrbk Stf; Var Cheerleading; High Hon Roll; Hon Roll; Pre-Law.

PCSOLYAR, CHAD; Quigley HS; Baden, PA; (Y); Art Clb; Aud/Vis; Church Yth Grp; Stage Crew; Yrbk Stf; Tennis; Trk; JC Awd; FL Inst Tech; Aviatn Mgmt.

PEACE, RICHARD; Punxsutawney Area SR HS; Punxsutawney, PA; (Y); Elec Tech.

PEACE, TAMMY; Homer Center JR SR HS; Indiana, PA; (Y); 23/116; French Clb; FBLA; Library Aide; Varsity Clb; Chorus; School Play; Yrbk Stf; Sftbl; Hon Roll; Jr NHS; Home Econ Awd 86; U Pittsburgh; Psychlgy.

PEACE, TRACY; Dubois Area HS; Dubois, PA; (Y); Church Yth Grp; Intnl Clb; Chorus; Cheerleading; Sftbl; Hon Roll; IN U Of PA; Nrsng.

PEACOCK, ROBERT; Tunkhannock HS; Tunkhannock, PA; (S); 34/280; Chess Clb; Spanish Clb; JV Bsktbl; Var L Tennis; Hon Roll; Susque Hanna U; Bus Admin.

PEAK, SAM; New Castle SR HS; New Castle, PA; (S); 16/253; Band; Concert Band; Vllybl; NHS; Duquese; Pre-Law.

PEAK, SHELLEY; New Castle SR HS; New Castle, PA; (S); 21/253; AFS; Church Yth Grp; Spanish Clb; Stu Cncl; Hon Roll; Slippery Rock U; Elem Educ.

PEARCE, ANEYSHA; Fox Chapel HS; Pittsburgh, PA; (Y); 5/380; Cmnty Wkr; Hosp Aide; Key Clb; Chorus; JV Cheerleading; Cit Awd; High Hon Roll; NHS; J Alfred Wilner Scholar 86; Top 20 Schlrs Awd 86; PA ST U; Pre-Med.

PEARCE, GLENN; Wm Allen HS; Allentown, PA; (Y); 42/678; Cmnty Wkr; French Clb; Intnl Clb; Key Clb; Model UN; Stu Cncl; JV Var Socr; French Hon Soc; Hon Roll; NHS; 7th Pl AATF 84-85; Northwestern U; Intrnal Bus.

PEARCE, KENT V; Central York HS; York, PA; (Y); Am Leg Boys St; Boy Scts; Varsity Clb; Nwsp Stf; Rep Frsh Cls; Rep Stu Cncl; Var Capt Bsktbl; Var Cmnty Wkr2; Hon Roll; Bus.

PEARCE, LAURA; Bellwood Antis HS; Tyrone, PA; (Y); 27/128; FHA; Hosp Aide; Red Cross Aide; Spanish Clb; Sec SADD; VICA; Band; Mrchg Band; JV Var Fld Hcky; Sftbl; Vo-Tech JR Cls Pres 84-85; Vo-Tech SR Cls Sec 85-86; Nrsng.

PEARCE, SHEILA; Punxsutawney Area HS; Rossiter, PA; (Y); French Clb; Hosp Aide; Science Clb; Hon Roll; NHS; Prfct Atten Awd; IN U Of Penn; Tchr.

PEARL, JIM; Geibel HS; Connellsville, PA; (Y); Camera Clb; SADD; Bsbl; Bsktbl; Bowling; Ftbl; Ftbl All Conf 84-85; Bsktbl All Cnty MVP 84-85; Ftbl All Cnty, Bstkbl All Cnty, All Dist & All Sectn.

PEARMAN, TIMOTHY; Emmaus HS; Wescosville, PA; (Y); Key Clb; SADD; Chorus; JV Var Bsbl; Hon Roll; Jr NHS; NHS.

PEARN, DEANA L; Northampton Area SR HS; Northampton, PA; (Y); #16 In Class; AFS; Girl Scts; Hosp Aide; Leo Clb; Chorus; Church Choir; Color Guard; Nwsp Ed-Chief; Sftbl; High Hon Roll; Kutztown U; Math.

PEARSON, GUENTHER; Brookville Area HS; Brookville, PA; (S); 15/150; Boy Scts; Pres German Clb; Hon Roll; NHS; 1st Govs Schl Intl Studies 84; Ger-Amer Prtnrshp Prgrm 85; IN U; Bus Adm.

PEARSON, JANICE; Harbor Creek HS; Erie, PA; (Y); 5/204; Capt Color Guard; Yrbk Stf; Sec Frsh Cls; Sec Soph Cls; Sec Jr Cls; Sec Sr Cls; Rep Stu Cncl; JV Stat Bsktbl; L Trk; Pres NHS; Ednbr U Hnrs Schlrshp; Stu Choice Cmncmnt Spkr; Grad Awds; Edinboro U PA; Art Ed.

PEARSON, LISA; Hempfield Area HS; Jeannette, PA; (Y); Church Yth Grp; Pep Clb; Spanish Clb; Church Choir; High Hon Roll; Hon Roll; Jr NHS.

PEARSON, LORI; Benton JR SR HS; Orangeville, PA; (Y); 13/54; Church Yth Grp; Keywanettes; Ski Clb; Teachers Aide; Stage Crew; Stat Bsktbl; Var Sftbl; Hon Roll; NHS; Natl Spn Cont 84; Century 21 Awd Typng 85; Century 21 Awd Acctng 86; Oral Roberts U; Mid East Studs.

PEARSON, MICHELE; Bensalem HS; Bensalem, PA; (Y); High Hon Roll; Hon Roll; Bus Sec.

PEARSON, SCOTT; Ford City HS; Russell, PA; (Y); 20/154; Band; Golf; Hon Roll; NHS; 3rd OH ST Mandolin Cntst, 4th OH ST Guitar Flatpicking Cntst 85; Fnlst PA Bluegrass Bnd Cntst 84.

PEASLEY, COLETTE; Danville Area HS; Danville, PA; (Y); French Clb; Girl Scts; NFL; Speech Tm; Nwsp Rptr; JV Sftbl; Hon Roll; Prfct Atten Awd; Grl Scout Gold Awd 85; JV Ltr Sftbl 85; 3rd Pl Prose Husky Forn Comptn 86; Bloomsburg U PA; Mass Cmmnctns.

PEAVY, ROBYNNE; Penn Wood HS; Aldan, PA; (Y); 30/310; Orch; Nwsp Rptr; Nwsp Stf; Rep Stu Cncl; Var Tennis; JV Vllybl; High Hon Roll; Hon Roll; Home & Schl Assn Awd 86; Dstngshd Hon Roll Stu 85-86; St Josephs U; Intl Rltns.

PEBLER, HEIDI; Penn Hills HS; Pittsburgh, PA; (Y); German Clb; Ski Clb; Band; Concert Band; Drill Tm; Soph Cls; Stu Cncl; High Hon Roll; Hon Roll; Carnegie Solo Comptn 1st Oboe 84; Intl Rel.

PECHATSKO, VICTORIA; Fairchance-Georges SR HS; Uniontown, PA; (Y); 25/160; Cmnty Wkr; Drama Clb; Hosp Aide; School Play; Stage Crew; High Hon Roll; Hon Roll; IN U; Bus.

PECK, DONNA; Juniata HS; Mifflintown, PA; (Y); Drama Clb; Spanish Clb; Chorus; Flag Corp; Mrchg Band; School Play; Yrbk Stf; Sftbl; High Hon Roll; NHS; Child Dvlpmnt.

PECK, JEANNINE; Nazareth Acad; Feasterville, PA; (Y); Cmnty Wkr; Spanish Clb; VP Soph Cls; JV Cheerleading; Var Tennis; Advertising.

PECK, MARION; Mc Connellsburg HS; Mcconnellsburg, PA; (Y); 4/80; Varsity Clb; Mrchg Band; Nwsp Stf; Yrbk Ed-Chief; Pres Frsh Cls; VP Soph Cls; Var Bsktbl; Var Trk; High Hon Roll; Sec VP NHS; Pres Acdmc Schlrshp Slippery Bk U 86; All Am HS Stu Awd; Slippery Rock U; Med Lab Tech.

PECK, STEVEN; Blue Mountain Acad; Spencer, MA; (Y); #4 In Class; Church Yth Grp; Radio Clb; Ski Clb; Varsity Clb; Nwsp Rptr; Yrbk Stf; JV Bsbl; Vllybl; High Hon Roll; Prfct Atten Awd; Andrws U; Grphc Arts.

PECKMAN, WILLIAM; Elizabeth Forward HS; Mckeesport, PA; (Y); 32/304; Var Capt Bsktbl; Var Capt Ftbl; Hon Roll; NHS; Rotary Awd; All Cnfrnc Ftbll; Chsn Cmncmnt Spkr 3rd Team All-Amer Ftbll 86; All-ST Ftbll Schlrshp TX A & M 86; TX A & M U; Bus.

PECKYNO, ROBERT; Monessen HS; Monessen, PA; (Y); 3/90; Boy Scts; French Clb; JA; Chorus; Capt Tennis; High Hon Roll; NHS; Amer Lgn Awd 84; PMEA Western Dist Chorus 85; Hugh O Brian 85; Monessen JR Tamburitzans 86; Duquesne U; Pre-Med.

PECORA, JAMES J; Mount Lebanon HS; Pittsburgh, PA; (Y); 60/530; Sec Frsh Cls; Sec Soph Cls; VP Jr Cls; Sec Sr Cls; Im Socr; Hon Roll; Ntl Merit SF; Engrng.

PECORA, MISSY; Bradford Central Christian HS; Bradford, PA; (Y); 3/27; NFL; Pep Clb; SADD; Chorus; Nwsp Sprt Ed; Yrbk Ed-Chief; Stu Cncl; High Hon Roll; Jr NHS; NHS; Achvt Awd Recogntn Of Outstdng Accmplshmnt 86; Stu Cncl Awd Schlrshp 86; Englsh Awd Schlrshp 86; Psych.

PECORARO, TERRI; Burrell HS; Lower Burrell, PA; (Y); 47/210; Cmnty Wkr; JA; Library Aide; Pep Clb; PAVAS; Radio Clb; Spanish Clb; Chorus; Church Choir; Capt Color Guard; Jrnlsm.

PECSKO, JEROME; Uniontown Area HS; Uniontown, PA; (Y); 87/321; Boy Scts; VP Pres Church Yth Grp; Spanish Clb; Teachers Aide; Stage Crew; Var Trk; Hon Roll; CA U PA; Industrl Mgmt Tech.

PECUKONIS, KATHLEEN; Wyalusing Valley HS; Wyalusing, PA; (Y); Hosp Aide; Ski Clb; Spanish Clb; Cheerleading; Trk; Hon Roll; Nrsg.

PEDANO, MONICA A; Merion Mercy Acad; Merion, PA; (Y); French Clb; VP GAA; Library Aide; Office Aide; Pep Clb; Science Clb; Service Clb; Chorus; Variety Show; Var Bsktbl; Chrstn Srv Awd 85 & 86; Sprtsmnshp Awds 84-86; Bus Adm.

PEECHATKA, MICHELLE; Pocono Mountain HS; Stroudsburg, PA; (Y); 25/300; Ski Clb; SADD; Chorus; Trs Concert Band; Trs Mrchg Band; School Musical; Swing Chorus; Hon Roll; NHS; Pres Church Yth Grp; Black Blt In Tang Soo Do Karate 85; Hm Econmcs Awd 86; Weiler Brush Schlrshp 86; PA ST U.

PEEL, JACKIE; East Juniata HS; Mc Alisterville, PA; (Y); 15/94; Church Yth Grp; School Play; Yrbk Stf; Bsktbl; Score Keeper; Socr; Sftbl; Hon Roll; Messiah Coll; Elem Ed.

PEELING, TIM; Northeastern HS; Mt Wolf, PA; (Y); Band; Trs Sr Cls; Stu Cncl; Bsktbl; Tennis; NHS; Boy Scts; Church Yth Grp; Exploring; JA; Egl Sct 86; Acctnt.

PEET, DEBBIE; The Baptist HS; Hop Bottom, PA; (Y); Trs Sec Church Yth Grp; Office Aide; Var Bsktbl; Cit Awd; Hon Roll; Keystone Chrstn Ed Assn 2nd Pl Piano Comp 84-85; PA Tlnts For Christ 2nd Pl Piano Comp 85; Baptist Bible Coll; Elem Ed.

PEET, MICHAEL; Old Forge HS; Old Forge, PA; (Y); Off Soph Cls; Stu Cncl; Var Golf; Hon Roll; Comp Prog.

PEFFER, BONNIE; Mt Plesaant Area HS; Norvelt, PA; (Y); French Clb; GAA; Red Cross Aide; Band; Concert Band; Mrchg Band; Nwsp Bus Mgr; Nwsp Rptr; Crs Cntry; Swmmng.

PEFFLEY, AMMON; Mechanicsburg Area HS; Mechanicsburg, PA; (Y); 17/311; Var L Bsbl; Var L Bsktbl; Var L Socr; High Hon Roll; NHS.

PEFFLEY, MIKE; Lebanon HS; Lebanon, PA; (Y); 10/300; Cmnty Wkr; German Clb; Key Clb; Pres Ski Clb; Varsity Clb; Ed Yrbk Ed-Chief; Var Bsktbl; Var Tennis; Im Wt Lftg; Hon Roll; Key Club Star Awd Bsktbll 86; Elec Engr.

PEHANICH, DIANE; Old Forge HS; Old Forge, PA; (S); Scholastic Bowl; Yrbk Stf; High Hon Roll; NHS; Schlr Yr 86; Gregg Typng Awd 85; Marywood Coll; Mth Ed.

PEIFER, DAVID; Halifax HS; Halifax, PA; (Y); JV Bsbl; Theatre Arts.

PEIFFER, MARGIE; Towanda Area HS; Wysox, PA; (Y); 7/172; VP Church Yth Grp; Exploring; French Clb; FTA; SADD; Chorus; Concert Band; Mrchg Band; Stat Bsktbl; NHS; Elglsh.

PEILCHER, DAWN; Meyersdale JR SR HS; Meyersdale, PA; (S); Spanish Clb; Nwsp Rptr; Nwsp Stf; High Hon Roll; Hon Roll; Prfct Atten Awd.

PEIRCE, BARBARA; Abington SR HS; Glenside, PA; (Y); 163/535; Girl Scts; Hosp Aide; Latin Clb; Color Guard; Mrchg Band; Mgr Bsktbl; Mgr(s); Muhlenberg Coll; Socl Wrk.

PEKAREK, DONNA M; Donegal HS; Mt Joy, PA; (Y); Church Yth Grp; Hon Roll; Mthmtcs.

PEKARSKI, JO RENEE; Coudersport Area HS; Coudersport, PA; (Y); Church Yth Grp; French Clb; Band; Chorus; Concert Band; Mrchg Band; Pep Band; Stu Cncl; Var L Bsktbl; Var L Vllybl; Lock Haven U; Elem Educ.

PELAGATTI, JULIA; Harriton HS; Gladwyne, PA; (Y); Pep Clb; Nwsp Rptr; Yrbk Stf; Capt Fld Hcky; Mgr(s); Prfct Atten Awd; Main Line Womens Strike For Peace Essay Awd 86; Enrlmnt Challenge; Stu Advsr Awd Middlestates Ed 84; Northwestern; Psych.

PELAK, SANDRA; G A R Memorial HS; Wilkes Barre, PA; (S); 22/177; Library Aide; Stu Cncl; Trk; High Hon Roll; Hon Roll; NHS; Typing Cert 84.

PELES, JOE; Purchase Line HS; Starford, PA; (Y); Varsity Clb; High Hon Roll; Hon Roll.

PELES, KIMBERLY; Purchase Line HS; Commodore, PA; (Y); 11/123; VP FBLA; Sec SADD; Varsity Clb; Mrchg Band; Stage Crew; L Var Sftbl; JV Capt Vllybl; Hon Roll; NHS.

PELKA, TAMARA; Tunkhannock Area HS; Tunkhannock, PA; (Y); Church Yth Grp; Key Clb; Chorus; Score Keeper; Co-Capt Twrlr; Hon Roll; Bloomsburg U.

PELKOWSKI, TIM; Iroquois HS; Erie, PA; (Y); 5/149; Var Swmmng; JV Trk; High Hon Roll; Hon Roll; NHS; Ntl Merit SF; SAT Hnrs 85; Case Wstrn U Schlrshp 86; Case Western Rsrv U; Elec Engr.

PELLEGRINO, LEN; Council Rock HS; Churchville, PA; (Y); 25/845; Church Yth Grp; Cmnty Wkr; Computer Clb; Spanish Clb; Badmtn; Bsbl; Im Bsktbl; Coach Actv; Im Sftbl; Im Vllybl; PA ST; Engnrng.

PELLEGRINO, VALERIE A; Exeter Twp SR HS; Birdsboro, PA; (Y); 7/217; Drama Clb; Leo Clb; Chorus; Jazz Band; School Musical; School Play; High Hon Roll; NHS; Hosp Aide; Y-Teens; Cnty Chorus 84-86; Dist & Rgnl Chous 85.

PELLICANO, RACHEL; Lincoln HS; Ellwood City, PA; (Y); 39/163; FBLA; Lib Band; Concert Band; Mrchg Band; Orch; Powder Puff Ftbl; High Hon Roll; Hon Roll; Acad Achvt Awd 83; Clarion U Of PA; Math.

PELLICONE, PATRICIA; Archbishop Kennedy HS; Philadelphia, PA; (Y); Church Yth Grp; French Clb; Science Clb; Im Vllybl.

PELLIS, DREUX; Hempfield Area HS; Greensburg, PA; (Y); Art Clb; Pep Clb; Ski Clb; Spanish Clb; Rep Frsh Cls; Ftbl; Wt Lftg; Wrstlng; Hon Roll; Carnegie-Mellon; Dsgn Engr.

PELORO, LETIZIA A; Bishop Kenrick HS; Norristown, PA; (Y); Pres Church Yth Grp; Cmnty Wkr; Dance Clb; Hosp Aide; Mgr Office Aide; Spanish Clb; Var Vllybl; Natl Ldrshp & Svc Awd 86.

PELUZZO, CHRISTINA; St Basil Acad; Philadelphia, PA; (Y); 34/98; Spanish Clb; School Musical; Variety Show; Yrbk Stf; Lit Mag; Bsktbl; Tennis; Chem Engrng.

PENA, CAROL E; Winchester-Thurston HS; Pittsburgh, PA; (Y); Hosp Aide; Spanish Clb; Chorus; School Musical; Yrbk Rptr; Lit Mag; Sec Trs Jr Cls; Var L Lcrss; Ntl Merit SF; Semifin Natl Hispanic Schlr Awd Prog 85; Stu Of Month Gen Fed Of Womens Clb 85; Physician.

PENA, MARISOL; Mt Pleasant Area HS; Mt Pleasant, PA; (Y); GAA; Latin Clb; Mat Maids; Var Trk; Im Vllybl; Hon Roll; NHS; Rotary Awd; Chiropractor.

PENCEK, MATTHEW; Tunkhannock HS; Tunkhannock, PA; (S); 20/280; Aud/Vis; Pres Church Yth Grp; Drama Clb; School Play; Nwsp Sprt Ed; JV Golf; JV Tennis; Hon Roll; NHS; JV Bsktbl; Rotry Ldrshp Camp 85; TV Comm.

PENDLE, MATTHEW; Harry S Truman HS; Levittown, PA; (Y); 50/600; Temple U; Arch.

PENDLETON, CHARLES; Perry Traditional Acad; Pittsburgh, PA; (Y); 76/135; Boy Scts; Hon Roll; Smthfld Yng Bsktbl League Chmpns 85-86; U NC; Comp Rpr.

PENECALE, GINA; Upper Moreland HS; Hatboro, PA; (Y); 64/253; Rep Key Clb; Chorus; Color Guard; Mrchg Band; Rep Frsh Cls; Rep Soph Cls; Rep Jr Cls; Rep Stu Cncl; Trk; Capt Twrlr; Trck Suburban League-Hnrb Mntn-100 M Hurdles 86; Bus.

PENGLASE, CAROLYN; Central Bucks East HS; Doylestown, PA; (Y); Band; Mrchg Band; Orch; School Musical; School Play; Yrbk Stf; Var L Trk; High Hon Roll; Hon Roll.

PENKROT, AMY; Lake-Lehman HS; Shavertown, PA; (Y); 13/121; Key Clb; Ski Clb; Capt Cheerleading; High Hon Roll; NHS; French Clb; SADD; School Play; Nwsp Stf; Yrbk Stf; Bus.

PENLAND, CLAUDE; Archbishop Carroll HS; Wayne, PA; (Y); 9/165; Latin Clb; Science Clb; Var L Wrstlng; Off NHS; Ntl Merit Ltr; Mth Outstndg Achvt Awd 86; Sci Outstndg Achvt Awd 86; Mth Outstndg Achvt Awd 86; Johns Hopkins U; Mth Sci.

PENMAN, JUANITA; Punxsutawney Area SR HS; Punxsutawney, PA; (Y); Pres Church Yth Grp; Debate Tm; Hosp Aide; Radio Clb; SADD; Fshn Merch.

PENNELL, JULIE; Slippery Rock Area HS; Slippery Rock, PA; (Y); 12/172; Church Yth Grp; German Clb; Intnl Clb; Band; Pep Band; Nwsp Stf; Yrbk Stf; Trk; NHS; Ntl Merit Ltr; Hnr Butler Cnty Band 85; Slippery Rock U; Cmmrcl Recrtn.

PENNER, GARY; Upper Moreland HS; Hatboro, PA; (Y); 3/253; Jazz Band; Mrchg Band; School Musical; Symp Band; NHS; Ntl Merit Ltr; Band; Concert Band; High Hon Roll; Trumpet Soloist Awd 86; District Band & Orch 85; District Band & Orch 86; Doctor.

PENNINGTON, JAMES V; Sharpsvsille SR HS; Shaprsville, PA; (Y); VP Church Yth Grp; Cmnty Wkr; Thesps; Nwsp Rptr; Hon Roll; NHS; Bst Acctg I Stdnt Awd; Acdmc Achvt Awd; PA ST U; Brdcst Jrnlsm.

PENNOCK, MARK; Fort Le Boeuf HS; Waterford, PA; (Y); 17/167; Boy Scts; Pres Church Yth Grp; Computer Clb; Bowling; Im Vllybl; High Hon Roll; PA ST Behrend; Acctg.

PENNYPACKER, LISA; Emmaus HS; Macungie, PA; (Y); Art Clb; Hosp Aide; VP Pep Clb; Teachers Aide; Chorus; School Musical; Yrbk Stf; JV Bsktbl; Var Cheerleading; JV Fld Hcky; Bstr Clb Sprts Awd 86; LCCC; Cmmrcl Art.

PENNYPACKER, MICHELE; Pottstown SR HS; Pottstown, PA; (Y); 27/238; Exploring; French Clb; JA; Key Clb; Lansdale Schl Bus; Accntng.

PENO, MELISSA; Cowanesque HS; Westfield, PA; (Y); French Clb; FFA; FHA; Pep Clb; Rep Stu Cncl; Sftbl; Trk; Hon Roll; Lock Haven U; Prim Educ.

PENROD, DIANNA; Windber Area HS; Windber, PA; (Y); Office Aide; Chorus; Hon Roll; Stu Of Mnth 86.

PENROD, WENDY; Windber Area HS; Windber, PA; (S); Ski Clb; Band; Color Guard; Concert Band; Flag Corp; Mrchg Band; JV Vllybl; High Hon Roll; NHS; Med.

PENROSE, ROBERT; United JR SR HS; New Florence, PA; (Y); 35/157; Trs Church Yth Grp; Band; Chorus; Church Choir; Mrchg Band; Var Capt Ftbl; Var L Trk; Hon Roll; NHS; Dist Regnl Chorus 86; IUP; Bio.

PENROSE, SEAN; St John Neumann HS; Philadelphia, PA; (Y); 102/357; Ftbl; Sci.

PENSENSTADLER, ELAINE; Ambridge HS; Ambridge, PA; (Y); Church Yth Grp; Dance Clb; Chorus; Church Choir; School Play; Variety Show; JV Vllybl; French Clb; Pep Clb; Hon Roll; Librl Arts.

PENSIS, BOBBI; Charleroi Area JR SR HS; Charleroi, PA; (Y); Trs French Clb; Office Aide; Ski Clb; SADD; Nwsp Rptr; Nwsp Stf; Yrbk Stf; Stu Cncl; Mgr Trk; NHS.

PENTZ, MONICA; York Co Vocational Technical HS; Dover, PA; (Y); VICA; Stu Cncl; Bsktbl; Trs NHS; PA ST U; Mech Dfrtng.

PENZONE, SANDY; Scranton Central HS; Scranton, PA; (Y); Art Clb; Ski Clb; Spanish Clb; VP Soph Cls; Sftbl; Prfct Atten Awd; Spanish NHS; U Of Scranton; Phy Thrpy.

PEOPLES, MARLENE; Hempfield SR HS; Grapesville, PA; (Y); VP FBLA; Ski Clb; JV Bsktbl; JV Vllybl; Cit Awd; High Hon Roll; Hon Roll; Bradford; Acctg.

PEPERAK, CINDY; Connellsville Area HS; Connellsville, PA; (Y); 9/550; Pres GAA; Pres Pep Clb; Yrbk Stf; Var L Bsktbl; Var L Sftbl; Var L Vllybl; French Hon Soc; High Hon Roll; Jr NHS; NHS.

PEPONIDIS, CORINNA; Sacred Heart HS; Pittsburgh, PA; (Y); Art Clb; Nwsp Stf; Yrbk Stf; Im Vllybl; High Hon Roll; Hon Roll; U Of Ptsbrg; Vet.

PEPPLE, MICHELE; Everett Area HS; Everett, PA; (Y); Varsity Clb; Band; Chorus; Sec Soph Cls; Hst Sr Cls; Stu Cncl; Var L Socr; Var L Sftbl; Var L Vllybl; VP NHS; PA ST; Bus Adm.

PERCHERKE, JAMES; North Star HS; Boswell, PA; (S); #1 In Class; Math Clb; Scholastic Bowl; Ski Clb; Stu Cncl; Golf; Hon Roll; Mu Alp Tht; Dist V Golf Champ 85-86; Natl Sci Merit Awd 85-86; Chem Engrng.

PERCOSKY, KATHY; Forest Hills HS; Windber, PA; (Y); 7/158; Hosp Aide; Pep Clb; Y-Teens; Chorus; Nwsp Rptr; JV Var Bsktbl; High Hon Roll; Hon Roll; Jr NHS; Spanish NHS; U Of Pittsburgh; Dent.

PERCOSKY, RENEE L; Danville Area HS; W Hazleton, PA; (Y); Red Cross Aide; Ski Clb; Spanish Clb; SADD; Nwsp Stf; Yrbk Stf; Var Powder Puff Ftbl; Var JV Sftbl; High Hon Roll; Phys Ther.

PERCY, ELAINE; Grove City Area HS; Volant, PA; (Y); 8/189; FBLA; Key Clb; Concert Band; Mrchg Band; Stat Bsktbl; High Hon Roll; NHS; Bus.

PERDEW, DEE; Monaca JR-SR HS; Monaca, PA; (Y); Church Yth Grp; Library Aide; Red Cross Aide; School Musical; Nwsp Ed-Chief; Yrbk Sprt Ed; Var Co-Capt Cheerleading; Hon Roll; Alg II Awd 84; Pittsburgh U; Math Educ.

PERDICK, JEFF; Catasauqua HS; N Catasauqua, PA; (Y); 11/111; Varsity Clb; Var L Bsbl; Var L Ftbl; Hon Roll; NHS; Pres Acad Ftns Awd 86; US Nat Ldrshp Merit Awd 86; Intl Frgn Lng Awd 86; U Of FL; Elec Engrng.

PERDUE, JEFFREY; Shenango HS; New Cattle, PA; (Y); Varsity Clb; Band; Var L Bsbl; Bsktbl; Im Coach Actv; Var L Ftbl; Wt Lftg; Theil Coll; Envrnmnt Sci.

PERDUE, TINA; North East HS; North East, PA; (Y); 70/149; Latin Clb; Pep Clb; Var Cheerleading; Behrend Coll.

PERECHINSKY, JOSEPH; Lakeland JR SR HS; Jermyn, PA; (S); Aud/Vis; Library Aide; Deisal Mech.

PERETIN, JOE; Baldwin HS; Pittsburgh, PA; (Y); Church Yth Grp; Bsktbl; Mgr(s); Score Keeper; High Hon Roll; Hon Roll; Bus.

PEREZ, DELTON; Blue Mountain Acad; Waterbury, CT; (Y); Art Clb; Camera Clb; Chess Clb; Latin Clb; Radio Clb; Teachers Aide; Acpl Chr; Drill Tm; Flag Corp; Symp Band; Med.

PEREZ, GEMMA; Geibel HS; Connellsville, PA; (Y); Pep Clb; Ski Clb; Rep Soph Cls; Sec Jr Cls; VP Sr Cls; Cheerleading; French Hon Soc; High Hon Roll; Hon Roll; NHS.

PEREZ, JENNIFER; Pennsbury HS; Yardley, PA; (Y); 6/775; Spanish Clb; Rep Stu Cncl; Var Cheerleading; Var Socr; JV Var Trk; Hon Roll; NHS; Dance Clb; Chorus; Stage Crew; GE Ldrshp Cnfrnc TMOT 85; Cert Excllnc Spnsh U Of Salmnca Spain 85; Awd Outstndgprtcptn Frgn Lang 86; Arch.

PERFECKY, MARTA; Abington HS; Glenside, PA; (Y); French Clb; Latin Clb; Rep Jr Cls; Mgr(s); Socr; Trk; Art Shows; La Salle U.

PERGOSKY, JAMES CHARLES; Hazleton SR HS; Hazleton, PA; (Y); 31/385; Drama Clb; VP Leo Clb; Ski Clb; Pres SADD; Band; Chorus; Church Choir; Concert Band; Drill Tm; Jazz Band; Northeastern U; Pharm.

PERHOSKY, RONALD; Langley HS; Pittsburgh, PA; (Y); JV Ftbl; JV Wt Lftg; High Hon Roll; Jr NHS; Prfct Atten Awd; U Of Pittsburgh; Chem Engr.

PERICH, MICHELE; South Allegheny JR SR HS; Mc Keesport, PA; (S); 15/184; Church Yth Grp; Trs Computer Clb; Exploring; French Clb; Office Aide; Y-Teens; Band; Concert Band; Mrchg Band; School Musical; Phys Ther.

PERINI, KENDRA; Lebanon Catholic HS; Lebanon, PA; (Y); 20/80; Civic Clb; Service Clb; Spanish Clb; Yrbk Stf; Rep Stu Cncl; L Bowling; Cheerleading; Hon Roll; Paralegal.

PERINIS, MARY; Mt Lebanon HS; Pittsburgh, PA; (Y); Cmnty Wkr; Dance Clb; Capt Drill Tm; School Musical; High Hon Roll; NEDT Awd; Pres Schlr; Amrcn U Pres Schlrshp 86; Mem Ryl Acad Of Dncng 82; Actvts Key & Grd 86; Amrcn U; Pltcl Sci.

PERKA, THOMAS W; Shaler Area HS; Pittsburgh, PA; (Y); 102/518; Spanish Clb; Hon Roll; Spanish NHS; Optmtry.

PERKINS, BONNIE; Nazareth Acad; Philadelphia, PA; (Y); Pres Latin Clb; Hon Roll; Nrsng.

PERKINS, MARTIN; Glen Mills Schls; Concordville, PA; (S); Church Yth Grp; Computer Clb; Drama Clb; FCA; Stu Cncl; Bsktbl; Ftbl; Var Trk; Var Capt Wt Lftg; Hon Roll; GED Stu Mth 85; SAT Stu Mth 85; Kerney Cup Awd-Pwr Lftng 85; Mgmt Infrmtn.

PERKINS, MISSY; Hempfield Area SR HS; Greensburg, PA; (Y); Capt Flag Corp; Nwsp Ed-Chief; Nwsp Rptr; Var L Swmmng; Hon Roll; Prfct Atten Awd; Hempfield Enrchmnt Pgm 79-87.

PERKINS, STACY; Seneca HS; Erie, PA; (Y); Spanish Clb; School Musical; Yrbk Phtg; Yrbk Stf; JV Stat Bsktbl; Var Sftbl; Var JV Vllybl; Hustle Awd Sftbl 86; Pres Physcl Ftns Awd 85-86; Behrend Coll; Hotel Mgmt.

PERKO, NICOLE M; Mars Area SR HS; Mars, PA; (Y); 5/150; Pres German Clb; Stage Crew; Yrbk Stf; High Hon Roll; NHS; Engnrng.

PERKOSKY, JOHN; Shaler Area HS; Pittsburgh, PA; (S); Var Wrstlng; High Hon Roll; NEDT Awd; Rotary Awd; Outstndng Schlr-Athlt 83-84.

PERLINGER, DEANNA; Norwin SR HS; N Huntingdon, PA; (Y); 115/550; AFS; German Clb; Pep Clb; SADD; Band; Color Guard; Mat Maids; Hon Roll; Radlgy.

PERO, JEFF; Upper Moreland HS; Willow Grove, PA; (Y); 12/267; JV Bsbl; Var Trk; Var Capt Wrstlng; High Hon Roll; NHS; Pres Schlr; Wrstlng Suburban One 1st Tm All-Lgue 85-86; Top Acctng I & II Stu Awd 86; Bucknell U; Acctng.

PEROTTI, THOMAS; Bishop Egan HS; Bensalem, PA; (Y); 40/229; German Clb; Latin Clb; Library Aide; Office Aide; Red Cross Aide; Im Bsktbl; JV Var Ftbl; High Hon Roll; Hon Roll; Distngshd Achvmnt Awd Engl 85; Drexel U; Mech Engrng.

PERRETTA, JOHN; New Brighton SR HS; New Brighton, PA; (Y); 65/154; VP Computer Clb; JA; JV Var Bsbl; JV Var Bsktbl; High Hon Roll; Hon Roll; Clarion U; Bus Admin.

PERRIN, LOIS; Northern Bedford County HS; Loysburg, PA; (Y); Aud/Vis; Ski Clb; SADD; Band; Chorus; Trs Sr Cls; Var Capt Bsktbl; Var L Cheerleading; L Trk; Var Capt Vllybl; Dist 5 Enfrnlympcs Chmpn 86; PA ST U; Wldlife Tech.

PERRINE, MELISSA; Laural Highlands SR HS; Uniontown, PA; (Y); Math Clb; Math Tm; Spanish Clb; Band; Color Guard; Concert Band; Capt Flag Corp; Mrchg Band; Nwsp Rptr; Nwsp Stf; Uniontown Schl Of Nrsng.

PERRINS, GERALD; Pittston Area HS; Pittston, PA; (Y); 29/365; Key Clb; Science Clb; Off Frsh Cls; Off Soph Cls; Ftbl; Trk; Hon Roll; NHS; Acadmc All Amern 86; Penn ST.

PERRY, ABBY; Freedom HS; Bethlehem, PA; (Y); 135/445; Hosp Aide; Science Clb; Hon Roll; Art Awd Clay Sclpture 83-84; Penn ST; Cmmrcl Art.

PERRY, BRIAN; Towanda Area HS; Towanda, PA; (Y); 14/170; Cmnty Wkr; Letterman Clb; Ski Clb; Spanish Clb; Varsity Clb; Trs Frsh Cls; Trs Soph Cls; VP Jr Cls; VP Sr Cls; L Bsbl; Rtry Ldrs Cmp Prtcpnt 84; Pres Physcl Ftnss Awd 85-86; Bsktbl Vrsty Outstndng Offnsv Plyr 86; Lafaytt Coll; Prelaw.

PERRY, CAROL; Big Spring HS; Newville, PA; (Y); 60/190; Trs 4-H; Nwsp Phtg; Nwsp Rptr; Nwsp Stf; Var L Crs Cntry; Stat Trk; Rptr 4-H Awd; Hon Roll; Rotary Awd; Wmns Clb JR Of Mnth 86; Prsdntl Physcl Ftns Awd 86; Comm.

PERRY, DALENE; South Park HS; Library, PA; (Y); 3/203; Color Guard; Powder Puff Ftbl; Sftbl; Trk; High Hon Roll; NHS; NEDT Awd; Chubb Ins Schlrshp 86; Penn ST U; Aero Engrng.

PERRY, DORIE; Warwick HS; Lititz, PA; (Y); 52/230; Library Aide; Teachers Aide; Nwsp Rptr; Im Vllybl; High Hon Roll; Hon Roll; Sec Educ.

PERRY, ELISABETH; Danville Area SR HS; Danville, PA; (Y); Debate Tm; Drama Clb; French Clb; NFL; Ski Clb; School Play; Pres Frsh Cls; High Hon Roll; Kiwanis Awd; NEDT Awd; Bucknell U; Intl Rltns.

PERRY, KEN; Kennett Cons HS; Mendenhall, PA; (Y); 14/154; Boy Scts; Ed Yrbk Stf; Rep Jr Cls; VP Sr Cls; Rep Stu Cncl; High Hon Roll; Hon Roll; Weightmans Prfrmnc Ctr 5 Yr Awd 85; Elec Engrng.

PERRY, KRISTINE; Penn Hills SR HS; Pittsburgh, PA; (S); 18/760; Hosp Aide; Ski Clb; Spanish Clb; Varsity Clb; Yrbk Stf; Var Cheerleading; Powder Puff Ftbl; Tennis; High Hon Roll; NHS; Englsh Encllnc Awd 86; PA ST; Optmtrst.

PERRY, LEAH; Cardinal Dougherty HS; Cheltenham, PA; (Y); 4/747; Cmnty Wkr; Yrbk Stf; Fld Hcky; High Hon Roll; NHS; PA City Schlrshp 86; La Salle Chrstn Brothrs Grnt 86; Profcncy Awds:Advncd Spnsh, Engl, AP, 85 & 86; St Josephs U; Corprt Law.

PERRY, MICHELLE J; Trinity HS; Washington, PA; (Y); Church Yth Grp; Chorus; Church Choir; Hon Roll; Gymstc Trphy 75-77; Mngmnt.

PERRY, RENEE; Punxsutawney Area HS; Punxsutawney, PA; (Y); Computer Clb; French Clb; Band; Concert Band; Mrchg Band; Yrbk Stf; Gifted Prgm 82-86; Stu Helping Others-Tutor In French 85-86; Chatham Coll; Econ.

PERRY, STEPHEN; Bishop Guilfoyle HS; Altoona, PA; (Y); Pep Clb; Red Cross Aide; Service Clb; Ski Clb; Band; Jazz Band; Rep Jr Cls; Stu Cncl; Var L Ftbl; NHS.

PERRY, TIMOTHY; Downingtown SR HS; Downingtown, PA; (Y); Boy Scts; Computer Clb; School Musical; Stage Crew; Hon Roll; West Chester U; Comp Sci.

PERSI, LISA; Aliquippa HS; Aliquippa, PA; (S); 1/163; Pres Chess Clb; Church Yth Grp; Math Tm; Concert Band; Mrchg Band; Pep Band; Bausch & Lomb Sci Awd; High Hon Roll; Lion Awd; Hst NHS; Intl Frgn Lang Awd 84; Cert Merit PA Soc Profssnl Engrs 84; Bio.

PERSING, DI ANN; Line Mountain HS; Shamokin, PA; (Y); 3/109; Art Clb; Computer Clb; Drama Clb; Math Clb; Chorus; Drill Tm; School Musical; Swing Chorus; Bausch & Lomb Sci Awd; Cit Awd; Highest Average In Physics 86; Bloomsburg U; Math.

PERSON, ROD; Steel Valley HS; Homestead, PA; (Y); Latin Clb; Hon Roll; Prfct Atten Awd; 3rd Pl Art Cntst 85; 2nd Pl Art Cntst 86; Rcrdng Engr.

PERSUDA, JANET; Charleroi Area SR HS; Charleroi, PA; (Y); Chorus; Church Choir; Color Guard; Jazz Band; Ed Nwsp Stf; Hon Roll; NHS; Stdnt Tutr; Acctg.

PERSUN, SHERRY; Highlands SR HS; Tarentum, PA; (Y); Exploring; Rep Soph Cls; Rep Jr Cls; Jr NHS; NHS; Acad All Am 86; Chroprctc.

PERUGINI, SAM; Holy Ghost Prep; Philadelphia, PA; (S); Aud/Vis; Latin Clb; Science Clb; Teachers Aide; Band; School Play; Hon Roll; NHS; Latin Awd Nom 85-86; Social Studies Awd Nom 86; Envrnmntl Sci.

PESI, CHRISTINE; Frazier HS; Star Junction, PA; (Y); Trs Church Yth Grp; Drama Clb; Library Aide; Spanish Clb; Band; Color Guard; Mrchg Band; School Play; High Hon Roll; Elem Educ.

PESTA, LAURA; York Catholic HS; Shrewsbury, PA; (Y); Debate Tm; French Clb; Hosp Aide; Pep Clb; Teachers Aide; Chorus; School Musical; Nwsp Rptr; Yrbk Rptr; Hon Roll; Svc Awd 83; Pres Scholar Awd U Scranton 86; U Scranton; Hstry.

PETA, DOUGLAS; B Reed Henderson HS; West Chester, PA; (S); 11/349; JCL; Nwsp Rptr; Rep Frsh Cls; Rep Jr Cls; JV Bsbl; Im Bsktbl; Hon Roll.

PETCOS, A HELEN; Deer Lakes JR SR HS; Curtisville, PA; (Y); Church Yth Grp; Computer Clb; Drama Clb; Hosp Aide; Church Choir; School Play; Variety Show; Var Stat Bsktbl; Trk; Hon Roll; Engrng.

PETE, DEBBIE; Lock Haven SR HS; Lock Haven, PA; (Y); Art Clb; French Clb; Keywanettes; Service Clb; SADD; Temple Yth Grp; Chorus; Variety Show; Rep Stu Cncl; Var Cheerleading; Soc Wrk.

PETE, JAMES; Owen J Roberts SR HS; Spring City, PA; (Y); German Clb; Band; Mrchg Band; Symp Band; Bus Mgt.

PETE, MATTHEW; Bishop Mccort HS; Johnstown, PA; (Y); Cmnty Wkr; Chorus; Var L Bsbl; Var L Ice Hcky; High Hon Roll; Hon Roll; NHS; Engrng.

PETER, PRISCILLA; Cedar Grove Christian Acad; Philadelphia, PA; (Y); Church Yth Grp; Teachers Aide; Band; Church Choir; Concert Band; High Hon Roll; Hon Roll; NHS; Lit Mag; Natl Math League Schl Wnr For Algebra II 86; Temple U; Comp Sci.

PETERMAN JR, LANCE; Downingtown HS; Exton, PA; (S); #28 In Class; Church Yth Grp; Pres Model UN; Ski Clb; Rep Jr Cls; Im Bsktbl; Var L Ftbl; JV Im Tennis; High Hon Roll; NHS; NEDT Awd; Cvl Engrng.

PETERMAN, SHARI; Hughesville HS; Benton, PA; (Y); 15/136; Key Clb; Chorus; Hon Roll; NHS; Ski Clb; Green & White Sawd 84-85; Elem Ed.

PETERMAN, TANYA; Slippery Rock Area HS; Slippery Rock, PA; (Y); 4/180; Church Yth Grp; Nwsp Rptr; Yrbk Stf; Trs Jr Cls; Score Keeper; High Hon Roll; NHS; Intnl Clb; Pep Clb; Chorus; Slippery Rock U; Elem Ed.

PETERS, ANGELA; Crestwood HS; Wapwallopen, PA; (Y); Girl Scts; Hosp Aide; Library Aide; Pep Clb; Ski Clb; Im Cheerleading; JV Fld Hcky; JV Var Socr; High Hon Roll; Hon Roll; Slvr Ldrshp Awd Grl Scts 86; 10 Yr Awd Grl Scts 86; Job At Mc Dnlds 85-86; Luzerne Cmnty Coll; RN.

PETERS, BRETT; Somerset Area HS; Somerset, PA; (Y); English Clb; German Clb; High Hon Roll; Hon Roll; Acctng.

PETERS, BRONSON; Northwestern Le High HS; Germansville, PA; (Y); Church Yth Grp; Cmnty Wkr; Computer Clb; Letterman Clb; Varsity Clb; Stage Crew; Var Crs Cntry; Var Trk; JV Var Wrstlng; Hon Roll; Leag & Dist Trck Qulfr 4th Pl Caty 3200 R 86; Leag & Dist Wrstlng Qlfr 85-86; 2nd Pl NW Trnmnt 84-85; PA ST U; Engrng.

PETERS, CHRIS; Emmaus HS; Wescosville, PA; (Y); 50/495; JA; Var Capt Bsbl; Hon Roll; Jr NHS; NHS; Ntl Merit Ltr; Engrng.

PETERS, DAN; Fort Leboeuf HS; Waterford, PA; (Y); 16/167; Exploring; Band; Concert Band; Jazz Band; Mrchg Band; Pep Band; Nwsp Rptr; Capt Vllybl; High Hon Roll; NHS; Stanley-Proto Ind Tools Cont 1st Pl 86; W PA Ind Art Fair 2nd Pl 85; Engrng.

PETERS, DAWN; Belle Vernon Area HS; Belle Vernon, PA; (Y); Exploring; NFL; Ski Clb; Nwsp Rptr; Yrbk Stf; Sec Soph Cls; Sec Jr Cls; Stu Cncl; Powder Puff Ftbl; Sftbl; 2nd Pl Essay Wnnr 84; Coll; Pre-Law.

PETERS, ERIC; Moon Area S HS; Coraopolis, PA; (Y); 6/335; Aud/Vis; JA; Math Tm; Jazz Band; Symp Band; Trs Frsh Cls; Gov Hon Prg Awd; Church Yth Grp; Cmnty Wkr; 1st Pl Alghny Cnty Comp Fair 85; Estes Rcket Corp Dsgn Of Mnth Awd 85; Crng-Mellon; Elec Engrng.

PETERS, FRANK; Harborcreek HS; Harbor Creek, PA; (Y); 9/228; Cmnty Wkr; Yrbk Phtg; High Hon Roll; Hon Roll; Harborcreek Vlntr Fire Dept 83-86; Emergency Med Tech 86; Engrng.

PETERS, JAMES; Northampton Area SR HS; Bethlehem, PA; (Y); 92/467; Aud/Vis; DECA; FBLA; Office Aide; Speech Tm; Teachers Aide; High Hon Roll; FBLA 2nd Pl Wnnr Entrprnrshp 86; DECA 2nd Pl Wnnr Finc Crdt 85-86; Schlrshp Jhnsn Whls Stu Yr 86; Hsptlty.

PETERS, JOANNE; Middleburg Joint HS; Middleburg, PA; (Y); 21/132; Varsity Clb; Band; Nwsp Stf; Yrbk Stf; VP Frsh Cls; VP Soph Cls; Pres Jr Cls; Pres Sr Cls; Bsktbl; Coach Actv; Sftbl MVP 85; Sftbl Hustle Awd 86; Elem Educ.

PETERS, KELLIE; Fort Le Boeuf HS; Waterford, PA; (Y); 24/167; Nwsp Stf; Off Frsh Cls; Off Soph Cls; Off Jr Cls; Pres Sr Cls; Stu Cncl; High Hon Roll; Hon Roll; US Stu Cncl Awd 85; Gannon U Of PA; Prlgl.

PETERS, MELINDA M; Middletown Area HS; Middletown, PA; (Y); 20/166; FCA; Key Clb; SADD; Chorus; Drill Tm; Var Gym; Var Twrlr; Hon Roll; Var Lttr Gymnstcs 84; Cert From Harrisburg Arts Magnet Schl 85; Internshp For Comm GPU Nuclear TMI; Comm.

PETERS, MELISSA; Mid Valley HS; Dickson City, PA; (Y); Church Yth Grp; Hon Roll; Accntng.

PETERS, MICHELE; Valley View JR SR HS; Jessup, PA; (Y); 2/195; Church Yth Grp; Cmnty Wkr; French Clb; Latin Clb; High Hon Roll; NHS; Prfct Atten Awd; Acdmc Excllnc Awd 85-86; U Of Scranton; Psych.

PETERS, RANDALL; Susquenita HS; Duncannon, PA; (S); 8/158; Chess Clb; Church Yth Grp; Quiz Bowl; Rep Jr Cls; Rep Stu Cncl; L Var Crs Cntry; Var Trk; Im Wrstlng; Hon Roll; NHS; Demolay; Pen ST; Engrng.

PETERS, STEPHANIE; Quigley High HS; Freedom, PA; (Y); Am Leg Aux Girls St; Church Yth Grp; Trs 4-H; Speech Tm; Band; Powder Puff Ftbl; Capt Twrlr; Hon Roll; Oper Prom Grad 86; Hands Acrs Am 86; Fnlst Cnty Jr Miss Pgnt 86; U Of Pittsburgh; Pre Med.

PETERS, STEPHEN; Parkland HS; Orefield, PA; (Y); 82/464; Boy Scts; Camera Clb; Chess Clb; Church Yth Grp; Drama Clb; JA; Science Clb; High Hon Roll; Hon Roll; NHS; Boy Scts Amer Life Awd 85; Sci.

PETERS, THOMAS; Forest Hills SR HS; South Fork, PA; (Y); U Of Pittsburgh; Cvl Engrng.

PETERS, WENDY; Hanover SR HS; Hanover, PA; (Y); Pres Pep Clb; Red Cross Aide; Band; Concert Band; Jazz Band; Mrchg Band; Orch; School Play; Stage Crew; JV Capt Cheerleading; Harcum JC; Fshn Mrchndsng.

PETERSEN, SHANNON CHRISTOPHER; Lancaster Catholic HS; Lancaster, PA; (Y); Varsity Clb; Bsktbl; Ftbl; Trk; Acctg.

PETERSEN, STEPHANIE; Garden Spot HS; Narvon, PA; (Y); 10/204; Trs Drama Clb; Q&S; Chorus; School Play; Stage Crew; Ed Yrbk Rptr; Rep Jr Cls; High Hon Roll; Hon Roll; Jr NHS; Blue Bll Lnss Clb Schlrshp 86; Amrcn Bus Wmns Assoc Schlrshp 86; Estrn Lncstr Cnty Educ Assoc Schlrshp; Elizabethtown Coll; Cmmnctns.

PETERSON, ALAN; Mckeesport HS; White Oak, PA; (Y); 26/350; Church Yth Grp; JA; Mrchg Band; Sec Orch; School Musical; Rep Stu Cncl; High Hon Roll; Hon Roll; Jr NHS; NHS; Sci Fair 83-84; Sci Fair 85; PA ST; Engrg.

PETERSON, ANDREW; Franklin Regional HS; Murrysville, PA; (Y); AFS; Church Yth Grp; Computer Clb; JA; Ski Clb; Stat Bsktbl; JV Var Crs Cntry; JV Trk; U Of NC At C H; Polit Sci.

PETERSON, BRAD; Marion Center Area HS; Home, PA; (S); 20/170; Latin Clb; SADD; Varsity Clb; Var Ftbl; Var Wt Lftg; High Hon Roll; NHS; PA ST U; Engrng.

PETERSON, CANDACE; Glendale JR SR HS; Irvona, PA; (Y); 16/73; VP Chorus; Capt Color Guard; Yrbk Phtg; Pres Stu Cncl; Capt L Bsktbl; Stat Ftbl; Powder Puff Ftbl; Capt L Sftbl; Hon Roll; NHS; Best Defensive Plyr Sftbl 86; Hgst Batting Avg Sftbl 86; Fash Inst Pitt; Fash Merch.

PETERSON, CHRIS ANN; Mc Keesport SR HS; White Oak, PA; (Y); 24/339; AFS; Hosp Aide; JV Band; Mrchg Band; Symp Band; JV Bsktbl; Powder Puff Ftbl; High Hon Roll; NHS; Nrs.

PETERSON, JEFF; Connellsville HS; Cnlsvle, PA; (Y); Church Yth Grp; Drama Clb; Band; Jazz Band; Mrchg Band; Pep Band; School Musical; Symp Band; Penn ST; Elec Engrng.

PETERSON, JOHN; Creswtwood HS; Nuangola, PA; (Y); Ski Clb; JV Trk; Naval Acad; Pilot.

PETERSON, JOHN; Greater Latrobe SR HS; Latrobe, PA; (Y); Boy Scts; Church Yth Grp; JCL; Latin Clb; Hon Roll; Byu; Microbiology.

PETERSON, KARYN; Rockwood Area HS; Rockwood, PA; (S); 5/95; Trs Intnl Clb; Band; Chorus; Rep Stu Cncl; Var Cheerleading; Var Sftbl; JV Vllybl; High Hon Roll; Ntl Merit Schol; Intl Trade.

PETERSON, KRISTA; Wellsboro Area HS; Wellsboro, PA; (Y); 6/154; Art Clb; French Clb; Pep Clb; Band; Yrbk Stf; Bsktbl; Crs Cntry; Trk; Intl Bus.

PETERSON, KRISTEN; Dallastown Area HS; Dallastown, PA; (Y); Art Clb; Camera Clb; Varsity Clb; Color Guard; Nwsp Phtg; Capt Cheerleading; L Trk; 7 Presdntl Physcl Ftns Awds; YMCA Natl Gymnstcs Mt 83; Beauty Pgnts 84-85; Trck 3rd Co, 4th Dist 84-85.

PETERSON, MAREE; Plum HS; Pittsburgh, PA; (Y); Church Yth Grp; JA; Math Clb; Math Tm; High Hon Roll; NHS; Trk; FBLA; Deans Schlrshp 85-86; BYU; Math.

PETERSON, MARY; Southmoreland SR HS; Scottdale, PA; (Y); Sec Church Yth Grp; Sec 4-H; Library Aide; Pep Clb; Spanish Clb; Teachers Aide; Trk; 4-H Awd; Bradford School; Comp Pgrm.

PETERSON, VIVIAN; Plum SR HS; Pittsburgh, PA; (Y); Church Yth Grp; Library Aide; Chorus; Hon Roll; Penn ST; Accntng.

PETEY, MARK; Center HS; Monaca, PA; (Y); 5/180; Am Leg Boys St; Church Yth Grp; Cmnty Wkr; Spanish Clb; Stage Crew; Yrbk Rptr; Yrbk Stf; High Hon Roll; Hon Roll; NHS; PA ST Exec Scholar 86; Acad Excllnce Spn II 84; Cert Beaver Cnty Hocky Assn 83; PA ST; Chem Engrng.

PETHERICK, KIM; Lackawanna Trl HS; Dalton, PA; (Y); 14/92; Rep Sec Church Yth Grp; Cmnty Wkr; Hon Roll; U Of Scranton; Math Prof.

PETHTEL, KIM; Linesville HS; Linesville, PA; (Y); 3/71; Am Leg Aux Girls St; Pep Clb; Ski Clb; SADD; Rep Stu Cncl; Var L Bsktbl; Im Coach Actv; Var L Sftbl; Var Vllybl; DAR Awd; U S Army Schlr/Athlt 86; Fml Athlt Of Yr 86; Schlrshps-Egan, Tny Dnghia, LCS Fclty Memrl, Rby Mrsh El; Mercyhurst Coll; Sprts Med.

PETITJEAN, BETH; Governor Mifflin HS; Shillington, PA; (Y); 34/280; Exploring; Hosp Aide; Nwsp Rptr; Lit Mag; Hon Roll; PA Free Entrpse Week Lock Haven U 85; Attnd Brks Lrsthp Wk 85; Am Crrnty Stg Mngr Aplha/Omege Plyrs; Tech Thtr Arts Coll; Stg Mngr.

PETKO, NANETTE; Spring-Ford SR HS; Royersford, PA; (S); 10/230; Trs German Clb; Sr Cls; Stu Cncl; Var L Bsktbl; Fld Hcky; Score Keeper; Sftbl; Hon Roll; Jr NHS; NHS; Distngshd Schlr Awd 85-86; Ursinus Schlrshp Awd 85-86; Ursinus Coll.

PETLIKOWSKI, LISA; East HS; West Chester, PA; (S); DECA; FBLA; SADD; Nwsp Stf; Yrbk Phtg; DECA Awd 6th Pl Food Mrktng Fld 85; 1st Pl Plus 2 Mdllns 86; W Chester U; Bus Mgmt.

PETLIKOWSKI, RENEE; East HS; West Chester, PA; (Y); 81/395; High Hon Roll; Hon Roll; Hm Ec Awd 85-86; West Chester U; Bus Adm.

PETNER, LISA; St Hubert HS; Philadelphia, PA; (Y); 22/367; Office Aide; Spanish Clb; Yrbk Stf; High Hon Roll; Hon Roll; Psych.

PETRAGLIA, DENISE; Cardinal O Hara HS; Drexel Hill, PA; (Y); 11/772; Church Yth Grp; French Clb; Service Clb; Varsity Clb; Yrbk Stf; Lit Mag; Var L Swmmng; High Hon Roll; Hon Roll; NHS; All Catholic Swmng 84-85.

PETRAKOVICH, BOB; Mount Pleasant Area HS; Mount Pleasant, PA; (Y); Cmnty Wkr; French Clb; Library Aide; Ski Clb; Band; JV Bsktbl; JV Var Ftbl; Var Capt Ftbl; Im Sftbl; JV Trk; S PA Intrschlr Hcky All Str Tm 85-86; Keystone ST Gms Hcky Tryts 85; U Of MI; Ntrtnl Exprt.

PETRATUS, JUDITH; Carmichaels Area HS; Rices Landing, PA; (Y); 6/108; French Clb; Office Aide; Varsity Clb; Chorus; Cheerleading; NHS; Psych.

PETRAVICH, ALAN; Pine Grove Area HS; Pine Grove, PA; (Y); Drama Clb; Chorus; School Musical; Rep Jr Cls; Rep Stu Cncl; God Cntry Awd; Hon Roll; NEDT Awd; Prfct Atten Awd; Jacobs Church Cncl Sec 86; Bio.

PETRELLI, GINA; Plum SR HS; New Kensington, PA; (Y); 90/415; Aud/Vis; Exploring; FHA; Library Aide; Ski Clb; Stage Crew; Hon Roll; Trvl Agnt.

PETRILAK, JOHN; Pen Argyl SR HS; Pen Argyl, PA; (Y); Chess Clb; Exploring; Ski Clb; Off Frsh Cls; Stu Cncl; Im Bsbl; Im Bsktbl; Var L Ftbl; Var Trk; Hon Roll; Lions Clb Ldrshp Smnr Dstrct 14u 86; 2nd Pl Nat Hstry Dy Muhlenberg Coll 86; Engrng.

PETRILLA, DOUGLAS; Central Bucks HS West; Doylestown, PA; (Y); 39/383; Am Leg Boys St; Mathletes; Model UN; Scholastic Bowl; Nwsp Bus Mgr; Cit Awd; NHS; Ntl Merit Schol; Pres Schlr; Church Yth Grp; Ntl Sci Olympd Chem; Spkr House Mdl Cngrs; U DE U Merit Schlrshp; U Delaware; Econ.

PETRILLA, STAN; North Star HS; Hooversville, PA; (Y); Art Clb; FCA; Math Clb; Varsity Clb; Var L Bsbl; Var L Bsktbl; Hon Roll; Stanley Davis Meml Awd 86; WV U.

PETRILLI, DENISE; St Marys Area HS; Saint Marys, PA; (Y); Boys Clb Am; Sec Frsh Cls; Sec Soph Cls; JV L Cheerleading; Var L Sftbl; Modeling.

PETRILLI, ROGER; St Marys Area HS; St Marys, PA; (Y); Varsity Clb; Var Capt Crs Cntry; Trk; High Hon Roll; NHS; Pres Schlr; PA ST U; Comp Sci.

PETRILLO, DENISE M; South Allegheny JR SR HS; Glassport, PA; (Y); Sec Camera Clb; Sec Church Yth Grp; French Clb; JA; Office Aide; Y-Teens; Powder Puff Ftbl; Var Trk; Hon Roll; Prfct Atten Awd; Accntng.

PETRILLO, MATTHEW; E L Meyers HS; Wilkes Barre, PA; (Y); Boy Scts; Ski Clb; Chorus; Var L Swmmng; Hon Roll; Cmmnctns.

PETRILLO, TRACEY; Farrell Area HS; Farrell, PA; (Y); Letterman Clb; Teachers Aide; Varsity Clb; Yrbk Stf; Lit Mag; Capt Var Cheerleading; NHS; Amer Lg Awd 83; Legal Asst.

PETRISHEN, NICK; Highland SR HS; Natrona Hts, PA; (Y); Im Bsktbl; Jr NHS; Schltc Achvt Awd 85.

PETRISIN JR, GERALD J; Clairton HS; Clairton, PA; (Y); Am Leg Boys St; High Hon Roll; Am Leg Schl Awd 83; Pol Sci.

PETRITSCH, KELLIE; Cardinal Brennan HS; Shenandoah, PA; (Y); 8/60; Spanish Clb; Art Clb; Dance Clb; Band; Co-Capt Cheerleading; Hon Roll; Spanish NHS; Spnsh Achvt Awd 85; Both JV & Vrsty Ltr Chrldg 84-85; Penn ST; Pharm.

PETRO, BETH; Canon-Mc Millan SR HS; Canonsburg, PA; (Y); 96/350; Church Yth Grp; Dance Clb; Ski Clb; Yrbk Stf; JV Sftbl; Var Tennis; Var Trk; Hon Roll; Spanish NHS; Awd Excllnc Lng Stu 86; Slippery Rock U; Sec Educ.

PETRO, CHERYL; Canon Mc Millan HS; Canonsburg, PA; (Y); 103/371; Church Yth Grp; Latin Clb; Varsity Clb; Band; Concert Band; Mrchg Band; JV Bsktbl; Var Sftbl; Hon Roll; Bnd Fstvl Awd 84; Orchstra Fstvl Awd 84; Excptnl Musicnshp 84; Music.

PETRO, CHRISTINE; Ringgold HS; Donora, PA; (Y); Church Yth Grp; Ski Clb; VP Stu Cncl; Gym; Hon Roll; NHS; Sci Math Hnr Soc Sec 85-86; Interact Clb 85-86.

PETRO, MISSY; Mc Keesport HS; White Oak, PA; (Y); 6/339; Church Yth Grp; Cmnty Wkr; French Clb; Office Aide; Yrbk Ed-Chief; Yrbk Rptr; Yrbk Stf; Rep Stu Cncl; Mgr Powder Puff Ftbl; High Hon Roll; Penn ST; Child Psych.

PETROFF II, PETER; California Area HS; California, PA; (Y); 7/103; Church Yth Grp; Pep Clb; Science Clb; Nwsp Rptr; Yrbk Stf; Rep Stu Cncl; Var L Ftbl; Score Keeper; Hon Roll; All Conf, Dist, Cnty Post Gazette Ftbl All Star 85-86; Co-MVP Ftbl 85-86; Bio Sci.

PETROLE, CHRIS; Marian Catholic HS; Tresckow, PA; (S); 2/114; Aud/Vis; Camera Clb; Chess Clb; Church Yth Grp; French Clb; Radio Clb; Scholastic Bowl; Ski Clb; School Play; Rep Frsh Cls; Aerontcl Engr.

PETRORE, TOM; Greater Johnstown HS; Johnstown, PA; (Y); Boy Scts; Computer Clb; JA; Math Clb; Spanish Clb; Stat Bsktbl; Var Tennis; Hon Roll; Law.

PETROSKE, JENNIFER; Ringgold HS; Donora, PA; (Y); Math Clb; Science Clb; Chorus; Hon Roll; Nrsng.

PETROSKI, APRIL; Bishop O Reilly HS; Dallas, PA; (Y); 4/109; Drama Clb; FBLA; Math Clb; Ski Clb; Chorus; School Play; Sec Frsh Cls; Sec Soph Cls; Sec Jr Cls; Stu Cncl; JR Acad Of Sci 1st Reg 2nd St 83-86; U Of Scranton; Bio.

PETROSKI, MEG; Seton Catholic HS; Wyoming, PA; (Y); Church Yth Grp; Ski Clb; School Musical; Variety Show; Cheerleading; Sftbl; Tennis; High Hon Roll; Hon Roll; Seton Catholic HS Schlrshp 82; Ntl Hnr Soc 84; LCBA Schlrshp Comptn Semfnlst 86; Luzerne Cnty CC; Pre-Phrmcy.

PETROSKI JR, RAYFORD; Wyoming Valley West HS; Edwardesville, PA; (Y); 58/358; Church Yth Grp; Quiz Bowl; Science Clb; Yrbk Stf; Crs Cntry; Trk; High Hon Roll; Hon Roll; NHS; U Scranton; Pre-Med.

PETROSKY, MICHAEL; Norwin SR HS; N Huntingdon, PA; (Y); Letterman Clb; Math Clb; Ski Clb; Spanish Clb; Var L Socr; JV Wrstlng; Hon Roll; PA ST; Engrng.

PETROSKY, SHERRI; Greater Latrobe SR HS; Latrobe, PA; (Y); 51/335; Pres Church Yth Grp; High Hon Roll; Hon Roll; Natl Art Hnr Socty; IN U Of PA; Elem Ed.

PETROSKY, WANDA; Greater Latrobe SR HS; Latrobe, PA; (Y); 9/335; Pres Church Yth Grp; JCL; French Hon Soc; High Hon Roll; NHS; Pres Schlr; IN U; Elem Ed.

PETROZZI JR, JOHN; St Josephs Preparatory Schl; Medford Lakes, NJ; (Y); Camera Clb; Dance Clb; Letterman Clb; Spanish Clb; Varsity Clb; L Golf; Socr; Wrstlng; High Hon Roll; Hon Roll; Catholic Lge Mdl In Crew 85 Awd In Crew; Ecnmcs.

PETRUNA, JOE; Homer Center HS; Coral, PA; (Y); Church Yth Grp; French Clb; Library Aide; Concert Band; Mrchg Band; School Musical; Yrbk Stf; Hon Roll; Jr NHS; NHS.

PETRUSH, JOHN R; Laurel Highlands HS; Puyallup, WA; (Y); Art Clb; French Clb; JA; Ski Clb; Pres Frsh Cls; VP Stu Cncl; Var Bsbl; Cheerleading; Var L Golf; Hon Roll; U WA; Engrng.

PETRUZZELLI, JOHN PAUL; Archbishop Ryan H S For Boys; Philadelphia, PA; (Y); 10/431; VP Church Yth Grp; SADD; Ed Nwsp Stf; Dnfth Awd; Elks Awd; NHS; Pres Schlr; Sal; Cmnty Wkr; Hugh O Brian Yth Found; St Josephs U; Sec Ed.

PETRY, GREGORY; Bishop Shanahan HS; Cochranville, PA; (Y); 71/218; Boy Scts; Chorus; School Musical; Var L Crs Cntry; Var L Trk; Aerospc Engr.

PETRY, JEFFREY; Bishop Shanahan HS; Cochranville, PA; (Y); 60/219; Boy Scts; Chorus; School Musical; Swing Chorus; Egl Sct 85; Mst Imprvd Chrl Stu 83-84; Chemcl Engrng.

PETTIGREW, MARCIA; Susquenita HS; Duncannon, PA; (Y); French Clb; Library Aide; Ed Yrbk Stf; Hon Roll; NEDT Awd.

PETTINATO, MARY ELIZABETH; Bishop Hannan HS; Scranton, PA; (Y); Spanish Clb; Rep Stu Cncl; Hon Roll; Computer Clb; Natl Piano Auditns 82 & 85; ST Stu Natl Piano Auditns 83 & 86; Awds Excllnc-Alg II/Trig 86; PA ST U; Arch Engrng.

PETTIT II, JACK B; Washington HS; Columbia, SC; (S); 11/167; Key Clb; Letterman Clb; Ski Clb; Spanish Clb; Jazz Band; Symp Band; JV Socr; Var Tennis; High Hon Roll; Hon Roll; Hgh Hnr Rl 83-84; U SC; Pre-Law.

PETTIT, TIM; Central Bucks HS West; Doylestown, PA; (Y); Boy Scts; Church Yth Grp; Chorus; Variety Show; JV Crs Cntry; Var L Wrstlng; Hon Roll; Eagle Scout 86; 2nd Team All Bux-Mont Wrstlng 86; Succsfly Cmpltd Gnrl Elec Prgm-Twn Mtng On Tmrw 85; Sprots Med.

PETTKO, LISA M; Mon Valley Catholic HS; Belle Vernon, PA; (S); 5/102; Ski Clb; Spanish Clb; Nwsp Ed-Chief; Rep Soph Cls; Trs Jr Cls; High Hon Roll; NHS; Spanish NHS; Rcpnt U Schlrshp Duquesne U; Duguesne U; Phrmcy.

PETTY, BRYAN; North Allegheny SR HS; Allison Park, PA; (Y); 157/605; Art Clb; Boy Scts; Exploring; French Clb; U Pittsburgh; Elect Engr.

PETTY, DAVID; Mt Lebanon HS; Pittsburgh, PA; (Y); Orch; School Musical; Hon Roll; PA Dist 1 Hnrs Band 85; Adv Plcmnt Hist 85-86 & Frnch 86-87; Three Rvrs Yng Peopls Orch 85-86; Comp Sci.

PETULLA, MISSY; Oil City HS; Oil City, PA; (Y); Varsity Clb; Variety Show; Im Var Cheerleading; Stat Wrstlng; High Hon Roll; Hon Roll; NHS.

PETUSKY, MIKE; Scranton Prep; Scranton, PA; (Y); 59/192; Var JV Bsbl; High Hon Roll; Hon Roll; Ecnmcs.

PEYAKOVICH, DANIELLE; Blue Mountain HS; Orwigsville, PA; (Y); 1/243; Exploring; Quiz Bowl; Chorus; Trs Soph Cls; Chrmn Stu Cncl; Var Cheerleading; French Hon Soc; Gov Hon Prg Awd; Mu Alp Tht; NHS; PA Govnrs Schl Sci 85; Ldrshp Awd 86; Susquehanna; Bus Admin.

PEYTON, KELLY; Shaler Area SR HS; Pittsburgh, PA; (Y); 31/517; Office Aide; Teachers Aide; Yrbk Stf; Hon Roll; NHS; Outstndg Spnsh I Avhvmnt 85; Marshall U; Optmtry.

PEYTON, SHELLEY; West Allegheny HS; Mcdonald, PA; (Y); #6 In Class; Pres Sec Church Yth Grp; Chorus; Capt Color Guard; Madrigals; High Hon Roll; Jr NHS; NHS; Ntl Merit Ltr; Acdmc All-Amer Awd 84-85; Gftd Prog.

PEZ, ANN; Benton Area JR SR HS; Stillwater, PA; (Y); Library Aide; Varsity Clb; Flag Corp; Mrchg Band; Rep Stu Cncl; Var Bsktbl; Var Fld Hcky; Sftbl; Elks Awd; Hon Roll; Wllmsprt WACC; Bus.

PEZZANO, MARK; Archbishop Ryan HS For Boys; Philadelphia, PA; (Y); Rep Frsh Cls; Holy Family Coll; Mgt.

PFAFF, CRAIG; Neshaminy SR HS; Levittown, PA; (Y); 129/750; Boy Scts; Var Capt Gym; Socr; Elks Awd; Hon Roll; Med.

PFAFF, GRETCHEN; Elk County Christian HS; St Marys, PA; (Y); Letterman Clb; Varsity Clb; Bowling; Cheerleading; The Linda Bolden Mem Awd-Excllnc Chrldng 86; St Marys Beauty Acad; Beauticn.

PFAFF, JILL; Elk County Christian HS; St Marys, PA; (Y); Letterman Clb; Varsity Clb; Stu Cncl; Var Capt Cheerleading; Hon Roll; Abnormal Phych.

PFEFFER, DAVID; Bishop Mc Devitt HS; Willow Grove, PA; (Y); 58/351; Boy Scts; Church Yth Grp; Bowling; Var Ftbl; High Hon Roll; Hon Roll; Kiwanis Awd; Highst GPA Sci Math & Relgn 82-86; MCCC; Med Lab Tech.

PFEIFER, ELLEN; Mt Pleasan T HS; Mt Pleasant, PA; (Y); French Clb; Ski Clb; Color Guard; Mrchg Band; Nwsp Stf; High Hon Roll; Hon Roll.

PFEIFER, MELISSA; Hempfield Area HS; Greensburg, PA; (Y); Camera Clb; Computer Clb; French Clb; Pep Clb; Nwsp Rptr; Nwsp Stf; Yrbk Phtg; Yrbk Stf; Jr NHS; Prfct Atten Awd; Phys Ther.

PFEIFFER, DEBBY; Marion Center HS; Marion Ctr, PA; (Y); Pres FNA; Science Clb; Band; Concert Band; Stage Crew; VP Frsh Cls; VP Soph Cls; VP Stu Cncl; Swmmng; Hon Roll.

PFEIFFER, JOHN DAVID; Saucon Valley HS; Bethlehem, PA; (Y); 4/171; Boy Scts; Scholastic Bowl; Chorus; Trs Stu Cncl; Capt Socr; Tennis; DAR Awd; Lion Awd; NHS; Ntl Merit Ltr; Hugh O Brien Yth Fndtn Ambssdr 84; 4-Yr Army ROTC Schlrshp 86; Cornell U; Engrng.

PFEIFFER, KARL; Northern Chester Co Vo Tech; Malvern, PA; (Y); Boy Scts; Wrstlng; Egl Sct 82; Hnr Rll 84.

PFEIFFER, LORIE; Hopewell HS; Aliquippa, PA; (Y); 63/280; Pres Church Yth Grp; DECA; JA; Chorus; Powder Puff Ftbl; Sftbl; High Hon Roll; Hon Roll; DECA; Spanish Clb; Bradford Bus Schl; Retail Mgt.

PFEUFER, KELLY; Elk County Christian HS; St Marys, PA; (Y); 24/88; Letterman Clb; Varsity Clb; Sec Jr Cls; Sec Sr Cls; Bsktbl; Var L Tennis; Var Trk; Hon Roll; NHS.

PFISTER, BRIAN D; A W Beattie-North Allegheny HS; Sewickley, PA; (S); VP DECA; 1st Pl DECA Food Mrktng Spvr Lvl Dist 85; 1st Pl DECA Food Mrktng Dist 86; Dist Ed Clb Amer Mktng; Allegheny CC; Retail Mrktng.

PFISTERER, KARIN BETH; Palisades JR SR HS; Upper Black Eddy, PA; (S); Chorus; Madrigals; School Musical; School Play; Variety Show; Sec Stu Cncl; Var L Cheerleading; Hon Roll; AFS; Church Yth Grp; Bcks Cnty Msc Fstvl 18th Chr Soprano 85; Rgnl Pres FBLA 85-86; Psychlgy.

PFLIEGLER, SCOTT; Freedom HS; Bethlehem, PA; (Y); 116/445; Comp.

PFLUEGER, JEFF; Blue Mt HS; Auburn, PA; (Y); 14/226; Boy Scts; Var Ftbl; Var Wt Lftg; Hon Roll; Hghst Mth Avg Voctnl Cur 86; Army.

PFROGNER, KIMBERLY; Mt Pleasant Area HS; Mt Pleasant, PA; (Y); 14/243; German Clb; GAA; Pres VICA; Mgr(s); Vllybl; NHS; Mt Pleasant Area SR HS Vrsty Schlstc 86; Schlrshp Westmorland Cnty Fed Wmns Awd 86; Stu Of Mnth 85; ICM Schl Bus; Med Off Assist.

PFUHL, NANCY; Gr Johnstown HS; Johnstown, PA; (Y); French Clb; Ski Clb; Mrchg Band; Trs Jr Cls; Sec Sr Cls; L Tennis; High Hon Roll; NHS.

PHAM, CHIEU; Manheim Township HS; Lancaster, PA; (Y); Church Yth Grp; Science Clb; Trk; Vllybl; High Hon Roll; Hon Roll; NHS; Prfct Atten Awd; Stu Of Mnth 84; Drexel; Elec Engrng.

PHAM, THIEP; Kutztown SR HS; Kutztown, PA; (Y); Aud/Vis; Computer Clb; Science Clb; Band; Concert Band; Mrchg Band; Trk; High Hon Roll; Prfct Atten Awd; Sec Dance Clb; Kutztwn U; Comp Sci.

PHANCO, THOMAS WAYNE; Chief Logan Joint HS; Mc Clure, PA; (Y); Church Yth Grp; FFA; SADD; Chorus; Trk; Wrstlng; High Hon Roll; OH Diesel Tech; Aviatn Engnr.

PHARR, LISA; Bensalem SR HS; Bensalem, PA; (Y); 38/538; Key Clb; ROTC; Nwsp Rptr; High Hon Roll; Hon Roll; NHS; Beaver Coll Schlrshp 85-86; Beaver Coll; Elem Educ.

PHAYRE, JENIFER; Chichester HS; Boothwyn, PA; (Y); Model UN; SADD; Chorus; School Musical; School Play; Nwsp Rptr; Yrbk Stf; Stu Cncl; Schlrshp Frm Amrcn Lgn 86; Ntl JR Hon Soc 83; NEDT S Awd 83; W Chester U.

PHEASANT, HOLLI; Williamsburg HS; Williamsburg, PA; (Y); 2/62; Church Yth Grp; Pres VP 4-H; Sec FFA; Band; Ed Nwsp Stf; Yrbk Stf; Capt Cheerleading; Bausch & Lomb Sci Awd; High Hon Roll; NHS; FFA Kystn Deg 86; Srptmst Yth Ctznshp Awd Blr Cnt 3rd 85-86; Deklb Ag Awd 86; Juniata Coll; Pre-Med.

PHELAN, KATIE; Franklin Regional HS; Murrysville, PA; (Y); AFS; Library Aide; Ski Clb; Spanish Clb; Stage Crew; JV Cheerleading; Trk; High Hon Roll; Intl Bus.

PHELAN, MARK; Saegertown HS; Saegertown, PA; (Y); 34/125; SADD; Bsktbl; Golf; Vllybl; Hon Roll; Jr NHS; NHS; Ltrd Bsktbl 85-86.

PHELAN, PAULA; Saegertown HS; Meadville, PA; (Y); 11/117; Letterman Clb; Spanish Clb; Varsity Clb; Hon Roll; Jr NHS; JV Var Sftbl; JV Var Vllybl; Paralegal.

PHILIPS, CURT; Karns City HS; Chicora, PA; (Y); 5/116; Church Yth Grp; Exploring; Golf; Hon Roll; NHS; Licensed Arch.

PHILIPS, CURTIS; Karns City HS; Chicora, PA; (Y); 5/116; Church Yth Grp; Exploring; Golf; Hon Roll; NHS; Archt.

PHILLIPPE, LUCIEN; Cheltenham HS; Wyncote, PA; (Y); 140/360; Science Clb; Rep Soph Cls; Im Badmtn; Im Bsktbl; JV Ftbl; JV Gym; JV Trk; Athl Ftnss Awd 86; French II Hnrs 1st Smstr 84; Engr.

PHILLIPPI, JEFFREY; Rockwood Area HS; Rockwood, PA; (Y); Spanish Clb; Trk; Wrstlng; Hon Roll; Dist 5 Wrstlng Champ 85-86; PA All Star Wrstlng Tm 84-86; Slippery Rock U; Physcl Thrpy.

PHILLIPS, A BENJAMIN M; Moravian Acad; Allentown, PA; (Y); 12/55; Pres Computer Clb; Science Clb; Ski Clb; Teachers Aide; Nwsp Ed-Chief; Nwsp Rptr; Nwsp Stf; Off Frsh Cls; Off Soph Cls; Off Jr Cls; Sci Awd 86; Tutorial Awd 84; Johns Hopkins U; Elect Engr.

PHILLIPS, ABBEE; Neshaminy HS; Langhorne, PA; (Y); 54/728; Ski Clb; SADD; Temple Yth Grp; Chorus; Concert Band; Jazz Band; Rep Stu Cncl; JV Fld Hcky; Mgr(s); Hon Roll; Amer Lgn Awd 83-84; Physl Thrpst.

PHILLIPS, ANDREW JOHN; Punxsutawney Area HS; Rochester Mills, PA; (Y); Art Clb; Science Clb; Varsity Clb; Var L Bsbl; Var L Ftbl; French Clb; Variety Show; Hon Roll; Pre-Med.

PHILLIPS, ANN MARIE; Catasauqua HS; Catasauqua, PA; (Y); 7/128; Church Yth Grp; Drama Clb; Ski Clb; School Musical; School Play; Lit Mag; Rep Soph Cls; Rep Jr Cls; Rep Sr Cls; Hon Roll; Ntl Sci Merit Awd 85; Ind Psychlgst.

PHILLIPS, BENJAMIN; Susquehanna Township HS; Harrisburg, PA; (Y); 3/160; Am Leg Boys St; Rep Key Clb; Letterman Clb; Math Tm; Model UN; Speech Tm; Thesps; Varsity Clb; VP L Bsbl; High Hon Roll; Hugh O Brian Yth Ldrshp Smnr 85; STEP Semnr For Top Engrng Prspcts At Purdue U 86; U Of Notre Dame; Engrng.

PHILLIPS, BETHANY; James M Coughlin HS; Wilkes Barre, PA; (Y); #1 In Class; Orch; Nwsp Stf; High Hon Roll; Jr NHS; NHS; Ntl Merit Schol; NEDT Awd; Val; Georgetown U; Interprtr.

PHILLIPS, BRENNA; Bellefonte Area HS; Bellefonte, PA; (Y); Church Yth Grp; Spanish Clb; Var JV Cheerleading; Vllybl; Hon Roll; Penn ST U; Scndry Educ.

PHILLIPS, CALVIN; Canton JR SR HS; Marsh Hill, PA; (Y); 15/125; Church Yth Grp; French Clb; Science Clb; Teachers Aide; Ftbl; Trk; Hon Roll; Ltrmns Clb 84-85; Psych.

PHILLIPS, CHERYL; Elizabeth-Forward HS; Elizabeth, PA; (Y); 1/325; Debate Tm; 4-H; JA; NFL; Pep Clb; Ed Yrbk Stf; Cheerleading; High Hon Roll; NHS; Spanish NHS; Dncng 14 Yrs 1st Pl Awd 84 & 86; Hmnties Awd U Of Pittsburgh 85; Prtl Schlrshp J Casablancas Ctr 86; Law.

PHILLIPS, CHRISTIAN; South Philadelphia HS; Philadelphia, PA; (Y); 215/643; Boy Scts; Church Yth Grp; Teachers Aide; JV L Bsbl; Im Vllybl; US Naval Aviatr.

PHILLIPS, CHRISTOPHER J; Corry Area HS; Corry, PA; (Y); 115/200; Pres Aud/Vis; Boy Scts; Church Yth Grp; Pres Radio Clb; Ski Clb; Var L Bsktbl; Var L Crs Cntry; Var L Mgr(s); Var L Trk; Altr Boy; Embry-Riddle Aerontcl U; Offcr.

PHILLIPS, DAVID; Meyers HS; Wilkes Bare, PA; (Y); Church Yth Grp; German Clb; Chorus; Church Choir; Swmmng; Trk; Hon Roll; Phys Ther.

PHILLIPS, DAVID E; Waynesburg Central HS; Waynesburg, PA; (Y); Art Clb; Camera Clb; Chess Clb; Computer Clb; French Clb; Letterman Clb; Bsktbl; Crs Cntry; Trk; Hon Roll; Marin Bio.

PHILLIPS, DAWN; Tunkhannock HS; Tunkhannock, PA; (S); Aud/Vis; Spanish Clb; Color Guard; Flag Corp; JV Bsktbl; Hon Roll; Law.

PHILLIPS, DENNIS; Franklin JRSR HS; Franklin, PA; (Y); Church Yth Grp; Band; Concert Band; Jazz Band; Mrchg Band; Pep Band; High Hon Roll; Hon Roll; Pres Chrch Yth Grp 85-86; VP Band 86-87; Photo.

PHILLIPS, DONALD; Brownsville Area HS; Grindstone, PA; (S); 9/225; VICA; Wrstlng; Awd 3rd Pl Vica, ST Compttn & Diesel Mech 86; OH Diesel Inst; Diesel Mech.

PHILLIPS, DWIGHT; Carmichaels Area HS; Nemacolin, PA; (Y); 17/102; Ski Clb; Spanish Clb; High Hon Roll; Hon Roll; NHS; Penn ST; Arspc Engrng.

PHILLIPS, GARY; Danville HS; Riverside, PA; (Y); 82/204; Boy Scts; Drama Clb; Red Cross Aide; Spanish Clb; School Play; Nwsp Rptr; Var Capt Bowling; Eagle Scout 84; Amer Lgn Good Ctzn Citation 85; PA House Of Rep Good Ctznshp Citation 85; Sociology.

PHILLIPS, JACQUELYN; Harry S Truman HS; Levittown, PA; (Y); Church Yth Grp; Girl Scts; Band; Mrchg Band; Trk; Hon Roll; NHS; Prfct Atten Awd; Psychology.

PHILLIPS, JANET; Waynesburg Central HS; Waynesburg, PA; (S); Sec VP DECA; Trs Library Aide; High Hon Roll; Hon Roll; Bradford DECA Schlrshp-Top 5 Fnlst 86; Bradford DECA Schlrshp Wnnr 86; Bradford Busnss Schl; Retl Mgmt.

PHILLIPS, JENNIFER; Carmilhaels Area HS; Carmichaels, PA; (Y); 22/110; Band; Drm Mjr(t); Ski Clb; Spanish Clb; SADD; Concert Band; Mrchg Band; Cheerleading; Twrlr; DAR Awd; Bus Mgmnt.

PHILLIPS, JOEL; Simon Gratz HS; Philadelphia, PA; (S); 20/341; Debate Tm; JA; Library Aide; Office Aide; Pep Clb; Chorus; Off Frsh Cls; Off Soph Cls; Pres Jr Cls; VP Sr Cls; E Strousberg U; Comp Sci.

PHILLIPS, JOHN H; West York HS; York, PA; (Y); 27/200; Am Leg Boys St; Boy Scts; Church Yth Grp; German Clb; JA; Yrbk Stf; JV Var Vllybl; Hon Roll; The Citadel; Elec Engrng.

PHILLIPS, JULIE; Chambersburg Area SR HS; Chambersburg, PA; (Y); 160/640; AFS; Pres Church Yth Grp; Drama Clb; Key Clb; Band; Chorus; Church Choir; Concert Band; Flag Corp; Mrchg Band; Elem Ed.

PHILLIPS, KRISTEN; North Allegheny HS; Wexford, PA; (Y); 149/605; Church Yth Grp; Band; Concert Band; Mrchg Band; Pep Band; School Musical; School Play; Symp Band; Variety Show; Hon Roll; Mid E Music Fstvl & Allegheny Vly Honrs Bnd 84-85; Hon Ment Pgh Alliance Cntst 85; Music Schlrshp 86; Slippery Rock U; Music.

PHILLIPS, KRISTI; East SR HS; West Chester, PA; (Y); Cmnty Wkr; FBLA; Hosp Aide; Hst JCL; Latin Clb; Capt Color Guard; School Musical; Stage Crew; Yrbk Rptr; Hon Roll; St Eberharda Schlrshp-Neumann Coll; Chester Cnty Hosp Svc Volunteer Awd 86; Neumann Coll; Commctns.

PHILLIPS, LAURIE; Franklin JR SR HS; Franklin, PA; (Y); Aud/Vis; Church Yth Grp; Library Aide; Office Aide; Ski Clb; Spanish Clb; Var L Cheerleading; Stat Wrstlng; Hon Roll; ICM Schl Bus; Bus.

PHILLIPS, LEEANN; Penn Cambria HS; Cresson, PA; (Y); Drama Clb; Ski Clb; Spanish Clb; VP Frsh Cls; Bsktbl; JV Cheerleading; Vllybl; High Hon Roll; Hon Roll; NHS.

PHILLIPS, LINDA; Carmichaels Area SR HS; Carmichaels, PA; (S); Ski Clb; Sec Spanish Clb; Band; Chorus; Capt Color Guard; Mrchg Band; Trs Sr Cls; Stu Cncl; NHS; Ntl Merit Ltr; PA ST University Pk; Bus Adm.

PHILLIPS, LYNN; Windber Area HS; Windber, PA; (Y); Math Clb; Ski Clb; L Capt Bsktbl; Var L Sftbl; Var L Vllybl; High Hon Roll; Hon Roll; Church Yth Grp; Computer Clb; GAA; Hgst Grade Alg II 85-86; Dist Bsktbl Freethrw 83-84; BMX 85-86; U Pittsburgh; Hlth.

PHILLIPS, MICHAEL E; Monaca HS; Monaca, PA; (Y); 1/76; Pres FBLA; VICA; Nwsp Ed-Chief; Yrbk Stf; Stu Cncl; Mgr(s); Lion Awd; NHS; Val; 1st Plc VICA Comp Prog Comptn Dist ST Lvls 86; Pres Acad Ftnss Awd Wnnr 86; Wnnr Amer Legn Schshp 86; Robert Morris Coll; Bus Inf Sys.

PHILLIPS, NED; E L Meyers HS; Wilkes Barre, PA; (Y); 23/140; Church Yth Grp; Spanish Clb; Chorus; Church Choir; Crs Cntry; Swmmng; Trk; NEDT Awd; BYU; Crmnl Jstc.

PHILLIPS, NEIL; Cheltenham HS; Laverock, PA; (Y); 21/365; Debate Tm; Science Clb; Rep Soph Cls; Rep Jr Cls; Var Socr; French Hon Soc; Ntl Merit Ltr; NEDT Awd; 1st Dist PJAS Comp 85; 2nd St PJAS Comp 85; 2nd DE Vlly Sci Comp 86.

PHILLIPS, PAUL; Plum Boro SR HS; Pittsburgh, PA; (Y); Boy Scts; Camera Clb; Exploring; Letterman Clb; Political Wkr; School Play; Nwsp Phtg; Yrbk Phtg; Yrbk Stf; Coach Actv; Rifle Tm 2 Ltrs Vrsty; U KY; Phys Ther.

PHILLIPS, PAULA; St Maria Goretti HS; Philadelphia, PA; (Y); 33/426; GAA; Variety Show; Rep Soph Cls; Rep Jr Cls; Sec Sr Cls; Stu Cncl; Var L Vllybl; High Hon Roll; NHS; Church Yth Grp; Natl Soc Stud Olym Awd 85&86; Cabrini Coll; Cmmnctns.

PHILLIPS, RICKY; Philipsburg-Osceola SR HS; West Decatur, PA; (Y); 52/219; Crs Cntry; Wt Lftg; Wrstlng; God Cntry Awd; Hon Roll; Martial Arts Purple Blet Goshin Jutsu 82-85; Annapolis; Ofcr Training.

PHILLIPS, ROCHELLE; El Meyers HS; Wilkes Barre, PA; (Y); Church Yth Grp; Soph Cls; Bsktbl; Fld Hcky; Trk; High Hon Roll; Hon Roll; Jr NHS; NHS; Spanish NHS; Scholar Coll Discovery Pgm Kings Coll 86; Dist Wnnr Mile Relay 85; Ed.

PHILLIPS, SAMUEL; Middletown Area HS; Middletown, PA; (Y); Hon Roll; Radlgy Tech.

PHILLIPS, SCOTT; Bethel Park SR HS; Bethel Park, PA; (Y); Orch; School Musical; Rep Soph Cls; Var L Swmmng; High Hon Roll; Hon Roll; NHS; Wnnr Natl Hist Day 83-84; Stu Prince 84-85; VA ST; Pre-Med.

PHILLIPS, SHARON; St Maria Goretti HS; Philadelphia, PA; (Y); 31/426; Church Yth Grp; Dance Clb; Trs GAA; Mathletes; Math Clb; Science Clb; Teachers Aide; Stage Crew; Var Tennis; VP NHS; French Awd Hon Mntn 85; Ntl Hist & Gov Awd 85; Drexel U; Comm.

PHILLIPS, TAMMY; Philipsburg-Osceola Area SR HS; Philipsburg, PA; (Y); 43/250; Church Yth Grp; Pep Clb; Ski Clb; SADD; Yrbk Stf; Bsktbl; Sftbl; Vllybl; Hon Roll; Educ.

PHILLIPS, TAMMY YVONNE; Burgettstown HS; Burgettstown, PA; (Y); Church Yth Grp; Cmnty Wkr; FHA; GAA; Girl Scts; Library Aide; Office Aide; Teachers Aide; Chorus; Church Choir; Nrsg.

PHILLIPS, TODD; Hughesville HS; Muncy, PA; (Y); 10/150; VP Church Yth Grp; Bsbl; Bsktbl; Im Vllybl; NHS; Grn & White Awd 84-86; Law Enfrcmnt.

PHILLIPS JR, WILLIAM G; Windber Area HS; Windber, PA; (Y); 12/128; Church Yth Grp; Bsbl; Bowling; Golf; High Hon Roll; NHS; Stu Mnth 84; Med.

PHILLIS, JUDITH; Ft Cherry HS; Mc Donald, PA; (S); 1/131; Church Yth Grp; Math Clb; Science Clb; Trs Varsity Clb; Band; Chorus; Drm Mjr(t); Capt Sftbl; Twrlr; Capt Vllybl.

PHILPOTT, JEAN; Hampton HS; Allison Pk, PA; (Y); 4/225; Church Yth Grp; Ski Clb; Church Choir; Mrchg Band; Symp Band; Rep Stu Cncl; Capt L Crs Cntry; L Trk; NHS; Pres Schlr; Westinghse Sci Hnrs Inst Lect Series 85-86; Astronmy Apprentcshp 85-86; Mid East Hnrs Band 84-85; Cornell U; Aero Sp Engr.

PHOUTTHASINH, DAWN; York County Vo-Tech; York, PA; (Y); Exploring; FBLA; FNA; Hosp Aide; Math Tm; Service Clb; Teachers Aide; VICA; Sec Soph Cls; Hon Roll; RN.

PIA, ELIZABETH; Downingtown SR HS; Downingtown, PA; (S); 22/527; Dance Clb; GAA; Spanish Clb; Teachers Aide; JV Var Cheerleading; Var Trk; Twrlr; High Hon Roll; NHS; Spnsh Cert 82-83; Phy Fit Pres Awds 82-83; Ldrshp, Acadmc & Chrldg Awds 85-86; TEMPLE; Hlth Fld.

PIA, RENATO; Downingtown HS; Downingtown, PA; (Y); 112/510; Art Clb; Letterman Clb; Yrbk Stf; Ftbl; Trk; Wt Lftg; Wrstlng; Gov Hon Prg Awd; Hon Roll; Schlstc Art Awds Ntl Recog 86; 1st Pl One Artst Shw 86; Cngrsmns Mdl Of Mrt In Art 85-86; Pratt Inst; Illstrtn.

PIANO, BRET; Hatboro-Horsham HS; Hatboro, PA; (Y); JV Socr; Var Tennis; Hon Roll.

PIATT, HOWARD SCOTT; Lock Haven SR HS; Lock Haven, PA; (Y); Boy Scts; Chess Clb; Church Yth Grp; Model UN; School Play; Nwsp Rptr; JV Socr; Hon Roll; Lock Haven ST U; Eng.

PICARD, LAUREN; Carlyntan HS; Carnegie, PA; (Y); French Clb; Drill Tm; VP Jr Cls; L Trk; High Hon Roll; NHS; Amer Legn Awd 83-84; Math.

PICCA, KIMBERLY; Valley View JR SR HS; Archbald, PA; (Y); 5/201; Nwsp Stf; Ed Yrbk Ed-Chief; Sec Stu Cncl; Capt Cheerleading; Var Trk; Elks Awd; High Hon Roll; Sec NHS; Prfct Atten Awd; Pres Schlr; Dist II 100 M Track Champ 86; Schlr Yr 86; USCA 2nd Indvl Chrldng Awd 85; Penn ST U; Pre-Law.

PICCOLINO, JOHN; Bishop Hannan HS; Scranton, PA; (Y); 17/122; Bowling; Hon Roll; Excllnc Alg II/Trig 85-86; Hnrbl Mntn Chem & Comp Pgmg 85-86.

PICCOLO, BRONWYN; St Marys Area HS; Saint Marys, PA; (Y); 54/301; Hosp Aide; Red Cross Aide; Band; Concert Band; Mrchg Band; Stage Crew; Rep Stu Cncl; Mgr(s); Timer; Stat Trk; Nrsng.

PICCOLOMINI, MARLA; Laurel Highlands HS; Uniontown, PA; (Y); 84/349; Art Clb; Office Aide; Pep Clb; Nwsp Stf; DAR Awd; Hon Roll; Jr NHS; Phy Thrpy.

PICHIARELLO, MARY BETH; Bishop O Hara HS; Dunmore, PA; (S); 1/113; French Clb; Latin Clb; Nwsp Rptr; Yrbk Stf; High Hon Roll; NHS; Prfct Atten Awd; Hugh Obrien Cntrl PA Ldrshp Smnr 85; Lwyr.

PICHLER, JENNIFER; St Marys Area HS; Kersey, PA; (Y); 29/301; Church Yth Grp; Girl Scts; Hosp Aide; JA; Varsity Clb; Yrbk Stf; Var Cheerleading; Var JV Trk; Hon Roll; Psych.

PICK, KRISTINE; Delaware Valley HS; Dingmans Fy, PA; (S); Church Yth Grp; Drama Clb; Band; Concert Band; Jazz Band; School Musical; School Play; Var Capt Bsktbl; High Hon Roll; NHS; PA Govr Schl Semi-Fnlst Pian 84 & 85; PA Regnsl Schl Fnlst Pian 84; Pike Cnty JR Ms 86; Muscl Entertnr.

PICKARD, JENNIFER; Scranton Prep Schl; Archbald, PA; (Y); 25/200; Nwsp Stf; Yrbk Stf; Swmmng; Trk; Jr NHS; NHS; Ntl Merit Ltr; Law.

PICKENHEIM, TIMOTHY; North Pcono HS; Moscow, PA; (S); 4/240; Church Yth Grp; Trs JA; Band; Concert Band; Mrchg Band; Nwsp Stf; Var Trk; High Hon Roll; NHS; Engrng Penn ST; Aerospc Engr.

PICKERSGILL, JANET; Penncrest HS; Media, PA; (Y); Church Yth Grp; Office Aide; Drill Tm; School Musical; Variety Show; AFS; Yrbk Stf; Hon Roll; NHS; U Of DE; Elem Ed.

PICKETT, DEBORAH; Wyalusing Valley JR SR HS; Laceyville, PA; (Y); FBLA; Ski Clb; Spanish Clb; SADD; Yrbk Stf; High Hon Roll; Hon Roll; VP Frsh Cls; VP Soph Cls; VP Jr Cls; Dustrct All Str Sftbl 85-86; Cnty JR Ms Fnlst 86-87; Biochem.

PICKETT, KIM; Elkland Area HS; Elkland, PA; (Y); 8/88; French Clb; High Hon Roll; NHS; Acadmc Lttr; Acadmc All Am; Teaching Frgn Languages.

PICKETT, KIMBERLY; Cowanesque Valley HS; Westfield, PA; (S); 8/88; French Clb; Hon Roll; NHS; Ntl Merit Ltr; Bus Clb; Acad All Amer; Frgn Lang.

PICKUP, JULIE; Purchase Line HS; Commodore, PA; (Y); 30/130; Church Yth Grp; French Clb; FBLA; Pep Clb; Ski Clb; Band; Bsktbl; Gym; Twrlr; Hon Roll; IN U PA; Econ.

PICKUP, KATHLEEN; Archbishop Ryan H S For Girls; Philadelphia, PA; (Y); 26/475; Am Leg Aux Girls St; Pres JA; Yrbk Phtg; Rep Sr Cls; Stu Cncl; Im Bsktbl; NHS; Art Clb; French Clb; Q&S; Engl, Wrld Cult, Art Certs Of Merit 83; Art Cert Of Merit 84; Penn ST U; Comm.

PIDA, DAVID; North Penn HS; Blossburg, PA; (Y); 8/67; Church Yth Grp; VP Key Clb; Pres Varsity Clb; Concert Band; Bsbl; Bsktbl; High Hon Roll; Pres Schlr; Prom Committee Chrmn 86; Stu Cncl Stu Forum Rep 85-8l; Le Moyne Coll; Bus.

PIDGEON, CHRIS; Sacred Heart HS; Carbondale, PA; (Y); 1/42; Chess Clb; FBLA; Trs Spanish Clb; Var L Bsktbl; High Hon Roll; NHS; Library Aide; Teachers Aide; Chorus; Full Schlrshp To HS 83-87; Lehigh; Pre-Law.

PIDGEON, MARY T; Sacred Heart HS; Carbondale, PA; (Y); 13/57; Scholastic Bowl; Spanish Clb; Var L Bsktbl; High Hon Roll; NHS; Ntl Merit Ltr; Computer Clb; Hosp Aide; Latin Clb; Full Scholar 82; Pres Acad Fit Awd 86; Bishops Awd Yth Ministry 86; U Scranton; Biol.

PIE, MARK; Geibel HS; Connellsville, PA; (Y); Boy Scts; Church Yth Grp; French Clb; Science Clb; Ski Clb; Var L Ftbl; Wt Lftg; French Hon Soc; Hon Roll; Cardio Surgry.

PIECHNICK, CRAIG; Canon Mc Millan SR HS; Canonsburg, PA; (Y); 1/390; Computer Clb; French Clb; Varsity Clb; Yrbk Stf; VP Trs Stu Cncl; Var Bsbl; Var Capt Ftbl; Var Wrstlng; High Hon Roll; NHS; Natl Journlsm Awd 83; Pre Med.

PIEKANSKI, CHARLIE; Tunkhannock Area HS; Dallas, PA; (Y); Boy Scts; Church Yth Grp; FCA; Latin Clb; Letterman Clb; Spanish Clb; VP Sr Cls; Var Bsbl; Var Ftbl; Var Wt Lftg; Outstndng Offnsv Linemn 85; WY Vly Conf Chmpns Bsbl 86; Trphy 1000 Lb Clb 86; Lwyr.

PIERCE, BETH; Union Area Middle HS; New Castle, PA; (Y); 20/60; French Clb; Hosp Aide; Library Aide; Band; Mrchg Band; Pep Band; Nwsp Stf; Stat Trk; Hon Roll; NHS; Tp Quartile 85-86.

PIERCE, JIM; Canon Mc Millan SR HS; Canonsburg, PA; (Y); Ski Clb; Stage Crew; Trk; Hon Roll.

PIERCE, OLIVIA; Cedar Crest HS; Lebanon, PA; (Y); 59/305; Church Yth Grp; French Clb; Pep Clb; Band; Concert Band; Mrchg Band; Vllybl; Hon Roll; Hnr Bnqt 86; U Of MD; Arch.

PIERCE, R MATSON; Danville Area HS; Danville, PA; (Y); VP Church Yth Grp; Computer Clb; French Clb; Key Clb; Ski Clb; Yrbk Sprt Ed; Rep Stu Cncl; Var Socr; Var Tennis; Susquehanna Vly All Star Soccer Tm 84-86.

PIERCE, SCOTT E; Rocky Grove HS; Franklin, PA; (Y); 28/95; Chess Clb; Church Yth Grp; French Clb; Band; Concert Band; Jazz Band; Pep Band; School Musical; Stage Crew; Var JV Bsktbl; Dist Band 85 & 86.

PIERCE, SHERRI; West Mifflin Area HS; W Mifflin, PA; (Y); 11/330; Exploring; Hosp Aide; Office Aide; Concert Band; Mrchg Band; JV Powder Puff Ftbl; High Hon Roll; Hon Roll; Jr NHS; NHS; Elem Educ.

PIERCE, STEPHANIE LYNE; Solanco HS; Kirkwood, PA; (Y); FTA; JA; Teachers Aide; Lit Mag; Var Crs Cntry; Im Vllybl; Hon Roll; Masonic Awd; Elem Ed.

PIERCE, SUSAN; Montour HS; Coraopolis, PA; (Y); Dance Clb; Rep Stu Cncl; Var Gym; High Hon Roll; NHS; Montour GATE Prgm 83-86.

PIERCE, VANESSA; Troy SR HS; Col X Rds, PA; (Y); Letterman Clb; Mgr Bsktbl; Capt Trk; Lion Awd; Troy Bus & Prof Wmns Orgnztn 86; Rep Troy Schl At Renovo Flmng Foliage 85; Pres Of UMYF 85-86; Corning Cmnty Coll; Acctg.

PIERMATTEO, VICTORIA; Upper Merion Area HS; King Of Prussia, PA; (Y); 29/320; Sec German Clb; Intnl Clb; Math Tm; Model UN; Chorus; Yrbk Stf; Rep Stu Cncl; Im Vllybl; High Hon Roll; NHS; Acdmc Awd 84&85; German Awd High Av 84; Finance.

PIERRE, MICHELE; North Pocono HS; Moscow, PA; (Y); 8/236; Church Yth Grp; Girl Scts; Chorus; Church Choir; Pres Concert Band; Pres Mrchg Band; Sec Orch; School Musical; High Hon Roll; NHS; Dist, Regnl Orch 83-86; Dist Chorus 86; Girl Scout Slvr Awd 83; Mus Ed.

PIERZGA, PATRICIA; Notre Dame HS; Nazareth, PA; (Y); Color Guard; Flag Corp; High Hon Roll; Hon Roll; Prfct Atten Awd; U Of Scrntn; Comm Media.

PIESHEFSKI, SUSAN; Mid-Valley Secondary Ctr; Throop, PA; (Y); Ski Clb; VICA; Cheerleading; High Hon Roll; Hon Roll; Csmtlgst.

PIETRANTONIO, LISA; Sharon SR HS; Sharon, PA; (Y); Shenago Vly Schl; Secr.

PIETROCARLO, LAURIE; Morrisville HS; Morrisville, PA; (Y); FBLA; School Musical; Yrbk Stf; Trs Soph Cls; Trs Jr Cls; Trs Sr Cls; Cheerleading; Sftbl; Hon Roll; NHS; Bulldog Awd Chrldng 84-86; Mst Dedctd Sftbll Plyr 85-86; Mst Conscnts Bst Attd 85-86; Bradford Bus Schl; Commnctns.

PIETROLAJ, TRICIA; Mid-Valley HS; Throop, PA; (Y); Ski Clb; Nwsp Phtg; Nwsp Rptr; Nwsp Stf; Cheerleading; Mgr Ftbl; Mgr(s); Vllybl; Mgr Wrstlng; Bus Adm.

PIETROPAOLO, VINCE; Shaler HS; Glenshaw, PA; (Y); 51/517; Ski Clb; Sftbl; Hon Roll; Engineering.

PIETRUSEWICZ, ELAINE; Peters Township HS; Mc Murray, PA; (Y); 12/250; Church Yth Grp; Hosp Aide; Church Choir; Drill Tm; Mrchg Band; Wrstlng; High Hon Roll; NHS; Spanish NHS; Hrt Srgn.

PIFER, MICHAEL; Meadville Area SR HS; Meadville, PA; (Y); 67/291; Ski Clb; SADD; Off Sr Cls; Stu Cncl; Ice Hcky; IN U PA; Bus.

PIFER, RODNEY; Punxsutawney Area HS; Reynoldsville, PA; (Y); Church Yth Grp; Band; Mrchg Band; Hon Roll; Triangle Tech; Crpntry.

PIFER, ROSS; Punxsutawney Area HS; Reynoldsville, PA; (Y); 8/238; Church Yth Grp; Variety Show; Yrbk Stf; Rep Stu Cncl; L Crs Cntry; L Trk; DAR Awd; 4-H Awd; Pres NHS; Rotary Awd; PA ST U; Agribus.

PIGHETLI, GINA; Bald Eagle Area HS; Howard, PA; (Y); Aud/Vis; Library Aide; Spanish Clb; Teachers Aide; Bsktbl; Gym; Mat Maids; Powder Puff Ftbl; High Hon Roll; Bio.

PIGMAN, MATTHEW; Peters Township HS; Bridgeville, PA; (Y); Church Yth Grp; Lit Mag; Ice Hcky; Tennis; High Hon Roll; Hon Roll; Acad All Str Hcky Tm; Bucknell U; Psychol.

PIGZA, JENNIFER; Bishop Carroll HS; Ebensburg, PA; (S); 5/104; Ski Clb; Pres SADD; Yrbk Stf; Rep Stu Cncl; L Vllybl; Hon Roll; Pres NHS; NEDT Awd; Duquesne U; Jrnlsm.

PIHIOU, GEORGE; Ganon Mc Millian HS; Canonsburg, PA; (Y); Church Yth Grp.

PIKE, BRADLEY A; Altoona Area HS; Altoona, PA; (Y); Art Clb; Computer Clb; French Clb; Lit Mag; Off Stu Cncl; HS Pblc Lbrary Art Cntst-1st Pl Wtrclr 85; HS Wmns Clb Art Cntst-3rd Pl Wtrclr 85; Air Force; Comp Sci.

PIKULSKY, RICHELLE; Uniontown Area SR HS; Uniontown, PA; (Y); 9/287; JA; Spanish Clb; Capt Drill Tm; Trs Jr Cls; Trs Sr Cls; Stu Cncl; Stat Swmmng; High Hon Roll; NHS; Achvrs Awd JA 85; Phrmcy.

PILARSKI, LORRAINE; Mercy Vocational HS; Philadelphia, PA; (Y); 1/20; Hosp Aide; Nwsp Ed-Chief; Ed Nwsp Stf; Hon Roll; Prfct Atten Awd; Merit Awd 83-85; Punctuality Awd 83-86.

PILEWSKI, JULIE; Venango Christian HS; Oil City, PA; (Y); 3/36; Sec Frsh Cls; Trs Sr Cls; Rep Stu Cncl; Stat Score Keeper; VP NHS; NEDT Awd.

PILLA, MARY JO; St Maria Goretti HS; Philadelphia, PA; (Y); 143/390; Orch; Hon Roll; Katharine Gibbs Bus Schl; Sec.

PILLAR, SAMANTHA; Saint Francis Acad; Allentown, PA; (Y); 7/20; Church Yth Grp; Drama Clb; Hosp Aide; Sec VP JA; Service Clb; Chorus; School Musical; Hon Roll; PA JR Acad Sci Cmptn 2nd, 1st Rgn 85 & 86; PA JR Acad Sci Cmptn 2nd ST 86; HSTRC Presrvtn.

PILLER, TIM; Bradford Area HS; Bradford, PA; (Y); JV Bsktbl; Var L Ftbl; Vllybl; Wt Lftg; Hon Roll; Flg Ftbl Trphy, Ftbl Awds, Voolbl Awds 82-83 & 84-86; Wghtlftng Awd 86; Wldlf Mgmt.

PILLITTERI, JANINE; Seneca Valley HS; Mars, PA; (Y); French Clb; Pep Clb; Ski Clb; SADD; Yrbk Stf; Rep Stu Cncl; Co-Capt Cheerleading; Gym; Hon Roll; NHS; 3 Yr Schlrshp Awd 86; IN U PA.

PILOTTI JR, WILLIAM L; Bishop Shanahan Catholic HS; Coatesville, PA; (Y); PA ST; Med.

PILSTON, REBECCA; Highlands SR HS; Tarentum, PA; (Y); Intnl Clb; Trs Key Clb; Office Aide; Band; Color Guard; Concert Band; Drill Tm; Mrchg Band; Jr NHS; NHS; U Of Pittsburgh; Law.

PINCHER, BETH; Altoona Area HS; Altoona, PA; (Y); Spanish Clb; Chorus; Orch; Cheerleading; Penn ST; Med Tech.

PINCHOT, DANIEL; Ambridge Arca HS; Freedom, PA; (Y); Pep Clb; Red Cross Aide; Spanish Clb; Chorus; Church Choir; Mrchg Band; School Musical; Stage Crew; Variety Show; Hon Roll; Accptd Dist 5 Dist Chorus Fstvl & Hon Chorus Fstvl 84-86; Penn ST U; Tele Cmmnctns.

PINCKNEY, CHARLYENE; Engineering & Science HS; Philadelphia, PA; (Y); 27/147; Pres Church Yth Grp; Cmnty Wkr; Drama Clb; Chorus; Church Choir; Variety Show; Yrbk Stf; High Hon Roll; Hon Roll; NHS; Natl Hnr Socty 84-86; Meritrous Stds; Temple U; Bio.

PINCKNEY, SHERILYNN KAYE; Northwestern SR HS; Girard, PA; (Y); 42/148; Church Yth Grp; Model UN; Spanish Clb; Chorus; Church Choir; Trk; Southwestern Assy God Coll; Bus.

PINDER, MICHELE D; Mt St Joseph Acad; Philadelphia, PA; (Y); 33/127; French Clb; JA; Church Choir; Nwsp Rptr; Nwsp Stf; Sec Trs Jr Cls; French Hon Soc; Hon Roll; NHS; NEDT Awd; Stu Natl Achvt Pgm-Outstndng Ngro Stus 85; Natl Frnch Hnr Soc 84-86; Artcl-Philadelphia Dly Nws 84; Bus.

PINER, CHERYL; Northeast HS; Philadelphia, PA; (Y); Girl Scts; Hon Roll; Nrsng.

PINKERTON, ANDRE; Williams Valley HS; Tower City, PA; (Y); 21/112; Art Clb; Ski Clb; Bowling; High Hon Roll; Hon Roll; Acad All Amer 84-85.

PINKETT, SEAN; Chester HS; Chester, PA; (Y); 7/314; German Clb; Mathletes; Math Clb; Dnfth Awd; High Hon Roll; Hon Roll; Charles A Giles Plaque 86; Most Distngushd Trig Stu 86; John Joseph Pyzowski Awd 86; PA ST U; Math.

PINKHAM, TODD; Somerset Area SR HS; Somerset, PA; (Y); 31/239; Art Clb; Church Yth Grp; English Clb; PAVAS; Ski Clb; Trs Spanish Clb; Var Tennis; Gov Hon Prg Awd; High Hon Roll; Hon Roll; Yng Amer Crtve Patrtc Art Awd 86; Millie Matthew Memrl Art Awd 83-84; PA Gov Schl Of Art 85; Art.

PINKNEY, PENNY; Bethlehem Center SR HS; Marianna, PA; (Y); #43 In Class; Civic Clb; Drama Clb; 4-H; Spanish Clb; Teachers Aide; Band; Church Choir; 4-H Awd; Hon Roll; Mercy Schl Of Nrsg; Nrsg.

PINKO, KATHLEEN; John S Fine SR HS; Nanticoke, PA; (S); 12/244; Ski Clb; Chorus; Yrbk Phtg; Yrbk Stf; Capt Fld Hcky; High Hon Roll; NHS; NEDT Awd; Kings College; Commctns.

PINSKER, MATTHEW; J P Mc Caskey HS; Lancaster, PA; (Y); 8/471; Capt Debate Tm; Capt Quiz Bowl; Nwsp Stf; JV Var Ftbl; Elks Awd; NCTE Awd; NHS; Exploring; NFL; Speech Tm; Schlstc Writing Aed 86; PA Trial Lawyers-Lincoln Douglass Debate 86; PA Gov Schl Intl Rel 85; Harvard U.

PINTER, WENDY; Owen J Roberts HS; Spring City, PA; (Y); Service Clb; Band; Concert Band; Mrchg Band; School Musical; Stage Crew; Score Keeper; Hon Roll; York Coll Of PA.

PINTI, KIM; Sharon SR HS; Sharon, PA; (Y); French Clb; Hosp Aide; Var L Cheerleading; Im Diving; Var Gym; Im Swmmng; Im Trk; Hon Roll; Penn ST U; Med.

PINTO, MARY JO; Windber Area HS; Windber, PA; (Y); Church Yth Grp; Drama Clb; French Clb; Math Clb; Band; Concert Band; Mrchg Band; School Play; Hon Roll; NHS; Indiana U Of PA.

PIOCQUIDIO, LISA; Aliquippa HS; Aliquippa, PA; (S); Exploring; French Clb; Hosp Aide; Band; Mrchg Band; Pep Band; Yrbk Rptr; Trs Jr Cls; Twrlr; High Hon Roll; Indstrl Arts Clb-1st Pl Sfty Postr 85; Indstrl Art Clb-3rd Pl Multi-Clr Prntg 85; Duquesne U; Pre-Law.

PIORKOWSKI, RITA; Lakeland JR SR HS; Jermyn, PA; (S); 31/149; FBLA; Hosp Aide; Yrbk Phtg; Yrbk Stf; Hon Roll; U Of Scranton; Mrktng.

PIOTROWICZ, BRIAN; Archbishop Wood HS; Southampton, PA; (Y); 62/282; Church Yth Grp; Bsktbl; Hon Roll; Bio.

PIOTROWSKI, CHARLE-LENE; Central Catholic HS; Allentown, PA; (Y); 60/212; Hosp Aide; Spanish Clb; Y-Teens; Chorus; Var Bsktbl; Var Crs Cntry; Score Keeper; Stat Sftbl; Im Vllybl; Hon Roll; Psychlgy.

PIPER, CARMEL; Ligonier Valley SR HS; Latrobe, PA; (Y); 1/150; Pres Church Yth Grp; Pres Band; Chorus; School Musical; School Play; Yrbk Stf; Var Trk; High Hon Roll; NHS; Ntl Merit Ltr; Arch Engr.

PIPER, CHARLES; Central HS; Roaring Spring, PA; (Y); 4/186; Church Yth Grp; Cmnty Wkr; Varsity Clb; Stage Crew; JV Bsbl; Hon Roll; Mltry; Aviation.

PIPER, CHARLOTTE; Deer Lakes JR SR HS; Cheswick, PA; (Y); Drama Clb; Sec Trs SADD; School Play; Nwsp Rptr; Nwsp Stf; Yrbk Stf; Cheerleading; Score Keeper; Trk; Masonic Awd; Spec Educ.

PIPER, DIANA LYNN; Liqonier Valley SR HS; Latrobe, PA; (Y); 19/164; AFS; Yrbk Stf; Rep Stu Cncl; Var JV Cheerleading; Hon Roll; COCA Chrmn; Latrobe Area Hosp Vlntr; Duquesne U; Phrmcy.

PIPER, EDITH; Meadow Brook Christian Schl; Matteson, IL; (S); 2/12; FTA; Pep Clb; Spanish Clb; SADD; Chorus; Church Choir; Cheerleading; Capt Socr; Hon Roll; NHS; Ensmble Awd 85; Dstngshd Spn Awd 85; Stu Of Mtnh 85; Elem Ed.

PIPER, MICHELLE LEE; Greater Labrobe SR HS; Latrobe, PA; (Y); Sec Pres Church Yth Grp; Sec Exploring; JA; Library Aide; Office Aide; Pep Clb; Chorus; School Play; Hon Roll; Bradford Bus Schl; Retl Mgmt.

PIPER, RICHARD; Center HS; Monaca, PA; (Y); 19/184; Am Leg Boys St; JA; Letterman Clb; Scholastic Bowl; Spanish Clb; Varsity Clb; Bowling; Var Capt Golf; Hon Roll; Jr NHS; Geneva Coll Schlr Awd 86; Geneva Coll; CPA.

PIPER, TONI; Pie Forge Acad; Chesterfield, VA; (S); Band; Church Choir; Bausch & Lomb Sci Awd; High Hon Roll; NHS; Eng High Honor Awd 85; French High Honor Awd 85; US Hstry Excllnt Schlrshp 85; Howard U; Gyn/Ob.

PIPER, TONYA; Greencastle Antrium HS; Greencastle, PA; (Y); Band; Concert Band; Var Capt Cheerleading; Stat Sftbl; High Hon Roll; Hon Roll; Make-Up Dsgn.

PIPKINS, CHRIS; York Catholic HS; York, PA; (Y); Church Yth Grp; Cmnty Wkr; Exploring; Chorus; Church Choir; School Play; Hon Roll; Comm.

PIRAGAS, DONALD; Old Forge HS; Old Forge, PA; (S); Ski Clb; Spanish Clb; Frsh Cls; JV Var Bsbl; JV Capt Bsktbl; Ftbl; Golf; Wt Lftg; Hon Roll; NHS.

PIRAINO, LEE; Lakeland JR SR HS; Jermyn, PA; (S); 14/150; French Clb; FHA; Rep Stu Cncl; Hon Roll; Psych.

PIREAUX, KELLIE; Charleroi Area JR SR HS; N Charleroi, PA; (Y); Pres French Clb; Hosp Aide; Office Aide; Sec Varsity Clb; Stu Cncl; Stat Bsktbl; Sftbl; High Hon Roll; NHS; TTOS Athltc Awd Local Comm Recognition 86; Medical.

PIRNICK, BETH; Clearfield Area HS; Clearfield, PA; (S); 29/318; Key Clb; Ski Clb; Spanish Clb; SADD; Church Choir; Concert Band; Mrchg Band; High Hon Roll; Hon Roll; Gannon U; Phar.

PIROCH, JOSEPH; Meadville Area SR HS; Meadville, PA; (Y); 4/356; Debate Tm; French Clb; German Clb; JCL; Latin Clb; Math Clb; NFL; Socr; High Hon Roll; Hon Roll.

PIROLLI, STACY; Saint Maria Goretti HS; Philadelphia, PA; (Y); 23/426; Church Yth Grp; Office Aide; Spanish Clb; Nwsp Ed-Chief; High Hon Roll; NHS; Pres Schlr; Hosp Aide; Speech Tm; Stu Cncl; Newspaper Gen Exc Awd 85-86; Editoria Editor 84-85; Psnsh Hnrbl Ment Awd 84-85; Beaver Coll; Pre-Law.

PIROLLO, SALVATORE; John Neumann HS; Philadelphia, PA; (Y); 185/338; Computer Clb; Dance Clb; Ski Clb; Teachers Aide; Temple; Bus Law.

PIRRO, DANA; Saegertown Area HS; Saegertown, PA; (Y); 12/117; SADD; Chorus; Color Guard; Flag Corp; Mrchg Band; Swing Chorus; Hon Roll; NHS; Presdntl Acadmc Fitness Awd 86; Grove City Coll; Bio.

PIRROTTA, ELIZABETH A; Peters Township HS; Mcmurray, PA; (Y); 6/246; Trs Key Clb; Thesps; Orch; Ed Yrbk Stf; NHS; St Schlr; Service Clb; Spanish Clb; Church Choir; School Musical; Phila Coll Txtls & Sci Mrt Schlrshp 86-87; Wstnghs Fmly Schlrshp Wnnr 86; Wrld Affrs Cncl 85-86; Phila Coll Txtls & Sci; Fash.

PIRROTTA, KATHRYN; Peters Township HS; Mc Murray, PA; (S); Sec Intnl Clb; NFL; Science Clb; Jazz Band; Mrchg Band; High Hon Roll; NHS; Church Yth Grp; Debate Tm; Key Clb; Carnegie-Mellon Solo Cmptn Euphnm Wnnr 85; 1st Pl PA ST JR Sci Acad 85; 4th Pl PA Frnscs Extmprns.

PIRRUNG, DAVID; Northern Potter HS; Ulysses, PA; (Y); 10/62; French Clb; German Clb; Varsity Clb; School Play; Nwsp Stf; Yrbk Bus Mgr; Pres Soph Cls; Pres Jr Cls; Pres Sr Cls; Var Capt Bsktbl; AFROTC Scholar 86; Rochester Inst Tech; Sci.

PISANO, ANGIE; Ambridge Area HS; Ambridge, PA; (Y); Sec Church Yth Grp; German Clb; Girl Scts; Pep Clb; Band; Concert Band; Mrchg Band; Off Jr Cls; Var Trk; JV Vllybl.

PISANO, FRANCENE; Wyoming Area HS; Exeter, PA; (Y); Art Clb; FHA; Ski Clb; Yrbk Stf; Trk; Marywood Coll; Psych.

PISARCHICK, MARY BETH; Brockway Area HS; Brockway, PA; (Y); 1/109; GAA; Varsity Clb; Nwsp Sprt Ed; Yrbk Ed-Chief; Var Capt Cheerleading; Var Capt Vllybl; DAR Awd; High Hon Roll; NHS; Rotary Awd; Amer Leg Awd 83; Ntl Chrldrs All Amer Chrldrs 85; USCAA Chrldng Awd 86; PA ST U; Engrng.

PISARCHICK, TAMMY; Linesville HS; Linesville, PA; (Y); 60/89; DECA; SADD; Rep Stu Cncl; Mgr(s); Vllybl; Edinboro U; Preschl Tchr.

PISAREK, RENEE; Mc Keesport SR HS; Coulter, PA; (Y); 54/362; Cheerleading; Powder Puff Ftbl; Trk; High Hon Roll; Hon Roll; U Pttsbrgh.

PISAREK, THERESA; St Paul Cathedral HS; Pittsburgh, PA; (Y); Church Yth Grp; FBLA; Library Aide; Nwsp Rptr; Nwsp Stf; Yrbk Stf; Rep Frsh Cls; Stu Cncl; Cheerleading; Stenographer I Awd FBLA Rgn 24 86; Bst Bus Stu, Bst Typng & Bst Shrthnd 86; Hlth.

PISARSKI, CINDY; Forest Hills HS; Summerhill, PA; (Y); Library Aide; NFL; Nwsp Stf; Capt Trk; Cit Awd; DAR Awd; NHS; Trk Awd 86; Hmntrn Clb 85; Treas & Pres 86; Schl Msct 86; CA U Of PA; Med Tech.

PISKURA, KIM; Bishop Mc Cort HS; Johnstown, PA; (Y); German Clb; Pep Clb; Chorus; Church Choir; Nwsp Ed-Chief; Nwsp Rptr; Nwsp Stf; High Hon Roll; Hon Roll; Cmmnctns.

PISTNER, CHRIS; Johnsonburg Area HS; Johnsonburg, PA; (S); 14/90; Camera Clb; Varsity Clb; Yrbk Stf; Rep Jr Cls; Trs Stu Cncl; Trk; Var L Vllybl; Hon Roll; Sec NHS; Ldrshp Awd 85; Acad All Amer 85; St Bonaventure UELEM Ed.

PISTNER, KIMBERLY; St Marys Area HS; St Marys, PA; (Y); 20/290; Hosp Aide; VP Stu Cncl; JV Var Bsktbl; Bowling; JV Var Sftbl; JV Var Vllybl; Hon Roll; NHS; Pres Schlr; U Pittsburgh; Phys Thrpy.

PISTORIA, LISA; Deer Lakes JR SR HS; Gibsonia, PA; (Y); Computer Clb; Drama Clb; French Clb; Office Aide; Pep Clb; Varsity Clb; School Play; Stage Crew; Variety Show; Stu Cncl; IN U PA; Math.

PISTORIA, MIKE; Upper Perkiomen HS; Pennsburg, PA; (Y); 2/250; Pres Debate Tm; Concert Band; Mrchg Band; Pep Band; L Trk; High Hon Roll; Pres NHS; PMEA Regn VI Band And Orch 85; 1st EEAC Schlr Rsrch Papr Cntst 86; 4th Yth Debts On Enrgy 86; Med.

PISTORIUS, LORI; Karns City HS; Chicora, PA; (Y); Chorus; Variety Show; Trs Sr Cls; Trs Stu Cncl; Stat Bsktbl; JV Var Cheerleading; Cit Awd; High Hon Roll; Hon Roll; Trs NHS; U Pittsburgh; Nrsng.

PISZCZOR, JENNIFER; Uniontown Area SR HS; New Salem, PA; (Y); 20/320; Am Leg Aux Girls St; FNA; Pres Letterman Clb; Stu Cncl; JV Bsktbl; Var L Sftbl; CC Awd; High Hon Roll; NHS; Pres Schlr; Dan R Kovar Schlrshp 86; Army Schlr Athlt Awd 86; Penn ST U; Nrsng.

PITASSI, ELIZABETH; Canevin HS; Coraopolis, PA; (Y); Church Yth Grp; Cmnty Wkr; Dance Clb; Hosp Aide; Chorus; Church Choir; Drill Tm; School Musical; School Play; Powder Puff Ftbl; Carlow Coll; Engl.

PITCHOK, CARISSA; Seton-La Salle Regional HS; Clairton, PA; (Y); 4/232; Math Tm; SADD; Band; Concert Band; Mrchg Band; Mgr(s); Mgr Socr; High Hon Roll; Pres NHS; Dgls C Very Awd 86; St Vncnt Coll Acdmc Schlrshp & Ldrshp Schlrshp 86; Wshngtn & Jfrsn Schlr 86; St Vncnt Coll; Chmstry.

PITMAN, WILLIAM; Wilmington Area HS; New Wilmington, PA; (S); 8/122; Boy Scts; Chess Clb; Latin Clb; Math Tm; Spanish Clb; Nwsp Rptr; Crs Cntry; Hon Roll; Band; Concert Band; PMEA Hnrs Bnd 83-85; Elec Engr.

PITRELLI, RICK; Lincoln HS; Ellwood City, PA; (Y); Church Yth Grp; French Clb; Letterman Clb; Band; Concert Band; Pep Band; JV Bsbl; JV L Ftbl; Hon Roll.

PITTA, GINA; Carlisle HS; Carlisle, PA; (Y); German Clb; Latin Clb; Ski Clb; Spanish Clb; Flag Corp; Mrchg Band; Sftbl; Swmmng; Trk; Church Yth Grp; Pre-Med.

PITTAS, ANN-MARGARET; Brentwood HS; Pittsburgh, PA; (S); 32/130; Dance Clb; Nwsp Stf; Ed Yrbk Stf; Sec Jr Cls; Sec Sr Cls; Stu Cncl; Capt Twrlr; High Hon Roll; Hon Roll; NHS; Bus Career Devlpmnt Pgm Rep 86; Robert Morris Coll; Bus Cmmncts.

PITTMAN, CHERYL; Middletown Area HS; Middletown, PA; (Y); Dance Clb; 4-H; French Clb; GAA; Chorus; Gym; Swmmng; Trk; Vllybl; Hon Roll; Point Park Coll; Dance.

PITTMAN, DANA; Simon Gratz HS; Philadelphia, PA; (Y); Church Yth Grp; Hosp Aide; Teachers Aide; VP Church Choir; Acctg.

PITTMAN, JENNIFER; Abington Heights North Campus HS; Clarks Summit, PA; (Y); 80/266; Church Yth Grp; Hosp Aide; SADD; Chorus; Fld Hcky; Capt Trk; Abngtn Hts Booster Clb Schlrshp 86; Geisinger Schl Of Nrsng; Nrsng.

PITTMAN, WENDY; Gettysburg SR HS; Gettysburg, PA; (Y); 26/238; Varsity Clb; Band; Concert Band; Jazz Band; Mrchg Band; Orch; Capt Sftbl; Hon Roll; M Hereter Mem Schlrshp In Msc 86; N L Ramer Tchng Schlrshp 86; Mlrsvl U PA; Msc.

PITTSMAN, JEFFREY; Mid-Valley HS; Olyphant, PA; (Y); Var Bsbl; Var Bsktbl; Var Ftbl; Var Wt Lftg; Hon Roll.

PITZ, GARY; Hempfield HS; Mountville, PA; (Y); 15/430; Im L Bsktbl; Var L Ftbl; Var Trk; Hon Roll; NHS; I Dare You Ldrshp Awd; Elec Engrng.

PITZER, JEFF; New Castle SR HS; New Castle, PA; (S); 19/253; AFS; VP Church Yth Grp; Math Tm; Ski Clb; Spanish Clb; Stat Bsktbl; Var L Tennis; Hon Roll; Natl Acadmc Games.

PITZER, KEVIN; New Castle SR HS; New Castle, PA; (S); 17/253; Spanish Clb; JV Wrstlng; Hon Roll; Ftbl Trnr.

PITZER, MICHELE; Wilmington Area HS; New Wilmington, PA; (Y); 27/122; Church Yth Grp; Drill Tm; Sec Soph Cls; Sec Jr Cls; Stu Cncl; Var Gym; Powder Puff Ftbl; Hon Roll; Drama Clb; Library Aide; Homecoming Court 84; Princess Of Prom 86; Real Est.

PIVIROTTO, VICKIE; West Allegheny HS; Oakdale, PA; (Y); FBLA; Nwsp Rptr; Nwsp Stf; Yrbk Bus Mgr; Yrbk Ed-Chief; Yrbk Rptr; Yrbk Stf; VP Rep Stu Cncl; JV Bsktbl; Hon Roll; Rtry Yth Ldrshp Awd 86; Westminster; Psychlgy.

PIZZELLA, JUSTIN; Springdale HS; Cheswick, PA; (Y); 2/125; Spanish Clb; Nwsp Rptr; Rep Stu Cncl; Var L Socr; Gov Hon Prg Awd; High Hon Roll; VP NHS; Prfct Atten Awd; Spanish NHS; All WPIAL All-Stars Mem 86; USSF Rgstrd Referee 85-86; USYSA Wstrn PA Select Team Mem 85-86; Engrng.

PIZZI, MARK; Arch Bishop Carroll HS; Havertown, PA; (Y); 25/170; JV Ftbl; JV Var Wrstlng; Hon Roll; Jr NHS; Engrng.

PIZZICA, LORI; Plum SR HS; Pittsburgh, PA; (Y); Dance Clb; Hosp Aide; Service Clb; Drill Tm; Yrbk Stf; Pom Pon; High Hon Roll; NHS; Phys Ther.

PLACE, MARY; Grove City Area SR HS; Grove City, PA; (Y); 15/154; Church Yth Grp; Thesps; Mrchg Band; School Musical; Sec Soph Cls; L Var Bsktbl; Elks Awd; High Hon Roll; JP Sousa Awd; NHS; Rotary Clb Awd 86; Bus Profssnl Wmn Awd 86; John Carroll U; Pre-Law.

PLACEK, TRACY; Our Lady Of The Sacred Heart Acad; Coraopolis, PA; (Y); 11/68; Church Yth Grp; Pep Clb; Band; Chorus; Church Choir; School Musical; Nwsp Stf; Yrbk Stf; Im Bowling; Im Vllybl; Edinboro; Med Tech.

PLACK, MATTHEW; Susquehanna Township HS; Harrisburg, PA; (Y); 30/155; Model UN; Quiz Bowl; Teachers Aide; Varsity Clb; Yrbk Rptr; Pres Frsh Cls; Var Crs Cntry; Var Trk; NHS; Pol.

PLANT, BETSY; Shaler Area SR HS; Glenshaw, PA; (Y); Hon Roll; Physcl Thrpy.

PLANTS, GINA; Hollidaysburg Area SR HS; Hollidaysburg, PA; (Y); 6/352; Church Yth Grp; SADD; Yrbk Stf; High Hon Roll; NHS; Liberty U; Psych.

PLASCO II, ROBERT M; Bishop Hoban HS; Laflin, PA; (Y); 33/190; Boy Scts; Exploring; FBLA; Latin Clb; VP Soph Cls; VP Jr Cls; Var L Ftbl; Eagle Scout 83; U Of Pittsburgh.

PLASHA, BRUCE; Kutztown Area HS; Kempton, PA; (Y); Boy Scts; 4-H; Var Ftbl; Var Trk; Var Wrstlng; 4-H Awd; Hon Roll; Riflt Tm-Vrsty Shooting 84-87.

PLASHA, WAYNE W; Lower Moreland HS; Huntingdon Valley, PA; (S); Capt Debate Tm; German Clb; NFL; Science Clb; Yrbk Stf; Rep Stu Cncl; NHS; Stu Advsry Cncl 84-85; U Of VA; Law.

PLASSIO, SHELLY; Yough SR HS; Irwin, PA; (Y); FBLA; Ski Clb; JV Bsktbl; Var Sftbl; Bus.

PLASTERER, GARRI; Cumberland Valley Christian HS; Waynesboro, PA; (Y); 3/20; Church Yth Grp; Cmnty Wkr; Hosp Aide; Library Aide; Office Aide; Political Wkr; Chorus; School Musical; Nwsp Ed-Chief; Var JV Cheerleading; Acad All Amer 83; Pres Achvt 86; Intl Frgn Lng 83.

PLATOW, BETH; Council Pack HS; Washington Crossi, PA; (Y); 126/845; Church Yth Grp; Girl Scts; Spanish Clb; Mgr(s); Powder Puff Ftbl; Score Keeper; Swmmng; Im Wt Lftg; Hon Roll; U Of Richmond; Lang.

PLATT, ERIKA; Indiana Area SR HS; Indiana, PA; (Y); Debate Tm; Model UN; NFL; Chorus; Nwsp Rptr; Nwsp Stf; Socr; High Hon Roll; NHS; Ntl Merit Ltr; Dist Wnnr Intl Rtry Clb Lts For Peace Cntst 86; 1st Pl Edtrl Wnnr Lcl Cntst For Gaztt 86; Intl Studis & Langs; Intl Stds.

PLATT, LISA; Berlin Brothers Valley HS; Berlin, PA; (Y); Trs French Clb; SADD; Band; Color Guard; Concert Band; Var Cheerleading; Hon Roll.

PLATZ, DEAN; Fairview HS; Fairview, PA; (Y); Boy Scts; Pres Church Yth Grp; Off Varsity Clb; Ftbl; Capt Wrstlng; NHS; Grove City Coll; Sec Ed Math.

PLAVECSKY, DEBRA J; Lincoln HS; Ellwood City, PA; (Y); 17/166; French Clb; Sec Y-Teens; L Co-Capt Bsktbl; L Capt Crs Cntry; Powder Puff Ftbl; L Capt Trk; High Hon Roll; Hon Roll; NHS; Trk & Fld ST 85 & 86; Rook Scholar Pitt 86; Pittsburgh U.

PLAZA, MARIA; Fort Leboeuf HS; Waterford, PA; (Y); Church Yth Grp; Drama Clb; 4-H; Sec FFA; Model UN; Capt Quiz Bowl; Hon Roll; Pres Schlr; Penn ST.

PLEBAN, CHRIS; Weatherly Area HS; Weatherly, PA; (S); 2/56; FBLA; Letterman Clb; Spanish Clb; Trs Jr Cls; Stu Cncl; Bsbl; Golf; High Hon Roll; NCTE Awd; Penn ST; Engr.

PLESSINGER, ANGELA D; Mc Connellsburg HS; Needmore, PA; (Y); 5/81; Church Yth Grp; Varsity Clb; Chorus; Var L Bsktbl; Var L Trk; Var L Vllybl; NHS; Pres Schlr; Drama Clb; English Clb; Outstndng Schlstc Achvt In Amrcn Hstry; ST Trck & Fld Chmpn In 300 Intrmdt Hrdls; Mltry Srvc; Intlgnc.

PLESSINGER, DOUGLAS C; Altoona Area HS; Altoona, PA; (Y); 22/683; French Clb; Band; Concert Band; Jazz Band; Pep Band; Golf; Hon Roll; NHS; Acad Achvt Awd 86; Northeastern; Pharm.

PLESZ, LISA; Hempfield SR HS; New Stanton, PA; (Y); Pres Church Yth Grp; Office Aide; Pep Clb; Ski Clb; Capt Drm Mjr(t); Lion Awd; Prfct Atten Awd; Bradford Schl Bus; Bus.

PLETCHER, ALLEN; Rockwood Area HS; Rockwood, PA; (Y); Im Bsktbl; Var Socr; Var Trk; Hon Roll; Rifle Marksmnshp Awds 84; Drftg.

PLETCHER, SHAWN; Meyersdale Area HS; Meyersdale, PA; (S); Spanish Clb; Aerontcl.

PLETCHER, VALERIE; Southmoreland SR HS; Ruffsdale, PA; (Y); 29/222; Latin Clb; Sec Trs Band; Chorus; Church Choir; Concert Band; Drm Mjr(t); Jazz Band; Mrchg Band; Pep Band; Stage Crew; Engr.

PLEVELICH, CHERYL; Greensburg Central Catholic HS; Greensburg, PA; (Y); 10/243; VP AFS; Hosp Aide; Yrbk Ed-Chief; Yrbk Stf; VP Soph Cls; VP Jr Cls; High Hon Roll; Sec NHS; Chorus; Im Bsktbl; Westinghse Sci Hnrs Inst Cert Achvt 85-86; Jrnlsm Awd 85-86; U Pittsburgh; Elect Engr.

PLEWA, JOHN; Penn Cambria HS; Cresson, PA; (Y); Ski Clb; Spanish Clb; SADD; Bsbl; Bsktbl; Ftbl; Golf; Wt Lftg; Hon Roll; NHS.

PLISCOTT, KAREN; John S Fine HS; Nanticoke, PA; (S); 10/247; Girl Scts; Library Aide; Ski Clb; L Chorus; Yrbk Stf; High Hon Roll; NHS; Luzerne Cnty CC; Bus Adm.

PLISHKA, ROBERT; Scranton Prep; Old Forge, PA; (Y); Boy Scts.

PLITT, DARIN; Hanover HS; Hanover, PA; (Y); 2/138; Chess Clb; Church Yth Grp; Cmnty Wkr; Bsbl; Trk; Wrstlng; Bausch & Lomb Sci Awd; High Hon Roll; Sal; Elks Teen Of Mnth 86; Geneva Coll; Elec Engrng.

PLOCINIK, LYNDA; Rochester Area HS; Rochester, PA; (Y); 22/97; Church Yth Grp; Girl Scts; JA; Church Choir; Off Concert Band; Jazz Band; Off Mrchg Band; Orch; Var L Trk; NHS; Dist V Band 85-86; Beavr Cnty Hnrs Band 85-86; Grove City Coll; Gentc Engrng.

PLOMSKI, STEPHANIE; Shamokin Area HS; Shamokin, PA; (Y); Camera Clb; Key Clb; Pep Clb; Science Clb; Varsity Clb; Mrchg Band; Yrbk Sprt Ed; Yrbk Stf; L Var Bsktbl; L Var Vllybl; X-RAY Tech.

PLONSKI, LAURA; Carbondale Area HS; Carbondale, PA; (Y); 5/160; FBLA; Ski Clb; Spanish Clb; Band; Concert Band; Mrchg Band; High Hon Roll; NHS.

PLOTKIN, MICHAEL; Scranton Central HS; Scranton, PA; (Y); Ski Clb; Temple Yth Grp; Varsity Clb; Band; Wrstlng.

PLOTNER, JAMES; Sharpsville Area HS; Sharpsville, PA; (Y); Aud/Vis; Letterman Clb; Science Clb; Spanish Clb; Varsity Clb; Stage Crew; Var L Bsbl; Var L Ftbl; Var Wt Lftg; Var Wrstlng; Miami U Of FL; Sprts Med.

PLOTNER, MARK; Punxsutawney Area HS; Punxsutawney, PA; (Y); 30/243; French Clb; FBLA; Variety Show; Rep Sr Cls; High Hon Roll; Hon Roll; Sec Trs NHS; Rotary Boy Of Mnth 86; Mary Ann Irvin Schlrshp 86; Gannon U; Pre-Law.

PLOWEY, JEFFREY M; Hampton HS; Allison Pk, PA; (Y); Church Yth Grp; Exploring; Ski Clb; JV Bsbl; JV Var Ice Hcky; High Hon Roll; Hon Roll; Ntl Merit Ltr; U Of Pittsburgh; Pre-Med.

PLUBELL, JOHN E; West Branch Area HS; Karthaus, PA; (Y); Schl Of Comp Tech; Comp.

PLUCIENNIK, BETSY; Scranton Preparatory Schl; Scranton, PA; (Y); 36/192; Dance Clb; Chorus; Stage Crew; VP Rep Soph Cls; VP Rep Jr Cls; Var Capt Cheerleading; Trk; High Hon Roll; NHS; Fash Dsgn.

PLUMB, JENNIFER; Saint Benedict Acad; Erie, PA; (Y); 8/64; Church Yth Grp; Office Aide; Q&S; Color Guard; Stage Crew; Yrbk Stf; Sec Pres Stu Cncl; Cheerleading; Hon Roll; NHS; Elect Engr.

PLUMLEY, MARY; J R Masterman HS; Philadelphia, PA; (Y); 28/30; Var Capt Bowling; Office Aide; School Play; Hahneman U; Chls Psychlgst.

PLUMMER, DONALD M; Owen F Roberts HS; Phoenixville, PA; (S); 2/291; JA; Letterman Clb; Chorus; School Musical; Off Soph Cls; Off Jr Cls; Stu Cncl; Socr; Trk; Vllybl; Rutgers Coll; Physcs.

PLUMMER, JEAN; Conrad Weiser HS; Robesonia, PA; (Y); 6/184; Drama Clb; Ed JCL; VP Key Clb; Chorus; School Musical; Ed Lit Mag; High Hon Roll; NHS; Ntl Merit Ltr; School Play; Key Clbbr Of Mnth Awd 85 & 86; Smmr Enrich Pgm Schlrshp 85; Acad Pin 84 & 85; Englsh.

PLUMMER, KRISTIN; Lackawanna Trail HS; Laplume, PA; (Y); 4-H; French Clb; Ski Clb; Flag Corp; Madrigals; School Musical; Yrbk Stf; Cheerleading; Elem Ed.

PLUSHANSKI, JESSE; Kutztown Area HS; Kutztown, PA; (Y); Boy Scts; VP 4-H; Var Ftbl; Var Trk; High Hon Roll; Hon Roll; Chem.

PLUTA, BRENDA; Mc Connellsburg HS; Mcconnellsburg, PA; (Y); Sec FHA; Band; Color Guard; Hon Roll; Jr NHS.

PLYLER, BONNIE; Runxsutawney Area HS; Punxsutawney, PA; (Y); Trs Church Yth Grp; FBLA; Band; Concert Band; Mrchg Band; Pep Band; Hon Roll; Prfct Atten Awd; Csmtlgy.

POALL, AMY; George Washington HS; Philadelphia, PA; (Y); 105/790; Yrbk Stf; Var Cheerleading; NHS; U CO; Lib Arts.

POCH, SCOTT; Governor Mifflin HS; Sinking Spring, PA; (Y); 62/280; Exploring; German Clb; Band; Concert Band; Jazz Band; Mrchg Band; Orch; Stage Crew; Bsbl; Bowling.

POCRATSKY, RAYMOND; Mount Pleasant Area SR HS; Mt Pleasant, PA; (Y); VP Church Yth Grp; French Clb; Quiz Bowl; Chorus; Var Bsktbl; Var Ftbl; Im Sftbl; French Hon Soc; Outstndng Alter Svc Awd 84; U Pittsburg; Mortury Sci.

PODBIELSKI, TODD; Cathedral Prep; Erie, PA; (Y); Camera Clb; Stage Crew; Yrbk Phtg; Var Trk; JV Wrstlng; Hon Roll; Mech Engrng.

PODLESNY, CHRISTINE; Manheim Central HS; Manheim, PA; (Y); 84/237; DECA; Office Aide; Color Guard; Drill Tm; Mrchg Band; VP Jr Cls; VP Sr Cls; Cheerleading; Coach Actv; Rotary Awd; Fshn Mrchndsg.

PODOLAK, GREG; Crestwood HS; Mountaintop, PA; (Y); Library Aide; Concert Band; Jazz Band; Mrchg Band; Pep Band; Symp Band; High Hon Roll; Hon Roll; Ntl Merit SF; NEDT Awd; Wilkes Coll; Engrng.

PODYARSKI, MARK; Central Buck East HS; New Hope, PA; (Y); Ski Clb; Var Bsbl; Var Ftbl; JV Tennis; Ntl Merit Ltr.

POE, AUDREY; Peters Township HS; Finleyville, PA; (Y); 19/230; NHS; Spanish NHS.

POE, BRANDON; Mechanicsburg Area SR HS; Mechanicsburg, PA; (Y); 39/311; Church Yth Grp; Ski Clb; Orch; Yrbk Stf; Socr; Trk; Wrstlng; High Hon Roll; NHS.

POEHLMANN, KAREN; St Basil Acad; Philadelphia, PA; (Y); German Clb; Hosp Aide; Pres Soph Cls; Pres Jr Cls; Pres Sr Cls; Pres Stu Cncl; Var Bsktbl; Sftbl; Nrs.

POERIO, JANINE; Southmoreland HS; Scottdale, PA; (Y); 80/213; JCL; Latin Clb; Office Aide; Ski Clb; Color Guard; Nwsp Stf; Lit Mag; Sec Jr Cls; Stu Cncl; CC Awd; Ldrshp Dev Prgm 84; California U Of Pa:Elem Edctn.

POFFEL, ANGELA; Vicentian HS; Allison Park, PA; (Y); 7/60; Teachers Aide; School Musical; High Hon Roll; Hon Roll; Psych.

POFI, SUSAN; Penn Hills HS; Pittsburgh, PA; (Y); French Clb; Mrchg Band; Var L Crs Cntry; Powder Puff Ftbl; Var L Swmmng; Var L Trk; Kiwanis Awd; SAR Awd.

POGGI, MICHELLE; Somerset Area HS; Somerset, PA; (Y); 7/239; English Clb; French Clb; JA; Chorus; High Hon Roll; NHS; Hon Roll; Am Legion Aux Essay Awd 1st,3rd Pl 86; Ltr Acad Achvt 86; Frnch Cretv Wrtng Awd 2nd Pl 86.

POGODA, LAUREL; Mon Valley Catholic Schl; Charleroi, PA; (Y); Drama Clb; Pep Clb; Ski Clb; Spanish Clb; Chorus; Nwsp Rptr; Cheerleading; Hon Roll; Natl Hist/Govt Awd 83; Indiana U PA; Bus Admin.

POGOZELEC, TERESA; Lincoln HS; Wampum, PA; (Y); 33/163; Band; Church Choir; Concert Band; Mrchg Band; Bowling; Powder Puff Ftbl; Sftbl; Trk; High Hon Roll; Prfct Atten Awd; Robert Morris Coll; CPA.

POGOZELSKI, SUSAN; Moon Area HS; Coraopolis, PA; (Y); Sec VP French Clb; Hon Roll; 5th In Bus Engl Cmptn-FBLA Conf 86; PA ST; Acctg.

POGUE, RANDALL D; Bishop Kenrick HS; Norristown, PA; (Y); VP Science Clb; Spanish Clb; Nwsp Phtg; Nwsp Rptr; Yrbk Stf; Wt Lftg; Wrstlng; Bus Adm.

POHLOT, MARYLOU; Bentworth SR HS; Bentleyville, PA; (Y); Dance Clb; Pres VP FHA; Band; Drill Tm; Mrchg Band; Yrbk Stf; WA Hosp Schl Nrsng; Nrsng.

POIESZ, BARBARA; Chichester SR HS; Boothwyn, PA; (Y); 16/270; Camera Clb; Church Yth Grp; Drama Clb; Pep Clb; SADD; School Musical; Nwsp Phtg; Yrbk Phtg; Cmnty Wkr; Cheerleading; Peer Group Cnslr 84-86; PA ST; Bus.

POINELLI, JENNIFER; Dubois Area HS; Penfield, PA; (Y); 10/280; Chorus; Mrchg Band; School Musical; Hon Roll; Hst NHS; Atnd Clarion U Smr Acad 86; Mem Pupil Enrchmt Prgm.

POKOMO, JACKIE; Monessen HS; Monessen, PA; (Y); 3/87; Model UN; Yrbk Ed-Chief; Off Stu Cncl; Twrlr; High Hon Roll; NHS; Penn ST U; Engrg.

POKRAJAC, STEPHEN; Bethel Park SR HS; Bethel Park, PA; (Y); Ski Clb; Var L Ftbl; Var L Trk; Im Wt Lftg; Var JV Wrstlng; Prfct Atten Awd; Phys Thrpy.

POLAKOVICH, PAULA; Freedom HS; Allentown, PA; (Y); 154/445; Pep Clb; Band; Concert Band; Mrchg Band; Symp Band; Crs Cntry; Hon Roll; Band Awd Frshmn, Sphmr & JR Yrs; Psych.

POLAND, JOANNA; Red Land HS; York Haven, PA; (Y); 64/275; Church Yth Grp; 4-H; Spanish Clb; Drill Tm; Hon Roll; Med.

POLANOWSKI, JOSEPH; Hanover Area JR SR HS; Ashley, PA; (Y); 5/186; JV Var Bsbl; JV Var Bsktbl; Var Golf; High Hon Roll; Jr NHS; NHS; Wilkes-Barre Cmps Advsry Bd Schlrshp; PA ST Wilkes Barre; Mech Eng.

POLANSKY, G MICHAEL; Bellefonte HS; Bellefonte, PA; (Y); 42/278; Church Yth Grp; Drama Clb; PAVAS; Spanish Clb; SADD; Thesps; Acpl Chr; Chorus; School Musical; School Play; Upward Bound Rep; Mansfield; Cmmnctns.

POLANSKY, JUDITH E; Nativity B V M HS; New Phila, PA; (Y); 18/99; Math Clb; Ski Clb; Drill Tm; Mgr(s); Hon Roll; Yrbk Stf; Pres Schlr; Art Clb; Chess Clb; French Clb; Hghst Achvt-Trig, Alg I & Engl; Phila Coll/Phrmcy & Sci; Phrmcy.

POLASKI, TIMOTHY; Mercyhurst Prep; Erie, PA; (Y); 10/150; Boy Scts; Ltr Rowing; 1st Pl Reg, 2nd Pl ST PA VR Acad Sci; Engrng.

POLCHIN, DAVID; Hazleton HS; Hazleton, PA; (Y); 20/400; Church Yth Grp; Ski Clb; Teachers Aide; Bsktbl; Crs Cntry; Trk; High Hon Roll; NHS; Prsdnts Acadmc Ftns Awd 86; Army Rsrvst; Penn ST; Engr.

POLCHINSKI, PATRICK; Kiski Area HS; Leechburg, PA; (Y); Band; Jazz Band; Mrchg Band; Symp Band; Trk; High Hon Roll; Hon Roll; Top Ten Awd 84; Engrng.

POLENS, ARLENE; Penn Hills SR HS; Pittsburgh, PA; (S); 228/762; Aud/Vis; Yrbk Stf; Stu Cncl; Vllybl; Hon Roll; Lamp Of Knwldg 85-86; Law.

POLIN, SCOTT; Council Rock HS; Richboro, PA; (Y); Aud/Vis; Chess Clb; Temple Yth Grp; Hon Roll; Prfct Atten Awd; PA ST U; Bus Adm.

POLINSKI, CINDY; Johnsonburg Area HS; Wilcox, PA; (Y); Camera Clb; Computer Clb; Nwsp Ed-Chief; Nwsp Rptr; Yrbk Phtg; Rep Frsh Cls; Bsktbl; Elks Awd; NHS; Accoc Retarded Ctzns Elk Co 86; Penn ST U Park; Psych.

POLINSKY, TRACY; Greater Latrobe HS; Latrobe, PA; (Y); 16/344; Church Yth Grp; German Clb; Hosp Aide; Band; NHS; Ntl Merit Ltr; Pres Schlr; Med Explorers; Germn Hnr Soc; Delta Kappa Gamma Scholar; IN U PA; Ed.

POLIS, ADAM; Central Bucks High School East; Warrington, PA; (Y); Rep Frsh Cls; Rep Jr Cls; Hon Roll; Jr NHS; NHS; Yrbk JR Class Ed 85-86; Brandeis U; Math.

POLITZ, JANINE; G A R Memorial HS; Wilkes Barre, PA; (S); 34/177; Band; Chorus; Concert Band; Capt Flag Corp; Jazz Band; Nwsp Stf; Bsktbl; Sftbl; NHS.

POLITZA, PAUL; Bellwood-Antis HS; Tyrone, PA; (Y); 13/110; Varsity Clb; VICA; Acpl Chr; Chorus; Church Choir; School Musical; Swing Chorus; Variety Show; Bsktbl; Hon Roll; Cnty, Dist, Regnl Chorus 83-86; PA ST; Arch Tech.

POLIZZI, ROSARIA; Elizabethtown HS; Elizabethtown, PA; (Y); Church Yth Grp; FFA; Hon Roll; Harrisburg Area CC; Bus.

POLK, CAROL; Elmer L Meyers HS; Wilkes-Barre, PA; (S); Key Clb; Ski Clb; Chorus; Nwsp Bus Mgr; Yrbk Stf; JV Fld Hcky; Var Score Keeper; JV Sftbl; Hon Roll; Jr NHS; Wilkes Coll; Nrsng.

POLKA, MIKE; Franklin HS; Franklin, PA; (Y); 60/230; Letterman Clb; JV Bsbl; JV Bsktbl; L Golf; Hon Roll; Acctg.

POLKA, THOMAS; Apollo Ridge HS; Apollo, PA; (Y); Band; Concert Band; Mrchg Band; Pep Band; Hon Roll; Lttred Band 85; USAFA; Elctrncs.

POLKINGHORN, CHRIS; Clearfield Area HS; Clearfield, PA; (Y); Church Yth Grp; Drama Clb; Tennis; High Hon Roll; Hon Roll; Marjorie Keast Bell Scholar 86; Central PA Bus Sch6; Supv Mgmt.

POLKIS, ERIC M; Northgate HS; Pitsburgh, PA; (Y); Am Leg Boys St; Math Tm; Capt Ftbl; Var Capt Swmmng; Wt Lftg; Cit Awd; Hon Roll; Acad All Amer 85-86; Carnegie-Mellon U; Humants.

POLKOWSKI, STEPHEN; Strath Haven HS; Media, PA; (Y); Boy Scts; FBLA; Nwsp Phtg; Nwsp Stf; Rep Soph Cls; Var Crs Cntry; Im Socr; Trk; High Hon Roll; Opt Clb Awd; BSA Eagle Awd 86; Order Of Arrow 84; Engrng.

POLLACK, AMEE; Lower Moreland HS; Huntingdon Valley, PA; (S); 20/214; Art Clb; Church Yth Grp; French Clb; Key Clb; Political Wkr; Red Cross Aide; Scholastic Bowl; JV Var Fld Hcky; Var Mgr(s); JV Trk; Aelantic Pfc Math Lgu Awd 83; Josten Ldrshp Awd Cndt 86; Frgn Exhng Prog France 85; Bus.

POLLACK, ANNE; Bishop Hafey HS; Freeland, PA; (Y); Church Yth Grp; Civic Clb; Cmnty Wkr; 4-H; Letterman Clb; Science Clb; Spanish Clb; Band; Yrbk Stf; Bowling; PA U; Secondary Edu.

POLLARD, DENNIS B; Northeast HS; Philadelphia, PA; (Y); 49/600; Capt Debate Tm; Chrmn Model UN; NHS; Spanish NHS; Chess Clb; Sec Church Yth Grp; Hosp Aide; JA; Office Aide; Chorus; Raoul Wallenberg Humntrn Awd 86; Goodwl Rep Senegal & Israel 85; Penn ST; Engrng.

POLLETTA, JULIE; Our Lady Of The Sacred Heart HS; Aliquippa, PA; (Y); 3/74; NFL; Hst Frsh Cls; Hst Soph Cls; Hst Jr Cls; Hst Sr Cls; Var L Sftbl; Var L Vllybl; NHS; U Notre Dame; Mech Engrg.

POLLEY, NICOLE; Western Wayne HS; Lk Ariel, PA; (Y); 55/153; French Clb; VP FBLA; Hon Roll; Awd Outstndng Svc & Ldrshp FBLA 86; 1st Plc Accntng II FBLA Rgnl Conf 86; Bloomsburg U; Accntng.

POLLIARD, JACKIE; Brockway Area HS; Brockway, PA; (Y); Math Clb; English Clb; Flag Corp; Bsktbl; Acctnt.

POLLICK, JEFF; Berwick Area SR HS; Berwick, PA; (Y); Boy Scts; French Clb; Band; Concert Band; Mrchg Band; Nwsp Stf; Yrbk Stf; Swmmng; X-Ray Tech.

POLLICK, TRACEY; Punxsutawney Area SR HS; Punxsutawney, PA; (Y); 63/243; Pres Church Yth Grp; Hosp Aide; Spanish Clb; Band; Drm Mjr(t); Orch; Variety Show; Rep Stu Cncl; Mgr(s); Hon Roll; Mary Ann Irving Schlrshp 86; Acad All Amer 85; Nat Bsktbl Awd 85; PA ST U; Scndry Educ.

POLLINS, SCOTT; Manheim Township HS; Lancaster, PA; (Y); 12/325; JA; Chrmn Key Clb; Nwsp Stf; Lit Mag; Im Bsktbl; L Crs Cntry; Var Trk; High Hon Roll; Pre-Law.

POLLISINO, MEG; Moshannon Valley HS; Houtzdale, PA; (Y); Art Clb; Pep Clb; Band; Chorus; Concert Band; Mrchg Band; Pep Band; School Play; Stage Crew; Music Prodctn.

POLLOCK, DAVID; Hampton HS; Allison Pk, PA; (Y); 40/250; Church Yth Grp; Exploring; French Clb; Ski Clb; Yrbk Phtg; Pres Sr Cls; Var L Swmmng; Hon Roll; Ambassador Hugh O Brien Yth Fndtn Ldrshp Smnr 85; Bus.

POLLOCK, JANET S; Tamaqua Area HS; Tamaqua, PA; (Y); Church Yth Grp; Civic Clb; Dance Clb; Drama Clb; Girl Scts; Band; Church Choir; Mrchg Band; Twrlr; God Cntry Awd; Pre Law.

POLLOCK, LORI; Harbor Creek HS; Erie, PA; (Y); 30/204; Pres AFS; Model UN; JV Vllybl; Hon Roll; NHS; U Pittsburgh; Span.

POLLOCK, MELANIE; Karns City Area HS; Parker, PA; (Y); Pres Church Yth Grp; Sec Teachers Aide; Church Choir; Nwsp Ed-Chief; Nwsp Rptr; Hon Roll; Worthy Advsr Intl Ordr Of Rnbw For Grls-Chicora Assmbly No 160 85; Duboise Bus Coll; Lgl Secy.

POLLOCK, STEPHANIE; Henderson HS; West Chester, PA; (S); 20/349; Ski Clb; Spanish Clb; Rep Frsh Cls; Rep Soph Cls; Var Fld Hcky; Var Lcrss; Hon Roll; Spanish NHS; 2nd Tm All Chesmont Field Hcky 85; Engrng.

POLOGROT, MIKE; Mt Pleasant Area HS; Mount Pleasant, PA; (Y); Boy Scts; Latin Clb; Ski Clb; Band; Concert Band; Mrchg Band; Var Trk; Hon Roll; Engr.

POLOGRUTO, ELIZABETH; Mt Plesant Area HS; Mt Pleasant, PA; (Y); 60/250; FBLA; German Clb; GAA; Hosp Aide; Red Cross Aide; Band; Concert Band; Mrchg Band; Mat Maids; High Hon Roll; Hosp Aid Svc Awd 84; Head Start Vlnt Awd 83; Typng Cert 86; CA U; Elem Ed.

POLOVINA, AMY; Yough SR HS; Irwin, PA; (Y); 45/224; Sec Trs Church Yth Grp; Drama Clb; French Clb; Girl Scts; Library Aide; Band; Chorus; Concert Band; Mrchg Band; School Play; Cnty Band 83 & 85; G S Slvr & Gld Awd 83 & 86; Ed.

POLOVITCH, NADINE; Mid Valley HS; Throop, PA; (Y); Drama Clb; Pep Clb; School Play; Stage Crew; Nwsp Stf; JV Cheerleading; Hon Roll; Penn ST; Dietitian.

POLSENBERG, LISAROSE; Lebanon Catholic HS; Palmyra, PA; (Y); Key Clb; Library Aide; Ski Clb; SADD; Chorus; Stage Crew; Elem Ed.

POLSKY, STEWART M; William Allen HS; Allentown, PA; (Y); 18/556; Key Clb; Temple Yth Grp; Im Bsktbl; Hon Roll; NHS; Pres Schlr; Spanish NHS; Outstndng Acad Achvt Awd 85; Acad Ltr 85; William Allen Stu Adv Schlrshp 86; Muhlenburg Coll; Pre-Med.

POLYMENAKOS, NICHOLAS; Upper Darby HS; Upr Darby, PA; (Y); Band; Concert Band; Jazz Band; Mrchg Band; Orch; Ice Hcky; High Hon Roll; Hon Roll; Eng.

POLZER, ROBERT J; Allentown Central Catholic HS; Coplay, PA; (Y); 8/224; Computer Clb; Exploring; Math Clb; Office Aide; Science Clb; School Musical; Nwsp Stf; High Hon Roll; NHS; Pres Coplay Stu Govt Day 86; Gallas F Wukits Meml Awd Germ 86; Air Prods And Chem Achvt Awd 86; Muhlenberg Clg; Rdlgy.

POMFRET, ELLEN; Country Day School Of The Sacr Heart; Devon, PA; (S); Chorus; Stage Crew; Rep Stu Cncl; Var Bsktbl; Var Fld Hcky; Var Lcrss; Hon Roll; Natl Merit Sci Awd-Bio 84-85; Natl Merit Sci Awd-Chem 85-86.

POMPE, MICHELLE; Murgettstown Area JRSR HS; Burgettstown, PA; (Y); Church Yth Grp; French Clb; Office Aide; Ski Clb; Soph Cls; Jr Cls; Stu Cncl; Cheerleading; Hon Roll; Occupational Therapy.

POMPEO, ALEXIS; Our Lady Of The Sacred Heart; W Aliquippa, PA; (Y); 23/74; Pep Clb; Capt Cheerleading; Hon Roll; NHS; Cmnty Wkr; Stu Cncl; Sftbl; Hghst Avg Spnsh IV & Engl IV Rbbns 86; Gannon U; Psychlgy.

POMPEY, DAWN; Lackawanna Trail HS; Nicholson, PA; (Y); 6/86; 4-H; Hosp Aide; Ski Clb; Chorus; Sec Frsh Cls; Trs Soph Cls; Trs Stu Cncl; Cheerleading; Var Capt Fld Hcky; Wt Lftg; U Of Scranton; Pre-Med.

POMPLAS, CRAIG T; La Salle College HS; Warminster, PA; (Y); 4/230; School Play; Nwsp Ed-Chief; Yrbk Rptr; Yrbk Stf; Lit Mag; High Hon Roll; NHS; Ntl Merit Ltr; Brown U Awd Engl 85; HOBY Conf Rep 84; Georgetown U; Intl Rltns.

POMROY, JILL; Donegal HS; Mount Joy, PA; (Y); Church Yth Grp; Dance Clb; Band; Church Choir; Concert Band; Mrchg Band; Pep Band; School Play; Cheerleading; Bus.

PONCELET, STEPHEN; Schuylkill Haven HS; Schuylkill Haven, PA; (S); 32/92; SADD; Var L Ftbl; Im Wt Lftg; Hon Roll; Ofnsve Lineman Wk 85; Dfnsve Lineman Wk 85; TV Brdcstng.

PONDISH, MARIA; Panther Valley HS; Nesquehoning, PA; (Y); 27/130; Drama Clb; Library Aide; Trs Band; Pres Chorus; Concert Band; Drm Mjr(t); School Musical; Nwsp Stf; Lit Mag; Hon Roll; US Marines Sempr Fidelis Awd-ExclInc In Music 86; Pres Acad Ftns Awd 86; H W Evans Meml Awd Music 86; West Chester U; Music Educ.

PONIATOWSKI, CAROLINE; Fort Le Boeuf HS; Erie, PA; (Y); 30/169; Ski Clb; Rep Soph Cls; Rep Jr Cls; High Hon Roll; Hon Roll; Psychlgst.

PONSOCK, RONALD; Bishop Egan HS; Levittown, PA; (Y); 28/229; Exploring; Office Aide; Science Clb; Rep Soph Cls; Rep Jr Cls; Rep Sr Cls; Stu Cncl; High Hon Roll; Hon Roll; Bio, Chem & Physics Awds; Delaware Valley Coll; Hortcltur.

PONTANI, DEANNA; Penns Manor HS; Penn Run, PA; (Y); 6/99; VP Pres FBLA; Chorus; School Musical; Yrbk Stf; Trs Jr Cls; Trs Stu Cncl; Capt Var Cheerleading; High Hon Roll; Hon Roll; NHS; 2nd Pl Awd Bus Mth FBLA Comptn 85; 5th Pl Awd Acctng I FBLA Comptn 86; IN U PA; Bus Ed Tchr.

PONTIN IV, JOHN F; Spring-Ford HS; Royersford, PA; (S); 19/261; Computer Clb; English Clb; German Clb; Letterman Clb; Ski Clb; Varsity Clb; Var L Bsbl; Var Capt Bsktbl; High Hon Roll; NHS.

PONTIOUS, HOPE; Ridgway Area HS; Ridgway, PA; (S); 8/125; Drama Clb; Yrbk Phtg; Cheerleading; Stat Vllybl; High Hon Roll; Hon Roll; Hmcmng Queen 85-86; Comp Pgmmng.

PONTZER, HEIDE; St Marys Area HS; Kersey, PA; (Y); 26/290; Band; Mrchg Band; Stat Trk; Hon Roll; NHS; Pres Schlr; Outstndng Stu 86; Outstndng Engl,Sportscstr 86; Penn ST U; Brdcst Jrnlsm.

PONTZER, MELISSA; St Marys Area HS; Kersey, PA; (Y); 4/290; Cmnty Wkr; Girl Scts; Hosp Aide; Hon Roll; NHS; Psych.

POOLE, HOLLY; Harbor Creek HS; Erie, PA; (Y); Pres AFS; SADD; Var Swmmng; Hon Roll; NHS; Intl Rltns.

POPALIS, BRUCE; Shenandoah Valley HS; Shenandoah, PA; (S); 12/100; Church Yth Grp; Political Wkr; Yrbk Stf; Stu Cncl; Var L Bsbl; Var L Bsktbl; Im Vllybl; High Hon Roll; NHS; Pre-Law.

POPE JR, BOB W; James Buchanan HS; St Thomas, PA; (Y); Am Leg Boys St; FFA; Flag Corp; Var Crs Cntry; Var Mgr(s); Var Trk; High Hon Roll; Hon Roll; NHS; Boy Scts; Good Citznshp Awd 86; Star Chap Farmer 84; Star Greenhand 83; Penn ST; US Army.

POPE, DALE; Mc Keesport SR HS; Mc Keesport, PA; (Y); 52/380; NFL; Speech Tm; Pres Acpl Chr; School Musical; School Play; Nwsp Phtg; Nwsp Rptr; Natl Schl Chorl Awd 86; Pres Acdmc Fit Awd 86; Tuquesne U; Cmmnctns.

POPECK, ROBYN; Crestwood HS; Mountain Top, PA; (Y); Art Clb; Ski Clb; Var Cheerleading; Hon Roll; French Clb; Letterman Clb; Yrbk Stf; Rep Frsh Cls; Rep Soph Cls; Rep Jr Cls; JR Olympcs Mdls, Trck & Fld Awds 84-85; Kings Coll; Chld Psych.

POPENDIEKER, KEITH; Deer Lakes HS; Cheswick, PA; (Y); Church Yth Grp; Exploring; Varsity Clb; School Musical; School Play; Stage Crew; Im Bsktbl; Var Socr; Hon Roll; The Pennsylvania Junior Academy Of Science 85; Pitt; Elec Engr.

POPIELARZ, BARBARA; Merion Mercy Acad; Phila, PA; (Y); Camera Clb; Spanish Clb; Chorus; Variety Show; Hon Roll; Villanova; Cmnctns.

POPIELSKI, JEFFREY D; North Hills HS; Pittsburgh, PA; (Y); 1/500; Exploring; Mrchg Band; Symp Band; NHS; Ntl Merit Ltr; Val; Rice Mem Schlrshp 86; Rensselaer Sci Mdl 85; Pres Acad Ftnss Awd 86; GA Inst Tech; Chem Engrng.

POPIES, JOHN; Central Catholic HS; Pittsburgh, PA; (Y); Church Yth Grp; JA; Ski Clb; VP Jr Cls; Engrg.

POPLAWSKI, ANDREA; Seton Catholic HS; Dupont, PA; (Y); Key Clb; Ski Clb; School Play; Yrbk Stf; Var Cheerleading; Sftbl; Capt Tennis; Hon Roll; PA ST U; Accntng.

POPPERT, MICHELE; Cheltenham HS; Glenside, PA; (Y); 77/365; Church Yth Grp; Chorus; Rep Soph Cls; Rep Jr Cls; Rep Stu Cncl; Powder Puff Ftbl; Var Sftbl; Frgn Lang Hnr Rl 84-86; All Area Sftbl Tm 86; Intl Bus.

POPRIK, DAN; Highlands HS; Brackenridge, PA; (Y); 20/280; Am Leg Boys St; Key Clb; JV Bsktbl; Capt Crs Cntry; Capt Tennis; High Hon Roll; Jr NHS; NHS.

PORATH, MICHAEL; Corry Area HS; Corry, PA; (Y); 45/212; French Clb; Off Jr Cls; JV Var Bsktbl; Var Crs Cntry; Im Golf; Vrsty Lttr & Vrsty Jckt 85-86; Marietta Coll; Prrlm Engrng.

PORCARELLI, ROBERT; Mercersburg Acad; Mercersburg, PA; (Y); Rep Stu Cncl; Bsktbl; Var Socr; JV Var Tennis; Hon Roll; Lincoln Intermdry Unit Rep 85-86; Med.

PORETTA, CHERYL; Saucon Valley SR HS; Hellertown, PA; (Y); FFA; Office Aide; Tennis; Hon Roll; Northampton Cnty CC; Secy.

PORRECA, JULIA; Academy Of Notre Dame; Drexel Hl, PA; (Y); #2 In Class; Drama Clb; School Play; Stage Crew; Nwsp Stf; Yrbk Stf; Socr; Sftbl; High Hon Roll; Gen Excllnc Awd 86; Spnsh Awd 86; U Of Richmond; Bus.

PORRECCA, STEVE; Upper Merion HS; King Of Prussa, PA; (Y); 35/321; Math Tm; Var JV Bsbl; Var JV Socr; Hon Roll.

PORT, MOSES; Altoona Area HS; Altoona, PA; (S); Key Clb; Math Clb; Math Tm; Pres Science Clb; Pres Spanish Clb; VP Temple Yth Grp; Var Bsktbl; Var Tennis; Jr NHS; NHS; David Ira Giller Mem Awd Outstndg Confirmand 86; Natl Yth Ldrshp Cncl Awd 86; Liberal Arts.

PORTER, ANDRA; Chichester SR HS; Marcus Hook, PA; (Y); French Clb; Stat Ftbl; Mgr(s); Hon Roll; Jr NHS; NHS; Prfct Atten Awd; PA ST U; Mth.

PORTER, ANDREA L; Center HS; Monaca, PA; (Y); Camera Clb; Exploring; Hosp Aide; VP Latin Clb; Sec Frsh Cls; Mgr(s); Powder Puff Ftbl; Score Keeper; Hon Roll; NHS; Giftd & Talented Pgm 83-86; Pre-Med.

PORTER, ANNETTA; Harrisburg HS; Harrisburg, PA; (S); 5/386; Cmnty Wkr; Library Aide; Office Aide; Chorus; Church Choir; Yrbk Stf; High Hon Roll; Hon Roll; Trs NHS; Sci Fair Awd 1st Pl 84; Chrch Keybd Dist Comp 2nd Pl 86; Eastern Nazarene Coll; Music.

PORTER, BRYAN; Unionville HS; Kennett Sq, PA; (Y); 12/300; Church Yth Grp; Band; Church Choir; Orch; School Musical; Var L Socr; High Hon Roll; NHS; Opt Clb Awd; Biochem.

PORTER, CHERYL DIANE; Nazareth Acad; Trevose, PA; (Y); German Clb; Library Aide; Hon Roll; Prfct Atten Awd; Penn St; Counslr Hndcppd Chldrn.

PORTER, CHRIS; Clearfield Area HS; Hyde, PA; (Y); Boy Scts; Church Yth Grp; Key Clb; Ftbl; Wt Lftg; High Hon Roll; Hon Roll; Armed Frcs; Elctncs.

PORTER, CHRISTINE L; Mc Guffey HS; Claysville, PA; (Y); 52/206; German Clb; Model UN; Varsity Clb; Chorus; School Musical; Yrbk Stf; Rep Soph Cls; Sec Jr Cls; Var L Tennis; Hon Roll; IN U Of PA; Comm Media.

PORTER, DAVID; Freeport Area HS; Freeport, PA; (Y); Concert Band; Mrchg Band; School Musical; JV Var Bsktbl; JV Var Ftbl; Var Trk; High Hon Roll; NHS; Pres Schlr; St Vincent Coll; Bio.

PORTER, DIANNA; Mary Fuller Frazier HS; Dawson, PA; (Y); Quiz Bowl; VICA; High Hon Roll; Hon Roll; Dir List 85-86; Nursing.

PORTER, GENEVIEVE; Nazareth Acad; Yardley, PA; (Y); Debate Tm; Latin Clb; Math Clb; NFL; VP Speech Tm; Band; Orch; Lit Mag; Im Bsktbl; Opt Clb Awd; 2nd Pl Intl Optimist Ortrcl Cont 85; ST Qlfr PA Spch Trnmnt Natl Forn Lg 86; Naval Offcr.

PORTER, JENNIFER; Cocalico HS; Stevens, PA; (Y); Art Clb; Chess Clb; Church Yth Grp; Var Cheerleading; Hon Roll; Eagl Clsscl Alls Str Chrldr 85; Secy.

PORTER, LAURA; St Nobert HS; Philadelphia, PA; (Y); 1/383; Church Yth Grp; Ed Nwsp Stf; Yrbk Rptr; Ed Lit Mag; Var Swmmng; High Hon Roll; VP Jr NHS; VP NHS; Ntl Merit SF; Val; Bus.

PORTER, MICHAEL; Northern Bedford County HS; Hopewell, PA; (Y); 9/98; Pres Church Yth Grp; FBLA; Model UN; SADD; Varsity Clb; Var L Bsbl; Var L Ftbl; Var L Wrstlng; Hon Roll; NHS; Cvl Engr.

PORTER, NOELLE; Lewisburg Area HS; Lewisburg, PA; (Y); 27/165; 4-H; French Clb; Band; Chorus; Mrchg Band; School Musical; Yrbk Stf; Tennis; Trk; Hon Roll; Mt Holyoke Coll; Psychology.

PORTER, ROSEMARIE; Lenape AVTS HS; Ford City, PA; (Y); Pep Clb; Spanish Clb; High Hon Roll; Hon Roll; Data Procssr.

PORTER, SUSAN; Freeport HS; Freeport, PA; (S); 1/170; Pres Church Yth Grp; FBLA; Church Choir; Mrchg Band; VP Frsh Cls; VP Soph Cls; Sec Stu Cncl; Var JV Bsktbl; Trk; High Hon Roll; Acctgg.

PORTER, SUSAN; Southmoreland SR HS; Scottdale, PA; (Y); 23/216; Church Yth Grp; Library Aide; Office Aide; Pep Clb; Ski Clb; Spanish Clb; Teachers Aide; Chorus; Sftbl; Spanish NHS; IN U Penn; Acctg.

PORTERFIELD, SHELIA; Sharon HS; Sharon, PA; (Y); Art Clb; Pres Schlr; Hosp Aide; Chorus; Mdlng.

PORTERFIELD, STEPHANIE; Connellsville Area SR HS; Connellsville, PA; (Y); FNA; Hosp Aide; Red Cross Aide; Chorus; Bowling; Sftbl; Swmmng; Tennis; Vllybl; Hon Roll; RN.

PORTUGALLO, STEFANIE M; Lincoln HS; Ellwood City, PA; (Y); 63/163; Ski Clb; Spanish Clb; Y-Teens; Chorus; School Musical; VP Stu Cncl; Co-Capt Cheerleading; Powder Puff Ftbl; Sftbl; Trk; Svc Awd 84-86; Betty Yahn Nsng Scholar 86; U Edinboro; Nrsng.

POSA, MICHELE; Shade HS; Central City, PA; (Y); 3/64; Scholastic Bowl; Spanish Clb; Chorus; Nwsp Stf; Yrbk Ed-Chief; Pres Frsh Cls; Stu Cncl; Sftbl; Hon Roll; VP NHS; Outstndng Achvt Acad Bio 84; Sci.

POSDON, MARIA; Western Wayne HS; Waymart, PA; (Y); 22/150; Exploring; Pres FBLA; High Hon Roll; Guilds H S Diplm Paderewski 86; Memrl Gld Medl & Schlrshp Amer Coll Of Musicns; Marywood Coll.

POSEL, CHRISTINE; Seneca Valley SR HS; Mars, PA; (Y); 41/370; SADD; Hon Roll.

POSEY, HEATHER; Gov Mifflin SR HS; Reading, PA; (Y); Capt Flag Corp; Capt Mrchg Band; School Musical; Stage Crew; Y-Teens; Hon Roll; Unfd Achvmnt Awd 86; Penn ST; Pre-Med.

POSEY, KAREN; Peters Twp HS; Mc Murray, PA; (Y); Church Yth Grp; Drill Tm; Yrbk Stf; JV Var Cheerleading; High Hon Roll; Hon Roll; Ltr & Pin Drll Tm 84-85; Prom Comm 85.

POSEY, SHAWN; Slippery Rock HS; Butler, PA; (Y); 69/171; Am Leg Boys St; Boys Clb Am; Pep Clb; Var Bsbl; Var L Ftbl; Hnrb Mntn All-Conf Ftbl 85; Elec Engrng.

POSEY, VICKI RENEE; Harrisburg HS; Harrisburg, PA; (Y); 35/386; Var Capt Bsktbl; Var Capt Fld Hcky; Var Capt Sftbl; Var Capt Tennis; High Hon Roll; Hon Roll; NHS; PA Clbs Fml Athlt Of Yr 85-86; Mst Outstndng Schlr Athlt 85-86; U S Army Rsrv Ntl Schlr/Ahtlt Awd 86; Blmsbrg U; Pltcl Sci.

POSIVAK, STEPHEN; St Josephs Prep Schl; Philadelphia, PA; (Y); 23/246; Service Clb; Rep Concert Band; Jazz Band; Pep Band; Crs Cntry; Score Keeper; Timer; Trk; High Hon Roll; Law.

POSPISTLE, STEVE; Hempfield Area SR HS; Greensburg, PA; (Y); Computer Clb; High Hon Roll; Hon Roll; Rotary Awd; Wstmrlnd Intrmdt Unit 7 Comp Cont 2nd Pl 85; IUP Physcs Achvmnt Awd 86; Penn ST U; Mchncl Engrng.

POSSENTI, TIMOTHY E; Sun Valley HS; Aston, PA; (Y); 35/320; DECA; Varsity Clb; Bsktbl; Ftbl; Ftbl Scholar TU 86; Temple U; Acctng.

POSSESSKY, LAURA; Bethel Park HS; Bethel Park, PA; (Y); Church Yth Grp; Dance Clb; Pres Thesps; Chorus; School Musical; Yrbk Ed-Chief; Ed Yrbk Stf; Cheerleading; NHS; Drama Clb; Pittsburgh U Provost Day Schlrshp Finlst 86.

POST, VICKIE; Seneca HS; Union City, PA; (Y); Yrbk Ed-Chief; Yrbk Stf; Var Cheerleading; Hon Roll; Wild Clb Treas 85-86; Acad All Am 83-84; Bus.

POSTANCE, JENNIFER; Waynesboro HS; Quincy, PA; (Y); Library Aide; Ski Clb; Nwsp Sprt Ed; Yrbk Rptr; Yrbk Stf; Mat Maids; Johns Hopkins Schltc Tlnt Srch 82; Frnch.

POSTICK, MICHAEL; Minersville Area HS; Pottsville, PA; (Y); 3/108; Exploring; Ski Clb; Spanish Clb; Stage Crew; JV Wrstlng; High Hon Roll; NHS; Schlstc Achvmnt Awd; Penn ST U; Comp Sci.

POSTIE, DESIREE; Marian Catholic HS; Delano, PA; (Y); 35/115; Art Clb; Girl Scts; Office Aide; SADD; Mc Ann Schl Bus; Commercial Art.

POSTLEWAITE, HEATHER; Seneca HS; Erie, PA; (Y); Church Yth Grp; FBLA; Teachers Aide; Band; Concert Band; Mrchg Band; Pep Band; Yrbk Stf; Hon Roll; Clrk Typst 2nd Pl FBLA 85-86; J H Thompson; Med Sec.

POSTREICH, LESLIE; Tyrone Area HS; Tyrone, PA; (Y); DECA; Library Aide; Sec VICA; Chorus; Hon Roll; Outstndg Stu Distrbtv Educ 85-86; Fashion Merchandising.

POSTUPAK, ANNE; Hamburg Area HS; Hamburg, PA; (Y); 18/152; Latin Clb; Spanish Clb; Chorus; Yrbk Bus Mgr; Mgr Fld Hcky; Mgr(s); Score Keeper; Sftbl; Hon Roll; NHS; Acad Awd Chem Study 85; U Scranton; Phys Thrpy.

POTERO, TIMOTHY; St Josephs Prep; Philadelphia, PA; (Y); 53/235; Cmnty Wkr; Nwsp Rptr; Yrbk Rptr; Rep Soph Cls; Rep Stu Cncl; L Golf; JV Socr; Var Trk; High Hon Roll; Yth Am Pol Sys 86; Ntl Latin Ex 85-86; Pol Sci.

POTOCHAR, ROBERT; Greater Johnstown HS; Johnstown, PA; (Y); Chess Clb; French Clb; Ftbl; Hon Roll; U S Military Acad; Engrng.

POTOCHNIK, CHRISTINA; Churchill HS; Turtle Creek, PA; (Y); 23/224; Hosp Aide; JA; Q&S; Yrbk Ed-Chief; Mgr(s); High Hon Roll; Hon Roll; Kent ST U; Jrnslm.

POTOCHNIK, ROSANNE; Mohawk JR SR HS; Bessemer, PA; (S); 3/128; Church Yth Grp; VP French Clb; School Musical; Yrbk Ed-Chief; DAR Awd; High Hon Roll; NHS; Chess Clb; FBLA; School Play; Amer Lgn Awd 83; Flg Awd 82; Frnch Crtfcts Mrt 83-86; Art Inst Of Pittsburgh; Vsl Cmm.

POTOCKI, TIMOTHY J; North Allegheny HS; Wexford, PA; (Y); 260/640; Am Leg Boys St; JA; Radio Clb; ROTC; Trk; Rotary Awd; SAR Awd; Retrd Ofcr Assoc Mdl 85; Air Frc Assoc Mdl 86; AFROTC 4-Yr Coll Schlrp 86; Penn St U; Elec Engr.

POTOKA, JUDI; Mt Pleasant SR HS; Mt Pleasant, PA; (Y); 2/245; Cmnty Wkr; Drama Clb; English Clb; GAA; JA; Red Cross Aide; Science Clb; Ski Clb; Color Guard; Nwsp Ed-Chief; Law Schlrshp 86; U Of Pittsburgh; Pre-Law.

POTTEIGER, DARRELL; Cumberland Valley Christgian Schl; Orrstown, PA; (S); Church Yth Grp; Varsity Clb; Pres Soph Cls; Pres Jr Cls; Pres Sr Cls; Var Bsbl; JV Var Bsktbl; Var Socr; Hon Roll; Algebra I & II Awd 84-85; Spnsh Awd I & II 84-85; Gods Bible Coll; Bible.

POTTER, BETH; Slippery Rock Area HS; Slippery Rock, PA; (Y); Concert Band; School Musical; Nwsp Rptr; Nwsp Stf; Yrbk Stf; Rep Stu Cncl; High Hon Roll; Hon Roll; NHS; Dance Clb; FL ST U; Law.

POTTER, EDYTHE E; Jamestown HS; Jamestown, PA; (Y); 4/54; Service Clb; Spanish Clb; Capt Drill Tm; Sec Soph Cls; Sec Jr Cls; Rep Stu Cncl; Hon Roll; Voice Dem Awd; Guest Page Hse Rep 86; Psychlgy.

POTTER, ERIN; Fairview HS; Erie, PA; (Y); 25/151; Sec French Clb; Ski Clb; Teachers Aide; Var Crs Cntry; Hon Roll.

POTTER, JENNIFER; Villa Maria Acad; Erie, PA; (S); 9/135; VP Church Yth Grp; French Clb; Model UN; PAVAS; Political Wkr; Capt Quiz Bowl; School Musical; Stu Cncl; NHS; NEDT Awd; Teresa Burns Frnch Schlrshp 85; PA Hgher Ed Asst Agncy Cert Of Mrt 85; IN U Of PA; Frnch.

POTTER, MARY JANE; Unionville HS; Chadds Ford, PA; (Y); Exploring; 4-H; FBLA; Girl Scts; JA; Nwsp Rptr; Yrbk Stf; DAR Awd; High Hon Roll; NHS; 1st Pl Prlmntry Prcdr FBLA 86; John Hopkins; Med.

POTTS, BECKY; Clearfield Area HS; Clearfield, PA; (Y); Key Clb; Spanish Clb; L Capt Cheerleading; Hon Roll.

POTTS, DEBBIE; Cardinal O Hara HS; Brookhaven, PA; (Y); 37/740; Cmnty Wkr; JV Trk; Hon Roll; NHS; DE Cnty Sci Fair Awd Hnbl Mntn 85; Wesley Acdmc Schlrshp 86; Hnbl Mntn Art Awd 86; Wesley Coll; Acctg.

POTTS, SHELLIE; Everett Area HS; Artemas, PA; (Y); Computer Clb; FBLA; FHA; SADD; Varsity Clb; Chorus; Yrbk Stf; Sec Sr Cls; Sftbl; Hon Roll; Bus.

POTUCEK, STEPHEN; Freeland HS; Freeland, PA; (Y); 2/95; Trs Computer Clb; Spanish Clb; Pres Band; Yrbk Stf; Pres Stu Cncl; Var Capt Bowling; Var Tennis; JV Elks Awd; Hon Roll; Elks JR Citizen Of Yr 86; Engrng.

POTUTSCHNIG, TISHA; Glendale JR SR HS; Flinton, PA; (Y); 10/98; Church Yth Grp; Science Clb; Band; Chorus; Drm Mjr(t); Stat Sftbl; Hon Roll; NHS; Elem Ed.

POULTER, KATHLEEN LYNN; Indiana SR HS; Indiana, PA; (Y); 23/325; VP Church Yth Grp; Girl Scts; Key Clb; Band; Chorus; Church Choir; Concert Band; Hon Roll; Var Bsktbl; Var Cheerleading; Finalist Of IN Cnty Jr Miss Cntst 86; Gannon U; Bus Admin.

POVERNICK, DENISE; St Basil Acad; Philadelphia, PA; (Y); Computer Clb; Drama Clb; Pres German Clb; Madrigals; School Musical; School Play; Variety Show; Bsktbl; Gym; Socr; 3rd Pl-Sci Fair-Ursinus Coll 85; 3rd Pl-Sci Fair-U Of Phrmcy & Sci 85; Law.

POWELL, AMY; New Brighton HS; New Brighton, PA; (S); Church Yth Grp; DECA; GAA; Girl Scts; Hosp Aide; JA; Library Aide; Chorus; Church Choir; Hon Roll; 4th Pl Deca Dist Comptn 86; Advstng Svcs; Advstng.

POWELL, ANTHONY J; Mcguffey HS; Washington, PA; (Y); 10/200; French Clb; Model UN; Pep Clb; Varsity Clb; Yrbk Phtg; Rep Jr Cls; Rep Stu Cncl; Var Tennis; High Hon Roll; NHS; Outstndng Stu Awd 83-85; Natl Fnlst Sci Essy Awd 86; Pres Acadmc Ftnss Awd 86; Allegheny Clg; Chem.

POWELL, BRIAN; West Middlesex HS; W Middlesex, PA; (Y); 12/110; Science Clb; Spanish Clb; Bsbl; Bsktbl; Wt Lftg; Penn ST; Bio.

POWELL, CAROL; Hamburg Area HS; Shoemakersville, PA; (Y); 36/152; Library Aide; Spanish Clb; SADD; Color Guard; Hon Roll; NHS; Alvernia Coll; Phy Thrpy Asstnt.

POWELL, CHRIS; Perkiomen HS; Rahns, PA; (Y); Am Leg Boys St; Letterman Clb; Varsity Clb; Band; Concert Band; Rep Stu Cncl; JV Bsbl; JV Bsktbl; Var Ftbl; Envrmntl Engrng.

POWELL, CHRISTINA; Western Wayne HS; Lake Ariel, PA; (Y); Yrbk Stf; Trs Jr Cls; Sftbl; Tennis; Vllybl; Hon Roll; NHS; Law.

POWELL, CHRISTOPHER; Center HS; Aliquippa, PA; (Y); 51/184; Yrbk Sprt Ed; Pres Jr Cls; Pres Sr Cls; L Crs Cntry; L Trk; Hon Roll; NHS; Spanish Clb; Varsity Clb; Nwsp Rptr; Govrnrs Schl For Arts Semi-Fnlst 85; Pres Stu Forum 85-86; Ctr Twnshp Bd Of Educ Cert Awd 86; Edinboro U; Art.

POWELL, CHUCK; Council Rock HS; Holland, PA; (Y); 18/845; Rep Frsh Cls; High Hon Roll; NHS; Cmptr Engrng.

POWELL, CINDY; Delone Catholic HS; Mc Sherrystown, PA; (Y); Model UN; School Musical; Nwsp Ed-Chief; Yrbk Sprt Ed; VP Bowling; Rep Soph Cls; Var Cheerleading; Hon Roll; NHS; Adms Cnty Jnr Miss-Wnnr 85-86; IN U Of PA; Accntng.

POWELL, COURTNEY E; Lakeview HS; Stoneboro, PA; (Y); 15/120; Drama Clb; Intnl Clb; Band; Chorus; Church Choir; Concert Band; Mrchg Band; Pep Band; School Play; Yrbk Stf; Stu Athlt Awd 86; Mst Imprvd Bsktbl Plyr 86; Mercer Corinty Schlstc Hall Of Fm 86; Fshn Inst Pittsburgh; Fshn.

POWELL, DAVID; John S Fine HS; Nanticoke, PA; (Y); High Hon Roll; Cert Of Prfcncy Accntng, Bus Math & Typwrtng 86; Accntng.

POWELL, DAVID D; Mt Lebanon HS; Pittsburgh, PA; (Y); 30/531; Pep Clb; Science Clb; SADD; Band; Concert Band; Drm Mjr(t); Mrchg Band; Pep Band; Symp Band; High Hon Roll; Hons Dist I & Reg I Bands For PMEA 85-86; Asst Drum Mjr In Band 85-86; Instmntlst Mags Muscnshp Awd; Grove City Coll; Pre-Med.

POWELL, JINX; Chief Logan HS; Lewistown, PA; (Y); Pep Clb; Spanish Clb; SADD; Varsity Clb; Trs Jr Cls; Var L Bsktbl; Var L Fld Hcky; Var L Trk; Office Aide; Nwsp Stf; PA ST Upwrd Bnd Prgm; Ms Tn Intl Schrlshp Pgnt USA; Pblc Rltns.

POWELL, KIMBERLY; Farrell Area HS; Farrell, PA; (Y); Spanish Clb; Band; Chorus; Concert Band; Mrchg Band; Pep Band; Stage Crew; Nwsp Rptr; Nwsp Stf; Stat Bsktbl; Pittsburgh U; Spcl Ed.

POWELL, KRISTAN; Jefferson-Morgan HS; Jefferson, PA; (Y); 12/127; Art Clb; Varsity Clb; Pres Frsh Cls; VP Rep Stu Cncl; Var Capt Cheerleading; Trk; Hon Roll; Spnsh Awd 84-86; Girls ST 86; Hmcmnt Crt 83-85.

POWELL, MELANIE; Penn Hills SR HS; Pgh, PA; (S); 130/762; AFS; Church Yth Grp; Cmnty Wkr; Drama Clb; JA; Key Clb; Office Aide; Political Wkr; Science Clb; Spanish Clb; PTA Schlrshp Awd 86; W Liberty ST Coll WV; Bus Adm.

POWELL, PATRICK; North East HS; North East, PA; (Y); 25/145; Boy Scts; Church Yth Grp; FBLA; Letterman Clb; Varsity Clb; Crs Cntry; Trk; Hon Roll; NHS; Pres Schlr; Mst Outstndng Stu Spnsh II, Engl II, Bus Law 84, 85 & 86; OH ST U; Airln Pilot.

POWELL, RANDY; Redbank Valley HS; New Bethlehem, PA; (Y); Pres Church Yth Grp; Trk; Clarion U.

POWELL, SAM; John S Fine SR HS; Nanticoke, PA; (Y); Pres Church Yth Grp; SADD; VICA; High Hon Roll; Hon Roll; Bishops Awd 86; Cert Comptncy Shop Awd Wilkes Barre Vo Tech 86.

POWELL, STACEY; East SR HS; West Chester, PA; (Y); 129/429; Hosp Aide; Pep Clb; Chorus; JV Var Cheerleading; Swmmng; Twrlr; Cmmnctns.

POWELL, THOMAS; Hazleton SR HS; Hazleton, PA; (Y); 86/360; Office Aide; Hon Roll; Penn ST; Law Enfrcmnt.

POWELL, TRACEY; Quaker Valley HS; Fair Oaks, PA; (Y); German Clb; Math Tm; Chorus; School Musical; High Hon Roll; NHS; Hgh Acad Achvt Awd 84; 1st Pl MLK Essy Cntst 84.

POWERS, LORI A; Bishop Shanahan HS; Exton, PA; (Y); 14/214; Cmnty Wkr; Debate Tm; Hosp Aide; Bsktbl; Var Socr; Var Swmmng; Var Tennis; Hon Roll; NHS; Dr Julius Margolis Memrl Schlrshp 86-87; Villanova; Nrsng.

POWERS, MICHELE; Lock Haven HS; Lock Haven, PA; (Y); Spanish Clb; Drill Tm; Yrbk Stf; Trk; Bus Adm.

POWERS, ROBERT; Neshaminy HS; Langhorne, PA; (Y); 70/750; Am Leg Boys St; Cmnty Wkr; Red Cross Aide; Chorus; Concert Band; Jazz Band; Nwsp Stf; Yrbk Stf; Bsbl; JV Var Socr; Amer Legion Schl Medal Awd; PA U Princeton; Engrng.

POWERS, T; Cumberland Valley HS; Mechanicsburg, PA; (Y); Key Clb; Model UN; PAVAS; Stage Crew; Swmmng; Hon Roll; Ntl Merit SF; Natl Art Hnr Scty 84-86; U Of Pittsburgh; Chem.

POWERS, TERRY; Poahs HS; Philipsburg, PA; (Y); 50/250; Church Yth Grp; Letterman Clb; Ski Clb; Trs Frsh Cls; Trs Stu Cncl; Var Capt Ftbl; DAR Awd.

POWLEY, CAROLINE K; Altoona Area HS; Altoona, PA; (S); 8/683; Computer Clb; German Clb; Key Clb; Spanish Clb; Jr NHS; NHS; NEDT Awd; Natl Mert Sachlrshp Cmdtn 85; PA Hghr Ed Asstnc Agncy Cert Mert 85.

POWLEY, KRIS; Central Dauphin HS; Harrisburg, PA; (Y); Key Clb; Chorus; Yrbk Rptr; Yrbk Stf; JV Var Cheerleading; Var Vllybl; Hon Roll; Athlt Of Wk-Twice-Vllybl 85; 2nd All Star Tm-Vllybl 85; Penn ST; Bus Adm.

POZESKY, ROBERT; Archibishop Wood HS; Huntingdon Vly, PA; (Y); 43/282; Church Yth Grp; Cmnty Wkr; German Clb; Political Wkr; Church Yth Grp; Var L Ftbl; Swmmng; Hon Roll; Schl Sci Fair Gld Mdl 85; DE Vly Sci Far Hon Mntn 85; Bcks Cnty Sci Fair 2nd Pl 86; Engrng.

PRAISNER, TINA; Meadville SR HS; Meadville, PA; (Y); Church Yth Grp; French Clb; Hosp Aide; Key Clb; Hon Roll; Med Fld.

PRALL, STACY L; North Allegheny SR HS; Pittsburgh, PA; (Y); 29/605; Off Frsh Cls; Off Church Yth Grp; Off Jr Cls; Off Sr Cls; Stu Cncl; Powder Puff Ftbl; Hon Roll; NHS; Pres Schlr; IN U Hnrs Schlrshp 86; Distngshd Achvt Awd Physcl Educ 86; IN U.

PRASAD, RAJEEV; Scranton Preparator Schl; Laflin, PA; (Y); 12/192; Church Yth Grp; Ski Clb; Var L Tennis; High Hon Roll; Med.

PRASCHAK, PAULA; Riverside JR SR HS; Taylor, PA; (Y); 39/175; Art Clb; VP Drama Clb; School Musical; School Play; Variety Show; Rep Jr Cls; Var Co-Capt Cheerleading; Hon Roll; Nrs.

PRATHER, DIANE; Susquehanna Township HS; Harrisburg, PA; (Y); 78/165; Pep Clb; Nwsp Stf; Yrbk Stf; Rep Sr Cls; Rep Stu Cncl; Poems Pblshd Ltry Jrnl HACC 85 & 86; Hampton U; Arch.

PRATHER, DOUGLAS EARL; Maplewood HS; Centerville, PA; (Y); 1/124; Aud/Vis; Pres Trs Church Yth Grp; Math Tm; Quiz Bowl; Spanish Clb; Bausch & Lomb Sci Awd; DAR Awd; Elks Awd; High Hon Roll; Lion Awd; PA Soc Profssnl Engrs Awd; PA ST U; Bus Admin.

PRATHER, TINA; Titusville SR HS; Titusville, PA; (Y); Hosp Aide; Spanish Clb; High Hon Roll; Hon Roll; Prfct Atten Awd; Sec.

PRATHER, WILLIAM; Hempfield HS; Lancaster, PA; (Y); Spanish Clb; Chorus; School Play; Nwsp Stf; Bsktbl; Golf; Tennis; Hon Roll; Bus.

PRATKANIS, JOE; Kiski Area HS; Vandergrift, PA; (Y); Spanish Clb; Band; Jazz Band; Mrchg Band; Symp Band; High Hon Roll; NHS; Amercn Lgn Awd 83-84; Tp 10 83-84.

PRATT, BARBARA; Wissahickon HS; Norristown, PA; (S); AFS; Trs Art Clb; Office Aide; Ski Clb; Color Guard; Drill Tm; Flag Corp; Mrchg Band; Nwsp Stf; Yrbk Stf; Amer U WA DC; Intl Lawyer.

PRATT, JEFF; Hanover SR HS; Hanover, PA; (Y); Varsity Clb; Lit Mag; JV Bsbl; Var L Ftbl; Var L Trk; Hon Roll; NEDT Awd; Mining Engrng.

PRATT, RON; Middletown Area HS; Harrisburg, PA; (Y); Yrbk Stf; Var Ftbl; Wt Lftg; JV Wrstlng; Rotary Stu 86; Lock Haven U; Sclgy.

PRATT, SHARON; Burgettstown JR SR HS; Burgettstown, PA; (Y); 10/150; Pres 4-H; Band; Chorus; Concert Band; Mrchg Band; Symp Band; 4-H Awd; Hon Roll; Jr NHS; Drama Clb; Accntng.

PRATT, SHEILA MARIE; Langley HS; Pittsburgh, PA; (Y); 35/281; Girl Scts; Spanish Clb; Nwsp Rptr; High Hon Roll; Hon Roll; Prfct Atten Awd; Outstndng Bus Stu 85-86; Stu Who Grew Most 86; U Pittsburgh; Mktg.

PRATT, THOMAS; Geibel Memorial HS; Connellsville, PA; (Y); Church Yth Grp; Varsity Clb; Rep Jr Cls; VP Stu Cncl; Var Capt Bsbl; Var Capt Bsktbl; Hon Roll; MVP Bsktbll Tm 86; All Cnty & All Sec Bsktbll 86; Tchng.

PRATT, WILLIAM A; Conemaugh Twp Area HS; Hollsopple, PA; (S); 5/101; Ski Clb; Nwsp Ed-Chief; High Hon Roll; Hon Roll; 1st & 2nd Pl In Schlstc Quiz 84; Engrng.

PRAWDZIK, BRENDA; Lakeland JR-SR HS; Carbondale, PA; (S); 47/147; FHA; Yrbk Stf; Pres Frsh Cls; Var Bsktbl; Capt Sftbl; DAR Awd; Hugh O Brien Ldrshp Awd 84; Marywood Coll; Spec Ed.

PRAZENICA, PATRICK; St Joseph HS; Natrona Hts, PA; (Y); 14/55; Rep Frsh Cls; Var Bsbl; Var L Bsktbl; NEDT Awd; Duquesne U Parish Grant 86; St Joseph Sci Fair 3rd Overall, 2nd Comp Sci 84; Duquesne U; Bus.

PRAZNIK, KATHLEEN; North Allegheny HS; Pittsburgh, PA; (Y); Church Yth Grp; Exploring; Yrbk Stf; Jr Cls; JV Fld Hcky; 3rd Pl JR Acad Of Sci; CO ST U; Education.

PREATE, DON; Scranton Preparatory Schl; Waverly, PA; (Y); 11/192; Cmnty Wkr; Drama Clb; Chorus; School Musical; School Play; Rep Jr Cls; Rep Stu Cncl; L Bowling; Im Ftbl; High Hon Roll; Natl Greek Exam Awd High Hnr 86; U Of Scranton; Pre Med.

PREAUX, CHERYL ELIZABETH; Canon Mc Millan HS; Cecil, PA; (Y); French Clb; FBLA; Library Aide; Chorus; Tennis; Acctng.

PREBISH JR, JOHN J; Penn Cambria HS; Cresson, PA; (Y); Am Leg Boys St; Art Clb; Rep Frsh Cls; Rep Soph Cls; JV Capt Bsktbl; Var L Ftbl; Trk; Im Vllybl; Wt Lftg; Pres Phys Fitness Awd 84.

PREBLE, JOSEPH; Frankford HS; Philadelphia, PA; (Y); 8/453; Orch; Nwsp Bus Mgr; Nwsp Rptr; Var Stat Bsbl; Im Sftbl; Hon Roll; NHS; Thole Essay Wnnr 85; Dr D F Maxwell Mem 86; 2nd Math 84; Drexel U; Info Sys Anlys.

PREBLE, MAUREEN; Technical HS; Scranton, PA; (Y); 25/215; FBLA; Color Guard; Var Pom Pon; Hon Roll; Prfct Atten Awd; Co Op Office Ed; Sec.

PREBOSNYAK, KAREN; Freedom SR HS; Bethlehem, PA; (Y); 145/456; Art Clb; Chorus; Yrbk Stf; Powder Puff Ftbl; Twrlr; Med Tech.

PREGMON, TANYA; Old Forge HS; Old Forge, PA; (Y); 18/70; FNA; Hosp Aide; Ski Clb; Spanish Clb; Yrbk Ed-Chief; Capt Cheerleading; Pom Pon; Hon Roll; Spanish NHS; Nrsng.

PREISLER, VICTORIA JO; Freedom HS; Bethlehem, PA; (Y); 32/445; Art Clb; Church Yth Grp; Pep Clb; Spanish Clb; Church Choir; Stage Crew; JV Var Mgr(s); JV Sftbl; Hon Roll; NHS; Penn ST; Vet.

PREMENTINE, BETSY; Butler Area SR HS; Butler, PA; (Y); VP Exploring; French Clb; JA; SADD; Thesps; Chorus; Drill Tm; Jr NHS; Intl Thspns 86; Acctg.

PRENDERGAST, JILL; Archbishop Kennedy HS; Philadelphia, PA; (Y); 7/176; Aud/Vis; Nwsp Rptr; Rep Stu Cncl; Var Crs Cntry; Var Trk; Hon Roll; NHS; Church Yth Grp; Cmnty Wkr; Dance Clb; MVP Cross Cntry 85; Schlrshp Lebanon Vly Coll Comm-Yth Schlrs Prog 86; Vp For Cmnty Svc Corps 86-87; Comm.

PRENDERGAST, STACY; Henderson HS; W Chester, PA; (S); 20/346; Church Yth Grp; Spanish Clb; School Musical; Rep Stu Cncl; Cheerleading; Lcrss; Hon Roll; NHS; Spanish NHS; Fnlst Grls Spkg Cntst; JR New Century Club West Chester Stdnt Declmtn Cntst 3rd Pl; IN U Of PA; Cmmnctns.

PRENNI, TRACY; Saltsburg JR-SR HS; Saltsburg, PA; (Y); 3/93; Trs Ski Clb; Varsity Clb; Nwsp Stf; Yrbk Stf; Sec Jr Cls; Stu Cncl; Var Cheerleading; Var Sftbl; DAR Awd; High Hon Roll.

PREPUTNICK, ERIC; Central Dauphin HS; Harrisburg, PA; (Y); 8/373; Church Yth Grp; Exploring; Key Clb; Stage Crew; Yrbk Rptr; Yrbk Stf; Jr Cls; Im Vllybl; High Hon Roll; NHS; Pre-Law.

PRESANT, JANET E; Council Rock HS; Churchville, PA; (Y); 181/800; Church Yth Grp; Drama Clb; SADD; School Musical; School Play; Var Mgr(s); Hon Roll; Prfct Atten Awd; Tchr.

PRESCHUTTI, BETH; Lakeland HS; Olyphant, PA; (Y); 4-H; FHA; SADD; Yrbk Stf; Var L Cheerleading; Var Trk; 4-H Awd; Hon Roll; PA ST; Bus.

PRESCHUTTI, CRAIG; Valley View HS; Archbald, PA; (Y); 28/200; Ski Clb; Spanish Clb; Varsity Clb; Stu Cncl; Bsbl; Bsktbl; Ftbl; Golf; Hon Roll; Temple U; Bus Mgmt.

PRESCOTT, KRISTIE; Lower Dauphin HS; Palmyra, PA; (Y); Ski Clb; Yrbk Stf; Var Cheerleading; Hon Roll; Schltc Art Awd 86; Cmmrcl Dsgn.

PRESLOID, DAVID; Spring-Ford HS; Oaks, PA; (Y); 32/256; Spanish Clb; Hon Roll; Comp Sci.

PRESLOID, JOSEPH; Punxsutawney Area HS; Punxsutawney, PA; (Y); VP Varsity Clb; Nwsp Stf; Pres Jr Cls; Trs Sr Cls; Var L Bsktbl; Var L Ftbl; Var L Trk; Rotary Awd; OH Northern; Phrmcy.

PRESOGNA, CHRISTINE; Villa Maria Acad; Erie, PA; (Y); Hosp Aide; Cert Apprctn Vlntr Hmt Med Ctr 86; Gannon U; Nrsng.

PRESS, SHERRIE; Pennsbury HS; Philadelphia, PA; (Y); Drama Clb; Spanish Clb; Chorus; School Play; Yrbk Phtg; Yrbk Stf; Hon Roll; NHS; Bus.

PRESSLEY, SHELLEY; Manheim Township HS; Lancaster, PA; (Y); 2/325; Church Yth Grp; Church Choir; Yrbk Ed-Chief; Yrbk Stf; Lit Mag; JV Tennis; High Hon Roll; NHS; Lbrl Arts Educ.

PRESTASH, MELISSA; John S Fine SR HS; Nanticoke, PA; (Y); Mgr Trk; High Hon Roll; York Coll Of PA; Psych.

PRESTON, LESLIE; Perry Traditional Acad; Pittsburgh, PA; (Y); 4/124; German Clb; Trk; High Hon Roll; NHS; Robert Morris Coll; Acctng.

PRESUTTI, MICHELLE; Western Beaver HS; Midland, PA; (Y); Computer Clb; Library Aide; Office Aide; Chorus; Bowling; Cheerleading; Trk; Wt Lftg; Hon Roll; Trival Pursuit Clb 84-85.

PRESUTTI, NANCY MANGANARO; Riverview HS; Oakmont, PA; (Y); Church Yth Grp; Hosp Aide; Band; Concert Band; Jazz Band; Mrchg Band; Pom Pon; Gov Hon Prg Awd; Hon Roll; Allegheney Vly Hnrs Bnd 84 & 85; Spec Ed.

PRESUTTI, PAMELA; Western Beaver HS; Midland, PA; (Y); 19/90; Chorus; Jazz Band; Nwsp Stf; Yrbk Ed-Chief; Trk; NHS; Embry-Riddle; Arspc.

PRETE, TODD; Plum SR HS; Pittsburgh, PA; (Y); Church Yth Grp; DECA; Letterman Clb; SADD; Varsity Clb; Var L Bsktbl; Var L Ftbl; Var L Trk; Var Wt Lftg; Hon Roll; IN U Of PA; Bus.

PRETEROTI, PETE; Canon Mc Millan SR HS; Canonsburg, PA; (Y); 118/357; Chess Clb; Church Yth Grp; Varsity Clb; Band; Church Choir; Concert Band; Var Crs Cntry; Var Swmmng; Var Trk; Hon Roll; Ambassodor Coll Pasdna CA.

PRETTI, LUANN; Du Bois HS; Penfield, PA; (Y); 69/287; Office Aide; Varsity Clb; Chorus; Yrbk Stf; Sec Soph Cls; Cheerleading; Hon Roll.

PREVITE, ANTHONY; Bishop Shanahan HS; Coatesville, PA; (Y); 40/219; Hon Roll.

PREVOST, JONET; Penn Center Acad; Philadelphia, PA; (S); Dance Clb; Drama Clb; Chorus; School Play; Variety Show; Yrbk Stf; Pres Soph Cls; Rep Stu Cncl; VP L Bsktbl; Hon Roll; Art.

PREZKOP, MARK; Bishop Hannan HS; Scranton, PA; (Y); 20/123; Boys Clb Am; French Clb; Bsbl; High Hon Roll; Hon Roll; Jr NHS; NHS; Pres Schlr; Pres Schlrshp 86; John & Lucille Guzey Schlrshp U Of Scrntn 86; Pres Ftns Awd 85-86; U Of Scranton; Sci.

PRIBICKO, JON; Homer Center JR SR HS; Homer City, PA; (Y); 19/109; Varsity Clb; Band; Mrchg Band; Nwsp Stf; Trk; High Hon Roll; NHS; Superior Achvt & Excllnc Rcgntn Awd In Physcs 86; IN U Of PA; Chem.

PRICE, ADAM; Spring Grove Area SR HS; Thomasville, PA; (Y); 14/222; French Clb; Band; School Musical; Swing Chorus; Var Mgr(s); Var Capt Swmmng; NHS; Pres Schlr; Yrk Dsptch Acdmc All Strs 86; Music Bstr Schlrshp 86; U SC; Engl.

PRICE, AMY; Harbor Creek HS; Erie, PA; (Y); Capt Mrchg Band; Variety Show; VP Frsh Cls; VP Soph Cls; VP Jr Cls; VP Sr Cls; Stu Cncl; Capt Pom Pon; VP Church Yth Grp; Chorus; Hmcmng Queen ST Fnlst 85; Govnrs Schl Arts Semi-Fnlst 85.

PRICE, BECKY; Slippery Rock Area HS; Portersville, PA; (Y); 20/172; Sec Trs Church Yth Grp; Intnl Clb; JCL; Political Wkr; Band; Chorus; Concert Band; Rep Stu Cncl; Hon Roll; NHS; Chrch Dist Mscl Tm 86; Olvt Nzrn Coll; Elem Ed.

PRICE, DARYL; Canon-Mc Millan HS; Canonsburg, PA; (Y); Chess Clb; Latin Clb; Varsity Clb; Crs Cntry; Wt Lftg; Capt Wrstlng; Washington; Econ.

PRICE, DEBBIE; Windber Area HS; Windber, PA; (Y); 5/112; Off Church Yth Grp; Drama Clb; VP French Clb; Girl Scts; Scholastic Bowl; Band; Church Choir; Concert Band; Jazz Band; Mrchg Band; Pres Acad Ftns Awd 86; Cert Hnr Acad 83-86; Stu Mnth 83-86; IN U; Bus Law.

PRICE, HEATHER; Canon Mc Millan HS; Canonsburg, PA; (Y); 39/390; Cmnty Wkr; Latin Clb; Ski Clb; Varsity Clb; Yrbk Stf; Sftbl; Swmmng; High Hon Roll; Pre-Med.

PRICE, HOLLY; Central Dauphin HS; Harrisburg, PA; (Y); 28/355; Ski Clb; Chorus; Orch; Nwsp Ed-Chief; Yrbk Bus Mgr; Yrbk Stf; Tennis; DAR Awd; Hon Roll; Jr NHS.

PRICE, JENNIFER; Wyalusing Valley HS; Dushore, PA; (Y); 19/150; Church Yth Grp; 4-H; Spanish Clb; VP Soph Cls; Trs Sr Cls; Bsktbl; Trk; Vllybl; 4-H Awd; High Hon Roll; Tyler Memrl Schlrshp 86; Prom Queen 86; Bsktbl Awd 86; Lycoming Coll; Nrs.

PRICE, KATHLEEN; Penn Hills SR HS; Pittsburgh, PA; (S); 18/800; Ski Clb; Spanish Clb; Yrbk Stf; Stu Cncl; High Hon Roll; Hon Roll; Jr NHS; NHS; PA ST U; Bus.

PRICE, KRISTI; State College SR HS; State College, PA; (Y); Church Yth Grp; Office Aide; Ski Clb; SADD; Stu Cncl; Var Cheerleading; Var Powder Puff Ftbl; Im Socr; Im Trk; Im Vllybl; Pres US Pony Clb 83-86; Rsrv Chmpn Schlng Jmpr AHSA 86; Penn ST U; Anml Biosci.

PRICE, PAMELA; Harbor Creek HS; Erie, PA; (Y); Capt Drill Tm; Variety Show; Stu Cncl; Bsktbl; Crs Cntry; Sftbl; Hon Roll; VP NHS; 1st All Cnty Ptchc In Sftbl 86; Hnrb Mntn In Sftbl 85.

PRICE, ROBERT H; Perkiomen Valley HS; Collegeville, PA; (Y); SADD; Stage Crew; Yrbk Stf; VP Frsh Cls; Trs Soph Cls; Rep Jr Cls; Rep Stu Cncl; Hon Roll; Ursinus Coll; Bus Admn.

PRICE, ROBYN; Cumberland Valley Christian Schl; Chambersburg, PA; (S); Church Yth Grp; Yrbk Stf; Var Capt Bsktbl; Var Capt Cheerleading; Var Sftbl; Hon Roll; Ntl Merit Ltr; Extraordinary Christ Stu Amer 84-85; Booster Clbs Fml Athlet Yr 85; Liberty U; Elem Ed.

PRICE, STEPHANIE; Philipsburg-Osceola Area HS; Sandy Ridge, PA; (Y); Girl Scts; SADD; Band; Chorus; Church Choir; Stage Crew; JV Bsktbl; Var JV Sftbl; Crmnl Justice.

PRICE, SUSAN; Danville SR HS; Washingtonville, PA; (Y); Church Yth Grp; French Clb; FHA; Girl Scts; Library Aide; Temple Yth Grp; Chorus; Church Choir; School Musical; School Play; Semnry Grad 86; Bloomsburg U; Hndcppd Ed.

PRICHARD, JILL; Harbor Creek HS; Erie, PA; (Y); 2/222; Pres 4-H; Model UN; Varsity Clb; Concert Band; Mrchg Band; Variety Show; Rep Stu Cncl; Stat Sftbl; Var L Swmmng; NHS.

PRICHARD, LISA; Carrick HS; Pittsburgh, PA; (S); Cmnty Wkr; French Clb; Q&S; School Play; Nwsp Stf; Yrbk Stf; High Hon Roll; Hon Roll; Med.

PRICHARD, STEPHANIE; Mercy Vocational HS; Philadelphia, PA; (Y); Hosp Aide; Vllybl; Cosmetlgy Tchr.

PRIEBE, KRISTEN; Upper Darby HS; Drexel Hill, PA; (Y); Church Yth Grp; Drill Tm; Flag Corp; Mrchg Band; JV Lcrss; JV Swmmng; High Hon Roll; Hon Roll; Prfct Atten Awd; Nrsng.

PRIESTER, RODNEY; Dayton HS; Templeton, PA; (Y); 25/52; Aud/Vis; Library Aide; Hon Roll; Archtctr.

PRIMAK, LARA; Juniata HS; Mifflintown, PA; (Y); Chorus; Nwsp Stf; Yrbk Stf; JV Tennis; Bausch & Lomb Sci Awd; High Hon Roll; NHS; Pres Schlr; Voice Dem Awd; Susquehanna U; Biochem.

PRIMAK, NATALIE; Juniata HS; Mifflintown, PA; (Y); Quiz Bowl; Nwsp Stf; Yrbk Stf; Gym; Trk; Hon Roll.

PRIMAVERA, CATHERINE; Conemaugh Twp Area HS; Hollsopple, PA; (Y); 18/106; Church Yth Grp; Drama Clb; Q&S; Spanish Clb; Chorus; Flag Corp; Nwsp Rptr; Yrbk Stf; Sftbl; DAR Awd; Bus & Prfsnl Wmns Clb Grl Mnth 86; Duquesne U; Pre-Law.

PRIMAVERA, MICHELE; Saint Basil Acad; Phila, PA; (Y); Art Clb; Church Yth Grp; Cmnty Wkr; Spanish Clb; Chorus; Church Choir; School Musical; Variety Show; JV Bowling; JV Score Keeper; Bus Mngmnt.

PRIMO, MICHELLE; Monaca JR SR HS; Monaca, PA; (Y); 16/95; Am Leg Aux Girls St; Exploring; Sec Pres Library Aide; Red Cross Aide; Spanish Clb; School Musical; Sftbl; High Hon Roll; Hon Roll; NHS; Church Chrs 84-85; Pep Clb 84-86; Gannon U; Pre Med.

PRIMROSE, SCOTT; East Stroudsburg HS; E Stroudsburg, PA; (Y); 17/225; Boy Scts; VP Church Yth Grp; Cmnty Wkr; Sec Exploring; Ski Clb; Yrbk Stf; High Hon Roll; Pocono Wrtrs Awd For Sci Fiction 85; Lafayette Coll; Elec Engrng.

PRIMUS, GUY W; Penn Hills HS; Verona, PA; (Y); French Clb; Science Clb; Concert Band; Mrchg Band; Rep Stu Cncl; Engrng.

PRINCE, TONYA; Frankford HS; Philadelphia, PA; (Y); Am Leg Aux Girls St; Church Yth Grp; Dance Clb; Girl Scts; Band; Flag Corp; Yrbk Stf; Coach Actv; Twrlr; Cit Awd; Law.

PRINCIPE, TAMI; St Marys Area HS; Saint Marys, PA; (Y); Band; Concert Band; Stage Crew; Var Trk; Spec Ed.

PRINDLE, ROBERT; Tech Memorial HS; Erie, PA; (Y); 5/365; Math Tm; Chrmn Model UN; Var L Crs Cntry; Var Tennis; High Hon Roll; Kiwanis Awd; NHS; Presdntl Acadmc Achvt; Cmnty Svc Awd; Gld Key Awds-Scl Stds, Math & Data Prcssng; Penn ST-BEHREND; Engrng.

PRINGLE, DEBRA; Bald Eagle-Nittany HS; Salona, PA; (Y); 47/130; Hosp Aide; Pep Clb; Mat Maids; JV Sftbl; Hon Roll; Lee & Bessie Graham Schlrshp 86; Clinton Cnty Med Aux Schlrshp 86; Jersey Shore Hosp Schlrshp 86; Centre Cnty Area Vo Tech; Nrsg.

PRINKEY, GEORGIA; Southmoreland SR HS; Scottdale, PA; (Y); 42/230; Pep Clb; VICA; Chorus; Church Choir; Prfct Atten Awd; Dntl Hygnst.

PRISCO, DANIELLE; Forest City Regional HS; Pleasant Mount, PA; (Y); 2/52; Letterman Clb; Ski Clb; Spanish Clb; Var Sftbl; JV Var Vllybl; High Hon Roll; NHS; Rensselaer Mdl 85-86; Natl Sci Merit Awd 84-85; Lehigh U; Engrng.

PRISK, KATHRYN; Curwensville Area HS; Curwensville, PA; (Y); Church Yth Grp; FBLA; Band; Chorus; Concert Band; Mrchg Band; Nwsp Stf; Twrlr; Hon Roll; SECR.

PRISTAS, CLIFFORD P; Greater Latrobe SR HS; Latrobe, PA; (Y); 120/350; Boy Scts; Band; Chorus; Concert Band; Jazz Band; Mrchg Band; Pep Band; School Musical; Stage Crew; Symp Band; Dist I Hnrs Band Trombn Cnty Dist-Rgnl Band 85-86; Dist Orchstra 85-86; Duquesne; Music Ed.

PRISTAS, HEIDI; North Star HS; Stoystown, PA; (Y); 7/124; AFS; Art Clb; FCA; Ski Clb; Chorus; Off Stu Cncl; NHS; Stu Actn For Educ 84-86; Lioness Grl Of Mnth 86; Seton Hill Coll; Biol.

PRISTASH, DAWN; Spring Ford SR HS; Monte Clare, PA; (S); 26/258; Spanish Clb; Hon Roll; NHS; Dstngshd Spnsh Awd 84; Crtfct Art Mrt 84; PA ST Coll; Psych.

PRITCHARD, CATHERINE M; North Catholic HS; Pittsburgh, PA; (Y); 2/265; Church Yth Grp; Capt Debate Tm; Hosp Aide; NFL; Sec Speech Tm; Stage Crew; Nwsp Ed-Chief; Nwsp Stf; NHS; Soc Wmn Engrs; Wrld Affrs Cncl Sistr Cty Yth Rep Shffld Englnd 85; Zappa Awd Physcl Sci.

PRITCHARD, JACK; Church Farm Schl; Paoli, PA; (Y); 4/23; Aud/Vis; Chess Clb; JA; Science Clb; Chorus; Church Choir; School Play; Nwsp Stf; Rep Jr Cls; Rep Stu Cncl; Hampden-Sydney; Sci.

PRITCHARD, MELINDA; Southmoreland SR HS; Scottdale, PA; (Y); 31/216; Church Yth Grp; German Clb; Office Aide; Pep Clb; Ski Clb; Spanish Clb; Chorus; School Musical; Nwsp Stf; Lit Mag; Penn ST; Sec Ed.

PRITTS, BRENDA; Salisbury-Elklick HS; Meyersdale, PA; (Y); 6/35; Church Yth Grp; Band; Chorus; Concert Band; Mrchg Band; Yrbk Stf; Trs Soph Cls; Score Keeper; High Hon Roll; Hon Roll; Vly Forge Chrstn Coll; Ministry.

PRITTS, DEBORAH; Connellsville Area SR HS; Normalville, PA; (Y); Computer Clb; VICA; Nwsp Rptr; Nwsp Stf; VP Jr Cls; Hon Roll; Slvr & Brnz Mdl Opn & Clsng Crmnes Vica 85-86; 3rd Pl Plqu Pblc Spkng Cntst Vica 86; Comp Opr.

PRITTS, KRISTEEN; Somerset Area SR HS; Somerset, PA; (Y); Art Clb; Spcl Awd-Outstndg JR Cafeteria Stu 86; 2 Awds Art Clb 86; Pittsburg Beauty Acad; Csmtlgy.

PRITTS, RALPH; Salisbury Elk-Lick JR HS; Salisbury, PA; (Y); 13/35; Drama Clb; Band; Yrbk Stf; Bsbl; Bsktbl; Score Keeper; Socr; Hon Roll; Ntl Merit Ltr; Police.

PRITTS, SUSAN L; Hempfield HS; Hunker, PA; (Y); Camera Clb; Swmmng; Shrn Gnrl Hosp 83-84; Bus Mngmnt.

PROBERT, DAVID J; MMI Preparatory Schl; Hazelton, PA; (Y); Art Clb; Boy Scts; Camera Clb; Church Yth Grp; Pep Clb; JV L Bsbl; Var L Crs Cntry; Hon Roll; NEDT Awd; 1st Pl Anmtd Flm 85-86; Area Music Awd Cncrt Socty 86; USC; Flm Mkg.

PROBST, MOLLY; Northern York County HS; Dillsburg, PA; (Y); 28/223; Church Yth Grp; French Clb; Off Band; Chorus; Church Choir; Concert Band; Jazz Band; Mrchg Band; School Musical; Hon Roll; Tri-M Music Hnr Soc 86; Dist Bands, Dist Orch 84-85; Rgnl Band 84; Music.

PROCH, CAROLYN A; Kiski Area HS; Avonmore, PA; (Y); 5/388; Math Clb; Band; Mrchg Band; Symp Band; Rep Frsh Cls; Rep Jr Cls; High Hon Roll; NHS; Acad Ltr; Top Ten; U Pittsburgh; Math.

PROCHNAU, TIMOTHY; William Allen HS; Allentown, PA; (Y); 30/559; Trs Church Yth Grp; Exploring; Band; Concert Band; Mrchg Band; Orch; Hon Roll; Jr NHS; NHS; Engr.

PROCOPIO, MICHAEL; Northwestern Lehigh HS; Kempton, PA; (Y); 33/158; Exploring; Teachers Aide; School Musical; School Play; Yrbk Phtg; Var L Crs Cntry; Var L Trk; Hon Roll; NEDT Awd; IN U Physics Testng Comptn; PA ST U; Comp Sci.

PROCOVICH, MICHAEL T; Rochester Area HS; Rochester, PA; (Y); Teachers Aide; VICA; Stage Crew; Ftbl; Tennis; Trk; Wt Lftg; Hon Roll; NHS; Prfct Atten Awd; Devry Inst Technology; Elec Eng.

PROCTOR, EVANNA; William Penn SR HS; York, PA; (Y); 3/321; SADD; Color Guard; Mrchg Band; Orch; NHS; Ntl Merit Schol; Pres Schlr; Camera Clb; Pep Clb; Chorus; Pres Schlrshp Wilson Coll 85-86; Acadmc All Star 85-86; Hnr Grad 85-86; Wilson Coll; Bio.

PROCTOR, JOSEPH; John Harris Campus HS; Harrisburg, PA; (S); 4/457; Pep Clb; Nwsp Rptr; VP Bsktbl; High Hon Roll; Hon Roll; NHS; Ntl Merit Ltr; Bus Mngmnt.

PROCTOR, LESLIE RENEE; Penn Trafford HS; Trafford, PA; (Y); Pres Church Yth Grp; Church Choir; NHS; Gold Slvr & Brnze Mdl Spch, Art, & Instrmntl Music Regnl Yth Comptn 85; Duquesne U; Bus Admin.

PROCTOR, WILLIS; Corry Area HS; Corry, PA; (S); Boy Scts; Church Yth Grp; French Clb; Library Aide; Math Tm; Radio Clb; SADD; VICA; Yrbk Stf; Wrstlng; Mach Shop.

PROFIT, ANGELA; Mount Carmel Area HS; Mt Carmel, PA; (Y); 11/185; Key Clb; Spanish Clb; Nwsp Rptr; Yrbk Stf; Var Bsktbl; High Hon Roll; NHS; Spanish NHS.

PROFY, JOE; Holy Ghost Prep; Newtown, PA; (S); Political Wkr; Spanish Clb; Nwsp Stf; Bsbl; Bsktbl; Hon Roll; NHS.

PROIETTO, DENISE; Pittston Area HS; Dupont, PA; (Y); 34/348; Science Clb; VICA; Tennis; Hon Roll; NHS.

PROKARYM, NOREEN; Lackawanna Trail HS; Factoryville, PA; (Y); 1/85; Computer Clb; Stu Cncl; Sftbl; French Hon Soc; NHS; Val; Bst Of Cls-WBRE TV 28 86; Marywood Coll; Med Tech.

PROKOP, MICHAEL; Archbishop Kennedy HS; Conshohocken, PA; (Y); Aud/Vis; Boy Scts; Cmnty Wkr; Rep Stu Cncl; Trk; Hon Roll; SR Patrol Ldr BSA 85-86; JR Stu Yr Karate 84; Genetics.

PROLEIKA, SUZANNE; Wyoming Valley West HS; Forty Fort, PA; (Y); 7/386; French Clb; Orch; Lit Mag; High Hon Roll; NHS; NEDT Awd.

PRON, JOHN; Minersville Area HS; Pottsville, PA; (Y); 32/124; German Clb; Ski Clb; Rep Stu Cncl; JV Bsbl; Var L Ftbl; Var L Wrstlng; US Air Force; Accntng.

PROSEK, MARIANNE LYNN; Mc Dowell SR HS; Erie, PA; (Y); 33/529; Cmnty Wkr; Model UN; Mrchg Band; Yrbk Stf; Sec Frsh Cls; JV Trk; Hon Roll; NHS; Exploring; Pep Clb; Outstndng HS Achvt 85; Outstndng Runner 85-86; Cert Of Aprctn From Untd Way 84; Grv Cty Coll; Bio-Med Engr.

PROSKE, NICOLE; Elk County Christian HS; Ridgway, PA; (S); Art Clb; Church Yth Grp; Dance Clb; Girl Scts; Ski Clb; JV Cheerleading; L Tennis; High Hon Roll; NEDT Awd; Amer Lgn Awd 83; U Of Pittsburgh; Phrmcy.

PROSPER, MARIE JEANINE; Our Lady Of The Sacred Heart HS; Aliquippa, PA; (Y); 15/73; Debate Tm; Pep Clb; Chorus; Nwsp Rptr; CCBC Beaver Cnty; Med Sec.

PROSS, ELLEN; Nazareth Acad; Philadelphia, PA; (Y); VP Debate Tm; VP NFL; Nwsp Stf; Hon Roll; Awds Of Excllnc Various Pieces Of Prose 83-4; Poetry NFL 84-5; Accntnt.

PROSSER, JAMES; Central Bucks West HS; Doylestown, PA; (Y); 15/400; Boy Scts; Camera Clb; Cmnty Wkr; Ski Clb; SADD; Acpl Chr; Church Choir; School Play; Var L Bsbl; Var Ftbl; Duke U; Pre-Med.

PROTZ III, MICHAEL; Blue Ridge HS; Hallstead, PA; (Y); 1/100; Pep Clb; Concert Band; Drm Mjr(t); Jazz Band; Mrchg Band; JV Var Bsktbl; Var L Vllybl; Bausch & Lomb Sci Awd; High Hon Roll; VP NHS; PA ST U; Pre-Med.

PROUT, SUSAN; Manheim Central HS; East Petersburg, PA; (Y); Church Yth Grp; Teachers Aide; Jazz Band; Mrchg Band; Rptr Jr Cls; Rptr Sr Cls; Trk; Hon Roll; VFW Awd; 4-Way Test Awd; Yth Fit Achvt Awd; Lancaster Gen Hosp Schl; Nrsg.

PROVANCE, SCOTT; Uniontown Area SR HS; Mill Run, PA; (Y); 88/349; Drama Clb; Library Aide; Band; Concert Band; Jazz Band; Mrchg Band; School Play; French Hon Soc; High Hon Roll; Hon Roll; Cnty Band 83-86; Sectn Of Yr 85; Sctn Ldr 85-86; Grove City Coll; Comp Sys.

PROVINS, CATHLEEN A; Bethel Park SR HS; Bethel Park, PA; (Y); 7/520; Latin Clb; Library Aide; Office Aide; JV Bsktbl; Var Powder Puff Ftbl; JV Sftbl; High Hon Roll; Sec NHS; Pres Ftns Awd 86; Penn ST; Nrsng.

PROVOST, CHRISTINE; Shady Side Acad; Pittsburgh, PA; (Y); Drama Clb; PAVAS; Chorus; School Musical; Stage Crew; Rep Soph Cls; Var L Cheerleading; Var L Swmmng; Trk; Hon Roll; Chatham Coll Mrt Schlrshp 86; Mt Holyoke Coll; Intl Pol.

PROWEL, BRAIN; Butler SR HS; Butler, PA; (Y); Office Aide; Hon Roll; CAP; Chorus; Trk; Optmtry.

PROWELL, JODI; Northeast)rn HS; Mt Wolf, PA; (Y); 17/149; Band; Chorus; Rep Sr Cls; Var Bsktbl; Mgr(s); Var Tennis; Var Vllybl; Hon Roll; NHS; AFS; MVP Vlybl 84; Phrmcy.

PROX, KAREN; Peters Twp HS; Mc Murray, PA; (Y); Dance Clb; Drill Tm; School Play; Yrbk Stf; JV Mgr(s); Var Pom Pon; Powder Puff Ftbl; JV Score Keeper; Var Trk; Hon Roll; Best Smile 85; Nrsng.

PRPIC, MLADEN; Connellsville Area HS; Cnlsvle, PA; (Y); Camera Clb; Chess Clb; Computer Clb; Ski Clb; School Musical; School Play; Socr; Swmmng; Carnegie; Cmptr Sci.

PRUCE, SHERRI; Canon-Mc Millan HS; Canonsburg, PA; (Y); 31/340; Pep Clb; Spanish Clb; Drm Mjr(t); Tennis; Twrlr; High Hon Roll; NHS; Prfct Atten Awd; Spanish NHS; Washington & Jefferson.

PRUE, SCOTT; Mt Pleasant Area SR HS; Norvelt, PA; (Y); Boy Scts; JA; Ski Clb; Band; Concert Band; Mrchg Band; Im JV Bsktbl; Im Ftbl; Prfct Atten Awd; Air Force; Pilot.

PRUM, PISET ANG; Lebanon SR HS; Lebanon, PA; (Y); 58/266; French Clb; Latin Clb; Spanish Clb; Teachers Aide; Nwsp Rptr; Nwsp Stf; Yrbk Rptr; Yrbk Stf; Tennis; Hon Roll; Drexel U; Intr Dsgn.

PRUNER, AMY; Marion Center Area HS; Chambersvl, PA; (Y); Hosp Aide; Varsity Clb; JV Var Cheerleading; VP Hlth OCC Stu Amrca, Deleg ST Hlth OCC Stu Amrca Conf 85-86; Mt Aloysius; Srgcl Tech.

PRUNTY, LESLIE A; Bethel Park SR HS; Bethel Park, PA; (Y); 58/515; Band; Concert Band; Mrchg Band; Symp Band; Yrbk Stf; Var Bsktbl; Var Powder Puff Ftbl; Var Capt Sftbl; Var Capt Vllybl; Hon Roll; All Tourn Sftbll Tm In WPWFSL 85; Pst Gazettes S Grls Sftbll All Str Tm 86; Advert Sftbll Tm 86; OH U.

PRUSKI, TOM; Bentworth HS; Scenery Hill, PA; (Y); Art Clb; Hon Roll; Schlrp 84; Elect Engr.

PRUSS, KIM; Western Wayne HS; Sterling, PA; (Y); Church Yth Grp; 4-H; Mgr(s); Mat Maids; Score Keeper; Psych.

PRUTZER, CARLA; Perkiomen Valley HS; Perkiomenville, PA; (Y); 11/187; Varsity Clb; JV Var Bsktbl; Var Tennis; High Hon Roll; Hon Roll; Lion Awd; NHS; Presdntl Acadmc Ftns Awd 85-86; Hrlysvl Ins Compns Coll Schlrshp 86; Bus & Prfsnl Wmns Clb Grl Of Mnth; Shippensburg U PA; Crmnl Jstc.

PRY, LISA; Clearfield Area HS; Mineral Springs, PA; (Y); 25/300; Church Yth Grp; Key Clb; Spanish Clb; High Hon Roll; NHS; Pres Acad Ftnss Awd 86; ICM Schl Of Bus; Med Ofc Asst.

PRYER, DARIN; West Catholic HS For Boys; Phila, PA; (Y); 65/203; Pres Sec Boys Clb Am; Library Aide; Cit Awd; Yth Of Yr For Boys Clubs Of City Of Phila 86; ST Fnlst For Yth Of Yr 86; Dr Charles Drew Mem Awd 86; Temple U; Communications.

PRYLE, BARBARA A; Penn Hills SR HS; Pittsburgh, PA; (Y); 64/798; FFA; VICA; Acpl Chr; Chorus; School Musical; High Hon Roll; Hon Roll; NHS; Linton Super People Awd Voctnl Svcs 84; Camp Knowledge Awd 83-86; Cert Recgntn Exc 86; Hnr Rl; Floral Designer.

PRYNDA, MICHELE; Carbondale Arca HS; Simpson, PA; (Y); 16/150; Ski Clb; Spanish Clb; Var Cheerleading; Var L Trk; Hon Roll; 3 Time Wnr Pres Phys Ftnss Awd 84-86; 2 Time Wnr YMCA Gymnstcs Awd 84-85; Mst Sprtd Vrsty Chrldng 86; Acctng.

PRYOR, MARIA; E L Meyers HS; Wilkes-Barre, PA; (Y); Office Aide; Nwsp Rptr; Nwsp Stf; Yrbk Phtg; Yrbk Stf; Var L Trk; Vllybl; Hon Roll; Spanish NHS; Art Clb; Antnl Inst Of Art; Phtgrphy.

PRYOR, ROSS; Valley HS; Arnold, PA; (Y); Pep Clb; Spanish Clb; Varsity Clb; Concert Band; Mrchg Band; JV Var Bsktbl; JV Ftbl; JV Var Trk; High Hon Roll; Hon Roll; Drum Capt 86-87; Air Force; Bus Mgmt.

PRYOR, SARAH; Waynesboro Area SR HS; Blue Ridge Smt, PA; (Y); Camera Clb; Church Yth Grp; Hosp Aide; Chorus; High Hon Roll; Hon Roll; York Coll; Nrsng.

PRZYBYLEK, ANDREW; North Allegheny HS; Allison Park, PA; (S); Cmnty Wkr; Pres Rep DECA; FBLA; Pres JA; Variety Show; Rep Jr Cls; Rep Sr Cls; Stu Cncl; Bsbl; Wt Lftg; 3rd Pl ST DECA Comptn 85; 2nd Pl ST DECA Comptn 86; 2 Time Natl Cntndr DECA 85-86; Bus.

PRZYWARA, LISA; John S Fine HS; W Nanticoke, PA; (Y); 30/256; Ski Clb; Chorus; Yrbk Stf; Rep Stu Cncl; Mgr(s); High Hon Roll; X Ray Tech.

PSOLKA, MAX; Northern York HS; Dillsburg, PA; (Y); 2/210; Var L Ftbl; Var L Trk; High Hon Roll; NHS; Val; Math Awd 86; MVP Fld & Trck 85-86; Acdmc All-Str 86; The Johns Hopkins U; Bio-Med.

PSZENICZNY, CHARLOTTE; Northwest JR SR HS; Benton, PA; (Y); 21/105; Computer Clb; FHA; Red Cross Aide; Science Clb; SADD; Church Choir; VP Stu Cncl; Bsktbl; High Hon Roll; Hon Roll; Env Ed Awd 86; Max Mac Gralo Thomas Alva Edison Awd 86; Slippery Rock U; Env Ed.

PTASZKIEWICZ, BETH; Highlands HS; Natrona Hgts, PA; (Y); Cmnty Wkr; Hosp Aide; Office Aide; Nwsp Ed-Chief; Yrbk Stf; Stu Cncl; Cheerleading; Trk; Jr NHS; Prfct Atten Awd; Elem Ed.

PUAL, SUSAN; Upper Dauphin Area HS; Elizaebthville, PA; (Y); 7/110; Exploring; Chorus; Capt Drill Tm; School Musical; Yrbk Stf; Stu Cncl; High Hon Roll; Pres NHS; Church Yth Grp; Jhn Hll Schlrshp 86; Susquehanna U; Plctcl Sci.

PUCEL, DANETTE; Ringgold HS; Monongahela, PA; (Y); Ski Clb; Band; Bsbl; Bsktbl; U Of Pittsburgh; Sprts Med.

PUCHALSKI, BARBARA; St Huberts HS; Philadelphia, PA; (Y); 60/367; Cmnty Wkr; Dance Clb; Red Cross Aide; Spanish Clb; Teachers Aide; Cheerleading; Gym; Wt Lftg; Hon Roll; NHS; Frankford Nrs Schl; Nrsng.

PUCHALSKI, STANLEY; Ather Judge HS; Philadelphia, PA; (Y); 50/410; Church Yth Grp; Math Clb; Service Clb; Stu Cncl; Ftbl; Trk; Wt Lftg; Hon Roll; NHS.

PUCKEY, STEVE; Yough SR HS; W Newton, PA; (Y); Boy Scts; VP Church Yth Grp; French Clb; Ski Clb; Yrbk Stf; JV Var Bsbl; Hon Roll; NHS.

PUCKLY, FRANCINE; Corry Area HS; Corry, PA; (S); 1/219; Model UN; Church Choir; Concert Band; Jazz Band; Mrchg Band; Var L Crs Cntry; Var L Trk; High Hon Roll; Ntl Merit Schol; Bus & Profssnl Womns Grl Mnth 85-86; Cornell U; Nutrtnl Biochem.

PUDLAK, JOSEPH P; Bethel Park SR HS; Bethel Park, PA; (Y); Am Leg Boys St; Boy Scts; Church Yth Grp; Band; Concert Band; Mrchg Band; School Musical; Symp Band; Hon Roll; Senator Keystone Boys ST 86; Nationally Ranked Competitive Water Skier; OH Northern; Pharmacy.

PUDLOWSKI, HEATHER; Lackawanna Trl JR SR HS; Hummelstown, PA; (Y); 12/98; Camera Clb; Spanish Clb; Co-Capt Color Guard; Lit Mag; JV Sftbl; Hon Roll; NHS; Mst Otstndng Grd Awd 86; Pres Physcl Ftnss Awd 84-86; Harrisburg Area CC; Pblc Rltns.

PUETTE, DEBORAH S; Mc Dowell SR HS; Erie, PA; (Y); 7/546; Dance Clb; French Clb; Model UN; Ski Clb; School Musical; School Play; Stu Cncl; Cheerleading; Tennis; Cit Awd.

PUFFINBURGER, TRACY; New Brighton HS; New Brighton, PA; (Y); Art Clb; Computer Clb; Library Aide; Chorus; Trs Frsh Cls; Rep Stu Cncl; JV Tennis; Hon Roll; Prom Comm & Xmas Danc Comm; Tri-Hi-Y & GAA; Sundy Schl Tchr; Vactn Bibl Schl Tchr; Air Force.

PUGAR, ELIZABETH; North Catholic HS; Pittsburgh, PA; (Y); 21/301; Cmnty Wkr; FNA; Pep Clb; School Musical; Sec Frsh Cls; Sec Jr Cls; Rep Sr Cls; Sec Stu Cncl; JV Capt Cheerleading; Elks Awd; Hmcmng Queen; Duquesne U; Nrsng.

PUGH, DAVE; Purchase Line HS; Dixonville, PA; (Y); Pres Church Yth Grp; French Clb; FBLA; Letterman Clb; Spanish Clb; SADD; Varsity Clb; Mgr Bsktbl; L Trk; Hon Roll; IN U; Acctg.

PUGH, DIANE; Chambersburg Area SR HS; Stockton, CA; (Y); 29/638; AFS; Drama Clb; Concert Band; Mrchg Band; Var Crs Cntry; Var Trk; High Hon Roll; Cit Awd; High Hon Roll; Service Clb; Sec CSF 83-84; Lovers Lang Lit Group 85-86; Shippensburg US Frgn Lang Comptn 2nd Pl 85-86; UC Berkeley; Clincl Psych.

PUGH, JEFFREY; Tunkhannock Area HS; Tunkhannock, PA; (S); 5/330; Church Yth Grp; FCA; German Clb; Letterman Clb; JV Ftbl; Var Vllybl; Hon Roll; NHS; Rotary Awd; Soc Dist Am HS Stu 85; Acdmc All Am 85; Dickinson Coll; Law.

PUGH, REBECCA; Fannet-Metal HS; Dry Run, PA; (S); Sec Church Yth Grp; Drama Clb; Band; Chorus; Church Choir; Concert Band; Mrchg Band; School Play; Var Cheerleading; Hon Roll; Shippensburg; Drama.

PUGLIESE, CATERINA; Dunmore HS; Dunmore, PA; (Y); 10/155; Hosp Aide; Letterman Clb; Yrbk Stf; Trs Jr Cls; Trs Sr Cls; Stu Cncl; Var Bsktbl; Var Cheerleading; Jr NHS; NHS; Med.

PUGLISE, ANDREW J; Quigley HS; Aliquippa, PA; (Y); 1/112; Math Tm; Pres Soph Cls; Pres Jr Cls; Pres Sr Cls; L Swmmng; Gov Hon Prg Awd; High Hon Roll; NHS; Ntl Merit SF; Comp Engrng.

PUGLISI, MELANY P; HS For Engineering & Science; Philadelphia, PA; (Y); 26/184; Drama Clb; Teachers Aide; School Musical; Stage Crew; Yrbk Rptr; Im Ftbl; Im Ice Hcky; Wt Lftg; High Hon Roll; FL Inst Of Tech; Chem Engrng.

PUHLMAN, POLLY; Bethel Park SR HS; Bethel Pk, PA; (Y); Office Aide; Drm Mjr(t); School Musical; Variety Show; Twrlr; High Hon Roll; Modernettes Baton Twrlg Corp Wnrs Wrld & Natl Twrlg Titles & Show Titls 78-85; Early Chldhd.

PUKACH, JENNIFER; Quigley HS; Aliquippa, PA; (S); 24/103; Hosp Aide; Band; Concert Band; Mrchg Band; Pep Band; Nwsp Stf; Yrbk Stf; Powder Puff Ftbl; High Hon Roll; Hon Roll; Ntrtn.

PULASKI, BETH; St Maria Goretti HS; Philadelphia, PA; (Y); 14/426; Church Yth Grp; Capt Mathletes; Capt Math Tm; Science Clb; Spanish Clb; Stage Crew; Gov Hon Prg Awd; High Hon Roll; NHS; Natl JR Sci & Humanities Symposium 86; Carnegie-Mellon U; Micro Bio.

PULFORD, ERIN; Carrick HS; Pittsburgh, PA; (S); French Clb; Girl Scts; Hosp Aide; Q&S; School Musical; School Play; Nwsp Stf; Mgr(s); Powder Puff Ftbl; U Of Pittsburgh; Ed.

PULITI, ANGELA; Red Land HS; New Cumberland, PA; (Y); 41/275; Ski Clb; SADD; Yrbk Stf; Off Frsh Cls; Off Soph Cls; Off Jr Cls; Off Sr Cls; Rep Stu Cncl; Var Capt Cheerleading; Gym; Biomchncs.

PULKOWNIK, FRANK; West Greene HS; Wind Ridge, PA; (Y); FFA; Letterman Clb; Varsity Clb; School Play; Var L Bsbl; Var L Bsktbl; Var L Ftbl; Var Wt Lftg; Hon Roll; NHS; Acdmc All Am Awd 85-86; Penn ST U Fayette; Electrncs.

PULLI, JENNIFER L; North Penn HS; Hatfield, PA; (Y); Church Yth Grp; Pep Clb; Band; Mrchg Band; Off Frsh Cls; Rep Soph Cls; Rep Jr Cls; Rep Stu Cncl; Bsbl; Cheerleading; Chrldng Cptn 83-84; Prom Comm Chrpsn 83-84; Prfmng Stage Awd 84-85; Art.

PULLIAM, JENNIFER; Homer Center HS; Homer City, PA; (Y); Church Yth Grp; Band; Concert Band; Mrchg Band; School Play; Stu Cncl; Homer City Band Boosters Schlrshp 86; IN U PA; Elem Ed.

PULLIN, PATRICIA; Interboro HS; Norwood, PA; (S); French Clb; JCL; Latin Clb; Yrbk Bus Mgr; Rep Soph Cls; Rep Jr Cls; High Hon Roll; NHS.

PULLO, MELISSA; Pius X HS; Roseto, PA; (Y); School Musical; Sftbl; High Hon Roll; Hon Roll; NHS; Bus.

PULLO, TRACY; St Maria Goretti HS; Philadelphia, PA; (Y); 6/390; Cmnty Wkr; Exploring; GAA; Mathletes; Rep Soph Cls; Rep Jr Cls; Rep Sr Cls; Hon Roll; NHS; Prfct Atten Awd; Acad All Amer Awd 84; USLMA Ldrshp Awd 85; Alg Awd 84; U Of PA; Law.

PULTYNOVICH, LISA; Our Lady Of Lourdes Regional HS; Shamokin, PA; (Y); AFS; Cmnty Wkr; Debate Tm; Drama Clb; Sec FBLA; Library Aide; Pep Clb; Chorus; Capt Drill Tm; School Play; Bloomsburg U; Ofc Admin.

PUMO, VICTOR; Council Rock HS; Washington Cros, PA; (Y); 80/845; Var Socr; Hon Roll; NHS.

PUNCHELLO, CATHARINE; Pennsbury HS; Morrisville, PA; (Y); Exploring; Intnl Clb; Yrbk Stf; Stu Cncl; Im Bowling; Hon Roll; PA ST Plc Yth Wk 86; Law Enfrcmnt.

PUNCHELLO, VALERIE; Pennsbury HS; Morrisville, PA; (Y); 1/712; Mathletes; Scholastic Bowl; Orch; Yrbk Ed-Chief; Lit Mag; NHS; Ntl Merit Schol; School Musical; Hon Roll; Rotary Awd; Phi Beta Kppa Key 86; Morrisvl Rotry Stu Mth 85; Bucks Cnty Engrs Stu Yr 85; Princeton U; Physcst.

PUNT, SANDRA; Downingtown HS; Exton, PA; (Y); Church Yth Grp; Drama Clb; Pep Clb; Ski Clb; Spanish Clb; Chorus; School Musical; Bowling; Mgr(s); Hon Roll; Merit Diploma Spn 83; Daisy Chain Grad 85; York Coll; Nrsng.

PUPI, ROBERT; Monaca JR SR HS; Monaca, PA; (Y); 1/90; School Musical; JV Var Bsktbl; JV Var Ftbl; High Hon Roll; NHS; Prfct Atten Awd; Governs Schl Sci Altrnt 86; High Q Team 86; Premed.

PUPO, MARY; Penn Cambria SR HS; Cresson, PA; (Y); Pres Trs Church Yth Grp; Trs Girl Scts; Spanish Clb; Co-Capt Color Guard; Rep Stu Cncl; JV Bsktbl; Var Sftbl; JV Vllybl; High Hon Roll; Hon Roll; PA Cambria Hnr Scty 85-86; Mst Outstndng Frnch Stu 83-84; PA ST U; Engrng.

PURBAUGH, BARBARA; Meyersdale HS; Garrett, PA; (Y); FFA; Hon Roll; NHS; Greenhand Awd 85; Chptr Frmr 86; Writer.

PURCELL, AMY; Villa Maria Acad; Erie, PA; (Y); 2/130; Cmnty Wkr; Science Clb; Spanish Clb; High Hon Roll; Hon Roll; NHS; NEDT Awd; Pres Schlr; Hnr Grad 85-86; Gannon Sci Engr Awd 84-85; Acad Schlrshp 85-86; Gannon U; Med.

PURCELL, DAWN; Reading SR HS; Reading, PA; (Y); 74/638; Exploring; Hon Roll; Edwin Youse Schlrshp Awd 86; Pres Acad Fit Awd 86; Reading Area CC; Nrsng.

PURCELL, KELLY; Shamokin Area HS; Shamokin, PA; (Y); 33/241; Drama Clb; Girl Scts; Pep Clb; Science Clb; Band; Score Keeper; PA ST U; Microbio.

PURCELL II, MARY LYNN O T C; Solebury Schl; New Hope, PA; (S); 1/40; Camera Clb; Yrbk Phtg; Yrbk Stf; Im Swmmng; High Hon Roll; Val; Bst Clss Chnl 6 Tv Prog 86; Fshn Inst Of Tech; Fshn Edtr.

PURCELL, VINCENT; Our Lady Of Lourdes HS; Shamokin, PA; (Y); AFS; Sec Camera Clb; Pres Church Yth Grp; Band; Mrchg Band; Pep Band; Stu Cncl; Bsktbl; Wt Lftg; JV Var Wrstlng; Cert Of Merit Schlstc Phtgrphy Awds 85-86; Acctng.

PURDY, ANNE MARIE; Bethel Christian Schl; Erie, PA; (S); 1/12; Church Yth Grp; Chorus; Orch; Stu Cncl; Sftbl; Vllybl; High Hon Roll; JC Awd; Acadmc Excllnc Awd; Bible Schlr Awd; Mst Imprvd Vlybl; Sci.

PURDY, TERI; Lackawanna Trail JR-SR HS; Factoryville, PA; (Y); 3/97; 4-H; FHA; Drill Tm; 4-H Awd; NHS; Outstndng Band Stu 85; Band Cptn 86-87; Flag Co Cptn 85; Med Tech.

PURINTON, KIMBERLY; Tunkhannock HS; Tunkhannock, PA; (Y); VP Church Yth Grp; VP JA; Spanish Clb; Nwsp Bus Mgr; Rep Soph Cls; Rep Jr Cls; Rep Sr Cls; Cit Awd; NHS; Chess Clb; Pres Acadmc Ftns Awd 86; Baptist Bible Coll; Elem Ed.

PURNER, AMY; Cardinal O Hara HS; Media, PA; (Y); 272/877; Debate Tm; Hosp Aide; Golf; Swmmng; Tennis; 4-H Awd; Equestrian Riding,Champ/Resere Champ JR Equitatrian, Pleasure Horse, JR & Chldrn 84-86; Rosemont Coll; Accntng.

PURSEL, VICTORIA; Columbia-Montour Area HS; Catawissa, PA; (Y); VICA; JV Cheerleading; Hon Roll; Csmtlgst.

PURTA, LORI; North Pocono HS; Moscow, PA; (S); 11/250; Library Aide; Pep Clb; Ski Clb; Trk; High Hon Roll; NHS; Spn.

PURVIS, GREGORY J; Allentown Central Catholic HS; Whitehall, PA; (Y); 25/200; Church Yth Grp; Ski Clb; Im Bsktbl; Im Fld Hcky; Capt Var Tennis; Hon Roll; MVP Tnns Tm 85-86; Penn St; Engr.

PURVIS, JENNIFER; Seneca Valley HS; Evans City, PA; (Y); Church Yth Grp; Drama Clb; Pres Thesps; Acpl Chr; Chorus; Church Choir; Madrigals; School Musical; High Hon Roll; Hon Roll; Westminster Fcoll Hons Choir 85; PA ST Chorus 86; All Eastern Performing Groups 87; Slippery Rock U; Music Therapy.

PURYEAR, TERRI; Beaver Area JR SR HS; Beaver, PA; (Y); 20/179; Hosp Aide; Natl Beta Clb; Ski Clb; Score Keeper; Tennis; Trk; High Hon Roll; Hon Roll; Acctg.

PUSATERI, THERESA; Bishop Hannan HS; Scranton, PA; (Y); 2/122; Church Yth Grp; Debate Tm; Scholastic Bowl; Sec Spanish Clb; Speech Tm; Chorus; Church Choir; High Hon Roll; NHS; Maxima Cum Laude Natl Latin Exam 84; Vet.

PUSCAVAGE, KIMBERLY; Pittston Area SR HS; Pittston, PA; (Y); Computer Clb; Key Clb; Science Clb; Ski Clb; Band; L Swmmng; Hon Roll.

PUSHCHAK, THERESA; Seneca HS; Erie, PA; (Y); 16/160; French Clb; Yrbk Stf; VP Frsh Cls; VP Soph Cls; Pres Stu Cncl; JV Bsktbl; JV Sftbl; JV Vllybl; Hon Roll; Prfct Atten Awd; Prnt, Stu, Tchr Untd Schlrshp 86; Gannon U; Bio.

PUSHWA, VALERIE; Greensburg Central Catholic HS; Greensburg, PA; (Y); 91/250; Pep Clb; Ski Clb; Lit Mag; L Tennis; Var Trk; High Hon Roll; Hon Roll; Carnegie Mellon U; Mech Engr.

PUSKAR, PHILIP; Mount Pleasant Area HS; Mt Pleasant, PA; (Y); 75/250; German Clb; Var L Bsktbl; Ftbl; Hon Roll; Lang Clb Wnnr 3rd German Play 86; Johnson & Wales Coll; Hotel Mgm.

PUTHENPURACKAL, TINA; Owen J Roberts HS; Pottstown, PA; (S); 5/267; Hosp Aide; Yrbk Rptr; NHS; Phy Ther.

PUTMAN, HEIDI; North Star HS; Stoystown, PA; (Y); 10/124; FCA; Hosp Aide; Math Clb; Band; Chorus; Concert Band; Hon Roll; NHS; CPA Altruism Awd 86; Otstndng Cndy Strpr Awd 83 & 86; Amer Lgn Schl Awd 86; St Francis Coll; Nrsng.

PUTNAM, ELLEN; Warren Area HS; Warren, PA; (Y); Ski Clb; Acpl Chr; Madrigals; School Musical; Nwsp Rptr; High Hon Roll; Jr NHS; NHS; PA Gvrnrs Schl For Arts 86; PA Cncl Tchrs Englsh Awd 84; Amer Lgn Aux Essay Cntst Awd 86; Anthropology.

PUTT, RHONDA; Hamburg Area HS; Shoemakersville, PA; (Y); FBLA; German Clb; SADD; Hon Roll; Acad Awd In Amer Cultures 85-86; Kutztown U; Acctng.

PUTT, TERRY; Boiling Springs HS; Boiling Spgs, PA; (Y); 2/105; Concert Band; Mrchg Band; Var L Bsbl; Var L Bsktbl; Var L Socr; High Hon Roll; Hon Roll; NHS; Rotary Awd.

PUTZ, KIMBERLY ANN; Norwin SR HS; North Huntingdon, PA; (Y); 125/556; Leo Clb; Letterman Clb; Library Aide; Pep Clb; Ski Clb; Spanish Clb; SADD; Chorus; Im Bsktbl; Var Bowling; Bowlg Proprutrs Schlrshp 83-84; Stu Cncl Schlrshp 86; Robert Morris Clg; Bus Adm.

PUZIO, STEPHEN; Wyoming Valley West HS; Plymouth, PA; (Y); 89/410; Ski Clb; Hon Roll.

PYLE, AMY; Palmyra Area HS; Palmyra, PA; (Y); #87 In Class; Spanish Clb; Teachers Aide; Cheerleading; Hon Roll; Mgmt.

PYLE, BARBARA FAYE; Solanco HS; Quarryville, PA; (Y); Church Yth Grp; FBLA; Varsity Clb; Var Capt Cheerleading; High Hon Roll; Hon Roll; NHS; Prfct Atten Awd; Acctg.

PYLE, CHRISTINE; Northwestern HS; Cranesville, PA; (Y); 26/163; Art Clb; Church Yth Grp; Pep Clb; Chorus; Hon Roll; Ntl Merit Ltr; Prfct Atten Awd; Cert Merit Outstndng Achvt 86; Awd Jump Rope Heart 84-86; Edinboro ST Coll; Art.

PYLE, CONNIE; Solanco HS; Quarryville, PA; (Y); 6/234; Radio Clb; Teachers Aide; Acpl Chr; Chorus; School Musical; High Hon Roll; Lion Awd; NHS; Pres Schlr; Exploring; Lanc Lebanon Cnty Chorus 84-86; PMEA Prfrmnc Solanco Chorl 86; Outstndng Stdnt Awds 83-86; Lebanon Valley Coll; Elem Ed.

PYLE, RANDY; Heritage Christian Acad; Erie, PA; (Y); 1/15; Camera Clb; Church Yth Grp; Computer Clb; FCA; German Clb; Office Aide; Ski Clb; Band; Stage Crew; Yrbk Phtg; Natl Schlr Athlt Awd 85; Oral Roberts U; Acctng.

PYLE, SUE; Ford City HS; Ford City, PA; (Y); 26/153; AFS; Drama Clb; German Clb; Hosp Aide; Yrbk Stf; Frsh Cls; Jr Cls; Vllybl; Hon Roll; NHS; PA ST; Intl Stds.

PYLE, YANCE D; Center Area HS; Monaca, PA; (Y); Boy Scts; Church Yth Grp; Civic Clb; Ftbl; God Cntry Awd; Hon Roll; Prfct Atten Awd; Offcr In Svc.

PYLES, DARLA; Beth-Center HS; Waynesburg, PA; (Y); GAA; Ski Clb; Spanish Clb; Varsity Clb; Stu Cncl; Cheerleading; Score Keeper; Hon Roll; IN U Of PA; Elem Educ.

PYLES, STEVE; Northern Lebanon HS; Lebanon, PA; (Y); 49/177; Chess Clb; School Play; Rep Sr Cls; Rep Stu Cncl; L Golf; JV L Socr; Var L Sftbl; Im Wt Lftg; Var L Wrstlng; Hon Roll; Tmstrs Lcl 771 Wrstlng Trnmnt 98 Lb Chmp 86; Amer Allnc Hlth, Physcl Educ,Rcrtn & Dance Achvt Awd 85; Penn ST; Psych.

PYLES, TAASHA NIKOL; Bermudian Springs HS; East Berlin, PA; (Y); Band; Chorus; Concert Band; Madrigals; Mrchg Band; School Musical; Swing Chorus; Sec Jr Cls; Stu Cncl; Capt Cheerleading.

PYSH, DAVID; Beth-Center HS; Richeyville, PA; (Y); 35/160; Boy Scts; Church Yth Grp; English Clb; JA; Spanish Clb; Band; Coach Actv; High Hon Roll; Hon Roll; CA U; Computer Sci.

PYSH, SANDRA; Carlynton HS; Carnegie, PA; (Y); French Clb; German Clb; Band; Chorus; Drm Mjr(t); Mrchg Band; Yrbk Phtg; Bsktbl; Swmmng; Hon Roll; U Pittsburgh; Chem.

QUACKENBOS, MELISSA; Hatboro-Horsham SR HS; Horsham, PA; (Y); 3/270; Hosp Aide; Intnl Clb; Key Clb; Color Guard; Drm Mjr(t); Mrchg Band; NHS; Intl Bus.

QUADER, MELISSA; Burgettstown JR-SR HS; Atlasburg, PA; (Y); Church Yth Grp; Ski Clb; Spanish Clb; Band; Symp Band; Var Capt Cheerleading; Hon Roll; NHS; Phy Asst.

QUAGLIARIELLO, ANTONIA; West Catholic Girls HS; Philadelphia, PA; (Y); 4/250; Drama Clb; Mathletes; NFL; Nwsp Rptr; Nwsp Sprt Ed; NHS; Hghst Gen Avg Religion 86; Hghst Gen Avg Hstry 86; Forenscs Awd 84.

QUAGLIERI, LISA; Gateway HS; Monroeville, PA; (Y); 152/508; Chorus; Var JV Cheerleading; Score Keeper; Trk; Physcl Thrpst.

QUAID, RONALD; Central Dauphin East HS; Harrisburg, PA; (Y); 52/251; French Clb; Chorus; Bsktbl; Hon Roll; Jr NHS; Bio.

QUALTERS, AMY; Mc Keesport Area HS; Mckeesport, PA; (Y); Church Yth Grp; Acpl Chr; Band; Church Choir; Concert Band; Mrchg Band; Pep Band; School Musical; Symp Band; Rep Frsh Cls; Dist I Hnrs Choir 85; Elem Ed.

QUATRANI, PAUL; Archbishop Carroll HS; Ardmore, PA; (Y); 12/162; SADD; Stage Crew; Off Sr Cls; High Hon Roll; Hon Roll; NHS; Hlth Sci.

QUATTROCK, MARK; Governor Mifflin SR HS; Kenhorst, PA; (Y); 86/325; Nwsp Stf; Jr Cls; Stu Cncl; Hon Roll; Kutztown; Hstry.

QUEAR, PAULA; Freedom HS; Bethlehem, PA; (Y); 100/445; Cmnty Wkr; French Clb; VP JA; Chorus; School Musical; Hon Roll; JR Exec Awd Holding Ofc As VP 84; W Chester U; Child Psych.

QUEEN, JOYCE; Moshannon Valley JR SR HS; Irvona, PA; (Y); 4/128; Church Yth Grp; Spanish Clb; Band; Chorus; Concert Band; Mrchg Band; Pep Band; High Hon Roll; Hon Roll; NHS; Jacob W George Memrl Schlrshp 86; IN U Of PA; Nrsng.

QUEER, FENNA; Rockwood SR HS; Rockwood, PA; (S); 22/98; Church Yth Grp; Ski Clb; Spanish Clb; Band; Chorus; Drm Mjr(t); Mrchg Band; Yrbk Stf; Rep Jr Cls; Rep Stu Cncl; Mth Awd 83-84; Pittsburgh Tech; Cmprtzd Drftng.

QUEL, JENNIFER; Gateway HS; Monroeville, PA; (Y); Pres Church Yth Grp; Band; Chorus; Church Choir; Var Capt Swmmng; Hon Roll; Hnrs Fund Schlrshp 86; Clarion U; Secndry Ed.

QUENZER, DONNA L; East Pennsboro HS; W Fairview, PA; (Y); Art Clb; Church Yth Grp; Chorus; Nwsp Rptr; JV Bsktbl; JV Var Crs Cntry; JV Powder Puff Ftbl; JV Sftbl; JV Var Trk; Fmly & Chldrns Svc Awd-1st Pl Prose 85-86; Miss Amercn Coed Pgnt Fnlst 84-85; U S Air Force; Fnancl Mngmt.

QUENZLER, ANGIE; Central Dauphin HS; Harrisburg, PA; (Y); Church Yth Grp; Hon Roll; NHS; Eastern College; Elem Educ Tchr.

QUERIO, ANDREA M; Highlands SR HS; Brackenridge, PA; (Y); Art Clb; Church Yth Grp; FBLA; FHA; Chorus; Yrbk Stf; Jr NHS; Pres Physcl Ftns Awd 84; Intr Dsgnr.

QUICK, DIANA; Blairsville SR HS; Blairsville, PA; (Y); Office Aide; Chorus; School Musical; Stat Bsktbl; Stat Sftbl; NHS; High Hon Roll; NHS; Prfct Atten Awd; Presdntl Acdmc Fitness Awd 86.

QUICK, JOEY; State College SR HS; State College, PA; (Y); Church Yth Grp; Cmnty Wkr; Hosp Aide; Library Aide; Teachers Aide; Chorus; School Musical; School Play; Hon Roll; PA ST UED.

QUICK, KATHRYN S; Wyoming Seminary HS; Harveys Lake, PA; (Y); 6/84; Pres SADD; School Musical; Stage Crew; Nwsp Rptr; High Hon Roll; NCTE Awd; Ntl Merit SF; PA Govnrs Schl For Intl Studies 85; Concours Natl De Francais-Hnrbl Mentn, 4th & 2nd Pl 82-84; Psych.

QUICK, PAUL; Danville Area HS; Danville, PA; (Y); 20/204; Chess Clb; CAP; Band; Crs Cntry; Trk; High Hon Roll; NHS; Amer Lg ST Polc Yth Wk 86; Crimnl Justc.

QUICK, PAULA; Danville SR HS; Danville, PA; (Y); 8/163; Church Yth Grp; Pres FHA; Latin Clb; Teachers Aide; High Hon Roll; NHS; NEDT Awd; Prfct Atten Awd; Soroptimist Citznshp Awd; Acadmc Schlrshp; Misericordia; Elem Educ.

QUIGLEY, ALICIA; Phoenixville Area HS; Phoenixville, PA; (Y); Church Yth Grp; Key Clb; Pep Clb; Sec SADD; School Musical; Nwsp Rptr; Rep Soph Cls; High Hon Roll; Jr NHS; NHS; Comm.

QUINLAN, CLARE MARIE; Fox Chapel HS; Aspinwall, PA; (Y); Church Yth Grp; German Clb; SADD; PA ST U; Econ.

QUINN, ADAM; St Marys Area HS; St Marys, PA; (Y); Boy Scts; Bsktbl; Ftbl; Golf; NHS; Pres Schlr; Eagle Scout Awd ,6; Syracuse U; Bio.

QUINN, BILL; Kennedy Christian HS; W Middlesex, PA; (Y); 23/98; Science Clb; Ski Clb; Spanish Clb; Concert Band; Jazz Band; Mrchg Band; School Musical; Var Golf; Im Vllybl; Hon Roll; Cath Dghtrs Of Amer Ptry Cont 84; Pa JR Acad Of Sci 85; Susquehanna; Inter Bus.

QUINN, HEATHER; Chartiers Valley HS; Heidelberg, PA; (Y); Drama Clb; SADD; School Musical; School Play; Nwsp Ed-Chief; Rep Stu Cncl; NHS; Regnl Pres Greater Pittsburgh Bnai Brith Yth Orgnztn 85-86; SR Ofcr Of Schls Teen Inst 85-87; Interntl Jrnlst.

QUINN, HEATHER; Freeport HS; Sarver, PA; (S); 15/170; Church Choir; Mrchg Band; School Musical; Stu Cncl; Var Bsktbl; Trk; High Hon Roll; Psych.

QUINN, HELEN; Trinity HS; Washington, PA; (Y); 149/374; Art Clb; Pres VP Girl Scts; Hosp Aide; Key Clb; Office Aide; Pep Clb; Chorus; Flag Corp; Grl Sct Slvr Ldrshp Awd 83; Grl Sct Slvr Awd 83; Grl Sct Gld Ldrshp Awd 85-86; Sawyer; Med Asst.

QUINN, JULIE; Fairview HS; Fairview, PA; (Y); Dance Clb; Pep Clb; School Play; Capt Cheerleading; Pom Pon; Psych.

QUINN, LAURIE; Pleasant Valley HS; Saylorsburg, PA; (Y); Drama Clb; VP Exploring; SADD; Chorus; School Play; Yrbk Bus Mgr; Yrbk Stf; Rep Stu Cncl; Var Fld Hcky; Envrmntl.

QUINN, LISA; Butler SR HS; Butler, PA; (Y); Chorus; Hon Roll; Butler County CC; Nrsng.

QUINN, MARY G; Cardinal O Hara HS; Springfield, PA; (Y); 133/750; Computer Clb; Dance Clb; French Clb; Girl Scts; Pep Clb; Var Capt Cheerleading; Im Vllybl; Hon Roll; Prfct Atten Awd; St Josephs U; Fin.

QUINN, MATTHEW; St Josephs Preparatory Schl; W Trenton, NJ; (Y); Spanish Clb; Speech Tm; JV Swmmng; Im Wt Lftg; Fairfield; Law.

QUINN, RACHEL; Reading Central Cath; Oley, PA; (Y); Drama Clb; Pres Library Aide; NFL; Band; School Musical; School Play; JV Cheerleading; Hon Roll; Drama.

QUINN, SUSAN; Bishop Kenrick HS; Norristown, PA; (Y); GAA; Service Clb; Nwsp Stf; Rep Frsh Cls; Rep Soph Cls; Rep Jr Cls; Rep Sr Cls; Stu Cncl; Bsktbl; Fld Hcky; All Cthlc Brls Bsktbll 83-84; Sci.

QUINN, THOMAS; Henderson HS; West Chester, PA; (S); 8/349; Cmnty Wkr; JCL; Latin Clb; Varsity Clb; Variety Show; Nwsp Rptr; Lit Mag; Capt L Golf; High Hon Roll; 1st Tm All Ches-Mont Golf Tm 85; JR Golf Champ 85.

QUINNEY, COLLEEN; Chichester SR HS; Boothwyn, PA; (Y); Model UN; Red Cross Aide; SADD; Nwsp Rptr; VP Soph Cls; Pres Jr Cls; VP Stu Cncl; Capt Cheerleading; Trk; Hon Roll; Stu Cncl Svc Awd 86; Outstndg Athlt Awd 86; Miss T E E N Contestant PA 86; W Chester U.

QUINT, LESLIE; North Allegheny SR HS; Wexford, PA; (Y); Art Clb; Nwsp Stf; Lit Mag; Fld Hcky; Hon Roll; Jr NHS; Gov Schl Arts 85; Pre Coll Art Schlrshp 86; Distngushd Achvt Awd 85; Art.

QULI, FARHAT; MMI Prep; Mountaintop, PA; (S); Art Clb; Ski Clb; Rep Soph Cls; Var Bsbl; Var Crs Cntry; High Hon Roll; Hon Roll; NHS; Ntl Merit Ltr; Spanish NHS; 2nd Pl Amer Chmcl Assn Cntst 86; 2nd Pl Kngs Coll Spnsh Cntst 85; 3rd Pl Ntl Spnsh Cntst 85.

QUORESIMO, CATHERINE; Saegertown HS; Meadville, PA; (Y); 16/130; Computer Clb; Letterman Clb; Varsity Clb; Band; Variety Show; JV Var Bsktbl; Var JV Vllybl; High Hon Roll; Hon Roll; Bus.

RAAB, CHERYL; Northampton SR HS; Walnutport, PA; (Y); 9/495; AFS; FTA; Chorus; School Musical; School Play; Stage Crew; Var L Tennis; God Cntry Awd; High Hon Roll; NHS; God & Lf Awd 86; Mxd Vcl Ensmbl 84-87; Elem Educ.

RABATIN, JULIE; Mary Fuller Frazier HS; Perryopolis, PA; (Y); 4-H; Mrchg Band; Stat Vllybl; Hon Roll; Chem.

RABBERMAN, DEBBIE; Council Rock HS; Newtown, PA; (Y); Band; Concert Band; Jazz Band; Mrchg Band; Orch; Pep Band; School Musical; Symp Band; Stat Bsbl; Spec Educ.

RABBERMAN JR, ROBERT C; Hatboro-Horsham HS; Hatboro, PA; (Y); 50/300; Nwsp Rptr; Nwsp Sprt Ed; Nwsp Stf; Trs Soph Cls; Socr; Trk; Cnslng Awd Plq 84; Mchncl Drwng Awd Plq 85; Archtctr.

RABE, DAN; Belle Vernon Area HS; Belle Vernon, PA; (Y); Ski Clb; Band; Jazz Band; Pep Band; Hon Roll; CA U Of PA; Elec Engr.

RABITS, JENNIFER; Bishop Guilfoyle HS; Altoona, PA; (Y); 42/110; Art Clb; Church Yth Grp; Dance Clb; French Clb; Science Clb; SADD; Y-Teens; Mrchg Band; Capt Pom Pon; Hon Roll; Penn ST U; Sci.

RABOLD, TAMELA; Eastern Lebanon County HS; Newmanstown, PA; (Y); Church Yth Grp; Cmnty Wkr; Library Aide; Chorus; Color Guard; Drill Tm; Yrbk Stf; Off Jr Cls; Score Keeper; Hon Roll; Mt Ida Coll; Travel.

RABURN, LORI; Lincoln HS; Philadelphia, PA; (Y); 23/500; Church Yth Grp; FHA; Hosp Aide; Office Aide; JV Var Badmtn; Mgr(s); Timer; Frankford Schl Nrsg; Nrs.

RABUTINO, DAWN; St Maria Goretti HS; Philadelphia, PA; (S); 5/402; Church Yth Grp; Intnl Clb; Mathletes; Service Clb; Nwsp Stf; High Hon Roll; NHS; Contnentl Math Leag Awd 85; Frnch Awd 84; Med.

RACE, LYNETTE; Northeast Bradford HS; Rome, PA; (Y); FHA; SADD; Yrbk Ed-Chief; Yrbk Stf; Stu Cncl; Hon Roll.

RACE, PATRICIA; Norwin SR HS; N Huntingdon, PA; (Y); Pres Church Yth Grp; French Clb; Girl Scts; Pep Clb; VICA; Band; Chorus; Concert Band; Mrchg Band; Orch; Accntng.

RACHO, JEFF; MMI Prep Schl; Hazleton, PA; (S); Computer Clb; School Play; Variety Show; Pres Frsh Cls; Rep Jr Cls; Var Bsbl; JV Golf; Hon Roll; NHS; US Military Acad Workshop 86.

RACHWAL, MARTHA; Nazareth Acad; Philadelphia, PA; (Y); Lit Mag; Sec Frsh Cls; Hon Roll; Prfct Atten Awd; 1st Pl Plsh Ortrcl Cntst 86; Phila Coll; Fshn Mrchndsng.

RACICH, DANA; Archbishop Kennedy HS; Conshohocken, PA; (Y); 30/160; Rep Jr Cls; Rep Stu Cncl; Var Fld Hcky; Var Trk; Hon Roll.

RACICOT, ARTHUR; Carson Long Military Inst; Drayton Plains, MI; (S); 5/45; ROTC; Varsity Clb; Im Bsbl; Var L Socr; Var L Tennis; Im Vllybl; High Hon Roll; Hon Roll; Goodwill & Meritime Svc Awd 83-84; Rungers 84-86; Brown Belt Koei Kan Karate; MA Inst Tech; Mech Engrng.

RACINE, BRIAN; Hamburg Area HS; Hamburg, PA; (Y); 5/164; Pres French Clb; Library Aide; Ski Clb; Yrbk Stf; Stu Cncl; Socr; Tennis; French Hon Soc; High Hon Roll; NHS; Acad Achvt Awd Bio 84; Acad Achvt Awds Alg II & Geom 85-86; Mensa Intl 85; Swarthmore Coll; Mth.

RACITI, LINDA; Bishop Kenrick HS; Norristown, PA; (Y); 6/305; Church Yth Grp; Drama Clb; Office Aide; Science Clb; Band; Yrbk Stf; High Hon Roll; NHS; Dance Clb; Intnl Clb; Acad Excllnce Lang 83-84; Hugh O Brien Fndtn Fnlst 84-85; Schl Guid Ofce Aid 85-86; Bus.

RACSOK, DAWN M; Freedom SR HS; Bethlehem, PA; (Y); Drama Clb; Hosp Aide; JA; Library Aide; Teachers Aide; Thesps; Acpl Chr; Chorus; School Play; Stage Crew; Northampton Comm Coll; Trvl.

RACZKOWSKI, JOHN; Canton HS; Roaring Br, PA; (Y); Aud/Vis; Boy Scts; French Clb; Letterman Clb; JV Bsktbl; Cit Awd; Hon Roll; Williamsport Area CC; Auto Bdy.

RADATTI, MICHELE M; Archbishop Kennedy HS; Conshohocken, PA; (Y); Library Aide; Office Aide; Pep Clb; Yrbk Phtg; Yrbk Stf; Stu Cncl; Mgr(s); Score Keeper; Sftbl; High Hon Roll; Prfsnl Cosmtlgst.

RADCLIFFE, DAVID; Brockway Area HS; Brockway, PA; (Y); 5/109; VP Jr Cls; Pres Sr Cls; Var Crs Cntry; DAR Awd; High Hon Roll; NHS; Prfct Atten Awd; Colonial Dames Of Am Schrlshp 86; Hugh O Brien Found 84; Cornell U; Human Ecolgy.

RADELET, MATT; Langley HS; Pittsburgh, PA; (Y); 10/279; Capt Crs Cntry; Timer; Socr; Swmmng; Var Trk; Wt Lftg; Cit Awd; High Hon Roll; Hon Roll; Rotary Awd; Pres Fit Awd 83-86; U Pittsburgh; Civil Engrng.

RADELLA, MARJORIE; Quigley HS; Mars, PA; (S); 6/112; Math Tm; Chorus; Stat Bsktbl; L Crs Cntry; Mgr Powder Puff Ftbl; Co-Capt Tennis; Trk; High Hon Roll; Jr NHS; Lion Awd; US Army Schlr Athlt; Mrty Kndr Jr Mrl Awd; Trck & Fld MVP; Gannon U; Biolgy.

RADER, DAVE; Liberty HS; Bethlehem, PA; (Y); 14/475; Math Clb; High Hon Roll; Amrcn Invtnl Mthmtcs Exam Part 86; Econ.

RADER, ERIC; Seneca Valley HS; Evans City, PA; (Y); 10/366; Aud/Vis; Church Yth Grp; VP JA; Im Bsktbl; Hon Roll; NHS; JR Achvt Achvr Awd, D Carnegie, Rotary Schlrshps 86; Grove City Coll; Engrng.

RADINOVSKY, LISA M; Penn Manor HS; Lancaster, PA; (Y); 2/311; VP Hst Thesps; School Musical; Stage Crew; VP Sr Cls; NHS; Ntl Merit SF; Debate Tm; Hon Roll; Opt Clb Awd; Spanish NHS; Stu Mnth Awd 84-85; Ntl Piano Plyng Audtns Local,Dist,ST 81-85; Harvard Smr Schl Stu Pgm 85; Millersville U; Lib Arts.

RADLEY, DANA; Hazleton HS; Hazelton, PA; (Y); Church Yth Grp; Cmnty Wkr; Hosp Aide; Office Aide; Scholastic Bowl; Spanish Clb; Var Trk; Readng Hosp Schl/Nrsng; Nrsng.

RADOMSKI, DAVID F; Lansdale Catholic HS; Chalfont, PA; (Y); 5/222; Aud/Vis; Pres Church Yth Grp; Nwsp Rptr; Var Socr; High Hon Roll; NHS; Ntl Merit SF; Smmr Sci Sem USAF Acad 85; Cert Dstnctn Natl Sci Olympd 83 & 84; Cert Merit PA Hghr Ed Assn Agcy 85; Aero Engrng.

RADOVICH, MICHELLE; Springdale HS; Springdale, PA; (Y); Art Clb; Spanish Clb; Yrbk Stf; Stat Bsktbl; Coach Actv; JV Capt Vllybl; High Hon Roll; Hon Roll; Prfct Atten Awd; Nw Knsngtn Police Dept Trng Pgm Awd 86; Crmnlgy.

RADWICK, THOMAS A; Downingtown SR HS; Exton, PA; (Y); 70/525; Nwsp Rptr; Ed Yrbk Stf; Rep Sr Cls; Stu Cncl; Bsktbl; Var Capt Tennis; Hon Roll; NCTE Awd; NEDT Awd; Compete Penn StPCTEA 86; Syracuse U; Comm.

RADY, NOELLE; Our Lady Of The Sacred Heart HS; Aliquippa, PA; (Y); 20/63; Church Choir; School Musical; Cheerleading; Pep Clb; Variety Show; Nwsp Stf; Fshn Dsgn.

RADY, STEPHANIE; St Clair Area HS; St Clair, PA; (Y); FHA; Math Clb; Ski Clb; Nwsp Rptr; Nwsp Stf; Yrbk Rptr; Yrbk Stf; Mu Alp Tht; NHS; NEDT Awd; Math.

RADYN, MARK; Franford HS; Philadelphia, PA; (Y); 146/430; Aud/Vis; Church Yth Grp; English Clb; FBLA; German Clb; ROTC; SADD; Concert Band; School Play; Jr Cls; Temple Coll; Army.

RADZIMINSKI JR, DENNIS; Shaler Area HS; Pittsburgh, PA; (Y); 137/517; JV Bsbl; Var JV Swmmng; Hon Roll; Arch.

RADZWILKA, DIANNE AMY; Wyoming Area HS; Wyoming, PA; (Y); 17/247; Church Yth Grp; German Clb; Key Clb; Nwsp Stf; Tennis; High Hon Roll; Hon Roll; Jr NHS; NHS; Ntl Cncl Yth Ldrshp 85-86; Pomeroys Tnbrd 84-85; U Of Pittsburgh; Math.

RAE, BARBARA; Jayre Area HS; Sayre, PA; (Y); Spanish Clb; SADD; Ed Lit Mag; Lincoln Tech Inst; Drftng.

RAEZER, KARA; Marple Newtown HS; Newtown Square, PA; (Y); Art Clb; Drama Clb; Ski Clb; Thesps; Drill Tm; Nwsp Rptr; VP Stu Cncl; Trk; High Hon Roll; NHS; 1st Pl Wrtng Awd 84; Writing.

RAFALKO, JESSICA; James M Coughlin HS; Wilkes-Barre, PA; (Y); Drama Clb; 4-H; Band; Orch; School Play; Swmmng; NHS; Trustees Schlrshp 86; Phila Coll Of Phrmcy; Phrmcy.

RAFEEW, CHRISTINE; Chartiers Valley HS; Bridgeville, PA; (Y); 81/343; Art Clb; Camera Clb; Varsity Clb; Var L Bsktbl; L Trk; U Of Pittsburgh; Med.

RAFFAELE, CHRISTINE; Peters Township HS; Mc Murray, PA; (S); Speech Tm; Concert Band; Mrchg Band; Free Entrprs Week Schlrshp 85; Scndry Ed.

RAFFEINNER, TIM; Saint Marys Area HS; Kersey, PA; (Y); 5/300; Debate Tm; JA; High Hon Roll; NHS; Most Outstndg JR-SOC Stud 86.

RAFFERTY, EMMETT; Beth-Center SR HS; Vestaburg, PA; (Y); Civic Clb; Drama Clb; School Play; Nwsp Ed-Chief; Nwsp Phtg; Nwsp Stf; High Hon Roll; Hon Roll.

RAFFERTY, KATHLEEN; Hampton HS; Gibsonia, PA; (Y); 2/260; 4-H; Concert Band; Drill Tm; Mrchg Band; Symp Band; Pom Pon; 4-H Awd; High Hon Roll; NHS; Allegheny Vly Hnrs Band 83-84; PA Music Edctrs Assn Dist I Band 84; Grad Marshl 86; Pre-Law.

RAGAN, BEVERLY; Slippery Rock Area HS; Prospect, PA; (Y); FBLA; Intnl Clb; Pep Clb; SADD; High Hon Roll; Hon Roll; NHS; Bus.

RAGAN, CHARLES E; West Allegheny HS; Oakdale, PA; (Y); 1/213; Church Yth Grp; Math Tm; Lit Mag; High Hon Roll; NHS; Ntl Merit SF; Acad Tm 84; Lions Clb Stu Mnth 85; Engrng.

RAGAN, JYMSE; St Marie Goretti HS; Philadelphia, PA; (Y); Girl Scts; JA; Vllybl; Hon Roll; Temple U; Med.

RAGAN, STACEY; Lampeter-Strasburg HS; Strasburg, PA; (Y); 6/160; Var Bsktbl; Hon Roll; NHS; Burrones Schlr 86; Engrng.

RAGAZZONE, ANGELA; St Basil Acad; Philadelphia, PA; (Y); German Clb; GAA; Pep Clb; Varsity Clb; Fld Hcky; Sftbl; Duqisne U; Sci.

RAGER, DAVID; Greater Johnstown HS; Johnstown, PA; (Y); Art Clb; VP Sec Church Yth Grp; Math Clb; Spanish Clb; Hon Roll; NHS; Compu Sci.

RAGER JR, DAVID R; Grove City HS; Grove City, PA; (Y); 42/154; Aud/Vis; Church Yth Grp; Office Aide; Teachers Aide; Chorus; Church Choir; School Play; High Hon Roll; Hon Roll; Choral Awd 84-85; Med.

RAGNELLI, DINA; Northwester Lehigh HS; Germansvile, PA; (Y); 7/185; Ski Clb; Drm Mjr(t); Sec Stu Cncl; Mgr(s); Twrlr; High Hon Roll; NHS; Prfct Atten Awd; Engl Literature Essy Cntst Wnnr; Fshn Mrchndsng.

RAGNI, GREGORY; Bethlehem Catholic HS; Bethlehem, PA; (S); 15/229; Math Tm; Model UN; NFL; Political Wkr; Scholastic Bowl; Pres Jr Cls; Pres Stu Cncl; Golf; Tennis; Church Yth Grp; Le High U Ldrshp Awd; Polit Sci.

RAGO JR, ROBERT V; St John Neumann HS; Philadelphia, PA; (Y); 138/338; Chorus; Im Bsktbl; Pierce JC; Accntng.

RAGO, SHERRY; Penn Hills SR HS; Pittsburgh, PA; (Y); Exploring; Hosp Aide; Sec JA; VP Pres Science Clb; Ski Clb; Spanish Clb; Mrchg Band; Off Stu Cncl; High Hon Roll; NEDT Awd; Merit Diploma In Spnsh 83-84; U Of Pittsburgh; Med.

RAGONA, ROBERT; Western Wayne HS; Lk Ariel, PA; (Y); 50/147; FBLA; Hon Roll; Dist Wnnr NE Intrmdiate Unit Comp Cntst 86; Mltry Police.

RAHM, BRENDA; Bishop Guilfoyle HS; Altoona, PA; (Y); 26/131; GAA; Stu Cncl; Var Bsktbl; Score Keeper; Var Sftbl; Timer; Hon Roll; Prfct Atten Awd; Grls Bsktbl PA ST Schmpnshp Team 84; Dist AAA Chmpshp Team 84-86; Bus Admn.

RAHN, TINA; Waynesboro Area SR HS; Waynesboro, PA; (Y); Girl Scts; Ski Clb; Band; Chorus; Concert Band; Mrchg Band; School Musical; Swing Chorus; Rep Jr Cls; High Hon Roll; Grl Scts Slvr Ldrshp Awd & Slvr Awd; Phys Ther.

RAHN, VICKIE L; Muhlenberg HS; Reading, PA; (Y); Trs Exploring; Concert Band; Drm Mjr(t); Sec School Musical; Var L Bsktbl; Var L Sftbl; Bausch & Lomb Sci Awd; NHS; Jazz Band; Mrchg Band; Outstndng Math Engl & Acad Stud; Math.

RAICH, ANTOINETTE; Greater Johnstown HS; Johnstown, PA; (Y); Pres Spanish Clb; Pres Band; Concert Band; Mrchg Band; Orch; Yrbk Stf; Var Vllybl; Hon Roll; NHS; Prfct Atten Awd.

RAIFSNIDER, TINA; Exeter Township SR HS; Reading, PA; (Y); 13/207; Hosp Aide; Band; Concert Band; Flag Corp; Orch; Off Soph Cls; Off Jr Cls; Off Sr Cls; Off Stu Cncl; High Hon Roll; Ithaca Col6; Phy Thrpy.

RAILEY, REBECCA; Beaver Valley Christian Acad; Beaver, PA; (Y); Debate Tm; Drama Clb; Speech Tm; School Play; Variety Show; Nwsp Rptr; Nwsp Stf; Yrbk Phtg; Yrbk Rptr; Yrbk Stf; Public Reltns.

RAINEY, JODY; Penns Manor HS; Penn Run, PA; (Y); 29/99; Cmnty Wkr; Varsity Clb; Var L Bsktbl; Var L Ftbl; Var L Trk; Hon Roll; Prfct Atten Awd; 2nd Tm Cnty Offnsv Ftbl 85-86; All Star Tm Bsktbl 85-86; Hnrbl Mntl Bsktbl 85-86; Comm.

RAINEY, KURTIS; Simon Gratz HS; Philadelphia, PA; (Y); Office Aide; Var L Trk; DAR Awd; Hon Roll; Electrical Engineering.

RAINEY, LISA; Purchase Line HS; Hillsdale, PA; (Y); 4/109; 4-H; French Clb; Pep Clb; SADD; Twrlr; High Hon Roll; Hon Roll; Jr NHS; NHS; Ntl Merit Ltr; IN Eve Gazette Edtrl Wrtng Cont 2nd Pl 85, 3rd Pl 86; PTSA Reflctns Lit Cont 2nd Pl 85; IN U PA; Pre-Med.

RAINEY, PATRICIA; Blairsville SR HS; Blairsville, PA; (Y); Church Yth Grp; Band; Capt Color Guard; Concert Band; Stat Bsktbl; L Vllybl; Hon Roll; NHS; Ptsbrgh Bty Coll; Spcl Cosmtlgy.

RAINSBERGER, HEATHER; Hampton HS; Allison Park, PA; (Y); Sec Church Yth Grp; French Clb; Hosp Aide; JV Cheerleading; Pom Pon; Stat Trk; High Hon Roll; Hon Roll.

RAISLEY, MICHAEL L; Seneca Valley HS; Harmony, PA; (Y); 31/374; Church Yth Grp; ROTC; Lit Mag; Bsktbl; Ftbl; Capt Socr; Penn ST; Wildlife Tchngly.

RAJAN, RAVIKANTH ROB; Central HS; Philadelphia, PA; (Y); 16/230; Chess Clb; Cmnty Wkr; Office Aide; Teachers Aide; Var Wrstlng; High Hon Roll; Philip Batzer Prze For Schlrshp 86; Penn ST; Med Doctor.

RAJASENAN, DEEPA; Lincoln HS; Ellwood City, PA; (Y); 4/170; Service Clb; Spanish Clb; Temple Yth Grp; Y-Teens; Stu Cncl; High Hon Roll; NHS; NEDT Awd.

RAJECKI, SUZANNE; General Mc Lane HS; Mckean, PA; (Y); Art Clb; Exploring; German Clb; Teachers Aide; Powder Puff Ftbl; High Hon Roll; Hon Roll; NHS.

RAJNIK, MICHAEL; Cumberland Valley HS; Camp Hill, PA; (Y); 12/550; Spanish Clb; Var L Bsbl; Var L Bsktbl; High Hon Roll; Hon Roll; Engrng.

RAK, LINDA; Vincentian HS; Glenshaw, PA; (Y); Church Yth Grp; Rep Jr Cls; Hon Roll; Prfct Atten Awd; Penn ST; Arch.

RAKE, DOUGLAS RAYMOND; Northern Cambria HS; Barnesboro, PA; (Y); JV Bsktbl; JV Var Ftbl; Hon Roll; Francis Coll; Elem Ed.

RAKENTINE, DIRK; Waynesboro Area SR HS; Waynesboro, PA; (Y); 166/363; Boy Scts; Cmnty Wkr; VICA; Hon Roll; Thiel Coll; Auto Body.

RAKER, ROBERT; South Park HS; Library, PA; (Y); Exploring; Socr; High Hon Roll; Hon Roll; Johnson & Walles; Culnry Arts.

RAKOS, DAVID; Lehighton Area HS; Lehighton, PA; (Y); 1/215; Scholastic Bowl; School Play; Bausch & Lomb Sci Awd; NHS; Val; Debate Tm; 4-H; Chorus; JV Ftbl; CC Awd; ST Chmpn Olympc Mind Tm 84-85; Comenius Schlrshp 86; Moravian Coll; Pre Med.

RALSTON, KAREN; Du Bois Area HS; Dubois, PA; (Y); Band; Chorus; Church Choir; Concert Band; Drill Tm; Mrchg Band; School Musical; Swing Chorus; Twrlr; Bus.

RALSTON, THOMAS J; Old Forge HS; Old Forge, PA; (Y); Aud/Vis; Mgr Concert Band; Mgr Mrchg Band; Orch; School Musical; Mgr School Play; Mgr Stage Crew; Var Golf; JV Var Score Keeper; Penn ST; Elec Engrng.

RAM, SUJATA; Butler SR HS; Butler, PA; (Y); 64/771; Church Yth Grp; Debate Tm; Drama Clb; Hosp Aide; JA; Orch; Stu Cncl; Tennis; Hon Roll; Jr NHS; Sydnod U Trinity Presbyterian Church Appalachian 86; Bucknell U; Bio.

RAMA, JOHN; Mid Valley HS; Dickson City, PA; (Y); Pres Aud/Vis; Computer Clb; VP Drama Clb; Library Aide; School Play; Stage Crew; Nwsp Phtg; Nwsp Rptr; Nwsp Stf; Rep Soph Cls; De Vry Tech Schl; Data Sys Repr.

RAMBEAU, DAVID H; Portage Area HS; Cassandra, PA; (Y); 19/121; Varsity Clb; L JV Ftbl; Im Socr; Hon Roll; NHS; Elec Engrng.

RAMBEAU, DAWN RENEE; Portage Area HS; Cassandra, PA; (Y); Teachers Aide; Chorus; School Musical; Hon Roll; Schl Of Commerce; Accntnt.

RAMBERGER, ERIC; Halifax Area HS; Halifax, PA; (Y); 17/117; Trs FFA; Varsity Clb; Rep Stu Cncl; Var Capt Bsbl; Var L Ftbl; Wt Lftg; Hon Roll.

RAMBO, DENISE; Ambridge HS; Baden, PA; (Y); Church Yth Grp; SADD; Thesps; Chorus; Church Choir; School Musical; School Play; Variety Show; Tennis; Hon Roll; Messiah Coll; Acctg.

RAMER, STEVE; Upper Moreland HS; Hatboro, PA; (Y); 87/276; Boy Scts; Church Yth Grp; Ski Clb; Stage Crew; Yrbk Phtg; Yrbk Rptr; Yrbk Stf; Lit Mag; Ftbl; Ntl Merit Ltr; PA ST U; Film.

RAMEY, ROBIN; Ringgold HS; Monongahela, PA; (Y); Church Yth Grp; Computer Clb; Office Aide; Varsity Clb; Pres Band; Pres Church Choir; Nwsp Rptr; Yrbk Stf; Rep Jr Cls; Var JV Cheerleading; Phys Therapy.

RAMFOS, RORK; Franklin HS; Franklin, PA; (Y); 50/220; German Clb; Varsity Clb; Frsh Cls; Soph Cls; Jr Cls; Sr Cls; Stu Cncl; Var Bsktbl; Var L Ftbl; Var Capt Trk; Grove City; Pltcl Sci.

RAMIREZ, LUIS; Harry S Truman HS; Bristol, PA; (Y); School Musical; Sec Jr Cls; VP Sr Cls; Rep Stu Cncl; Var Socr; Trk; Wt Lftg; Hon Roll; Pres NHS; Pres Of Natl Hon Soc 86-87; Electrical Engineering.

RAMIREZ, TERRI; Norwin SR HS; Westmoreland City, PA; (Y); Computer Clb; Teachers Aide; Powder Puff Ftbl; Trk; Vllybl; Vllybl Awd 85-86; Trck Awd 85; Crmnlgy.

RAMOS, AMELIA; Thomas A Edison HS; Philadelphia, PA; (Y); #11 In Class; Church Choir; Hon Roll; Drexel U; Elec Engrs.

RAMOS, CARLOS; Thomas Edison HS; Philadelphia, PA; (Y); #1 In Class; Church Yth Grp; Lit Mag; Stu Cncl; High Hon Roll; Hon Roll; NHS; Engrng.

RAMOS, TIMOTHY; The Hill Schl; Pottstown, PA; (Y); Sec Trs Drama Clb; Latin Clb; Thesps; Stage Crew; Var Ftbl; Var Lcrss; Ntl Merit SF; Bus.

RAMSAY, KARLYN; Albert Gallatin SR HS; Smithfield, PA; (Y); 1/140; Am Leg Aux Girls St; Spanish Clb; Color Guard; Concert Band; Mrchg Band; High Hon Roll; NHS; Acdmc All-Amer At Lrg Div Awd 86; Case Wstrn Rsrv U Smmr Law Symposia 86; Law.

RAMSEY, KEITH; Warwich HS; Lititz, PA; (Y); 26/247; Am Leg Boys St; Computer Clb; Varsity Clb; Bsbl; Bsktbl; Ftbl; High Hon Roll; NHS; Dr Grosh Schlrshp 86; Dana Zimmerman Awd 3 Vrsty Lttrs In Sr Yr; Rotary Ldrs Conf 85; IVP.

RAMSEY, MICHELLE; Ambridge Area HS; Ambridge, PA; (Y); French Clb; Pep Clb; Spanish Clb; Band; Concert Band; Mrchg Band; Symp Band; Rep Soph Cls; Rep Jr Cls; Hon Roll; Robert Morris Coll; Sec Adm.

RAND, MICHELLE; Nazareth Acad; Philadelphia, PA; (Y); Cmnty Wkr; Pres German Clb; Model UN; Chorus; School Musical; Hon Roll; NHS; Ntl Merit Ltr; Partial 4-Yr Schlrshp Nazareth Acad 83; Pltcl Sci.

RANDALL, BECKY; Coudersport JR SR HS; Coudersport, PA; (Y); 4/84; VP Church Yth Grp; French Clb; Varsity Clb; Sec Band; Chorus; Var JV Bsktbl; Var Trk; JV Var Vllybl; High Hon Roll; NHS; 30 Point Lttr 86.

RANDALL, JEFFREY TODD; Garden Spot HS; Narvon, PA; (Y); 8/218; Drama Clb; Chorus; Stage Crew; Yrbk Phtg; Trs Stu Cncl; Crs Cntry; Socr; L Trk; NHS.

RANDALL, KIMBERLY; Mc Keesport Area SR HS; Mckeesport, PA; (Y); 137/339; Church Yth Grp; FBLA; Library Aide; Diving; Powder Puff Ftbl; Swmmng; Sawyer; Exec Sec.

RANDAZZO, JEFF; Wyoming Area HS; W Wyoming, PA; (Y); 68/281; 4-H; Bsbl; Crs Cntry; Golf; Wrstlng; PIAA Wrstlng Rgnl Qlfr 3rd Pl 84-85; 1st Pl Glf Tourn Dispatch Cup 85-86; Forestry.

RANDAZZO, RENEE; Wyoming Area SR HS; W Pittston, PA; (Y); French Clb; Key Clb; Yrbk Stf.

RANDIG, SHARYN; South Allegheny HS; Elizabeth, PA; (S); Exploring; Pres Girl Scts; Y-Teens; Chorus; Powder Puff Ftbl; Hon Roll; NHS; Prfct Atten Awd; GS Slvr Awd 83; Ntl Sci Awd 85.

RANDIS, PAM; Hazleton SR HS; Drums, PA; (Y); Drama Clb; Band; Mrchg Band; Var L Trk; Hon Roll; Frgn Lng Orgnztn 85-86; Dgrs Clb 85-86; Brbzn Schl Mdlng 85; Penn ST U; Elec Engr.

RANDLE, TAMMY; York County Vo Tech; York, PA; (Y); JA; VICA; Band; JV Cheerleading; Hon Roll; Prfct Atten Awd; Phys Ftnss Awd 85; York College; Nrsg.

RANDLES, KATHLEEN; Saint Hubert HS; Philadelphia, PA; (Y); 85/367; Cmnty Wkr; Office Aide; Chorus; School Musical; Hon Roll; Prfct Atten Awd; Holy Family Coll; Tchr.

RANDOLPH, CURTIS; Danville SR HS; Danville, PA; (Y); Ski Clb; Rep Frsh Cls; Rep Soph Cls; Rep Stu Cncl; Var L Bsktbl; Var L Golf; Var L Trk; Hon Roll; Graham F Stvns Crtsy Awd 84; WY Smnry; Marine Bio.

RANDOLPH, SHERI; John Harris HS; Harrisburg, PA; (Y); Cmnty Wkr; Band; Concert Band; Orch; Stu Cncl; Trk; Hon Roll; Prfct Atten Awd; Mdrn Miss Schlrshp Pagent 85; Bus.

RANGEL, VICTOR; Lincoln HS; Ellwood City, PA; (Y); Church Yth Grp; Spanish Clb; Off Frsh Cls; Off Soph Cls; Var L Bsbl; Var L Socr; Hon Roll; Pittsburgh; Optometry.

RANGI, SATBIR; Clarion Area HS; Clarion, PA; (Y); Church Yth Grp; Trs Sec FCA; Hosp Aide; Band; Color Guard; Drill Tm; Variety Show; Yrbk Stf; Twrlr; Hon Roll; Capt Rifl Twrlng Sqd 86; Pre-Law.

RANIERI, PAM; Freeport SR HS; Freeport, PA; (Y); Church Yth Grp; Library Aide; Color Guard; Yrbk Stf; Vllybl; Hon Roll.

RANIOWSKI, ELISH; Punxsutoawney HS; Punxsutawney, PA; (Y); 106/238; Spanish Clb; Chorus; Church Choir; Variety Show; Nwsp Stf; Stat Wrstlng; Mary Ann Irving Schlrshp 86; Gannon U; Pre-Law.

RANK, MARK; Red Lion SR HS; Red Lion, PA; (Y); 25/337; Varsity Clb; Bsktbl; L Var Golf; Var L Swmmng; Hon Roll; St Schlr; Susquehanna U Schlrp Hnrs Prog 86; Susquehanna U; Engl.

RANKIN, CONNIE; Carmichaels SR HS; Carmichaels, PA; (Y); #30 In Class; Boy Scts; Mrchg Band; Im High Hon Roll; Im Hon Roll; VICA; Pittsburgh Bty Acad; Csmtlgy.

RANKIN, JANET; Punxsutawney Area HS; Punxsutawney, PA; (Y); French Clb; Var L Cheerleading; JV Vllybl; Phys Educ.

RANKIN, KAREN; Belle Vernon Area HS; Belle Vernon, PA; (Y); Ski Clb; Nwsp Stf; Rep Frsh Cls; Rep Soph Cls; Rep Jr Cls; Cheerleading; Powder Puff Ftbl; Vllybl; Hon Roll; NHS; Pharm.

RANKIN, RACHEL; California Area HS; Calif, PA; (Y); 1/109; Pres Drama Clb; School Play; Nwsp Ed-Chief; VP Soph Cls; Pres Jr Cls; Trs Stu Cncl; Score Keeper; High Hon Roll; Pres NHS; Pep Clb; Engrng.

RANONE, KELLY; Center HS; Monaca, PA; (Y); Church Yth Grp; Exploring; German Clb; Church Choir; Concert Band; Mrchg Band; Orch; Pep Band; Hon Roll; NHS; German Straight A Awd 83-86.

RANSDORF, JOI; Montoursville HS; Montoursville, PA; (Y); 50/177; Sec German Clb; Ski Clb; Varsity Clb; School Musical; Rep Frsh Cls; Co-Capt Var Cheerleading; Mgr(s); Powder Puff Ftbl; Socr; NHS; Bloomsburg U; Elem Ed.

RANSIL, DONNA; Villa Maria Acad; Erie, PA; (S); French Clb; NFL; PAVAS; Variety Show; Nwsp Stf; Stu Cncl; Crs Cntry; Trk; Vllybl; High Hon Roll; Acad Achvt 84; Recgntn Accmplshmnt Graphic Arts 85; 1st Pl Caligrphy Cntst; Bus Mgmt.

RAO, DIANE; Villa Maria Academy For Girls; Erie, PA; (Y); 38/135; Girl Scts; NFL; PAVAS; Spanish Clb; Speech Tm; Church Choir; School Musical; Nwsp Stf; Hon Roll; NHS; Gannon U.

RAO, VANI; Mechanicsburg Area SR HS; Mechanicsburg, PA; (Y); 3/311; High Hon Roll; Hon Roll; NHS; 3rd Pl R10 Arriba Chptr AATSP Spnsh Exm 84; 2nd Pl AHSME 86; Acctng.

RAPACH, CHRIS; Bishop Oreilly HS; Kingston, PA; (Y); Civic Clb; Cmnty Wkr; Drama Clb; English Clb; Model UN; NFL; Service Clb; Nwsp Rptr; Yrbk Stf; Lit Mag; Penn ST U Behrend; Comm.

RAPACIK, CHRISTIE; Bishop Mc Cort HS; Johnstown, PA; (Y); 10/129; Math Clb; Radio Clb; Band; Orch; School Play; Stage Crew; Yrbk Stf; Rep Sr Cls; High Hon Roll; NHS; Eagle Schlrshp Awd Washington & Jefferson Coll 86; Rgnl Band 85&86; Dist Orch 85&86; Washington & Jefferson; Bus Adm.

RAPE, LISA; Seneca Valley HS; Zelienople, PA; (Y); 194/352; Duquesue U; Phrmcst.

RAPSEY, JEANNA; Cedar Cliff HS; Camp Hill, PA; (Y); Camera Clb; Cmnty Wkr; French Clb; Key Clb; Stage Crew; Cheerleading; Fld Hcky; Sftbl; Trk; Hon Roll; PA ST U; Ed.

RARICK, SUSAN; Tamaqua Area HS; Tamaqua, PA; (Y); 5/200; Drama Clb; Concert Band; Mrchg Band; Yrbk Ed-Chief; Sec Jr Cls; Pres Stu Cncl; Capt Twrlr; High Hon Roll; NHS; VP Spanish NHS; Top Span Stu 85-86; Law.

RAS, JOANN; GAR Memorial HS; Wilkes Barre, PA; (S); 33/177; Library Aide; Office Aide; Ski Clb; Band; Chorus; Concert Band; Drm Mjr(t); Mrchg Band; Stage Crew; Nwsp Stf; Cosmetology.

RASH, DIANA; Central Dauphin East HS; Steelton, PA; (Y); Church Yth Grp; FBLA; Pep Clb; Mrchg Band; Yrbk Stf; Lock Haven U; Spch Cmmnctns.

RASMUS, TIM; West Perry SR HS; Landisburg, PA; (Y); 25/285; Church Yth Grp; Computer Clb; School Play; Variety Show; Var Trk; Theatre.

RASO, ROSEMARIE; Ambridge Area HS; Ambridge, PA; (Y); Church Yth Grp; Pep Clb; Rep Soph Cls; Rep Jr Cls; Rep Stu Cncl; JV Cheerleading; Hon Roll; Elem Educ.

RASPEN, JANICE; Hanover Area JR SR HS; Wilkes-Barre, PA; (Y); 21/156; Model UN; Band; Chorus; Concert Band; Jazz Band; Mrchg Band; Yrbk Stf; High Hon Roll; NHS; NEDT Awd; Wilkes Coll; Nrsg.

RATCHFORD, DONALD; Bishop Carroll HS; Ebensburg, PA; (S); 20/102; Yrbk Stf; VP Soph Cls; Pres Jr Cls; Pres Sr Cls; Stu Cncl; Hon Roll; NEDT Awd.

RATESIC, ERIN; Norwin SR HS; N Huntingdon, PA; (Y); 20/577; Sec Frsh Cls; VP Soph Cls; VP Jr Cls; VP Sr Cls; Rep Stu Cncl; Var L Crs Cntry; Var L Diving; Var L Trk; NHS; Ntl Merit Ltr; Financing.

RATH, DEBBIE; Solanco SR HS; Quarryville, PA; (Y); 120/238; Varsity Clb; Flag Corp; Yrbk Stf; Var JV Mgr(s); JV Trk; Elem Ed.

RATHMAN, CLAYTON LINCOLN; Ephrata SR HS; Ephrata, PA; (Y); Var Ftbl; Wt Lftg; JV Var Wrstlng; Civil Engr.

RATICA, ARLENE; Greensburg Central Catholix HS; Greensburg, PA; (Y); Church Yth Grp; Hosp Aide; Chorus; High Hon Roll; Med.

RATICO, PAUL; Pennsbury HS; Levittown, PA; (Y); French Clb; Letterman Clb; Varsity Clb; JV Bsbl; Var Socr; JV Wrstlng; Im Bsktbl; Im Bowling; Im Golf; Prfct Atten Awd; Pharm.

RATJAVONG, SAYSAVATH; Pequea Valley HS; Gordonville, PA; (Y); Art Clb; Church Yth Grp; Computer Clb; Pep Band; Stage Crew; Variety Show; Rep Stu Cncl; Hon Roll; Prfct Atten Awd; Arch.

RATKOVICH, MARCY; Center Area HS; Aliquippa, PA; (Y); 40/184; German Clb; Letterman Clb; Varsity Clb; Nwsp Stf; Yrbk Stf; Trs Stu Cncl; Im Bowling; Var L Vllybl; Hon Roll; NHS; PA ST U; Frgn Svc.

RAU, STEPHEN; Franklin Regional SR HS; Delmont, PA; (Y); 23/323; Boy Scts; Church Choir; Var L Crs Cntry; Var L Trk; High Hon Roll; NHS; USAF ROTC 4 Yr Schlrshp 86; USAF Accad Appntmnt 86; Vigil Hnr 86; U S Air Force Acad; Rsrch-Devlp.

RAUB, DEVLYN; Souderton Area HS; Tylersport, PA; (Y); 19/420; Cmnty Wkr; Chorus; Color Guard; Off Stu Cncl; Score Keeper; Hon Roll; Jr NHS; NHS; Prfct Atten Awd; German Awd; Psych.

RAUBAUGH, TERRI; Connellsville Area SR HS; Connellsville, PA; (Y); 30/550; Band; Chorus; Church Choir; Concert Band; Mrchg Band; Orch; Pep Band; School Musical; Symp Band; High Hon Roll; PMEA Dist 1 Hnrs Band 83-86; Educ.

RAUCH, DAWN; Souderton Area HS; Telford, PA; (Y); 15/350; Church Yth Grp; Rep Sr Cls; Rep Stu Cncl; JV Stat Bsktbl; Var Fld Hcky; Var Sftbl; Hon Roll; NHS; Outstndng Frnch Stu 83; Tucker Hake Mem Awd Mth 86; Excllnce Acad & Ctznshp Awd 86; Ursinus Coll; Mth.

RAUCH, KEVIN P; Northampton Area SR HS; Walnutport, PA; (Y); 3/480; Math Clb; Model UN; Scholastic Bowl; High Hon Roll; NHS; Ntl Merit SF; Voice Dem Awd; Astrophscs.

RAUCH, STARR; Northwestern Lehigh HS; New Tripoli, PA; (Y); 20/163; Church Yth Grp; Pres Capt Drm Mjr(t); Yrbk Stf; Capt Twrlr; High Hon Roll; Hon Roll; NHS; Prfct Atten Awd; Mst Outstndng Majrtte; Engl, Germn Awds 85-86; Kutztown U PA; Engl Tchr.

RAUCHUT, SHAWN; Palmyra Area HS; Annville, PA; (Y); French Clb; Yrbk Stf; Jr Cls; Sr Cls; Stu Cncl; Socr; Trk; High Hon Roll; Yrbk Ed-Chief; Yrbk Rptr; People To People Ambsdr Prgm 85 & 86; Bus.

RAUDENBUSH, GREGORY E; Pine Grove Area HS; Pine Grove, PA; (Y); 5/120; Am Leg Boys St; Quiz Bowl; ROTC; Varsity Clb; School Play; Nwsp Stf; Stu Cncl; L Bsktbl; Capt Bowling; Awd Hghst Male Grd Pnt Aver 85-86; Pennstate U; Nuclear Engrng.

RAUPP, JEFFREY; Plymouth-Whitemarsh HS; Lafayette Hill, PA; (Y); 32/320; Exploring; Math Clb; JV Bsbl; Capt Swmmng; High Hon Roll; Mu Alp Tht; Ntl Merit Ltr; Engrng.

RAUPP, MARIE; Harry S Truman HS; Levittown, PA; (Y); 12/625; Drama Clb; Concert Band; Mrchg Band; School Musical; Stu Cncl; Fld Hcky; Capt Socr; High Hon Roll; NHS; Schlr Athlete Awd 86; Rcvd Fac Schlrshp 86; Villanova U; Engl.

RAUSCH, BOBBI JO; Annville Cleona HS; Cleona, PA; (Y); FBLA; Chorus; Fld Hcky; Score Keeper; Hon Roll; NHS.

RAUSCH, THOMAS; Tulpehocken Area HS; Bernville, PA; (S); 15/115; Boy Scts; Pres FFA; Band; School Musical; Stage Crew; Var Capt Bsbl; Var Socr; Hon Roll; NHS; Agri-Bus Mngmnt.

RAUSCHER, LINDA; Lower Moreland HS; Huntingdon Valley, PA; (S); Church Yth Grp; Cmnty Wkr; French Clb; Key Clb; Science Clb; School Play; JV Crs Cntry; Var Swmmng; JV Trk; Hon Roll; Bio.

RAUTZAHN, JEFFRY; Williams Valley HS; Williamstown, PA; (Y); 2/102; Pres Jr Cls; Golf; Pres NHS; Church Yth Grp; Band; Chorus; Church Choir; Concert Band; Dstct X Chrs 83-86; Rgn V Shrs 83-86; PMEA All ST Chrs 83-85; PA ST U; Cmptr Sci.

RAVENSCRAFT, ROY; German Township HS; Mc Clellandtown, PA; (Y); Pres Art Clb; French Clb; Band; Chorus; Concert Band; Yrbk Stf; VP Soph Cls; Pres Sr Cls; Rep Stu Cncl; Hon Roll; West VA U; Music Ed.

RAY, DEBBIE; Monessen JR SR HS; Monessen, PA; (Y); Library Aide; Teachers Aide; Stage Crew; Stu Cncl; Hon Roll; Tchng.

RAY, JACQUELINE; Merion Mercy Acad; Phila, PA; (Y); 8/80; French Clb; Mathletes; Science Clb; Service Clb; Chorus; Church Choir; School Musical; Hon Roll; NHS; Music Scholar 83.

RAY, JONNA; Moniteau HS; W Sunbury, PA; (Y); Church Yth Grp; Pres Girl Scts; Ski Clb; Band; Chorus; Church Choir; Jazz Band; Variety Show; Score Keeper; Hon Roll; Math.

RAY, MARGO; Farrell SR HS; Farrell, PA; (Y); 10/120; French Clb; Key Clb; Letterman Clb; Sec Trs Varsity Clb; School Play; JV Bsktbl; Var Capt Vllybl; French Hon Soc; High Hon Roll; NHS; Penn ST; Law.

RAY, ROCHELLE; Montour HS; Mckees Rocks, PA; (Y); Church Yth Grp; Band; Concert Band; Jazz Band; Mrchg Band; Rep Soph Cls; Rep Jr Cls; High Hon Roll; NHS; US Achvt Acad Awd 84 & 85; Ntl Ldrshp & Srvc Awd 85; US Bus Ed Awd 84; Westminster; Acctng.

RAYBA, VIRGINIA; Northern Cambria HS; Marsteller, PA; (Y); 14/115; Band; Capt Color Guard; Concert Band; Mrchg Band; Yrbk Stf; Stu Cncl; Hon Roll; Hst NHS.

RAYER, THOMAS J; Marple-Newtown HS; Broomall, PA; (Y); Boy Scts; Chess Clb; Im Bsktbl; Im Ice Hcky; Rugby Tm B All Star Tm 86 84-85 & 85-86; Chess Red Rose Lancaster Trnmt 1st Pl 85; Penn ST; Aeronautical Engr.

RAYMOND, JUDY; West Branch Area HS; Drifting, PA; (S); 5/113; Office Aide; Spanish Clb; Teachers Aide; Chorus; Flag Corp; Yrbk Stf; High Hon Roll; NHS; Bus Awd 86; Acctnt.

RAYMOND, KEN; Northwestern SR HS; Albion, PA; (Y); Art Clb; Pres Church Yth Grp; Computer Clb; Nwsp Rptr; Nwsp Stf; Hon Roll; Ard Awd Nazarene Dist Fstvl Life 84; Edinboro U PA; Pol Sci.

RAYMOND, ROBERT; York Catholic HS; York, PA; (Y); 20/200; FBLA; Spanish Clb; Varsity Clb; School Play; Nwsp Rptr; Ftbl; Wt Lftg; High Hon Roll; NHS; Prfct Atten Awd; Acctng.

RAYMONT, DOREEN; Ford City HS; Ford City, PA; (Y); Hosp Aide; Office Aide; Spanish Clb; VICA; Rep Stu Cncl; High Hon Roll; IN U Of PA; Nrsng.

RAYNER, JOHN; St John Neumann HS; Philadelphia, PA; (Y); Computer Clb; SADD; Engrng.

RAZZAVO, CHRIS; Archbishop Kennedy HS; Philadelphia, PA; (Y); English Clb; Stu Cncl; Mgr(s); Hon Roll; Jrnlsm.

RAZZI, LARRY; Upper Darby SR HS; Upper Darby, PA; (Y); Var Bsbl; JV Ftbl; High Hon Roll; Hon Roll; Law.

REA, KELLY; Seneca HS; Union City, PA; (Y); 7/144; Band; Concert Band; Mrchg Band; Orch; High Hon Roll; Hon Roll; Pres Acad Achvt Awd 86.

REA, TIM; Upper Perkiamen HS; Pennsburg, PA; (Y); 24/249; VP Church Yth Grp; Computer Clb; Band; Concert Band; Jazz Band; Mrchg Band; Orch; Pep Band; Variety Show; Var L Socr; Bucks & Mntgmry Cnty Band 85 & 86; Sprtsmnshp Awd-Vrsty Sccr 85 & 86; Rtry Ldrshp Cmp Neidig 86; Comp Sci.

REA, TIMOTHY A; Boiling Springs HS; Boiling Springs, PA; (Y); 2/109; Capt Debate Tm; Pres Sr Cls; Var Capt Bsbl; Var Capt Socr; High Hon Roll; Pres NHS; Ntl Merit SF; Pres Church Yth Grp; Political Wkr; Capt Quiz Bowl; PA Intl Stud Gvrnrs Schl 85; PA Hugh O Brian Intl Ldrshp Smnr Ambssdr 84; IVY-LEAGUE U; Econ.

READ, KIM; Warren Co Christian HS; Warren, PA; (S); 1/3; Pres Church Yth Grp; Chorus; Yrbk Stf; Rep Stu Cncl; Var Stat Bsktbl; Var Sftbl; Capt Var Vllybl; High Hon Roll; Prfct Atten Awd; Vllybl All Star Tm 85; Acctg.

READ, LISA; Clearfield HS; Woodland, PA; (Y); 9/298; Church Yth Grp; Hosp Aide; Spanish Clb; High Hon Roll; NHS; Sawvel Schlrshp Thiel Coll 86; Elizabeth Stewart Schlrshp Thiel Coll 86; Thiel Coll; Bio.

READLER, WENDY; Berwick Area SR HS; Wapwallopen, PA; (Y); 17/203; Cmnty Wkr; Key Clb; Library Aide; Nwsp Stf; Yrbk Stf; Rep Stu Cncl; Var Fld Hcky; Hon Roll; NHS; Prfct Atten Awd; Achvt Awd Outstndng Merit Lions Clb Schlrshp 86; PA ST U; Comp Sci.

REAGAN, LAURA; Technical HS; Scranton, PA; (Y); Art Clb; Church Yth Grp; Psych.

REAGLE, DOUGLAS; Franklin JR SR HS; Franklin, PA; (Y); Church Yth Grp; German Clb; Varsity Clb; Band; Concert Band; Var Bsbl; Im Bsktbl; Var Ftbl; Var Wt Lftg; Cit Awd; Brd Schl Dir Awd 84-86; Med.

REAHM, AIKO MALYNDA; Everett Christian Acad; Osterburg, PA; (S); 3/7; Rep Church Yth Grp; Band; Yrbk Stf; Sec Sr Cls; Var Bsktbl; Var Vllybl; Hon Roll; Prfct Atten Awd; Acad Excllnc 85; Penn ST U; Scndry Math Educ.

REAM, SHANNON; Lebanon SR HS; Lebanon, PA; (Y); German Clb; Pep Clb; Varsity Clb; Y-Teens; Fld Hcky; Wt Lftg; Hon Roll; Psychlgy.

REAP, BRIDGET; Coughlin HS; Laflin, PA; (Y); 30/385; Var Fld Hcky; Var Sftbl; High Hon Roll; Jr NHS; NHS; NEDT Awd; U Of Scranton; Comp Sci.

REAP, MICHAEL; Catasauqua HS; Catasauqua, PA; (Y); 24/146; Drama Clb; VICA; Stage Crew; Bsktbl; Ftbl; Lincoln Tech Inst; Comp Sci.

REARDON, DAVE; Central Dauphin HS; Harrisburg, PA; (Y); 45/400; Varsity Clb; Band; Yrbk Stf; Swmmng; Trk; Vllybl; Hon Roll; All ST Swmmng Tm 86; Ntl Top YMCA Swmmng Times 85-86; NISCA ST Top 10 Awd 86; Cornell; Pre-Law.

REARDON, PAMELA L; Peters Township HS; Mc Murray, PA; (Y); 23/260; Pep Clb; Science Clb; Ski Clb; Band; Drill Tm; Mrchg Band; Yrbk Stf; Stu Cncl; Stat Bsktbl; Stat Sftbl; Women Sci & Engr 85; PA JR Acad Sci 2nd Pl Awd 84; PA Free Entrpr Wk Lock Haven U 84; Engr.

REARICK, DENISE; Shikellamy HS; Sunbury, PA; (Y); Church Yth Grp; French Clb; Hosp Aide; SADD; Teachers Aide; Band; Color Guard; Drill Tm; Mrchg Band; Var Score Keeper; Messiah Temple; Pre-Med.

REASINGER, SUSAN; Mt Lebanon HS; Venetia, PA; (Y); Color Guard; Powder Puff Ftbl; Cert Of Merit Heart Assn 84-85; Math.

REASNER, DONNA LEE; Bishop Neumann HS; Williamsport, PA; (Y); 5/46; Cmnty Wkr; Drama Clb; Hosp Aide; Chorus; Yrbk Stf; Stat Bsktbl; DAR Awd; High Hon Roll; Lion Awd; NHS; Alumni Awd 86; Catholic Daughter Awd 86; Bloomsburg U Schlrs Pgm 86; Bloomsburg U; Med Tech.

REASNER, RONDA; South Williamsport SR HS; S Wmspt, PA; (Y); Church Yth Grp; Pres Leo Clb; Office Aide; Varsity Clb; Color Guard; Flag Corp; Var Cheerleading; Swmmng; Trk; Hon Roll; Phys Therpy Vlntr 85-86; Varsty Ltr Trk; Bloomsburg U; Phys Thrpy.

REAVER, CONNIE; Littlestown HS; Littlestown, PA; (Y); Art Clb.

REBARCHAK, JOSEPH; James M Coughlin HS; Wilkes-Barre, PA; (Y); Ftbl; Capt Trk; Hon Roll; Jr NHS; NHS; Pres Acad Fit Awd 85-86; 3rd Pl Javelin Dist Trk 85-86; 2nd Pl Javelin Dist Trk 84-85; Bloomsburg U; Comp Info Sys.

REBECK, CINDY; Our Lady Of The Sacred Heart HS; Coraopolis, PA; (Y); Pep Clb; School Play; Yrbk Phtg; Pres Jr Cls; Pres Stu Cncl; Var Bsktbl; Var Sftbl; NHS; PA JR Acad Sci 84; Kent ST U; Prfssnl Pilot.

REBER, MIKE; Middletown Area HS; Middletown, PA; (Y); 30/178; Latin Clb; Vllybl; Hon Roll; Golf Conf Finals; Latin Fest 1st Pl Awd 84-85; Bsktbl Mid Penn Conf Tm 85-86; Golf Grill Conf & Dist; Bus.

REBERT, DANIEL QUENTIN; York Vocational Tech; York, PA; (Y); Var L Wrstlng; 1st Pl Art Directions 86 Dsgn 86; Pblshd Work Natl Mag Fangoria 86; Sbjct Artcle In York Daily Record; Specl Effect Artist.

REBICH, E TODD; Rochester Area HS; Rochester, PA; (Y); 15/108; Am Leg Boys St; Ski Clb; SADD; Stage Crew; Trs Frsh Cls; Trs Soph Cls; Trs Jr Cls; Pres Stu Cncl; Capt Var Bsbl; L Var Bsktbl; Allegheny Coll; Pol Sci.

REBICH, KELLY; Charleroi JR SR HS; Charleroi, PA; (Y); French Clb; Office Aide; Ski Clb; Chorus; Capt Color Guard; Capt Drill Tm; Capt Flag Corp; Stu Cncl; Wrthy Advsr-H S Rnbw Grls 84; Psychlgy.

REBICH, LYNETTE M; Center HS; Aliquippa, PA; (Y); 92/188; Church Yth Grp; Cmnty Wkr; Office Aide; Pep Clb; Spanish Clb; SADD; Band; Concert Band; Drill Tm; Mrchg Band; Wrthy Advsr Intl Order Rainbow Grls 86; Co-Capt All Amer Pom Pon Sqd 86; Cert Partcptn All Amer 85; Clarion; Spch Thrpy.

REBOK, TRAVIS; Chambersburg Area SR HS; Chambersburg, PA; (Y); 57/641; Band; Concert Band; Mrchg Band; Orch; Symp Band; Im Bsbl; Var Im Bsktbl; Im Ftbl; Hon Roll.

REBUCK, CRAIG; Line Mountain HS; Klingerstown, PA; (S); 40/120; Band; Concert Band; Mrchg Band; Stage Crew; JV Var Bsktbl; Am Musicl Found Band Hnr 85; All Am Hall Fame Band Hnr 85; Twin Vly SR Band Festvl 86; PA ST U; Acctng.

REBUCK, PEGGY SUE; Shippensburg Area SR HS; Shippensburg, PA; (Y); 36/230; Cmnty Wkr; Var Vllybl; High Hon Roll; Hon Roll; Lion Awd.

REBUCK, RICH; Shippensburg SR HS; Shippensburg, PA; (Y); 5/225; Am Leg Boys St; Varsity Clb; Trs Jr Cls; Trs Sr Cls; JV Crs Cntry; Var Trk; Im Vllybl; High Hon Roll; NHS; Bucknell U; Chem.

REBUCK, TINA; Lock Haven HS; Lock Haven, PA; (Y); Computer Clb; FTA; Spanish Clb; JV Bsktbl; Diving; Golf; Sftbl; Spanish NHS; Math Tchr.

RECCEK, ANTHONY; Saugon Valley SR HS; Hellertown, PA; (Y); 22/146; Ntl Soc Studies Olymp 84; Coll St Francis De Sales; Bio.

RECH, AARON; East SR HS; West Chester, PA; (S); Boy Scts; DECA; Ski Clb; Ftbl; Mgr(s); Var Trk; Dist DECA Fnlst 3rd 2nd 86; West Chester U; Bus.

RECHEL, WENDY; Lock Haven SR HS; Lock Haven, PA; (Y); Church Yth Grp; Pres FBLA; Band; Chorus; Church Choir; Color Guard; Mrchg Band; Variety Show; JV Bsktbl; Business.

RECHLICZ, NINA; Abington Heights HS; Clarks Summit, PA; (Y); Ski Clb; Concert Band; Trs Soph Cls; Socr; Sftbl; Swmmng; Hon Roll; NHS; Girl Scts; Mrchg Band; Med Careers Club-Treas 84-86; Natl Hist Day-3rd Pl 83-84; Muhlenberg Coll; Pre Med.

RECKLESS, DIANE; Upper Moreland HS; Willow Grove, PA; (Y); 30/270; Church Yth Grp; Key Clb; Mrchg Band; Stu Cncl; Capt Crs Cntry; Trk; High Hon Roll; NEDT Awd; Calvin Coll; Bio.

RECKTENWALD, MARK; Brentwood JR SR HS; Pittsburgh, PA; (S); 14/132; Church Yth Grp; Pep Clb; Stage Crew; Yrbk Stf; Rep Jr Cls; VP Stu Cncl; Var L Ftbl; Var Trk; High Hon Roll; NHS; U Of Pittsburgh; Elec Engr.

RECKUS, JANET ALEXIS; Harry S Truman HS; Levittown, PA; (Y); 31/576; Pres Debate Tm; Drama Clb; NFL; Pres Speech Tm; Band; Concert Band; Stu Cncl; High Hon Roll; Rotary Awd; Ntl Frnscs Leag Fnls; St Jsphs U Vlgr Dbtng Soc Schlrshp; Cthlc Frnscs Fnls; St Josephs U; Law.

RECROSIO, PAUL; Chartiers Valley HS; Pittsburgh, PA; (Y); 14/303; Letterman Clb; Ski Clb; Varsity Clb; Nwsp Sprt Ed; JV Bsbl; Var Capt Wrstlng; NHS; Aero Engrng.

RECTOR, INGRID S; Lawrence County Co-Tech; New Castle, PA; (Y); 45/245; Church Yth Grp; Cmnty Wkr; Pres 4-H; French Clb; Teachers Aide; VICA; Church Choir; Concert Band; Mrchg Band; Hon Roll; A Crown Banner Trophy Outstndng Stu 85; Comp Exc Cert Awds 84-85; 2nd Pl Medalion 86; Fash Merch.

RECTOR, TAMARA M; Central Bucks East HS; Pipersville, PA; (Y); 41/459; Church Yth Grp; Trs Drama Clb; Hosp Aide; Political Wkr; Band; Yrbk Stf; Cit Awd; Hon Roll; Ntl Merit Ltr; Close Up Study Of Govt Wash DC 85; Band & Flag Corp Awds 82-85; Gwynedd-Mercy Coll; Nrs.

RECUPERO, FRANK; Northern HS; Dillsburg, PA; (Y); 42/209; Church Yth Grp; Hon Roll; Accntnt.

REDD, MICHAEL; Fort Cherry HS; Mc Donald, PA; (S); Computer Clb; Drama Clb; Math Clb; Science Clb; Ski Clb; Pres Varsity Clb; L Bsktbl; L Ftbl; High Hon Roll; NHS.

REDDIN JR, JAMES J; Northeast Catholic HS; Philadelphia, PA; (Y); 135/362; Pres Stu Cncl; Var Socr; Rep Soph Cls; Hon Roll; 2nd Hnrs 84-86; Civl Engrng.

REDDING, DAVID; Cumberland Valley Christian Schl; Chambersburg, PA; (S); 1/17; Varsity Clb; Pres Jr Cls; Var Socr; Hon Roll; NHS.

REDDING, MARK; Hanover HS; Hanover, PA; (Y); Chess Clb; Computer Clb; Stat Bsktbl; Ntl Merit Ltr; Am Leg Awd 83; Intl Rel.

REDDINGTON, ED; Clearfield HS; Clearfield, PA; (Y); 14/360; Stu Cncl; Var L Ftbl; Var Trk; JV L Wrstlng; High Hon Roll; NHS; French Clb; Key Clb; Ski Clb; Spanish Clb; Military Sci.

REDINGTON, PATRICIA; Seton Catholic HS; Avoca, PA; (Y); 30/96; Hosp Aide; Key Clb; Mathletes; Teachers Aide; Soph Cls; Jr Cls; Sr Cls; Stu Cncl; Bsktbl; JV Cap Mathletes 84; Mst Dedicated Stu Cncl 86; Misericordia; Occ Thrpy.

REDISH, JOHN; Penn-Trafford HS; Jeannette, PA; (Y); AFS; Pres Spanish Clb; School Play; Nwsp Ed-Chief; Yrbk Stf; Im Vllybl; Spanish.

REDLICH, BETH; Hempfield Area SR HS; North Miami Bch, FL; (Y); Spanish Clb; Trs Temple Yth Grp; Varsity Clb; Rep Stu Cncl; Var L Tennis; High Hon Roll; Hon Roll; Jr NHS; NHS; Spanish NHS.

REDMOND, BRENDA; Northwest Area HS; Shickshinny, PA; (Y); 21/108; Computer Clb; French Clb; High Hon Roll; Hon Roll; Upward Bound-Wilkes Coll 84-86; Penn ST; Mech Engrng.

REDMOND, CHRISTINE; Harbor Creek HS; Erie, PA; (Y); 4/225; Office Aide; Color Guard; Yrbk Rptr; Yrbk Stf; Stu Cncl; Diving; Mgr(s); L Sftbl; Swmmng; High Hon Roll; Bus Admn.

REDMOND, LISA; California Area HS; California, PA; (Y); Pep Clb; Chorus; Mrchg Band; JV Tennis; Twrlr; JV Vllybl; High Hon Roll; Sec NHS; Pre Med.

REDUZZI, TRACY; Pen Argyle Area HS; Pen Argyl, PA; (Y); 14/129; Ski Clb; Varsity Clb; Sec Jr Cls; JV Var Cheerleading; High Hon Roll; Hon Roll; Moravian Coll; Pre-Law.

REDZENSKY, CAROL; Moshannon Valley HS; Ramey, PA; (Y); 1/130; Pres Spanish Clb; Band; Chorus; Concert Band; Capt Flag Corp; Mrchg Band; Pep Band; Bausch & Lomb Sci Awd; High Hon Roll; Pres NHS; Renssalear Mth & Sci Awd 86; Dist Band & Chorus 86.

REED, BRENDA; Punxsutawney Area HS; Punxsuta, PA; (Y); 14/238; Pres Church Yth Grp; French Clb; Math Tm; Band; Color Guard; Jazz Band; Variety Show; Hon Roll; NHS; BPW Grl Mth 85; PHEAA Cert Merit; Geneva Coll; Cmnctns.

REED, CHARLES; Boyertown Area SR HS; Boyertown, PA; (Y); 8/472; Aud/Vis; Math Tm; Stage Crew; Lit Mag; High Hon Roll; Ntl Merit Ltr; 3rd Berks Cnty Stu Art Cntst 86; Sci.

REED, CHERYL L; Henderson HS; West Chester, PA; (S); 4/349; JV Var Cheerleading; Hon Roll; Spanish NHS.

REED, DAWN; Waynesboro SR HS; Waynesboro, PA; (Y); 18/321; Cmnty Wkr; FTA; Intnl Clb; Service Clb; Stat Mat Maids; High Hon Roll; NHS; Math Achvt Awd 84; Lock Haven U; Cmmnctns.

REED, DENISE; Montour HS; Mckees Rocks, PA; (Y); Girl Scts; Concert Band; Mrchg Band; Frsh Cls; Jr Cls; Powder Puff Ftbl; Ntl Poetry Anthlgy 85; Clarion U; Spcl Ed.

REED, EILEEN; Franklin Area JR SR HS; Franklin, PA; (Y); FBLA; Hosp Aide; Band; Chorus; Concert Band; Pep Band; Variety Show; Yrbk Stf; Score Keeper; Hon Roll; 2nd Gold Cup PFMC Music Festiral 86; Psychology.

REED, ERIC S; Cedar Crest HS; Lebanon, PA; (Y); 20/320; School Musical; Stu Cncl; JV Bsktbl; Var Socr; Var Vllybl; Hon Roll; NHS; Church Yth Grp; FCA; Pep Clb; Part People Hg Scl Ambas Pgm 85; Attnd Rot Ldrshp Conf 86; Pl 7th Natl JR Olym Sabre Fncng Champ 85; Lib Arts.

REED, KATRINA; Williamsport Area HS; Williamsport, PA; (Y); 98/518; Key Clb; Ski Clb; Chorus; Color Guard; Rep Sr Cls; Tennis; Frgn Rltns.

REED, KEVIN; Mid Valley HS; Olyphant, PA; (Y); Church Yth Grp; Computer Clb; Drama Clb; School Musical; School Play; Stage Crew; Rep Frsh Cls; Rep Soph Cls; Rep Jr Cls; Rep Sr Cls; Acad All Amer 84 & 85; PA Coll; Pharm.

REED, KIMBERLY; Tamaqua Area HS; Tamaqua, PA; (Y); #4 In Class; German Clb; Q&S; Nwsp Rptr; Nwsp Stf; Yrbk Stf; Pom Pon; High Hon Roll; Hon Roll; Jr NHS; NHS; Cntry III Lcl Schlrshp Wnnr 85-86; Hugh O Brian Smnr Rep 83-84; Fshr Memrl Schlrshp 85-86; Elizabethtown Coll.

REED, LISA; Bishop Mc Devitt HS; Highspire, PA; (Y); Math Tm; Im FBLA; Mgr Tennis; Harrisburg Area CC; Bus Admn.

REED, MARY; Hopewell SR HS; Aliquippa, PA; (Y); French Clb; Girl Scts; Band; Concert Band; Jazz Band; Mrchg Band; Pep Band; Variety Show; Powder Puff Ftbl; Hon Roll; Silver Awd Girl Scouts 83; Worthy Advsr, Grand Usherette, Intrntl Order Of Rainbow For Girls 82-85; ICM Schl Of Bus; Travel.

REED, MICHAEL; Northern Bedford County HS; Woodbury, PA; (Y); 2/100; Pres FBLA; Pres SADD; VP Stu Cncl; Var Capt Bsbl; Var Capt Bsktbl; Var L Ftbl; High Hon Roll; NHS; Church Yth Grp; Math Clb; MVP Bsktbl/Bsbl, PA Math Lg Jr Hi Scorer; Hlth.

REED, MICHAEL; Williams Valley JR SR HS; Wiconisco, PA; (S); 4/117; Pres VP Church Yth Grp; Chorus; Church Choir; High Hon Roll; Hon Roll; NHS; Susquehanna U; Theol.

REED, MICHELLE; Kishacoquillas HS; Milroy, PA; (Y); 8/144; French Clb; FBLA; Mgr Capt Mrchg Band; Var Capt Cheerleading; Twrlr; High Hon Roll; NHS; Prfct Atten Awd; Library Aide; Office Aide; Majorette Pa Allstate Lions Bnd 85-86; Schlstc Chrldng Awd 86; Accntng.

REED, PAMELA; Penn Cambria HS; Ashville, PA; (Y); Church Yth Grp; French Clb; Hosp Aide; Variety Show; Psychlgy.

REED, STEPHANIE; Allegheny Clarion Valley HS; Emlenton, PA; (Y); 4/97; Varsity Clb; Drm Mjr(t); VP Stu Cncl; Var Bsktbl; L Trk; 4-H Awd; High Hon Roll; NHS; Pres Frsh Cls; Capt L Cheerleading; Hugh O Brian Ldrshp Smnr 85; PA Assn Frmr ST Smnr 84; James Madison U; Math.

REED, TRACY; Punxsutawney Area HS; Punxsutawney, PA; (Y); 19/238; Pres French Clb; Math Tm; Science Clb; Varsity Clb; Yrbk Stf; Trk; Co-Capt Vllybl; Elks Awd; Hon Roll; NHS; MVP Vlybl; Mry Ann Irvn Schlrshp; Grl Of Mo Bus & Pfrsnl Wmns Awd; Washington & Jefferson; Med.

REED, TRINA; Penn Cambria HS; Cresson, PA; (Y); Trs FBLA; Stat Vllybl; Accntng.

REED, VICKIE JEAN; Punxsutawney Area SR HS; Punxsutawney, PA; (Y); 51/238; Church Yth Grp; Drama Clb; 4-H; French Clb; Office Aide; Acpl Chr; Chorus; Church Choir; School Musical; Hon Roll; PA Police Acad; Law.

REED, WILEY; Cathedral Prep; Erie, PA; (Y); 14/216; Trs Church Yth Grp; Debate Tm; Ski Clb; Trs Church Choir; JV Socr; High Hon Roll; Hon Roll; Latin Hnr Awd 84-85.

REED, WILLIAM L; Du Bois Area HS; Troutville, PA; (Y); Varsity Clb; VP L Mgr(s); Im Vllybl; Hon Roll; Engrng.

REEDER, JANE; Northern York HS; Dillsburg, PA; (Y); 7/201; Computer Clb; Chorus; Yrbk Ed-Chief; Yrbk Stf; Rep Sr Cls; High Hon Roll; Acad All-Star 86; Correspondent To Two Newspprs 86; Prsdntl Acad Fitns Awd 86; Penn ST U; Bus Admin.

REEDER, JENNIFER; Danville SR HS; Danville, PA; (Y); 9/207; Sec Church Yth Grp; Exploring; Key Clb; Latin Clb; JV Var Bowling; Gym; High Hon Roll; NHS; NEDT Awd; Biol.

REEDER, MIKE; Lampeter-Strasburg HS; Strasburg, PA; (Y); Aud/Vis; FBLA; School Musical; School Play; Stage Crew; Var Crs Cntry; Var Trk; Var Wt Lftg; Bloomsburg U; Tch Hrng Imprd.

REEDER, SANDRA; Bishop Kenrick HS; Norristown, PA; (Y); JV Trk; JV Vllybl.

REEDY, LISA; South Western HS; Hanover, PA; (Y); 17/205; Sec Key Clb; Color Guard; Yrbk Rptr; Rep Jr Cls; Off Sr Cls; JV Fld Hcky; Hon Roll; NHS; Stu Of Mnth 86; E TN ST U.

REES III, JAMES W; Ridley HS; Ridley Pk, PA; (Y); 107/427; Drama Clb; Bowling; Hon Roll; Engrng.

REES, TOBY; The Hill Schl; Mclean, VA; (Y); Boy Scts; Cmnty Wkr; French Clb; JA; Model UN; Ski Clb; Var Socr; Var Swmmng; JV Trk; Bus.

REES, WALTER; Otto-Eldred JR SR HS; Eldred, PA; (Y); Varsity Clb; Chorus; Yrbk Phtg; Yrbk Sprt Ed; Yrbk Stf; Ftbl; Trk; High Hon Roll; Hon Roll; Engrng.

REESE, BRIAN; Governor Mifflin HS; Reading, PA; (Y); 11/300; Church Yth Grp; Band; Concert Band; Jazz Band; Mrchg Band; Orch; School Musical; High Hon Roll; NHS; JV Crs Cntry; Unifd Achvt Awd 85 & 86; Penn ST; Engrng.

REESE, JENNIFER; Bellefonte Area HS; Bellefonte, PA; (Y); 63/232; Letterman Clb; SADD; Varsity Clb; Band; Concert Band; Mrchg Band; Rep Jr Cls; L Bsktbl; L Sftbl; Hon Roll; Bloomsburg U; Mktng.

REESE, KELLY; Kennedy Christian HS; Farrell, PA; (Y); 24/98; Spanish Clb; Color Guard; Drill Tm; Stage Crew; Im Bsktbl; U Of Pittsburgh; Psych.

REESE, KELLY; Spring-Ford SR HS; Mont Clare, PA; (S); 2/275; Spanish Clb; Orch; Nwsp Rptr; Var L Bsktbl; Var L Sftbl; Hon Roll; NHS; Marine Bio.

REESE, KIMBERLY; Spring-Ford HS; Mont Clare, PA; (S); 3/240; Exploring; Ski Clb; Spanish Clb; Var L Socr; L Capt Sftbl; JETS Awd; VP NHS; Ntl Merit Ltr; U Of PA; Pedtrcs.

REESE, KIMBERLY; Wyoming Valley West HS; Kingston, PA; (Y); 104/410; French Clb; Key Clb; Library Aide; Ski Clb; Rep Stu Cncl; Cheerleading; Im Vllybl; Hon Roll; Moravian Coll; Psych.

REESE, LISA; Baldwin SR HS; Pittsburgh, PA; (Y); 164/531; Hon Roll.

REESE, LORI; Danville SR HS; Danville, PA; (Y); Latin Clb; Band; Concert Band; Mrchg Band; Gayann Cotner Bus Awd 86.

REESE, RACHEL M; Trinity HS; Washington, PA; (Y); 110/373; Art Clb; Camera Clb; Key Clb; Office Aide; Pep Clb; Score Keeper; Sprt Of Frndlinss-May Day 86; Indiana U Of PA; Soc Wk.

REESE JR, WILLIAM F; Mc Guffey HS; Washington, PA; (Y); 29/216; Church Yth Grp; Spanish Clb.

REEVE, JOCELYN; Council Rock HS; Holland, PA; (Y); 215/845; Church Yth Grp; Hosp Aide; Church Choir; Mrchg Band; Symp Band; Hon Roll; Med.

REEVES, BRIAN; Northwestern Lehigh HS; New Tripoli, PA; (Y); Ski Clb; JV Bsktbl; Var Ftbl; Trk; Wt Lftg; U Of Pittsburgh; Elec Engrng.

REEVES, GEORGE; Harry S Truman HS; Levittown, PA; (Y); Yrbk Stf; Stu Cncl; Ftbl; Hon Roll; Temple U; Engrng.

REFFITT, DARIN M; Carson Long Inst; Colmar, PA; (Y); 3/40; Drama Clb; ROTC; Speech Tm; Chorus; School Play; Variety Show; Yrbk Stf; Lit Mag; Hon Roll; Pre-Law.

REGA, CASANDRA FAY; Mt Pleasant Area HS; Mt Pleasant, PA; (Y); French Clb; VICA; Yrbk Phtg; Yrbk Stf; Soph Cls; Rep Stu Cncl; High Hon Roll; Comp Prgmmr.

REGA, DEBRA; Spring-Ford HS; Royersford, PA; (S); 8/230; French Clb; Lit Mag; Rep Sr Cls; JV Sftbl; Im Vllybl; High Hon Roll; NHS; Church Yth Grp; Pep Clb; Score Keeper; Dstngshd Schlr Awd 86; Penn ST U; Nuclear Engr.

REGA, JOANNE; Spring Ford SR HS; Royersford, PA; (S); 5/258; German Clb; Score Keeper; JV Tennis; High Hon Roll; NHS; Top German Stu 85-86; Comm.

REGAL, SHANE; Northern HS; Lewisberry, PA; (Y); 45/209; Art Clb; Church Yth Grp; Letterman Clb; Spanish Clb; Varsity Clb; Chorus; Jazz Band; School Musical; Stage Crew; Var Bsbl; Accntg.

REGAN, COLLEEN; Bishop Hannan HS; Scranton, PA; (Y); French Clb; Lackawanna JC; Sec Sci.

REGAN, TIMOTHY; Scranton Preparitory Schl; Scranton, PA; (Y); Boys Clb Am; Cmnty Wkr; Off Jr Cls; Off Sr Cls; Bsbl; Bsktbl; U Of Scranton; Pre Law.

REGAS, MICHELLE; Avonworth HS; Sewickley, PA; (Y); Im Fld Hcky; ICM Schl Bus; Sec Sci.

REGINA, RON; Canon-Mc Millan HS; Bridgeville, PA; (Y); French Clb; Chorus; Trk; Vllybl; Wrstlng; High Hon Roll; Hon Roll; St Vincent Coll Chlng Pgm Partial Prsdntl Schlrshp 86.

REGITZ, CRAIG S; Conestoga Valley HS; Leola, PA; (Y); 25/258; Church Yth Grp; Orch; Stage Crew; Stu Cncl; Capt Wrstlng; High Hon Roll; Hon Roll; NHS; 2nd Tm All-Star Lancastr Lebnon Wrstlng League 86; Gettysburg Coll; Chem.

REGITZ, GRETA; Penn-Trafford HS; Jeannette, PA; (Y); AFS; Spanish Clb; Nwsp Rptr; Hon Roll; Educ.

REGNA, RANDY; Lincoln HS; Ellwood City, PA; (Y); 79/163; Art Clb; Church Yth Grp; Computer Clb; Exploring; German Clb; Trk; Wrstlng; Jameson Mem Hosp Schl Of Nrsng.

REGOLI, BEN; Valley HS; New Kensington, PA; (Y); 16/202; Leo Clb; Trs Ski Clb; Varsity Clb; Rep Stu Cncl; Var Bsbl; JV Bsktbl; Hon Roll; NHS; Shamey Athltc Schltc Awd 86; Stud Of The Mnth 86; Engrng.

REGOTTI, KAREN; Yough SR HS; Smithton, PA; (Y); Trs DECA; Ski Clb; Band; Westmorland CC; Real Est.

REHRIG, ANTHONY J; Palmerton Area HS; Palmerton, PA; (Y); Am Leg Boys St; Church Yth Grp; Cmnty Wkr; Var JV Bsbl; JV Ftbl; Var Golf; Var Mgr(s); Sftbl; Hon Roll; Hnrb Mntn-Bsbl Cntrfld 86; LCCC; Tchng.

REIBSON, CHRISTY; Sullivan County HS; Forksville, PA; (Y); School Play; Stu Cncl; JV Var Vllybl; Hon Roll; NHS.

REICH, DEBBIE; Beaver JR SR HS; Beaver, PA; (Y); 64/177; Pep Clb; Ski Clb; Powder Puff Ftbl; Resrvtnst.

REICH III, JOHN H; Cedar Crest HS; Lebaon, PA; (Y); 14/305; Debate Tm; Pep Clb; Quiz Bowl; Trs Frsh Cls; Trs Soph Cls; Crs Cntry; Trk; Vllybl; NHS; Woodmn Wrld Amer Hstry Awd 84; Cornell U; Htl Adm.

REICHARD, DIANNE; Reynolds HS; Greenville, PA; (Y); 4/170; Latin Clb; Library Aide; Math Clb; Varsity Clb; Chorus; Pres Frsh Cls; Pres Sec Stu Cncl; Var Capt Vllybl; Hon Roll; NHS; Bst Offnsv Plyr Awd Vllybll 85-86; Grove City Coll.

REICHENBACH, TANDI; East Juniata HS; Mc Alisterville, PA; (Y); 43/87; Chess Clb; Church Yth Grp; FHA; Band; Chorus; Mrchg Band; Cheerleading; Twrlr; Ntl Merit Ltr; Chrldng Merit Awd 84-86; SR Standout Chrldng 86-87; Radiologic Tech.

REICHENBAUGH, GAIL; Lower Dauphin HS; Hummelstown, PA; (Y); 11/230; VP Church Yth Grp; Varsity Clb; Sec Soph Cls; Sec Jr Cls; Rep Stu Cncl; Capt Var Cheerleading; JV Var Sftbl; Var Tennis; High Hon Roll; Sec NHS; Penn ST U; Indstrl.

REICHMAN, LYNNE MARIE; Wallenpaupack Area HS; Greentown, PA; (Y); 7/149; Am Leg Aux Girls St; NFL; Band; High Hon Roll; Jr NHS; NHS; Church Yth Grp; Debate Tm; Science Clb; Chorus; Womns Clb Stdnt Tailrg Comptn 2nd & 3rd ST 85-86; Natl Sci Olympd Tm 86; JR Hnr Grd 86; Htl Mgmt.

REID, AMY; Vincentian HS; Pittsburgh, PA; (Y); Dance Clb; Drama Clb; Library Aide; Office Aide; Teachers Aide; Lib Chorus; School Play; Stage Crew; Hon Roll; Prfct Atten Awd; Robert Morris Clg; Cmptr Sci.

REID, BRIAN; Cardinal Doughertyh HS; Phila, PA; (Y); 205/747; Church Yth Grp; Computer Clb; Yrbk Stf; Hon Roll; John Mc Kee Schlrshp 86; Union League Of Philadelphia Schlrshp 86; Temple U; Accntng.

REID, FELICIA LYNNETTE; Chester HS; Chester, PA; (Y); Church Yth Grp; Pep Clb; Band; Church Choir; Drill Tm; VP Frsh Cls; VP Soph Cls; VP Jr Cls; Pres Sr Cls; Prfct Atten Awd; Cmmnctns.

REID, LAURA; Uniontown HS; Chalkhill, PA; (Y); Drama Clb; German Clb; Key Clb; Ski Clb; Thesps; Nwsp Rptr; School Play; Hon Roll; UNC; Marine Bio.

REID, RICHARD; Springdale HS; Cheswick, PA; (Y); 14/160; Computer Clb; FBLA; Spanish Clb; VP Stu Cncl; Var Capt Bsktbl; Var Capt Tennis; High Hon Roll; Hon Roll; Trs NHS; Washington & Jefferson Schlrshp 86-87; MVP Bsktbl 85-86; Schlr/Athl Awd-US Army Rsrv 86; Bus.

REIDER, LYLE; Elizabethtown Area HS; Bainbridge, PA; (Y); 42/227; Boy Scts; Pres Church Yth Grp; Ski Clb; Band; Concert Band; Drm Mjr(t); Jazz Band; Mrchg Band; Variety Show; Var Bsbl; Penn ST U; Elctrnc Engr.

REIDINGER, TODD; Danville HS; Danville, PA; (Y); 30/170; Spanish Clb; Bsktbl; Crs Cntry; Trk; High Hon Roll; Hon Roll; NHS; Trk Ltr 84-86; Crs Cntry Ltr 84-85; Spn Awd 83 & 86; U Pittsburgh; Phrmcy.

REIDLER, JEANNETTE; Bethlehem Catholic HS; Upr Black Eddy, PA; (Y); Mgr Wrstlng; Hon Roll; Sci.

REIFENSTEIN, RICK; Deer Lakes JR SR HS; Tarentum, PA; (Y); 2/10; Church Yth Grp; Drama Clb; Letterman Clb; SADD; Varsity Clb; School Musical; School Play; Stage Crew; Variety Show; Crs Cntry; Theater.

REIFF, MELANIE; Cedar Cliff HS; New Cumberland, PA; (Y); 41/272; Key Clb; Ski Clb; Spanish Clb; Stage Crew; Var Tennis; JV Vllybl; High Hon Roll; NHS; Pres Schlr; Spanish NHS; Shippensburg U; Sec Ed.

REIFF, RAY; Ephrata HS; Stevens, PA; (Y); Vrsty Ltr Rifl 85; Marn Bio.

REIGH, PAMELA; Altoona Area HS; Altoona, PA; (S); Trs Key Clb; Ski Clb; Speech Tm; Band; Chorus; Concert Band; Flag Corp; Mrchg Band; School Musical; Variety Show; Sci Awd 84; PA ST U; Biolgy.

REIGHARD, TRICIA; Forest Hills HS; Sidman, PA; (Y); 1/160; Art Clb; Trs Pep Clb; Chorus; Nwsp Stf; Stu Cncl; Bausch & Lomb Sci Awd; Jr NHS; Lion Awd; Spanish NHS; Stu Yr 83-84; Chem.

REIGHLEY, CHRISTOPHER LEE; Wilson SR HS; West Lawn, PA; (Y); Computer Clb; Leo Clb; Band; Chorus; Concert Band; Drm Mjr(t); Jazz Band; Mrchg Band; Orch; Pep Band; PA Grnd Chmpn Bndmstrs Assoc 85; Slost Rnggld Bnd 85-86; Morehead ST U; Msc Prfrmnc.

REIGLE, PATRICIA; Central Catholic HS; Reading, PA; (Y); 28/125; Art Clb; Trs Church Yth Grp; GAA; Office Aide; Pep Clb; Chorus; Church Choir; Color Guard; School Musical; Stage Crew; Top Shorthand,Acctng,Typng Cls; Manor JC; Exec Sec.

REIGNER, BARBARA ANN; Boyertown HS; Barto, PA; (Y); 8/500; Am Leg Aux Girls St; Church Yth Grp; Computer Clb; German Clb; Nwsp Rptr; Rep Soph Cls; Rep Jr Cls; JV Fld Hcky; JV Lcrss; L Trk; Ntl Hnr Soc 85-86; Lndscpg.

REIHART, MICHELLE; Juniata Valley HS; Huntingdon, PA; (Y); 12/72; Am Leg Aux Girls St; Sec Trs FHA; Library Aide; Pep Clb; Speech Tm; Chorus; Nwsp Rptr; Rep Stu Cncl; JV Cheerleading; Masonic Awd; Nrsng.

REIHART, ROBERT E; Juniata Valley HS; Alexandria, PA; (Y); 3/77; Boy Scts; Letterman Clb; School Play; Yrbk Stf; VP Sr Cls; Var L Bsbl; Var L Bsktbl; Var L Ftbl; High Hon Roll; Pres NHS; Schlr Athlt, Gd Sprtsmnshp, Mth & Sci Awds 86; PA ST U; Engrng.

REILEY JR, DAVID; Somerset Area HS; Somerset, PA; (Y); 2/239; French Clb; JA; Math Tm; Jazz Band; Orch; Trs Stu Cncl; Pres NHS; SADD; High Hon Roll; SAR Awd; PA Gvrnrs Schl Sci 86; All-ST Orchstra PA 85-86; Schlstc Quiz Tm 86.

REILLY, ANN; Canevin HS; Pgh, PA; (Y); 8/183; Church Yth Grp; FBLA; Trs Girl Scts; Chorus; Church Choir; School Musical; Pres Jr Cls; Pres Sr Cls; High Hon Roll; Pres NHS; PA ST.

REILLY, GRAHAM; Central Bucks East HS; Lahaska, PA; (Y); Boy Scts; Ski Clb; Stu Cncl; Var L Socr; JV Tennis; JV L Trk; Hon Roll; Jr NHS; NHS; Inter Cnty Trvlng Sccr Tm 82-86.

REILLY, JAY G; Hempfield Area SR HS; Greensburg, PA; (Y); 1/650; Pres Camera Clb; Math Tm; NFL; Jazz Band; Nwsp Phtg; Yrbk Phtg; Var Trk; French Hon Soc; Trs Jr NHS; Pres NHS; PA Gvrnrs Sci Schl 84; 1st Pl ST Radio Anncng Cmptn 85.

REILLY, JOANNA; Central HS; Scranton, PA; (Y); 27/300; Art Clb; French Clb; Quiz Bowl; Scholastic Bowl; Varsity Clb; Yrbk Stf; Var Bsktbl; Var Sftbl; Var Trk; French Hon Soc; GNB Schlrshp 86; Penn ST; Pre-Law.

REILLY, JOHN; Pulisades HS; Kintnersville, PA; (Y); 13/178; Math Clb; Math Tm; Science Clb; Lit Mag; JV Bsktbl; Var Crs Cntry; Im Socr; Var Capt Trk; Im Vllybl; Im Wt Lftg; Lioness Schlrshp 86; James Wolfinger Mem Schlrshp 86; Ron Bozzuto Mem Schlrshp 86; U PA; Pre-Vet.

REILLY, KERRI; Freedom HS; Bethlehem, PA; (Y); 18/445; Intnl Clb; Pep Clb; Trs Spanish Clb; SADD; Band; Orch; High Hon Roll; VP NHS; Intl Rltns.

REILLY, KERRIANNE O; Forest City Regional HS; Union Dale, PA; (Y); 2/62; Scholastic Bowl; Spanish Clb; School Musical; Yrbk Stf; Stu Cncl; Stat Socr; VP NHS; Rotary Awd; Sal; Semi-Fnlst-Educ Cmmnctns Schlrshp 86; U Of PA; Psych.

REILLY, RONILYN; Hempfield Area HS; Greensburg, PA; (Y); 60/647; Art Clb; Pep Clb; Concert Band; Mrchg Band; School Musical; Nwsp Stf; Trk; High Hon Roll; Hon Roll; Ski Clb; 1st Pl Gannon U Poetry Cntst 86; Schlrshp John Casablancas Modelng Agncy 86; Gannon U; Comm Arts.

REILLY, SHARON; Our Lady Of Sacred Heart HS; Coraopolis, PA; (Y); Church Choir; School Musical; Variety Show; Cheerleading; Socr; Sftbl; Math Awd 84; Bus Mgmt.

REILLY, SUE; Harry S Truman HS; Levittown, PA; (Y); Church Yth Grp; Var Cheerleading; CC Awd; Hon Roll; Stu Ldrshp; Bus.

REIM, MEG; Villa Maria Acad; Fairview, PA; (Y); 21/143; Cmnty Wkr; Hosp Aide; Model UN; Ski Clb; Crs Cntry; Swmmng; Trk; High Hon Roll; NHS; Ntl Merit Ltr; Mission Clb 86-87; PA ST U; Bus.

REIMAN, MICHAEL; Northern Potter HS; Genesee, PA; (S); Varsity Clb; School Play; Nwsp Sprt Ed; Yrbk Sprt Ed; Pres Stu Cncl; Var Socr; Var Trk; High Hon Roll; NHS; Ntl Merit Ltr; MVP Trk 85; Oct Stu 85; PA ST U; Pre-Law.

REIMER, ANNMARIE; Northampton SR HS; Walnutport, PA; (S); 15/475; Nwsp Bus Mgr; Nwsp Rptr; Yrbk Stf; JV Bsktbl; Var L Fld Hcky; Var L Sftbl; High Hon Roll; Trs NHS; Pres Schlrshp Allentown Coll 86-87; Grl Of Mnth 86; Allentown Coll; Math.

REIMER, SHERI; Bangor Area SR HS; Bangor, PA; (Y); 6/188; Varsity Clb; Chorus; Color Guard; School Musical; Tennis; High Hon Roll; Jr NHS; NHS; Bangor Elks Yth Schlrshp Awd 86; Penn ST Hazelton Campus.

REIN, SUZANNE; Little Flower HS For Girls; Philadelphia, PA; (Y); 109/413; Cmnty Wkr; Church Choir; Lit Mag; Marywood Coll; Elem Educ.

REINECKE, RACHEL A; Emmaus HS; Macungie, PA; (Y); 71/479; Color Guard; Mrchg Band; Orch; Pep Band; Symp Band; JP Sousa Awd; Dist PMEA Band 86; Regn V PMEA Band 86; Qlfd PA All ST Band 86; Temple U; Music Educ.

REINER, DAVID; Latrobe SR HS; Latrobe, PA; (Y); 140/431; German Clb; Stage Crew; Stat Bsktbl; High Hon Roll; Hon Roll; Prfct Atten Awd; Comp Prgrmmng.

REINER, DENISE; Line Mountain HS; Leck Kill, PA; (Y); VP Church Yth Grp; Sec 4-H; Key Clb; Varsity Clb; Stu Cncl; Var Bsktbl; Var Sftbl; 4-H Awd; Prfct Atten Awd; Stage Crew; Athltc Trainng.

REINER, DREW; Upper Moreland HS; Willow Grove, PA; (Y); 3/275; Church Yth Grp; Key Clb; School Musical; Sec Stu Cncl; Var Capt Crs Cntry; Var Capt Trk; High Hon Roll; NHS; Athlte Schlr, Outstndng Stu Awd, & Whte Memrl Schlrhp Awds 86; MVP Crss Cntry & Wntr Trck; US Naval Acad; Engrng.

REINERT, KAREN; Elizabethtown Area HS; Elizabethtown, PA; (Y); 87/245; Church Yth Grp; Hosp Aide; Teachers Aide; Chorus; Church Choir; Orch; Yrbk Stf; Elem Ed.

REINERT, LISA; Kutztown Area HS; Lenhartsville, PA; (Y); 22/150; Pres Church Yth Grp; Trs 4-H; Sec FFA; Hosp Aide; Library Aide; Quiz Bowl; Chorus; School Musical; Stage Crew; Yrbk Stf; Nrsg.

REINERT, TARA; Brandywine Heights HS; Bechteleseville, PA; (Y); 31/126; Band; Drm Mjr(t); Mrchg Band; Bsktbl; Nrsg.

REINHARD, DIANA; Northampton SR HS; Northampton, PA; (S); 87/475; AFS; Acpl Chr; Chorus; Nwsp Ed-Chief; Stu Cncl; Bsktbl; Var L Fld Hcky; JV Sftbl; Var L Trk; Hon Roll; E PA Legue Hnbl Mntn All-Star Fld Hockey 84-85; Nov Girl Of Mnth By Northampton Bus & Prof Wmn 85-86; IN U; Comm.

REINHARD, HEATHER; Brandywine Heights HS; Macungie, PA; (Y); 7/98; Var Sftbl; Var Tennis; High Hon Roll; NHS; Pres Acad Ftnss Awd 86; Kutztown U; CPA.

REINHARD, PENNY J; Whitehall HS; Whitehall, PA; (Y); 125/257; Am Leg Aux Girls St; Aud/Vis; Chorus; Drill Tm; Mrchg Band; School Musical; Stage Crew; Yrbk Stf; Stu Cncl; Capt Pom Pon; Millersville; Soc Wrk.

REINHART, CURTIS; Solanco HS; Kirkwood, PA; (Y); 12/268; Ski Clb; Spanish Clb; Varsity Clb; Band; Concert Band; Jazz Band; Mrchg Band; Trs Soph Cls; Trs Jr Cls; Trs Sr Cls; Solanco Sclhr Awd 83; PA ST U; Bus Adm.

REINHART, KATHY; Marian HS; Jim Thorpe, PA; (S); 13/114; Church Yth Grp; Chorus; Variety Show; Nwsp Rptr; Nwsp Stf; Yrbk Stf; Var Sftbl; Hon Roll; Spanish NHS.

REININGER, VICKI; Greater Johnstown HS; Johnstown, PA; (Y); French Clb; Math Clb; Band; Concert Band; Drm Mjr(t); Mrchg Band; Orch; Var Sftbl; Hon Roll; NHS; Countty Band & Orchestra 84; IUP; Music Ed.

REINKE, TERESA; Leechburg Area HS; Leechburg, PA; (Y); 12/82; Band; Concert Band; Mrchg Band; Pep Band; Var Bsktbl; Var Sftbl; Hon Roll; 1st Fed MVP Awd-Bsktbl 85-86.

REINSEL, DAN; Rocky Grove HS; Oil City, PA; (Y); Aud/Vis; CAP; Exploring; High Hon Roll; Hon Roll; Frstry.

REINSEL, KRISTI; Hampton HS; Allison Pk, PA; (Y); 35/255; Church Yth Grp; Cmnty Wkr; Hosp Aide; NFL; Yrbk Rptr; Stu Cncl; Trk; High Hon Roll; Debate Tm; Political Wkr; Outstndg Acad Achvt Awd 83-85; 2nd Pl Dist Natl Hstry Day Comp 84-85.

REINSHAGEN, SHELLY; Upper Moreland HS; Hatboro, PA; (Y); 57/253; Key Clb; Letterman Clb; Varsity Clb; Sftbl; Vllybl; NHS; Acctng.

REISINGER, STACY; Seneca Valley HS; Harmony, PA; (Y); 139/342; Teachers Aide; Chorus; Hon Roll; Miss PA USA Pgnt 86; Model.

REISNER, DANNY; Moravion Acad; Allentown, PA; (Y); Math Tm; Model UN; Ski Clb; Variety Show; Nwsp Sprt Ed; Yrbk Phtg; Var Crs Cntry; DAR Awd; High Hon Roll; Hon Roll; Dartmouth Book Awd 86; Cum Laude Socy 86; Engl Awd 86.

REISS, CAROL; Butler Area SR HS; Butler, PA; (Y); Exploring; Chorus; Drm & Bgl; Lawyer.

REISS, ERIC D; William Allen HS; Allentown, PA; (Y); 91/576; Church Yth Grp; Jr NHS; PA ST U; Engrng.

REISS, MARK; Montour HS; Pittsburgh, PA; (Y); Art Clb; Stage Crew; JV Bsbl; L Ftbl; Hon Roll; Cmrcl Art.

REITANO, ANNETTE; Neshaminy HS; Levittown, PA; (Y); 50/782; SADD; Chorus; Drm Mjr(t); School Musical; Sec Pres Stu Cncl; Var Fld Hcky; High Hon Roll; NHS; Prfct Atten Awd; Dance Clb; Outstndng Stu Srvc Schl 82-83; Outstndng Stu Srvc Schl 83-84; Chem Engr.

REITANO, JILL; St Maria Goretti HS; Philadelphia, PA; (Y); 143/426; Hon Roll; Prfct Atten Awd; Steno Cert 85; Sec Studies Cert 85-86; Katharine Gibbs; Sec Fld.

REITER, DAVE; Marion Center Area HS; Marion Center, PA; (S); 1/174; Pres Church Yth Grp; Trs Band; JV Var Crs Cntry; Var Trk; High Hon Roll; NHS; Intnl Clb; Science Clb; SADD; Cert Of Merit-Coll Of Engrng At Gannon U 85; Dist Band & Chorus 85; HS Gradtn Oranist 84-85; Banking.

REITER, STEVE; Pine Grove Area HS; Pine Grove, PA; (Y); 15/120; Am Leg Boys St; Varsity Clb; Band; Concert Band; Mrchg Band; School Play; Stage Crew; JV L Bsktbl; Var L Ftbl; Im Sftbl; Elec Engnrng.

REITH, DAVID W; Bethel Park SR HS; Bethel Park, PA; (Y); French Clb; Mrchg Band; Symp Band; Rep Frsh Cls; High Hon Roll; NHS; Pres Schlr; John Leroy Awd Exc Compstn 83; Exc Frnch 83; High Hnrs 83; PA ST; Bus Mgmt.

REITLER, ROBERT; Norwin HS; N Huntingdon, PA; (Y); Letterman Clb; Spanish Clb; JV Im Bsbl; Var JV Ftbl; JV Trk; Wt Lftg; Engr.

REITMEYER, KRISTEN; Bishop Hafey HS; Nuremberg, PA; (Y); Drama Clb; PAVAS; Ski Clb; Orch; School Play; Yrbk Stf; Lit Mag; Stu Cncl; Hon Roll.

REITZ, BETH ANN; Daniel Boon JR-SR HS; Douglassville, PA; (Y); 2/148; Drama Clb; Chorus; Concert Band; Drm Mjr(t); School Play; Yrbk Stf; High Hon Roll; VP NHS; Ntl Merit SF; Sal; Berks Cnty Choir 83-86; Dstrct X Chrs 86; Boston U; Occptnl Thrpy.

REITZ, DOUG; State College Area SR HS; State College, PA; (Y); 147/550; Church Yth Grp; French Clb; Science Clb; Hon Roll; PA ST U; Telecmmnctns.

REKUS, PAM; Central Dauphin HS; Harrisburgh, PA; (Y); Girl Scts; Teachers Aide; Chorus; Flag Corp; Madrigals; Orch; School Musical; High Hon Roll; Hon Roll; NHS; PTA Awd Eclln French 84.

RELLER, JENNIFER; Pensbury HS; Morrisville, PA; (Y); Church Yth Grp; Science Clb; Chorus; Soph Cls; Jr Cls; Fld Hcky; Vllybl; Hon Roll; NHS; Prfct Atten Awd; Bucks Cnty Sci Sem Accptnc 86; PA Free Entgrprs Wk Accptnc 86; Sbrbn 1 All Leag Hcky Tm Hon Ment 86; Lehigh; Math.

REMAKER, PHILLIP; High Schl Of Engineering And Science; Philadelphia, PA; (S); 2/200; Computer Clb; Math Tm; Science Clb; Band; Hon Roll; NHS; Ntl Merit SF; Prfct Atten Awd; PJAS Sci Fairs Rgnl & ST Lvl 84-85; DE Vlly Rgnl Sci Fairs 85-86; PECO Eeac Comp Bwl 84; U Of PA; Comp Sci.

REMALEY, JASON; Lock Haven SR HS; Castanea, PA; (Y); Key Clb; Model UN; Spanish Clb; Nwsp Stf; L Var Bsktbl; Hon Roll; NHS; NEDT Awd; Jrnlsm.

REMALEY, MICHAEL; Middleburg Joint HS; Middleburg, PA; (Y); 30/130; Chorus; Concert Band; Drm Mjr(t); Mrchg Band; School Musical; School Play; Stage Crew; Nwsp Rptr; Yrbk Phtg; Hon Roll; Profssnl Prod-Snd Music 84; Dist Chorus Dist, Rgnl 86; Semi-Fnlst-Govs Schl Arts 85 & 86; Theatr Art.

REMALEY, PAULA; Lehighton Area HS; Parryville, PA; (Y); FBLA; Chorus; Color Guard; School Play; Pres Soph Cls; VP Sr Cls; Trs Stu Cncl; Sftbl; Lehigh Comm Coll; Occpntl Thrpy.

REMALY, MICHAEL; W Allegheny HS; Oakdale, PA; (Y); 30/250; Science Clb; Spanish Clb; Varsity Clb; Chorus; Nwsp Stf; Stu Cncl; Var Ftbl; Trk; Wt Lftg; High Hon Roll.

REMALY, MIKE; West Allegheny HS; Oakdale, PA; (Y); 30/300; Spanish Clb; Varsity Clb; Chorus; Rep Stu Cncl; Var Ftbl; Trk; Wt Lftg; High Hon Roll; Hon Roll; Cert Achvt Bio Olympics 83-84 & 85-86; Chorus Achvt Awds 83-85; USAF Acad; Med.

REMATT, MICHAEL; Cambria Heights HS; Carrolltown, PA; (Y); 34/183; Cmnty Wkr; Computer Clb; Ski Clb; JV Bsktbl; Im Bowling; Var Ftbl; Im Sftbl; Hon Roll; NHS; Penn ST; Engrng.

REMBERT, DANNY; Carlynton HS; Pittsburgh, PA; (Y); Church Yth Grp; JV Ftbl; Var Trk; Hon Roll.

REMICH, NICOLE; Sheffield HS; Clarendon, PA; (Y); 3/75; Drama Clb; SADD; Drm Mjr(t); Mrchg Band; School Musical; School Play; Cheerleading; High Hon Roll; NHS; Voice Dem Awd.

REMLEY, PAUL; Benton Area JR SR HS; Benton, PA; (Y); Mgr Band; Chorus; Yrbk Stf.

RENALD, RENEE; Bethlehem Catholic HS; Bethlehem, PA; (Y); Cheerleading; Keystone Coll; Hotl Mgmt.

RENDA, SUSAN; Cahrtiers Valley HS; Pittsburgh, PA; (Y); 70/343; Ski Clb; Acpl Chr; Drill Tm; School Musical; Yrbk Stf; Cheerleading; NHS; IN U; Cmmnctns.

RENDOS, KAREN M; Ambridge Area HS; Baden, PA; (Y); Pep Clb; VP Trs Spanish Clb; Mrchg Band; Pres Stu Cncl; Capt Pom Pon; High Hon Roll; NHS; Ambsdr For Hnds Across Amer 86; U Ptsbrgh; Comp Tech.

RENDULIC, LISA; Belle Vernon Area HS; Belle Vernon, PA; (Y); 114/272; Drama Clb; Library Aide; NFL; Speech Tm; Band; Concert Band; Mrchg Band; Pep Band; School Play; Stage Crew; Persuasive Spkng Awd 86; CA U-PA; Gen Spch Cmmnctns.

RENKERT, MICHAEL; The Hill Schl; Elverson, PA; (Y); 4-H; FBLA; Letterman Clb; Model UN; Ski Clb; Spanish Clb; Varsity Clb; Yrbk Bus Mgr; Bsktbl; JV Var Crs Cntry; Skeet Tm 83-86; Cornell U; Mktng.

RENNIE, DAVID; Northampton Area HS; Northampton, PA; (Y); Church Yth Grp; High Hon Roll; Hon Roll.

RENNING, RUTH; Punxsutawney Area HS; Punxsutawney, PA; (Y); Drama Clb; Band; Chorus; Mrchg Band; Pep Band; School Musical; School Play; Yrbk Stf; Hon Roll; Concert Band; Comp Grphcs Engrng Wrkshp IA ST 86; PA ST; Indstrl Engrng.

RENNINGER, BRADLEY; Juniata HS; Mifflintown, PA; (Y); Varsity Clb; JV Bsbl; JV Wrstlng; Hon Roll; NHS; Elec.

RENNINGER, CATHERINE; Ringgold SR HS; Monongahela, PA; (Y); 52/349; Church Yth Grp; Computer Clb; Drama Clb; JA; School Musical; School Play; Variety Show; Ed Nwsp Ed-Chief; Yrbk Phtg; Yrbk Stf; JA Dist Achvr Yr, Dist Bst Slsprsn 84; JA Prfct Atten 83-85; Carnegie Mellon U; Drama.

RENNINGER, GRETCHEN; Nazareth Area HS; Wind Gap, PA; (Y); 20/240; Cmnty Wkr; Pres 4-H; Key Clb; Ski Clb; Band; Concert Band; Stage Crew; Yrbk Stf; Var L Vllybl; High Hon Roll; Pre Med.

RENNINGER, MICHELE; Holy Name HS; Kenhorst, PA; (Y); 15/117; Pep Clb; Q&S; Science Clb; Yrbk Rptr; Yrbk Stf; Im Bowling; Trk; High Hon Roll; NHS; Trustees Awd Albright Coll 86-87; Albright Coll.

RENNINGER, SCOTT A; Middleburg HS; Kreamer, PA; (Y); 3/115; Am Leg Boys St; German Clb; Var Bsktbl; High Hon Roll; NHS; Pres Fit Awd 86; Chem Awd Hgh Schltc Achvt 86; Hstry Awd Hgh Schltc Achvt 86; Penn ST U; Engrng.

RENNINGER, SHANAN; Lock Haven SR HS; Beech Creek, PA; (Y); Art Clb; Drama Clb; Nwsp Stf; Mat Maids; Var L Trk; Pre Law.

RENNINGER, TERESA L; Lewistown Area HS; Lewistown, PA; (Y); 12/247; AFS; Church Yth Grp; Drama Clb; 4-H; Pep Clb; Service Clb; Spanish Clb; Chorus; School Musical; Yrbk Ed-Chief; Faculty Commtt Outstndng Stu Schrlshp 86; Geisnger Med Cntr Schl; RN.

RENNIX, BETH; Unionville HS; Unionville, PA; (Y); Church Yth Grp; Exploring; 4-H; Nwsp Phtg; Yrbk Phtg; Yrbk Stf; Sftbl; 4-H Awd; Hon Roll; Nrsng.

RENSA, CAROL; Coughlin HS; Wilkes Barre, PA; (Y); 13/350; FBLA; Band; Concert Band; Jazz Band; Mrchg Band; Orch; Pep Band; Symp Band; Hon Roll; JP Sousa Awd; Dist Band 84-86; Rgnl Band 85-86; FBLA RLC 1st Pl-Acctng II 86; PA ST U; Music.

RENTZEL, AMY ELIZABETH; West York Area SR HS; York, PA; (Y); 14/191; Church Yth Grp; VP JA; VP SADD; Church Choir; Mrchg Band; Symp Band; Yrbk Stf; High Hon Roll; Hon Roll; NHS; Cert Merit Schlstc Wrtng Awds, Ntl Piano Aud, LIU Smnr Acad Poetry Cls 86; Brigham Young U; Geolgy.

RENTZEL, ROBIN; Central York SR HS; York, PA; (Y); 22/248; Sec Pres Church Yth Grp; Varsity Clb; Flag Corp; Mrchg Band; Yrbk Stf; Stu Cncl; Var JV Bsktbl; High Hon Roll; Hon Roll; Sec NHS; Shippensburg U.

RENZO, ZANE; Lock Haven SR HS; Lock Haven, PA; (Y); Boy Scts; Chess Clb; Church Yth Grp; Cmnty Wkr; Letterman Clb; Ed Ski Clb; Chorus; Wt Lftg; Elec Technen.

RENZULLI, CHRIS; Cardinal O Hara HS; Newtown Square, PA; (Y); Chess Clb; Dance Clb; JA; Varsity Clb; School Musical; School Play; Bsbl; Wrstlng; Saint Josephs U; Bus.

REPASKY, RENEE; Philipsburg Osceola Area HS; Philipsburg, PA; (Y); 23/250; Art Clb; Sec Library Aide; Mrchg Band; Co-Capt Twrlr; Hon Roll; U Of CA Los Angeles; Pre-Med.

REPICI, MICHELE; Padua Acad; Aston, PA; (Y); Cmnty Wkr; JV Sftbl; JV Swmmng; Hon Roll; Acntng.

REPLOGLE, ALLEN; Northern Bedford County HS; New Enterprise, PA; (Y); Acpl Chr; Band; Chorus; Concert Band; Jazz Band; Mrchg Band; Pep Band; School Musical; Swing Chorus.

REPLOGLE, LISA; Spring Cove Central HS; Martinsburg, PA; (Y); Pres Church Yth Grp; Computer Clb; Drama Clb; FCA; SADD; Chorus; School Play; Stu Cncl; Var L Trk; Ntl Merit Schol; PA ST; Bus Adm.

REPOSH, DANIEL; James M Coughlin HS; Wilkes Barre, PA; (Y); 16/365; Aud/Vis; Chess Clb; Computer Clb; Math Clb; Math Tm; Band; Orch; Nwsp Rptr; High Hon Roll; Jr NHS; Physcs.

REPOUSIS, ANGELO; Upper Darby HS; Upper Darby, PA; (Y); 18/576; JA; High Hon Roll; Hon Roll; Pres Schlr; Villanova Schlrshp 86; Villanova U; Bio.

REPPAR, GREGORY A; Chartiers Valley HS; Pittsburgh, PA; (Y); 21/343; Ski Clb; Varsity Clb; Var L Bsbl; Var Im Bsktbl; Var Capt Ftbl; Var L Trk; High Hon Roll; NHS; US Naval Acad; Engrng.

REPPERT, ANGELA; Allentown Central Catholic HS; Northampton, PA; (Y); Spanish Clb; Chorus; Mrchg Band; Stat Score Keeper; Capt Twrlr; Hon Roll; PSYCH.

REPPERT, LISA; Louis E Dieruff HS; Allentown, PA; (Y); 48/325; Pres Band; Chorus; Concert Band; Pres Mrchg Band; Nwsp Rptr; Sec Stu Cncl; Mgr(s); Var Sftbl; Cit Awd; Hon Roll; Outstndng Achvt Studnt Cncl, 15th Cngrsnl Dist Awd For Ctznshp & Zeswitz Awd Musc Ldrshp 85-86; NCACC; Liberal Arts.

REPPERT, MELISSA; Allen HS; Allentown, PA; (Y); 27/586; Key Clb; Letterman Clb; Spanish Clb; Varsity Clb; Yrbk Stf; Rep Frsh Cls; Rep Soph Cls; Rep Jr Cls; Stu Cncl; Var L Crs Cntry; MVP Gymnstcs 84; Ntl Hnr Soc 86; PA ST; Sprts Med.

REPPERT, SHAWN; Hamburg Area HS; Shoemakersville, PA; (Y); 14/154; Camera Clb; Library Aide; Yrbk Ed-Chief; Trs Sr Cls; Var L Bsktbl; Var L Trk; Hon Roll; Rep NHS; J Griffiths Mem Awd 86; Inter-Clb Cncl 85-86; Drexel U; Mech Engrng.

RESAVAGE, CINDY; Wyoming Valley West HS; Swoyersville, PA; (Y); Band; Chorus; Concert Band; Mrchg Band; Orch; School Musical; Cit Awd; High Hon Roll; NHS; Prfct Atten Awd; Philadelphia Coll; Pharmacy.

RESCHER, MARK; Central Catholic HS; Pittsburgh, PA; (Y); 7/268; School Musical; School Play; Stage Crew; High Hon Roll; Hon Roll; NHS; Ntl Merit Ltr; Dance Clb; Latn Hnr Soc; Washingtn Wrkshps; Cornell U Smmr Coll.

RESEK, PETER; Reynolds HS; Fredonia, PA; (Y); Church Yth Grp; FFA; VICA; Stage Crew; Capt Ftbl; Wt Lftg; Pres Of Electric Shop 86-87; Treas Of Electric Shop 85-86.

RESINSKI, MARIA; Archbishop Wood HS; Hatboro, PA; (Y); 125/255; Cmnty Wkr; French Clb; Service Clb; Nwsp Rptr; Nwsp Stf; W Chester U; Elem Ed.

RESINSKI, REBECCA E; Penn Cambria SR HS; Loretto, PA; (Y); 1/200; Drama Clb; French Clb; Spanish Clb; Speech Tm; SADD; High Hon Roll; Hon Roll; NHS; Ntl Merit SF; Schlrshp PA Gov Schl For The Arts 85.

RESNICK, AILEEN J; Council Rock HS; Richboro, PA; (Y); 2/755; Aud/Vis; Drama Clb; VP Temple Yth Grp; Chorus; Stage Crew; High Hon Roll; NHS; Ntl Merit SF; Bucks Cty Chors 85; Stanford; Biol.

RESNICK JR, CHARLES E; Saltsburg JR SR HS; Saltsburg, PA; (Y); Ski Clb; SADD; Varsity Clb; Stage Crew; Yrbk Stf; Var L Bsktbl; Var L Ftbl; Trk; Off Stu Cncl; High Hon Roll; Pres Phy Fit Awd 86.

RESNIK, SUSAN; Mc Keesport SR HS; White Oak, PA; (Y); 38/380; AFS; Church Yth Grp; German Clb; Acpl Chr; School Musical; Nwsp Stf; Capt Swmmng; NHS; Pres Acdmc Fit Awd 85-86; Mc Keesport Area HS Schlstc Awd 85-86; Indiana U Of PA; Elem Educ.

RESSER, KORI; Northeastern HS; Manchester, PA; (Y); 7/149; Hosp Aide; Yrbk Bus Mgr; Yrbk Ed-Chief; Yrbk Rptr; Yrbk Sprt Ed; Yrbk Stf; Var Capt Tennis; High Hon Roll; Hon Roll; NHS; Millersvl U; Bio.

RESSLER, BARBARA; Fairview HS; Fairview, PA; (S); 113/185; French Clb; Band; Church Choir; Concert Band; Sec Mrchg Band; Pres Orch; Pep Band; School Musical; Hon Roll; Duquesne U; Music Ed.

RESTA, LYNN; Western Beaver HS; Industry, PA; (Y); 12/83; Trs Church Yth Grp; Pep Clb; Chorus; Nwsp Ed-Chief; Yrbk Stf; Stat Sftbl; L Vllybl; Cit Awd; Hon Roll; NHS; Acctg.

RESTANEO, STACEY; St Paul Cathedral HS; Pittsburgh, PA; (S); 4/62; Drama Clb; Girl Scts; Ski Clb; Color Guard; School Play; Nwsp Stf; Yrbk Stf; Sec Jr Cls; Var Cheerleading; High Hon Roll; Ntl Hstry Day-2nd Pl 85; PA ST U; Bio.

RESTUCCIA, NADINE; Pittston Area HS; Pittston, PA; (Y); FNA; Key Clb; Ski Clb; Pres Jr Cls; Hon Roll; NHS; Bio.

RESTUCCIA, NATALIE; Pittston Area SR HS; Pittston, PA; (Y); 3/330; FNA; Key Clb; Math Clb; Yrbk Ed-Chief; High Hon Roll; Hon Roll; Jr NHS; NHS; Prfct Atten Awd; U Of Scranton; Pre-Med.

RESURRECCION, ROSEMARIE; Lower Moreland HS; Huntingdon Valley, PA; (S); German Clb; Key Clb; Red Cross Aide; Chorus; Orch; School Musical; Yrbk Stf; JV Var Fld Hcky; JV Var Lcrss; Hon Roll.

RESUTA, KENNY; Bishop Hafey HS; Hazleton, PA; (Y); Var JV Bsktbl; Var L Golf; Hon Roll; Syracuse; Bus.

RESZKOWSKI, LYNN; Venango Christian HS; Oil City, PA; (Y); 3/40; Cmnty Wkr; Pep Clb; Pres Frsh Cls; Var L Bsktbl; Var Score Keeper; Var L Sftbl; Var L Vllybl; High Hon Roll; NHS; NEDT Awd; PA Free Enterprs Wk 85; Phy Thrpy.

RETALLACK, DIANE; Cathllic HS; Lancaster, PA; (Y); 2/203; JCL; Service Clb; Yrbk Stf; JV Fld Hcky; Hon Roll; NHS; Pres Schlr; Sal; Stat Mgr(s); Tuit Schlrshp 86-87; Alumni Assn Awd 86; Ntl Ltn Exm Cum Laude 83-84, 86; Widener U; Bio.

RETHERFORD, CHRISTINE A; Manheim Township HS; Lancaster, PA; (Y); Cmnty Wkr; JA; Library Aide; JV Socr; High Hon Roll; Hon Roll; Engrng.

RETHI, AMY JO; Marion Center Area HS; Clymer, PA; (S); Church Yth Grp; 4-H; Intnl Clb; Office Aide; SADD; Drill Tm; 4-H Awd; High Hon Roll; Hon Roll; Jr NHS; Pblc Rltns Awd 84-85.

RETORT, PATRICK; Springdale HS; Harwick, PA; (Y); 35/121; Church Yth Grp; Im L Bsktbl; Var L Ftbl; Hon Roll.

RETTER, CINDY; Kiski Area HS; Vandergrift, PA; (Y); JA; Teachers Aide; Chorus; High Hon Roll; Hon Roll; IN U PA; Teachr.

RETTER, HEIDI; Northeast Bradford HS; Warren Center, PA; (Y); 2/85; Am Leg Aux Girls St; Church Yth Grp; Band; Chorus; Hst Soph Cls; VP Stu Cncl; Var Cheerleading; Bausch & Lomb Sci Awd; High Hon Roll; VP NHS; Pre-Med.

RETTINER, PATRICIA; Line Mountain HS; Dalmatia, PA; (Y); 8/109; Am Leg Aux Girls St; Drama Clb; Girl Scts; VP Ski Clb; Trs Varsity Clb; Nwsp Sprt Ed; Var Capt Fld Hcky; Cit Awd; Hon Roll; Lion Awd; Natl Sci Olympd 85; Am Leg Aux Awd 83; 1st Cls Girl Sct 83; Geisinger Med Ctr Schl; RN.

REUSS, KARLA; Pen Argyl Area SR JR HS; Nazareth, PA; (Y); FBLA; Off Jr Cls; Cheerleading; Powder Puff Ftbl; Sftbl; Trk; Var Capt Twrlr; East Stroudsburg.

REUSS, LAURA; Upper Darby SR HS; Upr Darby, PA; (Y); 10/629; Band; Concert Band; Mrchg Band; Orch; Pep Band; School Musical; Symp Band; Sftbl; High Hon Roll; Hon Roll; Genetcs.

REUTHER, KEN; North Pocono HS; Moscow, PA; (S); 15/250; Band; Mrchg Band; VP Orch; School Musical; High Hon Roll; Trs NHS; Natl Sci Merit Awd 85; Penn ST; Engrng.

REVAK, MICHELLE; Sto-Rox SR HS; Mc Kees Rocks, PA; (Y); 18/149; Boys Clb Am; French Clb; Hosp Aide; JA; Library Aide; SADD; Nwsp Rptr; Nwsp Stf; Yrbk Ed-Chief; Yrbk Stf; U CA San Diego; Psych.

REVIELLO, KEITH; Scraonton Prep Schl; Scranton, PA; (Y); Boys Clb Am; Exploring; Spanish Clb; Stage Crew; Var Ftbl; Wt Lftg; U Of Scranton.

REVILLA, JUAN A; Strath Haven HS; New York, NY; (Y); Spanish Clb; Varsity Clb; Trs Frsh Cls; JV Bsktbl; JV Var Ftbl; Var Capt Trk; Cit Awd; High Hon Roll; Hon Roll; Spanish NHS; Wesleyan U; Med.

REXA, CHRISTINE; St Francis Acad; Pittsburgh, PA; (S); 1/35; Chorus; Co-Capt Cheerleading; High Hon Roll; Recvd Awd Takg Frnch Tst PITT 84-85; Med Asst.

REXROTH, LYNNELLE; York County Area Vo-Tech; Mt Wolf, PA; (Y); Art Clb; Church Yth Grp; Cmnty Wkr; VICA; Chorus; Hon Roll; 1st Wldlif Ill, 2nd Sngl Color Ad Layout 86; Hgh Scr Cmmrcl Art Achvt 85-86; Cmmrcl Artst.

REYBITZ, JEFFREY; Freedom HS; Bethlehem, PA; (Y); 107/445; Art Clb; Camera Clb; Exploring; Ski Clb; Var Bsbl; Im Bsktbl; JV Ftbl; Hon Roll.

REYERSON, CHRISTINE; Unionville HS; West Chester, PA; (Y); JV Bsktbl; Var L Fld Hcky; Var L Lcrss; Im Powder Puff Ftbl; High Hon Roll; Jr NHS; NHS; A Grd In Every Discipline 84.

REYES, IRIS; Olney HS; Philadelphia, PA; (Y); JV Cheerleading; Chrldg Awd 84-85; Awd Of Merit 84; Temple U; Nrsg.

REYNARD, MICHELLE; Parkland SR HS; Breinigsville, PA; (Y); Sec Church Yth Grp; VP 4-H; Leo Clb; Church Choir; Color Guard; Chrmn Frsh Cls; 4-H Awd; Hon Roll; Lion Awd; Kutztown U PA; Phyclgy.

REYNOLDS, BARBARA; Sayre Area HS; Athens, PA; (Y); Spanish Clb; Yrbk Stf; Score Keeper; Trk; Hon Roll; Elem Ed.

REYNOLDS, DANIEL; Bishop O Reilly HS; Dallas, PA; (Y); Thesps; Chorus; School Play; Pres Jr Cls; Var Socr; Hon Roll; NHS; Rotary Awd; Church Yth Grp; Debate Tm; Natl Congrssnl Yth Leadrshp Conf 86; CDA Essay Contst-2nd Pl Div 2 84; Theology.

REYNOLDS, ERIN; Our Lady Of The Sacred Heart HS; Aliquippa, PA; (Y); 9/75; Girl Scts; NFL; School Play; Yrbk Stf; VP Frsh Cls; VP Soph Cls; Crs Cntry; DAR Awd; NHS; Pres Schlr; Pres Schlrshp 86; Girl Sct Awd 85; Lewis Cpln Hmn Rltns Awd 86; Lambuth Coll Jackson.

REYNOLDS, GREGORY M; Neshannock HS; New Castle, PA; (Y); 14/99; Aud/Vis; Church Yth Grp; Library Aide; Teachers Aide; Capt Crs Cntry; Trk; NHS; Walmo Lions Schlrshp 86; Grove Cty Coll Schlrshp 85-87; Grove Cty Coll.

REYNOLDS, KATHY; Central HS; Martinsburg, PA; (Y); 15/187; Girl Scts; Library Aide; Ski Clb; Band; Yrbk Stf; Hon Roll; NHS; Rotary Essay Cont 3rd Pl 86; JR Acad Sci Hnrb Mntn 86; Silv Awd Grl Scouts 84.

REYNOLDS, KELLY; Charleroi Area HS; Charleroi, PA; (Y); Church Yth Grp; Hosp Aide; Office Aide; Ski Clb; SADD; PA ST; Nrsg.

REYNOLDS, KELLY; Hempfield HS; Landisville, PA; (Y); 44/430; Letterman Clb; Varsity Clb; Sec Frsh Cls; Diving; Gym; Swmmng; Hon Roll; Lehigh U; Arts Engr.

REYNOLDS, KEVIN; Bethlehem Catholic HS; Bethlehem, PA; (Y); Church Yth Grp; Var Bsbl; Var Bsktbl; Hon Roll; NHS; Engrng.

REYNOLDS, PAMELA; Clarion-Limestone HS; Clarion, PA; (Y); 25/88; Intnl Clb; VP Chorus; VP Rep Stu Cncl; Var Cheerleading; Stat Ftbl; Var Trk; Drama Clb; French Clb; SADD; Rep At NASC Conf 85; Sr High Cnty Chorus 84-85; Clarion U Of PA; Comm.

REYNOLDS, SUSAN; Danville SR HS; Danville, PA; (Y); 85/202; Sec Church Yth Grp; FBLA; FHA; Hosp Aide; Pres SADD; Color Guard; Rep Stu Cncl; JV Bowling; Hon Roll; Prfct Atten Awd; Gregg Shorthnd Speed Tst Awd 85-86; Stu Govt Assn Awd 85-86; Peer Cnslr.

REYNOLDS, VICTORIA A; Abington HS; Meadowbrook, PA; (Y); 72/535; Varsity Clb; Rep Sr Cls; Rep Stu Cncl; Fld Hcky; Lcrss; Pres Acadmc Fitnss Awd 86; Cornell; Art.

REZNICK, MELISSA; Hazleton HS; Hazleton, PA; (Y); Spanish Clb; Color Guard; NHS; Spanish NHS; Orch; Yrbk Stf; Sociology.

REZZEMINI JR, HARRY L; Parkland SR HS; Fogelsville, PA; (Y); 12/459; JCL; Trs Key Clb; Political Wkr; Chorus; Lit Mag; Stu Cncl; High Hon Roll; NHS; Ntl Merit SF; Drama Clb; Semfnlst Crtv Wrtng PA Govs Schl For The Arts 86; Bst Wrtr Allegheny Coll Smmr Wrtng Prog 85; Engl.

RHAD, ANGELA; St Francis Acad; Pittsburgh, PA; (S); Math Tm; Nwsp Stf; Rep Frsh Cls; Rep Soph Cls; Var L Bsktbl; Var L Vllybl; High Hon Roll; NEDT Awd; Prfct Atten Awd; WPIAL Bsktbl Clss A Champ 85; Acadmc All Amer 85; Robert Morris Coll; Bus Adm.

RHEA, HEATHER; Purchase Line HS; Dixonville, PA; (Y); 21/111; French Clb; Chorus; Concert Band; Drm Mjr(t); VP Mrchg Band; VP Frsh Cls; VP Soph Cls; VP Jr Cls; Hon Roll; Vet Assist.

RHED, DAN; Brockway Area JR SR HS; Brockport, PA; (Y); 23/87; Boy Scts; God Cntry Awd; Hon Roll.

RHEE, MAGGIE; MMI Prep Schl; Mountaintop, PA; (Y); Art Clb; German Clb; Ski Clb; Yrbk Stf; JV Bowling; JV Crs Cntry; Sftbl; Hon Roll; German Hon Soc 85-86; PA JR Acad Of Sci.

RHEE, YUN SUN C; MMI Preparatory Schl; Mountain Top, PA; (S); Art Clb; Chess Clb; Church Yth Grp; Cmnty Wkr; Debate Tm; Drama Clb; Model UN; Science Clb; Ski Clb; Acpl Chr; Music.

RHEIN, PATTY; Sch Haven Area HS; Sch Haven, PA; (S); Am Leg Aux Girls St; Church Yth Grp; Dance Clb; FNA; SADD; Chorus; School Play; Var Cheerleading; Co-Capt Gym; Hon Roll; PA ST U; Nrsg.

RHEN, ROD; Pine Grove Area HS; Pine Grove, PA; (Y); 2/126; Varsity Clb; Nwsp Sprt Ed; Rep Stu Cncl; Bsbl; Bsktbl; Ftbl; Wt Lftg; Cit Awd; Hon Roll; Pres NHS; All Co Dfnsve Back Ftbl 85.

RHIEW, BETTY; Scranton Preparatory Schl; Clarks Green, PA; (Y); 4/197; Orch; Lit Mag; Var Cheerleading; Var Tennis; Var L Trk; High Hon Roll; NHS; Ntl Merit SF; Pa Govrnrs Schl Sci 86; Dist Orchstra 84-86; Med.

RHIEW, RICHARD; Scranton Preparatory Schl; Clarks Green, PA; (Y); 8/196; Orch; School Musical; Var Tennis; High Hon Roll; Hon Roll; NHS; Cmnd Stu Natl Mrt Schlrshp Prog 84; Hon Men Amer Chem Scty Tst 85; Cert Regntn IN U Physcs Tst 86; U Of PA; Bio.

RHINEHART, WILLIAM C; Shi Kellamy HS; Sunbury, PA; (Y); 36/316; Trs FBLA; Library Aide; Spanish Clb; Yrbk Bus Mgr; Yrbk Ed-Chief; Yrbk Stf; JV Bowling; Hon Roll; Nicholas B Ottaway Fndtn Schlrshp 86; $50 Svngs Bond Frm Bus Ed Dept 86; Blmsbrg U PA; CPA.

RHINES, AMANDA; Hopewell HS; Aliquippa, PA; (Y); 22/245; Exploring; German Clb; Spanish Clb; Band; Chorus; Hst Sr Cls; Stat Vllybl; NHS; Trs Church Yth Grp; Concert Band; Grl Scout Gold Awd 86; Rep Model Congress WA DC 86; Pol Sci.

RHOAD, GALEN; Northern Lebaron HS; Fredericksburg, PA; (Y); Aud/Vis; Boy Scts; Church Yth Grp; Band; Concert Band; Drill Tm; Jazz Band; Mrchg Band; Pep Band; Yrbk Phtg; Outstndng Acadmc Achvt Awd 86.

RHOADES, GLENN; Yough SR HS; Smithton, PA; (Y); Cmnty Wkr; ROTC; Var L Trk; Hon Roll; NHS; Boy Scts; Pep Clb; Hnry Yth Pres Natl Eagle Sct Assc & Eagle Sct Schlrp 85; US Army Rsrv 86; Order Of The Arrow 84; ROTC; Pre-Med.

RHOADES, JENNIFER; Line Mountain HS; Dalmatia, PA; (Y); 20/109; Am Leg Aux Girls St; FBLA; Hosp Aide; Varsity Clb; Concert Band; Nwsp Rptr; Rep Stu Cncl; Bsktbl; Fld Hcky; Sftbl; Millersville U; Spec Educ.

RHOADES, RICH; Brookville Area HS; Brookville, PA; (Y); 14/145; Chess Clb; Nwsp Rptr; Nwsp Stf; Bsktbl; L Trk; Hon Roll; NHS; Cmnctn Art.

RHOADES JR, WILLIAM; Homer Center HS; Homer City, PA; (Y); 17/106; Aud/Vis; Nwsp Sprt Ed; Sr Cls; Rep Stu Cncl; Hon Roll; Jr NHS; Kiwanis Awd; NHS; Ntl Merit Schol; Pres Schlr; PA JR Acad Of Sci 6 Yr Prsrvrnc Awd 86; Indiana U Of PA; Mrktng.

RHOADS, GRETCHEN; Warwick HS; Lititz, PA; (Y); 19/237; Thesps; Chorus; Drm Mjr(t); Mrchg Band; Orch; School Musical; Sec Sr Cls; Cheerleading; Sec NHS; Drama Clb; Schl Brd Rep 85-86; Drama.

RHOADS, ROBERT; Palmyra Area HS; Palmyra, PA; (Y); VP Church Yth Grp; JV Var Bsbl; JV Im Ftbl; High Hon Roll; Hon Roll; Ftbl Defnsv Plyr Of Yr 84.

RHODES, DAYNA; Dover Area HS; Dover, PA; (Y); 45/475; Church Yth Grp; Girl Scts; Band; Chorus; Concert Band; Mrchg Band; Yrbk Stf; Hon Roll; Spec Ed.

RHODES, DEBORAH LYNN; Warren Area HS; Warren, PA; (Y); French Clb; Hosp Aide; Chorus; Yrbk Stf; Trk; Hon Roll; Slvr Bee Awd 82-83; Clarion U PA; Mktg.

RHODES, JULIE; Tyrone Area HS; Tyrone, PA; (Y); Key Clb; Chorus; JV Cheerleading; High Hon Roll; Hon Roll; Jr NHS.

RHODES, KELLY; Windker HS; Windber, PA; (Y); 6/112; NHS; Hosp Aide; Ski Clb; Chorus; Color Guard; Yrbk Phtg; Yrbk Stf; Stu Cncl; Trk; High Hon Roll; Stu Mnth 84-86; Stu Yr 85; U Pittsburgh; Phys Thrpy.

RHODES, MARY JANE; Meadowview Christian Acad; Elysburg, PA; (S); Church Yth Grp; Library Aide; Chorus; Im Bsktbl; Im Socr; Hon Roll; Val; Nwsp Rptr; Nwsp Stf; Im Crs Cntry; 1st Pl ACE ST Stu Cnvntn Essy Wrtg Competn & 3rd Pl Shrt Stry Competn 85; 1st Pl Schl Sci Fair 84.

RHODES, MICHAEL; Central HS; Roaring Spring, PA; (Y); Art Clb; Chess Clb; Computer Clb; Ski Clb; Varsity Clb; Var L Bsbl; Var Golf; Vllybl; Hon Roll; Pttsbrg Inst Of Avonics; Panels.

RHODES, ROBERT; Roxborough HS; Philadelphia, PA; (Y); Aud/Vis; Computer Clb; High Hon Roll; NHS; Drexel; Elec.

RHODES, SANDRA; Otto-Eldred JR SR HS; Smethport, PA; (Y); 9/76; Band; Concert Band; Pres Mrchg Band; School Musical; Yrbk Stf; Hon Roll; NHS; Prfct Atten Awd; Mc Donalds All-Amer Mrchng Band 85; Semper Fidelis Aws For Musical Excllnc 86; Slippery Rock U; Pol Sci.

RHODES, TAMMY; Brookville Area HS; Brookville, PA; (Y); Art Clb; Church Yth Grp; FNA; Library Aide; Band; Flag Corp; Flag Corp; Mrchg Band; School Musical; Nrs.

RHODES, TINA; California Area HS; Elco, PA; (Y); Drama Clb; JA; Pep Clb; Ski Clb; Drill Tm; Mrchg Band; School Play; Nwsp Rptr; Yrbk Stf; 1st, 2nd, & 3rd Pl Span Cont 84-85; JR Stage 85-86; CA U; Psychology.

RHODES, WILLIAM J; Community Preparatory Acad; Erie, PA; (S); 1/7; Computer Clb; Yrbk Stf; Rep Stu Cncl; Hon Roll; Prfct Atten Awd; Hnr Grd 83-86; Chi-Rho Scty 84-86; Crusaders 83-86; Mercyhurst; Comp Sci.

RHODY, SCOTT; Minersville Area JR SR HS; Minersville, PA; (Y); French Clb; Ski Clb; SADD; School Play; Stage Crew; Var L Bsbl; Var L Bsktbl; Ftbl; Hon Roll.

RHONE, HOLLY; Susquehanna Comm HS; Susquehanna, PA; (Y); Church Yth Grp; 4-H; Girl Scts; Trs Soph Cls; Rep Stu Cncl; Cheerleading; Score Keeper; Sftbl; Hm Ec Awd 86; Nellie Jane De Witt BPW Clb 86; Empire Beauty Schl; Cosmtlgy.

RHONE, JEFF; Clearfield Area HS; Clearfield, PA; (S); Band; Chorus; Concert Band; Mrchg Band; Orch; Pep Band; School Musical; Swing Chorus; Variety Show; Chr Dist,Regnl And ST Altrnt 85-86; Edinboro U; Musc.

RHONE, LEANNE; Susquehanna Community HS; Starrucca, PA; (Y); Church Yth Grp; Ski Clb; Band; Chorus; Concert Band; Mrchg Band; Cheerleading; Crs Cntry; Trk; Ntl Merit Ltr; Art Thrpy.

RHUDY, KIM; Hanover HS; Hanover, PA; (Y); Church Yth Grp; Pep Clb; Chorus; Church Choir; Yrbk Rptr; Yrbk Stf; High Hon Roll; Hon Roll; Art.

RHYNER, SARAH; Bishop Guilfoyle HS; Altoona, PA; (S); Church Yth Grp; Science Clb; Ski Clb; Speech Tm; SADD; Teachers Aide; Band; Co-Capt Drill Tm; Mrchg Band; Yrbk Stf.

RHYU, JAMES; Lower Moreland HS; Huntingdon Valley, PA; (S); Church Yth Grp; VP Jr Cls; Var Socr; Var Trk; Im Wt Lftg; Var Wrstlng; Hon Roll; John Hopkens Schlrsp Smmr Prog 83; Stu Forum Rep 85-86; Cnty Math Pre Fous Yth Prog 83-85; Bus.

RIAL, HUGH; Highlands HS; Natrona Heights, PA; (Y); Pres Church Yth Grp; Trs 4-H; Band; VP Chorus; Concert Band; Mrchg Band; School Musical; Swing Chorus; Variety Show; Hon Roll; Pittsburgh Civic Light Opera Ministare 86; Mus Theater.

RIBBLE, CHARLES; Souderton HS; Schwenksville, PA; (Y); Aud/Vis; Boy Scts; Camera Clb; Church Yth Grp; 4-H; Quiz Bowl; Ski Clb; Band; School Musical; Stage Crew; Bloomsburg ST Coll; Bus.

RICCI, ALEX; Upper Moreland HS; Huntingdon Vly, PA; (Y); Key Clb; Rep Frsh Cls; Trs Soph Cls; Trs Jr Cls; Trs Sr Cls; Trs Stu Cncl; Var Bsbl; Var Socr; Var Trk; U Of CA Santa Barbara; Law.

RICCI, CYNDI; Bishop O Reilly HS; Kingston, PA; (Y); 4-H; Drill Tm; 4-H Awd; Hon Roll; Hosp Aide; Chorus; Stage Crew; Luzerne Cnty CC; Pthlgy.

RICCIO, MICHAEL; St Josephs Prep Schl; Philadelphia, PA; (Y); Boy Scts; Computer Clb; Mathletes; L Var Bowling; 1st Pl St Joes U Rgnl Pgmmng Cntst 86; Comp Sci.

RICCIO, RICHARD; Hazleton SR HS; Hazleton, PA; (Y); Teachers Aide; Chorus; Stage Crew; Sec Stu Cncl; Bsktbl; Ftbl; Trk; NHS; Williamsport Area CC; Equip Op.

RICCITELLI, DINA; Quigley HS; Aliquippa, PA; (S); 17/112; Exploring; Math Tm; Pep Clb; Chorus; Church Choir; Nwsp Stf; Stu Cncl; Cheerleading; Coach Actv; Swmmng; Ntl Hnr Roll 86; Acadmc All Amercn 86; Duquesne U; Phrmcy.

RICCO, PAMELA; Bishop Hafey HS; Hazleton, PA; (Y); 41/129; French Clb; Color Guard; French Hon Soc; Cert Of Merit Outstndng Perfmce French II 84-85; French.

RICE, ANITA; Abington Senior HS; Abington, PA; (Y); JV Fld Hcky; Lion Awd; Lions Clb Awd Fr Ovrcmng Grt Hndicp 86; Bus Adm.

RICE, BECKY; Southmoreland SR HS; Scottdale, PA; (Y); French Clb; Pep Clb; Teachers Aide; VICA; Chorus; Yrbk Ed-Chief; Rep Stu Cncl; JV Cheerleading; Var Powder Puff Ftbl; Var Sftbl; PBA; Beauty Prof.

RICE, DONNA; Wyoming Area HS; W Wyoming, PA; (Y); 2/210; VP Church Yth Grp; Ski Clb; Co-Capt Capt Color Guard; Hon Roll; Psych.

RICE, JEN S; Quakerton SR HS; Quakertown, PA; (Y); Art Clb; Church Yth Grp; Chorus; JV Fld Hcky; JV Tennis; JV Trk; Hon Roll; Bluffton Coll; Econ.

RICE, JENNIFER; Ephrata SR HS; Ephrata, PA; (Y); 31/280; Trs Church Yth Grp; Exploring; Spanish Clb; Band; Concert Band; JV Fld Hcky; Var L Sftbl; Var L Tennis; Hon Roll; Aerontcl Engrng.

RICE, JILL; Tyrone Area HS; Tyrone, PA; (Y); 36/179; Church Yth Grp; Cmnty Wkr; SADD; Varsity Clb; Var Capt Bsktbl; Score Keeper; Sftbl; Elks Awd; High Hon Roll; Hon Roll; PTO Schlrshp 86; Alpha Delta Kappa Schlrshp 86; Lycoming Coll; Elem Educ.

RICE, JOHN; Peters Township HS; Mcmurray, PA; (Y); Var JV Ftbl; U Of Pittsburgh; Bus.

RICE, KEITH; Shenandoah Valley HS; Shenandoah, PA; (S); 1/100; Rptr Yrbk Stf; Trs Sr Cls; Trs Stu Cncl; JV Var Bsktbl; L Ftbl; Wt Lftg; High Hon Roll; Trs NHS; 1st Tm All Cnty Offnsv Grd & Dfnsv Tckl 85; Schlr Athl 85; Marine Biolgst.

RICE, LYNNETTE; Plum SR HS; Pittsburgh, PA; (Y); FBLA; FHA; Girl Scts; Color Guard; Yrbk Stf; Var L Trk; Hon Roll.

RICE, MARCY; Susquehanna Comm HS; Susquehanna, PA; (Y); 4/75; Yrbk Ed-Chief; Pres Frsh Cls; Pres Soph Cls; Pres Jr Cls; Pres Sr Cls; Sec Stu Cncl; Capt Cheerleading; Powder Puff Ftbl; Hon Roll; NHS.

RICE, MARGARET; Susquehanna Community HS; Susquehanna, PA; (S); Yrbk Ed-Chief; Pres Soph Cls; Pres Jr Cls; Pres Sr Cls; Sec Stu Cncl; Capt Cheerleading; Var Trk; High Hon Roll; NHS; Ntl Merit Ltr; Philadelphia Coll; Phrmcst.

RICE, NANCE; Pocono Mt HS; Tobyhanna, PA; (Y); Church Yth Grp; Girl Scts; SADD; JV Powder Puff Ftbl; High Hon Roll; Hon Roll; Harvard; Law.

RICE, RUSSELL; Pennsbury HS; Yardley, PA; (Y); Boy Scts; Church Yth Grp; Stage Crew; Var Bowling; Hon Roll; Accntng.

RICE, SIRENA; Hollidaysbug SR HS; Hollidaysburg, PA; (Y); 5/349; Church Yth Grp; Color Guard; Concert Band; Mrchg Band; Yrbk Bus Mgr; Yrbk Phtg; Yrbk Stf; High Hon Roll; Jr NHS; NHS; Pres Schrlshp Liberty U 86; Liberty U.

RICE, SUSAN; Susquenita HS; Duncannon, PA; (S); Yrbk Sprt Ed; Stu Cncl; Fld Hcky; Trk; Hon Roll; Bloomsburg Coll; Dentl Hyg.

RICEDORF, STEPHANIE; Donegal HS; Mount Joy, PA; (Y); 5/165; Varsity Clb; Rep Frsh Cls; JV Bsktbl; Var Sftbl; Var L Tennis; Hon Roll; NHS.

RICEVUTO, JOANNE; West Chester East HS; West Chester, PA; (Y); 80/396; Sec Jr Cls; Sec Sr Cls; Stu Cncl; JV Bsktbl; Var Fld Hcky; JV Trk; Hon Roll; Spanish NHS; Prsdnt Of Spnsh Natl Hnr Society 84-86; W Chester U; Math.

RICH, CHERYL; Nazareth Acad; Philadelphia, PA; (S); 17/121; Cmnty Wkr; Hosp Aide; NFL; Spanish Clb; L Speech Tm; Off Church Choir; Pres Frsh Cls; Stu Cncl; Var Tennis; Hon Roll; Holy Redeemer Hosp Awd 84; Early Childhd Ed.

RICH, ERIC; Jersey Shore Area SR HS; Jersey Shore, PA; (Y); Computer Clb; FBLA; Science Clb; Ski Clb; Band; Bloomsburg; Geology.

RICH, JANET; Newport HS; Newport, PA; (Y); Girl Scts; Band; Chorus; Concert Band; Jazz Band; Mrchg Band; School Musical; School Play; Swing Chorus; Hon Roll; Modern Music Masters 83-86; VP Band 85-86; Shippensburg U; Mrktng.

RICH, WENDY JEAN; Lewisburg Area HS; Lewisburg, PA; (Y); 2/175; Am Leg Aux Girls St; Church Yth Grp; VP Acpl Chr; School Musical; School Play; Trs Lit Mag; Var Cheerleading; NHS; Chorus; JV Tennis; PA Gov Schl Arts 86.

RICHARD, CHRISTINE; Shaler Area HS; Glenshaw, PA; (Y); 32/521; Hosp Aide; JA; Trs SADD; Rep Frsh Cls; Rep Soph Cls; Rep Jr Cls; High Hon Roll; NEDT Awd; Natl Sci Olympd Bio 84-86; Miss Amer Coed Pgnt PA Fnlst 86; Pltcl Sci.

RICHARD, KATIE; Newport HS; Wila, PA; (Y); Pres Church Yth Grp; Sec 4-H; Teachers Aide; Band; Concert Band; Mrchg Band; School Play; Yrbk Stf; JV Sftbl; Hon Roll; Tri-M Hstrn 85; PYEA VP 85.

RICHARD, MELISSA; Crestwood HS; White Haven, PA; (Y); FBLA; Chorus; Score Keeper; Sftbl; Hon Roll; NEDT Awd; Geo.

RICHARDS, ALESIA; Bradford Central Christian HS; Bradford, PA; (Y); Drama Clb; Pep Clb; Ski Clb; SADD; Nwsp Stf; Rep Stu Cncl; Var Bsktbl; Var Sftbl; Hon Roll; Jr NHS; Elem Tchr.

RICHARDS, B KEITH; New Brighton HS; New Brighton, PA; (Y); 23/154; Band; Concert Band; Jazz Band; Mrchg Band; School Play; Nwsp Rptr; High Hon Roll; Hon Roll; Pres Schlr; U Pittsburgh; Phrmcy.

RICHARDS, CRAIG; Bald Eagle Area HS; Howard, PA; (Y); Boy Scts; Church Yth Grp; Trk; Wrstlng; Valley Forge; Pastor.

RICHARDS, GRETCHEN; East Stroudsburg HS; E Stbg, PA; (Y); 43/225; Church Yth Grp; Girl Scts; Hosp Aide; Office Aide; Pep Clb; Red Cross Aide; Band; Concert Band; Mrchg Band; Pep Band; Lds Axlry Vtrns Frgn Wrs US Ldrshp Ctn 84-85; Grl Sct Slvr Awd 83-84; 2 Cert Of Merit; Scdry Ed.

RICHARDS, JEANNE; Danville SR HS; Danville, PA; (Y); 115/202; Exploring; Latin Clb; Red Cross Aide; SADD; Rep Frsh Cls; Hon Roll; Radiology.

RICHARDS, KAREN L; E L Meyers HS; Wilkes-Barre, PA; (Y); 20/146; Girl Scts; Chorus; Church Choir; VP Jr Cls; VP Sr Cls; DAR Awd; NHS; Art Clb; Church Yth Grp; Dance Clb; PA Gvrnrs Schl Arts In Dance Schlrshp 84; ARTS Ntl Semi Fnlst Modern Dance 86; Ntl Schstc Art Awd 86; Juilliard School; Dance.

RICHARDS, KELLY; Schuylkill Valley HS; Reading, PA; (Y); 20/126; Concert Band; Capt Bsktbl; L Fld Hcky; Sftbl; L Trk; Capt Vllybl; Hon Roll; NHS; SICO Schlrshp Millersville U 86; Partl Schlrshp Bsktbl 86; Millersville U; Bio.

RICHARDS, KRISTY L; Mcconnellsburg HS; Mc Connellsburg, PA; (Y); 1/80; Pres Church Yth Grp; Pres Band; Chorus; Drm Mjr(t); Nwsp Stf; Trs Sr Cls; Var L Trk; Gov Hon Prg Awd; Ntl Merit Schol; Val; Cornell U; Zoology.

RICHARDS, MARK; Laurel Valley HS; New Florence, PA; (Y); 4/87; Scholastic Bowl; VP Varsity Clb; Chorus; School Play; Stu Cncl; Var L Bsbl; Var L Bsktbl; Var L Ftbl; Hon Roll; NHS; 3rd German Prose Humanities Day 85.

RICHARDS, MEREDITH A; North Allegheny HS; Pittsburgh, PA; (Y); 124/605; Church Yth Grp; JA; Library Aide; Chorus; Variety Show; Socr; Hon Roll; Indiana U PA; Nrs.

RICHARDS, PIPER; Moshannon Valley HS; Brisbin, PA; (Y); 15/120; Ski Clb; Band; Chorus; Church Choir; Mrchg Band; Orch; Pep Band; Stage Crew; High Hon Roll; Hon Roll; Exec Sec.

RICHARDS, RAHN; Tri-Valley JR SR HS; Hegins, PA; (Y); 17/77; Boy Scts; Drama Clb; School Musical; Yrbk Phtg; Hst Jr Cls; Var L Ftbl; Im Sftbl; Im Wt Lftg; JV Wrstlng; NEDT Awd; Lge All Star Tm-Ftbl 85; Hampden-Sydney; Pre Med.

RICHARDS, RALPH; Marian HS; Mahanoy City, PA; (Y); 13/114; Church Yth Grp; Cmnty Wkr; Math Clb; Spanish Clb; SADD; Rep Frsh Cls; Pres Soph Cls; Rep Jr Cls; Stu Cncl; Bsbl; Ftbl; Yth Grp Advsr; Rep Allentown Diocese; Stu Cncl; St Trooper.

RICHARDS, RENEE; Northern SR HS; Dillsburg, PA; (Y); 3/209; Sec French Clb; Yrbk Phtg; Yrbk Sprt Ed; Rep Sr Cls; Var L Bsktbl; Var L Sftbl; French Hon Soc; High Hon Roll; Ntl Merit Ltr; Rotary Awd; Pre Vet.

RICHARDS, TONY; Johnstown HS; Johnstown, PA; (Y); Musicians Institute; Music.

RICHARDSON, CHRIS; W Middlesex Area HS; W Middlesex, PA; (S); 4/110; Church Yth Grp; Office Aide; Spanish Clb; Off Stu Cncl; Bsktbl; CC Awd; High Hon Roll; Jr NHS; NHS; Spanish NHS; SPAN Stu 85-87; Pilot.

RICHARDSON, DARLINDA; Chester HS; Chester, PA; (Y); Church Yth Grp; 4-H; Girl Scts; Hosp Aide; Library Aide; Office Aide; Teachers Aide; Chorus; Church Choir; Drill Tm; Bus Admn.

RICHARDSON, DORIS; Williamsburg HS; Williamsburg, PA; (Y); Church Yth Grp; FFA; FNA; Nwsp Rptr; Nrsng.

RICHARDSON, ERIC A; Bishop Kenrick HS; Collegeville, PA; (Y); 5/311; Mathletes; Rep Frsh Cls; Rep Soph Cls; Rep Jr Cls; Pres Stu Cncl; Var Capt Swmmng; Var Tennis; DAR Awd; NHS; Opt Clb Awd; Rotry Schlrshp Attgend Camp Neidig 86; Norristown Exchange Clubs Yth Of Yr 86.

RICHARDSON JR, JOHN A; Harry S Truman HS; Croydon, PA; (Y); SADD; JV Socr; Hon Roll; Temple U; Comp.

RICHARDSON, KAREN; Palisades HS; Kintnersville, PA; (Y); Drama Clb; Spanish Clb; Varsity Clb; Acpl Chr; Chorus; Madrigals; School Musical; School Play; Stage Crew; Swing Chorus.

RICHARDSON, MARY; J P Mc Caskey HS; Lancaster, PA; (Y); 1/439; VP Pres AFS; Cmnty Wkr; Capt Dance Clb; Speech Tm; Variety Show; Nwsp Rptr; Ed Yrbk Stf; Ed Lit Mag; Rep Stu Cncl; High Hon Roll; Ntl Hnr Soc Schlrshp 86; PA Govrns Schl Intl Stds 85; Amer Lgn Awd 86; Williams Coll; Envrnmntl Sci.

RICHARDSON, RUTH; Laurel Highlands SR HS; Uniontown, PA; (Y); Trs Church Yth Grp; Chrmn FBLA; JA; Office Aide; Teachers Aide; Band; Concert Band; Mrchg Band; Nwsp Stf; Sec Soph Cls; Robert Morris-Carthage; Bus Adm.

RICHARDSON, TINA; Mc Keesport Area HS; White Oak, PA; (Y); 17/350; Church Yth Grp; Exploring; Office Aide; Band; Concert Band; Mrchg Band; Symp Band; Cit Awd; High Hon Roll; Hon Roll; Semper Fidelis Schrlshp 86; IN U; Math.

RICHART, MICHELLE; Muncy HS; Muncy, PA; (Y); Church Yth Grp; Pep Clb; Trs Spanish Clb; Varsity Clb; Band; Chorus; School Musical; Co-Capt Cheerleading; Hon Roll; Spanish NHS; Wrthy Advsr Of Rnbw 85; Sophmr-Hstrn 85; Air Force.

RICHBERG, MARK H; Central HS; Philadelphia, PA; (Y); 22/225; Varsity Clb; Rep Sr Cls; JV Var Ftbl; JV Var Tennis; Hon Roll; Ntl Merit SF.

RICHES, JONATHAN S; Philadelphia Montgomery Christ Acad; Pipersville, PA; (Y); 1/41; Ed Nwsp Stf; Ed Lit Mag; VP Trs Stu Cncl; High Hon Roll; NHS; Pres Schlr; Rotary Awd; Val; Cmnty Wkr; Band; Philmonts SR Sci Awd-Outstndg Perfm Sci 86; SR Hstry Awd-Showing Keen Interest In Hstry 86; PA ST U; Vet.

RICHEY, MARCIA; Ringgold SR HS; Monongahela, PA; (Y); 1/320; Church Yth Grp; Computer Clb; Girl Scts; Office Aide; Service Clb; Chorus; Stu Cncl; High Hon Roll; NHS; Val; $250 From Firehall 86; WV U; Mech Engrng.

RICHMOND, ANN; Steelton-Highspire HS; Highspire, PA; (Y); 19/94; Church Yth Grp; VP FBLA; Girl Scts; Office Aide; Trk; Hon Roll; Outstndng Bus Stud Of The 2nd Mrkng Prd 86; Horrizburg Area Cmnty Cll; Acct.

RICHMOND, JAY; Mahanoy Area HS; Mahanoy City, PA; (Y); Ski Clb; Stage Crew; Variety Show; Rep Soph Cls; Stu Cncl; Im Bsktbl; Var L Ftbl; Var L Trk; Wt Lftg; JV Wrstlng.

RICHMOND, SHARON; Trinity HS; Washington, PA; (Y); 53/374; Debate Tm; Exploring; Key Clb; Math Tm; Pep Clb; Ski Clb; Speech Tm; High Hon Roll; Hon Roll; NEDT Awd; Accntng.

RICHMOND, W JAY; Mc Guffey HS; Claysville, PA; (Y); 10/201; Boy Scts; Church Yth Grp; Letterman Clb; Model UN; Pep Clb; VP Spanish Clb; Varsity Clb; Var L Golf; High Hon Roll; NHS; Acad All-Amer 86; Cert Of Awd For Outstndng Prfmnc 86; Tchng.

RICHTER, NANCI; Phil-Mont Christian Acad; North Hills, PA; (Y); Church Yth Grp; Teachers Aide; Chorus; Church Choir; Concert Band; Hon Roll; JV Bsktbl; JV Var Fld Hcky; Eastern Coll; Accntng.

RICHTER, PENNY; Springdale HS; Springdale, PA; (Y); 15/114; FBLA; GAA; Acpl Chr; Score Keeper; Vllybl; High Hon Roll; Hon Roll; Outstdng Perf Typng II 86; 2nd Pl FBLA Rgnl Bus Math Cmptn 85; 15th Pl FBLA ST Bus Math Cmptn 85; New Kensington Commercial; Acct.

RICHTER, STACEY; Annville-Cleonna HS; Annville, PA; (S); 6/121; Model UN; Varsity Clb; School Musical; Nwsp Rptr; Lit Mag; Fld Hcky; Trk; NHS; Ntl Merit Ltr; Wodsmn Of Wrld Amercn Hstry Awd 84; Schltc Wrtng Awd-Hnrb Mntn 85; PA Gvrnrs Schl Arts-Semi Fnlst 85; Engl.

RICHTER, TAMMY; Connellsville SR HS; Normalville, PA; (Y); Library Aide; Hon Roll; Spanish NHS; German Natl Hnr Scty 85-86; U Of Pittsburgh.

RICHWINE, MARK; Northern York County HS; Dillsburg, PA; (Y); 11/209; VP Band; Pres Chorus; VP Concert Band; Jazz Band; VP Mrchg Band; Orch; School Musical; Symp Band; High Hon Roll; Hon Roll.

RICK II, DAVID T; Hamburg Area JR SR HS; Hamburg, PA; (Y); Latin Clb; VP Spanish Clb; Rep Sr Cls; VP Stu Cncl; JV Var Bowling; JV Im Socr; Hon Roll; NHS; Dance Clb; Acadmc Ltr Awd Wrld Cult 84-85; Acadmc Lttr Awd Am Hist 85-86; JR Clss Spirt Awd 86; Socl Stu Ed.

RICKARD, CHELENE; Penn-Trafford HS; Irwin, PA; (Y); 74/344; FBLA; Chorus; JV Sftbl; Var Trk; High Hon Roll; Hon Roll; Cert Of Prfcncy 85-86.

RICKARD, JENNIFER D; Curwensville HS; Curwensville, PA; (Y); DECA; Hosp Aide; Drama Clb; FNA; Library Aide; Chorus; Mat Maids; 3rd Pl Comptn DECA 86; Candystriper Hat 84-85; Bradford Bus Coll; Bus Mgt.

RICKENBACH, MARK G; Schuylkill Valley HS; Reading, PA; (Y); 10/126; Aud/Vis; Quiz Bowl; School Musical; Stage Crew; Var L Trk; Vllybl; Bausch & Lomb Sci Awd; High Hon Roll; NHS; Pres Schlr; USAF; Physics.

RICKENBAUGH, JOELLE; East Juniata HS; Mcalistervl, PA; (Y); Chess Clb; Chorus; School Musical; Yrbk Phtg; Rep Jr Cls; Rep Stu Cncl; Fld Hcky; Stat Ftbl; Hon Roll; Snowball Princess 83-84; May Day Attdnt 83-84; Empire Beauty Schl; Csmtlgy.

RICKERT, JENNIFER; Bishop Kenrick HS; Norristown, PA; (Y); Cmnty Wkr; French Clb; Political Wkr; Science Clb; Ski Clb; School Play; Variety Show; Hon Roll; Villanova; Bus.

RICKERT, JILL; Meadville Area SR HS; Meadville, PA; (Y); Chorus; Concert Band; Nwsp Stf; Var L Socr; Hon Roll; PA Dist II Chrs Fstvl 85 & 86; Music.

RICKETTS, CONSTANCE; Moshannon Valley JR SR HS; Irvona, PA; (Y); 4-H; Hosp Aide; Spanish Clb; Chorus; Church Choir; IN U; Nrsng.

RICKLES, NATHANIEL; Cheltenham HS; Philadelphia, PA; (Y); 59/365; Debate Tm; Hosp Aide; Temple Yth Grp; Stage Crew; Nwsp Rptr; Score Keeper; Timer; Rep Stu Cncl; Hugh O Brien Ldrshp Seminar 85; Awd Excellnce Religious HS 85; Confirmatn Religious Educ Pres Clss 86; Med.

RICKMAN, SHELLEY; Lakeview HS; Mercer, PA; (Y); FHA; Library Aide.

RICOTTA, PENNY; Conemaugh Township HS; Davidsville, PA; (Y); 23/105; JA; Ski Clb; VP Chorus; Flag Corp; School Play; Nwsp Stf; Lit Mag; Stu Cncl; Score Keeper; Hon Roll; Clarion U; Elem Tchr.

RIDDELL, SHERRI; Montgomery Area JR-SR HS; Allenwood, PA; (Y); Church Yth Grp; French Clb; Varsity Clb; Band; Concert Band; Drm Mjr(t); Sec Soph Cls; Sec Jr Cls; Var Bsktbl; NHS; Lock Haven U PA; Elem Ed.

RIDDELL, TONYA; Belle Vernon Area HS; Belle Vernon, PA; (Y); Pres Church Yth Grp; Pep Clb; Pres Chorus; Church Choir; Hon Roll; Pittsburgh U; Nrsng.

RIDDLE, DAVID M; Westmont Hilltop HS; Johnstown, PA; (Y); 7/142; Am Leg Boys St; Church Yth Grp; Band; Concert Band; Drm Mjr(t); Jazz Band; Mrchg Band; JV Bsktbl; High Hon Roll; JP Sousa Awd; U Of Pittsburgh.

RIDDLE, MITCHELL A; Red Lion SR HS; Red Lion, PA; (Y); 29/340; Boy Scts; Varsity Clb; Soph Cls; Jr Cls; VP Sr Cls; VP Stu Cncl; Socr; Capt Tennis; Trs NHS; Rotary Awd; Lebanon Vly Smmrs Schlrs Pgm 85; PA ST U; Med.

RIDENHOUR, MARY BETH; Gettysburg Area SR HS; Gettysburg, PA; (Y); 2/238; Church Yth Grp; Church Choir; Orch; Sal; Trs German Clb; Model UN; School Musical; Hon Roll; NHS; Juniata Coll; Bio.

RIDENOUR, KRISTIN; Southmoreland SR HS; Scottdale, PA; (Y); 40/243; French Clb; Hosp Aide; Pep Clb; Ski Clb; Concert Band; Mrchg Band; Socr; Sftbl; Bus Adm.

RIDER, CLINT; Bellefonte HS; Pleasant Gap, PA; (Y); German Clb; Im Fld Hcky; Var L Tennis; High Hon Roll; Acad Achvt Pin 84-85; Bloomsburg U; Acctng.

RIDER, LINETTA; Juniata HS; Mifflintown, PA; (Y); Church Yth Grp; Girl Scts; Band; Chorus; Stage Crew; Rep Stu Cncl; High Hon Roll; Hon Roll; NHS; Church Choir; Tri-M Mdrn Msc Mstrs 86; Elem Educ.

RIDER, TAMMY; Bellefonte SR HS; Pleasant Gap, PA; (Y); Library Aide; SADD; Hon Roll; Exec Asst.

RIDGELL, TRISSA; Seneca Valley SR HS; Mars, PA; (Y); Drama Clb; JA; Drill Tm; Mrchg Band; School Play; Symp Band; Nwsp Stf; Capt Pom Pon; Hon Roll; NHS; Hugh O Brian Ldrshp; Amer Yth Symph; Butler Cnty JR Miss Fnlst; Pre-Med.

RIDGEWAY, DEAN; Shaler HS; Allison Pk, PA; (Y); 163/517; JA; Rifle Tm Var 84-85&85-86; Shaler Art Show Arch Dsgn 3rd 86; Shaler Art Show Wood Wrkng 1st 85; Arch.

RIECKS, SHANNON; Beth Center HS; Clarksville, PA; (Y); 25/167; Ski Clb; Spanish Clb; Rep Jr Cls; Socr.

RIEDE, VICCI; Grove Cty HS; Grove City, PA; (Y); 6/185; Sec Key Clb; Science Clb; School Play; Yrbk Stf; Rep Stu Cncl; JV Var Cheerleading; High Hon Roll; NHS; Church Yth Grp; Winter Festival Court 85-86; Sci.

RIEDEL, RICHARD; W B Saul HS; Phialelphia, PA; (Y); 75/166; Boy Scts; Cmnty Wkr; Red Cross Aide; Service Clb; Off Sr Cls; Prfct Atten Awd; Eagle Scout 85; Ad Alatre Dei Religious Awd 83; Agriculture.

RIEDEL, SEAN; J P Mc Caskey HS; Lancaster, PA; (Y); 5/450; Variety Show; Rep Stu Cncl; Var Socr; JV Wrstlng; Hon Roll; NHS; Bus.

RIEDEL, TED; Red Land HS; New Cumberland, PA; (Y); 3/275; Am Leg Boys St; Quiz Bowl; Spanish Clb; Im Vllybl; High Hon Roll; Spanish NHS; Natl Spn Exam 1st Cntrl PA Regn, 3rd Overall Natn 84-85, 1st Cntrl PA Regn 85-86; Spg Lang Cont; Lehigh U; Engrng.

RIEDER, MARC; Greensburg Central Catholic HS; Greensburg, PA; (Y); Boy Scts; Church Yth Grp; Var Bsbl; JV Bsktbl; Var Ice Hcky; Var Mgr(s); Var Socr; Im Tennis; High Hon Roll; Hon Roll; Bus Econ.

RIEDY, DANIEL; William Allen HS; Allentown, PA; (Y); Cmnty Wkr; Exploring; Pres JA; JCL; Latin Clb; Quiz Bowl; Jr NHS; Prfct Atten Awd; PA ST; Mech Engr.

RIEDY, MARK; William Allen HS; Allentown, PA; (Y); 102/606; ROTC; Ski Clb; JV Var Bsbl; JV Var Bsktbl; Var Golf; Hon Roll; Naval Acad; Nvl Aviation.

RIEGER, MICHELLE; Shikellamy SR HS; Sunbury, PA; (Y); Church Yth Grp; French Clb; FBLA; L Capt Fld Hcky; L Capt Sftbl; L Trk; Hon Roll; Prom Qn 86; Hmcmg Ct 86; Bst Drssd SR Girl 86; Med Trnscrptnst.

RIEGER, PAUL; Notre Dame HS; Stroudsburg, PA; (Y); School Musical; School Play; Nwsp Rptr; Rep Jr Cls; VP Stu Cncl; Var Bsbl; Var Bsktbl; Var Socr; Hon Roll; NHS; Best Offensive Player ESU Soccer Camp 85; Holy Cross; Bio.

RIEGNER JR, DANIEL J; Seton La Salle HS; Pittsburgh, PA; (Y); Boy Scts; Church Yth Grp; Cmnty Wkr; Exploring; Ftbl; Hon Roll; Arch.

RIEGNER, LORI L; Pottstown SR HS; Pottstown, PA; (S); 10/183; Drama Clb; French Clb; Latin Clb; Thesps; Acpl Chr; Chorus; Color Guard; Mrchg Band; School Musical; School Play; Allentown Coll; Theatr.

RIEHL, GARY; Hamburg Area HS; Strausstown, PA; (Y); Hon Roll; Elctrncs.

RIEHL, ROSE; Dequea Valley HS; Kinzers, PA; (Y); 24/142; AFS; Color Guard; Stage Crew; Yrbk Stf; Rep Soph Cls; Off Stu Cncl; Fld Hcky; Gym; Hon Roll; Social Wrk.

RIEK, MELISSA; Bishop Mc Cort HS; Johnstown, PA; (Y); Latin Clb; Chorus; School Musical; School Play; High Hon Roll; Hon Roll; Mu Alp Tht; NHS; Mt Aloysius JC; Travel.

RIEKER, MICHAEL; Annville-Cleona HS; Cleona, PA; (Y); CAP; Cmnty Wkr; German Clb; Hosp Aide; Red Cross Aide; Stage Crew; Crs Cntry; Hugh O Brian Ldrshp Semnr Ambssdr 85; Cvl Air Patrl Billy Awd Natl Awd 86; Emrgncy Nrsg.

RIENDEAU, RALPH; Father Judge HS; Philadelphia, PA; (S); 37/403; Church Yth Grp; Swmmng; Hon Roll; NHS; Metrlgy.

RIEPPEL, KIM; Cowanesque Valley HS; Cowanesque, PA; (S); 6/96; VP Church Yth Grp; French Clb; Letterman Clb; Quiz Bowl; SADD; Varsity Clb; Stat Bsktbl; Mgr(s); Score Keeper; Var Tennis; Stu Of Mnth 85; Chrch Awd 84; Lycoming Coll; Accntg.

RIES, CATHYANN; Nazareth Acad; Philadelphia, PA; (Y); German Clb; Girl Scts; Sec Math Clb; Chrmn NFL; Speech Tm; Variety Show; NHS; Ntl Merit Ltr; Prfct Atten Awd; Schlrshp Nazareth Acad 83; Schlrshp St Huberts 83.

RIESMEYER, TERESA; Seneca Valley SR HS; Evans City, PA; (Y); SADD; VP Thesps; School Musical; School Play; Stage Crew; High Hon Roll; Hon Roll; NHS; Church Yth Grp; Church Choir; Bst Stg Mgr 85; Bst Acrts & Thspn 86; Allghny Coll; Psych.

RIFE, BRIAN; Phoenixville Area HS; Phoenixville, PA; (Y); Key Clb; Varsity Clb; School Musical; Var Bsktbl; Var Ftbl; Var Wt Lftg; Hon Roll; Jr NHS; NHS; Acdmc All Amer.

RIFKIN, STACEY; Wyoming Valley West HS; Kingston, PA; (Y); 14/424; FBLA; Key Clb; Ski Clb; VP Temple Yth Grp; Chorus; Var L Cheerleading; High Hon Roll; Hon Roll; NHS; Ntl Cncl Yth Ldrshp 86-87; Biochem.

RIFUGIATO, LYNNE; Penn Hills HS; Pittsburgh, PA; (Y); 150/800; Cmnty Wkr; French Clb; Hon Roll; Natl Svc Ldrshp Awd 86; John Carroll U; Psych.

RIGATTI, BRIAN; Highlands SR HS; Natrona Hts, PA; (Y); 7/277; Key Clb; Varsity Clb; Var L Ftbl; Var L Trk; NHS; Natl Sci Merit Awd 85-86; Acad All Amer 85-86; Pres Acad Fit Awd 85-86; U Pittsburgh; Pre-Med.

RIGBY, LAUREL; Corry Area HS; Spring Creek, PA; (S); 21/216; Band; Concert Band; Mrchg Band; Pep Band; Yrbk Stf; High Hon Roll; French Clb; Girl Scts; Yrbk Phtg; Acctng.

RIGGAR, AMY; Connellsville Area SR HS; S Connellsville, PA; (Y); 72/500; DECA; Pep Clb; Jr Cls; 7th Pl Wnnr DECA Dist 3 Cmpttn 85.

RIGGIN, BETH; Connellsville SR HS; Dawson, PA; (Y); 66/550; Church Yth Grp; FBLA; FTA; Office Aide; Chorus; Yrbk Stf; High Hon Roll; Hon Roll; Seton Hill Coll; Elem Educ.

RIGGIN, ROBERT; Uniontown HS; Smock, PA; (Y); Spanish Clb; High Hon Roll; Hon Roll; Spanish NHS; Military.

RIGGINS, FRANK; Lake-Lehman HS; Shavertown, PA; (Y); Church Yth Grp; Ski Clb; Band; Concert Band; Jazz Band; Mrchg Band; Symp Band; NHS; Hon Roll; Jr NHS; PMEA Dist IX Band 86; PMEA Regn IV Band 86; JR Deacon Huntsville Chrstn Church 84-86; PA ST U; Engrng.

RIGGLE, APRIL; Ford City JR SR HS; Ford City, PA; (Y); Drama Clb; 4-H; Spanish Clb; VICA; Color Guard; Rep Soph Cls; Twrlr; Hon Roll; 3rd Pl VICA Opnng & Clsng Ceremonies 86; Pittsburgh Beauty Acad; Csmtlgy.

RIGGLE, BECKY; Trinity HS; Washington, PA; (Y); Church Yth Grp; Civic Clb; German Clb; Office Aide; Pep Clb; Nwsp Stf; PA ST; Bus Admn.

RIGGLE, CARRIE L; Leechburg Area HS; Leechburg, PA; (Y); Drama Clb; Band; Concert Band; Mrchg Band; Variety Show; Nwsp Rptr; Nwsp Stf; Yrbk Rptr; Yrbk Stf; JV Var Cheerleading; Comm.

RIGGS, DENNIS; Mc Guffey HS; Washington, PA; (Y); German Clb; Crs Cntry; Church Yth Grp; School Play.

RIGNEY, AISLING B; Allentown Central Catholic HS; Allentown, PA; (Y); 5/224; Am Leg Aux Girls St; Trs French Clb; Math Clb; Rep Jr Cls; Trs Stu Cncl; Var L Cheerleading; High Hon Roll; NHS; Prfct Atten Awd; James F Martin Memrl Awd Frnch 86; Socty Womn Engrs Cert Merit Hnr Sci & Math 86; U Of Notre Dame; Bus Adm.

RIGOT, GREGG; Central Catholic HS; W Mifflin, PA; (Y); 80/260; Art Clb; Ski Clb; Varsity Clb; Var Golf; Hon Roll; Church Yth Grp; Exploring; Im Bsktbl; Im Bowling; Im Crs Cntry; Hole In One Awd Golf 85; Bowling Lgue 3 Gme Hgh Srs 84; Pre Law.

RIHN, JILL; Shaler HS; Allison Pk, PA; (Y); 4-H; Office Aide; JV Mgr(s); JV Score Keeper; JV Timer; JV Vllybl; 4-H Awd; High Hon Roll; Typng Awds 85; Hrs Shwng Awds 83-86; Hmcmng Cmt 86-87; U FL; Marine Bio.

RIKER, CANDACE; Upper Dublin SR HS; Maple Glenn, PA; (Y); 27/307; Aud/Vis; Church Yth Grp; Cmnty Wkr; Radio Clb; JV Lcrss; JV Tennis; High Hon Roll; Hon Roll; NHS.

RILATT, JOSEPH F; Henderson HS; West Chester, PA; (Y); 94/348; Cmnty Wkr; JV Var Bsktbl; Coach Actv; Var L Trk; Im Vllybl; Hon Roll; Math.

RILEY, DIANE; Gettysburg SR HS; Gettysburg, PA; (Y); Art Clb; French Clb; Yrbk Stf; Hon Roll; Drm Mjr(t); Mgr(s); Cert Of Merit Schlstc Art 86; Outstdng SR Artist 86; Philadelphia Coll Of Art; Illst.

RILEY, JEFFREY; Solanco HS; Quarryville, PA; (Y); 17/250; Chess Clb; Varsity Clb; Co-Capt Socr; Hon Roll; NHS; NRTOC Schlrshp 86; Rtry Stu Of Mnth 86; 3 Slnc Schlr Awds 83; Villanova U; Hstry.

RILEY, KEVIN; Pocono Central Catholic HS; Scotrun, PA; (Y); 11/31; Am Leg Boys St; Service Clb; School Musical; Yrbk Phtg; Pres Frsh Cls; Rep Soph Cls; Pres Jr Cls; Pres Stu Cncl; Bsbl; Bsktbl; ACCNTNT.

RILEY, KIM; Waynesburg Central HS; Waynesburg, PA; (Y); French Clb; Pep Clb; Pres Chorus; Swing Chorus; High Hon Roll; Prfct Atten Awd; Frndlst Awd In Chorus 84-86; Bus.

RILEY, LESLIE; Penn Hills SR HS; Pittsburgh, PA; (S); 22/765; French Clb; Science Clb; Ski Clb; Varsity Clb; Yrbk Stf; Rep Stu Cncl; Var L Cheerleading; Var L Trk; High Hon Roll; NHS; U Of Ptsbrgh; Physcl Thrpy.

RILEY, LYNDA; Notre Dame Acad; Norristown, PA; (Y); Debate Tm; Hosp Aide; Mathletes; Thesps; Chorus; School Play; Pres Soph Cls; Pres Jr Cls; Im Lcrss; Hon Roll; PA Natl Teengr Music Awd 85; Tlnt Amer Grnd Wnnr 85; PA Natl Teengr Frnscs Awd 85; U Of Richmond; Voice Prfrmnc.

RILEY, PAMELA; Carmichaels Area HS; Carmichaels, PA; (Y); 27/129; Band; Chorus; Concert Band; Mrchg Band; Stat Bsktbl; Score Keeper; High Hon Roll; NHS; Acadmc All Amer 86; WV Career Coll; Acctng.

RILEY, RYAN; Wyoming Valley West HS; Luzerne, PA; (Y); Band; Chorus; Concert Band; Jazz Band; Mrchg Band; Radio Clb; Stage Crew; Musicianship Awd 86; Berklee Coll Music; Perfrmnce.

RILEY, TWYLA; South Phila HS; Philadelphia, PA; (Y); Church Yth Grp; Cmnty Wkr; Dance Clb; Hosp Aide; Library Aide; Office Aide; Varsity Clb; Chorus; Church Choir; Drill Tm; Amer Fndtn For Negro Affairs 83-85; Jefferson Hosp Pgm 86; Amherst U; Child Psych.

RILEY, WILLIAM; Monsignor Bonner HS; Lansdowne, PA; (S); 11/333; Pres Church Yth Grp; Cmnty Wkr; VP Intnl Clb; Model UN; Service Clb; Stage Crew; Nwsp Stf; Hon Roll; NHS; Acadmc Excllnc-AP US Hstry; Scotts Hi-Q; Bus.

RIMBY, STEVE; Exeter Twp SR HS; Reading, PA; (Y); Aud/Vis; Boy Scts; Church Yth Grp; Computer Clb; Drama Clb; Radio Clb; Varsity Clb; Band; School Musical; School Play; Eagle Scout Pending 86; God & Country Awd 85; Broadcasting.

RIMEL, CHRIS; Mt Pleasant Area HS; Acme, PA; (Y); Chess Clb; Latin Clb; Yrbk Stf; Im Bsktbl; Im Sftbl; Im Vllybl; Hon Roll; St Vincent Coll; Pre-Med.

RIMMEY, JILL S; State College Area SR HS; State College, PA; (Y); Cmnty Wkr; Dance Clb; Drama Clb; Ski Clb; Chorus; JV Cheerleading; High Hon Roll; Hon Roll; Rep Frsh Cls; Rep Soph Cls; Dnc Schlrshp Allghny Dnc Co 84; Bio.

RIMMEY, SUSAN; Bellefonte Area HS; Mingoville, PA; (Y); Trs Church Yth Grp; High Hon Roll; Nrsg.

RINALDI, CARMELLA; Bishop O Hara HS; Dunmore, PA; (Y); 5/124; French Clb; Latin Clb; Science Clb; High Hon Roll; NHS; Penn ST; Med.

RINALDI, LISA; Marple Newtown SR HS; Newtown Square, PA; (Y); 125/369; Hosp Aide; Chorus; Rptr Nwsp Rptr; Yrbk Bus Mgr; Soph Cls; Stu Cncl; Hon Roll; Jr NHS; Ithaca Coll; Communications.

RINALDIS, TIZIANA; Bishop Mc Devitt HS; Harrisburg, PA; (S); 4/200; VP French Clb; Q&S; Ed Yrbk Stf; Rep Frsh Cls; Rep Soph Cls; Rep Jr Cls; Rep Sr Cls; Rep Stu Cncl; Cheerleading; Acadmc All Amer; Penn ST; Engrng.

RINDGEN, PAMELA; Wyoming Area SR HS; Harding, PA; (Y); Sec Trs Church Yth Grp; Cmnty Wkr; 4-H; German Clb; Ski Clb; 4-H Awd; Scraton U; Pre Med.

RINEER, DIANA; Solanco SR HS; Quarryville, PA; (Y); FBLA; Red Cross Aide; Ski Clb; Band; Chorus; Church Choir; Color Guard; Madrigals; Orch; School Musical; Solanco Schlr Music 84-85; Outstndng Stdnt Orch 84-85; U Of TN; Bus.

RINEER, MICHAEL; Ephrata SR HS; Ephrata, PA; (Y); Chess Clb; Church Yth Grp; German Clb; JA; Chorus; School Musical; School Play; Stage Crew; Var L Golf; Hon Roll; J Harry Hibshman Schlrshp 86; Wolf Fndtn Ed Schlrshp 86; Pres Acdmc Fit Awd 86; Penn ST U; Comp Sci.

RINEHART, CHRISTINE; Great Hope Baptist Schl; Shermansdale, PA; (S); 1/4; Church Yth Grp; Teachers Aide; Yrbk Bus Mgr; Hon Roll; Yrbk Stf; JV Cheerleading; Var Vllybl; Med Sec.

RINEHART, KIM; Emmaus HS; Macungie, PA; (Y); 102/492; Exploring; Key Clb; Spanish Clb; Concert Band; Drm & Bgl; Mrchg Band; School Musical; JV Fld Hcky; Hon Roll.

RINEHART, LORA; New Freedom Christian HS; Railroad, PA; (Y); 3/7; Church Yth Grp; Debate Tm; Drama Clb; Teachers Aide; Chorus; Var Capt Sftbl; Var Capt Vllybl; Hon Roll; NHS; Maranatha Bapt Bible Coll; Educ.

RINEHIMER, DAVID; John S Fine HS; Wapwallopen, PA; (Y); Cmnty Wkr; Hon Roll; Elec Engr.

RINGER, KAREN; Plum SR HS; Pittsburgh, PA; (Y); Exploring; French Clb; Band; Chorus; Concert Band; Mrchg Band; Hon Roll; NHS; NEDT Awd; Prfct Atten Awd; Vet Med.

RINGER, KEITH; Mc Guffey HS; Claysville, PA; (Y); Spanish Clb; JV Var Bsbl; Hon Roll; NHS; Mary Noss Schlrshp U Of CA 87; California U Of PA; Cmptr Mgmt.

RINGLABEN, PATRICIA; West Hazleton HS; W Hazelton, PA; (Y); Church Yth Grp; FBLA; Office Aide; Hon Roll.

RINGSDORF, WILLIAM; Downingtown SR HS; Exton, PA; (Y); 24/580; Drama Clb; Ski Clb; Chorus; School Musical; School Play; NHS; JA; Spanish Clb; Church Choir; Masonic Awd; Engrng.

RIOS, JOANN; Liberty HS; Bethlehem, PA; (Y); Boys Clb Am; Dance Clb; Drama Clb; 4-H; Library Aide; Pep Clb; Spanish Clb; Teachers Aide; Band; Chorus; Lab Technlgy.

RIOTTO, ANDREA; Nativity Bum HS; Pottsville, PA; (Y); Math Clb; Chorus; Drm Mjr(t); Stage Crew; Kutztown Coll; Art Educ.

RIPKA, LUCINDA DAWN; Bellefonte Area HS; Bellefonte, PA; (Y); High Hon Roll; Hon Roll; Fshn Merch.

RIPLEY, NATALIE; Coudersport JR SR HS; Coudersport, PA; (Y); 17/82; Drama Clb; French Clb; Variety Show; Nwsp Stf; Yrbk Stf; Pres Sr Cls; Rep Stu Cncl; Var Score Keeper; Hon Roll; NHS; PA ST U; Bus Admn.

RIPPEON, JACQUELINE; Littlestown HS; Littlestown, PA; (Y); 9/120; Church Yth Grp; FBLA; Church Choir; Color Guard; Yrbk Stf; High Hon Roll; Hon Roll; Library Aide; Teachers Aide; Chorus; Hnr Star Missionettes Girls Yth Grp 85; Pres, VP & Treas Yth Group 84-86; Treas FBLA 85-86; Mgt.

RIPPIN, RICHARD; Greater Johnstown HS; Johnstown, PA; (Y); Art Clb; Chess Clb; Church Yth Grp; Key Clb; Var L Bsbl; Rdlgst Tech.

RIPPLE, MICHAEL; Seneca Valley SR HS; Harmony, PA; (Y); 50/350; VP JA; JV Bsktbl; Var Golf; Coll Of William & Mary; Bus.

RISBON, PATRICIA; Cambria Heights HS; Patton, PA; (Y); ROTC.

RISCH, FREDERICK J; Wyoming Area HS; Harding, PA; (Y); Cmnty Wkr; German Clb; High Hon Roll; Hon Roll; NHS; Finance.

RISHEL, SUSAN M; East Juniata HS; Thompsontown, PA; (Y); 20/94; Band; Pres Chorus; Capt Var Cheerleading; Var Capt Twrlr; Trs Library Aide; Concert Band; Mrchg Band; School Musical; School Play; Variety Show; Natl Chorl Awd 86; PA All ST Lions Band 85-86; Dist Chorus & Band 85-86; Regnl Chorus 86; Point Park Coll; Psych.

RISHEL, WENDY S; Millville HS; Bloomsburg, PA; (Y); 18/76; Am Leg Aux Girls St; Hosp Aide; Band; School Play; Sec Jr Cls; Sec Sr Cls; Var Cheerleading; Var Sftbl; Stat Wrstlng; Kiwanis Awd; West Chester U; Phych.

RISHELL, GAIL; Wilmington Area HS; New Bedford, PA; (S); Trs Church Yth Grp; Drama Clb; French Clb; Girl Scts; Office Aide; Church Choir; Nwsp Rptr; Nwsp Stf; Var Sftbl; Var Trk; Vllybl All-Star From Tri-Cnty 85; Trck Lttrs 84-85; Anthrplgy.

RISHELL, SUSAN ANN; New Brighton HS; New Brighton, PA; (Y); 27/154; Trs 4-H; GAA; Varsity Clb; Var L Tennis; 4-H Awd; High Hon Roll; Hnr Grad 86; Presdntl Acadmc Ftne Awd 86; Claron U Of PA; Chem.

RISHKO, TARA; Allentown Central Catholic HS; Allentown, PA; (Y); 2/210; Am Leg Aux Girls St; Math Clb; School Play; Var Cheerleading; High Hon Roll; NHS; PSPA 1st Awd Lght Poetry 85; Aerospc Engnrng.

RISKO, RHONDA; Pittston Area SR HS; Pittston, PA; (Y); 98/385; Art Clb; Hosp Aide; Library Aide; Teachers Aide; Chorus; Tennis; Hon Roll; Frncs Hook Schlrshp Fnd 85-86; Nrs.

RISSER, BRIAN; Elizabethtown Area HS; Elizabethtown, PA; (Y); 6/234; Teachers Aide; VP Varsity Clb; Stu Cncl; Bsbl; Ftbl; Wrstlng; Jr NHS; NHS; Bio.

RISSINGER, ELLEN F; Conrad Weiser Area Schl District; Robesonia, PA; (Y); 16/184; Sec JCL; Band; Chorus; Church Choir; Concert Band; Mrchg Band; Orch; School Musical; School Play; NHS; Cnty, Dist, & Region Chorus 86; Cnty & Dist Band 86; Berks Cnty Womans Clb Piano Competition 1st Pl 85; Music.

RISSINGER, MICHAEL S; Conrad Weiser Area HS; Robesonia, PA; (Y); 26/139; Church Yth Grp; Computer Clb; Chorus; Church Choir; School Musical; Bsbl; Bowling; Golf; Hon Roll; Berks Co Chorus 84-86; 2nd Pl Berks Co Invdl Bwlng Chmpshp 86; Conrad Weisers Bst Defsv Bsbl Plyr 86; Bloomsbrg U; Accntng.

RISSMILLER, JILL B; Hamburg Area HS; Hamburg, PA; (Y); 63/162; Church Yth Grp; German Clb; Chorus; Jazz Band; School Musical; School Play; Yrbk Stf; Pres Stu Cncl; Hon Roll; Philadelphia Coll Of The Arts.

RITCHEY, DANA; Mars HS; Valencia, PA; (Y); Pres GAA; Varsity Clb; Trs Soph Cls; Rep VP Stu Cncl; Capt Bsbl; Var Capt Bsktbl; Var Capt Vllybl; High Hon Roll; NHS; Jeff Danner Schlrshp 86; Amer Legion Awd 81-82; Homecoming Queen 85-86; U Of Pittsburgh.

RITCHEY, DAWN ANNETTE; Tussey Mountain HS; Saxton, PA; (Y); AFS; Sec Drama Clb; Band; Chorus; Church Choir; Concert Band; Mrchg Band; Pep Band; Nwsp Rptr; Nwsp Stf; Mt Aloysius JC; Ocptnl Thrpst.

RITCHEY, JIM; Baldwin HS; Pittsburgh, PA; (Y); 150/535; Church Yth Grp; High Hon Roll; Hon Roll; Natl Art Hnr Soc; Med Fld.

RITCHEY, JULIE; Chief Logan HS; Mcclure, PA; (Y); Art Clb; Sec Church Yth Grp; German Clb; Key Clb; Pep Clb; Yrbk Stf; Sftbl; Trk; Twrlr; Hon Roll; May Stu Of Mnth 84; Cont In PA Mdrn Miss Pgnt 86; Crmnl Law.

RITCHEY, PATTY; Union HS; Rimersburg, PA; (Y); SADD; Yrbk Stf; Pep Clb; Stu Cncl; Sal; Val; Modern Miss Teen Scholar Pag 85; Prom Comm 84-85; ICM Schl Bus; Med Office Asst.

RITCHEY, REBECCA L; Hollidaysburg Area HS; Hollidaysburg, PA; (Y); 30/350; French Clb; Library Aide; Hon Roll; NHS; Penn ST; Bio.

RITCHEY, SHARON; Bangor Area SR HS; Bangor, PA; (Y); Church Yth Grp; Chorus; Church Choir; L Concert Band; Mrchg Band; School Musical; Sec Trs Nwsp Rptr; High Hon Roll; NHS; Pres Schlr; Messiah Coll Deans Schlrshp 85-86; Bonger Area Ed Assn Schlrshp Ed 86; PA Govrnr Schl Arts 85; Messiah Coll; Elem Ed.

RITCHIE, JOSEPH; Dayton JR-SR HS; Smicksburg, PA; (Y); 5/50; Band; Drm Mjr(t); Yrbk Ed-Chief; Sec Sr Cls; JP Sousa Awd; NHS; 4-H; Chorus; Concert Band; Semper Fidelis Music Awd 86; Mbr All-St Lions Band-PA 86; Smmr Happngs-IUP 84; Indiana U PA; Music Ed.

RITCHIE, RONNA LEAH; Dayton JR/Sr HS; Smicksburg, PA; (Y); 13/52; VP Pres 4-H; Band; Mrchg Band; School Musical; Nwsp Stf; Pres VP Stu Cncl; Bsktbl; 4-H Awd; Hon Roll; NHS; Outstndng 4-H Grl Awd 84; Cmmnctns.

RITENOUR, CAROL; Laurel Valley HS; New Florence, PA; (Y); Pres AFS; VP Band; Chorus; Concert Band; Drm Mjr(t); Jazz Band; School Play; Nwsp Stf; Yrbk Stf; Capt Tennis; Co Band & Chorus; Indiana U PA; Elem Educ.

RITENOUR, DEREK; Southmoreland HS; Scottdale, PA; (Y); 20/230; Letterman Clb; Pres Math Clb; Office Aide; Ski Clb; Spanish Clb; Trs Frsh Cls; Trs Soph Cls; L Var Ftbl; L Var Trk; Spanish NHS; Juniata Fndrs Awd 86; Juniata; Acctg.

RITKO, AMYEE; Greater Johnstown HS; Johnstown, PA; (Y); German Clb; Pep Clb; Ski Clb; SADD; Rep Stu Cncl; Cheerleading; Hon Roll; U Pittsburgh; Mth.

RITTENHOUSE, MICHELLE; Corry Area HS; Corry, PA; (S); 47/212; Library Aide; Hon Roll; Hnr Roll 85; Accntng.

RITTER, ANNA E; Gateway SR HS; Monroeville, PA; (Y); 65/431; Church Yth Grp; French Clb; Ski Clb; School Play; JV Stat Bsktbl; Mgr(s); JV Trk; Stat Vllybl; French Hon Soc; High Hon Roll; Pres Acad Ftnss Awd 86; Carlow Coll; Librl Arts.

RITTER, BRIAN; Salisbury HS; Alletown, PA; (Y); Church Yth Grp; Cmnty Wkr; Computer Clb; JA; Bsktbl; Hon Roll; Polc Ath Bowling Lg Hgh Avg 85-86; 4th Pl Lehigh Vly Masters Bowling 86; PA ST; Comp Tech.

RITTER, DENISE; West Perry HS; Loysville, PA; (Y); #4 In Class; Church Yth Grp; Girl Scts; Var Bsktbl; High Hon Roll; Hon Roll; Jr NHS; NHS; Prfct Atten Awd; Data Prcsng Stu Of Quarter 86; HACC; Systm Anlyst.

RITTER, KIRK L; Warren Area HS; Clarendon, PA; (Y); Church Yth Grp; FCA; Acpl Chr; Church Choir; Madrigals; School Musical; Variety Show; High Hon Roll; Jr NHS; Bio.

RITTER, TAMMY; Henderson HS; Exton, PA; (S); 6/348; Church Yth Grp; French Clb; JCL; Var Bsktbl; Var Vllybl; French Hon Soc; Hon Roll; Educ.

RITTER, WILLIAM; Ephrata SR HS; Ephrata, PA; (Y); 45/220; Church Yth Grp; Band; Chorus; Church Choir; Jazz Band; Mrchg Band; Orch; School Musical; Nwsp Stf; Var L Bsbl; Kutztown U; Cmmnctns.

RITTERSON, CHRISTOPH C; Gettysburg SR HS; Gettysburg, PA; (Y); Am Leg Boys St; Drama Clb; PAVAS; School Musical; School Play; Var Socr; Rotary Awd; VP Frsh Cls; Rtry Ldrshp Cnfrnc 86; Cnty Cmmsnr 86; Pr Cnslr 86; Hstry.

RITTINGER, RICHARD; Wyoming Valley W HS; Forty Fort, PA; (Y); Trs Key Clb; Ski Clb; Stage Crew; Rep Jr Cls; JV Bsbl; Im Bsktbl; Capt L Socr; Im Vllybl; High Hon Roll; Hon Roll; PA Dist Distngshd Key Clb Treas Awd 85-86; PA ST U; Engrng.

RITTS, KELLY; Dallas SR HS; Trucksville, PA; (Y); Art Clb; Office Aide; Yrbk Stf; Penn ST; Bus.

RITZ, MARY; W Hazelton HS; W Hazleton, PA; (S); 14/191; Sec Church Yth Grp; Cmnty Wkr; Capt Scholastic Bowl; SADD; Capt Color Guard; Nwsp Stf; Yrbk Ed-Chief; High Hon Roll; NHS; VFW Awd; 1st Poster Cntst 83; PA ST U Hazelton; Phys Thrpy.

RITZ, MONA; Bradford Area HS; Bradford, PA; (Y); 35/276; Rep AFS; Pres Church Yth Grp; Band; Chorus; Jazz Band; Mrchg Band; Pep Band; Yrbk Stf; Rep Stu Cncl; Var L Crs Cntry; Acctng.

RITZ, PATTI; Punxstawney HS; Punxsutawney, PA; (Y); 96/238; French Clb; FBLA; GAA; Spanish Clb; Variety Show; Nwsp Stf; Stat Crs Cntry; Stat Trk; Prfct Atten Awd; Dubois Bus Coll; Med Sec.

RITZERT, JERRY; Lincoln HS; Ellwood City, PA; (Y); Cmnty Wkr; Letterman Clb; Ski Clb; Spanish Clb; Var Ftbl; Wt Lftg; Wrstlng; Hon Roll; ST Polc Ofcr.

RITZIE, PAMELA; Seton Catholic HS; Dupont, PA; (Y); Art Clb; Chorus; School Play; Variety Show; Yrbk Phtg; Yrbk Stf; Bsktbl; Rochester Inst Tech; Photo.

RITZMAN, CHRISTINE; Pequea Valley HS; Paradise, PA; (Y); Church Yth Grp; Varsity Clb; Band; Chorus; Concert Band; Mrchg Band; School Musical; Crs Cntry; Hon Roll; NHS.

RIVENBURGH, LINDA; Susquehanna Comm JR SR HS; Thompson, PA; (S); Ski Clb; Band; Chorus; Concert Band; Mrchg Band; Powder Puff Ftbl; Csmtlgy.

RIVERSO, JOANN; Ste Maria Goretti HS; Philadelphia, PA; (Y); 130/469; French Clb; Library Aide; Math Clb; Teachers Aide; Stage Crew; Off Frsh Cls; Off Soph Cls; Ed Stu Cncl; Cheerleading; High Hon Roll; Radlgy.

RIVKIN, BILL; Abington SR HS; Roslyn, PA; (Y); 73/532; Church Yth Grp; Var Bowling; JV Var Lcrss; JV Var Socr; Im Vllybl; GBCA Arch Dsgn & Constrctn Cont Merit Awd 85 & 86; U DE; Civl Engnrg.

RIZEN, MICHAEL; Lower Moreland SR HS; Huntingdon Vly, PA; (S); VP Soph Cls; Var L Diving; Var L Socr; JV Var Trk; DAR Awd; High Hon Roll; Hon Roll; Kiwanis Awd; NHS; Pres Physcl Ftnss Awd; Spnsh Mrt Awd; Soc Studs Achvt Awd 84.

RIZOR, BILL; West Allegheny SR HS; Imperial, PA; (Y); 8/218; Math Tm; Science Clb; Var Ftbl; Var Trk; Var Wt Lftg; High Hon Roll; NHS; Ntl Merit Ltr; U Pitts; Pre-Med.

RIZZARDI, LISA; Warren Area HS; Warren, PA; (Y); Church Yth Grp; French Clb; Girl Scts; Hosp Aide; Office Aide; Y-Teens; Yrbk Stf; Hon Roll; New Process Co Bus Awd 86; Erie Bus Cntr; Arln/Trvl Svc.

RIZZARDI, PAUL; Pocono Mountain HS; Swiftwater, PA; (Y); 11/300; JV Socr; Hon Roll; NHS; Natl Sci Olympd Awd Biolgy Olympd 84-85; Archtctr.

RIZZI, ANNEMARIE; Nazereth Acad; Philadelphia, PA; (Y); German Clb; NFL; Yrbk Stf; Hon Roll; NHS; Schlrshp Moore Coll Art Smmr Cls 86; Law.

RIZZO, COURTNEY P; Peters Twp HS; Venetia, PA; (Y); Stu Cncl; JV Cheerleading; L Trk; Hon Roll; Mercyhurst Coll; Sprts Med.

RIZZO, DONNA; Pittston Area SR HS; Pittston, PA; (Y); 18/365; Key Clb; Math Clb; Yrbk Stf; Score Keeper; Hon Roll; NHS; Pharm.

RIZZO, KAREN; Penn-Trafford HS; Trafford, PA; (Y); Hosp Aide; Latin Clb; Color Guard; Prfct Atten Awd; Nrsg.

RIZZO, KELLY; Knoch JR & SR HS; Saxonburg, PA; (Y); German Clb; Pep Clb; Band; Chorus; Capt Drill Tm; School Musical; School Play; Yrbk Stf; Sr Cls; Stu Cncl; Wstmnstr Coll; Psychlgy.

RIZZO, RACHELLE; Winchester Thurston HS; Pittsburgh, PA; (Y); AFS; Church Yth Grp; GAA; Ski Clb; Rep Stu Cncl; Var L Sftbl; Var L Tennis; Intrntl Bus.

RIZZUTO, JAMES; York Vo-Tech; York, PA; (Y); VICA; Diesel Inst Of Amer; Diesel Mch.

RIZZUTO, PAULA; Yhork Catholic HS; York, PA; (Y); Church Yth Grp; Varsity Clb; Im JV Bsktbl; Var Crs Cntry; Var JV Mgr(s); Im Sftbl; Var JV Trk; JV Vllybl; Hon Roll; SF Spch Festvl 84-85; Mrktng.

ROACH, CONCETTA; Troy SR HS; Towanda, PA; (Y); Art Clb; Camera Clb; Computer Clb; Debate Tm; FTA; Library Aide; Teachers Aide; Yrbk Phtg; Yrbk Stf; Drama Clb; Type A Thon Leukemia Scty Amrc 84.

ROACH, PATRICK; Council Rock HS; Newtown, PA; (Y); 51/845; Drama Clb; School Play; Stage Crew; Hon Roll; NHS; Vet.

ROACH, TERESA; Grove City SR HS; Grove City, PA; (Y); 47/195; Pres VP Church Yth Grp; Pres Trs Ski Clb; Band; Church Choir; Yrbk Ed-Chief; Sec Soph Cls; Var Capt Cheerleading; Powder Puff Ftbl; Var L Trk; Var Capt Vllybl.

ROADMAN, LORI; Mount Pleasant Area HS; Acme, PA; (Y); 12/253; Church Yth Grp; Latin Clb; Band; Concert Band; Mrchg Band; Yrbk Stf; Hon Roll; NHS; Math.

ROAN, JONATHAN; Bellefonte Area HS; Bellefonte, PA; (Y); Swmmng; Wt Lftg; High Hon Roll; Hon Roll; Electronics.

ROBA, ANTHONY C; Bishop Egan HS; Bensalem, PA; (Y); Computer Clb; School Musical; School Play; Stage Crew; Bsktbl; Vllybl; High Hon Roll; Hon Roll; Comp Sci Awd 85&86; Physics Awd 86; Drexel U; Comp Sci.

ROBACKER, KRISTEN; Freedom SR HS; Bethlehem, PA; (Y); 92/456; Trs Drama Clb; French Clb; German Clb; Pep Clb; VP SADD; School Play; Trs Frsh Cls; Trs Stu Cncl; L Capt Fld Hcky; Hon Roll.

ROBB, JANINE; Kiski Area HS; Vandergrift, PA; (Y); French Clb; Pep Clb; Chorus; Yrbk Stf; VP Stu Cncl; High Hon Roll; Pres Schlr; Top Ten Awd 84; Schlstc Awd 84; Cert Of Mrt Acdmc Exclnc 86; Accntng.

ROBB, KATHY; Manheim TWP HS; Lancaster, PA; (Y); 75/325; Cmnty Wkr; JA; Y-Teens; School Musical; School Play; Stage Crew; Variety Show; Lit Mag; Hon Roll; Solost-Synchrnzd Swmmng; Partcptn Awd Swmmng; Elem Educ.

ROBB, RUTH; Penn Trafford HS; Jeannette, PA; (Y); Church Yth Grp; FBLA; SADD; Band; Concert Band; Mrchg Band; High Hon Roll; Hon Roll; Prfct Atten Awd; 1st Pl Bus Math Awd FBLA 85; CA U Of PA; Acctg.

ROBB II, WILLIAM D; Lock Haven SR HS; Lock Haven, PA; (Y); Drama Clb; School Play; Stu Cncl; Var Trk; Var Wrstlng; Engr Drwg Awd 85-86; Lehigh U; Arch Dsgn.

ROBBINS, JEAN; Connellsville SR HS; Connellsville, PA; (Y); 47/500; Church Yth Grp; Library Aide; School Musical; School Play; Stage Crew; Var Capt Vllybl; High Hon Roll; Jr NHS; NHS; German Clb; German Hon Soc 84-86; Penn ST U; Arspc Engrn.

ROBBINS, MARY; Coudersport HS; Coudersport, PA; (Y); Varsity Clb; Band; Chorus; Yrbk Stf; Bsktbl; Trk; Vllybl; Hon Roll; NHS; Mth.

ROBBINS, MICHELLE; Clearfield Area HS; Clearfield, PA; (Y); 21/292; Speech Tm; Band; Chorus; Concert Band; Mrchg Band; Orch; Swing Chorus; Stat Wrstlng; High Hon Roll; Hon Roll; Grove City Coll; Elem Ed.

ROBEL, MIKE; Conneaut Lake HS; Conneaut Lake, PA; (Y); SADD; Band; Concert Band; Mrchg Band; Nwsp Stf; Off Stu Cncl; L Capt Bsbl; Bsktbl; Im Mgr Vllybl; Hon Roll; Bus.

ROBERSON, HELENE; Harry S Truman HS; Levittown, PA; (Y); #49 In Class; Hosp Aide; Spanish Clb; Temple Yth Grp; Band; Concert Band; Mrchg Band; Stu Cncl; JV Var Socr; Hon Roll; Phys Thrpy.

ROBERTS, AMY; Fort Le Boeuf HS; Waterford, PA; (Y); 45/180; Letterman Clb; Model UN; Pep Clb; Ski Clb; Varsity Clb; Band; Concert Band; Mrchg Band; School Musical; School Play; Trck & Chrldg Capt 86; Penna Free Entrprs Wk 85; Edinboro U; Elem Ed.

ROBERTS, CAROL E; Central Dauphin East HS; Swatara, PA; (Y); 2/271; Trs German Clb; Latin Clb; Concert Band; Jazz Band; Mrchg Band; Orch; School Musical; Swmmng; High Hon Roll; JETS Awd; Ltr Swmmng 85-86; Faculty Sci Awd 83-84; Acad Stu Mnth 85; Engrng.

ROBERTS, CINDY; Ferndale Area HS; Johnstown, PA; (Y); 5/57; Leo Clb; SADD; Pres Jr Cls; Pres Sr Cls; Stu Cncl; Capt Twrlr; Cit Awd; High Hon Roll; Trs NHS; Lions Clb Stu Mnth 86; Bus Prof Womens Clb 86; Svc Awd 86; U Pittsburgh.

ROBERTS, ELAINE; Charlerio JR SR HS; N Charleroi, PA; (Y); Science Clb; Spanish Clb; SADD; Concert Band; Mrchg Band; Nwsp Stf.

ROBERTS, ELIZABETH; Wyoming Valley West HS; Kingston, PA; (Y); Rep Frsh Cls; Rep Soph Cls; Rep Jr Cls; Var Fld Hcky; JV Sftbl; Im Vllybl; Cit Awd; High Hon Roll; NHS; Prfct Atten Awd.

ROBERTS, JAMES C; GAR Memorial HS; Wilkes Barre, PA; (S); 4/187; German Clb; Letterman Clb; Stage Crew; Rep Stu Cncl; Stat Bsktbl; Var L Crs Cntry; Mgr(s); Score Keeper; Var L Trk; High Hon Roll; Bloomsburg U; Mass Comm.

ROBERTS, KENNY; Ther Mercersburg Acad; Mc Lean, VA; (Y); Lit Mag; Var L Diving; Church Yth Grp; Computer Clb; FBLA; Ski Clb; Var Crs Cntry; JV Trk; Hon Roll; 2nd Dgre Brwn Blt Tae Kwon Do 84; Hon Frm Dptmt Of Air Frc & Ptnt Off Soc 83; Dvng Awds 86; Cmptr Engrng.

ROBERTS, LEIGH SUZANNE; Lower Moreland HS; Huntingdon Valley, PA; (S); Exploring; German Clb; Key Clb; Science Clb; Pres Temple Yth Grp; Rep Jr Cls; Var Tennis; Timer; Med.

ROBERTS, LORI; Abington Heights HS; Clarks Summit, PA; (Y); Pres Church Yth Grp; Band; Church Choir; Mrchg Band; Var Sftbl; Nrsng.

ROBERTS, MARIE; Sacred Heart HS; Carbondale, PA; (Y); FBLA; Library Aide; Var Capt Bsktbl; Sftbl; Hon Roll; NHS; Ntl Merit Ltr; Kystn JC; Rdlgy.

ROBERTS, MARY BETH; Hopewell Area HS; Aliquippa, PA; (Y); 15/240; Latin Clb; Rep Band; Mrchg Band; Rep Frsh Cls; Rep Soph Cls; Rep Jr Cls; Stat Var Bsktbl; Var JV Sftbl; High Hon Roll; NHS; Beaver Cnty Schlstc Athl All Strs 85-86; Band Ltr 3 Yrs; Duquesne U; Pharm.

ROBERTS, MELISA; Nazareth Area HS; Nazareth, PA; (Y); Key Clb; Yrbk Stf; Hon Roll; Psych.

ROBERTS, SHELLEY A; Vincentian HS; Pittsburgh, PA; (Y); 5/58; Q&S; Chorus; Rep Frsh Cls; Sec Soph Cls; L Fld Hcky; Mgr(s); High Hon Roll; Hon Roll; NHS; PA ST U; Lib Arts.

ROBERTS, STEPHEN; Mt Pleasant Area HS; Mt Pleasant, PA; (Y); Nwsp Sprt Ed; Bsbl; Hon Roll; Nwspapr Sprts Edtr 86-87; Hnr Rl 85-86; Bsbl 84-85.

ROBERTS, STEVEN; Hopewell Area HS; Aliquippa, PA; (Y); 89/267; Exploring; German Clb; Band; Concert Band; Mrchg Band; Pep Band; Var L Ftbl; Wt Lftg; Hon Roll; St Francis Coll Of PA; Sclgy.

ROBERTS, TIM; Reynolds HS; Greenville, PA; (Y); 23/147; VP Church Yth Grp; Spanish Clb; VICA; Stat Bsktbl; Im Score Keeper; Hon Roll; 3rd Pl Dist 10 Voctnl Indstrl Clbs Amer Skill Olympcs 86; Mercer Cnty Vo-Tech; Carpntry.

ROBERTS, TOM; Beaver Area JR SR HS; Beaver, PA; (Y); FCA; JA; VP Jr Cls; VP Sr Cls; L Ftbl; Powder Puff Ftbl; L Trk; Wt Lftg; Dnfth Awd; Hon Roll; Phrmcy.

ROBERTS, TONY; Unionville HS; Coatesville, PA; (Y); 91/300; Ski Clb; Soroptimist; Sftbl; High Hon Roll; Hon Roll; Cmmrcl Pilot.

ROBERTSON, BETH; Meadville Area SR HS; Meadville, PA; (Y); 34/306; Girl Scts; Red Cross Aide; SADD; Chorus; Yrbk Stf; High Hon Roll; Hon Roll; NHS; Prfct Atten Awd; Pres JA; Grad Dale Carnegie Course 85; Stu Achvt 85; 2nd,3rd Pl Spnsh Frgn Lang Comptn 85-86.

ROBERTSON, BRIAN; Hazleton HS; Hazleton, PA; (Y); Ski Clb; Nwsp Ed-Chief; Var L Crs Cntry; Var L Trk; HHS Jrnlsm Awd 86; Penn ST; Sprts.

ROBERTSON, CRAIG; Manheim Central HS; Manheim, PA; (Y); 74/268; Orch; School Musical; Yrbk Phtg; Yrbk Rptr; Yrbk Stf; Crs Cntry; Socr; Tennis; Trk; Cit Awd; 4 Way Tst Awd & Lions Club Outstndng Ldrshp Awd 86; Gannon U; Mech Engrng.

ROBERTSON, JIM; East Alleghany HS; N Versailles, PA; (Y); 1/200; Chess Clb; Computer Clb; Math Clb; Math Tm; Science Clb; Ski Clb; Hon Roll; NHS; PA PTA Cltrl Arts-Rflctns-Lit Rgnl & Cnty Wnnr 85-86; Coll In H S Pgm-Pttsbrgh U 85-86; Lwyr.

ROBERTSON, KELLY; St Marys Area HS; St Marys, PA; (Y); 3/290; Model UN; Varsity Clb; Var L Crs Cntry; Var Swmmng; Var Capt Trk; High Hon Roll; NHS; Pres Schlr; Cmnty Wkr; Drama Clb; PA Gvrnrs Schl Intl Stds 85; Army Athlt Schlr Awd 86; Susquehanna U; Pre-Med.

ROBESON, CANDICE; Bristol JRSR HS; Bristol, PA; (Y); 11/102; Computer Clb; Drama Clb; Office Aide; Red Cross Aide; Varsity Clb; Band; Concert Band; Mrchg Band; Orch; School Play; Berkley Schl Of Bus 86; Bristol Demo Assoc 86; Berkeley Schl; Comp Accntng.

ROBIDOUX, DAVID; Muhlenberg SR HS; Reading, PA; (Y); Boy Scts; Band; Concert Band; Jazz Band; Mrchg Band; Pep Band; School Musical; Sec Stu Cncl; JV Socr; Var Wrstlng; Eagle Scout Rank 85; Music Prfrmnc.

ROBIDOUX, RAYMOND A; Milton Hershey HS; Hershey, PA; (Y); 4/130; Am Leg Boys St; Library Aide; Service Clb; Yrbk Rptr; Yrbk Stf; Lit Mag; Rep Stu Cncl; Mgr(s); High Hon Roll; NHS.

ROBINSON, AMY; Towanda Area HS; Towanda, PA; (Y); Church Yth Grp; Letterman Clb; Chorus; Madrigals; Yrbk Stf; Swmmng; Trk; Vllybl; Hon Roll; NHS; NVP Vlybl 86; Dist IV Swmng Champ 5 Times 83-86; Outstndng Music Awd 86; Comm.

ROBINSON, CHRISTINE; State College Area HS; State College, PA; (Y); Art Clb; Trs Model UN; Thesps; Lit Mag; Hon Roll; Lion Awd; Ntl Merit Ltr; NEDT Awd; Alpha Ambulnc Clb 86; Frannie Awd Thspns 86; PA ST U; Psych.

ROBINSON, DANIEL D; Conneaut Lake HS; Conneaut Lake, PA; (Y); Letterman Clb; Math Clb; Pep Clb; Spanish Clb; SADD; Varsity Clb; Rep Frsh Cls; Rep Stu Cncl; Var Bsbl; Var Bsktbl; Bus.

ROBINSON, DENISE; Simon Gratz HS; Philadelphia, PA; (Y); Hon Roll; Prfct Atten Awd; Gym Prprtn Awd 80; Reddathn Awd 83; Hrdst Wrkng Stu Awd 82.

ROBINSON, ERIK; Frankford HS; Philadelphia, PA; (Y); Boys Clb Am; Chess Clb; Church Yth Grp; Church Choir; JV Bsktbl; Cit Awd; Edwin R Popper Mem Awd.

ROBINSON, HEATHER; St Maria Goretti HS; Philadelphia, PA; (Y); Church Yth Grp; Civic Clb; Cmnty Wkr; Hosp Aide; Capt Mathletes; Math Clb; Math Tm; School Musical; Lit Mag; Rep Jr Cls; 4 Mrt Awd Vlntr Svc St Agnes Med Ctr 81-85; Math Lge Awd 86; Awd Prtcptn Yth Pltcl Systm Sympsm 86; Temple U; Nrsng.

ROBINSON, KARA; Altoona Area HS; Altoona, PA; (Y); Cmnty Wkr; Trs PAVAS; Spanish Clb; Speech Tm; Chorus; School Musical; School Play; Variety Show; Rep Frsh Cls; Hon Roll; Med.

ROBINSON, KELLIE; St Basil Acad; Philadelphia, PA; (S); 6/97; Church Yth Grp; Cmnty Wkr; French Clb; Math Clb; Science Clb; Service Clb; Chorus; High Hon Roll; Ntl Merit Ltr; 2nd St Hubert Acadmc Decthln 83; Prtl Schlrshp St Basil Acadm 83-Pres; Math.

ROBINSON, KELLY; Merion Mercy Acad; Phila, PA; (Y); 16/72; Cmnty Wkr; Mathletes; Pres Sec Science Clb; Chorus; Yrbk Phtg; Im Bsktbl; JV Fld Hcky; Hon Roll; NHS; Prfct Atten Awd; Cum Laude-Latin Comptn 84; Sprtsmnshp Awd 84-86; Med.

ROBINSON, MATT; Chief Logan HS; Lewistown, PA; (Y); 18/204; Boy Scts; CAP; Debate Tm; Ski Clb; Chorus; Stage Crew; Jr Cls; High Hon Roll; NHS; Ntl Merit SF; Lttr Acdmc Prfrmnc 84; PA ST Sci Olympian 84-85.

ROBINSON, MATTHEW; Fort Le Baeuf HS; Erie, PA; (Y); Exploring; FCA; Var L Bsbl; JV Var Bsktbl; High Hon Roll; NHS; 1st Pl Wstrn PA Indstrl Arts Fair 86, 3rd Pl 85; Bio.

ROBINSON, PAMELA; Schenley HS; Pittsburgh, PA; (S); 19/150; Dance Clb; French Clb; Key Clb; Natl Beta Clb; Pep Clb; PAVAS; Temple Yth Grp; Chorus; School Play; Stage Crew; Chem Awd 84; Alpha Kappa Alpha Essy Cntst Wnnr 84; U Of Pittsburgh; Chem.

ROBINSON, SHELLEY; Western Wayne HS; Lake Ariel, PA; (Y); 4-H; Girl Scts; SADD; Band; Concert Band; Jazz Band; Drill Tm; School Musical; Hon Roll; NHS; Stu Of Fortnight Awd 85.

ROBINSON, SHERRY; Hollidayburg SR HS; Duncansville, PA; (Y); 40/351; Church Yth Grp; JA; Library Aide; Spanish Clb; Teachers Aide; Varsity Clb; Chorus; Church Choir; Orch; Variety Show; Airln Stewdss.

ROBINSON, STEVE; Mechanicsburg SR HS; Mechanicsburg, PA; (Y); 37/315; Jazz Band; Sec Mrchg Band; School Play; Symp Band; Nwsp Rptr; Yrbk Phtg; Hon Roll; Dist Band 85-86; Commencmnt Spkr 86; Louis Armstrong Jazz Awd 86; IN U PA; Jrnlsm.

ROBINSON JR, THOMAS V; Central HS; Philadelphia, PA; (Y); Trk; Wt Lftg; Ntl Merit SF; Bus Adm.

ROBINSON, TRACEY E; West Catholic For Girls; Philadelphia, PA; (Y); 33/256; Church Yth Grp; Dance Clb; Hosp Aide; Spanish Clb; Orch; School Play; High Hon Roll; Hon Roll; Nrsg.

ROBINSON, VICKI; Union Area HS; New Castle, PA; (Y); 33/72; Art Clb; Church Yth Grp; French Clb; Library Aide; Pep Clb; Spanish Clb; Chorus; Nwsp Phtg; Nwsp Stf; Yrbk Stf; Interior Design.

ROBISON, PATRICIA; Shaler Area SR HS; Pittsburgh, PA; (Y); Church Yth Grp; Exploring; Hosp Aide; Office Aide; Chorus; Church Choir; Hon Roll; Shadyside Hosp Schl Nrsg; Nrsg.

ROBL, PAUL; Greater Latrobe HS; Latrobe, PA; (Y); 93/407; Cmnty Wkr; Letterman Clb; Varsity Clb; Var L Bsbl; Im Bsktbl; Coach Actv; Var L Ftbl; Wt Lftg; High Hon Roll; Hon Roll; Bus.

ROBLEDO, VIVIAN; Freedom HS; Bethlehem, PA; (Y); 67/402; Church Yth Grp; Spanish Clb; Var Vllybl; Hon Roll; 1st Tm All-Str Vllybl 84; Pres Acdmc Ftns Awd 86; US Army Rsrv Natl Schlr/Athlt Awd 86; E Stroudsburg U; Comp Sci.

ROBLES, PACIANITA; Freedom HS; Bethlehem, PA; (Y); Exploring; Latin Clb; Spanish Clb; Chorus; School Musical; Cheerleading; Trk; Hon Roll; Nrsng.

ROBOSKI, CORIENNE; Mt Penn HS; Santa Clara, CA; (Y); 29/76; FBLA; GAA; Intnl Clb; Y-Teens; Yrbk Phtg; Dnfth Awd; Hon Roll; NHS; Camera Clb; Church Yth Grp; Pomeroys Teen Bd Rep 85-86; U Of CA; Pre-Med.

ROBSOCK, MARY ANN; Berwick Area SR HS; Berwick, PA; (Y); Church Yth Grp; VP Band; Chorus; VP Concert Band; Drm Mjr(t); Jazz Band; VP Mrchg Band; Swing Chorus; JP Sousa Awd; NHS; Columbis Cnty Bnd Dist Bnd Regnl Band 85-86; Dist Chorus Reg Chorus 86; Amer Legn Awd 84; Music Ed.

ROBSON, KRISTEN; Scranton Preparatory Schl; Scranton, PA; (Y); 1/190; Nwsp Rptr; Nwsp Stf; Var L Cheerleading; Var L Tennis; NHS; Val; Dance Clb; Political Wkr; High Hon Roll; Schlrshp Hnr Rev Edw Baxter SJ U Scranton, Schlr Yr 86; Holy Cross Coll Alumni Bk Awd 85; U Scranton; Pre-Med.

ROBUCK, TANIA; Altoona Area HS; Altoona, PA; (S); 27/683; French Clb; FHA; Hon Roll.

ROCCO, DOMINICK; Mid-Valley HS; Throop, PA; (Y); Pres VICA; Hon Roll; PA ST; Elec.

ROCCO, FRANCIS; Central Christian HS; Reynoldsville, PA; (Y); Computer Clb; Ski Clb; SADD; Law.

ROCHE, DIANE R; Gateway HS; Monroeville, PA; (Y); Church Yth Grp; Dance Clb; Ski Clb; SADD; Chorus; Teen Inst Ldrshp 85-86; Pres TRES CHIC Hm Ec Clb 85-86; Tstmstrs Yth Ldrshp 86; Point Park; Thtr Arts.

ROCHE, WENDY S; Crestwood HS; Mountaintop, PA; (Y); Exploring; Hosp Aide; Ski Clb; Yrbk Stf; Stu Cncl; Cheerleading; Crs Cntry; Trk; High Hon Roll; All Amer Chrldr 84-85; Trck & Fld Dist Wnnr 84-85; Pharm.

ROCHENY, ELIZABETH; Sacred Heart HS; Carbondale, PA; (Y); 9/45; Cmnty Wkr; Office Aide; Teachers Aide; Chorus; School Musical; School Play; High Hon Roll; Hon Roll; Sci.

ROCK, MICHELE; Mt Pleasant HS; Greenburg, PA; (Y); GAA; Ski Clb; Band; Mrchg Band; Sec Frsh Cls; Trk; Trvl.

ROCK, NERISSA T; Bedford SR HS; Bedford, PA; (Y); FBLA; Chorus; School Musical; Trs Sr Cls; Co-Capt Cheerleading; Twrlr; Hon Roll; Acadmc Al-Amer Awd 85; Natl Ldrshp-Svc Awd 86; Profssnl Singr-Actrss.

ROCK, TIMOTHY; Ambridge Area HS; Baden, PA; (Y); 1/300; Pres German Clb; Pep Clb; Quiz Bowl; Stu Cncl; Var Bsbl; Var L Crs Cntry; High Hon Roll; NHS; PA Govrnr Schl Sci 86; U S Air Force Acad Smmr Sci Semnr 86; Aerosp Engrng.

ROCKEFELLER, JILL; Pennsbury HS; Fairless Hills, PA; (Y); Spanish Clb; Band; Concert Band; Mrchg Band; Fld Hcky; JV Sftbl; Kutztown U; Bus.

ROCKEMORE, MARIE; Simon Gratz HS; Philadelphia, PA; (S); Church Yth Grp; Church Choir; Hon Roll; Prfct Atten Awd; William Penn Chrtr Coll Prep Awd 85; Perfect Attndnc Awd 82; Mrtrs Hnr Roll 86; Temple U; Pre-Law.

ROCKENSTEIN, AMY; Butler SR HS; Butler, PA; (Y); VP DECA; FBLA; SADD; Thesps; WV U; Law.

ROCKEY JR, DONALD; Carlisle SR HS; Carlisle, PA; (Y); JV L Bsbl; Im L Bsktbl; Im L Ftbl; Hon Roll; Vet Med.

ROCKEY, LISA; Hughesville HS; Hughesville, PA; (Y); 10/145; Church Yth Grp; Trs Key Clb; Ski Clb; VP Band; Drm Mjr(t); Mrchg Band; School Musical; Var Trk; Hon Roll; PA ST U; Bio.

ROCKMULLER, STEVE; Cash HS; Pittsburgh, PA; (Y); 48/500; Church Yth Grp; Ski Clb; Spanish Clb; Temple Yth Grp; VP Rep Frsh Cls; VP Rep Soph Cls; Golf; Im JV Socr; Hon Roll; Pres Schlr.

ROCKOVICH, BRIAN; Hazleton HS; Hazleton, PA; (Y); Computer Clb; Drama Clb; FBLA; JA; Scholastic Bowl; Stage Crew; Im Bsktbl; Hon Roll; Comp.

ROCKWELL, MEG; Bentworth SR HS; Amity, PA; (Y); Church Yth Grp; FHA; Library Aide; Red Cross Aide; Science Clb; Teachers Aide; Mgr Band; Mgr Concert Band; Mgr Drill Tm; Mgr Mrchg Band; Amer Leg Awd8cnty Chorus; CA U PA; Phy Thrpy.

ROCKWOOD, CHRIS; Trinity HS; Carlisle, PA; (Y); 23/144; French Clb; School Musical; School Play; Rep Stu Cncl; L Var Bsktbl; L Var Socr; L Var Trk; Hon Roll; NEDT Awd; Church Yth Grp; Athlt Of Yr 86.

RODA, ROBERTA; North Hills SR HS; Pittsburgh, PA; (Y); Key Clb; Chorus; Capt Cheerleading; Diving; Mgr(s); Swmmng; High Hon Roll; Hon Roll; U Of Pittsburgh; Psychlgy.

RODAVICH, ROD; Waynesburg Central HS; Waynesburg, PA; (Y); 8/200; Letterman Clb; Ski Clb; Spanish Clb; Bsbl; Bsktbl; Golf; NHS; Top 10 Stu; PA ST Earth & Sci Awd 85-86; Acadmc All Amercn 85-86; PA ST U; Elec Engrng.

RODDY, KELLY; East Pennsboro Area HS; Enola, PA; (Y); German Clb; Girl Scts; Hosp Aide; Bsktbl; Fld Hcky; High Hon Roll; Hon Roll; Prfct Atten Awd; Math.

RODDY, REBECCA; Bethel Christian HS; Erie, PA; (S); 1/16; Chorus; School Play; Variety Show; Yrbk Stf; Pres Jr Cls; Pres Sr Cls; Capt Bsktbl; Capt Vllybl; High Hon Roll; Val; Bible Schlr Awds 83-84; Soc Distnqushd Amer Stu 84-85; Gannon U; Elem Ed.

RODENHORN, WESLEY; Punxsutawney HS; Punxsutawney, PA; (Y); Var JV Bsbl; Var JV Ftbl.

RODESAUGH, WILLIAM; Cedar Grove Christian Acad; Philadelphia, PA; (Y); 3/45; Church Yth Grp; Band; Chorus; Nwsp Ed-Chief; Sec Trs Frsh Cls; Sec Trs Soph Cls; Trs Jr Cls; JV Bsbl; Stat Bsktbl; Var Crs Cntry; Hgst Avg Chem,Hist,Alg II 86; Chem.

RODGER, HEIDI; Northeastern HS; York, PA; (Y); Ski Clb; Varsity Clb; Band; Mrchg Band; Fld Hcky; Trk; Millersville U; Elem Ed.

RODGERS, BRUCE; Wilmington Area HS; New Wilmington, PA; (S); 6/123; Trs Church Yth Grp; Computer Clb; Drama Clb; Spanish Clb; Band; School Play; Stage Crew; High Hon Roll; Hon Roll; NHS.

RODGERS, DENISE; Owen J Roberts HS; Pottstown, PA; (Y); JA; Drill Tm; Yrbk Stf; Rep Soph Cls; Rep Jr Cls; JV Bsktbl; JV Lcrss; Hon Roll; Nrsng.

RODGERS, JAY; Allegeny Clarion Valley HS; St Petersburgh, PA; (Y); 12/105; Spanish Clb; Grove City Coll; Acctg.

RODGERS, KEIRSTEN; Parkland HS; Allentown, PA; (Y); 145/459; Debate Tm; Key Clb; School Musical; Nwsp Rptr; Yrbk Stf; Stu Cncl; Stat Bsbl; Twrlr; Jr Prom Queen 85; US Hist Day Rgnl 2nd Pl Awd 84; Geologist.

RODGERS, LAURA; Hempfield Area SR HS; Seekonk, MA; (Y); 13/657; French Clb; Latin Clb; Ski Clb; Nwsp Stf; Yrbk Stf; Lit Mag; High Hon Roll; Jr NHS; NHS; U Of Pittsburgh; CAS.

RODGERS, MATT; Palmyra HS; Palmyra, PA; (Y); Church Yth Grp; Chorus; Church Choir; Nwsp Rptr; Rep Stu Cncl; JV Ftbl; Var Trk; JV Wrstlng; Music Thrpy.

RODGERS, REBECCA; Chief Logan HS; Lewistown, PA; (Y); Art Clb; Concert Band; Drm Mjr(t); Mrchg Band; Yrbk Stf; JV Bsktbl; Var Trk; PA ST Schlstc Art Merit Awd 86; 1st Pl Design-An-Ad Cntst 86; Cmmrcl Art.

RODGERS, SUSAN; Grove City HS; Grove City, PA; (Y); Hosp Aide; Key Clb; Science Clb; Band; Concert Band; Mrchg Band; Var JV Cheerleading; Im Tennis; Hon Roll; PA ST U Hzltn; Physcl Thrpst.

RODGERS, TAMMI K; Rocky Grove HS; Reno, PA; (Y); 10/91; Pres Church Yth Grp; Girl Scts; Hosp Aide; Band; Chorus; Pep Band; High Hon Roll; Hon Roll; Acdmc ExclInc Awd 83-85; Physcn.

RODGERS, TERRY L; Girard HS; Girard, PA; (Y); Am Leg Boys St; Church Yth Grp; Spanish Clb; VP Varsity Clb; Trs Frsh Cls; VP Soph Cls; Var L Bsbl; Var Bsktbl; High Hon Roll; Hon Roll; VP-VRSTY Clb; Top 10% Cls; Ltr-All Cnty Bsbl & Bsktbl; Hnr Rll; Hgh Hnr Rll; Coach Lttl Leag Bsbl; PA ST U; Bus Adm.

RODGERS, TUESDAE; Franklin HS; Cochranton, PA; (Y); 21/240; Church Yth Grp; Cmnty Wkr; German Clb; Hosp Aide; Pres Service Clb; Rep Stu Cncl; Var Swmmng; High Hon Roll; Hon Roll; NHS; Shcl Brd Dir Awd 85 & 86; Kung Fu Ylw Blt 85-86; Psych.

RODGERS, VERONICA; St Maria Goretti HS; Philadelphia, PA; (Y); 60/435; Cmnty Wkr; French Clb; VP Sr Cls; VP Stu Cncl; High Hon Roll; Hon Roll; NHS; Prfct Atten Awd; Camp Fr Inc; Concrnd Blacernen Inc Awd 86; Yth Cngrs 85-86; La Salle U; Poli Sci.

RODGERS, WENDY; Penridge SR HS; Pipersville, PA; (Y); Art Clb; Church Yth Grp; French Clb; Yrbk Stf; Cheerleading; Fld Hcky; Hon Roll; Baylor Univ; Fash Dsgn.

RODICHOK, JOSEPH; Williams Valley JR/SR HS; Williamstown, PA; (Y); 7/120; Boy Scts; Chorus; Concert Band; Jazz Band; Mrchg Band; Symp Band; JV Bsktbl; Var JV Ftbl; Hon Roll; NHS; Aerospace Engrng.

RODICK, DAVID; Hazleton HS; Drums, PA; (Y).

RODKEY, MARIE; Bishop Guilfoyle HS; Altoona, PA; (S); 15/150; Church Yth Grp; VP Spanish Clb; SADD; Church Choir; Yrbk Stf; Sec Jr Cls; Rep Stu Cncl; JV Var Cheerleading; High Hon Roll; VP Trs NHS; Ntl Physcl Ed Awd; IN U Of Penna; Food Svc Mgmt.

RODLAND, JEFF; Harbor Creek HS; Erie, PA; (Y); Model UN; Chorus; Yrbk Ed-Chief; Yrbk Stf; Rep Sr Cls; Elem Teach.

RODRIGUES, MARK; Mt Lebanon HS; Mt Lebanon, PA; (Y); 120/519; Chess Clb; CAP; Exploring; Service Clb; Ski Clb; Varsity Clb; Band; JV Socr; High Hon Roll; Hon Roll.

RODRIGUEZ, CARLOS; Elizabeth Forward HS; Elizabeth, PA; (Y); 10/315; Church Yth Grp; Exploring; Varsity Clb; Stage Crew; Ftbl; Wt Lftg; High Hon Roll; NHS; Chem.

RODRIGUEZ, GLADYS; Mastbaum A V T HS; Philadelphia, PA; (Y); 31/379; Sec Church Yth Grp; Math Clb; Office Aide; Spanish Clb; Church Choir; Yrbk Stf; Im Vllybl; High Hon Roll; Hon Roll; FBLA; Awd From Aspira Clb Treas 86; Ldrshp Mdl 85; Med.

RODRIGUEZ, KAREN; Bristol JR SR HS; Bristol, PA; (Y); Drama Clb; Spanish Clb; Color Guard; Mrchg Band; School Musical; Variety Show; Var Crs Cntry; Var Trk; Hon Roll; BAL 100 Mtr Grls Hurdle Champ 86; BAL Girls Trpl Jump Champ 85; All Area Track & Field 85; Bucks Cnty CC; Music.

RODRIGUEZ, ROGELIO C; Moon SR HS; Corapolis, PA; (Y); Sec Trs Computer Clb; Math Tm; Rep Stu Cncl; JV Socr; High Hon Roll; Hon Roll; U Of Pittsburgh; Engrg.

RODRIGUEZ, THOMAS D; Mon Valley Catholic HS; Belle Vernon, PA; (S); 10/102; Spanish Clb; Var L Bsktbl; Coach Actv; Var L Ftbl; L Golf; Powder Puff Ftbl; Wt Lftg; NHS; Spanish NHS; 2nd Pl Spnsh Prose Humnts Day 85; Dayton ST; Bus.

RODRIGUEZ, TIM; Monongahela Valley Catholic HS; Belle Vernon, PA; (Y); 8/83; Spanish Clb; Varsity Clb; Variety Show; Var L Bsktbl; JV Ftbl; Var L Golf; Powder Puff Ftbl; NHS; Spanish NHS; Hugh O Brien 84-85; Bus Mgmnt.

RODRIQUEZ, DANIEL; Northampton SR HS; Walnutport, PA; (Y); Boy Scts; Exploring; SADD; Var Crs Cntry; Var Trk; AF Pilot.

RODZINAK, VANESSA; Lake-Lehman HS; Hunlock Creek, PA; (Y); 3/140; Church Yth Grp; SADD; High Hon Roll; Jr NHS; NHS; Century 21 Typwrtg Awd 85.

ROE, RHONDA; Penn-Trafford HS; Trafford, PA; (Y); Pres 4-H; Hosp Aide; Math Clb; Political Wkr; Church Choir; Variety Show; Nwsp Stf; VP Diving; 4-H Awd; Hon Roll; Math Schlrshp 85; 4-H Qn Attndnt 85; Mod Dance Awd 85; Arch Engr.

ROEBER, PATRICK; Bethel Park HS; Bethel Park, PA; (Y); Ftbl; Socr; Trk; All Conf Ftbl Kicker 85; Dapper Dan All Star Sccr Game 85; Bowling Gree ST U; Bus.

ROEBUCK, MICHAEL; Mapletown HS; Dilliner, PA; (Y); 1/92; Boy Scts; Nwsp Stf; Yrbk Stf; Trs Jr Cls; High Hon Roll; NHS; Ntl Merit Ltr; Summr Schl Grad 85-86.

ROEHL, ANDREA; Exeter SR HS; Reading, PA; (Y); 16/227; Drama Clb; Ski Clb; Y-Teens; Band; Rep Jr Cls; Rep Stu Cncl; Cheerleading; High Hon Roll; JC Awd; NHS; Law.

ROEHRIG, THEODORE; Marple Newtown SR HS; Newtown Square, PA; (Y); 3/360; Pres Math Clb; Math Tm; Variety Show; Nwsp Stf; Rep Stu Cncl; Var Crs Cntry; Im Ice Hcky; Im Vllybl; NHS; High Hon Roll; PA Cncl Teachrs Of Math 1T Pl 86; BP Oil Acad Awd 86; Soc Studies Locl Poltcs Awd 86; Lehigh U; Civil Engrng.

ROELKE, GREGORY; Red Lion SR HS; York, PA; (Y); 66/337; Boy Scts; Church Yth Grp; JV Ftbl; Var Swmmng; High Hon Roll; Hon Roll; Hnr Stu 86; IN U; Elect Engr.

ROESCH, MAUREEN; Bishop Guilfoyle HS; Altoona, PA; (S); 3/129; Art Clb; Church Yth Grp; German Clb; Chorus; Trs Jr Cls; Rep Stu Cncl; Bsktbl; High Hon Roll; Hon Roll; Penn ST; Bus.

ROESCH, MICHELLE; Bishop Guilfoyle HS; Altoona, PA; (Y); 13/108; Art Clb; Cmnty Wkr; German Clb; Sec Stu Cncl; Rep Jr Cls; JV Var Bsktbl; Hon Roll; Penn ST U; Bus.

ROESHORE, HEIDI; Annville-Cleona HS; Annville, PA; (Y); Band; Chorus; Concert Band; Mrchg Band; Orch; Pep Band; Jr NHS; NHS; Goldey Beacom; Acctg.

ROESKE, NICOLE; Cedar Crest HS; Lebanon, PA; (Y); German Clb; Pep Clb; Vllybl; Hon Roll; Booster Clb Hnr Bnqt 86; Millersville; Bus.

ROESSING, DOUG; Allegheny Clarion Valley HS; Parker, PA; (Y); 8/108; Aud/Vis; Varsity Clb; Var Bsktbl; Var Ftbl; Var Golf; Var Trk; Hon Roll; 4 Yr NROTC Schlrshp Wnr 86; Pres Acadmc Fitnss Awd 86; PA ST U Univ Pk; Arch Engrng.

ROG, STACIE; Manheim Township HS; Lancaster, PA; (Y); 43/327; Church Yth Grp; Girl Scts; Chorus; VP Mrchg Band; School Musical; Variety Show; Yrbk Stf; Trs Soph Cls; Rep Stu Cncl; Hon Roll; Mrchng Bnd Sctn Ldr 85-86; Ten Yr Grl Scout Awd 86; Cnty, Dstrct & R Gnl Chorus & Cnty & Dstrct Bnd; Law.

ROGALA, AMIE; Strath Haven HS; Wallingford, PA; (Y); Art Clb; Mathletes; Yrbk Rptr; Yrbk Stf; High Hon Roll; Hon Roll; Mu Alp Tht; Grapevine Advsry Cncl 85-86; Vrsty Arts Let 86; Assnt Actvty Dir Of The Wallingfore Nrsng Hm 85-86.

ROGALEWICZ, ROGER; West Scranton HS; Scranton, PA; (Y); 75/265; Boy Scts; Cmnty Wkr; Political Wkr; Nwsp Rptr; Rep Jr Cls; Bsbl; Ftbl; Hon Roll; Lackawanna JR Coll; Law.

ROGAN, DEBRA; St Marys Area HS; St Marys, PA; (Y); 32/290; Camera Clb; 4-H; Library Aide; Varsity Clb; Var L Gym; Var L Tennis; Var L Trk; High Hon Roll; Hon Roll; Pres Schlr; U Of FL-GAINSVL; Pre-Vet Med.

ROGAN, KELLI; Trinity HS; Carlisle, PA; (Y); 2/140; Drama Clb; French Clb; Pep Clb; Ski Clb; Stage Crew; Yrbk Stf; JV Socr; JV Trk; High Hon Roll; NHS; Patriot News Wrtg Cert Merit 86; Pre-Med.

ROGAN, KELLY M; Penn Hills SR HS; Verona, PA; (Y); 33/762; Ski Clb; Spanish Clb; VP Drill Tm; Sr Cls; Stu Cncl; Pom Pon; Powder Puff Ftbl; High Hon Roll; NHS; Penn ST U; Bus Admn.

ROGERS, ANTOINETTE; Philadelphia-Montgomery Chrstn Academy; Philadelphia, PA; (Y); VP Church Yth Grp; Church Choir; Trs Sr Cls; High Hon Roll; Hon Roll; NHS; JV Bsktbl; Charles E Ellis Grant & Schlrshp Fund 82-87; White-Williams Fndtn 83-87; Med.

ROGERS, EDWARD; Farrell SR HS; Farrell, PA; (Y); Science Clb; Spanish Clb; Var L Vllybl; Engrng.

ROGERS, KIMBERLY ANNE; Shippensburg Area SR HS; Shippensburg, PA; (Y); 2/250; Am Leg Aux Girls St; Girl Scts; SADD; Band; School Musical; School Play; Stu Cncl; Fld Hcky; Cit Awd; NHS; Slctd Attnd Lhugh Obrien Yth Smnr 85; Smi-Fnlst Jpn US Senate Schlrshp; Ecnmcs.

ROGERS, MARY FRANCES; Bishop O Hara HS; Elmhurst, PA; (Y); Church Yth Grp; Latin Clb; Science Clb; Teachers Aide; Chorus; Church Choir; School Musical; Hon Roll; Keystone JC; Bio.

ROH, SUNNY; Philadelphia High Schl For Girls; Philadelphia, PA; (Y); Pres Church Yth Grp; Teachers Aide; Orch; Stu Cncl; Var Fld Hcky; Var Lcrss; Var Tennis; Hon Roll; Intr Dsgn.

ROHAL, TODD; Avella Area HS; W Middletown, PA; (Y); French Clb; Nwsp Stf; VP Soph Cls; Pres Jr Cls; VP Stu Cncl; Hon Roll.

ROHLAND, BRYAN; Middleburg HS; Middleburg, PA; (Y); Computer Clb; Band; Jazz Band; Socr; Vllybl; Wrstlng; NHS; Concert Band; Madrigals; Mrchg Band; Tri-Valley Leag All-Star Wrstlng 85-86; Acadmc Achvt 85-86; Mst Imprvd Wrstlr Awd 85-86; Arch.

ROHLAND, JACK; Freeport Area HS; Sarver, PA; (S); Var JV Ftbl; Var Trk; High Hon Roll; Hon Roll.

ROHM, SHERRY; Shamokin Area HS; Shamokin, PA; (Y); 54/239; Church Yth Grp; Varsity Clb; Trs Band; Pep Band; Var L Bsktbl; Var Trk; Hon Roll; Comp Pgmmr.

ROHN, KHALIL; Mastbaum AVTS; Philadelphia, PA; (Y); 5/321; Chess Clb; Math Clb; Math Tm; Nwsp Sprt Ed; Var Capt Ftbl; Var Capt Trk; High Hon Roll; NHS; Natl Schlr/Ath Awd U S Army 86; Congressnl Merit Awd 86; Distngshd Engrng Draftng Awd 86; Temple U; Mech Engr.

ROHRBACH, ERIKA; Liberty HS; Bethlehem, PA; (Y); 20/391; German Clb; Model UN; Church Choir; Mrchg Band; Orch; Lit Mag; Rep Frsh Cls; Capt Var Tennis; NHS; Grad Speaker 86; Morris E Black Schlrsph 86; Ursinus Coll; Physcn.

ROHRBACH, TAMMY; Brandywine Heights HS; Mertztown, PA; (Y); 4/101; Stage Crew; Yrbk Stf; Sec Jr Cls; Sec Sr Cls; Pres Stu Cncl; Capt Fld Hcky; Var Trk; Cit Awd; DAR Awd; Sec NHS; US Air Force Acad; Aernctl Eng.

ROHRBAUGH, KIMBERLY A; Central York SR HS; York, PA; (Y); Church Yth Grp; Band; Concert Band; Mrchg Band; Orch; School Musical; Symp Band; Hon Roll; Ambssdrs Of Musc Europ Tr 85; Millersville U; Elem Ed.

ROHRBAUGH, TIMOTHY; Southwestern HS; Hanover, PA; (Y); 17/225; Drm & Bgl; Drm Mjr(t); Jazz Band; Mrchg Band; Orch; Pep Band; Symp Band; Tennis; JP Sousa Awd; NHS; Westchester U; Music Ed.

ROHRER, BARBARA; Solanco HS; Quarryville, PA; (Y); 1/230; Church Yth Grp; Letterman Clb; Pep Clb; Varsity Clb; Band; Chorus; Concert Band; Drm Mjr(t); Mrchg Band; Orch; Rotary Stu Of The Mnth 85; Soroptomist Good Citznshp Awd 86; Ursinus Coll; Chem.

ROHRER, CHRISTOPHER; Donegal HS; Marietta, PA; (Y); Boy Scts; Church Yth Grp; German Clb; Rep Stu Cncl; Var Crs Cntry; Var Trk; Var Vllybl; Var Wt Lftg; Var Wrstlng; Cit Awd; Lfsvng 82; Egl Sct 80; Ordr Arrow 81; Penn ST; Mech Engr.

ROHRER, DARRYL; Lampeter-Strasburg HS; Lancaster, PA; (Y); 52/157; FFA; VICA; Rep Jr Cls; Hon Roll; Greenhand Degree 83-84; Chapter Farmer Award 84-85; Vo Tech Honor Roll 85-86; Diesel Mech Schl; Diesel Mech.

ROHRER, KERRY; Solanco HS; Quarryville, PA; (Y); 8/250; Church Yth Grp; Drama Clb; Spanish Clb; Chorus; Church Choir; School Play; Stage Crew; Yrbk Rptr; Yrbk Stf; High Hon Roll; Hlth Awd Schlr 84.

ROHRER, LELA; Pequea Valley HS; Paradise, PA; (Y); 60/130; Trs Varsity Clb; Band; Pres Chorus; Mrchg Band; School Musical; Ed Yrbk Phtg; VP Sr Cls; Var Fld Hcky; Var Gym; Var Sftbl; Commnctns.

ROHRER, MICHELE; Manheim Central HS; Lititz, PA; (Y); 4/265; Church Yth Grp; 4-H; Red Cross Aide; Band; Chorus; Orch; Yrbk Ed-Chief; Var Tennis; NHS; Ntl Merit Ltr; Engl, Home Ec Awds 84; 4 Way Tst Awd 86; Messiah Coll.

ROHRER, WENDY S; Solanco HS; Quarryville, PA; (Y); 22/215; Church Yth Grp; Teachers Aide; Band; Concert Band; Jazz Band; Mrchg Band; Orch; School Musical; Nwsp Stf; Fld Hcky; Millersville U; Spec Ed.

ROKE, LISA; John S Fine HS; Glen Lyon, PA; (Y); Am Leg Aux Girls St; Girl Scts; Key Clb; Library Aide; Model UN; Speech Tm; Chorus; Yrbk Stf; Swmmng; Hon Roll; Am Lung Assoc Awd 81; Penn ST.

ROKOSKY, DAVE; Du Bois Area HS; Dubois, PA; (Y); Art Clb; Ski Clb; Arch.

ROLAND, JAMIE; Bishop Guilfoyle HS; Altoona, PA; (Y); Church Yth Grp; SADD; Band; Chorus; Concert Band; Mrchg Band; Pres Pep Band; Variety Show; Hon Roll; NHS; Mscl Thtre.

ROLAND, KEVIN; Our Lady Of The Sacred Heart HS; Pittsburgh, PA; (Y); 1/65; Computer Clb; School Musical; Stage Crew; Bowling; Socr; Hon Roll; NHS; Engrng.

ROLES, ELIZABETH; Blacklick Valley HS; Nanty Glo, PA; (S); 5/80; Church Yth Grp; Cmnty Wkr; FBLA; Girl Scts; Library Aide; Office Aide; OEA; Ski Clb; Rep Frsh Cls; Rep Soph Cls; Grad Barbizon Modlg Schl 82; Fnlst Miss Amer Co Ed Pagnt 84; Bus.

ROLINSKI, ANTHONY M; Penn Hills SR HS; Pittsburgh, PA; (Y); 159/797; Aud/Vis; Office Aide; Science Clb; Spanish Clb; Off Jr Cls; Off Sr Cls; Stu Cncl; JV Bsbl; Wt Lftg; High Hon Roll; U Of Pittsburgh; Bio.

ROLLA, BONNIE; Central HS; Scranton, PA; (Y); 7/285; Debate Tm; Drama Clb; French Clb; Drill Tm; School Play; Yrbk Stf; VP Sr Cls; Pres Stu Cncl; Cheerleading; Hon Roll; Amer Busnsswmns 86; Disabled Amer Vets Schlrp 86; Francis Clarke Awd 86; Bucknell U; Tchr.

ROLLIN, KRISTIN DONELL; Elizabeth Forward SR HS; Elizabeth, PA; (Y); 10/317; Pres Church Yth Grp; Q&S; Drm Mjr(t); Jazz Band; School Musical; Nwsp Ed-Chief; High Hon Roll; NHS; Pres Schlr; Non-Music Major Flute Schlrshp U SC 86; PA Music Edu Assoc Dist & Rgn Bands 86; PA Lions All ST Bd; U SC; Pharmacy.

ROLLMAN, JOHN; Shamokin Area HS; Shamokin, PA; (Y); 20/241; German Clb; Science Clb; Varsity Clb; Var Capt Ftbl; Var Capt Wrstlng; High Hon Roll; Hon Roll; NHS; Vars Wrstlng Ltr & Capt; Vars Ftbl Ltr & Capt.

ROLLY, SHAUN; Deer Lakes JR-SR HS; Gibsonia, PA; (Y); Drama Clb; Concert Band; Mrchg Band; Pep Band; School Play; Stage Crew; Variety Show; Yrbk Rptr; Yrbk Stf; Trk; Buhl Sci Cntrs Awd Comp Sci 83; Indiana U Of PA; Comp Sci.

ROMAN, JAMES; West Mifflin Area HS; W Mifflin, PA; (Y); Band; Concert Band; Jazz Band; Mrchg Band; Orch; Pep Band; Symp Band; Hon Roll; FL Intl U; Elec Engrng.

ROMAN, JOE; Burgettstown Area HS; Paris, PA; (Y); Ski Clb; Spanish Clb; Ftbl; Hon Roll; Penn ST U; Bus Admn.

ROMAN, RICHARD; Valley View HS; Jessup, PA; (Y); Church Yth Grp; Bsktbl; Trk; Hon Roll; U Scranton; Arch Engr.

ROMAN, TRACEY; Saint Hubert HS; Philadelphia, PA; (Y); 183/367; Camera Clb; Girl Scts; Hosp Aide; Teachers Aide; Ntl Sci Merit Awds 84; Hlth Awd St Hbrt 85; Rsprtry Thrpst.

ROMANCE, JANNETTE; Western Wayne HS; Aldenville, PA; (Y); 18/138; Pres 4-H; FBLA; Church Choir; Mrchg Band; VP Soph Cls; Pres Jr Cls; Rep Stu Cncl; JV VP Bsktbl; Hon Roll; NHS; Hosp Admin.

ROMANCHOCK, PAUL; Windber Area HS; Windber, PA; (Y); 17/130; Sec Soph Cls; VP Jr Cls; Rep Sec Stu Cncl; Var L Bsktbl; Var L Ftbl; Hon Roll; NHS; All Cnty Ftbl Tm-Top Dist Passer; All Lge-Bsktbl Tm; Bsktbl Tm-St Qtrfnlst; Sprts Thrpy.

ROMANELLI, AL; Coatesville Area HS; Coatesville, PA; (Y); Ftbl; Wt Lftg; Wrstlng; Hon Roll; NHS; Wrstlng/Mst Take Downs/Awd 86; Penn ST U; Bus.

ROMANI, JANINE; Chichester HS; Boothwyn, PA; (Y); 38/293; Nwsp Stf; Yrbk Stf; Cheerleading; Hon Roll; Penn St U.

ROMANI, MARCELLA; Greater Johnstown HS; Johnstown, PA; (Y); 3/268; Thesps; Concert Band; Mrchg Band; School Musical; Stat Sftbl; High Hon Roll; Pres NHS; Math Tm; Band; Pep Band; Fred M Glosser Scholar Awd 86; Stu Mnth Exch Clb 85-86; PA ST U JR Sci Sympsm 85; PA ST U.

ROMANIC, MARY LYNNE; St Marys Area HS; Byrnedale, PA; (Y); 6/301; Sec Stu Cncl; Var Trk; High Hon Roll; NHS; Cert Of Merit In Spanish 85-86; 1st Pl Typist 84-85.

ROMANIK, RICK; Blairsville SR HS; Blairsville, PA; (Y); Art Clb; French Clb; Swmmng; Trk; Wt Lftg; Wrstlng; High Hon Roll; Hon Roll; Vale Tech.

ROMANISHAN, BOBBI JO; Nazareth Area SR HS; Wind Gap, PA; (Y); 20/241; Art Clb; Girl Scts; JV Fld Hcky; High Hon Roll; Hon Roll; Kiwanis Awd; Schlstc Art Awd 86; Art Illus.

ROMANO, AMELIA; Pocono Mountain HS; Tobyhanna, PA; (Y); Church Yth Grp; Hosp Aide; Library Aide; Science Clb; Hon Roll; Prtcl Nrsng Pgm 83; West Chester; Nrsng.

ROMANO, DEBBIE; St Maria Goretti HS; Philadelphia, PA; (Y); Cmnty Wkr; Exploring; GAA; Intnl Clb; Math Clb; Pep Clb; Pres Service Clb; Spanish Clb; Band; Chorus.

ROMANO, JEFFREY; Hampton HS; Gibsonia, PA; (Y); Ski Clb; Rep Stu Cncl; Var L Socr; High Hon Roll; Hon Roll; French Clb; Rep Frsh Cls; Rep Soph Cls; Rep Jr Cls; JV Ftbl.

ROMANO, KENNETH A; Father Judge HS; Philadelphia, PA; (S); 37/403; Office Aide; Band; School Musical; School Play; Hon Roll; NHS; Philadelphia Inquir Schlrshp Asstnc Awd 83; Holy Family Coll; Intntl Bus.

ROMANO, MARIA; Bishop Kenrick HS; Norristown, PA; (Y); 11/307; Cmnty Wkr; French Clb; Mathletes; Math Clb; Scholastic Bowl; Science Clb; Nwsp Rptr; Mgr(s); Trk; Hon Roll; French Awd 85; Phar.

ROMANOSKI, DEB; Shamokin Area HS; Shamokin, PA; (Y); 28/244; German Clb; Letterman Clb; Sec Band; Sec Concert Band; Rep Soph Cls; Rep Stu Cncl; Capt Cheerleading; Var L Trk; Var Vllybl; Hon Roll; Medcl Technlgy.

ROMANOSKY, MICHAEL; Norristown Area HS; Norristown, PA; (S); 19/583; DECA; Pres FBLA; Key Clb; Ski Clb; Pres Frsh Cls; Pres Soph Cls; JV Bsbl; Hon Roll; Bus Adm.

ROMANOWSKI, MARY ELAINE; Scranton Tech; Scranton, PA; (Y); 6/257; FBLA; Yrbk Stf; High Hon Roll; Hon Roll; Jr NHS; Trs NHS; Bus Co-Op Of Yr Awd 86; 1st Hnrs Bus 86; Natl Hnr Soc Scholar 86; NE Inst Of Ed; Trvl.

ROMBALDI, CHRISTINA; Deer Lakes JR-SR HS; Tarentum, PA; (Y); Drama Clb; Ski Clb; School Play; Stage Crew; Pres Frsh Cls; Pres Soph Cls; Pres Jr Cls; Stu Cncl; Hon Roll; NHS; IUP; Crim Jstc.

ROMBERGER, JULIE; Annville Cleona HS; Annville, PA; (Y); 25/125; Girl Scts; Varsity Clb; Var JV Fld Hcky; Mat Maids; JV Sftbl; Jr NHS; NHS; Leader Corp 84-86; Central Penn; Chldcre Mgmt.

ROMBOLA, LISA; Bishop Mc Devitt HS; Glenside, PA; (Y); 61/351; Church Yth Grp; Dance Clb; Drama Clb; Intnl Clb; Band; Concert Band; Mrchg Band; Orch; School Musical; Hon Roll; Tlnt Fnlst Miss Natl Tnagr Metro Phila 84; Tlnt Fnlst Modern Miss PA 85; Southeastern Acad; Trvl.

ROMEO, ANITA; Center HS; Monaca, PA; (Y); Spanish Clb; Band; Concert Band; Drm Mjr(t); Mrchg Band; School Musical; High Hon Roll; Hon Roll; NHS; Swckly Symphny Orch 84-86; Slvr Awd Grl Scts 84; Med Tech.

ROMEO JR, DOMINIC P; Chambersburg Area SR HS; Fayetteville, PA; (Y); 130/641; Letterman Clb; Ski Clb; Band; Drm & Bgl; Jazz Band; Mrchg Band; Diving; Var L Socr; Var L Trk; Hon Roll; U Of Pittsburgh; Pre-Med.

ROMESBURG, DEBRA; Rockwood Joint HS; Rockwood, PA; (S); 10/100; Church Yth Grp; Computer Clb; Band; Chorus; Church Choir; Concert Band; Mrchg Band; Yrbk Sprt Ed; Yrbk Stf; JV Var Bsktbl; Grls Phy Ed Awd 84-85; U Of Pittsburg; Crmnlgy.

ROMEU, DIANA LORENA; Germantown Acad; N Wales, PA; (Y); Intnl Clb; Ski Clb; Spanish Clb; Yrbk Sprt Ed; Var Capt Fld Hcky; Var L Lcrss; Hon Roll; Pres Frsh Cls; Cit Awd; Yrbk Art Edtr 85-86; Upr Schl Art Prze 86; Stanford U; Intl Rel.

ROMICH, TAMMY; Scranton Central HS; Scranton, PA; (Y); Church Yth Grp; French Clb; JA; Concert Band; Mrchg Band; Psych.

ROMIG, KIMBERLY; Shippensburg Area SR HS; Orrstown, PA; (Y); 6/226; Concert Band; Mrchg Band; Orch; School Musical; High Hon Roll; NHS; Srch Excllnce Schlrshp 86; Millersville U; Math.

ROMIG, TOM; Hamburg Area HS; Hamburg, PA; (Y); 61/155; Church Yth Grp; SADD; Stu Cncl; Bsbl; Bsktbl; Socr; Trk; Coaches Roundtable 84-85; Hamburg Booster Tour MVP 85.

ROMIGH, KELLY; Sewickley Acad; Beaver, PA; (Y); 11/70; Church Yth Grp; French Clb; Key Clb; Speech Tm; Chorus; School Play; Nwsp Ed-Chief; Nwsp Rptr; Ed Nwsp Stf; Sec Stu Cncl; Jrnlsm.

ROMMES, JILL; Deer Lakes HS; Gibsonia, PA; (Y); Church Yth Grp; Drama Clb; French Clb; Mrchg Band; School Play; Pom Pon; Hon Roll.

RONAN, DANA; Bishop Guilfoyle HS; Altoona, PA; (S); 15/129; Church Yth Grp; Y-Teens; Trs Frsh Cls; Rep Stu Cncl; Cheerleading; High Hon Roll; Hon Roll; JR Hmncng Ct Rep 85-86; PA ST U; Optmtry.

RONAN, JOE; Bishop Kenrick HS; Norristown, PA; (Y); Ftbl; Wt Lftg; Wrstlng; Bus Admin.

RONDINELLI, LISA B; Bangor Area SR HS; Bangor, PA; (Y); 40/212; Pres Church Yth Grp; Varsity Clb; Concert Band; School Musical; Chorus; Church Choir; Variety Show; Var Bsktbl; Var Fld Hcky; High Hon Roll; Kathryn & Walter Speck Schlrshp 86; Queen Of Bangor Fr Dept 100 Anniv 86; Educ Assoc Schlrshp 86; Geisinger Med Ctr; Nrsng.

RONEY, MARCIE; Punxsutawney Area HS; Punxsutawney, PA; (Y); Cmnty Wkr; Hosp Aide; Teachers Aide; Band; Concert Band; Drill Tm; Mrchg Band; Var Twrlr; Hon Roll.

RONTZ, TRISHA; Jim Thorpe HS; Jim Thorpe, PA; (S); 2/99; Chorus; Nwsp Sprt Ed; Yrbk Phtg; Sec Stu Cncl; Var Capt Bsktbl; Var L Sftbl; Var L Vllybl; DAR Awd; Lion Awd; Pres NHS; PA JR Sci & Humnts Sympsm PSU 85; JR Rotrn 86; Muhlenberg Coll; Acctg.

RONZANO, ROBERT; Council Rock HS; Holland, PA; (Y); JV Ftbl; L Trk; Im Vllybl; Im Wt Lftg; High Hon Roll; Hon Roll; Penn ST; Math.

ROOF, REGINA; Cedar Crest HS; Lebanon, PA; (Y); Am Leg Aux Girls St; Drama Clb; Pres 4-H; German Clb; Pep Clb; SADD; Cit Awd; 4-H Awd; Hon Roll; Ray Clodoveo Accrdn Bnd Pres 85; Psychlgy.

ROOFNER JR, FRANKLIN D; Leechburg Area HS; Vandergrift, PA; (Y); Aud/Vis; Speech Tm; Band; Concert Band; Drm & Bgl; Mrchg Band; Pep Band; Yrbk Stf; Trs Jr Cls; Capt Im Vllybl; VFW Natl Champnshp 84; Bnd Tchr.

ROOK, MICHELLE; Butler Area SR HS; Butler, PA; (Y); Church Yth Grp; FBLA; Chorus; School Musical; Rep Soph Cls; Var L Gym; Pennsylvania Mdrn Miss Pgnt 4th Rnnr Up 84; Ushers Clb Pres 86-87; Bus Admn.

ROONEY, ELIZABETH; Vincentian HS; Pi Tsburgh, PA; (Y); 28/56; Cmnty Wkr; Hosp Aide; VP Trs NFL; Service Clb; Chorus; Natl Sci Olympd Tst 2nd, 3rd 84 & 86; Natl Fornscs Leag 85; Fornscs Degre Hnr, Excllnc 85 & 86.

ROONEY, KARIN; Manheim Central HS; Manheim, PA; (Y); 17/241; VP Church Yth Grp; Band; Chorus; Pres Church Choir; Orch; School Musical; Yrbk Stf; Tennis; High Hon Roll; NHS; L Kent Buhl Crt Awd 86; Brdcst Jrnlsm.

ROONEY, WILLIAM; Faith Community Christian Schl; Pittsburgh, PA; (S); 1/36; Aud/Vis; Church Yth Grp; Computer Clb; NEDT Awd.

ROOP, GINA; Cardinal O Hara HS; Aston, PA; (Y); 30/790; VP Church Yth Grp; Cmnty Wkr; Pres French Clb; FNA; Library Aide; Rep Stu Cncl; Var Cheerleading; High Hon Roll; Jr NHS; NHS; Bus.

ROOS, COLETTE; E L Meyers HS; Wilkes Barre, PA; (Y); Church Yth Grp; Key Clb; Ski Clb; Chorus; Flag Corp; Yrbk Stf; Vllybl; Hon Roll; Cmnty Wkr; Drama Clb; Cty Spnsrd Sftbl 82-86; Educ.

ROOS, RHONDA; Manheim Central HS; Manheim, PA; (Y); Drill Tm; Capt Flag Corp; Mrchg Band; Nwsp Rptr; Off Jr Cls; Off Sr Cls; Sec Stu Cncl; Capt Fld Hcky; Trk; Dnfth Awd; Phy Fit Awd; 4-Way Tst Awd; Amrcn Music Awd Tr Part; Shippensburg U; Intl Fnc.

ROOS, ROSEMARY; Cumberland Valley HS; Mechanicsburg, PA; (Y); 183/522; Church Yth Grp; Dance Clb; Key Clb; Ski Clb; Spanish Clb.

ROOT, JODY; Middleburg Joint HS; Middleburg, PA; (Y); Boys Clb Am; FCA; FHA; Varsity Clb; Drill Tm; Var Bsktbl; Var Score Keeper; Var Sftbl; Var Trk; Typwrtng Cert 83; JV Ltr Trk 83; Vrsty Ltr & Jacket Trk 85; Spec Ed.

ROPER, CHARLES; Coatesville SR HS; Coatesville, PA; (Y); 15/535; Debate Tm; Acpl Chr; Chorus; Jazz Band; Stage Crew; Yrbk Ed-Chief; VP Jr Cls; Ftbl; Var Wrstlng; High Hon Roll; Philadelphia Coll; Mdrn Music.

ROPER, THERESA A; Mon Valley Catholic HS; Finleyville, PA; (S); 8/110; Ski Clb; Chorus; Stu Cncl; French Hon Soc; VP NHS; Homecmng Qn And Chrstms Qn 85-86; Raqtbl Tm,Pep Clb 85-86; Meals On Whls 85-86; Seton Hill Clg; Fash Dsngr.

ROPON, KARRIE; Quigley HS; Fair Oaks, PA; (Y); Camera Clb; Cmnty Wkr; Church Choir; Drill Tm; Mrchg Band; Yrbk Stf; Stat Bsktbl; JV Var Cheerleading; Mgr(s); Powder Puff Ftbl; Spd & Accuracy Typng I Awd 85 & 86; Soc Wrkr.

RORICK, DONNA; Technical HS; Scranton, PA; (Y); Letterman Clb; Pep Clb; Orch; Rep Stu Cncl; Var L Cheerleading; Var L Crs Cntry; Var Capt Trk; God Cntry Awd; Dist Orchstra 85-86; Maywood Coll; Musical Thrpy.

RORICK, MICHELLE; Central HS; Scranton, PA; (Y); Cmnty Wkr; Dance Clb; Spanish Clb; Chorus; Cheerleading; Trk; Bus Mgt.

ROSA-BIAN, LINDA; Bishop Mc Devitt HS; Willow Grove, PA; (Y); 68/351; Cmnty Wkr; Intnl Clb; Service Clb; Nwsp Rptr; Nwsp Stf; Yrbk Stf; Lit Mag; Prfncy Awd In Englsh II; Lsrhsp Awd For Italian III & IV; Temple U.

ROSADO, JOHN; Roxborough HS; Philadelphia, PA; (Y); Office Aide; Chorus; School Play; Nwsp Rptr; Rep Stu Cncl; Var Bsbl; Var Ftbl; Var Socr; Var Capt Swmmng; DAR Awd; Root Awd 86; St Josephs U; Hstry Tchr.

ROSAGE, LISA; Bishop Mc Cort HS; Johnstown, PA; (Y); Sec Latin Clb; Pep Clb; Teachers Aide; Band; Concert Band; Drm Mjr(t); Mrchg Band; Vllybl; High Hon Roll; NHS; Novak Awd 83; Acad All Amer 86; Edinboro; Ed.

ROSANELLI, CHRISTINA L; Pennridge HS; Dublin, PA; (Y); 112/436; VP Trs 4-H; Library Aide; Var L Gym; 4-H Awd; Cnty Fshn Revu 82 83 & 85; Lock Haven U; Comp Sci.

ROSATI, RICHARD; Girard Academic Music Program; Philadelphia, PA; (Y); 5/51; Chorus; Color Guard; School Musical; School Play; Ed Nwsp Stf; Yrbk Rptr; Ed Yrbk Stf; Lit Mag; Hon Roll; NHS; Geomtry Awd 83084; Acdmc Plus Mdl Of Hnr Awd; Phldlpha Coll Txtl/Sci; Dsgnr.

ROSATO, ANTHONY; B Redd Henderson HS; West Chester, PA; (S); 16/362; Cmnty Wkr; Spanish Clb; Nwsp Rptr; High Hon Roll; VP NHS; Spanish NHS; Penn ST; Bus.

ROSATO, MARIA; Saint Maria Goretti HS; Philadelphia, PA; (Y); 49/402; VP Church Yth Grp; French Clb; GAA; Math Clb; Stage Crew; Hon Roll; Sec NHS; Prfct Atten Awd; Actvts Off; Bus.

ROSBOROUGH, VICKIE; Monessen HS; Monessen, PA; (Y); 8/87; French Clb; JA; Teachers Aide; Band; Nwsp Rptr; Twrlr; High Hon Roll; NHS; Past Wrthy Advsr Rainbw Grls 85 & 86; Past Grnd Usherett Rainbw Grls 86; Slippery Rock; Elem Ed.

ROSCH, CAREN A; Quakertown Comm SR HS; Quakertown, PA; (Y); 45/289; Band; Chorus; Drm Mjr(t); Nwsp Stf; Yrbk Stf; Var L Bsktbl; Var L Fld Hcky; Var L Sftbl; Hon Roll; NHS; Silvr Mdl Sftbl Thrw 83; Spinlon Ind Ctznshp Awd 86; Bloomsburg U; Bus Admn.

ROSCHE, RUTH; Elizabeth-Forward HS; Elizabeth, PA; (Y); 1/312; German Clb; Ski Clb; Nwsp Phtg; Yrbk Phtg; High Hon Roll; VP NHS; Val; WVU Achvt Schlrshp 86; Outstdng Chem St 86; Pres Acad Ftnss Awd 86; WV U; Mech Engrng.

ROSCIOLI, KEN; Wilson Area HS; Easton, PA; (S); 9/149; Church Yth Grp; Variety Show; Pres Jr Cls; Stu Cncl; L Capt Ftbl; Swmmng; L Trk; L Capt Wrstlng; High Hon Roll; Hon Roll; Stu Of Mnth 85; Outstndng Stu Athlt 86; Stu Of Wk 86; PA ST U; Archtctrl Engrng.

ROSCOE, JEANNE; Lourdes Regional HS; Elysburg, PA; (Y); 19/95; AFS; GAA; Capt Pep Clb; Spanish Clb; Yrbk Stf; Im Score Keeper; Hon Roll; Thompson Inst; Med Ofc Asst.

ROSCOE, WILLIAM; Hempfield Area HS; Jeannette, PA; (Y); Boys Clb Am; Boy Scts; French Clb; Pep Clb; Teachers Aide; Varsity Clb; Im Bsktbl; JV Im Ftbl; Im Socr; Im Vllybl; Bio.

ROSE, BRENDA; A Leboeuf HS; Erie, PA; (Y); Ski Clb; Rep Stu Cncl; JV Var Cheerleading; Sftbl; Trk; Hon Roll; Physcl Ftnss Awd 84-86; Hnr Roll Awd 84; Chrldng Awd 84-85; Penn ST Behrend Coll; Med Fld.

ROSE, BRENDA; Freedom Area HS; Rochester, PA; (Y); FCA; Pep Clb; Ski Clb; SADD; Trs VICA; Band; Chorus; Var JV Cheerleading; Sftbl; Hon Roll; Cosmtlgst.

ROSE, CRAIG; Scranton Prepatory Schl; Scranton, PA; (Y); 88/192; Boys Clb Am; Letterman Clb; Service Clb; L Bsktbl; L Golf; High Hon Roll; Hon Roll.

ROSE, CRIS; West Scranton HS; Scranton, PA; (Y); #17 In Class; Capt Pom Pon; Hon Roll; Jr NHS.

ROSE, JEFFREY; Cathedral Prep; Erie, PA; (Y); Model UN; NFL; Speech Tm; Var Tennis; High Hon Roll; NHS; Ntl Merit Ltr.

ROSE, JIM; Belle Vernon Area HS; Belle Vernon, PA; (Y); 15/272; Debate Tm; Drama Clb; NFL; Speech Tm; Band; Mrchg Band; Pep Band; School Play; Nwsp Bus Mgr; Nwsp Rptr; Stu Mnth Womens Clb Am 86; Westmoreland Cty Band 83; 2nd Trophy Spkng 85; IN U; Comm.

ROSE, LYNDA; East Pennsboro HS; Enola, PA; (Y); 3/180; Church Yth Grp; GAA; VP Latin Clb; Var Bsktbl; Var Diving; Var Fld Hcky; Var Trk; High Hon Roll; Hon Roll; NHS; Dcknsn Coll Smr Schl Schlrshp 86; Mst Vlbl Track 85; 3 All Star Hcky Teams 85-86; Law.

ROSE, LYNDA; Rockwood Area HS; Confluence, PA; (S); AFS; Trs Church Yth Grp; Intnl Clb; Band; Chorus; School Play; Yrbk Ed-Chief; High Hon Roll; Hon Roll; NHS; Swyr Schl; Trvl.

ROSE, PETER; Bellefonte Area HS; Bellefonte, PA; (Y); Penn ST; Electronics.

ROSE, SHARON; Harbor Creek HS; Erie, PA; (Y); 1/228; Trs Model UN; Trs Band; Pep Band; Variety Show; Trs Sr Cls; Var Bsktbl; Gov Hon Prg Awd; Hon Roll; Trs NHS; Bio.

ROSE, TAMMY; Central Cambria HS; Portage, PA; (S); 11/209; Art Clb; French Clb; FBLA; Color Guard; Mgr(s); Score Keeper; Mgr Swmmng; High Hon Roll; Hon Roll; Acctnt.

ROSEBERRY, ERIN; Chambersburg Area SR HS; Marion, PA; (Y); 226/641; Cmnty Wkr; Drama Clb; School Musical; Yrbk Phtg; Ed Yrbk Stf; JV Crs Cntry; AFS; Church Yth Grp; Spanish Clb; American U; Intl Rltns.

ROSEBERRY, LORI; Central York SR HS; York, PA; (Y); 13/239; Church Yth Grp; Teachers Aide; Varsity Clb; Yrbk Stf; Mgr Trk; High Hon Roll; Hon Roll; NHS; Pres Schlr; Acad Let & Svc Bar 85-86; Vrsty Let 85; York Coll; Bus Admin.

ROSEMAN, LYNN ANN; Yough HS; W Newton, PA; (Y); 62/226; French Clb; Ski Clb; Band; Mrchg Band; Nwsp Rptr; Nwsp Stf; Yrbk Stf; Hon Roll; NHS; Jrnlsm Awd 86; Schlstc Achvmnt Awd 86; Mascot Sprts Awd 86; U Of Pittsburgh; Bus.

ROSEMAN, PATTI; Sallcon Valley HS; Bethlehem, PA; (Y); Rep Stu Cncl; JV Var Fld Hcky; JV Sftbl; High Hon Roll; Hon Roll; Elmntry Ed.

ROSEMAS, NICK; Forest Hills HS; South Fork, PA; (Y); Church Yth Grp; Spanish Clb; Spanish NHS.

ROSEMEIER, RANDAL; Monongahela Valley Catholic HS; Cokeburg, PA; (Y); 6/83; Trs Frsh Cls; Trs Soph Cls; Trs Jr Cls; Trs Sr Cls; Trs Stu Cncl; Var L Bsbl; Var L Bsktbl; NHS; Spanish NHS; Aerspc Engr.

ROSEN, DEBORAH; Center HS; Aliquippa, PA; (Y); 10/183; Band; Concert Band; Drm Mjr(t); Mrchg Band; Hon Roll; NHS; Outstndng Stu Awd Spanish I & II 83-84; WV U; Accntng.

ROSEN, FRED; Pennsbury HS; Yardley, PA; (S); 42/729; Band; Concert Band; Drm Mjr(t); Jazz Band; Mrchg Band; Orch; Pep Band; School Musical; High Hon Roll; NHS; Valdctrn Confrmtn Cls 84; MD U; Dentstry.

ROSEN, JOEL; Bensalem HS; Bensalem, PA; (Y); Aud/Vis; Temple Yth Grp; Varsity Clb; Var JV Bsktbl; Var JV Mgr(s); Var JV Score Keeper; High Hon Roll; Hon Roll; Acctg.

ROSEN, KENNETH; High School Of Engineering Science; Philadelphia, PA; (S); 3/184; Computer Clb; Math Tm; Nwsp Ed-Chief; Yrbk Stf; High Hon Roll; Kiwanis Awd; Pres NHS; Ntl Merit SF; 1st Kiwanis Math Mrthn Tm 82-83; Drew U.

ROSEN, NELSON G; High Schl Of Engineering & Science; Philadelphia, PA; (Y); Boy Scts; Chess Clb; Pres Computer Clb; Var Mgr(s); High Hon Roll; NHS; Ntl Merit SF; PA Jr Acad Sci ST & Rgnl 1st Awd 85; Rennselaer Polytec Ins; Elctrnc.

ROSENBERG, JEFFREY; Breed Henderson HS; West Chester, PA; (S); 10/357; Scholastic Bowl; Ski Clb; Nwsp Stf; Rep Stu Cncl; JV Tennis; Hon Roll; NHS; Acad Achvt Awd 84-85; Duke U; Med.

ROSENBERG, LAWRENCE; Kennett HS; Chadds Ford, PA; (Y); Radio Clb; Nwsp Ed-Chief; Yrbk Stf; Hst Jr Cls; Hst Sr Cls; Var L Bsktbl; Var L Crs Cntry; Var L Tennis; Sec NHS; Spnsh Awd; Lbrl Arts.

ROSENBERGER, BRIAN; Punxsutawney HS; Smicksburg, PA; (Y); Ftbl; Wt Lftg.

ROSENBERGER, BRIAN; Souderton HS; Telford, PA; (Y); 76/355; Rep Capt Soph Cls; Rep Capt Jr Cls; Rep Stu Cncl; Var Capt Socr; Var L Trk; Hon Roll; Amer Inst For Frgn Study 86; Avid Skier, Camper & Weight Training; Sci.

ROSENBERGER, DEBRA; Susquenita HS; Duncannon, PA; (S); 9/183; VP Church Yth Grp; Cmnty Wkr; Quiz Bowl; Acpl Chr; Band; Drill Tm; School Musical; School Play; High Hon Roll; NEDT Awd; Hghst Ranking Girl In Cls 83-84; Hnrs Choir 86; Cnty Chorus 85 & 86; Relgn.

ROSENBERGER, JOHN; Waynesboro Area SR HS; Waynesboro, PA; (Y); Boy Scts; Var Bsbl; Eagl Sct Awd 85.

ROSENBERGER, JULIE; Marion Center Area HS; Home, PA; (S); 20/170; VP FNA; Intnl Clb; Science Clb; Band; Concert Band; Mrchg Band; Pep Band; Sec Jr Cls; Rep Stu Cncl; Stat Swmmng; Radlgy.

ROSENBERGER, MELISSA; Central Bucks HS West; Chalfont, PA; (Y); 10/495; Concert Band; Rep Frsh Cls; Var L Cheerleading; Fld Hcky; High Hon Roll; Hon Roll; Jr NHS; Bucks County Cncl Arts Awd 83.

ROSENBERRY, TAMI; Connellsville Area SR HS; Normalville, PA; (Y); 31/550; Church Yth Grp; Office Aide; Chorus; Church Choir; School Musical; French Hon Soc; High Hon Roll; Ntl Bible Quzzng 86; Outstndng Frnch Stu Awd 84; Nrs Aide 83-86.

ROSENELLA, DEBORAH; Dunmore HS; Dunmore, PA; (Y); 5/150; French Clb; Yrbk Sprt Ed; Var Bsktbl; Var L Trk; High Hon Roll; NHS; Elem Ed.

ROSENER, DOUGLAS; Lower Dauphin HS; Palmyra, PA; (Y); 62/217; Band; Chorus; Church Choir; Concert Band; Drm & Bgl; Jazz Band; Mrchg Band; Orch; JP Sousa Awd; Thesps; Music Actvty Tuitn Schlrshp 86; Prsdntl Acdmc Ftnss Awd 86; Outstndg Male Band Stu 85; PA ST U; Music Educ.

ROSENGRANT, LORI; West Scranton HS; Scranton, PA; (Y); 2/262; Latin Clb; Ski Clb; Nwsp Stf; Yrbk Ed-Chief; Capt Cheerleading; Score Keeper; Trk; High Hon Roll; NHS; Elem Tchr.

ROSENSTEEL, DANA; Altoona Area HS; Altoona, PA; (Y); Off JA; JV L Crs Cntry; Var Capt Trk; MVP Track Tm 84-85 & 85-86; 5th PIAA St Champs High Jump 84-85; Penn ST U; Sprts Ther.

ROSENSTIEHL, ALICIA; Cardinal O Hara HS; Upland, PA; (Y); 74/772; Cmnty Wkr; Spanish Clb; Teachers Aide; School Musical; Hon Roll; Prfct Atten Awd; Schlstc Awd; Radiology.

ROSH, SHARON; Sayre Area HS; Sayre, PA; (Y); Spanish Clb; High Hon Roll; Hon Roll; Prfct Atten Awd; Baton Twrlng 83-86; Dncg 83; Alfred St Coll; Florcltr.

ROSIAK, JON; Lackawanna Trail HS; Nicholson, PA; (Y); Ski Clb; VP Frsh Cls; Var Bsbl; Var Ftbl; Phys Ed.

ROSIAK, KIM; E L Meyers HS; Wilkes-Barre, PA; (S); 16/161; Key Clb; Ski Clb; Yrbk Stf; High Hon Roll; Hon Roll; Jr NHS; NHS; NEDT Awd; Spanish NHS; U Of Scranton; Pre-Med.

ROSICK, DEBBIE; John S Fine HS; Glen Lyon, PA; (Y); Pres Key Clb; Model UN; Ski Clb; Chorus; Flag Corp; Yrbk Stf; High Hon Roll; NHS; Susquehanna U; Pre-Med.

ROSIEK, STEVEN G; Seneca Valley SR HS; Mars, PA; (Y); Boy Scts; Chess Clb; Hon Roll; Indstrl Engr.

ROSIER, AMY; Spring Grove SR HS; Spring Grove, PA; (Y); 14/227; Chorus; Church Choir; Jazz Band; Symp Band; Nwsp Rptr; Sec Soph Cls; Tennis; High Hon Roll; NHS; Schrlshp Wooster Coll 86; Schlrshp Penn ST 86; Wilson Coll; Intl Rel.

ROSPIGLIOSI, CESAR; Tunkhannock Area HS; Tunkhannock, PA; (Y); 2/330; Key Clb; Chorus; Trs Jr Cls; JV Golf; Var L Swmmng; Cit Awd; Hon Roll; Trs NHS; Sal; Rotary Leadrshp Camp 84; Natl Hispanic Schlrs Awd Semi-Fnlst 86; U Of ME Giftd Studtns Pgm 85; MIT; Physics.

ROSS, AIMEE D; Millville Area HS; Orangeville, PA; (Y); 27/72; Church Yth Grp; Pep Clb; Sr Cls; Cheerleading; Capt Fld Hcky; Socr; Cit Awd; Band; Gym; Most Vlbl Ofnsv Plyr 85; Soc Dstngshd HS Stu 86; Phys Ed Awd & Girl Of Month 86; Prom Qn 86; East Stroudsburg; Phys Educ.

ROSS, AMY; Washington HS; Washington, PA; (S); 40/157; French Clb; Key Clb; Spanish Clb; SADD; Yrbk Stf; Hon Roll; Airln Stew.

ROSS, ANGELA; Sacred Heart HS; Cheswick, PA; (Y); French Clb; Math Clb; Nwsp Stf; Hon Roll; NHS; Pres Schlr; JR Volunteer 84; Cert Merit 1st Yr Alg Cont 83; Cert Merit Westminster Coll Mth Comp 85; IN U Of PA; Comp Sci.

ROSS, BRIAN; Crestwood HS; Mountaintop, PA; (Y); Var L Ftbl; Var L Wrstlng; Hon Roll; NEDT Awd; Engnrng.

ROSS, CHRISTINA; Sto-Rox SR HS; Mckees Rocks, PA; (Y); 17/149; Hosp Aide; Library Aide; Office Aide; Red Cross Aide; Chorus; Yrbk Stf; Hon Roll; OVGH Schl Of Nrsg; Nrsg.

ROSS, CHRISTOPHER; Downingtown SR HS; Downingtown, PA; (S); 7/527; Letterman Clb; Spanish Clb; SADD; Band; Concert Band; Mrchg Band; Var Tennis; High Hon Roll; Hon Roll; NHS; All Chestmont Dbls-Hnr Mntn 85; Tomorrows Ldrs Conf 85; US Naval Acad; Nclr Engr.

ROSS, DANA; Shenango HS; New Castle, PA; (Y); 5/117; Trs Church Yth Grp; Capt Drill Tm; School Play; VP Sr Cls; Trs Stu Cncl; Var Gym; Cit Awd; NHS; Rotary Awd; Spts Med.

ROSS, DEBBY; Marple Newtown SR HS; Broomall, PA; (Y); Church Yth Grp; Cmnty Wkr; Debate Tm; Drama Clb; Service Clb; School Musical; Stage Crew; Variety Show; Nwsp Stf; Ed Yrbk Stf; Ldr Human Rel Comm 86-87; FL; Law.

ROSS, DENISE; Hopewell SR HS; Aliquippa, PA; (S); 18/250; Church Yth Grp; Cmnty Wkr; Exploring; Latin Clb; Spanish Clb; Stage Crew; Yrbk Stf; Rep Soph Cls; Rep Jr Cls; High Hon Roll; Med.

ROSS, DENISE L; Greater Works Acad; Pittsburgh, PA; (Y); 8/36; Church Yth Grp; Service Clb; Yrbk Stf; Rep Stu Cncl; High Hon Roll; Hon Roll; CC Of Alleg Heny Cnty Hnr Schlrshp 86; Grove Cty Coll; Comp Sci.

ROSS, DONNA J; Kishacoquillas HS; Milroy, PA; (Y); 23/144; Church Yth Grp; Cmnty Wkr; French Clb; Chrmn Spanish Clb; High Hon Roll; Hon Roll; Acad Ltr Hgh Hnr Roll 85-86; Hnr Stu Mdlln 85-86; Spn Achvt Success Card 85-86; Tchr.

ROSS, ELLEN; Cumberland Valley HS; Mechanicsburg, PA; (Y); Girl Scts; Ski Clb; JV Cheerleading; Hon Roll; Girl Scts Gld Awd 86; 1st Plc Arts Fest Prntmkng 86; Physcl Thrpy.

ROSS, ERICA; Nazareth Acad; Philadelphia, PA; (Y); 10/118; Sec Cmnty Wkr; German Clb; NFL; Orch; Yrbk Stf; Off Stu Cncl; JV Var Bsktbl; High Hon Roll; NHS; Prfct Atten Awd; Excllnc Awd Prose Readg Frnscs 83-84; Sci.

ROSS, GEORGE; Brownsville HS; Grindstone, PA; (Y); Drama Clb; Var Bsbl; Var Bsktbl; Cit Awd; DAR Awd; High Hon Roll; NHS; Pres Schlr; MVP Bsbl; Labette CC; Crmnl Just.

ROSS, JAMES; Elk County Christian HS; St Marys, PA; (S); 1/89; Letterman Clb; Ski Clb; Bowling; Crs Cntry; Trk; High Hon Roll; PA ST U; Engrng.

ROSS, JENNIFER; West Scranton HS; Scranton, PA; (Y); 16/260; French Clb; Letterman Clb; Ski Clb; Var Cheerleading; L Var Crs Cntry; Mat Maids; Var L Trk; High Hon Roll; Jr NHS; NHS; Lit Awd 2nd Pl 84.

ROSS, KATRINA; Carmichaels Area HS; Carmichaels, PA; (S); #12 In Class; Library Aide; Ski Clb; Spanish Clb; Jr Cls; High Hon Roll; Hon Roll; NHS; Pre Law.

ROSS, LISA; West Scranton HS; Scranton, PA; (Y); 10/253; Latin Clb; Red Cross Aide; Yrbk Ed-Chief; Trs Jr Cls; Trs Sr Cls; Cheerleading; Hon Roll; Jr NHS; NHS; PTA Ltry Awd 83; U Of Scrntn; Acctng.

ROSS, MICHAEL; Trinity HS; Washington, PA; (Y); 8/374; Art Clb; Math Tm; Speech Tm; JV Bsktbl; JV Ftbl; Var L Tennis; NHS.

ROSS, MICHELE RAE; Troy SR HS; Troy, PA; (Y); 49/174; Trs Church Yth Grp; Letterman Clb; Sec Pep Clb; Ski Clb; Concert Band; Yrbk Stf; Var Cheerleading; Var Sftbl; Capt Twrlr; NHS; Keystone Grls ST Rep 86; Orgnztnl Cmmnctns.

ROSS, PAM; Marion Center Area HS; Marion Center, PA; (S); 12/161; Pres 4-H; Latin Clb; Library Aide; Varsity Clb; Band; VP Jr Cls; Swmmng; 4-H Awd; High Hon Roll; NHS; Ntl 4-H Cngrss 85; Intl Rltns.

ROSS, PHIL; Cheltenham HS; Elkins Pk, PA; (Y); 88/365; Science Clb; Rep Jr Cls; Var Lcrss; Speak In Front Of Schlbrd; Bus.

ROSS, ROBERT MATTHEW; Bethlehem Center SR HS; Brownsville, PA; (Y); 19/156; Church Yth Grp; Spanish Clb; CA U; Soclgy.

ROSS, SCOTT; Abington Heights HS; Clarks Summit, PA; (Y); 1/271; Boy Scts; Ski Clb; Pres Band; Chorus; Drm Mjr(t); Pres Mrchg Band; Var JV Socr; High Hon Roll; NHS; Sci.

ROSS, SHANNON; Chartiers Houston HS; Washington, PA; (Y); Church Yth Grp; 4-H; Library Aide; Office Aide; Stu Cncl; 4-H Awd; Hon Roll; Voice Dem Awd; Bob Evans Wnnr 84; Pblc Rltns.

ROSS, STEVEN; Harrisburg HS; Harrisburg, PA; (Y); Church Yth Grp; Cmnty Wkr; Exploring; FCA; FBLA; JA; ROTC; Science Clb; Teachers Aide; Church Choir; Mc Cullough Mem Church Yth Yr Awd 86; Sci.

ROSS, SUSAN; Corry Area HS; Corry, PA; (S); 26/212; Church Yth Grp; Chorus; Off Jr Cls; Hon Roll; Gannon U; Bnkng.

ROSS, TAMMY; Leechburg Area HS; Leechburg, PA; (Y); Church Yth Grp; Band; Chorus; Concert Band; Jazz Band; Mrchg Band; Pep Band; Yrbk Stf; Hon Roll; Cnty Band 85 & 86; Dist Band 85 & 86; Rgnl Band 85; Duquesne U; Music Educ.

ROSS III, WILLIAM H; St Josephs Prep Schl; Philadelphia, PA; (Y); 6/231; Debate Tm; JCL; High Hon Roll; Ntl Merit SF; Prfct Atten Awd; Natl Greek Exam Awd Hghst Hnr 83-86; Natl Latin Exam Awd Magna Cum Laude 84-86; Crew Cath Lg Champnshp; MIT; Bus Mgmt.

ROSSETTI, RENAE; Yough SR HS; Sutersville, PA; (Y); Art Clb; GAA; Ski Clb; Stu Cncl; Badmtn; Bsktbl; Golf; Powder Puff Ftbl; Sftbl; Vllybl; Vllybll Lttr 86; Jr Olympics Sftbll 85; ASA Tourn; Slippery Rock U; Phys Educ.

ROSSEY, RE NAE; Clarion-Limestone HS; Corsica, PA; (Y); 2/57; Church Yth Grp; Hon Roll; NHS; Prfct Atten Awd; Cert Of Profcncy Shrthnd I 86; Exceptnl Achvmnt Awd Fine Arts 86; Clarion U.

ROSSEY, WILLIAM D; Methacton SR HS; Collegeville, PA; (Y); Debate Tm; Key Clb; Library Aide; Ski Clb; Yrbk Stf; JV Ftbl; Var Trk; Penn St Acad Dcthln Tm 86; Scrd 2nd Ntn Scl Sci Tst At Acad Dcthln Natl Chmpnshp 86; Millersville U; Secndry Educ.

ROSSI, ARTHUR; Penn Hills HS; Verona, PA; (Y); Boys Clb Am; Church Yth Grp; JA; Chorus; Ftbl; Trk; Hon Roll; Robotcl Engr.

ROSSI, CHRISTINA; St Maria Goretti HS; Philadelphia, PA; (Y); 46/396; Art Clb; Church Yth Grp; Cmnty Wkr; Office Aide; Lit Mag; Rep Stu Cncl; High Hon Roll; Pep Clb; Rep Soph Cls; Rep Jr Cls; Moore Coll Art Prtflo Schlrshp 86; Hsn Coll Art Smmr Schlrshp 85; Moore Coll Of Art; Fshn Illstrn.

ROSSI, ELIZABETH ANN; Easton Area HS; Easton, PA; (Y); 11/460; Am Leg Aux Girls St; Church Yth Grp; Ski Clb; Orch; School Play; Var Crs Cntry; Var Trk; Hon Roll; Jr NHS; Sec NHS; Yng Pepls Phlhrmnc-Lehgh Vly 83-87.

ROSSI, JAUDIE; Gbg Central Catholic HS; Jeannette, PA; (Y); French Clb; Ski Clb; Crs Cntry; Socr; Trk; High Hon Roll; NHS; Law.

ROSSI, JODI; Greenburg Central Catholic HS; Jeannette, PA; (Y); AFS; French Clb; Pep Clb; Ski Clb; Im Var Crs Cntry; Var Socr; Im Sftbl; Var L Trk; Im Vllybl; High Hon Roll; Frgn Rel.

ROSSI, LEAH; Bentworth HS; Bentleyville, PA; (Y); Letterman Clb; Ski Clb; Spanish Clb; Varsity Clb; School Play; Rep Soph Cls; Rep Jr Cls; Stu Cncl; Cheerleading; Vllybl; Bradford; Accntng.

ROSSI, LISA; Hopewell SR HS; Aliquippa, PA; (Y); 33/295; FBLA; Spanish Clb; Stu Cncl; Powder Puff Ftbl; High Hon Roll; Hon Roll; NHS; Ntl Merit Ltr; Johnson & Wales Schlrshp 85; Fut Sec Am Schlrshp 86; Johnson & Wales Coll; Acctg.

ROSSI, MICHAEL; St John Neumann HS; Philadelphia, PA; (Y); #49 In Class; Chorus; La Salle U; Comp Sci.

ROSSI, TERESA; Hopewell SR HS; Aliquippa, PA; (Y); Sec Church Yth Grp; French Clb; Hosp Aide; Library Aide; Spanish Clb; Trk; JV Var Vllybl; Hon Roll; Forgn Stud.

ROSSINO, JEANETTE; Marian Catholic HS; Jim Thorpe, PA; (Y); 20/120; Church Yth Grp; SADD; Thesps; Chorus; Church Choir; School Musical; High Hon Roll; Civic Clb; Cmnty Wkr; Drama Clb; St Davids Scty Schuylkill & Carbon Cntys 86; Vocal Schlrshp #1 Soprano Vclst In Cnty 85-86; Sec Ed.

ROSSMILLER, SUZANNE; Father Geibel Catholic HS; Donegal, PA; (Y); Church Yth Grp; Drama Clb; School Musical; School Play; Stage Crew; Lit Mag; VP Soph Cls; High Hon Roll; NHS; Spanish NHS; Math Educ.

ROSSO, ANITA; Uniontown Area SR HS; Uniontown, PA; (Y); 37/287; VP French Clb; Concert Band; Nwsp Rptr; Nwsp Stf; Co-Capt Cheerleading; French Hon Soc; Hon Roll; Psych.

ROSSO, MICHAEL; Brownsville Area HS; Fairbank, PA; (S); 4/225; Church Yth Grp; Computer Clb; Var Capt Bsktbl; Var Capt Bowling; High Hon Roll; Jr NHS; NHS; Outstndng Stu 82-83; Engrg.

ROTCHFORD, TANYA; Ferndale HS; Johnstown, PA; (Y); 14/57; GAA; Ski Clb; SADD; Chorus; Cheerleading; Vllybl; Hon Roll; JC Awd; U Pittsburgh Johnstown; Psych.

ROTERING, CHRISTINE D; Mifflinburg Area HS; Mifflinburg, PA; (Y); 19/152; Am Leg Aux Girls St; French Clb; Hosp Aide; Key Clb; SADD; High Hon Roll; NHS; Mrn Bio.

ROTH, DAVID; Big Spring HS; Newville, PA; (Y); Chess Clb; Ski Clb; Band; Concert Band; Var Bsbl; Var Crs Cntry; Var Swmmng; Engr.

ROTH JR, GLENN; Freedom HS; Bethlehem, PA; (Y); 83/390; Chess Clb; Band; Jazz Band; Symp Band; Hon Roll; David Gngld Schlrshp 86; U Of Ptsbrgh; Pltcl Sci.

ROTH, I LEROY; Governor Mifflin SR HS; Shillington, PA; (Y); 3/280; Church Yth Grp; FBLA; Trs Key Clb; Model UN; Q&S; Yrbk Stf; Rotary Awd; Aud/Vis; French Clb; Varsity Clb; Gvnrs Schl Of Intl Stdys 86; Summa Cum Laude On Ntl Latn Ntl Exam 86.

ROTH, KURT; Sharpsville Area HS; Sharpsville, PA; (Y); Boy Scts; Camera Clb; Chorus; Stage Crew; L Trk; Wrstlng.

ROTH, LISA; Garden Spot HS; New Holland, PA; (Y); Church Yth Grp; Drama Clb; German Clb; PAVAS; Acpl Chr; Chorus; Church Choir; School Musical; School Play; Stage Crew; Altrnt PA Gvrnrs Schl Arts 86; Cnty Chrs 85 & 86; West Chester U; Music.

ROTH, MIKE; Penn Hills SR HS; Pittsburgh, PA; (Y); 29/750; Church Yth Grp; Computer Clb; Math Clb; Spanish Clb; Im Bsktbl; Score Keeper; High Hon Roll; Compu Sci Engrng.

ROTH, SHARON; Norristown Area HS; Norristown, PA; (Y); 35/428; Church Yth Grp; DECA; Intnl Clb; Orch; Symp Band; Var Lcrss; Var Capt Swmmng; NHS; Pres Schlr; U DE; Bio.

ROTH, THERESA; General Mc Lane HS; Mckean, PA; (Y); Church Yth Grp; Computer Clb; Red Cross Aide; Teachers Aide; Chorus; Hon Roll; U Of Dayton.

ROTHBAUER, JOE; West Mifflin Area HS; W Mifflin, PA; (Y); 35/370; Var Trk; Var High Hon Roll; NHS; Grove City Coll; Chem Engr.

ROTHENBACH, TRICIA; Germantown Acad; Hatboro, PA; (Y); Off Frsh Cls; Sec Soph Cls; JV Fld Hcky; Var L Sftbl; Var L Swmmng; NHS; PIAA Top Ten Awd Swmg 84-85; All Suburban I Leag Swmg 84-85; All Area 1st Tm Sftbl 84; Pre-Med.

ROTHENBERGER JR, JAMES; Levanon Catholic HS; Lebanon, PA; (Y); Cmnty Wkr; Exploring; Band; Concert Band; Mrchg Band; Clwn Mnstry Cmnty Srv Awd 83; Air Force; Smll Bus.

ROTHERMEL, BETH; Millersburg Area HS; Millersburg, PA; (S); 1/63; VP Chorus; Nwsp Ed-Chief; Yrbk Stf; VP Sr Cls; Trs Stu Cncl; Co-Capt Cheerleading; Powder Puff Ftbl; NHS; Voice Dem Awd; Natl Mrt Lttr Of Cmmndtn 85; Distngshd Hnr Rll 83-85.

ROTHERMEL, DAVID C; Mechanicsburg Area SR HS; Mechanicsburg, PA; (Y); 74/310; Boy Scts; Church Yth Grp; Computer Clb; Spanish Clb; Band; Chorus; Church Choir; Concert Band; Orch; JV Stat Ftbl; Williamsport CC; Diesel Tech.

ROTHERMEL, ELAINE; Mechanicsburg SR HS; Mechanicsburg, PA; (Y); Church Yth Grp; GAA; Drill Tm; Sec Sr Cls; Var Bsktbl; Var Fld Hcky; Lock Haven U; Sprts Med.

ROTHRA, DANIEL; Williamsport Area HS; Cogan Sta, PA; (Y); Church Yth Grp; Chorus; Bsktbl; Hon Roll; Acctg.

ROTHROCK, DAWN E; Dallas HS; Shavertown, PA; (Y); 8/198; Church Yth Grp; Flag Corp; Stage Crew; Stat Bsktbl; Stat Fld Hcky; Mgr(s); High Hon Roll; NHS; Ntl Merit SF; Drama Clb; Engl Dept Awd 84-85; Math.

ROTONDO, DIANE; East SR HS; West Chester, PA; (Y); 24/378; Pres Exploring; VP JA; Acpl Chr; School Musical; Nwsp Rptr; Var Capt Vllybl; High Hon Roll; NHS; Church Yth Grp; SADD; Chick-Fil-A Schlrshp; Stu Cncl Schlrshp; Syracuse U; Avtg.

ROTONDO, NADINE; Upper Merion Area HS; Bridgeport, PA; (Y); 60/350; Cmnty Wkr; VP Jr Cls; Stu Cncl; Fld Hcky; Lcrss; Trk; Opt Clb Awd; Prfct Atten Awd; Villanova; Eng.

ROTTINA, DONNA; Hatboro-Horsham HS; Horsham, PA; (Y); Church Yth Grp; VP Intnl Clb; Key Clb; SADD; Mrchg Band; Var Lcrss; Capt Twrlr; Hon Roll; All Buxmont League Team La Crosse 86; Ctznshp Awd 86; Millersville U; Bio.

ROTZ, DARCI; Red Lion Area SR HS; Red Lion, PA; (Y); 93/330; Church Yth Grp; Library Aide; Varsity Clb; Flag Corp; Mrchg Band; Mgr(s); Swmmng; Timer; Hon Roll; Frnsc Sci.

ROUB, ANNETTE; Central HS; Martinsburg, PA; (Y); 4-H; FNA; JA; Chorus; Church Choir; School Musical; Rep Stu Cncl; High Hon Roll; Hon Roll; Acadmc Outstndng Schltc Achvt 84; High Phys Ftnss Awd 84; Altoona Hosp; RN.

ROUDA, RANDALL S; Dubois Area HS; Dubois, PA; (Y); 14/270; Boy Scts; Debate Tm; Chorus; School Musical; High Hon Roll; NHS; Ntl Merit SF; Johns Hopkins U Ctr Tlntd Yth 83-84; Genetic Engr.

ROUGH, STEPHANIE; Bloomsburg SR HS; Bloomsburg, PA; (Y); 29/146; 4-H; Band; Concert Band; Jazz Band; Mrchg Band; School Musical; Hon Roll; Educ.

ROUPE, TERESA; Waynesburg Central HS; Mt Morris, PA; (Y); Drama Clb; French Clb; Chorus; Nwsp Stf; Var Bsktbl; Var Sftbl; Hon Roll; Comp.

ROUPP, MELISSA; Canton Area JR SR HS; Ralston, PA; (Y); 4/120; Trs AFS; Church Yth Grp; French Clb; Chorus; Hon Roll; Sec NHS.

ROUSCHE, KATHLEEN T; Montoursville HS; Montoursville, PA; (Y); 8/177; French Clb; Pres Key Clb; Ski Clb; School Musical; Stu Cncl; Var L Bsktbl; Mgr(s); Powder Puff Ftbl; Socr; French Hon Soc; Mntlly Gftd Tlntd Pgm; Rusinus Coll; Bio.

ROUSE, BRIGITTE; North Allegheny SR HS; Pittsburgh, PA; (Y); DECA; Exploring; Pep Clb; Spanish Clb; Band; Stu Cncl; Im JV Cheerleading; Hon Roll; Dstngsheed Achvrs Awd Bus, Hnrs Wrtng 86; U Pittsburgh; Bus.

ROUSE, JENNIFER SUSAN; Arch Wood High School Girls; Warminster, PA; (Y); 106/259; Pres Church Yth Grp; Cmnty Wkr; Hosp Aide; Service Clb; Spanish Clb; Variety Show; Yrbk Stf; Rep Soph Cls; Rep Sr Cls; Rep Stu Cncl; 3rd Yr Of Spnsh 85; Gen Excllnc Rev Jsph D Dghtry 83; Bucks Cnty Comm Coll; Lbrl Arts.

ROUSE, LORI; East Allegheny HS; N Versailles, PA; (Y); Dance Clb; French Clb; Pep Clb; Ski Clb; Church Choir; Rep Soph Cls; Rep Jr Cls; Trk; Camera Clb; Church Yth Grp; Cert For Completing 8 Week Biomedical Program At Pitts School Of Medicine 86; U Of Pittsburgh; Pharmacy.

ROUSE, REGINALD; Abraham Lincoln HS; Philadelphia, PA; (Y); 9/440; Boy Scts; Trs Church Yth Grp; Math Tm; Lit Mag; Cit Awd; High Hon Roll; Hon Roll; Jr NHS; Synod Of Trinity Schlrshp Grant 86; William H Boerckel Mem Awd For Prof In Math 86; Merit In Sci 86; Clark U; Comp Sci.

ROUSH, CHRIS; Trinity HS; Washington, PA; (Y); German Clb; Hon Roll; Pres Fit Awd 84; Washington & Jefferson; Bio.

ROUSH, JUDY LEE; Fort Le Boeuf HS; Waterford, PA; (Y); 34/188; 4-H; Band; Color Guard; Concert Band; 4-H Awd; Hon Roll.

ROUT, MICHAEL; St John Neumann HS; Philadelphia, PA; (Y); 88/321; Computer Clb; Pres Spanish Clb; Var L Ftbl; Im Vllybl; St John Neumann Awd 85-86; Drexel U; Elec Engrng.

ROUTE, DENNY; Canton Area HS; Ralston, PA; (Y); French Clb; Letterman Clb; Var L Ftbl; Wt Lftg; Var L Wrstlng; DAR Awd; Hon Roll; Ed.

ROUTE, TINA; Liberty HS; Liberty, PA; (Y); Pres German Clb; Trs Jr Cls; Trs Sr Cls; Trs Stu Cncl; Var JV Bsktbl; Sftbl; Var JV Vllybl; Hon Roll; Keystone JR Coll; Trvl Agnt.

ROUVIERE, MICHELLE; Hopewell Memorial SR HS; Imperial, PA; (Y); 70/269; Pres Church Yth Grp; Band; Church Choir; Drm Mjr(t); L Powder Puff Ftbl; Var L Wt Lftg; High Hon Roll; French Clb; SADD; PA ST U; Psych.

ROUZER, EVONNE N; East Stroudsburg HS; E Stroudsburg, PA; (Y); 2/191; Drama Clb; Concert Band; Mrchg Band; Pep Band; School Play; Stu Cncl; High Hon Roll; NHS; Sal; Social Studies Awd 84; IN U Of PA; Poli Sci.

ROVINSKY, DAVID; Bishop O Reilly HS; Swoyersville, PA; (Y); 1/106; Debate Tm; Political Wkr; Spanish Clb; Rep Stu Cncl; Stat Bsbl; High Hon Roll; NHS; Ntl Merit SF; Sal; Spanish NHS; Laurentian Schrlshp; Outstndng Grad 86; Acad Hnr Medallions 86; St Lawrence U; Intl Law.

ROVINSKY, SUSAN; Lakeland JR SR HS; Olyphant, PA; (Y); Spanish Clb; Yrbk Stf; VP Frsh Cls; Rep Jr Cls; Rep Sr Cls; Rep Stu Cncl; Capt Bsktbl; Capt Sftbl; Hon Roll; Marwood Coll; Educ.

ROVITO, LORI; Northern SR HS; Dillsburg, PA; (Y); 19/223; Drama Clb; Speech Tm; Teachers Aide; JV Var Cheerleading; Trk; Hon Roll; Penn ST; Vet Med.

ROWE, CYNTHIA A; Millersburgh Area HS; Millersburg, PA; (Y); 7/60; Chorus; Color Guard; Jazz Band; Mrchg Band; Rep Stu Cncl; Var Cheerleading; Twrlr; High Hon Roll; Hon Roll; Voice Dem Awd; Kathryn Glbrt Music Awd 86; SR Clr Grd Awd 86.

ROWE, DARA; Big Spring HS; Carlisle, PA; (Y); 8/186; Church Yth Grp; Pep Clb; Yrbk Stf; Stat JV Bsktbl; Mgr Crs Cntry; Mgr Swmmng; JV Trk; High Hon Roll; Trs NHS; Acctng.

ROWE, DAVE; Central Bucks W HS; Doylestown, PA; (Y); 176/483; Cmnty Wkr; 4-H; German Clb; Rep Soph Cls; Im Capt Lcrss; JV Wrstlng; Ntl Merit Ltr.

ROWE, DONALD CRAWFORD; Chestnut Ridge SR HS; Schellsburg, PA; (S); 12/107; VP Camera Clb; FBLA; Speech Tm; Chorus; Church Choir; Nwsp Ed-Chief; Nwsp Phtg; Yrbk Phtg; Var Bsktbl; Dnfth Awd; Messiah Coll; Radio.

ROWE, JAMES; Harbor Creek HS; Erie, PA; (Y); 18/228; Boy Scts; Computer Clb; 4-H; Yrbk Stf; JV Var Ftbl; Cit Awd; 4-H Awd; NHS; BSA Eagle W/Bronze & Gold Palms 85; Cngrsnl Awd Merit 85.

ROWE, KAREN; Marple Newtown SR HS; Broomall, PA; (Y); Yrbk Phtg; Rep Jr Cls; Rep Stu Cncl; Hon Roll; Prfct Atten Awd; Bus Adm.

ROWE, KIMBERLY; Hopewell HS; Aliquippa, PA; (Y); Pres VP Exploring; Latin Clb; Band; Concert Band; Jazz Band; Mrchg Band; Pep Band; Stage Crew; NHS; Bio.

ROWE, LINDA; Chestnut Ridge HS; Schellsburg, PA; (S); 6/142; Spanish Clb; Band; Concert Band; Jazz Band; Nwsp Phtg; Nwsp Rptr; Nwsp Stf; High Hon Roll; Hon Roll; NHS; Messiah Coll; Elem Ed.

ROWE, SUSAN; Elk Lake HS; Meshoppen, PA; (Y); 4/100; Art Clb; Library Aide; Band; Chorus; Concert Band; Mrchg Band; High Hon Roll; Hon Roll; Comp Sci.

ROWKER, KELLIE; Crestwood HS; Mountaintop, PA; (Y); 22/190; Yrbk Stf; Trs Stu Cncl; Var L Bsktbl; Var L Bowling; Var L Cheerleading; Var L Crs Cntry; Var L Fld Hcky; Var L Sftbl; High Hon Roll; NHS; Keystone ST Games 86; Sports Med.

ROWLAND, AMY; Big Spring HS; Carlisle, PA; (Y); 5/187; Pep Clb; Nwsp Rptr; Yrbk Ed-Chief; Yrbk Stf; Sec Frsh Cls; Powder Puff Ftbl; JV Socr; Var Swmmng; JV Trk; High Hon Roll; Womens Clb Jr Of Month 85; Foreign Lang.

ROWLAND, DEBRA; Karns City HS; Chicora, PA; (Y); 41/110; FCA; Concert Band; JV Var Vllybl; Hgh Scorer Vllybl Troph 84; Penn ST; Wldlf Tech.

ROWLAND, NOREEN; Unionville Chadds Ford HS; Kennett Square, PA; (Y); 18/269; Acpl Chr; Chorus; Concert Band; Orch; School Musical; School Play; Hon Roll; NHS; Ntl Merit Ltr; SADD; Levan P Smith Memrl 86; Hewlett Packard Co Emplyee Schlrshp 86; 2nd Rnnr Up Unionvl Hrvst Qn Pagnt 85; Westchester U Of PA; Music Ed.

ROWLAND, SIOBHAN; Unionville HS; Kennett Sq, PA; (Y); 85/287; Hosp Aide; Acpl Chr; Chorus; School Musical; Trk; Church Yth Grp; Exploring; Color Guard; Mrchg Band; Nwsp Stf; Medcl Tech.

ROWLES, CHARLES; Coughlin HS; White Haven, PA; (Y); Aud/Vis; Church Yth Grp; Nwsp Stf; Hon Roll; Jr NHS; NHS; Pres Schlr; PA ST U; Comp Sci.

ROWLES, DAWN; East Juniata HS; Mcalistervl, PA; (Y); Chess Clb; Yrbk Phtg; Yrbk Sprt Ed; Yrbk Stf; Var L Bsktbl; Var L Fld Hcky; Var L Trk; Hon Roll.

ROWLES, GEO; Clearfield Area HS; Clearfield, PA; (Y); 125/363; Aud/Vis; Church Yth Grp; Cmnty Wkr; Debate Tm; Drama Clb; Key Clb; PAVAS; Spanish Clb; Band; Chorus; Tgeen Volntr Of Yr Awd 85; Thlgy.

ROWLES, JANE; Clearfield Area HS; Clearfield, PA; (Y); Church Yth Grp; French Clb; Sec Key Clb; Ski Clb; Band; Chorus; Stat Bsktbl; Hon Roll; Anna Aeillo Mem Scholar Awd 86; U Pittsburgh; Pre-Phrmcy.

ROWLES, RAY; Brockway Area JR SR HS; Brockport, PA; (Y); 2/90; Church Yth Grp; Varsity Clb; VP Jr Cls; Var L Ftbl; Cit Awd; High Hon Roll; Hst NHS; Ntl Merit Ltr; Naval Nuclr Pwr Pschl; Nucl Pwr.

ROWLEY, JEN; Strath Haven HS; Swarthmore, PA; (Y); VP Church Yth Grp; Church Choir; School Musical; Stage Crew; JV Var Tennis; Cmnty Wkr; French Clb; German Clb; JV Lcrss; Natl Frnch Cont Wnnr 84-86; Classcl Studs.

ROWLEY, JULIE ANN; Mount Saint Joseph Acad; Abington, PA; (Y); Hosp Aide; Sec Sr Cls; Bsktbl; Sftbl; French Hon Soc; Hon Roll; NHS; NEDT Awd; Cum Laude Natl Latin Exam 82-84; Excllnc Engl III IV 84-86; Villanova U; Nrsng.

ROY, LYNDA; Beaver Falls HS; Deland, FL; (Y); French Clb; FBLA; Drm Mjr(t); Stat Sftbl; Capt Twrlr; High Hon Roll; Hon Roll; NHS; Natl Voctnl Tech Hnr Soc 85-86.

ROYALL, TIMOTHY J; Cathedral Prep; Erie, PA; (Y); 28/230; Boy Scts; Camera Clb; Church Yth Grp; Drama Clb; Exploring; Speech Tm; Teachers Aide; Thesps; Band; Chorus; U Of Pittsburgh; Phy Thrpy.

ROYCE, CHRISTINE A; Wes Scranton HS; Scranton, PA; (S); 13/287; Aud/Vis; Quiz Bowl; Scholastic Bowl; Band; Concert Band; Drm Mjr(t); Mrchg Band; Orch; School Musical; Yrbk Phtg; 1st Chr Flute 84-86; U Of S; Med Tech.

ROYCE, DANIELLE; Susquehanna Comm HS; Susquehanna, PA; (Y); Ski Clb; Color Guard; Sec Frsh Cls; VP Soph Cls; VP Jr Cls; Var Cheerleading; JV Powder Puff Ftbl; Var Trk; JV Var Vllybl; Frederick Lawrence; Mdlng.

ROYCROFT, BECKY; Fairchance Georges JR SR HS; Fairchance, PA; (Y); 30/160; Church Yth Grp; FHA; School Play; Stage Crew; Trs Jr Cls; Cheerleading; High Hon Roll; Hon Roll; VP Jr NHS; IUP; Fshn Mrchndng.

ROYCROFT, JENNIFER; Fairchance-Georges JR SR HS; Fairchance, PA; (Y); 10/150; French Clb; Hosp Aide; Nwsp Stf; Yrbk Stf; Hst Soph Cls; Trs Jr Cls; Trs Sr Cls; JV Var Cheerleading; VP NHS; WV U; Psychlgy.

ROYER, BETSEY A; Cocalico HS; Stevens, PA; (Y); 20/200; Pres Sec Church Yth Grp; Pres Trs 4-H; Hosp Aide; Rep Stu Cncl; Var Cheerleading; JV Fld Hcky; 4-H Awd; High Hon Roll; Hon Roll.

ROYER, KAREEN; Benton Area JR/SR HS; Stillwater, PA; (Y); 6/41; Keywanettes; Flag Corp; Nwsp Stf; Yrbk Stf; Stu Cncl; Bsktbl; Hon Roll; Trs NHS; Century 21 Typng Awd 84; Century 21 Accntng Awd 85; IN U PA; Bus Ed.

ROYER, LUCY; Freedom HS; Bethlehem, PA; (Y); 148/445; Cmnty Wkr; German Clb; Sec Intnl Clb; Band; Color Guard; Drill Tm; Drm & Bgl; Mrchg Band; Pep Band; Hon Roll; Shippensburg; Pre-Law.

ROYER, MELISSA; Northern Bedford County HS; Roaring Spg, PA; (Y); FBLA; Band; Chorus; Drm Mjr(t); Jazz Band; Swing Chorus; Nwsp Sprt Ed; Bsbl; Bsktbl; Outstndng Majorette 85-86; Katharine Gibbs; Exec Sec.

ROYER, MELYNDA; Ephrata SR HS; Ephrata, PA; (Y); Pres Stu Cncl; Capt Var Fld Hcky; Powder Puff Ftbl; Hon Roll; :Advrtsng.

ROYLE, LEIGH; West Hazleton HS; W Hazleton, PA; (S); 19/204; Y-Teens; Stu Cncl; L Capt Bsktbl; Hon Roll; NHS; Bus Ed.

ROYSTER, SAMUEL; Pine Forge Acad; Pine Forge, PA; (S); 2/60; Library Aide; Chorus; Church Choir; Yrbk Bus Mgr; Trs Jr Cls; Cit Awd; High Hon Roll; Prfct Atten Awd; Oakwood Coll; Evnglst Mnstr.

ROYSTON, AMY; Richland HS; Mars, PA; (Y); AFS; Ski Clb; Chorus; Trk; Hon Roll; School Musical; Old Dominion U.

ROZELL, MICHAEL; Connellsville Area SR HS; Connellsville, PA; (Y); Pres Church Yth Grp; Chorus; Mrchg Band; Orch; School Musical; Swing Chorus; Variety Show; High Hon Roll; Jr NHS; NHS; Cast Of Up With People 86-87; Herb Dugan & Pearl Keck Music Schlrshp 86; Music Educ.

ROZELLE, ERIC J; Corry Area HS; Corry, PA; (Y); 2/186; Aud/Vis; Church Yth Grp; Pres German Clb; Library Aide; Church Choir; High Hon Roll; NHS; Pres Schlr; Sal; Rotry Clb By Mnth 86; Penn ST Behrend; Engrng.

ROZETAR, JOHN; Minersville Area HS; Llewellyn, PA; (Y); STEVENS Technel Schl; Machnst.

ROZIC, PAUL; Quigley HS; Conway, PA; (S); 12/120; Math Tm; JV Bsbl; L Bsktbl; L Golf; High Hon Roll; NHS; Typng Awd 86; Aerospc Engrng.

ROZINSKY, JANALEE; Mt Pleasant Area HS; Mt Pleasant, PA; (Y); Church Yth Grp; GAA; Office Aide; Teachers Aide; Chorus; Nwsp Stf; High Hon Roll; Hon Roll; Bus Stu Mnth 85; Bus Careers Inst; Scrtrl.

ROZMAN, JOHN; West Allegheny HS; Oakdale, PA; (Y); Spanish Clb; Chorus; JV Var Bsbl; South Hills Area Schl Dist Assoc Awd 86; IN U; Comp Sci.

ROZMAN, ROBERT; Quigley HS; Baden, PA; (S); 13/110; Church Yth Grp; Letterman Clb; Math Tm; JV Bsbl; JV Bsktbl; French Hon Soc; High Hon Roll; Hon Roll; Jr NHS; NHS; Penn ST U; Cvl Engrng.

ROZWADOWSKI, JOHN; Cathedral Prepatory Schl; Erie, PA; (Y); 35/263; Chess Clb; Model UN; Ski Clb; Stu Cncl; Im Church Yth Grp8; Cheerleading; Var L Socr; JV Trk; NHS; Clarkson U; Engrng.

RUBACKY, ANN MARIE; Hazleton SR HS; Hazleton, PA; (Y); Office Aide; Color Guard; Mrchg Band; High Hon Roll; Hon Roll; PA ST U; Bus Adm.

RUBANO, DIANA A; Bethel Park HS; Bethel Park, PA; (Y); FBLA; Capt Var Cheerleading; Powder Puff Ftbl; High Hon Roll; Jr NHS; NHS; Ntl Merit Ltr; Duquesne U; Phrmcy.

RUBENSTEIN, MARLENE; Mt Lebanon HS; Pittsburgh, PA; (Y); 93/514; Dance Clb; Office Aide; Temple Yth Grp; Capt Drill Tm; Rep Stu Cncl; Trk; High Hon Roll; Pres Schlr; Activities Key 86; United Jewish Fed Scholar 86; PA ST U.

RUBERTELLI, ROBIN; William Allen HS; Allentown, PA; (Y); Pres GAA; Ski Clb; Var JV Fld Hcky; JV Sftbl; Hon Roll; Bus.

RUBIN, BENJAMIN; Cheltenham HS; Elkins Pk, PA; (Y); 52/360; Band; Jazz Band; Mrchg Band; Orch; School Musical; Symp Band; Pres Stu Cncl; Var Lcrss; JP Sousa Awd; Ntl Merit SF; Staller Coll; Htl Mgmt.

RUBIN, JOE; Church Farm Schl; Chevy Chase, MD; (Y); 2/25; Chess Clb; Ski Clb; Nwsp Stf; JV Var Socr; JV Swmmng; Var Tennis; JV Wrstlng; Hon Roll; Bus.

RUBINO, MARY JO; Wyoming Area HS; Wyoming, PA; (Y); 7/260; Drama Clb; French Clb; Key Clb; Chorus; Hon Roll; NHS; Pltcl Sci.

RUBINO, NANCY; St Marys Area Public HS; Saint Marys, PA; (Y); Art Clb; Pttsburg Art Inst; Int Dsgn.

RUBINO, TONY; Beaver Area HS; Beaver, PA; (Y); 37/177; Sec JCL; Ski Clb; School Musical; Yrbk Bus Mgr; VP Stu Cncl; JV Ftbl; Var Tennis; Hon Roll; Church Yth Grp; Latin Clb; U Of Pittsburgh; Dntstry.

RUBISH, BARB; Frazier Mem JR SR HS; Perryopolis, PA; (Y); Cmnty Wkr; Drama Clb; FNA; Hosp Aide; Library Aide; Trs Chorus; High Hon Roll; Hon Roll; Peer Tutor 85-86; Nrsng.

RUBY, MONICA LYNN; Indiana Area SR HS; Indiana, PA; (Y); French Clb; Hosp Aide; Key Clb; Pep Clb; Chorus; Color Guard; Nwsp Rptr; Im Bsktbl; High Hon Roll; Hon Roll; Acctnt.

RUCHAK, JOHN; Bishop O Hara HS; Dunmore, PA; (S); 20/124; Computer Clb; Drama Clb; JA; Spanish Clb; School Musical; Nwsp Stf; Yrbk Phtg; Bowling; Hon Roll; Prfct Atten Awd; Scty Dist Amer Stu 83-85; Ntl Ldrshp Awd 82-85; Bishop O'hara Ntl Hnr Scty 84-85; U Of Scranton; Comp Sci.

RUCKER, SARA; New Castle SR HS; New Castle, PA; (S); 12/253; Spanish Clb; Trk; Hon Roll; Art.

RUCZHAK, JEANNE; Octorara Area HS; Christiana, PA; (Y); 46/161; Church Yth Grp; Cmnty Wkr; FTA; Pres Library Aide; Service Clb; SADD; Teachers Aide; Hon Roll; Prfct Atten Awd; Silv Poet Awd 86; Hnrb Mntn Peac Awarenss Cont Solutions World Hunger 86; Spec Ed.

RUDA, JOHNINE; North Allegheny HS; Wexford, PA; (Y); 136/642; Dance Clb; Ski Clb; Band; Drill Tm; Yrbk Stf; Hon Roll; Spanish NHS.

RUDA, MARY; Lake-Lehman HS; Hunlock Creek, PA; (Y); Office Aide; Spanish Clb; SADD; Varsity Clb; Cheerleading; Trk; Vllybl; Jr NHS; Scrtrl.

RUDAR, STACEY; Ringgold HS; Venetia, PA; (Y); Church Yth Grp; Library Aide; Office Aide; Usherette 83; Interact Clbh 86; JE Prom Cmte 85; CA U Of PA; Early Chldhd.

RUDDICK, DEBBI; Pleasant Valley HS; Saylorsburg, PA; (Y); Art Clb; Drama Clb; School Play; Nwsp Stf; Hon Roll; Writng.

RUDDY, JOHN; Scranton Prep; Dunmore, PA; (Y); 86/190; Ski Clb; Bsbl; Var Ftbl; Trk; Vllybl; Wt Lftg; Wrstlng; U Of Scranton; CPA.

RUDEGEAIR, EMILY; Cedar Crest HS; Lebnaon, PA; (Y); Debate Tm; French Clb; Pep Clb; Band; Concert Band; Drm & Bgl; Jazz Band; Mrchg Band; Orch; Pep Band; Cedar Crest Silver Mdllnst Awd; Pltcl Sci.

RUDEK, RAYMOND; Moon SR HS; Coraopolis, PA; (Y); 16/304; Trs Key Clb; Yrbk Phtg; Yrbk Sprt Ed; Trs Soph Cls; Trs Jr Cls; L Socr; L Swmmng; L Trk; High Hon Roll; NHS; Buhl Sci Fair Awd Wnnr Auto Engrs 86; PS Dist Outstndng Treas Awd For Key Clb.

RUDIC, RADU DANIEL; Upper Dublin HS; Ambler, PA; (Y); 3/350; JA; Orch; Im Bsbl; Im Bsktbl; Var Tennis; Wt Lftg; NHS; Biol.

RUDICK, MARY; Penn Trafford HS; Jeannette, PA; (Y); AFS; Girl Scts; Hosp Aide; Latin Clb; VICA; Concert Band; Mrchg Band; Hon Roll; Cnsrvtn Law Enfrcmnt.

RUDISILL, ALAN; Mt Carmel Area JR-SR HS; Mt Carmel, PA; (Y); 8/136; Key Clb; Math Tm; Ski Clb; Spanish Clb; School Play; Rep Stu Cncl; Var Bsktbl; Var Crs Cntry; High Hon Roll; NHS; Deppen Schlrshp Bucknell U 86; Bucknell U Lewisburg PA; Elec.

RUDISLL, ANN; Mt Carmel Area JR SR HS; Mt Carmel, PA; (Y); Key Clb; Latin Clb; Pep Clb; Spanish Clb; Chorus; School Musical; School Play; Nwsp Stf; Stu Cncl; Cheerleading.

RUDMAN, MARY BETH; Connellsville HS; Connellsville, PA; (Y); 77/500; Church Yth Grp; Civic Clb; Office Aide; Service Clb; SADD; Band; Chorus; Concert Band; Mrchg Band; Pep Band; Montefiore Hosp Schl Radlgy.

RUDNICK, ANDREW G; Unionville HS; Chadds Ford, PA; (Y); 1/255; Hosp Aide; Library Aide; Math Clb; Temple Yth Grp; Stage Crew; Rep Soph Cls; Var L Trk; Mu Alp Tht; Ntl Merit SF; Val; Penn ST; Pre-Med.

RUDNIK, MICHAEL; Hempfield Area SR HS; Jeannette, PA; (Y); German Clb; ROTC; Ftbl; Golf; High Hon Roll; Hon Roll; Psychlgy.

RUDOCK, CHRIS; Solanco HS; Nottingham, PA; (Y); 52/235; Teachers Aide; Hon Roll; Mltry.

RUDOLPH, JACQUELINE; Richland HS; Gibsonia, PA; (Y); Drama Clb; Swing Chorus; Pres Jr Cls; VP Stu Cncl; Capt L Tennis; Debate Tm; Red Cross Aide; Chorus; School Musical; Nwsp Rptr; Lib Arts.

RUDOLPH, KIRSTEN; Northern Potter HS; Genesee, PA; (Y); 1/66; French Clb; Varsity Clb; School Play; Nwsp Ed-Chief; Yrbk Ed-Chief; Sec Soph Cls; Sec Sr Cls; Var Capt Cheerleading; Bausch & Lomb Sci Awd; High Hon Roll; PA ST U; Psych.

RUDOLPH, LARA; Rocky Grove HS; Franklin, PA; (Y); 5/93; VP Trs Church Yth Grp; French Clb; Office Aide; Service Clb; SADD; Chorus; School Musical; Sec Jr Cls; Stu Cncl; JV Cheerleading; Elem Educ.

RUDOLPH, NICOLE C; The Ellis Schl; Edgewood, PA; (Y); Pres Drama Clb; Intnl Clb; School Play; Ed Yrbk Stf; Rep Stu Cncl; High Hon Roll; Ntl Merit SF; Service Clb; Nwsp Rptr; Stage Crew; Virginia P Stevenson Awd Hstry 85; Provosts Day Comptn Fnlst Frnch 85; Natl Frnch Cntst 5th Pl 85.

RUDOLPH, SCOTT; Richland HS; Wexford, PA; (Y); Cmnty Wkr; French Clb; Chorus; Rep Frsh Cls; Rep Soph Cls; Rep Jr Cls; Var L Bsktbl; Coach Actv; Var L Ftbl; Var L Trk; CA ST; Comp Tech.

RUDOLPH, SHELBY; Sheffield Area JR SR HS; Sheffield, PA; (Y); Church Yth Grp; Pep Clb; VP SADD; Varsity Clb; School Play; Sec Soph Cls; Off Stu Cncl; JV Var Cheerleading; Mat Maids; Stat Trk; Hmcmng Attendnt 84-86.

RUDOLPH, THEODORE; Cardinal O Hara HS; Springfield, PA; (Y); German Clb; Ski Clb; School Musical; School Play; Stage Crew; Hon Roll; Prfct Atten Awd; IEE Engrng Awd 85; Excllnce Awd DE Cnty Sci Fair 85; Excllnce Awd DE Vly Sci Fair 86; Comp Engrng.

RUDOWSKY, MICHAEL; West Mifflin Area HS; W Mifflin, PA; (Y); 5/338; Sec Science Clb; Concert Band; Drm Mjr(t); Jazz Band; Mrchg Band; Nwsp Stf; Rep Soph Cls; Rep Jr Cls; High Hon Roll; NHS; Cmptr Sci.

RUDY, SCOTT M; Charleroi JR SR HS; Charleroi, PA; (Y); Art Clb; Science Clb; Ski Clb; Art Inst; Vsl Comm.

RUDY, TAMMI L; William Penn HS; Harrisburg, PA; (S); 54/386; FBLA; Office Aide; Pep Clb; HACC; Bus Admin.

RUELA, ANTHONY; Bethlehem Catholic HS; Bethlehem, PA; (Y); 35/221; SADD; Varsity Clb; Bsktbl; Var Socr; Gov Hon Prg Awd; Hon Roll; JETS Awd; NHS; Prfct Atten Awd; Wentworth Inst; Aerontcl Maint.

RUEV, CASSANDRA; Ringgold HS; Donora, PA; (Y); Church Yth Grp; Dance Clb; Hosp Aide; Band; Chorus; Church Choir; Concert Band; Mrchg Band; JV Var Vllybl; Hon Roll; Douglas Schl Of Bus; Prof Sec.

RUFF, CHRISTINE; Bethel Park SR HS; Pittsburgh, PA; (Y); Church Yth Grp; FHA; Key Clb; Im Bsktbl; Cheerleading; Mgr(s); Pom Pon; Powder Puff Ftbl; Im Sftbl; NHS.

RUFF, JENNIFER; Lower Moreland HS; Huntingdon Valley, PA; (S); Drama Clb; Key Clb; Acpl Chr; Chorus; Concert Band; Drill Tm; Pep Band; School Musical; Hon Roll; NHS; JR Womens Club Music Stu Mnth 84; U Of PA; Phy.

RUFFER, ROBYN L; Reading SR HS; Reading, PA; (S); 3/650; Church Yth Grp; Pres Debate Tm; VP JA; VP Model UN; Q&S; Madrigals; Nwsp Ed-Chief; Supt Schlstc Rcgntn 83-86; Outstndng Feml Stu 83.

RUFFIN, JANENE; Abp John Carroll HS; Wayne, PA; (Y); 95/212; Cmnty Wkr; Library Aide; SADD; Varsity Clb; School Play; Lit Mag; Rep Soph Cls; Pres Sr Cls; Var Capt Trk; Prfct Atten Awd; Law.

RUFFLEY, TRACIE LYNN; Greencastle-Antrim HS; Greencastle, PA; (Y); 99/176; Am Leg Aux Girls St; Stu Cncl; Stat Bsktbl; Cheerleading; Im Vllybl; Hon Roll; Accntng.

RUFFNER, KRISTINE; Derry Area SR HS; Derry, PA; (Y); 5/255; Letterman Clb; Ski Clb; Sec Chorus; Yrbk Bus Mgr; Stu Cncl; JV Bsktbl; Cheerleading; Var Capt Vllybl; Rotary Awd; Westmoreland County CC All Star Vllybll Camp Tm 84; U Of Pittsburgh.

RUGGERI, DAVID; Norwin SR HS; N Huntingdon, PA; (Y); Computer Clb; DECA; Nwsp Stf; JV Bsbl; L Ftbl; L Trk; Im Wt Lftg; Hon Roll; DECA Dstrct Cmptn 2nd Pl 85; DECA Dstrct Cmptn 4th Plc Rstrn Mrktng 86; Ecnmcs.

RUGGERY, KATHLEEN; Bishop Guilfoyle HS; Altoona, PA; (S); 21/150; Chorus; Yrbk Ed-Chief; Sec Jr Cls; VP Sr Cls; Rep Stu Cncl; Capt JV Bsktbl; Capt JV Cheerleading; Tennis; High Hon Roll; VP NHS; Ntl Phy Ed Awd 86; Penn ST U; Elem Ed.

RUGGIA, TINA; Bensalem SR HS; Bensalem, PA; (Y); 50/564; Teachers Aide; Pres Frsh Cls; Rep Sr Cls; Rep Stu Cncl; Stat Bsktbl; Var Fld Hcky; Var Capt Sftbl; High Hon Roll; NHS; Rep Soph Cls; 3-D Awd-Sftbl 86; West Chester U; Bus Admin.

RUGGIERO, TRICIA; Bishop Hafey HS; Sugarloaf, PA; (Y); Drama Clb; French Clb; Hosp Aide; School Play; French Hon Soc; Hon Roll.

RUGGLES, LORI; Central HS; E Freedom, PA; (Y); FBLA; Yrbk Stf; Trk; Hon Roll; Bus Eng Awd 86; Exec Sec.

RUGOLA, AMY; Brownsville Area HS; Allison, PA; (S); 13/225; Computer Clb; Drama Clb; Library Aide; Math Clb; SADD; Band; Mrchg Band; Variety Show; Vllybl; High Hon Roll; Susquehanna Un; Ansthslgst.

RUHF, BECKY; Brandywine Heights HS; Topton, PA; (Y); Band; Concert Band; Mrchg Band; JV Var Fld Hcky; Hon Roll; Prfct Atten Awd; Penn ST; Bus Mgmt.

RUHF, MICHAEL; Freedom HS; Bethlehem, PA; (Y); 134/445; Boy Scts; Science Clb; Band; Concert Band; Jazz Band; Mrchg Band; Eagl Sct 84; Lehigh U; Bio.

RUHL, CYNTHIA; Annville-Cleona HS; Cleona, PA; (Y); 1/121; FBLA; Girl Scts; Math Tm; Quiz Bowl; Varsity Clb; Band; Chorus; Concert Band; Mrchg Band; Pep Band; PA St Champ-Amer Lgn Ortrcl Cntst 86; Pres Acadmc Ftns Awd 86; Gsmber Ortrcl Cntst Wnr 86; James Madison U VA; Econ.

RULLO, CHRISTINE; Ringgold HS; Monongahela, PA; (Y); Computer Clb; Girl Scts; Ski Clb; Arch.

RUMBAUGH, RICHARD; Laurel HS; Volant, PA; (Y); #22 In Class; Boy Scts; Pres Ski Clb; Wolves Clb Schlrshp 86; PA ST U; Elec Engr.

RUMBAUGH, SUSAN; Shippensburg SR HS; Shippensburg, PA; (Y); 25/227; Band; Chorus; Concert Band; Jazz Band; Mrchg Band; School Musical; School Play; Dnfth Awd; High Hon Roll; Mnstrm Schlrshps 86; Rtry Clb Schlrshp 86; Cvc Clb Schlrshp 86; Shippensburg U; Erly Chldhd Edu.

RUMBERGER, ANNE L; Garnet Valley HS; Glen Mills, PA; (Y); French Clb; Varsity Clb; Stu Cncl; Var Bsktbl; Var Sftbl; Var Vllybl; Hon Roll; Rotary Awd; Library Aide; Office Aide; Peer Cnslng-Grp Ldr; Frgn Exchg Clb; Mktng.

RUMBLE, BETH; Brandywine Heights HS; Mertztown, PA; (Y); 15/126; Church Yth Grp; Band; Concert Band; Jazz Band; Mrchg Band; Pep Band; High Hon Roll; NHS; Erly Chldhd Ed.

RUMELFANGER, RICHARD; Hickory HS; Hermitage, PA; (Y); 11/175; Boy Scts; Varsity Clb; Chorus; School Musical; Stage Crew; Nwsp Rptr; Stu Cncl; Bsktbl; Crs Cntry; NHS; Phrmcy.

RUMMEL, JEANETTE; Blacklick Valley JR SR HS; Belsano, PA; (S); 1/90; Varsity Clb; Yrbk Sprt Ed; Yrbk Stf; Var Capt Bsktbl; Var Capt Sftbl; Hon Roll; Sec NHS; Acad All Amer 83-85.

RUMMEL, JULIE; Everett Christian Acad; Everett, PA; (S); Church Yth Grp; Band; Chorus; Church Choir; Yrbk Stf; Pres Jr Cls; VP Stu Cncl; Capt Bsktbl; Capt Vllybl; NHS; Hghst Overall Avg 84-85; Acad Excllnc 84-85; Engl Awd 84-85; Lee Coll.

RUMMEL, ROY; Littlestown HS; Hanover, PA; (Y); #23 In Class; Church Yth Grp; JV Ftbl; JV Wrstlng; Hon Roll; Engrng.

RUMMEL, TERRI; Penns Manor HS; Glen Cambell, PA; (Y); Camera Clb; FNA; Girl Scts; Band; Concert Band; Mrchg Band; High Hon Roll; Hon Roll; Prfct Atten Awd; RN.

RUMMELL, BARB; Johnstown HS; Johnstown, PA; (Y); Art Clb; Church Yth Grp; 4-H; School Musical; Hon Roll; Prfct Atten Awd; Cmrcl Artst.

RUMNEY, JOHN; Marion Center Area HS; Rossiter, PA; (S); Latin Clb; Chorus; High Hon Roll; Hon Roll; NHS; Med.

RUMP, RACHEL S; Serra Catholic HS; Port Vue, PA; (Y); 6/127; AFS; Band; Yrbk Stf; Powder Puff Ftbl; French Hon Soc; Hon Roll; NHS; NEDT Awd; PA ST U; Bus Adm.

RUMSKEY, CHERIE L; Waynesburg Central HS; Waynesburg, PA; (Y); Church Yth Grp; Office Aide; Spanish Clb; Nwsp Stf; VP Frsh Cls; Pres Soph Cls; VP Jr Cls; VP Cheerleading; High Hon Roll; Waynesburg Clg; Bus.

RUNAS, RICHARD; Deer Lakes HS; Gibsonia, PA; (Y); 45/190; Art Clb; Drama Clb; PAVAS; Political Wkr; Ski Clb; SADD; School Musical; School Play; Var Crs Cntry; L Var Trk; Carnegie Mellon Pre Coll Art Prog 84-85; SF Gvrnr Schl Arts 85; Carnegie Mellon; Fine Art.

RUNDLE, SCOTT; Waynesboro Area HS; Waynesboro, PA; (Y); 15/392; Church Yth Grp; Band; Concert Band; Jazz Band; Mrchg Band; School Musical; High Hon Roll; NHS; Math Tchr.

RUNGE, REBECCA; Octorara Area HS; Cochranville, PA; (Y); 15/171; Math Clb; Concert Band; Jazz Band; Mrchg Band; Var Bsktbl; Var Fld Hcky; Var Trk; High Hon Roll; Hon Roll; NHS; Elizabethtown Coll; Math.

RUNK, KARENA; Fannett Metal HS; Willow Hill, PA; (Y); VP DECA; Sec Varsity Clb; Color Guard; Mrchg Band; Rep Jr Cls; Trs Stu Cncl; Co-Capt Bsktbl; Cheerleading; Var Capt Sftbl; Hon Roll; Tm MVP Awd Sftbl 85-86.

RUNKLE, CAROL; Schuylkill Haven HS; Schuylkill Haven, PA; (S); 5/77; Church Yth Grp; German Clb; Science Clb; SADD; Nwsp Rptr; Cheerleading; Hon Roll; Phrmcy.

RUNSHAW, BONNIE; Shippensburg Area SR HS; Shippensburg, PA; (Y); FBLA; High Hon Roll; Schlstc Art Awd 81; Hon Stu Awd 86; Sec.

RUNYON, CHRISTINA; Big Spring HS; Carlisle, PA; (Y); Pep Clb; SADD; Rep Jr Cls; Trs Sr Cls; Rep Stu Cncl; Cheerleading; Pom Pon; Powder Puff Ftbl; Vllybl; Hon Roll; Sportsmnshp Vllybl 85-86; Shippensburg U; Crimnl Justc.

RUPEIKS, NADINE; Council Rock HS; Newtown, PA; (Y); Art Clb; Church Yth Grp; 4-H; Key Clb; Church Choir; Yrbk Stf; Cheerleading; 4-H Awd; Hon Roll; Grad From Rssn Prsh Schl Vldctrn 85; Lang.

RUPERT, ALETA; Yough HS; W Newton, PA; (Y); Pep Clb; Ski Clb; VICA; Yrbk Stf; Stu Cncl; Var Co-Capt Cheerleading; Powder Puff Ftbl; Hon Roll; Cosm.

RUPERT, CHRISTOPHER; Tussey Mountain HS; Saxton, PA; (Y); 29/97; Nwsp Stf; Yrbk Stf; Var L Bsktbl; Var L Trk; Hon Roll; Penn ST; Elec Engrng.

RUPERT, JOYCE; Hughesville HS; Hughesville, PA; (Y); 7/136; Library Aide; Teachers Aide; Hon Roll; NHS; Green & White Awd 86; Ed.

RUPERT, THERESA; Ford City HS; Ford City, PA; (Y); 15/160; Church Yth Grp; Hosp Aide; Spanish Clb; Rep Soph Cls; Rep Jr Cls; Var Bsktbl; Var Sftbl; High Hon Roll; NHS; Interpreter.

RUPP, JESSICA; Ephrata SR HS; Ephrata, PA; (Y); German Clb; Pep Clb; Rep Frsh Cls; Rep Jr Cls; Rep Stu Cncl; Var Bsktbl; Hon Roll; Lancaster Schl Cosmetlogy; Cmst.

RUPP, KENDRA; Scranton Prep; Jermyn, PA; (Y); 53/192; Drama Clb; Chorus; School Musical; School Play; Sftbl; Trk; High Hon Roll; NHS; Bus.

RUPP, LISA; Danville HS; Riverside, PA; (Y); 22/163; FHA; Chorus; Lit Mag; High Hon Roll; Gayann Cotner Bus Awd 86; SR Bus Clb Tres 86.

RUPP, LYNN; St Benedict Acad; Erie, PA; (Y); 1/63; Quiz Bowl; Yrbk Stf; Lit Mag; Pres Frsh Cls; Rep Stu Cncl; Var L Bsktbl; Var L Sftbl; High Hon Roll; Hon Roll; Pres NHS; Acad Schlrshp St Bendict Acad 84; Natl Cncl Tchrs English Awd 86; Highest Acad Achvt Awds 84 & 85 & 86; Phys Therapy.

RUPP, SHENANN; General Mc Lane HS; Waterford, PA; (Y); 12/220; Aud/Vis; German Clb; Band; Chorus; Concert Band; Flag Corp; Mrchg Band; Stage Crew; Hon Roll; Intrmntlst Mag Music Awd 84; H S Acad Dstnctn Awd 84; Edinboro U; Pre-Law.

RUPP, SUZETTE; Yough HS; Yukon, PA; (Y); French Clb; Mgr Band; Chorus; Yrbk Ed-Chief; High Hon Roll; Hon Roll; NHS; Variety Show; Wstmrlnd Cnty Chorus 85-86; Dstrct I & Rgn I Chorus 85-86; IN U PA; Bus Adm.

RUPP, TIM; Scranton Preparatory Schl; Simpson, PA; (Y); 26/192; Chorus; School Musical; Yrbk Stf; Rep Frsh Cls; Var L Swmmng; Var L Trk; Im Vllybl; High Hon Roll; Hon Roll; NHS; Ntl Hnr Scty & Track 85-86; Sprts Med.

RUPPEL, KARA; Turkeyfoot Valley Area HS; Confluence, PA; (S); 4/53; Ski Clb; Varsity Clb; Chorus; Nwsp Phtg; Nwsp Rptr; Yrbk Rptr; Stu Cncl; Var Capt Cheerleading; High Hon Roll; NHS; Jrnlsm.

RUPPERT, KIMBERLY; Dover Area HS; Dover, PA; (Y); Girl Scts; Hosp Aide; Color Guard; Stat Bsbl; L Twrlr; Cert Of Merit 83-84; Physicl Terapy.

RUPPERT, TONY; Eastern HS; York, PA; (Y); 25/123; JA; Trs Varsity Clb; Var Capt Ftbl; Wt Lftg; High Hon Roll; Hon Roll; Jr NHS; Outstndng Paper Carrier Yr 83; Stu Mnth 85; York Coll; Resp Thrpy.

RUSCIO, BRAD; Altoona Area HS; Altoona, PA; (Y); Band; Concert Band; Mrchg Band; Stage Band 82-83; Phrmctcl.

RUSH, AMY; Washnington HS; Washington, PA; (S); 8/155; French Clb; FNA; Letterman Clb; Library Aide; Varsity Clb; Band; Concert Band; Jazz Band; Mrchg Band; Rep Frsh Cls; Sports Med.

RUSH, JAMES; Mahonoy Area HS; New Boston, PA; (Y); Ski Clb; JV VP Bsbl; Im Bsktbl; NHS.

RUSH, KAREN; Cumberland Valley HS; Camp Hill, PA; (Y); 116/551; Key Clb; Nwsp Rptr; Lit Mag; Sec Frsh Cls; VP Soph Cls; Rep Jr Cls; Hon Roll; Church Yth Grp; German Clb; Ski Clb; Hugh O Brien Leadrshp-Honorary Awd 85; Germn Achvt Awd 84 & 85; Top 40-Miss Teenage Amer Contst 85; James Madison U; Communctns.

RUSH, KELLY; Carmichaels Area HS; Carmichaels, PA; (Y); 20/101; Ski Clb; Trs Spanish Clb; Band; Capt Color Guard; Hon Roll; Acad All Amer 85-86; JR Standing Comm Treas 85-86.

RUSH, STEVE; Cathedral Preparatory Schl; Erie, PA; (Y); 71/216; JV Trk; Gannon U; Bus.

RUSH, TRACY; Kiski Area HS; Apollo, PA; (Y); Hosp Aide; Spanish Clb; Band; Yrbk Stf; High Hon Roll; Hon Roll; Upj; Physcl Ther.

RUSHTON, JENNIFER; North East Prep Schl; Philadelphia, PA; (S); Temple U; Lang.

RUSHTON, MARK; Northeast Catholic HS; Philadelphia, PA; (Y); 60/390; Aud/Vis; Varsity Clb; Rep Jr Cls; Rep Stu Cncl; Capt Var Wrstlng; High Hon Roll; Hon Roll; NHS; Acctng.

RUSINKO, MARLENE; South Allegheny HS; Elizabeth, PA; (S); 102/184; Church Yth Grp; French Clb; Office Aide; Y-Teens; Band; Concert Band; Jazz Band; Mrchg Band; Orch; Pep Band.

RUSK, BILL; Canton JR-SR HS; Grover, PA; (Y); Chrmn Aud/Vis; Computer Clb; Science Clb; High Hon Roll; Hon Roll; Natl Socl Study Olympd Awd 85-86; Comp Pgmng.

RUSLAVAGE, ROBERT; Clarion Area HS; Clarion, PA; (Y); Yrbk Stf; Trs Soph Cls; Stu Cncl; Bsktbl; Ftbl; Trk; Hon Roll; NHS; Mech Engrg.

RUSNAK, CAROLYN; Cambria Heights HS; Hastings, PA; (Y); 5/180; Ski Clb; Concert Band; Mrchg Band; Nwsp Stf; Yrbk Phtg; Trs Sr Cls; Sec NHS; NEDT Awd; Acad All Amer 86; Mst Spirited 86; IN U PA; Secndry Ed.

RUSNAK, DIANE; Panther Valley HS; Summit Hill, PA; (Y); 11/131; Color Guard; Nwsp Rptr; Yrbk Stf; Sftbl; High Hon Roll; Hon Roll; NHS; Rotary Awd; Pres Acdmc/Ftns Awd; Lit & Hlth Awds; PA ST U; Acctg.

RUSNAK, SUSAN E; General Mc Lane HS; Mckean, PA; (Y); 23/240; French Clb; German Clb; Hosp Aide; Chorus; School Musical; Nwsp Ed-Chief; Nwsp Rptr; Lit Mag; Off Stu Cncl; JV Bsktbl; Hnrd Outstndg Ldr Amer Assoc U Women 86; Engl.

RUSNOCK, PAULA; Donegal HS; Mt Joy, PA; (Y); 28/164; Band; Concert Band; Mrchg Band; Var Bsktbl; Var JV Fld Hcky; Var Sftbl; Im Vllybl; Hon Roll; Vrsty Bsktbl 83-84; Law.

RUSNOCK, ROBERT; Bishop Hafey HS; Hazleton, PA; (Y); Boy Scts; Exploring; Spanish Clb; Band; Concert Band; Orch; Church Yth Grp; Dist/Reg Orchstra 85-86; Radio Brdcstng.

RUSS, AMY; Mc Keesport Area HS; Mc Keesport, PA; (Y); 10/396; Exploring; Q&S; Concert Band; Mrchg Band; Orch; School Musical; Powder Puff Ftbl; High Hon Roll; NHS; Duquesne U; Phrmcy.

RUSSELL, BRAD; Clearfield Area HS; Clearfield, PA; (Y); Chess Clb; Cmnty Wkr; French Clb; Science Clb; SADD; Yrbk Stf; JV Im Bsktbl; Im Ftbl; JV Tennis; Im Vllybl; Phy Thrpy.

RUSSELL, CATHERINE; Venango Christian HS; Oil City, PA; (Y); 5/43; Model UN; Radio Clb; Nwsp Rptr; Yrbk Bus Mgr; Yrbk Rptr; Yrbk Stf; Var Stat Bsktbl; Stat Ftbl; Var JV Sftbl; Var Capt Vllybl; U Of Pittsburgh; Phy Thrpy.

RUSSELL, JEANINE; Mt Pleasant Area HS; Mount Pleasant, PA; (Y); 3/253; Sec Church Yth Grp; GAA; Girl Scts; Latin Clb; Ski Clb; Trs Band; Church Choir; Trs Concert Band; Jazz Band; Trs Mrchg Band; Arch.

RUSSELL, KRISTIN; Highlands SR HS; Brackenridge, PA; (Y); Trs Church Yth Grp; Cmnty Wkr; Hosp Aide; Intnl Clb; Key Clb; Library Aide; Office Aide; Varsity Clb; Band; Color Guard; Duquesne U Mid East Hnrs Band 85-86; Alleghany Coll; Hosp Adm.

RUSSELL, LISA; Pennsylvania Manor HS; Indiana, PA; (Y); Pres SADD; Acpl Chr; Band; Chorus; Drill Tm; School Musical; Nwsp Bus Mgr; Sec Stu Cncl; Church Yth Grp; Dance Clb; Regnl And ST Awd Acctg I And II 85-86; Jr Miss Contstnt 85; Most Outstndng SR 86; Carlow College; Acctg.

RUSSELL, RENEE; Hanover Area HS; Wilkes Barre, PA; (Y); Hosp Aide; Key Clb; Red Cross Aide; Band; Bsktbl; Var Trk; Hon Roll; Nrsng.

RUSSELL, RICHARD; Altoona Area HS; Altoona, PA; (S); 20/683; Drama Clb; PAVAS; Science Clb; Ski Clb; Chorus; Drm Mjr(t); School Musical; Trk; NHS; Am Leg Schl Awd 82; Mid ST Band Scholar Awd 83; Juniata Coll; Bus.

RUSSELL, SHARON; Mechanicsburg Area SR HS; Mechanicsburg, PA; (Y); 7/300; Drama Clb; NFL; Chorus; Orch; High Hon Roll; JC Awd; NHS; Church Yth Grp; SADD; Teachers Aide; Grl Sct Gold Awd 84; Comm Sr Awd 86; Excell In Actng Awd 86; Millersville U; Elem Educatn.

RUSSELL, SHERRI; Carrich HS; Pittsburgh, PA; (S); Speech Tm; Chorus; School Musical; School Play; Cit Awd; Princeton U; Ltrtre.

RUSSELLO, CHARLES; West Scranton SR HS; Scranton, PA; (Y); High Hon Roll; Hon Roll; NHS; Musicn.

RUSSEY, MICHELLE; Huntington Area HS; Huntingdon, PA; (Y); Pres Church Yth Grp; German Clb; Concert Band; Mrchg Band; School Play; Hon Roll; Quiz Bowl; Ski Clb; Band; Church Choir; PA Bandmasters Assn Awd Of Most Musical Progress 84-85; Presdntl Physcl Ftnss Awd 85-86; Intl Relations.

RUSSIN, MICHAEL; New Castle HS; New Castle, PA; (S); 4/253; AFS; VP French Clb; SADD; Concert Band; Pep Band; Rep Frsh Cls; Rep Soph Cls; Rep Jr Cls; Gov Hon Prg Awd; High Hon Roll; Westmister Hnrs Band 84.

RUSSO, LINDA; Abp Prendergast HS; Havertown, PA; (Y); 42/361; Hon Roll; NHS; Ski Clb; Sec SADD; Stage Crew; Var Fld Hcky; Var Sftbl; Immaculata Coll Half Tuition Schlrshp 86; Immaculata Coll; Bio.

RUSSO, LISA; Quaker Valley SR HS; Sewickley, PA; (Y); 24/167; Church Yth Grp; German Clb; Hosp Aide; Science Clb; Band; Stage Crew; Lit Mag; JV Var Socr; Var L Sftbl; Mrchg Band; Amer Grmn Fld Exchnge Pgm 86; Bio.

RUSSO, MARIA; Bishop Kenrick HS; Norristown, PA; (Y); 66/295; Art Clb; Science Clb; Ski Clb; Spanish Clb; Yrbk Stf; Fshn Dsgn.

RUSSO, MICHAEL; Bishop Kenrick HS; Norristown, PA; (Y); Computer Clb; Science Clb; Ski Clb; Hon Roll; Opt Clb Awd; Comp.

RUSSO III, RALPH J; Bishop Kenrick HS; Norristown, PA; (Y); 61/273; Church Yth Grp; Cmnty Wkr; Office Aide; Pres Stu Cncl; Crs Cntry; Trk; NHS; Prfct Atten Awd; Rotary Awd; Aud/Vis; Samuel & Rebecca Kardon Fndtn 86; Svc Awd 86; PA ST; Comp Sci.

RUSSO, SAL; St John Neumann HS; Philadelphia, PA; (Y); 70/338; Prfct Attdnc 83-84; Wnng Pstr Cntst Math Wk 83-84; Drexel; Elec Engrng.

RUSSO, SHAWN; Karns City JR SR HS; Parker, PA; (Y); 36/116; Spanish Clb; Rep Stu Cncl; Var L Trk; Hon Roll; Chroprctcs.

RUSSO, TANYA; Monessen HS; Monessen, PA; (Y); 16/87; French Clb; Mrchg Band; Stage Crew; Yrbk Stf; Stu Cncl; High Hon Roll; Hon Roll; Jr NHS; IN U Of PA; Accntng.

RUSSO, THOMAS P; Archbishop John Carroll HS; Wayne, PA; (Y); 13/162; Quiz Bowl; Band; Nwsp Rptr; Nwsp Stf; Tennis; Hon Roll; NHS; Crrll Ln Schl Ppr Awd 86; Hon Soc 85-86; Bus.

RUST, JULIE; Red Land HS; Lewisberry, PA; (Y); 20/275; Debate Tm; French Clb; Concert Band; Mrchg Band; School Musical; Symp Band; French Hon Soc; High Hon Roll; Hon Roll; Excllnc Music Awd 85-86.

RUSYNYK, JULIA; Cenral Dauphin HS; Harrisburg, PA; (Y); Band; Mrchg Band; Hon Roll; NHS; Lbrl Arts.

RUTANARUGSA, TRIPET; Lancaster Mennonite HS; Bronx, NY; (Y); Church Choir; Eastern Mennonite Coll; Comp Sc.

RUTH, MICHAEL; Christopher Dock HS; Souderton, PA; (Y); 34/92; Red Cross Aide; School Play; Im Badmtn; JV Bsbl; Var Mgr Bsktbl; Var Capt Socr; Im Vllybl; Im Wt Lftg; Im Wrstlng; Hon Roll; 2nd Tm Bicntl Athlc Lgu Soccer 83-84; 2nd Tm BAL Vrsty Soccer 84-85; 1st Tm 85-86; Ursinus Coll; Pre Med.

RUTH, PEGERON; Churchill HS; Rankin, PA; (Y); 76/220; VP 4-H; Church Choir; Var Vllybl; 4-H Awd; Hon Roll; Stu Dnc Tchr Awd 82; Real Estat.

RUTH, STEPHANIE; Schuylkill Valley HS; Mohrsville, PA; (Y); 19/126; FBLA; JA; Var L Crs Cntry; Var L Trk; Var Vllybl; Hon Roll; NHS; Pres Schlr; Top Cmmrcl Stdnt Awd 86; PYEA Mst Contrbtn Awd 86; Gld SV Top 10 Pct Clss 86.

RUTH, WILLIAM; Conrad Weiser HS; Womelsdorf, PA; (Y); 10/149; Church Yth Grp; Yrbk Stf; Var Capt Bsktbl; Hon Roll; Lion Awd; U S Army Rsrv Schlr/Athlt Awd 86; Grove Cty Coll; Chem Engrng.

RUTHERFORD, BUD; Northampton SR HS; Walnutport, PA; (Y); SADD; Pres Sr Cls; Var Socr; L Trk; Var Wt Lftg; Meterlgy.

RUTHERFORD, MAYA; Springside Schl; Philadelphia, PA; (Y); Church Yth Grp; Nwsp Phtg; Nwsp Rptr; Nwsp Stf; Lit Mag; VP Frsh Cls; Pres Soph Cls; JV Badmtn; Fld Hcky; Lcrss; Brown U Engl Awd 86; PA Govrnrs Schl For Arts 86; High Hnrs Engl Art 85; Hgh Hnrs Engl Art Hist Ltn 86; Engl.

RUTHIG, LISA; Pottstown SR HS; Pottstown, PA; (S); 6/183; Drama Clb; Hosp Aide; Ski Clb; School Play; Ed Lit Mag; High Hon Roll; Hon Roll; NHS; Ntl Merit SF; Church Yth Grp; Natl Hstry Day 1st Dist, 2nd ST, 4th Natl; Clss Essy Cntst 1st; Bio.

RUTKOSKI, SCOTT; Crestwood HS; Mountaintop, PA; (Y); Cmnty Wkr; Letterman Clb; Red Cross Aide; Ski Clb; Stu Cncl; Bsbl; Ftbl; Wt Lftg; High Hon Roll; NHS; BS Bio.

RUTKOSKY, CHARLENE; Millville Area HS; Millville, PA; (Y); FBLA; Library Aide; Band; Chorus; High Hon Roll; Hon Roll; NHS; Accntng.

RUTKOWSKI, JOSEPH; Upper Perkiomen HS; Red Hill, PA; (Y); 37/198; Cmnty Wkr; Band; Concert Band; Jazz Band; Mrchg Band; Pep Band; Stage Crew; 4-H Awd; High Hon Roll; Hon Roll; Sec Band 86; 1st Chr Awd Concrt Band 85-86; Allentwn Bus Schl; Mngmt.

RUTKOWSKI, LISA; Forest City Regional HS; Forest City, PA; (Y); 12/60; Letterman Clb; Sec Band; Concert Band; Jazz Band; Mrchg Band; Sec Jr Cls; Rep Stu Cncl; Var Score Keeper; Var Sftbl; Var Vllybl; Awd For 2nd Tm All-Star Vllybl/Sftbl 85-86; Mdl For Wnng Dist 12 Vllybl 85-86; Var Ltrs & Jckt; Biochemstry.

RUTT, DARYL; Mount Calvary Christian HS; Mt Joy, PA; (S); 3/12; Camera Clb; Nwsp Phtg; Yrbk Phtg; VP Sr Cls; Rep Stu Cncl; Var Bsbl; Stat Bsktbl; Stat Socr; Hon Roll; Comp Sci.

RUTTER, BRIAN; Middletown Area HS; Middletown, PA; (Y); US Marines.

RUTTER, CHAD; Central York HS; York, PA; (Y); 44/244; 4-H; Varsity Clb; Rep Stu Cncl; Var L Ftbl; Var L Vllybl; Wrstlng; High Hon Roll; Hon Roll; NHS; Opt Clb Awd; Pre Med.

RUTZ, KEVIN B; Allentown Central Catholic HS; Allentown, PA; (Y); 27/220; Pres Church Yth Grp; Drama Clb; Math Clb; SADD; Im Fld Hcky; Cit Awd; Hon Roll; NHS; Rep Soph Cls; Lee Iacocca Ldrshp Awd & Altrsm Awd 86; Villanova U; Finc.

RUVOLO, LISA; Middletown Area HS; Middletown, PA; (Y); 31/165; Varsity Clb; Band; Concert Band; Mrchg Band; Yrbk Phtg; Yrbk Stf; Var Socr; Var Sftbl; PA ST U; Bus Adm.

RUZYC, IWONA; Nazareth HS; Bensalem, PA; (Y); 2/123; Spanish Clb; VP Orch; Yrbk Stf; VP Frsh Cls; Sec Soph Cls; Prfct Atten Awd; Pres Plsh Clb 85-86; 1st Pl Awd Plsh Oratorical Cnst 84; Temple U; Dental Hygiene.

RUZZI, VINCENT; Strath Haven HS; Wallingford, PA; (Y); Aud/Vis; Church Yth Grp; Library Aide; Science Clb; Teachers Aide; Stage Crew; Wrstlng; Hon Roll; Natl Yth Phys Fit Awd Maarine Corps Lg 84 & 85.

RYAN, ANNE; Clearfield HS; Clearfield, PA; (Y); Church Yth Grp; French Clb; Nwsp Stf; JV Var Bsktbl; Var L Sftbl; Hon Roll; Math.

RYAN, BRIDGET; Susquehanna Community HS; Susquehanna, PA; (S); Band; Mrchg Band; Var Trk; Twrlr; JV Vllybl; Hon Roll; Prfct Atten Awd; Data Prcssng.

RYAN, CHRIS; Technical HS; Scranton, PA; (Y); Art Clb; Ski Clb; Stage Crew; Nwsp Stf; Yrbk Stf; Cheerleading; Sftbl; Swmmng; Trk; Achvt In Art Schlrshp Awd 83; Am Educ Wk Art Awd 84; Business Mgmt.

RYAN, COLLEEN; Seton Catholic HS; Pittston, PA; (Y); Drama Clb; Ski Clb; School Play; Yrbk Stf; Hon Roll; Luzerne County CC; Acctg.

RYAN, COURTNEY; Wissahickon HS; Gwynedd, PA; (Y); Rep JCL; Off Latin Clb; Orch; School Musical; Lit Mag; Var Crs Cntry; Var Trk; Cit Awd; Jr NHS; NHS; Drwg & Paint Awd 85; Oil Paint Awd 86; Soc Stud II Awd 86; Lib Art.

RYAN, DESMOND; St Josephs Prep; Narberth, PA; (Y); Church Yth Grp; Model UN; Spanish Clb; SADD; Im Bsktbl; Im Ftbl; Im Powder Puff Ftbl; High Hon Roll; Hon Roll; Med.

RYAN, DONALD; Boiling Springs HS; Boiling Spgs, PA; (Y); 4/110; Science Clb; Band; Yrbk Stf; Var Bsbl; Var Bsktbl; Var Ftbl; High Hon Roll; Lion Awd; NHS; L Whitcomb Awd 82-83; Moravian Coll; Physc.

RYAN, ERIC J; Beaver Area JR-SR HS; Worthington, OH; (Y); 7/190; Boy Scts; Camera Clb; French Clb; VP JA; Yrbk Phtg; JV Var Ftbl; Mgr(s); JV L Swmmng; JV Var Trk; High Hon Roll; Schlstc Achvt Awd 85; Orthpdc Srgn.

RYAN, FRANK; Meyersdale Area HS; Meyersdale, PA; (Y); French Clb; Yrbk Stf; Var L Bsbl; JV Bsktbl.

RYAN, GWYNNE OONAGH; Strath Haven HS; Swarthmore, PA; (Y); Church Yth Grp; Quiz Bowl; SADD; Teachers Aide; Capt Flag Corp; Symp Band; Ed Nwsp Stf; Ed Yrbk Stf; Lit Mag; Mgr(s); U PA.

RYAN, JOHN; Greater Johnstown HS; Johnstown, PA; (Y); Band; Mrchg Band; Hon Roll.

RYAN, JUDY; West Catholic Girls HS; Phila, PA; (Y); Church Yth Grp; Cmnty Wkr; Cheerleading; Coach Actv; Hon Roll; Pierce JC; Fash Merch.

RYAN, KELLIE; Clearfield Area HS; Clearfield, PA; (Y); Debate Tm; Band; Orch; Swing Chorus; Nwsp Sprt Ed; Yrbk Stf; Rep Stu Cncl; JV Vllybl; NHS; PMEA Reg III Bnd 86; Law.

RYAN, KELLY; Shaler Area SR HS; Allison Pk, PA; (Y); 76/517; Girl Scts; Hosp Aide; SADD; Chorus; Flag Corp; School Musical; School Play; Nwsp Rptr; Yrbk Stf; Hon Roll; NEDT Top 10 Pct Awd 84; Grl Scout Silvr Ldrshp Awd 85; Cmmnty Svc Awd 84; Intl Studies.

RYAN, KEN; Grove City Area HS; Grove City, PA; (Y); 30/190; Thesps; Church Choir; Concert Band; Drm Mjr(t); Mrchg Band; School Musical; School Play; Swing Chorus; Crs Cntry; Hon Roll; Music.

RYAN, LISA ANN; York Suburban HS; York, PA; (Y); 20/190; Trs Church Yth Grp; Chrmn FBLA; Pres Sec JA; Concert Band; Mrchg Band; Yrbk Stf; Hon Roll; Lion Awd; Phyllis Hoke Lehman Mem Awd/Bus Curriculum 86; Most Outstndng Sr Awd 86; Highes GPA Acctg II 86; PA ST U; Actg.

RYAN, MOLLY; Northgate HS; Pittsburgh, PA; (Y); 13/153; Math Tm; School Musical; School Play; Nwsp Stf; Yrbk Stf; High Hon Roll; Hon Roll; U Of Pittsburgh; Lbrl Arts.

RYAN, RACHEL; Minersville Area HS; Minersville, PA; (Y); Church Yth Grp; SADD; Pres Jr Cls; Capt Var Crs Cntry; Var L Sftbl; Hon Roll; Prfct Atten Awd; German Clb; Ski Clb; Varsity Clb; WNEP Sprtstr Of Wk 86; JR Garland 86; Physcl Ftnss Awd 86; Bucknell; Cmmnctns.

RYAN, REGINA; Geibel HS; Connellsville, PA; (Y); Drama Clb; Pep Clb; Ski Clb; SADD; Stage Crew; Yrbk Stf; Lit Mag; French Hon Soc; High Hon Roll; Prfct Atten Awd; Elem Tchr.

RYAN, SEAN; St Josephs Prep HS; Philadelphia, PA; (Y); French Clb; Yrbk Stf; Jr Cls; Bsktbl; Diving; Ftbl; Mgr(s); Natl Sports Fest 85; USA JR Natl Rowing Tm 86; St Josephs Prep Crw 83-87; Vrsty 85-87; Medicine.

RYAN, SEAN D; Chestnut Hill Acad; Philadelphia, PA; (Y); 6/44; Political Wkr; Jazz Band; School Play; Stage Crew; Nwsp Ed-Chief; Var L Socr; High Hon Roll; Ntl Merit SF; Church Yth Grp; Band; Intl Diplomacy.

RYAN, TIMOTHY; Cathedral Prepatory Schl; Erie, PA; (Y); 92/216; Latin Clb; Band; Concert Band; Mrchg Band; Hon Roll.

RYBKA, MICHELLE; South Allegheny HS; Port Vue, PA; (S); French Clb; FNA; Office Aide; Y-Teens; Band; Mrchg Band; School Play; Nwsp Stf; Sec Soph Cls; Off Jr Cls; Vet Sci 84-85; Animal Behaviol Pittsburgh Zoo 85; Vet Med.

RYCERZ JR, ANTHONY; Bald Eagle Area HS; Bellefonte, PA; (Y); 4/212; Concert Band; Jazz Band; Mrchg Band; School Musical; School Play; Rep Stu Cncl; Im Mgr Bsktbl; High Hon Roll; JP Sousa Awd; NHS; Pres Acad Ftnss Awd 85-86; SR Awd 86; AAUW Awd 85; Slippery Rock U PA; Bio.

RYDER, ELIZABETH; North Allegheny Senior HS; Sweickley, PA; (Y); 152/630; Red Cross Aide; Pres Service Clb; Stu Cncl; Cheerleading; Hon Roll; U Pittsburgh; Psychlgst.

RYDER, HEATHER; Blue Mountain Acad; Allentown, PA; (Y); Church Yth Grp; Teachers Aide; Bsktbl; Sftbl; Vllybl; Wt Lftg; Hon Roll; Prfct Atten Awd; Med.

RYDESKI, P THOMAS; Plum HS; Pittsburgh, PA; (Y); Computer Clb; Ski Clb; Band; Jazz Band; Mrchg Band; Pep Band; School Musical; Symp Band; Tennis; JP Sousa Awd; Schlrshp Duquesne U Music 86; Dist Band & Hnrs 84-86; 1 Yr All ST Band & Natl Hnrs Band Hall Fm 85-86; Duquesne U; Music.

RYDOCK, KIRSTEN M; Elizabethtown Area HS; Elizabethtown, PA; (Y); Trs Church Yth Grp; Hosp Aide; Model UN; Church Choir; School Play; Yrbk Stf; NHS; Ntl Merit Ltr; Rdlgc Tech.

RYDZEWSKI, MICHELLE; Hazleton HS; Hazleton, PA; (Y); Chess Clb; Drama Clb; French Clb; SADD; Band; Concert Band; Drill Tm; Jazz Band; Pres Mrchg Band; Orch; Lackawanna JC; Comp.

RYLAND, TODD; Eastern Labanon County HS; Myerstown, PA; (Y); Capt Var Bsbl; Var L Bsktbl; Capt Var Socr; Hon Roll; NHS; Pres Schlr; Rotary Awd; Pres Acdmc Ftns Awd 86; U S Army & Ntl Soccer Coaches Assn Of Amer MVP 86; E Strdsbrg U; Sprts Med.

RYLEY, THOMAS R; Northeast Catholic HSFB; Philadelphia, PA; (Y); Crs Cntry; Mgr(s); Timer; Trk; L Hon Roll; Prfct Atten Awd; Psyctrst.

RYNO, SHERRY LYNN; Solanco SR HS; Quarryville, PA; (Y); 7/229; FBLA; Red Cross Aide; Spanish Clb; Teachers Aide; Yrbk Stf; Sec Bsbl; Pom Pon; JV Trk; High Hon Roll; Hon Roll; Sico Schlrshp 86; Millersville U; Elem Educ.

RYS, JOE; Cathedral Prep; Erie, PA; (Y); 40/220; Boy Scts; Church Yth Grp; Model UN; Rep Soph Cls; Rep Jr Cls; Rep Stu Cncl; Var L Ftbl; Var JV Wt Lftg; JV Wrstlng; Hon Roll; Rcvd Hnr Cards 84-86; 1st Trophies Schl Boxing Tourn 84-86; SC U; Acctg.

RYZNER, KENNETH; Council Rock HS; Newtown, PA; (Y); 147/845; VP Drama Clb; Chorus; School Musical; School Play; Stage Crew; Clnry Arts.

RZESZOTARSKI, TRACEY M; Sullivan County HS; Dushore, PA; (Y); VP FBLA; Color Guard; Mrchg Band; Nwsp Stf; Yrbk Bus Mgr; Yrbk Stf; Pres Frsh Cls; Rep Stu Cncl; Capt Cheerleading; Hon Roll; Awd In Shrthnd & Typg 85-86; Williamsport Schl/Cmrc; Med Sec.

SAAB, KARA LYNN M; Salisbury HS; Allentown, PA; (Y); 34/138; Cmnty Wkr; GAA; Girl Scts; Key Clb; Varsity Clb; Band; Bsktbl; Tennis; Hon Roll; MVP Tennis Awd 84-86; ST Tennis Tour 85-86; Law.

SAAR, WENDY; Abington Hts HS; Dalton, PA; (Y); 58/271; Pres Church Yth Grp; Chorus; Church Choir; Rep Jr Cls; Rep Sr Cls; Sec Stu Cncl; Stat Bsktbl; Hon Roll; Engl.

SABADOS, LANCE; Shazler Area HS; Allison Pk, PA; (Y); 70/517; JA; Ski Clb; Rep Frsh Cls; Rep Soph Cls; Rep Stu Cncl; JV Var Bsbl; JV Var Socr; Hon Roll; Natl Sci Olympd Tst Hnrbl Mntn 86; ELEC Engr.

SABANOS, GERRI; Crestwood HS; Mountaintop, PA; (Y); 29/223; DECA; High Hon Roll; Hon Roll; NHS; Crim Justice.

SABATASSE, TINA; Burgettstown Area JR-SR HS; Burgettstown, PA; (Y); 13/172; Sec Pres French Clb; Ski Clb; Speech Tm; Band; Concert Band; Mrchg Band; Symp Band; Hon Roll; Jr NHS; NHS; Climax Schrlshp Awd 86; Distngushd Schrlshp Awd 86; Pres Schrlshp Kent ST 86; Kent ST U; Int Desgn.

SABATELLA, ERIC; Valley View JR SR HS; Peckville, PA; (Y); 10/200; Computer Clb; Latin Clb; Scholastic Bowl; Spanish Clb; JV Bsbl; Var Vllybl; High Hon Roll; Hon Roll; Hnrbl Mntn Natl Spnsh Exm 85; Pres Physcl Ftns SR Merit 85-86; Natl Hnr Scty 85-87; Engrng.

SABATELLA, SHERRI; Valley View HS; Peckville, PA; (Y); #8 In Class; Spanish Clb; VP Soph Cls; VP Jr Cls; VP Sr Cls; VP Rep Stu Cncl; Capt Cheerleading; High Hon Roll; Hon Roll; NHS; Stu Mnth Eng 85; Moreau Schlrshp Kings Coll 86-87; Kings Coll; Acctng.

SABATINO, MARIA; E L Meyers HS; Wilkes Barre, PA; (Y); 8/161; Key Clb; Ski Clb; Chorus; Orch; Yrbk Stf; Sec Stu Cncl; Capt Cheerleading; Tennis; NHS; Spanish NHS; Penn ST; Bus.

SABER, JANET; Hampton HS; Gibsonia, PA; (Y); 11/223; Rep Jr Cls; Rep Sr Cls; Var Cheerleading; Robert Morris Coll; Bus Adm.

SABICH, SUSAN; Hempfield Area HS; Greensburg, PA; (Y); 25/656; Ski Clb; Spanish Clb; Band; Mrchg Band; Stat Bsktbl; Jr NHS; NHS; Spanish NHS; Wstnghse Sci Hnrs Inst 86; U Pittsburg; Pharm.

SABINO, KATRINA; Shenango JR SR HS; New Castle, PA; (Y); #48 In Class; Varsity Clb; Bsktbl; Trk; Crs Cntry; Hon Roll; Mst Imp Trk & Fld Athlt Trphies 84-86; 1st Pl Feml 2 Ml Humn Race 1st Feml Run Hope 86; Wildlf.

SABO, GEMA; Coatesville Area SR HS; Coatesville, PA; (Y); French Clb; JA; Mathletes; Office Aide; Teachers Aide; Chorus; School Musical; Sftbl; Wt Lftg; Ntl Merit Ltr; Cathryn Gibbs; Legal Sec.

SABOL, CHRISTINE ELIZABETH; Shikellamy HS; Sunbury, PA; (Y); 9/351; French Clb; Girl Scts; Nwsp Rptr; Yrbk Stf; VP NHS; Pres Schlr; Gir Sct Gld Awd 85; East Stroudsburg U; Hlth Rcds.

SABOL, CHRISTY; Carmichaels Area HS; Carmichaels, PA; (Y); Dance Clb; GAA; SADD; Varsity Clb; Band; Concert Band; Mrchg Band; Stu Cncl; JV Var Cheerleading; Hon Roll; Chsn Coal Queen Cand For Carmichaels 86; Art Insti Of PA; Fshn Merc.

SABOL, ELIZABETH; William Allen HS; Allentown, PA; (Y); 26/559; German Clb; VP JA; Concert Band; Mrchg Band; Orch; Rep Jr Cls; Hon Roll; Jr NHS; NHS; Summo Cum Hnr Scholar Awd 86; Bus Adm.

SABOL, JEFF; Bethel Park SR HS; Bethel Park, PA; (Y); Letterman Clb; Varsity Clb; Rep Stu Cncl; JV Bsbl; Var Bsktbl; Var Ftbl; Hon Roll; NHS; Prfct Atten Awd; Bowling Green U; Law Enfrcmnt.

SABOL, PATRICIA; Marian HS; Nesquehoning, PA; (Y); 1/115; Service Clb; Nwsp Stf; French Hon Soc; High Hon Roll; Trs NHS; Math & Sci Bowl 3rd Pl 86; NE PA Natl Frnch Cntst 3rd Pl & Hon Ment 85-86.

SABOL, STEPHEN; Uniontown Area HS; Uniontown, PA; (Y); JA; Spanish Clb; Spanish NHS; Phrmcy.

SABOL, SUZANNE; Penn Hills SR HS; Pittsburgh, PA; (Y); 1/750; Drama Clb; VP JA; Office Aide; Science Clb; Spanish Clb; School Play; VP Stu Cncl; High Hon Roll; NCTE Awd; Pitt/Provost Day Free Cls Wnnr 86; U Of PITTSBURGH; Engrng.

SABOL, TRACY L; Fort Leboeuf HS; Erie, PA; (Y); 10/169; Church Yth Grp; Dance Clb; Rep Jr Cls; JV Cheerleading; Sec Ftbl; Trk; High Hon Roll; Miss PA U S Teen Pgnt Awd 84; Penn ST U; Indstrl Engrng.

SABOURIN, PAUL; Pennsbury HS; Morrisville, PA; (S); Church Yth Grp; Drama Clb; Pep Clb; PAVAS; SADD; Acpl Chr; Band; Chorus; Concert Band; Jazz Band; Drma Comptn Actng Awd 84; Cnty Chrs 85.

SACANE, JOSEPH; Charleroi Area HS; Charleroi, PA; (Y); Boy Scts; Church Yth Grp; Pres Exploring; JA; God Cntry Awd; Eagle Scout 86; Altare Dei Awd; Comp Sci.

SACCANI, DINO; Parkland HS; Allentown, PA; (Y); 88/415; VP Debate Tm; School Play; VP Soph Cls; Rep Stu Cncl; Hon Roll; Ntl Merit Ltr; PA Hghr Ed Asst Agncy Cert Merit 85; U Richmond; Econ.

SACCO, SHARON; Butler Area HS; Butler, PA; (Y); English Clb; Latin Clb; Library Aide; Chorus; Rep Frsh Cls; Rep Soph Cls; Stu Cncl; Gym; Vllybl; Clarion U; Psych.

SACCO, TODD; Moon SR HS; Coraopolis, PA; (Y); 39/329; Boy Scts; CAP; Concert Band; Jazz Band; Mrchg Band; Symp Band; Rep Stu Cncl; Var Trk; Var L Wrstlng; Ntl Merit SF; Cadet Of Yr Cvl Air Ptrl 84; Earhart Awd Cvl Air Ptrl 85; Cvl Air Ptrl Flght Schlrshp 86; Washington & Jefferson; Psychlg.

SACCONE, JIM; Bishop Mc Cort HS; Johnstown, PA; (Y); 7/124; Math Clb; Math Tm; Chorus; Pres Sr Cls; Bsbl; Ftbl; Wt Lftg; NHS; Army Schlr Athltc Awd 86; Appntd-U S Mltry Acad 86; West Point.

SACH, LOIS; Sun Valley HS; Brookhaven, PA; (Y); 6/309; Pres Drama Clb; Band; Chorus; Yrbk Ed-Chief; Swmmng; Sec NHS; Church Yth Grp; Computer Clb; Intnl Clb; SADD; Hugh O Brien Ldrshp Awd 84; Ntl Chorus Awd 86; Mc Cabe Schlrshp Swrthmr Coll 86; Swrthmr Coll; Music.

SACHON, SEAN; Calvary Baptist Schl; Nesquehoning, PA; (S); 1/4; Computer Clb; Science Clb; School Play; Socr; Trk; High Hon Roll; Val; Chess Clb; Church Yth Grp; Chorus; Best Of Show/Sci Fair 82-84; Hstry Proj 1st Pl 85; Math Comptnt 1st Pl 82-83.

SACHS, ROBERT; Hazleton HS; Drums, PA; (Y); 44/300; High Hon Roll; Hon Roll; Penn ST; Engrng.

SACHS, SARAH; Manheim Central SR HS; Manheim, PA; (Y); Crtvty Cert Outstndg Prtcptn 86; Fshn Dsgn.

SACIK, MICHAEL; Ford City JRSR HS; Ford City, PA; (Y); Church Yth Grp; Spanish Clb; VICA; Chorus; Stu Cncl; Bsbl; Bsktbl; Scholastic Bowl; 3rd ST SR Little Lg 84; 4th ST SR Little Lg Bsbl 85; 2nd WPIAL & 2nd ST HS Bsbl 86; Pro Baseball.

SADAKA, RONDA E; Abington Heights HS; Clarks Summit, PA; (Y); 42/270; French Clb; Hosp Aide; SADD; Rep Lit Mag; Rep Soph Cls; Rep Trs Jr Cls; Trs Stu Cncl; High Hon Roll; Jr NHS; NHS; Vlntr Yr Untd Cereb Plsy Merit Awd 86; Mst Valued Wrkr Diabets Msclr Dis Carnvls 82; Bio.

SADAVAGE, JEFFERY; Mid-Valley HS; Olyphant, PA; (Y); Var Capt Bsbl; Var JV Bsktbl; Var Capt Ftbl; JV Im Wt Lftg; JV Hon Roll; JV NHS; JV Prfct Atten Awd; Law.

SADECKY, BETH; Highlands HS; Tarentum, PA; (Y); 47/273; Church Yth Grp; Color Guard; Concert Band; Flag Corp; Mrchg Band; Rep Stu Cncl; Trk; Jr NHS; NHS; Indiana U PA; Elmntry Ed.

SADECKY, JAMES; Highlands HS; Natrona Hts, PA; (Y); Cmnty Wkr; Key Clb; Band; Concert Band; Mrchg Band; Stage Crew; Trk; Hon Roll; Kiwanis Awd; PA ST U.

SADENWASSER, JON A; Center Area HS; Aliquippa, PA; (Y); Chess Clb; German Clb; Varsity Clb; Var L Bsbl; Hon Roll; NHS; German Awd 4.0 Avg; Engrng.

SADLEK, JIM; Waynesburg Central HS; Waynesburg, PA; (Y); Ski Clb; Spanish Clb; Concert Band; Golf; Wrstlng; Hon Roll; WVU; Engrng.

SADLER, NANNETTE A; Monongahela Valley Catholic HS; Chareroi, PA; (Y); 11/82; Trs FBLA; Spanish Clb; Chorus; Nwsp Stf; Yrbk Stf; Spanish NHS; CA U PA; Math.

SADLER, ROBERT; Wilmington Area HS; Volant, PA; (S); 14/125; Church Yth Grp; Computer Clb; Drama Clb; Spanish Clb; Stage Crew; JV Bsktbl; Var L Golf; Var L Trk; Hon Roll; Aerosp Engr.

SADLIK, LOLA ANN; Little Flower Catholic HS; Philadelphia, PA; (Y); 6/415; Church Choir; Orch; Yrbk Ed-Chief; High Hon Roll; Prfct Atten Awd; Pres Schlr; German Clb; Service Clb; Teachers Aide; School Musical; Grmn Avg Hon Mntn Awd 86; Colonial Hstrcl Soc Essy Cntst Hon Mntn 85; Chestnut Hill Coll; Spec Ed.

SADLOWSKI, CYNTHIA; Holy Name HS; Reading, PA; (Y); Pep Clb; JV Var Cheerleading; JV Mgr(s); Fshn Merch.

SADORF, JOHN A; Bristol HS; Bristol, PA; (Y); 8/102; FCA; School Play; Stage Crew; Yrbk Sprt Ed; VP Pres Stu Cncl; Bsbl; Capt Ftbl; Trk; Hon Roll; NHS; Susquehanna U; Physcl Thrpy.

SADOWSKI, CHRISTIE; Butler HS; Butler, PA; (Y); Boy Scts; Dance Clb; Exploring; JA; Math Tm; Office Aide; Spanish Clb; SADD; Teachers Aide; Drill Tm; Pres JA Co 85-86.

SADOWSKI, DANIEL; Central Catholic HS; Fleetwood, PA; (Y); Boy Scts; Camera Clb; Ftbl; Trk; Wt Lftg.

SADOWSKI, SHEILA; Freedom HS; Bethlehem, PA; (Y); 141/456; French Clb; Pep Clb; Chorus; Cheerleading; Var Powder Puff Ftbl; Var Twrlr; Hon Roll; Mrchg Band; Jr Miss Dance PA 1st Rnr Up 84; Dnc Edctrs Amer Sr Solo 1st Pl 84; DEA Natl Perf Arts Chmpshps Rnrup; Cmmnctns.

SAEGER, ALISON; Emmaus HS; Wescosville, PA; (Y); 13/493; Stu Cncl; Var Crs Cntry; Var Fld Hcky; Var Trk; High Hon Roll; Hon Roll; NHS; Ntl Merit SF; E PA Conf Champ 1st Pl 85-86; Trk And Fld Champ 1st 86; Bio Chem.

SAELER, MICHELE; Butler Area SR HS; Butler, PA; (Y); Church Yth Grp; Cmnty Wkr; Exploring; Hosp Aide; Band; Var Gym; Charles E Wilkin Awd 86; Natl Piano Plyng 82; Shadyside Hosp Schl; Nrsng.

SAFFEL, JOHN; Cannon Mc Millan SR HS; Canonsburg, PA; (Y); Chess Clb; Exploring; Chorus; Hon Roll; Waynesburg Coll; Psychol.

SAFKA, SCOTT; John S Fine HS; Nanticoke, PA; (Y); Letterman Clb; Ski Clb; Band; Concert Band; Mrchg Band; Orch; Variety Show; Golf; Trk; High Hon Roll; Math.

SAFSTROM, MICHELLE J; Annville-Cleona HS; Cleona, PA; (S); 22/121; FBLA; Mrchg Band; Yrbk Ed-Chief; Var L Cheerleading; Mat Maids; NHS; Bus Admn.

SAGERS, HEATHER; Chichester HS; Linwood, PA; (Y); 150/350; Drama Clb; Sec French Clb; Pres FTA; SADD; Band; Chorus; Mrchg Band; School Musical; Yrbk Stf; Stu Cncl; West Chester U; Educ.

SAGUSKY, JEANA; Nativity BVM HS; Minersville, PA; (Y); French Clb; Stage Crew; Penn ST; Bus Adm.

SAIA, FRANCES; St Maria Goretti HS; Philadelphia, PA; (Y); 40/426; VP Church Yth Grp; French Clb; Hosp Aide; Teachers Aide; Hon Roll; NHS; Prfct Atten Awd; Algebra II Achvmnt Awd 84-85; Activities Rep 83-84; Hahnemann U; Nrsng.

SAIN, ARLENE; Brookville Area HS; Brookville, PA; (Y); 9/150; Key Clb; Trs Varsity Clb; Stu Cncl; Capt Im Bsktbl; Var L Swmmng; Var L Trk; Pres Jr NHS; VP NHS; Pres Church Yth Grp; Trs Pep Clb; US Marine Corps Distgshd Athlt Awd 85fBAHS Undrclsmn Athlt Of The Yr Awd 86; Arch.

SAJNANI, RAVI; Catasauqua HS; Catasauqua, PA; (Y); Computer Clb; Kutztown Coll; Math.

SAKANICH, KERRY; Steel Valley HS; West Homestead, PA; (S); 11/240; Church Yth Grp; Flag Corp; Mrchg Band; Nwsp Stf; Yrbk Stf; Stu Cncl; High Hon Roll; Hon Roll; NHS; Penn ST U; Spec Educ.

SAKERKA, SHEILA; Washington HS; Washington, PA; (S); Spanish Clb; Hon Roll; Acadmc Achvt 83; WA Schl Of Nrsng; Med.

SAKULICH, AMY; Abington Heights HS; Clarks Summit, PA; (Y); VP Church Yth Grp; Ski Clb; Off Band; Off Mrchg Band; JV Var Bsktbl; Trk; Hon Roll; NHS; Russian Essay Olympiad Bronze & Silver Mdls 83-85; U Of Scranton; Pre Med.

SALAK, DAVID; Lakeland HS; Carbondale, PA; (Y); Johnson Tech Inst; Carpentry.

SALAK, JANE; Western Wayne HS; Waymart, PA; (Y); 2/140; SADD; Pres Soph Cls; JV Bsktbl; Vllybl; Jr NHS; NHS; Prfct Atten Awd; Elem Educ.

SALAK, LISA; Shaler Area HS; Glenshaw, PA; (Y); 37/517; Office Aide; Nwsp Rptr; Nwsp Stf; Stu Cncl; High Hon Roll; Hon Roll; Spanish NHS.

SALAK, MIKE; Western Wayne HS; Waymart, PA; (Y); Church Yth Grp; FBLA; School Play; Pres Frsh Cls; Trs Stu Cncl; Bsktbl; Var L Tennis; High Hon Roll; Trs NHS; Prfct Atten Awd; Am Lg Awd 83; Wayne Co Chldrn & Yth Svcs Advsry Brd 85-86 & 86-87; Pre-Law.

SALAMA, TAHANI; West Philadelphia Cath Girls HS; Upper Darby, PA; (Y); 56/240; Church Yth Grp; Drama Clb; French Clb; Library Aide; Office Aide; Teachers Aide; Church Choir; Concert Band; High Hon Roll; Hon Roll; Exemplry Stu Awd.

SALAMANDRA, MARK; Pennsbury HS; Yardley, PA; (Y); JV Bsbl; JV Bsktbl; JV Ftbl; Air Force; Bio.

SALAMONE, CHRISTINE; Upper Darby HS; Drexel Hill, PA; (Y); Cmnty Wkr; Spanish Clb; Bsktbl; Sftbl; Hon Roll; Colleen Nolan Awd 84.

SALANDRO, DEANNA; Greater Latrobe HS; Latrobe, PA; (Y); 96/337; High Hon Roll; St Vincetn Coll; Acctg.

SALATA, CHRISTINE; Bishop Hafey HS; Hazleton, PA; (Y); 3/129; Ski Clb; Spanish Clb; Y-Teens; Stu Cncl; Var L Cheerleading; High Hon Roll; NHS; Spanish NHS; Schlrshp Bishop Hafey HS 83-87; Ed.

SALATA, MARK; James M Coughlin HS; Wilkes Barre, PA; (Y); 35/355; Aud/Vis; Chess Clb; Computer Clb; Hosp Aide; Chorus; Variety Show; Crs Cntry; JV Ftbl; Trk; Var L Vllybl; Bio.

SALAZAR, TINA; MMI Prep Schl; Hazleton, PA; (S); 8/35; Art Clb; Hosp Aide; Science Clb; Ski Clb; School Play; JV Bowling; Var Crs Cntry; Var Tennis; High Hon Roll; Hon Roll; HOBY Ldrshp Rep MMI 84-85; Regnl & ST Awds PA JR Acad Sci 83-86; Locl Music Comp Awd; Psych.

SALAZER, DENISE; Bishop Hafey HS; Hazleton, PA; (Y); Church Yth Grp; Cmnty Wkr; Spanish Clb; Y-Teens; Stat Bsbl; Mgr(s); Score Keeper; Stat Sftbl; High Hon Roll; Hon Roll; Hghst Avg Alg II 86; Century 21 Typgwrtg Awd 86; Penn ST U.

SALCI, SALVATORE; Grand Army Republic HS; Wilkes Barre, PA; (S); 12/150; Aud/Vis; Camera Clb; Teachers Aide; Nwsp Phtg; Ftbl; Wt Lftg; Hon Roll; NHS; Outstndg Vocatnl Stu Williamsport Coll 85-86; Vo Tech Schl E Northmptn Cnty Dist I Vica Comp 85; Wilkes Coll; Crim Just.

SALDI, SHERI; Valley View JR SR HS; Archbald, PA; (Y); FBLA; Spanish Clb; Nwsp Rptr; Nwsp Stf; Yrbk Stf; Var Trk; Vllybl; High Hon Roll; Hon Roll; NHS; Marywood Coll; Accntng.

SALDUKAS, JANICE; Shenandoah Valley JR & SR HS; Shenandoah, PA; (Y); Pep Clb; Teachers Aide; Variety Show; Yrbk Stf; Rep Frsh Cls; JV Bsktbl; JV Crs Cntry; Var Capt Sftbl; High Hon Roll; Hon Roll; Acdmc All Amer Athlete 84; Wilkes Coll; Compu Sci.

SALEM, KEN; Bishop Mc Cort HS; Johnstown, PA; (Y); Letterman Clb; Ski Clb; Spanish Clb; Nwsp Rptr; L Ftbl; JV Trk; Pep Clb; Chorus; School Musical; School Play; Bus.

SALERNO, CONNIE; Bishop Hannan HS; Scranton, PA; (Y); 28/141; Art Clb; French Clb; Hon Roll; NHS; Wilkes COLL; Sci.

SALES, RENITA E; Germantown HS; Philadelphia, PA; (Y); Library Aide; Math Clb; Office Aide; Pres Frsh Cls; Var Tennis; Var Trk; Hon Roll; NHS; Ntl Merit Ltr; Prfct Atten Awd; U Of CA-LOS Angeles; Chem.

SALIGA, BARBARA L; Blairsville SR HS; Blairsville, PA; (Y); 10/126; Band; Concert Band; Mrchg Band; Sftbl; High Hon Roll; NHS; Prfct Atten Awd; Pres Acadmc Ftnss Awd 86; Westmoreland CC; Sec Sci.

SALINE, MARK; Cameron County HS; Emporium, PA; (Y); 25/89; IN U; Accntng.

SALINE, NONA; St Marys Area HS; Kersey, PA; (Y); Computer Clb; Yrbk Stf; JV L Cheerleading; Im Vllybl; Stat Wrstlng; Schlstc Awd Speech 86; X-Ray Tech.

SALKELD, BRETT; Cumberland Valley HS; Mechanicsburg, PA; (Y); Church Yth Grp; Cmnty Wkr; Key Clb; Red Cross Aide; Var L Swmmng; Im Wt Lftg; Hon Roll; Water Polo V Let Capt 83-87; US Naval Acad; Sci.

SALKELD, COURTNEY; United HS; Seward, PA; (Y); 76/157; Library Aide; Nwsp Ed-Chief; Ed Nwsp Stf; Yrbk Stf; Lit Mag; Var Bsbl; JV Var Bsktbl; Stat Ftbl; Hon Roll; Prfct Atten Awd; Brdcstng.

SALLACK, DAWN; Johnsonburg Area HS; Johnsonburg, PA; (S); Camera Clb; Band; Concert Band; Drm & Bgl; Drm Mjr(t); Mrchg Band; Yrbk Phtg; Yrbk Stf; Stat Wrstlng; Dist Band 84; Dist & Regional Band 85.

SALLASH, ROBERT; Freedom HS; Bethlehem, PA; (Y); Church Yth Grp; JV Var Bsktbl; Var L Vllybl; Im Wt Lftg; Hon Roll; Math.

SALLIS, ROXANNE; Western Beaver HS; Industry, PA; (Y); Art Clb; Church Yth Grp; Drama Clb; FHA; Library Aide; Chorus; Church Choir; Nwsp Stf; Bowling; Var L Trk; Pre-Phrmcy.

SALLO, TONY; Central Catholic HS; Pittsburgh, PA; (Y); Bus.

SALMONSEN, XANA; Central Bucks East HS; Warrington, PA; (Y); 10/487; Church Yth Grp; Library Aide; Yrbk Stf; Fld Hcky; Lcrss; DAR Awd; Hon Roll; Pres Schlr; Centrl Bucks Chmbr Commrc Studio Art Awd 86; Grove City Coll; Socl Wrk.

SALOOM, CHARLENE R; Mt Pleasant Area SR HS; Mount Pleasant, PA; (Y); Trs Sec 4-H; Latin Clb; Band; Drm Mjr(t); Jazz Band; Mrchg Band; Yrbk Stf; High Hon Roll; NHS; Mid East Music Fstvl 86; Lib Arts.

SALOPEK, EDWARD; Norwin HS; N Huntingdon, PA; (S); Art Clb; Spanish Clb; School Play; Yrbk Stf; High Hon Roll; Hon Roll; Jr NHS; NHS; Art I Awd Strght A 84-85; Pharm.

SALOSKY, JENNIFER; Mapletown HS; Bobtown, PA; (Y); 8/74; FTA; Ski Clb; Varsity Clb; Trs Sr Cls; Cheerleading; Vllybl; Hon Roll; NHS; WV U.

SALOUM, SAMANTHA; Ford City HS; Ford City, PA; (Y); Church Yth Grp; Spanish Clb; Drill Tm; Off Soph Cls; Off Jr Cls; Off Sr Cls; Stu Cncl; Bus Mgmt.

SALSBERRY, LORI; Trinity HS; Washington, PA; (Y); Band; Concert Band; Jazz Band; Mrchg Band; Pep Band.

SALSGIVER, LORI; Altoona Area HS; Altoona, PA; (Y); Church Yth Grp; German Clb; Library Aide; Vllybl; High Hon Roll; Hon Roll.

SALTER, CRISTEN; Solebury Schl; Delray Beach, FL; (S); Drama Clb; Q&S; Nwsp Ed-Chief; Nwsp Stf; Crs Cntry; Sftbl; Hon Roll; Spnsh Tutor 85-86; Brdcst Jrnlsm.

SALTER, SEAN; Cardinal O Hara HS; Havertown, PA; (Y); Stage Crew; Temple; Pre-Law.

SALUJA, SUNIL KUMAR; Central Catholic HS; Pittsburgh, PA; (Y); 10/258; Debate Tm; Exploring; 4-H; NFL; Political Wkr; Red Cross Aide; Science Clb; Speech Tm; Temple Yth Grp; Im Bsktbl; 1st Pl Bio Awd PA Sci Acad 85-86; 9th Pl Debate Cathlc Natnl Tournmnt 85-86; Natnl Forensic Leag; U Of MI; Med.

SALVA, JOHN W; Dunmore HS; Dunmore, PA; (Y); 51/155; Boy Scts; Church Yth Grp; Computer Clb; French Clb; JA; Stage Crew; Nwsp Rptr; Trk; Hon Roll; NHS; Jr Achvmnt Slsmn Of Yr NE Pa 86; Eagle Scout With Bronze, Gold & Silver Palms 84-86; PA ST U; Lib Arts.

SALVATI, LOUIS; Lincoln HS; Ellwood City, PA; (Y); 33/162; Church Yth Grp; Ski Clb; Spanish Clb; Chorus; Capt Bowling; Prfct Atten Awd; Anapolis; Aviation.

SALVATORE, CHRISTOPHER; Donegal HS; Maytown, PA; (Y); 18/151; Math Tm; JV Capt Bsktbl; JV Var Ftbl; High Hon Roll; Hon Roll; NHS; Rotary Awd; Spanish NHS; Junes Boy Mnth 85-86; Millersville U; Math.

SALVATORE, DINA; Hampton HS; Allison Pk, PA; (Y); Drill Tm; Cheerleading; Powder Puff Ftbl; High Hon Roll; Hon Roll; Accntng.

SALVIA, ELISE; Villa Maria Acad; Erie, PA; (Y); Art Clb; Church Yth Grp; Dance Clb; PAVAS; Ski Clb; Cheerleading; Coach Actv; Gym; JV Socr; Hon Roll; Penn ST; Art.

SALVIA, JACQUELINE; Pennsbury HS; Yardley, PA; (Y); Chorus; Rep Jr Cls; Swmmng; Makefield Polce Explr 85-86; Synchrzd Swmng 83-86; PA ST Champ Duet & Team Keystone ST Games 84-86; Sports.

SAMARAS, ROULA; St Mana Goretti HS; Philadelphia, PA; (Y); 17/407; Church Yth Grp; Cmnty Wkr; French Clb; GAA; Teachers Aide; Stage Crew; High Hon Roll; Hon Roll; NHS; Ntl Merit Schol; Ntl Merit Ldrshp Awd 86.

SAMEK, ELIZABETH; George HS; Edison, NJ; (Y); Cmnty Wkr; Key Clb; Chorus; School Musical; Nwsp Rptr; Trs Frsh Cls; Rep Stu Cncl; Cheerleading; JV Tennis; Hon Roll; Pres, Dorm Council; ADVERT.

SAMER, ANTHONY W; Allentown Central Catholic HS; Allentown, PA; (Y); 11/231; Church Yth Grp; Ski Clb; Yrbk Rptr; Pres Jr Cls; Pres Stu Cncl; High Hon Roll; NHS; Ntl Merit SF; Drama Clb; JA; Pltcl Sci.

SAMES, D JASON; Bentworth SR HS; Bentleyville, PA; (Y); 13/150; Ski Clb; Band; Concert Band; Mrchg Band; Stage Crew; High Hon Roll; NHS; Elect Engr.

SAMICK, ROBERT; Ridway Area HS; Ridgway, PA; (Y); 10/127; Var L Bsktbl; Hon Roll; NHS; Pres Acad Fit Awd 85-86; Lock Haven U; Comp Sci.

SAMILA, LOVEY; Canon Mc Millan SR HS; Canonsburg, PA; (Y); 43/371; Cmnty Wkr; High Hon Roll; Trophy 9th Grade 3 Yrs Hon Roll 84; Lgl Sec.

SAMMARCO, TIMOTHY STEVEN; Cambria Heights SR HS; Patton, PA; (Y); 7/200; Var L Bsbl; Var Ftbl; Var L Wrstlng; Hon Roll; NHS; Ntl Merit Ltr; Sci.

SAMMARTINO, MARK; Bethel Park HS; Bethel Park, PA; (Y); 200/530; Band; Rep Frsh Cls; Rep Soph Cls; Rep Jr Cls; Capt Var Ftbl; Wt Lftg; 5 Schlrshp Offrs-Ftbl 86; Mercyhurst Coll; Comp.

SAMONSKY IV, JOHN H; Titusville Ares SR HS; Titusville, PA; (Y); Chorus; Jazz Band; Mrchg Band; School Musical; School Play; Var Swmmng; High Hon Roll; NHS; Ntl Merit Ltr; Boy Scts; Music Awd 86; U PA; Chem.

SAMPLE, DAVID; Penn Hills HS; Pittsburgh, PA; (Y); 39/760; German Clb; Ski Clb; Var Crs Cntry; Var Trk; High Hon Roll; NHS; Army Schrl Athlete 86; PA ST U; Ceramic Engr.

SAMPLE, REUEL; Fairview HS; Fairview, PA; (Y); Pres Church Yth Grp; Cmnty Wkr; Sec VP Drama Clb; Band; Church Choir; Mrchg Band; School Musical; VP Pres Stu Cncl; Lion Awd; NHS; Ntl Latin Hnr Soc 86; Music Boostrs Svc Awd 86; Grove City Coll; Prsbythn Mnstr.

SAMPLE JR, WILLIAM R; Central Catholic HS; Pittsburgh, PA; (Y); JV Var Bsbl; Im Bsktbl; Im Ftbl; SPRTS Med.

SAMPLES, JOHN; Knoch JR SR HS; Butler, PA; (Y); Pres FBLA; Pres German Clb; VP Math Clb; Sec Science Clb; School Play; Nwsp Stf; Yrbk Stf; Bsktbl; Ftbl; Score Keeper; MS ST U; Chem Engr.

SAMPSELL, STEVE; Montgomery Area HS; Allenwood, PA; (Y); 5/63; Boy Scts; Nwsp Sprt Ed; Yrbk Stf; Pres Stu Cncl; Var L Bsktbl; Var L Ftbl; Var L Trk; Cit Awd; Hon Roll; Lion Awd; Am Leg Awd 86; PA ST U; Jrnlsm.

SAMPSON, ROBERT; Center HS; Monaca, PA; (Y); Exploring; German Clb; Varsity Clb; Stage Crew; Bowling; Score Keeper; L Trk; Hon Roll; Law.

SAMPSON, TIMIKO; University HS; Philadelphia, PA; (Y); Cmnty Wkr; Hosp Aide; Badmtn; Score Keeper; Vllybl; Prfct Atten Awd; Math Lab 86; Job Srch 86.

SAMS, LAURA; Penn Wood HS; Darby, PA; (Y); 4/297; Drama Clb; Band; Chorus; Church Choir; Concert Band; Mrchg Band; Orch; Trs Soph Cls; Sec Jr Cls; Rep Sr Cls; Outstndng Eng And Chem 84-85; Outstndng Phys Wrd Proc And Adv Frnch 86; Bucknell U; Chem.

SAMUEL, ROBERT E; Abington Hts HS; Clarks Summit, PA; (Y); 50/270; Boy Scts; Pres Radio Clb; JV Wrstlng; NHS; Church Yth Grp; Hon Roll; Eagl Sct Awd 86; Engrng.

SAMUELS, DENNIS; Upper Moreland HS; Willow Grove, PA; (Y); German Clb; Ski Clb; Color Guard; Drm & Bgl; Mrchg Band; Pep Band; Symp Band; Bio Sci.

SAMUELS, JILL; Pittston Area HS; Duryea, PA; (Y); Ski Clb; Swmmng; High Hon Roll; Hon Roll; NHS; Bus Admin.

SANCHEZ, CHRISTINE; Keystone Oaks HS; Pittsburgh, PA; (Y); Hosp Aide; Spanish Clb; Y-Teens; Hon Roll; PA Dance Alloy 86; Sahde Sisters Dance 11 Yrs Prfct Attndnc 75-86; CPA.

SANCHEZ, MICHAEL; Salisbury HS; Allentown, PA; (Y); 42/138; Church Yth Grp; Varsity Clb; Bsbl; Bsktbl; Crs Cntry; Colonial Lg & Dist Champ Var Bsbl Tm 86; Arch Desgn.

SANDELSTEIN, TAMMY; Academy HS; Erie, PA; (S); 6/185; French Clb; Pres Temple Yth Grp; Capt Color Guard; Camera Clb; Mrchg Band; Sec Jr Cls; High Hon Roll; Jr NHS; NHS; US Ntl Band 85; USNMA Awd; Health.

SANDERS, BLAKE; Franklin Regional HS; Murrysville, PA; (Y); 71/338; Sec AFS; JA; VP Thesps; Chorus; School Musical; School Play; Stage Crew; Swing Chorus; Hon Roll; Cnty Chorus PMEA 85&86; Hnr Thspn 86.

SANDERS, CHRISTY L; Neshannock HS; New Castle, PA; (Y); 24/99; Church Yth Grp; Library Aide; Office Aide; Ski Clb; Cheerleading; Cit Awd; Prfct Atten Awd; Svc Awd; Hockey-Ice Sktng Clb; Guidance Aide; WV Wesleyan; Fash Merch.

SANDERS, DEVIN; Shikellamy HS; Northumberland, PA; (Y); 15/301; Church Yth Grp; French Clb; Teachers Aide; Chorus; Concert Band; Jazz Band; Mrchg Band; School Musical; School Play; Hon Roll; Bus.

SANDERS, JANE; York Catholic HS; York, PA; (Y); Dance Clb; 4-H; French Clb; FBLA; Chorus; School Musical; Yrbk Stf; Hon Roll; Pres Acad Ftnss Awd 86; Coll Of PA; Engl.

SANDERS, LYNN; Bentworth HS; Eighty Four, PA; (Y); 7/138; Pres Church Yth Grp; Ski Clb; Varsity Clb; VP Stu Cncl; Var L Sftbl; Vllybl; High Hon Roll; Hon Roll; NHS.

SANDERS, MARGARET; Cedar Crest HS; Lebanon, PA; (Y); French Clb; Girl Scts; Pep Clb; Band; Concert Band; Mrchg Band; Pep Band; Schlstc Hnr Bnqut 85&86; Psych.

SANDERS, MELANIE; Hempfield HS; Lancaster, PA; (Y); 2/400; Pres Church Yth Grp; VP Science Clb; Chorus; Nwsp Rptr; Var Bsktbl; Stat Sftbl; VP NHS; Ntl Merit Ltr; Sal; Stu Of Mnth 84 & 86; Philadelphia Coll; Phrmcy.

SANDERS, MELISSA; Conrad Weiser HS; Robesonia, PA; (Y); 9/140; Key Clb; Library Aide; Pep Clb; Teachers Aide; Nwsp Rptr; Nwsp Sprt Ed; Pres Sr Cls; Stu Cncl; Capt Var Bsktbl; Capt Var Fld Hcky; Athltc Schlrshp U Of IA Fld Hcky; Lns Clb Schlrshp 86-87; U Of IA; Educ.

SANDERS, MICHELE; Mc Guffey HS; Prosperity, PA; (Y); 3/200; German Clb; Rep Sr Cls; High Hon Roll; NHS; Sal; WA & Jefferson Schlrs Awd 86; Acad All Amer 85-86; WA & Jefferson Alumni Awd 86; WA & Jefferson Coll.

SANDERS, PHILIP; Littlestown HS; Littlestown, PA; (Y); 7/149; Pres FCA; Varsity Clb; School Play; Yrbk Sprt Ed; Var L Bsbl; Var L Crs Cntry; Bausch & Lomb Sci Awd; Cit Awd; VP NHS; Pres Schlr; Amer H S Math Exam 1st Pl 85-86; PA ST U; Math.

SANDERS, SANDRA R; Kennedy Christian HS; Wheatland, PA; (Y); 6/98; VP Church Yth Grp; Hosp Aide; Science Clb; Nwsp Ed-Chief; Yrbk Ed-Chief; Pres Soph Cls; Var Capt Vllybl; High Hon Roll; Schlrs Pgm 86; Schlrshp Setoo Hills Ldrshp Dev Wrkshp 85; St Elizabeth Ann Seton Schlrshp 84; Pediatrcs.

SANDERS, TOM; Moon Area HS; Coraopolis, PA; (Y); 46/330; Stat JV Bsktbl; Var Crs Cntry; Var L Trk; Stat Vllybl; Hon Roll; Engrg.

SANDERSON JR, NED; Pennsbury HS; Valdosta, GA; (Y); Church Yth Grp; Drama Clb; French Clb; SADD; Acpl Chr; Chorus; Church Choir; School Musical; Swmmng; Trk; Bkcs Cnty Chrl Soc Schlrshp 86; 1st & 2nd Pl Cnty Chrs 84-86; Soc Sci.

SANDERSON, PATRICIA; Wyalusing Valley HS; Sugar Run, PA; (Y); Am Leg Aux Girls St; 4-H; Band; Chorus; Concert Band; Drm Mjr(t); Mrchg Band; Orch; School Musical; Church Yth Grp; Spch Ther.

SANDERSON, REBECCA; Otto-Eldred HS; Rixford, PA; (Y); Girl Scts; Band; Chorus; Concert Band; Mrchg Band; Bsktbl; Olean Bus Inst; Lgl Secty.

SANDMAN, BRAD; Council Rock HS; Holland, PA; (Y); 120/845; Mrchg Band; Engrng.

SANDS, CHUCK; Tunkhannock Area HS; Tunkhannock, PA; (Y); FCA; French Clb; Band; Church Choir; Concert Band; Mrchg Band; Trs Sr Cls; Bsbl; Ftbl; JC Awd; Archt.

SANDS, JODI L; Norristown HS; Norristown, PA; (Y); DECA; FBLA; GAA; Key Clb; Ski Clb; Yrbk Stf; Shipensburg U.

SANDS, KIM; Shenandoah Valley JR SR HS; Shenandoah, PA; (Y); 12/108; Library Aide; Chorus; Color Guard; Nwsp Stf; Yrbk Stf; Capt Crs Cntry; Trk; Hon Roll; NHS; Elem Ed.

SANDS, VINCENT J; New Castle SR HS; New Castle, PA; (Y); Office Aide; Spanish Clb; Speech Tm; SADD; Varsity Clb; Nwsp Rptr; Pres Sr Cls; Pres Stu Cncl; JV Var Ftbl; Var Trk; Amrcn Lgn Essy Awd Wnnr 86; Aerospc Engnrng.

SANDS IV, WILLIAM; Upper Perkiomen HS; Pennsburg, PA; (Y); 5/249; Rep Church Yth Grp; VP Debate Tm; Pres Radio Clb; Acpl Chr; Band; Var Socr; JC Awd; Trs NHS; Aud/Vis; Computer Clb; Comp Bowl 85-86; Sci Fr 1st,3rd 84-85; Elec Engr.

SANDY, AMY; Homer Center HS; Lucerne Mines, PA; (Y); French Clb; SADD; Band; Chorus; Concert Band; Stu Cncl; Hon Roll.

SANFORD, LESLIE; Beaver Area JR SR HS; Beaver, PA; (Y); French Clb; Chorus; Fash Inst; Fash Merch.

SANFORD, MICHAEL G; Mc Dowell HS; Erie, PA; (Y); 20/615; Am Leg Boys St; Boy Scts; Church Yth Grp; Exploring; German Clb; Spanish Clb; Var JV Ftbl; Cit Awd; High Hon Roll; Hon Roll; Acdmc All Amer 85; Engrng.

SANFORD, SHEILA; Heritage Christian Acad; Erie, PA; (S); Sec Church Yth Grp; Drama Clb; Hosp Aide; Office Aide; Teachers Aide; Stage Crew; Nwsp Stf; Outstndg Stu Awd 85; Ntl Yth Magzn Artcl 86.

SANGER, MATTHEW K; Strath Haven HS; Swarthmore, PA; (Y); Cmnty Wkr; German Clb; Hosp Aide; School Play; Rep Soph Cls; JV Crs Cntry; JV Swmmng; JV Trk; Ntl Merit SF; Amercn Assoc Tchrs Germn 85 & 86.

SANGMEISTER, EDWARD; Bensalem HS; Bensalem, PA; (Y); Church Yth Grp; German Clb; Varsity Clb; Swmmng; Wt Lftg; Hon Roll; PA ST; Engrg.

SANKARAN, SHEILA; Wissahickon HS; Norristown, PA; (S); 2/276; Pres Art Clb; Chorus; Nwsp Rptr; JV Crs Cntry; JV Trk; High Hon Roll; NHS; Opt Clb Awd; Sal; Hosp Aide; Statistcn.

SANKO, CAROLYN E; Marian Catholic HS; Hazleton, PA; (Y); Capt L Bsktbl; Capt L Sftbl; Allentown Coll; Med Tech.

SANKS, ZETA; Hempfield HS; Landisville, PA; (Y); Varsity Clb; Band; Chorus; Concert Band; Orch; School Musical; Stu Cncl; Var Capt Trk; High Hon Roll; NHS; U Of MD; Bus Admin.

SANNER, CHRISTINE; Rockwood Area HS; Markleton, PA; (S); Church Yth Grp; 4-H; Office Aide; Trs Jr Cls; JV Var Bsktbl; Var L Sftbl; Hon Roll; NHS; Presdntl Physcl Ftnss Awd 85; Casselman Chrg SR High Yth Grp Pres 85-86; Mt Zion Utd Methodist 81; Accntnt.

SANSIG, BRENDA; Connellsville Area HS; Dunbar, PA; (Y); 5/550; Drm Mjr(t); Jazz Band; Mrchg Band; School Musical; Symp Band; Bsktbl; French Hon Soc; High Hon Roll; NHS; Band; Engrng Schlrshp U Pittsbrgh 86; Govrs Schl Music 86; PM EA Hnrs Band 84-85; U Of Pittsburgh; Music.

SANTANA, LUIS; Mastbaum Voc Tech Schl; Philadelphia, PA; (Y); Boy Scts; VICA; Pres Frsh Cls; Carpntry.

SANTANGELO, MEREDYTH; New Brighton HS; New Brighton, PA; (Y); 5/160; Am Leg Aux Girls St; GAA; Drm Mjr(t); Yrbk Ed-Chief; Cheerleading; Capt L Trk; Twrlr; DAR Awd; Pres Schlr; Beaver Cnty Jr Ms Pgnt 86; Kent ST U; Law.

SANTANILLO, A CHRISTINE; Manheim Township HS; Lancaster, PA; (Y); JV Var Fld Hcky; JV L Swmmng; Bloomsburg U; Occptnl Thrpy.

SANTARELLI, DIANE; Ambridge Area HS; Ambridge, PA; (Y); Cmnty Wkr; French Clb; Pep Clb; Red Cross Aide; Yrbk Ed-Chief; Ed Yrbk Stf; High Hon Roll; Hon Roll; Elem Ed.

SANTARELLI, RAYMOND; St Josephs Prep; Philadelphia, PA; (Y); Exploring; Spanish Clb; Im Bsktbl; Im Ftbl; High Hon Roll; Prfct Atten Awd; Hnry Schlrshp 83; Excel Lang Arts 83; Perf Atten 82-83; Bus.

SANTELLI, ANTHONY; East Stroudsburg Area HS; E Stroudsburg, PA; (Y); 15/204; Art Clb; Dance Clb; Drama Clb; FBLA; Spanish Clb; Band; Chorus; Color Guard; Concert Band; School Play; Natl Hnrs Banq 86; Cls 1965 Scholar Awd 86; E Stroudsburg U; Theatre.

SANTELLO, JEFFREY; Elizabeth Forward HS; Monongahela, PA; (Y); Golf; Hon Roll; Hnr Stdnt Awd, Perf Atten Awd 83-84; Phy Ftnss Awd 82-84; Radiolgy.

SANTIAGO, CANDIDA; Edison HS; Philadelphia, PA; (Y); Church Yth Grp; Computer Clb; Library Aide; Office Aide; Cit Awd; High Hon Roll; Hon Roll; Pres Schlr; Rotary Awd; Corp 72-73; Most Imprvd Stu 80-81; Temple U; Exec Sec.

SANTIAGO, DANIEL; Lutheran HS; Philadelphia, PA; (Y); Church Yth Grp; Debate Tm; Nwsp Stf; Dctr.

SANTIAGO, ODILLE; Morrisville HS; Morrisville, PA; (Y); 4/105; Church Yth Grp; Band; School Musical; Ed Nwsp Ed-Chief; Nwsp Rptr; Sec VP Stu Cncl; Cheerleading; Twrlr; Hon Roll; Jr NHS; Intl Frgn Lang Awd 85-86; Attndg Pres Clssrm Yng Amer 85-86; Attndg Sci Acad 86; Berkeley U; Med.

SANTILLI, ANTHONY; Hopewell HS; Aliquippa, PA; (Y); 45/256; Church Yth Grp; Spanish Clb; Chorus; Variety Show; Stu Cncl; Var Bsbl; Coach Actv; JV Ftbl; Var Tennis; High Hon Roll; Embry Riddle U; Aerontcs.

SANTILLO, CORRI; Lincoln HS; Ellwood City, PA; (Y); Church Yth Grp; JA; Y-Teens; Chorus; Yrbk Stf; Powder Puff Ftbl; Var L Trk; Hon Roll; Bradford; Retail Mgmt.

SANTINI, DAVID; California Area HS; California, PA; (Y); 27/101; Church Yth Grp; Cmnty Wkr; German Clb; Variety Show; Nwsp Rptr; Nwsp Stf; Off Sr Cls; Tennis; Hon Roll; Masonic Awd; Amer Legion Awd 85; Meritorious Srv Awd 85; ST Chaplin, Treas & Order Of De Molay 85-86; CA U; Theology.

SANTOLI, BETH; Highlands SR HS; Natrona Hts, PA; (Y); 12/277; Church Yth Grp; Key Clb; Tennis; NHS; Prfct Atten Awd; Pres Girl Scts; Intnl Clb; Office Aide; Westringhse Sci Hnr Inst 85-86; Grl Sct Gld Awd 85; Commnbcmnt Spkr 86; PA ST; Psych.

SANTOLI, LAURIE; Bishop Hannan HS; Scranton, PA; (Y); 1/122; Cmnty Wkr; Hosp Aide; Math Clb; Scholastic Bowl; Trs Spanish Clb; High Hon Roll; NHS; VFW Awd; Teachers Aide; Bishop Hannan Scholar 83-86; Amer Lg Essay Awd 85.

SANTORA, STEPHEN; Abington SR HS; Roslyn, PA; (Y); 61/540; Boys Clb Am; Church Yth Grp; Varsity Clb; Rep Stu Cncl; Bsbl; Bsktbl; Lcrss; Socr; Swmmng; Cit Awd; Roslyn Boys Clb Marsden Mem Schlrshp 86; Inter Cnty Under 19 Select Soccr Tm 86; U DE; Bio Sci.

SANTOS, NURIA LISA; Bishop Shanahan HS; West Chester, PA; (Y); 65/218; Church Yth Grp; Dance Clb; Pep Clb; Rep Jr Cls; Stu Cncl; JV Var Fld Hcky; Var Trk; Hon Roll; U Delaware; Sci.

SANTOS, ROBERTO; Pottsgrove HS; Pottstown, PA; (Y); 3/229; Math Tm; Nwsp Stf; Yrbk Stf; Lit Mag; Hon Roll; Graphic Dsgn.

SANTOS, TYRONE J; Dover Area HS; Dover, PA; (Y); 82/241; Varsity Clb; Pres Soph Cls; Pres Jr Cls; Pres Sr Cls; Capt L Bsktbl; Coach Actv; Capt L Ftbl; Capt L Trk; High Hon Roll; Computer Clb; Stu Forum 85-86; Pa ST U; Med.

SANTRY, BRYAN; Council Rock HS; Newtown, PA; (Y); 137/845; FBLA; Pres Ski Clb; Var L Bsktbl; JV Crs Cntry; JV Ftbl; Im Lcrss; Var L Tennis; Im Vllybl; Hon Roll; Banqt Hnrs 10 Yrs Comm & Schl Bsktbl & Summr Coachg 86; Fnce.

SANZI, DAVID; Somerset Area SR HS; Somerset, PA; (Y); 92/239; English Clb; JA; L Band; Concert Band; Mrchg Band; Pep Band; Stu Cncl; L Ftbl; Powder Puff Ftbl; Wt Lftg; Bus.

SAPERS, TAMARA; Central Bucks High School East; Warrington, PA; (Y); Ski Clb; Temple Yth Grp; Chorus; Yrbk Stf; High Hon Roll; Hon Roll; Jr NHS; Hon Acdmc Achvt Awd 83-84; Acdmc Achvt Ltr 85-86; Gld Acdmc Achvt Pin 83-84; Law.

SAPP, CHRISTINE; Wilmington Area JR SR HS; Volant, PA; (S); 5/102; Drama Clb; Office Aide; Spanish Clb; Band; Stu Cncl; Powder Puff Ftbl; JV Var Score Keeper; High Hon Roll; Sec NHS; Rotary Awd; Vrsty Ltr; Band; Acadmc Achvt Awd; Spch Pathlgy.

SAPP, DEBBIE; Marion Center HS; Marion Center, PA; (Y); 10/174; FHA; Pep Clb; Q&S; SADD; Yrbk Phtg; Yrbk Rptr; Yrbk Sprt Ed; High Hon Roll; Hall Patrol As Chosen By V Principal 85-86; Journalism.

SAPUTSKI, DENISE; Mt Alvernia HS; Pittsburgh, PA; (S); 7/65; Boys Clb Am; Computer Clb; Science Clb; High Hon Roll; Hon Roll; NHS; U Ptsbrg; Nrsng.

SARABOK, JEFF; Palmyra Area HS; Palmyra, PA; (Y); 16/200; Drama Clb; Quiz Bowl; Chorus; Church Choir; School Play; Stage Crew; Stu Cncl; Crs Cntry; Trk; High Hon Roll; PA ST; Bus Adm.

SARACHEK, LIZ; Parkland SR HS; Allentown, PA; (Y); 91/415; Camera Clb; Cmnty Wkr; Drama Clb; Hosp Aide; Key Clb; Leo Clb; Library Aide; Office Aide; Q&S; Band; Stu Dir Schl Plays 86; Tisch Schl Art; Wrtr.

SARAHS, KIM; Technical HS; Scranton, PA; (Y); Band; Nwsp Phtg; Nwsp Rptr; Im Cheerleading; Im Sftbl; Med Secy.

SARAJIAN, CHRIS; Pocono Mountain HS; Henryville, PA; (Y); 50/330; Computer Clb; French Clb; Pep Clb; Ski Clb; Rep Frsh Cls; Rep Soph Cls; Var L Ftbl; Var Capt Tennis; High Hon Roll; Hon Roll; Cornell U; Mngmnt.

SARGENT, GREG; Neshaminy HS; Langhorne, PA; (Y); 120/730; Spanish Clb; Socr; JV Trk; Hon Roll; Jr NHS.

SARGENT, JILL; Mid Valley Secondary Ctr; Dickson City, PA; (Y); Art Clb; Computer Clb; Temple Yth Grp; Rep Jr Cls; Rep Sr Cls; Hon Roll; Army; Ntlgnce.

SARGENT, PAMELA JEAN; Girard Alliance Christian Acad; Broken Arrow, OK; (Y); 1/13; Off Church Yth Grp; Drama Clb; Chorus; Trs Church Choir; Concert Band; Drill Tm; Mrchg Band; School Play; Nwsp Stf; Cheerleading; PA Free Enterprize Wk 84; Rhema Bible Trng Ctr; Yth Min.

SARISKY, BRIAN; Notre Dame HS; Easton, PA; (Y); 4/95; Exploring; High Hon Roll; NHS; Prfct Atten Awd; Outstndng Effrt Trigonmtry 85-86; Engrng.

SARNECKI, KIMBERLY; Coughlin HS; Plains, PA; (Y); 62/342; Ski Clb; SADD; VP Jr Cls; VP Sr Cls; Var L Fld Hcky; Hon Roll; Bsktbl; Stat Swmmng; NHS; Band; Wilkes Coll; Law.

SARNOSKI, TRICIA; Benton Area HS; Orangeville, PA; (Y); Church Yth Grp; Cmnty Wkr; Drama Clb; FTA; Keywanettes; Chorus; School Musical; School Play; Stage Crew; Score Keeper; Elem Tchr.

SAROCKY, DENEEN; Greensburg Central Cath; N Huntingdon, PA; (Y); Rep Frsh Cls; Rep Stu Cncl; Bus.

SARRIS, CHRISTINE; Bishop O Reilly HS; Kingston, PA; (Y); 3/106; French Clb; Math Clb; Chorus; Co-Capt Flag Corp; Stage Crew; Pres Jr Cls; Stu Cncl; French Hon Soc; High Hon Roll; NHS; PA Jr Acad Of Sci; Lock Haven U; Math.

SARSFIELD, DEBRA; Hempfield Area HS; Hunker, PA; (Y); 42/657; VP Church Yth Grp; FBLA; Pep Clb; Ski Clb; Capt Color Guard; Mrchg Band; High Hon Roll; Hon Roll; NHS; U Pittsburgh; Bus Mgmt.

SARSFIELD, SHANNON; West Allegheny HS; Coraopolis, PA; (Y); JA; Ski Clb; SADD; School Play; Nwsp Stf; Yrbk Stf; Lit Mag; Bsktbl; Powder Puff Ftbl; Hon Roll; Prblm Slvng Bowl 1st Pl 86; Gftd & Tlntd Educ 83-86; Hote Mgmnt.

SARVER, CHERYL; Knoch HS; Saxonburg, PA; (Y); Computer Clb; Exploring; Chorus; Madrigals; High Hon Roll; NHS; Tlnt Awd In Miss Saxonburg Pgnt 86; 7 Pl Ribbons In Cmptve Gynmastcs 86; Fashion Merch.

SARVER, DAN; Mt Lebanon HS; Pittsburgh, PA; (Y); Boy Scts; Ski Clb; Spanish Clb; Varsity Clb; Rep Frsh Cls; JV Bsbl; Var JV Golf; JV Ice Hcky; Var JV Wrstlng; High Hon Roll; IN U Of PA; Fin.

SARVER, HOLLY; Brockway Area HS; Brockway, PA; (Y); Church Yth Grp; Drama Clb; Chorus; Capt Drill Tm; School Play; Sec Rep Stu Cncl; Capt Twrlr; Comm.

SARVER, TAMMY; Bishop Mc Cort HS; Johnstown, PA; (Y); German Clb; Pep Clb; Nwsp Ed-Chief; Nwsp Rptr; Nwsp Stf; High Hon Roll; Mu Alp Tht; NHS; Cmnty Wkr; Soroptimist; Fnlst Cambria Somerset JR Miss 85-86; Tribune Democ Jrnlsm Awd 86; U Of Pittsburgh; Engl.

SARVEY, KELLIE; Slippery Rock Area HS; Prospect, PA; (Y); 25/215; Church Yth Grp; Intnl Clb; Pep Clb; SADD; Varsity Clb; Yrbk Stf; Bsktbl; Crs Cntry; Trk; Hon Roll.

SASALA, KELLY; Sharon SR HS; Sharon, PA; (Y); Art Clb; French Clb; Letterman Clb; Varsity Clb; Band; Concert Band; Flag Corp; Mrchg Band; Swmmng; Hon Roll; Crmnl Justc.

SASALA, THOMAS; Homer Center; Coral, PA; (Y); 11/96; French Clb; School Musical; School Play; Stage Crew; Nwsp Phtg; Yrbk Phtg; Ftbl; High Hon Roll; Jr NHS; NHS; Elec Engr.

SASALA, TIM; Homer Ctr; Coral, PA; (Y); 2/96; Boy Scts; Church Yth Grp; Varsity Clb; Chorus; School Play; Nwsp Rptr; Yrbk Rptr; Var Trk; Jr NHS; NHS; Psych.

SASLO, CHARLENE; Lakeland JR SR HS; Mayfield, PA; (Y); 2/145; FBLA; Sec FHA; SADD; Drill Tm; Yrbk Stf; High Hon Roll; Hon Roll; NHS; Schltc Schlrshp 86; Natl Sci Merit Awd, Natl Ldrshp Awd 86; Penn ST U; Admin Of Jstc.

SASS, LAURELLE; Ambridge Area HS; Ambridge, PA; (Y); 90/265; Cmnty Wkr; Hosp Aide; Office Aide; Pep Clb; Cheerleading; Trk; Hon Roll; CC Beaver Cnty; Bus Mgmt.

SASSAMAN, DARYL; Cameron County HS; Emporium, PA; (Y); 10/91; Boy Scts; German Clb; Varsity Clb; Yrbk Phtg; JV Var Ftbl; L Trk; L Wrstlng; Hon Roll; Prfct Atten Awd; Cmnty Wkr; Dist IX Wrstlng Chmpn 85; Military.

SASSAMAN, SHELLEY; Danville HS; Danville, PA; (Y); Pep Clb; Trs Sr Cls; Off Stu Cncl; Capt Cheerleading; Var Fld Hcky; Mat Maids; Trk; West Chester U.

SASSAMAN, WILLIAM K; Liberty HS; Bethlehem, PA; (Y); 40/475; Computer Clb; Hon Roll; Muhlenberg; Scndry Educ.

SASSELLI, AMY; South Park HS; Library, PA; (Y); 21/215; Rep Frsh Cls; Rep Soph Cls; Rep Jr Cls; Rep Sr Cls; JV Bsktbl; Powder Puff Ftbl; Trk; High Hon Roll; Hon Roll; NHS; U Pittsburgh; Med Tech.

SASSELLI, MARLO; South Park HS; Library, PA; (Y); Office Aide; Yrbk Stf; Mgr(s); Score Keeper.

SASTOKAS, BRYAN; Kennedy Christian HS; Sharpsville, PA; (Y); Science Clb; Nwsp Sprt Ed; Pres Frsh Cls; Trs Soph Cls; Trs Sr Cls; Rep Stu Cncl; Var L Bsktbl; Var L Trk; Hon Roll; PA Jnr Acad Of Sci 84 & 85; MVP 1st Rnd Hoyle Tourn-Bsktbl 86; U Of Notre Dame IN; Pre-Med.

SATCHELL, NICOLA; St Maria Goretti HS; Philadelphia, PA; (Y); Orch; School Musical; JV Cheerleading; Hon Roll; NHS; Temple; Phys Ther.

SATELL, GREG; Harriton HS; Narberth, PA; (Y); Var Ftbl; Var Capt Wrstlng; Most Imrpoved Wrstlng 86; Med.

SATKOWSKI, BARBARA; Pittston Area HS; Avoca, PA; (Y); 11/365; High Hon Roll; Hon Roll; NHS; PA St U; Accntg.

SATO, NAOMI; Southern Columbia HS; Bloomsburg, PA; (Y); Key Clb; Chorus; School Play; JV Fld Hcky; Socr; High Hon Roll; NHS; Prfct Atten Awd; UNC.

SATTERLEE, KAREN; Saegertown HS; Saegertown, PA; (Y); 24/124; SADD; Im Mgr Crs Cntry; Hon Roll; Jr NHS; Bus Adm.

SAUDER, J MICHAEL; Manheim Township HS; Lancaster, PA; (Y); 32/325; Church Yth Grp; Computer Clb; Orch; High Hon Roll; Hon Roll; Chem.

SAUDER, SHARI; Manheim Central HS; Lititz, PA; (Y); 18/253; Mrchg Band; Yrbk Stf; Rep Frsh Cls; Rep Soph Cls; Rep Jr Cls; Rep Sr Cls; Rep Stu Cncl; JV Var Cheerleading; JV Var Fld Hcky; NHS; Hnr Rll 84-86; 4-Way Tst Awd 86; Messiah Coll.

SAUER, CARLA; Strath Ahven HS; Wallingford, PA; (Y); Pres Church Yth Grp; Cmnty Wkr; French Clb; Intnl Clb; Office Aide; Ski Clb; SADD; Teachers Aide; Chorus; School Musical; PA ST U.

SAUER, JANETTA; Lakeview HS; Sandy Lake, PA; (S); 11/120; 4-H; Girl Scts; Intnl Clb; School Play; Capt Cheerleading; Crs Cntry; Trk; NHS; Bradford Bus Schl; Accntng.

SAUERS, BRIAN; Central Bucks E HS; Warrington, PA; (Y); Boy Scts; Chorus; Yrbk Stf; Rep Frsh Cls; Trs Jr Cls; Stu Cncl; Var L Trk; JV Var Wrstlng; God Cntry Awd; Hon Roll; Penn ST U; Psych.

SAUL, LORIE; Christopher Dock HS; Gilbertsville, PA; (Y); Exploring; Chorus; Church Choir; School Play; Nwsp Ed-Chief; Nwsp Phtg; Nwsp Rptr; Nwsp Sprt Ed; Nwsp Stf; Lit Mag; Wrtrs Awd 86; Forgn Lang Awd 86; Temple U; Jrnlsm.

SAULA, SUSAN; Hempfield SR HS; Madison, PA; (Y); 26/720; Pres Spanish Clb; Stu Cncl; High Hon Roll; Jr NHS; Kiwanis Awd; NHS; Trs Spanish NHS; Alg II Awd 84; Phy Thrpy.

SAUNDERS, BETH; Fairview HS; Fairview, PA; (Y); 22/180; French Clb; Yrbk Stf; Trk; Hon Roll; Pitt; Nrsg.

SAUNDERS, DAVID; Westinghouse HS; Pittsburgh, PA; (Y); Concert Band; Mrchg Band; Var Tennis; Wt Lftg; Hon Roll; Math.

SAUNDERS, RON; Grove City HS; Grove City, PA; (Y); L Ftbl; L Wrstlng; High Hon Roll; Sci.

SAUNDERS, VON ERIC; Springfield HS; Laverock, PA; (Y); 28/139; Boy Scts; Church Yth Grp; Model UN; Band; Chorus; Church Choir; Concert Band; Orch; Stu Cncl; Bsbl; Syracuse U; Pre-Med.

SAUNDERS, WILFORD; Central Bucks East HS; Pipersville, PA; (Y); Capt Church Yth Grp; Drama Clb; Library Aide; Political Wkr; Ski Clb; Yrbk Stf; Ntl Merit Ltr; Histry.

SAURMAN, MADISON Y; Council Rock HS; Newtown, PA; (Y); Boy Scts; Church Yth Grp; Bsbl; Bowling; Golf; Wrstlng; Hon Roll; Aerontcl Engrng.

SAUTTER, CHERYL; Pocono Mountian HS; Long Pond, PA; (Y); 16/320; Pep Clb; Red Cross Aide; Teachers Aide; Var L Cheerleading; Var L Trk; Hon Roll; NHS; Physics Olympics 2nd Pl 86; Edinboro Summer Acad 83-85; Comm Fundraising, Svc, Soc Activities 84-87; Comp Sci.

SAVAGE, BRENDA; Plum SR HS; Pittsburgh, PA; (Y); Dance Clb; JA; School Play; Yrbk Stf; Forbes Rd E Area Vo Tech Schl Cosmtlgy Hnrs 86; Cosmtlgst.

SAVAGE, KIMBERLY; Benton Area JR/SR HS; Benton, PA; (Y); 3/39; 4-H; Chorus; Church Choir; Concert Band; Nwsp Stf; Yrbk Stf; Stu Cncl; Var Bsktbl; 4-H Awd; NHS; Presdntl Acadmc Ftns Awd 85-86; Marjorie Faust Memrl Awd 86; Columbia Cnty Fdrtn Wmns Clbs Awd 86; Penn ST U; Arch Engrng.

SAVAGE, REBECCA L; Highlands SR HS; Brackenridge, PA; (Y); Girl Scts; Hosp Aide; Key Clb; Library Aide; SADD; Concert Band; Mrchg Band; Pep Band; Cit Awd; Hon Roll; Phrmcy.

SAVAGLIO JR, ITALO R; Central Dauphin East HS; Harrisburg, PA; (Y); Art Clb; Exploring; Latin Clb; Science Clb; Stage Crew; Variety Show; Off Stu Cncl; Ice Hcky; Hon Roll; Jr NHS; PA ST U; Microbio.

SAVER, JULIE; Plum SR HS; Pittsburgh, PA; (Y); AFS; Pres French Clb; FHA; Hosp Aide; Band; Flag Corp; Mrchg Band; Symp Band; Stat Socr; Stat Trk; Phys Ther.

SAVERCOOL, APRIL; Pius X HS; Pen Argyl, PA; (Y); 8/35; Pep Clb; Varsity Clb; Nwsp Rptr; Nwsp Stf; Yrbk Stf; Stat Bsktbl; Var Cheerleading; Powder Puff Ftbl; Amer Bus Awd; Amer Hist Awd; Pius X Typing Awd; Churchmans Bus Schl; Lgl Sec.

SAVIDGE, CHRISTINE; Danville HS; Danville, PA; (Y); Cmnty Wkr; Band; Church Choir; Concert Band; Jazz Band; Mrchg Band; Pep Band; Var L Crs Cntry; Im Socr; Var L Trk; Liberty Baptist Coll; Ed.

SAVIDGE, CRAIG; Lebanon HS; Lebanon, PA; (Y); 16/266; Computer Clb; Concert Band; Jazz Band; Mrchg Band; Hon Roll; Aud/Vis; Church Yth Grp; French Clb; Band; Church Choir; Comp Sci.

SAVIDGE, TERESA; Williamsport Area HS; Williamsport, PA; (Y); Key Clb; Spanish Clb; Chorus; School Musical; Capt Cheerleading; Teachers Aide; Pres Acad Ftnss Awd 86; Chrldg Advsrs Awd 86; Duquesne U; Pol Sci.

SAVIDGE, WAYDE; Danville HS; Danville, PA; (Y); JV Var Bsbl; Var JV Bsktbl; JV Var Ftbl; Var Golf.

SAVIGNANO, ERIC; Tunkhannock Area HS; Tunkhannock, PA; (S); 56/300; Church Yth Grp; FCA; Spanish Clb; Im JV Bsktbl; Var L Crs Cntry; Im Var Trk; Hon Roll; NHS; Elec Engr.

SAVOCCHIA, MICHELLE; New Castle SR HS; New Castle, PA; (S); 21/236; AFS; Library Aide; Spanish Clb; Nwsp Rptr; Hon Roll; NHS; Cmntns.

SAVOY, HAKIM; W B Saul Agriculture HS; Philadelphia, PA; (Y); 32/120; Dance Clb; FFA; Quiz Bowl; Acpl Chr; Capt Bsktbl; Capt Im Ftbl; Capt Im Sftbl; Philadelphia Fndtn Schlrshp 86; DE Vly Coll; Food Sci.

SAWA, AMY; Ringgold HS; Donora, PA; (Y); 19/340; Church Yth Grp; Band; Concert Band; Mrchg Band; Rep Jr Cls; Sftbl; High Hon Roll; Hon Roll; NHS; Dsgnd & Won 1st In Mid Mon Vly Trnst Assoc Bus Logo 86; Art Awds 82-86; Hnr Cords At Grad 86; CCAC; Data Prcssng Spclst.

SAWDEY, LORI K; Great Valley SR HS; Malvern, PA; (Y); 44/258; CAP; SADD; Trs Chorus; Concert Band; Mrchg Band; Pep Band; School Musical; High Hon Roll; NHS; Drama Clb; Miss Amer Co-Ed Pgnt 86; Intl Wnnr Natl Guild Piano Tchrs Aud 86; Natl Wnnr Natl Guild Piano Tchrs Aud; Law.

SAWIN, ELIZABETH A; Girard HS; Girard, PA; (Y); Am Leg Aux Girls St; Church Yth Grp; Model UN; Teachers Aide; Varsity Clb; Band; Var L Bsktbl; Var L Crs Cntry; Var L Trk; Cit Awd; Darn Nice Kid Awd 86; Girard Ath Boosters Scholar 86; PA Free Enterprise Wk 85; PA ST; Frgn Svc.

SAWKA, LINDA; Shenandoah Valley HS; Shenandoah, PA; (Y); 7/99; Pep Clb; Yrbk Phtg; Yrbk Stf; JV Var Cheerleading; Pom Pon; High Hon Roll; Hon Roll; Stu Of Mnth 86; Bloomsburg U; Mrktng.

SAWKA, RAELIN; Bethlehem SR HS; Denbo, PA; (Y); 14/165; Civic Clb; Drama Clb; Exploring; Band; Concert Band; Mrchg Band; Nwsp Ed-Chief; High Hon Roll; Hon Roll; Eng.

SAWKA, SUE; North Pocono HS; Lake Ariel, PA; (Y); FBLA; Orch; Hon Roll; Marywood.

SAWYER JR, WILLIAM; Interboro SR HS; Prospect Park, PA; (Y); Aud/Vis; Camera Clb; Nwsp Phtg; Vllybl; DE County CC; Bus.

SAX, DOROTHA; Seneca HS; Erie, PA; (Y); Computer Clb; 4-H; FBLA; JV Var Cheerleading; Hon Roll; Trivia Clb Vp 85-86; 3rd Pl Shrthnd Comptn 86; Bus.

SAXE, TINA MARIE THERESA; Pleasant Valley HS; Stroudsburg, PA; (Y); Rep Church Yth Grp; Drama Clb; Girl Scts; Library Aide; Pep Clb; Ski Clb; SADD; Chorus; Stage Crew; Yrbk Phtg; Cert Pocono Wrtrs Cntst 85; Penn ST U; Pedtrcn.

SAXON, SAMANTHA; Hampton HS; Gibsonia, PA; (Y); French Clb; VP JA; L Socr; Hon Roll; Model NATO 85; Phrmcst.

SAY, DEBORAH; Ford City JR & SR HS; Ford City, PA; (Y); 39/154; Trs Church Yth Grp; Computer Clb; Trs 4-H; Chorus; Church Choir; School Musical; Yrbk Stf; Frsh Cls; Soph Cls; French Hon Soc; Smmr Happngs 86; ST Fnlst 4-H Blu Form Nclothg 86; Bus Mgmt.

SAYERS, CONSTANCE S; Clarion-Limestone Area HS; Summerville, PA; (Y); 15/100; Drm Mjr(t); Yrbk Ed-Chief; Sec Frsh Cls; Sec Soph Cls; Sec Jr Cls; Twrlr; Hon Roll; NHS; Corsica Jfrsn Cnty Fire Queen 85; Miss Clarion Hemisphere 86; Instrctr Brkvl Bckaroos Batn Corp 86; Clarion U Of PA; Pol Sci.

SAYERS, MELISSA; Hempfield HS; Lancaster, PA; (Y); Dance Clb; Yrbk Stf; Powder Puff Ftbl; High Hon Roll; Hon Roll; Bus.

SAYLOR III, JAMES M; Conemaugh Twp Ara HS; Davidsville, PA; (Y); JA; Q&S; School Play; Nwsp Phtg; Nwsp Rptr; Nwsp Stf; Yrbk Phtg; Yrbk Stf; Hon Roll; Lion Awd; Penn ST; Elec Engrng.

SAYLOR, JILL; Williamsburg HS; Williamsburg, PA; (Y); FNA; Teachers Aide; Band; Chorus; Concert Band; Mrchg Band; Pep Band; Yrbk Stf; Church Yth Grp; Drama Clb; Newspaper Editor 86-87; HOBY Found Rep 84-85; Elem Ed.

SAYLOR, MICHAEL; Tunkannock Area HS; Tunkhannock, PA; (Y); Hon Roll; Lincoln Tech Inst; Elec Tech.

SAYLOR, TRICIA; Conemaugh Twp Area HS; Johnstown, PA; (Y); Office Aide; Pep Clb; Pres VP Stu Cncl; Capt Cheerleading; Katherine Gibb Schl; Sec.

SAYRE, JENNIE; Chestnut Ridge SR HS; New Paris, PA; (Y); 23/115; Teachers Aide; Band; Concert Band; Jazz Band; Mrchg Band; Nwsp Phtg; Var L Socr; Hon Roll; NHS; Grad Hnrs 86; Lock Haven U; Sco Wrks.

SBARRA, PAUL; St John Newmann HS; Philadelphia, PA; (Y); 84/338; Ftbl; Hon Roll; Bus Mgmt.

SCAFF, DAVID; Lock Haven HS; Loganton, PA; (Y); Intnl Clb; Key Clb; Spanish Clb; Band; Variety Show; Yrbk Stf; Socr; High Hon Roll; Lion Awd; NEDT Awd; Spec Library Svc Awd Outstndng Svc 84; Lions Clb Intl Yth Exch Australia 86; Med.

SCAFFIDI, DONNA; Abington SR HS; Phila, PA; (Y); 57/508; High Hon Roll; Hon Roll; La Salle U; Bus Admin.

SCALERCIO, NANCY; Ambridge HS; Ambridge, PA; (Y); Hosp Aide; Pep Clb; Red Cross Aide; Spanish Clb; SADD; Band; Concert Band; Mrchg Band; Pep Band; School Musical; Pittsburgh U; Nrsng.

SCALES, JOHN; Greensburg Central Catholic HS; Greensburg, PA; (Y); 50/210; Ski Clb; Im Bsktbl; Var L Socr; Im Sftbl; Var Trk; Im Capt Vllybl; High Hon Roll; Hon Roll; Frnch Drawng Drama Awd 86; Northwestern; Pre-Law.

SCALISE, NANCY; Villa Maria Acad; Erie, PA; (Y); Art Clb; Cmnty Wkr; FBLA; FHA; Hosp Aide; JA; Red Cross Aide; Ski Clb; School Musical; Yrbk Bus Mgr; Bus Mgmnt.

SCALZO, KRISTA; Loyalsock Township HS; Williamsport, PA; (Y); Church Yth Grp; French Clb; Letterman Clb; Ski Clb; Varsity Clb; Variety Show; Nwsp Rptr; Trs Soph Cls; VP Jr Cls; Var Bsktbl; Ldng Batter-Sftbl 85.

SCANDALE, FRANK; Canon Mc Millan SR HS; Canonsburg, PA; (Y); Nwsp Stf; Yrbk Stf; Pres Frsh Cls; VP Jr Cls; VP Sr Cls; Rep Stu Cncl; JV Trk; High Hon Roll; Hon Roll; WA; Med.

SCANDLE, BETHANY L; Shamokin Area HS; Sunbury, PA; (Y); 49/196; Sec Drama Clb; Key Clb; Speech Tm; Sec Varsity Clb; Pres Stu Cncl; Var Cheerleading; Var L Diving; Var L Swmmng; Capt Var Trk; Pres Ftns Awd 86; Photo Awd 86; Prom Cmmttee 85.

SCANGA, BILL; Highlands SR HS; Tarentum, PA; (Y); Church Yth Grp; Intnl Clb; Band; Concert Band; Jazz Band; Mrchg Band; Pep Band; Stu Cncl; Socr; Prfct Atten Awd; Grnd Prz Vlly Nws Dsptch Create-An-Ad Cntst 82; Alle-Kiski Hnrs Band 85&86; U Of Pittsburgh; Engnrng.

SCANLAN, BARRY; Biship Carroll HS; Cresson, PA; (S); 15/102; Aud/Vis; Chorus; Church Choir; Im Bowling; Hon Roll; NEDT Awd; Music Stdnt Mnth 84; Penn ST U; Engrng.

SCANLAN, PATRICK; Blue Mountain HS; Schuylkill Haven, PA; (Y); 5/226; Quiz Bowl; Chorus; Nwsp Sprt Ed; Rep Stu Cncl; Var L Crs Cntry; Hon Roll; Mu Alp Tht; NHS; NEDT Awd; Boy Scts; Latn Hnr Soc; Eagl Rank-Boy Scts 84; US Navy; Nuclr Engrng.

SCANLAN, SUE; Saint Basil Acad; Philadelphia, PA; (Y); Church Yth Grp; German Clb; GAA; Math Clb; Varsity Clb; Nwsp Rptr; Nwsp Sprt Ed; Lit Mag; Socr; Hon Roll; Ntl Jrnlsm Awd 86; Phila Incntv Awd 84; NEDT Awd 83; Lasalle U; Tchr.

SCANLON, FRANK C; Mid-Valley HS; Throop, PA; (Y); 17/100; Boy Scts; Cmnty Wkr; SADD; Concert Band; Bsbl; Hon Roll; Ntl Merit Ltr; VFW Awd; Bsbl MVP RBI Ldr Throop Teener 85; Engrng.

SCANLON, JAMES P; Venango Christian HS; Shippenville, PA; (Y); Pep Clb; Spanish Clb; Band; Pep Band; School Musical; Var Socr; Clarion U; Intl Bus.

SCANLON, NICOLLE; Bethel Park HS; Bethel Pk, PA; (Y); DECA; FBLA; Powder Puff Ftbl; High Hon Roll; 5th Pl-Apprl & Accssrs-DECA Career Conf 86; St Awd-DECA Career Conf 86; Chld Psych.

SCANLON, RICHARD E; New Brighton HS; New Brighton, PA; (Y); 21/154; Computer Clb; Band; Concert Band; Jazz Band; Mrchg Band; Orch; Pep Band; Symp Band; High Hon Roll; Clarion U PA; Acctg.

SCANLON, SHARON; State College Area SR HS; State College, PA; (Y); 19/580; Band; Yrbk Rptr; High Hon Roll; Ntl Merit Ltr; PA ST U; Sci.

SCANNAPIECO, RAYMOND; Archbishop Carroll HS; King Of Prussia, PA; (Y); 16/162; High Hon Roll; NHS; Chem Awd; US Hstry Awd; Drexel U; Engrng.

SCARBOROUGH, TRACY; Williamsport Area HS; Williamsport, PA; (Y); Cmnty Wkr; Band; Concert Band; Mrchg Band; Symp Band; Hon Roll; Prfct Atten Awd; Ltr Cmmndtn Engl Dept Excllnt Achvmt 85-86; Peer Hlpr 86-87; Bus Adm.

SCARCELLA, VANESSA; Hazleton HS; Hazleton, PA; (Y); 22/350; Drama Clb; Exploring; Pep Clb; Thesps; Chorus; School Play; Stage Crew; Nwsp Stf; Yrbk Stf; High Hon Roll; PA ST U; Engnrng.

SCARDUZIO, ADELINA; St Maria Goretti HS; Philadelphia, PA; (Y); 27/426; Mathletes; Math Clb; High Hon Roll; NHS; Prfct Atten Awd; Acad Mdl For Italian II, III & IV 84-86; Pres Acad Ftnss Awd 86; Sons Of Italy Schlrshp 86; Temple U; Pre-Med.

SCARFUTTI, STACY; Highlands SR HS; Natrona Hts, PA; (Y); Drama Clb; Intnl Clb; Key Clb; Color Guard; School Play; Stu Cncl; Tennis; Trk; Jr NHS; NHS; Pre-Med.

SCARPARI JR, EDWARD A; Elizabeth Forward HS; Elizabeth, PA; (Y); Church Yth Grp; Exploring; French Clb; JA; JV Bsbl; Var L Crs Cntry; Var L Trk; High Hon Roll; NHS; Rotary Awd; John Glenn Meml Schlrshp 86; Musikingum College; Math.

SCARSELLONE, RICHARD; Aliquippa HS; Aliquippa, PA; (S); 22/154; Boy Scts; Pres DECA; Pres Band; Mrchg Band; Pep Band; Crs Cntry; Trk; Wrstlng; High Hon Roll; Hon Roll; CCBC; Bus Mgmt.

SCATTON, FRANCINE; Hazleton HS; Hazleton, PA; (Y); 119/388; Drama Clb; Office Aide; Color Guard; Nwsp Rptr; Crs Cntry; Hon Roll; RN.

SCATTON, MICHELLE; Hazleton SR HS; Kelayres, PA; (Y); 49/388; Intnl Clb; Thesps; Stage Crew; Stu Cncl; Drama Clb; Chorus; School Musical; School Play; Nwsp Stf; Tennis; Hnrbl Ment; Sclstc Arts Awd Wilkes Barre 86; Banking.

SCAVUZZO, LAURA; Emmaus HS; Emmaus, PA; (Y); 7/530; AFS; French Clb; Symp Band; High Hon Roll; NHS; Lttl Svn Litrary Cntst-Awd Of Crtcs Chc 84; Engl.

SCEKERES, DON; Mt Pleasant Area SR HS; United, PA; (Y); Debate Tm; French Clb; German Clb; Var L Golf; Var L Trk; High Hon Roll; Yth Commtte Paiesk Cncl; Comp.

SCHAAF, PAUL; Penn Hills SR HS; Verona, PA; (Y); AFS; Boy Scts; Drama Clb; JA; Science Clb; Spanish Clb; School Musical; School Play; Yrbk Stf; Tennis; Eagle Scout Awd 86; Pres Clsrm 86; Comp Engr.

SCHACH, CRYSTAL; Pine Grove Area HS; Pine Grove, PA; (Y); ROTC; Varsity Clb; Chorus; Var Sftbl; Hon Roll; Cert Awd Art 86; Kutztown U; Comm Dsgn.

SCHACHTE, MICHAEL; Greensburg Central Catholic HS; United, PA; (Y); High Hon Roll; NHS.

SCHAD, CHRISTINE; South Park HS; Library, PA; (Y); 9/204; L Tennis; L Trk; High Hon Roll; NHS; Bus.

SCHADDER, CINDY; Hazleton HS; Hazleton, PA; (Y); 4/377; Drama Clb; Hosp Aide; Chorus; Color Guard; Mrchg Band; Yrbk Bus Mgr; Cheerleading; High Hon Roll; NHS; NEDT Awd; Kings Coll Spnsh Cntst 2nd Pl & 3rd Pl 83 & 84; Schlstc Art Cmptn Gld Key Fnlst 86; PA ST U; Pre-Med.

SCHADE, ERIC; The Christian Acad; Aston, PA; (Y); 1/95; Church Yth Grp; Cmnty Wkr; Computer Clb; Exploring; Red Cross Aide; Teachers Aide; Chorus; Socr; Wt Lftg; High Hon Roll; Chem Awd Encclnc 86; A Hnr Roll 4 Trms 84-86; Chem Engrng.

SCHADLER, JILL; Perkiomen Valley HS; Perkiomenville, PA; (Y); Cmnty Wkr; Variety Show; Pres Jr Cls; Rep Stu Cncl; Co-Capt Cheerleading; JV Fld Hcky; JV Var Lcrss; High Hon Roll; Hon Roll; NHS; Am Legn Cert Schl Awd 84; Stu Mnth 84; Bus Adm.

SCHAEFER, DAVID; Mohawk HS; Bessemer, PA; (Y); Trs Spanish Clb; Bsbl; Var Capt Ftbl; Wt Lftg; High Hon Roll; Hon Roll; NHS; Ntl Merit Schol; Comp Tech.

SCHAEFER, IAN T; John Piersol Mc Caskey HS; Lancaster, PA; (Y); 7/450; Computer Clb; Math Clb; Chorus; Hon Roll; NHS; Ntl Merit Ltr; Sertoma Essay Wnnr 83-84; Merrill Lynch Esy Fnlst 84-85; Archtctr.

SCHAEFER JR, JIM; St Marys Area HS; Saint Marys, PA; (Y); 97/301; Band; Chorus; Concert Band; Drm & Bgl; Drm Mjr(t); Jazz Band; Mrchg Band; Orch; Pep Band; Stage Crew; JV No Bnd 85; Vrsty Ltr Bnd 86; IN U Of PA; Music.

SCHAEFER, MARK; Sullivan County HS; Dushore, PA; (Y); 3/92; Math Tm; Yrbk Stf; Var L Bsbl; Var L Bsktbl; Var L Crs Cntry; Pres NHS; Presdntl Acadmc Awd 86; Math Awd 86; Penn ST U Univ Pk; Engrng.

SCHAEFER, WILLIAM E; Cardinal Dougherty HS; Philadelphia, PA; (Y); 16/747; Church Yth Grp; Pres German Clb; Service Clb; School Play; Nwsp Rptr; Nwsp Stf; Stu Cncl; DAR Awd; High Hon Roll; Jr NHS; Cert Of Acadmc Pro Alg And Hist 83-86; St Josephs U Schlrshp 86; La Salle U Chrstn Bros Grant 86; St Josephs U; Acctg.

SCHAEFFER, CASSIE; Ford City HS; Ford City, PA; (Y); 29/154; Cmnty Wkr; Sec Drama Clb; VP Spanish Clb; Chorus; Capt Drm Mjr(t); Mrchg Band; School Play; Rep Soph Cls; Rep Sr Cls; Rep Stu Cncl; Nrsng.

SCHAEFFER, DONNA; Pine Grove Area HS; Pine Grove, PA; (Y); Chorus; Flag Corp; School Musical; Yrbk Stf; Pres Frsh Cls; Pres Soph Cls; Pres Jr Cls; Pres Sr Cls; Stu Cncl; Var Vllybl; Amer Legn Aux Good Ctznshp Awd 84; Grnd Ofcr Intl Ordr Rainbw 85-86.

SCHAEFFER, LORI; Emmaus HS; Emmaus, PA; (Y); Sec Church Yth Grp; Hosp Aide; Spanish Clb; SADD; Chorus; Church Choir; School Musical; Rep Frsh Cls; Bsktbl; Sftbl; Messiah Coll; Elem Ed.

SCHAEFFER, MARIA; Nativity BVM HS; Pottsville, PA; (Y); 10/98; Church Yth Grp; French Clb; Yrbk Stf; Off Frsh Cls; Rep Jr Cls; Sec Stu Cncl; Sftbl; Hon Roll; NHS; Stu Mnth 86; Peer Cnslng 86-87; Acctng.

SCHAEFFER, SHERRY; Cocalico HS; Denver, PA; (Y); Cmnty Wkr; Hosp Aide; Red Cross Aide; Spanish Clb; VICA; JV Tennis; High Hon Roll; Hon Roll; Prfct Atten Awd; Willow St Vo Tech; Nrsg.

SCHAFER, BILL; Schuylkill Haven HS; Schuylkill Haven, PA; (Y); 11/99; FCA; Pres German Clb; SADD; Capt Bsbl; VP Ftbl; Hon Roll; Sch Hvn Rtry Schlrshp 86; Sch Hvn Educ Assoc Schlrshp 86; Sch Hvn Prnt-Tchrs Orgnztn Schlrshp 86; Lincoln Tech Inst; Elctrncs.

SCHAFER, KEITH; Franklin HS; Franklin, PA; (Y); 42/220; Boy Scts; Drama Clb; Pres French Clb; Ski Clb; Chorus; Church Choir; Madrigals; Swing Chorus; High Hon Roll.

SCHAFER, MARISA; Penn Hills SR HS; Pittsburgh, PA; (Y); 80/700; Office Aide; Spanish Clb; Teachers Aide; Yrbk Stf; Var L Bsktbl; High Hon Roll; Hon Roll; Sawyer Schl; Htl/Mtl Mgmt.

SCHAFFER, ERIC; Ridley SR HS; Morton, PA; (Y); 47/427; Church Yth Grp; Cmnty Wkr; Bsbl; Ftbl; Hon Roll; Comp Engr.

SCHAFFER, JAMES S; Upper Bucks Chrst Schl; Allentown, PA; (Y); 17/26; Boy Scts; Church Yth Grp; Exploring; 4-H; Band; Chorus; Concert Band; Mrchg Band; Swing Chorus; Jazz Band; Eagle Scout Awd 86; Maranatha Bapt Bible Coll; Educ.

SCHAFFER, KERRY R; Quakertown Community SR HS; Quakertown, PA; (Y); 24/289; Rep Varsity Clb; Pres Stu Cncl; Var L Sftbl; Capt L Vllybl; Im Wt Lftg; Hon Roll; Jr NHS; NHS; Pres Schlr; SAR Awd; Bus & Profssnl Wmns Clb Awd 86; Joseph S Neidig Awd 86; U Of Delaware; Fshn Merch.

SCHALL, HAROLD; Butler HS; Butler, PA; (Y); VP JA; Math Tm; Spanish Clb; SADD; Hon Roll; Trs Jr NHS; Trs NHS; Bus.

SCHALL, KENNETH; Bishop Carroll HS; Hastings, PA; (S); 20/102; Boy Scts; Spanish Clb; JV Bsktbl; Im Bowling; Var Ftbl; High Hon Roll; Hon Roll; Acctng.

SCHALLES, LISA; Pittston Area HS; Duryea, PA; (Y); Science Clb; Ski Clb; Trk; Dntl Assist.

SCHAMBERGER, DANIEL; Emmaus HS; Emmaus, PA; (Y); 69/493; Exploring; German Clb; Hon Roll; Jr NHS; NHS; Stu Ath Trainer Awd 84-85; Allegheny Coll; Wildlf Mgr.

SCHAMING, CARA; Uniontown SR HS; Uniontown, PA; (Y); Spanish Clb; Nrsng.

SCHAMING, MICHAEL; Aliquippa HS; Aliquippa, PA; (S); Comp Sci.

SCHANCK, SARAH; Freedom HS; Bethlehem, PA; (Y); 100/465; French Clb; Pep Clb; PAVAS; Chorus; Var Pom Pon; Var Powder Puff Ftbl; Hon Roll; Amer Music Abrd Touring Choir 85-86; Music Ed.

SCHANE, TAMMY; North Pocono HS; Moscow, PA; (S); 4/250; Chorus; Nwsp Stf; Yrbk Ed-Chief; Yrbk Stf; Lit Mag; Stu Cncl; High Hon Roll; NHS; IUP; Jrnlsm.

SCHANK, RACHEL; Norwin SR HS; N Huntingdon, PA; (Y); 182/556; Trs FBLA; Office Aide; Teachers Aide; Off Band; Church Choir; Concert Band; Jazz Band; Off Mrchg Band; Lttrd Band 85-86; Bradford Bus Schl; Sec.

SCHANTZ, JUSTINE; Perkiomen Valley HS; Spg Mt, PA; (Y); Model UN; Mrchg Band; Stat Bsbl; VP Capt Cheerleading; Crs Cntry; High Hon Roll; Hon Roll; VP NHS.

SCHAPPELL, LISA; Hamburg Area HS; Hamburg, PA; (Y); 42/150; German Clb; SADD; Chorus; School Musical; Rep Stu Cncl; Hon Roll; Grmn Ntl Hnr Soc 86; Acadmc Ltr-Grmn 85 & 86.

SCHAPPELL, TANYA; Kutztown Area HS; Kutztown, PA; (Y); 10/167; Chorus; Concert Band; Drill Tm; Pres Sr Cls; Sec Stu Cncl; JV Var Bsktbl; JV Var Fld Hcky; High Hon Roll; NHS; Pop Chorus; Bus.

SCHARBA, TRACI; Sharon SR HS; Sharon, PA; (Y); Dance Clb; Pres Spanish Clb; School Play; Nwsp Stf; Rep Stu Cncl; Var Cheerleading; Hon Roll; Spanish NHS; Child Psych.

SCHARNBERGER, ROBERT C; Penn Manor HS; Millersville, PA; (Y); 1/311; Chess Clb; Drama Clb; Math Tm; Quiz Bowl; Thesps; Jazz Band; School Musical; School Play; NHS; Ntl Merit SF; Math.

SCHATZ, KAREN; Elk County Christian HS; St Marys, PA; (Y); #22 In Class; Cmnty Wkr; Intnl Clb; Ski Clb; SADD; Yrbk Stf; Stat Bsktbl; JV Vllybl; Hon Roll; Cls Hnrs; Sec Ed.

SCHAUB, GARY; South Hills HS; Pittsburgh, PA; (Y); 5/180; Boy Scts; Spanish Clb; Nwsp Stf; Rep Jr Cls; Capt Tennis; Wt Lftg; High Hon Roll; NHS; Prfct Atten Awd; Rotary Awd; Alumni Assn Schlrshp 86; Pres Acadmc Fit Awd 86; Carnegie-Mellon U; Info Sys.

SCHAUB, HELEN; Saint Paul Cathedral HS; Pittsburgh, PA; (Y); Drama Clb; Hosp Aide; NFL; Political Wkr; Nwsp Stf; Yrbk Stf; Mgr(s); High Hon Roll; NHS; NEDT Awd; Arab Stdy.

SCHAUER, STACEY; Brandywine Heights HS; Topton, PA; (Y); 20/124; Hosp Aide; Concert Band; Mrchg Band; Nwsp Sprt Ed; Yrbk Rptr; JV Var Fld Hcky; Hon Roll; NHS; Intl Stds.

SCHAUT, LUCY; St Marys HS; Saint Marys, PA; (Y); Hosp Aide; Yrbk Stf; JV Cheerleading; Hon Roll; Penn ST U; Psych.

SCHAWALLER, INGRID; Muncy HS; Muncy, PA; (Y); 10/72; French Clb; Bsktbl; Tennis; Vllybl; Hon Roll; NHS; Pres Acdmc Fit Awd 86; Hghst Avg Chem Awd Grl 86; PA ST U; Psych.

SCHAWINSKI, ROBERT; Our Lady Of The Sacred Heart HS; Mckees Rocks, PA; (Y); 9/59; Computer Clb; Debate Tm; NFL; Speech Tm; School Musical; School Play; Bowling; Socr; High Hon Roll; Hon Roll; Psych.

SCHEER, MARYALICE; Plum Sr HS; Pittsburgh, PA; (Y); AFS; French Clb; FTA; Library Aide; Q&S; Science Clb; Ski Clb; Nwsp Ed-Chief; Lit Mag; FHA; Hlth Clsrm Awd 84; Lit Clsrm Awd 85-86; Family Reltns Clsrm Awd; IN U Of Penna; Elem Ed.

SCHEETZ, DEBBIE; Liberty HS; Bethlehem, PA; (Y); 76/475; Art Clb; Church Yth Grp; Hosp Aide; Spanish Clb; Hon Roll; Intr Dsgn.

SCHEIDEL, AMY PATRICIA; Owen J Roberts HS; Glenmoore, PA; (Y); 41/287; Church Yth Grp; JCL; Letterman Clb; Chorus; Yrbk Sprt Ed; Yrbk Stf; Stu Cncl; L Capt Trk; Im Vllybl; Hon Roll; Villanova U; Librl Arts.

SCHEIER, ROBERT; Upper Merion SR HS; Bridgeport, PA; (Y); 51/321; Art Clb; Cmnty Wkr; Letterman Clb; Math Clb; Math Tm; Varsity Clb; JV Var Bsbl; Im Bsktbl; Var Bowling; Im Vllybl; Art Proj On Handbk 86; Arch Engrng.

SCHEIFELE, ROB; Salisbury HS; Allentown, PA; (Y); Debate Tm; JV Bsktbl; VP L Socr; Hon Roll; PA JR Acad Of Sci 1st Pl Rgnl Cmptn 86; PA JR Acad Of Sci 2nd Pl 86; Hugh O Brian Yth Fndtn 85.

SCHEITHAUER, MARIA; Our Lady Of Lourdes Regional HS; Marion Heights, PA; (Y); 24/96; AFS; Library Aide; Pep Clb; VP Service Clb; Spanish Clb; Yrbk Stf; Hon Roll; Ind Psychlgst.

SCHEIVERT, ANDREA; Cardinal O Hara HS; Gradyville, PA; (Y); 92/748; French Clb; Office Aide; Fld Hcky; Tennis; Hon Roll; Lion Awd; Villanova; Commerce.

SCHELER, FREDERICK; Cathedral Preparatory HS; Erie, PA; (Y); 70/244; French Clb; Model UN; Ski Clb; BAMBA; Econ.

SCHELL, DEBORAH; Cedar Grove Christian Acad; Philadelphia, PA; (Y); Church Yth Grp; Sftbl; Cit Awd; Hon Roll.

SCHELL, DOUG; Cedar Grove Acad; Philadelphia, PA; (Y); 4/43; Church Yth Grp; Computer Clb; Band; Concert Band; Nwsp Rptr; Yrbk Stf; Bsbl; Bsktbl; Score Keeper; High Hon Roll; Pre-Med.

SCHELL, EDWARD; Norwin SR HS; Irwin, PA; (Y); 30/577; AFS; Church Yth Grp; Math Clb; Spanish Clb; L Ftbl; JV Wrstlng; High Hon Roll; Jr NHS; Spanish NHS; Carnegie Mellon U; Chem Engr.

SCHELL, ELIZABETH; Clearfield Area HS; Clearfield, PA; (Y); 82/330; Spanish Clb; SADD; Band; Chorus; Concert Band; Mrchg Band; Orch; Var Stat Diving; Var Swmmng; Var Twrlr; Arch.

SCHELL, JENNI; Cedar Cliff HS; Camp Hill, PA; (Y); 48/250; Sec Key Clb; Spanish Clb; Chorus; Stu Cncl; JV Var Cheerleading; Var Gym; Var Trk; Hon Roll; Spanish NHS; All Amer Chrldr 85-86; Educ.

SCHELL, RAYMOND K; Schuylkill Valley HS; Leesport, PA; (Y); 22/126; Var L Tennis.

SCHELL, STEPHANIE; Berwick Area HS; Nescopeck, PA; (Y); 55/202; Cmnty Wkr; VP Key Clb; Library Aide; Pres Natl Beta Clb; Chorus; Nwsp Stf; Yrbk Phtg; Yrbk Stf; Lit Mag; Var L Sftbl; Penn ST; Medcl.

SCHELLENBERGER, SANDRA; Greater Works Acad; Pittsburgh, PA; (Y); 1/36; Church Yth Grp; Service Clb; Ski Clb; Yrbk Ed-Chief; Rep Stu Cncl; Var Capt Cheerleading; Var Capt Vllybl; High Hon Roll; Val; Grove City Coll; Elec Engrng.

SCHELLER, CRAIG; Avonworth HS; Pittsbg, PA; (Y); Nwsp Rptr; Nwsp Stf; Yrbk Stf; Rep Stu Cncl; L Ftbl; Im Wt Lftg; Var L Wrstlng; High Hon Roll; Hon Roll; INDIANA U Of PA.

SCHELLER, JASON; Le Dieruff HS; Allentown, PA; (Y); 17/351; Drama Clb; ROTC; Band; Chorus; Church Choir; Concert Band; Drill Tm; Drm & Bgl; Jazz Band; Mrchg Band; Ltr Of Cmmndtn NMSQT 85; AFROTC 4-Yr Schlrshp 86; Boston U; Aerontcl Engrng.

SCHELLER, MICHAEL J; Brentwood HS; Pittsburgh, PA; (Y); 2/130; Church Yth Grp; Pep Clb; Yrbk Phtg; Yrbk Sprt Ed; Stu Cncl; L Crs Cntry; L Trk; DAR Awd; NHS; Ntl Merit SF; Cvl Engrng.

SCHELLHAMER, CHRIS D; Northwestern Lehigh HS; Slatington, PA; (Y); L Bsbl; L Bsktbl; L Crs Cntry; High Hon Roll; Hon Roll; German I & II Acad Awds 85-86; Stu Of Mnth 85; Art Cert Hnr Awd 86; German.

SCHELLHAMER, KAREN; Northwestern Lehigh HS; New Tripoli, PA; (Y); 5/163; Chorus; JV Fld Hcky; Stat Ftbl; JV Sftbl; NHS; Stu Mnth 86; Kutztown U; Med Tech.

SCHELLIN, KAREN M; Emmaus HS; Emmaus, PA; (Y); 1/479; French Clb; Key Clb; Trs Soph Cls; Trs Jr Cls; Trs Sr Cls; Swmmng; DAR Awd; High Hon Roll; NHS; Ntl Merit SF; Hugh O Brian Ldrshp Smnr Ambssdr; PIAA ST Chmpn & ST Rcrd Hldr Swmmng; All Amer HS Swmmr; U Of VA.

SCHENCK, ANDREW; Henderson HS; West Chester, PA; (S); 14/336; Boy Scts; Pres Spanish Clb; Nwsp Sprt Ed; VP Sr Cls; Stu Cncl; Var Socr; Var Capt Wrstlng; Hon Roll; NHS; Pres Spanish NHS; Acad Awd 85; Outstndg Achvt Awd Sctng 84; Elec Engr.

SCHENCK, BETH; Milton Area HS; New Columbia, PA; (Y); 35/213; Latin Clb; Band; Chorus; Church Choir; Color Guard; Concert Band; Mrchg Band; Yrbk Stf; Rep Jr Cls; Powder Puff Ftbl; Nrsg.

SCHENTZEL, ADAM; William Allen HS; Allentown, PA; (Y); FBLA; Im Bsktbl; JV Ftbl; Var Powder Puff Ftbl; Im Socr; Trk; PA ST U; Bus.

SCHEPIAN, ANITA; Phila Montgomery Christian Acad; Oreland, PA; (Y); 5/41; Sec Church Yth Grp; Teachers Aide; VP Acpl Chr; Church Choir; Var Tennis; High Hon Roll; Hon Roll; Sec Trs NHS; Deans Schrlshp 86; Instrumntl Music Awd 86; Athletic Awd Tennis; Messiah Coll; Music Ed.

SCHERER, KIM; Nazareth Area SR HS; Bethlehem, PA; (Y); 25/239; Hosp Aide; JA; Band; Concert Band; Drill Tm; Jazz Band; Mrchg Band; Art Clb; Church Yth Grp; Computer Clb; Gftd Prgm Hnrs Prgm; Dist 10 Band 85; Stu Dor Band Pres 86; IN U; OB Nrse.

SCHERER, LYNN; Pottsgrove HS; Pottstown, PA; (Y); German Clb; Latin Clb; Science Clb; Varsity Clb; Yrbk Sprt Ed; Rep Stu Cncl; Var Fld Hcky; Var Sftbl; Hon Roll; NHS; 1st Tm Au Ches Mont 85; Bio.

SCHERFEL, JENNIFER; Harry S Truman HS; Levittown, PA; (Y); Church Yth Grp; Mathletes; Pep Clb; Trs Jr Cls; Stu Cncl; Var Im Bsktbl; Var Sftbl; Var Trk; High Hon Roll; Hon Roll; Temple U; Dntl.

SCHERFEL, LISA; Ambridge HS; Ambridge, PA; (Y); 35/265; Church Yth Grp; Pep Clb; Spanish Clb; SADD; Teachers Aide; Pres Sr Cls; JV L Trk; Twrlr; Hon Roll; NHS; U Of Pittsburgh; Psychlgy.

SCHERFEL, SUE ELLEN; Ambridge Area HS; Ambridge, PA; (Y); Church Yth Grp; Exploring; Hosp Aide; Rep Pep Clb; Red Cross Aide; Spanish Clb; Drill Tm; Rep Jr Cls; Trk; Hon Roll; Dietetics.

SCHERMERHORN, GAIL; Phil Montgomery Christian Acad; Ardsley, PA; (Y); Church Yth Grp; Chorus; Stage Crew; Yrbk Phtg; JV Var Sftbl; Widener U; Nrsg.

SCHEUNEMAN, JOAN; Scranton Technical HS; Scranton, PA; (S); 1/247; Church Yth Grp; VP FBLA; Q&S; Scholastic Bowl; Church Choir; Nwsp Stf; Hon Roll; Jr NHS; VP NHS; Val; Comp Sci.

SCHEURING, LISA; Shaler Area HS; Pittsburgh, PA; (Y); 27/517; Spanish Clb; Concert Band; Drill Tm; Mrchg Band; Symp Band; Variety Show; Nwsp Rptr; Rep Frsh Cls; High Hon Roll; Sec Spanish NHS; Nrs.

SCHIAVI, MICHAEL; Chartiers Valley HS; Pittsburgh, PA; (Y); Drama Clb; Library Aide; Thesps; School Musical; School Play; Stage Crew; NHS; Ntl Merit SF; Spnsh.

SCHIED, DAVID M; Central Bucks West HS; Chalfont, PA; (Y); 75/383; Hon Roll; Jazz Band; Var L Socr; Var Swmmng; Var Trk; Shippensburg U; Bus.

SCHIEDT, LIZ; Pennsbury HS; Morrisville, PA; (Y); VP Church Yth Grp; Intnl Clb; Band; Concert Band; Mrchg Band; Hon Roll; Prfct Atten Awd; Educ.

SCHIFANO, ANTHONY; Old Forge HS; Old Forge, PA; (S); 14/69; Yrbk Phtg; Yrbk Stf; Sec Jr Cls; Sec Sr Cls; Hon Roll; NHS; Gregg Typg Awd; H S Ldr Duquesne U; U Pittsburgh; Phrmcy.

SCHILDT, STEVE; Central Bucks East HS; Pipersville, PA; (Y); Cmnty Wkr; Ski Clb; Var L Bsbl; Var L Ftbl; Trk; Wt Lftg; Bausch & Lomb Sci Awd; High Hon Roll; NHS; Prfct Atten Awd; Stu Sci Trnng Pgm Chem Phldlph Coll Txtls Sci 86; Leg Hnrs Sbrbn Ftbl Assctn 86; Chmstry.

SCHILL, LANE; Johnsonburg Area HS; Johnsonburg, PA; (Y); 24/88; Nwsp Stf; Ftbl; Trk; Prfct Atten Awd; Var Lttr Track 85 & 86; Gannon U; Robotics Tech.

SCHILLING, ALICE; Marian Catholic HS; Coaldale, PA; (Y); 10/115; Church Yth Grp; Pres 4-H; Hosp Aide; Service Clb; SADD; Nwsp Stf; Yrbk Ed-Chief; High Hon Roll; NHS; Pres Spanish NHS; Bio-Med.

SCHIMONSKY, LORALEI; Brownsville SR HS; Brownsville, PA; (S); 5/235; Church Yth Grp; Trs Hosp Aide; Library Aide; Math Clb; Office Aide; SADD; Band; Church Choir; Concert Band; Mrchg Band; Stu Of Mnth 86; Acdmc All-Amer Schlr 85-86; Natl Ldrshp & Svc Awd 86; Carlow Coll; Accntng.

SCHIMONSKY, LORILYN; Brownsville Area HS; Brownsville, PA; (S); 15/220; Sec Hosp Aide; Latin Clb; Library Aide; Math Clb; Office Aide; SADD; Band; Yrbk Stf; NHS; Rotry Clb; Carlow Clg.

SCHINDLER, RICHARD; Marple Newtown HS; Broomall, PA; (Y); Boy Scts; Var L Tennis; U Of MD; Mrktng.

SCHIRNHOFER, BRENDA; Steel Valley HS; Munhall, PA; (S); 18/243; Trs Key Clb; Band; Concert Band; Jazz Band; Mrchg Band; Pep Band; JV Bsktbl; High Hon Roll; Hon Roll; NHS; Duquesne; Phrmcy.

SCHIRRA, AMY; Faith Community Christian Schl; Mc Murray, PA; (S); 1/29; Church Yth Grp; Ski Clb; Teachers Aide; Rep Stu Cncl; JV Cheerleading; Dnfth Awd; High Hon Roll; NHS; NEDT Awd; Ed.

SCHITTLER, LINDA; Brandywine Heights Area HS; Alburtis, PA; (Y); Pep Clb; Chorus; Color Guard; Flag Corp; Hon Roll; E Stroudsburg U; Music Educ.

SCHLACK, BOBBI; Shenandoah Valley JR SR HS; Shenandoah, PA; (Y); 4/108; Debate Tm; Office Aide; Pep Clb; Yrbk Stf; Im Score Keeper; Im Vllybl; French Hon Soc; High Hon Roll; Hon Roll; Float Commttee 83-86.

SCHLACK, MICHAEL; Beaver Area SR HS; Beaver, PA; (Y); Church Yth Grp; FCA; German Clb; Latin Clb; Ski Clb; Chorus; JV Bsbl; JV Var Ftbl; Powder Puff Ftbl; Slippery Rock U; Acctg.

SCHLASTA, DEBORAH; Lakeland JR SR HS; Jermyn, PA; (S); 30/147; Pres VP FHA; Letterman Clb; Var Capt Cheerleading; Hon Roll; Tele Comm.

SCHLEGEL, CHRISTOPHER; Devon Prep Schl; Ardmore, PA; (Y); Boy Scts; Church Yth Grp; Hosp Aide; School Play; Nwsp Rptr; Rep Frsh Cls; VP Rep Jr Cls; Var L Bsbl; Hon Roll; NEDT Awd; Ad Altari Dei Medl Boy Scts Amer 84; Ordr Arrw Assc 84.

SCHLEGEL, DENISE; Cocalico SR HS; Denver, PA; (Y); 4/170; Quiz Bowl; Teachers Aide; Chorus; School Musical; School Play; Stage Crew; Off Sr Cls; High Hon Roll; Trs NHS; Library Aide; Fair Qun 86; Bio.

SCHLEGEL, HOLLY; Northeastern SR HS; Manchester, PA; (Y); Dance Clb; Chorus; JV Var Bsktbl; Var Sftbl; High Hon Roll; Hon Roll; NHS; 1st Pl Awd Essy What My Family Means To Me Yk Cnty 85; Cmmnctns.

SCHLEGEL, JON; Richland HS; Gibsonia, PA; (Y); 36/183; Aud/Vis; Church Yth Grp; Stage Crew; JV Bsbl; Var Ftbl; Wt Lftg; Var Wrstlng; High Hon Roll; Coach Actv; Clarion ST U; Bus Adm.

SCHLEGEL, LYNDA; Shikellamy HS; Sunbury, PA; (Y); 67/316; Sec Church Yth Grp; German Clb; Girl Scts; Chorus; Concert Band; Mrchg Band; Variety Show; Rep Stu Cncl; Cheerleading; Hon Roll; Engl.

SCHLEGEL, MARC; Norwin SR HS; N Huntingdon, PA; (Y); 74/557; French Clb; Letterman Clb; Var JV Bsktbl; JV Ice Hcky; Var L Socr; Hon Roll; Zoolgy.

SCHLEGEL, SANDRA; Fleetwood HS; Fleetwood, PA; (Y); #6 In Class; Trs Band; Chorus; Concert Band; Mrchg Band; Stage Crew; Trs Stu Cncl; Var Bsktbl; Capt Var Tennis; Hon Roll; NHS; Shippensburg ST Coll; Acctg.

SCHLEICHER, CAROL; Catasauqua HS; Catasauqua, PA; (Y); 1/125; Drama Clb; Sec VP Band; School Musical; Rep Stu Cncl; Cit Awd; God Cntry Awd; Hon Roll; VP NHS; Val; Shippensburg U; Psych.

SCHLEINITZ, DANIELLE; Kennett HS; Kennett Sq, PA; (Y); 2/154; Pres Service Clb; Nwsp Stf; Yrbk Stf; Pres Frsh Cls; Var Fld Hcky; Swmmng; Gov Hon Prg Awd; NHS; Rotary Awd; Rep Soph Cls; Wellesley Bk 86; Intl Rltns.

SCHLEITER, MICHELLE DENISE; Ambridge Area HS; Ambridge, PA; (Y); 29/265; Sec Church Yth Grp; VP German Clb; Rep Pep Clb; Drill Tm; Off Jr Cls; Off Sr Cls; Stu Cncl; Pom Pon; Hon Roll; NHS; Am Leg Awd 82; U Pittsbrgh; Phrmcy.

SCHLENER, KIMBERLY A; Saucon Valley SR HS; Bethlehem, PA; (Y); Church Yth Grp; French Clb; Girl Scts; Hosp Aide; Ski Clb; Band; Church Choir; Concert Band; Mrchg Band; Hon Roll; Amer Leg Aux Essay Awd 2nd 83; Penn ST; Vet Med.

SCHLESSMAN, JAMIE L; Wilson SR HS; Sinking Spring, PA; (Y); 1/286; Sec Aud/Vis; French Clb; Scholastic Bowl; Trs Band; Chorus; Lit Mag; High Hon Roll; Sec NHS; Ntl Merit SF; Psych.

SCHLEY, MERRITT LYNN; Mercyhurst Prep; Erie, PA; (Y); Art Clb; Drama Clb; French Clb; School Musical; School Play; Yrbk Stf; Pblc Rltns.

SCHLICK, DENIELLE LA RUE; Pottstown HS; Pottstown, PA; (Y); 45/238; French Clb; Pre-Vet.

SCHLIMM, CHRISTINE; Elk County Christian HS; St Marys, PA; (Y); 20/97; Sec Hosp Aide; Intnl Clb; Library Aide; Yrbk Stf; Hon Roll; Stackpole Corp Schlrshp 86; Bu Bois Bus Coll; Legal Sec.

SCHLOSBERG, YVONNE; Gateway SR HS; Monroeville, PA; (Y); Exploring; Hosp Aide; Chorus; Color Guard; School Play; Yrbk Stf; Off Frsh Cls; Off Soph Cls; Trk; NHS.

SCHLOSS, JUDEANNE; Cardinal O Hara HS; Eddystone, PA; (Y); 129/780; Computer Clb; School Play; Nwsp Stf; Yrbk Stf; O Haras Fall Show Publcty 85-86; Mth.

SCHLOSSER, AMY; Richland HS; Wexford, PA; (Y); 32/183; Church Yth Grp; Chorus; Bsktbl; Sftbl; Vllybl; Hon Roll; Pittsburgh Post Gazette N Hills News Rec Sftbl 86; PIAA Fnls 2nd St Vllybll 86; MVP Sftbll 84.

SCHLOSSER, KEVIN; Cathedral Prep; Erie, PA; (Y); 40/216; Sec Sr Cls; Im Bsktbl; JV Ftbl; Var Trk; Msgr Hastings Awd 83; Boxing Awd 86; Duke U; Pilot.

SCHLOSSER, MATTHEW A; Abington Heights HS; Clarks Summit, PA; (Y); 17/275; Boy Scts; Church Yth Grp; Band; Mrchg Band; Hon Roll; NHS; Rotary Awd; Eagle Scout 86; German Cntst 3rd Pl Kings Coll 85; Patrol Ldr; Ntl Scout Jamboree; Engrng.

SCHLOTT II, JOHN R; Gateway SR HS; Pitcairn, PA; (Y); 25/440; Boy Scts; Church Yth Grp; Exploring; German Clb; School Play; JV Ftbl; Mgr(s); High Hon Roll; U Pittsburgh Engrng Scshlrshp 86; Lamp Knowledge Awd 84 & 85; U Pittsburgh; Chem Engrng.

SCHLOTTER, LAUREN; East Allegheny HS; N Versailles, PA; (Y); Church Yth Grp; French Clb; Sec Band; Concert Band; Mrchg Band; Orch; Yrbk Stf; Var Trk; Hon Roll; Prfct Atten Awd; Ultra Snd Tech.

SCHMADER, DEBBIE; North Clarion HS; Lucinda, PA; (Y); 5/100; Office Aide; Spanish Clb; Stage Crew; Yrbk Ed-Chief; Yrbk Stf; Sec Bsktbl; Cheerleading; Var Timer; JV Im Trk; High Hon Roll.

SCHMADER, GRETTA; Clarion Area HS; Shippenville, PA; (Y); Band; Chorus; Concert Band; Mrchg Band; Pep Band; Var L Bsktbl; Var Trk; JV Im Vllybl; Comp Prgrmg.

SCHMADER, LISA; Sheffield Area JR-SR HS; Clarendon, PA; (Y); Drama Clb; Varsity Clb; Concert Band; Jazz Band; Mrchg Band; School Musical; School Play; Stat Bsktbl; Var Cheerleading; Hon Roll; Big 30 Chrldr 86-87; Vrsty Ltrs Bnd Chrldng Station & Drama 83-86; Mercyhurst Coll; Chld Dev.

SCHMALDIENST, TERRY; Allentown Central Catholic HS; Whitehall, PA; (Y); Art Clb; Pep Clb; Spanish Clb; Flag Corp; Hon Roll; Kutztown U; Advrtsg.

SCHMALDINST, PAUL; Emmaus HS; Zionsville, PA; (Y); 52/486; Computer Clb; Exploring; German Clb; JCL; NHS; Ntl Merit SF; Biomedical Engrng.

SCHMECK, KELLY; Exeter SR HS; Reading, PA; (Y); 10/200; Exploring; Y-Teens; Chorus; High Hon Roll; Jr NHS; NHS; Ernst & Whinney Accntng Awd 86; Outstndg Math Awd 86; Elizabethtown Coll; Accntnt.

SCHMEHL II, LARRY; Tulpehocken HS; Bethel, PA; (Y); Church Yth Grp; Chorus; Church Choir; School Musical; Variety Show; JV Var Tennis; Cmmrcl Art.

SCHMID, E CHRISTOPHER; Archbishop Wood For Boys HS; Southampton, PA; (Y); 75/282; Im Bsbl; Im Bsktbl; JV Ice Hcky.

SCHMID, TRACEY; Knoch JR SR HS; Butler, PA; (Y); Church Yth Grp; Jazz Band; Mrchg Band; Pep Band; Stage Crew; Symp Band; High Hon Roll; NHS; Drama Clb; Band; Accptd To Boston Coll Experience 86; Mid East Music Conf At Duquesne U; 86fhnrs Band At Westmnstr 86; Acctng.

SCHMIDT, CHRIS; Ambridge HS; Baden, PA; (Y); 49/265; Soph Cls; Jr Cls; Sr Cls; Trk; High Hon Roll; Hon Roll; U Pittsburgh; Pharm.

SCHMIDT, ERIC WILLIAM; Hempfield HS; Manheim, PA; (Y); 72/418; Band; Mrchg Band; Hon Roll; Bus.

SCHMIDT, JACQUELINE; Palisades JR/SR HS; Ferndale, PA; (Y); 6/177; Rep Sec 4-H; Lit Mag; Var L Crs Cntry; Var L Trk; Hon Roll; Jr NHS; NHS; Ntl Merit SF; Am Leg Aux Girls St; Library Aide; Bucks Cnty Intrmed Unit 22 Sci Semnr; Prevet Stds.

SCHMIDT, JEANNINE; Cambridge Springs HS; Conneautville, PA; (Y); 12/102; Sec 4-H; Pep Clb; Sec Spanish Clb; VP Band; Church Choir; Pres Concert Band; VP Mrchg Band; Pep Band; Yrbk Phtg; Yrbk Rptr; Edinboro U; Bio.

SCHMIDT, JOHN; Lakeland Jr - SR HS; Clarks Summit, PA; (Y); JA; Variety Show; Rep Jr Cls; Var Bsbl; Hon Roll; Cmmnctns.

SCHMIDT, MARGARET; Bishop Conwell HS; Fairless Hls, PA; (Y); 39/254; GAA; Q&S; Yrbk Ed-Chief; Yrbk Stf; Mgr(s); Swmmng; Var Capt Vllybl; Hon Roll; Prfct Atten Awd; Serv & Ldrshp Acad Awd; Acad All Amer; Phila Classical Soc Cum Laude; U Of Scranton; Hstry.

SCHMIDT, MARISA; Upper Darby HS; Drexel Hill, PA; (Y); 50/660; Cmnty Wkr; Spanish Clb; Orch; School Musical; Yrbk Stf; Mgr(s); JV Trk; Hon Roll.

SCHMIDT, RACHAEL; Little Flower Catholic HS Girls; Philadelphia, PA; (Y); 153/395; Church Yth Grp; Cmnty Wkr; Office Aide; ROTC; Band; Church Choir; Color Guard; VP Orch; Stage Crew; Swmmng; Schlrshp To Take Coll Music 86; VP Of Orch 86-87; Awd For Srvce Chrch & Cmnty 86; Temple U; Music.

SCHMIDT, RICHARD; Marple Newtown SR HS; Broomall, PA; (Y); Boy Scts; Science Clb; Band; Concert Band; Mrchg Band; Pep Band; School Musical; Variety Show; Nwsp Stf; Hon Roll; Bio.

SCHMIDT, ROBERT; Cambridge Springs HS; Saegertown, PA; (Y); 34/104; 4-H; Pep Clb; Pres Spanish Clb; 4-H Awd; Hon Roll; Church Yth Grp; SADD; Yrbk Stf; Var L Bsktbl; Var L Ftbl; Favrte Ftbl Plyr Awd 85; Intlgnce.

SCHMIDT, STACEY; Carrick HS; Pittsburgh, PA; (S); Camp Fr Inc; Church Yth Grp; School Musical; Yrbk Stf; Bus.

SCHMIDT, TAMMY; Northwestern HS; Girard, PA; (Y); 26/160; French Clb; Pep Clb; Teachers Aide; Chorus; Stage Crew; Yrbk Phtg; Yrbk Rptr; Yrbk Stf; JV Vllybl; Hon Roll; Frnch Awd 83-84.

SCHMIDT JR, WILLIAM A; West Forest HS; Pleasantville, PA; (Y); Chess Clb; Varsity Clb; School Play; VP Frsh Cls; VP Soph Cls; Bsktbl; Capt Socr; 4-H Awd; High Hon Roll; Hon Roll; Accntng.

SCHMIEG, RICK; Towanda Area HS; Towanda, PA; (Y); Band; Chorus; Concert Band; Mrchg Band; Swing Chorus; Elks Awd; Drctrs Awd In Music 86; Amer Lgn Awd 83; Radio Brcstng.

SCHMIELER, ROB; Moniteau HS; Harrisville, PA; (Y); Computer Clb; Science Clb; Spanish Clb; Ftbl; Trk; Hon Roll; Slppry Rock U; Mrn Bio.

SCHMIGEL, CHRIS; Avonworth HS; Pittsbg, PA; (Y); Hosp Aide; JA; Sec Service Clb; Stat Bsktbl; Mgr(s); Score Keeper; Stat Socr; Stat Sftbl; High Hon Roll; Hon Roll; Hghst Semstr Pts Spn 84; Sewickley Hosp Schl; RN.

SCHMINKY, JONNIE; Upper Dauphin Area HS; Elizabethville, PA; (Y); 30/100; Trs Church Yth Grp; Chorus; School Musical; Yrbk Stf; Mgr Trk; Twrlr; Mgr Twrlr; Hon Roll; Mary Margaret Nestor Schlrshp 86; 80 NBTA Btn Twrlng Awds 82-86; B Hnrs 86; IN U; Occptnl Thrpy.

SCHMITT, BETH; Norht Hills HS; Pittsburgh, PA; (Y); JV Var Bsktbl; JV L Sftbl; JV L Vllybl; Outstndng Female Athlt 86; Fl Sftbl Schlrshp-Sthrn IL 86; Sthrn IL; Athltc Trnng.

SCHMITT, ERIC; Highlands Ssr HS; Natrona Hts, PA; (Y); L Mgr Bsktbl; Brown Awd Grad Pt Avg 84-86; Industry.

SCHMITT, MICHELLE; Oliver HS; Pittsburgh, PA; (Y); Yrbk Stf; Hon Roll; Schlrshp Franco Bea Acad 86; VICA Stff; Franco Beauty Acad; Csmtlgst.

SCHMITT, PAMELA; Technical Memorial HS; Erie, PA; (Y); 32/349; Spanish Clb; Nwsp Phtg; Yrbk Phtg; Yrbk Stf; Acctnt.

SCHMITTNER, JOHN; St Joseph Prep; Philadelphia, PA; (S); 23/200; Camera Clb; Debate Tm; Pep Clb; Pres Science Clb; Nwsp Ed-Chief; Yrbk Stf; Rep Jr Cls; Tennis; NHS; Ntl Merit Ltr; Prep Schlr Awd 82-86; Best Tennis Plyr 85-86; Prep Svc Awd Edtr Schl Nwspr 85; Pre-Med.

SCHMOKE, TAMMY; Cameron County HS; Sinnamahoning, PA; (Y); Hon Roll; Ntl Bus Hon Soc 84-86.

SCHMONDIUK, RENAE; East Allegheny HS; Wall, PA; (Y); Sec Church Yth Grp; Girl Scts; Ski Clb; Concert Band; Mrchg Band; Yrbk Stf; Off Soph Cls; Off Jr Cls; Twrlr; NHS; Pre-Med.

SCHMOUDER, LON; Liberty HS; Liberty, PA; (Y); Church Yth Grp; Pep Clb; Stage Crew; Var Bsktbl; Var Tennis; Hon Roll; NHS.

SCHMOUDER, TINA; North Penn HS; Arnot, PA; (Y); Camera Clb; Drama Clb; Trs Key Clb; Yrbk Stf; Stat Trk; Hon Roll; NHS; NEDT Awd; Library Aide; Frgn Lang Clb; Ready Wrtng Cntst; Yslippery Rock U; Biolgcl Rsrch.

SCHMOYER, BETH; Freedom HS; Easton, PA; (Y); 158/445; Art Clb; German Clb; Band; Concert Band; Mrchg Band; Pep Band; Symp Band.

SCHMOYER, JASON; Northwestern Lehigh HS; Germansvile, PA; (Y); 17/126; Service Clb; Yrbk Stf; Trs Frsh Cls; VP Rep Stu Cncl; Ftbl; Capt Wrstlng; Cit Awd; Dnfth Awd; High Hon Roll; Hon Roll; Engl Awds 84-85; HOBY Ldrshp 84; Alt NROTC Scholar 86; VA Military Inst; Econ.

SCHMOYER, KIMBERLY; Liberty SR HS; Bethlehem, PA; (Y); Camera Clb; Church Yth Grp; Cmnty Wkr; Drama Clb; School Play; Stage Crew; High Hon Roll; Hon Roll; Sci.

SCHMUCK, TERRY; York County Area Voc Tech Schl; Glen Rock, PA; (Y); Varsity Clb; VICA; Bsbl; Hon Roll.

SCHNABEL, BARBARA; Upper Perkiomen HS; Green Lane, PA; (Y); Rep Stu Cncl; Cheerleading; Powder Puff Ftbl; Trk; Hon Roll; Chorus; Yrbk Stf; Rep Sr Cls; AHSA Natl Horse Of Yr 83-84; PHSA Horse Hi Score Awd 83-84; AHSA/Insilco Horse Of Yr Zone II 83-84; Bus Mgmt.

SCHNARRENBERGER, ROBIN; North Catholic HS; Pittsburgh, PA; (Y); 26/301; French Clb; Pep Clb; Ski Clb; Var Capt Cheerleading; High Hon Roll; NHS; Church Yth Grp; Cmnty Wkr; FCA; JA; PA ST U; Pre Med.

SCHNECK, BARBRA J; Pine Grove Area HS; Pine Grove, PA; (Y); 9/118; Church Yth Grp; Exploring; Varsity Clb; Chorus; Church Choir; Mrchg Band; Yrbk Stf; Rep Frsh Cls; Rep Sr Cls; Rep Stu Cncl; Snowflake Princess Rep 86; Bloomsburg U; Nrsng.

SCHNECK, SUSAN; Washington HS; Washington, PA; (S); Stu Cncl; Capt Crs Cntry; L Trk.

SCHNEE, KAREN; Lampeter-Strasburg HS; Lancaster, PA; (Y); 21/158; Sec Church Yth Grp; Thesps; Band; Chorus; Church Choir; Concert Band; Madrigals; Mrchg Band; School Musical; Var Trk; Vrsty Chrldng 84-86; U Of DE; Physcl Thrpy.

SCHNEIDER, CHRISTINE M; York Catholic HS; York, PA; (Y); French Clb; Pep Clb; Color Guard; Rep Frsh Cls; Rep Sr Cls; Bsbl; High Hon Roll; Hon Roll; Sec NHS; Clr Grd Rep In Our Music Assn 87; Peer Cnslr 10 11 & 12 Core Membr 11 & 12 85-87; SR Ensmble 87; Millersville U; Sec Ed.

SCHNEIDER, EDWARD; North Catholic HS; Philadelphia, PA; (Y); 132/362; Chess Clb; Var Wrstlng.

SCHNEIDER, GREG; St Marys Area HS; St Marys, PA; (Y); Var L Bsbl.

SCHNEIDER, HEATHER; Plymouth Whitemarsh HS; Lafayette Hill, PA; (Y); Aud/Vis; Camera Clb; Cmnty Wkr; Hosp Aide; Ski Clb; SADD; Mrchg Band; Stage Crew; Off Soph Cls; Off Jr Cls; Acad Hnrs 84-85; Telecomm.

SCHNEIDER, HELGA; Palmyra SR HS; Palmyra, PA; (Y); Church Yth Grp; Library Aide; Pep Clb; SADD; Chorus; Yrbk Stf; Cheerleading; Sftbl; Trk; Hon Roll; Bus Adm.

SCHNEIDER, JENNIFER T; Kiski Area HS; Apollo, PA; (Y); Math Tm; Political Wkr; Q&S; Chorus; Nwsp Rptr; High Hon Roll; VP NHS; Ntl Merit SF; BPW Girl Of Mnth 85; Ldrshp Sem Schlrshp 85; Bus.

SCHNEIDER, JOE; Council Rock HS; Holland, PA; (Y); Var Socr; JV Swmmng; Var Trk; High Hon Roll; Hon Roll; Pre-Med.

SCHNEIDER, JOHN; Elk County Christian HS; St Marys, PA; (S); 10/100; Varsity Clb; JV Bsktbl; Var L Crs Cntry; Var L Trk; Hon Roll; NEDT Awd; Penn ST Berhend; Engrng.

SCHNEIDER, LORI; Oil City SR HS; Oil City, PA; (Y); Varsity Clb; Chorus; Var L Bsktbl; L Crs Cntry; Trk; Vllybl; Hon Roll; Phy Asst.

SCHNEIDER, MARIANNE; Archbishop Prendergost HS; Sharon Hl, PA; (Y); 70/360; French Clb; Office Aide; Orch; Yrbk Stf; Temple U.

SCHNEIDER, MARYBETH; Archbishop Wood HS; Huntingdon Vly, PA; (Y); 42/268; Church Yth Grp; Cmnty Wkr; German Clb; Yrbk Stf; Hon Roll; La Salle U; Bus Adm.

SCHNEIDER, MELANIE DAEL; Central York SR HS; York, PA; (Y); 1/239; Cmnty Wkr; Scholastic Bowl; Ski Clb; Varsity Clb; Flag Corp; Mrchg Band; Nwsp Stf; Yrbk Stf; Lit Mag; Var Trk; Mst Outstndg Engl Stu 86; Cmmncmnt Spkr 86; York Dspatch Acad All Stars 86; Duke U; Pre-Med.

SCHNEIDER, MICHELLE; Mercyhurst Preparatory Schl; Harborcreek, PA; (Y); 30/150; French Clb; Hosp Aide; Pres Spanish Clb; Lit Mag; Var L Cheerleading; JV Capt Vllybl; Hon Roll; NHS; Inter Discplnry Studies.

SCHNEIDER, RAYMOND; West Chester East HS; West Chester, PA; (Y); Ftbl; Wt Lftg; Northampton Area CC; Mortuary.

SCHNEIDER, SCOTT; St Marys Area HS; St Marys, PA; (Y); 101/303; Boys Clb Am; Bsbl.

SCHNEIDER, SUSAN; Taylor Allderdice HS; Pittsburgh, PA; (Y); 58/456; Hosp Aide; JA; Temple Yth Grp; High Hon Roll; Hon Roll; Acadmc Ltr 84-86; PA ST.

SCHNEIDER, TIM; Kiski Area SR HS; Apollo, PA; (Y); Exploring; Mgr(s); Trk; High Hon Roll; Pre Med.

SCHNELL, MISTY; Karns City HS; Karns City, PA; (Y); 23/113; JV Var Bsktbl; Var Crs Cntry; Var Trk; JV Var Vllybl; Hon Roll; Band; Mst Dedicated Trck 85.

SCHNEPP, KIMBERLY; Sto-Rox HS; Mc Kees Rocks, PA; (Y); 26/160; Pep Clb; Red Cross Aide; Cheerleading; VFW Awd; U Pittsburgh; Acctng.

SCHNESSEL, FERN; Scranton Prep; Carbondale, PA; (Y); 93/192; JA; VP Temple Yth Grp; Stage Crew; Nwsp Stf; Yrbk Phtg; Trk; Comm.

SCHNETZKA, TERESA; York County Area Vo-Tech Schl; Brodbecks, PA; (Y); Girl Scts; JA; VICA; JV Fld Hcky; Hon Roll; 1st & 2nd Pl Dstrct Cmptn Cmmrcl Art 85 & 86; 2 Yrs Art Coll Crs 84-86; Art.

SCHNOKE, LYNDA; Cedar Crest HS; Lebanon, PA; (Y); Lib Band; Concert Band; Jazz Band; Sec Mrchg Band; Pep Band; Millersville ST Coll; Elem Ed.

SCHNORR, JAMES; York Catholic HS; York, PA; (Y); Church Yth Grp; AFS; Pep Clb; Spanish Clb; Varsity Clb; Bsbl; Bsktbl; Hon Roll; Bus.

SCHOCK, MARCINE; Charleroi Area HS; N Charlaroi, PA; (Y); Office Aide; Acctng.

SCHOCK, MICHAEL; Northwestern Lehigh HS; Slatington, PA; (Y); Pres Sec Church Yth Grp; Band; Concert Band; Mrchg Band; Pep Band; Yrbk Stf; JV Bsbl; Hon Roll; PA ST U; Bus Mngmt.

SCHODOWSKI, CECILIA; Holy Name HS; Wernersville, PA; (Y); 6/115; VP Church Yth Grp; Drama Clb; Chorus; Church Choir; School Musical; Yrbk Stf; Trk; High Hon Roll; NHS; Typ I Awd, Yrbk Svc Awd 85; Elizabethtown; Math.

SCHOELKOPF, DONALD; Columbia HS; Columbia, PA; (Y); 9/86; Varsity Clb; Nwsp Sprt Ed; Bsktbl; Capt Ftbl; Capt Trk; Hon Roll; Jr NHS; Pres NHS; Ntl Merit Ltr; Prfct Atten Awd; M S Groft Schlrshp 86; Mlsrvl U.

SCHOENBERGER, DAWN; Liberty HS; Bethlehem, PA; (Y); 145/396; Church Yth Grp; Hosp Aide; Chorus; Church Choir; H S 12-Spclly Tlntd Grp Of Sngrs 86.

SCHOENBERGER, STEVE; Downingtown HS; Downingtown, PA; (S); 19/527; Trs German Clb; Letterman Clb; Ski Clb; Im Bsktbl; Var L Ftbl; Im Lcrss; Var Trk; Im Wt Lftg; Hon Roll; NHS; Eco.

SCHOENEBERGER, TODD; Pen Argyl HS; Wind Gap, PA; (Y); 6/117; Church Yth Grp; Band; Concert Band; Drm Mjr(t); Jazz Band; Mrchg Band; Yrbk Stf; High Hon Roll; Jr NHS; NHS; Rensselaer Math & Sci Awd 86; Nclr Engrng.

SCHOENEMAN, APRIL; West Allegheny HS; Oakdale, PA; (Y); 9/203; Church Yth Grp; Exploring; Chorus; Drill Tm; High Hon Roll; NHS; U Pittsburgh; Biolgcl Sci.

SCHOFFLER, GERRY; Little Flower HS; Philadelphia, PA; (Y); 35/450; Aud/Vis; Camera Clb; Cmnty Wkr; Pres French Clb; Pres FBLA; Office Aide; Science Clb; Service Clb; Rep Stu Cncl; Hon Roll; Pres Acdmc Fit Awd 86; Cert Cmmndtn Bus Ed Currclm Comm 86; PA ST U; Mktg.

SCHOFFSTALL, JEANNETTE; Steelton-Highspire HS; Steelton, PA; (Y); Hosp Aide; Spanish Clb; Teachers Aide; Band; Capt Color Guard; Concert Band; Yrbk Stf; Hon Roll; JC Awd; Rotary Awd; Hugh Obrian Ldrshp Conf 85; Rotary Ldrshp Smnr 86; Hugh Obrian Ldrshp Conf Reunion Cmmtt Sec 86; Paralegal.

SCHOK, TINA MARIE; Interboro HS; Essington, PA; (Y); Am Leg Aux Girls St; French Clb; Key Clb; Nwsp Rptr; Yrbk Stf; Sec Pres Stu Cncl; Var Bsktbl; Var Fld Hcky; Var Sftbl; Cit Awd; Hugh O Brian Yth Fndtn Awd 85; Del Val All Lg Hon Awd Fld Hcky 85; Acdmc All Amrcn Hon 86; Vet Med.

SCHOLL, ERIC; Freedom HS; Bethlehem, PA; (Y); 83/404; Computer Clb; Yrbk Bus Mgr; Yrbk Stf; Ntl Merit Ltr; Lehigh U; Engrng.

SCHOLL, GREG J; Avonworth HS; Pittsburgh, PA; (Y); 8/98; Church Yth Grp; Latin Clb; Nwsp Ed-Chief; Pres Sr Cls; Var L Ftbl; High Hon Roll; Hon Roll; NHS; Ntl Merit SF; Wt Lftg; Schlr Athlt Cert Of Hnr 85-86; Pittsburgh Press N All Star Spcl Tms/Ftbl 85-86; Smmr Intern Mallon U.

SCHOLL, MICHELE; Altoona Area HS; Altoona, PA; (Y); 86/680; Pres Church Yth Grp; Rep Cmnty Wkr; Pres German Clb; Pep Clb; School Play; Stage Crew; Nwsp Ed-Chief; Nwsp Rptr; Nwsp Stf; Lit Mag; Ricks Coll-Rexburg ID; Hstry.

SCHOLODER, MIKE; Elk County Christian HS; St Marys, PA; (S); JA; Ski Clb; Yrbk Stf; Lit Mag; Bowling; Hon Roll; Ntl Ldrshp Merit Awds 86; Penn ST U; Mech Engr.

SCHOLTZ, KEVIN J; Greater Johnstown HS; Johnstown, PA; (Y); 56/268; Band; Chorus; Concert Band; Drm Mjr(t); Jazz Band; Mrchg Band; School Musical; Tennis; Hon Roll; PA ST Chorus 85; U Pittsburgh; Comp Sci.

SCHOMAKER, ANJI; Souderton HS; Telford, PA; (Y); 4-H; Chorus; Hon Roll; Opt Clb Awd; Dental Asst.

SCHON, JANICE; Montoursville Area HS; Williamsport, PA; (Y); 12/174; Art Clb; German Clb; Key Clb; High Hon Roll; Hon Roll; German Hon Soc 87.

SCHONDER, JOHN; Shaler Area HS; Glenshaw, PA; (Y); 38/538; Chess Clb; Spanish Clb; Rep Frsh Cls; Rep Soph Cls; Bausch & Lomb Sci Awd; High Hon Roll; NHS; NEDT Awd; Rotary Awd; Spanish NHS; Am Chem Soc Chem Competition 1st Pl; PA JR Acad Sci ST 2nd Pl; Civil Engr Soc, Special Awd; Gannon U; Med.

SCHONDER, MATT; Shaler Area HS; Glenshaw, PA; (Y); 47/517; Exploring; Im Sftbl; Im Tennis; Var L Vllybl; Hon Roll; (EDT 84; Natl Sci Olympd 86.

SCHOSSER, MARY; Lakeview HS; Sandy Lake, PA; (S); 4/120; Church Yth Grp; Girl Scts; Intnl Clb; Band; Concert Band; Mrchg Band; Pep Band; School Play; Yrbk Stf; NHS; Slippery Rock U; Elem Educ.

SCHOTT, RYAN; Galeton Area HS; Galeton, PA; (Y); 5/35; Boy Scts; Church Yth Grp; Band; Chorus; Church Choir; Mrchg Band; School Play; JV Var Bsbl; JV Var Bsktbl; JV Var Socr; Natl Sci Olympd Awd 84-85; PA Dist 4 Bsktbl Chmps 85-86; Phrmcy.

SCHRACK, SUSAN; Northern York County HS; Dillsburg, PA; (Y); 33/207; Drama Clb; Hosp Aide; NFL; Band; Chorus; Drm Mjr(t); Mrchg Band; School Musical; School Play; High Hon Roll; West Chester U; Medcl Prof.

SCHRADER, GREG; William Allen HS; Allentown, PA; (Y); 47/550; Key Clb; Letterman Clb; Ski Clb; Varsity Clb; Pres Stu Cncl; Swmmng; Hon Roll; NHS; Ntl Merit SF; Outstndng HS Swimming Awd Allen 84-85&85-86; Penn ST U; Sprts Med.

SCHRAM, LANETTE; Moshannon Valley HS; Smithmill, PA; (Y); 41/124; Drama Clb; Letterman Clb; Pep Clb; SADD; Varsity Clb; Band; Chorus; School Play; Stat Bsktbl; Capt Cheerleading; Dubois Bus COLL; Exec Sec.

SCHRAM, PERRY; Norwin HS; Norwin, PA; (Y); 79/550; Math Clb; ROTC; Ski Clb; Bsbl; Var L Wrstlng; Penn ST; Aerospc Engrng.

SCHRAMM, DOROTHY; Palisades HS; Coopersberg, PA; (Y); 2/170; AFS; Am Leg Aux Girls St; Dance Clb; Drama Clb; Ski Clb; Thesps; School Play; Yrbk Stf; Hon Roll; Sal; Air Force; Navigation.

SCHRAMM, MARY; Cardinal O Hara HS; Swarthmore, PA; (Y); 33/772; Church Yth Grp; Hosp Aide; Service Clb; Band; Concert Band; Mrchg Band; School Musical; High Hon Roll; NHS; French Clb; Cardinal O Hara Sci Fair 2nd Pl 84; DE Cty Sci Fair 2nd Pl 84; Elizabethtown; Occuptn Thrpy.

SCHRAMM, ROBERT; Notre Dame HS; E Stroudsburg, PA; (Y); 1/38; School Musical; School Play; Nwsp Ed-Chief; Nwsp Rptr; Hon Roll; Opt Clb Awd; Amr Lgn Essy Cntst 84; Lw Dy Moot Crt Cmptn 86.

SCHRANN, LEANN; Sayre Area HS; Sayre, PA; (Y); 3/116; School Play; Pres Sr Cls; JV Var Bsktbl; Var L Trk; JV Var Vllybl; Bausch & Lomb Sci Awd; Cit Awd; DAR Awd; VP NHS; Sal; Elmina Coll Key Awd 85; Robert E Douglas Athltc Mem Awds 86; U S Army Rsrv Awds 86; Bloomsburg U; Sec Educ.

SCHRANTZ, SCOTT; Freedom HS; Bethlehem, PA; (Y); 59/426; Varsity Clb; VICA; Im Bsbl; Im Bsktbl; Vllybl; High Hon Roll; Prfct Atten Awd; PA Teen King 85; Teen Pres 86; 2nd Pl Dist UICA Weldng Cntst 86; Welding.

SCHRECENGAST, AMBER; Chief Logan HS; Lewistown, PA; (Y); Art Clb; Key Clb; Varsity Clb; Pres Frsh Cls; VP Stu Cncl; Var Cheerleading; L Trk; High Hon Roll; PA Govnrs Sch Of Art 86; Cnty & Dist Chorus & Special Choral Grps; PA ST; Art.

SCHRECENGOST, LISA J; Sto-Rox HS; Mc Kees Rocks, PA; (Y); 13/153; French Clb; Letterman Clb; Office Aide; Nwsp Ed-Chief; Yrbk Stf; Sec Frsh Cls; Sec Soph Cls; JV Var Cheerleading; Cit Awd; High Hon Roll; Pittsburgh Tech; French.

SCHRECONGOST, TINA; Lenape Vo Tech Schl; Freeport, PA; (Y); 10/265; Pres Computer Clb; Sec 4-H; FFA; German Clb; Pres SADD; Rptr VICA; Nwsp Stf; Yrbk Stf; Rep Soph Cls; Pres Jr Cls; Wstrn Regn VP VICA 86-87; Outstndng 4-H Awd 85; Natl VICA Conf ST Offcr 86; U Pittsburg; Phrmcy.

SCHREINER, ERIC; Bishop Kenrick HS; Norristown, PA; (Y); 57/300; Mathletes; Ftbl; Hon Roll; Prfct Atten Awd; Temple U; Civil/Cnstrctn Engr.

SCHREMP, DOUG; Radnor HS; Wayne, PA; (Y); Boy Scts; Band; Jazz Band; Cit Awd; High Hon Roll; Var Capt Swmmng; JV Trk; Engrng.

SCHREVELIUS, KARISA; Owen J Roberts HS; Chester Springs, PA; (S); 21/267; Band; Mrchg Band; School Musical; Rep Frsh Cls; Rep Jr Cls; Sec Stu Cncl; DAR Awd; Hon Roll; Trs NHS; Intl Reltns.

SCHRIVER, JIM; Selinsgrove Area HS; Selinsgrove, PA; (Y); 35/215; Trs Spanish Clb; Chorus; School Musical; School Play; Sr Cls; Var L Socr; Var Tennis; Church Yth Grp; Varsity Clb; Band.

SCHRIVER, KIMBERLY B; Peters Township HS; Mc Murray, PA; (Y); 34/230; Aud/Vis; Church Yth Grp; Cmnty Wkr; Exploring; Key Clb; Yrbk Ed-Chief; Yrbk Stf; High Hon Roll; Hon Roll; Hlth Care Adm.

SCHROCK, JOHN E; Somerset HS; Friedens, PA; (Y); 24/240; FCA; Math Clb; Concert Band; Jazz Band; Mrchg Band; Stage Crew; JV Ftbl; Var Capt Trk; JV Wrstlng; High Hon Roll; Schl Rcrds Track 86; Track & Field Coaches Awd 86; Pres Phy Fitness Awd 82-86; Messiah Coll; Engrng.

SCHROCK, MICHAEL; Somerset Area SR HS; Somerset, PA; (Y); German Clb; Math Clb; Trk; Hon Roll; NHS; Advncd Electrnc.

SCHROCK JR, ROBERT; Meyersdale Area HS; Garrett, PA; (Y); 10/83; Pres FFA; L Ftbl; NHS; FFA Scholar 86; Sheldon Bowman Mem Scholar 86; Frostburg ST; Acctng.

SCHROECK, MARY BETH; Saint Benedict Acad; Erie, PA; (Y); Church Yth Grp; Teachers Aide; Yrbk Stf; Var Tennis; NHS; Ntl Bus Hnr Scty 85-86; Lois B Hanlin Bus Schlrshp 85-86; Bus.

SCHROEDER, CHRISTINE; Downingtown HS; Exton, PA; (Y); 29/560; Intnl Clb; Ski Clb; Spanish Clb; Orch; Rep Stu Cncl; Fld Hcky; NHS; NEDT Awd; Church Yth Grp; GAA; Awd Schlrshp Ald Chem Co Grmny 84; Intrnl Stds.

SCHROEDER, DAVID M; Trinity HS; Carlisle, PA; (Y); 5/120; Spanish Clb; Yrbk Stf; Im Bsktbl; Capt Var Socr; Ntl Merit SF; Summer Sci Smnr At US Naval Acad 85; Engnrng.

SCHROEDER, THOMAS; Springford HS; Royersford, PA; (S); 9/258; Am Leg Boys St; Church Yth Grp; Var L Ftbl; Trk; Wt Lftg; High Hon Roll; NHS; Acadmclly 1st 9th Grd 84; Engl Wrtg Awd 85-86; Schlrshp PA Amer Legn Keystn Boys ST Cmp Stdy Govt 86; Genetc Engr.

SCHROETTNER, ANDREA; Nazareth Area SR HS; Nazareth, PA; (Y); Aud/Vis; Church Yth Grp; GAA; Key Clb; Library Aide; Yrbk Stf; High Hon Roll; Hon Roll; Phy Thrpst.

SCHROPE, ELIZABETH; Williams Valley JR SR HS; Williamstown, PA; (Y); 14/100; Aud/Vis; Girl Scts; Quiz Bowl; Chorus; Pres Jr Cls; JV Bsktbl; High Hon Roll; Hon Roll; NHS; Rotary Stu Of The Yr Pres Ftns Awd 86; Mary Margaret Nestor Fndtn Schlrshp 86; David Hollenbach 86; Geisinger Med Ctr Schl; Nrsng.

SCHROPP, MARYBETH; Bishop Mc Deritt HS; Harrisburg, PA; (S); 23/200; Church Yth Grp; French Clb; FBLA; Service Clb; Band; Yrbk Stf; Stat Bsbl; Stat Bsktbl; Bowling; Coach Actv; FBLA Mnthly Stu Awd 85; FBLA Rgnl Typng Awd 85; Villa Julie Coll; Prlgl.

SCHROTH, TRACI; Butler SR HS; Fenelton, PA; (Y); Computer Clb; German Clb; ROTC; Teachers Aide; Chorus; Church Choir; Nwsp Stf; Hon Roll; Jr NHS; Slippery Rock U; Psych.

SCHUBERT, AMY; Henderson HS; Westchester, PA; (S); 11/349; Church Choir; Fld Hcky; Lcrss; Sec French Hon Soc; Hon Roll; 1st Tm All-Leag Fld Hcky 84 & 85; Lib Arts.

SCHUBERT, DAVID L; Seneca Valley HS; Evans City, PA; (Y); 19/356; Boy Scts; Pres Exploring; ROTC; SADD; Thesps; Tennis; NHS; Am Leg Boys St; School Play; V-Rifle Tm Ltr/Wnr/Cap 85-86; Eagle Scout 84; JROTC Sup Cadet Awd 86; PA ST U; Nuclr Engrng.

SCHUBERT, HEIDI; Boyertown Area SR HS; Boyertown, PA; (Y); 156/472; Library Aide; Office Aide; Chorus; Variety Show; JV Cheerleading; Cit Awd; Hon Roll; Secretrl Fld.

SCHUBERT, PATRICIA; Villa Maria Acad; Downingtown, PA; (Y); 29/100; Church Yth Grp; Drama Clb; Hosp Aide; Ski Clb; Spanish Clb; School Play; Yrbk Rptr; Cheerleading; Tennis; Trk; Villanova U; Nrsng.

SCHUCKER, KATHY; Kutztown Area HS; Kempton, PA; (Y); 15/149; Church Yth Grp; Band; Chorus; Color Guard; Concert Band; Drill Tm; Flag Corp; Mrchg Band; High Hon Roll; NHS.

SCHUCKER, SCOTT A; Cedar Cliff HS; Camp Hill, PA; (Y); 25/249; Church Yth Grp; German Clb; Key Clb; Model UN; Ski Clb; SADD; School Play; Tennis; Vllybl; High Hon Roll; Ger Hnr Soc; Sci.

SCHUCOLSKY, SHARON; Peters Twp HS; Mc Murray, PA; (Y); Drill Tm; Yrbk Stf; Stu Cncl; Var L Swmmng; Pre-Law.

SCHUDA, STEPHEN J; Central Catholic HS; Pittsburgh, PA; (Y); Boy Scts; Computer Clb; Im Bsktbl; Im Ftbl; JV Var Vllybl; Hon Roll; John Corroll U; Bnkng.

SCHUELLER, JOHN C; Tulpehocken Area HS; Bernville, PA; (Y); 5/105; Church Yth Grp; Computer Clb; Band; Pep Band; Mgr(s); JV Socr; JV Tennis; Hon Roll; NHS; Tylephocken Schlr Awd 86; Berks Cty Smmr Enrchmnt Comp 85; Ag.

SCHUETTLER, MICHAEL; Nativity B V M HS; Pottsville, PA; (Y); Computer Clb; Spanish Clb; Lincoln Tech; Comp.

SCHUG, JEANNETTE; Charleroi HS; Charleroi, PA; (Y); 3/179; High Hon Roll; NHS; IN U PA; Acctg.

SCHUHL, CATHLEEN; Little Flower Catholic HS For Girls; Philadelphia, PA; (Y); 11/413; Cmnty Wkr; Office Aide; Nwsp Stf; Yrbk Rptr; Yrbk Stf; Off Soph Cls; Off Sr Cls; Stu Cncl; Capt Trk; Cit Awd; Cngrssnl Mdl Outstndng Schlrshp, Schl Invlvmnt, & Cvc Prd 86; Pres Acad Ftnss Awd 86; U Of Scranton; Phys Thrpy.

SCHULD, MICHELLE; Downington SR HS; Downingtown, PA; (Y); 102/563; Aud/Vis; Church Yth Grp; Cmnty Wkr; French Clb; Intnl Clb; Ed Yrbk Ed-Chief; Yrbk Stf; High Hon Roll; Hon Roll; Temple U; Cmmnctns.

SCHULER, JOSEPH; Bishop Egan HS; Levittown, PA; (Y); 17/225; VP Church Yth Grp; Spanish Clb; Yrbk Ed-Chief; Im Mgr Bsktbl; Var Lcrss; Im Mgr Vllybl; Hon Roll; NHS; Full Tuitn Schlrshp U Scrntn 86; A Marlyn Moyer Schlrshp 86; Scranton U; Accnting.

SCHULLER, SCOTT; United HS; New Florence, PA; (Y); 59/157; Church Yth Grp; CAP; Computer Clb; Chorus; Swing Chorus; Lit Mag; Ftbl; Mgr(s); Trk; Wrstlng; Engrng.

SCHULTE, GEORGIA; Burgettstown Area HS; Burgettstown, PA; (Y); 6/175; Ski Clb; Concert Band; Mrchg Band; Pep Band; Symp Band; High Hon Roll; Jr NHS; NHS; Cert Hnr 86; Diploma Merit 86; Robert Morris Acad Schlrshp 86; Robert Morris Coll; Bus Admin.

SCHULTE, JEAN; Midland HS; Midland, PA; (Y); 1/37; Latin Clb; Concert Band; Jazz Band; Trs Mrchg Band; Yrbk Stf; Rep Frsh Cls; Rep Soph Cls; Rep Jr Cls; Trs Stu Cncl; Mgr Bsktbl; Acad All Am Awd 86; Stu Cncl Acad Schlr Awd 86; Math Achvt Awds 83-85; Pre-Med.

SCHULTE, SANDY; Burgettstown Area HS; Burgettstown, PA; (Y); 10/175; Ski Clb; Concert Band; Mrchg Band; Pep Band; High Hon Roll; NHS; Cert Of Hnr 86; Diploma Of Merit 86; Robt Orris Acad Schlrshp 86; Robt Morris Col6; Bus Admin.

SCHULTHEIS, BETH; Central HS; Scranton, PA; (Y); Church Yth Grp; Church Choir; Orch; Hon Roll; Jr NHS; Early Chld Ed.

SCHULTHEIS, CHRISTINE; Kiski Area HS; Leechburg, PA; (Y); Debate Tm; Pres French Clb; Math Tm; Capt Spanish Clb; Mrchg Band; Stu Cncl; Var Trk; 4-H Awd; High Hon Roll; Acadmc Ltr 85-86; Poltcl Sci.

SCHULTHEIS, DARLENE; Mount Pleasant HS; Mt Pleasant, PA; (Y); Pres Church Yth Grp; Pep Clb; Chorus; High Hon Roll; Hon Roll.

SCHULTHEIS, REBECCA L; Gateway HS; Monroeville, PA; (Y); 7/465; Science Clb; Ed Lit Mag; Ntl Merit Ltr; Pres Schlr; Rotary Awd; St Schlr; Exploring; Math Tm; Band; Mrchg Band; Natl Soc Profsnl Engrs Auxlry Schlrshp 86; Westnghse Sci Tlnt Srch Hnr Grp 86; PA Music Ed ST Band; Lafayette Coll; Chem Engrng.

SCHULTZ, ANDREW; Salem Christian Schl; Zionsville, PA; (S); 1/10; Church Yth Grp; Nwsp Stf; Yrbk Stf; VP Stu Cncl; Capt Socr; High Hon Roll; Ntl Merit Ltr; Val; Distng Chrst HS Stu 85-86; Cert Of Merit SAT Scores 85; PA Coll Of Bible; Missions.

SCHULTZ, ANGELA; Exeter HS; Reading, PA; (Y); Cmnty Wkr; Drama Clb; Y-Teens; Concert Band; Flag Corp; School Musical; Stu Cncl; Fld Hcky; Leo Clb; Variety Show.

SCHULTZ, BILL; South Allegheny JR SR HS; Mckeesport, PA; (Y); 15/185; Church Yth Grp; Spanish Clb; Rep Soph Cls; Bsbl; Hon Roll; Ntl Merit Ltr; Sci Fair Wnnr 83-84; Music.

SCHULTZ, CHRISTIAN; General Mc Lane HS; Mc Kean, PA; (Y); 22/240; Am Leg Boys St; Letterman Clb; Spanish Clb; Chorus; Var L Bsktbl; Var L Ftbl; Var Capt Trk; Wt Lftg; NHS; Defns Awd 84; Dist Mdl Trk 86; Pre Med.

SCHULTZ, CHRISTINE; Plum SR HS; Pittsburgh, PA; (Y); 110/378; Boy Scts; Dance Clb; FHA; Office Aide; Chorus; Capt Flag Corp; Hon Roll; Elem Ed.

SCHULTZ JR, DAVID C; Nazareth Area HS; Nazareth, PA; (Y); 15/237; Key Clb; JV Bsbl; Var L Bsktbl; Var Ftbl; Im Golf; Im Wt Lftg; High Hon Roll; Hon Roll; NHS; Chem.

SCHULTZ, ELAINE M; Heritage Christian Acad; Berwick, PA; (S); Art Clb; Church Yth Grp; Computer Clb; FHA; Office Aide; OEA; Teachers Aide; Church Choir; School Play; Yrbk Stf; Scrptr Memrztn.

SCHULTZ, JENNIFER; Governor Mifflin HS; Shillington, PA; (Y); #98 In Class; Spanish Clb; Y-Teens; Fld Hcky; PA Schl Of Arts; Interior Dsgn.

SCHULTZ, JOYCE; Canon-Mc Millan SR HS; Eighty Four, PA; (Y); Cmnty Wkr; VP 4-H; FBLA; Office Aide; Political Wkr; Chorus; JV Trk; 4-H Awd; High Hon Roll; Hon Roll; Bradford; Bus.

SCHULTZ, KAREN; Spring Grove SR HS; Spring Grove, PA; (Y); 8/222; Ski Clb; Drill Tm; Mrchg Band; Orch; School Play; Stat Bsktbl; JV Vllybl; High Hon Roll; Hon Roll; NHS; Blackburn College; Spch.

SCHULTZ, KAREN L; Salisbury HS; Allentown, PA; (Y); 1/160; Debate Tm; Exploring; Model UN; High Hon Roll; NHS; Ntl Merit SF; PA Gvrns Schl For Arts Poetry; Ntl Gld Audtns Spr Rtng In Piano; Englsh.

SCHULTZ, KARLYN; Strong Vincent HS; Eire, PA; (Y); 20/164; Yrbk Stf; Sec Sr Cls; Capt Cheerleading; NHS; U Of Pittsburgh; Chld Psychlgy.

SCHULTZ, KENNETH; Freedom HS; Bethlehem, PA; (Y); 8/456; Chess Clb; VP JA; Capt Math Tm; Capt Scholastic Bowl; Science Clb; Rep Stu Cncl; Hon Roll; NHS; PA Governors Sci Schl 86; Eagle Scout 86; Engr.

SCHULTZ, LAURIE A; St Pius X HS; Red Hill, PA; (S); 4/161; VP Church Yth Grp; French Clb; FBLA; Nwsp Stf; Cheerleading; Tennis; Trk; High Hon Roll; NHS; Sci.

SCHULTZ, LYNAIA; Pennsbury HS; Levittown, PA; (Y); Intnl Clb; Nwsp Rptr; Rep Soph Cls; Bsktbl; JV Fld Hcky; JV Var Mgr(s); JV Var Timer; Hon Roll; Stu Of Month 84.

SCHULTZ, MICHAEL; Bishop Egan HS; Levittown, PA; (S); 6/243; Pres Church Yth Grp; Pres Sr Cls; Stu Cncl; Var L Ftbl; Var L Trk; NHS; Computer Clb; Wt Lftg; High Hon Roll; Schlr Athl Awd Ftbl 85-86; U S Stdnt Cncl Awd 85-86; U S Naval Academy; Elec Engrng.

SCHULTZ, SCOTT; Lake-Lehman HS; Shavertown, PA; (Y); 65/145; Letterman Clb; Ski Clb; JV Bsbl; Var Ftbl; Var Trk; Gettysburg Coll.

SCHULTZ, SHERRI; Seton-La-Salle HS; Pittsburgh, PA; (Y); 39/248; Church Yth Grp; Dance Clb; Stage Crew; Mat Maids; High Hon Roll; Tudor; Accntng Awd; Chairperson Big Sisters; Duguesne U; Accntng.

SCHULTZ, STEVEN; Lower Moreland HS; Huntingdon Valley, PA; (S); 68/214; FBLA; German Clb; Var Capt Tennis; Hon Roll; MVP Tnns Tm 85; 39th Pl Tennis Assoc; Accntng.

SCHULTZ, STEVEN; Saegertown HS; Springboro, PA; (Y); FFA; Varsity Clb; Pres Jr Cls; Pres Stu Cncl; Im Crs Cntry; Var L Ftbl; Im Wt Lftg; Var L Wrstlng; Hon Roll; NHS; Engrg.

SCHULTZ, SUSAN; Ambridge HS; Baden, PA; (Y); 4-H; French Clb; Pep Clb; Jr Cls; Hon Roll.

SCHULTZE, ROBERT; Penn Hills SR HS; Verona, PA; (S); 1/797; Church Yth Grp; Pres Exploring; Sec Trs German Clb; Ski Clb; Chorus; School Musical; NHS; NEDT Awd; Val; Provost Schlrshp; U Ptsbrgh; Doctor.

SCHULZ, LINDA; Cheltenham HS; Glenside, PA; (Y); 112/365; Church Yth Grp; Capt Color Guard; JV L Sftbl; Var L Swmmng; Suburban I Amer Div Brst Strk Champ & All Leag 2nd Tm Swmg Recog Of Commndtn 85-86; Phy Ed.

SCHULZ, STEVEN; Unionville HS; West Chester, PA; (Y); Church Yth Grp; Intnl Clb; Ski Clb; Acpl Chr; Chorus; Boy Scts; Madrigals; Camp Fr Inc; Bowling; Hon Roll; Chem.

SCHULZ, TRACY; Lakeview HS; Stoneboro, PA; (S); 2/120; AFS; Church Yth Grp; VP Exploring; Intnl Clb; Band; Chorus; Concert Band; Mrchg Band; Pep Band; School Play; Rotarian Yth Ldrshp Westminster Coll 85; Slippery Rock U; Accntg.

SCHUMACHER, LAUREN; Salisbury SR HS; Allentown, PA; (Y); 19/138; Church Yth Grp; Drama Clb; VP Key Clb; School Musical; Rep Stu Cncl; Var L Bsktbl; Var L Fld Hcky; Var JV Sftbl; High Hon Roll; Hon Roll; Engl.

SCHUMACHER, LISA; Bishop Hafey HS; Milnesville, PA; (Y); Exploring; 4-H; French Clb; Library Aide; Pep Clb; Teachers Aide; Y-Teens; Hon Roll; Accntng Awd 86.

SCHUMACHER, LISA; Frazier HS; Perrypolis, PA; (Y); GAA; Yrbk Stf; Sftbl; Prfct Atten Awd; Robert Morris; Med Tech.

SCHUMAKER, STEPHANIE; Hamburg Area JR SR HS; Hamburg, PA; (Y); 2/150; Sec Church Yth Grp; Rep German Clb; Yrbk Stf; Pres Jr Cls; Var Bsktbl; Var Fld Hcky; High Hon Roll; NHS; Natl Grmn Hnr Scty 85-86; Math.

SCHUMAN, TERESA; Bishop Mccort HS; Mesa, AZ; (Y); German Clb; Band; Color Guard; Orch; High Hon Roll; NHS; Mu Alp Tht; Arizona ST U; Bus.

SCHUMANN, DARCI; Pennsbury HS; Levittown, PA; (Y); German Clb; SADD; Yrbk Stf; Hnr Docmnt Dstngshd Prfrmnc Grmn 83-85; Amer Coll Appld Arts; Fshn Mrch.

SCHUMANN, JOHN; Minersville Area HS; Minersville, PA; (Y); Art Clb; VP Aud/Vis; Ski Clb; VICA; High Hon Roll; Penn ST U; Elec Engrng.

SCHUMANN, KRISTEN A; Manheim Township HS; South Woodstock, CT; (Y); Acpl Chr; Chorus; Church Choir; Concert Band; Mrchg Band; Orch; School Musical; Church Yth Grp; Swing Chorus; Symp Band; Yng Mscl Artsts Cmptn 83; LLMA Chrs Fstvl 86; Dstrct Chrs Fstvl 86.

SCHUPBACH, STEPHANIE; Peters Township HS; Mcmurray, PA; (Y); 11/245; Intnl Clb; NFL; Speech Tm; Teachers Aide; High Hon Roll; Hon Roll; Kiwanis Awd; NHS; Spanish NHS; U Of OK; Psych.

SCHUR, NEIL; Cheltenham HS; Elkins Pk, PA; (Y); 28/365; Capt Debate Tm; Drama Clb; JCL; SADD; School Musical; School Play; Ed Nwsp Stf; Pres Soph Cls; Sec Stu Cncl; Hon Roll; 4 Sevens Comm 85-86; Stdnt Forum 85-86; Law.

SCHUSTER, DARIA; West Scranton HS; Scranton, PA; (Y); 9/253; Capt Debate Tm; Pres Exploring; Letterman Clb; Spanish Clb; Speech Tm; Sec Thesps; Yrbk Stf; Stu Cncl; Var Capt Swmmng; High Hon Roll; Lns Clb Schlrshp 86; Penn ST; Bus Admin.

SCHUSTER, DAVE; Northwestern SR HS; Edinboro, PA; (Y); 13/169; Church Yth Grp; JA; Rep Jr Cls; Rep Sr Cls; Sec Stu Cncl; Capt Var Bsbl; Var Ftbl; Wt Lftg; Var Wrstlng; Hon Roll; 2nd All-Cnty Ftbll; Hnrbl Mntn All-Cnty Bsbll; Cmmnctns.

SCHUSTER, FRANK; W Scranton HS; Scranton, PA; (Y); Art Clb; Boys Clb Am; Camera Clb; Ski Clb; Yrbk Phtg; Wrstlng; Acctg.

SCHUSTER, JENNIFER; Ringgold HS; Monongahela, PA; (Y); Hon Roll; Fash Dsgnr.

SCHUTZ, SUSANNA; Nazareth Acad; Churchville, PA; (S); German Clb; Chorus; Orch; School Musical; Sec Soph Cls; Sec Jr Cls; Sec Sr Cls; Hon Roll; Sec NHS; 3rd Prz 3rd Yr Germn Amer Assn Tchrs Of German 83; Hnbl Mntn 4th Yr Germn AATG Tst 84; Villanova U; Intl Bus.

SCHWAB, BRENT; Manheim Township HS; Lancaster, PA; (Y); Chess Clb; Church Yth Grp; High Hon Roll; Hon Roll; MVP Chess Tm 83-86; Engrng.

SCHWAB, DAN; Susquehanna Twp HS; Harrisburg, PA; (Y); 6/187; Hst Key Clb; Capt Math Tm; Ski Clb; Varsity Clb; Yrbk Sprt Ed; Diving; Swmmng; Capt Tennis; NHS; Ntl Merit Ltr; Bus.

SCHWAB, GRETCHEN; Council Rock HS; Newtown, PA; (Y); 35/756; Church Yth Grp; German Clb; Band; Concert Band; Drm Mjr(t); Mrchg Band; Pep Band; School Musical; Symp Band; DAR Awd; Band Cnty, Dist, Regnl 86; Grove City Coll; Intl Bus.

SCHWAB, KIMBERLY; Oil City SR HS; Oil City, PA; (Y); 29/241; 4-H; Acpl Chr; Chorus; School Musical; Yrbk Stf; Hon Roll; Ntl Merit Ltr; Pres Schlr; Washington Coll; Psychlgy.

SCHWAB, SUSAN; Fort Cherry HS; Mc Donald, PA; (S); Drama Clb; FNA; Math Clb; Science Clb; Spanish Clb; Thesps; Varsity Clb; School Play; Sftbl; Hon Roll; Nrs.

SCHWAB, WILLIAM; Fort Le Boeuf HS; Waterford, PA; (Y); 10/170; Rep Stu Cncl; Var L Ftbl; Im Vllybl; Capt L Wrstlng; High Hon Roll; NHS; Prfct Atten Awd; Stu Cncl Acdmc Achvmnt Awd 84-86; Lawyer.

SCHWABENBAUER, SHEILA; North Clarion HS; Tylersburg, PA; (Y); Drama Clb; Mrchg Band; Bsktbl; Vllybl; Church Yth Grp; Spanish Clb; Color Guard; School Play; Yrbk Stf; Hon Roll.

SCHWANDT, CHRISTOPHER; Souderton Area SR HS; Harleysville, PA; (Y); Drama Clb; Intnl Clb; Band; Concert Band; Jazz Band; Mrchg Band; Orch; Pep Band; Stage Crew; Symp Band; Mechncl Archt Engr.

SCHWARE, JOEL; Central Catholic HS; Allentown, PA; (Y); 25/200; Math Clb; Math Tm; JV Bsbl; Ntl Merit Ltr; Penn ST U; Aero Engr.

SCHWARTZ, ADAM; Allen HS; Allentown, PA; (Y); Cmnty Wkr; Pres Key Clb; Trs Frsh Cls; Rep Stu Cncl; Var Socr; Hon Roll; Pol Sci.

SCHWARTZ, ADRIANE; St Maria Goretti HS; Philadelphia, PA; (Y); 107/426; Wedener U; Psych.

SCHWARTZ, JEFF; Boiling Springs HS; Boiling Spgs, PA; (Y); 1/120; Band; Jazz Band; Var L Ftbl; Var Trk; High Hon Roll; NHS; Ntl Merit SF; Engrng.

SCHWARTZ, JOHN; Hazleton HS; Mcadoo, PA; (Y); 37/373; Leo Clb; Sec Ski Clb; Stu Cncl; Bsbl; Ftbl; Elks Awd; NHS; Michael M Minor Schlstc Achvt Awd 86; Michael Ruggiero Cls 65 Awd 86; Temple U; Arch.

SCHWARTZ, KIMBERLY; John S Fine HS; Glenlyon, PA; (Y); 23/242; Key Clb; High Hon Roll; Luzerne Cnty CC; Dntl Hyg.

SCHWARTZ, LAURIE; Chapel Christian Acad; Pottstown, PA; (S); Library Aide; Pep Clb; Chorus; School Play; Yrbk Stf; Var Capt Cheerleading; Hon Roll; 2nd Pl Ntl Spch Cmptn 85; Liberty U; Tch Spch.

SCHWARTZ, LISA; Marple-Newtown SR HS; Broomall, PA; (Y); 14/360; Sec Temple Yth Grp; School Play; Ed Yrbk Stf; Rep Sr Cls; Stu Cncl; Var JV Vllybl; High Hon Roll; Hon Roll; VP Jr NHS; NHS; Soc Wmn Engrs Awd Merit 86; PYO Awd Merit Outstndng Svc 86; MN Adult Schl Awd Merit Svc 86; Cornell U; Mech Engrng.

SCHWARTZ, MARC; St John Neumann HS; Philadelphia, PA; (Y); 48/338; Dance Clb; FBLA; JA; Quiz Bowl; Radio Clb; Spanish Clb; VP Frsh Cls; Rep Soph Cls; Rep Jr Cls; Rep Sr Cls.

SCHWARTZ, RENEE; Southmoreland SR HS; Scottdale, PA; (Y); 20/218; Art Clb; CAP; Color Guard; Drill Tm; Stage Crew; Rep Sr Cls; Stu Cncl; Powder Puff Ftbl; Socr; Latin Clb; Civil Air Patrol Billy Mitchell Awd 86; Pres Acad Fit Awd 85-86; Stu Mnth Awd 85-86; IN U PA; Bio.

SCHWARTZ, SUSAN; Navitity B V M HS; New Philadelphia, PA; (Y); 7/98; Church Yth Grp; Sec Spanish Clb; Yrbk Stf; High Hon Roll; Hon Roll; NHS; Prfct Atten Awd; Hghst Achvt Wrld Cultures 85; Awd Cert PA JR Acad Sci 85; Excllnce Spn I 84; Hghst Achvt Hlth 86; Hlth/Rest Mgmt.

SCHWARTZ, SYDNEY ANNE; South Park HS; Pittsburgh, PA; (Y); Drama Clb; Ski Clb; Color Guard; Swmmng; High Hon Roll; Hon Roll; 3 Yr Ltr Vars Swmmng; Ltr Color Grd; Grove City Coll; Lit.

SCHWARTZ, THERESA; West Scranton HS; Scranton, PA; (Y); Office Aide; Keystone JC; Bus Adm.

SCHWARTZER, STACEY; Saint Huberts HS; Philadelphia, PA; (Y); 146/367; JA; Holy Family Coll; Accntng.

SCHWARZ, FRANCES; Hopewell HS; Aliquippa, PA; (Y); Hosp Aide; Latin Clb; Wrstlng; Hon Roll; Beaver County CC; Lgl Sec.

SCHWARZ, JANE; St Paul Cathedral HS; Pittsburgh, PA; (Y); Science Clb; Chorus; Nwsp Rptr; High Hon Roll; NHS; Prfct Atten Awd; Natl Hstry Day 2nd Pl Regnl 86; Natl Hstry Day ST Excllnt Ratg 86; Yrbk Layout Edtr.

SCHWARZBAUER, KRISTINA; Cedar Cliff HS; Camp Hill, PA; (Y); 155/272; Art Clb; German Clb; Yrbk Ed-Chief; Gym; Hon Roll; Schlstc Awds 86; Maryland Isnt; Art Hstry.

SCHWEIDLER, GLENN; Arch Bishop Wood For Boys; Warminster, PA; (Y); 136/282; Varsity Clb; Rep Soph Cls; Rep Jr Cls; JV Ftbl; Var L Trk; Hon Roll; La Salle; Pharmcy.

SCHWEINGRUBER, ERIC; Cedar Crest HS; Lebanon, PA; (Y); 1/325; Pep Clb; Band; Church Choir; Concert Band; Jazz Band; Mrchg Band; Orch; Pep Band; School Musical; Rep Frsh Cls; 1st Chair Cornet-Natl Band Assn & HS Hnrs Cncrt Band 86; All St Band 86; Music.

SCHWEISS, KATHERINE J; Sharpsville HS; Sharpsville, PA; (Y); Am Leg Aux Girls St; Yrbk Stf; Pres Frsh Cls; Pres Soph Cls; Pres Jr Cls; Pres Sr Cls; Stu Cncl; L Var Bsktbl; Dnfth Awd; Hon Roll; Bus.

SCHWEITZER, AMY; Central Cambria HS; Ebensburg, PA; (Y); 19/189; Church Yth Grp; Hosp Aide; Band; Concert Band; Jazz Band; Mrchg Band; Pep Band; High Hon Roll; Hon Roll; Nat Hnr Rll 85; IN U; Educ Excptnl Prsns.

SCHWEIZER, LISA; Ridley SR HS; Folsom, PA; (Y); 68/427; Church Yth Grp; FBLA; Chorus; Drill Tm; Flag Corp; Mrchg Band; Hon Roll; Ldrshp Awd Future Sec 86; FBLA ST Chapter 5th Pl 8l; Katherine Gibbs Bus Schl; Sec.

SCHWENK, ALLAN; Muncy HS; Muncy, PA; (Y); 1/75; Drama Clb; Math Tm; School Musical; Trs Jr Cls; Rep Stu Cncl; Bausch & Lomb Sci Awd; NHS; Ntl Merit Schol; Pres Schlr; Val; PA ST U; Pre-Med.

SCHWENK, DAVID A; Wyoming Valley West HS; Swoyersville, PA; (Y); Am Leg Boys St; Boy Scts; Cmnty Wkr; Exploring; Latin Clb; Orch; School Musical; School Play; Ftbl; Vllybl; Natl Latin Hnr Scty; Pre-Med.

SCHWENTKER, ANN R; Lower Dauphin SR HS; Hummelstown, PA; (Y); 5/218; Cmnty Wkr; Dance Clb; Chorus; Orch; School Musical; Ed Lit Mag; Rep Frsh Cls; Rep Soph Cls; Rep Jr Cls; Rep Sr Cls; Natl Cnsl Eng Tchrs Achvt Awd 85; PA Gov Schl Sci 85; Med.

SCHWERIN, ERIC; Cheltenham HS; Melrose Pk, PA; (Y); 30/360; JCL; Latin Clb; Temple Yth Grp; Band; Concert Band; Yrbk Ed-Chief; NEDT Awd; PJAS 1st Pl Rengl 2nd Pl ST 85; Law.

SCHWERIN, MARK; Moon SR HS; Corapolis, PA; (Y); JA; Band; Mrchg Band; Bsbl; Bsktbl; Crs Cntry; High Hon Roll; Hon Roll; NHS; Ntl Merit Ltr.

SCIALABBA, JOHN M; Penn Hills SR HS; Pittsburgh, PA; (Y); 142/762; Chess Clb; French Clb; JA; Tennis; High Hon Roll; Hon Roll; Jr NHS; Lamp Of Knowldg Awds 85-86; PA ST U; Elec Engr.

SCIANDRA, LOUIS; Pittston Area HS; Pittston, PA; (Y); Art Clb; Aud/Vis; Key Clb; Letterman Clb; Bsbl; L Bsktbl; High Hon Roll; Hon Roll; NHS; FNA; Wght Lftg Champ Of Schl 86.

SCIBELLI, CHRIS; Cedar Crest HS; Lebanon, PA; (Y); 3/305; German Clb; Pep Clb; JV Bsktbl; L Golf; Var Trk; High Hon Roll; NHS; Yth Schlrs Inst Lbnn Vlly Coll 86; Moleculr Bio.

SCIORTINO, CHRISTOPHER R; William Penn SR HS; York, PA; (Y); 11/303; JA; Bsbl; Bsktbl; Golf; Hon Roll; Jr NHS; NHS; Prfct Atten Awd; Pres Schlr; Dante Comm Ed Scholar 86; Shippensburg U; Acctg.

SCIPIONI, CATHY; Freedom HS; Bethlehem, PA; (Y); JA; Red Cross Aide; VICA; Mgr(s); Hon Roll; 2nd Pl Vo-Tech Schl In Style Shwcs 86; Csmtlgy.

SCIRANKO, MICHELE; Everett Area HS; Everett, PA; (S); 10/114; Sec Drama Clb; SADD; VP Band; Chorus; Drm Mjr(t); School Play; Trs Soph Cls; Hon Roll; NHS; Schlstc Awd 84-85; Acadmc All Amer Stdnt 84; Juniata Coll; Pre-Law.

SCIULLI, CARLA; Saint Paul Cathedral HS; Pittsburgh, PA; (S); 9/60; FBLA; Pep Clb; Chorus; Nwsp Stf; Yrbk Stf; Frsh Cls; Cheerleading; Sftbl; Hon Roll; Brdfrd Bus Schl; Exec Scrtry.

SCIULLO, NANCY; St Paul Cathedral HS; Pittsburgh, PA; (Y); 16/54; Camera Clb; Exploring; JA; Nwsp Stf; Yrbk Stf; Rep Stu Cncl; Bio.

SCLAN, SUSAN; Council Rock HS; Richboro, PA; (Y); Drama Clb; Hosp Aide; Temple Yth Grp; Chorus; Hon Roll; Penn ST U; Nrsng.

SCOBLICK, LOU ANN; Bishop O Hara HS; Archbald, PA; (S); French Clb; Latin Clb; Letterman Clb; Varsity Clb; Nwsp Sprt Ed; Capt L Bsktbl; Sftbl; High Hon Roll; Hon Roll; NHS.

SCOLNIK, CHRISSA J; Strath Haven HS; Wallingford, PA; (Y); Art Clb; Co-Capt Dance Clb; Chorus; Concert Band; Orch; School Musical; Nwsp Rptr; Rep Stu Cncl; Cheerleading; Hon Roll; Art Dir Of Actvties Cncl 85-87; Comm Art.

SCOPEL, DARREN; Ford City HS; Ford City, PA; (Y); Pres Church Yth Grp; Pres Key Clb; School Musical; VP Jr Cls; Stu Cncl; JV Bsktbl; Var Ftbl; Var Trk; High Hon Roll; NHS; Bio.

SCOPELLITI, DEBI; Scranton Central HS; Scranton, PA; (Y); Church Yth Grp; Dance Clb; Drama Clb; French Clb; NFL; Speech Tm; Yrbk Stf; Cheerleading; High Hon Roll; Jr NHS; Pre-Med.

SCORAN, CATHY; Portage Area HS; Portage, PA; (Y); Chorus; Drm Mjr(t); Stat Bsktbl; Trk; Slippery Rocks; Psych.

SCORSONE, JOSEPH; Cardinal O Hara HS; Broomall, PA; (Y); 16/772; Spanish Clb; Im Bsktbl; Prtcptd Natl Spnsh Cont 85-86.

SCORZA, LARI; Charleroi SR HS; Charleroi, PA; (Y); Science Clb; SADD; Varsity Clb; Yrbk Ed-Chief; Rep Jr Cls; Trs Stu Cncl; Swmmng; Bausch & Lomb Sci Awd; High Hon Roll; NHS; Dentstry.

SCOTT, DIONNE; Carlisle SR HS; Harker Hts, TX; (Y); 9/400; Church Yth Grp; French Clb; Varsity Clb; Lit Mag; Mgr(s); Trk; Vllybl; High Hon Roll; Hon Roll; NHS; Rcgntn Urban Leag Acad Achvt 86.

SCOTT, DONNA; Gettysburg SR HS; Gettysburg, PA; (Y); 39/283; Band; Concert Band; Mrchg Band; Capt Twrlr; Hon Roll; Prfct Atten Awd; Gov Energy Educ Awd 85.

SCOTT, DU JUAN; St John Neumann HS; Philadelphia, PA; (Y); 6/321; Spanish Clb; Chorus; Bsktbl; Trk; High Hon Roll; Hon Roll; Jr NHS; NHS; Spanish NHS; Rutgers U; Bus.

SCOTT, JENNY; Bentworth HS; Eighty Four, PA; (Y); 4-H; Varsity Clb; Mgr(s); Score Keeper; Sftbl; Hon Roll; CA ST COLL; Elem Ed.

SCOTT, KAREN; S P H S Motivation HS; Philadelphia, PA; (Y); Church Yth Grp; Hosp Aide; Library Aide; Teachers Aide; Church Choir; Variety Show; Hon Roll; Jr NHS; Prfct Atten Awd; Frnch I & II Awds 84 & 85; U Of PA Acad Achvt Schlrshps 84-86; Morgan ST U; Sclgy.

SCOTT, LAURENCE; Baldwin HS; Pittsburgh, PA; (Y); Speech Tm; Trk; Hon Roll; Mdsg.

SCOTT, LISA; Swissvale HS; N Braddock, PA; (Y); 53/175; Pres Church Yth Grp; Library Aide; Spanish Clb; Y-Teens; Acpl Chr; Pres Church Choir; Swing Chorus; High Hon Roll; Hon Roll; Walter Hart Schlrshp, A M Minney Schlrshp 86; PTSA Schlrshp 86; Clarion U Of PA; Psych.

SCOTT, MARCY; Pennsylvania Manor HS; Clymer, PA; (Y); 6/102; SADD; Chorus; School Musical; High Hon Roll; Hon Roll; NHS; IN U; RN.

SCOTT, MARY; Slippery Rock Area HS; Slippery Rock, PA; (Y); 6/200; Intnl Clb; Pep Clb; Spanish Clb; School Play; Yrbk Bus Mgr; Yrbk Stf; Rep Stu Cncl; Var Capt Stu Cncl; Var Capt Cheerleading; High Hon Roll; 1st Womens Grnd Champ Red Belt Div 85-86; Grnd Champ Chrldng 85-86; Cert Instrctr Trainee Tackwondo 86; Pre Med.

SCOTT, MICHELLE; Chester HS; Chester, PA; (Y); Spanish Clb; Hon Roll; Teachers Aide; School Musical; Fld Hcky; Outstndng Stdnt Yr 86; Stdnt Mnth Awd 86; Spnsh Awd 85-86; Widener U; RN.

SCOTT, REBECCA; Cambria Heights HS; Ebensburg, PA; (Y); 14/189; Library Aide; Q&S; Teachers Aide; Band; Concert Band; Jazz Band; Mrchg Band; Nwsp Bus Mgr; Nwsp Stf; High Hon Roll; Jr Ltr March/ Cncrt Band; Sr Jackett Mrch/Cncrt Band; Indiana U PA; Chldhd Educ.

SCOTT, RICHARD; Southmoreland HS; Scottdale, PA; (Y); 2/213; Math Clb; Ski Clb; Concert Band; Jazz Band; Mrchg Band; Stu Cncl; Var Tennis; French Hon Soc; NHS; Sal; Stu Of The Mnth Awd; Penn State U; Elec Engrng.

SCOTT, SHARON; Little Flower H S For Girls; Philadelphia, PA; (Y); 35/398; Exploring; German Clb; Office Aide; Service Clb; Drill Tm; Sec Stu Cncl; Var Cheerleading; Hon Roll; Stu Ldrshp Awd 85-86; Nrsng Schl; Nrsng.

SCOTT, SUSAN; Mechanicsburg Area SR HS; Mechanicsburg, PA; (Y); 36/311; Band; Chorus; Church Choir; Concert Band; Mrchg Band; Orch; Symp Band; High Hon Roll; Hon Roll; Prfct Atten Awd; Communictn Disordrs.

SCOTT, WILLIAM; Juniata HS; Mifflintohn, PA; (Y); Church Yth Grp; Band; Jazz Band; Mrchg Band; Orch; School Musical; Bsbl; Bsktbl; Hon Roll; Prfct Atten Awd; PA ST U.

SCOTTI, STACEY; Bensalem HS; Bensalem, PA; (Y); Rep Frsh Cls; Trs Soph Cls; Var JV Cheerleading; Stat Ftbl; Mgr(s); Mat Maids; Var Socr; Stat Wrstlng; High Hon Roll; Hon Roll; Vet.

SCRABIS, LYNN; Sto-Rox SR HS; Mc Kees Rocks, PA; (Y); #1 In Class; Office Aide; Chorus; Nwsp Rptr; Nwsp Stf; Var JV Cheerleading; Hon Roll; NEDT Awd; Jrnlsm.

SCRAFFORD, BRETT; Troy Area HS; Columbia Cross Rd, PA; (Y); Church Yth Grp; Band; Chorus; Church Choir; Concert Band; Mrchg Band; Swing Chorus; Variety Show; Nwsp Rptr; Nwsp Stf; Dist Chorus 86; Mansfield U; Music.

SCRIBNER, ERICA; Iroquois HS; Erie, PA; (Y); 27/140; Art Clb; Model UN; Sec Varsity Clb; Concert Band; Pep Band; Bsktbl; Cheerleading; Sftbl; Vllybl; Brk Schl Asst Rcrd Bsktbl 85-86; All Cnty 1st Tm Chc 85-86.

SCRIPPS, MARK; Burrell HS; Lower Burrell, PA; (Y); French Clb; JA; Spanish Clb; Socr; L Capt Wrstlng; High Hon Roll; Hon Roll; Jr NHS; NHS; VFW Awd; Pre-Med.

SCRUTCHINS, JOAN; Hopewell SR HS; Aliquippa, PA; (S); 17/260; Church Yth Grp; Exploring; German Clb; Latin Clb; Band; Church Choir; Concert Band; Rep Frsh Cls; JV Var Cheerleading; High Hon Roll; Pre Med.

SCRUTON, SHARI; Hempfield HS; Lancaster, PA; (Y); English Clb; Hosp Aide; Sec Varsity Clb; Nwsp Stf; Rep Stu Cncl; JV Bsktbl; L Crs Cntry; JV Fld Hcky; L Trk; Hon Roll; Engr.

SCULL, STEVEN; Reading SR HS; Reading, PA; (Y); Yrbk Stf; Var Bsbl; Var Bsktbl; Merit Roll 84-86; Student Athlete Awd 83-84; Printing.

SCULLI, MONICA L; Cardinal O Hara HS; Springfield, PA; (Y); 28/772; Cmnty Wkr; French Clb; Hosp Aide; Lit Mag; Hon Roll; NHS; H S Schltc Awd-Frnch IV 86; Ntl Frnch Cntst Cert Of Merit 86; Prncpls Awd-Acadmc Exclnc 85 & 86.

SCULLIN, MEAGHEN; Kennedy Christian HS; Adamsville, PA; (Y); 39/ 98; Art Clb; Church Yth Grp; Pep Clb; Spanish Clb; Var Capt Bsktbl; Vllybl; Pre-Med.

SCULLY, MICHAEL; Penn Hills HS; Pittsburgh, PA; (Y); Boy Scts; Church Yth Grp; Letterman Clb; Ski Clb; Spanish Clb; Varsity Clb; Ice Hcky; Hon Roll; Genetics.

SCULLY, MICHAEL; South Philadelphia HS; Philadelphia, PA; (Y); Acpl Chr; Band; Concert Band; Orch; School Play; Stage Crew; Stu Cncl; Bsbl; Crs Cntry; Trk; Awd Band & Orch 82-84; Art Awd 83-84; Pfct Atten 81-82; Clarion; Art.

SCULLY, SUZANNE; Warren Area HS; Warren, PA; (Y); Church Yth Grp; French Clb; Hosp Aide; Chorus; Color Guard; Var Swmmng; Stat Trk; High Hon Roll; Hon Roll; Jr NHS; Silver B Citznshp Awd 84; La Salle U; Educ.

SCULLY, TRACI; Skikellamy HS; Sunbury, PA; (Y); 15/315; Debate Tm; NFL; Speech Tm; NHS; Sentate Of PA Proclmntn Of Cngrdltns For Wnng States-Lincoln Douglas Dbt; Susquehanna U; Elem Ed.

SCURRY, BRENDA; Franklin HS; Franklin, PA; (Y); 57/242; Church Yth Grp; GAA; JV Bsktbl; L Sftbl; L Swmmng; JV Trk; Hon Roll; Brd Schl Dir Awd 84-85; Flagler U; Cmmnctns.

SCUTCHALL, VANESSA; Northern Bedford County HS; Hopewell, PA; (Y); Pres VP Church Yth Grp; FBLA; Pres VP FBLA; Hosp Aide; Math Clb; Math Tm; Pep Clb; SADD; Varsity Clb; Band; REA Rep To Washington DC Yth Tour 86; Sfall Foliage Pgnt 85; JR Class Escort 86; Phy Thrpy.

SEABOLD, LYNETTE; Milton Area SR HS; Milton, PA; (Y); 106/214; Art Clb; 4-H; Sec FHA; Hosp Aide; Latin Clb; Library Aide; Yrbk Stf; Trk; Sml Drfs Fmly Fnd Schlrshp 86; Nrsng Hm Vlntr Awd Ovr 500 Hrs 84; Carlow Coll; Nrs.

SEABURN, ROBIN; Lincoln HS; Wampum, PA; (Y); 55/162; Drama Clb; Girl Scts; Key Clb; Y-Teens; Chorus; High Hon Roll; Hon Roll; Nrsng.

SEAKS, TIM; Dover Area HS; Dover, PA; (Y); Chess Clb; Church Yth Grp; FCA; JA; Chorus; Church Choir; Sftbl; Hon Roll; Sftbl MVP-NRTHRN Subrbn Leag 84.

SEAMAN, DANIEL; East Juniata HS; Richfield, PA; (Y); 12/86; Boy Scts; Concert Band; Mrchg Band; Trs Soph Cls; Trs Jr Cls; Var L Socr; Var L Trk; God Cntry Awd; Hon Roll; Modern Music Masters 84-86; Order Of Arrow 84-86; Compu Elec.

SEAMAN, DANIEL; Newport HS; Newport, PA; (S); VP Church Yth Grp; Quiz Bowl; Chorus; Church Choir; School Musical; School Play; Swing Chorus; Stu Cncl; JV Bsktbl; High Hon Roll; Pltcl Sci.

SEAMAN, DAVID; Newport HS; Newport, PA; (S); 3/100; Church Yth Grp; Quiz Bowl; Chorus; Church Choir; School Musical; School Play; Swing Chorus; Rep Stu Cncl; JV Bsktbl; NHS; Mod Music Masters 84; Law.

SEAMAN, LESLI; Gettysburg SR HS; Gettysburg, PA; (Y); 23/248; Thesps; L Band; Pres VP Chorus; Concert Band; Jazz Band; Mrchg Band; Hon Roll; NHS; AFS; N Louise Ramer Future Tchr Scholar 86; Millersville U; Elem Ed.

SEAMAN, PETE; Liberty HS; Bethlehem, PA; (Y); 131/475; Church Yth Grp; Y-Teens; Band; Concert Band; Mrchg Band; Nwsp Stf; Bsbl; Var Golf; JV Wrstlng; Hon Roll; Cmmnctns.

SEANOR, JENNIFER; Riverview HS; Verona, PA; (Y); French Clb; Office Aide; Co-Capt Color Guard; Concert Band; Yrbk Stf; Jr Cls; Sr Cls; Stat Ftbl; High Hon Roll; Hon Roll; Gov Energy Awd 83.

SEARCY, CATHY; Council Rock HS; Newtown, PA; (Y); Band; Chorus; Jazz Band; Mrchg Band; Orch; Symp Band; Hon Roll; NHS; Simon Ford Music Schlrshp 86; Cnty, Dist & Reg Band 84-86; Cnty & Dist Orchstra 85-86; Temple U; Music.

SEARLE, NICOLA; Unionville HS; West Chester, PA; (Y); 81/300; Church Yth Grp; Girl Scts; Millersville U; Elmtry Ed.

SEARLS, COLEEN; Meadville SR HS; Meadville, PA; (Y); 31/300; Church Yth Grp; Pres Hosp Aide; Spanish Clb; Speech Tm; Rep Jr Cls; Stat Sftbl; High Hon Roll; Hon Roll; 2nd Pl Natl Hstry Day Dist Cont 85; Natl Coke Bowling Tourn Dist Qualifier 86; Phy Thrpst.

SEAVER, ROBIN; West Allegheny HS; Clinton, PA; (Y); 50/150; Church Yth Grp; FBLA; JA; Spanish Clb; Powder Puff Ftbl; Hon Roll; SHASDA Awd 86.

SEAVEY, VALERIE; Archbishop Prendergast HS; Collingdale, PA; (Y); 137/361; Office Aide; Spanish Clb; School Musical; Im Bowling; JV Gym; Prfct Atten Awd.

SEBASTIAN, MYRA A; W Phila Univ City HS; Philadelphia, PA; (Y); 8/310; Office Aide; Teachers Aide; Nwsp Stf; Badmtn; Trk; Vllybl; Hon Roll; NHS; White Williams Schlrs 83-86; Old Dominion U; Nrsng.

SEBASTIANI, CARLOS; Scranton Prep; Jessup, PA; (Y); 55/192; Cmnty Wkr; Im Bsbl; Im Bsktbl; Var L Trk; High Hon Roll; Hon Roll; Vet Sci.

SEBASTINELLI, RONNIE; Valley View JR SR HS; Jessup, PA; (Y); 50/ 205; Church Yth Grp; Cmnty Wkr; Pep Clb; Spanish Clb; Yrbk Stf; Var Ftbl; Var Trk; Var Wt Lftg; Ftbl Capt 83; Trck Capt 84; Phys Ther.

SEBELIN, DEBBIE; Jim Thorpe SR HS; Jim Thorpe, PA; (S); 21/101; Nwsp Rptr; Yrbk Ed-Chief; Stu Cncl; Bsktbl; Fld Hcky; Sftbl; Vllybl; Hon Roll; NHS; Vllybl MVP 84; Rotry Intl; Cedar Crest Coll.

SEBES, PAMELA; Ringgold HS; Finleyville, PA; (Y); Trs Band; Concert Band; Mrchg Band; Nwsp Rptr; Nwsp Stf; Rep Soph Cls; Rep Jr Cls; Hon Roll; Girl Scts; Library Aide; Christy Mc Aulif Essay ST Liberty 86; Odd Fellows Essay Cntst 86; Flrst.

SECHLER, CRAIG; Cheif Logan HS; Lewistown, PA; (Y); 27/194; Spanish Clb; Varsity Clb; Variety Show; Ed Yrbk Stf; Stu Cncl; Var Ftbl; Var Trk; Var Wt Lftg; High Hon Roll; Hon Roll; Stdnt Mnth 85; Acadmc Ltr 84; Bio.

SECHLER, SCOTT; Rockwood Area HS; Rockwood, PA; (Y); Spanish Clb; Chorus; Variety Show; Var L Bsbl; Var L Bsktbl; Var L Golf; Hon Roll; Boys SR Hi Phys Fitns Awd 84-86; Bus Mngmnt.

SECOR, ANNA; State College Area SR HS; State College, PA; (Y); Intnl Clb; Model UN; Nwsp Ed-Chief; Yrbk Ed-Chief; Ed Lit Mag; French Hon Soc; High Hon Roll; Kiwanis Awd; Ntl Merit SF; PA Govs Schl For Arts 85; Oberlin Coll; Creatv Wrtg.

SECREST, TROY; Mount Union Area HS; Shirleysburg, PA; (Y); Frsh Cls; Church Yth Grp; Jr Cls; Ftbl; Trk; Wrstlng; Capts Ldrshp Awd Wrstlng 85-86.

SECRISKEY, KATHY; Forest Hills SR HS; Sidman, PA; (Y); Pep Clb; Band; Chorus; Concert Band; Mrchg Band; Hon Roll.

SEDDON, CHERYL; Lock Haven HS; Castanea, PA; (Y); German Clb; Nwsp Stf; Hm Ecnmcs.

SEDIVA, KAREN; Marian Catholic HS; Summit Hill, PA; (S); 22/123; Church Yth Grp; Exploring; Ski Clb; Spanish Clb; School Play; Yrbk Stf; Hon Roll; NHS; Spanish NHS; Nrsng.

SEDLIAK, JUDE; Roman Catholic HS; Philadelphia, PA; (S); 1/150; Computer Clb; High Hon Roll; Hon Roll; NHS; Prfct Atten Awd; Thlgy, Engl, Latin, Wrld Cltr & Sci Awds 83-84; Bio, Thlgy, Wrld Cltr Awds 84-85; U Of PA; Bus.

SEDOR, STEPHANIE; Bishop Carroll HS; Revloc, PA; (S); 4/103; GAA; PAVAS; Ski Clb; Spanish Clb; Trs Frsh Cls; Var Capt Cheerleading; L Trk; Hon Roll; NHS; Radlgy.

SEDOWSKY, CHRISTINE; Perkiomen Valley HS; Collegeville, PA; (Y); Office Aide; Sec SADD; Yrbk Stf; Rep Jr Cls; Rep Stu Cncl; Cheerleading; Hon Roll; Art Awd 85-86; Natl Merit Scholar 83-84; Pre-Med.

SEEBACHER, BRIAN; Gateway SR HS; Monroeville, PA; (Y); 129/348; JV Ftbl; JV Trk; JV Vllybl; Capt Wt Lftg; 3rd Bdybldng Chmpshp 86.

SEEDS, MEGAN; Cardinal O Hava HS; Broomall, PA; (Y); 25/775; VP Church Yth Grp; Office Aide; Chorus; Church Choir; School Musical; Stage Crew; Yrbk Ed-Chief; Hon Roll; NHS; 2nd Plc Math DE Vlly Sci Fr 85-86.

SEELEY, BRENDA; Lake-Lehman HS; Dallas, PA; (Y); Capt Pep Clb; SADD; Capt Cheerleading; Stat Mgr(s); Capt Pom Pon; Stat Score Keeper; Stat Trk; Hon Roll; Jr NHS; Phy Thrpy.

SEELEY, BRENDA; Spring-Ford SR HS; Royersford, PA; (Y); 56/263; Hosp Aide; Spanish Clb; Mrchg Band; Yrbk Phtg; Stu Cncl; Mgr Bsktbl; Trk; Writer Of Yr Engl Class 84-86; US Navy; Comm.

SEELEY, TIMOTHY; Trinity HS; Mechanicsburg, PA; (Y); Boy Scts; Drama Clb; School Play; Rep Frsh Cls; Rep Soph Cls; Stu Cncl; JV Im Bsktbl; Var Capt Socr; Var Trk; Im Vllybl; Cmnctns.

SEEM, ALAN; Riverview HS; Oakmont, PA; (Y); 1/120; Boy Scts; Varsity Clb; VP Band; Concert Band; Jazz Band; Mrchg Band; Stu Cncl; Var Bsktbl; Var Capt Golf; High Hon Roll.

SEES III, JOSEPH; Danville Area HS; Danville, PA; (Y); 23/161; Ski Clb; Var Ftbl; CAP; Var Trk; Elks Awd; Hon Roll; Valerie Walton Woods Mem Schlrshp 86; Burknell U; Comp Sci.

SEES, NEDD RANDALL; Danville Area HS; Danville, PA; (Y); Mrchg Band; Church Yth Grp; Concert Band; Jazz Band; Var L Bowling; Var L Socr; Var L Trk; Hon Roll; Comp Prog.

SEESE, MICHAEL; Brownsville Area HS; Brownsville, PA; (Y); CA U Of PA; Electrcl Engr.

SEESE, SIOBHAN; Gwynedd Mercy Acad; Huntingdon Vly, PA; (Y); Cmnty Wkr; GAA; Varsity Clb; Yrbk Stf; Fld Hcky; Lcrss; Tennis; Villanova U; Accntng.

SEESE, TAMMY; Chestnut Ridge HS; New Paris, PA; (S); 11/107; Pres 4-H; Speech Tm; Teachers Aide; Chorus; Nwsp Rptr; Nwsp Stf; Off Jr Cls; Bsktbl; NHS; Rural Elec Yth Tour WA 85; PA Farmers Assn Yth Tour 85; PA Assn Farmers Coop Yth Learn 84; Conemaugh Vly Schl; Nrsng.

SEESHOLTZ, KIMBERLY; Bishop Mc Cort HS; Johnstown, PA; (Y); 6/ 133; German Clb; Girl Scts; Math Clb; Spanish Clb; Concert Band; Mrchg Band; Orch; High Hon Roll; NHS; Spanish NHS; Outstndng Stud Awd For Hnrs Spnsh II 86; U Of Pittsburgh; Elem Ed.

SEESHOLTZ, WENDY; Berwick Area SR HS; Berwick, PA; (Y); 4-H; Chorus; Cheerleading; Trk; 4-H Awd; Equine Mgmt.

SEGAL, STEPHANIE; Pennsbury HS; Yardley, PA; (Y); Church Yth Grp; Spanish Clb; School Play; Nwsp Rptr; Yrbk Stf; Swmmng; High Hon Roll; NHS; VP Of Frgn Lang Clb 86-87; Rock Crusher Awd 86; St Fnlst In Bloomsburg Lang Compttn 84-85; Lang.

SEGAL, SUZANNE; Ft Le Boeuf HS; Erie, PA; (Y); 2/184; Debate Tm; French Clb; Model UN; Variety Show; Rep Sr Cls; Im Gym; High Hon Roll; NHS; Prfct Atten Awd; Sal; Stu Cncl Schlrshp; Lloyd Veit Schlrshp; Outstndng French Stu Awd; Penn ST Behrend.

SEGAL, TARA A; Abington SR HS; Huntingdon Vly, PA; (Y); PAVAS; Service Clb; Temple Yth Grp; School Musical; Rep Stu Cncl; Swmmng; Natl Acad Of Arts-Schlrshp In Dance Smmr 85; Bucks Cnty Dance Co 82-86; NE Rgnl Ballet Assoc; NUY Tisch Schl Of Arts; Dncr.

SEGAL, TEDDI A; Springside Schl; Philadelphia, PA; (Y); Dance Clb; Drama Clb; Acpl Chr; Chorus; Jazz Band; School Musical; School Play; Nwsp Stf; JV Vllybl; Hon Roll; Engl Hnrs; NYU; Music.

SEGAN, SCOTT; Nazareth Area SR HS; Nazareth, PA; (Y); Computer Clb; VICA; High Hon Roll; Hon Roll; Outstndng Sr Of Yr Awd In Elec Tech 86; Elec Tech.

SEGER, TAMMY; Curwensville HS; Grampian, PA; (Y); DECA; Hosp Aide; Ski Clb; Chorus; Stage Crew; Nwsp Stf; Frsh Cls; Soph Cls; Jr Cls; Vllybl; Business.

SEGESSENMAN, JENNIFER; Biglerville HS; Arendtsville, PA; (Y); 10/83; Art Clb; Church Yth Grp; Band; Mrchg Band; Pep Band; Yrbk Stf; JV Bsktbl; High Hon Roll; NHS; Ntl Sojourners Ltry Awd 86; Chrprctr.

SEGIN, ROSALIE; Belle Vernon Area HS; Belle Vernon, PA; (Y); Band; Hon Roll; CA ST U; Education.

SEGLETES, PATRICIA; Archbishop Kennedy HS; Philadephia, PA; (Y); Girl Scts; Hon Roll; Mktng.

SEGUIN, LINDA; State College Area SR HS; State College, PA; (Y); Art Clb; Library Aide; Radio Clb; Concert Band; Mrchg Band; Symp Band; Faculty Schlr Awd 86; PA ST U.

SEGUINOT, JUAN; Mastbaum Jules Avts HS; Philadelphia, PA; (Y); Church Yth Grp; DECA; Latin Clb; Band; School Musical; JV Bsktbl; Cit Awd; Hon Roll; Temple U Philadelphia; Cptr Sci.

SEIBEL, DAVID J; Lewistown Area HS; Lewistown, PA; (Y); Pres Church Yth Grp; FCA; Letterman Clb; Varsity Clb; Concert Band; School Musical; JV Bsktbl; Var Ftbl; Var Golf; Var Trk; MVP Trk 86; Cedarville Coll.

SEIBERT, BETH; Cedar Crest HS; Lebanon, PA; (Y); French Clb; Latin Clb; Pep Clb; Band; Church Choir; Concert Band; Orch; Cheerleading; Diving; Socr; Dntst.

SEIBERT, CHRISTIE; Peters Township HS; Library, PA; (Y); SADD; Varsity Clb; Capt Drill Tm; Nwsp Stf; Lit Mag; VP Soph Cls; Pres Jr Cls; Stu Cncl; L Trk; Spanish NHS; WVU Jrnlsm Cntst Fnlst Sprts Wrtg 86; Suprstr Drll Tm Fnlst Suprstr Grl 85; Peters Twnshp Drll Tm 84; Cmmnctns.

SEIBERT, DANIEL L; Mountain View Christian Schl; Elizabethtown, PA; (S); 1/9; Chorus; Pres Jr Cls; Pres Sr Cls; Var L Bsktbl; Var Capt Socr; High Hon Roll; NHS; Val; Bob Jones U; Acctng.

SEIBERT, MICHELLE; Central Dauphin HS; Harrisburg, PA; (Y); 60/ 386; Chorus; Stu Cncl; Stat Swmmng; Im Vllybl; Hon Roll; Comm.

SEID, ALAN; Churchill HS; Pittsburg, PA; (Y); 29/187; Exploring; Service Clb; Ski Clb; Band; Concert Band; Mrchg Band; Orch; Rep Stu Cncl; High Hon Roll; Hon Roll; PA ST; Elect Engr.

SEIDA, SHARON; Bishop Hoban HS; Wilkes-Barre, PA; (Y); Computer Clb; FBLA; Math Clb; Stage Crew; Im Bowling; Im Tennis; Im Vllybl; High Hon Roll; Mu Alp Tht; NHS; Mitrani Schlrshp 86; Bloomsburg U; Cmptr Sci.

SEIDEL, HENRY; Hamburg Area HS; Lenhartsville, PA; (Y); 10/152; Pres 4-H; Pres FFA; SADD; Var L Bsbl; Var L Bowling; 4-H Awd; High Hon Roll; Hon Roll; Pres NHS; Natl Grange Yth Rep Awd Wnnr 86; Penn ST U; Ag Engrng.

SEIDERS, DANA; Mc Connelsburg HS; Mc Connellsburg, PA; (Y); 2/80; English Clb; Varsity Clb; Chorus; School Musical; School Play; Capt Gym; High Hon Roll; NHS; Sal; Nwsp Stf; Pres Acad Ftnss Awd 86; Pharm.

SEIGER, GEORGE; Bensalem HS; Bensalem, PA; (Y); JV Var Socr.

SEIGHMAN, ROXANN; Ringgold HS; Monongahela, PA; (Y); Chorus; Hon Roll.

SEILER, ANGELE; Pennsbury HS; Morrisville, PA; (Y); Cmnty Wkr; Yrbk Stf; Bausch & Lomb Sci Awd; NHS; Intnl Clb; Hon Roll; IN U Of PA Physics Testing Comptn; Pharm.

SEILER, DEANNA; Bishop Guilfoyle HS; Altoona, PA; (S); 41/149; Hosp Aide; Spanish Clb; Nrsng.

SEILUS, CHRIS; Upper Darby HS; Drexel Hill, PA; (Y); Hosp Aide; Office Aide; Stat Bsktbl; Mgr(s); Hon Roll; Temple; Criminal Law.

SEIPPELE, ANNE; St Benedict Acad; Erie, PA; (Y); #19 In Class; Pep Clb; Stage Crew; Variety Show; Rep Stu Cncl; Capt Cheerleading; Var JV Sftbl; Hon Roll; NHS; Crmnl Justc.

SEISCIO, JILL; Pottsgrove HS; Pottstown, PA; (Y); #3 In Class; Debate Tm; German Clb; Latin Clb; Pep Clb; Science Clb; Ski Clb; Varsity Clb; School Musical; School Play; Yrbk Stf; U Of PA.

SEITZ, RENEE; Mary Fuller Frazier HS; Perryopolis, PA; (Y); Ski Clb; Spanish Clb; Mrchg Band; Nwsp Rptr; Stat Bsktbl; Var Cheerleading; Spanish NHS; WVU.

SEJVAR, JIM; Franklin Regional HS; Murrysville, PA; (Y); AFS; JA; Band; Mrchg Band; JV Crs Cntry; Var L Swmmng; High Hon Roll; NHS; Pre-Med.

SEKEL, CHRISTINE M; Meadville Area SR HS; Meadville, PA; (Y); Church Yth Grp; Spanish Clb; Church Choir; Orch; Hon Roll; Wolves Clb Schlrshp 86; Ruby Mrsh Edred Schlrshp 86; Duquesne U; Crprt Law.

SEKELIK, DONALD; Chartiers Valley HS; Carnegie, PA; (Y); Church Yth Grp; JV Bsbl; Pittsburgh; Engr.

SEKELSKY, STEPHEN; Norwin HS; Westmoreland City, PA; (Y); 6/550; Computer Clb; German Clb; Math Clb; High Hon Roll; Lion Awd; NHS; Sci Outstndng Stu Awd 83; Hist Olympd 3rd Pl 85; 1st Comptr Prog Cntst 85-86; 2nd Comptr Progmg Cnsts; Rensselaer Polytech; Elec Engrg.

SEKERA, TAMMY; Riverview HS; Verona, PA; (Y); Office Aide; Band; Capt Color Guard; Concert Band; Mrchg Band; Yrbk Stf; Rep Jr Cls; Powder Puff Ftbl; High Hon Roll; NEDT Awd; ASETS Prog Forbes Rd E AVTS 86; Robert Morris; Mrktng.

SEKERAK, RENEE; Brownsville Area HS; Merrittstown, PA; (S); 7/200; French Clb; Mathletes; Trs Ski Clb; Concert Band; Drm Mjr(t); Jazz Band; Mrchg Band; Yrbk Bus Mgr; Yrbk Stf; Off Frsh Cls; Stu Of Month Rotary Clb 86; U Of MD; Archt.

SEKOL, LAUREL; Crestwood HS; Mountaintop, PA; (Y); 41/223; Ski Clb; Drm Mjr(t); Nwsp Phtg; Trs Frsh Cls; Var Twrlr; High Hon Roll; Hon Roll; NEDT Awd; Chem.

SEKULA II, FRANK J; Central Catholic HS; Newkensington, PA; (Y); 21/268; High Hon Roll; NHS; Latin Clb; Pres Frsh Cls; Pres Soph Cls; VP Jr Cls; Rep Stu Cncl; Swmmng; Natl Latn Hnr Socty 84-86; Max Adlscnt Potntls 84-86; Acctg.

SELBY, JULIE; Freedom HS; Easton, PA; (Y); 96/445; Church Yth Grp; Drama Clb; German Clb; Girl Scts; Hosp Aide; JA; Pep Clb; ROTC; Chorus; Stage Crew; Communications.

SELDOMRIDGE, BONNY; Brandywine Heights HS; Mertztown, PA; (Y); 4-H; Band; Concert Band; Psych.

SELGRATH, CHRIS; Bishop Mc Devitt HS; Abington, PA; (Y); 38/395; French Clb; Rep Frsh Cls; Rep Soph Cls; Rep Jr Cls; Rep Sr Cls; Bsbl; Bsktbl; Crs Cntry; Trk; Hon Roll; Loyola Coll; Pre-Med.

SELL, BRENDA; Cambria Heights HS; Carrolltown, PA; (Y); Art Clb; ROTC; Nwsp Stf; Yrbk Stf; Im Bsbl; Im Swmmng; Var Trk; Im Vllybl; Art Inst Phg; Cmmrcl Art.

SELL, MELINDA; Littlestown HS; Littlestown, PA; (Y); 19/142; Chorus; Concert Band; Mrchg Band; School Musical; Swing Chorus; Ed Yrbk Stf; VP Frsh Cls; VP Soph Cls; VP Jr Cls; VP Sr Cls; Partcptd Jr Miss Pagnt Adams Cnty 85; Keystone JC; Early Chldhd Ed.

SELLECK, MARK N; Clarion-Limestone HS; Clarion, PA; (Y); 1/86; Am Leg Boys St; Intnl Clb; Letterman Clb; Varsity Clb; Pres Jr Cls; Rep Stu Cncl; Golf; Trk; NHS; Val; Harvard; Bus.

SELLERS, DAVID; Red Lion Area HS; Felton, PA; (Y); 25/330; Sec Trs Church Yth Grp; Library Aide; Science Clb; Chorus; Church Choir; School Play; High Hon Roll; Hon Roll; NHS; Rotary Awd; U Of DE; Chem Engrng.

SELLERS, JULIE; Central Dauphin East HS; Harrisburg, PA; (Y); 19/249; Church Yth Grp; Drill Tm; Drm Mjr(t); Mrchg Band; Off Jr Cls; Off Sr Cls; Gym; Hon Roll; NHS; Stu Cncl; Mst Otstndg Acad Stu Pnbrk Brgh 86; George Mason U; Nrsng.

SELLERS, LESLIE; York Catholic HS; York, PA; (Y); 27/150; Pres French Clb; FBLA; Color Guard; Nwsp Stf; Cheerleading; Mgr(s); Hon Roll; NHS; Pres Schlr; IN U Of PA; Finance.

SELLERS, TINA; East Juniata HS; Thompsontown, PA; (Y); 3/97; Varsity Clb; Sec Band; Sec Concert Band; Sec Mrchg Band; School Musical; Var L Cheerleading; Var L Trk; High Hon Roll; NHS; Stu Of Mnth Sptmbr 85; Pres Acad Ftns Awd 86; Hnr Stu 86; PA ST U.

SELLMAN, PATRICIA; Upper Merion SR HS; King Of Prussia, PA; (Y); 39/322; Var Fld Hcky; Var Lcrss; NHS; Phys Thrpy.

SELTZER, LYNN; Benton Area JR SR HS; Benton, PA; (Y); 12/45; Keywanettes; Color Guard; Trs Soph Cls; Trs Jr Cls; Hon Roll; NHS; Acctg.

SELWAY, MICHAEL; Trinity HS; Washington, PA; (Y); 25/374; Church Yth Grp; Cmnty Wkr; FBLA; Letterman Clb; L Var Bsbl; L Var Bsktbl; L Var Ftbl; Wt Lftg; High Hon Roll; Hon Roll; Bus Admin.

SELZNICK, SANDFORD; Hempfield Area SR HS; Greensburg, PA; (Y); 30/730; Computer Clb; Drama Clb; Mathletes; Ski Clb; Jazz Band; School Play; Yrbk Stf; NHS; Ntl Merit Ltr; VP Spanish NHS.

SEMAN, KAREN; Gateway SR HS; Mornoeville, PA; (Y); 38/435; Church Yth Grp; FBLA; Band; Chorus; Concert Band; JV Var Cheerleading; High Hon Roll; NHS; PA ST U; Pltcl Sci.

SEMAN, KATHLEEN; Norwin SR HS; N Huntingdon, PA; (Y); 91/557; Ski Clb; SADD; Outstndg Art I Stu 85; Outstndg Ski Club Stu 85; Indiana U Of PA; Rsprtry Thrpy.

SEMBHI, TARVINDER; Wilson Area HS; Easton, PA; (S); 1/150; Model UN; Ski Clb; Capt Socr; Trk; Wt Lftg; NHS; Soccer Schlr Athlete 85-86; PA ST U; Engrng.

SEMBOWER JR, JOHN; Penn Hills SR HS; Pittsburgh, PA; (Y); JV Var Bsbl; Hon Roll; Bus.

SEMENZA, GINA; Old Forge HS; Old Forge, PA; (Y); Ski Clb; Spanish Clb; Rep Frsh Cls; Stu Cncl; Cheerleading; High Hon Roll; Hon Roll; Jr NHS; Phrmcy.

SEMIC, BETH; Central Dauphin East HS; Harrisburg, PA; (Y); Pres Church Yth Grp; Chorus; Rep Frsh Cls; Sec Soph Cls; Sec Jr Cls; Sec Sr Cls; Var Cheerleading; Hon Roll; Jr NHS; NHS; Chrldng Chrldr 85-86; Corp Lawyer.

SEMISCH, BRUCE; The Hill Schl; Newtown Sq, PA; (Y); Camera Clb; Pres Computer Clb; JA; Model UN; Ski Clb; Yrbk Phtg; Capt Diving; Im Tennis; Hon Roll.

SEMMELROTH, LAURA; Merion Mercy Acad; Drexel Pk, PA; (Y); Camera Clb; French Clb; PAVAS; Service Clb; Stage Crew; Yrbk Rptr; Yrbk Stf; Natl Art Hnr Soc 86; Drexel U; Intrior Dsgn.

SEMMER, HEIDI ANNE; Greenville HS; Greenville, PA; (Y); 2/160; VP Thesps; Chorus; Yrbk Ed-Chief; JV Tennis; High Hon Roll; VP NHS; Ntl Merit SF; Sal; Public Spkng 86; Wellesley Coll; Law.

SEMPLE, EDWARD; Mt Union Area HS; Mt Union, PA; (Y); Am Leg Aux Girls St; Im Bsktbl; Hon Roll; South Hills Bus Schl; Accntng.

SEN GUPTA, SHELIA M; Meadville Area SR HS; Meadville, PA; (Y); 3/279; Trs French Clb; Science Clb; High Hon Roll; NHS; Prfct Atten Awd; Pres Schlr; PA ST; Accntng.

SENA, LYNNETTE D; Elk Lake HS; Meshoppen, PA; (Y); 4/108; Ski Clb; Hon Roll; ELEA Schltc Achvt Awd 84-86; Outstndng Cmmrcl Stu 85-86; Wilkes Coll; Acctng.

SENDZIK, JAMES; Portage Area HS; Portage, PA; (S); 3/122; Trs Church Yth Grp; Pres 4-H; Varsity Clb; Trs Stu Cncl; Var L Ftbl; Im Socr; Var L Wrstlng; 4-H Awd; High Hon Roll; NHS.

SENES, DANIEL M; Lower Merion HS; Wynnewood, PA; (Y); Chess Clb; Latin Clb; Math Tm; Nwsp Rptr; Ed Nwsp Stf; Hon Roll; NHS; Ntl Merit SF; Cert De Merite Concours Ntl De Francais 83; Liberal Arts Coll; Ed.

SENF, RAQUEL; Methacon SR HS; Audubon, PA; (Y); Chorus; Color Guard; Mrchg Band; Swing Chorus; Hon Roll; P A Gvnrs Schl Fr Arts 85; Otstdng Artst Awd 84-85; Art.

SENFT, ALBERT; West York Area HS; York, PA; (Y); 55/191; Church Yth Grp; Varsity Clb; Mrchg Band; Symp Band; Var Capt Crs Cntry; Var Capt Trk; Bus Adm.

SENIOR, ELIZABETH; Du Bois Central Christian HS; Falls Church, PA; (Y); Camera Clb; Trs FBLA; Nwsp Phtg; Nwsp Rptr; Var Bsktbl; Art Clb; Pep Clb; Science Clb; Falls Creek Fire Queen 86; Williamsport CC; Culnry Art.

SENKA, TOM; Seneca Valley HS; Harmony, PA; (Y); Letterman Clb; Ski Clb; Varsity Clb; Bsbl; Bsktbl; Golf; Optmtry.

SENNETT, RANDI A; Bishop Hoban HS; Wilkes-Barre, PA; (Y); Church Yth Grp; Computer Clb; Latin Clb; Math Clb; Var L Diving; Var L Swmmng; High Hon Roll; NHS; Bloomsburg U; Chem Engr.

SENNICK, SUSAN; Wyoming Area HS; Exeter, PA; (Y); Church Yth Grp; Key Clb; Q&S; Capt Color Guard; Nwsp Ed-Chief; Pres Stu Cncl; Stat Swmmng; Hon Roll; Blmsbrg U; Comm.

SENOFONTE, KARRIE; Scranton Prep; Clarks Summit, PA; (Y); Drama Clb; Letterman Clb; Pep Band; School Play; Sec Frsh Cls; Rep Soph Cls; Var Cheerleading; Var Pom Pon; JV Trk; Penn ST; Law.

SENOTT, AIMEE; Punxsutawney Area HS; Rossiter, PA; (Y); 93/237; Variety Show; Nwsp Stf; Yrbk Stf; Mgr(s); Sftbl; Trvl Schl.

SENSABAUGH, PAULA; Purchase Line HS; Commodore, PA; (Y); 12/128; Church Yth Grp; VP FBLA; Chorus; Church Choir; Concert Band; Drm Mjr(t); Pres Mrchg Band; School Play; Yrbk Stf; High Hon Roll; Mst Outstndng Bus Stu Awd 85-86; Acad All Amer Stu 85; Sec.

SENSEBAUGH, SCOTT; Hollidaysburg JR & SR HS; Duncansville, PA; (Y); 75/355; Boy Scts; French Clb; Var Trk; Im Vllybl; Acdmc Accelerated Cls Eng & Hist; Comp Sci.

SENSENIG, GLEN; Pequea Valley HS; Narvon, PA; (S); Var Crs Cntry; Var Wrstlng; 2 Time Sectnl Rnnr Up-Wrestlng 85-86; 1st Team Leag All Star-Wrestlng 86; Marine Corps.

SENSENIG, LARRY; Cocalico HS; Reinholds, PA; (Y); Aud/Vis; Camera Clb; Chess Clb; Church Yth Grp; Drama Clb; Science Clb; SADD; School Play; Stage Crew; Hon Roll.

SENSENIG, STEVEN; Coatesville Area SR HS; Parkesburg, PA; (Y); 27/492; Church Yth Grp; Spanish Clb; SADD; Pres Band; Chorus; Church Choir; Pep Band; School Musical; High Hon Roll; NEDT Awd; Phila Coll Bible; Music.

SENSER, GREGORY J; M M I Prep; Mountaintop, PA; (Y); Aud/Vis; Chess Clb; Ski Clb; Variety Show; Var L Bsbl; Im Socr; NEDT Awd; PA JR Acad Of Sci 2nd & 3rd Reg Awds 84 & 85 & 86; Bus.

SENSS, SUSAN; St Maria Goretti HS; Philadelphia, PA; (Y); Church Yth Grp; Hosp Aide; Chorus; School Musical; VP Stage Crew; Nwsp Phtg; Nwsp Stf; Hon Roll; PA ST U; Microbio.

SENTIPAL, RHONDA; Burgettstown JR SR HS; Slovan, PA; (Y); 41/191; Church Yth Grp; Science Clb; Spanish Clb; Yrbk Stf; High Hon Roll; Hon Roll; Slippery Rock U; Cmmnctns.

SENTIWANY, TERRY; Weatherly Area HS; White Haven, PA; (Y); Art Clb; Church Yth Grp; Drama Clb; FBLA; FFA; Pep Clb; Ski Clb; VICA; Band; Chorus; Voc Ind Clbs Of Amer-Extmpry Spkng Dist 85-86; Tempel; Biomed Eqpt.

SEPESKY, DOUGLAS; Belle Vernon Area HS; Belle Vernon, PA; (Y); 74/272; Ski Clb; Band; Trs Soph Cls; Trs Jr Cls; Trs Sr Cls; Trs Stu Cncl; JV Ftbl; Powder Puff Ftbl; Capt Swmmng; Vllybl; IN U Of PA; Finc.

SEPESY, NATALIE; Bethlehem-Center SR HS; Brownsville, PA; (Y); Dance Clb; Color Guard; Hon Roll; CA U Of PA; Elem Ed.

SEPITKO, CAMIE; Charleroi Area HS; Charleroi, PA; (Y); Pres Cmnty Wkr; FBLA; Spanish Clb; Band; Off Stu Cncl; Twrlr; Hugh Obrien Ldrshp Awd 84; REACH Gftd Pgm 80-86; Soc Edtr-Schl Nwspr; CA U Of PA; Athltc Trnr.

SEPRISH, LISA; Bald Eagle Area HS; Snow Shoe, PA; (Y); French Clb; Hosp Aide; Library Aide; Yrbk Stf; Var Cheerleading; Natl Sci Olympd Awd; JR Ex Comm 85-86; PA ST; Pre Med.

SERA, KATHLEEN; Pequea Valley HS; Gap, PA; (Y); 3/140; AFS; Church Yth Grp; Drama Clb; Acpl Chr; Band; Chorus; Mrchg Band; School Musical; School Play; Cheerleading; Paridise Rotary Clb Stu Of The Mnth 86; West Chester U; Nrsng.

SERAFIN, CAROLYN; Bishop Mc Cort HS; Johnstown, PA; (Y); Cmnty Wkr; German Clb; Math Clb; Pep Clb; Chorus; Church Choir; Yrbk Stf; Vllybl; High Hon Roll; Mu Alp Tht.

SERAFIN, JOE; Venango Christian HS; Oil City, PA; (Y); 5/42; Model UN; Rep Frsh Cls; Rep Jr Cls; VP Stu Cncl; L Bsktbl; Capt Ftbl; JV Vllybl; NHS; Pres Schlr; Army Res Schlr Ath Awd 86; Archbishop Gannon Mdl Gen Acad Excllnce 86; Gannon U; Pre-Med.

SERAFIN, KATHEY; Pleasant Valley HS; Kunkeltown, PA; (Y); Band; Chorus; Concert Band; Drm & Bgl; Drm Mjr(t); Mrchg Band; School Musical; Church Yth Grp; Ski Clb; Rep Frsh Cls; Dist 10 Band Frnch Horn 2nd Chair 86; Hnr Band & Hnr Chorus 86; Band Awd 86; Music.

SERAFIN, MICHAEL; Berwick Area SR HS; Nescopeck, PA; (Y); SADD; JV Wrstlng; Hon Roll; NHS; Bloomsburg; Tchng.

SERAFIN, TASO; Upper Darby HS; Upper Darby, PA; (Y); 19/730; Boy Scts; Church Yth Grp; German Clb; Rep Frsh Cls; Rep Soph Cls; JV Ftbl; JV Var Lcrss; Im Wt Lftg; JV Wrstlng; High Hon Roll; Sci Schlrshp Temple U 86; U Of PA; Actrl Sci.

SERAFINI, STEFANI; Chambersburg Area SR HS; Chambersburg, PA; (Y); Latin Clb; Letterman Clb; Pep Clb; Political Wkr; Varsity Clb; Yrbk Sprt Ed; Yrbk Stf; Rep Jr Cls; Rep Stu Cncl; Var L Bsktbl.

SERGI, RUTH ANN; Moon HS; Coraopolis, PA; (Y); 34/304; Church Yth Grp; Church Choir; Mrchg Band; Symp Band; Var Capt Diving; JV Gym; Var Capt Socr; Hon Roll; Spanish.

SERHIENKO, AMY; Phoenixville Area HS; Phoenixville, PA; (Y); 21/194; Key Clb; Office Aide; Band; Jazz Band; Variety Show; Trk; Hon Roll; Kiwanis Awd; NHS; Pres Schlr; Susan Anita Gutkowski Mem Scholar 85-86; Outstndng Svc Awd 85-86; Westchester U; Soc Sci.

SERISH, LISA; Burgettstown Area JR-SR HS; Burgettstown, PA; (Y); 27/146; Drama Clb; French Clb; SADD; Chorus; Yrbk Stf; Hon Roll; Jr NHS; NHS; Physcl Thrpy.

SERNAK, SUE; Weatherly Area HS; Weatherly, PA; (S); 5/70; FBLA; FHA; Band; Mrchg Band; Rep Trs Soph Cls; Var Capt Bsktbl; Score Keeper; Sftbl; Hon Roll; 1st Tm All Area Bsktbl 84-85; Cnty Bnd 84-85; Phy Thrpy.

SERNIK, JILL; Reynolds HS; Greenville, PA; (Y); 43/150; Pres Church Yth Grp; Latin Clb; Math Clb; Science Clb; Score Keeper; Hon Roll; NEDT Awd; 3rd Pl In The Cngrsnl Art Cmptn 86; Art Edu.

SEROKA, MIKE; Marian HS; New Ringgold, PA; (S); 25/114; Pres 4-H; Quiz Bowl; Band; Concert Band; Variety Show; 4-H Awd; High Hon Roll; Hon Roll; Med Prof.

SERRAO, MARTINA; Penn Hills HS; Pittsburgh, PA; (Y); Exploring; Science Clb; Spanish Clb; Band; Concert Band; Mrchg Band; Yrbk Stf; Stu Cncl; High Hon Roll; Jr NHS; U Of Pittsburgh; Med.

SERVICE, JENNIFER; Bethel Park SR HS; Bethel Park, PA; (Y); 1/500; Drama Clb; Intnl Clb; VP NFL; Sec Thesps; School Musical; School Play; High Hon Roll; NHS; ST-WIDE Frnscs Trnmnt 85; 1st Pl In HI At NC Frnscs Trnmnt 85; 1s Pl In HI At Mrcr Frnsc Trnmnt 86; Chmstry.

SESCILLA, MARK; Lampeter-Strasburg HS; Willow St, PA; (Y); 13/160; Thesps; Band; Chorus; Drm Mjr(t); Jazz Band; Madrigals; NHS; Church Yth Grp; Cmnty Wkr; Concert Band; Burrowes Schlr Awd Music, Rotary Club Stu Mnth 85-86; PA Gov Schl Arts 86; Mus.

SESSA, ANDREA; Quaker Valley HS; Sewickley, PA; (Y); #6 In Class; Drama Clb; French Clb; Pres Chorus; School Play; Nwsp Stf; Sec Jr Cls; Cheerleading; Var L Socr; Swmmng; Var L Trk.

SESSO, ANDREW; W Scranton SR HS; Scranton, PA; (Y); 84/250; Art Clb; Boys Clb Am; Pep Clb; Ski Clb; Spanish Clb; Band; Concert Band; Jazz Band; Mrchg Band; Pep Band; Air Force Acad; Spc Sci.

SESSOMS, KERRINE; Germantown HS; Philadelphia, PA; (Y); Girl Scts; Hosp Aide; Spanish Clb; Chorus; Church Choir; Hon Roll; UCLA; Pre-Med.

SESTI, MELISSA; Ambridge Area HS; Baden, PA; (Y); Am Leg Aux Girls St; Church Yth Grp; Office Aide; Pep Clb; Var Sftbl; Var L Vllybl; High Hon Roll; NHS; Beaver Cnty JR Ms Pgnt 86; Med.

SETH, SHARON; Neshannock JR-SR HS; New Castle, PA; (Y); 37/102; Exploring; Hosp Aide; Library Aide; Pep Clb; Teachers Aide; Gannon U; Pre-Med.

SETHMAN, PAMELA; Norwin SR HS; N Huntingdon, PA; (Y); FBLA; Library Aide; Regnl FBLA-1ST Pl Typing 85; Westmoreland Cnty CC; Busnss.

SETTLEMYER, JONATHAN; Jersey Shore SR HS; Jersey Shore, PA; (Y); Boy Scts; Pres Church Yth Grp; Band; Chorus; School Play; Rep Soph Cls; Swmmng; Hon Roll; NHS; Bio Sci.

SETTNEK, SHARON; Hampton HS; Allison Park, PA; (Y); 7/205; L Bsktbl; L Sftbl; L Vllybl; High Hon Roll; NHS; Female Athlete Of Yr 86; U Of Pittsburgh; Math.

SETTNEK, SUE; Gateway SR HS; Pitcairn, PA; (Y); DECA; Art Inst Pittsburgh; Fshn Merch.

SETTO, PAULA R; Canon Mc Millan HS; Canonsburg, PA; (Y); Church Yth Grp; Office Aide; Varsity Clb; Band; Chorus; Var Pom Pon; JV Sftbl; Trk; High Hon Roll; Hon Roll; Washngtn Hosp Schl-Nrsng; Nrsng.

SETTY, VENKATESHKUMAR P; Geibel HS; Connellsville, PA; (Y); Science Clb; Ski Clb; SADD; Temple Yth Grp; Nwsp Ed-Chief; Yrbk Stf; VP Frsh Cls; JV Crs Cntry; JV Trk; High Hon Roll; Spanish Merit Awd; Engrng.

SEVERA, JENNIFER; Highlands SR HS; Brackenridge, PA; (Y); 2/277; Sec Key Clb; Chorus; Mgr Mrchg Band; School Play; Nwsp Ed-Chief; High Hon Roll; NHS; Pres Schlr; Sal; Carnegie-Mellon U Sal Scholar 86; U Pittsburgh Hnrs Convoctn 85; Carnegie-Mellon U; Writing.

SEVERCOOL, BECKY; Lackawanna Trail HS; Factoryville, PA; (Y); 6/92; Ski Clb; Chorus; Madrigals; School Musical; Variety Show; Yrbk Stf; French Hon Soc; Hon Roll; NHS; Hnrb Mntn Natl Frnch Cont 84-85; Jrnlst.

SEVERNAK, SHARLENE; Wyoming Area SR HS; W Wyoming, PA; (Y); 11/250; French Clb; Key Clb; Nwsp Rptr; Nwsp Stf; Stu Cncl; Co-Capt Sftbl; High Hon Roll; NHS; Bloomsbrg U; Math.

SEVERO, JOSEPHINE; St Maria Goretti HS; Philadelphia, PA; (Y); 7/390; Cmnty Wkr; Mathletes; Math Clb; Science Clb; Service Clb; Nwsp Phtg; Nwsp Stf; High Hon Roll; NHS; Ntl Merit Schol; Honorable Mention Sci 83-85, Engl 85, Latin 84; Natl Math League Stu Awd 85; Pre Med.

SEVERSON, BRIAN P; Danville HS; Danville, PA; (Y); Ski Clb; Spanish Clb; Var L Bsktbl; Var L Socr; Var L Trk; High Hon Roll; Hon Roll; NHS; Pres Schlr; Dtsch Fmly Schlrshp 86; Mst Otstndng Male Athlt 86; 1st Tm All-Str Sccr, Hnrbl Mntn Bsktbll 86; U Of Pittsburgh; Phycl Educ.

SEVICK, DENISE; South Hills Christian HS; Monongahela, PA; (Y); 3/14; Church Yth Grp; Pep Clb; Variety Show; Nwsp Stf; Yrbk Stf; Capt Cheerleading; Hon Roll; Church Yth Grp; Chorus; Editor Chrch Yth Ltr 86; Geneva Coll; Engl.

SEWOCK, BONNIE; Canon Mc Millon SR HS; Canonsburg, PA; (Y); High Hon Roll; Hon Roll; Bus.

SEXTON, KELYNDA; Wm Penn SR HS; York, PA; (Y); 51/321; Library Aide; Rep Soph Cls; Rep Sr Cls; Hon Roll; Lincoln U Scholar 86-87; Lincoln U Fndrs Awd 86-87; Lincoln U; Engl.

SEXTON, LAURA; Palmyra Area HS; Palmyra, PA; (Y); Drama Clb; Service Clb; Spanish Clb; Band; Chorus; Concert Band; Jazz Band; Mrchg Band; Off Stu Cncl; Stat Wrstlng; MUSIC.

SEXTON, SCOTT; Cardinal O Hara HS; Glenolden, PA; (Y); 286/776; Computer Clb; JV Bsbl; JV Ftbl; PA ST Coll; Comp.

SEYBERT, CRAIG; Columbia-Montour Vo-Tech; Berwick, PA; (Y); Camera Clb; VICA; Nwsp Phtg; Stu Cncl; High Hon Roll; NHS; Schl Nwspr Photogrphy Edtr 85-86; Graphic Arts.

SEYDL, JON L; Moravian Acad; Easton, PA; (Y); Cmnty Wkr; 4-H; Library Aide; Model UN; Orch; Yrbk Stf; Hon Roll; Ntl Merit SF; Art Hist.

SEYFERT, SUE; Hamburg Area JR SR HS; Hamburg, PA; (Y); 7/155; German Clb; SADD; Band; Church Choir; School Musical; Yrbk Stf; Var Tennis; High Hon Roll; Hon Roll; NHS; Engr.

SEYKOSKI, KIMBERLY A; Charleroi Area HS; Charleroi, PA; (Y); Church Yth Grp; Sec French Clb; Trs Concert Band; Mrchg Band; Ed Nwsp Stf; Hon Roll.

SEYMOUR, CHAD; Fort Le Boeuf HS; Waterford, PA; (Y); 33/168; Computer Clb; Exploring; Ski Clb; Im Vllybl; High Hon Roll.

SEYMOUR, KIMBER; Waynesburg Central HS; Mt Morris, PA; (Y); Trs Church Yth Grp; Pres 4-H; Trs FHA; Spanish Clb; SADD; Chorus; Church Choir; Madrigals; Swing Chorus; Nwsp Bus Mgr; Blue Merit Awd 4 H 83-86; 4 H Perf Attndnce Awd 84-85; WV U; Prof Horse Tranr.

SEYMOUR, MARYANN; Central HS; Scranton, PA; (Y); Exploring; FNA; JA; Hon Roll; Jr NHS; PA ST; Nrs.

SFEREDES, JOANNA; St Hubert HS; Philadelphia, PA; (Y); 12/367; Church Yth Grp; Computer Clb; Chorus; Church Choir; Orch; School Musical; Hon Roll; NHS; Prfct Atten Awd; Cert Of Acadmc Merit In British Lit 86 & In Phys Sci 84; Cert Music Orch 84 & 86; Bus Adm.

SFORZA, LAURA; Kiski Area HS; Vandergrift, PA; (Y); FBLA; JA; Teachers Aide; Chorus; Color Guard; High Hon Roll; Hon Roll; Medcl Asst.

SGRICCIA, MATTHEW; Freeport SR HS; Freeport, PA; (Y); Var L Bsbl; Var L Bsktbl; NHS; Penn ST U Pk; Engrng.

SHAAK, CHRISTOPHER; Lebanon Catholic HS; Annville, PA; (Y); Boy Scts; Church Yth Grp; Cmnty Wkr; Ftbl; Prz Money Wrtg Papr Fair Housing 86; Yth Cty Govt Prog As Crmnl Detctv 86; IN U Of PA; Crmnlgy.

SHABLIK, KIM; Norwin SR HS; North Huntington, PA; (Y); Trs Band; Concert Band; Jazz Band; Mrchg Band; U Of Pittsburgh; Bus.

SHADE, DIANE; Cocalico HS; Denver, PA; (Y); Sec FBLA; Girl Scts; Concert Band; Mrchg Band; Mat Maids; High Hon Roll; Hon Roll; 4th Pl Steno I FBLA Rgnl Cmptn 86; Mdcl Secy.

SHADE, ROBERT; Red Land HS; Lewisberry, PA; (Y); 69/277; Church Yth Grp; Computer Clb; Crs Cntry; Swmmng; Trk; Wt Lftg; Hon Roll; Prfct Atten Awd; Varsty Ltr Track, Crss Cntry 84-85; JV Ltr Crss Cntry 84-85; Old Dominion U; Aero Space Eng.

SHADLE, DOUGLAS; South Western HS; Hanover, PA; (Y); Concert Band; Jazz Band; Mrchg Band; Pep Band; Symp Band; Tennis; High Hon Roll; Hon Roll; NHS; Rotary Awd; PA ST U; Elec Engnrng.

SHAFER JR, JACK; Crestwood HS; Wapwallopen, PA; (Y); Math Clb; Ski Clb; L Bsbl; Capt Socr; High Hon Roll; NHS; Church Yth Grp; Cmnty Wkr; Exploring; Stage Crew; 90th Pct Nedt Scores 83-84; Penn ST; Elec Engrng.

SHAFER, MATTHEW; Huntingdon Area HS; Huntingdon, PA; (Y); 1/210; Key Clb; Stat Bsktbl; Var L Tennis; Var L Wrstlng; High Hon Roll; Pres NHS; NEDT Awd; Pres Schlr; Val; Voice Dem Awd; PA Govrs Schl For Intl Studies 86; Pres Classroom For Yng Amer 86; Amer U; Intl Studies.

SHAFER, TRIESTE; Hazelton HS; Hazleton, PA; (Y); Cmnty Wkr; Office Aide; Pep Clb; SADD; Y-Teens; Sec Sr Cls; Pres Stu Cncl; Var Capt Cheerleading; Awd Outstndng Chrldr Elzbthtwn Coll 86; Mbr Awd Wnnng Chrldng Sqd 86; Phys Ed.

SHAFFER, AMY; Cardinal O Hara HS; Springfield, PA; (Y); 9/772; Church Yth Grp; Service Clb; Spanish Clb; Yrbk Stf; High Hon Roll; Hon Roll; NHS; Spanish NHS; Cert Merit Ntl Spnsh 84-85; Bus.

SHAFFER, BONNIE; Western Wayne HS; Lake Ariel, PA; (Y); 18/149; Sec 4-H; Hosp Aide; Hon Roll; Gifted Program; PA ST; Health Planning.

SHAFFER, BRENDA; Somerset Area SR HS; Somerset, PA; (Y); 46/239; Art Clb; Church Yth Grp; English Clb; JA; Spanish Clb; Varsity Clb; Band; Concert Band; Mrchg Band; Rep Stu Cncl; Drum Mjr Tam O Shanters 85-86; Tri-Hi-Y 86; Coll; Accntnt.

SHAFFER, BRIDGETTE; Shanksville-Stonycreek HS; Central City, PA; (S); 8/31; Am Leg Aux Girls St; School Play; Yrbk Stf; Pres Jr Cls; Pres Sr Cls; Dnfth Awd; Hon Roll; NHS; Spanish NHS; USA Teen Mis Schlrshp Pgnt 2nd Rnnr-Up; JR Miss Pgnt; Bio.

SHAFFER, CAROLYN; Hyndman Middle SR HS; Hyndman, PA; (Y); Library Aide; Spanish Clb; Teachers Aide; Chorus; Color Guard; Color Guard 84; Chorus; Tchrs Aide; Bus.

SHAFFER, CHRISSY; Meyersdale Area HS; Hyndman, PA; (Y); FBLA; Library Aide; Office Aide; Band; Chorus; Color Guard; Concert Band; Yrbk Stf; Cit Awd; Rep Stu Cncl; Bus.

SHAFFER, DARRELL; Shikellamy HS; Camp Hill, PA; (Y); Hon Roll; Outstndng Nwspr Carrier Of Yr 83 & 84; Hrsbrg Area CC; Fd Srv Mngmnt.

SHAFFER, DONNA; Blacklick Valley HS; Twin Rocks, PA; (S); 8/90; Art Clb; German Clb; Ski Clb; Varsity Clb; Var Capt Bsktbl; Var Capt Sftbl; Hon Roll; NHS; Seton Hill Coll; Medcl Tchnlgy.

SHAFFER JR, EDWARD; Tunkhannock Area HS; Tunkhannock, PA; (S); Boy Scts; VP Science Clb; Chorus; Var Diving; Var Golf; Var Swmmng; Cit Awd; Hon Roll; NHS; Spanish Clb; Rotry Ldr Camp 85; Bus Mgmt.

SHAFFER, ERIC; Dover Area HS; Dover, PA; (Y); 49/287; Boy Scts; Band; Chorus; Jazz Band; Mrchg Band; Socr; Trk.

SHAFFER JR, JAMES M; Montgomery Area Schl District; Montgomery, PA; (Y); 1/65; French Clb; High Hon Roll; NHS; Ntl Merit Ltr; Elec Engrng.

SHAFFER, JENNIFER; Forest City Regional HS; Pleasant Mount, PA; (Y); 2/55; German Clb; Letterman Clb; Band; Jazz Band; VP Jr Cls; Pres Stu Cncl; JV Capt Vllybl; High Hon Roll; NHS; Wrtr.

SHAFFER, JOAN; Northern HS; Dillsburg, PA; (Y); 40/209; Church Yth Grp; Band; Chorus; Church Choir; Concert Band; Jazz Band; Mrchg Band; School Musical; French Hon Soc; Hon Roll; Tri M Music Hnr Soc 86; Music.

SHAFFER, JODI; Mo Hawk JR SR HS; Wampum, PA; (Y); Sec Church Yth Grp; French Clb; Band; Chorus; Church Choir; Concert Band; Jazz Band; Mrchg Band; Swing Chorus; Beaver Cnty CC; Nrsng.

SHAFFER, JULIE; Marion Center Area HS; Creekside, PA; (Y); Church Yth Grp; VICA; Yrbk Stf; High Hon Roll; Hon Roll; Kittanning Bty Schl; Csmtlgst.

SHAFFER, KEVIN; Dover HS; Dover, PA; (Y); 24/300; Church Yth Grp; Var JV Bsktbl; High Hon Roll; Hon Roll; Optmtrst.

SHAFFER, KIMBERLY; Council Rock HS; Churchville, PA; (Y); 7/845; Dance Clb; Hosp Aide; Office Aide; Hon Roll; NHS; Ntl Merit Ltr; Prfct Atten Awd.

SHAFFER, KRISTEN; Quigley HS; New Brighton, PA; (S); 22/113; Band; Flag Corp; Jazz Band; Mrchg Band; Powder Puff Ftbl; Trk; Hon Roll; NHS; Trig Awd 85; Ldrshp Merit Awd 85-86.

SHAFFER, LISA; Frazier HS; Perryopolis, PA; (Y); Pres FNA; Hosp Aide; Flag Corp; Trs Mrchg Band; Yrbk Stf; Jr Cls; High Hon Roll; Hon Roll; Jr NHS; Prfct Atten Awd; U Of Pittsburgh; Nrsg.

SHAFFER, LISA; Jefferson-Morgan JR SR HS; Jefferson, PA; (Y); 26/88; Art Clb; Church Yth Grp; Hosp Aide; Spanish Clb; Yrbk Stf; DAR Awd; Hon Roll; Gftd Prog 83-86; Sld Coal Dncr 86; Phys Thrpy.

SHAFFER, LORI; Elderton JR SR HS; Spring Church, PA; (Y); 18/99; Drama Clb; Spanish Clb; Varsity Clb; Color Guard; Mrchg Band; School Play; Yrbk Phtg; Yrbk Stf; Var Capt Cheerleading; High Hon Roll; IN U; Acctng.

SHAFFER, MARC; Solanco HS; Quarryville, PA; (Y); 24/235; Church Yth Grp; Trs Varsity Clb; Band; Rep Jr Cls; Var Ftbl; Var Trk; NHS; Rotary Awd; Concert Band; Jazz Band; Vrsty Indr Trck; Cnty Symphnc Band; 2 Awds Cnty Sci Fair; Grove City Coll; Engnrng.

SHAFFER, MARY; Warwick HS; Rothsville, PA; (Y); 31/234; AFS; Church Yth Grp; Yrbk Stf; Lit Mag; Trk; High Hon Roll; NHS; Ple-Ple Stu Ambsdr 85; Shippensburg U.

SHAFFER, MELISSA; Eastern Lancaster County HS; Morgantown, PA; (Y); German Clb; Library Aide; High Hon Roll; Hon Roll; Jr NHS; Cngrss Bndstg Exchng Stu Grmny 85-86; Bio.

SHAFFER, MICHELLE; Seneca Valley HS; Zelienople, PA; (Y); Church Yth Grp; Cmnty Wkr; Band; Church Choir; Concert Band; Mrchg Band; Pep Band; Symp Band; Hon Roll; Psych.

SHAFFER, ROBERT; Kiski Area HS; Apollo, PA; (Y); VP Key Clb; Varsity Clb; Rep Frsh Cls; Rep Soph Cls; Rep Jr Cls; Rep Stu Cncl; Var L Ftbl; L Trk; Wt Lftg; High Hon Roll; Top 10 Awd 84.

SHAFFER, RON; Jeffermon Morgan HS; Jefferson, PA; (Y); 3/85; Varsity Clb; Pres Jr Cls; VP Sr Cls; Stu Cncl; Var L Bsbl; Var L Bsktbl; Bausch & Lomb Sci Awd; NHS; Magna Cum Laude Ntl Lat Exm 86; Acad All Amer; Engrng.

SHAFFER, RUTH; Grove City SR HS; Grove City, PA; (Y); 15/199; Church Yth Grp; Cmnty Wkr; FNA; Key Clb; Im Vllybl; High Hon Roll; Hon Roll; Grove City Coll; Socl Wrk.

SHAFFER, SHANNON; Hyndman HS; Hyndman, PA; (Y); 1/39; Spanish Clb; Varsity Clb; Band; Chorus; Yrbk Stf; Var Tennis; High Hon Roll; Jr NHS; Trs NHS.

SHAFFER, STEPHANIE; Indiana Area SR HS; Indiana, PA; (Y); 49/299; Office Aide; Red Cross Aide; Spanish Clb; Color Guard; Mrchg Band; High Hon Roll; Hon Roll; Jr NHS; Prsdntl Acadmc Ftns Awd 86; IUP Physcs Awd 86; IN U; Med Tech.

SHAFFER, TONI; Conemaugh Valley HS; Summorholl, PA; (Y); Church Yth Grp; JA; Library Aide; Pep Clb; SADD; Trk; Vllybl; Prfct Atten Awd; Outstndg Achvt Awd Vllybl 83-84; Bus.

SHAFFER, TRACY; Westmont Hilltop HS; Johnstown, PA; (Y); 24/142; Art Clb; Church Yth Grp; Pres Chorus; Church Choir; Color Guard; School Musical; Yrbk Stf; L Cheerleading; Hon Roll; NHS; Harcum JC; Legal Secy.

SHAFFER, WALLY; Marion Center HS; Creekside, PA; (Y); Pres Church Yth Grp; Intnl Clb; Office Aide; Science Clb; SADD; Varsity Clb; L Bsbl; L Bsktbl; L Ftbl; Hon Roll.

SHAFFER, WENDY; Shanksville Stonycreek HS; Central City, PA; (S); 5/34; Church Yth Grp; Office Aide; Band; Chorus; Church Choir; Mrchg Band; Nwsp Rptr; Nwsp Stf; Sec Frsh Cls; Sec Soph Cls; NYACK; Psych.

SHAFFER, WILLIAM; Chestnut Ridge SR HS; Imler, PA; (S); 3/142; Church Yth Grp; Nwsp Stf; Mgr(s); High Hon Roll; NHS; Voice Dem Awd; U Miami; Engrng.

SHAFRANCIH, MARK; Kishacoquillas HS; Milroy, PA; (Y); 4/144; French Clb; Varsity Clb; Stu Cncl; Bsbl; Capt Ftbl; Capt Wrstlng; High Hon Roll; Trs NHS; Outstndng Wrstlr-Dist VI 86; Rod Tate Wrstlng Awd 86; Outstndng Wrstlr-Chrstms Tourn 85; PA ST U; Mech Engr.

SHAH, AMEETA; Montour SR HS; Mckees Rocks, PA; (Y); Exploring; Band; Concert Band; Mrchg Band; High Hon Roll; Hon Roll; Sec NHS; Temple Yth Grp; Biomed Engr.

SHAH, ASHESH; Wissahickon HS; Norristown, PA; (S); 6/277; Computer Clb; VP Intnl Clb; Model UN; Trs Frsh Cls; High Hon Roll; Hon Roll; NHS; Debate Tm; Math Clb; Stage Crew; 2 Acad Ltrs 84 & 85; Elec Engrng.

SHAH, DIPAN; Spring-Ford HS; Royersford, PA; (S); 8/258; Am Leg Boys St; German Clb; Library Aide; Radio Clb; Teachers Aide; Var Tennis; Hon Roll; NHS; Pre-Med.

SHAH, JAHNAVI; Spring-Ford SR HS; Royersford, PA; (Y); 52/234; Computer Clb; French Clb; Hosp Aide; Library Aide; Red Cross Aide; SADD; Varsity Clb; Mgr(s); Bckwltr Schlrshp 86; Sprtstrnr 84-86; Anchr Clb 84-86; West Chester U; Chem.

SHAH, PAMIRA; Wyomissing Area HS; Wyomissing Hills, PA; (S); 1/125; Exploring; Sec Intnl Clb; Spanish Clb; Yrbk Stf; Var Capt Bsktbl; Var Capt Fld Hcky; High Hon Roll; NHS; Val; Drama Clb; Harvard; Pre-Law.

SHAKOSKE, AMY; Fox Chapel HS; Pittsburgh, PA; (Y); Stat Bsbl; JV Capt Cheerleading; High Hon Roll; Hon Roll; Trck Awd; WV U; Bus.

SHALIKASHVILI, AMY; Carlisle SR HS; Carlisle, PA; (Y); 7/348; Church Yth Grp; Mrchg Band; Rep Stu Cncl; Var L Gym; High Hon Roll; NHS; Rtry Ldrshp Conf 86; Math.

SHALKOWSKI, DEBRA; Louis E Dieruff HS; Allentown, PA; (Y); 3/321; Art Clb; Drama Clb; Concert Band; Sec Trs Mrchg Band; School Play; Rptr Yrbk Stf; Rep Frsh Cls; Jr NHS; NHS; Instmntl Music Clb Schlrshp 86; Outstndng Art Awd, Hghst Hon Awd 86; Tyler School Art Temple U; Art.

SHALL, MARCIA; Sheffield Area JR SR HS; Sheffield, PA; (Y); 5/98; Church Yth Grp; Pep Clb; SADD; Varsity Clb; Chorus; Church Choir; Capt Cheerleading; Trk; High Hon Roll; NHS; Chrldr Big 30 Charities Ftbl Gm 86; Grad Hnr Stdnt 86; JETS Acadmc Tm 86; Clarion U; Bus.

SHALLENBERGER, JANE; Connellsville SR HS; Vanderbilt, PA; (Y); 227/484; Sec Church Yth Grp; Pres Sec 4-H; Library Aide; Office Aide; Pep Clb; Chorus; Church Choir; Stage Crew; Yrbk Rptr; Yrbk Stf; Bus Mngmt.

SHAMES, JONINA F; Beth Jacob HS; Cherry Hill, NJ; (Y); Teachers Aide; Band; School Play; Stage Crew; Nwsp Ed-Chief; Rep Frsh Cls; Trs Soph Cls; Hon Roll; NEDT Awd; 3rd Pl Ntl Crtv Wrtg Cont 85; 1st Pl Jewish Hertg Crvt Wrtg Cont 85; Stern Coll Max Stern Schlrs Pgm; Stern Coll For Wmn; Comp Sci.

SHAMITIS, RENEE; Central Catholic HS; Herminie, PA; (Y); AFS; Church Yth Grp; Exploring; High Hon Roll; NHS; Sci.

SHANDRA, EDW; Seton Catholic HS; Pittston, PA; (Y); 17/100; Key Clb; Letterman Clb; Spanish Clb; Yrbk Stf; Rep Soph Cls; Rep Jr Cls; Rep Sr Cls; Pres Stu Cncl; Bsbl; Bsktbl; Awd Excllngn Ballfield & Clssrm 86; Wilkes Coll; Engrng.

SHANE, PATRICIA; Hazleton HS; Mc Adoo, PA; (Y); 15/377; Sec Drama Clb; Sec Trs Intnl Clb; Pres Leo Clb; Chorus; School Musical; Trk; French Hon Soc; NHS; SF Cnty JR Miss Pgnt, Scroptmst Intl Ctznshp 85-86; Penn ST U; Comm.

SHANEBROOK, SCOTT; New Oxford SR HS; Mcsherrystown, PA; (Y); 20/187; Boys Clb Am; Debate Tm; FBLA; FTA; JA; SADD; Varsity Clb; Rep Stu Cncl; High Hon Roll; Prfct Atten Awd; Bus.

SHANER, DAWN; Bayertown Area SR HS; Gilbertsvl, PA; (Y); Aud/Vis; SADD; Stage Crew; Stu Cncl; Var Fld Hcky; Var Lcrss; Trk; Cit Awd; High Hon Roll; Sec NHS.

SHANER, SANDRA; Ford City JR/SR HS; Ford City, PA; (Y); ROTC; Spanish Clb; Band; Chorus; Color Guard; Flag Corp; Mrchg Band; Stage Crew; Nwsp Rptr; Rep Frsh Cls.

SHANER, SYD; Plum SR HS; Pittsburgh, PA; (Y); 9/383; Chess Clb; Computer Clb; JA; Math Tm; VP Science Clb; Band; School Play; High Hon Roll; NHS; Prfct Atten Awd; 1st Pl Comp Fiar Ed Dept 85; Math.

SHANK, DEAN P; Bermudian Springs HS; East Berlin, PA; (S); 29/80; Pres Sec FFA; Church Choir; School Musical; Rep Stu Cncl; Im Wt Lftg; Hon Roll; FFA Kystn Frmr Degree, Chptr Ldrshp Awd & De Kalb Agrcltrl Acmplshmnt Awd 86; PA ST Mont Alto; Frst Tech.

SHANK, EDWARD; Bellwood-Antis HS; Bellwood, PA; (Y); Art Clb; French Clb; Chorus; School Musical; Nwsp Stf; Twrlr; Wt Lftg; Art Instrctn Schls MN 81; USAF; Arch.

SHANK, LARRY; Elizabethtown Area HS; Elizabethtown, PA; (Y); 73/248; Church Yth Grp; FFA; Library Aide; Hon Roll; NHS; Accntng.

SHANK, RANDALL; Ephrata SR HS; Ephrata, PA; (Y); 4/250; Trs Church Yth Grp; Library Aide; Mathletes; Math Tm; Quiz Bowl; Radio Clb; Nwsp Ed-Chief; Gov Hon Prg Awd; High Hon Roll; NHS; 4th Pl Intl Sci Fair-Chem 86; Comp Sci.

SHANK, STACEY; Cumberland Valley Christian Schl; Chambersburg, PA; (S); Art Clb; Sec Jr Cls; Var L Sftbl; Cit Awd; Hon Roll; NHS.

SHANKLE, ERIC; Harmony HS; Cherry Tree, PA; (Y); Ski Clb; Stage Crew; Yrbk Stf; Bsbl; Bsktbl; Hon Roll; Audio Engr.

SHANLEY, ISABEL; Pocono Central Catholic HS; Mt Pocono, PA; (S); 6/22; Art Clb; Pep Clb; Pres VP Service Clb; Ski Clb; Yrbk Stf; Rep Stu Cncl; Capt Var Fld Hcky; DAR Awd; Sec NHS; Exc Typng Awd,Acctng Awd; Schl Spirit Awd; Millersville U; Ed.

SHANNON, BRIAN; Wilmington Area HS; New Wilmington, PA; (S); 5/121; Church Yth Grp; Cmnty Wkr; Hosp Aide; Letterman Clb; Red Cross Aide; Varsity Clb; Pres Soph Cls; Pres Jr Cls; Rep Stu Cncl; Var L Bsbl.

SHANNON, COLLEEN; Brockway Area HS; Brockway, PA; (Y); 11/91; Art Clb; Debate Tm; Drama Clb; Rep Stu Cncl; Var L Mgr(s); JV Vllybl; Elem Ed.

SHANNON, DARCY; Chambersburg Area SR HS; Chambersburg, PA; (Y); FNA; Latin Clb; Drm Mjr(t); JV Twrlr; Hon Roll; RN.

SHANNON, JEFF; Lancaster Christian HS; Lancaster, PA; (Y); 12/24; Church Yth Grp; Drama Clb; Band; Concert Band; School Play; Yrbk Stf; Var Bsbl; Var Bsktbl; Hon Roll.

SHANNON, LINDA; Pittston Area HS; Pittston, PA; (Y); 88/240; Key Clb; Chorus; Trk; Radlgc Tech.

SHANNON, PATRICK; Wilmington Area HS; New Wilmington, PA; (S); 4/108; Church Yth Grp; Cmnty Wkr; Hosp Aide; Key Clb; Letterman Clb; Red Cross Aide; Spanish Clb; Varsity Clb; Band; Concert Band; Westminister Coll; Pre-Med.

SHANTON, ERIK M; William Allen HS; Allentown, PA; (Y); JCL; Model UN; Political Wkr; School Play; Rep Frsh Cls; Rep Soph Cls; Rep Jr Cls; Sr Cls; L Trk; Pres Schlr; Allntwn Schlmns Schlrshp 86; Cert Cum Ld Hgh Scrng In Ntl Ltn Exm 85 & 86; 2nd Pl Awd Egg Drop 86; PA ST U; Ed.

SHANTZ, CATHLEEN; Penn Hills HS; Pittsburgh, PA; (Y); #1 In Class; Church Yth Grp; Office Aide; Spanish Clb; Varsity Clb; Var Bsktbl; Score Keeper; Var Vllybl; High Hon Roll; Prfct Atten Awd; Ver Important Persn Awd 85; All Trny Tm Vllybl 86; Envrnmntl Sci.

SHANTZ, DAWN; Owen J Roberts HS; Parker Ford, PA; (Y); #50 In Class; Church Yth Grp; GAA; Chorus; School Musical; Soph Cls; Fld Hcky; Lcrss; Vllybl; Hon Roll; Ntl Hnr Scty 84-86; Lebanon Valley Coll; Comp Sci.

SHAPIRO, MARC; Lower Moreland HS; Philadelphia, PA; (S); 2/228; Computer Clb; Mathletes; Science Clb; Lit Mag; High Hon Roll; NHS; Sal; Rnslr Math & Sci Awd 85; 1st Pl Amer HS Math Exam 85; PA Math Team 85; Physics.

SHAPIRO, SIOUXSIE; Performing Arts Schl Of Phila; Philadelphia, PA; (Y); Drama Clb; PAVAS; Political Wkr; Teachers Aide; School Play; Lit Mag; Rep Soph Cls; NYU; Drama.

SHAPPELL, MICHELE; Schuylkill Haven Area; Schuylkill Haven, PA; (Y); SADD; Chorus; Mrchg Band; School Musical; Sec Frsh Cls; Sec Jr Cls; Sec Sr Cls; Sec Pres Stu Cncl; Capt Cheerleading; Trk; Hnr Grd 85; Bryland Beauty Acad; Cosmtlgy.

SHAPPELL, TAMMY; Milton Area HS; Milton, PA; (Y); 29/202; Color Guard; JV Var Bsktbl; Sr Cls; Hon Roll; NHS; Phys Thrpy.

SHARDY, JENNIFER; Reynolds HS; Fredonia, PA; (Y); Hosp Aide; Latin Clb; Science Clb; Chorus; School Musical; NHS; Ntl Merit Schol; NEDT Awd; Acdmc All-Amrcn 85-86; Grove City Coll; Pre-Med.

SHARER, BRIAN; Liberty HS; Bethlehem, PA; (Y); 72/475; Chess Clb; Scholastic Bowl; Chorus; School Musical; School Play; Nwsp Rptr; Lit Mag; Hon Roll; Ecology.

SHARGA, MICHELLE; Wm Allen HS; Allentown, PA; (Y); 34/604; GAA; Key Clb; Ski Clb; Varsity Clb; Yrbk Stf; Off Sr Cls; Var L Fld Hcky; Capt Var Sftbl; Hon Roll; NHS; Schl Rep Athletic Cncl; Pre Med.

SHARIF, RUQAIYA; St Joseph Acad; Dover, PA; (Y); 1/20; High Hon Roll; Voice Dem Awd; Mrt Awd Englsh 85-86; Schlrshp Awd 85; Dickinson Coll; Pltcl Sci.

SHARKEY, CHERYL; West Scranton HS; Scranton, PA; (Y); Red Cross Aide; Ski Clb; School Play; Stu Cncl; Hon Roll; Jr NHS; NHS; Medcl Lab Technlgs.

SHARMA, SANDEEP; Cathedral Prep; Erie, PA; (Y); 39/220; French Clb; Letterman Clb; Ski Clb; SADD; JV Socr; Var Capt Tennis; High Hon Roll.

SHARP, DAVID W; Bethel Park HS; Bethel Park, PA; (Y); 64/518; CC Allegheny County; Crmnlgy.

SHARP, GREG; Manheim Central HS; Manheim, PA; (Y); 50/210; Church Yth Grp; Band; Concert Band; Jazz Band; Mrchg Band; Pep Band; High Hon Roll; Hon Roll; Etown Coll; Acctng.

SHARP, LISA; Central-York SR HS; York, PA; (Y); German Clb; Girl Scts; Y-Teens; Color Guard; Flag Corp; Nwsp Stf; Yrbk Stf; Cheerleading; Swmmng; Twrlr; Accounting.

SHARP, MICHELE; Kiski Area HS; Avonmore, PA; (Y); Math Clb; Math Tm; SADD; Band; Jazz Band; Mrchg Band; Symp Band; High Hon Roll; NHS; Church Yth Grp; Johnny Murphy Music Awd 84; Top 10 Cls 84; Elec Engr.

SHARP, RICK; Rocky Gorve HS; Franklin, PA; (Y); 30/93; Aud/Vis; Boys Clb Am; Church Yth Grp; SADD; Band; Crs Cntry; Var Tennis; Acctg.

SHARPE, JOSEPH; Marian Catholic HS; Tamaqua, PA; (Y); Scholastic Bowl; SADD; Nwsp Rptr; Nwsp Stf; Bsbl; Bsktbl; Var Ftbl; Penn ST; Engrng.

SHARPE, KIMBERLEY; Clarion Area HS; Shippenville, PA; (Y); Cmnty Wkr; Sec Trs FTA; Girl Scts; Political Wkr; Chorus; Variety Show; Ed Yrbk Stf; Hon Roll; NHS; Prof Polit Sci.

SHARROW, MARK; Southern Columbia Area HS; Catawissa, PA; (Y); Boy Scts; Church Yth Grp; 4-H; Pep Clb; Red Cross Aide; Teachers Aide; Church Choir; Rep Stu Cncl; Forestry.

SHARTLE, BRENDA; Saegertown HS; Meadville, PA; (Y); Art Clb; Church Yth Grp; Spanish Clb; SADD; Church Choir; Hon Roll; Guilford Tech CC; RN.

SHARY, TIMOTHY M; The Harrisburg Acad; Middletown, PA; (Y); Drama Clb; Capt Quiz Bowl; Stage Crew; Nwsp Stf; Sec Sr Cls; Stat Crs Cntry; Hon Roll; PA Govnrs Schl Arts Crtv Wrtng 85; Schlstc Wrtng Awds 85-86; Humanities.

SHATTO, JOHN; Central Dauphin HS; Harrisburg, PA; (Y); Computer Clb; Var Bsbl; JV Bsktbl; Var L Trk; Hghst Scr AHSME Tst 86; Comp Prog.

SHATZ, ELLYN; Upper Dublin HS; Willow Grove, PA; (Y); Camera Clb; Intnl Clb; JA; Office Aide; Science Clb; Temple Yth Grp; Nwsp Rptr; Yrbk Phtg; Yrbk Rptr; Yrbk Stf; Meritorious Achvt Awd Gratz Coll 86; Pediatrician.

SHATZ, REBECCA; Coudersport JR SR HS; Coudersport, PA; (Y); 6/87; Pres VP 4-H; French Clb; Flag Corp; Yrbk Stf; Stat Bsktbl; 4-H Awd; High Hon Roll; Hon Roll; NHS; Nice AIC 85; Schrlshp Intl Exc 86; Med.

SHATZER, JASON; Waynesboro Area SR HS; Waynesboro, PA; (Y); Art Clb; Stage Crew; Nwsp Phtg; Nwsp Stf; Yrbk Phtg; Rep Stu Cncl; Im Bowling; Var Socr; Im Sftbl; Im Vllybl; Penn ST U; Archtctrl Engrng.

SHATZER, MELANIE; Laurel Valley JR SR HS; New Florence, PA; (Y); 12/87; VP AFS; Pres Church Yth Grp; Hosp Aide; Varsity Clb; Nwsp Ed-Chief; Yrbk Stf; VP Stu Cncl; Var L Sftbl; Var L Vllybl; Hon Roll; U Of Pittsburgh; Nrsng.

SHATZER, VICKI R; Greencastle Antrim HS; Greencastle, PA; (Y); Church Yth Grp; Girl Scts; Political Wkr; Church Choir; Var L Bsktbl; Var L Sftbl; 3rd Prz Ins Ci Fair 83-84; Ltrs In Bsktbl & Sftbl 86; PA St; Vtrnry Med.

SHAUGHNESSY, CHRISTINE; West Scranton HS; Scranton, PA; (Y); 50/250; Boys Clb Am; Dance Clb; Debate Tm; Letterman Clb; NFL; Red Cross Aide; Ski Clb; Spanish Clb; Speech Tm; Nwsp Stf; Elem Educ.

SHAULIS, STEVE; Ligonier Vallly SR HS; Laughlintown, PA; (Y); JV Bsktbl; Var Ftbl; Penn ST U; Arch.

SHAULL, MIKE; Boiling Springs HS; Boiling Spgs, PA; (Y); Boy Scts; Band; Jazz Band; Mrchg Band; Symp Band; Nwsp Stf; Var L Socr; Var L Trk; Hon Roll; Aud/Vis; Boy Scout Citatn 82.

SHAW, BRIAN; Philipsburg-Osceola Area HS; West Decatur, PA; (Y); 61/250; Am Leg Boys St; Letterman Clb; Pres Band; Concert Band; Yrbk Stf; Stu Cncl; Var L Ftbl; Wt Lftg; Hon Roll; NEDT Awd; PA ST; Mech Engrng.

SHAW, BRIAN; South Allegheny HS; Mc Keesport, PA; (S); 3/184; Exploring; German Clb; Quiz Bowl; Sec Trs Science Clb; Trk; High Hon Roll; Hon Roll; Allegheny Sngr Rsrch Inst Sci Comp 1st Pl 86; PA Govnrs Schl Art Semi-Fin 85; 3 Rvrs Art Fstvl Bnnr; Archit.

SHAW, DALE; Philipsburg-Osceola HS; West Decatur, PA; (Y); 87/240; Church Yth Grp; Yrbk Stf; Stu Cncl; Var Bsbl; Hon Roll; Bus.

SHAW JR, DALE; Highlands SR HS; Tarentum, PA; (Y); Pres Church Yth Grp; Rep Stu Cncl; L Var Ftbl; L JV Trk; Wt Lftg; High Hon Roll; Jr NHS; Pres NHS; Human Relatns Comm 83-86; Clemson; Elec Engrng.

SHAW, DAWN; Hempfield Area SR HS; Irwin, PA; (Y); Chorus; Church Choir; Concert Band; Jazz Band; School Musical; Exploring; Band; Mrchg Band; Stage Crew; Cit Awd; Dist U Hnrs Choir 85; IUP; Music.

SHAW, DONNA M; Scranton Central HS; Scranton, PA; (Y); 1/298; Cmnty Wkr; Political Wkr; Orch; Stage Crew; Yrbk Phtg; Rep Stu Cncl; High Hon Roll; Jr NHS; NHS; Ntl Merit SF; PA Gvrns Sci Schl 84; Nvl ROTC Schlrshp 85; U Of PA; Med.

SHAW, ELIZABETH; Manheim Central SR HS; Penryn, PA; (Y); Church Yth Grp; Chorus; Church Choir; Orch; School Musical; Var L Bsktbl; Dnfth Awd; Hon Roll; NHS; Pres Schlstc & Ftns Awd 85-86; Schlrshp Womens Club 86; U DE; Entomology.

SHAW, HEATHER; Portersville Christian Schl; Mars, PA; (Y); Chorus; Church Choir; Cheerleading; Wt Lftg; Hon Roll; NHS.

SHAW, JENNY; Frazier HS; Perryopolis, PA; (Y); High Hon Roll; Cosmotology.

SHAW, KELLI; Central HS; E Freedom, PA; (Y); Church Yth Grp; FBLA; Bsktbl; Score Keeper; Varsity Clb; Yrbk Stf; Rep Stu Cncl; Sftbl.

SHAW, KEVIN; Clearfield Area HS; Bigler, PA; (Y); 4-H; FFA; High Hon Roll; Hon Roll; Cngrssnl Schlr 86; Acdmc All Amer 85.

SHAW, KIM; Lackawanna Trail HS; Factoryville, PA; (Y); Camera Clb; Church Yth Grp; JA; Ski Clb; Chorus; Church Choir; School Musical; Stu Cncl; JV Sftbl; Hon Roll; Nrsg.

SHAW, LATHEA; Highlands SR HS; Tarentum, PA; (Y); Church Yth Grp; Library Aide; Teachers Aide; Church Choir; Church Yth Grp; Jr Cls; Hon Roll; Jr NHS; Suprntdt Advsry Comm 8086; Humn Rel Comm 79-86; Bus.

SHAW, MARCIE; New Castle HS; New Castle, PA; (S); 20/236; AFS; Letterman Clb; NFL; Drill Tm; Nwsp Sprt Ed; Rep Sr Cls; Rep Stu Cncl; L Bsktbl; NHS.

SHAW, MARK ANDREW; Keystone Oaks HS; Pittsburgh, PA; (Y); Boy Scts; Chess Clb; Church Yth Grp; Exploring; Pres Spanish Clb; L Var Bsktbl; L Var Golf; NHS; Pres Schlr; Spnsh Intrnl Frgn Lng Awd 86; Egl Schlrshp Entrprnrl Stds Prgrm 86; MVP Vrsty Bsktbll 86; WA & Jefferson Coll; Accntng.

SHAW, MARTHA; Grove City HS; Volant, PA; (Y); Sec Church Yth Grp; Cmnty Wkr; French Clb; Science Clb; Chorus; Church Choir; High Hon Roll; Hon Roll; Natl Hstry Day 1st Pl Dist & Regnl 83-84, Hnrb Mntn 84-85; Choral Ltr 85-86; Westminster Coll; Elem Ed.

SHAW, MELINDA; General Mclane HS; Edinboro, PA; (Y); Spanish Clb; Teachers Aide; Yrbk Stf; High Hon Roll; Hon Roll.

SHAW, PEGGY; Central Dauphin East HS; Harrisburg, PA; (Y); 6/250; Chorus; Concert Band; Orch; School Musical; Trs Sr Cls; Var L Tennis; High Hon Roll; Trs NHS; Rotary Awd; Joseph Ciara Memrl Music Awd 85-86; Jody D Smith Memrl Schlrshp Awd 85-86; Cnty, Dist, Regnl Chorus 85; Mansfield U; Math.

SHAW, SETH; Manheim Central HS; Penryn, PA; (Y); 46/237; Debate Tm; Library Aide; Bsbl; L Bsktbl; Coach Actv; L Ftbl; Vllybl; Wt Lftg; Hon Roll; Rotary Awd; Comp Sci.

SHAW, TIMOTHY; Clearfield Area HS; Bigler, PA; (Y); 107/301; VICA; High Hon Roll; Hon Roll; Wmsport CC; Elec Engrng.

SHAW, VIRGINIA; Carninal O Hara HS; Springfield, PA; (Y); 131/772; Latin Clb; Band; Concert Band; Mrchg Band; Pep Band; School Musical; Hon Roll; West Chester U; Music.

SHAWALUK, MARYANN; St Basil Acad; Phialdelphia, PA; (Y); 30/100; Cmnty Wkr; Drama Clb; Spanish Clb; Im Cheerleading; Hon Roll; Fll Schlrshp 82-86; Villanova U; Nrsng.

SHAWARYN, MARLA; St Basil Acad; Philadelphia, PA; (S); Church Yth Grp; Cmnty Wkr; French Clb; Latin Clb; Science Clb; Chorus; Madrigals; Bsktbl; Clark U; Psychlgy.

SHAWGO, REBECCA; Lakeview HS; Sandy Lake, PA; (S); 6/120; Intnl Clb; Library Aide; Color Guard; School Play; Nwsp Stf; Cheerleading; Trk; Twrlr; NHS; Art Inst Of Pitts; Fshn Merch.

SHAWLEY, GRETCHEN; Hollidaysburg Area HS; Duncansville, PA; (Y); 26/351; Church Yth Grp; French Clb; Chorus; Im Vllybl; Gov Hon Prg Awd; High Hon Roll; Hon Roll; NHS; Phrmcst.

SHAWVER, CATHY; West Snyder HS; Mcclure, PA; (Y); Trs FNA; Yrbk Stf; Rep Frsh Cls; Rep Soph Cls; Rep Jr Cls; Sec Stu Cncl; JV Mgr Bsktbl; JV Capt Fld Hcky; Hon Roll; NEDT Awd; Psych.

SHAY, DAVID; Freedom HS; Bethlehem, PA; (Y); 5/445; Pres Church Yth Grp; Math Tm; Band; Concert Band; Mrchg Band; Hon Roll; NHS; Ntl Merit Ltr; 3rd Plc PA Jr Acad Sci ST Sci Fr 84; Plcd Le High U Math Cntst 86; Moravian; Math.

SHEA, JENNIFER; Warren Area HS; Warren, PA; (Y); Church Yth Grp; Varsity Clb; School Musical; Yrbk Bus Mgr; Rep Stu Cncl; Sftbl; Vllybl; Hon Roll; Jr NHS; Rep Jr Cls; Schl Apprctn Awd 86; Outstndng Achvmnt Physcl Educ 86; Penn ST U; Telecomm.

SHEA, RICHARD; Northern Cambria HS; Barnesboro, PA; (Y); 62/115; Var L Bsbl; JV Var Ftbl; Var Wt Lftg; St Frncs Coll.

SHEA, SHERRY; Tunkhannock HS; Tunkhannock, PA; (S); 23/330; Cmnty Wkr; Drama Clb; German Clb; Latin Clb; Stage Crew; Rep Jr Cls; Bsktbl; Trk; Hon Roll; NHS; Acadmc Al-Amer 84-85; Lycoming Coll; Pre-Med.

SHEA, TINA; Technical HS; Scranton, PA; (Y); JA; Pep Clb; Chorus; Var Crs Cntry; Var Trk.

SHEA, WILLIAM T; Henmpfield Area SR HS; Greensburg, PA; (Y); 40/657; Boy Scts; Nwsp Rptr; Nwsp Sprt Ed; Nwsp Stf; High Hon Roll; Hon Roll; Jr NHS; NHS; Wartburg Coll Regents Schlrshp 86; Pres Acad Ftnss Awd 86; Hnr Grad Awd 86; Wartburg Coll; Comm.

SHEADER, SCOTT; Sto-Rox SR HS; Mc Kees Rocks, PA; (Y); Boys Clb Am; School Play; Stage Crew; Nwsp Rptr; Var Capt Ftbl; Trk; Wt Lftg; Hon Roll; NEDT Awd; High Hon Roll; Art Cont 83-85; Electrl Engrng.

SHEAFFER, ANNMARIE; Owen J Roberts HS; Elverson, PA; (Y); Church Yth Grp; Drama Clb; French Clb; Pep Clb; SADD; Band; Chorus; Stu Cncl; Var Cheerleading; Hon Roll; Miss Natl Teen Ager Fnlst Trophy 85-86; Metro Philadelphias Miss Hospitality Teen Ager 85-86; Temple U; Dental Hygienist.

SHEAFFER, DIANE; Central Dauphu East SR HS; Harrisburg, PA; (Y); 26/289; Chorus; Concert Band; Mrchg Band; VP Frsh Cls; Var Cheerleading; Var Mgr(s); Var Vllybl; Hon Roll; Jr NHS; NHS; Radiation Thrpy Tech.

SHEAFFER, JENNIFER; Greenwood HS; Millerstown, PA; (S); 3/70; ROTC; Band; Chorus; Concert Band; Flag Corp; Mrchg Band; Pep Band; School Musical; School Play; Nwsp Rptr; Hugh O Brian Ldrshp Awd 85; Cert Recgntn Outstndng Svc Commonwlth 84.

SHEAFFER, KEITH; Greenwood HS; Millerstown, PA; (Y); Cmnty Wkr; 4-H; Band; Concert Band; Mrchg Band; Yrbk Stf; Rep Soph Cls; Trk; Cit Awd; 4-H Awd; Hgst Money Rais For CROP 82-86; 4-H JR Ldrshp Awd 80-85; 4-H Ldr 86; Drexel U; Arch.

SHEAFFER, KIMBERLY RUTH; Manheim Central HS; Manheim, PA; (Y); Church Yth Grp; School Musical; School Play; Yrbk Stf; Off Sr Cls; JV L Fld Hcky; Mgr L Trk; Hon Roll; Cert Mrn Bio Shrt Stdy 83; Yth Ftnss Awd 86; ABWA Schlrshp 86; U Of DE; Spcl Educ.

SHEAFFER, LAURA; Carlisle HS; Carlisle, PA; (Y); Sec Church Yth Grp; Ski Clb; Color Guard; Mrchg Band; Nwsp Rptr; Hon Roll; Spn Rvr Anthlgy Actrs 85; Plyd Piano 81-86; Psych.

SHEAFFER, MATTHEW; South Western HS; Hanover, PA; (Y); Art Clb; Letterman Clb; Varsity Clb; Nwsp Stf; Yrbk Stf; Trk; Elks Awd; Leo Lawler Trk & Fld Scholar 86; Yrk Cnty Trk & Fld Hnr Roll 86; 6th Pl Ephrata Relays 86; PA Schl Arts; Comm Art.

SHEAHAN, KELLI ANN; Little Flower HS; Philadelphia, PA; (Y); 40/380; Church Yth Grp; Trk; Second Hons 84-86.

SHEAHAN, KELLY; Franklin Regional HS; Murrysville, PA; (Y); AFS; Church Yth Grp; Pres 4-H; JA; Q&S; Chorus; School Play; Trk; 4-H Awd; High Hon Roll; Equine Sci.

SHEALER, RONALD C; Gettysburg HS; Gettysburg, PA; (Y); Golf; Trk; Wt Lftg; Wrstlng; Hon Roll; Millersville; Inds Arts.

SHEALY, STEVE; Ambridge Area HS; Baden, PA; (Y); German Clb; Pep Clb; Jazz Band; Mrchg Band; Pep Band; School Play; Symp Band; JP Sousa Awd; Lion Awd; All ST Orchstra 85-86; Marine Corp Semper Fidelis Awd 86.

SHEARER, DAVID C; Butler Area SR HS; Butler, PA; (Y); Boy Scts; Exploring; JA; Math Clb; Im Bsktbl; Var Crs Cntry; Var Trk; Hon Roll; Jr NHS; Ski Clb; Pres Acadmc Ftnss Awd 86; Grove City Clg; Elec Engrg.

SHEARER, JONI; Jersey Shore Area SR HS; Linden, PA; (Y); Church Yth Grp; Computer Clb; French Clb; Library Aide; Lit Mag; Gov Hon Prg Awd; High Hon Roll; Hon Roll; Law.

SHEARER, JUD; E L Meyers HS; Wilkes-Barre, PA; (Y); 3/141; Ski Clb; Chorus; Pres Jr Cls; Pres Sr Cls; Rep Stu Cncl; Var Crs Cntry; Var Trk; Hon Roll; Jr NHS; NHS; E Mennonite Coll.

SHEARER, LISA; Exeter Twp HS; Birdsboro, PA; (Y); Leo Clb; Band; Camera Clb; Orch; Alvernia; Bus Adm.

SHEARER, LOIS; Carlisle SR HS; Carlisle, PA; (Y); Hosp Aide; Rep Frsh Cls; Rep Soph Cls; Rep Sr Cls; Im L Cheerleading; Var L Mgr(s); L Trk; Im JV Vllybl; Hon Roll; Bloomsburg U; Elem Educ.

SHEARER, MARCY L; Waynesboro Area SR HS; Waynesboro, PA; (Y); 33/341; Chorus; Yrbk Ed-Chief; High Hon Roll; NHS; Waynesboro Coll Clb Schlrshp 86; Exectve Cncl Mbr 86; Franklin Cnty Honey Queen 85; Shippensburg U; Crmnl Jstce.

SHEARER, MARK J; Red Land HS; Etters, PA; (Y); 17/275; Pres Church Yth Grp; Chorus; Church Choir; School Musical; Var Ftbl; Wt Lftg; French Hon Soc; High Hon Roll; Sec NHS; Acpl Chr; Engrng.

SHEARER, PETER W; Belle Vernon Area HS; Belle Vernon, PA; (Y); Church Yth Grp; Var L Bsktbl; Var L Ftbl; Hon Roll; Prfct Atten Awd; Amer Lgn Schl Awd 83.

SHEARER II, RODNEY; Spring Grove SR HS; Spg Grove, PA; (Y); 30/315; Chess Clb; Chorus; Church Choir; Ftbl; Trk; Hon Roll; Schl Schlstc Point Awd 85-86; Nrotc; Biochem.

SHEARER, TODD; Canon Mc Millan Schl; Canonsburg, PA; (Y); Church Yth Grp; French Clb; Letterman Clb; Varsity Clb; Crs Cntry; Trk; NHS; U Pittsburgh; Engr.

SHEARER, TOM; Mc Connellsburg HS; Mc Connellsburg, PA; (Y); FFA; Pep Clb; Varsity Clb; Var Bsbl; Var Bsktbl; Var Socr; High Hon Roll; Hon Roll.

SHEARMAN, SCOTT; Windber Area HS; Windber, PA; (Y); Yrbk Stf; Var L Bsbl; JV Im Bsktbl; Hon Roll; Bus Admin.

SHECKMAN, SAMUEL P; Cheltenham HS; Elkins Park, PA; (Y); 22/365; Nwsp Rptr; Yrbk Stf; JV Im Bsktbl; JV Socr; Im Vllybl; French Hon Soc; Hon Roll; PA JR Acad Sci Awd 85; Hortense-Alvin Greenberg Awd 85; Advrtsng.

SHEDLOCK, DENISE; Moshannon Valley JR SR HS; Ramey, PA; (Y); Hosp Aide; Pep Clb; Red Cross Aide; Spanish Clb; Band; Chorus; Concert Band; Mrchg Band; Pep Band; Nrsng.

SHEDRICK, PAMELA; Langley HS; Pittsburgh, PA; (Y); Hosp Aide; Yrbk Stf; Vllybl; Hon Roll; TN ST U; Pre-Med.

SHEEHAN, AMY; Kennedy Christian HS; Brookfield, OH; (Y); Pep Clb; Spanish Clb; Band; Concert Band; Mrchg Band; Pep Band; Im Vllybl; Hon Roll; Nrsng.

SHEEHAN, CHRISTA; Cardinal O Hara HS; Springfield, PA; (Y); 10/772; Band; Concert Band; Mrchg Band; Orch; School Musical; Nwsp Phtg; Nwsp Sprt Ed; High Hon Roll; NHS; Rotary Awd; PA Jr Acad Of Sci-2nd 85; Maxima Cum Laude-2nd Pl 86; Intl Rltns.

SHEEHAN, ESTELLA; Little Flower Catholic HS For Girls; Philadelphia, PA; (Y); 10/415; VP French Clb; Stage Crew; Rep Stu Cncl; Var L Bowling; Hon Roll; NHS; Prfct Atten Awd; Church Yth Grp; Computer Clb; Hosp Aide; Soc Stu Acdmc Awd, Pres Acdmc Ftns Awd 86; Hnbl Mntn Sci Fari 84; Temple U; Mgt Info Systems.

SHEELEY, CALLIANNE; Carlisle SR HS; Carlisle, PA; (Y); 4/8; Art Clb; Lit Mag; High Hon Roll; Hon Roll; Govnrs Schl For Arts 85; Tuitn Schlrshp BYU 86; Frnch Awd 86; BYU; Flm.

SHEELY, BARB; Cedar Cliff HS; Mechanicsburg, PA; (Y); Camera Clb; Key Clb; Latin Clb; SADD; Co-Capt Flag Corp; Rep Stu Cncl; Im Bowling; Hon Roll; Prfct Attndnc 84-85; Air Force; Med.

SHEERER, JOHN; Fox Chapel HS; Pittsburgh, PA; (Y); Boys Clb Am; Church Yth Grp; Exploring; Chorus; Rep Frsh Cls; Rep Soph Cls; VP Bsktbl; Im Ftbl; Im Sftbl; Cmmnctns.

SHEESLEY, GEORGETTA; Punxsutawney Area HS; Punxsutawney, PA; (Y); Pres FBLA; Band; Mrchg Band; Trk; Legl Aid.

SHEESLEY, KIM; West Allegheny HS; Coraopolis, PA; (Y); Church Yth Grp; FBLA; Library Aide; Spanish Clb; SADD; VICA; Rep Stu Cncl; Hon Roll; Huntingdon Daily News Superior Staffer Awd 85-86; Johnstown Tribune Jrnlst Awd 86; Penn ST U; Jrnlsm.

SHEESLEY, LISA; Marion Center Area HS; Indiana, PA; (Y); 46/160; FBLA; SADD; Varsity Clb; Color Guard; Yrbk Stf; Trs Jr Cls; Trs Sr Cls; Score Keeper; Hon Roll; JR Accntng Awd; In U PA; Bu Adm.

SHEETS, ERIN; Soegertown HS; Meadville, PA; (Y); 1/125; VP Church Yth Grp; VP Sec 4-H; Quiz Bowl; Ski Clb; Pres Band; Yrbk Ed-Chief; Jr NHS; NHS; Varsity Clb; Concert Band; Sale Carnegie Cls Schlrshp Wnr 86; Allegheny Coll Smr Schl Schlrshp Wnr 86; Chem.

SHEETS, PAMELA J; Waynesburg Central HS; Nantucket, MA; (Y); 21/206; Pres VP 4-H; French Clb; Letterman Clb; Office Aide; Ski Clb; Church Choir; Color Guard; Nwsp Stf; Yrbk Stf; L Var Bsktbl; Girls Track Ideal Squad 86; Mentor Prog Bryant Coll 86; PA ST Sci Fair,2nd Pl Physics 86; Bryant Coll; Hotel & Rest Mgt.

SHEETS, REBECCA; Sullivan County HS; Muncy Valley, PA; (Y); 8/92; Sec Church Yth Grp; Key Clb; Sec Concert Band; Jazz Band; Mrchg Band; Pep Band; Yrbk Ed-Chief; Hon Roll; NHS; Acctng.

SHEETS, SCOTT; North Star HS; Stoystown, PA; (Y); Aud/Vis; FCA; Chorus; School Musical; School Play; Stage Crew; Yrbk Phtg; Trs Stu Cncl; Trk; Hon Roll; Tv Brdcstng.

SHEETZ, RANDY; Cumberland Valley HS; Mechanicsburg, PA; (Y); Arch.

SHEFFER, JANA; Newport HS; Newport, PA; (S); Chorus; Yrbk Stf; JV Var Cheerleading; Lanc Genrl Hosp Schl Of Nursng.

SHEFFER, TRAVIS; Dover Area HS; Dover, PA; (Y); Boy Scts; FFA; Stage Crew; Hon Roll; FFA Outdr Rec 84-85; FFA Fsh & Wldlfe Mgmt 85-86; FFA ST Conv 17th Wildlife Cont 85-86; Penn ST; Wldlfe Biol.

SHEFFIELD, DAWN; Lancaster Counrty Day HS; Lancaster, PA; (Y); Cmnty Wkr; Teachers Aide; School Play; Yrbk Stf; Lit Mag; Var Bsktbl; JV Fld Hcky; High Hon Roll; Hon Roll; NHS; Vet-Sci.

SHEFFIELD, JESSICA; East Juniata HS; Mcalisterville, PA; (Y); 1/100; Drm Mjr(t); School Musical; Yrbk Stf; VP Soph Cls; Pres Jr Cls; Pres Stu Cncl; Var Bsktbl; Var Fld Hcky; High Hon Roll; NHS; Penn ST U; Chem.

SHEFFIELD, SHELLY MARIE; Moon Area SR HS; Moon Township, PA; (Y); Church Yth Grp; Computer Clb; GAA; SADD; School Musical; Var Crs Cntry; Var L Trk; Hon Roll; Chorus; Church Choir; Blck Incentv Schlrshp 86-87; Aliquippa Wmns Achvt Clb Outstdng Sprng Stu 86; PA ST U; Comp Sci.

SHEFFIELD, TANYA; Montour HS; Mckees Rocks, PA; (Y); Computer Clb; Drama Clb; Spanish Clb; Variety Show; Hon Roll; Prfct Atten Awd; Pres Schlr; Dance Clb; Spec Cngrssnl Sem 85; U Pittsburgh; Vet Med.

SHEFFLER, LYNN; New Castle SR HS; New Castle, PA; (S); 19/236; Pres Church Yth Grp; Computer Clb; Girl Scts; SADD; Band; Mrchg Band; Nwsp Rptr; NHS; Blackburn Coll Hnr Awd 85; Engl Dept Awd 83; 2nd Pl ST Jr Acad Sci 85; Medcl Tech.

SHEHAN, STEPHANIE; Central HS; Roaring Spg, PA; (Y); Church Yth Grp; Cmnty Wkr; VP FBLA; GAA; Varsity Clb; Capt Band; Chorus; Capt Color Guard; JV Bsktbl; Pres JV Sftbl; Law Day Schlrshp 86; Katharine Gibbs; Lgl Sec.

SHEHY, DARLA; Wilmington Area HS; Pulaski, PA; (Y); 36/123; Church Yth Grp; Sec 4-H; Girl Scts; Sec Key Clb; Pres Latin Clb; Chorus; Church Choir; 4-H Awd; Hon Roll; Penn ST U; Nrsng.

SHEIDY, MELISSA; Elizabethtown Area HS; Elizabethtown, PA; (Y); Church Yth Grp; Office Aide; Church Choir; Stu Cncl; Cheerleading; Powder Puff Ftbl; U Miami; Wldlf Bio.

SHELDON, ERIK; Carmichaels Area HS; Crucible, PA; (Y); 50/126; Aud/Vis; Church Yth Grp; Drama Clb; Library Aide; Ski Clb; Spanish Clb; SADD; Band; School Play; Stage Crew; Waynesburg Coll; Cmnctns.

SHELDON, TRACEY; Southmoreland HS; Scottdale, PA; (Y); Church Yth Grp; Dance Clb; Drama Clb; French Clb; Latin Clb; Office Aide; Pep Clb; Ski Clb; Chorus; School Musical; Wn Rtry Clb Awd Essy On Peace 86; IN U Of PA; Mrktng.

SHELEHEDA, MICHELLE; Bethel Park SR HS; Bethel Park, PA; (Y); Chorus; School Musical; VP Capt Cheerleading; High Hon Roll; NHS; Hotl & Restrnt Mgmt.

SHELHAMER, BEV; Seneca HS; Erie, PA; (Y); 10/135; Pres Church Yth Grp; Office Aide; Color Guard; Concert Band; School Play; Stage Crew; Rep Stu Cncl; Hon Roll; NHS; Pres Schlr; Erie Bus Ctr Schlrshp 86; Erie Bus Center; Med Sec.

SHELLENBERGER, AMY J; Milton Area SR HS; Milton, PA; (Y); 15/207; Sec Trs Key Clb; Pres VP Spanish Clb; Hst Varsity Clb; Yrbk Stf; Var Crs Cntry; Var Trk; NHS; Booster Clb Schlrshp 86; Dickinson Coll; Bio.

SHELLENBERGER, PARRISH; Juniata HS; Port Royal, PA; (Y); Computer Clb; Varsity Clb; Trk; Vllybl; Wrstlng; Hon Roll; Golden Hammer Awd Best Wood Project 85; Lincoln Tech; Drafting.

SHELLENBERGER, TAMMY; Juniata HS; Mifflintown, PA; (Y); Camera Clb; FHA; Varsity Clb; School Play; Yrbk Phtg; JV Cheerleading; Var JV Sftbl; Im Vllybl; Hon Roll; Awd JV Lttrf Sftbl 85; Awd JV Lttr Chrldng 84-85; ACCNTNG.

SHELLENHAMER, STACY; Palmyra SR HS; Palmyra, PA; (Y); 33/200; Hosp Aide; Quiz Bowl; Twrlr; Hon Roll; West Chester Nrsng Sch; Nrsng.

SHELLER, MELINDA; Bishop Guilfoyle HS; Altoona, PA; (S); 8/149; Hosp Aide; Ski Clb; Yrbk Phtg; Yrbk Stf; Off Sr Cls; Rep Stu Cncl; Var Cheerleading; High Hon Roll; Hon Roll; Sec NHS; PA ST U; Nrsng.

SHELLEY, JENNIFER; Taylor Allderdice HS; Pittsburgh, PA; (Y); Hosp Aide; High Hon Roll; Hon Roll; Jr NHS; Ntl Merit Ltr; Bio.

SHELLEY, LISA; Warwick HS; Lititz, PA; (Y); 34/240; Office Aide; Varsity Clb; Bsktbl; Fld Hcky; Mgr(s); Hon Roll; NHS; Church Yth Grp; Library Aide; Outstndg Bus Stu Awd; Rcrd Exprs Athl Wk; Bus.

SHELLHAMER, DEBRA C; Northwestern Lehigh HS; Germansville, PA; (Y); 8/132; Am Leg Aux Girls St; Intnl Clb; Quiz Bowl; Varsity Clb; Pres Soph Cls; Pres Jr Cls; Pres Sr Cls; Stu Cncl; Bsktbl; Fld Hcky; All-STR Sr Fld Hcky Plyr 86; All-Str Sr Sftbl Plyr 86; Pres Acdmc Physcl Ftns Awd 86; Bloomsburg U; Accntng.

SHELLHAMER, PAMELA; Parkland HS; Orefield, PA; (Y); 53/459; Church Yth Grp; Latin Clb; Leo Clb; Chorus; Church Choir; School Musical; Swing Chorus; High Hon Roll; Hon Roll; NHS; Nrsng.

SHELPMAN, TRACY; Bethel Park SR HS; Bethel Park, PA; (Y); FBLA; Chorus; JV Powder Puff Ftbl; Var Sftbl; JV Vllybl; 5th Pl Data Prcssng Concepts FBLA Sprng Ldrshp Conf 86; Real Est.

SHELTMAN, WILLIAM; Lewisburg Area HS; W Milton, PA; (Y); French Clb; Spanish Clb; Band; Chorus; School Musical; Trk; Bus Adm.

SHELTON, ERNEST; Germantown HS; Philadelphia, PA; (Y); Band; Var Bsbl; Hon Roll; Prfct Atten Awd 83; Cultural Grp 83; Georgetown U; Bus Adm.

SHELTON, PAGE; Unionville HS; Chadds Ford, PA; (Y); 90/300; Varsity Clb; Rep Sr Cls; Var L Bsktbl; Var L Fld Hcky; High Hon Roll; Hon Roll; Art Clb; Camera Clb; Church Yth Grp; French Clb; Slctd Xmas Trnmnt All Str Bsktbl, All Str SCCL & Kystn ST Gms Fld Hcky 85.

SHELTON, TAWNYA; Octorara Area HS; Cochranville, PA; (Y); 13/161; Church Yth Grp; Chorus; Yrbk Bus Mgr; Yrbk Ed-Chief; Yrbk Rptr; Yrbk Stf; JV Var Fld Hcky; Var Sftbl; Hon Roll; NHS; Chester Cnty Stu Forum 85-87; Resp Ther.

SHELVEY, JIM; Meadville SR HS; Meadville, PA; (Y); 56/354; Hon Roll; Natl Ftns Awd 85-86; Acctng.

SHEMANSKI, SEAN; Liberty HS; Bethlehem, PA; (Y); Var L Socr; Hon Roll; Chem.

SHEMELUK, JOHN ROBERT; Interboro HS; Prospect Park, PA; (S); 46/263; AFS; Key Clb; Pres Chorus; Concert Band; Jazz Band; Mrchg Band; VP Stu Cncl; Var Capt Bsbl; NHS; Rotary Awd; Dist Band XII 85 & 86; Rgnl Band VI 86; W Chester U; Mus Educ.

SHENCK, JONI; Cedar Cliff HS; New Cumberland, PA; (Y); 97/295; German Clb; Sec Key Clb; Cheerleading; Var Crs Cntry; Var Trk; Hon Roll; Vrsty Ltr Trck & 5th Pl Dist 84-85; Vrsty Ltr Crss Cntry 84-85; Bus Mgmt.

SHENK, CAROL R; Lancaster Mennonite HS; Manheim, PA; (Y); Sec Church Yth Grp; Cmnty Wkr; Teachers Aide; Trs Acpl Chr; Nwsp Stf; Yrbk Stf; Im Sftbl; High Hon Roll; Sec NHS; Ntl Merit Sf; Goshen Coll; Nrsng Ed.

SHENK, ERIC; Manheim Central HS; Manheim, PA; (Y); Band; Chorus; Concert Band; Jazz Band; Mrchg Band; School Musical; School Play; VP L Trk; Hon Roll; Bst Male Lead Prfrmnc 86; 4-Way Tst Awd 86; Chem Engrng.

SHENK, RODNEY; Manheim Central SR HS; Manheim, PA; (Y); Church Yth Grp; Hon Roll; Wild Life Mgmnt.

SHENOSKY, DON; Punxsutawney HS; Punxsutawney, PA; (Y); French Clb; Math Tm; Varsity Clb; Band; Concert Band; Mrchg Band; Pep Band; Variety Show; Ftbl; Wt Lftg; PA ST U; Nclr Engrng.

SHEPARD, BONNIE; Mount Carmel Area JR SR HS; Kulpmont, PA; (Y); Trs FNA; Key Clb; Red Cross Aide; Spanish Clb; Concert Band; Mrchg Band; Nwsp Rptr; Nwsp Stf; Hon Roll; FTA; Lgsltv Cmmnty Svc Awd 86.

SHEPARD, NANCY; Cocalico HS; Stevens, PA; (Y); 70/171; Sec Church Yth Grp; Hst FBLA; Church Choir; School Musical; Hon Roll; Prfct Atten Awd; Art Clb; Computer Clb; 4-H; Eastern Mennonite; Elem Tchr.

SHEPHARD, GRETCHEN; Farrell HS; Farrell, PA; (Y); 16/87; Sec Church Yth Grp; French Clb; Science Clb; Band; Chorus; VP Church Choir; Stat Swmmng; L Trk; PA Free Entrprs Wk 86; Dist Chrs 86; Polit Sci.

SHEPHARD, KIMBERLY; Corry Area HS; Corry, PA; (S); Church Yth Grp; French Clb; Trs SADD; Trs Y-Teens; Drm Mjr(t); Mrchg Band; Yrbk Ed-Chief; JV Cheerleading; Phys Ther.

SHEPHERD, DONNA; Governor Mifflin HS; Shillington, PA; (Y); 12/274; Hosp Aide; Band; Concert Band; Mrchg Band; School Musical; Trk; Vllybl; Hon Roll; Jr NHS; NHS; Elem Ed.

SHEPHERD, MELISA; Oxford Area HS; Lincoln Universit, PA; (Y); 5/161; Pres FTA; Yrbk Sprt Ed; Hon Roll; NHS; SICO Fndtn Scholar 86; Art Mst Outstndg 84-86; Ind Art Mst Outstndg 86; Millersville U; Art Ed.

SHEPHERD, PATRICIA; Kiski Area HS; Vandergrift, PA; (Y); 6/388; VP JA; Math Tm; SADD; Chorus; Yrbk Ed-Chief; Elks Awd; High Hon Roll; NHS; Ntl Merit Ltr; Pres Schlr; Duquesen U Schlrs Awd 86; Leechburg Lioness Clb Schlrshp 86; Vandergirft Women Clb Schrshp 86; Duquesne U; Bus Adm.

SHEPPARD, KIM; Moniteau HS; Butler, PA; (Y); Church Yth Grp; French Clb; SADD; Band; Chorus; Concert Band; Jazz Band; Mrchg Band; Hon Roll; Clrn U; Chld Psychlgy.

SHEPTOCK, MARYBETH; Bethlehem Catholic HS; Bethlehem, PA; (Y); Exploring; Key Clb; School Play; Yrbk Stf; Cheerleading; Hon Roll; Bus Admin.

SHERANKO, RONALD; Laurel Highlands SR HS; Hopwood, PA; (Y); 37/365; Pres Church Yth Grp; Spanish Clb; Chorus; Church Choir; School Musical; High Hon Roll; Jr NHS; Penn ST Fayette.

SHERBINE, ERIC; Portage Area HS; Portage, PA; (S); 15/122; Varsity Clb; Trs Soph Cls; Trs Jr Cls; Capt Var Ftbl; JV Var Wrstlng; NHS; U Of Pittsburgh; Comp Sci.

SHERBONDY, BETH; Yough SR HS; W Newton, PA; (Y); French Clb; FBLA; Band; Concert Band; Mrchg Band; NHS; Prfct Atten Awd; Wstmrlnd Cnty Cmnty Coll; Acctg.

SHERBONDY, BILL; Mt Pleasant Area HS; Norvelt, PA; (Y); Var L Bsbl; Var L Ftbl; Wt Lftg; Hon Roll; All-Western Pa Legion Basebll Team 86; Distct 31 Legion Battin Title 86.

SHERBONDY, MARY J; Bethel Park SR HS; Bethel Park, PA; (Y); Church Yth Grp; DECA; Key Clb; Sec NFL; Speech Tm; JV Powder Puff Ftbl; JV Sftbl; Hon Roll; Kiwanis Schlrshp Frm Bthl Pk Kiwanis 86; Dgr Dstnctn Ntl Frnsc League 86; CA U Of PA; Spch Pthlgy.

SHERFY, BETH; Elizabethtown Area HS; Elizabethtown, PA; (S); 13/221; Pres Church Yth Grp; Acpl Chr; Band; Chorus; Church Choir; Concert Band; Mrchg Band; Orch; NHS; Commnty Muscls 81-85; PMEA Dist And Regnl Orch 84-86; Psych.

SHERIDAN, JOHN; Hershey HS; Hummelstown, PA; (Y); 8/209; Math Tm; Ski Clb; Band; Mgr Stage Crew; Variety Show; JV Bsktbl; High Hon Roll; NHS; Spanish NHS; Church Yth Grp; Rnsslr Plytchnc Inst Math & Sci Awd 85-86; Engrng.

SHERIDAN, STACEY; Tonkhannock Area HS; Dalton, PA; (S); 50/280; French Clb; Science Clb; Acpl Chr; School Play; Diving; Fld Hcky; Trk; Hon Roll; Kiwanis Awd; NHS; Le Concrs Natnle 84 & 85; Frgn Rltns.

SHERIF, HASSAN H; Valley Forge Military Acad; Malvern, PA; (Y); Am Leg Boys St; Nwsp Ed-Chief; Frsh Cls; Stu Cncl; Dnfth Awd; High Hon Roll; NHS; Opt Clb Awd.

SHERIFF, CHRIS; Minersville Area HS; Minersville, PA; (Y); Im Bsktbl; JV Var Ftbl; JV Var Wt Lftg.

SHERIFF, HEATHER; Eastern York HS; York, PA; (Y); 17/175; Varsity Clb; Sec Band; Drm Mjr(t); Jazz Band; Mrchg Band; Trs Frsh Cls; Trs Jr Cls; Trs Sr Cls; Var Capt Bsktbl; Var Capt Trk; Rotary Ldrshp Conf 86; Bio.

SHERIN, STEVEN LOUIS; Northeast HS; Philadelphia, PA; (Y); 1/600; JA; Math Tm; Scholastic Bowl; Stage Crew; Cit Awd; High Hon Roll; Hon Roll; NHS; Ntl Merit Ltr; St Schlr; Full Tuition Schlrshp To U Of PA 86; Mensa Essy Cont Winner 86; Alumni Gold Mdl Ranked 1st 86; U Of PA; Computer Science.

SHERLOCK, JENNIFER; Huntingddon Ara HS; Huntingdon, PA; (Y); 30/230; Hosp Aide; Key Clb; Teachers Aide; Yrbk Stf; JV Fld Hcky; JV Sftbl; Var L Vllybl; Hon Roll; NEDT Awd.

SHERMAN, BRIAN; Wellsboro Area SR HS; Wellsboro, PA; (Y); 2/130; Trs German Clb; Pep Clb; Pres Band; Concert Band; Jazz Band; Mrchg Band; Rep Stu Cncl; 4-H Awd; High Hon Roll; NHS; Music Ed.

SHERMAN, DARLENE; Mansfield HS; Mansfield, PA; (S); 7/98; Pres Ski Clb; Band; Chorus; Concert Band; Mrchg Band; Yrbk Stf; Sec Stu Cncl; Var Swmmng; Var Tennis; Dnfth Awd; Yth Ldrs Of Tomorrow 85-86; Miss Flaming Foliage 85; Bus & Prof Wmn Girl Of Mnth 86; Nrsng.

SHERMAN, JAMES; Northern Potter JR SR HS; Westfield, PA; (Y); 2/83; Computer Clb; German Clb; Math Tm; Quiz Bowl; Teachers Aide; JV Socr; Trk; High Hon Roll; NHS; PA Gov Schl Ag 86; Comp Sci.

SHERMAN, KIMBERLY; Brookville Area HS; Brookville, PA; (Y); 20/145; Church Yth Grp; French Clb; FTA; Key Clb; Pep Clb; Varsity Clb; Chorus; Capt Drm Mjr(t); School Musical; Sec Soph Cls; Phrmcy.

SHERMAN, MARY ANNE; Central Christian HS; Du Bois, PA; (Y); 5/43; Church Yth Grp; Exploring; SADD; Chorus; Nwsp Rptr; Nwsp Stf; Var Crs Cntry; High Hon Roll; Hon Roll; NHS; Natl Hnr Soc 86; Awd Most Imprvd Crss Cntry 86; Mercyhurst Clg; Htl/Rest Mgmt.

SHERMAN, MICHELLE; Bald Eagle Nittany HS; Mill Hall, PA; (Y); 21/130; Key Clb; Trs Frsh Cls; Elks Awd; High Hon Roll; Hon Roll; NHS; Prsdntl Acdmc Ftnss Awd 85-86; Sec.

SHERNISKY, DIANE; Mon Valley Catholic HS; Belle Vernon, PA; (Y); Band; Mrchg Band; Concert Band; Stage Crew; Variety Show; Yrbk Bus Mgr; Yrbk Phtg; Stat Bsktbl; Score Keeper; Csmtlgy.

SHERO, GERARD; Central Cambria HS; Ebensburg, PA; (S); 8/190; Science Clb; Band; Hst Frsh Cls; Hst Soph Cls; Hst Jr Cls; Hst Sr Cls; Var L Bsbl; Var L Bsktbl; High Hon Roll; Hon Roll; IN U; Chem.

SHERRER, RICHARD; Leechburg HS; Leechburg, PA; (Y); 27/82; Chorus.

SHERRETTS, CATHY; Sharon HS; Sharon, PA; (Y); French Clb; Hosp Aide; Latin Clb; Band; Color Guard; Flag Corp; Sftbl; Hon Roll.

SHERRICK, LISA; Northwest Area HS; Shickshinny, PA; (Y); 12/120; Computer Clb; Pres Soph Cls; Pres Jr Cls; Pres Sr Cls; Sec Stu Cncl; JV Var Cheerleading; Sftbl; Hon Roll; Natl Hnr Soc Treas 85-86; Stu Cncl Awd 85; Gourmet Clb 85-86; Phil Coll Of Phrmcy-Sci; Phrmcy.

SHERRICK, RACHAEL; Southmoreland SR HS; Scottdale, PA; (Y); 36/230; VP Church Yth Grp; Cmnty Wkr; Spanish Clb; Church Choir; JV Var Bsktbl; Powder Puff Ftbl; Spanish NHS; Psych.

SHERRY, ANGELA; North Allegheny HS; Pittsburg, CA; (Y); 157/641; Boy Scts; Church Yth Grp; Cmnty Wkr; Drama Clb; Pres JA; Temple Yth Grp; High Hon Roll; Hon Roll; Jr NHS; NHS; BYU; Psych.

SHERRY, ANISE; Northern Cambria HS; Barnesboro, PA; (Y); Cmnty Wkr; French Clb; Spanish Clb; Nwsp Phtg; Nwsp Stf; Yrbk Phtg; Yrbk Rptr; Yrbk Stf; Stu Cncl; Vllybl; VFW Schlrshp 83 & 84; IN U; Offc Admin.

SHERRY, DAWN A; Cambria Heights HS; Carrolltown, PA; (Y); 27/177; NFL; Ski Clb; Chorus; Yrbk Stf; Var Trk; NHS; Ntl Merit Sf; NEDT Awd; Concert Band; JV Bsktbl; Acad All-American 86; Indiana U Of PA; Spch Pthlgy.

SHERRY, KATHLEEN; Hanover HS; Hanover, PA; (Y); Art Clb; Trs Church Yth Grp; Band; Chorus; Concert Band; Mrchg Band; Orch; School Musical; School Play; Nwsp Stf; Dist Orchstra 83-86; Penn ST; Engr.

SHERRY, LYNN; Northern Cambria HS; Barnesboro, PA; (Y); Spanish Clb; Chorus; High Hon Roll; Hon Roll; Spanish NHS; Stenoscript Awd 86; IN U; Elem Educ.

SHERRY, REGIS; Cambria Heights HS; Ashville, PA; (Y); Hon Roll; Acadmc All Amrcn 86; Hons 90 Avg 85-86; PA ST Altoona; Accntng.

SHERTZER, JERE; Lancaster Christian HS; Lancaster, PA; (Y); 5/28; Church Yth Grp; 4-H; Pres Soph Cls; JV Bsbl; Var Socr; 4-H Awd; High Hon Roll; Hon Roll; Outstdng Stu Awd Assn Of Christian Schls Intl 85-86; Pastorial Stds.

SHERWIN, HEATHER; Bishop Carroll HS; Cherry Tree, PA; (S); 15/108; Ski Clb; Band; Concert Band; Mrchg Band; Pep Band; NHS; NEDT Awd; Pre-Law.

SHERWIN, KIMBERLY; Emmaus HS; Allentown, PA; (Y); 106/492; Church Yth Grp; French Clb; JA; SADD; Varsity Clb; Var Bsktbl; Var Fld Hcky; JV Trk; Hon Roll; Jr NHS; Ed.

SHERWIN, ROBERT; Canevin HS; Pittsburgh, PA; (Y); 34/176; Sec VP Church Yth Grp; FBLA; Varsity Clb; School Play; Nwsp Rptr; Nwsp Sprt Ed; Stu Cncl; JV Var Bsktbl; Hon Roll; Prfct Atten Awd; Schlr Athl Awd 86; Penn Jr Acadmy Of Sci 2nd Awd 84 & 85.

SHERWOOD, BRIAN; Pocono Mountain HS; Canadensis, PA; (Y); Computer Clb; Stage Crew; Socr; Mth.

SHERWOOD, DEIDRE; Crestwood HS; Mountaintop, PA; (Y); FHA; Hosp Aide; Hon Roll.

SHERWOOD, MELISSA; Otto-Eldred JR-SR HS; Eldred, PA; (Y); Pres Pep Clb; Varsity Clb; Chorus; Swing Chorus; Nwsp Stf; Yrbk Stf; Sec Stu Cncl; Cheerleading; Trk; MST Vlb Chrldr Awd 85; Spcl Educ.

SHERWOOD, RHONDA; Blacklick Valley HS; Belsano, PA; (S); Ski Clb; Band; Yrbk Stf; Hon Roll; NHS; Psychlgy.

SHETROMPH, CAROL; Hempfield HS; East Petersburg, PA; (Y); Church Yth Grp; Dance Clb; Red Cross Aide; Chorus; School Musical; School Play; Nwsp Bus Mgr; Sr Cls; Var L Cheerleading; Hon Roll; U Of Delaware; Psych.

SHETTERLY, STEVEN; Millersburg Area HS; Millersburg, PA; (Y); Church Yth Grp; Pres 4-H; Quiz Bowl; Band; Mrchg Band; Hon Roll; NHS; Vtrnrn.

SHETTY, NINA; Quigley HS; Beaver, PA; (Y); Hosp Aide; Math Tm; Capt NFL; Nwsp Rptr; Yrbk Stf; Sec Soph Cls; Capt L Tennis; High Hon Roll; NHS; Ntl Cngrssnl Schlr 86; Hugh O Brian Ldrshp Awd 85; Pre Med.

SHETZLINE, JESSICA; Harry S Truman HS; Bristol, PA; (Y); French Clb; Library Aide; Yrbk Stf; Stu Cncl; Im Golf; Hon Roll; Prfct Atten Awd; Bus Mgmt.

SHEWACK, LORI; West Hazleton HS; W Hazleton, PA; (Y); VP FBLA; Hon Roll; Data Entry.

SHEWAN, KATE; Saint Benedict Acad; Erie, PA; (Y); 41/63; Chorus; Concert Band; Jazz Band; Mrchg Band; Variety Show; JV Cheerleading; Var Crs Cntry; Var Socr; Var Tennis; Edinboro U; Spec Ed.

SHICK, ANDREA K; Homer Center HS; Homer City, PA; (Y); 30/106; FBLA; Library Aide; Varsity Clb; Trs Concert Band; Mrchg Band; Hst Sr Cls; Capt Bsktbl; Trk; Twrlr; Hon Roll; Band Booster Schlrshp 86; Robert Morris Coll; Bus Ed.

SHICK, ERIC; Union HS; Rimersburg, PA; (Y); SADD; L Bsktbl; L Trk; Prfct Atten Awd; Fin.

SHIDELEFF, ROBERT; Bensalem HS; Bensalem, PA; (Y); Model UN; Swmmng; High Hon Roll; Outstndng Swimmer 86; Elec Engrng.

SHIDERLY, HEIDI; Sharon HS; Sharon, PA; (Y); 2/196; Drama Clb; Varsity Clb; Band; Swmmng; Tennis; Kiwanis Awd; NHS; Sal; Church Yth Grp; Pres Girl Scts; Holiday Rambler Rcrtnl Vehicle Clb Schlrshp 1st Plc 86; Century III Ldrshp Awd 85; Grove City Coll PA; Intl Bus.

SHIDERLY, RONALD; Mohawk Area JR SR HS; New Castle, PA; (S); Church Yth Grp; Var L Ftbl; Var L Trk; Hon Roll; NHS; Med.

SHIEL, DONNA; Burgettstown Area JR SR HS; Burgettstown, PA; (Y); 3/172; Sec Church Yth Grp; Teachers Aide; Chorus; Church Choir; School Musical; High Hon Roll; Jr NHS; Lion Awd; NHS; Tony Pappas Mem Schlrp 86; Fclty Recog Schlrp Robert Morris Coll 86; Bus Awd 86; Robert Morris Coll; Bus Ed.

SHIELDS, ALLISON; Abp Prendergast HS; Havertown, PA; (Y); 11/361; Mathletes; Ski Clb; Coach Actv; VP Gym; Hon Roll; Millersville U; Marine Bio.

SHIELDS, ERIC; Altoona Area HS; Altoona, PA; (Y); VP Church Yth Grp; Drama Clb; JA; Speech Tm; School Play; Nwsp Rptr; Stu Cncl; Sales Clb Achvt 85; Acctng.

SHIELDS, JENNIFER; Brookville Area HS; Summerville, PA; (Y); 5/147; FTA; German Clb; Band; Chorus; Jazz Band; School Musical; Nwsp Rptr; Nwsp Stf; Jr NHS; NHS; Jffrsn Cntry Dairy Prncss Alt 86-87; Dairy Ambssdrs 85; Clarion U PA; Spcl Educ.

SHIELDS, LORIANNE; Pittston Area SR HS; Hughestown, PA; (Y); 65/348; Church Yth Grp; Computer Clb; Drama Clb; Girl Scts; Key Clb; Science Clb; Ski Clb; Yrbk Stf; Hon Roll; PRMCY.

SHIELDS, RICHARD; Northeast Catholic HS; Philadelphia, PA; (Y); 19/356; Bsbl; Hon Roll.

SHIENBAUM, ALAN J; Lower Moreland SR HS; Huntingdon Valley, PA; (S); Debate Tm; Science Clb; Ed Nwsp Stf; Var Tennis; Albrght Coll Rdng PA; Med.

SHIFFER, ANGEL; Minersville Area HS; Minersville, PA; (Y); FBLA; Band; Concert Band; Drm Mjr(t); Mrchg Band; School Musical; Ed Yrbk Stf; Capt Crs Cntry; High Hon Roll; Hon Roll; Minersville Area Scholar Fund 86; Kutztown U; Elem Ed.

SHIFKO, PAUL A; Jeannette SR HS; Jeannette, PA; (Y); 21/144; Am Leg Boys St; Pres Church Yth Grp; French Clb; Var Golf; Outstndng Nwspr Carrier Of Yr 85; Frnch Clb Trip To France 84; Clarion; Secndry Educ.

SHILEY, WILLIAM; Williams Valley JR SR HS; Williamstown, PA; (Y); 12/105; Band; Concert Band; Jazz Band; Mrchg Band; Symp Band; Var L Bsbl; Var L Golf; High Hon Roll; Hon Roll; IUP; Acctg.

SHILKRET, TRACY; Neshaminy HS; Langhorne, PA; (Y); 7/740; Church Yth Grp; Nwsp Ed-Chief; Capt Var Bsktbl; Var Fld Hcky; Var Socr; High Hon Roll; Hon Roll; NHS; Hulmeville Soccer Clb Annual Achv Awd 86; Bus.

SHILLADAY, MARK; Pottsgrove HS; Pottstown, PA; (Y); 30/229; Math Tm; Concert Band; Jazz Band; Mrchg Band; Tennis; Wrstlng; Hon Roll; NHS; Spanish Clb; Band; Dist Region Band; ST Orch; Aeronutcs.

SHILLING, ALICE; Marian HS; Coaldale, PA; (S); 4/114; Church Yth Grp; 4-H; Hosp Aide; Service Clb; Nwsp Rptr; Yrbk Stf; Im Trk; 4-H Awd; High Hon Roll; NHS; Phrmcst.

SHILLING, CAROLE; Waynesboro Area SR HS; Waynesboro, PA; (Y); 30/380; Church Choir; Yrbk Stf; Rep Soph Cls; Sec Sr Cls; Rep Stu Cncl; Var Trk; Var Capt Vllybl; Cit Awd; Hon Roll; NHS.

SHILLINGER, TRACY; Gateway SR HS; Monroeville, PA; (Y); 120/508; Pep Clb; Twrlr; Accntnt.

SHIMCHOCK, FRANCINE; Curwensville Area HS; Olanta, PA; (Y); Camera Clb; 4-H; French Clb; VP FBLA; Nwsp Stf; Cert Pblc Acctnt.

SHIMEL, RHONDA; Philipsburg-Osceola HS; Philipsburg, PA; (Y); Pep Clb; Band; Chorus; Concert Band; Flag Corp; Mrchg Band; Nwsp Stf; Accntng.

SHIMEL, TINA; Curwensville Area HS; Curwensville, PA; (Y); FBLA; Nwsp Stf; Var JV Sftbl; Hon Roll; NHS.

SHIMER, KIMBERLY ANN; Easton Area HS; Easton, PA; (Y); Am Leg Aux Girls St; Drama Clb; NFL; School Musical; Nwsp Stf; Yrbk Stf; Cit Awd; NHS; Cmptr In Ntl Cthlc Frnsc Lg Ntl Cmptn 85-86; 4th Pl Ntl Hstry Day Essy Cmptn 85-86; Comm.

SHIMMEL, VANESSA; Clearfield Area HS; Clearfield, PA; (Y); 64/315; Spanish Clb; Bsktbl; Mat Maids; Sftbl; Hon Roll; Wrestlerette 83-86; Pres Stdnt Cncl 82-83; Special Olympic Aid 86; Acctng.

SHINDEL, ANGELA; Eastern York JR SR HS; York, PA; (Y); 34/159; Chorus; Flag Corp; Nwsp Rptr; Yrbk Ed-Chief; Yrbk Stf; Hon Roll; Central Penn Bus Schl; Phy Thry.

SHINDLER, ALANA L; Garden Spot HS; New Holland, PA; (Y); Church Yth Grp; Var Sftbl; Hon Roll.

SHINKE, STEPHEN W; South Side Beaver HS; Hookstown, PA; (Y); 7/93; Am Leg Boys St; SADD; Varsity Clb; Chorus; School Play; Yrbk Ed-Chief; Stat Bsktbl; Stat Trk; NHS; High Hon Roll; Pres Acad Ftns Awd 86; Ntl Hstry & Govt Ad 86; Slippery Rock U Of PA; Math.

SHINN JR, RICHARD J; Bishop Kenrick HS; Norristown, PA; (Y); 14/270; Capt Bsktbl; Var Socr; JV Trk; NHS; NROTC Schlrshp Alt 86-87; Villanova U; Bus Admin.

SHINSKY, ANNETTE; Brownsville Area HS; Grindstone, PA; (Y); 49/220; Intnl Clb; Church Choir; High Hon Roll; Hon Roll; Church Yth Grp; CA U PA; Mth.

SHINSKY, COLEEN; Canon-Mc Milliam SR HS; Canonsburg, PA; (Y); Art Clb; Hosp Aide; Library Aide; Chorus; Drm Mjr(t); School Play; Mgr(s); Socr; Trk; Hon Roll; Majrt Trophy 84, Ltr 86; Nrsng.

SHINSKY, DAVID A; Geibel HS; Uniontown, PA; (Y); Lit Mag; VP Frsh Cls; VP Soph Cls; VP Jr Cls; VP Stu Cncl; Var Bsbl; JV Var Bsktbl; JV Var Crs Cntry; Var Golf; Hon Roll; CA U PA; Brdcstng.

SHINSKY, RACHEL; Hempfield HS; Lancaster, PA; (Y); Aud/Vis; Cmnty Wkr; Q&S; Teachers Aide; Nwsp Rptr; Nwsp Stf; Yrbk Ed-Chief; Yrbk Rptr; Yrbk Stf; Quill & Scroll NHS Jrnlsts 85-87; Franklin & Marshall; Bus Adm.

SHIPANGA, DENEENE N; Germantown HS; Philadelphia, PA; (Y); Church Yth Grp; Dance Clb; Hosp Aide; Library Aide; Chorus; Yrbk Stf; High Hon Roll; Hon Roll; Sec NHS; Cert Of Achvt Awd-Prtcptn Sem Yth & The Amer Polit Sys 86; PA Sst U; Nrs.

SHIPE, ANDREW; Shikellamy HS; Sunbury, PA; (Y); 3/319; Am Leg Boys St; Pres Sr Cls; JV Wrstlng; Hon Roll; NHS; U S Military Acad; Elec Engrng.

SHIPE, DIANE; Knoch HS; Saxonbug, PA; (Y); Band; Concert Band; Mrchg Band; Pep Band; School Musical; Symp Band; High Hon Roll; Hon Roll; Wrtng.

SHIPE JR, WARREN; Shikellamy HS; Sunbury, PA; (Y); Var L Bsbl; JV Bsktbl; Var L Ftbl; Wt Lftg; Hon Roll; Athlt Wk Bsbll 86; Accntnt.

SHIPE, WENDY; Shikellamy HS; Sunbury, PA; (Y); 3/316; Am Leg Aux Girls St; Pres Church Yth Grp; Spanish Clb; Rep Jr Cls; Capt Crs Cntry; Capt Trk; Hon Roll; NHS; Sal; Chorus; Northern Central Bnk Math Awd 86; E Stroudsburg U; Med Tech.

SHIPHERD, KRISTEN M; Fairview HS; Fairview, PA; (Y); 13/152; German Clb; Speech Tm; JV Tennis; High Hon Roll; Hon Roll; Archlgy.

SHIPIERSKI, STEPHEN; Greater Nanticoke Area HS; Wanamie, PA; (Y); Swmmng.

SHIPLEY, ANGELA; Freedom HS; Bethlehem, PA; (Y); 14/462; High Hon Roll; Hon Roll; Jr NHS; NHS; Bethlehem Fine Arts Commsn Hnrb Mntn 86; PA JR Acad Sci 1st Pl Sci Fair 84; Livingston U Scholar 86; Med Illstrtn.

SHIPLEY, RAY; Central HS; Philadelphia, PA; (Y); 83/225; Boy Scts; Church Yth Grp; Var Bsbl; JV Crs Cntry; Hon Roll; Temple; Comm.

SHIPLEY, WAYNE; West Allegheny HS; Oakdale, PA; (Y); 42/204; Cmnty Wkr; Nwsp Rptr; Nwsp Sprt Ed; Nwsp Stf; Yrbk Sprt Ed; Yrbk Stf; Crs Cntry; Trk; Jr NHS; IN U Of PA.

SHIPMAN, DAVE; Mechanicsburg Area SR HS; Mechanicsburg, PA; (Y); 53/313; Boy Scts; Ski Clb; Nwsp Phtg.

SHIPP, DIANE; Towanda Area SR HS; Towanda, PA; (Y); FBLA; Spanish Clb; Varsity Clb; School Play; Yrbk Stf; VP Frsh Cls; Pres Soph Cls; Pres Jr Cls; Pres Sr Cls; Stu Cncl; Outstndng Schlstc Achvt In Accntng II 85-86; 3rd Runner-Up In Hmcmng Ct 85; PA ST U; Bus Admin.

SHIPULA, STEVEN; Jamestown HS; Jamestown, PA; (Y); Boy Scts; VICA; School Play; OH Diesel; Auto Elctrncs.

SHIREY, ANITA; United HS; Robinson, PA; (Y); 78/157; Art Clb; French Clb; Pep Clb; Ski Clb; SADD; Chorus; Mgr(s); Stat Vllybl; Hon Roll; Vllybll Lttr 85-86; Bio.

SHIREY, BARBARA; Clearfield Area HS; Frenchville, PA; (Y); 9/302; High Hon Roll; NHS; Ntl Merit Ltr; Sal; PA ST U; Arch.

SHIREY, BRENDA; Marion Center HS; Marion Ctr, PA; (Y); FBLA; Sec FNA; Latin Clb; Pep Clb; Science Clb; Flag Corp; Mrchg Band; Orch; Stage Crew; Sec Stu Cncl; Sports Lttr 84-85 & 85-86; Stu Pride Awd 83-84; Dubois Bus Schl; Med Secr.

SHIREY, BRENT; Union HS; Rimersburg, PA; (Y); 1/77; Nwsp Rptr; Yrbk Rptr; Trs Stu Cncl; Bsktbl; Ftbl; Trk; High Hon Roll; Pres NHS; Pres Schlr; Val; US Army Rsrv Natl Schlr/Athlt Awd 86; Mellon Bnk Schlrshp Awd 86; Grove City Coll; Elctrcl Engr.

SHIREY, GINA; Freeport Senior HS; Sarver, PA; (S); Church Yth Grp; Pres 4-H; Mrchg Band; Pep Band; Symp Band; Yrbk Bus Mgr; Bsktbl; Trk; 4-H Awd; High Hon Roll; Hugh O Brien Ldrshp Sem 85; Summer Happenings In Marine Bio IUP 85.

SHIREY, GRETCHEN J; Central Columbia HS; Orangeville, PA; (Y); DECA; FHA; Teachers Aide; Hon Roll; Bus.

SHIREY, MICHAEL; Laurel Valley HS; New Florence, PA; (Y); 5/77; Art Clb; Boy Scts; Camera Clb; Pres Church Yth Grp; Scholastic Bowl; Science Clb; Band; Chorus; Church Choir; Concert Band; Eagle Scout 85; Bio II Awd 85; Semper Fidelis Awd 86; PA ST; Chem Engnrng.

SHIREY, SAM; Mechanicsburg HS; Mechanicsburg, PA; (Y); Pres Frsh Cls; Pres Soph Cls; Rep Jr Cls; Trs Sr Cls; Stu Cncl; Var Bsbl; Var Bsktbl; JV Ftbl; James Madison U; Ecnmcs.

SHIREY, SUSAN; Clarion Area HS; Clarion, PA; (Y); Band; School Musical; Swing Chorus; Ed Yrbk Stf; Trs Jr Cls; Rep Trs Stu Cncl; Stat Trk; High Hon Roll; Hon Roll; NHS; Sci.

SHIREY, SUSAN; Kiski Area HS; Saltsburg, PA; (Y); Girl Scts; VICA; Im Vllybl; High Hon Roll; Hon Roll; PA ST; RN.

SHIRING, STEVE; Western Beaver JR SR HS; Beaver, PA; (S); Jazz Band; Mrchg Band; Symp Band; VP Soph Cls; Trs Jr Cls; Rep Stu Cncl; Var L Bsktbl; Golf; High Hon Roll; NHS; Japan-US Senate Schlrshp 85; Engr.

SHIRK, KAREN; Garden Spot HS; Martindale, PA; (Y); Church Yth Grp; JV Fld Hcky; Powder Puff Ftbl; Hon Roll; Jr NHS; Nrsng.

SHIRK, LINDA; Baldeagle-Nittany HS; Beech Creek, PA; (Y); Library Aide; Teachers Aide; Color Guard; Nwsp Rptr; Gym; Sftbl; Hon Roll.

SHIRK, VALERIE; Lancaster Christian HS; Reinholds, PA; (Y); #8 In Class; Art Clb; Church Yth Grp; Drama Clb; Yrbk Stf; Var Bsktbl; JV Cheerleading; Var Score Keeper; Var Vllybl; Hon Roll; Socl Wrk.

SHISSLER, DAVID; Shalam Christian Acad; Newburg, PA; (Y); 1/26; Church Yth Grp; Acpl Chr; School Musical; Yrbk Stf; Rep Stu Cncl; Im Ftbl; High Hon Roll; Hon Roll; Prfct Atten Awd; Masca Bible Quizzing-2nd Pl 84; Masca Bible Quizzing-1st Pl 85; Oral Roberts U; Bus.

SHIVELY, NICOLE; Milton SR HS; Milton, PA; (Y); 51/202; Computer Clb; Trs Sec Intnl Clb; Varsity Clb; Drill Tm; Mrchg Band; Yrbk Stf; Off Soph Cls; Off Jr Cls; Sec Stu Cncl; Co-Capt Cheerleading; Navy; Flight Atten.

SHIVELY, SARAH ABIGAIL; Phoenixville Area HS; Phoenixville, PA; (Y); 38/180; Key Clb; Office Aide; Ski Clb; Drill Tm; Soph Cls; Sftbl; Vllybl; Hon Roll; Gftd & Tlntd Assoc Of MD 81-83; WV U; Frnch.

SHIVERDECKER, PAMELA L; Bethel Park HS; Pittsburgh, PA; (Y); 5/520; Church Yth Grp; Exploring; JA; Off Band; Drill Tm; Mrchg Band; Orch; School Musical; Symp Band; Powder Puff Ftbl; General Assmbly 85-86; VA Tech; Archtctr.

SHIVES, DANNY; Southern Fulton HS; Warfordsburg, PA; (Y); Church Yth Grp; Band; Chorus; School Play; L Bsbl; L Bsktbl; L Mgr(s); Hon Roll; Marines Reserves; Engrng.

SHIVES, MICHAEL; Berwick Area SR HS; Berwick, PA; (Y); 15/219; Camera Clb; Church Yth Grp; Key Clb; Band; Hon Roll; NHS; Prfct Atten Awd; Biochem.

SHLIKAS, JOSEPH E; Shamokin Area HS; Shamokin, PA; (Y); 74/241; Drama Clb; Letterman Clb; Sec Pep Clb; Thesps; Varsity Clb; Variety Show; Pres Stu Cncl; Capt Trk; Wrstlng; Voice Dem Awd; Psychlgy.

SHOBER, JOAN; Marian HS; Summit Hill, PA; (S); 2/123; Pres French Clb; Library Aide; Yrbk Stf; Off Stu Cncl; Capt Twrlr; Pres French Hon Soc; High Hon Roll; NHS; Ntl Phy Ed Awd 84-85; US Stdnt Cncl Awd 85-86; Phy Thrpy.

SHOCKEY, JODI; Portersville Christian Schl; Butler, PA; (Y); Church Yth Grp; Speech Tm; Chorus; Var L Bsktbl; Var L Vllybl; Wt Lftg; High Hon Roll; Jr NHS; Geneva.

SHOCKEY, SALLY; Portage Area HS; Portage, PA; (Y); Band; Chorus; Church Choir; Concert Band; Jazz Band; Mrchg Band; Orch; Pep Band; Variety Show; Hon Roll; U Of PA.

SHOEMAKER, BARRY RAY; Dover Area HS; Dover, PA; (S); 17/227; Church Yth Grp; Cmnty Wkr; Chorus; Church Choir; School Play; Var Socr; JV Wrstlng; Hon Roll; NHS; Renaissance Chrl Grp 84-87; Chem.

SHOEMAKER, BRYAN; Butler SR HS; Butler, PA; (Y); Church Yth Grp; Cmnty Wkr; Office Aide; Political Wkr; Ski Clb; Spanish Clb; SADD; Band; Concert Band; Jazz Band; IN U Of PA; Optmtry.

SHOEMAKER, CHARLENE; Du Bois Area SR HS; Dubois, PA; (Y); 3/281; VP Sec Church Yth Grp; Teachers Aide; Chorus; Church Choir; Swing Chorus; Vllybl; High Hon Roll; VP NHS; German Clb; Intnl Clb; Math.

SHOEMAKER, CHRIS; Wyalusing Area HS; New Albany, PA; (Y); 14/152; JV Bsbl; Var Wrstlng; High Hon Roll; Hon Roll; Williamsport CC; Auto Tech.

SHOEMAKER, LYNNE; Philipsburg-Osceola Area HS; Philipsburg, PA; (Y); 13/247; Ski Clb; Concert Band; Mrchg Band; School Musical; Hon Roll; NHS; Prfct Atten Awd; Elem Ed.

SHOEMAKER, MARK; Greater Latrobe SR HS; Latrobe, PA; (Y); 49/411; Pres Church Yth Grp; French Clb; Var Socr; High Hon Roll; Hon Roll; Educ Tchr.

SHOEMAKER, SAUNDRA; Hempfield SR HS; Greensburg, PA; (Y); Church Yth Grp; Pep Clb; VICA; Band; Color Guard; Mrchg Band; Hon Roll; Pittsburg Beauty Acad; Cosmetlg.

SHOEMAKER, THERESA; B Ishop Guilfoyle HS; Altoona, PA; (Y); Cmnty Wkr; German Clb; Science Clb; Yrbk Stf; Soph Cls; Jr Cls; Stu Cncl; Cheerleading; 2nd Pl Wnnr Poetry 86; IN U; Med Assist.

SHOENFELT, SUSAN; Bishop Guilfoyle HS; Altoona, PA; (S); 22/129; Girl Scts; Red Cross Aide; Science Clb; SADD; Church Choir; Concert Band; Flag Corp; High Hon Roll; Hon Roll; Silver Awd Girl Scouts 84; Marian Medl Awd 84.

SHOEPE, RICHARD; West Hazleton HS; Sugarloaf, PA; (Y); Church Yth Grp; FBLA; Var Bsbl; Coach Actv; Hon Roll; Accntnt.

SHOFFLER, CHRISTINA; Our Lady Of Lourdes Regional HS; Elysburg, PA; (Y); 53/95; AFS; French Clb; Library Aide; Nwsp Stf; Rep Soph Cls; Rep Sr Cls; JV Sftbl.

SHOFFNER, DANIEL JOSEPH; Meadville Area SR HS; Meadville, PA; (Y); 110/306.

SHOFFSTALL, LESLIE; Venango Christian HS; Seneca, PA; (Y); 4/42; Pep Clb; Chorus; Ed Yrbk Stf; High Hon Roll; Hon Roll; NHS; Prfct Atten Awd; Pres Acad Ftnss Awd 86; Chem Oplympcs 86; U Pittsburgh; Pharm.

SHOLLENBERGER, MELISSA; Exeter HS; Reading, PA; (Y); JA; Red Cross Aide; Varsity Clb; VICA; Chorus; Stage Crew; Bowling; Mrt Roll 3 Qtrs 86; Hnr Roll 1 Qtr 83; Reading; Nrsng.

SHOMPER, CAROL; Millersburg Area HS; Millersburg, PA; (Y); Capt Drill Tm; Mrchg Band; Nwsp Stf; Yrbk Stf; Powder Puff Ftbl; High Hon Roll; Sec.

SHONDECK, RUDY; Deer Lakes SR HS; Creighton, PA; (Y); Var Ftbl; Hon Roll; Heating.

SHONK, STEVE; Ephrata SR HS; Ephrata, PA; (Y); 23/257; Church Yth Grp; Exploring; Trs FBLA; Trs JA; High Hon Roll; Hon Roll; NHS; Millersville ST U; Accntng.

SHOOK, DENNIS C; Butler SR HS; Butler, PA; (Y); Exploring.

SHOOP, AIMEE; Halifax Area HS; Halifax, PA; (S); 5/100; Sec FBLA; Chorus; Drill Tm; Nwsp Rptr; Ed Yrbk Stf; High Hon Roll; NHS; Sec Church Yth Grp; Drama Clb; Sec Conf Yth Minstrs Cncl 85-86; Harrisbrg Dist Yth 85-86; Harrisburg CC; Acctg.

SHOOP, HEATHER; Halifax Area HS; Halifax, PA; (Y); 13/100; Drama Clb; Sec FNA; SADD; School Musical; Yrbk Sprt Ed; Rep Stu Cncl; Stat Bsbl; Capt Cheerleading; Hon Roll; Art Inst Of Philadelphia; Int D.

SHOOP, JOHN; Riverview HS; Oakmont, PA; (Y); AFS; Church Yth Grp; FCA; Varsity Clb; Capt Bsbl; Capt Bsktbl; Capt Ftbl; CAP; East-Sub Ftbl All Stars 85; Minster.

SHOOP, KATHY; Saegertown HS; Meadville, PA; (Y); 3/124; Church Yth Grp; Girl Scts; Hon Roll; Phrmycst.

SHOOP, ROXANNE; Donegal HS; Mt Joy, PA; (Y); 2/170; Church Yth Grp; GAA; Latin Clb; Varsity Clb; JV Fld Hcky; Var L Sftbl; High Hon Roll; Hon Roll; NHS; Prfct Atten Awd; Dntl Hygn.

SHOOP, TRICIA; Halifax HS; Halifax, PA; (Y); 14/104; Hosp Aide; Chorus; JV Cheerleading; Twrlr; Hon Roll; Physcl Thrpst.

SHORE, CAROL RACHEL; George Washington HS; Philadelphia, PA; (Y); 17/750; Ed Yrbk Stf; Var Gym; Elks Awd; Trs French Hon Soc; NHS; Trs French Clb; SADD; Yrbk Bus Mgr; Rep Sr Cls; Phila JR Miss 86; U Of PA; Bus.

SHORE, CHRISTINE A; Mc Connellsburg HS; Mc Connellsburg, PA; (Y); Art Clb; Chess Clb; Sec Pres Church Yth Grp; Debate Tm; Trs Drama Clb; English Clb; Chorus; School Play; Nwsp Stf; Hon Roll; French Awd 85-86; Hogerstown Bus Coll; Bus Adm.

SHORE, KIMBERLEY; Mechanicsburg Area SR HS; Macon, GA; (Y); 29/321; Girl Scts; Quiz Bowl; Speech Tm; SADD; High Hon Roll; Hon Roll; NHS; Ntl Merit Ltr; Penfield Schlrshp Mercer U 86; Washington Wrkshp Part 85; French.

SHORE, PAUL; Cheltenham HS; Cheltenham, PA; (Y); 15/380; Cmnty Wkr; Capt Math Tm; Model UN; Red Cross Aide; Orch; School Musical; Var Lcrss; JV Swmmng; Hon Roll; Ntl Merit SF; 1st Pl Delaware Vlly Sci Fair 85; Williams Coll Book Awd 86; Mem Johns Hopkins Tlnt Search 83-86; Biomed.

SHORE, REGINA; St Huberts HS; Philadelphia, PA; (Y); 277/367; Dance Clb; Girl Scts; Jazz Band; Beaver Clg; Comp Sci.

SHORT, BRIAN; Marion Center Area HS; Home, PA; (Y); Church Yth Grp; 4-H; FFA; Band; Concert Band; Mrchg Band; Ftbl; Hon Roll; PA ST; Meats Ind.

SHORT, DONNA; Seneca Valley HS; Harmony, PA; (Y); Church Yth Grp; Varsity Clb; Mrchg Band; Symp Band; Nwsp Stf; Rep Frsh Cls; Capt Var Sftbl; Hon Roll; Slippery Rock U; Phys Ed.

SHORTEN, KEVIN; Roman Catholic HS; Philadelphia, PA; (S); 11/133; Red Cross Aide; Varsity Clb; Yrbk Stf; Var Capt Bsbl; Bsktbl; Hon Roll; Ntl Merit Ltr; Temple U; Acctg.

SHORTENCARRIER, RENEE; Cambria Heights SR HS; Hastings, PA; (Y); 4/190; Dance Clb; Ski Clb; Band; Concert Band; Mrchg Band; Yrbk Ed-Chief; VP Jr Cls; Stu Cncl; Trk; Hon Roll.

SHOSTEK, AMY; Chartiers Valley HS; Carnegie, PA; (Y); Cmnty Wkr; Ski Clb; Varsity Clb; Var L Crs Cntry; Var L Trk; NHS; Civic Clb; Chorus; Tennis; Dist Wnr Natl PTA Essay Cntst 86; Spec Ed.

SHOTWELL, DIANA; Elizabeth Forward HS; Elizabeth, PA; (Y); Church Yth Grp; Exploring; Hosp Aide; Spanish Clb; Band; Flag Corp; Nwsp Stf; Hon Roll; Gftd And Talntd Ed 84-86; Emplyd Biddle Chiro Clnc 85-86; Med.

SHOUP, BRIAN J; Bethe Park SR HS; Pittsburgh, PA; (Y); Aud/Vis; VP JA; Stage Crew; JR Achvt Dale Carnegie Crs Schlrshp 85-86; NY Inst Of Tech; Cmmnctn Arts.

SHOUP, CAROLINE; Millville Area HS; Orangeville, PA; (Y); Pres Church Yth Grp; Spanish Clb; Chorus; Capt Drm Mjr(t); School Musical; School Play; JV Fld Hcky; Var Sftbl; Hon Roll; NHS.

SHOUP, TAMMY; Saltsburg JR-SR HS; Saltsburg, PA; (Y); DECA; Pep Clb; SADD; Chorus; High Hon Roll; Hon Roll; Sec DECA; EXEC Sec.

SHOUPE, DENISE; Kiski Area HS; Avonmore, PA; (Y); Pep Clb; Spanish Clb; Varsity Clb; High Hon Roll; Hon Roll; VFW Awd; Var Bsktbl; Var L Vllybl; Top 10 84; Prsdntl Awd 84-86; Penn ST; Nrsng.

SHOVER, DAWN; Mechanicsburg Area SR HS; Mechanicsburg, PA; (Y); Church Yth Grp; Acpl Chr; Chorus; Church Choir; Mrchg Band; Orch; Symp Band; Variety Show; Nwsp Stf; Hon Roll; 1st Pl Schl Tlnt Shw 86; Cnty Chorus 82, 84 & 85; Messiah Coll; Pre-Vet Med.

SHOWALTER, JEANINE; Cocalico HS; Denver, PA; (Y); Church Yth Grp; FBLA; Pres Drm Mjr(t); Chorus; Concert Band; Mrchg Band; School Musical; High Hon Roll; NHS; Pres Schlr; Schrlshp George Washington U 86; VFW Ladies Aux Schrlshp 86; Pres Acad Ftns Awd; George Washington U; Biomed Eng.

SHOWERS, JENNI; Du Bois Area SR HS; Dubois, PA; (Y); 56/285; Cmnty Wkr; English Clb; School Play; Yrbk Stf; Trs Jr Cls; Trs Sr Cls; Rep Stu Cncl; Stat Bsbl; Stat Bsktbl; Hon Roll; Stdnt Wk 86; Spnsh.

SHPON, ARETA; Villa Maria Acad; Erie, PA; (Y); Girl Scts; Model UN; PAVAS; Swmmng; High Hon Roll; NHS; Ntl Merit SF.

SHRADER, AMY; West York HS; York, PA; (Y); Church Yth Grp; JA; Pres Spanish Clb; Teachers Aide; Nwsp Stf; Rep Stu Cncl; Mgr Bsbl; Var Fld Hcky; JV Tennis; Hon Roll; Bus.

SHRADER, WILLIAM; Lakeland HS; Jermyn, PA; (S); 41/180; Spanish Clb; Band; Mrchg Band; Bus.

SHRAWDER, NICOLE; Millersburg Area; Millersburg, PA; (Y); 10/80; Sec French Clb; Yrbk Ed-Chief; Stu Cncl; Bsktbl; Capt Cheerleading; Powder Puff Ftbl; Swmmng; Trk; High Hon Roll; NHS; Princeton U; Arch.

SHRECK, MARK; Milton Area HS; W Milton, PA; (Y); Computer Clb; German Clb; Rep Stu Cncl; Var Ftbl; PA Nwspr Pblshers Assn Carrier Yr 85; Comp Sci.

SHREFFLER JR, DONALD; Conemaugh Twp Area HS; Holsopple, PA; (Y); Aud/Vis; Church Yth Grp; Cmnty Wkr; JA; Lttr For Track 86; Accntng.

SHREFFLER, SHAWN; West Perry HS; Blain, PA; (Y); 31/216; Church Yth Grp; Computer Clb; Trs Spanish Clb; Yrbk Stf; Rep Stu Cncl; Var L Bsbl; Var Capt Bsktbl; Var L Ftbl; Hon Roll; Acdmc All Amer 86-87; Mrn Bio.

SHREFFLER, SUSAN; Oil City SR HS; Franklin, PA; (Y); 30/256; Church Yth Grp; Hosp Aide; Band; Concert Band; Jazz Band; Mrchg Band; Pep Band; Swmmng; Hon Roll; Radlgy.

SHREIBER, DAVID; Central Bucks HS East; Warrington, PA; (Y); Capt Quiz Bowl; Capt Scholastic Bowl; Band; Golf; High Hon Roll; Hon Roll; NHS; Sci Clb 85-86; Comp Pgmg Awd 83-84; Crtv Wrtg Awd 83-84; Bio.

SHREVE, LINDA; G A R Memorial HS; Wilkes Barre, PA; (S); 1/187; Church Yth Grp; FBLA; High Hon Roll; Hon Roll; Jr NHS; NHS.

SHREVE, REBEKAH; E L Meyers HS; Wilkes Barre, PA; (Y); Church Yth Grp; FBLA; Chorus; Art Clb; Acctng.

SHRIVER, MATTHEW; Eastern Lancaster County HS; New Holland, PA; (Y); JV Trk; JV Wrstlng; Hon Roll.

SHRIVER, MICHELLE A; Trinity HS; Mechanicsburg, PA; (Y); Drama Clb; Pep Clb; Spanish Clb; Chorus; Church Choir; School Musical; Nwsp Rptr; JA; Thesps; Stage Crew; Cmmnctns.

SHRIVER, WENDY; Waynesburg Central HS; Waynesburg, PA; (Y); FCA; Spanish Clb; Nwsp Stf; Yrbk Stf; Var L Trk; JV Var Vllybl; Hon Roll; Aud/Vis; Church Yth Grp; GAA; Ideal Sqd Membr 85; Vllybl Tm 3rd 86; 3rd Highjmp Qlfrs And Rgnsl 86; OH ST U; Advtsg.

SHROFF, DEVEN V; George Washington HS; Philadelphia, PA; (Y); 22/769; Boy Scts; Hosp Aide; Intnl Clb; Mathletes; Math Clb; SADD; Yrbk Stf; JV Crs Cntry; High Hon Roll; Hon Roll; Eagle Scout 83; Phrmctcl Awd PRIME Pgm 85; Temple U; Biochem.

SHRUM, ROBERT; Quigley HS; Ambridge, PA; (Y); 17/102; Yrbk Stf; Pres Soph Cls; Pres Jr Cls; Var Capt Golf; NHS; Art Awd 84; SADD 86.

SHUBER, MICHAEL; Norwin SR HS; N Huntingdon, PA; (Y); 266/586; Church Yth Grp; Computer Clb; Exploring; 4-H; German Clb; Math Clb; Math Tm; SADD; JV Bsbl; JC Awd; Vo-Tech Indstrl Clbs Amer 86; Royal Rangers 86; Crmnlgy.

SHUBERT, KAREN; James M Coughlin HS; Wilkes Barre, PA; (Y); 112/355; Pom Pon; Hon Roll; Jr NHS; Law.

SHUBERT, STEVEN; Waynesboro Area HS; Waynesboro, PA; (Y); Boy Scts; VP Church Yth Grp; Drama Clb; Chorus; School Musical; School Play; Swing Chorus; Nwsp Rptr; JV Crs Cntry; Var JV Wrstlng; Order Arrow 85; Scout Yr 84; Ecology Cnslr-BSA 85 & 86; Huntington Coll; Guitar.

SHUE, ALLEN; York Catholic HS; York, PA; (Y); French Clb; Rep Band; Concert Band; Jazz Band; Mrchg Band; Pep Band; Im Bsktbl; Var Socr; Hon Roll.

SHUEY, BILL; Central Dauphin East HS; Harrisburg, PA; (Y); Ski Clb; Chorus; Pres Stu Cncl; Golf; Socr; Vllybl; Hon Roll; Jr NHS; NHS; Prfct Atten Awd; Bus Adm.

SHUEY, MICHELLE; Lebanon Christian Acad; Ono, PA; (S); Church Yth Grp; Drama Clb; Hosp Aide; Chorus; Church Choir; Yrbk Stf; Pres Frsh Cls; Pres Soph Cls; Alg I & II Awd 83-84 & 84-85; Hist Awd 83-84 & 84-85.

SHUFRAN, DONALD; Bradford Area HS; Bradford, PA; (Y); Nwsp Stf; JV Golf; Var L Tennis; High Hon Roll; Jr NHS; NHS; Rotary Awd; Mth Acad Excllnc Awd 84; 99th Prcntl NEDT 85; Amer Chem Soc Awd 86.

SHUGAR, JEFF; Brockway Area HS; Brockway, PA; (Y); Varsity Clb; Var L Wrstlng; JV Ftbl; Capt Socr; Vocational Explrs 85-86.

SHUGARTS, ERIC; Brookville Area HS; Brookville, PA; (Y); 61/141; Ftbl; Clarjon U; Criminology.

SHUK, TODD; Central Dauphin East HS; Harrisburg, PA; (Y); Debate Tm; Band; Chorus; Jazz Band; Mrchg Band; Stage Crew; Golf; Hist Teacher.

SHULDINER, SARIT; Hillel Academy Of Pittsbrg; Pittsburgh, PA; (S); Drama Clb; Hosp Aide; Chorus; School Play; VP Stu Cncl; High Hon Roll; Acad All-Amer 85; Stern Coll For Women; Pre-Med.

SHULER, HALLIE; Muncy HS; Muncy, PA; (Y); 2/80; French Clb; Political Wkr; Varsity Clb; Pres Jr Cls; Bsktbl; Tennis; High Hon Roll; NHS; Hopwood Scholar 86; Bio & Home Ec Hnr 85; Chem & Soc Hnr 86; Bio.

SHULMAN, IVY; Council Rock HS; Holland, PA; (Y); Chorus; School Play; Stage Crew; Hon Roll; NHS.

SHULOCK, BARRY J; Monongahela Valley Catholic HS; Courtney, PA; (S); 1/102; Cmnty Wkr; FBLA; School Play; Ed Nwsp Stf; Stat Ftbl; Sec French Hon Soc; NHS; Ntl Merit Ltr; Century III Ldr 85; Frnch Prose Awd U Of Pittsburgh Humnts Day 85; Law.

SHULTZ, BRIAN; Laurel Highlands SR HS; Uniontown, PA; (S); 8/365; Church Yth Grp; FBLA; Math Tm; CC Awd; High Hon Roll; Jr NHS; NHS; NEDT Awd; Pittsburgh U Provost Day Fnlst 85; Engr.

SHULTZ, CAROLE A; Danville Area HS; Danville, PA; (Y); 103/202; Church Yth Grp; FCA; French Clb; Ski Clb; Chorus; Yrbk Stf; Bowling; Mat Maids; High Hon Roll; Hon Roll; Bloom U; Soclgy.

SHULTZ, ELIZABETH EYRE; Lackawanna Trail HS; Factoryville, PA; (Y); 9/86; Scholastic Bowl; Acpl Chr; Band; Pres Madrigals; Stu Cncl; Bsktbl; Hon Roll; NHS; Pres Schlr; 1st Pl Dist Chorus 85-86; Ntl Choral Awd 86; Barnard Coll; Bio.

SHULTZ, ERIC; West Hazleton HS; Drums, PA; (Y); Spanish Clb; SADD; Ftbl; Wt Lftg; Hon Roll; PA ST U; Engrng.

SHULTZ, FRANCIS J; Center Area HS; Aliquippa, PA; (Y); 35/186; Am Leg Boys St; German Clb; Letterman Clb; Varsity Clb; Bsbl; Ftbl; Wt Lftg; Hon Roll; NHS; Cntr Ftbl Mthrs Schlrshp Wnnr 86; Ftbl Capt 86; Ltr Wnnr Ftbl 84-86; Duquesne U; Law.

SHULTZ, JEFFERY; Altoona Area HS; Altoona, PA; (Y); 35/683; Drama Clb; Im Ftbl; Im Trk; High Hon Roll; Hon Roll; Presdntl Acad Fitness Awd 85-6; Juniata Coll; Pre-Med.

SHULTZ, KARLA; Danville Area HS; Danville, PA; (Y); Church Yth Grp; 4-H; French Clb; Red Cross Aide; Concert Band; Mrchg Band; High Hon Roll; NHS; Intl Day-Blmsbrg U-2nd Pl Frnch Awd 85; Ntl Ltn Exm-Mxma Cum Laude Awd 86; Frgn Lang.

SHULTZ, LISA; Mt Pleasant Area SR HS; Southwest, PA; (Y); 24/241; GAA; Office Aide; Teachers Aide; Concert Band; Mrchg Band; Nwsp Stf; Hon Roll; NHS; Pres Schlr; Rotary Awd; Bus Clb Mbr 84-86; Hmnties Day 85-86; JR Hgh Yrbk Typst 85-86; Bradford Schl; Rtl Mgmt.

SHULTZ, MARLENE; Tyrone Area HS; Tyrone, PA; (S); FBLA; Key Clb; SADD; Color Guard; Mrchg Band; Off Soph Cls; Off Jr Cls; Trk; Wrstlng; NHS.

SHULTZ, MIKE; York County Vo-Tech HS; York Haven, PA; (Y); 24/406; Church Yth Grp; VICA; Im Bsbl; Var L Ftbl; Im Wt Lftg; Hon Roll; Diesl Mech.

SHUMAKER, JENNIFER; West Greene HS; Sycamore, PA; (S); Drama Clb; Sec French Clb; Library Aide; Ski Clb; Chorus; School Musical; School Play; Yrbk Stf; Stat Trk; High Hon Roll.

SHUMAKER, JULIE; Meadville Area SR HS; Meadville, PA; (Y); Hosp Aide; Key Clb; Ski Clb; Socr; Hon Roll; Rotary Awd; Intl Stds.

SHUMAKER, MELINDA; West Greene HS; Rogersville, PA; (Y); Church Yth Grp; Dance Clb; FBLA; FHA; Girl Scts; Pres Library Aide; School Musical; Yrbk Sprt Ed; Trs Frsh Cls; Rep Stu Cncl; Century 21 Acctng Awd Profcncy 85-86; Acctng.

SHUMAN, ALAN; Lewisburg Area HS; Lewisburg, PA; (Y); 40/170; Chess Clb; French Clb; JV Crs Cntry; Var L Trk.

SHUMAN, BENJAMIN; H S Of Engineering & Sci; Philadelphia, PA; (Y); Math Tm; Model UN; Political Wkr; Science Clb; High Hon Roll; NHS; Pres Acad Fit Awd 86; Distngshd Studies 84 & 85; PA ST U; Bio.

SHUMEK JR, GEORGE; Montour HS; Mckees Rocks, PA; (Y); Boys Clb Am; Church Yth Grp; ROTC; Lit Mag; Socr; High Hon Roll; Hon Roll; IN U Of PA; Crmnlgy.

SHUPE, TERESA; Saucon Valley SR HS; Hellertown, PA; (Y); Church Yth Grp; Drama Clb; French Clb; Library Aide; Office Aide; Chorus; School Play; Nwsp Rptr; JV Sftbl; Trk; Elem Ed.

SHURILLA, JEFFREY; Brandywine Hts Area HS; Alburtis, PA; (Y); 38/150; JV Bsktbl; Var Golf; Hon Roll.

SHUSTER, LAURIE; Archbishop Ryan HS For Girls; Philadelphia, PA; (Y); 20/475; Girl Scts; Library Aide; Q&S; Teachers Aide; Yrbk Sprt Ed; Yrbk Stf; Var Fld Hcky; JV Trk; Hon Roll; Phldlpha Cty Schlrshp 86; St Jsphs U Schlrshp 86; Chrst Brthrs Grnt 86; St Jsphs U; Lbrl Arts.

SHUSTER, STEPHANIE; Hempfield Area SR HS; Irwin, PA; (Y); Computer Clb; Hosp Aide; Trs Ski Clb; Spanish Clb; Color Guard; High Hon Roll; Hon Roll; Jr NHS; Spanish NHS; Outstndg Spnsh Stu Awd; Nrsng.

SHUTT, IVY; Bloomsburg Christian HS; Danville, PA; (Y); 1/8; Church Yth Grp; Chorus; Nwsp Ed-Chief; Pres Jr Cls; Pres Sr Cls; Socr; High Hon Roll; Val; Deans List Schlrshp Eastern Nazarene Coll 86; Presdntl Acadmc Ftnss Awd 86; Eastern Nazarene Coll; DR.

SHUTT, KERRI; Hempfield SR HS; Bovard, PA; (Y); Pep Clb; Ski Clb; Sftbl; Cheerleading; Tech.

SHUTTA, LISA; Northwest Area HS; Shickshinny, PA; (Y); 2/119; Computer Clb; Var Capt Cheerleading; High Hon Roll; NHS; NEDT Awd; Prfct Atten Awd; PA ST U; Comp Sci.

SHUTTER, ROBIN; Lebanon SR HS; Lebanon, PA; (Y); 43/266; German Clb; Pep Clb; Teachers Aide; Color Guard; Mrchg Band; School Musical; Sftbl; Hon Roll; Archlgy.

SHUTTLEWORTH, JOHN; Unionville HS; Chadds Ford, PA; (Y); 8/269; Ski Clb; Rep Frsh Cls; Rep Soph Cls; Rep Jr Cls; Var Lcrss; High Hon Roll; Jr NHS; NHS; Ntl Merit Ltr; NEDT Awd; PA ST U; Aero Sp Engr.

SHUTTLEWORTH, STACY; Conestoga Valley HS; Leola, PA; (Y); 14/256; Art Clb; Service Clb; Stage Crew; Tennis; Hon Roll; Merit Awd Schlstc Art Awd 85; Gold Key Ntls Schlstc Art Awds 86; Stu Mnth; Art Schl; Graphic Art.

SHUTTY, MICHAEL; Bishop Carroll HS; Hastings, PA; (Y); Boy Scts; Spanish Clb; Bsktbl; Ftbl; Trk; Essay Wnnr Fut Of Computers 1st Pl; Hnrs Engl; Advncd Clsses; U Pittsburgh; Biol.

SHWALLON, CHRIS; Brownsville Area HS; W Brownsville, PA; (Y); 35/222; SADD; Rep Frsh Cls; Var Bsktbl; Mgr(s); Var Sftbl; Stat Wrstlng; High Hon Roll.

SHWALLON, MICHAEL; Bethlehem Center HS; Richeyville, PA; (Y); Boy Scts; Church Yth Grp; Ad Altare Dei 84; Art.

SHWALLON, TAMMY; Uniontown HS; Uniontown, PA; (Y); Pres Church Yth Grp; Dance Clb; Drama Clb; FBLA; Pep Clb; Teachers Aide; Chorus; Drill Tm; School Musical; School Play; Usheretts; Acctnt.

SIA, ELIZABETH; William Penn HS; Harrisburg, PA; (S); 10/442; Hon Roll; Prfct Atten Awd; Typg Speed Awd 84 & 85; Harrisburg Area CC; Accntng.

SIATKOSKY, SCOTT; Plum SR HS; Pittsburgh, PA; (Y); Church Yth Grp; JV Bsbl; Im Sftbl; Im Vllybl; High Hon Roll; NHS; PA ST U; Biogentcs.

SIBERSKI, SCOTT; Wyoming Valley West HS; Plymouth, PA; (Y); Church Yth Grp; Chorus; School Musical; Rep Soph Cls; VP Sr Cls; Ftbl; Socr; Dist 9 Chorus Fest 86; Sunday Indepndt All Star Socr Team 1st Team 86; MVP Awd US Army Socr 86; US Coast Guard; Elec Engrng.

SIBERT, WILLIAM; Hershey HS; Hershey, PA; (Y); Boy Scts; Church Yth Grp; Var L Ftbl; Hon Roll; Acctng Awd 86; Valparaiso U; CPA.

SIBETO, JACQUELINE; New Castle SR HS; New Castle, PA; (S); 11/253; Church Yth Grp; High Hon Roll; Hon Roll; Acctnt.

SIBIK, MICHELLE; Kiski Area HS; Apollo, PA; (Y); FBLA; Ski Clb; Band; Color Guard; Mrchg Band; Pep Band; Symp Band; Bradford School; Legl Sec.

SIBLEY III, WILLIAM; Faith Christian Schl; Stroudsburg, PA; (Y); VP Jr Cls; Pres Sr Cls; Stat Bsbl; Stat Bsktbl; Stat Sftbl; Bkpng Awd JR & SR Yr 85-86; Bible Awd JR & SR Yr 85-86; Messiah Coll; Bkpng.

SICA, KEVIN; Cardinal Dougherty HS; Philadelphia, PA; (Y); 44/747; Church Yth Grp; Stu Cncl; High Hon Roll; Hon Roll; NHS; La Salle; Acctng.

SICHAK, DAVID; Butler SR HS; Lyndora, PA; (Y); Exploring; Bsbl; Im Bsktbl; U Of Pgh; Engrng.

SICHAK, ROBERT; Hopewell SR HS; Aliquippa, PA; (Y); 64/260; Boys Clb Am; Boy Scts; German Clb; High Hon Roll; Hon Roll; Phrmcy.

SICHERI, MICHELE; Brockway Area HS; Brockway, PA; (Y); FBLA; Ski Clb; Varsity Clb; Band; Concert Band; Capt Flag Corp; VP Frsh Cls; VP Soph Cls; Pres Jr Cls; Capt Vllybl; Robert Morris; Trvl Agnt.

SICHERI, SHEILA; Ford City HS; Ford City, PA; (Y); 10/160; Capt Drill Tm; Yrbk Stf; Off Frsh Cls; Off Soph Cls; Off Jr Cls; Pres Sr Cls; Pres Stu Cncl; Tennis; High Hon Roll; NHS; Rotary Yth Ldrshp Awds 86; U Pittsburgh; Nrs Anesth.

SICHKO, KRISTIN; Canon Mc Millan HS; Canonsburg, PA; (Y); Latin Clb; Ski Clb; Band; Concert Band; Mrchg Band; High Hon Roll; Goucher Coll; Psychlgy.

SICKLER, TED M; Wyalusing Valley HS; Wyalusing, PA; (Y); 10/150; Band; Orch; School Musical; Rep Stu Cncl; Cit Awd; High Hon Roll; NHS; Cmnty Wkr; Drama Clb; Library Aide; HOBY Found Ldrshp Awd 85; Altrnte Penn Gov Schl Arts 85; Free Enterprise Wk Schlrshp 86; Bus Adm.

SICKLES, SCOTT C; North Hills HS; Pittsburgh, PA; (Y); 105/493; Chrmn Am Leg Boys St; Library Aide; Pres NFL; Chrmn Speech Tm; Thesps; School Play; Nwsp Rptr; Ed Lit Mag; High Hon Roll; Hon Roll; Natl Forensic Lg Degree Of Spcl Distinction 86; U Of Pittsburgh; Psychology.

SIDOR, GEORGE; Lincoln HS; Ellwood City, PA; (Y); 9/179; Computer Clb; German Clb; Concert Band; Mrchg Band; School Musical; High Hon Roll; Geneva Coll SAT Schlrshp; Geneva Coll; Elec Engnrng.

SIDORIAK, JOHN; Tamaqua Area HS; Tamaqua, PA; (Y); 35/109; Boy Scts; Church Yth Grp; Ski Clb; Var L Bsbl; Im Bsktbl; Var L Ftbl; JV Trk; Im Wt Lftg; JV Wrstlng; French Hon Soc; Penn ST; Ophthalmlgy.

SIDOW, RICHARD; Geibel HS; Connellsville, PA; (Y); Pres Church Yth Grp; Pep Clb; Ski Clb; SADD; School Play; Rep Jr Cls; High Hon Roll; Pres NHS; Prfct Atten Awd; VP Spanish NHS.

SIEBER, SHELBY; East Juniata HS; Mcalisterville, PA; (Y); 8/90; Pres Church Yth Grp; JV Ftbl; Wt Lftg; High Hon Roll; Hon Roll; NHS; Prfct Atten Awd; Pre-Med.

SIECK, FRANK; Mahanoy Area HS; Mahanoy, PA; (Y); Church Yth Grp; School Play; Stage Crew; Variety Show; JV Bsbl; JV Im Bsktbl; Hon Roll; PA ST U; Bus & Fnc.

SIECK, WINSTON; Franklin Regional HS; Export, PA; (Y); 186/328; Chess Clb; Church Yth Grp; Ski Clb; Ftbl; Var L Ice Hcky; Hon Roll; Tri ST Amateur Hockey Assn Acad Awd 85-86; USAF Acad; Pilot.

SIECKO, LORI ANN; Berwick Area SR HS; Berwick, PA; (Y); 10/202; Drama Clb; Color Guard; Mrchg Band; Yrbk Ed-Chief; Stu Cncl; Trk; Hon Roll; Trs NHS; Voice Dem Awd; Cmnty Wkr; Natl Piano Playing Auditions 83-86; Catholic War Vets Oratorical Cntst Wnnr 86; Schlrshp Discvry Prog; Villanova U; Communications.

SIEDLECKI, PATRICIA; Carlynton HS; Carnegie, PA; (Y); German Clb; VP L Trk; High Hon Roll; Hon Roll; NHS; Prfct Atten Awd; Bio.

SIEFRING, LEO; Valley View JR SR HS; Peckville, PA; (Y); 46/200; Church Yth Grp; VP Science Clb; Trs Band; Trs Concert Band; Trs Jazz Band; Trs Mrchg Band; Trs Pep Band; Itln Clb-Treas 86; Ply Taps-VFW & Amercn Leg 84-86; Plyd For Prade Of Chmpns 85; Psychlgy.

SIEFRING, SUZANNE; Valley View JRSR HS; Peckville, PA; (Y); 47/201; Church Yth Grp; Latin Clb; Spanish Clb; Varsity Clb; Band; Chorus; Concert Band; Drill Tm; Drm Mjr(t); Jazz Band; Scranton ST Hosp; Rdgrphc Tech.

SIEGAL, STEPHANIE; Central HS; Scranton, PA; (Y); 17/290; Cmnty Wkr; French Clb; Ski Clb; Y-Teens; Yrbk Phtg; Yrbk Rptr; Coach Actv; Fld Hcky; Lcrss; Vllybl; Mc Gill U; Mgmt.

SIEGEL, ALEXANDER; Manheim Central HS; Manheim, PA; (Y); Church Yth Grp; Cmnty Wkr; Band; Concert Band; Symp Band; Cert Of Recgntn-Cncrt Band 86; Hstry Prof.

SIEGEL, ANGIE; North Clarion JR SR HS; Tionesta, PA; (Y); Varsity Clb; Trk; Hon Roll; Prfct Atten Awd; Dstrct Track 84, 85 & 86; ST Trck Altrnt 84-85.

SIEGEL, CINNAMON; North Clarion HS; Lucinda, PA; (Y); Chorus; Cheerleading; Mgr(s); Score Keeper; Scrtrl.

SIEGEL, JOEY; North Clanon HS; Lucinda, PA; (Y); Church Yth Grp; Var JV Cheerleading; Stat Trk; Spanish Clb; Church Choir; Score Keeper.

SIEGEL, TINA; North Clarion HS; Venus, PA; (Y); 3/86; Church Yth Grp; Cmnty Wkr; Drama Clb; French Clb; SADD; Band; Chorus; School Musical; School Play; Variety Show; Edtr Chf 3 ST Pblctn PA Brdsd 86-87; Pres Chrch Yth Grp 85-87; Crspndng Secty JR Hstrns PA 86-87; Penn ST U; Psych.

SIEGFRIED, CHRIS; West Hazleton HS; Drums, PA; (Y); Church Yth Grp; Letterman Clb; SADD; Var L Ftbl; Var L Wrstlng; Bus Mgmt.

SIEGFRIED, JANET; Unionville HS; West Chester, PA; (Y); 17/300; Church Yth Grp; Concert Band; Rep Stu Cncl; Var Bsktbl; Var Sftbl; Var Vllybl; High Hon Roll; Jr NHS; NHS; NEDT Awd; Hstry.

SIEGL, LORI J; Methacton SR HS; Norristown, PA; (Y); 59/336; Hosp Aide; Library Aide; Chorus; Off Jr Cls; Off Sr Cls; Powder Puff Ftbl; Mgr Tennis; High Hon Roll; Beaver Coll Schlrshp 86; Stu Athltc Trnr Of Yr 86; Pres Acdmc Fit Awd 86; Beaver Coll; Phy Ther.

SIEGRIST, BRENDA; Northern Lebanon HS; Jonestown, PA; (Y); 8/175; Trs Church Yth Grp; Trs Varsity Clb; Mrchg Band; Sec Soph Cls; Sec Jr Cls; Sec Sr Cls; Var L Fld Hcky; Sec NHS; January Stu Of The Month 86; Widener U; Htl & Restrnt Mgmt.

SIEGRIST, KRISTEN; Northern Lebanon HS; Jonestown, PA; (Y); Church Yth Grp; Varsity Clb; Band; School Play; VP Jr Cls; Rep Stu Cncl; JV Cheerleading; Var Fld Hcky; Hon Roll; NHS; Trvl Agnt.

SIERER, KARLA; Williams Valley JR SR HS; Williamstown, PA; (Y); Church Yth Grp; 4-H; Girl Scts; Church Choir; JV Var Bsktbl; 4-H Awd; Grand Champ Horse Div Dauphin Cnty 82-85; Wilson Coll; Vet Sci.

SIERS, TAMI; New Oxford HS; Hanover, PA; (Y); Dance Clb; Drama Clb; SADD; Band; Chorus; Color Guard; Concert Band; Flag Corp; Mrchg Band; Stage Crew; Music.

SIEVERT, DAVID; Kutztown Area HS; Lenhartsville, PA; (Y); 30/151; School Play; Bsbl; Bsktbl; Ftbl; Trk; High Hon Roll; NHS; Elctrcl Engr.

SIFORD, AMY E; Red Lion Area SR High; York, PA; (Y); 45/372; JCL; Varsity Clb; Chorus; School Musical; Cheerleading; Diving; Trk; Hon Roll; Sec Frsh Cls; Rep Jr Cls; Law.

SIGGERS, CHRISTINE; New Castle SR HS; New Castle, PA; (S); 5/253; VP Sec AFS; JA; Letterman Clb; VP Spanish Clb; Rep Stu Cncl; Var L Trk; Vllybl; High Hon Roll; NHS; Fut Phys Club Secry 85-86; Med.

SIGMUND, MARIBETH; Lock Haven SR HS; Woolrich, PA; (Y); Church Yth Grp; German Clb; Yrbk Stf; Mat Maids; Trk; Hon Roll; NHS; Math.

SIGNORE, PATRICK H; Penn Hills HS; Verona, PA; (Y); Hon Roll; Arch.

SIKET, MELISSA; Abingotn Heights HS; Clarks Summit, PA; (Y); 124/271; Dance Clb; Letterman Clb; Ski Clb; Stu Cncl; Var L Cheerleading; Fash Merch.

SIKORA, DANIEL; Trinity HS; Washington, PA; (Y); Church Yth Grp; Hon Roll; U Of Pittsburgh; Cvl Engr.

SIKORA, JOANNE; Butler Area SR HS; Butler, PA; (Y); FBLA; Hosp Aide; Office Aide; SADD; Color Guard; School Play; Cheerleading; Hon Roll; Jr NHS; U Of Ptsbrgh; Phrmcy.

SIKORA, NANCY; Hampton HS; Allison Pk, PA; (Y); Powder Puff Ftbl; Hon Roll.

SIKORA, SCOTT E; Oley Valley HS; Oley, PA; (Y); 4/250; School Play; Pres Soph Cls; Pres Jr Cls; Var L Socr; Var L Trk; Gov Hon Prg Awd; High Hon Roll; Pres NHS; Quiz Bowl; Scholastic Bowl; PA Gov Schl Sci Schlrshps 85; US Dept Energy Spr Comp Hnrs Pgm Schl 86; MIT; Comp Engrng.

SIKORSKI, ANN MARIE; South Allegheny HS; Liberty Boro, PA; (S); French Clb; Sec FNA; Hosp Aide; Y-Teens; Band; Chorus; Nwsp Stf; Powder Puff Ftbl; Trk; Hugh O Brian Yuth Fdtn 84; Dist Chorus 82-84.

SIKORSKI, CINDY S; Chartiers Valley HS; Carnegie, PA; (Y); 10/340; Trs Church Yth Grp; GAA; Ski Clb; Varsity Clb; Var L Sftbl; Var L Tennis; NHS; Gannon U; Fmly Med.

SIKORSKI, TAMMIE; Carlynton HS; Carnegie, PA; (Y); Yrbk Phtg; Yrbk Stf; Trk.

SIKRA, MARY; Bangor Area HS; Bangor, PA; (Y); 1/180; Hosp Aide; School Musical; School Play; Rptr Yrbk Stf; Var Cheerleading; Var Fld Hcky; Var Trk; High Hon Roll; Jr NHS; NHS; Outstndng Bio Awd 85; Pltcl Sci.

SILBER, JONATHAN L; Harriton HS; Penn Valley, PA; (Y); Chess Clb; Computer Clb; Debate Tm; French Clb; JA; Pres Math Tm; Model UN; Political Wkr; Science Clb; Temple Yth Grp; Wesleyan U; Philosophy.

SILDRA, DANIELLE; Aliquippa HS; Aliquippa, PA; (S); Church Yth Grp; French Clb; Hosp Aide; Band; Concert Band; Mrchg Band; Pep Band; Symp Band; Off Jr Cls; Hon Roll; Dist V Band 85-86; Bio.

SILFIES, JEFFREY DENNIS; Bethlehem Catholic HS; Bethlehem, PA; (Y); 38/220; Aud/Vis; Cmnty Wkr; Math Tm; Red Cross Aide; Stage Crew; Nwsp Sprt Ed; Rep Sr Cls; Var L Golf; High Hon Roll; NHS; Frgn Lang Clb Treas; Moravian Coll.

SILFIES, KELLY JO; Nazareth Area SR HS; Tatamy, PA; (Y); 3/123; Church Yth Grp; Key Clb; Church Choir; Drill Tm; Mrchg Band; Off Stu Cncl; L Twrlr; NHS; Pres Schlr; High Hon Roll; Hnr Grad, Cmmncmnt Spkr, Boston U Schlrshp 86; Boston U; Marine Sci.

SILFIES, SHERYL; Bethlehem Catholic HS; Bethlehem, PA; (Y); Red Cross Aide; Ski Clb; Trs Band; Concert Band; Mrchg Band; Psychlgy.

SILIMPERI, ANNEMARIE; Nazareth Area SR HS; Bethlehem, PA; (Y); 19/231; Rep Soph Cls; Stu Cncl; L Fld Hcky; Stat Mgr(s); Mat Maids; Var Trk; Hmcmng Crt 86; Muhlenberg Coll; Intl Bus.

SILKO, KATHY; Blairsville SR HS; Blairsville, PA; (Y); 8/126; Color Guard; Bsktbl; Sftbl; High Hon Roll; Hon Roll; NHS; Westmoreland Co CC; Rtlng Mngt.

SILKO, MICHELE; Blairsville SR HS; Blairsville, PA; (Y); 33/131; Teachers Aide; NHS.

SILLERS, AMY; Carlynton JR SR HS; Pittsburgh, PA; (Y); 20/160; Church Yth Grp; French Clb; Girl Scts; Band; Church Choir; Concert Band; Mrchg Band; Symp Band; High Hon Roll; Hon Roll; Bio.

SILLIMAN, JANET; Bishop Hafey HS; Beaver Meadows, PA; (Y); 8/129; German Clb; Ski Clb; Ed Yrbk Ed-Chief; Lit Mag; JV Bsktbl; L Sftbl; High Hon Roll; NHS; Psych.

SILLMAN, STEPHANIE; General Mc Lane HS; Edinboro, PA; (Y); Art Clb; SADD; Teachers Aide; VICA; Chorus; Yrbk Ed-Chief; Yrbk Phtg; Yrbk Stf; Hon Roll; Commrcl Artist.

SILOCK, JOSEPH; Hazleton HS; Hazleton, PA; (Y); 58/340; Cmnty Wkr; Im Golf.

SILVA, MIKE; Dunmore HS; Dunmore, PA; (Y); Cmnty Wkr; French Clb; Science Clb; Ski Clb; Trk; Hon Roll.

SILVANO, DENEEN; Bishop Shanahan HS; W Chester, PA; (Y); 41/218; Dance Clb; Swmmng; Accntng.

SILVASY, ROBERT; W Mifflin Area HS; Whitaker, PA; (Y); 41/318; Exploring; Teachers Aide; Stat Bsktbl; Timer; L Wrstlng; High Hon Roll; Hon Roll; NHS; Penn ST; Engnrng.

SILVER, LYNDA; Penn Wood HS; Darby, PA; (Y); Girl Scts; Flag Corp; Comp Tech.

SILVER, MICHAEL ANDREW; Dover Area HS; Dover, PA; (Y); 2/200; Library Aide; Capt Scholastic Bowl; Rep Stu Cncl; Var Socr; VP NHS; Ntl Merit SF; Sal; Computer Clb; Princpls Awd Outstndng SR 86; PA Govrnrs Schl Sci 85; Acadmc All-Star 86; Carnegie-Mellon U; Comp.

SILVERI, ALBERT; Holy Name HS; Wyomissing, PA; (Y); Church Yth Grp; Library Aide; Pep Clb; Science Clb; Nwsp Rptr; Nwsp Stf; Var L Ftbl; Var L Trk; Sci Fair 4th Pl Physcs 85; Dist Qlfr Trck & Fld 85 & 86; Bio Engrng.

SILVERMAN, ALLISON; Cheltenham HS; Elkins Pk, PA; (Y); 6/365; Teachers Aide; Ed Yrbk Stf; JV Fld Hcky; Var Gym; JV Lcrss; Ntl Merit Ltr; U Of PA Alumni Bk Awd 86; 2nd Pl PJAS JRT Acad Of Sci 85; Cert Of Prfrmnc Natl Ed Dev Tests 85; Liberal Arts.

SILVERMAN, ISAAC E; Lower Merion HS; Wynnewood, PA; (Y); VP Temple Yth Grp; Yrbk Ed-Chief; Var Crs Cntry; JV Var Tennis; Pres French Hon Soc; NCTE Awd; Ntl Merit SF; Math Tm; Orch; Nwsp Rptr; Gratz Coll Dist Stu Awds Jewish Stds 82-86; Lankenau Med Ctr Intern 85; Natl Frnch Cert Merit 83-84; Biochem.

SILVESTER, BETH; Pennsbury HS; Yardley, PA; (Y); Chorus; Flag Corp; Madrigals; Yrbk Stf; Rep Soph Cls; Rep Jr Cls; Var Trk; Im Vllybl; Hon Roll; Cnty Choir; Talent Show-Singing; Brigham Young U.

SILVESTER, DAVID; Richland HS; Gibsonia, PA; (S); French Clb; VP JA; NFL; Jazz Band; Mrchg Band; Orch; School Musical; Ed Nwsp Stf; NHS; High Hon Roll; 1st Pl AIU Comp Fair 83, 84 & 85; Cmnctns.

SILVESTRI, JACQUELINE; Central Bucks HS East; Doylestown, PA; (Y); Drama Clb; School Musical; Yrbk Stf; Var Capt Mat Maids; Hon Roll; Jr NHS; Library Aide; Ski Clb; Color Guard; School Play; Hnr Roll Lttr Issd For Mkng 85-86; Athltc Awd Vrsty Lttr Bar For Chrldng 85-86.

SILVEY, KAREN R; Chichester SR HS; Aston, PA; (Y); Capt Dance Clb; GAA; Model UN; SADD; Band; Concert Band; Jazz Band; Mrchg Band; School Musical; School Play; W Chester U; Bio.

SILVEY, LOIS ANN; Juniata Valley HS; Alexandria, PA; (Y); 1/77; Church Yth Grp; Speech Tm; Church Choir; School Play; Nwsp Rptr; Rep Stu Cncl; Cit Awd; Pres NHS; Val; VP Pep Clb; All St Chorus 86; Pres Acadmc Ftnss Awd 86; Amer Lgn Awd 86; Bryan Coll; Elem Ed.

SILVIUS, TODD; Parkland HS; Allentown, PA; (Y); 166/459; Im JV Bsktbl; Var Golf; JV Socr; Var L Trk; Acctg.

SIMAO, STEVEN; Emmaus SR HS; Allentown, PA; (Y); 15/497; Spanish Clb; Chorus; Orch; School Musical; Rep Stu Cncl; Bsktbl; High Hon Roll; Hon Roll; NHS; Trvl.

SIMARI, DEBRA; Mohawk Area HS; Hillsville, PA; (Y); Church Yth Grp; Latin Clb; Band; Sec Jr Cls; Capt Cheerleading; Powder Puff Ftbl; Hon Roll; Hlth Srvs.

SIMARI, GERI LYNN; Mohawk HS; Hillsville, PA; (Y); Church Yth Grp; VP Latin Clb; Office Aide; Concert Band; Mrchg Band; School Musical; School Play; Var Bsktbl; JV Cheerleading; Powder Puff Ftbl; Slippery Rock U; Phys Ther.

SIMCHICK, WILLIAM; Hanover Area HS; Askam, PA; (Y); Key Clb; SADD; Bowling; Tennis; Trk; Vllybl; Hon Roll; Penn ST U; Nclr Engr.

SIMCOX, CORI J; Lock Haven SR HS; Farrandsville, PA; (Y); 4-H; Chorus; Concert Band; Variety Show; Cheerleading; L Trk; 4-H Awd; High Hon Roll; Hon Roll; NHS; ST 4-H Achvt Days Blue Rbbn 85; 3rd Pl ST Hrse Shw 85.

SIMCOX, MICHAEL WAYNE; Clearfiel Area HS; Clearfield, PA; (Y); 71/315; Wt Lftg; JV Var Wrstlng; Hon Roll; Rep Demolay Awd 86; Comp Draftng.

SIMEONE, DAVID; Penn SR HS; Pittsburgh, PA; (S); 18/790; Boy Scts; Exploring; German Clb; High Hon Roll; NHS; U Of Pittsburgh; Engrng.

SIMINGTON, CHRISTINA; Altoona Area HS; Altoona, PA; (S); Church Yth Grp; French Clb; Science Clb; Var Cheerleading; JV Crs Cntry; JV Sftbl; Var Trk; Jr NHS; NHS; Typng Awd 83; Duquesne; Pham.

SIMINICK, DYANN; Sharon SR HS; Sharon, PA; (Y); 52/196; Office Aide; Spanish Clb; SADD; Stage Crew; Nwsp Rptr; Nwsp Stf; Stu Cncl; Hon Roll; Spanish NHS; Acad Boosters Ltr For GPA 85-86; Edinboro U Of PA; Psychol.

SIMINICK, LEEAN; Sharon SR HS; Sharon, PA; (Y); 64/209; Drama Clb; Office Aide; Spanish Clb; School Play; Nwsp Stf; Stu Cncl; Edinboro U.

SIMKISS, COLLEEN; St Basil Acad; Richboro, PA; (S); GAA; Spanish Clb; Chorus; Frsh Cls; Soph Cls; Jr Cls; Stu Cncl; Ntl Merit Schol; Cmmcrl Art.

SIMKO, KAREN; Coughlin HS; Laflin, PA; (Y); Cheerleading; Hon Roll; Jr NHS.

SIMMONS, AISHAH; Philadelphia High Schl For Grls; Philadelphia, PA; (Y); 150/395; Drama Clb; Trs Intnl Clb; Chrmn Service Clb; Teachers Aide; Chorus; Nwsp Stf; Trs Stu Cncl; Rep Jr Cls; Judicial Aide 86; Law.

SIMMONS, BRENDA; Punxsutawney Area SR HS; Punxsutawney, PA; (Y); Hosp Aide; Math Tm; Varsity Clb; Variety Show; Capt L Cheerleading; Hon Roll; Art Clb; Im Bsktbl; Var Tennis; Var Trk; Schlrshp Cert 83-86; Comp Sci.

SIMMONS, BRYON; Susquenita HS; Duncannon, PA; (S); 12/153; Chorus; Bsktbl; Ftbl; Wt Lftg; High Hon Roll; Hon Roll; Jr NHS; NHS.

SIMMONS, DOUG; Grove City HS; Grove City, PA; (Y); 2/179; Pres French Clb; Soph Cls; Var Capt Bsktbl; Var Capt Ftbl; Var Trk; Elks Awd; High Hon Roll; Sec NHS; Ntl Merit Ltr; Opt Clb Awd; Cooper Engy Svcs Schlrshp 86; U S Air L O Barnes Schlrshp Awd 86; KDKA TV-2 Extrra Effrt Awd Wnnr 86; Cornell U; Law.

SIMMONS, HEATHER; Merion Mercy Acad; Phila, PA; (Y); French Clb; Pres Spanish Clb; Chorus; Nwsp Bus Mgr; Nwsp Ed-Chief; Nwsp Rptr; French Hon Soc; High Hon Roll; Pres NHS; Qul & Scrl Awd 86; Ntl Plcmnt AATF Frnch Cntst 85-86; Ntl Plcmnt AATSP Spnsh Cntst 86; LANG.

SIMMONS, LISA MARIE; Hamburg Area JR SR HS; Shoemakersville, PA; (Y); 8/152; Sec Trs Church Yth Grp; French Clb; Chorus; School Musical; Yrbk Stf; French Hon Soc; High Hon Roll; NHS; Acadmc Awds Frnch III & IV 85-86; Outstndng Frnch Sr Stu 86.

SIMMONS, LORI; Hanover Area HS; Wilkes Barre, PA; (Y); 38/167; Hosp Aide; Key Clb; Ski Clb; Im Bowling; Jr NHS.

SIMMONS, MICHELLE; Mercyhurst Preparatory Schl; Erie, PA; (Y); Key Clb; Q&S; Ski Clb; Yrbk Ed-Chief; Gym; Socr; Vllybl; NHS; Rotary Awd; Jr Natls Womens Crew Camp 85; Rotary Intl Exchange Stu 86-87; Bucknell U.

SIMMONS, OMAR; Simon Gratz HS; Philadelphia, PA; (Y); Church Yth Grp; ROTC; Teachers Aide; Prfct Atten Awd; Comp Pgmr.

SIMMONS, PAUL; Henderson HS; West Chester, PA; (S); 19/380; Ski Clb; Spanish Clb; Bsbl; Wrstlng; High Hon Roll; Hon Roll; NHS; Ntl Merit SF; Acdmc All Am 86; Aerontcl Engrng.

SIMMONS, TINA; Cowanesque Valley HS; Knoxville, PA; (Y); Computer Clb; Sec SADD; Chorus; Rep Stu Cncl; Var Cheerleading; Var Vllybl; Hon Roll; Athl Schlr Awds 84-86; Exec Secy.

SIMMONS, YOLANDA; University HS; Philadelphia, PA; (Y); Church Yth Grp; Dance Clb; Debate Tm; Girl Scts; Pep Clb; Speech Tm; Variety Show; Nwsp Ed-Chief; Nwsp Rptr; Nwsp Stf; Crtv Wrtng Awd 85-86; Dbtn Gm Hnr Crtfcts 84-86; Lincoln U; Chld Psychlgsts.

SIMMS, PAMELA; Faith Community HS; Elizabeth, PA; (S); 3/45; Church Yth Grp; Dance Clb; French Clb; Library Aide; Office Aide; Pep Clb; Yrbk Stf; JV Cheerleading; Var Tennis; High Hon Roll; Baylor TX; Pre Law.

SIMMS, SHELLEY Y; Philadelphia High Schl For Girls; Philadelphia, PA; (Y); 6/264; Political Wkr; Chorus; VP Jr Cls; Pres Sr Cls; Capt Fld Hcky; Elks Awd; NHS; Am Leg Aux Girls St; Church Yth Grp; Cmnty Wkr; Brown U Alum Club Phila Schlrhsp 86; Flwshp Senegal, Africa, Israel Smmr 85; PA Gov Schl Sci 84; Brown U; Pol Sci.

SIMMS, SUSAN; Upper Darby HS; Drexel Hl, PA; (Y); JV Var Bsktbl; JV Var Fld Hcky; Var Sftbl; Hon Roll; Kiwanis Awd; Hosp Aide; Yrbk Stf; Lcrss; Sftbl All Cntrl All Star Team 85; MVP JV Bsktbl 84-85; Physcl Thrpst.

SIMON, DAVID; Canon Mc Millian HS; Canonsburg, PA; (Y); Band; Trk; Vllybl; Hon Roll; Muscn.

SIMON, JEANNINE; Connellsville Area SR HS; Vanderbilt, PA; (Y); VP Church Yth Grp; Pep Clb; Stage Crew; Nwsp Rptr; Nwsp Stf; High Hon Roll; Tri-Hi-Y 85-86.

SIMON, KATHLEEN; Villa Joseph Marie HS; Hatboro, PA; (Y); 5/50; Church Yth Grp; Library Aide; Science Clb; Variety Show; Hon Roll; NEDT Awd; Prfct Atten Awd; Pres Acad Ftnss Awd 86; Ls Salle U; Pol Sci.

SIMON, MARCI; Liberty HS; Bethlehem, PA; (Y); 29/500; French Clb; Key Clb; Library Aide; Temple Yth Grp; Rep Soph Cls; Stu Cncl; Mgr(s); Hon Roll; NHS.

SIMON III, MICHAEL; St John Neumann HS; Philadelphia, PA; (Y); #9 In Class; Dance Clb; Science Clb; Band; Concert Band; Jazz Band; School Musical; Stage Crew; Rep Frsh Cls; Rep Soph Cls; Rep Jr Cls; Gld Mdl Band 83-86; Sns Of Itly Custodus Pacis Ldg Schlrshp 86; Ntl Hnr Soc Stu Cncl 83-86; La Salle U; Bus.

SIMON, MICHELE; Canevin HS; Pittsburgh, PA; (Y); FBLA; Var L Bsktbl; Hon Roll; Psych.

SIMON, MICHELE; Little Flower Catholic HS; Philadelphia, PA; (Y); Church Yth Grp; Teachers Aide; Church Choir; Orch; Music.

SIMON, PAUL; Council Rock HS; Richboro, PA; (Y); 40/820; Boy Scts; Im Bsktbl; High Hon Roll; Hon Roll; Ntl Merit Ltr; Engrng.

SIMON, SHAWN A; Center Area HS; Monaca, PA; (Y); 5/188; Am Leg Boys St; Pres German Clb; School Musical; Nwsp Ed-Chief; Pres Sr Cls; Var Bsbl; Im Bsktbl; Im Bowling; NHS; Center Area Gifted Pgm 85-86.

SIMON, THOMAS; Greensburg Central Catholic HS; Greenburg, PA; (Y); 50/250; High Hon Roll; Hon Roll; Comp Sci.

SIMON, VICKIE; Upper Ublin HS; Ft Washington, PA; (Y); 4/337; Pres Sec Intnl Clb; Temple Yth Grp; Nwsp Stf; Yrbk Stf; Rep Sr Cls; Stu Cncl; Stat Bsbl; High Hon Roll; Pres NHS; Ntl Merit Ltr; Cert Cash Awd From Lge Of Wmns Vtrs 85-86; Cert From PA Hghr Ed Asst Agncy 85-86; Pres Ftnss Awd 86; Duke U; Pol Sci.

SIMONS, BRIAN; HS For Creative & Performing Arts; Philadelphia, PA; (S); Dance Clb; Drama Clb; Thesps; School Play; Rep Stu Cncl; Hon Roll; Cert Merit Stu Cncl; Cert Merit Perfrmnce A Soldiers Play; Theatre.

SIMONS, JENNA; Spring-Ford HS; Royersford, PA; (Y); 49/256; French Clb; FBLA; Hosp Aide; Ski Clb; Rep Soph Cls; Rep Jr Cls; Rep Stu Cncl; Var Bsktbl; Var L Lcrss; Hon Roll; Educ.

SIMONS, KEVIN; Honesdale JR SR HS; Honesdale, PA; (Y); Band; Chorus; Mrchg Band; Stage Crew; Rep Frsh Cls; Rep Soph Cls; Rep Jr Cls; Rep Stu Cncl; Crs Cntry; Trk; Cmmnctns.

SIMPSON, ALLYSON; Washington HS; Washington, PA; (S); 14/155; Trs French Clb; Key Clb; Letterman Clb; Rep Frsh Cls; Rep Soph Cls; Rep Jr Cls; Score Keeper; VP Tennis; DAR Awd; High Hon Roll; Nrsng.

SIMPSON, AMY; Methacton SR HS; Norristown, PA; (Y); Church Yth Grp; Hosp Aide; Chorus; Rep Frsh Cls; Rep Soph Cls; Rep Jr Cls; JV Lcrss; JV Trk; Hon Roll; Philadelphia Coll Of Pharm.

SIMPSON, BETH; Marion Center HS; Marion Center, PA; (S); FBLA; Band; Chorus; Drill Tm; Mrchg Band; Swing Chorus; Jr NHS; NHS; Majorette-Lions Pride Drl Team.

SIMPSON, BRIAN; Carlisle SR HS; Carlisle, PA; (Y); Boy Scts; Band; Concert Band; Mrchg Band; Hon Roll; Cert Acdmc Excllnc 86; CASAC Sci Fair & CASEF Sci Fair SR Div 86; Bus Adm.

SIMPSON, DONELLA; Churchill HS; Pittsburgh, PA; (Y); 49/260; JA; Q&S; SADD; Band; Concert Band; Drm Mjr(t); Mrchg Band; Orch; School Musical; Yrbk Ed-Chief; Mdls Bus Upward Bound 84; 1st Pl Trophy Drum Mjr Camp 85; Sec Treas JA 84; PA ST U; Bus Mgmt.

SIMPSON, DOROTHY; Freeport Area HS; Sarver, PA; (S); School Play; Rep Jr Cls; Im Cheerleading; High Hon Roll; Hon Roll; Marine Bio Smmr Happening 85; U Pittsbrgh; Vet.

SIMPSON, FRED; Blairsville SR HS; Blairsville, PA; (Y); High Hon Roll; NHS; Phys Ther.

SIMPSON, HEATHER; Monaca HS; Monaca, PA; (Y); JA; Library Aide; Pep Clb; Concert Band; School Musical; Yrbk Stf; Capt Twrlr; Hon Roll; JC Awd; NHS; Bio Stdy Pgm Gnva Coll 86; JR Ms Fnlst Bvr Co PA 86; Fnlst Gov Schl Arts 85; Med.

SIMPSON, JOEL DAVID; Ford City SR HS; Ford City, PA; (Y); 17/151; Aud/Vis; Pres Church Yth Grp; Rep Chorus; Yrbk Phtg; Rep Stu Cncl; High Hon Roll; Indiana U PA; Cmmnctns.

SIMPSON, KELLY; Moniteau JR SR HS; W Sunbury, PA; (Y); Exploring; Spanish Clb; Band; Chorus; Concert Band; Jazz Band; Mrchg Band; Pep Band; Yrbk Phtg; Nrsng.

SIMPSON, LISA; Labanon Catholic HS; Cleona, PA; (Y); 12/76; German Clb; JV Capt Bsktbl; Var Capt Sftbl; FCA; FHA; Yrbk Stf; Im Vllybl; Ntl Merit Ltr; Srvd In City Govt Day 86; Christian Athl & MVP Sftbl 86; Psychol.

SIMPSON, LORI; James M Coughlin HS; Wilkes Barre, PA; (Y); Drama Clb; Chorus; Color Guard; Orch; School Play; Variety Show; Pom Pon; Hon Roll; Jr NHS; NHS; Orchstra Awd 83-84; PA ST U; Elem Educ.

SIMPSON, MICHELE; Mc Guffey HS; Prosperity, PA; (Y); 41/202; Church Yth Grp; Spanish Clb; Tennis; Hon Roll; Psych.

SIMPSON, MICHELLE L; West Hazleton HS; Conyngham, PA; (S); FTA; Library Aide; Ski Clb; Spanish Clb; Stu Cncl; Var L Trk; NHS; Millersville U; Elem Educ.

SIMPSON, ROSEMARIE; St Maria Goretti HS; Philadelphia, PA; (Y); 88/389; Pres Church Yth Grp; GAA; Mathletes; Hon Roll; Charles E Ellis Schlrshp 83-87; Villanova; Comp.

SIMPSON, SAMUEL; Pine Forge Acad; Brooklyn, NY; (Y); Band; Church Choir; Stu Cncl; Cit Awd; Hon Roll; NHS; Bus Mgmt.

SIMS, JAMES; Bethel Park HS; Bethel Park, PA; (Y); Letterman Clb; Varsity Clb; Variety Show; JV Bsbl; Var Bsktbl; Var L Ftbl; Wt Lftg; Latin Clb; Band; Var Bsktbl; Bus.

SIMS, SANDRA; Freedom HS; Bethlehem, PA; (Y); 5/404; Sec Band; Concert Band; Mrchg Band; Sec Orch; Pep Band; Symp Band; Hon Roll; NHS; PMEA Dist Band 84-86; Dist Orchstr 86; PMEA Reg Band 85-86; Reg Orchstr 86; All ST Orchstr 86; Penn ST U.

SIMS, SEIJUN; Talyor Allderdice HS; Pittsburgh, PA; (Y); Boys Clb Am; Cit Awd; High Hon Roll; Hon Roll; Ntl Merit Ltr; Pres Of Soc Stud Cls 83; Valubl Stu 84; PITT; Engrng.

SIMS, TAYLOR; Waynesboro Area SR HS; Waynesboro, PA; (Y); Ski Clb; Rep Frsh Cls; Rep Soph Cls; Rep Jr Cls; High Hon Roll; Hon Roll; Stu Cnsrvtn Assn 86; Frstry.

SIMS, THERESA; Engineering And Science HS; Philadelphia, PA; (Y); 8/177; Civic Clb; Cmnty Wkr; Science Clb; Church Choir; Off Frsh Cls; Soph Cls; Pres Jr Cls; Off Stu Cncl; High Hon Roll; Hon Roll; Soc Of Women Engrs Cert Of Merit 86; Hon & Rise Schlrshp From U Of DE 86; U Of DE; Chem Engrng.

SINCAVAGE, ANN; Pocono Central Catholic HS; Blakeslee, PA; (S); 11/29; Art Clb; Pep Clb; Ski Clb; Chorus; Church Choir; Trs Frsh Cls; VP Soph Cls; VP Jr Cls; Stu Cncl; Var JV Bsktbl; Sci Awd 83-84; Soc Distngushd Am HS Stu; Boyt-Pittsburgh; Trvl Bus.

SINCLAIR, CATHY; Archbishop Wood For Girls; Willow Grove, PA; (Y); 72/259; Band; Concert Band; Jazz Band; Mrchg Band; Orch; Rep Soph Cls; Twrlr; Jack Lynch Mem Spirit Awd In Bnd 86; St Cyril Prsh Awd Of Exc In Msc 86; Holy Fmly Coll; Crmnl Jstc.

SINCO, MICHAEL; Crestwood HS; Mountaintop, PA; (Y); 12/200; Letterman Clb; Varsity Clb; Bsbl; Ftbl; Wt Lftg; High Hon Roll; Hon Roll; NHS; All Schltc 2nd Bases 86.

SINES, RICHARD; Strong Vincent HS; Erie, PA; (Y); 18/182; Chess Clb; Church Yth Grp; Cmnty Wkr; Trk; High Hon Roll; Lee Coll; Hstry.

SINES, SHELLY; Strong Vincent HS; Erie, PA; (Y); 36/164; Church Yth Grp; Office Aide; Chorus; Church Choir; Vllybl; Hon Roll; Cosmotlgy.

SINGER, AMY; E L Meyers HS; Wilkes Barre, PA; (Y); 4/148; German Clb; Girl Scts; Hosp Aide; Concert Band; Jazz Band; Mrchg Band; Orch; NHS; NEDT Awd; Pres Schlr; Dstrct & Rgnl Bnds 83-85; Dstrct Orchstra 83-84; Phil Coll Of Phrmcy & Sci Trst Schlrshp 85; Phil Coll Phrmcy; Phrmcst.

SINGER, DOUGLAS; Lebanon SR HS; Lebanon, PA; (Y); 1/270; Pres Computer Clb; German Clb; Band; L Bsktbl; Capt L Crs Cntry; L Trk; Bausch & Lomb Sci Awd; High Hon Roll; NHS; Val; US Army Res Schlr Ath 86; Outstndng Mth Awd 86; Outstndng Chem Awd 86; Lehigh U; Engrng.

SINGER, GREGORY; Radnor HS; Villanova, PA; (S); Boy Scts; JV Capt Debate Tm; Model UN; NFL; Quiz Bowl; Speech Tm; High Hon Roll; NHS; Comp.

SINGER, LISA; Lincoln HS; Ellwood City, PA; (Y); 48/169; French Clb; Ski Clb; Y-Teens; Chorus; School Musical; Yrbk Stf; Cheerleading; Powder Puff Ftbl; High Hon Roll; Hon Roll; Westminster Coll; Acctg.

SINGER, WENDY; Altoona Area HS; Altoona, PA; (S); 5/683; Office Aide; Q&S; Spanish Clb; SADD; VP Temple Yth Grp; Nwsp Rptr; Yrbk Ed-Chief; Lit Mag; Jr NHS; NHS.

SINGH, REETA; Cedar Cliff HS; Camp Hill, PA; (Y); 14/272; Debate Tm; Hosp Aide; Soroptimist; Pres Frsh Cls; Rep Soph Cls; Trs Jr Cls; Pres Sr Cls; NHS; German Clb; Letterman Clb; John Hall Fndtn Schlrshp 86; Grmn Nat Hnr Soc 85-86; Gvrnrs Schl Intl Stds 85; PA St U; Engrng.

SINGH, SUMEET; Clarion Area HS; Clarion, PA; (S); 1/80; FHA; FTA; Hosp Aide; Yrbk Stf; High Hon Roll; Pres NHS; Amer Lgn Essay Cont Awd 85; Clarion U.

SINGHOSE, LINDA; Mars Area SR HS; Valencia, PA; (Y); 9/160; GAA; Office Aide; Pep Clb; Spanish Clb; Varsity Clb; JV Var Bsktbl; Sftbl; High Hon Roll; NHS; Awd For Excellence In Business Skills 86; Butler Cnty Comm Coll; Accntng.

SINGLETARY, NICOLE; Aliquippa HS; Aliquippa, PA; (Y); French Clb; Band; Concert Band; Mrchg Band; Pep Band; Off Jr Cls; Off Sr Cls; Cheerleading; Trk; Hon Roll; Law.

SINGLETON, KIRSTEN LEIGH; Penn Hills SR HS; Pittsburgh, PA; (Y); Church Yth Grp; French Clb; Hosp Aide; Letterman Clb; Varsity Clb; Drill Tm; Mrchg Band; Stu Cncl; Hst Pom Pon; Swmmng; Lamp Of Learning 85-86; Advncd Lfsvg/Lifegrdg, 1st Aid, CPR Cert 86; Nrsg.

SINGLETON, STEVEN; Highlands HS; Natrona Heights, PA; (Y); Exploring; PA ST U; Mech Engr.

SINGLETON, TAMMY; Franklin JR SR HS; Utica, PA; (Y); Pres Trs Church Yth Grp; Pres Sec 4-H; Trs Spanish Clb; Cheerleading; Crs Cntry; Capt Trk; 4-H Awd; High Hon Roll; Hon Roll; Spansh Lang Awd 86; Schl Dirctrs Awd 86; Slippery Rock U; Poltcl Sci.

SINGLEY, MISSY; Biglerville HS; York, PA; (Y); 29/85; Computer Clb; FHA; German Clb; Girl Scts; Library Aide; Band; Chorus; Church Choir; Color Guard; Concert Band; Gd Sprtsmnshp Grls Sftbl 79; Gd Sprtmnshp Grls Sftbl 80.

SINGO, CHRISTIANN; Connellsville HS; Dunbar, PA; (Y); Bsktbl; Drctrs Lst Vo-Tech 86; Pittsburgh Barber Sch; Cosmtlgy.

SINGRELLA JR, VINCENT D; Plymouth-Whitemarsh HS; Conshohocken, PA; (Y); Boy Scts; Computer Clb; Concert Band; Jazz Band; Mrchg Band; Pep Band; Stage Crew; Hon Roll; Jr NHS; Drexel Schlrshp 86-87; Drexel U; Sftwr Engrng.

SINHA, LUNA; Moon SR HS; Coraopolis, PA; (Y); Cmnty Wkr; French Clb; Key Clb; Office Aide; Teachers Aide; Tennis; Vllybl; High Hon Roll; Hon Roll; NHS; Penn ST U; Genetc Engrng.

SINICKI, KAREN; Seneca Valley HS; Mars, PA; (Y); Pres Church Yth Grp; Hosp Aide; SADD; Hon Roll; Lion Awd; Teachers Aide; Mrchg Band; School Musical; Symp Band; Yrbk Stf; Med.

SINKO, JOHN; Ringgold HS; Monongahela, PA; (Y); Church Yth Grp; Hon Roll; PTA Cultrl Arts Awd 3rd Pl Litrtr 85; Duquesne U; Microbio.

SINOPOLI, KRISTA; Sharon SR HS; Sharon, PA; (Y); 45/162; Aud/Vis; Church Yth Grp; Girl Scts; Office Aide; Spanish Clb; Teachers Aide; Pres Jr Cls; Tri Hi Y; Pre-Schl Tchr.

SIPE, RICK; Philipsburg-Osceola Area HS; Osceola Mills, PA; (Y); 137/245; Chess Clb; Political Wkr; Band; Concert Band; Mrchg Band; JV Crs Cntry; Hon Roll; Allsopp Awd Music 84; Pre-Law.

SIPES, MARIE; Central York SR HS; York, PA; (Y); 59/248; VP JA; Office Aide; Varsity Clb; Nwsp Stf; Yrbk Stf; Stat Bsbl; Mgr(s); Mgr Wrstlng; Hon Roll; St Schlr; Rapid Amer Schlrshop 86; Shippensburg U; Bus Admin.

SIPPY, KINTA; Saegertown HS; Saegertown, PA; (Y); 4/124; Church Yth Grp; Ski Clb; Spanish Clb; Chorus; Rep Stu Cncl; Hon Roll; Jr NHS; NHS.

SIRAVO, DINA MARIE; Little Flower Catholic HS For Girls; Philadelphia, PA; (Y); 39/413; Pres Chorus; School Musical; School Play; Nwsp Ed-Chief; Hon Roll; NHS; Prfct Atten Awd; Pres Schlr; Drama Clb; French Clb; Stu Prsnnl 86; Rcgntn Awd Quill & Scroll Soc 86; Outstndg Srv Awd 86; Temple U; Brdscst Journlsm.

SIRAVO, LUCIA; St Hubert Catholic HS; Philadelphia, PA; (Y); 3/369; Hosp Aide; Nwsp Ed-Chief; Cit Awd; DAR Awd; High Hon Roll; Hon Roll; NHS; Ntl Merit Ltr; Tmpl U Pres Awd 86; Awd-Hghst Acadmc Avg-Engl 85; Awd-Hghst Acadm Avg Stdy Itln 83-86; Temple U; Phrmcst.

SIRIANNI, GINA M; Kennedy Christian HS; Brookfield, OH; (Y); 1/100; Latin Clb; Drill Tm; Yrbk Stf; Rep Stu Cncl; Im Bsktbl; Var Capt Cheerleading; Im Vllybl; Hon Roll; NHS; NEDT Awd; Amer H S Mth Exam Awd 83; Natl Hnr Rl.

SIRKO, MARYBETH; Forest Hills HS; Summerhill, PA; (Y); 14/156; Spanish Clb; Band; Concert Band; Mrchg Band; Orch; Hon Roll; Spanish NHS; IN U PA; Dietetics.

SIROKI, LAURA; Elizabeth Forward HS; Elizabeth, PA; (Y); Church Yth Grp; Cmnty Wkr; Library Aide; SADD; Teachers Aide; Chorus; Yrbk Stf; Bsktbl; Vllybl; Hon Roll; Nrsng.

SIROTA, STEVEN T; Blackhawk HS; Darlington, PA; (Y); 20/275; Boy Scts; Church Yth Grp; Band; Concert Band; Jazz Band; Mrchg Band; Symp Band; VP Sr Cls; Bsbl; Crs Cntry; Engrng.

SISAK, SUZANNE R; Fairview HS; Fairview, PA; (Y); 2/183; French Clb; Jazz Band; Mrchg Band; Orch; School Musical; High Hon Roll; NHS; Ntl Merit SF; Drama Clb; Prin Dble Bass ST Orchestra 85; Math, Sci Medal RPI 85; Jets & ACS Chmlympcs Sci Teams 85; Ortho.

SISITKI, JAMES; United HS; Robinson, PA; (Y); 46/157; Camera Clb; Church Yth Grp; French Clb; Math Clb; Var L Bsbl; Var L Bsktbl; Var L Ftbl; Var Wt Lftg; Hon Roll.

SISKIND, ADRIENNE; Solebury Schl; Yardley, PA; (S); Acpl Chr; Chorus; Madrigals; School Play; Lit Mag; Vllybl; Wt Lftg; High Hon Roll; Hon Roll; Ntl Merit Ltr; Geo & Calc Awds 84 & 85; Spcl Math Awd 86; Phys Aed; Rochester Inst Tech; Math.

SISKO, FRANK; Homer-Center HS; Homer City, PA; (Y); 39/90; Boy Scts; Camera Clb; French Clb; Ski Clb; Varsity Clb; School Play; Nwsp Phtg; Nwsp Sprt Ed; Yrbk Phtg; Yrbk Sprt Ed; IN Cnty Hon Mntn Ftbl 85; Plyr Wk Ftbl 85; Engrng.

SITAR, SHAWN; Abington Heights North Campus HS; Clarks Green, PA; (Y); 47/271; Boy Scts; Exploring; Ftbl; Trk; Hon Roll; NHS; Prfct Atten Awd; Abington Hts Triathln Indvdls Wnr 86; Biol.

SITEK, SCOTT; Catherdral Prep; Erie, PA; (Y); Band; Concert Band; Jazz Band; Mrchg Band; Comp Sci.

SITES, DORRIEANN B; Carrick HS; Pittsburgh, PA; (Y); Church Yth Grp; Exploring; Q&S; Stage Crew; Nwsp Stf; Var Sftbl; High Hon Roll; Hon Roll; MVP Sftbl-Overbrook Cmmnty 84 & 85; U Of Pittsburgh; Phys Ther.

SITES, JAMES; Fairfield HS; Fairfield, PA; (Y); 9/42; FCA; Spanish Clb; Band; Concert Band; Jazz Band; Mrchg Band; Pep Band; School Play; JV Var Bsbl; JV Var Bsktbl; Mt Alto Campus; Frstry.

SITES, KATHERINE; Pennsbury HS; Morrisville, PA; (Y); 7/820; Cmnty Wkr; Trs Pres Debate Tm; German Clb; Intnl Clb; Trs Pres NFL; Trs Pres Speech Tm; Rep Stu Cncl; Hon Roll; NHS; Prfct Atten Awd; Intl Rel.

SITKO, JEFFFREY; Saint Pius X HS; Douglassville, PA; (S); 15/139; Science Clb; Off Sr Cls; Stu Cncl; Var L Bsktbl; L Var Golf; High Hon Roll; NHS; Opt Clb Awd; Villanova U; Elec Engrng.

SITLER, SUSAN; Saint Hubert HS; Philadelphia, PA; (Y); 155/367; Office Aide; Chorus; School Musical.

SITOSKI, CAROL; Hazleton HS; Drums, PA; (Y); 7/400; Church Yth Grp; Capt Dance Clb; Drama Clb; English Clb; Leo Clb; Science Clb; Chorus; School Musical; School Play; Variety Show; Top 10 Stu 86; Penn ST U; Chem Engrg.

SIUNIAK, STEPHANIE; Blacklick Valley JR SR HS; Nanty Glo, PA; (Y); 19/91; Camera Clb; Library Aide; Ski Clb; Varsity Clb; Nwsp Stf; JV Var Cheerleading; Var Score Keeper; Var Sftbl; JV Vllybl; Hon Roll; TUP.

SIVEL, TRACY; Archbishop Kennedy HS; Plymouth, PA; (Y); 16/186; French Clb; Mathletes; Nwsp Rptr; Yrbk Stf; Rep Jr Cls; Rep Sr Cls; Fld Hcky; Vllybl; Hon Roll; Pres NHS; Whitemarsh Bus Assn & Cathlc Philapitrn Schlrshps 86; Knghts Columbus Svc Awd; La Salle U; Mktg.

SIVILICH, KURT R; Berwick Area SR HS; Berwick, PA; (Y); 80/286; Band; Concert Band; Jazz Band; Mrchg Band; Orch; Var Swmmng; God Cntry Awd; Prfct Atten Awd; Boy Scts; Church Yth Grp; Dist Orch 86; Dist Band 86; Regn Band 86; Arch Engrng.

SIWINSKI, DAVID R; Archbishop Ryan High Schl For Boys; Philadelphia, PA; (Y); 1/431; Church Yth Grp; JA; Nwsp Rptr; Var Capt Crs Cntry; Var Capt Trk; High Hon Roll; VP NHS; Computer Clb; Mathletes; Mst Outstndng Schlr Athlt; Truste Schlrshp-Le High U; Al-Cathlc Mile; Le Hgh U; Chemcl Engrng.

SIWINSKI, DENISE ELIZABETH; Archbishop Ryan HS For Girls; Philadelphia, PA; (Y); 1/491; Am Leg Aux Girls St; Church Yth Grp; Q&S; VP Science Clb; Spanish Clb; Nwsp Stf; Var L Crs Cntry; Var L Trk; NHS; Prfct Atten Awd; Cummultv Rank 1 84-86; Ldrshp Semnrs-Hugh O Brien Yth Fndtn, Twn Mtng Tmmrrw, PA Entrprs Wk 85 & 86.

SIWULA, LISA; Southmoreland HS; Scottdale, PA; (Y); 18/218; German Clb; Office Aide; Nwsp Stf; Lit Mag; ALPHA Gftd Stu Pgm 82-86; Grmn Ntl Hon Soc 83-86; Robert Morris Coll; Acctg.

SIZEMORE, CAROL; Solanco SR HS; Peach Btm, PA; (Y); Spanish Clb; Teachers Aide; Varsity Clb; Band; Concert Band; Mrchg Band; Var L Crs Cntry; Var L Trk; High Hon Roll; NHS; Phys Ed.

SKAFF, TOM; E L Meyers HS; Wilkes Barre, PA; (Y); Letterman Clb; Chorus; Yrbk Stf; Stu Cncl; Bsbl; Bsktbl; Ftbl; Hon Roll; Ftbl Schlrshp 86-87; Bloomsburg U.

SKALA, BETH; Conemaugh Township HS; Johnstown, PA; (S); 7/101; Drama Clb; NFL; Band; Color Guard; Flag Corp; School Play; Nwsp Stf; Lit Mag; Rep Stu Cncl; Hon Roll; Psychlgy.

SKALAMERA, TINA; St Maria Goretti HS; Philadelphia, PA; (Y); 43/390; VP Church Yth Grp; GAA; Mathletes; Math Clb; Spanish Clb; Teachers Aide; High Hon Roll; Hon Roll; Jr NHS; NHS; Math.

SKALNIAK, DAVID B; South Side Catholic HS; Pittsburgh, PA; (S); School Play; Nwsp Ed-Chief; Trs Frsh Cls; Trs Soph Cls; Trs Jr Cls; Trs Sr Cls; Stu Cncl; Bowling; NHS; Hstry Awd; U Of Pittsburgh; Cmptr Scir.

SKANDERSON, PAUL; Springdale HS; Springdale, PA; (Y); Spanish Clb; Band; Concert Band; Jazz Band; Mrchg Band; Pep Band; Bsbl; Bsktbl; Socr; Hon Roll; Washington Jefferson Coll; Optm.

SKAPYAK, MICHAEL; Old Forge HS; Old Forge, PA; (S); Var Bsbl; Var JV Bsktbl; Hon Roll; NHS.

SKARBEK, MARY; Punxsutawney Area HS; Walston, PA; (Y); 23/238; Church Yth Grp; FNA; GAA; Hosp Aide; Science Clb; Church Choir; Variety Show; Hon Roll; NHS; Bsktbl Queen 86; IN U; Nrsng.

SKARIOT, SUSAN; Trinity HS; Washington, PA; (Y); Church Yth Grp; Exploring; Hosp Aide; Key Clb; Office Aide; Pep Clb; Teachers Aide; Hon Roll; Occptnl Thrpy.

SKARUPA, KAREN; Fort Cherry HS; Mcdonald, PA; (Y); Cmnty Wkr; Computer Clb; Drama Clb; Exploring; French Clb; FNA; Library Aide; Math Clb; Science Clb; Ski Clb; Lfgd 85-86; PTSA Acadmc Achvt Awd 85; Scuba Dvr; Sewickley Valley; Nrsg.

SKARUPSKI, CHRISTOPHER; Cathedral Prep; Erie, PA; (Y); 8/244; Camera Clb; Model UN; Crs Cntry; JV Trk; JV Wrstlng; High Hon Roll; Ntl Merit Ltr.

SKELDING, KIM; Our Lady Of Lourdes HS; Mt Carmel, PA; (Y); 11/100; Pres Cmnty Wkr; Pres Library Aide; Sec PAVAS; Spanish Clb; Thesps; School Play; Nwsp Ed-Chief; Stu Cncl; Hon Roll; Ntl Spch Drama Awd; Comm Diocesan Pro Life Actvties; Best Perf Drama Comptn; Franklin; Pre-Med.

SKELTON, BRENDA; Tyrone Area HS; Tyrone, PA; (Y); Chorus; Powder Puff Ftbl; High Hon Roll; Hon Roll; PA ST U; Real Est.

SKELTON, MICHELLE; Waynesburg Central HS; Waynesburg, PA; (Y); AFS; Church Yth Grp; French Clb; Natl Beta Clb; Ski Clb; Sec Jr Cls; Stu Cncl; Stat Crs Cntry; Make It W/Wool Model Awd; Fashn Mrchndsng.

SKERKOSKI, BECKY; South Allegheny HS; Glassport, PA; (S); 1/164; Sec French Clb; Y-Teens; Band; School Musical; Nwsp Stf; Yrbk Sprt Ed; Off Jr Cls; Off Sr Cls; Rep Stu Cncl; Trs NHS; IN U Of PA; Accntng.

SKERLEC, DEBRA; Western Beaver HS; Industry, PA; (Y); Drama Clb; 4-H; VP JA; Band; Nwsp Rptr; Sec Frsh Cls; Pres Soph Cls; Sec Stu Cncl; Cheerleading; Sftbl; JR Exec & Achvr Awds JA 85-86; Fnlst VP Prod JA 85-86; Bst Sales Prsn Beaver Vly JA 85-86; Georgetown U; Intl Law.

SKERLEC, LYNNE; Beaver JR-SR HS; Beaver, PA; (Y); German Clb; Hosp Aide; JCL; Key Clb; Stu Cncl; Cheerleading; Hon Roll; JC Awd; NHS; Bvr Cntys JR Miss 86; Fnlst Gov Schl Dnce 84; Altrnt Gov Schl Dnce 85; U Pittsburgh; Physcl Thrpy.

SKERO, TIM; Sharon HS; Sharon, PA; (Y); 44/239; Aud/Vis; Civic Clb; Latin Clb; Office Aide; Nwsp Stf; Golf; Gov Hon Prg Awd; Jr NHS; NHS; Ntl Merit Schol; Army; Med.

SKIBA, JOE; Susq Comm HS; Susquehanna, PA; (Y); Camera Clb; Chess Clb; Drama Clb; School Play; Stage Crew; Yrbk Stf; Capt Crs Cntry; Trk.

SKIBINSKI, GREG; Wyoming Area HS; W Wyoming, PA; (Y); Church Yth Grp; Math Clb; JV Bsktbl; Var Trk; Hon Roll.

SKIBO, LORI; Wilson HS; Easton, PA; (S); Drama Clb; Sec Band; Chorus; Concert Band; School Musical; Nwsp Ed-Chief; Yrbk Ed-Chief; Tennis; Hon Roll; NHS; Acad All Amer Schlr 86; Temple U; Jrnlsm.

SKIDMORE, SHERRY; Greater Johnstown HS; Johnstown, PA; (Y); Church Yth Grp; Drama Clb; NFL; Chorus; Church Choir; School Musical; School Play; Swing Chorus; Variety Show; Nwsp Rptr; Solo Hnr Nazarene Yth Intl Gld Mdl Vocl 84; Forn Awds 85 & 86; Poet Awd E Naz Coll 84; WVU; Theatr.

SKIDMORE, THOMAS; Gateway SR HS; Monroeville, PA; (Y); 27/508; Exploring; Ski Clb; High Hon Roll; NHS; PA ST U; Bus Adm.

SKIFF, MARCI; Warren Area HS; Warren, PA; (Y); Church Yth Grp; German Clb; Office Aide; Ski Clb; Varsity Clb; Var Crs Cntry; Var Sftbl; Var Trk; High Hon Roll; Hon Roll; Dist X-Cntry Champ, X-Cntry St Qlfr 85; Track St Qlfr 86; Houghton Coll; Psych.

SKILANE, RICHARD; South Moreland SR HS; Mt Pleasant, PA; (Y); VICA; Htng.

SKINNER, TAMI; Cowanesque Valley HS; Westfield, PA; (S); 2/85; Pres Ski Clb; Pres Concert Band; Yrbk Ed-Chief; Sec Stu Cncl; Cheerleading; High Hon Roll; NHS; Sal; Chess Clb; German Clb; Dist 8 Band 84-85; Schlr Athlete Awd 83-85; Le Cercle Moderne Poetry Awd 85; Grove City Coll; Comm Arts.

SKIRCHAK, CONNIE; Crestwood HS; Wapwallopen, PA; (Y); 14/210; High Hon Roll; NHS; Ntl Merit Ltr; NEDT Awd; Kings Coll; Acctng.

SKOBEL, MICHELLE; Bethlehem-Center SR HS; Millsboro, PA; (Y); 24/156; Art Clb; Church Yth Grp; Civic Clb; Spanish Clb; Band; High Hon Roll; Hon Roll; Stu Of Mnth 85; Clrcl.

SKOLNEKOVICH, SCOTT; Moon Area HS; Coraopolis, PA; (Y); Church Yth Grp; Exploring; FBLA; JA; Rep SADD; Nwsp Stf; Rep Stu Cncl; Var Capt Bsktbl; Hon Roll; Acctng.

SKORKA, MICHAEL; Trinity HS; Camp Hill, PA; (Y); French Clb; Ski Clb; Spanish Clb; Yrbk Stf; Var L Crs Cntry; Var L Trk; Yth In Govr.

SKORNICKEL, MICHAEL; Carrick HS; Pittsburgh, PA; (S); 90/315; German Clb; Sec JA; Library Aide; School Musical; Hon Roll; U Of Pittsburgh; Mod Lang.

SKOTEK, MICHELLE; Marian Catholic HS; Mcadoo, PA; (Y); 46/115; Church Yth Grp; Service Clb; SADD; Yrbk Stf; Penn St; Phys Thrpy Asst.

SKOWRON, MICHELE; Central Catholic HS; Reading, PA; (Y); Pep Clb; Spanish Clb; Chorus; Color Guard; Mrchg Band; Vllybl; Oceangrphy.

SKOWRONSKI, GINA; Archbishop Kennedy HS; Philadelphia, PA; (Y); Hon Roll; Prfct Atten Awd; Moore Coll Of Art 86; Gft Cert Frm La Belle Ami 86; Cert For Stsfctry Cmpltn Of Sat Crs In Engl & Mth; Chestnut Hill; Hlth.

SKRIPKAR, LYDIA; Penn-Trafford HS; Jeannette, PA; (Y); 81/328; FBLA; Office Aide; Teachers Aide; VICA; High Hon Roll; Hon Roll; Prfct Atten Awd; Data Proc.

SKUBIC, JOHN; Foret City Regional HS; Forest City, PA; (Y); Computer Clb; Ski Clb; Spanish Clb; Socr; High Hon Roll; Hon Roll; Army; Avionic Navigatn.

SKUL, ANDREA; Lincoln HS; Ellwood City, PA; (Y); 6/163; French Clb; Hosp Aide; Office Aide; Yrbk Stf; Powder Puff Ftbl; Stat Trk; High Hon Roll; NHS; Pres Acad Fit Awd 86; Lions Clb Stu Mnth 86; Ushers Clb; Gannon U; Biochem.

SKUSE, MARK; Corry Area HS; Corry, PA; (S); High Hon Roll; Mth.

SKWERES, JEFF; West Mifflin Area HS; West Mifflin, PA; (Y); Exploring; Var JV Ftbl; Hon Roll; Jr NHS; NHS; Natl Hnr Soc 83-86; Engrng.

SKWIRUT, ANTHONY; Sun Valley HS; Aston, PA; (Y); 25/285; Variety Show; Nwsp Rptr; Lit Mag; JV Bsbl; Capt Var Socr; Var Tennis; Var Trk; Hon Roll; Textiles Sci Schlrshp 86-87; Phil Coll; Acctng.

SLABACH, TRISH; Cocalico HS; Adamstown, PA; (Y); GAA; Var Cheerleading; Trk; Ct Rprtr.

SLABINSKI, ROSE MARY; James M Coughlin HS; Hudson, PA; (Y); Church Yth Grp; French Clb; Ski Clb; Jr NHS; NHS; Wilkes Coll; Nrsng.

SLABY, STACY; Shamokin Area HS; Shamokin, PA; (Y); 18/247; Drama Clb; German Clb; Key Clb; Pep Clb; Science Clb; Yrbk Stf; Trs Jr Cls; Var Cheerleading; Pom Pon; High Hon Roll; Pschlgy.

SLACHTA, KATHLEEN; Cardinal O Hara HS; Aston, PA; (Y); 189/772; Church Yth Grp; Service Clb; Trk; Hon Roll; Prfct Atten Awd; Psych.

SLADE, DAVID; Shanksville-Stonycreek HS; Stoystown, PA; (S); 3/31; Pres Church Yth Grp; Teachers Aide; Band; Chorus; Church Choir; Mrchg Band; Nwsp Rptr; Nwsp Stf; Var Hon Roll; Pres NHS; Acad Scholar Messiah Coll 86-87; Messiah Coll; Christian Ed.

SLAGLE, ALLEN; Juniata HS; E Waterford, PA; (Y); Church Yth Grp; School Musical; Variety Show; Im Vllybl; High Hon Roll; Hon Roll; NHS; Pres Schlr; Hgh Schltc Awd 81-86; Drftng.

SLAGLE, LORI; Ford City HS; Ford City, PA; (Y); AFS; Art Clb; Chorus; Off Frsh Cls; Stu Cncl; Capt Twrlr; Hon Roll; Wilma Boyd; Flight Attendnt.

SLAGLE, MISTY; Clarion-Limestone HS; Clarion, PA; (Y); Sec French Clb; Intnl Clb; Varsity Clb; Sec Soph Cls; Bsktbl; Capt Cheerleading; Trk; Vllybl; Hon Roll; NHS; Dist Track Champ Triple,Long Lump 84-86; Track MVP 85-86.

SLAGLE, ROBERT; Shawango HS; New Castle, PA; (Y); 63/119; Boy Scts; Exploring; French Clb; Varsity Clb; L Jr Cls; Var L Ftbl; L Trk.

SLANE, WENDY; Blue Mountain HS; Pottsville, PA; (Y); Rep Stu Cncl; Var Cheerleading; Var Diving; Var Swmmng; High Hon Roll; Hon Roll; Ltn Hnr Scty 86.

SLATER, CRAIG; Lakeview HS; Stoneboro, PA; (Y); Church Yth Grp; DECA; Off Intnl Clb; Library Aide; VICA; School Play; Stage Crew; Brdfrd Schl Bus; Rtl Mngmnt.

SLATER, GERALD; North East HS; Northeast, PA; (Y); Exploring; Quiz Bowl; Band; Concert Band; Mrchg Band; Pep Band; School Musical; Hon Roll; U Pittsburgh; Engrng.

SLATER, JEFFREY; Carson Long Military Acad; Philadelphia, PA; (Y); 3/36; Drama Clb; Letterman Clb; School Play; Nwsp Stf; Yrbk Stf; Frsh Cls; Soph Cls; Jr Cls; Sr Cls; Stu Cncl; Senate Awd Pol Sci 85-86; Clark Lee Holman Medl Outstndng Mltry Ldrshp & Char 85-86; NM Mltry Acad; Pltcl Sci.

SLATES, MICHAEL; Fort Cherry HS; Mc Donald, PA; (S); Pres Church Yth Grp; Drama Clb; Ski Clb; Thesps; Chorus; Church Choir; School Play; Nwsp Sprt Ed; Yrbk Stf; Math Clb; Cnty Chorus; Penn ST; Comm.

SLATOFF, JEFFERSON D; Pennsbury HS; Morrisville, PA; (Y); Church Yth Grp; German Clb; Intnl Clb; SADD; Concert Band; Jazz Band; Mrchg Band; School Musical; Var Ftbl; Var Swmmng.

SLAVEK, JENNIFER; Souderton Area HS; Telford, PA; (Y); Band; Drm Mjr(t); Mrchg Band; School Play; Sr Cls; Stu Cncl; Cheerleading; Mgr(s); Hon Roll; NHS; Drexel U; Arch Engr.

SLAVIC, RONNIE; Laurel HS; Uniontown, PA; (Y); 98/346; Church Yth Grp; Letterman Clb; Office Aide; VP Frsh Cls; VP Stu Cncl; JV Bsktbl; Var L Ftbl; Arch Drwng Dsgn Awd 86; Pittsburgh Tech Inst; Arch.

SLAVICK, TAMMIE; Conemaugh Valley JR/SR HS; Johnstown, PA; (Y); French Clb; Pep Clb; Varsity Clb; Bsktbl; Sftbl; Vllybl; NHS.

SLAVISH, CHARLA; G A R Memorial HS; Wilkes Barre, PA; (S); 15/187; French Clb; Library Aide; Chorus; Yrbk Stf; Rep Stu Cncl; Stat Bsktbl; Var Cheerleading; Hon Roll; Jr NHS; NHS; Vet Med.

SLAVITSKO, DAVE; E L Meyers HS; Wilkes Barre, PA; (Y); 15/167; Red Cross Aide; Chorus; Var L Ftbl; Wt Lftg; Hon Roll; Jr NHS; NHS; NEDT Awd; Spanish NHS.

SLAYMAKER, MICHAEL; Lampeter-Strasburg HS; Strasburg, PA; (Y); 1/158; Church Yth Grp; Pres Thesps; Varsity Clb; Band; School Musical; Pres Jr Cls; Rep VP Stu Cncl; Var L Ftbl; High Hon Roll; NHS; Amer Chemcl Soc Sci Awd 86; Rotry Clb Stu Mth 86; Engrng.

SLAYTON, MICHAEL; Center HS; Monaca, PA; (Y); 39/180; Boy Scts; German Clb; Varsity Clb; Var L Bsbl; Im Bsktbl; Im Bowling; Hon Roll; Prfct Atten Awd; Stu Cncl Scholar Awd 86; PA ST; Elec Engrng.

SLEASMAN, APRIL; Connellsville Area SR HS; Indian Head, PA; (Y); 96/484; Pres Church Yth Grp; FTA; Teachers Aide; Chorus; Church Choir; School Musical; Trs Jr Cls; Trs Sr Cls; Hon Roll; Prfct Atten Awd; David C Guhl Schlrshp 86; Messiah Coll; Elem Ed.

SLEBODNIK, CATHY; Bishop O Hara HS; Dunmore, PA; (S); 20/124; Latin Clb; Science Clb; Spanish Clb; High Hon Roll; NHS; Psych.

SLEDINSKI, JULIE; West Scranton JR HS; Scranton, PA; (Y); Church Yth Grp; Latin Clb; Church Choir; School Play; Yrbk Stf; Pom Pon; Hon Roll; Marywood Coll; Comm.

SLEEGER, CAROL; Upper Darby HS; Drexel Hl, PA; (Y); Cmnty Wkr; Girl Scts; Red Cross Aide; JV Var Lcrss; High Hon Roll; Hon Roll; CPA.

SLEIGHT, JEANNETTE; Unionville HS; Kennett Sq, PA; (Y); 32/300; Dance Clb; Intnl Clb; SADD; Chorus; Orch; School Musical; Variety Show; Nwsp Bus Mgr; Nwsp Rptr; Nwsp Stf.

SLEITH, SHELLY; Yough SR HS; West Newton, PA; (Y); 19/226; Church Yth Grp; Ski Clb; Spanish Clb; Im Badmtn; Gym; Im Vllybl; High Hon Roll; Hon Roll; NHS; U Pittsburgh; Bio.

SLENN, BRAD; Abington SR HS; Huntington Valley, PA; (Y); 37/535; Pres Latin Clb; Model UN; Yrbk Stf; Rep Jr Cls; Rep Sr Cls; Trs Stu Cncl; Var Socr; Sec NHS; Nwsp Stf; Hon Roll; Ntl Latn Magnu Cum Laude; Wrld Affrs Frum Clb; Amnesty Intl; U TX; Bus.

SLENN, MURRAY; Abington SR HS; Huntigton, PA; (Y); 35/540; Intnl Clb; Latin Clb; Nwsp Stf; Yrbk Sprt Ed; Im Bsktbl; Lcrss; Socr; Jr NHS; U Of TX Austin; Bus Admin.

SLETNER, LAURA; Delaware Valley HS; Milford, PA; (Y); 26/130; Drama Clb; Ski Clb; Chorus; School Musical; Cheerleading; Pom Pon; Hon Roll.

SLEVIN, JEFFREY; Shady Side Acad; Pittsburgh, PA; (Y); 20/110; Crs Cntry; Socr; Trk; High Hon Roll; Hon Roll; Spanish Clb; Cum Laude Soc; Spnsh Awd; Air Force.

SLICHTER, CHANDA; Hamburg Area HS; Shoemakersville, PA; (Y); 5/150; Library Aide; Ski Clb; Spanish Clb; Speech Tm; School Musical; Soph Cls; Stu Cncl; Cheerleading; High Hon Roll; NHS; Acadmc Awd In Psych 86; Acadmc Awd In Plane Geom 85; Merit Cert In Spanish 86; Psych.

SLICK, LESLIE; Manheim Township HS; Lancaster, PA; (Y); 130/320; Key Clb; Var L Bsktbl; Var Crs Cntry; Powder Puff Ftbl; Var L Trk; Hon Roll; 3 Yr Ltr Awd Trk; Psych.

SLIFKO, LISA; Beaver Area HS; Beaver, PA; (Y); FCA; French Clb; Pep Clb; Ski Clb; Sftbl; Vllybl; High Hon Roll; Hon Roll; Pres Acdmc Ftns Awd 85-86; U Ptsbrgh; Engrng.

SLIFKO, STEVE; Forest Hills SR HS; Salix, PA; (Y); Church Choir; Golf; Hon Roll; U Of Pittsburgh; Acctng.

SLIKE, WILLIAM; Eastern Lebanon County HS; Myerstown, PA; (Y); 2/199; Teachers Aide; Var Capt Bowling; Var L Golf; Cit Awd; High Hon Roll; NHS; Pres Schlr; Rotary Awd; Sal; Awd Advncd Comp Pgmng 86; Cmncmt Spkr 86; Bwlng Tm MVP 86; Penn ST U; Engrng.

SLIMICK, JILL; Highlands HS; Tarentum, PA; (Y); Exploring; Hosp Aide; VP JA; Office Aide; Jr Cls; Rep Stu Cncl; Mgr(s); High Hon Roll; Jr NHS; NHS; US Achvt Acad Natl Sci Merit Awd 84; US Achvt Acad Natl Ldrshp & Sci Awd 85; Pre-Med.

SLINGHOFF, CHRISTINE; East HS; West Chester, PA; (Y); 20/384; Church Yth Grp; Rep Jr Cls; Rep Sr Cls; Var Tennis; Var Trk; High Hon Roll; Hon Roll; NHS; Trs Spanish NHS; U Richmond; Bus.

SLINGLUFF, ALBERT; Shankville Stoneycreek HS; Central City, PA; (S); 10/31; Pres Church Yth Grp; Quiz Bowl; VP Band; Chorus; School Play; Nwsp Rptr; Rep Stu Cncl; JV Var Bsktbl; Hon Roll; NHS; Penn ST; Ag Engrng.

SLIPKO, KRISTINA; Hopewell HS; Aliquippa, PA; (Y); 37/249; Church Yth Grp; Dance Clb; JA; Library Aide; Spanish Clb; Drill Tm; Flag Corp; Yrbk Stf; Powder Puff Ftbl; Trk; ACCTG.

SLIVENSKY, KATIE; Quigley HS; Baden, PA; (Y); Pep Clb; Drill Tm; Yrbk Stf; Mgr(s); Powder Puff Ftbl; Carlow Coll; Soclgy.

SLIWINSKI, JANICE; Montour HS; Mckees Rocks, PA; (Y); Church Yth Grp; Church Choir; Concert Band; Mrchg Band; Mgr(s); High Hon Roll; NHS; Prfct Atten Awd; Nrsng.

SLOAN, HOWARD; Union Area HS; Edingburg, PA; (Y); 4/72; Dance Clb; Rep French Clb; Chorus; Madrigals; JV Bsbl; Stat Bsktbl; Stat Ftbl; Hon Roll; Blue Ribbon Sq Dance 84-85; Slippery Rock U; Ed.

SLOAN, MELISSA; Monieau JR SR HS; Eau Claire, PA; (Y); 26/132; Drama Clb; Exploring; Spanish Clb; Nwsp Rptr; Nwsp Stf; Yrbk Stf; Stat Trk; Gannon U; Fam Med.

SLOANE, GEORGINA; Pottstown SR HS; Pottstown, PA; (Y); 15/183; Pres French Clb; Service Clb; VP Frsh Cls; Off Soph Cls; Off Jr Cls; Off Sr Cls; Stu Cncl; Fld Hcky; NHS; Pres Schlr; Amer Assoc U Wmn Schlrp; Cabot Chem Co Schlrp; Hist Awd At Wyndcroft; Franklin & Marshall; Chem Engrg.

SLOAT, DEBBI; High Point Baptist Acad; Birdsboro, PA; (S); 1/19; Sec Trs Church Yth Grp; School Play; Sec Trs Soph Cls; Sec Trs Jr Cls; JV Var Bsktbl; JV Var Cheerleading; Hon Roll; Ntl Merit Ltr; Elem Educ.

SLOBOZIEN, MARY; Conemaugh Township Area HS; Hollsopple, PA; (Y); 4/102; Drama Clb; Yrbk Sprt Ed; Var Jr Cls; Var Sr Cls; Hon Roll; Lion Awd; NHS; Technel Dir Of Schl Play 85-86; Stu Dir Of Schl Musical 85-86; Woodman Of World Soc Hist Awd 85-86; Shippensburg U; Accntng.

SLOCUM, CINDY; Lake Lehman HS; Dallas, PA; (S); 47/174; SADD; Band; Color Guard; Mrchg Band; Bsktbl; Fld Hcky; Sftbl; Hon Roll; NHS; All Star Sftbl 84-86; Sunday Indpndnt Nwsp All Star Sftbl Tm 84-86; Outstndng Sftbl Plyr 86; Bloomsburg U; Elem Ed.

SLOCUM, DEANNA; Susquehanna Community HS; Thompson, PA; (Y); 17/76; SADD; Teachers Aide; Chorus; Stu Cncl; Cheerleading; French Hon Soc; High Hon Roll; Hon Roll; Ntl Sci Mrt Awd 85-86; Schlrshp Awd From Lcl Tchrs Orgnztn 86; Mansfield U; Elmntry Ed.

SLOCUM, SUSIE; Lake-Lehman HS; Dallas, PA; (S); Aud/Vis; Church Yth Grp; Computer Clb; FTA; GAA; JA; Letterman Clb; Ski Clb; SADD; Teachers Aide; Keystone ST Games Field Hcky 85; All Schltc Sftbl All Star Tm 85-86; All Schltc Hcky All Star 84-86; Soc Sci.

SLOMOUITZ, JACQUELINE; Coughlin HS; Plains, PA; (Y); Computer Clb; French Clb; Office Aide; Ski Clb; Teachers Aide; Bsktbl; Crs Cntry; Tennis; Vllybl; Hon Roll; Temple U; Pre Dntstry.

SLONAKER, TIMOTHY J; York Suburban HS; York, PA; (Y); Ski Clb; Varsity Clb; Band; Rep Soph Cls; Rep Jr Cls; JV Var Ftbl; Var L Trk; Im Wt Lftg.

SLOSS, DOUGLAS; Lower Moreland HS; Huntingdon Valley, PA; (S); 60/214; Church Yth Grp; FBLA; Science Clb; JV Socr; Hon Roll; Hmcmng King 85-86; U FL; Chem.

SLOTHER, SHAWN; Titusville SR HS; Titusville, PA; (Y); 4/201; Art Clb; French Clb; High Hon Roll; Hon Roll; Lion Awd; NHS; Pres Schlr; Bst Show Pntng Cnty Art Shw 85; Bst Shw Sculptr Cnty Art Shw 85; 2nd Plc Regnls Womens Clb Art Cnst 86; Prototype Sculptor.

SLOTHER, TIMOTHY; Warrior Run Area HS; Watsontown, PA; (Y); VICA; JV Var Bsbl; JV Ftbl; Edward Roodarmell Awd-Drftng 86; U S Air Force; Arch.

SLOVAK, TAMMY; New Brighton HS; New Brighton, PA; (Y); 69/154; Computer Clb; GAA; Girl Scts; Pres JA; Spanish Clb; Mrchg Band; Nwsp Stf; Hon Roll; Color Guard; Trk; JA Achiver Awd, JA Sales Club Awd 86; U Tampa; Econ.

SLOWIK, CHRISTINE; Cardinal Dougherty HS; Ohila, PA; (Y); 240/747; Church Yth Grp; Office Aide; Stat Im Bsktbl; Mgr(s); Timer; Im Vllybl; Prfct Atten Awd.

SLUCHER, DAWN; Trinity HS; Falls Church, VA; (Y); Camp Fr Inc; Church Yth Grp; VP FHA; Hosp Aide; Drill Tm; Flag Corp; Sec Jr Cls; Opt Clb Awd; OK ST U; Bus Admin.

SLUSSER, JENNIFER; Chambersburg Area SR HS; Chambersburg, PA; (Y); German Clb; Science Clb; Hon Roll; Physcl Thrpy.

SLUSSER, KENT; Central Columbia HS; Berwick, PA; (Y); 9/174; Trs Church Yth Grp; Math Tm; Church Choir; High Hon Roll; Hon Roll; Kiwanis Awd; NHS; Soc Stud Key Awd 86; Pres Acdmc Ftnss Awd 86; Ntl Hnr Scty Schlrshp 86; Bloomsburg U; Comp Sci.

SLUSSER, KURT; Central Columbia HS; Berwick, PA; (Y); 7/174; Pres Church Yth Grp; Church Choir; High Hon Roll; Hon Roll; NHS; Hester Bowman Mem Scholar 86; NHS Scholar 86; Pres Acad Fit Awd Pgm 86; Bloomsburg U; Acctng.

SLUTTER, CHARLEEN; Pen Argye Area HS; Pen Argyl, PA; (Y); 24/129; Computer Clb; German Clb; Band; Chorus; Capt Color Guard; Concert Band; Capt Mrchg Band; Orch; Yrbk Stf; Ltr Flags 83-84; Concert Marchng Band 83-84; Band Orch Pins 85-86; Math.

SLYHOFF, KIM; Council Rock HS; Churchville, PA; (Y); Girl Scts; Chorus; Stu Cncl; Coach Actv; Swmmng; Hon Roll; Prfct Atten Awd; Social Sci.

SMAIL, MICHAEL; Trinity Christian Schl; East Pittsburgh, PA; (S); 1/6; Church Yth Grp; School Play; Yrbk Ed-Chief; Pres Sr Cls; Var Bsktbl; Hon Roll; NHS; Val; Calvin Coll; Ed.

SMAIL, MICHELE; Apollo-Ridge HS; Spring Chruch, PA; (Y); 11/164; Exploring; German Clb; JA; Math Clb; Band; Madrigals; Pep Band; Yrbk Stf; Hon Roll; NHS; PA ST; Aerospc Engrng.

SMAIL, SUZAN; Keystone HS; Knox, PA; (Y); 1/125; Church Yth Grp; Letterman Clb; Yrbk Stf; Rep Stu Cncl; Stat Bsktbl; Capt L Trk; Bausch & Lomb Sci Awd; High Hon Roll; NHS; Val; Lutheran Brotherhood Scholar 86; H J Crawford Mem Scholar 86; Grl Scout Gold Awd 84; Grove City Coll; Elem Ed.

SMAIL, TIMOTHY; Penn Trafford HS; Irwin, PA; (Y); 23/328; Pres French Clb; Intnl Clb; JA; Ski Clb; Teachers Aide; VP Soph Cls; Im Badmtn; Im Bsktbl; High Hon Roll; Hon Roll; Hnrs Oration Grad 86; PA ST; Engrng.

SMAKULA, PHILIP; Conemaugh Township Area HS; Holsopple, PA; (Y); 36/101; Church Yth Grp; Spanish Clb; Co-Capt Varsity Clb; Var Capt Bsbl; Var L Ftbl; Im Wt Lftg; Hon Roll.

SMALE, CAROLYN R; Owen J Roberts HS; Pottstown, PA; (S); 17/225; Var Diving; Hon Roll.

SMALE, MARY; Bangor Area SR HS; Bangor, PA; (Y); FBLA; Pep Clb; Ski Clb; Mgr Fld Hcky; High Hon Roll; Jr NHS; NHS; Teachers Aide; Cntry 21 Accntng Awd 86; 3rd Pl FBLA Typing II Cntst 86; Bus Awd 86; Northampton CC; Sec Sci.

SMALLEY, JOSEPH; Northeast Catholic HS; Philadelphia, PA; (Y); 80/400; French Clb; Yrbk Stf; Var Ftbl; Var Wt Lftg; Hon Roll; NHS; Sec SR Cls 87; La Salle; Lwyr.

SMALLS, LORI; James M Coughlin HS; Wilkes-Barre, PA; (Y); FBLA; Yrbk Stf; Var Cheerleading; Hon Roll; Jr NHS; Sec NHS; Pres Acadmc Ftnss Awd 86; Luzerne Cnty CC; CPA.

SMART, DONNELL RAE; Aliquippa HS; Aliquippa, PA; (Y); 50/135; SADD; Band; Concert Band; Mrchg Band; Yrbk Stf; Score Keeper; Sftbl; Hon Roll; Travel.

SMARTNICK, TYRONE; Mt Pleasant Area HS; Mt Pleasant, PA; (Y); Church Yth Grp; Drama Clb; FFA; Teachers Aide; School Play; Crs Cntry; Trk; High Hon Roll; FFA Stu Mnth 86; Penn St; Ornmntl Hrtcltr.

SMATHERS, STACY; Clarion Area HS; Clarion, PA; (Y); 15/100; Church Yth Grp; FCA; Pres FHA; Pep Clb; Chorus; Sec Jr Cls; Sec Stu Cncl; Var Capt Cheerleading; Hon Roll; NHS; Natl Rurl Elect Yth Tar 86; Law.

SMAY, HEATHER; Knoch JR SR HS; Saxonburg, PA; (Y); Pres Church Yth Grp; Sec Science Clb; Drill Tm; Orch; School Musical; High Hon Roll; NHS; Young Womanhd Recgntn Awd 86; Dist Orchestra 85; Johns-Hopkins; Med.

SMAY, TED; Forest Hills School Dist; Ehrenfeld, PA; (Y); 42/124; Drama Clb; Ski Clb; Pres Band; Concert Band; Jazz Band; Pres Mrchg Band; School Musical; Stage Crew; L Golf; Hon Roll.

SMAY, TONYA; Spring Grove Area SR HS; York, PA; (Y); 2/220; Trs Pres Church Yth Grp; Drama Clb; Hosp Aide; JA; Ski Clb; Yrbk Stf; Mgr Vllybl; High Hon Roll; NHS; Sal; PA Cert Of Merit For SAT Scr 85; Artwrk In PA Lgsltv Schl Art Exhbt Hrsbrg 86; RI Schl Dsgn; Grphc Arts.

SMEAD, PAIGE; Williamsport HS; Williamsport, PA; (Y); Art Clb; Church Yth Grp; Drama Clb; FHA; Girl Scts; Library Aide; Band; Chorus; Church Choir; Concert Band; Intr Dsgnr.

SMEAL, BETH; West Branch HS; Hawk Run, PA; (Y); 17/113; Science Clb; Spanish Clb; Pres VICA; Chorus; Trs Jr Cls; Trs Sr Cls; Rep Stu Cncl; Im Vllybl; Hon Roll; Medcl Secy.

SMEDLEY, JANA; Lock Haven SR HS; Lock Haven, PA; (Y); Spanish Clb; Chorus; Variety Show; Rep Stu Cncl; Var Cheerleading; Chrldr 10 Yrs; Sprts Brdcstr.

SMELKO, KAREN; Punxsutawney Area HS; Reynoldsville, PA; (Y); French Clb; Yrbk Stf; Mgr(s); Hon Roll; Indiana U PA; Fshn Merch.

SMELTZ, DALE E; Upper Dauphin Area HS; Lykens, PA; (S); 17/100; 4-H; Sec Rptr FFA; Chorus; Hon Roll; NHS; PA ST; Pltry Tech & Mgmt.

SMELTZ, KANE; Line Mountain HS; Dornsife, PA; (Y); Computer Clb; Varsity Clb; Var Ftbl; Var Capt Wrstlng; Hon Roll; Chiroprctr.

SMELTZER, AMIE; Penn Cambria HS; Cresson, PA; (Y); 40/215; Drama Clb; French Clb; Ski Clb; Chorus; Hon Roll; Eductn.

SMELTZER, MELANIE; Jersey Shore HS; Linden, PA; (Y); 4-H; Ski Clb; Rep Stu Cncl; 4-H Awd; Hon Roll; Hnrd Schl Nwspr Horseshw Champ 85; US Equest; Fin.

SMELTZER, ROBERT E; West York Area HS; York, PA; (Y); 8/207; Varsity Clb; Mrchg Band; Symp Band; Var L Ftbl; Hon Roll; NHS; Prfct Atten Awd; Temple U.

SMELTZER, SEAN; Hempfield Area HS; Youngwood, PA; (Y); Ski Clb; Band; Concert Band; Jazz Band; Mrchg Band; Bsktbl; Tennis; High Hon Roll; Jr NHS; NHS; PA ST U; Engrng.

SMERDEL, PAUL; Central Catholic HS; Pittsburgh, PA; (Y); 48/268; Art Clb; Var L Bsktbl; Var L Ftbl; Hon Roll; NHS; Cmmrcl Art.

SMERECZNIAK, KARYN; Jefferson-Morgan HS; Clarksville, PA; (S); 3/107; Dance Clb; Drama Clb; Band; Nwsp Rptr; Yrbk Ed-Chief; Sec Trs Stu Cncl; Var L Cheerleading; Wt Lftg; VP NHS; Chmstry.

SMERECZNIAK, SCOTT; Jefferson Morgan HS; Clarksville, PA; (Y); 2/89; Art Clb; SADD; Band; Concert Band; Yrbk Phtg; Yrbk Stf; Rep Jr Cls; Var Trk; High Hon Roll; NHS; Acadmc All Amer Awd 86; Architecture.

SMERROSKIE, DAWN; Our Lady Of Lourdes Regional HS; Shamokin, PA; (Y); AFS; Pres 4-H; Girl Scts; Pep Clb; PAVAS; Spanish Clb; SADD; Varsity Clb; Chorus; Mrchg Band; U Scranton; Physcl Ther.

SMETAK, ROB; Norwin SR HS; Irwin, PA; (Y); 96/550; Letterman Clb; Spanish Clb; Yrbk Ed-Chief; Coach Actv; Capt Var Socr; Prtcptd Dapper Dan Soccer Clssc Pittsburgh 85; Stu Of PA All ST Tm Sccr 85; Ply Amer Sccr Ambssdr 86; U Of Pittsburgh; Pre Dntl.

SMETANA, BOBBY; Big Spring HS; Newville, PA; (Y); Aud/Vis; Im Bowling; Im Tennis; Hon Roll; Astronomy.

SMETANA, PETER; Hazleton HS; Hazleton, PA; (Y); 62/385; Quiz Bowl; Spanish Clb; Teachers Aide; Stage Crew; Hon Roll; Grphcs Dsgn.

SMICHERKO, DONNA L; Scranton Preparatory Schl; Old Forge, PA; (Y); 28/190; Drama Clb; Sec Exploring; Chorus; School Musical; Cheerleading; Trk; High Hon Roll; Hon Roll; NHS; Excllnc Medls-Grk, Latn, Germn 84 & 85; Ursinus Coll; Med.

SMIGIEL, FRANK A; Allentown Central Catholic HS; Coopersburg, PA; (Y); 3/240; Drama Clb; Math Clb; Q&S; Nwsp Ed-Chief; Lit Mag; Hon Roll; NHS; Ntl Merit SF; PA Stu Press Assn Keystone Awd Wnnr; Engl Lit.

SMIHAL, EUGENE; Windber Area HS; Windber, PA; (Y); 21/128; Sec Church Yth Grp; VP Exploring; Capt Band; Chorus; Capt Mrchg Band; VP Stage Crew; Var Stat Bsbl; Im Bowling; Trk; Hon Roll; Bus Enterprs Wk Schlrshp 86; U Pittsburgh; Phrmtsts.

SMILEY, DAVE; Steel Valley HS; Munhall, PA; (Y); Exploring; Chorus; Bsktbl; Ftbl; Swmmng; Wt Lftg; Hon Roll; Amateur Astronomers 85-86.

SMILEY, MARNIE; Altoona HS; Altoona, PA; (Y); Drama Clb; Spanish Clb; VICA; Chorus; School Play; Stage Crew; Variety Show; Rep Stu Cncl; Var L Cheerleading; Var L Trk; Drftng.

SMINK, DAVID M; Conestoga HS; Berwyn, PA; (Y); 8/408; Trs Soph Cls; Stu Cncl; JV Bsbl; Var Capt Ice Hcky; Cit Awd; Pres NHS; Ntl Merit SF; Most Likely Succeed 82-85; Orthopedic.

SMINK, ED; Shamokin Area HS; Shamokin, PA; (Y); Key Clb; Spanish Clb; SADD; Varsity Clb; Rep Trs Stu Cncl; Var L Bsbl; Var JV Bsktbl; Var L Crs Cntry; Im Vllybl; High Hon Roll; Pres Physcl Fitnss Awd 86; Mechncl Engrng.

SMITH, ADAM; Bald Eagle Area HS; Bellefonte, PA; (Y); 18/200; Church Yth Grp; Bsbl; Im Bowling; High Hon Roll; Engl, Hist, Acad Alg II Awds 84; Fishrs Mgmnt.

SMITH, ALISA; Gateway SR HS; Monroeville, PA; (Y); Cmnty Wkr; Exploring; JA; Chorus; Hon Roll; Cert Maintng Hnr Roll 83; U Pittsburgh; Chem.

SMITH, AMBY; Reading Central Catholic HS; Boyertown, PA; (Y); Aud/Vis; 4-H; Drill Tm; Variety Show; Yrbk Stf; Stat Bsbl; JV Var Fld Hcky; JV Score Keeper; Nrs.

SMITH, AMY; Canon-Mc Millan HS; Mcdonald, PA; (Y); FBLA; JA; Office Aide; Hon Roll; Bus.

SMITH, AMY; Mt Union Area JR SR HS; Mt Union, PA; (Y); French Clb; FBLA; GAA; Stage Crew; Im Bowling; Elizabethtown; Elem Ed.

SMITH, AMY S; Waynesboro SR HS; Waynesboro, PA; (Y); 95/363; Pep Clb; Chorus; Hon Roll; York Coll PA; Accntng.

SMITH, ANNETTE; Annville-Cleona HS; Cleona, PA; (Y); Cmnty Wkr; VP FBLA; Office Aide; SADD; Chorus; Nwsp Stf; Lit Mag; Hon Roll; Jr NHS; NHS; Med Sec.

SMITH, ANTHONY; Carlisle SR HS; Carlisle, PA; (Y); 22/411; Boy Scts; Sec Sr Cls; Pres Stu Cncl; High Hon Roll; Hon Roll; NHS; SAR Awd; Carlisle Civic Clb Stu Mnth 85; Troop 160 Scout Yr 82; Engrng.

SMITH, AUDREY; Lehigh Christian Acad; Plymouth, PA; (S); 1/12; Church Yth Grp; Church Choir; Pres Sr Cls; Rep Stu Cncl; Var Bsktbl; Var L Sftbl; Var Vllybl; Hon Roll; NHS; Eastern Coll; Bio.

SMITH, BARB; Allegheny Clarion Valley HS; Dubois, PA; (Y); 26/105; Pres GAA; Var L Vllybl; Principals List 1st & Ind Nine Wks; Dubois Bus Coll; Med Sec.

SMITH, BARB; Manheim Central HS; Manheim, PA; (Y); 49/237; Teachers Aide; Stage Crew; Pres Jr Cls; Pres Sr Cls; Rep Stu Cncl; Var Bsktbl; Im Powder Puff Ftbl; Var Sftbl; Var Tennis; Var Trk; 4 Way Tst Awd 86; Phsy Ftns Awd 84-85-86; Shippensburg; Accntng.

SMITH, BARBARA; Carlisle SR HS; Carlisle, PA; (Y); 23/406; Church Yth Grp; Debate Tm; 4-H; Yrbk Stf; Lit Mag; 4-H Awd; Hon Roll; NHS; Lehigh U.

SMITH, BECKY; Delone Catholic HS; Mc Sherrystown, PA; (Y); 4/168; Radio Clb; Yrbk Stf; Cheerleading; Vllybl; High Hon Roll; NHS; Top 10% Awd; Pres Acad Ftns Awd; US Chrldng Awd; Penn ST; Psychlgy.

SMITH, BELINDA; Canton JR-SR HS; Canton, PA; (Y); 49/124; Letterman Clb; Yrbk Stf; Var Cheerleading; Sec Sci.

SMITH, BETSY; E L Meyers HS; Wilkes Bare, PA; (Y); Trs Key Clb; Chorus; Yrbk Stf; Trs Jr Cls; Trs Sr Cls; Rep Stu Cncl; Stat Bsktbl; L Fld Hcky; L Sftbl; Hon Roll; Elem Ed.

SMITH, BOBBI SUE; Bethel Park SR HS; Bethel Park, PA; (Y); Church Yth Grp; Var Capt Crs Cntry; Var Capt Trk; Hon Roll; Phys Therapy.

SMITH, BRIDGET; Portage Area HS; Portage, PA; (Y); Church Yth Grp; Drama Clb; Varsity Clb; Band; Color Guard; Mrchg Band; School Play; Variety Show; Stu Cncl; Score Keeper; Presdnts Physcl Fttnss 85-86 & 84-85 & 83-84; Indiana; Crmnl Just.

SMITH, BRYAN DAVID; Spring-Ford HS; Rogersford, PA; (S); 7/208; Boy Scts; Radio Clb; Band; Concert Band; Drm Mjr(t); Jazz Band; Mrchg Band; Trk; NHS; Ntl Merit Ltr; Smmr Scntfc Semnr US Air Frc Acad 86; Rotry Clb Ldrshp Cmp 86; US Air Frc Acad; Aerntcl Engr.

SMITH, CARL; Wyalusing Valley HS; New Albany, PA; (Y); Boy Scts; Trs Church Yth Grp; Pres Computer Clb; German Clb; Hon Roll; Continental Math Leag 1st Pl 84; Comp Sci.

SMITH, CHARLES; E L Meyers HS; Wilkes Barre, PA; (Y); 16/161; Chorus; Yrbk Stf; Rep Stu Cncl; Var L Ftbl; Var L Swmmng; Var Trk; Hon Roll; Jr NHS; NHS; Spanish NHS.

SMITH, CHRIS; Frankford HS; Philadelphia, PA; (Y); 4/365; JV Var Bsbl; Hon Roll; Drexel U Phila PA; Elec Engrng.

SMITH, CHRIS; Williamsburg HS; Williamsburg, PA; (Y); Camera Clb; FBLA; FFA; Teachers Aide; Color Guard; Pres Frsh Cls; Pres Soph Cls; Rep Stu Cncl; JV Var Bsktbl; JV Var Cheerleading; Elem Ed.

SMITH, CHRISTINE; Hempfield HS; Landisville, PA; (Y); Band; Concert Band; Mrchg Band; Orch; Nwsp Stf; Hon Roll; Hempfield Ed Assoc Schlrp 86; Frmrs 1st Bnk Awd 86; Elizabethtown Coll; Bus Adm.

SMITH, CHRISTINE; St Marys Area HS; Trenton, NJ; (Y); JV L Bsktbl; Var Sftbl; Hon Roll; NHS; Penn ST U.

SMITH, CHUCK; South Williamsport HS; S Williamsport, PA; (Y); Boy Scts; German Clb; JA; Im Mgr Bsktbl; JV Var Tennis; Wt Lftg; Hon Roll; Williamsport Area CC Bus Awds 86; Acctg.

SMITH, COLLEEN A; Bishop Hodan HS; Wilkes Barre, PA; (Y); FBLA; Ski Clb; Chorus; Cheerleading; US Achvmt Acad 85; Med Scrtry.

SMITH, CONNIE; Central HS; Martinsburg, PA; (Y); 27/182; VP Church Yth Grp; Drama Clb; Library Aide; VICA; Color Guard; Hon Roll; Pittsburgh Bty Acad; Csmtlgst.

SMITH, CONNIE; Danville SR HS; Danville, PA; (Y); 80/205; Church Yth Grp; Exploring; FBLA; Hosp Aide; Latin Clb; Pep Clb; Chorus; JV Cheerleading; Gym; Powder Puff Ftbl; Soclgy.

SMITH, COURTNEY; Hanover SR HS; Hanover, PA; (Y); 10/104; Band; Trs Soph Cls; VP Jr Cls; VP Sr Cls; Rep Stu Cncl; JV Var Bsktbl; Hon Roll; NHS; Varsity Clb; Chorus; Stu Schl Brd Rep 85-87; NEDT Awd 85; Red Crss Bldmbl Vlnteer 86; Arntcl Engr.

SMITH, DANIEL JAY; Central HS; Martinsburg, PA; (Y); 12/186; Drama Clb; FCA; Ski Clb; Varsity Clb; Chorus; Var L Ftbl; Var Capt Tennis; Natl Choral Awd 86; Central Hnr Soc 84-86; Tnns MVP 86; IN U Of PA; Math Engr.

SMITH, DARLEEN; Mercyhurst Prep; North East, PA; (Y); Church Yth Grp; Cmnty Wkr; Hosp Aide; Intnl Clb; Nwsp Rptr; Ed Yrbk Ed-Chief; Yrbk Phtg; Yrbk Stf; Var L Bsktbl; Exchange Stu; Natl Ldrshp & Serv Awd; Academic All Amer; Canisius Coll; Intl Rltns.

SMITH, DAVID; Beaver Area JR SR HS; Beaver, PA; (Y); Band; Concert Band; Mrchg Band; High Hon Roll; Hon Roll; NHS; Pres Schlr; Geneva Coll; Mth.

SMITH, DAVID; Bensalem HS; Bensalem, PA; (Y); Boy Scts; Acpl Chr; Band; Chorus; Church Choir; Madrigals; School Musical; Swing Chorus; Im Golf; JV Var Socr; Pre-Med.

SMITH, DAVID; Butler SR HS; Butler, PA; (Y); French Clb; Math Tm; Ski Clb; Band; Concert Band; Jazz Band; Mrchg Band; Orch; Pep Band; Symp Band; Westminster Hnrs Band 84-85; Pitt; Elctrcl Engrng.

SMITH, DAVID T; Phoenixville Area HS; Phoenixville, PA; (Y); 1/200; Boy Scts; Scholastic Bowl; Rep Soph Cls; Pres Stu Cncl; Var Tennis; Capt Var Wrstlng; Gov Hon Prg Awd; NHS; Ntl Merit SF; PIAA Wrstlng Rgnl Qulfr; Harvrd Bk Prz; G E Town Meetng On Tomorrow; Chem Engr.

SMITH, DAWN; Cheltenham HS; Laverockk, PA; (Y); 77/365; Hosp Aide; Political Wkr; VP Jr Cls; Ntl Merit SF; NEDT Awd; Church Choir; Color Guard; Mentally Gftd Prgrm; Bus & Prof Wmns Clb Yth Org Phila; Ec.

SMITH, DEBBIE L; Yough SR HS; Rillton, PA; (Y); 16/263; Sec Computer Clb; Library Aide; Pep Clb; Capt Color Guard; Mrchg Band; High Hon Roll; Hon Roll; NHS; Acad All Amer 86.

SMITH, DEBRA; Greater Johnstown HS; Johnstown, PA; (Y); 24/286; Var Capt Twrlr; High Hon Roll; NHS; Prfct Atten Awd; Schlrshp To Cambria-Rowe Bus Coll 86; Outstndng Accntng Awd For Schl 86; Cambria-Rowe Bus Coll; Accntng.

SMITH, DEBRA; Our Lady Of The Sacred Heart HS; Coraopolis, PA; (Y); 6/75; NFL; SADD; School Play; Yrbk Stf; Sec Frsh Cls; Pres Soph Cls; Pres Sr Cls; Trs NHS; Voice Dem Awd; NOPA Scholar 86; WA & Jefferson; Psych.

SMITH, DONNA; Greater Johnstown HS; Johnstown, PA; (Y); Church Yth Grp; French Clb; Speech Tm; W PA Nrsng Schl; Nrsng.

SMITH, DONNA; Wyoming Area HS; W Pittston, PA; (Y); Girl Scts; Ed Yrbk Stf; Stu Cncl; Var Sftbl; French Hon Soc; Hon Roll; Kiwanis Awd; Trs French Clb; Key Clb; Yth Mnstry Awd; Key Clbbr Mnth Awd; 17 Magzn Teen Brd; U Of Pittsburgh; Occptnl Thrpy.

SMITH, DOREEN; Northeast HS; North East, PA; (Y); 25/149; AFS; FBLA; Nwsp Stf; Hon Roll; Newbury Coll Schlrshp Boston MA 86; Newbury Coll Bostn; Trvl-Toursm.

SMITH, DORINE; High Point Baptist Acad; Mohnton, PA; (S); 1/28; Spanish Clb; VP Jr Cls; Cheerleading; Sftbl; Vllybl; High Hon Roll.

SMITH, DWIGHT; Danville SR HS; Danville, PA; (Y); Exploring; FBLA; Ski Clb; Spanish Clb; Band; Mrchg Band; Pep Band; School Play; Gym; Hon Roll; Psyclgy.

SMITH, EILEEN; Bishop Hafey HS; Milnesville, PA; (Y); 23/128; Trs French Clb; Science Clb; Y-Teens; Drill Tm; Cheerleading; Sftbl; Hon Roll; Prfct Atten Awd; JR Acad Sci 84-85; Bloomsburg Coll; Accntng.

SMITH, ERICA; Academy Of The New Church; Forest Park, GA; (Y); Church Yth Grp; Natl Beta Clb; Band; Concert Band; Symp Band; Hon Roll; Jr NHS; Grmn Excllnc Awd 85-86.

SMITH, ERICA; Greensburg Central Catholic HS; Latrobe, PA; (Y); AFS; JCL; Ski Clb; Im Sftbl; Var Trk; Im Vllybl; Hon Roll; Psych.

SMITH, ERIKA; Lakeland HS; Jermyn, PA; (Y); FHA; Cheerleading; Hon Roll; Medcl Asst.

SMITH, FRANK; Upper Moreland SR HS; Hatboro, PA; (Y); 47/256; Aud/Vis; Key Clb; Var Socr; High Hon Roll; Hon Roll; Pres Acad Ftnss Awd 86; Moravian COLL; Bus.

SMITH, GEORGETTA LYN; Mary Fuller Frazier Memorial HS; Grindstone, PA; (Y); VICA; Band; Concert Band; Mrchg Band; Yrbk Stf; Mgr(s); Stat Vllybl; Hon Roll; Dirctrs List At Tech 85-86; Jr High Cnty Bandk 83; Aprl Stu Of The Mnth At Tech 86; Sr Awd-Data Procsng; Schl Of Comp Tech; Bus Prog.

SMITH, GLENDA; West Hazleton JR/SR HS; West Hazleton, PA; (Y); 21/207; FTA; Yrbk Stf; Pres Stu Cncl; Pres Stu Cncl; Mgr(s); Trk; Millersville U; Bus Adm.

SMITH, GREGG; Owen J Roberts HS; St Peters, PA; (Y); Church Yth Grp; JA; Var Bsbl; JV Bsktbl; JV Ftbl; Im Ice Hcky; Im Sftbl; Im Vllybl; Im Wt Lftg; Ntl Merit Ltr; All Strs Bsbl 84; Crmnlgy.

SMITH, GREGORY D; Ambridge Area HS; Baden, PA; (Y); Am Leg Boys St; Boy Scts; Pres VP Church Yth Grp; Trs German Clb; VP Stu Cncl; L Var Gym; Gov Hon Prg Awd; High Hon Roll; NHS; SAR Awd; Order Of Arrow BSA 84; Engrng.

SMITH, H JOEL; Bethel Park SR HS; Bethel Park, PA; (Y); 52/515; Aud/Vis; Church Yth Grp; Science Clb; Rep Sr Cls; Var L Socr; High Hon Roll; NHS; Pres Schlr; Navy ROTC 4 Ur Schlrshp 86; Purdue U; Engrng.

SMITH, HEATHER; Du Bois Area HS; Reynoldsville, PA; (Y); 30/272; Church Yth Grp; German Clb; Color Guard; Mrchg Band; Stage Crew; Swmmng; High Hon Roll; Hon Roll; Carnegie Mellon; Comp.

SMITH, HEATHER; Vinceton HS; Bradford Woods, PA; (Y); 4/70; Math Tm; Service Clb; Teachers Aide; Variety Show; Capt JV Cheerleading; Hon Roll; NHS; Rep Frsh Cls; 2nd Natl Sci Olympiad Chem 84-85; 2nd Jr Acad Sci; Ms Teen Pittsburgh Pgnt 85; Cardiology.

SMITH, HEATHER; Wissahickson HS; Penllyn, PA; (Y); Computer Clb; Debate Tm; Drama Clb; Office Aide; Political Wkr; Speech Tm; Pep Band; School Musical; School Play; Key Clb; Intl Scholar Awd 86; Intl Bus.

SMITH, HEIDI; Faith Baptist Christian Acad; Levittown, PA; (Y); 1/4; Church Yth Grp; Computer Clb; Drama Clb; Chorus; Church Choir; School Play; Yrbk Ed-Chief; Yrbk Phtg; Yrbk Sprt Ed; Im JV Bsktbl; Prncpls Awd 86; St Francis Schl Nursing; Nrsng.

SMITH, HOWARD; Bensalem HS; Bensalem, PA; (Y); JV Socr; Var Swmmng; Hon Roll; Law.

SMITH, JACKIE; Northern Cambria HS; Spangler, PA; (Y); Drama Clb; NFL; Ski Clb; Chorus; Church Choir; Mrchg Band; School Play; Variety Show; Nwsp Rptr; Nwsp Stf; Natl Schl Choral Awd 86; Outstdng Drama Stu 86; Dist & Rgnl Chorus 84-86; Pittsburgh Fash Inst; Buyer.

SMITH, JACQUELINE; Brandywine Heights HS; Alburtis, PA; (Y); Girl Scts; Hosp Aide; JA; Rep Jr Cls; Rep Sr Cls; Fld Hcky; Trk; High Hon Roll; Pres Schlr; Womns Clb Schlrshp & Awd 86; Phil Coll Of Pharm & Sci.

SMITH, JAMES; West Hazleton HS; W Hazleton, PA; (Y); 47/250; Varsity Clb; Band; Mrchg Band; Var L Bsktbl; Trk; Hon Roll; Rotary Awd; Bus Admin.

SMITH III, JAMES H; St James HS; Brookhaven, PA; (Y); 8/135; Var L Bsbl; Var Bsktbl; JV Ftbl; French Hon Soc; Hon Roll; Spelling & Speech Awd 84; 2nd Hnrs Awd 84-85; Sports Med.

SMITH, JAMI; Du Bois Area HS; Brockway, PA; (Y); Hon Roll; NHS.

SMITH, JAMIE; Lower Moreland HS; Huntingdon Valley, PA; (S); 62/214; Drama Clb; French Clb; FBLA; Sec Key Clb; Library Aide; Temple Yth Grp; School Musical; Stage Crew; Yrbk Stf; Var Tennis; U Of Pitts; Spch Thrpst.

SMITH, JANICE R; Gateway Christian Schl; Kutztown, PA; (S); 2/11; Church Yth Grp; Drama Clb; Girl Scts; Chorus; Nwsp Rptr; Yrbk Stf; Rep Stu Cncl; Vllybl; Eastern Mennonite Coll.

SMITH, JARETT; Academy Of The New Church; Freeport, PA; (S); 3/42; Church Yth Grp; Computer Clb; Pres Trs 4-H; Yrbk Stf; Var Capt Crs Cntry; Ftbl; JV Ice Hcky; L Trk; High Hon Roll; Carneigie Mellon U; Elec Engrng.

SMITH, JEFF; Bishop Mc Corr HS; Johnstown, PA; (Y); Ski Clb; Spanish Clb; Chorus; Bsktbl; Trk; High Hon Roll; Hon Roll; Spanish NHS; Bus Mgmt.

SMITH, JEFF; New Brighton Area HS; New Brighton, PA; (Y); Hon Roll; Engrng.

SMITH, JENNIFER; Central Bucks East HS; Wycombe, PA; (Y); 65/468; Hosp Aide; Flag Corp; Hon Roll; Psych.

SMITH, JENNIFER; Loyalsock HS; Montoursville, PA; (Y); 4/120; Key Clb; Spanish Clb; Chorus; Yrbk Ed-Chief; Yrbk Stf; VP Stu Cncl; Mgr(s); Tennis; Hon Roll; NHS; Awds Spnsh, Alg I, Psych, Spnsh II, Spnsh III Knght Awd; U PA; Mrktg.

SMITH, JENNIFER; Plum SR HS; Pittsburgh, PA; (Y); 125/378; Church Yth Grp; JA; Spanish Clb; SADD; Church Choir; Hon Roll; Mathematics.

SMITH, JENNY; Waynesburg Central HS; Waynesburg, PA; (Y); Trs Church Yth Grp; Spanish Clb; Chorus; Church Choir; Nwsp Ed-Chief; Stat Trk; High Hon Roll; NHS; NEDT Awd; Spanish NHS; Fstvl Lf Awd 85 & 86; Outstndng Chrl Awd 84; Waynesburg Coll.

SMITH, JESSIE; Wyoming Valley West HS; Forty Fort, PA; (Y); #11 In Class; Key Clb; Band; Concert Band; Mrchg Band; Stu Cncl; Swmmng; High Hon Roll; NHS; Prfct Atten Awd; Bus.

SMITH, JILL; Punxsutawney Area HS; Punxsutawney, PA; (Y); #13 In Class; Math Tm; Science Clb; Varsity Clb; Band; Concert Band; Mrchg Band; Variety Show; Capt Trk; Twrlr; High Hon Roll; Allegheny Coll.

SMITH, JOANNE; Catasququa HS; Catasauqua, PA; (Y); 14/142; Drama Clb; Ski Clb; Stage Crew; Stu Cncl; Hon Roll; NHS; Allentown Schl Of Csmtlgy.

SMITH, JODEEN; Blair County Christian HS; Duncansville, PA; (S); 1/4; Church Yth Grp; Ed Nwsp Sprt Ed; Trs Jr Cls; Var Trk; High Hon Roll; Bob Jones U; Mth.

SMITH, JOHN S; Thomas Jefferson HS; Pittsburgh, PA; (Y); 24/265; Am Leg Boys St; Exploring; Sec JCL; Mrchg Band; Nwsp Rptr; Bsktbl; Trk.

SMITH, JOSEPH; Windber Area HS; Windber, PA; (Y); Jr Cls; Stu Cncl; Var Bsbl; High Hon Roll; Hon Roll; NHS.

SMITH, JUDY; Hempfield Area HS; Madison, PA; (Y); Pep Clb; Spanish Clb; Rep Stu Cncl; High Hon Roll; Hon Roll; Jr NHS; Spanish NHS; Rnkd Top 3-Grdtng Mdlng Cls 85; Psychlgy.

SMITH, JULIE; Brockway Area HS; Brockport, PA; (Y); 10/90; Band; Concert Band; Co-Capt Flag Corp; Mrchg Band; Pep Band; Hon Roll.

SMITH, KARLA; Lewistown Area HS; Mcveytown, PA; (Y); 8/256; Sec Chorus; Sec Concert Band; Drm Mjr(t); Sec Mrchg Band; School Musical; High Hon Roll; NHS; PA ST U; Elem Educ.

SMITH, KAROL A; Octorara Area HS; Parkesburg, PA; (Y); Church Yth Grp; FBLA; Church Choir; School Musical; Nwsp Rptr; VP Jr Cls; Pres Rep Stu Cncl; Im Mgr(s); NHS; Cmnty Wkr; Odd Fllws & Rbkhs Annl UN Yth Plgrmg 85; Syracuse U; Pre-Law.

SMITH, KATHERINE; Harrisburg HS; Harrisburg, PA; (Y); 13/450; ROTC; Chorus; Color Guard; Yrbk Stf; Cheerleading; Swmmng; Hon Roll; Schlstc Excllnc & Hon Cadet & Dstngshd Cadet NJROTC 86; Nrsng.

SMITH, KATHY; Carlynton HS; Pittsburgh, PA; (Y); Office Aide; Drill Tm; Rep Frsh Cls; Rep Jr Cls; L Pom Pon; Vllybl; Stat Wrstlng; High Hon Roll; Hon Roll; Ldrshp Awd 86; Math.

SMITH, KELLI; Penn Hills HS; Pittsburgh, PA; (Y); French Clb; Ski Clb; Stu Cncl; High Hon Roll; NHS; U Of Pgh Schlrshp 86-91; Awd Eng 83-84; Chem Awd 86; U PA; Phar.

SMITH, KELLI; Strath Haven HS; Wallingford, PA; (Y); Church Yth Grp; Hosp Aide; Var L Swmmng; L Stat Vllybl; Hon Roll; Spec Ed.

SMITH, KELLYANN; Bishop Kenrick HS; Norristown, PA; (Y); 20/295; Cmnty Wkr; Spanish Clb; Powder Puff Ftbl; Trk; Hon Roll; Law.

SMITH, KEVIN WESLEY; Mmi Prep; Mountaintop, PA; (Y); 5/32; Computer Clb; Debate Tm; Model UN; Natl Beta Clb; Ed Yrbk Phtg; Stat Bsktbl; Mgr(s); Mgr(s); Score Keeper; Im Vllybl; Century III Ldrs 85; Presdntl Clsrm 85; U Of Chicago; Poli Sci.

SMITH, KIMBERLY; Lampeter-Strasburg HS; Strasburg, PA; (Y); 35/158; Chorus; Church Choir; School Musical; JV Fld Hcky; JV Capt Sftbl; Church Yth Grp; Band; Concert Band; Mrchg Band; School Play.

SMITH, KRISTEN; Milton SR HS; Milton, PA; (Y); Pres Soph Cls; Pres Jr Cls; Varsity Clb; Bsktbl; Crs Cntry; Powder Puff Ftbl; NHS.

SMITH, KRISTIN; Jenkintown HS; Jenkintown, PA; (S); Nwsp Stf; Trs Soph Cls; Fld Hcky; Lcrss; Hon Roll; Jr NHS; NHS; Spanish NHS.

SMITH, KRISTIN; Northeast Bradford HS; Rome, PA; (Y); 13/79; VP 4-H; Pres FHA; Varsity Clb; Yrbk Stf; Sec Jr Cls; Sec Sr Cls; JV Bsktbl; Var Cheerleading; 4-H Awd; 5th Pl Scripps Howard Natl Spllg Bee 83; Hum Rel.

SMITH, KRISTIN ANN; Thomas Jefferson HS; Clairton, PA; (Y); 88/254; Exploring; French Clb; Hosp Aide; Office Aide; Teachers Aide; Yrbk Stf; Hon Roll; Stu Svc Awd VP 85-86; Stu Svc Awd Schl Ofce 85-86; Slippery Rock U; Elem Ed.

SMITH, LARRY; Slippery Rock HS; Prospect, PA; (Y); Church Yth Grp; Intnl Clb; Pep Clb; Chorus; Concert Band; Mrchg Band; Pep Band; Symp Band.

SMITH, LAURA; Meadville Area SR HS; Meadville, PA; (Y); Hosp Aide; Key Clb; Office Aide; Ski Clb; Chorus; Nwsp Stf; Yrbk Stf; Stu Cncl; Hon Roll; NHS; Med.

SMITH, LESLIE; Chambersburg Area SR HS; Fayetteville, PA; (Y); Key Clb; Red Cross Aide; Rep Varsity Clb; Yrbk Bus Mgr; Yrbk Ed-Chief; Sec Soph Cls; Sec Jr Cls; Sec Sr Cls; Pres Stu Cncl; Var Capt Cheerleading; U Of Pittsburgh; Bio.

SMITH JR, LESLIE; Brockway Area HS; Brockway, PA; (Y); Pres Church Yth Grp; Varsity Clb; Concert Band; Mrchg Band; Pep Band; Pres Frsh Cls; Var Capt Bsktbl; DAR Awd; High Hon Roll; VP NHS.

SMITH, LINDA; Bald Eagle Area HS; Howard, PA; (Y); French Clb; SADD; Chorus; Flag Corp; Mrchg Band; School Play; Nwsp Stf; JV Bsktbl; Im Fld Hcky; Powder Puff Ftbl; UTSA; Elem Tchr.

SMITH, LISA; Eastern Lebanon County HS; Newmanstown, PA; (Y); Art Clb; Chorus; Stage Crew; Schltc Art Awds 84; Cert Merit Art Show; Millersville U.

SMITH, LISA; Hempfield HS; New Stanton, PA; (Y); Church Yth Grp; Drama Clb; Girl Scts; Hosp Aide; VICA; Chorus; Church Choir; Jazz Band; School Play; Variety Show; County Chorus 85; Nrsng.

SMITH, LISA; Manheim Central HS; Manheim, PA; (Y); GAA; Band; Chorus; Fld Hcky; Sftbl; Hon Roll; Air Force; Nursng.

SMITH, LISA; Northwestern HS; Cranesville, PA; (Y); 27/164; Chorus; Capt Color Guard; Mrchg Band; School Musical; Stage Crew; Sec Yrbk Stf; JV Trk; Hon Roll; Ntl Merit Ltr; Indiana U PA; Psychol.

SMITH, LISA S; South Side Catholic HS; Pittsburgh, PA; (S); 3/46; Cmnty Wkr; Red Cross Aide; School Play; Nwsp Stf; Yrbk Ed-Chief; Stu Cncl; Hon Roll; Pres NHS; Political Wkr; Natl Awd Of Exclnc 84-85; High Avrg Eng Awd; U Of Pittsburgh; Psych.

SMITH, LORI; Catasauqua HS; Catasauqua, PA; (Y); 39/128; Church Yth Grp; Drama Clb; Lit Mag; Stu Cncl; Bsktbl; Fld Hcky; Modlg Wrk; Bloomsburg; Nrsg.

SMITH, LORI; Venango Christian HS; Oil City, PA; (Y); 7/36; Model UN; Rep Frsh Cls; Rep Soph Cls; Rep Jr Cls; VP Sr Cls; Rep Stu Cncl; JV Bsktbl; Score Keeper; Var Sftbl; Stat Wrstlng; Bus Admn.

SMITH, LUANNE; Warren Area HS; Warren, PA; (Y); Church Yth Grp; French Clb; Library Aide; Pres Soroptimist; Chorus; Im Gym; Im Trk; Hon Roll; Pres Physcl Ftns Awd 82-83.

SMITH, MACE; Penn Cambria SR HS; Lilly, PA; (Y); Capt Ftbl; Penn ST; Comp Sci.

SMITH, MAGGIE; Fox Chapel Area HS; Pittsburgh, PA; (Y); 19/342; Key Clb; Ski Clb; School Musical; Yrbk Stf; Golf; Powder Puff Ftbl; High Hon Roll; Hon Roll; NHS; Cum Laude In Ntl Ltn Exam.

SMITH, MARIA; Eastern HS; York, PA; (Y); 31/169; SADD; Drm Mjr(t); Yrbk Rptr; Yrbk Stf; Rep Soph Cls; Rep Stu Cncl; JV Capt Cheerleading; Im Gym; Var Mgr(s); Hon Roll; Elem Tchng.

SMITH, MARITA JAYNE; Waynesburg Central HS; Waynesburg, PA; (Y); 11/190; Letterman Clb; Natl Beta Clb; Ski Clb; Spanish Clb; Var Capt Cheerleading; High Hon Roll; Lion Awd; NHS; Hmcmng Attendnt 82; U Pittsburgh; Pub Rel.

SMITH, MARK; Southern Huntingdon County HS; Rockhill Furnace, PA; (Y); Chess Clb; Computer Clb; Varsity Clb; Bsbl; Ftbl; Powder Puff Ftbl; Wt Lftg; Bausch & Lomb Sci Awd; Cit Awd; Dnfth Awd; Natl Ldrshp & Svc Awd 85-86; Mid Penn Ftbl All Strs 85; Elctrcl Engrng.

SMITH, MARY LOU; John S Fine HS; Glen Lyon, PA; (Y); 50/251; Hosp Aide; Key Clb; Ski Clb; Chorus; Yrbk Stf; Var Mgr Ftbl; Var Mgr(s); Hon Roll; Phys Thrpy.

SMITH, MATTHEW; Saegertown HS; Saegertown, PA; (Y); Ski Clb; Varsity Clb; Variety Show; Rep Stu Cncl; Bsbl; Ftbl; Wt Lftg.

SMITH, MEGAN; Harrisburg Acad; Carlisle, PA; (Y); 14/31; Drama Clb; English Clb; Quiz Bowl; Chorus; School Play; Nwsp Ed-Chief; Ed Lit Mag; JCL; Latin Clb; Orch; Lebanon Vly Coll Yth Schlrs Pgm Scholar 86; SF Gov Schl Arts 86; Summa Cum Laude Natl Latin Exam 84; Engl.

SMITH, MELISSA; Du Bois Area SR HS; Penfield, PA; (Y); 4/277; Church Yth Grp; Pep Clb; Science Clb; Teachers Aide; Chorus; Flag Corp; Mrchg Band; DAR Awd; High Hon Roll; Trs NHS; Sci Awd 83-84; Bio II Awd, Nice Kid Awd 85-86; Penn ST.

SMITH, MELISSA; Hanover HS; Hanover, PA; (Y); 5/104; Red Cross Aide; Band; Concert Band; Drm Mjr(t); Jazz Band; Mrchg Band; Nwsp Stf; Cheerleading; Hon Roll; NHS.

SMITH, MELISSA YEAGER; Villa Maria HS; Eighty Four, PA; (Y); Cmnty Wkr; French Clb; Thesps; Acpl Chr; Chorus; School Musical; Nwsp Rptr; Stu Cncl; Im Sftbl; Drama Clb; PMEA Midwestern Dist 5 Choral Fest 86; Villanova U; Communications.

SMITH, MICHAEL; Mc Guffey HS; Claysville, PA; (Y); Pres 4-H; Var Bsktbl; Var Tennis; 4-H Awd; Hon Roll; Prfct Atten Awd; Bus.

SMITH, MICHAEL; Punxsutawney Area HS; Punxsutawney, PA; (Y); Varsity Clb; Bsktbl; Trk; Spanish Clb; Phy Thrpy.

SMITH, MICHAEL A; Milton Hershey Schl; King Of Prussia, PA; (Y); Am Leg Boys St; Yrbk Ed-Chief; Yrbk Sprt Ed; Yrbk Stf; Lit Mag; VP Sr Cls; Var L Ftbl; Var L Trk; Var L Wrstlng; Hon Roll; Stu Ldrshp Soc 86; Rtgrs U; Med.

SMITH, MICHAEL D; York Suburban HS; York, PA; (Y); 4/191; Church Yth Grp; Concert Band; Mrchg Band; School Musical; Yrbk Stf; Hon Roll; JETS Awd; NHS; Acdmc Awd Top 5% Cls 84-86; Engr.

SMITH, MICHAEL J; Port Allegany HS; Port Allegany, PA; (Y); 3/118; Boy Scts; French Clb; Band; Chorus; Concert Band; Mrchg Band; School Musical; School Play; Yrbk Stf; NHS; Penn Yrk Chmcl Scty Chmstry Awd 85; Army Sci Aawd Of Exc At Rgnl Fair 84; Dcknsn Coll; Gntc Engrng.

SMITH, MICHAEL P; Red Lion SR HS; Red Lion, PA; (Y); 25/326; Boy Scts; Nwsp Stf; Hon Roll; Physics.

SMITH, MICHELE; Cowanesqua Valley HS; Sabinsville, PA; (S); 5/85; Computer Clb; Concert Band; Mrchg Band; Yrbk Ed-Chief; Yrbk Stf; JV Bsktbl; Stat Vllybl; High Hon Roll; NHS; All Amer Acad 84-85; Williamsport Schl Commerce; Bus.

SMITH, MICHELE; Kittanning SR HS; Worthington, PA; (Y); 34/224; Church Yth Grp; French Clb; FHA; Hosp Aide; Jr Cls; Bsktbl; Cheerleading; Hon Roll; NHS; IN U Of PA; Bus Mgmt.

SMITH, MICHELLE; Annville-Cleona HS; Lebanon, PA; (Y); FBLA; Office Aide; Chorus; Stat Bsbl; Stat Bsktbl; Score Keeper; Bus.

SMITH, MICHELLE; Lancaster Catholic HS; Lancaster, PA; (Y); Church Yth Grp; Model UN; Varsity Clb; Nwsp Rptr; Yrbk Stf; Crs Cntry; Fld Hcky; Trk; St Francis Coll; Librl Arts.

SMITH, MISSY; Newport HS; Newport, PA; (Y); 20/90; Varsity Clb; Var Fld Hcky; JV Sftbl; 1st Tm All Star Fld Hcky 84; 2nd Tm All Star Fld Hcky 85; Bst Dfnsive Plyr Fld Hcky 85; Bus.

SMITH, NANETTE; Central Cambria HS; Ebensburg, PA; (S); 1/217; VP Art Clb; Red Cross Aide; Band; Drm Mjr(t); Trk; High Hon Roll; Hon Roll; Prfct Atten Awd; Office Aide; IN U Of PA; Nrsng.

SMITH, NEIL; Littlestown HS; Littlestown, PA; (Y); 58/120; Mrchg Band; Crs Cntry; Prfct Atten Awd; PA ST.

SMITH, NICOLE; St Maria Goretti HS; Philadelphia, PA; (Y); 168/370; Exploring; GAA; Hosp Aide; Service Clb; Hon Roll.

SMITH, OWEN B; Academy Of The New Church; Glenview, IL; (Y); 2/38; Speech Tm; School Musical; Variety Show; Pres Jr Cls; Stu Cncl; L Bsbl; L Ftbl; NHS.

SMITH, PAM; South Allegheny HS; Elizabeth, PA; (S); 1/183; Y-Teens; Band; Concert Band; Jazz Band; Mrchg Band; Pep Band; Powder Puff Ftbl; High Hon Roll; Hon Roll; US Bus Educ Awd 85.

SMITH, PAMELA; Bangor HS; Mt Bethel, PA; (Y); Pep Clb; Varsity Clb; Pres Band; Concert Band; Drill Tm; Mrchg Band; Pep Band; Pres Stu Cncl; Twrlr; Hon Roll; Musicns Union Awd 86; Mst Outstndg SR Bandfront 86; Nathan Branch Scholar 86; Wilkes Coll; Bus Adm.

SMITH, PAMELA; Blue Mountain Acad; Limekiln, PA; (Y); Band; Chorus; Gym; Sftbl; Vllybl; Andrews U; Bus.

SMITH, PAMELA; Moon SR HS; Coraopolis, PA; (Y); Key Clb; Q&S; Yrbk Ed-Chief; Yrbk Phtg; Hon Roll; Jrnlsm Stu Of Smster 85; Photojrnlsm.

SMITH, PAMELA A; Creative & Performing Arts HS; Philadelphia, PA; (Y); 17/130; Dance Clb; PAVAS; Rep Soph Cls; Hon Roll; NHS; Smmr Schlrshp PA Govrnr Schl Arts 85; Schlrshp Six Wks CIGNA Cmmnctns 86; Chatham Coll; Lib Arts.

SMITH, PATRICIA; Avon Grove HS; W Grove, PA; (Y); 6/179; SADD; Band; Concert Band; Mrchg Band; School Play; Nwsp Stf; Yrbk Stf; Lit Mag; Sec Jr Cls; Sec Sr Cls; Eng Achvt Awd; Phys Educ Awd; Jrnlsm.

SMITH, PAULA; Oxford Area HS; Nottingham, PA; (Y); Office Aide; Band; Chorus; Capt Color Guard; Drm Mjr(t); Mrchg Band; Nwsp Phtg; Nwsp Rptr; Nwsp Stf; Var Fld Hcky; Frnk J Mchls Schlrshp 86-87; Nwsp-Schl-Schlrshp Awd 86; IN U Of PA; Photojrnlsm.

SMITH, PENNY; State College Area SR HS; Lemont, PA; (Y); 3/490; Church Yth Grp; German Clb; Concert Band; Var Diving; Im Powder Puff Ftbl; Var Sftbl; Var Capt Tennis; Cit Awd; High Hon Roll; NEDT Awd; James H Snyder Stu/Ath Awd 86; Fclty Schlr 86; Bruce E Knox Yth Awd 85; Cornell U; Russn.

SMITH, PROMISE; GAR Memorial HS; Wilkes Barre, PA; (S); 8/187; French Clb; Hosp Aide; Office Aide; Ski Clb; Chorus; Stage Crew; Cheerleading; God Cntry Awd; High Hon Roll; Hon Roll.

SMITH, RAMONA; Grove City Area HS; Grove City, PA; (Y); 37/195; Church Yth Grp; FBLA; Orch; High Hon Roll; Hon Roll; Elem Ed.

SMITH, RANDALL; Council Rock HS; New Hope, PA; (Y); 27/755; Boy Scts; Drama Clb; Exploring; Chorus; Church Choir; Hon Roll; NHS; Ntl Merit Ltr; Church Yth Grp; Intnl Clb; Ordr Of Arrw 84; Eagl Awd BSA 86; Ltrmn Selct Chrs 86; Bio.

SMITH, REBECCA; Altoona Area HS; Altoona, PA; (Y); GAA; Spanish Clb; SADD; Chorus; Sec Frsh Cls; Var L Gym; Mgr(s); Hon Roll; Pre-Med.

SMITH, REBECCA; St Marys Area HS; Saint Marys, PA; (Y); 5/293; Hosp Aide; Band; Mrchg Band; Rep Stu Cncl; JV Var Crs Cntry; Trk; Hon Roll; NHS; Pre-Med.

SMITH, RENEE M; Penn Cambria HS; Gallitzin, PA; (Y); Drama Clb; Spanish Clb; Variety Show; Rep Jr Cls; Var Capt Cheerleading; Coach Actv; Hon Roll; Asst Dance Instrctr 84-87; Presdntl Physcl Ftnss Awd 84-86; Cambrie Somerset JR Miss Fnlst 86-87; IN U Of PA; X-Ray Technology.

SMITH, RHONDA; Westinghouse HS; Pittsburgh, PA; (Y); GAA; Jazz Band; Mrchg Band; Trk; JA; Band; Concert Band; Drm & Bgl; Bsktbl; Bowling; Bowling A 205 Game 85; Set Record For Long Jump 86; Lincoln U; Physical Therapist.

SMITH, ROBBI; Weatherly Area HS; Weatherly, PA; (Y); 27/61; Art Clb; Boy Scts; Church Yth Grp; VICA; Crs Cntry; Hon Roll; Elec Cert CCVATS-VICA; Valley Forge Chrstn Coll; Rbtcs.

SMITH, ROBERT; Churchill HS; Pittsburgh, PA; (Y); 23/188; Church Yth Grp; Exploring; Key Clb; Trs Band; Trs Concert Band; Jazz Band; Trs Mrchg Band; Sec Trs Orch; School Musical; High Hon Roll; Natl Conf Chrstns Jews Wrkshp 85; Engrng.

SMITH, ROBERT; Southmoreland SR HS; Alverton, PA; (Y); Church Yth Grp; Math Clb; Spanish Clb; Masonic Awd; St Vincent Coll; Engrng.

SMITH JR, ROGER; West Chester East HS; West Chester, PA; (Y); 100/397; JA; Pep Clb; SADD; Rep Frsh Cls; Rep Stu Cncl; Var Ftbl; Var Lcrss; Cit Awd; Hon Roll; Kiwanis Awd; Drexel U; Engrng Mgr.

SMITH, RONALD; Lakeland HS; Jermyn, PA; (Y); French Clb; SADD; L Ftbl; Wt Lftg; Hon Roll; RI Schl Of Design; Archtctr.

SMITH, RONNA RAE; Freeport Area Joint HS; Sarver, PA; (S); Drama Clb; Band; School Musical; School Play; Pres Frsh Cls; Rep Soph Cls; Trs Jr Cls; Stu Cncl; VP Cheerleading; Mgr(s); U Pittsburgh; Phys Ther.

SMITH, RYAN; Butler Area SR HS; Butler, PA; (Y); 52/777; French Clb; Var Bsktbl; JV Crs Cntry; Im Ftbl; Var Swmmng; Hon Roll; Grove City; Engr.

SMITH, SANDY; Corry Area HS; Corry, PA; (Y); Band; Concert Band; Mrchg Band; Var L Trk; Edinboro U Of PA; Bio.

SMITH, SANDY; St Marys Area HS; Weedville, PA; (Y); 34/300; Sec Trs Church Yth Grp; Girl Scts; Band; Chorus; Concert Band; Mrchg Band; High Hon Roll; Hon Roll; Benettes Vly Lions Clb Schlrshp 86; IN U Of PA; Math.

SMITH, SHANNON; Sacred Heart HS; Jermyn, PA; (Y); FBLA; Spanish Clb; Teachers Aide; Chorus; School Musical; Rep Jr Cls; High Hon Roll; NHS.

SMITH, STEFANIE; Upper Darby HS; Drexel Hill, PA; (Y); 30/629; Church Yth Grp; Cmnty Wkr; French Clb; Office Aide; Y-Teens; Yrbk Stf; Stu Cncl; Var Capt Gym; High Hon Roll; Hon Roll; Sci Awd 84; Hm Ec Awd 84; Boston U; Mktg.

SMITH, STEPHANIE C; The Shipley Schl; Philadelphia, PA; (Y); 8/69; Church Yth Grp; Dance Clb; Church Choir; School Musical; Yrbk Ed-Chief; Lit Mag; Fld Hcky; Lcrss; Wt Lftg; Natl Achvt Semi-Fnlst 85-86; Biomed Engr.

SMITH, STEPHEN M; Central HS; Philadelphia, PA; (Y); 73/248; Hon Roll; Ntl Merit Ltr; Hosp Aide; Teachers Aide; Var Trk; Schlstc Acad Schlrp 85; 7th St United Meth Chrch; Med.

SMITH, STEVE; Southern Fulton HS; Warfordsburg, PA; (Y); Boy Scts; Church Yth Grp; FBLA; FFA; Chorus; Yrbk Stf; JV L Bsktbl; Var L Trk; Hon Roll; Penn ST; Cvl Engr.

SMITH, SUSAN; Charleroi Area SR HS; Charleroi, PA; (Y); 6/180; Science Clb; Ski Clb; Spanish Clb; Varsity Clb; Chorus; Rep Stu Cncl; Var JV Cheerleading; High Hon Roll; Hon Roll; VP NHS; NSMA 86; Homecmng Court 85; Speers Civics Club Schlrshp 86; WV U; Physcl Thrpy.

SMITH, SUSAN; St Paul Cathdral HS; Pittsburgh, PA; (S); 8/53; Dance Clb; FBLA; Library Aide; NFL; Service Clb; School Play; Nwsp Stf; Yrbk Stf.

SMITH, SUZANNE; Littlestown SR HS; Littlestown, PA; (Y); 46/100; Church Yth Grp; Rptr FBLA; Intnl Clb; Office Aide; Teachers Aide; Chorus; Hon Roll; Comp.

SMITH, SUZANNE; Saint Basil Acad; Philadelphia, PA; (Y); Drama Clb; Latin Clb; Madrigals; JV Var Bsktbl; Hon Roll; FBLA; Acpl Chr; Chorus; Acad Schlrshp St Basil Acad 83; 3rd Philadelphia Hstrcl Soc Essay Cntst 85; Natl Engl Mrt Awd 86; Psych.

SMITH, TAMMI; Butler SR HS; Prospect, PA; (Y); Church Yth Grp; German Clb; JA; Office Aide; Mrchg Band; Symp Band; Butler CC; Math.

SMITH, TAMMY; Blairsville SR HS; Blairsville, PA; (Y); Art Clb; Chess Clb; Church Yth Grp; Library Aide; Office Aide; Teachers Aide; Chorus; School Play; High Hon Roll; Hon Roll; Am Hrt Assoc Awds 85-86; Float Cmmttee Awd 85-86; NYU; Bus Admn.

SMITH, TAMMY; Clearfield Area HS; Clearfield, PA; (Y); 45/230; French Clb; VICA; Sftbl; Vllybl; High Hon Roll; Hon Roll; VICA Dist 7 Skll Olympcs-1st Pl Data Entry 85-86; Cert Of Recog-ST Data Entry 5th Pl 85-86; ICM; Comp.

SMITH, TAMMY; Punxsutawney Area HS; Punxsutawney, PA; (Y); Church Yth Grp; Math Tm; Spanish Clb; Hon Roll.

SMITH, TERRI; Brandywine HS; Alburtis, PA; (Y); 4-H; Tennis; Trk; Hon Roll; Art.

SMITH, TERRY; Bethel Park HS; Bethel Park, PA; (Y); Concert Band; JV Ftbl; Hon Roll.

SMITH, TINA M; Brandywine Heights HS; Mertztown, PA; (Y); 1/126; Sec Pres FBLA; Band; Concert Band; Mrchg Band; High Hon Roll; NHS; Prfct Atten Awd; Church Yth Grp; Pep Band; 1st Pl ST Ldrshp Cnfrnc, FBLA Entrprshp I 84; 1st Pl ST FBLA Accntg I, Atnd NLC 86; Bloomsburg U; Accntng.

SMITH, TODD; Pennsbury HS; Fairless Hills, PA; (Y); Im Bsktbl; Var Wrstlng; Hon Roll; NHS.

SMITH, TRACEY; Punxsutawney Area HS; Punxsutawney, PA; (Y); French Clb; FNA; Hosp Aide; Band; Flag Corp; Mrchg Band; Yrbk Stf; Hon Roll; Intl Bus.

SMITH, TRACY; Boyertown HS; Bechtelsville, PA; (Y); Church Yth Grp; SADD; VICA; Rep Soph Cls; Stat Socr; JV Sftbl; Prfct Atten Awd.

SMITH, TRACY; Coudersport JR SR HS; Coudersport, PA; (Y); Church Yth Grp; Varsity Clb; Nwsp Rptr; Nwsp Stf; Yrbk Stf; Golf; L Trk; High Hon Roll; Hon Roll; Troph 2nd Pl 3200 Mtrs Dist Trck 86; Sci.

SMITH, TRACY; Fairfield HS; Rouzerville, PA; (Y); 11/58; Cmnty Wkr; FBLA; Varsity Clb; Chorus; Nwsp Rptr; Nwsp Stf; Yrbk Stf; Fld Hcky; Sftbl; High Hon Roll; Chrs Awd 86; FBLA Futur Bus Ldr Of Am Pin 84, Ofcr 84; Lock Haven U; Soc Wrk.

SMITH, TRICIA; Chestnut Ridge HS; New Paris, PA; (S); 9/142; Band; Nwsp Sprt Ed; VP Frsh Cls; VP Soph Cls; VP Stu Cncl; Var L Sftbl; Var Twrlr; Var L Vllybl; Hon Roll; NHS.

SMITH, TROY R; Butler HS; Butler, PA; (Y); Spanish Clb; Stage Crew; Rep Frsh Cls; Rep Soph Cls; Var Crs Cntry; JV Var Trk; Hon Roll.

SMITH, VICKI; Lower Moreland HS; Huntingdon Valley, PA; (S); 57/214; FBLA; Pep Clb; Pres Chorus; Church Choir; Capt Color Guard; Madrigals; School Musical; Twrlr; Hon Roll; NHS; Penn ST; Parlgl.

SMITH, VICKIE; Mt Pleasant HS; Mt Pleasant, PA; (Y); 9/250; Spanish Clb; Pres Jr Cls; Sec Stu Cncl; Var Cheerleading; Hon Roll; Nrsng.

SMITH, WENDI; Lincoln HS; Ellwood City, PA; (Y); 77/170; AFS; Church Yth Grp; Key Clb; Chorus; Flag Corp; Stat L Crs Cntry; L Mgr(s); Powder Puff Ftbl; Fshn.

SMITH, WENDY; Pleasant Valley HS; Kunkletown, PA; (Y); 1/233; Math Tm; Ski Clb; Varsity Clb; VP Jr Cls; Stu Cncl; Var L Cheerleading; Trk; High Hon Roll; Top 20 In Cls; Top Hstry Studnt; Top Sci Studnt; Perfct Attndnc.

SMITH, WENDY E; Crestwood HS; Wapwallopen, PA; (Y); VP Key Clb; Red Cross Aide; SADD; Nwsp Stf; Yrbk Ed-Chief; Yrbk Stf; Trs Soph Cls; Stu Cncl; Stat Bsktbl; Stat Vllybl; 1st Pl Litry Div; Marist Coll; Comms.

SMITH, WILLIAM; Greater Johnstown HS; Johnstown, PA; (Y); Hon Roll; Acctg.

SMITH, YVONNE; Our Lady Of Lourdes Regional HS; Shamokin, PA; (Y); 33/94; AFS; French Clb; Pep Clb; Chorus; Hon Roll; Nrsng.

SMITHBURGER, KIMBERLY; Uniontown HS; Gibbon Glade, PA; (Y); Church Yth Grp; French Clb; Girl Scts; Church Choir; School Play; Sec Frsh Cls; Var Bsktbl; French Hon Soc; High Hon Roll; Hon Roll; Hnrb Mntn Calif U For Frnch Comptn 84; Duffs Business Inst; Prof Sec.

SMITHMYER, ANN; Bishop Carroll HS; Loretto, PA; (S); 11/109; Pep Clb; SADD; Rep Stu Cncl; L Crs Cntry; L Trk; Hon Roll; NHS; Hugh O Brian Ldrshp Smnr 85; Cross Cntry Ski Clb; Hlth Sci.

SMITHNOSKY, MARK; Hopewell HS; Aliquippa, PA; (Y); Boy Scts; Chorus; School Musical; Rep Stu Cncl; Hon Roll; Am Leg Boys St; Var Im Bsbl; Im Ftbl.

SMOCK, DONNA; Palmyra Area SR HS; Palmyra, PA; (S); DECA; Hosp Aide; Spanish Clb; Yrbk Stf; Hon Roll; 5th Pl Dist Cmptn Rstrnt Mgmt Emplyee Lvl 86; Own Boutique.

SMOKER, CAROL; Pequea Valley HS; Intercourse, PA; (Y); AFS; Computer Clb; Sec FBLA; GAA; Varsity Clb; Mrchg Band; Stage Crew; Capt JV Bsktbl; Var Fld Hcky; Hon Roll; Vrsty Fld Hockey Certs 85 & 86; JV Fld Hockey Certs 83 & 84; FBLA-4TH Pl Certs 85 & 86.

SMOKER, JOHN; Butler Area HS; Butler, PA; (Y); Church Yth Grp; Cmnty Wkr; Exploring; JA; Library Aide; Office Aide; Nwsp Ed-Chief; Nwsp Rptr; Nwsp Stf; Yrbk Stf; Yrbk Rptr; Achvt Banker Yr 86; IN U; Acctng.

SMOKER, KEN; Northern Potter HS; Genesee, PA; (Y); 1/80; German Clb; Math Tm; Varsity Clb; Soph Cls; Jr Cls; Stu Cncl; Bsktbl; Bausch & Lomb Sci Awd; High Hon Roll; NHS; Enrichmnt Pgm 84-86.

SMOKER, MICHAEL S; Eastern Lancaster County HS; New Holland, PA; (S); Boy Scts; VP 4-H; FFA; Var Crs Cntry; JV Var Wrstlng; High Hon Roll; Hon Roll; Eagle Sct 86; FFA Awds 83-86; Meat Cttr.

SMOLENAK, ELLYSE E; Nazareth Area SR HS; Nazareth, PA; (S); 6/248; Church Yth Grp; Ski Clb; Flag Corp; Jazz Band; Mrchg Band; High Hon Roll; NHS; Nazareth HS Gftd Prgm 84-86; Lawyr.

SMOLKE, HEATHER; Our Lady Of Lourdes Regional HS; Shamokin, PA; (Y); 15/101; AFS; Drama Clb; School Play; Capt JV Cheerleading; Hon Roll; Cmnty Wkr; Library Aide; Pep Clb; Political Wkr; Spanish Clb; Accntng.

SMOLKO, TIM; Bishop Carroll HS; Ebensburg, PA; (Y); Church Yth Grp; Computer Clb; Spanish Clb; Band; Concert Band; Mrchg Band; Hon Roll; Amer Lgn Essy Cntst Wnnr 86; IN U Of PA; Comp Sci.

SMOLKO, TOM; Red Land HS; New Cumberland, PA; (Y); 2/275; VP Spanish Clb; SADD; Yrbk Stf; Pres Sr Cls; Rep Stu Cncl; Var Bsbl; Var Golf; High Hon Roll; NHS; VP Spanish NHS; Comp Engrng.

SMOLSKIS, KAREN; Minersville Area HS; Pottsville, PA; (Y); 7/121; German Clb; Sec Frsh Cls; Sec Soph Cls; Sec Jr Cls; Capt Bsktbl; Var Crs Cntry; Var Sftbl; High Hon Roll; NHS; JR Garlnd Grp 86; Sftbl All Star 86.

SMOYER, ANDREW; Upper Moreland HS; Hatboro, PA; (Y); 20/260; Boy Scts; Church Yth Grp; Key Clb; Off Jr Cls; Socr; Trk; NHS.

SMURL, PAMELA; Wyoming Valley West HS; Plymouth, PA; (Y); Hosp Aide; Key Clb; Pep Clb; Chorus; School Musical; School Play; Stu Cncl; High Hon Roll; Hon Roll; NHS; Excllnt Attndnc Awds 83 & 85; Luzerne Cnty CC; Nrsg.

SMYDO, JOE; Bentworth HS; Scenery Hill, PA; (Y); Ski Clb; School Play; Yrbk Ed-Chief; Off Jr Cls; Pres Sr Cls; Sec Stu Cncl; Hon Roll; NHS; Prom King 86; Brdcst Jrnlsm.

SMYERS, BERTRAND; North Catholic HS; Glenshaw, PA; (Y); 28/264; Art Clb; Church Yth Grp; Pres German Clb; Rep Frsh Cls; Var Bsbl; Var L Bsktbl; Var Capt Ftbl; Hon Roll; NHS; Ntl Merit Ltr.

SMYERS, DAVID C; Hungtindon Area HS; Huntingdon, PA; (Y); 6/223; Am Leg Boys St; Ski Clb; JV Tennis; Var Trk; JV Wrstlng; High Hon Roll; NHS; NEDT Awd.

SNARE, ERIC; Lincoln HS; Ellwood City, PA; (Y); #1 In Class; Art Clb; Boy Scts; Drama Clb; Exploring; Spanish Clb; Chorus; School Musical; School Play; Stu Cncl; High Hon Roll; Math.

SNARE, LORI; Hollidaysburg SR HS; Duncansvillle, PA; (Y); Church Yth Grp; Spanish Clb; SADD; Chorus; School Musical.

SNARE, ROBERT; Tussey Mountain HS; Saxton, PA; (Y); Var Capt Ftbl; Var L Trk; Scrty Spclst.

SNAVELY, MICHAEL; Beaver Area JR SR HS; Beaver, PA; (Y); Church Yth Grp; FCA; JCL; Latin Clb; Chorus; Church Choir; Stu Cncl; Ftbl; Trk; High Hon Roll; Phrmcy.

SNEDEKER, ANN MARIE; Scranton Central HS; Scranton, PA; (Y); Spanish Clb; Hon Roll; Jr NHS.

SNEDEKER, WENDY; Canon Mcmillan SR HS; Eighty Four, PA; (Y); Chess Clb; Church Yth Grp; Ski Clb; Varsity Clb; Yrbk Stf; Var L Sftbl; Im Vllybl; High Hon Roll; Hon Roll; Elem Ed.

SNEE, JAMES; Mid-Valley HS; Olyphant, PA; (Y); Church Yth Grp; Var Bsktbl; Var Golf; Var Wt Lftg; Hon Roll; Miss Lbrty Essay Cntst Wnnr 86; Spanish Merit Awd 85; Scranton U; Crmnl Justice.

SNEE, MICHELLE; West Greene HS; Wind Ridge, PA; (Y); Dance Clb; School Musical; School Play; Nwsp Stf; Yrbk Stf; Pres Stu Cncl; VP Sec Mat Maids; Twrlr; Hon Roll; NHS; Acadmc Excllnce Cert In German 84-86; Psych.

SNEE, THOMAS; Plum HS; Pittsburgh, PA; (Y); Spanish Clb; Varsity Clb; Band; Var L Bsbl; Var L Bsktbl; Golf; Im Trk; Hon Roll; Bus.

SNEERINGER, JO ANN; Delone Catholic HS; Hanover, PA; (Y); 39/168; Pres Chorus; VP Concert Band; Jazz Band; VP Mrchg Band; School Musical; NHS; Natl Schl Choral Awd 86; Excllnc Music 86; Prednt l Acad Fitns Awd 86; Top 10 Pct Cls 86; Mansfield U; Music Ed.

SNELBAKER, KEVIN; Northeastern SR HS; Manchester, PA; (Y); Boy Scts; Exploring; Ski Clb; JV Bsbl; JV Var Vllybl; JV Wrstlng; Hon Roll.

SNELBECKER, KAREN A; Springfield Twp HS; Wyndmoor, PA; (Y); 1/138; Computer Clb; German Clb; Math Tm; Nwsp Rptr; Yrbk Stf; Lit Mag; Rep Stu Cncl; Var JV Trk; Ntl Merit SF; Val; Am Assoc Tchrs Germny Study Trip 85; Lngstcs.

SNELICK, LAURA; St Marys Area HS; St Marys, PA; (Y); 6/301; Camera Clb; Debate Tm; Girl Scts; Hosp Aide; Yrbk Stf; Var L Cheerleading; Mgr(s); Score Keeper; Var JV Swmmng; Timer; Nrsng.

SNESAVAGE, JOSEPHINE; JR SR Williams Valley HS; Wiconisco, PA; (Y); Computer Clb; Pep Clb; Rep Frsh Cls; Rep Stu Cncl; Sftbl; Hon Roll; PA ST; Acctng.

SNIEGOWSKI, JOHN; Scranton Tech; Scranton, PA; (Y); 2/242; Camera Clb; French Clb; FBLA; Letterman Clb; Quiz Bowl; Scholastic Bowl; Ski Clb; Nwsp Phtg; Yrbk Phtg; Pres Stu Cncl; NROTC Schlrshp 86; Penn ST; Pre Med.

SNODGRASS, STEVEN; Gateway SR HS; Monroeville, PA; (Y); 28/500; Church Yth Grp; ROTC; Var Bsktbl; High Hon Roll; German Iii Hnr 85-86; Bio Hnr 84-85; Penn St; Math.

SNOOK, BRYAN; West Snyder HS; Beaver Spring, PA; (Y); 1/96; Am Leg Boys St; Boy Scts; Pres Sr Cls; Stu Cncl; Wrstlng; NHS; NEDT Awd; Computer Clb; Science Clb; Varsity Clb; Ntl Yng Ldrs Cnfrnc 86; PA Free Entrprs Week 86.

SNOOK, JACQUELINE; Waynesboro SR HS; Blue Ridge Summit, PA; (Y); Am Leg Aux Girls St; JCL; Latin Clb; Service Clb; Nwsp Rptr; Var L Crs Cntry; Var L Trk; High Hon Roll; NHS; Mont Alto Acad Schrlshp 86; Fnlst Mis Ntl Teen Ager Pagnt 86; Dictnry Interntl Bio 86; PA ST U; Bus Adm.

SNOVER, AMY J; Danville Area HS; Danville, PA; (Y); 1/169; Drama Clb; Sec 4-H; VP French Clb; Key Clb; School Play; Gym; Mat Maids; 4-H Awd; Pres NHS; Ntl Merit SF; Yng Amercn 85; Cnty Outstndg 4-Her 85; PA ST U; Vet.

SNYDER, AMY; Milton Area HS; Milton, PA; (Y); 56/213; VP Spanish Clb; Yrbk Stf; Trs Soph Cls; Trs Jr Cls; Bsktbl; Cheerleading; Powder Puff Ftbl; Trk; Bus.

SNYDER, AMY; Philadelphia Montgomery Christ Acad; Horsham, PA; (Y); Church Yth Grp; Acpl Chr; Chorus; School Play; JV Var Fld Hcky; High Hon Roll; Hon Roll; NHS.

SNYDER, ANDREA; East Juniata HS; Richfield, PA; (Y); 4/90; Band; Concert Band; Mrchg Band; Ed Yrbk Ed-Chief; Sftbl; High Hon Roll; Hon Roll; NHS; Vet Sci.

SNYDER, BARBIE; Liberty JR SR HS; Trout Run, PA; (Y); Pres Church Yth Grp; Pres 4-H; FHA; Sec German Clb; Sec Pep Clb; Pres Stu Cncl; Capt Cheerleading; Hon Roll; NHS; Chrldng MVP 84-86; Natl Frgn Lang Awd 84-86; Natl Ldrshp-Svc Awd 86; Radlgy.

SNYDER, BILL; Hampton HS; Allison Park, PA; (Y); 11/224; Spanish Clb; Bsktbl; High Hon Roll; Hon Roll; NHS; YMCA All Abrms Awd, MVP Bsktbl, All Star 86; Westminster Coll; Acctg.

SNYDER, BRIAN; Freedom HS; Bethlehem, PA; (Y); 120/450; German Clb; Pep Clb; Hon Roll; Law.

SNYDER, BRYAN; Salisbury HS; Bethlehem, PA; (Y); Exploring; Stage Crew; Rep Stu Cncl; Var Ftbl; Var Trk; Var Wrstlng; Hon Roll; Oceanography.

SNYDER, CAMI; Line Mountain HS; Dornsife, PA; (Y); 5/112; Hosp Aide; Sec Varsity Clb; Drill Tm; Nwsp Rptr; Nwsp Stf; Trs Sr Cls; Rep Stu Cncl; Bsktbl; Sftbl; High Hon Roll; Penn ST; Radiolgcl Tech.

SNYDER, CARLA; Shikellamy HS; Sunbury, PA; (Y); Band; Concert Band; Mrchg Band; Bloomsburg U Of PA; Chem.

SNYDER, CRAIG; Bethel Park HS; Bethel Park, PA; (Y); Band; Concert Band; Jazz Band; Mrchg Band; Orch; Symp Band; Variety Show; Yrbk Stf; Prfct Atten Awd; PMEA Dist I Hnrs Band 85.

SNYDER, DAN; Titusville HS; Titusville, PA; (Y); 12/205; Church Yth Grp; SADD; Varsity Clb; Chorus; School Musical; Rep Stu Cncl; L Var Bsbl; L Var Bsktbl; L Var Ftbl; L Var Trk; Class Orator 86; Penn ST U; Hosp Adm.

SNYDER, DIONNE; Kishacoquillas HS; Belleville, PA; (Y); Church Yth Grp; Computer Clb; Library Aide; Spanish Clb; Variety Show; Yrbk Stf; Bowling; Mat Maids; Sftbl; Hon Roll; PA ST Altoona Cmps; Bus Adm.

SNYDER, DONNA; Millersburg Area HS; Millersburg, PA; (S); 6/82; Pres Church Yth Grp; French Clb; Church Choir; Yrbk Stf; High Hon Roll; Hon Roll; Natl Sci Mrt Awd 84; Natl Frgn Lang Awd 84; Natl Ldrshp Mrt Awd 85; Frnch Intrprtr.

SNYDER, DWIGHT; Shanksville-Stonycreek HS; Berlin, PA; (Y); Church Yth Grp; DECA; Var Bsbl; JV Var Bsktbl; Trk; Wt Lftg; Pres Crpntry Clss Vo-Tech Schl.

SNYDER, GRACE E; South Park HS; Library, PA; (Y); 26/203; Church Yth Grp; Nwsp Stf; Rep Jr Cls; Rep Sr Cls; Bowling; Capt Var Cheerleading; Powder Puff Ftbl; Hon Roll; Allegheny Coll; Psychlgy.

SNYDER, HELEN M; Reading SR HS; Reading, PA; (Y); 217/620; Church Yth Grp; FBLA; Library Aide; Office Aide; Chorus; Modeling.

SNYDER, HOLLY; Governor Mifflin HS; Shillington, PA; (Y); 61/266; Trs Church Yth Grp; Girl Scts; Concert Band; Mrchg Band; Var Bowling; Hon Roll; Drill Tm; Pep Band; Achvt Awd 84; Hotl Mgmt.

SNYDER, JAMI; Coudersport Area JR SR HS; Coudersport, PA; (Y); 2/100; French Clb; Varsity Clb; Band; Concert Band; Mrchg Band; VP Soph Cls; Bsktbl; DAR Awd; High Hon Roll; NHS; Phrmcy.

SNYDER, JEFF; North Star HS; Boswell, PA; (Y); Cit Awd.

SNYDER, JODY; Shanksville-Stonycreek HS; Friedens, PA; (Y); 13/32; Church Yth Grp; Sec Trs 4-H; Sec FHA; Library Aide; Office Aide; Spanish Clb; Chorus; Color Guard; School Play; Nwsp Stf; Hm Ecnmcs Awd 86; Seton Hill Coll; Acctg.

SNYDER, JODY; Tri-Valley HS; Valley View, PA; (S); Church Yth Grp; Rptr DECA; Rep Stu Cncl; Var Capt Cheerleading; Sftbl; High Hon Roll; Fash Coordntr.

SNYDER, JOYCE; Nazareth Area SR HS; Stockertown, PA; (Y); 25/249; Computer Clb; Ski Clb; Band; Concert Band; Jazz Band; Mrchg Band; Orch; Hon Roll; Amer Hnrs Music 84-86; Dist Bnd 85-86; Regnl Bnd 86; Comp.

SNYDER, JULIE; Brookville Area HS; Brookville, PA; (Y); Church Yth Grp; French Clb; German Clb; Key Clb; Pep Clb; Spanish Clb; Teachers Aide; Chorus; Church Choir; Drm & Bgl.

SNYDER, KATHY; Ford City HS; Ford City, PA; (Y); #4 In Class; Camera Clb; Computer Clb; Spanish Clb; Rep Jr Cls; Rep Sr Cls; High Hon Roll; NHS; PA JR Acad Sci Comp 84-86; IN U PA; Bus.

SNYDER, KATHY; Shikellamy HS; Northumberland, PA; (Y); Chorus; Mrchg Band; JV Fld Hcky; Slippery Rock U; Bus.

SNYDER, KELLY; Engineering & Science; Philadelphia, PA; (S); 4/150; Chess Clb; NHS; 2nd Pl-Alpha Delta Kappa Wrtng Prtfolio Compt 85; Comp Sci & Engrng Conf Spkspsn 85; Haverford; Law.

SNYDER, KELLY; West Snyder HS; Mcclure, PA; (Y); 5/93; Yrbk Stf; VP Jr Cls; VP Sr Cls; Rep Stu Cncl; Mgr(s); Stat Socr; High Hon Roll; Hon Roll; Sec NHS; NEDT Awd.

SNYDER, LAUREL F; Southwestern HS; Hanover, PA; (Y); AFS; Church Yth Grp; Girl Scts; Chorus; Church Choir; Mrchg Band; School Musical; Hon Roll.

SNYDER, LORI; Spring Grove SR HS; York, PA; (Y); 46/289; Church Yth Grp; Nwsp Rptr; Nwsp Stf; High Hon Roll; Hon Roll.

SNYDER, LORI; York Suburban SR HS; York, PA; (Y); 1/197; Concert Band; Nwsp Sprt Ed; Var Capt Bsktbl; Var Capt Tennis; Trs NHS; Val; Church Yth Grp; Cmnty Wkr; Pep Clb; Yrk Cnty JR Miss 85-86; Otstndng Englsh, Mth & Physcs Stu 85; YCIAA All Cnty Bsktbl & Cnty Chp 85-86; Johns Hopkins U; Math.

SNYDER, MARGIE; Elizabethtown Area HS; Bainbridge, PA; (Y); Chorus; Nwsp Stf; Yrbk Stf; Rep Soph Cls; Rep Stu Cncl; Var Cheerleading; Var Sftbl; Fash Merch.

SNYDER, MAURA K; Wilmington Area HS; New Wilmington, PA; (Y); 36/101; Office Aide; Spanish Clb; Nwsp Rptr; Nwsp Stf; Lit Mag; Sec Jr Cls; Sec Sr Cls; Stu Cncl; JV Var Powder Puff Ftbl; Im Sftbl; Slippery Rock U; Comm.

SNYDER, MELISSA; Muhlenberg HS; Reading, PA; (Y); Cmnty Wkr; Hosp Aide; Band; Chorus; Color Guard; Concert Band; Capt Flag Corp; Mrchg Band; School Musical; Variety Show.

SNYDER, MICHELE; Greencatle-Antrim HS; Waynesboro, PA; (Y); Band; Concert Band; Hon Roll; 2nd Pl Sci Fair Chem 85; Hagerstown Bus Coll; Bus Adm.

SNYDER, MICHELE; Upper Dauphin Area HS; Lykens, PA; (Y); 21/105; Art Clb; Computer Clb; Girl Scts; Math Clb; Chorus; School Play; Stage Crew; Rep Stu Cncl; Trk; NHS; John Hall Scholar 86; Mary Margaret Nestor Fndtn Scholar 86; Harrisburg Area CC; Nuclr Med.

SNYDER, MICHELLE; Southern Columbia Area HS; Elysburg, PA; (Y); 14/41; Church Yth Grp; Cmnty Wkr; FCA; Hosp Aide; Church Choir; Yrbk Stf; Mgr Powder Puff Ftbl; Hon Roll; NHS; Exploring; Grgg Typng Awd Achvt 84-85; Nrsng.

SNYDER, NANCY; Purchase Line HS; Mahaffey, PA; (Y); 12/124; Church Yth Grp; French Clb; School Play; Nwsp Rptr; Sec Soph Cls; Rep Stu Cncl; Hon Roll; PTA Lit 1st Pl Wnnr 84.

SNYDER, PATRICIA; Solanco HS; Quarryville, PA; (Y); 14/235; Art Clb; 4-H; Pep Clb; Ski Clb; Varsity Clb; Church Choir; Nwsp Rptr; Nwsp Stf; Capt VP Cheerleading; Powder Puff Ftbl; Phys Ed Awd 84; Hlth Ed Awd 84; Hstry Awd 85; Franklin & Marshall; Eng.

SNYDER, RICHARD; Elizabeth Forward HS; Mckeesport, PA; (Y); AFS; Debate Tm; Drama Clb; Intnl Clb; Ski Clb; Spanish Clb; Concert Band; Mrchg Band; Nwsp Rptr; Hon Roll; PA ST U; Indstrl Engrng.

SNYDER, ROBBIE; Moniteau HS; Boyers, PA; (Y); #31 In Class; Boy Scts; Church Yth Grp; Exploring; Spanish Clb; Bsbl; Mgr(s); Trk; Wt Lftg; God Cntry Awd; Hon Roll; Slippery Rock U; Geolgy.

SNYDER, SHANE; Red Lion SR HS; Felton, PA; (Y); Computer Clb; German Clb; JA; Science Clb; Orch; Hon Roll; Penn ST U; Pre-Med.

SNYDER, SHARON; Garden Spot HS; East Earl, PA; (Y); Library Aide; Chorus; Stage Crew; High Hon Roll; Hon Roll; Jr NHS; NHS; Bus.

SNYDER, SHAWN; Mt Pleasant Area SR HS; Acme, PA; (Y); German Clb; High Hon Roll; Hon Roll; Acad All-Amer 85.

SNYDER, SHAWNIE; Southern Huntingdon Co HS; Shade Gap, PA; (Y); 22/119; FBLA; GAA; SADD; Ed Yrbk Stf; Powder Puff Ftbl; Hon Roll; Hgrstwn Bus Coll; Med Rcptnst.

SNYDER, STEPHANIE; Manheim Central HS; Manheim, PA; (Y); 11/237; Church Yth Grp; Chorus; Church Choir; Yrbk Stf; Capt L Crs Cntry; JV Fld Hcky; L Var Trk; High Hon Roll; NHS; Ntl Merit Ltr.

SNYDER, STEVE; Tulpehocken HS; Myerstown, PA; (Y); 5/102; Church Yth Grp; Socr; Tennis; NHS; Engrng.

SNYDER, SUSAN; Parkland HS; Breinigsville, PA; (Y); 15/462; Church Yth Grp; Pres 4-H; Chorus; Color Guard; Stage Crew; 4-H Awd; High Hon Roll; NHS; Prfct Atten Awd; Central Penn Business Schl.

SNYDER, SUSAN; Wilmington Area HS; New Wilmington, PA; (Y); Church Yth Grp; Ski Clb; Nwsp Stf; Stu Cncl; Gym; Powder Puff Ftbl; Hon Roll; Nwsppr Artist 84-85; Prom Dcrtng Comm 85-86; Columbus Coll Of Art; Art.

SNYDER, TAMMY; Blue Mountain HS; Friedensburg, PA; (S); Pres DECA; 5th Pl PA Rstrnt Mrktng Cmptn 86; Bus Mngmnt.

SNYDER, TERRI; New Castle HS; New Castle, PA; (Y); 24/234; Girl Scts; Pep Clb; Ski Clb; Band; Drill Tm; Mrchg Band; Rep Frsh Cls; Rep Soph Cls; Rep Jr Cls; Stu Cncl; Hnry Histrc Soc 85; Gannon Schlrshp Merit 86; Gannon U; Pre-Phrmcy.

SNYDER, TIMOTHY; Ford City JR SR HS; Ford City, PA; (Y); Boy Scts; Church Yth Grp; VP Drama Clb; Chorus; School Play; Nwsp Rptr; Stu Cncl; Bsktbl; Crs Cntry; Trk; Stu Actvts Awd 85-86; Smmr Happeng Schlrshp 85; Track,Cross Cty Ltr 86; IN U; Comm.

SNYDER, TINA; Shamokin Area HS; Paxinos, PA; (Y); 115/245; Drama Clb; Pep Clb; Science Clb; Ski Clb; Concert Band; Mrchg Band; Var Swmmng; Var Trk; Im Vllybl.

SNYDER, TRACEY; Laurel Valley HS; New Florence, PA; (Y); Art Clb; Cmnty Wkr; Library Aide; Hon Roll; Ocie Kuhar Mem Schlrshp 86; Carlow Coll; Nrsng.

SNYDER, WENDY; Milton SR HS; Milton, PA; (Y); Library Aide; Office Aide; Williamsport Area CC; Sec.

SNYDER, WILLIAM; William Allen HS; Allentown, PA; (Y); Chess Clb; Church Yth Grp; German Clb; Church Choir; Hon Roll; NHS; Ntl Merit SF; Marine Bio.

SNYDER, WILLIAM J; Somerset SR HS; Somerset, PA; (Y); 83/239; English Clb; Letterman Clb; Varsity Clb; Var Bsbl; Var Ftbl; Hon Roll; Accounting.

SOARES, DAVID; Bethlehem Catholic HS; Hellertown, PA; (Y); 25/180; Cmnty Wkr; Exploring; Var Socr; High Hon Roll; NHS; Aircrft Maintenance Engr.

SOBCZAK, KELLY; Bethel Park HS; Bethel Park, PA; (Y); Drama Clb; Sec FBLA; Hosp Aide; VP JA; Co-Capt Powder Puff Ftbl; High Hon Roll; Hon Roll; NHS; 3rd Pl FBLA Typng Cntst 85-86.

SOBECKY, STACIE; Greater Johnstown HS; Johnstown, PA; (Y); Church Yth Grp; German Clb; Library Aide; Pep Clb; Scholastic Bowl; Nwsp Rptr; Nwsp Stf; Stu Cncl; Hon Roll; Chem.

SOBINSKY, MARSHA; Mt Pleasant Area HS; Norvelt, PA; (Y); 28/253; German Clb; Concert Band; Mrchg Band; Yrbk Stf; JV Var Bsktbl; High Hon Roll; Math.

SOBOLEWSKI, ANGELIC; Berwick Ssr HS; Berwick, PA; (Y); Key Clb; Chorus; Color Guard; Yrbk Stf; Library Aide; RN.

SOBON, DANNA; Avonworth HS; Pittsburgh, PA; (Y); AFS; VP French Clb; Band; Church Choir; High Hon Roll; NHS; Excllnc Stanford Achvt Tst 86.

SOBOTA, BRET; Biglerville HS; Biglerville, PA; (Y); 3/82; Letterman Clb; Yrbk Ed-Chief; L Ftbl; L Trk; Wrstlng; NHS; Pres Schlr; Wt Lftg; Jr NHS; Am Lgn Awd 86; LV Stck Sci Awd 86; Chmstry Crtfct Mrt 85; Penn ST U; Pre-Med.

SOCK, STEPHEN; Bensalem SR HS; Bensalem, PA; (Y); Debate Tm; Var Bsbl; JV Bsktbl; JV Ftbl; High Hon Roll; Hon Roll; NHS; Ntl Merit Ltr.

SOCKMAN, BETH A; Bucktail Area HS; Renovo, PA; (Y); 2/75; 4-H; Key Clb; Band; Drill Tm; Pres Soph Cls; VP Jr Cls; Pres Sr Cls; Var Bsktbl; JV Cheerleading; High Hon Roll; Penn ST U; Sec Math Tchr.

SOCKO, DENISE; Southern Columbia Area HS; Catawissa, PA; (Y); Hosp Aide; Chorus; School Play; Yrbk Stf; High Hon Roll; Hon Roll; NHS; Prfct Atten Awd; Awd Outstndng Achvmnt Comp Math 86; Phrmcy.

SOCOSKI, CHRISTINA; Philipsburg-Osceda HS; Osceola Mills, PA; (Y); Art Clb; Drama Clb; Thesps; Band; Chorus; Church Choir; Concert Band; Mrchg Band; School Musical; School Play; Performing Arts.

SODA, GORDON; Plymouth-Whitemarsh HS; Norristown, PA; (Y); 125/375; Cmnty Wkr; Concert Band; Powder Puff Ftbl; Var Socr; Hon Roll; Mst Imprvd Plyr Sccr 83; Cert Of Merit Sccr 85; Bloomsbury U Of PA; Acctg.

SODERGREN, KATHRYN; Bellefonte Area HS; Bellefonte, PA; (Y); 11/217; Band; Chorus; Concert Band; Mrchg Band; School Musical; Yrbk Stf; Var Crs Cntry; Var Trk; Hon Roll; NHS; Phi Beta Kappa Awd PA ST Chptr 86; PA ST U; Spec/Elem Ed.

SOFFA, MELISSA; Bethlehem Catholic HS; Bethlehem, PA; (Y); 3/201; Church Yth Grp; Hosp Aide; Key Clb; Red Cross Aide; Scholastic Bowl; SADD; Im Fld Hcky; High Hon Roll; Trs NHS; Algebra & German Awds 84; German Awd 85; 3d Pl Manhrs Awd At PA Dist 86; Psych.

SOFFRONOFF, JOHN; Pius X HS; Pen Argyl, PA; (Y); 1/33; Church Choir; Yrbk Bus Mgr; Rep Jr Cls; Var Bsbl; Var Capt Ftbl; Var Wrstlng; High Hon Roll; Lion Awd; NHS; Moravian Coll.

SOFORIC, VANESSA; Geibel HS; Scottdale, PA; (Y); Drama Clb; Library Aide; Pep Clb; School Musical; Stage Crew; Yrbk Stf; JV Sftbl; Real Est.

SOFRANKO, BOB; Mt Pleasant Area HS; Mt Pleasant, PA; (Y); Latin Clb; Spanish Clb; Yrbk Stf; Im Bsktbl; L Tennis; Im Vllybl; Hon Roll; Bus Admn.

SOHL, LORI ANN; Mercyhurst Preparatory Schl; Erie, PA; (Y); Tennis; Hon Roll; NHS; PA JR Acad Sci 1st Pl Regnl & 2nd Pl ST Awds 83; Teeng Actn Clb Cmmnty Svc 82-84; Guilford Coll; Bio.

SOHMER, LINDA; Archbishop Carroll Girls HS; Devon, PA; (Y); 53/216; Pres Church Yth Grp; Service Clb; Socr; Swmmng; High Hon Roll; Hon Roll; Cthlc Ntl Trng Inst For Ldrshp & Srv 85; U Of Delaware.

SOHN, GENIE; Shady Side Academy; Martins Ferry, OH; (Y); English Clb; French Clb; Sec Trs Spanish Clb; Band; Chorus; Nwsp Stf; Yrbk Stf; JV Sftbl; Var L Swmmng; Var Tennis; Ntl Merit Awd 85; 2nd Pl-Grand Concours Frnch Cont Of Pittsburgh 84, 3rd Pl Rgn 83; Georgetown U; Med.

SOHN, TAE-HO; Marple Newtown SR HS; Newtown Square, PA; (Y); Boy Scts; Chess Clb; Church Yth Grp; Computer Clb; Math Tm; Science Clb; JV Tennis; High Hon Roll; Hon Roll.

SOHNS, LORI J; Lakeland HS; Olyphant, PA; (S); 2/168; Girl Scts; VP JA; Spanish Clb; VP Band; Stu Cncl; High Hon Roll; Hon Roll; Chorus; Awd Achvt Joans Dance Studios 85; Intermed Music Stdy Natl Keybrd Art Assn 83; Dist Chrs 85; Psych.

SOHYDA, NICK; Canon Mc Millan HS; Muse, PA; (Y); 90/396; Church Yth Grp; Cmnty Wkr; Varsity Clb; Rep Frsh Cls; L Ftbl; Wt Lftg; VFW Awd; Volunteer Firefighter; Civil Engrng.

SOKACH, MARY ELIZABETH; Wyoming Area HS; W Pittston, PA; (Y); 15/247; Church Yth Grp; Trs Key Clb; Capt Color Guard; Rep Stu Cncl; High Hon Roll; Kiwanis Awd; Lion Awd; NHS; Cmnty Wkr; Girl Scts; Hugh O Brian Ldrshp Awd 84; Natl Cncl Yth Ldrshp 85; Beaver Coll; Phy Thrpy.

SOKOLOSKI, CHERYL; Bishop O Reilly HS; Luzerne, PA; (Y); Ski Clb; Spanish Clb; Chorus; Church Choir; Mrchg Band; School Musical; Stage Crew; Hon Roll; NEDT Awd; Luzerne County CC; Bus Admin.

SOKOLOSKI, EDWARD; Lakeland HS; Olyphant, PA; (Y); 33/145; JV Bsbl; L Bsktbl; Capt Ftbl; Hon Roll; NHS; Rochester Natl Scholar; U Rochester; Ed.

SOKOLOSKI, PAUL; Shamokin Area HS; Shamokin, PA; (Y); 44/239; Aud/Vis; Boy Scts; Camera Clb; Drama Clb; Key Clb; Science Clb; School Musical; Var Swmmng; God Cntry Awd; Hon Roll; Bucknell U; Engrng.

SOKOLOW, EILEEN; Northeast HS; Philadelphia, PA; (Y); Chorus; VP Frsh Cls; Temple; Jrnlsm.

SOKOLOWSKI, ROBERT; St Josephs Prep; Moorestown, NJ; (Y); Lit Mag; Ftbl; Trk; Hon Roll; Pol Sci.

SOLAREK, LINDA; Bradford Area HS; Bradford, PA; (Y); AFS; Band; Concert Band; Drm Mjr(t); Mrchg Band; Pep Band; Var Cheerleading; Hon Roll; Lion Awd; Slippery Rock U; Athletic Trnng.

SOLBERG, ANDREW; Biglerville HS; Aspers, PA; (Y); 40/80; Computer Clb; Ftbl; Tennis; Comp Sci.

SOLBERG, SONJA; Millersburfg Area HS; Millersburg, PA; (Y); 6/60; Church Yth Grp; French Clb; Spanish Clb; Teachers Aide; Chorus; Church Choir; School Musical; Nwsp Sprt Ed; Yrbk Ed-Chief; Off Stu Cncl; Liberty U; Elem Ed.

SOLER, MERARI; Thomas A Edison HS; Philadelphia, PA; (Y); Church Yth Grp; DECA; Teachers Aide; Band; Church Choir; Hon Roll; Tmpct Ser Prct Atten 86; Exmplry Demo In Jb Develpmnt 86; Temple U CC; Hnd Comm.

SOLI, MICHAEL; Cathedral Prep; Erie, PA; (Y); 49/216; Church Yth Grp; Spanish Clb; Band; Chorus; Church Choir; Concert Band; Mrchg Band; Orch; School Musical; School Play; Thtr.

SOLIS, PETER; Seneca Valley SR HS; Evans City, PA; (Y); VP Ski Clb; Nwsp Phtg; Ed Yrbk Phtg; Arch.

SOLIT, DAVID; Cheltenham HS; Elkins Pk, PA; (Y); 16/365; Yrbk Stf; Lit Mag; Rep Stu Cncl; Var Golf; Var Ice Hcky; JV Tennis; Ntl Merit Ltr; Rnslr Math & Sci Awd 86; Hnrs By Ntl Assn Of Bio Tchrs 86; 1st Pl In Sci Fair 86; Pre-Med.

SOLKA, STACEY; Sacred Heart HS; Pittsburgh, PA; (Y); Church Yth Grp; Cmnty Wkr; Computer Clb; Chorus; Variety Show; Nwsp Rptr; Nwsp Stf; Trs Frsh Cls; Capt Im Vllybl; Comm.

SOLOMON, DANIEL; Bishop Mc Cort HS; Johnstown, PA; (Y); Drama Clb; Key Clb; Math Clb; Pres Frsh Cls; Pres Soph Cls; Var Capt Bsktbl; Var Golf; All Tourn Tm U Pitts At Johnstown Holiday Tourn, Dir Girls Parochial Sccr Lg 85; John Carroll U; Law.

SOLOMON, KEITH; Penn-Trafford HS; Level Green, PA; (Y); 24/363; Varsity Clb; Im Bsktbl; Capt JV Ftbl; Var L Wrstlng; High Hon Roll; NHS.

SOLOMON, KIM; Derry Area HS; Derry, PA; (Y); 40/255; AFS; Math Clb; Office Aide; Chorus; Stage Crew; Stu Cncl; Cheerleading; High Hon Roll; Hon Roll; Tourism.

SOLOW, JORDAN; Winchester-Thurston HS; Pittsburgh, PA; (Y); Ed Nwsp Ed-Chief; Ed Yrbk Ed-Chief; Ed Lit Mag; Skidmore Coll Alumnae Art Awd 85; The Plaid Art Awd 85; Hnrb Mntn Three Rivers Arts Fest 84; RI Schl Desgn.

SOLSMAN, DEBRA; Dunmore HS; Dunmore, PA; (Y); 26/155; Church Yth Grp; FBLA; Chorus; Capt Pom Pon; High Hon Roll; Hon Roll; NHS; Eiln Fnnrty Mem Awd Bus 86; Awd Bus Eng ST Of PA Ftr Bus Ldrs 86; Prf Oper.

SOLT, AUDREY; Brandywine Heights HS; Mertztown, PA; (Y); 17/144; Church Yth Grp; Band; Chorus; Church Choir; Concert Band; Jazz Band; Mrchg Band; Pep Band; School Play; Sec Frsh Cls; Cnty Dist Rgnl Chorus 85 & 86; Music Educ.

SOLTESZ, JENNIFER; Richland HS; Gibsonia, PA; (Y); AFS; Aud/Vis; Cmnty Wkr; School Musical; Stage Crew; Hon Roll; PA ST; Rcrtnl Thrpy.

SOLTIS, CAROLE; W Branch Area HS; Hawk Run, PA; (Y); 20/112; Science Clb; Spanish Clb; Teachers Aide; Varsity Clb; Chorus; Yrbk Stf; Var Sftbl; Im Vllybl; Hon Roll; NHS; S Hills Bus Schl; Micro-Comps.

SOLTIS, JOAN; Schoglkill Valley HS; Leesport, PA; (Y); 23/127; VP FTA; Teachers Aide; Chorus; Concert Band; Nwsp Stf; Yrbk Stf; Var Capt Bsktbl; Crs Cntry; Var Capt Trk; Vllybl; Wmns Clb Leesport Awd 86; Outstndng Feml Athlt Rotry Medl 85-86; PA Yth Educ Assn Awd 86; Kutztown U; Cmnctns.

SOLTIS, KIMBERLY; Connellsville Area SR HS; Connellsville, PA; (Y); Hon Roll; Sawyer Schl; Hlth.

SOMA, EILEEN; Bishop Hannan HS; Scranton, PA; (Y); 20/131; Church Yth Grp; Drama Clb; SADD; Chorus; Orch; School Musical; Hon Roll; NHS; Exclnce In Engl, Wrld Cltrs & Orchstra 83-84; Hnrb Mntn Wrld Cltrs Ii & Orchstra 84-85; Exclnce Soc 86; U Of Scranton; Med.

SOMANATH, SUNITHA; Bethel Park HS; Pittsburgh, PA; (Y); French Clb; FBLA; Teachers Aide; Stage Crew; Yrbk Rptr; Yrbk Stf; Hon Roll; PA ST; Pre-Dentl Med.

SOMENSKY, FRANI; St Hubert HS For Girls; Philadelphia, PA; (Y); 137/342; CAP; French Clb; Office Aide; Teachers Aide; Var L Fld Hcky; Var L Trk; Hon Roll; Prfct Atten Awd; Leg Hnr 84; Billy Mitchell Awd 84; Amiela Earhart Awd 85; USAF Acad; Psychlgy.

SOMERS, REBECCA; Bald Eagle Area HS; Milesburg, PA; (Y); Church Yth Grp; Varsity Clb; Acpl Chr; Chorus; Concert Band; Mrchg Band; Nwsp Stf; Stu Cncl; Hon Roll; Prfct Atten Awd; Most Athlc Awd Yth Camp 85-86; 1st Pl Photogrphy ST Awd 86; Dist Band & Dist Chourus 86; Lee Coll; Bus.

SOMERVILLE, JAMES A; Hopewell HS; Aliquippa, PA; (Y); 110/245; Computer Clb; Spanish Clb; Bowling; Vllybl; Hon Roll; God Cntry Awd; Pharmacy.

SOMERVILLE, STEVE; Purchase Line HS; Cherry Tree, PA; (Y); 3/127; Trs Varsity Clb; Pres Jr Cls; Pres Sr Cls; Stu Cncl; Capt Bsktbl; Capt Ftbl; Trk; Dnfth Awd; High Hon Roll; NHS; Line Ed Assoc Schlrshp 86; Bus Prof Womens Schrlshp 86; PA ST U; Engrng.

SOMMARIVA, ROSEMARY; Butler Area SR HS; Butler, PA; (Y); Church Yth Grp; FBLA; JA; Science Clb; Spanish Clb; Bus.

SOMMER, ANN; Meadville Area SR HS; Meadville, PA; (Y); Church Yth Grp; French Clb; Key Clb; NFL; Office Aide; Pep Clb; Ski Clb; Speech Tm; Chorus; Church Choir.

SOMMER, GREGORY; Bethlehem Catholic HS; Bethlehem, PA; (S); 16/220; Church Yth Grp; Key Clb; Math Tm; Ski Clb; School Musical; Rep Sr Cls; Var Ftbl; Var Capt Socr; High Hon Roll; NHS; Chem.

SOMMER, JOHN; St Josephs Prep HS; Philadelphia, PA; (Y); French Clb; Latin Clb; Off Frsh Cls; Off Jr Cls; Stu Cncl; Var Golf; Var Socr; JV Trk; Bus.

SOMMER, SCOTT; Kennard-Dale HS; New Park, PA; (Y); Church Yth Grp; Pres Varsity Clb; School Musical; Trs Jr Cls; Trs Sr Cls; L Bsbl; L Bsktbl; L Socr; Trs NHS; Knnrd-Dale Stu Of Mnth For Acads 86.

SOMMERS, DENVER; Mt Pleasant Area SR HS; Mt Pleasant, PA; (Y); 13/253; German Clb; JV Wrstlng; High Hon Roll; Hon Roll; NHS; Pres Acdmc Ftns Awd 85-86; Hesston Coll; Aviation.

SOMMERS, RICHARD; Pottstown HS; Pottstown, PA; (S); 3/238; Key Clb; Spanish Clb; Yrbk Stf; High Hon Roll; NHS; Biochem.

SOMMERS, SUZANNE; Panther Valley HS; Summit Hill, PA; (Y); 9/106; Church Yth Grp; Math Clb; Sftbl; Swmmng; High Hon Roll; NHS; Education.

SON, ANGELA; Upper Dublin HS; Ambler, PA; (Y); 23/307; Church Yth Grp; Cmnty Wkr; Trs VP FBLA; Intnl Clb; Orch; Yrbk Bus Mgr; Lit Mag; Fld Hcky; Lcrss; Jr NHS.

SONG, JAE; Harrisburg HS; Harrisburg, PA; (S); Boys Clb Am; Chess Clb; ROTC; Science Clb; Drill Tm; Bsbl; Socr; Tennis; Hon Roll; NHS; Yth Yr Boys Clb 84; Rotry Ldrshp Conf 85; Tmeple U; Intnatl Bus.

SONNEBORN, TRICIA; Upper Dublin SR HS; Oreland, PA; (Y); 75/322; Art Clb; Varsity Clb; Band; Yrbk Stf; Stu Cncl; Bowling; Crs Cntry; Swmmng; Trk; Lion Awd.

SONNEN, DAVID; Conrad Weiser HS; Richland, PA; (Y); 5/184; Sec Church Yth Grp; Trs Pres 4-H; JCL; Key Clb; 4-H Awd; High Hon Roll; Hon Roll; NHS; PA Quester Schlrshp 84; Hstry.

SONNENBERG, DALE; Cathedral Prep; Erie, PA; (Y); Church Yth Grp; NFL; Spanish Clb; Speech Tm; Y-Teens; Bsktbl; Bowling; Score Keeper; Sftbl; Vllybl.

SONNON, SCOTT; Northern Lebanon HS; Fredericksburg, PA; (Y); 28/115; Art Clb; Computer Clb; Band; Chorus; School Musical; School Play; Stage Crew; Ftbl; Wt Lftg; Compu Sci.

SONON, ANDREW E; Penn Hills SR HS; Pittsburgh, PA; (Y); 96/616; Am Leg Boys St; Boy Scts; Computer Clb; Science Clb; Band; Mrchg Band; Rep Stu Cncl; High Hon Roll; Hon Roll; NEDT Awd; Eagle Scout 86; PA ST Semi-Fnlst-Cmptr On-Line LIN TEL Stu Srch Off 86; Bus.

SONSINI, TAMMY; Aliquippa HS; Aliquippa, PA; (S); Church Yth Grp; Dance Clb; Drama Clb; Exploring; French Clb; FNA; Band; Concert Band; Pep Band; School Play; U Of Pittsburgh; Anstst.

SONSTEIN, AMY; Upper Dublin HS; Ambler, PA; (Y); 51/307; Math Tm; Pres SADD; Varsity Clb; Orch; Var L Crs Cntry; Var L Trk; Hon Roll; Jr NHS; Prfct Atten Awd; Slct Prtcp Mntgmry Cnty Intrmdt Unts Intsv Spnsh 86; 2 Mle Run Indr Rcrd 86; 1st Tm Crss Cntry.

SONTHEIMER, NADINE; Bethel Park SR HS; Bethel Park, PA; (Y); 136/515; Girl Scts; Hosp Aide; Key Clb; Teachers Aide; Band; Yrbk Stf; Off Soph Cls; Off Jr Cls; Pres Stu Cncl; Powder Puff Ftbl; E Carolina U; Nursing.

SOO HOO, LEA; Northern Lebanon HS; Lebanon, PA; (Y); 1/174; Math Tm; Model UN; Band; Chorus; School Play; Trk; Hon Roll; NHS; Frgn Lang Clb; Lebanon Vly Yth Schlrs Chem Pgm; U PA; Bus.

SOO HOO, PATRICK; Church Farm Schl; New York, NY; (Y); 1/30; German Clb; JV Var Socr; Im Sftbl; JV Var Wrstlng; High Hon Roll; Hon Roll; NHS; Amer Chmcl Soc Awd 86; Indstrl Arts Awd 84; Hghst Acadmc Avg Schl 86; Sci.

SOOS, ANGELA; Owen J Roberts HS; Spring City, PA; (Y); 4-H; FBLA; JA; Yrbk Stf; Bsktbl; Diving; Vllybl; 4-H Awd; Hon Roll; Eastern Coll; Interpretor.

SOPKO, BETH; Ambridge Area HS; Baden, PA; (Y); Pep Clb; Spanish Clb; Band; Church Choir; Concert Band; Mrchg Band; Pep Band; Symp Band; Hon Roll; Acctg.

SOPKO, SHARON; Bethlehem Catholic HS; Bethlehem, PA; (Y); 23/219; Key Clb; Mrchg Band; Orch; Yrbk Stf; High Hon Roll; NHS; Pres Schlr; Amer Assn Of U Wmn Schlrshp 86; Outstndng Achvt In Typng 85; PA ST U; Mcrbdgy.

SORANNO, THOMAS; Bishop Ohara HS; Peckville, PA; (S); 12/124; Am Leg Boys St; Boy Scts; Computer Clb; Drama Clb; Spanish Clb; Chorus; School Musical; High Hon Roll; JETS Awd; NHS; Eagle Scout 85; Excllnc Physics-PA Jr Acad Of Sci 85; Engrng.

SORBER, AMY; Greater Latrobe HS; Greensburg, PA; (Y); Letterman Clb; Pep Clb; Capt L Bsktbl; L Crs Cntry; Capt L Tennis; Hon Roll; Nancy Rogers Otstndng Woman Ahlt Yr 86; WA Cngrssnl Smnr Reprsntv 86; VA Tech; Bus.

SORENSEN, FRANK; Cardinal O Hara HS; Rutledge, PA; (Y); 120/800; Rep Frsh Cls; Rep Soph Cls; Capt L Golf; High Hon Roll; Hon Roll; Naval Acad.

SORG, JACQUELINE; St Marys Area HS; Weedville, PA; (Y); Cmnty Wkr; Library Aide; Service Clb; Yrbk Stf; Hon Roll; Kiwanis Awd; NHS; Outstndng JR Bus 84-85; Stackpole Corp Schlrshp 86; PA ST U; Accntng.

SORICK, GRETCHEN; Pocono Central Catholic HS; Canadensis, PA; (Y); Art Clb; Church Yth Grp; Pep Clb; School Musical; Sec Soph Cls; Capt Cheerleading; Sftbl; High Hon Roll; Hon Roll; NHS; MVP Awd Chrldng 84-85; Chem Awd/Svc Awds/Rlgn Awd 85-86; Nrsng.

SORKIN, RACHEL; Haverford Twp SR HS; Havertown, PA; (Y); 30/485; Speech Tm; Variety Show; Nwsp Rptr; Ed Lit Mag; NHS; Ntl Merit SF; Wm Garrett Awd 85; Lbrl Arts.

SORRENTINO, ERIC GEORGE DAVID; Manor HS; Ft Relvior, VA; (Y); Church Yth Grp; Computer Clb; Hosp Aide; Chorus; Church Choir; Stage Crew; Im Wt Lftg; Hon Roll; NEDT Awd; Acad Achvt Engl III; Acad Achvt Wrld Cult; U VA; Adol Psych.

SORTMAN, TRINA; Shikellamy SR HS; Sunbury, PA; (Y); 92/327; Sec Church Yth Grp; Girl Scts; Pres Spanish Clb; Drill Tm; Hon Roll; Spanish NHS; Penn ST Coll; Spn Tchr.

SOSKO, JEFF; Mt Pleasant Area HS; Mount Pleasant, PA; (Y); 50/253; German Clb; Var L Ftbl; Im Trk; Var L Wrstlng; Hon Roll.

SOSSMAN, ERIK L; Bethel Park HS; Bethel Park, PA; (Y); Am Leg Boys St; Spanish Clb; Rep Frsh Cls; Rep Jr Cls; Var L Socr; Var L Tennis; High Hon Roll; NHS; Lib Arts.

SOSSONG, TOM; North Pocono HS; Moscow, PA; (Y); Cmnty Wkr; Ski Clb; Band; Concert Band; Mrchg Band; Orch; High Hon Roll; Hon Roll; U Of Scranton; Phrmcy.

SOTAK, AMY L; Bethlehem Ctr; Brownsville, PA; (Y); 2/156; Drama Clb; Spanish Clb; Varsity Clb; School Play; Yrbk Stf; Stu Cncl; Var L Bsktbl; Var Vllybl; High Hon Roll; NHS; Sprts Mgmt.

SOTAK, KATHLEEN; Parkland HS; Schnecksville, PA; (Y); Key Clb; Stu Cncl; Hon Roll; NHS; Natl Merit Schlrshp 86; PA ST U; Chem Engrg.

SOTO, EDWIN; Bensalem HS; Trevose, PA; (Y); Pres Church Yth Grp; Acpl Chr; Chorus; Church Choir; Madrigals; Mrchg Band; School Play; Var Capt Ftbl; Var Capt Wrstlng; Boy Scts; Comp Pgm.

SOTO, MARYBELL; Pottstown SR HS; Pottstown, PA; (S); 13/238; Art Clb; JV Fld Hcky; JV Lcrss; Var Score Keeper; High Hon Roll; Hon Roll; Jr NHS; NHS; Sectrl.

SOTOSKY, JOE; Windber Area HS; Windber, PA; (Y); Ftbl; U Pittsburgh; Comm.

SOTTILE, LOUISE; Bishop Hannan HS; Scranton, PA; (Y); French Clb; JA; Rep Frsh Cls; Rep Soph Cls; Bowling; Hnrb Mntn Theol III 86; Excllnce Eng I 84; Cert Stu Cncl 84; Marywood Coll; Elem Ed.

SOUBIK, KRISTINA; Lourdes Regional HS; Kulpmont, PA; (Y); 16/98; Service Clb; Spanish Clb; Church Choir; Nwsp Stf; Yrbk Stf; Hon Roll; Prfct Atten Awd; Spanish NHS; Pottsville Nrsng Schl; Nrsng.

SOUCHAK, KRISTIN; Mahanoy Area HS; Mahanoy City, PA; (Y); Church Yth Grp; Drama Clb; Chorus; Church Choir; Mrchg Band; School Play; Variety Show; Sec Jr Cls; Var Cheerleading; Var Sftbl; Engl.

SOUCHOCK, SHERYL; Gwynedd Mercy Acad; Harleysville, PA; (Y); Band; Chorus; School Musical; School Play; Variety Show; Var Lcrss; JV Tennis; Excllnc In Chem 84; Magna Cum Laude Latn 84; Band Awd 86; Ursinus College.

SOUDER, DAVID; Father Judge HS; Philadelphia, PA; (S); 8/417; Chess Clb; German Clb; Latin Clb; Mathletes; Math Clb; Math Tm; Nwsp Rptr; Im Bsktbl; Im Ftbl; High Hon Roll; Optmst Clb Essy Wnr 86; Drexel U; Elec Engr.

SOUDERS, JOSEPH; Middletown Area HS; Middletown, PA; (Y); 13/181; Church Yth Grp; Library Aide; Yrbk Stf; Ftbl; Trk; Wt Lftg; Wrstlng; High Hon Roll; Jr NHS; NHS; Acdmc All-Amer 86.

SOUDERS, MARTHA; Archbishop Ryan High Schl For Girls; Philadelphia, PA; (S); 328/494; Camp Fr Inc; Church Yth Grp; Exploring; Office Aide; Service Clb; Church Choir; Schlrp Trip To Engl For Study 84; Tn Of Mnth CYO 86.

SOUDERS, MELISSA; Halifax Area HS; Halifax, PA; (Y); 23/100; Drama Clb; Trs FHA; Chorus; Color Guard; Mrchg Band; Yrbk Sprt Ed; Yrbk Stf; Sec Rep Stu Cncl; Var JV Bsktbl; Hon Roll; Srv Awd Ftr Hmmkrs Of Amer 86; JV & Vrsty Awd Ltr In Bsktbl 85-86; Air Frc; Rdlgy.

SOUDERS, MICHELLE; Steelton-Highspire HS; Highspire, PA; (Y); 14/94; French Clb; Sec FBLA; Spanish Clb; Teachers Aide; JV Cheerleading; Hon Roll; NHS; VBLA Regnls-3rd Pl Accntng II 86; Harrisburg Area CC; Bus Admin.

SOULCHECK, JILL; Greater Johnstown Vo-Tech; Johnstown, PA; (Y); 99/320; Dance Clb; DECA; Ski Clb; Chorus; Hon Roll; NHS; 6th Pl Awd DECA Dist Comptn 84-85; Bradford Business Schl; Lgl Scy.

SOUTHARD, HEIDI; Fairview HS; Eric, PA; (Y); 52/190; German Clb; Hosp Aide; Varsity Clb; Nwsp Ed-Chief; Yrbk Stf; Rep Stu Cncl; Cheerleading; Coll Wooster; Psychlgy.

SOUTHERLING, E ANDREW; Farther Judge HS; Jenkintown, PA; (S); 25/410; Chess Clb; German Clb; SADD; Yrbk Stf; Rep Frsh Cls; Rep Soph Cls; Var Bsbl; Var Socr; Cit Awd; NHS; Law.

SOUTHERN, TRACEY; Moshannon Valley JR SR HS; Madera, PA; (Y); Letterman Clb; Band; Chorus; Pep Band; Sec Frsh Cls; Sec Soph Cls; Sec Jr Cls; Sec Sr Cls; Off Stu Cncl; Bsktbl; Du Bois Bus Coll; Med Sec.

SOWASH, MARLENE; Grove City Area HS; Grove City, PA; (Y); 16/199; Church Yth Grp; Sec FBLA; Thesps; Band; Concert Band; Mrchg Band; Pep Band; School Play; Stage Crew; NHS; Grove City Coll; Accntng.

SOWERS, LISA; Grove City SR HS; Grove City, PA; (Y); 5/197; VP Key Clb; Concert Band; Mrchg Band; School Play; Ed Yrbk Stf; Cheerleading; Powder Puff Ftbl; High Hon Roll; NHS; Rotary Awd.

SOWERS, MATTHEW; Pequea Valley HS; Paradise, PA; (Y); 10/135; Church Yth Grp; Stage Crew; NHS; Physics.

SOWERS, TAMMY; Kiski Area HS; Vandergrift, PA; (Y); Church Yth Grp; Cmnty Wkr; Pep Clb; Nwsp Rptr; Nwsp Stf; Yrbk Stf; Stat Bsktbl; Hon Roll; Clarion U.

SOWINSKI, ROBERT; Catasauqua HS; Catasauqua, PA; (Y); 4/130; Bsktbl; Crs Cntry; Trk; Hon Roll; NHS; Engrng.

SOWKO, ROBERT; South Alleheny HS; Glassport, PA; (Y); 19/177; Aud/Vis; Boy Scts; VP Church Yth Grp; Dance Clb; Exploring; French Clb; Science Clb; Trk; Hon Roll; NHS; Buhl Sci Fair Hnrbl Mntn 86; Amer Wldng Soc Awd 86; Alcoa Found Awd 86; Indstrl Arts.

SOXMAN, ALAN; Plum SR HS; New Kensington, PA; (Y); Church Yth Grp; Cmnty Wkr; Computer Clb; VP JA; Science Clb; SADD; High Hon Roll; Hon Roll; NHS; Spec Clsrm Awds 84-86; JR Achvt Sls Awd 84-86; Carnegie Mellon; Aerontcl Engr.

SOYSTER, DAVID; Strath Haven HS; Wallingford, PA; (Y); Church Yth Grp; Office Aide; Yrbk Phtg; High Hon Roll; Hon Roll; Wallingford Swarthmore Ed Assoc Schrlshp 86; PA ST U; Mech Engr.

SOYSTER, VALERIE; State College Area HS; State College, PA; (Y); 111/568; Rep Soph Cls; Var Capt Cheerleading; Var Swmmng; Hon Roll; Crtfct Achvmnt 86; Pwr Of Paws Awd 83-86; Nrsng.

SOZA, DANIEL; Cornell HS; Coraopolis, PA; (Y); Church Yth Grp; Spanish Clb; Nwsp Rptr; Golf; Score Keeper; High Hon Roll; NHS; Bd Of Admin Coraopolis Meth Chrch 85-86; Asst Coach Grls Sftbl Kiwanis Leag 86; Sci.

SPACHT, GLORIA; Cambria Heights HS; Patton, PA; (Y); 39/180; Church Yth Grp; Cmnty Wkr; Library Aide; Chorus; Church Choir; Yrbk Stf; Mat Maids; Hon Roll; Hnrb Mntn Jhnstwn Cptr Ntl Orgnztn For Wmn 86; IUP; Nrs.

SPADA, JASON; Cathedral Prep; Erie, PA; (Y); Spanish Clb; Im Swmmng; High Hon Roll; Hon Roll.

SPADAFORA, KRISTEN L; Mon Valley Catholic HS; Monongahela, PA; (S); 16/102; Hosp Aide; Pep Clb; Spanish Clb; Band; Church Choir; Concert Band; Drm Mjr(t); Mrchg Band; Pep Band; Variety Show; Cert Merit Fred J Millers Clinics Fld Commnder 84; Natl Bnd Assn Outstndg Music Cmprs Awd 85; Phys Ther.

SPADARO, ANTHONY; West Catholic Boys HS; Phila, PA; (Y); 20/205; Mathletes; Yrbk Stf; Var Socr; Hon Roll; Prfct Atten Awd; 2nd Tm All Cathlc Sccr Tm 85-86; Temple U; Bus Mngmnt.

SPADARO, JOHN; Carlynton HS; Carnegie, PA; (Y); Political Wkr; Capt Var Socr; Var Tennis; Im Vllybl; Hon Roll.

SPADELL, SUSAN; Crestwood HS; Wh Haven, PA; (Y); 103/226; Church Yth Grp; FBLA; FHA; VICA; Hon Roll.

SPAGNOLA, JANET; South Allegheny JR SR HS; Glassport, PA; (Y); Sec Band; Concert Band; Jazz Band; Mrchg Band; Pep Band; School Musical; Sec Soph Cls; Pres Jr Cls; High Hon Roll; NHS; Pres Acad Ftnss Awd; U Of Pittsburgh; Elem Educ.

SPAGNOLO, BETH; Richland HS; Wexford, PA; (Y); Band; Concert Band; Drm Mjr(t); Mrchg Band; High Hon Roll; Var Jr Cls; Sec Stu Cncl; Var L Bsktbl; Capt Powder Puff Ftbl; Var L Tennis.

SPAHR, DAMION; Hanover SR HS; Hanover, PA; (Y); 5/104; Aud/Vis; Church Yth Grp; School Play; Stage Crew; Yrbk Stf; VP Stu Cncl; JV Bsbl; Var Golf; Hon Roll; NEDT Achvt Awd 85; Prom Chrprsn 86; Lcl Anti Drnk-Drvng Cmpgn 86; Bio-Med Engrng.

SPAHR, LISA; Northern HS; Wellsville, PA; (Y); 12/200; French Clb; French Hon Soc; High Hon Roll; Hon Roll; Hnr Ltr & Bar 83; Hnr Bar 84-85; Hnr Lmap Pin-Dstngshd Hnr 86; PA ST U; Comp Sci.

SPAID JR, DONALD; United HS; Blairsville, PA; (Y); 4/127; VP Chess Clb; Pres Math Clb; VP Jr Cls; VP Sr Cls; Var L Ftbl; Var L Trk; Var L Wrstlng; High Hon Roll; Schlr Ath Awd 86; Pres Acad Fit Awd 86; PA ST U; Secndry Ed.

SPAK, ANN; Punxsutawney Area HS; Reynoldsville, PA; (Y); Church Yth Grp; French Clb; FBLA; Band; Concert Band; Mrchg Band; Twrlr; Frnch.

SPALLINO, CHRISTOPHER; Charleroi Area HS; Charleroi, PA; (Y); Ski Clb; Rep Stu Cncl; JV Im Bsktbl; Var Trk; High Hon Roll; NHS; Natl Sci Merit Awd 85; PA ST; Publc Rel.

SPANGLER, BRIAN; Rockwood Area HS; Rockwood, PA; (S); 24/97; High Hon Roll; Hon Roll; NHS; Triangle Tech; Mech Drftng/Desg.

SPANGLER, DANE; Governor Mifflin SR HS; Reading, PA; (Y); 29/273; Var L Ftbl; Hon Roll; Lfgrd & Cert Wtr Sfty Instr 86; Arch.

SPANGLER, DENNIS; Hampton HS; Allison Pk, PA; (Y); 77/255; Ski Clb; Var L Bsbl; Hon Roll; MVP Bsbl 86.

SPANGLER, JASON; Rockwood Area HS; Rockwood, PA; (S); 13/97; Church Yth Grp; Band; Rep Stu Cncl; High Hon Roll; Hon Roll; NHS; Voctnl.

SPANGLER, LISA; Rockwood Area HS; Rockwood, PA; (S); 2/95; Church Yth Grp; Spanish Clb; Band; Chorus; Church Choir; Mrchg Band; School Play; Yrbk Stf; Rep Jr Cls; Rep Stu Cncl; Amer Music Fndtn-Band Hnrs 85; Pres Phys Ftnss 85 & 86.

SPANGLER, LORIE; Northeastern SR HS; Dover, PA; (Y); AFS; Church Yth Grp; Exploring; FBLA; Chorus; Church Choir; Palmers Schl; Med Recept.

SPANIK, LOREN; Highlands HS; Brackenridge, PA; (Y); Hosp Aide; Key Clb; Office Aide; Yrbk Stf; Sftbl; High Hon Roll; Jr NHS; NHS; Allegheny Vly Hosp Staff Dev; Nrsg.

SPANOS, CHRIS; Northampton SR HS; Northampton, PA; (Y); Boy Scts; Church Yth Grp; CAP; VFW Awd; Embry Riddle; Aero.

SPARAGNA, GENEVIEVE; Elk Lake HS; Friendsville, PA; (Y); 2/100; Drama Clb; Scholastic Bowl; Sec Chorus; School Musical; School Play; Swing Chorus; Yrbk Phtg; High Hon Roll; Sal; MA Inst Of Technlgy; Biomed En.

SPARBER, JENNIFER; Greater Latrobe HS; Latrobe, PA; (Y); 16/350; Church Yth Grp; French Clb; JA; Band; Bsktbl; French Hon Soc; High Hon Roll; NHS; Ntl Merit SF; Pres Schlr; Wttnbrg U Schlr; Ltrb Bus Wmn Acctg Awd; Wttngbrg U; Acctg.

SPARE, KIM; Brockway Area HS; Brockport, PA; (Y); 10/209; Thesps; Varsity Clb; Band; Chorus; Flag Corp; School Play; Yrbk Stf; Rep Stu Cncl; Golf; Hon Roll; Grove City Coll; Bus Educ.

SPARGO, TODD A; Tussey Mt HS; Riddlesburg, PA; (Y); Drama Clb; Pres SADD; Band; Chorus; Drm Mjr(t); School Play; Trs Stu Cncl; Hon Roll; NHS; Slippery Rock U; Comp Tech.

SPARVERO, LOUIS J; Fox Chapel Area HS; Pittsburgh, PA; (Y); Chess Clb; Math Clb; Math Tm; Nwsp Stf; Rep Jr Cls; High Hon Roll; Mu Alp Tht; NHS; Ntl Merit SF; Boy Scts; Amer Chmcl Soc-3rd Pl Awd 85; Chem.

SPATAFORE, PHIL; Apollo-Ridge HS; N Apollo, PA; (Y); 48/180; Chess Clb; French Clb; Letterman Clb; Ski Clb; Varsity Clb; Band; Bsbl; Bsktbl; Ftbl; Hon Roll; CA U PA; Urban Rec.

SPATARO, SHAWN A; Hyndam Middle HS; Hyndman, PA; (Y); 13/56; Church Yth Grp; Pep Clb; Spanish Clb; Varsity Clb; Chorus; Trs Frsh Cls; Trs Soph Cls; Pres Sr Cls; Rep Stu Cncl; L Socr; Ntl Hnr Soc Awd 86; Alleg CC; Elec Engr.

SPATOLA, KEVIN; Hamburg Area HS; Hamburg, PA; (Y); Yrbk Stf; Rep Stu Cncl; Var L Bsbl; JV Bsktbl; Var Ftbl; Hon Roll; Acadmc Ltr Awd-Plane Geom 85-86; Engrng.

SPAULDING, JONATHAN; Fort Le Boeuf HS; Erie, PA; (Y); 19/184; Spanish Clb; Band; Concert Band; Mrchg Band; Nwsp Stf; High Hon Roll; Hon Stu Pin 86; U Pittsburgh; Med.

SPAYD, CARL; Muhlenberg SR HS; Laureldale, PA; (Y); Service Clb; Mgr Trs Stage Crew; Var L Bowling; Hon Roll; NHS; Prfct Atten Awd; Outstndng Engl Awd 83-85; HS Cnty Chmpshp Tm 86; All Cnty Bwlng Tm 86; Math.

SPAYD, SANDRA; Hamburg Area HS; Hamburg, PA; (Y); Pres French Clb; Library Aide; Stat Bsktbl; Cheerleading; Hon Roll; Acad Ltr Awd Wrld Cultrs 84-85; Acad Awd Amer Cultrs 85-86; Pierce JC; Fash Merch.

SPEACE, AMY; Williamsport Area HS; Williamsport, PA; (S); #20 In Class; Sec Church Yth Grp; Key Clb; Chorus; Mrchg Band; School Musical; Swing Chorus; Lit Mag; NHS; Latin Clb; Acpl Chr; PA Govnrs Schl For Arts 85; PA Schl Press Assn Poet & Fictn 2 Keystones 85-86; 1st Pl Natl Spn Exam; Eastman Schl Music; Music.

SPEAK, STEVEN; Quaker Valley HS; Sewickley, PA; (Y); Boy Scts; Drama Clb; Key Clb; Political Wkr; Thesps; School Play; God Cntry Awd; PA Dist Outstndg Key Clb Lt Gov 85-86; PA Dist Key Clb Gov 86-87; Law.

SPEAR, MAUREEN; Bishop Hannan HS; Scranton, PA; (Y); Chorus; JV Cheerleading; High Hon Roll; Hon Roll; Hnrb Mntn Wrld Cltrs II; Exclnce In Frnch I & Alg II; Hnrb Mntn Chem & Engl III; Med.

SPEAREN, JOHN; Mapletown HS; Bobtown, PA; (Y); 13/85; Boys Clb Am; Varsity Clb; Band; Concert Band; Jazz Band; Mrchg Band; Var L Bsbl; Var L Ftbl; Wt Lftg; High Hon Roll; Mst Outstndng Music 84; Ldr WPAL Dbls & Runs Btd In Bsbl 86; Elec Engr.

SPEARMAN, CANTRICE HOPE; Roxborough HS; Philadelphia, PA; (Y); Church Yth Grp; Cmnty Wkr; Library Aide; Office Aide; Red Cross Aide; Teachers Aide; Chorus; Church Choir; Color Guard; Rep Soph Cls; Root Awd 83; Katherine Gibbs Schl; Comp Prcs.

SPEARS, MICHAEL; Lourdes Regional HS; Shamokin, PA; (Y); 26/99; Key Clb; Spanish Clb; Varsity Clb; Nwsp Stf; VP Soph Cls; VP Jr Cls; Var Bsktbl; Var Ftbl; Hon Roll; NHS; Duquesne U; Jrnlsm.

SPECHT, LEONARD; Susquenita HS; Duncannon, PA; (Y); Boys Clb Am; Boy Scts; 4-H; Band; Concert Band; Mrchg Band; Capt Socr; Trk; Hon Roll; Physcs.

SPECHT, MICHELLE; Greensburg Central Catholic HS; Mt Plasant, PA; (Y); Debate Tm; Ski Clb; SADD; Band; Rep Soph Cls; Stu Cncl; Im Sftbl; Im Trk; Im Vllybl.

SPECHT, SHANNON LEE; Tri-Valley HS; Hegins, PA; (Y); Pres Church Yth Grp; Pres Ski Clb; Sec Trs SADD; Sec Chorus; Concert Band; Drm Mjr(t); School Musical; VP Stu Cncl; Var L Cheerleading; Var L Vllybl; Hugh Obrien Outstndng Awd 84; Schylkill Cnty Chorus 85; Certified Life Guard & WSI Instructor 86; Lock Haven U; Med.

SPECK, RYAN; Mc Guffey HS; Washington, PA; (Y); 29/200; Boy Scts; German Clb; Yrbk Stf; NHS; Stu Rcgntn Awd 84&85; California U PA; Comp Sci.

SPECTOR, JILL; Springfield Township HS; Wyndmoor, PA; (Y); Aud/Vis; Library Aide; Sec Political Wkr; Temple Yth Grp; Chorus; Hon Roll; Spanish Clb; Bus.

SPECTOR, LARRY; Abington HS; Huntingdon Valley, PA; (Y); 28/535; Band; Nwsp Stf; Stu Cncl; Capt Swmmng; High Hon Roll; NHS; Pres Schlr; B Douglas McDevitt Mem Swmmng 86; U Of DE; Med.

SPEELMAN, VERONICA; Connellsville Area HS; Connellsville, PA; (Y); Trs Camera Clb; Office Aide; SADD; Chorus; Stage Crew; Rep Stu Cncl; High Hon Roll; Sawyer Schl; Bus.

SPEER, SHARON; Central Bucks West HS; Chalfont, PA; (Y); 18/386; VP Church Yth Grp; Sec Civic Clb; Acpl Chr; Chorus; Off Sr Cls; NHS; Pres Schlr; Soc Wmn Engrg Hghst Hon 86; YFU-FMC Smmr Schlrp To Netherlnds 84; Cnty Choir 85-86; PA St U; Sci.

SPEERHAS, TIMOTHY D; Western Beaver JR SR HS; Midland, PA; (Y); 4/80; Drama Clb; Nwsp Rptr; Yrbk Stf; Rep Stu Cncl; Capt Bsktbl; High Hon Roll; NHS; Pres Schlr; Keystone Boys ST 85; U Schlrshp 86; Athlt Awd 86; Duquesne U; Phrmcy.

SPEHAR, SHARON; N Allegheny SR HS; Pittsburgh, PA; (Y); 103/642; Ed Church Yth Grp; Hosp Aide; NFL; Hon Roll; Jr NHS; NHS; Frnch Awd Outstndng Stu; Hnrb Mntn X-Mas Card Cont; Gov Schl Art PA SF; Comm Art.

SPEICHER, BRENDA; Hempfield Area HS; Greensburg, PA; (Y); Pres French Clb; Rep Frsh Cls; Stu Cncl; JV Capt Cheerleading; High Hon Roll; Hon Roll; Jr NHS; Bus Finance.

SPEIGLE, NANCY; North Star HS; Boswell, PA; (Y); VP Church Yth Grp; FCA; Hosp Aide; Sec Math Clb; Cit Awd; High Hon Roll; Lion Awd; NHS; Rotary Awd; Pres Acad Ftnss Awd 86; Hon Mntn PTO Essy Cntst 86; E Mennonite Coll; Nrsg.

SPEISER, NANCY; New Hope-Solebury HS; New Hope, PA; (S); Band; Concert Band; Mrchg Band; Pep Band; School Musical; Rep Frsh Cls; Rep Soph Cls; Off Stu Cncl; Cheerleading; Hon Roll; Natl Hnr Scty 84-86; Hnrs Engl 80-86; Frnch.

SPELGATTI, CHERYL; Elizabethtown Area HS; Elizabethtown, PA; (Y); 10/237; Church Yth Grp; Spanish Clb; Varsity Clb; Var JV Cheerleading; Mgr(s); Var JV Pom Pon; Powder Puff Ftbl; NHS; Spanish NHS; Computer Clb; Med.

SPENCE, AMY; Penn Hills HS; Pittsburgh, PA; (S); Church Yth Grp; Library Aide; Trs Spanish Clb; Pres Acpl Chr; Church Choir; Capt Drill Tm; School Musical; Nwsp Stf; Chrmn Sr Cls; Stu Cncl; Minrty Schlrshp 86; Tuitn Schlrshp 86; U Of Dayton; Musc.

SPENCE, BECKY; Marion Center Area HS; Home, PA; (S); 1/168; Intnl Clb; Varsity Clb; Color Guard; Rep Stu Cncl; Var Diving; Var Gym; High Hon Roll; Jr NHS; NHS; Engrng.

SPENCE, CRYSTAL; Crestwood HS; Mountaintop, PA; (Y); FBLA; Co-Capt Cheerleading; Crs Cntry; Gym; Trk; Star Beauty Acad.

SPENCE, MARSHA; Marion Center Area HS; Creekside, PA; (S); 4/148; Church Yth Grp; Trs FBLA; Latin Clb; Library Aide; SADD; Teachers Aide; High Hon Roll; NHS; 1st Pl Acctng FBLA Rgnl Comptn 85; Sec.

SPENCER, AMY; York Catholic HS; York, PA; (Y); 7/166; French Clb; Chorus; Concert Band; Jazz Band; School Play; Nwsp Stf; Im Sftbl; Var L Trk; High Hon Roll; NHS; Hgh Scorer PSAT/NMSQT; Jrnlsm Awd; Aerospc Engrng.

SPENCER, CHARLES; Curwensville Area HS; Grampian, PA; (Y); Drama Clb; French Clb; Letterman Clb; Thesps; School Play; Stage Crew; Bsktbl; Ftbl; Golf; Penn ST; Psych.

SPENCER, DON; Lake-Lehman HS; Dallas, PA; (Y); Church Yth Grp; Letterman Clb; Var L Bsbl; Var L Ftbl; Var L Golf; Im Wt Lftg; Var L Wrstlng; Hon Roll; Srvy Engrng.

SPENCER, ERICK; Quigley HS; Mars, PA; (Y); Math Clb; JV Ftbl; Var Capt Wrstlng; Hon Roll; Bus.

SPENCER, JOHN; Canevin HS; Imperial, PA; (Y); 60/183; Ski Clb; School Musical; Yrbk Sprt Ed; Trs Stu Cncl; Var L Bsbl; Var L Ftbl; Hon Roll; Supr Achvt & Prof Test 84-85; Sci Dept Svc 85-86; Recruitmnt Pgm Svc 85-86; U Dayton; Sys Anlyst.

SPENCER, JOHN; Tunkhannock Area HS; Tunkhannock, PA; (Y); Band; Concert Band; Jazz Band; Mrchg Band; Var Bsbl; Hon Roll; NHS; Norm Ball Memrl Bsbl Schlrshp; Coachs Awd-Bsbl; Lttrmns Awd; Penn ST; Engrng.

SPENCER II, JOHN W; Owen J Roberts HS; Chester Spgs, PA; (Y); 14/252; Aud/Vis; Boy Scts; Library Aide; Var Swmmng; Hon Roll; NHS; Pres Schlr; Bucknell U; Ecmncs.

SPENCER, KEITH L; Troy SR HS; Canton, PA; (Y); 56/174; Am Leg Boys St; Letterman Clb; Varsity Clb; JV Var Bsbl; L Var Ftbl; Wt Lftg; Hon Roll; NHS.

SPENCER, SHANNON; Central Dauphin East HS; Harrisburg, PA; (Y); French Clb; Band; Chorus; Mrchg Band; School Musical; Variety Show; Nwsp Stf; Stu Cncl; Cheerleading; Twrlr; Comp Baton Twlr 1200 Trphys & 250 Mdls; Pre-Med.

SPENCER, STACEY; Wyalusing Valley JR SR HS; New Albany, PA; (Y); 23/153; Church Yth Grp; FBLA; German Clb; Chorus; Hghst Grd Pt Avg Bus Curriculum 86; 5th FBLA Cmptn Tstng Bus Engl 86; Pensacola Christian Coll; Bus.

SPENCER, SUSAN; Bishop Mc Devitt HS; Wyncote, PA; (S); 79/361; Camp Fr Inc; Church Yth Grp; Debate Tm; French Clb; NFL; SADD; School Play; Rep Frsh Cls; Rep Soph Cls; Powder Puff Ftbl; All-Str Bsktbl CYO; 4th Plc Tm PCFL; Spksprsn Cmpfr 85 Convntn KS; Commnctn.

SPENNATI, AMY; Aliquippa HS; Aliquippa, PA; (S); Art Clb; Drama Clb; French Clb; Band; Yrbk Stf; Rep Jr Cls; Cheerleading; Hon Roll; Aud/Vis; Church Yth Grp; U Pittsburgh; Elec Engr.

SPERANZA, PATRICK; Blairsville SR HS; Black Lick, PA; (Y); 7/130; Concert Band; Mrchg Band; Pep Band; School Musical; JV Golf; Var Trk; High Hon Roll; NHS; Prfct Atten Awd; Boy Scts; Schlr Ath; Gannon U; Mech Engr.

SPERLING, WENDI; Neshaminy HS; Trevose, PA; (Y); SADD; Varsity Clb; Yrbk Stf; Stu Cncl; Bsktbl; Mgr(s); Score Keeper; Swmmng; Tennis; Hon Roll; Bus.

SPERTZEL, SUSAN; Mechanicsburg Area SR HS; Mechanicsburg, PA; (Y); 99/311; Key Clb; Bsktbl; Mgr(s); Trk; Hon Roll.

SPICHER, CAROL; Ephrata SR HS; Ephrata, PA; (Y); 15/216; Pres Church Yth Grp; VP DECA; Pep Clb; Teachers Aide; Church Choir; Mgr(s); Vllybl; Hon Roll; NHS; Soc Distngshd Amer HS Stu 85 & 86; ENC Hnr Schlrshp 86; Hibshman Schlrshp 86; Estrn Nazarene Coll; Comp Sci.

SPICHER, DANA; Du Bois Area HS; Reynoldsville, PA; (Y); 48/280; Varsity Clb; Chorus; Vllybl; Hon Roll; Prfct Attndnc Awd 86; Mst Imprvd Athlt Swm Tm 83-84; Prsdntl Acdmc Ftns Awd 86; IN U Of PA; Crmnlgy.

SPICHIGER, LEA; Seneca HS; Northeast, PA; (Y); 19/173; Pres 4-H; Concert Band; Drill Tm; Mrchg Band; Orch; Yrbk Ed-Chief; Yrbk Stf; Co-Capt Pom Pon; Trk; 4-H Awd; Presdntl Ftns; Physcl Thrpy.

SPICKERMAN, NANCY; New Brighton Area SR HS; New Brighton, PA; (Y); 39/154; Church Yth Grp; Chorus; Flag Corp; School Play; Hon Roll; Pres Acad Ftns Awd 85-86.

SPIEGEL, ERIK; Mc Keesport Area HS; Mckeesport, PA; (Y); 84/339; Stage Crew; L Ftbl; L Trk; Wstrn PA Indstrl Arts Fair; Engrng.

SPIEWAK, JOSEPH; Father Judge HS; Philadelphia, PA; (Y); 76/403; Stage Crew; Im Bowling; JV Crs Cntry; Drexel U; Comp Sci.

SPIGELMYER, LEE; Selinsgrove Area HS; Selinsgrove, PA; (Y); Church Yth Grp; Drama Clb; Spanish Clb; Thesps; Band; Chorus; Church Choir; School Musical; School Play; Nwsp Rptr; Dist Chorus.

SPIGELMYER, TERESA; West Chester East HS; West Chester, PA; (Y); Hosp Aide; JCL; Color Guard; Hon Roll; Intrmrl Flr Hcky 84-86; Immaculata Coll; Nrsng.

SPILLERS, WENDE; Kiski Area HS; Apollo, PA; (Y); Girl Scts; Jazz Band; Mrchg Band; Pep Band; Symp Band; High Hon Roll; Hon Roll; Thiel Coll; Med.

SPILLMAN, SUE; Hatboro-Horsham HS; Hatboro, PA; (Y); 45/280; SADD; Var Fld Hcky; JV Sftbl; Cit Awd; High Hon Roll; NHS; Hugh O Brian Yth Ldrshp Smnr 84-85; Bio Awd 84-85; Cmrcl Artst.

SPINA, CHRISTINA; Canon Mc Millan HS; Canonsburg, PA; (Y); Library Aide; Ski Clb; Stage Crew; Nwsp Phtg; Nwsp Rptr; Yrbk Stf; Sftbl; Trk; Hon Roll; Cosmtlgy.

SPINALE, JOHN; Montour HS; Pittsburgh, PA; (Y); 7/308; Computer Clb; NFL; SADD; Powder Puff Ftbl; Var Socr; Var Wt Lftg; High Hon Roll; NHS; Ntl Merit SF; Fermi Awd Physcs 86; JR Acad Of Sci 86; Natl Sci Wk Hon 86; Med.

SPINAZZOLA, MARIA; Windber Area HS; Windber, PA; (Y); 13/112; Pres Library Aide; NFL; Sec Speech Tm; Concert Band; Mrchg Band; Sec School Play; Nwsp Rptr; Rep Stu Cncl; Var Vllybl; Hon Roll; Maple Princs 85-86; Stu Mth 83-86; CA U Of PA; Therputc Recreatn.

SPINDLER, DONNA; Scranton Central HS; Scranton, PA; (Y); Sec Girl Scts; JA; Orch; JV Bsktbl; Var Trk; Wilkes Coll; Acctnt.

SPINELLA, CHERYL; Mt Pleasant Area SR HS; Mt Pleasant, PA; (Y); Exploring; Girl Scts; Latin Clb; Band; Concert Band; Jazz Band; Mrchg Band; Rep Jr Cls; JV Var Bsktbl; Stat Mat Maids; Nrsng.

SPINELLI, DIANE; Shaler Area HS; Pgh, PA; (Y); 125/650; French Clb; JA; DAR Awd; High Hon Roll; Hon Roll; Jonell Schl Awd 84; Duquesne U; Mgr.

SPINELLI, JENNIFER; Highlands SR HS; Natrona Hts, PA; (Y); 4/280; Intnl Clb; Key Clb; Office Aide; Mrchg Band; Swmmng; High Hon Roll; Jr NHS; VP NHS; PA Jr Acad Of Sci Awd 86; Achvmnt Acad Awd Sci & Math 86; Chemistry.

SPIRITO, EUGENE J; La Salle College HS; Lafayette Hl, PA; (Y); 80/250; Capt Ftbl; Trk; Wt Lftg; Hon Roll; Villanova; Bus.

SPIRKO, JENNIFER; Mt Pleasant Area SR HS; Mt Pleasant, PA; (Y); GAA; Hosp Aide; Band; Concert Band; Mrchg Band; Yrbk Stf; Hon Roll; WCCC; Bus Mgmt.

SPISAK, CRAIG; Greensburg Central Catholic HS; W Newton, PA; (Y); Ski Clb; JV Var Bsbl; Var L Wrstlng; Hon Roll; ASVAB Tst Scr 94 86; Penn St U; Mech Engrg.

SPISAK, SAMANTHA; Greater Johnstown HS; Johnstown, PA; (Y); Church Yth Grp; Library Aide; Ski Clb; Spanish Clb; Jazz Band; Mrchg Band; Orch; Yrbk Phtg; Jr Cls; Hon Roll; Edinboro U; Photogrphy.

SPISHOCK, AMY; Downingtown HS; Exton, PA; (Y); GAA; Ski Clb; Spanish Clb; Chorus; L Bsktbl; Var Trk.

SPISHOCK, TERRI; Upper Darby HS; Upper Darby, PA; (Y); 121/649; Drill Tm; Orch; Cheerleading; Jr NHS; Delaware County CC; Psych.

SPLAIN, JOHN M; Columbia Boro JR SR HS; Columbia, PA; (Y); 2/84; Boy Scts; Pres Drama Clb; Band; Stage Crew; Nwsp Stf; Yrbk Phtg; Trs Stu Cncl; NHS; Ntl Merit SF; Eagle Scout 85; Acad All Am 85; Outstndng Physic Stu Yr 85; Physics.

SPOCK, SHAWN; Shamokin Area HS; Shamokin, PA; (Y); Boy Scts; Camera Clb; Chess Clb; Computer Clb; Science Clb; Ski Clb; Spanish Clb; SADD; Yrbk Stf; Crs Cntry.

SPOHN, KRISTIN; Aliguippa JR SR HS; Aliquippa, PA; (S); 5/154; Church Yth Grp; Exploring; French Clb; Math Tm; Concert Band; Mrchg Band; Yrbk Stf; Off Jr Cls; Off Sr Cls; Timer; Miss PA Teen USA Cont 85; Indiana U Of PA; Psych.

SPOLAR, RENEE; Ambridge Area HS; Baden, PA; (Y); Am Leg Aux Girls St; Pep Clb; Off Spanish Clb; Yrbk Stf; Mat Maids; JV Sftbl; JV Vllybl; High Hon Roll; Hon Roll; Mth.

SPONDIKE, JOHN; Sharpsville Area HS; Sharpsville, PA; (S); 48/120; Aud/Vis; Drama Clb; Thesps; Varsity Clb; Chorus; Concert Band; Jazz Band; School Musical; Stage Crew; Rep Stu Cncl; All Str Tm Ftbl 85-86; Radio/TV Brdcstng.

SPONSLER, LORI; Altoona Area HS; Altoona, PA; (Y); Band; Mrchg Band; Orch; Stu Cncl; Twrlr; Psych.

SPONSLER, ROBYN; Altoona Area HS; Altoona, PA; (S); 24/683; Band; Concert Band; Drm Mjr(t); Rep Sr Cls; Twrlr; NHS; U Of Pittsburgh; Phy Therapy.

SPOONHOUR, COREY; Chambersburg Area SR HS; Chambersburg, PA; (Y); Church Yth Grp; German Clb; Off Jr Cls; Var Bsbl; Var Bsktbl; High Hon Roll; Air Force Acad; Offcr.

SPORER, CATHY; Rocky Grove HS; Franklin, PA; (Y); 7/83; Library Aide; Chorus; School Musical; Ed Yrbk Stf; Frsh Cls; Stat Bsbl; Var Golf; Var Vllybl; NHS; Pres Acdmc Ftns Awd 85-86; PA ST U; Pre-Law.

SPORER, JULIE; Rocky Grove HS; Franklin, PA; (Y); 3/93; Library Aide; Var Golf; L Score Keeper; L Sftbl; JV Vllybl; High Hon Roll; VP NHS; Grls Golf Chmp-Dist 10 84-85; Grls St Golf Qlfr 83-85; Grls Golf-Dist 10 5th Pl 83.

SPORNER, DIANE; Elk County Christian HS; St Marys, PA; (Y); 21/80; Hosp Aide; Library Aide; Trs SADD; Yrbk Stf; Off Jr Cls; Stu Cncl; Hon Roll; Rotary Awd; Law Enfrcmnt.

SPOSSEY, CHERI; Uniontown Area HS; Ohiopyle, PA; (Y); 6/340; Computer Clb; French Clb; Mathletes; Pres Ski Clb; Nwsp Stf; Yrbk Stf; Stat Trk; French Hon Soc; VP NHS; St Vincent Ldrshp & Acdmc Schlrshps 86; St Vincent Coll; Bus Mgt.

SPOTTS, BETH; Penns Manor HS; Penn Run, PA; (Y); Q&S; Chorus; School Musical; Nwsp Bus Mgr; Nwsp Rptr; Nwsp Stf; High Hon Roll; NHS; NEDT Awd; Tribune Democrat Schltc Jrnlst Awd 86; Photo Clb 85-86; In U PA; Jrnlsm.

SPOTTS, DALE; Line Mountain HS; Dalmatia, PA; (Y); Church Yth Grp; Computer Clb; Lincoln Tech Inst; Elec.

SPOTTS, JEFF; Southern Columbia Area HS; Shamokin, PA; (Y); Church Yth Grp; Hosp Aide; Band; Chorus; Church Choir; School Play; Hon Roll; Messiah.

SPOTTS JR, RICHARD D; Seneca Valley SR HS; Renfrew, PA; (Y); 119/356; Art Clb; Drm & Bgl; Bsbl; Hon Roll; Art Awd Clmbia Schltc Prss Assoc 1st Awd Ill 83-84; Plbctn Rdr Rvw Clmbia Schltc Prss Assoc 85-86; U Of Pittsburgh; Engrng.

SPOTTS, STACEY K; Milton SR HS; Milton, PA; (Y); Spanish Clb; Varsity Clb; Band; Chorus; Concert Band; Yrbk Stf; Sec Soph Cls; Sec Jr Cls; Off Sr Cls; Stu Cncl; Dreifuss Schlrshp 86; Grad Spkr 86; Schlr Athlete Awd 86; Penn ST U; Bus.

SPOTTS, VINCENT J; Seneca Valley HS; Renfrew, PA; (Y); 13/372; Art Clb; Math Tm; Drm & Bgl; Var Bsbl; High Hon Roll; Hon Roll; NHS; Schltc Cert Awd Acad Achvt 84-85; Schltc Awd Acad Achvt 85-86; U Pittsburgh; Engrng.

SPOTTS, YVETTE; Elizabethtown Area HS; Elizabethtown, PA; (Y); Church Yth Grp; Church Choir; Mrchg Band; Yrbk Stf; Mgr(s); Twrlr; Reading Hosp Schl Of Nrsng; RN.

SPRAGUE, JEFFREY W; Cumberland Valley HS; Mechanicsburg, PA; (Y); 15/505; Church Yth Grp; Spanish Clb; Nwsp Rptr; Rep Stu Cncl; Hon Roll; NHS; Amer Legn Schlstc Awd 86; Acadmc Ltr Top 24 Clss 86; Balfour Awd Achvt Hstry 86; Le Tourneau Coll; Aviatn.

SPRAGUE, TAMMY; Du Bois Area HS; Du Bois, PA; (Y); Chorus; Capt Color Guard; Hon Roll; Clarion U; Elem Educ.

SPRANKLE, CONNIE; Elderton JR SR HS; Spg Church, PA; (Y); Camera Clb; Drama Clb; Library Aide; Science Clb; Spanish Clb; Band; Color Guard; Concert Band; School Play; Yrbk Phtg; Schlrshp For Full Paid Tuition To Pittsburgh Bty Acad 86; Pittsburgh Bty Acad; Bty Cltr.

SPRANKLE, DANE; Penns Manor HS; Penn Run, PA; (Y); Varsity Clb; Stage Crew; Ftbl; Trk; Hon Roll.

SPRANKLE, RONDA; Bellwood Antis HS; Altoona, PA; (Y); SADD; Chorus; School Musical; School Play; Variety Show; Lit Mag; Hon Roll; Chem Awd 85-86; K Pin 83-84; Tchg.

SPRAY, THOMAS R; Chartiers Valley HS; Pittsburgh, PA; (Y); 56/365; Nwsp Rptr; Nwsp Sprt Ed; Im Ice Hcky; Hnrbl Mntn Sprts Wrtng Awd Td 2nd Plc 86; Syracuse U; Tv-Radio.

SPRENGEL, SCOTT; Carlisle SR HS; Carlisle, PA; (Y); 4/410; Chorus; Concert Band; Jazz Band; Mrchg Band; Orch; School Musical; High Hon Roll; NHS; Dst Band 85-86; Eagle Sct 83; Arch.

SPRENKLE, GREG; Biglerville HS; Aspers, PA; (Y); 24/86; Church Yth Grp; Varsity Clb; L Bsbl; L Ftbl; L Trk; L Wrstlng; Hon Roll; Phys Ed.

SPRENKLE, LISA; Northeastern HS; Manchester, PA; (Y); Ski Clb; Sec Chorus; Color Guard; Off Frsh Cls; Trs Soph Cls; Trs Jr Cls; Cheerleading; High Hon Roll; Hon Roll; NHS; AP Engl Adv Plcmnt; Comm.

SPRENKLE, MELISSA; Waynesboro Area HS; Waynesboro, PA; (Y); Church Yth Grp; Library Aide; Pep Clb; Band; Chorus; Church Choir; Concert Band; Mrchg Band; Nwsp Stf; Bowling; Secy.

SPRESSER, REBECCA; Mc Keesport Area HS; Mckeesport, PA; (Y); 3/339; AFS; Pres Church Yth Grp; Concert Band; Mrchg Band; Orch; Symp Band; Hon Roll; NHS; Ntl Merit Ltr; Exploring; Med.

SPRING, PENNY; Hughesville HS; Muncy Valley, PA; (Y); 7/132; Am Leg Aux Girls St; Pres Church Yth Grp; 4-H; Sec Key Clb; Chorus; Rep Jr Cls; Cit Awd; DAR Awd; High Hon Roll; Sec NHS; Green & White Awd; Cedar Crest Coll; Engl.

SPRINGER, CHARLES; Cardinal Dougherty HS; Phila, PA; (Y); 5/774; Exploring; Latin Clb; Nwsp Stf; L Golf; High Hon Roll; NHS; Pres Schlr; St Josephs UPRE-MED.

SPRINGER, DEBRA; Oxford Area HS; Oxford, PA; (Y); 18/161; FTA; Sec Band; Chorus; Drm Mjr(t); Jazz Band; JV Var Vllybl; Hon Roll; JP Sousa Awd; NHS; Church Yth Grp; Rotary SR Mnth 86; Elizabeth M Krendal Memrl Schlrshp 86; Millersville U; Elem Ed.

SPRINGER, MARY; Fort Cherry HS; Bulger, PA; (Y); 32/130; Cmnty Wkr; Drama Clb; Math Clb; Science Clb; Varsity Clb; Chorus; Drill Tm; School Play; Yrbk Stf; NHS; Carlow Coll; Elem Ed.

SPRINGMAN, JILL; Montoursville Area HS; Montoursville, PA; (Y); Sec Church Yth Grp; Exploring; FBLA; German Clb; Stat Bsktbl; Var Tennis; Hon Roll; NHS; Pres Acad Fit Awd 86; Chrissie Mayr Awd 86; Bloomsburg U; Acctg.

SPRINGMAN, JULIE; Beaver HS; Beaver, PA; (Y); 40/200; Sec German Clb; Pep Clb; Chorus; Nwsp Rptr; Var Swmmng; Capt Twrlr; Pres Schlr; Slippery Rock U; Elem Ed.

SPROULL, NADINE; Punxsutawney HS; Punxsutawney, PA; (Y); Church Yth Grp; Spanish Clb; Varsity Clb; Y-Teens; Band; Church Choir; Jazz Band; Mrchg Band; Pep Band; Variety Show; IN U; Speech Thrpy.

SPROW, MICHAEL; Governor Mifflin HS; Shillington, PA; (Y); 13/285; Varsity Clb; JV Im Bsktbl; JV Var Socr; Var Trk; High Hon Roll; JC Awd; Gvnr Mifflin Hnr Soc 86; Shillington Rotary Clb Boy Of Month 86.

SPRUMONT, MARIE; Steel Valley HS; Munhall, PA; (Y); 8/207; Exploring; Girl Scts; JCL; Pres Key Clb; Band; Concert Band; Rep Mrchg Band; NHS; Slvr Str Grl Scts 83; Bus Adm.

SQUADRITO, DARIA; St Maria Goretti HS; Philadelphia, PA; (Y); 111/409; Computer Clb; FBLA; Key Clb; Letterman Clb; Mathletes; Spanish Clb; SADD; Hon Roll; Accntng.

SQUILLANTE, SHEILA; St Maria Goretti HS; Philadelphia, PA; (Y); 80/390; GAA; JA; Mathletes; Math Clb; Math Tm; Spanish Clb; Teachers Aide; Nwsp Rptr; School Play; Variety Show; Hon Men Awd Bus; Tri M Music Hnr Soc; Comm.

SQUIRE, RAMONA; Germantown HS; Philadelphia, PA; (Y); Boys Clb Am; Church Yth Grp; Dance Clb; Drama Clb; Girl Scts; Church Choir; School Play; Stage Crew; VP Jr Cls; Hon Roll; Charles Elliss Schlrship 83-84; Communications.

SRBINOVICH, MICHAEL; Mapletown HS; Bobtown, PA; (Y); 8/84; Chess Clb; French Clb; Letterman Clb; Varsity Clb; Var L Bsbl; Var L Bsktbl; Var L Ftbl; High Hon Roll; Hon Roll; Sec NHS; Vrsty Bsbl MVP Awd 84-85; Accntng.

SRINIVASAN, VASANTHI; Upper Darbyl HS; Upper Darby, PA; (Y); 45/629; Cmnty Wkr; Rep Frsh Cls; Rep Soph Cls; High Hon Roll; Hon Roll; Distngshd Hnr Rll 84-86; U Of VA; Engrng.

SRIVASTAVA, BOB; Penn Trafford HS; Export, PA; (Y); Chess Clb; French Clb; Yrbk Stf; Hon Roll; Prfct Atten Awd; Elec Engr.

ST AMANT, KELLY; Rocky Grove HS; Franklin, PA; (Y); 22/92; Church Yth Grp; Hosp Aide; Band; Chorus; Concert Band; Pep Band; Yrbk Stf; Stu Cncl; Var L Vllybl; Hon Roll; Penn ST; Mngmnt.

ST CLAIR, JILL; Langley HS; Pittsburgh, PA; (Y); 56/278; Dance Clb; Drama Clb; Color Guard; Drill Tm; Drm Mjr(t); Mrchg Band; School Musical; School Play; Yrbk Stf; Pres Frsh Cls; Penn ST-BEAVER; Psychlgy.

ST CLAIR JR, RICHARD; Frankford HS; Philadelphia, PA; (Y); Yrbk Stf; High Hon Roll; Hon Roll; NHS; Prfct Atten Awd; Drexel; Comp Sci.

ST CLAIR JR, ROBERT; Southern Huntingdon County HS; Blairs Mills, PA; (Y); 4/118; Rptr FBLA; Pres Spanish Clb; Band; Chorus; Concert Band; Jazz Band; Mrchg Band; School Musical; Yrbk Stf; Trs NHS; Hnr Rl 84-86; VFW Essay Awd 86; Supr Staffer Awd Schl Nswpr 86; Shippensburg U.

STAAB, RACHEL; Carlynton HS; Carnegie, PA; (Y); Church Yth Grp; French Clb; Hosp Aide; Yrbk Stf; Swmmng; Hon Roll; Duquesne U.

STABILE, MICHELE; Canevin HS; Carnegie, PA; (Y); 6/183; Co-Capt Drill Tm; Jazz Band; School Play; Nwsp Ed-Chief; High Hon Roll; Pres Schlr; Loyola Coll.

STABILE III, PAUL F; Canon Mac Millan HS; Canonsburg, PA; (Y); 55/390; Spanish Clb; L Tennis; JV Wrstlng; High Hon Roll; Hon Roll; CA ST Lang Cntst 85-86; Duquesne U; Comm.

STABS, STEVEN; Cedar Crest HS; Cornwall, PA; (Y); 11/363; German Clb; Pep Clb; Im Vllybl; Hon Roll; NHS; Ntl Merit Ltr; Hrmn Esnhr Fmly Schlrshp 86; PA ST U; Chem Engnrng.

STACEY, ROBERT; Altoona Area HS; Altoona, PA; (S); Political Wkr; Q&S; Nwsp Ed-Chief; Nwsp Rptr; Lit Mag; Stu Cncl; Var Crs Cntry; Var Trk; Ntl Merit Ltr; NEDT Awd; Pre-Law.

STACHACZ, JAMES; Bishop O Hara HS; Dickson City, PA; (S); 13/129; Church Yth Grp; Cmnty Wkr; Pep Clb; Ski Clb; Chorus; High Hon Roll; Hon Roll; NHS; Prfct Atten Awd; Meteorlgy.

STACHEL, WENDY; Scranton HS; Scranton, PA; (Y); Pres VP Soph Cls; Pres Girl Scts; Spanish Clb; Band; Concert Band; Mrchg Band; Yrbk Phtg; Yrbk Stf; Stat Swmmng; Hon Roll; Finc.

STACKHOUSE, KRISTIN; Pen Argyl HS; Nazareth, PA; (Y); 25/166; Pep Clb; Ski Clb; Spanish Clb; SADD; Varsity Clb; Chorus; Cheerleading; Sftbl; Hon Roll; Prfct Atten Awd; Bloomsburg U; Elem Ed.

STACKONIS, CLIFFORD; GAR Memorial HS; Wilkes Barre, PA; (S); 4/177; Church Yth Grp; Ski Clb; Rep Stu Cncl; Capt Tennis; High Hon Roll; NHS; Penn St; Engr.

STACKPOLE, JULIE; Central Bucks East HS; Furlong, PA; (Y); Band; Hon Roll; Frgn Lang.

STACKPOLE, PATRICK; Elk Christian HS; St Marys, PA; (Y); 39/80; Aud/Vis; Library Aide; Model UN; Office Aide; Ski Clb; Bowling; Ftbl; Golf; L Wrstlng; High Hon Roll; Marine Vtrnrn.

STADE, WILLIAM R; Strath Haven HS; Wallingford, PA; (Y); Church Yth Grp; Exploring; Red Cross Aide; Ski Clb; Spanish Clb; JV Capt Bsktbl; Var Socr; Var Socr; Im Wt Lftg; Hon Roll; Stu Advsry Cncl 85, 86; Bldmble Chrmn 84-86; Acadmc Vrsty Ltr 84-86.

STADTMILLER, SHARON; Technical Memorial HS; Erie, PA; (Y); 7/365; Yrbk Stf; High Hon Roll; NHS; Ntl Hnr Scty 85-86; Comp.

STADTMUELLER, TERESA; Harborcreek HS; Erie, PA; (Y); 8/228; VP AFS; 4-H; Model UN; Mrchg Band; Mgr Variety Show; High Hon Roll; Hon Roll; NHS; Ntl Merit Ltr; Concert Band; Rtry Yth Lead Awd Cnfrnc; Pltcl Scnc.

STAFF JR, DAVID; Butler Area SR HS; Butler, PA; (Y); 90/731; Church Yth Grp; Exploring; Chorus; Church Choir; Stage Crew; Swing Chorus; Butler Cnty Cmnty Clg; Metro.

STAFFA, JAMES; James M Coughlin HS; Hudson, PA; (Y); 35/355; Drama Clb; Key Clb; School Play; Yrbk Stf; NHS; Phrmcy.

STAFFORD, CHRISTIE; Canon-Mc Millan HS; Clearwater, FL; (Y); Church Yth Grp; Acpl Chr; Chorus; Church Choir; High Hon Roll; Hon Roll; Washington Cnty Chorus 84-86; Hm Ec Awd 83-84; Dntl Asst.

STAFFORD, DARLENE MARIE; Norristown Area HS; Norristown, PA; (Y); Church Yth Grp; FBLA; Teachers Aide; VICA; Chorus; Church Choir; Variety Show; Hon Roll; Prfct Atten Awd; Montgomery CC; Comp.

STAFFORD, JAMES; Reynolds HS; Greenville, PA; (Y); L Bsktbl; Wt Lftg; High Hon Roll; Hon Roll; Pres Schlr; Mercer Cnty Vo-Tech Data Prcsng SR Of Yr 86; PA ST; Comp Sci.

STAGER, STACY; Bishop Carroll HS; Portage, PA; (S); 18/102; Cmnty Wkr; Pep Clb; Ski Clb; Spanish Clb; Off Jr Cls; Mgr Cheerleading; Hon Roll; Bus.

STAGGERS, MARCY; Southmoreland HS; Alverton, PA; (Y); Church Yth Grp; French Clb; Ski Clb; Church Choir; Comp.

STAHERSKI, MARCIA L; Penn Manor HS; Conestoga, PA; (Y); Varsity Clb; Rep Jr Cls; Rep Sr Cls; JV Var Bsktbl; JV Var Tennis; Hon Roll; NHS; Mst Outstndng Fml Hlth Physcl Ed Stu 86; Shippensburg U.

STAHL IV, CHARLES H; W Mifflin Area HS; W Mifflin, PA; (Y); Ski Clb; Band; Mrchg Band; Tennis; Wrstlng; Hon Roll; Church Yth Grp; Key Clb; Variety Show; Trk; Naval Acad; Aviator.

STAHL, JESSICA; Meyersdale Area HS; Meyersdale, PA; (S); Trs Spanish Clb; Concert Band; Yrbk Stf; Sec Stu Cncl; JV Var Bsktbl; Stat Ftbl; Var Sftbl; Var Vllybl; NEDT Awd; Mrchg Band; Smrst All Cnty Sftbl Tm-Hnrb Mntn & 2nd Tm; Penn ST U; Comm.

STAHL, SUE; Somerset Area SR HS; Somerset, PA; (Y); 69/239; English Clb; Trs Spanish Clb; Stu Cncl; Mgr Bsktbl; Hon Roll; Commun.

STAHL, SUSAN; Holy Name HS; Sinking Spring, PA; (Y); VP JA; Sec Office Aide; Band; Capt Drill Tm; School Musical; Lit Mag; Rep Stu Cncl; Dale Carnegie Schlrshp Human Relat 85; March Dimes Hosp Intenshp Schlrshp 85; Regotn & Svc Awd 86; St Francis; Med.

STAHL, TERRY; Mt Pleasant Area HS; Acme, PA; (Y); 75/243; Chess Clb; Church Yth Grp; French Clb; Library Aide; High Hon Roll; Hon Roll.

STAHLE, RACHEL; Dallastown Area HS; Dallastown, PA; (Y); 28/353; Am Leg Aux Girls St; Church Yth Grp; Church Choir; Nwsp Ed-Chief; Lit Mag; High Hon Roll; Hon Roll; Art Clb; Cmnty Wkr; Pep Clb; Multi Lvl Sci Fair Wnnr 84; Dmstc Exchng 86; Stu Of Mnth 85; Clarion U PA; Engl.

STAHLER, KATRINA; Tamaqua Area HS; Andreas, PA; (Y); 13/180; Church Yth Grp; Drama Clb; Pres 4-H; Library Aide; Nwsp Stf; Hon Roll; NHS; Grmn Ntl Hnr Soc 85-86; Bio.

STAHLER, LAURA; New Freedom Christian HS; New Freedom, PA; (S); 2/9; Church Yth Grp; Debate Tm; German Clb; Church Choir; Bsktbl; Score Keeper; Socr; Sftbl; Vllybl; Hon Roll; 8th Pl Schl Sci Fair Hon Men 86; Hon Recog Submit Art Drwg 85; Tchg.

STAHLER, SARAH; Lehigh Christian Acad; Slatington, PA; (S); 4/14; Sec Church Yth Grp; Chorus; Sftbl; Capt Vllybl; Hon Roll; Alg II Bible 84-85; Outstndng Christian Test 84-85; Natl Math Awd 84-85; Pinebrook JC; Math.

STAHLEY, DEBORAH L; Perkiomen Valley HS; Schwenksville, PA; (Y); VP Church Yth Grp; 4-H; Girl Scts; Model UN; VP SADD; Teachers Aide; Band; Church Choir; Concert Band; Mrchg Band; Stu Of Mo 84; Ithaca; Biology.

STAHLMAN, DANIEL; Punxsutawney Area HS; Punxsutawney, PA; (Y); Church Yth Grp; CAP; French Clb; Math Tm; Science Clb; Teachers Aide; Im Bsktbl; JV Golf; Hon Roll; NHS; Comp Sci.

STAHLMAN, JOSEPH; Oil City HS; Oil City, PA; (Y); 35/260; German Clb; Im Wrstlng; Intl Bus.

STAHLSMITH, JULIE; Freeport Area SR HS; Worthington, PA; (S); 14/170; Hosp Aide; Nwsp Rptr; Yrbk Stf; High Hon Roll; Grove City Coll; Elem Ed.

STAHOVEC, MARIA; Bishop O Reilly HS; Dallas, PA; (Y); 1/106; JP Sousa Awd; Sec NHS; Ntl Merit Ltr; Val; Chorus; Pres Concert Band; Pres Jazz Band; Pres Mrchg Band; Stage Crew; Schlrshp Penn ST 86; Penn ST; Actural Sci.

STAHOVIAK, APRIL; Moniteau JR ST HS; Karns City, PA; (Y); Pres Church Yth Grp; Drama Clb; French Clb; Band; Concert Band; Mrchg Band; School Musical; Nwsp Stf; Ed Lit Mag; Cit Awd.

STAINS, BRENT; Greencastle-Antrim HS; Chambersburg, PA; (Y); Church Yth Grp; French Clb; Rep Soph Cls; VP Jr Cls; Rep Stu Cncl; JV Bsbl; JV Bsktbl; Hon Roll; Cert Achvmnt Outstndng Wrk Physcl Sci 84; Cert Achvmnt A Avg Wrld Cltrs 84; Engr.

STAIRS, ANN; Hempfield HS; Monheim, PA; (Y); 125/418; Church Yth Grp; 4-H; Sec Varsity Clb; Yrbk Phtg; Rep Frsh Cls; Hst Soph Cls; Hst Jr Cls; Hst Sr Cls; JV Bsktbl; Var L Crs Cntry; Hugh O Brian Yth Ldrshp Conf 85; People To People 86; Bus.

STAKE, BRAD; Chambersburg Area SR HS; Chambersburg, PA; (Y); 23/648; Orch; Tennis; High Hon Roll; Hon Roll; Instctr-Chambersburg Area Recrtn Dept Ten Cmp Smmrs 85 & 86; Shippensburg U; Bus Admin.

STAKELBEAK, FRED; Cardinal Dougherty HS; Phila, PA; (Y); 278/756; Am Leg Boys St; Church Yth Grp; FCA; Office Aide; SADD; Rep Soph Cls; Trs Sr Cls; Stu Cncl; Var Bsktbl; Var Ftbl; Crwprsn Month Mc Donalds 86; Temple U; Crmnl Just.

STALES, PAUL; Mastbaum AVTS HS; Philadelphia, PA; (Y); High Hon Roll; Hon Roll; Engnrng.

STALINSKY, RICKI; Allderdice HS; Pittsburgh, PA; (Y); French Clb; JCL; Latin Clb; Temple Yth Grp; Nwsp Ed-Chief; Mgr(s); Vllybl; Hon Roll; Vol Hosp 83-84; Genertns Tgthr 85-86; Ed.

STALLONE, KAREN M; Bristol JR/SR HS; Bristol, PA; (Y); 19/102; Sec Civic Clb; Dance Clb; Drama Clb; Sec Intnl Clb; Political Wkr; Yrbk Bus Mgr; Trs Sr Cls; Hst Stu Cncl; Capt Cheerleading; Capt Pom Pon; Free Entrprs Fllwshp Pgm 85; Vly Forge Freedms Fndtn 85; Trvl Clb Schlrshp 86; Moravian Coll; Hstry.

STALNAKER, ANN; West Greene HS; New Freeport, PA; (Y); FFA; SADD; Nwsp Rptr; Yrbk Rptr; Hon Roll; Oratory Awd 84; German I Awd 85; Art Educ.

STALSITZ, KRISTIN; Allentown Central Catholic HS; Emmaus, PA; (Y); 56/210; Church Yth Grp; French Clb; Math Clb; Pep Clb; Ski Clb; Rep Frsh Cls; Rep Sr Cls; Rep Stu Cncl; Im Mgr Vllybl; Hon Roll; 2nd Pl PA JR Acad Of Sci 84; Bus.

STALTER, LORI; Tamagua Area HS; Andreas, PA; (Y); Band; Chorus; Concert Band; Jazz Band; Mrchg Band; Score Keeper; Trk; Hon Roll; Kutztown U; Bus Mgmt.

STAM, MELISSA; Cardinal O Hara HS; Glenolden, PA; (Y); 108/740; Church Yth Grp; Cmnty Wkr; French Clb; Service Clb; School Musical; School Play; Yrbk Stf; Hon Roll; VP Comm Ser Corps; Immclta Coll Acdmc Schlrshp; Yth & The Pltcl Sys Smnr At Lasalle Coll; Immaculata Coll; Hstry.

STAMBAUGH, DENISE; Hatboro-Horsham HS; Hatboro, PA; (Y); 47/300; Trs Key Clb; Band; Concert Band; Jazz Band; Mrchg Band; Variety Show; Pre-Med.

STAMBAUGH, ERIC; Northern JR/SR HS; Wellsville, PA; (Y); 15/210; Chorus; Church Choir; School Musical; Stage Crew; JV Socr; French Hon Soc; Hon Roll; Engrng.

STAMBAUGH, KAREN; York Catholic HS; Dover, PA; (Y); 13/166; Pep Clb; Spanish Clb; Varsity Clb; Chorus; School Musical; Var Trk; JV Vllybl; High Hon Roll; Hon Roll; NHS; Concert Choir; Orthodontics.

STAMBAUGH, LISA; Central York SR HS; Emigsville, PA; (Y); 26/248; Church Yth Grp; Hosp Aide; JA; Chorus; Yrbk Stf; Trk; Hon Roll; NHS; Pres Acdmc Ftns Awd 85-86; Marine Corps Lg St Schlrhsp 85-86; Lancaster Genl Hosp Schl; Nrsng.

STAMBAUGH, PAIGE; Homburg Area HS; Strausstown, PA; (Y); Church Yth Grp; French Clb; Hosp Aide; Ski Clb; Spanish Clb; SADD; Yrbk Stf; Hon Roll; JV Bsktbl; JV Fld Hcky; Sci.

STAMBAUGH, STEVE; Central SR HS; York, PA; (Y); Pep Clb; Ski Clb; Capt L Socr; Hon Roll; Arch Engrng.

STAMETS, DAWN; Elkland Area HS; Osceola, PA; (Y); Church Yth Grp; Trs Sec Dance Clb; Pres VP 4-H; Pres Sec French Clb; SADD; Yrbk Rptr; Yrbk Stf; 4-H Awd; High Hon Roll; Hon Roll; Vet.

STAMM, TAMMY; Milton SR HS; Milton, PA; (Y); 30/213; Intnl Clb; Color Guard; School Musical; Nwsp Stf; Yrbk Stf; Rep Jr Cls; Rep Stu Cncl; Var Capt Cheerleading; JV Fld Hcky; Acctng.

STANCAVAGE, ROBINANNE; Mt Carmel Area JR/SR HS; Mt Carmel, PA; (Y); 8/168; Key Clb; Spanish Clb; Nwsp Rptr; Nwsp Stf; Lit Mag; Var L Bsktbl; Var L Sftbl; High Hon Roll; NHS; Ntl Merit Ltr; Outstndng Defnsv Awd Sftbll; OM Tm 2nd Plc ST Comptn Mousembl; OM Tm 2nd Plc Regnl Comp; Bucknell U; Engr.

STANCZAK, GREGORY C; Harbor Creek HS; Erie, PA; (Y); 20/206; Church Yth Grp; Band; Concert Band; Mrchg Band; Pres Pep Band; Variety Show; Hon Roll; VP NHS; Ntl Merit Ltr; Kent ST U Pres Schlrshp; Kent ST U; Psych.

STANCZAK, KIMBERLY; Pittston Area SR HS; Inkerman, PA; (Y); 62/365; French Clb; Ski Clb; Sftbl; X-Ray Tech.

STANEK, JENNIFER; Mt Pleasant Area HS; Woodbridge, VA; (Y); Debate Tm; Latin Clb; Library Aide; Ed Nwsp Stf; Im Vllybl; High Hon Roll; Hon Roll; Trs NHS; Psych.

STANEK, ROSS; Farrell Area HS; Farrell, PA; (Y); Var English Clb; French Clb; Pres Science Clb; Varsity Clb; Yrbk Rptr; Rep Frsh Cls; Rep Stu Cncl; JV Var Bsktbl; High Hon Roll; NHS; Comp.

STANFORD, ANTHONY; Thomas A Edison HS; Philadelphia, PA; (Y); Art Clb; Church Yth Grp; FCA; Church Choir; Lyons Inst; Elec Tech.

STANFORD, STACEY; Purchase Line HS; Burnside, PA; (Y); Church Yth Grp; Cmnty Wkr; FBLA; Chorus; School Musical; Spanish Clb; Gym; Hon Roll; NSMA Sci Awd; Gym Shw; Physcl Thrpy.

STANGE, REBECCA; Clarion-Limestone HS; Strattanville, PA; (Y); 3/85; Sec Band; School Play; Lit Mag; Sec Jr Cls; Pres Sr Cls; Var L Cheerleading; NHS; Ntl Merit SF; Hgh Obrn Yth Ldrshp Awd 885; Rtry Yth Ldrshp Awd 86.

STANGIL, TERRY; Northwestern Lehigh HS; Schnecksville, PA; (Y); German Clb; Yrbk Stf; Var Bsbl; Co-Capt Ice Hcky; Hon Roll; Lock Haven U; Athltc Trnng.

STANICKYJ, LISA; St Basil Acad; Philadelphia, PA; (Y); German Clb; GAA; Chorus; Im Bsktbl; Ntl Merit Ltr; Charles Ellis Schlrshp Fnd 84 & 85; Pre-Med.

STANIEC, ALYCIA; Nazareth Acad; Langhorne, PA; (Y); Church Yth Grp; VP Cmnty Wkr; Q&S; Nwsp Ed-Chief; Im Bsktbl; Dnfth Awd; NHS; Jrnlsm Awd 86; U Of PA; Med.

STANISLAW, LAURA; Southmoreland HS; Everson, PA; (Y); Sec Trs German Clb; Pep Clb; Ski Clb; Yrbk Stf; Rep Stu Cncl; Var Powder Puff Ftbl; Var Sftbl; Humanities German Rcltn Awd 84; German Natl Hnr Soc 85-86; California U Of PA; Elem Ed.

STANISLAWCZYK, PETER; Governor Muffin HS; Shillington, PA; (Y); 22/300; Varsity Clb; Im Bsbl; Im Bsktbl; Var Trk; Var L Wrstlng; Hon Roll; Pre-Dntl.

STANKO, SAMANTHA; Sheffield Area JRSR HS; Tiona, PA; (Y); 19/96; FBLA; Varsity Clb; Concert Band; Pep Band; School Musical; Pres Mat Maids; Stat Wrstlng; Hon Roll; NHS; VFW Awd; Jamestown Bus Coll; Acctng.

STANLEY, KATCHA; Elizabethtown Area HS; Rheems, PA; (Y); 25/250; Varsity Clb; Rep Soph Cls; Stu Cncl; Bsktbl; Var JV Fld Hcky; Var JV Sftbl; Wt Lftg; Hon Roll; NHS; Most Imprvd Fld Hcky Awd 84-85; NY U; Intl Finance.

STANLEY, SHEILA; St Pius X HS; Royersford, PA; (Y); French Clb; Nwsp Rptr; Nwsp Stf; Rep Frsh Cls; Var Cheerleading; Hon Roll.

STANSKI, STAN; James M Coughlin HS; Plains, PA; (Y); Art Clb; Aud/Vis; Camera Clb; Chess Clb; Variety Show; Var L Ftbl; CC Awd; Ntl Schlstc Photo Porfolio Fnlst 85; Art Design Schlrshp 86; Keystone Pres Schrlshp 86; Temple U; Graphic Design.

STANTON, FREDERICK; Susquehanna Community HS; Susquehanna, PA; (S); Hon Roll; NHS.

STANTON, KELLY; Wyalusing Valley HS; Wyalusing, PA; (Y); 20/152; Camera Clb; Ski Clb; Spanish Clb; Stat Bsbl; Capt Twrlr; Hon Roll; NHS; Rotary Awd; Trs Frsh Cls; Trs Soph Cls; Psych.

STANTON II, LUTHER; Wilson Area HS; Easton, PA; (S); 1/138; Computer Clb; Exploring; Model UN; Capt Scholastic Bowl; Ed Yrbk Stf; Score Keeper; High Hon Roll; NHS; Lehigh U; Elec Engr.

STANULIS, BARBARA; Wyoming Area SR HS; Yatesville, PA; (Y); Church Yth Grp; French Clb; Color Guard; Flag Corp; Rep Stu Cncl; High Hon Roll; NHS.

STANULIS, JACQUELINE; Wyoming Valley West HS; Swoyersville, PA; (Y); Girl Scts; Science Clb; Teachers Aide; Chorus; School Musical; Bsktbl; Ftbl; L Mgr(s); High Hon Roll; Hon Roll; LCCC; Nrsg.

STANWOOD, GREGG; Archbishop Kennedy HS; Conshohocken, PA; (Y); 5/170; Service Clb; Trk; Hon Roll; Spnsh Awd 85-86.

STAPH, ALLISON; Pocono Mountain SR HS; Pocono Pines, PA; (Y); JA; Math Tm; Pep Clb; Chorus; Yrbk Stf; Trk; Wt Lftg; Hon Roll; Ntl Chem Olympd Fnlst 84; Outstndng VP Prdctn Yr 85; Fnlst Rssl C Hghs Splng Bee 85; West Chestere U; Comp Sci.

STAPLETON, MARY ANN; United HS; Indiana, PA; (Y); 34/129; Art Clb; Pres FBLA; Pep Clb; Ski Clb; Drill Tm; Trs Jr Cls; High Hon Roll; Hon Roll; Prfct Atten Awd; 1st Pl Rgn 3 Comp Ms FBLA 86; 3rd Pl Rgn 3 Comp Clerk Typist 85; IN U Of PA; Accntng.

STAPLETON, MAUREEN; Central Bucks High School East; Doylestown, PA; (Y); 37/468; Church Yth Grp; Natl Beta Clb; Service Clb; School Musical; Nwsp Rptr; Rep Stu Cncl; Var Capt Crs Cntry; Var Trk; High Hon Roll; Hon Roll; Hgh Obrn Yth Fndtn 85.

STARCESKI, MARY; St Francis Acad; Pittsburgh, PA; (S); 6/34; Chorus; School Play; Rep Frsh Cls; Rep Soph Cls; Rep Jr Cls; Pres Stu Cncl; Var Capt Vllybl; High Hon Roll; NHS; PA ST U; Cmmnctns.

STARCHVILLE JR, THOMAS F; Windber HS; Windber, PA; (S); 3/113; Drama Clb; NFL; Acpl Chr; Concert Band; Jazz Band; Mrchg Band; School Play; Yrbk Ed-Chief; Rep Jr Cls; Var L Golf; Stu Of Yr 84; Stu Of Mnth; Penn ST U; Aerspc Engrng.

STARK, ROBERT; Norwin SR HS; N Huntingdon, PA; (Y); 77/560; Pres Computer Clb; VP Band; Chorus; Concert Band; Jazz Band; Mrchg Band; Stage Crew; 2nd Pl-PA Intrmdt Comp Pgmmng Cntst 84; Outstndng Musicn 86; Comp Sci.

STARK, SARAH; Tunkhannock Area HS; Mehoopany, PA; (S); 28/320; Pres Sec 4-H; Yrbk Bus Mgr; Crs Cntry; Trk; 4-H Awd; Hon Roll; Bloomsburg; Elem Ed.

STARK, SEAN; Saucon Valley SR HS; Hellertown, PA; (Y); Library Aide; PAVAS; Band; Bowling; L Ftbl; Swmmng; L Trk; Wt Lftg; L Wrstlng; Prfct Atten Awd; Phy Ed.

STARK, TODD; General Mc Lane HS; Edinboro, PA; (Y); Boy Scts; Ski Clb; Spanish Clb; Pres Chorus; School Musical; Swing Chorus; Swmmng; High Hon Roll; Hon Roll; NHS; Ltr Chrus 86; PA ST U; Engrng.

STARMACK, THOMAS J; West Mifflin Area HS; W Mifflin, PA; (Y); 53/317; Pres Church Yth Grp; Ftbl; Capt Golf; Hon Roll; SAT Math Awd 86; U Dayton; Sec Educ.

STARNER, MELISSA; Pocono Mountain HS; Tannersville, PA; (Y); 7/328; Pres Frsh Cls; Pres Soph Cls; Pres Jr Cls; Rep Stu Cncl; JV Var Fld Hcky; Trk; High Hon Roll; Hon Roll; NHS; Stu Ldrshp Awd 83-84.

STARNER, TAMALA; Southwestern HS; Hanover, PA; (Y); 7/207; Church Yth Grp; Chorus; Church Choir; Flag Corp; Mrchg Band; School Musical; Hon Roll; NHS; Pres Acdmc Fit Awd 86; Stu Rtrn 86; Cert Of Schlstc Rcgntn Frm Exchng Clb Of Hanover 86.

STARR, CHRISSY; Brockway Area HS; Brockway, PA; (Y); 18/87; Chorus; Nwsp Ed-Chief; Nwsp Rptr; Nwsp Stf; Hon Roll; Cert Of Prfcncy Accntng 85-86; Clarion U Of PA; Accntng.

STARR, JEAN; Saint Maria Goretti HS; Philadelphia, PA; (S); 3/450; Sec Trs Church Yth Grp; VP Service Clb; Nwsp Rptr; Rep Soph Cls; Rep Jr Cls; Pres Sr Cls; Im Bsktbl; High Hon Roll; NHS; Prfct Atten Awd; Spnsh, Ltn, & Engl Awds 83-85; Cthlc Yth Orgnztn Awds 83-85; Natl Trnng Inst Ldrshp & Serv Awd 83; Intl Bus.

STARR, MARIE; Kiski Area HS; New Kensington, PA; (Y); Drama Clb; FBLA; SADD; Chorus; School Musical; School Play; Stage Crew; Nwsp Stf; Yrbk Stf; High Hon Roll; D Youville Coll; Nrsng.

STARR, MARYANNE; Central Backs East HS; Buckingham, PA; (Y); Ski Clb; Band; Yrbk Stf; Cheerleading; Swmmng; Hon Roll; Jr NHS; Soclgy.

STARR, PATRICK; Freedom HS; Bethlehem, PA; (Y); Boy Scts; Church Yth Grp; Cmnty Wkr; Hosp Aide; Pep Clb; Political Wkr; JV Socr; JV Tennis; Emery-Riddle Schl Aviatn; Aero.

STARRUICK, KELLY A; West Hazleton HS; West Hazleton, PA; (S); 3/192; FNA; Spanish Clb; Capt Cheerleading; Trk; NHS; Penn ST U.

STAS, ERIC A; Emmaus HS; Macungie, PA; (Y); 3/479; German Clb; JA; Key Clb; Yrbk Sprt Ed; Var Crs Cntry; High Hon Roll; NCTE Awd; NHS; Ntl Merit Ltr; Voice Dem Awd; William & Mary; Law.

STASH, SUSANNE; Lake Lehman HS; Shavertown, PA; (Y); 13/161; Cmnty Wkr; French Clb; Key Clb; SADD; School Play; Nwsp Stf; Ed Yrbk Stf; Var Fld Hcky; Stat Vllybl; High Hon Roll; Accntng.

STASICK, ANDREA; Lincoln HS; Ellwood City, PA; (Y); 49/180; Church Yth Grp; Hosp Aide; Spanish Clb; Y-Teens; Pres Chorus; School Musical; Rep Stu Cncl; JV Var Cheerleading; Powder Puff Ftbl; Sftbl; PA Dist 5 & Rgn 1 Chorus 86; Hlth.

STASIK, PAUL; Carrick HS; Pittsburgh, PA; (S); Boy Scts; Church Yth Grp; CAP; English Clb; French Clb; Stage Crew; Rep Stu Cncl; Var JV Vllybl; Hon Roll; West Point Acad; Avtn.

STASKO, PAMELA; Steel Valley HS; W Homestead, PA; (Y); 44/250; Trs Church Yth Grp; Varsity Clb; Var L Tennis; Stat Vllybl; Bus.

STASSEL, DEBBIE; West Catholic Girls HS; Philadelphia, PA; (Y); 56/240; JA; Spanish Clb; Var Cheerleading; Hon Roll; Katherine Gibbs Bus Schl; Bus.

STASSI, PHIL; Neshaminy HS; Langhorne, PA; (Y); 170/752; Var L Tennis; Hon Roll; Rcgntn Excllnc Artwork Dist Arts Fest 83-86; Rep Schl Suburban I Dble Tnns Tourn 86; No 1 Sngls Tnns; Physcl Thrpy.

STATES, BRIAN; York Vo Tech; York, PA; (Y); 7/436; Church Yth Grp; VICA; Band; Rep Jr Cls; Crs Cntry; Var L Trk; VP NHS; Rotary Awd; Elec.

STATES, CHARLES; Huntingdon Area HS; Huntingdon, PA; (Y); 34/218; Am Leg Boys St; Church Yth Grp; 4-H; Band; Mrchg Band; Trk; Coast Guard Acad.

STATES, KARIN; Dubois Area HS; Dubois, PA; (Y); 5/285; Church Yth Grp; Band; Concert Band; Jazz Band; Mrchg Band; School Musical; Stat Bsktbl; Hon Roll; NHS; Dist Band 86; Houghton-NY; Cmmnctns.

STAUB, D DEETTE; Delone Catholic HS; Hanover, PA; (Y); Debate Tm; Library Aide; Rep Frsh Cls; Sec Jr Cls; Var L Cheerleading; Hon Roll; NHS; Soph Homecomg Queen 84; U S Chrldr Achvt Awd 86; Nrs.

STAUB, RENE G; New Oxford SR HS; Mcsherrystown, PA; (Y); 24/220; Am Leg Boys St; Art Clb; Teachers Aide; Chorus; Concert Band; Drm Mjr(t); School Musical; Var Trk; Hon Roll; 1st Pl Locl Handicppd Poster 86; 2nd Lvl Govnrs Art Schl 85; Cer Merit Patriot News Poems 84; Art Dir.

STAUB, RICHARD; Northern York County HS; Wellsville, PA; (Y); 21/200; Chess Clb; Var Mgr(s); Hon Roll; NHS; Pres Acad Ftns Awd 86; Lck Hvn U Of PA; Engrng.

STAUDT, SHEILA; Mount Alvernia HS; Pittsburgh, PA; (S); Church Yth Grp; French Clb; VP JA; Nwsp Rptr; Trs Frsh Cls; Trs Soph Cls; Trs Jr Cls; Hon Roll; NHS; U Of PITTSBURGH.

STAUDT, TODD; Troy Area HS; Troy, PA; (Y); 1/142; Letterman Clb; Ski Clb; Bsktbl; Ftbl; Bausch & Lomb Sci Awd; Hon Roll; NHS; Pres Schlr; Val; Acad All-Amer 84-86; Pres Natl Hnr Soc 86; Co Cptn Ftbl & Bsktbl Tms 85-86; Air Force Acad.

STAUFFER, AMY; Hanover SR HS; Hanover, PA; (Y); 31/137; Church Yth Grp; Band; Chorus; Church Choir; Concert Band; Jazz Band; Mrchg Band; Orch; School Musical; Swing Chorus; Frmr Bnk Bus Ed Schlrshp 86; Lwr Dist 7 Band Fstvl 85 & 86; PA Ambssdrs Of Music 85; Goldey Beacom Coll; Acctg.

STAUFFER JR, BYRON G; Connellsville Area SR HS; Connellsville, PA; (Y); 19/550; Church Yth Grp; Cmnty Wkr; School Musical; Stage Crew; Rep Stu Cncl; Var L Ftbl; Im Wt Lftg; High Hon Roll; NHS; Spanish NHS; Outstndng 1st Tm Entr,Natl Hist Day CMU 86; Aerospace Engr.

STAUFFER, DAVID; North Penn HS; Lansdale, PA; (Y); 118/696; VP 4-H; Acpl Chr; Pres Chorus; Church Choir; Madrigals; Orch; Swing Chorus; Nwsp Rptr; Yrbk Rptr; VP Frsh Cls; Summr Music Schl Schlrshp 83-84; IN U; Music.

STAUFFER, ERIKA; Central Columbia HS; Nescopeck, PA; (Y); 40/180; Hosp Aide; Sec Key Clb; Ski Clb; Varsity Clb; Sec Jr Cls; Rep Stu Cncl; Var JV Cheerleading; Var Fld Hcky; Ftbl; Var Capt Trk; Hmcmng Queen 85; Prom Ct 86; West Chester U; Athltc Trng.

STAUFFER, GREGORY; Elk County Christian HS; St Marys, PA; (Y); 4/97; Varsity Clb; JV Bsktbl; Var L Ftbl; Var Mgr(s); Var Trk; High Hon Roll; Boy Scts Eagle Awd 86; Bishop Mcmanaman Awd 86; Magna Cum Laude 86; Penn ST U; Engrng.

STAUFFER, JOHN; St Marys Area HS; St Marys, PA; (Y); Boy Scts; Red Cross Aide; Var Bsktbl; Tennis; Hon Roll; NHS; Pres Schlr; Eagle Scout 85; Syracuse U; Elec Engrng.

STAUFFER, JULIE; Benton Area JR-SR HS; Benton, PA; (Y); 3/53; Keywanettes; Capt Flag Corp; School Play; Pres Soph Cls; Off Stu Cncl; Co-Capt Cheerleading; Fld Hcky; Hon Roll; Jr NHS; NHS; Gregg Speed Typng Awd 85; Named To Columbia Cnty All-Star Fld Hocky Tm 85-86; Smi-Fnlst Miss Teen 86; Comp.

STAUFFER, KAREN; Boyertown Area SR HS; Barto, PA; (S); 1/450; Nwsp Ed-Chief; Var L Bsktbl; High Hon Roll; NHS; Church Yth Grp; Computer Clb; Nwsp Phtg; Nwsp Rptr; Yrbk Rptr; Bowling; Outstndng Acad Achvt Awd; Intern-Local Paper 84-85; Mbr Stu Board 85; Jrnlsm.

STAUFFER, KIRK THOMAS; Manheim Township HS; Lancaster, PA; (Y); 89/325; JV Ftbl; Hon Roll; Acctg.

STAUFFER, LINDA; Fleetwood Area HS; Fleetwood, PA; (Y); 10/116; Chorus; Concert Band; Jazz Band; Mrchg Band; Pep Band; School Musical; Yrbk Stf; Sec Pres Stu Cncl; Fld Hcky; High Hon Roll; Culinary Arts.

STAUFFER, PHILIP H; Elizabethtown Area HS; Elizabethtown, PA; (Y); 17/240; Math Tm; Mrchg Band; Var Capt Crs Cntry; Var Trk; NHS; Ntl Merit Schol; U S Naval Acad Summer Smnr 85; Intl Trade Diplomat.

STAUFFER, ROBERT; Northern Cambria HS; Barnesboro, PA; (Y); 25/126; Church Yth Grp; Spanish Clb; School Play; Variety Show; Pres Frsh Cls; Pres Jr Cls; Stu Cncl; High Hon Roll; Hon Roll; Frnscs 85-86; Hstry Day Dist Wnnr 84-85; U Of FL; Bio.

STAUFFER, SUE; Allentown Central Catholic HS; Allentown, PA; (Y); 19/230; Intnl Clb; Pep Clb; Service Clb; Color Guard; High Hon Roll; NHS; Forgn Lang.

STAUFFER, TIM; Upper Moreland HS; Hatboro, PA; (Y); 2/270; Off Boy Scts; Off Church Yth Grp; Band; Var L Bsbl; Var L Socr; Cit Awd; God Cntry Awd; Pres NHS; Ntl Merit SF; Rotary Awd; Boy Sct JR Ldrshp In Amer Awd 85; Congrssnl Schlrs Natl Yth Ldrshp Conf 86; Engrng.

STAUFFER, TRACY; Emmaus HS; Emmaus, PA; (Y); 12/475; Church Yth Grp; French Clb; VP L Bsktbl; VP L Fld Hcky; JV L Sftbl; VP L Trk; High Hon Roll; Hon Roll; Jr NHS; NHS; Hnrs Grad 86; Loyola; Comm.

STAWARZ, MARGARET; Windber Area HS; Windber, PA; (Y); French Clb; Library Aide; Math Clb; Rep Stu Cncl; Var L Bsktbl; Coach Actv; Var L Sftbl; Trk; Twrlr; Hon Roll; Grls Bsktbl-Al Trny Tm Rockwd 85; Chem.

STAWITZ, ERIC; Cumberland Valley HS; Camp Hill, PA; (Y); Aud/Vis; Boy Scts; Church Yth Grp; German Clb; Ski Clb; Var Mgr(s); JV Socr; Attnmnt Of Eagle Sct Rnk 85.

STAYMATES, MERI; Kiski Area HS; Export, PA; (Y); Pres Church Yth Grp; Pep Clb; Spanish Clb; Varsity Clb; Cheerleading; Sftbl; Vllybl; High Hon Roll; NHS; Pres Schlr; Pre-Med.

STEADLE, ROBINN; Lake Lehman HS; Harveys Lake, PA; (Y); 18/152; Ski Clb; Band; Concert Band; Mrchg Band; Yrbk Stf; Stat•Socr; Mgr Wrstlng; High Hon Roll; Hon Roll; Jr NHS; Dist Band Stu 85-86; Arch.

STEADMAN, HEATHER; Conrad Weiser JS HS; Robesonia, PA; (Y); 30/184; Drama Clb; JCL; Key Clb; Teachers Aide; Chorus; School Musical; Yrbk Stf; Lit Mag; Bowling; Hon Roll; Key Clbr Of Mnth Awd 86; 2nd Pl Berks Cnt Y Pstr Cntst 84; Psych.

STEADMAN, TINA; Windber Area HS; Windber, PA; (Y); Church Yth Grp; Band; Concert Band; Jazz Band; Mrchg Band; Stage Crew; Sftbl; Vllybl; Hon Roll; IUP; Acctnt.

STEALS, TYRONE T; Aliquippa SR HS; Aliquippa, PA; (Y); Var Bsktbl; Hon Roll.

STEAR, SHERRI; Maron Center HS; Home, PA; (Y); 66/170; Trs Church Yth Grp; FNA; Hosp Aide; Sec Latin Clb; Pep Clb; Science Clb; SADD; Varsity Clb; School Play; Stage Crew; IN U; RN.

STEARNS, KRISTINA; Conneaut Lake HS; Conneaut Lake, PA; (Y); Church Yth Grp; Spanish Clb; VP Band; Concert Band; Mrchg Band; Pep Band; Variety Show; JV Sftbl; Im Vllybl; Hon Roll; Soc Wrk.

STEBBINS, JOHN; Mereyhurst Prep; Erie, PA; (Y); 27/165; Trs Pres Church Yth Grp; Computer Clb; French Clb; Library Aide; Ski Clb; Nwsp Stf; Pres Soph Cls; Trs Sr Cls; French Hon Soc; NHS; Carnegie Mellon U; Econ.

STEBBINS, MARK; Purchase Line HS; Glen Campbell, PA; (Y); Varsity Clb; School Play; Nwsp Phtg; Nwsp Stf; Var L Bsktbl; Ftbl; Elec Engr.

STEBBINS, MICHELLE; Central York SR HS; York, PA; (Y); Ski Clb; Varsity Clb; Concert Band; Mrchg Band; Symp Band; Yrbk Stf; Fld Hcky; Trk; 4-H Awd; Hon Roll; Awd PTSA Rflctns Scheme 85; Vet Asst.

STEBBINS, SONJA; Newport HS; Newport, PA; (Y); 4-H; Chorus; School Musical; School Play; Sec Stu Cncl; JV Var Bsktbl; JV Var Fld Hcky; JV Var Sftbl; Law Enfrcmnt.

STEBELSKI, MARY; Bethlehem Catholic HS; Bethlehem, PA; (Y); 12/200; Key Clb; Library Aide; Yrbk Stf; Stat Bsktbl; Im Fld Hcky; NHS; 2nd Pl Indvdl Manhours PA Dist Key Clb 85-86; Engrng.

STEC, BEVERLY; Spring Ford SR HS; Spring City, PA; (Y); 11/256; German Clb; Band; Concert Band; Mrchg Band; Rep Sr Cls; JV Var Cheerleading; Capt Twrlr; Hon Roll; NHS; Opt Clb Awd.

STEC, DAVE; Scranton Central HS; Scranton, PA; (Y); AFS; Exploring; Hosp Aide; Band; Jazz Band; Mrchg Band; Orch; Symp Band; JV Var Bsbl; JV Bsktbl; Genetic Engrng.

STECK, TAMARA; Norwin SR HS; N Huntingdon, PA; (Y); 66/557; FBLA; Chorus; Color Guard; Var L Bsktbl; Var Sftbl; Hon Roll; NHS; Cert Of Achvt Sftbl Leag 83 & 84; Ntl Sftbl Chmpnshp 84; Bradford Bus Schl; Lgl Sec.

STECKER, TAWNY M; Mercersburg Acad; Raleigh, NC; (Y); 14/124; Dance Clb; Stage Crew; Lit Mag; Swmmng; Trk; Hon Roll; All Amer Swmmng 83-86; Lit Clb 86; A V Mc Clain Art Awd 86; Kenyon Coll; Bio.

STECKLINE, CHRISTOPHER; Abington SR HS; Roslyn, PA; (Y); Boy Scts; FBLA; JV Bsbl; Var Swmmng; Radio-TV Sprts Brdcstng.

STEELE, ALISSA; Coatesville Area SR HS; Coatesville, PA; (Y); 58/480; Sec Leo Clb; Ski Clb; Spanish Clb; Off Soph Cls; Trs Sr Cls; Stu Cncl; Var L Lcrss; Var Tennis; Phrmcst.

STEELE, BRIAN; Youngsville HS; Pittsfield, PA; (Y); Spanish Clb; Rep Jr Cls; Rep Stu Cncl; JV Var Bsktbl.

STEELE, DAVE; Berwick Area SR HS; Berwick, PA; (Y); 90/190; Aud/Vis; Church Yth Grp; Cmnty Wkr; Key Clb; Ski Clb; Varsity Clb; Nwsp Sprt Ed; Yrbk Sprt Ed; Bsbl; Bsktbl; Bloomsburg U; Mass Comm.

STEELE, DOUGLAS; Henderson SR HS; West Chester, PA; (Y); Cmnty Wkr; Ftbl; Trk; Wt Lftg; Rotary Awd; Lincoln U Upward Bound Prog 85-86; Wnnr Mc Les Amies Fndtn Shclrshp 86; VP Mc Black Stu Union 86; PA ST U; Bio.

STEELE, FELICIA ANN; Quaker Valley SR HS; Sewickley, PA; (Y); Am Leg Aux Girls St; Spanish Clb; Chorus; School Musical; Cheerleading; Gym; Pom Pon; Trk; High Hon Roll; Hon Roll; Spnsh Bus.

STEELE, JENNIFER; Northern Bedford HS; Everett, PA; (Y); FBLA; Band; Concert Band; Mrchg Band; Stat Sftbl; Hon Roll; Century 21 Accntng Pin & Typng Cert 8 6; Gregg Shrthd Awd 86.

STEELE, KENDRICK; John Harris Campus; Harrisburg, PA; (Y); 38/488; Boys Clb Am; Band; Concert Band; Mrchg Band; Hon Roll; Engrng.

STEELE, LISA; Williams Valley HS; Joliett, PA; (Y); 6/100; Chorus; Yrbk Stf; Sec Sr Cls; Hon Roll; NHS; John Hall Schlrshp 86; Harrisburg Area CC; Comp Pgmr.

STEELE, LU ANN; Central Dauphin HS; Harrisburg, PA; (Y); 42/385; Nwsp Stf; Var L Fld Hcky; Var L Gym; Hon Roll; Jr NHS; NHS; Amer Mensa.

STEELE, SUSAN; Lock Haven SR HS; Castanea, PA; (Y); French Clb; Model UN; Service Clb; Chorus; Stat Bsktbl; Var Socr; High Hon Roll; NHS; Ntl Hist & Gvnmnt Awd 86; Bio-Chem.

STEELE, TERESA; Punxsutawney HS; Punxsutawney, PA; (Y); French Clb; FBLA; GAA; Math Tm; Yrbk Stf; Var Tennis; Var Trk; Twrlr; Hon Roll; Chld Dvlmpnt.

STEFAN, TODD; Pennsbury HS; Fairless Hills, PA; (Y); Spanish Clb; Var Capt Bsbl; Bsktbl; Capt Ftbl; Hon Roll; NHS; Academic All American 85; LOS Angeles Dodgers Baseball Camp MVP 86; Sports Med.

STEFANEK, MICHAEL; Marian Catholic HS; Tamaqua, PA; (Y); 30/120; Ski Clb; School Play; JV Bsktbl; Hon Roll; Scndry Educ.

STEFANISKO, MARK; Marian HS; Mcadoo, PA; (Y); 65/115; Im Ftbl; PA ST U; Elec Engrng.

STEFANIW, MATTHEW; Harriton HS; Villanova, PA; (Y); Socr; Hon Roll; Aerosp Engrng.

STEFANO, KEN; Connellsville Area SR HS; Connellsville, PA; (Y); 3/480; VP Chess Clb; Pep Clb; VP Science Clb; Ski Clb; SADD; Band; Jazz Band; Mrchg Band; Pep Band; School Musical; Hnrs Band; Robert P Mc Luckey Memrl Schlrshp; Carnegie Mellon U; Elec Engrng.

STEFF, PAUL A; Western Beaver JR SR HS; Industry, PA; (Y); 8/82; Band; Jazz Band; Mrchg Band; Symp Band; High Hon Roll; Hon Roll; NHS; Church Yth Grp; Concert Band; Nwsp Stf; Mid-East All Star Band 84-86; Beaver Cnty Hnrs Band 84, 86; Geneva Coll; Lwyr.

STEFFEN, CHRISTY; Beaver Area HS; Beaver, PA; (Y); Spanish Clb; Yrbk Stf; Powder Puff Ftbl; Swmmng; High Hon Roll; Hon Roll; Acadmc Achvt Awd-Tp 10 Prct Cls 85; Phrmcy.

STEFFENS, PAUL A; Germantown Acad; Ft Washington, PA; (Y); 1/120; Church Yth Grp; Math Clb; Var Bsbl; Var Bsktbl; Var Socr; Var Tennis; Cit Awd; High Hon Roll; NHS; Ntl Merit SF; Advncd Math Awd 84; Chem Awd 84; Natl H S Math Exm 85; Math.

STEFFY, ANN; Cedar Crest HS; Lebanon, PA; (Y); Art Clb; Church Yth Grp; Drama Clb; French Clb; Pep Clb; Orch; Im Socr; Var Swmmng; Im Bausch & Lomb Sci Awd; Hon Roll; Carnegie-Mellon U; Art.

STEFFY, CHRISTINA; Hempfield HS; E Petersbg, PA; (Y); 9/460; Church Yth Grp; Drama Clb; Band; Chorus; Church Choir; High Hon Roll; Hon Roll; NHS; Lancaster-Lebanon County Chorus 84-86; Dist V Chorus 84-86; Modern Music Masters Soc 85-86; Psychlgy.

STEFFY, DANA; Punxsutawney Area HS; Punxsutawney, PA; (Y); FBLA; Bsbl; Stat Bsktbl; Stat Wrstlng; Socl Wrkr.

STEFFY, MARIJO; Exeter SR HS; Reading, PA; (Y); Sec Leo Clb; Y-Teens; Band; Concert Band; Mrchg Band; Rep Jr Cls; Rep Stu Cncl; Var Tennis; Hon Roll.

STEFL, PHYLLIS; Connellsville Area HS; Scottdale, PA; (Y); 188/438; Art Clb; Pres VP Church Yth Grp; Cmnty Wkr; Hosp Aide; VICA; Church Choir; Hon Roll; Dirs List N Fayette Area Vo-Tec Sch 85-86; HOSA 83-86; 2nd Pl St Lvl HOSA Bowl 85-86; Westmoreland Cnty CC; Med Secy.

STEGENGA II, DAVID I; Chartiers-Houston HS; Houston, PA; (Y); French Clb; Band; Concert Band; Jazz Band; Mrchg Band; Bsbl; Bsktbl; High Hon Roll; Hon Roll; WA & Jefferson; Bio.

STEGER, HEIDI; Mercyhurst Preparatory Schl; Erie, PA; (Y); 76/160; French Clb; Var Socr; Hon Roll; Gannon U; Lwyrs Asst.

STEGMAN, RICHARD; Hampton HS; Allison Pk, PA; (Y); 5/255; Chess Clb; Exploring; Concert Band; Drm Mjr(t); Mrchg Band; Pep Band; Stage Crew; Symp Band; High Hon Roll; NHS; UNC; Astrnmy.

STEHL, SHARON; Harry S Truman HS; Levittown, PA; (Y); 31/576; Cmnty Wkr; Yrbk Stf; Stu Cncl; Gym; High Hon Roll; Hon Roll; NHS; Prfct Atten Awd; Physcl Ftns Awd 84-86; Bus.

STEIBING, LISA; Hazleton SR HS; Hazleton, PA; (Y); 20/374; Leo Clb; Color Guard; High Hon Roll; NHS; Penn ST U; Mdcl Tech.

STEIGERWALT, AMY; Red Land HS; New Cumberland, PA; (Y); 34/275; Latin Clb; Band; Concert Band; Jazz Band; Hst Mrchg Band; Orch; Symp Band; Swmmng; Trk; Hon Roll; Arch.

STEIGERWALT, JUDITH; Nazareth Area SR HS; Nazareth, PA; (Y); VP Drama Clb; School Musical; Nwsp Ed-Chief; Yrbk Rptr; Off Stu Cncl; Capt L Cheerleading; Hon Roll; Church Yth Grp; Key Clb; Thesps; Richard J Schmoyer Mem Awd Jrnlsm 86; Fnlst PA Gvnrs Schl Arts & Thea 85; Temple U; Jrnlsm.

STEIMEL, KIRK; Owen J Roberts HS; Pottstown, PA; (S); 18/301; Band; Chorus; Concert Band; Mrchg Band; School Musical; School Play; Variety Show; Hon Roll; NHS; Math Ed.

STEIN, BONNIE; Wyoming Valley West; Forty Fort, PA; (Y); Church Yth Grp; Band; Chorus; Mrchg Band; Orch; School Musical; Yrbk Stf; Lit Mag; Hon Roll; NEDT Awd; Mrchnb Bnd Squad Ldr 85-86; Temple U; Cmnctns.

STEIN, BRIAN; Bensalem HS; Bensalem, PA; (Y); Cmnty Wkr; Temple Yth Grp; Varsity Clb; Socr; Trk; High Hon Roll; NHS; ST Certifies Emergcy Med Tech 86; Tres-Sigma Alph Rho Intl Fraturnity 86; Sigma Alpha Wnnr Mth 85-84; Physician.

STEIN, CHERYL; Montour HS; Mc Kees Rocks, PA; (Y); Radio Clb; Yrbk Stf; Rep Stu Cncl; Capt Cheerleading; Var Powder Puff Ftbl.

STEIN, JEANNE; Meadville Area SR HS; Meadville, PA; (Y); 10/350; Church Yth Grp; Chorus; Church Choir; Pres Jr Cls; Stu Cncl; Vllybl; High Hon Roll; Dist Regnl & ST Chrs; Natl Stu Cncl Awd Recip.

STEIN, JEFF; Crestwood HS; Mountaintop, PA; (Y); Boy Scts; Ski Clb; Ftbl; Golf; Trk; Lwyr.

STEIN, JENNIFER; Akiba Hebrew Acad; Philadelphia, PA; (Y); Cmnty Wkr; Temple Yth Grp; Var Mgr(s); Var Socr; Mgr Wrstlng.

STEIN, MELISSA S; Upper Dublin HS; Dresher, PA; (Y); 7/307; Aud/Vis; Camera Clb; Intnl Clb; Yrbk Stf; Lit Mag; NHS; Prfct Atten Awd; Stdnt Wk Acdmc 86.

STEIN, MICHELLE; Ambridge Area HS; Ambridge, PA; (Y); German Clb; Pep Clb; Red Cross Aide; SADD; Band; Color Guard; Off Jr Cls; Stu Cncl; High Hon Roll; NHS; Math.

STEIN, WADE; Red Lion Area SR HS; Red Lion, PA; (Y); 58/330; Varsity Clb; JV Var Mgr(s); Hon Roll.

STEINBACH, KRISTY; Manheim Twp HS; Lancaster, PA; (Y); Cmnty Wkr; Hosp Aide; Key Clb; Library Aide; Red Cross Aide; Nwsp Phtg; Nwsp Rptr; Nwsp Stf; Lit Mag; Stu Cncl; U DE; Bus Admin.

STEINBACHER, MELISSA; Montoursville Area HS; Montoursville, PA; (Y); German Clb; Spanish Clb; School Musical; Mgr(s); Powder Puff Ftbl; Travel.

STEINBERG, REBECCA; Plymouth Whitemarsh HS; Norristown, PA; (Y); 41/375; Hosp Aide; Math Clb; Concert Band; Mrchg Band; Stu Cncl; Lcrss; Swmmng; High Hon Roll; Hon Roll; Mu Alp Tht; Yth Educ Assoc Pub Rel Chrmn 85-86; Phys Ther.

STEINBRING, MICHELE LEA; Greater Johnstown HS; Johnstown, PA; (Y); German Clb; Chorus; Nwsp Rptr; VP Jr Cls; Pres Sr Cls; Trs Stu Cncl; Var Bsbl; Var Vllybl; Hon Roll; NHS; All Am Schlr Awd 86; Stu Cncl Awd 85-86; Ltr Bsktbl Vlybl 84-86; Nrs.

STEINBROOK, JENNIFER; Springside Schl; Philadelphia, PA; (Y); 4/45; Yrbk Phtg; Trs Sr Cls; Var Capt Bsktbl; Var Co-Capt Socr; Co-Capt Capt Sftbl; Hon Roll; Cum Laude Soc; Wellesley Bk Awd.

STEINHAUER, R DOUGLAS; Warwick HS; Lititz, PA; (Y); 61/219; Camera Clb; Science Clb; SADD; Teachers Aide; Thesps; Varsity Clb; Band; Concert Band; Mrchg Band; Orch; Slna Cox-Eshelmn Ptry Awd 85-86; Fture Co Clmnst Schl Nwspaper 84-85; Tmple U Of PA; Jrnlsm.

STEINIGER, WILLIAM; Notre Dame HS; Stourdsburg, PA; (Y); 4/37; Am Leg Boys St; Chess Clb; Drama Clb; Exploring; Red Cross Aide; Stage Crew; Yrbk Stf; VP Stu Cncl; Var Socr; DAR Awd; ROTC Schlrshp 86; Northeastern U; Bus.

STEININGER, LAURIE; Coughlin HS; Laflin, PA; (Y); Ski Clb; Hon Roll; NHS; Bloomsburg U; Elem Ed.

STEININGER, VALARIE; Northeastern HS; Manchester, PA; (Y); Ski Clb; Chorus; Boy Scts; Yrbk Stf; Sec Sr Cls; Rep Stu Cncl; JV Var Bsktbl; Var Trk; Hon Roll; NHS; Bloomsburg U Of PA; Nrsng.

STEINKAMP, KAREN; Moon SR HS; Coraopolis, PA; (Y); Exploring; JA; Chorus; Hon Roll; NHS; Flght Attndng.

STEINKOPF, MARY; Elizabeth Forward HS; Elizabeth, PA; (Y); PAVAS; SADD; Acpl Chr; School Musical; Rep Jr Cls; Var L Swmmng; Var L Trk; High Hon Roll; NHS; Prfct Atten Awd; Carnegie Mellon; Drama.

STEINMILLER, SAMANTHA; Waynesburg Central Greene HS; Pine Bank, PA; (Y); Church Yth Grp; Dance Clb; Natl Beta Clb; Pep Clb; Spanish Clb; Y-Teens; Cheerleading; Trk; Hon Roll; Outstndng Wrkmnshp Awd/In Make It With Wool 86; Phrmicst.

STEITZ, FRANCIS C; Archbishop Kennedy HS; Ambler, PA; (Y); 6/180; Drama Clb; Pres Intnl Clb; Socr; Trk; Pres NHS; Frst Hnrs 84-86; Engr.

STELACONE, LEE; Wyoming Area HS; Wyoming, PA; (Y); 42/260; Key Clb; Chorus; Color Guard; Sec Sr Cls; Aud/Vis; French Clb; Sec Soph Cls; Sec Jr Cls; Rep Stu Cncl; Trk; Dist Chorus 83-86; Penn ST U; Librl Arts.

STELLA, BEVERLY; Hatboro Horsham HS; Horsham, PA; (Y); FBLA; SADD; JV Bsktbl; Coach Actv; Var Tennis; Vllybl; Cit Awd; Hon Roll; Temple U; Acctg.

STELLE, BRENDA; Harborcreek JR SR HS; Erie, PA; (Y); 22/210; Church Yth Grp; ROTC; Drill Tm; Nwsp Ed-Chief; Cit Awd; DAR Awd; Hon Roll; NHS; VFW Awd; Army & Air Force Schlrshp 86; Gannon U; Chem.

STELLITANO, LEONARD J; Penn Hills HS; Pittsburgh, PA; (Y); 49/735; Am Leg Boys St; Aud/Vis; Spanish Clb; Var Crs Cntry; High Hon Roll; Hon Roll; NHS; Trundell Schlrshp-VA Military Inst 86-87; VA Military Inst; Engrng.

STELLWAGEN, ROBIN; Neshaminy HS; Trevose, PA; (Y); 207/730; Chorus; Yrbk Stf; Stat Wrstlng; Hon Roll; Concert Choir 85-87; Math.

STELMACK, CAROLYN; St Francis Acad; Mc Murray, PA; (S); Drama Clb; Red Cross Aide; Chorus; Church Choir; School Play; Nwsp Stf; High Hon Roll.

STELTER, JAMES; Shenango HS; Wampum, PA; (Y); 37/127; Chorus; JV Var Bsbl; Im Bsktbl; Im Vllybl; PA ST.

STELTZ, WENDY MONICA; Upper Perkiomen HS; Pennsburg, PA; (Y); Am Leg Aux Girls St; Hosp Aide; Band; Chorus; Concert Band; Co-Capt Flag Corp; Mrchg Band; Variety Show; Mgr(s); Hon Roll; Kutztown U; Elem Ed.

STELZER, SCOTT; Upper Dublin HS; Ambler, PA; (Y); 7/307; Cmnty Wkr; FBLA; Intnl Clb; Letterman Clb; Quiz Bowl; Scholastic Bowl; Temple Yth Grp; Varsity Clb; Nwsp Rptr; Nwsp Stf.

STEMMLER, ROBERT; North Star HS; Boswell, PA; (Y); Art Clb; Church Yth Grp; Drama Clb; FCA; 4-H; Spanish Clb; Chorus; School Play; 4-H Awd; Hon Roll; Art Cirrclm Awd 85-86; Cazenovia Clg; Commcl Dsgn.

STEMPA, LOUISE; Panther Valley HS; Nesquehoning, PA; (Y); 16/129; Trs Library Aide; Ski Clb; Church Choir; Mrchg Band; Yrbk Bus Mgr; Trk; Twrlr; Hon Roll; NHS; Geissinger Med Ctr Schl; Nrs.

STENGEL, DARREN; N Hills HS; Pittsburgh, PA; (Y); Library Aide; PAVAS; Prfct Atten Awd; Edinbrgh Flm Awd 84-85; Dublin Intrnatl Flm Festvl 2nd Pl 85; Natl Flm Festvl 84 & 86; Pittsburgh U; Archlgy.

STENGER, MARY; State College Area SR HS; State College, PA; (Y); 29/488; Church Yth Grp; Dance Clb; Ski Clb; Concert Band; Yrbk Stf; Sec Frsh Cls; Rep Stu Cncl; High Hon Roll; Faclty Schrl 86; Miss Talnt Schrlshp 85; Kalamazoo Coll; Bio.

STENNETT, JACKIE; Ford City HS; Manorville, PA; (Y); 34/151; AFS; Chorus; Rep Frsh Cls; Var Capt Bsktbl; Var Sftbl; SR Plaque Bsktbl & Sftbl 86.

STENZEL, KIM; Chartiers Valley HS; Bridgeville, PA; (Y); Dance Clb; GAA; School Musical; Math.

STEPANIUK, KIMBERLY; Bishop Conwell HS; Morrisville, PA; (Y); 27/254; Q&S; Nwsp Stf; Bsktbl; Socr; Sftbl; Cit Awd; Hon Roll; Art Clb; Dance Clb; GAA; Wnnr Energy Poster Cont Phila Elec Co 82-83; Wnnr Essay Cont-What Makes Amer Great 84; Moore Coll Of Art; Cmmrcl Art.

STEPHEN, DENISE; Minersville HS; Pottsville, PA; (Y); 7/119; Cmnty Wkr; Computer Clb; JA; Library Aide; Natl Beta Clb; Pep Clb; Scholastic Bowl; Ski Clb; Spanish Clb; SADD; Schlr Athlt 86; Robert P Morgan Awd 86; Mr Edward Brady Awd 86; Shippensburg U; Sec Bio Eductn.

STEPHENS, AMY; Rocky Grove HS; Franklin, PA; (Y); 1/93; Church Yth Grp; SADD; Chorus; Yrbk Stf; Stat Vllybl; High Hon Roll; Pres NHS; Rotary Awd; Med.

STEPHENS, DAN; Trinity Area HS; Washington, PA; (Y); 12/374; Math Clb; Concert Band; Jazz Band; Mrchg Band; VP Sr Cls; Tennis; High Hon Roll; Hon Roll; NHS; Nclr Engrng.

STEPHENS, JEFFREY D; Lakeland HS; Jermyn, PA; (S); 31/149; Exploring; Crs Cntry; Hon Roll; Millersville U; Comp Sci.

STEPHENS, JENNIFER L; Strath Haven HS; Swarthmore, PA; (Y); Pres Church Yth Grp; GAA; Intnl Clb; Mrchg Band; Orch; Var Fld Hcky; Var Trk; DAR Awd; NHS; Natl Hnrs Orchstra 86; Sesqucntnl Schlrshp 86; Physcl Thrpy.

STEPHENS, KATHLEEN M; Blacklick Valley HS; Nanty-Glo, PA; (Y); 19/60; Drama Clb; Pres German Clb; NFL; Speech Tm; Band; Chorus; Concert Band; Mrchg Band; Pep Band; School Play; Forensic Awd 86; IN U PA; Med Tech.

STEPHENS, KELLY L; Reading SR HS; Reading, PA; (S); 27/610; Sec Debate Tm; Sec German Clb; Trs Model UN; Yrbk Stf; NHS; 1st Plc Berks Sci Fr Med & Hlth 85; Natl Pno Plyng Adtns Dstrct Mbr 85.

STEPHENS, MAX; Hickory HS; Farrell, PA; (Y); 59/175; German Clb; Varsity Clb; Band; Concert Band; Jazz Band; Mrchg Band; Orch; Pep Band; Hon Roll; Jr NHS; Lettermen Jacket 84; Let In Trk 86; Mercer Cnty All Star Jazz Band 86; Penn ST; Accntng.

STEPHENS, W MARK; Punxsutawney Area HS; Sprankles Mls, PA; (Y); 103/238; Boy Scts; Ftbl; Mercyhurst; Med Techncn.

STEPHENSON, AIMEE; Chapel Christina Acad; Schwenksville, PA; (S); Drama Clb; Chorus; Church Choir; School Musical; School Play; Yrbk Stf; Stu Cncl; L Cheerleading; Hon Roll; Sacred Piano 2nd In ST 84; Drmtc Interp ST Wnnr 85; Bob Jones U; Piano Mjr.

STEPKE, DAVID; Hampton HS; Allison Park, PA; (Y); 26/228; Cmnty Wkr; Ski Clb; Spanish Clb; Im Bsbl; JV Crs Cntry; Var L Ice Hcky; Im Sftbl; High Hon Roll; Hon Roll; Pres Schlr; St Bnvntr U; Bus Mngmnt.

STEPNOWSKI, DIANE M; Upper Merion HS; King Of Prussia, PA; (Y); Key Clb; Rep Jr Cls; Rep Sr Cls; Var Cheerleading; Coach Actv; Hon Roll; NHS; Delta Kappa Gamma Socty Intl Recrtmt Grnt Alpha Alpha ST 86; Temple U Pres Awd 86; Temple U; Erly Chldhd Ed.

STEPPE, CHRISTINE; Hazleton SR HS; Hazleton, PA; (Y); FBLA; Girl Scts; Hosp Aide; Key Clb; Office Aide; Yrbk Stf; Mgr(s); Mgr Swmmng; Hon Roll; Awd Of Cmmndtn For Outstndng & Loyal Svc Vlntrd In Hosp 84; Cert Of Apprctn In Vlntr Svc In Cmnty 84; Bus.

STERANKO, MICHAEL; Chartiers Valley HS; Carnegie, PA; (Y); 11/303; Church Yth Grp; Ski Clb; Varsity Clb; Bsbl; Crs Cntry; Jr NHS; Engrng.

STERLING, SHANNON; Saegertown Area HS; Saegertown, PA; (Y); 13/124; Am Leg Aux Girls St; SADD; Varsity Clb; Color Guard; Drill Tm; Var L Mgr(s); Vllybl; High Hon Roll; Co Rep Yth NPTPC 86; Actg.

STERMER, ANNETTE; Cowanesque Valley HS; Knoxville, PA; (S); 8/93; Computer Clb; Drama Clb; Letterman Clb; School Play; Capt Bsktbl; L Trk; L Vllybl; Ntl Sci Merit Awd 84.

STERNER, JEFFERY; Northeastern HS; Mt Wolf, PA; (Y); Ski Clb; Acpl Chr; Chorus; Jazz Band; Golf; Vllybl; Hon Roll; Penn ST U; Engrng.

STERNER, KIM; Emmaus HS; Macungie, PA; (Y); 97/463; Pres Church Yth Grp; VP FHA; Key Clb; Hon Roll; Pedtrc Nrsng.

STERNER, MATTHEW; Benton Area JR/SR HS; Orangeville, PA; (Y); Drama Clb; Key Clb; Ski Clb; Band; Chorus; Concert Band; Jazz Band; Mrchg Band; School Musical; School Play; Sound Amrc Hon Band & Chorus 86; Centruy 2 Typng Awd 86; Air Force.

STERNER, MICHAEL; Brandywine Heights Area HS; Fleetwood, PA; (Y); Boy Scts; Band; Concert Band; Mrchg Band; Pep Band; NHS; PA ST U; Elec Engrng.

STERNER, ROBERT; Spring Grove SR HS; Spg Grove, PA; (Y).

STEROWSKI, SHARON JULIA; Benton Area JR/SR HS; Stillwater, PA; (Y); 8/52; Chorus; Co-Capt Color Guard; Mrchg Band; School Musical; School Play; Nwsp Ed-Chief; Nwsp Rptr; High Hon Roll; NHS; Swing Chorus; Cent 21 Typg Awd 85; Aerospc Engrg.

STERRETT, ANDY; St Marys Area HS; Kersey, PA; (Y); Boys Clb Am; JV Bsktbl; Hon Roll.

STESSNEY, TIMOTHY; Altoona Area HS; Altoona, PA; (Y); Art Clb; Computer Clb; Ski Clb; Crs Cntry; High Hon Roll; NEDT Awd; PA ST U.

STETTLER, LE ANNE; Kutztown Area HS; Kutetown, PA; (Y); 13/151; Band; Chorus; Church Choir; Concert Band; Jazz Band; Mrchg Band; School Musical; JV Var Fld Hcky; High Hon Roll; NHS; Zeswitz Music Awd 83-84; Kempton Dutch Queen Cont Miss Congnlty 86; PA All ST Lions Band 85-86; Navy; Band Dirctr.

STETZAR, STACEY; W Scranton HS; Scranton, PA; (Y); 7/253; Latin Clb; Church Choir; School Play; Nwsp Stf; Yrbk Stf; Cheerleading; High Hon Roll; Jr NHS; NHS; 2nd Hnrs Ltn SR Hnrs Awds 85-86; Ldrshp Schlrshp Estrn Coll 4 Yrs 86; Eastern Coll St Davids; Pre-Law.

STEUER, KELLY; Mercy Vocational HS; Philadelphia, PA; (Y); Chess Clb; Church Yth Grp; Church Choir; Nwsp Ed-Chief; Coach Actv; Mgr(s); Mat Maids; Score Keeper; Vllybl; Hon Roll; Sec.

STEUP, CLAYTON ROBERT; Quaker Valley SR HS; Edgeworth, PA; (Y); Art Clb; Church Yth Grp; Exploring; German Clb; Latin Clb; Var Bsktbl; Golf; JV Var Socr; Tennis; Hon Roll; Bio.

STEVENS, ALISA; Schenley HS; Pittsburgh, PA; (S); 17/160; Dance Clb; French Clb; JA; Pep Clb; School Play; Rep Sr Cls; Co-Capt Cheerleading; High Hon Roll; Hon Roll; Carlow Coll; Med.

STEVENS, DOUGLAS; Pottstown HS; Pottstown, PA; (Y); Boy Scts; Cmnty Wkr; Debate Tm; Letterman Clb; Nwsp Stf; Capt L Bsbl; L Ftbl; Hon Roll; Prfct Atten Awd; All Chestmont Lg Ftbl 85-86; Bsbl Ltr 84-86; Bus Adm.

STEVENS, HEATH; Meadville Area SR HS; Meadville, PA; (Y); Latin Clb; Hon Roll; Wooster.

STEVENS, KATHLEEN; Dover Area HS; Dover, PA; (Y); 137/240; Church Yth Grp; Drama Clb; Acpl Chr; Chorus; Church Choir; Cheerleading; Mat Maids; Tennis; Hon Roll; Erly Chldhd Ed.

STEVENS, KELLI; Taylor Allderdice HS; Pittsburgh, PA; (Y); 11/410; Computer Clb; Math Tm; Chorus; Orch; High Hon Roll; NCTE Awd; NHS; Ntl Merit SF; Prfct Atten Awd; Natl Achvt SF 85; Musicn.

STEVENS, LEIGH; Bellefonte Area HS; Bellefonte, PA; (Y); Trs French Clb; Girl Scts; Hosp Aide; Ski Clb; SADD; Chorus; Rep Frsh Cls; Rep Soph Cls; Rep Jr Cls; Capt JV Cheerleading; Mktg.

STEVENS, LENORE; Center HS; Aliquippa, PA; (Y); Exploring; Latin Clb; Spanish Clb; Pres Stu Cncl; Var Mgr(s); Hon Roll; NHS; Fmly Med.

STEVENS, MICHELE; North Pocono HS; Lake Ariel, PA; (S); 31/250; Trs Church Yth Grp; Band; Church Choir; Concert Band; Mrchg Band; Orch; School Musical; Hon Roll; NHS; Med.

STEVENS, MICHELLE; General Mc Lane HS; Edinboro, PA; (Y); 10/210; French Clb; Letterman Clb; SADD; Sec Chorus; Jazz Band; Swing Chorus; JV Var Cheerleading; JV Var Vllybl; High Hon Roll; NHS; Dstrct, Rgnl & St Chorus 86; Bio.

STEVENS, WENDY; Bellwood-Antis HS; Altoona, PA; (Y); Church Yth Grp; Chorus; Church Choir; School Musical; Variety Show; Nwsp Stf; Yrbk Stf; DAR Awd; Hon Roll; VP NHS; Lncstr Bible Coll; Elem Ed.

STEVENSON, DALE; Solanco HS; New Providence, PA; (Y); Var L Crs Cntry; Var L Trk; Hon Roll; Grad Gold Collor 86; Rotary Stu Mnth 86; Rose Hulman Inst Of Tech; Physc.

STEVENSON, DEAN; Grace Christian Schl; Myerstown, PA; (S); 1/10; Drama Clb; Spanish Clb; Band; Chorus; Church Choir; Concert Band; Jazz Band; School Play; Yrbk Stf; Var Bsbl; Fruit Of The Spirit Schlrshp 84-85; Distngsh Christn Hgh Schl Stu 84-85; Coaches Awd 84-85; Messiah Coll; Englsh Educ.

STEVENSON, ERIC; Chartiers Valley HS; Carnegie, PA; (Y); Cmnty Wkr; Letterman Clb; Ski Clb; Varsity Clb; Pres Stu Cncl; Crs Cntry; Mgr Fld Hcky; Capt L Ice Hcky; Ntl Merit Ltr; Ice Hcky MVP, Most Imprvd 84-86; Ice Hcky Keyston Games 86.

STEVER, MEG; Tyrone Area HS; Tyrone, PA; (Y); Church Yth Grp; Key Clb; Office Aide; SADD; Varsity Clb; Band; Concert Band; Mrchg Band; Var Capt Cheerleading; Stat Trk; Hmcmng Prncss 84-85; Bio.

STEWARD, YVONNE; Central HS; Martinsburg, PA; (Y); 3/175; Church Yth Grp; FCA; FTA; GAA; Varsity Clb; Yrbk Bus Mgr; VP Stu Cncl; Co-Capt Bsktbl; L Trk; Drama Clb; Sci Awd 86; Steward Athltc Schlr Awd 86; IN U Of PA; Educ For Excptnl.

STEWART, AMY; Fannett-Metal HS; Doylesburg, PA; (S); Camera Clb; Drama Clb; Chorus; Chorus; Concert Band; Mrchg Band; JV Sftbl; Hon Roll; Drftg.

STEWART, ANDREW M; Cardinal Daugherty HS; Phila, PA; (Y); 131/747; German Clb; Mrchg Band; Var Capt Golf; Hon Roll; Golf MVP Awd 83; 2nd Hnrs Schltc; La Salle U; Bus Admin.

STEWART, ANGELA; Karns City HS; Bruin, PA; (Y); 4/113; Trs FCA; SADD; L Teachers Aide; School Play; JV Var Bsktbl; L Trk; JV Var Vllybl; Hon Roll; NHS; Ntl Merit Ltr; Butler Cty Miss Fnlst 86; Grove City Coll; Med.

STEWART, BETH; Carlynton HS; Carnegie, PA; (Y); #35 In Class; Nwsp Rptr; Rep Frsh Cls; Rep Soph Cls; Rep Stu Cncl; JV Var Cheerleading; JV Var Swmmng; High Hon Roll; Hon Roll; Pittsbgh Bty Acad; Csmtlgy Mgmt.

STEWART, BONNIE; Wilmington Area HS; New Wilmingtn, PA; (Y); 38/101; Exploring; FBLA; Key Clb; Latin Clb; Chorus; Church Choir; School Musical; Stage Crew; Hon Roll; Dist Chorus 84; Westminster Clg; Accntng.

STEWART, CONSTANCE; Northwestern Lehigh HS; Schnecksville, PA; (Y); Var Cheerleading; Var Mgr(s); High Hon Roll; Hon Roll; Muhlenberg; Para-Legal.

STEWART, DAPHNE A; Central Dauphin East HS; Dauphin, PA; (Y); 19/274; Sec Trs Church Yth Grp; Chorus; Capt Flag Corp; Orch; Yrbk Stf; Hst Soph Cls; High Hon Roll; Hon Roll; Jr NHS; NHS; Chem Engr.

STEWART, DAVID; Canon Mc Millan HS; Canonsburg, PA; (Y); 36/400; Church Yth Grp; Exploring; Latin Clb; Ski Clb; Timer; Trk; Wrstlng; Hon Roll; Elctrncs.

STEWART, DIANA; West Greene SR HS; New Freeport, PA; (S); 1/109; Science Clb; SADD; Teachers Aide; Concert Band; Mrchg Band; Nwsp Rptr; Yrbk Stf; High Hon Roll; Grmn Awd; All Cnty Band; Bst Geoglst Awd Sci Fair; Waynesburg Coll; Math.

STEWART, ERICKA; Strong Vincent HS; Erie, PA; (Y); 45/164; GAA; Band; Chorus; Madrigals; Mrchg Band; Variety Show; Yrbk Stf; Rep Stu Cncl; Bsktbl; Bowling; Trck & Fld MVP 85; Bus.

STEWART, HEIDI; Bradford Area HS; Bradford, PA; (Y); AFS; Ski Clb; Trs SADD; Chorus; Trk; Twrlr; Hon Roll; Mdcl Explrs Boy Scouts Of Amer Pres 86-87; Cert Of Atndnc To Mnsfld Rdy Wrtng Cntst 84; PA ST U; Rhbltn Ed.

STEWART, HELEN; Oliver HS; Pittsburgh, PA; (Y); 4-H; Office Aide; ROTC; Trk; High Hon Roll; Hon Roll; Bradford Schl Of Bus; Accntg.

STEWART, JACQUELINE; Waynesburg Central HS; Waynesburg, PA; (Y); 4-H; Girl Scts; Hosp Aide; Library Aide; Band; Color Guard; Mrchg Band; Capt Twrlr; Hon Roll; Acctnt.

STEWART, JAMES; Bensalem SR HS; Bensalem, PA; (Y); FCA; FBLA; FFA; Letterman Clb; OEA; SADD; Varsity Clb; Ftbl; Var Capt Wrstlng; High Hon Roll; Acctng.

STEWART, JODI; Council Rock HS; Churchville, PA; (Y); 180/759; Church Yth Grp; Girl Scts; Hosp Aide; Intnl Clb; Key Clb; Church Choir; Flag Corp; Mrchg Band; Im Powder Puff Ftbl; Grove City Coll; Pre-Med.

STEWART, KENNETH; Meyersdale HS; Meyersdale, PA; (Y); French Clb; Yrbk Stf; JV Var Bsktbl; Golf; Swmmng; Tennis; L Trk; 1st & 3rd Pl JR Olympcs 86; Alleghany CC; Acctg.

STEWART, KEVIN; United HS; Homer City, PA; (S); 4/157; Aud/Vis; Chess Clb; Church Yth Grp; Chorus; Church Choir; High Hon Roll; Hon Roll; Jr NHS; NHS; Ntl Merit Ltr; Marine Bio Quest 86 ARIN 86; Comp Engr.

STEWART, LISA; West Greene HS; Graysville, PA; (Y); Trs Letterman Clb; Trs Varsity Clb; School Musical; Nwsp Stf; Yrbk Stf; Stu Cncl; VP Capt Cheerleading; Var L Trk; Var VP Vllybl; High Hon Roll; Fnlst Intl Chrldng Comptn 85; Qlfd Rgnl Comptn Trck/Fld 86.

STEWART, LISA; West Phila Catholic Girls HS; Philadelphia, PA; (Y); 14/245; Trs French Clb; Service Clb; Chorus; School Play; Cheerleading; High Hon Roll; Hon Roll; Sec NHS; Semi Fnlst Mayors Cty Schlrshp Prgm 86; Exmplry Stu Awd 86; Pres Awd Physcl & Acadexcllnc 86; Gwynedd-Mercy Coll; Radlgc Tech.

STEWART, MARK; Meadville Area SR HS; Meadville, PA; (Y); Church Yth Grp; Latin Clb; Im Socr; High Hon Roll; Hon Roll; Prfct Atten Awd; John Carroll U; Bus Admnstrtn.

STEWART, MARY JO; Knoch JR-SR HS; Saxonburg, PA; (Y); Debate Tm; Library Aide; Speech Tm; Band; Mrchg Band; Pep Band; Symp Band; Mgr(s); Hon Roll; Voice Dem Awd; Villa Maria Coll; Nrsng.

STEWART, MELINDA; Waynesburg Central HS; Mt Morris, PA; (Y); Ski Clb; VP Spanish Clb; Chrmn Y-Teens; Nwsp Rptr; Hon Roll; WV U; Architctr.

STEWART, NICOLE DEE; Ephrata HS; Akron, PA; (Y); 27/235; German Clb; Trs Service Clb; Trk; Hon Roll; Pres Schlr; Hibshman Schlrsh P86; Hnr Grad 86; York Coll; Child Psychlgy.

STEWART, RACHEL; York County Area Vo-Tech; York, PA; (Y); #2 In Class; Church Yth Grp; Church Choir; Color Guard; Jr Cls; High Hon Roll; Hon Roll; NHS; Rotary Awd; VP HOSA 84-85, Pres 85-86; RN.

STEWART, REBECCA; Southern Columbia Area HS; Catawissa, PA; (Y); Church Yth Grp; Computer Clb; Hon Roll; Math.

STEWART, RICHARD; Mc Keesport Area HS; Mckeesport, PA; (Y); 5/339; Church Yth Grp; German Clb; L Swmmng; L Trk; High Hon Roll; Provost Day Math Test 86; Rookie Of Yr Swim Tm 84; MVP Church Vllybl 86; Carnegie Mellon U; Engr.

STEWART, ROBERT; Greensburg-Salem HS; Greensburg, PA; (Y); AFS; Boy Scts; Church Yth Grp; 4-H; German Clb; Band; Concert Band; Mrchg Band; High Hon Roll; Hon Roll; Johnson & Wales; Chef.

STEWART, STACY; Marion Center Area HS; Marion Ctr, PA; (Y); Church Yth Grp; FBLA; FHA; FNA; Service Clb; Chorus; Capt Color Guard; Nwsp Stf; Pres Stu Cncl; Hon Roll; IN U PA; Htl Mgmnt.

STEWART, THERESA; Cardinal O Hara HS; Newtown Square, PA; (Y); Camera Clb; Church Yth Grp; Computer Clb; Spanish Clb; Yrbk Phtg; Yrbk Stf; Hon Roll; NHS; West Chester U; Elem Ed.

STEWART, VIRGINIA; Waynesburg Central HS; Mt Morris, PA; (Y); 17/200; French Clb; Band; Concert Band; Mrchg Band; Hon Roll; Biol II Awd; Melvina Haugen Scholar; PTT Scholar Mt Morris Stu; WVU; Nrsg.

STEWART, WILLIAM; Trnity HS; Carlisle, PA; (Y); 2/150; Church Yth Grp; French Clb; Political Wkr; Red Cross Aide; Var Capt Socr; Im Sftbl; Var Trk; Im Vllybl; High Hon Roll; NHS; Mid-Penn Cnfrnc 1600 Mtr Rn Chmpn Trck 86; Mid-Penn 2nd Tm All-Str Sccr 84.

STEYER, TERRENCE; Springdale HS; Cheswick, PA; (Y); 4/136; Hosp Aide; Band; Jazz Band; Nwsp Ed-Chief; High Hon Roll; Lion Awd; NHS; Church Yth Grp; Drama Clb; German Clb; Allegheny Coll Schlrs Awd, Bro Neal Gldn Awd, Chevron-Reach Schlrshp 86; Allegheny Coll; Med.

STIADLE, PATRICK; Montgomery Area HS; Montgomery, PA; (Y); 6/63; Drama Clb; French Clb; PAVAS; Thesps; Chorus; Church Choir; Madrigals; School Musical; School Play; Swing Chorus; Dist & Regnl Chorus 86; Pre-Med.

STICH, CATHERINE; Penn Cambria SR HS; Loretto, PA; (Y); L Bsktbl; Var Capt Sftbl; Hon Roll; Comp Oper.

STICKER, MARISA; Forest City Regional HS; Pleasant Mt, PA; (Y); 6/60; German Clb; Hon Roll; NHS; Ntl Merit Schol.

STICKLE, JENNY; Butler SR HS; Butler, PA; (Y); Church Yth Grp; Girl Scts; Chorus; Drm & Bgl; Stat Swmmng; Hon Roll; Messiah Coll; Chrstn Ed.

STICKLER, CYNTHIA; Northern Lebanon HS; Jonestown, PA; (Y); Varsity Clb; Color Guard; VP Soph Cls; Sec Sr Cls; Rep Stu Cncl; Var Cheerleading; Hon Roll; NHS; Art Clb; Pep Clb.

STICKLER, STEPHEN; Washington HS; Washington, PA; (S); Boy Scts; Church Yth Grp; Cmnty Wkr; Letterman Clb; Ski Clb; Spanish Clb; Band; Yrbk Stf; VP Frsh Cls; Stu Cncl; Engrng.

STICKLEY, LAURA A; Owen J Roberts HS; Elverson, PA; (S); 13/291; High Hon Roll; Hon Roll; Anchor Clb 85-86; Villanova; Englsh.

STICKLIN, DANIELLE; Danville Area HS; Danville, PA; (Y); Key Clb; SADD; Sec Jr Cls; Var L Crs Cntry; Mat Maids; Trk; Hon Roll; Trs NHS; Acdmc All Amer 84; Med.

STIEDLE, HELGA; Governor Mifflin SR HS; Reading, PA; (Y); 1/320; Varsity Clb; Y-Teens; Chorus; Bsktbl; Fld Hcky; Trk; Vllybl; Hon Roll; Pres NHS; Bio.

STIER, JOHN; Penn Hills SR HS; Verona, PA; (Y); 97/762; Spanish Clb; High Hon Roll; Hon Roll; NHS; Duquesne U Competv Schlrp 86-87; SR Cls Schlrp 86-87; Lamp Of Knwldg Awd 84-86; Duquesne U; Bus.

STIFEL, ELIZABETH; Winchester-Thurston HS; Pittsburgh, PA; (Y); Church Yth Grp; Latin Clb; Library Aide; Thesps; Chorus; School Musical; Stage Crew; Nwsp Phtg; Lit Mag; Pres Sr Cls; Outstndng Latin Stu 86; Outstndng Geo Stu 84; Assoc Artist Pittsburgh Schlrshp 86; Arts.

STIFFEY, BRIAN; Hempfield Area HS; Greensburg, PA; (Y); Letterman Clb; Pep Clb; Ski Clb; L Ftbl; Wt Lftg; L Wrstlng.

STIFFLER, BETH; Penn Cambria SR HS; Lilly, PA; (Y); 28/214; Spanish Clb; Band; Chorus; Concert Band; Mrchg Band; Hon Roll; Villa Maria Coll; Med Tech.

STIFFLER, GREG; Claysburg Kimmel HS; Queen, PA; (S); 19/73; Church Yth Grp; FFA; Band; Mrchg Band; High Hon Roll; Hon Roll; PA Forest Fire Fghtng Trng Awd 85; Cmmnwlth PA DER Cnsvrvtn Awd & Blue Knb YCL Smmr Fstvl Trng 84; Wldlf Mgmt.

STIFFLER, KAROLYN; Central HS; Martinsburg, PA; (Y); 53/188; Cmnty Wkr; FBLA; Chorus; School Musical; Hon Roll; Altoona Schl Commerce; Med Sec.

STIFFLER, KIMBERLY; Chestnut Ridge HS; New Paris, PA; (Y); Church Yth Grp; Girl Scts; Trs Jr Cls; Trs Sr Cls; Sec Stu Cncl; Stat Score Keeper; Capt Socr; Stat Trk; Var Vllybl; Hon Roll; Elem Tchr.

STIFFLER, KRISTINE; Quigley HS; Aliquippa, PA; (Y); 30/103; Chorus; Mrchg Band; Cheerleading; Powder Puff Ftbl; Twrlr; DAR Awd; Hon Roll; Band; Toastmstrs Of Am 84-85; Rythmc Typg Cert 85-86; Typg Profcncy Cert 86; ICM Schl Of Bus; Bus Admn.

STIGERWALT, KELLY; Milton Area SR HS; New Columbia, PA; (Y); Church Yth Grp; FTA; Spanish Clb; Band; Concert Band; Mrchg Band; Hon Roll; NHS; Bloomsburg U; Bus.

STILES, CAROL; Penns Manor HS; Clymer, PA; (Y); 4/102; SADD; Chorus; Concert Band; Jazz Band; Mrchg Band; School Musical; High Hon Roll; Hon Roll; NHS; Prfct Atten Awd.

STILES, GRANT; Western Wayne HS; Lake Ariel, PA; (Y); 4-H; Trs FFA; Natl Beta Clb; JV Var Wrstlng; 4-H Awd; Prfct Atten Awd; Entmlgy.

STILL, KIRSTEN; Freedom HS; Bethlehem, PA; (Y); German Clb; Pep Clb; Science Clb; Ski Clb; Band; Concert Band; Mrchg Band; School Musical; Symp Band; Stu Cncl; Moravian Coll Schlrshp 86; U Of DE; Bus.

STILLIONS, JERRY; Kiski Area HS; E Vandergrift, PA; (Y); Chorus; Dist Chorus; Mixed Chorus; Boys Glee Clb; Cnty Chorus; Jazz Rock; Sound Tech; Cncrt Chior; Hydraulic Engr.

STILLMAN, CRAIG; Pennsbury HS; Morrisville, PA; (Y); 101/729; Nwsp Phtg; Yrbk Phtg; Capt JV Ftbl; Im Vllybl; NHS; Pres Schlr; IN U Physcis Awd; U Denver; Acctng.

STILTS, RANDY; Elkland Area HS; Osceola, PA; (S); 7/79; Chess Clb; French Clb; Varsity Clb; L Socr; L Trk; High Hon Roll; Hon Roll; NHS; Penn ST U; Engr.

STIM, SUSAN K; Upper Dublin SR HS; Maple Glen, PA; (Y); 50/350; Church Yth Grp; Intnl Clb; Varsity Clb; Concert Band; Symp Band; Powder Puff Ftbl; Co-Capt Socr; Co-Capt Swmmng; NHS; Hmcmg Qn 85-86; Johns Hopkins U.

STIMAKER, MICHELE; Belle Vernon Area HS; Belle Vernon, PA; (Y); 194/272; Pep Clb; Variety Show; Sec Frsh Cls; Pres Soph Cls; Pres Jr Cls; Sec Sr Cls; Stu Cncl; JV Var Cheerleading; Powder Puff Ftbl; Sftbl; Rcvd Lttrs In Chrldng 83-86; Rcvd Plaques Chrldng 85-86; Rcvd Outstndng Chrldr Awd At Cmp 85-86; ICM Schl; Med Asstnt.

STINE, SANDRA; Downingtown SR HS; Chester Springs, PA; (S); 31/574; German Clb; VP GAA; Trs Jr Cls; Trs Sr Cls; Rep Stu Cncl; Var Fld Hcky; JV Capt Lcrss; High Hon Roll; NHS; NEDT Awd.

STINE, SHARON; Bellefonte Area HS; Howard, PA; (Y); Church Yth Grp; Computer Clb; Hon Roll; Schlrshp Soph 84-85; S Hills Bus Schl; Bookkeeper.

STINE, SUSAN C; Dover Area HS; Dover, PA; (Y); Church Yth Grp; Varsity Clb; Chorus; Color Guard; Trs Frsh Cls; Off Stu Cncl; Var Capt Cheerleading; Co Capt Colrgrd-2 Yrs; Central PA Bus Schl.

STINEDURF, SHAWN; West Middlesex HS; New Wilmington, PA; (S); 15/127; Office Aide; Bsktbl; Wt Lftg; High Hon Roll; Hon Roll.

STINER, KIM LEA; Mc Shannan Valley HS; Houtzdale, PA; (Y); 58/134; JA; Red Cross Aide; VP VICA; Band; Color Guard; Concert Band; Mrchg Band; Pep Band; Yrbk Phtg; Yrbk Stf; Upwrd Bnd Hnr & Prtcptn Awd 84-86; U2CA Prtcptn Awd For Cnvntns 86; Music Awd 86; Dubois Campus; Mgmt.

STINSON, RENITA; Trinity HS; Washington, PA; (Y); Pres Church Yth Grp; Civic Clb; Key Clb; Sec Church Choir; Drill Tm; Rep Sr Cls; Stu Cncl; Var Capt Trk; Cit Awd; St Champ Track 86; WV U; Child Psych.

STIPANOVICH, MIKE; Mc Keesport Area HS; White Oak, PA; (Y); 15/339; German Clb; Var Capt Ftbl; Var Capt Trk; High Hon Roll; NHS.

STITELER, TRACEY; Marion Center Area HS; Indiana, PA; (Y); FHA; FNA; Latin Clb; Pep Clb; SADD; Band; Concert Band; Mrchg Band; JV Trk; Nrsng.

STITELY, SUZANNE; Norwin SR HS; Irwin, PA; (Y); 257/576; Ski Clb; Spanish Clb; Pres Color Guard; Mrchg Band; Nwsp Rptr; Hon Roll; Jr NHS; Lttr Awd; IN U Of PA; Fash Mdsg.

STITES, SHANNON; Elizabethtown Area HS; Elizabethtown, PA; (Y); Dance Clb; French Clb; Band; Concert Band; Orch; Im Vllybl; Awd Early Status Adm Elizabethtown Coll 85-86; Elizabethtown Coll; Psychlgy.

STITLEY, JULIE; Shikellamy HS; Sunbury, PA; (Y); 4/301; Church Yth Grp; Intnl Clb; VP Spanish Clb; Band; Concert Band; Jazz Band; Mrchg Band; Hon Roll; VP NHS; Awd Band 86; Pre Law.

STITT, DEE; Elderton HS; Ford City, PA; (Y); 10/99; Varsity Clb; Yrbk Phtg; Trs Soph Cls; Trs Sr Cls; Trs Stu Cncl; Var Capt Bsktbl; Var L Sftbl; Var Capt Vllybl; High Hon Roll; NHS; Elizabeth Stewart Hon Schlrps 86; Armstrong Cnty Sprts Hl Of Fm Inductee 86; Thiel Coll; Accntg.

STITT, JAN; Purchase Line HS; Clymer, PA; (Y); Sec Church Yth Grp; VP French Clb; Drill Tm; Pres Frsh Cls; Pres Soph Cls; Pres Jr Cls; Pres VP Stu Cncl; JV Capt Vllybl; Hon Roll; RN.

STITZINGER, SHARON M; Mc Dowell HS; Erie, PA; (Y); 6/546; German Clb; Model UN; Chorus; School Musical; Rep Sr Cls; Capt Var Crs Cntry; Var L Gym; Var L Trk; Hon Roll; Kiwanis Awd; Chem Awd 85; Model UN Scholar 85; PA Cert Merit 85; SIGMA Awd Mth 83; Allegheny Coll; Bio.

STIVASON, MICHAEL; Apollo-Ridge HS; Apollo, PA; (Y); Pres Ski Clb; Varsity Clb; Capt Ftbl; Wt Lftg; Hon Roll; Lion Awd; NHS; Louise Nelson Scholar 86; Al Abrams Top Wstrn PA Schlr Ath 86; US Army Nathl Schlr Ath Awd 86; Carnegie Mellon; Comp Sci.

STOCK, JAMES; Susquehanna Township HS; Harrisburg, PA; (Y); 36/155; Church Yth Grp; 4-H; Teachers Aide; Hon Roll; Prfct Atten Awd; Dauphin Cnty Ctzns Crime Prevntn Cnsl 86; Forestry.

STOCK, JOSEPH; Bishop Carroll HS; Nanty Glo, PA; (S); 25/103; Church Yth Grp; SADD; Church Choir; L Bsbl; L Bsktbl; Golf; Hon Roll; Ntl Merit Ltr; NEDT Awd; Pitt; Physcl Thrpy.

STOCKDALE, HOLLY; Jefferson-Morgan HS; Jefferson, PA; (Y); Drm Mjr(t); Art Clb; Computer Clb; Office Aide; Spanish Clb; Band; Color Guard; Drm Mjr(t); Mrchg Band; Rep Frsh Cls; Gregg Shorthnd & Typing Awd 85-86; Band Ltr 85-86; Bradford Bus Schl; Exec Sec.

STOCKDALE, JIM; Punxsutawney SR HS; Punxsutawney, PA; (Y); Hon Roll; Wldlf Tech.

STOCKE, LAURA E; Penn Hills HS; Pittsburgh, PA; (Y); 1/797; Drama Clb; French Clb; Concert Band; Jazz Band; Mrchg Band; Orch; School Musical; NHS; Ntl Merit SF; Church Yth Grp; PMEA Hnrs Bnd 84-85; Ntl Flute Choir 85; Duquesne U; Music Ed.

STOCKETT, NOEL; Belle Vernon Area HS; Belle Vernon, PA; (Y); Pres Church Yth Grp; Cmnty Wkr; Pep Clb; Band; Concert Band; Mrchg Band; Pep Band; High Hon Roll; Hon Roll; NHS; Outstndng Hlth Stu Awd & Outstndng Sci Stu Awd 84; Nrsng.

STOCKMAN, MATT; Canon Mc Millan SR HS; Wash, PA; (Y); 52/357; Varsity Clb; School Musical; Bsbl; Co-Capt Bsktbl; High Hon Roll; Athltc Trainer-Stu; Schl Spirit Awd; U Of Pittsburgh; Sprts Med.

STOCKSLAGER, CHRIS; Littlestown HS; Littlestown, PA; (Y); 35/135; Varsity Clb; Stage Crew; Im Bsbl; Var Bsktbl; Var Ftbl; Im Sftbl; Im Tennis; Var Trk; Im Vllybl; Im Wt Lftg; Bus Admin.

STODDARD, KAREN; Central Christian HS; Duboise, PA; (Y); Varsity Clb; Rep Jr Cls; Var L Bsktbl; Var Crs Cntry; Var Sftbl; NHS; Nrsg.

STOE, CHRISTY; Lancaster Country Day Schl; Lancaster, PA; (Y); Cmnty Wkr; Hosp Aide; Model UN; Pres Natl Beta Clb; Office Aide; Yrbk Stf; Chorus; Bsktbl; Fld Hcky; Sftbl; Boston Coll; Smmr Exprnce 86; Coaches Awd Bstkbll 86; Coaches Awd Sftbll 85; Law.

STOECKLE JR, BOB; Fort Cherry JR SR HS; Midway, PA; (Y); 7/128; Aud/Vis; Math Clb; Science Clb; Varsity Clb; Nwsp Stf; Tennis; High Hon Roll; NHS; Henry King Stanford Schlrp 86; U Miami; Cinema.

STOFFAN, CYNTHIA; Corry Area HS; Columbus, PA; (S); 3/215; Pres Church Yth Grp; Spanish Clb; Band; Concert Band; Mrchg Band; Stu Cncl; High Hon Roll; Bus Adm.

STOFFIERE, RICHARD; Elizabeth Forward HS; Elizabeth, PA; (Y); Aud/Vis; Ski Clb; Stage Crew; Var L Golf; Var L Swmmng; Hon Roll; Advncd Plcmnt Am Hist 85-86; PA ST U; Arspc Engrng.

STOGNER, JENNY; Lewisburg HS; Lewisburg, PA; (Y); Church Yth Grp; VP Band; Chorus; Drm Mjr(t); Mrchg Band; VP Orch; Socr; Tennis; NHS; Spanish NHS; Arion Awd-Band 84-85; MI ST U; Music Thrpy.

STOHL, HOLLYLYNNE; Mt Pleasant Area HS; Mt Pleasant, PA; (Y); Dance Clb; FTA; GAA; Nwsp Ed-Chief; Var Cheerleading; Coach Actv; Mat Maids; Wrstlng; High Hon Roll; Hon Roll; Theatre Arts.

STOIANOFF, JENNIFER; Chief Logan HS; Mcclure, PA; (Y); Church Yth Grp; Office Aide; Service Clb; Spanish Clb; Hon Roll; Bus.

STOKER JR, JAMES; South Park HS; Pittsburgh, PA; (Y); Band; Concert Band; Jazz Band; Mrchg Band; High Hon Roll; Hon Roll; USAF Acad; Ofcr.

STOKES, SHARON; Dallas SR HS; Trucksville, PA; (Y); Hosp Aide; Chorus; Hon Roll; Nrsng.

STOLARCZYK, CAROL; Archbishop Kennedy HS; Conshohocken, PA; (Y); Pep Clb; Chorus; Hon Roll; Acdmc Awd Acctg, Phila Natl Bk Awd Acctg 86; VA Commnwealth U; Finance.

STOLTZ, SCOTT; Bishop Guilfoyle HS; Altoona, PA; (Y); 26/117; VP German Clb; Chorus; Stu Cncl; Var Bsbl; JV Bsktbl; PA ST U; Htl Mngmnt.

STOLTZFUS, BETH; Octorara HS; Gap, PA; (Y); Church Yth Grp; Math Clb; Ski Clb; SADD; Band; Concert Band; Jazz Band; Mrchg Band; Pep Band; Pres Soph Cls; Intl Bus.

STOLTZFUS, PATTI; Pequea Valley HS; Kinzers, PA; (Y); FBLA; Sec Yrbk Stf; Rep Frsh Cls; Rep Soph Cls; Rep Jr Cls; Rep Sr Cls; Sec Stu Cncl; Gym; Sftbl; NHS; Bloomsburg U; Acctg.

STOLZE, BRIAN; Avella Area HS; Burgettstown, PA; (Y); French Clb; Letterman Clb; Speech Tm; Variety Show; Trs Soph Cls; Trs Jr Cls; Mgr Bsktbl; JV Mgr Ftbl; Hon Roll; Wnr Of Lip-Sync Cntst 85-86; Chem.

STONE, ANE; Aliquippa HS; Aliquippa, PA; (S); Natl Beta Clb; Church Choir; Pres Frsh Cls; Stu Cncl; Capt Var Bsktbl; Capt L Trk; Var Vllybl; Hon Roll; Most Imprvd Plyr Awd Bsktbl 85-86.

STONE, BARBARA; Monaca JR-SR HS; Monaca, PA; (Y); 10/80; Pep Clb; Red Cross Aide; Sec Jr Cls; Pres Stu Cncl; Golf; Hon Roll; NHS; Nrsng.

STONE, DANIEL BENJAMIN; Warren Area HS; Buffalo, NY; (Y); 21/300; Art Clb; Camera Clb; Chess Clb; French Clb; Nwsp Stf; Cit Awd; High Hon Roll; Hon Roll; Jr NHS; NHS; Acad Lttr Awd 85-86; Gldn Grgn Ctznshp Awd 86; Gldn Key Schltc Art Awd 86; Rochester Inst; Bus.

STONE, DAVID; Blue Mountain Acad; Waverly, PA; (S); Band; Church Choir; Stu Cncl; Hon Roll; 2nd Pl Insprtnl Cat Norma Youngberg Mem Poetry Cont 86; Theolgy.

STONE, DEANNA; New Castle SR HS; New Castle, PA; (Y); Intnl Clb; Office Aide; Pep Clb; SADD; Y-Teens; Band; Mrchg Band; Vllybl; Comp Sci.

STONE, GINNY; Norwin HS; N Huntingdon, PA; (Y); 96/557; German Clb; Office Aide; Chorus; Nwsp Rptr; Yrbk Stf; Stu Cncl; Trk; Educ.

STONE, JOE; James M Caughlin HS; Wilkes Barre, PA; (Y); 38/368; Hon Roll; NHS; ROTC Schlrshp 85-86; PA ST U; Aero Sp Engr.

STONE, JON; Marple Newtown HS; Broomall, PA; (Y); Debate Tm; Ski Clb; Variety Show; Golf; Socr; Tennis; High Hon Roll; Hon Roll; NHS; Pre Dntstry.

STONE, KRISTENA MAREE; Warren Area HS; Warren, PA; (Y); Pres Church Yth Grp; Spanish Clb; Concert Band; Jazz Band; Mrchg Band; Orch; Pep Band; School Musical; School Play; Stat Bsbl; Outstndng Instrmntlst Awd 86; Philomel Clb Scholar 86; Duquesne U; Music Thrpy.

STONE, LISA; Susquenita HS; New Bloomfield, PA; (S); 12/153; Hon Roll; NHS; Harrisburg Area CC; Data Proc.

STONE, MELISSA; Moon SR HS; Coraopolis, PA; (Y); Church Yth Grp; Drama Clb; Key Clb; Stage Crew; Variety Show; Crs Cntry; Trk; Hon Roll; Grphc Arts.

STONE, ROSEMARY; California Area HS; Daisytown, PA; (Y); Drama Clb; JA; Pep Clb; Band; Concert Band; Mrchg Band; Nwsp Stf; Yrbk Stf; Hon Roll; Chem Engr.

STONEBROOK, JEFFREY; Penn Hills HS; Verona, PA; (Y); VP Computer Clb; German Clb; Letterman Clb; Science Clb; Teachers Aide; Varsity Clb; Var L Golf; Var L Tennis; High Hon Roll; Hon Roll; Penn St; Elec Engr.

STONEKING, KATHY; Waynesburg Central HS; Waynesburg, PA; (Y); 1/210; Church Yth Grp; Cmnty Wkr; French Clb; Natl Beta Clb; High Hon Roll; Lion Awd; NHS; NEDT Awd; Pres Schlr; Val; PA ST U; Bus.

STONEKING, MICHELLE; Mapletown JR SR HS; Mt Morris, PA; (Y); Yrbk Stf; Vllybl; High Hon Roll; Hon Roll.

STONER, BECKY; Biglerville HS; Biglerville, PA; (Y); #38 In Class; Church Yth Grp; Chorus; Nwsp Stf; Mgr Ftbl; Mgr(s); Auto Tech.

STONER, JODIE; Blair County Christian HS; Ebensburg, PA; (Y); 2/4; Church Yth Grp; Dance Clb; Teachers Aide; Band; Chorus; Concert Band; Mrchg Band; Pep Band; Nwsp Ed-Chief; Nwsp Stf; U Pitts; Elect Engr.

STONER, KAREN; Southmoreland SR HS; Scottdale, PA; (Y); 2/250; French Clb; Drm Mjr(t); Mrchg Band; Powder Puff Ftbl; French Hon Soc; NHS; Comp.

STONER, LORI; York Suburban HS; York, PA; (Y); 56/192; Church Yth Grp; Hosp Aide; Latin Clb; School Play; Rep Frsh Cls; Rep Sr Cls; L Cheerleading; Tennis; Hon Roll; Hmcmng Queen 85; Bloomsburg U; Med Tech.

STONER, SUSAN; Altoona Area HS; Altoona, PA; (S); French Clb; PAVAS; Chorus; Concert Band; School Musical; School Play; Rep Jr Cls; Jr NHS; Ntl Merit Ltr; NEDT Awd; French Awd 83-84; Pediatrics.

STONFER, DENICE; Frazier JR SR HS; Newell, PA; (Y); Mrchg Band; Bsktbl; Band; Yrbk Sprt Ed; Yrbk Stf; Trs Jr Cls; Sftbl; Twrlr; High Hon Roll; NHS; All Cnty Bsktbl 85-86.

STONGE, TAMMY; Northern York HS; Dillsburg, PA; (Y); Church Yth Grp; Band; Church Choir; Concert Band; Mrchg Band; Socr; Trk; Music.

STOOK, ADRIENNE ANN; G A R Memorial HS; Wilkes Barre, PA; (S); 20/177; FBLA; Library Aide; Office Aide; Pep Clb; Ski Clb; Chorus; Cheerleading; Hon Roll; Jr NHS; NHS; Typing Awds 84-85; Flight Attndnt.

STOOPS, KIM; Slippery Rock Area HS; Harrisville, PA; (Y); 26/177; Church Yth Grp; Intnl Clb; Pep Clb; Spanish Clb; Thesps; Mrchg Band; Stage Crew; Trk; Hon Roll; Marine Bio.

STOOPS, SHEILA; Susquenita HS; Duncannon, PA; (S); 17/200; 4-H; French Clb; Leo Clb; Flag Corp; Yrbk Stf; NHS; HACC; Paralgl.

STOPPERICH, TODD; Canon Mc Millan SR HS; Canonsburg, PA; (Y); Sr Cls; Stu Cncl; Wt Lftg; Wrstlng; High Hon Roll; Hon Roll; WA & Jefferson.

STORCH, ANNE; Cedar Crest HS; Lebanon, PA; (Y); 57/306; Drama Clb; French Clb; Model UN; Pep Clb; School Musical; Socr; Tennis; Hon Roll; People To People HS Stu Ambsdr Pgm 85; Intl Rltns.

STOREY, JENNIFER; Peters Township HS; Mc Murray, PA; (Y); Band; Drill Tm; Mrchg Band; Yrbk Stf; Pom Pon; JV Trk; Comm.

STORIONE, MARIA; St Maria Goretti HS; Philadelphia, PA; (Y); 122/390; Hon Roll; Psych.

STORM, EILEEN; Downington HS; Exton, PA; (S); 25/527; Pres Computer Clb; Spanish Clb; Yrbk Stf; Sec Rep Stu Cncl; High Hon Roll; NHS; Rotary Awd; Millersville U; Comp Sci.

STORMS, ERIC; Altoona Area HS; Altoona, PA; (S); Sec Chess Clb; Church Yth Grp; CAP; Spanish Clb; Color Guard; Rep Jr Cls; Off Sr Cls; JV L Bsbl; CO U; Aeronauticl Engrng.

STORMS, JENNIFER; Spring-Ford HS; Royersford, PA; (S); 28/231; FBLA; Trs Sr Cls; Bsktbl; L Fld Hcky; L Lcrss; Hon Roll; Pres NHS; Ithaca Coll; TV Cmnctns.

STORTI, CORINNE; Norristown Area HS; Norristown, PA; (Y); Hosp Aide; Teachers Aide; VICA; Chorus; High Hon Roll; Hon Roll; Prfct Atten Awd; Students Club 85; Super Citizen Awd 83; Outstanding Student Awd For Good Grades 86; Certified Health Asst.

STORTI, JESSICA; Union Area HS; New Castle, PA; (Y); 14/66; Library Aide; Office Aide; Trs Color Guard; Nwsp Stf; Yrbk Ed-Chief; Stat Trk; Hon Roll; NHS; Acadmc All Amer 86; Pres Acadmc Ftns Awd 86; Slipper Rock U.

STOSHAK, SUSAN; Bishop Hoban HS; Sugar Notch, PA; (Y); 9/198; French Clb; Math Clb; Ski Clb; Speech Tm; Cheerleading; Hon Roll; Mu Alp Tht; NHS; Frnch Awd 83-84; Hnr Rl 82-86; PA ST U; Engrng.

STOTKA, LISA; Hopewell HS; Aliquippa, PA; (S); 12/260; Trs German Clb; Chorus; Sec Frsh Cls; Sec Soph Cls; Co-Capt Cheerleading; Powder Puff Ftbl; Tennis; Trk; High Hon Roll; Excelled Pgm; SF Miss Beaver Co Jr Miss Pgm Jaycees 86; Med Explorers Aliquippa Hosp 85-86; Duquesne U; Pharm.

STOUDT, JILL K; Owen J Roberts HS; Spring City, PA; (S); 6/261; Trs Service Clb; Concert Band; Rep Frsh Cls; Rep Soph Cls; Rep Jr Cls; JV Lcrss; Co-Capt Tennis; High Hon Roll; Hon Roll; NHS; Athltc Awds-Tennis Letters 82-85; U Of Pittsburgh; Biolgcl Sci.

STOUDT, RICHARD; Allentown Central Catholic HS; Whitehall, PA; (Y); 36/210; Church Yth Grp; Math Clb; Band; Golf; Phrmcy.

STOUFFER, GINGER; Chambersburg Area SR HS; Chambersburg, PA; (Y); 1/620; Pres Girl Scts; Library Aide; Concert Band; Jazz Band; Orch; High Hon Roll; Girl Scout Silver Awd; Bus.

STOUFFER, JASON; Connellsville Area SR HS; Scottdale, PA; (Y); 110/650; Chess Clb; JV Wrstlng; Liberty U; Math.

STOUFFER, LAWRENCE; Greater Latrobe SR HS; Latrobe, PA; (Y); 47/419; CAP; Ski Clb; Mgr(s); DAR Awd; French Hon Soc; High Hon Roll; Hon Roll; Church Yth Grp; French Clb; Gen Willim Billy Mitchell Awd Civil Air Patrol 85; PA Wing Flt Schlrshp Civil Air Patrol 86; Air Force; Pilot.

STOUFFER, MICHELE; Greencastle Antrim HS; Greencastle, PA; (Y); Band; Chorus; Concert Band; Mrchg Band; Sec Soph Cls; Sec Jr Cls; Var Capt Cheerleading; Score Keeper; Stat Sftbl; Swmmng; Sectrl.

STOUGH, JACQUELINE; York County Area Vo-Tech; York, PA; (Y); 29/391; Computer Clb; Library Aide; Concert Band; Jazz Band; Mrchg Band; High Hon Roll; Hon Roll; Outstndng Dental Stdnt Awd 86; Hlth Occptns Stdnts Of America 83-86; Dental Assistant.

STOUGH, MICHELLE; Dover HS; Dover, PA; (Y); Church Yth Grp; Cmnty Wkr; Girl Scts; Hosp Aide; Acpl Chr; Band; Chorus; Church Choir; Concert Band; Jazz Band; Girls Trk Tm Champions-YCIAA AAA Dist A Champions 85; Temple U; Physcl Thrpy.

STOUT, KITTY; Mercyhurst Prep; Erie, PA; (Y); 4/150; JCL; Spanish Clb; Thesps; Acpl Chr; Sec Chorus; Pep Band; School Musical; Hon Roll; NHS; Yth For Undrstndng Am Ovrseas 86; Musc Thrpy.

STOUT, SHERRI; Troy Area HS; Columbia Cross Rd, PA; (Y); 7/144; Sec VP Church Yth Grp; Sec 4-H; SADD; Color Guard; Mrchg Band; L Bsktbl; Score Keeper; Trk; Hon Roll; NHS; Outstndng Span Awd 84-85; John Jay Coll; Police Sci.

STOUT, TAYLORINA; Yough SR HS; Herminie, PA; (Y); 27/250; Church Yth Grp; Church Choir; School Play; High Hon Roll; Hon Roll; NHS; Ntl Engl Merit Awd 86.

STOVAR, MARTIN; Penn Trafford HS; Trafford, PA; (Y); 19/338; Varsity Clb; Band; Var L Bsktbl; Var Capt Ftbl; Hon Roll; NHS; Pres Schlr; Carnegie Mellon U; Indstrl Mgmt.

STOVER, BRENNAN; York Catholic HS; York, PA; (Y); 50/175; Cmnty Wkr; Spanish Clb; Varsity Clb; Band; Concert Band; Mrchg Band; Symp Band; Bsktbl; Ftbl; Hon Roll; Law.

STOVER, MELISSA; Middleburg Joint HS; New Berlin, PA; (Y); 46/132; Art Clb; FBLA; FHA; Key Clb; Ski Clb; SADD; Stage Crew; JV Cheerleading; DAR Awd; Hon Roll; 3rd Sch Art Shw 86; Art School; Comm Art.

STOVER, SEAN; Wilmington Area HS; New Wilmington, PA; (S); 1/102; Drama Clb; Spanish Clb; Band; Mrchg Band; Pep Band; School Musical; School Play; Stage Crew; High Hon Roll; NHS; Lions All ST Band 85-86; AF Acad; Aeronaut Engrng.

STOVER, SHERRY; Palmyra Area SR HS; Campbelltown, PA; (Y); 9/200; SADD; Drm Mjr(t); Yrbk Stf; Var Tennis; High Hon Roll; NHS; Ntl Merit Ltr; Amer Lg Essay Awd 86; Chem Engrng.

STOY, BILL; Somerset Area SR HS; Somerset, PA; (Y); 16/239; English Clb; French Clb; Math Clb; Varsity Clb; Var L Bsbl; Var JV Bsktbl; JV Golf; Wt Lftg; High Hon Roll; NHS; Bus.

STOYER, DEAN; Susquehanna Township HS; Harrisburg, PA; (Y); 59/162; German Clb; Varsity Clb; Chorus; Concert Band; Jazz Band; Mrchg Band; Nwsp Sprt Ed; Yrbk Sprt Ed; Var Bsbl; Var Ftbl; Jrnlsm.

STRACHAN, BILL; Norwin SR HS; Irwin, PA; (Y); 62/550; Church Yth Grp; Debate Tm; Leo Clb; Letterman Clb; NFL; Pep Clb; Ski Clb; SADD; Stu Cncl; Var L Socr; Grove City Coll; Pre-Law.

STRACHAN, LAURIE; Western Beaver HS; Midland, PA; (Y); 17/80; Church Yth Grp; Band; Concert Band; Drm Mjr(t); Mrchg Band; Symp Band; Yrbk Stf; Im Bsktbl; Var L Trk; High Hon Roll; Slippery Rock U; Bus.

STRACHAN, RONDA; Quaker Valley HS; Sewickley, PA; (Y); Chrmn Spanish Clb; Chorus; School Musical; Gym; Swmmng; High Hon Roll; Kiwanis Awd; NCTE Awd; NHS; Dance Mstrs PA Schlrshp 85; Outstndng Vclst Chorus 84; Choreogrphr & Lead Role Schl Mscl 85-86; Psych.

STRAHL, BESSIE; Hempfield SR HS; New Stanton, PA; (Y); Cmnty Wkr; Hosp Aide; Ski Clb; Spanish Clb; Concert Band; Mrchg Band; Hon Roll; Jr NHS; Spanish NHS; High Hon Roll; Lock Haven U; Chem.

STRAHLEY, LISA; Huntingdon Area HS; Huntingdon, PA; (Y); Exploring; Hosp Aide; Key Clb; Political Wkr; SADD; Teachers Aide; Trk; Prom Comm Orgnzr 85-86; Homeroom Rep 83-86; Spec Olympcs 83-86; Merch.

STRAIT, CHRIS; Mc Connellsburg HS; Harrisonville, PA; (Y); Church Yth Grp; Pres 4-H; Pres FFA; High Hon Roll; Animal.

STRAIT, DARLENE; Otto-Eldred JR SR HS; Duke Center, PA; (Y); Church Yth Grp; Exploring; Chorus; Church Choir; Nwsp Stf; Hon Roll; Mech Drwng.

STRAIT, DEBBIE; Mc Connellsburg HS; Hustontown, PA; (Y); Church Yth Grp; Chorus; High Hon Roll; Hon Roll; Tn Temple U; Elem Educ.

STRAIT, JANET; Mc Connellsburg HS; Mcconnellsburg, PA; (Y); Art Clb; FHA; Stage Crew; Yrbk Ed-Chief; Var L Vllybl; DAR Awd; High Hon Roll; Hon Roll; Jr NHS; NHS; Accntng.

STRAIT, WENDY L; Southern Fulton HS; Warfordsburg, PA; (Y); Church Yth Grp; French Clb; Pres FHA; Chorus; Nwsp Stf; Stat Bsbl; Co-Capt Cheerleading; Twrlr; Hon Roll; NHS; Acdmc All Am Math & French 86; Plaque Announcing 86; Shipensburg U; Math.

STRAKA, JOEL W; Sewickley Acad; Sewickley, PA; (Y); 1/61; VP Key Clb; Rep Pres Stu Cncl; Var Capt CC Awd; Var L Socr; Var Capt Wrstlng; Hon Roll; Ntl Merit SF; Williams Coll Bk Awd 85; Brown U Bk Awd 85; MVP Wrestling 83 & 85; Bio.

STRAMARA, MIKE; Manheim Township HS; Lancaster, PA; (Y); Church Yth Grp; Key Clb; Ski Clb; Im Bsbl; Var Ftbl; Im Golf; Var Swmmng; Var Tennis; Im Vllybl; Hon Roll; Bus.

STRANDQUEST, MICHELE; Greater Johnstown SR HS; Johnstown, PA; (Y); Church Yth Grp; Ski Clb; Spanish Clb; Chorus; Yrbk Stf; Trk; Hon Roll; NHS; Pres Physcl Ftnss Awd 85-86; Marine Bio.

STRANGE, MEGHAN; Nazareth Acad; Huntington Vly, PA; (S); Drama Clb; Latin Clb; Chorus; Church Choir; Orch; School Musical; School Play; Jr NHS; Nazareth Acad Vcl Schlrshp 83; Prfrmng Arts.

STRANK, PAULA; Conemaugh Valley JR SR HS; Johnstown, PA; (Y); 22/120; French Clb; Library Aide; Office Aide; Pep Clb; Nwsp Rptr; Yrbk Ed-Chief; Yrbk Phtg; Trs Jr Cls; Hon Roll; NHS; FHA Awd 84; Phys Educ Awd 86; Sec.

STRANO, JOHN; St John Neumann HS; Pheladelphia, PA; (Y); 57/320; Computer Clb; Spanish Clb; Yrbk Ed-Chief; Yrbk Phtg; Im Ftbl; Im Vllybl; Drexel U; Elec Engr.

STRANZL, LORI; William Allen HS; Allentown, PA; (Y); 51/576; GAA; Pres Service Clb; Varsity Clb; Ed Yrbk Ed-Chief; Var L Bsktbl; Var L Fld Hcky; Var L Sftbl; NHS; MVP Fld Hcky 86; Carol Weil Mem Schlrshp 86; Big A Bstr Clb Schlrshp 86; PA ST U.

STRASSER, JEFF; Cathedral Prep; Erie, PA; (Y); 25/236; Church Yth Grp; Im Bsktbl; Im Vllybl; MVP Bsktbl; Gannon U; Pre Pharmcy.

STRATTON, TONYA; Waynesburg Central HS; Waynesburg, PA; (Y); 42/207; Letterman Clb; Library Aide; Office Aide; Score Keeper; Var Sftbl; High Hon Roll; Hon Roll; Cert Recog Hstry 85-86; Acctg.

STRATTS, GEORGE; Archbishop Carroll HS; Newtown Sq, PA; (S); 4/166; Pres Soph Cls; Pres Jr Cls; Var Ftbl; Var Trk; Var Wt Lftg; High Hon Roll; Jr NHS; Soph Rep HOBY Ldrshp Sem 85; Close Up Fndtn 86; 2nd Tm All Cath Ftbl 85; Civl Engrng.

STRAUB, JULIE; Elk County Christian HS; St Marys, PA; (Y); Varsity Clb; Sec Soph Cls; Rep VP Stu Cncl; Var Capt Bsktbl; Var L Crs Cntry; Var Stat Trk; JV Vllybl; High Hon Roll; Stdnt Athl Awd; U S Army Resrv Natl Schlr Athl Awd; Math.

STRAUB, KATHLEEN M; Bethel Park SR HS; Bethel Park, PA; (Y); 20/515; Hosp Aide; Crs Cntry; Trk; NHS; St Joan Arc Medallion Vol Svc 85; Ntl Eng Merit Awd 84; Phi Delta Kappa Dist Schrlshp Wnnr 86; Boston Coll; Spcl Ed.

STRAUB, KEVIN; Scranton Technical HS; Scranton, PA; (Y); Boys Clb Am; VICA; Badmtn; Bsbl; Bowling; Ftbl; Sftbl; Vllybl; Wt Lftg; Hon Roll; Won The WNEP Tv 16 Nwsgme 3 Times 85-86; I Attnd Voc Tech Schl 84-86; Johnsons Tech Schl; Auto Body.

STRAUB, LINDA; Fort Le Boeuf HS; Erie, PA; (Y); Camera Clb; Hosp Aide; Model UN; Spanish Clb; Nwsp Rptr; Rep Jr Cls; Var Trk; Var Vllybl; High Hon Roll; Hon Roll; Hrtg Chrst Acad Cert Of Awd For Scrptr Memory 84; Piano Exc Awd For Recitals 83 & 84; Dntstry.

STRAUB, MARK; Cathedral Prep Schl; Erie, PA; (Y); 81/216; Church Yth Grp; Ski Clb; Im Bsktbl; Var L Wrstlng; Outstndng Nwsp Carrier Yr 85; PA ST; Bus Adm.

STRAUB, PETER; Elk County Christian HS; St Marys, PA; (S); Boy Scts; Varsity Clb; Pres Frsh Cls; Pres Soph Cls; Pres Jr Cls; Pres Cmnty Wkr; Var L Bsktbl; Trk; Hon Roll; NHS.

STRAUB, TAMMY; Elk County Christian HS; St Marys, PA; (S); 10/80; Hosp Aide; Ski Clb; Yrbk Stf; JV Var Bsktbl; Var Trk; JV Vllybl; High Hon Roll; NEDT Awd; Phrmcy.

STRAUSBAUGH JR, EARL; Spring Grove SR HS; Spg Grove, PA; (Y); AFS; Boy Scts; Cmnty Wkr; 4-H; FFA; Girl Scts; SADD; VICA; Bsbl; NHS; Dubois; Wldlf Technlgy.

STRAUSER, DEBORAH; Keystone JR-SR HS; Cranberry, PA; (Y); 2/125; FBLA; Hosp Aide; Letterman Clb; Color Guard; Var L Bsktbl; High Hon Roll; NHS; Prfct Atten Awd; Sal; Gannon U; Pedtrcs.

STRAUSS, DAVID; John Piersol Mccaskey HS; Lancaster, PA; (Y); AFS; Drama Clb; Q&S; School Play; Nwsp Rptr; Yrbk Stf; Lit Mag; Socr; Hon Roll; NCTE Awd; Engl Tutorng 85; Theatrics 85; Engl.

STRAUSS, LESLIE; Northern Lebanon HS; Jonestown, PA; (Y); 27/177; Trs Church Yth Grp; FCA; Pres Trs 4-H; Color Guard; Mrchg Band; JV Bsktbl; 4-H Awd; Hon Roll; Chorus; Swing Chorus; Lebanon Co Teen Cncl Vp; Lebanon Co Horse Bowl Cptn; Psych.

STRAUSS, MARY GRACE; Centger HS; Aliquippa, PA; (Y); Exploring; Hosp Aide; Rep Band; Yrbk Ed-Chief; Trs Soph Cls; Rep Stu Cncl; Capt Rep Twrlr; Hon Roll; Jr NHS; Prfct Atten Awd; Outstndng Majorette Of Yr 85-86; Gftd Cmptrs & Gftd Art 83-87; Cndystrpng 100 Hr Vlntr Pin 86; U Of PA; Bus.

STRAUSSER, BETH; Phoenixville Area HS; Phoenixville, PA; (Y); Key Clb; Scholastic Bowl; Chorus; School Musical; Hon Roll; NHS; Church Yth Grp; Cmnty Wkr; Pep Clb; Quiz Bowl; Dist Chorus Awd 86; Latn II III Awd 85-86; Bio Awd 85; Librl Arts.

STRAUSSER, DAFFNEY; Millville Area HS; Millville, PA; (Y); Church Yth Grp; Spanish Clb; School Play; JV Fld Hcky; High Hon Roll; Hon Roll; Nrsg.

STRAUSSER, TODD; Danville SR HS; Danville, PA; (Y); FFA; Bsbl; Ftbl; Wt Lftg; Wrstlng; DE Valley; Ag.

STRAW, AMY; Du Bois Area HS; Grampian, PA; (Y); Office Aide; Mat Maids; Score Keeper; Hon Roll; Jr Attndnt In Coronation Ct; Dubois Bus Coll; Accntng.

STRAW, MICHELLE; Warwick HS; Lititz, PA; (Y); 26/237; Pres Trs Church Yth Grp; Computer Clb; Elks Awd; High Hon Roll; Hon Roll; NHS; Stu Mnth Womans Clb 86; Millersville U; Elem Ed.

STRAWLEY, FAITH; Sun Valley HS; Aston, PA; (Y); 45/319; Science Clb; Band; Chorus; Concert Band; Jazz Band; Mrchg Band; Variety Show; Swmmng; Hon Roll; Jr NHS; Schlrshp Luzerne Music Ctr NY 84; Cigna Schlrshp Priv Stdy Music 84-86; Dist II Orch 84; Temple U; Lwyr.

STRAWN, SUSAN; Punxsutawney Area HS; Punxsutawney, PA; (Y); 4-H; French Clb; Varsity Clb; Band; Flag Corp; Variety Show; Capt Twrlr; 4-H Awd; IUP; Elem Ed.

STRAYER, CHRISTINA; Montgomery JR SR HS; Allenwood, PA; (Y); Yrbk Stf; Cit Awd; High Hon Roll; NHS; Local Govt Day Borough Mgr 84; Annual Bus Educ Symposm 85-86; 1st Cls Prem Lycmng Cnty Fair Prnt Mkng; Teachng.

STRAYER, DODIE JO; Shippensburg Area HS; Shippensburg, PA; (Y); Computer Clb; Drama Clb; FBLA; Chorus; Capt Color Guard; School Musical; Cheerleading; Hon Roll; Lion Awd; Hnr Stu 86; Central PA Bus Schl; Acctg.

STRAYER, LANCE; Upper Dauphin Area HS; Gratz, PA; (Y); 6/112; Chess Clb; Church Yth Grp; Rep Frsh Cls; Hon Roll; Cert Achvt German 86; Cert Achvt Bio & Wrld Cultures 85; Elctrnc Engrng.

STRAYER, PATRICK; Chambersburg Area SR HS; Fayetteville, PA; (Y); 13/602; Church Yth Grp; Rep Frsh Cls; Bsbl; Var Bsktbl; Ftbl; Sftbl; High Hon Roll; Hon Roll; Ntl Merit Ltr; Law.

STRAYER, SHELLEY; Chestnut Ridge HS; Schellsburg, PA; (S); 18/142; Office Aide; Ski Clb; Band; Concert Band; Mrchg Band; Nwsp Rptr; Ed Nwsp Stf; Stu Cncl; Var Sftbl; Hon Roll; Duquesne U; Phrmcy.

STRAZISAR, ANTHONY; South Park HS; Library, PA; (Y); 3/185; Church Yth Grp; Exploring; FBLA; JA; JV Var Bsktbl; JV Ftbl; L Tennis; Var Trk; High Hon Roll; NHS.

STRECKER, WENDY; Ambridge Area HS; Baden, PA; (Y); 110/270; 4-H; German Clb; Girl Scts; Pep Clb; Quiz Bowl; Band; Chorus; Concert Band; Mrchg Band; Orch; Nrsg.

STREDNAK, CHRISTINA; Mount Pleasant Area HS; Acme, PA; (Y); 7/254; GAA; Nwsp Stf; VP Frsh Cls; VP Soph Cls; VP Jr Cls; VP Sr Cls; Capt L Cheerleading; CC Awd; High Hon Roll; VP NHS; Ntl Math Awd 85-86; Rotary Awd; Indiana U PA; Speech Pthlgy.

STREETT, KAREN; Kennard Dale HS; Fawn Grove, PA; (Y); 9/130; German Clb; Varsity Clb; Chorus; Church Choir; Yrbk Stf; Capt L Crs Cntry; Capt L Trk; Hon Roll; NHS; NEDT Awd; 15th ST X-Cntry 86; Yth Tour To Washington 86; Pre-Med.

STREHL, MARY BETH; Lebanon Christian Acad; Lebanon, PA; (S); 1/8; Church Yth Grp; Drama Clb; Chorus; School Musical; Yrbk Stf; VP Jr Cls; VP Sr Cls; Vllybl; Hon Roll; Prfct Atten Awd; Ex Libris Awd 85; Engl & Hstry Awds 85; Lbrl Arts.

STRELECKY, BETH; Upper Perkiomen HS; Pennsburg, PA; (Y); 30/242; Cmnty Wkr; Powder Puff Ftbl; JV Sftbl; Hon Roll; Hnrbl Mntn Mntgmry Cnty Sci Fair; Scnd Pl Mntgmry Cnty Sci Fair; Hnrbl DE Vlly Sci Fair; Blgy.

STRELETZKY, LINDA; Bethlehem Catholic HS; Bethlehem, PA; (Y); 17/223; Church Yth Grp; Key Clb; Red Cross Aide; Church Choir; High Hon Roll; NHS; Pres Acad Fit Awd 86; PA ST U; Cmmnctns.

STREMMEL, CELESTE; Hanover SR HS; Hanover, PA; (Y); 25/138; Hosp Aide; Band; Chorus; Concert Band; Jazz Band; Mrchg Band; Orch; School Musical; School Play; Yrbk Stf; Florence De Haven Stick Scholar 86; H Elizabeth Spangler Scholar 86; Sheetz Scholar 86; Reading Hosp Schl Nrsg; Nrsg.

STRICKER, ROBERT; Newport HS; Newport, PA; (Y); 35/100; Varsity Clb; Var Bsbl; Var Ftbl; Var Wrstlng; Hon Roll; Slippery Rock; Aerospc Sci.

STRICKLAND, COREY; Owen J Roberts HS; Pottstown, PA; (Y); 2/300; Pres Church Yth Grp; VP JA; Latin Clb; Quiz Bowl; Concert Band; Mrchg Band; Stage Crew; Hon Roll; NHS; Bio.

STRICKLAND, KAREN; Archbishop Wood Girls HS; Doylestown, PA; (Y); 10/250; Var Capt Bsktbl; Var Capt Fld Hcky; JV Var Sftbl; High Hon Roll; Hon Roll; Awds Acad Profcncy Chem, Alg II, & Soc Stus 85-86; Drexel U; Chem.

STRIKER, KELLY; Clearfield Area HS; Clearfield, PA; (Y); 61/301; Hon Roll; Gregg Shorthand Spec Achvt Awd 84-85; Dubois Bus Coll; Acctg.

STRINE, NANCY; S Fayette HS; Bridgeville, PA; (S); 8/93; Pres Church Yth Grp; Drama Clb; Ski Clb; Varsity Clb; Nwsp Rptr; Sec Nwsp Stf; Yrbk Stf; Bsktbl; Sftbl; Vllybl; Mono Gram Clb 83-86; Slippery Rock; Math Tchr.

STRINGER, PENNEY; Governor Mifflin HS; Reading, PA; (Y); 2/250; JA; Varsity Clb; Orch; School Musical; Pres Jr Cls; VP Stu Cncl; Bsktbl; Tennis; JV Trk; Sec NHS; Wellesly Coll Awd 86; Unified Point Awd 85 & 86; Pre-Med.

STRINGER, TIM; Tyrone Area HS; Tyrone, PA; (Y); Boy Scts; Varsity Clb; Var L Bsbl; JV Bsktbl; Var L Ftbl; Wt Lftg; Hon Roll.

STRITTMATTER, KIM; Trinity HS; Eighty Four, PA; (Y); Art Clb; Camera Clb; German Clb; GAA; Pep Clb; Var Cheerleading; Hon Roll; Arch.

STRNISA, CHRIS; Canon-Mc Millan HS; Canonsburg, PA; (Y); Spanish Clb; Var Bsktbl; Var Ftbl; Hon Roll; Spanish NHS.

STROBEL, ANDREW; St Pius X HS; Pottstown, PA; (S); Mathletes; Science Clb; Var L Bsbl; Im Stat Bowling; High Hon Roll; Trs NHS; Ntl Merit SF; Prfct Atten Awd; Val; Engrng.

STROBEL, BERNIE; Pittston Area SR HS; Duryea, PA; (Y); French Clb; Bsktbl; Sftbl; High Hon Roll; Hon Roll; NHS.

STROBEL, BRIAN; Moniteau HS; W Sunbury, PA; (Y); 7/128; Spanish Clb; Var L Ftbl; Var Trk; Hon Roll; PA ST U; Engnrg.

STROBEL, JOANNE; Liberty HS; Bethlehem, PA; (Y); 73/500; Dance Clb; Library Aide; Varsity Clb; Band; Mrchg Band; Rep Frsh Cls; Var Mat Maids; JV Var Score Keeper; Var Wrstlng; Hon Roll; Eng Hnr 85-87; German Hnr 87; Zoology.

STROCK, CHRISTOPHER; Holy Name HS; Wyomissing, PA; (Y); 20/120; Pep Clb; Im Bowling; Var Ftbl; Ntl Merit SF; Pre-Med.

STROCK III, DAVID J; Owen J Roberst HS; Pottstown, PA; (S); 15/291; Letterman Clb; Rep Soph Cls; Var Bsbl; Var Bsktbl; Var Ftbl; High Hon Roll; Hon Roll; NHS; Dr.

STROCKOZ, SCOTT; Pivs X HS; Pen Argyl, PA; (Y); 4/38; NFL; Varsity Clb; Stage Crew; Var Bsbl; Var Capt Bsktbl; Hon Roll; NHS; Ntl Merit Ltr; MVP Bsktbl 84-86; Bus.

STROHECKER, JEANETTE; Reading Central Catholic HS; Reading, PA; (Y); Art Clb; Hosp Aide; Office Aide; Pep Clb; Mrchg Band; School Play; Stat Bsktbl; Var Fld Hcky; Mat Maids; Stat Wrstlng; ST Fnlst Miss Coed Amer 86; Kent ST; Arch Engrng.

STROHECKER, JILL; Central Dauphin HS; Harrisburg, PA; (Y); 50/320; Exploring; Ski Clb; Chorus; Crs Cntry; Tennis; Twrlr; Cit Awd; Hon Roll; NHS; Pltcl Sci.

STROHECKER, JOEL; Milton SR HS; Milton, PA; (Y); German Clb.

STROHECKER, LYNN; Slippery Rock Area HS; Slippery Rock, PA; (Y); 17/187; Church Yth Grp; Girl Scts; Chorus; Mrchg Band; Pep Band; Variety Show; God Cntry Awd; Hon Roll; NHS; 3rd Pl Butler Cty Consrvtn Schl 85; PA ST; Mgmt.

STROHECKER, PHILIP; Mohawk JR-SR HS; New Castle, PA; (S); #1 In Class; Boy Scts; Latin Clb; Band; Concert Band; Mrchg Band; Pep Band; School Musical; Trk; High Hon Roll; Sec NHS; Acdmc Awd 86; Cert Eductnl Dvlpmnt Ntl 84; Cert Of Merit Wstmnstr Coll Hnrs Band 86; Comp Engnrng.

STROHM, MATT; Central Dauphin HS; Harrisburg, PA; (Y); Cmnty Wkr; Science Clb; Teachers Aide; Nwsp Rptr; Stat Ftbl; Wrstlng; NHS; Pres Schlr; Christopher Knauss Sci Awd 86; John Hall Schlrshp 86; Juniata Coll; Med Doc.

STROHM, MAUREEN; Nazareth Acad; Philadelphia, PA; (Y); Hosp Aide; Service Clb; Cheerleading; Sftbl; Embry Riddle Aerntcl U; Avtn Mg.

STROJEK, LESLIE; Ambridge Area HS; Ambridge, PA; (Y); Pep Clb; Red Cross Aide; Spanish Clb; Band; Concert Band; Jazz Band; Mrchg Band; Symp Band; Off Jr Cls; Off Sr Cls; Bus.

STROJNY, KATHERINE; West Mifflin Area HS; W Mifflin, PA; (Y); Ski Clb; Orch; Hon Roll; Penn ST; Elem Tchr.

STROKA, CONNIE; Tunkhannock HS; Tunkhannock, PA; (S); 26/305; VP Swmmng; Ski Clb; Rep Soph Cls; Rep Jr Cls; Sec Bsktbl; Var Fld Hcky; Cit Awd; NHS; Comp Technlgy.

STROLL, GEORGE; Newport JR SR HS; Liverpool, PA; (Y); Art Clb; FFA; Chorus; School Musical; School Play; Stage Crew; Yrbk Stf; Trk; Hon Roll; PYEA 87; Shppnsbrg U; Thtr.

STROLL, STACEY; Middletown Area HS; Middletown, PA; (Y); 10/185; Library Aide; School Play; Nwsp Stf; Tennis; Hon Roll; NHS; Ldies Auxlry Of The Elks Nrsng Schlrshp 86; York Coll Of PA; Nrsng.

STROLLO, JOSEPH; Archbishop Wood HS; Langhorne, PA; (Y); 66/282; Cmnty Wkr; Latin Clb; SADD; Rep Frsh Cls; Rep Soph Cls; Bowling; Math.

STROMEI, JOE; Cornell HS; Coraopolis, PA; (Y); Church Yth Grp; Drama Clb; JA; Pep Clb; Band; Drm Mjr(t); Jazz Band; Mrchg Band; Pep Band; School Play; Robert Morris Coll; Marktng.

STRONG, ASHLEY; Villa Maria Acad; Erie, PA; (Y); 56/133; Chorus; Stu Cncl; Mgr(s); JV Socr; Im Vllybl; Hon Roll; Tp Scr JR Cls Mth Cntst 86; Cmmnctns.

STRONG, CONNIE; Brookville Area HS; Reynoldsville, PA; (Y); 21/150; VP French Clb; Sec Key Clb; Varsity Clb; Chorus; Trs Soph Cls; Sec Jr Cls; Stu Cncl; Var L Trk; Hon Roll; Sec NHS; Phys Thrpy.

STRONG, EDWARD; Penns Manor HS; Penn Run, PA; (Y); Church Yth Grp; Cmnty Wkr; Stage Crew; Var L Trk; High Hon Roll; Hon Roll; NEDT Awd; U Of Pittsburgh; Phrmcy.

STRONG, GEORGE; Quaker Valley HS; Sewickley, PA; (Y); 5/160; Church Yth Grp; Key Clb; Spanish Clb; Chorus; Trs Soph Cls; Off Stu Cncl; Var Bsbl; Var Capt Socr; High Hon Roll; NHS; US Rgn I Olympc Dev Tm Sccr 85-86.

STRONY, RONALD; Bishop Ohara HS; Olyphant, PA; (S); Exploring; Ski Clb; Rep Frsh Cls; Rep Stu Cncl; JV Var Bsbl; High Hon Roll; Hgh Hnr Roll 84-86; Pre-Med.

STROPE, ANGELA; Jefferson-Morgan JR SR HS; Waynesburg, PA; (Y); 16/88; Church Yth Grp; Cmnty Wkr; Yrbk Stf; High Hon Roll; Hon Roll; Gregg Shrthnd Awd 86; CA U Of PA-INTL Day Awd 84-86; Slippery Rock U.

STROPE, LISA; Mc Guffey HS; Taylorstown, PA; (Y); 20/210; Art Clb; Church Yth Grp; Pep Clb; Varsity Clb; Pres Soph Cls; Rep Jr Cls; Rep Sr Cls; Var Powder Puff Ftbl; Var Sftbl; Var L Tennis; Stdnt Rcgntn; U Pittsburgh Johnstown; Acctg.

STROPE, REBECCA; E L Meyers HS; Wilkes Bare, PA; (Y); Sec Church Yth Grp; German Clb; Girl Scts; Spanish Clb; Chorus; Church Choir; Orch; Nwsp Rptr; Nwsp Stf; Jr NHS; Crtv Wrtng.

STROTHER, KIMBERLY; Westmont Hilltop HS; Johnstown, PA; (Y); 58/160; Trs Key Clb; Chorus; Church Choir; School Musical; Yrbk Stf; Var Debate Tm; Var Tennis; High Hon Roll; Fshn Dsgn.

STROUD, ALISA R; South Hills HS; Pittsburgh, PA; (Y); 9/300; Church Yth Grp; Dance Clb; Exploring; Library Aide; Drill Tm; Yrbk Rptr; Sec Jr Cls; VP Sr Cls; Cit Awd; Hon Roll; Wiberforce U; Bus Adm.

STROUD, AMY; Burgettstown Area JR SR HS; Avella, PA; (Y); French Clb; Ski Clb; Band; Stat Bsktbl; Score Keeper; High Hon Roll; Jr NHS; NHS; Ntl Merit Schol; Nrsng.

STROUD, BETH; Lake-Lehman HS; Sweet Valley, PA; (Y); 1/140; Trs Church Yth Grp; Yrbk Stf; Bausch & Lomb Sci Awd; High Hon Roll; Jr NHS; NHS; Physcl Thrpst.

STROUD, GARY; Towanda Area SR HS; Towanda, PA; (Y); Art Clb; Boys Clb Am; Boy Scts; Camera Clb; VICA; Stu Cncl; Bsbl; Bsktbl; Ftbl; Sftbl; Bradfd Cnty Area Voctnl Tech Schl-Mst Advncd 1st, 2nd Yr Stu 84-85 & 85-86; Williamsport; Bldng Constrctn.

STROUMBAKIS, NICHOLAS C; Slippery Rock Area HS; Slippery Rock, PA; (Y); Church Yth Grp; Exploring; French Clb; JCL; Latin Clb; Math Tm; Concert Band; Mrchg Band; Rep Stu Cncl; NHS; PA ST U; Med.

STROUP, ALICE; South Williamsport Area HS; S Williamsport, PA; (Y); 17/140; Computer Clb; Key Clb; Varsity Clb; Color Guard; Stu Cncl; Var Capt Bsktbl; Var L Sftbl; Hon Roll; Al-Star Tms Trnmnt-Bsktbl 85; 1st Tm Al-Conf Bsktbl 86; Trnmnt MVP Sftbl 86; Fshn Mrchndsng.

STROUP, CHRISTOPHER; Williams Valley HS; Williamstown, PA; (S); Chorus; Variety Show; Var L Ftbl; Wt Lftg; Hon Roll; Prfct Atten Awd; Outstndng Nwsppr Carrier Yr 84; Pottsvll Republ Carrier Mnth 84; Spippensburg; Comp Engrng.

STROUSE, KAREN; Louis E Dieruff HS; Allentown, PA; (Y); 15/327; ROTC; Yrbk Bus Mgr; Var L Golf; Var Powder Puff Ftbl; Var L Sftbl; Hon Roll; NHS; Air Force ROTC Schlrshp 86; Hnry 1st Defndrs Awd 86; Penn ST U; Aerosp Engrng.

STROZYK, KATHLEEN; Canton Area JR SR HS; Canton, PA; (Y); Church Yth Grp; Letterman Clb; Rep Stu Cncl; Var Bsktbl; L Var Sftbl; Var Vllybl; Pres Awd Phys Ftns.

STRUBIN, JUSTINE; South Western HS; Hanover, PA; (Y); AFS; Aud/Vis; Hosp Aide; Red Cross Aide; Ski Clb; Nwsp Ed-Chief; Nwsp Stf; Rep Frsh Cls; Var Cheerleading; Chestnut Hill Coll.

STRUBINGER, KRIS; Central Columbia HS; Bloomsburg, PA; (Y); Cmnty Wkr; German Clb; Key Clb; Red Cross Aide; Nwsp Stf; Yrbk Stf; Sec Stu Cncl; Var Swmmng; Stat Trk; Hon Roll; Temple U; Spch Pathology.

STRUBLE, DEBI; Hempfield SR HS; Jeannette, PA; (Y); French Clb; Hosp Aide; Library Aide; Ski Clb; Nwsp Stf; Elem Ed.

STRUCK, CANDICE; Upper Dublin HS; Oreland, PA; (Y); 32/307; Cmnty Wkr; Varsity Clb; Im Bsktbl; Im Fld Hcky; JV Capt Socr; Var Sftbl; Var Tennis; NHS; Prfct Atten Awd.

STRUNK, KRISTIE; Shamokin Area HS; Shamokin, PA; (Y); Drama Clb; Key Clb; Chrmn Pep Clb; Science Clb; Ski Clb; Varsity Clb; Band; Drill Tm; Yrbk Stf; Rep Church Yth Grp; Rdlgy Tech.

STRUNK, LISA; Tunkhannock Area HS; Tunkhannock, PA; (S); 4/328; Church Yth Grp; Trs Key Clb; Scholastic Bowl; Spanish Clb; Var Tennis; Cit Awd; Hon Roll; NHS; Wilkes Coll; Math Tchr.

STRZESIESKI, MARTHA; Highlands SR HS; Natrona Hgts, PA; (Y); Cmnty Wkr; Computer Clb; DECA; German Clb; Hosp Aide; Library Aide; Office Aide; Radio Clb; Pep Band; Stage Crew; Brdcstng.

STUART, JANELLE; Butler Area SR HS; Butler, PA; (Y); Office Aide; VP SADD; High Hon Roll; Hon Roll; Schlrshp Econo Schl Part Of Smmr 84-85; Grove City Coll; Psych.

STUART, JENNIFER; Mercyhurst Preparatory Schl; Erie, PA; (Y); Art Clb; French Clb; Pres Model UN; Chorus; Church Choir; School Play; Nwsp Stf; Yrbk Stf; Hon Roll; NHS; Best Soph Artist 84-85; Grphc Dsgn.

STUART, ROBERT; Northeastern SR HS; Mt Wolf, PA; (Y); 20/149; Boy Scts; Computer Clb; Exploring; Ski Clb; Chorus; Bowling; Tennis; Hon Roll; NHS; Pres Schlr; York County Merit Schlrshp 86; York College ; Acctg.

STUBANAS, DIEDRE; Spring-Ford SR HS; Montclare, PA; (S); 23/258; German Clb; Var L Fld Hcky; Var L Lcrss; L Trk; High Hon Roll; NHS; Millersville U; Math.

STUCCIO, FRED; Scranton Prep; Pittston, PA; (Y); 166/197; Var Ftbl; Wt Lftg; Trk; Vllybl; Hon Roll.

STUCK, ERIC T; Freeport Area HS; Sarber, PA; (Y).

STUCK III, WILLIAM; Chief Logan HS; Yeagertown, PA; (Y); 44/199; Boy Scts; German Clb; Variety Show; Var Mgr Ftbl; Mgr(s); Elks Awd; God Cntry Awd; Gov Hon Prg Awd; Hon Roll; Millersville ST Coll; Ind Art.

STUCKEY, HEATHER; Annville-Cleona HS; Annville, PA; (Y); 25/105; Church Yth Grp; Pres FBLA; Office Aide; SADD; Varsity Clb; School Musical; Yrbk Stf; Var Co-Capt Cheerleading; NHS; FBLA Clerk Typst II Awd 1st Pl 85; Teen Yr Awd Chrch Yth Grp 84; Drama Awd 2nd Pl Natls 84; Goldey Beacom Coll; Sec.

STUCKEY, MELINDA; Cameron County HS; Emporium, PA; (Y); 35/86; Church Yth Grp; Computer Clb; French Clb; FHA; Girl Scts; Office Aide; Sec Chorus; Yrbk Stf; Sec Frsh Cls; Stat Bsktbl; Psych.

STUCKEY, TOM; Newport HS; Newport, PA; (Y); Spanish Clb; Varsity Clb; Var L Bsbl; Var L Ftbl; Im Wt Lftg; Hon Roll; Bus Adm.

STUDENT, JOSEPH D; West Hazleton HS; W Hazelton, PA; (Y); 5/230; Capt Quiz Bowl; Capt Scholastic Bowl; SADD; Nwsp Ed-Chief; Yrbk Stf; Rep Jr Cls; High Hon Roll; Voice Dem Awd; Pres Clssrm Selectn 87; PA JR Acad Of Sci 83-85; Can Do Indstrl Stu Dir 86; Pol Sci.

STULGINSKAS, NICOLE; Steel Valley HS; Munhall, PA; (Y); 15/207; High Hon Roll; Hon Roll; Jr NHS; NHS; Med.

STULL, DAWN MARIE; Bishop Mc Cort HS; Johnstown, PA; (Y); 5/129; German Clb; Pep Clb; Ski Clb; Yrbk Stf; Vllybl; High Hon Roll; Mu Alp Tht; NHS; Rotary Awd; Duquesne U; Pharm.

STULL, DON; Shanksville-Stonycreek HS; Shanksville, PA; (S); Boy Scts; Church Yth Grp; Band; Concert Band; Mrchg Band; Nwsp Phtg; Nwsp Sprt Ed; Pres Stu Cncl; Mgr Bsbl; Mgr Bsktbl; Penn ST; Aerosp Engrng.

STULL, KATHRYN; Wyoming Valley West; Edwardsville, PA; (Y); 41/401; French Clb; Sec Math Clb; Yrbk Stf; Lit Mag; Hon Roll; NHS; NEDT Awd; Natl Frnch Cntst Mrt Awd 84-85; Genrl Hosp Schl Rdlgc Tech; Rdl.

STULL, MONICA; Geibel HS; Scottdale, PA; (Y); Drama Clb; Pep Clb; Spanish Clb; School Musical; School Play; Stage Crew; High Hon Roll; Prfct Atten Awd; Spanish NHS; NEDT Awd; PJAS Awd 85; Comm.

STUMP, DANIEL; Juniata HS; Mifflintown, PA; (Y); Computer Clb; Hon Roll; NHS; Shippensburg U; Mgmt.

STUMP, LORI; Juaniata HS; Mifflintown, PA; (Y); JV Fld Hcky; JV Sftbl; Var Trk; Hon Roll; NHS; Shippensburg U; Chem.

STUMP, WENDY; Elizabethtown Area HS; Newville, PA; (Y); German Clb; Stage Crew; JV Powder Puff Ftbl; Art.

STUMPF, KELLY; Trinity HS; Washington, PA; (Y); Camera Clb; German Clb; Pep Clb; Nwsp Phtg; Trk; Nrsng.

STUMPF, STACY; Blairsville SR HS; Blairsville, PA; (Y); 4/129; Pres Church Yth Grp; Band; Chorus; Concert Band; School Musical; Rep Stu Cncl; Cheerleading; High Hon Roll; NHS; Pres Schlr; Hugh O Brien Yth Ldrshp Smnr 84; 2/10 Schlrshp 86; Delta Kappa Gamma Rcrtmnt Grnt 86; IN U Of PA; Sec Englsh Educ.

STUMPFF, RENEE; Du Bois Area SR HS; Dubois, PA; (Y); 28/256; Church Yth Grp; Varsity Clb; Band; Chorus; Mrchg Band; School Musical; Yrbk Stf; Rep Stu Cncl; Var Capt Crs Cntry; Swmmng; Stackpole 80th Annvrary Scholar 86; VA Polytech Inst; Biochem.

STUMPO, JEFF; Westmont Hilltop HS; Johnstown, PA; (Y); Pres Key Clb; Ski Clb; Chorus; Capt Var Bsbl; Ftbl; Ellwood Ailes Awd Outstndng Bsbl Plyr 85-86; IN U; Pre-Law.

STUMPO, PAULALEE; St Huberts Catholic HS; Philadelphia, PA; (Y); 40/367; Office Aide; Bsktbl; Trk; Hon Roll; Prfct Atten Awd; 1st Anl Katherine Kibbs Ldrshp Awd Futr Secys 86; Typng I 86; Katherine Gibbs; Crt Stenogrphy.

STUPI, JANE; Mechanicsburg Area SR HS; Mechanicsburg, PA; (Y); 84/311; Color Guard; Flag Corp; Mgr(s); Score Keeper; Mgr Stat Swmmng; Hon Roll; Natl Art Hnr Soc 84-86; Chem Engrng.

STURCHAK, DANNY; Bentworth HS; Bentleyville, PA; (Y); Letterman Clb; Varsity Clb; Off Jr Cls; Ftbl; Wt Lftg; Wrstlng; Hon Roll; Mech Engr.

STURDEVANT, KERRI; Sheffield Area JR SR HS; Sheffield, PA; (Y); Chorus; Drm Mjr(t); School Musical; School Play; Yrbk Phtg; Stu Cncl; JV Cheerleading; Var Sftbl; Var JV Vllybl; Hon Roll; Cnstnt & Fnlst In Miss Alleghany Highland Schlrshp Pgnt 86; Cntstnt In Sheffield Sesquicentennial 86; U Of Pittsburgh; Nrsng.

STURDEVANT, SHARON; Fort Le Boeuf HS; Waterford, PA; (Y); 9/167; Sec Church Yth Grp; Computer Clb; Sec Girl Scts; Model UN; Band; Concert Band; Jazz Band; Mrchg Band; Yrbk Stf; High Hon Roll; PMEA Dist II & Region II Band 85-86; Hugh O Brien Yth Sem 85; Cmmnctns.

STURGEON, KIMBERLY; West Allegheny HS; Oakdale, PA; (Y); 26/206; Church Yth Grp; VP Chorus; Capt Mrchg Band; Trs Frsh Cls; VP Soph Cls; VP Jr Cls; High Hon Roll; NHS; Spanish Clb; Trs Frsh Cls; Cntry III Ldrshp Awd Wnnr 86; Pres Acdmc Ftns Awd 86; Chrs Awd Wnnr 86; IN U PA; Engl.

STURGES, AMY; Wellsboro Area HS; Wellsboro, PA; (Y); 4-H; French Clb; Hosp Aide; Ski Clb; Trs SADD; Chorus; Ed Yrbk Stf; Hon Roll; Packer Fndtn Schlrshp 86; IN U Of PA; Psych.

STURGIS, SCOTT; Tamaqua Area HS; Tamaqua, PA; (Y); 15/190; Nwsp Stf; Var Trk; Hon Roll; Pres Spanish NHS; NHS; Ntl Merit Ltr; PA ST U Smmr Hnrs Acdmy Stdnt 86.

STURIALE, LISA; Kiski Area HS; Avonmore, PA; (Y); 20/388; Church Yth Grp; FBLA; Math Clb; Pep Clb; Church Choir; Concert Band; Capt Drm Mjr(t); Mrchg Band; Off Frsh Cls; High Hon Roll; Bell-Avon Alumni Schlrshp 86; PA ST U.

STURKIE, SANDY; Norwin HS; N Huntingdon, PA; (Y); FBLA; Pep Clb; Chorus; Powder Puff Ftbl; Hon Roll; Bst Drssd 86; 2nd Pl Imprptu Spkg 84-86; Pres Chrs 84-85; Bradford; Sec.

STUTZ, SHEREEN; Penn Trafford HS; Irwin, PA; (Y); 25/324; Boys Clb Am; Pres Church Yth Grp; JA; Ski Clb; Spanish Clb; Im JV Sftbl; Hon Roll; NHS; Duquesne U Smmr Intgrtd Hnrs Prog 85; Duquesne U Schl Of Pharmacy.

STUTZMAN, ANDREW; Tri-Valley HS; Valley View, PA; (Y); Art Clb; Boy Scts; Church Yth Grp; Computer Clb; Exploring; Ski Clb; School Musical; Yrbk Phtg; Rep Stu Cncl; JV Var Bsktbl; Natl Coll Recrtng Assoc Ftbl 86; Fitnessgrm Pres Cncl On Phys Fit & Sprts 85-86.

STUTZMAN, ANDREW K; Cedar Cliff HS; New Cumberland, PA; (Y); Var Bsbl; Var L Ftbl; Var L Wrstlng; Hon Roll; Boy Scts; Church Yth Grp; Varsity Clb; Var Trk; Pres Acadmc Ftnss Awd 86; Drexel U; Commrc.

STUTZMAN, BETH; United HS; Seward, PA; (Y); 3/128; Drama Clb; Math Clb; Band; Chorus; Concert Band; Mrchg Band; School Musical; High Hon Roll; Hon Roll; Marines Semper Fidelis Awd For Music 86; IN U Of PA; Music Educ.

STUTZMAN, LEE ANN; Rockwood Area HS; Somerset, PA; (S); Office Aide; Band; Chorus; Yrbk Stf; Hon Roll; NHS; Sec AFS; Church Yth Grp; Teachers Aide; Maple Princess Contstn & Miss Congnlty 85-86; Jubilee Queen 2nd Rnnr Up 84-85; County Chorus; Med.

STUTZMAN, TIFFANY; Seneca HS; North East, PA; (Y); Church Yth Grp; GAA; Yrbk Stf; Var Bsktbl; Sftbl; Var Vllybl; Hon Roll; Trpl Crwn Awd 86; Pltcl Sci.

STYBORSKI, CARLA; Meadville Area SR HS; Meadville, PA; (Y); 68/306; JA; Key Clb; Ski Clb; Spanish Clb; Color Guard; Mrchg Band; Yrbk Stf; Hon Roll.

STYCHE, TRICIA; Elizabeth Forward HS; Elizabeth, PA; (Y); Exploring; Spanish Clb; Color Guard; Yrbk Stf; Stat Bsktbl; Im Cheerleading; Stat Var Swmmng; High Hon Roll; NHS; Aud/Vis; Gftd & Tlntd Prgm GATE; Ntrtn.

STYER, YVONNE; Philadelphia HS For Girls; Philadelphia, PA; (Y); Teachers Aide; Drill Tm; Nwsp Rptr; Yrbk Stf; Stu Cncl; JV Sftbl; JV Vllybl; NYU; Pre Law.

STYERS, ADAM; Lewisburg Area HS; New Columbia, PA; (Y); Spanish Clb; Soph Cls; Stu Cncl; Bsktbl; Cheerleading; Ftbl; Tennis; Trk; Hon Roll; J P M Schlrshp-Accntng 86; GA Southern Coll.

STYERS, BRENDA; Lock Haven SR HS; Lock Haven, PA; (Y); FBLA; VP Library Aide; Hon Roll; Most Improved Stu Upward Bound 85; Accountant.

STYPULA, KIM; Mt Lebanon HS; Pittsburgh, PA; (Y); 286/416; Art Clb; Church Yth Grp; Cmnty Wkr; SADD; Lit Mag; Hon Roll; Elem Educ.

STYS, DEANNA; Trinity HS; Washington, PA; (Y); 22/374; German Clb; Math Clb; Color Guard; Drm Mjr(t); Mrchg Band; Twrlr; High Hon Roll; Hon Roll; NEDT Awd; Mst Outstndng Majorette 85-86; Sports Med.

STYSKIN, JULIE; Butler SR HS; Butler, PA; (Y); JA; Spanish Clb; Speech Tm; SADD; Pres Temple Yth Grp; Rep Soph Cls; Var Trk; Hon Roll; U Of PA; Pharm.

SU, YEECHUN; Upper Dublin HS; Ft Washington, PA; (Y); 20/318; Camera Clb; Hosp Aide; Intnl Clb; Yrbk Stf; Lit Mag; JV Bowling; NHS; Ntl Merit Ltr; Science Clb; Aud/Vis; Sci Fairs 1st & 2nd Awds 85; Psych.

SUBASIC, LORI LYNN; Hickory HS; Hermitage, PA; (Y); 10/185; Math Clb; Service Clb; Chorus; Concert Band; Mrchg Band; Orch; Pep Band; School Musical; Nwsp Stf; NHS.

SUBE, RENEE S; West Hazleton HS; W Hazleton, PA; (S); 40/191; FTA; Spanish Clb; Band; Concert Band; Drm Mjr(t); Jazz Band; Mrchg Band; Pep Band; School Musical; Hon Roll; Dist Band 84-85; Penn ST U; Nrs.

SUBRAMANIAN, SHARDA; Clarion Limestone HS; Clarion, PA; (Y); French Clb; Sec FHA; Girl Scts; JA; Library Aide; Band; Nwsp Rptr; Score Keeper; JV Sftbl; JV Vllybl; Microbio.

SUCHAR, MIKE; Bethel Park HS; Pittsburgh, PA; (Y); Chess Clb; FBLA; Math Tm; JV Bsktbl; Im Trk; High Hon Roll; Jr NHS; NHS; Prfct Atten Awd; Spanish NHS; Top 100 Math Test Won Free Course Pittsburgh U; Civil Engr.

SUCHY, LAURA A; Bethel Park HS; Bethel Park, PA; (Y); 26/520; French Clb; Band; Concert Band; Mrchg Band; Orch; Symp Band; Powder Puff Ftbl; Wt Lftg; High Hon Roll; Hon Roll; Dist Orch; PA ST U; Acctng.

SUCKLE, RICHARD; Cheltenham HS; Cheltenham, PA; (Y); 48/365; Nwsp Stf; Var L Bsktbl; Var Capt Golf; Mrktng Stu Hnrs 86; Pltcl Stdys.

SUDIK, MELINDA; Philipsburg-Osceola HS; Philipsburg, PA; (Y); 27/245; Church Yth Grp; Cmnty Wkr; Letterman Clb; Ski Clb; SADD; Thesps; Chorus; School Musical; School Play; Stage Crew; Cntr Cnty Jr Miss Cntstnt 86-87; Mdrn Miss Cntstnt 85; Miss PA Natl Tngr Cntstnt 84; Clarion U Of PA; Accntng.

SUDOL, BRANDY; Danville SR HS; Danville, PA; (Y); 34/202; Exploring; Key Clb; Ski Clb; Rep Stu Cncl; Var Capt Cheerleading; Var Fld Hcky; Var Trk; High Hon Roll; Nrsng.

SUEHR, JILL; Burgettstown JR SR HS; Clinton, PA; (Y); Art Clb; Ski Clb; Acctg.

SUEHR, MARY; Montour HS; Mckees Rocks, PA; (Y); 4/275; VP Pres JA; Math Tm; Trk; High Hon Roll; Hon Roll; NHS; Pres Schlr; Dale Carnegie Schlrshp 85; Provost Schlrshp-U Pittsbrgh 86; JR Achvt Schlrshp 86; U Of Pittsburgh; Arts, Sci.

SUHY, DAVID A; Bethel Park HS; Bethel Park, PA; (Y); Church Yth Grp; Jazz Band; Mrchg Band; Variety Show; High Hon Roll; Kiwanis Awd; Pres Schlr; Lions Clb Acad Schlrshp Awd 86; John R Leroy Wrtng Awd Fin; Founder-Aspiring Med Achvrs; U Of Pittsburgh; Med.

SUJANSKY, SUSAN; Somerset Area SR HS; Somerset, PA; (Y); 23/239; German Clb; NFL; Band; Mrchg Band; Yrbk Stf; Sec Stu Cncl; Tennis; Trk; High Hon Roll; NHS; Engrng.

SUKAL, MICHAEL; Brownsville Area HS; La Belle, PA; (S); 8/225; Drama Clb; Ski Clb; Rep Jr Cls; Var L Bsbl; Var L Ftbl; High Hon Roll; NHS; VP Rotary Awd; Engrng.

SUKAY, MISSY; Greensburg Salem HS; Greensburg, PA; (Y); Pres Sec 4-H; French Clb; Hosp Aide; Pep Clb; Ski Clb; Teachers Aide; Chorus; Nwsp Stf; Yrbk Stf; Stu Cncl; William J Borbonus Sprtsmnshp 84-85; Bus Admin.

SUKENIK, LEANNE; Johnstown HS; Johnstown, PA; (Y); JA; Chorus; Nwsp Rptr; Yrbk Phtg; Yrbk Rptr; Hon Roll; NHS; Cambria Rowe Bus Coll; Acctg.

SUKITS, SHERRY; Perry Traditional Acad; Pittsburgh, PA; (Y); Church Yth Grp; Nwsp Sprt Ed; Var L Swmmng; Var L Tennis; High Hon Roll; Hon Roll; VP NHS; Prfct Atten Awd; Soc Wrkr.

SULAK, MARY; Fairchance Georges HS; Uniontown, PA; (Y); Art Clb; Spanish Clb; Speech Tm; SADD; Chorus; Hon Roll.

SULIK, GAYLE; Williamsport Area HS; Williamsport, PA; (S); Hosp Aide; Acpl Chr; Band; Chorus; High Hon Roll; Hon Roll; Church Yth Grp; Exploring; Key Clb; Church Choir; Dist & Rgnl Chorus 85; Ithaca Coll; Phys Thrpy.

SULIKOWSKI, MIRANDA; Pennsbury HS; Fairless Hills, PA; (S); DECA; Cert Of Achvt Jrnl Wrtg 85; 9th Apprl And Access Dist DECA 86; Bucks County CC; Crtv Wrtg.

SULLIVAN, KATHLEEN; Nortre Dame Of Green Pond HS; Easton, PA; (Y); 3/88; Office Aide; Pep Clb; Frsh Cls; Soph Cls; Sr Cls; Bsktbl; Crs Cntry; Mgr(s); Trk; High Hon Roll; Stu Forum 86; Sunday Schl Tchr 85-86; Teen Cncl Alcohlism 86.

SULLIVAN, KELLEY; Middletown Area HS; Middletown, PA; (Y); 25/200; Church Yth Grp; Band; Concert Band; Flag Corp; Mrchg Band; Yrbk Stf; JV Bsktbl; Vllybl; Hon Roll; NHS; Millersville U; Bus.

SULLIVAN, MICHELLE; St Hubert HS; Philadelphia, PA; (Y); Art Clb; Church Yth Grp; Hon Roll; Rep Soph Cls; Rep Stu Cncl; Ells Grnt Schlrshp; Ntl Hon Soc; Bus.

SULLIVAN, NEIL; Bishop Mc Devitt HS; Harrisburg, PA; (S); 28/202; Q&S; Band; VP Chorus; Church Choir; Madrigals; School Musical; Nwsp Ed-Chief; Yrbk Ed-Chief; Rep Frsh Cls; NHS; Allentown Coll; Bus Comm.

SULLIVAN, PATTY; Perkiomen Valley HS; Schwenksville, PA; (Y); Trs SADD; Var Diving; JV Fld Hcky; JV Lcrss; Hon Roll; Textile Dsgn.

SULLIVAN, PAUL; Pennridge HS; Perkasie, PA; (Y); 129/435; Boy Scts; JV L Socr; Bloomsburg U; Bus.

SULLIVAN, ROBERT; Devon Preparatory Schl; Paoli, PA; (Y); 7/35; Cmnty Wkr; Computer Clb; Radio Clb; Nwsp Ed-Chief; High Hon Roll; NHS; NEDT Awd; Prtl Schlrshp Ursinus Coll 86; Prtl Schlrshp To ST Josephs U 86; Schlstc Awds Chem, Math, Bio 84-86; Ursinus Coll; Engnrng.

SULLIVAN, SHAWN; Crestwood HS; Mountaintop, PA; (Y); Sec Math Clb; Ski Clb; School Play; Yrbk Stf; Cheerleading; Crs Cntry; Gym; Trk; High Hon Roll; Jr NHS; Bio.

SULOUFF, CHRISTINE; Shikellamy HS; Northumberland, PA; (Y); 151/320; Church Yth Grp; Pres 4-H; VICA; Chorus; Mrchg Band; 4-H Awd; Jr Miss Pineknttr 83; Rainbw Wrthy Advsr 84; 4-H Teen Cncl Sec, Tres 85-86; Central PA Bus Schl; Phys Thrp.

SULTAGE, C NICOLE; Tyrone Area HS; Tyrone, PA; (Y); 49/197; Am Leg Aux Girls St; Church Yth Grp; Computer Clb; FNA; Keywanettes; Pep Clb; SADD; Chorus; Church Choir; High Hon Roll; PSU; Nrsng.

SULTZER, MARCY; Mt Pleasant Area SR HS; Mt Pleasant, PA; (Y); Church Yth Grp; Cmnty Wkr; Pres French Clb; PAVAS; SADD; Chorus; Church Choir; Variety Show; Yrbk Bus Mgr; Var L Cheerleading; Schlrshp Frnch Clb 86; PMEA Dist 1 Chrs Fstvl 84 & 86; PMEA Reg 1 Chrs Fstvl 86; Frnch.

SUMAN, ROBERT; Derry Area SR HS; Blairsville, PA; (Y); Letterman Clb; Ski Clb; Yrbk Stf; Var L Bsbl; Bsktbl; Var L Ftbl; JV Vllybl; Hon Roll; Hnrbl Mntl Al-Area Ftbl Tm 85; Al-Sec Bsbl Tm-Pitchr 85-86; IN Gazzetteld Bsbl Tm-Pitchr/6-0 85-86; Sprts Medcn.

SUMMERLY, LYNN C; Mc Keesport Area HS; White Oaks, PA; (Y); Pres Church Yth Grp; Band; Concert Band; Mrchg Band; Orch; School Musical; School Play; Symp Band; Rep Stu Cncl; Var Bsktbl; Mid East Fest Duquesne U 84-85; Miss PA Amer Co Ed Modl & Evng Wear Wnnr 86; Cmmnctns.

SUMMERS, ANGELA; Tussey Mountain HS; Robersdale, PA; (Y); AFS; Ski Clb; Pres SADD; Band; Church Choir; Concert Band; Mrchg Band; Sec Pres Stu Cncl; Cheerleading; Cit Awd; Lock Havon U; Elem Ed.

SUMMERS, BRYAN; Curwensville Area HS; Grampian, PA; (Y); Art Clb; Chess Clb; FFA; Prfct Atten Awd; Greenhand Awd Voc Ag 85; Chptr Frmr Voc Ag 86; Dept Envrnmntl Rsrcs Awd 86.

SUMMERS, CHARLISA; Annville Cleona HS; Annville, PA; (Y); Rptr FBLA; Hosp Aide; Model UN; SADD; Chorus; Drill Tm; Stu Cncl; Mat Maids; NHS; NEDT Awd; FBLA 2nd Pl Dist Comp, Bus Eng 85; FBLA 1st Pl Dist Comp, Job Intrvw 86; 8th Pl ST Comp Job Invw 86; U Of Pittsburg; Pre Med.

SUMMERS, KATHY; Elizabethtown Area HS; Elizabethtown, PA; (Y); 61/237; Office Aide; Flag Corp; Capt JV Cheerleading; JV Mgr(s); Powder Puff Ftbl; Var Tennis; Psych.

SUMMERS, LAURA; Lock Haven SR HS; Lock Haven, PA; (Y); Church Yth Grp; VP FHA; Spanish Clb; Chorus; School Musical; Nwsp Stf; Cheerleading; Tennis; Trk.

SUMMERS, MELISSA; Octorara Area HS; Kinzers, PA; (Y); Church Yth Grp; Hosp Aide; Science Clb; SADD; Nrsng.

SUMMERSON, VALARIE; Cameron County HS; Sinnamahoning, PA; (Y); Library Aide; Spanish Clb; Teachers Aide; Prfct Atten Awd; Interior Desgn.

SUMMERVILLE, DEBIE; Gateway SR HS; Monroeville, PA; (Y); 98/460; VP DECA; Trs Exploring; FBLA; Ski Clb; Off Soph Cls; Trs Jr Cls; Off Sr Cls; Stu Cncl; Hon Roll; Rotary Yth Ldrshp; 3rd Pl FBLA Dist Comp Acctg II; FBLA ST Comp; U Dayton; Acctnt.

SUMMERVILLE, SHARON; Keystone HS; Knox, PA; (Y); 7/125; Library Aide; Yrbk Stf; JV Stat Bsktbl; Stat Trk; French Hon Soc; L High Hon Roll; Hon Roll; Pres NHS; Prfct Atten Awd; Geogrphy Awd 83; IN U Of PA; Scdndry Ed.

SUMNER, THERESA; North Western HS; Albion, PA; (Y); 25/164; VP Church Yth Grp; School Musical; Pres Soph Cls; Pres Jr Cls; Pres Sr Cls; JV Var Bsktbl; Coach Actv; JV Var Sftbl; Hon Roll; Cmnctns.

SUNDARJI, KARIMA; Ephrata SR HS; Ephrata, PA; (Y); 8/300; Nwsp Bus Mgr; Nwsp Ed-Chief; Sec Frsh Cls; Sec Soph Cls; Sec Jr Cls; Sec Sr Cls; Rep Stu Cncl; Hon Roll; Sec NHS.

SUNDAY, TRACY; Tyrone Area HS; Tyrone, PA; (Y); 4-H; FBLA; Office Aide; Pep Clb; Chorus; Hon Roll; South Hills Bus Schl; Lgl Secy.

SUNDER, SUE; J S Fine HS; Nanticoke, PA; (Y); Nwsp Rptr; Nwsp Stf; Powder Puff Ftbl; High Hon Roll; Hon Roll; Bus Mth Awd 90 & Btr Aver 85-86; Acctg Awd 15 & Btr Aver 84-85; LCCC; Bus Mgmt.

SUNDERLAND, ERIKA; Freedom Area HS; New Brighton, PA; (Y); 5/160; Church Yth Grp; Trs French Clb; Math Tm; Nwsp Ed-Chief; Yrbk Stf; Sec Sr Cls; Stu Cncl; DAR Awd; NHS; Drama Clb; Carlow Presdntl Schlrshp 85-86; Carlow Coll; Nrsng.

SUNDERMAN, REBECCA LYNN; Center HS; Aliquippa, PA; (Y); 31/186; German Clb; Pres Girl Scts; Band; Drm Mjr(t); Mrchg Band; Trk; High Hon Roll; Hon Roll; NHS; Rep Stu Cncl; Girl Sct Gold Awd 85; NC ST U; Chem Engrg.

SUNDY, GEORGE; Chartiers Valley HS; Bridgeville, PA; (Y); Letterman Clb; Varsity Clb; Var L Bsbl; Var L Ftbl; Hon Roll; NHS; Engrng.

SUNG, HUGH J; Penn Center Acad; Bala Cynwyd, PA; (Y); 2/30; Pres Stu Cncl; NHS; Sal; Arts Rcgntn & Tlnt Srch Fnlst 86; Curtis Inst Music Schlrshp-Piano 81; Curtis Inst Music; Music.

SUNSERI, DEBBIE; Moon SR HS; Coraoplis, PA; (Y); JA; Yrbk Phtg; Yrbk Stf; CC-ALLEGHENY County; Pedlgy.

SUNSERI, ROSE; Cambria Hgts HS; Patton, PA; (Y); Church Choir; Concert Band; Mrchg Band; Yrbk Rptr; Yrbk Stf; Hon Roll; U Of Pittsburgh; Nursing.

SUPPA, PAUL; East Allegheny HS; N Versailles, PA; (Y); 70/209; Boy Scts; Church Yth Grp; CAP; ROTC; Ski Clb; SADD; Ftbl; Swmmng; Wt Lftg; Hon Roll.

SURABIAN, MICHAEL; Liberty HS; Bethlehem, PA; (Y); 131/491; French Clb; Thesps; School Musical; School Play; Stage Crew; Variety Show; Yrbk Stf; Lit Mag; Var Tennis; Yng Wrtrs Awd 85-86; William Shakespeare Awd 85-86; Stage Crw Awd 85-86; Ntl Hstry Day-2nd Pl 84-85; Hofstra U; Theatr Arts.

SURAN, JUSTIN; Cumberland Valley HS; Camp Hill, PA; (Y); 1/540; Debate Tm; Quiz Bowl; Lit Mag; JV Tennis; High Hon Roll; NHS; Schlstc Gld Key Wrtng 85-86; Govrs Schl Intl Stud U PA 85; Govrs Schl Sci Carnegie Mellon U 86.

SURBER, LAURA; Connelsville Area HS; Champion, PA; (Y); Library Aide; Radio Clb; Ski Clb; Teachers Aide; Yrbk Stf; VP Jr Cls; Pres Sr Cls; Stu Cncl; Var L Tennis; High Hon Roll; German Hnr Scty 86; U Of PA.

SURDICK, LYNN; Bishop O Hara HS; Dickson City, PA; (S); Art Clb; Camera Clb; French Clb; NFL; School Play; High Hon Roll; Church Yth Grp; Pep Clb; Church Choir; Gld Key Art-Symblc Outstndng Achvt 85; Excllnc Oral Intrprtn Cert 83; Genrl Excllnc Art 83 & 85; Occptnl/Recrtnl Thrpy.

SURGENT, JEFFREY; Central Catholic HS; Pittsburgh, PA; (Y); 120/360; English Clb; JA; Math Clb; Spanish Clb; Im Ftbl; Hon Roll; NHS; Spanish NHS; Robert Morris; Bus Admin.

SURKOVICH, NANCY; Moshannon Valley HS; Houtzdale, PA; (Y); 25/120; Pep Clb; Ski Clb; Spanish Clb; SADD; Chorus; Concert Band; Flag Corp; Pep Band; Nwsp Stf; Stat Bsktbl; Altrnt Yth Schlrs Prgm 86; Fash Merch.

SURMA, JON ERIC; Mt Pleasant Area HS; Mt Pleasant, PA; (Y); Art Clb; CAP; Exploring; Letterman Clb; Ski Clb; VICA; JV Bsktbl; L Var Golf; L Var Trk; Wt Lftg; WCCC; Arch.

SUROVEC, TRAVIS; Bald Eagle Area HS; Clarence, PA; (Y); 32/200; Concert Band; Jazz Band; Mrchg Band; High Hon Roll; Hon Roll; Prfct Atten Awd.

SUROWIEC, GERALYN; Scranton Prep; Clarks Summit, PA; (Y); 6/192; Chorus; School Musical; High Hon Roll; Am Clsscl League; Ntl Jr Clsscl; Greek Ex High Hnr 86; Bus.

SURRENA, LISA; Ft Le Boeuf HS; Waterford, PA; (Y); Dance Clb; Debate Tm; SADD; Varsity Clb; Variety Show; Sec Soph Cls; Pres Jr Cls; Var Cheerleading; JV Var Pom Pon; Stat Score Keeper; Mrt Achvmnt Piano 84; Mst Creatv Pep Rlly Rtn Chrldng Cmp 83; Pre-Med.

SURRENA, SHANAN; Franklin HS; Grove City, PA; (Y); 22/220; Office Aide; Spanish Clb; Variety Show; Frsh Cls; Soph Cls; Jr Cls; Cheerleading; High Hon Roll; NHS; Schl Dirctrs Awd 84-86.

SUSKO, JOANNE; Salisbury Township SR HS; Allentown, PA; (Y); 1/151; Exploring; FBLA; DAR Awd; High Hon Roll; Trk; Pres Schlr; Val; Soropt Fndtn Yth Ctzrnshp Awd 86; Outstndg Bus Stu 86; Elizabethtown FBLA Scholar Awd 86; DAR; Elizabethtown Coll; Acctg.

SUSTRIK, ROBIN; Mc Guffey HS; W Finley, PA; (Y); Church Yth Grp; 4-H; FFA; 4-H Awd; German Clb; Office Aide; Church Choir; Color Guard; FFA Profcncy Awds Grdng & Pub Spkng 84-86; 4-H Gld Awd 85; FFA Ldrshp WA Conf Prog Schlrp 86; Penn St U; Ag Engrg.

SUTCAVAGE, BETH A; Dallas SR HS; Trucksville, PA; (Y); 37/194; Art Clb; Drama Clb; Chorus; Yrbk Stf; Acdmc Rcgntn Art Awd 84-86; Luzerne CC; Cmmrcl Art.

SUTER, MARK H; Fort Cherry HS; Bulger, PA; (S); Art Clb; Computer Clb; Math Clb; Science Clb; Ski Clb; Rep Soph Cls; JV Var Wrstlng; High Hon Roll; Varsity Clb; Presdntl Physcl Ftns Awd 84-85; Achvt Physcl Ftns Awd 83-84; Engr.

SUTER, SCOTT; Southmoreland HS; Ruffsdale, PA; (Y); 30/218; Latin Clb; Spanish Clb; Crs Cntry; Score Keeper; Tennis; Natl Knowldgmstr Open Tm 86; Hist Rangers 86; Classics Clb 85-86; Pittsburgh Tech Inst:Compu Dsg.

SUTKOWSKI, BEVERLY; Lincoln HS; Ellwood City, PA; (Y); 14/162; Church Yth Grp; French Clb; Y-Teens; Chorus; School Musical; Pom Pon; NHS; 4-H; Drill Tm; School Play; Snr Drmtcs 85-86; Ushers Clb 85-86; Duquesne; Phrmcy.

SUTORKA, MARK; Lakeland HS; Carbondale, PA; (Y); Art Clb; Band; Concert Band; Jazz Band; Stage Crew; Symp Band; Variety Show; Vllybl; Socr; PA ST U; Psych.

SUTORKA, MICHELLE; Highlands HS; Natrona Hts, PA; (Y); Church Yth Grp; Girl Scts; Band; Mrchg Band; Symp Band; Jr NHS; NHS; JR Natl Hnr Soc; Natl Hnr Soc; Mid-East Hnrs Band; Bradford Bus Schl; Exec Sec.

SUTT, LARRY; Altoona Area HS; Altoona, PA; (Y); German Clb; Trk; Hon Roll; PA ST U; Dntst.

SUTTER, DAREN; Lincoln HS; Ellwood City, PA; (Y); #4 In Class; Key Clb; Ski Clb; Bowling; Hon Roll.

SUTTMILLER, SHAWN; Greater Johnstown HS; Johnstown, PA; (Y); Chess Clb; German Clb; VP JA; Trk; Hon Roll.

SUTTON, BETH; Beaver Area JR SR HS; Beaver, PA; (Y); Church Yth Grp; French Clb; Pep Clb; Teachers Aide; Band; Boy Scts; Concert Band; Mrchg Band; High Hon Roll; Hon Roll; 1st Plc Mtls Cmptv Ice Sktng 79-86; Psych.

SUTTON, DONNA; Benton Area JR SR HS; Benton, PA; (Y); 9/40; FTA; Keywanettes; Ski Clb; Chorus; Color Guard; Capt Flag Corp; School Musical; School Play; Yrbk Stf; Var Capt Cheerleading; Natl Engl Merit Awd 86; US Chrldr Achvt Awd 85; Cntry 21 Accntg Awd 84; Bloomsburg U; Accntnt.

SUTTON, JACK C; Saegertown HS; Saegertown, PA; (Y); 28/117; Boy Scts; Church Yth Grp; SADD; Hon Roll; Crawford County Area Vo-Tech.

SUTTON, JAMES; Avon Grove HS; West Grove, PA; (Y); 50/150; Boy Scts; Church Yth Grp; Debate Tm; Exploring; SADD; Band; Concert Band; Mrchg Band; School Musical; School Play; W Grove Frmrs Clb Schlrshp 86; New London Grange Schlrshp 86; PA ST U; Ornmntl Horticltr.

SUTTON, KERRY; Stroudsburg HS; Stroudsburg, PA; (Y); 92/233; Pep Clb; Spanish Clb; Varsity Clb; Yrbk Sprt Ed; Sec Frsh Cls; Var JV Cheerleading; High Hon Roll; Hon Roll; U AL; Fshn Mrchndsng.

SUTTON, LAURA; Central Bucks East HS; Doylestown, PA; (Y); Ski Clb; Chorus; Cheerleading; Mgr(s); Score Keeper; L Socr; Timer; Hon Roll; Intl Bus.

SUTTON, RAMONA; Fairchance JR SR HS; Fairchance, PA; (Y); Church Yth Grp; FHA; JV Bsktbl; Hon Roll; Marine Bio.

SUTTS, ANNARIE; Monongahela Valley Catholic HS; Monongahela, PA; (S); 17/102; French Clb; Pep Clb; Band; Chorus; Church Choir; Mrchg Band; French Hon Soc; U Pittsburgh; Nrsng.

SUWAN, SASI; Freeport SR HS; Sarver, PA; (S); 1/200; English Clb; School Play; Stage Crew; Ed Nwsp Rptr; Yrbk Rptr; Stat Bsktbl; High Hon Roll.

SUWOLITCH, TONYA; Marion Center HS; Dixonville, PA; (Y); 56/169; Latin Clb; Library Aide; Pep Clb; Q&S; SADD; School Play; Variety Show; Yrbk Rptr; Yrbk Stf; High Hon Roll; IUP; Med Lab Tech.

SUYDAM, ERIC; Hemfield HS; E Petersburg, PA; (Y); Elec.

SUZICH, NATALIE; Moon SR HS; Coraopolis, PA; (Y); 15/329; German Clb; JA; Key Clb; Trs Chorus; Nwsp Ed-Chief; Nwsp Rptr; Nwsp Stf; Hst Sr Cls; Stu Cncl; Var Sftbl; Jrnlsm.

SVITAK, LISA MARIE; Little Flower Catholic HS For Girls; Philadelphia, PA; (Y); 60/430; Church Yth Grp; Cmnty Wkr; Dance Clb; GAA; Stage Crew; Yrbk Stf; Cheerleading; Coach Actv; Hon Roll; Law.

SVITEK, JOHN L; Canon Mac Millan SR HS; Canonsburg, PA; (Y); Chess Clb; Latin Clb; Science Clb; Tennis; Chem Engr.

SVITKO, DREW; South Allegheny HS; Port Vue, PA; (Y); 27/168; Math Clb; Math Tm; Scholastic Bowl; Spanish Clb; Stage Crew; Stu Cncl; Golf; Hon Roll; NHS; Am Leg Schl Awd 83; PA ST; Corp Law.

SWAB, KIM; Clarion-Limestone HS; Brookville, PA; (Y); Spanish Clb; Varsity Clb; Drill Tm; Pom Pon; Trk; Vllybl; Clarion U; Elem Ed.

SWAB III, MELVIN; Upper Dauphin Area HS; Elizabethville, PA; (Y); 19/112; Boy Scts; Im Vllybl; Hon Roll; Crimnl Justice.

SWAILES, SHIELA; Shalom Christian Acad; Willow Hill, PA; (Y); Pres Church Yth Grp; FHA; Hon Roll; NEDT Awd; Wilson Coll; Vet.

SWALLOW, JAMES; Northeast Catholic HS; Philadelphia, PA; (Y); 68/398; JV Bsktbl; Hon Roll; Outstanding Awd For German 84-85; Drexel U; Bus Mgnt.

SWAN, ANNE M; Warwick HS; Lititiz, PA; (Y); 50/285; Art Clb; Trs Varsity Clb; Fld Hcky; Swmmng; Trk; Carnegie-Mellon U Natl Art Schlrshp 86; Carnegie Mellon U; Art.

SWANEY, VAN; Seneca Valley HS; Zelienople, PA; (Y); 6/43; Concert Band; Mrchg Band; Orch; Pep Band; Symp Band; Nwsp Rptr; Ed Lit Mag; French Hon Soc; Jr NHS; NHS; Acad Achvt Awd 85; Pre-Med.

SWANGER, TRICIA; Mechanicsburg Area HS; Mechanicsburg, PA; (Y); 91/311; Pres Spanish Clb; SADD; Hon Roll; 15th PA Spnsh 84; 2nd Schl Essay 84; Elem Ed.

SWANGO, KELLI; Charleroi Area SR HS; Charleroi, PA; (Y); Science Clb; Ski Clb; Spanish Clb; Chorus; Drill Tm; Capt Twrlr; Hon Roll; Robert Morris; Radlgy.

SWANIK, CHARLES B; Mohawk HS; Wampum, PA; (Y); FBLA; Ski Clb; Sec Sr Cls; L Ftbl; Capt Trk; Im Wt Lftg; Prfct Atten Awd; 1st Pl IBM & USS Steel Awds Buhl Sci Fair 86; 9th Pl PIAA Trk & Fld Champs 86; Penn ST; Adm.

SWANK, BRIAN; Knoch HS; Butler, PA; (Y); 12/254; Church Yth Grp; Science Clb; Varsity Clb; Var L Bsktbl; JV Var Ftbl; High Hon Roll; Hon Roll; NHS; Med.

SWANK, KATHI; Southmoreland SR HS; Scottdale, PA; (Y); 17/241; Yrbk Stf; Stu Cncl; Powder Puff Ftbl; CC Awd; French Hon Soc; High Hon Roll; Pres Schlr; Rotary Awd; Church Yth Grp; Miss Christmas Seal Amer Lung Assoc Scholar 85; U Pittsburgh; Bus.

SWANK, KRISTINA; Slippery Rock Area HS; Butler, PA; (Y); German Clb; Intnl Clb; Pep Clb; Band; Concert Band; Drm Mjr(t); Mrchg Band; School Musical; Nwsp Stf; High Hon Roll; Dist V Band, Rgnl Band 86; Mus Educ.

SWANK, LORI; Berlin Brothersvalley HS; Somerset, PA; (Y); Church Yth Grp; 4-H; FBLA; GAA; SADD; Nwsp Rptr; Var Capt Bsktbl; Var L Sftbl; Var L Vllybl; 4-H Awd.

SWANKLER, CLIFFORD; Everett Christian Acad; Bedford, PA; (Y); Church Yth Grp; Debate Tm; Political Wkr; Band; Yrbk Stf; JV Bsktbl; Mst Imprvd In Schl 85-86; Mst Imprvd In Char 85-86.

SWANSON, ERIC; General Mc Lane HS; Mckean, PA; (Y); 2/250; Var L Tennis; NHS; German Clb; Letterman Clb; Teachers Aide; Var Golf; High Hon Roll; Hon Roll; Mvp Tnns Team 86; All-Cnty Tnns 86; Engrng.

SWANSON, JIM; Warren Area HS; Warren, PA; (Y); Church Yth Grp; Spanish Clb; Band; Concert Band; Drm Mjr(t); Mrchg Band; Socr; Trk; Vllybl; High Hon Roll; Mrt Hnrs 5 Times-Rcvd Ltr 84-85; Mrt Hnrs 6 Times-Rcvd Pine For Ltr 85-86.

SWANSON, KELLY; State College Area HS; State College, PA; (Y); 15/500; Church Yth Grp; Concert Band; Yrbk Rptr; Rep Stu Cncl; JV Bsktbl; Socr; High Hon Roll; Frsh Cls; Im Vllybl; ST Coll Area Schl Dist Faculty Schlr 86; Concours Nationale De Francais Cert 86; Frgn Lang Awd 86; Bryn Mawr Coll; Pol Sci.

SWANSON, KERRY; Punxsutawney HS; Punxsutawney, PA; (Y); CAP; Nwsp Ed-Chief; Nwsp Phtg; Nwsp Stf; Yrbk Phtg; Yrbk Stf; Var Bsktbl; Hon Roll; NHS; VFW Awd.

SWANSON, KRISTEN E; Mercyhurst Prep Schl; Erie, PA; (Y); Dance Clb; Drama Clb; French Clb; Trs Key Clb; Ski Clb; Thesps; School Musical; School Play; NHS; PA HS Spch Lgs All ST Cast Awd 86; Ltr Commndtn Gov SAT Scores Awd 85; 1st & 2nd Pl JR Acad Sci; Barnard Coll; Theatre.

SWANSON, MICHELE; Clearfield Area HS; Woodland, PA; (Y); 3/306; Church Choir; Mrchg Band; High Hon Roll; NHS; Acad All-Amer 86; Prncpls List 86; PA Acad Of Csmtlgy; Csmtlgy.

SWANSON, STEPHEN; Harbor Creek HS; North East, PA; (Y); 7/203; Boy Scts; Mrchg Band; Pep Band; School Play; Rep Jr Cls; Pres Rep Sr Cls; L Swmmng; L Trk; L Wrstlng; NHS; Eagle Scout 86; Grove City Coll; Chem Engr.

SWARNER, LORIE; Downingtown SR HS; Downingtown, PA; (Y); Church Yth Grp; Teachers Aide; Band; Color Guard; Concert Band; Jazz Band; Mrchg Band; Rep Frsh Cls; Wrstlng; Hon Roll; Kutztown ST Coll; Elem Educ.

SWARTWOOD, ANNETTE; Cowanesque Valley HS; Westfield, PA; (S); 9/87; 4-H; German Clb; Hosp Aide; VP Letterman Clb; VP Ski Clb; Varsity Clb; Sec Band; Chorus; Concert Band; Jazz Band; Schlr Athlete 84; Nrsng.

SWARTZ, AMY; Susquehanna Comm JR SR HS; Starrucca, PA; (Y); Church Yth Grp; 4-H; Girl Scts; Hosp Aide; Band; Concert Band; Mrchg Band; Bsktbl; Score Keeper; Accntng.

SWARTZ, ANDY; Northeastern HS; York, PA; (Y); 9/160; Computer Clb; French Clb; Varsity Clb; Chorus; Bsbl; Socr; Vllybl; High Hon Roll; Hon Roll; NHS; Penn ST; Comp Engrng.

SWARTZ, DEBBIE; Littlestown HS; Hanover, PA; (Y); 38/149; Band; Chorus; Concert Band; Mrchg Band; Swing Chorus; Rep Sr Cls; Sec Stu Cncl; Capt Cheerleading; Outstndng Pianst 86; Arion Fndtn Awd 86; Pres Schlrshp Kystn 86; Keystone; Htl Mgt.

SWARTZ, KIM; Old Forge HS; Old Forge, PA; (Y); Cmnty Wkr; Exploring; Ski Clb; Pre Law.

SWARTZ, KIMBERLY; Susquenita HS; Duncannon, PA; (S); 10/185; Cmnty Wkr; School Musical; Hon Roll; Merit Awd Algebra II 84-85; Vet.

SWARTZ, KRISTIN L; Northeastern SR HS; York, PA; (Y); 19/159; Band; Chorus; Concert Band; Mrchg Band; Yrbk Stf; Rep Frsh Cls; Off Sr Cls; Capt L Bsktbl; L Var Trk; NHS; Most Promsng Athlt & Outstndng Permr-Track 83-86; Most Imprvd Defnsv Plyr-Bsktbl 85-86; Accntng.

SWARTZ, MARY; Saltsburg JR-SR HS; Saltsburg, PA; (Y); DECA; GAA; Ski Clb; Varsity Clb; School Musical; Stage Crew; Bsktbl; Sftbl; Vllybl; Hon Roll; Bus Mgmt.

SWARTZ, MATT; Potstown HS; Pottstown, PA; (Y); 38/238; Key Clb; Var Bsbl; Var Bsktbl; Var Ftbl; DAR Awd; Hon Roll; Bus.

SWARTZ, MICHAEL TODD; Hollidaysburg Area HS; Duncansville, PA; (Y); Church Yth Grp; Teachers Aide; Army.

SWARTZ, RANDI; Brookville Area HS; Brookville, PA; (Y); 53/144; Church Yth Grp; French Clb; FHA; FTA; Office Aide; Chorus; Mrchg Band; Orch; Sec Lit Mag; JV Trk; Sec.

SWARTZ, STACY; Brookville Area HS; Brookville, PA; (Y); Am Leg Aux Girls St; German Clb; SADD; Band; School Musical; Im Sftbl; Hon Roll; NHS; Venango Campus; RN.

SWARTZ, TINA; Sheffield Area HS; Sheffield, PA; (Y); 16/90; Church Yth Grp; FCA; Letterman Clb; Pep Clb; SADD; Varsity Clb; Trs Frsh Cls; Cheerleading; Mat Maids; High Hon Roll; IN U PA.

SWARTZ, TODD; Sheffield Area HS; Sheffield, PA; (Y); Church Yth Grp; Stage Crew; JV Ftbl; JV Wrstlng; High Hon Roll; US Army.

SWARTZENTRUBER, SONYA D; Belleville Mennonite HS; Belleville, PA; (Y); 2/9; Chorus; School Play; Yrbk Stf; Cheerleading; Fld Hcky; Mgr(s); Dnfth Awd; High Hon Roll; NHS; Sal; Hesston Coll; Bus Data Proc.

SWARTZLANDER, GREG; Cumberland Valley HS; Carlisle, PA; (Y); Aud/Vis; Band; Drm & Bgl; Jazz Band; Mrchg Band; Orch; Symp Band; L Trk; Wt Lftg; Hon Roll; Hnr Carrier Patriot News Co 84; Awd Excllnce GV Schls Band 84 & 85; Tele-Cmmnctns.

SWASING, LIORIE; Glendale HS; Coalport, PA; (Y); Nwsp Stf; Yrbk Phtg; Yrbk Rptr; Yrbk Stf; Sec Sr Cls; Var Church Yth Grp; Var Powder Puff Ftbl; Var Score Keeper; L Sftbl; Hon Roll.

SWASTA, BETH; Center HS; Aliquippa, PA; (Y); 16/175; German Clb; Rep Concert Band; Rep Mrchg Band; Pep Band; Hon Roll; NHS; Prfct Atten Awd; Med Tech.

SWATSKI, LORI; Mt Caremel Area JR SR HS; Kulpmont, PA; (Y); 9/138; Girl Scts; Latin Clb; Pep Clb; Q&S; Spanish Clb; Nwsp Rptr; Nwsp Stf; High Hon Roll; NHS; Natl Hstry Awd 85; Lock Haven U; Lwyr.

SWATSWORTH, PAULA; Laurel Valley HS; Seward, PA; (Y); 17/87; AFS; Color Guard; Mrchg Band; Yrbk Stf; Hon Roll; Accntng.

SWATSWORTH, SUSAN; Troy HS; Columbia Cross Rd, PA; (Y); 2/144; Church Yth Grp; Church Choir; School Play; Stu Cncl; Cit Awd; NHS; Pres Schlr; Drama Clb; VP Soph Cls; VFW Awd; Schlrshp Challenge Tm 86; Rhonda Gene Kelley Mem Awd 86; Ryon Hettich Mem Awd 86; Bob Jones U; Pre-Med.

SWAUGER, VAN; Beaver Area JR SR HS; Beaver, PA; (Y); Church Yth Grp; FCA; JCL; Latin Clb; Bsbl; L Bsktbl; High Hon Roll; Hon Roll; Pblc Rel.

SWEATMAN, PATRICIA A; B Reed Henderson HS; W Chester, PA; (Y); 45/335; Church Yth Grp; Office Aide; Q&S; Scholastic Bowl; Nwsp Bus Mgr; Var Crs Cntry; Var Lcrss; High Hon Roll; NHS; Spanish NHS; All Ches-Mont Leag Crs-Cntry Mbr 85-86; Acad Cmptn Tm Mbr 85-86; James Madison U; Htl Mgmt.

SWEDER, JANINE; Lakeland HS; Jermyn, PA; (S); 36/146; Sec Frsh Cls; Sec Soph Cls; Sec Jr Cls; Capt Pom Pon; Hon Roll; Penn ST; Bus Adm.

SWEDER, MAURA; Lakeland JR SR HS; Jermyn, PA; (S); 24/160; Spanish Clb; Cheerleading; Bus Admin.

SWEELEY, JOE; Marple Newtown SR HS; Broomall, PA; (Y); Art Clb; Chess Clb; Church Yth Grp; Var Ftbl; Var Capt Trk; Hon Roll.

SWEENEY, ANN; Central HS; Scranton, PA; (Y); Church Yth Grp; German Clb; Ski Clb; Hon Roll; Psychtry.

SWEENEY, EDWARD J; St Josephs Preparatory Schl; Philadelphia, PA; (Y); 10/260; Nwsp Stf; Yrbk Stf; Im Bsktbl; Im Ftbl; Im Ice Hcky; Im Score Keeper; High Hon Roll; Hon Roll; NHS; PRRP Schlr; Outstndng Acad Prfmnc Awd; Instrml Awd; Engrng.

SWEENEY, GLENN A; Pennsbury HS; Morrisville, PA; (Y); Cmnty Wkr; Stage Crew; Var L Swmmng; Im Vllybl; Engrng.

SWEENEY, JULIE; Northwestern HS; W Springfield, PA; (Y); Pep Clb; Drill Tm; Rep Frsh Cls; Sec Soph Cls; Hst Sr Cls; Rep Stu Cncl; Powder Puff Ftbl; Hon Roll; Bus Leg Sec.

SWEENEY, KATE; Red Lion Area SR HS; York, PA; (Y); 50/372; Varsity Clb; Rep Frsh Cls; VP Soph Cls; Sec Jr Cls; JV Var Cheerleading; Hon Roll; Hugh O Brien Yth Fndtn 85; PA ST U; Elem Ed.

SWEENEY, KATHE; Pius X HS; E Bangor, PA; (Y); 1/27; Am Leg Aux Girls St; Church Yth Grp; Yrbk Ed-Chief; Pres Stu Cncl; Bausch & Lomb Sci Awd; Dnfth Awd; NHS; Dance Clb; Pep Clb; 3rd Rnnr Up Miss PA Teen Pagnt 86; Miss PA Teen Schlrshp Awd 86; Chem Awd 86; Pol Sci.

SWEENEY, KATHLEEN; Archbishop Prendergast HS; Drexel Hill, PA; (Y); 57/361; Spanish Clb; Capt Crs Cntry; Trk; Hon Roll; Spanish NHS; West Chester U; Bus.

SWEENEY, KATHLEEN; West Scranton HS; Scranton, PA; (Y); Dance Clb; Ski Clb; SADD; Yrbk Stf; Rep Stu Cncl; Hon Roll; Marywood; Psych.

SWEENEY, MAUREEN E; Indiana Area SR HS; Indiana, PA; (Y); 12/298; Church Yth Grp; Model UN; VP Red Cross Aide; Band; Nwsp Ed-Chief; High Hon Roll; NCTE Awd; NHS; Sec Debate Tm; Q&S; PA Govrnrs Schl For Intnl Studies 85; Schls & Scribes New Correspondent 84-86; Intl Studies.

SWEENEY, TERRY; Karns City HS; Bruin, PA; (Y); Chorus; Hon Roll.

SWEET, ANITA; Fairchance George JR SR HS; Smithfield, PA; (Y); Church Yth Grp; Cmnty Wkr; FHA; Library Aide; Y-Teens; Band; Concert Band; Mrchg Band; School Musical; Nwsp Stf; Bus.

SWEET, ERIC; Cowanesque Valley HS; Middlebury Center, PA; (S); 7/100; Boy Scts; Rptr FFA; Wrstlng; Hon Roll; NHS; Eagle Awd 84; Acdmc Ltr 84; Air Force; Law Enfrcmnt.

SWEET III, ROBERT D; Chestnut Ridge HS; Alum Bank, PA; (S); 19/140; Church Yth Grp; Ski Clb; Ftbl; Hon Roll; NHS; Vet.

SWEETY, MELISSA; Saint Piusx HS; Pottstown, PA; (S); 3/161; FBLA; Letterman Clb; Rep Frsh Cls; Off Soph Cls; Rep Jr Cls; Stu Cncl; Var L Fld Hcky; Var L Sftbl; High Hon Roll; NEDT Awd.

SWEIGANT, LYNETT; Pequea Valley HS; Gordonville, PA; (Y); 42/139; Church Yth Grp; Drama Clb; Church Choir; School Play; High Hon Roll; Hon Roll; Hstry.

SWEIGARD, CHERYL; Upper Dauphin Area HS; Millesburg, PA; (Y); 3/112; Church Yth Grp; Band; Chorus; Concert Band; Jazz Band; Mrchg Band; Yrbk Stf; Hon Roll; NHS; Rotary Awd; Lancaster Gnrl Hosp Schl; Nrs.

SWEIGART, CHERYL; Pequea Vly HS; Gordonville, PA; (Y); 10/138; Varsity Clb; Chorus; Mrchg Band; Pres Frsh Cls; Pres Soph Cls; Bsktbl; Fld Hcky; Sftbl; Hon Roll; NHS; Soc Wrk.

SWEIGART, KIMBERLY NOEL; Lampeter-Strasburg HS; Willow Street, PA; (Y); Am Leg Aux Girls St; Concert Band; Mrchg Band; School Musical; Yrbk Stf; JV Bsktbl; Bausch & Lomb Sci Awd; NHS; Pres Art Clb; Band; Grnd Chmpn Lncstr Sci & Engr Fair 86; PA Gvrns Schl Sci 86; Gld Ky Schlstc Wrtng Awd 85.

SWEIGART, TRACY LYNN; Ephrata HS; Stevens, PA; (Y); Pep Clb; Teachers Aide; Color Guard; Drill Tm; Mrchg Band; Trk; Hon Roll; J Harry Hibshman Schlrshp 86-87; Schl Comp Tech; Bus.

SWEIGERT, EDWARD; Marian Catholic HS; Brockton, PA; (Y); Boy Scts; Church Yth Grp; Teachers Aide; Bsbl; Ftbl; Wt Lftg; Ftbl Coachs Awd 85; Merit Achvt Awd 83.

SWEINHART, JENNIFER; Boyertown Area SR HS; Boyertown, PA; (Y); 9/400; Drama Clb; SADD; Chorus; School Play; Variety Show; Rep Frsh Cls; Var Fld Hcky; Var Lcrss; High Hon Roll; Hon Roll; Psychlgy.

SWEITHELM, RICHARD; Canton HS; Roaring Branch, PA; (Y); Trs FFA; FFA Best Prj Awd $30 86; Agri Mgmt.

SWEITZER, DAVID; Connellsville Area SR HS; Mt Pleasant, PA; (Y); Band; Jazz Band; Mrchg Band; Pep Band; School Musical; Soph Cls; Sr Cls; Stu Cncl; USAF.

SWEITZER, LISA; York County Area Vo Tech; Thomasville, PA; (Y); 8/406; Yrbk Stf; Yrbk Stf; Rep Soph Cls; Rep Jr Cls; Stu Hlth Occptn Stu Amer; Rprtr Hlth Occptn Stu Amer; NRSNG.

SWEN, CRAIG; Hopewell SR HS; Aliquippa, PA; (Y); Church Yth Grp; Chorus; Var Bsbl; Var Bsktbl; Var Golf; Var Socr.

SWENSEN, JILL; Shady Side Acad; Pittsburgh, PA; (Y); Letterman Clb; Radio Clb; Ski Clb; Spanish Clb; SADD; Bsktbl; Tennis; Trk; Hon Roll; Ntl Merit Ltr; Beginning Spanish Awd 85; Arch.

SWENSON, HEIDI; George Washington HS; Philadelphia, PA; (Y); Church Yth Grp; Cmnty Wkr; Girl Scts; Hosp Aide; JA; Red Cross Aide; Var Bowling; JV Sftbl; Pre-Med.

SWENSON, JULIE; Harmony HS; Cherry Tree, PA; (Y); Ski Clb; Teachers Aide; Band; Chorus; Color Guard; Concert Band; Trs Nwsp Stf; Rep Stu Cncl; Var L Cheerleading; Var Sftbl; IN U Of PA; Foods/Nutrtn.

SWENSON, NEIL K; Germantown Friends Schl; Philadelphia, PA; (Y); Cmnty Wkr; School Play; Nwsp Ed-Chief; Var Crs Cntry; Var Trk; Ntl Merit SF; Harvard Clb Awd 85; Schl Latin Awd 83; Schl Hist Awd 84.

SWEPPENHEISER, BRENDA; Tunkhannock Area HS; Tunkhannock, PA; (Y); Drama Clb; Pep Clb; Stage Crew; Var Cheerleading; Var Trk; Hon Roll; ST Cvl Svc Cert Awd; Bloomsburg U; Acctg.

SWETAVAGE, DONNA; Shennandoah Valley HS; Shenandoah, PA; (Y); 37/100; Color Guard; Drill Tm; Yrbk Stf; Vllybl; Cit Awd; Pottsville Hosp Schl Nrsng; Nrs.

SWIATKOWSKI, CHRISTINE; Central Christian HS; Falls Creek, PA; (Y); Chorus; Yrbk Bus Mgr; Yrbk Ed-Chief; High Hon Roll; Hon Roll; NHS; Acad Exc Engl 85-86; PA ST; Bus.

SWICK, APRIL; Riverside HS; Beaver Falls, PA; (Y); Church Yth Grp; Pres 4-H; VP Letterman Clb; Varsity Clb; Band; Concert Band; Mrchg Band; Sftbl; L Trk; 4-H Awd; Mth Tchr.

SWIDZINSKI, CONNIE; Butler SR HS; Butler, PA; (Y); 4-H; FBLA; Hosp Aide; Spanish Clb; Teachers Aide; 4-H Awd; Hon Roll; Jr NHS; NHS; Slippery Rock U; Elem Educ.

SWIEGARD, MONICA; Freedom HS; Bethlehem, PA; (Y); 67/445; Church Yth Grp; Var Crs Cntry; Hon Roll; Nrsng.

SWIERCZYNSKI, SHARON; Annville-Cleona HS; Annville, PA; (S); 2/114; VP French Clb; Model UN; Sec SADD; Chorus; Church Choir; Madrigals; Ed Nwsp Stf; Lit Mag; Sec NHS; NEDT Awd; Am Legion Essay Awd 84-85; Woodmen World Life Ins Hist Awd 83-85; Dentstry.

SWIERCZYNSKI, TARA; Central HS; Philadelphia, PA; (Y); Model UN; SADD; Teachers Aide; Orch; School Musical; Co-Capt Rep Frsh Cls; Hon Roll; Psychlgy.

SWIERINGA, SCOTT; New Hope-Solebury HS; Lahaska, PA; (Y); Art Clb; Church Yth Grp; FBLA; Ski Clb; Teachers Aide; School Play; Hon Roll; Bus Admin.

SWIFT, AARON; Clearfield Area HS; Clearfield, PA; (Y); Rep FFA; Pres VICA; Im Bowling; JV Var Ftbl; JV Swmmng; Cit Awd; Hon Roll; ST For FFA Interview Cont 84; VICA Dist VII Skill Olympics 86; Electronics Teachers.

SWIFT, BRIAN; Central Dauphin HS; Harrisburg, PA; (Y); 35/325; Hon Roll; NHS; Ntl Merit Ltr; Engrng.

SWIFT, IAN; Wissahickon HS; Blue Bell, PA; (S); 31/276; Math Clb; Varsity Clb; Off Jr Cls; Var Capt Crs Cntry; Var Capt Trk; Acadmc Schlrshp-Philadelphia Coll Of Txtl & Sci 86-87; Philadelphia Coll; Chem.

SWIFT, JEFF; Carmichaels Area HS; Nemacolin, PA; (Y); 22/101; Letterman Clb; Spanish Clb; Varsity Clb; Nwsp Rptr; Var Bsbl; Var L Ftbl; Var L Wrstlng; Hon Roll; Acctnt.

SWIGART, KAREN; Lenape Area Vocational Tech; Worthington, PA; (Y); French Clb; VICA; Stu Cncl; Vllybl; Comp Sci.

SWIMLEY, TOM; Cowanesque Valley HS; Knoxville, PA; (Y); Boy Scts; Chorus; JV Ftbl; Hon Roll; VFW Awd; Frstry.

SWINCHOCK, SCOTT; Trinity HS; Mechanicsburg, PA; (Y); JV Ftbl; Var Trk; Law.

SWINDELL, IVA; Mc Connellsburg HS; Needmore, PA; (Y); FHA; Library Aide; Hgrstwn JC; Nrsng.

SWINDELL, TERESA; Huntingdon Area HS; James Creek, PA; (Y); Church Yth Grp; 4-H; Church Choir; Concert Band; Mrchg Band; Yrbk Stf; Hon Roll.

SWINEFORD, DAVID; Brookville Area HS; Brookville, PA; (Y); 39/141; Art Clb; Exploring; German Clb; Varsity Clb; Var L Ftbl; Var Trk; Hon Roll; Art Inst Pittsburgh; Cmmrcl Art.

SWINEHART, LISA; Nothern York HS; Dillsburg, PA; (Y); 50/210; Church Yth Grp; 4-H; Stu Cncl; Bsktbl; Powder Puff Ftbl; Hon Roll; Crim Jstc.

SWINGLE, FRED; Carbondale Area JR-SR HS; Carbondale, PA; (Y); French Clb; German Clb; Science Clb; Ski Clb; Im Timer; Trk; Elec Engrng.

SWINGLER, DENISE; George Westinghouse HS; Pittsburgh, PA; (Y); 14/211; Exploring; Drill Tm; Yrbk Sprt Ed; High Hon Roll; Hon Roll; NHS; Barbara Stannard Schlrshp 86; Spelman Coll; Phrmcy.

SWISHER, MARGARET; Eastern York HS; York, PA; (Y); Varsity Clb; School Musical; Sec Frsh Cls; Var L Crs Cntry; Var L Trk; Drama Clb; Ski Clb; Chorus; JV L Cheerleading; Jr NHS; $900 Schlrshp From York Cnty JR Miss Gnt 2nd Rnnr Up 86; Pres Physcl Ftns Awd 83-85; Brians Run 83; U Of Pittsburgh; Bus Admin.

SWISHER, SUSAN; Downingtown HS; Coatesville, PA; (Y); 156/501; German Clb; Yrbk Phtg; Yrbk Stf; Im Bowling; JV Lcrss; High Hon Roll; Hon Roll; Outstndng Bus Stu 86; Goldey Beacom Coll; Wrd Info Pr.

SWITALSKI, LORI ANN; North Catholic HS; Glenshaw, PA; (Y); Church Yth Grp; French Clb; German Clb; Pres Hosp Aide; Color Guard; School Musical; Sftbl; Joan Of Arc Mdlln Grl 85; IN U Of PA; Accntn.

SWITZER, GLORIA; Redbank Valley HS; Fairmount City, PA; (Y); FHA; Spanish Clb; Yrbk Stf; L Trk; High Hon Roll; Hon Roll; NHS; Clarion U Of PA; Elem Educ.

SWOAGER, FRANCINE; West Allegheny HS; Imperial, PA; (Y); Drama Clb; German Clb; Stage Crew; Hon Roll; Engrng.

SWOBODA, KIM; Coughlin HS; Plains, PA; (Y); Cmnty Wkr; Hosp Aide; Library Aide; Cheerleading; Crs Cntry; Trk; High Hon Roll; NHS; Misercordia; Occ Thrpy.

SWOGGER, MARCIE; Bellwood-Antis HS; Tyrone, PA; (Y); FBLA; Sec Key Clb; Spanish Clb; Varsity Clb; Chorus; School Musical; Chrmn Cheerleading; Gym; Trk; Wt Lftg; 1st Pl Wnr Danc Mstrs Cmptn Grp 84 & 85; 3-Tm Trck Ltrmn 84-86; Presdntl Physcl Ftns Awd 84; Penn ST; Danc.

SWOPE, ALLEN; Altoona Area HS; Altoona, PA; (Y); Boy Scts; Band; Concert Band; Jazz Band; Mrchg Band; Orch; Pep Band; School Musical; Variety Show; Var L Swmmng; Penn ST; Pre-Med.

SWOPE, CHRIS; Cedar Crest HS; Lebanon, PA; (Y); Art Clb; Church Yth Grp; ROTC; Band; Concert Band; Drm & Bgl; Mrchg Band; Bsbl; Ice Hcky; Wt Lftg; Hornsburg Area CC; Aviatn.

SWOPE, GARY; Cumberlan Valley Christian HS; Waynesboro, PA; (S); 1/20; Church Yth Grp; Yrbk Ed-Chief; Cit Awd; High Hon Roll; Hnr Soc Amer Chrstn Schls 83-86; PA ST; Mth.

SWOPE, JUDI; Elizabethtown Area HS; Elizabethtown, PA; (Y); Church Yth Grp; Library Aide; Lbrary Aide Cert 84-85; Pionr Grls Awds 84-86; Stdied Piano-7 Yrs; Sectrl Wrk.

SWOPE, MICHAEL; Tussey Mt HS; Robertsdale, PA; (Y); Boy Scts; Church Yth Grp; Varsity Clb; Var Bsktbl; Var Ftbl; Hon Roll; NHS; Altoona; Acctg.

SWOPE, RANDALL; Du Bois Area SR HS; Luthersburg, PA; (Y); 22/264; Trs Church Yth Grp; 4-H; VP FFA; Hon Roll; NHS; Ind Arts Awd 86; Stu Of Wk 86; Hnrs Awd 86; Penn ST Dubois; Animal Biosci.

SWOPE, THOMAS; Central Cambria HS; Ebensburg, PA; (S); 10/194; Computer Clb; Rep Stu Cncl; Capt Crs Cntry; Capt Cheerleading; Capt Swmmng; Capt Trk; High Hon Roll; VP Sr Cls; Dist VI Crss Cntry Chmp 85.

SWORD, STACIE; Harmony HS; Westover, PA; (Y); 4/48; Sec Band; Concert Band; Drill Tm; Mrchg Band; Nwsp Stf; Yrbk Ed-Chief; Yrbk Stf; Rep Stu Cncl; Pre-Law.

SYBERT, BRENDA; Karns City HS; Chicora, PA; (Y); Mnstry.

SYDNOR, ANDREA C; Dobbins AVTS HS; Philadelphia, PA; (Y); 15/483; Church Yth Grp; Math Clb; Math Tm; Church Choir; Yrbk Stf; Rep Soph Cls; Rep Jr Cls; Rep Sr Cls; JV Vllybl; Hon Roll; Cty Wd Bl Schlrshp 83; Hayre Schlrshp Awd 86; Tp 25 Cls Stus 86; NC A & T; Elec Engrng.

SYLVES, LORI L; United HS; New Florence, PA; (Y); 34/160; Trs Art Clb; Camera Clb; Ski Clb; Chorus; Jazz Band; Yrbk Stf; Var L Cheerleading; Var L Trk; NHS; Presdnts Phy Ftns Awd; U Pittsbrgh Johnstwn; Nrsng.

SYLVESTER, JEANETTE; Everett Area HS; Everett, PA; (Y); Church Yth Grp; GAA; Spanish Clb; Varsity Clb; Concert Band; Mrchg Band; Stu Cncl; Socr; Hon Roll; Spanish NHS; U S Music Ambass Tour 86; Clemson U; Nrsg.

SYMONIES, PATRICIA; Sacred Heart HS; Carbondale, PA; (Y); 1/56; Capt Scholastic Bowl; VP Stu Cncl; Var Cheerleading; Var Capt Tennis; Bausch & Lomb Sci Awd; Val; French Clb; NFL; Natl Schlr And Athlt Awd Army Rsrv 86; Pres Acadmc Ftnss Awd 86; Franklin & Marshall; Aero Engrg.

SYPOLT, CYNTHIA; Kiski Area HS; Apollo, PA; (Y); Church Yth Grp; Teachers Aide; Chorus; Church Choir; Yrbk Stf; VP Frsh Cls; Rep Jr Cls; Stu Cncl; Cheerleading; Sftbl; Bus Admin.

SYPUT, TIM; Highlands SR HS; Natrona Hts, PA; (Y); Exploring; Rep Frsh Cls; Hon Roll; PA ST; Chem Engrng.

SYRYTO, BRENDA; North Pocono HS; Moscow, PA; (S); 24/244; Church Yth Grp; Exploring; Girl Scts; JA; Flag Corp; Yrbk Stf; Lit Mag; Rep Stu Cncl; NHS; JR Achvts Outstndg Yng Bus Woman 86; U Scranton; Acctg.

SYSYN, NICOLA; North Clarion Area HS; Tylersburg, PA; (Y); 16/88; Drama Clb; Spanish Clb; Chorus; School Play; Yrbk Stf; Stat Bsktbl; JV Cheerleading; NEDT Awd; Pratt; Advrtsg.

SZABADOS, ANDREA J; Tunkhannock Area HS; Tunkhannock, PA; (Y); 24/315; Dance Clb; 4-H; Hosp Aide; Office Aide; Chorus; School Musical; Hon Roll; Jr NHS; Mst Imprvd SR Stu Of Yr 86; Keystone JC; Human Svcs.

SZABO, JULIE; Franklin Reg SHS HS; Export, PA; (Y); 16/328; French Clb; Pres JA; Spanish Clb; Thesps; Color Guard; Nwsp Stf; Yrbk Ed-Chief; High Hon Roll; NHS; Ntl Merit SF; Intl Bus.

SZABO, KATHLEEN A; East HS; Erie, PA; (Y); Am Leg Aux Girls St; French Clb; Model UN; Y-Teens; Yrbk Sprt Ed; Yrbk Stf; Stu Cncl; NHS; Wolves Club Schlrshp 86; Christian Ldr Inst Erie PA 85; Gannon U; Bus.

SZAJDEK, GARY; Northeast Catholic HS; Philadelphia, PA; (S); 11/390; Office Aide; Teachers Aide; Stage Crew; Im Bsbl; Im Bsktbl; Im Var Bowling; JV Golf; High Hon Roll; Hon Roll; Jr NHS; Temple Schl Of Pharmacy; Sci.

SZALA, JAMES D; Conemaugh Township HS; Johnstown, PA; (Y); 8/105; Varsity Clb; Hon Roll; JC Awd; NHS; C T Trib Democrat Athl Schlr Awd, US Army Rsrve Natl Schlr Athl Awd 86; U Pittsburagh; Engrng.

SZANYI, NEIL; Liberty HS; Bethlehem, PA; (Y); 4/475; Church Yth Grp; Math Tm; Band; Chorus; Church Choir; Orch; School Play; L Var Swmmng; High Hon Roll; NHS; Dartmouth Clg Clb Book Awd 86; Physcs.

SZCZEPANIAK, KAREN; Archbishop Kennedy HS; Philadelphia, PA; (Y); #17 In Class; Cmnty Wkr; Teachers Aide; Stu Cncl; JV Var Trk; Hon Roll; NHS; Art Awd Excllnce 86; Fine Arts.

SZCZEPANSKI, CRAIG; Council Rock HS; Churchville, PA; (Y); 46/845; Church Yth Grp; Drama Clb; School Musical; School Play; Stage Crew; Im Gym; Hon Roll; NHS; Frnch Clss For Bst Accent 86; Drama Clb Cert, Lttr & Star 83-86.

SZCZUBLEWSKI, SUSAN; Mount Alvernia HS; Pittsburgh, PA; (S); 5/69; Church Yth Grp; French Clb; Chorus; Var Capt Cheerleading; Swmmng; Vllybl; High Hon Roll; Hon Roll; NHS; Prfct Atten Awd.

SZCZYPIORSKI, SCOTT; Plymouth Whitemarsh HS; Conshohocken, PA; (Y); Art Clb; Office Aide; Nwsp Ed-Chief; Nwsp Stf; Lit Mag; Hon Roll; Prfct Atten Awd; Young Masters Consortium For The Arts Internship 86; Art.

SZEKERESH, LYNN; Central Cambria HS; Johnstown, PA; (Y); 12/225; Art Clb; Hosp Aide; Ski Clb; Band; Crs Cntry; Swmmng; Trk; Hon Roll; Law.

SZEMENYEI, STEPHEN; Freedom HS; Bethlehem, PA; (Y); 77/445; Band; Concert Band; Mrchg Band; JV Var Bsktbl; Hon Roll.

SZEPESI, MICHELLE; Connellsville Area HS; S Connellsville, PA; (Y); Band; Color Guard; Mrchg Band; Symp Band; Cheerleading; Hon Roll; Med.

SZEWCOW, MARK; Central Catholic HS; Pittsburgh, PA; (Y); 61/268; Letterman Clb; Varsity Clb; Var Bowling; Hon Roll; NHS; U Pittsburgh; Comp Pgmr.

SZEWCZYKOWSKI, MICHAEL; Cathedral Prep; Erie, PA; (Y); 59/216; Var Bsktbl.

SZEWYZKOWSKI, MICHAEL; Catherdral Prep; Erie, PA; (Y); 50/258; Var Bsktbl; Bus.

SZIMINSKI, TAMMY; Burgettstown Area HS; Bulger, PA; (Y); 54/173; Drill Tm; Yrbk Stf; Sec Stu Cncl; Point Park Coll; Jrnlsm.

SZMAL, MELISSA; John S Fine SR HS; Nanticoke, PA; (Y); 109/256; Cmnty Wkr; Exploring; Hosp Aide; Key Clb; Library Aide; Red Cross Aide; SADD; Chorus; Yrbk Stf; Twrlr; Nrsng.

SZMUC, RACHEL; Rockwood Area HS; Somerset, PA; (S); 8/95; 4-H; Rptr FHA; NFL; Office Aide; Speech Tm; Chorus; 4-H Awd; Hon Roll; NHS; Natl Forn Lg Awd 84; Schltc Awds Outstndng Schltc Achvt 83-85; Typng Awd 85; Sec.

SZOLIS, LEIGH A; Richland HS; Wexford, PA; (Y); 66/195; Art Clb; Nwsp Stf; Yrbk Stf; Rep Stu Cncl; Powder Puff Ftbl; Hon Roll; French Clb; Girl Scts; Hosp Aide; Score Keeper; Bus Admin.

SZOPIAK, PAUL L; Chartiers Valley HS; Pittsburgh, PA; (Y); CAP; Cmnty Wkr; Im JV Ice Hcky; Nvl Pilot.

SZTROIN, KIMBERLY; Mary Fuller Frazier Memorial HS; Perropolis, PA; (S); Library Aide; Band; Color Guard; Score Keeper; Stat Sftbl; Hon Roll; Prom Comm 84-85; Carnegie Mellon U Chem Olympcs 85; Phrmcy.

SZUGYE, TINA; Kennedy Christian HS; Farrell, PA; (Y); 15/98; Pep Clb; Spanish Clb; Im Bsktbl; High Hon Roll; Elizabeth Seton Schlrshp Awd 83; Bus Mgt.

SZURA, JEFFREY; Wyoming Area SR HS; Wyoming, PA; (Y); 79/247; French Clb; Kings Coll; Crmnl Justc.

SZUSZCZEWICZ, BRENDA; Nazareth Academy; Philadelphia, PA; (Y); 47/118; Cmnty Wkr; Service Clb; Orch; Lit Mag; Tennis; Hon Roll; Ntl Merit Ltr; Jazz Band; Stage Crew; U Of S FL; Atty.

SZYMANSKI, BETHANN; North Hills SR HS; Pittsburgh, PA; (Y); 190/435; Exploring; Girl Scts; Hosp Aide; JA; Library Aide; Office Aide; Chorus; Hon Roll; Library Awd 84; Chorus Awd 84; Bradford Schl Of Bus; Bus.

SZYMANSKI, THOMAS; Peabody HS; Pittsburgh, PA; (S); 5/235; L Band; L Concert Band; L Jazz Band; L Mrchg Band; L Orch; L Pep Band; L Symp Band; Cit Awd; High Hon Roll; NHS; All City Hnrs Bnd 83-86; Cntrs For Mscly Tlntd Awd 83-86; U Ptsbrg; Pre-Med.

SZYMECKI, JULIE; Harborcreek HS; Erie, PA; (Y); 25/240; Church Yth Grp; Sec Model UN; Political Wkr; Temple Yth Grp; Yrbk Stf; Sec Soph Cls; Rep Stu Cncl; Var Mgr(s); JV Trk; Hon Roll; Slippery Rock U; Psychlgy.

SZYMKOWSKI, BETH; Nazareth Acad; Philadelphia, PA; (Y); French Clb; VP Intnl Clb; Model UN; Service Clb; Var Bsktbl; Im Bowling; JV Var Fld Hcky; Hon Roll; Schlrshp 4 Yr Nzrth 83; Schlrshp Hussian Schl Of Art 85; Gldn Ky Awd Phila Coll Of Art 85; Engnrng.

SZYNAL, MIKE; Technical HS; Scranton, PA; (Y); VICA; Wldng.

TABACCHI, TRICIA; Deer Lakes HS; Cheswick, PA; (Y); Drama Clb; Varsity Clb; Trs Frsh Cls; Trs Soph Cls; Trs Jr Cls; Var Capt Cheerleading; Acctng.

TABARRINI, TARA; Old Forge HS; Old Forge, PA; (S); Office Aide; Ski Clb; Im Sftbl; Hon Roll; Jr NHS; NHS; Gregg Typng Awd 85 & 86.

TABASSO, CARMEN; St Maria Goretti HS; Philadelphia, PA; (Y); 25/400; Pres Church Yth Grp; VP Cmnty Wkr; Intnl Clb; Math Tm; Model UN; Spanish Clb; Nwsp Rptr; Rep Soph Cls; Rep Jr Cls; Rep Sr Cls; Villanova; Pre-Med.

TABATABAI, ALI; Lower Merion HS; Narberth, PA; (Y); 1/343; Math Tm; Nwsp Bus Mgr; Nwsp Ed-Chief; Stu Cncl; Var Crs Cntry; Var Trk; French Hon Soc; High Hon Roll; Ntl Merit Schol; Pres Schlr; Harvard; Med.

TABINOWSKI, BRIAN; Seneca Valley SR HS; Mars, PA; (Y); Church Yth Grp; Bsbl; Bowling; High Hon Roll; Hon Roll; PA ST U; Elec Engrng.

TABISH, DOUGLAS; Springdale HS; Cheswick, PA; (Y); 1/135; Am Leg Boys St; Boy Scts; German Clb; Rep Stu Cncl; Var JV Socr; High Hon Roll; Pres NHS; Ntl Merit Ltr; Eagle Scout 86; Hugh O Brian Yth Fndtn 85; Princeton; Elec Engr.

TABRON, JUDITH L; Chambersburg Area SR HS; Scotland, PA; (Y); 10/610; Pres Boy Scts; JCL; NFL; Chorus; Ed Lit Mag; NCTE Awd; NHS; Ntl Merit Schol; Pres Schlr; Voice Dem Awd; Brown U Bk Awd Excllnc Engl 85; Bryn Mawr Coll; Clsscs.

TACELOSKY, ANTHONY; Marian Catholic HS; Mahanoy, PA; (S); 7/114; Church Yth Grp; Cmnty Wkr; Stu Cncl; Var Im Bsktbl; Var Im Ftbl; Cit Awd; High Hon Roll; NHS; Spanish NHS; Letterman Clb; Engrng.

TACELOSKY, MARIA; Marian HS; Mahanoy City, PA; (S); 14/123; Church Yth Grp; Library Aide; Red Cross Aide; Drill Tm; School Play; Stu Cncl; JV Bsktbl; Twrlr; Hon Roll; NHS; Hugh O Brien Yth Fndtn Ldrshp Awd; Pre-Dnstry.

TACELOSKY, TONY; Marian HS; Mahanoy City, PA; (Y); 9/115; Church Yth Grp; Math Clb; Red Cross Aide; Spanish Clb; SADD; Stage Crew; Variety Show; Off Frsh Cls; Stu Cncl; JV Var Bsktbl; Elec Engrng.

TACHOVSKY, DEBORAH; Bethlehem Catholic HS; Bethlehem, PA; (Y); 13/214; Concert Band; Mrchg Band; Pep Band; High Hon Roll; NHS; Awd Highst Averg Engl III; Awd Highst Averg Thelgy III; Managemnt.

TACZAK, MARCY L; Avella Area JR-SR HS; Burgettstown, PA; (Y); 4/74; Am Leg Aux Girls St; FBLA; Ski Clb; Color Guard; Yrbk Stf; Sec Sr Cls; High Hon Roll; Hon Roll; NHS; 4-H; Clmx Mlybdnm Schlrshp 86; Robert Morris Coll; Accntng.

TADDY, MARCY; Ambridge HS; Ambridge, PA; (Y); 53/265; Church Yth Grp; Drama Clb; Pep Clb; Drill Tm; Jr Cls; Sr Cls; Coach Actv; Gym; Pom Pon; Hon Roll; Bridger Belle Cptn 84 & 86; Jrnlsm Awd 86; WPGL Chmpnshp Gymnst 83-84; Kent ST U; Chld Psych.

TAFANI, FRAN; Bishop O Reilly HS; Forty Fort, PA; (Y); Latin Clb; Band; Chorus; Mrchg Band; Nwsp Stf; Yrbk Stf; DAR Awd; MD Coll; Fshn Mrchndsng.

TAFEL, DIANE; Council Rock HS; Churchville, PA; (Y); 162/845; Cmnty Wkr; Coach Actv; JV Var Powder Puff Ftbl; L Var Sftbl; Hon Roll; Suburban I All Leag 2nd Tm Sftbll 86; 3rd & 2nd Pl ST Sch Sftbll 85-86; Educ.

TAFFERA, LIANE; Bishop O Reilly HS; Larksville, PA; (Y); Church Yth Grp; Drama Clb; Spanish Clb; Chorus; School Musical; School Play; Variety Show; Rep Frsh Cls; Spanish NHS; Drama.

TAFFERA, NANCY ANNE; Bishop O Hara HS; Olyphant, PA; (Y); Dance Clb; Hosp Aide; Nwsp Rptr; Nwsp Sprt Ed; Nwsp Stf; Rep Frsh Cls; JV Cheerleading; Otstndng Svc & Dedctn Pro-Life Clb; U Scranton; Accnt.

TAFT, KEN; William JR JR HS; Millerton, PA; (Y); Hon Roll; Mech Drawing Ii Awd 86; Corning CC; Drftsmn.

TAFT, STEVEN; Wissahickon HS; Blue Bell, PA; (S); 14/276; Boys Clb Am; German Clb; Trs Varsity Clb; Rep Jr Cls; Rep Stu Cncl; JV Ftbl; JV Lcrss; Var Socr; JV Wrstlng; AM Legion Awd Schlr 83; Bucknell U; Chem.

TAGGART, ELIZABETH; Northern Chester County Tech Schl; Phoenixville, PA; (Y); Church Yth Grp; Library Aide; Pep Clb; Radio Clb; Ski Clb; School Play; Nwsp Rptr; Yrbk Stf; Jr Cls; Stu Cncl; Bus Admn.

TAGGART, STEPHANIE; Washington HS; Washington, PA; (S); Church Yth Grp; French Clb; FNA; Hosp Aide; Key Clb; Letterman Clb; Library Aide; Ski Clb; Spanish Clb; SADD.

TAGLIABOSKI, LARIE; Bald Eagle Area HS; Bellefonte, PA; (Y); Varsity Clb; Yrbk Stf; Im Var Bsktbl; L Var FCA; L Var Trk; Hon Roll; NHS.

TAGLIENTE, DON; Clearfield HS; Clearfield, PA; (Y); Camera Clb; French Clb; Band; Chorus; Concert Band; Jazz Band; Mrchg Band; Orch; Nwsp Phtg; Yrbk Phtg.

TAGLIERI, DENISE; New Brighton Area HS; New Brighton, PA; (Y); 6/149; Computer Clb; GAA; Trs Girl Scts; Band; Concert Band; Jazz Band; Mrchg Band; Trk; Bnd Dir Awd 86; U Of Pittsburgh; Phrmcst.

TAGLIERI, VINCENT J; Father Judge HS; Philadelphia, PA; (S); 26/403; Boy Scts; Cmnty Wkr; French Clb; Yrbk Stf; Var Crs Cntry; Ftbl; Var Capt Trk; High Hon Roll; NHS; Brotherhood Ordr Arrw 84; La Salle U; Acctng.

TAGTMEIR, ELIZABETH; Interboro SR HS; Prospect Park, PA; (Y); Hosp Aide; Key Clb; Rep Soph Cls; Rep Jr Cls; Stu Cncl; Chld Psych.

TAHANEY, PAMELA; Harry S Truman HS; Levittown, PA; (Y); SADD; Band; Concert Band; Mrchg Band; Orch; Off Stu Cncl; Hon Roll; NHS; Var Awd Lttr Pin 85; Var Awd Lttr Pin & Bar 86; Psychology.

TAIKO, KRISTIN; Mahanoy Area HS; Barnesville, PA; (Y); Pres Church Yth Grp; Chorus; Church Choir; Comp Fld.

TAINTON, TRACY L; Lakeview HS; Sandy Lake, PA; (S); 5/119; Church Yth Grp; FCA; Sec FHA; Intnl Clb; Chorus; School Play; Nwsp Stf; NHS; Clarion U PA; Bus.

TAKAC, KRISTIN; Hempfield SR HS; Greensburg, PA; (Y); Art Clb; German Clb; Pep Clb; Ski Clb; Spanish Clb; Color Guard; Tennis; High Hon Roll; Hon Roll; Bst Smile 86; IN U Of PA; Hlth Fld.

TAKAC, MARK; Moon HS; Corapolis, PA; (Y); Var Socr; Im Vllybl; Hon Roll; Penn ST U; Mchncl Engrng.

TAKACH, DANA; Thomas Jefferson HS; Pittsburgh, PA; (Y); 39/259; Drama Clb; Thesps; Yrbk Stf; Powder Puff Ftbl; Lttr-Theatre Arts 84; Ytbk Staff Cert Awd 86; Clarion U Of PA; Cmnctns.

TAKACH, SARA; Lakeland Jr SR HS; Carbondale, PA; (Y); FHA; Ski Clb; Concert Band; Mrchg Band; Sec Bsktbl; Var Cheerleading; JV Var Score Keeper; Sec Trk; Hon Roll; Mrktg.

TAKACS, MARY B; Bishop Carroll HS; Ebensburg, PA; (S); 14/102; French Clb; Pep Clb; Ski Clb; Yrbk Stf; Bsktbl; Bowling; Hon Roll; All Tourny Tm Bsktbl 82-83; Outstndng Bio Stdnt Awd 83-84; St Francis Coll; Bio.

TAKAYAMA, YUKO; Upper St Clair HS; Pittsburgh, PA; (Y); JV Vllybl; Hon Roll; NHS; Eng.

TAKEI, NICOLLE; Clarion HS; Shippenville, PA; (Y); Chorus; Mrchg Band; School Musical; Variety Show; Yrbk Phtg; Yrbk Stf; L Capt Bsktbl; Var L Vllybl; Hon Roll; NHS; JR Acad Of Sci 1st Pl ST Lvl 84; Mst Vlbl Plyr Vllybl 85; Micro Bio.

TALARICO, ALEX; North Pocono JR SR HS; Moscow, PA; (Y); Ski Clb; Stage Crew; JV Bsktbl; JV Var Score Keeper; Var L Vllybl; Hon Roll; Bar Vlybl Awd 86; Reflctns Cntst 84; Scranton U; TV Brdcstng.

TALARICO, JUDY; Canon-Mc Millan SR HS; Canonsburg, PA; (Y); Office Aide; Spanish Clb; High Hon Roll; Spanish NHS; Med Sec.

TALARICO, NICOLE; Bentworth HS; Bentleyville, PA; (Y); Girl Scts; Ski Clb; Band; Mrchg Band; Twrlr; Vllybl; Hon Roll; Sci.

TALATY, PALLAVI C; Methacton SR HS; Audubon, PA; (Y); 17/341; Spanish Clb; Chorus; Color Guard; Trk; High Hon Roll; Kiwanis Awd; NHS; Schlrshp To Govrs Schl-Arts 84-85; Methacton Outstndg Achvt Awds; Outstndg Artst Of Yr Awd; PA ST U; Bio.

TALBOT, KIMBERLY LYN; Philadelphia-Montgomery Chrstn Acad; Philadelphia, PA; (Y); Church Yth Grp; Var Fld Hcky; Var Trk; Cit Awd; High Hon Roll; Hon Roll; Wmns Trck & Fld Var Mip 84; Wmns Trck & Fld Var Mvp 85.

TALERICO, TAMMY; Hopewell SR HS; Aliquippa, PA; (Y); Church Yth Grp; Cmnty Wkr; Drama Clb; French Clb; School Play; Hon Roll; Elem Ed.

TALKO, GREGG; Penn Cambria HS; Lilly, PA; (Y); Letterman Clb; Ski Clb; Spanish Clb; Pres Frsh Cls; Bsbl; Bsktbl; Ftbl; Golf; Wrstlng; Hon Roll; U Of Pittsburgh; Pre-Law.

TALLAKSEN, STEPHANIE; Northampton HS; Northampton, PA; (Y); AFS; Library Aide; Chorus; Yrbk Stf; Sec Sr Cls; Rep Stu Cncl; Powder Puff Ftbl; Trk; Wt Lftg; Hon Roll; Cedar Crest Coll; Nrsng.

TALLMAN, JOHN; Hatboro-Horsham HS; Hatboro, PA; (Y); Art Clb; Model UN; Nwsp Rptr; Nwsp Stf; Art Dept Awd; Hghst Hons Art Awd; Prom 85-86 Cvr Dsgn; Philadelphia Coll/Arts; Art Ed.

TALLON, LAURA; Cardinal O Hara HS; Springfield, PA; (Y); Cmnty Wkr; Girl Scts; Spanish Clb; School Musical; Score Keeper; Hon Roll; NHS; Chestnut Hill Coll; Elem Educ.

TALLON, REGINA; Cardinal O Hara HS; Springfield, PA; (Y); Church Yth Grp; Cmnty Wkr; Dance Clb; GAA; Girl Scts; JA; Office Aide; Service Clb; Spanish Clb; Varsity Clb; Comm Art.

TALONE, STEPHANIE; Connellsville SR HS; Connellsville, PA; (Y); 76/550; Band; Chorus; Mrchg Band; School Musical; Symp Band; High Hon Roll.

TALOTTA, ANGEL; St Maria Goretti HS; Philadelphia, PA; (Y); 21/402; Art Clb; Aud/Vis; Pres Cmnty Wkr; GAA; Math Clb; Pres Model UN; Lit Mag; Rep Frsh Cls; Rep Soph Cls; Hon Roll; Jewlr.

TALUBA, DENISE; James M Coughlin HS; Wilkes Barre, PA; (Y); 24/355; High Hon Roll; Hon Roll; NHS; Penn ST; Comp Acctnt.

TAMARKIN, SUSAN; York Suburban SR HS; York, PA; (Y); 13/187; Pep Clb; Ski Clb; Yrbk Stf; Pres Soph Cls; Rep Jr Cls; Sec Stu Cncl; Var Capt Cheerleading; Var Trk; Hon Roll; NHS; Top Histry Stu Awd 85.

TAMBLYN, KRISTI; South Allegheny HS; Port Vue, PA; (Y); FNA; Band; Concert Band; Mrchg Band; Nwsp Bus Mgr; Cheerleading; High Hon Roll; Hon Roll; NHS; Prfct Atten Awd; SR Band Awd 86; Paralegl.

TAMBURO, JORGEANN; Valley HS; Arnold, PA; (Y); 27/206; AFS; Hosp Aide; Sec Pep Clb; Varsity Clb; Chorus; Capt Color Guard; Concert Band; Yrbk Sprt Ed; Var Score Keeper; Stat Vllybl; Fnlst JR Miss Pgnt 86; Dist Chrus 86; Penn ST U; Sprts Med.

TAMBURRO, DAVID; Springdale HS; Springdale, PA; (Y); Boy Scts; Church Yth Grp; German Clb; Jazz Band; Sec Trs Mrchg Band; JV Bsktbl; Var Tennis; High Hon Roll; NHS; Band; Allegheny Kiski Hon Bnd 85; Law.

TAMINO, JOSEPH; Plum SR HS; Pittsburgh, PA; (Y); 59/378; Letterman Clb; Spanish Clb; JV Ftbl; Var Trk; High Hon Roll; Hon Roll; Prfct Atten Awd; U Of Pittsburgh; Sci.

TAMMARIELLO, STEVEN; General Mc Lane HS; Edinboro, PA; (Y); 40/230; Church Yth Grp; German Clb; Letterman Clb; Office Aide; Varsity Clb; Band; Concert Band; Flag Corp; Mrchg Band; Var L Bsbl; Edinboro U PA; Bio.

TAMMARO, DOUG; Lincoln HS; Ellwood City, PA; (Y); 32/170; Church Yth Grp; Cmnty Wkr; Latin Clb; Yrbk Stf; Stu Cncl; Hon Roll; Pres Soph Cls; Pres Jr Cls; Pres Sr Cls; Var L Bsktbl; Rotry Yth Ldrshp Awds Smnr 86; Sec Educ.

TAMMARO, MARIA; Lincoln HS; Ellwood City, PA; (Y); 20/166; French Clb; Y-Teens; Powder Puff Ftbl; High Hon Roll; Hon Roll; Med.

TAMOSAUSKAS, RONA; Avonworth HS; Pittsbg, PA; (Y); 11/96; Yrbk Stf; Lit Mag; Var Bsktbl; Coach Actv; Mgr(s); Cit Awd; High Hon Roll; Hon Roll; NHS; Northboros Yth Awd 85; Schlr/Athlt Awd 84-86; Acctng.

TAN, LY VOUCH; Juniata HS; Mifflintown, PA; (Y); Church Yth Grp; Computer Clb; Var Sftbl; Im Vllybl; High Hon Roll; NHS; Prfct Atten Awd; Schltc J 84-86; Pre-Med.

TAN, VIRAK; Elizabethtown Area HS; Elizabethtown, PA; (Y); 6/221; JV Bsktbl; Var L Socr; Var L Trk; NHS; Pres Schlr; Boy Of Mnth 86; Desire Awd Socr 86; EAEA Scholar 86; MA Inst Tech; Engrng.

TANCREDI, ANNE E; Penncrest HS; Media, PA; (Y); 19/293; Pres Church Yth Grp; School Musical; Pres Frsh Cls; Rep Soph Cls; Off Jr Cls; Rep Sr Cls; Pres Stu Cncl; Var Lcrss; High Hon Roll; Pres NHS; Century III Ldrshp Scholar 86; Schl Svc Awd 85; Rotary Ldrshp Conf 85, Cnslr 86; HOBY Ldrshp Fndtn 84; Ithaca Coll; TV/Radio.

TANEY, KELLY; John S Fine HS; Wapwallopen, PA; (Y); 91/251; Sec Church Yth Grp; Red Cross Aide; Yrbk Stf.

TANNEHILL, MARK; South Allegheny HS; Liberty, PA; (Y); Political Wkr; Var JV Bsbl; Hon Roll.

TANNEHILL, ROB; Belle Vernon Area HS; Belle Vernon, PA; (Y); Aud/Vis; Ski Clb; Band; Concert Band; Variety Show; Rep Jr Cls; Rep Stu Cncl; Im Bsbl; Var L Ftbl; Im Golf; Jrnlsm.

TANNER, ANGELA; Wm Allen HS; Allentown, PA; (Y); 65/615; Exploring; Hosp Aide; Sec JA; Spanish Clb; Chorus; Color Guard; Hon Roll; NHS; Spanish NHS; Pre-Med.

TAORMINA JR, ANTHONY F; Beaver Area HS; Beaver, PA; (Y); Ski Clb; Off Stu Cncl; Bsbl; Ftbl; Mgr(s); Trk; Hon Roll; Robt Morris Coll; Acctng.

TAPIA, BRENDA; Wyoming Area SR HS; Exeter, PA; (Y); 23/280; FBLA; Hosp Aide; High Hon Roll; Hon Roll; NHS; Mc Cann Bus Schl; Acctng.

TAPPER, JACOB; Akiba Hebrew Acad; Merion, PA; (Y); Art Clb; Debate Tm; Drama Clb; French Clb; Political Wkr; SADD; School Play; Nwsp Ed-Chief; Yrbk Stf; JV Pres Stu Cncl; Yehudit Herschkowitz Mem Awd 84; U Of PA Bk Awd 86; Yth Ldrshp Awd 86; Politics.

TARABRELLA, CHRISTINA; Elizabeth Forward HS; Elizabeth, PA; (Y); Dance Clb; Latin Clb; Yrbk Stf; Sec Soph Cls; Sec Jr Cls; Var L Cheerleading; Var L Swmmng; Var Trk; High Hon Roll; Hon Roll; Seven Springs Dance Comptn Rnnr-Up 86; Natls Smmr Dance Fest Canada Wnnr 86.

TARAMELLI, CHRISTINE; Valley View JR & SR HS; Jessup, PA; (Y); 15/200; FBLA; Spanish Clb; Yrbk Stf; Hon Roll; NHS; U Of Scranton; Fmly Study.

TARANTINO, JAMES; Penn Hills HS; Hillsborough, NC; (Y); Computer Clb; Exploring; Spanish Clb; Chorus; Rep Soph Cls; Rep Jr Cls; Hon Roll; U NC; Cmptr Sci.

TARAS, GREGORY A; Panther Valley HS; Lansford, PA; (Y); 11/106; Am Leg Boys St; ROTC; Color Guard; Hon Roll; NHS; Engrng.

TARAS, KRISTEN; Bentworth HS; Bentleyville, PA; (Y); 20/150; Ski Clb; Yrbk Stf; Soph Cls; Jr Cls; Sr Cls; Stu Cncl; Hon Roll; Attndnt Hmcmg Ct 85; Prom Ct 86; Capt-Majorette 85-87; Brdcstng.

TARAS, MATTHEW; Panter Valley HS; Coaldale, PA; (Y); 22/129; Pres Schlr; Acctg Awd 86; Lehigh CC; Acctg.

TARASI, MICHELE; Riverview HS; Verona, PA; (Y); 26/100; AFS; French Clb; Ski Clb; Varsity Clb; Nwsp Rptr; Yrbk Stf; Stu Cncl; Var L Cheerleading; Var L Sftbl; High Hon Roll; Westminster Coll; Pre-Med.

TARASUK, FRED; Mapletown JR SR HS; Dilliner, PA; (Y); 1/75; Aud/Vis; Varsity Clb; Rep Jr Cls; Var Bsktbl; Bausch & Lomb Sci Awd; High Hon Roll; NHS; Pres Schlr; Val; PA ST Fayette Campus Adv Bd Schlrshp 86; PA ST; Engrng.

TARBART, MAUREEN; Hanover SR HS; Hanover, PA; (Y); SADD; Teachers Aide; JV Fld Hcky; High Hon Roll; Hon Roll; Frshmn Hmcmg Rep 83-84; Acctnt.

TARBERT, DEBBIE; York Catholic HS; York, PA; (Y); 11/167; Pep Clb; VP Spanish Clb; Chorus; School Musical; School Play; Stage Crew; Nwsp Rptr; Mgr(s); High Hon Roll; Hon Roll; Essy Awd Amer Legn Yrk Post 127 Essy Nuclr Enrgy Is It Wrth It 86; Prsnnl Mgmt.

TARBOX, LORI; Canton HS; Canton, PA; (Y); Yrbk Stf; Csmtlgy.

TARCSON, TIM; Central Christian HS; Du Bois, PA; (Y); Exploring; Varsity Clb; Nwsp Ed-Chief; Nwsp Stf; VP Sr Cls; Var Bsbl; Var L Bsktbl; Crs Cntry; Var Socr; Hon Roll.

TARLECKY, AMY; Bloomsburg SR HS; Bloomsburg, PA; (Y); 80/150; Pep Clb; Varsity Clb; Chorus; Capt Var Cheerleading; Var Powder Puff Ftbl; Im Vllybl.

TARLEY, TINA; Beth Center HS; Millsboro, PA; (Y); 37/168; Ski Clb; Spanish Clb; Varsity Clb; Yrbk Stf; Sec Jr Cls; Off Stu Cncl; Cheerleading; Hon Roll; IN U Of PA; Bus.

TARNOSKY, JERRY; Canevin HS; Carnegie, PA; (Y); 54/127; Bowling; Socr; Hon Roll; Bus.

TARQUINIO, LISA; Villa Maria Acad; Erie, PA; (Y); 11/133; Art Clb; Church Yth Grp; Girl Scts; Hosp Aide; PAVAS; Color Guard; Yrbk Ed-Chief; Trs Sr Cls; Sftbl; High Hon Roll; Bus.

TARQUINIO, SUZANNE; Canevin HS; Coraopolis, PA; (Y); 22/190; Service Clb; Ski Clb; Sec Concert Band; Sec Mrchg Band; Orch; Pep Band; School Musical; Rep Stu Cncl; Hon Roll; Music Awd 83, 85 & 86; Outstndng Acadmc Achvt Presdntl Acadmc Ftns Awd 86; Cert Schlstc Excllnc 83-84; IN U Of PA; Elem Ed.

TARR, ELIZABETH; United HS; New Florence, PA; (Y); Pep Clb; Ski Clb; Chorus; Color Guard; Yrbk Stf; Rep Stu Cncl; Capt Cheerleading; Powder Puff Ftbl; Trk; Hon Roll; Acctng.

TARR, GABRIELE; Central Bucks West HS; Doylestown, PA; (Y); 27/495; Intnl Clb; SADD; Hon Roll; Prfct Atten Awd; Arch.

TARTAL, GEORGE; Southmoreland HS; Mt Pleasant, PA; (Y); 8/240; French Clb; French Hon Soc; NHS; Mchncl Engrng.

TARTAL, LORI; Southmoreland HS; Scottdale, PA; (Y); 5/245; French Clb; Pep Clb; Ski Clb; JV Powder Puff Ftbl; French Hon Soc; NHS; Hghst Scr Ntl Math Tst 85.

TARTLINE, SALLY A; Red Land HS; Mechanicsburg, PA; (Y); 1/242; Pres French Clb; Quiz Bowl; Spanish Clb; Pres Jr Cls; French Hon Soc; Hst NHS; Pres Spanish NHS; Band; Chorus; Concert Band; Schlrshp PA Govrnrs Schl Intl Stds Smmr 85; Ntl Spnsh Hnr Soc Stdy Tour 85; Century III Ldrshp Awd; Dickinson Coll; Intl Rltns.

TASHJIAN, NANCY; Upper Merian Area HS; King Of Prussia, PA; (Y); 54/310; JV Fld Hcky; Bus Admn.

TASKER, HEATHER; Delaware County Christian Schl; Berwyn, PA; (Y); 6/78; Math Tm; Chorus; School Play; Var JV Mgr(s); DECA; NHS; Church Yth Grp; Drama Clb; Math Clb; Awd Cert Excllnc Natl Endowmt Humanities 85; Cert Merit Am Assn Of Tchrs O Germ & Honrbl Mention 86; Science.

TASKER, TIM; Pennsburg HS; Yardley, PA; (Y); 93/729; German Clb; Intnl Clb; Red Cross Aide; Ski Clb; Lit Mag; Socr; Tennis; Hon Roll; NHS; Pres Schlr; Pres Acadmc Ftns Awd 86; Penn ST; Bus Adm.

TATE, DANA; Upper Merion HS; King Of Prussia, PA; (Y); Concert Band; Mrchg Band; Sec Frsh Cls; Sec Soph Cls; Sec Jr Cls; Sec Sr Cls; Capt Bsktbl; Cheerleading; Powder Puff Ftbl; JV Capt Sftbl; Stdnt Mnth Rotary Clb 84; Bus.

TATE, KRIS; Bradford Central Christian HS; Bradford, PA; (Y); Var L Bsktbl; Pep Clb; Ski Clb; SADD; Yrbk Phtg; Yrbk Stf; Sec Frsh Cls; Sec Soph Cls; Stat Mgr(s); Vrsty Ltr Bsktbl 85-86; Sprts Med.

TATE, LAURA R; Elizabethtown Area HS; Elizabethtown, PA; (Y); 20/221; Cmnty Wkr; Model UN; Teachers Aide; Ed Yrbk Stf; Var L Fld Hcky; Im Powder Puff Ftbl; NHS; Ntl Merit SF; Penn ST; Bus Adm.

TATE, SCOTT A; South Side Area HS; Hookstown, PA; (Y); 2/123; Am Leg Boys St; Boy Scts; VP Stu Cncl; Stat Bsktbl; Stat Ftbl; High Hon Roll; NHS; Ntl Merit Ltr; Aero.

TATMAN II, LESTER; St Josephs Prep HS; Philadelphia, PA; (Y); Church Yth Grp; Mathletes; Chorus; Var JV Bowling; Trk; Hon Roll; Natl Greek Exam High Hnrs 85-86; Phys Thrpy.

TATRAI, GAILINN; Charleroi HS; Charleroi, PA; (Y); Ski Clb; Varsity Clb; Church Choir; Off Soph Cls; Sec Jr Cls; Var JV Cheerleading; U Of Pittsburgh; Comm.

TATSAK, BARBARA; Dayton JR SR HS; Templeton, PA; (Y); Computer Clb; Library Aide; Chorus; Color Guard; VP Jr Cls; Rep Stu Cncl; Stat Sftbl; High Hon Roll; NHS; Hugh O Brian St Ldrshp Awd 85; Comp Oprtns.

TAUCHER, FRANK; Burgettstown Area HS; Burgettstown, PA; (Y); Church Yth Grp; French Clb; Ski Clb; Speech Tm; Varsity Clb; Var L Bsbl; Var Ftbl; Im Sftbl; Hon Roll; Jr NHS; Pilot.

TAULANE III, JOHN; Saint Josephs Prep; Huntingdon Vly, PA; (Y); JV Bsktbl; Var Capt Socr; Var Trk; Hon Roll; Outstndng Stu Awd Adcmc & Svc 85; Amer Lgn Awd 83.

TAVALSKY, CINDY; Greater Johnstown HS; Johnstown, PA; (Y); Cmnty Wkr; Drama Clb; German Clb; Pep Clb; Ski Clb; SADD; Y-Teens; School Play; Var L Cheerleading; Hon Roll; Penn ST; Phy Ed.

TAVARES, JOHN; South Western HS; Hanover, PA; (Y); 20/206; Computer Clb; Hon Roll; NHS; Elec Engrng.

TAYLOR JR, B THEODORE; Pequea Valley HS; Gordonville, PA; (Y); Chess Clb; Church Yth Grp; French Clb; Library Aide; Office Aide; Chorus; Church Choir; Hon Roll; Math.

TAYLOR, BONNIE; Seneca Valley HS; Harmony, PA; (Y); Drama Clb; JA; Latin Clb; Varsity Clb; Chorus; Church Choir; School Musical; School Play; Stage Crew; Trk.

TAYLOR, BRETT; North Penn HS; North Wales, PA; (Y); Aud/Vis; Dance Clb; Drama Clb; Chorus; School Play; Stage Crew; Rep Frsh Cls; Rep Soph Cls; Rep Jr Cls; JV Gym; Spring Garden Coll; Bus Mangmnt.

TAYLOR, CHELSEA; Juniata HS; Mifflintown, PA; (Y); Aud/Vis; Drama Clb; Varsity Clb; Chorus; School Play; Yrbk Stf; Rep Stu Cncl; Cheerleading; High Hon Roll; NHS; Schlstc J 85-86; Dntl Hygn.

TAYLOR, CHERIE; Germantown HS; Philadelphia, PA; (Y); Church Yth Grp; Sec Church Choir; Var Sftbl; Hon Roll; NHS; Dstngshd Stu; Meritorious Stu; Franklin & Marshall; Cmmrcl Art.

TAYLOR, CHERYL; Bensalem HS; Bensalem, PA; (Y); JV Sftbl; Var Swmmng; Hon Roll; Prfct Atten Awd; JR & SR Cls Rep Seminar Bucks Cnty Chamber Cmmrc 86-87; Phys Therpy.

TAYLOR, DARLA ANN; Redbank Valley HS; Mayport, PA; (Y); 6/125; Hon Roll; Redbank Vly Acad Hnr Soc 85-86; Pres Acad Fit Awd 86; Clarion U PA; Secndry Ed.

TAYLOR, DAVID N; Huntingdon Area HS; Huntingdon, PA; (Y); Am Leg Boys St; Church Yth Grp; Key Clb; Political Wkr; School Play; Stat Bsbl; Gov Hon Prg Awd; Ntl Merit Ltr; Pres Schlr; Voice Dem Awd; Dickinson Coll; Pol Sci.

TAYLOR, DAWN; Western Wayne HS; Moscow, PA; (Y); FBLA; Flag Corp; Trk; Hon Roll; Prfct Atten Awd; Bandfront & Track SR Athletic Awd 84-86; FBLA Awd 82-86.

TAYLOR, DEBBIE; Geibel HS; Connellsville, PA; (Y); Drama Clb; Pep Clb; Ski Clb; SADD; School Musical; School Play; Cheerleading; High Hon Roll; Hon Roll.

TAYLOR, DEBBIE; Lourdes Regional HS; Shamokin, PA; (Y); Girl Scts; Hosp Aide; Sec Library Aide; Service Clb; Teachers Aide; Chorus; Church Choir; School Play; Nwsp Stf; Swmmng.

TAYLOR, ELIZABETH H; Cardinal O Hara HS; Aston, PA; (Y); 118/772; Church Yth Grp; Cmnty Wkr; Service Clb; JV Var Crs Cntry; JV Var Trk; Hon Roll; Prfct Atten Awd; Penn ST; Bus Adm.

TAYLOR, ERIN; Trinity Area HS; Washington, PA; (Y); 200/373; Art Clb; Off Camera Clb; Key Clb; Office Aide; Pep Clb; Ski Clb; Off Stu Cncl; Sftbl; Trk; Duquesne U; Elem Ed.

TAYLOR III, GEORGE L; Lampeter Strasburg HS; Strasburg, PA; (Y); AFS; Church Yth Grp; Varsity Clb; Rep Frsh Cls; Rep Stu Cncl; Var Capt Bsktbl; Var Capt Socr; Wt Lftg; Chorus; All Star Sccr Tm, Bsktbl 85.

TAYLOR, JACKIE; G A R Memorial HS; Wilkes-Barre, PA; (Y); Boy Scts; Church Yth Grp; Cmnty Wkr; Computer Clb; Key Clb; Ski Clb; Varsity Clb; Church Choir; School Musical; School Play; Comp Mgmt.

TAYLOR JR, JAMES E; Altoona Area HS; Altoona, PA; (Y); Band; Concert Band; Drm & Bgl; Jazz Band; Mrchg Band; Pep Band; Symp Band; JV Trk; Engrng.

TAYLOR, JEFF; Clearfield HS; Clearfield, PA; (Y); Trs 4-H; VP FFA; Hon Roll.

TAYLOR, JEFF; Jamestown HS; Jamestown, PA; (Y); 6/53; Varsity Clb; Wrstlng; High Hon Roll; Hon Roll.

TAYLOR, JENNIFER; Bethleham Catholic HS; Bath, PA; (Y); Art Clb; Physcl Thrpy.

TAYLOR, JENNIFER; Warren Area HS; Warren, PA; (Y); 1/280; Am Leg Aux Girls St; Math Tm; Science Clb; Mrchg Band; Stu Cncl; Cit Awd; DAR Awd; High Hon Roll; NHS; Val; Amer Soc Of Mtls Schlrshp 86; J D Paramlee Math Awd 86; GA Inst Of Tech; Aerospc Engrg.

TAYLOR, JIM; Penn Trafford HS; Jeannette, PA; (Y); 40/325; Chess Clb; Capt Computer Clb; Service Clb; Concert Band; Jazz Band; Mrchg Band; JV Im Bsktbl; Im Ftbl; VP L Tennis; High Hon Roll; Sci Hnrs Inst 86; PA ST; Elect Engrg.

TAYLOR, JOHN A; Mount Carmel Area HS; Mt Carmel, PA; (Y); Key Clb; Ski Clb; Spanish Clb; JV Bsktbl; Ftbl; Var Tennis; Hon Roll; Mt Carmel Area Fforensics Tm 85-86; Knights Of Columbus Cncl 85-86; Emergncy Rm Volntr 86; Notre Dame; Pre Med.

TAYLOR, JOSEPH; Geibel HS; Connellsville, PA; (Y); Church Yth Grp; Science Clb; Spanish Clb; Bsktbl; Ftbl; Wt Lftg; Hon Roll; Prfct Atten Awd; Teaching.

TAYLOR, KAREN; Kennett HS; Toughkehamon, PA; (Y); 58/156; French Clb; Model UN; Pep Clb; Ski Clb; Varsity Clb; Chorus; Mrchg Band; Yrbk Stf; Var Capt Cheerleading; Pom Pon; Elizabethtown Coll; Bus.

TAYLOR, KEITH; Chester HS; Chester, PA; (Y); Boys Clb Am; Var Capt Bsktbl; JV Ftbl; Hon Roll.

TAYLOR, KELLY; Saucon Valley SR HS; Bethlehem, PA; (Y); 12/145; Drm Mjr(t); Var L Swmmng; High Hon Roll; NHS; Prmry Educ.

TAYLOR, KEVIN; Neshaminy HS; Trevose, PA; (Y); 66/752; Chorus; Church Choir; Jazz Band; School Musical; Yrbk Stf; JV Socr; Var Tennis; High Hon Roll; Hon Roll; NHS; Schl Ltrsd Music 84-86; Schl Ltr Vrsty Ten 85-86; Mech Engrng.

TAYLOR, KRISTIN; Red Lion Area SR HS; Red Lion, PA; (Y); 54/327; Varsity Clb; Yrbk Stf; Mgr(s); Timer; Trk; Hon Roll; U Of DE; Bio.

TAYLOR, LAURA; Strathhaven HS; Rose Valley, PA; (Y); Art Clb; Church Yth Grp; Dance Clb; Hosp Aide; School Musical; Yrbk Stf; Rep Stu Cncl; Capt Cheerleading; Trk; Hon Roll; Comm.

TAYLOR, LAURA ANN; Chartiers Valley HS; Pittsburgh, PA; (Y); 150/343; Church Yth Grp; Pep Clb; Ski Clb; SADD; Varsity Clb; Rep Stu Cncl; Cheerleading; Powder Puff Ftbl; U Of Pittsburgh; Pre-Law.

TAYLOR, MAUREEN; Shippensburg Area SR HS; Shippensburg, PA; (Y); 13/214; Art Clb; Trs Leo Clb; Chorus; Trk; High Hon Roll; NHS; Schlrshp Rcgntn Dnr 84-86; Pres Acad Ftns Awd 86; 4 Yr HS Choir Awd 82-86; Frnkln Cnty Vo-Tech Schl; Nrsg.

TAYLOR, MAURICE; Gar Memorial HS; Wilkes-Barre, PA; (Y); Boy Scts; Church Yth Grp; Cmnty Wkr; Drama Clb; French Clb; Key Clb; Letterman Clb; Ski Clb; Varsity Clb; Chorus; ROTC; Comp Engr.

TAYLOR, MEGAN; Liberty HS; Bethlehem, PA; (Y); 70/575; Drama Clb; French Clb; Key Clb; Service Clb; Thesps; Yrbk Stf; Lit Mag; Fld Hcky; Mgr(s); High Hon Roll; Intl Bus.

TAYLOR, NANCY; Swissvale HS; Pittsbuirgh, PA; (Y); 30/205; German Clb; Hosp Aide; Y-Teens; Acpl Chr; Yrbk Stf; Capt Bowling; Hon Roll; NHS; Ntl Merit Ltr; Vlntr Awds & Trphy 85 & 86; Nrsng.

TAYLOR, RACHEL; Shady Side Acad; New Kensington, PA; (Y); Church Yth Grp; Girl Scts; Letterman Clb; SADD; Capt Cheerleading; JV Gym; VP Mgr(s); Ntl Merit SF; Engl.

TAYLOR, RICHARD G; East Allegheny HS; Wilmerding, PA; (Y); 3/209; Am Leg Boys St; Trs French Clb; Trs Frsh Cls; Sr Cls; Stat Bsktbl; Pres NHS; Opt Clb Awd; Prfct Atten Awd; U Merit Schlrshp 86; Schl Of Engrng Hon Schlrshp 86; 1st Pl Lit Cultural Arts Cntst 86; U Of Pittsburgh; Engng.

TAYLOR, SARA; Huntingdon Area HS; Huntingdon, PA; (Y); 19/203; Sec Church Yth Grp; Hosp Aide; Teachers Aide; Chorus; Yrbk Stf; High Hon Roll; NHS; Pres Schlr; Messiah Coll; Med Tech.

TAYLOR, SCOTT; Archbishop Carroll HS; Havertown, PA; (Y); 15/162; Boy Scts; Cmnty Wkr; Red Cross Aide; Yrbk Stf; JV L Trk; High Hon Roll; Hon Roll; Jr NHS; NHS; Im Bsktbl; Outstndng Achvt Awd Compostn & Brit Lit 85-86; Sci.

TAYLOR, SCOTT; Elk County Christian HS; St Marys, PA; (Y); Boys Clb Am; Office Aide; Varsity Clb; Off Frsh Cls; Ftbl; Wrstlng; Hon Roll; St Bonaventure; Comp Sci.

TAYLOR, SHANI; Burrell SR HS; Lower Burrell, PA; (Y); AFS; Church Yth Grp; Spanish Clb; Stage Crew; Hon Roll; Jr NHS; Chem.

TAYLOR, SHERI; Slippery Rock Area HS; Butler, PA; (Y); 43/177; VP 4-H; Intnl Clb; Pep Clb; Spanish Clb; Varsity Clb; Band; Mrchg Band; Variety Show; Nwsp Stf; Stat Bsbl; Penn ST; Law.

TAYLOR, STARLETTE; New Brighton HS; New Brighton, PA; (Y); 7/146; Spanish Clb; Chorus; Color Guard; High Hon Roll; Hon Roll; Intl Frgn Lng Awd 85; Bradford Bus Schl; Acctng.

TAYLOR, TAMI; Peters Township HS; Mcmurray, PA; (Y); Church Yth Grp; Hosp Aide; Rep Frsh Cls; Rep Soph Cls; Rep Jr Cls; Stu Cncl; Var Gym; Mgr(s); Trk; High Hon Roll; Kent ST U; Eng.

TAYLOR, TAMMY; Lincoln HS; Ellwood City, PA; (Y); 59/167; Cmnty Wkr; Exploring; Hosp Aide; Office Aide; Y-Teens; Yrbk Stf; Var Bsktbl; Var Powder Puff Ftbl; Stat Trk; Hon Roll; Slippery Rock U; Med Tech.

TAYLOR, TODD; Juniata HS; Mifflintown, PA; (Y); 1/160; Varsity Clb; Chorus; School Musical; Yrbk Stf; Var Capt Bsktbl; Var Capt Socr; Tennis; High Hon Roll; VP NHS; Rotary Awd; Stu Mnth 85; Distngshd Hnr Stu 86; Gannon U; Family Med.

TAYLOR, TOM; Altoona Area HS; Altoona, PA; (Y); 102/682; Ftbl; Wrstlng; Penn ST; Elec Engrng.

TAYLOR, TRACIE; Aliquippa JR SR HS; Aliquippa, PA; (Y); Bsktbl; Cheerleading; Hon Roll; Sewickly Nrsng Acad; Nrsng.

TAYLOR, TRALICE; Simon Gratz HS; Philadelphia, PA; (Y); Cmnty Wkr; Library Aide; Lcrss.

TAYLOR, VALERIE; Waynesburg Central HS; Waynesburg, PA; (Y); DECA; 4-H; FFA; Var 4-H Awd; Bradford Bus Schl; Rtl Mgmt.

TAYLOR, VANIA; Archbishop Kennedy HS; Philadelphia, PA; (Y); Church Yth Grp; Hon Roll; Mbr Momento Muscl Ensmble Sngr, Dncr; Temple U; Voice.

TAYLOR, YONNA; Canton Area HS; Canton, PA; (Y); 1/122; VP Church Yth Grp; Sec 4-H; Mrchg Band; Rep Frsh Cls; Sec Soph Cls; Sec Jr Cls; Trs Stu Cncl; Cit Awd; High Hon Roll; NHS; Cls Magazine Drive Chrmn 85; Hghst Mth & Engl Grade Awd 84; Milligan Coll; Elem Ed.

TAYLOR-KATZAMAN, KAREN; Palmyra Area SR HS; Campbelltown, PA; (Y); 57/186; Teachers Aide; Chorus; Swing Chorus; High Hon Roll; Hon Roll; Hndcppd Chldrn.

TAYMAN, MICHAEL; Moon SR HS; Coraopolis, PA; (Y); Exploring; Mathletes; ROTC; Spanish Clb; Rep Soph Cls; Rep Jr Cls; Stu Cncl; Coach Actv; Im Ice Hcky; Im Vllybl; Army ROTC Schlrshp; Embry Riddle U; Aerontcl Engr.

TEA, JULIE; Richland HS; Gibsonia, PA; (S); 1/210; Cmnty Wkr; French Clb; NFL; Red Cross Aide; Speech Tm; Chorus; School Musical; Swing Chorus; Variety Show; Nwsp Rptr; 2nd Pl Dist Fnls-Infrmtv Spkg 84-85; Plaud At Frnsc ST Fnls-Infrmtv Spkg 84-85; Stu To Schl Bd 83-84; U Of PA; Cmmnctns.

TEAGUE, CAROL; Chambersburg Area SR HS; Chambersburg, PA; (Y); 8/546; Cmnty Wkr; Ed JCL; Latin Clb; Political Wkr; Concert Band; Mrchg Band; Var L Crs Cntry; Var L Trk; Elks Awd; Sec NHS; Wake Forest U; Intl Rltns.

TEAL, LORI; Penn Wood SR HS; Darby, PA; (Y); 47/314; Drama Clb; School Play; Nwsp Ed-Chief; Rep Stu Cncl; Var Mgr(s); Var L Vllybl; High Hon Roll; Hon Roll; Jr NHS; Prfct Atten Awd; Otstndng Achvmnt Psychlgy Awd 86; Cnscnts Achvmnt Awd 83; Widener U; Psychlgy.

TEAL, REBECCA ELLEN; South Western HS; Hanover, PA; (Y); 3/206; Key Clb; Yrbk Ed-Chief; Tennis; Elks Awd; NHS; Pres Schlr; Rotary Awd; Goldn Galleon Yrbk Awd 86; Exch Clb Top 10 Clss Awd 86; Acadmc Achvt Awd 82-86; Shippensburg U; Acctg.

TEANG, TYMO; S Philadelphia High Motivation Schl; University Park, PA; (Y); 13/585; Camera Clb; Church Yth Grp; Cmnty Wkr; Exploring; Office Aide; Teachers Aide; Trk; French Hon Soc; Hon Roll; Prfct Atten Awd; White Williams Fndtn Scholar 86; Robert Freeman & Edward Goldman Awd 86; Thomas Jefferson U Hnr 85; PA ST U; Bus Adm.

TEASDALE, TROY; Meadville Area SR HS; Meadville, PA; (Y); 143/344; Church Yth Grp; VICA; JV Var Vllybl; Hon Roll; Robert Raikes Diplma 85-86; Electncs.

TEATINO, THEDRA; Canon Mc Millan SR HS; Hendersonville, PA; (Y); Art Clb; Drama Clb; French Clb; School Play; Stage Crew; Hon Roll; Washington Coll; Pre-Law.

TECK, TRACEY; St Paul Cathedral HS; N Braddock, PA; (Y); 21/55; Church Yth Grp; FBLA; Library Aide; Pep Clb; Church Choir; Mrchg Band; Yrbk Stf; Cheerleading; Hon Roll; Cert Excllnc Natl Hstry Day 86; Robert Morris Coll; Acctg.

TEDESCO, ANGELA; Cornell Educational Ctr; Coraopolis, PA; (Y); Church Yth Grp; Exploring; JA; Band; Concert Band; Mrchg Band; Pep Band; Nwsp Stf; Yrbk Stf; High Hon Roll; Pitt U; Mech Engrng.

TEDORA, LISA; Altoona Area HS; Altoona, PA; (Y); Trs 4-H; German Clb; Scholastic Bowl; Concert Band; Jazz Band; Mrchg Band; Orch; School Musical; Nwsp Stf; Off Frsh Cls; PA ST U; Astrspc.

TEES, STACY; St Basil Acad; Philadelphia, PA; (Y); Dance Clb; French Clb; Hosp Aide; Science Clb; Yrbk Stf; Im Socr; Hon Roll; Natl Engl Merit Awd; Pre Med.

TEETER, DANIEL; Brockway Area HS; Brockway, PA; (Y); 2/109; Varsity Clb; Rep Stu Cncl; Var L Bsbl; Cit Awd; DAR Awd; High Hon Roll; Trs NHS; Ntl Merit Ltr; Pres Schlr; Sal; Snorky Morris Awd 86; Amercn Lgn Schl Awd 86; John Klees Memrl Awd 86; U Of PA.

TEETER, GLENN; Peters Township HS; Venetia, PA; (Y); Var L Crs Cntry; Var L Wrstlng; Prfct Atten Awd; Aviation.

TEETERS, BRAD; Brandywine HS; Topton, PA; (Y); Boy Scts; VICA; Vllybl; High Hon Roll; Prfct Atten Awd; Arch.

TEETS, ROBIN; Sharon HS; Sharon, PA; (Y); Spanish Clb; Stu Cncl; Hon Roll; Bus.

TEFFT, ANDREW; North East HS; North East, PA; (Y); 3/151; Concert Band; Mrchg Band; Pep Band; NHS; Ntl Merit SF; Church Yth Grp; Latin Clb; Band; School Musical; High Hon Roll; Regnl Band 86; Penn ST Frshmn Excllnc Awd 86; PA ST U; Chem Eng.

TEFFT, SHANNON; Karns City Area JR/SR HS; Chicora, PA; (Y); 3/120; FCA; Pep Clb; SADD; Stage Crew; Nwsp Ed-Chief; VP Trk; Stat Vllybl; Hon Roll; NHS; Pres Schlr; Schltc Achvt Ltr 86; PA ST U; Biochem.

TEHANSKY, STEVE; Southern Columbia HS; Elysburg, PA; (Y); Varsity Clb; Pres Frsh Cls; Rep Stu Cncl; Var Capt Ftbl; Wt Lftg; Wilkies Coll; Bus Adm.

TELEMKO, FRANK; Sacred Heart HS; Carbondale, PA; (Y); 24/50; Computer Clb; FBLA; Ski Clb; Bsbl; Bsktbl; Ftbl; Golf; Vllybl; Bloomsburg; Advrtsg.

TELENKO, JOHN E; Elizabethtown Area HS; Elizabethtown, PA; (Y); Am Leg Boys St; Boy Scts; Ski Clb; Lit Mag; Off Stu Cncl; Var Capt Socr; Var Capt Wrstlng; Hon Roll; Lion Awd; NHS; Juniata Coll; Math.

TELENKO, MICHELLE; Elizabethtown Area HS; Elizabethtown, PA; (Y); 69/250; Pres Church Yth Grp; GAA; Hosp Aide; Ski Clb; Drm Mjr(t); Mgr(s); Powder Puff Ftbl; Var Tennis; Twrlr; Wt Lftg; Drexel U; Hotel.

TELEPO, ALLEN D; Bangor Area HS; Bangor, PA; (Y); 2/190; Am Leg Boys St; Computer Clb; Office Aide; Yrbk Sprt Ed; JV Bsbl; Var Bsktbl; High Hon Roll; NHS.

TELESHA, CHRIS; Mid-Valley HS; Dickson City, PA; (Y); Nwsp Rptr; Nwsp Stf; Bus Admn.

TELESZ, KEVIN; Old Forge HS; Old Forge, PA; (Y); JV Bsbl; Var Ftbl; Accntng.

TEMEL, CHRISTINE; Linesville HS; Espyville, PA; (Y); Church Yth Grp; Drama Clb; 4-H; German Clb; Office Aide; Pep Clb; Ski Clb; SADD; School Play; Trs Soph Cls; Bus.

TEMPLE, JOY; Harry S Truman HS; Levittown, PA; (Y); Church Yth Grp; Library Aide; Cheerleading; Trk; Hon Roll; Bucks Cnty CC; Bus.

TEMPLE, PATRICK; Millville Area HS; Millville, PA; (Y); Church Yth Grp; Nwsp Stf; Yrbk Stf; Rep Stu Cncl; Var Bsktbl; Var Socr; Elks Awd; Hon Roll; Spch Awd Bst Spkr 84-85; 1st Tm All-Lg All Str Sccr 5 Cnty Lg 85-86; Kystn ST Gms Sccr 85-86; Bus Admin.

TEMPLIN, BRIAN; Tunkhannock HS; Tunkhannock, PA; (S); 14/275; Computer Clb; Ski Clb; Crprte Law.

TEMPLIN III, STANTON A; Eastern Lebanon County HS; Richland, PA; (Y); 1/185; SADD; School Musical; Swing Chorus; Pres Stu Cncl; L Bsbl; L Bsktbl; L Socr; L Trk; Bausch & Lomb Sci Awd; VP NHS; GA Inst Of Tech; Chem Engrng.

TEN BROECK, LESLIE A; Conestoga SR HS; Strafford, PA; (Y); 152/408; Church Yth Grp; Drama Clb; Chorus; Orch; School Musical; School Play; Swing Chorus; Variety Show; Tri County Concert Assn-1st Pl Vocl 85; Combs Coll Vocl Comptn-Fnlst 85; Lead In Opera 86; Moravian Coll; Music Perfrmnc.

TENELLY, KATHY; North Pocono HS; Moscow, PA; (Y); 32/247; Church Yth Grp; Dance Clb; Ski Clb; Rep Stu Cncl; Var L Cheerleading; Var Trk; High Hon Roll; Hon Roll; NHS; Voice Dem Awd; Literary Awd 83; Temple; Bus Mgmt Admin.

TENER, TRILBY JO; Cheltenham HS; Laverock, PA; (Y); JV Var Bsktbl; JV Var Sftbl; Var Tennis; NEDT Awd; Ntl Engl Tchr Essay; Med.

TENGES, TRACEY; Pen Argyl Area HS; Nazareth, PA; (Y); 19/117; Yrbk Stf; JV Bsktbl; JV Bowling; Var Mgr(s); Var Powder Puff Ftbl; Var Score Keeper; Mgr Var Trk; High Hon Roll.

TENNANT, JACQUELINE; William Penn HS; Philadelphia, PA; (Y); Girl Scts; Teachers Aide; Band; Off Sr Cls; Cheerleading; Wt Lftg; Bnd Awd 85-86; Outstndng Bus Awd 85-86; Law.

TENNANT, RENEE; Waynesburg Central HS; Spraggs, PA; (Y); Church Yth Grp; Drama Clb; Spanish Clb; Color Guard; School Play; Mgr Stage Crew; Nwsp Stf; High Hon Roll; Hon Roll; WV U; Elem Schl Tchr.

TENNANT, SARA; Waynesburg Central HS; Brave, PA; (Y); Library Aide; Natl Beta Clb; Red Cross Aide; SADD; VICA; Off Jr Cls; Off Sr Cls; Hon Roll; Nrsng.

TEOLI, STEPHANIE; Newport HS; Newport, PA; (S); Nwsp Ed-Chief; Nwsp Rptr; Off Jr Cls; VP Stu Cncl; Stat Bsktbl; Var Fld Hcky; JV Sftbl; Hon Roll; Phy Thrpy.

TEPEDINO, FILOMENA; Bethel Park SR HS; Pittsburgh, PA; (Y); FBLA; JA; NFL; High Hon Roll; Hon Roll; U Pittsburgh; Com Psci.

TEPPER, STEVEN; Father Judge HS; Philadelphia, PA; (S); 44/403; Cmnty Wkr; Letterman Clb; Varsity Clb; Crs Cntry; Trk; Hon Roll; NHS; All-Cathl Crss Cntry 85-86; Allentown Coll.

TERCHICK, LEIGH; Gateway SR HS; Monroeville, PA; (Y); 23/434; Band; Chorus; Mrchg Band; Yrbk Stf; Capt Var Cheerleading; High Hon Roll; Hon Roll; NHS; Pres Acad Ftns Awd 86; PA ST U; Bus Admn.

TERESHKO, OLGA J; Hempfield Area SR HS; Greensburg, PA; (Y); Band; Concert Band; Orch; Nwsp Rptr; Nwsp Stf; Yrbk Stf; High Hon Roll; Hon Roll; Jr NHS; Read Mag Writing Awd Hnbl Mntn 83; Carnegie-Mellon U.

TERESKA, TODD; Liberty HS; Bethlehem, PA; (Y); 81/500; Church Yth Grp; Trs Band; Concert Band; Jazz Band; Mrchg Band; Orch; School Musical; Temple U; Med.

TERMIN, SHELLI; Penn-Trafford HS; Irwin, PA; (Y); Sec Church Yth Grp; JCL; Latin Clb; Bsktbl; Sftbl; Vllybl; High Hon Roll; Hon Roll; NHS; Cmmnty Action Pgm Awd 86.

TEROTTA, TINA; Scranton Preparatory Schl; Old Forge, PA; (Y); 24/192; Church Yth Grp; Dance Clb; Drama Clb; Exploring; Sec NFL; Political Wkr; Sec Speech Tm; Lib Chorus; Church Choir; School Musical; Gold Medal Spnsh 85-86; Pre Law.

TERRACCINO, ANGELA; Hazleton HS; Hazelton, PA; (Y); 46/488; Pep Clb; Y-Teens; Chorus; High Hon Roll; Rep Stu Cncl; Var Capt Cheerleading; Im Gym; Im Vllybl; Hgh Hnr Roll 85-86; Drexel U; Arch Engr.

TERRANA, ROSEMARY; Pittston Area HS; Pittston, PA; (Y); 35/348; Church Yth Grp; French Clb; FNA; Hosp Aide; JA; Key Clb; Political Wkr; Chorus; High Hon Roll; Hon Roll; Dietcn.

TERRANOVA JR, LEONARD J; St Josephs Preparatory Schl; Philadelphia, PA; (Y); Cmnty Wkr; Spanish Clb; Prep Schlr Awd 83-86; IM Sprts 83-86; Sr Prom Comm 86; Bus Adm.

TERRIJONI, NORMAN; Mc Keesport Area HS; White Oak, PA; (Y); 14/385; Church Yth Grp; German Clb; Office Aide; Band; Capt Bowling; Wt Lftg; High Hon Roll; NHS; Pres Schlr; Grove City Coll; Engrng.

TERRILL, ROBERT; Cathedral Prep; Erie, PA; (Y); Hon Roll.

TERRONI, CHRISTOPHER M; Council Rock HS; Holland, PA; (Y); Capt Swmmng; Hon Roll; Kiwanis Awd; Pres Awd Brzy Pnt Swm Clb 86; Dedctn Awd 84-85; Mst Imprvd Swmmr Mtl Tghnss Awd 85-86; Engrng.

TERRY, ANN MARIE; Elk County Christian HS; St Marys, PA; (Y); 25/98; Cheerleading; Vllybl; High Hon Roll; Hon Roll; Edinboro U; Elem Ed.

TERRY, CHAS; Cardinal O-Hara HS; Media, PA; (Y); 7/740; Church Yth Grp; PAVAS; Band; Concert Band; Jazz Band; Mrchg Band; Pep Band; School Musical; Variety Show; Yrbk Ed-Chief; Ntl Merit Fnlst 86; Bnd Pres 86; Ntl Hnr Soc 86; U Of PA; Pre Med.

TERRY, LISA-ANN; Marian Catholic HS; Lansford, PA; (S); Pres Church Yth Grp; Exploring; Hosp Aide; Spanish Clb; Teachers Aide; School Play; Hon Roll; Spanish NHS; Phrmcy.

TERWILLIGER, JULIE; Allegheny Clarion Valley HS; Emlenton, PA; (Y); FHA; Drill Tm; School Play; Rep Stu Cncl; Chef.

TERZICH, MIKE; West Mifflin HS; West Mifflin, PA; (Y); Key Clb; Varsity Clb; Var L Bsbl; JV Bsktbl; Var L Golf; Hon Roll; Comp Sci.

TESAURO, TINA; Laurel Highlands SR HS; Lemont Fce, PA; (Y); French Clb; JA; Ski Clb; Band; Chorus; Mrchg Band; Sftbl; Trk; Vllybl; PA ST; Dntl Hyg.

TESCHNER, SANDY; Upper Moreland HS; Willow Grove, PA; (Y); Church Yth Grp; Dance Clb; German Clb; Ski Clb; Variety Show; Gym; Score Keeper; Socr; Sftbl; Trk; German Soc Of PA Hon Mntn Perf In Germ 86; Amer Assn Tchrs Germ Inc Hon Mntn 3rd Lvl Germ 86; Penn ST Coll; German.

TESEO, MARILU; Cardinal O Hara HS; Morton, PA; (Y); 91/740; Camera Clb; Cmnty Wkr; Acpl Chr; Chorus; Church Choir; School Musical; School Play; Stage Crew; Yrbk Stf; Tennis; U Of Pittsburgh; Phys Thrpy.

TESORIERO, DENISE; Kennedy Christian HS; Tempe, AZ; (Y); 27/100; Spanish Clb; Varsity Clb; Flag Corp; Hon Roll; NHS; Presdntl Acadmc Ftns Awd 86; AZ ST U; Psychlgy.

TESSITORE, DAN; Central Bucks HS West; Warrington, PA; (Y); 77/495; Boy Scts; Cmnty Wkr; Exploring; JV Ftbl; Cit Awd; Hon Roll; Eagle Scout 84; Union Lge & Amer Lgn Ctznshp Awd 85; KC Yth Ctznshp Awd 86; Finance.

TESTA, DENISE M; Kiski Area HS; Apollo, PA; (Y); German Clb; Pep Clb; Band; Concert Band; Mrchg Band; Yrbk Stf; Capt Var Bsktbl; Var L Trk; Twrlr; DAR Awd; W PA Schl Hlth Tech; Phrmcy Te.

TESTA, KRISTI; Burgettstown Area JR SR HS; Burgettstown, PA; (Y); 64/172; Ski Clb; Spanish Clb; Band; Chorus; Drill Tm; Yrbk Stf; Stu Cncl; Hon Roll; SR Stu Of Yr Dncng Awd 83; Drl Tm All Star Perfrmr 85; Seton Hill Coll; Nrs.

TESTA IV, VINCENT JAMES; Burgettstown Area JR SR HS; Burgettstown, PA; (Y); 2/173; Ski Clb; Spanish Clb; Band; Yrbk Phtg; Var L Tennis; High Hon Roll; Jr NHS; NHS; Sal; Yrbk Stf; Climax Schrlshp Fnlst 86; Diplomo Merit 86; Embry Riddle; Aeronutcl Engr.

TETANICH, PAULA; Bishop Guilfoyle HS; Altoona, PA; (S); 6/119; VP Hosp Aide; Spanish Clb; Band; Chorus; Concert Band; Mrchg Band; High Hon Roll; Hon Roll; Hlth.

TETREAULT, KEVIN; Dunmore HS; Dunmore, PA; (Y); 49/150; Computer Clb; Ski Clb; Spanish Clb; Stage Crew; JV Bsktbl; Var Swmmng; JV Trk; PA ST; Biomed.

TEUFEL, GREG; Wyoming Valley West HS; Kingston, PA; (S); Chess Clb; Church Yth Grp; Ski Clb; Lit Mag; Var L Crs Cntry; Var L Swmmng; Var L Trk; Cit Awd; High Hon Roll; NHS; Pre-Law.

TEWELL, JULIE; Waynesburg Cntrl HS; Waynesburg, PA; (Y); 9/204; Pres AFS; French Clb; Nwsp Ed-Chief; Nwsp Rptr; Yrbk Stf; JV Capt Vllybl; NHS; NEDT Awd; Camera Clb; Library Aide; Outstndng SAT Awd; Outstndng Engl 12 C Awd; Edwin B Corday Hist Awd; WV U; Phrmcy.

TEWELL, LAURA; South Williamsport HS; S Williamsport, PA; (Y); 13/150; Leo Clb; Pep Clb; Ski Clb; Varsity Clb; Sec Soph Cls; Sec Jr Cls; Stu Cncl; Capt Cheerleading; High Hon Roll; NHS; Accntng.

TEXTER, DOUG; Cathedral Prep; Erie, PA; (Y); 6/230; Debate Tm; Exploring; Band; Concert Band; Lit Mag; High Hon Roll; Kiwanis Awd; Pres Schlr; Rotary Awd; U Of PA; Intl Stud.

THACH, THEIM VAN; West Catholic High For Boys; Phila, PA; (Y); 2/215; Intnl Clb; Mathletes; Variety Show; Yrbk Sprt Ed; Off Soph Cls; High Hon Roll; Hon Roll; Jr NHS; NHS; Prfct Atten Awd; Phldlpha City Schlrshp 86; W Cthlc Sltrn Awd 86; Drxl U 86; Drxl U; Engrng Sci.

THAELER, KAREN; Meadville Area SR HS; Meadville, PA; (Y); 31/344; Drama Clb; Spanish Clb; Chorus; Crs Cntry; Trk; High Hon Roll; Hon Roll; Treas HS Sorority Miramar 86-87; Capt Of Crss Cntry Tm 86-87; Penn ST U; Landscape Architect.

THAIK, RICHARD; Emmaus HS; Wescosville, PA; (Y); Chess Clb; Computer Clb; Exploring; Math Tm; High Hon Roll; Jr NHS; NHS; Ntl Merit Ltr; Amer Compu Sci Leag All Star Tm 85; 2nd Pl ACSL Indvdl All Star Cntst 86; Elec Engrng.

THALER, JULIA; Wilson Area HS; Easton, PA; (S); 2/160; VP Church Yth Grp; Lib Chorus; Trs Concert Band; Jazz Band; Trs Mrchg Band; Sftbl; Co-Capt Tennis; High Hon Roll; Jr NHS; Sec NHS; Juniata Coll; Mth.

THARP, MICHAEL D; Central Bucks HS West; Doylestown, PA; (Y); 4/426; VP Intnl Clb; Model UN; Political Wkr; Ski Clb; Pres Frsh Cls; Pres Stu Cncl; Rotary Awd; Boy Scts; Church Yth Grp; Debate Tm; Wrld Afrs Clb; Rtry Cmp Neidig Ldrshp Camp; D Boone Fndtn Schlrshp Awd; Prnctn U; Intl Fnc.

THATCHER, KATHLEEN ELEANOR; East Stroudsburg HS; East Stroudsburg, PA; (Y); 8/243; Ski Clb; JV Fld Hcky; JV Sftbl; JV Tennis; High Hon Roll; Hon Roll; VP NHS; Acad Schlrshp Awd 84-87; PA Free Enterprise Week 86; Bus Adm.

THAYER, ELAINE; Garnet Valley HS; Nashville, TN; (Y); 27/162; Church Yth Grp; VP French Clb; Rep JA; Varsity Clb; Rep Stu Cncl; Fld Hcky; Capt Sftbl; Hon Roll; Powder Puff Ftbl; Jr NHS; Phys Ed Achvt Awd 86; Geneva Schlr Awd 86; Geneva Coll; Cnslng.

THEAL, BARBARA; Manheim Central HS; Manheim, PA; (Y); 60/241; Nwsp Stf; Stu Cncl; Bsktbl; Var Capt Fld Hcky; Trk; Hon Roll; Lion Awd; Bowling; Coachs Awd Bsktbll 84-85; MIP Trck 85; All Star Hon Ment 85; Elem Ed.

THEINER, IMMANUEL H; Taylor Allderdice HS; Pittsburgh, PA; (Y); 13/376; Computer Clb; Math Tm; Nwsp Stf; High Hon Roll; NHS; Wstnghse Sci Hnrs Inst 85-86; Russian Clb; Frisbee Clb; Carnegie-Mellon U; Chem Engr.

THEORGOOD, JILLIAN; Moon HS; Corapolis, PA; (Y); Teachers Aide; Soph Cls; Jr Cls; Crs Cntry; Hon Roll; Gold Medal Pittsburg; CA Trk Jesse Owens 84; Jinroads Prog 86; Medcl.

THERIT, TRACEY; Littlestown HS; Hanover, PA; (Y); 5/120; Speech Tm; Chorus; School Musical; School Play; VP Frsh Cls; VP Soph Cls; Rep Stu Cncl; High Hon Roll; Pres NHS.

THERRIAT, MICHAEL P; Pocono Mt HS; Scotrun, PA; (Y); Cmnty Wkr; Exploring; 4-H; Ski Clb; Rep Jr Cls; Im Bsbl; JV Var Ftbl; Im Lcrss; Im Sftbl; Im Wt Lftg; Stdnt Tutrg Prog Awd 86; U Of FL; Law Enfrcmt.

THI, UT VO; Mc Caskey HS; Lancaster, PA; (Y); 23/468; AFS; Church Yth Grp; JA; Q&S; Church Choir; Orch; Lit Mag; Vllybl; Hon Roll; Jr NHS; Farm & Home Fndtn Scholar Awd 86; ABWA Lancaster Chrtr Chptr Scholar 86; Lancaster Towne Clb Scholar; Lancaster Gen Hosp; Nrsng.

THIEL, VICKI; Council Rock HS; Washington Crossi, PA; (Y); 58/845; Church Yth Grp; Trs Stu Cncl; JV Tennis; French Hon Soc; Hon Roll; Jr NHS; NHS; Math.

THIELE, JACKIE; Freeport SR HS; Sarver, PA; (Y); Mrchg Band; Capt Twrlr; Hon Roll; PA ST; Radiology.

THIELER, DOLLY; Connellsville Area SR HS; Mt Pleasant, PA; (Y); Chess Clb; Hosp Aide; Nwsp Rptr; High Hon Roll; Hon Roll; 4 Yr Perf Attndnc Awd; Nrs Hlpr SR Yr; RN.

THIEMANN, ERIC; Highlands HS; Tarentum, PA; (Y); 76/280; Boy Scts; Pres Church Yth Grp; Socr; Trk; Hon Roll; Nvy Plt.

THIERWECHTER, LORI; Cedar Crest HS; Lebanon, PA; (Y); Pep Clb; Spanish Clb; School Musical; Tennis; Trk; High Hon Roll; Hon Roll; NHS; Ntl Merit SF; Cmmndtn PHEAA 86; Millersville U; Forgn Lang.

THILKER, STEVEN; Interboro HS; Norwood, PA; (Y); Yrbk Phtg; Trk; Hon Roll; PA Inst Of Tech; Elec Engr.

THINNES, MICHELE; North Penn HS; Hatfield, PA; (Y); 83/678; Church Yth Grp; Key Clb; Yrbk Stf; Rep Jr Cls; JV Cheerleading; Powder Puff Ftbl; JV Sftbl; Hon Roll; NHS; Prfct Atten Awd; Villanova; Engrng.

THOM, REBECCA; Punxsutawney Area HS; Punxsutawney, PA; (Y); L Crs Cntry; L Trk; MVP Cross Cntry 84 & 85; High Pnt Trk 84 & 85.

THOMA, WILLIAM; Blle Vernon Area HS; Belle Vernon, PA; (Y); 47/272; Exploring; JA; Office Aide; Trk; High Hon Roll; Hon Roll; NHS; Ntl Merit SF; Hnr Awds 85; CA U PA; Prof Wrtng.

THOMAN, JEFF; Conestoga Valley HS; Leola, PA; (Y); 9/256; Chorus; JV Bsktbl; Var Socr; Var Tennis; Hon Roll; Ntl Merit Ltr; Stu Of Mnth, April 86; Engrng.

THOMAN, MICHAEL J; Susquehannock HS; Seven Valleys, PA; (Y); 7/228; Rep Jr Cls; Im Tennis; High Hon Roll; Hon Roll; JETS Awd; Ntl Merit SF; Prfct Atten Awd; Rotary Awd; AHSME Amer Math Cmptn-Wnnr 85-86; IN U Of PA Physcs Tstg Cmptn Wnnr 85-86; Aeronaut Engr.

THOMAS, AIMEE; Old Forge HS; Old Forge, PA; (Y); Computer Clb; Hosp Aide; Political Wkr; Spanish Clb; Rep Stu Cncl; Capt Bsktbl; Sftbl; Hon Roll; 6th Leadng Scorer Cty Girls Bsktbl 86; E Stroudsburg; Tchr.

THOMAS, ALICIA; Columbia Montour Area Vo Tech; Catawissa, PA; (Y); Trs FFA; Teachers Aide; VICA; Hon Roll; NHS; FFA WA Ldrshp Conf Prgrm 85; Intervw Cont Bronz Emblm Awd 86; FFA Publc Speakng Cont 1st Pl 86; Williamsport Area CC; Hortcltr.

THOMAS, ANDREA; Aliquippa SR HS; Aliquippa, PA; (S); 13/154; Exploring; French Clb; Church Choir; Yrbk Stf; VP Soph Cls; Pres Jr Cls; Pres Sr Cls; Rep Stu Cncl; Hon Roll; NHS.

THOMAS, BOB; E L Meyers HS; Wilkes Barre, PA; (Y); 27/160; Church Yth Grp; Ski Clb; Chorus; Ftbl; Trk; Wrstlng; Hon Roll; NHS.

THOMAS, BRIAN; Pittston Area HS; Pittston, PA; (Y); Church Yth Grp; FNA; Key Clb; Ski Clb; Ftbl; Trk; Wt Lftg; Hon Roll; Devry Inst Of Tech; Elctrncs.

THOMAS, CATHERINE; Manheim Central HS; Manheim, PA; (Y); 64/241; Model UN; Concert Band; Mrchg Band; Nrsng.

THOMAS, CHRISTINA L; Harborcreek HS; Erie, PA; (Y); 27/204; Church Yth Grp; Computer Clb; Band; Concert Band; Mrchg Band; High Hon Roll; Hon Roll; NHS; Ntl Merit Ltr; GTE Pres Hnrs Schlrshp 86-87; Edinboro U; Engrng.

THOMAS, CORINNE; Bishop Hoban HS; Wilkes Barre, PA; (Y); 100/230; FBLA; Latin Clb; JV Var Cheerleading; Hon Roll; Accntng Bus Cmptn 86; Accntng.

THOMAS, DEAN; Ephrata SR HS; Ephrata, PA; (Y); 22/257; Church Yth Grp; Ski Clb; Var L Socr; Hon Roll; Carnegie-Mellon U; Auto Dsgn.

THOMAS, DEBORAH R; Perry Traditional Acad; Pittsburgh, PA; (Y); 5/124; Church Yth Grp; German Clb; Var Swmmng; High Hon Roll; NHS; Scrtrl.

THOMAS, DEBORAH R; Unionville HS; Kenneth Sq, PA; (Y); Art Clb; Camera Clb; Varsity Clb; Yrbk Stf; Rep Frsh Cls; Rep Jr Cls; Stu Cncl; Var Bsktbl; Var Fld Hcky; Var Sftbl; Mrktng.

THOMAS, DEREK R; Unionville HS; Kennett Square, PA; (Y); 5/269; Church Yth Grp; FBLA; Acpl Chr; Chorus; School Musical; Sr Cls; Ftbl; High Hon Roll; Jr NHS; Ntl Merit Schol; Dr Julius Margolis 86-89; Unionvle Comm Schlrshp 86; Sun Co Schrlshp 86-89; Cornell U; Engrng.

THOMAS, ESTHER; Shikellamy HS; Sunbury, PA; (Y); 7/315; Girl Scts; Spanish Clb; Chorus; Capt Color Guard; Capt Drill Tm; Yrbk Stf; Hon Roll; Jr NHS; Kiwanis Awd; NHS; Bloomsburg U; Acctg.

THOMAS JR, FRED; Columbia Montoor Area Vo-Tech; Catawissa, PA; (S); 2/226; Computer Clb; Math Tm; Scholastic Bowl; VICA; Rep Stu Cncl; High Hon Roll; NHS; Prfct Atten Awd; Math Bowl 85-86; ST Sci Olympcs 85-86; Comp Engrng Tech.

THOMAS, GAIL; Downingtown SR HS; Downingtown, PA; (Y); FBLA; Yrbk Stf; High Hon Roll; Hon Roll; Engl Dept Awd 86; DE CC; Bus Mgmt.

THOMAS, HOLLY L; Mifflinburg Area HS; Mifflinburg, PA; (Y); 6/169; Drama Clb; German Clb; Library Aide; Nwsp Stf; Var L Gym; High Hon Roll; NHS; Ntl Merit Ltr; Prfct Atten Awd; 4th Pl Patriotic Essay Cmptn; PA Math League Cert Of Merit; Hnrb Mtn Pi Mu Epsilon Awd; Bucknell U; Math.

THOMAS, JAMES; Gateway SR HS; Monroeville, PA; (Y); 66/450; Camera Clb; School Play; Yrbk Stf; Hon Roll; Pres Schlr; Pres Acdmc Fit Awd 86; Penn ST; Bus Adm.

THOMAS, JAMES P; Bloomsburg HS; Bloomsburg, PA; (Y); 40/150; Am Leg Boys St; Band; Concert Band; Bsbl; Bsktbl; Var Ftbl; Mrchg Band; Cmmnctns.

THOMAS, JAMI; Millville Area HS; Bloomsburg, PA; (Y); Church Yth Grp; Spanish Clb; School Play; Fld Hcky; Sftbl; Twrlr; NHS; Hon Roll.

THOMAS, JEFF; Cedar Cliff HS; Camp Hill, PA; (Y); Nwsp Bus Mgr; Nwsp Ed-Chief; Nwsp Rptr; Nwsp Stf; Off Frsh Cls; Off Soph Cls; Off Jr Cls; Off Sr Cls; Stu Cncl; Ftbl; Ptrt Nws Co Jrnlsm Achvt Awd 86; Wnnr Gld Key Schlstc Wrtng Awds Shrt Stry 86; Cert Merit Schlstc Wrtn; U Pittsburgh; Bus.

THOMAS, JOHN; Bald Eagle Area HS; Howard, PA; (S); 1/202; Aud/Vis; Boy Scts; Church Yth Grp; Library Aide; Nwsp Rptr; Lit Mag; Im Bowling; Cit Awd; High Hon Roll; NHS; Student Of The Month 86; PA ST U; Pre-Med.

THOMAS, JOHN; Bethel Park HS; Bethel Pk, PA; (Y); Rep Frsh Cls; JV Ftbl; Hon Roll; Engrng.

THOMAS, JULIE; Aliquippa SR HS; Aliquippa, PA; (S); 6/140; Sec Art Clb; Church Yth Grp; Pres Am Leg Aux Girls St; Hosp Aide; Sec Aud/Vis; Pep Band; Rptr Yrbk Stf; Stu Cncl; Hon Roll; Exploring.

THOMAS, KEITH; Ephrata SR HS; Akron, PA; (Y); Letterman Clb; Ski Clb; Varsity Clb; Stage Crew; Var Socr; JV Wrstlng; High Hon Roll; Hon Roll; Badmtn; Bsbl; Water Skng Wthin Top 200 Slalom Skiers In Wrld 86; PA St Slalom & Trick Champ 85; Rollins Coll; Bus.

THOMAS, KEITH; Upper Merion Area HS; King Of Prussa, PA; (Y); Math Tm; Variety Show; Hon Roll; Prfct Atten Awd; Muscn.

THOMAS, KELLY; Nativity B V M HS; Port Carbon, PA; (Y); Church Yth Grp; Spanish Clb; Chorus; Variety Show; Rptr Nwsp Rptr; Rotary Awd; Pres Acad Ftns Awd 86; Kutztown U.

THOMAS, KENNY; Churchill HS; Braddock, PA; (Y); 41/224; Church Yth Grp; Stu Cncl; Var Trk; High Hon Roll; Hon Roll; Hnr Roll Awd 83-85; Woodlnd Hills Ed Assoc Awd 86; U Of Pittsburgh; Elec Engr.

THOMAS, KIMBERLY; Sacred Heart HS; Carbondale, PA; (Y); 5/45; Cmnty Wkr; Drama Clb; Ski Clb; Spanish Clb; Teachers Aide; Nwsp Stf; High Hon Roll; Jr NHS; NHS; Law.

THOMAS, KIMBERLY; St Marys Area HS; St Marys, PA; (Y); Drama Clb; JA; Library Aide; Color Guard; Yrbk Stf; Hon Roll; Outstndng Jr In Art 85; Golumbic Mem Art Awd 86; Pres Acad Ftnss Awd 86; Mercyhurst Coll; Intr Dsgn.

THOMAS, LAWRENCE; Burgettstown JR-SR HS; Bulger, PA; (Y); VP Church Yth Grp; VP SADD; Pres Mrchg Band; Yrbk Phtg; Rep Stu Cncl; Var L Tennis; JV Wrstlng; Jr NHS; NHS; Hon Roll; U S Navy; Nclr Pwr.

THOMAS, LEIGHTON; Littlestown HS; Hanover, PA; (Y); 8/121; Varsity Clb; Var L Bsbl; Var L Bsktbl; Im Ftbl; Var Capt Golf; Im Tennis; High Hon Roll; Hon Roll; NHS; Comp Bus.

THOMAS, LESLIE LYNNE; Villa Maria Acad; Erie, PA; (Y); 60/145; Church Yth Grp; Model UN; Var Crs Cntry; Capt Trk; Hon Roll; Nrsng.

THOMAS, LISA; Bishop Mc Cort HS; Johnstown, PA; (Y); Sec Exploring; NFL; Pep Clb; Speech Tm; Chorus; Nwsp Rptr; Nwsp Stf; Yrbk Stf; High Hon Roll; Hon Roll; Sprts Med.

THOMAS, LISA; Deer Lakes HS; Cheswick, PA; (Y); Drama Clb; School Play; Nwsp Stf; Sec Soph Cls; Sec Jr Cls; Rep Stu Cncl; JV Var Cheerleading; Vllybl; Hon Roll; NEDT Awd; TV Brdcstr.

THOMAS, MARY ELIZABETH; Norwin SR HS; N Huntingdon, PA; (S); 54/550; French Clb; Chorus; School Play; Nwsp Ed-Chief; Sec Stu Cncl; JV Jr Cls; Var Socr; JV Trk; Hon Roll; NHS; Outstndng Stdnt Drama Awd 83-84; Oustndng Stdnt Cncl Awd 83-85; Comm.

THOMAS, MARY ROSE; Sacred Heart HS; Pittsburgh, PA; (Y); FBLA; JA; Pep Clb; Ski Clb; Spanish Clb; Yrbk Bus Mgr; Hon Roll; IN U; Acctng.

THOMAS, MATT; Garden Spot HS; New Holland, PA; (Y); Boy Scts; Exploring; German Clb; Library Aide; Band; Chorus; Mrchg Band; Socr; Hon Roll; Chem.

THOMAS, MICHAEL; Hempfield HS; Columbia, PA; (Y); 108/432; Boy Scts; Church Yth Grp; Chorus; Concert Band; Mrchg Band; Orch; School Musical; Trk; Engr.

THOMAS, NANCY E; Williamsport Area HS; Williamsport, PA; (Y); Latin Clb; Ed Lit Mag; NCTE Awd; Ntl Merit Ltr.

THOMAS, PAMELA; Pine Grove Area HS; Tremont, PA; (Y); Drama Clb; Chorus; School Musical; Yrbk Sprt Ed; Rep Jr Cls; Rep Stu Cncl; JV Vllybl; Hon Roll; NHS; PA Free Entrps Wk Schlrshp 86; Nrsg.

THOMAS, PATRICIA J; Haverford SR HS; Havertown, PA; (Y); 90/480; Church Yth Grp; Spanish Clb; Band; Church Choir; Concert Band; Mrchg Band; Pep Band; Symp Band; Variety Show; Dist Band 85-86; Indiana U Of PA; Compu Sci.

THOMAS, REBECCA; Fairview HS; Erie, PA; (Y); French Clb; Ski Clb; Teachers Aide; Varsity Clb; Rep Soph Cls; Rep Sr Cls; Sec Stu Cncl; Tennis; Trk; Hon Roll; Rotary Yth Ldrshp Awd 86; Liberal Arts.

THOMAS, ROBERT J; West Allegheny HS; Oakdale, PA; (Y); 13/220; Pres Church Yth Grp; Drama Clb; Math Tm; Trs Band; Chorus; Trs Concert Band; Drm Mjr(t); Jazz Band; Trs Mrchg Band; School Play; Hugh O Brien Ldrshp Awd 85.

THOMAS, RUTH; Blue Ridge HS; New Milford, PA; (Y); 7/110; Church Yth Grp; German Clb; Chorus; Var L Mat Maids; Var Sftbl; High Hon Roll; Trs NHS; David Hwang Memrl Awd.

THOMAS, SANDRA; Central Cambria HS; Ebens, PA; (S); 10/189; Pres French Clb; Science Clb; Ski Clb; Speech Tm; Off Stu Cncl; Bsktbl; Capt Cheerleading; Trk; Penn ST U; Law.

THOMAS, SARA; Blue Ridge HS; New Milford, PA; (Y); Church Yth Grp; German Clb; Chorus; Orch; Hon Roll; NHS; Elem Ed.

THOMAS, SCOTT; Wyoming Valley West HS; Larksville, PA; (Y); 83/385; Boy Scts; Church Yth Grp; Library Aide; Rep Frsh Cls; Bsbl; JV Bsktbl; Var L Vllybl; Hon Roll; Zoolgy Clb; AZ ST U; Cvl Engrng.

THOMAS, SEAN BARKLEY; Abraham Lincoln HS; Philadelphia, PA; (Y); FCA; Math Clb; Spanish Clb; Band; Variety Show; Nwsp Stf; Var Bsktbl; Coach Actv; Var Ftbl; Var Socr; MIP Awd Vrsty Bsktbl 85; All Keystone Conf Hon Mntn Bsktbl 85; Demnstrtd Extra Effrt In Acad 83-86; UCLA; Math.

THOMAS, TAMMY; Owen J Roberts HS; Phoenixville, PA; (S); 13/269; Church Yth Grp; Hosp Aide; Church Choir; JV Sftbl; Trk; Vllybl; High Hon Roll; NHS; Liberty U.

THOMAS, VERONICA; Frankford HS; Philadelphia, PA; (Y); Dance Clb; Math Clb; Office Aide; Church Choir; School Play; Bsktbl; Cheerleading; Swenson Skill Ctr; Nrsg.

THOMAS, VONCILE; Franklin Learning Center HS; Philadelphia, PA; (Y); Cmnty Wkr; Exploring; FNA; Hosp Aide; Red Cross Aide; Hon Roll; Schlrshp The Synod Of Trinity 86; Schl Alpha Bettes Sorority 86; Howard U; Med Tech.

THOMAS, WILLIAM; Brownsville Area HS; Republic, PA; (S); 10/225; Computer Clb; Drama Clb; Mathletes; Math Clb; Math Tm; SADD; School Play; Variety Show; Nwsp Rptr; Frsh Cls; Bus Admin.

THOMASON JR, BRUCE; Saint James Catholic HS; Brookhaven, PA; (Y); 25/140; Stage Crew; JV Bsbl; JV Bsktbl; Im Fld Hcky; Hon Roll; Prfct Atten Awd; Draftng II Awd 86; Theolgy IV Awd 86; Conduct Awd 82-86; PA Coll; Int Desgnr.

THOMPKINS, ADRIENNE; High School Of Engineering & Science; Philadelphia, PA; (Y); 106/186; Office Aide; Teachers Aide; Variety Show; Yrbk Stf; Mgr(s); Trk; Vllybl; Cit Awd; Prfct Atten Awd; Philly Tchrs Fed Awd-2nd Pl 86; Hm & Schl Assn-$75 Bond Spprtng Schl 86; Rcrdsn-Vcks $3000 Schlrshp 86; Penn ST U; Bus Admin.

THOMPKINS, DEENA; Chester HS; Chester, PA; (Y); Church Yth Grp; Latin Clb; Pep Clb; Chorus; Church Choir; Co-Capt Color Guard; School Play; Cit Awd; High Hon Roll; NHS; Pico Schlrshp 86; Ltn Awds 85-86; Penn ST; Cmptr Sci.

THOMPKINS, JOMARGA; Taylor Allderdice HS; Pittsburgh, PA; (Y); Church Yth Grp; Exploring; Intnl Clb; Spanish Clb; Vllybl; Hon Roll; Prsdntl Phys Ftns Awd 86; Sci Awd 83; Howard U; Bus.

THOMPSON, ALEXANDER; Pottsgrove HS; Pottstown, PA; (Y); 62/229; Church Yth Grp; Spanish Clb; Varsity Clb; Band; Concert Band; Mrchg Band; Pep Band; JV Var Bsktbl; Var L Trk; Hon Roll; Ldrshp Camp 85-86.

THOMPSON, ALICE; Mount Calvary Christian Schl; Mt Joy, PA; (S); Church Yth Grp; Chorus; School Play; Nwsp Stf; Yrbk Stf; Cheerleading; Sftbl; Hon Roll; NHS; Math Awds, Ntl Hstry & Gvrnmnt Awds & Intl Frgn Language Awd 86.

THOMPSON, ALISHA R; Engineering And Science HS; Philadelphia, PA; (S); 9/229; Church Yth Grp; Drill Tm; Rep Frsh Cls; Rep Soph Cls; Rep Jr Cls; Hon Roll; Jr NHS; NHS; Prfct Atten Awd; Hnrbl Mntn Crisis Intrvntn Drgs 83; PA Rgnl Intro Minrts To Engrg 83; Matron Sunbeams Of Eastrn Star; Drexel U; Matls Engr.

THOMPSON, ANGELA M; Harrisburg HS; Harrisburg, PA; (Y); #93 In Class; Aud/Vis; Latin Clb; Color Guard; Stage Crew; Yrbk Phtg; Rep Stu Cncl; Hon Roll; Hnr Rl 85-86; Achvt Acad 85-86; TELECOMM.

THOMPSON, BECKY; Hopewell SR HS; Aliquippa, PA; (Y); Cmnty Wkr; Latin Clb; Chorus; JV Bsktbl; High Hon Roll; Hon Roll; Phy Thrpy.

THOMPSON, BONNIE; Fox Chapel HS; Cheswick, PA; (Y); 68/322; Church Yth Grp; Ski Clb; Varsity Clb; Band; Drill Tm; JV Cheerleading; Var Fld Hcky; High Hon Roll; Hon Roll; Peer Tutr Eng Comp 85-86; Lbrl Arts.

THOMPSON, BRENT; Souderton Area HS; Telford, PA; (Y); Band; Concert Band; Jazz Band; Mrchg Band; School Musical; Hon Roll.

THOMPSON, BRIAN E; Leechburg Area HS; Leechburg, PA; (Y); 20/82; VP JA; Nwsp Sprt Ed; Yrbk Stf; L Ftbl; Capt Vllybl; Wt Lftg; Blu Dvl Ftbl Attd Awd 84; Mst Dec Wght Lftr 85; WV U; Bus.

THOMPSON, CANDICE; Chester HS; Chester, PA; (Y); Library Aide; Mathletes; Yrbk Stf; High Hon Roll; Hon Roll; Prfct Atten Awd; Balla Dance Awd & Jaz Dance 86; W Chester U; Comp Sci.

THOMPSON, CANDY; Clearfield Area HS; Clearfield, PA; (Y); FCA; Hosp Aide; Sftbl; High Hon Roll; Hon Roll; Clearfield Vo-Tech; RN.

THOMPSON, DANA; Kennedy Christian HS; Mercer, PA; (Y); French Clb; Sftbl; Hon Roll; Pittsburgh ST U; Phrmcy.

THOMPSON, DANA C; Octorara Area SR HS; Parkesburg, PA; (Y); 13/171; Church Yth Grp; Math Clb; Band; Concert Band; Jazz Band; Capt Mrchg Band; Pres Jr Cls; Pres Sr Cls; Rep Stu Cncl; Var Capt Bsktbl; MVP Bsktbl 85 & 86; MVP Vllybl 86; U Of CO Boulder; Phy Thrpy.

THOMPSON, DAVID; The Baptist HS; Clarks Summit, PA; (S); 1/16; Church Yth Grp; Chorus; Church Choir; Orch; Pres Bsktbl; Var Bsktbl; Var Capt Socr; High Hon Roll; Val; Rep Stu Cncl; Talents For Christ-1st Pl Writing-ST Levl 85; Baptist Bible Coll; Seminary.

THOMPSON II, DAVID C; Kennedy Christian HS; Transfer, PA; (Y); 19/100; Boy Scts; Latin Clb; Bowling; NHS; St Hyacinth Coll; Philosophy.

THOMPSON, DAVID N; Red Lion Area SR HS; Airville, PA; (Y); 60/337; Am Leg Boys St; Symp Band; Band; Concert Band; Jazz Band; Mrchg Band; Orch; Pep Band; DAR Awd; High Hon Roll; Drexel U; Matl Engrng.

THOMPSON, DIANA; Clearfield Area HS; Clearfield, PA; (Y); Church Yth Grp; Library Aide; Office Aide; SADD; Teachers Aide; VICA; JV Sftbl; Im Vllybl; High Hon Roll; Hon Roll.

THOMPSON, DONALD; Sharpsville Area HS; Sharpsville, PA; (S); Varsity Clb; Var L Socr; Var Trk; VICA; Hon Roll; USAF; Refrigeration.

THOMPSON, DONNA; Washington HS; Washington, PA; (Y); 15/150; Church Yth Grp; Drama Clb; Key Clb; Letterman Clb; Library Aide; Spanish Clb; SADD; School Play; Yrbk Stf; Tennis; NHS 85-86; Grace Coll.

THOMPSON, DOROTHY V; Lower Bucks Christian Acad; Hulmeville, PA; (Y); 4/26; Varsity Clb; Yrbk Stf; VP Jr Cls; VP Sr Cls; Stat Bsbl; JV Var Cheerleading; High Hon Roll; Hon Roll; Schlrshp Bucks Cnty CC 86; Yrbk Awd 86; Drexel U; Bus.

THOMPSON II, GARY I; Linesville HS; Linesville, PA; (Y); 14/80; Mrchg Band; Hon Roll; VFW Awd; German Clb; SADD; VP Concert Band; VP Jazz Band; VP Pep Band; Nwsp Stf; VP Band; Yth Tour WA 86; Dist Band 86; Edinboro Coll; Comp Pgmmng.

THOMPSON, JEFFREY; Cameron County HS; Emporium, PA; (Y); 1/86; Church Yth Grp; Computer Clb; Math Clb; Office Aide; Spanish Clb; Teachers Aide; School Musical; School Play; Yrbk Stf; Bausch & Lomb Sci Awd; Sci.

THOMPSON, JODI; Bellefonte HS; Bellefonte, PA; (Y); 45/232; Church Yth Grp; Band; Chorus; Jazz Band; Mrchg Band; Stu Cncl; Tennis; Hon Roll; Fshn Mrchndsng.

THOMPSON, JODI; Elk County Christian HS; Johnsonburg, PA; (S); Church Yth Grp; Model UN; Yrbk Stf; High Hon Roll; Penn ST U; Bus Adm.

THOMPSON, JOHN; East Juniata HS; Mc Alisterville, PA; (Y); 9/100; Church Yth Grp; Math Tm; Chorus; School Musical; JV Var Bsbl; JV Var Bsktbl; JV Var Ftbl; Lion Awd; NHS; Rotary Awd; Shippensburg U; Mathg.

THOMPSON, JOHN; Wilmington Area HS; Volant, PA; (Y); 23/123; VP Spanish Clb; Lit Mag; Ftbl; Hon Roll; Gannon; Law.

THOMPSON, JOHN HENRY; Penncrest HS; Media, PA; (Y); 27/329; Civic Clb; School Play; Variety Show; Nwsp Stf; Yrbk Stf; Pres Frsh Cls; Off Soph Cls; Pres Jr Cls; Pres Sr Cls; Stu Cncl; Hugh O Brien; Clos-Up; Natl Hnr Scty; Polt Sci.

THOMPSON, JOYCE; Norwin SR HS; Aroara, PA; (Y); SADD; VICA; Chorus; Church Choir; Orch; 3rd Pl Lcl VICA Cmtpn Fd Svc Trds 86; Htl Rest Mgmt.

THOMPSON, KATHLEEN; South Park HS; Pittsburgh, PA; (Y); 3/220; Church Yth Grp; JA; Concert Band; Var L Bsktbl; Var L Crs Cntry; Var L Trk; NHS; Ntl Merit Ltr; Mrchg Band; High Hon Roll; Carnegie Museum Of Ntl Hist Sci Awd 86; Schl Of Music Awd 85-86; AP Chem Schl Awd 86.

THOMPSON, LAUREL; Hatboro-Horsham SR HS; Horsham, PA; (Y); 39/270; Church Yth Grp; Debate Tm; Pep Clb; Teachers Aide; Soph Cls; Jr Cls; Bsktbl; Fld Hcky; Lcrss; Hon Roll; Elem Ed.

THOMPSON, LISA J; Blairsville SR HS; Blairsville, PA; (Y); 15/131; Church Yth Grp; Band; Capt Drm Mjr(t); School Musical; Stu Cncl; Capt Twrlr; High Hon Roll; NHS; Prfct Atten Awd; Cnty Jr Ms Fnlst; PA ST U; Nrsng.

THOMPSON, LORI; Sharpsville Area HS; Sharpsville, PA; (Y); Dance Clb; Library Aide; Teachers Aide; Mgr(s); Hon Roll; Crselnr Drctr.

THOMPSON, MARCY; Connellsville Area HS; Connellsville, PA; (Y); 29/550; VP Computer Clb; Pep Clb; School Musical; VP Soph Cls; Pres Jr Cls; Var Cheerleading; Sftbl; Swmmng; High Hon Roll; Spanish NHS.

THOMPSON, MARK; Holy Ghost Prep Schl; Philadelphia, PA; (S); Nwsp Rptr; Nwsp Stf; Lit Mag; NHS; Great Books Prog Achvt Awd 86; Cert Of Awd Svc To Flame 86; Jrnlsm.

THOMPSON, MIKE; Penn Trafford HS; Irwin, PA; (Y); Im Bsktbl; Im Ftbl; Im Socr; Im Sftbl; Prfcny Awd In Acctng 85-86; IN U Of PA; Acctnt.

THOMPSON, MILLIE; Central HS; Roaring Sprg, PA; (Y); 26/175; FBLA; High Hon Roll; Hon Roll; Legal Sec.

THOMPSON, PAM; Plymouth-Whitemarsh HS; Plymouth Mtg, PA; (Y); Church Yth Grp; Rep Soph Cls; Rep Jr Cls; Rep Sr Cls; Rep Stu Cncl; JV Capt Fld Hcky; Var Lcrss; Im Powder Puff Ftbl; Hon Roll; Sbrbn I All League 1st Team In La Crosse 86; Gene Gisburne Mem Awd For Lacrosse 86; Acdmc Achvt 84-86; Bus.

THOMPSON, PAULINE; Berwick Area SR HS; Wapwallopen, PA; (Y); Dance Clb; Drama Clb; FBLA; Key Clb; Math Clb; School Play; Nwsp Rptr; Ed Nwsp Stf; Boy Scts; Ed Lit Mag; Nrsng Aide; Nrtheastrn PA Scholar Dancer 85-86; Natl Pag Wnnr 85-86; Meteorlgy.

THOMPSON, RAEGAN; Oil City Area SR HS; Oil City, PA; (Y); 12/250; Church Yth Grp; Hosp Aide; Acpl Chr; Color Guard; Drill Tm; School Musical; Variety Show; Yrbk Stf; High Hon Roll; Hon Roll; Math Awd 83-84; Messiah Coll; Phys Thrpy.

THOMPSON, SCOTT; Pine Grove Area HS; Pine Grove, PA; (Y); 47/127; Boy Scts; Varsity Clb; Chorus; School Play; Trs Soph Cls; Trs Jr Cls; Trs Sr Cls; Stu Cncl; JV Ftbl; Var Wrstlng; Stu Forum; Eagle Scout 84; Cptn Vrsty Wrstlng 86.

THOMPSON, STEPHANIE; Kennard-Dale HS; Stewartstown, PA; (Y); Church Yth Grp; French Clb; Pep Clb; Ski Clb; Varsity Clb; Chorus; School Musical; JV Var Cheerleading; JV Var Mgr(s); Hon Roll; Elizabethtown Hnrs Choir 85; Bus Adm.

THOMPSON, SUSAN; Pennsbury HS; Yardley, PA; (Y); Church Yth Grp; French Clb; Chorus; Church Choir; Orch; Yrbk Stf; Hon Roll; NHS.

THOMPSON, TAMMY; Freeport Area SR HS; Sarver, PA; (S); 22/170; Church Yth Grp; German Clb; GAA; Spanish Clb; Bsktbl; Sftbl; High Hon Roll; Grove City; Teacher.

THOMPSON, TERRI; Lock Haven HS; Beech Creek, PA; (Y); Art Clb; Church Yth Grp; Cmnty Wkr; French Clb; Hosp Aide; Library Aide; Red Cross Aide; Nwsp Rptr; Stu Cncl; Mgr(s).

THOMPSON, TERRY; Central HS; Roaring Sprg, PA; (Y); 22/184; FCA; Ski Clb; Varsity Clb; Var L Bsbl; Im Bsktbl; Var Golf; Im Vllybl; Hon Roll; Coaches Achvt Awd Bsbl 86; Pittsburgh Inst; Avia Electrncs.

THOMPSON, THARREN; First Baptist Church Acad; Reynoldsville, PA; (Y); 2/8; Church Yth Grp; Band; Church Choir; Concert Band; Mrchg Band; School Musical; Stage Crew; DAR Awd; Hon Roll; Sal; Schl Awd Outstndng Inst Music Awd 86; Acclrtd Chrstn Ed 1st Pl Awd Radio Scrpt Natl Conv 86; Philadelphia Coll Of Bibl; Mssn.

THOMPSON, THOMAS; Owen J Roberts HS; Elverson, PA; (Y); 35/292; Letterman Clb; School Musical; L Var Bsbl; Var L Ftbl; Im Mgr Ice Hcky; Im Mgr Vllybl; Im Mgr Wt Lftg; Cit Awd; God Cntry Awd; NHS; Elec Engrng.

THOMPSON, TRACEY; Shaler Area HS; Pittsburgh, PA; (Y); 165/517; Church Yth Grp; Debate Tm; Hon Roll; Elem Educ.

THOMPSON, TRUDI CHRISTINA; Berwick Area SR HS; Wapwallopen, PA; (Y); Art Clb; FBLA; Girl Scts; Library Aide; Office Aide; Stage Crew; Lit Mag; Tennis; Prfct Atten Awd; Offc Aide US Army; Explorers Past US Army; US Army.

THOMS, RICHARD; Chambersburg Area SR HS; Chambersburg, PA; (Y); Boy Scts; Church Yth Grp; Spanish Clb; JV Var Socr; Var Trk; Hon Roll; Prfct Atten Awd; Ordr Of Arrw 86; Egl Sct Awd 86; US Army Bsc Tning 86; Airforce Acad; Elec Engrng.

THOMSON, ELLIE; Central Columbia HS; Orangeville, PA; (Y); 18/183; Cmnty Wkr; Key Clb; Ski Clb; Spanish Clb; School Musical; School Play; Off Stu Cncl; Bsktbl; Swmmng; Tennis; Pres Schlr Awd 86; Perfct Attndc Awd 86; Loc Schlrshp Awd 86; Ursinus College; Sci.

THOMSON, LAURA; Plum SR HS; Pittsburgh, PA; (Y); Pres DECA; Varsity Clb; Var L Vllybl; DECA 1st Pl ST Comptn, Tp 20 Natl Cmptn 86; Pittsbrgh Zoo Vlntr 86; Sftbl Trnmt Tm 86; Mrktng.

THORNE, JAMES; Ford City JR SR HS; Ford City, PA; (Y); 5/145; Off Boy Scts; Computer Clb; Concert Band; Drm Mjr(t); Mrchg Band; Pep Band; Crs Cntry; Trk; NHS; Capt YMCA Swm Tm 82-83; Mech Engr.

THORNTON, CHRISTOPHER W; Bishop Mc Devitt HS; Harrisburg, PA; (Y); 7/183; Church Yth Grp; Concert Band; Jazz Band; Mrchg Band; Pep Band; Bsbl; Bsktbl; Cit Awd; High Hon Roll; Engrng.

THORNTON, JIM; Ridley SR HS; Folsom, PA; (Y); Drama Clb; Thesps; Chorus; School Musical; School Play; Stage Crew; Nwsp Phtg; Nwsp Stf; Intntnl Thspian Soc; Peer Cnslng; Cmmnctns.

THORNTON, JODY; Old Forge HS; Old Forge, PA; (S); Ski Clb; Nwsp Phtg; Capt Sftbl; Hon Roll; NHS.

THORNTON, LISA; Carbondale Area HS; Simpson, PA; (Y); French Clb; FBLA; Flag Corp; Sftbl; Tennis; French Hon Soc; High Hon Roll; Jr NHS; PA ST; Engrng.

THORNTON, MICHELE; Annville-Cleona HS; Lebanon, PA; (S); 15/121; FBLA; Varsity Clb; Band; Chorus; Yrbk Stf; Cheerleading; Sftbl; Twrlr; NHS; Latin Excllncy Awd 84-85; Girl Of Mnth 85-86; Pre-Med.

THORNTON, TODD; Pine Grove Area HS; Pine Grove, PA; (Y); Am Leg Boys St; Rep Stu Cncl; JV Bsktbl; Var Ftbl; NEDT Awd; Varsity Clb; Stage Crew; Im Bsbl; Im Trk; Im Vllybl; Cnty Studnt Frm Rep; Gftd Studnt Prog; Arch.

THORP, PAM; Curwensville Area HS; Grampian, PA; (Y); Church Yth Grp; Drama Clb; French Clb; Nwsp Stf; Yrbk Ed-Chief; Golf; High Hon Roll; NHS; Dist IX Girls Golf Champ 85; Jrnlsm.

THORPE, BRENNA; Trinity HS; Washington, PA; (Y); #13 In Class; Drama Clb; Temple Yth Grp; School Play; Var L Trk; High Hon Roll; Hon Roll; NHS; Pep Clb; Variety Show; A Govs Schl For Arts 85; Dist, Regnl & State Orchstrs 83-84; Music.

THORPE, CHRISTOPHER D; Mercer Area HS; Mercer, PA; (Y); 8/111; Church Yth Grp; Computer Clb; Math Tm; Science Clb; Varsity Clb; NHS; PA ST U; Elec Engrng.

THORSEN, ROBERT; Upper Moreland HS; Willow Grove, PA; (Y); Church Yth Grp; Key Clb; Stu Cncl; Bowling; Swmmng; Tennis; USC; Mrn Bio.

THORSETT, KRISTEN; North Penn HS; Lansdale, PA; (Y); Drama Clb; School Play; Lit Mag; Rep Frsh Cls; Var Gym; Var Powder Puff Ftbl; High Hon Roll; Hon Roll; Vrsty Ltr Gymnstcs 83-84; U Of MN; Jrnlsm.

THOUROT, LORI A; Lampeter-Strasburg HS; Willow St, PA; (Y); VP Thesps; Acpl Chr; Trs Chorus; Madrigals; School Musical; Trs Nwsp Rptr; Sec Frsh Cls; Sec Soph Cls; Sec Jr Cls; Sec Sr Cls; Hmcmb Qn; Cnty Chrs 3 Yrs; Prom Cmmttee; Shippensburg U; Cmmnctns.

THRASH, ERIC; Berwick Area SR HS; Berwick, PA; (Y); VP Soph Cls; VP Jr Cls; Rep Stu Cncl; Var Bsbl; L Wrstlng; Hon Roll; NHS; Comm.

THRASHER, LISA; Connellsville SR HS; Cnlvle, PA; (Y); Art Clb; Church Yth Grp; Dance Clb; Drama Clb; Library Aide; Chorus; Church Choir; Yrbk Stf; Stu Cncl; Wt Lftg; Durbins; Secy.

THROWER, STEPHANIE; Knoch JR SR HS; Saxonburg, PA; (Y); AFS; JA; Chorus; Madrigals; School Play; Lit Mag; Crs Cntry; Trk; Hon Roll.

THUCH, SOCHITRA; Ephrata SR HS; Ephrata, PA; (Y); PA ST U; Elec Engrng.

THURANSKY, JENNIFER L; Greensburg Central Catholic HS; West Newton, PA; (Y); French Clb; JA; JCL; Letterman Clb; Political Wkr; Yrbk Stf; L Bsktbl; L Trk; Capt Vllybl; Hon Roll; WA & Jefferson; Bus.

THYREEN, JENNY; Waynesburg Central HS; Waynesburg, PA; (Y); Church Yth Grp; VP French Clb; Letterman Clb; Jazz Band; Yrbk Phtg; Rep Stu Cncl; Trk; Vllybl; High Hon Roll; NHS.

TIANO, SUSAN L; Nazareth Acad; Norristown, PA; (Y); NFL; Service Clb; Teachers Aide; School Musical; Lit Mag; Capt Cheerleading; Var Sftbl; High Hon Roll; NHS; GAA; Socratic Awd 86; PA Coll; Phrmcy.

TIBBETTS, TRACEY; Cameron County HS; Emporium, PA; (Y); 11/91; Church Yth Grp; German Clb; Band; Chorus; Church Choir; Concert Band; Mrchg Band; Hon Roll; Debate Tm; Delta Epsilon Phi 86; Music.

TIBEL, ALYSIA; Pittston Area HS; Dupont, PA; (Y); French Clb; Yrbk Stf; Score Keeper; Vllybl; John Hopkins U Tlnt Srch 82; Semi Fnlst Teen Magz Mdl Srch 85; Kings Coll; Finance.

TIBERIO, JOANNA; Western Beaver HS; Industry, PA; (Y); Mrchg Band; Symp Band; Yrbk Ed-Chief; Yrbk Stf; Sec Jr Cls; Twrlr; Cit Awd; Hon Roll; NHS; Finlst In Beaver Cnty Jr Ms Pgm 86; Patrcpnt In Beaver Cnty Hnrs Band 85-86; Leg Sec.

TICE, PAMELA MAE; Bellefonte HS; Bellefonte, PA; (Y); 47/212; Band; Chorus; Concert Band; Mrchg Band; Rep Frsh Cls; Rep Soph Cls; Rep Stu Cncl; Dntl Asst Awd 86; Nwsppr Carrier Of Mnth 85; Centre Bus Schl; Exec Sec.

TICE, SARAH; Delaware County Christian Schl; Havertown, PA; (Y); Church Yth Grp; Chorus; Church Choir; Sec Soph Cls; VP Pres Stu Cncl; Var Capt Bsktbl; Var Capt Fld Hcky; JV Var Sftbl; High Hon Roll; NHS; Home Econmcs.

TIDD, MICHELLE; General Mc Lane HS; Mckean, PA; (Y); 8/236; Art Clb; German Clb; Office Aide; JV Cheerleading; Powder Puff Ftbl; JV Var Sftbl; JV Var Vllybl; High Hon Roll; Hon Roll; NHS; Fav Undrclssmn 86; Art Prjcts Accptd ST U Art Shw 86; SR Advsr Pln Gen Mcln 86; PA ST; Art.

TIELLE, DAVID; Pittston Area HS; Pittston, PA; (Y); 30/365; Exploring; French Clb; Key Clb; Ski Clb; Band; Jazz Band; Mrchg Band; NHS; Acad All Amer 86.

TIERS, MELISSA; Liberty HS; Bethlehem, PA; (Y); 71/502; French Clb; Chorus; Hon Roll; Prncpls Awd 85; Bus Mrktng.

TIESENGA, TAMMY; Christian School Of York; York, PA; (S); Speech Tm; Chorus; Church Choir; Stu Cncl; Var Bsktbl; Capt Var Cheerleading; Score Keeper; Var Sftbl; Chlrdng MVP 85; Spch.

TIETJEN, ROBERT C; Honesdale HS; Honesdale, PA; (Y); Aud/Vis; Computer Clb; Hosp Aide; Letterman Clb; Ski Clb; Y-Teens; Yrbk Phtg; Bsktbl; JV Var Ftbl; Wt Lftg; Jrnlsm.

TIGER, MELISSA; Cannon Mc Millan HS; Canonsburg, PA; (Y); FBLA; Girl Scts; Pep Clb; Yrbk Stf.

TIGHE, STEVEN; Spring-Ford SR HS; Schwenksville, PA; (S); 11/255; Church Yth Grp; JV Var Bsbl; JV Bsktbl; Coach Actv; Score Keeper; Hon Roll; NHS; Athltc Trainer,Bsbl,Bsktbl Cert 85-86; Physcl Thrpy.

TILGHMAN, GREGORY S; Northeast HS; Philadelphia, PA; (Y); 208/690; Church Yth Grp; Math Clb; Ski Clb; Church Choir; Gym; Instrmntl Music Piano 84 & 85; U Pittsburgh; Elec Engrng.

TILLOTSON, TERRY; Corry Area HS; Spartansburg, PA; (Y); Boy Scts; Chess Clb; 4-H; Band; Concert Band; Mrchg Band; School Play; Edinboro Coll; Acctg.

TIMBLIN, BECKY; Bald Eagle Area HS; Howard, PA; (Y); Chorus; Sec Jr Cls; Sec Sr Cls; Rep Stu Cncl; Var L Cheerleading; Var L Mgr(s); Var Powder Puff Ftbl; Var Trk; Var Wt Lftg; Miss Bald Eagles Ct 86-87; PA ST U; Adv.

TIMCHAK, ALICE ANN; North Allegheny HS; Sewickley, PA; (Y); 136/642; School Play; Var L Gym; CC Awd; Hon Roll; Pitt Coll; Occptnl Thrpy.

TIMKO, LISA; Our Lady Of The Sacred Heart HS; W Aliquippa, PA; (Y); Hosp Aide; Pep Clb; Church Choir; School Musical; Yrbk Stf; Pres Jr Cls; Pres Stu Cncl; Var Capt Cheerleading; Hon Roll; NHS; Acad All Amer Schlr Awd 85-86; Hghst Overall Avg Spn 83-86; Bus.

TIMM, MARIA; Abington SR HS; Glenside, PA; (Y); 61/535; Concert Band; Mrchg Band; School Musical; Off Sr Cls; Stu Cncl; Sftbl; Hon Roll; NHS; 1st Pl Kathrine Gibbs Typng Cont 85; Dirtrs Awd Outstndng Dedc Instrmntl Music 86; W Eugene Stull Awd; Villanova U; Comp Sci.

TIMM JR, WILLIAM; Schuylkill Haven Area HS; Schuylkill Haven, PA; (S); 28/100; Church Yth Grp; Science Clb; Teachers Aide; Chorus; Church Choir; Concert Band; Mrchg Band; Pep Band; School Musical; Hon Roll; 1st Pl Adv Bio Fair 85; Peer Educ 85-86; Enrichment Stu 82-86; Penn ST U; Bio.

TIMMERMAN, SCOTT; Lincoln HS; Ellwood City, PA; (Y); 16/170; Spanish Clb; Var L Bsktbl; Var L Ftbl; High Hon Roll; Hon Roll; Jr NHS; NHS; Leadership Award 85-86; Scholar Athlete Award 85; Med.

TIMMINS, LORI; Delone Catholic HS; Hanover, PA; (Y); 2/169; Drama Clb; Library Aide; Yrbk Ed-Chief; Rep Jr Cls; Rep Sr Cls; High Hon Roll; NHS; Sal; Hmcmng Cmmtte; Prm Cmmtte; Villanova U; Bus Adm.

TIMMS, DARYL; Seneca Valley SR HS; Harmony, PA; (Y); Church Yth Grp; L Bsbl; L Bsktbl; Crs Cntry; Ftbl; L Tennis; High Hon Roll; Hon Roll; NHS; Engrng.

TIMNEY, ELIZABETH; Western Beaver HS; Industry, PA; (Y); Pres Church Yth Grp; Band; Chorus; Church Choir; VP Sr Cls; Stu Cncl; Pom Pon; Cit Awd; Hon Roll; NHS; Wilma Boyd Career Schl; Airlns.

TIMON, KATHERINE; Villa Maria Acad; Erie, PA; (Y); 8/133; Aud/Vis; Model UN; Yrbk Stf; NHS; Acctng.

TIMS, WENDY; Middletown Area HS; Middletown, PA; (Y); 90/166; Church Yth Grp; Girl Scts; Band; Chorus; Church Choir; Concert Band; Drm & Bgl; Jazz Band; Orch; Music Tchr.

TINCLER, ROSE IRENE; Venango Christian HS; Kill Devil Hills, NC; (Y); 4/43; Art Clb; Math Tm; Chorus; Madrigals; Nwsp Stf; Yrbk Stf; Rep Sr Cls; Stu Cncl; Capt Cheerleading; Hon Roll; NC ST U; Math.

TINDALL, LESLIE; Peqwa Valley HS; Gap, PA; (Y); AFS; Sec Drama Clb; Girl Scts; Chorus; Color Guard; School Musical; Yrbk Bus Mgr; High Hon Roll; NHS; Bucknell U; Erly Chldhd Ed.

TINDALL, STEVEN M; Thomas Jefferson HS; Pittsburgh, PA; (Y); 1/255; French Clb; Capt Bsktbl; Capt Socr; NCTE Awd; Pres NHS; Val; AFS; Debate Tm; Im Coach Actv; Var Trk; Chem Olympcs Slvr Mdl 83-84; Yale Coll; Comp Sci.

TINGLE, HELENE; Tyrone Area HS; Tyrone, PA; (Y); 46/182; Am Leg Aux Girls St; French Clb; Spanish Clb; Chorus; Color Guard; High Hon Roll; Hon Roll; Letter Senator Being Slctd Keystone Girls ST 86.

TINKEY, BETH; Rockwood Area HS; Rockwood, PA; (S); 5/92; AFS; Office Aide; Speech Tm; Chorus; Concert Band; Mrchg Band; Yrbk Stf; Sec NHS; Stenogrphy Awd Shrthnd 85; 2nd Bus Cls 83-85; Robert Morris Coll; Bus Adm.

TINKEY, LORI; Connellsville Area HS; Indian Head, PA; (Y); Art Clb; Church Yth Grp; VICA; Church Choir; Hon Roll; Dirs Lst 84-86; Pitts Bty Acad Grnsbrg; Btcn.

TINKEY, WENDY; Canon-Mc Millan HS; Canonsburg, PA; (Y); 67/360; Hon Roll.

TINNEY, MARJORIE; W Catholic Girls HS; Philadelphia, PA; (Y); 60/240; French Clb; Nwsp Rptr; Yrbk Rptr; Stu Cncl; Cheerleading; Cmnty Wkr; Debate Tm; Temple.

TIRDEL, DAVID; Valley HS; New Kensington, PA; (Y); Drama Clb; Pep Clb; Trs Ski Clb; Spanish Clb; SADD; Varsity Clb; Band; Chorus; Concert Band; Mrchg Band.

TIRNAUER, JUDD; Upper Merion Area HS; Gulph Mills, PA; (Y); 18/340; French Clb; Math Clb; Math Tm; Rep Frsh Cls; Var Bsbl; Var Tennis; High Hon Roll; Hon Roll; Pre Med.

TIRPAK JR, DAVID B; Northern Chester Co Technical Schl; Phoenixville, PA; (Y); Hon Roll; Elec Tech.

TIRPAK, JUSTINE M; William Allen HS; Allentown, PA; (Y); 49/576; Cmnty Wkr; Leo Clb; Political Wkr; Ski Clb; Yrbk Stf; Powder Puff Ftbl; Hon Roll; Jr NHS; NHS; Pres Schlr; Outstndng Schltc Achvt 85; Temple U Pres Awd 86; Schl Scholar 86; Temple U; Cmmnctns.

TITTELMAYER, JANET LYNN; George Washington HS; Philadelphia, PA; (Y); 7/769; Chrmn Red Cross Aide; Science Clb; Off Chorus; School Musical; Yrbk Ed-Chief; High Hon Roll; Pres NHS; Church Yth Grp; Cmnty Wkr; Drama Clb; Natl Yth Sci Camp 85; Pres Clssrm 86; Am Legn Awd 86; Drexel U; Bio.

TITUS, GREG; Sharpsville Area HS; Sharpsville, PA; (Y); 44/129; Aud/Vis; Church Yth Grp; Library Aide; Spanish Clb; Stage Crew; JV Var Bsktbl; Im Crs Cntry; Var L Trk.

TITUS, GREG; Tamaqua Area HS; Tamaqua, PA; (Y); 17/180; Church Yth Grp; Drama Clb; Science Clb; Band; Church Choir; Concert Band; Mrchg Band; School Musical; School Play; Coach Actv; Air Force Smmr Sci Sem 86; Lehigh; Math.

TITUS, JANET; Tunkhannock Area HS; Tunkhannock, PA; (Y); Library Aide; Office Aide; Ski Clb; Spanish Clb; Band; Concert Band; Mrchg Band; Hon Roll; Comp.

TITZELL, MELISSA; Cumberland Valley HS; Mechanicsburg, PA; (Y); 11/522; L Rep Church Yth Grp; Hosp Aide; Ski Clb; Chorus; Co-Capt Color Guard; Mrchg Band; Stage Crew; Hon Roll; NHS; Dickinson Coll Smr Schlrshp Cmptr Sci 86; Penn Questers Hstry Prjct U Of PA 84; Frnch Achvmnt Awds.

TKACH, STACEY; North Hills HS; Pittsburgh, PA; (Y); Dance Clb; Hosp Aide; Latin Clb; Sec Band; Concert Band; Capt Drm Mjr(t); Mrchg Band; Sec Symp Band; JV Cheerleading; Capt L Twrlr; U Pittsburgh; Phys Thrpy.

TKACIK, KRISTIN; Franklin Regional HS; Murrysville, PA; (Y); AFS; Church Yth Grp; Ski Clb; Color Guard; Drill Tm; Yrbk Stf; God Cntry Awd; High Hon Roll; Hon Roll; Pre Med.

TKATCH, LAURA; Ambridge Area SR HS; Baden, PA; (Y); 6/280; Capt Drill Tm; School Musical; Elks Awd; High Hon Roll; JC Awd; Jr NHS; Lion Awd; NHS; French Clb; Library Aide; Natl Band Assn Awd Ldrshp 84; Grl Mnth 85; Geneva Coll; Jrnlsm.

TOBER, JENNIFER A; Upper Moreland SR HS; Willow Grove, PA; (Y); 69/253; Chorus; School Musical; School Play; Lit Mag; Mgr(s); JV Socr; JV Trk; Hon Roll; Stu Consrvtn Assoc 85; Acting.

TOBIAS, BETH; Cumberland Valley HS; Boiling Springs, PA; (Y); French Clb; FBLA; Intnl Clb; Key Clb; Pep Clb; PAVAS; SADD; School Musical; Church Yth Grp; German Clb; ICF Natl Cheering Champnshp 85; Cnty Orch Fest 84; Acctng.

TOBIAS, JOY; Beaver County Christian HS; Darlington, PA; (Y); Church Yth Grp; Pres Trs 4-H; Band; Chorus; Church Choir; High Hon Roll; Church & Sunday Schl Pianist 83-86; Mus Educ.

TOBIN, ANN MARIE; Nazareth Acad; Philadelphia, PA; (Y); Church Yth Grp; Cmnty Wkr; Hosp Aide; Q&S; Spanish Clb; Ed Lit Mag; Hon Roll; NHS; Quill & Scroll Society 86; Commendation For Outstanding Performance On Sat 86; St Josephs U; Eng.

TOBIN, KIRSTI; Bishop Shanahan HS; Chadds Ford, PA; (Y); 22/218; Cmnty Wkr; Ski Clb; Fld Hcky; Trk; High Hon Roll; Hon Roll.

TOBIN, ROBERT; Fort Cherry HS; Mc Donald, PA; (S); Aud/Vis; Church Yth Grp; Math Clb; Science Clb; Spanish Clb; Chorus; Church Choir.

TOBIN, TIMOTHY; Mahanoy Area HS; Gilberton, PA; (Y); Church Yth Grp; Band; Variety Show; Bsktbl; Ftbl; Trk; God Cntry Awd; High Hon Roll; Hon Roll; NHS; Optometry.

TOBOZ, STEPHEN; Lock Haven HS; Lock Haven, PA; (Y); Spanish Clb; Chorus; Stage Crew; Variety Show; Yrbk Stf; Pres Frsh Cls; Im Bsbl; Im Bsktbl; Var L Ftbl; Im Socr; Mst Imprvd Wrstlr Awd 84-85; Vrsty Ftbl Outstndng Bck Awd 85; US Naval Acad; Sprts Med.

TOBUREN, KELLY; Manheim Central HS; Manheim, PA; (Y); Library Aide; Office Aide; Teachers Aide; Stage Crew; Jr Cls; Sr Cls; Stu Cncl; Cheerleading; Crs Cntry; Pom Pon; Stu Mnth 85; Dentl Asst Scholar 86; Willow St Vo-Tech; Dentl Asst.

TOCA, FREDERICK; Quigley HS; Mars, PA; (Y); Boy Scts; Church Yth Grp; JA; Math Clb; SADD; Trk; Wrstlng; Hon Roll; LEAD Prog Bus Adm; Xavier U LA; Pre-Law.

TOCCO, AMY; Highlands SR HS; Natrona Hts, PA; (Y); 16/274; Hosp Aide; Intnl Clb; Varsity Clb; Var L Bsktbl; Var Capt Tennis; High Hon Roll; NHS; Prfct Atten Awd; Acdmc All Amer Awd 86; Athltc Acadmc Awd 86; Sci Merit Awd Ntl 86; Slippery Rock U; Elem Ed.

TOCCO, ERIC; Highlands SR HS; Natrona Heights, PA; (Y); Am Leg Boys St; Key Clb; Speech Tm; Stu Cncl; Golf; Socr; Tennis; Trk; Jr NHS; Trs NHS; Gld Awds; Keystn Boys ST 86.

TOCZYLOWSKI, CAROL; Villa Maria Acad; Erie, PA; (Y); 18/125; Church Yth Grp; Computer Clb; Model UN; PAVAS; Chorus; Church Choir; Ntl Merit Ltr; Tresa Burns Art Schlrshp; Penn St Behrend Jrs Day.

TODD, AMY LYNN; Conestoga Valley HS; Lancaster, PA; (Y); 38/255; Yrbk Stf; Twrlr; Lion Awd; Prof Scrtries Intl Schlrshp 86; Lncstr Cnty Lgl Scrtries Schlrshp 86; C V Schl Str Shrthnd & Typng Awd; Central Penn Bus Schl; Lgl Asst.

TODD, GLENN; Ringold HS; Finleyville, PA; (Y); Am Leg Boys St; JA; Law.

TODD, HENRY; New Hope-Solebury HS; New Hope, PA; (S); 4/66; Ski Clb; Nwsp Rptr; Yrbk Stf; Pres Frsh Cls; Trs Soph Cls; Pres Jr Cls; Rep Stu Cncl; High Hon Roll; NHS; Cert De Merite; Treas Natl Hnr Socty; Peer Facilatr; Pol Sci.

TODD, JEFFREY; Susq Comm HS; Susq, PA; (S); JA; Hon Roll; Jr NHS; NHS.

TOKAR, BRAD; Ft Cherry HS; Mc Donald, PA; (S); 4/120; Stage Crew; Bsbl; Bsktbl; Ftbl; Sftbl; Wt Lftg; Wrstlng; High Hon Roll; Jr NHS; NHS; All ST Team; MVP Ftbl-OH Valley Conf All Stars 85-86.

TOKARCIK, JOHN; Conneaut Lake HS; Conneaut Lake, PA; (Y); Boy Scts; Drama Clb; Spanish Clb; SADD; JV Crs Cntry; Im Vllybl; Hon Roll; Air Frc.

TOKAREK, KRISTEN; Freeport Area HS; Sarver, PA; (S); Drama Clb; Band; Concert Band; Jazz Band; Mrchg Band; School Musical; Symp Band; Rep Stu Cncl; Cheerleading; High Hon Roll; IN U Of PA; Pre-Vet.

TOKI, KAREN; Windber Area HS; Windber, PA; (Y); Drama Clb; Ski Clb; Rep Soph Cls; Rep Jr Cls; Sec Stu Cncl; Capt Co-Capt Cheerleading; Trk; Vllybl; High Hon Roll; Stu Of Mnth 85; PA ST Altna Cmps; Tchr.

TOLAN, NOELLE; Dunmore HS; Dunmore, PA; (Y); Am Leg Boys St; Yrbk Phtg; Sec Jr Cls; Sec Sr Cls; Sec Stu Cncl; JV Var Cheerleading; High Hon Roll; Hon Roll; Jr NHS; NHS; Med.

TOLASSI, MICHAEL; North Penn HS; Lansdale, PA; (Y); 171/651; Boy Scts; VICA; Hon Roll; NHS.

TOLBERT, JOEL; Upper Moreland HS; Willow Grove, PA; (Y); Church Yth Grp; Band; Church Choir; Concert Band; Jazz Band; Mrchg Band; Trk; High Hon Roll; Hon Roll; Dist Bnd 85; Temple U; Bus.

TOLERICO, MICHELE; Hazleton SR HS; Hazleton, PA; (Y); FBLA; Flag Corp; Mrchg Band; Hon Roll; FBLA 4th Pl Off Procdur 86; Hmcmng Queen 86; Hazleton; Radlgy.

TOLERICO, RICH; West Hazleton HS; Drums, PA; (Y); 45/250; Church Yth Grp; Scholastic Bowl; Ski Clb; SADD; Varsity Clb; Pres Stu Cncl; Var L Bsbl; Var L Ftbl; Elks Awd; Hon Roll; Schl Spirt Awd 85; Sci.

TOLIVER, WALTER; Saint Josephs Prep; Philadelphia, PA; (Y); Church Yth Grp; Exploring; Library Aide; Rep Stu Cncl; Bsktbl; Ftbl; JV Var Mgr(s); JV Var Score Keeper; Stat L Trk; High Hon Roll; Williams Coll Bk Awd 86; Ntl Attic II Grk Exm With Merit 86; Ntl Attic I Grk Exm With Merit 85; Corp Lwyr.

TOLL, CURTIS; Marple Newtown SR HS; Broomall, PA; (Y); 7/367; Boy Scts; Civic Clb; Capt Debate Tm; Stu Cncl; High Hon Roll; Hon Roll; Jr NHS; NHS; Rotary Awd; Mert Schlrshp U Of Pittsburgh 86; Mrt Schlrshp Brandeis U 86; U Of Pittsburgh; Pol Sci.

TOLTESI, SUZANNE; Freedom HS; Bethlehem, PA; (Y); 89/445; Cmnty Wkr; Color Guard; Drill Tm; Flag Corp; Hon Roll; Penn ST; Elem Ed.

TOMANCHEK, MICHAEL; Hazleton HS; Hazleton, PA; (Y); Computer Clb; Scholastic Bowl; High Hon Roll; PA ST U; Engnrng.

TOMARI, CHRIS; Emmaus HS; Macungie, PA; (Y); Latin Clb; Spanish Clb; Band; Nwsp Stf; JV Mgr(s); JV Score Keeper; Hon Roll; Med.

TOMARO, MARY ANN; Connellsville Area HS; Cnlvle, PA; (Y); 36/440; Pres Church Yth Grp; Pres Band; Chorus; Church Choir; Mrchg Band; School Musical; Symp Band; High Hon Roll; NHS; Spanish NHS; Anchor Hocking Schlrhsp 86; U Of Pittsburgh; Nrsng.

TOMASELLO, DENISE; South Allegheny HS; Liberty Boro, PA; (S); Office Aide; Y-Teens; Band; Concert Band; Mrchg Band; Powder Puff Ftbl; Hon Roll; Bradford Bus Schl; Fshn Mrchnds.

TOMASIC, JOANNE ELEN; West Mifflin Area HS; W Mifflin, PA; (Y); Boy Scts; Church Yth Grp; Office Aide; Science Clb; Teachers Aide; Concert Band; Mrchg Band; Orch; Rep Frsh Cls; Rep Soph Cls; Chem Engrng.

TOMASIC, MARIANNE; Jeannette SR HS; Jeannette, PA; (Y); Drama Clb; French Clb; Ski Clb; School Play; Stat Bsktbl; JV Trk; JV Vllybl; High Hon Roll; Hon Roll; Engl.

TOMASO, JULIE R; Bishop Mc Devitt HS; Harrisburg, PA; (Y); 28/203; Art Clb; Service Clb; Ski Clb; Chorus; Madrigals; School Play; Var Cheerleading; Swmmng; Hon Roll; NHS; Bst Show Juried Art Exhbt 85; 2nd Pl Oil Pntg 84; 2nd Pl Sci Fair & Hnrbl Mntn 84; Art.

TOMASOFSKY, JUDITH; West Scranton HS; Scranton, PA; (Y); Drama Clb; Spanish Clb; Thesps; Flag Corp; Pres Orch; School Musical; School Play; NHS; Trophy 1st Chair Cello; Natl Schl Orch Assoc Awd; Silk Tm Flag Twirling Awd; Marywood Coll; Psych.

TOMASZEWSKI, JEFF; Ambridge Area HS; Freedom, PA; (Y); Am Leg Boys St; Chess Clb; Church Yth Grp; Cmnty Wkr; Math Clb; Spanish Clb; SADD; Crs Cntry; Trk; High Hon Roll; Rep PA Mntgmry Lions Intl Yth Cmp 86; Nmd Hon Lt Col AL ST Militia 86; Elec Engr.

TOMB, DOUGLAS; Greater Johnstown HS; Johnstown, PA; (Y); Boy Scts; Church Yth Grp; Band; Hist.

TOMCIK, LORI; South Allegheny HS; Glassport, PA; (S); VP Church Yth Grp; German Clb; Pres Y-Teens; Band; School Musical; Off Jr Cls; Off Sr Cls; Rep Stu Cncl; High Hon Roll; Hon Roll; IN U PA; Cmptr Sci.

TOMCZAK, PATTY; Linesville HS; Linesville, PA; (Y); 24/70; Church Yth Grp; German Clb; Chorus; Mgr(s); Score Keeper; Stat Vllybl; Hon Roll; Church Choir; Linesville Msc Bstrs Schlrshp 86; Edinboro U Of PA; Elem Educ.

TOMCZYNSKI, MARK; Northeast Catholic HS; Philadelphia, PA; (S); 1/317; Sec Cmnty Wkr; Dance Clb; Science Clb; Nwsp Stf; Yrbk Stf; High Hon Roll; NHS; Latin Awd-Fluncy 84; U Of PA; Pre-Med.

TOMECSKO, KIMBERLY; Canon Mc Millan SR HS; Canonsburg, PA; (Y); 5/342; Science Clb; Drill Tm; Yrbk Ed-Chief; Yrbk Stf; Bsktbl; Cheerleading; Pom Pon; High Hon Roll; NHS; Spanish NHS; PA ST U; Math.

TOMECSKO, MARCI; Canon Mc Millan SR HS; Canonsburg, PA; (Y); Office Aide; Flag Corp; Var L Swmmng; High Hon Roll; Hon Roll; Spanish NHS.

TOMKO, CHRISTINE M; Norwin SR HS; N Huntingdon, PA; (Y); 180/550; Girl Scts; Letterman Clb; Library Aide; Office Aide; Pep Clb; SADD; Yrbk Stf; Stu Cncl; Bsktbl; Capt Var Socr; Tm Sprt Fld Awd 84; Am Legn Best Defnsv Plyr 85; High Excllnc, Ldrshp And Enthusm Tm Sprit Awd 85; Carlow College; Bus Mgmt.

TOMKO, KERRIE; West Middlesex HS; Sharon, PA; (S); French Clb; Concert Band; Mrchg Band; Cheerleading; Hon Roll.

TOMKO, MICHELLE; Bensalem HS; Bensalem, PA; (Y); Office Aide; Pres Jr Cls; Pres Sr Cls; Stu Cncl; Var Capt Cheerleading; Most Spirited In Cheerldng 83-84; Most Valuable 84-85; Med Tech.

TOMKO, STEPHEN VINCENT; Mc Keesport Area HS; White Oak, PA; (Y); French Clb; Drm Mjr(t); Mrchg Band; Pep Band; School Musical; Stage Crew; Symp Band; Rep Stu Cncl; Trk; Hon Roll; Bus.

TOMLINSON, MELISSA; Faith Christian Schl; E Stroudsburg, PA; (S); 1/11; Pres VP Church Yth Grp; Library Aide; Chorus; Church Choir; Yrbk Rptr; Pres Jr Cls; Var Capt Bsktbl; JV Cheerleading; JV Var Sftbl; Var Capt Vllybl; Schlr Athl Awd 85; Dstngshd Christian HS Stu 86; Intl Christian Hnr Soc 84-86; Bloomsburg U; Bio.

TOMLINSON, WENDY; Downingtown SR HS; Downingtown, PA; (Y); 31/623; Office Aide; Chorus; Nwsp Stf; High Hon Roll; Hon Roll; NHS; PA ST; Nrsng.

TOMLJANOVIC, ANTHONY; Bishop Mc Cort HS; Johnstown, PA; (Y); French Clb; Latin Clb; Letterman Clb; Math Clb; School Play; Yrbk Ed-Chief; Yrbk Sprt Ed; Bsktbl; Var L Ftbl; Wt Lftg; Athltc Schlrshp Ftbl; Outstndng Male Of Grad Cls 86; Prncpls Awd For Outstndng Svc To Schl 86; Lafayette Coll; Bio.

TOMLJANOVIC, CHARLES; Bishop Mc Cort HS; Johnstown, PA; (Y); Art Clb; Math Clb; Math Tm; Chorus; Hon Roll; Natl Sci Olympd-Physics 86.

TOMMASIN, LISA; Canon-Mc Millan SR HS; Canonsburg, PA; (Y); Church Yth Grp; Drama Clb; Hosp Aide; Latin Clb; Library Aide; Office Aide; School Play; Stage Crew; Yrbk Stf; Nursing.

TOMPKINS, BETH; George Washington HS; Philadelphia, PA; (Y); 278/797; FNA; Hosp Aide; Intnl Clb; Hon Roll; Masonic Awd; Prfct Atten Awd; Abington Hosp Schl Nrsng Scholar 86; Abington Mem Hosp Schl; Nrsng.

TOMPKINS, CHRISTOPHER; Donegal HS; Mt Joy, PA; (Y); 1/160; Yrbk Stf; Pres Sr Cls; Var L Bsbl; Im Bsktbl; Var L Ftbl; Im Socr; NHS; Opt Clb Awd; Spanish NHS; Val; Coaches Assn Scholar 86; Ed Assn Scholar 86; Merit Scholar Awd 86; Bucknell U; Elec Engrng.

TOMPKINS, IVY LYN; Unionville HS; Kennett Square, PA; (Y); 128/300; Church Yth Grp; Rep Soph Cls; Trs Rep Jr Cls; Sec Stu Cncl; Trk; Hon Roll; Jr NHS; Homecomg Rep 85-86; Mktg.

TOMPKINS, KATHY; South Williamsport Area HS; Duboistown, PA; (Y); Art Clb; French Clb; FBLA; Leo Clb; Library Aide; Office Aide; Chorus; Color Guard; Var Trk; Twrlr; Williamsport Area CC; Med.

TOMSIC III, JOHN; New Brighton Area HS; New Brighton, PA; (Y); Computer Clb; French Clb; Ftbl; Tennis; Wt Lftg; High Hon Roll; Hon Roll; Pre-Med.

TONER, AIMEE; Cardinal O Hara HS; West Chester, PA; (Y); 45/740; Dance Clb; Drama Clb; School Musical; School Play; Hon Roll; NHS; Hnr Rl 85-86; Boston Coll; Nrsng.

TONEY, SHAWN; Valley HS; New Kensington, PA; (Y); 20/224; CAP; Key Clb; Leo Clb; Science Clb; Ski Clb; Spanish Clb; SADD; Bsbl; Trk; Wt Lftg; Elizabeth Stewart Schlrshp, Cmbr Cngrs Awd Wrtrs; OH U; Bio.

TONKIN, DAVID; Brookville Area HS; Emporium, PA; (Y); 5/150; Varsity Clb; Var Bsktbl; Var L Crs Cntry; Var L Trk; High Hon Roll; Hon Roll; NHS; Dist Chmp Trck 85-86; 4 ST Trk Chmpnshps85-86.

TONKIN, WILLIAM; Marion Center HS; Indiana, PA; (Y); Aud/Vis; Camera Clb; Chess Clb; Varsity Clb; Band; Concert Band; Mrchg Band; School Musical; Stu Cncl; Ftbl; IN U PA; Crimnlgy.

TONOFF, BARRY; Steelton-Highspire HS; Steelton, PA; (Y); 1/99; Model UN; Spanish Clb; School Musical; Lit Mag; Hon Roll; NHS; Voice Dem Awd; Crtv Wrtng Clb Awd Poetry 85-86; Mltry Ord WW Citatn 85; Intl Rel.

TONTY, PAMELA JANE; Mercyhurst Prep; Erie, PA; (Y); 3/150; Church Yth Grp; Girl Scts; Key Clb; Pep Clb; VP Spanish Clb; Rep Jr Cls; Bsktbl; Cheerleading; Sftbl; Hon Roll; Tresa Burns Schlrshp 85 & 86; Natl Merit Awd 86; Acdmc All Am 86; Educ.

TOOKES, MARK; Midland HS; Midland, PA; (Y); 6/40; Am Leg Boys St; Sec Church Yth Grp; VP Latin Clb; Chorus; Church Choir; Yrbk Ed-Chief; L Bsktbl; L Ftbl; CC Awd; Cit Awd; Am Leg Awd 84; Mdlnd ST Rnnr Ups Bsktbl 85; Mdlnd Sec C Hamps Bsktbl 86; Bus Mgnt.

TOOLE, DEBORAH ANN; Valley View HS; Peckville, PA; (Y); 21/200; Church Yth Grp; VP French Clb; Trs Chorus; Rep Stu Cncl; Capt Cheerleading; JV Sftbl; Var Trk; Var Vllybl; NHS; Prfct Atten Awd.

TOOLE, PADRAIC; Fox Chapel HS; Cheswick, PA; (Y); 86/322; Im Crs Cntry; L Trk; JV Wrstlng; Hon Roll; AKC Champ Dog 85; MAPS Ldrshp Training U Pittsburgh 84-85; Natl Latin Exam Outstndng Cert 86; Psych.

TOOLE, PATRICIA; Pittston Area SR HS; Pittston, PA; (Y); 61/319; Church Yth Grp; Computer Clb; Drama Clb; Math Clb; Science Clb; Ski Clb; Variety Show; Yrbk Stf; Hon Roll; Prfct Atten Awd; Cert Achvt Citizens Voice 86; USAF; Invntry Mgt Spec.

TOOMEY, DENNIS; Lebanon Catholic HS; Lebanon, PA; (Y); Aud/Vis; Debate Tm; Spanish Clb; VICA; School Play; Variety Show; Bsbl; Bsktbl; Golf; Timer.

TOONDER, BRIAN; Movduian Acad; Allentown, PA; (Y); Ski Clb; Spanish Clb; Chorus; Variety Show; Golf; Tennis; High Hon Roll; Hon Roll; Aero Engr.

TOONE, ROBERT; Unionville HS; Kennett Sq, PA; (Y); 5/300; Cmnty Wkr; Scholastic Bowl; Nwsp Rptr; Var L Bsktbl; JV Tennis; High Hon Roll; Mu Alp Tht; NHS; Ntl Merit Ltr.

TOPAR, DAVID; Penns Manor HS; Alverda, PA; (Y); Church Yth Grp; SADD; Band; Chorus; Concert Band; Mrchg Band; School Musical; Hon Roll.

TOPAZ, RHONDA; Lawer Moreland HS; Huntingdon Valley, PA; (S); 48/216; FBLA; Var Capt Cheerleading; Var Tennis; Hon Roll; Hmcmng Qun 86; Bus.

TOPOR, RICHARD M; Moon Area HS; Coraopolis, PA; (Y); Ftbl; Wt Lftg; Wrstlng.

TOPPER, TAMMY; Littlestown SR HS; Hanover, PA; (Y); Color Guard; Mrchg Band; Yrbk Stf; Sec Frsh Cls; Sec Soph Cls; Sec Jr Cls; Sec Sr Cls; Sec Stu Cncl; JV Sftbl; Var Tennis; Schlrshp For Being Sprt Of JR Mss Wnr 86; Trvl Agnt.

TORBOLI, LISA; Trinity HS; Washington, PA; (Y); 10/374; Pep Clb; Var Crs Cntry; Var L Trk; High Hon Roll; Sports Med.

TORELLI, AMY; Moon SR HS; Coraopolis, PA; (Y); 29/306; Trs Church Yth Grp; Cmnty Wkr; FBLA; German Clb; Key Clb; Mgr(s); JV Vllybl; Hon Roll; NHS; Bus.

TORGENT, PAULA; Highlands SR HS; Brackenridge, PA; (Y); Girl Scts; Hosp Aide; Intnl Clb; Key Clb; SADD; Band; Chorus; Drm Mjr(t); Var L Swmmng; NHS; Girl Scout Slvr Awd 85; Phrmcy.

TORIELLO, CHRISTINA; Nazareth Acad; Holland, PA; (Y); Cmnty Wkr; French Clb; Pep Clb; Church Choir; VP Soph Cls; Pres Jr Cls; Var Cheerleading; High Hon Roll; Hon Roll; Georgetown; Jrnlsm.

TORKOS, KATHY; Mc Keesport SR HS; Mckeesport, PA; (Y); 8/380; Library Aide; Office Aide; Stu Cncl; Cheerleading; Trk; Vllybl; High Hon Roll; Trs NHS; Rotry Hnr Stu 85-86; Clg Clb Schlrshp 86; Army Resrv Schlr Athlt Awd 86; PA ST; Chem Engrg.

TORMEY, MICHELLE; Clearfield Area HS; Woodland, PA; (Y); Girl Scts; Hosp Aide; Office Aide; High Hon Roll; Hon Roll; Dubois Bus Coll; Med Secy.

TORNICHIO, JONI; Canon Mc Millan SR HS; Canonsburg, PA; (Y); 33/400; Art Clb; English Clb; Rep Latin Clb; Q&S; Ed Nwsp Stf; Yrbk Rptr; Ed Yrbk Stf; Rep Stu Cncl; Hon Roll; Prfct Atten Awd; PTA Art Exllnce 84; U Of Pittsburg; Doctor.

TORO, ANGELA; Frankford HS; Philadelphia, PA; (Y); Cmnty Wkr; German Clb; High Hon Roll; Hon Roll; Hgh Hnr Roll 84-85.

TORO, CHRISTOPHER; Bishop Hannan HS; Old Forge, PA; (Y); 13/128; Debate Tm; Spanish Clb; Nwsp Rptr; Crs Cntry; Hon Roll; NHS; Duquesne U; Fnce Prof.

TOROCKIO, DANA; Greater Latrobe SR HS; Latrobe, PA; (Y); Letterman Clb; Library Aide; Pep Clb; Yrbk Stf; VP Soph Cls; Rep Stu Cncl; Var L Cheerleading; Var JV Mat Maids; High Hon Roll; Hon Roll; Elementary Educ.

TOROK, KRISTY; Monessen HS; Monessen, PA; (Y); 2/87; Teachers Aide; Nwsp Rptr; Yrbk Rptr; Stu Cncl; Twrlr; High Hon Roll; VP NHS; Sal; Chorus; Mrchg Band; Carol Naccarato Schlrshp Awd; Monessen Yth Educ Assn-Asst Treas; Brdcstng Stf Mgr; Ushers Clb; IN U Of PA; Elem Ed.

TORPEY, DREW; Northeast Catholic HS; Philadelphia, PA; (Y); Hosp Aide; ROTC; Varsity Clb; JV Bsbl; JV L Ftbl; JV L Wrstlng; Hon Roll; Actvties Awd; Expert Small Bore Rifle; Lib Arts.

TORQUATO, THERESA; Shade HS; Central City, PA; (Y); 14/73; FBLA; Ski Clb; Varsity Clb; Chorus; Nwsp Phtg; Yrbk Stf; Off Stu Cncl; Var L Bsktbl; Var Trk; Hon Roll; Natl Acctg Awd 85; Montgomery CC; Psych.

TORRES, MYRNELITH; Little Flower HS; Philadelphia, PA; (Y); Camera Clb; French Clb; Stu Mnth & Yr Alg 85-86; 2nd Hnrs 84-86; 1st Hnrs 83-84; Dentstry.

TOSH, BRIAN; Beaver Area SR HS; Beaver, PA; (Y); 14/179; Church Yth Grp; Pres French Clb; Band; Jazz Band; Mrchg Band; School Musical; JV Bsktbl; Var Swmmng; Var Capt Tennis; High Hon Roll; Acadmc Awd Sch 85 & 86.

TOSOLT, JOSEPH; Scranton Preparatory Schl; Moosic, PA; (Y); Boy Scts; Jazz Band; Im JV Ftbl; Im Var Trk; Im JV Wt Lftg; Boys Clb Am; Band; Variety Show; Eagle Awd 85; Bus.

TOSSONA, COREEN; Wissahickon SR HS; Norristown, PA; (S); 21/276; Art Clb; Drama Clb; School Play; Yrbk Stf; Sftbl; NHS; PA ST U; Comm.

TOTANI, KRISTAN; Pen Argyle Area HS; Pen Argyl, PA; (Y); Church Yth Grp; Math Clb; Pep Clb; Spanish Clb; Var Powder Puff Ftbl; JV Sftbl; Prfct Atten Awd; An Aidein The Special Olympics 85; Churchmans Schl Bus; Bus Admin.

TOTH, BETH ALISON; Ringgold HS; Monongahela, PA; (Y); 52/325; FNA; Office Aide; Service Clb; Ski Clb; Chorus; School Play; Nwsp Stf; Ed Yrbk Ed-Chief; Yrbk Stf; Stu Cncl; Mercy Hostp Schl Nrsg; Nrsg.

TOTH, DEBORAH; Lakeland JR SR HS; Olyphant, PA; (Y); 41/151; Pres Sec Church Yth Grp; Varsity Clb; Church Choir; Rep Stu Cncl; Var L Bsktbl; Coach Actv; Var L Sftbl; Rep Vllybl; Hon Roll; Penn ST U; Phys Ed.

TOTH, GAYLE; Belle Vernon Area HS; Belle Vernon, PA; (Y); Art Clb; Ski Clb; Yrbk Ed-Chief; Capt Cheerleading; Hon Roll; Court Stengrphr.

TOTH, JANET; Peters Twp HS; Mcmurray, PA; (Y); 51/250; Church Yth Grp; Girl Scts; Varsity Clb; Rep Stu Cncl; Var Swmmng; High Hon Roll; Hon Roll; Arch.

TOTH, JOHN; Northampton SR HS; Northampton, PA; (S); Chess Clb; VICA; High Hon Roll; NHS; Milwaukee Schl-Engrng; Comp Sci.

TOTH, KIM; Tunkhannock Area HS; Factoryville, PA; (Y); 53/320; Aud/Vis; German Clb; Rep Soph Cls; Rep Sr Cls; Capt L Bsktbl; Cit Awd; Hon Roll; Band; Concert Band; Mrchg Band; Frgn Exchng Clb 85; All Star Cnfrnc Bsktbl Tm 86; Vrsty Bsktbl Mst Dedctd Awd 86; Wilma Boyd Career Schl; Airline.

TOTH, MATTHEW; Yough SR HS; Smithton, PA; (Y); 1/224; Church Yth Grp; Computer Clb; Ski Clb; Spanish Clb; Trk; High Hon Roll; NHS; Ntl Merit Ltr; Val; Pres Schlrshp; Schlstc Awd 85-86; Washington Jefferson Coll; Phys.

TOTH, MICHELE; Liberty HS; Bethlehem, PA; (S); 26/417; School Musical; School Play; Nwsp Ed-Chief; Yrbk Ed-Chief; Sec Jr Cls; Sec Sr Cls; Twrlr; Hon Roll; Drama Clb; Library Aide; Cntry III Ldr 85; Cohen Tripship 3 Wk Exch Stu Japan 85; Syracuse U; Engl Comm.

TOTH, MICHELLE; Hazelton HS; Hazleton, PA; (Y); 117/392; Church Yth Grp; FNA; Scholastic Bowl; Yrbk Stf; Var L Bsktbl; Var L Sftbl; Wilkes Coll; Nrsng.

TOUBO, MICHELLE; Moshannon Valley JR SR HS; Madera, PA; (Y); 28/133; Church Yth Grp; Spanish Clb; SADD; Varsity Clb; School Play; Yrbk Stf; Var Co-Capt Cheerleading; Hon Roll; Spirit Awds Chrldng 84-86; PA ST U; Psych.

TOUVELL, CHARLENE; Brookville Area HS; Brookville, PA; (S); 6/142; Key Clb; Chorus; Orch; Stu Cncl; High Hon Roll; Hon Roll; Jr NHS; Natl Hstry Day Cntst Awd Wnnr 81-85; Anchr & Rprtr Actn Kds Nws 82-85; Comm.

TOVEN, NIKI; Punxsutauney SR HS; Anita, PA; (Y); Chess Clb; Dance Clb; Girl Scts; Band; Chorus; Color Guard; Variety Show; Stat Bsbl; Stat Wrstlng; Prfct Atten Awd.

TOWER, CRAIG; Moon Area HS; Coraopolis, PA; (Y); 58/360; Church Yth Grp; Exploring; Letterman Clb; Var L Bsktbl; JV Crs Cntry; Var L Trk; Hon Roll; All Str Tm Bsktbl Tourn 84; Hnbl Mntn All Sectn Tm Bsktbl 86; Mth.

TOWERS, MARY ANN; Cardinal Brennan HS; Ashland, PA; (Y); 27/50; Church Yth Grp; Library Aide; Chorus; Color Guard; School Musical; Yrbk Stf; Score Keeper; Sftbl; Vllybl; Hon Roll; Outstndng Achvt Awds 84-86; Nrsng.

TOWNER, SARAH R; Cumberland Valley HS; Camp Hill, PA; (Y); 15/505; Orch; School Musical; Hon Roll; NHS; Tchrs Assc Schlrshp 86; JR Wednsdy Clb Schlrshp 86; Natl Schl Orchestra Awd 86; U Of Richmond; French.

TOWNSEND, JILL; Neshaming HS; Penndel, PA; (Y); 5/756; Cheerleading; Gym; Mgr(s); Sftbl; High Hon Roll; Hon Roll; NHS; Gymnght Chrldrs 84-86; Lawyer.

TOWNSEND, RESHA; Kiski Area HS; Vandergrift, PA; (Y); Am Leg Aux Girls St; Pep Clb; Chorus; Pres Frsh Cls; Sec Soph Cls; Rep Stu Cncl; JV Capt Cheerleading; Hon Roll.

TOY, GAIL; North East HS; Northeast, PA; (Y); 28/150; AFS; FBLA; VP FHA; Office Aide; Chorus; Color Guard; Drill Tm; Nwsp Stf; Capt Pom Pon; Hon Roll; Robert Morris Coll; Mktg.

TOY, TIM; Freedom HS; Bethlehem, PA; (Y); Drama Clb; German Clb; Political Wkr; Chorus; School Play; Pres Soph Cls; Pres Stu Cncl; Ice Hcky; Socr; Hon Roll.

TRACE, ROB; Pottstown HS; Pottstown, PA; (Y); 40/200; Jazz Band; Nwsp Stf; Yrbk Stf; Lit Mag; Off Soph Cls; Off Jr Cls; Off Sr Cls; Stu Cncl; Var Capt Bsbl; Hon Roll; Westchester U.

TRACEY, SONJA LA RUE; New Oxford SR HS; New Oxford, PA; (Y); FBLA; FNA; Red Cross Aide; Stage Crew; Hon Roll; Gregg Typng Awd 85; Acad Excllnc Awd 86; May Day Exhbt Rbbns 85-86; Comp Op.

TRACHTENBERG, DAVID; Upper Moreland HS; Huntingdon Valley, PA; (Y); 22/270; Aud/Vis; Camera Clb; Drama Clb; Im Socr; High Hon Roll; NHS; Media Svc Awd 84-86; U CA-LOS Angeles; Radio.

TRACY, CINDY; Tamaqua Area HS; Tamaqua, PA; (Y); 14/168; Library Aide; Q&S; Nwsp Sprt Ed; Var JV Bsbl; French Hon Soc; NHS; Abe Hassan Memrl Schlrshp 86; Schlstc Jrnlst Yr 86; Top Engl Stu 86; Millersville U; Math.

TRACY, TIMOTHY S; Chartiers Valley HS; Pittsburgh, PA; (Y); 111/366; Ski Clb; Varsity Clb; Var Golf; Capt Ice Hcky; Var Tennis; MVP Hocky Plyr 85 & 86; Wstrn PA Tp 20 Hcky Plyr 85 & 86; MVP PA ST AA Chmpnshp Hcky Game 86; Nrthestrn U Boston MA; Bus.

TRAGGIAI, REGINA; Knoch JR SR HS; Cabot, PA; (Y); Church Yth Grp; Cmnty Wkr; Chorus; Concert Band; Jazz Band; Madrigals; Mrchg Band; Orch; School Musical; High Hon Roll; Butler Cnty JR Miss Finlst 86-87; Mid E Music Conf At Duquesne Univ 86; Butler Cnty All Star Band 86; Elizabethtown; Music Therapy.

TRAGO, ANN; Carbondale Area JR SR HS; Carbondale, PA; (Y); 4/150; Art Clb; FBLA; Pres Science Clb; Ski Clb; Spanish Clb; Varsity Clb; JV Var Fld Hcky; NHS; FBLA Ldrshp Cnfrnc 85; U Of Scranton; Pschlgy.

TRAIN, TIMOTHY; Delaware County Christian HS; Newtown Sq, PA; (Y); 21/78; Math Tm; Speech Tm; Chorus; Church Choir; Concert Band; Madrigals; Variety Show; Im Gym; High Hon Roll; Hon Roll; Erly Bach Mdl Ntl Guld Adtns 85; Dstngshd Chrstn HS Stu Awd 85-86; 1st Pl Dorothy Sutton Pino Comptn.

TRAINA, LORI; Solanco HS; Kirkwood, PA; (Y); Teachers Aide; Yrbk Phtg; Bsktbl; Trk; Hon Roll; Trvl Trng.

TRAINOR, BELINDA; Lebanon Catholic HS; Grantville, PA; (Y); 30/62; Library Aide; Var Bowling; Hon Roll; Harrisburg Area CC; Data Proc.

TRAMA, LAURA; W Scranton HS; Scranton, PA; (Y); 31/215; Debate Tm; Drama Clb; NFL; Speech Tm; Thesps; School Play; Pom Pon; Hon Roll; NHS; Mrywd Coll; Psych.

TRAN, CUONG; Allentown Central Catholic HS; Allentown, PA; (Y); Chess Clb; Math Tm; Nwsp Stf; Yrbk Stf; Rep Soph Cls; VP Jr Cls; VP Stu Cncl; Var Crs Cntry; Hon Roll; Dntstry.

TRAN, DUNG; Souderton Area HS; Philadelphia, PA; (Y); Art Clb; Church Yth Grp; French Clb; Chorus; Nwsp Stf; Yrbk Stf; Lit Mag; Fld Hcky; Trk; Hon Roll; Dplm Merit For Spnsh 85; Cert Of Achvt Music 83; Dr & Mrs George Stimmel Schlrshp 86; Penn ST U; Tchr.

TRAN, NGA; J P Mc Caskey HS; Lancaster, PA; (Y); 60/473; AFS; 4-H; FBLA; 4-H Awd; Hon Roll; Prfct Atten Awd; Accntng.

TRAN, NGA; West Catholic Girls HS; Philadelphia, PA; (Y); 5/240; French Clb; Mathletes; Orch; Yrbk Stf; Hon Roll; NHS; U Of PA; Hlth Svc Admn.

TRAN, THANH; Central Bucks East HS; Warrington, PA; (Y); Church Yth Grp; Mathletes; JV Socr; NHS; Engrng.

TRAN, THU HA; West Catholic HS For Girls; Philadelphia, PA; (Y); 10/240; French Clb; FBLA; Mathletes; Church Choir; Variety Show; Capt Vllybl; High Hon Roll; Hon Roll; NHS; Prfct Atten Awd; Vllybl 1st Tm Plyr 84-86; Frnscs Tm 83-84; Ldrshp For Ftr Secys 86; Bus Admin.

TRAN, THUY; Harrisburg HS; Harrisburg, PA; (S); 12/386; Intnl Clb; Math Clb; Science Clb; Stu Cncl; NHS; PA ST U; Med.

TRAN, TRANG; Marian Catholic HS; Lansford, PA; (Y); 20/115; Pep Clb; Chorus; Drill Tm; Mrchg Band; Yrbk Stf; Pres French Hon Soc; Hon Roll; NHS; Towson U; Accptnl Thrpy.

TRAN, YEN; West Phila Cath Girls HS; Philadelphia, PA; (Y); 40/285; Debate Tm; Varsity Clb; Orch; Vllybl; Hon Roll; Med.

TRANGUCH, KATY; Bishop Hafey HS; Hazleton, PA; (Y); 40/130; Church Yth Grp; Spanish Clb; SADD; Y-Teens; Yrbk Stf; Rep Frsh Cls; Rep Soph Cls; Rep Jr Cls; Pres Stu Cncl; Var Capt Bsktbl; All Area 2nd Tm Bsktbl 86; Wmns Sprts Fndtn All Star Awd 86; Spec Ed.

TRANSEAU, STACEY; South Williamsport SR HS; Williamsport, PA; (Y); Key Clb; Leo Clb; Spanish Clb; Band; Stu Cncl; Sftbl; Trk; Hon Roll.

TRAPANI, JOSEPHINE J; Bishop O Hara HS; Dunmore, PA; (Y); 24/125; Drama Clb; Latin Clb; Ski Clb; Spanish Clb; Chorus; Rep Jr Cls; JV Var Cheerleading; High Hon Roll; Hon Roll; NHS; Marywood; Nrsng.

TRAPNELL, STEPHEN STEVE; Manheim Township HS; Lancaster, PA; (Y); 38/313; Church Yth Grp; Cmnty Wkr; Church Choir; Nwsp Rptr; Ed Lit Mag; High Hon Roll; Lebanon Vly Coll Pres Ldrshp Schlrp & Hnrs Prog 86-87; Lebanon Valley Coll; Lib Arts.

TRAPP, JILL; Northwestern Lehigh HS; Germansville, PA; (Y); Hosp Aide; SADD; School Play; Sec Stu Cncl; Cheerleading; Coach Actv; Twrlr; Hon Roll; Acad All Amer 86; US Stu Cncl Awd 86; Kutztown U; Erly Chldhd Elem Ed.

TRAPP, WILLIAM; Bethlehem Catholic HS; Bethlehem, PA; (Y); Ski Clb; Stage Crew; Rep Jr Cls; Rep Stu Cncl.

TRASK, SCOTT; Mechanicsburg Area SR HS; Mechanicsburg, PA; (Y); 29/311; CAP; Exploring; Trk; High Hon Roll; Hon Roll; NHS; Ntl Merit Ltr; Pro Race Drvr.

TRASK, TINA; Central Catholic HS; Whitehall, PA; (Y); Math Clb; L Crs Cntry; Im Ftbl; Var L Sftbl; Var Tennis; High Hon Roll; Hon Roll; Pltcl Sci.

TRAUB, KENNY; Hazleton SR HS; Hazleton, PA; (Y); Aud/Vis; Var L Bsbl; Ftbl; St Joseph Hosp; Radlgy.

TRAUGER, SCOTT; Liberty HS; Bethlehem, PA; (Y); 100/510; Ski Clb; Var Ftbl; Im Wt Lftg; Penn ST; Engrng.

TRAUGH, DANIELLA; Berwick SR HS; Berwick, PA; (Y); VP Church Yth Grp; Hosp Aide; Pep Clb; Yth Ftns Achvt Awd 84-86; Phys Thrpy.

TRAUNER, MARYELLEN; Shaler Area HS; Allison Pk, PA; (Y); 36/545; Office Aide; Ski Clb; Variety Show; High Hon Roll; Rotary Awd; Hlth Ocup Stu Of Amer 84-86; 1st Wnnr Medl Lab Asst 86; Mercy Hosp Schl Nrsg; Nrsg.

TRAUTERMAN, JAMES; Seneca Valley SR HS; Evans City, PA; (Y); Church Yth Grp; Trs 4-H; 4-H Awd; Physics.

TRAUTLEIN, THOMAS J; Central Dauphin East HS; Harrisburg, PA; (Y); Pres Church Yth Grp; Ski Clb; Chorus; School Musical; Rep Jr Cls; Var Socr; Im Vllybl; Hon Roll; Rotary Awd; Best Actor Drama Festvl 84.

TRAUTMAN, CINDY; Elco HS; Myerstown, PA; (Y); 22/179; VP Chorus; Color Guard; Rep Mrchg Band; Bsktbl; Sftbl; Tennis; Trk; Rotary Awd; MVP-BSKTBL; All Cnty Tm-Bsktbl; Mst Wins-Tnns.

TRAUTMAN, KIMBERLY A; Central HS; E Freedom, PA; (Y); Var L Cheerleading; Exec Secy.

TRAUTMAN, SHELLY; Sto-Rox SR HS; Mc Kees Rocks, PA; (Y); Boys Clb Am; FBLA; Y-Teens; Yrbk Phtg; Yrbk Stf; Trs Jr Cls; Art Awd, Good Mnnrs Awd 80-81; Crt Steno.

TRAUTZ, THOM; Northeast Catholic HS; Philadelphia, PA; (Y); 2/362; Mathletes; Science Clb; Chorus; Concert Band; Mrchg Band; NHS; Al-Cthlc Band Hnr 84; Grmn II Tp Stu Awd 86; Scintst.

TRAVERS, COLLEEN; Merion Mercy Acad; Havertown, PA; (Y); 34/87; Church Yth Grp; French Clb; Office Aide; Science Clb; Service Clb; Variety Show; High Hon Roll; Hon Roll; Awds Champnshp Irish Dncng; Villanova U; Accntg.

TRAVIS, KATRINA; Frankford HS; Philadelphia, PA; (Y); Red Cross Aide; Service Clb; Rep Soph Cls; Sec Jr Cls; Pres Sr Cls; Rep Stu Cncl; Var Fld Hcky; JV Sftbl; Var Tennis.

TRAVIS, MICHAEL; Dayton HS; Smicksburg, PA; (Y); Varsity Clb; Band; Chorus; School Musical; Sr Cls; Bsbl; Bsktbl; Ftbl; Hon Roll; NHS; U Of Pittsburgh; Engrg.

TRAYLOR, TONYA; University City HS; Philadelphia, PA; (Y); JA; School Play; Jr Cls; Cheerleading; Hon Roll; Charles E Ellis Scholar Fndtn 82-84; Pep Pgm Outstndng Achvt Awd 85-86; Bus Adm.

TREASTER, CHRIS; Chief Logan HS; Yeagertown, PA; (Y); Trs Spanish Clb; Varsity Clb; Rep Stu Cncl; JV Var Bsbl; JV Var Ftbl; Prfct Atten Awd; Acctg.

TREECE, GEORGIA; Mapletown JR SR HS; Greensboro, PA; (Y); GAA; Varsity Clb; Yrbk Stf; Rep Soph Cls; Rep Jr Cls; Rep Stu Cncl; Var Capt Cheerleading; Im Vllybl; Hon Roll; Hmcmng Ct Atten 85; PA Commercial Inc; Bus Adm.

TREESE, JASON; Lewisburg Area HS; Lewisburg, PA; (Y); Church Yth Grp; Science Clb; Spanish Clb; Rep Frsh Cls; Rep Soph Cls; Var Bsktbl; L Socr; Jr NHS; NHS; Ntl Merit Ltr; Pre-Med.

TREFELNER, RICHARD A; Leechburg Area HS; Leechburg, PA; (Y); 9/70; Pres Church Yth Grp; Drama Clb; Concert Band; Mrchg Band; Pep Band; Yrbk Stf; L Bsbl; L Bsktbl; Hon Roll; Hnr Grad 86; Leechburg Area Mthrs Clb Scholar 86; Leechburg Ed Assn Scholar 86; IN U PA; Acctng.

TREFFINGER, CHRISTINE A; Upper Perkiomen HS; East Greenville, PA; (Y); Am Leg Aux Girls St; Band; Concert Band; Mrchg Band; Stu Cncl; Stat Bsbl; Var Powder Puff Ftbl; JV Sftbl; Var Capt Swmmng; Hon Roll; Millersville U; Earth Sci Tchr.

TREGO, CHRISSY; Downingtown HS; Glenmoore, PA; (Y); 117/563; French Clb; GAA; Ski Clb; Concert Band; Yrbk Stf; Rep Stu Cncl; Var Capt Fld Hcky; Var Lcrss; Hon Roll; NHS; 2 Yr Vrsty Lacross Awd 86.

TREGO, PAM; Downingtown SR HS; Downingtown, PA; (Y); Library Aide; Nwsp Rptr; Var Fld Hcky; Var Trk; Gvt.

TREIBER, CELESTE; Bethlehem Catholic HS; Bethlehem, PA; (Y); Key Clb; Ski Clb; Ed Yrbk Stf; Stat Bsbl; Var Crs Cntry; High Hon Roll; Bus.

TREIBLE, LISA; Pius X HS; Bangor, PA; (Y); 12/32; Drama Clb; Lib 4-H; Pep Clb; School Play; Nwsp Rptr; Nwsp Stf; Yrbk Rptr; Yrbk Stf; Var Cheerleading; 4-H Awd; Kings Coll; Hlth Cr Mngmnt.

TREIMAN, PHILIP; Lower Moreland HS; Huntingdon Valley, PA; (S); Pres Science Clb; Band; Concert Band; Jazz Band; Mrchg Band; Pep Band; Nwsp Stf; High Hon Roll; Hon Roll; NHS; Med.

TREJCHEL, SHIRLEY; St Benedict Acad; Erie, PA; (Y); 5/63; Am Leg Aux Girls St; Quiz Bowl; Variety Show; Rep Stu Cncl; Bsktbl; Sftbl; Hon Roll; Ntl Hnrs Soc Schlrshp 83; Soc Studys Awd 85; Lois Hanlin Dahlkemper Bus Schlrshp 84.

TRELLA, MARK; Monaca JR SR HS; Monaca, PA; (Y); 18/90; School Musical; Sec Jr Cls; Var Bsktbl; Var L Ftbl; Hon Roll; Prfct Atten Awd; Gannon Pitt; Physcl Ther.

TRELLI, JOSEPH A; Plymouth-Whitemarsh HS; Miquon, PA; (Y); Boy Scts; Rep Stu Cncl; Var L Ftbl; Wt Lftg; High Hon Roll; Hon Roll; Ordr Of Arrow Chptr 85; Ad Altare Dei Awd 86; Wrld Consvtn Awd 86; Biochem.

TREMBA, MICHAEL; Redbank Valley HS; New Bethlehem, PA; (Y); 12/120; Drama Clb; French Clb; School Play; Stage Crew; Hon Roll; Acad Hnr Soc 85-86; PA ST U; Advrtsng.

TREMEWEN, SUSAN; Archbishop Wood H S For Girls; Holland, PA; (Y); 51/248; Mathletes; Capt Band; Capt Concert Band; Capt Mrchg Band; School Musical; Variety Show; Hon Roll; Prfct Atten Awd; Acctg I Mdl 86; All Cath Bnd 86; Villanova; Bus.

TREMITIERE, DOUGLAS; William Penn SR HS; York, PA; (Y); 5/348; Church Yth Grp; French Clb; School Musical; Stu Cncl; Swmmng; NHS; Rotary Exchange Progrm 83-84; Georgetown U; Foreign Svc.

TRENKLE, MELANIE; Bishop Mccort HS; Johnstown, PA; (Y); 33/155; German Clb; Pep Clb; Ski Clb; Chorus; School Musical; Nwsp Stf; Yrbk Stf; Sec Jr Cls; Sec Sr Cls; Hon Roll; Penn ST; Physcl Thrpy.

TRENT, RICHARD; Glendale JR SR HS; Coalport, PA; (Y); 27/86; Church Yth Grp; Cmnty Wkr; Science Clb; Mgr Band; Mgr Concert Band; Mgr Mrchg Band; Pep Band; Yrbk Stf; Hon Roll; JP Sousa Awd; USMC.

TRENTLY, ALLAN; Mid Valley HS; Olyphant, PA; (Y); Boy Scts; Chess Clb; Computer Clb; Wt Lftg; Cit Awd; Hon Roll; Eagle Sct 86; U Of Scrntn; Forestry.

TRESKY, MARIAN; Quigley HS; Mars, PA; (S); Math Clb; Nwsp Rptr; High Hon Roll; NHS; Toastmastrs Publc Spkng Awd 84; Exprt Rhymthmc Typng Cert 85; Psychlgy.

TRESSA, SHARON; J M Coughlin HS; Plains, PA; (Y); 42/355; Church Yth Grp; French Clb; Nwsp Rptr; Yrbk Stf; Socr; High Hon Roll; Hon Roll; Jr NHS; NHS; Hopwood Smmr Schlrshp Pgm 86; Art.

TRESSLER, DEBRA ANN; Elderton JR SR HS; Spring Church, PA; (Y); 5/100; Church Yth Grp; Pres Spanish Clb; Varsity Clb; Color Guard; Stu Cncl; Sftbl; Vllybl; High Hon Roll; NHS; Pres Acad Ftnss Awd 86; IN U Penn; Crmnlgy.

TRESSLER, DIANE; Belleponte SR HS; Bellefonte, PA; (Y); Pres Church Yth Grp; Var L Sftbl; Im Vllybl; Hon Roll.

TRESSLER, JAMES; Bald Eagle Nittany HS; Lamar, PA; (Y); 1/125; Model UN; Rep Stu Cncl; Bausch & Lomb Sci Awd; High Hon Roll; Trs NHS; Val; Kathleen A Golden Govt Awd 86; Pres Acad Ftns Awd 86; Superior Dlgtn-Mdl UN 85; Lock Haven U; Crmc Engrng.

TRESSLER, SUSAN; Millersburg Area HS; Millersburg, PA; (Y); French Clb; Mrchg Band; Yrbk Bus Mgr; Powder Puff Ftbl; Hon Roll; NHS; Mid Penn Bnk Scholar 86; Geraldine Seal Mem Scholar 86; Harrisburg Area CC; Med Lab.

TRETTEL, KRISTAN; Mercy Hurst Prep; Erie, PA; (Y); Am Leg Aux Girls St; Exploring; Rep Jr Cls; Trs Sr Cls; Rep Stu Cncl; JV Var Cheerleading; Hon Roll; Yth Fr Undrstndng Exchng Stu To England 86.

TREXLER, DENISE; William Allen HS; Allentown, PA; (Y); 69/604; Service Clb; Varsity Clb; Yrbk Stf; Rep Jr Cls; Rep Stu Cncl; Var Bsktbl; Var Trk; Hon Roll; Jr NHS; NHS; Honrbl Mention Mc Cormick Book Awds 86; Polit Sci.

TREXLER, MELISSA; Northampton HS; Northampton, PA; (Y); 41/461; Chorus; JV Fld Hcky; JV Trk; Hon Roll; NHS; Muhlenberg Coll; Pre-Med.

TREXLER, TODD; Southern Lehigh HS; Coopersburg, PA; (Y); 21/225; VP Varsity Clb; Capt Band; Capt Concert Band; Co-Capt Bsbl; Co-Capt Ftbl; High Hon Roll; NHS; 2nd-Tm All Str Bsbl 85; 2 Hnrbl Mntns Ftbl Placekckr 83 & 84; Penn ST.

TRIANTAFILLOU, GREG; Upper Darby HS; Upper Darby, PA; (Y); Pres Church Yth Grp; Dance Clb; Office Aide; Rep Frsh Cls; Rep Stu Cncl; JV Bsktbl; Hon Roll; Youth Pres Of Argeriniotico Soc 85; Pres Of GOYA 85; Chrmn Of The Bd Of Argeriniotico 86; Temple; Bus Admin.

TRIBUIANI, MELISSA; Upper Darby HS; Upper Darby, PA; (Y); 14/629; Hosp Aide; Service Clb; Spanish Clb; Teachers Aide; Yrbk Stf; Rep Jr Cls; JV Trk; High Hon Roll; Drama Clb; Red Cross Aide; Spnsh III Awd 86; Amer Stds Awd 86; Med.

TRICE, SCOTT; Mt Pleasant Area HS; Mt Pleasant, PA; (Y); Chess Clb; Band; Wrstlng; High Hon Roll; Hon Roll.

TRICE, TRACEY; Greensburg Central Catholic HS; Mt Pleasant, PA; (Y); Church Yth Grp; Cmnty Wkr; Exploring; Im Sftbl; JV Trk; High Hon Roll; NHS; Med.

TRICHON, JEFF; Council Rock HS; Holland, PA; (Y); 40/845; Church Yth Grp; Spanish Clb; Concert Band; Mrchg Band; Pep Band; Tennis; Hon Roll; NHS; Duke U; Math.

TRICK, MICHELLE; Cocalico HS; Reinholds, PA; (Y); 2/169; Computer Clb; Library Aide; Quiz Bowl; Band; Chorus; Concert Band; Mrchg Band; School Play; High Hon Roll; Prfct Atten Awd; Soc Stu Grp Awd 84-85 & 85-86; Frgn Lang Awd, Modern Miss Schlrshp Pgnt 85-86; Juniata Coll; Soc Wrk.

TRICKER, ANGELA S; Bellefonte Area SR HS; Bellefonte, PA; (Y); 2/237; Band; Flag Corp; Mrchg Band; Var Cheerleading; Var Trk; Im Vllybl; High Hon Roll; Hon Roll; NHS; Scholar Awd 83 & 84; Dentstry.

TRICOLO, TONI LYNN; Mohawk JR SR HS; Edinburg, PA; (Y); Church Yth Grp; Trs FBLA; Latin Clb; Pep Clb; Band; Concert Band; Mrchg Band; Mgr School Musical; Mgr School Play; Stu Cncl; Entrepreneurship Awd For FBLA 85; Youngstown ST U; Elem Educ.

TRIDICO, ANTHONY; Quigley HS; Midland, PA; (S); 16/115; Church Yth Grp; Math Tm; Science Clb; Service Clb; Band; Concert Band; Var L Bsktbl; Var L Golf; High Hon Roll; NHS; PA JR Acad Of Sci 3rd Pl; Svc Awd; Hstry Awd; Chem.

TRIETSCH, IRITH; Cheltenham HS; Cheltenham, PA; (Y); Latin Clb; Science Clb; School Musical; Lit Mag; NHS; Ntl Merit SF; Drama Clb; JCL; Acpl Chr; Sci Fair 85; Marian Cum Laude Natl Latn Exm 86; Vet Med.

TRIGONA, ANTHONY; Bishop Mc Cort HS; Johnstown, PA; (Y); Cmnty Wkr; Ski Clb; High Hon Roll; Hon Roll; Mu Alp Tht; NHS.

TRIMARKI, MICHAEL D; Burgettstown JR SR HS; Burgettstown, PA; (Y); French Clb; Science Clb; Ski Clb; Speech Tm; SADD; Yrbk Stf; Pres Stu Cncl; Sec Trs Jr NHS; NHS; Voice Dem Awd; Bus Adm.

TRIMBATH, LINDA; Danville SR HS; Danville, PA; (Y); Drama Clb; Intnl Clb; Latin Clb; School Play; Stage Crew; Nwsp Rptr; Socr; Hon Roll; Photo.

TRIMMEL, DOREEN; Plymouth-Whitemarsh HS; Conshohocken, PA; (Y); 26/334; High Hon Roll.

TRIMMER, HEATHER; Northern York County HS; Lewisbury, PA; (Y); 89/223; French Clb; Band; Chorus; Color Guard; Concert Band; Drill Tm; Mrchg Band; Stat Bsktbl; Powder Puff Ftbl; Twrlr; HACC; Med Lab Tech.

TRIMPEY, FRED; Clearfield Area HS; Frenchville, PA; (Y); Boy Scts; Church Yth Grp; Cmnty Wkr; Exploring; VICA; High Hon Roll; Hon Roll; Pres Schlr; Elec Engr.

TRINH, HOA C; Mc Caskey HS; Lancaster, PA; (Y); 15/450; Cmnty Wkr; Service Clb; Orch; Frsh Cls; Trs Soph Cls; Trs Stu Cncl; JV Tennis; Hon Roll; Jr NHS; NHS; Carnegie-Mellon U; Bio-Medical.

TRINIDAD, TRACIE; Philipsburg-Osceola HS; Philipsburg, PA; (Y); 90/214; Letterman Clb; Ski Clb; SADD; Yrbk Stf; Capt Cheerleading; Stat Crs Cntry; Stat Vllybl; Btty Crckr Awd; DAR Awd; Prfct Atten Awd; Recrtn Drctr.

TRIOLI, LISA MARIE; Archbishop Kennedy HS; Philadelphia, PA; (Y); 14/187; Cmnty Wkr; Hosp Aide; Chorus; Hon Roll; Trs NHS; Prfct Atten Awd; Rlgn Awd; Spsh Awd; Temple U; Psych.

TRIPONEY, CARRIE; Clearfield Area HS; Hyde, PA; (S); 50/320; Church Yth Grp; French Clb; Speech Tm; Band; Chorus; Orch; School Musical; School Play; Swing Chorus; High Hon Roll; Good Citznshp Awd 84; Music.

TRIPP, COURTNEY; West Chester East HS; West Chester, PA; (Y); Boy Scts; Pres Church Yth Grp; JA; Letterman Clb; Ski Clb; Chorus; Church Choir; School Musical; Nwsp Stf; Im Bsktbl; BYU; Aerosp Engrng.

TRITT, JULIE; Big Spring SR HS; Plainfield, PA; (Y); Pep Clb; Rep Jr Cls; Pres Sec Stu Cncl; Var Capt Cheerleading; Im Vllybl; Hon Roll; Spnsh Schlrshp-Live/Tour Spain-Spnsh Heritage 85; Polit Sci.

TRITT, SUSAN; Boiling Springs HS; Boiling Spgs, PA; (Y); Sec Trs Band; Chorus; Concert Band; Jazz Band; Mrchg Band; Nwsp Stf; Var Trk.

TROFIN, IRINA; Abington HS; Glenside, PA; (Y); 60/528; Key Clb; Spanish Clb; Stu Cncl; Hon Roll; NHS; Temple U.

TROIANI, ANNMARIE; Quigley HS; Midland, PA; (Y); Church Yth Grp; Girl Scts; Math Tm; Pep Clb; Swing Chorus; Sec Jr Cls; Im Bowling; Powder Puff Ftbl; Var Tennis; Stat Wrstlng; Awd Prnsl Excllnce, Msntry Team, Musi Cmnstry, Stu Orgnzd Svc 86; Awd Flk Grp 85; Psych.

TROILO, LOUIS; Cardinal O Hara HS; Springfield, PA; (Y); 58/772; Aud/Vis; Pep Clb; Im Bsktbl; Var Tennis; Im Vllybl; High Hon Roll; NHS; Comp Sci Schlstc Achvt Awd 86; 1st Pl Spgfld Twnshp Tennis Tourn Mens B 86; Amkor Karate Outstndng 85; Bus.

TROMBETTA, CHRISTOPHER; Aliquippa HS; Aliquippa, PA; (Y); Church Yth Grp; Exploring; Rep Sr Cls; Wrstlng; Med.

TROMBINO, ANGELIQUE; Susquehanna Township HS; Harrisburg, PA; (Y); Art Clb; Drama Clb; English Clb; Church Choir; Madrigals; School Musical; Hon Roll; Ntl Merit Schol; Opt Clb Awd; Church Yth Grp; Pres Susqhnna Tnsp Ptry Clb 86-87; Publctn In Accolds 86; Carnegie-Mellon U; Eng Comp.

TROMBLEY JR, THEODORE; Hatboro-Horsham SR HS; Hatboro, PA; (Y); Computer Clb; JV Bsbl; L Socr; JV L Wrstlng; Cit Awd; Hon Roll; Elec Engrng.

TRONCONE, JANET; Villa Marie Acad; Erie, PA; (Y); Church Yth Grp; Trk; NHS; PA ST Behrend; Pre Law.

TROOP, BILL; Manheim Central HS; Lititz, PA; (Y); 85/255; Stu Cncl; Ftbl; Im Vllybl; Wt Lftg; Var Wrstlng; Hon Roll; 4 Wy Tst Awd 86; MI Iron Man Awd Wstlng 85-86; Dstrct Wrsltng Champ 86.

TROSIEK, JOHN; German SR HS; Mc Clellandtown, PA; (Y); 3/78; DAR Awd; High Hon Roll; Hon Roll; Jr NHS; NHS; Val; Stu Of Mnth 83 & 85; Pres Acad Ftns Awd 86; US Army; Aircrft Elctrncs.

TROSS, ANGELA; Bishop Hannan HS; Old Forge, PA; (Y); 7/130; Cmnty Wkr; Red Cross Aide; Chorus; High Hon Roll; NHS; Nrsng.

TROST, DEBORAH; Ringgold HS; Monongahela, PA; (Y); Church Yth Grp; Band; Concert Band; Sec Mrchg Band; Mgr(s); Swmmng; Tennis; U Pitt; Nrsng.

TROST, KELLY; Mercy Hust Prep; Erie, PA; (Y); 19/150; Art Clb; Vllybl; PA JR Acad Sci PJAS 84; Psych.

TROSTLE, DEBRA; Hempfield HS; E Petersburg, PA; (Y); 45/350; Sec Church Yth Grp; Science Clb; High Hon Roll; Hon Roll; 1st Pl For Rugbraiding At Ephrata Fair & Manheim Farm Show 84; 3rd Pl Rugbrading PA ST Farm Show 85; Chemistry.

TROSTLE, ROBERT; Altoona Area HS; Altoona, PA; (Y); Band; Concert Band; Pep Band; Mchncl Eng.

TROTMAN, CISSY; Avon Grove HS; West Chester, PA; (Y); 25/150; Pres 4-H; Pres FNA; Pres Girl Scts; Hosp Aide; Library Aide; Flag Corp; Yrbk Phtg; Rep Stu Cncl; Capt Cheerleading; High Hon Roll; Girl Sct Slvr Star Awd 82; 4-H Co-Op Dlgt 83; Avon Grove Phohtgrphy Awd 84; Penn ST; Wildlife Bio.

TROTT, JUDITH; The Baptist HS; Clarks Summit, PA; (Y); Church Yth Grp; Cmnty Wkr; Chorus; Church Choir; Rep Frsh Cls; Rep Soph Cls; Rep Stu Cncl; Var Bsktbl; Var Cheerleading; Im Socr; Baptist Bible Coll; Paralgl.

TROTT, MATTHEW; Cathedral Prep; Erie, PA; (Y); 25/218; NFL; Speech Tm; Im Bsktbl; Var L Ftbl; Im Vllybl; High Hon Roll; Hon Roll; V Bxng 86; Teenage Actn Clb; PA ST U; Engrng.

TROTTA, ADRIENNE; New Castle HS; New Castle, PA; (Y); 69/272; AFS; Drama Clb; English Clb; NFL; Pep Clb; SADD; Chorus; Color Guard; Drill Tm; Mrchg Band; YABA Bowling Awds 80-86; U VA; Comm.

TROTTA, ALEX; Bishop Guilfoyle HS; Altoona, PA; (S); 5/149; Boy Scts; Pep Clb; VP Science Clb; Ski Clb; Acpl Chr; Band; Chorus; Concert Band; Mrchg Band; Pep Band; Amer Lgn Awd 82; Yth Ldrshp Awd 84; Villanova; Bus.

TROTTA, KRISTIN; Charleroi Area HS; Monongahela, PA; (Y); Library Aide; Nwsp Stf; Hon Roll; Hsptlty Clb 83-86; Tri-C Club 85-86; Hlth Career 84; CA U Of PA; Acctg.

TROTTER, BRUCE; Northwestern Lehigh HS; Kempton, PA; (Y); Ski Clb; Varsity Clb; Bsktbl; Ftbl; Trk; Hon Roll; Engrng.

TROTTINI, CHRISTINE; Wyoming Area HS; Exeter, PA; (Y); 13/247; Church Yth Grp; Dance Clb; Hosp Aide; Key Clb; Sec Spanish Clb; Yrbk Stf; Trs Soph Cls; Cheerleading; Gym; Trk; Natl Yth Salute 86; Kings Coll; Hstry.

TROUP, BRIAN; Marion Center JR SR HS; Marion Center, PA; (Y); FBLA; VICA; Hon Roll; Stu Pride Awd 83; Army; Law Enfrcmnt.

TROUP, DEANNA; West Snyder HS; Beaver Springs, PA; (Y); 28/93; 4-H; FBLA; Varsity Clb; Band; Chorus; Drm Mjr(t); Yrbk Stf; Pres Stu Cncl; Cheerleading; Sftbl; Elem Ed.

TROUT, ANDREW; Northern Lebanon HS; Lebanon, PA; (Y); 30/177; Church Yth Grp; FCA; Varsity Clb; Var L Ftbl; Var L Trk; Wt Lftg; Im Wrstlng; 3rd Pl Schl Math Test 84-85; Military Acad; Nuclear Engrng.

TROUT, BEVERLY; Penn-Trafford HS; Claridge, PA; (Y); VICA; Nwsp Rptr; High Hon Roll; Hon Roll; Church Yth Grp; FBLA; Library Aide; Comm Action Prog Awd 83; W TC ST U; Comp Inform Systms.

TROUT, TERESA; Greater Latrobe SR HS; Greensburg, PA; (Y); Library Aide; Concert Band; Drm Mjr(t); Mrchg Band; Symp Band; Variety Show; Nwsp Stf; Twrlr; High Hon Roll; Bus Typg Awd 86; Bus.

TROUTMAN, CRAIG; Bradford Area HS; Bradford, PA; (Y); Aud/Vis; Church Yth Grp; School Play; Bsbl; Bowling; Hon Roll; Prfct Atten Awd; Awd For Outstndng Perf-Accntng 86; Penn ST; Accntng.

TROUTMAN, DIANE; Conrad Weiser JR SR HS; Myerstown, PA; (Y); Art Clb; 4-H; Latin Clb; Chorus; School Musical; Tennis; Hon Roll; Art.

TROUTMAN, HEIDI; Phil-Mont Christian Acad; Philadelphia, PA; (Y); Hosp Aide; Library Aide; Teachers Aide; Acpl Chr; Chorus; Church Choir; Madrigals; School Play; Fld Hcky; High Hon Roll; Ntl Hnr Scty.

TROUTMAN, JOHN; W Hazleton SR HS; Conyngham, PA; (Y); 65/205; Drama Clb; Stage Crew; VP Bsktbl; Var JV Ftbl; Im Vllybl; High Hon Roll; Hon Roll; Auburn; Jrnlsm.

TROUTMAN, JOY; Meyersdale Area HS; Hyndman, PA; (S); Church Yth Grp; French Clb; Band; Concert Band; Mrchg Band; L Vllybl; Wt Lftg; Hon Roll; Law.

TROUTMAN, TOM; Reynolds HS; Greenville, PA; (Y); 6/150; Latin Clb; Math Clb; Science Clb; Pres Band; Concert Band; Jazz Band; Mrchg Band; Pep Band; Nwsp Stf; NHS; U Of Ptsbrgh; Pre-Dnstry.

TROXELL, GREG; Blairsville SR HS; Blairsville, PA; (Y); 54/123; Boy Scts; Exploring; Ski Clb; Varsity Clb; School Musical; Rep Stu Cncl; JV Var Bsktbl; JV Var Ftbl; Im Swmmng; Im Tennis; Pres Phys Fit Awd; Marine Bio.

TROXELL, MICHELE; Glendale HS; Glasgow, PA; (Y); 8/98; Trs Band; Mrchg Band; Pep Band; Yrbk Stf; Stu Cncl; Var Capt Bsktbl; Hon Roll; NHS; The Instrmnltst Mgz Mscnshp 85 & 86.

TROXELL, PAULA; Tailor Allderdice HS; New Wilmington, PA; (Y); Church Yth Grp; Vllybl; Cit Awd; High Hon Roll; NHS; Govnrs Schl For Ag 86; Forestry.

TROY, DOUG; Somerset Area SR HS; Friedens, PA; (Y); 108/239; Trs Church Yth Grp; English Clb; JA; Office Aide; Varsity Clb; Band; Rep Stu Cncl; Var L Bsbl; L Ftbl; Im Wt Lftg; Bill Halverson Mem Awd Sprtsmanship 83.

TROZZOLILLO, MARIA; Bishop Hannon HS; Scranton, PA; (Y); Church Yth Grp; French Clb; Hosp Aide; Latin Clb; Math Clb; Church Choir; High Hon Roll; Cert Excllnc Engl I, Cltrs, Sci, Ltn I & II, Frnch I & Math 85-86; Cert Hnrbl Mntn Music Rlgn 85-86.

TRUAX, HOLLY; Cardinal Ohara HS; Chester, PA; (Y); 86/772; Church Yth Grp; Dance Clb; Spanish Clb; School Musical; Hon Roll; NHS; Chmstry.

TRUE, ANNE MICHELLE; Greencastle Antrim HS; Greencastle, PA; (Y); 37/135; Library Aide; Chorus; High Hon Roll; Hon Roll; Hagerstown Bus Coll; Accntng.

TRUFFA, MELISSA; Leechburg Area HS; Leechburg, PA; (Y); Drama Clb; Chorus; School Play; Nwsp Ed-Chief; Yrbk Stf; VP Soph Cls; Rep Stu Cncl; Hon Roll; NHS; Phrmcy.

TRUJILLO, DAVID; Neshaminy HS; Langhorne, PA; (Y); 100/752; Camera Clb; Computer Clb; Drama Clb; Exploring; Radio Clb; Band; Concert Band; Mrchg Band; Stage Crew; Im Bsktbl; Achvt Awd Exc Alg 84; U PA; Chem.

TRULLENDER, RENEE; Hollidaysburg Area SR HS; Altoona, PA; (Y); 37/346; French Clb; Intnl Clb; SADD; Teachers Aide; Chorus; School Musical; Nwsp Stf; French Hon Soc; Hon Roll; NHS; H-Pin 80-83; Indiana U Of PA; Journlsm.

TRUMBAUER, ERIC; Emmaus HS; Emmaus, PA; (Y); 22/493; Cmnty Wkr; Chrmn Band; Chrmn Concert Band; Chrmn Mrchg Band; Pep Band; Im Sftbl; Im Vllybl; Hon Roll; Jr NHS; NHS; JV Ltr Band 86; Engrng.

TRUMBAUER, WENDY; Owen J Roberts HS; Pottstown, PA; (Y); Church Yth Grp; JA; Service Clb; Band; Concert Band; Mrchg Band; Hon Roll; Prfct Atten Awd; Temple U; Phy Thrpy.

TRUMP, ANDREA; Eastern Lebanon County HS; Myerstown, PA; (Y); 2/184; Sec Stu Cncl; Fld Hcky; Trk; Elks Awd; Sec NHS; Ntl Merit Ltr; Rotary Awd; Sal; Voice Dem Awd; Army Reserve Scholar Athlete 86; Carnegie Mellon U; Chem Engrng.

TRUONG, DO; Elizabethtown HS; Elizabethtown, PA; (Y); Hon Roll; JETS Awd; NHS; Prfct Atten Awd; Plymouth AAA Trbl Shootg 86; PA ST U; Mech Engrng.

TRUONG, HOAI NAM; J P Mc Caskey HS; Lancaster, PA; (Y); 232/450; AFS; JA; Yrbk Phtg; Yrbk Stf; Socr; Timer; Vllybl; Hon Roll; Intl Rltns.

TRUSHOVIC, PAT; West Allegheny HS; Oakdale, PA; (Y); 50/210; Spanish Clb; Bsbl; Ftbl; Hon Roll; Prfct Atten Awd; Pre Law.

TRUSOW, GEORGINE; St Clair Area HS; St Clair, PA; (Y); 6/84; Trs FHA; Sec Math Clb; Quiz Bowl; Ski Clb; Nwsp Rptr; Yrbk Ed-Chief; VP Sr Cls; Twrlr; Hon Roll; NHS; PTA Schlrshp Grnt 86; Stu Of Mnth 86; Bloomsburg U; Rdlgc Tech.

TRUSSLER, SHARI; The Baptist HS; Clarks Summit, PA; (Y); 1/16; Library Aide; Chorus; Church Choir; Yrbk Rptr; Yrbk Stf; Bsktbl; Capt Cheerleading; High Hon Roll; Ntl Merit Ltr; 2nd Pl ST Sci Awd 85; Law.

TRUZZI, FRANK; Canon Mc Millan SR HS; Eighty Four, PA; (Y); ROTC.

TRYBEND, BRIAN; Canon Mc Millan HS; Canonsburg, PA; (Y); 5/370; Latin Clb; Ski Clb; Ed Yrbk Stf; Bsktbl; Ftbl; Wt Lftg; High Hon Roll; Natl Yth Ldrshp Cert Merit 86; WA & Jefferson; Pre-Med.

TRYBUS, TIM; Portage Area HS; Portage, PA; (S); 10/118; Cmnty Wkr; Varsity Clb; Stu Cncl; Var Bsbl; Var Capt Bsktbl; Var Ftbl; Im Vllybl; High Hon Roll; Hon Roll; NHS; Bus Admin.

TRYNOSKY, KIMBERLY; Pine Grove Area HS; Pine Grove, PA; (Y); Am Leg Aux Girls St; VP SADD; Varsity Clb; School Musical; School Play; Nwsp Stf; Yrbk Ed-Chief; Hst Sr Cls; Rep Stu Cncl; Capt JV Cheerleading; Engrng.

TRYON, CHRISTOPHER; Central HS; Scranton, PA; (Y); Ski Clb; Crs Cntry; Golf; Trk; Comp Sci.

TRYPUS, JOHN; Cambridge Springs HS; Cambridge Springs, PA; (Y); JV Var Bsktbl; JV Ftbl.

TRZECIAK, SHAWN; Highlands HS; Natrona Hts, PA; (Y); Art Clb; Drama Clb; Pres Intnl Clb; Office Aide; Spanish Clb; School Play; Stage Crew; Var L Bsbl; JV Bsktbl; Var JV Wt Lftg; Brown Awds 3.0-3.5 GPA 85-86.

TSAI, KAREN; Gateway HS; Monroeville, PA; (Y); Computer Clb; FBLA; PAVAS; Band; Concert Band; Mrchg Band; School Play; Symp Band; High Hon Roll; NHS; U Of CA Berkeley; Ecnmcs.

TSCHOPP, SHAWNEE; Susquenita HS; Marysville, PA; (Y); Drama Clb; Leo Clb; SADD; Chorus; Flag Corp; School Musical; Off Frsh Cls; Hon Roll; US Ntl Art Awd, 3rd Yuth Art Day 86; Fash Dsgn.

TSELEPIS, NICHOLAS; California Area HS; California, PA; (Y); Drama Clb; JA; Ski Clb; Stage Crew; Hon Roll; Prfct Atten Awd; CA U Of PA; Comp.

TSHITEYA, MIREILLE; State College Area SR HS; State College, PA; (Y); 158/483; Art Clb; French Clb; Juniata Coll; Compu Sci.

TSONG, EDITH L; State College Area SR HS; State College, PA; (Y); 50/505; Trs Art Clb; Lit Mag; Var Crs Cntry; Var Diving; Var Trk; Im Vllybl; High Hon Roll; Hon Roll; Prfct Atten Awd; PA Govs Schl Of Arts 85; PA ST Stu Intrnshp Fluid & Hydrdynmcs 85; Regnl Schlstc Art Awd 85; U Of Chicago; Asian Stds.

TSOUROS, ZOITSA; Owen J Roberts HS; Pottstown, PA; (Y); Church Yth Grp; FCA; Letterman Clb; Ski Clb; School Musical; School Play; Yrbk Bus Mgr; Yrbk Stf; Rep Frsh Cls; Rep Soph Cls.

TUBBS, DONALD M; Du Bois Area HS; Du Bois, PA; (Y); Dance Clb; Band; Chorus; Church Choir; Concert Band; Mrchg Band; School Musical; School Play; Swing Chorus; Variety Show; Natl Schl Choral Awd, Frederick Chopin Piano Awd 86; Duquesne U; Piano/Voice.

TUBBS, MELISSA; Curwensville Area HS; Curwensville, PA; (Y); Drama Clb; Pres FNA; Chorus; JV Bsktbl; JV Var Tennis; Im Vllybl; Ntl Phy Ed Awd 83; Intr Decrtr.

TUBBS, ROBBIE; First Baptist Church Acad; Curwensville, PA; (Y); Church Yth Grp; Chorus; Mrchg Band; Var Bsktbl; DAR Awd; Hon Roll; Hardworker Awd 83-84.

TUBRIDY, JENNIFER A; Seneca Valley SR HS; Zelienople, PA; (Y); AFS; Hosp Aide; Math Tm; Ski Clb; SADD; Stage Crew; Symp Band; Yrbk Sprt Ed; Ed Yrbk Stf; High Hon Roll; Carneigie Mellon U; Ind Adm.

TUCCI, TERESA; Corry Area SR JR HS; Columbus, PA; (S); Civic Clb; 4-H; Girl Scts; Office Aide; Spanish Clb; Chorus; School Play; Trk; JV Vllybl; 4-H Awd; Med.

TUCKER, BELINDA; Mc Connellsburg HS; Harrisonville, PA; (Y); 3/80; Art Clb; Chorus; Stage Crew; Nwsp Stf; Yrbk Stf; Stat Trk; High Hon Roll; Hon Roll; NHS; Pres Schlr; Phila Coll Of Textiles & Sci.

TUCKER, COURTNEY; Cardinal O Hara HS; Ridley Pk, PA; (Y); 192/772; Spanish Clb; Lit Mag; Hon Roll; Jrnlsm.

TUCKER, MONIQUE; Aliquippa HS; Aliquippa, PA; (Y); Library Aide; Office Aide; VICA; Hon Roll; Cert Of Achvt 85-86; Voc Ind Clbs Of Am Dist 8 VICA Comp 85-86; Armed Forces; Airline Reserv.

TUDOR, TROY; Sheffield Area JR SR HS; Sheffield, PA; (Y); 3/95; Library Aide; Ski Clb; Band; Concert Band; Jazz Band; High Hon Roll; NHS; Wmns Clb Math Schlrshp 86; CETA Comp Prog Awd 83; Comp Tech.

TUFF, SARA E; Gettysbug SR HS; Gettysburg, PA; (Y); 27/246; Hosp Aide; Variety Show; Yrbk Bus Mgr; Rep Soph Cls; Hon Roll; NHS; 1st Quintile SR Class 86; Shippensburg U; Bus Adm.

TUFFIE, TRICIA; Hopewell HS; Aliquippa, PA; (Y); Drama Clb; JA; Latin Clb; Band; Concert Band; Mrchg Band; Pep Band; Yrbk Sprt Ed; Yrbk Stf; Powder Puff Ftbl; CCBC; Med Tech.

TUKLOFF, STACY; Henderson HS; West Chester, PA; (Y); 57/333; Cmnty Wkr; VP SADD; School Musical; Yrbk Phtg; Sec Soph Cls; Sec Jr Cls; JV Capt Cheerleading; Var Lcrss; Hon Roll; Spanish NHS; Flght Trng Schlrshp 86; J Davis-Walton Grls Spkng Cntst 1st Pl 84; Cert Spprt Outstndng Bld Srvce 86; CA ST U; Radio.

TULANOWSKI, KAREN; Sauderton Area HS; Harleysville, PA; (Y); 63/345; Aud/Vis; School Play; Nwsp Rptr; Nwsp Stf; Cheerleading; Hon Roll; Chrldng Co-Capt 85-86; NCA Camp Chrldng Awds 85; Nrs.

TULIO, LOUISE; Bishop Kenrick HS; Collegeville, PA; (Y); 57/292; Pep Clb; Drill Tm; Nwsp Stf; Yrbk Stf; Mgr(s); Hon Roll; Prfct Atten Awd; Cmnty Wkr; Spanish Clb; Band; Prm Chrprsn 86; Hmcmng Chrprsn 83-86; Guidanc Aid/Cnslr 85-86; Temple U; Sprts Info.

TULLAR, COURTNEY; Avonworth JR/SR HS; Pittsbg, PA; (Y); AFS; Drama Clb; VP French Clb; Chorus; School Musical; School Play; Stage Crew; Var Swmmng; High Hon Roll; NHS; Intl Bus.

TULLIO, ANNE; Villa Maria Acad; Erie, PA; (Y); FBLA; Stu Cncl; Bsktbl; Sftbl; Vllybl; Hon Roll; NHS; Pres Schlr; St John Baptist Outstndg Alumni Awd 86; NW Jaycees City Cnty All Star Bsktbl 86; St John Fisher Coll; Bus Mgmt.

TULLOCK, CHRISTEN; Liberty HS; Bethlehem, PA; (Y); 183/535; FBLA; Spanish Clb; Lit Mag; Hon Roll; Fshn Mrchndsng.

TUMAN, JOHN; Northeast Catholic HS; Philadelphia, PA; (Y); 120/372; Band; Chorus; Concert Band; Mrchg Band; Rep Frsh Cls; Rep Soph Cls; Rep Jr Cls; Hon Roll.

TUNMER, LYNN; MMI Prep Schl; Mountaintop, PA; (Y); Art Clb; Cmnty Wkr; Ski Clb; School Play; Nwsp Rptr; Nwsp Stf; Yrbk Rptr; Yrbk Stf; Var Cheerleading; Var Crs Cntry; PA JR Acad Of Sci Awd 83-84; Athltc Awd 84-86; Merit Awd Achvt Art 84-86; Fshn Illstrtn.

TUNNELL, SCOTT; Middletown Area HS; Middletown, PA; (Y); 13/162; Varsity Clb; Yrbk Stf; VP Jr Cls; Var Socr; Var Tennis; Hon Roll; NHS; Rotary Awd; Acadmc All Am 85-86; Bus.

TUNNEY, MAUREEN; Avonworth HS; Pittsbg, PA; (Y); French Clb; SADD; Band; School Play; Yrbk Rptr; Yrbk Stf; Lit Mag.

TUOHY IV, EDWARD ROBERT; Council Rock HS; Newtown, PA; (Y); 12/845; Church Yth Grp; Hosp Aide; Im Bsktbl; VP L Ftbl; Im Vllybl; Im Wt Lftg; High Hon Roll; NHS; Ntl Merit Schol; Med.

TURANO, LISA; Carbondale Area JR SR HS; Carbondale, PA; (Y); Art Clb; French Clb; FBLA; Ski Clb; High Hon Roll; Hon Roll; Katharine Gibbs Schl; Bus.

TURCHANIK, TANYA; Hanover Area JR/SR HS; Wilkes Barre, PA; (Y); Key Clb; Band; Concert Band; Jazz Band; Mrchg Band; Var L Bsktbl; Hon Roll; Jr NHS; NHS; Comp Sci.

TURCHETTI, JOE; Cumberland Valley HS; Camp Hill, PA; (Y); 28/522; Boy Scts; Spanish Clb; Var Bsktbl; Crs Cntry; Var Trk; Hon Roll; NHS; Egl Sct 85; Cert Of Excllnc-Frgn Lang 84-86; Accntng.

TURCHI, JOSEPH; Plymouth-Whitemarsh HS; Norristown, PA; (Y); 102/350; VP Frsh Cls; Rep Soph Cls; Var Ftbl; Wt Lftg; Hon Roll; JR Natl Hon Soc 82-83; Schlrshp Awd 80-81; Agronomy.

TURCHIAROLO, MARIO J; Archbishop John Carroll For Boys; Philadelphia, PA; (Y); Band; Mrchg Band; Nwsp Stf; High Hon Roll; Hon Roll; Jr NHS; NHS; Nwsppr Awd 83; Svc Awd Natl Hnr Socty 86; Pres Acadmc Fit Awd 86; Temple U; Cmmnctns.

TUREK, JILL; Shenandoah Valley HS; Shenandoah, PA; (Y); 23/108; Pep Clb; Trs Band; Chorus; Concert Band; Mrchg Band; Pep Band; Ed Nwsp Stf; Yrbk Stf; Wt Lftg; Hon Roll; Cert Excptnl Wrk Frnch 85.

TUREK, PAMELA; Shenandoah Valley HS; Shenandoah, PA; (Y); 18/108; Dance Clb; Pep Clb; VP Band; Chorus; Church Choir; Pep Band; Ed Nwsp Stf; Yrbk Stf; Wt Lftg; Hon Roll; Crtfct Mrt Excptnl Wrk Frnch 86; Bloomsburg U.

TURIK, KRISTIE; West Branch Area HS; Drifting, PA; (S); 4/150; Church Yth Grp; Science Clb; Band; Mrchg Band; Hon Roll; Bio.

TURINSKI, STEVE; Hanover Area HS; Wilkes Barre, PA; (Y); Var L Bsbl; Var L Ftbl; Hon Roll; Jr NHS; NHS; Engr.

TURK, ANITA; Allegheny Clarion Valley HS; Emlenton, PA; (Y); 3/100; Sec Trs Church Yth Grp; French Clb; Band; Chorus; Concert Band; Var L Bsktbl; Var L Trk; Var L Vllybl; High Hon Roll; NHS; Duquesne; Phrmcy.

TURK, BRAD; Shenango HS; New Castle, PA; (Y); Boy Scts; Letterman Clb; Office Aide; Yrbk Stf; JV Var Bsbl; Capt Var Bsktbl; Coach Actv; Crs Cntry; Ftbl; Trk.

TURK, LISA; Shenango JR SR HS; New Castle, PA; (S); 3/112; French Clb; Drill Tm; School Play; Nwsp Stf; Yrbk Stf; Pres Jr Cls; VP Stu Cncl; Var Trk; Im Vllybl; High Hon Roll; Ntl Engl Merit Awd 86; Ntl Sci Merit Awd 86; Arch.

TURK, ROB; Meadville Area SR HS; Meadville, PA; (Y); 49/290; Church Yth Grp; Latin Clb; Im Bsktbl; Var L Crs Cntry; Var L Trk; Hon Roll.

TURKO, SANDY; Mid-Valley HS; Olyphant, PA; (Y); Church Yth Grp; French Clb; Rep Jr Cls; JV Cheerleading; Hon Roll; Penn ST U; Hlth.

TURLEY, JAN M; Radnor HS; Bryn Mawr, PA; (Y); 33/276; Church Yth Grp; Exploring; Band; Church Choir; Concert Band; Drm Mjr(t); Orch; High Hon Roll; NHS; Ntl Merit SF; Cert Merit Commnwlth PA 85; Hood Coll; Bus.

TURLEY, LAURA; John S Fine SR HS; Nanticoke, PA; (Y); Am Leg Aux Girls St; Sec Key Clb; Capt Speech Tm; SADD; Mgr Mrchg Band; Nwsp Ed-Chief; Yrbk Stf; L Crs Cntry; Hon Roll; NEDT Awd; PA Key Club Oratorical Winner 86; Amer Lgn Inter District Oratorical Awd 85-86; Communications.

TURLEY, NANCY; John S Fine HS; Nanticoke, PA; (Y); 24/252; Chorus; Nwsp Rptr; Nwsp Sprt Ed; Nwsp Stf; Yrbk Rptr; Yrbk Stf; Cheerleading; Swmmng; Trk; High Hon Roll.

TURLIP, MARY ELLEN; Bishop O Hara HS; Archbald, PA; (Y); 37/124; Pres FNA; Latin Clb; Spanish Clb; Chorus; Lib Church Choir; Bsktbl; Vllybl; 1st Plc Rgnl & ST Jr Acad Sci Chem 85; Schlrshp Amer Bus Wmns Assoc 86; Marywood Coll; Nrsng.

TURNBACH, TIM; Hazelton SR HS; Hazleton, PA; (Y); 35/390; Church Yth Grp; JV Bsktbl; High Hon Roll; Hon Roll; Cmnty Wkr; Ski Clb; Nwsp Rptr; Nwsp Stf; Yrbk Stf; NHS; Elec Engr.

TURNBAUGH, GENA; Newport HS; Newport, PA; (Y); Art Clb; Hon Roll; Hnrble Mntn On Cvrd Brdge Plate Prnt 84-85; Prtcpnt Rbbn For Pstl Of Ldy On The Couch 84-85.

TURNBULL, MARK; Saltsburg JR SR HS; Saltsburg, PA; (Y); Boy Scts; Church Yth Grp; VICA; Chorus; Stage Crew; JV Trk; Var Wrstlng; Hon Roll; Voctnl Indstrl Tchr.

TURNER, AUDREY; Dowingtown SR HS; Glenmoore, PA; (Y); 12/563; German Clb; GAA; Ski Clb; Band; Chorus; Co-Capt Flag Corp; Var L Lcrss; NHS; NEDT Awd; Psychlgy.

TURNER, BETSY; Canton HS; Roaring Branch, PA; (Y); 9/100; Church Yth Grp; Band; Chorus; Nwsp Stf; Var Cheerleading; Hon Roll; NHS; Pres Schlr; Canton Mfg Schlrshp 86; Cindy Daniels Mem 86; Mansfield U; Elem Educ.

TURNER, CYNTHIA; Plymouth Whitemarsh HS; Norristown, PA; (Y); Band; Chorus; Concert Band; Jazz Band; Mrchg Band; Orch; School Musical; Hon Roll; Arch Design.

TURNER, JENNIFER; Lake-Lehman HS; Dallas, PA; (Y); 4/140; Key Clb; SADD; Yrbk Stf; Var L Fld Hcky; High Hon Roll; Jr NHS; NHS; Ntl Merit Ltr; Boston Coll; Intl Law.

TURNER, JOSEPH; Father Judge RC HS; Philadelphia, PA; (S); 9/450; Chess Clb; Church Yth Grp; Cmnty Wkr; German Clb; Latin Clb; Mathletes; Yrbk Sprt Ed; JV Bsbl; Capt Bsktbl; Hon Roll; Villanova; Elec Engrng.

TURNER, KIMBERLY; Mercyhurst Prep Schl; Erie, PA; (Y); Church Yth Grp; Girl Scts; Key Clb; Service Clb; Chorus; Yrbk Stf; Stu Cncl; Hon Roll; NHS.

TURNER, MARQUETTE W; Central Catholic HS; Pittsburgh, PA; (Y); Cmnty Wkr; Teachers Aide; Chorus; Im Bsktbl; Im Ftbl; Ntl Merit Ltr; Psych.

TURNER, SCOTT; Coughlin HS; Wilkes Barre, PA; (Y); Jazz Band; Mrchg Band; Lion Awd; NHS; Drama Clb; Band; Chorus; Orch; Jr NHS; NEDT Awd; Acad All Amer 85-86; PA ST U; Microbio.

TURNER, SCOTT; Fairview HS; Erie, PA; (Y); Varsity Clb; Var Ftbl; Var L Trk; Var Wt Lftg; Hon Roll; Bus.

TURNER, SHAWN; Southern Fulton HS; Warfordsburg, PA; (Y); 1/77; Church Yth Grp; FBLA; FFA; Var L Trk; PA ST U; Civil Engr.

TURNER, STEPHANIE; Germantown HS; Philadelphia, PA; (Y); Library Aide; Office Aide; Teachers Aide; Crs Cntry; Trk; DE ST Coll; Accntng.

TURNER, STEPHEN; Carson Long Military Acad; Lansdowne, PA; (Y); 5/41; Debate Tm; Library Aide; ROTC; School Play; Nwsp Rptr; Lit Mag; Sec Jr Cls; Var Stat Bsbl; Im Sftbl; Im Vllybl; Penn ST Clg; Crtcl Langs.

TURNER, TRACIE; Forest City Regional HS; Pleasant Mt, PA; (Y); 8/68; Drama Clb; Library Aide; Spanish Clb; SADD; Band; Chorus; Concert Band; Jazz Band; Mrchg Band; School Musical; Dist Chrs 84-86; Schlrshp Katherine Gibbs 86; Bus Schl Awd Acad Merit, Intrvw, & Fincl Need; Katherine Gibbs Bus Sch; Music.

TURNER, TRENT; Lock Haven SR HS; Lock Haven, PA; (Y); 6/247; Church Yth Grp; Trs Key Clb; VP Frsh Cls; Pres Soph Cls; Var L Wrstlng; High Hon Roll; NHS; Biol Awd 85; Lock Haven U Of PA; Hlth Sci.

TURNS, ROBIN; Mapletown HS; Bobtown, PA; (Y); 16/74; FTA; GAA; Library Aide; SADD; Varsity Clb; Yrbk Ed-Chief; Yrbk Stf; Var Cheerleading; High Hon Roll; Hon Roll; Hghst Acad Ablty On Chrldg Sqd 85-86; Mgmt.

TURNSEK, RUDY S; Jeannette SR HS; Jeannette, PA; (Y); Am Leg Boys St; Spanish Clb; Var Ftbl; Var Trk; Wt Lftg; High Hon Roll; Hon Roll; Waynesburg Coll; Biochem.

TURSKE, MICHAEL; Carlynton HS; Carnegie, PA; (Y); L Trk; High Hon Roll; NHS; Ntl Merit SF; Pitt Provosts Day Awd Schlrshp 86; U Of Pittsburgh; Elctrcl Engr.

TURZAK, CARA; Kennedy Christian HS; Sharpsville, PA; (Y); 2/98; Sec Latin Clb; Service Clb; Band; Mrchg Band; Stu Cncl; JV Bsktbl; Var Cheerleading; Var L Crs Cntry; Mat Maids; Var L Trk; Pre-Med.

TURZO, TIM; Souderton HS; Harleysville, PA; (Y); SADD; Pres Jr Cls; Stu Cncl; Ftbl; Socr; Trk; Wrstlng; Hon Roll; PA ST U.

TUSTIN, K BRUCE; Ridley HS; Ridley Park, PA; (Y); 1/420; Capt Scholastic Bowl; Var L Bsbl; Capt L Ice Hcky; High Hon Roll; NHS; Pres Schlr; Sal; Aud/Vis; Math Clb; Nwsp Sprt Ed; Brown Englsh Awd 85; Yale U.

TUTERA, DAVID A; Duquesne HS; Duquesne, PA; (Y); Pres Band; JP Sousa Awd; Pres Concert Band; Pres Jazz Band; Pres Mrchg Band; Mgr Stage Crew; Hon Roll; PMEA Dist I Bnd Awd 86; PMEA Rgnl Bnd Awd 86; JR & SR Hall Of Fame Awds 84-86; Pt Park Coll; Bus.

TUTOROW, JAMES A; Council Rock HS; St Clair Shores, MI; (Y); 263/779; Drama Clb; Acpl Chr; Band; Chorus; Orch; School Musical; School Play; Stage Crew; Var L Ftbl; Var JV Trk; Bowling Green ST U; Theatre.

TUTRONE, EDWARD; Pocono Mt HS; Pocono Pines, PA; (Y); Aud/Vis; Ski Clb; Stage Crew; Hon Roll; Law.

TUTTLE, CHRISTINE; St Marys Area HS; Benezett, PA; (Y); Cmnty Wkr; 4-H; High Hon Roll; NHS; Penn ST; Hotl Mgmt.

TUTTLE, LAUREN; Steel Valley HS; Munhall, PA; (Y); Band; Concert Band; Drill Tm; Mrchg Band; Bsktbl; Sftbl; U Of Pittsburgh.

TUTTLE, WAYNE; Harbor Creek HS; Erie, PA; (Y); Church Yth Grp; Letterman Clb; Office Aide; Varsity Clb; Yrbk Stf; Ftbl; Trk; Vllybl; Wt Lftg; Wrstlng; Anderson Coll; Phys Ed.

TUTTON, DARYL; Delaware County Christian Schl; Newtown Sq, PA; (Y); Church Yth Grp; Trs Drama Clb; Math Clb; School Play; Stage Crew; Score Keeper; JV Var Socr; JV Var Trk; High Hon Roll; Hon Roll; Dstngshd Chrstn HS Stud ACSI 85-86; Clemson; Engrng.

TWADDLE, SHARON; Greensburg Central Catholic HS; Greensburg, PA; (Y); 54/249; Pep Clb; Ski Clb; Yrbk Stf; High Hon Roll; Washington & Jefferson Coll Grand 86-87; WA & Jefferson Coll; Bio.

TWARDOWSKI JR, JOHN; James M Coughlin HS; Plains, PA; (Y); Math Tm; Band; Hon Roll; Jr NHS; Lion Awd; NHS; Rtry Int Dst 741 Ldrs Cmp 85; Phila Coll Phrmcylnd Sci; Phrmc.

TWARDOWSKI, ROBERT; Northeast Catholic HS; Philadelphia, PA; (Y); 3/362; Mathletes; Science Clb; NHS; Frnch Awd For Top Stu 85-86; NE Catholic Cert Of Excellence 83-86; Cert Of Comp Bowl 85-86; Drexel U; Comp Sci.

TWARDZIK, JENNIFER; Salisbury HS; Allentown, PA; (Y); 53/135; Cmnty Wkr; Key Clb; Y-Teens; Chorus; Nwsp Stf; Yrbk Stf; Rep Jr Cls; Var Crs Cntry; Var Trk; Im Wt Lftg; Mhtnbrg Coll; Elem Ed.

TWARYONAS, NICHOLE; Lebanon HS; Lebanon, PA; (Y); 8/285; Pres French Clb; Varsity Clb; Pres Orch; School Musical; Rep Jr Cls; Var JV Mgr(s); JV Socr; Var JV Sftbl; Wt Lftg; Hon Roll; Bst Frnch Awd I-II 84-85; Frnch.

TWENTIER, ANN; Lincoln HS; Portersville, PA; (Y); 25/165; AFS; Drama Clb; 4-H; Key Clb; Y-Teens; Chorus; High Hon Roll; Hon Roll.

TWIST, TODD; Milton SR HS; Milton, PA; (Y); 67/202; Boy Scts; VP Church Yth Grp; Band; Concert Band; Mrchg Band; God Cntry Awd.

TWITMYER, ROBERT; The Haverford Scshl; St Davids, PA; (S); 15/78; Chorus; Nwsp Rptr; Yrbk Phtg; Yrbk Rptr; Pres Sec Stu Cncl; Var L Bsbl; Var L Ftbl; Im Wt Lftg; Hon Roll; Ntl Merit Ltr; Free Entrprs Fllwshps 85; Warden Prz Attndnc Duty 85; Thomas A Newhall Prz Ldrshp 83.

TWYMAN, NICHELLE; Altoona Area HS; Altoona, PA; (Y); 32/691; German Clb; PAVAS; Spanish Clb; Color Guard; Mrchg Band; Nwsp Sprt Ed; Yrbk Stf; Var JV Vllybl; NHS; Pres Schlr; U Notre Dame; Pre-Med.

TWYMAN, TYRONE; Kennett HS; Kennett Square, PA; (Y); Rep Varsity Clb; Capt Bsktbl; Capt Socr; Capt Trk; Im Vllybl; Hon Roll; Prfct Atten Awd; Rotary Awd; All-League Sccr 84-85; All-League Bsktbl 85-86; Dist Track Fnlst 86; Vly Forge Mltry JR Coll; Engrg.

TYCENSKI, PATRICIA; Merion Mercy Acad; Penfield Downs, PA; (Y); 26/73; Cmnty Wkr; Hosp Aide; Mathletes; Science Clb; Service Clb; Spanish Clb; Chorus; Yrbk Ed-Chief; Bsktbl; Im Swmmng; Physcl Thrpy.

TYCHINSKI, BRUCE; Altoona Area HS; Altoona, PA; (Y); Speech Tm; Band; Concert Band; Drm & Bgl; Jazz Band; Mrchg Band; Orch; School Musical; Symp Band; Trs Frsh Cls; PA Gov Schl Arts, All ST Orch 86; IN U PA Hnrs Band 84-85; Tromb Perf.

TYGER, BRETT; Marion Center Area HS; Creekside, PA; (S); 17/164; Intnl Clb; SADD; Varsity Clb; Stage Crew; Bsbl; High Hon Roll; Hon Roll; Jr NHS; NHS; Acadmc All Amer 84; Penn ST; Elctrcl Engrng.

TYGER, TONYA; Punxsutawney HS; Glen Campbell, PA; (Y); Church Yth Grp; Sec 4-H; FNA; Hosp Aide; 4-H Awd; Acctnt.

TYLOSKY, SANDI; Ambridge Area HS; Ambridge, PA; (Y); Pep Clb; Red Cross Aide; Yrbk Stf; Jr Cls; JV Var Cheerleading; Hon Roll; Slippery Rock U; Elem Educ.

TYMA, JONATHAN; Ambridge HS; Freedom, PA; (Y); Am Leg Boys St; Math Clb; Spanish Clb; Yrbk Stf; Var L Ftbl; Var Trk; Wt Lftg; Gov Hon Prg Awd; High Hon Roll; NHS; PA Govnrs Schl Ag 86; Pre-Med.

TYPOVSKY, KELLY; CA Area HS; Daisytown, PA; (Y); Science Clb; High Hon Roll; Bus Mngmnt.

TYSINGER, MELINDA; Waynesboro Area SR HS; Blue Ridge Smt, PA; (Y); Church Yth Grp; Ski Clb; Band; Chorus; Church Choir; Concert Band; Mrchg Band; Swing Chorus; Computer Clb; Library Aide; John Hopkins Talent Srch 82; Coperate Law.

TYSON, ELAINE; Northern Lebanon HS; Annville, PA; (Y); 44/200; Concert Band; Mrchg Band; School Musical; School Play; Swing Chorus; Variety Show; Var JV Fld Hcky; Var Wt Lftg; NHS; Musc Perf.

TYSON, JEFF; Henderson HS; West Chester, PA; (S); 11/349; Church Yth Grp; JCL; Service Clb; Ski Clb; JV Lcrss; JV Socr; French Hon Soc; Prfct Atten Awd; Latin Hnr Soc 85.

TYSON, MARK; Hatboro-Horsham HS; Hatboro, PA; (Y); Church Yth Grp; FCA; SADD; Variety Show; Var Ftbl; Var Trk; Im Wt Lftg; Temple U; Sales.

TYSON, MISSY; Kennedy Christian HS; Sharon, PA; (Y); 8/100; French Clb; Pep Clb; Varsity Clb; Band; Chorus; Capt Drill Tm; Yrbk Stf; Im Bsktbl; NHS; Pres Schlr; Egan Schlrshp 86; Excllnc Frnch 86; Mercyhurst.

TYSON, SUSAN; Kutztown Area HS; Kutztown, PA; (Y); Sec FHA; School Play; Mgr Bsktbl; Mgr Stat Fld Hcky; Mgr(s); High Hon Roll; NHS; Psych.

TYTKE, WILLIAM; Steel Valley HS; Munhall, PA; (Y); 16/207; Cmnty Wkr; Var Ftbl; Wt Lftg; High Hon Roll; Hon Roll; NHS; Embry Riddle; Engr.

TZANAKIS, MATT; West Mifflin Area HS; W Mifflin, PA; (Y); 3/300; Ski Clb; L Bsbl; High Hon Roll; Jr NHS; NHS; Indiana U Of PA Physcs Tstng Comptn 86; Penn ST; Engrg.

TZITZIFAS, ZOIS; Upper Darby HS; Upr Darby, PA; (Y); Church Yth Grp; JA; High Hon Roll; Accntng 1 Awd 85-86; Hnr Stu 85-86; CPA.

UBER, MOLLY; St Marys Area HS; St Marys, PA; (Y); Church Yth Grp; Hon Roll; NHS; Messiah; Med.

UBER, PHIL; Grove City HS; Grove City, PA; (Y); 33/195; Art Clb; Aircraft Mech.

UBERTI, MICHELLE; Du Bois Area HS; Penfield, PA; (Y); Church Yth Grp; 4-H; Girl Scts; Varsity Clb; Yrbk Stf; Stu Cncl; Capt Var Cheerleading; Gym; Hon Roll; Gannon U; Pre-Med.

UBRIACO, THOMAS J; Pennsbury HS; Yardley, PA; (Y); Church Yth Grp; Computer Clb; Rep Stu Cncl; Im Bsktbl; Cheerleading; Var Socr; Im Sftbl; Im Tennis; Outstndng Mdfldr Awd For Sccr 84-85; Bus.

UCMAN, TENA; Elizabeth Forward HS; Elizabeth, PA; (Y); Pep Clb; Ski Clb; Spanish Clb; Nwsp Stf; Yrbk Stf; Spanish NHS; Psych.

UDANI, MANISHA NALIN; Bethal Park SR HS; Bethel Park, PA; (Y); 1/515; Rep French Clb; Rep Stu Cncl; High Hon Roll; NHS; Val; Ptry Pblshd Amer Ptry Anthlgy & Bst Nw Pts 86; Wstnghs Sci Hons Inst Stu; Pennsylvania ST U; Med.

UDELL, HARRAN; Upper Dublin HS; Ambler, PA; (Y); 80/307; Temple Yth Grp; Varsity Clb; Var JV Bsbl; Var L Bowling; JV L Socr; Bus.

UDICIOUS, MELISSA; Central Catholic HS; Allentown, PA; (Y); Church Yth Grp; Chorus; Variety Show; Var Capt Bsktbl; Var Capt Crs Cntry; Var Capt Sftbl; High Hon Roll; Hon Roll; Army Rsrvs Schlr Athl Awd 86; Sftbl & X-Cntry 1st Tm All-Conf & All-Str 84-86; Sftbl 2nd Tm 85-86; Spec Ed.

UDOH, MONIQUE; Upper Moreland HS; Willow Gr, PA; (Y); VP Church Yth Grp; Pres Church Choir; Rep Stu Cncl; Var Bsktbl; Chrch Fmly Of Yr Awd 86; Smmr Intnsv Frgn Lang Prgm Awd 86; Spellman Coll; Arch.

UFBERG, DAVID; Parkland HS; Allentown, PA; (Y); 21/472; Cmnty Wkr; Math Tm; SADD; Rep Soph Cls; VP Stu Cncl; Capt L Socr; Var L Trk; High Hon Roll; NHS; Ntl Merit Ltr; Blck Blt Tae Kwan Doe Karate 83; Lehigh Vly All Str Slct Sccr Tm Goalkpr 86; Mst Courgs Athl Awd 86; Med.

UFFELMAN, JON; Mansfield JR & SR HS; Mansfield, PA; (S); Drama Clb; Band; Chorus; Mrchg Band; School Musical; VP Stu Cncl; Tennis; High Hon Roll; NHS.

UHLMAN, LORI; Connecut Valley HS; Linesville, PA; (Y); 32/71; GAA; Sec Trs Pep Clb; Color Guard; Yrbk Ed-Chief; Yrbk Phtg; Yrbk Sprt Ed; Stu Cncl; Stat Vllybl; Air Force.

UKRYN, HEATHER JOY; Hempfield SR HS; Irwin, PA; (Y); AFS; Camera Clb; French Clb; Ski Clb; Spanish Clb; Band; French Hon Soc; Jr NHS; NHS; Englsh-Hstry Hnrs Clss 83-86; The American U; Intl Bus.

ULAN, DONNA; Northwestern SR HS; Albion, PA; (Y); #5 In Class; VP Camera Clb; Science Clb; Concert Band; Mrchg Band; Pres Yrbk Ed-Chief; Yrbk Phtg; Hon Roll; NHS.

ULANOSKI, JAMES; Greenwood HS; Liverpool, PA; (S); 7/63; Boy Scts; Church Yth Grp; Red Cross Aide; Band; Chorus; Church Choir; Concert Band; Mrchg Band; School Musical; Trk; Penn ST.

ULERY JR, JAMES M; Greensburg Central Catholic HS; Latrobe, PA; (Y); 15/244; AFS; Boy Scts; Chess Clb; Church Yth Grp; Drama Clb; Ski Clb; Acpl Chr; Chorus; School Musical; School Play; Wstnghse Hon Inst 86; St Vincent Coll; Med.

ULICHNEY, DREW; Pocono Mountain HS; Mt Pocono, PA; (Y); 7/325; Scholastic Bowl; Rep Soph Cls; JV Var Bsktbl; Var Golf; Var Socr; Var Trk; Bausch & Lomb Sci Awd; DAR Awd; Hon Roll; NHS.

ULINSKI, DONNA; Pennsbury HS; Yardley, PA; (Y); Church Yth Grp; German Clb; Intnl Clb; Chorus; School Musical; Yrbk Sprt Ed; Yrbk Stf; Var Fld Hcky; Var Socr; Im Vllybl; Phys Ftns 84-85.

ULJON, HEATHER; Elk County Christ; St Marys, PA; (S); Dance Clb; Drama Clb; Ski Clb; Swing Chorus; Variety Show; Yrbk Stf; Stat Bsktbl; Hon Roll; NEDT Awd; Cmnty Wkr; Advrtsng.

ULLOM, TARA; Jefferson Morgan JRSR HS; Clarksville, PA; (S); 8/100; Spanish Clb; Varsity Clb; Yrbk Stf; Rep Frsh Cls; Rep Stu Cncl; Var L Cheerleading; Cit Awd; Hon Roll; CA U Of PA; Psych.

ULMER, BARB; Bellefonte HS; Bellefonte, PA; (Y); Trs Church Yth Grp; Hon Roll; Secy.

ULMER, CHRIS; Mohawk Area JR SR HS; Enon Valley, PA; (Y); Church Yth Grp; 4-H; Girl Scts; Latin Clb; Pep Clb; Band; Church Choir; Concert Band; Mrchg Band; School Musical; Sci.

ULMER, MICHAEL; Dubois Area Sr HS; Du Bois, PA; (Y); 34/277; Pres Church Yth Grp; Ski Clb; Varsity Clb; School Play; Yrbk Stf; Var Ftbl; Var Capt Socr; Im Wt Lftg; High Hon Roll; Hon Roll; Aeronaut Engrng.

ULMER, TAMMY; Jersey Shore Area SR HS; Jersey Shore, PA; (Y); Church Yth Grp; FBLA; German Clb; Sftbl; Hon Roll; Acctng.

ULRICH, SUSAN; Lebanon Christian Acad; Lebanon, PA; (S); Drama Clb; 4-H; Chorus; Church Choir; School Musical; School Play; Yrbk Stf; Pres Soph Cls; Sec Sr Cls; JV Var Sftbl.

ULTMAN, SHARI K; State College Area Alternative Program; State College, PA; (Y); Nwsp Rptr; Ntl Merit SF; Amer Assoc U Wmn Awd For Acadmc Excllnc 85; Cert Merit-Cmmn Wlth PA 85; Engl.

UMBAUGH, PATRICIA; Punxsutawney Area SR HS; Punxsutawney, PA; (Y); 4-H; 4-H Awd; Hrs Trnr.

UMBENHAUER, ANN; Northern Lebanon HS; Fredericksburg, PA; (Y); 4-H; Teachers Aide; Varsity Clb; Bsktbl; Fld Hcky; Hon Roll; Church Yth Grp; Chorus; School Musical; Sftbl; Lebanon Cnty Soc Of Frm Wmn Schlrshp 86; Vrsty Ltr 83-86; Ntl Ed Ctr; Exec Secy.

UMBENHAUER, NEIL; Pine Grove Area HS; Pine Grove, PA; (Y); Am Leg Boys St; Varsity Clb; Band; Concert Band; Jazz Band; Mrchg Band; Pep Band; Nwsp Rptr; Rep Frsh Cls; Rep Jr Cls; ; Frstry.

UMBENHAUR II, WILLIAM; Saint Clair Area HS; St Clair, PA; (Y); 4/85; VP Drama Clb; Math Tm; Ski Clb; Varsity Clb; Stage Crew; Nwsp Rptr; Yrbk Sprt Ed; Pres Jr Cls; Pres Sr Cls; Sec Stu Cncl; MVP Bsbl Team 86; Brian Picciolo Awd Ftbl 85; Engrng.

UMBENHOUER, SEAN; Hamburg Area HS; Shoemakersville, PA; (Y); Church Yth Grp; Pres German Clb; VP Band; Concert Band; Jazz Band; Mrchg Band; Pep Band; Var Bsbl; Var Socr; Hon Roll; Schlstc Awd Am Hist 86; Comp Sci.

UMBERGER JR, GLENN; Northern Lebanon HS; Jonestown, PA; (Y); 82/178; Church Yth Grp; Office Aide; SADD; Teachers Aide; School Play; Var Trk; Shppnsbrg U; Mth.

UMBERGER, LEE; Eastern Lebanon County HS; Womelsdorf, PA; (Y); Band; Church Choir; Jazz Band; Mrchg Band; High Hon Roll; JP Sousa Awd; NHS; Pres Schlr; Church Yth Grp; Srvc Abv Slf Awd 86; Otstndng Sphmr & SR Music 84-86; U Of DE; Math.

UMBRIAC, MICHAEL; MMI Preparatory Schl; Hazleton, PA; (S); Trs Computer Clb; Nwsp Stf; High Hon Roll; JETS Awd; NHS; Ntl Merit Ltr; NEDT Awd; Ski Clb; School Play; U Of PA Alumnae Assn Merit Awd 86; Alpha Kappa Chaptr German Natl Hnr Soc 86; 1st Pl MII Open Hs Pro; Aerosp Engrng.

UMHOLTZ, PAM; Tyron Area HS; Tyrone, PA; (Y); FBLA; Pep Clb; SADD; Varsity Clb; Band; Chorus; Color Guard; Bsktbl; Powder Puff Ftbl; Sftbl.

UMPHREY, PATTI L; Canon Mc Millan SR HS; Strabane, PA; (Y); Cmnty Wkr; Exploring; Hosp Aide; Latin Clb; Science Clb; Band; Concert Band; Drill Tm; Mrchg Band; L Pom Pon; U Of Pittsburgh; Pharm.

UMSTEAD, KELLY; Freedom HS; Easton, PA; (Y); 10/404; Church Yth Grp; French Clb; JA; High Hon Roll; Hon Roll; NHS; Pres Acad Ftns Awds Pgm 86; Blmsbrg U Schlr Pgm 86; Marco & Louise Mitrani Schlrp 86; Bloomsburg U; Erly Chldhd Educ.

UMSTEAD, LYN; Middleburg HS; Middleburg, PA; (Y); 7/120; Pres Chorus; VP Concert Band; VP Mrchg Band; Stage Crew; Nwsp Stf; Ed Yrbk Stf; Stu Cncl; Var Cheerleading; Hon Roll; NHS; Susquehanna Vly Band 84-86; MVP Chrldng 85.

UNDERKOFFLER, TERI; Williams Valley HS; Tower City, PA; (Y); Band; Chorus; Church Choir; Concert Band; Flag Corp; Mrchg Band; Symp Band; Trs Jr Cls; Hon Roll; Mrchng Band Sweater 86; Chorus Sweater 85; Stu Sec 86; Thompson Inst; Exec Sec.

UNDERWOOD, SEAN; Simon Gratz HS; Philadelphia, PA; (Y); Concert Band; Mrchg Band; Cornell; Comp.

UNGER, DIANE; Salisbury HS; Allentown, PA; (Y); 61/130; Hosp Aide; Color Guard; Mrchg Band; Rep Jr Cls; Smr Plygrnd Instrctr 86; Lancaster Gnrl Hosp; RN.

UNGER, HEIDI MICHELE; Moon SR HS; Coraopolis, PA; (Y); 19/330; Dance Clb; Concert Band; Mrchg Band; Symp Band; Rep Stu Cncl; Capt Cheerleading; Capt Twrlr; Cit Awd; High Hon Roll; NHS; 1st Rnnr Up Miss Natl Teen Pag 84; Ctznshp Awd Scholar Eckerd Coll 84; IN U PA; Bus.

UNGER JR, JAMES G; Kenneth HS; Chadds Ford, PA; (Y); Boy Scts; Letterman Clb; Pres Radio Clb; School Play; Nwsp Stf; Rep Sr Cls; Var L Trk; Var L Wrstlng; Yrbk Stf; Hon Roll; Acad Comp Tm MVP 85-86; Milman E Prettyman Sprtsmnshp Awd 85-86; The Citadel; Polit Sci.

UNGER, KELLY; Hopewell SR HS; Clinton, PA; (Y); 30/260; Pres 4-H; German Clb; Band; Yrbk Stf; Stu Cncl; Capt Powder Puff Ftbl; Trk; Wt Lftg; 4-H Awd; High Hon Roll; Gneva Coll Hnr Schlr Awd 86; I Dare You Awd 85; Geneva Coll.

UNIEJEWSKI, EDWARD; Trinity HS; Washington, PA; (Y); 130/374; JV Var Bsbl; Var Golf; Hon Roll; West Liberty ST Coll; Phys Edu.

UNSIL, O; J P Mc Caskey HS; Lancaster, PA; (Y); AFS; Pres JA; Band; Chorus; Sec Stu Cncl; Var Cheerleading; Trk; Cit Awd; Hon Roll; Bus Admin.

UNVARSKY, JEAN; GAR Memorial HS; Wilkes Barre, PA; (S); 21/177; FBLA; Library Aide; Yrbk Bus Mgr; Yrbk Stf; Var Sftbl; Hon Roll; Jr NHS; NHS; LCCC; Bnkng.

UPDIKE, CHARLES; Pennsbury HS; Levittown, PA; (Y); Chess Clb; Computer Clb; French Clb; Mathletes; Math Clb; Scholastic Bowl; Hon Roll; NHS; Pres Schlr; AHSME Mth Exam Fin 86; ARML All PA Mth Tm 4th Pl 86; Mth, Comp Sci, Comp Lab Asst Awds 86; PA ST U; Mth.

UPDYKE, THERESA; St Huberts High School For Girls; Philadelphia, PA; (Y); 46/367; Church Yth Grp; Cmnty Wkr; Stage Crew; Nwsp Stf; Yrbk Stf; Lit Mag; Hon Roll; NHS; Prfct Atten Awd; Hnrbl Mntn Natl Ptry Cntst 84-86; Rcmmndtn Cmmntry Srv 85; Temple U; Physcl Thrpy.

UPPERMAN, KELLY; Chambersburg Area SR HS; Chambersburg, PA; (Y); French Clb; Girl Scts; Hosp Aide; NFL; Nwsp Stf; Yrbk Stf; Lit Mag; Masonic Awd; VFW Awd; Voice Dem Awd; Jrnlsm.

UPPERMAN, LINDA; Yough SR HS; W Newton, PA; (Y); 9/226; French Clb; Hosp Aide; Band; Chorus; Camp Fr Inc; Jazz Band; Mrchg Band; High Hon Roll; NHS; Fr Excllncy Cert 86; Hnr Stu Awd 86; U Pittsburgh; Bio.

URAM, DIANE; Lakeland HS; Mayfield, PA; (S); 24/152; FHA; Var JV Cheerleading; Hon Roll; Prfct Atten Awd; Marywood; Nrsg.

URANOWSKI, GAIL; John S Fine HS; Nanticoke, PA; (Y); 24/251; Chorus; Mgr(s); Swmmng; High Hon Roll; NHS; Chrs Awd Medl 85; Acad All Amer 86; Med.

URBAN, GAIL; Steel Valley HS; Munhall, PA; (Y); 21/233; Exploring; JCL; Office Aide; Church Choir; High Hon Roll; Hon Roll; NHS; Interboro Coll Clb Schlrp 86; Hist Soc Essay Awd 86; Penn St; Elem Ed.

URBAN, IAN; Conestoga SR HS; Wayne, PA; (Y); Var L Golf; Var L Tennis; Hon Roll; U Of Vt; Elec Engrng.

URBAN, KENNETH; Cedar Crest HS; Lebaon, PA; (Y); 75/300; Latin Clb; Pep Clb; JV Var Bsktbl; Mansfield U; Math Stats.

URBAN, LAURA L; Athens HS; Athens, PA; (Y); 2/150; Sec Soph Cls; Rep Stu Cncl; Var L Bsktbl; Var Sftbl; Var L Trk; Var L Vllybl; Hon Roll; Pres NHS; Ntl Merit SF; Cert Merit High Ed Assist Agncy 85; Engrng.

URBAN, PATRICK W; Panther Valley HS; Coaldale, PA; (Y); 14/106; Am Leg Boys St; Boy Scts; Political Wkr; ROTC; Church Choir; Color Guard; Yrbk Stf; God Cntry Awd; Hon Roll; ROTC Battallion Cmdr LTC 86-7; Comm.

URBAN, RACHEL; Hershey HS; Hershey, PA; (Y); 21/196; Camera Clb; Var L Bsktbl; Mgr Fld Hcky; Co-Capt Var Trk; High Hon Roll; Hon Roll; Natl Merit Finalist; Origami Club Fndr & Pres 84-86; Treva Disc Schlrshp; Rutgers U Douglass Coll; Langs.

URBAN, SHAUN; Somerset SR HS; Friedens, PA; (Y); Var Ftbl; Engnr.

URBANI, LORI; Sto-Rox SR HS; Mc Kees Rocks, PA; (Y); 30/145; French Clb; Office Aide; Sec Chorus; School Play; Nwsp Rptr; JV Var Bsktbl; Hon Roll; Trs Frsh Cls; Sec Soph Cls; Sec Jr Cls; Law.

URBANOWICZ, ALAN; Cardinal Brennan HS; Ashland, PA; (Y); 19/50; Spanish Clb; Var Bsbl; Var Bsktbl; Engrng.

URBANSKI, CONNIE; Pius X HS; Stroudsburg, PA; (Y); 7/32; Office Aide; Pep Clb; School Musical; Nwsp Stf; Yrbk Stf; Mgr Ftbl; High Hon Roll; NHS; Acdmc All Amer 84-85; Pre-Law.

URBANY, LISA M; Trinity HS; Washington, PA; (Y); Debate Tm; VP Key Clb; NFL; Pep Clb; Ski Clb; Speech Tm; Flag Corp; Mrchg Band; High Hon Roll; Hon Roll; U Pittsburgh; Physcl Thrpy.

URICH, MICHAEL; West Perry SR HS; Elliottsburg, PA; (Y); 17/217; Church Yth Grp; Pres Computer Clb; Spanish Clb; Trs Varsity Clb; Trs Soph Cls; Stu Cncl; Var L Bsbl; Var L Bsktbl; Var L Socr; Trs NHS; PA ST; Engnrng.

URITZ, PETER; Pittston Area HS; Pittston, PA; (Y); Art Clb; Church Yth Grp; Red Cross Aide; Jazz Band; Hon Roll; Wilkes Coll; Music.

URSIC, TRACY; West Allegheny HS; Imperial, PA; (Y); 16/197; Drama Clb; Chorus; Psych.

URSIDA, BETH; Big Beaver Falls HS; Beaver Falls, PA; (Y); AFS; VP Church Yth Grp; JA; Q&S; Concert Band; Mrchg Band; Yrbk Stf; Sftbl; L Tennis; High Hon Roll; Hghst Hon Awd 86; Hstry Awd Win Pc Clb 86; Gannon U; Med Tech.

URSINE, LORETTA; Windber Area HS; Windber, PA; (Y); 25/110; Chorus; Stu Cncl; Cheerleading; Trk; Hon Roll; Sec NHS; IN U Of PA; Fshn Merch.

URSO, DENISE; Peters Twp HS; Mc Murray, PA; (Y); Cmnty Wkr; Exploring; Intnl Clb; Key Clb; Spanish Clb; Concert Band; Mrchg Band; School Play; Hon Roll; NHS; Natl Sci Olympiad Bio 84; Natl Sci Olympiad Chem 85; Amer Lit Awd 85.

URSO, JON; North Allegeheny SR HS; Pittsburgh, PA; (Y); DECA; FBLA; JA; Ski Clb; Rep Frsh Cls; Rep Soph Cls; Rep Jr Cls; Rep Stu Cncl; Ftbl; Socr; DECA Dstrct, ST & Ntl Lvl Awds In Rtsrnt Mngmnt 85 & 86; Purdue; Rstrnt Mngmnt.

URSO, MARIA; Mid-Valley HS; Throop, PA; (Y); Chorus; Crs Cntry; Hon Roll; Air Force.

USAITIS, ROBERT; Wyoming Valley West HS; Kingston, PA; (S); 15/410; Key Clb; Ski Clb; Rep Stu Cncl; L Swmmng; Var Trk; Cit Awd; French Hon Soc; High Hon Roll; NHS; NEDT Awd; Intl Frgn Lang Awd 86; Pre-Med.

USNER, CHRISTINE; Ephrata SR HS; Ephrata, PA; (Y); Sec Church Yth Grp; Band; Concert Band; Mrchg Band; Orch; School Musical; Symp Band; Tennis; Hon Roll; J Harry Hibshman Schlrshp 86; Lehigh Data Proc Inst; Comp Prg.

USSIA, JOSEPH P; Bethel Park SR HS; Bethel Park, PA; (Y); 131/515; JA; Rep Frsh Cls; Rep Soph Cls; U Pittsburgh; Engrng.

USUKA, DENISE M; Upper Dauphin Area HS; Lykens, PA; (Y); 10/105; Sec Church Yth Grp; PAVAS; Mrchg Band; School Musical; School Play; Yrbk Stf; Capt Twrlr; NHS; Pres Schlr; Rotary Awd; Yth Schlrs Chmstry 85; U Of Pittsburgh; Lawyer.

UTLEY, SUSAN E; Moravian Acad; Bethlehem, PA; (Y); Church Yth Grp; Hosp Aide; Chorus; School Play; Symp Band; Variety Show; Yrbk Stf; Lit Mag; Var Crs Cntry; JV Fld Hcky; Smmr-6 Wk Trp To Englnd UK 86; Paper Rt.

VACCARI, NATALIE; Ringgold SR HS; Finleyville, PA; (Y); 18/319; Pres Church Yth Grp; Pres Library Aide; Band; Chorus; Church Choir; Concert Band; Mrchg Band; Orch; School Musical; Nwsp Rptr; U Schlrs Awd Duquesne U 85; Math, Sci Hnr Scty Hgh Hnrs Awd 85-86; Duquesne U; Psych.

VACCONE, MICHELLE; Strath Haven HS; Wallingford, PA; (Y); Church Yth Grp; Ski Clb; Spanish Clb; Chorus; School Musical; Variety Show; Hon Roll; CYO Tlnt Awd 81-82; Patriotsm & Svc To Cmnty Awd 81-82.

VACHARAT, MELISSA; Cheltenham HS; Melrose Pk, PA; (Y); Gym; Sftbl; Tennis; Phys Fit Awd 85 & 86; Bus.

VACHINO, JOHN A; Scranton Prep; Taylor, PA; (Y); 40/190; Pep Clb; Ftbl; Trk; Wt Lftg; High Hon Roll; Hon Roll; NHS; Prfct Atten Awd; U Scrntn; Pltcl Sci.

VACLAVIK, STEVEN; Upper Dauphin Area HS; Millersburg, PA; (Y); 9/111; Varsity Clb; Band; Chorus; Church Choir; School Musical; School Play; Var JV Ftbl; Hon Roll; NHS; Rotary Stu Of Mnth & Ldrshp Conf; Penn ST U; Aerospc Engrg.

VAHALY, PERRY; Belle Vernon Area HS; Belle Vernon, PA; (Y); Pres Exploring; Political Wkr; Red Cross Aide; Ski Clb; Var L Ftbl; Var L Swmmng; Im Wt Lftg; Boy Scts; Pres JA; SADD; Pres Of Year Jr Achvt 85-86; Eagle Scout 84; U Pittsburgh; Pre Med.

VAHANIAN, MELISSA; Mercyhurst Prep HS; Erie, PA; (Y); 56/150; School Play; Yrbk Ed-Chief; Yrbk Stf; Var L Cheerleading; Var Powder Puff Ftbl; Cert Merit Excllnc Frnch 84-85; Hnbl Mntn Bouqt Arts 85-86.

VAHEY JR, BRIAN; Kennett HS; Landenberg, PA; (Y); 6/154; Boy Scts; Science Clb; Yrbk Ed-Chief; Yrbk Phtg; Rep Stu Cncl; Im Bsktbl; JV Crs Cntry; Var Trk; Hon Roll; NHS; PA Gov Schl Sci Alt 86; Mech Engrng.

VAIL, MICHELLE; Lakeland Jr SR HS; Jermyn, PA; (Y); 16/143; Pres FBLA; FHA; Drill Tm; Yrbk Stf; Hon Roll; NHS; Northeast Inst Of Educ; Lgl Sec.

VAJDIC, DIANE; Bishop Mc Devitt HS; Bressler, PA; (Y); 53/210; Art Clb; Mgr Mgr(s); Hon Roll; 3rd Pl-All Yeas In Art 86; St Vincents Coll; Dsgn.

VALCARCEL, ANN; North Allegheny SR HS; Pittsburgh, PA; (Y); Church Yth Grp; Cmnty Wkr; Hon Roll; Jr NHS; NHS; Dstngshd Achvt Awd Chem 84-85; Dstngshd Achvt Awd World Cultures 84-85; Dstngsd Achvt Awd Engl 85-86; Bus.

VALDERRAMA, WENDY; Wyoming Seminary Prep Schl; Shavertown, PA; (Y); Cmnty Wkr; Hosp Aide; Pep Clb; Ski Clb; Spanish Clb; Chorus; Stage Crew; Yrbk Stf; JV Bsktbl; JV Var Mgr(s); Med.

VALE, PAULA; Elmer L Meyers HS; Wilkes Barre, PA; (Y); 10/160; FBLA; Key Clb; Office Aide; Yrbk Stf; Rep Stu Cncl; Var Capt Swmmng; High Hon Roll; Jr NHS; Trs NHS; Spanish NHS; Presdntl Acad Ftns Awd 86; Hofstra U; Lbrl Arts.

VALE, SHARI; E L Meyers HS; Wilkes Barre, PA; (Y); 9/160; Key Clb; Temple Yth Grp; Chorus; Yrbk Ed-Chief; Stu Cncl; Fld Hcky; Hon Roll; NHS; NEDT Awd; Spanish NHS; Phrmcy.

VALENCIA, KATHY; Mahanoy Area HS; Barnesville, PA; (Y); 18/122; Rptr FFA; Yrbk Stf; Var L Trk; High Hon Roll; Hon Roll; Gino Capone Memrl Schlrshp 86.

VALENTE, CLAIRE M; Radnor HS; Rosemont, PA; (Y); 1/280; Trs Drama Clb; Exploring; Math Tm; Model UN; Quiz Bowl; School Play; Ed Lit Mag; NCTE Awd; Ntl Merit SF; Val; Brown U Eng Awd 85; Mt Holyoke Math,Sci Awd 85; Natl Cntst 3rd ST 85; Hist.

VALENTI, DEBORAH; Norwin SR HS; Westmoreland City, PA; (Y); Hosp Aide; Library Aide; Math Clb; Spanish Clb; Yrbk Stf; Hon Roll; NHS; Westmoreland County CC; Nrsng.

VALENTI, JAMES; Penn Hills SR HS; Pittsburgh, PA; (S); 18/897; Pres German Clb; Ski Clb; Varsity Clb; Capt Ice Hcky; Cit Awd; High Hon Roll; Jr NHS; NHS; 3 1/2 Yr AFROTC Schlrshp 86; Jr Ctzn Of Yr 86; PA ST U; Astronautics.

VALENTI, MARK; New Castle HS; New Castle, PA; (S); 13/236; Computer Clb; Ski Clb; Band; Concert Band; Var L Ftbl; Trk; Hon Roll; US Naval Acad; Aerospace Engr.

VALENTINE, HOPE; Pottstown SR HS; Pottstown, PA; (S); 5/238; French Clb; Key Clb; Spanish Clb; Church Choir; Pres Frsh Cls; Sec Soph Cls; Trs Jr Cls; Rep Stu Cncl; Var Cheerleading; NHS; Phrmcy.

VALENTINE, KEVAN M; Tamaqua Area SR HS; Tamaqua, PA; (Y); 64/191; Boy Scts; Church Yth Grp; French Clb; Pep Clb; Science Clb; Rep Frsh Cls; Rep Soph Cls; Rep Stu Cncl; L Ftbl; French Hon Soc; Brigham Young U; Bus Mgmt.

VALENTINE, LAURA; Pleasant Valley HS; Columbia, NJ; (Y); 25/171; Library Aide; SADD; Chorus; Rep Jr Cls; Rep Sr Cls; Score Keeper; Easter Seals Schrlshp 86; Pres Acad Ftns Awd 86; Cum Laude 86; County Coll Morris; Nrsng.

VALENTINO, ANGELA; Saint Maria Goretgti HS; Philadelphia, PA; (Y); 96/390; Hosp Aide; Hon Roll; Charles E Ellis Scholar 85-86; 2nd Hnrs 85-86; Peirce JC; Crt Rptr.

VALENTINO, JENNIFER; Bethel Park HS; Bethel Pk, PA; (Y); Drama Clb; JA; Chorus; School Musical; Cheerleading; Diving; Powder Puff Ftbl; Trk; High Hon Roll; Hon Roll; Musicl Thtr.

VALENZO, WILLIAM J; Lancaster Catholic HS; Lancaster, PA; (Y); 51/218; Church Yth Grp; Teachers Aide; Varsity Clb; Var L Bsbl; Var L Ftbl; Hon Roll; KC Schlrshp 86; Hnrb Mntn Lancaster Lebaon Leag Ftbl All Star 86; West Chester U; Sports Med.

VALERI, AMY; Bellwood-Antis HS; Bellwood, PA; (Y); 9/127; Chorus; Church Choir; Concert Band; School Musical; Variety Show; Ed Nwsp Rptr; Capt Twrlr; High Hon Roll; NHS; Bus Profsnl Womens Girl Mnth 86; PA ST U.

VALERIANO, DEENA R; Oley Valley HS; Oley, PA; (Y); 41/163; Pres Pep Clb; School Musical; Pres Soph Cls; Pres Jr Cls; Sec Stu Cncl; Var Co-Capt Cheerleading; Var Sftbl; Twrlr; Smile Cont Fin 83-84; Athltc Assn Offcr 84-86; Feature Twirler 85-86; Dntl Hygn.

VALINE, CRAIG; Forest Hills HS; Salix, PA; (Y); Ski Clb; Chorus; JV Wrstlng; High Hon Roll; Hon Roll; U Of Pittsburgh.

VALLA, ANNA; Charleroi Area JR SR HS; Charleroi, PA; (Y); 8/180; Science Clb; Ski Clb; Spanish Clb; Sec Soph Cls; Sec Jr Cls; Sec Sr Cls; VP Stu Cncl; DAR Awd; High Hon Roll; Hon Roll; Mary Noss Frshmn Scholar 86; CA U PA; Spn.

VALLE, BRENDA DALLA; Everett Area HS; Everett, PA; (S); Drama Clb; Spanish Clb; Varsity Clb; Sec Band; Trs Sr Cls; Cheerleading; Sec NHS; Penn ST U; Spec Ed.

VALVANO, JOSEPH CHRISTOPHER; West Side Vo-Tech; Hunlock Creek, PA; (Y); Var L Ftbl; Var Wt Lftg; High Hon Roll; PA ST; Arch Engr.

VAN, CHERYL; Delaware Valley SR HS; Milford, PA; (Y); Drama Clb; Ski Clb; SADD; Chorus; School Musical; Yrbk Ed-Chief; Lit Mag; Crs Cntry; High Hon Roll; NHS.

VAN BLARGAN, ROBERT; Northampton SR HS; Danielsville, PA; (S); Computer Clb; Nwsp Stf; JV Socr; Hon Roll; Comptr Sci.

VAN CLEVE, JACQUI; Bristol JR SR HS; Bristol, PA; (Y); Aud/Vis; Cmnty Wkr; Trs Intnl Clb; Capt Color Guard; Ed Yrbk Stf; Natl Hstrcl Scty Philadelphia 85; Vly Frg Frdm Fdn Smnr 86; Advrstng Exec.

VAN DER LEE, FRANCES; Canon-Mcmillan SR HS; Canonsburg, PA; (Y); 30/371; Church Yth Grp; French Clb; FBLA; Nwsp Stf; French Hon Soc; High Hon Roll; Hon Roll; Prfct Atten Awd; C H A M P S Awd 84; Bradford; Sec.

VAN DERLICK, JODI; G A R Memorial HS; Wilkes Barre, PA; (S); 14/177; Sec Church Yth Grp; FBLA; Hosp Aide; Chorus; Church Choir; Hon Roll; NHS; Ntl Merit Ltr; Accntng.

VAN DEWARK, SHERRIE; Sayre Area HS; Sayre, PA; (Y); 31/119; Nwsp Rptr; Nwsp Stf; Lit Mag; Trs Sr Cls; Hon Roll; Joyce Beck Mem Awd 86; Bloomsburg ST U; Sec Ed.

VAN DUYNE, STEVEN; Bishop Kenrick HS; Norristown, PA; (Y); 89/317; Wt Lftg; Villanova U; Nclr Engnrng.

VAN FLEET, BRIAN; Lackawann Trail HS; Dalton, PA; (Y); 10/83; Scholastic Bowl; Pres Frsh Cls; Var L Ftbl; High Hon Roll; Lion Awd; NHS; Presdntl Acadmc Ftns Awd 86; Hghst Math Awd 86; Acadmc Al-Amer Schlr 86; Penn ST; Bus Mgmt.

VAN HORN, ANN M; Mifflinburg Area HS; New Berlin, PA; (Y); 12/169; Am Leg Aux Girls St; Sec 4-H; Pres Mrchg Band; Yrbk Ed-Chief; Stu Cncl; Var L Fld Hcky; Var L Sftbl; High Hon Roll; NHS; Church Yth Grp; SVL All Star 1st Tm Fld Hcky 84-86; Acadmc And Athltc Schlrshp 86; Catawba Clg; Sprts Med.

VAN HORN, LORI; Marion Center Area HS; Creekside, PA; (Y); 4-H; FBLA; Office Aide; Science Clb; Chorus; Orch; 4-H Awd; Jr NHS; NHS; Gregg Typng I Awd 85; Gregg Typng II Awd 86; Bus.

VAN HORNE, JO LYNN; Altoona Area HS; Altoona, PA; (S); 26/683; Pres Sec Church Yth Grp; German Clb; Hosp Aide; Concert Band; Orch; Rep Frsh Cls; Rep Sr Cls; Var L Swmmng; NHS; NEDT Awd; IN U Of PA; Med Tech.

VAN NATTA, MICHEL L; Central Dauphin HS; Harrisburg, PA; (Y); 21/386; Varsity Clb; Off Frsh Cls; Off Soph Cls; Off Jr Cls; Off Sr Cls; Trs Stu Cncl; Var Cheerleading; Var Swmmng; Var Capt Trk; Im Vllybl; Peopl To Peopl H S Stu Ambssdr 85; Physcl Thrpy.

VAN ORMER, STEVEN; Cambra Heights HS; Gilroy, CA; (Y); 31/171; Band; Mrchg Band; Pep Band; Yrbk Stf; Hon Roll; NHS; Acdmc All-Amer 86.

VAN ROEKEL II, RICHARD P; Waynesboro SR HS; Waynesboro, PA; (Y); 57/381; Hon Roll; Law Enfrcmnt.

VAN SCYOC III, JOHN; Big Spring HS; P Lainfield, PA; (Y); 1/189; Computer Clb; Quiz Bowl; Band; Concert Band; Mrchg Band; High Hon Roll; NHS; Outstndg In Physcs Awd 86; Acad Bnd Awd 86; Elec Engrg.

VAN SICKLE, SCOTT; Uniontown HS; Uniontown, PA; (Y); 42/296; Boys Clb Am; Cmnty Wkr; 4-H; Trs German Clb; Varsity Clb; Var L Bsbl; Var L Bsktbl; Tennis; High Hon Roll; Church Yth Grp; Master Cnclr De Molay Masonic 83; German Hnr Soc 84; Alderson-Broaddus Grant; Alderson Broaddus; Bus Admin.

VAN SKIVER, DAVID; Northeast Catholic HS; Philadelphia, PA; (Y); JV Bsbl.

VAN TASSEL, TRACY; New Brighton SR HS; New Brighton, PA; (Y); 53/146; Library Aide; VICA; Chorus; Rep Stu Cncl; Capt JV Cheerleading; Trk; High Hon Roll; Hon Roll; Stu Of Wk; Fshn Merchndsng.

VAN VLIET, LAUREN S; Wellsboro SR HS; Wellsboro, PA; (Y); French Clb; Hosp Aide; Sec Band; Chorus; Drm & Bgl; School Musical; Trk; High Hon Roll; NHS; Pep Clb; BPW Girl Of Month Feb 86; SSMH Health Career Schlrshp 86; Phy Ed Awd 86; Drivers Ed Awd 86; U Of Pittsburgh; Phrmcy.

VAN VOORHIS, GREGG; Franklin Regional HS; Murrysville, PA; (Y); Boy Scts; Pres Church Yth Grp; Ski Clb; Band; Bsktbl; Var L Crs Cntry; God Cntry Awd; Hon Roll; NHS; JA; Eagle Scout 86; Polit Sci.

VAN WHY, AMY; Grand Army Of The Republic Memorial; Wilkes Barre, PA; (S); 7/180; Exploring; Hosp Aide; Key Clb; Band; Chorus; Concert Band; Drm Mjr(t); Orch; Tennis; High Hon Roll; Typng I Awd 85; Pre-Med.

VAN WHY, NANCY; E L Meyers HS; Wilkes-Barre, PA; (S); 24/166; Hosp Aide; Sec Key Clb; Ski Clb; Chorus; Yrbk Stf; Capt Cheerleading; L Sftbl; Hon Roll; NHS; Spanish NHS; Outstndng Typng Awd 85; PA ST U; Cmmnctns.

VAN WYE, GRETCHEN; Cumberland Valley HS; Mechanicsburg, PA; (Y); 16/550; Cmnty Wkr; Debate Tm; SADD; Band; School Musical; School Play; Ed Lit Mag; Rep Stu Cncl; Hon Roll; NHS.

VANATTA, BOB; Johnsonburg Area HS; Johnsonburg, PA; (S); 9/88; Varsity Clb; Nwsp Stf; Var Ftbl; L Trk; Hon Roll; Prfct Atten Awd; Comp Engrng.

VANCE, DANIELLE; St Maria Goretti HS; Philadelphia, PA; (Y); 123/390; Orch; School Musical; Lit Mag; Communications.

VANDEGRIFT, CHERYL; Neshaminy HS; Levittown, PA; (Y); 208/730; Church Yth Grp; Bsktbl; Sftbl; Mgr(s); Bus.

VANDEGRIFT, CHRISTOPHER; Archbishop Kennedy HS; Gwynedd Valley, PA; (Y); 25/187; Cmnty Wkr; Ski Clb; Rep Jr Cls; Trs Sr Cls; Stu Cncl; JV Bsktbl; Capt Crs Cntry; Capt Trk; Hon Roll; NHS; US Marine Corps Dstngshd Athl Awd 86; U Of Pittsburgh; Cvl Engrng.

VANDEGRIFT, PAUL; Archbiship Kennedy HS; Gwynedd Vly, PA; (Y); 14/169; Rep Frsh Cls; Var Crs Cntry; Var Trk; Hon Roll; Trs NHS; Philadelphia Inqr Athl Wk 86; Futr Olympn Awd Olympc Clb 86; Exch Clb MVP Awd 86.

VANDERHOOF, ALISA; Corry JR SR HS; Corry, PA; (S); 17/215; VICA; Plcd 1st VICA Cmptn 86; Pittsbrgh Beauty Acad; Csmtlgy.

VANDERMARTIN, LISA; Nativty BVM HS; Pottsville, PA; (Y); Aud/Vis; French Clb; Drill Tm; Stat Bsktbl; Capt Bowling; Score Keeper; Hon Roll; Lebanon Valley Coll; Rdlgy.

VANDERVOORT, KARYN; Line Mountain HS; Rebuck, PA; (Y); 12/109; 4-H; Ski Clb; Nwsp Stf; Trs Frsh Cls; Rep Stu Cncl; Fld Hcky; Sftbl; Elks Awd; Hon Roll; NHS; Pres Phys Ftns Awd, Natl Sci Olympiad 85; Am Leg Cert Schl Awd 86; Shippensburg U; Mktg.

VANDEWATER, KEVIN; Peters Township HS; Venetia, PA; (Y); Church Yth Grp; Varsity Clb; Pres Stu Cncl; Var L Bsbl; Var L Bsktbl; Var L Ftbl; High Hon Roll; Hon Roll; Stu Adv Commtte 85-86.

VANDIVER, CLAUDINE; St Huberts HS; Philadelphia, PA; (Y); 100/367; Dance Clb; School Play; Stu Cncl; Crs Cntry; Hon Roll; Prfct Atten Awd; Cert Merit Hghst Grade Avg Related Arts 85; Accntg.

VANDYKE, KEN; Ambridge Area HS; Baden, PA; (Y); Am Leg Boys St; Boy Scts; Exploring; French Clb; Band; Concert Band; Mrchg Band; School Musical; Variety Show; Var L Trk; Robert Morris Coll; Accntng.

VANDZURA, DANIEL; Lewistown HS; Lewistown, PA; (Y); 37/276; AFS; Boy Scts; Pres 4-H; Key Clb; Chorus; School Musical; Yrbk Phtg; Pres Soph Cls; Pres Stu Cncl; 4-H Awd; PA ST U; Law.

VANEK, DENNIS; Valley HS; New Kensington, PA; (Y); 12/201; Exploring; Science Clb; Ski Clb; Spanish Clb; Varsity Clb; Var L Ftbl; Var L Trk; NHS.

VANEMAN, TIMOTHY; Bishop Mc Cort HS; Johnstown, PA; (Y); Exploring; Letterman Clb; Chorus; Jr Cls; Ftbl; Wt Lftg; Hon Roll; Physcl Ther.

VANKIRK, CYNTHIA; Frazier HS; Perryopolis, PA; (Y); Church Yth Grp; Drama Clb; Library Aide; Band; Chorus; Concert Band; Mrchg Band; Pep Band; School Play; Yrbk Phtg; Chld Psychlgst.

VANLEW, DEBRA; Downingtown SR HS; Downingtown, PA; (Y); 77/600; Church Yth Grp; Band; Mrchg Band; Bowling; Mgr(s); Score Keeper; High Hon Roll; Hon Roll; Katherine Gibbs; Secy.

VANNATTEN, RENEE; Union Area HS; New Castle, PA; (Y); 18/66; Library Aide; Spanish Clb; Y-Teens; Nwsp Stf; Yrbk Stf; High Hon Roll; NHS; Pep Clb; Acdmc All Amer 86; Pres Acdmc Ftns Awd 86; Jms Mem Schl Of Nrs; Nrs.

VANNUCCI, DAVE; Frazier HS; Fayette City, PA; (Y); Spanish Clb; Yrbk Phtg; Ftbl; Gym; CA ST U; Bus Adm.

VANNUCCI, KAREN; Lancaster Catholic HS; Landisville, PA; (Y); 10/220; Trs Service Clb; Soroptimist; Varsity Clb; JV Bsktbl; Var L Fld Hcky; Var L Sftbl; Hon Roll; NHS; Bus Dptmnt Schlrshp Elzbthtwn Coll 86; Mst Valble Plyr Softbl 86; US Army Rsrve Ntl Schrl Ath Awd 86; Elizabethtown Coll; Acctg.

VANORSDALE, TAMMY; Elkland Area HS; Elkland, PA; (Y); Church Yth Grp; Drama Clb; Band; Concert Band; Jazz Band; Yrbk Bus Mgr; Trs VP Stu Cncl; JV Var Vllybl; High Hon Roll; SADD; Soccr Homecmng Honr 85; NTL W Champnshp For Vllybl Stu 85; Math.

VANOVER, DOUGLAS; York County Area Vo Tech; York, PA; (Y); Church Yth Grp; Computer Clb; VICA; JV Swmmng; Hon Roll; Prfct Atten Awd; Penn ST U; Comp Sci.

VANPELT, JODY; Benton Area JR SR HS; Benton, PA; (Y); 10/50; Church Yth Grp; Keywanettes; Pres Band; Sec Trs Chorus; School Musical; Stu Cncl; JV Var Cheerleading; Var Fld Hcky; Hon Roll; NHS; Triple Trio; Mixed Ensmbl; Phys Thrpy.

VARADHACHARY, ARUN; Council Rock HS; Newtown, PA; (Y); 104/900; Var Capt Swmmng; German Clb; Orch; Hon Roll; Pre-Med.

VARADY, JOSEPH; Owen J Roberts HS; Phoenixville, PA; (Y); Aud/Vis; Camera Clb; Computer Clb; Latin Clb; Varsity Clb; School Play; Stage Crew; Yrbk Phtg; Yrbk Stf; JV Ftbl; Lat Natl Hnr Soc 84-86; Bus.

VARALLO, DEANNA; St Maria Goretti HS; Philadelphia, PA; (Y); French Clb; GAA; Mathletes; Chorus; School Musical; Stage Crew; Rep Soph Cls; Bsktbl; Cheerleading; Mgr(s); Engr.

VARALLO, LEE; Abington SR HS; Huntingdon Valley, PA; (Y); 114/550; Hosp Aide; Library Aide; Ski Clb; Spanish Clb; Yrbk Stf; Rep Jr Cls; Rep Sr Cls; Hon Roll; Jr NHS; NHS; Phila Coll Textile; Textile Mkt.

VARANO, MONICA; Albert Gallatine HS; Pt Marion, PA; (Y); VP FHA; Office Aide; Band; Concert Band; Drm Mjr(t); Mrchg Band; Pep Band; Yrbk Stf; Twrlr; Hon Roll; Sawyers Schl; Rsrvtnsts.

VARANO, THERESA MARIE; Mount Carmel Area JR SR HS; Kulpmont, PA; (Y); 18/140; Am Leg Aux Girls St; Key Clb; Latin Clb; Band; Mrchg Band; Nwsp Rptr; JV Cheerleading; Var L Trk; High Hon Roll; NHS; Phys Ther.

VARAVETTE, KEVIN; Western Beaver HS; Industry, PA; (Y); Hon Roll; ICM Pittsburgh; Accntng.

VARECHA, ARLENE; Midland HS; Midland, PA; (Y); Latin Clb; Drill Tm; Bsktbl; Sftbl; High Hon Roll; Hon Roll; Navy.

VARGAS, RANDALL T; Du Bois Area HS; Dubois, PA; (Y); Computer Clb; Varsity Clb; Rep Cmnty Wkr; JV Var Bsbl; JV Var Ftbl; Im Tennis; Im Vllybl; JV Var Vllybl; Hon Roll; Bus Mngmnt.

VARGESON, MIKE; Cowanesque Valley HS; Little Marsh, PA; (Y); 48/92; Drama Clb; FFA; Letterman Clb; Ski Clb; Varsity Clb; School Play; Var Ftbl; Wt Lftg; Hnrbl Ment All-Stars Ftbl 85; Edinboro U.

VARGO, DEBORAH JO; Mary Fuller Frazier HS; Star Junction, PA; (S); Drama Clb; FNA; Ski Clb; School Play; Stu Cncl; Bsktbl; Cheerleading; Score Keeper; Sftbl; High Hon Roll; Hosp Adm.

VARGO, LORI; Frazier HS; Fayette City, PA; (Y); Sec FNA; Hosp Aide; Ski Clb; Color Guard; Nwsp Stf; Yrbk Stf; Rep Soph Cls; Rep Jr Cls; Rep Sr Cls; Rep Stu Cncl; Med.

VARGO, ROBERT; Nazareth Area SR HS; Nazareth, PA; (Y); 4/231; Church Yth Grp; High Hon Roll; Hon Roll; Lion Awd; NHS; Pres Schlr; Rotary Awd; Wilkes Coll; Chmstry.

VARILLO, JOSEPH; Neshaminy HS; Langhorne, PA; (Y); 39/700; Variety Show; High Hon Roll; Hon Roll; NHS; Prfct Atten Awd; Merit Awds 84-86; Penn ST; Elec Engrng.

VARLEY, JODI; Steel Valley HS; Munhall, PA; (Y); #9 In Class; Band; Concert Band; Mrchg Band; Hon Roll; NHS; Govrs Schl For Ag 86; Vet.

VARNER, DIANE; Middletown Area HS; Middletown, PA; (Y); Church Yth Grp; Model UN; Color Guard; Mrchg Band; Nwsp Stf; Computer Clb.

VARNER, JASON D; Cambridge Springs HS; Cambridge Springs, PA; (Y); 18/119; Boy Scts; Chess Clb; Pres Church Yth Grp; French Clb; Library Aide; Model UN; Quiz Bowl; SADD; Concert Band; Mrchg Band; Bst 1st Yr Deleg Modl Legsltr 84-85; Pres Area Yth Fllwshp 86-87; Amer Socty H S Stdnts 86-87; Elctrcl Engrng.

VARNER, KEITH; Forest Hills HS; Johnstown, PA; (Y); 38/156; Church Yth Grp; L Var Bsbl; Hon Roll; Jr NHS; U Of Pittsburgh; Chrprctr.

VARNER, LAURA; Steel Valley HS; West Homestead, PA; (S); 15/233; Key Clb; High Hon Roll; Hon Roll; NHS; Robert Morris Coll; Bus Adm.

VARNER, MICHELLE RAYNE; Seneca Valley SR HS; Harmony, PA; (Y); Church Yth Grp; JA; SADD; Symp Band; Var L Cheerleading; Mgr(s); Hon Roll; NHS; Varsity Clb; Am Yth Semnr Japan 86; Elem Educ.

VARNER, PAULA; Trinity HS; Washington, PA; (Y); Camera Clb; JA; Key Clb; Library Aide; Office Aide; Pep Clb; FL Coll; Counclng.

VARNER, SAM; Clearfield Area HS; Clearfield, PA; (Y); Church Yth Grp; Band; Chorus; Concert Band; Mrchg Band; School Musical; High Hon Roll; Hon Roll; Music.

VARNER, SHANE; East Juniata HS; Mcalisterville, PA; (Y); 7/95; Church Yth Grp; Varsity Clb; Rep Frsh Cls; Pres Soph Cls; VP Jr Cls; VP Stu Cncl; Var Bsbl; Var Bsktbl; Var Capt Ftbl; Hon Roll; US Air Force Acad; Engrng.

VARZALY, DANIELLE; Abington Heights HS; Clarks Summit, PA; (Y); 27/266; Church Yth Grp; Dance Clb; Drama Clb; Ski Clb; Varsity Clb; Band; Chorus; Concert Band; Mrchg Band; School Musical; Drexel U; Elctrcl Engrng.

VASBINDER, ERIN; Purchase Line HS; Clymer, PA; (Y); Church Yth Grp; FBLA; Band; Church Choir; Concert Band; Mrchg Band; Pep Band; School Play; Hon Roll; Cnty Band 84; Dist Band 85; Cnty Band 86; Music Educ.

VASBINDER, HEATHER; Butler Area SR HS; Butler, PA; (Y); FBLA; Thesps; Swing Chorus; VP Soph Cls; Rep Stu Cncl; Hon Roll; Travl.

VASICAK, KIM; West Side Vo-Tech HS; Larksville, PA; (Y); 4/155; Sec Trs FBLA; Yrbk Ed-Chief; Yrbk Stf; Sec Soph Cls; Var Capt Vllybl; High Hon Roll; Hon Roll; Yth Salute 85; Kings Coll; Comp.

VASKO, CYNTHIA; Freedom HS; Bethlehem, PA; (Y); 33/445; Art Clb; JA; Science Clb; VICA; Hon Roll; NHS; Westchester U; Micro-Bio.

VASQUEZ, MARIA; Jules E Mastbaum Voc Tech; Philadelphia, PA; (Y); Teachers Aide; JV Vllybl; Hon Roll; Paralegal Lawyer.

VATTIERI, TERESA; Saint Huberts Catholic HS; Philadelphia, PA; (Y); 7/367; Camera Clb; Mathletes; Yrbk Stf; High Hon Roll; Hon Roll; NHS; Prfct Atten Awd; Cmnty Svc Corp Rcgntn 85-86; Triest Colloqum 86; Advrtsng.

VAUGHAN, DAVID; Pottsgrove SR HS; Pottstown, PA; (Y); 56/229; Chess Clb; Church Yth Grp; Key Clb; Hon Roll; Amer Lgn Schl Awd 83; Cert Of Excllnc-Drftg 86; Drexel U; Arch Engrng.

VAUGHAN, LAURA; Sullivan County HS; Lopez, PA; (Y); 11/91; Church Yth Grp; Drama Clb; Nwsp Rptr; L Bsktbl; Capt Cheerleading; L Vllybl; NHS; Am Leg Aux Girls St; VP Key Clb; Nwsp Stf; Spirit Jr Miss Awd 85; MVP Vllybl, Vlybl All Star 86; La Roche Coll; Bio.

VAUGHN III, CHARLES PAUL; Susquehanna Township HS; Harrisburg, PA; (Y); Var JV Bsktbl; Var L Trk; Bus Admin.

VAUGHN, JEFFREY; Philipsburg-Osceola SR HS; Sandy Ridge, PA; (Y); 14/250; Boy Scts; Chess Clb; Church Yth Grp; Ftbl; God Cntry Awd; Hon Roll; NHS; NEDT Awd; BSA Eagle 86; Cert Lfgrd; Engrng.

VAUGHN, SALLY; Huntingdon Area HS; Huntingdon, PA; (Y); Key Clb; Yrbk Stf; Mgr(s); JV Vllybl; Forgn Lang.

VAUGHT, GAIL; York Catholic HS; York, PA; (Y); Spanish Clb; Varsity Clb; Chorus; Var JV Bsktbl; Var L Trk; Var L Vllybl; High Hon Roll.

VAUX, SHERRY; Philipsburg-Osceola Area HS; Philipsburg, PA; (Y); 105/250; Drama Clb; Thesps; Chorus; School Play; Stage Crew; Nwsp Stf; JV Sftbl; PA ST U; Actg.

VAVRICK, MICHELLE; Dunmore HS; Dunmore, PA; (Y); Computer Clb; FBLA; Ski Clb; Spanish Clb; Nwsp Rptr; Yrbk Stf; Bowling; Twrlr; High Hon Roll; Jr NHS; Math.

VAYANSKY, TOM; Mon Valley Catholic HS; Belle Vernon, PA; (Y); 10/80; AFS; Church Yth Grp; Letterman Clb; Radio Clb; Var L Socr; Penn St.

VAYDA, RON; Swissvale HS; Pittsburgh, PA; (Y); French Clb; ROTC; Ski Clb; Bsbl; JV Vllybl; Wrstlng; French Hon Soc; Hon Roll; NHS; Aviation.

VAYDOVICH, TINA; Uniontown Area HS; Waltersburg, PA; (Y); 25/326; VP Spanish Clb; Band; Stu Cncl; High Hon Roll; Jr NHS; Trs NHS; Pres Schlr; Spanish NHS; Helen Brice Schlrshp 86; Svc Awd 86; St Vincent; Lwyr.

VAZZANA, EVERETT; North Catholic HS; Pittsburgh, PA; (Y); 37/301; German Clb; Math Tm; School Play; Bsbl; Var Capt Socr; Hon Roll; NEDT Awd; ROTX Schlrshp 86-90; Case W Rsrv U; Elec Engrng.

VEARD, CHRISTINE; Cornell HS; Coraopolis, PA; (Y); 8/81; Color Guard; Stage Crew; Nwsp Ed-Chief; Yrbk Ed-Chief; Var Cheerleading; Swmmng; High Hon Roll; Hon Roll; Jr NHS; NHS; Penn ST U; Chem Engrng.

VECCHIO, TINA; Mapletown JR R HS; Dilliner, PA; (Y); Aud/Vis; GAA; Library Aide; Ski Clb; Varsity Clb; Yrbk Stf; Rep Soph Cls; Sec Jr Cls; Rep Stu Cncl; Timer; Exec Secty.

VEERAPPAN, VEENA; Altoon Area HS; Altoona, PA; (S); 6/682; Pres Computer Clb; French Clb; Math Clb; NFL; Science Clb; Orch; Jr NHS; Trs Sec NHS; Frnch Awd 83; Comp Sci.

VEET, LISA; Bishop Mc Divitt HS; Middletown, PA; (S); 3/200; Cmnty Wkr; Drama Clb; Pres French Clb; Service Clb; Chorus; Rep Soph Cls; Pres Jr Cls; VP Sr Cls; High Hon Roll; NHS; Holy Cross Coll Bk Awd; Outstndng Schlrshp Ldrshp 85; St Josephs U; Lib Arts.

VELEZ, NOEL; Central Dauphin East HS; Harrisburg, PA; (Y); Ski Clb; Im Ice Hcky; JV L Socr; Im Vllybl; Hon Roll; Crmnl Jstce.

VELISARIS, ELAINE; Canon Mc Millan SR HS; Canonsburg, PA; (Y); Pres Church Yth Grp; Chess Clb; Trs French Clb; Office Aide; VP Chorus; School Musical; Yrbk Ed-Chief; Yrbk Stf; Stu Cncl; DAR Awd; Med.

VELLONE, TONY; Bishop Guilfoyle HS; Altoona, PA; (Y); Art Clb; Chess Clb; Church Yth Grp; Ski Clb; Chorus; Coach Actv; Ftbl; Vllybl; High Hon Roll; Hon Roll; PA ST; Law.

VELMER, KELLY; South Park HS; Library, PA; (Y); 18/200; Concert Band; Mrchg Band; Powder Puff Ftbl; Twrlr; High Hon Roll; Hon Roll; NHS; Awd Outstndng Acdmc Achvt 86; Pres Acdmc Fit Awd 86; U Pitts; Bio Sci.

VENAFRA, TINA; Abp Wood For Girls; Warminster, PA; (Y); Cmnty Wkr; Var Socr; Church Yth Grp; German Clb; Office Aide; Var Trk; Hon Roll; Pres Schlr; Knghts Of Clmbs Awd Sccr 85-86; US Army Ntl Coaches Assis Sccr MVP Awd 86; B Grnt & Stu Grnt; Barry U Miami; Allied Hlth.

VENARCHICK, KELLY; Danville SR HS; Danville, PA; (Y); SADD; Chorus; JV Bsktbl.

VENART, ELLEN E; Methacton HS; Collegeville, PA; (Y); 11/350; Drama Clb; French Clb; Red Cross Aide; Chorus; School Musical; School Play; Lit Mag; Rep Sr Cls; High Hon Roll; NHS; U Of DE; Cmmnctns.

VENARUCCI, RAEMIE; Seton Catholic HS; Pittston, PA; (Y); 9/92; Key Clb; Stat Mathletes; Ski Clb; Yrbk Stf; Var Capt Cheerleading; L Sftbl; L Tennis; High Hon Roll; NHS; Intl Frgn Lang Awd Frnch 85; US Chrldr Achvt Awd 86; YMCA Gym Tm 85-86; Med.

VENDITTO, DANIEL N; Louis E Dieruff HS; Allentown, PA; (Y); 87/327; Art Clb; Drama Clb; FBLA; Ski Clb; School Play; Yrbk Phtg; Yrbk Rptr; Yrbk Stf; Rep Stu Cncl; Powder Puff Ftbl; Philadelphia Coll; Fshn Mdsng.

VENEY, VICKY; Greater Johnstown HS; Johnstown, PA; (Y); JA; Pep Clb; SADD; Im JV Cheerleading; JV Trk; Bus Mgmt.

VENEZIA, MARY JO; Gwynedd Mercy Acad; Collegeville, PA; (Y); 17/69; Church Yth Grp; Service Clb; Nwsp Stf; Stu Cncl; Fld Hcky; Sftbl; Tennis; High Hon Roll; Trs NHS; Hghst Avg In Frnch Gold Mtl Awd 85-86; Fnlst In Montgmry Cnty JR Miss 85-86; Philadelphia Coll; Phrmcy.

VENNUM, MICHAEL K; Montour SR HS; Coraopolis, PA; (Y); 16/277; JA; Math Tm; NFL; Political Wkr; ROTC; Off Mrchg Band; NHS; Pres Schlr; Voice Dem Awd; PA ST U; Pre-Med.

VENO, ARTHUR; Mid-Valley HS; Dickson City, PA; (Y); Ski Clb; Capt Ftbl; Im Vllybl; Var Wt Lftg; Capt Wrstlng; Big 11 Cnfrnc Ftbl All-Star 85 & 86; Phys Thrpst.

VENSEL, KATHLEEN S; Mc Guffey HS; W Alexander, PA; (Y); 18/200; German Clb; Pep Clb; Spanish Clb; Chorus; Var L Bsktbl; Capt Powder Puff Ftbl; L Sftbl; High Hon Roll; NHS; Ntl Merit Schol; Pres Wheeling Coll Schlrshp, Wheeling News Rgstr Teen Wk 86; Acdmc All Am 86; Wheeling Coll.

VENTURI, GINA; Crestwood HS; Mountaintop, PA; (Y); FBLA; Hosp Aide; Ski Clb; School Play; Var Trk; NEDT Awd; Early Chldhd Educ.

VENTURO, JOE; Moon Area SR HS; Coraopolis, PA; (Y); 34/304; Band; Concert Band; Jazz Band; Mrchg Band; Symp Band; Stat Swmmng; Trk; Im Vllybl; PTA Spnsrd Wrtng Cmptn 1st Pl Awd 85.

VENUTO, ANN; Bishop Shanahan HS; Kennett Square, PA; (Y); 55/215; Pres Sec Church Yth Grp; Pep Clb; Var Cheerleading; JV Var Sftbl; Hon Roll; NHS; Bus Admin.

VENUTO, TOM; Central Columbia HS; Bloomsburg, PA; (Y); Church Yth Grp; Bowling; Bloomsbrg U; Physcl Ftnss.

VERBA, MICHAEL; Saucon Valley SR HS; Hellertown, PA; (Y); 19/148; French Clb; Hosp Aide; Band; Jazz Band; Mrchg Band; Pep Band; School Play; Var L Swmmng; Hon Roll; Chem.

VERBONITZ, KIM; Central Catholic HS; Whitehall, PA; (Y); 3/210; French Clb; Intnl Clb; Math Clb; Service Clb; Rep Jr Cls; Stu Cncl; JV Bsktbl; Var L Crs Cntry; High Hon Roll; NHS; PSPB Engl Awd 2nd Awd 86; 1s Tpl St & Rgnls PJAS 85; Crss-Cntry 1st Pl Dist Team 85.

VERCUSKY, WAYNE; William Allen HS; Allentown, PA; (Y); 41/651; Art Clb; Letterman Clb; Varsity Clb; Lit Mag; Wrstlng; Hon Roll; NHS; Socr; Grad Hnrs 85-86; Adv Plcmt Stdo Art Prog 85-86; PA ST U; Art.

VERDUCI, CARMELA A; Bishop Shanahan HS; Westchester, PA; (Y); Drama Clb; Quiz Bowl; Chorus; Nwsp Stf; Yrbk Stf; Hon Roll; Rep Schl Archdiocesan Bus Comp 85-86; Accntng.

VEREB, MELISSA; Villa Maria Acad; Erie, PA; (Y); 23/133; Trs Service Clb; Ski Clb; Stage Crew; Yrbk Phtg; High Hon Roll; Hon Roll; NHS; NEDT Awd.

VERES, LORA; Canon-Mc Millan HS; Canonsburg, PA; (Y); Church Yth Grp; Drama Clb; FBLA; Hosp Aide; Office Aide; Ski Clb; School Play; Sftbl; High Hon Roll; Hon Roll; Canon Mc Millan Ed Assoc Schlrshp 86; Duffs Bus Inst; Crt Stenogrphr.

VERESPEY, PEGGY; Scranton Central HS; Scranton, PA; (Y); 91/310; Cmnty Wkr; Dance Clb; Exploring; French Clb; Hosp Aide; Red Cross Aide; Ski Clb; Yrbk Stf; Var L Pom Pon; Bloomsburg U; Spch Pthlgy.

VERGENES, DENISE; Sto-Rox SR HS; Mc Kees Rocks, PA; (Y); 11/149; Church Yth Grp; Office Aide; Color Guard; Flag Corp; Yrbk Stf; Capt Pom Pon; Hon Roll; Mgmt.

VERHOLY, KIM; Louis E Deruff HS; Allentown, PA; (Y); 33/323; Trs Key Clb; Lib Band; Concert Band; Jazz Band; Mrchg Band; Nwsp Rptr; Nwsp Stf; Hon Roll; Jr NHS; NHS; Schl Store Awds, Top Hnr Grad 86; Harcum JC; Anml Hlth Tech.

VERHOVSEK, HOLLI; Bishop Mc Cort HS; Johnstown, PA; (Y); Hosp Aide; Math Clb; Church Choir; Color Guard; Mrchg Band; Orch; High Hon Roll; NHS; U Of Pittsburgh; Bus Mngmnt.

VERICA, CHRIS; Archbishop Carroll For Girls; Havertown, PA; (Y); 14/217; Sec Church Yth Grp; French Clb; Rep Soph Cls; VP Jr Cls; Trs Stu Cncl; Sftbl; High Hon Roll; Hon Roll; NHS; Widener U Schl Of Htl/Rest Mgm.

VERLEST, ROCHELLE; Wilmington Area HS; New Wilmington, PA; (S); 9/101; Sec French Clb; Nwsp Ed-Chief; Yrbk Stf; Stu Cncl; Var L Cheerleading; Var L Gym; Powder Puff Ftbl; Hon Roll; NHS; Early Chldhd Educ.

VERMEULEN, TROY; Tunkhannock Area HS; Dushore, PA; (S); 17/340; FCA; German Clb; Letterman Clb; Rep Jr Cls; Var Capt Vllybl; Hon Roll; NHS; Ntl Merit Ltr; Acad All Amer 84-85; Penn ST; Physics.

VERMILLION, LEN; Blacklick Valley HS; Nanty Glo, PA; (Y); Library Aide; Spanish Clb; Varsity Clb; Bsktbl; Hon Roll; U Pittsburgh; Comp Sci.

VERNA, LORI; Norwin SR HS; N Huntingdon, PA; (Y); 113/546; Girl Scts; Spanish Clb; Hon Roll; St Vincent Coll; Psych.

VERNATI, LINDA; Bishop Kenrick HS; Norristown, PA; (Y); 30/305; Cmnty Wkr; Hosp Aide; Ski Clb; School Play; JV Crs Cntry; Hon Roll; Chsnt Hill Wmns Schlrshp Awd; Villanova U; Nrsng.

VERNER, CORAL; Mc Guffey HS; Washington, PA; (Y); 41/210; Church Yth Grp; French Clb; Concert Band; Mrchg Band; Trk; Hon Roll; Am Lg Essay Awd 86; WV Wesleyan Coll; Chemistry.

VERNICK, CHRIS; Jenkintown HS; Jenkintown, PA; (Y); 14/50; Chess Clb; Quiz Bowl; Ski Clb; School Musical; Yrbk Phtg; VP Soph Cls; Pres Jr Cls; Pres Sr Cls; Pres Rep Stu Cncl; Bsbl; $500 Schlrshp For Outstndng Citizenship 86; U Of DE; Intl Bus.

VERNON, SARA E; Central Bucks H S East; Doylestown, PA; (Y); Chorus; Concert Band; Mrchg Band; Cit Awd; DAR Awd; NHS; Ntl Merit SF; Church Yth Grp; Band; Church Choir; Congrssnl Schlr Natl Young Ldrs Conf 85; Dist & Regnl Band 85.

VERONESI, DAVID; Belle Vernon Area HS; Belle Vernon, PA; (Y); Church Yth Grp; Church Choir; Pres Soph Cls; Pres Jr Cls; Rep Stu Cncl; High Hon Roll; Hon Roll; NHS.

VERRILL, MICHAEL; Governor Mifflin HS; Mohnton, PA; (Y); 28/269; Church Yth Grp; JA; Model UN; Varsity Clb; Chorus; School Musical; Stage Crew; Symp Band; Var Crs Cntry; Var Swmmng; Unified Points Awd 85 & 86; Champnshp Trk Awd 85 & 86; Var Jacket Awd 85; U VA; Bus Adm.

VERRILLA, MARLO; Penn Hills HS; Pittsburgh, PA; (Y); 91/762; AFS; French Clb; Lit Mag; Crs Cntry; High Hon Roll; Hon Roll; Jr NHS; Barbara Freya Mem Schlrshp 86; Prsdntl Acdmc Ftnss Awd 86; U Of Cincinnati; Arch.

VERSZYLA, JEFFREY; Quigley HS; Sewickley, PA; (Y); 26/138; Letterman Clb; Math Tm; VP Soph Cls; Coach Actv; Ftbl; Tennis; Wrstlng; Cit Awd; French Hon Soc; Hon Roll; Cmnctns.

VERVANIC, BARTHOLOMEW J; Brownsville Area HS; Merrittstown, PA; (Y); Drama Clb; French Clb; Letterman Clb; Ski Clb; Yrbk Phtg; Trs Jr Cls; Var L Ftbl; Var Trk; Hon Roll; West Point; Engr.

VERWEY, REBECCA; Saint Josephs Acad; Lancaster, PA; (Y); Science Clb; Nwsp Rptr; Nwsp Stf; Sec Frsh Cls; Sec Soph Cls; Im Bowling; JV Sftbl; 2nd Hghst Avg-Bus Engl, Antmy & Physlgy & Engl II 86; Bus Adm.

VESEK, DAN; E L Meyers HS; Wilkes Barre, PA; (Y); Church Yth Grp; Computer Clb; German Clb; Ski Clb; Wt Lftg; Wrstlng; Hon Roll; Htl Rest Mgmt.

VESOTSKI, LISA; Butler SR HS; Butler, PA; (Y); Cmnty Wkr; Red Cross Aide; Ski Clb; Spanish Clb; Sec Soph Cls; Rep Stu Cncl; JV Capt Cheerleading; Stat Trk; High Hon Roll; Hon Roll; Bus.

VESSELS, RONALD; Cardinal Dougherty HS; Phila, PA; (Y); 224/747; Church Yth Grp; Chorus; Church Choir; High Hon Roll; Hon Roll; Prfct Atten Awd; Eastern Coll; Comp Sci.

VETRO, ANITA; Archbisoph Prendergast HS; Folcroft, PA; (Y); 70/361; Office Aide; Service Clb; SADD; Stage Crew; Nwsp Stf; Mgr Swmmng; Natl Bus Hnr Soc 85-86; Archdcse Phila Bus Cmptn Acctg Ii 86; Keystone Business Schl; Acctg.

VETROVEC, DAVID K; Dover Area HS; Dover, PA; (Y); 36/247; Am Leg Boys St; JA; Library Aide; ROTC; Ftbl; Ntl Merit SF; Memphis ST U; Intl Stud.

VEYCHEK, JOSEPH; Norwin SR HS; N Huntingdon, PA; (Y); Boy Scts; 4-H; Capt Golf; 4-H Awd; Hon Roll; Jr NHS; Elect Engr.

VICARIO, GINA; St Maria Goretti HS; Philadelphia, PA; (Y); 36/426; Rep Church Yth Grp; Cmnty Wkr; JA; Math Clb; Office Aide; Teachers Aide; Lit Mag; High Hon Roll; CSC Hmrm Rep 83; Achvt Awd 86; Spec Hon Dedctn 84; Bloomsburg U; Nrsng.

VICARIO, JULIE; Kennedy Christian HS; Sharon, PA; (Y); 29/98; Latin Clb; Pep Clb; Drm Mjr(t); Nwsp Stf; Trs Frsh Cls; Rep Stu Cncl; Im Bsktbl; Capt Cheerleading; L Twrlr; Var Vllybl; Nrsng.

VICCARI, GINA; Lincoln HS; Wampum, PA; (Y); VP Camera Clb; Key Clb; Ski Clb; Y-Teens; Chorus; Coach Actv; Powder Puff Ftbl; Var Capt Trk; CC Awd; Hon Roll; Key Club Intl Presdncy Awd 86.

VICCARO, JAMES; Cumberland Valley HS; Mechanicsburg, PA; (Y); Bsbl; Bsktbl; Ftbl; Lcrss; Vllybl; Photo Clb 87; Photo.

VICTOR, EDWARD; Brownsville HS; Hiller, PA; (Y); 21/220; Hon Roll; U CA; Comp Systms Mngmnt.

VICTOR, THOMAS; Brownsville Area HS; Hiller, PA; (Y); 31/220; Hon Roll; Archry Clb 86; CA U Of PA; Bus Adm.

VICTOR, TINA; Bentworth HS; Bentleyville, PA; (Y); VP Church Yth Grp; 4-H; FHA; Girl Scts; Ski Clb; Chorus; School Play; Stage Crew; JV Bsktbl; Hon Roll; Jrnlsm.

VICTORY, THERESA; Kutztown Area HS; Kutztown, PA; (Y); Sec Church Yth Grp; Hosp Aide; Office Aide; Color Guard; School Play; Yrbk Stf; Swmmng; Var Tennis; High Hon Roll; Hon Roll; Aoluance Lifesaving Cert 85; C P R Cert 86; Bus.

VIDIC, ELIZABETH; Moniteau JR SR HS; W Sunbury, PA; (Y); Ski Clb; Spanish Clb; Concert Band; Mrchg Band; Nwsp Rptr; Bsktbl; Stat Trk; Hon Roll.

VIERKORN, KRISTIN; General Mc Lane HS; Edinboro, PA; (Y); 32/221; Girl Scts; Spanish Clb; Band; Concert Band; Mrchg Band; Symp Band; JV Sftbl; NHS; Edinboro U.

VIGHETTI, STEPHEN; Cheltenham HS; Glenside, PA; (Y); 70/365; Capt JV Socr; Spanish NHS.

VIGNA, BILL; Leechburg Area HS; Leechburg, PA; (Y); 29/85; Drama Clb; Library Aide; Band; Nwsp Stf; Yrbk Stf; Var L Ftbl; Im Vllybl; Telecmnctns.

VIKOREN, SUSANNE; Central Bucks East HS; Holicong, PA; (Y); Debate Tm; Acpl Chr; Chorus; Nwsp Stf; Rep Jr Cls; VP Stu Cncl; Var L Tennis; Hon Roll; NHS; Val; Pre-Law.

VILA, JENNIFER; Annville-Cleona HS; Annville, PA; (Y); Church Yth Grp; French Clb; Acpl Chr; Band; Madrigals; Mrchg Band; Ed Yrbk Stf; Var L Tennis; NHS; Psychlgy.

VILCHOCK, TAMARA; Old Forge HS; Old Forge, PA; (S); Ski Clb; Hon Roll; NHS; Spanish NHS; Law.

VILCKO, KENNETH; Hazleton HS; Drums, PA; (Y); Boy Scts; FBLA; Hon Roll; Air Force; Law Enfrcmnt.

VILLA, DONELL A; Coudersport JRSR HS; Emporium, PA; (Y); 2/79; FHA; Varsity Clb; Band; Chorus; Cheerleading; Trk; Vllybl; NHS; Pres Schlr; Rotary Awd; Army Rsrve Schlr/Ath Awd 86; 30 Pt Ltr Excllnce Acad Athltcs & Extra-Curr Pursuits 85; Penn ST U; Rehab Ed.

VILLA, LAUREN; Clearfield Area HS; Clearfield, PA; (Y); 25/300; Church Yth Grp; Trs Spanish Clb; Band; Mrchg Band; Orch; Var Im Crs Cntry; Var Swmmng; Var L Trk; High Hon Roll; Dance Clb; Miss Co Ed Teen Pgnt 85-86.

VILLAFANIA, MINETTE; Baldwin HS; Pittsburgh, PA; (Y); 20/535; Math Clb; Orch; JV Vllybl; High Hon Roll; VP NHS; U Pittsburgh; Phrmcy.

VILLALPANDO, CAMILLE; Sacred Heart HS; Pittsburgh, PA; (Y); 1/150; Drama Clb; Spanish Clb; Chorus; Jazz Band; School Musical; School Play; Stage Crew; Variety Show; High Hon Roll; Ntl Merit Ltr.

VILLANOVA, DEBBIE J; Hempfield HS; New Stanton, PA; (Y); French Clb; Pep Clb; Ski Clb; Pep Band; Yrbk Stf; Rep Frsh Cls; Rep Stu Cncl; Var Cheerleading; Im Gym; French Hon Soc; WV U; Physcl Thrpy.

VILLARI, MARNIE; Saint Maria Goretti HS; Philadelphia, PA; (Y); 14/390; Camp Fr Inc; Church Yth Grp; Cmnty Wkr; Drama Clb; 4-H; GAA; Intnl Clb; Mathletes; Math Clb; Science Clb; Pre-Med.

VIMISLICKY, SHAWN; Mt Pleasant Area HS; Mt Pleasant, PA; (Y); Boy Scts; German Clb; Letterman Clb; Science Clb; Bsktbl; Crs Cntry; Capt L Tennis; Trk; Vllybl; Hon Roll; Natl Sci Mrt Awd 85; Med Tech.

VINCENT, DIANE; Wilmington Area HS; Slippery Rock, PA; (Y); Drama Clb; Spanish Clb; Trk; Vllybl.

VINCENT, ERIN; Slippery Rock Area HS; Slippery Rock, PA; (Y); 25/172; Pep Clb; Intnl Clb; Spanish Clb; Band; Mrchg Band; Orch; Nwsp Stf; Rep Stu Cncl; Hon Roll; Slippery Rock U; Secndry Ed.

VINCENT, EVA SUE; Pequea Valley HS; Gap, PA; (Y); 10/121; AFS; Church Yth Grp; JA; Chorus; Concert Band; Jazz Band; Madrigals; Mrchg Band; School Musical; School Play; Magna Cum Laud 86; Pres Acad Ftns Awd 86; Am Assoc Physcs Tchrs Outstndng Stu Yr 86; U DE; Math.

VINCENT, JOHN; Riverview HS; Oakmont, PA; (Y); Drama Clb; French Clb; Jazz Band; School Play; Yrbk Stf; High Hon Roll; Hon Roll; Rado.

VINCENTI, TRACY; Burgettstown JR SR HS; Burgettstown, PA; (Y); Art Clb; Computer Clb; GAA; Office Aide; Ski Clb; Spanish Clb; Chorus; Hon Roll; Hmcmng Crt 86; Prm Crt 86; Cmps Lf 86; Robert Morris Coll; Bus Admn.

VINCI, DONNA; St Maria Goretti HS; Philadelphia, PA; (Y); 83/309; Art Clb; Cheerleading; Itln Hnrs 82-84.

VINCI, KAREN; Sto-Rox SR HS; Mc Kees Rocks, PA; (Y); Church Yth Grp; Cmnty Wkr; Exploring; FBLA; Office Aide; Teachers Aide; Pres Band; Pres Mrchg Band; Yrbk Stf; Pres Soph Cls; Duquense U; Bus.

VINDIVICH, DIANE; Frazier HS; Perryopolis, PA; (S); Drama Clb; Band; Pres Chorus; Jazz Band; Mrchg Band; School Play; Yrbk Bus Mgr; Yrbk Stf; Hon Roll; NHS; Bus Adm.

VINEIS, BONNIE; Morrisville HS; Morrisville, PA; (Y); Band; Concert Band; Mrchg Band; Pep Band; Ed Yrbk Stf; Off Sr Cls; Bausch & Lomb Sci Awd; Hon Roll; Jr NHS; NHS; Walter A Steene Awd 86; Wmns Engrng Math & Sci Awd 86; Hgh Achvt Eng Lit, Chmstry & Grmn II 86; Drexel U; Mtrls Engrng.

VINGLAS, ORIANA; Penn Cambria HS; Portage, PA; (Y); Drama Clb; Ski Clb; Chorus; JV Cheerleading; High Hon Roll; Hon Roll; Duquesne; Pre-Law.

VINH, BINH; Chambersburg HS; Chambersburg, PA; (Y); 44/585; French Clb; Ski Clb; JV Socr; L Tennis; Hon Roll; Kiwanis Awd; Lion Awd; NHS; JV Trk; Minorty Schlrshp 86; Altruism Awd/Trvlrs Protective Assoc 86; Penn ST; Elec Engr.

VINOSKI, JULIANNE; Connellsville Area HS; Connellsville, PA; (Y); 40/500; Cmnty Wkr; Library Aide; Band; Concert Band; Mrchg Band; Sftbl; Trk; High Hon Roll; Hon Roll; Connellsville Girls Ftbl Schlrshp 86; Anchr Glass Containr Corp Schlrshp 86; Acadmc Excllnc Germ Hnry; PA ST U; Bus Adm.

VINROE, BRADEN E; Red Land HS; New Cumberland, PA; (Y); 28/285; CAP; Computer Clb; Exploring; Im Bowling; Hon Roll; Bushido Karate Clb 85-86; PA Game News Mag Drawng Publctn 84; Schl Acad Achvt Awd 84-85; PA ST U; Aerospc Engr.

VINSKOFSKI, KELLY; W Scranton HS; Scranton, PA; (Y); 18/270; Dance Clb; French Clb; Hosp Aide; Ski Clb; Nwsp Stf; Yrbk Stf; Stu Cncl; Sftbl; High Hon Roll; NHS; Scranton U; Med.

VIOLA, ANN MARIE; Scranton Prep; Old Forge, PA; (Y); 37/190; Cmnty Wkr; Church Choir; Sec Concert Band; Jazz Band; Orch; Sec Pep Band; School Musical; High Hon Roll; Hon Roll; U Scranton; Phrmcy.

VIOLA, JASON; Archbishop Kennedy HS; Philadelphia, PA; (Y); Boys Clb Am; Civic Clb; Cmnty Wkr; Hon Roll; Union Leag Awd 85; Temple U; Mathmtcs.

VIOLA, MICHAEL; Father Judge HS; Philadelphia, PA; (Y); 37/359; Aud/Vis; Cmnty Wkr; FCA; Varsity Clb; Nwsp Stf; Im Bsktbl; Var Capt Socr; Cit Awd; Hon Roll; NHS; 1st Tm All-Cthlc Sccr 85-86; 3rd Tm All-Cty Sccr 85-86; Villanova U; Bus.

VIOLA, VINNIE; Bradford Central Christian HS; Bradford, PA; (Y); 5/28; Key Clb; SADD; Pres Jr Cls; Sec Stu Cncl; Var Bsbl; Var Bsktbl; Hon Roll; NHS; Stage Crew; Jr NHS; PA Math Lg Achvt Awd 85; USAF Acad CO Spgs; Hlth Sci.

VIROSTEK, DENISE; Kiski Area HS; Leechburg, PA; (Y); French Clb; Math Tm; Pep Clb; Science Clb; Ski Clb; Spanish Clb; Chorus; High Hon Roll; NHS; Band; Top 10 84; Acad Ltr 84-86.

VIRUS, LISA; Upper Perkiomen HS; Barto, PA; (Y); 80/250; Yrbk Stf; VP Frsh Cls; Pres Soph Cls; Pres Jr Cls; JV Var Cheerleading; Var Capt Fld Hcky; Var Capt Trk; Hon Roll; PA Dist I Champ 200 Meter Dash 86; PA ST Champ 6th Pl 200 Meter Dash 86; Physical Therapy.

VISH, ALBERT; Butler HS; Butler, PA; (Y); German Clb; JV Bsbl; Hon Roll; IN U Of PA.

VISHNESKI, KELLY; Downingtown SR HS; West Chester, PA; (Y); FTA; Library Aide; Office Aide; Spanish Clb; SADD; Teachers Aide; Chorus; Nwsp Rptr; Yrbk Stf; Var Sftbl; IN U PA; Home Ec.

VISHNISKY, WAYNE; Valley View JR SR HS; Archbald, PA; (Y); 11/200; Spanish Clb; High Hon Roll; Hon Roll; Spnsh Merit Awd 83-86; Acadmc Excllnc Awd 83-86.

VISSOTSKI, CARLA; Coughlin HS; Plains, PA; (Y); 83/342; Hosp Aide; Ski Clb; Cmnty Wkr; Capt Var Cheerleading; Capt Var Fld Hcky; Mgr(s); Var Sftbl; Swmmng; Hon Roll.

VISWANATHAN, AKILA; Geibel HS; Connellsville, PA; (Y); 1/75; Drama Clb; Science Clb; Ski Clb; Trs Stu Cncl; Var Cheerleading; Pres French Hon Soc; High Hon Roll; NHS; NEDT Awd; Pres Schlr; PA Govrnrs Schl-Intl Stds 85; PA Govrnrs Schl-The Sciences 86; Wstnghse Jnr Sci Tlnt Srch Awd 86; Med.

VISWANATHAN, SRI; Cedar Crest HS; Lebanon, PA; (Y); 22/326; School Musical; High Hon Roll; Cmnty Wkr; Dance Clb; Drama Clb; French Clb; Pep Clb; Band; Concert Band; Mrchg Band; Ppl To Ppl Hgh Schl Ambsdr 85; Hon Bnqt 85-86; Geargetown Intl Rltns Prgm 86; Intl Rltns.

VITALE, ANTHONY; Belle Vernon Area HS; Belle Vernon, PA; (Y); Letterman Clb; Ski Clb; Spanish Clb; Ftbl; Wt Lftg; Wrstlng; Hon Roll; Civl Engr.

VITALE, JOHN; Spring-Ford SR HS; Pottstown, PA; (Y); 70/268; German Clb; Spanish Clb; Bsbl; Ftbl; Trk; Vllybl; Wt Lftg.

VITALE, KAREN; St Cyril Acad; Danville, PA; (Y); 2/13; French Clb; Sec Key Clb; Math Tm; Quiz Bowl; Chorus; School Play; Nwsp Rptr; Trs Frsh Cls; Rep Soph Cls; VP Jr Cls; Coll Discvry Pgm Schlrshp Kings Coll 86; Russian Lang.

VITELLI, MARK; Pittston Area HS; Pittston, PA; (Y); 97/348; Ski Clb; JV Ftbl; JV Wrstlng; Hon Roll; Medicine.

VITH, DENISE; West Allegheny HS; Cora, PA; (Y); 38/218; Drama Clb; Band; Color Guard; Concert Band; Mrchg Band; School Play; Swmmng; Twrlr; Hon Roll; Pittsburgh U; Syst Anal.

VITKAUSKAS, DAVID J; Southern Columbia Area HS; Bloomsburg, PA; (Y); JV Bsktbl; Hon Roll; NHS; Engrng.

VITTI, LOIS M; Penn Hills SR HS; Pittsburgh, PA; (Y); French Clb; Political Wkr; Pres Science Clb; Ski Clb; Spanish Clb; Trs Jr Cls; Stu Cncl; Gym; High Hon Roll; Hon Roll; Pres Schlrshp Amer U 86; Natl Hnr Socty 85-86; Schlrshp Cours Chatham Coll 85; American U; Intl Bus.

VITUSZYNSKI, LAURA; Cedar Crest HS; Lebanon, PA; (Y); 183/306; Cmnty Wkr; FTA; Girl Scts; Key Clb; Pep Clb; Spanish Clb; SADD; Band; Chorus; Church Choir.

VIVELO, RENEE; Union Area HS; New Castle, PA; (Y); 19/66; Library Aide; Pep Clb; Spanish Clb; Y-Teens; Nwsp Stf; Yrbk Stf; Rep Frsh Cls; Cheerleading; High Hon Roll; Hon Roll; Pres Acdmc Ftns Awd.

VIVIAN, KENDRA; Saegertown HS; Meadville, PA; (Y); 6/125; Church Yth Grp; Ski Clb; Spanish Clb; Drm Mjr(t); Mrchg Band; Yrbk Stf; Hon Roll; NHS; Queen 85; Psych.

VIVIAN, SHARON; Wyoming Valley West HS; Kingston, PA; (Y); Key Clb; Yrbk Stf; Lit Mag; High Hon Roll; Hon Roll; Jr NHS; NHS; NEDT Awd; Ski Clb; Wilkes Coll; Accntng.

VIVINO, MELINA; Penn Hills SR HS; Pittsburgh, PA; (Y); French Clb; FBLA; Yrbk Stf; Stu Cncl; Bsktbl; High Hon Roll; Hon Roll; Grgg Shrthnd Awd 86; Lmp Knwldg Awd 83-86; Supe Prsn Awd Sci 84; PA ST U; Bus Mgmt.

VIVIS, LISA; Bishop Mc Cort HS; Parkhill, PA; (Y); Art Clb; VP Church Yth Grp; Latin Clb; Pep Clb; Chorus; Yrbk Stf; Sftbl; Trk; High Hon Roll; Hon Roll.

VIZZA, TERESA; Monessen JR SR HS; Monessen, PA; (Y); 1/97; Church Yth Grp; French Clb; Sec Band; Sec Concert Band; Sec Mrchg Band; Nwsp Rptr; Rep Frsh Cls; Trs Soph Cls; Bausch & Lomb Sci Awd; High Hon Roll; Union Carbide Schlr 86.

VLASNIK, JON; Meadville Area SR HS; Meadville, PA; (Y); 21/244; Ski Clb; Bsbl; Bowling; Ftbl; Wt Lftg; Hon Roll; NHS; Pharmacy.

VO, PHAT; Harrisburg HS; Harrisburg, PA; (Y); 48/453; ROTC; Drill Tm; Socr; Tennis; Trk; U Of FL; Arch.

VOCI, FRANK; St Josephs Prep; Cherry Hill, NJ; (Y); Camera Clb; School Play; Rep Frsh Cls; Rep Soph Cls; Sec Stu Cncl; Slvr Mdl Acdmc Excllnc 84-85; Hon Ment All Catholic Tm 86; :Aerospace Engrng.

VODA, MICHELLE; Wyalusing Valley JR SR HS; Laceyville, PA; (Y); 8/155; Trs Church Yth Grp; 4-H; Sec Girl Scts; Hosp Aide; Library Aide; Spanish Clb; Band; Chorus; Hst Sr Cls; NHS; Grace Ide Memrl Awd 86; Ladies Aide Schlrshp 86; Hnbl Mntn Rsrv Grnd Champ & Sev Blu Rbbns 4-H 84; U Of PA ST; Microbio.

VODENICHAR, JENNY; Slippery Rock Area HS; Slippery Rock, PA; (Y); 13/172; 4-H; German Clb; Pep Clb; Band; Nwsp Stf; Cheerleading; 4-H Awd; Hon Roll; NHS; Ntl Merit SF; Penn ST; Med.

VOEGHTLY, CARLA; Johnstown Vo-Tech; Johnstown, PA; (Y); JA; Key Clb; VICA; Var L Bsktbl; Var L Vllybl; NHS; Rotary Awd; Robert H Kifer Schlr Athlete Awd 86; WV U; Phy Thrpy.

VOELKL, DAWNA; Avonworth JR SR HS; Pittsburgh, PA; (Y); 1/100; Church Yth Grp; Latin Clb; Y-Teens; Yrbk Bus Mgr; Ed Lit Mag; Stat Bsktbl; Var L Socr; High Hon Roll; NHS; Ntl Merit SF; Buhl Sci Fr Awd Gen Sci Catgry 83-84; N Boroughs Yth Awd 85-86; Mst Valbl Offnsv Plyr Sccr 85-86; Pre-Med.

VOGEL, CLAUDINE L; Mars Area SR HS; Mars, PA; (Y); 18/154; Church Yth Grp; Hosp Aide; Flag Corp; Ed Yrbk Stf; Rep Soph Cls; Rep Jr Cls; Rep Sr Cls; Stat Trk; NHS; Rotary Awd; Rotary Yth Ldrshp Awd 85; Susquehanna U.

VOGEL, JAMES L; Montour HS; Mc Kees Rocks, PA; (Y); 43/277; Band; Chorus; Concert Band; Jazz Band; Mrchg Band; School Musical; Stage Crew; High Hon Roll; Hon Roll; Arion Awd-Musicl Achvt-Dedctn Instrmntl Music Pgm 86; Duquesne U; Music Ed.

VOGEL, JOE; Carrick Pa; Pittsburgh, PA; (S); Chorus; Church Choir; School Musical; Stage Crew; Variety Show; Hon Roll; Nrsg.

VOGEL, PEGGY; Clearfield HS; Clearfield, PA; (S); Trs Key Clb; Spanish Clb; Band; Chorus; Concert Band; Mrchg Band; Orch; Pep Band; L Bsktbl; L Trk; Nursng.

VOGEL, SHARON K; Vincentian HS; Pittsburgh, PA; (Y); Drama Clb; GAA; Library Aide; Ski Clb; School Play; Stage Crew; Nwsp Rptr; Yrbk Stf; VP Soph Cls; Sec Jr Cls; Duquesne U; Phrmcy.

VOGEL, VALARIE; Shady Side Acad; Monroeville, PA; (Y); Drama Clb; French Clb; Hosp Aide; School Musical; Nwsp Stf; JV Sftbl; Tennis; NHS; Ntl Merit Ltr; Johns Hpkns U Tlnt Srch Ntl, Reg & ST Awds 83; Washingtn & Jefferson Coll; Med.

VOGELSANG, BECKY; Littlestown HS; Littlestown, PA; (Y); DECA; VP Sec FBLA; Office Aide; Teachers Aide; Hon Roll; Rgn Ldrshp Cnfrnce FBLA 85; Pres Physcl Ftns Awd 84-85; Acctng.

VOGRIN, AMY; Vincenntian HS; Pittsburgh, PA; (Y); Church Yth Grp; Service Clb; Variety Show; Yrbk Stf; Im Badmtn; JV Var Bsktbl; JV Tennis; Im Vllybl; Astnt Bsktbl Coach Grls Grd Schl 84 & 85; PA ST; Hlth Care.

VOGRIN, DAVID; Marple-Newtown HS; Newtown Square, PA; (Y); Church Yth Grp; FCA; Yrbk Stf; Ftbl; Var Capt Golf; JV Tennis; Hon Roll; Ecnmcs.

VOIT, MICHAEL; Shaler HS; Glenshaw, PA; (Y); 167/517; FBLA; Ski Clb; Spanish Clb; Rep Frsh Cls; Rep Soph Cls; Rep Jr Cls; Var L Ftbl; Ice Hcky; Trk; Wt Lftg; Ftbl Ldng Ground Gainer 86; Weight Lftng Record 85; Ice Hcky Cptn 86-87; Bus.

VOIT, TIMOTHY; Cheltenham HS; Cheltenham, PA; (Y); Boy Scts; Symp Band; Jr Cls; Trk; Geogrphy.

VOITHOFER, LORI; Fairchance Georges SR HS; Smithfield, PA; (Y); Church Yth Grp; Drama Clb; Chorus; Church Choir; School Play; Hon Roll.

VOLANSKI, SHARON ANN; Northwest HS; Benton, PA; (Y); 17/108; Computer Clb; French Clb; Var Capt Trk; High Hon Roll; NHS; Aud/Vis; Chorus; Hon Roll; PA ST U; Ptrlm Engr.

VOLCHKO, GERRI; Cornell HS; Coraopolis, PA; (Y); 1/87; Pres French Clb; Pres Sec Key Clb; Band; Color Guard; Yrbk Rptr; Co-Capt Cheerleading; High Hon Roll; NHS; Ntl Merit Ltr; Psych.

VOLINGAVAGE JR, ANTHONY; Bishop Hoban HS; Shickshinny, PA; (Y); 46/189; Computer Clb; Latin Clb; Ski Clb; Hon Roll; Comp Applctns Awd 86; Kings Coll; Comp Sci.

VOLK, PAMELA J; Manheim Township HS; Lancaster, PA; (Y); Key Clb; Chorus; Stage Crew; Mgr(s); Hon Roll; Pres Citation Yth Grp 79-86; U MD; Microbio.

VOLLMER, DARCY; St Marys Area HS; Saint Marys, PA; (Y); Band; Concert Band; Mrchg Band; Stage Crew; Nwsp Rptr; Nwsp Stf; Score Keeper; Swmmng; Vllybl; Hon Roll; Nrsng.

VOLLMER, JODI L; Beaver Area JR SR HS; Beaver, PA; (Y); 14/193; VP Sec German Clb; JCL; Key Clb; Pep Clb; Ski Clb; Chorus; Powder Puff Ftbl; High Hon Roll; Hon Roll; VP NHS; Acdmc Hnr Awd 84-86; Pres Acdmc Fit Awd 85-86; Hnr Grad 86; Westminster Coll; Intl Bus.

VOLOSIN JR, ROBERT ANDREW; Mt Carmel Christian Schl; Connellsville, PA; (Y); Church Yth Grp; Drama Clb; School Play; Pres Sr Cls; Var Bsktbl; Var Socr; Hon Roll; Pres Schlr; Var Sftbl; TN Temple U; Bus.

VOLPE, BONNIE; Scranton Central HS; Scranton, PA; (Y); 79/278; Ski Clb; Trk; Hon Roll; U Of Scranton; Cmnctns.

VOLPE, DAVID; Greensburg Central Catholic HS; Greensburg, PA; (Y); Aud/Vis; Church Yth Grp; Exploring; Hosp Aide; JCL; Library Aide; Office Aide; Concert Band; Mgr Mrchg Band; Hon Roll; Pre Med.

VOLPE, KRISTINA M; Bishop Kenrick HS; Norristown, PA; (Y); 25/293; Sec Spanish Clb; Stu Cncl; Cheerleading; Hon Roll; Trs NHS; Rotary Awd; WBIC News Chrprsn; U Of Scranton; Acctng.

VOLZ, KELLY; Seneca Valley HS; Evans Cty, PA; (Y); Pres Church Yth Grp; Library Aide; ROTC; Yrbk Stf; Bsktbl; Score Keeper; Sftbl; DAR Awd; High Hon Roll; Hon Roll; Rtrd Offcrs Assn Awd-Mltry Excllnc 84-5; Rsrv Offcrs Assn Awd 85-6; Amer Lgn Awd Mltry Excllnc 85-6; Butler County CC; Accntng.

VOMMARO, JOHN; Strong Vincent HS; Erie, PA; (Y); 32/164; Church Yth Grp; Var Bsbl; Hon Roll; Edinboro U; Bus.

VON CAMPBELL, TIMOTHY; Shenango HS; New Castle, PA; (Y); 37/112; Church Yth Grp; Cmnty Wkr; Im Bsktbl; JV Crs Cntry; Stat Mgr(s); Im Trk; Hon Roll; Jr NHS; Bus Mgt.

VON DREAU, JAYNE E; Williamsport Area HS; Williamsport, PA; (Y); Chorus; Concert Band; Mrchg Band; Symp Band; Lock Haven; Sprts Med.

VON HOFEN, JANE; Quaker Valley SR HS; Edgeworth, PA; (Y); Church Yth Grp; Spanish Clb; Band; Concert Band; Mrchg Band; Symp Band; Bsktbl; Hon Roll; Accnt.

VON SCHLICHTEN, DAVID; Bangor Area SR HS; Bangor, PA; (Y); 3/194; Band; Chorus; Concert Band; Jazz Band; Mrchg Band; School Musical; School Play; Jr NHS; NHS; Boy Scts; Most Outstndng Bandsman Awd 84-86; Band Pres 86-87; PA Govrns Schl For The Arts 86; Drew U; Humanities.

VONDERCRONE, LINDA A; Lansdale Catholic HS; Hatfield, PA; (Y); Drama Clb; FBLA; SADD; Y-Teens; Nwsp Rptr; Nwsp Stf; Lit Mag; Var Powder Puff Ftbl; Var Swmmng; Im Vllybl; Temple U; Jrnlsm.

VORA, SANJAY; Plum SR HS; Pittsburgh, PA; (Y); Church Yth Grp; Cmnty Wkr; Exploring; Var L Tennis; High Hon Roll; NHS; PA ST U; Aerospc Engnrng.

VORACHEK, LAURA; Marple Newton HS; Newtown Square, PA; (Y); Debate Tm; Hosp Aide; JCL; Hst Latin Clb; Trs Service Clb; Ski Clb; Nwsp Stf; Yrbk Stf.

VORE, ANDREW; Trinity HS; Washington, PA; (Y); 29/374; Math Tm; Var L Bsbl; Var L Ftbl; High Hon Roll.

VORKAPICH, RODNEY; Steelton-Highspire HS; Steelton, PA; (Y); 2/94; Chess Clb; Church Yth Grp; Yrbk Stf; Pres Stu Cncl; Bsbl; Bsktbl; High Hon Roll; NHS; Sal; Rensselaer Mdl For Excllnc In Math & Sci 85; Pres Acad Fitns Awd 86; U S Army Rsrve Natl Schlr 86; Wake Forest U; Chem.

VOSEFSKI, THERESA; Northampton Area SR HS; Bath, PA; (Y); Aud/Vis; Office Aide; SADD; Rep Stu Cncl; Var Tennis; High Hon Roll; Hon Roll; Jr NHS; NHS; Bloomsburg; Psych.

VOSSEN, KAREN; Gateway SR HS; Monroeville, PA; (Y); 2/450; Exploring; Math Tm; Model UN; Science Clb; Church Choir; Jazz Band; Mrchg Band; Rep Stu Cncl; Ntl Merit Ltr; Sal; Wstnghse Fmly Schlrshp 86; PA Gvrnrs Schl For The Scis 85; 2nd Pl In Gntcs Slppry Rck U Bio Olympc 86; U Of Notre Dame; Med Dr.

VOUGHT, BETH; Harry S Truman HS; Levittown, PA; (Y); 66/570; Var Crs Cntry; Var Trk; Hon Roll; Subrbn I All-Lg 2nd Tm Wmns X-Cntry 85-86; Soc Wrk.

VOUGHT, SHERRY; Pen Argyl SR HS; Pen Argyl, PA; (Y); Pep Clb; Varsity Clb; Chorus; Sec Frsh Cls; Sec Soph Cls; L Bsktbl; JV Cheerleading; L Fld Hcky; Mgr(s); Trk; Med Tech.

VOYTEK, KAREN; Uniontown Area HS; Uniontown, PA; (Y); 17/325; Church Yth Grp; Spanish Clb; Yrbk Stf; High Hon Roll; NHS; Spanish NHS; Bnkng Prfsn.

VOYTEK, WILLIAM; Frazier HS; Perryopolis, PA; (Y); French Clb; Math Clb; Rep Soph Cls; Im Bsktbl; U AK-FAIRBANKS; Engrng.

VOYTON, FRANCINE; John S Fine HS; Glen Lyon, PA; (Y); Yrbk Phtg; Yrbk Stf; Hon Roll.

VOYTON, GENE; John S Fine HS; Nanticoke, PA; (Y); Varsity Clb; Bsbl; Ftbl; Trk; Wt Lftg; High Hon Roll; NHS; Engrg.

VOZEL, LISA; Norwin SR HS; North Huntingdon, PA; (Y); 6/550; Art Clb; Computer Clb; Exploring; Math Clb; Spanish Clb; Chorus; Nwsp Phtg; Cheerleading; 4-H Awd; Top Ten Cls 85-86; Achvt Acad Sci Awd 85-86; Carnegie Mellon U; Comp Sci.

VRABEL, JEANNETTE; Nativity B V M HS; Minersville, PA; (Y); 26/98; Aud/Vis; FNA; Spanish Clb; Stat Bsktbl; Capt Bowling; Stat Sftbl; Hon Roll; Bowling Trphy Hgh Hndcap, Hgh Game, Hgh Series 84; Htl-Mtl Mgmt.

VRABEL, PAUL L; Whitehall HS; Whitehall, PA; (Y); Am Leg Boys St; Boy Scts; Computer Clb; High Hon Roll; Hon Roll; Penn ST U; Arch.

VRANA, LARA; Penns Manor HS; Clymer, PA; (Y); 9/102; Sec Varsity Clb; Yrbk Stf; Bsktbl; Vllybl; High Hon Roll; Hon Roll; NHS; IN U; Media Comm.

VRANA, TOM; West Allegheny HS; Coraopolis, PA; (Y); 4/250; Computer Clb; Mathletes; Math Tm; Chorus; Crs Cntry; Trk; High Hon Roll; NHS.

VRCEK, TARIS; Sto-Rox HS; Mc Kees Rocks, PA; (Y); 4/149; Church Yth Grp; Exploring; Math Tm; Im Ftbl; Var Trk; Hon Roll; Prfct Atten Awd; Nedt High Score Awd 85; RPI; Aerosp Engrng.

VREDENBURG, DEBBIE; Laurel HS; New Castle, PA; (Y); 20/104; Church Yth Grp; 4-H; Yrbk Stf; Sec Trs Jr Cls; Sec Sr Cls; Rep Stu Cncl; Sftbl; Hon Roll; Awd GPE 86; Grad Hnrs 86; Hncmng Queen Cand 86; Slippery Rock U; Psych.

VRESILOVIC, JOHN; Homer Center HS; Coral, PA; (Y); 3/94; French Clb; Varsity Clb; Var Capt Ftbl; Var Capt Trk; High Hon Roll; Hon Roll; Jr NHS; NHS; NEDT Awd; Prfct Atten Awd; Compltn Smmr Happening Marine Bio Awd 85; Stanford U; Marine Bio.

VROMAN, JEFF; Moshannon Valley JR SR HS; Houtzdale, PA; (Y); Church Yth Grp; Letterman Clb; SADD; Varsity Clb; Var L Ftbl.

VU, HUNG; Downington SR HS; Exton, PA; (S); 29/527; Boy Scts; Im Bowling; Im Tennis; JV Trk; Im Vllybl; Im Wt Lftg; L Hon Roll; NHS; Hnr Rll Awd 83-84; Cert-Natl Hnr Soc 84-85; Stu Of Mnth 85-86; Surgery.

VU, LEQUYEN; Olney HS; Philadelphia, PA; (Y); Math Clb; Math Tm; Teachers Aide; Hon Roll; NHS; Prfct Atten Awd; Top 7 Phila HS MAA Cont 86; Won Sci Rsrch At Hahnamann U 86; Won Schlrshp Smmr PA ST U Math 86; Drexel U; Sci Engr.

VU, TUAN NGOC; Olney HS; Philadelphia, PA; (Y); 6/575; Drama Clb; Math Tm; School Play; Hon Roll; Kiwanis Awd; Trs NHS; Cty Of Phila Schlrshp 86; Sprng Grdn Coll; Comp Engrng Te.

VUCELICH, DANICE; Plum SR HS; Pittsburgh, PA; (Y); Dance Clb; Ski Clb; Chorus; Church Choir; Capt Drill Tm; School Musical; Yrbk Bus Mgr; Yrbk Stf; Hon Roll; NHS; Duquesne U; Phrmcy.

VUGRINCIC, SUZETTE; Plum SR HS; Pittsburgh, PA; (Y); Sec French Clb; Band; Mrchg Band; Orch; School Musical; Symp Band; Hon Roll; Bus Adm.

VUJNOVICH, DIANE; Center HS; Aliquippa, PA; (Y); 48/193; Sec Church Yth Grp; Dance Clb; German Clb; Latin Clb; Library Aide; Quiz Bowl; Speech Tm; Concert Band; Orch; Hon Roll; Ger Cult Cont 3rd Pl 86; Penn ST; Rsrch Chem.

VUKELICH, CYNTHIA; Deer Lakes JR/SR HS; Russellton, PA; (Y); Drama Clb; French Clb; Ski Clb; School Musical; School Play; Stage Crew; Stat Socr; Twrlr; Hon Roll; NEDT Awd; IN U PA; Intl Bus.

VUKMANIC, TODD J; Bishop Mc Devitt HS; Bressler Steelto, PA; (Y); 6/180; Am Leg Boys St; Church Yth Grp; Rep Frsh Cls; Pres Soph Cls; Rep Jr Cls; Var JV Bsktbl; JV Ftbl; Wt Lftg; Hon Roll; NHS; Red Cross Comndtn For Choking Rescue 85; Vet Med.

VUKMIROVICH, JENNIFER; Hopewell Memorial SR HS; Aliquippa, PA; (Y); Hosp Aide; Hon Roll; Psych.

VULLO, TAMARA ANN; Riverside JR SR HS; Taylor, PA; (Y); Art Clb; Pres Drama Clb; Ski Clb; Chorus; School Musical; School Play; Variety Show; Rep Stu Cncl; JV Var Cheerleading; L Trk; Girls Track-All Arnd High Scorer 85; Studnt Commtt Rep To Middle ST Evaluators 85; Specl Eductn.

VUONO, JOHN; Ringgold HS; Monongahela, PA; (Y); Stat Bsktbl; Var L Tennis; Hon Roll; NHS; Acctg.

WABLE, STACEY; Salisbury-Elk Lick HS; Salisbury, PA; (S); Art Clb; Church Yth Grp; School Play; Nwsp Rptr; Nwsp Stf; Yrbk Stf; Var Capt Cheerleading; Var Sftbl; Hon Roll; Bus Adm.

WACHOB, ELLEN; Punxsutawney Area HS; Punxsutawney, PA; (Y); Church Yth Grp; Trs FBLA; Band; Color Guard; Yrbk Stf; Hon Roll; NHS; 2nd Pl Clrk Typst II Regn FBLA Comp 86; Bus.

WACHOB, TODD; Punxsutawney Area HS; Punxsutawney, PA; (Y); 47/238; Band; Concert Band; Mrchg Band; Pep Band; Variety Show; Hon Roll; Mary Ann Irvin Schlrp 86; JV Colonna Bnd Awd 86; Penn ST U Dubois; Meteorlgy.

WACHS, BOB; Yough SR HS; Sutersville, PA; (Y); Bus.

WACIK, CHRISTINE ANN; Freedom HS; Bethlehem, PA; (Y); 188/445; Pep Clb; Science Clb; Chorus; Rep Stu Cncl; Var Trk; Hon Roll; MVP Trk 4x100 Meter Relay 84-85 & 85-86; Patriot Awd 85-86; Childhd Ed.

WADDELL, LORI; Spring Ford SR HS; Collegeville, PA; (Y); 1/227; Exploring; French Clb; Band; Stu Cncl; Var Fld Hcky; Var Lcrss; Ntl Merit Ltr; Val; Cit Awd; DAR Awd; Genl Electric STAR Schlrhsp 86; PA Gov Schl Sci 85; Dist & Rgnl Band 85 & 86; Cornell U; Vet.

WADDING, BARBARA; Penns Manor HS; Indiana, PA; (Y); 14/99; Spanish Clb; Band; Concert Band; Flag Corp; Mrchg Band; Hon Roll; Prfct Atten Awd; Clarion; Pre-Law.

WADDING, NICK; Hopewell HS; Aliquippa, PA; (Y); 49/295; Church Yth Grp; German Clb; Var L Bsbl; Var L Socr; High Hon Roll; Bsbl 1st Tm All Sectn 85; Soccer Captn 85; Grove City Coll; Math.

WADE, KIRK; Canon Mcmillan HS; Canonsburg, PA; (Y); 150/356; Church Yth Grp; Letterman Clb; Science Clb; Ski Clb; Varsity Clb; Var JV Bsktbl; Im JV Ftbl; Capt Socr; Vllybl; Masonic Awd; MVP Natl Soccr Coaches Amer & US Army 86; Slippery Rock U; Bio.

WADHWANI, GEETA; Bethleham Ctr; Brownsville, PA; (Y); Dance Clb; Spanish Clb; Varsity Clb; School Play; Yrbk Stf; Stu Cncl; Cheerleading; Hon Roll; Homecoming Queen 85; Amer Legion Awd 83-84; Bus Admin.

WADSWORTH, BILL; Shaler Area HS; Glenshaw, PA; (Y); 229/538; Boy Scts; Church Yth Grp; JA; Ski Clb; VICA; Hon Roll; Prfct Atten Awd; Engnrng.

WADSWORTH, JEFF; Connellsville Area HS; Scottdale, PA; (Y); Church Yth Grp; Office Aide; JV Bsbl; JV Ftbl; Wt Lftg; High Hon Roll; U Pittsburgh; Phrmcy.

WADSWORTH, MICHELLE; Forest Hills SR HS; South Fork, PA; (Y); 1/156; Am Leg Aux Girls St; Drama Clb; Scholastic Bowl; Chorus; Church Choir; School Musical; Nwsp Rptr; Hon Roll; Jr NHS; Sec Pres NHS; Occuptnl Thrpy.

WAFFORD, IVY MELISSA; Philadelphia High School For Girls; Philadelphia, PA; (Y); 33/285; Trs Church Yth Grp; Girl Scts; Library Aide; VP Church Choir; Nwsp Rptr; Trs Jr Cls; VP Sr Cls; Im Bowling; Var Tennis; Hon Roll; Natl Achvt Schlr 86; Fnlst Smithkline Beccklman Corp Mth Cont 84; Yth Cncrned Blk Men In 86; U A; Eng.

WAGAMAN, HEIDI N; Susquehanna Township HS; Harrisburg, PA; (Y); 1/155; Art Clb; Dance Clb; Library Aide; Yrbk Stf; Rep Jr Cls; Rep Stu Cncl; Bausch & Lomb Sci Awd; High Hon Roll; Rotary Awd; Schltc Art Awd Cert Merit 86; Bio.

WAGAMAN, JODI; Spring Grove SR HS; Codorus, PA; (Y); 10/285; Band; Concert Band; Jazz Band; Mrchg Band; Orch; School Musical; High Hon Roll; Hon Roll; Nrsng.

WAGAMAN, LISA; Waynesboro Area HS; Waynesboro, PA; (Y); JCL; Yrbk Stf; Trs Rep Stu Cncl; JV Var Bsktbl; JV Cheerleading; Hon Roll; NHS; U Miami; Engrng.

WAGMAN, ALLAN; Wissahickon SR HS; Ambler, PA; (S); 25/276; Art Clb; Computer Clb; Math Clb; Model UN; Nwsp Rptr; Hon Roll; NHS; Gold Medal Econ 1st All ST PA Ntl Acadmc Dcthln; Hnrbl Mntn Ntl Hist Day; JR Wrld Affrs Cncl; Bio Med Engr.

WAGNER, ALAN; Huntingdon Area HS; Huntingdon, PA; (Y); Computer Clb; Drama Clb; Band; Concert Band; Mrchg Band; Bsbl; Schuylkill; Compu Tech.

WAGNER, AMANDA J; State College Area HS; State College, PA; (Y); 13/480.

WAGNER, AMY; Palmyra Area SR HS; Palmyra, PA; (Y); 25/198; Drama Clb; French Clb; Chorus; Flag Corp; Jazz Band; Sec Stu Cncl; Stat Bsktbl; JV Trk; Hon Roll; Ntl Merit SF; Bus.

WAGNER, BENJAMIN B; Williiam Allen HS; Allentown, PA; (Y); 40/542; Boy Scts; Scholastic Bowl; Band; Nwsp Stf; Lit Mag; NHS; Ntl Merit Ltr; JV Bsktbl; Im Bowling; Chess Clb; Fndrs Scholar Messiah Coll 86; Deans Scholar Messiah Coll 86; Messiah Coll; Missionary.

WAGNER, CATHERINE; B Reed Henderson HS; West Chester, PA; (S); 6/348; VP JCL; VP Latin Clb; Quiz Bowl; Rep Jr Cls; Rep Stu Cncl; French Hon Soc; High Hon Roll; Ntl Merit SF; Natl Latin Exm-Maxima Cm Laud 84; Intnatl Rltns.

WAGNER, DALE; Uniontown Area HS; Markleysburg, PA; (Y); Exploring; VP JA; Math Tm; Spanish Clb; High Hon Roll; Jr NHS; NHS; Meritrs Serv Awd 85; Outstndng Sci Stu 85; Outstndng Eng Stu 85; NC ST; Elec Engrg.

WAGNER, DEBRA; Bald Eagle Nittany HS; Mill Hall, PA; (Y); 7/132; Key Clb; Spanish Clb; Varsity Clb; Variety Show; Rep Stu Cncl; Var Sftbl; Var Vllybl; Hon Roll; Jeff & Susan Smth Schlrshp 86; Ntl Rsrvs Awd Mdl Acdmcs Athltcs 86; Awd Bus Frm Svgs & Ln 86; IN U Of PA; Intl Trd.

WAGNER, GREGORY; Sacred Heart HS; Jermyn, PA; (Y); 6/47; Ski Clb; Pres Frsh Cls; Pres Soph Cls; Pres Jr Cls; Stu Cncl; JV Bsktbl; Hon Roll; NHS; Acad All Am; U Scrntn; Med.

WAGNER, GRETA; Spring-Ford HS; Royersford, PA; (S); 15/263; French Clb; Yrbk Stf; Tennis; NHS.

WAGNER, JUDY; Central York HS; York, PA; (Y); 45/224; Drama Clb; Pep Clb; School Musical; Nwsp Stf; Yrbk Stf; Cheerleading; Hon Roll; Bus Admin.

WAGNER, JUDY; Sheffield Area HS; Sheffield, PA; (Y); Art Clb; Church Yth Grp; Drama Clb; Pep Clb; Ski Clb; SADD; Varsity Clb; Band; Bsktbl; Score Keeper.

WAGNER, KRISTIN; Annville-Cleona HS; Jonestown, PA; (Y); VP Church Yth Grp; Varsity Clb; Co-Capt Color Guard; Madrigals; School Musical; Sec Frsh Cls; Sec Soph Cls; Tennis; VP Jr NHS; NHS; Phy Thrpy.

WAGNER, LAURA J; Christian School Of York; East Berlin, PA; (Y); 1/39; Church Yth Grp; Concert Band; School Play; Rep Stu Cncl; Var Cheerleading; High Hon Roll; Ntl Merit Ltr; Pres Schlr; Intl Distngshd Stu 86; Lancaster Bible Clg.

WAGNER, LIESL; Lock Haven SR HS; Woolrich, PA; (Y); German Clb; Concert Band; Variety Show; L JV Cheerleading; Stat Trk; NEDT Awd; PA ST U; Math.

WAGNER, LORI; Johnstown Chrst Schl; Windber, PA; (Y); 4/17; Church Yth Grp; Drama Clb; Pep Clb; Chorus; Yrbk Bus Mgr; Yrbk Stf; JV Var Cheerleading; Cit Awd; Hon Roll; Englsh Awd, Spnsh Awd, Pnmnshp Awd 84-85; Elem Educ.

WAGNER, MARTHA; Bethel Park SR HS; Bethel Park, PA; (Y); 27/515; Church Yth Grp; Band; Church Choir; Mrchg Band; School Musical; Symp Band; Variety Show; High Hon Roll; NHS; VA Tech; Engnrng.

WAGNER, MATTHEW; Downington SR HS; Downingtown, PA; (S); 9/527; Boy Scts; VP Computer Clb; Ski Clb; Spanish Clb; Teachers Aide; Concert Band; Rep Stu Cncl; Capt Bowling; High Hon Roll; NHS; Rotarys Tomorrows Ldrs Conf 85; Gen Elec Town Meet 84; NEDT Awd 83; Comp Sci.

WAGNER, MICHELLE; Lewistown Area HS; Lewistown, PA; (Y); AFS; Church Yth Grp; French Clb; Key Clb; Ski Clb; Varsity Clb; Band; Concert Band; Mrchg Band; Rep Frsh Cls; Therapeutic Sci.

WAGNER, PATRICIA; Plymouth-Whitemarsh HS; Conshohocken, PA; (Y); 150/362; Rep Frsh Cls; Rep Soph Cls; Rep Jr Cls; Capt Cheerleading; Powder Puff Ftbl.

WAGNER, ROB; Emmaus HS; Wescosville, PA; (Y); Computer Clb; Key Clb; Var L Swmmng; Hon Roll; Jr NHS; NHS; VA Plytech Inst; Archt.

WAGNER, ROBERT; Notre Dame HS; Easton, PA; (Y); Aud/Vis; Lib Band; Lib Concert Band; School Musical; School Play; Stage Crew; Prfct Atten Awd; Lock Haven U.

WAGNER, ROBERT; Old Forge HS; Old Forge, PA; (Y); 2/12; Boy Scts; Church Yth Grp; Ski Clb; VICA; Crs Cntry; Trk.

WAGNER, ROBERT; Plymouth Whitemarsh HS; Plymouth Mtg, PA; (Y); 33/337; Chess Clb; Math Clb; Concert Band; Jazz Band; Mrchg Band; Pep Band; High Hon Roll; NHS; Outstndng Soph-Hugh O Brien Yth Foundtn 84-85; Elec Engrng.

WAGNER, ROBIN; Northern Lebanon HS; Lebanon, PA; (Y); 35/170; Cmnty Wkr; Pres SADD; Band; Chorus; Pep Band; School Musical; NHS; Hon Roll; Library Aide; PMEA Dist Bnd 85 & 86; Peer Counslng 85 & 86.

WAGNER, ROBYN; Freedom SR HS; Bethlehem, PA; (Y); 95/465; Aud/Vis; German Clb; Pep Clb; Mgr Chorus; Hon Roll; Psych.

WAGNER, SEAN; St John Neumann HS; Philadelphia, PA; (Y); 115/338.

WAGNER, SHARON; Cedar Crest HS; Lebanon, PA; (Y); Church Yth Grp; 4-H; Chorus; Orch; Crs Cntry; Trk; 4-H Awd; High Hon Roll; NHS; French Clb; Outstndg Chors 86; Northampton; Dntl Hygnst.

WAGNER, SHARON; Marion Center Area HS; Beyer, PA; (S); 17/170; FNA; Hosp Aide; Latin Clb; VICA; Drill Tm; Mrchg Band; Twrlr; High Hon Roll; NHS; Fshn Merch.

WAGNER, STACY; Neshannock HS; New Castle, PA; (Y); Math Tm; NFL; Band; Capt Drill Tm; School Musical; School Play; Nwsp Stf; Yrbk Stf; High Hon Roll; Pres NHS; Svc & Hnr Awds 84-86; Forensic Awds 85-86; Socl Psych.

WAGNER, TAMMIE; Richland HS; Gibsonia, PA; (Y); Sec AFS; Library Aide; VICA; High Hon Roll; Hon Roll; Jr NHS; NHS; U Of Pittsburgh; Nrsng.

WAGNER, TAMMY; North Clarion HS; Venus, PA; (Y); 23/85; Church Yth Grp; Cmnty Wkr; French Clb; Stage Crew; Trk; Ed.

WAGNER, TERESA; Annville-Cleona HS; Annville, PA; (Y); Church Yth Grp; FBLA; Office Aide; Varsity Clb; Band; Chorus; Mrchg Band; JV Fld Hcky; Mgr(s); Mat Maids; Bus.

WAGNER, THOMAS; Newport JR SR HS; Newport, PA; (Y); 22/97; Church Yth Grp; Computer Clb; Chorus; School Musical; School Play; Stage Crew; Swing Chorus; Yrbk Stf; Hon Roll; Mdrn Music Mstrs Tri-M; Math.

WAGNER JR, THOMAS E; Juniata HS; Mifflintown, PA; (Y); 1/156; Yrbk Stf; Hon Roll; NHS; April Stu Of Mnth 86; Dstngshd Hon Stu 86; Outstndng Stu In Mth Sci & Spnsh 86; Shippensburg U; Cmptr Sci.

WAGNER, TRACY; Moon SR HS; Coraopolis, PA; (Y); Camera Clb; Computer Clb; Girl Scts; JA; Rep Stu Cncl; Hon Roll; Film Club 85-86; Phy Sci.

WAGNER, TRACY; Ringgold HS; Finleyville, PA; (Y); Ski Clb; Y-Teens; Drill Tm; Variety Show; Rep Soph Cls; Pom Pon; Powder Puff Ftbl; Trk; Hon Roll; Natl Math Sci Hnr Soc 84-86; Temple; Bio Chem.

WAGNER, WESLEY W; Line Mountain HS; Rebuck, PA; (Y); 15/109; Pres Art Clb; Pres Church Yth Grp; Nwsp Stf; Yrbk Phtg; Yrbk Stf; Rep Hst Sr Cls; Elks Awd; Hon Roll; Kiwanis Awd; Pres NHS; 5th, 6th & 8th Annl Lgsltv Schl Art Exbtns 83-86; Yng Amer Awd 86; Pres Physcl Ftns Awd 83-85; Marion Coll; Art.

WAGNER, WILLIAM; Lakeland JR SR HS; Jermyn, PA; (S); 8/168; Art Clb; Church Yth Grp; 4-H; JA; Library Aide; Concert Band; Mrchg Band; Pep Band; High Hon Roll; Hon Roll.

WAGSTAFF, CATHARINE; William Allen HS; Allentown, PA; (Y); Exploring; Hst FBLA; Chorus; School Play; Vllybl; Hon Roll; Jr NHS; Pope Pius XII Relg Awd 85; Grn Cir Clb Sec 85-86; Contmpry Affrs Clb 85-86; Lehigh County CC; Med Sec.

WAHL, CORIN; Shade HS; Stoystown, PA; (Y); Church Yth Grp; Band; Chorus; Church Choir; Rep Stu Cncl; Hon Roll; Radio.

WAHL, SUZANNE; Pequea Valley HS; Gap, PA; (Y); 15/127; AFS; Girl Scts; JA; Chorus; Mrchg Band; Stage Crew; JV Fld Hcky; Hon Roll; NHS; Cum Laude 86; Millersville Coll; Elem Educ.

WAHL, TINA; Shade HS; Cairnbrook, PA; (Y); Church Yth Grp; Cmnty Wkr; FFA; Ski Clb; Band; Chorus; Church Choir; Mrchg Band; Hon Roll; Somerset Cnty FFA Cntst Intrvw 1st 86; Degree Chapter Frmr FFA 86; Outstndng Bgnnng Hrtcltrlst 85; EMT-PARAMEDIC.

WAHLER, MIKE; Marion Center Area HS; Indiana, PA; (S); 18/148; Church Yth Grp; Pres Band; Pres Concert Band; Pres Mrchg Band; Mgr Stage Crew; Bsbl; High Hon Roll; Hon Roll; NHS; U S Air Force Acad; Aeron Engrn.

WAHLERS, RICK; Council Park HS; Churchville, PA; (Y); 148/845; Church Yth Grp; Concert Band; JV Socr; Im Vllybl; JV Wrstlng; Hon Roll.

WAIDA, SCOTT; Reynolds HS; Fredonia, PA; (Y); 2/160; Latin Clb; Letterman Clb; Math Clb; Science Clb; Varsity Clb; Rep Stu Cncl; L Ftbl; L Trk; Im Wt Lftg; Hon Roll; Engr.

WAITE, ALLISON; Huntingdon Area HS; Huntingdon, PA; (Y); 40/225; French Clb; FHA; Key Clb; Letterman Clb; SADD; Chorus; Concert Band; Mrchg Band; Yrbk Stf; Var Bsktbl; Ntl Sci Awd 84&85; Bio.

WAITE, DARREN; Hampton HS; Gibsonia, PA; (Y); Arch.

WAITE, SHERRY A; Clearfield Area HS; Clearfield, PA; (Y); Cheerleading; Comm.

WAITKUS, SUSAN; Tamaqua Area SR HS; Tamaqua, PA; (Y); Girl Scts; Q&S; Band; Chorus; Flag Corp; Nwsp Ed-Chief; Nwsp Rptr; French Hon Soc; Hon Roll; Eng.

WAJLER, BONITA J; Neshannock HS; New Castle, PA; (Y); 33/104; Office Aide; Ski Clb; Teachers Aide; Chorus; School Musical; Stage Crew; Nwsp Rptr; Nwsp Stf; Trs Soph Cls; Trs Jr Cls; Superior & Outstndg Prfrmnc Chrldng 82-86; Art Inst Pttsbrgh; Vsl Cmmnctns.

WAKIYAMA, SHARON; Blue Mountain HS; Orwigsburg, PA; (Y); 2/225; Capt Quiz Bowl; Band; Concert Band; Yrbk Stf; Rep Stu Cncl; Var Capt Crs Cntry; Var L Swmmng; Var L Trk; French Hon Soc; High Hon Roll; Army Schlr Athltc 86; Mu Alpha Theta Sec 86; Tri-Hi-Y Soph Rep 83-84; Kutztown; Math.

WALASIK, JOHN; Bethel Park HS; Bethel Park, PA; (Y); Church Yth Grp; DECA; Key Clb; Var JV Bsbl; High Hon Roll; NHS; Ntl Merit Ltr; Schlr Athlt 85-86; Presdntl Acad Fitns Awd 86; OH ST U.

WALBORN, CINDI; South Williamsport Area HS; Williamsport, PA; (Y); 52/158; JA; Library Aide; Chorus; School Musical; Stage Crew; Variety Show; Yrbk Rptr; Yrbk Stf; Hon Roll; Photo.

WALBURN, LISA; Canton Jr-SR HS; Canton, PA; (Y); 14/100; Sec Var Aud/Vis; Sec Var Church Yth Grp; French Clb; Letterman Clb; Chorus; Concert Band; Var L Cheerleading; High Hon Roll; Exploring; Girl Scts; Miss PA US Tn ST Fnlst 85; Outstndng Acdmc Achvmnt Awd 86; Nclr Med.

WALBURN, TINA; Canton Area HS; Canton, PA; (Y); 5/100; Church Yth Grp; Band; Chorus; Concert Band; Jazz Band; Mrchg Band; Nwsp Rptr; Cheerleading; Sec NHS; Ntl Merit Ltr; Geisinger Schl Nrsng; Nrsng.

WALDEN, BENJAMIN; Gateway SR HS; Morneoville, PA; (Y); 247/326; Varsity Clb; Chorus; Capt Ice Hcky; Var Trk; Im Wt Lftg; Var Wrstlng; IN U Of PA; Mktg.

WALDMAN, CHRISTINE; South Willimsport HS; S Williamsport, PA; (Y); 42/140; Key Clb; Leo Clb; Spanish Clb; Band; Rep Stu Cncl; JV Score Keeper; JV Sftbl; Var Tennis; Var Trk; Hon Roll; Comp Sci.

WALDO, L SCOTT; Bethel Park SR HS; Bethel Park, PA; (Y); 90/520; Science Clb; Ski Clb; Var L Crs Cntry; Var L Trk; Elks Awd; High Hon Roll; Hon Roll; Lion Awd; Pres Acadmc Ftns Awd 86; U Of Pittsburgh; Engrng.

WALDSCHMIDT, MICHELLE; Chambersburg Area SR HS; Chambersburg, PA; (Y); 165/641; Church Yth Grp; JCL; Chorus; Church Choir; Lit Mag; Rep Soph Cls; Rep Jr Cls; Swmmng; Hon Roll; AFS; Biochem.

WALEFF, VALERIE; Elizabethtown Area HS; Elizabethtown, PA; (Y); 15/220; Church Yth Grp; Yrbk Stf; JV Bsbl; Var Powder Puff Ftbl; NHS; Pres Schlr; Duquesne U; Phrmcy.

WALEGA JR, CHESTER J; Midvalley HS; Dickson City, PA; (Y); VICA; Hon Roll; Johnson Schl Tech; Elec Tech.

WALEGA, LYNDA; Vo-Tech Wood St HS; New Castle, PA; (Y); PAVAS; Ski Clb; Sec Jr Cls; Hon Roll; Atty.

WALES, JAMES; Dayton JR SR HS; Templeton, PA; (Y); 3/50; Science Clb; Chorus; Pres Jr Cls; Pres Sr Cls; Rep Stu Cncl; Var Bsbl; Var Ftbl; Var High Hon Roll; NHS; Pres Acadmc Ftnss Awd 85-86; Natl Schlr And Athltc Awd 86; Grove City Clg; Chem Engrg.

WALES, SHERI; Dallastown Area HS; Dallastown, PA; (Y); Church Yth Grp; JV Var Bsktbl; JV Var Cheerleading; Im Sftbl; Hon Roll; Presdntl Physcl Ftns Awd 83-85.

WALIZER, SHERRY; Bald Eagle Nittany HS; Mill Hall, PA; (Y); 13/132; German Clb; Key Clb; Model UN; Pep Clb; Ski Clb; Trs Soph Cls; Hon Roll; Pres Schlr; German Awd 86; Bloomsburh U; Med Tech.

WALKER, AARON; Cumberland Valley HS; Mechanicsburg, PA; (Y); Church Yth Grp; Key Clb; VP Latin Clb; Hon Roll; Chem Engrng.

WALKER, AMY; Moon SR HS; Corapolis, PA; (Y); 70/317; Church Yth Grp; German Clb; Band; Vllybl; Hon Roll; WVU.

WALKER, BRADLEY; William Penn SR HS; York, PA; (Y); Hon Roll; Bus Admn.

WALKER, BRYAN; Bishop Kenrick HS; Norristown, PA; (Y); 33/304; Science Clb; Rep Frsh Cls; Rep Soph Cls; Rep Jr Cls; Rep Sr Cls; Rep Stu Cncl; Var Bsbl; Var Ftbl; JV Socr; Hon Roll; Villanova; Engrng.

WALKER, CHRISTINA; New Hope-Solebury HS; New Hope, PA; (Y); 12/66; Art Clb; FBLA; FHA; Chorus; Nwsp Rptr; Trk; Hon Roll; NHS; Pres Schlr; North TX; Psych.

WALKER, COLLEEN; Blairsville SR HS; Blairsville, PA; (Y); 14/129; Trs Church Yth Grp; Varsity Clb; Band; Concert Band; Mrchg Band; Sec Stu Cncl; Capt Bsktbl; Vllybl; High Hon Roll; Sec NHS; Westmoreland Cnty CC; Med Sec.

WALKER, DAVID; Karns City HS; Fenelton, PA; (Y); 3/103; SADD; Chorus; Stage Crew; VP Jr Cls; Var Crs Cntry; L Trk; Cit Awd; High Hon Roll; NHS.

WALKER, DAWN; Upper Morelan DSR HS; Hatboro, PA; (Y); German Clb; School Play; Hon Roll; Nrs.

WALKER, DEANNA; Ford City JR SR HS; Ford City, PA; (Y); 12/150; Church Yth Grp; Chorus; Drill Tm; Yrbk Stf; Off Jr Cls; Off Sr Cls; Stu Cncl; Vllybl; High Hon Roll; NHS; Deans Schlrshp 86; Judson Coll; Hum Rel.

WALKER, DEBBY; Waynesburg Central HS; Waynesburg, PA; (Y); Pres Church Yth Grp; Trs French Clb; GAA; Letterman Clb; Rep Stu Cncl; Capt Bsktbl; Trk; Capt Vllybl; Hon Roll; All Trnmnt Tm Bsktbl 85; All Dist Hnrbl Mntn Bsktbl 85-86.

WALKER, ELIZABETH; Tunkhannock Area HS; Tunkhannock, PA; (Y); 33/330; Drama Clb; Pres German Clb; Key Clb; Concert Band; Jazz Band; Mrchg Band; School Musical; School Play; Stage Crew; JV Trk; Drama Club Awd 86; OH ST U; Genetics.

WALKER, FELICIA; Franklin Learning Ctr; Philadelphia, PA; (Y); Church Yth Grp; Dance Clb; JA; Variety Show; Cheerleading; Sftbl; Swmmng; Jr NHS; Prfct Atten Awd; Philadelphia Coll; Dance.

WALKER, GARY; Weatherly Area HS; Weatherly, PA; (S); 6/66; Aud/Vis; FBLA; FFA; Var L Bsbl; JV Var Bsktbl; High Hon Roll; Hon Roll; NHS.

WALKER, GREG; Johnstown HS; Johnstown, PA; (Y); Chess Clb; Ftbl; Slippery Rock U; Bio.

WALKER, JEAN; Avon Grove HS; Landenberg, PA; (Y); 17/171; Band; Drama Clb; Concert Band; Jazz Band; Mrchg Band; School Musical; School Play; Gym; JV Sftbl; High Hon Roll.

WALKER, JERRY; Hempfield Area HS; Ruffsdale, PA; (Y); 7/697; AFS; Art Clb; NFL; Spanish Clb; Church Choir; Yrbk Stf; Jr NHS; Kiwanis Awd; NHS; Spanish NHS; Englsh Hstry Hnrs Prgm 84-86; Hmpfld Enrchmnt Prgm 84-85; Archtctrl Engrng.

WALKER, KRISTINA; Blairsville SR HS; Blairsville, PA; (Y); 9/129; Band; Nwsp Rptr; Yrbk Stf; Var Trk; Var Twrlr; Var Vllybl; NHS; Sec Trs Church Yth Grp; Political Wkr; Pres Schlr; Am Hist Awd; Kenny Greene Mem Schlrshp; Quota Clb Schlrshp; IN U Of PA; Tv Brdcstng.

WALKER, LEE M; Cocalico HS; Denver, PA; (Y); 6/180; Church Yth Grp; Sec GAA; Co-Capt Var Cheerleading; Var Fld Hcky; High Hon Roll; Lion Awd; NHS; VFW Awd; Dance Clb; Im Badmtn; Teen Of Week 86; Stu Of Mnth 86; Homecomg Court, Prom Queen 85-86; All Star Chrldr 86; Gettysburg Coll; Psych.

WALKER, LISA; Shanksville Stonycreek HS; Friedens, PA; (S); Pres FHA; Pres Band; Chorus; School Play; Nwsp Rptr; Yrbk Stf; Sec Sr Cls; Pres Sec Stu Cncl; Capt Var Bsktbl; NHS; Stoystwn Lioness Clbs Grl/Mnth 86; UPJ.

WALKER, MARGARET; Academy Of The New Church; Bryn Athyn, PA; (Y); 2/35; Teachers Aide; School Musical; Pres Soph Cls; Pres Stu Cncl; Var L Fld Hcky; NHS; Pres Schlr; Cmnty Wkr; Ski Clb; Chorus; Hist Dept Awd 84; Histrcl Soc Awd 86; Theta Alpha Intl Awd 86; Acad New Church Coll; Law.

WALKER, MATTHEW WILLIAM; Rockwood Area HS; Rockwood, PA; (Y); Band; Concert Band; Mrchg Band; Stage Crew; Stu Cncl; Wrstlng; Hon Roll; Pres Drftng Cls Smrst Voc Tech Schl 84-85; Mech Drftr.

WALKER, MELINDA; Elizabethtown Area HS; Elizabethtown, PA; (Y); 85/249; Church Yth Grp; Hosp Aide; Library Aide; Sec Band; Church Choir; Concert Band; Mrchg Band; School Musical; School Play; Stage Crew; Phys Thrpy.

WALKER, MELISSA; Bensalem HS; Bensalem, PA; (Y); Cmnty Wkr; Band; Concert Band; Mrchg Band; Trs Jr Cls; JV Cheerleading; Var Mgr(s); Score Keeper; Hon Roll; NHS; Awd Partcptn JV Sccr; Awd Wrk Stdnt Vlntr; Awd Partcptn Stdnt Cncl; Pre-Lw.

WALKER, MELISSA; Big Spring HS; Newville, PA; (Y); Pres Sec 4-H; Chorus; Nwsp Phtg; Nwsp Rptr; Nwsp Stf; 4-H Awd; Hon Roll; Elem Ed.

WALKER, MICHAEL; Mount Union Area HS; Mount Union, PA; (Y); Spanish Clb; Var Golf; Vrsty Lttr Golf 85-86.

WALKER, MICHELLE L; Shenango HS; New Castle, PA; (Y); 43/112; Church Yth Grp; 4-H; Library Aide; Yrbk Stf; Hon Roll; NHS; Slippery Rock U; Elem Educ.

WALKER, REBECCA; Centre County Christian Acad; Pleasant Gap, PA; (S); 2/11; Hosp Aide; Chorus; Pres Soph Cls; Pres Jr Cls; Pres Sr Cls; Var Capt Bsktbl; Var Capt Socr; Var Sftbl; High Hon Roll; Sal; 3rd Ntl Sci Fair Wnnr 85; $500 Schlrshp-Centre Dly Tms Nwspr 86; Ctznshp Awd 86; Bob Jones U; Pre-Med.

WALKER, ROBERT; Punxutawney Area HS; Punxsutawney, PA; (Y); Church Yth Grp; Science Clb; Spanish Clb; Variety Show; Golf; Hon Roll; WV U; Animl Sci.

WALKER, SHAWN O; Warren Area HS; Warren, PA; (Y); Art Clb; French Clb; Acpl Chr; Chorus; Madrigals; Off Frsh Cls; Off Jr Cls; Golf; High Hon Roll; Prfct Atten Awd; Silver B Ctznshp Awd 84; Presdntl Ftns Awd 84; Biolgcl Sci.

WALKER, STACY; Mc Guffey HS; Washington, PA; (Y); 4-H; JA; Key Clb; Color Guard; Nwsp Stf; 4-H Awd; High Hon Roll; Hon Roll; NHS; Pres Schlr; Wrtr.

WALKER, TANYA; Homer-Center HS; Homer City, PA; (Y); Varsity Clb; Band; Chorus; Flag Corp; Mrchg Band; School Musical; Yrbk Stf; Stat Bsktbl; Var Vllybl; Hon Roll; Physcl Thrpist.

WALKER, TRACY; Penn Hills SR HS; Verona, PA; (Y); Library Aide; Powder Puff Ftbl; Hon Roll; Prfct Atten Awd; Slippery Rock U; Flght Attendnt.

WALKER, WENDY; Freeport Area SR HS; Freeport, PA; (Y); Church Yth Grp; Office Aide; Band; Church Choir; School Play; Yrbk Ed-Chief; Stat Trk; Hon Roll; Drama Clb; Yrbk Stf; Yrbk Prep Awd 84 & 86; Gannon U; Intl Studies.

WALKO, AMY; St Maria Goretti HS; Philadelphia, PA; (Y); 97/390; Cmnty Wkr; French Clb; Math Tm; Mrchg Band; Orch; Hon Roll; Athltc Star Awds; Austrln Math Comptn Westpac Awd 84; Accntng.

WALKO, H JOHN; West Allegheny HS; Oakdale, PA; (Y); 28/208; Boy Scts; Church Yth Grp; Drama Clb; Band; Chorus; Concert Band; Mrchg Band; Pep Band; School Play; High Hon Roll; GATE 82-86; Wnd Ensmble Mid-East Music Fstvl 86; Duquesne U; Music.

WALKOW, MARC; Seneca Valley SR HS; Harmony, PA; (Y); 12/356; Aud/Vis; Political Wkr; Ski Clb; Thesps; School Play; Nwsp Stf; High Hon Roll; NHS; Ntl Merit Ltr; Rotary Awd; Brd Drctrs Schl Cbl TV Sta 85-86; Prtl-Tuitn Schlrshp-Yale U Smmr Schls 85; Gftd & Tlntd Pgm 82-86; Swarthmore Coll-PA; Phlsphy.

WALKUP, DOUG; Upper Darby HS; Drexel Hl, PA; (Y); Aud/Vis; Lcrss; Swmmng; Hon Roll.

WALKUP, LINDA; Philadelphia Montgomery Christia; Willow Grove, PA; (Y); Church Yth Grp; Hosp Aide; Acpl Chr; Chorus; Church Choir; Cheerleading; Fld Hcky; Hon Roll; NHS; Physcl Thrpy.

WALL, KEVIN; Yough SR HS; Ruffsdale, PA; (Y); Boy Scts; Ski Clb; Band; Concert Band; Mrchg Band; Symp Band; Trk; Bus Mgmt.

WALL, RAYMUND; Bensalem HS; Bensalem, PA; (Y); Church Yth Grp; Cmnty Wkr; Political Wkr; Varsity Clb; Rep Frsh Cls; Rep Soph Cls; Rep Jr Cls; Coach Actv; Var JV Socr; Hon Roll; Bus.

WALLACE, CAROLYN; Harry S Truman HS; Levittown, PA; (Y); Band; Concert Band; Mrchg Band; Rep Stu Cncl; Var Cheerleading; Var Socr; Hon Roll; Nrsng.

WALLACE, CLAUDE; Lutheran HS; Philadelphia, PA; (Y); 2/16; Boy Scts; Church Yth Grp; Nwsp Sprt Ed; Yrbk Sprt Ed; Rep Frsh Cls; Rep Soph Cls; Rep Jr Cls; Var JV Bsktbl; Vllybl; Hon Roll; Hghst Avg Algbr II, Englsh III & Histry Of Art I 85-86; US Air Force; Tele Comm.

WALLACE, GEORGINE; Wayreboro Area HS; Fayetteville, PA; (Y); Am Leg Aux Girls St; JCL; Library Aide; Rep Jr Cls; VP Sr Cls; Rep Stu Cncl; High Hon Roll; Hon Roll; NHS; Voice Dem Awd; XXIII Wrld Affrs Smnr 86; Polit Sci.

WALLACE, JOHN; Penn Trafford HS; Irwin, PA; (Y); 190/324; Stage Crew; Im Badmtn; Im Bsktbl; Im Ftbl; Im Score Keeper; Im Sftbl; Im Tennis; Im Vllybl; High Hon Roll; Hon Roll; Washington & Jefferson; Accntng.

WALLACE, LIBBY; Conneaut Lake HS; Atlantic, PA; (Y); Church Yth Grp; Drama Clb; Trs 4-H; Spanish Clb; SADD; Chorus; School Musical; Nwsp Rptr; 4-H Awd; Hon Roll; PA ST U; Bus.

WALLACE, LISA; South Park HS; Library, PA; (Y); Church Yth Grp; Exploring; Office Aide; Band; Mrchg Band; Orch; Yrbk Stf; Hon Roll; Tutorng Svc 85-86; Schl Svc Awd 85-86; Spd Typng Awd 83-84; Westminster Coll; Math.

WALLACE, LISA; Wilmington Area HS; Pulaski, PA; (Y); Drama Clb; French Clb; Key Clb; Spanish Clb; Band; Mrchg Band; Powder Puff Ftbl; Hon Roll; Clarion U; Elem.

WALLACE, MICHAEL; Altoona Area HS; Altoona, PA; (Y); Church Yth Grp; Computer Clb; Key Clb; Spanish Clb; Varsity Clb; Band; Concert Band; Orch; Variety Show; Lit Mag; Dist 6 Dbls Champn Tnns 86; Mst Outstndng Plyr 86; MVP 2 Yrs Row 85-86; Biochem.

WALLACE, MIKE; Central Bucks East HS; Furlong, PA; (Y); Ski Clb; Band; Var Capt Crs Cntry; Var Socr; Capt Var Trk; Hon Roll; Kiwanis Awd; Prfct Atten Awd; Crss Cntry Rkie Of The Yr 84; X-Cntry Most Vlble Plyr 86; U Of Delaware; Engrng.

WALLACE, ROMAN; St James Catholic HS; Chester, PA; (Y); 49/140; Computer Clb; Var Capt Trk; JV Im Bsktbl; Var JV Crs Cntry; Prncpsl Awd, PCL Trck & Fld & MVP Del Cnty 85-86; All Delco, All Cthlc ST Champ MVP Tck & Fld; MD U; Bus.

WALLACE, SHAWN; Hempfield Area SR HS; Greensburg, PA; (Y); #41 In Class; Var L Ftbl; JV Socr; Var L Trk; French Hon Soc; High Hon Roll; NHS; Ntl Merit Ltr; Prfct Atten Awd; Lloyd Allshouse Awd 83-84.

WALLACE, SUSAN; Henderson HS; West Chester, PA; (Y); 140/360; JCL; Latin Clb; Ski Clb; SADD; Flag Corp; JV Golf; Var Mgr(s); Var Score Keeper; JV Sftbl; JV Vllybl.

WALLACE, SUZANNE; Central Cambria HS; Colver, PA; (Y); Church Yth Grp; FBLA; Key Clb; Library Aide; Chorus; Church Choir; Var JV Mgr(s); Hon Roll; Chorus Awd 85; Library Sci.

WALLANDER, R RUSSELL; State College Area HS; Boalsburg, PA; (Y); 67/568; Church Yth Grp; Band; Elks Awd; High Hon Roll; Vo Tech Englsh Awd 85; Hgh Vo Tech Hnr Roll 85-86; PA ST U; Engr.

WALLEN, KARL; MMI Preparatory Schl; Hazelton, PA; (Y); Cmnty Wkr; FBLA; Pep Clb; Science Clb; Ski Clb; VP Jr Cls; High Hon Roll; Hon Roll; NEDT Awd; Art Clb; Hnrbl Ment Ntl Spnsh Comptn 84-85; Dentstry.

WALLEY, MATTHEW; Quigley HS; Aliquippa, PA; (S); 3/115; Math Tm; VP Soph Cls; Var L Ftbl; Var Trk; Var L Wrstlng; High Hon Roll; Spnsh & Hstry Awds 83-85.

WALLICK, DUSTIN; Eastern York HS; Wrightsville, PA; (Y); Pres Church Yth Grp; Band; Concert Band; Jazz Band; Mrchg Band; Pep Band; Trk; Wrstlng; Hon Roll; Marine Bio.

WALLICK, SHARON; North Pocono HS; Moscow, PA; (Y); Library Aide; Hon Roll; NHS; Pre Schl Tchr.

WALLS, GARY TROY; Marion Center HS; Marion Ctr, PA; (Y); Chess Clb; French Clb; Intnl Clb; Spanish Clb; Trk; Cit Awd; Hon Roll; Spnsh Awd 84-85; Frnch Awds 84-85; Publc Rel 84; IUP; Engr.

WALLS, GREGG; Ambridge Area HS; Ambridge, PA; (Y); Sec Church Yth Grp; French Clb; SADD; Chorus; L Ftbl; Wt Lftg; CPA.

WALLS, JAIMI; Strath Haven HS; Wallingford, PA; (Y); Church Yth Grp; Ski Clb; Teachers Aide; Yrbk Stf; Stu Cncl; Stat Bsktbl; Stat Am Leg Boys St5; Var Sftbl; JV Vllybl; Hon Roll; Towson ST U; Grphc Dsgn.

WALLS, ORVILLE; William Penn Charter Schl; Philadelphia, PA; (Y); FCA; Ski Clb; Pres Soph Cls; VP Jr Cls; VP Sr Cls; Pres Stu Cncl; Var Ftbl; Var Trk; Var Wrstlng; Dentstry.

WALLS, TAMI; Aliquippa HS; Aliquippa, PA; (S); #10 In Class; Exploring; Pres French Clb; Band; Yrbk Stf; Off Sr Cls; NHS; Spch Pathlgst.

WALMER, ERIC; Lancaster Country Day Schl; Elizabethtown, PA; (Y); Church Yth Grp; Cmnty Wkr; Hst Drama Clb; Exploring; Chorus; School Musical; School Play; Stage Crew; Variety Show; Bsbl; Athlete Of Yr Awd & Mvp For Soccer 86; MVP For Soccer & Capt 85; Capt For Bsktbl 86.

WALNOCK, MICHELE; Louis E Dieruff HS; Allentown, PA; (Y); FBLA; ROTC; Chorus; Rep Soph Cls; JV Var Cheerleading; Hon Roll; Allentown Hosp/Radiolgy; Radlgy.

WALP, KIM; Emmaus HS; Macungie, PA; (Y); 5/490; Key Clb; Band; Chorus; Color Guard; Jazz Band; Mrchg Band; Trs Sec Pep Band; Trs Sec School Musical; High Hon Roll; NHS; Engr.

WALSH, ALAN J; La Salle College HS; Huntingdon Vly, PA; (Y); 35/240; Band; Concert Band; Nwsp Ed-Chief; Yrbk Stf; Var L Bsbl; NHS; Franklin Clg; Jrnlsm.

WALSH, BRIAN; Bishop Kenrick HS; Norristown, PA; (Y); 45/295; JV Trk; Opt Clb Awd; Acctng.

WALSH, BRIAN; Emmaus HS; Macungie, PA; (Y); 9/496; Model UN; Quiz Bowl; Scholastic Bowl; Spanish Clb; Im Bsbl; Im Socr; High Hon Roll; Hon Roll; Jr NHS; NHS.

WALSH, CHARLES; Shady Side Acad; Pittsburgh, PA; (Y); 38/112; Boys Clb Am; Chess Clb; Letterman Clb; Math Tm; SADD; Yrbk Rptr; Rep Frsh Cls; VP Jr Cls; Var Ftbl; JV Lcrss; Yale Awd 85; Centenl Awd 86; Amherst Col; Medcn.

WALSH, DONNA; Bishop O Hana HS; Dickson City, PA; (S); 2/113; French Clb; Latin Clb; Chorus; JV Cheerleading; High Hon Roll; NHS; Prfct Atten Awd.

WALSH, GREGORY; Wissahicken HS; N Wales, PA; (S); 23/280; Key Clb; Math Clb; Ski Clb; Off Sr Cls; Golf; Wt Lftg; High Hon Roll; Hon Roll; Jr NHS; Penn ST U; Engr.

WALSH, KATHLEEN; Abington Heights HS; Clarks Summit, PA; (Y); 123/253; Church Yth Grp; Dance Clb; Ski Clb; Stage Crew; Rep Soph Cls; Rep Jr Cls; Rep Stu Cncl; L Diving; Mgr(s); Stat Trk; PA ST; Intl Area Studies.

WALSH, KATHLEEN M; Penn Hills HS; Verona, PA; (Y); French Clb; Science Clb; Stu Cncl; Mgr Trk; Hon Roll; U SC; Psych.

WALSH, LAURA; Seneca Valley HS; Zelienople, PA; (Y); Variety Show; Sec Soph Cls; Var Pom Pon; Hon Roll; Acadmc Achvt Awd 84-85; Psych.

WALSH, LAURA; Villa Maria Acad; Lansdowne, PA; (Y); 7/96; Library Aide; Ed Yrbk Stf; JV Lcrss; Pres Sec French Hon Soc; High Hon Roll; NHS; Ntl Merit Ltr; Chester Cnty Acad Comp Tm Mem 85-86; Natl Tchers Awd For Excllc Frnch 86; Cornell U; Urbn Dev.

WALSH, LAURENE; Center Area HS; Monaca, PA; (Y); 20/188; Sec Exploring; German Clb; Drill Tm; Socr; High Hon Roll; Hon Roll; NHS; Trp Germany Frndshp Connctn Exchng Stu 86; Gftd Stu Prog Comp Prog 83-86; Penn ST; Psychology.

WALSH, MARIANN; Susquenita HS; Halifax, PA; (S); 20/153; French Clb; Trs FBLA; Leo Clb; Drill Tm; Mrchg Band; Yrbk Stf; NHS; Cntrl PA Bus Schl; Lgl Asstnt.

WALSH, MAUREEN; Seneca Valley HS; Renfrew, PA; (Y); Ski Clb; Varsity Clb; Stu Cncl; L Var Bsktbl; L Var Crs Cntry; Var L Swmmng; L Trk; Hon Roll; NHS; Church Yth Grp; Cmnty Sftbl All-Stars 84-87; Sftbl Tm-1st Pl 84, 85; Phys Thrpy.

WALSH, MICHAEL; B Reed Henderson HS; West Chester, PA; (Y); Boy Scts; Westchester Schl Dist Flying Lssns Schlrshp 85; Air Force ROTC; Pilot.

WALSH, MICHAEL; Lebanon Catholic HS; Lebanon, PA; (Y); 13/82; Boy Scts; Debate Tm; German Clb; Key Clb; Library Aide; Science Clb; Var Bsbl; JV Var Bsktbl; Var Golf; Im Socr; Notre Dame; Chem Engrng.

WALSH, MIKE; Bishop Ohara HS; Dickson City, PA; (Y); 13/119; Var Bsbl; Var Bsktbl; High Hon Roll; NHS; Space Engrng.

WALSH, PAMELA; Abraham Lincoln HS; Philadelphia, PA; (Y); 28/400; Church Yth Grp; Girl Scts; JV Sftbl; Var Swmmng; Hon Roll; Temple U; Bus Ed.

WALSH, PAULA; Mary Fuller Frazier Mem HS; Perryopolis, PA; (Y); Church Yth Grp; Chorus; Yrbk Stf; High Hon Roll; Hon Roll; Jr NHS; NHS; Prfct Atten Awd; US Bus Educ Awds 83-86; Sec.

WALSH, SUSAN; Archbishop Prendergast HS; Glenolden, PA; (Y); 102/363; Computer Clb; FBLA; Intnl Clb; Key Clb; Office Aide; Political Wkr; Radio Clb; Ski Clb; Teachers Aide; Yrbk Stf; Westchester U.

WALSH, THOMAS; Council Rock HS; Newtown, PA; (Y); 18/845; Ski Clb; Concert Band; Im JV Bsbl; JV Var Bsktbl; NHS; Rotary Awd; Med.

WALSH, WILLIAM; Bishop Hannan HS; Scranton, PA; (Y); Drama Clb; Ski Clb; Orch; Golf; Hon Roll; Hon Mntn Algbra II Trgnmtry, Amer Cltrs 86; Excllnc Soclgy 86; Penn ST; Bus.

WALSKI, MICHAEL; Wyoming Valley West HS; Swoyersville, PA; (Y); 3/300; Am Leg Boys St; Chess Clb; Math Clb; High Hon Roll; NHS; NEDT Awd; 3rd Hghst Avg 85-86; Hon Ment Kings Coll Spnsh Cntst 86; Engrng.

WALTEMIRE, DEBRA; Blacklick Valley JR SR HS; Ebensburg, PA; (S); 3/90; Varsity Clb; Yrbk Sprt Ed; Yrbk Stf; Var Capt Bsktbl; VP Capt Sftbl; Hon Roll; Pres NHS; Acad All Amer 84-85; Cambria Rowe; Bus Mgmnt.

WALTENBAUGH, LESLIE SUSAN; Apollo-Ridge SR HS; Apollo, PA; (Y); 30/164; FBLA; FNA; VP JA; Library Aide; Nwsp Stf; Hon Roll; IN U PA; Jrnlsm.

WALTER, BRIAN; Big Spring HS; Newville, PA; (Y); Ski Clb; Stu Cncl; Powder Puff Ftbl; Socr; Hon Roll; Pres Phys Ftns Awd 85-86; Cvl Engrng.

WALTER, CHRISTINE L; North Allegheny HS; Pittsburgh, PA; (Y); 198/605; Mrchg Band; Lit Mag; Frsh Cls; Soph Cls; Sr Cls; Hon Roll; Miami U OH; Comm.

WALTER, ELIZABETH; Concmough Township Area HS; Hollsopple, PA; (Y); 1/105; Church Yth Grp; Key Clb; Scholastic Bowl; Soroptimist; Band; Concert Band; Ed Yrbk Stf; Ed Lit Mag; Bausch & Lomb Sci Awd; Cit Awd; Heffly Meml Schlrshp 86; Pres Acadmc Ftns Awd 86; Am Legn Schlrshp Mdl 86; U Of Pittsburg; Sec Educ.

WALTER, JENNIFER; Greater Johnstown HS; Johnstown, PA; (Y); French Clb; JA; Library Aide; NFL; Ski Clb; Band; Chorus; Concert Band; Mrchg Band; School Musical.

WALTER, KATHRYN; Norwin SR HS; N Huntingdon, PA; (Y); FBLA; Office Aide; Chorus; Var L Trk; Yth Fitness Achv Awd 86; Exprt Rhythmc Typing Cert 85; Legal Sec.

WALTER, LYNESIA; Shanksville Stonycreek HS; Stoystown, PA; (S); 2/31; Trs FHA; Sec Spanish Clb; Concert Band; Mrchg Band; School Play; Yrbk Stf; Stu Cncl; Vllybl; Sec NHS; Pres Spanish NHS; Pre-Vet.

WALTER, MARK; Carlynton HS; Carnegie, PA; (Y); Nwsp Stf; High Hon Roll; Hon Roll; Ntl Merit Ltr; Pres Schlr; Outstndng Engl Stu 86; Mst Talented Wrtr 86; U Pittsburgh; Author.

WALTER, MARK; Nazareth Area SR HS; Nazareth, PA; (Y); 50/241; Boy Scts; Camera Clb; Chess Clb; Trs Exploring; Band; Jazz Band; Mrchg Band; Yrbk Stf; Hon Roll; Electrcl Engrng.

WALTER, MICHAEL; Millersburg Area HS; Millersburg, PA; (S); 4/62; Ski Clb; School Musical; Trs Sr Cls; Ftbl; Hon Roll; Phrmcy.

WALTER, NOLITA; Westside Christian Schl; Dover, PA; (Y); Art Clb; Church Yth Grp; Y-Teens; Chorus; Church Choir; School Play; Yrbk Stf; Var Bsktbl; Fld Hcky; Hon Roll; Teen Tlnt Schlrshp 86; Vly Forge Christian Coll; Voice.

WALTER, TARA; Nazareth Acad; Langhorne, PA; (Y); German Clb; Yrbk Stf; Hon Roll; Cmmndtn Ltr Stuart Cntry Day Schl 83; Hlf Tuition Scholar Nazareth Acad 83-86; Part Scholar Villa Vict; Mth.

WALTER, TIMOTHY; Upper Darby HS; Drexel Hl, PA; (Y); 7/561; Band; Orch; Co-Capt Crs Cntry; Trk; High Hon Roll; Ntl Merit Ltr; Pres Schlr; Harvard Bk Clb Awd 85; Carnegie Mellon U.

WALTERMIRE, CRAIG; Rockwood HS; Rockwood, PA; (S); Church Yth Grp; 4-H; FFA; Band; Chorus; Mrchg Band; 4-H Awd; Hon Roll; NHS; Star Chptr Farmr 85; Keystone Frmr Degr 85; 4 Entrprz Proj Bk Gld Mdl ST 85; Ag.

WALTERMYER, CHRISTINE; Northern Lebanon HS; Jonestown, PA; (Y); 22/166; Art Clb; Church Yth Grp; Chorus; School Musical; School Play; Nwsp Stf; Tennis; Hon Roll; Kutztown U; Art Mjr.

WALTERS, ANDREA; Mon Valley Catholic HS; Elrama, PA; (Y); 22/82; Church Yth Grp; Girl Scts; SADD; Pres Band; Nwsp Stf; Yrbk Sprt Ed; Yrbk Stf; Off Jr Cls; Stu Cncl; Powder Puff Ftbl; Physcs A Avrg 85-86; IN U Of PA; Msc.

WALTERS, DAVE; Wilmington Area HS; Edinburg, PA; (S); 12/122; Church Yth Grp; Var L Crs Cntry; Var L Trk; NHS; Ntl Merit Ltr; Hon Roll; Spanish Clb; Mech Engrng.

WALTERS, DIANNE; Cocalico HS; Denver, PA; (Y); Church Yth Grp; Girl Scts; Band; Chorus; Church Choir; Concert Band; Mrchg Band; School Musical; School Play; NHS; Amer Bus Womens Schlrshp 86; Cocalico Clss Schlrshp 86; Vocal Music Awd 86; Franklin Marshall Coll; Bio.

WALTERS, ERIK; Carson Long Inst; Lancaster, PA; (Y); 4/41; Chess Clb; Debate Tm; Varsity Clb; Chorus; Sec Frsh Cls; Rep Stu Cncl; JV Bsktbl; Var Socr; Var Trk; Hon Roll; Hghst Achvt Mltry Fld 85-86; Physcl Ftnssawd 82-86; Penn ST; Intl Pltcs.

WALTERS, JAMES; Springdale HS; Springdale, PA; (Y); Off Frsh Cls; Bsktbl; Var Socr; High Hon Roll; Hon Roll; Acad Games 84-87; U Of Pittsburgh; Comp Sci.

WALTERS, JEANNETTE; Gateway SR HS; Monroeville, PA; (Y); 59/430; Drama Clb; PAVAS; Chorus; Church Choir; School Play; Yrbk Rptr; Yrbk Stf; High Hon Roll; Church Yth Grp; Godspl Tourng Grp 83-84; Drama.

WALTERS, JO ELLA; Johnsonburg Area HS; Johnsonburg, PA; (S); 4/90; Camera Clb; Sec Varsity Clb; Capt Var Bsktbl; Var L Tennis; DAR Awd; High Hon Roll; VP NHS; Acadmc Al-Amer Awd 84-85; US Ldrshp Merit Awd 84-86; St Bonaventure U; Biochem.

WALTERS, JUDY; Northampton SR HS; Northampton, PA; (Y); FTA; Band; Concert Band; Mrchg Band; High Hon Roll; Hon Roll; Hgst Avg Alg I 84; U Pittsburgh; Elem Ed.

WALTERS, KAREN; Elkland Area HS; Osceola, PA; (Y); 3/80; French Clb; Trs SADD; School Play; Rep Church Yth Grp; Var Capt Bsktbl; Sftbl; Swmmng; Var L Vllybl; High Hon Roll; NHS; NTL West Vllybl Champ Tm 85-86; PIAA Bsktbl Champ Tm 85-86; Prncpls Awd 3 Consec Hgh Hnr Rll 85-86; Penn ST U; Frnch.

WALTERS, KAREN LYNN; Canon Mc Millian SR HS; Muse, PA; (Y); 141/396; French Clb; Office Aide; Yrbk Stf; Twrlr; Hon Roll; U Of Ptsbrg; RN.

WALTERS, LORI; Upper Dublin HS; Maple Glen, PA; (Y); Temple Yth Grp; Band; Chorus; Concert Band; Mrchg Band; Orch; School Musical; Symp Band; Hon Roll; NHS; PA ST U; Ed.

WALTERS, LOWELL; Northern Bedford County HS; Bakers Summit, PA; (Y); Church Yth Grp; Library Aide; Chorus; Church Choir; School Musical; Swing Chorus; Nwsp Ed-Chief; Yrbk Phtg; Hon Roll; NHS; Liberty U; Hstry.

WALTERS, REBECCA; Youngsville HS; Irvine, PA; (Y); French Clb; FBLA; Color Guard; Flag Corp; School Play; Co-Capt Trk; Vllybl; Hon Roll; Ltr Trck 84-86; Rcvd Mst Outstndng Rnnr Awd 85-86; Soc Svcs.

WALTERS, RHONDA E; Bodine HS For Intl Affairs; Philadelphia, PA; (Y); 25/96; Drama Clb; School Play; Nwsp Stf; JV L Badmtn; Var Bowling; Var Cheerleading; Vllybl; Hon Roll; NHS; Ntl Merit SF; Penn ST; Mktg.

WALTHER, DONALD E; Conestoga SR HS; Wayne, PA; (Y); 13/420; Debate Tm; French Clb; Am Leg Boys St; Intnl Clb; JV Crs Cntry; High Hon Roll; NHS; Ntl Merit SF; Aud/Vis; Chess Clb; Hugh O Brian Ldrshp Smnr Ambssdr 83; Cntry III Ldrshp Rep 85; ; Intl Bus Admin.

WALTIMYER, DENISE; Red Lion Area SR HS; Red Lion, PA; (Y); 3/70; Pres Church Yth Grp; Church Choir; Drill Tm; Hon Roll; Offcr Intl Ordr Rainbow Grls 84-86; ST Chmpn Valkyrie Drl Tm 85; Shippensburg U; Accntng.

WALTMAN, JEFFREY; Karns City HS; Chicora, PA; (Y); 21/113; Boy Scts; Exploring; Spanish Clb; Band; Mrchg Band; Pep Band; 4-H Awd; Bus.

WALTMAN, JEFFREY; South Williamsport Area HS; S Williamport, PA; (Y); 80/160; Camera Clb; French Clb; Ski Clb; Nwsp Phtg; Yrbk Phtg; Yrbk Stf; Socr; Tennis; PA ST U; Bus.

WALTMAN, MICHELLE L; Solanco SR HS; Quarryville, PA; (Y); Pres Church Yth Grp; Teachers Aide; Varsity Clb; Flag Corp; School Musical; Stu Cncl; JV Fld Hcky; Var L Trk; Hon Roll; JV Bsktbl; Schlastic Art Awd 85-86; Millersville U; Social Wrk.

WALTON, DAVID J; North Penn HS; N Wales, PA; (Y); Rep Stu Cncl; Var L Bsbl; Var L Ftbl; Im Wt Lftg; Hon Roll; NHS; MVP Bsbll 86; Bsbll Mst Prmsng Soph 84; All Bux Mont Bsbll 85-86; West Chester U; Intl Rltns.

WALTON, DIANE; North Hills HS; Pittsburgh, PA; (Y); 4/467; Church Yth Grp; VP Keywanettes; Chorus; High Hon Roll; NHS; Head Usher Cmmncmnt 86; GATE; Engrg Mgmt.

WALTON, DONYA L; John Harris HS; Harrisburg, PA; (Y); 12/473; Office Aide; Pep Clb; SADD; Chorus; Pres Frsh Cls; Pres Soph Cls; Pres Sr Cls; VP Stu Cncl; Hon Roll; NHS; Acctg.

WALTON, ELIZABETH; Strath Haven HS; Wallingford, PA; (Y); VP Church Yth Grp; Intnl Clb; School Musical; Variety Show; Ed Nwsp Phtg; Yrbk Phtg; Capt Cheerleading; High Hon Roll; Ntl Merit Ltr; Rotary Awd; Girl Scouts Silver Awd 83; Middlebury Coll.

WALTON, GORDY; Delaware County Christian HS; Wayne, PA; (Y); Church Yth Grp; Band; Chorus; Pep Band; High Hon Roll; Dstngshd Chrstn Stu Awd-Music 85-86; Bus.

WALTON, KENNETH; Solanco HS; Oxford, PA; (Y); 3/238; Church Yth Grp; Varsity Clb; Rep Stu Cncl; Var JV Bsbl; Var Capt Bsktbl; Var JV Socr; High Hon Roll; NHS; Pres Schlr; All-Sctn Bsktbl Plyr 85-86; Natl Schlr/Athlt 85-86; Elizabethton Coll; Math.

WALTON, LYNDA; Butler HS; Butler, PA; (Y); Church Yth Grp; Girl Scts; SADD; Co-Capt Drill Tm; School Musical; Variety Show; Jr NHS; NHS; Chem.

WALTON, MELINDA; John S Fine HS; Alden, PA; (Y); Ski Clb; Chorus; Nwsp Stf; Yrbk Stf; Hon Roll; Pre-Law.

WALTON, NICOLE; Berwick Area SR HS; Berwick, PA; (Y); Drama Clb; Trs Key Clb; Service Clb; Speech Tm; SADD; School Play; Stage Crew; Nwsp Bus Mgr; Nwsp Rptr; Nwsp Stf; 2nd Pl Awd-Vc Of Demcrcy 84-86; 4th Pl Awd-PA Schl Press Assn 85-86; Prof Wrtng.

WALTOS, LISA; Windber Area HS; Windber, PA; (Y); 26/114; Pep Clb; Color Guard; Sec Frsh Cls; Stu Cncl; Trk; Hon Roll; NHS; Bus Awds Shrthd & Typg 84-85; Stu Of Mnth Awds 84-86; Emplyee Of Mnth 85; Clrk Typst.

WALTZ, SUSAN; Blicklick Valley JR SR HS; Nanty Glo, PA; (S); 13/90; Cmnty Wkr; Pres Exploring; Office Aide; Teachers Aide; Capt Color Guard; Sec Soph Cls; Trs Jr Cls; Trk; Btty Crckr Awd; Hon Roll; Mt Aloysius-St Francis; Bus Adm.

WALZER, KEN; Fox Chapel SR HS; Glenshaw, PA; (Y); Band; Concert Band; Jazz Band; Mrchg Band; School Musical; Slippery Rock; Music.

WAMPLER, JEFFREY; Owen J Roberts HS; Pottstown, PA; (S); 40/200; Hon Roll; Engrng.

WAMPLER, SHERRI; Cedar Crest HS; Lebanon, PA; (Y); Nwsp Bus Mgr; Yrbk Bus Mgr; Yrbk Rptr; Yrbk Stf; Lit Mag; Hon Roll; German Clb; Pep Clb; Stage Crew; Txclgy.

WAMPLER, SUZANNE; Central Dauphin HS; Harrisburg, PA; (Y); Varsity Clb; Rep Frsh Cls; Rep Soph Cls; Rep Jr Cls; Var Capt Cheerleading; Var Gym; Var L Tennis; Trk; Im Vllybl; Acctg.

WANAMAKER, MARIE; Cheltenham HS; Elkins Pk, PA; (Y); Art Clb; Church Yth Grp; 4-H; Office Aide; PAVAS; Church Choir; JV Badmtn; JV Bsktbl; Hon Roll; Schlstc Art Awds 84; Yng Adlt Choir Awd 84; PAFA Yng Dcnts Awd 85; Bus.

WANCHISN, STACY; Marion Center HS; Marion Center, PA; (S); 7/200; 4-H; Latin Clb; Q&S; Band; Mrchg Band; Nwsp Rptr; Nwsp Stf; High Hon Roll; Hon Roll; NHS; PA Schl Prss Assn 2nd, 1st Artwrk 84-85; IUP Art-Theatr 85; Fndtns IUP Schl Wrkshp Wkend Art Ed 85; IN U Of PA Indiana PA; Art.

WANDEL, KELLY; Lake-Lehman HS; Dallas, PA; (S); 31/177; Var L Bsktbl; Var Capt Fld Hcky; Var Capt Sftbl; Hon Roll; NHS; U S Army Resrv Schlr Athl Awd 86; Achvt Schlrshp 86; Wilkes Deans Schlrshp 86; Wilkes Coll; Med Tech.

WANDTKE, ANN; Pen Argyl Area HS; Pen Argyl, PA; (Y); Drama Clb; Ski Clb; Band; Trs Orch; Stage Crew; Nwsp Rptr; NHS; Computer Clb; Spanish Clb; High Hon Roll; Gov Schl Arts PA 85; Dist, Rgnl, All-St Orch 85 & 86; Cngress Bundestag Yth Exch Schlrshp Germany 86.

WANG, RHODA Y; State College Area SR HS; State College, PA; (Y); Hosp Aide; Library Aide; Orch; Yrbk Ed-Chief; Yrbk Stf; Cit Awd; Hon Roll; Prfct Atten Awd; Fll Schlrshp PA Gvrnrs Schlr For The Arts 85; Wnnr Ntl Piano Gld Adtns 81-86; Peabody Cnsrvtry/Music; Piano.

WANGMAN, ANDREW; Ephrata SR HS; Ephrata, PA; (Y); 35/280; Chess Clb; German Clb; Intnl Clb; Quiz Bowl; Hon Roll; Grmn Clss Awd 85; Grmn Awd Mllrsvll U 85; Crtfct Mrt AATG 86; German.

WANJEK, CHRISTOPHER; Father Judge HS; Philadelphia, PA; (Y); 4/403; German Clb; Mathletes; Nwsp Rptr; Yrbk Rptr; Crs Cntry; Trk; Gov Hon Prg Awd; High Hon Roll; Jr NHS; NHS; Sons Of Italy Schlrshp 86; Outstndng Achvt Schlrshp 86; Pres Schlrshp 86; Temple; Pre-Med.

WANNER, STEPHEN; Emmaus HS; Emmaus, PA; (Y); 210/500; Key Clb; Latin Clb; SADD; Pres Frsh Cls; Off Soph Cls; Off Jr Cls; Pres Sr Cls; Pres Stu Cncl; Bus.

WANZIE, MONICA; Southern Columbia Area HS; Numidia, PA; (Y); Church Yth Grp; Red Cross Aide; Varsity Clb; Concert Band; Drm Mjr(t); Yrbk Stf; Trs Frsh Cls; Trs Soph Cls; Trs Jr Cls; Var L Fld Hcky; Phys Thrpy.

WAPINSKI, THERESA; Holy Name HS; Reading, PA; (Y); 1/115; Hosp Aide; Q&S; Science Clb; Spanish Clb; Yrbk Stf; High Hon Roll; NHS; Val; Mina Bauer Schlrshp 86; Penn ST U; Bus Admn.

WAPNER, BRIAN; Kishacoquillas HS; Reedsville, PA; (Y); 6/146; Chorus; Concert Band; Rep Stu Cncl; Var L Bsbl; Dnfth Awd; High Hon Roll; Sec NHS; Pres Schlr; Church Yth Grp; Ski Clb; PA ST SR Study Prog 85-86; Army ROTC 4 Yr Schlrshp 86; PA ST; Oper Mgmt.

WARBURTON, DENISE; Upper Dublin HS; Ambler, PA; (Y); 96/307; Hosp Aide; Im Powder Puff Ftbl; Foundrs Cp Cmptv Ice Sktr 84; Intrprtv Sktng Gld 82-84; South Atlntcs Fgr Sktg 82-83; Physcl Thrpy.

WARBURTON, JODI; Towanda Area HS; Towanda, PA; (Y); Trs Church Yth Grp; Drama Clb; FBLA; VP FTA; SADD; Chorus; Church Choir; Rep Stu Cncl; DAR Awd; Hon Roll; Rainbow Clb Stu/Musician/Offcr 85-86; Knutztown U; Elem Educ.

WARCHOL, KATHLEEN; Pennsbury HS; Yardley, PA; (Y); Church Yth Grp; Cmnty Wkr; French Clb; Hosp Aide; Band; Mrchg Band; Nwsp Stf; Yrbk Stf; Hon Roll; NHS.

WARD, AMY; Upper Merion HS; King Of Prussia, PA; (Y); 27/280; Mrchg Band; Fld Hcky; Powder Puff Ftbl; Socr; Hon Roll; Prfct Atten Awd; Pres Schlr; Mst Imprvd JV Sccr 83; Mst Vlbl JV Sccr 84; Cert Acadmc Excllnc Math 86; Widener U; Engrng.

WARD, AMY C; Lower Dauphin SR HS; Harrisburg, PA; (Y); Church Yth Grp; German Clb; Office Aide; Color Guard; Rep Frsh Cls; Rep Soph Cls; Rep Jr Cls; Hst Sr Cls; Rep Stu Cncl; Var Cheerleading; PA ST U; Bus.

WARD, BARB; Northwestern SR HS; E Springfield, PA; (Y); Mrchg Band; Trs Soph Cls; Trs Jr Cls; Trs Sr Cls; Sec Rep Stu Cncl; Bsktbl; Capt Pom Pon; Powder Puff Ftbl; Sftbl.

WARD, CHRISTINA; W Philadelphia Catholic Girls HS; Philadelphia, PA; (Y); 40/245; Latin Clb; Model UN; Speech Tm; School Play; Yrbk Stf; Cit Awd; DAR Awd; Prfct Atten Awd; Pres Clssrm For Yng Amer 84; Temple U; Pol Sci.

WARD, CHRISTINE; Saint Maria Goretti HS; Philadelphia, PA; (Y); Sec Church Yth Grp; French Clb; Math Clb; Hon Roll; NHS; Prfct Atten Awd.

WARD, CONSTANCE L; Lower Moreland HS; Huntingdon Vly, PA; (Y); 34/211; Key Clb; Red Cross Aide; Science Clb; SADD; Orch; Yrbk Stf; Trs Frsh Cls; Fld Hcky; Stat Swmmng; High Hon Roll; Acad All Amer Awd 85-86; Phila Schlrshp 85-86; Philadelphia Coll; Bio.

WARD, KATHLEEN; Brownsville Area HS; Grindstone, PA; (Y); Ski Clb; SADD; Band; Concert Band; Flag Corp; Mrchg Band; High Hon Roll; Hon Roll; Prfct Atten Awd; Bus Adm.

WARD, KEVIN JOSEPH; St John Neumann HS; Philadelphia, PA; (Y); 82/321; Chorus; Hon Roll; Music Awd 86; CC Phila; Law.

WARD, KIM; New Brighton SR HS; New Brighton, PA; (S); Pres DECA; GAA; Library Aide; Chorus; Color Guard; High Hon Roll; Hon Roll; Bus Mngmnt.

WARD, KIMBERLY; H S Of Engineering & Sci; Philadelphia, PA; (Y); 62/184; Church Yth Grp; Civic Clb; Cmnty Wkr; Hosp Aide; Library Aide; Math Clb; Pep Clb; Science Clb; Church Choir; Nwsp Rptr; Howard U; Pre-Med.

WARD, LINDA; Canton HS; Canton, PA; (Y); Church Yth Grp; Letterman Clb; Chorus; Church Choir; Flag Corp; Mrchg Band; Cheerleading; Crs Cntry; Trk; NHS; Clark Cummings Art Prz 84; Elem Educ.

WARD, LISA; Ephrata SR HS; Ephrata, PA; (Y); Camp Fr Inc; Latin Clb; Spanish Clb; JV Var Cheerleading; JV Var Crs Cntry; Im Gym; Im Vllybl; Hon Roll; Outstndng Spnsh Achvt Awd 85-86; U Of OK; Spnsh.

WARD, LONIE; Trinity HS; Washington, PA; (Y); JV Bsktbl; High Hon Roll; Hon Roll; Air Frc Acad; Srgry.

WARD, MARILYN L; Dallas SR HS; Dallas, PA; (Y); 2/197; Drama Clb; Hosp Aide; Chorus; Capt Drill Tm; School Musical; School Play; Yrbk Stf; Stu Cncl; Capt Pom Pon; High Hon Roll; Pres Acad Ftnss Awd; Dallas Lioness Bk Schlrshp; IUP; Appld Math.

WARD, MARK; York Catholic HS; York, PA; (Y); JV Ftbl.

WARD, SABINE; Belle Vernon Area HS; Belle Vernon, PA; (Y); Church Yth Grp; Teachers Aide; Band; Concert Band; Mrchg Band; JV Powder Puff Ftbl; Hon Roll; Prfct Atten Awd; Pitt U; Nrsg.

WARD, TAMMY; Western Beauer HS; Beaver, PA; (Y); Chorus; Stu Cncl; Twrlr; Cit Awd; Hon Roll.

WARD, VICKI; Sharon HS; Sharon, PA; (Y); 2/162; French Clb; Hosp Aide; Service Clb; Trs Sr Cls; JV Tennis; Hon Roll; NHS; NEDT Awd; J F Kennedy Hnrs Schlrshp $500 83; Amer Chem Scty Cert Of Merit 86; Finance.

WARD, VICTORIA; Cardinal O Hara HS; Newtown Sq, PA; (Y); 41/740; Dance Clb; Yrbk Stf; Trk; Im Vllybl; High Hon Roll; Hon Roll; Lion Awd; Cert Of Merit In French 83; Prncpls Awd Acadmc Excllnce 85-86; Ursinus Coll.

WARD, WANDA; Otto-Eldred JR SR HS; Eldred, PA; (Y); 7/88; Varsity Clb; Yrbk Stf; Var Bsktbl; High Hon Roll; Prfct Atten Awd; Ntl Engl Merit Awd 86; Acad All Am Large Div 86.

WARDEN, ANNE; Academy Of Notre Dame HS; Berwyn, PA; (Y); Church Yth Grp; Math Tm; Nwsp Rptr; Lit Mag; Pres Soph Cls; VP Jr Cls; VP Stu Cncl; Bsktbl; Socr; Tennis; Skiing; Ntl Engr Awd 83; PA Math League; U PA.

WARDEN, ROB; Fairview HS; Erie, PA; (Y); French Clb; Science Clb; Ski Clb; Varsity Clb; School Play; Rep Frsh Cls; L Socr; High Hon Roll; Hon Roll; NHS; Sci Dept Awd; SR Sccr Plyr Yr; Bucknell U; Premed.

WARDLE, BRIAN L; Upper Perkiomen HS; East Greenville, PA; (Y); Aud/Vis; Chorus; Church Choir; JV Bsktbl; JV Socr; Var L Tennis; High Hon Roll; Hon Roll; Biochem.

WARDLOW, TAMMY; Carbondale Area HS; Carbondale, PA; (Y); Art Clb; French Clb; Hosp Aide; Ski Clb; High Hon Roll; Hon Roll; Pre-Dntl.

WARE, HUNTER; Unionville HS; Kennett Sq, PA; (Y); 15/300; Sec Boy Scts; FBLA; Ski Clb; Var Trk; High Hon Roll; Jr NHS; NHS; Vrsty Acdmc Team 85-86; Pilot.

WAREHAM, GREGORY S; Gateway SR HS; Pitcairn, PA; (Y); 127/508; Am Leg Boys St; Hosp Aide; Nwsp Ed-Chief; Lit Mag; Off Frsh Cls; Off Soph Cls; Hst Jr Cls; Masonic Awd; PA Gvrnrs Schl Arts 85; Mst Outstndng Photo Gettysburg Yrbk Wrkshp 83; Utica Coll Syracuse U; Occ Ther.

WARF, JULIANE M; Ambridge Area HS; Baden, PA; (Y); 56/265; Church Yth Grp; Office Aide; Pep Clb; Jr Cls; Sr Cls; Hon Roll; PA ST U; Vet.

WARFEL, CINDY; Halifax Area HS; Halifax, PA; (S); 6/97; FHA; Teachers Aide; Vllybl; High Hon Roll; Hon Roll; NHS; Central PA Bus; Bus Mgt.

WARGO, DANEEN; Trinity HS; New Cumberland, PA; (Y); 16/145; Church Yth Grp; Pep Clb; Spanish Clb; High Hon Roll; Hon Roll; Cmmnctns.

WARGO, MICHELLE; Monongahela Vallaey Catholic HS; W Brownsville, PA; (Y); 3/81; Spanish Clb; Chorus; Drill Tm; School Musical; Variety Show; Stat Bsktbl; NHS; Spanish NHS; Concert Band; Powder Puff Ftbl; PA Acad Sci ST Awds 84-86; Sci Talnt Srch 86.

WARHOLAK, TERRI; Canon Mc Millan SR HS; Canonsburg, PA; (Y); 20/375; Latin Clb; Trs Science Clb; Trs Band; Concert Band; Drill Tm; Cheerleading; High Hon Roll; NHS; Mrchg Band; Ed Assn Scholar 86; Grl Scout Gold Awd 82; Purdue U; Bio.

WARHOLIC, MICHAEL; West Branch HS; Morrisdale, PA; (Y); 2/123; Trs Science Clb; Varsity Clb; Var L Bsbl; Var Co-Capt Bsktbl; Var Ftbl; Hon Roll; Pres NHS; Sal; U S Army Schlr Athlt Awd; Halden Johnson Mem Awd; Male Athlt & Schlr Of The Yr; Penn ST U; Engl.

WARMBRODT, SHARON; Johnsonburg Area HS; Johnsonburg, PA; (S); 1/100; Camera Clb; Nwsp Ed-Chief; Pres Frsh Cls; Capt Cheerleading; High Hon Roll; NHS; Amer Lgn Auxlry Awd 82; Flmng Foliag Pagnt 85; Penn ST Univ Park; Engrng.

WARME, REBECCA; State College Area SR HS; State College, PA; (Y); Art Clb; French Clb; Band; Sec Soph Cls; Trk; DAR Awd; High Hon Roll; Ntl Merit Ltr; Sci Merit & Engl Awds 86; Intr Dsgn.

WARNE, MATTHEW; Newport HS; Newport, PA; (S); 5/100; Church Yth Grp; Co-Capt Quiz Bowl; School Play; Pres Frsh Cls; Pres Soph Cls; Pres Jr Cls; Bsktbl; Ftbl; Wt Lftg; VP NHS; West Point; Engrng.

WARNER, AMY; Oil City SR HS; Oil City, PA; (Y); Band; Sec Chorus; Color Guard; Boy Scts; Capt Drill Tm; Capt Drm Mjr(t); Sec Mrchg Band; School Musical; School Play; Variety Show; Westminster Coll; Elem Educ.

WARNER, ANN; Bradford Central Christian HS; Bradford, PA; (Y); Letterman Clb; Library Aide; SADD; Var Golf; Stat Trk; Elem Educ.

WARNER, BOB; Scranton Tech; Scranton, PA; (Y); Boy Scts; Cmnty Wkr; Ski Clb; Ad Alteri Da Sctng 84.

WARNER, CATHY; Wyalusing Valley HS; Laceyville, PA; (Y); 7/150; Spanish Clb; VP Sr Cls; Rep Stu Cncl; Var Capt Sftbl; Var Capt Vllybl; High Hon Roll; Hon Roll; NHS; Sftbl-All Stars Ntl-Twn Tier All Star 84-86; Vllybl-All Star Ntl 86; Hnr Schlrshp-Acad 86; Coll Miserioordia; Rad Tech.

WARNER, DONNA; Norristown Area HS; Norristown, PA; (S); 22/525; Trs FBLA; High Hon Roll; Prof Secry.

WARNER, LORI; Sayre Area HS; Sayre, PA; (Y); Church Yth Grp; Girl Scts; Hosp Aide; Band; Chorus; Concert Band; Mrchg Band; Pep Band; Hon Roll; Prfct Atten Awd; Slctd Cnty Band 86; Psych.

WARNER, MELISSA; Sayre Area HS; Sayre, PA; (Y); 12/119; Church Yth Grp; Teachers Aide; Band; Chorus; Concert Band; Mrchg Band; Ed Lit Mag; Capt Var Sftbl; Im Vllybl; High Hon Roll; Richard Carl Etshman Exprmntl Concpts Meml Awd 86; Dr Charles H Osher Meml Awd 86; Mansfield U; Avtg Illstrtr.

WARNER, PATRICIA; Crestwood HS; Mountain Top, PA; (Y); 30/168; Girl Scts; Key Clb; Math Clb; Ski Clb; Y-Teens; Yrbk Stf; Rep Stu Cncl; JV Fld Hcky; JV Stat Vllybl; High Hon Roll; U Scranton; Pre-Med.

WARNER, RACHEL; Brugettstown JR SR HS; Burgettstown, PA; (Y); 17/173; Drama Clb; Library Aide; Science Clb; Chorus; Yrbk Stf; Hon Roll; Jr NHS; NHS; Pres Of Lib Clb; Blue Notes.

WARNER, RHONDA; Lewistown Area HS; Lewistown, PA; (Y); 20/262; AFS; Cmnty Wkr; Trs German Clb; Yrbk Sprt Ed; Cheerleading; High Hon Roll; NHS; Pres Schlr; Church Yth Grp; Key Clb; Lewistown Area Pnthr Princess 85-86; Penn ST U Upward Bound Prgm 83-86; Penn ST U; Indstrl Engr.

WARNER, SUSAN; Red Lion Area SR HS; Windsor, PA; (Y); 36/337; Pres VP Church Yth Grp; VP SADD; Chorus; Church Choir; School Musical; School Play; JV Var Trk; Hon Roll; Sec NHS; Millersville ST U; Elem Ed.

WARNER, WENDY ANN; Plum SR HS; Pittsburgh, PA; (Y); Pres Exploring; French Clb; Chorus; Hon Roll; Chld Care.

WARNETSKY, TRICIA; Valley View JR SR HS; Archbald, PA; (Y); 34/195; French Clb; Drill Tm; Swmmng; Trk; Vllybl; Hon Roll; Bio.

WARNICK, MARCIA; Butler SR HS; Butler, PA; (Y); Church Yth Grp; Exploring; French Clb; SADD; Church Choir; Concert Band; Mrchg Band; Swmmng; Hon Roll; Jr NHS; Dntl Hyg.

WARRACH, ANDREA; Immaculate Conception HS; Canonsburg, PA; (Y); 21/51; Art Clb; Nwsp Stf; Swmmng; Hon Roll; French Art 85; French 86; Parsons; Fshn Dsgn.

WARREN, ANNA; Springside Schl; Pillsbury, PA; (Y); Chorus; Nwsp Stf; Yrbk Stf; Pres Frsh Cls; JV Var Fld Hcky; Var Ice Hcky; Var Sftbl; JV Tennis; Gov.

WARREN, CHRISTOPHER; John S Fine HS; Alden, PA; (S); 2/242; Science Clb; Varsity Clb; Trk; High Hon Roll; NHS; Ntl Merit Ltr; NEDT Awd; Chem.

WARREN, JEFF; Linesville HS; Linesville, PA; (Y); 1/78; Pres German Clb; Pep Clb; SADD; Wt Lftg; High Hon Roll; Pres NHS; Prfct Atten Awd; Acad Challenge 85-86; Grove City Coll; Engrng.

WARREN, JODI; Canton Area JR SR HS; Canton, PA; (Y); Sec Church Yth Grp; 4-H; Library Aide; Chorus; Church Choir; Yrbk Stf; Hon Roll; Certf Porfcncy Accntng 86; 98 Grade Pnt Avg Yr; Sec.

WARREN, JULIE; Cowanesque Valley HS; Knoxville, PA; (S); 16/85; Hst French Clb; Letterman Clb; Library Aide; SADD; Band; Stat Mgr Trk; Hon Roll; NHS.

WARREN, KARIS; Pine Forge HS; Huntsville, AL; (S); 4/61; Hosp Aide; Teachers Aide; Chorus; School Play; Yrbk Ed-Chief; Sec Soph Cls; High Hon Roll; NHS; Cmnty Wkr; Red Cross Vlntr Pin 84-85; Psychlgy.

WARREN, KATHERINE; Kennard-Dale HS; Stewartstown, PA; (Y); 1/150; Church Yth Grp; School Play; Yrbk Ed-Chief; JV Var Cheerleading; Var Trk; Var Twrlr; Bausch & Lomb Sci Awd; High Hon Roll; NHS; French Clb; Attended PA JR Sci & Humanities Symposium; Math.

WARREN, KEVIN; Middletown Area HS; Middletown, PA; (Y); 83/181; Latin Clb; Model UN; Radio Clb; Boy Scts; FBLA; JCL; Band; Concert Band; Mrchg Band; Rep Stu Cncl; Pltcl Sci.

WARREN, MICHAEL E; Annville-Cleona HS; Annville, PA; (Y); 11/121; Acpl Chr; School Musical; School Play; Ed Yrbk Phtg; Yrbk Stf; NHS; Annville Rotary Clb Boy Of Mnth 86; Rochester Inst Tech; Comp Sci.

WARREN, RENEE L; Montrose Area HS; Montrose, PA; (Y); 27/174; Art Clb; Church Yth Grp; French Clb; French Hon Soc; High Hon Roll; Hon Roll; Library Aide; Chorus; Church Choir; School Play; Monday Evening Wmns Federated Clb Schlrshp 86; Honorary Cert Frnch Hghst Grd 86; Baptist Bible Coll; Elem Educ.

WARREN, SANDRA; Donegal HS; Mount Joy, PA; (Y); 40/166; Church Yth Grp; Pep Clb; Concert Band; Mrchg Band; School Play; Yrbk Stf; Rep Soph Cls; JV Cheerleading; Hon Roll; Lay Reader Chrch 83-87; PA ST U.

WARRENFELTZ, KRISTIN; Hempfield HS; Landisvile, PA; (Y); Office Aide; Chorus; Orch; School Musical; Nwsp Stf; Yrbk Stf; Hon Roll; Lncst Lebano Cnty Orchstr 86; Msc Vrsty Ltr 86; Bloomsburg U; Blgy.

WARREY, LISA; York Catholic HS; Thomasville, PA; (Y); 48/180; Church Yth Grp; Latin Clb; Pep Clb; Service Clb; Spanish Clb; Chorus; Nwsp Stf; Rep Sr Cls; JV Var Vllybl; Hon Roll; ROTC; Pharmcst.

WARRINER, MELISSA; Mansfield JR SR HS; Mansfield, PA; (S); OEA; Ski Clb; JV Cheerleading; Var Trk; Var L Vllybl; Hon Roll; Miss Maple Swthrt 85; Mansfield U; Law.

WARRINGTON, BOB; Henderson SR HS; Westchester, PA; (S); 18/349; Church Yth Grp; Computer Clb; Ski Clb; Nwsp Rptr; Bsbl; Ftbl; High Hon Roll; Hon Roll; Engrng.

WARRINGTON, GAIL; Cardinal O Hara HS; Folsom, PA; (Y); 34/776; Sec Church Yth Grp; Office Aide; Yrbk Stf; Im Vllybl; High Hon Roll; Hon Roll; Prfct Atten Awd; Vlybl Champ 85; Princ Acadmc Excllne Awd 85-86; Phys Ther.

WARSING, MELISSA; Shenango HS; New Castle, PA; (Y); Office Aide; Var Trk; Erie Bus Ctr; Air.

WARTELLA, CAROL; Nativity B V M HS; Pottsville, PA; (Y); Ski Clb; Spanish Clb; Chorus; Flag Corp; Variety Show; Yrbk Stf; Bowling; Hghst Achvt In Alg II 86; Bus.

WARUNEK, KIMBERLY; Old Forge HS; Old Forge, PA; (S); Church Yth Grp; Ski Clb; Spanish Clb; High Hon Roll; Hon Roll; NHS; Prfct Atten Awd; Physcl Ed Awd 84.

WARUNEK, KIMBERLY; Pittston Area SR HS; Dupont, PA; (Y); 30/380; Drama Clb; Key Clb; Math Clb; Ski Clb; Chorus; Swmmng; Hon Roll.

WARYANKA, JILL; Hempfield Area HS; Irwin, PA; (Y); French Clb; NFL; Rep Frsh Cls; Rep Stu Cncl; French Hon Soc; High Hon Roll; Jr NHS; Med.

WARZYNSKI, GARY; Penn Trafford HS; Export, PA; (Y); 4/362; Chess Clb; Church Yth Grp; FBLA; Ski Clb; Bsbl; Im Bsktbl; Im Ftbl; Im Sftbl; High Hon Roll; Sec NHS; Aeronutcl Engr.

WASALINKO, ALEX; Scranton Tech HS; Scranton, PA; (Y); Ski Clb; Penn ST U; Mchncl Engrng.

WASCO, MELANIE; Mon Valley CHS; Belle Vernon, PA; (Y); 7/82; Ski Clb; Spanish Clb; Teachers Aide; Color Guard; Powder Puff Ftbl; NHS; Spanish NHS; Merit Awd Spnsh II 84-85; Constrctn Modl Humanites Day 86.

WASELKO, DAVID; Kiski Area HS; Leechburg, PA; (Y); Boy Scts; Pres Church Yth Grp; JA; Pep Clb; SADD; Band; Concert Band; Jazz Band; Mrchg Band; Pep Band.

WASHINGTON, CHRISTOPHER; St James HS; Chester, PA; (Y); 45/140; Church Yth Grp; French Clb; Pep Clb; Teachers Aide; Yrbk Stf; Pres Schlr; Widener U; Bus Admn.

WASHINGTON, LEONARD; Trinity HS; Washington, PA; (Y); 76/374; Boy Scts; German Clb; Library Aide; Varsity Clb; Chorus; Church Choir; L Ftbl; L Trk; L Wt Lftg; UCLA; Pre-Med.

WASHINGTON, WENDY D; Conestoga SR HS; Berwyn, PA; (Y); 61/408; Pres VP Church Choir; Variety Show; Stat Mgr(s); Co-Capt Vllybl; Hon Roll; Black Incentive Grant 86; PA ST U.

WASHKO, EILEEN; Lakeland JR SR HS; Jermyn, PA; (S); 1/162; French Clb; GAA; Drm Mjr(t); Twrlr; Hon Roll.

WASHMON, JOHN; The Hill Schl; Brownsville, TX; (Y); Boy Scts; Church Yth Grp; Model UN; Ski Clb; Spanish Clb; Socr; Var Tennis; High Hon Roll; Hon Roll; Prfct Atten Awd.

WASHOWICH, WAYNE; Mc Keesport SR HS; White Oak, PA; (Y); Church Yth Grp; Cmnty Wkr; Exploring; Nwsp Rptr; Nwsp Stf; Pres Frsh Cls; Rep Soph Cls; Rep Jr Cls; Stu Cncl; L Ftbl; Mngmnt.

WASICKI, SHELLEY; Punxsutawney HS; Anita, PA; (Y); GAA; Letterman Clb; Spanish Clb; Varsity Clb; Var L Bsktbl; Var L Trk; Var L Vllybl; Bio.

WASIELEWSKI, SUZANN; Ft Le Boeuf HS; Waterford, PA; (Y); Dance Clb; Variety Show; Girl Scts; Chorus; JV Cheerleading; Hon Roll; Fshn Mrchndsng.

WASIL, MICHELLE; Geibel HS; Mcclellandtown, PA; (Y); Drama Clb; VP Spanish Clb; School Play; High Hon Roll; Hon Roll; VP Spanish NHS; Pre-Med.

WASILEWSKI, LISA; Hanover Area JR SR HS; Wilkes Barre, PA; (Y); Key Clb; Letterman Clb; Ski Clb; Color Guard; Yrbk Stf; Var Capt Bsktbl; Var L Sftbl; Im Swmmng; Var L Trk; Hon Roll; Physcl Thrpy.

WASILEWSKI, MIKE; Our Lady Of Lourdes HS; Kulpmont, PA; (Y); Sec Sr Cls; L Bsbl; Bsktbl; Ftbl; Score Keeper; Sftbl; Altar Boy; Wrks For Chrch Drng Smmr Mnths.

WASILKO, JENNIFER; Bishop Carroll HS; Barnesboro, PA; (S); 6/105; Drama Clb; NFL; Ski Clb; School Play; Stage Crew; Rep Soph Cls; High Hon Roll; NHS; NEDT Awd; Hugh O Brian Ldrshp Awd 84; Soc Of Distngshd Spch Drama Stu 85; Dickinson Coll; Intl Stds.

WASILOWSKI, SUSAN; Highlands SR HS; Natrona Hts, PA; (Y); Cmnty Wkr; FBLA; Hosp Aide; SADD; Chorus; Swing Chorus; Yrbk Stf; Hon Roll; NHS; Prfct Atten Awd; Brown Awds 83-86; Bradford Bus Schl; Acctng.

WASKO, LISA; Saint Hubert HS; Philadelphia, PA; (Y); 104/456; Church Yth Grp; Band; Chorus; Jazz Band; Orch; School Musical; Cmnty Wkr; Exploring; PAVAS; Radio Clb; Cathlc Dghts Of Amercs Div III Msc Sngwrtng Cty Cmptn 1st Plc & ST Cmptn 3rd Plc 86; Temple U; Music.

WASKO, SHAWN; Blairsville SR HS; Blairsville, PA; (Y); 5/131; Boy Scts; Church Yth Grp; Varsity Clb; JV Bsktbl; Var L Ftbl; Var L Trk; High Hon Roll; NHS; Chem Engr.

WASLEY, KEVIN F; Bishop O Hara HS; Archbald, PA; (Y); 37/127; CAP; French Clb; Latin Clb; Math Clb; Radio Clb; Hon Roll; Pres Schlr; Pres Schlrshp 86; U Of Scranton; Med Fld.

WASSENICH, AMY; William Allen HS; Allentown, PA; (Y); 1/553; Church Yth Grp; Drama Clb; German Clb; Model UN; Ski Clb; Chorus; Concert Band; Mrchg Band; Lit Mag; High Hon Roll; Mt Holyoke Bk Awd 86; Congrss-Bundestag Yth Exch Scholar 86; 2nd Pl Austrian Bk Awd Amer Assn Tchrs 86; United Wrld Coll; Intl Rel.

WASSON, PAUL; East HS; West Chester, PA; (S); Boys Clb Am; Cmnty Wkr; DECA; Outstndng Svc DECA 84-85; Cert Apprctn DECA 86; Acad Excllnce DECA 83-84; ST Awd Cert DECA 85-86; Westchester U; CPA.

WATENPOOL, SUSAN; North Allegheny SR HS; Ingomar, PA; (Y); JA; Chorus; Rep Jr Cls; Rep Stu Cncl; Vllybl; Pres Schlr; Stolle Corp Acad Schlrshp 85-86; Penn ST; Bus Admin.

WATERFIELD, DAVID; Lincoln HS; Ellwood City, PA; (Y); Boy Scts; Church Yth Grp; Cmnty Wkr; Band; Concert Band; Mrchg Band; Mgr Bsktbl; Bowling; Mgr Ftbl; Mgr(s); Comp.

WATERMAN, MICHAEL; Lock Haven SR HS; Lock Haven, PA; (Y); French Clb; Model UN; Nwsp Rptr; Var Bsktbl; High Hon Roll; Hon Roll; NHS; Dr David W Thomas Sr Mem Awd Chem 85-86; Sci.

WATERMAN, SCOTT; William Penn Charter HS; Philadelphia, PA; (Y); Debate Tm; VP Model UN; Political Wkr; Pres Science Clb; Pres Service Clb; Nwsp Rptr; Yrbk Bus Mgr; Rep Soph Cls; Off Jr Cls; Off Sr Cls; Thomas Jefferson U VA Awd 86; Essay Cont Wnnr 86; Yth Ldrshp Conf Lehigh U Rep 86; Forensic Law.

WATERS, JERE; Western Wayne HS; Waymart, PA; (Y); Sec FHA; Chorus; Concert Band; Drm Mjr(t); Mrchg Band; School Musical; Socr; High Hon Roll; JP Sousa Awd; PACE Prgm At T Jfrsn U Phldlpha 86; Blmsbrg U; Physcl Thrpy.

WATERS, KATHY; Central Dauphin HS; Harrisburg, PA; (Y); Aud/Vis; Debate Tm; Ski Clb; SADD; Chorus; Church Choir; Drm Mjr(t); School Musical; Trk; Voice Dem Awd; Law.

WATERS, LAURA; Bristol JR-SR HS; Bristol, PA; (Y); 1/90; Scholastic Bowl; Band; Concert Band; Mrchg Band; Orch; Yrbk Ed-Chief; Trs Jr Cls; High Hon Roll; Cmnty Wkr; Red Cross Aide; Soc Wmn Engrs Sci & Math Cert Merit 86; Bucks Cnty Sci Sem Cert 86; Chem Engrng.

WATERS, MICHELE; Juniata HS; Mifflin, PA; (Y); Drama Clb; Varsity Clb; Band; Chorus; School Play; Stage Crew; Yrbk Sprt Ed; JV Bsktbl; JV Var Cheerleading; Hon Roll; Juniata Coll; Elem Ed.

WATERS, NICHOLAS; Lincoln HS; Philadelphia, PA; (Y); Orch; Ftbl; Wt Lftg; Bus Mgmt.

WATERS, WENDI; Western Beaver HS; Industry, PA; (Y); Computer Clb; Library Aide; Office Aide; Chorus; Mrchg Band; Nwsp Stf; Yrbk Stf; Var Twrlr; Hon Roll; Outstndng Cmmrcl Stu Schlrshp & Awd 86; Scrtry.

WATKINS, ANNE; Ambridge Area HS; Baden, PA; (Y); 4/271; Am Leg Aux Girls St; French Clb; Sec German Clb; Hosp Aide; Pep Clb; Pres Service Clb; Stat Trk; High Hon Roll; Sec NHS; Seton Hill Ldrshp Smnrs Wmn 85; Penn ST U; Chem Engr.

WATKINS, BRAD; Towanda Area HS; Monroeton, PA; (Y); 22/134; Church Yth Grp; Letterman Clb; Spanish Clb; Var Bsbl; Var Bsktbl; Var L Golf; Hon Roll; Landscape Arch.

WATKINS, CHARLES; Wilkinsburg HS; Pittsburgh, PA; (Y); Hon Roll; Arch.

WATKINS, CONNIE; Southern Huntingdon Co HS; Three Springs, PA; (Y); Varsity Clb; Chorus; Sec Jr Cls; Stu Cncl; JV Fld Hcky; Powder Puff Ftbl; Dnfth Awd; Hon Roll; NHS; Ntl Merit Ltr; X-Ray Tech.

WATKINS, ERIC; Central Dauphin HS; Harrisburg, PA; (Y); Church Yth Grp; Cmnty Wkr; PAVAS; Variety Show; Ftbl; JV Var Trk; Vllybl; Hon Roll; Ltrs Track Tm 83-84; Bus Adm.

WATKINS, LYNDA; Hatboro-Horsham HS; Hatboro, PA; (Y); Model UN; Band; Chorus; Concert Band; School Musical; JV Bsbl; JV Sftbl; Tyler Schl Art; Art.

WATKINS, PENNY; Mansfield JR SR HS; Mansfield, PA; (S); Band; Chorus; Church Choir; Color Guard; Concert Band; Mrchg Band; Pep Band; Yrbk Stf; High Hon Roll; NHS; Mansfield U; Pre-Law.

WATKINS, SHAWN; Conemaugh Township HS; Holsopple, PA; (Y); 39/102; Var L Bsbl; JV Ftbl; Var L Wrstlng.

WATKINS, TAMMY; Southern Huntingdon HS; Cassville, PA; (Y); 4-H; FBLA; FHA; GAA; Spanish Clb; SADD; Varsity Clb; Band; Flag Corp; School Play; Lgl Secty.

WATKINS, TIM; Blairsville SR HS; Blairsville, PA; (Y); 37/124; Off Church Yth Grp; Varsity Clb; Var L Ftbl; Var L Trk; Var Wt Lftg; Var L Wrstlng; Hon Roll; Prfct Atten Awd; Aldo Ackerson Scholar 86; Thiel Coll; Physcs Tchr.

WATKINS, WILLIAM; California Area SR HS; Roscoe, PA; (Y); 2/95; Aud/Vis; Church Yth Grp; Science Clb; Var Mgr(s); High Hon Roll; NHS; Finance.

WATLEY, LEONARD B; Harry S Truman HS; Bristol, PA; (Y); Boy Scts; Church Yth Grp; Cmnty Wkr; JA; Library Aide; Math Clb; Math Tm; ROTC; Spanish Clb; SADD; Graduating Committee 86; U Of Villanova; Accounting.

WATROBA, ANNEMARIE; Ringgold HS; Donora, PA; (Y); 8/350; FNA; Hosp Aide; Office Aide; Service Clb; Ski Clb; Varsity Clb; Chorus; Rep Frsh Cls; Rep Soph Cls; Rep Jr Cls; Mrcy Hosp Schl Of Nrsng; Nrsng.

WATSON, CHRISTY; Derry Area SR HS; Latrobe, PA; (Y); 10/275; JA; Letterman Clb; Math Clb; Chorus; School Musical; School Play; Stu Cncl; Capt Cheerleading; Vllybl; High Hon Roll; U PA; Pre Med.

WATSON, DAVID N; New Brighton Area HS; New Brighton, PA; (Y); 17/154; Band; Concert Band; Jazz Band; Mrchg Band; Orch; School Musical; Symp Band; Rotary Awd; Rep Stu Cncl; High Hon Roll; SR All Amercn Hall Fame Band Hnrs 86; Acadmc Comptve Schlrshp Duquesne U 86-87; Music Schlrshp 86-87; Duquesne U; Music Educ.

WATSON, HEATHER; Trinity HS; Washington, PA; (Y); 7/374; Church Yth Grp; GAA; Key Clb; Letterman Clb; Pep Clb; Spanish Clb; Bsktbl; Crs Cntry; Tennis; Trk; All-Cnty All Str Bsktbl 85-86; Pttsbrgh Prss All-Str Bsktbl 85-86; Pre-Med.

WATSON, JAMES; Bald Eagle Area HS; Milesburg, PA; (Y); Varsity Clb; Crs Cntry; Var L Trk; Wt Lftg; Hon Roll; NHS; PA ST; Anml Bio Sci.

WATSON, JANICE; GAR Memorial JR SR HS; Wilkes Barre, PA; (S); 11/177; Church Yth Grp; Computer Clb; French Clb; Chorus; Church Choir; Rep Stu Cncl; Bsktbl; Sftbl; High Hon Roll; Hon Roll; Mst Imprvd Plyr Bsktbl 84-85; U Of CA; LA; Comp Sci.

WATSON, JOLENE; David B Olivery HS; Pittsburgh, PA; (Y); 9/219; Library Aide; Nwsp Rptr; Nwsp Stf; JV Sftbl; JV Vllybl; High Hon Roll; NHS; Ntl Merit SF; Ntnl Lng Arts Olympcs 84; Penn ST; Chem.

WATSON, MARC; Oxford Area HS; Oxford, PA; (Y); 64/190; Y-Teens; Chorus; Yrbk Stf; Capt Var Bsktbl; JV Ftbl; Var Tennis; Full Schlrshp Slppry Rck U PA 86; 2nd Pl Chstr Cty & PA ST Cnsrvtn Pstr Cntst 86; MVP JR Yr Bsktb; Slippery Rock U; Art.

WATSON, MARK W; Mapletown JR SR HS; Mapletown, PA; (Y); 3/80; Church Yth Grp; VP Ski Clb; Varsity Clb; Var L Bsbl; Im Bsktbl; Var L Ftbl; Wt Lftg; High Hon Roll; Hon Roll; VP NHS; Acctng.

WATSON, PATRICK; Avon Grove HS; West Grove, PA; (Y); Aud/Vis; Boy Scts; Chess Clb; Church Yth Grp; Cmnty Wkr; Computer Clb; DECA; FTA; Library Aide; Mathletes; E Stroudsburg U; Comptr Sci.

WATSON, THERESA; Eastern York HS; Wrightsville, PA; (Y); Church Yth Grp; Chorus; Church Choir; Color Guard; School Musical; Powder Puff Ftbl; High Hon Roll; Hon Roll; Trs Jr NHS; NHS; York Coll Of PA.

WATT, KATHERINE; Altoona Area HS; Altoona, PA; (Y); German Clb; Girl Scts; Hosp Aide; Chorus; Concert Band; Mrchg Band; Rep Stu Cncl; Mgr(s); High Hon Roll; Sea Cadt Yr 84; RN.

WATT JR, RONALD; Jamestown HS; Greenville, PA; (Y); VICA; Chorus; School Musical; Bsktbl; Golf; Hon Roll; Electroncs.

WATTS, HEATHER; Millville Area HS; Millville, PA; (Y); Band; Concert Band; Mrchg Band; School Play; Stat Bsbl; Stat Wrstlng; Hon Roll; VP Of Lbrty Clb 85-86; Tchng Deaf.

WATTS, JESSICA; Cocalico SR HS; Denver, PA; (Y); 28/179; Art Clb; Exploring; 4-H; Speech Tm; Varsity Clb; Pres Jr Cls; Trs Stu Cncl; JV Bsktbl; Im Tennis; Im Vllybl; Outstndg Teen Ldr 81-86; Bst Demnstrtn 86; 3rd Pl Lancaster Tstmstrs Intl Spch Cont 85; Engl.

WATTS, NATASHA; Pine Forge Acad; Capitol Heights, MD; (S); Capt Pep Clb; Church Choir; Nwsp Phtg; Trs Frsh Cls; Rep Soph Cls; Sec Stu Cncl; Cit Awd; Hon Roll; NHS; Wohelas Dorm Clb Offcr; Good Wrk Rcrd Awd; Columbia Union Coll; Acctng.

WAUGAMAN, JODI; Norwin HS; N Huntingdon, PA; (S); French Clb; Color Guard; Mrchg Band; Hon Roll; Jr NHS; Outstndg Stu Fr II 84; Hgh Achvt Phys Sci 83; Fash Merch.

WAUGH, JULIE; Milton Area SR HS; Milton, PA; (Y); Computer Clb; Trs Key Clb; Spanish Clb; Varsity Clb; Band; Yrbk Stf; Var JV Cheerleading; Var JV Fld Hcky; Hon Roll; NHS.

WAWROSE, DOROTHY; Huntingdon Area HS; Huntingdon, PA; (Y); 1/207; Drama Clb; Key Clb; Nwsp Stf; Yrbk Stf; Var Bsktbl; Var Trk; Bausch & Lomb Sci Awd; High Hon Roll; NHS; Pres Clsrm 85; U PA; Bio.

WAWRZYNSKI, ROCHELLE; Shenango JR SR HS; New Castle, PA; (Y); Yrbk Stf; Im Vllybl; Basic Arts Awd 86; Art Inst PA; Art.

WAX, NANCY; Allen HS; Allentown, PA; (Y); 60/600; Spanish Clb; Temple Yth Grp; Yrbk Stf; Stu Cncl; Vllybl; Hon Roll; NHS; Art Hon Awd Gld Key 83-84.

WAXLER, DYAN; Ambridge Area HS; Baden, PA; (Y); 28/296; Exploring; German Clb; SADD; Band; Concert Band; Mrchg Band; Pep Band; Symp Band; Im Sftbl; Hon Roll; PA ST U; Bio.

WAXMAN, FREDERIC; Upper Moreland HS; Cheltenham, PA; (Y); 35/276; French Clb; Key Clb; School Musical; School Play; Nwsp Stf; Rep Frsh Cls; Stu Cncl; Tennis; High Hon Roll; Hon Roll; Pres Acdmc Ftns Awd 86; U MD.

WAXMONSKY, DENISE; Bishop Hoban HS; Plains, PA; (Y); FBLA; Latin Clb; Ski Clb; Stu Cncl; Cheerleading; High Hon Roll; Hon Roll; NHS.

WAY, CHARLIE; Clearfield Area HS; Clearfield, PA; (Y); Church Yth Grp; SADD; JV Ftbl; Var Trk; Im Wt Lftg; Belong To Wld Trky Fedrtn Part Ntl Rfle Assn Mbr In Our Lcl Sportsmen Clb; Lock Haven U; Ed Tchr.

WAY, MICHELLE; Philipsburg/Osceola Area SR HS; Wallaceton, PA; (Y); 98/290; Church Yth Grp; Yrbk Stf; Stat Score Keeper; Hon Roll.

WAY, TODD B; State Colege Area SR HS; Lemont, PA; (Y); 4-H; Im Bsktbl; Ftbl; Im Vllybl; 4-H Awd; Hon Roll; PA ST U.

WAYES, AMY; Perkiomen Schl; Barto, PA; (Y); Ski Clb; Thesps; Varsity Clb; Chorus; Nwsp Ed-Chief; Yrbk Stf; Pres Jr Cls; VP Co-Capt Fld Hcky; Var Lcrss; Pres NHS; Dr James M Anders Awd 84; Norman Rockwill Bate Mrl Awd 86; Hillegass Jrnlsm Awd 86; Ursinus Coll; Hstry.

WAYNE, AILEEN; Cardinal Brennan HS; Girardville, PA; (Y); 7/52; Chorus; Rep Frsh Cls; Rep Jr Cls; Rep Sr Cls; Rep Stu Cncl; JV Twrlr; Hon Roll; Spanish NHS; School Play; Nwsp Stf; Engl I, Engl II 84-85; Wrld-Amer Cultr 84-85; Bio, Relgn II 85; Bloomsburg U; Elem Ed.

WAYNE, TINA; Altoona Area HS; Altoona, PA; (Y); VP Drama Clb; Key Clb; NFL; Ski Clb; VP Temple Yth Grp; School Musical; Variety Show; Yrbk Stf; Sec Sr Cls; Rep Stu Cncl; Cr Dscrvry Prgm Archt Harvard U 86; Steerng Cmmnt Yth Grp Intrnl 86; Archt.

WAYNEBERN, SCOTT; Upper Dublin HS; Dresher, PA; (Y); Nwsp Ed-Chief; Nwsp Rptr; Rep Stu Cncl; Bsktbl; Tennis; NHS; Ntl Merit SF; Spnsh Sll-Amrcn 85.

WAZENSKI, STEPHEN; Hanover Area HS; Wilkes Barre, PA; (Y); JA; Key Clb; Science Clb; Ski Clb; VP Jr Cls; L Golf; High Hon Roll; Kiwanis Awd.

WEACHTER, JAMES; Warwick HS; Elm, PA; (Y); Sec Varsity Clb; Var JV Bsbl; Im Bsktbl; Var JV Ftbl; Im Vllybl; Advrtsng.

WEACHTER, PETE; Warwick HS; Lititz, PA; (Y); Ski Clb; Chorus; Variety Show; Var L Socr; Hon Roll; Physcl Thrpy.

WEAKLAND, LEIGH ANN; Lewistown SR HS; Lewistown, PA; (Y); 11/247; Sec AFS; Key Clb; Trs Pep Clb; Ski Clb; Trs Boys Clb Am; School Musical; Sec Stu Cncl; Stat Trk; High Hon Roll; NHS; Shippensburg U PA; Acctg.

WEAKLAND, MICHELE; Harmony Area Schls; Cherry Tree, PA; (Y); Sec Church Yth Grp; Office Aide; Band; Chorus; Concert Band; Mrchg Band; Sec Jr Cls; Im Stat Bsktbl; Hon Roll; Prfct Atten Awd; Sec.

WEAKLAND, PAULA; Cambria Heights HS; Patton, PA; (Y); JV Bsktbl.

WEAKLAND, TAMMY; Tyrone Area HS; Tyrone, PA; (Y); Church Yth Grp; 4-H; Library Aide; Chorus; Coach Actv; Sftbl; Swmmng; 4-H Awd; Hon Roll; Reg Nrs.

WEALAND, ANDREA L; Cocalico HS; Stevens, PA; (Y); 1/200; Pres Church Yth Grp; Concert Band; Jazz Band; Pres Frsh Cls; Pres Soph Cls; Var Cheerleading; High Hon Roll; NHS; Acadmc All Amer 85; Intl Forgn Lang Awd 85; Sci.

WEATHERHOLTZ, RUSSELL; Conestoga Valley HS; Leola, PA; (Y); 10/247; High Hon Roll; Hon Roll; Stu Of The Month 86; SAGE 85-86; Math.

WEATHERLY, BRAD; Fairfield Area HS; Fairfield, PA; (Y); 13/42; Chess Clb; Spanish Clb; Varsity Clb; Var Socr; Var Trk; Hon Roll; Fld Comp.

WEATHERMAN, KEN; Mahanoy Area HS; Mahanoy City, PA; (Y); Im JV Bsktbl; Pittsburgh U; Dntstry.

WEATHERS, THOMAS; Cardinal O Hara HS; Media, PA; (Y); 107/772; JV Var Crs Cntry; Var Trk; Hon Roll; Aerospc Engrng.

WEAVER, AMY; Fairfield HS; Fairfield, PA; (Y); 7/51; Drama Clb; Band; School Musical; School Play; Yrbk Stf; Stat Bsktbl; Stat Sftbl; Stat Vllybl; High Hon Roll; Sec NHS; Shrthd Awds; Bus & Hghst GPA Bus Curclm; Secy.

WEAVER, AMY; Hollidaysburg Area HS; Newry, PA; (Y); Church Yth Grp; Cmnty Wkr; French Clb; Latin Clb; SADD; Teachers Aide; Chorus; Church Choir; Im Vllybl; DAR Awd; Modern Miss Schlrshp Pagnt Cert Achvt 86; Editor Genelgy Clb Cookbk Sec 84; Juniata Coll; Psychlgy.

WEAVER, ANNETTE; Palmyra HS; Annville, PA; (Y); Drama Clb; Spanish Clb; Varsity Clb; Chorus; Rep Frsh Cls; Rep Sr Cls; Stu Cncl; Stat Bsktbl; Var L Fld Hcky; JV Sftbl; Cmmnctns.

WEAVER, CHRISTOPHER; Lancaster Catholic HS; Lancaster, PA; (Y); 17/212; Boy Scts; Church Yth Grp; VP Model UN; Concert Band; Hst Mrchg Band; Pres Sr Cls; Bausch & Lomb Sci Awd; Hon Roll; NHS; Ntl Merit Ltr; Franklin/Marshall Coll; Engl Ed.

WEAVER, CINDY; Central Dauphin HS; Harrisburg, PA; (Y); Church Yth Grp; Pres Key Clb; Chorus; Yrbk Sprt Ed; Rep Jr Cls; JV Var Cheerleading; Trk; JV Var Vllybl; NHS; Journlsm Awd Patriot News 86; Queen Snow Court 83-84; Homecmng Court Rep 84-86; Mass Cmmnctns.

WEAVER, CLARE; Canon-Mc Millan HS; Canonsburg, PA; (Y); 28/356; French Clb; Latin Clb; JV Bsktbl; L Tennis; High Hon Roll; NHS; Acadmc Schlrshp 86; St Vincent Clg; Frng Lang.

WEAVER, DAVID; Canton Area HS; Roaring Branch, PA; (Y); 20/130; Art Clb; Pres Church Yth Grp; FCA; Band; Church Choir; Concert Band; Jazz Band; Mrchg Band; Sftbl; Hon Roll; Yth Plnr-4 Chrchs 85-86; Wrk Fl-Tm Fmly Farm; Scndry Math Tchr.

WEAVER, DAVID; Somerset Area SR HS; Somerset, PA; (Y); Church Yth Grp; Computer Clb; VP 4-H; Speech Tm; Band; Chorus; Church Choir; Concert Band; Mrchg Band; High Hon Roll; Chem Engr.

WEAVER, DIANE; Cocalico HS; Stevens, PA; (Y); 12/200; Trs Church Yth Grp; GAA; JV Var Bsktbl; JV Capt Fld Hcky; High Hon Roll; Hon Roll; Prfct Atten Awd.

WEAVER, DIANE; Danville SR HS; Danville, PA; (Y); 117/202; Exploring; Hosp Aide; Red Cross Aide; Spanish Clb; SADD; Chorus; Nwsp Stf; Yrbk Stf; JV Cheerleading; L Var Fld Hcky; Slippery Rock; Educ.

WEAVER, DIANNA; Blair County Christian Schl; E Freedom, PA; (S); 2/11; Church Yth Grp; 4-H; Yrbk Stf; Pres Sr Cls; Cheerleading; Sftbl; Trk; Vllybl; 4-H Awd; Pensacola Christian Coll; Edctn.

WEAVER, ELIZABETH; Abington HS; Meadowbrook, PA; (Y); 97/508; Church Yth Grp; Chorus; Yrbk Stf; Rep Stu Cncl; JV Tennis; Hon Roll; Econ.

WEAVER, ELMER B; Cambria Heights SR HS; Hastings, PA; (Y); 37/200; Boy Scts; Church Yth Grp; Cmnty Wkr; Letterman Clb; Chorus; Var L Bsktbl; Var L Ftbl; Var Wt Lftg; High Hon Roll; Hon Roll; WNCC Trophy 86; Tri-Cnty All Star 84-86; Christms All Trnmnt Tm 84-86; Accntng.

WEAVER II, HAROLD; Eastern Lebanon County HS; Myerstown, PA; (Y); JV Ftbl; NHS; Rotary Awd; Sal; Penn ST; Engrng.

WEAVER, JEFF; Punxsutawney Area HS; Timblin, PA; (Y); Varsity Clb; Var Ftbl; Var Trk; Air Force; Piloting.

WEAVER, JILL COURTNEY; Phila High Schools For Girls; Philadelphia, PA; (Y); 104/395; Church Yth Grp; Drama Clb; Office Aide; Chorus; School Musical; School Play; Stu Cncl; Zoolgst.

WEAVER, KEITH; Du Bois Central Christian HS; Reynoldsville, PA; (Y); Church Yth Grp; CAP; Computer Clb; Hosp Aide; Radio Clb; Nwsp Stf; Yrbk Stf; Socr; Trk; Hon Roll; Gen Billy Mitchell Awd Civil Air Patrol 86; Aeronautical Engr.

WEAVER, KEVIN S; Bald Eagle Area HS; Howard, PA; (Y); 1/250; CAP; Concert Band; Jazz Band; Mrchg Band; High Hon Roll; NHS; Ntl Merit SF; Val; Boy Scts; School Musical; 1s Army Rsrv; ROTC Schlrshp; Penn ST; Us Army.

WEAVER, LORA; Spring Grove SR HS; Codorus, PA; (Y); Drama Clb; Chorus; Orch; School Play; High Hon Roll; Hon Roll; Yth Grp Sec 84.

WEAVER, LORI; Dover Area HS; Dover, PA; (Y); Color Guard; Var Swmmng; Var Vllybl; Hon Roll.

WEAVER, MARK; Garden Spot HS; New Holland, PA; (Y); 1/250; Band; Concert Band; Jazz Band; Mrchg Band; Orch; School Musical; Bsbl; Socr; High Hon Roll; Hon Roll; Dist Band & Orchstra 86.

WEAVER, MELANE; Penn-Trafford HS; Trafford, PA; (Y); 105/350; Church Yth Grp; Girl Scts; Hosp Aide; JCL; Spanish Clb; Teachers Aide; Acpl Chr; Chorus; Yrbk Stf; Hon Roll.

WEAVER, MELISSA; Northwestern Lehigh HS; Germansville, PA; (Y); FNA; Capt Color Guard; Sec Stu Cncl; High Hon Roll; Hon Roll; NHS; Prfct Atten Awd; Stu Of Wk For Lcl Nespr 86; Bio Awd 85; Nrsng.

WEAVER, MELODIE; Grace Christian Schl; Myerstown, PA; (Y); 4/18; Church Yth Grp; FBLA; Chorus; Var L Sftbl; High Hon Roll; Hon Roll; Mst Outstndng Sftbl Plyr 86; Engl Awd 86; Phys Ed Awd 86.

WEAVER, MICHAEL; Canton Area JR SR HS; Roaring Branch, PA; (Y); 20/130; Art Clb; Church Yth Grp; Cmnty Wkr; FCA; Church Choir; Concert Band; Jazz Band; Variety Show; Hon Roll; Band.

WEAVER, MICHAEL; Conrad Weiser HS; Wernersville, PA; (Y); 52/192; Computer Clb; JCL; Latin Clb; Spanish Clb; JV Tennis; Var Trk; Compu Prg.

WEAVER, MICHELLE; Harbor Creek HS; Erie, PA; (Y); Dance Clb; Intnl Clb; ROTC; Drill Tm; Mrchg Band; Pom Pon; NJROTC Natl Acadmc Comptn 1st Pl 85; Chem.

WEAVER, MICHELLE; Littlestown HS; Littlestown, PA; (Y); Speech Tm; Teachers Aide; Color Guard; JV Bsktbl; Var JV Sftbl; Tennis.

WEAVER, PAMELA; Bald Eagle Area HS; Howard, PA; (Y); 20/201; SADD; Chorus; Church Choir; Variety Show; Yrbk Stf; Sec Sr Cls; Stu Cncl; Fld Hcky; Gym; Powder Puff Ftbl; Thomas Miles/Riversd Prsnl Devlpmt Awd 86; Howard Schl Cmnty Svc Awd 86; Horward Ares Schlstc Awd 86; Lock Haven U; Bus.

WEAVER, RENEE; Manheim Central HS; Manheim, PA; (Y); Church Yth Grp; Chorus; Church Choir; Var Capt Fld Hcky; Sftbl; Hon Roll; Yth Ftnss Achvt Awd 86; Dntl Hygn.

WEAVER, SHARI; Chambersburg Area SR HS; Chambersburg, PA; (Y); 39/641; Church Yth Grp; Key Clb; Library Aide; Office Aide; Pep Clb; Y-Teens; Fld Hcky; High Hon Roll; Hon Roll; Clarion U Clarion; Finc.

WEAVER, TAMMY; North Star HS; Boswell, PA; (Y); Church Yth Grp; Red Cross Aide; Band; Bsktbl; Trk; Mech Engr.

WEAVERLING, JILL; Tussey Mountain HS; Saxton, PA; (Y); AFS; Church Yth Grp; SADD; Chorus; Rep Jr Cls; Var Capt Cheerleading; Mgr(s); Mst Ldrshp For Grls Vrsty Bsktbl Chrldng 85-86; Cazenovia Coll; Intr Dsgn.

WEBB, HOPE; Lewistown Area HS; Lewistown, PA; (Y); Spanish Clb; Varsity Clb; JV Bsktbl; Var Fld Hcky; Var Sftbl; Hon Roll; Lock Haven U; Spec Ed.

WEBB, JODI; Nativity B V M HS; Cumbola, PA; (Y); 16/99; Chess Clb; Church Yth Grp; Library Aide; Color Guard; Nwsp Rptr; Yrbk Stf; High Hon Roll; Hon Roll; Govt Awd 86; PA Jnr Acad Of Sci-3rd 85; HS Sci Fair-2nd Pl 84-86.

WEBB, LAURA; Williamsburg HS; Williamsburg, PA; (Y); Church Yth Grp; French Clb; Band; Chorus; Concert Band; Mrchg Band; Yrbk Stf; Cheerleading; Twrlr; Hon Roll; Cnty Bnc 85; Cnty Chorus 85 & 86; PA ST U; Elem Tchr.

WEBB, STACEY; Berlin Brothers Valley HS; Berlin, PA; (Y); 17/90; French Clb; Trs Frsh Cls; Sec Soph Cls; Sec Jr Cls; Sec Rep Stu Cncl; Var Cheerleading; Stat Ftbl; French Hon Soc; Hon Roll; NHS; Elem Ed.

WEBB, SUSAN; Williamsburg HS; Williamsburg, PA; (Y); Church Yth Grp; FNA; Band; Concert Band; Flag Corp; Mrchg Band; Nwsp Rptr; Bsktbl; JV Vllybl; Hon Roll; Cnty Band 86; Physcl Thrpy.

WEBBER, AUDREY; Mercersburg Acad; Hickory, NC; (Y); Sec Spanish Clb; Yrbk Stf; Rep Soph Cls; L Crs Cntry; L Sftbl; High Hon Roll; Peer Grp Ldr 86-87; Prefect 86-87; Hist Awd 85-86.

WEBBER, JERRY; Big Spring HS; Newville, PA; (Y); 19/185; Church Yth Grp; Trs Ski Clb; JV Var Bsbl; High Hon Roll; Hon Roll; Bus Mgmt.

WEBBER, JULIE; Sharon HS; Sharon, PA; (Y); 49/196; Latin Clb; Band; Concert Band; Mrchg Band; Orch; Hon Roll; NHS; Edinboro U Of PA.

WEBBER, MATTHEW; Danville SR HS; Danville, PA; (Y); VP Computer Clb; Drama Clb; Key Clb; Ski Clb; Hst Soph Cls; Hst Jr Cls; Gym; Socr; Var L Trk; Wrstlng; Tchrs Awd; Gymnstcs Awd; Arch.

WEBER, BARBARA; Boyertown HS; Douglassville, PA; (Y); Teachers Aide; JV Cheerleading; Stat Trk; Twrlr; Hon Roll; Camp Fr Inc; Library Aide; Pep Clb; Drm Mjr(t); Variety Show; Nrs.

WEBER, BRADD; General Mc Lane HS; Edinboro, PA; (Y); 22/221; Var Golf; Var Wrstlng; Hon Roll; Ntl Merit Ltr; All Cnty Team Slctn Golf 85-86; All Cnty Team Slctn Wrstlng 85-86; Bus.

WEBER, JENNIFER; Parkland HS; Allntwn, PA; (Y); 21/432; Cmnty Wkr; Leo Clb; Chorus; School Musical; High Hon Roll; Hon Roll; NHS; Fin.

WEBER, KATHLEEN MARIE; Fort Le Boeuf HS; Waterford, PA; (Y); 6/174; Model UN; Band; Yrbk Stf; Sec Trs Jr Cls; Rep Sr Cls; Var L Cheerleading; Im Gym; High Hon Roll; NHS; Church Yth Grp; Pres Acad Achvt Awd 86; Grad Hgh Hnrs 86; Ft Le Boeuf Acad Achvt Awd 85 & 86; IN U PA; Biol.

WEBER, KEITH; West Scranton HS; Scranton, PA; (Y); 40/250; Letterman Clb; JV Var Bsktbl; Var Crs Cntry; JV Trk; Hon Roll; Jr NHS; NHS.

WEBER, LISA; Bentworth HS; Bentleyville, PA; (Y); 9/145; Church Yth Grp; FBLA; Concert Band; Flag Corp; Mrchg Band; VP Frsh Cls; VP Soph Cls; Var JV Bsktbl; High Hon Roll; NHS.

WEBER, MELISSA; Towanola Area HS; Towanda, PA; (Y); Trs GAA; Girl Scts; Trs Jr Cls; Stu Cncl; Var L Crs Cntry; Capt Pom Pon; Var L Trk; Hon Roll; NHS.

WEBER, PAULA; Calvary Baptist Christian Acad; Meadville, PA; (S); 2/5; Church Yth Grp; 4-H; Chorus; Yrbk Bus Mgr; Sec Jr Cls; Var L Bsktbl; Var L Vllybl; High Hon Roll; NHS; Sec Frsh Cls; Christ Athlete Awd 85.

WEBER, SHERI; Curwensville Area HS; Grampian, PA; (Y); Camera Clb; Chess Clb; French Clb; Nwsp Stf; Bsktbl; Sftbl; Vllybl; LSU.

WEBER, TAMMY; Centre County Christian Acad; Pleasant Gap, PA; (S); 1/11; Pres Church Yth Grp; Chorus; Sec Frsh Cls; Sec Soph Cls; Sec Jr Cls; Sec Sr Cls; Capt Cheerleading; High Hon Roll; Hon Roll; Val; Lock Haven U Pres Schlrshp 86; Schlrs In Ed Awd 86; Lock Haven U; Sec Ed.

WEBER, TIMOTHY W; Du Bois Area HS; Grampian, PA; (Y); 3/256; Letterman Clb; SADD; Chorus; Pres Sr Cls; Var L Bsbl; High Hon Roll; NHS; Pres Schlr; Church Yth Grp; John Klees Hnr Rll Athl Yr 85-86; U S Army Resrv Natl Schlr Athl Awd 85-86; PA ST U; Chem Engrng.

WEBER, VIRGINIA; Moon SR HS; Coraopolis, PA; (Y); Church Yth Grp; Hosp Aide; Key Clb; Var Im Swmmng; Var JV Vllybl; Physcl Thrpy.

WEBSTER, CHRISTOPHER SHAWNE; Mercy Vocational HS; Philadelphia, PA; (S); Church Yth Grp; VP FBLA; Yrbk Phtg; Rptr Yrbk Rptr; Rptr Yrbk Stf; Capt Sec Swmmng; Bus Ed Awd 84; Natl Sci Merit Awd 85; Comp Lit.

WEBSTER, DENISE; Grove City HS; Grove City, PA; (Y); 17/235; Church Yth Grp; Girl Scts; Library Aide; Band; Concert Band; Mrchg Band; Pep Band; Powder Puff Ftbl; Trk; High Hon Roll.

WEBSTER, LORETTA; Bellwood Antis JR SR HS; Bellwood, PA; (Y); L FFA; Hosp Aide; VICA; Chorus; Altoona Vo-Tech; Intr Dsgn.

WEBSTER, MICHAEL; Philipsburg-Osceola SR HS; Philipsburg, PA; (S); 4/250; Chess Clb; Church Yth Grp; Nwsp Stf; Hon Roll; Pre Med.

WEBSTER, SUSAN M; Norristwon Area HS; Norristown, PA; (S); 8/503; Church Yth Grp; Cmnty Wkr; Exploring; Intnl Clb; Yrbk Stf; High Hon Roll; Hon Roll; Eng Dept Awd 83-84, 85; Comm.

WEBSTER, WHITNEY N; Southern Leihigh HS; Center Valley, PA; (Y); 13/238; Aud/Vis; Dance Clb; Drama Clb; Madrigals; School Musical; Gov Hon Prg Awd; NHS; Chorus; School Play; High Hon Roll; Stdnt Forum Pres 85-86; Dist, Regnl & ST Chorus 85-86; Hugh O Brian Yth Ldrshp Semnr ILS Altrnt 84; Musical Theatr.

WECHSLER, FRANCIS; Allentown Central Catholic HS; Allentown, PA; (Y); 88/208; Church Yth Grp; JA; Math Clb; Rep Sr Cls; Stu Cncl; Var Bsktbl; Var Crs Cntry; Var Trk; MVP X-Cntry 85 & 86; All Star X-Cntry 86.

WEDDIGEN, RAYMOND; Bethlehem Catholic HS; Hellertown, PA; (Y); 20/200; High Hon Roll; Jr NHS; NHS; Gymnstcs Prog 84-87; Comp Sci.

WEDDLE, KATIE; Lebanon SR HS; Lebanon, PA; (Y); German Clb; Intnl Clb; Key Clb; SADD; Yrbk Stf; Stu Cncl; Var Capt Bsktbl; Var Capt Sftbl; Var L Tennis; Hon Roll; Bst Athl Yr 84; Dntl Hygenist.

WEDDLE, ROBERT J; Cedar Crest HS; Lebaon, PA; (Y); 13/300; Debate Tm; Latin Clb; Pep Clb; Spanish Clb; SADD; Trs Jr Cls; Trs Sr Cls; Var JV Ftbl; High Hon Roll; NHS; Atty.

WEDEKIND, BRENDA; Fairview HS; Fairview, PA; (Y); Varsity Clb; Var L Trk; Var L Vllybl; Hon Roll; Comp Sci.

WEDGWOOD, THOMAS; St Josephs Prep; Cherry Hill, NJ; (Y); Drama Clb; Stage Crew; Yrbk Stf; Var Swmmng; Green Ribbon-Natl Greek Exam 85-86; Arch.

WEEKS, BRUCE; Lake Lehman HS; Dallas, PA; (Y); High Hon Roll; Hon Roll; PA ST U; Wrtr.

WEEMS III, ADOLPHUS TREY; Central Dauphin East HS; Harrisburg, PA; (Y); Boys Clb Am; Boy Scts; Political Wkr; Ski Clb; School Play; Stage Crew; Rep Stu Cncl; Mgr Bsktbl; Im Vllybl; Hon Roll; Civil Engr.

WEESNER, RENEE; Annville Cleona HS; Lebanon, PA; (S); 6/105; Church Yth Grp; Girl Scts; Chorus; JV Bsktbl; Im Fld Hcky; Var Trk; NHS; NEDT Awd; Amer Lgn Essay Awd 85; Latin Excllnc Awd 85; Pre-Med.

WEGEMER, CARLA; St Marys Area HS; Saint Marys, PA; (Y); 57/301; Letterman Clb; Varsity Clb; Var Capt Bsktbl; Var Sftbl; JV Var Vllybl; Hon Roll; NHS; Elem Ed.

WEGERT, VICKI LYNN; Gateway SR HS; Pitcairn, PA; (Y); Pres Acpl Chr; Madrigals; School Musical; Swing Chorus; Ed Yrbk Stf; High Hon Roll; Lion Awd; NHS; Prfct Atten Awd; Pres Schlr; Prfct Attndnc Hnr 86; Lions Clb Schlrshp 86; Comm.

WEHNER, LAURA; Hampton HS; Gibsonia, PA; (Y); French Clb; Intnl Clb; Stu Cncl; Powder Puff Ftbl; Hon Roll; Frnch.

WEHR, DEBRA; Panther Valley HS; Summit Hill, PA; (Y); 27/110; Am Leg Aux Girls St; Ski Clb; Mrchg Band; Cheerleading; Trk; Med Tech.

WEHR, GAIL; Jim Thorpe Area HS; Jim Thorpe, PA; (S); 6/97; Computer Clb; FHA; German Clb; Chorus; School Play; Nwsp Rptr; Yrbk Rptr; High Hon Roll; NHS; Natl Assn Of Stu Organists 84; Bloomsburg; Comm.

WEHRER, JILL; Avella JR SR HS; Burgettstown, PA; (Y); Pres French Clb; Ski Clb; Nwsp Stf; Yrbk Stf; VP Frsh Cls; Var L Cheerleading; Pre-Law.

WEHRUNG, KEITH; Chestnut Ridge HS; Alum Bank, PA; (S); Boy Scts; Church Yth Grp; Scholastic Bowl; Band; Jazz Band; Mrchg Band; Ftbl; Wrstlng; Hon Roll; NHS; Comp Sci.

WEICKOSKY, STEVE; Nativity BVM HS; Middleport, PA; (Y); 41/98; Cmnty Wkr; Exploring; Mathletes; Math Clb; Nwsp Ed-Chief; Nwsp Rptr; Nwsp Sprt Ed; Nclr Physcst.

WEIDENBOERNER, KARL; Elk County Christian HS; St Marys, PA; (Y); 43/89; Boy Scts; Cmnty Wkr; German Clb; Intnl Clb; Red Cross Aide; SADD; Yrbk Stf; Im Bowling; JV Ftbl; God Cntry Awd; PA ST; Elec Engrng.

WEIDERHOLD, TRACEY; Harry S Truman HS; Levittown, PA; (Y); #51 In Class; Var Tennis; Hon Roll; Comp Proc.

WEIDINGER, TOM; Ambridge Area HS; S Heights, PA; (Y); Exploring; JA; Pep Clb; Rep Soph Cls; JV Bsbl; Var Golf; Hon Roll; Carpentry.

WEIDMAN, JAMES; Garden Spot HS; Bowmansville, PA; (S); 67/186; Boy Scts; VP Church Yth Grp; Rptr FFA; JV Bsbl; FFA 2nd Pl ST Pltry Cntst 83; FFA Gld Natl Pltry Cntst 83; PA ST; Ag.

WEIDMAN, JODI; Elizabethtown Area HS; Mt Joy, PA; (Y); Drama Clb; Thesps; Chorus; School Musical; School Play; Rep Stu Cncl; Var Capt Tennis; Var L Trk; Powder Puff Ftbl; Model UN; Comm.

WEIDNER, HEIDI; Sheffield HS; Sheffield, PA; (Y); 19/98; Varsity Clb; Trs Soph Cls; Trs Jr Cls; Trs Sr Cls; Var Bsktbl; Var Sftbl; Var Vllybl; Hon Roll; NHS; Hmcmng Qun 85; 1st Attndnt-Prom 86.

WEIDNER III, RICHARD L; Manheim Township HS; Lancaster, PA; (Y); 9/325; Boy Scts; Band; Concert Band; Jazz Band; Mrchg Band; Pep Band; Nwsp Rptr; High Hon Roll; NHS; Engrng.

WEIERBACH, ROBYN; Nortre Dame HS; Bethlehem, PA; (Y); 6/89; Pep Clb; Chorus; Church Choir; School Musical; Yrbk Stf; Rep Soph Cls; High Hon Roll; NHS; Rep Stu Cncl; Stat Bsktbl; High Hnr Frm Soc Women Engrs 86; Pres IN Vly Appaloosa Yth Clb 85-86; TX A&M U; Bio.

WEIERS, GRETCHEN CORINNE; Derry Area SR HS; Latrobe, PA; (Y); 26/255; AFS; Letterman Clb; Band; Chorus; School Musical; Yrbk Stf; Var L Bsktbl; Var L Vllybl; Mu Alp Tht; Pres Schlr; St Vincent Coll.

WEIGAND, TRACY; North Hills HS; Pittsburgh, PA; (Y); Keywanettes; Ski Clb; High Hon Roll; Hon Roll; HS Sci Fair 3rd Pl 84; Crmnlgy.

WEIGLE, JEFF; Iroquois HS; Erie, PA; (Y); 48/154; VP Church Yth Grp; Concert Band; Jazz Band; Pep Band; Bowling; JV Chrmn Ftbl; Trk; Wt Lftg; Wrstlng; Hon Roll; PA ST; Bus Admn.

WEIGLE, MONICA; New Oxford SR HS; Abbottstown, PA; (Y); 1/200; Pres Stu Cncl; Var Capt Bsktbl; Var L Fld Hcky; Var Capt Sftbl; Bausch & Lomb Sci Awd; High Hon Roll; Ntl Merit Ltr; Val.

WEIGNER, HENRY; Carlynton HS; Carnegie, PA; (Y); Aud/Vis; Church Yth Grp; Exploring; 4-H; Library Aide; Political Wkr; ROTC; SADD; Church Choir; Drm & Bgl; Aud/Visual Awd 83-86; Church Ldr 85; Future Ofcr Fellowship 84; Ministerial Wrk.

WEIGNER, MICHAEL B; Boyertown Area HS; Gilbertsville, PA; (Y); 15/435; Boy Scts; Church Yth Grp; Math Tm; Pres Stu Cncl; Ftbl; Trk; Cit Awd; High Hon Roll; NHS; Pres Schlr; Grad High Hnrs 86; Penn ST U; Aerospace Engrng.

WEIKEL, JOHN; Pennsbury HS; Morrisville, PA; (Y); Hon Roll.

WEIKERT, JODI; Biglerville HS; Biglerville, PA; (Y); 13/87; Girl Scts; Varsity Clb; Rep Stu Cncl; Bsbl; Bsktbl; Var L Fld Hcky; Ftbl; Trk; Wrstlng; Hon Roll; Phy Thrpy.

WEIKERT, LISA M; Huntingdon Area HS; Huntingdon, PA; (Y); 7/203; Political Wkr; Ski Clb; SADD; Ed Yrbk Stf; Var Capt Cheerleading; High Hon Roll; NHS; NEDT Awd; VFW Awd; Church Yth Grp; Pres Acdmc Fit Awd 85-86; 3 Yr Army ROTC Schlrshp 86; Franklin; Gov.

WEIL, PAMELA; Council Rock HS; Richboro, PA; (Y); 162/850; Socr; Hon Roll; Math.

WEILMINSTER JR, RICHARD J; South Williamsport HS; Williamsport, PA; (Y); 32/140; Band; Mrchg Band; Orch; Pep Band; Var L Socr; Var L Trk; Hon Roll; Bio.

WEIMER, AMY; Carmichaels Area HS; Carmichaels, PA; (S); 9/129; Office Aide; SADD; Color Guard; Flag Corp; Nwsp Stf; Rep Sr Cls; Rep Stu Cncl; High Hon Roll; Hon Roll; NHS; Edinboro U PA; Med Tech.

WEIMER, KEITH; Connellsville Area SR HS; Indian Head, PA; (Y); 23/500; French Hon Soc; High Hon Roll; Hon Roll; Jr NHS; NHS; Ntl Merit Ltr; Deike-Ryan Schlrshp 86; Allegheny COLL.

WEIMER, WAYNE; Rockwood Area HS; Somerset, PA; (Y); Church Yth Grp; Band; Chorus; School Play; Trk; Vllybl; Hon Roll; NHS; Toccoa Falls Coll; Mnstr.

WEINACHT, CHRISTINA; Beaver Area HS; Beaver, PA; (Y); Church Yth Grp; FCA; French Clb; Key Clb; Science Clb; Concert Band; School Play; Var Crs Cntry; Var Trk; Chorus; Geneva Coll; Bio-Chem.

WEINBERG, ELLEN; Altoona Area HS; Altoona, PA; (Y); Hosp Aide; Q&S; Yrbk Ed-Chief; L Cheerleading; L Tennis; Capt L Trk; Jr NHS; Ski Clb; Spanish Clb; Temple Yth Grp; Sunday Schl Tchr 85-87; Stu Cncl Adv Chrmn 86-87; Yrbk Cls Editor 85-86; Physcil Med.

WEINBERG, PAM; Upper Dublin SR HS; Dresher, PA; (Y); FBLA; Intnl Clb; Nwsp Rptr; Nwsp Stf; Yrbk Rptr; Yrbk Stf; Rep Frsh Cls; Rep Stu Cncl.

WEINBERGER, MICHAEL; Hillel Academy Of Pittsbgh; Pittsburgh, PA; (S); Temple Yth Grp; Yrbk Ed-Chief; VP Frsh Cls; Rep Jr Cls; Rep Stu Cncl; Var Socr; Hon Roll; NCSY & UJF Isreal Schlrshp 84-85; Carnegie-Mellon U; Ecnmcs.

WEINBERGER, ROXANNE; Western Wayne HS; Waymart, PA; (Y); 1/175; High Hon Roll; Jr NHS; Rep NHS; Superior Status Ntl Piano Plyng Aud 84-86; Wayne Cty Rep Miss Teen Schrlshp Pagnt 86; Marywood Coll; Music Thrpy.

WEINEL, DOTTI; South Allegheny HS; Mc Keesport, PA; (S); 5/185; Spanish Clb; Y-Teens; Drill Tm; Yrbk Stf; Off Jr Cls; Stu Cncl; Cheerleading; Powder Puff Ftbl; Twrlr; High Hon Roll; Accntnt.

WEINERT, CHRISTINE; Trinity HS; Enola, PA; (Y); Service Clb; Spanish Clb; School Musical; Nwsp Rptr; Rep Stu Cncl; Var JV Cheerleading; High Hon Roll; NHS; Ntl Merit SF; Cmnty Wkr; Natl Piano Guild Awd; Frgn Lang.

WEINGARTNER, BETSY; Shenango JR SR HS; New Castle, PA; (Y); 25/112; Church Yth Grp; VP French Clb; Nwsp Stf; Yrbk Stf; Pres Soph Cls; Rep Jr Cls; Rep Stu Cncl; JV Var Cheerleading; Var Sftbl; Hon Roll.

WEINHOLD, MELISSA; Hempfield HS; Lancaster, PA; (Y); 90/400; Millersville U; Tchr.

WEINSCHBENK, KATIE; Dunmore HS; Dunmore, PA; (Y); French Clb; Ski Clb; Var Cheerleading; Gym; High Hon Roll; NHS.

WEINSCHENK, KATIE; Dunmore HS; Dunmore, PA; (Y); 4/130; French Clb; Ski Clb; Var Cheerleading; Rep Gym; High Hon Roll; NHS.

WEINSTEIN, MARC; Upper Dublin HS; Dresher, PA; (Y); 10/300; FBLA; JA; Rep Jr Cls; Rep Sr Cls; Rep Stu Cncl; Im Bsktbl; JV Bowling; Var Golf; JV Tennis; High Hon Roll; Engl Exchng Stu 86; Bus & Finance.

WEINSTOCK, ROGER; Cheltenham HS; Elkins Pk, PA; (Y); 77/385; Cmnty Wkr; Intnl Clb; Science Clb; Teachers Aide; Temple Yth Grp; Stage Crew; Trk; High Hon Roll; Hon Roll; Prfct Atten Awd; Compu Sci.

WEINZEN, AMY; Monongahela Valley Catholic HS; Coal Center, PA; (Y); 33/102; Hosp Aide; Pep Clb; Chorus; Color Guard; Mrchg Band; Variety Show; Calif U PA; Phys Ther.

WEIR, CHRISTINE; Shikellamy HS; Sunbury, PA; (Y); French Clb; Chorus; JV Cheerleading; JV Var Tennis; Int Dsgn.

WEIR, DIA; Washington HS; Washington, PA; (S); Key Clb; Library Aide; Ski Clb; Spanish Clb; SADD; Sec Soph Cls; Rep Stu Cncl; Capt Var Cheerleading; L Var Tennis; Hon Roll; Psych.

WEIR, KIMBERLY; Danville SR HS; Danville, PA; (Y); 16/162; French Clb; Chorus; Rep Stu Cncl; VP Capt Bowling; Stat Trk; High Hon Roll; NHS; Stu Of Mnth Frgn Lang 86; Nicolas B Ottaway Awd 86; Acad & Music Schlrshps To Wittenberg U 86; Wittenberg U; Intl Rel.

WEIRBACH, SCOTT; Emmaus HS; Macungie, PA; (Y); Computer Clb; Stat Bsbl; Hon Roll; NHS; Sci.

WEIRICH, DEANNA; Pocono Mt HS; Pocono Lake, PA; (Y); Pep Clb; Q&S; Teachers Aide; Band; Chorus; Concert Band; Mrchg Band; Pep Band; School Musical; School Play; Geisinger; Nrsng.

WEIRICH, DEBRA; Northeastern HS; Manchester, PA; (Y); 22/153; Church Yth Grp; VP Exploring; Lib Band; Chorus; Church Choir; Concert Band; Mrchg Band; Sr Cls; Hon Roll; NHS; Orendorf Elem Schl Schlrshp 86; Earl & Einez Frey Schlrshp 86; York Coll; Thrptc Rcrtn.

WEIRICH, MATTHEW; Northeastern SR HS; Manchester, PA; (Y); 2/154; Trs Church Yth Grp; Varsity Clb; Var L Bsbl; Var L Bsktbl; Var L Socr; Var L Vllybl; High Hon Roll; NHS; Stu Mth 85; Arch.

WEIRICH, SCOTT; Conrad Weiser JR SR HS; Robesonia, PA; (Y); 6/138; JCL; Nwsp Stf; Yrbk Rptr; Stu Cncl; JV Golf; JV Tennis; High Hon Roll; Hon Roll; NHS; Ntl Merit SF; Swarthmore; Classics.

WEIRICH, WENDY; Cedar Crest HS; Lebanon, PA; (Y); FBLA; Pep Clb; Chorus.

WEIS, LEIGH; St Marys Area HS; Saint Marys, PA; (Y); Pres Church Yth Grp; Hosp Aide; Pep Clb; Chorus; Rep Stu Cncl; Capt Trk; Hon Roll; Brdcstng.

WEIS, MELISSA; Windber Area HS; Windber, PA; (Y); 2/130; Church Yth Grp; Pres Math Clb; Ski Clb; Nwsp Rptr; Nwsp Stf; Ed Yrbk Ed-Chief; Trs Stu Cncl; L Var Bsktbl; Var Sftbl; High Hon Roll; Stu Yr 84-86; Acad Achvt Wrld Cultures 85-86; Natl Hstry Awd 83-84; Med.

WEISBERGER, CAROLYN; Butler SR HS; Butler, PA; (Y); 45/800; Debate Tm; Trs Latin Clb; Model UN; NFL; Temple Yth Grp; Mrchg Band; Orch; Nwsp Ed-Chief; Yrbk Rptr; NHS; Stu Of Jr Satsmn Smr Schl 86; 3 Tm Wnr Natl Hist Day Prjct Awd 84-86; Intl Ldrshp Trng Conf 85; Ecnmcs.

WEISBROD, JACQUELINE; Lancaster Catholic HS; Lancaster, PA; (Y); Var Cheerleading; Church Yth Grp; Pep Clb; Varsity Clb; Band; Mrchg Band; School Musical; School Play; JV Fld Hcky; Elem Ed.

WEISBROD, PATRICIA; Steel Valley HS; W Homestead, PA; (Y); 14/240; Dance Clb; Key Clb; Drill Tm; Mrchg Band; Yrbk Ed-Chief; Yrbk Stf; Vllybl; High Hon Roll; Hon Roll; NHS.

WEISER, JOANNE; Cedar Crest HS; Rexmont, PA; (Y); French Clb; JA; Key Clb; Pep Clb; NHS; Scndry Educ.

WEISGARBER, KRISTI; Sharon HS; Sharon, PA; (Y); 17/200; Varsity Clb; Gym; Tennis; High Hon Roll; NHS; French Clb; Band; Concert Band; Mrchg Band; School Musical; Pres Physcl Ftns Awd.

WEISKOPFF, WENDY; Mansfield JR SR HS; Mansfield, PA; (S); #4 In Class; Church Yth Grp; Pep Clb; Chorus; Church Choir; Stage Crew; Yrbk Stf; Vllybl; High Hon Roll; Hon Roll; NHS; Mansfield U; Resprtry Thrpst.

WEISNER, DANIEL J; St Marys Area HS; St Marys, PA; (Y); Am Leg Boys St; Band; Concert Band; Mrchg Band; Var Capt Wrstlng; Hon Roll; NHS; Capt Awd Wrstlg 86; 4 Yr Lttrmn Awd Wrstlg 86; Dist Chmp Wrstlg 86; Penn ST; Engrng.

WEISNER, DARA; Lower Moreland HS; Huntingdon Valley, PA; (S); Drama Clb; French Clb; Key Clb; Chorus; Madrigals; School Musical; School Play; Capt Trk; High Hon Roll; NHS; Distngushd Hnr Rl 84-85; Outstndng Achvt Soc Studies 83-85; Med.

WEISNER, JOHN; St Marys Area HS; Saint Marys, PA; (Y); 26/301; Band; Mrchg Band; Trs Stu Cncl; Bsbl; Trk; Var L Wrstlng; High Hon Roll; NHS; ST Qlfr Wrstlg 86; Elk Cnty Govt Citation Wrstlg 86; Engrng.

WEISNER, RANDALL; Elk County Christian Schl; St Marys, PA; (Y); Model UN; SADD; Varsity Clb; Jazz Band; Mrchg Band; Pres Frsh Cls; Stu Cncl; Var L Wrstlng; High Hon Roll; ST Qlfr Wrstlng 86; Elk Co Gvt Ctn Wrstlng 86; MVP Schl Awd Wrstlng 85-86; Engr.

WEISS JR, DAVID P; Shaler Area SR HS; Glenshaw, PA; (Y); 123/538; Ski Clb; Concert Band; Drm Mjr(t); Jazz Band; Mrchg Band; Stage Crew; Symp Band; Mgr(s); Socr; Hon Roll; U Pittsburgh; Comp Sci.

WEISS, JAY; William Allen HS; Allentown, PA; (Y); 58/576; Pres Varsity Clb; Wt Lftg; Capt Wrstlng; Hon Roll; NHS; Allen Booster Clb Scholar Awd 86; Robert Mentzel Mem Scholar 86; Franklin & Marshall; Sports Med.

WEISS, JEANNE; Carlynton HS; Carnegie, PA; (Y); German Clb; Nwsp Rptr; Nwsp Stf; High Hon Roll; Hon Roll; NHS; Prfct Atten Awd; Grmn.

WEISS, JOHN; Manheim Township HS; Lancaster, PA; (Y); 5/325; Church Yth Grp; Computer Clb; Office Aide; Orch; High Hon Roll; NHS; Ntl Merit Ltr; Physics.

WEISS, KEN; Richland SR HS; Gibsonia, PA; (S); Debate Tm; Nwsp Ed-Chief; Var L Socr; Var Trk; High Hon Roll; Hnbl Mntn 3 Rvrs Arts Fest 85; Artstc Achvt Awd Sprg Arts Fest 85; Grphc Arts.

WEISS, MARK; Unionville HS; Kennett Square, PA; (Y); 4/269; Trs Church Yth Grp; Intnl Clb; Pres JA; SADD; Band; Chorus; Church Choir; Concert Band; Jazz Band; Orch; Unionvl Cmnty Schlrshp 86; Helen Cosson Awd-Solvng Pblms Peacfly, Logcly 86; Outstndng Voclst 86; Lafayette Coll; Medcn.

WEISS, SANDRA M; Altoona Area HS; Altoona, PA; (Y); Drama Clb; Speech Tm; SADD; Pres Temple Yth Grp; School Musical; School Play; Lit Mag; Jr NHS; NEDT Awd; Girl Scts; Prncpls Advsry Comm 85-86; Chld Psych.

WEISS, STEPHANIE; St Pius X HS; Pottstown, PA; (S); 68/161; Cmnty Wkr; Sec 4-H; Office Aide; School Musical; Nwsp Rptr; Yrbk Stf; Crs Cntry; Twrlr; 4-H Awd; High Hon Roll; PA Jr Acad Sci 1st Pl 84; Montgmry Co Sci Fair 3rd Pl, PJAS 3rd Pl 85; B Franklin Sci Fair Hnrbl Mnt; Vet.

WEISS, TAMMY; Bishop Hannan HS; Scranton, PA; (Y); Boys Clb Am; Girl Scts; VICA; High Hon Roll; Hon Roll; Gymnstc Awds; Excllnc In Mth; Exllnc In Thlgy; Nrsg.

WEISS, TOVA; Beth Jacob HS; Philadelphia, PA; (Y); Drama Clb; Nwsp Rptr; Rep Frsh Cls; Trs Soph Cls; VP Jr Cls; Rep Sr Cls; Columbia U; Acctng.

WEISSER, KRISTA; Lancaster Catholic HS; Lancaster, PA; (Y); 18/218; Hst Service Clb; Nwsp Ed-Chief; Rep Sr Cls; DAR Awd; NHS; Opt Clb Awd; Pres Schlr; Dance Clb; Drama Clb; Library Aide; Lancaster Dance Cmpny 84-86; Acad Schlrshp To Immaculate Coll 86; Lead In Play Which Won 1st Pl St 85; Immaculata Col6; Ecnmcs.

WEIST, KRISTI; Southern Fulton HS; Crystal Spg, PA; (Y); Computer Clb; French Clb; FHA; Chorus; Hon Roll.

WEIST, THOS; Redland HS; New Cumberland, PA; (Y); 47/275; Boy Scts; Acpl Chr; School Musical; Rep Stu Cncl; Ftbl; Trk; Wrstlng; Prfct Atten Awd; Hon Roll; Stage Crew; Schl Chorus Pres 86-87; Amer Music Abrd 84; Cnty & Dist Chorus 84-87; Air Force Acad; Engr.

WEITZEL, JENNY; Manheim Central HS; Manheim, PA; (Y); 19/241; VP JA; Model UN; Office Aide; Powder Puff Ftbl; Var L Sftbl; JV Tennis; JV Trk; High Hon Roll; NHS; Jr Achvmnts Brd Achvr Awd 86; Accntng.

WEITZMAN, MARTIN; Marple Newtown HS; Broomall, PA; (Y); 27/367; Chess Clb; Debate Tm; Math Tm; Yrbk Stf; Hon Roll; Jr NHS; NHS; Prfct Atten Awd; Bell Of PA Diamond ST Schlrshp 86; PA ST; Elect Engrg.

WELC, ROBERT; Mt Pleasant Area HS; Mt Pleasant, PA; (Y); 57/263; Latin Clb; Science Clb; Capt Var Bsktbl; 1st Tm Dist BB Plyr 86; U Of Pittsburgh; Phrmcy.

WELCH, CHARLENE; Morrisville HS; Morrisville, PA; (Y); 12/99; Dance Clb; Pres FBLA; Band; Drill Tm; Jr NHS; Sec NHS; Bradford Bus Schl; Bus.

WELCH, CHRISTOPHER D; Upper St Clair HS; Upper St Clair, PA; (Y); 18/350; Church Yth Grp; Q&S; Radio Clb; Thesps; Chorus; School Musical; Yrbk Rptr; Lit Mag; High Hon Roll; NHS; Engl.

WELCH, JENNIFER L; Nazareth Acad; Philadelphia, PA; (Y); 10/120; Cmnty Wkr; Dance Clb; Latin Clb; School Musical; School Play; Lit Mag; Hon Roll; Variety Show; Alumni Assn Schlrshp 86; Bio.

WELESKI, KAMMY; Knoch HS; Cabot, PA; (Y); Chorus; Church Choir; Mrchg Band; Stage Crew; Rep Frsh Cls; Rep Stu Cncl; L Twrlr; High Hon Roll; Hon Roll; Bus.

WELKER, JIM; Shaler Area HS; Pgh, PA; (Y); 15/520; Ski Clb; Jazz Band; Var Capt Crs Cntry; Var Trk; High Hon Roll; NHS; Rotary Awd; Spanish NHS; Acdmc All Amer 85; Natl Sci Olympd Tst Bio 84 & 86; Biochem.

WELLER, CHRISTAL; Chambersburg Area SR HS; Chambersburg, PA; (Y); Church Yth Grp; German Clb; Band; Chorus; Concert Band; Jazz Band; Mrchg Band; Hon Roll; Air Force.

WELLER, MARTIN; Boyertown Area HS; Gilbertsvl, PA; (Y); 179/485; SADD; Rep Frsh Cls; VP Soph Cls; VP Jr Cls; VP Sr Cls; Rep Stu Cncl; L Var Bsbl; JV Bsktbl; Cit Awd; Hon Roll; Boyrtwn Am Legn Bsbl Tm 84; 1st Tm All Chesmnt Bsbl 85-86; Tm Battg Titl Bsbl 85-86; Sprts Thrpy.

WELLER, RHONDA; Newport JR SR HS; Newport, PA; (Y); School Play; Yrbk Stf; JV Var Fld Hcky; Gym; Hon Roll; Comm Art.

WELLER, SHAWN; Southern Columbia HS; Elysburg, PA; (Y); Art Clb; Church Yth Grp; Var L Ftbl; Var JV Wt Lftg; High Hon Roll; Hon Roll; NHS; PA ST.

WELLES, JODELL; E L Meyers HS; Wilkes Barre, PA; (Y); 21/143; German Clb; Key Clb; Pep Clb; Chorus; Yrbk Stf; Sec Stu Cncl; Capt Cheerleading; Fld Hcky; Hon Roll; NHS; Outstndng Girl 86; Msrcrd Coll; Nrsng.

WELLIVER, LISA; Warrior Run HS; Watsontown, PA; (Y); 4/171; AFS; French Clb; Varsity Clb; School Musical; VP Jr Cls; Capt Cheerleading; Powder Puff Ftbl; NHS; Dist Choir 86; Winter Dance Ct 86; Bloomsburg U; Personnel Mgr.

WELLIVER, MARY; Hershey SR HS; Hummelstown, PA; (Y); 6/200; Church Yth Grp; Quiz Bowl; Scholastic Bowl; Chorus; Nwsp Ed-Chief; Var Bsktbl; Bausch & Lomb Sci Awd; High Hon Roll; NHS; Ntl Merit Ltr.

WELLMAN, JEFF; Unionville HS; Kennett Square, PA; (Y); 12/264; Church Yth Grp; Intnl Clb; Chorus; Church Choir; Concert Band; Drm Mjr(t); Jazz Band; Mrchg Band; School Musical; JV Crs Cntry; Spn Awd 84-86; Music Prtcptn Awd 86; Schl Key Awd 86; IA ST U; Mech Engrng.

WELLS, CHARLENE; Waynesburg Central HS; Waynesburg, PA; (Y); FFA; VICA; Trk; Csmtlgst.

WELLS, CHARLES A; Elizabethtown Area HS; Elizabethtown, PA; (Y); 60/230; Am Leg Boys St; Pres Church Yth Grp; Ski Clb; Teachers Aide; Var Socr; Var Trk; June By Of Mnth Spnsrd Rtry Int; Elizabethtown Coll; Bio.

WELLS, JAMES; Forest City Regional HS; Forest City, PA; (Y); 5/55; Var Bsktbl; Capt Golf; Var Socr; Vllybl; High Hon Roll; Hon Roll; NHS; Sccr-Mst Prmsng.

WELLS, JAMES; Tunkhanhock Area HS; Dalton, PA; (S); 22/334; Computer Clb; FFA; Hon Roll; NHS; 2 Publ Spkng Awds FFA 84-85; 2 Land Judgng Awds 83-84; Wildlife Awd 85; Clarkson; Mech Engrng.

WELLS, KRIS; Du Bois Area HS; Dubois, PA; (Y); 35/290; Cmnty Wkr; Hosp Aide; Intnl Clb; Yrbk Rptr; Yrbk Stf; Off Stu Cncl; Stat Bsktbl; U Of NC; Law.

WELLS, MARY; Seneca HS; Erie, PA; (Y); VP Church Yth Grp; Cmnty Wkr; Science Clb; Rep Stu Cncl; Stat Bsktbl; Var Crs Cntry; JV Trk; Hon Roll; NHS; Prfct Atten Awd; Phys Ther.

WELLS JR, THOMAS; Shamokin Area HS; Shamokin, PA; (Y); 11/240; Letterman Clb; Science Clb; Varsity Clb; Stu Cncl; Crs Cntry; Wrstlng; High Hon Roll; Hon Roll; Jr NHS; NHS.

WELSH, JEANETTE; West Mifflin Area HS; W Mifflin, PA; (Y); Ski Clb; Drill Tm; Trk; High Hon Roll; Hon Roll; Jr NHS; NHS; Pres Schlr; FTA Scholar 86; U Pittsburgh; Mth.

WELSH, KAREN; Garden Spot HS; New Holland, PA; (Y); 38/220; Church Yth Grp; Drama Clb; Chorus; Orch; School Musical; School Play; Stage Crew; Var Fld Hcky; Var Trk; High Hon Roll; Pblc Admn.

WELSH, KATHLEEN; Henderson HS; West Chester, PA; (Y); Hosp Aide; JCL; Latin Clb; Chorus; Stage Crew; Variety Show; Rep Jr Cls; Stu Cncl; Rdlgy.

WELSH, MELINDA K; Waynesboro SR HS; Waynesboro, PA; (Y); Church Yth Grp; Library Aide; Church Choir; Hon Roll; Capt Of Bible Qz Tm 85-86; Bus.

WELSH, THERESA; Cardinal Dougherty HS; Phila, PA; (Y); 200/747; Chorus; School Musical; School Play; High Hon Roll; Hon Roll; Temple U.

WELTE, MOLLIE; Penn Hills HS; Pittsburgh, PA; (S); 91/780; Church Yth Grp; French Clb; Girl Scts; VP Library Aide; Teachers Aide; School Musical; Yrbk Stf; Stu Cncl; Var Capt Gym; Trk; U Of Pittsburgh; Elec Engr.

WELTON, BOBBI; Karns City JR SR HS; Petrolia, PA; (Y); Model UN; Pep Clb; ROTC; SADD; Yrbk Stf; Cheerleading; Powder Puff Ftbl; Score Keeper; Vllybl; Pittsbrg Beauty Acad; Cosmtlgy.

WELTY, JAMES; Boiling Springs SR HS; Boiling Spgs, PA; (Y); Chorus; Concert Band; Jazz Band; Mrchg Band; VP Stu Cncl; L Socr; Capt Swmmng; HOBY Ldrshp Sem 85-86; Convention II Dely 86; Rotary Clb Ldrshp Sem 86; Pol Sci.

WELTY, RACHAEL; Purchase Line HS; Clymer, PA; (Y); SADD; Concert Band; Mrchg Band; Pep Band; Nwsp Stf; Twrlr; Hon Roll; Frgn Lang Clb VP 86 Pres 87; Acdmc All-Amer Awd 84; Cmmdrtts Drm & Btn Corp Co-Capt 81-84; Jrnlsm.

WENDEL, MICHAEL; Easter York HS; York, PA; (Y); Hon Roll; Cmptr Sci.

WENDEL, STEPHEN; St Marys HS; Saint Marys, PA; (Y); Boys Clb Am; JV Bsktbl; Im Ftbl; Var Wt Lftg.

WENDEL, TERRY; Blainsville SR HS; Blairsville, PA; (Y); Varsity Clb; Var Wrstlng; High Hon Roll; Marine Physcl Ftnss Awd 86; Vet.

WENEROWICZ, PAULA; St Benedict Acad; Erie, PA; (Y); 4/63; Camera Clb; Church Yth Grp; Q&S; Ski Clb; Yrbk Stf; Sec Jr Cls; Stu Cncl; Sftbl; High Hon Roll; Hon Roll; Acdmc Schlrshp 83; Spnsh Schlrshp 84-85; Bus Admin.

WENERSTROM, WENDY; Baldwin HS; Pittsburgh, PA; (Y); 109/549; Nwsp Stf; Yrbk Stf; Score Keeper; High Hon Roll; Hon Roll; OH U; Jrnlsm.

WENG, DAVID; Neshaminy HS; Feasterville, PA; (Y); 58/752; Cmnty Wkr; Chorus; High Hon Roll; Hon Roll; NHS; Church Yth Grp; Band; Jazz Band; Orch; School Musical; Tomorrows Ldrs Conf Rotary Intl 86; Mech Engr.

WENGER, ADRIENNE; Elizabeth Area HS; Elizabethtown, PA; (Y); Ski Clb; Ed Yrbk Phtg; Trs Frsh Cls; Trs Soph Cls; Trs Jr Cls; Rep Sr Cls; Stu Cncl; JV Bsktbl; Fld Hcky; Co-Capt Powder Puff Ftbl; MIP Sftbl 85; All Sctn & All Lge 1st Bsmn Sftbl 86; Penn ST U.

WENGER, JAY; Eastern Lebanon County HS; Richland, PA; (Y); 75/184; Church Yth Grp; Prfct Atten Awd.

WENGER, TIMOTHY; Manheim Central HS; Manheim, PA; (Y); 2/242; Trs Church Yth Grp; Yrbk Stf; Hon Roll; NHS; Chem I Awd 85 & 86; 4-Way Tst Awd 85-86.

WENGRAITIS, MATTHEW G; Archbishop Ryan H S For Boys; Philadelphia, PA; (Y); 4/429; Church Yth Grp; Yrbk Stf; JV Crs Cntry; JV Trk; High Hon Roll; NHS; Ntl Merit SF; Cmnty Wkr; Computer Clb; 1300 Clb Awd 85-86; Attnd PA Gvrnrs Schl Sci 86; Engrng.

WENGRAITIS, STEPHEN; Archbishop Ryan High School - Boys; Philadelphia, PA; (Y); 17/429; Service Clb; Yrbk Stf; Lit Mag; JV Crs Cntry; VP Trk; Hon Roll; NHS; Ntl Merit SF; Computer Clb; Schlrshp PA Gov Schl For Sci 86; Awd 3rd Pl Essay Cntst 85; Drexel U; Engrng.

WENGRYN, LOU ANN; Chartiers Valley HS; Carnegie, PA; (Y); 6/343; Pep Clb; Yrbk Rptr; Ed Yrbk Stf; Rep Frsh Cls; Rep Soph Cls; Rep Jr Cls; Rep Sr Cls; Rep Stu Cncl; Fld Hcky; High Hon Roll; Inlnd Steel Schlrshp 86; Pres Acdmc Ftns Awd Our Outstndng Acdmc Achvt 86; Wmn In Sci 3 Engrng Prgm 85; Carnegie Mellon U; Engrng.

WENNER, ANNAMARIA; Northwestern Lehigh HS; Kutztown, PA; (Y); Hosp Aide; SADD; Nwsp Sprt Ed; Yrbk Stf; Rep Stu Cncl; JV Bsktbl; Stat Fld Hcky; Var Trk; High Hon Roll; Hon Roll; Stu Of Mth 84-85; Stu Of Mth 85-86; Chld Psych.

WENNER, DARYL; Crestwood HS; Mountaintop, PA; (Y); Library Aide; High Hon Roll; Hon Roll; Prfct Atten Awd; Achvt Awd NEDT 85; PA Olympcs Mind Crtvty Awd 84; Tchng.

WENNER, J; South Wmspt HS; S Wmspt, PA; (Y); 112/140; Camera Clb; Computer Clb; JV Wrstlng; Engrng.

WENRICH, SCOTT; Northern Potter HS; Harrison Vly, PA; (Y); 18/67; German Clb; Varsity Clb; Nwsp Stf; Yrbk Stf; Var Trk; Capt Wrstlng; US Ntl Jrnlsm Awd 84-85; US Eng Awd 84-85; PA Fr Entrprse Wk Schlrshp 85; Lockhaven U; Plc Scnc.

WENSEL, CRAIG; Saint Marys Area HS; Saint Marys, PA; (Y); 27/330; Am Leg Boys St; Boy Scts; Var L Trk; Var L Wrstlng; Hon Roll; NHS; PA ST U; Aerospc Engrng.

WENTLING, AMY; Annville-Cleona HS; Annville, PA; (S); Aud/Vis; Sec Trs Church Yth Grp; Girl Scts; Varsity Clb; Chorus; School Musical; Fld Hcky; Var Sftbl; NHS; Ntl Ed Dev Test Awd 84.

WENTROBLE, TERRY; Penn Trafford HS; Trafford, PA; (Y); Spanish Clb; Hon Roll; Psych.

WENTZ, DARLENE; Bellefonte Area HS; Bellefonte, PA; (Y); 60/217; Pres German Clb; Girl Scts; Rep Soph Cls; Sec Jr Cls; Var Bsktbl; Im Powder Puff Ftbl; Im Vllybl; Silver, Gold Ldrshp Awds Girl Scouts 82; S Hills Bus Schl; Bus Adm.

WENTZ, DAWN; Spring Grove SR HS; Spring Grove, PA; (Y); 6/220; Church Yth Grp; Drill Tm; Mrchg Band; Nwsp Ed-Chief; Trs Soph Cls; Trs Jr Cls; Trs Sr Cls; High Hon Roll; Hon Roll; Trs NHS; 400 Pnt Schlstc Pin 86; Stu Mnth 86; Bloomsburg U; Bus Adm.

WENTZ, ERIK; Dover Area HS; Dover, PA; (Y); 35/276; Church Yth Grp; Church Choir; Socr; Trk; Wt Lftg; Hon Roll; PA ST; Bus Mgmt.

WENTZ, JIL; Hanover HS; Hanover, PA; (Y); 36/104; Varsity Clb; Band; Concert Band; Jazz Band; Mrchg Band; School Play; Var Capt Cheerleading; Sftbl; Trk; FASHION Mdse.

WENTZ, T J; State College Area HS; Pennsylvania Furn, PA; (Y); 35/567; Stu Cncl; JV Var Bsktbl; Var Golf; Im Golf; Powder Puff Ftbl; Cit Awd; High Hon Roll; Ntl Merit Ltr; Physcs.

WENTZ, TONYA; Pine Grove Area HS; Pine Grove, PA; (Y); 35/126; Hosp Aide; ROTC; Mrchg Band; Nwsp Ed-Chief; Yrbk Ed-Chief; Rep Soph Cls; Rep Jr Cls; Twrlr; Cit Awd; Hon Roll; Outstndng & Supr Cadt Awds 85-86; Scranton U; Phy Thrpst.

WENTZEL, ANN; Eastern Lebanon County HS; Myerstown, PA; (Y); Church Yth Grp; SADD; Mrchg Band; Off Soph Cls; Off Jr Cls; Off Sr Cls; Fld Hcky; Sftbl; Vllybl; Rotary Awd; Elizabethtown Coll; Educ.

WENTZEL, JOELLE; Saucon Valley SR HS; Hellertown, PA; (Y); 31/183; Church Yth Grp; VP Spanish Clb; Stage Crew; Var Capt Cheerleading; Var Trk; High Hon Roll; Hon Roll; Kutztown ST; Art Ed.

WENTZEL, LYNNE C; Exeter HS; Reading, PA; (Y); 33/207; Varsity Clb; Band; Orch; Stu Cncl; Bowling; Trk; Hon Roll; NHS; 4th Pl-Bwlng Tourn 86; Shippensburg U; Bus Adm.

WENTZEL, TAMARA; Waynesburg Central HS; Waynesburg, PA; (Y); 1/205; Church Yth Grp; Spanish Clb; Church Choir; Nwsp Ed-Chief; Rep Stu Cncl; Var Trk; Bausch & Lomb Sci Awd; NHS; NEDT Awd; Voice Dem Awd; Alg I 84; Hugh O Brian Ldrshp Semnr 85; Bio Sci Fair 85.

WENZEL, AMY ELIZABETH; North Allegheny SR HS; Pittsburgh, PA; (Y); 78/642; Church Yth Grp; Cmnty Wkr; Hosp Aide; JA; Mrchg Band; Rep Stu Cncl; Trk; Hon Roll; NHS; Gvrnr Comm Awd Emplymt Handcppd 85-86; Mech Engrng.

WENZEL, ROBERT; Montoursville HS; Montoursville, PA; (Y); Pres Key Clb; Letterman Clb; Var L Ftbl; Var L Trk; Cit Awd; High Hon Roll; Pres NHS; Ntl Merit Ltr; Cnty Crdntr Hugh O Brian Yth Fndtn 85; Pre-Med.

WENZLER, AMY; Hampton HS; Allison Pk, PA; (Y); Sec French Clb; Hosp Aide; Nwsp Rptr; Sec Nwsp Stf; Powder Puff Ftbl; Hon Roll; Hmcmng Ct; Intr Dsgn.

WEREB, MELISSA; West Middlesex HS; W Middlesex, PA; (S); 19/107; Nwsp Stf; Yrbk Stf; Art Schl Inst.

WERGIN, ROXANE; Ringgold HS; Donora, PA; (Y); Camp Fr Inc; Church Yth Grp; Varsity Clb; Chorus; Variety Show; JV Var Cheerleading; Vllybl; Sec Rotary Awd; Pitt Pittsburgh; Law.

WERKHEISER, CRAIG; Penargyl Area HS; Nazareth, PA; (Y); 18/129; Church Yth Grp; Band; Concert Band; Jazz Band; Mrchg Band; Orch; Hon Roll; Prfct Atten Awd; Marchng Band Sq Yr 85; Spnsh.

WERKHEISER, GINA LEA; Bishop Kenrick HS; Norristown, PA; (Y); 2/268; JV Bsktbl; Var Fld Hcky; Im Powder Puff Ftbl; Capt Var Vllybl; High Hon Roll; NHS; All Catholic Vlybl 84-86; Schlstc Ldrshp Awd 86; Theolgy Awd 84; Penn ST U; Bus.

WERKHEISER, YVONNE; Stroudsburg HS; Stroudsburg, PA; (Y); 9/235; Drama Clb; Spanish Clb; Chorus; School Musical; Swing Chorus; VP Jr Cls; Stu Cncl; DAR Awd; High Hon Roll; NHS; Loyola U; Drama.

WERKMEISTER, MICHAEL; West Allegheny HS; Oakdale, PA; (Y); 52/208; Church Yth Grp; Pres Chorus; Stage Crew; Stat Bsktbl; Capt Ftbl; Score Keeper; L Wt Lftg; Hon Roll; Dist Chorus; Hmcmng Ct; Prom Ct; PA ST.

WERLEY, ABBE L; Kutztown Area HS; Kutztown, PA; (Y); Am Leg Aux Girls St; Science Clb; Band; Chorus; Drill Tm; Drm Mjr(t); Yrbk Phtg; Var Capt Fld Hcky; High Hon Roll; NHS; Grimley Trust Schlrshp 86; Physcs/Bio Awd & Social Sci 86; Natl Hon Soc Awd 86; Juniata Coll; Pre Med.

WERLEY, DENISE; Hamburg Area HS; Hamburg, PA; (Y); 60/154; High Hon Roll; Hon Roll; Prfct Atten Awd; Vo-Tech Csmtlgy Stu Of Qtr 84-85; Hairdrssr.

WERNER, AMY; Richland HS; Gibsonia, PA; (Y); 22/182; NFL; Mrchg Band; Orch; Nwsp Stf; VP Soph Cls; Tennis; Vllybl; NHS; Bus.

WERNER, BILL; Connellsville SR HS; Champion, PA; (Y); 160/600; Aud/Vis; Church Yth Grp; Cmnty Wkr; Computer Clb; FBLA; Teachers Aide; Stage Crew; Nwsp Rptr; Nwsp Stf; Yrbk Rptr; CA ST; Accntng.

WERNER, HEIDI; Bensalem SR HS; Bensalem, PA; (Y); Church Yth Grp; French Clb; Teachers Aide; Trk; NHS; Bucks Cnty Sci Lgue 84; Penn ST U; Bus Admin.

WERNER, JAMES PAUL; Ambridge Area HS; Sewickley, PA; (Y); German Clb; Pep Clb; Red Cross Aide; Yrbk Bus Mgr; Ed Yrbk Stf; High Hon Roll; Jr NHS; Drug & Alchl Cmt; Geneva Coll; Law.

WERNER, MELISSA; Blue Mountain Acad; Tamaqua, PA; (Y); Drama Clb; Band; Chorus; Concert Band; Hon Roll; Comp Engrng.

WERNER, NOEL; Derry Area SR HS; New Alexandria, PA; (Y); 2/285; Chorus; School Play; High Hon Roll; Sal; Westminster Choir Coll-Merit Schlrshp 85; Dist Choir 86; Rgnl, ST Choirs-1st Chair, Bass II 86; Westmnstr Choir Coll; Pipe Orgn.

WERNER, SHAUN; Knoch JR SR HS; Cabot, PA; (Y); Trs Science Clb; Im JV Bsktbl; Im Ftbl; High Hon Roll; Hon Roll; NHS; High Achvt Awd Am Soc,Anthrplgy 85-86; USAF Acad; Engrng.

WERNER, TINA; Mt Calvary Christian Schl; Bainbridge, PA; (S); 1/11; Church Yth Grp; Teachers Aide; Chorus; School Play; Nwsp Sprt Ed; Yrbk Ed-Chief; Var L Cheerleading; Var L Sftbl; JV Vllybl; Hon Roll; Hmcmng Ct 85-86; Word Of Life Bible Inst; Jrnlsm.

WERNER, WENDY; Baldwin HS; Pittsburgh, PA; (Y); 80/535; Rep Jr Cls; Capt Swmmng; High Hon Roll; NHS; NEDT Awd; Swmnng Team MVP 86.

WERNI, HEATHER; Annville-Cleona HS; Annville, PA; (Y); Aud/Vis; Trs Church Yth Grp; FBLA; German Clb; Varsity Clb; Chorus; Co-Capt Drill Tm; Yrbk Ed-Chief; Trs Soph Cls; Fld Hcky; Spcl Educ.

WERSTLER, GREGORY; Exeter Twp HS; Reading, PA; (Y); 26/217; Pres Church Yth Grp; Drama Clb; Chorus; School Musical; School Play; Crs Cntry; Trk; Hon Roll; NHS; Theatr.

WERT, COREY; Milton Area SR HS; Milton, PA; (Y); Trs Computer Clb; VP Pres FBLA; Mgr Stage Crew; JV Var Golf; Stat Mgr(s); Stat Wrstlng; NHS; Church Yth Grp; Spanish Clb; Varsity Clb; Bloomsburg U; Comp Sci.

WERT, KEVIN; Halifax HS; Halifax, PA; (S); 1/102; Camera Clb; Church Yth Grp; Nwsp Phtg; Pres Frsh Cls; Pres Soph Cls; VP Jr Cls; VP Sr Cls; High Hon Roll; NHS; Val; Chem Awd 85; Wdmn Of Wrld Awd 82; PA ST U; Aerosp Engrng.

WERT, SHELLEY; Cedar Crest HS; Lebanon, PA; (Y); Church Yth Grp; Cmnty Wkr; Drama Clb; Pres French Clb; 4-H; Hosp Aide; Pep Clb; SADD; Pres Band; Color Guard; Pltcl Sci.

WERT, TAMMIA; Northern York County HS; Dillsburg, PA; (Y); 46/209; Church Yth Grp; German Clb; Key Clb; Latin Clb; Science Clb; Var Powder Puff Ftbl; Var Sftbl; JV Vllybl; Hon Roll; Engrng.

WERT, TAMMY S; Juniata HS; Port Royal, PA; (Y); Church Yth Grp; Drama Clb; School Musical; Yrbk Ed-Chief; Hon Roll; NHS; Pres Schlr; Shippensburg U; Math Educ.

WERTMAN, MICHELE; Montgomery Area JR SR HS; Montgomery, PA; (Y); Pres Church Yth Grp; Am Leg Boys St; Thesps; Chorus; Drill Tm; Mrchg Band; Nwsp Stf; Yrbk Phtg; Pres Soph Cls; Rep Stu Cncl; Chldrns Medcn.

WERTZ, JOAN; Butler Area SR HS; Butler, PA; (Y); Exploring; Band; Mrchg Band; Stu Cncl; High Hon Roll; Jr NHS; Bio Med.

WERTZ, MOLLY; Bellwood-Antis HS; Bellwood, PA; (Y); 11/136; Yrbk Stf; JV Fld Hcky; JV Mgr(s); NHS; Alleghany CC; Lab Tech.

WERTZ, RHONDA; Montgomery JR SR HS; Montgomery, PA; (Y); Church Yth Grp; French Clb; FBLA; Chorus; Color Guard; Yrbk Stf; JV Bsktbl; Var Tennis; Var Trk; Hon Roll.

WESCOE, MICHAEL; Parkland HS; Allentown, PA; (Y); 11/459; Var L Bsktbl; High Hon Roll; Hon Roll; NHS; Temple U; Bus Adm.

WESCOE, STACY; Liberty HS; Bethlehem, PA; (Y); 93/475; Library Aide; Band; Concert Band; Mrchg Band; Ed Nwsp Ed-Chief; Nwsp Rptr; Nwsp Stf; Var Church Yth Grp8; Var Sftbl; Hon Roll; Messiah Coll; Med Tech.

WESCOTT, CHRISSY; Unionville HS; Kennett Square, PA; (Y); Exploring; Pres 4-H; Ski Clb; Nwsp Rptr; Nwsp Stf; Hon Roll; Red Cross Bldmbl Awd 86; Bio.

WESLER, PATRICIA; Upper Merion HS; King Of Prussia, PA; (Y); Math Tm; Chorus; Hon Roll; JV & Var Crew Tm; Aerospc Engrng.

WESLEY, RICHARD S; Commodore Perry HS; Greenville, PA; (S); Art Clb; Church Yth Grp; 4-H; FFA; Math Tm; Band; Concert Band; Jazz Band; Mgr(s); Hon Roll; UCLA; Psych.

WESLEY, ROSEMARY; Scranton Technical HS; Scranton, PA; (S); Aud/Vis; Cmnty Wkr; Drama Clb; JA; Ski Clb; Chorus; Stage Crew; Nwsp Stf; Yrbk Stf; Lit Mag; Sprtswrtng Awd 84-85; Poetry Awds From World Of Poetry 83-85; Golden Poet Awd World Of Poetry 85-86; Pblc Rel.

WESNER, ALICE; West Hazleton HS; Tomhicken, PA; (Y); Church Yth Grp; Cmnty Wkr; Pres VP 4-H; Library Aide; Office Aide; SADD; Score Keeper; 4-H Awd; High Hon Roll; Prfct Atten Awd; Citatn Of Merit Muscular Dystrphy Assoc 84.

WESNER, MICHELLE; Marian Catholic HS; Tamaqua, PA; (S); 16/123; Hosp Aide; Library Aide; VP Concert Band; VP Mrchg Band; Nwsp Stf; Yrbk Stf; Trk; Hon Roll; NHS; Nrsg.

WESS, SANDRA; Forest Hills SR HS; Summerhill, PA; (Y); Art Clb; Church Yth Grp; Office Aide; Spanish Clb; Y-Teens; Nwsp Stf; Yrbk Stf; Tennis; High Hon Roll; Spanish NHS.

WESSNER, DEBRA; Kutztown Area HS; Lenhartsville, PA; (Y); 5/160; Pres Church Yth Grp; Chorus; Church Choir; Swing Chorus; High Hon Roll; NHS; Teen Voice Friedens 85-87; Sunday Schl Tchr 85-87; Spec Olympcs Vlntr 86; Yth Ministry.

WESSNER, IDA; School Haven HS; School Haven, PA; (S); Church Yth Grp; Teachers Aide; Band; Chorus; Concert Band; Mrchg Band; Pep Band; Nwsp Rptr; Yrbk Rptr; JV Sftbl; Geneva Coll; Eng Tchng.

WESSNER, RENEE; Annville Cleona HS; Lebanon, PA; (Y); 5/125; Church Yth Grp; SADD; Chorus; JV Bsktbl; Var Trk; Bausch & Lomb Sci Awd; Hon Roll; NHS; NEDT Awd; Westchester; Bio.

WESSNER, TAMMY; Hamburg Area HS; Hamburg, PA; (Y); Rep German Clb; Rep Stu Cncl; Var Sftbl; High Hon Roll; Hon Roll; NHS; Ntl Merit Schol; Pres Schlr; Germn NHS Sec & Treas 85-87; Acad Awd Alg II, Germn II, Chem 84-86; Acctng.

WEST, AARON M; William Penn HS; York, PA; (Y); Drama Clb; Pres JA; Chorus; Nwsp Ed-Chief; Off Frsh Cls; Trs Soph Cls; VP Jr Cls; Pres Sr Cls; Gov Hon Prg Awd; Hon Roll; PA Gov Schl Arts Schlrshp 85; Philadelphia Coll Arts; Theatre.

WEST, ANTHONY; Sayre HS; Sayre, PA; (Y); Camera Clb; Cmnty Wkr; Computer Clb; Dance Clb; Letterman Clb; Ski Clb; Varsity Clb; Variety Show; Var Ftbl; Var Trk; Wrestling, Track Awds 86; WY Semnry; Engrng.

WEST, CAROLINE; Fox Chapel Area HS; Pittsburgh, PA; (S); Nwsp Ed-Chief; Nwsp Sprt Ed; Lit Mag; L Var Swmmng; Dnfth Awd; Natl H S Inst Jrnlsm Nrthwstrn U 85; QUEST Pgm Gifted Stu; Lehigh U; Jrnlsm.

WEST, JOAN; Penn Trafford HS; Trafford, PA; (Y); Church Yth Grp; Drama Clb; Exploring; FBLA; Ski Clb; Spanish Clb; Varsity Clb; JV Im Bsktbl; Var Crs Cntry; JV Var Sftbl; Elem Ed.

WEST, LAURA; Wests Middlesex HS; W Middlesex, PA; (Y); FBLA; Spanish Clb; Teachers Aide; Concert Band; Mrchg Band; High Hon Roll; Hon Roll; Spanish NHS; 3rd Pl Office Proc Comp 86; Kent ST; Fshn Mrchndsg.

WEST, PAULA; Downingtown HS; Downingtown, PA; (S); 29/574; Church Yth Grp; French Clb; GAA; Pep Clb; Capt Varsity Clb; Pres Sr Cls; Rep Stu Cncl; Var Capt Tennis; Hon Roll; NHS; Stu Rep-Scndry Schl Recgntn Prgrm 85; Hmcmng Queen 85; NEDT Awd 83; Med.

WEST, RICK; Trinity HS; Washington, PA; (Y); FCA; FBLA; FFA; Letterman Clb; Varsity Clb; JV Ftbl; Wt Lftg; Var L Wrstlng; Hon Roll; Woody Yaw Awd Wrstlng 85-86; Waynesburg Coll; Bus Mgmt.

WESTBROOK, CYNTHIA; Elkland Area HS; Elkland, PA; (Y); SADD; Sec Frsh Cls; Trs Civic Clb; Rep Stu Cncl; Var Cheerleading; Var Tennis; Var Trk; High Hon Roll; Hon Roll; Trs NHS; Acctg.

WESTCOTT, STEVEN; St Joseph Prep Schl; Wyndmoor, PA; (Y); 90/270; Drama Clb; Library Aide; Church Choir; School Musical; School Play; Lit Mag; Im Bsktbl; Im Ftbl; Ntl Merit Ltr; PAVAS; Gold Mdl Natl Lang Arts Olympd 84; Cum Laude Awd Natl Latin Exam 85; Acad Scholar 83; Bus Adm.

WESTERMAN, MARK; Mc Guffey HS; Washington, PA; (Y); 30/200; Am Leg Boys St; Crs Cntry; Trk; Wrstlng; Hon Roll; Acdmc All-Amer 85; Gannon; Physcns Asst.

WESTFALL, MAUREEN; Susquehanna Comm HS; Susquehanna, PA; (S); Yrbk Ed-Chief; Pres Frsh Cls; VP Jr Cls; VP Sr Cls; Stu Cncl; Var Bsktbl; Var Cheerleading; Im Powder Puff Ftbl; Var Sftbl; JV Vllybl; Ntl Ldrshp Merit Awd 84-85; Ntl Sci Merit Awd 84-85; Acdmc All Amer 84-85; Bloomsburg; Accntng.

WESTON, MICHELE; Salisbury HS; Allentown, PA; (Y); Var L Bsktbl; Var L Sftbl; Mt Saint Marys Coll; Psych.

WESTON, TIM; Bald Eagle Area HS; Julian, PA; (Y); Hon Roll; Williamsport CC; Dairy Hrd Mgt.

WESTOVER, LYNN; Central Columbia HS; Lightstreet, PA; (Y); 23/177; Church Yth Grp; Cmnty Wkr; Exploring; Trs 4-H; German Clb; Key Clb; Hon Roll; Pres Schlr; Josephine Carpenter Mem Schlrshp 86; PA ST U; Engnrng.

WESTOVER, MICHAEL; Red Land SR HS; New Cumberland, PA; (Y); 91/275; French Clb; Latin Clb; Library Aide; Spanish Clb; Speech Tm; School Play; Hon Roll; Mdrn Lang.

WETMORE, BARBARA; East Stroudsburg HS; E Stroudsburg, PA; (Y); 11/225; Pres Church Yth Grp; VP Girl Scts; Mgr Band; Color Guard; Concert Band; Capt Mrchg Band; Pep Band; Stu Cncl; Trk; High Hon Roll; Math.

WETMORE, TAMARA; Riv Erview HS; Oakmont, PA; (Y); 10/118; Key Clb; Church Choir; Color Guard; Trk; Vllybl; High Hon Roll; NHS; NEDT Awd; Law.

WETTACH, ERIN; Deer Lakes JR SR HS; Gibsonia, PA; (Y); 1/175; Church Yth Grp; Cmnty Wkr; Exploring; Girl Scts; Chorus; Capt Flag Corp; Yrbk Stf; Gov Hon Prg Awd; High Hon Roll; Hon Roll; LEAPS Pgm Buhl Sci Cntr 85; Awd Wnr Pittsbrgh Rgnl Schl Sci & Engrng Fair 86; Gvrnrs Smmr Schl 86; Psych.

WETTERAU, FRED; Hazleton SR HS; Hazleton, PA; (Y); Boy Scts; Scholastic Bowl; Mgr Bsktbl; Bowling; Navys Nuclear Power Schl; Nclr.

WETZEL, ANDREA; Allentown Central Catholic HS; Allentown, PA; (Y); Cmnty Wkr; JV Im Bsktbl; Var Capt Vllybl; High Hon Roll; Hon Roll; Accntng.

WETZEL, ANGELA; Marion Center Area HS; Marion Center, PA; (S); 8/170; Church Yth Grp; Latin Clb; Q&S; Science Clb; Chorus; Flag Corp; Orch; Yrbk Ed-Chief; NHS.

WETZEL, BRENDA; Ryenolds HS; Fredonia, PA; (Y); 13/147; 4-H; Sec Latin Clb; Varsity Clb; Madrigals; Var L Crs Cntry; Var Mat Maids; Var L Trk; NHS; Church Yth Grp; Library Aide; Acdmc All-Amer Awd 84-85; U Of Pittsburgh; Physcl Thrpy.

WETZEL, CINDY; South Park HS; Library, PA; (Y); Swmmng; High Hon Roll; Hon Roll; Jrnlsm.

WETZEL, JULIE; Fairfield Area HS; Fairfield, PA; (Y); 12/42; Hosp Aide; Library Aide; Trs Spanish Clb; School Play; Nwsp Stf; VP Frsh Cls; Rep Sr Cls; Score Keeper; Vllybl; High Hon Roll.

WETZEL, MAYA CHRISTINE; Beaver Area JRSR HS; Beaver, PA; (Y); 63/177; FCA; French Clb; Nwsp Stf; Yrbk Stf; Lit Mag; Bsktbl; Sftbl; Vllybl; Girls Discus Schl Rcrd & Vrsty Ltr 86; Girl Scouts; Communctns.

WETZEL, NATALIE; Danville SR HS; Danville, PA; (Y); Church Yth Grp; VP FHA; SADD; Chorus; Color Guard; High Hon Roll; Hon Roll; Upward Bnd Prgm 84-86; Acctg.

WETZEL, VICKI; Western Wayne HS; Waymart, PA; (Y); 20/144; Drama Clb; JA; Band; Chorus; School Musical; Stage Crew; Rep Stu Cncl; Stat Mgr(s); Hon Roll; Computer Clb; PA ST U; Pre-Law.

WETZEL, WILLIAM; Curwensville HS; Curwensville, PA; (Y); Letterman Clb; Varsity Clb; Stage Crew; Var L Ftbl; Wt Lftg; Var L Wrstlng.

WEYAND, ANNE; St Hubert HS; Philadelphia, PA; (Y); 120/305; Camera Clb; Lit Mag; Htl Rest Mgmt.

WEYAND-BROWN, JULIE; Somerset Area SR HS; Somerset, PA; (Y); 7/211; VP JA; Varsity Clb; Band; Drm Mjr(t); Stu Cncl; Cheerleading; High Hon Roll; NHS; Pres Schlr; Michael M Messina Memrl Awd 86; Acctg.

WEYMAN, HEATHER; Seneca Valley SR HS; Harmony, PA; (Y); Church Yth Grp; Ski Clb; JV Bsktbl; Im Sftbl; High Hon Roll; Hon Roll; Most Imprvd Bsktbl Plyr 83; Trophs Sftbl 85; Rcvd A And B Awds 86.

WEYRAUCH, KAREN J; Penn Hills SR HS; Pittsburgh, PA; (S); 1/797; Trs AFS; French Clb; Ski Clb; Yrbk Stf; Stu Cncl; Pom Pon; High Hon Roll; NHS; Val; VIP Awd US Histry 84; Notre Dame U; Engr.

WHALEN, PAMELA; Pottstown SR HS; Pottstown, PA; (S); 15/238; French Clb; Key Clb; Yrbk Stf; Trs Frsh Cls; Rep Soph Cls; Rep Jr Cls; Var Tennis; High Hon Roll; Hon Roll; NHS; Hnrs Engl Pgm 85-86; Med Tech.

WHALEN, REGINA; Saint Hubert Catholic HS For Girls; Philadelphia, PA; (Y); 144/363; Cmnty Wkr; Hosp Aide; Intnl Clb; JA; Pep Clb; SADD; Stu Cncl; Hon Roll; NHS; Debate Tm; Temple U; Dntl Hygn.

WHALEN, SALLY; Delaware Valley HS; Milford, PA; (Y); 5/130; Trs Drama Clb; Latin Clb; Trs Chorus; School Musical; Nwsp Bus Mgr; Yrbk Ed-Chief; High Hon Roll; Pres NHS; Ntl Merit SF; Regional Schl For The Arts 84; Dist Chorus 85-86; Boston Coll; Engl.

WHALEN, TERESA; North Allegheny HS; Allison Park, PA; (Y); 40/610; Latin Clb; Ski Clb; Band; Rep Frsh Cls; Off Soph Cls; Stu Cncl; Capt L Socr; L Var Swmmng; NHS; U Of Pittsburgh; Physcl Thrpy.

WHALEY, DONNA; H S Of Engineering & Science; Philadelphia, PA; (Y); 72/188; Science Clb; Nwsp Stf; Rep Jr Cls; Var Cheerleading; Temple U; Lib Arts.

WHALEY, JANICE; Poine Forge Acad; Pine Forge, PA; (S); 8/63; FCA; Badmtn; Capt Bsbl; Tennis; Trk; Vllybl; High Hon Roll; NHS; Oakwood Coll; Pre-Med.

WHALLIN, SUSAN; Seneca Valley HS; Evans City, PA; (Y); ROTC; Chorus; Drill Tm; School Musical; School Play; Sftbl; Hon Roll; ROTC Supr Cadet 84-86; Military Order Wrld Wars 85-86; Law.

WHANN, TODD; Wissahickon HS; Broad Axe, PA; (S); 27/275; Var JV Ftbl; Wt Lftg; Cit Awd; Hon Roll; Prfct Atten Awd; 2nd Tm All Suburban I Ftbl 85; Outstndng Offnsve Lnmn Ftbl Tm 85.

WHARRAM, AMY; St Benedict Acad; Erie, PA; (Y); 6/63; Chorus; High Hon Roll; NHS; PA JR Acad Of Sci 1st Pl Rgnls & 2nd Pl ST 84; Trnsprtn, Trvl & Toursm.

WHARRY, ROBERT; Unionville HS; Kennett Square, PA; (Y); 43/269; Boy Scts; Exploring; Band; Concert Band; Jazz Band; Mrchg Band; Orch; Pep Band; School Musical; Hon Roll; Eagle Scout 84; U DE; Chem Engrng.

WHARTENBY, TRACEY; St Hubert HS; Philadelphia, PA; (Y); 11/383; Cmnty Wkr; Mathletes; Spanish Clb; Nwsp Rptr; Ed Nwsp Stf; Ed Yrbk Rptr; Mgr Swmmng; Hon Roll; NHS; Prfct Atten Awd; Comm Svc Awd; Math Awd; Bus.

WHEARY, JOHN; Lourdes Regional HS; Shamokin, PA; (Y); 27/100; Key Clb; Bsktbl; Coach Actv; Ftbl; Stu Of Mo 86; Pre Med.

WHEELER, AMY; Knoch HS; Butler, PA; (Y); Band; Concert Band; Mrchg Band; Pep Band; School Musical; School Play; Yrbk Stf; Hon Roll; Butler Cnty Jr Miss 87; Hotel Mgt.

WHEELER, CATHERINE; Wyoming Valley West HS; Plymouth, PA; (Y); 17/364; VP Church Yth Grp; Ski Clb; Chorus; School Musical; Lit Mag; Cit Awd; High Hon Roll; NHS; VFW Awd; Drama Clb; Pres Acad Ftns 86; Lebanon Valley Coll; Music Educ.

WHEELER, JILL; Annville-Cleona HS; Cleona, PA; (S); 13/121; Varsity Clb; School Musical; VP Frsh Cls; VP Soph Cls; VP Jr Cls; VP Sr Cls; Sec Stu Cncl; Stat Fld; Mat Maids; NHS; PENN ST; Math.

WHEELER, LORI; Scranton Preparatory Schl; Scranton, PA; (Y); 56/190; Cmnty Wkr; GAA; Latin Clb; Letterman Clb; Pep Clb; Service Clb; Spanish Clb; Bsktbl; Sftbl; High Hon Roll; Gld Mdl In Mth & Brnz Mdl In Physcs 86; Phila Coll Of Phrmcy; Phrmcy.

WHEELER, ROBYN; West Middlesex Area HS; Mercer, PA; (S); 11/111; Capt Flag Corp; High Hon Roll; Hon Roll; Jr NHS.

WHEELER, ROXANNE; North Star HS; Jennerstown, PA; (Y); 14/130; Church Yth Grp; FCA; Band; Concert Band; Drm Mjr(t); Mrchg Band; VP Soph Cls; JV Capt Cheerleading; Hon Roll; JC Awd; County Band 86; Southeastrn Acad.

WHEELER, SANDI; Sullivan County HS; Shunk, PA; (Y); 12/100; Office Aide; Rep Frsh Cls; Hon Roll; Typg Awd 85; Shrtland Awd 86; Psych.

WHEELER, STACY LYNN; Williams Valley JR SR HS; Williamstown, PA; (Y); Church Yth Grp; Cmnty Wkr; Drama Clb; Girl Scts; Spanish Clb; Teachers Aide; JV Var Bsktbl; Gov Hon Prg Awd; Prfct Atten Awd; VP Yth Trffc Sfty Cncl 86-88; Stu Gov Exec Brd 84-86; Pres Yth Trffc Sfty Cncl 86-87; Compu Prg.

WHEELER, TOM; N E Catholic HS; Philadelphia, PA; (Y); 80/362; Bsktbl; Coach Actv; Wt Lftg; Wrstlng; Hon Roll; La Salle.

WHELAN, LORI; Archbishop John Carroll HS; Bala Cynwyd, PA; (Y); 2/216; Mathletes; School Musical; Rep Sr Cls; Capt Var Crs Cntry; Capt Var Trk; High Hon Roll; Trs NHS; Cmnty Wkr; GAA; Rep Service Clb; Schlrshp St Joes Widener & Lehigh Acad & Ath 86; Pres Ftnss Aws 86; Hst Aver Rlgn,Hist,Sci 83-85; Lehigh Ufchem Engrng.

WHERTHEY, CHRISTOPHER; Neshannock HS; New Castle, PA; (Y); 6/113; Church Yth Grp; Band; Concert Band; Mrchg Band; Pep Band; Stage Crew; Trk; Hon Roll; NHS; Prfct Atten Awd; Bio.

WHETSTINE, LISA; Bellwood-Antis HS; Tyrone, PA; (Y); Key Clb; Ski Clb; Stu Cncl; Im L Bsktbl; JV Fld Hcky; Trk; Mt Aloysius; Trvl.

WHETSTONE, JODY; Chestnut Ridge SR HS; Manns Choice, PA; (Y); 12/126; Teachers Aide; Band; Concert Band; Mrchg Band; Stu Cncl; Bsktbl; Score Keeper; Sftbl; Hon Roll; NHS; Comp.

WHIELDON, LAURA; Blue Mt HS; New Ringgold, PA; (Y); 21/227; Church Yth Grp; Cmnty Wkr; SADD; Varsity Clb; Chorus; School Musical; Stu Cncl; JV Var Cheerleading; JV Var Crs Cntry; JV Var Trk; Outstndg Female Rnnr Yr; Ensmbl & Cnty Chorus; Sing Alma Mater At Games; Early Chldhd Ed.

WHIPKEY, MICHELLE; Uniontown Area HS; Ohiopyle, PA; (Y); 9/308; Church Yth Grp; Pres Sec 4-H; Chorus; Church Choir; School Play; French Hon Soc; High Hon Roll; Jr NHS; NHS; Pres Schlr; St Vincent Coll; Finc.

WHITAKER, B LEE; Downingtown Senior HS; Exton, PA; (Y); 52/563; Church Yth Grp; Ski Clb; Spanish Clb; Varsity Clb; Var L Bsbl; Var L Ftbl; High Hon Roll; Hon Roll; NHS; Am Leg Boys St; Ldrshp Awd 86; Co-Chair Ski Clb 86-87; Exclince Span I Awd 83-84; Pre-Med.

WHITAKER, MARK; East Pennsboro Area HS; Enola, PA; (Y); 21/197; Boy Scts; German Clb; Spanish Clb; Varsity Clb; Frsh Cls; Soph Cls; Sr Cls; Bsbl; Bsktbl; Coach Actv; PA Amer Acad Pediatrcs Poster Cont Wnr 84; Slippery Rock U; Mth Ed.

WHITAKER, MARK; Gateway SR HS; Monroeville, PA; (Y); Church Yth Grp; Ski Clb; Band; Concert Band; Jazz Band; Orch; Grove Cty Coll.

WHITAKER, WENDY; Carlynton JR SR HS; Carnegie, PA; (Y); 8/174; French Clb; Yrbk Stf; JV Var Bsktbl; Var Sftbl; Var Tennis; High Hon Roll; NHS; Band; Mrchg Band; Presdntl Acadmc Ftns Awd 85-86; Cert Of Merit-Outstndng Achvt-Engl 85-86; PA ST U; Chmcl Engrng.

WHITBECK, ANNE J; Saegertown Area HS; Saegertown, PA; (Y); 7/117; Band; Church Choir; Concert Band; Jazz Band; Mrchg Band; Variety Show; High Hon Roll; Hon Roll; NHS; Ntl Merit Ltr; Pres Acad Fit Awd; PA ST U; Pre-Med.

WHITCO, MICHELLE; Washington HS; Washington, PA; (S); 20/155; French Clb; Letterman Clb; Varsity Clb; Bsktbl; Tennis; High Hon Roll; Hon Roll; Physical Therapy.

WHITE, ALEX; Tulpehocken HS; Bernville, PA; (Y); 16/100; Computer Clb; L Bsktbl; L Trk; Mst Imprvd JV Plyr Bsktbl 84; U South Carolina; Comp Sci.

WHITE, ANITA; Johnstown Vo-Tech; Salix, PA; (Y); 54/320; Drama Clb; Hosp Aide; Library Aide; Pep Clb; VICA; Y-Teens; Pres Jr Cls; Pres Sr Cls; JV Cheerleading; Stat Crs Cntry; NAACP Awd For Outstndng Achvt In Acad,Athltcs,Ldrshp 85; Outstndng Achvt In Trk & Fld 86; US Army; Prevntv Med Spclst.

WHITE, BETH ANN; James M Coughlin HS; Wilkes-Barre, PA; (Y); Sec DECA; Girl Scts; Band; Concert Band; Mrchg Band; High Hon Roll; Jr NHS; NHS; Prfct Atten Awd; Pres Schlr; Outstndng SR Mktg Prog 86; Bus Mgmt.

WHITE, BRIAN D; Owen J Roberts HS; Spring City, PA; (S); 3/267; Boy Scts; Scholastic Bowl; Band; Mrchg Band; God Cntry Awd; High Hon Roll; Hon Roll; NHS; Eagle Scout 83; Chem Engrng.

WHITE, CAMERON; Waynesboro Area Senior HS; Waynesboro, PA; (Y); Pres Church Yth Grp; Concert Band; Jazz Band; Mrchg Band; Rep Soph Cls; Rep Jr Cls; L Bsktbl; Hon Roll; Band; Orch; Cnty Bnd; Cnty Orchstr.

WHITE, CARMEN; Belle Fonte HS; Bellefonte, PA; (Y); German Clb; Chorus; Mat Maids; JV Sftbl; Hon Roll; Nrsg.

WHITE, CHARZZI S; Montour HS; Coraopolis, PA; (Y); 93/274; Library Aide; Pep Clb; Yrbk Stf; JV Bsktbl; Capt Powder Puff Ftbl; High Hon Roll; Hon Roll; Intl Frgn Lng Awd 86; Bthny Coll; Spnsh.

WHITE, DEBBIE; Pennsbury HS; Morrisville, PA; (Y); 33/730; Church Yth Grp; Cmnty Wkr; Nwsp Stf; Yrbk Sprt Ed; JV Sftbl; Var Tennis; Hon Roll; NHS; Pres Schlr; SADD; IN U Of Pas Physcs Awd; PA ST; Vet-Med.

WHITE, DEBORAH A; Richland HS; Gibsonia, PA; (Y); 12/168; AFS; Cmnty Wkr; Chorus; L Concert Band; Mrchg Band; Rep Frsh Cls; Mgr Stat Bsktbl; Mgr(s); Capt Sftbl; High Hon Roll; Gannon U Sci & Eng Awd 84; Slippery Rock U; Pks Mgmt.

WHITE, DENISE M; Med-Valley HS; Olyphant, PA; (Y); 19/76; Exploring; Pep Clb; Ski Clb; Yrbk Stf; Cheerleading; High Hon Roll; Hon Roll; Jr NHS; NHS; Spanish NHS; Bloomsburg U; Bus.

WHITE, DIANNA; Harry S Truman HS; Bristol, PA; (Y); Stu Cncl; Im Sftbl; Hon Roll; Prfct Atten Awd; Bucks County CC; Bus Educ.

WHITE, DWAYNE; Lock Haven SR HS; Lock Haven, PA; (Y); Computer Clb; Model UN; Comp Sci.

WHITE, EDNA; Lewistown Area HS; Granville, PA; (Y); 24/262; AFS; Pres Trs 4-H; Key Clb; Trs Pep Clb; Ski Clb; Yrbk Phtg; Fld Hcky; Trk; High Hon Roll; NHS; Phrmcy.

WHITE, ERIC; Altoona Area HS; Altoona, PA; (S); 14/683; Chess Clb; French Clb; Math Clb; Math Tm; Band; Concert Band; Drm Mjr(t); Jazz Band; Mrchg Band; School Musical; IN U Hnrs Bnd 83-85; Mid ST Bnk Awd Acad Achvt 83; Mth & Fr Awd Hghst Avg 83; Penn ST U; Engrng.

WHITE, GLENN; Chief Logan HS; Lewistown, PA; (Y); 81/181; Art Clb; Computer Clb; JV Stat Bsktbl; Im Tennis; Schltc Art Awd Cert Of Merit 86; Arts Fest Awd 86.

WHITE, GREG; Gov Mifflin SR HS; Shillington, PA; (Y); 17/265; Spanish Clb; School Musical; Nwsp Rptr; Yrbk Rptr; VP Jr Cls; VP Stu Cncl; NHS; Rotary Awd; VFW Awd; Pres Wrkshp NASC Conf 84 & 86; Natl Assn Stu Cncls; Unified Points Awd 85 & 86; &ASC Conf Wrkshps; Comm.

WHITE, JACQUELYN S; Montour HS; Mc Kees Rocks, PA; (Y); Hosp Aide; Pep Clb; SADD; Lit Mag; Chrmn Jr Cls; Score Keeper; Vllybl; High Hon Roll; Acad Achvt Awd Wlrd Cult 86; Med.

WHITE, JENNIFER; Council Rock HS; Newtown, PA; (Y); Key Clb; Rep Stu Cncl; JV Fld Hcky; Ftbl; Var Socr; Sftbl; Im Vllybl; Hon Roll; U Of Hartford CT; Cmmnctns.

WHITE, JENNIFER; Northern Lebaron HS; Fredericksburg, PA; (Y); Church Yth Grp; Spanish Clb; Chorus; Color Guard; School Musical; JV Bsktbl; JV Var Sftbl; Hon Roll; Outstndng SR Band 86; Hghst Awd Hobby Cer 84; HACC; Bus Mgmnt.

WHITE, JENNIFER; Titusville HS; Titusville, PA; (Y); 193/241; Church Yth Grp; Girl Scts; VP Varsity Clb; Y-Teens; Chorus; School Musical; School Play; Rep Stu Cncl; Coach Actv; Score Keeper; Carlow Coll; Art Thrpy.

WHITE, JIM; Upper Merion Area HS; King Of Prussia, PA; (Y); 2/320; Boy Scts; Computer Clb; Yrbk Rptr; Var Bsktbl; Var Ftbl; Im Vllybl; Wt Lftg; Hon Roll; Rotary Awd; Natl Exchng Club Stu Mnth 86; Comp Sci.

WHITE, KATHLEEN; Mid-Valley Secondary HS; Olyphant, PA; (Y); Yrbk Stf; Hon Roll; Army; Comp Prgmr.

WHITE, KIMBERLY M; Northern Chester County Tech; Pottstown, PA; (S); DECA; VICA; 4th MDA Manual 85; 4th Finance & Credit Dist Comp 86; 4th Finance & Credit Wrttn Evnt St 86; Finance.

WHITE, KRISTIN; Puschase Lilne HS; Cherry Tree, PA; (Y); 11/118; Dance Clb; Drama Clb; French Clb; Pep Clb; Chorus; School Musical; School Play; Variety Show; Cheerleading; Hon Roll; Dnce Trphy & Scholar 79 & 83; Homecomg Court 86; Tch Dnce.

WHITE, LAURA LYNN; Pottsgrove HS; Pottstown, PA; (Y); Trs Church Yth Grp; Latin Clb; Math Tm; Science Clb; Varsity Clb; Church Choir; Trs Orch; Yrbk Stf; Rep Stu Cncl; Var Trk; Art.

WHITE, LEANN; Clearfield Area HS; Olanta, PA; (Y); #52 In Class; Church Yth Grp; French Clb; Library Aide; Office Aide; Band; Church Choir; Concert Band; Flag Corp; Mrchg Band; School Play; Acctng.

WHITE, LISA; Mt Pleasant SR HS; Latrobe, PA; (Y); Church Yth Grp; French Clb; GAA; Office Aide; Nwsp Stf; Hon Roll; California U Of PA.

WHITE, MARCI; Punxsutawney Area HS; Punxsutawney, PA; (Y); Church Yth Grp; Civic Clb; GAA; Letterman Clb; Pep Clb; Spanish Clb; SADD; Varsity Clb; Rep Frsh Cls; Rep Stu Cncl; Erly Chldhd Educ.

WHITE, MARLA; Hickory HS; Hermitage, PA; (S); 6/190; Letterman Clb; Service Clb; Varsity Clb; Chorus; Capt L Bsktbl; Capt L Cheerleading; Capt L Trk; NHS; Trs Spanish NHS; Brk Schl Recrd Scord 35 Pts Sngl Game Bsktbl & 1st Tm Mercer Cnty All Strs &3 2nd Leadg Scorer 84-85; Carnegie-Mellon U; Math.

WHITE, MEGAN; Owen J Roberts HS; Glenmore, PA; (Y); 36/270; Church Yth Grp; Band; Chorus; Church Choir; Color Guard; Mrchg Band; School Musical; VP Swmmng; Im Vllybl; Hon Roll; Elem Educ.

WHITE, MELINDA E; Lower Merion HS; Narberth, PA; (Y); Chorus; Variety Show; Hon Roll; 1st Pl Carey Rose Winshi Memrl Ballet Cmptn 84; Ballet Dncr.

WHITE, MELISSA; Shenango JRSR HS; New Castle, PA; (Y); Church Yth Grp; OEA; Drill Tm; Jazz Band; Hon Roll; Cosmetology.

WHITE, MICHELE; Mechanicsburg SR HS; Mechanicsburg, PA; (Y); 19/300; Chorus; Mrchg Band; Symp Band; Trk; High Hon Roll; NHS; Ntl Merit Ltr; Pres Schlr; Pres Schlr Bloomsburg U 86; Bloomsburg U; Biol.

WHITE, PETER; Mercy Vocational HS; Philadelphia, PA; (Y); Boy Scts; Drexel U; Elctrncs.

WHITE, RACHEL; Mechanicsburg Area SR HS; Mechanicsburg, PA; (Y); 31/311; Chorus; High Hon Roll; Hon Roll; NHS.

WHITE, ROBERT; G A R Memorial HS; Wilkes Barre, PA; (S); 10/187; Aud/Vis; Acpl Chr; Yrbk Stf; Rep Frsh Cls; Rep Jr Cls; Rep Stu Cncl; JV Ftbl; Wt Lftg; Var Wrstlng; Hon Roll.

WHITE, ROBERT; West Greene HS; Sycamore, PA; (S); 3/70; SADD; Varsity Clb; Yrbk Stf; Rep Sr Cls; Rep Stu Cncl; Bsbl; High Hon Roll; Hon Roll; NHS; Prfct Atten Awd; PA ST U; Engrng.

WHITE, ROBERT C; Penn Manor HS; Lancaster, PA; (Y); 45/301; Debate Tm; Library Aide; Q&S; Chorus; Nwsp Rptr; High Hon Roll; Hon Roll; Spanish NHS; Lancaster Genl Hosp Schl; Rdlgy.

WHITE, ROBERTA; Shenango JR SR HS; New Castle, PA; (Y); 8/112; Aud/Vis; Pres Church Yth Grp; French Clb; Teachers Aide; Band; Concert Band; Co-Capt Flag Corp; Jazz Band; Stage Crew; Yrbk Stf; Eng.

WHITE, ROBYN L; Taylor Allderdice HS; Pittsburgh, PA; (S); Church Yth Grp; Cmnty Wkr; Hosp Aide; JA; Q&S; Nwsp Bus Mgr; Nwsp Rptr; Socr; High Hon Roll; NHS; PA Free Enterprise Wk 85; Generations Together 85-86; Bus.

WHITE, SCOTT; Northeast Catholic HS; Philadelphia, PA; (Y); 50/390; Socr; Hon Roll; NHS; Ntl Merit Schol; Elec Engrng.

WHITE, SHARON; Strath Haven HS; Wallingford, PA; (Y); JV Cheerleading; Mgr(s); Hstry.

WHITE, SHERRY LYNN; Farrell HS; Farrell, PA; (Y); Library Aide; Spanish Clb; Chorus; Nwsp Rptr; Hon Roll; Comp Sci.

WHITE, TERI; Pennridge SR HS; Sellersville, PA; (Y); Girl Scts; Pres VICA; High Hon Roll; Hon Roll; Spnsh Stu Of Mnth 86; Comp Prog.

WHITE, TONIA; Mercy Vocational HS; Philadelphia, PA; (Y); Cmnty Wkr; Dance Clb; Girl Scts; Church Choir; Cty Of Philly Incentive 84-85 Awd; Svc Awd 84; Med Recs.

WHITE, TRICIA; Northeastern HS; Dover, PA; (Y); VP Sec Church Yth Grp; 4-H; Ski Clb; Teachers Aide; Chorus; Church Choir; Lit Mag; L Bsktbl; 4-H Awd; Voice Dem Awd; Dr Herm Gailey 4-H Meml Trophy 84.

WHITE, VINCENT; Fort Le Boeuf HS; Erie, PA; (Y); 31/179; Rep Soph Cls; Var L Ftbl; Var L Trk; High Hon Roll; Bio Mech.

WHITE, WENDY; The Christian Acad; Essington, PA; (Y); 23/64; Church Yth Grp; Library Aide; School Play; Yrbk Sprt Ed; Yrbk Stf; Var Vllybl; Hon Roll; DE Cnty CC; Natrl Sci.

WHITEBREAD, NANCY; Berwick Area SR HS; Berwick, PA; (Y); 64/183; Drama Clb; Pres VP 4-H; FBLA; Band; Chorus; Concert Band; Mrchg Band; School Play; Yrbk Stf; Path Essy Cntst 84; Mst Prmsing Musicn 83; Geisinger Schl Of Nrsng; Nrsng.

WHITEBREAD, ROBERT DAVID; Northwest Area HS; Shickshinny, PA; (Y); 14/108; Chess Clb; Computer Clb; French Clb; High Hon Roll; NHS; Voice Dem Awd; Travel Clb Treas 84-85; Voice Democracy Dist Wnnr 86; PA ST U; Aerosp Engr.

WHITEHEAD, CORI; Norwin SR HS; N Huntingdon, PA; (Y); 132/557; Letterman Clb; Pep Clb; SADD; VICA; Co-Capt Cheerleading; Hon Roll; Jr NHS; PA Miss All-Amer Chrldr Pgnt Miss Spirit & Bst Persnlty 86; Pittsburgh Beauty Acad; Cosme.

WHITEHEAD, THOMAS; Philipsburg Osceola SR HS; Philipsburg, PA; (Y); 31/250; Ski Clb; Stu Cncl; Bsbl; Bsktbl; NHS; Natl Honor Soc 86.

WHITELEY, CHERI; Kennett HS; Landenberg, PA; (Y); 55/154; FBLA; Girl Scts; Bus Adm.

WHITEMAN, CHRIS; Cathedral Prep; Erie, PA; (Y); 14/236; VP German Clb; Letterman Clb; Math Clb; Quiz Bowl; Band; Concert Band; Jazz Band; Orch; Vllybl; High Hon Roll; 1st Pl Slpry Rck Ntl Lnge 85; 2dn Pl Slpry Rck Ntl Lnge 86; Hnrble Mntn Slpry Rck Lng 86; PA ST At U Park; Accntg.

WHITEMAN, DAVID; Cathedral Prep; Erie, PA; (Y); 5/216; Model UN; Spanish Clb; Im Bsktbl; Golf; Im Vllybl; Penn ST; Bus Adm.

WHITEMAN, LISA; Elk County Christian HS; St Marys, PA; (S); Intnl Clb; Ski Clb; Rep Soph Cls; Var L Bsktbl; Var L Vllybl; High Hon Roll.

WHITEMAN, MICHAEL; Octorara Area HS; Christiana, PA; (Y); 15/161; Var L Crs Cntry; Var L Trk; Hon Roll; Arch.

WHITEMAN, SUSAN E; Central Bucks H S East; Hartsville, PA; (Y); 3/474; Church Yth Grp; Scholastic Bowl; Chorus; Madrigals; School Musical; School Play; High Hon Roll; Hon Roll; NHS; Ntl Merit SF; Dist & Regnl Choir 85.

WHITEMAN, TINA; Otto-Eldred HS; Rixford, PA; (Y); 7/90; Girl Scts; Library Aide; Nwsp Rptr; Hon Roll; Prfct Atten Awd.

WHITENIGHT, CYNTHIA; Hazleton SR HS; Hazleton, PA; (Y); Office Aide; Color Guard; Flag Corp; Mrchg Band; Trk; Hon Roll; St Joseph Med Ctr; Rdlgc Tech.

WHITENIGHT, JEFFREY; Benton Area JR-SR HS; Benton, PA; (Y); 4/61; Pres Church Yth Grp; 4-H; Sec Key Clb; VP Band; VP Chorus; VP Concert Band; Mrchg Band; School Musical; School Play; Pres Stu Cncl; Penn ST; Engr.

WHITESELL, SARAH E; Manhelm Township HS; Lancaster, PA; (Y); 2/314; Jazz Band; Orch; Nwsp Sprt Ed; Nwsp Stf; Stu Cncl; JV Fld Hcky; Trk; Hon Roll; NHS; Ntl Merit SF.

WHITFIELD, MELISSA; Somerset Area HS; Somerset, PA; (Y); Church Yth Grp; English Clb; German Clb; Pep Clb; Ski Clb; Spanish Clb; Chorus; Church Choir; Stu Cncl; Ntl Fed Musc Clbs 83; Piano Excl Awd Pittsburgh Ntl Fed; Meremec CC; Comms.

WHITING, MARY GRACE; Cameron County HS; Emporium, PA; (Y); Yrbk Stf; High Hon Roll; Hon Roll; Robert Morris Hnrs Scholar 86; Robert Morris Coll; Sport Mgmt.

WHITMAN, MARILEE; West Scranton SR HS; Scranton, PA; (Y); Drama Clb; Speech Tm; Band; Chorus; Church Choir; School Musical; School Play; SPEC Effcts Make-Up Artist.

WHITMAN, WILLIAM; Bishop O Hara HS; Olyphant, PA; (S); 6/124; Capt Bowling; High Hon Roll; NHS; Penn ST; Bus Adm.

WHITMER, CASSANDRA LYNN; Union HS; Rimersburg, PA; (Y); 3/74; Chorus; Nwsp Ed-Chief; Yrbk Stf; Sec Jr Cls; Var L Cheerleading; Capt Trk; Var L Vllybl; Hon Roll; NHS; Pres Schlr; Prom & Hmcmg Cts 86; Gannon U; Radlgc Tech.

WHITMER, JEFFREY L; Selinsgrove Area HS; Selinsgrove, PA; (Y); 5/224; Am Leg Boys St; Boy Scts; Church Yth Grp; Var Stat Bsktbl; Var L Crs Cntry; Cit Awd; High Hon Roll; NHS; Trk; Eagle Scout 86; Educ Assoc Schlrshp 86; PA ST U; Sport/Exercs Sci.

WHITMIRE, CATHIE; Moniteau HS; Petrolia, PA; (Y); 19/133; Drama Clb; Spanish Clb; Hon Roll; NHS; Capt Mbr Tm Spcl Olympns 82-86; Top Slprsn Spanish Clb 84-86; Edinbrough U; Accntng.

WHITMOYER, ALAN; Millville Area HS; Millville, PA; (Y); Church Yth Grp; Band; Chorus; Concert Band; Mrchg Band; School Musical; School Play; JV Bsktbl; JV Socr; Hon Roll; PA Music Edctrs Assn Dist Chrs 85-86; PMEA Dist Bnd, PMEA Rgnl Chorus 86; Carson-Newman Coll; Music.

WHITMYRE, WENDY; Milton SR HS; Milton, PA; (Y); Cmnty Wkr; Sec FHA; Library Aide; Office Aide; Red Cross Aide; Spanish Clb; Yrbk Stf; Hon Roll; Parmdc.

WHITNEY, DENNIS PATRICK; Harbor Creek HS; Harborcreek, PA; (Y); 12/204; Boy Scts; Stage Crew; Variety Show; JV Ftbl; Var L Trk; Var L Wrstlng; NHS; SAR Awd; Marine ROTC 4 Yr Scholar 86; Erie Rep PA Farmers Assn ST Sem 84; Purdue U; Engrng.

WHITSELL, JASON; Otto-Eldred HS; Eldred, PA; (Y); Chorus; School Musical; Hon Roll; Dstrct Chrs Mtls 84-86; Rgnl Chrs Mtl 84-86; ST Chrs Mtl 85-86; Comp Sci.

WHITT, DARYL J; Beaver Area JR-SR HS; Beaver, PA; (Y); 1/200; Boy Scts; German Clb; Pres Key Clb; School Play; Capt Socr; Swmmng; NHS; Ntl Merit SF; Eagl Sct 85; Clemson U; Chmcl Engr.

WHITTAKER, JIM; Cedar Crest HS; Lebanon, PA; (Y); 22/393; VP Latin Clb; Pep Clb; School Musical; Crs Cntry; Capt Swmmng; Hon Roll; NHS; Pres Schlr; Penn ST; Crmnl Jstc.

WHITTICK, JOHN; St John Neumann HS; Philadelphia, PA; (Y); 48/339; Chorus; Concert Band; Im Bsktbl; Hon Roll; Prfct Atten Awd; Temple U; Accntnt.

WHITTINGTON, AMY; Millville HS; Millville, PA; (S); VP Church Yth Grp; Church Choir; School Musical; Yrbk Phtg; VP Soph Cls; VP Jr Cls; Var Capt Cheerleading; Var Fld Hcky; High Hon Roll; NHS; Duke U; Math.

WHITTINGTON, DAWN; Cardinal O Hara HS; Chester, PA; (Y); Pres Church Yth Grp; Cmnty Wkr; Teachers Aide; Chorus; Church Choir; Variety Show; Rep Crs Cntry; Trk; Vllybl; Outstndng Dncr 86; Eastern Coll; Psych.

WHITTLE III, RANDOLPH G; Greater Johnstown HS; Johnstown, PA; (Y); 45/300; Debate Tm; Math Clb; Quiz Bowl; Ski Clb; Band; Concert Band; Jazz Band; Mrchg Band; Orch; Pep Band; IN U Bloomington Schlrshp 86-90; Natl Mus Camp Interlochen Schlrshp 85; 1st Chr Euphonium Mus Camp 85; IN U Bloomington; Orch Cond.

WHITTY, JOHN; Lincoln HS; Canada; (Y); AFS; Boy Scts; Spanish Clb; Socr; AFS To Portugal 86; Scl Wrk.

WHOOLERY, STACI; Fairchance-Georges JR-SR HS; Fairchance, PA; (Y); Drama Clb; French Clb; School Play; Stage Crew; Yrbk Rptr; Yrbk Stf; Score Keeper; Stat Wrstlng; High Hon Roll; Hon Roll.

WHORIC, BRIAN; Southmoreland SR HS; Scottdale, PA; (Y); Cmnty Wkr; VICA; WCCC; Paramedic.

WHORTON, JOHN; Dunmore HS; Dunmore, PA; (Y); Computer Clb; French Clb; Band; Concert Band; Mrchg Band; Nwsp Rptr; Nwsp Stf; Trk; Eng.

WHYE, BRENDA; Greater Works Acad; Mc Keesport, PA; (S); Pres Church Yth Grp; German Clb; Chorus; Church Choir; Yrbk Stf; Rep Jr Cls; Off Stu Cncl; Hon Roll; Jr NHS; Schlrshp Open Bible Coll 85; Yth Mnstry.

WHYTOSEK, EUGENE; Archbishop Wood HS; Ivyland, PA; (Y); 48/282; Spanish Clb; Var Ftbl; Spnsh Awd 85; Penn ST U; Bio.

WIAND, SAMUEL; Middletown Area HS; Middletown, PA; (Y); Am Leg Boys St; Boy Scts; Church Yth Grp; Hon Roll.

WIBECAN, NISSA; Solebury Schl; Brooklyn, NY; (S); Q&S; Nwsp Ed-Chief; Stu Cncl; High Hon Roll; Prosecuting Law.

WIBLE, SHARON L; Baldwin HS; Pittsburgh, PA; (Y); Pres Key Clb; Chorus; Jazz Band; School Musical; Rep Sr Cls; Rep Stu Cncl; Var Tennis; High Hon Roll; Trs NHS; Pres Schlr; U Pittsbrgh Provost Day Germ Lan Comp 85; Outstndng Key Club Pres Awd 86; AATG 84; William & Mary Coll; Pol Sci.

WIBLE, SUSAN; Bethel Park SR HS; Bethel Park, PA; (Y); Pres Church Yth Grp; Chorus; Church Choir; Drm Mjr(t); Swing Chorus; Variety Show; Yrbk Stf; Powder Puff Ftbl; Var Twrlr; Hon Roll; Psych.

WICK, CANDACE C; Butler Area SR HS; Butler, PA; (Y); AFS; Aud/Vis; Hosp Aide; Spanish Clb; Thesps; Jr NHS; Pres Schlr; Pres Schlrshp Amer U 86; Schltc Ltf Natl Jr Hnr Soc 84; The Amer U; Visual Comm.

WICK, JERILYN A; Quaker Valley HS; Sewickley, PA; (Y); 15/168; Q&S; Spanish Clb; Band; Nwsp Phtg; Nwsp Rptr; Nwsp Stf; Yrbk Phtg; Yrbk Rptr; Yrbk Stf; Lit Mag; Natl Acad Fit Awd 86; Pres Acad Fit Awd 86; Math Awd 86; Geneva Coll; Bus.

WICK, RICHARD; Upper Dublin HS; Ft Washington, PA; (Y); 187/351; Cit Awd; Hon Roll; Ntl Merit Ltr; Aud/Vis; Boy Scts; Camera Clb; Church Yth Grp; Computer Clb; Drama Clb; Intnl Clb; US Army.

WICKARD, DEBRA; Big Spring HS; Newville, PA; (Y); 28/198; Church Yth Grp; Hosp Aide; Band; Concert Band; Lit Mag; Hon Roll; Med.

WICKEL, SANDRALEE; North Pocono HS; Moscow, PA; (Y); Church Yth Grp; Cmnty Wkr; Capt Color Guard; Variety Show; Nwsp Ed-Chief; Nwsp Phtg; Nwsp Rptr; Nwsp Stf; VP Soph Cls; High Hon Roll; Keystone JC; Comm.

WICKERHAM, CATHERINE; Shady Side Acad; Pittsburgh, PA; (Y); 10/113; Pres German Clb; Acpl Chr; Chorus; Stage Crew; Ed Yrbk Stf; JV Tennis; Bausch & Lomb Sci Awd; High Hon Roll; Ntl Merit SF; German Awds 83-86; Cum Laude Soc 86; Haverford Coll.

WICKETT, MARCY; Johnsonburg HS; Johnsonburg, PA; (Y); 20/88; Letterman Clb; Library Aide; Varsity Clb; Capt Bsktbl; Score Keeper; Capt Vllybl; MVP Bsktbl 84-86; MVP Vlybl 84-86; Acad All Amer Schlrshp 85-86; Lock Haven.

WICKIZER, NANCY; Old Forge HS; Old Forge, PA; (S); Ski Clb; High Hon Roll; Jr NHS; NHS; Ntl Merit Ltr; Phrmcy.

WICKMAN, DEBORAH L; North Hills HS; Alpharetta, GA; (Y); Am Leg Aux Girls St; Cmnty Wkr; Exploring; Girl Scts; Hosp Aide; Pres JA; Letterman Clb; NFL; Sec Speech Tm; High Hon Roll; Vernon Metz Awd 86; Vlntr Svc Awd-250 Hrs 85; Natl Frnscs Leag 500 Pts Clb 86; U Of GA; Lwyr.

WICKMANN, CHRISTY; Zanareth Area HS; Nazareth, PA; (Y); 39/241; Church Yth Grp; Drama Clb; Key Clb; Band; Church Choir; Color Guard; Concert Band; Flag Corp; Mrchg Band; Pep Band; Clby Coll Wtrvl ME; Blngl Adm.

WIDDOWSON, LAURIE; Interboro HS; Norwood, PA; (S); AFS; Exploring; Latin Clb; SADD; Yrbk Stf; Off Sr Cls; Stu Cncl; JV Var Lcrss; Sec Jr NHS; NHS; Drewxel U; Comp Systms Mgmt.

WIDDUP, JEFFREY B; Waynesburg Central HS; Waynesburg, PA; (Y); 35/204; Cmnty Wkr; Letterman Clb; Spanish Clb; Stu Cncl; Bsbl; Ftbl; Hon Roll; FCA; Antmy, Physlgy Awd 86; 4 Ltrs Bsbll 83-86; 2 Ltrs Ftbl 84-85; Waynesburg Coll; Phrmcy.

WIDDUP, JOSEPH; Waynesburg Central HS; Waynesburg, PA; (Y); 20/205; Spanish Clb; Stu Cncl; Fld Hcky; Wt Lftg; Wrstlng; High Hon Roll; Hon Roll; Spnsh II Awd 84; Waynes Coll; Chem.

WIDMER, JEFFREY; Canevin HS; Bridgeville, PA; (Y); Church Yth Grp; Bsbl; Outstndng Stu; Jrnlsm.

WIDMYER, SCOTT; Sharon SR HS; Sharon, PA; (Y); Computer Clb; French Clb; Office Aide; Radio Clb; SADD; Hon Roll; Acadmc Excllnc Bio 85; Acadmc Achvt Upward Bnd Pgm 85; Astrnmy.

WIDRA, HOWARD; Cheltenham HS; Wyncote, PA; (Y); 29/385; DECA; Temple Yth Grp; Nwsp Rptr; Nwsp Stf; Yrbk Stf; Rep Stu Cncl; Im Bsktbl; Im Bowling; Lcrss; Var Capt Socr; Comet Trails Ldrshp Awd 84; Presdntl Clssrm Prtcptn 86.

WIEAND, LISA; Milton Area SR HS; Milton, PA; (Y); 21/600; Art Clb; Latin Clb; Chorus; School Musical; School Play; Ed Yrbk Ed-Chief; Stu Cncl; JV Fld Hcky; Hon Roll; NHS; NEMA 84; Nrsng.

WIECHECKI, KAREN; Governor Mifflin HS; Mohnton, PA; (Y); 22/300; Latin Clb; Library Aide; Y-Teens; Hon Roll; Prfct Atten Awd; High Hon Roll; Amer Clsscl Leag Latn Awd 84-85; Phildlphia Clsscl Soc Latn Awd 86; RN.

WIECZOREK, KEN; Father Judge HS; Philadelphia, PA; (Y); 1/360; Mathletes; Yrbk Stf; Im Mgr Bsktbl; JV L Crs Cntry; JV L Trk; High Hon Roll; Hon Roll; Jr NHS.

WIECZOREK, KENNETH; Father Judge HS; Philadelphia, PA; (S); 1/360; Mathletes; Yrbk Stf; Im Bsktbl; JV Crs Cntry; JV Trk; High Hon Roll; Hon Roll; NHS.

WIEDEMER, JOSEPH; Bishop Guilfoyle HS; Altoona, PA; (S); 1/145; JA; Red Cross Aide; Science Clb; Chorus; Rep Stu Cncl; High Hon Roll; Hon Roll; NHS; Pre-Med.

WIEDER, DARREN; Lower Moreland HS; Huntington Valley, PA; (S); Aud/Vis; Camera Clb; FBLA; Science Clb; Varsity Clb; Y-Teens; Trk; Bst Cmpr 83; Trk Novice Mdls 83; Photo Awd 85; Accntng.

WIELAND, WENDY S; Chartiers Valley HS; Pittsburgh, PA; (Y); Church Yth Grp; Exploring; FBLA; German Clb; VP JA; Library Aide; Pres Pep Clb; Ski Clb; Church Choir; Yrbk Phtg; Mss Metro Pttsbrgh Ntl Teen 86; 3rd Pl Jb Intrvw Rgnls FBLA 86; 4th Pl Mss PA Ntl Teen 86; Clarion U; Bus Admin.

WIELGOPOLSKI, DONNA MARIE; G A R Memorial HS; Wilkes Barre, PA; (S); 1/178; Letterman Clb; Office Aide; Chorus; Flag Corp; Nwsp Rptr; Var Capt Crs Cntry; L Twrlr; NHS; PA ST U; Chem Engrng.

WIELOCH, PATRICIA; Perry Traditional Acad; Pittsburgh, PA; (Y); 15/139; German Clb; Library Aide; Chorus; Nwsp Rptr; JV Var Vllybl; High Hon Roll; Hon Roll; OH Northern U; Phrmcy.

WIEMANN, KIMBERLY; Seneca Valley HS; Renfrew, PA; (Y); 8/369; Art Clb; Aud/Vis; Church Yth Grp; JA; Scholastic Bowl; Mrchg Band; Hon Roll; Lion Awd; Teachers Aide; Amer Legion Oratorical Cntst Wnnr Cnty & Dist Divs 86; Schlstc Achvmnt Awds 85-86; Wittenberg U; Teaching.

WIERMAN, MOLLY JEANNE; Hanover HS; Hanover, PA; (Y); 13/136; Red Cross Aide; Varsity Clb; Band; Orch; Trs Soph Cls; Trs Pres Stu Cncl; Bsktbl; Tennis; Vllybl; Hon Roll; PA ST U; Bus Adm.

WIEST, KELLY; Upper Dauphin Area HS; Lykens, PA; (Y); 4/112; Library Aide; Band; Chorus; Concert Band; Mrchg Band; JV Bsktbl; JV Sftbl; Hon Roll; NHS; Math Awd 83-85; RN.

WIEST, PATTY; Academy HS; Erie, PA; (S); Color Guard; Mrchg Band; Bowling; Sci.

WIGGINS, BOBBY; Spring-Ford HS; Pottstown, PA; (Y); 68/270; Boy Scts; Cmnty Wkr; Dance Clb; Drama Clb; German Clb; Political Wkr; Science Clb; Ski Clb; Varsity Clb; VP Frsh Cls; Pre-Med.

WIGGINS, WENDY; Meadville Area SR HS; Meadville, PA; (Y); Art Clb; Spanish Clb; Chorus; Var L Gym; Stat Mgr(s); Var L Swmmng; Var L Trk; High Hon Roll; Hon Roll; NHS; Point Park Coll; Bus Mngmnt.

WIGGINS, WILLIAM; Pennsburg HS; Yardley, PA; (Y); German Clb; JV Ftbl; Im Vllybl; Im Wt Lftg; JV Wrstlng; Cit Awd; Hon Roll; Bus.

WIGGLESWORTH, CRAIG; Dover Area HS; Dover, PA; (Y); 26/237; German Clb; Band; Chorus; Concert Band; Variety Show; Rep Frsh Cls; JV Var Socr; Var Tennis; Var Trk; Hon Roll; Music.

WIGMAN, MARILYNN; Bellwood-Antis HS; Altoona, PA; (Y); 40/118; Sec Hosp Aide; Key Clb; Trs Library Aide; Band; Chorus; School Musical; Fld Hcky; Trk; Church Yth Grp; JA; SR Hgh Cnty Band 85-86; Vlntr Svc Pin 86; IN U Of PA; Nrsng.

WIGTON, AMY; Wilmington Area HS; New Wilmington, PA; (Y); Church Yth Grp; Drama Clb; Office Aide; Spanish Clb; Church Choir; Stage Crew; Variety Show; Stat Bsktbl; JV Var Trk; JV Var Vllybl; 3rd Pl Team Bible Quzzng Chmpnshp 83; Trck Hon Roll 86.

WIKE, SHELLEY; Lebanon Catholic HS; Lebanon, PA; (Y); 7/76; FHA; Hosp Aide; Spanish Clb; Ed Yrbk Stf; Var L Bsktbl; Var Sftbl; Hon Roll; NHS; Ntl Merit Ltr; Prfct Atten Awd; Crtfct Hghst Avrg Spnsh Psychlgy 86; Rdlgy.

WILBERT, GEORGIA; Bensalem HS; Bensalem, PA; (Y); Cmnty Wkr; VP Key Clb; Office Aide; Political Wkr; Drill Tm; Rep Sr Cls; Wt Lftg; Hon Roll; Prfct Atten Awd; Promtn Petti Offcr 2nd Cls USNSCC 86; Wheaton Coll; Internl Stdies.

WILCHACKY, GLENN; Archbishopwood Boys HS; Richboro, PA; (Y); Var Golf; Accntng.

WILCOX, MARY; Highlands HS; Tarentum, PA; (Y); Exploring; Hosp Aide; Church Yth Grp; Library Aide; Chorus; Var Sftbl; Hon Roll; Prfct Atten Awd; Pres Phys Fit Awd 86; ICM Schl Bus; Psych.

WILCOX, SARA; Johnstown HS; Johnstown, PA; (Y); Hosp Aide; Math Clb; Speech Tm; Orch; Yrbk Ed-Chief; Rep Stu Cncl; High Hon Roll; NHS; 1st Pl Jostens Sem Jrnlsm Awd 85; 1st Pl Exchng Clb Freedom Shrine Awd 86; Hearing Ther.

WILCOX, SUSAN; Western Beaver HS; Industry, PA; (Y); 9/80; Pres FHA; Pep Clb; Sec SADD; Teachers Aide; Stu Cncl; Bsktbl; High Hon Roll; NHS; Pres Schlr; Indiana U PA; Home Econ.

WILDASIN, TOBY; South Western HS; Hanover, PA; (Y); 32/206; Church Yth Grp; VP Varsity Clb; School Play; Bsktbl; Capt Trk; Hon Roll; Jr NHS; NHS; Horticulture Schlrshp 86; Leo Lawler Mem Schlrshp 86; Mont Alto Penn ST; Forestry.

WILDAY, JENNIFER; Otto-Eldred HS; Eldred, PA; (Y); Church Yth Grp; Varsity Clb; Chorus; Variety Show; Nwsp Stf; Yrbk Stf; Stat Bsktbl; Var Gym; Var Trk; Awds-Trk & Gymnstcs 84-85; Cazenovia; Fash Merch.

WILDMAN, LISA; Sharon SR HS; Sharon, PA; (Y); Art Clb; Drama Clb; Spanish Clb; Thesps; School Musical; School Play; Var Cheerleading; Hon Roll; Art.

WILDS, STEFANIE; Norristown HS; Norristown, PA; (S); 17/485; Church Yth Grp; Key Clb; Ski Clb; Rep Frsh Cls; Rep Soph Cls; Rep Jr Cls; Rep Sr Cls; Pres Stu Cncl; Hon Roll; NHS; Lebanon Valley Coll; Bio.

WILDS, VESTA; Sacred Heart HS; Pittsburgh, PA; (Y); Church Yth Grp; Civic Clb; Cmnty Wkr; Exploring; Girl Scts; Hosp Aide; Library Aide; SADD; Y-Teens; Chorus; Ldrshp Awd 85 & 86; Politcs.

WILENZIK, ROSLYN; Central Bucks East HS; Doylestown, PA; (Y); Sec Frsh Cls; Sec Soph Cls; Sec Jr Cls; Var L Lcrss; Cit Awd; DAR Awd; Hon Roll; Jr NHS; NHS; German Clb; Amer Legn Awd Outstndng All Arnd Stdnt 84; Peer Cnslr 85-86.

WILEY, BRENDA; Lancaster Catholic HS; Lancaster, PA; (Y); 35/218; Pep Clb; Service Clb; Speech Tm; Bsktbl; Var Trk; Hon Roll; 1st Pl Local Hstry Day 83; Cum Laude Awd-Natl Latin Exam 85; 3rd Pl Hstry Day 85; Catholic U Of Amer; Pre-Law.

WILEY, JANET HAZEL; York County Vo Tech; Delta, PA; (Y); 137/408; SADD; Pres VICA; Vllybl; IASA; Lttr JV Vllybll; Pres B-Wk Cbntmkg Shp; Vica Advsrs; Prlmntrn York Vo-Tech SADD Chapt.

WILEY, JOHN; Mapletown HS; Bobtown, PA; (Y); Church Yth Grp; Wt Lftg; Wrstlng; Hon Roll; Electrncs.

WILEY, MARK; Solanco SR HS; Quarryville, PA; (Y); 79/245; Church Yth Grp; Varsity Clb; Acpl Chr; Chorus; Concert Band; Mrchg Band; School Musical; Capt Var Golf; High Hon Roll; Hon Roll; Mst Imprvd Sci Stdnt 85-86; Temple U; Pharm.

WILEY, TAMMY; Lincoln HS; Wampum, PA; (Y); 40/168; French Clb; Hosp Aide; Key Clb; Office Aide; Sec Bowling; Powder Puff Ftbl; Sftbl; High Hon Roll; Hon Roll; IN U PA; Med Tech.

WILFONG, MARIO; Bishop Mc Cort HS; Johnstown, PA; (Y); 10/133; Church Yth Grp; Letterman Clb; Math Clb; Math Tm; Var L Bsbl; Ftbl; High Hon Roll; Mu Alp Tht; NHS; Johnstown Tribune-Dem Paper Carrier Of Mnth 85; U Of Pittsburgh Chem Olympics 86; Acctng.

WILHELM, CHRISTOPHER; Upper Moreland HS; Willow Gr, PA; (Y); 13/256; Church Yth Grp; Trs Key Clb; Scholastic Bowl; VP Church Choir; Orch; Stu Cncl; Var Socr; Var Tennis; Trs NHS; U VA; Chem Engrng.

WILHELM, LISA; Chichester SR HS; Boothwyn, PA; (Y); Band; Chorus; Concert Band; Mrchg Band; Sftbl.

WILHELM, ROB; Steel Valley HS; Munhall, PA; (Y); 25/207; Cmnty Wkr; Letterman Clb; SADD; Varsity Clb; Var L Swmmng; Hon Roll; NHS; MVP H S Swmmng Athlt 85-86; All ST H S Swmmr 86; U Of NC-WILMINGTON; Mrn Bio.

WILHELM, TONYA; Montoursville HS; Montoursville, PA; (Y); 56/174; French Clb; Hosp Aide; Stu Cncl; Mgr(s); Powder Puff Ftbl; Trk; Hon Roll; Bus Mgmt.

WILINSKY, BRAD; Freedom HS; Bethlehem, PA; (Y); 162/456; Exploring; Yrbk Ed-Chief; Yrbk Phtg; Penn ST Bloomsburg; Pre Law.

WILK, JULIE; Glendale HS; Coalport, PA; (Y); 6/98; Pres Church Yth Grp; Science Clb; Co-Capt Drm Mjr(t); Nwsp Stf; Yrbk Stf; High Hon Roll; NHS; Voice Dem Awd; RN.

WILK, KATHIE; Shamokin Area HS; Shamokin, PA; (Y); 14/179; Church Yth Grp; Pep Clb; Science Clb; Varsity Clb; Yrbk Stf; Var L Swmmng; Var L Trk; Im Vllybl; High Hon Roll; Hon Roll; IN U; Nrsg.

WILK, NANCY; Shamokin Area HS; Shamokin, PA; (Y); Church Yth Grp; German Clb; Pep Clb; Science Clb; Varsity Clb; Yrbk Stf; Rep Jr Cls; Swmmng; Trk; Hon Roll; IN U Of PA; Rsprtry Ther.

WILKE, PHILIP; Peters Township HS; Mcmurray, PA; (Y); Intnl Clb; Science Clb; Spanish Clb; Var Swmmng; Var Tennis; High Hon Roll; Hon Roll; Prfct Atten Awd.

WILKERSON, DONALD; Girard Clg; Philadelphia, PA; (Y); 12/30; Camera Clb; Chess Clb; Computer Clb; Math Clb; Band; Sec Soph Cls; Sec Jr Cls; JV Var Bsbl; JV Bsktbl; Mgr Crs Cntry; Heat Treatng Mdl 85-86; U Pittsburgh; Mech Engrg.

WILKES, CHRISTINE; John S Fine HS; Sheatown, PA; (Y); 21/240; Varsity Clb; Chorus; Variety Show; Yrbk Stf; Var Capt Cheerleading; Swmmng; High Hon Roll; NHS; Acad All-Amer Awd 86; PA ST U; Elec Engrng.

WILKES, LAURA; York Catholic HS; York, PA; (Y); Varsity Clb; Nwsp Sprt Ed; Yrbk Rptr; Trk; Vllybl; High Hon Roll; NHS; Sctry Msc Assoc 86; Prtcpnt Dstrct 3 PIAA Trck Mt 86; Mrt Awd 86; Med.

WILKES, MARGARET; York Catholic HS; York, PA; (Y); 2/150; FBLA; Yrbk Stf; Trk; Vllybl; High Hon Roll; NHS; Sal; Spanish Clb; VP Varsity Clb; Chorus; York Cnty Trck Chmpsnshp Meet 86; PIAA Dstrct 3 Tck Met Mutple Mdlst 86; PIAA Tck Chmpshps 4th Pl 86; Bucknell U; Bus.

WILKINS, CHRISTOPHER; Bethel Park SR HS; Bethel Park, PA; (Y); 6/512; Boy Scts; Church Yth Grp; German Clb; SADD; Orch; School Musical; Off Jr Cls; Stu Cncl; God Cntry Awd; High Hon Roll; Eagle Scout 84; Bronze Palm 85; Rep To Schl Brd From Stu Cncl 85-86; ; Pittsburgh Ytth Symphony 85-86; Episcopal Mnstry.

WILKINS, JOE; Wilmington Area HS; Pulaski, PA; (Y); 29/122; Spanish Clb; Chorus; Hon Roll; Westminster; Mgmt.

WILKINS, KELLIE; Shenandoah Valley HS; Shenandoah, PA; (Y); Yrbk Sprt Ed; Off Stu Cncl; Capt Bsktbl; Var Sftbl; Hon Roll; NHS; Acad All Am 84-86; Float Cmmttee 84-86; Bus.

WILKINSON, DAN; Gettysburg SR HS; Gettysburg, PA; (Y); 58/243; Church Yth Grp; Pres VP FFA; Orch; Dnfth Awd; 4-H Awd; ST FFA Judgng Cont Bronze 84; Dekalb Awd 86; FFA Tractr Driving Cont 2nd Pl 85; People To People 86; Farming.

WILKINSON, DOUGLAS; Peters Township HS; Venetia, PA; (Y); 4/236; Church Yth Grp; Key Clb; Science Clb; Church Choir; Nwsp Stf; High Hon Roll; Hon Roll; NHS; Cert & Ltr Of Achvt 83-85; Vtrnry Med.

WILKINSON, JENNIFER; Bishop Conwell HS; Croydon, PA; (Y); 4/255; Cmnty Wkr; French Clb; Library Aide; Q&S; Service Clb; Yrbk Stf; Lit Mag; High Hon Roll; Hon Roll; NHS; Natl Sci Merit Awd; Natl Engl Merit Awd; Acdmc All Amer; Natl Hon Soc; Guidance Rep; Holy Family Coll; Bus Admin.

WILKINSON, RICHARD; Forest Hills HS; Mineral Pt, PA; (Y); 1/156; Scholastic Bowl; Thesps; Band; Concert Band; Jazz Band; Mrchg Band; NHS; Spanish NHS; Drama Clb; Stage Crew.

WILKINSON, WILLIAM; Forest Hills SR HS; Mineral Point, PA; (Y); 1/156; Scholastic Bowl; Speech Tm; Thesps; Band; Jazz Band; Nwsp Rptr; Pres Jr Cls; Stu Cncl; NHS; Jr NHS; Physcl Sci.

WILKS, DANIELLE; Greater Johnstown HS; Johnstown, PA; (Y); Key Clb; Chorus; Color Guard; Mrchg Band; Sec Pres Stu Cncl; Var L Trk; Capt Twrlr; JV Vllybl; High Hon Roll; NHS; Pres Physcl Ftns Awd 84-86; PA ST U; Engrng.

WILL, PHILIP; Somerset Area HS; Friedens, PA; (Y); 19/216; German Clb; High Hon Roll; Mu Alp Tht; NHS; Rnslr Schlrshp From PA ST 86; Pres Adcmc Ftns Awd 85-86; PA ST U; Engrng.

WILL, STEVEN; Middleburg HS; Middleburg, PA; (Y); 2/125; VP Band; Chorus; Concert Band; Jazz Band; Mrchg Band; High Hon Roll; NHS; Pres Schlr; Sal; Am Soc Mech Engnrs Civic Affairs Awd 86; Renssalaer Polytechnic Awd 85; Penn ST U; Mech Engrng.

WILLAIMS, DOUG; Gateway HS; Monroeville, PA; (Y); 30/500; Am Leg Boys St; Stu Cncl; Capt L Bsbl; Coach Actv; L Ftbl; Capt L Wrstlng; Cit Awd; High Hon Roll; NHS; Pres Schlr; NROTC 4 Yr Schlrshp Wnr 86-90; Garden City Wmns Clb Schlr Awd 86; Acadmc Fitnss Awd 86; PA ST U; Med.

WILLAMS, BETH; Bensalem HS; Bensalem, PA; (Y); French Clb; Key Clb; Chorus; Pom Pon; French Hon Soc; Hon Roll; Temple U; Wrtr.

WILLERT, PATRICIA; Cardinal O Hara HS; Woodlyn, PA; (Y); 83/740; Aud/Vis; VP Church Yth Grp; French Clb; Nwsp Stf; Rep Frsh Cls; Rep Soph Cls; Rep Jr Cls; Fld Hcky; Sftbl; NHS; PA ST U; Commuicative Arts.

WILLEY, ELAINE M; Quakertown Community SR HS; Quakertown, PA; (Y); Ski Clb; Sec Trs Chorus; School Musical; Rep Stu Cncl; Var Sftbl; Var Tennis; Hon Roll; Jr NHS; NHS; Pres Schlr; Stu Govt Awd 86; Fordham U; Lbrl Arts.

WILLHEIM, DAWN; Hanover SR HS; Hanover, PA; (Y); Church Yth Grp; SADD; Du Page; Hrtcltr.

WILLIAMS, ADRIENNE; Pen Argyl Area HS; Wind Gap, PA; (Y); 15/117; Red Cross Aide; Ski Clb; Var L Sftbl; High Hon Roll; Hon Roll; Bloomsburg U; Bus Admn.

WILLIAMS, AIMEE; New Hope Solebury HS; New Hope, PA; (Y); 9/78; Drama Clb; Pep Clb; Ski Clb; Spanish Clb; Band; JV Bsktbl; Var Cheerleading; Im Swmmng; Hon Roll; NHS; Span Awd 84; Home Economics 85; Penn ST.

WILLIAMS, ALISSA; New Brighton Area HS; New Brighton, PA; (Y); Exploring; Girl Scts; High Hon Roll; Hon Roll; Grl Sct Gld Awd 86; Auto Maintnc.

WILLIAMS, AMBER E; Unionville HS; Daphne, AL; (Y); 120/300; Church Yth Grp; JA; Church Choir; Nwsp Stf; High Hon Roll; Hon Roll.

WILLIAMS, ANISSA; Manheim Central HS; Manheim, PA; (Y); 17/237; Church Yth Grp; Chorus; Orch; High Hon Roll; NHS; 4-Way Tst Awd 86.

WILLIAMS, APRIL; Cheltenham HS; Loweroch, PA; (Y); Cmnty Wkr; Computer Clb; English Clb; Library Aide; Pep Clb; Band; Chorus; Sec Frsh Cls; Var Bsktbl; Coach Actv; Pre Med.

WILLIAMS, BENJAMIN C; Bishop Mc Devitt HS; Harrisburg, PA; (Y); 43/176; Computer Clb; Science Clb; Engrg.

WILLIAMS, BRENDA; Saegertown HS; Saegertown, PA; (Y); 11/116; Cmnty Wkr; Hosp Aide; Red Cross Aide; Band; Concert Band; Mrchg Band; Pep Band; Hon Roll; Presdntl Acadmc Ftns Awd 86; Meadvl Mdcl Ctr Auxlry Schlrshp 86; PA Rep Free Entrprs Wk 85; Allegheny Coll; Phrmcy.

WILLIAMS, CARA; Purchase Line HS; Clymer, PA; (Y); 5/123; Sec Pep Clb; Spanish Clb; Var Cheerleading; Hon Roll; NHS; Sec Frsh Cls.

WILLIAMS, CATHERINE; Old Forge HS; Old Forge, PA; (S); High Hon Roll; Hon Roll; NHS; Spanish NHS; Mdcl.

WILLIAMS, CHANTEL E; G A R Memorial HS; Wilkes Barre, PA; (S); Church Yth Grp; Teachers Aide; Drm Mjr(t); Twrlr; Hon Roll; NHS; Pres Stu Cncl; NHS Awd 85-86; Hnr Roll Awd 83-84; Wilkes Coll; Htl & Rstrnt Mgmt.

WILLIAMS, CHRIS; Upper Dublin HS; Oreland, PA; (Y); JA; Science Clb; Ski Clb; NHS; Comptd 36th Intl Sci & Engrng Fair 85; Prtcptd Alt 37th Intl Sci & Engrng Fair 86; Ntl Yth Wrld Wtr 86; Oceanography.

WILLIAMS, CHRISTINE KAY; Greencastle-Antrim HS; Greencastle, PA; (Y); 40/187; Cmnty Wkr; Yrbk Sprt Ed; Stat Bsbl; Hon Roll; NHS; Hagerstown Bus Coll; Med Scrtry.

WILLIAMS, CHRISTOPHER; Cardinal Brennan HS; Girardville, PA; (Y); 2/50; Camera Clb; L Ftbl; High Hon Roll; Spanish NHS; Elec.

WILLIAMS, CRAIG; Punxsutawney Area SR HS; Punxsutawney, PA; (Y); French Clb; FBLA; Math Tm; Hon Roll.

WILLIAMS, CURTIS; Trinity Christian HS; Pittsburgh, PA; (S); 2/6; German Clb; Hosp Aide; Acpl Chr; Stage Crew; Variety Show; VP Frsh Cls; VP Soph Cls; Rep Jr Cls; Pres Stu Cncl; Var L Bsktbl; NC A&T; Arch.

WILLIAMS, DANA; Pen Argyl Area HS; Pen Argyl, PA; (Y); 43/154; Art Clb; Pep Clb; Ski Clb; Chorus; Variety Show; JV Cheerleading; Powder Puff Ftbl; Hon Roll; Baum Schl Of Art Schlrshp 85-86; 2nd Pl Objects 3 Arts & Crfts Exhibit 84-85; Kutztown ST U; Cmmnctn.

WILLIAMS, DAWN; Philadelphia HS For Girls; Philadelphia, PA; (Y); Teachers Aide; Off Jr Cls; Tennis; Howard U; Dentstry.

WILLIAMS, DEBBIE; Downingtown SR HS; Exton, PA; (Y); 113/520; Church Yth Grp; SADD; Color Guard; Flag Corp; Mrchg Band; Rep Jr Cls; High Hon Roll; Hon Roll; Pre-Law.

WILLIAMS, DEBBIE; Highlands SR HS; Natrona Heights, PA; (Y); Hosp Aide; Concert Band; Mrchg Band; Pep Band; NHS; Gold Awds 84-85; Brown Awds 83-84 & 85-86; Temple U; Bio.

WILLIAMS, DEBORAH; Donegal HS; Mount Joy, PA; (Y); 1/164; Varsity Clb; Var L Bsktbl; Var L Fld Hcky; Var L Sftbl; High Hon Roll; Pres NHS; Delta Mu Sigma OME Awd; Acctng.

WILLIAMS, DIANE; Penn Trafford HS; Trafford, PA; (Y); Church Yth Grp; Drama Clb; GAA; Hosp Aide; Office Aide; Chorus; Color Guard; High Hon Roll; NHS; Prfct Atten Awd; PA ST.

WILLIAMS, DONNA; Sto-Rox SR HS; Mc Kees Rocks, PA; (Y); Chorus; Trs Soph Cls; Pres Jr Cls; Cit Awd; High Hon Roll; Hon Roll; Jr NHS; Cert Of Acdmc Achvmnt Engl & Civics 84; Temple U; Pre Law.

WILLIAMS, DOUG; Avonworth HS; Pittsbg, PA; (Y); 8/101; Civic Clb; Latin Clb; Yrbk Rptr; Ed Lit Mag; Var L Bsktbl; Cit Awd; High Hon Roll; NHS; Ntl Merit SF; Rotary Awd; Pttsbrgh Pst Gztt-Nwspapr Crrier Of Yr 85; U S Nvl Acad Smmr Smnr 86; Pltcl Sci.

WILLIAMS, H CLINTON; Mars Area SR HS; Mars, PA; (Y); Im Bsktbl; Im Ftbl; Im Sftbl; Im Vllybl; High Hon Roll; Hon Roll; Perfct Atten.

WILLIAMS, HEATHER; Belle Vernon Area HS; Belle Vernon, PA; (Y); Drama Clb; French Clb; JA; Pep Clb; High Hon Roll; NHS; Med.

WILLIAMS, HEIDI; Blair County Christian Schl; Duncansville, PA; (S); 1/11; Church Yth Grp; Teachers Aide; Chorus; Yrbk Ed-Chief; Yrbk Stf; VP Sr Cls; High Hon Roll; Prfct Atten Awd; Val; Keystn Chrstn Eductnl Assoc Bible Tstng 85.

WILLIAMS, JEFFERY; Wyalusing Valley HS; Wyalusing, PA; (Y); Boy Scts; Computer Clb; Spanish Clb; Band; Church Choir; Rep Stu Cncl; JV L Bsktbl; JV Ftbl; JV L Trk; High Hon Roll; Cert Hnrbl Mntn-Outstndng Sci Prjct US Army 86; Air Force Outstndng Achvt Awd-Outstndng Sci Prjct 86; Chem Engrng.

WILLIAMS, JERI D; Canon Mc Mc Millan HS; Canonsburg, PA; (Y); 43/390; French Clb; Y-Teens; Chorus; Church Choir; Yrbk Stf; Trk; High Hon Roll; Hon Roll; Prfct Atten Awd; Shasda Studnt Achvt Awd 86; Med.

WILLIAMS, JIM; Pennsbury HS; Levittown, PA; (Y); Var L Bsbl; Var L Ftbl; Purdue U; Envrnmtl Sci.

WILLIAMS, JOHN C; Panther Valley HS; Coaldale, PA; (Y); 2/110; Am Leg Boys St; ROTC; High Hon Roll; NHS; Prfct Atten Awd; Sal; Recipient Of The Rensselaer Awd For Outstndng Math & Sci 86; Adjutant & Trsr Panther Vly JROTC 85-86.

WILLIAMS, JULIET A; Central HS; Philadelphia, PA; (Y); 4/248; French Clb; Office Aide; Nwsp Rptr; Nwsp Stf; Yrbk Stf; Lit Mag; JV Swmmng; High Hon Roll; Ntl Merit SF; PA Histrcl Soc Essay Cntst 85; Cls Eng Awd 85; Brown U Bk Awd 85; Hist.

WILLIAMS, KAMLA; Little Flower HS; Philadelphia, PA; (Y); 98/448; German Clb; Tennis; Trk; Hon Roll; Csc, Blk Stdnt Leag, AFNA 83-84; Med.

WILLIAMS, KAREN; Butler Area SR HS; Renfrew, PA; (Y); Church Yth Grp; Exploring; Spanish Clb; Chorus; Swing Chorus; Mgr(s); Score Keeper; Timer; Stat Trk; Hon Roll.

WILLIAMS, KEITH; Pen Argyl HS; Pen Argyl, PA; (Y); 19/129; Letterman Clb; Science Clb; Varsity Clb; Bsktbl; Hon Roll; Chem Engrng.

WILLIAMS, KEITH; Trinity Christian HS; Pittsburgh, PA; (S); 3/16; Pres Frsh Cls; Pres Soph Cls; Trs Stu Cncl; Var L Bsktbl; Im Sftbl; Im Trk; Im Vllybl; High Hon Roll; Hon Roll; Jr NHS; Mst Imprvd Bsktbl Plyr 85; Bst Apprnce 85; Arch.

WILLIAMS, KELLI; Jamestown HS; Jamestown, PA; (S); 1/59; VP Spanish Clb; Varsity Clb; Band; Chorus; Church Choir; Pres Sr Cls; Rep Stu Cncl; Var L Bsktbl; High Hon Roll; NHS; Dist Band,Chorus 84-86; Regnl Chorus 86; PA ST U.

WILLIAMS, KELLY; Brandywine Heights HS; Mertztwn, PA; (Y); #7 In Class; Var Fld Hcky; Var Sftbl; NHS; 3 Yr Vrsty Sftbl Awd 86; Acctg I Awd 86; Amer Cult Awd 86; Med.

WILLIAMS, KELLY; Plum SR HS; Pittsburgh, PA; (Y); Dance Clb; Office Aide; Spanish Clb; SADD; Drill Tm; Yrbk Stf; Pom Pon; Sftbl; Trk; Hon Roll; Acctng.

WILLIAMS, KEN; Muhlenberg SR HS; Laureldale, PA; (Y); Boy Scts; Exploring; Band; Concert Band; Jazz Band; Mrchg Band; Orch; Pep Band; School Musical; Trk; Music Educ.

WILLIAMS, KERRY; New Hope-Solebury HS; New Hope, PA; (S); 5/64; AFS; Drama Clb; Chorus; Var Bsktbl; Var Fld Hcky; Var Sftbl; High Hon Roll; NHS; Prfct Atten Awd; School Musical; Spnsh, Frnch Awd 85; Mst Imprvd Sftbl 85; Biol.

WILLIAMS, KRISTIN; Bishop Shanlhan HS; W Chester, PA; (Y); 11/218; Hosp Aide; Band; Sec Chorus; Jazz Band; School Musical; NHS; PA Gov Schl For Arts Music Schlrshp 86; PA ST Chorus 86; Am Music Abroad Chorus 85.

WILLIAMS, LAURA; Cumberland Valley HS; Boiling Springs, PA; (Y); JV Fld Hcky; Hon Roll; Fshn Merch.

WILLIAMS, LORI; Moshannon Valley HS; Smithmill, PA; (Y); 12/164; Spanish Clb; SADD; Pres Band; Concert Band; Mrchg Band; Pep Band; Var Capt Bsktbl; Church Yth Grp; Girl Scts; Varsity Clb; Bus Admn.

WILLIAMS, LORI A; Lehighton Area HS; Lehighton, PA; (Y); 67/269; FHA; Hosp Aide; Color Guard; School Play; Nwsp Stf; Yrbk Stf; High Hon Roll; Hon Roll; Pre Law.

WILLIAMS, LYNNE; Waynesburg Central HS; Waynesburg, PA; (Y); 2/230; Trs Sec AFS; Sec Church Yth Grp; French Clb; Pres Girl Scts; French Hon Soc; NHS; NEDT Awd; Girl Scout Silver Awd 85; Alg,Engl Awd 86.

WILLIAMS, MARIA; Chambersburg Area SR HS; Chambersburg, PA; (Y); 102/641; Varsity Clb; Swmmng; Engrng.

WILLIAMS, MARK; Sharon HS; Sharon, PA; (Y); 44/210; Letterman Clb; Y-Teens; Bsbl; Ftbl; Hon Roll; Mercyhurst; Acctng.

WILLIAMS, MARQUETTE; Corry Area HS; Corry, PA; (S); 27/212; Drama Clb; French Clb; SADD; Band; Concert Band; Jazz Band; Mrchg Band; Pep Band; Psych.

WILLIAMS, MAUREEN; Wallenpaupack Area HS; Greentown, PA; (Y); Camera Clb; NFL; Ski Clb; Nwsp Sprt Ed; VP Stu Cncl; Var Capt Cheerleading; Crs Cntry; L Trk; Hon Roll; VFW Awd; Comm.

WILLIAMS, MELANIE; Conemaugh Township HS; Johnstown, PA; (Y); 2/101; Art Clb; Drama Clb; Var L Trk; Bausch & Lomb Sci Awd; French Hon Soc; Hon Roll; NHS; PA ST U; Lab Psychlgy.

WILLIAMS, MELINDA; Pen Argyl Area HS; Pen Argyl, PA; (Y); Computer Clb; German Clb; Math Clb; Yrbk Stf; JV Var Cheerleading; Hon Roll; Socl Work.

WILLIAMS, MELISSA; East Juniata HS; Richfield, PA; (Y); 14/96; Pres Jr Cls; Pres Stu Cncl; Var L Bsktbl; Var L Fld Hcky; Hon Roll; VFW Awd; Voice Dem Awd; Speech Tm; Varsity Clb; School Play; Outstndng Schltc Athlete 86; Outstndng Female Athlete 86; Dist Trk 84-86; Millersville U.

WILLIAMS, MELISSA; Yough HS; Yukon, PA; (Y); Debate Tm; VICA; Band; Church Choir; Concert Band; Drm Mjr(t); Mrchg Band; Symp Band; Nwsp Phtg; Nwsp Rptr; Graphic Communications Tchr.

WILLIAMS, MICHAEL; C A S HS; Chambersburg, PA; (Y); Varsity Clb; Off Sr Cls; Bsktbl; Ftbl; Trk; All Area Tm Ftbl 85-86; Ldng Tackler Ftbl Tm 85-86; Ldng Scorer Ftbl Tm 85-86; Business Mgmt.

WILLIAMS, MICHELE; Trinity HS; Mechanicsburg, PA; (Y); 15/144; French Clb; Pep Clb; Spanish Clb; Var Trk; Spanish NHS.

WILLIAMS, MICHELLE; Ambridge Area HS; Ambridge, PA; (Y); Cmnty Wkr; JA; Pep Clb; Red Cross Aide; Spanish Clb; SADD; School Musical; Stu Cncl; Hon Roll; OH ST U; Spec Ed Tchr.

WILLIAMS, NICOLE; William Allen HS; Allentown, PA; (Y); German Clb; JA; Band; Nwsp Stf; Hon Roll; Cmmnctns.

WILLIAMS, NOREEN; Saegertown HS; Meadville, PA; (Y); 25/125; French Clb; SADD; Varsity Clb; Rep Sec Stu Cncl; JV Var Cheerleading; JV Var Sftbl; Hon Roll; Pres Physcl Ftns Awd 83-86; Clarion U; Bus Adm.

WILLIAMS, PAMELA; Westinghouse HS; Pittsburgh, PA; (Y); Cmnty Wkr; Science Clb; Teachers Aide; Y-Teens; Chorus; Nwsp Rptr; Rep Stu Cncl; Var Vllybl; High Hon Roll; NHS; Cvl Engr.

WILLIAMS, PEGGY; Western Wayne HS; Lake Ariel, PA; (Y); 28/137; Hosp Aide; Yrbk Stf; Trs Soph Cls; Cheerleading; Vllybl; Hon Roll; Ntl Gftd Prgm 83-87.

WILLIAMS JR, PERRY K; Exeter Township HS; Reading, PA; (Y); 49/205; Varsity Clb; L Socr; L Trk; L Twrlr; L Wrstlng; Penn ST U.

WILLIAMS, PHILIP; Manheim Township HS; Lancaster, PA; (Y); 98/309; Cmnty Wkr; Bsktbl; Ftbl; Hon Roll; Bsktbl All Star 85-86; Millersville; Bus Adm.

WILLIAMS, PRISCILLA; Harry S Truman HS; Levittown, PA; (Y); 101/625; Church Yth Grp; ROTC; Church Choir; Capt Var Bsktbl; Var Capt Trk; Chorus; Nwsp Stf; Var Cheerleading; JV Fld Hcky; Hon Roll; ST 3rd Pl-Shot Put 85-86; Natl 5th Pl-Shot Put 86; Busnss Admin.

WILLIAMS, RANDI K; Lower Dauphin HS; Harrisburg, PA; (Y); Office Aide; Ski Clb; Stage Crew; Frsh Cls; Soph Cls; Jr Cls; Sr Cls; Cheerleading; High Hon Roll; Hon Roll; HAAC; Acctg.

WILLIAMS, RASHEED B; Martin Luther King HS; Philadelphia, PA; (Y); 52/350; Art Clb; PAVAS; Bsbl; Bsktbl; Ftbl; Natl Cnfrnc Artst Awd 86; Tri-ST Awd & Urbn Lg Prntng Awd 85-86; Phila CC; Art.

WILLIAMS, RICHARD; Scranton Technical HS; Scranton, PA; (Y); Art Clb; Boys Clb Am; Church Yth Grp; Exploring; FCA; Ski Clb; VICA; Bowling; Ftbl; Sftbl; Gld Key Awd 83-84; Pillsbury Bapt Coll; Pstrl Stds.

WILLIAMS, RICHARD; Wyoming Valley West HS; Kingston, PA; (Y); Church Yth Grp; Rep Stu Cncl; Var Ftbl; Var L Trk; Cit Awd; Hon Roll; NEDT Awd.

WILLIAMS, ROBERT; Harmony HS; Philipsburgh, PA; (Y); 28/43; VICA; Bsktbl; Im Ftbl; Im Vllybl; Prfct Atten Awd; Acctng.

WILLIAMS, ROSALYND; Penn Hills SR HS; Pittsburgh, PA; (Y); JA; Spanish Clb; Trk; High Hon Roll; Hon Roll; Prfct Atten Awd; Pre Med.

WILLIAMS, SHANI; Wyoming Area SR HS; Falls, PA; (Y); 14/268; French Clb; Key Clb; Stu Cncl; Capt Cheerleading; High Hon Roll; Natl Sci Olympiad 86; Cert Merit Am Hist 86; Sci.

WILLIAMS, SHANNON; Bethlehem Center SR HS; Clarksville, PA; (Y); Art Clb; Church Yth Grp; Spanish Clb; Church Choir; Off Soph Cls; Off Jr Cls; Trk; Hon Roll; Exec Sec.

WILLIAMS, SHANNON; Clearfield HS; Clearfield, PA; (Y); Church Yth Grp; Ski Clb; Spanish Clb; Band; Chorus; Church Choir; Score Keeper; Twrlr; Hon Roll.

WILLIAMS, SHELLEY; Nazareth SR HS; Nazareth, PA; (Y); Church Yth Grp; Key Clb; Church Choir; Ed Nwsp Stf; JV Sftbl; Hon Roll.

WILLIAMS, STEPHANIE; Emmaus HS; Zionsville, PA; (Y); Church Yth Grp; Cmnty Wkr; Dance Clb; Drama Clb; GAA; Key Clb; NFL; Speech Tm; SADD; Thesps; Cedar Crest; Dntl Hyg.

WILLIAMS, STEVEN; Bradford Central Christian HS; Bradford, PA; (Y); Key Clb; SADD; Yrbk Stf; Var L Bsbl; Var L Ftbl; Hon Roll; Ntl Merit Ltr; Ntl Sci Merit Awd 85-86; OBI; Acctg.

WILLIAMS, SUSAN; Swissvale HS; Pittsbuirgh, PA; (Y); 16/213; VP Church Yth Grp; French Clb; Hosp Aide; SADD; Teachers Aide; Y-Teens; Nwsp Rptr; Yrbk Stf; High Hon Roll; NHS; Biomedical Engrng.

WILLIAMS, TAMMY S; Jamestown HS; Hartstown, PA; (Y); Library Aide; Sec Spanish Clb; Sec Trs Varsity Clb; Band; Chorus; Concert Band; Mrchg Band; Pep Band; Stu Cncl; Var Bsktbl; Gannon U; Radiolgy.

WILLIAMS, TERRI; Tyrone Area HS; Altoona, PA; (Y); 4-H; FBLA; FFA; Service Clb; SADD; Varsity Clb; Chorus; VP Soph Cls; VP Jr Cls; Rep Stu Cncl; PA ST; Hrtcltr.

WILLIAMS, TERRY; Western Beaver HS; Industry, PA; (Y); 4-H; Chrmn SADD; Band; Concert Band; Jazz Band; Rep Stu Cncl; Var Bsbl; Var Trk; Var Wt Lftg; Comp Tech; Comp Prog.

WILLIAMS, THOMAS; Wyoming Valley West HS; Swoyerville, PA; (Y); Ski Clb; Im Ftbl; Hon Roll; Yrk Coll; Bhvrl Sci.

WILLIAMS, TODD; Clearfield HS; Woodland, PA; (Y); French Clb; Key Clb; Ski Clb; Sec Sr Cls; Capt Wrstlng; Hon Roll; 2 Time Dist & Regnl Champ Wrstgl 85-86; PIAA ST Wrstlg 85 & 86; Lock Haven U; Mth.

WILLIAMS, TRACEY; Conemaugh Township HS; Johnstown, PA; (Y); Var L Letterman Clb; Stage Crew; Nwsp Stf; Yrbk Stf; Sec Jr Cls; Sec Sr Cls; Rep Stu Cncl; Capt Var Bsktbl; Capt Powder Puff Ftbl; Capt Var Sftbl; Athltc Cncl Awd 86; Cone Twsp Rotary Awd 86; MIP Bsktbl 84-85; 1st Tm Al Cnty Sftbl 86; Stu Cncl Awd 86; Phy Thrpst.

WILLIAMS, TREVOR W; West Catholic High For Boys; Phila, PA; (Y); 25/217; Church Yth Grp; Cmnty Wkr; JA; Bsktbl; Ftbl; Hon Roll; Prfct Atten Awd; U Of Dayton Schlrshp 86-87; U Of MD; Accntng.

WILLIAMS, TROY; Manheim Central HS; Manheim, PA; (Y); JA; Rep Frsh Cls; Rep Soph Cls; Rep Jr Cls; Rep Sr Cls; Rep Stu Cncl; Var L Ftbl; Var L Trk; Var Wt Lftg; High Hon Roll; Electrncs Engrng.

WILLIAMS, WENDY; G A R Memorial HS; Wilkes Barre, PA; (S); Drama Clb; Key Clb; Chorus; Stage Crew; Hon Roll; NHS; Temple U; CPA.

WILLIAMS, WENDY; Harry S Truman HS; Levittown, PA; (Y); Rep Stu Cncl; Var Bsktbl; Var Capt Cheerleading; Coach Actv; Gym; Socr; JV Sftbl; Yth Ftns Achvt Awd 83; Buck Cnty CC; Bus.

WILLIAMS, WILLIAM F; Chambersburg Area SR HS; Chambersburg, PA; (Y); Art Clb; Letterman Clb; Varsity Clb; Var Capt Swmmng; Golden Key Awd Acrylics Scratchbrd & Self Portrait Schltc Art Awd 86; MD Inst; Fine Art.

WILLIAMSON, CHRIS; Greenwood HS; Liverpool, PA; (Y); Chorus; Color Guard; Drill Tm; Yrbk Stf; JV Cheerleading; High Hon Roll; Hon Roll; NHS.

WILLIAMSON, CHRISTINE; Tamaqua HS; Quakake, PA; (Y); Dance Clb; Drama Clb; Library Aide; Band; Chorus; Church Choir; Flag Corp; Mrchg Band; Stage Crew; Nwsp Stf; Phila Coll Textiles; Fash Dsgn.

WILLIAMSON, CRISTAL; Chester HS; Brookhaven, PA; (S); 55/384; Office Aide; Pep Clb; Yrbk Stf; Sec Sr Cls; Mgr Trk; Star Hnrs Prgm 86; Brdcstng.

WILLIAMSON, DAVID; East Stroudsburg Area HS; E Stroudsburg, PA; (Y); 25/245; Nwsp Rptr; Trs Soph Cls; Trs Jr Cls; Trs Sr Cls; Capt Ftbl; Var Wrstlng; Hon Roll; NHS; Rotary Awd; Cmnty Wkr; Acad All-Amer 84-86; Lbrl Arts.

WILLIAMSON, JIM; Philipsburg-Osceola HS; Philipsburg, PA; (Y); 89/250; Art Clb; Letterman Clb; SADD; Yrbk Stf; JV Bsbl; Var L Ftbl; Wt Lftg; JV Wrstlng; 1st Pl Awd Phlipsburg Hstrcl Art Soc 86; UIP Coll; Acad.

WILLIAMSON, MELANIE; Germantown HS; Philadelphia, PA; (Y); Church Yth Grp; French Clb; Hosp Aide; Library Aide; Teachers Aide; Crs Cntry; Var Trk; High Hon Roll; NHS; French Two Hghst Avg Awd 86; NYU; Law.

WILLIAMSON, MICHELLE; Saint Maria Gorett HS; Philadelphia, PA; (Y); 121/475; Math Clb; Teachers Aide; Lit Mag; Rep Soph Cls; Hon Roll; Awd Of Merit For Geom 84; Awd Of Merit For Algebra II 85; Allentown Coll; Accntng.

WILLIAMSON, REBECCA; Blacklick Valley JR SR HS; Nanty-Glo, PA; (S); 9/90; Pres Art Clb; Pres Church Yth Grp; Capt Drm Mjr(t); Yrbk Stf; VP Jr Cls; Sec Sr Cls; Rep Stu Cncl; Bsktbl; Sftbl; ICM Schl Bus; Med Asst.

WILLIAMSON, ROD; Burgettstown Area JR-SR HS; Burgettstown, PA; (Y); 8/176; Church Yth Grp; Chorus; Church Choir; School Musical; School Play; Stu Cncl; High Hon Roll; Jr NHS; Lion Awd; VP NHS; Natl Schl Choral Awd 85-86; Cert Of Hnr 85-86; U Of Pittsburgh; Chem Engrng.

WILLIAMSON, STEPHANNIE; Chambersburg Area HS; Chambersburg, PA; (Y); AFS; Church Yth Grp; Cmnty Wkr; FNA; Girl Scts; Spanish Clb; Sec SADD; Natl Advncd Piano Players Awd 84; Silver Awd Girl Sct 86; Med Tech.

WILLIAMSON, TIA NICOLE; George Westinghouse HS; Pittsburgh, PA; (S); 12/211; Office Aide; Drill Tm; Flag Corp; Variety Show; Yrbk Stf; Stu Cncl; Hon Roll; Acad All Amer 86; Comp Acctnt.

WILLIAMSON, VERNEL; Philipsburg-Osceola Area HS; Philipsburg, PA; (Y); 40/220; Church Yth Grp; Letterman Clb; Pep Clb; SADD; L Band; L Concert Band; L Mrchg Band; Nwsp Stf; Stu Cncl; Capt Cheerleading; Yng Wrtrs Awd 84; PA ST U; Cmnty Dvlpmnt.

WILLIS, AMANDA; Shamokin Area HS; Shamokin, PA; (Y); Pres Art Clb; Cmnty Wkr; Key Clb; Office Aide; Red Cross Aide; Varsity Clb; School Musical; Stage Crew; Variety Show; Nwsp Stf; Coal Twp Almni Assn Schlrshp Awd; Crnll U Schl Grnt; Hmcmng Queens Crt; Cornell U-Ithaca NY; Jrnlsm.

WILLIS, BRUCE; Lock Haven HS; Lock Haven, PA; (Y); 3/244; Model UN; VP Spanish Clb; Pres Band; Chorus; Jazz Band; Gov Hon Prg Awd; High Hon Roll; JP Sousa Awd; Sec NHS; Most Imprvd Soph Awd Band 83-84; Excllnce Humanities Awd, GAPS Cmmnty Svc Awd 85-86; Coll Wm & Mary; Anthropology.

WILLIS, LAURA K; Brookville Area HS; Brookville, PA; (Y); FTA; Varsity Clb; Hst Sec Chorus; Drill Tm; Swing Chorus; Yrbk Stf; Stat Bsktbl; Var Swmmng; Var Trk; Hst NHS; Pres Acdmc Ftns Awd 86; Pres Physcl Ftns Awd 85; Clarion U Of PA.

WILLIS, PAUL MICHAEL; Penn Hills SR HS; Pittsburgh, PA; (Y); Computer Clb; Spanish Clb; Band; Jazz Band; High Hon Roll; Hon Roll; NHS; U Of Ptsbrgh Schlrshp 85; Lamp Of Knwldg 84-86; U Of Ptsbrgh; Pre-Dntl.

WILLITS, RICH; Jersey Shore Area HS; Jersey Shore, PA; (Y); Art Clb; German Clb; Ski Clb; Varsity Clb; Var Bsbl; JV Wrstlng; Hon Roll; Outstndg Achvmnt Awd Scl Stds 85; Schlstc Art Awd Hrrsbrg Ptrt Nws 84; Cntrl PA Schlstc Art Awd 84; Bus Admi.

WILLMAN, ELIZABETH; Red Lion Area SR HS; Red Lion, PA; (Y); 5/327; Cmnty Wkr; Girl Scts; SADD; School Musical; School Play; High Hon Roll; Pres NHS; Ntl Merit Ltr; Pres Schlr; Mgr Fld Hcky; George Washington U Brd Of Trsts Hnr Schlrshp 86; George Washington U; Spch Lang.

WILLNER, TOM; Mansfield HS; Mansfield, PA; (S); French Clb; Chorus; Variety Show; Yrbk Stf; High Hon Roll; NHS; HOBY Fndtn PA Ldrshp Sem; Spce Tech.

WILLOW, TEDDI LEA; West Perry HS; Shermans Dale, PA; (Y); 21/190; Hon Roll; NHS; Pres Acad Fit Awd 86; Shippensburg; Elem Ed.

WILLS, JIM; Central York SR HS; York, PA; (Y); Boy Scts; JA; Concert Band; Mrchg Band; Symp Band; Yrbk Stf; JV Var Socr; Hon Roll; Band Achvt Awd 86; Aerontcl Engrng.

WILLS, TED; Altoona Area HS; Altoona, PA; (Y); Band; Mrchg Band; Hon Roll; Pres Physcl Ftns Awd 83-85; Elect Engr.

WILLSIE, KEITH; Warren Area HS; Russell, PA; (Y); German Clb; Math Tm; Scholastic Bowl; Hon Roll; Ntl Merit SF; M V Ball Awd 86; Homemkr Exten Schlrshp 86; UPB; Comp Sci.

WILLSON, KEVIN; Red Lion Area SR HS; Red Lion, PA; (Y); 30/337; Church Yth Grp; SADD; Varsity Clb; Stage Crew; High Hon Roll; Hon Roll; Var L Socr; York COLL PA; Bus Ed.

WILSON, ALICIA; Bellefonte HS; Bellefonte, PA; (Y); Varsity Clb; Band; Concert Band; Drm Mjr(t); Mrchg Band; Rep Jr Cls; Var L Gym; Var L Trk; High Hon Roll; NHS; PIAA ST Comptn 85; All Arnd Gymnstc Champ 85-86; 3rd Beam PIAA ST Comptn 86; Elem Ed.

WILSON, AMY; Scranton Central HS; Scranton, PA; (Y); Pres Church Yth Grp; NFL; Pres Speech Tm; Thesps; School Play; Mgr Stage Crew; Rep Stu Cncl; High Hon Roll; French Clb; All ST Cast Spch Leag 84-85; Intl Stdnt Ldrshp Inst 85-86; Comm.

WILSON, BARBARA; E L Meyers HS; Wilkes Barre, PA; (Y); Hosp Aide; Var Trk; Hon Roll; Jr NHS; Big Bro/Big Sis Pgm Schl 86-87; Nrsng.

WILSON, BARBARA; Montgomery Area JR SR HS; Montgomery, PA; (Y); Mrchg Band; Pres Jr Cls; Pres Sr Cls; Sec Stu Cncl; Capt Var Bsktbl; Var Trk; NHS; Church Yth Grp; French Clb; Thesps; MVP Bsktbl,Track 85-86; Best Offnsv Plyr Bsktbl 86; Lawyer.

WILSON, BETH; Emmaus HS; Wescosville, PA; (Y); 34/483; Sec Church Yth Grp; Girl Scts; Key Clb; Chorus; Hon Roll; NHS; Prfct Atten Awd; Girl Scouts God Hm & Cntry Awd 83; Silver Awd Girl Scouts 84; Gold Awd Girl Scouts 86; Lincoln Tech Inst; Drftng.

WILSON, BILL; N Pocono HS; Moscow, PA; (Y); Church Yth Grp; Ski Clb; Concert Band; Variety Show; Im Bsbl; Im Bsktbl; Var L Golf; Trk; Var L Vllybl; Accelerated Stu 82-86; Millerville U; Physcs.

WILSON, BRIAN; Selinsgrove Area HS; Selinsgrove, PA; (Y); 21/144; Art Clb; Letterman Clb; Spanish Clb; SADD; Chorus; JV Bsbl; JV Var Bsktbl; Var Crs Cntry; JV Ftbl; JV Var Mgr(s); Navy.

WILSON, BRIAN R; Shippensburg Area Sr HS; Newburg, PA; (Y); SADD; Band; Drm Mjr(t); Orch; School Musical; Variety Show; Swmmng; Lion Awd; NHS; Ntl Merit SF; Elec Engrng.

WILSON, BRYAN K; Cedar Cliff HS; New Cumberland, PA; (Y); 70/242; Var L Crs Cntry; Var Trk; High Hon Roll; Hon Roll; Ntl Merit Ltr; Engrng.

WILSON, CARLA; Elizabethtown Area HS; Elizabethtown, PA; (Y); 56/237; Art Clb; Church Yth Grp; Band; Chorus; Church Choir; Concert Band; Mrchg Band; Orch; Stage Crew; Var L Cheerleading; Intl Rltns.

WILSON, CAROLYN SUE; Huntingdon Area HS; Huntingdon, PA; (Y); 42/223; Trs French Clb; Church Yth Grp; Band; Concert Band; Mrchg Band; Hon Roll; Sci Stu Mnth.

WILSON, CATHY; Plum SR HS; Pittsburgh, PA; (Y); AFS; French Clb; Color Guard; Hon Roll; Penn ST; Bus.

WILSON, CHRIS; Mt Pleasant Area SR HS; Mt Pleasant, PA; (Y); Band; Concert Band; Mrchg Band; Pep Band; Im Bsktbl; Im Ftbl; Im Sftbl; Im Tennis; Im Vllybl.

WILSON, CHRISTINE; Elizabeth Forward HS; Elizabeth, PA; (Y); 76/312; Church Yth Grp; French Clb; Pres Chorus; School Musical; Yrbk Sprt Ed; Var Sftbl; Var Capt Vllybl; Hon Roll; Frgn Lang Schlrshp At Gannon U 85; PA Msc Edctrs Assn Dstrct Choir 86; Acdmc Schlrshp Gannon U 86; Gannon U; Intl Bus.

WILSON, CORINNE; Butler SR HS; Butler, PA; (Y); Church Yth Grp; Pres JA; Radio Clb; Spanish Clb; Church Choir; Yrbk Rptr; La Roche; Art.

WILSON, DAWN M; Mc Keesport Area HS; Mckeesport, PA; (Y); French Clb; Library Aide; Scholastic Bowl; School Play; Stage Crew; Variety Show; Hon Roll; Hgh Hnrs Grad 86; Mst Hlpfl Fml Awd 83-86; Edinboro U Of PA; Psych.

WILSON, DENNIS; Central Dauphin HS; Harrisburg, PA; (Y); 12/386; Boys Clb Am; Boy Scts; Church Yth Grp; Band; Chorus; Church Choir; Concert Band; Jazz Band; Madrigals; Mrchg Band; Coll Profssr.

WILSON, ELLEN; Wissahickon SR HS; Ambler, PA; (S); 47/277; Church Yth Grp; Key Clb; SADD; Varsity Clb; Rep Jr Cls; Stu Cncl; Var Capt Cheerleading; Capt Powder Puff Ftbl; L Trk; Hon Roll; Sub I All Lg Tm 85; PIAA Mdl Trk 85; Advrtsmnt.

WILSON, EVELYN; Blacklick Valley HS; Twin Rocks, PA; (S); 6/90; VP German Clb; Sec NFL; Concert Band; Mrchg Band; School Play; Yrbk Stf; Stat Trk; Hon Roll; NHS; German Natl Hnr Soc 84; U Of Pittsburgh; Phrmcst.

WILSON, GARY; Shaler Area SR HS; Glenshaw, PA; (Y); 245/517; Church Yth Grp; FHA; JA; Teachers Aide; Yrbk Phtg; Achvt Co Yr 85; Culinary Inst Am; Chef.

WILSON, JAMES; Roxborough HS; Philadelphia, PA; (Y); 60/330; Church Yth Grp; Chorus; Church Choir; Var L Bsbl; TN U; Aerspc Engr.

WILSON, JAMES; William Allen HS; Allentown, PA; (Y); 4/600; German Clb; Stage Crew; Lit Mag; Rep Jr Cls; High Hon Roll; NHS; Ntl Merit Ltr; Rep Soph Cls; Dartmouth Bk Awd 86; Physics Plympics Tm Cptn 86; Contmpry Affairs Clb 84-86.

WILSON, JANICE; Saegertown HS; Meadville, PA; (Y); 8/117; Pres Sec Church Yth Grp; Computer Clb; Spanish Clb; SADD; Band; Church Choir; Concert Band; Mrchg Band; Pep Band; Variety Show; Messiah Coll; Phys Ther.

WILSON, JENNIFER; Wyalusing Valley HS; Wyalusing, PA; (Y); 1/151; Pres VP Church Yth Grp; Scholastic Bowl; SADD; Chorus; School Musical; Var Crs Cntry; NHS; Drama Clb; Spanish Clb; Band; Pres Acad Fit Awd 86; Susquehanna U Blough Schlrp 86; Sr All-Amer Hl Of Fm Bnd Hnrs 86; Susquehanna U; Bus Admin.

WILSON, JODI; The Baptist HS; Clarks Summit, PA; (Y); 4/15; Chorus; Church Choir; School Musical; Yrbk Bus Mgr; Yrbk Ed-Chief; Bsktbl; Cheerleading; Socr; Hon Roll; Ntl Talents Christ 1st Pl Girls Voice 85; Cedarville Coll; Sec.

WILSON, KATHLEEN; Harbor Creek HS; Erie, PA; (Y); 67/228; Spanish Clb; Chorus; Var Trk; Northwest Inst; Cosmtlgy.

WILSON, KEN; Bethel Park SR HS; Bethel Park, PA; (Y); FBLA; JV Ftbl; Hon Roll.

WILSON, KENNETH; West Perry HS; Shermansdale, PA; (Y); 48/197; Spanish Clb; Varsity Clb; Rep Stu Cncl; Bsbl; Bsktbl; Ftbl; Hon Roll; Mid PA Div III All Star Bsbl 86; Natl Hstry & Govt Achvt Awd 85; US Army Res Schlr/Ath Awd 86; Lebanon Vly Coll; Comp Sci.

WILSON, LA WANDA; The Christian Acad; Chester, PA; (S); 8/68; Cmnty Wkr; Acpl Chr; Chorus; Sec Soph Cls; Pres Jr Cls; Var L Cheerleading; High Hon Roll; Hon Roll; Sec Trs NHS; Stu Of Mnth 86; Dstnghsd Chrstn HS Stu 86; Rutgers U; Ind Psych.

WILSON, MELISSA; Rochester Area HS; Rochester, PA; (Y); 4/96; DECA; Ski Clb; Nwsp Stf; Yrbk Ed-Chief; Yrbk Stf; JV Cheerleading; L Trk; Hon Roll; NHS; Beaver Cnty Tms Acadmc Al-Star 86 & 86.

WILSON, PAMELA; Altoona Area HS; Altoona, PA; (S); 23/683; Sec Church Yth Grp; VP SADD; Chorus; Church Choir; Socr; Sftbl; High Hon Roll; Hon Roll; NHS; School Musical; Cert Hon Men Cum Laude Outstndg Prfrmnce Natl Lat Exam 84; CVMH Schl Nrsg; BSN.

WILSON, PARRISH; South Philadelphia HS; Philadelphia, PA; (Y); Aud/Vis; Boy Scts; Church Yth Grp; Cmnty Wkr; Computer Clb; Dance Clb; 4-H; Radio Clb; Church Choir; Stu Cncl; Incentive Awd 85; Law.

WILSON, RENE; Carmichaels Area SR HS; Carmichaels, PA; (Y); 15/100; Am Leg Aux Girls St; Ski Clb; Spanish Clb; Varsity Clb; Band; Church Choir; Concert Band; Mrchg Band; Stu Cncl; Cheerleading; Jnr Stndng Cmmtte 85-86; Pres-Sdlty Of St Hugh Chrch; Accntng.

WILSON, SARAH TERI; Germantown HS; Philadelphia, PA; (Y); Mathletes; Teachers Aide; Sftbl; Hon Roll; Star Spnsh Awd 85; Rites Of Passg 86; Temple U; Comptr Sci.

WILSON, SCOTT; Saegertown HS; Santee, CA; (Y); Aud/Vis; Boy Scts; Exploring; Library Aide; Bsktbl; San Diego ST U; Telecmmnctns.

WILSON, SERENA; Reynolds HS; Greenville, PA; (Y); 32/132; Latin Clb; Library Aide; Math Clb; Science Clb; Nwsp Rptr; Med.

WILSON, SHANNON; Fairchance Georges SR HS; Fairchance, PA; (Y); Band; Concert Band; Mrchg Band; High Hon Roll; Hon Roll; Jr NHS.

WILSON, SHERYL L; Henderson HS; West Chester, PA; (Y); 104/342; JCL; Office Aide; Red Cross Aide; Ski Clb; Chorus; Yrbk Stf; Rep Soph Cls; Var JV Fld Hcky; Var Sftbl; Hon Roll; Bloomsburg U PA; Cmmnctns.

WILSON, STACEY; Norwin HS; N Huntingdon, PA; (Y); 181/550; Trs Ski Clb; SADD; Band; Jazz Band; Mrchg Band; Var Diving; Hon Roll; Indiana U Of PA; Accntg.

WILSON, STEVAN; Harrisburg Acad; Camp Hill, PA; (Y); Boy Scts; Church Yth Grp; Quiz Bowl; Trs Jr Cls; God Cntry Awd; Ntl Merit SF; Charles E Dahl Awd Outstndng Achvt Math And Sci 86; Math Cntst 1st 86; Coop Summr Schlrshp 86; Carnegie Mellon U; Engrg.

WILSON, THOMAS; Bethlehem Catholic HS; Bethlehem, PA; (Y); 14/201; Church Yth Grp; Key Clb; Math Tm; Model UN; NFL; Political Wkr; Scholastic Bowl; Nwsp Ed-Chief; Nwsp Rptr; Yrbk Stf; Pltcl Sci.

WILSON, ZANETTA; Jefferson-Morgan HS; Clarksville, PA; (Y); Intnl Clb; Spanish Clb; SADD; Church Choir; School Play; Variety Show; Yrbk Stf; Rep Jr Cls; Pres Sr Cls; Rep Stu Cncl; Gregg Typing Awd 85; WV U; Law.

WILT, AMBER LYNNE; Hollidaysburg Area SR HS; Duncansville, PA; (Y); Church Yth Grp; Pep Clb; Science Clb; Chorus; Church Choir; Orch; Trs Stu Cncl; Stat Bsktbl; Cit Awd; NHS; Messiah Coll; Bio.

WILT, CRYSTAL; Shippensburg Area SR HS; Shippensburg, PA; (Y); Cmnty Wkr; FBLA; FHA; Aud/Vis; Nwsp Rptr; Lit Mag; Cheerleading; High Hon Roll; NHS; Spanish NHS; Nrsng.

WILT, FAITH; Millersburg Area HS; Millersburg, PA; (Y); Church Yth Grp; Band; Stu Cncl; Bsktbl; Sftbl; Hon Roll; NHS; French Clb; Dist Band 86.

WILT, GREGORY; Mmi Preperatory Schl; Mountaintop, PA; (S); 5/32; Debate Tm; Model UN; VP Jr Cls; Rep Stu Cncl; Var L Bowling; JV Golf; VP Tennis; NHS; Ntl Merit Ltr; NEDT Awd; Bst Debator; Bst Assmbly; JETS Test Cert; Elec Engrng.

WILT, KIMBERLY ANN; Penn Cambria SR HS; Cresson, PA; (Y); 23/185; Drama Clb; NFL; Spanish Clb; Speech Tm; Band; JV Capt Cheerleading; Hon Roll; NHS; IN U Of PA; Cmmnctns.

WILTROUT, STEPHEN; Connellsville Area HS; Normalville, PA; (Y); 95/550; Church Yth Grp; Spanish Clb; Church Choir; L Trk; High Hon Roll; Hon Roll; Prfct Atten Awd; Ryl Rngrs Gld Mdl Achvmnt Rcpnt 83; Ryl Rngrs Natl Ryl Rngr Yr Cntstn 85; Upwrd Bnd Prgrm CA U 85.

WILTROUT, STEVE; Rockwood Area HS; Markleton, PA; (Y); Spanish Clb; Hon Roll; Sharp Shooter-Rifle Club 84-85; Army.

WILTSCHEK, WALTER; Christian School Of York; York, PA; (S); Rep Church Yth Grp; Ed Yrbk Stf; Trs Stu Cncl; High Hon Roll; Math Tm; Band; Nwsp Stf; Natl Hist Olym 1st Pl Soph Cls 85; Math Educ.

WINCEK, CATHLEEN; Penns Manor HS; Clymer, PA; (Y); FBLA; SADD; Band; Color Guard; Concert Band; Mrchg Band; Pep Band; Yrbk Stf; Rep Stu Cncl; Stat Trk; IN U Of PA; Elem Educ.

WINCEK, TINA; Penns Manor HS; Clymer, PA; (Y); 20/70; Church Yth Grp; French Clb; Girl Scts; SADD; Band; Concert Band; Drill Tm; Mrchg Band; Orch; Pep Band; PA ST; Elem Educ.

WINCK JR, DWIGHT; Everett Area HS; Breezewood, PA; (Y); Art Clb; Computer Clb; 4-H; JV Ftbl; Var Trk; Var Wrstlng; Hon Roll; Elctrcn.

WINDHORST, KELLY SUE; Chartiers Valley HS; Pittsburgh, PA; (Y); 11/336; Pres Church Yth Grp; Dance Clb; Pres FBLA; Golf; NHS; Pres Schlr; Pep Clb; Ski Clb; School Musical; Trk; PTA Schlrp 86; FBLA Rgnl Comptn 1st Pl Clrk Typst 2 86; Indiana U Of PA; Mgmt Inf Syst.

WINDISH, RICHARD; Saucon Valley SR HS; Hellertown, PA; (Y); 26/150; Concert Band; Jazz Band; Mrchg Band; Pep Band; Var L Bsktbl; Var L Ftbl; Var L Trk; High Hon Roll; Natl Athltc Merit Endrsmnt Svc 86; Engrng.

WINDLE, DIANE; Upper Darby HS; Lansdowne, PA; (Y); JV Bsktbl; JV Var Fld Hcky; JV Sftbl; Hon Roll; Elem Educ.

WINDSHEIMER, BENJAMIN; Burgettstown JR SR HS; Burgettstown, PA; (Y); 4-H; Ski Clb; Band; Concert Band; Mrchg Band; Pep Band; 4-H Awd; Hon Roll; Rookie Yr Bnd 84; Ag.

WINEBARGER, GLENDA; Northern Lebanon HS; Jonestown, PA; (Y); 45/166; VP Trs Church Yth Grp; Sec SADD; Band; Chorus; Church Choir; Concert Band; Mrchg Band; School Musical; School Play; Var Tennis; Home Econ.

WINEBARGER, JULIE; Northern Lebanon HS; Jonestown, PA; (Y); 1/167; Sec Church Yth Grp; Exploring; Color Guard; Mrchg Band; High Hon Roll; Hon Roll; Lion Awd; NHS; Grad Magna Cum Laude 86; Outstndng Stu Am Gov,Chem 85-86; Susquehanna U; Chem.

WINEBARK, LISA; Punysutawney Area HS; Rossiter, PA; (Y); Aud/Vis; Pres Church Yth Grp; Sec FBLA; Office Aide; Varsity Clb; Var Co-Capt Cheerleading; Hon Roll; Prfct Atten Awd.

WINEGRAD, GWYNETH N; Harriton HS; Penn Valley, PA; (Y); Nwsp Ed-Chief; Nwsp Rptr; Nwsp Stf; Ed Lit Mag; Var Capt Fld Hcky; JV Var Lcrss; Var Capt Swmmng; High Hon Roll; NHS; Ntl Merit SF; Phila Hockey Fstvl-Orlando 82; Natl Cncl Tchrs Eng Wrtg Cont 84; Wrt Poem For US Natrlztn Ceremony 84; Engl.

WINELAND, MARSHA; Meadville SR HS; Meadville, PA; (Y); 70/280; Letterman Clb; Nwsp Rptr; Rep Stu Cncl; Var Capt Swmmng; NHS; Reunir Sorty; OH Northern U; Pharm.

WINEY, DENISE; Garden Spot HS; New Holland, PA; (Y); 10/225; Church Yth Grp; Drama Clb; Quiz Bowl; Spanish Clb; Chorus; Church Choir; School Musical; Rep Jr Cls; JV Sftbl; Var Trk; Eastern Nazarene Coll; Psych.

WINFIELD, MICHAEL; Bethel Park SR HS; Bethel Park, PA; (Y); Acpl Chr; Chorus; School Musical; Swing Chorus; Variety Show; JV Ftbl; High Hon Roll; NHS.

WINFREE, SONJA; Ridley SR HS; Folsom, PA; (Y); 100/473; Church Yth Grp; Teachers Aide; Chorus; Drill Tm; Flag Corp; Mrchg Band; Yrbk Stf; Fld Hcky; Vllybl; Cit Awd; Elem Educ.

WINFREY, KEVIN; Morrisville HS; Morrisville, PA; (Y); 12/100; Quiz Bowl; Yrbk Rptr; Lit Mag; Pres Stu Cncl; Var Bsktbl; Var Ftbl; Hon Roll; Bus.

WINGARD, BARRY; Brookville Area HS; Brookville, PA; (Y); Pres Art Clb; Pres Church Yth Grp; French Clb; Library Aide; Church Choir; Stage Crew; Variety Show.

WINGARD, BOYD; Forest Hills SR HS; South Fork, PA; (Y); Art Clb; Ski Clb; Ftbl; Hon Roll; U Pittsburgh Johnstwn; Bus Mgmt.

WINGARD, KEVIN; West Middlesex HS; Sharon, PA; (S); #2 In Class; Pres Church Yth Grp; Chorus; Swing Chorus; Rep Stu Cncl; Var Bsbl; Var L Ftbl; High Hon Roll; Jr NHS; NHS; Spanish NHS.

WINGARD, SHELLY; Connellsvilel HS; Dunbar, PA; (Y); 38/484; Camera Clb; Church Yth Grp; Hosp Aide; Pep Clb; NHS; Prfct Atten Awd; Spanish NHS; Upward Bnd CA Coll, CA Pa 83-86; Hghst Achvt Sci 83-84; Hghst Achvt Engl 83-84; CA Coll; Accntng.

WINGARD, STEVEN; Millersburg Area HS; Millersburg, PA; (Y); Church Yth Grp; Varsity Clb; Church Choir; Yrbk Stf; Rep Frsh Cls; Rep Soph Cls; Rep Jr Cls; Bsktbl; Ftbl; Hon Roll; Geogrphy.

WINGER, JILL; Susquenita HS; Duncannon, PA; (S); 7/153; Sec Trs Spanish Clb; Chorus; Rep Stu Cncl; Capt Cheerleading; High Hon Roll; Hon Roll; NHS; NEDT Awd; Nrsng.

WINGERD, STEPHANIE; Chambersburg Area SR HS; Chambersburg, PA; (Y); 30/641; Sec Trs Church Yth Grp; JCL; Concert Band; Mrchg Band; High Hon Roll; JR Clsscl Leag Convtn 2nd Pl Grmmr Test 85; Accntng.

WINGERT, CHRISTOPHER; South Western HS; Hanover, PA; (Y); Pres Key Clb; Quiz Bowl; Varsity Clb; Yrbk Stf; Pres Frsh Cls; Pres Soph Cls; Rep Stu Cncl; JV Ftbl; Var Capt Tennis; Hugh O Brien Yth Ldrshp Ambsdr 85; Congsnl Yth Ldrshp 86.

WINGETT, JODI; Trinity HS; Washington, PA; (Y); Church Yth Grp; Concert Band; Mrchg Band; Trk; Prtcptd Cncrt Band & Mrchng Band; Srgcl Tech.

WINGROVE, ELISABETH; Mt Carmel Christian HS; Vanderbilt, PA; (Y); 1/5; Trs Church Yth Grp; Science Clb; Chorus; School Play; Stage Crew; Yrbk Ed-Chief; L Vllybl; Val; Church Choir; Hon Roll; 1st Pl Rgnl & ST KCEA Bible Memory Cmptn 85; 1st Pl Rgnl & St KCEA NT Bible Knwldg Cmptn 86; Bob Jones U; Pblshng.

WINKLEBLECH, AMY; Montrose Area HS; Montrose, PA; (Y); Church Yth Grp; French Clb; SADD; Band; Concert Band; Mrchg Band; Nwsp Stf; Yrbk Stf; Rep Stu Cncl; Messiah Coll; Behavrl Sci.

WINKLEBLECH, LISA; Bentworth HS; Finleyville, PA; (Y); 31/141; FBLA; Varsity Clb; Stu Cncl; Bsktbl; Robert Morris Coll; Acctg.

WINKLER, DANIEL; Kutztown Area HS; Kutztown, PA; (Y); Band; Jazz Band; Stu Cncl; High Hon Roll; Hon Roll; NHS; Rep Frsh Cls; VP Soph Cls; Rep Jr Cls; Var Socr; Elec Engrng.

WINKLER, DAVID; Governor Mifflin HS; Shillington, PA; (Y); 62/266; Computer Clb; Band; Concert Band; Jazz Band; Mrchg Band; Orch; Pep Band; Hon Roll; Cnty Band 83-84; Cnty Band-3 Outstndng Brass Solst Awds-Trmbn 84-85; Cnty Band 85-86; Engrng.

WINKLER, LARAINE; Fairview HS; Fairview, PA; (Y); Cmnty Wkr; Drama Clb; French Clb; German Clb.

WINKLER, ROBERT; Bangor Area SR HS; Bangor, PA; (Y); Rep Soph Cls; L Golf; High Hon Roll; Lion Awd; Army ROTC Scholar 86; PA Motor Truck Assn Scholar 86; Lehigh U Trustee Scholar 86; Lehigh U; Elec Engrng.

WINKOWSKI, DAVID; St Josephs Prep; Philadelphia, PA; (Y); Red Cross Aide; Var L Ftbl; Wt Lftg; High Hon Roll; Exemplary Stu Awd 84-85.

WINKOWSKI, ROBERT; Bethel Park SR HS; Pittsburgh, PA; (Y); Church Yth Grp; JV Bsktbl; Bowling Green ST U; Acctg.

WINNE, SUZANNE; Reading Central Catholic HS; Mt Penn, PA; (Y); Office Aide; Pep Clb; Spanish Clb; Chorus; Flag Corp; Mrchg Band; School Musical; School Play; Variety Show; Hon Roll; Reading Hosp Schl; Nrsng.

WINROW, KIP; Mansfield JR SR HS; Mansfield, PA; (S); Boy Scts; VP Key Clb; Ski Clb; Band; Trs Jr Cls; Rep Stu Cncl; Crs Cntry; Trk; High Hon Roll; NHS.

WINSHEIMER, LISA; William Penn SR HS; York, PA; (S); Hosp Aide; Pep Clb; Chorus; Church Choir; Jazz Band; Mrchg Band; Trs Orch; Symp Band; Jr NHS; Sec NHS.

WINSLOW, JONATHAN; Swissvale Of Woodland Hills Schl; Pittsburgh, PA; (Y); 9/193; VP French Clb; Model UN; Q&S; Varsity Clb; Acpl Chr; School Musical; Nwsp Ed-Chief; Nwsp Rptr; Nwsp Sprt Ed; Rep Soph Cls; Bahai Peace Essay 1st Pl 86; PA Gov Schl Intrntl Stds 85; Civic Clb Schlrshp 86; Dickinson Coll; Intrntl Stds.

WINTER, BETH ANN; Mccaskey HS; Lancaster, PA; (Y); 5/468; Sec Church Yth Grp; Sec Band; Jazz Band; DAR Awd; Hon Roll; NHS; Opt Clb Awd; Pres Schlr; VP Spanish NHS; Am Bus Womans Assoc Schrlshp 86; Dickinson; Pub Rel.

WINTER, GLENDA; Jersey Shore HS; Williamsport, PA; (Y); Church Yth Grp; Drama Clb; French Clb; FBLA; Rep Soph Cls; Mat Maids; Hon Roll; Scndry Ed.

WINTER, LISA; Jersey Shore Area HS; Williamsport, PA; (Y); Church Yth Grp; French Clb; FBLA; Model UN; Ski Clb; Chorus; Church Choir; Drm Mjr(t); School Musical; School Play; Mst Outstndg FBLA Mbr 85-86; Dist & Reg Chorus Fest 85-86; Vocal Perfmncs; Europe 86 Clb; Liberty U; Bus Admin.

WINTER, THERESA; Jersey Shore SR HS; Williamsport, PA; (Y); Cmnty Wkr; Drama Clb; FBLA; Girl Scts; Pep Clb; Rep Soph Cls; Rep Jr Cls; Mat Maids; High Hon Roll; Cert Merit Currnt Evnts 84; Walk A Thn Musclr Dystrphy 84-85; Penn ST U; Recrtnl Thrpy.

WINTERHALTER, ERIK; Mary Fuller Frazier HS; Dawson, PA; (Y); Spanish Clb; Ed Yrbk Phtg; Pres Jr Cls; Rep Stu Cncl; Im Capt Ftbl; Penn ST; Admin Of Justice.

WINTERMANTEL, MARY; Avonworth HS; Pittsbg, PA; (Y); 5/118; AFS; Pres French Clb; High Hon Roll; NHS; N Boroughs Intl Yth Awd 85; Stanford Achvt Test Cert 86; Sys Anlyst.

WINTERS, GUY; Bishop Kenrick HS; Marmora, NJ; (Y); 23/304; Cmnty Wkr; Debate Tm; Science Clb; Pres Spanish Clb; Nwsp Rptr; Nwsp Stf; Stu Cncl; JV Swmmng; JV Trk; Hon Roll; Lehigh; Accntng.

WINTERS, LISA; Shaler Area HS; Pittsburgh, PA; (Y); 179/538; Church Yth Grp; High Hon Roll; Hon Roll; Gregg Shorthnd Speed Awd 86; Sawyer Schl; Travl.

WINTERS, RODNEY; Brookville Area HS; Brookville, PA; (Y); Boy Scts; Pres Church Yth Grp; German Clb; Varsity Clb; School Musical; Pres Frsh Cls; VP Soph Cls; VP Jr Cls; Stu Cncl; L Var Ftbl; U PA; Ind Engrng.

WIRDZEK, ADAM; Connellsville HS; Acme, PA; (Y); 99/520; Cmnty Wkr; Drama Clb; Band; Chorus; Concert Band; Jazz Band; Mrchg Band; Orch; Pep Band; School Musical; PA ST Senate Citatn 85; Mc Donalds All Amer H S Mrchg Bnd, Jazz Bnd 85-86; PA Govnrs Schl Art 85; Berklee Coll Music; Music.

WIRICK, KIRSTIE; Windber Area HS; Windber, PA; (Y); Art Clb; Cheerleading; Hon Roll; Stu Of Mnth 85; Pres Physcl Ftns Awd 85; Bus.

WIRSCHAL, MARION A; Dallastown Area HS; York, PA; (Y); 36/332; Varsity Clb; Chorus; Crs Cntry; Trk; High Hon Roll; NHS; Pres Schlr; Ski Clb; School Play; Yrbk Stf; Pres Phys Fit Awds 80-85; YCIAA East Div Crs Cntry Champ 84; Dist III AAA Girls Trk Champ 84; Penn ST U; Bus Adm.

WIRTH, ED; East Pennsboro Area HS; Camp Hill, PA; (Y); 9/190; German Clb; Camp Fr Inc; Mrchg Band; School Musical; Stu Cncl; Socr; Trk; NHS; Dist Band; Lebanon Vly; Bio Chmstry.

WIRTH, GREG; Norwin HS; N Huntingdon, PA; (Y); 158/577; Church Yth Grp; German Clb; Letterman Clb; Rep Frsh Cls; JV Ftbl; Var L Trk; Var Wt Lftg; Prfct Atten Awd; 5th Pl Medl ST Comptn Pole Vlt 86; 5th Pl Medl WPIAL Fnls Pole Vlt 86.

WIRTH, JULIE; Shikellamy HS; Sunbury, PA; (Y); French Clb; German Clb; Yrbk Stf; Trs Frsh Cls; VP Soph Cls; Sec Stu Cncl; Cheerleading; Trk; Hon Roll; Shippensburg U; Bus Mgmt.

WIRTNER, MELANIE; Bethel Park HS; Bethel Park, PA; (Y); 112/519; Var L Swmmng; Hon Roll; All-Amrcn 100 Yd Bttrfly 85; All-Amrcn 200 Yd Freestyl & ST Chmpn 85&86; All-Amrcn 500 Yd Freestyl 86; Bio.

WISCOUNT, BETH; Pine Grove Area HS; Tremont, PA; (Y); School Musical; Yrbk Stf; Trs Frsh Cls; Rep Jr Cls; Im Mgr Ftbl; Im Mgr Tennis; Hon Roll; Accntng.

WISE, FAWN; Northwestern HS; Cranesville, PA; (Y); Church Yth Grp; Drama Clb; Chorus; School Play; Cheerleading; Trk; Hon Roll; Edinboro U; Psych.

WISE, JENNIFER; Pocono Mountain HS; Scotrun, PA; (Y); 50/278; Pep Clb; Band; Concert Band; Rep Frsh Cls; JV Var Fld Hcky; Var Powder Puff Ftbl; JV Var Trk; Hon Roll; Natl Guild Piano Adtns 83-84; Natl Sci Olympd 84-85; Atty.

WISE, KEVIN; Cocalico HS; Reinholds, PA; (Y); Camera Clb; Chess Clb; Computer Clb; Science Clb; Stage Crew; Var Trk; Wt Lftg; JV Wrstlng; Cert SS Wrk 85; Marine Sci Consrtm 85; Coast Guard.

WISE, LENORE; Plum SR HS; Murrysville, PA; (Y); 80/415; Pres Church Yth Grp; French Clb; Library Aide; Sec Chorus; Church Choir; School Musical; Hon Roll; Ntl Merit Ltr; Ntl Schl Chrl Awd 86; Brigham Yng U; Music Ed.

WISE, MILLICENT; Donegal HS; Marietta, PA; (Y); Church Yth Grp; Drama Clb; 4-H; Band; Concert Band; Mrchg Band; 4-H Awd; Attnd Rotary Intl Ldrshp Cmp 86; Pre-Law.

WISE, ONDA; Bellwood-Antis HS; Bellwood, PA; (Y); 4/118; Sec Church Yth Grp; Key Clb; Ski Clb; Varsity Clb; Trs Stu Cncl; Var Fld Hcky; Var Trk; Sec NHS; Stu Cncl Awd 86; Acad All Am 86; Acctng.

WISE, RICH; Riverview HS; Verona, PA; (Y); Hon Roll; Accntng.

WISELEY, COLLEEN; West Catholic Girls HS; Philadelphia, PA; (Y); 6/245; French Clb; School Play; Nwsp Stf; Pres Stu Cncl; L Bsktbl; DAR Awd; Hon Roll; NHS; Pres Schlr; Sal; Prsdntl Schlrshp Grnt 86; Acadmc Fitnss Awd 86; Sci Fair 2nd Pl 84; Phila Coll Text & Sci; Bus.

WISEMAN, ROBERT; St Josephs Prep; Philadelphia, PA; (Y); 23/239; Lit Mag; Im Bsktbl; JV Wrstlng; Hon Roll; Ntl Merit SF; PA; Engl.

WISHCHUK, MARYELLEN; Allentown Central Catholic HS; Allentown, PA; (Y); 31/231; Math Clb; Ski Clb; Yrbk Ed-Chief; Stu Cncl; Capt Sftbl; High Hon Roll; NHS; Church Yth Grp; Pep Clb; Trs Spanish Clb; Schlstc Schlrshp 86-90; PJAS 1st Plc Rgnls 3rd Plc ST 84; Bg Brthrs/Bg Sistrs Sftbl All-Strs 86; Mt St Marys Coll.

WISINSKI, MELANIE; Seneca HS; Erie, PA; (Y); Sec Church Yth Grp; Computer Clb; Pep Clb; Drill Tm; Sec Soph Cls; Sec Jr Cls; Var L Cheerleading; Hon Roll; Mercyhurst Coll; Accntng.

WISNIEWSKI, DENISE; Hatboro-Horsham SR HS; Horsham, PA; (Y); Church Yth Grp; 4-H; French Clb; Yrbk Phtg; Yrbk Stf; JV Cheerleading; Powder Puff Ftbl; Athltc Trng.

WISNIEWSKI, EDWARD; Iroquois JR SR HS; Erie, PA; (Y); 19/150; Church Yth Grp; Capt Computer Clb; Letterman Clb; Bowling; Var L Ftbl; Var L Ice Hcky; Var L Trk; Hon Roll; NHS; Natl Math Exm; Penn ST; Comp Sci.

WISNIEWSKI, JOHN; Hampton HS; Gibsonia, PA; (Y); 42/255; Church Yth Grp; JV Bsbl; L Ftbl; Hon Roll; Ntl Merit Ltr; Engrng.

WISNIEWSKI, LEONARD; Father Judge HS; Philadelphia, PA; (S); Cmnty Wkr; Mathletes; Red Cross Aide; Concert Band; Capt Mrchg Band; Ed Nwsp Stf; Var L Crs Cntry; Var L Trk; High Hon Roll; NHS; Mayfair Monarcus Char Awd 83; Union Lg Good Ctznshp Awd 84; Cert Merit Hgh SAT 85; Mth.

WISNIEWSKI, RAYMOND; North East Catholic HS; Philadelphia, PA; (Y); 53/312; Aud/Vis; Church Yth Grp; Jr NHS; NHS; Tv/Radio Brdcstng.

WISNIEWSKI, STACEY; Bishop Shanahan HS; West Chester, PA; (Y); 5/214; Hosp Aide; Mathletes; SADD; Yrbk Stf; Var Tennis; High Hon Roll; NHS; Office Aide; Varsity Clb; Julius Margolis Scholar Awd 85; MVP Ten 84-86; Toni Lee Mem Awd 85; Franklin & Marshall; Bio.

WISOR, JONATHAN; Phoenixville Area HS; Phoenixville, PA; (Y); 5/210; Church Yth Grp; Quiz Bowl; SADD; JV Trk; JV Wrstlng; High Hon Roll; Hon Roll; NHS; Mst Outstndng Stu Of Yr-Spnsh 85-86; Mst Outstndng Stu Of Yr-Drvrs Ed 85-86.

WISOR, SHANNONDEL; Clear Field HS; W Decatur, PA; (Y); Church Yth Grp; Cmnty Wkr; Dance Clb; JA; VICA; Var Bsbl; High Hon Roll; Hon Roll.

WISSER, JOAN; Northwestern Lehigh HS; New Tripoli, PA; (Y); 13/126; Pres 4-H; Sec Trs Band; Concert Band; School Play; Var Crs Cntry; JV Fld Hcky; JV Stat Trk; Hon Roll; NHS; 4-H Awd; Pres Acad Fit Awd 86; Kutztown U; Secndry Mth Ed.

WISSER, KIM; Hamburg Area HS; Hamburg, PA; (Y); 50/152; Pres Latin Clb; Library Aide; Ski Clb; Yrbk Stf; Stu Cncl; Fld Hcky; Trk; Hon Roll; Outstndng Latin 86; Acad Ltr Awd Latin 86; Millersville U.

WISSINGER, DONNA; Marion Center HS; Home, PA; (Y); 34/156; FBLA; Office Aide; Mrchg Band; Pres Frsh Cls; Pres Soph Cls; Pres Jr Cls; Stu Cncl; Co-Capt Twrlr; Hon Roll; Punysutawney Beauty Acad; Csmtg.

WISSLER, CHRISTA; Manheim Township HS; Lancaster, PA; (Y); Church Yth Grp; Y-Teens; JV Bsktbl; Im Sftbl; Hon Roll; Engl.

WISSLER, MICHELLE; Solanco HS; Quarryville, PA; (Y); 78/235; Varsity Clb; Concert Band; Jazz Band; Mrchg Band; Orch; Fld Hcky; Trk; High Hon Roll; Hon Roll; Nrsng.

WITCOSKI, JOHN C; Neshaminy HS; Levittown, PA; (Y); 14/735; Boy Scts; Chess Clb; Trs Service Clb; Orch; Nwsp Stf; Cit Awd; High Hon Roll; NHS; Eagle Sct 86; Pre-Med.

WITCOSKI, SUZANNA; Shenandoah Valley HS; Shenandoah, PA; (Y); 28/102; Yrbk Ed-Chief; Rep Soph Cls; VP Jr Cls; VP Sr Cls; VP Stu Cncl; Cheerleading; Gym; Sftbl; Hon Roll; Jr Spring Qn 85; 1st Degree Black Belt 83; Bloomsburg U.

WITHERELL, MELISSA; Warren Area HS; Warren, PA; (Y); 25/275; German Clb; Acpl Chr; Band; Orch; School Musical; School Play; Cit Awd; Jr NHS; England/Scotland Tour 85; Music Awd Outstndng Marchng Band 86; Pres Awd 86; Grove City Coll; Math.

WITHERITE, SHEREE; Bald Eagle Area HS; Snow Shoe, PA; (S); Church Yth Grp; Chorus; Church Choir; Yrbk Stf; Powder Puff Ftbl; High Hon Roll; Hon Roll; NHS; PA ST U; Bus Adm.

WITHROW, DENISE; Du Bois Area HS; Du Bois, PA; (Y); Chess Clb; Intnl Clb; Chorus; School Musical; Hon Roll; Snr Chrl Awd 86; Wilma Boyd Career Schl; Trvl.

WITIAK, ALISSA; Liberty HS; Bethlehem, PA; (Y); 33/475; Church Yth Grp; School Musical; Lit Mag; Rep Sr Cls; Var Swmmng; Var Capt Tennis; Var Trk; Hon Roll; Sec NHS; Key Clb; Rep Of Librty Hugh O Brien Yth Ldrshp Sem 85.

WITMER, AMY; Newport HS; Liverpool, PA; (Y); 4-H; FTA; Teachers Aide; Band; Color Guard; Mrchg Band; School Play; 4-H Awd; Hon Roll; NHS; Educ.

WITMER JR, GARY; East Pennsboro HS; Enola, PA; (Y); Latin Clb; Varsity Clb; Var L Ftbl; Var Trk; Var Wt Lftg; Var Wrstlng; Hon Roll; Prof Ftbl.

WITMER, LORRI; Manheim Township HS; Lancaster, PA; (Y); 199/325; Church Yth Grp; Color Guard; Mrchg Band; Var Trk; Hon Roll; Psych.

WITMER, MELISSA; Shikellamy HS; Sunbury, PA; (Y); French Clb; School Musical; School Play; Rep Jr Cls; Capt Cheerleading; Elem Tchr.

WITONSKY, SHELLEY; Montoursville HS; Montoursville, PA; (Y); Art Clb; French Clb; Ski Clb; Mrchg Band; School Musical; School Play; Powder Puff Ftbl; Trk; Twrlr; Phrmcy.

WITOWICH, MICHAEL D; Ambridge Area SR HS; Ambridge, PA; (Y); English Clb; French Clb; Pep Clb; Chorus; School Musical; Swing Chorus; Trk; Hon Roll; PMEA Hnrs Chorus 85; PMEA Dist V Chorus, Rgn I ST Chorus 85 & 86; IN U Of PA; Music Educ.

WITT, BRENT; Connellsville Area HS; Connellsville, PA; (Y); Church Yth Grp; Leo Clb; Library Aide; VICA; Chorus; School Musical; School Play; Var Crs Cntry; JV Trk; High Hon Roll; Fayette Cnty Rstrnt Assoc 86; Jhnsn & Wls Acad Schlrshp 86; Dstngshd Vstng Chf Schlrshp 86; Jhnsn & Wls Coll; Clnry Arts.

WITT, CATHERINE; Villa Maria Acad; Broomall, PA; (Y); 1/97; JCL; Capt Mathletes; Quiz Bowl; Scholastic Bowl; Yrbk Ed-Chief; Rep Jr Cls; Rep Sr Cls; Lcrss; Hon Roll; NCTE Awd; Mu Alpha Theta Pres; Latin Hnr Soc Pres 85-86; Natl Merit Scholar 86; Pres Scholar 86; Benf Hudson Schol; Chem.

WITT, NADINE; Harry S Truman HS; Levittown, PA; (Y); #65 In Class; Chorus; L Bsktbl; JV L Bowling; L Trk; Hon Roll; Chem.

WITTER, GINNY; Tunkhannock Area HS; Tunkhannock, PA; (Y); 86/320; Aud/Vis; German Clb; Girl Scts; Letterman Clb; Rep Jr Cls; Rep Sr Cls; Var Capt Fld Hcky; Var L Trk; Stat Wrstlng; Hon Roll; Acctng & Athltc Awd 86; MVP-CTZNS Voice All Strs, Fld Hcky, Unico All Strs, Tm Ldr All Stars 85; Shippensburg U; CPA.

WITTIG, ANDY; Exeter Twp SR HS; Reading, PA; (Y); 12/240; Key Clb; Letterman Clb; Varsity Clb; VP Soph Cls; Rep Jr Cls; Rep Sr Cls; Var Wrstlng; Hon Roll; Pres Jr NHS; Amer Lgn Awd 84; Mech Engrng.

WITTMAN, PAMELA; Catasauqua HS; Catasauqua, PA; (Y); 5/140; Am Leg Aux Girls St; Drama Clb; Hosp Aide; Ski Clb; Church Choir; Yrbk Stf; Trs Stu Cncl; Fld Hcky; Hon Roll; NHS; Acad All Am Awd 86; Ntl Sci Merita Wd 86; PA Coll; Toxiclgy.

WITTMANN, BRIAN; Northeastern HS; Manchester, PA; (Y); Chess Clb; JA; Hon Roll; NHS; PA ST U; Comp Pgmr.

WIVELL, NANCY; Spring Grove SR HS; Seven Valleys, PA; (Y); 41/285; Church Yth Grp; Nwsp Bus Mgr; Nwsp Stf; JV Bsktbl; JV Trk; High Hon Roll; Chld Devlpmnt.

WODARSKI JR, ROBERT; Plymouth White Marsh HS; Conshohocken, PA; (Y); Office Aide; Rptr VICA; Hon Roll; Williamsn Trd Schl; Mchn Shop.

WOEBER, TEENA K; North Allenghey SR HS; Wexford, PA; (Y); VP JA; Model UN; Variety Show; VP Trs Stu Cncl; Powder Puff Ftbl; Var L Socr; Hon Roll; NHS; Ntl Merit Schol; Eckerd Coll Pres Schlrshp 86; US Army Rsrv Natl Schlr/Athlt Awd 86; US Army Rsrv Natl Essy Cntst Wnr; Eckerd Coll; Intl Rltns.

WOELFLING, R JOHN; Cedar Crest HS; Lebanon, PA; (Y); French Clb; Pep Clb; Trk; Vllybl; Hon Roll; Arch.

WOESSNER, LORI S; Conrad Weiser HS; Robesonia, PA; (Y); 45/139; FBLA; Chorus; School Play; Var Cheerleading; Hon Roll; Acctg Awd 84-85; Performing Arts Philadelphia.

WOGINRICH, CHERIE; Northampton SR HS; Northampton, PA; (Y); 16/444; AFS; Leo Clb; Teachers Aide; Rep Stu Cncl; Bsktbl; Var Powder Puff Ftbl; Var Trk; High Hon Roll; Hon Roll; NHS; Bloomsburg U; Nrs.

WOITKO, KIMBERLY J; Hazleton HS; Hazleton, PA; (Y); Drama Clb; FBLA; Pep Clb; Ski Clb; School Musical; Yrbk Ed-Chief; Hon Roll.

WOJCIECHOWICZ, KAREN; John S Fine SR HS; Mocanaqua, PA; (Y); CAP; ROTC; Church Choir; High Hon Roll; Hon Roll; Ntl Merit Ltr; Acct I High Hnr Cert Awd 86; Bus Math II High Hnr Awd 86; Sec Awd 86; Bus Mgmt.

WOJCIECHOWSKI, THERESA; Mid Valley HS; Dickson City, PA; (Y); JA; Yrbk Stf; Coach Actv; Hon Roll.

WOJCIK, JULIE; Western Wayne HS; Aldenville, PA; (Y); Pres VP 4-H; Pres FFA; Concert Band; Mrchg Band; 4-H Awd; NHS; 4-H IFYE Ambssdr To Denmark 86; Vet.

WOJCIK, MICHAEL; St Pius X HS; Schwenksville, PA; (S); Science Clb; Ed Yrbk Phtg; Yrbk Rptr; Yrbk Stf; High Hon Roll; Hon Roll; NEDT Awd; Comptr.

WOJCIK, PAUL; South Allegheny HS; Port Voe, PA; (S); 30/170; Pres Band; Concert Band; Jazz Band; Mrchg Band; Pep Band; School Musical; Rep Jr Cls; Rep Sr Cls; Hon Roll; VP NHS; Med.

WOJNAKOWSKI, PAM; Villa Maria Acad; Erie, PA; (Y); 42/133; Civic Clb; Cmnty Wkr; Intnl Clb; Model UN; Ski Clb; Yrbk Rptr; Hon Roll; NHS; NEDT Awd; Bus.

WOJNAROWSKI, CAROLYN; Geibel HS; Scottdale, PA; (Y); Pres Girl Scts; Pep Clb; Ski Clb; Var L Sftbl; Hon Roll; Bus Mgmnt.

WOJNAROWSKI, DARLENE; West Greene HS; Wind Ridge, PA; (S); 7/72; Dance Clb; French Clb; Band; Chorus; Concert Band; Jazz Band; Mrchg Band; Trs Jr Cls; Trs Sr Cls; Sec Trs Stu Cncl; Hmcmg Qn 85; Dist Band 86; Cnty Band 83-86; U Of Pittsburgh; Elctrcl Engrng.

WOJTKOWSKI, TIM; Yough HS; West Newton, PA; (Y); 56/224; Spanish Clb; NHS; U Pittsburgh; Comp Sci.

WOLAND, DARLENE; Halifax Area HS; Halifax, PA; (S); 2/100; FBLA; Chorus; Color Guard; Drill Tm; Yrbk Stf; Powder Puff Ftbl; NHS; Prfct Atten Awd; Regn 15 FBLA 1st Pl Bus Engl 86; Mst Studious 86; Harrisburg Area CC; Acctng.

WOLBERT, WENDY; East Stroudsburg HS; E Stroudsburg, PA; (Y); 11/204; Art Clb; Cmnty Wkr; Concert Band; Jazz Band; Mrchg Band; Pep Band; Stu Cncl; Cit Awd; High Hon Roll; NHS; Smithfield Schlrshp 86; Band Parents Schlrshp 86; Flory Miller Awd 86; Kutctown U; Art Ed.

WOLCOTT, RICHARD; Harbor Creek HS; Erie, PA; (Y); 55/228; Computer Clb.

WOLCZAK, BARBARA; Pittston Area HS; Pittston, PA; (Y); 20/332; Church Yth Grp; Library Aide; Math Clb; Science Clb; Church Choir; Yrbk Stf; Stat Trk; High Hon Roll; NHS; Cert Of Achvt 83-86; Schlrshp Kings Clg 86; Pres Acadmc Ftns Awd 86; Kings College; Acctg.

WOLESAGLE, STEVE; Chichester SR HS; Boothwyn, PA; (Y); Spanish Clb; JV Bsktbl; Hon Roll; Jr NHS; Spanish NHS.

WOLF, ALBERT; Bethel Park HS; Bethel Park, PA; (Y); Science Clb; Orch; School Musical; Var L Swmmng; High Hon Roll; NHS; Mbr Pittsburgh Yth Symph Orch 85-86; PMEA Dist Orch 85-86.

WOLF, DARREN; Turtle Creek HS; N Braddock, PA; (Y); 3/189; Spanish Clb; Var L Ftbl; Var L Socr; Im Vllybl; Bausch & Lomb Sci Awd; High Hon Roll; Opt Clb Awd; Computer Clb; Exploring; ROTC 4-Yr Schlrshp 86; US Army Rsrv Natl Schlr/Athlt Awd 86; Carnegie Mellon U; Engrng.

WOLF III, DONALD HENRY; Palmyra Area HS; Palmyra, PA; (Y); 66/186; Aud/Vis; Boy Scts; Drama Clb; Band; Jazz Band; School Play; Yrbk Phtg; Trk; Hon Roll; US Naval Acad; Engrng.

WOLF, DOUGLAS; Selinsgrove Area HS; Selinsgrove, PA; (Y); 29/214; Spanish Clb; JV Ftbl; Im Vllybl; Hon Roll; Schl Lttr Hnr Roll 84-86.

WOLF, ELIZABETH; Big Spring HS; Carlisle, PA; (Y); 1/220; Trs Church Yth Grp; Varsity Clb; Chorus; Church Choir; VP Sr Cls; Var L Cheerleading; Powder Puff Ftbl; Var L Trk; NHS; Val; $4000 SICO Schlrshp; Gftd & Tlntd Pgm; Acadmc Lttr; Shippensburg U; Acctng.

WOLF, ERIC; Warwick HS; Lititz, PA; (Y); 13/235; Pres Model UN; High Hon Roll; NCTE Awd; NHS; Ntl Merit SF; Pres Schlr; 1st Prz Ntl Schlstc Wrtng Awds 86; Amherst Coll; Physcis.

WOLF, JENNIFER LYNN; James Buchanan HS; St Thomas, PA; (Y); 24/201; Church Yth Grp; Drama Clb; Chorus; Church Choir; Swing Chorus; Powder Puff Ftbl; Hon Roll; NHS; Cert Of Disngshd Serv Educ Musc Chrs 85-86; Point Park Clg; Dnc.

WOLF, JILL; Ephrata SR HS; Ephrata, PA; (Y); 49/257; Church Yth Grp; Cmnty Wkr; FFA; Church Choir; Vllybl; Hon Roll; Star Greenhnd Awd 86; Natl FFA 1st Yr Florcltr Awd 86; Natl FFA 3rd Pl Florcltr ST Wnnr 86; Williamsport CC; Florcltr.

WOLF, JOSEPH; Du Bois Area HS; Dubois, PA; (Y); #25 In Class; Church Yth Grp; German Clb; Band; Concert Band; Jazz Band; Mrchg Band; School Musical; School Play; Hon Roll; US Navy; Law Enfrcmnt.

WOLF, SCOTT; New Oxford HS; New Oxford, PA; (Y); 11/201; FCA; Varsity Clb; Rep Stu Cncl; Var Capt Bsbl; Var Capt Bsktbl; High Hon Roll; Outstndng Male Athlete 86; VMP Bsktbll 86; Athletic Training.

WOLFE, CATHY; Hanover SR HS; Hanover, PA; (Y); 9/137; Varsity Clb; Concert Band; Jazz Band; Mrchg Band; Var L Bsktbl; Var Capt Vllybl; High Hon Roll; Hon Roll; NHS; Rotary Awd; Vlybl MIP Awd; Vlybl Outstndng Plyr Awd; Messiah Coll; Math.

WOLFE, CHRISTINA; Bellwood Antis HS; Altoona, PA; (Y); Church Yth Grp; Sec SADD; Church Choir; School Musical; School Play; Sec Yrbk Stf; JV Var Cheerleading; High Hon Roll; NHS; Teachers Aide; Hghst Acadmc Engl Avg 84-85; Acclrtd Chrstn Educ Intl Cnvntn-1st Pl Awd-Radio Pgm 84-85; Liberty U-VA; Elem Educ.

WOLFE, CHRISTY; Northern Lebanon HS; Jonestown, PA; (Y); 12/174; Spanish Clb; Band; Chorus; Concert Band; Mrchg Band; School Musical; School Play; Hon Roll; SR Outstndg Engl 86; Bloomsburg U; Journlsm.

WOLFE, DAVID; Northern Lebanon HS; Annville, PA; (Y); 23/177; Church Yth Grp; FCA; Varsity Clb; Ftbl; Trk; Wrstlng; Hon Roll; Spanish NHS.

WOLFE, DEBORAH; Pennsbury HS; Morrisville, PA; (Y); Yrbk Phtg; Yrbk Stf; Hon Roll; Phila Art Inst; Photo.

WOLFE, HENRY; Elk Co Christian HS; St Marys, PA; (Y); 36/98; Pres Church Yth Grp; Office Aide; Red Cross Aide; Yrbk Ed-Chief; Off Jr Cls; Off Sr Cls; Rep Stu Cncl; Stat Mgr Bsktbl; Stat Mgr Ftbl; Robert Morris Coll; Bus Mgmt.

WOLFE, JEFF; Bellwood-Antis HS; Tyrone, PA; (Y); Art Clb; Church Yth Grp; JA; Ski Clb; Chorus; Stage Crew.

WOLFE, JENNY; Northern Lebanon HS; Jonestown, PA; (Y); VP 4-H; Varsity Clb; Var Capt Cheerleading; Trk; 4-H Awd; Foreign Lang Intrprtr.

WOLFE, JULIA; Elk County Christian HS; St Marys, PA; (S); Capt Vllybl; High Hon Roll; Action Interact Clb 82-86; Psych.

WOLFE, JULIE; Berwick Area SR HS; Berwick, PA; (Y); 12/219; Var Capt Bsktbl; Var Capt Fld Hcky; Var L Sftbl; High Hon Roll; NHS; Prss-Entrprs Athlt Wk Bsktbl & Sftbl 86; Mst Vlbl Plyr Prss-Entrprs All-Str Bsktnl Tm 86.

WOLFE, JULIE; Youngsville HS; Youngsville, PA; (Y); Ski Clb; SADD; Color Guard; Concert Band; Mrchg Band; Yrbk Stf; Sec VP Stu Cncl; Trk; Wt Lftg; Hon Roll.

WOLFE, KIMBERLY A; Garden Spot HS; New Holland, PA; (Y); Drama Clb; Chorus; Church Choir; Stage Crew; Hon Roll; Jr NHS; NHS; Mdcl Fld.

WOLFE, LISA ANN; North Allegheny SR HS; Mars, PA; (S); DECA; ROTC; Drill Tm; VFW Awd; Air Force Assoc Mdl 85; 2nd Pl Apprrl & Accssrs Dist DECA Cmptn 85 & 1st Pl 86; Rtl Mrchndsng.

WOLFE, LORI; Elk County Christian HS; St Marys, PA; (S); Cmnty Wkr; Library Aide; Office Aide; Political Wkr; SADD; Score Keeper; Stat Vllybl; High Hon Roll; NHS; Cathlc Dghtr Amer Poetry Cntst 83-84; Bus Admin.

WOLFE, MIKE; Cardinal O Hara HS; Glenolden, PA; (Y); French Clb; Pep Clb; Science Clb; JV L Ftbl; Hon Roll.

WOLFE, SUSAN; Annville-Cleona HS; Annville, PA; (S); 4/121; Math Tm; Pres Varsity Clb; Chorus; Yrbk Stf; Pres Frsh Cls; Var Bsktbl; Var Fld Hcky; Stat Ftbl; Var Trk; NHS; All Star Hcky Tm 84 & 85; Elem Ed.

WOLFE, TRACI; Marion Center Area HS; Indiana, PA; (Y); 47/168; SADD; Varsity Clb; Var Bsktbl; Var Sftbl; Var Vllybl; Hon Roll; Jr NHS; Sftbl MVP 85 & 86; Mst Imprvd Grls Bsktbl Plyr 85-86; 1st Tm Gztlnd Sftbl 85 & 86; Phys Ed.

WOLFE, TRACY; Northern Lebanon HS; Jonestown, PA; (Y); VP Exploring; German Clb; Varsity Clb; School Play; Tennis; MVP In Tnns 84-86; U Of Pittsburgh; Pysch.

WOLFF, MARGEE; Greensburg-Salem SR HS; New Alexandria, PA; (Y); 6/324; AFS; Drama Clb; Pres 4-H; German Clb; Girl Scts; VP Chorus; Church Choir; School Musical; Variety Show; Yrbk Stf; PA ST Outstndng 4-H Grl 85; PA ST 4-H Achvt Wnnr 85; 2nd Pl ST Pblc Spkng Cntst 85; Engl.

WOLFGANG, DEBBIE; Middletown Area HS; Middletown, PA; (Y); 28/196; FBLA; Library Aide; Band; Color Guard; Mrchg Band; School Play; High Hon Roll; Hon Roll; Harrisburg Area CC; Acctng.

WOLFGANG, LISA; Shikellamy HS; Sunbury, PA; (Y); 49/304; Am Leg Aux Girls St; VP Church Yth Grp; Trs Spanish Clb; VP SADD; Yrbk Stf; Hon Roll; Geisinger Med Ctr; Nrsng.

WOLFGANG JR, RAYMOND F; Central Dauphin HS; Harrisburg, PA; (Y); Church Yth Grp; Cmnty Wkr; Rep Sr Cls; Var Ftbl; Var Capt Trk; Im Vllybl; Awd Voluntrs Amer 85-86; Juniata Coll; Wildlife Consrvtn.

WOLFINGER, AIMEE; Avonworth JR SR HS; Pittsbg, PA; (Y); AFS; Nwsp Stf; Yrbk Stf; Rep Stu Cncl; Stat Bsbl; Cheerleading; High Hon Roll; Hon Roll; Awd Scoring In 90 Pct Or Above On Achvt Tests 85-86; Business.

WOLFORD, CHRISTY; Hillidaysburg Area SR HS; Hollidaysburg, PA; (Y); 56/351; Hon Roll.

WOLFORD, JUDY; Beaver Area HS; Beaver, PA; (Y); 14/177; Church Yth Grp; Cmnty Wkr; FCA; Hosp Aide; JCL; Key Clb; Latin Clb; Pep Clb; Rep Stu Cncl; Var Sftbl; Cls Awd; Accntng.

WOLGEMUTH, ERIC; Manheim Township HS; Lancaster, PA; (Y); Quiz Bowl; Band; Chorus; Church Choir; Orch; School Musical; Vllybl; Bausch & Lomb Sci Awd; High Hon Roll; NHS; Ntl Mrt Ltr Of Cmdtn 85; PA Hgr Ed Asstnc Agncy Cert Of Mrt 85; Weis Mrkts Emply Schlrshp 86; Johns Hopkins U; Nro Srgn.

WOLKO, SUZANNE; St Hubert Catholic HS; Philadelphia, PA; (Y); 14/364; Camera Clb; Service Clb; Teachers Aide; Stage Crew; JV Bowling; High Hon Roll; Hon Roll; NHS; Hghst Avg Acctg I 86; Cert Cmndtn Archdcs Bus Cntst 86; Acctg.

WOLLNER, JANINE; Mid-Valley HS; Dickson City, PA; (Y); Pep Clb; Ski Clb; Band; Chorus; Concert Band; Nwsp Stf; Bsktbl; Hon Roll; Diploma Of Merit Spnsh Cert 84-85; Cert Prtcptng Jump Rope For Heart 84; Med Sec.

WOLOSZYN, SHERRY; Lincoln HS; Wampum, PA; (Y); 34/167; Church Yth Grp; Key Clb; Y-Teens; Chorus; Church Choir; Powder Puff Ftbl; Tennis; Hon Roll; NEDT Awd.

WOLPINK, DEBORAH; Mary Fuller Frazier Memorial HS; Newell, PA; (Y); 8/122; Camp Fr Inc; High Hon Roll; Hon Roll; NHS; Westminster Coll H S Math Comptn 85; Bus Adm.

WOLTER, ERIC ENO; Mon Valley Cath HS; Charleroi, PA; (Y); 15/96; FBLA; VP JA; Ball ST U Muncie IN; Arch.

WOLZ, GREGORY; Center Area HS; Aliquippa, PA; (Y); Computer Clb; German Clb; SADD; Hon Roll; CPR Cert 84; U Pittsburgh; Elec Engrng.

WOMELDORF, CARMEN; Montgomery Area JR SR HS; Montgomery, PA; (Y); Sec 4-H; French Clb; Hosp Aide; Chorus; JV Var Bsktbl; 4-H Awd; High Hon Roll; Hon Roll; NHS; Bstkbl Hustle Awd 86; Med.

WOMER, KRISTIE; Loyalsock Township HS; Montoursville, PA; (Y); French Clb; Letterman Clb; Political Wkr; Sec Ski Clb; Varsity Clb; Variety Show; Nwsp Stf; Sec Frsh Cls; JV Bsktbl; Cheerleading; Psych.

WONDERLING, KELLY; Brookville Area HS; Brookville, PA; (Y); Church Yth Grp; Sec FTA; Key Clb; Varsity Clb; Yrbk Ed-Chief; Yrbk Stf; Var Trk; Var Capt Vllybl; Gannon U; Elem Tchr.

WONDERS, BRETT; Shanksville-Stonycreek HS; Central City, PA; (S); 3/31; Nwsp Ed-Chief; Stat Bsktbl; Hon Roll; U Of Pittsburgh; Bus Adm.

WONDOLOSKI, LESLIE; Southern Columbia HS; Elysburg, PA; (Y); Key Clb; Cheerleading.

WONG, ALICE; Girls HS; Philadelphia, PA; (Y); Teachers Aide; Badmtn; Hon Roll; Comp Sci.

WONG, CHUI-MEI; William Allen HS; Allentown, PA; (Y); 25/530; Trs Intnl Clb; JCL; Leo Clb; Model UN; Political Wkr; Yrbk Phtg; Rep Soph Cls; L Mgr(s); High Hon Roll; NHS; Lehigh U; Elec Engr.

WONG, DIONNE; Germantown HS; Philadelphia, PA; (Y); 10/435; Office Aide; Teachers Aide; High Hon Roll; Hon Roll; Jr NHS; NHS; Engr.

WONG, EDWIN; Perkomen Schl; Pennsburg, PA; (Y); 1/48; Thesps; Chorus; School Musical; School Play; Yrbk Stf; Socr; Tennis; High Hon Roll; Hon Roll; NHS; RPI Sci & Math Mdl 86; Gld Ky 85; Brnz Ky 86; U Of PA; Bus Admn.

WONG, WILBUR; Hampton HS; Gibsonia, PA; (Y); 15/205; Scholastic Bowl; Teachers Aide; Stage Crew; Bowling; High Hon Roll; Pres Schlr; PA Jr Acad Sci 85; Westinghouse Sci Hnrs Inst 86; PA ST U Frshmn Exclince Awd 86; Penn ST; Pre Med.

WOOD, BRAIAN; Towanda Area HS; Monroeton, PA; (Y); French Clb; Science Clb; SADD; Band; Chorus; Concert Band; Mrchg Band; Long Island U; Oceangrphy.

WOOD, DANIEL; Greater Johnstown SR HS; Johnstown, PA; (Y); JA; Band; Chorus; Concert Band; Jazz Band; Mrchg Band; Orch; Pep Band; School Musical; Rotary Awd.

WOOD, DAVID; Mid Valley HS; Dickson City, PA; (Y); Boy Scts; Church Yth Grp; Cmnty Wkr; Nwsp Rptr; Pres Frsh Cls; Pres Sr Cls; God Cntry Awd; High Hon Roll; NHS; Rotary Awd; Phrmcy.

WOOD, DAVID; Penn Wood HS; Yeadon, PA; (Y); 10/364; Boys Clb Am; Var Capt Bsbl; Var Ftbl; Var Wrstlng; Hon Roll; NHS; Prfct Atten Awd; 11th Outstndg Trig Stu; Bus Mngmnt.

WOOD, DOUG; Waynesburg Central HS; Waynesburg, PA; (Y); Art Clb; Boy Scts; 4-H.

WOOD, GREG; Marion Center Area HS; Home, PA; (S); 10/168; Intnl Clb; Varsity Clb; Band; Stu Cncl; Ftbl; Swmmng; Trk; High Hon Roll; NHS; Alt PA Gvnrs Schl Arts 84; Summr Music Scholar IUP 84; IN U; Bus Mgmt.

WOOD, JENNIFER ANN; Perry Township HS; Hummelstown, PA; (Y); Hosp Aide; Pep Clb; Stu Cncl; Cheerleading; Gym; Hon Roll; Giftd Pgm 82-86; Arch.

WOOD, JIM; Waynesburg Central HS; Waynesburg, PA; (Y); 32/210; Letterman Clb; Spanish Clb; SADD; Var L Bsbl; High Hon Roll; Hon Roll; Lion Awd; W VA U; Bus.

WOOD, JUSTIN; Northwestern HS; Springboro, PA; (Y); 18/146; Chess Clb; Church Yth Grp; Drama Clb; French Clb; Quiz Bowl; Thesps; Chorus; School Play; Stu Cncl; Hon Roll; Behrend PA ST; Accntng.

WOOD, KELLY; Marion Center Area HS; Indiana, PA; (S); 4/170; Church Yth Grp; FBLA; FNA; Hosp Aide; Intnl Clb; Library Aide; SADD; High Hon Roll; NHS; Pre-Med.

WOOD, KIMBERLY; Elderton HS; Shelocta, PA; (Y); Pres Church Yth Grp; Spanish Clb; Varsity Clb; Band; Concert Band; Mrchg Band; School Play; Yrbk Ed-Chief; Pres Frsh Cls; VP Jr Cls; IN U Of PA; Elem Educ.

WOOD, LORI; Central Bucks East HS; Doylestown, PA; (Y); 154/468; Mrchg Band; Hon Roll; Var JV Lcrss; Var Capt Swmmng; U Of NC; Marketing.

WOOD, MARY; Penncrest HS; Media, PA; (Y); School Play; Sec Sr Cls; JV Fld Hcky; Var Sftbl; Office Aide; Chorus; Variety Show; West Chester U; Elem Ed.

WOOD, MICHELE; Rocky Grove HS; Franklin, PA; (Y); 17/83; Library Aide; Chorus; Yrbk Stf; Var JV Bsktbl; Var JV Vllybl; High Hon Roll; Hon Roll; NHS; Acad Exc 83-86; Athl SR Awd 86; Edinboro U; Bus Adm.

WOOD, SHAWN; Corry Area HS; Corry, PA; (S); Aud/Vis; Church Yth Grp; Library Aide; Band; Concert Band; Stage Crew.

WOOD, SHERRY; Williams Valley HS; Tower City, PA; (S); 4/104; Chorus; Mrchg Band; Yrbk Ed-Chief; Hst Soph Cls; Hst Jr Cls; Pres Sr Cls; Sftbl; Hon Roll; Prfct Atten Awd; Rotary Awd; Rotary Stu Mth 86; Geisinger Medcl Ctr; RN.

WOOD, TAMMY S; Corry Area HS; Corry, PA; (S); 88/212; Church Yth Grp; Teachers Aide; Stat Bsktbl; Powder Puff Ftbl; Var L Trk; Var L Vllybl; Presntd Wreath Tmb Of Unk Soldr 83; Spec Olympc Volntr 84; Empl WWCB Radio For H S Brdcstng Cls 85; Brdcstng.

WOOD, TANIA; East Allegheny HS; N Versailles, PA; (Y); 25/200; Church Yth Grp; Exploring; Girl Scts; Science Clb; Concert Band; Mrchg Band; Orch; Swmmng; Trk; NHS; Girl Sct Gold Awd 86; Natl Hstry & Govt Awd 86; MVP Vrsty Swm Tm 86; Slippery Rock; Rec Ther.

WOOD, TERESA; Pequea Valley HS; Strasburg, PA; (Y); 17/138; Jazz Band; Mrchg Band; School Musical; Stage Crew; Fld Hcky; Hon Roll; NHS; FBLA; GAA; Hosp Aide; Lancaster Gen Sch Of Nrsng; Nrs.

WOOD, TODD; Philipsburg Osceola Area HS; Philipsburg, PA; (Y); 79/256; Var Bsktbl; Var Ftbl; Var Wt Lftg; IN U PA; Crmnlgy.

WOOD, TODD; Weatherly Area HS; White Haven, PA; (Y); Church Yth Grp; Band; Concert Band; Mrchg Band; Pep Band; JV Bsktbl; Var Golf; Hon Roll; Hgh Achvt Awd Chem 85; Hgh Achvt Algbra 86; PA ST U.

WOODBURN, BRETT; South Park HS; Library, PA; (Y); 3/203; VP Church Yth Grp; Drama Clb; Letterman Clb; Ski Clb; Thesps; Church Choir; School Musical; School Play; Ftbl; Mgr(s); Outstndg Stu Hist & Engl 86; Allegheny Coll Meadvl; Lib Arts.

WOODCOCK, MICHELLE; Altoona Area HS; Altoona, PA; (S); French Clb; Hosp Aide; Math Tm; Ski Clb; VP Speech Tm; Orch; Stu Cncl; Jr NHS; NHS; Concert Band; Amer Leg Awd 84.

WOODGATES, MICHAEL; Umiontown SR HS; Fairbanks, PA; (Y); VICA; Band; Mrchg Band; High Hon Roll; Hon Roll; Aerontcs.

WOODLEY, LYNN; Liberty HS; Bethlehem, PA; (Y); Church Yth Grp; Drama Clb; FBLA; German Clb; Girl Scts; JA; Library Aide; Teachers Aide; Chorus; Stage Crew; Dental Ast.

WOODLEY, RONALD; Liberty HS; Bethlehem, PA; (Y); 23/500; Exploring; French Clb; Political Wkr; Color Guard; Flag Corp; Mrchg Band; Pep Band; Stage Crew; Yrbk Stf; Hon Roll; Lehigh U; Cmptr Engr.

WOODLIEF, GREGORY; Waynesboro Area SR HS; Waynesboro, PA; (Y); 15/350; Boy Scts; Computer Clb; Capt Bowling; Wrstlng; Hon Roll; Orthodontist.

WOODMAN, MARY; Red Land HS; Etters, PA; (Y); 8/275; Spanish Clb; Color Guard; Mrchg Band; Off Frsh Cls; Off Soph Cls; Off Jr Cls; High Hon Roll; NHS; Rotary Awd; Spanish NHS; 1st Pl Essy Cntst Wnnr Rtry Ldrs Cnfrnc 86; Dickinson Coll; Law.

WOODRING, DANIEL; Philipsburg Osceola SR HS; Osceola Mills, PA; (Y); VICA; Yrbk Stf; L Bsktbl; JV Ftbl; Hon Roll; Mst Tlntd 83; U S Air Frc; Cmrcl Art.

WOODRING, DAWN A; Hershey SR HS; Hershey, PA; (Y); Church Yth Grp; Pep Clb; Church Choir; School Musical; Nwsp Rptr; Yrbk Stf; Lit Mag; Gym; Trk; Hon Roll; AAUW Reace Ptry Cntst 1st Pl 85; Schltc Wrtng Awds 85; Kysnr Poet Awd 85; PA ST U; Advrtsng.

WOODRING, DENISE; Waynesboro Area SR HS; Waynesboro, PA; (Y); Church Yth Grp; Office Aide; Pep Clb; Yrbk Phtg; Yrbk Sprt Ed; Stat Bsbl; Im Mgr Vllybl; High Hon Roll; Hon Roll; Voice Dem Awd; Voice Of Demcrcy-Lttr Of Cngrtltns Rep Terry Punt 85; Sndry Ed.

WOODRING, JIM; Tamaqua Area HS; Tamaqua, PA; (Y); Boys Clb Am; Leo Clb; Science Clb; Rep Soph Cls; JV Var Bsktbl; JV L Ftbl; Lib Arts.

WOODRING, LORI; Hazleton HS; Beaver Meadows, PA; (Y); French Clb; Y-Teens; Yrbk Stf; French Hon Soc; High Hon Roll; Hon Roll; NHS; Pres Schlr; Bloomsburg U; Soc Sci.

WOODRING, SHERRY; Cedar Crest HS; Lebanon, PA; (Y); 60/330; German Clb; Key Clb; Latin Clb; Pep Clb; Nwsp Rptr; Nwsp Stf; Yrbk Rptr; Yrbk Stf; JV Bsktbl; JV Fld Hcky.

WOODRING, STEVE; Harbor Creek HS; Erie, PA; (Y); Church Yth Grp; Computer Clb; Teachers Aide; JV Stat Ftbl; Hon Roll; NHS; Comp Tech.

WOODRING, TAMMY; Philipsburg-Osceola HS; Osceola Mills, PA; (Y); 65/250; Pres Pep Clb; SADD; Band; Stage Crew; Ed Nwsp Stf; Yrbk Stf; Rep Stu Cncl; Var Cheerleading; Ski Clb; Concert Band; Womns Clb Excllnc Hmmkg Awd 84; Pres Phy Fit Awd 84; Penn ST; Biochem.

WOODRUFF, KAYE; Danville SR HS; Danville, PA; (Y); 8/204; French Clb; Latin Clb; VP SADD; Ed Nwsp Stf; Capt Crs Cntry; Capt Trk; High Hon Roll; VP NHS; Acad All Am 84; Graham F Stephens Courtsy Awd 84; Sports Med.

WOODRUFF, KEITH; Danville HS; Danville, PA; (Y); Latin Clb; Hon Roll; Air Force.

WOODS, ANGELA; Northern Cambria HS; Barnesboro, PA; (Y); Drama Clb; Spanish Clb; Speech Tm; Chorus; School Play; Trk; High Hon Roll; NHS; Spanish NHS; Intl Frgn Lang Spnsh Awd 84; St Francis Coll; Psych.

WOODS, BONNIE; Seneca Valley SR HS; Mars, PA; (Y).

WOODS, CHERYL; Freedom Area HS; Conway, PA; (Y); 1/160; FCA; French Clb; Math Tm; Quiz Bowl; Service Clb; Yrbk Sprt Ed; Yrbk Stf; Soph Cls; Cheerleading; NHS; Hmcmng Ct 85; Jr Miss Pagnt Fnlst 85; Dept Awds Hnrs Chem,Frnch,Writng,Spch,Soc Sci 85-86; Bucknell U; Mgmt.

WOODS, CINDY; Emmaus HS; Macungie, PA; (Y); 4-H; Yrbk Phtg; Lit Mag; Hst Soph Cls; JV Fld Hcky; Mgr(s); Var L Tennis; High Hon Roll; NHS; Ntl Merit Ltr.

WOODS, CYNTHIA M; Bishop Kenrick HS; Norristown, PA; (Y); Cmnty Wkr; French Clb; Science Clb; Sec Service Clb; School Play; Hon Roll; Prfct Atten Awd; YWCA Ralston Fndtn Schlrshp 86; Allentown Coll St Francis.

WOODS, DIANNE; Union Area HS; New Castle, PA; (Y); Art Clb; Church Yth Grp; Dance Clb; French Clb; Hosp Aide; High Hon Roll; Hon Roll; 1st Pl PA ST Farm Shw Square Dance Commp 86.

WOODS, DONALD; St Josephs Preparatory Schl; Philadelphia, PA; (Y); Church Yth Grp; Cmnty Wkr; French Clb; Mathletes; Math Tm; Office Aide; Pep Clb; Service Clb; SADD; Teachers Aide; Cum Laude Natl Latin Exam 84-85; Mth.

WOODS, KAREN; Laurel JR SR HS; New Castle, PA; (Y); 34/104; Off SADD; Varsity Clb; Drm Mjr(t); Yrbk Stf; Rep Sr Cls; Off Stu Cncl; Var Capt Cheerleading; Powder Puff Ftbl; Trk; Prfct Atten Awd; Clarion U Of PA; Elem Educ.

WOODS, KERRY; Northern SR HS; Wellsville, PA; (Y); 57/200; Chess Clb; Color Guard; School Musical; Var Bsktbl; Hon Roll; Capital Clssrm Internshp Pgm 86; PA ST U; Bus Adm.

WOODS, LISA; South Western HS; Glen Rock, PA; (Y); AFS; Sec Church Yth Grp; 4-H; Key Clb; Yrbk Stf; JV Var Cheerleading; Shippensburg U; Cmnctns.

WOODS, LURETHA; Simon Gratz HS; Philadelphia, PA; (Y); #1 In Class; Hosp Aide; Teachers Aide; Hon Roll; NHS; Temple U; Nrsng.

WOODS, MICHAEL; Cardinal O Hara HS; Havertown, PA; (Y); 33/784; Aud/Vis; Latin Clb; Var Capt Crs Cntry; Var Trk; Hon Roll; NHS; Prfct Atten Awd; Med.

WOODSIDE, ANITA; Hughesville HS; Unityville, PA; (Y); 2/132; VP Pres Church Yth Grp; FTA; Teachers Aide; Cit Awd; Hon Roll; NHS; Sal; Grn & Wht Awd 86; Mary Ann Fox Schlrshp 86; Cmmnwlth Bnk & Trst Schlrshp 86; Lock Haven U; Spcl Educ.

WOODSIDE, WENDY; Ford City JR SR HS; Ford City, PA; (Y); 9/154; AFS; Sec Church Yth Grp; Trs Drama Clb; Trs German Clb; Hosp Aide; Chorus; Drm Mjr(t); Yrbk Stf; Rep Stu Cncl; L Sftbl; Arin Mntrshp Prgm 86; Bio.

WOODSON, CARMEN; Canon-Mc Millan HS; Canonsburg, PA; (Y); Latin Clb; Varsity Clb; Band; Church Choir; JV Cheerleading; Stat Var Crs Cntry; Sftbl; Var L Trk; High Hon Roll; Hon Roll; Hgh Hnr Roll 85-86; Hnr Roll 832-84; Trk Scholar & Ltrs 83-86; Med Tech.

WOODWARD, GREG; Hempfield HS; Greensburg, PA; (Y); Ski Clb.

WOODWARD, KATHY S; Southwestern HS; Hanover, PA; (Y); 84/209; Varsity Clb; Pres Frsh Cls; Rep Soph Cls; Rep Jr Cls; Rep Stu Cncl; Capt Bsktbl; VP Fld Hcky; Capt Trk; CC Awd; Cit Awd; Bsktbl Schlrshp Bloomsburg U 86; All Around Oustndg Femal Athl 86; Athlc Awds Track, Fld Hcky, & Bskbl; Bloomsburg U.

WOODWARD, KIMBERLY ANNE; Tamaquaarea HS; Tamaqua, PA; (Y); 30/200; Am Leg Aux Girls St; VP Pres French Clb; Capt Flag Corp; Nwsp Rptr; Rep Frsh Cls; Rep Soph Cls; Rep Jr Cls; Rep Sr Cls; Pres French Hon Soc; Hon Roll; Mst Prmsng Feat Stff 83-84; 1st Pl Awd PSPA Rvws 84-85, Feature 84-85; Fash Dsgn.

WOODWARD, LISA; Juniata HS; Honey Grove, PA; (Y); Boy Scts; Sec Church Yth Grp; Band; Chorus; Church Choir; Orch; Nwsp Rptr; High Hon Roll; Jr NHS; NHS; Band & Chrs Awd 83-84; Mod Music Masters Awd 84; Pre-Law.

WOODWORTH, TIMOTHY; Mc Keesport Area HS; Mckeesport, PA; (Y); 16/369; Boys Clb Am; Church Yth Grp; Cmnty Wkr; Teachers Aide; Pres Sr Cls; Rep Stu Cncl; Cit Awd; High Hon Roll; Hon Roll; Jr NHS; Ntl Hon Soc 86; Ltrd In Acdmc Prfmnc 83-84; Yrly Hon Rl 83-86; Engrng.

WOODY, JEANNE; Donegal HS; Mount Joy, PA; (Y); 42/160; Band; Mrchg Band; Yrbk Stf; Hst Frsh Cls; Hst Soph Cls; Hst Jr Cls; Hst Sr Cls; Rep Stu Cncl; JV Cheerleading; Hon Roll; Bus.

WOOLEVER, ERNEST J; North Pocono HS; Moscow, PA; (S); 10/239; Am Leg Boys St; Church Yth Grp; Debate Tm; Exploring; Scholastic Bowl; Stu Cncl; High Hon Roll; NHS; Rifle Letter; Penn ST U; Hstry.

WOOLEVER, LINDA L; Highlands SR HS; Church Hills, VA; (Y); 70/277; Church Yth Grp; Drama Clb; FNA; Key Clb; Office Aide; Chorus; Rep Frsh Cls; Prfct Atten Awd; Gld Awds Achvng; Brown Awds 86; U Of VA; Psychlgy.

WOOLFORD, TIM; Mechanicsburg Area SR HS; Mechanicsburg, PA; (Y); 72/350; Church Yth Grp; Cmnty Wkr; Key Clb; Ski Clb; Variety Show; Nwsp Bus Mgr; Nwsp Rptr; Nwsp Stf; JV Golf; Var L Tennis; Vlb Plyr Tennis 84-86; U MI; Bus Admnsrtn.

WOOLLAM, JEFF; Saint Clair Area HS; St Clair, PA; (Y); Letterman Clb; Ski Clb; Varsity Clb; Rep Jr Cls; VP Sr Cls; VP Stu Cncl; Var L Bsktbl; Var L Ftbl; Var Wt Lftg; Penn ST.

WOOLLEY, JENNIFER; Delaware Valley HS; Milford, PA; (Y); 8/160; Drama Clb; Ski Clb; School Musical; School Play; Stage Crew; Yrbk Stf; Var Fld Hcky; Hon Roll; NHS; Gold Key Awd Ntl Schlstc Arts Comp 85 & 86; Semi-Fnlst PA Governors Schl For Arts 84 & 85; Penn ST U; Graphic Dsgn.

WOOLSLAYER, LISA; Meyersdale Area HS; Meyersdale, PA; (Y); 1/80; Trs Church Yth Grp; Spanish Clb; Chorus; Concert Band; Mrchg Band; School Play; Yrbk Stf; NHS; Val; Voice Dem Awd; Intl Citznshp Awd; Penn ST U; Pre Med.

WOOMER, LORI; Chief Logan HS; Lewistown, PA; (Y); Spanish Clb; Band; Concert Band; Jazz Band; Mrchg Band; Pep Band; Yrbk Stf; JV Bsktbl; Trk; High Hon Roll; Ltr In Band 85; Acadmc Ltr 86.

WORCESTER, CAROL; Annville-Cleona HS; Annville, PA; (Y); FBLA; Chorus; Mrchg Band; School Musical; Stat Bsbl; Cheerleading; Shippensburg U; Acctg.

WORKMAN, ERIC; Wilkinsburg HS; Pittsburgh, PA; (Y); Boy Scts; Drama Clb; French Clb; Band; Concert Band; Mrchg Band; High Hon Roll; Hon Roll; AM Lgn Awd 84; Acdmc Achvt Awd 86; U Of Pittsburgh; Bio.

WORKMAN, LEASHELL; Central York SR HS; York, PA; (Y); Boys Clb Am; Church Yth Grp; Exploring; Hosp Aide; Intnl Clb; Band; Mrchg Band; Yrbk Bus Mgr; Hon Roll; Resp Ther.

WORLEY, DIANE; Fort Le Boeuf HS; Waterford, PA; (Y); 17/168; Art Clb; Nwsp Stf; Yrbk Stf; JV Bsktbl; Var L Sftbl; Var L Vllybl; High Hon Roll; Hon Roll.

WORLEY, ERIN; Du Bois Area HS; Du Bois, PA; (Y); 45/256; Sec Drama Clb; Library Aide; NFL; Thesps; Chorus; Concert Band; School Musical; School Play; Swing Chorus; Stu Cncl; Point Park Coll Dnc Asstncshp 86; Mdrn Miss PA Tlnt Wnr 85-86; Point Park Coll; Dnce.

WORLINE, LESLEY; Co Calico HS; Denver, PA; (Y); Church Yth Grp; GAA; Band; Concert Band; Mrchg Band; Off Soph Cls; Stu Cncl; Bsktbl; Sftbl; Hon Roll; Bst Athltc; Bus.

WORMLEY, CECILIA; Bishop Mc Devitt HS; Roslyn, PA; (Y); French Clb; Hosp Aide; Drill Tm; Stage Crew; Ed Nwsp Stf; Bowling; Trk; Abington Piloce Assn Scholar 86; Activity Awds 86; Immaculata Coll; Law.

WOROSZYLO, TRACY; Lincoln HS; Ellwood City, PA; (Y); Church Yth Grp; Hon Roll; Prfct Atten Awd.

WORRALL, LISA; Pottsgrove HS; Pottstown, PA; (Y); 19/229; Science Clb; Rep Spanish Clb; Teachers Aide; Varsity Clb; Stu Cncl; Var Cheerleading; Var Trk; Var Twrlr; Hon Roll; NHS; Elem Educ.

WORRELL, MICHELE; Harry S Truman HS; Levittown, PA; (Y); 47/684; Drama Clb; GAA; JA; Chorus; School Musical; Nwsp Rptr; Stu Cncl; Co-Capt Crs Cntry; Trk; Hon Roll; Kutztown U; Theater Arts.

WORSNICK, MICHELLE; West Scranton HS; Scranton, PA; (Y); 65/260; Spanish Clb; Flag Corp; Hon Roll; NHS; Nrsng.

WORST, BRIAN; Montour HS; Coraopolis, PA; (Y); Boy Scts; Church Yth Grp; JA; Hon Roll; Prfct Atten Awd; $200 Sales Clb Awd-JR Achvt 85 & 86; Dale Carnegie Schlrshp 86; IN U Of PA.

WORTHINGTON, CHANCE J; Hatboro-Horsham HS; Horsham, PA; (Y); 23/278; Ftbl; Wt Lftg; Wrstlng; Hon Roll; NHS; PA ST U; Comp Sci.

WORTMAN, JOSEPH D; St Marys Area HS; Kersey, PA; (Y); Boys Clb Am; Church Yth Grp; JV Var Bsktbl; Var L Ftbl; Im Wt Lftg; Hon Roll; NHS; Pres Schlr; Big 30 & Bucktail Confrnc All Star Team Ftbl 86; Bob Jones U; Accntng.

WOTEN JR, DAVID L; Ambridge Area SR HS; Baden, PA; (Y); Exploring; German Clb; Pep Clb; Band; Concert Band; Jazz Band; Mrchg Band; Pep Band; Vllybl; Hon Roll; USNA; Aerontcs.

WOTUS, DARIN; Gr Latrobe SR HS; Crabtree, PA; (Y); Church Yth Grp; Letterman Clb; L Bsbl; Hon Roll; Penn ST U; Engrng.

WOYSHNAR, JACK; Technical HS; Scranton, PA; (Y); 14/260; Church Yth Grp; Ski Clb; Hon Roll; NHS; PA ST; Elec.

WOYSHNAR, SUSAN; Scranton Central HS; Scranton, PA; (Y); 9/283; Cmnty Wkr; Pres French Clb; Ski Clb; Ed Yrbk Ed-Chief; High Hon Roll; Pres Schlrshp 86; U Of Scranton; Pharm.

WOZNIAK, CRAIG; Bishop Hafey HS; Conyngham, PA; (Y); 40/141; Chess Clb; Ski Clb; Spanish Clb; Teachers Aide; Stage Crew; Rep Stu Cncl; Im Bsktbl; Var L Ftbl; Var Trk; Hon Roll; Outstndg Plyr Ftbl 85.

WOZNIAK, LISA; Seton Catholic HS; Dupont, PA; (Y); 5/96; SADD; Chorus; Madrigals; School Musical; High Hon Roll; NHS; Pres Schlrshp To Msrcrd Coll 86; Cum Laude Cert In Ntl Latin Cntst 84 & 85; Spnsh Awd 86; Kings Coll; Intl Law.

WOZNIAK, ROBERT; Harriton HS; Bryn Mawr, PA; (Y); Model UN; Science Clb; Var Trk; Indr Trck Vrsty 84-86; Bus.

WOZNIAK, WENDY; Plum SR HS; Pittsburgh, PA; (Y); Dance Clb; Ski Clb; Spanish Clb; Drill Tm; Rep Jr Cls; Rep Sr Cls; Swmmng; Trk; Vllybl; Hon Roll; Phys Ther.

WRABEL, JOSEPH; Bishop Mc Devitt HS; Harrisburg, PA; (S); 3/228; Church Yth Grp; Letterman Clb; Stu Cncl; Co-Capt Bsbl; Ftbl; Wt Lftg; High Hon Roll; Hon Roll; NHS; Hugh O Brien Ldrshp Awd 84; St Josephs U; Accntng.

WRAZIEN, DAVID; Freedom HS; Bethlehem, PA; (Y); 37/404; Ski Clb; Yrbk Phtg; Yrbk Stf; Var Capt Golf; High Hon Roll; Hon Roll; Pres Acad Fit Awd 86; U DE; Mth.

WRENN, CHRISTINA; Northeast HS; Philadelphia, PA; (Y); JV Sftbl; Var Swmmng; Hon Roll; NHS; Temple U; Acctg.

WRESSELL, CHRISTINA; Villa Maria Academy; Erie, PA; (S); Ski Clb; Rep Soph Cls; Pres Jr Cls; High Hon Roll; Hon Roll; NHS; Sports Day Chrmn; VA U; Bus.

WRIGHT, AMY; Corry Area HS; Spartansburg, PA; (S); 22/212; Drama Clb; French Clb; Radio Clb; Band; Concert Band; Mrchg Band; High Hon Roll; Hon Roll; Comm.

WRIGHT, AMY; Newport JR/SR HS; Newport, PA; (Y); 10/98; Concert Band; Drm Mjr(t); Jazz Band; Mrchg Band; School Musical; Yrbk Stf; NHS; Spanish Clb; Teachers Aide; Hon Roll; Snd Of Amer Hnr Band 86; Uppr Dist 7 Cncrt Band 86; Mdrn Music Hrn Soc 85-86; Math.

WRIGHT, APRIL; Upper Merion HS; Bridgeport, PA; (Y); Computer Clb; School Musical; Capt Powder Puff Ftbl; Anthony Chiccino Mem Awd Schlrshp 86; Certf App Drama 86; Mllrsvl U; Physcs.

WRIGHT, BRENDA; Canton Area HS; Canton, PA; (Y); 12/100; Band; Chorus; Concert Band; Mrchg Band; DAR Awd; Hon Roll; JP Sousa Awd; Sec Soph Cls; Sec Jr Cls; Dist & Rgnl Band & Chorus 85 & 86; Cnty Band & Chorus 84-86; Mansfield U; Music Ed.

WRIGHT, BRIAN J; North Allegheny HS; Allison Pk, PA; (Y); 74/605; Yrbk Phtg; Capt L Diving; Hon Roll; Prfct Atten Awd; Prsdntl Acad Ftnss Awd 85-86; Pheaa Cert Of Merit 85; Alld Sgnl Ntl Schlrshp Fnlst 86; Allegheny Coll; Lbrl Arts.

WRIGHT III, CHARLES; Penn Hills SR HS; Pittsburgh, PA; (S); 142/800; Church Yth Grp; Pep Clb; Science Clb; Pres Spanish Clb; Pres Soph Cls; Pres Jr Cls; Pres Stu Cncl; Cit Awd; Hon Roll; Kiwanis Awd; PTA Schlrshp 86; SR Cls Schlrshp 86; Villanora; Pre Med.

WRIGHT, DENISE; St Basil Acad; Philadelphia, PA; (Y); Church Yth Grp; Computer Clb; Latin Clb; Math Clb; Thesps; Stage Crew; Prfct Atten Awd; Sec Ed.

WRIGHT, ERIC; Tunkhannock Area HS; Tunkhannock, PA; (Y); Capt Church Yth Grp; Var Bsbl; Var Wt Lftg; JV Wrstlng; Hon Roll; Pres Phy Fit Awd 86; Luzerne County CC; Crmnl Jstc.

WRIGHT, HAROLD; Chambersburg Area SR HS; Chambersburg, PA; (Y); 49/641; Church Yth Grp; Cmnty Wkr; FCA; Chorus; Church Choir; Var JV Bsktbl; Coach Actv; Im Ftbl; Score Keeper; Im Sftbl.

WRIGHT, JAMES; Chestnut Ridge HS; New Paris, PA; (S); 14/107; Boy Scts; Church Yth Grp; Exploring; Spanish Clb; Var L Bsktbl; Im Coach Actv; Var L Crs Cntry; Var L Trk; High Hon Roll; Hon Roll; Pittsburgh U; Chem.

WRIGHT, KAREN; Newport HS; Newport, PA; (Y); Office Aide; Yrbk Stf; Hon Roll; Prfct Atten Awd; Svc-Typst 85; Bus.

WRIGHT, KRIS; Carrick HS; Pittsburgh, PA; (Y); Stage Crew; Sftbl; Tennis; High Hon Roll; Partial Schlrshp Carnegie Mellon Pre-Coll Art Sch 84-85.

WRIGHT, LARRY; Homer Center JR SR HS; Homer City, PA; (Y); French Clb; SADD; Chorus; Church Choir; School Musical; School Play; Stage Crew; Swing Chorus; Yrbk Stf; NHS; Music.

WRIGHT, LENDINA F; Winchester-Thurston HS; Pittsburgh, PA; (Y); AFS; Dance Clb; GAA; Service Clb; Spanish Clb; Chorus; School Musical; School Play; Mgr(s); Crngie-Mlln U Pre-Coll Pgm Fn Arts 86; Semi-Fnlst Mss Blck Teen Pgnt 86; Psychlgst.

WRIGHT, LINDA C; Catasauqua HS; Catasauqua, PA; (Y); 7/150; FBLA; Hon Roll; Sec NHS; FBLA Rgnl Conf 86; Cert Of 3rd Pl Bus Law Test 86; Ntl Hnr Scty Insgna Ptch For Svc 86; Vrsty Ltr C 86; Moravian Coll; Pre-Law.

WRIGHT, LORI; Blue Mountain Acad; Gibsonia, PA; (Y); Church Yth Grp; Sec Computer Clb; Teachers Aide; Church Choir; Concert Band; Variety Show; Im Sftbl; Im Vllybl; Hon Roll; Outdoor Clb Pres 86; Hartland Coll; Hlth Care.

WRIGHT, LORINDA; Palisades HS; Ottsville, PA; (Y); 6/151; Math Tm; Lit Mag; L Crs Cntry; Trk; Cit Awd; NHS; Pres Schlr; Honor Roll 85-86; Elizabethtown Coll; Pre-Vet.

WRIGHT, MARCIE; Boyertown SR HS; Bally, PA; (Y); Art Clb; French Clb; Library Aide; Pep Clb; SADD; Chorus; Color Guard; Cit Awd; Hon Roll; Prfct Atten Awd; Temple U; Engl Tchr.

WRIGHT, MARK; Punxsutawney Area SR HS; Summerville, PA; (Y); CAP; Math Tm; Science Clb; Hon Roll; Engnrng.

WRIGHT, MICHELLE; Canton Area HS; Canton, PA; (Y); 8/124; Church Yth Grp; 4-H; Letterman Clb; Bsktbl; Sftbl; Vllybl; High Hon Roll; Hon Roll; NTL Vllybll Tm All Stars 85-86; Susquehanna U; Math.

WRIGHT, RICHARD; Perry Traditional Acad; Pittsburgh, PA; (Y); 37/130; Band; Mrchg Band; Mgr(s); Cit Awd; Hon Roll; U Of Pittsburgh; Mech Engrng.

WRIGHT, STEPHANIE; Newport HS; Middletown, PA; (Y); Exploring; FTA; Library Aide; Radio Clb; Nwsp Stf; Hon Roll; Ntl Merit Schol; PA ST U; Vet Med.

WRIGHT, TERESA; West Greene HS; Aleppo, PA; (Y); Church Yth Grp; FFA; SADD; Sftbl; Vllybl; Slmnshp Of Yr FFA 84-85; Bradford; Sec.

WRISBY, CORNELL; Pottstown SR HS; Pottstown, PA; (S); 18/238; French Clb; VP GAA; Key Clb; Spanish Clb; Var Bsktbl; Var Fld Hcky; Var Trk; Hon Roll; NHS; Sec Frsh Cls; UCLA; Pre-Law.

WROBLESKI, GARRY; Bishop O Hara HS; Dickson City, PA; (S); Exploring; Spanish Clb; VP Ftbl; High Hon Roll; Prfct Atten Awd; PA ST U; Med.

WROBLEWSKI, FRANK; Mahanoy Area HS; Mahanoy City, PA; (Y); Var JV Bsktbl; Hon Roll; NHS.

WROBLEWSKI, MIKE; Conrad Weiser HS; Wernersville, PA; (Y); 43/184; Aud/Vis; Spanish Clb; Chorus; School Musical; Mgr Stage Crew; Variety Show; Var Socr; JV Tennis; Var Wrstlng; Hon Roll; Jrnlsm.

WROBLEWSKI, TERRI; Seneca Valley SR HS; Evans City, PA; (Y); Chorus; Jazz Band; Mrchg Band; Symp Band; Nwsp Ed-Chief; Nwsp Rptr; Yrbk Stf; Lit Mag; NHS; Ntl Merit Ltr; Miss PA Coachmen 86; Grove City Coll; Cmmnctns.

WRONA, CHRISTINA; Saint Maria Goretti HS; Philadelphia, PA; (Y); 50/402; Camera Clb; French Clb; Mathletes; Stage Crew; Jr NHS; Prfct Atten 84-85; Temple; Med.

WRONA, LAURIE; Ambridge Area HS; Ambridge, PA; (Y); 52/365; Pep Clb; Red Cross Aide; Band; Concert Band; Mrchg Band; Pep Band; Stu Cncl; JV Bsktbl; Var L Tennis; Hon Roll; Penn ST U.

WU, PHAN; G W C HS Schl Of Engineer & Science; Philadelphia, PA; (S); 4/288; Yrbk Stf; Hon Roll; Prfct Atten Awd; Art Awd 85; Phrmcy.

WU, WENDY L; Villa Maria HS; Edgerton, OH; (Y); Cmnty Wkr; Library Aide; Ski Clb; Spanish Clb; School Musical; Nwsp Rptr; Yrbk Stf; Lit Mag; Stat Trk; Spanish NHS; Pre Med.

WUCHTER, TRAVIS M; Northampton Area SR HS; Northampton, PA; (S); 23/475; Art Clb; Cmnty Wkr; Model UN; VICA; Ed Yrbk Stf; Ftbl; Wt Lftg; Wrstlng; High Hon Roll; Allentown Coll; Psych.

WUENSCHEL, DANA; Carrick HS; Pittsburgh, PA; (S); Math Tm; Q&S; Ski Clb; Nwsp Stf; Yrbk Stf; Rep Stu Cncl; Powder Puff Ftbl; High Hon Roll; Sec Church Yth Grp; Exploring; Ambssdr HOBY Ldrshp Sem 85; ST Fin Miss Amer Co-Ed Pag 84; Pedtrcs.

WUFSUS, SHARON; Marian HS; Mahanoy City, PA; (S); 18/114; Church Yth Grp; Band; Church Choir; Concert Band; Mrchg Band; Pep Band; JV Bsktbl; Hon Roll.

WULFFRAAT, ANNE; Warren Area HS; Warren, PA; (Y); VP German Clb; Acpl Chr; Church Choir; Jazz Band; Madrigals; Mrchg Band; School Musical; School Play; Trk; Pres Schlr; U Of PA Schlr Cup 86; Ltrary Arts Awd Outstndg Wrtrs 84; Carnegie-Mellon U; Pre-Med.

WULKOWICZ, TINA S; Exeter HS; Reading, PA; (Y); 60/200; Exploring; Library Aide; Chorus; Merit Rl 85-86; Golden Egle Awd 85; Penn ST U; Acctg.

WUNDER, C ANDREW; Tyrone Area HS; Pt Matilda, PA; (Y); Pres Trs Church Yth Grp; Spanish Clb; SADD; Stage Crew; JV Var Ftbl; Var Trk; Wt Lftg; JV Wrstlng; High Hon Roll; Hon Roll; Sci Tchr.

WUNDER, GLENN; Spring-Ford HS; Royersford, PA; (Y); Boy Scts; Spanish Clb; Rep Stu Cncl; JV Bsbl; Var Ftbl; Wt Lftg; Capt Wrstlng.

WUNNER, RONALD; G A R Memorial HS; Wilkes Barre, PA; (S); 4/187; German Clb; Chorus; Off Jr Cls; Off Stu Cncl; Vllybl; Wt Lftg; Hon Roll; Jr NHS; NHS; FL ST U; Oceanogrphr.

WUNNER, SUSANNE; Mercyhurst Prepatory Schl; Erie, PA; (Y); French Clb; Hosp Aide; Sec Trs Model UN; Lit Mag; Stu Cncl; Hon Roll; Zoolgy.

WUORIO, SANDRA; Hanover Area HS; Wilkes Barre, PA; (Y); Chorus; Mrchg Band; School Play; Variety Show; Stu Cncl; Hon Roll; High Avg Comprhnsve Awd 86.

WURSTER, CHARLES; Clearfield Area HS; Clearfield, PA; (Y); Var Debate Tm; Var VP French Clb; Speech Tm; Band; Concert Band; Mrchg Band; Pep Band; School Musical; Stage Crew; Variety Show; Penn ST U; Lbrl Arts.

WUSLICH, DIANE; Dowingtown SR HS; Chester Springs, PA; (Y); Church Yth Grp; Ski Clb; Spanish Clb; Chorus; Fld Hcky; Mgr(s); High Hon Roll; Wm & Mry Wake Frst; Bus.

WUYSCIK, DENNIS R; Kiski Area HS; Apollo, PA; (Y); 31/388; Church Yth Grp; Key Clb; Math Clb; Pep Clb; Varsity Clb; Bsbl; Bsktbl; Ftbl; Wt Lftg; DAR Awd; Athletic Ftbl Schlrshp 86-90; Schlr Athlete Awd 86; Kiski Areas Male Athlete Yr 85-86; Bucknell U; Pol Sci.

WYANDT, MARY A; Greater Johnstown HS; Johnstown, PA; (Y); Church Yth Grp; Exploring; Pres VP Girl Scts; Church Choir; Yrbk Stf; High Hon Roll; NHS; Prfct Atten Awd; Silver Awd 85; Rock Girl Scout Cncls Bd Dir 86; U Pittsburgh; Physcl Thrpy.

WYATT JR, SAMUEL J; Chester HS; Chester, PA; (Y); 55/336; Quiz Bowl; Chorus; Yrbk Stf; Pres Jr Cls; Im L Bsbl; Im L Socr; Comp Progrmng Awd 85-86; Mourning Announcer 84-86; Acad Excllnce Chester-Upland Educ Assoc 85-86; Penn ST U; Pre Law.

WYBRANSKI, STANLEY; Northeast Catholic HS; Philadelphia, PA; (Y); 147/362; Bsktbl; Var Capt Crs Cntry; Var Capt Trk; Bus Mgmt.

WYCOFF, TERRI; Carrick HS; Pittsburgh, PA; (S); School Musical; Tennis; High Hon Roll; Hon Roll.

WYDA, LAURA; G A R Memorial HS; Wilkes Barre, PA; (S); Church Yth Grp; Band; Chorus; Concert Band; Jazz Band; Mrchg Band; Orch; Hon Roll; Jr NHS; NHS.

WYDILA, DAVID; Mt Carmel Area JR SR HS; Mt Carmel, PA; (Y); 2/168; French Clb; VP Key Clb; Latin Clb; Letterman Clb; Q&S; Nwsp Stf; Trs Soph Cls; Trk; High Hon Roll; NHS; Bucknell U; Elctrcl Engrng.

WYLER, RICHARD; Valley Forge Military Acad; Kensington, MD; (Y); German Clb; Nwsp Stf; Hon Roll; NHS; Amer Chem Soc 86; Engr.

WYLIE, GIST; Clarion Area HS; Clarion, PA; (Y); Church Yth Grp; Teachers Aide; L Trk; Debate Tm; Meteorlgy.

WYMAN, SCOTT; New Castle SR HS; New Castle, PA; (Y); 37/263; Church Yth Grp; Ski Clb; Var Ftbl; Var Wt Lftg; Hon Roll; Rep Stu Cncl; Engrng.

WYNINGS, TRACY; Boyertown Area SR HS; Boyertown, PA; (Y); FBLA; Pep Clb; Variety Show; Rep Stu Cncl; Var Capt Cheerleading; Cit Awd; Hon Roll; Bus Educ Ldrshp Awd 86; Katherine Gibbs; Bus Educ.

WYNN, DOUGLAS; Carmichaels Area HS; Carmichaels, PA; (S); 8/100; Drama Clb; Ski Clb; Pres Spanish Clb; Pres Band; Drm Mjr(t); School Play; Rep Jr Cls; NHS; Homecoming Court 85; Acad All-Amer 86; DAR Awds 84; Phrmcy.

WYNNE, JOSEPH; Canton Area JR SR HS; Canton, PA; (Y); 23/115; AFS; Aud/Vis; Church Yth Grp; Computer Clb; Variety Show; Mgr(s); Hon Roll; Rotary Awd; Hnrb Mntn Natl Soc Studs Olympd 86; Rotary Ldrs Camp 85; Engrng.

WYPA, LYNN; Lake Lehman HS; Shavertown, PA; (Y); 16/200; Church Yth Grp; Hosp Aide; Key Clb; Band; High Hon Roll; Hon Roll; Jr NHS; NHS; Legal.

WYSOCKI, SYLVIA; Danville HS; Danville, PA; (Y); Key Clb; Spanish Clb; Rep Frsh Cls; JV Var Cheerleading; Var Fld Hcky; JV Var Trk; High Hon Roll; Hon Roll; Coprt Law.

WYSOKINSKI, MICHELE; Pittston Area HS; Pittston, PA; (Y); 32/365; Church Yth Grp; Computer Clb; Drama Clb; Key Clb; Co-Capt Drill Tm; Sec Soph Cls; Swmmng; Hon Roll; NHS; Bus.

WYSONG, ALICE; The Christian Acad; Wilmington, DE; (S); 1/69; Church Yth Grp; Acpl Chr; Sec Chorus; Rep Stu Cncl; Capt Cheerleading; Fld Hcky; Sftbl; High Hon Roll; NHS; Val; Distngshd Christian H S Studnt-ACSI 85-86; Studnt Of Mnth 86; Grove City Coll.

WYSZYNSKI, DAVID; Father Judge HS; Philadelphia, PA; (Y); 121/358; Var Crs Cntry; Var Trk; Temple U; Arch.

WYTOVICH, ROMAN MICHAEL; Old Forge HS; Old Forge, PA; (Y); Church Yth Grp; Yrbk Stf; Hon Roll; Wdnr U; Bus Admin.

XAVIER, DORA; Salisbury HS; Allentown, PA; (Y); Drama Clb; Sec Key Clb; School Play; Rep Stu Cncl; Stat Ftbl; Score Keeper; High Hon Roll; Hon Roll; Lion Awd; Prfct Atten Awd; Bst Ldng Fml Role In Play 84-85; Bst Outstndg Stu Span II 84-85; Spec Ed.

XIONG, KA YOUA; Mercyhurst Prep HS; Erie, PA; (Y); 14/150; Cmnty Wkr; French Clb; Hosp Aide; Model UN; Chorus; Orch; School Musical; Lit Mag; High Hon Roll; NHS; Rnnr Up-Outstndng Carrier Of Yr 83; 3rd Pl Wnnr-Miss Hmong Pgnt 85-86; Intl Hmong Dncrs Awd 84.

YABLONSKI, JANINE; Lakeland HS; Olyphant, PA; (Y); Bsktbl; Sftbl; Bausch & Lomb Sci Awd; High Hon Roll; NHS; Hon Roll; Natl Merit Sci Awds-Chem 85, Bio & Physcs 86; Pres Acadmc Ftnss Awd 86; Schlumberger Schlrshp 86; PA ST U; Engrng.

YACABUCCI, JAN; Clearfield HS; Clearfield, PA; (S); Drama Clb; French Clb; Chorus; Concert Band; Mrchg Band; Orch; School Musical; Swmmng; Hon Roll.

YACAPSIN, GENE; Marian HS; Nesquehoning, PA; (Y); 45/120; JV Bsktbl; L Var Ftbl; Trk; Bus.

YACONI, GEORGE; Laurel Valley HS; New Florence, PA; (Y); 21/87; Boy Scts; NFL; Science Clb; Chorus; Concert Band; Jazz Band; Mrchg Band; Pep Band; Hon Roll; Order Of The Arrw 86; PA ST; Astronomy.

YACOVIELLO, MIKE; Moon SR HS; Coraopolis, PA; (Y); Exploring; JA; Letterman Clb; Varsity Clb; Im Bsktbl; JV Var Crs Cntry; Im Vllybl; Var L Wrstlng; High Hon Roll; Hon Roll; Penn ST; Chem Engr.

YACULAK, KIM; St Pius X HS; Pottstown, PA; (S); 8/182; FCA; French Clb; FBLA; FNA; Service Clb; Ski Clb; Nwsp Bus Mgr; Nwsp Sprt Ed; Off Frsh Cls; Off Soph Cls; Athl Of Mnth-Lcl ABC Clb Of Elk 86; 2nd Tm All Chesmont Hockey 85-86; Phys Educ.

YADUSH, JOSEPH; Northampton Area HS; Walnutport, PA; (S); Computer Clb; DECA; Hon Roll; Chaptr Treas 85-86; 3rd Pl Dist Awd Finance & Credit 85-86; Chruchmans Business Schl; Accnt.

YAGLA, BARBARA; Hempfield Area SR HS; Bovard, PA; (Y); Pep Clb; Spanish Clb; Yrbk Stf; Vllybl; High Hon Roll; Hon Roll; Jr NHS; NHS; Elec Engrng.

YAHNER, DAVID; Cambria Heights HS; Patton, PA; (Y); 4/200; Sec Soph Cls; Rep Jr Cls; Stu Cncl; Capt Ftbl; Capt Wrstlng; High Hon Roll; NHS; NEDT Awd 85; Engrng.

YAHNER, TRICIA; Altoona Area HS; Altoona, PA; (Y); Key Clb; Drill Tm; Penn ST; Comp Sci.

YAKICH, GREGORY; Central Catholic HS; Pittsburgh, PA; (Y); 75/275; Am Leg Boys St; Boy Scts; Exploring; Concert Band; Im Bowling; Im Ftbl; Im Socr; Im Wrstlng; Hon Roll; Natl Marble Champ 84; Am Leg Awd 83; County Marble Champ 81-84; Duquesne U; Acctg.

YAKIMICK, TAUSHA; Rockwood Area HS; Somerset, PA; (S); 4/95; Band; Chorus; School Play; Yrbk Stf; Rep Stu Cncl; High Hon Roll; PA ST U; Chem.

YAKUBOSKI, LISA; Hanover Area JR SR HS; Wilkes Barre, PA; (Y); Key Clb; SADD; Chorus; Color Guard; Mrchg Band; School Musical; High Hon Roll; Jr NHS; NHS; PA JR Acad Sci; Med Lab Tech.

YAKUPCIN, MARK; Delaware Valley HS; Matamoras, PA; (Y); Varsity Clb; Bsbl; Hon Roll; Sci.

YAKUPKOVIC, FRANCINE; Quigley HS; Aliquippa, PA; (Y); Exploring; VP Sec JA; Math Tm; SADD; Concert Band; Mrchg Band; Nwsp Stf; Mgr Bsbl; JV Bsktbl; Powder Puff Ftbl; Engrng.

YALCH, SHARON; John S Fine HS; Sheatown, PA; (S); 15/250; Hosp Aide; Chorus; Swmmng; High Hon Roll; NHS; Phy Thrpy.

YALE, DINA; Bishop Hafey HS; Hazleton, PA; (Y); Cmnty Wkr; Ski Clb; Y-Teens; Capt Cheerleading; Hon Roll; Int Design.

YAN, SANDY YEE-MAN; Mount Alvernia HS; Pittsburgh, PA; (S); Computer Clb; French Clb; Hosp Aide; Chorus; Yrbk Stf; Var Stat Bsktbl; High Hon Roll; NHS; Hghst Avg Awd 84; Chem & Engl Awds 85; Elctrcl Engr.

YANAK, BRENDA; St Marys Area HS; Saint Marys, PA; (Y); 1/301; Hon Roll; NHS; Outstndng Sci, Frgn Lang 86; PA Govs Schl Ag 86; Outstndng Ambssdr Wstrn PA Yth Ldrshp Semnr 85; Genetcs.

YANCHE, MICHELLE; Bishop Carroll HS; Nanty Glo, PA; (S); 1/104; Church Yth Grp; Drama Clb; NFL; Ski Clb; Pres Spanish Clb; High Hon Roll; Sec NHS; Ntl Merit Ltr; NEDT Awd; Pep Clb; Cross-Cntry Ski Club; Pre-Law.

YANCHUNAS, SEAN; Crestwood HS; Mountop, PA; (Y); Am Leg Boys St; Church Yth Grp; Cmnty Wkr; Science Clb; Ski Clb; JV Var Bsbl; Im Bsktbl; JV Var Ftbl; Im Tennis; JV Var Wt Lftg; Engrng.

YANCHUNAS, VICTOR; Crestwood HS; Mountaintop, PA; (Y); Church Yth Grp; Cmnty Wkr; Ski Clb; JV Var Bsktbl; Im JV Fld Hcky; JV Var Tennis; Var Trk; Im JV Wt Lftg; Hon Roll; Engrng.

YANCHUS, NANCY; Shady Side Acad; New Kensington, PA; (Y); Drama Clb; Letterman Clb; SADD; Chorus; School Musical; Yrbk Stf; Fld Hcky; Trk; Hon Roll; 3rd Pl Frnch Cntst; Engl.

YANCICH, LUANN; Brownsville Area HS; Brownsville, PA; (Y); Hosp Aide; Library Aide; Mathletes; Math Clb; Math Tm; SADD; Nwsp Stf; Off Soph Cls; Stu Cncl; Var Cheerleading; Nrsg.

YANCKELLO, TRACEY; Quaker Valley SR HS; Sewickley, PA; (Y); Dance Clb; French Clb; Chorus; School Musical; Stu Cncl; Bsktbl; Trk; Gov Hon Prg Awd.

YANCY, MARY; Upper Dublin HS; North Hills, PA; (Y); 109/320; Church Yth Grp; FBLA; Intnl Clb; Chorus; Church Choir; School Play; Stage Crew; Yrbk Stf; Rep Frsh Cls; Pres Soph Cls; Optmst Clb Schlrshp 86; Hrn Roll 84; Chestnut Hill Coll; Pre-Law.

YANEZ, JOSEPH; Norwin SR HS; N Huntingdon, PA; (Y); 11/547; Mathletes; Trs Math Clb; Math Tm; Spanish Clb; Var L Crs Cntry; High Hon Roll; NHS; Prfct Atten Awd; U Of PA; Chem Engrng.

YANICK, JEAN; John S Fine HS; Nanticoke, PA; (Y); Computer Clb; Girl Scts; SADD; VICA; Chorus; High Hon Roll; Hon Roll; Luzerne Cnty Comm; D P.

YANITY, MISSY; Marion Center Area HS; Marion Ctr, PA; (Y); Church Yth Grp; Hosp Aide; Chorus; Church Choir; Concert Band; Mrchg Band; Orch; Pep Band; Rep Stu Cncl; 4-H Awd; Ms Amercn Coed ST Fnlst 86; Dist Orchstra-2nd Violin 85; IUP; Mdcl Technlgy.

YANKANICH, THOMAS; Parkland SR HS; Orefield, PA; (Y); Rep Stu Cncl; JV Bsbl; JV Socr; Capt L Wrstlng; Hon Roll; Columbia U; Bus Admn.

YANKELITIS, MARY ANN; Bishop Hannan HS; Scranton, PA; (Y); 21/123; VP Exploring; VP Hosp Aide; Pres Ski Clb; Chorus; School Play; Stu Cncl; Hon Roll; NHS; Prfct Atten Awd; Pres Schlr; Mercy Hosp Vol Schlrshp 86; U Scranton; Nrsng.

YANKOWSKI, JEFF; Mount Pleasant Area HS; Mt Pleasant, PA; (Y); Cmnty Wkr; Ski Clb; Nwsp Sprt Ed; Var Bsbl; JV Bsktbl; High Hon Roll; Pre-Med.

YANN, KELLY; St Paul Cathedral HS; Pittsburgh, PA; (S); 3/55; Drama Clb; French Clb; School Play; Stage Crew; Nwsp Stf; Yrbk Stf; Mgr Vllybl; High Hon Roll; NEDT Awd; Prfct Atten Awd.

YANNACCI, DEAN; Kiski Area HS; Apollo, PA; (Y); Key Clb; Letterman Clb; Varsity Clb; Band; Rep Stu Cncl; Var Capt Ftbl; Wt Lftg; High Hon Roll; Hon Roll.

YANNACCI, MIKE; Yough SR HS; Yukon, PA; (Y); French Clb; Ski Clb; Rep Soph Cls; Stu Cncl; Ftbl; Hon Roll.

YANNACONE, TERESA; Cardinal O Hara HS; Media, PA; (Y); 91/772; Art Clb; Trs Church Yth Grp; Cmnty Wkr; Latin Clb; Library Aide; Pres Service Clb; Spanish Clb; Hon Roll; NHS; Prfct Atten Awd; Hnrb Mntn In Crdnl O Hara Sci Fair 86; 1st Pl DE Cnty Sci Fair 86; Physcl Thrpy.

YANNEY, LUCIE; Cedar Crest HS; Lebanon, PA; (Y); 40/306; Drama Clb; French Clb; Hosp Aide; JA; Pep Clb; School Musical; School Play; Hon Roll; Prfct Atten Awd; Boostr Clb Hnr Bnqt; Medcl Careers Clb; Erly Chldhd Educ.

YANOCHKO, ANNE MARIE; Bethlehem Catholic HS; Bethlehem, PA; (S); 20/215; Exploring; Girl Scts; Key Clb; Color Guard; Drill Tm; Mrchg Band; Nwsp Stf; Stat Bsktbl; Score Keeper; High Hon Roll; Vrsty Ltr-Mrchng Bnd/Drl Team 85; Rising Star Colorguard 85 & 86; Vtrnry Med.

YANOS, ROBERT; Owen J Roberts HS; Pottstown, PA; (Y); 84/270; Boy Scts; JV Socr; Hon Roll; Prfct Atten Awd; Engrng.

YANOSCSIK, MICHELLE; Homer Center SR HS; Homer City, PA; (Y); 2/96; French Clb; Hosp Aide; Library Aide; Varsity Clb; Nwsp Stf; Yrbk Stf; JV Bsktbl; Im Sftbl; Var Trk; Var Vllybl; Smmr Happenngs Marine Bio 85.

YANTEK, JOHN; Bentworth HS; Bentleyville, PA; (Y); Ski Clb; Spanish Clb; Varsity Clb; Pres Jr Cls; Var L Ftbl; Var L Wrstlng; Hon Roll; NHS; Natl Sci Merit Awd 84; Aerospace Engrng.

YANTKO, DENISE E; Uniontown Area SR HS; New Salem, PA; (Y); #32 In Class; Am Leg Aux Girls St; French Clb; Library Aide; French Hon Soc; High Hon Roll; NHS; Eberly Fndtn Schlrshp 86; Pres Acdmc Ftnss Awd 86; CA U Of PA; Accntng.

YANTOS, JENNIFER; Gettysburg SR HS; Gettysburg, PA; (Y); Library Aide; Chorus; Hon Roll; Prfct Atten Awd; Bus.

YAO, SUZANNE BRUNELLE; Kennedy Christian HS; Sharpsville, PA; (Y); 15/100; Trs Cmnty Wkr; VP Spanish Clb; Nwsp Rptr; Nwsp Stf; Yrbk Stf; VP Jr Cls; Rep Stu Cncl; Hon Roll; St Marys Coll; Engl.

YAP, ELEANOR; Abington SR HS; Abington, PA; (Y); 19/535; Camera Clb; Intnl Clb; Service Clb; Nwsp Stf; Rep Stu Cncl; High Hon Roll; Hon Roll; NHS; Pres Acad Ftns Awd 85-86; Prcvl R Rieder,Esq Awd 86; Tmpl U Pres Awd 86; Temple U Cambler Camp; Jrnlsm.

YAPLE, MARK; Lake-Lehman HS; Shickshinny, PA; (Y); 56/176; VP Jr Cls; Pres Sr Cls; Var L Ftbl; Var L Vllybl; Var L Wrstlng; Hon Roll; Millersville U; Acctng.

YAPLE, MARYLYN; Berwick Area SR HS; Berwick, PA; (Y); Library Aide; Red Cross Aide; Ski Clb; SADD; Chorus; Rep Stu Cncl; Var Capt Fld Hcky; Var Trk; Hon Roll; Rep Frsh Cls; Nrsg.

YARAMUS, KATHY; Aliquippa HS; Aliquippa, PA; (S); SADD; Off Jr Cls; Off Sr Cls; Capt Cheerleading; Sftbl; Hon Roll; NHS; Beaver Cnty CC; Nrsng.

YARAMUS, SAMUEL N; Aliquippa HS; Aliquippa, PA; (S); Church Yth Grp; Off Jr Cls; Ftbl; Wt Lftg; High Hon Roll; Aerontcs.

YARD, AMY; Rocky Grove HS; Franklin, PA; (Y); Sec 4-H; French Clb; Quiz Bowl; JV Var Cheerleading; Im Gym; JV Vllybl; 4-H Awd.

YARD, BETH ANN; Beaver Area SR HS; Beaver, PA; (Y); Art Clb; 4-H; German Clb; Key Clb; Pep Clb; Nwsp Rptr; Nwsp Stf; Lit Mag; Hon Roll; Connors ST Clg; Equine Studies.

YARD, CYNTHIA; Rocky Grove HS; Franklin, PA; (Y); 5/92; Library Aide; SADD; Variety Show; Rep Jr Cls; Rep Stu Cncl; JV Var Cheerleading; Var Crs Cntry; Gym; High Hon Roll; Hon Roll.

YARD, FREDERICK; Fort Le Boeuf HS; Waterford, PA; (Y); 8/174; Chess Clb; Church Yth Grp; Exploring; Model UN; Concert Band; Mrchg Band; Nwsp Phtg; Yrbk Ed-Chief; Yrbk Phtg; High Hon Roll; Acad Achvt Awd 84-85; Pres Acad Ftnss Awd 85-86; Rochester Inst Of Tech; Photogr.

YARGER, PENNY; Moshannon Valley JR SR HS; Houtzdale, PA; (Y); DECA; Library Aide; Hon Roll; Nrsng.

YARKANIN, STEVEN; Hazleton HS; Sugarloaf, PA; (Y); Computer Clb; FBLA; High Hon Roll; NHS; Shawn Zanolini Mem Awd 86; Air Force; Comp Prog.

YARNELL, SCOTT; Marple Newtown SR HS; Broomall, PA; (Y); Service Clb; Nwsp Bus Mgr; Nwsp Rptr; Rptr Sr Cls; Stu Cncl; JV Bsktbl; JV Lcrss; Socr; Hon Roll; NEDT Awd; Sato VP USY Chptr 86-87; World Affairs Cncl 86-87; Bus.

YARNELL, STACY; Chestnut Ridge SR HS; Alum Bunk, PA; (S); 21/142; Church Yth Grp; Dance Clb; Chorus; Church Choir; Pres Soph Cls; Pres Jr Cls; Off Stu Cncl; Twrlr; High Hon Roll; Hon Roll; PA ST Twirling & Mdlng Awd 85-86; Psych.

YARNES, MICHELE; Sacred Heart HS; Jermyn, PA; (Y); Church Yth Grp; Spanish Clb; Acpl Chr; Church Choir; Flag Corp; Var Bsktbl; Var JV Cheerleading; JV Crs Cntry; JV Score Keeper; Var Sftbl; Marywood; Lgl Asst.

YARRINGTON, BRIAN W; Wissahickon SR HS; Ambler, PA; (Y); 5/276; Boy Scts; Trs Spanish Clb; Varsity Clb; Var Socr; God Cntry Awd; High Hon Roll; NHS; Ntl Merit SF; Rep Stu Cncl; Ntl Merit Semi-Fnlst; Schl Wnnr Cntry III Ldr Prog 85; Hnr Awd Acad Excll; Eagle Scout 83.

YARTZ, VIC; Laurel Highlands HS; Hopwood, PA; (Y); Penn ST U; Music Engrng.

YASKO, D BRETT; Quacker Valley HS; Sewickley, PA; (Y); Math Clb; Lit Mag; Crs Cntry; Hon Roll; Pres Schlr; Syracuse U; Comm.

YASOFSKY, ANITA; Swissvale HS; Pittsburgh, PA; (Y); 29/175; Office Aide; Ski Clb; Spanish Clb; Varsity Clb; Y-Teens; Capt Drm Mjr(t); Nwsp Stf; JV Cheerleading; Hon Roll; NHS; PTSA Schrlshp 86; Robert Morris; Mrktng.

YASTREMSKI, ROBERT; Hanover Area HS; Ashley, PA; (Y); 9/182; Im Bsktbl; High Hon Roll; Jr NHS; NHS; Wilkes Barre Campus Advsry Bd Schlrshp Penn ST, Hanover Area Poetry Cntst 2nd Sr Div 86; Penn ST Wilkes Barre; Engrng.

YATCILLA, PETER; St Josephs Prep Schl; Philadephia, PA; (Y); Cmnty Wkr; Library Aide; Nwsp Stf; Im Bsktbl; Im Ftbl; Var Golf; High Hon Roll; Hon Roll; Work Scholar 83-87; Chem.

YATES, EDNARD; Hampton HS; Allison Pk, PA; (Y); #13 In Class; Church Yth Grp; FCA; French Clb; Ski Clb; Band; School Musical; Off Frsh Cls; Off Soph Cls; Off Jr Cls; Crs Cntry; Pole Vaulting Schlr Rcrd; St Ski Team; Arch.

YATSONSKY, ELLEN; Western Wayne HS; Lake Ariel, PA; (Y); 7/148; Church Yth Grp; Hosp Aide; Mgr(s); Score Keeper; Sftbl; VP Capt Tennis; High Hon Roll; Hon Roll; Jr NHS; NHS; US Navy/Army Rsrve Schlr/Athl Awd 86; Bloomsburg U; Bio.

YAUCH, JIM; Carrick HS; Pittsburgh, PA; (S); Letterman Clb; Nwsp Stf; Yrbk Stf; Ftbl; Wt Lftg; Hon Roll; Military.

YAUGER, MELISSA; Fairchance-Georges HS; Uniontown, PA; (Y); Band; Concert Band; Mrchg Band; Yrbk Stf; VP Frsh Cls; VP Jr Cls; Var Cheerleading; Var Twrlr; Var Hon Roll; Drama Clb; Med.

YAUNT, SARAH; Hampton HS; Allison Pk, PA; (Y); 19/220; Science Clb; SADD; Stage Crew; Trs Sr Cls; Ftbl; Powder Puff Ftbl; High Hon Roll; Trs NHS; Pres Schlr; French Clb; Wstnghs Sci Hnrs Inst 86; Wmn In Cnstrctn Schlrshp 86; PA ST; Engrng.

YAZWINSKY, JILL; Crestwood HS; Mountaintop, PA; (Y); Ski Clb; Teachers Aide; Twrlr; Hon Roll; Hosp Aide; Yrbk Stf; Spec Educ Tutor Hnr Awd 85-86; Majorette Co-Capt 85; Majorette Featr 86; Educ.

YEAGER, ALISSA; Northampton SR HS; Northampton, PA; (S); AFS; Model UN; SADD; Nwsp Rptr; Nwsp Stf; Trk; High Hon Roll; Hon Roll; Voic Of Democrcy Essy Cntst 3rd Pl 83 & 84; Rotry Clb Outstndng Schlstc Rcrd 86; Hlth Fld.

YEAGER, EDWARD; Cambria Heights HS; Carrolltown, PA; (Y); 98/200; Var L Bsbl; Var Capt Ftbl; Im Wt Lftg; Hon Roll; Bsbl All Trnmnt Tm; Tms Ldng Rushr-Ftbl Ttl Yds 1654; Temple; Elem Ed.

YEAGER, MICHAEL P; Cardinal O Hara HS; Clifton Heights, PA; (Y); 25/772; Church Yth Grp; Spanish Clb; Band; Concert Band; Drm Mjr(t); Mrchg Band; JV Bsbl; High Hon Roll; Hon Roll; NHS; Pal Athl Awd 84; Sci Fair Hnr Mntn 85; Nwscrrir Of Yr 84-85.

YEAGER, SUSAN R; North Allegheny SR HS; Pittsburgh, PA; (Y); 118/630; Yrbk Ed-Chief; Off Sr Cls; Stu Cncl; Cheerleading; Trk; Jr NHS; Ntl Merit SF; Pres Schlr; Bell Telephone Co Schlrshp 86; OH U Manasseh Ctlr Schlrshp 86; OH U Admsns W/Distnctn 86; OH U Hnrs Tutrl Coll; Telecomm.

YEAGER, TARA; William Allen High; Allentown, PA; (Y); 44/604; Church Yth Grp; Girl Scts; Leo Clb; Yrbk Stf; NHS; Ntl Merit Ltr; Exploring; Ski Clb; High Hon Roll; Hon Roll; Cthlc Mrn Mdl, Grl Scts Slvr Ldrshp & Slvr Awd 84; Temple; Phrmcy.

YEAGER, TERESA; Lakeview HS; Clarks Mills, PA; (S); 3/120; Girl Scts; Intnl Clb; Science Clb; Band; Concert Band; Mrchg Band; Pep Band; School Play; Nwsp Stf; NHS.

YEAGER, THOMAS; Farrell HS; Farrell, PA; (Y); 40/100; Art Clb; Drama Clb; English Clb; French Clb; Letterman Clb; Varsity Clb; Band; Chorus; Concert Band; Mrchg Band; NEDT 84; Penn ST.

YEAGER, TIMOTHY; Washington HS; Washington, PA; (S); 14/157; Band; Concert Band; Jazz Band; Mrchg Band; Symp Band; JV Var Wrstlng; High Hon Roll; Hon Roll; Cornell U; Chem Engnrng.

YEAGLEY, MICHAEL; Annville-Cleona HS; Cleona, PA; (S); 7/105; Band; Pres Chorus; Madrigals; School Musical; Var L Socr; Trs NHS; NEDT Awd; Trs Church Yth Grp; Math Tm; Dist Bnd 84 & 85; Dist Chrs 85 & 86; Lebanon Vly Coll Hnrs Bnd 84-86; Music.

YEAGLEY, PAM; Elizabethtown Area HS; Elizabethtown, PA; (S); 31/221; Church Yth Grp; 4-H; Teachers Aide; Pres Chorus; Concert Band; Mrchg Band; Orch; 4-H Awd; Messiah Coll Acad Scholar 86-87; Grl Mnth 86; Messiah Coll; Bus Adm.

YEAGY, MICHAEL; Northern SR HS; Dillsburg, PA; (Y); 79/209; Var Socr; IN U; Bus Mgmt.

YEANY, TANYA STORM; Redbank Valley JR SR HS; Mayport, PA; (Y); 13/125; Cmnty Wkr; FHA; Spanish Clb; Mrchg Band; School Play; Yrbk Phtg; Yrbk Stf; Sec Frsh Cls; Bskbtl; Score Keeper; Acadmc Schlrshp ORU 86-87; Outstndng Mjrtt Squad Capt 4 Yrs Awd 86; Phys Ftnss Awd 86; ORU; Pre-Law.

YEARICK, BOBBI JO; Lock Haven HS; Flemington, PA; (Y); 49/237; Art Clb; Spanish Clb; Lock Haven U; Scl Wrk.

YEARICK, JOHNNI; Bellefonte Area SR HS; Bellefonte, PA; (Y); 39/217; Church Yth Grp; VP German Clb; Band; Chorus; Mrchg Band; Rep Jr Cls; Rep Sr Cls; Rep Stu Cncl; Var Gym; Capt Twrlr; Beta Chi Iota, Phi Gamma Delta Soro Awd, Womens Clb Outstndngr Sr, Ms Keystone Cntrl Mjrte Comp 86; Eastenr IL U; German Educ.

YEARY, RAMONA; Owen J Roberts HS; Parkerford, PA; (Y); Letterman Clb; School Musical; Rep Frsh Cls; Var Capt Cheerleading; Var Swmmng; Var Trk; High Hon Roll; Outstndng Sr Schlr Awd 85-86; Temple U; Phy Therapy.

YECH, DONNA; Hanover Area JR SR HS; Wilkes Barre, PA; (Y); Key Clb; Yrbk Stf; L Sftbl; Trk; Vllybl; Hon Roll; NHS.

YECK, MICHELLE; Riverside HS; Moosic, PA; (Y); Dance Clb; Girl Scts; Hosp Aide; Ski Clb; Church Choir; Variety Show; Stu Cncl; Var Co-Capt Cheerleading; Trk; Hon Roll; Phy Thrpy.

YEDLICKA, TAMMY; Milton Hershey HS; Port Charlotte, FL; (S); 3/111; Band; Lit Mag; Stu Cncl; Cheerleading; Crs Cntry; Fld Hcky; L Stat Swmmng; Trk; High Hon Roll; NHS; Schlr Of Mnth 85; Chem.

YEDSENA, SUZANNE; Mahanoy Area HS; Mahanoy City, PA; (Y); Art Clb; Debate Tm; Drama Clb; Band; Pep Band; School Play; Variety Show; Yrbk Stf; Pres Frsh Cls; VP Soph Cls; PA ST-BLMSBRG; Law.

YEH, SABRINA; Henderson HS; W Chester, PA; (S); 3/348; Art Clb; Cmnty Wkr; Intnl Clb; Math Tm; Quiz Bowl; Ski Clb; Lit Mag; Fld Hcky; Trs French Hon Soc.

YEICH, BRIAN; Western Wayne HS; Lake Ariel, PA; (Y); 32/140; Boy Scts; Church Yth Grp; Var L Ftbl; Var L Trk; Im Wt Lftg; Hon Roll; PA ST; Forestry.

YEICH, KENNETH; Danville Area HS; Washingtonville, PA; (Y); Computer Clb; Ski Clb; Spanish Clb; Rep Frsh Cls; Trs Soph Cls; Trs Jr Cls; Rep Stu Cncl; Var Capt Bsbl; Var Capt Socr; JV Wrstlng; U Of MS; Comp Sci.

YEIGH, TRACY; Middleburg Joint HS; Kreamer, PA; (Y); 14/125; Trs German Clb; Ski Clb; Y-Teens; Chorus; Stage Crew; Cheerleading; Hon Roll; NHS.

YEISER, TINA; Eastern Lebanon County HS; Myerstown, PA; (Y); 64/159; Trs Sec Church Yth Grp; Band; Chorus; Concert Band; Pep Band; Off Soph Cls; Off Jr Cls; Acctg.

YELOVICH, JEAN; North Star HS; Stoystown, PA; (Y); 12/136; Political Wkr; Ski Clb; Band; Concert Band; Mrchg Band; School Play; Pres Sr Cls; Rep Stu Cncl; Trs NHS; Sec AFS; Hmnts Day-1st Pl Music Ovrall 85-86; 1st Rnnr-Up PA Mple Queen-Schlrshp 85-86; Franklin Coll; Engl.

YEN, DAVID; William Allen HS; Allentown, PA; (Y); 2/670; Pres Key Clb; Sec Pres Ski Clb; Ed Nwsp Stf; Rep VP Stu Cncl; Socr; Trk; Pres NHS; Ntl Merit SF; Rotary Awd; Boy Scts; Attnd HOBY Ldrshp Smnrs For E PA 85; Cntmpry Affairs Clb Trea 86-87; Vrsty Rifle Team Co-Cap 83-87; Cornell; Plstc Surgery.

YENCA, JULIANNE; Deer Lakes HS; Tarentum, PA; (Y); Church Yth Grp; Exploring; Speech Tm; Varsity Clb; Band; Color Guard; Mrchg Band; Pep Band; Stat L Trk; High Hon Roll; Frnch Ambssdr.

YENCHA, JOANNE; St Huberts HS; Philadelphia, PA; (Y); 15/367; Math Clb; Red Cross Aide; Teachers Aide; Hon Roll.

YENCHA, STEPHEN COREY; Lake Lehman HS; Shavertown, PA; (Y); Concert Band; Jazz Band; Mrchg Band; JV Vllybl; Comp Sci.

YENKEVICH, TANYA; MMI Preparatory Schl; Sugarloaf, PA; (S); 1/35; Debate Tm; Science Clb; Nwsp Stf; Yrbk Stf; High Hon Roll; NHS; Val; Art Clb; Drama Clb; Girl Scts; German Natl Hnr Scty Pres 86; PA JR Acad Sci 83-86; Rensselaer Medal Math & Sci 85; Bio.

YERACE, ELIZABETH; Norwin SR HS; N Huntingdon, PA; (S); 25/575; French Clb; Hosp Aide; Ski Clb; SADD; Chorus; Nwsp Rptr; Rep Stu Cncl; Var Vllybl; Hon Roll; NHS; MVP Edinboro Vllybl Camp 83-84; Med.

YERGER, BARBARA; Mount Penn HS; Mt Penn, PA; (Y); 12/76; Church Yth Grp; FTA; Model UN; Service Clb; Y-Teens; Band; Chorus; Flag Corp; Vllybl; NHS; Band, Chorus, Accompnmnt Svc Awd 86; FTA Svc Awd 86; Eastern; Bio.

YERGER, DOUGLAS; Conrad Weiser HS; Wernersville, PA; (Y); 1/137; Sec JCL; Chorus; Yrbk Sprt Ed; Trs Sr Cls; Bowling; VP NHS; Ntl Merit Ltr; Pres Schlr; Val; Computer Clb; NHS NASSP Schlrshp; GMI Engrng & Mgmt Inst; Engrng.

YERGER, KURT; Penn Wood HS; Lansdowne, PA; (Y); Church Yth Grp; Stage Crew; Var Socr; Var Tennis; Hon Roll; Prfct Atten Awd; Drexel U; Fin.

YERGER, YVONNE E; Schuylkill Valley HS; Leesport, PA; (Y); 36/131; Church Yth Grp; Church Choir; School Musical; JV Cheerleading; Var Fld Hcky; Var Sftbl; JV Trk; Var Vllybl; Hon Roll; NHS; PA ST U; Instrmntatn.

YERKEY, JENNIFER; Monongahela Vly Cath HS; Belle Vernon, PA; (Y); 13/84; Pres Art Clb; JA; Ski Clb; Band; Nwsp Rptr; Off Stu Cncl; JV Vllybl; French Hon Soc; High Hon Roll; NHS; All Amer Sci Awd 84; Phrmcy.

YESALAVAGE, CARL; Lake Land JR-SR HS; Mayfield, PA; (S); Var Bsbl; Var Golf; Hon Roll; Ntl Merit Ltr; Penn ST; Engrng.

YESALAVICH, LAURIE; Bishop O Hara HS; Dickson City, PA; (S); 5/124; Pres Church Yth Grp; French Clb; Hosp Aide; Ski Clb; School Musical; Nwsp Stf; Rep Stu Cncl; High Hon Roll; NHS; Phys Thrpy.

YESVILLE, MARYLOU; Pleasant Valley HS; Saylorsburg, PA; (Y); 11/233; VP Drama Clb; VP 4-H; JA; Capt Flag Corp; School Play; Rptr Nwsp Rptr; Yrbk Bus Mgr; Yrbk Ed-Chief; Jr NHS; NHS; Top Spanish Stu; Top 20 In Clss; Aeronautics.

YETTER, DAWN; Knoch HS; Marwood, PA; (Y); Church Yth Grp; Chorus; Var L Bsktbl; Sftbl; Trk; Hon Roll; Achvt Acad Awd 84-85; Allegheny Valley Hosp; Tech.

YETTER, TAMMY; Juniata HS; Mifflin, PA; (Y); Church Yth Grp; Drama Clb; Varsity Clb; Chorus; School Musical; School Play; Yrbk Stf; Var Sftbl; High Hon Roll; Hon Roll; Schltc Awd 84; Penn ST; Nrsng.

YETTER, TERESA; Juniata HS; Mifflintown, PA; (Y); Sec Band; Chorus; Concert Band; Mrchg Band; School Musical; School Play; Yrbk Stf; Mgr Bsktbl; Mgr(s); JV Sftbl; Radiolgc Tech.

YEZBAK, CHUCK; Union Area HS; Uniontown, PA; (Y); 18/370; Church Yth Grp; Pres French Clb; Letterman Clb; Yrbk Stf; VP Stu Cncl; Im Var Bsktbl; High Hon Roll; NHS; Key Clb; Mathletes; Ntl Frgn Lang Hnr Soc 85; Best Receiver Ftbl 84.

YI, CHUNG; Hatboro-Harsham SR HS; Horsham, PA; (Y); Model UN; VP Frsh Cls; Pres Jr Cls; Rep Stu Cncl; JV Socr; JV Tennis; High Hon Roll; Hon Roll; NHS; Prfct Atten Awd; Bio Awd; AP Comp Sci Awd; Aerosp Engrng.

YINGLING, MEGHAN P; Blairsville SR HS; Blairsville, PA; (Y); FBLA; JA; Ski Clb; Color Guard; Hon Roll; Bio.

YINGST, DONNA; Donegal HS; Mount Joy, PA; (Y); 43/100; Varsity Clb; Capt Color Guard; Yrbk Phtg; Rep Frsh Cls; Rep Soph Cls; Rep Jr Cls; Rep Sr Cls; Rep Stu Cncl; Var Capt Cheerleading; Millersville; Chld Psychlgy.

YINGST, LISA; Annville-Cleona HS; Annville, PA; (Y); Drama Clb; French Clb; Letterman Clb; Service Clb; Var Capt Crs Cntry; JV Var Trk; Hon Roll; NHS; Elmer Hafer Schlrshp Awd-Polic Fld/Amer Lgn 86; Polic Sci.

YINGST, STACY; Blue Mountain Acad; Quarryville, PA; (Y); Teachers Aide; Chorus; Sec Frsh Cls; Hon Roll; Vocal/Instrmntl Touring Grp-Praise Ensmbl 85-86; Secy Pgm 87; Phys Thrpy.

YINKEY, JULIE; Meyersdale Area HS; Meyersdale, PA; (Y); Church Yth Grp; Band; Concert Band; Mrchg Band; Nwsp Rptr; Hon Roll; NHS; US Achvt Acad Ldrshp 86; Pres Acad Fitness Awd 86.

YOCKEY, ERIC; Kittaning SR HS; Worthington, PA; (Y); Boy Scts; Band; Concert Band; Mrchg Band; Stage Crew; Hon Roll; Amer Legion Schl Awd.

YOCOM, BRADLEY; Carson Long Military Inst; Vincent, OH; (S); 4/46; Chess Clb; ROTC; School Play; Lit Mag; Im Sftbl; Im Vllybl; Hon Roll; Mjr Rodney P Grove Bio Medal 85; The Citadel; Pol Sci.

YOCUM, CAROLE; Marple Newton SR HS; Newtown Sq, PA; (Y); Service Clb; Yrbk Stf; Fld Hcky; Mgr(s).

YOCUM, JENNIFER A; Pennridge HS; Sellersville, PA; (Y); 32/436; Am Leg Aux Girls St; Library Aide; Nwsp Stf; Rep Frsh Cls; Sec Jr Cls; Rep Stu Cncl; Var L Cheerleading; High Hon Roll; NHS; Pres Schlr; Rutgers U; Pharmacy.

YOCUM, KAREN; Sun Valley HS; Aston, PA; (Y); Hon Roll; Widener U; Acctng.

YOCUM, LISA; West Perry HS; Shermans Dale, PA; (Y); 28/188; Spanish Clb; Varsity Clb; Chorus; Capt Color Guard; Mrchg Band; School Play; Yrbk Stf; JV Sftbl; Ntl Merit Ltr; Mst Outstndng JR Art 85-86; 1st, 2nd, 3rd Pl Awd Vsl Arts Prry Cnty Cncl Arts Cntst 85-86; Art.

YOCUM, RANDY E; Schuylkill Valley HS; Leesport, PA; (Y); 4/133; Exploring; Var L Bsbl; Var L Bsktbl; Var L Ftbl; Var L Vllybl; Wt Lftg; High Hon Roll; Hon Roll; NHS; Prfct Atten Awd; All St Ftbl Tm 86; All Berks-Lancaster Ftbl Tm 86; Rcvd Temples Pres Awd 86; Temple U; Phys Ther.

YODER, ANITA; Rockwood Area HS; Somerset, PA; (S); 11/95; Church Yth Grp; Computer Clb; Band; Chorus; Church Choir; Var Bsktbl; Var Sftbl; Hon Roll; Phys Educ.

YODER, BRADD; Souderton Area HS; Greenlane, PA; (Y); Aud/Vis; FCA; Quiz Bowl; Stage Crew; Pres Frsh Cls; VP Soph Cls; Rep Jr Cls; Pres Stu Cncl; Var Bsbl; Var Bsktbl; Rick Ball Memrl Awd-Ldrshp, Ctznshp 83; Union Leag Phildlphia Boys Awd 83; Engrng.

YODER, DARRIN; Kishacoquillas HS; Belleville, PA; (Y); 7/144; Pres Church Yth Grp; Computer Clb; Spanish Clb; Nwsp Rptr; Trs Jr Cls; Trs Sr Cls; Trs Stu Cncl; High Hon Roll; VP NHS; Stu Of Mnth 84; Mansfield U; Comp.

YODER, JEFF; Butler SR HS; Butler, PA; (Y); Am Leg Boys St; Exploring; FCA; JA; Ski Clb; Spanish Clb; Teachers Aide; School Musical; Rep Frsh Cls; Rep Soph Cls; JR Clb Chmpn Glf Btlr Cntry Clb 85; Mst Actv Stu Cncl JR Cls 86; Stu Cncl Cnfrnc Erie Mcdwll 86; Engrng.

YODER, KEITH; Conemaugh Twp Area HS; Davidsville, PA; (Y); 19/102; Pres Church Yth Grp; Drama Clb; Speech Tm; Band; Concert Band; Mrchg Band; School Musical; School Play; Hon Roll; Acdmc All Amer Awd 85-86; Bus Admin.

YODER, KELLY; Wilson SR HS; Wyomissing, PA; (Y); French Clb; Library Aide; Frsh Cls; Soph Cls; Cheerleading; Sftbl; Hon Roll.

YODER, LISA; Abington HS; Glenside, PA; (Y); 26/535; Latin Clb; Capt Flag Corp; Capt Mrchg Band; Hon Roll; NHS; Magna Cum Laude Natl Latin Exam 85; Highest Hnrs-Math/Sci Soc Women Engnrs 86; Lehigh U; Engrng.

YODER, LISA; Seneca Valley HS; Harmony, PA; (Y); Drama Clb; Pep Clb; Church Choir; School Play; Stage Crew; Nwsp Stf; Mgr Swmmng; Timer; Psychlgy.

YODER, PETER; Manheim Central HS; Manheim, PA; (Y); Boy Scts; Church Yth Grp; VICA; Band; Church Choir; Concert Band; Mrchg Band; Golf; God Cntry Awd; Hon Roll; Eagle Scout Awd 86; Elctrcl.

YODER, SHARON; Conemaugh Twp Area JR SR HS; Hollsopple, PA; (S); 12/101; Art Clb; Sec Trs Church Yth Grp; Drama Clb; School Play; Nwsp Stf; VP Soph Cls; Pres Jr Cls; Stu Cncl; Sftbl; Hon Roll; Natl Englsh Mrt Awd 86; Med.

YODER, STEVEN; Columbia-Montour Vo-Tech Schl; Nescopeck, PA; (Y); FFA; Letterman Clb; VICA; Var L Ftbl; Hon Roll; Plmng.

YOHA, THERESA; Gateway SR HS; Monroeville, PA; (Y); 75/509; Church Yth Grp; Cmnty Wkr; Ski Clb; Rep Frsh Cls; Rep Soph Cls; Rep Jr Cls; Rep Sr Cls; Rep Stu Cncl; Im JV Vllybl; Pitt U; Physcl Thrpst.

YOHE, DIANE; Dubois Area HS; Du Bois, PA; (Y); 14/267; Pres Church Yth Grp; Cmnty Wkr; SADD; Chorus; Church Choir; School Musical; Swing Chorus; Rep Stu Cncl; Stat Bsktbl; High Hon Roll; Spnsh Ed.

YOHE, GREGORY D; Gettysburg SR HS; Gettysburg, PA; (Y); Rep Frsh Cls; JV Bsktbl; JV Trk; Var Wrstlng; Pre-Med.

YOHN, AMY; Northern Lebanon HS; Jonestown, PA; (Y); 7/180; Cmnty Wkr; Library Aide; SADD; Chorus; Church Choir; School Musical; School Play; High Hon Roll; Hon Roll; NHS; Elem Educ.

YOHN, CARLA; Southern Huntingdon Co HS; Blairs Mills, PA; (Y); Church Yth Grp; FBLA; FHA; VP GAA; SADD; Varsity Clb; Band; Chorus; Church Choir; Concert Band; Bus Grphcs Awd 86; Bus Mrchndsng.

YOHN JR, JACK; Greenwood HS; Millerstown, PA; (S); Am Leg Boys St; Church Yth Grp; Nwsp Ed-Chief; Sec Frsh Cls; Sec Soph Cls; Rep Stu Cncl; Hon Roll; NHS; Schl Mascot 85-86; The Amer Legion Schl Awd 83; Zoology.

YOHO, MELISSA; New Castle SR HS; New Castle, PA; (S); 22/253; AFS; Church Yth Grp; Girl Scts; Spanish Clb; Mrchg Band; Var Trk; Im Vllybl; Hon Roll.

YOKIEL, MARGARET; Brownsville Area SR HS; Grindstone, PA; (Y); Church Yth Grp; Library Aide; SADD; Church Choir; Im Mgr Socr; Im Mgr Sftbl; Im Mgr Vllybl; Hon Roll; Nrsng.

YOKOPENIC, PAMELA; Hempfield Area SR HS; Greensburg, PA; (Y); 67/657; Ski Clb; Band; Sec Stu Cncl; Swmmng; Vllybl; High Hon Roll; Hon Roll; Jr NHS; French Clb; Concert Band; Duquesne U Comptv Schlrshp 86; Bell PA/Diamnd ST Tlphn 86; Duquesne U; Phrmcy.

YOMMER, MICHELLE; Meyersdale Area HS; Meyersdale, PA; (Y); Spanish Clb; Chorus; School Play; Nwsp Rptr; Yrbk Stf; Stat Bsktbl; Var L Cheerleading; Stat Wrstlng; NHS; Pres Schlr; Prs Phy Ftnss Awd 86; Juniata Coll; Psych.

YONKOSKI, CATHY; Forest Hills SR HS; Dunlo, PA; (Y); 1/167; Am Leg Aux Girls St; Nwsp Rptr; Yrbk Ed-Chief; Pres Stu Cncl; Dnfth Awd; Jr NHS; Pres NHS; Pres Schlr; Spanish NHS; Val; Heffly Memrl Schlrshp-U Of Pittsbrgh Johnstwn 86; Slovak Cathlc Sokol Schlrshp 86; Pres Acad Ftns Awd; U Of Pittsbrgh Jhnstwn; Cmnctns.

YONKOSKI, SHIRLEEN; Coughlin HS; Wilkes Barre, PA; (Y); 44/342; Cmnty Wkr; French Clb; Hosp Aide; Band; Concert Band; Mrchg Band; Yrbk Stf; High Hon Roll; Hon Roll; NEDT Test Hgh Scr; Psychlgy.

YONKOVITZ JR, ALBERT F; Steel Valley HS; Munhall, PA; (Y); 30/201; Church Yth Grp; Band; Mrchg Band; Rep Stu Cncl; Co-Capt Swmmng; Hon Roll; NHS; Bus.

YONKOVITZ, VICKI; Steel Valley HS; W Homestead, PA; (Y); 21/229; Concert Band; Drm Mjr(t); Flag Corp; Hon Roll; NHS; Pitt; Nrsng.

YOO, HONG; Fairview HS; Fairview, PA; (Y); 27/187; Science Clb; Ski Clb; Teachers Aide; Varsity Clb; Jazz Band; Var Crs Cntry; Var Trk; Hon Roll; Carnegie Mellon; Med.

YOO, LISA; Central Christian HS; Du Bois, PA; (Y); 1/40; Drama Clb; Pep Clb; Ski Clb; Varsity Clb; Chorus; School Play; JV Capt Cheerleading; Vllybl; Bausch & Lomb Sci Awd; High Hon Roll; Pre Med.

YORDY, DONALD; Hamefield SR HS; Columbia, PA; (Y); Pittsburgh U; Sci.

YORK, LAURA; North Pocono HS; Moscow, PA; (Y); Band; Concert Band; Mrchg Band; County Band 84; Hnrs Band 84; Geisinger Schl Nrsng; Nrsng.

YORNS, EDDIE; New Brighton HS; New Brighton, PA; (Y); 32/155; JA; Math Tm; Varsity Clb; Yrbk Stf; Bsbl; Bowling.

YOSKIN, MAURICE; Plymouth-Whitemarsh SR HS; Flourtown, PA; (Y); 10/360; Art Clb; Math Clb; Lit Mag; Trk; High Hon Roll; Ntl Merit Ltr; Sm-Fnlst Wnr Natl Spc Shttl Stu Invlvmnt Proj 84; Stu Of Mnth 83; 3rd In Sch Amer Math Exam 86; Biochem.

YOSLER, PAUL; Ambridge Area HS; Freedom, PA; (Y); German Clb; Intnl Clb; Pep Clb; Band; Hon Roll.

YOST, BETH; Our Lady Of Lourdes; Shamokin, PA; (Y); FBLA; Hosp Aide; Nwsp Stf; Yrbk Stf; Nrsg.

YOST, CAMMY; Pleasant Valley HS; Saylorsburg, PA; (Y); 12/233; Varsity Clb; Sec Frsh Cls; Sec Soph Cls; Sec Jr Cls; Var Cheerleading; Var Sftbl; High Hon Roll; Hon Roll; Top 20 83-85; Elem Educ.

YOST, CHRISTINE; Parkland SR HS; Allentown, PA; (Y); 86/462; Varsity Clb; L Sftbl; Capt Vllybl; Shippensburg U; Acctg.

YOST, CONNIE; Spring Ford SR HS; Spring City, PA; (Y); 22/237; Cmnty Wkr; German Clb; Hosp Aide; SADD; Band; Drill Tm; Hon Roll; Jr NHS; Gwynedd-Mercy Coll; Nrsng.

YOST, HEATHER; Greater Latrobe HS; Latrobe, PA; (Y); 98/337; AFS; Color Guard; Flag Corp; Ed Yrbk Stf; Mat Maids; High Hon Roll; Hon Roll; Business Careers Inst; Word Pro.

YOST, JAMIE; Mohawk Area HS; New Galilee, PA; (S); Church Yth Grp; French Clb; Ski Clb; Bsktbl; Crs Cntry; Powder Puff Ftbl; Sftbl; Trk; Hon Roll; NHS; V Ltr Track 84-86; Bio.

YOST, JODI; Northwestern Lehigh HS; Orefield, PA; (Y); Church Yth Grp; Varsity Clb; Nwsp Stf; Stu Cncl; Cheerleading; Trk; Hon Roll; Acctg.

YOST, SARAH L; Burrell SR HS; Lower Burrell, PA; (Y); VP Exploring; School Musical; School Play; L Diving; JV Var Trk; Capt Twrlr; High Hon Roll; Church Yth Grp; Drama Clb; Ski Clb; Allegheny-Kiski Valleys JR Miss Schlrshp86; Tlnt Schlrshp In Lcl & ST Pgnts 86; E Carolina U; Dance.

YOST, STEVEN E; Red Land HS; New Cumberland, PA; (Y); 30/245; Am Leg Boys St; Ski Clb; VP CAP; Stu Cncl; Im Bowling; Var Capt Socr; Trk; Im Vllybl; Cit Awd; Hon Roll; Prep Schlrshp-West Point 86; 4 Yr ROTC Schlrshp 86; Lehigh; Engrng.

YOTHERS, BOBBI; Mt Pleasant Area HS; Mt Pleasant, PA; (Y); German Clb; Concert Band; Mrchg Band; Pres Mat Maids; JV Var Score Keeper; Stat Wrstlng; Hon Roll; Intl Forgn Lang Awd Grmn 83-85; Phys Therapy.

YOTKO, CHRISTINE; Cardinal Brennen HS; Lavelle, PA; (Y); 6/65; 4-H; Library Aide; Pep Clb; Spanish Clb; Band; Chorus; Mrchg Band; School Musical; Soph Cls; Jr Cls; Inter Dsgn.

YOU, SONG C; Upper Darby HS; Upper Darby, PA; (Y); 20/550; Pres Intnl Clb; JA; Speech Tm; Im Ftbl; JV Lcrss; JV Tennis; Var Trk; NHS; Prfct Atten Awd; USAF Acad; Aerontcl Engrng.

YOUD, STEVEN J; Bradford Area HS; Bradford, PA; (Y); 7/320; Am Leg Boys St; Pres Soph Cls; Pres Sr Cls; Rep Stu Cncl; Var Capt Bsktbl; Var L Ftbl; Jr NHS; Pres NHS; NEDT Awd; Key Clb; Pres Mc Kean Cnty Mental Htlh Assn 85-87; US Air Force Acad; Aerontcl.

YOUELLS, AMY; Tunkhannock Area HS; Tunkhannock, PA; (S); 35/330; French Clb; VP Key Clb; Letterman Clb; Rep Jr Cls; Rep Sr Cls; Stat Bsktbl; Cit Awd; Hon Roll; NHS; Pre-Vet Med.

YOUELLS, TARA; Danville HS; Riverside, PA; (Y); French Clb; Sec SADD; Chorus; Var L Crs Cntry; Mat Maids; Timer; JV Trk; High Hon Roll; Hon Roll; Fshn Jrnlsm.

YOUGH, KAREN; Knoch HS; Saxonburg, PA; (Y); Church Yth Grp; School Play; Stage Crew; Nwsp Rptr; Nwsp Stf; Im Vllybl; French Hon Soc; High Hon Roll; Hon Roll; NHS.

YOUNG, AMY; Canon-Mc Millan HS; Canonsburg, PA; (Y); Office Aide; Sec Jr Cls; Sec Stu Cncl; L Cheerleading; Hon Roll; U Pittsburgh.

YOUNG, ANGUS; Johnstown HS; Johnstown, PA; (Y); CAP; Q&S; Acpl Chr; L Ice Hcky; Timer; Prfct Atten Awd; Scrub Club 86; Scrub Club Sprtsman Of Year 86; Volunteer Firefighter Of Year 85; U MD; Fire Prot Engr.

YOUNG, ANITA; West York Area HS; York, PA; (Y); 26/200; Trs Frsh Cls; Trs Soph Cls; Trs Jr Cls; JV Cheerleading; Var Vllybl; Hon Roll.

YOUNG, ANNETTE; Spring-Ford SR HS; Schwenksville, PA; (Y); 85/256; JV Fld Hcky; JV Lcrss; Hon Roll; Penn ST U; Sci.

YOUNG, ARICA; Little Flower HS For Girls; Philadelphia, PA; (Y); 42/398; Orch; School Play; Hon Roll; TV Arts & Sci Clb 84-86; Chpl Aids 84-86; Edsn Stu Cngrss 84-86; Intl Rltns.

YOUNG, BONNIE; Altoona Area HS; Altoona, PA; (Y); 11/683; Church Yth Grp; Computer Clb; Math Tm; Science Clb; Off Sr Cls; NHS; NEDT Awd; FBLA; German Clb; Spanish Clb; Wright Schl PTO Schlrshp 86; Pres Acad Fit Awd 86; HS Dipl In Soc Music 86; PA ST U; Chem Engrng.

YOUNG, BRENDA; Belle Vernon Area HS; Fayette City, PA; (Y); Pres 4-H; Pep Clb; Band; Mrchg Band; Powder Puff Ftbl; Sftbl; Cit Awd; Hon Roll; NHS.

YOUNG, CHARMAINE; George Washington HS; Philadelphi, PA; (S); Church Yth Grp; Dance Clb; DECA; Girl Scts; Hosp Aide; Model UN; Office Aide; Red Cross Aide; Church Choir; Wt Lftg; Lawyer.

YOUNG, CHRISTINE; Karns City HS; Chicora, PA; (Y); #8 In Class; Church Yth Grp; SADD; Chorus; Stage Crew; Capt Cheerleading; High Hon Roll; NHS; ICM Cruise Dir.

YOUNG, CHRISTINE; Pennsbury HS; Yardley, PA; (Y); Yrbk Stf; Frsh Cls; Soph Cls; Jr Cls; Ftbl; Hon Roll; NHS; Schlrshp Moore Coll Art 86; Advrtsng.

YOUNG, DEBRA; Jersey Shore Area HS; Linden, PA; (Y); Church Yth Grp; FBLA; Chorus; School Musical; Blmsbrg U; Accntng.

YOUNG, DENNIS; Bishop Kenrick HS; Norristown, PA; (Y); Science Clb; Nwsp Rptr; Nwsp Stf; Hon Roll; NHS.

YOUNG, DOUGLAS A; Everett Area HS; Breezewood, PA; (Y); Spanish Clb; Varsity Clb; Var Bsbl; Var Ftbl; NEDT Awd; US Army; Law Enf.

YOUNG, DOUGLAS A; Scranton Prep Schl; Clarks Summit, PA; (Y); Ski Clb; Var L Ftbl; Var L Trk; Var Wt Lftg; Hon Roll; Med.

YOUNG, GREG; Cedar Crest HS; Lebanon, PA; (Y); 7/303; German Clb; Pep Clb; Orch; School Musical; Bsktbl; Socr; High Hon Roll; Hon Roll; NHS.

YOUNG, GREG; Warwick HS; Lititz, PA; (Y); 56/222; Church Yth Grp; JV Var Ftbl; Im Vllybl; High Hon Roll; Hon Roll.

YOUNG, HOLLY; Elk County Christian HS; St Marys, PA; (Y); 42/80; Library Aide; Ski Clb; SADD; Yrbk Stf; Sec Stu Cncl; Bsktbl; Trk; Hon Roll; E Carolina U; Pysch.

YOUNG, JENNIFER; Pennsbury HS; Levittown, PA; (Y); Church Yth Grp; German Clb; Church Choir; School Musical; Trk; Hon Roll; NHS; U PA; Acctng.

YOUNG, JIM; Mechanicsburg Area SR HS; Mechanicsburg, PA; (Y); 10/313; Debate Tm; NFL; Ski Clb; Chorus; Yrbk Stf; Trs Frsh Cls; Rep Soph Cls; High Hon Roll; NHS; Duke.

YOUNG, JOHN; Monogahela Valley Catholic HS; Monessen, PA; (Y); 7/84; Rep Frsh Cls; VP Stu Cncl; Var Bsktbl; Var Golf; Spanish NHS; Engrng.

YOUNG, KAREN; Hickory HS; Sharpsville, PA; (Y); 2/175; Church Yth Grp; Math Clb; Service Clb; Chorus; NHS; Pres Schlr; Sal; Pres Spanish NHS; U Hnrs Schlrshp Duquesne U 85-86; Cert Mrt Amer Chem Scty 86; Duquesne U; Phrmcy.

YOUNG, KARLA; Spring-Ford SR HS; Royersford, PA; (Y); 80/248; Sec French Clb; Pep Clb; Ski Clb; Color Guard; Drill Tm; Yrbk Stf; Off Jr Cls; Off Sr Cls; Cheerleading; Wrstlng; Lcok Haven U Of PA; Phy Thrpy.

YOUNG, KAY; Central Dauphin HS; Harrisburg, PA; (Y); High Hon Roll; Hon Roll; NHS; Vet Med.

YOUNG, KENNETH B; Lock Haven HS; Lock Haven, PA; (Y); 4/260; VP French Clb; Trs Key Clb; Model UN; Trs Stu Cncl; Var Capt Socr; Trk; Hon Roll; VP NHS; Lions Clb Ctznshp Awd 86; Lock Haven Knghts Columbs Awd Exclnc 86; Coll Of William & Mary; Bus.

YOUNG, KIMBERLY; Penns Manor Joint JR SR HS; Penn Run, PA; (Y); Camera Clb; Cmnty Wkr; Chorus; Stu Cncl; Var Cheerleading; Prfct Atten Awd; Congress Bundestag Yth Enchng Prog 84; PHD Psychology.

YOUNG, KRISTIN; Harbor Creek HS; Erie, PA; (Y); Spanish Clb; Drill Tm; Mrchg Band; Variety Show; Yrbk Stf; Rep Soph Cls; Rep Jr Cls; Rep Stu Cncl; JV Var Bsktbl; Var L Sftbl.

YOUNG, KRISTIN; Troy HS; Troy, PA; (Y); 25/140; Church Yth Grp; Drama Clb; French Clb; Band; Church Choir; Concert Band; Mrchg Band; Pep Band; School Play; Nwsp Ed-Chief; All Cnfrnc In Bnd 85; PA ST Blmsbrg; Elem Ed.

YOUNG, LISA; Butler SR HS; Butler, PA; (Y); Off Church Yth Grp; GAA; Office Aide; Chorus; JV Lcrss; Im Vllybl; Stat Wrstlng; Hon Roll.

YOUNG, LISA; Conneaut Lake HS; Conneaut Lake, PA; (Y); Drama Clb; Girl Scts; Sec Spanish Clb; SADD; Chorus; School Play; Nwsp Phtg; Nwsp Rptr; Nwsp Stf; Yrbk Rptr; Slippery Rock U; Elem Ed.

YOUNG, MARK; Greater Johnstown HS; Johnstown, PA; (Y); Church Yth Grp; Spanish Clb; Band; Concert Band; Mrchg Band; Pep Band; Tennis; IN U Of PA; Elem Educ.

YOUNG, MELISSA; Cornell HS; Coraopolis, PA; (Y); 9/85; VP Church Yth Grp; Sec French Clb; JA; Concert Band; Mrchg Band; Stage Crew; Nwsp Stf; Yrbk Stf; High Hon Roll; Jr NHS; Bio.

YOUNG, MICHAEL; Neshamin HS; Levittown, PA; (Y); 62/702; JV Wrstlng; NHS; Temple U; Elec Engrng.

YOUNG, MISSY; Slippery Rock Area HS; Slippery Rock, PA; (Y); Intnl Clb; Pep Clb; Chorus; Stage Crew; Yrbk Stf; Rep Stu Cncl; Stat Bsktbl; Hon Roll; NHS; Soclgy.

YOUNG, RANDI S; Peters Twp HS; Mc Murray, PA; (Y); SADD; Drill Tm; Mrchg Band; Var Gym; Var Pom Pon; Spanish NHS.

YOUNG, SHAWN A; Northern York County HS; Dillsburg, PA; (Y); 63/200; Chess Clb; Computer Clb; Concert Band; Mrchg Band; Hon Roll; Millersville U; Physcs.

YOUNG, SHERRI; Kutztown Area HS; Kutztown, PA; (Y); 20/135; Church Yth Grp; Band; Chorus; Concert Band; Capt Drill Tm; School Play; Var JV Cheerleading; High Hon Roll; NHS; Kutztown Area HS Jr Miss; Law.

YOUNG, STACY; Hempfield HS; Lancaster, PA; (Y); 16/432; Hosp Aide; Teachers Aide; Band; Chorus; School Play; Nwsp Rptr; Stu Cncl; Hon Roll; NHS; Ntl Merit Ltr; Hnrs Cert-Cls For Gftd Stus Frnkln/Mrshl Coll 85; Intl Rltns.

YOUNG, SUSAN; Freeport SR HS; Sarver, PA; (Y); Band; Concert Band; Drill Tm; Mrchg Band; Pep Band; School Musical; Stage Crew; Nwsp Stf; Yrbk Stf; Capt Sftbl; Slippery Rock U; Spec Ed.

YOUNG, SUSAN ANN; Cedar Cliff HS; New Cumberland, PA; (Y); 2/242; Am Leg Aux Girls St; Trs Key Clb; Pres Model UN; Pres Soph Cls; Pres Jr Cls; Var Fld Hcky; Capt Trk; High Hon Roll; NHS; GAA; Latin Hnr Soc; Girls Nation-Amer Lgn Aux 86; Natl Affairs Delg 86; Pre-Med.

YOUNG, TODD; Greater Johnstown HS; Johnstown, PA; (Y); JA; Chorus; Nwsp Stf; Jr Cls; Tennis; High Hon Roll; Hon Roll; Prfct Atten Awd; Bus.

YOUNG, WENDY; Altonna Area HS; Altoona, PA; (S); Trs French Clb; VP JA; Math Clb; Y-Teens; Bsktbl; Sftbl; Hon Roll; PA ST U; Acctng.

YOUNGBLOOD, JEFFREY; Donegal HS; Mount Joy, PA; (Y); Red Cross Aide; Band; VP Sr Cls; JV Ftbl; Swmmng; Hon Roll; OK ST U; Engr.

YOUNKEN, MICHELLE; Waynesburg Central HS; Waynesburg, PA; (Y); Art Clb; Sec Church Yth Grp; Pres Natl Beta Clb; Spanish Clb; JV Cheerleading; High Hon Roll; NHS; Spanish NHS; Spnsh I Awd 83-84; Spnsh II Awd 84-85; Elem Educ.

YOUNKER, DEIDRA A; West Hazleton HS; Tresckow, PA; (Y); Library Aide; SADD; Chorus; Cheerleading; Penn ST U; Psychlgy.

YOUNKIN, VANESSA; Rockwood Area HS; Markleton, PA; (S); 23/96; Band; Chorus; Mrchg Band; Stu Cncl; High Hon Roll; Hon Roll; Jr NHS; NHS.

YOUNT, JAMES; Kiski Area HS; Vandergrift, PA; (Y); 13/378; Key Clb; Varsity Clb; Concert Band; Nwsp Stf; Var L Ftbl; Var L Trk; High Hon Roll; Lion Awd; Trs NHS; Ntl Merit Ltr; Russellton Medcl Group 1st Annual Schlrshp 86; PA ST U; Engrng.

YOURISH, BRADLEY; Deer Lake S HS; Cheswick, PA; (Y); 9/180; Bsktbl; High Hon Roll; NHS; Ntl Merit Ltr; W PA Ldrshp Sem 85; Gftd & Talent Enrchmnt Pgm 77-86; Med.

YOUSHOCK, SHARON; Mid-Valley HS; Dickson City, PA; (Y); Drama Clb; Girl Scts; Library Aide; Pep Clb; Chorus; Hon Roll; Bus.

YOUST, CRAIG; Reading SR HS; Reading, PA; (Y); 5/520; Key Clb; Model UN; Quiz Bowl; Pres Stu Cncl; Bsktbl; Hon Roll; NHS; William H Luden Schlrshp 86; Mr & Mrs Edwin S Youse Schlrshp 86; U Of NC; Med.

YOVETICH, BARBARA; Peters Township HS; Mc Murray, PA; (Y); Dance Clb; Thesps; Varsity Clb; Co-Capt Drill Tm; Orch; Cheerleading; Powder Puff Ftbl; Trk; High Hon Roll; Allegheny Coll.

YOW, LAURA; Strath Haven HS; Media, PA; (Y); Drama Clb; Intnl Clb; School Musical; School Play; JV Tennis.

YOWAN, GARY; Bethel Park HS; Pittsburgh, PA; (Y); JV Var Bsktbl; JV Var Ftbl; JV Trk; Im Var Wt Lftg; NHS; Engrng.

YOZVIAK, ANDREW; Greater Nanticoke Area HS; Nanticoke, PA; (Y); 13/251; Boy Scts; Band; Chorus; Concert Band; Mrchg Band; Orch; School Musical; Variety Show; Nwsp Stf; Rep Stu Cncl; Dist Regnl Band 85; Janet Heller Music Awd 86; Berkeley Coll; Music.

YUCHA, JENNIFER; Shikellamy HS; Sunbury, PA; (Y); 1/319; Am Leg Aux Girls St; French Clb; Sec Stu Cncl; Var Bsktbl; JV Sftbl; Bausch & Lomb Sci Awd; Pres NHS; Ntl Merit Ltr; Hug O Brian Yth Ldrshp Semnr Partcpt 85; Stdnt Membr Schl Brd 85-87; Acadmc All Amer 86; PA ST U; Math.

YUCHA, MARK P; Shikellamy HS; Sunbury, PA; (Y); 5/319; Am Leg Boys St; Var Bsktbl; Var Trk; Hon Roll; NHS; Voice Dem Awd; Acad All Amer 86; PA ST U.

YUCHA, SCOTT; Mt Carmel JR & SR HS; Mt Carmel, PA; (Y); 22/168; Boy Scts; Pres Key Clb; Spanish Clb; Concert Band; Jazz Band; Mrchg Band; Stu Cncl; Bsktbl; Var L Ftbl; Var Trk.

YUGOVICH, JACQUELINE C; United HS; Armagh, PA; (Y); 10/161; Ski Clb; High Hon Roll; Hon Roll; Prfct Atten Awd; Acad All Amer 86; Crimnlgy.

YUHANIAK, JOHN; Our Lady Of The Sacred Heart HS; Corapolis, PA; (Y); Art Clb; Computer Clb; Hon Roll; NHS; Jr-Sr Hist/Govt Econ Acdmc Awd, Jr-Sr Eng Acdmc Awd, Jr Religion Acdmc Awd 86; ICM Schl Bus; Comp Sci.

YUHAS, KATHLEEN; Pius X HS; Pen Argyl, PA; (Y); Hosp Aide; Pres Pep Clb; Varsity Clb; Church Choir; Var Capt Cheerleading; Lcrss; Hon Roll; 1st Tm All Star Chldr 83-85; Fshn Mdse.

YUHAS, MICHELLE; Greater Johnstown HS; Johnstown, PA; (Y); Pres Exploring; Hosp Aide; Band; Chorus; Church Choir; School Musical; Nwsp Stf; Yrbk Stf; Co-Capt Twrlr; Hon Roll; Hnrb Mntn Tribune Democrts Wrtng Cont 85; Jrnlsm.

YUHAS, SCOTT; Bishop Mc Cort HS; Davidsville, PA; (Y); Spanish Clb; Chorus; School Musical; Hon Roll; Good Citznshp Awd 83; U Of Pittsburg; Elec Engr.

YUHASZ, AMY; Rocky Grove HS; Franklin, PA; (Y); 14/92; VP Church Yth Grp; 4-H; Band; Chorus; Ed Yrbk Stf; Rep Stu Cncl; JV Var Bsktbl; Var L Sftbl; JV L Vllybl; Hon Roll; Sch Rep Hugh O Brien Ldrshp Semnr 85; Schlrshp 4-H Congrss PA ST 85-86; Clarion U Summr Acad 86; Poltcl Sci.

YUHOUSE, LISA; Mt Pleasant Area HS; Hunker, PA; (Y); German Clb; Hosp Aide; Library Aide; Ski Clb; Teachers Aide; Yrbk Phtg; Yrbk Rptr; Yrbk Stf; Rep Frsh Cls; VP Soph Cls; Pitt; RN.

YUN, SANG; Cedar Crest HS; Lebanon, PA; (Y); Sec Drama Clb; Pres French Clb; Quiz Bowl; Orch; School Musical; School Play; Tennis; Vllybl; Hon Roll; Pres NHS; Silv Medallion 86; Princeton U; Psych.

YUN, SCOTT; Churchill HS; Pittsburgh, PA; (Y); 25/188; JV Var Ftbl; JV Vllybl; Im Wt Lftg; High Hon Roll; Ntl Conf Christians Jews Ldrshp Traing Wrkshp 85; U PA; Mgmt.

YUNKUNIS, PATRICIA; Wyoming Area HS; W Pittston, PA; (Y); Key Clb; Color Guard; Yrbk Stf; Rep Frsh Cls; Math.

YURCHAK, KIRK; Liberty HS; Bethlehem, PA; (Y); Computer Clb; FBLA; High Hon Roll; Hon Roll; Le High U; Comp Sci.

YURCHAK, THOMAS; Pennridge HS; Sellersville, PA; (Y); Off Jr Cls; Off Sr Cls; JV Bsbl; L Ftbl; Im Vllybl; L Wrstlng; High Hon Roll; Hon Roll; Chcml Engrng.

YURCHO, JAMES; Hazelton HS; Hazleton, PA; (Y); 11/300; Church Yth Grp; High Hon Roll; NHS; Amrcn Lgn Cert Schl Awd 83; Outstndg Sci Stu 86; Prsdntl Acdmc Ftnss Awd 86; Rochester Inst Tech; Comp Sci.

YURCINA, ANGIE; Hopewell HS; Aliquippa, PA; (Y); Pres German Clb; Hosp Aide; Chorus; Rep Jr Cls; Hst Sr Cls; Stu Cncl; Powder Puff Ftbl; Boys Clb Am; SADD; Band; Aerontcs.

YUREK, LISA A; Norwin HS; N Huntingdon, PA; (Y); 98/550; AFS; Cmnty Wkr; Hosp Aide; Pep Clb; Spanish Clb; Hon Roll; VFW Awd; Suburban Womans Clb Schlrshp 86; VFW Schlrshp 86; Amer Legion & Deno Castelli Schlrshp 86; U Of Pittsburgh; Nrsng.

YURGATIS, SANDY; Wyalusing Valley HS; Laceyville, PA; (Y); Camera Clb; Church Yth Grp; FBLA; Trs Library Aide; Speech Tm; Rep SADD; Band; Chorus; Church Choir; Sec Stu Cncl; Bus Adm.

YURGOSKY, KEITH; Lakeland HS; Jermyn, PA; (S); 18/168; Bsbl; Bsktbl; Ftbl; Hon Roll; U Of Scranton; Accntng.

YURICH, ANDREA; Quigley HS; Midland, PA; (Y); Camera Clb; Church Yth Grp; Girl Scts; Hosp Aide; Chorus; Nwsp Phtg; Nwsp Stf; Yrbk Phtg; Yrbk Stf; JV Vllybl; PJAS Sci Awd 83-84; Bus.

YURICH, MIKE; South Allegheny HS; Port Vue, PA; (S); 20/180; VP French Clb; Scholastic Bowl; Concert Band; Jazz Band; Mrchg Band; School Musical; Rep Jr Cls; Rep Stu Cncl; Hon Roll; NHS; Carnegie Mellon U; Civil Engr.

YURICK, PAMELA J; Carmichaels Area HS; Carmichaels, PA; (S); 14/112; Sec French Clb; Varsity Clb; Rep Soph Cls; Rep Jr Cls; Rep Stu Cncl; JV Var Cheerleading; Hon Roll; NHS; Frnch Comp Awd From Ca U Of Pa 86; U Of Pittsburgh; Med.

YURICK, VICKI; St Huberts HS; Philadelphia, PA; (Y); 76/367; Cmnty Wkr; French Clb; Intnl Clb; Service Clb; Orch; Full Schlrshp Music Pathways Smmr Prgm Cmnty Clg Of Philadelphia 86; Music.

YURISH, MARK B; Freeland HS; Freeland, PA; (Y); 11/94; Chess Clb; Computer Clb; Yrbk Ed-Chief; Yrbk Stf; Stu Cncl; Im JV Bsktbl; Var L Crs Cntry; Var Tennis; NHS; Astrospc Engrng.

YURKANIN, AARON; Lakeland JR SR HS; Jermyn, PA; (S); 7/152; Art Clb; Camera Clb; Yrbk Stf; Stu Cncl; Crs Cntry; High Hon Roll; Hon Roll.

YURKANIN, LEANNE; Valley View JR SR HS; Archbald, PA; (Y); Church Yth Grp; French Clb; SADD; Drill Tm; Pom Pon; French Hon Soc; High Hon Roll; Hon Roll; NHS; U Of Scranton; Psych.

YURKANIN, MARGO; Lakeland JR SR HS; Jermyn, PA; (S); 27/161; FBLA; Ski Clb; Yrbk Ed-Chief; VP Frsh Cls; Sec Sr Cls; Var Cheerleading; Hon Roll; Sec.

YURKANIN, THOMAS KEVIN; Hazleton HS; Hazleton, PA; (Y); 109/376; Chorus; Stage Crew; Hon Roll; PA ST U; Scndry Educ.

YURKEWICZ, MICHAEL; Tech HS; Erie, PA; (Y); 32/349; Comp Repair.

YUSKO, MICHELLE; Hempfield Area SR HS; Greensburg, PA; (Y); GAA; Hosp Aide; Letterman Clb; Pep Clb; Ski Clb; Varsity Clb; Var L Trk; High Hon Roll; Hon Roll; Perfct Attndnc 82; U Of Pittsburgh; Nutrtn.

YUTKOWITZ, JONATHAN; Council Rock HS; Churchville, PA; (Y); 133/761; Yrbk Phtg; Yrbk Stf; JV Tennis; Hon Roll; U Of DE; Comp Sci.

YUTZLER, HEIDI; Upper Dublin SR HS; Maple Glen, PA; (Y); 6/337; Hosp Aide; Jazz Band; Mrchg Band; Symp Band; Yrbk Stf; Stu Cncl; DAR Awd; NHS; Opt Clb Awd; Raymond L Boyd Mem Scholar Stage Bnd 86; Pres Acad Fit Awd 86; Dickinson Coll; Med.

YUTZY, KYLE; Meyersdale Area; Meyersdale, PA; (S); Church Yth Grp; 4-H; Spanish Clb; Varsity Clb; Concert Band; Mrchg Band; Var Bsbl; Var Bsktbl; Amer Legion Aux Awd 82.

ZABELA, RENEE; Sto-Rox SR HS; Mc Kees Rocks, PA; (Y); VP Sec Church Yth Grp; Letterman Clb; Office Aide; Political Wkr; Yrbk Stf; Rep Stu Cncl; Cheerleading; Sftbl; Hon Roll; Sftbl MVP 85-86; 3rd Pl PA Sftbl Chmpnshp 86; WPIAL Strkots 86; Engrng.

ZABINSKI, MARK; Bellwood-Antis HS; Tyrone, PA; (Y); 41/128; Art Clb; Varsity Clb; School Play; Nwsp Phtg; Yrbk Phtg; L Ftbl; L Trk; Wt Lftg; L Wrstlng; Hon Roll; PA ST U; Mrktng Mngr.

ZABINSKI, RICHARD; Kiski Area HS; E Vandergrift, PA; (Y); 4/392; Jazz Band; Nwsp Ed-Chief; NHS; Church Yth Grp; Math Clb; Band; Mrchg Band; Orch; Pep Band; Symp Band; John Murphy Awd Musicl Excllnce 86; CA U Jazz Perfrmr Wk 86; U Schlr Duquesne U; Duquesne; Phrmcy.

ZABLOTNEY, MARSHA; Windber Area HS; Windber, PA; (Y); Chess Clb; Exploring; Math Clb; Chorus; Rep Stu Cncl; Hon Roll; Stu Mo Mrch 85, May 86; Ntl Stu Ldrshp Svc Awd USAA 84 & 85; Schlrshp Lbn Vly Coll 86; Elizabethtown Coll; Bio.

ZABODYN, CHRIS; Exeter Twp SR HS; Birdsboro, PA; (Y); #63 In Class; Church Yth Grp; Cmnty Wkr; JA; Varsity Clb; JV Bsbl; Im Bsktbl; Var Bowling; Im Ftbl; Im Lcrss; Var Socr; Ag.

ZACCARIA, CHARLES; Cardinal O Hara HS; Springfield, PA; (Y); 92/786; Var JV Bsbl; Im Bsktbl; Im Vllybl; High Hon Roll; Hon Roll; VA Tech; Aerospace Engrng.

ZACCONE, NATALIE; Canon-Mc Millan HS; Cecil, PA; (Y); Mgr(s); High Hon Roll; Hon Roll; Outstndng Hnr Roll Awd 83-84; Nrsng.

ZACHERL, ANNA; Knoch HS; Saxonburg, PA; (Y); Am Leg Aux Girls St; JA; Concert Band; Mrchg Band; Nwsp Ed-Chief; Nwsp Rptr; Stu Cncl; High Hon Roll; NHS; 4-H; Outstndng Stuco Rep Awd 86.

ZADAKIS, CHARLES; Trinity HS; Washington, PA; (Y); Boy Scts; Band; Nwsp Stf; High Hon Roll; Prfct Atten Awd; Outstndng Newspaper Carrier Yr 85; Hnrbl Ment Newspapers ST Lvl 85; Chem Engr.

ZADINSKI, MARY; Bethel Park SR HS; Pittsburgh, PA; (Y); Chorus; Drm Mjr(t); School Musical; Variety Show; Point Park Coll; Dance.

ZADRAVEC, BRENDA; Homer-Center JR SR HS; Graceton, PA; (Y); DECA; Drama Clb; French Clb; FBLA; Office Aide; Chorus; School Musical; Yrbk Stf; Cheerleading; Hon Roll; Pres Of Distributive Ed Club 86; Co-Cap Of Cheering Squad 86; Pont Park Coll; Brdcstng.

ZADROGA, JENNIFER; Bishop Kenrick HS; Norristown, PA; (Y); Cmnty Wkr; Science Clb; Ski Clb; School Play; JV Crs Cntry; Hon Roll.

ZAGALSKY, MICHELE; Upper Dublin HS; Ft Washington, PA; (Y); 32/320; Intnl Clb; Yrbk Stf; High Hon Roll; NHS; Pres Schlr; Penn ST University Park; Bus.

ZAGORSKI, DAVE; Lincoln HS; Ellwood City, PA; (Y); 18/162; Key Clb; Ski Clb; Bsbl; Ftbl; Trk; Wt Lftg; High Hon Roll; Hon Roll; NHS; Prfct Atten Awd.

ZAGORSKI, JACK; Holy Ghost Preparatory Schl; Bensalem, PA; (S); 1/81; Mathletes; Math Clb; Scholastic Bowl; Im Bsktbl; Im Ftbl; Var Capt Tennis; Im Vllybl; High Hon Roll; NHS; Ntl Merit Ltr.

ZAGORSKI, MARK S; Mc Dowell HS; Erie, PA; (Y); 10/546; Pep Clb; Quiz Bowl; Ski Clb; Yrbk Stf; Var Capt Crs Cntry; Var L Trk; Hon Roll; NHS; Ntl Merit SF; 7th Pl-Gannon U Frnch Comptn 85; Cert For Excllnc In Sci-Erie Engrs 85; Hnrs Cert 85; Intl Bus & Fin.

ZAGORSKI, STAN; Scranton Prep; Moscow, PA; (Y); 45/200; Church Yth Grp; Letterman Clb; Ski Clb; Varsity Clb; Band; Concert Band; Nwsp Sprt Ed; Bsbl; Bsktbl; Ftbl; U Scranton; Bio.

ZAGORSKI, TRACI; Seton La Salle HS; Pittsburgh, PA; (Y); 34/264; Boy Scts; Church Yth Grp; Pep Clb; Red Cross Aide; Ski Clb; High Hon Roll; Hon Roll; NHS; Physcl Thrpst.

ZAHAREWICZ, JEFF; Seton-Lasalle HS; Pittsburgh, PA; (Y); 10/232; Drama Clb; Math Clb; School Musical; Stage Crew; Nwsp Phtg; Nwsp Stf; High Hon Roll; NHS; Socl Stu Awd 82-83; PA ST U; Engrg.

ZAHARIS, KAREN; Nativity B V M HS; St Clair, PA; (Y); Art Clb; Variety Show; Yrbk Stf; JV Var Cheerleading; Hon Roll; Chld Psychlgy.

ZAHARKD, SANDRA; Vincentian HS; Gibsonia, PA; (Y); 3/65; Teachers Aide; Rep Soph Cls; Rep Jr Cls; Im JV Bsktbl; Var JV Fld Hcky; Im Var Sftbl; Im Var Vllybl; Hon Roll; Pres Jr NHS; NHS; Part In Sci Wrkshp Srs PA JR Acad Of Sci 84-85; Amrcn Chem Soc Cntst 84-85; Chem.

ZAHNISER, KIMBERLY; West Middlexex HS; W Middlesex, PA; (Y); Church Yth Grp; 4-H; Girl Scts; Spanish Clb; Band; Mgr Concert Band; Mgr Mrchg Band; Im Sftbl; Hon Roll; 3rd Cls Band Awd 86; JR Deaconess Hnr 84.

ZAHORCHAK, DONALD; Elderton JR SR HS; Shelocta, PA; (Y); 31/100; Spanish Clb; Varsity Clb; Pres Frsh Cls; Rep Stu Cncl; JV Var Bsktbl; JV Var Socr; Hon Roll; NHS; Penn ST; Elec Engrng Tech.

ZAIKOSKI, LEONARD; James M Coughlin HS; Wilkes-Barre, PA; (Y); 35/432; High Hon Roll; Jr NHS; NHS; Ntl Merit Schol; Penn ST U Acdmc Schlrshp 86; Pres Acdmc Ftns Awd 86; Ltr Commndtn 85; Penn ST U; Comp Sci.

ZAJAC, VERA; Central HS; Philadelphia, PA; (Y); 19/211; Office Aide; Bryn Mawr Coll; Law.

ZAJDEL, DAVID JOHN; Greater Johnstown Central SR HS; Johnstown, PA; (Y); VP French Clb; Math Clb; Quiz Bowl; Scholastic Bowl; Chorus; Church Choir; Hon Roll; NHS.

ZAJDEL, SUSAN; Johnstown HS; Johnstown, PA; (Y); 23/286; Math Clb; Spanish Clb; SADD; Color Guard; Sec Jr Cls; Sec Sr Cls; Capt Twrlr; Hon Roll; NHS; Prfct Atten Awd; Dir,Alumni Awd 85-86; IN U; Elem Ed.

ZAK, CHRISTINE; Valley HS; New Kensington, PA; (Y); Trs Science Clb; Ski Clb; Sec Varsity Clb; Chorus; VP Jr Cls; VP Sr Cls; Pres Stu Cncl; Capt Cheerleading; Capt Trk; Capt Vllybl; U S Army Rsrv Ntl Hnr Schlr/Athlt Awd 86; Art Awd 86; IN U Of PA; Physcl Ed.

ZAKRZEWSKI, WALTER; Roman Catholic HS; Philadelphia, PA; (S); Var Bsbl; Var Ftbl; Var Golf; Hon Roll.

ZAKRZWSKI, DAVID F; Bishop Carroll HS; Cresson, PA; (S); 17/109; Aud/Vis; Pep Clb; Spanish Clb; Hon Roll.

ZAKRZWSKI, JAMES; Bishop Carrell HS; Cresson, PA; (Y); Aud/Vis; PAVAS; Bowling; CA UW Of PA; Engrng.

ZALAR, AMY; Mapletown HS; Waynesburg, PA; (Y); 6/76; 4-H; GAA; Ski Clb; Varsity Clb; Nwsp Stf; Yrbk Stf; Var Sftbl; Im Vllybl; High Hon Roll; NHS.

ZALESKI, MATT; Pittston Area SR HS; Avoca, PA; (Y); Key Clb; Bsktbl; Vllybl; Hon Roll; Bsktbll 1st Tm All-Schlstc 85-86; Bsktbll Brnze Mdl At Keystone ST Games 86.

ZALESKY, MICHAEL; Archbishop Wood HS; Warminster, PA; (Y); 65/282; Rep Soph Cls; Rep Stu Cncl; JV Crs Cntry; JV Ftbl; High Hon Roll; NHS; Bus.

ZAMBETTI, KAREN; Pittston Area HS; Yatesville, PA; (Y); #18 In Class; Math Clb; Drill Tm; Stat Bsktbl; L Sftbl; Hon Roll; NHS; Prfct Atten Awd; Sec Key Clb; Accntnt.

ZAMBO, CHRISTINE; Notre Dame HS; Freemansburg, PA; (Y); 19/109; Art Clb; Varsity Clb; Yrbk Stf; Bowling; Sftbl; Hon Roll; Prfct Atten Awd; Grtst Achvt Algebra 84; Sci.

ZAMBONI, WILLIAM; Blacklick Valley JR SR HS; Nanty-Glo, PA; (S); 1/100; Library Aide; Ski Clb; Varsity Clb; Pres Stu Cncl; Var L Bsbl; Var L Bsktbl; Var L Ftbl; High Hon Roll; NHS; Acad All-Amer 85; IN Gazette 2nd Tm Ftbl 85; Apalachian Con Hnrb Mtn 85; U Of Pittsburgh; Engrng.

ZAMBROSKI, MICHELLE; Shenandoah Valley JR SR HS; Shenandoah, PA; (Y); Hosp Aide; Chorus; Color Guard; Co-Capt Drill Tm; Yrbk Stf; Var L Crs Cntry; Mgr(s); Sftbl; Psychol.

ZAMIEROSKI, MICHELLE; Villa Maria Acad; Erie, PA; (Y); 34/136; Model UN; Ski Clb; School Play; Off Frsh Cls; Off Soph Cls; Off Jr Cls; Off Sr Cls; Stu Cncl; Cheerleading; Trk; U Of Pittsburgh; Engrng.

ZAMPETTI, VICTOR; Danville SR HS; Danville, PA; (Y); 50/250; Aud/Vis; Church Yth Grp; VP Frsh Cls; VP Soph Cls; Var Ftbl; JV Trk; Im Wt Lftg; Var Wrstlng; High Hon Roll; Mth.

ZAMPOGNA, MARK; Harborcreek HS; Erie, PA; (Y); Boy Scts; Church Yth Grp; Band; Mrchg Band; Pep Band; Swmmng; Gov Hon Prg Awd; Ntl Merit Ltr; 3rd Pl PA Math Cntst 86; Ltrd In Swmmng & Band 86; Aerontc Engnrng.

ZAMULEVIC, DIANE; Southside Catholic HS; Pittsburgh, PA; (S); 15/48; Art Clb; Drama Clb; Science Clb; Sec Service Clb; Stage Crew; Yrbk Stf; Rep Jr Cls; Rep Sr Cls; Sftbl; Hon Roll; Rlgn Awd 85; U Of Pittsburgh; Bio.

ZANARDELLI, JILL; Mc Guffey HS; Washington, PA; (S); 35/210; French Clb; Chorus; School Musical; Yrbk Phtg; Yrbk Rptr; Yrbk Stf; L Trk; Hon Roll; Stu Recog Awd; IN U Of PA; Jrnlsm.

ZANARDELLI, LISA; Ringgold HS; Monongahela, PA; (Y); Drama Clb; Ski Clb; Spanish Clb; School Play; Stage Crew; Variety Show; Rep Soph Cls; Hon Roll; Chorus; Mgr(s); Sci & Math Hnr Soc; Outdoor Educ Club; Blue & Gold Club; Med.

ZANDE, JILL M; Radford Area HS; Lewis Run, PA; (Y); 3/310; AFS; Yrbk Stf; Cheerleading; Trk; High Hon Roll; Jr NHS; NHS; NEDT Awd; Aca Excllnc Awd 84; AFS Exchng Stu Smmr In Athens Greece 86; Marine Bio.

ZANGARI, MICHELA; Trinity HS; Camp Hill, PA; (Y); 60/120; Hosp Aide; Ski Clb; Spanish Clb; Chorus; School Musical; Yrbk Stf; Rep Stu Cncl; Cheerleading; Trk; Spanish NHS; Span.

ZANKEL, JAMES; Cornell HS; Coraopolis, PA; (Y); 13/55; Boys Clb Am; Exploring; VP Key Clb; Library Aide; Chorus; School Play; Stage Crew; Yrbk Sprt Ed; Yrbk Stf; Hon Roll; Acad Schrlshp 86; Johnson & Wales Coll; Arts.

ZANONI, TRICIA; Bishop Mc Cort HS; Jerome, PA; (Y); 2/133; Cmnty Wkr; Math Clb; Sec Spanish Clb; Band; Yrbk Stf; Pres Sr Cls; Var Socr; High Hon Roll; Sec NHS; Sec Spanish NHS; IN U Hnrs Band 84-85; Altrnt Govrnrs Schl Sci 86; Civic Band Alleghny Hrtland Band 84-85; Sci.

ZAPATA, WILLIAM; Garden Spot HS; New Holland, PA; (Y); 50/203; Spanish Clb; Rep Stu Cncl; JV Bsktbl; Var Capt Socr; Trk; High Hon Roll; Hon Roll; Jr NHS; NHS; Outstndng Fresh Track Awd; Minorities Amer; Shippensburg U; Bus Mgmt.

ZAPH, AARON; Mon Valley Catholic HS; Belle Vernon, PA; (Y); 19/90; Cmnty Wkr; Var Bsktbl; JV Ftbl; Var Golf; Hon Roll; Crml Just.

ZAPPACOSTA, BRONWYN; Bishop Shanahan HS; Coatesville, PA; (Y); Hon Roll.

ZAPPACOSTA, MARIA; Upper Darby HS; Upr Darby, PA; (Y); Church Yth Grp; Hosp Aide; Office Aide; Spanish Clb; SADD; Lit Mag; Rep Soph Cls; Rep Jr Cls; Var JV Vllybl; Hon Roll; Temple; Bus Mgmt.

ZAPPI, DEANNA; Mc Guffey HS; Claysville, PA; (Y); French Clb; JA; Sec Trs Pep Clb; Spanish Clb; Varsity Clb; Var JV Bsktbl; Var Sftbl.

ZAPPIA, ROBERT; Meadville Area SR HS; Meadville, PA; (Y); 97/344; Aud/Vis; Boy Scts; CAP; JCL; Latin Clb; Office Aide; SADD; French Hon Soc; 2nd Pl Local Hstry Day 85; USAF Acad; Astront.

ZAPPONE, JENNIFER; Greensburg Central Catholic HS; Latrobe, PA; (Y); 89/243; Pres 4-H; JCL; Nwsp Rptr; Nwsp Stf; Trk; High Hon Roll; Hon Roll; Prfct Atten Awd; U Of Pittsburgh; Phy Thrpy.

ZARECKY, MARC; Greenville SR HS; Greenville, PA; (Y); Spanish Clb; Chorus; Hghst Achvr Spnsh I 84; 3rd Pl Forgn Lang Comptn Westmnstr Coll 84; Comp Oprtr.

ZARY, JILL; Bethel Park SR HS; Bethel Park, PA; (Y); Drama Clb; Rptr FBLA; FHA; Chorus; School Musical; Variety Show; Yrbk Stf; Pom Pon; Powder Puff Ftbl; High Hon Roll; FBLA 3rd Pl Clerk Typst I 86.

ZASADA, SUSAN; Hanover Area JR SR HS; Ashley, PA; (Y); Key Clb; Yrbk Stf; Sftbl; Hon Roll; NHS; Luzern Cnty CC; Chld Dvlpmnt.

ZASLOFF, ANNE L; Taylor Allderdice HS; Pittsburgh, PA; (Y); 3/410; Math Tm; Temple Yth Grp; Acpl Chr; Nwsp Stf; JV Var Vllybl; High Hon Roll; NHS; Ntl Merit SF; Orch; Grand Concours Ntl De Francais-City & Tri-St 82 & 83; U Of Pittsburgh Prvst Day Comp Winner 85; Engl.

ZASTAWNIAK, JANICE; Springdale JR SR HS; Springdale, PA; (Y); JA; Acpl Chr; Nwsp Stf; Chrmn Jr Cls; Capt JV Cheerleading; High Hon Roll; Sec NHS; Pres Schlr; Hgh Hnr Awd 85 & 86; Gftd & Tlntd Ed 82-86; PA ST; Englsh.

ZATKIEWICZ, SANDY; Villa Maria Acad; Erie, PA; (Y); Church Yth Grp; Cmnty Wkr; Yrbk Rptr; Yrbk Stf; Rep Sr Cls; Rep Stu Cncl; JV Var Bsktbl; Im Fld Hcky; Im Socr; Im Vllybl; Bsktbl Sprts Cert, Metro Chmps, 2 Ptchs & Ltr 82-85; Chrmn Stu Cncl Mxr 85; Slippery Rock U; Elem Ed.

ZATRATZ, DENISE; Holy Name HS; Mohnton, PA; (Y); Camera Clb; Exploring; FBLA; Library Aide; Pep Clb; Hon Roll.

ZAUNICK, MICHAEL; Johnsonburg Area HS; Johnsonburg, PA; (S); 2/100; Camera Clb; Rep Frsh Cls; Off Stu Cncl; High Hon Roll; NHS; Prfct Atten Awd; Acad All Amer Awds 85; Acctg.

ZAVASKY, SHERI; Freeland HS; Freeland, PA; (Y); 6/96; FBLA; VP Pep Clb; Spanish Clb; School Play; Stu Cncl; Cheerleading; Sftbl; Hon Roll; NHS; Pres Schlr; Inlnd Cntnr Corp Schlrshp 86; U Of Scranton; Physcl Thrpy.

ZAVATSKI, GINA; Mc Guffey HS; Taylorstown, PA; (Y); 17/220; Church Yth Grp; JA; Pep Clb; Spanish Clb; Varsity Clb; Chorus; Yrbk Stf; Var Sftbl; Var Vllybl; Hon Roll; Occup Thrpy.

ZAVECZ, REGINA; Freedom HS; Bethlehem, PA; (Y); 4/117; French Clb; Pep Clb; Red Cross Aide; Chorus; School Musical; Nwsp Stf; Yrbk Stf; Var Pom Pon; Hon Roll; Trvl-Toursm.

ZAVETSKY, DAVID G; West Mifflin Area HS; W Mifflin, PA; (Y); 27/285; Exploring; Chorus; School Musical; Crs Cntry; Trk; High Hon Roll; Hon Roll; NHS; VFW Awd; Voice Dem Awd; Dist Chorus; Region Chorus; U Of S FL; Pre-Med.

ZAVITSKY, SUSAN; Hazleton HS; Drums, PA; (Y); 19/300; Church Yth Grp; Drama Clb; French Clb; FBLA; Leo Clb; French Hon Soc; Hon Roll; Cdt Clb Secy 86-87; Bus Admin.

ZAVODNICK, MINDI; Bensalem HS; Neshaminy Valley, PA; (Y); Pres Key Clb; Red Cross Aide; SADD; Teachers Aide; Nwsp Stf; Rep Stu Cncl; Var Stat Ftbl; Var Stat Wrstlng; Hon Roll; Var Mgr(s); Red Cross Development Center Scholarship For Leadership 86; Educ.

ZAWADA, JOHN; Central Catholic HS; Greensburg, PA; (Y); 14/250; Computer Clb; Exploring; JCL; Concert Band; Mrchg Band; High Hon Roll; NHS; Bus.

ZAWADZKI, CHAS; Dunmore HS; Dunmore, PA; (Y); 29/149; Ski Clb; JV Bsktbl; High Hon Roll; Hon Roll; Jr NHS; Hrt Fnd Drive 85; Blmsbrg Coll; Accntng.

ZAWISTOSKI, MARYBETH; Mercyhurst Prep; Erie, PA; (Y); 37/150; Church Yth Grp; French Clb; Chorus; Nwsp Phtg; Vllybl; Lit Mag; Yth Understndsg Schlrshp 86; Cmpus Ministry Stu Tm; Photojournlsm.

ZAZYCZNY, JOCELYN; Nazareth Acad; Philadelphia, PA; (Y); Church Yth Grp; Rep Stu Cncl; Bsktbl; Var Cheerleading; Coach Actv; Pom Pon; Tennis; Ntl Merit SF; Prfct Atten Awd; Philadelphia Coll Of Pharmacy.

ZBORAY, BRUCE; West Hazleton HS; W Hazleton, PA; (Y); Computer Clb; Latin Clb; Ski Clb; Ftbl; Wt Lftg; Comp Sci.

ZDANAVAGE, COREY; John S Fine SR HS; Nanticoke, PA; (S); 9/264; Varsity Clb; Rep Soph Cls; VP Bsbl; JV Bsktbl; High Hon Roll; VP NHS; Yth Fit Achvt Awd 84; Pres Phys Fit Awd 85; Math.

ZDANAVAGE, STACEY; Crestwood HS; Mountaintop, PA; (Y); Ski Clb; Stu Cncl; Bsbl; Ftbl; Wt Lftg; Bloomsburg U; Bio.

ZDRILICH, ERICA; Villa Maria HS; Poland, OH; (Y); French Clb; Key Clb; French Hon Soc; NHS; Ntl Merit Schol; NEDT Awd; Med.

ZDROSKY, GLORIA; Tussey Mountain HS; Saxton, PA; (Y); Trs Church Yth Grp; Nwsp Rptr; Sec Nwsp Stf; Powder Puff Ftbl; Vllybl; Civic Clb Awd 86; Tixan Tpc Nwsltr Awd 86; Csmtlgy.

ZEAFLA, RANDALL R; Williamsport Area HS; Williamsport, PA; (Y); 145/460; Church Yth Grp; Letterman Clb; Varsity Clb; Band; Concert Band; Jazz Band; Mrchg Band; Pep Band; Symp Band; Var L Bsbl; Barry Campbell Awd Prsnlty 86; Embry Riddle Aero U; Aero Sci.

ZEARING, SONYA R; Lower Dauphin HS; Harrisburg, PA; (Y); 20/217; Concert Band; Frsh Cls; Soph Cls; Jr Cls; Trs Sr Cls; Stat Bsbl; Cheerleading; JV Sftbl; NHS; Bus Adm.

ZEBRASKI, DAVID; Methacton HS; Norristown, PA; (Y); Boy Scts; Cmnty Wkr; Computer Clb; Exploring; SADD; Teachers Aide; VICA; Chem Ntl Olympiad 85-86; Drexel Inst Of Tech; Elec Engr.

ZEBROWSKI, CHRISTOPHER; St Pius X HS; Collegeville, PA; (S); Aud/Vis; JA; Mathletes; Science Clb; School Musical; Stage Crew; Socr; Hon Roll; Math.

ZECHMAN, DAVID; Hamburg Area HS; Strausstown, PA; (Y); Church Yth Grp; French Clb; Trs Chorus; Church Choir; School Musical; Swing Chorus; Yrbk Stf; NHS; Ntl Merit Ltr; Music Prfrmr.

ZEDEK, KIMBERLY KAYE; Northern Cambria HS; Herndon, VA; (Y); Church Yth Grp; Dance Clb; Chorus; Stage Crew; Yrbk Stf; Chrch Lector 83-86; Girls Chorus 86; Real Est.

ZEDOLIK, SUZANNE; Crestwood HS; Mountaintop, PA; (Y); Hosp Aide; Ski Clb; Yrbk Stf; Pres Stu Cncl; L Cheerleading; L Crs Cntry; Fld Hcky; L Trk; Hon Roll; Blmsbrg U Of PA; Elem Educ.

ZEEMAN, KIMBERLY; Northampton Area HS; Nazareth, PA; (Y); 18/444; AFS; Drama Clb; VP Leo Clb; Library Aide; SADD; Yrbk Stf; Cheerleading; High Hon Roll; Hon Roll; NHS; Med Tech.

ZEGAR, CATHY; Swissvale HS; Swissvale, PA; (Y); 7/205; Office Aide; Spanish Clb; Y-Teens; Band; Concert Band; Mrchg Band; Yrbk Stf; High Hon Roll; NHS; Spnsh Cert Merit 85; Chld Psychlgy.

ZEHNER, MICHELLE; Williamsburg HS; Williamsburg, PA; (Y); 5/62; Varsity Clb; Yrbk Stf; Capt Var Cheerleading; Tennis; Vllybl; Hon Roll; NHS; US Army Res Schlr Ath Awd 86; Microage Comp Strs Altoona Math Awd 86; Pepsi Cola Schlr Ath Awd 86; PA ST U; Comp Sci.

ZEHNER, PATRICIA; Wilmington Area HS; New Wilmington, PA; (Y); Drama Clb; Spanish Clb; Band; Concert Band; Mrchg Band; Nwsp Rptr; Nwsp Stf; Var JV Cheerleading; Var JV Powder Puff Ftbl; Var Trk.

ZEIDERS, ANNA; Carlisle SR HS; Carlisle, PA; (Y); Am Leg Aux Girls St; School Musical; Nwsp Ed-Chief; Rep Stu Cncl; Var L Fld Hcky; Var L Trk; Pres NHS; Church Yth Grp; Computer Clb; Pep Clb; PA Jr Acad Sci ST Comp 1st Plc 86; NACEL Frgn Exchng Prgrm 85; Stu Yth Frm 85-86.

ZEIDERS, BRENDA J; Central Dauphin HS; Harrisburg, PA; (Y); Church Yth Grp; Hosp Aide; Library Aide; Var L Cheerleading; Var L Fld Hcky; Var Gym; Im Vllybl; Hon Roll; Make-Up Artstry.

ZEIDERS, GENE; East Pennsboro HS; Enola, PA; (Y); Varsity Clb; JV Bsbl; Var Bsktbl; Var Golf; Var Swmmng; Var Tennis; Var Wrstlng; Hon Roll; Golf Plaques MVP 84-86; Swmmng Trophy 85-86; Cazenovia Coll; Carpenter.

ZEIDERS, JEAN; Tyrone Area HS; Tyrone, PA; (Y); Latin Clb; Teachers Aide; Mgr(s); Powder Puff Ftbl; Score Keeper; High Hon Roll; Hon Roll; NHS; Altonna Hosp Schlof Nrs; Nrs.

ZEIDERS, STEPHEN; Newport HS; Newport, PA; (Y); Bsbl; Bsktbl; Ftbl; Wt Lftg; Hon Roll; Law Enfrcmnt.

ZEIGLER, SHELLIE; Tyrone Area HS; Tyrone, PA; (Y); 11/197; Key Clb; Ski Clb; Yrbk Stf; Sec Sr Cls; Sec Stu Cncl; Var JV Cheerleading; Elks Awd; High Hon Roll; NHS; VP Spanish Clb; Presdntl Acad Fitness Awd 86; Herman A Freidman & Mary A Freidman Schlrshp 86; Grad Clss Hnrs Grp 86; PA ST U; Nutrition.

ZEIGLER, STEPHEN; Halifax Area HS; Halifax, PA; (S); 9/97; Camera Clb; Church Yth Grp; Drama Clb; Chorus; School Musical; Nwsp Phtg; Dnfth Awd; High Hon Roll; NHS; Messiah Coll; Math.

ZEILER, REBECCA; Marian HS; Mc Adoo, PA; (S); Church Yth Grp; Pep Clb; Ski Clb; Chorus; Drill Tm; Rep Soph Cls; Rep Jr Cls; Stu Cncl; High Hon Roll; Hon Roll; 30 Hr Adlt Typng Crs 84; Pres Physcl Ftns Awd 84; Law.

ZEILER, RICH; Bethel Park SR HS; Bethel Park, PA; (S); DECA; 4th Pl DECA Rest Mktng & Mgmt 86; PA ST; Mktng.

ZEIS, JENNIFER; Downingtown SR HS; Exton, PA; (Y); French Clb; Ski Clb; Yrbk Ed-Chief; High Hon Roll; NHS; Computer Clb; SADD; Band; Concert Band; Mrchg Band.

ZEISET, G ELAINE; Garden Spot HS; Denver, PA; (S); Sec Church Yth Grp; Sec FFA; Library Aide; Chorus; Church Choir; Hon Roll; Pub Spkg FFA Profcncy Awd 85; Lamb Prod FFA Profcncy Awd 84; Bus Mgmt.

ZEITLIN, ANDREW; Parkland SR HS; Allentown, PA; (Y); 37/415; Debate Tm; Drama Clb; JCL; Latin Clb; Math Tm; Scholastic Bowl; School Play; Crs Cntry; NHS; Ntl Merit Ltr; Frnch Hnr Awd 86; Pres Clssrm 85; Brandeis U; Lawyer.

ZELAHY, SANDY M; Plum SR HS; Plum Boro, PA; (Y); 38/415; FBLA; Q&S; Speech Tm; Nwsp Ed-Chief; Lit Mag; Stat Socr; High Hon Roll; Hon Roll; NHS; Pres Schlr; Pres Acad Fit Awd 86; SR Awd Typg Editor 86; Stu Tchg Awd Adlt Wrd Proc Cls 86; IN U PA; Bus Mgmt.

ZELASKO, JOSEPH; Freedom HS; Bethlehem, PA; (Y); 71/456; Acctng.

ZELENSKE, ANDREW; Mt Pleasant Area HS; Stahlstown, PA; (Y); Ski Clb; L Ftbl; Trk; Wrstlng; Prom Committee; Sprtmns Clb.

ZELESNIK, RICH; Ambridge Area HS; Ambridge, PA; (Y); Pep Clb; Red Cross Aide; Spanish Clb; SADD; CC Beaver Cnty; Air Trfc Cntrl.

ZELEZNIK, MATT; West Mifflin Area HS; W Mifflin, PA; (Y); 75/340; Computer Clb; Key Clb; Letterman Clb; Ski Clb; Varsity Clb; Band; Var L Bsktbl; Var L Ftbl; Var L Trk; Penn ST; Bus Mngmnt.

ZELINKA, LISA; Cowanesque Valley HS; Knoxville, PA; (Y); Drama Clb; French Clb; German Clb; Library Aide; Ski Clb; School Musical; Hst Frsh Cls; Hst Sr Cls; Rep Stu Cncl; Var Trk; Occ Thrpy.

ZELINSKY, KRISTYN; Ringgold HS; Finleyville, PA; (Y); Drama Clb; French Clb; Ski Clb; Band; Stage Crew; Variety Show; Yrbk Stf; Bsktbl; Score Keeper; IN U Penna; Physcl Thrpst.

ZELINSKY, TINA L; Northern Lehigh HS; Slatington, PA; (Y); Am Leg Aux Girls St; German Clb; Ski Clb; Variety Show; Rep Stu Cncl; Var Cheerleading; Stat Trk; Hon Roll; Jr Prom Ct 86; Med Adm.

ZELKO, DAVIAN; Latasaugua HS; Catasauqua, PA; (Y); Drama Clb; Hosp Aide; Color Guard; School Musical; Stage Crew; Twrlr; High Hon Roll; Hon Roll; Le High Cnty CC; Real Estate.

ZELLER, MARA J; William Allen HS; Allentown, PA; (Y); 60/556; Drama Clb; JCL; Latin Clb; Office Aide; JV Diving; Var L Swmmng; Hon Roll; Pres Schlr; Allen H S Advncmnt Fund Schlrshp 86; Muhlenberg Clg; Comm.

ZELLER, RUTH; Mid Valley HS; Throop, PA; (Y); 27/125; Dance Clb; Pep Clb; Yrbk Stf; VP Sr Cls; Cheerleading; Hon Roll; PA ST U; Bus Adm.

ZELLERS, DOUG; Scranton Central HS; Scranton, PA; (Y); Art Clb; Boy Scts; Ski Clb; Co-Capt Ftbl; Co-Capt Trk; Bio-Med.

ZELLERS, KARIN; Annville-Cleona HS; Lebanon, PA; (Y); 30/120; Trs Church Yth Grp; FBLA; Office Aide; Color Guard; Yrbk Stf; VP Mat Maids; Goldey Beacom Coll; Accntng.

ZELLERS, KRISTINE; Annville-Cleona HS; Annville, PA; (S); 1/127; Pres Church Yth Grp; Math Tm; Ed Yrbk Stf; Sec Jr Cls; Stat Ftbl; Cit Awd; Dnfth Awd; NHS; Acpl Chr; Chorus; Rensalaer Mth & Sci Awd 85; Rotary Grl Of Mnth 85; Wittenberg; Pre-Med.

ZELLERS, PAMELA; Penn Trafford HS; Jeannette, PA; (Y); FBLA; Spanish Clb; SADD; VICA; High Hon Roll; Hon Roll; Nrsng.

ZELLO, RICHARD; United HS; Indiana, PA; (Y); 28/130; Boy Scts; Pres Church Yth Grp; Drama Clb; FFA; Ski Clb; Jazz Band; Mrchg Band; School Musical; Hon Roll; Prfct Atten Awd; US Air Frc; Med.

ZELMAN, LISA; Dubois Area HS; Dubois, PA; (Y); 8/250; Stu Cncl; Stat Bsktbl; Hon Roll; NHS; Bio.

ZELMORE, JASON; Southmoreland SR HS; Mt Pleasant, PA; (Y); Aud/Vis; Letterman Clb; Ski Clb; Spanish Clb; Teachers Aide; Stage Crew; Rep Jr Cls; Pres Stu Cncl; Var Ftbl; Var Wrstlng; Ironman Wrstlng Awd 85-86; Yth Assoc Of Wrld Affairs VP 85-86; Slippery Rock U; Phys Educ Tchr.

ZELNO, JACQUELINE A; Slippery Rock Area HS; Slippery Rock, PA; (Y); Trs Intnl Clb; Pep Clb; Chorus; School Musical; Stage Crew; Pres Soph Cls; Pres Jr Cls; VP Sr Cls; Var Capt Trk; NHS; Law.

ZELT, SUSAN; St Marys Area HS; St Marys, PA; (Y); 28/300; Lion Awd; NHS; Boys Clb Am; Girl Scts; Varsity Clb; Var Tennis; JV Vllybl; Hon Roll; Pres Acad Fit Awd 86; PA ST U; Bio Chem.

ZEMA, CHRISTOPHER; Freeport HS; Sarver, PA; (S); 25/170; Varsity Clb; Rep Frsh Cls; Var L Bsbl; Var L Bsktbl; Var L Ftbl; Var Trk; High Hon Roll; Hon Roll; Arch.

ZEMA, MICHAEL S; Freeport SR HS; Freeport, PA; (Y); Letterman Clb; Pep Clb; Varsity Clb; Var L Ftbl; Im Ice Hcky; Var Capt Trk; Hon Roll; Pole Vault Reocrd 86; Slippery Rock U; Athltc Trainng.

ZEMA, WILLIAM; Freeport HS; Freeport, PA; (S); Church Yth Grp; Var L Ftbl; Var L Trk; High Hon Roll; Penn ST U; Law.

ZEMANTAUSKI, SUSAN; Nativity B V M HS; Pottsville, PA; (Y); 19/99; Cmnty Wkr; Nwsp Rptr; Nwsp Stf; JV Bsktbl; Capt Bowling; Var Sftbl; High Hon Roll; Hon Roll; Yng Amercn Bwlng Allnc Schlrshp 85-86; Hghst Achvt Awd-Antmy/Physlgy & Trig/Anlysis 85-86; Marywood Coll; Bio.

ZEMBA, DONNA M; Southmoreland HS; Mt Pleasant, PA; (Y); FFA; Spanish Clb; VICA; Chorus; Church Choir; Powder Puff Ftbl; Sftbl; Library Aide; Soil Water Mgmt AFFA Awd; Huntington Twirlltts; Hortcltur.

ZEMBLE, BETH; Lower Moreland HS; Huntingdon Valley, PA; (S); 3/215; Key Clb; Model UN; Office Aide; Science Clb; SADD; Temple Yth Grp; Acpl Chr; Chorus; Color Guard; Flag Corp; Miss PA Natl Teenagr 86; Natl Hnr Soc; PA Ambssdr HOBY Ldrshp Sem 84; Law.

ZEMETRO, JOHN; Hanvoer Area JR SR HS; Warrior Run, PA; (Y); 1/180; Bausch & Lomb Sci Awd; High Hon Roll; Hon Roll; Jr NHS; NHS; NEDT Awd.

ZENDRI, SHERRI; Elk County Christian HS; St Marys, PA; (S); Model UN; Thesps; Yrbk Stf; Sec Soph Cls; Rep Stu Cncl; Var Cheerleading; High Hon Roll; NHS; NEDT Awd; SAR Awd; PA ST U; Elect Engr.

ZEPKA, TERESA; Conemaugh Valley HS; Johnstown, PA; (Y); 14/121; French Clb; Girl Scts; Pep Clb; Speech Tm; Mrchg Band; Yrbk Stf; Co-Capt Twrlr; Hon Roll; Jr NHS; NHS.

ZERA, DEBORAH; Norwin HS; North Huntingdon, PA; (Y); 50/550; French Clb; Band; Concert Band; Mrchg Band; Trs Yrbk Stf; Hon Roll; Allegheny Coll; Pltcl Sci.

ZERANCE, GENE; Central Dauphin HS; Harrisburg, PA; (Y); 34/386; Ski Clb; Band; Concert Band; Mrchg Band; Stage Crew; Cit Awd; Hon Roll; NHS; Elect.

ZERANICK, DOREEN; Ambridge HS; Freedom, PA; (Y); French Clb; Pep Clb; Thesps; Chorus; Church Choir; Co-Capt Drill Tm; Mrchg Band; School Musical; Swing Chorus; Variety Show; Westminstr Hnrs Chorus 85; Dist V Chorus 86; Point Park Coll; Muscl Theatre.

ZERBE, LAURAL; Lock Haven SR HS; Lock Haven, PA; (Y); Pres FHA; Spanish Clb; Nwsp Rptr; Hon Roll.

ZERBE, MARLENE K; Shikellamy HS; Sunbury, PA; (Y); French Clb; Yrbk Stf; Sec Soph Cls; Sec Jr Cls; Sec Sr Cls; Stu Cncl; Cheerleading; Tennis; Hon Roll; NHS; Rtry Stu Mnth 86; Snbry Wmns Clb Swng Awd 86; Shikellamy Educ Assoc Schlrshp 86; Shippensburg U; Elem Educ.

ZERBE, NADINE; Shikellamy HS; Sunbury, PA; (Y); 14/315; Sec French Clb; Rep Key Clb; Chorus; Yrbk Stf; Sec Frsh Cls; Sec Soph Cls; Sec Stu Cncl; Var Cheerleading; Tennis; Hon Roll; Yng Amer 85; 2nd Pl Natl Frnch Cntst 85; NCA All Amer Fnlst 84; E Stroudsburg U; Pharm.

ZERBINI, LORI; Homer Center HS; Homer City, PA; (Y); French Clb; SADD; Sftbl; Vllybl; Hon Roll.

ZERBY, JUDY; Cowanesque Valley HS; Knoxville, PA; (S); 1/94; VP 4-H; VP Band; Trk; 4-H Awd; High Hon Roll; NHS; German Clb; Chorus; Amer Lgn Awd 83; Phy Ftnss Awd 85; Trvl/Trsm.

ZERFOSS, COLEEN; Somerset Area HS; Somerset, PA; (Y); 62/239; Church Yth Grp; German Clb; Church Choir; Concert Band; Mrchg Band; Var JV Trk; JV Var Vllybl; Hon Roll; Pep Clb; Bsktbl; Pres Physcl Ftns Awd 81-85; Hnr Roll Ltr 85-86; Accntng.

ZERFOSS, POLLY; Somerset Area SR HS; Somerset, PA; (Y); Church Yth Grp; Cmnty Wkr; NFL; Q&S; Stu Cncl; High Hon Roll; NHS; Art Clb; Drama Clb; English Clb; Catherine V Pfeiffer Memorial Awd Otstndng SR Grl 86; Pres Acad Ftns Awd 86; Tm Ed Pgms Fnlst 86; Misericordia Coll; Octnl Thrpy.

ZERFOSS, SUSAN; Somerset Area HS; Friedens, PA; (Y); 49/233; German Clb; JA; Math Clb; Q&S; Red Cross Aide; Yrbk Stf; Off Stu Cncl; High Hon Roll; NHS; Pres Schlr; Eagle Scholar 86; WA & Jefferson; Acctng.

ZERLA, ANDREW; Mc Guffey HS; Washington, PA; (S); 3/210; French Clb; Band; Jazz Band; Mrchg Band; Yrbk Stf; High Hon Roll; NHS; Prfct Atten Awd; Mid East Band Fest 86; WA Cnty Band 86; Grove City Coll; Mth.

ZERPHEY, TIMOTHY; Elizabethtown HS; Elizabethotwn, PA; (Y); Spanish Clb; Teachers Aide; Im Bsktbl; Var Capt Ftbl; Var Capt Trk; Ftbll Awd 86; Harry K Alwine Schlrshp 86; Shippensburg U.

ZESZUTEK, DAWN M; Canon Mc Millan HS; Cecil, PA; (Y); FBLA; Office Aide; Ski Clb; Stu Cncl; Cheerleading; Penn ST; Bus Adm.

ZESZUTEK, SUSAN; Canon Mc Millan HS; Cecil, PA; (Y); 90/376; Sec French Clb; Office Aide; Varsity Clb; JV Stu Cncl; Cheerleading; Hon Roll; U Pittsburgh; Nrsng.

ZETH, TINA; Claysburg-Kimmel HS; Claysburg, PA; (Y); 12/57; FBLA; Library Aide; Var Cheerleading; Hon Roll; Hghst Achvt Awd 86; Altoona Schl Of Commerce; Bus.

ZETTELMAYER, ERIK J; North Catholic HS; Pittsburgh, PA; (Y); 34/250; Am Leg Boys St; German Clb; JA; Ski Clb; Ice Hcky; Hon Roll; NHS; NEDT Awd; Corprt Law.

ZETTERHOLM, CATHERINE; Fairview HS; Erie, PA; (Y); Girl Scts; Concert Band; Jazz Band; Mrchg Band; Pep Band; Nwsp Stf; Mgr(s); Hon Roll; MI ST U; Psych.

ZETTLEMOYER, KURT; Towanda HS; Towanda, PA; (Y); Boy Scts; Church Yth Grp; Var Crs Cntry; Hon Roll; Wrtng.

ZETTLEMOYER, MICHAEL; Brandywine HS; Mertztown, PA; (Y); 18/126; Pres Band; Chorus; Church Choir; Concert Band; Mrchg Band; School Play; NHS; Rotary Camp NEIDIG Tomorrows Ldrs 86; Lions Clb Canadian Exchng Stu 84; Chem.

ZEVENEY, THERESA; Bishop Hoban HS; Mountain Top, PA; (Y); FBLA; Pres Latin Clb; Chorus; Concert Band; Jazz Band; Mrchg Band; Orch; Hon Roll; Duquesne U; Msc Thrpy.

ZGLINICKI, CHRIS; Merecy Voctnal; Philadelphia, PA; (Y); Chess Clb; JV Bowling; Indstrl Elec.

ZHOOKOFF, KIMBERLY; Donegal HS; Marietta, PA; (Y); 15/160; Church Yth Grp; Drama Clb; School Play; Rep Stu Cncl; Stat Bsktbl; Mgr(s); High Hon Roll; Franklin & Marshall Coll; Acctn.

ZIACIK, JACQUELYN; Freeport HS; Sarver, PA; (Y); Hosp Aide; Library Aide; Trk; Twrlr; Vllybl; High Hon Roll; NHS; Freeport Wmns Evng Clb Scholar 86; IN U PA; Elem Ed.

ZIBURA, MARYANN; Forest Hills HS; Beaverdale, PA; (Y); 8/170; Pres FBLA; Nwsp Rptr; Chrmn Yrbk Stf; Stu Cncl; Var L Tennis; NHS; Pres Schlr; Rotary Awd; Hosp Aide; Pep Clb; Schrlshp Medal Awd 86; Soc Studies Awd 86; Jayceettes VP 86; U Pittsburgh; Acctng.

ZICCARDI, MARY JO; West Catholic Girls HS; Philadelphia, PA; (Y); 12/250; Dance Clb; Mathletes; Orch; School Play; Nwsp Rptr; Ballet Des Juenes Scholar 84-87; Claro Mdlng Agncy Scholar 85; TV Rep Ballet Des Juenes 84 & 86-87; Julliard; Dancing.

ZICCARELLI, JOSEPH; North Catholic HS; Pittsburgh, PA; (Y); 5/302; Chess Clb; Church Yth Grp; Computer Clb; Math Clb; Math Tm; Ski Clb; Stage Crew; Trs Stu Cncl; NHS; Ntl Merit SF; Natl Merit Fnlst 86; Cornell U; Engrng.

ZIDAR, ELIZABETH; Seton-La Salle HS; Pittsburgh, PA; (Y); Church Yth Grp; Cmnty Wkr; Drama Clb; Ski Clb; Chorus; School Play; High Hon Roll; Hon Roll; Jr NHS; Acad Chem Awd 85.

ZIDEK, JEFFREY; Apollo-Ridge HS; N Apollo, PA; (Y); 2/164; French Clb; Yrbk Phtg; Gov Hon Prg Awd; Hon Roll; Lion Awd; NHS; Pres Schlr; Sal; PA Gov Schl Arts Photogrphy 85; Summr Hepening Arts Photogrphy 84; St Vincent Coll; Graphic Arts.

ZIEGLER, ALLAN; Northampton Area SR HS; Bath, PA; (Y); 11/465; Model UN; Pres Soph Cls; Pres Jr Cls; Pres Sr Cls; Rep Stu Cncl; JV Bsbl; Ftbl; Var Trk; Cit Awd; High Hon Roll; Apptmt US Navl Acad 86; US Navl Acad; Aerntcl Engr.

ZIEGLER, BARBARA; Nazareth Acad; Washington Crsg, PA; (Y); Rep German Clb; School Play; Pres Soph Cls; Rep Stu Cncl; Cheerleading; Fld Hcky; Socr; Capt Tennis; High Hon Roll; Hon Roll.

ZIEGLER, JIM; Pittston Area HS; Pittston, PA; (Y); Math Clb; Im Bsktbl; Var Golf; Var Tennis; NHS.

ZIEGLER, JOHN; Chambersburg Area SR HS; Sugarlane, TX; (Y); Church Yth Grp; Quiz Bowl; ROTC; Teachers Aide; Var Bsktbl; Var Ftbl; Im Vllybl; Hon Roll; NHS; TX Tech U; Archtctr.

ZIEGLER, JOHN; Northeastern HS; Mt Wolf, PA; (Y); Church Yth Grp; Ski Clb; Varsity Clb; Chorus; Var Bsbl; Var Bsktbl; Var Socr; Hon Roll; Athletic Trnr.

ZIEGLER, THERESA; Salisbury HS; Allentown, PA; (Y); FBLA; School Play; Yrbk Stf; Im Cheerleading; 1st Plc FBLA Comptn 86; Pres Chptr 14 FBLA 86-87; Schl Of Visual Arts; Art.

ZIEGMANN, DAWN MICHELLE; South Williamsport Area SR HS; S Wmspt, PA; (Y); 10/140; Hosp Aide; Key Clb; Band; Chorus; Concert Band; Mrchg Band; School Musical; Nwsp Ed-Chief; Nwsp Phtg; Nwsp Rptr; Spcl Educ Tchr.

ZIELINSKI, SHARON; Reading Central Catholic HS; Reading, PA; (Y); 3/102; Cmnty Wkr; Exploring; German Clb; Math Clb; Pep Clb; Chorus; Variety Show; Ed Yrbk Stf; Hon Roll; NHS; Thelma Staab Trst Fund Schlrshp Math 86; Excllnc Relgn 86; Excllnc Math 86; IN U Of PA; Math.

ZIEMBA, ANN MARIE; Bishop Hoban HS; Plains, PA; (Y); 8/231; FBLA; Latin Clb; Math Clb; Ski Clb; JV Var Bsktbl; JV Capt Cheerleading; High Hon Roll; Hon Roll; NHS; Phy Thrpy.

ZIEMBA, JENNIFER LYNN; Wallenpaupak Area HS; Greentown, PA; (Y); Hosp Aide; Library Aide; Office Aide; Band; Var Capt Cheerleading; Mgr Socr; Trk; Pres Phys Ftnss Awd; Bloomsburg; Psychtry.

ZIEMBA, KATHRYN; Saint Pius X HS; Spring City, PA; (S); 3/139; JA; Mathletes; Office Aide; School Musical; Nwsp Rptr; Trk; High Hon Roll; NEDT Awd; Prfct Atten Awd; Debate Tm; Yth Ldrshp Conf 85; Pol Sci.

ZIEMINSKI, SAMUEL; Northeast Catholic HS; Philadelphia, PA; (Y); 68/362; Computer Clb.

ZIEMKE, WAYNE; Deer Lakes JR SR HS; Gibsonia, PA; (Y); Church Yth Grp; Library Aide; SADD; Chorus; Church Choir; Cert Awd Acdmc Achvmnt 86; Oral Roberts U; Med.

ZIENTEK, ANGELA; Notre Dame HS; Bethlehem, PA; (Y); 5/73; Computer Clb; Math Clb; Yrbk Stf; Var Swmmng; Var Trk; Cit Awd; Hon Roll; Jr NHS; Pres NHS; Hnry Mntn-Latin II 84; Outstndng Effort-Engl III 85; Outstndng Achvt Religion IV 86; Chestnut Hill Coll; Pre-Med.

ZIFF, TINA MARIE; Springfield HS; Springfield, PA; (Y); SADD; Cheerleading; Lcrss; Trk; Hon Roll.

ZIGO, KARA; Highlands HS; Natrona Hts, PA; (Y); Art Clb; Intnl Clb; Library Aide; SADD; Nwsp Stf; Rep Stu Cncl; Var Capt Cheerleading; Var Gym; Var Tennis; Hon Roll; Seventeen Cover Girl Fnlst 86; Joseph Hornes Teen Bd 85-87; Drexel U; Fshn Dsgn.

ZILFOU, JACK; William Allen HS; Allentown, PA; (Y); Church Yth Grp; Math Clb; JV Ftbl; Wt Lftg; JV Wrstlng; Hon Roll; Jr NHS; NHS; Prfct Atten Awd; Pres Schlr; Rifle Varsity Ltr 86; Muhlenberg Coll; Bio-Physics.

ZIMMER, HEIDI; Montour SR HS; Mckees Rocks, PA; (Y); Church Yth Grp; Cmnty Wkr; Sec Trs Exploring; Hosp Aide; Concert Band; Mrchg Band; School Musical; Stage Crew; High Hon Roll; Band; Outstndng Acad Achvt German II 86; Bio.

ZIMMERMAN, AMIE; Lewisburg Area HS; Lewisburg, PA; (Y); 54/162; VP Sec Church Yth Grp; Pep Clb; Spanish Clb; L Var Bsktbl; L Var Sftbl; Hon Roll; Coaches Awd-Bsktbl 85; Dfnsve Plyr Of The Yr Sftbl 85; MVP Bsktbl 86; Shippensburg U; Sclgy.

ZIMMERMAN, AMY; Annville-Cleona HS; Lebanon, PA; (Y); Church Yth Grp; FBLA; Sec German Clb; Office Aide; Varsity Clb; Y-Teens; Chorus; Church Choir; School Musical; Yrbk Stf; Art Awd Gold Key 84; Bus.

ZIMMERMAN, ANDREA; Kutztown Area HS; Kutztown, PA; (Y); 36/170; Teachers Aide; Band; Chorus; Church Choir; Concert Band; Mrchg Band; School Play; Variety Show; Yrbk Stf; Rep Stu Cncl; Smile Cont Awd; Bloomsburg U; Child Psych.

ZIMMERMAN, BRENDA; Punxsutawney Area HS; Sykesville, PA; (Y); 32/252; Am Leg Aux Girls St; Church Yth Grp; Math Tm; Band; Concert Band; Mrchg Band; Pep Band; Symp Band; Hon Roll; Stu Of Mnth 84-85; Accntnt.

ZIMMERMAN, CHRISTIE; Geibel HS; Perryopolis, PA; (Y); Pres JA; Pep Clb; Sftbl; VP French Hon Soc; High Hon Roll; Hon Roll; Pres Of Yr For J A Chapter In Uniontown 85-86; Duquesne U; Psych.

ZIMMERMAN, CONNIE; Millersburg Area HS; Millersburg, PA; (S); Church Yth Grp; Cmnty Wkr; 4-H; French Clb; Concert Band; Jazz Band; Mrchg Band; Yrbk Stf; Rep Stu Cncl; High Hon Roll; Ldrshp Awd; Sci Chem Awd; Bryan Coll; Med.

ZIMMERMAN, CONSTANCE M; Forest Hills SR HS; South Fork, PA; (Y); 10/156; Drama Clb; Speech Tm; Thesps; Chorus; School Musical; School Play; Jr NHS; Lion Awd; Trs NHS; Ntl Merit Ltr.

ZIMMERMAN, DAPHNE; Cocalico HS; Stevens, PA; (Y); Church Yth Grp; 4-H; Hst FBLA; Teachers Aide; Chorus; Church Choir; JV Tennis; High Hon Roll; NHS; Prfct Atten Awd; Elem Educ.

ZIMMERMAN, DAVID; Archbishp Wood HS For Boys; Hatboro, PA; (Y); 29/282; Y-Teens; JV Ftbl; Hon Roll; St Thomas U; Acctng.

ZIMMERMAN, DAVID; Northwest Area HS; Hunlock Creek, PA; (Y); 1/108; Pres Church Yth Grp; Pres Computer Clb; SADD; Band; Church Choir; Yrbk Phtg; Trs Sr Cls; Rep Stu Cncl; Elks Awd; VP NHS; Rep Schl Bd 86; Stevens Inst Tech; Comp Sci.

ZIMMERMAN, DICK; Johnsonburg Area HS; Wilcox, PA; (S); Pres Soph Cls; Hon Roll; Trs NHS; Ntl Merit Ltr; Penn ST U; Engrng.

ZIMMERMAN, ERIC; Ephrate SR HS; Akron, PA; (Y); 6/236; Boy Scts; CAP; Science Clb; Bsktbl; Socr; Vllybl; Hon Roll; NHS; Pres Schlr; Chem-Physcs Outstndg Stu Awd 86; Embry-Riddle Aero U; Aero Engrn.

ZIMMERMAN, HOLLY; Garden Spot HS; New Holland, PA; (Y); GAA; SADD; Rep Stu Cncl; Bsktbl; Fld Hcky; Powder Puff Ftbl; Sftbl; Hon Roll; Lancaster Schl; Csmtlgy.

ZIMMERMAN, JENNIFER M; Penn Cambria HS; Cresson, PA; (Y); FBLA; Drm & Bgl; Hon Roll; Rdng Awd 83-84; Mrt Prtcpatn 1st Yr Alg I Cntst 86; Cvcs Awd 83-84; Accntnt.

ZIMMERMAN, KIM; Bensalem HS; Bensalem, PA; (Y); Var Cheerleading; Var Crs Cntry; JV Fld Hcky; Var Trk; High Hon Roll; Hon Roll.

ZIMMERMAN, LANCE; South Williamsport HS; S Williamsport, PA; (Y); 19/140; High Hon Roll; Accntng.

ZIMMERMAN, LISA; Hempfield Area SR HS; Greensburg, PA; (Y); Hosp Aide; JA; Pep Clb; Spanish Clb; SADD; Chorus; Mrchg Band; School Play; Variety Show; Bus Admin.

ZIMMERMAN, LORIE; Everett Area HS; Everett, PA; (S); Spanish Clb; Varsity Clb; Band; Concert Band; Mrchg Band; Var L Trk; Twrlr; Hon Roll; Spanish NHS; Computer Clb; Schl Record-3200 Meter Relay 85; Nursng.

ZIMMERMAN, MARK; Milton Area SR HS; Potts Grove, PA; (Y); Church Yth Grp; 4-H; Latin Clb; Band; Church Choir; Concert Band; Mrchg Band; Stu Cncl; Hon Roll; NHS; Susquehanna; Comm.

ZIMMERMAN, MICHEAL; Ephrata HS; Ephrata, PA; (Y); Chorus; School Musical; School Play; Stage Crew; Var Ftbl; Var Wrstlng; Hon Roll; Hibshman Schlrshp 86; Goshen Coll; Chem.

ZIMMERMAN, PAMELA JANE; Pine Grove Area HS; Pine Grove, PA; (Y); Am Leg Aux Girls St; ROTC; SADD; Capt Flag Corp; School Musical; Nwsp Rptr; Yrbk Stf; Rep Soph Cls; Rep Jr Cls; Stat Sftbl; Bus.

ZIMMERMAN, RACHEL; Hempfield HS; Lancaster, PA; (Y); 39/460; Cmnty Wkr; Hosp Aide; Red Cross Aide; Service Clb; Orch; High Hon Roll; Ntl Merit Ltr; Exploring; Girl Scts; Band; All Amer Yth Hnr Musician 84; Mrkt Resrch.

ZIMMERMAN, RANDY; Cocalico HS; Denver, PA; (Y); Pres Church Yth Grp; Var L Bsktbl; Im Vllybl; Hon Roll.

ZIMMERMAN, RON; Annville-Cleona HS; Annville, PA; (Y); Cmnty Wkr; Letterman Clb; Varsity Clb; School Musical; Stage Crew; Bsbl; Bsktbl; Coach Actv; Ftbl; Vllybl; Military Svc.

ZIMMERMAN, RONALD JASON; Mt Pleasant Area HS; Norvelt, PA; (Y); Latin Clb; Band; Concert Band; Mrchg Band; Stage Crew; Yrbk Stf; Rep Frsh Cls; Hon Roll; VP SR HS Band 85-86; Musicians Institute; Music.

ZIMMERMAN, SCOTT; Ambridge Area HS; Ambridge, PA; (Y); 53/265; Am Leg Boys St; German Clb; Pep Clb; Soph Cls; Pres Stu Cncl; Ftbl; Tennis; Hon Roll; Lion Awd; Lions Club Boy Mnth Dec 85; VA Tech; Elec Engr.

ZIMMERMAN, SHARON; Mantour HS; Coraopolis, PA; (Y); Boys Clb Am; Church Yth Grp; Ski Clb; Concert Band; Mrchg Band; Swmmng; High Hon Roll; Elem Educ.

ZIMMERMAN, STEPHEN; Cathedral Prep Schl; Erie, PA; (Y); 2/267; Debate Tm; NFL; Office Aide; Speech Tm; Im Bsktbl; Im Vllybl; High Hon Roll; Hon Roll.

ZIMMERMAN, THOMAS ERIC; Warwick HS; Lititz, PA; (Y); 15/237; Math Clb; Band; VP Mrchg Band; Orch; High Hon Roll; NHS; Ntl Merit SF; Pres Schlr; Oper Barnabas Opus Awd 85; Warwick Music Schlr 85; Grace Coll; Music.

ZIMMERMAN, WANDA; Kutztown HS; Lenhartsville, PA; (Y); 8/150; Chorus; Yrbk Stf; Var Bsktbl; Var Fld Hcky; JV Sftbl; High Hon Roll; NHS; Art.

ZIMMERS, AMY; Susquenita HS; Marysville, PA; (Y); Church Yth Grp; Pres Exploring; 4-H; Leo Clb; Pres Ski Clb; Spanish Clb; Teachers Aide; Chorus; Rep Jr Cls; Rep Stu Cncl; 2nd Pl Sci Fair 85; Mst Imprvd Swimmr 86; Pilot.

ZINGER, VICTORIA C; Boyertown Area SR HS; Boyertown, PA; (Y); 3/433; Am Leg Aux Girls St; Math Tm; Sec Band; Sec Concert Band; Sec Mrchg Band; School Musical; School Play; JV Tennis; Cit Awd; High Hon Roll; Gulack Fndtn Schlrshp 86; Schlstc Scrimmage Tm 83-86; Pres Acad Ftnss Awd 86; U Of PA; Bio.

ZINKHAM, TIM; Seneca Valley HS; Harmony, PA; (Y); Aud/Vis; Church Yth Grp; Computer Clb; Radio Clb; Stat L Bsbl; Im Bsktbl; Mgr(s); JV Trk; Im Wt Lftg; Hon Roll; 1st Yr Awd 86; Engrng.

ZINNI, LISA; Archbishop Kennedy HS; Philadelphia, PA; (Y); Stu Cncl; Hon Roll; Hghst Avrg Spnsh Cls 85; Bus.

ZINOBILE, ANGELA; Southern Huntingdon County HS; Mapleton Depot, PA; (Y); Pres GAA; SADD; Band; Chorus; School Musical; Yrbk Stf; Capt Bsktbl; L Fld Hcky; Powder Puff Ftbl; L Sftbl; Altillo Alumni Awd 86; Sidney J Mc Cormick Mrl Awd 86; Lockhaven U; Health Phy Ed.

ZIOGAS, ANTONIA; Elizabethtown Area HS; Elizabethtown, PA; (Y); Church Yth Grp; Model UN; Yrbk Bus Mgr; Yrbk Stf; JV Fld Hcky; JV Var Trk; Stage Crew; Stat Mgr(s).

ZIPNOCK, KRYSTAL; Mt Pleasant Area SR HS; Mt Pleasant, PA; (Y); French Clb; Cheerleading; GAA; Ski Clb; Teachers Aide; Sr Cls; Stu Cncl; Mat Maids; Hon Roll; U Of Pittsburgh; Psychlgy.

ZIPP, JOY; Harborcreek JR SR HS; Harbor Creek, PA; (Y); 27/228; Church Yth Grp; Model UN; Sec Frsh Cls; VP Soph Cls; VP Jr Cls; VP Sr Cls; Stu Cncl; Hon Roll; Pres NHS; Nrsng Adm.

ZISSIS, NIKKI; Freedom HS; Bethlehem, PA; (Y); 45/465; Camera Clb; Pep Clb; Color Guard; Hon Roll; Temple; Hlth.

ZITO, NANCY; Cameron County HS; Emporium, PA; (Y); 27/85; Cmnty Wkr; Spanish Clb; Band; Concert Band; Mrchg Band; Pep Band; Nwsp Ed-Chief; Yrbk Stf; Pres Trs Stu Cncl; Ftbl; Lifeguard 83-86; Mistress Ceremonies Hmcmng 85; Mst Schl Spirit 86; Lock Haven U; Sports Med.

ZIVKOVICH, ANNALEE; Carlynton JR SR HS; Carnegie, PA; (Y); Art Clb; French Clb; Ski Clb; Tennis; High Hon Roll; Pres NHS; PA ST U; Frnch.

ZMICH, KURT; B Reed Henderson HS; W Chester, PA; (Y); 24/349; Boy Scts; Lit Mag; JV Bsbl; Var JV Lcrss; Im Wt Lftg; NHS; Spanish NHS; PSAT Hgh Scorer Awd.

ZOBA, TRICIA A; Marian HS; Mc Adoo, PA; (Y); 3/115; Church Yth Grp; Chorus; Color Guard; Drill Tm; French Hon Soc; High Hon Roll; NHS; Bio.

ZOCK, FRANK; Portage Area HS; Portage, PA; (S); Church Yth Grp; Cmnty Wkr; French Clb; School Play; Im JV Bsbl; Im JV Bsktbl; High Hon Roll; NHS; Acadmc All Amercn; Sci.

ZOCK, KAREN; Bishop Carroll HS; Portage, PA; (S); 7/102; Drama Clb; Pep Clb; Ski Clb; Spanish Clb; SADD; Stage Crew; Yrbk Stf; JV Cheerleading; Var L Vllybl; High Hon Roll; U Pittsburgh; Elec Engrg.

ZOCK, LESLIE; Bishop Carroll HS; Portage, PA; (S); 13/110; Drama Clb; Pep Clb; Ski Clb; SADD; Church Choir; Stage Crew; JV Cheerleading; Var Vllybl; Hon Roll; Trs NHS; Ntn Ed Dvlpmnt Awd 83; Phy Thrpy.

ZODY, CRAIG H; Waynesboro Area SR HS; Waynesboro, PA; (Y); Church Yth Grp; Ski Clb; Band; Chorus; Concert Band; Jazz Band; Mrchg Band; School Play; Score Keeper.

ZOERKLER, FLORENCE; Frankford HS; Philadelphia, PA; (Y); 1/453; Drama Clb; Chorus; Concert Band; Jazz Band; Orch; Nwsp Ed-Chief; Yrbk Stf; High Hon Roll; NHS; Ntl Merit Ltr; Harleysville Insrnc Co Schlrshp 86; Philadelphia Coll Pharm & Sci Pres Schlrshp 85; Philadelphia Coll Pharm; Toxicl.

ZOLA, CHRISTINE M; Shaler Area HS; Pittsburgh, PA; (Y); 118/538; Office Aide; Speech Tm; Chorus; School Musical; Stage Crew; Yrbk Stf; Hon Roll; Rotary Awd; PA ST U; Chem.

ZOLA, CONNIE; Hazleton HS; Hazleton, PA; (Y); Church Yth Grp; Drama Clb; Pep Clb; Bsktbl; Cheerleading; Tennis; PA ST; Accntnt.

ZOLA, JAMES; Hazleton HS; Hazleton, PA; (Y); 10/375; Scholastic Bowl; Hon Roll; Pres Schlr; Spanish NHS; David Roman Schlrshp 86; S P Turnbach Awd 86; Renaissance Schlrshp 86; PA ST U; Bio.

ZOLA, SHARON; Hazleton HS; Hazleton, PA; (Y); 74/388; Service Clb; Bsktbl; Hon Roll.

ZOMAK, DEBORA ANN; Canon Mc Millan HS; Cecil, PA; (Y); Varsity Clb; Band; Chorus; Capt Color Guard; Concert Band; Drill Tm; Mrchg Band; Bsktbl; Var Sftbl; NHS; Mth.

ZOOK, CAPRICE; Juniata HS; Mifflintown, PA; (Y); 4-H; Chorus; Concert Band; Jazz Band; Mrchg Band; School Musical; NHS; Ntl Merit Ltr; Computer Clb; Sec Drama Clb; Outstndng Soph Bnd 85; Amer Lgn Essy Awd 85; Music.

ZOOK, KATHLEEN J; Camp Hill HS; Camp Hl, PA; (Y); Church Yth Grp; German Clb; Office Aide; Band; Concert Band; Jazz Band; Mrchg Band; Pep Band; Yrbk Stf; Outstndng Bus Stu Yr 86; Hgh Hon Roll 83-86; Sec Sci.

ZOOK, LONNA; Hollidaysburg Area SR HS; Hollidaysburg, PA; (Y); 61/368; Church Yth Grp; Varsity Clb; Nwsp Sprt Ed; Yrbk Stf; Pres Sr Cls; Var Capt Bsktbl; Var Crs Cntry; Var Capt Sftbl; Var Swmmng; Hon Roll; Delta Kappa Gamma Awd 86; Bst All Around Girl Awd 86; Outstndng Female Athlete 86; Lycoming Coll; Educ.

ZORANSKI, KYRA; Wyoming Valley West HS; Kingston, PA; (Y); Church Yth Grp; French Clb; Key Clb; Teachers Aide; Church Choir; Concert Band; Drm Mjr(t); Mrchg Band; School Musical; Rep Sr Cls; Wymng Vly W Band Prnts Assoc Awd 86; M Blcok 11 Yr Hnrum Schlrshp 86; Luzerne Cnty Mock Trl Cert 86; Penn St U; Pre-Law.

ZORE, CATHY; St Marys Area HS; Saint Marys, PA; (Y); Church Yth Grp; Cmnty Wkr; Girl Scts; Hosp Aide; Hon Roll; Grl Sct Gld Awd 85, Marion Awd 83; Psychrst.

ZORETICH, MARIA; Chester HS; Chester, PA; (Y); High Hon Roll; Katherine Gibbs Ldrshp Awd 86; Acadmc Achvt Awd 86; Outstndng Strght A Avg Bus Math 86; Katharine Gibbs; Sectrl.

ZORN, KATHERINE; General Mc Lane HS; Edinboro, PA; (Y); Church Yth Grp; Cmnty Wkr; Office Aide; High Hon Roll; Flgt Attndt.

ZOTOS, PETER; Bensalem HS; Bensalem, PA; (Y); Intnl Clb; Nwsp Stf; JV Var Tennis; High Hon Roll; Ntl Merit SF; Intl Bus.

ZUBRITSKI, TORI; John S Fine HS; Wanamie, PA; (Y); 18/256; Church Yth Grp; Varsity Clb; Yrbk Stf; Var Capt Bsktbl; Var L Sftbl; High Hon Roll; NHS; Physcl Thrpy.

ZUBRYD, JAMES; Hempfield Area SR HS; Irwin, PA; (Y); FFA; Band; OH ST; Dairy Sci.

ZUCCARELLO, MICHELLE; W C East HS; West Chester, PA; (Y); JV Var Cheerleading; Itln Hnr Soc 85 & 86; WC Bd Ed Outstndg Achvt Awd 86; WC Outstndg Svc Awd 86; West Chester U; Tchg.

ZUCCHERO, LORI; Moon SR HS; Coraopolis, PA; (Y); DECA; Chorus; Hon Roll; Competed In Dist For DECA 85-86; Robert Morris; Mgmt.

ZUCCO, LISA; Plum SR HS; Pittsburgh, PA; (Y); 85/378; Girl Scts; Spanish Clb; Band; Mrchg Band; School Play; Symp Band; Variety Show; Nwsp Rptr; Nwsp Stf; L Trk; Clsrm Awds Alg,Trig,Spnsh,Comp Litrcy And Bio 84-86; Vet Med.

ZUCZEK, MATTHEW; Bishop O Hara HS; Dickson City, PA; (S); 2/130; French Clb; Scholastic Bowl; School Musical; High Hon Roll; Sal; PA ST U; Corp Lwyr.

ZUESI, MARIBETH; Mon Alley Catholic HS; Monongahela, PA; (Y); 52/105; Pep Clb; Science Clb; Spanish Clb; Yrbk Bus Mgr; Yrbk Stf; Bsktbl; Cheerleading; Advrtsng.

ZUKAUCKAS, CRIS ANNE; Elizabeth Forward HS; Elizabeth, PA; (Y); 6/317; SADD; Mrchg Band; Hst Sr Cls; Capt Sftbl; Capt Twrlr; CC Awd; High Hon Roll; NHS; Church Yth Grp; Cmnty Wkr; Carnegie Inst Sci Rcgntn Awd 86; Miss PS US TEEN 86; Modeling 84-86; Penn ST U; Human Dev.

ZUKOSKI, JOSEPH; Hanover Area JR SR HS; Wilkes Barre, PA; (Y); 4-H; Key Clb; Band; Chorus; Concert Band; Mrchg Band; School Musical; Stu Cncl; Bowling; Gov Hon Prg Awd; Temple U; Jrnlsm.

ZUKOWSKI, CHRISTINE; Harbor Creek HS; Erie, PA; (Y); 6/204; Model UN; SADD; Var L Bsktbl; Coach Actv; Var L Sftbl; Hon Roll; NHS; Im Score Keeper; 1st Tm All Cnty Bsktbl; 1st Tm All Cnty Sftbl; Kystn ST Gms Sftbl 85, Bsktbl 86; Math.

ZULEWSKI, ELIZABETH; Nazareth Acad; Philadelphia, PA; (Y); German Clb; Hosp Aide; Red Cross Aide; Yrbk Stf; High Hon Roll; PA Coll; Pharmacy.

ZULICK, CYNDI; Butler SR HS; Butler, PA; (Y); Trs Church Yth Grp; Girl Scts; Spanish Clb; SADD; Chorus; Church Choir; Swmmng; Hon Roll; L Jr NHS; Natl Hnr Soc 86; Phys Ther.

ZUNDEL, CHRISTIE C; Hempfield Area SR HS; Greensburg, PA; (Y); 12/657; Sec Church Yth Grp; Cmnty Wkr; Drama Clb; Spanish Clb; Teachers Aide; Church Choir; Orch; Jr NHS; NHS; Pres Schlr; Debate Tm 2nd Pl Wnnr Humanities Day 86; Hempfield Hnr Grad 86; CA U; Spch Pathlgy.

ZUNDEL, DENISE; Greensburg Salem HS; New Alexandria, PA; (Y); 30/324; German Clb; Var L Bsktbl; Var L Crs Cntry; Var L Sftbl; Var L Vllybl; High Hon Roll; NHS; 4-H; Band; Hon Roll; Earl Ewing Awd-Outstndng Feml Athlt 86; Natl Athltc Schlrshp Soc Scndry Schls 86; Tp 10 Prcnt Schl 86; Salem Coll; Phy Ed.

ZUNG, MICHAEL; St Francis Prep; Arlington, VA; (Y); 1/36; Drama Clb; Church Choir; School Play; Variety Show; Nwsp Ed-Chief; Nwsp Stf; Sec Stu Cncl; JV Var Bsktbl; Im Mgr Sftbl; Im Mgr Tennis; NY U Trustee Schlrshp 86; William & Mary Coll; Intl Rltns.

ZUNGALI, SCOTT; Greater Johnstown SR HS; Johnstown, PA; (Y); Boy Scts; Pres Sec Church Yth Grp; JA; Spanish Clb; SADD; Nwsp Stf; Hon Roll; Comp Sci.

ZUNIGA, SCHEHERAZADA ELAINE; Clarion Area HS; Clarion, PA; (Y); 5/80; Sec Church Yth Grp; FCA; Chorus; Color Guard; School Musical; Variety Show; Yrbk Stf; Hon Roll; NHS; Robert L Wiberg Schlrshp $500 86; Bio Sci Awd 86; PA ST U; Human Dvlpmnt.

ZUPANCIC, GIGI; South Park HS; Pittsburgh, PA; (Y); Church Yth Grp; Teachers Aide; Im Bsktbl; Hon Roll.

ZUPANCIC, JOSEPH; Canon Mc Millan HS; Canonsburg, PA; (Y); 9/395; Exploring; Latin Clb; Varsity Clb; School Play; Var L Ftbl; Var L Trk; NHS; Pres Med Expl Club 85-86; Chem.

ZUPSIC, ROBERT; Center Area HS; Monaca, PA; (Y); 17/180; Am Leg Boys St; Camera Clb; Computer Clb; Spanish Clb; Band; Yrbk Bus Mgr; Yrbk Phtg; Yrbk Stf; Stu Cncl; NHS; Outstndng Accntnt Stu 86; Hnr Grad 86; PA ST U; Bus Admin.

ZURAT, KELLY; Bradford Area HS; Bradford, PA; (Y); Ski Clb; Chorus; School Play; Rep Jr Cls; Stu Cncl; Var Tennis; Im Vllybl; High Hon Roll; Hon Roll; NHS.

ZURAWSKI, REBECCA JANE; Cardinal O Hara HS; Media, PA; (Y); 179/740; Office Aide; Pres Acdmc Ftns Awd 86; Comp Oper.

ZURENDA, RICHARD; Punxsutawney HS; Punxsutawney, PA; (Y); Art Clb; Spanish Clb; Stage Crew; Crs Cntry; Wt Lftg; Hon Roll; OH Comp Schl; Comp Tech.

ZURKOVSKI, SUSAN A; Baldwin HS; Pittsburgh, PA; (Y); 3/531; Key Clb; School Musical; Nwsp Ed-Chief; Stu Cncl; NHS; John Carroll U Acad Scholar 86; Natl Hnr Soc Scholar 86; Albert Hilko Mem Scholar 86; John Carroll U; Eng.

ZURZOLO, TRACY; Upper Darby HS; Drexel Hill, PA; (Y); 11/506; Art Clb; Cmnty Wkr; Drama Clb; JA; Spanish Clb; Yrbk Stf; Lit Mag; Jr Cls; Sr Cls; Stu Cncl; Spanish & Engl Lang Awd; U Of PA; Engl.

ZVOCH, CYNTHIA; West Mifflin Area HS; W Mifflin, PA; (Y); 34/335; Church Yth Grp; Girl Scts; SADD; Off Jr Cls; Off Sr Cls; High Hon Roll; Hon Roll; Ntl Hstrcl Cmte 86; PTSA 84-86; Slvr Awd 84-85; Clarion U; Erly Chldhd.

ZVONAR, GREGORY; Mt Lebanon HS; Pittsburgh, PA; (Y); 50/493; Exploring; German Clb; Ski Clb; Im Vllybl; High Hon Roll; Nemra Schlrshp 86; Bata Base Pgm Yrbk 86; Virginia Tech; Elect Engr.

ZWEIER, SCOTT; Lebanon HS; Lebanon, PA; (Y); German Clb; Rep Frsh Cls; Rep Soph Cls; Rep Jr Cls; Var Tennis; High Hon Roll; NHS; Ntl Merit Ltr; Woodmn Wrld Life Ins Scty Awd Outstndng Profcncy US Hstry 85; Rensselaer Polytech Inst Awd 85.

ZWEIG, KELLY; Greater Nanticoke Area HS; Hunlock Creek, PA; (Y); Art Clb; Church Yth Grp; Chorus; Hon Roll; Nanticoke JR Womns Clb & Luzerne Cnty Fed Of Womn 1st Pl 86; Francis Hook Art Schlrshp Comptn PA 86; Art.

ZWIEBEL, LAURA A; Bishop Hoban HS; Wilkes Barre, PA; (Y); 10/230; Drama Clb; FBLA; Hosp Aide; Latin Clb; Chorus; School Musical; School Play; Cheerleading; Hon Roll; NHS; Vrsty Cheerleading Routines 86.

ZWOLENIK, CHERYL; Lancaster Catholic HS; Lancaster, PA; (Y); 93/215; Varsity Clb; Nwsp Rptr; Stat Bsktbl; Hon Roll; Penn ST York; Bus.

ZYCHOWSKI, KELLY; South Park HS; Pittsburgh, PA; (Y); Bsktbl; Coach Actv; Socr; Trk; Hon Roll; NHS; Sprts Med.

ZYGMUNT, SUSAN; Nazareth Acad; Philadelphia, PA; (Y); 12/122; Exploring; German Clb; Capt Hosp Aide; Acpl Chr; VP Chorus; Church Choir; School Musical; School Play; High Hon Roll; Hon Roll; 3rd Pl Polish Hrtg Soc Ptry Rctl 84; Gntc Rsrch.

DELA-WARE

Abrenica, Norlisa
Archmere Acad
Wilmington, DE

Adamczyk, Patricia
Newark HS
Newark, DE

Alfieri, Maria
Padua Acad
Wilmington, DE

Allen, Tracey
Smyrna HS
Smyrna, DE

Alvarez, Robert
Glasgow HS
Newark, DE

Anderson, III Angus E
Christiana HS
Newark, DE

Angel, Christina
Sussex Central HS
Millsboro, DE

Asbury, Shelia
William Penn HS
Bear, DE

Ash, Phillip
Indian River HS
Frankford, DE

Attix, Joyce
Milford HS
Lincoln, DE

Bacino, Kimberly
Dover HS
Dover, DE

Backus, Kelli
William Penn HS
New Castle, DE

Baffone, Marc
Salesianum HS
Newark, DE

Baker, Cheryl
Dover HS
Dover, DE

Barchock, Joyce
Concord Christian
Wilmington, DE

Barry, Kevin
William Penn HS
New Castle, DE

Barton, Loren
Newark HS
Newark, DE

Behan, Margaret Anne
Smyrna HS
Smyrna, DE

Bernhard, Lisa
Delcastle Tech HS
New Castle, DE

Berster, Michele Marie
Padua Acad
Wilmington, DE

Bethard, Christopher S
Caesar Rodney HS
Camden, DE

Betts, Michele
Cape Henlopen HS
Lewes, DE

Beyer, Greg
Newark HS
Newark, DE

Biden, Beau
Archmere Acad HS
Wilmington, DE

Blackwood, Raymond
Salesianum Schl
Wilmington, DE

Blazes, William J
St Marks HS
Newark, DE

Blessing, Rhonda Kay
Milford SR HS
Milford, DE

Bock, Pamela A
Dover HS
Dover, DE

Boush, Michael A
Salesianum Schl
Wilmington, DE

Bovankovich, Paul
St Marks HS
Newark, DE

Bowens, Marla
William Penn HS
New Castle, DE

Bozzo, Stephen
Archmere Acad
Wilmington, DE

Bradley, Kaeti E
Cape Henlopen HS
Harbeson, DE

Bradley, Kevin
Archmere Acad
Claymont, DE

Breault, Nancy Elizabeth
Howard Career Center HS
Wilmington, DE

Brown, Patrick
Salesianum Schl
Hockessin, DE

Bruck, Jeffrey
Salesianum Schl
Wilmington, DE

Brunozzi, Diana
Padua Acad
Wilmington, DE

Brynes, Pam
William Penn HS
New Castle, DE

Brzozowski, Michelle
Delcastle Technical
Wilmington, DE

Burchfield, Beth
Delcastle Technical
Wilmington, DE

Burns, Lisa Anne
William Penn HS
Newark, DE

Burns, Michael
Salesianum HS
Hockessin, DE

Butz, Nicole
St Marks HS
Newark, DE

Carlson, Kathleen
Lake Forest HS
Camden-Wyoming, DE

Carney, Christine
Seaford HS
Seaford, DE

Centrella, Lori
Archmere Acad
Newark, DE

Cerminaro, III Frank T
Delcastle Technical
Newark, DE

Chadwell, Jr Arthur
Woodbridge HS
Bridgeville, DE

Chelton, Melissa
Seaford SR HS
Seaford, DE

Chen, Beth
Archmere Acad
Wilmington, DE

Chudzik, Trina
St Marks HS
Wilmington, DE

Churilla, Monica
Milford SR HS
Milford, DE

Clark, Jeffrey
Smyrna HS
Kenton, DE

Cloyd, Jennifer Theresa
Brandywine HS
Wilmington, DE

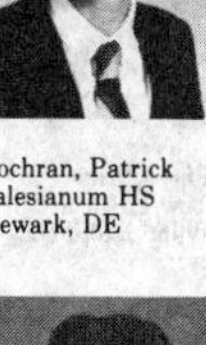

Cochran, Patrick
Salesianum HS
Newark, DE

Coggins, Claire
Archmere Acad
West Chester, PA

Collender, Stacie
St Marks HS
Wilmington, DE

Collins, Dale
Indian River HS
Frankford, DE

Collison, Beth
Lake Forest HS
Harrington, DE

Conner, Susan
Dover HS
Dover, DE

Consiglio, Amy Marie
Saint Marks HS
Newark, DE

Cook, Cathy
Seaford SR HS
Seaford, DE

Cordrey, Tabatha
Indian River HS
Dagsboro, DE

Corpus, Rachael
Caesar Rodney HS
Dover, DE

Counrtney, Jr James J
St Marks HS
New Castle, DE

Courtney, Jennifer
Saint Marys HS
New Castle, DE

Crescenzo, James
Alexis I Du Pont HS
Wilmington, DE

Critzer, Lisa
Padua Acad
Brookhaven, PA

Crockett, Don
Smyrna HS
Townsend, DE

Crouse, Michelle
Caravel Acad
Newark, DE

Cundiff, III Bruce T
Brandywine HS
Wilmington, DE

Cunha, Lisa
Caesar Rodney HS
Dover, DE

Curtis, Glen
Caesar Rodney HS
Camden, DE

Davis, Angelique
Wilmington HS
Wilmington, DE

Davis, Trina
Laurel Senior HS
Laurel, DE

Davolos, Stephanie
Archmere Acad
Wilmington, DE

Day, Nick
Cape Henlopen HS
Rehoboth, DE

De Vore, Lisa
Delmar HS
Delmar, MD

Deely, David
Salesianum School
For Boys
Wilmington, DE

Dettra, Mark
William Penn HS
New Castle, DE

Deveney, Michelle D
Claymont HS
Claymont, DE

Dickerson, Diana L
Dover HS
Dover, DE

Dickerson, Scott
Milford SR HS
Milford, DE

Dietz, Lorie
Newark HS
Newark, DE

Dimauro, Jr Michael
J
Mt Pleasant SR HS
Wilmington, DE

Dorsey, III Daniel
Richard
Howard Career Ctr
Wilmington, DE

Dowrick, Ed
Salesianum HS
Aston, PA

Dunsmore, Michelle
Glasgow HS
Newark, DE

Dupre, Shelley
Seaford SR HS
Seaford, DE

Durkin, Kevin
Archmere Acad
Brookhaven, PA

Eckbold, Janice
Delcaste Vo Tech
Wilmington, DE

Edwards, Cheryl
Wilmington HS
Wilmington, DE

Elliott, Christine
Indian River HS
Dagsboro, DE

Ellis, Andrew
Delmar JR SR HS
Delmar, DE

Ellis, Dawn
Dover HS
Dover, DE

Ellzy, Janelle
Wilmington HS
Wilmington, DE

Elswick, Robin
Laurel SR HS
Laurel, DE

Emerick, Kristen
John Dickinson HS
Wilmington, DE

Epps, Christina
Mount Pleasant HS
Wilmington, DE

Erling, Lisa
Saint Marks HS
West Grove, PA

Erskine, Brian M
Salesianum HS
Newark, DE

Farkas, Alexander P
Kent North
Camden, DE

Farmer, Kelly L
Thomas Mckean HS
Wilmington, DE

Farrelly, Laura
Laurel SR HS
Laurel, DE

Favazza, Yvette
Glasgow HS
Glendale Newark,
DE

Feeney, Brooke
Delmar HS
Delmar, MD

Figgs, Kimberly
Delmar HS
Delmar, DE

Fleetwood, III
Thomas C
St Marks HS
Wilmington, DE

Floyd, Jennifer
William Penn HS
New Castle, DE

Foltz, Becki
Mt Pleasant HS
Wilmington, DE

Ford, Yvette
Dover HS
Little Creek, DE

Fortuna, Maria G
Padua Acad
Philadelphia, PA

Foskey, Karen
Seaford SR HS
Seaford, DE

Foss, David
Alexis I Du Pont HS
Hockessin, DE

Foss, Lauren
A I Du Pont HS
Hockessin, DE

Foulk, Brian
Alexis I Du Pont HS
Hockessin, DE

Frallic, Debbie
Seaford SR HS
Seaford, DE

French, Missy
New Castle Baptist
Bear, DE

Frese, Paul
Dickinson HS
Wilmington, DE

Frey, Matthew
Delmar HS
Delmar, MD

Friedrich, Cheryl
Mount Pleasant HS
Wilmington, DE

Fuchs, Kira
Tower Hill Schl
Wilmington, DE

Fuller, Jerry
William Penn HS
New Castle, DE

Gable, Anne
St Marks HS
Newark, DE

Gaucher, Michael R
Thomas Mc Kean
Wilmington, DE

Gawinski, Teresa
St Elizabeth HS
Wilmington, DE

Geese, Janet
Newark SR HS
Newark, DE

Gempp, Steven
Salesignum HS
Hockessin, DE

Girardi, Andrew
St Marks HS
Wilmington, DE

Giuliani, Jennifer
Padua Acad
Newark, DE

Glaum, Mark C
Salesianum HS
Thorndale, PA

Golder, Lynn
Caesar Rodney HS
Magnolia, DE

Gopez, Melissa
Archmere Acad
Greenville, DE

Granito, Stefan
Saint Andrews Schl
Manasquan, NJ

Greenly, Jeff D
Milford SR HS
Milford, DE

Gregory, Matthew
Wilmington Friends
Wilmington, DE

Griffin, Cristi
John Dickinson HS
Newark, DE

Griffith, Julie
Brandywine HS
Wilmington, DE

Hahn, Robert
Salesianum Schl
Wilminton, DE

Hall, Brian L
Sussex Central SR
Millsboro, DE

Hall, Lareese
Concord HS
Claymont, DE

Halley, Christy
Alexis I Du Pont HS
Newark, DE

Hance, Lawrence
Salesianum HS
Wilmington, DE

Handsberry, Lisa
Smyrna HS
Smyrna, DE

Harper, Katherine
Claymont HS
Wilmington, DE

Harrell, Erica
William Penn HS
New Castle, DE

Harris, Sandra J
Christian
Tabernacle Acad
Georgetown, DE

Harwitz, Steven R
Concord HS
Wilmington, DE

Hill, Deesha
Dover HS
Dover, DE

Hitchens, Pamela
Laurel SR HS
Laurel, DE

Hodges, Ellen
Alexis I Dupont HS
Hockessin, DE

Holdren, Mike
William Penn HS
Bear, DE

Holladay, Robert
Indian River HS
Dagsboro, DE

Hood, Sabrina
Cape Henlopen HS
Milton, DE

Hopkins, Connie
Cape Henlopen HS
Milton, DE

Horgan, Neil
Archmere Acad
Wilmington, DE

Howe, Jr Richard O
Salesianum HS
Newark, DE

Hudson, Heather
Smyrna HS
Smyrna, DE

Hughes, Kelly
Padua Acad
Chadds Ford, PA

Hunt, Janine
William Penn HS
New Castle, DE

Inman, Melinda
Claymont HS
Claymont, DE

Iplenski, Genevieve
Dover HS
Hartly, DE

Jarrell, Jr Ralph
Wilmington
Christian Schl
Newark, DE

Jennings, Jack
Archmere Acad
Winston Salem, NC

Johnson, Jeffrey
Salesianum HS
Wilmington, DE

Johnson, Sherri
Seaford SR HS
Laurel, DE

Jones, Kim
Mc Kean HS
Wilmington, DE

Jones, Lisa
Caravel Acad
Newark, DE

Jordan, Brian
Indian River HS
Frankford, DE

Jordan, Karen
Caesar Rodney HS
Dover, DE

Joseph, Dawn
Delmar JR SR HS
Delmar, MD

Joyce, Robert
Salesianum HS
Wilmington, DE

June, Claudia
Milford SR HS
Milford, DE

Kellam, Jackie
Dover HS
Dover, DE

Kimble, Paula
Cape Henlopen HS
Lincoln, DE

King, Dawn
Seaford SR HS
Seaford, DE

Kiser, Sandra
Alexis I Du Pont HS
Hockessin, DE

Klein, Marc
Salesianum HS
Sewell, NJ

Klinge, Brian T
Salesianum Schl
Wilmington, DE

Kotowski, Michelle
R
St Marks HS
Wilmington, DE

Koutoufaris, Marcos
Dover HS
Dover, DE

Kral, Kim
William Penn HS
New Castle, DE

Krauss, III Granville
C
Claymont HS
Claymont, DE

Krewson, Stephanie
Wilmington Friends
Wilmington, DE

Kubicki, Barbara A
St Marks HS
West Grove, PA

Kulis, Mike
Archmere Acad
Boothwyn, PA

Lacava, Vincent
Archmere Acad
Claymont, DE

Lamb, K Scott
Concord HS
Wilmington, DE

Lambdin, Patrick M
Smyrna HS
Clayton, DE

Land, Harold
Newark HS
Newark, DE

Lantzy, Brian
Dover HS
Dover, DE

Larrimore, Amy
Seaford SR HS
Seaford, DE

Lauderbaugh, David
Dover HS
Dover, DE

Lee, Barbara
Brandywine HS
Wilmington, DE

Lemon, Bradley
Todd
Delmar JR SR HS
Delmar, MD

Leonardo, Edward
Salesianum HS
Parkside, PA

Lewis, Michelle
Christiana HS
New Castle, DE

Lillis, Brad
Salesianum HS
Wilmington, DE

Little, Amy C
Dover HS
Dover, DE

Little, D Renee
Dover HS
Dover, DE

Littleton, Angel
Sussey Central SR
Georgetown, DE

Luu, Nganha
Claymont HS
Claymont, DE

Lynch, Mary
Dover HS
Dover, DE

Makram, Maurice
Salesianum HS
Parkesburg, PA

Malaney, Lise
New Castle Baptist
New Castle, DE

Marquez, Paul
Smyrna HS
Smyrna, DE

Martens, Tammy
Seaford SR HS
Seaford, DE

Mascitti, Michelle
Pajvd Acad
Philadelphia, PA

Masino, Jr Thomas R
Caesar Rodney HS
Dover, DE

Maslanka, Francis C
Salesianum HS
Landenberg, PA

Massey, Heather L
Seaford SR HS
Bridgeville, DE

Matlusky, John
Salesianum Schl
Greenville, DE

Maximo, Victoria
Dover HS
Dover, DE

Mc Allister, Cheryl
St Marks HS
Newark, DE

Mc Cabe, Lori
Indian River HS
Ocean View, DE

Mc Cabe, Troy
Indian River HS
Selbyville, DE

Mc Ginnis, Sandy
Cape Henlopen HS
Lewes, DE

Mc Graw, Dawn
Glasgow HS
Newark, DE

Mc Guinness, Moira
Archmere Acad
Wilmington, DE

Mehan, Andrew
William Penn HS
New Castle, DE

Melson, Patricia L
Cape Henlopen HS
Lewes, DE

Melvin, Kellie
Dover HS
Dover, DE

Merrill, Anthony J
Indian River HS
Ocean View, DE

Michalcewiz, William W
Archmere Acad
Wilmington, DE

Mikeal, Konovia
Padua Acad
Wilmington, DE

Miller, Jr James W
Salesianum Schl
Townsend, DE

Miller, Lesli R
Sussex Central SR
Georgetown, DE

Miller, Lynn
Seaford SR HS
Seaford, DE

Milloy, Kimberly
Indian River HS
Bethany Bch, DE

Mills, Dennis I
Milford HS
Milford, DE

Mims, Rae
Dover HS
Dover, DE

Mitchell, Tonya
Indian River HS
Frankford, DE

Monaco, Meg
Archmere Acad
Wilmington, DE

Money, Brian
Smyrna HS
Clayton, DE

Mongeluzi, Donna
Padua Acad
Philadelphia, PA

Moore, Bill
Salesianum Schl
Aston, PA

Moore, Deena
Milford SR HS
Milford, DE

Morris, Lori
Delmar HS
Delmar, DE

Nelson, Gary
Sussex Central HS
Millsboro, DE

PHOTO NOT AVAILABLE

Nevdick, Heather
Dover HS
Scotts Valley, CA

O Connell, Ciara M
Archmere Acad
Wilmington, DE

O Neal, Annetta Lillian
Newark HS
Newark, DE

Oboryshko, Kathleen
John Dickinson HS
Wilmington, DE

Olsen, Arthur
Newark HS
Newark, DE

Pantuliano, Nancy
Padua Acad
New Castle, DE

Papa, Toni Nicole
Padua Acad
Philadelpia, PA

Parkinson, Lisa
Sussex Central HS
Millsboro, DE

Parramore, Jr James Wm
Indian River HS
Selbyville, DE

Parrott, Vicki K
Seaford HS
Seaford, DE

Parsons, David
Indian River HS
Selbyville, DE

Pasquarella, William
Salesisanum HS
Philadelphia, PA

Patchel, Steven J
Salesianum School For Boys
Kennett Square, PA

Pelaia, Maria Teresa
Padua Acad
Wilmington, DE

Perna, Kevin
William Penn HS
New Castle, DE

Pesce, Lucia
Padua Acad
Wilmington, DE

Pfeifer, Chris
Milford SR HS
Milford, DE

Pierce, D J
Archmere Acad
Wilmington, DE

Pileggi, Theresa M J
Archmere Acad
Chadds Ford, PA

Pitcher, Sandra L
Middletown HS
Townsend, DE

Pizzo, Stephanie
Padua Acad
Philadelpia, PA

Pope, Michael
Holy Cross HS
Milford, DE

Porter, Kevin J
John Dickinson HS
Wilmington, DE

Posdon, Amy
Dover HS
Dover, DE

Prillaman, Derek
Smyrna HS
Smyrna, DE

Purse, Vickie
Padua Acad
Wilmington, DE

Quigley, Melissa
Newark HS
Newark, DE

Reiss, Jr Robert J
Smyrna HS
Smyrna, DE

Reppert, Jocelyn
Caravel Acad
Elkton, MD

Riblett, Greg
Caesar Rodney HS
Dover, DE

Rider, Jay
Delmar JR SR HS
Laurel, DE

Rimmer, Chris
Milford HS
Milford, DE

Roberts, Debra
Dover HS
Dover, DE

Robinson, Jeff
Salesianum HS
Newark, DE

Roddy, Michael
Salesianum HS
Wilmington, DE

Rodgers, Charisse L
St Marks HS
Wilmington, DE

Rossell, Dana
St Marks HS
Wilmington, DE

Rust, Lowell
Alexis I Dupont HS
Wimington, DE

Scafaria, Jeffrey
Salesianum HS
West Chester, PA

Scarborough, Faith
Laurel SR HS
Laurel, DE

Schneider, Chrisie
New Castle Baptist
Newark, DE

Schreckengost, Dawn
William Penn HS
Middletown, DE

Schreckengost, Tricia
William Penn HS
Middletown, DE

Schwartz, Sherri
St Marks HS
Wilmington, DE

Shepeard, III Jesse T
William Penn HS
Wilmington, DE

Short, Stephen W
Sussex Central HS
Georgetown, DE

Sileo, Angela
Archmere Acad
Wallingford, PA

Smiley, Zyon
Dover HS
Dover, DE

Smith, Gordon
Caesar Rodney HS
Dover, DE

Smith, Kristina
St Marks HS
Hockessin, DE

Smith, Mark James
Dover HS
Dover, DE

Soctt, Kevin
Dover HS
Dover, DE

Solomon, Margaret
Padua Acad
Philadelphia, PA

Spengler, Ken
Caesar Rodney HS
Dover, DE

Spiker, Ted
St Marks HS
Wilmington, DE

Spink, Michael
Salesianum HS
Newark, DE

Spriggs, Stephany
Dover HS
Dover, DE

Starkey, Brenda
William Penn HS
New Castle, DE

Stein, Christopher L
Archmere Acad
Wilmington, DE

Stella, Roberto
Saint Marks HS
Wilmington, DE

Stellini, Stephanie
St Marks HS
Newark, DE

Stewart, Sharon
William Penn HS
Middletown, DE

Still, David
Salesianum Schl
Elsmere, DE

Stjohn, Cheree
Dover HS
Dover, DE

Stormer, Jeff
Smyrna HS
Clayton, DE

Sylvester, Lee
Christiana HS
New Castle, DE

Tall, Karen
Christiana HS
Newark, DE

Tatman, Cindy
Milford SR HS
Milford, DE

Taylor, Brian
William Penn HS
New Castle, DE

Taylor, Earl
Claymont HS
Wilmington, DE

Taylor, Kimberly
Delmar JR-SR HS
Delmar, MD

Thompson, Phillip
Indian River HS
Selbyville, DE

Throckmorton, Brian
Delmar JR SR HS
Delmar, DE

Tobin, Patricia
St Marks HS
Wilmington, DE

Tonogbanua, Arobert
Salesianum Schl
New Castle, DE

Torrance, Susan
Dover HS
Dover, DE

Totino, Megan L
Archmere Acad
Wallingford, PA

Towers, Michelle D
Seaford Christian
Denton, MD

Townsend, Ronnie
Indian River HS
Frankford, DE

Tritelli, Karen
Padua Acad
Wilmington, DE

Uldin, Linda
Christiana HS
Newark, DE

Urick, Greg
Dover HS
Dover, DE

Urion, Rebecca
Thomas Mc Keon
Wilmington, DE

Vagle, Kirk
John Dickinson HS
Newark, DE

Venables, Matia
Laurel SR HS
Laurel, DE

Vensel, Heidi
Caravel Acad
Newark, DE

Verma, Sandhya
Dover HS
Dover, DE

Viola, Todd Carlo
William Penn HS
New Castle, DE

Vivolo, Tina
Padua Acad
Wilmington, DE

Walls, Kathryn E
Wm Penn HS
New Castle, DE

Ward, Philip J
Concord HS
Wilmington, DE

Ward, Tom
Mount Pleasant HS
Wilmington, DE

Washington, Tammy
Christiana HS
Newark, DE

Weaver, Scott
Mt Pleasant HS
Wilmington, DE

Weber, Stacie N
Seaford Christian
Frankford, DE

Weiss, John A
Smyrna HS
Smyrna, DE

Weissgerber, Teri
Christiana HS
Newark, DE

Wherry, Matthew
Newark HS
Newark, DE

Whetzel, Patricia
Archmere Acad
Wilmington, DE

White, Tommi
Christiana HS
Newark, DE

Whitten, Kristin
Padua Acad
Hockessin, DE

Wicks, IV George
Smyrna HS
Smyrna, DE

Wilson, Dennis
Milford SR HS
Milford, DE

Wilt, Jr Charles E
Caear Rodney HS
Dover, DE

Windle, William
Dover HS
Hartly, DE

Wommack, J Brian
Brandywine HS
Wilmington, DE

Woods, Michael
Caravel Acad
Lincoln Univ, PA

Yerger, Brian
Salesianum HS
Newark, DE

Young, Jeffrey
Dover HS
Dover, DE

Zarkowski, Ed
Dover HS
Dover, DE

Zeisloft, Kari
Christiana HS
Newark, DE

Zevnik, Veroncee M
Mc Kean HS
Wilmington, DE

D.C.

Adams, Michelle
Woodrow Wilson SR
Washington, DC

Allen, Jacqueline
Ballou SR HS
Washington, DC

Argiro, Megan
Georgetown
Visitation Prep
Alexandria, VA

Asongwe, Alice
Woodrow Wilson SR
Washington, DC

Badrich, Marina
Immaculata Prep
Washington, DC

Baker, Monica
Duke Ellington
School Of The Arts
Washington, DC

Banks, III Charles
Dunbar SR HS
Washington, DC

Bararia, Vinay
Gonzaga Coll HS
Lanham, MD

Baron, Cristal J
Georgetown
Visitation HS
Washington, DC

Benn, Samuel
Ballou SR HS
Washington, DC

Benovil, Jacques A
The Duke Ellington
Schl Of The Arts
Washington, DC

Bradley, III William
G
Mc Kinley Tech HS
Washington, DC

Branch, Sarah
Eastern HS
Washington, DC

Brewton, Samantha
Immaculata Prep
Washington, DC

Brooks, James
Franklin
Calvin Coolidge SR
Washington, DC

Brooks, Marsha Ann
Calvin Coolidge HS
Washington, DC

Brown, Carolyn J
Duke Ellington Schl
Of The Arts
Upper Marlboro,
MD

Burbridge, Leilani
Sidwell Friends Schl
Washington, DC

Burnette, Anita
Theodore Roosevelt
Washington, DC

Burroughs, Alenda
Woodrow Wilson SR
Washington, DC

Butler, Scott P
Gonzaga College HS
Washington, DC

Caldwell, Paul C
Gonzaga College HS
Capital Heights, MD

Casey, Kenneth
Washington-Dix
Street Acad
Washington, DC

Chandler,
Dimeterice
Cardozo SR HS
Washington, DC

Clark, Connie
F W Ballou HS
Washington, DC

Cooper, Faith E
Dunbar SR HS
Washington, DC

Copeland, Kimberly
Howard D Woodson
SR HS
Washington, DC

Creighton, Maria
Roosevelt SR HS
Washington, DC

Crowley, Susan
Georgetown
Visitation Prep Schl
Washington, DC

Davis, Evette
Woodrow Wilson SR
Washington, DC

Dean, Janice
Coolidge HS
Washington, DC

Dickens, Tryphenia
Theodore Roosevelt
Washington, DC

Duvall, Robert
St Johns College HS
Gaithersburg, MD

Ellis, Kenneth M
Archbishop Carroll
Landover Hills, MD

Fisher, Ronell
Dunbar SR HS
Washington, DC

Fitzgerald, Marc
Archbishop Carroll
Capitol Hgts, MD

Ford, Regan
Woodrow Wilson SR
Washington, DC

Fox, Mark
United States
Senate Page Schl
Fairfax, VA

Fryar, Yvette
Benjamin Banneker
Washington, DC

Gibson, Julia L
Woodrow Wilson HS
Washington, DC

Gorsucl, Stephanie
Georgetown
Visitation Prep Schl
Falls Church, VA

Greene, Kelly A
Benjamin Banneker
Washington, DC

Grissett, Sidney
Archbishop Carroll
Mitchelleville, MD

Hamilton, Monique
Woodrow Wilson HS
Washington, DC

Hardy, Kiki
Eastern SR HS
Washington, DC

Harris, Teresa
Dunbar SR HS
Washington, DC

Henley, Alton J
Banneker Academis
S HS
Washington, DC

Hightower, Mark
De Matha Catholic
Washington, DC

Hill, Jacqueline D
Academy Of Notre
Washington, DC

Hyater, John E
Archbishop Carroll
Washington, DC

Jackson, Janet M
Central HS
Andrews Afb, DC

Johnson, Robert D
Benjamin Banneker
SR HS
Washington, DC

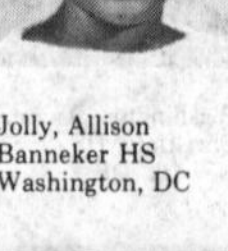

Jolly, Allison
Banneker HS
Washington, DC

Jones, Andrea
Theodore Roosevelt
SR HS
Washington, DC

Jones, Lisa
All Saints HS
Capitol Hts, MD

Kearney, Renee
Dunbar HS
Washington, DC

King, Conley B
Benjamin Banneker
Academic HS
Washington, DC

Lawson, Linda
Calvin Coolidge HS
Washington, DC

Ledbetter, Veronica
Cardozo HS
Forestville, MD

Legall, Shelley A
Benjamin Banneker
SR HS
Washington, DC

Littlejohn, Valerie
Eastern HS
Washington, DC

Lott, Marsha
Eastern HS
Washington, DC

Mathias, William T
Saint Anselms
Abbey Schl
Hyattsville, MD

Mc Crea, Nicole
Cardozo SR HS
Washington, DC

Milbourne,
Kimberly
H D Woodson SR
Washington, DC

Mitchell, Melissa
Benjamin Banneker
Washington, DC

Mosley, Paula
Ballou SR HS
Washington, DC

Mullins, George
Howard D Woodson
Washington, DC

Neil, Amaate
Gonzaga College HS
Washington, DC

Nichols, Brian
Woodrow Wilson HS
Washington, DC

Nutall, Dexter
Archbishop John
Carroll HS
Washington, DC

Parker, Rosalind
Woodrow Wilson SR
Washington, DC

Pate, Alexis
Woodrow Wilson HS
Washington, DC

Pilkerton, Joseph A
St Johns College HS
Potomac, MD

Pitts, Walter David
Ballou SR HS
Washington, DC

Posey, Michelle
Eastern HS
Washington, DC

Powe, Ralph
Benjamin Banneker
Washington, DC

Razza, III Joseph C
Banneher HS
Washington, DC

Ricks, Felicia
Woodrow Wilson HS
Washibgton, DC

Robinson, Diana
Calvin Coolidge HS
Washington, DC

Robinson, Lisa A
Frank Washinton
Ballou HS
Washington, DC

Robinson, Victoria
Woodrow Wilson SR
Washington, DC

Saunders, Anita
Benjamin Banneker
SR HS
Washington, DC

Scurlock, Tamara
Woodrow Wilson HS
Washington, DC

Seay, Dorothy
Eastern HS
Washington, DC

Smith, La Shonda L
Ballou SR HS
Washington, DC

Spohr, David
The Maret Schl
Washington, DC

Starks, Michelle
Paul Lawrence
Dunbar HS
Washington, DC

Stewart, Sean
Jerome
T Roosevelt HS
Washington, DC

Taylor, Arthur L
Duke Ellington Schl
Of The Arts
Washington, DC

Thomas, Dorothy C
Duke Ellington Schl
Of The Arts
Washington, DC

Thomas, Vickie R
Benjamin Banneker
SR HS
Washington, DC

Tillman, Charmin J
Benjamin Banneker
Academic HS
Washington, DC

Vessels, Derek
Calvin Coolidge HS
Washington, DC

Walker, Alison M
Benjamin Banneker
Washington, DC

Ward, Chris R
Gonzaga College HS
Alexandria, VA

Watson, Daryl
Dunbar SR HS
Washington, DC

Wells, Tomiko
T Roosevelt HS
Washington, DC

Westray, Maurice
Mackin HS
Washington, DC

Whitford, Angelina
Georgetown
Visitation Prep Schl
Rockville, MD

Wilkerson, Toni
Ballou SR HS
Washington, DC

Williams, Cynthia V
Frank W Ballou HS
Washington, DC

Williams, La Verne
C
Academy Of Notre
Washington, DC

Wilson, Juliette G
Benjamin Banneker
SR HS
Washington, DC

Wright, La Tanya D
Benjamin Banneke
Washington, DC

Wynne, Gary
Gonzaga College HS
Washington, DC

Young, Denise M
Immaculata
Preparatory Schl
Washington, DC

Yun, Joon K
St Albans Schl
Rockville, MD

MARYLAND

Abalahin, Andrew
Mt St Joseph HS
Glen Burnie, MD

Abbey, Jennifer
Marie
Connelly School Of
The Holy Child
Bethesda, MD

Abbott, Rebecca
Montrose Christian
Gaithersburg, MD

Abrams, Suzy
Rockville HS
Rockville, MD

Abrecht, Jr Douglas
F
Gov Thomas
Johnson HS
Frederick, MD

Abruscato, Gina
Thomas S Wootton
Potomac, MD

Absher, Billy
La Plata HS
Waldorf, MD

Acebal, Maria L
The Holton-Arms
Potomac, MD

Acosta, Donald J
Loyola HS
Dundalk, MD

Adam, Erdal
Fiendly HS
Ft Washington, MD

Adams, Jr Charles A
Bladensburg HS
Hyattsville, MD

Aderhold, Bruce
Thomas Stone HS
Waldorf, MD

Afanasieff, Lisa
Elizaveta
Immaculata College
Potomac, MD

Airey, Kathleen
Northern HS
Huntingtown, MD

Akers, Jeff
North Harford HS
Jarrettsville, MD

Akiyama, Taro
T S Wootton HS
Gaithersburg, MD

Alberts, Noreen M
Edgewood HS
Edgewood, MD

Alderson, Jr Michael
Great Mills HS
Lexington Park, MD

Alexander, Angie
La Plata HS
Bryantown, MD

Alexander, Beth
Gwynn Park HS
Brandywine, MD

Alexander, Michele
Great Mills HS
Leonardtown, MD

Alford, Jr Michael J
Frederick HS
Frederick, MD

Allen, Christopher
Northeast HS
North East, MD

Allen, Dale Eugene
Franklin HS
Owings Mls, MD

Allen, Douglas
Surrattsville HS
Clinton, MD

Allen, Jerome
Northern HS
Baltimore, MD

Aloupis, Sophia
Thomas Stone HS
Waldorf, MD

Alston, Thomas
Crossland HS
Capital Hgts, MD

Alt, Melissa
Westminster HS
Westminster, MD

Ama, Lynnette
Bowie HS
Bowie, MD

Amaya, Maritza
Albert Einstein HS
Silver Spring, MD

Amburgey, Alisha
Laplata HS
Bryantown, MD

Amiryzyan, Gemma
Laurel HS
Laurel, MD

Amos, Melissa L
Linganore HS
Ijamsville, MD

Andersch, Lisa
Hammond HS
Columbia, MD

Anderson, II Donald T
Gwynn Park SR HS
Clinton, MD

Anderson, Kari
Highland View Acad
Frederick, MD

Anderson, Kathy
Montgomery Blair
Silver Spring, MD

Anderson, Kirsten
Friendly SR HS
Ft Washington, MD

Anderson, Lakeshia
Oakland Mills HS
Columbia, MD

Anderson, Laurie
Archbishop Keough
Baltimore, MD

Anderson, Mark
Fairmont Heights
Landover Hills, MD

Anderson, Scott
Thomas Stone HS
Waldorf, MD

Andrew, John
St Michaels Senior
Easton, MD

Andrews, Eric
Fort Hill HS
Cumberland, MD

Andrews, Ranetta
Western HS
Baltimore, MD

Antoine, Romy I
Stone Rdg Cntry Dy Schl Of Th
Silver Spring, MD

Appel, Erik
Dulaney SR HS
Glen Arm, MD

Araujo, Augusto
Walter Johnson HS
Bethesda, MD

Arca, Lorraine
Archbishop Keough
Baltimore, MD

Archibald, Isabel Maria
Washington HS
Westover, MD

Arfaa, Babak E
John Carroll HS
Bel Air, MD

Argetakis, Angela
Patterson HS
Baltimore, MD

Arnold, Gina
Walter Johnson HS
Waldorf, MD

Arvin, Christie
Williamsport HS
Hagerstown, MD

Ash, David
Pikesville HS
Owings, MD

Ashford, Roslyn
Springbrook HS
Silver Spring, MD

Ashruf, Samia
Archbishop Keogh
Baltimore, MD

Ashruf, Sumera
Archbishop Keough
Baltimore, MD

Askew, Linda
Rockville HS
Rockville, MD

Auman, Matt
Parkside HS
Salisbury, MD

Austin, John
Cardinal Gibbons
Baltimore, MD

Avin, Jacquelyn
Sherwood HS
Ashton, MD

Baden, III Aubrey G
Queen Anne Schl
Riva, MD

Baik, Jennifer
Dulaney SR HS
Timonium, MD

Bailey, Brian
Thomas Stone HS
Hughesville, MD

Bailey, Cheryl
Archbishop Keough
Columbia, MD

Bailey, Ronald G
Largo HS
Capital Heights, MD

Baine, Kim
Thomas Stone HS
Waldorf, MD

Baisey, Debbie
Poolesville HS
Poolesville, MD

Baker, Daniel
Potomac SR HS
Temple Hills, MD

Baker, Danita
Thomas Stone HS
Lubbock, TX

Baker, David
Potomac SR HS
Temple Hills, MD

Baker, Nathan
Allegany HS
Cumberland, MD

Baldwin, Krista
Maurice J Mc Donough HS
Waldoff, MD

Balogh, Erika
Westminster SR HS
Westminster, MD

Bandell, Michael
Patterson SR HS
Baltimore, MD

Barber, Diane
Smithsburg HS
Smithsburg, MD

Barbour, Avon
Farimont Heights
Landover Hls, MD

Barnes, Kimberly R
Eleanor Roosevelt
Lanham, MD

Barnes, Melissa Elaine
Joppatowne HS
Edgewood, MD

Barnes, Sheila
Du Val HS
Landover, MD

Barr, Gillian R
Annapolis SR HS
Annapolis, MD

Bartels, John
Westminster SR HS
Westminster, MD

Bartholomew, Sara
Sherwood HS
Olney, MD

Bartlett, Catherine
Surrattsville HS
Clinton, MD

Barton, Lisa
Northern HS
Owings, MD

Basinger, Beth
Calvert HS
Prince Frederick, MD

Bateman, William
Calvert SR HS
Prince Frederick, MD

Bean, Paul A
Chopticon HS
Mechanicsville, MD

Beard, Renee
Patterson HS
Baltimore, MD

Becmer, Carolyn
La Plata HS
La Plata, MD

Becton, Stanwyn
De Matha Catholic
Lanham Seabrook, MD

Bedford, Kellie
Andover HS
Linthicum Hts, MD

Beeman, Amy
Valley HS
Barton, MD

Beeman, Tina
Valley HS
Barton, MD

Beers, Glen
Wicomico SR HS
Salisbury, MD

Behe, Paul Francis
Northern HS
Dunkirk, MD

Belen, Elaine
Archbishop Keough
Baltimore, MD

Bell, Marshall C
Randallstown SR
Owings Mills, MD

Bell, Patti
Grisfield HS
Marion, MD

Belton, Sharise
Forest Park HS
Baltimore, MD

Benbow, Arlene
Potomac SR HS
Temple Hills, MD

Benjamin, Maya
Wheaton HS
Rockville, MD

Bennett, Bradley
Saint Andrew's
Episcopal HS
Clinton, MD

Bennett, Coralie
Middletown HS
Middletown, MD

Benson, Walter
Fort Hill HS
Cumberland, MD

Berry, Stephanie
Renee
Western HS
Baltimore, MD

Bestpitch, Cathy
Takoma Acad
Silver Spring, MD

Biersay, Lisagaye
Wilde Lake HS
Far Rockaway, NY

Bilenki, Jennifer
Southern Garrett
Deer Pk, MD

Birckhead, Janeen L
Snow Hill HS
Snow Hill, MD

Birckhood, Judith
James M Bennett
SR HS
Wetipauin, MD

Bishop, Tammy
Snow Hill HS
Snow Hill, MD

Bivens, Matthew J
Sherwood HS
Olney, MD

Black, Karen
Thomas Stone HS
Waldorf, MD

Blackburn, Susan
Suitland HS
Forestvl, MD

Blackwell, Nancy
Walbrook SR HS
Baltimore, MD

Blake, Erin
Bishop Walsh HS
Cumberland, MD

Blakeslee, Julie
Mc Donough HS
Pomfret, MD

Bland, Stacey
Western HS
Baltimore, MD

Blaney, Michele
Marie
Liberty HS
Marriottsville, MD

Blank, Noelle
Montrose Christian
Kensington, MD

Blash, Steven J
Governor Thomas
Johnson HS
Frederick, MD

Block, Jonathan
Gaithersburg HS
Gaithersburg, MD

Blocker, III Ananias
Eleanor Roosevelt
Laurel, MD

Blubaugh, Jim
Flintstone HS
Oldtown, MD

Boboltz, Renee
Seneca Valley HS
Darnestown, MD

Boebel, Shelley
Franklin SR HS
Reisterstown, MD

Boesze, Astrid
Lauren SR HS
Laurel, MD

Bold, Sharon
Duval HS
Davidsonville, MD

Bolyard, Susan
Fort Hill HS
Cumberland, MD

Bonenberger,
William
Baltimore
Polytechnic Inst
Baltimore, MD

Bonsell, Jennifer
Fort Hill HS
Cumberland, MD

Bori, Denise
Connelly Schl Of
The Holy Child
Silver Spg, MD

Borsoni, Eric
Wilde Lake HS
Clarksville, MD

Bortnick, Marc
The Bullis Schl
Potomac, MD

Bounds, Holly
Parkside HS
Salisbury, MD

Bowe, Kimberly
W Nottingham Acad
Mitchellville, MD

Bower, Terri
Westminster HS
Finksburg, MD

Bowers, Brooks E
Du Val HS
Seabrook, MD

Bowman, Connie
Northern Garrett
Mchenry, MD

Bowman, Kris
La Plata HS
La Plata, MD

Boyd, Tammy Lynn
Gaithersburg HS
Gaithersburg, MD

Brady, Theresa
Dundalk SR HS
Baltimore, MD

Brady, Tim
Northern HS
Grantsville, MD

Brand, Steven
Renard
Eastern HS
Baltimore, MD

Brandenburg, Karin
Bowie HS
Bowie, MD

Brandon, Starcinda
Potomac HS
Suitland, MD

Branham, Antonio
Forestville HS
Suitland, MD

Branson, Leslie
Holton-Arms Schl
Washington, DC

Brawley, Charissa A
Gaithersburg HS
Gaithersburg, MD

Braxton, Tuawana
Porkdale HS
New Carrollton, MD

Bredenburg, David
E
North Carroll HS
Finksburg, MD

Brennan, Fred
La Plata HS
Bel Alton, MD

Briggs, Brian E
Mc Donough HS
White Plains, MD

Brody, Lisa
Wilde Lake HS
Columbia, MD

Brooks, Kathryn A
Sherwood HS
Olney, MD

Brown, Barry
Cardinal Gibbons
Baltimore, MD

Brown, Catherine
Forestville HS
Forestville, MD

Brown, Leesa
Takoma Acad
Takoma Park, MD

Brown, Lisa La
Ronda
Mercy High
Exemplary Schl
Baltimore, MD

Brown, Nichelle
St Marys Ryken HS
Loveville, MD

Brown, Ravi
Northern HS
Baltimore, MD

Brown, Rhonda
St Vincent Pallotti
Laurel, MD

Brown, Ronda
Easton HS
Trappe, MD

Brown, Ryan A
Oxon Hill HS
Ft Washington, MD

Brown, Sharon S
Du Val HS
Louisburg, NC

Brown, Susan
St Michaels SR HS
Bozman, MD

Brown, Timothy W
Damascus HS
Damascus, MD

Brown, Tracey
North Harford HS
Jarrettsville, MD

Brown, Trina
Maurice J Mc
Donough HS
Waldorf, MD

Bryan, Robin
Northern HS
Huntingtown, MD

Bryant, Cameron
Franklin HS
Glyndon, MD

Brzostek, Kathy
Institute Of Notre
Baltimore, MD

Buan, Erwin James
Northwestern SR
Lanham, MD

Buchanan, Emily
North East HS
Elkton, MD

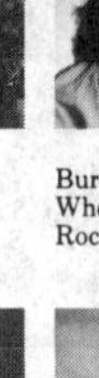

Buck, Paul
Annapolis HS
Annapolis, MD

Buckalew, Elizabeth C
Valley HS
Lonaconing, MD

Buley, Chris
The Bullis Schl
Gaithersburg, MD

Bullock, Brenda
Carroll Christian
Westminster, MD

Buob, Brenda K
Parkside HS
Salisbury, MD

Burch, Julie
Bowie HS
Bowie, MD

Burford, Wilhelmina
Baltimore
Polytechnic Inst
Baltimore, MD

Burkhardt, Keith
Dundalk HS
Baltimore, MD

Burley, Dionne
Southwestern HS
Baltimore, MD

Burnett, Carol
Wheaton HS
Rockville, MD

Burnette, Valerie
Parkville HS
Baltimore, MD

Burrell, Cheryl
Batlimore City Coll
Baltimore, MD

Burt, Thomas B
Loyola Blakefield
Baltimore, MD

Burton, Mike
Allegany HS
Cumberland, MD

Bush, Betty June
Bel Air HS
Bel Air, MD

Butler, Alfie G
Meade SR HS
Severn, MD

Butler, Brian
Fairmont Heights
Landover Hls, MD

Butler, Kimberly
Queen Annes
County HS
Grasonville, MD

Butler, Lori
Du Val SR HS
Seat Pleasant, MD

Butts, Sharyl
Magruder HS
Rockville, MD

Bynum, Edward
Friendly SR HS
Fort Washington, MD

Cabrera, Alice
Northwestern HS
Hyattsville, MD

Caine, Alexander
Potomae HS
Oxon Hill, MD

Caldejon, Marivi
Annapolis Area
Christian Schl
Annapolis, MD

Callahan, Mark
Easton HS
Easton, MD

Calloway, Lisa
Frederick HS
Frederick, MD

Cameron, Robert
Bullis Schl
Potomac, MD

Campagnoli, Patricia
Immaculate College
Rockville, MD

Campbell, Michelle
Parkdale HS
Riverdale, MD

Canaday, Terri L
North East HS
North East, MD

Cannon, Michelle Lynn
Sherwood HS
Olney, MD

Caples, Chandra
Dulaney HS
Cockeysville, MD

Carpenter, Frances
St Marys Ryken HS
Leonardtown, MD

Carr, Lashawn
Oxon Hill SR HS
Ft Washington, MD

Carrillo, Richard Laurence
Wicomico SR HS
Salisbury, MD

Carroll, Kimberly
Surrattsville HS
Clinton, MD

Carroll, Lesli
Surrattsville SR HS
Clinton, MD

Carroll, Wanda
Lackey HS
Bryans Rd, MD

Cartalla, David
Lackey HS
Bryans Rd, MD

Cartalla, Lillian
Lackey HS
Bryans Road, MD

Carter, Bricca
Calvert HS
Lusby, MD

Carter, Maria
Gaithersburg HS
Gaithersburg, MD

Carter, Sherrill
Suitland HS
Capitol Heights, MD

Casseday, Cathleen
Allegany HS
Cumberland, MD

Castle, Elaine
Notre Dame Prep
Timonium, MD

Catignani, Caryn
Bowie HS
Bowie, MD

Catlin, Jacqueline
Lackey HS
Bryans Rd, MD

Cavanaugh, Shelley
Surrattsville HS
Clinton, MD

Cessna, Bruce
Flintstone HS
Clearville, PA

Chakrabarty, Prabir
Good Counsel HS
Brookeville, MD

Champ, Timothy Bernard
Lakcey SR HS
Nanjemoy, MD

Chance, Lisa
Hammond HS
Jessup, MD

Chandler, Harold
Takoma Acad
Washington, DC

Chavis, Tandra
High Point HS
Beltsville, MD

Chen, Shante S
Walt Whitman HS
Potomac, MD

Cheng, Leigh K
Winston Churchill
Potomac, MD

Chervenak, Patrick
Maurice J Mc
Donough HS
Waldorf, MD

Cheshire, Wendy
Bruce HS
Westernport, MD

Cheung, Nancy
Walter Johnson HS
Potomac, MD

Chick, Stephen M
Valley HS
Hopewell, VA

Childs, Cheryl
Bladensburg HS
Seat Plsnt, MD

Chlumsky, Shannon
Parkville HS
Balt, MD

Chodnicki, Jennifer
Patapsco HS
Baltimore, MD

Choe, Steven
Liberty HS
Sykesville, MD

Chrisman, Craig M
Thomas Stone HS
Hughesville, MD

Christ, Jason J
Mc Donough HS
Pomfret, MD

Christian, Thomas D
Woodlawn HS
Baltimore, MD

Christmas, Colleen
Connelly Schl Of The Holy Child
Chevy Chase, MD

Chrzanowski, III Stanley R
Glen Burnie HS
Glen Burnie, MD

Chun, Hyesin
James M Bennett SR HS
Salisbury, MD

Chunn, Brenda S
Old Mill SR HS
Millersville, MD

Ciamacca, Magdalena
Catonsville HS
Baltimore, MD

Cissel, Susette
Rising Sun HS
Rising Sun, MD

Clarke, Lisa Renee
Fort Hill HS
Cumberland, MD

Claude, Tonya
Montgomery Blair
Silver Spring, MD

Clements, Jr Thomas
La Plata HS
La Plata, MD

Clough, Patrick D
Riverdale Baptist
Laurel, MD

Coates, Monica A
Randallstown SR
Randallstown, MD

Coble, Elizabeth
Surrattsville SR HS
Clinton, MD

Coble, Lawrence
The Bullis Schl
Potomac, MD

Cockerell, Daniel
Thomas S Wootton
Rockville, MD

Cockerham, Gene P
Aberdeen HS
Aberdeen, MD

Cody, Scott W
Frederick HS
Frederick, MD

Coffin, Britt
Takoma Acad
Brinklow, MD

Coffman, Annette
Northern HS
Dunkirk, MD

Coker, Karen
Seton HS
Baltimore, MD

Colaciello, Debbie
Gwynn Park HS
Brandywine, MD

Coleman, Christy
Beall HS
Frostburg, MD

Colley, Marlo
Snow Hill HS
Stockton, MD

Combs, Michelle
Ft Hill HS
Cumberland, MD

Combs, Shari
Fort Hill HS
Cumberland, MD

Conaway, Shelly
Wicomico SR HS
Parsonburg, MD

Connelley, Angie
Calvert HS
Huntingtown, MD

Connors, Robert William
Seneca Valley HS
Gaithersburg, MD

Coogen, Michael
Good Counsel HS
Rockville, MD

Cook, Gretchen
Oakland Mills HS
Columbia, MD

Cook, Jeff
Clear Spring HS
Clear Spg, MD

Cooke, Christie
High Point HS
W Hyattsville, MD

Cooke, II Colin
La Plata HS
La Plata, MD

Coontz, II David
La Plata HS
Waldorf, MD

Cooper, III Clinton
Snow Hill HS
Stockton, MD

Cooper, Stacy
Great Mills HS
St Inigoes, MD

Copaken, Jennifer R
Winston Churchill
Potomac, MD

Corrigan, Leslie
Archbishop Keough
Glen Burnie, MD

Cotton, Cynthia L
Western HS
Baltimore, MD

Cotton, Heather
North Harford HS
Jarrettsville, MD

Couch, Erica
Northern HS
Friendsville, MD

Covington, Damian
De Matha Catholic
Washington, DC

Cox, Chris
Crossland SR HS
Suitland, MD

Cox, Jr Woody E
La Plata HS
La Plata, MD

Craemer, Mark
Milford Mill HS
Balt, MD

Craig, Lorrie
Regina HS
Hyattsville, MD

Cravaritis, George
Gaithersburg HS
Gaithersburg, MD

Crawford, Larry
Williamsport HS
Fairplay, MD

Creaturo, Kelly
La Plata HS
Waldorf, MD

Creighton, Heather
Frederick HS
Frederick, MD

Crockett, Mary
Pocomoke HS
Pocomoke, MD

Cromwell, Jewel
Northwestern HS
Baltimore, MD

Cross, John H
North Caroline HS
Denton, MD

Crossland, Edward
Valley HS
Frostburg, MD

Crouch, Mary
Queen Annes Co HS
Chester, MD

Crowder, Christopher S
Albert Einstein HS
Wheaton, MD

Crowell, Courtney
Laurel HS
Laurel, MD

Crowley, Sharon
Eastern Vo Tech
Baltimore, MD

Crownover, IV Arthur
Gwynn Park HS
Clinton, MD

Crum, William
Brunswick HS
Brunswick, MD

Culbreath, Jr Walter L
Potomac SR HS
Oxon Hill, MD

Cummings, Shandra
Suitland HS
Forestville, MD

Cunningham, Cheryl
Forestville HS
Capitol Heights, MD

Cunningham, Keli
Dulaney SR HS
Cockeysville, MD

Cunningham, Michelle
Thomas Stone HS
Waldorf, MD

Cuppy, Lawrence
Mc Donough HS
Waldorf, MD

Curran, Megan
Archbishop Keough
Ellicott City, MD

Curran, Michael
Gaithersburg HS
Gaithersburg, MD

Curry, Jr Thomas
Capcata HS
Newburg, MD

Curtis, Mary
St Johnsd At
Prospect Hall HS
Gaithersburg, MD

D Alonzo, Joseph
Centennial HS
Ellicott, MD

Dabbs, Michelle
North Harford HS
Street, MD

Dacquel, Lorelei
Northwestern HS
Hyattsville, MD

Daley, Richard
Central HS
District Hgts, MD

Daly, David
La Plata HS
Kingman, AZ

Daly, Sarah
Rockville HS
Rockville, MD

Dang, An
Parkville HS
Balt, MD

Daniel, Barbara
Western SR HS
Glen Burnie, MD

Daniel, Leslie
Regina HS
Washington, DC

Daniels, Darlene R
Oxon Hill HS
Ft Washington, MD

Darling, Robyn
Queen Annes
County HS
Chester, MD

Daugherty, Michael Todd
Arundel HS
Odenton, MD

Davidson, Dawn
Northern HS
Dunkirk, MD

Davies, Tanya
Great Mills HS
Lex Pk, MD

Davis, Deandra
Parkdale HS
Silver Spring, MD

Davis, Deborah J
Mt Hebron HS
Ellicott City, MD

Davis, Dorothy
Thomas Stone HS
Waldorf, MD

Davis, Melissa A
Valley HS
Barton, MD

Davis, Suzanne L
Camp Spring
Christian HS
Waldorf, MD

Dawson, Michael
John Carroll HS
Perryville, MD

Day, Dawn
Brunswick HS
Brunswick, MD

Days, Christie
Fairmont Heights
Cheverly, MD

De George, James J
Loyola HS
Columbia, MD

De Loatch, Margaret C
Springbrook HS
Silver Spring, MD

De Pollar, Sherri L
Magruder HS
Gaithersburg, MD

De Simone, Elinka
John Carroll HS
Aberdeen, MD

Deaver, Beth
Elkton HS
Elkton, MD

Decker, David
Wicomico SR HS
Salisbury, MD

Deegan, Kathleen
Elizabeth Seton HS
Rockville, MD

Del Pino, John A
Montgomery Blair
Takoma Park, MD

Deneen, Matthew
Allegany HS
Cumberland, MD

Dennenberg, Beth
Dulaney SR HS
Cockeysville, MD

Detwiler, Mark
Pocomoke HS
Pocomoke, MD

Dickson, Bob
Highland View Acad
Frederick, MD

Dietz, Patricia
Institute Of Notre Dame HS
Baltimore, MD

Dilgard, Vickie
Southern HS
Oakland, MD

Dipietri, Patricia
Surrattsville HS
Clinton, MD

Disharoon, Kerry Sue
Loch Raven SR HS
Baltimore, MD

Diuguid, Duncan
Walt Whitman HS
Bethesda, MD

Dixon, Dwayne B
Centennial HS
Ellicott City, MD

Dixon, Jill
Patapsco HS
Baltimore, MD

Dodson, David
Francis Scott Key
Union Bridge, MD

Doll, Richard
Centennial HS
Columbia, MD

Donahue, Tommy
Calvert HS
Pr Frederick, MD

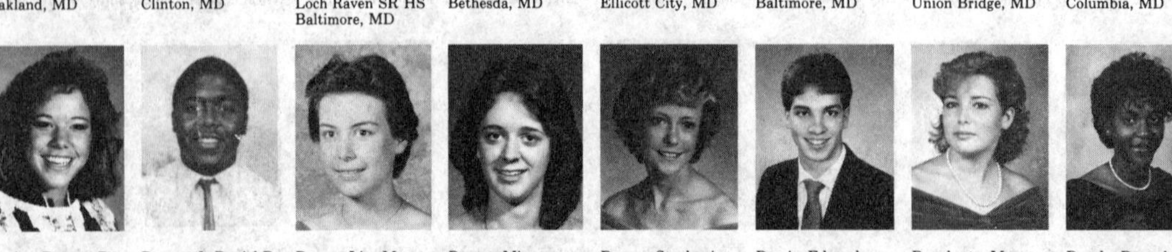

Donaldson, Davina
Regina HS
W Hyattsville, MD

Dooley, Deanna R
Sherwood HS
Brookeville, MD

Dorsey, Jr Daniel R
Mount Saint Joseph
Baltimore, MD

Dorsey, Lisa M
South Carroll HS
Sykesville, MD

Dorsey, Missy
St Marys Ryken HS
Prince Frederick, MD

Dorsey, Stephanie
Washington SR HS
Westover, MD

Dorsie, Edward
De Matha Catholic
Adelphi, MD

Dougherty, Mary Pat
Frederick HS
Frederick, MD

Dowdy, Raquel
North East HS
Elkton, MD

Doxzen, Mary
Western HS
Baltimore, MD

Dradrach, Iwona
Gaithersburg HS
Gaithersburg, MD

Draheim, Cheryl
Northern HS
Huntingtown, MD

Drake, D Craig
De Matha Catholic
Washington, DC

Drenner, Jr Dennis A
Mc Donough HS
Catonsville, MD

Driscoll, Sharon L
St Maria Goretti HS
Hagerstown, MD

Dryden, Rebecca
Mc Donough HS
Waldorf, MD

Dubas, Kevin
The John Carroll
Abingdon, MD

Duckworth, Lori
Beall HS
Frostburg, MD

Duffy, Bruce
Pocomoke HS
Pocomoke, MD

Dulin, Pamela
Easton HS
Cordova, MD

Duncan, Christopher
Mt St Joseph HS
Laurel, MD

Dunsen, Dana
Western HS
Baltimore, MD

Ealy, Stacey L
Hammond HS
Columbia, MD

Earle, Tamala
Western HS
Baltimore, MD

Eaton, Ronald
Northern HS
Baltimore, MD

Eckler, Rhonda
Great Mills HS
Lexington Prk, MD

Eckstorm, Lisa Ann
Elizabeth Secton HS
Greenbelt, MD

Edmiston, Deborah
Overlea HS
Baltimore, MD

Edwards, Richard I
High Point HS
Adelphi, MD

Egan, Erin
Walt Whitman HS
Bethesda, MD

Ehmig, Maryann
Mount De Sales
Baltimore, MD

Ellis, Doretha
Eastern HS
Baltimore, MD

Ellis, Erin
Liberty HS
Eldersburg, MD

Ellis, Steve B
Gaithersburg HS
Gaithersburg, MD

Emley, Meg
Mcdonough HS
Pt Tobacco, MD

Eng, Dennis
Laurel HS
Laurel, MD

Engen, Britt
Montrose Christian
Rockville, MD

Ennis, Dean
Pocomoke HS
Pocomoke, MD

Eno, Jackie
Surrattsville HS
Clinton, MD

Escalante, Angeli A
Archbishop Keongh
Baltimore, MD

Ettman, Alyson
Thomas S Wootton
Potomac, MD

Etzler, Janice M
Capital Lutheran
Sanderland, MD

Evans, Aaron S
Oxon HS
Andrews AFB, DC

Evans, Ann Marie
Gaithersburg HS
Gaithersburg, MD

Evans, Jr Dale Estel
Southern Garret Co
Mtn Lake Pk, MD

Evans, David
Gaithersburg HS
Gaithersburg, MD

Evans, Linda
Maurice J Mc
Donough HS
Waldorf, MD

Evans, Sherrell E
Western HS
Baltimore, MD

Everett, Gertrude
Trudy
Easteau HS
Baltimore, MD

Everly, Kelly
North Kagerstown
Hagerstown, MD

Eyler, Scot
Catoctin HS
Thurmont, MD

Facchina, Paul
Maurice J Mc
Donough HS
La Plata, MD

Facello, Michael
Eastrn Vocational
Technical HS
Baltimore, MD

Fair, Brian
Linganore HS
Ijamsville, MD

Fairfax, Katie
St Marys Ryken HS
Lexington Park, MD

Fanflik, Patricia
Wheaton HS
Rockville, MD

Farley, Ronald
Patterson HS
Baltimore, MD

Farmer, Mary
Rebecca
Governor Thomas
Johnson HS
Frederick, MD

Farmer, Steven
Governor Thomas
Johnson HS
Frederick, MD

Farra, Julie
Wicomico SR HS
Salisbury, MD

Fedd, Denise
Northern SR HS
Baltimore, MD

Feldman, Christina
V
Institute Of Notre
Baltimore, MD

Feliciano, Melissa K
Friends School Of
Baltimore, MD

Felsen, Martin
Barrie HS
Seabrook, MD

Fenner, II Robert L
Mc Donogh HS
Ellicott City, MD

Fenwick, Steve
St Marys Ryken HS
Leonardtown, MD

Feola, Lauren
Damascus HS
Gaithersburg, MD

Ferguson, Alonda
Trinette
Fairmont Heights
Landover Hills, MD

Ferguson, Laurie
Elizabeth Seton HS
Riverdale, MD

Ferguson, Mark
Perryville HS
Port Deposit, MD

Fila, Sandra
Archbishop Krough
Glen Burnie, MD

Filipowicz, Miriam
Severn Schl
Severna Pk, MD

Finck, Jennifer
Dundalk HS
Baltimore, MD

Fisch, Suzanne
Dulaney HS
Timonium, MD

Fishburne, Edward
The Bullis Schl
Rockville, MD

Fisher, Christina
Eleanor Roosevelt
Lanham, MD

Fisher, Terri Lynn
Lansdowne HS
Baltimore, MD

Fishter, Colleen
Riverdale Baptist
Davidsonville, MD

Fister, Lorena
Northwestern HS
Mt Rainier, MD

Flannery, John
North Hagerstown
Hagerstown, MD

Fleishell, Jennifer
Glenelg HS
Woodbine, MD

Fleishell, Karen
Glenelg HS
Woodbine, MD

Fleming, Katharine
Lee
Queen Anne Schl
Washington, DC

Fleming, Verna Jean
South Carroll HS
Mt Airy, MD

Flerlage, Lovie
Maurice J Mc
Donough HS
Waldorf, MD

Flesher, James R
La Plata HS
La Plata, MD

Flinn, Michael
St Marys Ryken HS
Lusby, MD

Flint, Heidi
Eastern Vo Tech
Baltimore, MD

Flower, Todd
James M Bennett
SR HS
Hebron, MD

Fogg, Erika
Friendly SR HS
Ft Washington, MD

Foos, Sheri
Central HS
Andrews AFB, DC

Ford, Janeen Viona
Cambridge-South Dorchester HS
Cambridge, MD

Forrest, James
St Marys Ryken HS
Ridge, MD

Fosco, Maria
Surrattsville SR HS
Clinton, MD

Fotia, Kelli L
Edgewood HS
Edgewood, MD

Fountain, Monique
Elizabeth Seton HS
Lanham, MD

Fowler, Candy
Thomas Stone HS
Waldorf, MD

Fowler, Craig
Outhern Garrett HS
Swanton, MD

Fowler, Janice
Brunswick HS
Brunswick, MD

Fowler, Tiffany
Northern HS
Dunkirk, MD

France, Robert
N Hagerstown HS
Hagerstown, MD

Frank, Jennifer L
Damascus HS
Clarksburg, MD

Franklin, Josette
Central SR HS
Forestville, MD

Franz, Beth
Lansdowne HS
Baltimore, MD

Freburger, Eric
Patterson HS
Baltimore, MD

Free, Cynthia
Catoctin HS
Thurmont, MD

Freeman, Kara
Crossland HS
Camp Spgs, MD

French, Farabe
Washington HS
Westover, MD

Frere, Kevin
Mc Donough HS
White Plains, MD

Fridovich, Laura A
The Holton-Arms
Silver Spring, MD

Friedman, Alex
The Park Schl
Baltimore, MD

Friedman, Brendon
Bullis Schl
Rockville, MD

Friend, Stephen
Southern Garrett
Swanton, MD

Frier, Simone
Notre Dame Prep
Baltimore, MD

Fujii, Karen
Oxon Hill HS
Ft Washington, MD

Fulghum, Kimberly E
Queen Anne Schl
Davidsonville, MD

Funk, Lauri Ann
Fallston HS
Fallston, MD

Furr, Kevin
Wicomico SR HS
Delmar, MD

Gaalaas, Dean
Northwestern HS
Hyattsville, MD

Gagnon, Debbie
Thomas Stone HS
Waldorf, MD

Gallagher, Leslie
St Marys Ryken HS
Leonardtown, MD

Gancayco, James
Georgetown Prep
Bethesda, MD

Ganni, Dina
Thomas Stone HS
Waldorf, MD

Garges, Kathy
Thomas S Wootton
Rockville, MD

Garland, Randy
Liberty HS
Finksburg, MD

Garner, Pamela
La Reine HS
Temple Hills, MD

Garnett, Cheryl
Patterson HS
Baltimore, MD

Gast, Barbara
Eastern Vocational
Baltimore, MD

Gastilo, Philip Anthony
Oxon Hill HS
Fort Washington, MD

Gatling, Ryan
Pocomoke HS
Pocomoke, MD

Gaus, Van
Ft Hill HS
Cumberland, MD

Gauthier, Danielle
St Marys Ryken HS
Prince Frederick, MD

Gawler, Bob Richard
Montgomery HS
Rockville, MD

Gayle, Carolyn
Archbishop Keough
Columbia, MD

Gayon, Kim
Mc Donough HS
Welcome, MD

Gehr, Theresa
Joppatowne HS
Edgewood, MD

Gehrig, Jr John F
Westminster HS
Westminster, MD

Genys, Victoria M
Bishop Walsh HS
Frostburg, MD

George, Robert Kevin
Queen Annes Co HS
Chester, MD

Gerwig, Kathleen
Notre Dame Prep
Baltimore, MD

Gerwin, Daniel J
C E S Jewish Day
Bethesda, MD

Gibbons, James
Northeast HS
Elkton, MD

Gibson, Corella
Milford Mill SR HS
Balt, MD

Gibson, Donna
Parkdale HS
Riverdale, MD

Gilbert, Allyson
Crossland SR HS
Ft Washington, MD

Gilbert, Jennifer
Oakland Mills HS
Columbia, MD

Gill, Ginny
Mc Donough HS
White Plains, MD

Gillan, Karen
Westminster HS
Westminster, MD

Gilpin, Kristina
Fort Hill HS
Cumberland, MD

Given, Donna
North East HS
Elkton, MD

Glascoe, III William O
Crossland HS
Fort Washington, MD

Glasgow, Gregory
Friendly SR HS
Ft Washington, MD

Glass, Lisa
Francis Scott Key
Taneytown, MD

Glass, Trudy F
Francis Scott Key
Taneytown, MD

Glenn, Michael Darin
Randallstown HS
Randallstown, MD

Glinsky, Cynthia
North Harford HS
White Hall, MD

Glover, Katherine
The Bullis HS
Mclean, VA

Gnidziejko, Robin
Mercy HS
Towson, MD

Godfrey, Geoffrey R
Hereford HS
Millers, MD

Goldblatt, Jeff
The Bullis Schl
Potomac, MD

Goldburn, Sharon
The Catholic HS Of
Baltimore, MD

Goldsmith, Tina
La Plata HS
Hughesville, MD

Goldstein, Marc
Thomas S Wootton
Potomac, MD

Gomer, Stephanie
Beall HS
Frostburg, MD

Goodwin, Laura E
Howard HS
Elkridge, MD

Gordon, David
Leonardtown HS
Hollywood, MD

Goss, Judith M
Sherwood HS
Olney, MD

Goto, David M
Fairmont Heights
Tuxedo, MD

Gould, Suzanne M
Laurel HS
Laurel, MD

Govotsos, Panagiotis
Demetrius
Linganore HS
Monrovia, MD

Grace, Douglas
Elkton HS
Elkton, MD

Grade, Sheryl R
Baltimore
Polytechnic Inst
Baltimore, MD

Granger, Tim
North East HS
N East, MD

Grant, Donald
Potomac SR HS
Oxon Hill, MD

Gray, Angie
Northern HS
Huntingtown, MD

Gray, Greta
Oxon Hill SR Hill
Ft Washington, MD

Gray, Sheenequa
Forestville SR HS
Forestville, MD

Green, Melissa
Bethesda-Chevy
Chase HS
Silver Spg, MD

Green, Ricky
Brunswick HS
Point Of Rocks, MD

Green, Shelly
Allegany HS
Cumberland, MD

Greenberg, Michael
Lawrence
Rockville HS
Rockville, MD

Greenwood,
Timothy
North Carroll HS
Hampstead, MD

Greenwood-Bright,
Phyllis
Roland Park
Country Schl
Baltimore, MD

Gregory, Jonathan
M
John F Kennedy HS
Rockville, MD

Gresser, Shawn E
Baltimore Actors
Theatre Conserva
Lutherville, MD

Grey, Matthew W
Loyola HS
Towson, MD

Griffin, Karen
Mt Hebron HS
Ellicott City, MD

Griffin, Retha
Carole
Kenwood SR HS
Baltimore, MD

Griffith, Amy
Beall HS
Frostburg, MD

Grimes, Ryan
Brunswick HS
Jefferson, MD

Grimm, Jennifer
Fort Hill HS
Cumberland, MD

Gross, Shawn Marie
Joppatowne HS
Joppa, MD

Groves, Tiffany
Sherwood HS
Brookeville, MD

Grzelakowski,
Edward
Gaithersburg HS
Gaithersburg, MD

Guadalupe, Phil
Laurel HS
Laurel, MD

Guevara, Abby
Faith Christian Schl
Waldorf, MD

Hadden, Grant
Westminster HS
Finksburg, MD

Hall, Marlon R
High Point HS
Beltsville, MD

Ham, Dawn
North East HS
Elkton, MD

Hamman, Kristen
Thomas Stone HS
Waldorf, MD

Hammond,
Kimberly
Parkside HS
Pittsville, MD

Hanford, Elizabeth
Great Mills HS
Lex Pk, MD

Hankinson, Aretha
Col Zadok Magruder
Rockville, MD

Hann, Caroline
Bishop Walsh HS
Frostburg, MD

Hannan, Bryan
Loyola-Blakefield
Baltimore, MD

Hardy, Michael
Friendly SR HS
Tantallon, MD

Hare, Kellie
Ft Hill HS
Cumberland, MD

Harfeld, Marc
Saints Peter & Paul
Greensboro, MD

Hargrove, Valencia
Leonardtown HS
Hollywood, MD

Harkins, Noelle
Landis
Parkside HS
Salisbury, MD

Harney, Michelle
Crossland HS
Camp Springs, MD

Harrigan, Nicholas
P
Damascus HS
Gaithersburg, MD

Harris, Chad
La Plata HS
La Plata, MD

Harris, Marieca
Saint Michaels SR
Easton, MD

Harris, Susan
North Harford HS
Jarrettsville, MD

Harrison, Elizabeth
Roland Park
Country Schl
Lutherville, MD

Harrison, Jeanne E
The Bullis Schl
Great Falls, VA

Hartford, Alexander
N
Charles W
Woodward HS
Rockville, MD

Hartman, Megan
Allegany HS
Lavale, MD

Hash, Lori
Elkton Christian
Newark, DE

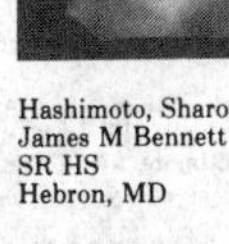
Hashimoto, Sharon
James M Bennett
SR HS
Hebron, MD

Hasker, David Allen
Camp Springs
Christian Schl
Temple Hills, MD

Haskins, Stephanie
St Michaels HS
Bozman, MD

Hatcher, Tara
Walkersville HS
Loveland, OH

Hawk, Jennifer
Fort Hill HS
Cumberland, MD

Hay, Angela
Francis Scott Key
Westminster, MD

Hayden, Melonique
B
Takoma Acad
Silver Spring, MD

Hayman, Jane
Wicomico SR HS
Salisbury, MD

Haywood, Karen
Fort Hill HS
Cumberland, MD

Healy, Jennifer Ann
Chesapeake HS
Pasadena, MD

Hebron, Danny
The Bullis Schl
Fredericksburg, VA

Heckman, Jodie
Bishop Walsh HS
Keyser, WV

Heinbaugh, Susan
Estern Vocational
Tech HS
Baltimore, MD

Heinerichs, Jr Don
Kenwood SR HS
Baltimore, MD

Heinlein, Tina M
Brooklyn Park JR
SR HS
Baltimore, MD

Heinselman, Kurt
Westminster SR HS
Westminster, MD

Heller, John
North Hagerstown
Hagerstown, MD

Hemming, Bernie
St Marys Ryken HS
Waldorf, MD

Henegar, Amy
Riverdale Baptist
Laurel, MD

Henrichsen, Sonya
R
La Plata HS
Waldorf, MD

Henson, Jr David W
Waldorf Christian
Waldorf, MD

Hepburn, Shannon
James M Bennett
SR HS
Salisbury, MD

Hernandez, Jr
Carlos
Springbrook HS
Silver Spring, MD

Herndon, Glenn
Mount Hebron HS
Ellicott City, MD

Hersberger, Dee
Carroll Christian
Westminster, MD

Hickey, Donna
Springbrook HS
Silver Spring, MD

Highsmith, Rhonda
Crossland HS
Camp Springs, MD

Hightower, Anthony
Loyola Blakefield
Baltimore, MD

Higson, Sonya
Fort Hill HS
Cumberland, MD

Hilgenberg, Janet
La Reine HS
Suitland, MD

Hill, Renee Michele
Springbrook HS
Silver Spring, MD

Hill, Sherita A
Eleanor Roosevelt
Upper Marlboro,
MD

Hill, Stacy
Oakland Mills HS
Columbia, MD

Hilton, Kathy
Allegany HS
Cumberland, MD

Himelright, Laura
Glenelg HS
Mt Airy, MD

Hines, Deborah L
Elizabeth Seton HS
Upper Marlboro,
MD

Hirshman, Linda
Crossland HS
Ft Washington, MD

Hobbs, Deanne
Catoctin HS
Thurmont, MD

Hobbs, Diane
Liberty HS
Sykesville, MD

Hoch, Bryant
Parkdale HS
Riverdale, MD

Hoff, Michelle
Northern HS
Huntingtown, MD

Hoffman, David L
Glenelg HS
Ellicott City, MD

Hoffman, Lisa
Wicomico SR HS
Salisbury, MD

Hoffman, Michelle L
Meade SR HS
Hanover, MD

Hoffman, Robin
Washington HS
Wenona, MD

Hogan, Cindy
Northern HS
Owings, MD

Hogan, Jon P
Largo HS
Forestville, MD

Hollins, James
Friendly SR HS
Ft Washington, MD

Holman, Angela
Francis Scott Key
Uniontown, MD

Holmes, Sherri
Potomac HS
Temple Hills, MD

Holmes, III
Theodore Ted
Friendly SR HS
Ft Washington, MD

Hooker, Iris
Towanda
Eastern HS
Baltimore, MD

Hopkins, Michele
Lee
Westminster HS
Westminster, MD

Hosfeld, Michelle
Williamsport HS
Hagerstown, MD

Hotchkiss, Stephen
Beall HS
Frostburg, MD

Houser, Scott
Westminster HS
Westminster, MD

Houzouris, Adrienne
John Carroll HS
Havre De Grace,
MD

Howard, Cheryl
Liberty HS
Eldersburg, MD

Howard, Holly
Magruder HS
Derwood, MD

Howell, Cherie
Acad Of The Holy
Silver Spring, MD

Howell, Jr Robert J
Mt St Joseph HS
Elliot City, MD

Hu, Peggy
Walter Johnson HS
Kensington, MD

Hughes, Angela
Northwestern HS
Avondale, MD

Hughes, Kevin L
Loyola HS
Catonsville, MD

Hughes, Mica
Oakland Mills HS
Columbia, MD

Hui, Eric C
John F Kenndy HS
Silver Spring, MD

Hunter, Michele
Seneca Valley HS
Gaithersburg, MD

Hunter, Tammy
Northwestern HS
Lewisdale, MD

Hunter, Yolanda
Oakland Mills HS
Columbia, MD

Hurley, Tammy J
Mardela HS
Hebron, MD

Huseman,
Christopher S
La Plata HS
La Plata, MD

Hutt, Michele C
James M Bennet SR
Salisbury, MD

Hyman, Betty
Forest Park SR HS
Baltimore, MD

Hyman, Elyse
Glenelg HS
Ellicott City, MD

Ifert, Danette
Linganore HS
Mt Airy, MD

Ifkovits, Jill
Bowie SR HS
Bowie, MD

Imes, Marc
Lackey HS
Laplata, MD

Ingerman, Brett
Mc Donogh Schl
Baltimore, MD

Insley, Kim
Cambridge South
Dorchester HS
Cambridge, MD

Insley, Misty
Parkville HS
Baltimore, MD

Introcaso, Mary C
Cambridge-South Dorchester HS
Church Crk, MD

Irvin, Darron
Gaithersburg SR HS
Gaithersburg, MD

Isles, Erica
Takoma Acad
Silver Spring, MD

Israel, Jasmine
Takoma Acad
Silver Spgs, MD

Izat, Donna
Bishop Walsh Middle HS
Lavale, MD

Jacks, Lawrence
Northern HS
Owings, MD

Jackson, Dena
Regina HS
Washington, DC

Jackson, Kristy
Westminster HS
Sykesville, MD

Jackson, Lydia
La Plata HS
Issue, MD

Jackson, Robert
Gaithersburg HS
Gaithersburg, MD

Jackson, Tabby
Frederick HS
Fairmont, WV

Jacobs, Lisa Marie
Walkersville HS
Walkersville, MD

Jacobs, Melinda
Highland View Acad
Hagerstown, MD

Jacobs, Molly
Sherwood HS
Olney, MD

Jago, Wendi
Great Mills HS
Great Mills, MD

James, Douglas Brant
Queen Annes County HS
Centreville, MD

James, Lisa
Damascus HS
Dickerson, MD

James, Stephanie
Academy Of The Holy Names
Wheaton, MD

Jamison, John David
Elkton SR HS
Elkton, MD

Jarman, Holly
Northwestern HS
Hyattville, MD

Jarrah, Ayman
Bullis HS
Rockville, MD

Jayne, Robyn
Kent County HS
Rock Hall, MD

Jenkins, Deborah
Elizabeth Seton HS
Washington, DC

Jenkins, Erynn
Bowie HS
Bowie, MD

Jennings, Pamela
Lackey HS
Bryans Rd, MD

Jessup, Richard
Gaithersburg HS
Gaithersburg, MD

Johng, Steven
Loyola Blakefield
Baltimore, MD

Johnson, III D Christopher
Northwestern HS
Baltimore, MD

Johnson, George
La Plata HS
Waldorf, MD

Johnson, Heather
Queen Annes Co HS
Queenstwn, MD

Johnson, Helene
Sherwood HS
Silver Spg, MD

Johnson, Ingrid
Academy Of The Holy Names
Beltsville, MD

Johnson, Karen M
Middletown HS
Middletown, MD

Johnson, Kathy
Poolesville JR SR
Dickerson, MD

Johnson, Kobi
Takoma Acad
Burtonsville, MD

Johnston, Chad
West Nottingham
Pt Deposit, MD

Johnston, Mary M
Immaculata College
Washington, DC

Jones, Bronte
Cambridge-South Dorchester HS
Cambridge, MD

Jones, Cary
Laplata HS
Mount Victoria, MD

Jones, Charles
Gwynn Park SR HS
Upper Marlboro, MD

Jones, Heather
Magruder/ Gaithersburg HS
Gaithersburg, MD

Jones, Hervoyna
Walbrook SR HS
Baltimore, MD

Jones, Jr James M
Westminster HS
Eldersburg, MD

Jones, Jennifer
Wilde Lake HS
Columbia, MD

Jones, Kevin
Crossland HS
Seat Pleasant, MD

Jones, Latonia
Baltimore City
Baltimore, MD

Jones, Melissa
Mount De Sales
Pasadena, MD

Jones, Natalie
Parkside HS
Salisbury, MD

Jones, Scott
Capitol Christian
Edgewater, MD

Jones, Sharilyn
Gaithersburg HS
Gaithersburg, MD

Jones, Sharon
Archbishop Keough
Severn, MD

Jones, Teresa
Surrattsville HS
Clinton, MD

Jordan, Elaine S
S River SR HS
Davidsonville, MD

Jordan, Sandra
Queen Ames Co HS
Chestertown, MD

Jozwick, Kimberly
Patapsco HS
Baltimore, MD

Jubb, Thomas Patrick
Williamsport HS
Willamsport, MD

Justice, Tricia
Wicomico SR HS
Salisbury, MD

Kahn, Brenda
Seneca Valley HS
Germantown, MD

Kallas, Terry Leigh
Eleanor Roosevelt
Laurel, MD

Kallon, Abdul
Bladensburg HS
Landover Hills, MD

Kamiru, Njoki
Northwestern HS
Hyattsville, MD

Kang, Sarah
The Garrison Forest
Reisterstown, MD

Kaouris, Demetrios
Wicomico SR HS
Salisbury, MD

Kapfhammer, David
Frederick HS
Clarksburg, MD

Kareem, Quanita
Balto Polytechnic Inst HS
Baltimore, MD

Karpiak, Veronica
Old Mill SR HS
Glen Burnie, MD

Katzke, Robin
Sherwood HS
Brookeville, MD

Kavanaugh, Margie
Allegany HS
Cumberland, MD

Kayoumy, Roya
Walter Johnson HS
Bethesda, MD

Keeley, Kellyanne
Connelly School Of The Holy Child
Bethesda, MD

Keeney, Raymond E
La Plata HS
La Plata, MD

Kehr, Diane
Capitol Christian
Upper Marlboro, MD

Keister, Patricia Anne
Charles W Woodward HS
Kensington, MD

Keith, Jeffrey A
Thomas Stone HS
Waldorf, MD

Kelley, Tamra
Southern Garrett
Oakland, MD

Kelly, Jill Suzanne
Dundalk SR HS
Baltimore, MD

Kennedy, Gary Michael
Seneca Valley HS
Gaithersburg, MD

Kennedy, Kerri
Archbishop Keough
Baltimore, MD

Kerr, Jr James H
Howard HS
Columbia, MD

Kershner, David
Williamsport HS
Hagerstown, MD

Kilmon, Michael
St Michaels SR HS
St Michaels, MD

Kim, Min
Eleanor Roosevelt
Seabrook, MD

Kim, Moonsu
Walt Whitman HS
Silver Spring, MD

Kim, Phil
Seneca Valley HS
Gaithersburg, MD

Kim, Teresa
Archbishop Keough
Baltimore, MD

Kines, Stephanie Ann
Linganore HS
Monrovia, MD

King, Jr James
Prospect Hall HS
Frederick, MD

King, Sharon
Maurice J Mc Donough HS
Waldorf, MD

Kingwell, Ken
Dulaney SR HS
Timonium, MD

Kirkland, Jr Charles B
Largo HS
Upper Marlboro, MD

Kirksey, Warren
Northwestern HS
Hyattsville, MD

Kirtinitis, Jolie
Glenelg HS
Glenelg, MD

Kisielewski, Constance
John Carroll HS
Fallston, MD

Kittel, Jim
Smithsburg HS
Hagerstown, MD

Klaff, Cheryl
Charles E Smith Jewish Day Schl
Rockville, MD

Klapka, D Monique
Notre Dame Prep
Baltimore, MD

Klebe, Rachel
Sherwood HS
Olney, MD

Kline, Kelli
Fort Hill HS
Cumberland, MD

Kline, Kristin Ann
Elkton HS
Elkton, MD

Kline, Monica
Allegany HS
Cumberland, MD

Klopcic, J Thaddeus
John Carroll HS
Bel Air, MD

Knapton, Mary A
C Milton Wright HS
Churchville, MD

Knight, Randall
Allegany HS
Cumberland, MD

Knippenberg, Ranae
Bishop Walsh HS
Cumberland, MD

Knisley, Susan
Allegany HS
Cresaptown, MD

Knittle, Mandy
St Pauls Schl For
Phoenix, MD

Knott, Vicki
Queen Anne Schl
Bowie, MD

Knowles, Cecily
Liberty HS
Westminster, MD

Koenig, Tanya
Great Mills HS
Great Mills, MD

Kokoski, Jennifer Rosemary
Archbishop Keough
Ellicott, MD

Kolbfleisch, Susie
Northern HS
Accident, MD

Kopit, Wendy
Rockville HS
Rockville, MD

Kornak, Eugene P
Archbishop Curley
Baltimore, MD

Kovach, Darin M
Washington HS
Princess Anne, MD

Krauch, Kelly S
Linganore HS
Monrovia, MD

Krauch, Michael Rene
Easton HS
Easton, MD

Krigbaum, Kim
Brunswick HS
Brunswick, MD

Krush, Paul
Chopticon HS
Mechanicsville, MD

Kuhar, Tom
Sparrow Point HS
Baltimore, MD

Kulp, William
Wicomico SR HS
Salisbury, MD

Kutner, Kara
Mount De Sales Academy HS
Baltimore, MD

Kwah, Marjorie
John Carroll Schl
Havre De Grace, MD

La Barre, Deirdre A
Rockville HS
Rockville, MD

La Mothe, Tammy Jo Ann
St Marys Nyken HS
Waldorf, MD

La Parle, Francis
Allegany HS
Cumberland, MD

Lamb, Irene
Great Mills HS
Lexington Park, MD

Lamonica, Lisa
Walkersville HS
Walkersville, MD

Lander, Dawn Melody
Rising Sun HS
Conowingo, MD

Lane, Sandra I
Hammond HS
Jessup, MD

Lanham, Kristen
Maurice J Mc Donough HS
Waldorf, MD

Lapidario, Jr Renato
Bishop Walsh HS
Cumberland, MD

Lardizabal, Lisa
Smithsburg SR HS
Hagerstown, MD

Larranaga, Virginia
The Bullis Schl
Gaithersburg, MD

Lasley, Felicia
Suitland HS
District Height, MD

Laurie, Mark
Aberdeen HS
Aberdeen, MD

Lavelle, Michael T
Eleanor Roosevelt
Largo, MD

Lavett, Deena
Regina HS
Washington, DC

Lawrence, Tracy
Forest Park HS
Baltimore, MD

Lay, Stephen E
Lackey SR HS
La Plata, MD

Layne, Donna
John Carroll HS
Monkton, MD

Le, Bao Loc
Albert Einstein HS
Silver Spring, MD

Le Blanc, Jr Donald J
Glenelg HS
Wodbine, MD

Leber, Michael
De Matha Catholic
Potomac, MD

Ledger, Darla Dee
Catoctin HS
Thurmont, MD

Lee, Alicia
Elizabeth Seton HS
Landover, MD

Lee, Crystal
Sparrows Point
Middue SR HS
Baltimore, MD

Lee, Kenneth
Thomas Stone HS
Waldorf, MD

Lee, Shana
Lackey HS
Welcome, MD

Lee, Soo
Magruder HS
Derwood, MD

Lee, Stacey
Carver Vo-Tech HS
Baltimore, MD

Lee, Tawanna
Northwestern SR
Baltimore, MD

Lees, Tanya
Maurice J
Mcdonough HS
La Plata, MD

Legates, Kevin
Wicomico SR HS
Salisbury, MD

Lehman, Richard A
Thomas Stone HS
Brandywine, MD

Lenhart, Marilyn
Gov Thomas
Johnson HS
Thurmont, MD

Lenhoff, Leslie
Mercy HS
Cockeysville, MD

Leonard, Lori
Takoma Acad
Takoma Park, MD

Leonardo, John L
Loyola HS
Timonium, MD

Lese, Christa
Bishop Walsh HS
Cumberland, MD

Lester, John
La Plata HS
Waldorf, MD

Lett, Laura E
Centennial HS
Ellicott City, MD

Lewis, Diane
Hammond HS
Laurel, MD

Lewis, Michelle E
Parkdale HS
Landover, MD

Lewis, Sheri
Crossland HS
Capitol Hts, MD

Libby, Gene
Calvert HS
St Leonard, MD

Lichtenfels, Mike
Elkton HS
Elkton, MD

Lied, Cheryl-Ann
North East HS
Elkton, MD

Lightner, Yarina
Carver Vocational
Tech HS
Baltimore, MD

Liller, Dwayne
Southern Garrett
Oakland, MD

Lin, Ephraim
Pauchung
Winston Churchill
Potomac, MD

Littrell, Joyce
Governor Thomas
Johnson HS
Frederick, MD

Liu, Sherrie
Perry Hall HS
Kingsville, MD

Liverman, Heath
Maurice J Mc
Donough HS
White Plains, MD

Loar, Angie
Bishop Walsh HS
Cumberland, MD

Lockard, Mary Anne
Northeast HS
North East, MD

Lockett, Staci Lyne
Forest Park HS
Baltimore, MD

Lolli, Jennifer
Frederick HS
Frederick, MD

Lomax, Christine
Dunbar HS
Baltimore, MD

Lore, Lynn
Friendly HS
Ft Washington, MD

Lott, Jr Fred
Dematha Catholic
Riverdale, MD

Louie, Linda Faye
Hammond HS
Columbia, MD

Lovick, Jennifer
Denise
Suitland HS
District Hts, MD

Lowe, Glenda
Mardela HS
Sharptown, MD

Lowe, L Michael
North Harford HS
Whiteford, MD

Lubitz, Jessica L
Eleanor Roosevelt
Laurel, MD

Luchinsky, Howard
Pikesville HS
Balto, MD

Luhn, Melissa
Heritage Acad
Middletown, MD

Lunsford, Lisa
John F Kennedy HS
Silver Spring, MD

Luppino, Christine
Gaithersburg HS
Gaithersburg, MD

Lusby, Lisa
Gov Thomas
Johnson HS
Frederick, MD

Luthe, Joey
Mount Hebron HS
Ellicott City, MD

Lyons, Kristin
Noelle
North Harford SR
Jarrettsville, MD

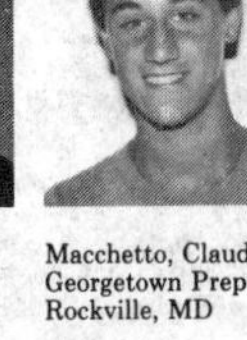
Macchetto, Claudio
Georgetown Prep
Rockville, MD

Macqueen, Ruth C
Towson HS
Towson, MD

Madigan, Kelley
John Carroll Schl
Forest Hill, MD

Magenau, Gail
South River HS
Davidsonville, MD

Maggio, Joseph
Patterson High
School HS
Baltimore, MD

Mahaffey, Jr Wayne
David
De Matha Catholic
Bowie, MD

Maher, Tina
Great Mills HS
Nas Pax River, MD

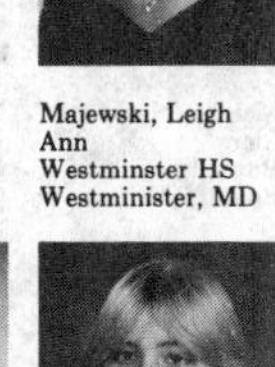
Majewski, Leigh
Ann
Westminster HS
Westminister, MD

Malachi, Lori
Regina HS
Washington, DC

Malat, Jonathan
Loyola HS
Baltimore, MD

Mallery, Scott
Mt Savage HS
Mt Savage, MD

Mallory, Nancy
Rockville HS
Rockville, MD

Malone, Chad
Beall HS
Frostburg, MD

Manimbo, Michele
Laurel HS
Laurel, MD

Manley, Tracy
Kent County HS
Still Pond, MD

Manning, Sean
Lackey HS
Indian Head, MD

Maralit, Marie
La Reine HS
Camp Springs, MD

Marconi, Lisa
Northern HS
Carney, MD

Marcos, Alexis
La Plata HS
Waldorf, MD

Margaronis, Demetrios P
West Nottingham
Alfred, NY

Marple, Richard
Southern Garrett
Oakland, MD

Marquis, Sandra
Maurice J Mc Donough HS
La Plata, MD

Marshall, Anita M
Catoctin HS
Thurmont, MD

Marshall, Vicki
Dundalk SR HS
Baltimore, MD

Marsteller, Brenda
Hereford HS
Freeland, MD

Martin, Pamela
Crossland HS
Camp Springs, MD

Martin, Traci
Southern Garrett
Oakland, MD

Martin, Wendy
North Carroll HS
Manchester, MD

Martof, Tanya E
Oxon Hill Science & Technology Ctr
Suitland, MD

Marzullo, Christopher
Calvert Hall College
Baltimore, MD

Mason, Dawn
Seton HS
Baltimore, MD

Mason, Deborah
Gaithersburg HS
Gaithersburg, MD

Massey, Amanda
Pocomoke HS
Pocomoke, MD

Mathias, Andrea
Snow Hill HS
Stockton, MD

May, Gena L
Oxon Hill SR HS
Ft Washington, MD

Mayes, Darron Renard
Friendly HS
Ft Washington, MD

Mayo, Monica L
Regina HS
Hyattsville, MD

Mc Allister, Paul
Du Val SR HS
Lanham, MD

Mc Bride, Jim
Frederick HS
Fred, MD

Mc Callin, Trina
Dundalk HS
Baltimore, MD

Mc Cammon, Jr Gary R
Perry Hall HS
Kingsville, MD

Mc Carron, Mary Agnes
Institute Of Notre
Baltimore, MD

Mc Clain, Tonya
Kent County HS
Chestertown, MD

Mc Clintock, Erin
La Plata HS
Hughesville, MD

Mc Cormick, Margaret
La Reine HS
Temple Hills, MD

Mc Coy, Jennifer
Allegany HS
La Vale, MD

Mc Cully, Christine
Thomas Stone HS
Hughesville, MD

Mc Donald, Lisa
Maurice J Mc Donough HS
Waldorf, MD

Mc Donald, Shandra L
Seneca Valley HS
Potomac, MD

Mc Dowell, Christie
North Hagerstown
Hagerstown, MD

Mc Elhone, Thomas
Parkside HS
Eden, MD

Mc Elwee, Mark
Mount Saint Joseph
Catonsville, MD

Mc Farland, Tricia
Bishop Walsh HS
Flintstone, MD

Mc Faul, Kelly
Patapsco HS
Baltimore, MD

Mc Gonnigal, J Bruce
Loyola HS
Towson, MD

Mc Gruder, Shawn Shyrlena
Centennial HS
Columbia, MD

Mc Guigan, Jennie
St Marys Ryken HS
Indian Head, MD

Mc Guire, Tracey
Chapticon HS
Mechanicsville, MD

Mc Kee, Danette
Hancock HS
Hancock, MD

Mc Kenzie, Stacey Linn
Allegany HS
Cresaptown, MD

Mc Kenzie, Terri
North Hagerstown
Hagestown, MD

Mc Kenzie, Wendy
Chopticon HS
Waldorf, MD

Mc Millan, Charmel
Crossland HS
Ft Washington, MD

Mc Millan, Dawn
Smithsburg HS
Ft Ritchie, MD

Mealo, Anthony
Northwestern HS
U Park, MD

Meilhammer, Deborah
James M Bennett SR HS
Salisbury, MD

Meneses, Reginald B
Loyola HS
Catonsville, MD

Meng, James
Pikesville SR HS
Baltimore, MD

Merella, Maureen Clare
Bowie HS
Bowie, MD

Merena, Theresa Marie
Glen Burnie HS
Glen Burnie, MD

Merkel, Kathleen
Elizabeth Seton HS
Bowie, MD

Miller, Carla
Allegany HS
Front Royal, VA

Miller, Chris
Cambridge South Dorchester HS
E New Market, MD

Miller, Cindy Marie
Governor Thomas Jefferson HS
Frederick, MD

Miller, Dawn
Bishop Walsh HS
Cumberland, MD

Miller, Penny
Francis Scott Key
New Windsor, MD

Miller, Stephen
Perryville HS
Pt Deposit, MD

Mills, Cheryl
Clear Spring HS
Big Pool, MD

Mills, Jennifer Lynn
Fort Hill HS
Cumberland, MD

Mills, Kate Dorinda
Gaithersburg HS
Gaithersburg, MD

Mills, Terri
Maurice J Mc Donough HS
White Plains, MD

Minnick, Adora
Allegany HS
Cumberland, MD

Mintz, Darryn
Montgomery Blair
Silver Spring, MD

Mitchell, Christopher
Loch Raven HS
Baltimore, MD

Mitchell, Curtis M
Gaithersburg HS
Gaithersburg, MD

Mitchell, Karla
Western HS
Baltimore, MD

Mitchell, Sally
Gaithersburg HS
Gaithersburg, MD

Mittan, Cheryl
Thomas Stone HS
Waldorf, MD

Moist, Natalie
Frederick HS
Frederick, MD

Mondell, Carolyn
Sherwood HS
Olney, MD

Montgomery, Danell
Fort Hill HS
Cumberland, MD

Moore, Michael
Bladensburg HS
Landover, MD

Moran, Glenn
Cardinal Gibbons
Baltimore, MD

Moreland, Dannyl M
Allegany HS
La Vale, MD

Moretti, Paul Joseph
Gaithersburg HS
Gaithersburg, MD

Morgan, Jodi
Martin Spalding HS
Glen Burnie, MD

Morgan, Kara Charles W
Woodward HS
Rockville, MD

Morgan, Martha E
Baltimore Polytechnic Inst
Baltimore, MD

Morris, III Charles E
Loyola HS
Baltimore, MD

Morris, Jr James G
Parkside HS
Parsonsburg, MD

Morris, John
Thomas S Wootton
Potomoc, MD

Morris, Richard
Thomas S Wooton
Potomac, MD

Morris, Ron
Parkside HS
Pittsville, MD

Morris, Suzi
Frederick HS
Frederick, MD

Morrison, Fabian
Northwestern HS
Baltimore, MD

Mortimer, Ed
Wilde Lake HS
Columbia, MD

Moulton, Vernell
Paul Laurence Dunbar HS
Baltimore, MD

Moultrie, Chelsea
Crossland HS
Ft Washington, MD

Moxley, Stephanie A
Damascus HS
Damascus, MD

Moyer, Brian
Surrottsville HS
Clinton, MD

Moylan, III Charles E
Friends Schl
Baltimore, MD

Muhlhausen, Rose
Centennial HS
Ellicott City, MD

Mullican, Lynn M
Fairmont Heights
New Carrollton, MD

Mulvihill, Grace
The Bullis Schl
Bethesda, MD

Murnane, Matt
Parkville HS
Baltimore, MD

Murphy, Crawford
Saints Peter & Paul
Cambridge, MD

Murphy, Damiana K
Stone Ridge Country Day Schl
Cheltenham, MD

Murphy, Jeffrey Scott
Cambridge South Dorchester HS
Cambridge, MD

Murphy, Yo Landa L
Governor Thomas Johnson HS
Frederick, MD

Murray, Bridget
Archbishop Keough
Severn, MD

Murray, Carol
Queen Annes County HS
Wye Mills, MD

Murtaugh, Dawn
Northwestern HS
Riverdale, MD

Myers, Michele
Notre Dame Prep
Towson, MD

Nagy, Katrina
Thomas Stone HS
Waldorf, MD

Nagy, Sandra Lee
Oxon Hill Science & Tech Ctr Ohhs
Fort Washington, MD

Narula, Jasmine
Thomas S Wootton
Gaithersburg, MD

Neal, Curtis G
High Point HS
Beltsville, MD

Neave, Tracy
Thomas Stone HS
Waldorf, MD

Needleman, Alyssa
Parkside HS
Salisbury, MD

Nelson, Jennifer
Wheaton HS
Silver Spring, MD

Nelson, Julia L
Wicomico SR HS
Salisbury, MD

Nelson, Mark
Brunswick HS
Brunswick, MD

Nesler, Richard Lee
Central HS
Forestville, MD

Neuman, Doug
The Bullis Schl
Potomac, MD

Newsome, Tina L
Eleanor Roosevelt
Lanham, MD

Nicholson, Isaac
Snow Hill HS
Snow Hill, MD

Nixon, Christine
Thomas S Wootton
Gaithersburg, MD

Nixon, Steven
Fort Hill HS
Cumberland, MD

Nock, Kim
Wicomico SR HS
Salisbury, MD

Noonkester, Jacqueline
C Milton Wright HS
Bel Air, MD

Norman, Kimberly S
Mc Donough HS
Waldorf, MD

Norris, Bronna
St Marys Ryken HS
Bryantown, MD

Norris, Kathy
Allegany HS
Cumberland, MD

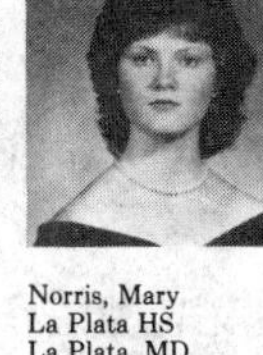
Norris, Mary
La Plata HS
La Plata, MD

Nugent, James
Friendly HS
Ft Washington, MD

O Donoghue, John
Elkton HS
Elkton, MD

O Toole, Jr Richard James
Patterson HS
Baltimore, MD

Oatway, Chris
Walter Johnson HS
Bethesda, MD

Ochoa, David
Catoctin HS
Thurmont, MD

Oh, Ju Hyoun
Loyola HS
Timonium, MD

Olewnik, Richard
De Matha Catholic
Washington, DC

Oliver, Jean
Northern HS
Catonsville, MD

Olsen, Jennifer Lynn
Joppatowne HS
Joppa, MD

Ore, Monica
Crossland HS
Suitland, MD

Ortt, Jr Richard
Parkville HS
Baltimore, MD

Otterbein, James
Mt Saint Joseph HS
Baltimore, MD

Outten, Michael J
Delmar HS
Delmar, MD

Pabis, Leah Melaney
Havre De Grace HS
Darlington, MD

Palacios, Stephen
Good Counsel HS
Kensington, MD

Palmer, Alan Jay
Bethesda Chevy Chase HS
Chevy Chase, MD

Palmer, Ron
Fallston HS
Fallston, MD

Palomo, Joyce
North Hagertown
Hagerstown, MD

Pankey, Fontella
Oxon Hill SR HS
Oxon Hill, MD

Papavasiliou, John A
Loyola HS
Timonium, MD

Paretzky, Jessica C
Thomas S Wootton
Potomac, MD

Park, Kathy
Allegany HS
Cumberland, MD

Park, Sooky
Seneca Valley HS
Gaithersburg, MD

Park, Jr William R
Allegany HS
Cresaptown, MD

Parker, Donald D
Colonel Zadok Magruder HS
Rockville, MD

Parks, Donna M
Parkside HS
Salisbury, MD

Parks, George T
Cardinal Gibbons
Baltimore, MD

Parry, Kimberly
Cambridge-South Dorchester HS
Crapo, MD

Parsapour, Mitra
Seneca Valley HS
Darnestown, MD

Parsons, James
De Matha Catholic
Greenbelt, MD

Parsons, III Lane W
Mc Donough HS
White Plains, MD

Partrich, Ellen Richard
Montgomery HS
Derwood, MD

Partridge, Stephanie
Surrattsville HS
Clinton, MD

Pascoe, Todd
Takoma Acad
Spokane, WA

Patchak, Jennifer
Notre Dame Preparatory Schl
Timonium, MD

Patterson, Dylan
The Bullis Schl
Bethesda, MD

Pattison, Scot
Du Val SR HS
Bowie, MD

Patton, Nanette
Seneca Valley HS
Germantown, MD

Patton, Tracy
Westminster HS
Finksburg, MD

Patzer, Karin
Howard HS
Ellicott City, MD

Paulikas, Nicole
Linganore HS
Ijamsville, MD

Peak, Bonnie
Westminster SR HS
Westminster, MD

Peck, Kendra
Allegany HS
Cumberland, MD

Pecunes, Doreen
Dulaney SR HS
Cockeysville, MD

Pekar, Anthony
Dematha HS
Hyattsville, MD

Pennepacker, Lenny
Sparrows Point HS
Baltimore, MD

Pensky, Jason
Bullis HS
Potomac, MD

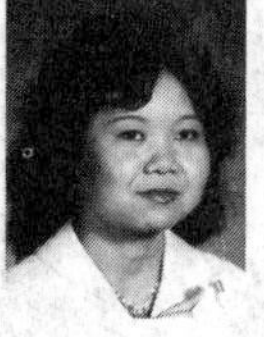
Peou, Voucheng
Parkdale HS
Riverdale, MD

Perez, Arelys
Gaithersburg HS
Gaithersburg, MD

Perez, Maria
Georgetown Vistiation Prep Schl
Silver Spring, MD

Perina, Raquel
Connelly School Of The Holy Child
Washington, DC

Perkins, Carrie Alene
Largo HS
Bowie, MD

Perrot, Rosemarie
Dundalk HS
Baltimore, MD

Perry, Dierdre
Crossland HS
Camp Springs, MD

Persiani, Jimmy
Crossland HS
Camp Spgs, MD

Petonbrink, Mark
Glenelg HS
Sykesville, MD

Petty, Elisabeth
Oldfields HS
Washington, DC

Pfeiffer, Mary E
Bel Air SR HS
Bel Air, MD

Phears, Vanessa
Oakland Mills HS
Columbia, MD

Phillips, Gina
North Dorchester
Vienna, MD

Phipps, Holly
Dulaney SR HS
Timonium, MD

Pickett, Jay
Westminster HS
Westminster, MD

Pierce, Shawn
Kenwood SR HS
Balto County, MD

Pilarski, Jerri Lynn
Mercy HS
Baltimore, MD

Pinder, III William D
Elkton HS
Elkton, MD

Pio Roda, Claro
Mc Donogh Schl
Lutherville, MD

Pleasants, Angela Michele
John F Kennedy HS
Silver Spring, MD

Pleines, C Lisa
Randallstown SR
Baltimore, MD

Plummer, Jenny
North Hagerstown
Hagerstown, MD

Poe, Nichelle A
Central HS
Suitland, MD

Poindexter, Thomas
Thomas S Wootton
Rockville, MD

Pomerantz, Phyllis M
Winston Churchill
Potomac, MD

Pontius, Katie
Heritage Acad
Clear Spring, MD

Pope, Lydia
Crossland HS
Temple Hills, MD

Portch, Kevin T
Paint Branch HS
Silver Spring, MD

Poser, Toby
Mc Donogh Schl
Baltimore, MD

Poston, Janice
Thomas S Wootton
Rockville, MD

Pouncey, Karen
Calvert HS
Solomons, MD

Powers, Karen E
Smithsburg HS
Ft Ritchie, MD

Prangley, Michael
De Matha Catholic
Bowie, MD

Prendergast, Hope
Bishop Walsh HS
Cumbuerland, MD

Price, III John H
Parkville HS
Baltimore, MD

Price, Linnea V
Middletown HS
Braddock Heights, MD

Price, Mimi
Archbishop Keough
Balt, MD

Price, Sonia
Forestville HS
Suitland, MD

Prillman, Carlos
Fairmont Heights
Lanham, MD

Pritchard, Jenny
Friendly HS
Ft Washington, MD

Proctor, Michelle
Hammond HS
Jessup, MD

Pugh, Junnette
Gwynn Park HS
Accokeek, MD

Purcell, Lisa
Suitland HS
Forestville, MD

Pusey, Jennifer
James M Bennett
SR HS
Salisbury, MD

Putman, Ronni
Governor Thomas
Johnson HS
Frederick, MD

Pyatt, Elizabeth J
Milford Mill HS
Baltimore, MD

Queen, Daryl W
Old Mill SR HS
Severn, MD

Quinlan, John
Bernard
Severn Schl
Bowie, MD

Quitiguit, Eunice
Notre Dame
Preparatory HS
Pikesville, MD

Raible, Jennifer
Bishop Walsh HS
Cumberland, MD

Rain, Michele
Franklin SR HS
Owings Mills, MD

Ramos, Sylvia A
Gaithersburg HS
Gaithersburg, MD

Ramsey, Carol
Northwestern HS
Hyattsville, MD

Rapisarda, Gina
John Carroll HS
Bel Air, MD

Rascon, Jeffrey Lee
Northern SR HS
Huntingtown, MD

Rasmussen, Ethel
Hereford HS
Monkton, MD

Ratliff, Bridgette
Potomac HS
Temple Hills, MD

Rausch, Karen
Western HS
Baltimore, MD

Rawlings,
Kimberleigh
St Pauls Schl For
Baltimore, MD

Redd, Robert
Magruder HS
Rockville, MD

Reed, Laura
Laurel HS
Roanoke, VA

Reese, Chris
Gaithersburg HS
Gaithersburg, MD

Reese, Mike
Middletown HS
Middletown, MD

Reeser, Cindra
Williamsport HS
Williamsport, MD

Reid, Laura
La Plata HS
Waldorf, MD

Reid, Steven G
St Pauls Schl
Baltimore, MD

Reitz, Kimberly
Notre Dame
Preparatory Schl
Towson, MD

Renner, Todd
Thomas Stone HS
Waldorf, MD

Reno, Christina Lea
Arundel SR HS
Odenton, MD

Resh, Joey
Williamsport HS
Hagerstown, MD

Retoma, Rachelle
Notre Dame
Preparatory Schl
Baltimore, MD

Reynolds, Robin
Parkside HS
Eden, MD

Rhodes, Meredith K
Gov Thomas
Johnson HS
Frederick, MD

Rice, Nicole
Allegany HS
Cumberland, MD

Rice, Ulysses
Potomac HS
Suitland, MD

Richards, John
Seneca Valley HS
Gaithersburg, MD

Richardson, Dawn
Mt De Sales Acad
Baltimore, MD

Richardson, Regina
Westminster HS
Finksburg, MD

Richardson, Stacey
Laurel HS
Laurel, MD

Richmond, Paula
Adele
Gwynn Park HS
Accokeek, MD

Riddick, Tiffany
Western SR HS
Baltimore, MD

Rife, Stefanie
Walkersville HS
Woodsboro, MD

Riggin, Tammy
North Carroll HS
Manchester, MD

Riley, Julie
North East HS
North East, MD

Rini, Donnell
Frederick HS
Frederick, MD

Rippeon, Karin
Frederick HS
Frederick, MD

Ritchey, Melissa
Rockville HS
Rockville, MD

Ritter, Maria
Regina HS
Silver Spring, MD

Rivera, Grace
Gaithersburg HS
Gaithersburg, MD

Roach, Jackie
Surrattsville HS
Clinton, MD

Roane, Marc W
Paint Branch HS
Silver Spring, MD

Roberts, Derek Jay
St Michaels SR HS
St Michaels, MD

Roberts, Thomas
Brunswick HS
Knoxville, MD

Robertson, Scott
Catonsville HS
Baltimore, MD

Robeson, Michael
Northern HS
Frostburg, MD

Robinette, Sherrie
Fort Hill HS
Cumberland, MD

Robinson, Anita
Rising Sun HS
Rising Sun, MD

Robinson, Christine
Wicomico SR HS
Salisbury, MD

Robinson, Heather
Gaithersburg HS
Gaithersburg, MD

Robinson, Joanna
Cambridge South
Dorchester HS
Cambridge, MD

Robinson, Lori S
Springbrook HS
Silver Spring, MD

Robinson, Michael
Broadneck SR HS
Annapolis, MD

Robinson, Tawana
Gwynn Park HS
Cheltenham, MD

Roca, Katherine
Centennial HS
Columbia, MD

Roche, Winifred J
Cambridge-South
Drochester HS
Cambridge, MD

Rochester, B J
Takoma Acad
Takoma Park, MD

Rock, Dawn
Western SR HS
Baltimore, MD

Rock, Lilda
Bethesda Chevy
Chase HS
Bethesda, MD

Rodavitch, Ann
Notre Dame Prep
Baltimore, MD

Rodney, Robin
Kent County HS
Chestertown, MD

Rohe, Anne Renee
Queen Annes
County HS
Stevensville, MD

Rolapp, Juliane
Bullis Schl
Darnestown, MD

Romano, Nino
Frederick HS
Clarksburg, MD

Roper, Belinda
Elkton HS
Elkton, MD

Roseman, Jeffrey
Thomas Stone HS
Waldorf, MD

Rosenstein, Judi
Thomas S Wootton
Rockville, MD

Ross, Suki
Surratsville HS
Clinton, MD

Rothage, David
Broadneck SR HS
Annapolis, MD

Rovine, Timothy J
John Carroll HS
Abingdon, MD

Rowe, II G Kenneth
Mcdonough HS
Waldorf, MD

Rowe, Stephanie
Delaney HS
Timonium, MD

Rowland, Dwayne
North Hagerstown
Hagestown, MD

Ruark, Steven
Sts Peter & Paul HS
Cambridge, MD

Rubin, Allan
Parkside SR HS
Salisbury, MD

Rudolph, Kathryn
Oxon Hill HS
Ft Washington, MD

Ruffin, Kelvin T
De Matha Catholic
Mitchellville, MD

Ruhl, Johna
Allegany HS
Cumberland, MD

Rumbarger, Richard
Charles
Winston Churchill
Potomac, MD

Rummel, Julie
North Hagerstown
Hagestown, MD

Rummel, Kelli Lynn
Bowie HS
Bowie, MD

Ruth, Dana
Queens Annes
County HS
Chester, MD

Ryan, Beth
Notre Dame Prep
Cockeysville, MD

Saadi, Cindi
Bowie HS
Bowie, MD

Sacks, Mary
Harford Vo-Tech
Forest Hill, MD

Sadanala,
Rajakumar
Takoma Acad
Takoma Park, MD

Salazar, Jere
St Vincetn Pallotti
Lanham, MD

Sales, Robert
Dulaney SR HS
Phoenix, MD

Sallese, Kelli A
The Institute Of
Notre Dame
Baltimore, MD

Sampson, Victoria
La Plata HS
White Plains, MD

Sanders, Jeff
Heritage Acad
Hagerstown, MD

Sandler, David
Walter Johnson HS
Bethesda, MD

Sapp, Anna
Gaithersburg HS
Gaithersburg, MD

Saralegui, Gisele
Winston Churchill
Potomac, MD

Sastro, Resa
Barnadiwa
Wheaton HS
Wheaton, MD

Saum, Andrea
Liberty HS
Sykesville, MD

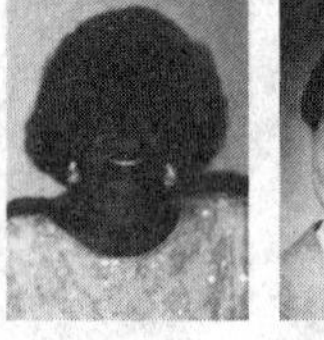
Saunders, Gail
Northwestern SR
Baltimore, MD

Savage, David C
Southern Garrett
Mountain Lake Pk,
MD

Saveleski, Karen
Broadneck SR HS
Annapolis, MD

Savia, Jolynn
La Plata HS
La Plata, MD

Savoy, Thomas
Lackey HS
Bryans Road, MD

Schaum, Charles
Eastern Voc Tech
Baltimore, MD

Scheinberg, Jason
Thomas S Wootton
Rockville, MD

Scheiner, David
Elkton HS
Elkton, MD

Scheiner, Mike
Elkton HS
Elkton, MD

Schenendorf, John
Noah
Gaithersburgh HS
Gaithersburg, MD

Schmidt, Karen
Mc Donough HS
Bryantown, MD

Schmitz, Mike
Magruder HS
Derwood, MD

Scholtz, Kristin
Institute Of Notre
Baltimore, MD

Schreder, Brandon
Cardinal Gibbons
Baltimore, MD

Schultz, Bonnie
Westminister HS
Westminster, MD

Schwartz, Jeffrey I
Mc Donogh Schl
Owings Mills, MD

Scott, III Leon F
Bishop Mc Namara
Temple Hills, MD

Scott, Wilton W
Springbrook HS
Silver Spring, MD

Seeber, Alyson
St Marys Ryken HS
Colonial Bch, VA

Seiter, Jane I
Rising Sun JR SR
Rising Sun, MD

Seitz, Nikki
Thomas Stone HS
Waldorf, MD

Selser, Jr Alan
Parkside HS
Salisbury, MD

Senft, David
Laplata HS
Waldorf, MD

Seto, Paul
Suitland HS
District Height, MD

Sexton, Geoff
Gwynn Park HS
Cheltenham, MD

Seymour, Sandra
Archbishop Keough
Balt, MD

Shank, Mike
Smithsburg HS
Hagerstown, MD

Shannon, Kathy
High Point SR HS
Beltsville, MD

Shawhan, Peter S
Springbrook HS
Silver Spring, MD

Shearer, Linda
Rockville HS
Rockville, MD

Shell, Brenda K
Eleanor Roosevelt
Laurel, MD

Sheng, Chain
Charles Woodward
Rockville, MD

Shepardson, Keith
Northern HS
Owings, MD

Sherr, Susan
Pikesville HS
Balto, MD

Sherwood, Tracy
Ft Hill HS
Cumberland, MD

Sheskin, Lisa
Rockville HS
Rockville, MD

Shirodkar, Sheela
Archbishop Keough
Baltimore, MD

Short, Heather
Parkville HS
Baltimore, MD

Short, Sean
Du Val HS
Lanham, MD

Shortall, Mary
SS Peter & Paul HS
Trappe, MD

Shrestha, Sushma
Fairmont Height HS
Hyattsville, MD

Shropshire, Sonya
Wilde Lake HS
Columbia, MD

Shryock, Susan
Smithsburg HS
Hagerstown, MD

Sibiga, Jennifer
Joan
North Carroll HS
Hampstead, MD

Siegel, Diana
Eleanor Roosevelt
Upper Marlboro,
MD

Simmons, Sharone
Lackey HS
Marbury, MD

Simpson, Kathleen
Ellen
Elizabeth Seton HS
Lanham-Seabrook,
MD

Simpson, Patricia
Regina HS
Greenbelt, MD

Sims, Amy
Crossland SR HS
Forestville, MD

Sinclair, Nicole
Takoma Acad
Adelphi, MD

Singh, Michael
Takoma Acad
Takoma Park, MD

Sion, Roger
Georgetown Prep
Rockville, MD

Six, Bobbi Jo
Francis Scott Key
Taneytown, MD

Skidmore, Nancy C
Wheaton HS
Wheaton, MD

Skidmore, Wendy
Gaithersburg HS
Gaithersburg, MD

Skrypzak, Karen
St Vincent Pallotti
Silver Spring, MD

Slagle, Mary
Brunswick HS
Knoxville, MD

Slavin, Tracy L
Rockville HS
Rockville, MD

Sliger, Kimberly
Soouthern Garrett
Oakland, MD

Small, Frank
Colonel Zadok
Magruder HS
Derwood, MD

Small, John Cota
Col Zador Magruder
Rockville, MD

Small, Patricia
Academey Of The
Holy Cross
Silver Springs, MD

Smith, Andy
Thomas S Wootton
Potomac, MD

Smith, Daniel
John Carroll Schl
Forest Hill, MD

Smith, Delisa
Friendly HS
Fort Washington,
MD

Smith, Donna D D
Potomac HS
Suitland, MD

Smith, Eric
Potomac HS
Temple Hills, MD

Smith, Jesse
Glenelg HS
Mt Airy, MD

Smith, Jr John R
Gaithersburg HS
Gaithersburg, MD

Smith, Jonathan
MT ST Joseph HS
Baltimore, MD

Smith, Keith
John Carroll HS
Havre De Grace,
MD

Smith, Kira M
Stone Ridge HS
Washington, DC

Smith, Lee Ann
Fort Hill HS
Cumberland, MD

Smith, Robin
Potomac HS
Suitland, MD

Smith, Shana
Riverdale Baptist
Upper Marlboro,
MD

Smith, Shanon
Centennial HS
Columbia, MD

Smith, Stephanie
Clear Spring HS
Hagerstown, MD

Smith, Tammy
Forestville HS
Suitland, MD

Smith, Tony
Frederick HS
Frederick, MD

Smith, Vanessa
Frederick HS
Frederick, MD

Smith, Wendy
Severna Park SR
Arnold, MD

Snead, Carla E
Montgomery Blair
Silver Spg, MD

Snodderly, Kim
Patapsco HS
Baltimore, MD

Snowden, Louis J
Edgewood SR HS
Edgewood, MD

Snyder, Cori
Pikesville HS
Balto, MD

Snyder, John
Fort Hill HS
Cumberland, MD

Snyder, Mark G
Gaithersburg HS
Gaithersburg, MD

Sokoloski, Carole T
Poolesville JR SR
Poolesville, MD

Spector, Ellen
Thomas S Wootton
Potomac, MD

Spencer, Shanan
Fort Hill HS
Cumberland, MD

Stachura, Michael
Lackey HS
Nanjemoy, MD

Stafford, Misty
Fort Hill HS
Cumberland, MD

Stancill, Stacey G
John Carroll HS
Bel Air, MD

Stanley, Michelle
St Vincent Pallotti
Laurel, MD

Staples, Julia
Queen Anne HS
Upper Marlboro,
MD

Starbird, Melinda
Mc Donough HS
White Plains, MD

Starbuck, Michelle
Lareine HS
Upper Marlboro,
MD

Starghill, Skylar
St Frances-Charles
Hall HS
Baltimore, MD

Stauffer, Andrew M
Linganore HS
Monrovia, MD

Steele, Carolyn
Frederick Douglass
Upper Marlboro,
MD

Steele, Tammy L
Mount Savage HS
Mt Savage, MD

Stefancic, Andrea
Linganore HS
Monrovia, MD

Stemmler, Martin B
German Schl
Potomac, MD

Stepanske, Nancy
Takoma Acad
Silver Spgs, MD

Stephens, Leslie B
Large HS
Upper Marlboro, MD

Stephens, Sam
Brunswick HS
Jefferson, MD

Stephens, Wanda
Bladensburg SR HS
Brentwood, MD

Stern, Andra
Charles W
Woodward HS
Rockville, MD

Stets, Robert J
Magruder HS
Rockville, MD

Stevens, Jennifer
Lynn
Middletown HS
Smithsburg, MD

Stevens, Julie
Northern Garrett
Grantsville, MD

Stevens, Kathy
Hammond HS
Columbia, MD

Stevenson, Kelly M
Williamsport HS
Hagerstown, MD

Stewart, Geoff
Seneca Valley HS
Gaithersburg, MD

Stewart, Shannon
Bowie HS
Bowie, MD

Stigall, Michelle
Archbishop Keough
Cartonsville, MD

Stiles, Andrew A
Damascus HS
Clarksburg, MD

Still, Amy
Cambridge-South
Dorchester HS
Cambridge, MD

Stonebraker, Alan T
Sherwood HS
Silver Spr, MD

Stoney, III Clement
Patrick
Fallston HS
Fallston, MD

Strausser, Kristin
Maurice J Mc
Donough HS
Waldorf, MD

Strother, Felicia
Potomac SR HS
Temple Hills, MD

Strother, Jacqueline
Regina HS
Washington, DC

Stuart, Jeffrey
Bowie HS
Bowie, MD

Sukachevin,
Chulachak
Takoma Acad
Silver Spring, MD

Summers, Linda
Brunswick HS
Jefferson, MD

Sutton, Patricia A
Loch Raven HS
Baltimore, MD

Sutton, Shana
Sherwood HS
Ashton, MD

Sutton, III William
Gaithersburg HS
Gaithersburg, MD

Symes, Maria
Gunston Schl
Virginia Bch, VA

Szilagyi, Sherry Ann
Eleanor Roosevelt
Laurel, MD

Szwed, Rose
St Marys Ryken HS
White Plains, MD

Talbert, Cheryl
Thomas Stone HS
Bryantown, MD

Tamres, Suzanne E
Northwestern HS
Baltimore, MD

Tan, Kimberly
Notre Dame
Preparatory Schl
Fallston, MD

Tarburton, Todd
Laplata HS
Hughesville, MD

Tavenner, Karen
High Point HS
Beltsville, MD

Taylor, III John C
Milford Mill HS
Balt, MD

Taylor, Kimberly
Western HS
Baltimore, MD

Taylor, Lesley
Washington SR HS
Eden, MD

Taylor, Shannon
Snow Hill HS
Snow Hill, MD

Taylor, Stephen
Montgomery Blair
Silver Spg, MD

Taylor, Timberly P
Walbrook SR HS
Baltimore, MD

Taylor, Yulanda
Oakland Mills HS
Columbia, MD

Tedesco, Joey
Cambridge South
Dorchester HS
Cambridge, MD

Temmermeyer, II
William F
Lackey HS
Bryans Road, MD

Ternent, John
Valley HS
Lonaconing, MD

Ternent, Mark
Valley HS
Lonaconing, MD

Terry, Garrett
Northern HS
Owings, MD

Thomas, Amy
Kent County HS
Worton, MD

Thomas, Ann
Southwestern SR
No 412 HS
Baltimore, MD

Thomas, David
Gov Thomas
Johnson HS
Frederick, MD

Thomas, Diane R
Williamsport HS
Hagerstown, MD

Thomas, Erin M
Sherwood HS
Ashton, MD

Thomas, Lizzie
Northwestern HS
Hyattsville, MD

Thomas, Richard
Friendly SR HS
Ft Washington, MD

Thomas, Suzie
Northwestern HS
Hyattsville, MD

Thomas, Tanya
Walter Johnson HS
Bethesda, MD

Thomas, Tracy
Allgany HS
Cresaptown, MD

Thompson, Debra
Thomas Stone HS
Waldorf, MD

Thompson, Lorie
Perryville HS
Perry Point, MD

Thompson, Mary
Anne
La Plata HS
La Plata, MD

Thorne, Charles A
Maurice J Mc
Donough HS
Waldorf, MD

Thornton, Mike
Surrattsville SR HS
Clinton, MD

Thune, Diana
Snow Hill HS
Snow Hill, MD

Tice, Lorie
Magruder HS
Derwood, MD

Tillmann, Amy
Liberty HS
Sykesville, MD

Tine, Gregory
Westminster HS
Westminster, MD

Tippett, Kelly
Lackey HS
White Plains, MD

Tittle, Kara
Oxon Hill HS
Ft Washington, MD

Toadvine, Theodore
James M Bennett
SR HS
Hebron, MD

Toder, Carol
Lackey HS
Indian Head, MD

Tom, Stephen
Linganore HS
Mt Airy, MD

Trader, Lori
Pocomoke HS
Pocomoke, MD

Trego, Nancy Kay
North East HS
Elkton, MD

Trenum, Gary Joe
Valley HS
Barton, MD

Tribbe, Michael E
Loyola HS
Baltimore, MD

Truitt, Jill
James M Bennett
SR HS
Salisbury, MD

Trumpower, David
Clear Spring HS
Clear Spg, MD

Tse, Aileen
Gaithersburg HS
Gaithersburg, MD

Tucker, Garrett
Capitol Christian
Lothian, MD

Tull, Gregory
Maurice Mc
Donough HS
White Plains, MD

Tunstall, Patricia D
Capital Lutheran
Washington, DC

Turner, Daryl
Laurel HS
Laurel, MD

Turner, Michael
Paul
Beall HS
Frostburg, MD

Turner, Shannan
Wheaton HS
Wheaton, MD

Tymiuk, Maria
The Catholic HS Of
Baltimore, MD

Ulen, Eisa N
Western HS
Baltimore, MD

Underwood,
Elizabeth S
Riverdale Baptist
Riverdale, MD

Uphold, Teri
Fort Hill HS
Rawlings, MD

Upole, Rebecca
Southern Garrett
Mt Lake Park, MD

Urian, Michael
Oakland Mills HS
Columbia, MD

Utermahlen, Jr
William
Francis Scott Key
Taneytown, MD

Vache, Suzanne C
John Carroll HS
Havre De Grace,
MD

Van Buren,
Stephanie
Magruder HS
Gaithersburg, MD

Van Dien, Jacquelyn
St Marys Piyken HS
Waldorf, MD

Vance, Martina
Southern Garrett
Mt Lake Pk, MD

Vance, Serena
Andover HS
Glen Burnie, MD

Vanskiver, Thomas
Southrew HS
Baltimore, MD

Velarde, David
Joseph
Walkersville HS
Walkersville, MD

Verga, Greg
Maurice J Mc
Donough HS
Port Tobacco, MD

Verrico, Bradley J
Elkton HS
Elkton, MD

Vest, Robert
Frederick HS
Clarksburg, MD

Vicendese, James
Loyola HS
Ellicott City, MD

Vickers, W Judd
Cambridge South
Dorchester HS
Cambridge, MD

Victor, Cecelia
Archbishop Keough
Catonsville, MD

Victor, Sujatha
Takoma Acad
Takoma Park, MD

Vincent, Wm
Northwestern HS
Hyattsville, MD

Vines, Letetia
Surrettsville SR HS
Clinton, MD

Vinick, Carole
Magruder HS
Olney, MD

Wagner, Karen
Laurel HS
Laurel, MD

Wahl, Stephanie
Dulaney SR HS
Cockeysville, MD

Wainwright, Cheryl
Western SR HS
Baltimore, MD

Walker, Greg
Thomas Stone HS
Waldorf, MD

Walker, Jenifer
Brunswick HS
Jefferson, MD

Wall, William
Governor Thomas
Johnson HS
Frederick, MD

Walsh, Chris
North Carroll HS
Hampstead, MD

Walsh, Colleen
Westminster HS
Westminster, MD

Walsh, Dennis
Loyola HS At
Baltimore, MD

Walsh, Pamela
St Johns At
Prospect Hall
Frederick, MD

Walston, Mark
Pocomoke HS
Pocomoke City, MD

Walters, Michelle S
Towson HS
Towson, MD

Ward, John
Fort Hill HS
Cumberland, MD

Ward, Joseph
La Plata HS
Charlotte Hall, MD

Ward, Melissa
La Plata HS
La Plata, MD

Ward, Jr Nathaniel
Snow Hill HS
Snow Hill, MD

Ware, Rita
Wicomico SR HS
Salisbury, MD

Warner, Cheryl N
Francis Scott Key
Westminster, MD

Warren, Danielle
Mc Donough HS
La Plata, MD

Warren, Simon
Rockville HS
Rockville, MD

Warrington, Carol
Parkside HS
Pittsville, MD

Wash, Ronald Loren
Thomas Stone SR
Waldorf, MD

Washington,
Jennifer
Bladensburg HS
Capitol Hts, MD

Washington,
Timothy
Crossland HS
Camp Springs, MD

Watanabe, Leslie
Michele
Charles W
Woodward HS
Rockville, MD

Waters, Nicol
Snow Hill HS
Snow Hill, MD

Watkins, Angela
Western SR HS
Baltimore, MD

Watkins, Tonya
Eastern HS
Baltimore, MD

Watkinson, Eric
Parkville HS
Baltimore, MD

Watson, Cheryl
Thomas Stone HS
Waldorf, MD

Watson, Karen
Mardela HS
Hebron, MD

Watson, Lynn
Sherwood HS
Olney, MD

Watson, Michelle Geneen
Eleanor Roosevelt SR HS
Lanham, MD

Waugh, William E
Maurice J Mc Donough HS
White Plains, MD

Way, Robin
Maurice J Mc Donough HS
White Plains, MD

Weakland, Sheila
Smithsburg HS
Cascade, MD

Weaver, Kristi
Walkersville HS
Walkersville, MD

Weaver, Lance
Valley HS
Barton, MD

Webb, Deborah
Lackey HS
White Plains, MD

Webb, Steven
Perryville HS
Colora, MD

Webber, Paula L
Surrattsville HS
Clinton, MD

Weeks, Wendy L
Mt Lake Independent Baptis
Loch Lynn, MD

Weems, Kristal T
Oxon Hill HS
Ft Washington, MD

Weems, Jr William E
Calvert HS
Port Republic, MD

Weese, Brian
Calvert Christian
Dunkirk, MD

Weible, Kerri Lynn
Bohemia Manor HS
Earleville, MD

Weiner, Marci A
Largo HS
Bowie, MD

Weiner, Neal
Thomas S Wootton
Rockville, MD

Weinhouse, Brett A
Baltimore Actors Theatre Conserve
Baltimore, MD

Weirick, Sharon M
Wicomico SR HS
Parsonsburg, MD

Weitzel, Jennifer
Potomac HS
Temple Hills, MD

Wells, Sharese
La Reine HS
Washington, DC

Welsh, Kristen E
Loch Raven HS
Glen Arm, MD

Welty, Tony
West Nottingham
Palestine, TX

Wenger, Lance Cole
The Bullis Schl
Bethesda, MD

Wessel, Donna
Kent County HS
Worton, MD

Westbrook, Joyce Harper
Perryville HS
Perryville, MD

Westmore, Michelle
Regina HS
Camp Springs, MD

Wharton, Michael A
Wicomico SR HS
Salisbury, MD

Wheaden, Tonya
Forest Park SR HS
Baltimore, MD

Wheatley, Anthony
Laurel HS
Laurel, MD

Wheatley, Paul
Milford Mill SR HS
Balt, MD

Wheeler, David
Francis Scott Key
Union Bridge, MD

Whitaker, Angela M
Eleanor Roosevelt
Adelphi, MD

Whitaker, Cindy
La Reine HS
Suitland, MD

White, Dina
Wicomico SR HS
Salisbury, MD

White, Elizabeth
Westminster HS
Westminster, MD

White, Jennifer C
Lareine HS
Accokeek, MD

White, Lisa
Oxon Hill SR HS
Fort Washington, MD

White, Rachelle
Walbrook SR HS
Baltimore, MD

Whitfield, Jr Guilford Arthur
Takoma Acad
Silver Spring, MD

Whitford, Wendy
La Plata HS
Charlotte Hall, MD

Whitt, Lillian Danielle
Crossland HS
Camp Springs, MD

Whittier, Timothy
Hammond HS
Columbia, MD

Wilder, Claude H
Eleanor Roosevelt
Silver Spring, MD

Wiles, Dale
Catoctin HS
Emmitsburg, MD

Wiley, Betty
Smithsburg HS
Smithsburg, MD

Wilhelm, Angela
Thomas Stone HS
Waldorf, MD

Wilhelm, Kirsten
Cambridge-South Dorchester HS
Cambridge, MD

Wilkerson, Laura
Gaithersburg HS
Gaithersburg, MD

Willey, Annmarie
Easton SR HS
Easton, MD

Williams, Andrea Nicole
Western SR HS
Baltimore, MD

Williams, II Daniel
Northwestern HS
Mt Rainier, MD

Williams, Jennifer
Surrattsville SR HS
Clinton, MD

Williams, John S
Elkton HS
Elkton, MD

Williams, Katrina
Mc Donough HS
Pomfret, MD

Williams, Quentin
Potomac HS
Temple Hills, MD

Williams, Scott
Friendly HS
Ft Washington, MD

Williams, Valerie
Du Val SR HS
Landover, MD

Wills, Bethany
St Marys HS
Annapolis, MD

Wills, Jill
Dundalk HS
Baltimore, MD

Wills, Lisa
Oxonhill High SR
Ft Washington, MD

Willsey, Angie
Takoma Acad
Silver Spgs, MD

Wilson, Dawn
Winston Churchill
Potomac, MD

Wilson, Kevin Clair
Hammond HS
Columbia, MD

Wilson, Stacey
Crisfield HS
Crisfield, MD

Wilson, Whitney
Walt Whitman HS
Bethesda, MD

Wilt, Jodi
Southern Garrett
Oakland, MD

Windsor, Jr Larry V
Cambridge-South Dorchestger HS
Toddville, MD

Witt, Jr Ray
Fort Hill HS
Cumberland, MD

Wizda, Sharyn
Western HS
Baltimore, MD

Wolf, Douglas
T S Woottan HS
Rockville, MD

Wolf, Kristin M
Academy Of The Holy Cross
Rockville, MD

Wolford, Heather
Allegany HS
Cresaptown, MD

Wong, Rebecca
Northwestern HS
Hyattsville, MD

Wood, Preston
Chopticon HS
Mechanicsville, MD

Woodward, Eric
Maurice J Mc Donough HS
Waldorf, MD

Wooten, Jennifer
Arundel HS
Crofton, MD

Wray, Terry
Great Mills HS
Monterey, CA

Wright, Sean
Parkdale HS
Lanham, MD

Wright, Tammera
High Point HS
Beltsville, MD

Wudarski, Julie
Catoctin HS
Thurmont, MD

Wycliffe, Joy John
Northwestern HS
Hyattsville, MD

Wynkoop, Patti
Wheaton HS
Wheaton, MD

Yesudian, Dayanthi
Takoma Acad
Beltsville, MD

Yoder, Debby
Northern Garrett
Grantsville, MD

York, Cathy
Joppatowne HS
Joppa, MD

Young, Cynthia
Valley HS
Midland, MD

Young, James
Fort Hill HS
Cumberland, MD

Young, Jill
Bishop Walsh HS
Cumberland, MD

Young, Kristin Taylor
Takoma Acad
Silver Spring, MD

Young, Melissa
Dulaney SR HS
Lutherville, MD

Young, Nancy Lynn
La Reine HS
Largo, MD

Young, Pamela
Calvert HS
Pr Frederick, MD

Younger, Cynthia
Institute Of Notre
Baltimore, MD

Yuffee, Michael
Walt Whitman HS
Bethesda, MD

Zahn, Jr Richard S
Catonsville HS
Catonsville, MD

Zannino, Salvatore V
Our Lady Of Pompei HS
Baltimore, MD

Zebarth, Laura
Mc Donough HS
White Plains, MD

Ziegler, Robert
Crossland SR HS
Upper Marlboro, MD

Zielinski, Maurita
Seneca Valley HS
Gaitherstown, MD

Ziler, Paula
Allegany HS
Cumberland, MD

Zimmerman, Deborah
Suitland HS
District Hts, MD

Zinkhan, Vickie
Joppatowne HS
Edgewood, MD

Zinn, Keven
Calvert HS
Lusby, MD

Zuretti, Cheryl
South Carroll HS
Mt Airy, MD

NEW JERSEY

Abalos, Veronica
Columbia HS
S Orange, NJ

Abbott, Chris B
Pleasantville HS
Absecon, NJ

Abbruzzese, Alisa
Washington Township HS
Turnersville, NJ

Abramo, Teddy
Hudson Catholic HS
Hoboken, NJ

Abrams, Martin
Garden State Acad
Willingboro, NJ

Achenbach, Debbie
St Mary HS
E Brunswick, NJ

Ackerman, Michael
Indian Hills HS
Franklin Lks, NJ

Ackroyd, Elizabeth
West Milford Township HS
West Milford, NJ

Acosta, Grisel
Norh Bergen HS
North Bergen, NJ

Acton, Thomas
Clifton HS
Clifton, NJ

Adams, Allison
Villa Victoria Acad
Trenton, NJ

Adams, Jim
Hamilton H S East
Hamilton Sq, NJ

Adams, Kelly
Absegami HS
Egg Hbr, NJ

Adams, Kim
Williamstown HS
Williamstown, NJ

Adams, Mark
Steinert HS
Hamilton Sq, NJ

Adams, Scott
Burlington City HS
Edgewater Park, NJ

Adamson, Linda
Wildwood HS
Wildwood, NJ

Adanas, Vahram
Memorial HS
West New York, NJ

Addis, Kirk S
BCVT Medford
Medford, NJ

Adelsberg, Risa
Solomon Schechter Day Schl
Livingston, NJ

Adlakha, Mona
Randolph HS
Randolph, NJ

Adlassnig, Sharon
South Plainfield HS
S Plainfield, NJ

Afflitto, Charlene
Verona HS
Verona, NJ

Agnolet, Jeanine
Queen Of Peace HS
Lyndhurst, NJ

Agostini, Francesca
Parsippany Hills HS
Parsippany, NJ

Agostino, Joseph
Secaucus HS
Secaucus, NJ

Agoston, David
Oratory Catholic
Montville, NJ

Agrifolio, Mary Lynn
West Essex HS
Fairfield, NJ

Aguilera, Alicia
St Mary Of The Assumption HS
Hillside, NJ

Aker, Gregory
Linden HS
Linden, NJ

Akgun, Altay
Pope John XXIII Reg HS
Hopatcong, NJ

Akian, Berj
Belleville SR HS
Belleville, NJ

Albano, Peter
Verona HS
Verona, NJ

Albert, Janice Lynn
Kingsway Regional
Swedesboro, NJ

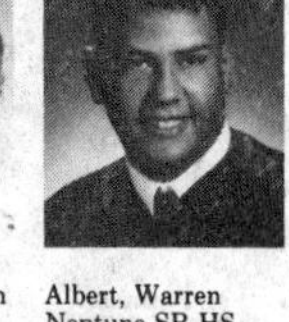
Albert, Warren
Neptune SR HS
Neptune, NJ

Alberty, Angela
Monsignor Donovan
Toms River, NJ

Aldana, Allyson
Pope John XXIII
Regional HS
Newton, NJ

Alder, Keith
West Essex HS
Upper Montclair, NJ

Alderton, Todd
Saint Joseph
Regional HS
Rivervale, NJ

Aleman, Denise L
Neptune SR HS
Neptune, NJ

Alessi, Kelly
Hamilton High West
Trenton, NJ

Alexander, Mary Jo
Red Bank Catholic
Rumson, NJ

Algeier, Susan Janet
Hackensack HS
Maywood, NJ

Alicea, Samuel
Vineland SR HS
Vineland, NJ

Allen, Andrea
Plainfield HS
Plainfield, NJ

Allen, Arlene
Clayton HS
Clayton, NJ

Allen, Chris
Hamilton High West
Trenton, NJ

Allen, Kia
Wilwood Catholic
Cape May, NJ

Allen, Nicole
Holy Cross HS
Willingboro, NJ

Allen, Paul
John F Kennedy HS
Metuchen, NJ

Alper, Curt
Matawan Regional
Holmdel, NJ

Altera, Rose Marie
West Essex Regional
Fairfield, NJ

Alvez, Debbie
Dwight Morrow HS
Englewood, NJ

Amaker, Harris
Rahway HS
Rahway, NJ

Ambardar, Meenakshi
Westfield SR HS
Westfield, NJ

Ambardar, Para
Westfield HS
Westfield, NJ

Amberg, John
Middletown South
Leonardo, NJ

Amon, Elizabeth
Hopewell Valley
Central HS
Hopewell, NJ

Anderson, Adrienne
Mount Saint Mary
S River, NJ

Anderson, Cynthia
Millville SR HS
Heislerville, NJ

Anderson, Derek
North Brunswick
Township HS
N Brunswick, NJ

Anderson, Edward
Kingsway Regional
Mickleton, NJ

Anderson, Melody
Park Bible Acad
Carneys Pt, NJ

Andia, Sandra
Mater Dei HS
Middletown, NJ

Andolpho, Denene
Mater Dei HS
Middletown, NJ

Andreeko, Andrew A
Warren Hills Reg
Hackettstown, NJ

Andrian, Theresa
Brick Memorial HS
Brick Town, NJ

Angelica, John
Don Bosco Prep HS
N Haledon, NJ

Angerole, Beth
Wall Twp HS
Sea Girt, NJ

Angulo, E Michael
Moorestown HS
Mt Laurel, NJ

Anilo, Ralph
Scotch Plains
Fanwood HS
Fanwood, NJ

Aninipot, Roderick L
Hudson Catholic HS
Jersey City, NJ

Anthony, Dwayne
Asbury Park HS
Asbury Pk, NJ

Anton, Doug
Ramsey HS
Saddle River, NJ

Antonelli, Vincent
James Caldwell HS
Caldwell, NJ

Antoshak, Ann C
Northern Valley
Regional H
Closter, NJ

Antunes, Lisa Marie
Mother Seton
Regional HS
Hillside, NJ

Anuszkiewicz, Nicholas S
Brick Township HS
Bricktown, NJ

Appio, Maryeileen
Passaic Valley HS
W Paterson, NJ

Apy, Melissa
Red Bank Regional
Red Bank, NJ

Aquino, Joanna M
Sussex County
Vo-Tech HS
Lake Stockholm, NJ

Arasin, Jo Anne
Saint James HS
Carneys Point, NJ

Archer, Steven T
Ridge HS
Basking Ridge, NJ

Arciszewski, Christine
South River HS
South River, NJ

Aretz, Tracie
Vineland SR HS
Vineland, NJ

Argue, Robin
Central Regional HS
Bayville, NJ

Arico, Frank
Morris Catholic HS
Rockaway, NJ

Arky, Lauren
East Brunswick HS
E Brunswick, NJ

Arlaus, Richard
Clifton HS
Clifton, NJ

Armenio, Peter J
De Paul Diocesan
Wayne, NJ

Armstrong, James M
Delbarton Schl
Madison, NJ

Arnold, Donna
Toms River North
Toms River, NJ

Arocho, Tammy Lee
Emerson HS
Union City, NJ

Aron, Julie
West Milford HS
Newfoundland, NJ

Aronsohn, William John
Ramapo HS
Wyckoff, NJ

Arthur, Shannon
Middletown HS
Middletown, NJ

Asaro, Margaret H
Hopewell Valley
Central HS
Hopewell, NJ

Asbrand, James
Hamilton HS East
Hamilton Sq, NJ

Ashton, Patricia Lynne
Pemberton
Township HS II
Browns Mills, NJ

Asselta, Thomas
Delsea Regional HS
Newfield, NJ

Astuni, Ann M
E Brunswick HS
East Brunswick, NJ

Atlee, Edward
Highland Regional
Clementon, NJ

Attanasio, Scott
Queen Of Peace HS
Nutley, NJ

Augustin, Nathalie
Union Catholic
Regional HS
Scotch Plains, NJ

Auld, William
Bound Brook HS
Bound Brook, NJ

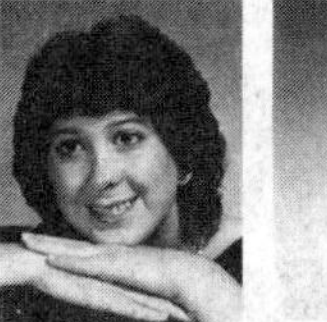

Auletto, Lisa
Secaucus HS
Secaucus, NJ

Aumueller, Cheryl
Central Jersey
Christian HS
Manasquan, NJ

Aurigemma, Sean J
River Dell SR HS
Oradell, NJ

Austin, Shelton L
St Marys Hall
Doane Acad
Willingboro, NJ

Avant, Ila Little
Frank H Morrell HS
Irvington, NJ

Avella, Carrie
Morris Knolls HS
Denville, NJ

Aymer, Valerie
Columbia HS
S Orange, NJ

Ayvaz, Ahmet
Hawthorne HS
Hawthorne, NJ

Azzolina, Andrea
North Hunterdon
Clinton, NJ

Babics, Catherine
East Brunswick HS
East Brunswick, NJ

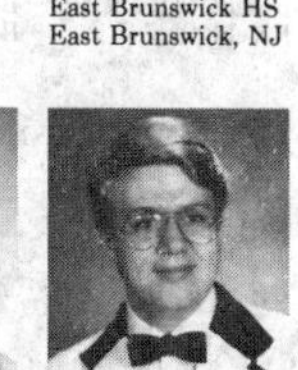

Babilino, Gina
Our Lady Of Mercy
Turnersvile, NJ

Baccarella, Michele
Holy Family Acad
Bayonne, NJ

Bach, Tami L
Paul VI HS
Blackwood, NJ

Backman, David
West Morris Central
Long Valley, NJ

Bacungan, Teofilo
Lower Cape May
Regional HS
N Cape May, NJ

Bagby, Elsa
Cumberland
Regional HS
Bridgeton, NJ

Bagin, Cathy
Washington Twp
Turnersville, NJ

Bagley, Michelle
Teaneck HS
Teaneck, NJ

Bagwell, Robin T
Neptune SR HS
Neptune, NJ

Baham, II Paul M
Hudson Catholic HS
Union City, NJ

Bahamon, Martha
East Side HS
Newark, NJ

Bailey, Christine
Verona HS
Verona, NJ

Bailey, T Jason
East Brunswick HS
East Brunswick, NJ

Bailey, Tyrone
Camden HS
Camden, NJ

Baker, Cecilia
Red Bank Catholic
Long Branch, NJ

Baker, Jodi
Spotswood HS
Milltown, NJ

Baker, Kim Yvette
Dwight Morrow HS
Englewood, NJ

Baker, Thomas
Steinert HS
Trenton, NJ

Baldanza, Sal
Christian Brothers
Manasquan, NJ

Baldwin, Brian
Wall HS
Sea Girt, NJ

Balik, Amy
Hunterdon Central
Ringoes, NJ

Ball, Jr Earle
William
Toms River H S
Toms River, NJ

Ball, Lisa Anne
Manasquan HS
Spring Lk, NJ

Ballard, Lori Ann
Piscataway HS
Piscataway, NJ

Ballon, Andrea
North Brunswick
Township HS
N Brunswick, NJ

Balzer, Claudia
Chatham Twp HS
Chatham Twp, NJ

Banasiak, III
Stephen J
Rahway HS
Rahway, NJ

Bangash, Shireen
Saddle River Day
Ridgewood, NJ

Banker, Danny
Lakeland Regional
Haskell, NJ

Banks, Andrew D
Seton Hall Prep
Cedar Grove, NJ

Bannister, Robert P
Cherodii HS
Atco, NJ

Barabas, Kimberly
Shore Regional HS
W Long Branch, NJ

Barall, Allan
Parsippany HS
Parsippany, NJ

Baranowski, Faith
Hackettstown HS
Hackettstown, NJ

Barash, Sara
Scotch Plains
Fanwood HS
Westfield, NJ

Barbara, Dan
Washington
Township HS
Turnersville, NJ

Barbarisi, Louis
West Essex HS
Roseland, NJ

Barber, Tracy
Cumberland
Regional HS
Bridgeton, NJ

Barbossa, David
Hudson Catholic HS
Jersey Cty, NJ

Barge, Angelique
Camden HS
Camden, NJ

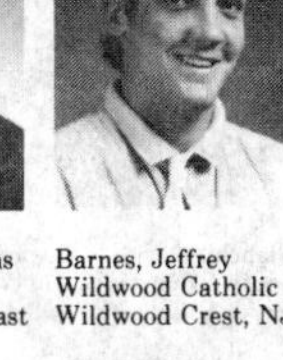

Barge, James
South River HS
South River, NJ

Barlow, Thomas
Spotswood HS
Spotswood, NJ

Barlow, III Thomas
B
Toms River HS East
Toms River, NJ

Barnes, Jeffrey
Wildwood Catholic
Wildwood Crest, NJ

Barnes, Michele S
Vernon Township
Glenwood, NJ

Barnett, Robert
Overbrook Regional
Lindenwold, NJ

Barr, Stephanie
Wayne Hills HS
Wayne, NJ

Barrett, Tracy
Scotch Plains
Fanwood HS
Fanwood, NJ

Barsky, Dennis
Cliffside Park HS
Fairview, NJ

Bartel, Brian
Middletown HS
Middletown, NJ

Bartiromo, Louis C
Lenape Valley
Regional HS
Stanhope, NJ

Bartolo, Marca
Leigh
Montclair School Of
Performing Arts
Montclair, NJ

Basaviah, Preetha
Montville Township
Montville, NJ

Bassman, Lori C
Cherry Hill HS East
Cherry Hill, NJ

Bastos, Cristina
Riverside HS
Riverside, NJ

Bate, Linda
Fair Lawn HS
Fair Lawn, NJ

Bates, Virginia
Logan
Brick Township
Mem HS
Brick, NJ

Batra, Monty S
Pennsville HS
Pennsville, NJ

Batts, Joseph K
Science HS
Newark, NJ

Bauer, Renee
Manchester
Regional HS
North Haledon, NJ

Baumann, Jr Daniel
Roselle Catholic HS
Roselle Pk, NJ

Bautz, Jennifer
Bloomfield SR HS
Bloomfield, NJ

Bayard, Brad
Cinnaminson HS
Cinnaminson, NJ

Bayles, Tanya
Bishop Eustace
Preparatory Schl
Haddon Heights, NJ

Beadle, La Rae
Scotchplains
Fanwood HS
Scotchplains, NJ

Beal, Jimmy
Eastern HS
Voorhees, NJ

Beale, Lisa
St Rose HS
Brick, NJ

Beard, IV Timothy
D
Ridge HS
Basking Ridge, NJ

Beato, Louis R
Nottingham HS
Trenton, NJ

Beavers, Hedy
Our Lady Of Good
Newark, NJ

Beck, Jackie
Morris Catholic HS
Succasunna, NJ

Becker, Pamela
B R East HS
Martinsville, NJ

Becker, Tiffany
Cherokee HS
Marlton, NJ

Beckerman, Natalie
Rancocas Valley
Regional HS
Mt Holly, NJ

Beckett, Dorothea
Holy Cross HS
Medford, NJ

Beer, Carolyn
Toms River HS
Toms River, NJ

Belcastro, Debbie
Lenape Valley
Regional HS
Andover, NJ

Belcher, Sue
Hunterdon Central
White House Stati,
NJ

Belem, Paula
Mother Seton
Regional HS
Hopelawn, NJ

Bell, Debra
Mainland Regional
Northfield, NJ

Bello, Natalie
St Dominic Acad
Jersey City, NJ

Belum, Suzan
Cherry Hill East HS
Cherry Hill, NJ

Bendinger, Jean
Marie
Bishop Eustace Prep
Haddonfield, NJ

Benesh, Sandra
Washington
Township HS
Sewell, NJ

Bennett, Anthony
Burlington City HS
Burlington, NJ

Bennett, David
Middletown South
Leonard, NJ

Benowitz, David B
Leonia HS
Leonia, NJ

Bensel, Eric
Pitman HS
Pitman, NJ

Benshoff, Kim
Spotswood HS
Spotswood, NJ

Benson, Robert E
Palmyra HS
Beverly, NJ

Benthin, Guy
North Hunterdon
Hampton, NJ

Benzell, Kimberly
Beth
Red Bank Catholic
Holmdel, NJ

Berardi, Paula
Kittatinny Regional
Newton, NJ

Berberich, Christine
Southern Regional
Barnegat, NJ

Beresin, Craig W
Cherry Hill HS East
Cherry Hill, NJ

Berg, Debra
Hightstown HS
East Windsor, NJ

Berg, Kelly
West Morris Central
Long Valley, NJ

Berger, Peter G
Sayreville War
Memorial HS
Parlin, NJ

Bergeron, Liesl
Randolph HS
Randolph, NJ

Bergheimer, William
Warren
Frank H Morrell HS
Irvington, NJ

Bergman, Kristine
Howell HS
Howell, NJ

Berish, II William S
Hamilton High
Trenton, NJ

Berkes, Cheryl
Cherry Hill East HS
Cherry Hill, NJ

Berliner, Roberta
W Morris Mendham
Brookside, NJ

Bernardino, Jan
Somerville HS
Somerville, NJ

Bernatavicius,
Albert
Holy Cross HS
Cinnaminson, NJ

Bernstein, Scott
Hightstown HS
E Windsor, NJ

Berruti, John
Brick Township HS
Brick, NJ

Berry, Stephanie
Holy Cross HS
Mount Laurel, NJ

Bertekap, Robert L
Woodbridge HS
Fords, NJ

Best, Stacey R
Frank H Morrell HS
Irvington, NJ

Betts, Nicole
Eastside HS
Paterson, NJ

Beukema, Michelle
West
Windsor-Plainsbor
Princeton Jct, NJ

Beveridge, Stacie
Pennsville Memorial
Salem, NJ

Bevis, Blaine R
The Pennington
Princeton Junctn,
NJ

Biagi, Susan
Our Lade Of Mercy
Vineland, NJ

Bianchi, David
South Brunswick
North Brunswick,
NJ

Bianchi, Terry
Woodstown HS
Woodstown, NJ

Biase, Denise
West Essex Regional
Roseland, NJ

Biberica, Joyce
Cliffside Park HS
Cliffside Pk, NJ

Bielavitz, Thomas C
Parsippany HS
Parsippany, NJ

Bien, Elaine
Bridgewater-Raritan
HS West
Bridgewater, NJ

Bieniaszewski, Irene
Mother Seton
Regional HS
Union, NJ

Bigley, Kristine
Paul VI HS
Haddon Heights, NJ

Bilal, Brian
Plainfield HS
Plainfield, NJ

Bill, Jennifer
Woodstown HS
Monroeville, NJ

Billies, Kevin A
St Joseph Regional
Oradell, NJ

Binaco, Debbie
Middletown HS
Middletown, NJ

Binder, Charles
Cumberland
Regional HS
Bridgeton, NJ

Binns, Jr Russell
Wm
Brick Township HS
Mantoloking, NJ

Biondi, Janette M
Scotch Plains
Fanwood HS
Scotch Plains, NJ

Biramontes, Joyce
Frank H Morrell HS
Irvington, NJ

Birdsong, Vicki
Hillside HS
Hillside, NJ

Birmingham, Eileen
Manalapan HS
Englishtown, NJ

Bischoff, Amiee
Mater Dei HS
Middletown, NJ

Bishop, Meredith
Louise
West Milford
Township HS
West Milford, NJ

Bisogno, Joseph
Toms River H S
Toms River, NJ

Bittenbinder, Susan
Point Pleasant
Borough HS
Pt Pleasant, NJ

Bitz, Jennifer
Ramapo Regional
Wyckoff, NJ

Bixby, Diane A
Ocean City HS
Woobbine, NJ

Blaese, Niccole
Northern Burlington
Co Reg HS
Columbus, NJ

Blair, Valerie
Cumberland
Regional HS
Bridgeton, NJ

Blake, Elizabeth
Haddonfield
Memorial HS
Haddonfield, NJ

Blake, Janine
Mainland Regional
Linwood, NJ

Blake, Jennifer
Mahwah HS
Mahwah, NJ

Blake, Scott J
Wallkill Valley Reg
Franklin, NJ

Blakovich, Patricia
L
Bayonne HS
Bayonne, NJ

Blanchard, Lauren
Hunterdon Central
Flemington, NJ

Blaney, Annemarie
Neptune SR HS
Neptune, NJ

Blanks, Donald R
Rahway HS
Rahway, NJ

Blatt, Kyrabeth
Mahawak HS
Mahwah, NJ

Bleacher, II Edward
Notre Dame HS
Kingston, NJ

Blejwas, Amy
Bridgewater-Raritan
East HS
Bridgewater, NJ

Blejwas, Mark
Bridgewater Raritan
East HS
Bridgewater, NJ

Blemings, Daniel
Vorhees HS
Califon, NJ

Blich, Jacqueline
Morris Catholic HS
Mine Hill Dover, NJ

Bloch, Colleen
Scotch
Plains-Fanwood HS
Scotch Pl, NJ

Bloch, Robert I
Ridgefield Memorial
Ridgefield, NJ

Bloodgood, David
Manasquan HS
Spring Lake Hts, NJ

Bloom, David
Parsippany HS
Parsippany, NJ

Blount, Jr Dennis
Lee
Memorial HS
West New York, NJ

Blum, Kenny
Colonia HS
Colonia, NJ

Blysak, Jennifer
West Morris Central
Long Valley, NJ

Boccia, Jeff
Northern Valley
Rgnl HS Ol
Old Tappan, NJ

Bockholt, Tracy
Bernards HS
Dallas, TX

Boehmer, Darcie
Toms River HS
Beachwood, NJ

Boehmler, Joel A
Moorestown HS
Delran, NJ

Boelhower, Susan
Nottingham HS
Mercerville, NJ

Boepple, Leanne J
Westwood HS
Westwood, NJ

Bogda, Michele
Notre Dame HS
Trenton, NJ

Boland, Kate
Morris Catholic HS
Montville, NJ

Boland, Kathleen
Immaculate
Conception HS
West Orange, NJ

Bolanowski, Richard
Oratory Prep
Cranford, NJ

Bolden, Darwin
Secaucus HS
Secaucus, NJ

Bonado, Lorenzo
Shore Regional HS
W Long Branch, NJ

Bonfigli, Richard M
Washington Twp
Turnersville, NJ

Bonhard, Kirk
Hudson Catholic HS
Jersey City, NJ

Bonnet, Deborah C
Morris Knolls HS
Denville, NJ

Bonzek, Anne
Hamilton HS West
Trenton, NJ

Bookholdt, III
Dewey P
Hamilton H S North
Trenton, NJ

Boos, Deborah
Midland Prk HS
Newfoundland, NJ

Boos, Karen
Scotch
Plains-Fanwood HS
Fanwood, NJ

Booth, Christine
Lynn
Butler HS
Bloomingdale, NJ

Borden, Stephanie
St Cecilia HS
Englewood, NJ

Bornstad, Christen
M
Roselle Catholic HS
Elizabeth, NJ

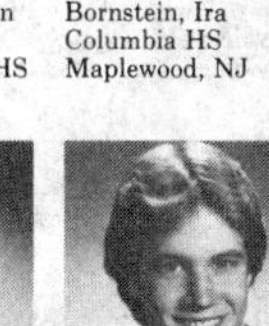
Bornstein, Ira
Columbia HS
Maplewood, NJ

Borota, Nick A
Florence Township
Memorial HS
Roebling, NJ

Borstelmann, Carrie
Kinnelon HS
Kinnelon, NJ

Boscia, Anne Marie
Mother Seton
Regional HS
Westfield, NJ

Bosco, Martin
Gloucester County
Christian Sch
Newfield, NJ

Bosler, Scott
Gloucester Coutny
Christian Schl
Mantua, NJ

Bosley, Mark
Monsienor Donovon
Long Beach Twp,
NJ

Bosley, Rachael
Monsignor Donovan
Long Beach Twp,
NJ

Bostic, Ebony L
Delran HS
Delran, NJ

Boston, Stacey M
Henry Snyder HS
Jersey City, NJ

Boswell, Scott D
St Josephs HS
Piscataway, NJ

Boszak, Dawn
Hamilton High West
Yardville, NJ

Bosze, Joan A
Carteret HS
Carteret, NJ

Bosze, Judee
Carteret HS
Carteret, NJ

Botkin, Brian
Manalapan HS
Englishtown, NJ

Bottitto, Lisa
Essey Catholic Girls
Union, NJ

Boudoughian, Alice
Pascack Hills HS
Woodcliff Lk, NJ

Boulazeris, Joanna
Atlantic City HS
Ventnor City, NJ

Boulware, Sheila
Renee
Stuart Country Day
Piscataway, NJ

Bouvier, Steven
Penns Grove HS
Pedricktown, NJ

Bowers, Steven
Bound Brook HS
S Bound Brook, NJ

Boyadjian, Mark
Brick Township HS
Brick, NJ

Boyd, Christina
Kingsway Regional
Swedesboro, NJ

Boyle, Georgeanne
Lakewood HS
Lakewood, NJ

Boyles, Erike
Hudson Catholic HS
Irvington, NJ

Bozolus, Cheryl
Roselle Catholic HS
Union, NJ

Bradley, Timia
Holy Spirit HS
Atlantic City, NJ

Bradshaw, Sean
Riverside HS
Riverside, NJ

Brand, Diana
Brick Township HS
Brick Town, NJ

Brandt, Jennifer
Woodbridge HS
Woodbridge, NJ

Brantley, Bryant H
Pennsville Memorial
Pennsville, NJ

Breault, Sharon
Brick Township HS
Brick Town, NJ

Breazeale, Lee
Hamilton High West
Trenton, NJ

Bredehoft, Anastasia
Ann
Toms River HS
Toms River, NJ

Bredehoft, Mary
Alice
Toms River North
Toms River, NJ

Breheny, Ann Marie
Manville HS
Manville, NJ

Brennan, Tara
Queen Of Peace HS
Lyndhurst, NJ

Brescia, Michael M
Saint Josephs HS
Fords, NJ

Brett, Jessica
Vineland HS
Vineland, NJ

Brett, Susie L
Abraham Clark HS
Roselle, NJ

Briante, Susan C
Scotch Plains
Fanwood HS
Fanwood, NJ

Bricker, Susan
Piscataway HS
Piscataway, NJ

Brickley, Tara
Bishop George Ahr/
St Thomas
Edison, NJ

Bridger, Elizabeth
Hopewell Valley
Central HS
Hopewell, NJ

Brierley, Suzanne
Toms River HS
Toms River, NJ

Brietenstine, Lynn L
Burlington County
New Lisbon, NJ

Briggs, Scott A
Montgomery HS
Belle Mead, NJ

Brillantes, Rosanna
Oak Knoll HS
Short Hills, NJ

Brimley, George
East Side HS
Paterson, NJ

Brinamen, Maribeth
Mount Olive HS
Flanders, NJ

Briscoe, Monica
Haddonfield
Memorial HS
Haddonfield, NJ

Broadnax, Christine
Westside HS
Newark, NJ

Broadwater, Michael
Millville SR HS
Millville, NJ

Brockman, Melissa
Lakewood HS
Lakewood, NJ

Broder, Helen A
Morristown Beard
Short Hills, NJ

Broderick, Colleen
Manchester
Township HS
Lakehurst, NJ

Brodka, Robert
Paramus Catholic
Boys HS
Garfield, NJ

Brokaw, Bradford
Red Bank Regional
Little Silver, NJ

Bronstein, Jamie L
The Pingry Schl
Succasunna, NJ

Brooks, Tonya
Penns Grove HS
Penns Grove, NJ

Brougham, Jr
Thomas J
Rahway HS
Rahway, NJ

Broughman, Jo Ann
Clayton HS
Clayton, NJ

Brower, Pam
Midland Park HS
Midland Park, NJ

Brown, Aurelia
John F Kennedy HS
Willingboro, NJ

Brown, Carmelita
Clifton HS
Clifton, NJ

Brown, Cheryl A
Mc Corristin
Catholic HS
Trenton, NJ

Brown, Corbin
Williamstown HS
Williamstown, NJ

Brown, Heidi
Lakewood HS
Lakewood, NJ

Brown, Jen
Lakeland Regional
Ringwood, NJ

Brown, Lars
Belvidere HS
Belvidere, NJ

Brown, Loretta
Roselle Catholic HS
Roselle, NJ

Brown, Patricia
Union Catholic
Regional HS
Elizabeth, NJ

Brown, Richard
Monsignor Donovan
Jackson, NJ

Brown, Teleea
Lakewood HS
Lakewood, NJ

Brown, Tracey
Millville SR HS
Port Norris, NJ

Brown, Wendy
Salem HS
Salem, NJ

Brown, III William
E
Somerville HS
Somerville, NJ

Browne, Lorrie
Union Catholic
Regional HS
Scotch Plains, NJ

Brozek, Jeff
Bridgewater-Raritan
HS East
Bridgewater, NJ

Bruce, Eric Brendan
Mater Dei HS
Middletown, NJ

Bruh, Ronald W
The Peddle Schl
E Windsor, NJ

Bruno, Angela M
Cinnaminson HS
Cinnaminson, NJ

Bruno, Marianne
Wall HS
Wall Township, NJ

Brunswon, Tammy
Highland Park HS
Highland Park, NJ

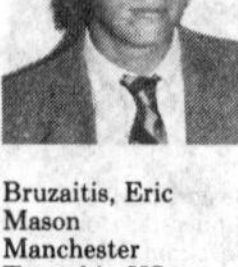
Bruzaitis, Eric
Mason
Manchester
Township HS
Toms River, NJ

Brzozowski, James
Manasquan HS
Spring Lake Hts, NJ

Bucci, Christopher
Morris Catholic HS
Oakridge, NJ

Buck, John
South Branswick HS
Dayton, NJ

Buckley, Ellen
St Rose HS
Sea Girt, NJ

Buckley, Kevin
Roselle Catholic HS
Elizabeth, NJ

Budden, Ray
Burlington City HS
Burlington, NJ

Budziski, Patricia
Dover HS
Mine Hill, NJ

Buffington, Melissa
New Milford HS
New Milford, NJ

Buler, Kelley J
Delran HS
Delran, NJ

Bullock, Calandra
Holy Spirit HS
Pleasantville, NJ

Bullock, Ryan
Pemberton Twp HS
Pemberton, NJ

Bulvanoski, Christina
Matawan HS
Matawan, NJ

Bunch, Michele
Marylawn Of The Oranges HS
Newark, NJ

Bundy, Erica S
Elizabeth HS
Elizabeth, NJ

Buoncristiano, Patricia
St Pius X HS
Metuchen, NJ

Buonocore, Dawn M
Brick Memorial HS
Bricktown, NJ

Buranich, Rayna
Piscataway HS
Piscataway, NJ

Burchell, Robert
Hamilton HS East
Hamilton Sq, NJ

Buren, Marcy
Raritan HS
Hazlet, NJ

Burger, Tracy
Hunterdon Central
Whitehouse Sta, NJ

Burgess, Carol A
Haddonfield Memorial HS
Haddonfield, NJ

Burke, Cynthia
Washington Township HS
Turnersville, NJ

Burke, Maureen
Saint Rose HS
Neptune, NJ

Burke, Pam
John P Stevens HS
Edison, NJ

Burklow, Timothy M
Pequannock Township HS
Pompton Plains, NJ

Burnham, John
Ocean Township HS
Ocean, NJ

Burnham, Yvette
Manalapan HS
Englishtown, NJ

Burns, Gregory E
Westwood HS
Westwood, NJ

Burt, Mary
Paulsboro HS
Gibbstown, NJ

Burton, Lauren
John F Kennedy HS
Paterson, NJ

Burzynski, Tamara
Toms River HS East
Toms River, NJ

Bush, Jacqueline R J
Bridgewater-Raritan High Schl West
Bridgewater, NJ

Bushell, Jr John T
Central Regional HS
Seaside Park, NJ

Busse, G Dirk
Colonia HS
Colonia, NJ

Bussie, Alvin
John F Kennedy HS
Paterson, NJ

Butler, Christina
Oak Knoll Schl
Jersey City, NJ

Butler, Gwendolyn
Kittatinny Regional
Middleville, NJ

Butler, Nicole
Red Bank Catholic
Farmingdale, NJ

Butler, Stephanie
Cherry Hill HS
Cherry Hill, NJ

Butte, Atul Janardhan
Cherry Hill HS East
Cherry Hill, NJ

Buzzelli, Pasquale
St Peters Prep
Jersey City, NJ

Byers, Jr Jesse Edward
Edgewood SR HS
Sicklerville, NJ

Byk, Kimberley
Mt Saint Mary Acad
Watchung, NJ

Byrd, Kandy
Hillside HS
Hillside, NJ

Byrd, Kimberly Denise
Abraham Clark HS
Roselle, NJ

Byrd, Tanya
Franklin HS
Somerset, NJ

Byrne, Kathleen
West Orange HS
W Orange, NJ

Byrne, Kelly M
Academy Of The Sacred Heart HS
Hoboken, NJ

Byrne, Kevin
St Josephs HS
South Amboy, NJ

Byrne, Lisa
Southern Regional
Cedar Run, NJ

Byrne, Sue Ann
St John Vianney HS
Manalapan, NJ

Bysterbusch, Ryan
Eastern Christian
Hawthorne, NJ

Cabalu, Ray
West Essex SR HS
N Caldwell, NJ

Cabatic, Jeannette
Mount Saint Dominic Acad
Bloomfield, NJ

Cagande, Consuelo
Pope John XXII HS
Sparta, NJ

Cagnetta, Robert
Verona HS
Verona, NJ

Cahill, Arla
Randolph HS
Randolph, NJ

Cain, Carolyn
Absegami HS
Absecon, NJ

Cain, Jenni
Williamstown HS
Williamstown, NJ

Calamita, Jaclyn
Wayne Hills HS
Wayne, NJ

Califano, Andy
Middlesex HS
Middlesex, NJ

Callahan, Dawn
West Morris Central
Long Valley, NJ

Callahan, Jonathan Matthew
Dwight Englewood
Leonia, NJ

Calvert, Edward
Cresskill HS
Cresskill, NJ

Calvo, John
St Mary HS
Passaic, NJ

Camaligan, III Cosme Ruel G
James J Ferris HS
Jersey City, NJ

Cameron, Heather
Marris Knolls HS
Butler, NJ

Cameron, Robert
Ramapo Regional
Wyckoff, NJ

Cameron, Robert W
Mountain Lakes HS
Mountain Lakes, NJ

Caminiti, Melissa
Paramus HS
Paramus, NJ

Camlin, Robert
Wayne Hills HS
Wayne, NJ

Cammilleri, Roxanne
Mary Help Of Christians Acad
Clifton, NJ

Campanella, Barbara Jeanne
Sterling HS
Stratford, NJ

Campanella, Christopher J
Christian Brothers
Matawa, NJ

Campbell, Cynthia
North Brunswick Twsp HS
N Brunswick, NJ

Campbell, Debbi
St Jammes HS
Salem, NJ

Campisano, Gina Marie
Wayne Valley SR
Wayne, NJ

Canada, Christopher M
Johnson Regional
Clark, NJ

Canady, Steve
Roselle Catholic HS
Roselle, NJ

Canahuate, Yolimar
Bishop Eustace Prep
Marlton, NJ

Cancila, Gregory
St James HS
Gibbstown, NJ

Candelino, Cheryl
Roselle Cath
Roselle, NJ

Candon, Christa
Union Catholic HS
Clark, NJ

Cane, Joanne
Parsippany HS
Parsippany, NJ

Canizares, Lourdes
Memorial HS
West New York, NJ

Cannon, Kolleen
Mater Dei HS
Middletown, NJ

Capalbo, Kim
Highland Regional
Erial, NJ

Capitano, Rosanne
Roselle Catholic HS
Roselle, NJ

Capobianco, James M
Saddle Brook HS
Saddle Brook, NJ

Capozzi, Joseph J
Ridgefield Memorial
Ridgefield, NJ

Cappola, Thomas
Dwight-Englewood
Middletown, NJ

Cappuccio, Donna
Wayne Hills HS
Wayne, NJ

Capraro, Suzanne
Woodbridge HS
Woodbridge, NJ

Caprio, Beth
Jackson Memorial
Jackson, NJ

Caputo, Bob
Toms River HS East
Toms River, NJ

Capuzzi, Albert
Morris Catholic HS
Morris Plains, NJ

Caravela, Joseph
James Caldwell HS
W Caldwell, NJ

Caravela, Thomas
James Caldwell HS
West Caldwell, NJ

Caravella, Peter
West Essex Regional
Fairfield, NJ

Carbonara, Michael
De Paul HS
Fairfield, NJ

Carbone, Carl Michael
Lyndhurst HS
Lyndhurst, NJ

Card, Douglas
Middletown HS
Highlands, NJ

Cardone, Anthony
Dover HS
Mine Hill, NJ

Carey, David
Roselle Catholic HS
Roselle, NJ

Carey, Patricia
St Rose HS
Spring Lake, NJ

Carlton, Karen
Morris Catholic HS
Parsippany, NJ

Carnathan, Mary Therese
Mt Olive HS
Flanders, NJ

Carri, Suzanne
Egg Harbor Township HS
Linwood, NJ

Carrow, Theresa
Pualsboro HS
Paulsboro, NJ

Carrozza, Paul
St Joseph Regional
Pearl River, NY

Carruth, Kevin
Haddon Heights HS
Lawnside, NJ

Carswell, III Jasper Lee
St Pius X Reginol
Plainfield, NJ

Carswell, John E
Allentown HS
Clarksburg, NJ

Carter, Jr Donald P
Seton Hall Prep
Newark, NJ

Carter, James
Deran HS
Delran, NJ

Carter, Saundra Frank H
Morrel-Irvington HS
Newark, NJ

Caruso, Katie
Wildwood Catholic
Cape May Ch, NJ

Carvajal, Luz Elena
Memorial HS
West New York, NJ

Casale, Michael
James Caldwell HS
Caldwell, NJ

Casavina, Louis R
River Dell SR HS
River Edge, NJ

Cashman, Janet
Chatham Twp HS
Chatham Twp, NJ

Casseus, Sandra
Essec Catholic Girls
Irvington, NJ

Cassidy, Heather
Glassboro HS
Glassboro, NJ

Cassidy, Linda
Kittatinny Regional
Newton, NJ

Castagno, Louis
Hudson Catholic HS
Jersey Cty, NJ

Castro, Nancy
Montclair Kimberley
Newark, NJ

Caswell, Jamell Ahmad
John F Kennedy HS
Willingboro, NJ

Cattell, Megan
Clayton HS
Clayton, NJ

Cauda, Lisa
Montville Twp HS
Pine Brook, NJ

Cautillo, Eugene J
Union Catholic Regional HS
Linden, NJ

Cavacier, Buck
Atl City HS
Margate, NJ

Cavalero, Catherine
Kittatinny Regional
Newton, NJ

Cece, Jennifer
Union HS
Union, NJ

Celentano, Vincent F
Lakewood HS
Lakewood, NJ

Celeste, Catherine
Wayne Valley HS
Wayne, NJ

Cerrato, Chris A
Vernon Township
Sussex, NJ

Chait, David
East Brunswick HS
E Brunswick, NJ

Chalian, Maral
Toms River HS
Glendale, CA

Chalson, Erica
North Brunswick Township HS
N Brunswick, NJ

Chance, Angelita
Pemberton HS II
Pemberton, NJ

Chandler, Christine
Cresskill HS
Cresskill, NJ

Chandler, Garrett
Gloucester County
Christian HS
Deptford, NJ

Chaney, Kendis
Monsignor Donovan
Seaside Heights, NJ

Chang, Steven
Parisippany HS
Parsippany, NJ

Charette, Gabrielle
Mount Saint Mary
Fanwood, NJ

Chase, Victoria
Southern Regional
Harvey Cedars, NJ

Cheddar, Christina
Woodbridge HS
Port Reading, NJ

Cherichella, Robert
Wood-Ridge HS
Wood-Ridge, NJ

Chervil, Balaguer
Memorial HS
West New York, NJ

Chester, Charlotte
Ann
Arthur P Schalick
Elmer, NJ

Chew, George
Cumberland
Regional HS
Bridgeton, NJ

Chimes, Michael J
Hightstown HS
E Windsor, NJ

Chin, Sabrina
Ramapo HS
Wyckoff, NJ

Chipman, Kathleen
B
Delsea Regional HS
Newfield, NJ

Choe, Jennifer
Newark Acad
Randolph, NJ

Choff, Jeffrey
Christian Brothers
Little Silver, NJ

Choi, Han Wook
The Lawrenceville
Pompton Lakes, NJ

Chordas, Darryl
South River HS
S River, NJ

Chou, Joseph H
Lawrenceville Schl
Cranbury, NJ

Choudhury, Sambhu
N
The Pingry Schl
Parsippany, NJ

Chrisco, Hillary
E Orange HS
East Orange, NJ

Christensen, Tara
Woodbridge HS
Wodbridge, NJ

Christian, Taynia
Lincoln HS
Jersey City, NJ

Christians, Jill
Rutherford HS
Rutherford, NJ

Christie, David
Andrew Michael
Bayley-Ellard
Catholic Regionl HS
Basking Ridge, NJ

Christopher, Frank
L
John F Kennedy HS
Willingboro, NJ

Chu, Alice
Westfield HS
Westfield, NJ

Chu, Keith C
Hillsborough HS
Belle Mead, NJ

Chu, Margaret
Dwight-Englewood
Englewood Cliffs,
NJ

Chuliver, Anthony
Holy Cross HS
Delran, NJ

Chun, Sam H
Moorestown HS
Moorestown, NJ

Chung, David
Riverside HS
Riverside, NJ

Chung, Joon
Northern Valley
Regional HS
Harrington Pk, NJ

Chung, Scott
Cresshill HS
Cresskill, NJ

Cialini, Mike
Atlantic City HS
Margate, NJ

Ciavatta, Chris
Neptune HS
Ocean Grove, NJ

Cibenko, Michael T
High Point Regional
Branchville, NJ

Ciccarelli, Steven T
Hopatcong HS
Hopatcong, NJ

Cichon, Suzie
Newton HS
Newton, NJ

Cichowski, Joseph
Rahway HS
Rahway, NJ

Cieciuch, Veronica
St Dominic Acad
Secaucus, NJ

Cignarella, Jr
Robert C
Watchung Hills
Regional HS
Warren, NJ

Ciliento, David
Pinelands Regional
Tuckerton, NJ

Ciperski, Jill
Wayne Hills HS
Wayne, NJ

Cipriani, Lydia
Park Ridge HS
Park Ridge, NJ

Cirello, Vincent
Anthony
Fair Lawn HS
Fair Lawn, NJ

Ciubinski, George
Lakewood HS
Lakewood, NJ

Ciufo, Lisa M
Watchung Hills
Regional HS
Warren, NJ

Civil, Richard
Wayne Hills HS
Wayne, NJ

Clair, Susan
St John Vianney HS
Colts Neck, NJ

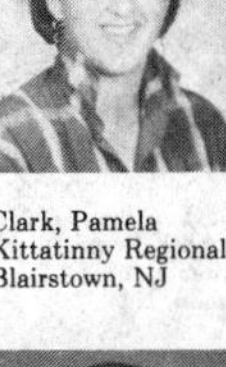

Clark, George B
Hackensack HS
Hackensack, NJ

Clark, Jonathan A
Governor Livingston
Reg HS
Berkeley Heights,
NJ

Clark, Pamela
Kittatinny Regional
Blairstown, NJ

Clark, Patty
Parsippany HS
Lk Hiawatha, NJ

Clark, Shannon
Essex Catholic Girls
East Orange, NJ

Clark, Sharon
Bridgewater-Raritan
East HS
Bridgewater, NJ

Clark, Tammy
Camden HS
Camden, NJ

Clarke, Heather
North Warren
Regional HS
Blairstown, NJ

Clarke, Shaune
Highland HS
Sicklerville, NJ

Clauss, Craig
Westwood Regional
Westwood, NJ

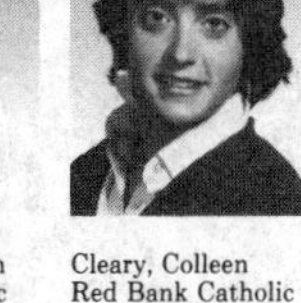

Clauss, Laurie
Salem HS
Salem, NJ

Clayton, David
Wood-Ridge HS
Wood-Ridge, NJ

Clayton, Kenneth
Paterson Catholic
Regional HS
Paterson, NJ

Cleary, Colleen
Red Bank Catholic
Brielle, NJ

Clement, John
Arthur L Johnson
Clark, NJ

Cloughley, Barbara
Dover HS
Dover, NJ

Clour, Randy
Salem HS
Salem, NJ

Coakley, Jeffrey
Roselle Catholic HS
Elizabeth, NJ

Cobb, Lavern
Burlington County
Vo-Tech HS
Willingboro, NJ

Cocca, Michael
St Peters
Preparatory HS
Jersey City, NJ

Coceano, Thomas
Saint Marys Hall
Doane Acad
Willingboro, NJ

Cogan, William E
Paul Vi Regional HS
Clifton, NJ

Cohen, III Arthur L
W
Lower Cape May
Regional HS
Cape May, NJ

Cohen, Eric
Fair Lawn HS
Fair Lawn, NJ

Cohen, Jeremy
James Caldwell HS
W Caldwell, NJ

Cohen, Jonathan
Bridgwater Raritan
East HS
Bridgewater, NJ

Cohen, Linda
Pompton Lakes HS
Pompton Lakes, NJ

Cohen, Neil
Shore Regional HS
W Long Branch, NJ

Cohen, Sharyn
John F Kennedy HS
Willingsboro, NJ

Coilparampil, Baiju
Orange HS
Orange, NJ

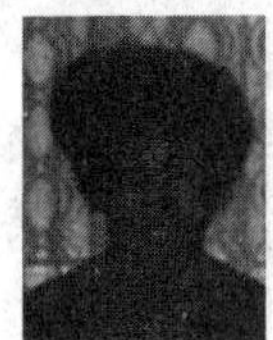
Coke, Donna
Vailsburg HS
Newark, NJ

Colclough, Rezena
Henry Snyder HS
Jersey City, NJ

Cole, Jeffrey
Eastside HS
Paterson, NJ

Cole, Lisa
Central Regional HS
S Toms River, NJ

Cole, Lisa Ann
Hackettstown HS
Hackettstown, NJ

Coleman, Patrice
Trenton Central HS
Trenton, NJ

Coleridge, Jennifer
Hunterdon Central
Flemington, NJ

Colletti, Roylene
N Warren Regional
Blairstown, NJ

Colligan, Jeanne
De Paul HS
Wayne, NJ

Collini, Amy
Pope John XXIII
Sparta, NJ

Collins, Edward
Harris
Red Bank Regional
Little Silver, NJ

Collins, Michelle
Triton Regional HS
Laurel Springs, NJ

Colomy, Heidi
Sacred Heart HS
Newfield, NJ

Colucci, James A
Wayne Valley HS
Wayne, NJ

Comegys, Susan
Holy Cross HS
Edgewater Park, NJ

Concialdi, Amy
Toms River HS East
Toms River, NJ

Congedo, Michael
Pascack Hills HS
Montvale, NJ

Coniglio, Natalie M
Notre Dame HS
Trenton, NJ

Conklin, Christie
Toms River HS
Toms River, NJ

Conlon, Stephanie
Sayreville War
Memorial HS
Parlin, NJ

Connolly, Martin
Seton Hall Prep
S Orange, NJ

Connor, Margaret
Indian Hills HS
Oakland, NJ

Conover, Theresa
Pemberton Twp H S
Pemberton, NJ

Constantin, Beth
Kittatinny Regional
Newton, NJ

Conza, John P
Burlington Co Voc
Pemberton, NJ

Coogan, John
St Peters Prep Schl
Upr Montclair, NJ

Cook, Gorden T
Hopewell Valley
Central HS
Pennington, NJ

Cook, Heather
Toms River HS East
Toms River, NJ

Cook, Mark
North Warren
Regional HS
Blairstown, NJ

Cook, Sheri
Mount St Mary
Milltown, NJ

Cook, Victoria
Brunah HS
Beverly, NJ

Cooke, Paul
De Paul Diocesan
Wayne, NJ

Coon, Jane
Jackson Memorial
Jackson, NJ

Cooper, Jr Thomas
E
Brick HS
Brick Town, NJ

Corbett, Melissa
Monsignor Donovan
Toms River, NJ

Corbett, Thomas
Monsignor Donovan
Bayville, NJ

Cordeiro, Jr Robert
St Mary HS
Spotswood, NJ

Corman, Lili
Roselle Catholic HS
Elizabeth, NJ

Cornejo, Debbie
Paterson Catholic
Regional HS
Paterson, NJ

Coronato, Thomas
Lenape Valley
Regional HS
Sparta, NJ

Corrado, Anna M
Spotswood HS
Spotswood, NJ

Correll, Gregory
Brick Township HS
Brick, NJ

Cortes, Raul
Woodrow Wilson HS
Camden, NJ

Cory, Chris
Manasquan HS
Belmar, NJ

Costanzo, Michael V
Watchung Hills
Regional HS
Warren, NJ

Courtright, Ralph
Sussex City
Vocational-Tech HS
Franklin, NJ

Coutinho, Albert
Seton Hall Prep
Newark, NJ

Covino, John
John F Kennedy
Memorial HS
Iselin, NJ

Cowell, Matt Alan
Westfield SR HS
Westfield, NJ

Cowgill, Kathryn
Kittatinny Regional
Newton, NJ

Cowgill, Kevin R
Kittatinny Regional
Newton, NJ

Cowherd, James
Oakcrest HS
Mays Landing, NJ

Cox, Holly Mari
Florence Twp Mem
Roebling, NJ

Coyne, Colleen
Neptune SR HS
Neptune, NJ

Coyne, Thomas
James Caldwell HS
W Caldwell, NJ

Crammer, Scott B
Northern Burlington
Regional HS
Columbus, NJ

Crane, Brian E
Admiral Farragut
Colts Neck, NJ

Crawford, Lisa
Tahoe
Dwight Morrow HS
Englewood, NJ

Cray, Ann Marie
Rutherford HS
Rutherford, NJ

Creegan, Michael
Don Bosco Prep
N Haledon, NJ

Cresti, Anthony
North Brunswick
Township HS
N Brunswick, NJ

Crisci, Dana
Ocean Township HS
Ocean, NJ

Croce, Stephen L
Ewing HS
Trenton, NJ

Cromonic, Debra D
Phillipsburg HS
Phillipsburg, NJ

Cronenwett, Donna
Hightstown HS
E Windsor, NJ

Croom, Lisa
Frank M Morrell
Irvington, NJ

Cross, Annemarie
Queen Of Peace HS
Kearny, NJ

Crossland, Bonnie
Atlantic City HS
Ventnor, NJ

Crotty, John
Christian Brothers
Spring Lake, NJ

Crouch, Kathleen
Jackson Memorial
Jackson, NJ

Crump, Cecil
Lawrence
The Vail-Deane
School HS
Newark, NJ

Cruz, Magdala C
St Joseph Of The
Palisades HS
West New York, NJ

Cruz, Sonia
Oakcrest HS
Elwood, NJ

Cruz, Suzy
Memorial HS
W New York, NJ

Csastellitto, Caroline
Immaculate
Conception HS
N Bergen, NJ

Cudnik, Denise
Hamilton High West
Yardville, NJ

Cummings, April
Anita
Garden State Acad
Massapequa, NY

Cummings, Pamela
Holy Family Acad
Bayonne, NJ

Cummings, Scott
Bayonne HS
Bayonne, NJ

Cummins, Maureen
Bishop George HS
Plainfield, NJ

Cummiskey, Peggy
Mother Seton
Regional HS
Clark, NJ

Cunniff, Keith
Nutley HS
Nutley, NJ

Cunningham, Allison
Paul VI HS
Pine Hill, NJ

Cunningham,
Matthew E
Red Bank Catholic
W Allenhurst, NJ

Cunnius, Colleen
South Hunterdon R
Lambertville, NJ

Cupon, Leanne N
Phillipsburg HS
Alpha, NJ

Curotto, James
Sayreville War
Memorial HS
Sayreville, NJ

Currie, Walter
Toms River H S
Toms River, NJ

Curry, Dawn
West Essex Regional
N Caldwell, NJ

Curtis, Glenn
Deptfort Township
Deptford, NJ

Curtsinger, Eva
Rancocas Valley Reg
Mt Holly, NJ

Cyrlin, Lance
Somerville HS
Somerville, NJ

Czebieniak, Daniel J
Spotswood HS
Millton, NJ

Czerepak, Jr Jan F
St Joseph Regional
Elmwood Park, NJ

D Amato, Joelle
Southern Regional
Barnegat, NJ

D Amico, John F
Montgomery HS
Belle Mead, NJ

D Apolito, Paul
Christian Brothers
Little Silver, NJ

D Uva, Gennaro
North Arlington HS
N Arlington, NJ

Dagbusan, Honey
Darlene C
Piscataway HS
Piscataway, NJ

Daggett, Aaron
Marc
Middletown HS
Red Bank, NJ

Dagostino, Leonardo
Holy Spirit HS
Atlantic City, NJ

Dallaportas, Patty
Manasquan HS
Belmar, NJ

Danckwerth, Kim
Wayne Valley HS
Wayne, NJ

Daniel, Gregory
Wardlaw-Hartridge
Cranford, NJ

Daniels, Jennifer
Weequahic HS
Newark, NJ

Daniels, Kim
Atlantic City HS
Ventnor, NJ

Darby, Christopher
Teaneck HS
Teaneck, NJ

Darchi, Debbi
Central Regional HS
Bayville, NJ

Darcy, Frank
Brick Town HS
Brick Town, NJ

Daren, Heather
Hamilton HS
Trenton, NJ

Darling, Ronald
Montville Township
Montville, NJ

Daudelin, Donnalee
Belleville HS
Belleville, NJ

Davenport, Jennifer
Hunterdon Central
Flemington, NJ

Davenport, Ted
Mount Olive HS
Flanders, NJ

David, Charmain
Mother Seton
Regional HS
Rahway, NJ

Davidson, Guy A
Pitman HS
Pitman, NJ

Davidson, Shannon
Toms River HS
Toms River, NJ

Davies, Judy
Bayley-Ellard HS
New Providence, NJ

Davis, Colleen
Toms River HS
Toms River, NJ

Davis, Eric
Highland Park HS
Highland Park, NJ

Davis, Glen D
Pennsville Memorial
Pennsville, NJ

Davis, Gregg S
Sayreville War
Memorial HS
Parlin, NJ

Davis, Lesley
Bridgewater Raritan
H S East
Bridgewater, NJ

Davis, Nancy
Malcolm X Shabazz
Newark, NJ

Davis, Paul
Spotswood HS
Milltown, NJ

Dawkins, Richard
Toms River North
Toms River, NJ

Dawson, Kelly
Spotswood HS
Spotswood, NJ

Day, Jr James
Christian Bros Acad
Colts Neck, NJ

De Dolce, Dawn
Marie
St Mary HS
Kearny, NJ

De Filippis, Eileen
Manchester
Regional HS
Haledon, NJ

De Filippis, Maria
Wood-Ridge HS
Wood-Ridge, NJ

De Groot, Allison
Kittatinny Regional
Newton, NJ

De Guardiola, Susan
Ridgewood HS
Ridgewood, NJ

De Hart, Renee
Mother Seton
Regional HS
Irvington, NJ

De La Cruz, Anne
Bishop George Ahr
Edison, NJ

De La Cruz, Michael S
Perth Amboy HS
Perth Amboy, NJ

De Maio, Douglas
West Morris
Mendham HS
Mendham, NJ

De Marco, Edward
Monroe Twp HS
Jamesburg, NJ

De Noia, Daria
Toms River High
School North
Toms River, NJ

De Sane, David
Christian Brothers
Ocean, NJ

De Shong, Brian
Christian Brothers
Middletown, NJ

De Simone, Elizabeth
Northern Valley
Regional HS
Closter, NJ

De Simone, Simone
Lacey Township HS
Forked River, NJ

De Sopo, James A
Passaic Valley
Regional HS
W Paterson, NJ

De Stefano, Chris
Spotswood HS
Spotswood, NJ

De Vincentis, Richard
Toms River North
Toms River, NJ

De Witte, Pamela
Clifton HS
Midland Pk, NJ

Degaetano, Arthur
Don Bosco Prep
Ramsey, NJ

Degan, Missy
Phillipsburg HS
Phillipsburg, NJ

Deignan, Johanna
St Rose HS
Farmingdale, NJ

Dejneka, Matthew
Hunterdon Central
Stockton, NJ

Del Duca, Gary V
Governor Livingston
Regional HS
Berkeley Hts, NJ

Delle, Andrejs M
Arthur L Johnson
Regional HS
Clark, NJ

Demaria, Laura
Holy Family Acad
Bayonne, NJ

Dembowski, Gregory
St Peters HS
Milltown, NJ

Demchak, Danielle Lee
St Marys
Hall-Doane Acad
Florence, NJ

Deming, Susan
Manalapan HS
Manalapan, NJ

Demm, Carolyn
Morris Catholic HS
Morris Plains, NJ

Dempsey, James
Rutgers Preparatory
Milltown, NJ

Denny, Adrienne
East Brunswick HS
E Brunswick, NJ

Depalma, John C
Mt Olive HS
Budd Lake, NJ

Deppenschmidt, Erika
Glassboro HS
Glassboro, NJ

Desmond, Mary Ellen
St John Vianney HS
Manalapan, NJ

Desopo, Carmine
Willingboro HS
Willingboro, NJ

Deutsch, Jill
Delran HS
Delran, NJ

Devlin, Jr James F
Rancocas Valley
Regional HS
Mt Holly, NJ

Dezutti, Kelly
Cherry Hill West
Cherry Hill, NJ

Di Bella, Joseph M
Sayreville War
Memorial HS
Parlin, NJ

Di Bianca, Suzanne
Holy Spirit HS
Margate, NJ

Di Carlo, Francine
Morris Catholic HS
Boonton, NJ

Di Enna, Michele L
Haddonfield
Memorial HS
Haddonfield, NJ

Di Giacomo, Missy
Mainland Regional
Northfield, NJ

Di Giovanna, Sean M
West Windsor/
Plainsboro HS
Princeton Junctn

Di Joseph, Robert
Cumberland
Regional HS
Bridgeton, NJ

Di Legge, Theresa
East Brunswick HS
E Brunswick, NJ

Di Paolo, Jr Joe
Sussex County
Sparta, NJ

Di Pietro, Donette
Holy Spirit HS
Pleasantville, NJ

Dias, David
Livingston HS
Livingston, NJ

Diaz, Victor
Central HS
Newark, NJ

Diaz, William A
Roselle Catholic HS
Union, NJ

Dickerson, Bruce Lawrence
New Brunswick HS
New Brunswick, NJ

Dickerson, Valley M
Orange HS
Orange, NJ

Didgeon, Nadine
Benedictine Acad
Clark, NJ

Diedrichs, Joakin
Cresskill HS
Cresskill, NJ

Dieffenbach, Krista
Morris Catholic HS
Morris Plains, NJ

Diekhaus, Richard
Secaucus HS
Secaucus, NJ

Diertl, Robert
Montville HS
Towaco, NJ

Dieter, Brian
Victory Christian
Williamstown, NJ

Dietrich, Paul E
Ocean City HS
Petersburg, NJ

Dileo, Russell
Palmyra HS
Palmyra, NJ

Diller, Rebekah R
Monmouth Regional
Tinton Falls, NJ

Dillon, Joe
Butler HS
Butler, NJ

Dimeo, Traci
Cumberland
Regional HS
Bridgeton, NJ

Dionisio, Rommel
Morristown-Beard
Parsippany, NJ

Dittmann, Christine
Wood-Ridge HS
Wood-Ridge, NJ

Dittmeier, Kristi
Toms River HS East
Toms River, NJ

Dixon, Sheri
Mary Lawn Of The
Oranges HS
E Orange, NJ

Dobrowolski, Jillian
Toms River HS East
Toms River, NJ

Dobrowolski, Suzanne J
Hopewell Valley
Central HS
Pennington, NJ

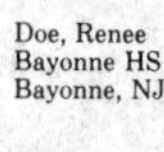
Doe, Renee
Bayonne HS
Bayonne, NJ

Doherty, Sheila
Elizabeth HS
Elizabeth, NJ

Doherty, Teresa
Williamstown HS
Williamstown, NJ

Doktorski, Joe
Steinert HS
Hamilton Sq, NJ

Dolan, Suzanne K
Villa Walsh Acad
Bernardsville, NJ

Dollberg, Dave
West Essex SR HS
Fairfield, NJ

Dollinger, Betsy L
Newark Acad
Randolph, NJ

Dombeck, Michelle
Brurian HS
Hillside, NJ

Donahue, Stephanie
St John Vianney HS
Colts Neck, NJ

Donar, Pamela
Roselle Catholic HS
Roselle, NJ

Doner, Lenore
Hackettstown HS
Hackettstown, NJ

Donnelly, John T
Atlantic Christian
Ventor, NJ

Donnelly, Patrick
Notre Dame HS
Princeton, NJ

Donohoe, Heidi
Ridge HS
Basking Ridge, NJ

Donovan, Lori
Piscataway HS
Piscataway, NJ

Doorly, Sean J
Seton Hall
Preparatory Schl
Caldwell, NJ

Dorofee, Cheryl
Highland Regional
Sicklerville, NJ

Dorschler, Richard
C
Hackettstown HS
Hackettstown, NJ

Doscher, Mark E
Don Bosco Prep
Waldwick, NJ

Dossena, Colleen
Hackettstown HS
Great Meadows, NJ

Doyle, Kathleen
Sayreville War
Memorial HS
Parlin, NJ

Doyle, Theresa
Mount Saint Mary
Scotch Plains, NJ

Draddy, Nina
Lacey Twp HS
Forked River, NJ

Drain, Nancy
Washington
Township HS
Turnersville, NJ

Draina, Bonnie
S Hunterdon Reg
Lambertville, NJ

Drangula, Drew
Holy Cross HS
Roebling, NJ

Drapkin, Paola T
Ocean Township HS
Ocean, NJ

Dravis, Stephen
Roselle Catholic HS
Roselle, NJ

Drayton, Lisa
Red Bank Catholic
Tinton Falls, NJ

Dreiss, Steven
Secaucus HS
Secaucus, NJ

Drexler, Jr Harry J
Lacey Tgownship
Forked River, NJ

Driscoll, Cheryl
Pinelands Regional
Pakertown, NJ

Driscoll, Tim
Mt Olive HS
Budd Lake, NJ

Driver, Audrey M
Hopewell Vly
Central HS
Pennington, NJ

Drosos, Eva
Dover HS
Dover, NJ

Drosos, Helen
Dover HS
Dover, NJ

Drzik, E Kevin
Cinnaminson HS
Cinnaminson, NJ

Du Bois, Jeffrey T
Cumberland
Christian Schl
Estell Manor, NJ

Du Bois, Lisa
Maranatha Christian
Acad HS
Freehold, NJ

Dubroski, Alison M
Union Catholic
Regional HS
Roselle, NJ

Duespohl, Kristen
Overbrook Regional
SR HS
Pine Hill, NJ

Duffus, Kevin
St Joseph Regional
Northvale, NJ

Dukiet, Linda
John P Stevens HS
Edison, NJ

Dulog, Max
St Pius X HS
Edison, NJ

Dunich, Jennifer
South River HS
S River, NJ

Dunkiel, Brian
Pascack Valley
Regional HS
Rivervale, NJ

Dunn, Wayne
High Point Regional
Sussex, NJ

Dupree, Jr Frank L
Middletown HS
Middletown, NJ

Durham, Jr Eddie L
John F Kennedy HS
Willingboro, NJ

Durkac, David
Neptune SR HS
Neptune, NJ

Durkin, Deidre
North Arlington HS
N Arlington, NJ

Dusheck, Brian
Toms River High
School East
Toms River, NJ

Dutkiewicz, Stephen
St Peters Prep Schl
Jersey City, NJ

Duve, Mark F
Warren Hill
Regional SR HS
Washington, NJ

Dygos, Richard
West Milford HS
West Milford, NJ

Dziezawiec, Joy
Mary Help Of
Christians Acad
Paterson, NJ

Ealer, James G
Hunterdon Central
Whitehouse Statn,
NJ

Eastmond, Patti
St John Vianney HS
Union Beach, NJ

Eccleston, Mary
Ellen
Our Lady Of Mercy
Cherry Hill, NJ

Echo, Jennie
Brick Memorial HS
Brick Town, NJ

Eckert, Kevin
Brick Twp HS
Brick, NJ

Edmond, Bobbi
Holy Spirit HS
Pleasantville, NJ

Edwards, Jr James
Bridgewater-Raritan
HS East
Bridgewater, NJ

Edwards, Laura
Paramus HS
Paramus, NJ

Effenberger, Kristin
West Essex HS
Roseland, NJ

Eger, Deana
Mainland Regional
Somers Pt, NJ

Egger, Amy S
West Essex SR HS
Roseland, NJ

Ehrhardt, Julia
Mother Seton
Redgional HS
Springfield, NJ

Ehrola, Alix
Pt Pleasant Boro
Pt Pleasant Boro,
NJ

Eichler, Maria
Paramus Catholic
Cliffside Pk, NJ

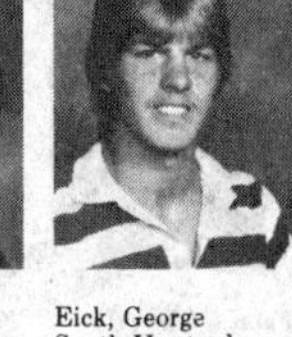
Eick, George
South Hunterdon
Regional HS
Lambertville, NJ

Ekberg, Lisa
Blair Acad
Danville, PA

El-Kharboutly,
Tarek
Toms River HS
Toms River, NJ

Elashewich,
Jeannine
Hunterdon Central
Edinburg, VA

Ellerbee, Angelique
Pleasantville HS
Pleasantville, NJ

Ellerbusch, Gary
Roselle Park HS
Roselle Park, NJ

Elliott, Kathy
Jackson Memorial
Jackson, NJ

Ellis, Cheryl
Pleasantville HS
Pleasantville, NJ

Ellis, Thomas B
Immaculata HS
Martinsville, NJ

Ellison, Kimberly
Sherly
Hillside HS
Hillside, NJ

Elmo, Charles
Lodi HS
Lodi, NJ

Embley, Greg
Hamilton High West
Trenton, NJ

Emenecker, Gary
Maple Shade HS
Maple Shade, NJ

Emiliani, Nancy
East Brunswick HS
E Brunswick, NJ

Emmer, Robert A
Lacey Township HS
Forked River, NJ

Engelbert, Keith P
Collingswood HS
Collingswood, NJ

England, Kimberley
Delaware Valley
Regional HS
Asbury, NJ

Englehart, Brian
Hackettstown HS
Hackettstown, NJ

Engstrom, Kristin
Mercer Christian
Hightstown, NJ

Enright, Jackie
Red Bank Catholic
Middletown, NJ

Entwistle, Suzanne
Clifton HS
Clifton, NJ

Ephrat, Dina
Cliffside Park HS
Cliffside Pk, NJ

Epps, Denise
Malcolm X Shabazz
Newark, NJ

Epps, Sharice
Orange HS
Orange, NJ

Epstein, Craig
Fair Lawn HS
Fair Lawn, NJ

Ercolino, Gino
Shore Regional HS
W Long Branch, NJ

Ericksen, Sharon
Bridgewater Raritan
HS East
Pluckemin, NJ

Escurra, Monica
Paterson Catholic
Regional HS
Paterson, NJ

Eskilson, Patricia
Washington Twp
Turnersville, NJ

Esmurdoc, Carolina
Frances
Oak Knoll Schl
Elizabeth, NJ

Espinosa, Rosario
Millburn SR HS
Short Hills, NJ

Espiritu, Alexander
Bayonne HS
Bayonne, NJ

Esposito, Mike
Parsippany HS
Lk Hiawatha, NJ

Esposito, Tamara
Louise
Hackettstown HS
Hackettstown, NJ

Estelle, Eddie
Lakewood HS
Lakewood, NJ

Evans, John M
Cherokee HS
Marlton, NJ

Evans, Kim
Holy Cross HS
Burlington, NJ

Evans, Laura
Holy Cross HS
Florence, NJ

Faccone, John
Bishop George Ahr
Scotch Plains, NJ

Faggello, John
St Jposephs
Regional HS
Teaneck, NJ

Faggello, Lisa
Teaneck HS
Teaneck, NJ

Fahey, Sean
Point Pleasant Boro
Point Pleasant, NJ

Fahy, Scott J
Don Bosoo Prep
Ridgewood, NJ

Fairbanks, III
Marshall L
Manchester Twp HS
Lakehurst, NJ

Fajardo, Jose
Saint Peters Prep
Jersey City, NJ

Falco, Noel
Elizabeth-Jane
Collingswood SR HS
Oaklyn, NJ

Falconer, Samantha
Clifford J Scott HS
E Orange, NJ

Fallahee, Kevin
Christian Brothers
Middletown, NJ

Fallan, Kristen
Bishop George Ahr
Perth Amboy, NJ

Fallon, Kerrie
Phillipsburg HS
Phillipsburg, NJ

Fallon, Kevin
Christian Brothers
Ocean Twnshp, NJ

Fals, Jaime
Hudson Catholic HS
Union City, NJ

Farina, Terri L
Phillipsburg HS
Phillipsburg, NJ

Farley, Christopher
Bishop AHR HS
Iselin, NJ

Farren, Mary
St Rose HS
Spring Lake, NJ

Farruggio, Jami
Lowy
Ocean Township HS
Wanamassa, NJ

Fata, Jane
Bayley Ellard
Regional HS
E Hanover, NJ

Fatum, Judi
Pemberton Twp HS
Browns Mills, NJ

Faubert, Jeff
Phillipsburg HS
Phillipsburg, NJ

Fausey, Laura
Middle Township
Cape May C H, NJ

Fears, Christopher
Scotch
Plains-Fanwood HS
Scotch Plains, NJ

Febres, Gloria I
Morris Knolls HS
Denville, NJ

Fehn, Kristina
Morristown HS
Morristown, NJ

Feith, Karen
Howell HS
Howell, NJ

Felcone, Thomas
Ewing HS
Trenton, NJ

Feldman, David
Martin
Bridgewater-Raritan
H S West
Bridgewater, NJ

Fell, Paul
Newton HS
Newton, NJ

Fenster, Mitchell
Bridgewater-Raritan
H S East
Martinsville, NJ

Fergus, Troy E
University HS
Newark, NJ

Fernandez, Eleanor
Glassboro HS
Glassboro, NJ

Fernandez, Jr
Lorenzo
Sayreville War
Memorial HS
Parlin, NJ

Fernandez, Rosa
St Aloysius HS
Jersey City, NJ

Fernandez, Roscel
Woodbridge HS
Pt Reading, NJ

Ferrante, Louis
Hackensack HS
Hackensack, NJ

Ferrara, Cathy-Jo
Kearny HS
Kearny, NJ

Ferrari, Terri
Cresskill HS
Cresskill, NJ

Ferraro, Catherine
Union HS
Union, NJ

Ferraro, Richard A
Manalapan HS
Englishtown, NJ

Ferreira, Dina
Wayne Hills HS
Wayne, NJ

Fesenko, John
Hamilton HS West
Trenton, NJ

Fettner, Holly
Spotswood HS
Spotswood, NJ

Fezzuoglio, Toni
Cherry Hill HS
Cherry Hill, NJ

Fiedler, Tracy
Atlantic City HS
Margate, NJ

Figueroa, Bill
Piscataway HS
Piscataway, NJ

Filipow, Nancy
Chatham HS
Chatham, NJ

Finch, II Lester G
Hamilton West HS
Trenton, NJ

Fincken, Heidi
Kittatinny HS
Newton, NJ

Findley, Barry
Lenape Valley
Regional HS
Stanhope, NJ

Finegan, Wendy
Hopewell Valley
Central HS
Pennington, NJ

Fink, Carolyn
Westfield SR HS
Westfield, NJ

Finkelstein, Jeff
Montville HS
Montville, NJ

Finkelstein, Mark
Highstown HS
E Windsor, NJ

Finlay, Shannon
Brick Township HS
Brick Town, NJ

Fischer, Christine
Passaic Valley HS
Little Falls, NJ

Fittipaldi, Susan
Franklin HS
Somerset, NJ

Fitzgerald, Colleen
Oak Knoll HS
Short Hills, NJ

Fitzhenry, Daniel
St Peters Prep
Bayonne, NJ

Fitzpatrick, Daniel
De Paul Diocesan
Wayne, NJ

Fitzsimmons, Carole
Ann
Mahwah HS
Mahwah, NJ

Flaherty,
Dianna-Jean
Palisades Park JR
SR HS
Palisades Pk, NJ

Fleckenstein, Donna
Woodstown HS
Woodstown, NJ

Fletcher, Jackie
Dover HS
Dover, NJ

Fletcher, Janice
East Brunswick HS
E Brunswick, NJ

Florento, Veroni C
St Mary HS
Jersey City, NJ

Flores, Bill
South Hunterdon
Regional HS
Lambertville, NJ

Flores, Jr Lamberto
O
Union Catholic Reg
Elizabeth, NJ

Flowers, Christina
Kingsway Regional
Mickleton, NJ

Floyd, Debbie
Clearview Regional
Sewell, NJ

Flynn, Kimberly
Hackettstown HS
Hackettstown, NJ

Fogarty, Lori
Monsignor Donovan
Howell, NJ

Folio, Kim
St John Vianney HS
Colts Neck, NJ

Foltz, Lisa
Southern Regional
Manahawkin, NJ

Fong, Clinton
Parsippany HS
Parsippany, NJ

Ford, Carolyn
Kearny HS
Kearny, NJ

Ford, Darlene
Westfield HS
Westfield, NJ

Ford, Jerod
Newton HS
Newton, NJ

Fortis, Stephen F
Absegami HS
Egg Harbor City, NJ

Fortna, Carl
Elizabeth HS
Elizabeth, NJ

Fortunato, John E
Christian Brothers
Freehold, NJ

Foster, Helen L
Lenape Valley
Regional HS
Andover, NJ

Fowler, Stephen
Bayonne HS
Bayonne, NJ

Fox, Heather
Wall HS
Manasquan Park,
NJ

Fox, Heather Anne
Northern Valley
Regional HS
Haworth, NJ

Foxson, Jennifer
Wallkill Valley
Regional HS
Hamburg, NJ

Foy, Jason
Dwight Morrow HS
Englewood, NJ

Fralinger, Nancy
Cumberland
Regional HS
Bridgeton, NJ

Frank, Raymond
Northern Valley Reg
Old Tappan, NJ

Frankel, Mollissa
Montville HS
Pine Brook, NJ

Franklin, Bryon
Anthony
Plainfield HS
Plainfield, NJ

Franklin, Melissa
Belvidere HS
Belvidere, NJ

Franklin, Stacia
Parsippany HS
Parsippany, NJ

Franks, Ralph
Robert
Highland Regional
Blackwood, NJ

Frasier, Marva
Victoria
Dwight Morrow HS
Englewood, NJ

Freda, Anthony
Newton HS
Newton, NJ

Freed, Laurence T
Highland Park HS
Highland Park, NJ

Fretz, Bonnie
Pennsville Memorial
Pennsville, NJ

Fretz, Pam
Lower Cape May
Regional HS
N Cape May, NJ

Freund, Howard
Union HS
Union, NJ

Fricke, Lisa
Hunterdon Central
Flemington, NJ

Fricks, Melinda
Toms River North
Toms River, NJ

Frie, Jr Paul
Delsea Regional HS
Monroeville, NJ

Friedrich, Stephen Charles
Sparta HS
Sparta, NJ

Fromkin, Russell
East Brunswick HS
E Brunswick, NJ

Fry, Jennifer
Buena Regional HS
Newfield, NJ

Fry, Richard
Pitman HS
Pitman, NJ

Fryar, Virginia
Mother Seton Regional HS
Newark, NJ

Fuchs, Robyn
Hillsborough HS
Somerville, NJ

Fugazzi, Michelle
N Hunterdon HS
Flemington, NJ

Fuhrer, Cynthia
Clearview Regional
Mantua, NJ

Fulda, Karen L
Bulleville HS
Belleville, NJ

Fuller, Chris
Scotch Plains Fanwood HS
Scotch Plains, NJ

Fuller, Marc R
Scotch Plains-Fanwood HS
Scotch Plains, NJ

Fulton, III Bernard B
Atlantic Friends
Atlantic City, NJ

Funk, Karen
Hamilton High School East
Hamilton Square, NJ

Furgiuele, Catherine
Lenape Valley Regional HS
Andover, NJ

Furmanski, William L
Haddon Hgts HS
Haddon Heights, NJ

Fusco, Laura Lee
Passaic Valley HS
W Paterson, NJ

Fye, Vianna
West Milford HS
Hewitt, NJ

Gade, Carla
James Caldwell HS
Caldwell, NJ

Gadsden, Robert H
Dwight Morrow HS
Englewood, NJ

Gahwyler, Brian
Mahwah HS
Mahwah, NJ

Gaibor, Harry
St Peters Prep
Jersey City, NJ

Gaines, Jennifer
Lakewood HS
Lakewood, NJ

Galaida, Robert
Bishop George Ahr
Perth Amboy, NJ

Galatro, Bryan
Glen Rock JR SR
Glen Rock, NJ

Galbraith, Aimee
Palmyra HS
Beverly, NJ

Gallagher, Keith
St John Vianney HS
Manalapan, NJ

Gallagher, Kelly
Toms River HS
Toms River, NJ

Gallagher, Kendra Elaine
Middletown South
Lincroft, NJ

Gallagher, Michele
Holy Spirit HS
Linwood, NJ

Gallagher, Nancy
Manalapan HS
Englishtown, NJ

Gallagher, Patrick W
Haddon Township
Westmont, NJ

Gallenagh, Elizabeth
Waldwick HS
Waldwick, NJ

Galliker, Jenny
Palisades Park JR/SR HS
Palisades Park, NJ

Gallo, Sabina
Cliffside Park HS
Cliffside Pk, NJ

Gambhir, Manisha
Westmilford HS
West Milford, NJ

Gandy, Michelle
Bridgeton HS
Newport, NJ

Gangadharan, Sidhu P
Parisippany Hills
Parsippany, NJ

Gara, Stephen
Newark Acad
Morristown, NJ

Garay, Carolyn
Red Bank Catholic
Middletown, NJ

Garbis, Christine
Montville Township
Montville, NJ

Garcia, Delilah
Red Bank Catholic
Oakhurst, NJ

Garcia, Joel
Memorial HS
W New York, NJ

Garcia, Marisol
Queen Of Peace HS
Newark, NJ

Garcia, Raul
Saint Josephs HS
Old Bridge, NJ

Gardner, Jeffrey
Piscataway HS
Piscataway, NJ

Gardner, Lynn Ann
Dover HS
Mine Hill, NJ

Garmont, Glenn
Seton Hall Prep
Newark, NJ

Garner, Reina
Freehold Township
Freehold, NJ

Garoppo, Valerie
Delsea Regional HS
Newfield, NJ

Garrick, Geralynn D
David Brearley Regional HS
Kenilworth, NJ

Garrison, Renetta
Plainfield HS
Plainfield, NJ

Garry, Michelle
Roselle Catholic HS
Elizabeth, NJ

Garzon, Ernesto
Morris Hills HS
Rockaway, NJ

Gasperini, Lisa
Shore Regional HS
West Long Branch, NJ

Gaston, Jerri
East Orange HS
East Orange, NJ

Gaudioso, Peter A
West Milford Twp
West Milford, NJ

Gaughan, Sean A
Northern Burlington County Regional
Allentown, NJ

Gavazzi, Melinda
Bridgewater-Raritan H S West
Bridgewater, NJ

Gavin, Stephen
North Bergen HS
North Bergen, NJ

Gazell, Dawn
Brick Township HS
Brick, NJ

Gebell, Thomas
Passaic Valley HS
Little Falls, NJ

Gedrys, Kris
Red Bank Catholic
Red Bank, NJ

Gehm, Heather
West Essex Regional
Fairfield, NJ

Geiger, Steve
Mt Olive HS
Flanders, NJ

Geissler, Wayne
St John Vianney HS
Hazlet, NJ

Gelin, Abdullahat
Don Bosco Prep
Garfield, NJ

Gelormini, Carol
James Caldwell HS
W Caldwell, NJ

Gemski, Peter F
West Milford HS
West Milford, NJ

Genoble, Leona
Montville HS
Montville, NJ

Genoese, Jodi
Madison HS
Madison, NJ

Genthe, David
Spotswood HS
Spotswood, NJ

Genthe, Thomas
Sportsood HS
Spotswood, NJ

Gentile, Andrew
Washington
Township HS
Turnersville, NJ

Gentile, Kristin
Millville SR HS
Millville, NJ

Genus, Michael
Holy Cross HS
Burlington, NJ

Genzale, Thomas
Pope John XXIII
Oak Ridge, NJ

George, Robert
Steinert HS
Hamilton Sq, NJ

George, Stephanie
Ambassador
Christian Acad
Turnersville, NJ

Geraldo, Maria
Emerson HS
Union City, NJ

Gerckens, John
Northern Valley
Regional HS
Old Tappan, NJ

Gerhauser, Jude E
Toms River High
School South
Beachwood, NJ

Gerkens, Francis
Vernon Township
Highland Lks, NJ

Geronimo, Vito
St Joseph Regional
Congers, NY

Geyer, Howard L
The Frisch Schl
West Orange, NJ

Ghumman,
Kulwinder
Mother Seton
Regional HS
Carteret, NJ

Gialanella, Frank
Livingston HS
Livingston, NJ

Giampetro, Andrew
Eastern HS
Voorhees, NJ

Giangiordano,
Richard
Shawnee HS
Medford, NJ

Giannantonio, Joe
Palisades Park HS
Palisades Pk, NJ

Gibbs, Jr Rudolph P
Rahway HS
Rahway, NJ

Gibson, Elizabeth
Anne
Bayley Ellard
Regional HS
Milton, NJ

Gibson, Stacey
Salem HS
Salem, NJ

Giddens, Gail
Metuchen HS
Metuchen, NJ

Giercyk, Christine F
Parsippany HS
Lake Hiawatha, NJ

Gilbert, Eileen
Montclair HS
Bloomfield, NJ

Gilbert, Evelyn
Red Bank Catholic
Tinton Falls, NJ

Gilbert, Timothy C
Middletown HS
Lincroft, NJ

Gill, Nishat
North Brunswick
Township HS
N Brunswick, NJ

Gillespie, Christian
River Dell HS
River Edge, NJ

Gimon, Patricia
Clifton HS
Clifton, NJ

Ginsberg, Susan
Piscataway HS
Piscataway, NJ

Girardi, Ellen
Buena Regional HS
Landisville, NJ

Giuliano, Concetta
Vineland SR HS
Vineland, NJ

Giuliano, Jill
Middlesex HS
Middlesex, NJ

Glass, Adam
Middletown South
Middletown, NJ

Glass, Colleena
Central Regional HS
Bayville, NJ

Gleman, Meg
Toms River HS
Beachwood, NJ

Glemser, Michelle
Central Jersey
Christian Schl
Asbury Park, NJ

Glencamp, Jr
Timothy
Plainfield HS
Plainfield, NJ

Glenn, Chrissy
Point Pleasant
Borough HS
Point Pleasant, NJ

Glenn, Tokar
Elizabeth
Southern Regional
Beach Haven, NJ

Gleyzer, Janette
New Milford HS
New Milford, NJ

Glover, Jimmy
Metuchen HS
Metuchen, NJ

Glover, Troy
East Orange HS
Irvington, NJ

Glowienka, Cynthia
Ocean City HS
Ocean City, NJ

Glueck, Richrd A
West Milford
Township HS
W Milford, NJ

Godown, Jr Arthur
R
South Hunterdon
Regional HS
Lambertville, NJ

Godown, Charles
South Hunterdon
Regional HS
Lambertville, NJ

Goerke, Christine
Union Catholic
Regional HS
Hillside, NJ

Goff, Jr Michael J
Woodstown HS
Alloway, NJ

Gold, Jennifer Anne
Hunterdon Central
Flemington, NJ

Gold, John E
Cherry Hill H S
Cherry Hill, NJ

Golday, David
Christopher
Ocean City HS
Ocean City, NJ

Goldberg, Scott M
James Calswell HS
W Caldwell, NJ

Goldelman, Alex
Jonathan Dayton
Regional HS
Springfield, NJ

Golden, Jr Alfred
James
Red Bank Catholic
Colts Neck, NJ

Golden, Rich
Delsea Regional HS
Glassboro, NJ

Goldman, Michele
Hanover Park HS
East Hanover, NJ

Goldman, Steven
Fairlawn HS
Fair Lawn, NJ

Golhar, Atul
Hillsborough HS
Bellemead, NJ

Golliday, Danielle
Bridgewater-Raritan
East HS
Bridgewater, NJ

Golubieski, Karen
Marie
Oak Knoll HS
Murray Hill, NJ

PHOTO
NOT
AVAILABLE

Gomez, Gabriela
Secaucus HS
Secaucus, NJ

Gomez, Stephen
St Peters Prep
Bayonne, NJ

Gomory, Pamela
Abraham Clark HS
Roselle, NJ

Goncalves, Deborah
Ann
Jackson Memorial
Morganville, NJ

Gonzalez, Celeste
Buena Regional HS
Collings Lks, NJ

Gonzalez, Herminia
Bayonne HS
Bayonne, NJ

Gonzalez, Kenneth
Perth Amboy HS
Perth Amboy, NJ

Gonzalez, Maria
Teresa
Columbia HS
Maplewood, NJ

Gonzalez, Miguel
Ramapo HS
Franklin Lakes, NJ

Goode, Nicole
Clifford J Scott HS
E Orange, NJ

Goodman, India
Hackensack HS
Hackensack, NJ

Goodridge, Philip
Washington
Township HS
Turnersville, NJ

Goodwyn, James
Clifford J Scott HS
Newark, NJ

Gordon, Lovell
Hackettstown HS
Hackettstown, NJ

Gordon, Susan
Phillipsburg HS
Phillipsburg, NJ

Gordy, Kathleen
Atlantic City HS
Atlantic City, NJ

Gorman, Tamela
Hunterdon Central
Flemington, NJ

Gormley, Sue Ann
Scotch Plains
Fanwood HS
Scotch Plains, NJ

Graessle, Cynthia
Toms River H S
Toms River, NJ

Graham, Dori Laine
N Burlington Co
Reg HS
Allentown, NJ

Granda, Angela
Manalapan HS
Englishtown, NJ

Grandberry, Cindy
Hillside HS
Hillside, NJ

Grandilli, Cristina
St John Vianney HS
Marlboro, NJ

Granelli, Kevin R
St Peters Prep
Kearny, NJ

Grant, Danny
Montville HS
Towaco, NJ

Grant, Tony
Edgewood Regional
SR HS
Sicklerville, NJ

Grasmick, III Louis
F
Haddon Township
Westmont, NJ

Graumann, Christel
M
Kittatinny Regional
Newton, NJ

Gravatt, Jill
Kathryn
Bordentown
Regional HS
Bordentown, NJ

Gray, Victoria E
Southern Regional
Manahawkin, NJ

Graybush, Marc
Randolph HS
Randolph, NJ

Graziano, Lisa
Rutherford HS
Rutherford, NJ

Green, Kenneth L
Teaneck HS
Teaneck, NJ

Green, Noah
Middletown HS
Middletown, NJ

Greene, Chantel
Plainfield HS
Plainfield, NJ

Greene, Jennifer
Middletown H S
Middletown, NJ

Greenway, Robert
St Joseph Regional
Monroe, NY

Greenwood, Tracey
Wildwood Catholic
Wildwood Crest, NJ

Greer, Lisa
Pleasantville HS
Pleasantville, NJ

Grieco, Annamaria
Mount Saint
Dominic Acad
Bloomfield, NJ

Griefer, Brian
Wallington HS
Wallington, NJ

Griffith, Patricia
Cumberland
Regional HS
Bridgeton, NJ

Grilk, Andrew H
West Milford HS
West Milford, NJ

Grim, Katherine
Delaware Valley
Regional HS
Milford, NJ

Grimes, Karol
St Cecilia HS
Eanglewood, NJ

Grimes, Tami
Essex Catholic Girls
East Orange, NJ

Griner, Pamela
Cumberland
Regional HS
Bridgeton, NJ

Grissom, Karen
Mt Olive HS
Flanders, NJ

Groder, Jill Ellen
Middletown HS
Middletown, NJ

Groff, Denise Lynn
Cumberland
Regional HS
Bridgeton, NJ

Groff, Jr Richard W
Phillipsburg HS
Phillipsburg, NJ

Gross, Nancy L
Holy Spirit HS
Cologne, NJ

Grossman, Lisa
Hillsborough HS
Belle Mead, NJ

Grove, Scott
South Brunswick
Kendall Pk, NJ

Grunstra, Gregg C
Hackensack HS
Maywood, NJ

Grzybowski, Melissa
Mater Dei HS
Atlantic Highlnds,
NJ

Guage, Joseph
St John Vianney HS
Aberdeen, NJ

Guarino, Carolyn
Elizabeth HS
Westfield, NJ

Guarino, Joy Lynn
Gill/St Bernards HS
Warren, NJ

Gudicello, Lynette
Shore Regional HS
Oceanport, NJ

Guear, Christopher
Hamilton High Schl
Trenton, NJ

Guerra, Jr Nicanor
D
Marist HS
Jersey City, NJ

Guerriero, Suzanne
Toms River East HS
Toms River, NJ

Guidry, Kevin G
Gloucester Catholic
Mantua, NJ

Guiliano, Gerald
Cliffside HS
Fairview, NJ

Gumienny, Jill
John F Kennedy HS
Iselin, NJ

Gunderman,
Christine
Phillipsburg HS
Phillipsburg, NJ

Gupta, Rajeew
Franklin Twp HS
Somerset, NJ

Gurskis, Grace-Anne
J
Toms River East HS
Toms River, NJ

Gurtcheff, Gary
Haddon Twp HS
Westmont, NJ

Gustis, Jennifer
West Milford HS
W Milford, NJ

Gutierrez,
Christopher
St Marys HS
Sayreville, NJ

Gutierrez, Juan J
Roselle Catholic HS
Elizabeth, NJ

Gutierrez, Loreto
Bayonne HS
Bayonne, NJ

Guy, Jr Terry R
Freehold Twp HS
Freehold, NJ

Gwal, Anita
Cherry Hill H S
Cherry Hill, NJ

Gyure, Richard
Dover HS
Mine Hill, NJ

Gyure, Russell
Dover HS
Mine Hill, NJ

Haag, Jeni
Point Pleasant
Beach HS
Lavallette, NJ

Haag, Kristine
Catherine
Westfield SR HS
Westfield, NJ

Haas, Ed
Absegami HS
Cologne, NJ

Hackett, Steven
Holy Spirit HS
Absecon, NJ

Hadley, Rakeim
The Pennington
Newtonville, NJ

Hagan, Joseph
Gloucester City JR
SR HS
Brooklawn, NJ

Hagenbarth,
Michael
Paulsboro HS
Gibbstown, NJ

Hagofsky, Linda
Louise
Jacksmon Memorial
Jackson, NJ

Hague, Kristine M
East Brunswick HS
East Brunswick, NJ

Haines, Carole Lynn
Toms River HS East
Normandy Bch, NJ

Hale, Karen
Parsippany HS
Lake Hiawatha, NJ

Halifko, Jodi
Woodbridge HS
Hopelawn, NJ

Hall, Catherine
Red Bank Catholic
Spring Lake, NJ

Hall, Christine
Union HS
Union, NJ

Hall, Jeffrey
Parsippany HS
Lake Hiawatha, NJ

Hall, Robert S
Ewing HS
Trenton, NJ

Hallman, Brian
Holy Spirit HS
Absecon, NJ

Hallman, Darren L
Wallkill Valley
Regional HS
Budd Lake, NJ

Haluska, Ann-Marie
Rahway HS
Rahway, NJ

Hamilton, Robbie
Mt Olive HS
Budd Lake, NJ

Hammer, Frank
Parsippany HS
Lake Hiawatha, NJ

Hammer, Michael
Parsippany HS
Lk Hiawatha, NJ

Hampton, Kelly
Holy Family Acad
Bayonne, NJ

Hampton, Kesha
Henry Snyder HS
Jersey City, NJ

Hanbicki, Aubrey
Hunterdon Central
Three Bridges, NJ

Hanclich, Cathy
Hawthorne HS
Hawthorne, NJ

Hand, Jennifer
Summit HS
Summit, NJ

Hanes, Robert
Bihsop AHR HS
Carteret, NJ

Hanigan, Bill
Pompton Lakes HS
Pompton Lakes, NJ

Hanke, Craig
Waldwick HS
Waldwick, NJ

Hann, Trudy
South Hunterdon
Regional HS
Lambertville, NJ

Hanna, Frederick A
St Peters Prep
Jersey City, NJ

Hannan, Judith E
Haddonfield
Memorial HS
Haddonfield, NJ

Hannon, Madeline
Union Catholic
Regional HS
Cranford, NJ

Hanvey, Forrest R
Northern
Highlands Reg HS
Upper Saddle Rv,
NJ

Haran, Sean T
Christian Brothers
Middletown, NJ

Hardenburg, Alan W
Jefferson Township
Wharton, NJ

Hardman, Kim
Colonia SR HS
Colonia, NJ

Hardy, Cathy
Bridgeton Public HS
Bridgeton, NJ

Hargrove, Tamica
Frank H Morrell HS
Vailsburg, NJ

Harker, Cynthia
Northern Burlington
Columbus, NJ

Harnett, John F
Sussex Vo-Tech
Blairstown, NJ

Harper, Cynthia
Cumberland
Regional HS
Seabrook, NJ

Harper, Kristin
Chatham Twp HS
Chatham Twp, NJ

Harrell, Tammie
John F Kennedy HS
Paterson, NJ

Harris, Costas
Dover HS
Dover, NJ

Harris, Dawn E
Paulsboro HS
Gibbstown, NJ

Harris, Kelly
Pemberton Twp HS
II HS
Pemberton, NJ

Harris, Koret Ann
Garden State Acad
Amityville, NY

Harris, Monica L
John F Kennedy HS
Willingboro, NJ

Harrison, Dean
Atlantic City HS
Margate, NJ

Hartley, Scott R
Bordentown
Regional HS
Bordentown, NJ

Hartsuiker,
Elizabeth
Clifton HS
Clifton, NJ

Hartz, Chris
Washington Twp
Turnersville, NJ

Harvey, Alyssa
Jackson Memorial
Jackson, NJ

Harvey, Robert T
Vineland HS
Vineland, NJ

Hassler, Brian
Christian Brothers
Jackson, NJ

Hastings, Jon
Williamstown HS
Williamstown, NJ

Hatcher, Suzanne
Over Brook Reg SR
Berlin, NJ

Hawkins, Sabrina B
Highland Park HS
Highland Park, NJ

Hayes, Cynthia
Atlantic City HS
Atlantic City, NJ

Hayes, Tracy Lyn
Overbrook Regional
SR HS
Clementon, NJ

Haynor, Kelly
Christine
Haddonfield Mem
Haddonfield, NJ

Haze, Jonathan
Randolph HS
Randolph, NJ

Hazen, Timothy J
West Milford
Township HS
West Milford, NJ

Healey, Mark A
West Morris Central
Long Valley, NJ

Healy, Leigh Ann
Westfield HS
Westfield, NJ

Heaney, Nicole
Manchester HS
North Haledon, NJ

Hedgeman, Crispus
FM
Arthur P Schalick
Bridgeton, NJ

Hedin, Debbie
Middletown HS
Lincroft, NJ

Heffernan, Rachel
Holy Cross HS
Moorestown, NJ

Heflich, Laurie
Wood-Ridge HS
Wood-Ridge, NJ

Hegg, Eric L
Morristown HS
Morristown, NJ

Heilweil, Sharon
West Essex HS
Fairfield, NJ

Hein, Chip
Newe Milford HS
New Milford, NJ

Hein, Tiffany
Hightstown HS
Colorado Springs, CO

Heintz, Matthew
Middlesex HS
Middlesex, NJ

Heinze, Margaret
Bridgewater-Raritan HS West
Bridgewater, NJ

Helwig, Donna
Lower Cape May Regional HS
N Cape May, NJ

Hendrickson, Beth
Manasquan HS
Spg Lk Hts, NJ

Hendrickson, L Andrew
Christian Brothers
Freehold, NJ

Hengeli, Lauri
Hunterdon Central
Whitehouse Statio, NJ

Henne, Michele
Montville Twsp HS
Montville, NJ

Henry, Jennifer
Neptune SR HS
Neptune City, NJ

Henry, Lisa A
Hamilton High East
Hamilton Sq, NJ

Henson, Chavella
North Brunswick Township HS
N Brunswick, NJ

Herbert, Amy
North Brunswick
N Brunswick, NJ

Hernandez, Jr David
Orange HS
Orange, NJ

Hernandez, Maria
Good Counsel HS
Newark, NJ

Herr, Liz
Saint John Vianney
Holmdel, NJ

Herring, David
Spotswood HS
Spotswood, NJ

Hess, James
Maple Shade HS
Maple Shade, NJ

Heyman, Russell
Parsippany Hills HS
Morris Plains, NJ

Heyward, Timothy
Central HS
Newark, NJ

Hicks, Michael
Pleasantville HS
Pleasantville, NJ

Hicks, Stephanie C
East Orange HS
East Orange, NJ

Higgs, Marcia
Wildwood HS
Wildwood, NJ

Hill, Charles A
West Essex SR HS
Roseland, NJ

Hill, Rebekah
Bishop George Ahr
Piscataway, NJ

Hill, Vincent
Frank H Morrell HS
Irvington, NJ

Hilla, Brian
Manasquan HS
Brielle, NJ

Hinze, Peter C
Boonton HS
Lincoln Park, NJ

Hipko, Tracy
Spotswood HS
Milltown, NJ

Hirshkind, Kiera
Academy Of St
Morris Plains, NJ

Hitch, Marcius
Pleasantville HS
Sicklerville, NJ

Hitchner, Gretchen
Woodstown HS
Alloway, NJ

Hittner, Leigh
Livingston HS
Livingston, NJ

Hjul, Elizabeth
Toms River HS
Norway

Hoden, Lisa
Pinelands Regional
Manahawkin, NJ

Hoffman, Debbie
Hamilton HS East
Trenton, NJ

Hoffman, Steve
Highstown HS
East Windsor, NJ

Hoffman, William
Point Pleasant Boro
Point Pleasant, NJ

Hofsess, Scott
Waldwick HS
Waldwick, NJ

Hogan, Richard
Neptune HS
Neptune, NJ

Holcombe, Jr George
Absegami HS
Absecon, NJ

Holden, Stephanie
Middletown HS
Middletown, NJ

Hollister, Bridget
Vineland HS
Vineland, NJ

Holloway, Derrick
Hillside HS
Hillside, NJ

Holloway, Rodrick
Roselle Catholic HS
Roselle, NJ

Holmes, Gina
Holy Spirit HS
Atlantic City, NJ

Holmes, Patricia
Lenape Valley Regional HS
Netcong, NJ

Holmes, Sue
Delsea Regional HS
Newfield, NJ

Holobowski, William F
H G Hoffman HS
S Amboy, NJ

Holowachuk, Stacie
Wayne Hills HS
Wayne, NJ

Holtje, Scott
Hudson Catholic Regional HS
Secaucus, NJ

Honohan, Matthew J
Paramus HS
Bayville, NJ

Hooks, Kiesha
Marylawn Of The Oranges HS
E Orange, NJ

Hoolko, Cheryl
Livingston HS
Livingston, NJ

Hooper, Sandra
University HS
Newark, NJ

Hoover, Lynn Christine
South River HS
South River, NJ

Hoover, Soritta Fay
Penns Grove HS
Carneys Point, NJ

Hopkins, Kevin
Pope John XXIII Regional HS
Sparta, NJ

Hopkins, Michael
Gloucester City HS
Gloucester, NJ

Hopkins, Michele
Arthur P Schalick
Elmer, NJ

Hopler, Tracy
Morris Knolls HS
Rockaway, NJ

Horner, Stephanie
Hightstown HS
Cranbury, NJ

Horowitz, Elana
Manalapan HS
Englishtown, NJ

Horsey, Paul
Oakcrest HS
Mays Landing, NJ

Horton, Lori
Delran HS
Delran, NJ

Horvath, Dawn
Toms River North
Toms River, NJ

Housman, Tammy
Monsignor Donovan
Lakewood, NJ

Howard, Kathleen
Holy Cross HS
Bordentown, NJ

Howard, Laura
Vail-Deane HS
Roselle Park, NJ

Howard, Nancy
Burlington City HS
Edgewater Park, NJ

Howell, Wade C
Kittatinny Regional
Newton, NJ

Howells, Bill
Sayreville Way
Memorial HS
Sayreville, NJ

Howland, Anne
Southern Regional
Barnegat, NJ

Hoyt, Justin
Indian Hills HS
Franklin Lakes, NJ

Hratko, Thomas
Jackson Memorial
Jackson, NJ

Hsu, Lillian
Scotch
Plains-Fanwood HS
Scotch Plains, NJ

Huang, Gene
Parsippany Hills HS
Lake Hiawatha, NJ

Hubbard, Bonnie R
Park Bible Acad
Pennsgrove, NJ

Huebner, Matthew
Southern Regional
Manahawkin, NJ

Huebsch, Julie
Boonton HS
Boonton, NJ

Huegel, Holly
Mary Help Of
Christians Acad
Clifton, NJ

Hugelmeyer,
Donnalee
Bishop Ahr HS
Woodbridge, NJ

Hughes, Brian
Saint John Vianney
Hazlet, NJ

Hughes, David E
Pope John XXIII
Reg HS
Andover, NJ

Hughes, Jeffrey J
Hanover Park HS
Florham Park, NJ

Hughes, Kevin
Middletown HS
Middletown, NJ

Hughes, Tami
Pennsville Memorial
Salem, NJ

Hulitt, Sherri
Bridgeton HS
Bridgeton, NJ

Humes, Lisa
Overbrook HS
Lindenwold, NJ

Humphreys, Michael
Penns Grove HS
Penns Grove, NJ

Hunt, Keith
Rahway SR HS
Rahway, NJ

Hunt, Nancy
Hamilton HS East
Hamilton Sq, NJ

Hunt, Thomas
Hunterdon Central
Readington, NJ

Hunter, Nancy
Hightstown HS
East Windsor, NJ

Hunter, Sharon
Jefferson Township
Oak Ridge, NJ

Hurff, Sandra
Paulsboro HS
Gibbstown, NJ

Hutchcraft, Lisa
Wayne Valley HS
Wayne, NJ

Hutchinson, Jack
Palmyra HS
Palmyra, NJ

Hutchinson, Marie J
Villa Victoria Acad
Trenton, NJ

Hutchison, Heidi
Egg Harbor Twp HS
Mays Landing, NJ

Hutchison, Monica
Bloomfield SR HS
Bloomfield, NJ

Hutton, Holly A
Asbury Park HS
Asbury Park, NJ

Hwang, Amanda
Parsippany HS
Parsippany, NJ

Hyatt, Carolyn
Midland Park HS
Midland Park, NJ

Hyland, Sherry
Mahwah HS
Mahwah, NJ

Hyland, Susan
North Plainfield HS
N Plainfield, NJ

Hymer, Lori
A P Schalick HS
Newfield, NJ

Iannazzone, Al
North Bergen HS
North Bergen, NJ

Iannuzzi, Michele
Holy Cross HS
Delran, NJ

Iglesias, Jose
Kearny HS
Kearny, NJ

Ihasz, Elizabeth
Phillipsburg HS
Alpha, NJ

Ilardi, Vanessa
Mount Saint
Dominic Acad
N Caldwell, NJ

Ilnseher, Michael
Toms River High
School South
Toms River, NJ

Indico, Sandy
Cumberland
Regional HS
Bridgeton, NJ

Ingram, Sandy
Triton Regional HS
Blackwood, NJ

Insabella, Glenda M
Union Catholic
Regional HS
Fanwood, NJ

Inteso, Michael
Toms River HS East
Toms River, NJ

Ippolito, Joann
Bridgewater Raritan
West HS
Bridgewater, NJ

Isaacs, Susan
Hillside HS
Hillside, NJ

Isajiw, Tamara
Kittatinny Regional
Newton, NJ

Isakoff, Steven
Highland Park HS
Highland Park, NJ

Iuliano, Lucia
Garden State Acad
Parrotsville, TN

Ivins, Dulcey
Lakewood HS
Lakewood, NJ

Jachna, Bozena
Parsippany HS
Parsippany, NJ

Jackson, Hillary
West
Windsor-Plainsbor
Princeton Jct, NJ

Jackson, Keith R
Teaneck HS
Teaneck, NJ

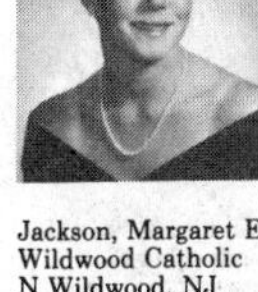

Jackson, Margaret E
Wildwood Catholic
N Wildwood, NJ

Jackson, Tracey
Lynn
Hackensack HS
Hackensack, NJ

Jacobs, Bruce
East Brunswick HS
East Brunswick, NJ

Jacobs, Kelly
Hamilton High Schl
Mercerville, NJ

Jacobs, Michael
Washington
Township HS
Turnersville, NJ

Jacobus, Jacqueline
Belleville HS
Belleville, NJ

Jacoby, Brian
Manalapan HS
Manalapan, NJ

Jacoby, Stacey
Kittatinny Regional
Newton, NJ

Jajal, Sanjay
W L Dickinson HS
Jersey City, NJ

Jakes, Gregory
Woodrow Wilson HS
Camden, NJ

Jakub, James
Red Bank Catholic
Eatontown, NJ

James, Sherwin
Dover HS
Dover, NJ

James, Tyrone
Sacred Heart HS
Clayton, NJ

Janeczek, Susan
East Brunswick HS
E Brunswick, NJ

Janoczkin, Michele
South River HS
S River, NJ

Janz, Stacey Patricia
Perth Amboy HS
Perth Amboy, NJ

Jarratt, Kirra L
The Pingry Schl
Westfield, NJ

Jaruszewski, Joseph J
Notre Dame HS
Hamilton Sq, NJ

Jawny, Tatiana
Oak Knoll Schl
Essex Fells, NJ

Jeffers, W James
Delsea Regional HS
Glassboro, NJ

Jeffries, Paul C
Montville Township
Pine Brook, NJ

Jelinek, Margaret
Freehold Township
Freehold, NJ

Jengehino, Susan
Cumberland Regional HS
Bridgeton, NJ

Jenkins, Denise
Holy Spirit HS
Absecon, NJ

Jenkins, Tina
Cherokee HS
Marlton, NJ

Jennings, David
Queen Of Peace HS
N Arlington, NJ

Jernee, Debra
Neptune SR HS
Neptune City, NJ

Jimenez, Wilfredo
East Side HS
Newark, NJ

Jo, Anna
Burlington City HS
Edgewater Park, NJ

Jobson, Stephanie
Palmyra HS
Palmyra, NJ

Joe, Gwynetta
Benedictine Acad
Newark, NJ

Joelson, Laine
Westfield HS
Westfield, NJ

John, Mary
St Pius X Regional
Edison, NJ

Johnson, Amy D
Asbury Park HS
Asbury Park, NJ

Johnson, Clint
Ridge HS
Basking Ridge, NJ

Johnson, Craig A
Plainfield HS
Plainfield, NJ

Johnson, Cristina
Mary Help Of Christians Acad
Paterson, NJ

Johnson, Erik N
West Windsor-Plainsbor
Princeton Jct, NJ

Johnson, James R
Pennsville Memorial
Pennsville, NJ

Johnson, Jill L
Plainfield HS
Plainfield, NJ

Johnson, Lisa
Holy Cross HS
Willingboro, NJ

Johnson, Mark R
Millburn HS
Millburn, NJ

Johnson, Michael
Maple Shade HS
Maple Shade, NJ

Johnson, Ola
Red Bank Catholic
Neptune, NJ

Johnson, Robert
Arthur P Schalick
Elmer, NJ

Johnson, Thaddeus R
Union HS
Vauxhall, NJ

Johnson, Trisha
Calvary Acad
Brick, NJ

Johnson, Yasmin
Weequahic HS
Newark, NJ

Johnston, Annmarie
Eastern Regional
Gibbsboro, NJ

Johnston, Carolyn
St John Vianney HS
Englishtown, NJ

Johnston, Kimberly
Mahwah HS
Mahwah, NJ

Joho, Brian
Abraham Clark HS
Roselle, NJ

Jones, Candice Starr
Union HS
Union, NJ

Jones, Carol
Alma Prep
Somerville, NJ

Jones, Kris
Mt St John Acad
Basking Ridge, NJ

Jones, Margaret
Linden HS
Linden, NJ

Jones, Pamela
Clifford J Scott HS
E Orange, NJ

Jones, Randolph L
Piscataway HS
Piscataway, NJ

Jones, Scott
Bishop George Ahr/ St Thomas Aquinas
Edison, NJ

Jordan, Maureen
Haddon Township
Oaklyn, NJ

Jose, Stephanie
Manalapan HS
Englishtown, NJ

Joseph, Marlene
Plainfield HS
Plainfield, NJ

Jost, Daniel
Manasquan HS
Manasquan, NJ

Joyce, Maureen
Paul VI Regional
Cedar Grove, NJ

Justis, Glenn P
Henry P Becton Regional HS
E Rutherford, NJ

Kadezabek, Lauren
Hunterdon Central
Flemington, NJ

Kahlenberg, David
Hun School Of
Yardley, PA

Kahn, Allen
Perth Amboy HS
Perth Amboy, NJ

Kain, III Philip G
Bridgewater-Raritan High Schl West
Bridgewater, NJ

Kaiser, John
Southern Regional
Barnegat, NJ

Kalisch, Kimberly
Bishop George Ahr
Woodbridge, NJ

Kaller, Richard P
Morristown HS
Convent Station, NJ

Kalnins, Andis
Wood-Ridge HS
Wood-Ridge, NJ

Kane, Jackie
Holy Cross HS
Moorestown, NJ

Kaplan, Alyssa
River Dell SR HS
River Edge, NJ

Kaplan, Eric J
Paramus HS
Paramus, NJ

Kaplan, Marc
Highstown HS
East Windsor, NJ

Kaplan, Paul
Freehold Township
Freehold, NJ

Kappmeier, Gregory
Hudson Catholic HS For Boys
N Bergen, NJ

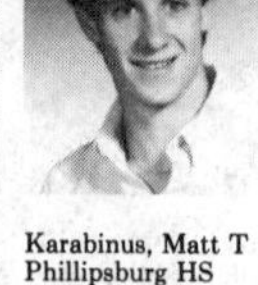
Karabinus, Matt T
Phillipsburg HS
Stewartsville, NJ

Karadis, Pauline
Villa Victoria Acad
Wrightstown, NJ

Karagias, Dimitra
Manasquan HS
Brielle, NJ

Karbane, Marci
Morris Knolls HS
Rockaway, NJ

Karkowski, Andrea
Toms River H S
Toms River, NJ

Karns, Gennifer
Lenape Valley
Regional HS
Stanhope, NJ

Karsevar, Danny
Atlantic City HS
Margate, NJ

Kasaks, Tara
Westfield SR HS
Westfield, NJ

Katchen, Deborah
Mount Olive HS
Budd Lake, NJ

Katz, Michael
Freehold Twp HS
Freehold, NJ

PHOTO
NOT
AVAILABLE

Kauffman, Kimberly
S
Hopewell Valley
Central HS
Titusville, NJ

Kaufman, Daniel
Academic HS
Jersey City, NJ

Kawalec, Jill
Immaculata HS
N Plainfield, NJ

Kay, Honaire
Roxbury HS
Princeton Jct, NJ

Kays, Monica
Hunterdon Central
Felmington, NJ

Kearney, Susan
Red Bank Regional
Little Silver, NJ

Kearns, Jr Paul C
Bergen Catholic HS
Teaneck, NJ

Keenan, Kim
Rahway HS
Rahway, NJ

Keenan, Marie
Lenape Valley Reg
Stanhope, NJ

Keene, Elizabeth
Middletown HS
Navesink, NJ

Kehoe, Patrick
Bishop George Ahr
Perth Amboy, NJ

Keith, Sharonda
Central HS
Newark, NJ

Keller, Laura
Manasquan HS
Belmar, NJ

Kelley, Colleen
Scotch
Plains-Fanwood HS
Fanwood, NJ

Kelley, Jak
Jackson Memorial
Jackson, NJ

Kelligrew, Susan
Bouton
Summit HS
Summit, NJ

Kellum, Tracy Lynn
Salem HS
Salem, NJ

Kelly, Gregory J
Ocean City HS
Marmora, NJ

Kelly, Janine Y
Fort Lee HS
Fort Lee, NJ

Kelly, John J
St Joseph Regional
Garnerville, NY

Kelly, Larissa
Teaneck HS
Teaneck, NJ

Kelly, Tara
Holy Cross HS
Medford, NJ

Kenerson, Kara
Jean
Hawthorne HS
Hawthorne, NJ

Kennedy, Karen
St John Vianney HS
Hazlet, NJ

Kennedy, Susan
Bishop George Ahr
Fords, NJ

Kennedy-Jansen,
Thomas
Paul VI HS
Deptford, NJ

Kenney, Margaret L
Cinnaminson HS
Cinnaminson, NJ

Kenny, Michael
Toms River HS
Pine Beach, NJ

Kent, Tara Anne
Pop John XXIII HS
Vernon, NJ

Kerish, John F
Vineland HS
Vineland, NJ

Kerstner, Christine
Newton HS
Andover, NJ

Kicera, Michael J
Hillside HS
Hillside, NJ

Kiesznowski, Sheri
Anne
St John Vianney HS
Freehold, NJ

Kim, Choong
St Peters
Preparatory HS
Rutherford, NJ

Kimball, Darren
East Brunswick HS
E Brunswick, NJ

Kimble, Linda
Gloucester HS
Gloucester, NJ

King, Christine
Eastern HS
Berlin, NJ

King, Glenn R
Lacey Twp HS
Forked River, NJ

King, Linda
Roselle Catholic HS
Roselle Pk, NJ

King, Russell
Delaware Valley
Regional HS
Frenchtown, NJ

King, Sarah
East Brunswick HS
E Brunswick, NJ

King, Tara
Howell HS
Howell, NJ

Kinney, Ricky W
Sussex County Vo
Tech HS
Montague, NJ

Kinsey, Latrice
Sharell
University HS
Newark, NJ

Kipp, Amy
Scotch
Plains-Fanwood HS
Scotch Plains, NJ

Kirby, Adrianne
Woodbridge HS
Woodbirdge, NJ

Kirk, Bonnie
Union HS
Union, NJ

Kirk, Karen
South River HS
S River, NJ

Kirsch, Lori
Ocean Township HS
W Deal, NJ

Kirschner, Susan
Mt Olive HS
Flanders, NJ

Kirstein, Laurie
Dwigght Englewood
Fort Lee, NJ

Kiss, Ildiko
Sussex Vo-Tech
Franklin, NJ

Kittrell, Doug
Florence Tnp
Memorial HS
Roebling, NJ

Kleiman, Dennis
Cherry Hill HS
Cherry Hill, NJ

Klein, Deena
Highstown HS
East Windsor, NJ

Klein, Kevin
Morris Catholic HS
Denville, NJ

Klein, Lawrence J
East Brunswick HS
E Brunswick, NJ

Klein, Leiann
Manalapan HS
Manalapan, NJ

Klein, Tamara
Washington
Township HS
Turnersville, NJ

Klein, Timothy E
Freehold Regional
New Egypt, NJ

Kleinman, Jonathan
West
Windsor-Plainsbor
Plainsboro, NJ

Klele, Michael
Secaucus HS
Secaucus, NJ

Klotz, Tammy
Bordentown
Regional HS
Cookstown, NJ

Klug, David
Kittatinny Regional
Newton, NJ

Klukososki, Lisa
South Plainfield HS
S Plainfield, NJ

Kmech, Kendra
Secaucus HS
Secaucus, NJ

Knapp, Kirstina D
Union HS
Union, NJ

Knauss, Liane
Hightstown HS
E Windsor, NJ

Knight, Stephanie
East Orange HS
E Orange, NJ

Knutelsky, Stephen
P
Wallkill Valley
Regional HS
Franklin, NJ

Kochansky, Krissy
Monmouth Regional
Tinton Falls, NJ

Kochka, Thomas
Wayne Valley HS
Wayne, NJ

Kochon, Juliann
Bergenfield HS
Bergenfield, NJ

Koetting, Jacquelyn
Paramus HS
Paramus, NJ

Kohler, Scott
Seton Hall Prep
Eatontown, NJ

Kolecki, Chris
Gateway Regional
Woodbury Hts, NJ

Kompa, Jill
Woodstown HS
Woodstown, NJ

Konek, James
Timothy
Spotswood HS
Spotswood, NJ

Konnick, Mark
Paulsboro HS
Gibbstown, NJ

Konopsky, Lisa M
Howell HS
Howell, NJ

Kopaz, Robert
Highland Regional
Blackwood, NJ

Korach, Stacy
Weehawken HS
Weehawken, NJ

Korchick, Robyn
Mc Corristin
Catholic HS
Yardley, PA

Korshalla, Paula
South River HS
S River, NJ

Koscienski, III
Walter F
St Thomas Aquinas/
Bishop Georg Ahr
Edison, NJ

Kotch, Troy
Bridgewater-Raritan
H S East
Bridgewater, NJ

Kotsiris, Lisa
Arthur P Schalick
Bridgton, NJ

Kotulich, Deborah
Bridgewater-Raritan
West HS
Bridgewater, NJ

Kovacs, Maria A
Paul VI HS
Waterford, NJ

Kovatch, Jeff
Wayne Hills HS
Wayne, NJ

Kovitz, Adam Jay
Hightstown HS
East Windsor, NJ

Kowalsky, Vicky
Freehold Township
Freehold, NJ

Koyen, Jeff
Parsippany HS
Parsippany, NJ

Koza, Margie
Passaic Valley HS
Totowa, NJ

Kozak, Michael J
Hamilton HS West
Trenton, NJ

Kozlowski, Dawn
Wall HS
Wall, NJ

Kozub, Deanna
Holy Cross HS
Burlington, NJ

Krafts, Andrew
Roxbury HS
Succasunna, NJ

Kramarchuk, Roman
A
Clifton HS
Clifton, NJ

Krause, Kimberly
Matawan Regional
Matawan, NJ

Krell, Justine
Passaic Valley
Regional HS
Little Falls, NJ

Kress, Mary
St John Vianney HS
Freehold, NJ

Kretiv, Beth Ann
Toms River H Schl
Toms River, NJ

Kricena, Susie
Midland Park HS
Midland Park, NJ

Krueger, Tricia
Lynn
Mc Corristin HS
Trenton, NJ

Kuehn, Jeffrey S
Sussex County
Vo-Tech HS
Vernon, NJ

Kugler, Craig W
Woodstown HS
Woodstown, NJ

Kuhn, Roger
H G Hoffman HS
South Amboy, NJ

Kukowski, Wendy
Holy Family Acad
Bayonne, NJ

Kulaga, Mark
St Rose HS
Spring Lake, NJ

Kuleba, Theodore J
Middletown HS
Belford, NJ

Kumagai, Tomomi
Indian Hills HS
Oakland, NJ

Kunze, Gretchen
Shore Regional HS
Sea Bright, NJ

Kupersmith,
Roseanne
Ocean Township HS
Oakhurst, NJ

Kurlychek, Anthony
Manchester
Regional HS
Prospect Pk, NJ

Kurman, Sheri
Woodstown HS
Alloway, NJ

Kurokawa, Shin
Holy Spirit HS
Margate, NJ

Kuznitz, Kim
Arthur L Johnson
Regional HS
Clark, NJ

Kwaak, Kathryn
Red Bank Catholic
Englishtown, NJ

Kwan, Karen
Matawan Regional
Aberdeen, NJ

Kwiatkowski,
Michelle
Woodbridge HS
Fords, NJ

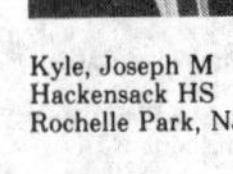
Kyle, Joseph M
Hackensack HS
Rochelle Park, NJ

La Badia, Jill
Indian Hills HS
Oakland, NJ

La Bar, Jr Richard
S
Pope John XXIII
Vernon, NJ

La Couture, Tamara
Holy Cross HS
Lumberton, NJ

La Terra, Vince
Mainland Regional
Northfield, NJ

Labrum, Josette A
Lenape Valley HS
Sparta, NJ

Lacatena, Michele
Kinnelon HS
Kinnelon, NJ

Laccitiello, Dawn
Nutley HS
Nutley, NJ

Lacher, Britt
Franklin HS
Somerset, NJ

Lachtman, David
Manalapan HS
Englishtown, NJ

Laczhazy, Robert S
Phillipsburg
Catholic HS
Phillipsburg, NJ

Lafferty, Dawn
Overbrook SR HS
Pine Hill, NJ

Lahiff, Michael
Cresskill HS
Cresskill, NJ

Laino, Kelly A
East Brunswick HS
E Brunswick, NJ

Lake, Walter
Warren County
Phillipsburg, NJ

Lal, Sangeeta
Glen Rock JR SR
Glen Rock, NJ

Lalbahadur, Videsh
Academic HS
Jersey City, NJ

Lalli, Candice M
Highland Regional
Clementon, NJ

Lambert, Kathleen
Notre Dame HS
Trenton, NJ

Lamberton, Jim
Waldwick HS
Waldwick, NJ

Lamborne, Renee
Holy Cross HS
Marlton, NJ

Lambusta, Gina
Brick Township HS
Brick Town, NJ

Lamparello, Michael J
Rutherford HS
Rutherford, NJ

Lamzaki, Dimas
Palisades Park JR SR HS
Palisades Park, NJ

Lancaster, Jr Allen
Lenape Valley
Regional HS
Andover, NJ

Lance, Alice
Hun Schl Of
High Bridge, NJ

Landini, Lee C
Randolph HS
Randolph, NJ

Landis, Steve
Pennsville Memorial
Pennsville, NJ

Landrigan, Kathy
North Bergen HS
North Bergen, NJ

Langbein, Tammy
Edgewood SR HS
Sicklerville, NJ

Langel, Heather
Livingston HS
Livingston, NJ

Langford, Virginia
Lower Cape May
Regional HS
W Cape May, NJ

Langley, George
Cumberland
Regional HS
Rosenhayn, NJ

Lanier, Albert
Asbury Park HS
Asbury Park, NJ

Lanz, Sabrina
Chatham Township
Chatham Twp, NJ

Lanza, Dañielle
Manalapan HS
Englishtown, NJ

Lanzerotti, Louis D
Madison HS
New Vernon, NJ

Lanzisera, Rosa
Toms River H S
Toms River, NJ

Lapidus, Lisa
Bridgewater-Raritan
East HS
Bridgewater, NJ

Laracy, Rich
Point Pleasant Boro
Point Pleasant, NJ

Larsen, Robby
Lenape Valley
Regional HS
Stanhope, NJ

Larson, Patricia
Mater Dei HS
Hazlet, NJ

Laschiver, Igor
Academic HS
Jersey City, NJ

Lasser, Sandy
Bayley Ellard HS
Morristown, NJ

Lassiter, Michael J
Northern Burlington
Co Reg HS
Mc Guire Afb, NJ

Latz, Glen
Pascack Valley HS
River Vale, NJ

Laufer, Glenn
Central Regional HS
Seaside Pk, NJ

Laughery, Carroll
Academic HS
Jersey City, NJ

Lavan, Michele
St John Vianney HS
Hazlet, NJ

Lavender, Joshua
North Brunswick
Twp HS
N Brunswick, NJ

Lavine, Josh
Montville HS
Towaco, NJ

Lavinson, Melissa
Princeton Day Schl
Princeton, NJ

Law, Christine
De Paul Diocesan
Ringwood, NJ

Law, Colleen
Villa Victoria Acad
W Trenton, NJ

Law, Patricia
Middle Township
Avalon, NJ

Lawrence, David C
Kittatinny Regional
Newton, NJ

Lawrence, David J
Jeferson Twp HS
Milton, NJ

Lawson, Ava M
Kingsway Regional
Swedesboro, NJ

Lawson, Jr Ervin V
Cumberland
Regional HS
Bridgeton, NJ

Laycock, Holli
Mt Olive HS
Flanders, NJ

Lazar, Michael
Queen Of Peace HS
North Arlington, NJ

Lazzara, Janelle
Paramus Catholic
Teaneck, NJ

Le Borgne, Jr
William
Wallington HS
Wallington, NJ

Leach, Joseph J
Hackettstown HS
Hackettstown, NJ

Leahy, Allison
Spotswood HS
Spotswood, NJ

Leahy, Dennis
Wilwood Catholic
Avalon, NJ

Leddy, Denise
Wall HS
Manasquan, NJ

Lee, Cho
N V R H S Old
Tappan HS
Harrington Pk, NJ

Lee, John
Ocean Township HS
Ocean, NJ

Lee, Lisa
Dover HS
Dover, NJ

Lee, Mark T
Whippany Park HS
Whippany, NJ

Lee, Morris S
Millburn HS
Short Hills, NJ

Lee, Suzanne
Gloucester Catholic
Bellmawr, NJ

Lee, Sylvia
Lincoln HS
Jersey City, NJ

Lee, Wm
Bloomfield HS
Bloomfield, NJ

Lehman, Christine
Belleville HS
Belleville, NJ

Leiseca, Edward
Memroail HS
West New York, NJ

Leishman, James
Don Bosco
Technical HS
Paterson, NJ

Leitch, Denise
Jackson Memorial
Jackson, NJ

Leiva, Michael J
Ridgefield Park HS
Little Ferry, NJ

Lembo, Nicholas
Don Bosco Prep
Franklin Lakes, NJ

Leming, Emily
Summit HS
Summit, NJ

Lemm, Sandra
West Essex Regional
Fairfield, NJ

Lemma, Brian
Overbrook Regional
SR HS
Clementon, NJ

Lemp, Debra
St John Vianney HS
Hazlet, NJ

Lemp, Kathryn
St John Vianney HS
Hazlet, NJ

Lenart, John
Toms River HS East
Toms River, NJ

Lenczycki, Nicole
Atlantic Friends
Linwood, NJ

Lengenfelder,
Jeannie
Villa Victoria Acad
Hamilton, NJ

Lenosky, Larissa
West Essex HS
Fairfield, NJ

Lenox, Kevin P
West
Windsor-Plainsbor
Princeton Jct, NJ

Lenz, Cheryl
Morris Knolls HS
Denville, NJ

Leo, Gerald
Monsignor Donovan
Brick, NJ

Leonard, Antoinette
St John Vianney HS
Hazlet, NJ

Leonard, Robert
Don Bosco Prep HS
Hillsdale, NJ

Lesky, Kathleen M
Cranford HS
Cranford, NJ

Lev, Eli
Wayne Hills HS
Wayne, NJ

Levy, Marc
Cherry Hill HS East
Cherry Hill, NJ

Lewis, Andrea
Clifford J Scott HS
E Orange, NJ

Lewis, Brian T
Morris Knolls HS
Long Valley, NJ

Lewis, Heather
Southern Regional
Manahawkin, NJ

Lewis, Helena D
Orange HS
Orange, NJ

Lewis, Steve
Brick HS
Brick Town, NJ

Lewis, Tracee
Union Catholic
Regional HS
Newark, NJ

Lewis, Yvette
Teaneck HS
Teaneck, NJ

Leyva, Maria
St Marys HS
Elizabeth, NJ

Li, Tongying Esther
Parsippany Hills HS
Parsippany, NJ

Liauw, Julita
Ramapo HS
Wyckoff, NJ

Libonati, Dana
Freehold Twp HS
Farmingdale, NJ

Librizzi, Roy
Pinelands Regional
Tuckerton, NJ

Librojo, Donata
Academic HS
Jersey City, NJ

Licciardiello, Dona
Mount Olive HS
Budd Lake, NJ

Liebig, Michelle
Deanna
Sussex Cty Voc
Tech Schl
Sussex, NJ

Liedl, Jeffrey M
Hillsborough HS
Somerville, NJ

Lifshey, Adam
Cherry Hill HS
Cherry Hill, NJ

Ligeralde, Davidson
Glen Ridge HS
Glen Ridge, NJ

Liggett, Robert W
Bishop George Ahr
Edison, NJ

Lightcap, Kristine
Belvidere HS
Phillipsburg, NJ

Ligos, Mark
West Morris Central
Long Valley, NJ

Lilley, Michelle
Freehold Boro HS
Freehold, NJ

Lilore, Jennifer
Parsippany HS
Parsippany, NJ

Lim, Eugene
Hillsborough HS
Somerville, NJ

Lin, Edward
Wall HS
Wall, NJ

Lindsay, Kathleen
Mary
Lyndhurst HS
Lyndhurst, NJ

Lindsey, Lucinda M
St Dominic Acad
Jersey City, NJ

Lindsey, Michele
Holy Cross HS
Mapleshade, NJ

Linenberg, Karen
Ann
Westfield SR HS
Westfield, NJ

Linnehan, Mary
Jane
Marlboro HS
Morganville, NJ

Lippai, Stephen P
Woodbridge HS
Fords, NJ

Lisk, Richard
St John Vianney HS
Union Beach, NJ

Liskiewicz, Lori
Queen Of Peace HS
N Arlington, NJ

Liu, Minetta
Kent Place Schl
Florham Park, NJ

Lo Cascio, Anthony
J
Lakeland Regional
Haskell, NJ

Lo Giudice, Maria D
North Brunswick
Township HS
N Brunswick, NJ

Lobb, Sherry
Buena Regional HS
Newfield, NJ

Locascio, Michael
Westfield SR HS
Westfield, NJ

Lockhart, Antoinette
Snyder HS
Jersey City, NJ

Locko, Dana
Hamilton High West
Trenton, NJ

Logan,
Mary-Frances
Red Bank Catholic
Neptune, NJ

Logoyda, Debbie
H G Hoffman HS
South Amboy, NJ

Loizeaux, Nicholas
Scotch
Plains-Fanwood HS
Scotch Plains, NJ

Lombardi, Jodi
Cherry Hill HS
Cherry Hill, NJ

Lombardo, Carolyn
Monsignor Donovan
Lakewood, NJ

Londoner, Corey
River Dell SR HS
Oradell, NJ

Lonegan, Stacey
Spotswood HS
Spotswood, NJ

Long, Jeffrey
Camden Catholic
Cherry Hill, NJ

Lopez, Maria
Cristela
Memorial HS
North Bergen, NJ

Lopez, Roberto
Teaneck HS
Teaneck, NJ

Lopez, Sandra
Saint Dominic Acad
N Bergen, NJ

Lopus, Nancy
West Essex SR HS
Essex Fells, NJ

Lord, David
Hightstown HS
E Windsor, NJ

Lorentz, Alison
Voorhees HS
Califon, NJ

Lorenzo, Michelle
North Bergen HS
North Bergen, NJ

Lott, Virginia D
Wayne Hills HS
Wayne, NJ

Lowe, Scott
Phillipsburg HS
Phillipsburg, NJ

Loyd, Patrick
St Peters/Christian
Lorton, VA

Lozea, Scott
Freehold Township
Freehold, NJ

Lucas, Denene
Teaneck HS
Teaneck, NJ

Lucca, Carolyn
Hammonton HS
Hammonton, NJ

Lucca, Tracy
St Joseph HS
Hammonton, NJ

Lucchesi, Arthur
Washington
Township HS
Sewell, NJ

Lucia, Joseph R
Red Bank Catholic
Eatontown, NJ

Ludwick, Melissa
Gloucester City JR
R HS
Gloucester, NJ

Ludwig, James D
Toms River HS
Toms River, NJ

Ludwig, Jens O
Lenape HS
Mt Laurel, NJ

Lugo, Sandra
Abbegami HS
Absecon Hlds, NJ

Lumby, Jeffrey S
Rancocas Valley
Regional HS
Mt Holly, NJ

Lund, Christian
Hackettstown HS
Belvidere, NJ

Lund, Suzanne
Denise
Teaneck HS
Teaneck, NJ

Lunney, Kelly P
Middletown HS
Leonard, NJ

Luongo, Lisa
Belleville HS
Belleville, NJ

Luppino, Cathy
Bayonne HS
Bayonne, NJ

Lutz, Kevin
Millville SR HS
Millville, NJ

Lutz, Kimberly
Rancocas Valley
Regional HS
Mt Holly, NJ

Luzar, Tina
Middlesex HS
Middlesex, NJ

Lynch, Jennifer
Toms River North
Toms River, NJ

Lynch, Norene
Franklin HS
Somerset, NJ

Lynes, David
St Marys
Hall-Doane Acad
Cherry Hill, NJ

Lyons, Lisa
Toms River High
School East
Toms River, NJ

Maat, Stacey Ann
Hackensack HS
S Hackensack, NJ

Mac Farran, Carrie
A
Mahwah HS
Mahwah, NJ

Mac Millan, Eric W
Mendham HS
Chester, NJ

Mac Neil, Jocelyn
Chatham Township
Chatham, NJ

Mac Taggart, Ethan
Seton Hall Prep
S Orange, NJ

Macaluso, Robert
Westfield HS
Westfield, NJ

Macaulay, Melissa
Phillipsburg HS
Phillipsburg, NJ

Macavoy, Jr Robert
Francis
Arthur L Johnson
Reg HS
Clark, NJ

Macdonald, Michelle
Delaware Valley
Regional HS
Milford, NJ

Machado, Elizabeth
Piscataway HS
Piscataway, NJ

Mackey, Murae
Red Bank Catholic
Manalapan, NJ

Macpherson, Paul
Mahway HS
Mahwah, NJ

Madamba, Aaron
Pinelands Regional
Mystic Island, NJ

Maddocks, Brian K
Pennsville Memorial
Pennsville, NJ

Magbalon, Michael J
Camden Catholic
Cherry Hill, NJ

Magnabousco,
Robert
Hackensack HS
Maywood, NJ

Magos, Deanna
Washington Twp
Sewell, NJ

Maguocchetti,
Catherine
Dover HS
Dover, NJ

Maher, Maureen
Bishop George Ahr
Edison, NJ

Maher, Wendy
Westfield HS
Westfield, NJ

Mahoney, Kevin
Hillsborough HS
Somerville, NJ

Mahony, Danny
Queen Of Peace HS
Rutherford, NJ

Maiello, Thomas
Bayonne HS
Bayonne, NJ

Majewski, Chet
Woodbridge HS
Fords, NJ

Majmudar, Parag
Bloomfieldd HS
Bloomfield, NJ

Major, Victoria
Waldwick HS
Waldwick, NJ

Mako, Eva
Burl Co Vo-Tech
Roebling, NJ

Makowski, Kim
Weehawken HS
Weehawken, NJ

Malatesta, Alicia
Neumann Prep HS
Paterson, NJ

Maldonado, Ivette
John F Kennedy HS
Paterson, NJ

Maldony, Maura
Mother Seton Reg
Edison, NJ

Malesich, Richard C
Camden Catholic
Cherry Hill, NJ

Mallek, Gregory S
Bernards HS
Bernardsville, NJ

Mallett, Jr Arthur N
Middletown North
Port Monmouth, NJ

Maloney, Cathy
Lodi HS
Lodi, NJ

Mancinelli, Diana
Washington
Township HS
Turnersville, NJ

Mancuso, William
Parsippany HS
Lk Hiawatha, NJ

Mango, Wayne J
Triton HS
Blackwood, NJ

Mangone,
Christopher A
Hillsborough HS
Belle Mead, NJ

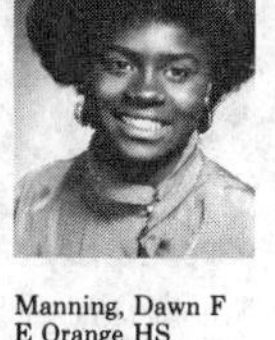
Manning, Dawn F
E Orange HS
E Orange, NJ

Manskopf, Britta
Rutherford HS
Rutherford, NJ

Manzella, Dawn
John F Kennedy HS
Willingboro, NJ

Maraziti, Jacqueline
Chatham Township
Chatham Twp, NJ

Marblestone, Alan
Parsippany HS
Parsippany, NJ

Marcel, Joseph R
Kittatinny Regional
Newton, NJ

Marcozzi, David E
Bishop Eustace Prep
Cinnaminson, NJ

Marcus, Nina
Hightstown HS
E Windsor, NJ

Marder, Melissa
Holy Cross HS
Browns Mills, NJ

Marhoefer, Michelle
A L Johnson
Regional HS
Clark, NJ

Marin, Gladys M
Essex County
Voc-Tech HS
Newark, NJ

Marinelli, Jon
Hackettstown HS
Hackettstown, NJ

Marinkovic, Petrija
Mary Help HS
Paterson, NJ

Marino, Josephine
Nutley HS
Nutley, NJ

Marino, Michael
West Essex SR HS
Fairfield, NJ

Marino, Susan
Pascack Hills HS
Woodcliff Lk, NJ

Marino, Theresa
Summit HS
Morristown, NJ

Markle, Nicole
Middlesex HS
Middlesx, NJ

Markley,
Christopher
Washington
Township HS
Sewell, NJ

Markovich, Michael
Toms River North
Toms River, NJ

Markowitz, Eric
Arthur L Johnson
Clark, NJ

Marks, Robin
East Brunswick HS
E Brunswick, NJ

Markulic, Lori A
Sayreville War
Memorial HS
Sayreville, NJ

Markus, Debbie
High Point Regional
Sussex, NJ

Marmaras, Irene
Belleville HS
Belleville, NJ

Marmora, Joseph B
St Joseph Regional
Upper Saddle Rive,
NJ

Marques, Anabela
East Side HS
Newark, NJ

Marrella, Jacquelyn
Holy Cross HS
Marlton, NJ

Marrero, Nicole
South Hunterdon
Lambertville, NJ

Marroni, Beth
Toms River H S
Toms River, NJ

Marsh, Amy
Neptune SR HS
Neptune City, NJ

Marshall, Dini
Lakewood Prep
Lanoka Harbor, NJ

Martin, Alyson
Hunterdon Central
Whitehouse Sta, NJ

Martin, Douglas M
Neptune SR HS
Neptune, NJ

Martin, Edward
Westfield HS
Westfield, NJ

Martin, Jr Elliott B
St Josephs HS
E Brunswick, NJ

Martin, John
Toms River HS East
Toms River, NJ

Martin, Kathy A
Kittatinny Regional
Newton, NJ

Martin, Kim
Our Lady Of Mercy
Girls Acad
Millville, NJ

Martin, Sandrine
Oak Knoll School Of
The Holy Child
South Orange, NJ

Martin, Sherri
Notre Dame HS
Hamilton Sq, NJ

Martinelly, Michelle
Red Bank Regional
Shrewsbury, NJ

Martinez, Maria
North Bergen HS
North Bergen, NJ

Martinez, Maria
Our Lady Of Good
Newark, NJ

Martini, Julia
Notre Dame HS
Lawrenceville, NJ

Martino, Jennifer
Arthur L Johnson
Reg HS
Clark, NJ

Martirano, Michael
Queen Of Peace HS
Kearny, NJ

Martopana, Teresa
Notre Dame HS
Trenton, NJ

Martz, Michelle
Marie
Hun Schl Of
Frederick, MD

Marzano, Lisa
Montville HS
Towaco, NJ

Masella, Joe
Fair Lawn HS
Fair Lawn, NJ

Masilang, Maria B
Holy Rosary Acad
Jersey City, NJ

Massaro, Tricia
Southriver HS
South River, NJ

Masso, Jessica Ann
St Joseph HS
Atco, NJ

Masterson, Brian
Sacred Heart HS
Cedarville, NJ

Mastropaolo,
Frances
Lodi HS
Lodi, NJ

Matarazzo, Christine
Manchester
Regional HS
North Haledon, NJ

Matarazzo, Jim
West Essex HS
N Caldwell, NJ

Mathis, Robin
John F Kennedy HS
Willingboro, NJ

Mathur, Atul D
Boonton HS
Lincoln Park, NJ

Matonis, Laura
Mother Seton
Reional HS
Edison, NJ

Matsuda, Hiroko
River Dell Reg HS
Oradell, NJ

Mattes, Gregory
Hunterdon Central
Whitehouse Sta, NJ

Matthai, Meru Ann
Belleville HS
Belleville, NJ

Matthews, Laura
Lakewood HS
Lakewood, NJ

Mattone, John
St John Vianney HS
Aberdeen, NJ

Maute, Michelle
Holy Cross HS
Cinnaminson, NJ

May, Arnold P
Cherry Hill HS East
Cherry Hill, NJ

May, Joseph C
South River HS
S River, NJ

Mayer, Lisa
Linden HS
Linden, NJ

Mayer, Nicholas
Hudson Catholic
Secaucus, NJ

Mayes, Karen
St Anthony HS
Jersey City, NJ

Mayes, Tom
Dover HS
Dover, NJ

Mayrina, Kathrine M
Hillside HS
Hillside, NJ

Mazurowski, Peter
North Warren Regional HS
Edmond, OK

Mazza, Stephanie
Millville SR HS
Millville, NJ

Mazzerina, Keith
Passaic Valley Regional HS
West Paterson, NJ

Mazzoni, Randall
Vineland HS
Vineland, NJ

Mc Auley, Margaret
Oak Knoll Schl
S Orange, NJ

Mc Breen, Kelley
St John Vianney HS
Freehold, NJ

Mc Bride, Ellen
Wildwood Catholic
Cape May, NJ

Mc Cabe, Jennifer
Kinnelon HS
Kinnelon, NJ

Mc Cabe, Michele
Egg Harbor Twp HS
Linwood, NJ

Mc Cahill, Jay W
Dover HS
Dover, NJ

Mc Carron, Diana
Asbury Park HS
Bradley Beach, NJ

Mc Carthy, Kerry
Waldwick HS
Waldwick, NJ

Mc Carthy, Susan
Arthur L Johnson
Clark, NJ

Mc Cartney, Meghan
Rutherford HS
Rutherford, NJ

Mc Caulley, Patrice
Holy Spirit HS
Longport, NJ

Mc Clammy, James I
West Windsor-Plainsbor
Princeton, NJ

Mc Clenahan, John
St John Vianney HS
Aberdeen, NJ

Mc Closkey, Dawn
Burlington County Vo- Tech
Edgewater Pk, NJ

Mc Connell, Stacey
Middlesex HS
Middlesex, NJ

Mc Cracken, Kelly
Roselle Catholic HS
Elizabeth, NJ

Mc Crae, Wanda
East Orange HS
East Orange, NJ

Mc Cray, Joyce
Central Jersey Christian Schl
Wall, NJ

Mc Daniel, Michael D
University HS
Newark, NJ

Mc Dermott, Sean P
Don Bosco Prep HS
Stony Pt, NY

Mc Devitt, Tara
Bayonne HS
Bayonne, NJ

Mc Donald, Keeley
Roxbury HS
Landing, NJ

Mc Donald, Marc
Dwight Morrow HS
Englewood, NJ

Mc Donald, Patrick
Christian Brothers
Springlake, NJ

Mc Donnell, Stacey
Mount Saint Mary
Spotswood, NJ

Mc Fillin, Terri
Holy Spirit HS
Margate, NJ

Mc Geary, Kerry Anne
Westfield SR HS
Westfield, NJ

Mc Gee, Kimberly
Memorial HS
Cedar Grove, NJ

Mc Gill, Gretchen Ann
Bloomfield SR HS
Bloomfld, NJ

Mc Ginty, James
Toms River HS
Toms River, NJ

Mc Glynn, Christy
Mainland Regional
Northfield, NJ

Mc Gowan, Shawn
Holy Spirit HS
Absecon, NJ

Mc Grogan, William
Parsippany Hills HS
Parsippany, NJ

Mc Guire, Stephen
South Hunterdon Regional HS
Lambertville, NJ

Mc Hugh, Steven Elliot
Hackettstown HS
Hackettstown, NJ

Mc Indoe, Kathy
Bogota HS
Bogota, NJ

Mc Inerney, Susan D
Central Jersey Christian Schl
Elberon, NJ

Mc Iver, Delenia
Clifford J Scott HS
E Orange, NJ

Mc Kean, Julie
Red Bank Catholic
Middletown, NJ

Mc Keever, Kathleen
Lyndhurst HS
Lyndhurst, NJ

Mc Kegney, Krissy
River Dell Reg HS
River Edge, NJ

Mc Kendrick, Dina Marie
North Brunswick Township HS
North Brunswick

Mc Kenna, David
Queen Of Peace HS
N Arlington, NJ

Mc Kenna, Kathleen
Saint Rose HS
Brick Town, NJ

Mc Kinley, Leon
Henry Snyder HS
Jersey City, NJ

Mc Lain, Susan
Bricktownship HS
Brick Town, NJ

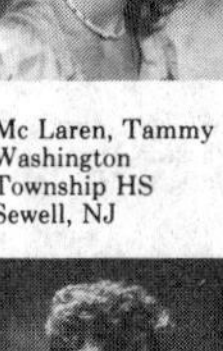
Mc Laren, Tammy
Washington Township HS
Sewell, NJ

Mc Laughlin, Colette
Bayonne HS
Bayonne, NJ

Mc Laughlin, Dawn
Bloomfield HS
Bloomfield, NJ

Mc Mahon, Theresa
Bishop George Ahr
Colonia, NJ

Mc Manus, Majella
Paul VI Regional
Bloomfield, NJ

Mc Michael, Maria M
Audubon HS
Audubon, NJ

Mc Namara, Heather
Haddon Heights HS
Barrington, NJ

Mc Namara, Jeffrey
Arthur P Schalick
Centerton, NJ

Mc Neil, Laura
Mt St Mary Acad
Edison, NJ

Meara, Jacqueline
Hamilton High West
Trenton, NJ

Mears, Mary Beth
Glassboro HS
Glassboro, NJ

Mechler, Robert T
New Milford HS
New Milford, NJ

Meehan, Barbara Ann
Bishop George Ahr
Edison, NJ

Meixner, Paul
South Plainfield HS
S Plainfield, NJ

Mele, Staci
Monsignor Donovan
Lakewood, NJ

Melnick, Melissa
Wall HS
Sea Girt, NJ

Melton, Kirsten
Mainland Regional
Northfield, NJ

Melzak, Lori
Raritan HS
Hazlet, NJ

Mendez, Osvaldo M
Eastside HS
Paterson, NJ

Mendonca, Francisco M
East Side HS
Newark, NJ

Mendoza, Maria
Oak Knoll Schl Of The Holy Child
Livingston, NJ

Mendum, Charles
Lakewood HS
Lakewood, NJ

Menendez, Alex
Secaucus HS
Secaucus, NJ

Menendez, J Lyle
Princeton Day Schl
Princeton, NJ

Mercado, Jerry B
Our Lady Of Good Counsel HS
Newark, NJ

Merighi, Lisa
Buena Regional HS
Richland, NJ

Merkle, Robert
Oratory Prep
New Providence, NJ

Merola, Stephen
Parsippany Hills HS
Morris Plains, NJ

Merrigan, Thoa
Toms River South
Beachwood, NJ

Merritt, Tina
Montville Township
Towaco, NJ

Mesday, Maureen
Notre Dame HS
Trenton, NJ

Messner, Alisa
Red Bank Regional
Interlaken, NJ

Meszaros, Kenneth
Hamilton HS East
Hamilton Sq, NJ

Meyer, Melanie
Hunterdon Central
White House Stati, NJ

Mezzanotte, Christopher
North Warren Regional HS
Blairstown, NJ

Miah, Kahlu A
Eastern Regional
West Berlin, NJ

Michalski, Maria
Freeehold Township
Freehold, NJ

Michel, Erich
Bogota HS
Bogota, NJ

Michura, Lisa
Neumann Prep
North Caldwell, NJ

Mikesell, Corinne
Parsippany HS
Parsippany, NJ

Milane, Joseph E
Marist HS
Bayonne, NJ

Miliote, Anthony
Manalapan HS
Manalapan, NJ

Miller, Andrea
Pitman HS
Pitman, NJ

Miller, Benjamin S
Killatinny Regional
Hainesville, NJ

Miller, Jr Clinton W
Neptune HS
Neptune City, NJ

Miller, Faith
Pleasantville HS
Pleasantville, NJ

Miller, Korey B
Saddle Brook HS
Saddle Brook, NJ

Miller, Kristen
Red Bank Catholic
Manasquan, NJ

Miller, Lynn
Essex Catholic Girls
Newark, NJ

Miller, Michelle
Hamilton West HS
Yardville, NJ

Miller, Nichelle
Kingsway Regional
Woodstown, NJ

Miller, Sandee
Middletown H S
Leonardo, NJ

Miller, Scott
Delran HS
Delran, NJ

Miller, Scott
Toms River HS
Toms River, NJ

Miller, Sean
Holy Cross HS
Edgewater Park, NJ

Miller, Stace
Garden State Acad
Andover, NJ

Miller, Tracy T
Chatham Twp HS
Chatham, NJ

Milley, Rodney
Williamstown HS
Williamstown, NJ

Millilo, Richard
Holy Cross HS
Cinnaminson, NJ

Min, Charleene
Hopewell Valley Central HS
Princeton, NJ

Min, John
Middlesex HS
Middlesex, NJ

Mindnich, Gretchen
Red Bank Regional
Little Silver, NJ

Minervini, Frank A
Hudson Catholic HS
Hoboken, NJ

Minervini, Tina
St John Vianney HS
Englishtown, NJ

Minichiello, Gabriel
Hudson Catholic HS
Jersey City, NJ

Minicucci, Patricia Anne
De Paul Diocesan
Pompton Lakes, NJ

Minieri, Michael A
Union HS
Union, NJ

Minitee, Tabrina
Hillside HS
Hillside, NJ

Miragliotta, Tina
Kittatinny Regional
Newton, NJ

Miranda, Antonio
Roselle Catholic HS
Elizabeth, NJ

Mirandi, Vincent
Whippany Park HS
Whippany, NJ

Mirzai, Hossein
Washington Township HS
Sewell, NJ

Mischak, Dana Lynn
Villa Victoria Acad
Yardley, PA

Misyak, Patti
Dover HS
Mine Hill, NJ

Mitchell, Audra
Southern Regional
Manahawkin, NJ

Mitchell, Brenda
Jackson Memorial
Jackson, NJ

Mitchell, Denise L
Delaware Valley Regional HS
Milford, NJ

Mitchell, Laura
Millville SR HS
Millville, NJ

Mitchell, Martin
Cherokee HS
Marlton, NJ

Mitchell, Romonita
Eastside HS
Paterson, NJ

Molina, Annabella
Hoboken HS
Hoboken, NJ

Molnar, Alyssa
Chatham Township
Chatham Twp, NJ

Monaco, Amy
Riverdell Regional
Oradell, NJ

Monaco, Anthony
Toms River HS
Toms River, NJ

Monagle, Kevin D
Camden Catholic
W Berlin, NJ

Moncrief, Craig
Holy Spirit HS
Ocean City, NJ

Moncrief, Erica
Toms River HS
Beachwood, NJ

Monego, Carl
Pope John XXIII
Hewitt, NJ

Montana, III
William
Vineland HS
Vineland, NJ

Montanaro, Lara
Holy Cross HS
Riverside, NJ

Montanez, Antonio
Vineland SR HS
Vineland, NJ

Monteleone,
Joyceann
Ocean City HS
Ocean View, NJ

Moody, Lisa
Lakewood HS
Lakewood, NJ

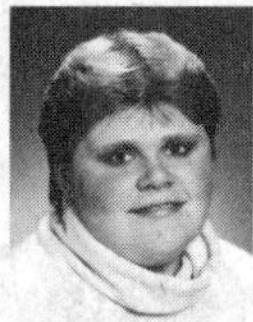
Moore, Meghan
De Paul Diocesan
Kinnelon, NJ

Moore, Ron
Pinelands Regional
Tuckerton, NJ

Moore, Ronald
Cumberland
Regional HS
Bridgeton, NJ

Moore, Sandra
Woodstown HS
Woodstown, NJ

Moore, Susan
Lyndhurst HS
Lyndhurst, NJ

Moore, Teresa
Eastside HS
Paterson, NJ

Moore, Tracy
Roms Rivers E HS
Toms River, NJ

Moos, Veronica
Highland Regional
Sicklerville, NJ

Moran, Elizabeth N
Teaneck HS
Teaneck, NJ

Morash, Tim
Hunterdon Central
White House Stati,
NJ

Morchower,
Matthew B
Millburn HS
Short Hills, NJ

Mordwin, Drew
James Caldwell HS
Caldwell, NJ

Morea, Joseph
Northern Valley
Regional HS
Northvale, NJ

Moreland, Gloria L
John F Kennedy HS
Willingboro, NJ

Moreno, Amparo
Memorial HS
W New York, NJ

Moreno, Linda
Manalapan HS
Englishtown, NJ

Morgan, Laura
No Bruns Township
N Brunswick, NJ

Morgan, Tonette
Weequahic HS
Irvington, NJ

Morgner, Melissa A
Kittatinny Regional
Branchville, NJ

Morris, April J
Edgewood Reg SR
Sicklerville, NJ

Morris, Crystal L
Archeray HS
Camden, NJ

Morris, Dave
Hightstown HS
East Windsor, NJ

Morris, Gwendolyn
S
Cumberland
Regional HS
Bridgeton, NJ

Morris, Jean F
Moorestown HS
Moorestown, NJ

Moses, Denise
Essex Catholic Girls
Newark, NJ

Moses, Robert
Northern Valley Reg
Northvale, NJ

Mosley, Robert J
West Windsor
Plainsboro HS
Plainsboro, NJ

Mostello, David
West
Windsor-Plainsbor
Princeton Jct, NJ

Mostello, Diane B
West
Windsor-Plainsbor
Princeton Junct, NJ

Mostofizadeh,
Djavad
South Hunterdon
Lambertville, NJ

Motomal, Elaine
Piscataway HS
Piscataway, NJ

Mourey, Mary
Burlington City HS
Beverly, NJ

Mraz, Carole
Paul VI Regional
Nutley, NJ

Mueller, Chuck
Westfield HS
Westfield, NJ

Muench, Nadine
Rancocas Valley
Regional HS
Mt Holly, NJ

Mugno, Albert M
Don Bosco HS
W Paterson, NJ

Muhlhauser, Kristin
Pope John XXIII
Milford, PA

Mulford, Robert
Glassboro HS
Pitman, NJ

Mullen, Kevin
Florence Twp Mem
Roebling, NJ

Mullen, Ty
Salem HS
Salem, NJ

Muller, Edward
Kittatinny Regional
Newton, NJ

Mulligan, Joycelyn
Shore Regional HS
Sea Bright, NJ

Mundell, Jr Thomas
Neptune SR HS
Neptune, NJ

Mundo, George
Memorial HS
West New York, NJ

Munech, Tom
Don Bosco Prep HS
N Haledon, NJ

Munoz, Yvette
Mother Seton
Regional HS
Irvington, NJ

Munson, T Eugene
Triton Regional HS
Somerdale, NJ

Munson, Todd
Washington Twp
Turnersville, NJ

Muracco, Stephen
Washington
Township HS
Turnersville, NJ

Murdoch, Karen
Spotswood HS
Spotswood, NJ

Murphy, Dina
Florence Twp Mem
Roebling, NJ

Murphy, Pamela
Raritan HS
Hazlet, NJ

Murphy, Tom
North Warren
Regional HS
Blairstown, NJ

Murray, Tim
Bishop George Ahr
Iselin, NJ

Murzenski, Michael
Lenape Valley Reg
Andover, NJ

Musser, Erica Lynn
Williamstown HS
Williamstown, NJ

Muth, Robert
Mount Olive HS
Hackettstown, NJ

Muzaffar, Ayesha
Friends Schl
Woodstown, NJ

Myers, Irene
Rochelle
Gloucester City JR
SR HS
Gloucester, NJ

Myers, Jill Suzette
Villa Victoria Acad
Trenton, NJ

Myers, Lisa
Our Lady Of Mercy
Wmstown, NJ

Nadel, John
Middletown H S
Belford, NJ

Nadell, Stacey
Matawan Regional
Matawan, NJ

Nagler, Anastasia
Ambassador
Christian Acad
Gibbstown, NJ

Nanayakkara,
Abigail
Villa Victoria Acad
Ewing, NJ

Nanfara, Ralph John
Holy Spirit HS
Atlantic City, NJ

Naples, Bethann
Hamilton High West
Trenton, NJ

Napodano, Gina
Passaic Valley HS
W Paterson, NJ

Nastasi, Billy
Wildwood HS
N Wildwood, NJ

Natale, Laura
Shore Regional HS
Oceanport, NJ

Nathan, Edward
Manalapan HS
Englishtown, NJ

Navallo, Dawn E
N Brunswick Twp
N Brunswick, NJ

Naylor, Bonnie
Riverside HS
Riverside, NJ

Negron, Eva M
Frank H Morrell HS
Irvington, NJ

Negron, Marilyn
Our Lady Of Good
Newark, NJ

Negron, Rose
Franklin HS
Somerset, NJ

Neidich, Wendy
Holy Cross HS
Edgewater Pk, NJ

Nelsen, Gregg
Red Bank Catholic
Red Bank, NJ

Nelson, Sherri
Weequahic HS
Newark, NJ

Nelson, Simone
West Essex SR HS
North Caldwell, NJ

Neral, John
Christian Brothers
Pt Pleasant Bch, NJ

Nesler, Mark
Piscataway HS
Piscataway, NJ

Nesta, Julianne
Bloomfield SR HS
Bloomfield, NJ

Newhard, Stefanie
St James HS
Pennsville, NJ

Newman, Jeff
Burlington City HS
Burlington, NJ

Nguyen, Phong
Academic HS
Jersey City, NJ

Nguyuza, Mc Neal H
Pascock HS
Montvale, NJ

Nichols, Catherine
Saint James HS
Mickleton, NJ

Nicol, Lia
Manasquan HS
Brielle, NJ

Nicoletti, Richard C
Whippany Park HS
N Ft Myers, FL

Nicoll, Pamela R
Middlesex County
Voctnl & Tech HS
Spotswood P O, NJ

Nicolosi, Joanne
De Paul HS
Wayne, NJ

Niedermaier, Scott
Hamilton West HS
Trenton, NJ

Nielsen, Tracey
S Hunterdon
Regional HS
Lambertville, NJ

Nieto, Michael K
Christian Brothers
Hazlet, NJ

Nieves, Gladys
James J Ferris HS
Jersey City, NJ

Nieves, Sonia
Oakcrest HS
Elwood, NJ

Nilla, Eric
East Brunswick HS
E Brunswick, NJ

Nizamoff, Steve
Toms River High
School North
Toms River, NJ

Noble, Jennifer
Northern Highlands
Montclair, NJ

Noel, Cassandra
East Brunswick HS
E Brunswick, NJ

Nol, Lina
Morris Catholic HS
Pine Brook, NJ

Nolan, John P
Moorestown HS
Moorestown, NJ

Nolan, Michael
St John Vianney HS
Hazlet, NJ

Nordman, Glenn
Park Ridge HS
Park Ridge, NJ

Novak, Karen
Spotswood HS
Spotswood, NJ

Novella, Joseph
Pennsauken SR HS
Pennsauken, NJ

Novellino, Gina
Woodbridge HS
Fords, NJ

Novembre, Carmine
Morris Catholic HS
Flanders, NJ

Nugent, Edward
Paramus HS
Paramus, NJ

Nunez, Harry S
Memorial HS
West New York, NJ

Nussbaum, Mindy Rae
Parsippany Hills HS
Parsippany, NJ

Nusz, Nanci
West Essex Regional
N Caldwell, NJ

O Boyle, Jeffrey M
Morris Knolls HS
Denville, NJ

O Boyle, Timothy F
West Orange HS
W Orange, NJ

O Donnell, David
Bridgeton HS
Bridgeton, NJ

O Donnell, Mark C
Oratory Prep
Mountain Lakes, NJ

O Dowd, Brian
Morris Catholic HS
Montville, NJ

O Keefe, Karen
Notre Dame HS
Mercerville, NJ

O Leary, June
St Marys HS
S Amboy, NJ

O Leary, Kathi-Ann
Waldwick HS
Waldwick, NJ

O Rourke, Colleen
Dover HS
Dover, NJ

O Rourke, Molly
Summit HS
Summit, NJ

Oakes, Eileen
Mainland Regional
Northfield, NJ

Obal, Kathleen
Pascack Valley HS
Hillsdale, NJ

Obertubbesing, Mary Ann
Middletown South
Leonardo, NJ

Occhipinti, Bridget
Butler HS
Butler, NJ

Occhipinti, Natalie M
Paterson Catholic R H HS
Paterson, NJ

Oconnor, Shivaun
Immaculate
Conception HS
Secaucus, NJ

Oeskovic, Sue L
Middlesex HS
Middlesex, NJ

Olah, Anissa
Lower Cape May
Regional HS
N Cape May, NJ

Olander, Dale
Wall HS
Wall, NJ

Oliver, Albert C
Burlngton Township
Burlington, NJ

Oliver, Honora Ann
Newton HS
Newton, NJ

Oliveri, Joseph
Wayne Valley HS
Wayne, NJ

Oliveri, Mary E
Saint James HS
Gibbstown, NJ

Olivero, Noel
Toms River HS
Toms River, NJ

Olivo, Charles
Cherry Hill HS
Cherry Hill, NJ

Olsen, Shannon
Matawan Regional
Matawan, NJ

Olson, Eric S
Neumann Prep
Ringwood, NJ

Olson, Tammy
Manasquan HS
Boynton Beach, FL

Olsson, Karen
Mainland Regional
Linwood, NJ

Ombalsky, Sandra
Belleville HS
Belleville, NJ

Onacilla, Susan
Shore Regional HS
Oceanport, NJ

Oneill, Kelly
Mainland Regional
Somers Point, NJ

Onorevole, Kevin
Nutley HS
Nutley, NJ

Onori, James
Hudson Catholic HS
Jersey City, NJ

Ontko, Carol
Delaware Valley
Regional HS
Milford, NJ

Ontko, Mary
Delaware Valley
Regional HS
Milford, NJ

Onufrow, Michael J
Kinnelon HS
Kinnelon, NJ

Orciuoli, Kim
Livingston HS
Livingston, NJ

Ordonez, Ivan
North Bergen HS
North Bergen, NJ

Orfanakos, George
Wayne Valley HS
Wayne, NJ

Orlando, II Joseph
M
Parsippany HS
Parsippany, NJ

Ormsby, Thomas
St John Vianney HS
Englishtown, NJ

Orrick, Annemarie
Middletown HS
Red Bank, NJ

Orsini, Dana
Voorhees HS
Glen Gardner, NJ

Ortega, Arnel V
St Peters Prep Schl
Jersey City, NJ

Ortolf, Kirsten
Cumberland
Regional HS
Bridgeton, NJ

Oslick, Jeffrey
Westfield HS
Westfield, NJ

Ossowski, David
Jackson Mrmotial
Jackson, NJ

Otero, Susan
St John Vianney HS
Marlboro, NJ

Ott, Brian
Gloucester Co
Christian Schl
Turnersville, NJ

Ott, Christine N
Howell HS
Howell, NJ

Ottaviano, Charles
Maple Shade HS
Maple Shade, NJ

Otten, Theodore
St James HS
Paulsboro, NJ

Oughourli, Diana
Manchester Reg HS
Prospect Pk, NJ

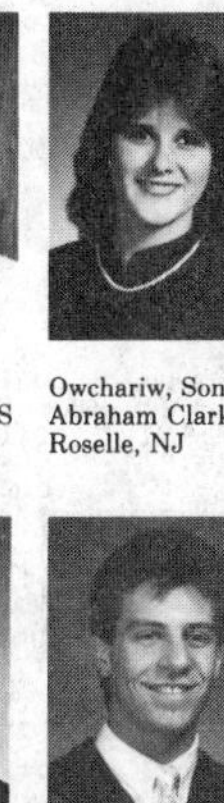
Owchariw, Sonia
Abraham Clark HS
Roselle, NJ

Owens, Anita
Irvington HS
Irvington, NJ

Owensby, Jennifer
Weehawken HS
Weehawken, NJ

Oxley, Renae
Gateway Reginal HS
National Park, NJ

Ozer, Esra
Hopewell Valley
Central HS
Pennington, NJ

Pachana, Joann
Oak Knoll Schl
Newark, NJ

Paddon, Eric
Chatham Twp HS
Chatham, NJ

Padilla, Mayra
Holy Family Acad
Bayonne, NJ

Page, Glenn
Pascack Hills HS
Woodcliff Lk, NJ

Pagels, Joseph
Hamilton East
Trenton, NJ

Pagliughi, Marty
Holy Spirit HS
Brigantine, NJ

Pagtalunan, Honesto
Woodbridge HS
Fords, NJ

Paleschic, Cami
Pennsville Memorial
Pennsville, NJ

Paleschic,
Christopher
Woodstown HS
Woodstown, NJ

Palmer, Anne
Whitney
West Morris
Mendham HS
Mendham, NJ

Palmieri, Cynthia
West Essex HS
Fairfield, NJ

Palmieri, Jr Vincent
J
Southern Regional
Barnegat, NJ

Palus, Mark
Indian Hills HS
Franklin Lks, NJ

Pancione, Danielle
Mt St Mary Acad
Piscataway, NJ

Panzera, Paul
Hillsborough HS
Belle Mead, NJ

Papanikolas,
Anastasios
Neptune SR HS
Neptune, NJ

Paparo, Dominic
Overbrook Regional
Pine Hill, NJ

Pappas, Eleni
St Dominic Acad
Bayonne, NJ

Parcells, Trish
Boonton HS
Lincoln Park, NJ

Pardo, Danielle A
Hanover Park HS
Florham Park, NJ

Parducci, Judith
Edgewood Regional
SR HS
Berlin, NJ

Paredes, Alessio
Joseph
Paul VI HS
Passaic, NJ

Paredes, Emigdio
Garden State Acad
N Bergen, NJ

Parent, Clifford
Hamilton High
School West
Trenton, NJ

Parise, Lori
Mount Saint Mary
Plainfield, NJ

Parisi, David
Ridgefield Park HS
Little Ferry, NJ

Park, Jane
Eastern HS
Voorhees, NJ

Parkes, Chris
Mater Dei HS
Middletown, NJ

Parks, Kathleen
Bishop George Ahr
Edison, NJ

Parks, Stacey
Waldwick HS
Waldwick, NJ

Parrillo, Christine
Wayne Valley HS
Wayne, NJ

Parrish, Thomas J
Roselle Catholic HS
Union, NJ

Parry, Debra
Bishop George Ahr
Colonia, NJ

Parsio, Anthony
Penns Grove HS
Carneys Point, NJ

Parsley, Craig
Salem HS
Salem, NJ

Parsons, Alleana
A P Schalick HS
Bridgeton, NJ

Parsons, Sandra S
Somerville HS
Somerville, NJ

Pasqua, John
Anthony
Oratory Catholic
Madison, NJ

Passanante, Jane E
Middlesex HS
Middlesex, NJ

Passarelli, Daniel F
N Plainfield HS
N Plainfield, NJ

Pastakia, Hettle
Colonia HS
Colonia, NJ

Patel, Amal
Middletown South
Lincroft, NJ

Patel, Mukesh
North Bergen HS
North Bergen, NJ

Patel, Nilesh P
Sayreville War
Memorial HS
Parlin, NJ

Pattabhi, Ruth
John F Kennedy
Memorial HS
Colonia, NJ

Patten, Cynthia M
Passaic Valley
Regional HS
Totowa, NJ

Patten, Thomas
Christian Brothers
Freehold, NJ

Patterson,
Elizabethann
Lakewood HS
Lakewood, NJ

Patterson, Rodney
Barringer HS
Newark, NJ

Paul, James
Trenton Central HS
Trenton, NJ

Paullin, Lisa
Deptford Township
Deptford, NJ

Pavincich, Marilyn
St Rose HS
Spring Lake, NJ

Pawson, David J
Lawrence HS
Lawrenceville, NJ

Payne, Jacqueline
Ann
Wayne Valley HS
Wayne, NJ

Paz, Cathy
Clifton HS
Clifton, NJ

Peace, Linda
Orange HS
Orange, NJ

Pecci, Lisa
Mary Help Of
Christians Acad
Paterson, NJ

Pedersen, Caroline
M
Middletown High
School South
Lincroft, NJ

Pedersen, Dan
Clearview HS
Richwood, NJ

Peek, Patricia
North Bergen HS
North Bergen, NJ

Peluso, Marlo
Watchung Hills
Regional HS
Gillette, NJ

Pemberton, Ron
Highland Regional
Somerdale, NJ

Pena, Becki
Memorial HS
West New York, NJ

Penn, Tammatha
Louise
Cumberland
Regional HS
Bridgeton, NJ

Pennell, Arthur
Toms River H S
South Toms River,
NJ

Pensabene, Cynthia
Cherry Hill HS
Cherry Hill, NJ

Penswater, John J
Holy Cross HS
Delran, NJ

Peraino, Renee
Toms River High
School North
Toms River, NJ

Pereira, Isabel
Immaculate
Conception HS
Newark, NJ

Peretti, Brenda
Vineland SR HS
Vineland, NJ

Perez, Arthur
Jackson Memorial
Jackson, NJ

Perfilio, Julie
Scotch Plains
Fanwood HS
Scotch Plains, NJ

Perkins, II Eddie L
Burlington City HS
Burlington, NJ

Perrine, Jr
Frederick L
South Plainfield HS
S Plainfield, NJ

Perrino, Dina
St John Vianney HS
Matawan, NJ

Perry, Dean
Bishop Eustace Prep
Medford, NJ

Perry, Thomas W
Christian Brothers
W Keansburg, NJ

Persel, Kenneth
Monsignor Donovan
Toms River, NJ

Perugini, Laura
Buena Regional HS
Richland, NJ

Pesci, Christine
Union Catholic
Regional HS
Roselle Park, NJ

Petersen, Michael
Toms River HS S
Beachwood, NJ

Peterson, Amy
Cherry Hill HS
Cherry Hill, NJ

Peterson, Edward
Middle Township
Cape May C H, NJ

Peterson, Katy
West Milford Twp
West Milford, NJ

Peterson, Pamela
Monsignor Donovan
Brick, NJ

Peterson, Tara Lee
De Paul HS
Butler, NJ

Petner, Gina
Manalapan HS
Englishtown, NJ

Petracca, Dawn
St Patricks HS
Elizabeth, NJ

Petrecca, Karen
Queen Of Peace HS
Newark, NJ

Petro, Robert
Washington Twp
Turnersville, NJ

Petron, Elena
Verona HS
Verona, NJ

Petrovic, Justine
Manville HS
Manville, NJ

Petruccelli, Michael
Cresskill HS
Cresskill, NJ

Petruzzi, Deborah
Washington
Township HS
Sewell, NJ

Petry, Heidi
Spotswood HS
Milltown, NJ

Pettiford-Chandler,
Aaron
Hillside HS
Hillside, NJ

Pettinelli, Gina
Phillipsburg HS
Alpha, NJ

Pfeiffer, Constance
Spotswood HS
Spotswood, NJ

Pfenninger, Peggy
South Hunterdon
Regional HS
Lambertville, NJ

Pfuelb, Pamela S
Chatham HS
Chatham, NJ

Phares, Joel
Cinnaminson HS
Cinna, NJ

Philbin, Kelly
Bishop Eustace Prep
Blackwood, NJ

Phillips, Debra
Lynn
Toms River HS East
Toms River, NJ

Phillips, Randi
Fair Lawn SR HS
Fair Lawn, NJ

Phillips, Robert
Manville HS
Manville, NJ

Piano, Joann
River Dell SR HS
Oradell, NJ

Piccone, Anthony
Paul VI HS
Atco, NJ

Pichinson, Daniel L
Highland Park HS
Highland Park, NJ

Pickels, Angela
Mary Help Of
Christians Acad
Paterson, NJ

Piekarz, Suzanne
Clifton HS
Clifton, NJ

Pierce, Teresa
Phillipsburg HS
Phillipsburg, NJ

Piestor, Daniel W
Steinert HS
Hamilton Square,
NJ

Pietkewicz, Melissa
Matawan Regional
Matawan, NJ

Pietro, Laura
Central Regional HS
Bayville, NJ

Pietrykoski,
Elizabeth
Bloomfield SR HS
Bloomfield, NJ

Pilewski, Kimberly
Linden HS
Linden, NJ

Pinkowitz, David A
Madison Central HS
Old Bridge, NJ

Pinnella, Kevin
Toms River HS
Toms River, NJ

Pinoski, Jr Paul
Wash Twp HS
Sewell, NJ

Pippi, Michele
Kittatinny Regional
Newton, NJ

Pisack, Robert
Bridgewater Raritan
HS West
Bridgewater, NJ

Piskadlo, Bryan
Ramapo Regional
Wyckoff, NJ

Pitcher, Brian S
Pemberton HS
Pemberton, NJ

Pittakas, Mina
Wildwood Catholic
N Wildwood, NJ

Pittman, Jody
Vailsburg HS
Newark, NJ

Pizzuto, Julie
Gateway Regional
Woodbury Heights,
NJ

Pladdys, Laureen
N Bergen HS
N Bergen, NJ

Planchard, Steven
Chatham Twp HS
Chatham, NJ

Plastine, Laura
Secaucus HS
Secaucus, NJ

Poat, Robbin
West Milford Twp
W Milford, NJ

Poblete, Christine
St John Vianney HS
Marlboro, NJ

Pockell, Lori Ann
Eastern HS
West Berlin, NJ

Pocklembo, Ann
Marie E
John P Stevens HS
Edison, NJ

Polasky, Christopher
Howell HS
Howell, NJ

Pole, Nnamdi
Hightstown HS
E Windsor, NJ

Polese, Mary
Brick Memorial HS
Brick, NJ

Polesuk, Eric
Parisppany HS
Parsippany, NJ

Policano, Marianne
Paramus Catholic
Girls Regionl HS
Elmwood Pk, NJ

Police, Cherie
Dover HS
Dover, NJ

Poling, Jeffrey M
Keyport HS
Keyport, NJ

Poliniak, Susan
Holy Cross HS
Willingboro, NJ

Polk, Sylvia S
Glen Rock JR SR
Glen Rock, NJ

Pollack, Joan
East Brunswick HS
E Brunswick, NJ

Pollak, Deborah
Bridgewater-Raritan
HS East
Bridgewater, NJ

Pomanelli, Diane
Madison HS
Madison, NJ

Pompeo, Mario
James Caldwell HS
W Caldwell, NJ

Ponstingel, Laura
Mary Help Of
Christians Acad
Paterson, NJ

Pontoriero, Joseph
Seton Hall Prep
Newark, NJ

Poplawski, Lorraine
Cresskill HS
Cresskill, NJ

Popper, Mindy
Toms River High
School North
Toms River, NJ

Poreda, Stanley
Burlington County
Riverside, NJ

Porro, Jeanine
Rutherford HS
Rutherford, NJ

Porter, Kent R
Frank H Morrell HS
Irvington, NJ

Porter, Michael N
Shawnee HS
Medford, NJ

Portilla, Pedro J
Passaic HS
Passaic, NJ

Post, Lauren T
Sayreville War
Memorial HS
Parlin, NJ

Post, Megan Anne
Our Lady Of Mercy
Marmora, NJ

Powers, Barbara
Paul VI Regional
Upper Montclair,
NJ

Powers, Denise
Pascack Valley HS
Hillsdale, NJ

Prachthauser,
Jonathan D
Morris Town HS
Morristown, NJ

Prasad, Sudhes
Jackson Memorial
Jackson, NJ

Prater, Hillary L
Neptune SR HS
Neptune, NJ

Preckajlo, Joseph
St Peters
Preparatory Schl
Elizabeth, NJ

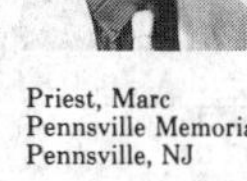

Prehodka, Bethany
North Warren
Regional HS
Blairstown, NJ

Prescott, William
Don Bosco HS
Hawthorne, NJ

Press, Michele
Pennsville Memorial
Pennsville, NJ

Preston, Doreen
Arthur P Schalick
Elmer, NJ

Preston, Edwin W
Riverside HS
Delanco, NJ

Prettyman, Chris
Mother Seton
Regional HS
Carteret, NJ

Price, Michelle
Raritan HS
Hazlet, NJ

Priest, Marc
Pennsville Memorial
Pennsville, NJ

Prieto, Hector
Memorial HS
West New York, NJ

Prieto, Laura
Mount Saint Mary
Westfield, NJ

Principe, Tammy
Arthur P Schalick
Elmer, NJ

Priola, Stephen J
Parsippany HS
Parsippany, NJ

Pritchett, Christine Y
Moorestown HS
Moorestown, NJ

Pritsch, Donna
Middletown High School South
Lincroft, NJ

Proano, Elke
Hackensack HS
Hackensack, NJ

Probst, Eric
Don Bosco Prep
Oakland, NJ

Profito, David
Green Brook HS
Green Brook, NJ

Prongay, Michele
St John Vianney HS
Aberdeen, NJ

Prout, Maureen
Marylawn Of The Oranges HS
Maplewood, NJ

Provost, Kellie
Hackettstown HS
Belvidere, NJ

Prudenti, Deborah
Mt Olive HS
Flanders, NJ

Pruess, Douglas R
Franklin HS
Somerset, NJ

Prunk, Rob
Don Bosco Prep HS
Park Ridge, NJ

Przecha, Lorie Anne
Hamilton H S East
Hamilton Square, NJ

Psillos, Lauren
North Plainfield HS
N Plainfield, NJ

Puckett, Jennifer
North Plainfield HS
N Plainfield, NJ

Puma, Joyce
Bridgewater-Raritan H S East
Bound Brook, NJ

Purdue, Kristen
Pinelands Regional
Tuckerton, NJ

Puri, Puneet K
Cherry Hill East HS
Cherry Hill, NJ

Puscian, Lisa
Eastern HS
Voorhees, NJ

Puttbach, Kenneth
Parsippany HS
Parsippany, NJ

Qayyum, Basit
Roselle Catholic HS
Hillside, NJ

Quattromini, Christine
Immaculate Conception HS
N Arlington, NJ

Quick, Jim
South Hunterdon Reg HS
Lambertville, NJ

Quinn, A Robyn
Bridgeton HS
Bridgeton, NJ

Quinn, Erin
Millville SR HS
Millville, NJ

Quirk, Jacqueline
Middletown HS
Middletown, NJ

Rabuano, Lisa
Mary Help Of Christians Acad
Paterson, NJ

Racciatti, Joanne
South Hunterdon Regional HS
Lambertville, NJ

Radigan, Debra
Notre Dame HS
Cranbury, NJ

Radtke, Letitia C
Westfield SR HS
Westfield, NJ

Rae, Christopher D
Ridgewood HS
Ridgewood, NJ

Raffay, Russell
Lenape Valley Regional HS
Stanhope, NJ

Rago, Christopher
Washington Township HS
Sewell, NJ

Ragolia, Stacia E
Northern Highlands Regional HS
Upper Saddle Rvr, NJ

Raichel, Robert
Clifton HS
Clifton, NJ

Rain, Kimberly
Woodstown HS
Elmer, NJ

Ramos, Idalisse
Our Lady Of Good Counsel HS
Newark, NJ

Ramos, Vanessa
Roselle Catholic HS
South Plainfield, NJ

Rand, Mindy
Passaic HS
Passaic, NJ

Randazzo, Jr Ludwig
Passaic HS
Passaic, NJ

Randolph, Monique
Kent Place Schl
Irvington, NJ

Rangel, Lorraine
North Arlington HS
N Arlington, NJ

Rao, Benjamin
Park Ridge HS
Park Ridge, NJ

Rao, Deanna
Park Ridge HS
Park Ridge, NJ

Rapp, Ilana
Sayreville War Memorial HS
Sayreville, NJ

Raskas, Robert
East Brunswick HS
E Brunswick, NJ

Rathbun, Rollin
Manville HS
Manville, NJ

Rattay, Dan
Morris Catholic Schl
Rockaway, NJ

Rattay, Tom
Morris Catholic HS
Rockaway, NJ

Rauh, III George A
Piscataway HS
Piscataway, NJ

Raven, Karen
Overbrook Regional SR HS
Berlin, NJ

Raven, Sharon
Bruriah HS For
Old Bridge, NJ

Rayauskas, Maria Anne
Wildwood Catholic
Wildwood Crest, NJ

Reagan, Michelle
Toms River High School East
Toms River, NJ

Reamer, III Raymond V
Don Bosco Preparatory HS
Fairlawn, NJ

Reardon, Eileen
Red Bank Regional
Little Silver, NJ

Rector, Kim
Piscataway HS
Piscataway, NJ

Redavid, John
Morris Catholic HS
Succasunna, NJ

Reddick, IV William J
Seton Hall Prep
Union, NJ

Reed, Elizabeth
Shore Regional HS
W Long Branch, NJ

Reed, Joy
A P Schalick HS
Bridgeton, NJ

Reed, Robbin
Overbrook Regional SR HS
Berlin, NJ

Reedy, Lance
The Pennington
Rocky Hill, NJ

Rehman, Tracy
Williamstown HS
Williamstown, NJ

Reho, James
St Josephs Preparator
Staten Island, NY

Rehse, Denis
Lenape Valley Regional HS
Stanhope, NJ

Reid, Amee
Kingsway Regional
Mullica Hill, NJ

Reid, Juliet
East Side HS
Wyckoff, NJ

Reid, Monee
Vailsburg HS
Newark, NJ

Reid, Scott D
Haddon Heights HS
Cherry Hill, NJ

Reilly, III Charles
Joseph
Overbrook SR HS
Pine Hill, NJ

Reinhold, Robyn
Pinelands Regional
Tuckerton, NJ

Reinke, Michael G
Secancus HS
Secaucus, NJ

Reiziss, Phyllis
Freehold Township
Howell, NJ

Relota, Josip
Bayley-Ellard
Regional HS
Chatham, NJ

Remazowski, Lisa
Queen Of Peace HS
N Arlington, NJ

Rendeiro, Maria
Queen Of Peace HS
Lyndhurst, NJ

Renshaw, April
Overbrook Regional
Pine Hill, NJ

Renwick, Ian
Wayne Hills HS
Wayne, NJ

Renz, Patricia
Holy Cross HS
Cinnaminson, NJ

Repert, Johanna
Red Bank Catholic
Freehold, NJ

Resch, Lori
Wayne Hills HS
Raleigh, NC

Restaino, Gary
Metuchen HS
Metuchen, NJ

Rettas, George
Dover HS
Dover, NJ

Rettig, Lisa
Manalapan HS
Englishtown, NJ

Rever, Scott
Unio HS
Union, NJ

Reyes, Deana
Central Reyes HS
Ocean Gate, NJ

Reynik, Laura S
Ramsey HS
Ramsey, NJ

Reynolds, L Bentley
High Point Regional
Branchville, NJ

Reynolds, Roseann
Orange HS
Orange, NJ

Rhoades, Beth
Parsippany Hills HS
Boonton, NJ

Ribeiro, Nancy
Kearny HS
Kearny, NJ

Ricardo, Alex
Freehold Township
Freehold, NJ

Riccardi, Jerry
Burlington City HS
Edgewater Pk, NJ

Rice, Angela
Jackson Memorial
Jackson, NJ

Richards, Michelle
Bishop George Ahr/
St Thomas HS
Plainfield, NJ

Richards, Scott
Highland HS
Laurel Spgs, NJ

Richards, Vanessa C
Jackson Memorial
Jackson, NJ

Richards, Jr Vernon
G
Seton Hall Prep
Newark, NJ

Richardson, Amy
North Plainfield HS
N Plainfield, NJ

Richmond, Fredrick
Teaneck HS
Teaneck, NJ

Richmond, Kelly
Hightstown HS
E Windsor, NJ

Ricke, Thomas
Morris Catholic HS
Bridgewater, NJ

Rickert, David
Toms River HS East
Toms River, NJ

Ridgway, Paul H
Cumberland
Regional HS
Bridgeton, NJ

Ridolfo, Rod
Montville Township
Montville, NJ

Rieder, Elizabeth
Union HS
Union, NJ

Rieser, Terri
Middle Township
Avalon, NJ

Rigsbee, Audrey
Camden HS
Camden, NJ

Riley, Kimberly
Red Bank Catholic
Neptune, NJ

Rilveria, Marjorie
St Marys HS
Sayreville, NJ

Rimili, David
Hamilton High West
Yardville, NJ

Rinkel, Patricia A
Sussex County
Montague, NJ

Rinkowski, Kim
Pinelands Regional
Tuckerton, NJ

Riola, Cheryl
Union Catholic
Regional HS
Hillside, NJ

Rise, Wendy
Shore Regional HS
Oceanport, NJ

Riseley, Mitzi K
Barnstable Acad
Hawthorne, NJ

Rispoli, Victor
Arthur L Johnson
Clark, NJ

Rittenhouse,
Elizabeth
Point Pleasant
Borough HS
Point Pleasant, NJ

Rivera, Jr Angel
David
Westfield HS
Westfield, NJ

Rivera, Eddie
Hoboken HS
Hoboken, NJ

Rivera, John J
Memorial HS
W New York, NJ

Rivera, Katherine
Emerson HS
Union City, NJ

Rivera, Tony
River Dell SR HS
River Edge, NJ

Rivers, Tiffany
University HS
Newark, NJ

Rizzo, Christine
Ocean City HS
Sea Isle City, NJ

Rizzo, Frank
St James HS
Gibbstown, NJ

Roach, Gary
Middle Township
Rio Grande, NJ

Roberts, Beverly
Plainfield HS
Plainfield, NJ

Roberts, Carole
Melissa
Middletown HS
Belford, NJ

Roberts, Charlene
Hillside HS
Hillside, NJ

Roberts, Lisa
Elmwood Park
Memorial HS
Elmwood Pk, NJ

Roberts, Tina J
Middle Township
Dennisville, NJ

Robertson, Corwin
Dwight Morrow HS
Englewood, NJ

Robertson, Janet
A P Schalick HS
Bridgeton, NJ

Robertson, Scott C
The Pingry Schl
Scotch Plains, NJ

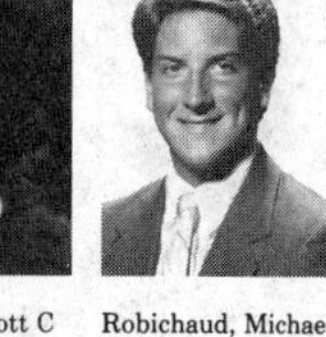
Robichaud, Michael
Verona HS
Verona, NJ

Robinson, Brett
Dwight Englewood
Englewood, NJ

Robinson, Janelle A
Pascack Valley
Regional HS
Hillsdale, NJ

Robinson, Joel D
Haddon Heights HS
Haddon Heights, NJ

Robinson, Mary
Middle Twp HS
S Seaville, NJ

Robinson, Stefanie
Parsippany HS
Parsippany, NJ

Robison, Bill
Northern Burlington
C R HS
Bordentown, NJ

Roccato, Daria
Washington
Township HS
Turnersville, NJ

Rocker, Brandon F
Memorial HS
Leonia, NJ

Rodrigues, Tony
Elizabeth HS
Elizabeth, NJ

Rodriguez, Anthony
L
Bishop George Ohr
Colonia, NJ

Rodriguez, Carmela
Trueba
East Side HS
Newark, NJ

Rodriguez, Hector
Good Counsel HS
Newark, NJ

Rodriguez, Jessica
Dover HS
Dover, NJ

Rodriguez, Maribel
Trenton HS
Trenton, NJ

Rodriguez, Raymond
Monsignor Donovan
Lakewood, NJ

Rodriguez, Jr
Samuel
Vineland HS
Vineland, NJ

Rodriguez, Theodore
North Bergen HS
North Bergen, NJ

Rogalski, Ellie
MSGR Donovan HS
Island Heights, NJ

Rogers, Linda
Bishop George Ahr
Perth Amboy, NJ

Rogers, Monica
Neptune SR HS
Neptune, NJ

Rogers, Scott
Ridge HS
Basking Ridge, NJ

Rohrs, Sabrina C
Matawan Regional
Aberdeen, NJ

Rojas, Giovanni
Eastside HS
Paterson, NJ

Rolon, Nick
North Bergen HS
North Bergen, NJ

Roman, Maria
Mercedez
Essex Co Vo Tech
Newark, NJ

Romanello, Theresa
St John Vianney HS
Matawan, NJ

Romaniw, Janis
James Caldwell HS
West Caldwell, NJ

Romano, Frances
Marie
Bayonne HS
Bayonne, NJ

Romano, John
Bayley-Ellard
Regional HS
Morristown, NJ

Rood, Hal
West Morris Central
Long Valley, NJ

Rooney, Sean
Northern Burlington
Regional HS
Trenton, NJ

Roque, Aldrin
Clifton HS
Clifton, NJ

Rorro, Mary
Villa Victoria Acad
Trenton, NJ

Rosado, Jane
Peth Amboy HS
Perth Amboy, NJ

Rosamilia, Salvatore
N
Kearny HS
Kearny, NJ

Rosander, David
Timothy Christian
Piscataway, NJ

Rosania, Jewel
Scotch Plains
Franwood HS
Scotch Plains, NJ

Rosasco, John
Neptune SR HS
Neptune, NJ

Roscher, Jeffrey A
Hunterdon Central
Flemington, NJ

Rose, Brandon
Brick Township HS
Brick, NJ

Rose, Lisa Beth
Governor Livingston
Regional HS
Berkeley Hts, NJ

Roseberry, Janel
Gloucester Co
Christian HS
Monroeville, NJ

Rosenberg, Linda
Diane
Cresskill HS
Cresskill, NJ

Rosenberg, Rachel
Morris Knolls HS
Denville, NJ

Rosenfarb, Jason
Randolph HS
Randolph, NJ

Rosensweig, Sara
Highstown HS
E Windsor, NJ

Ross, Alese
Cherry Hill HS
Cherry Hill, NJ

Ross, Bruce Evan
Paramus HS
Paramus, NJ

Ross, James
Hamilton H S West
Trenton, NJ

Ross, Scott
Bridgewater-Raritan
E HS
Bridgewater, NJ

Ross, Stacy
Holy Cross HS
Delran, NJ

Ross, Stephanie
E Orange HS
E Orange, NJ

Rossi, Anne Marie
Riverside HS
Delanco, NJ

Rossi, Lisa
St Peters HS
Somerset, NJ

Rossi, Louise
Clifton HS
Clifton, NJ

Rosso, Paola
Marylawn Of The
Oranges HS
E Orange, NJ

Roth, Sandra Lee
Bayley Ellard Reg
Whippany, NJ

Rothery, Richard
Wall HS
Wall, NJ

Rothschild,
Bradford
Solomon Schechter
Day Schl
Plainfield, NJ

Rothstein, Donna
West Milford
Township HS
West Milford, NJ

Rotunda, Domenica
West Essex Regional
Fairfield, NJ

Rouse, Tamika D
Camden Catholic
Camden, NJ

Rowand, Melinda
Sterling HS
Laurel Springs, NJ

Rowe, Michael J
Don Bosco Prep
N Haldeon, NJ

Rowley, Michael
Highstown HS
E Windsor, NJ

Royce, Laura
Kittatinny Regional
Newton, NJ

Rozas, III Ramon
Butler HS
Butler, NJ

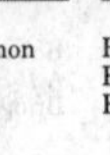
Rozo, Teresa
Butler HS
Butler, NJ

Rubio, Ramon
Mon Mouth
Regional HS
Eatontown, NJ

Ruditsky, Sue
Mt Olive HS
Budd Lake, NJ

Rudolph, Steven A
Collingswood HS
Collingswood, NJ

Ruela, Anthony J
Carteret HS
Carteret, NJ

Ruiz, Raoul
Bloomfield SR HS
Bloomfield, NJ

Ruscingno, Donna
Ridgefield Park HS
Little Ferry, NJ

Rush, Daryn E
Phillipsburg HS
Stewartsville, NJ

Russell, Carl
Hightstown HS
Hightstown, NJ

Russell, Steve
Salem HS
Salem, NJ

Russo, Jeana
Lodi HS
Lodi, NJ

Russo, Joann
Phillipsburg HS
Phillipsburg, NJ

Russo, Mariclaire
Sacred Heart HS
Vineland, NJ

Rust, Tara
Woodstown HS
Alloway, NJ

Ruszala, Greg
St Thomas Aquinas/
Bishop Ahr
Colonia, NJ

Ruth, Keith
Elmwood Park
Memorial HS
Elmwood Pk, NJ

Ruvo, Scott J
Pope John XXIII
Sparta, NJ

Ruyak, Craig
Hamilton High East
Hamilton Sq, NJ

Ryan, III John T
Seton Hall Prep
New Providence, NJ

Ryerson, Anne
Morris Catholic HS
Boonton, NJ

Saam, Bill
Voorhees HS
Hampton, NJ

Sabarese, Ted
Christian Brothers
Colts Neck, NJ

Sabbath, Joseph W
Pequannock
Township HS
Pompton Plains, NJ

Saber, Kristine L
Williamstown HS
Williamstown, NJ

Sabo, Stephanie
Ann
Morris Hills
Regional HS
Wharton, NJ

Sacco, Louis W
Buena Regional HS
Richland, NJ

Sacco, Mark
South Plainfield HS
S Plainfield, NJ

Sadhar, Amrit
Mother Seton
Regional HS
Hillside, NJ

Sadler, Elise
Woodrow Wilson SR
Camden, NJ

Sadovy, David J
Hamilton HS North
Trenton, NJ

Sagrestano, Kenneth
Bridgewater-Raritan
East HS
Bridgewater, NJ

Saks, Jeffrey
Abraham Clark HS
Roselle, NJ

Salayi, Jennifer
Mater Dei HS
Middletown, NJ

Salgado, Jr
Fernando
Watchung Hills
Regional HS
Gillette, NJ

Salgado, Margarit
Perth Amboy HS
Perth Amboy, NJ

Salko, Thomas
Bayley-Ellard HS
Whippany, NJ

Sallata, Suzanne
Atlantic City HS
Ventnor, NJ

Sallee, Paul W
Middletown HS
Middletown, NJ

Salmon, Laura
Diane
Pompton Lakes HS
Pompton Lakes, NJ

Salters, Audra
Linden HS
Linden, NJ

Salvaggio, Ralph J
Dwight Morrow HS
Englewood, NJ

Salvatore, Allison
Clayton HS
Clayton, NJ

Salvatore, Mary
Beth
Bishop Ahr HS
Belle Meade, NJ

Samalis, Jennifer
Red Bank Catholic
Loch Arbour, NJ

Samuel, Loleta
Lincoln HS
Jersey City, NJ

Sanchez, Celso
Highland Park HS
Highland Park, NJ

Sanchez, Igmara
Our Lady Of Good
Newark, NJ

Sanchez, Pedro
St Joseph Of The
Palisades HS
Union City, NJ

Sanders, Elizabeth
Parsippany Hills HS
Mt Tabor, NJ

Sandrue, Darrell
Hackettstown HS
Long Valley, NJ

Sanney, Stacie
Hopewell Valley
Central HS
Hopewell, NJ

Santana, Julissa
Katherine
Paul VI Regional
Passaic, NJ

Santilli, Lynn
Rancocas Valley
Regional HS
Mount Holly, NJ

Santino, Janine
Emerson JR SR HS
Emerson, NJ

Santonastaso, Ralph
North Plainfield HS
N Plainfield, NJ

Santora, Scott
Wayne Hills HS
Wayne, NJ

Santoro, Chuck
Paramus HS
Paramus, NJ

Santos, Nuno
St Peters Prep
Newark, NJ

Santos, Regina
Red Bank Regional
Union Bch, NJ

Saraco, Arlene
Bishop Ahr/St
Thomas HS
Colonia, NJ

Sasso, Robert
Lodi HS
Lodi, NJ

Sauers, Amanda
Williamstown HS
Williamstown, NJ

Saulog, Aimee E
St Pius X Regional
Piscataway, NJ

Saums, Kathryn
Hunterdon Central
Flemington, NJ

Sauter, Luisa P
Holy Family Acad
Bayonne, NJ

Savery, II Charles
Haddonfield
Memorial HS
Haddonfield, NJ

Savitsky, Anne P
Pascack Valley HS
River Vale, NJ

Sawaged, Raid
Hudson Catholic HS
Jersey Cty, NJ

Sawhney, Roger Anu
Wardlaw-Hartridge
Edison, NJ

Saylor, Debra
Washington
Township HS
Turnersville, NJ

Scaglione, Kristin
St Pius Regional HS
Dunellen, NJ

Scales, Tara
Marylawn Of The
Oranges HS
E Orange, NJ

Scalpati, Carroll
Ocean Township HS
Ocean, NJ

Scanlon, Jr Robert
A
Don Bosco Prep HS
Fairlawn, NJ

Scanzera, Beth
Bloomfield HS
Bloomfield, NJ

Scarani, Gia
Sacred Heart HS
Bridgeton, NJ

Schaefer, Jennifer
Hunterdon Central
Whitehouse Sta, NJ

Schafer, Dean J
Seton Hall Prep
Kenilworth, NJ

Schafer, Gene
Paramus Catholic
Boys HS
Rochelle Pk, NJ

Scharpf, Eric
Christian Brothers
Colts Neck, NJ

Schechter, Kim
Bridgewater Raritan
H S East HS
Bridgewater, NJ

Scheinthal, Lisa
Montville Township
Pine Brook, NJ

Schipsi, Lisa
Paul VI HS
Somerdale, NJ

Schipske, Monica P
Delsea Regional HS
Franklinville, NJ

Schlatmann, Raymond
Lakewood HS
Lakewood, NJ

Schlosser, Sandra
Timothy Christian
Warren, NJ

Schmidig, Brian
Henry P Becton Reg
East Rutherford, NJ

Schmidt, Christy A
St John Vianney HS
Bricktown, NJ

Schmitt, Robert
Northern Valley-Old
Tappan HS
Old Tappan, NJ

Schnabel, Greg
E Brunswick HS
E Brunswick, NJ

Schnabolk, Howard
Red Bank Catholic
Ocean, NJ

Schneck, Thomas W
Camden Catholic
Medford, NJ

Schneider, Brian
Hackettstown HS
Hackettstown, NJ

Schneider, Doron
Summit HS
Summit, NJ

Schneider, Michele
Middlesex HS
Middlesex, NJ

Schneider, Nancy
Butler HS
Bloomingdale, NJ

Schnell, Brian
Ridgefeld Park HS
Ridgefield Pk, NJ

Schnepp, Libby
Bishop Eustace Prep
Pennsauken, NJ

Schnitzer, Lori
Linden HS
Linden, NJ

Schoch, Gail
Washington Twp
Turnersville, NJ

Schoenberger, Wendi
Fair Lawn HS
Fair Lawn, NJ

Schoenwald, Ellen
Colonia HS
Colonia, NJ

Schonenberger, Simone
Park Ridge HS
Park Ridge, NJ

Schoonmaker, Jack
Brick HS
Brick, NJ

Schorr, Heather
West Morris
Mendram HS
Brookside, NJ

Schott, Darlene
Mahwah HS
Mahwah, NJ

Schroetter, Thomas
Mater Dei HS
Hazlet, NJ

Schubel, Liam
Freehold Township
Freehold, NJ

Schubiger, Scott
Lacey Township HS
Forked River, NJ

Schuler, Kristin
Scotch
Plains-Fanwood HS
Fanwood, NJ

Schulz, James
Hamilton HS
Yardville, NJ

Schuyler, Deborah
East Orange HS
E Orange, NJ

Schwartz, Abbe
Hackettstown HS
Hackettstown, NJ

Schwarz, Cathy
Franklin HS
Princeton, NJ

Schwietering, Barbra
Colonia HS
Colonia, NJ

Schworn, Lisa
Brick Township HS
Brick Town, NJ

Sciancalepore, Lawrence
Hoboken HS
Hoboken, NJ

Sciarrone, Denise
Passaic Valley HS
Little Falls, NJ

Scillieri, Joseph J
Pompton Lakes HS
Pompton Lakes, NJ

Sciretta, Michael
Scott
Bishop George AHR
Old Bridge, NJ

Scola, Robin M
Mahwah HS
Mahwah, NJ

Scott, Christopher P
Absegami HS
Oceanville, NJ

Scott, Gregory A
Holmdel HS
Holmdel, NJ

Scott, Jeffrey R
Sayreville War
Memorial HS
Parlin, NJ

Scribellito, David
Toms River HS East
Toms River, NJ

Seals, Heather
Mt Olive HS
Budd Lake, NJ

See, Jennifer
Mother Seton
Regional HS
Carteret, NJ

Seliger, Raymond
Wildwood Catholic
Avalon, NJ

Seligman, Erik
Ranapo HS
Wyckoff, NJ

Sen, Aparup
Waldwick HS
Waldwick, NJ

Sepanic, Jennifer
Audubon HS
Audubon, NJ

Seri, Angela
Pinelands Regional
Egg Harbor, NJ

Sessa, Sandra
Columbia HS
Maplewood, NJ

Setter, Catherine
Haddonfield
Memorial HS
Haddonfield, NJ

Severino, William
North Bergen HS
Ridgefield, NJ

Sewall, Lindsey D
Haddon Township
Haddonfield, NJ

Sexton, Michele
Saint Rose HS
Spring Lake Hgts, NJ

Shady, Kathryn
Point Pleasant
Beach HS
Lavallette, NJ

Shaffer, Ronald
Overbrook Regional
Berlin, NJ

Shah, Sonal
Dickinson HS
Jersey City, NJ

Shand, Eileen
Toms River East HS
Toms River, NJ

Shandor, Jennifer
Belvidere HS
Phillipsburg, NJ

Shannon, Thomas
Rutgers Prep
Berkeley Hts, NJ

Sharar, Linda
Dorothy
Glen Rock HS
Glen Rock, NJ

Sharkey, Greg
Toms Rive HS
Toms River, NJ

Sharkey, Kathleen
Pope John XXIII
Regional HS
Oak Ridge, NJ

Sharkey, Kim
Brick Township HS
Brick, NJ

Sharp, Martha Joy
Hunterdon Central
Grand Rapids, MI

Sharpe, Rhonda
Cumberland
Regional HS
Bridgeton, NJ

Shaughnessy,
Maureen
Bishop George Ahr
Colonia, NJ

Shaughnessy, Sara
St Rose HS
Point Pleasant, NJ

Shaw, Deborah Jean
Haddonfield
Memorial HS
Haddonfield, NJ

Shaw, Kelly
Manalapan HS
Manalapan, NJ

Shaw, Tracee
Freehold Township
Freehold Twp, NJ

Shea, Michael
Christian Brothers
Brielle, NJ

Shears, Tracey
Holy Cross HS
Browns Mills, NJ

Sheikh, Muhammad
Dickinson HS
Jersey, NJ

Shelton, Tanya
Pennsauken HS
Delair, NJ

Shepard, Michael
Wayne Hills HS
Wayne, NJ

Shepherd, Kimberly
Delaware Valley
Regional HS
Milford, NJ

Sheppard, Edward
Hudson Cath
Jersey Cty, NJ

Sheppard, Mignon
Lacordaire Acad
Newark, NJ

Sheppard, Sean P
Notre Dame HS
Kendall Park, NJ

Sherma, Shirvan
Marie
Our Lady Of Mercy
Mays Landing, NJ

Sherman, Jeanine
St John Vianney HS
Matawan, NJ

Sherman, Jonathan
M
Livingston HS
Livingston, NJ

Sherrier, William
Rahway HS
Rahway, NJ

Shick, Hubert
Cinnaminson HS
Cinnaminson, NJ

Shimshak, Randi
Bayonne HS
Bayonne, NJ

Shindler, Carol
Bridgeton HS
Bridgeton, NJ

Shipley, Helene
Spotswood HS
Spotswood, NJ

Shontz, Karen
Northern Burlington
Co Reg HS
Vincentown, NJ

Shrekgast, Greg
Wall HS
Wall Twp, NJ

Shuback, Harry J
Morris Hills HS
Wharton, NJ

Shue, John Madison
Columbia HS
South Orange, NJ

Shue, Susanna G
Phillipsburg HS
Phillipsburg, NJ

Shupack, Michelle L
South Plainfield HS
So Plainfield, NJ

Shustack, Kimberly
Colonia HS
Colonia, NJ

Sickels, Dawn M
Matawan Regional
Matawan, NJ

Sidaros, Maged
Marist HS
Jersey City, NJ

Siggins, Lisa
High Point Regional
Branchville, NJ

Silikovitz, Harvey
W Orange HS
W Orange, NJ

Silletti, Jason J
Bergen Catholic HS
Bogota, NJ

Silverman, Erika
St Peters HS
Kendall Park, NJ

Simmonds, Dale
Orange HS
Orange, NJ

Simmons, Faith C
Edgewood Regional
SR HS
Berlin, NJ

Simmons, Julie
Belvidere HS
Belvidere, NJ

Simonelli, Emilia
Shore Regional HS
W Long Branch, NJ

Simonelli, James
High School East
Toms River, NJ

Simons, Gregory
East Brunswick HS
East Brunswick, NJ

Simpkins, Barbara
Riverside HS
Delanco, NJ

Sims, Elizabeth
Red Bank Regional
Little Silver, NJ

Sinatra, Rocco
Lacey Township HS
Forked River, NJ

Sinclair, Jennifer
Vernon Township
Vernon, NJ

Singer, Scott
Raritan HS
Hazlet, NJ

Singh, Raj R
Moorestown Friends
Willingboro, NJ

Sinha, Parakh
Wardlaw-Hartridge
Colonia, NJ

Sinnott, Adrienne
Academic HS
Jersey City, NJ

Sinopoli, Cheryl
Rutherford HS
Rutherford, NJ

Siracusa, Christine
Red Bank Catholic
Middletown, NJ

Sirak, Stacie A
Holy Cross HS
Beverly, NJ

Sirangelo, Mary
St Marys HS
Parlin, NJ

Sitler, Pamela
Phillipsburg HS
Phillipsburg, NJ

Siwy, Cherish
S Hunterdon
Regional HS
Lambertville, NJ

Skeens, Scott J
Warren Hills
Regional SR HS
Broadway, NJ

Skewes, William A
Ridgewood HS
Ridgewood, NJ

Sklenar, Mark J
Wayne Valley HS
Wayne, NJ

Skrenta, Elizabeth
Ann
Wallington HS
Wallington, NJ

Skroce, Meri
Cliffside Park HS
Cliffside Pk, NJ

Slack, Thomas H
Cherry Hill HS East
Cherry Hill, NJ

Slate, Jason
Ocean Township HS
Oakhurst, NJ

Slattery, Stephen
Morris Catholic HS
Succasunna, NJ

Sloan, Debra
Cherry Hill West
Cherry Hill, NJ

Sloss, Mark A
Neptune SR HS
Neptune, NJ

Small, Jackie
Linden HS
Linden, NJ

Smetana, Deborah
Pope John Xx111
Andover, NJ

Smetana, Matthew J
Pope John XXIII
Andover, NJ

Smith, Alissa
Hamilton High
School North
Trenton, NJ

Smith, Anita
Abraham Clark HS
Roselle, NJ

Smith, Craig
Christian Brothers
Red Bank, NJ

Smith, Craig D
Teaneck HS
Teaneck, NJ

Smith, Dawn
Phillipsburg HS
Phillipsburg, NJ

Smith, Donald
Holy Cross HS
Delran, NJ

Smith, Doug
Brick Township HS
Brick Town, NJ

Smith, Earlyne
Weequahic HS
Newark, NJ

Smith, Ernest
Nathaniel
Teaneck HS
Teaneck, NJ

Smith, Estelle M
Delaware Valley
Regional HS
Milford, NJ

Smith, Jennifer
Toms River N HS
Toms River, NJ

Smith, Julia M
Jonathan Dayton
Reg HS
Mountainside, NJ

Smith, Kathy
Toms River HS
Toms River, NJ

Smith, Kimberly
Hackettstown HS
Great Meadows, NJ

Smith, Lori
Ocean Township HS
Oceantwp, NJ

Smith, Lynne
Mainland Regional
Hatfield, PA

Smith, Monica
Metuchen HS
Metuchen, NJ

Smith, Pamela M
Plainfield HS
Plainfield, NJ

Smith, Stacey
St Joseph HS
Collingslakes, NJ

Smith, Susan
Edgewood Regional
SR HS
Atco, NJ

Smith, William
Cinnaminson HS
Cinnaminson, NJ

Snyder, Kerri
Mount Saint Mary
Dunellen, NJ

Snyder, Terri
Millville SR HS
Heislerville, NJ

Soety, John J
Monroe Township
Spotswood, NJ

Sofield, Kevin
Ocean Township HS
Oakhurst, NJ

Sofroney, Sandra
Atlantic Christian
Ocean View, NJ

Sokalski, Elizabeth
Union HS
Unin, NJ

Sokolowski, Carol
St John Vianney HS
Morganville, NJ

Solan, Joe A
Mount Olive HS
Flanders, NJ

Sollog, II John
Joseph
Middletown HS
Red Bank, NJ

Solomon, Jonathan
Freehold Twp HS
Farmingdale, NJ

Soni, Rita
Mt Olive HS
Flanders, NJ

Sorrentino, Susan
East Brunswick HS
E Brunswick, NJ

Spafford, Maryann
Matawan Regional
Aberdeen, NJ

Spahr, Renee
Secaucus HS
Secaucus, NJ

Span, Henry A
Westfield SR HS
Westfield, NJ

Sparks, Christy
Lower Cape May
Regional HS
Cape May, NJ

Sparrock, Anne
Ocean Twp HS
Wayside, NJ

Sparta, Karen
West Milford
Township HS
Hewitt, NJ

Speed, Bonnie
Lakeland Regional
Ringwood, NJ

Speer, Karen
Hightstown HS
Hightstown, NJ

Speller, Crystal D
Union Catholic
Regional HS
Newark, NJ

Spenger, Gregg W
Bound Brook HS
Bound Brook, NJ

Spigner, Charlene
Hillside HS
Hillside, NJ

Spina, Michael
Delsca Regional HS
Franklinville, NJ

Spinello, Erin
Queen Of Peace HS
Kearny, NJ

Spitaletta, Alex
Emerson HS
Union City, NJ

Spitzberg, Erin
East Brunswick HS
Watchung, NJ

Spitzer, Matthew C
Millburn SR HS
Short Hills, NJ

Spooner, Erica
Lakewood HS
Lakewood, NJ

Spoto, Glenn
Montville Township
Montville, NJ

Sprague, John
Pinelands Regional
Tuckerton, NJ

Sprague, Linda
Nottingham HS
Wrightstown, NJ

Spreen, Julie K
Hawthorne HS
Hawthorne, NJ

Spuler, Steve
Delran HS
Delran, NJ

Squiccimarra, Lynn
Spotswood HS
Spotswood, NJ

Sribar, Valentin T
John P Stevens HS
Edison, NJ

Stagliano, Theresa
Bishp Ahr-St
Thomas Quinas HS
Perth Amboy, NJ

Stahlberger, William
H
Bridgeton HS
Bridgeton, NJ

Stamos, Deidre
Red Bank Catholic
Brielle, NJ

Stankiewicz,
Michael D
Millburn HS
Short Hills, NJ

Stanley, Tawanna
Plainfield HS
Piscataway, NJ

Stanz, Brian
Washington
Township HS
Sewell, NJ

Stanziano, Darren
St Peter's Prep
Jersey City, NJ

Stanzione, Jennifer
Toms River HS East
Toms River, NJ

Starkey, Beth
Steinert HS
Hamilton Square,
NJ

Staruch, Todd
Union HS
Union, NJ

Stasi, Evamarie
Roselle Catholic HS
Elizabeth, NJ

Stauffer, Ricky
Vineland HS
Vineland, NJ

Steed, Deirdre
St John Vianney HS
Colts Neck, NJ

Stefanchik, John A
Princeton HS
Princeton, NJ

Steglitz, Brian D
Columbia HS
South Orange, NJ

Stein, Valarie A
Belvidere HS
Phillipsburg, NJ

Steiner, Anita
John P Stevens HS
Edison, NJ

Steinhauer, Mary
Bridgeton HS
Newport, NJ

Stemmer, Tammy
Lynn
Rancocas Valley
Regional HS
Mount Holly, NJ

Sterling, Jr Francis
X
Morris Knolls HS
Dover, NJ

Stern, Lawrence
Madison Central HS
Old Bridge, NJ

Stevens, Brian
Middletown High
School South
Red Bank, NJ

Stevenson, Joe
Anthony
Camden HS
Camden, NJ

Stewart, Allan
Queen Of Peace HS
North Arlington, NJ

Stewart, John
Salem HS
Salem, NJ

Stewart, Pamela
Camden HS
Camden, NJ

Stibitz, David M
Southern Regional
Manahawkin, NJ

Stocker, Gerard
Toms River East HS
Toms River, NJ

Stoecker, Michael
North Bergen HS
Guttenberg, NJ

Stojalowsky, Laszlo
J
St Josephs
Preparatory Semina
Trenton, NJ

Stokes, Bernadette
Hillside HS
Hillside, NJ

Stone, Kevin
Red Bank Catholic
Freehold, NJ

Stonebraker, Dave
Christian Brothers
Bricktown, NJ

Storch, Susan
Manalapan HS
Manalapan, NJ

Storck, Colleen
Paterson Catholic
Regional HS
Paterson, NJ

Strahle, Robert E
West
Windsor-Plainsbor
Robbinsville, NJ

Stramaglia,
Christopher
Saddle River Day
Cliffside Park, NJ

Straten, Thomas
Hoboken HS
Hoboken, NJ

Straup, Renee
Overbrook Reg SR
Lindenwold, NJ

Strehle, Melissa
Jackson Memorial
Jackson, NJ

Strickland, Tamika
L
Edgewood HS
Sicklerville, NJ

Strong, Mary Louise
Hunterdon Central
Flemington, NJ

Suarez, Joyceann
Lodi HS
Lodi, NJ

Suillivan, Barbara
Morris Catholic HS
Lk Hiawatha, NJ

Sullivan, Chandra
Yvette
Vailsburg HS
Newark, NJ

Sullivan, John
Christian Brothers
Manalapan, NJ

Sulzinsky, John G
St Joseph HS
Milltown, NJ

Sun, Edmond
Jackson Memorial
Jackson, NJ

Sundararaj, Suja
South Brunswick
Kendall Park, NJ

Suppa, Stephanie
Ocean Township HS
Ocean Township, NJ

Surman, Lori
Lenape HS
Indian Mills, NJ

Sussna, Tracy
Lakewood HS
Lakewood, NJ

Sutton, Rita
Mainland Regional
Northfield, NJ

Sutton, Stacey
Hamilton H S East
Hamilton Sq, NJ

Swartz, Christine L
Whippany Park HS
Morris Plains, NJ

Swartz, Jr Harold J
Pleasantville HS
Pleasantville, NJ

Swayze, Bill
Dover HS
Dover, NJ

Sweeney, Kathleen
Holy Cross HS
Riverside, NJ

Sweitzer, Joseph H
The Pilgrim Acad
Northfield, NJ

Swezey, Wayne W
Midland Park HS
Midland Park, NJ

Swieconek, April
Delaware Valley
Regional HS
Milford, NJ

Swift, Patrick
Hudson Catholic HS
Jersey City, NJ

Swon, Kimberly A
West Morris
Mendham HS
Brookside, NJ

Swope, Nancy Ann
Mahwah HS
Mahwah, NJ

Sydlowski, Barb
BRHS-WEST HS
Bridgewater, NJ

Szabo, Gabriella
North Warren
Regional HS
Delaware, NJ

Szatkowski, Sean
North Plainfield HS
N Plainfield, NJ

Szczepaniak, Nancy
Matawan Regional
Matawan, NJ

Szep, Kristina
Franklin HS
Somerset, NJ

Szewczuk, John
Toms River HS
Toms River, NJ

Szilassy, Paul
Washington Twp
Turnersville, NJ

Szumski, Cindy
South River HS
South River, NJ

Szymanski, Ellen
Oak Knoll School Of
Bedminster, NJ

Tabacchi, Michael
Manalapan HS
Englishtown, NJ

Tabaka, Joelle L
Clifton HS
Clifton, NJ

Tabar, Jeffrey
A P Schalick HS
Bridgeton, NJ

Tabs, Daniel
West Essex SR HS
N Caldwell, NJ

Tafaro, Maria
West Essex Regional
N Caldwell, NJ

Tahan, Michelle
Paul VI Regional
Clifton, NJ

Talone, Paul J
Triton Regional HS
Runnemede, NJ

Talpas, Chris
Phillipsburg HS
Phillipsburg, NJ

Tambone, Michael
Middlesex HS
Middlesex, NJ

Taranto, Mary
Ramapo Regional
Wyckoff, NJ

Tarasevitsch, Nina L
Woodbridge SR HS
Iselin, NJ

Tardiff, Dean
Notre Dame HS
Hamilton Sq, NJ

Tarzy, James B
Cherokee HS
Marlton, NJ

Taylor, Amy Suzanne
Kittatinny Regional
Newton, NJ

Taylor, Holly
Wildwood HS
N Wildwood, NJ

Taylor, Kelly
Delsea Regional HS
Franklinville, NJ

Taylor, Robert
East Brunswick HS
E Brunswick, NJ

Taylor, Tanya M
Newark Acad
S Orange, NJ

Teat, Tanya
Marylawn Of The Oranges HS
S Orange, NJ

Tedeschi, Lisa
Cranford HS
Cranford, NJ

Tedesco, Michelle K
Monsignor Donovan
Whiting, NJ

Teevan, Martin
Christian Brothers
Holmdel, NJ

Teich, Tammy D
Montville HS
Pine Brook, NJ

Telesh, John
Hopatcong HS
Hopatcong, NJ

Temple, Patrick
Jefferson Township
Oakridge, NJ

Tencza, William
St Ros HS
Neptune City, NJ

Teri, Anthony
Bayonne HS
Bayonne, NJ

Terrell, Brenda Sheree
Red Bank Catholic
Neptune, NJ

Testa, Susan E
Buena Regional HS
Landisville, NJ

Teter, Thomas
St Augustine Prep
Vineland, NJ

Teti, Donna Marie
Pennsauken HS
Pennsauken, NJ

Thaxton, Cheryl
Immaculate Conception HS
East Orange, NJ

Theriault, Mark
Holy Cross HS
Riverton, NJ

Thomas, Carol
Westfield SR HS
Westfield, NJ

Thomas, Christine
Bayonne HS
Bayonne, NJ

Thomas, Denne
John F Kennedy HS
Willingboro, NJ

Thompson, Ann
Metuchen HS
Metuchen, NJ

Thompson, Carol
Eastside HS
Paterson, NJ

Thompson, Elda
Vailsburg HS
Newark, NJ

Thompson, Tina
Middletown South
Highlands, NJ

Thorne, Lisa
Shore Regional HS
Oceanport, NJ

Thorp, George
Cloucester Catholic
Brooklawn, NJ

Thorpe, Jennifer
Toms River East HS
Toms River, NJ

Throm, Colin C
Montgomery HS
Skillman, NJ

Tice, Janet
Burlington City HS
Burlington, NJ

Tierney, Michael
Holy Spirit HS
Ventnor, NJ

Tighe, Kevin
St John Vianney HS
Hazlet, NJ

Tillman, Carla
Middlesex HS
Middlesex, NJ

Tilton, Cori
Woodstown HS
Elmer, NJ

Tilton, Monica
Red Bank Catholic
Old Bridge, NJ

Timko, Donna
Spotswood HS
Milltown, NJ

Timonera, Mayda
Washington Township HS
Sewell, NJ

Tindell, Shannan
Benedictine Acad
Newark, NJ

Tirella, Michael
Butler HS
Butler, NJ

Tirenin, Michael
Hopewell Valley Central HS
Trenton, NJ

Todd, Jeffrey
Linden HS
Linden, NJ

Todd, Margaret
Lower Cape May Regional HS
N Cape May, NJ

Toland, Kimberly
Holy Spirit HS
Atlantic City, NJ

Tolbert, Valencia Ninette
Trenton Central HS
Trenton, NJ

Tolmayer, Robert J
Rancocas Valley Regional HS
Mt Holly, NJ

Tomarchio, Brian
Washington Township HS
Turnersville, NJ

Tomkovich, Celeste
Manalapan HS
Manalapan, NJ

Toner, Eileen
Roselle Catholic HS
Roselle, NJ

Toney, Quandal
Abraham Clark HS
Roselle, NJ

Tool, Kristina
Southern Regional
Beach Haven, NJ

Torres, Alexander
St John Vianney HS
Freehold, NJ

Torres, Edwin
Christian Brothers
Freehold, NJ

Torres, Lisa Marie
Paramus Catholic Girls Regionl HS
Fair Lawn, NJ

Torres, Ty A
Point Pleasant Beach HS
Point Pleasnt Bch, NJ

Torruellas, Madeline R
Camden County Voc Trade Schl
Camden, NJ

Torsiello, Bryon
Rutherford HS
Rutherford, NJ

Tortorelli, Raymond
Audubon HS
Mt Ephraim, NJ

Tovar, Adrianne
Bayonne HS
Bayonne, NJ

Towey, Cara L
Northern Valley HS
Harrington Park, NJ

Traeger, Geoffrey
Lenape Valley Regional HS
Andover, NJ

Travers, Christopher
Cedar Grove Memorial HS
Cedar Grove, NJ

Treacy, Shelley Ann
Shore Regional HS
Oceanport, NJ

Tredici, Frank
Bishop AHR HS
Edison, NJ

Tretina, Marcel
Mater Dei HS
Union Beach, NJ

Triano, Edwin
Queen Of Peace HS
Kearny, NJ

Trilone, Donna
Manville HS
Manville, NJ

Trilone, Kelly A
Manville HS
Manville, NJ

Triola, Stacey
Bridgewater-Raritan
H S East
Bridgewater, NJ

Trivedi, Sunil J
West Milford HS
West Milford, NJ

Troiano, Laurie
North Bergen HS
N Bergen, NJ

Troller, Mark
Wallington HS
Wallington, NJ

Troller, Scott
Wallington HS
Wallington, NJ

Troumees, Linda
Cumberland
Regional HS
Bridgeton, NJ

Trovato, Sandra
Morris Knolls HS
Dover, NJ

Trudeau, Michael
Oakcrest HS
Mays Landing, NJ

Trueman, Jennifer P
Sussex Co Vo-Tech
Hamburg, NJ

Truong, Tri M
Monroe Township
Spotswood, NJ

Tucker, Lloyd A
Hopewell Valley
Central HS
Hopewell, NJ

Tuers, Jody
Shore Regional HS
W Long Branch, NJ

Tuers, Kipp
Shore Regional HS
W Long Branch, NJ

Tumser, Keith
Fair Lawn HS
Fair Lawn, NJ

Tuohy, John
Christian Brothers
Aberdeen, NJ

Turner, Bill
Atlanitc Christian
Mays Landing, NJ

Turner, Jonathan M
Toms River High
School East
Toms River, NJ

Turner, Matthew
Morris Catholic HS
Flanders, NJ

Turner, Steve
Sacred Heart HS
Vineland, NJ

Tuttle, April
Middletown HS
Leonard, NJ

Twohy, Mary Sue
St John Vianney
Regional HS
Aberdeen, NJ

Tyhanic, Kurt
Pinelands Regional
Tuckerton, NJ

Tyler, Philip
Clifford J Scott HS
E Orange, NJ

Tylicki, Donna
Linden HS
Linden, NJ

Tymkow, Tammy
Marie
Toms River South
Beachwood, NJ

Uibelhoer, Denise
Roselle Catholic HS
Roselle Park, NJ

Urbano, Frank L
Toms River H S
Toms River, NJ

Urbano, Michael A
Passaic HS
Passaic, NJ

Urbay, Olivette
Memorial HS
West New York, NJ

Urion, Alice
Woodstown HS
Woodstown, NJ

Uron, Rebecca M
Edgewood Regional
SR HS
Waterford, NJ

Usarzewicz, Mark J
St Peters Prep
Bayonne, NJ

Ustin, Karen
Montville Township
Pine Brk, NJ

Vaclavicek, Renee
Immaculate
Conception HS
Little Falls, NJ

Valaveris, Anna
Hackensack HS
Hackensack, NJ

Valente, Michael
Sayreville War
Memorial HS
Parlin, NJ

Valentine, Michael
Pope John XXIII
Oak Ridge, NJ

Valian, David
Linden HS
Linden, NJ

Vallabhaneni,
Surendra
East Brunswick HS
E Brunswick, NJ

Valverde, Kenneth
David
Perth Amboy HS
Perth Amboy, NJ

Van Dyke, Tracy
Ramapo HS
Franklin Lakes, NJ

Van Gronigen,
Joseph
Paul VI HS
Glendora, NJ

Van Horn, Denise
Delsea Regional HS
Franklinville, NJ

Van Orden, Ann
Marie
Dover HS
Mine Hill, NJ

Van Steen, Leslie
Pemberton
Township H S II
Browns Mills, NJ

Van Winkle, Debby
Passaic Valley HS
W Paterson, NJ

Van Winkle, James
Hudson Catholic HS
Secaucus, NJ

Vanaman, Robert
Millville SR HS
Millville, NJ

Vance, Bonnie
Holy Spirit HS
Margate, NJ

Vandenberg, Loretta
Monteville
Township HS
Towaco, NJ

Vander Meer,
Debbie
Toms River High
School South
Toms River, NJ

Vandermark, Anne
Hightstown HS
Cranbury, NJ

Vannest, Aymee
Secaucus HS
Secaucus, NJ

Vasser, Edward
Holy Spirit HS
Margate, NJ

Vaughan, Marnie
Hightstown HS
East Windsor, NJ

Vaughn, Joel
Freehold Twp HS
Freehold, NJ

Vega, Juanita
Arts HS
Newark, NJ

Veit, Jr Richard F
South Plainfield HS
So Plnfld, NJ

Velardi, Ronica
Toms River High
School South
Toms River, NJ

Velasco, Julian
Bishop Ahr St
Thomas Aquinas HS
Perth Amboy, NJ

Velasquez, Brenda
Middletown H S
Lincroft, NJ

Velazquez, Dionisio
D
North Bergen HS
North Bergen, NJ

Veleber, Allison
Eastern Christian
Towaco, NJ

Velez, Deborah
Pennsville Memorial
Pennsville, NJ

Velez, Elsie
Frank H Morrell HS
Irvington, NJ

Velez, Mary Jo G
West Orange HS
W Orange, NJ

Veltre, Adam John
Bishop George AHR
Old Bridge, NJ

Veltri, Gregory
Lodi HS
Lodi, NJ

Verhille, Lori
Washington
Township HS
Sewell, NJ

Verhoeven, Michelle
Mahwah HS
Mahwah, NJ

Versaci, Frederick
Hudson Catholic HS
Hoboken, NJ

Viereck, Charles A
Paulsboro HS
Gibbstown, NJ

Vij, Anil
Hudson Catholic HS
Jersey City, NJ

Villa, John
St Joseph Regional
Pearl River, NY

Villamaria, Edward
N
Teaneck HS
Teaneck, NJ

Villani, Ginalyn
Piscataway HS
Piscataway, NJ

Villasenor, Anne P
Bishop Eustace Prep
Seaford, DE

Vilord, Kimberly
Washington Twp
Turnersville, NJ

Vinkman, Victor
Olav
Parsippany HS
Parsippany, NJ

Vita, Jr Andrew S
Don Bosco Prep
Hawthorne, NJ

Vitale, Deborah
St Rose HS
Spring Lake, NJ

Vitali, Dominique
Glen Ridge HS
Glen Ridge, NJ

Vivenzio, Augie
St John Vianney HS
Morganville, NJ

Vivona, David
St John Vianney HS
Colts Neck, NJ

Voegeli, Christine
Hightstown HS
Cranbury, NJ

Vogeding, Mark
Edward
Paulsboro HS
Paulsboro, NJ

Vogel, Jeffrey
Manasquan HS
Brielle, NJ

Vogel, Jr Robert A
Randolph HS
Randolph, NJ

Vogt, Charlton
Paul VI HS
Barrington, NJ

Vogt, Tracey
Passaic Valley HS
Little Falls, NJ

Vogt, III William
Hamilton High East
Trenton, NJ

Voit, Beth
St James HS
Pennsville, NJ

Vosseller, David
Middlesex HS
Middlesex, NJ

Voulgaris, Dorothea
Fair Lawn HS
Fair Lawn, NJ

Vovchik, Victoria
Northern Valley
Regional HS
Harrington Pk, NJ

Vrsalovic, Tanja
Wallington HS
Wallington, NJ

Vydro, Carolee
St Mary HS
Passaic, NJ

Waddy, Gene C
Neptune SR HS
Neptune, NJ

Wade, Tracy Lynn
Immaculata HS
Middlesex, NJ

Wade, Yolanda C
Kent Place Schl
Newark, NJ

Wadsack, Jennifer
Chatham Twp HS
Chatham Twp, NJ

Waer, Carolyn
Susan
Audubon HS
Audubon, NJ

Wagner, Chris
Toms River HS East
Toms River, NJ

Wagner, Edward W
Westwood HS
Westwood, NJ

Wagner, Kirsten
Watching Hills
Regional HS
Warren, NJ

Wahlberg, Susan
Midland Park HS
Ho-Ho-Kus, NJ

Wain, Mary Frances
Newton HS
Newton, NJ

Wainwright, Scott
Christian Brothers
Brielle, NJ

Waiters, Katrina
Marylawn HS
Irvington, NJ

Wakefield, Wendy
Leigh
Hanover Park HS
E Hanover, NJ

Walker, Anita
Trenton Central HS
Trenton, NJ

Walker, Isabella
Secaucus HS
Secaucus, NJ

Walker, Tracy
Edison Vocational &
Technical HS
Elizabeth, NJ

Wallen, Amy Susan
Millville SR HS
Millville, NJ

Waller, Sabrina
Ewing HS
Trenton, NJ

Walling, Theresa
Middletown High
School South
Red Bank, NJ

Walsh, Aimee
Glen Rock HS
Glen Rock, NJ

Walstrom, Mary
Central Regional HS
Bayville, NJ

Walters, Joseph T
Maple Shade HS
Maple Shade, NJ

Walters, Thomas
Maranatha Christian
Marlboro, NJ

Wampler, Paul
Westfield SR HS
Westfield, NJ

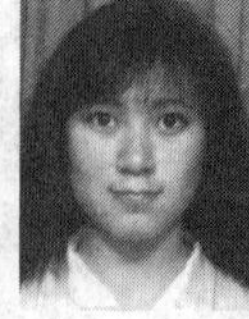

Wang, Hui
St Dominic Acad
Jersey City, NJ

Wang, Linda
Watchung Hills
Regional HS
Warren, NJ

Wardell, Charles
West Orange HS
W Orange, NJ

Warfield, Charles
Penns Greove HS
Carneys Point, NJ

Warner, Marc D
Lawrence HS
Lawrenceville, NJ

Warren, Melissa
Abraham Clark HS
Roselle, NJ

Washington,
Kassandra J
Pemberton Twp HS
Pemberton, NJ

Wastell, Charlotta
Bridgeton HS
Bridgeton, NJ

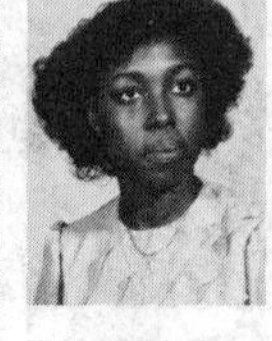

Waters, Nichelle
Camden HS
Camden, NJ

Waters, Tutasi
Marylawn Of The
Newark, NJ

Watson, Dawn
Paulsboro HS
Gibbstown, NJ

Watson, Lovie
Overbrook Regional
SR HS
Berlin, NJ

Watson, Richard F
Edgewood Regional
Sicklerville, NJ

Wavershak, Rose
Toms River HS East
Toms River, NJ

Webb, Michelle
Scotch
Plains-Fanwood HS
Scotch Plains, NJ

Weber, Susan
New Milford HS
New Milford, NJ

Weber, Tammy
Cumberland
Regional HS
Bridgeton, NJ

Weed, Mark
Union HS
Union, NJ

Weedon, Earl
Red Bank Catholic
Neptune, NJ

Weems, Michael
South River HS
S River, NJ

Weems, Richard K
Atlantic City HS
Ventnor, NJ

Weil, Jill Stacie
Union HS
Union, NJ

Weinberger, Beth
Overbrook Regional
Berlin, NJ

Weiner, David M
Westfield SR HS
Westfield, NJ

Weinstein, Kenneth
West Essex SR HS
Fairfield, NJ

Weinstein, Michael
Gill St Bernards HS
New Vernon, NJ

Weir, Dawn
John P Stevens HS
Edison, NJ

Weisert, Thomas
Seton Hall
Prepartory Schl
Hillside, NJ

Weisman, Lawrence
J
Jame Caldwell HS
W Caldwell, NJ

Weiss, Edward V
Monroe Township
Spotswood, NJ

Weiss, Karen
Spotswood HS
Milltown, NJ

Weitzman, Richard
Glen Rock HS
Glen Rock, NJ

Welch, Anthony S
Willingboro HS
Willingboro, NJ

Welsh, Margaret
Mary Help Of
Christians Acad
Suffern, NY

Welsh, Michael P
Mater Dei HS
Highlands, NJ

Wessner, Gregory
Burlington City HS
Edgewater Park, NJ

West, Steve A
Hackettstown HS
Hackettstown, NJ

Wetz, Ryan
Middletown South
Middletown, NJ

Whalen, Lachlan
Kittatinny Regional
Stillwater, NJ

Whetstone, Brian
High Point Regional
Sussex, NJ

White, Jeanne K
Morris Catholic HS
Parisippany, NJ

White, Leslie
Edison HS
Edison, NJ

White, Randy
Paulsboro HS
Paulsboro, NJ

White, Valerie
Denise
Millville SR HS
Millville, NJ

Whiteside, Kelly
Bishop Ahr HS
East Brunswick, NJ

Whiting, Terri
Clayton HS
Clayton, NJ

Whitman, Sherry
Arthur L Johnson
Regional HS
Clark, NJ

Wicke, Robert
Bishop Ahr HS
Edison, NJ

Wieczorek, Lisa
Middlesex HS
Middlesex, NJ

Wiedmann, James
Hillsborough HS
Belle Mead, NJ

Wieland, Kristine D
The Peddie Schl
E Windsor, NJ

Wieland, Ruth M
Pascack Valley HS
Hillsdale, NJ

Wiemer, Michael J
Atlantic City HS
Ventnor, NJ

Wiener, Andrew
Ocean Township HS
Ocean, NJ

Wiener, Kim
Glen Rock JR SR
Glen Rock, NJ

Wierciszewski,
Edward
Secaucus HS
Secaucus, NJ

Wilder, Lisa M
Willingboro HS
Willingboro, NJ

Wiley, Reginald D
Westfield HS
Westfield, NJ

Wilkes, Dawn
Teaneck HS
Teaneck, NJ

Will, Carolyn
Washington
Township HS
Turnersville, NJ

Willard, Randy
South Hunterdon
Regional HS
Lambertville, NJ

Williams, Jacqueline
Rahway HS
Rahway, NJ

Williams, Jeana
University HS
Newark, NJ

Williams, Jo Anne
Piscataway HS
Piscataway, NJ

Williams, Kamili
Immaculate
Conception HS
East Orange, NJ

Williams, Larry
Jackson Memorial
Jackson, NJ

Williams, Lori
Neptune SR HS
Neptune, NJ

Williams, Lucette
Ann
Ramsey HS
Ramsey, NJ

Williams, Marcia Y
Lawrence HS
Lawrenceville, NJ

Williams, Rachel
Garden State Acad
Paterson, NJ

Williams, Sandra
Lynn
Lodi HS
Lodi, NJ

Williamson, Gregg
West Essex SR HS
N Caldwell, NJ

Willis, Allen
Bridgeton HS
Bridgeton, NJ

Willman, Chris
Oakcrest HS
Mays Landing, NJ

Wilson, Amy
Ridge HS
Liberty Corner, NJ

Wilson, Cynthia J
Phillipsburgh HS
Phillipsburg, NJ

Wilson, Debra
Southern Regional
Barnegat, NJ

Wilson, Denise
Hamilton HS West
Trenton, NJ

Wilson, Dennis
Absegami HS
Absecon, NJ

Wilson, Kelly
Burlington City HS
Burlington, NJ

Wilson, Robin
Columbia HS
Maplewood, NJ

Wilson, Jr William
L
Wayne Hills HS
Wayne, NJ

Winans, Lori
Morris Knolls HS
Denville, NJ

Wingfield, Christine
Benedictine Acad
Orange, NJ

Winkler, Suzanne
Bridgewater Raritan
Bridgewater, NJ

Winsick, Jody
Secaucus HS
Secaucus, NJ

Wiser, Mark
Wayne Valley HS
Wayne, NJ

Wishart, Kimberly
Buena Regional HS
Milmay, NJ

Wittlinger, Linda
Hopewell Valley
Central HS
Pennington, NJ

Woelfle, Chris
Monsignor Donovan
Jackson, NJ

Wolf, III Robert D
Christian Brothers
Interlaken, NJ

Wolfberg, Mark
Montville Township
Towaco, NJ

Wolfsen, Julie
St John Vianney HS
Keyport, NJ

Wong, Betty
Cherry Hill HS
Cherry Hill, NJ

Wood, Kristen E
Hopewell Valley
Central HS
Pennington, NJ

Wood, Robyn
Linden HS
Linden, NJ

Wood, Tony
Hackettstown HS
Hackettstown, NJ

Woodring, Corey
Wallington HS
Cranford, NJ

Woollums, Michelle
Kearny HS
Kearny, NJ

Woolston, Tina
Marie
Burl Co Vo-Tech
Edgewater Pk, NJ

Woroniecka, Julita
Wm L Dickinson
Jersey City, NJ

Worthington, Jr
Gary
Overbrook Regional
W Berlin, NJ

Worthington,
Marjorie G
Hopewell Valley
Central HS
Pennington, NJ

Worthy, Bridget
Lakewood HS
Lakewood, NJ

Wozney, Kim
Waldwick HS
Waldwick, NJ

Woznicki, Tricia
Johnson Regional
Clark, NJ

Wright, Christina
Moon
James Caldwell HS
Caldwell, NJ

Wright, Lisa A
Mainland Regional
Somers Point, NJ

Wright, Lisa R
Northern Burlington
Co Reg HS
Wrightstown, NJ

Wurst, Eileen
Clifton HS
Clifton, NJ

Wyche, Todd B
Rancocas Valley
Regional HS
Mt Holly, NJ

Wymbs, Brian
Wood-Ridge HS
Wood-Ridge, NJ

Wymbs, Kevin
Middletown HS
Red Bank, NJ

Wyrough, Kelly E
Hamilton High West
Trenton, NJ

Xanthacos, Athena
Lakewood HS
Lakewood, NJ

Yaccarino, Chryssa
Ocean Township HS
Wayside, NJ

Yagozinski, Steven
Pope John XXIII
Lk Hopatcong, NJ

Yalong, Maria Fides
P
Bayonne HS
Bayonne, NJ

Yang, Arlene
Livingston HS
Livingston, NJ

Yang, Jing
Neptune SR HS
Neptune, NJ

Yarosh, Anthony J
Spotswood HS
Milltown, NJ

Yarusi, Stephanie
Central Regional HS
Seaside Park, NJ

Yeh, David M Y
Tenafly HS
Tenafly, NJ

Yesenosky, Mike
Passaic Valley Reg
West Patterson, NJ

Yesuvida, John
Linden HS
Linden, NJ

Yi, Heidi
Matawan Regional
Matawan, NJ

Yorio, Diana
Highland Park HS
Highland Park, NJ

Young, Audrey
Central HS
Newark, NJ

Young, Karin
Morris Knolls HS
Denville, NJ

Young, Susan
Middletown High
School South
Middletown, NJ

Younger, III Eugene
L
Arts HS
Newark, NJ

Younus, Zainab N
Washington
Township HS
Sewell, NJ

Yu, Eric T
Wayne Valley HS
Wayne Township,
NJ

Yuasa, Yoshiaki
West Essex SR HS
N Caldwell, NJ

Yun, Soojin
Linden HS
Linden, NJ

Zagorski, Sandy
Ocean Twp HS
Wayside, NJ

Zahorsky, Matthew
J
Wall HS
Allenwood, NJ

Zakroff, Stephen
Holy Cross HS
Cinnaminson, NJ

Zaleski, Erika
Union HS
Union, NJ

Zambrano, Anna
Villa Victoria Acad
Titusville, NJ

Zamora, Donald A
Lenape Valley
Regional HS
Andover, NJ

Zamora, Haydee M
St Joseph Of The
Palisades HS
North Bergen, NJ

Zampaglione,
Francine
Paulsboro HS
Gibbstown, NJ

Zapf, Edward
Southern Regional
Barnegat, NJ

Zapico, Anthony M
Kearny HS
Kearny, NJ

Zarelli, Leigh
Scotch Plaines
Fanwood HS
Scotch Plains, NJ

Zariczny, Lily
Holy Family Acad
Bayonne, NJ

Zavolas, Eva Lynn
Arthur L Johnson
Clark, NJ

Zdzienicki, Tara
St Marys HS
S Amboy, NJ

Zeller, Holly
Rancocas Valley
Regional HS
Medford, NJ

Zeller, Lisa
Chatham Township
Chatham, NJ

Zellers, Kathleen
Sussex Co Vo-Tech
Sussex, NJ

Zglobicki, Christine
Union Catholic
Regional HS
Colonial, NJ

Zick, Patricia
Toms River HS East
Toms River, NJ

Zilai, Mark
St Rose HS
Brielle, NJ

Zirrillo, Vincent
Red Bank Catholic
Long Branch, NJ

Zubar, Victor W
Sussex Vo-Tech HS
Highland Lakes, NJ

Zucca, Louise
Ernestine
Lacey Township HS
Forked River, NJ

Zuccarino, Jr Ralph
St Augustine Prep
Cardiff, NJ

Zukowski, Gregory A
De Paul HS
Wayne, NJ

Zuniga, Alexander
Arthur L Johnson
Reg HS
Clark, NJ

Zurlo, Laura
Highland Reg HS
Blackwood, NJ

PENNSYLVANIA

Aaron, Kelly Lynn
B Reed Henderson
West Chester, PA

Abadilla, Angela
Ambridge Area HS
Baden, PA

Abbadini, Angela
Brownsville Area HS
Brownsville, PA

Abbott, Kristen
Uniontown Area HS
Smock, PA

Abbruzzi, Mia
Saint Maria Goretti
Philadelphia, PA

Abeleda, Maria
Cedar Crest HS
Lebanon, PA

Abramason, Lisa
Lower Merion HS
Philadelphia, PA

Abrams, Karen
Akiba Hebrew Acad
Wyndmoor, PA

Abrams, Rosannette
Sayre Area HS
Sayre, PA

Abrams, Susan
St Maria Goretti HS
Philadelphia, PA

Abramson, Marla
Lower Moreland HS
Huntingdon Valley, PA

Abruzzo, Joseph
Roman Catholic HS
Philadelphia, PA

Abt, Eileen
The Harrisburg
Hershey, PA

Abt, Suzanne
Harrisburg Acad
Hershey, PA

Acker, Ron
Manheim Township
Lancaster, PA

Ackerman, Christine
Abington Heights
Clarks Summit, PA

Ackerman, Christine
St Huberts HS
Philadelphia, PA

Ackerman, John
Freedom HS
Easton, PA

Ackerman, R
Christian
Danville Area HS
Danville, PA

Ackinclose, Tim
Frazier HS
Fayette City, PA

Adair, John
Valley Forge
Military Acad
Glen Burnie, MD

Adamczak, Paul
Allentown Central
Catholic HS
Allentown, PA

Adametz, Greg
Belle Vernon Area
Belle Vernon, PA

Adams, Aida M
Phila HS Of
Engineering And Sci
Philadelphia, PA

Adams, Amber
Bishop Hannan HS
Scranton, PA

Adams, Kevin
Thomas
John S Fine SR HS
Nanticoke, PA

Adams, Olivia A
St Maria Goretti HS
Philadelphia, PA

Adams, Pam
Upper Dauphin
Area HS
Lykens, PA

Adams, Pam
West Middlesex JR
SR HS
Mercer, PA

Adams, Philip M
Pocono Mountain
Tannersville, PA

Adams, Tamara
Greater Works Acad
Monroeville, PA

Addis, John
Bradford Area HS
Derrick City, PA

Adelson, Susan
Coughlin HS
Laflin, PA

Advincula, Arnold P
Bishop Neumann
Lock Haven, PA

Adzentoivich, Ernie
Mahanoy Area HS
New Boston, PA

Agosto, Lisette M
St Hubert Catholic
Philadelphia, PA

Aiello, Michelle
Bishop Hafey HS
Hazleton, PA

Ainsley, Marcia
Connellsville Area
Normalville, PA

Aita, Kim
St Marie Goretti HS
Philadelphia, PA

Akhtar, Saadia R
Schenley HS
Teachers Center
Pittsburgh, PA

Akings, Sharon
Avon Grove HS
West Grove, PA

Alam, Anthony
Quigley HS
Aliquippa, PA

Albaugh, Karen
Venango Christian
Oil City, PA

Albert, Myrna
Northern HS
Dillsburg, PA

Albertson, Jr Dennis
E
Benton Area HS
Orangeville, PA

Albrecht, Lori
James M Coughlin
Wilkes-Barre, PA

Albrecht, Loriann
West Scranton SR
Scranton, PA

Albright, Christine
Central HS
E Freedom, PA

Albright, Deb
Central HS
Martnsburg, PA

Alcaraz, Lori
Shenandoah Valley
JR SR HS
Shenandoah, PA

Alcaro, Rosemary L
Saint Hubert HS
Philadelphia, PA

Alderfer, Tiffany
Souderton Area HS
Harleysville, PA

Alexander, Christina
St Pius X HS
Phoenixville, PA

Alexander, Richard
West Scranton HS
Scranton, PA

Alexander, Terri
Northern SR HS
Wellsville, PA

Aley, William T
Seneca Valley SR
Evans City, PA

Alfer, Anne
Penn Hills SR HS
Pittsburgh, PA

Alford, Tammie
Aliquippa SR HS
Aliquippa, PA

Algar, Daniel
Tunkhannock HS
Tunkhannock, PA

Allen, David
Oxford Area HS
Cochranville, PA

Allen, Donald R
Redhawk Valley HS
New Bethlehem, PA

Allen, Jr John J
Neshaminy HS
Langhorne, PA

Allen, Rhonda
Abington HS
Willow Grove, PA

Alleva, David
Quentin
Upper Moreland HS
Hatboro, PA

Allison, Belinda
Mc Guffey HS
Claysville, PA

Allison, Stephanie
Union Area HS
New Castle, PA

Allsman, Francis
Cardinal O Hara HS
Media, PA

Allwardt, Sylvia
Conrad Weiser HS
Wernersville, PA

Almony, Patricia J
Emmaus HS
Zionsville, PA

Aloisio, Jonathan
Kennett HS
Kennett Sq, PA

Alston, Crystal
Chester HS
Chester Twp, PA

Alterio, Kelli
Bellefonte HS
Bellefonte, PA

Altland, Angela
Christian Schl Of
York, PA

Altman, David
Shenango JR-SR HS
New Castle, PA

Alvarez, Laurie
Monongahela Vly
Catholic HS
Donora, PA

Alwine, Eugene
Conemaugh
Township Area HS
Hollsopple, PA

Amann, Stephanie
Villa Maria Acad
Erie, PA

Amato, Jonna
Big Spring SR HS
Newville, PA

Ambrose, Dana
Bentworth HS
Cokeburg, PA

Ambrose, Tracy
Charleroi Area HS
Charleroi, PA

Amelotte, Stacie
Eastern York HS
York, PA

Ament, Sandra
Highlands SR HS
Natrona Hts, PA

Amershek, Neil
Our Lady Of
Lourdes HS
Elysburg, PA

Ames, Mary Jo
Crestwood HS
Mountaintop, PA

Ames, William
Tamaqua Area HS
New Ringgold, PA

Ammon, Michele F
Souderton Area HS
Schwenksville, PA

Amos, Julie
Burgettstown JR SR
Slovan, PA

Amos, Shelly
West Green Md SR
Sycamore, PA

Amos, Sherry
West Greene Md SR
Sycamore, PA

Amspacher, Wendy
Central York SR HS
York, PA

Andersen, Stephen
M
Red Lion Area SR
Red Lion, PA

Anderson, Andy
Central SR HS
York, PA

Anderson, Diana
West Mifflin Area
W Mifflin, PA

Anderson, George
Bentworth HS
Bentleyville, PA

Anderson, Karen
Connellsville Area
SR HS
Connellsville, PA

Anderson, Kelly
Churchill HS
Braddock, PA

Anderson, Kristine
Mon Valley Catholic
Donora, PA

Anderson, Lee
Ambridge SR HS
Ambridge, PA

Anderson, Lenni
California Area SR
California, PA

Anderson, Mark
Dover Area HS
Dover, PA

Anderson, Mary
Lancaster Christian
Lancaster, PA

Anderson, Melissa
Coatesville SR HS
Downingtown, PA

Anderson, Michele L
Red Lion Area SR
Red Lion, PA

Anderson, Michelle
L
Mc Guffey HS
Washington, PA

Anderson, Niccola
Phila H S For Girls
Philadelphia, PA

Anderson, Shawn
Clearfield Area HS
Clearfield, PA

Anderson, Traci
Penn-Trafford HS
Harrison City, PA

Anderson, Wayne
Hershey SR HS
Hummelstown, PA

Anderson Miller,
Gregory
Kutztown Area HS
Kutztown, PA

Andes, Jennifer
Danville SR HS
Danville, PA

Ando, Susan
Blacklick Valley HS
Nanty Glo, PA

Andretti, Barbie
Nazareth SR HS
Nazareth, PA

Andrews, Joy
Parkland HS
Orefield, PA

Andrews, Kenya
South Philadelphia
Philadelphia, PA

Andrews, Melissa
Bishop Guilfoyle HS
Altoona, PA

Andrews, Sean
Girard Collge
Philadelphia, PA

Angelo, Philip
Downingtown SR
Downingtown, PA

Angelucci,
Christopher B
St Josephs Prep
Philadephia, PA

Angeny, Barry
Downingtown SR
Downingtown, PA

Antes, James
West Catholic HS
Philadelphia, PA

Anthony, Denise
Bishop Guilfoyle HS
Altoona, PA

Anthony, IV Edward
Mason
Hampton HS
Allison Park, PA

Anthony, Jennifer
Bishop Shanahan
Kennett Sq, PA

Anthony, Ray
Northampton Area
SR HS
Northampton, PA

Anthony, Shelly A
High Schl Of
Engineering
Philadelphia, PA

Antonini, Michelle
Hopewell HS
Aliquippa, PA

Apgar, Anders
Manheim Twp HS
Lancaster, PA

Apgar, Joseph
Louis E Dieruff HS
Allentown, PA

Apolinario, Ethel E
Abington SR HS
Rydal, PA

Aponte, Carmelo
Thomas A Edison
Philadelphia, PA

Appleby, Jim
Mechanicsburg Area
SR HS
Mechanicsburg, PA

Aracri, Joseph
Canevin HS
Pittsburgh, PA

Aragon, Bryon
Bethlehem Catholic
Bethlehem, PA

Arhangelsky, Barbara
J S Fine SR HS
W Nanticoke, PA

Armbrust, Donald
Penn Trafford HS
Irwin, PA

Armold, Melissia
Donegal HS
Marietta, PA

Armstrong, Cathy
Chester HS
Chester, PA

Armstrong, David
Rockwood Area HS
Rockwood, PA

Armstrong, Michele
Unionville HS
Chadds Ford, PA

Armstrong, Roger
Solance HS
Willow St, PA

Arndt, Chris
Emmaus HS
Emmaus, PA

Arnold, Allison
Central SR HS
York, PA

Arnold, Jr James R
Lebanon Catholic
Hershey, PA

Arnold, Lisa
Trinity Christian
Pittsburgh, PA

Arnold, Troy
Red Lion Area SR
Red Lion, PA

Arrigo, Chuck
Carlynton JR SR
Pittsburgh, PA

Artymowicz, Richard
Chichester SR HS
Linwood, PA

Ashbaugh, Gina
Clarion Limeston
Strattanville, PA

Ashby, Tom
Central Bucks H S
Warrington, PA

Ashford, Nina
Freedom HS
Bethlehem, PA

Ashman, Laura
Westmont Hilltop
Johnstown, PA

Ashmore, Todd
Trinity HS
Washington, PA

Ashton, Kirk
Meadville Area HS
Meadville, PA

Asman, Dawn
North East Bradford
Rome, PA

Aspinall, Susan Elaine
Bethel Park HS
Bethel Park, PA

Astrab, Patricia
Mc Keesport Area
Mckeesport, PA

Athanasion, Constance
St Francis Acad
Bethelehem, PA

Atkins, Angela Lynn
Donegal HS
Maytown, PA

Atkins, Rama
Creative & Performing Arts HS
Philadelphia, PA

Attman, Michael E
Archbishop Ryan HS For Boys
Philadelphia, PA

Auer, Tim
Connellsville SR HS
Mt Pleasant, PA

Aultman, Lori
Frazier HS
Perryopolis, PA

Aultz, Tammie
Somerset Area SR
Somerset, PA

Aumack, James
Blue Mt Acad
Hamburg, PA

Aumack, Sherry
Blue Mt Acad
Hamburg, PA

Auman, Mike
Conrad Weiser HS
Robesonia, PA

Aument, Brenda
Lampeter Strasburg
Strasburg, PA

Ausman, Michele
S Park HS
Library, PA

Austin, Teresa
North Allegheny HS
Ingomar, PA

Axline, Brenda
Towanda Area HS
Towanda, PA

Ayers, Mark
State College Area
Boalsburg, PA

Aymong, Nicole
Mercyhurst Prep
Erie, PA

Azinger, Tim
Kiski Area HS
Saltsburg, PA

Babinchak, John
Shenandoah Valley
Shenandoah, PA

Babjack, Lisa
Langley HS
Pittsburgh, PA

Baccamazzi, Lisa
Windber Area HS
Windber, PA

Bachman, Nate
Mt Leabanon SR
Mt Lebanon, PA

Bachman, Stephanie
Northern Lebanon
Lebanon, PA

Badman, Cynthia R
Phoenixville Area
Phoenixville, PA

Baggett, Timothy
Northeast Catholic
Philadelphia, PA

Bagshaw, Rhonda
Ambridge Area HS
Freedom, PA

Bagwell, Brett Edward
Quaker Valley HS
Sewickley, PA

Bahl, Monish
Riverview HS
Oakmont, PA

Baier, Frank H
Jersey Shore SR HS
Williamsport, PA

Bailey, Gary
Clearfield Area HS
Clearfield, PA

Bailey, Gregory M
Meadville Area SR
Meadville, PA

Bailey, Monica
Chester HS
Chester, PA

Bailey, Steve
Manheim Township
Lancaster, PA

Bailey, Tracy
Philipsburg-Osceola Area HS
Philipsburg, PA

Bailey, Valerie
Cedar Crest HS
Lebanon, PA

Baines, David
Chief Logan HS
Yeagertown, PA

Baird, Kathy
Bellefonte Area HS
Pleasant Gap, PA

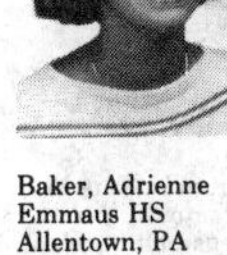
Baker, Adrienne
Emmaus HS
Allentown, PA

Baker, Amy B
Wallenpaupack Area
Greentown, PA

Baker, Christine
Central York SR HS
York, PA

Baker, Corri
Altoona Area HS
Altoona, PA

Baker, Gloria
Red Land HS
New Cumberland, PA

Baker, Kelly
Punxsutawney Area
Punxsutawney, PA

Baker, Rhonda
Center HS
Monaca, PA

Baker, Suzanne
Canon Mcmillan SR
Canonsburg, PA

Baker, Tammy
Lower Dauphin HS
Elizabethtown, PA

Baker, Teresa
Du Bois Area HS
Dubois, PA

Bakowski, Brian
South Side Catholic
Pittsburgh, PA

Balawejder, Janet
Gateway SR HS
Monroeville, PA

Baldwin, James
Mc Keesport Area
SR HS
White Oak, PA

Balendy, Michelle
Scranton Technical
Scranton, PA

Balestrieri, Teresa
Canevin Catholic
Pittsburgh, PA

Balin, Stacey
Lincoln HS
Ellwood, PA

Ball, Denise
Central York SR HS
York, PA

Ball, Elizabeth
Ringgold HS
Monongahela, PA

Balliet, Deborah
Ann
Hollidaysburg Area
SR HS
Hollidaysburg, PA

Balogh, Chaz
Meyers HS
Wilkes Barre, PA

Balsley, Matt
Saltsburg JR/SR HS
Saltsburg, PA

Balthaser, Beverly
Scotland Schl
Girardville, PA

Baltrush, Michael J
Neshaminy HS
Langhorne, PA

Baluta, David
Northwest Area JR
SR HS
Shickshinny, PA

Bamberger, Marc
Southern Lehigh HS
Coopersburg, PA

Banas, J Michael
Chartiers Valley HS
Presto, PA

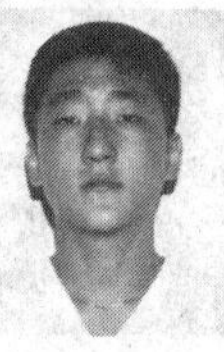
Bang, John
Marple Newtown
Newton Sq, PA

Bango, Lisa
Bishop Mc Cort HS
Johnstown, PA

Bankes, David
Col-Mont Vo-Tech
Berwick, PA

Banks, Jade
Harrisburg HS
Harrisburg, PA

Banks, Tammy
Forest Hills SR HS
Salix, PA

Banner, Paul
Venango Christian
Fryburg, PA

Bannon, Allison
Council Rock HS
Wycombe, PA

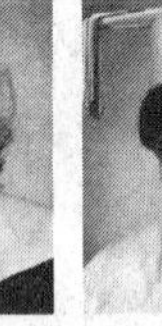
Banse, Susan
Perkiomen Valley
Collegeville, PA

Barats, Patti
Bensalem HS
Bensalem, PA

Barbaro, Pamela
General Mc Lane
Edinboro, PA

Barber, Greg Daniel
Laurel Highland SR
Hopwood, PA

Barber, William
Mt Pleasant Area
Mt Pleasant, PA

Barbour, Jr Michael
Hempfield Area SR
Greensburg, PA

Barchfeld, Terry
Gateway SR HS
Monroeville, PA

Barclay, Dana
Uniontown Area SR
Uniontown, PA

Bard, Cynthia
Ambridge Area HS
Ambridge, PA

Bare, Sean
Hershey HS
Hershey, PA

Barei, Michele
West Phila Catholic
Philadelphia, PA

Bargerstock, Cathy
A
Central Christian
Du Bois, PA

Barker, Jonathan
Emmaus HS
Emmaus, PA

Barker, Maura
Mount Lebanon HS
Pittsburgh, PA

Barker, Timothy
Muhlenberg HS
Reading, PA

Barkley, Ronald
Mt Pleasant Area
SR HS
Mt Pleasant, PA

Barkocy, Gary
Bishop Egan HS
Washington Cros,
PA

Barna, Sandra
Lakeland HS
Jermyn, PA

Barner, Jodell
Sheffield Ares
JR-SR HS
Sheffield, PA

Barnes, R Andrew
Mc Guffey HS
West Alexander, PA

Barnes, Vicki
Shade HS
Central City, PA

Barnett, Brian
Shippensburg SR
Shippensburg, PA

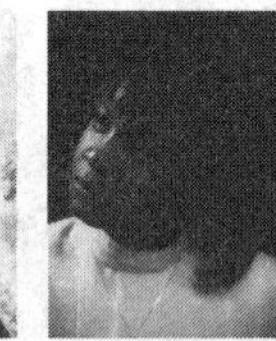
Barnett, Kendra
Overbrook HS
Philadelphia, PA

Barnhart, Melissa
North East HS
North East, PA

Barnhart, Stephen
Southern Fulton HS
Warfordsburg, PA

Barnhart, II Thomas
L
Cocalico HS
Denver, PA

Barnovsky, Ronald
A
New Castle SR HS
New Castle, PA

Baron, Leonard
Laurel Highlands
SR HS
Uniontown, PA

Baron, Tamara
Steel Valley HS
Munhall, PA

Baronti, Tanya L
North Allegheny SR
Wexford, PA

Barr, Leslie
Pequea Valley HS
Gap, PA

Barr, Paula
Marion Center HS
Home, PA

Barr, Vicky
Connellsville Area
Champion, PA

Barrall, Richard
Liberty HS
Bethlehem, PA

Barrett, Robert
Warwick HS
Lititz, PA

Barry, Gayle
Northgate JR/SR
Pittsburgh, PA

Barry, Michelle
Cardinal Brennan
Frackville, PA

Bartel, Scott
Reynolds HS
Greenville, PA

Bartel, Shelly A
Commodore Perry
Hadley, PA

Barth, Debra
Harry S Truman HS
Levittown, PA

Barthlow, Thomas E
Northern Lehigh HS
Neffs, PA

Bartholomew,
Kristina
Bethlehem Catholic
Bethlehem, PA

Bartholomew,
Michael
Northampton Area
Bath, PA

Bartis, Sarah
Peters Township HS
Mc Murray, PA

Bartles, Kimberly L
Yough SR HS
Irwin, PA

Bartlett, Jeff
Canton JR SR HS
Canton, PA

Bartnicki, Tara M
Scranton
Preparatory Schl
Old Forge, PA

Bartolacci, Paulette
Notre Dame HS
Easton, PA

Bartow, Susan
Boyertown Area SR
Boyertown, PA

Basile, Andrew
The Hill Schl
Douglassville, PA

Baskerville, Keyva L
Dobbins A V T HS
Philadelphia, PA

Bass, George
Steelton-Highspire
Steelton, PA

Bates, Jill
Greensburg Central
Catholic HS
Greensburg, PA

Bates, Kevin
Derry Area SR HS
Pitcairn, PA

Bates, Matthew J
Mansfield JR-SR
Mansfield, PA

Batshon, Brigitte S
Valley HS
New Kensington,
PA

Bauduin, Rachel
Avella Area JR SR
Avella, PA

Baughman, David
Moshannon Valley
Houtzdale, PA

Baughman, Jennifer
J
Canon Mc Millian
Eight Four, PA

Bauman, John
Pittston Area HS
Duryea, PA

Baumgardner, Sherri
Forest Hills HS
South Fork, PA

Bautz, Amy
Mon Valley Catholic
New Eagle, PA

Baxter, Stephanie L
Monongahela Valley
Catholic HS
Monongahela, PA

Bayer, Jennifer
Montour HS
Mckees Rocks, PA

Bayliss, Todd
Wilson HS
W Lawn, PA

Baylor, Robyn
Lorraine
Archbishop John
Carroll Girls HS
Philadelphia, PA

Baynard, Jr
Raymond
Pine Forge Acad
Pine Forge, PA

Bazala, Stephanie
Marion Center HS
Ernest, PA

Beach, John
Troy SR HS
Granville Summit,
PA

Beachell, Beth
Northern Lebanon
Grantville, PA

Beagle, Brian
Linesville HS
Linesville, PA

Beaken, Stacy
Greater Latrobe SR
Latrobe, PA

Beam, Dennis
Hazleton SR HS
Hazleton, PA

Beard, Christopher
Palmyra Area HS
Palmyra, PA

Beard, Ronald
Cowanesque Valley
Knoxville, PA

Beauchamp, Maria
Saint Pius X HS
Gilbertsville, PA

Bechtel, Kathy
Spring Grove SR HS
Hanover, PA

Beck, Cheryl L
North Hills HS
Pittsburgh, PA

Beck, Douglas E
Fleetwood Area HS
Hamburg, PA

Beck, Jeffrey F
La Salle College HS
Hatfield, PA

Beck, John H
Loyalsock Township
Williamsport, PA

Beck,
Kristine-Marie
Spring Grove Area
Codorus, PA

Beck, Laura
Belle Vernon Area
Belle Vernon, PA

Beck, Michelle
York County
Vocational Tec
York, PA

Beck, Patricia Ann
Ambridge HS
Sewickley, PA

Becker, Kim
Delone Catholic HS
Hanover, PA

Becker, Richard
Abraham Lincoln
Philadelphia, PA

Becse, Sylvia
Canon Mcmillan SR
Canonsburg, PA

Bedford, Kristin
Du Bois Area HS
Reynoldsville, PA

Bedics, Kathleen M
Notre Dame HS
Bethlehem, PA

Bedits, Hope
Bethel Park SR HS
Bethel Park, PA

Beener, Christy
North Star HS
Boswell, PA

Beers, Mark
Susquenita HS
New Bloomfield, PA

Begonia, Michael
Norwin SR HS
N Huntingdon, PA

Behrend, Robt
Chettenham HS
Melrose Pk, PA

Belak, Brett
Norwin HS
N Huntinbdon, PA

Belcastro, Lea
St Maria Goretti HS
Philadelphia, PA

Belfiore, Jeffrey
Canon Mc Millan
SR HS
Cecil, PA

Belin, Wendy
Cedar Crest HS
Lebanon, PA

Bell, Bruce
Unionville HS
Chadds Ford, PA

Bell, Coleen Ryan
Freeland HS
Freeland, PA

Bell, Jonathan
Central Bucks East
Warrington, PA

Bell, Sandra
East Brady/Lenape
Chicora, PA

Bell, Sherri
Saltsburg JR SR HS
Saltsburg, PA

Bell, Tammy
Clearfield Area HS
Woodland, PA

Bellano, Cesare P
Marple-Newtown
SR HS
Broomall, PA

Belli, Richard
Aliquippa HS
Aliquippa, PA

Bellissimo, Joseph S
Mohawk Area HS
Wampum, PA

Bello, Frank
Hampton HS
Allison Pk, PA

Belus, Christina
Sharon SR HS
Sharon, PA

Benamati, Robert
Bishop Carroll HS
Spangler, PA

Bender, Greg
Riverside HS
Beaver Falls, PA

Bender, Jeanette
Ephrata SR HS
Ephrata, PA

PHOTO
NOT
AVAILABLE

Bender, John
Hillidays Burg Area
Altoona, PA

Bender, Renee
Cambria Heights HS
Carrolltown, PA

Bendis, Brian
Apollo-Ridge HS
Saltsburg, PA

Benedetto, Deborah
St Maria Goretti HS
Philadelphia, PA

Benedict, Kelli
Solanco HS
New Providence, PA

Benegasi, Bernadette
Mohawk HS
Bessemer, PA

Benini, Kristina
Somerset Area HS
Sipesville, PA

Benjamin, Kimberly
Warwick HS
Lititz, PA

Benko, Angela S
Ephrata SR HS
Ephrata, PA

Benn, Lisa
Du Bois SR HS
Dubois, PA

Bennardo, Lisa
Mt Alvernia HS
Pittsburgh, PA

Benner, Bill
Titusville HS
Centerville, PA

Benner, Christopher
Williamsport Area
Williamsport, PA

Benner, Denise
Shikellamy HS
Sunbury, PA

Benner, Tammy
Waynesboro Area SR HS
Waynesboro, PA

Bennett, Rochanda
William Penn HS
Philadelphia, PA

Bennett, Susan M
Mc Keesport SR HS
Mc Keesport, PA

Bennett, Valerie Kay
Blairsville SR HS
Blairsville, PA

Beno, Cathy
Trinity HS
Washington, PA

Bensavage, Todd
Wyalusing Valley
Wyalusing, PA

Bensinger, Kim
Blue Mountain HS
Sch Haven, PA

Benson, Julie
Butler SR HS
Renfrew, PA

Benson, Sue
Palmyra Area SR
Palmyra, PA

Benson, Tricia L
Sharon HS
Sharon, PA

Benz, Jr Jerome V
Bishop Hafey HS
Conyngham, PA

Benz, Shauna
Charleroi JR SR HS
N Charleroi, PA

Benzo, Celeste A
Pen Hills SR HS
Verona, PA

Beppler, Cherilee
Scranton Central
Scranton, PA

Beranek, Jennifer
Southmoreland HS
Scottdale, PA

Berardinelli, James
Altoona Area HS
Altoona, PA

Berdine, Denise
Canon-Mc Millan
Eighty Four, PA

Berdis, Joe
Swissvale HS
Pittsburgh, PA

Berenbaum, Daniel
Council Rock HS
Richboro, PA

Berestecki, Louis J
Yough SR HS
W Newton, PA

Berezansky, Susan
West Allegheny HS
Clinton, PA

Berger, Colleen
Governor Mifflin HS
Mohnton, PA

Berger, Dan
Ambridge Area HS
Ambridge, PA

Berger, Kelli
Pennsbury HS
Fairless Hills, PA

Berger, Lisa
Spring Grove SR HS
Thomasville, PA

Berger, Melissa
Cheltenham HS
Melrose Pk, PA

Berger, Ruth
Greater Johnstown SR HS
Johnstown, PA

Bergerstock, Steve
Milton SR HS
Milton, PA

Bergman, Kristi
Scranton Preparatory Schl
Scranton, PA

Berkebile, Tracy
North Star HS
Boswell, PA

Berkey, April R
N Star HS
Boswell, PA

Berkheiser, David
Berwick Area HS
Berwick, PA

Berkstresser, Shawn
Mc Connellsburg HS
Mcconnellsburg, PA

Berlin, Eric
Manheim Central
Manheim, PA

Berlin, Samantha
Lower Moreland HS
Huntingdon Valley, PA

Berlinger, Kristen
Upper Moreland HS
Willow Gr, PA

Bernadowski, Bobbi
California Area SR
California, PA

Bernard, Elisa
Nazareth Acad
Philadelphia, PA

Bernard, Jenny
Central Dauphin HS
Harrisburg, PA

Bernard, Paul M
Yough SR HS
Madison, PA

Bernardo, Mark
Windber Area HS
Windber, PA

Bernoski, Tricia
Wyoming Valley West HS
Larksville, PA

Berrettini, Susan
Wyoming Valley West HS
Forty Fort, PA

Berrier, Anne
Lewistown Area HS
Lewistown, PA

Berry, Victoria N
Penn Wood HS
Lansdowne, PA

Berzinsky, Clarissa
Greater Johnstown
Johnstown, PA

Berzonski, James
Hampton HS
Gibsonia, PA

Best, Barbara
Chartiers Valley HS
Presto, PA

Bethard, Marijane
Upper Moreland HS
Willowgrove, PA

Betler, Marianne
Mc Guffey HS
Claysville, PA

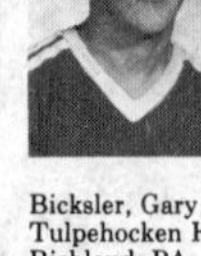

Betz, Brian
Berwick Area SR
Wapwallopen, PA

Beucher, Beth
Geibel HS
Connellsville, PA

Bey, Cameron
Schenley Teacher
Pittsburgh, PA

Bhavsar, Neha
Montour HS
Mckees Rocks, PA

Biagetti, Lisa
Seton-Lasalle HS
Pittsburgh, PA

Bianchi, Danielle
Valley View JR SR
Peckville, PA

Biblehimer, Holly
Montoursville HS
Montoursville, PA

Bicer, Jeffrey
St Pius X HS
Pottstown, PA

Bickel, Paul
Parkland SR HS
Allentown, PA

Bicksler, Gary
Tulpehocken HS
Richland, PA

Biebel, Edward
Holy Ghost Prep
Philadelphia, PA

Bieber, Rabecca
Burgettstown Area
JR SR HS
Burgettstown, PA

Bieber, Susan K
Upper Merion Area
King Of Prussia, PA

Biedzinski, Mary
Baldwin HS
Pittsburgh, PA

Bieranoski, Melissa
Kiski Area HS
New Kensington, PA

Biernesser, Darlene
Fox Chapel Area HS
Pittsburgh, PA

Bieser, Tina
Cowanesque Valley
Middlebury Ctr, PA

Biggans, Karen
St Huberts HS
Philadelphia, PA

Biggs, Scott
Moshannon-Valley
JR SR HS
Brisbin, PA

Bilger, Lisa
Solanco HS
Christina, PA

Billet, Michael
Dover Area HS
Dover, PA

Billets, Jerilyn
Abington Hts HS
Clarks Summit, PA

Billotte, Melissa L
Clearfield HS
Frenchville, PA

Biltgen, Renee
North Allegheny HS
Allison Pk, PA

Binelli, Karin
Boyertown Area SR
Boyertown, PA

Bingaman, Carole
James Buchanan HS
Mercersburg, PA

Binkley, Cindy
Pleasant Valley HS
Saylorsburg, PA

Biondi, John
Lincoln HS
Ellwood City, PA

Birch, Mariette
Homer-Center HS
Homer City, PA

Bird, Brian
Danville Area SR
Danville, PA

Birenbaum, Joanne
Robert E Lamberton
Philadelphia, PA

Birmingham, Beth
Little Flower HS
Philadelphia, PA

Bish, Melanie
Clarion Area JR SR
Shippenville, PA

Bishop, Alison
State College Area
SR HS
State College, PA

Bishop, David
Seton Lasalle HS
Pittsburgh, PA

Bishop, Holly
Marple Newtown SR
Newtown Sq, PA

Bishop, Melissa
Annville-Cleona HS
Cleona, PA

Bissaillon, Stephanie
Mt Carmel Area JR
SR HS
Mt Carmel, PA

Bistline, Melinda
Donegal HS
Mount Joy, PA

Bitner, Joseph A
Lock Haven SR HS
Blanchard, PA

Bittner, Christine
Meyersdale Area HS
Meyersdale, PA

Bittner, Richard
Meyersdale Area HS
Meyersdale, PA

Bixler, Lynn
Hanover SR HS
Hanover, PA

Black, Debbie
Coudersport JR SR
Coudersport, PA

Black, Donna
Tussey Mountain
Saxton, PA

Black, Douglas
Charleroi Area JR
SR HS
Charleroi, PA

Black, Jana
York Suburban HS
York, PA

Black, Jodi
Big Spring HS
Carlisle, PA

Black, Torie
Wilkinsburg JR SR
Wilkinsburg, PA

Blackhurst, Jill
Washington HS
Washington, PA

Blackwell, Nancy
Central HS
Philadelphia, PA

Blackwell, Shari
H S Of Engineering
And Science
Philadelphia, PA

Blaine, Alyssa
Greater Latrobe HS
Latrobe, PA

Blair, Michelle
Fairfield Area HS
Fairfield, PA

Blake, Elaine
Roxborough HS
Philadelphia, PA

Blake, Taige
Liberty HS
Bethlehem, PA

Blanco, Terry
Central Bucks HS
Mechanicsville, PA

Blannett, Jr Albert
P
Hanover Area JS SR
Ashley, PA

Blaskowitz, Rick
Lincoln HS
Ellwood City, PA

Blazer, Kevin
Greensburg Central
Catholic HS
N Huntingdon, PA

Blckstone, Tracey
Harrisburg HS
Harrisburg, PA

Blicha, John
Canon-Mc Millan
SR HS
Eighty Four, PA

Bliss, Eric
Oxford Area HS
Oxford, PA

Bliss, Laurie
S R U HS
Gillett, PA

Blocker, II Walter
Louis
Creative &
Performing Arts HS
Philadelphia, PA

Blodgett, Stacey
Canon-Mac Millan
SR HS
Canonsburg, PA

Bloom, Cynthia
United HS
Blairsville, PA

Bloom, Dawn
Harry S Truman HS
Fairless Hills, PA

Bloom, Marc
Central HS
Philadelphia, PA

Blosnick, Steven
West Allegheny HS
Imperial, PA

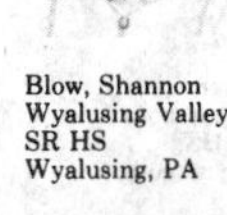
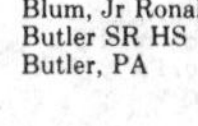

Blow, Shannon
Wyalusing Valley JR
SR HS
Wyalusing, PA

Blue, Melissa
Cheltenham HS
Elkins Pk, PA

Blue, Reginald
Northwestern
Lehigh HS
Germansvile, PA

Blum, Mark
Carson Long Inst
Vestal, NY

Blum, Jr Ronald
Butler SR HS
Butler, PA

Boccella, Erica
Amata
The Oakland Schl
Pittsburgh, PA

Bochnak, Kathy
Allentown Central
Catholic HS
Allentown, PA

Bock, Wendy
Bethel Park SR HS
Bethel Park, PA

Boden, Marian
West Perry SR HS
Landisburg, PA

Bodine, Heather
Unionville HS
Kennett Square, PA

Bodkin, Heather
Cardinal O Hara HS
Springfield, PA

Bodnar, Lisa Marie
Allentown Central
Catholic HS
Whitehall, PA

Boehmler, Britt
Hazleton HS
Hazleton, PA

Boehringer, C
Shawn
Gov Mifflin SR HS
Reinholds, PA

Boettcher, Edward
John
Abington Hgts HS
Clarks Summit, PA

Boggs, Dianna
German SR HS
Mc Clellandtown,
PA

Bogner, Michelle
Lebanon HS
Lebanon, PA

Bogo, Roxanne J
Canon-Mc Millan
Eighty Four, PA

Bogozi, Lori
Albert Gallatin SR
Masontown, PA

Bogush, Stephen
Southern Columbia
Area HS
Elysburg, PA

Boheen, Erica
Central Buck High
School East
Doylestown, PA

Bohner, Amy P
Central Bucks West
Warrington, PA

Bohner, Andrew
Emmaus HS
Emmaus, PA

Bohner, Tara
Bishop Shanahan
Boothwyn, PA

Bohr, Andrew C
Northeastern HS
Manchester, PA

Bohusch, Katherine
M
Mc Dowell HS
Erie, PA

Bojarski, Clare
Montour HS
Corapolis, PA

Bolli, Craig
Harry S Truman HS
Levittown, PA

Bollinger, Becky
Mechanicsburg SR
Mechanicsburg, PA

Bollinger, Bonnie
Richland HS
Gibsonia, PA

Bollman, Robert
Northern Bedford
County HS
Loysburg, PA

Bolye, Brenda
Wilmington Area
New Wilmington,
PA

Bomboy, Bob
Northwest Area JR
SR HS
Shickshinny, PA

Bonano, Matthew
Pius X HS
Bangor, PA

Bond, Carrie
Kutztown Area HS
Kempton, PA

Bonenberger, Jr
Kenneth J
Bishop Egan HS
Levittown, PA

Bonfiglio, John
Hatboro Horsham
Horsham, PA

Bonita, John
James M Coughlin
Plains, PA

Bonner, George
Mercy Vocational
Philadelphia, PA

Bonney, Christine
Liberty HS
Bethlehem, PA

Bonney, Jason
Boyertown HS
Boyertown, PA

Bonney, Lisa
Wilson Area HS
W Easton, PA

Bonnici, Mark S
William Allen HS
Allentown, PA

Book, Jr Joseph
Mount Union Area
Newton Hamilton,
PA

Boonswang, Ab
Notre Dame HS
Easton, PA

Boose, Stuart D
Henderson SR HS
West Chester, PA

Booz, Steven
Oxford Area HS
Nottingham, PA

Boozer, Kellie J
Elizabethtown Area
Elizabethtown, PA

Border, Heath
Millersburg HS
Millersburg, PA

Bordo, Karen
Old Forge HS
Old Forge, PA

Borosh, Ossie
Lower Merion HS
Philadelphia, PA

Borosky, Patricia
Carbondale Area HS
Simpson, PA

Borriello, Salvatore
St John Neumann
Philadelphia, PA

Borsch, Sandra
Susan
Strath Haven HS
Rutledge, PA

Borzillo, Keith
Owen J Roberts HS
Parkerford, PA

Botyrius, Tony
Wyoming Area SR
Wyoming, PA

Boulton, Krista
Moshannon Valley
JR SR HS
Houtzdale, PA

Bourg, Michelle
Canon Mc Millan
Muse, PA

Bovard, Don
Meadville Area SR
Meadville, PA

Bowen, Leslie
Juniata HS
Port Royal, PA

Bowen, Lynn
Beaver Area JR-SR
Beaver, PA

Bowen, Robert
Byrne
Susquehannock HS
Shrewsbury, PA

Bower, Jr Stanley L
Milton Area Joint
SR HS
Milton, PA

Bower, Thomas
Ford City HS
Ford City, PA

Bowers, Carol
Butler SR HS
Butler, PA

Bowers, Jodi
Punysutawney Area
Punxsutawney, PA

Bowers, Julie A
Academy HS
Erie, PA

Bowlen, Larry
Fairchance-Georges
Smithfield, PA

Bowlen, Richard
Waynesburg Central
Brave, PA

Bowman, John D
York Suburban HS
York, PA

Bowman, Lorin
Meadville Area SR
Meadville, PA

Bowman, Marty
Homer Center HS
Indiana, PA

Bowmer, Derek
Scotland School For
Vetrans Children
Philadelphia, PA

Bowser, Scott
Kettanning HS
Worthington, PA

Boyanowski, Tracy
Greencastle Antrim
Greencastle, PA

Boyd, Gregg
Oxford Area HS
Oxford, PA

Boyd, Kerri
Oxford Area HS
Oxford, PA

Boyden, John
Upper Darby HS
Lansdowne, PA

Boyer, Claire M
Shamokin Area HS
Gowen City, PA

Boyer, Kelly
Waynesboro Area
SR HS
Waynesboro, PA

Boyer, Kelly
Rhonda
Pine Grove Area HS
Pine Grove, PA

Boykin, Tony
Chester HS
Chester, PA

Bracco, Jennifer
Clearfield HS
Clearfield, PA

Brachman, Noel
Council Rock HS
Newtown, PA

Bracy, Cheryl
Parkland HS
Allentown, PA

Bradbury, Ruth
Hoepwell HS
Aliquippa, PA

Bradford, Mary
ST Huberts HS For
Philadelphia, PA

Bradica, John
Belle Vernon Area
Belle Vernon, PA

Bradley, Bernice
St Huberts HS
Philadelphia, PA

Bradley, Cynthia
Lakeland HS
Mayfield, PA

Bradley, Helene
Nazareth Academy
Phila, PA

Bradley, Leanne
Moon SR HS
Maryville, TN

Bradmon, Tara L
Laurel Highlands
SR HS
Uniontown, PA

Brady, Coreen
Saltsburg JR SR HS
Saltsburg, PA

Brady, Matthew
Lincoln HS
Fombell, PA

Brady, Temple
Mauk
Punxsutawney Area
SR HS
Punxsutawney, PA

Brady, Todd
Danville SR HS
Danville, PA

Bramer, William
Scott
Perkiomen HS
Glendale, CA

Brandon, Nichole
Shaler Area HS
Pittsburgh, PA

Brandon, Veronica
A
Creative &
Performing Arts HS
Philadelphia, PA

Brandt, Lurene
Cedar Crest HS
Lebanon, PA

Brandt, Suzanne
Central Dauphin
East HS
Harrisburg, PA

Brantner, Wendy
Altoona Area HS
Altoona, PA

Brate, Christine
Central Bucks HS
Doylestown, PA

Bratton, Darwin
Greenwood HS
Millerstown, PA

Brauchle, Kimberly
Allentown Central
Catholic HS
Allentown, PA

Braun, Jeffrey
General Mc Lane
Mckean, PA

Bray, Janis
Hazleton SR HS
Mcadoo, PA

Bray, Lora
Mc Keesport SR HS
Mckeesport, PA

Bredel, Ed
Bethel Park SR HS
Pittsburgh, PA

Breen, Jennifer
East Pennsboro
Area HS
Camp Hill, PA

Breinich, Todd
Emmaus HS
Emmaus, PA

Breitenstein, Brett
Moon SR HS
Coraopolis, PA

Brelsford, David
E L Meyers HS
Wilkes Barre, PA

Brennan, Carolyn
Bethlehem Catholic
Bethlehem, PA

Brenneman,
Kathleen
Butler Area SR HS
Butler, PA

Brenneman, Sherry
Greencastle-Antrim
State Line, PA

Breslin, Mary
Cardinal O Hara HS
Havertown, PA

Breslin, Mike
Cardinal O Hara HS
Clifton Hts, PA

Breustedt, III
Samuel K
Bensalem HS
Bensalem, PA

Brewer, Danielle
Com/Area HS
Spartansburg, PA

Brewer, Holly
Albert Gallatin SR
Masontown, PA

Brewin, Lauryn K
Hershey SR HS
Hershey, PA

Brezeale, Christina
Marie
Grace Christian Schl
Reading, PA

Bridge, Kim
Hampton HS
Allison Pk, PA

Bridy, Katie
Our Lady Of
Shamokin, PA

Brigati, Jacqueline
Cardinal Dougherty
Philadelphia, PA

Briggs, Dayna
South Park HS
Library, PA

Briggs, Gwen
John Piersol
Mccaskey HS
Lancaster, PA

Briggs, Jr Raymond
Bald Eagle Nitnany
Beech Creek, PA

Briggs, Sarah
Yough SR HS
Smithton, PA

Bright, William
St James Catholic
Bensalem, PA

Brightbill, Kevin
Spring-Ford HS
Schwenksville, PA

Brill, Kathleen
Turtle Creek HS
Turtle Creek, PA

Brininger, Shawn
Lewisburg Area HS
Winfield, PA

Brinker, Diane
Cardinal Ohara HS
Springfield, PA

Brinkos, Amy J
Mc Keesport Area
White Oak, PA

Brion, Steve
North Penn HS
Blossburg, PA

Brisgone, Robert
Monsignor Bonner
Aldan, PA

Brittain, Christina
Benton Area JR-SR
Stillwater, PA

Britton, Monique
Phila H S For Girls
Philadelphia, PA

Brna, Ruth
Ringgold SR HS
Monongahela, PA

Broadwell, Cathy
Cardinal O Hara HS
Glenolden, PA

Brobst, Jim
Millville Area HS
Millville, PA

Brodbeck, Bethel
Dover Area HS
Dover, PA

Brodecki, David
Bensalen HS
Bensalem, PA

Broderick, Tina
Ilene
Conestoga Valley
Lancaster, PA

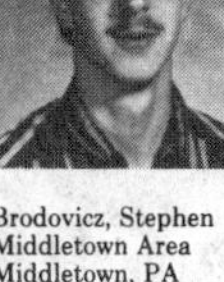
Brodovicz, Stephen
Middletown Area
Middletown, PA

Brodsky, Jay
Shaler Area SR HS
Glenshaw, PA

Brogan, Beth
Cardinal Ohara HS
Swarthmore, PA

Brogan, Marti
Meyers HS
Wilkes Barre, PA

Bromfield, Pamela
Downingtown SR
Exton, PA

Bronowicz, Sharon
Shaler Area SR HS
Pittsburgh, PA

Brookes, Wendy
Unionville HS
Chadds Ford, PA

Brooks, Cathy A
Lower Merion HS
Merion, PA

Brooks, Debra L
Shaler Area SR HS
Pittsburgh, PA

Brooks, Ken
Greensburg Central
Catholic HS
N Huntingdon, PA

Brooks, Mark
Solanco HS
Holtwood, PA

Brooks, Tina
J P Mc Caskey HS
Lancaster, PA

Brooks, Troy
Corry Area HS
Corry, PA

Broscious, Kellie
Clearfield HS
Clearfield, PA

Browder, Karyn
Meadville Area SR
Meadville, PA

Brown, Anna
North Penn HS
North Wales, PA

Brown, Beth
Canton JR SR HS
Canton, PA

Brown, Cynthia
Phila High School
For Girls
Philadelphia, PA

Brown, Dawn
Penn-Trafford HS
Jeannette, PA

Brown, Dawn
Westinghouse HS
Pittsburgh, PA

Brown, Donna
Wyoming Valley
West HS
Kingston, PA

Brown, Douglas G
Coudersport Area
Coudersport, PA

Brown, Elizabeth A
William Allen HS
Allentown, PA

Brown, Gail J
Mt Lebanon HS
Pittsburgh, PA

Brown, Janene
Creative And
Performing Arts
Philadelphia, PA

Brown, Jennifer
Bishop Guilfoyle HS
Altoona, PA

Brown, June
Wyoming Valley
West HS
Kingston, PA

Brown, Keith
Canon-Mc Millan
SR HS
Muse, PA

Brown, Kim
Wyoming Valley
West HS
Larksville, PA

Brown, III Leonard
G
Solanco HS
Kirkwood, PA

Brown, Matthew
New Castle SR HS
New Castle, PA

Brown, Michele
Franklin HS
Cochranton, PA

Brown, Rachel
Warrior Run HS
Turbotville, PA

Brown, Ryan
Belle Vernon Area
Belle Vernon, PA

Brown, Sean
Calvary Baptist
Indiana, PA

Brown, Shanequa
Harrisburg HS
Harrisburg, PA

Brown, Sherri
St Maria Goretti HS
Philadelphia, PA

Brown, Stacy L
Governor Mifflin SR
Mohnton, PA

Browning, Scott
Saint Pius X HS
Stowe, PA

Brownlee, Jonelle
Kennedy Christian
Burghill, OH

Brubaker, Benjamin
Homer Center HS
Homer City, PA

Brubaker, Kevin A
York Country Day
York, PA

Bruce, Anna
Seneca HS
Wattsburg, PA

Bruecken, Barbara
Shaler Area SR HS
Pittsburgh, PA

Brumbaugh, William
Tussey Mountain
Cassville, PA

Brunetti, Kenneth
West Catholic HS
Philadelphia, PA

Brungess, Barbara
Owen J Roberts HS
Spring City, PA

Bruni, Colette
Chichester HS
Boothwyn, PA

Brunner, Jeff
Boyertown HS
Gilbertsvl, PA

Bruno, Bernard A
Crestwood HS
Mountaintop, PA

Bruno, Brad
Norwin HS
N Huntingdon, PA

Bruno, Robert S
Bethel Park SR HS
Pittsburgh, PA

Bryan, Nicolle
James M Coughlin
Wilkes Barre, PA

Bryan, Patrick
John S Fine HS
Nanticoke, PA

Bryan, Todd
Waynesboro HS
Waynesboro, PA

Bryant, Lesley
Manheim Central
SR HS
Lititz, PA

Bryant, Richann
Bethel Park HS
Bethel Pk, PA

Bryner, Kelly
Juniata HS
Mifflin, PA

Bryner, Sarah J
Washington HS
Washington, PA

Bucci, Lori
Blacklick Valley JR
SR HS
Belsano, PA

Buchanan, Jennifer
L
Churchill HS
Pittsburgh, PA

Bucher, Greg
Warwick HS
Lititz, PA

Buchholz, Michele
Cardinal O Hara HS
Aston, PA

Buck, Angela
Clfd Area HS
Woodlands, PA

Buckles, Angella
Downingtown SR
Downingtown, PA

Budacki, Stephanie
New Brighton Area
SR HS
New Brighton, PA

Buday, Gretchen
Villa Maria HS
Poland, OH

Buehler, Christine
M
Cedar Crest HS
Lebanon, PA

Bufalini, Carol
Ambridge Area HS
Ambridge, PA

Buffington, Travis
Waynesboro Area
SR HS
Waynesboro, PA

Bugda, James
Hazleton HS
Hazleton, PA

Bukowski, Kira
Shenandoah Valley
Shenandoah, PA

Bula, Jacquelyn
Villa Maria Acad
Erie, PA

Bulebosh, Beth
Bethel Park HS
Pittsburgh, PA

Bundy, Madelyn
Marie
St Maria Goretti HS
Philadelphia, PA

Bunn, Karen
Greater Johnstown
Johnstown, PA

Bunting, Thomas
Arch Bishop Ryan
HS For Boys
Philadelphia, PA

Burba, Christine
Purchase Line HS
Arcadia, PA

Burch, Melissa
Archbishop
Prendergast HS
Prospect Park, PA

Burch, William
Bellwood-Antis HS
Bellwood, PA

Burchett, Nica
Trinity HS
Washington, PA

Burd, Scott
Brownsville Area HS
Brownsville, PA

Burdett, Laurie
Pittston Area HS
Pittston, PA

Burdge, Shannon
W Snyder HS
Mcclure, PA

Burdyn, III William
E
Bishop O Hara HS
Dickson City, PA

Burgess, Chris
Bethel Park SR HS
Bethel Pk, PA

Burgess, Jeanine
St Marys Area HS
St Marys, PA

Burgos, Naomi
Little Flower
Catholic HS Fo
Philadelphia, PA

Burke, Ron
Penns Manor HS
Heilwood, PA

Burke, Ronald
Bethlehem-Center
SR HS
Fredericktown, PA

Burke, Sheila
Lakeland HS
Clarks Summit, PA

Burkeen, Michael
Salisbury HS
Allentown, PA

Burkhardt, Debbie
North Clarion HS
Lucinda, PA

Burnett, Wendy
Pottstown HS
Pottstown, PA

Burney, Nathaniel
Valley Forge
Military Acad
Fairfax, VA

Burnley, Jennifer
Pottstown HS
Pottstown, PA

Burns, Leah
Northern SR HS
Dillsburg, PA

Burns, Lee Anne
Albert Gallatin SR
Lake Lynn, PA

Burns, Susan
Penn Trafford HS
Irwin, PA

Burskey, Barbara L
Cambria Heights HS
Carrolltown, PA

Busch, Laura
Chief Logan HS
Burnham, PA

Bush, Gary
Windber Area HS
Windber, PA

Bush, Krista
Penn Trafford HS
Jeannette, PA

Bushko, Holly
John S Fine SR HS
Nanticoke, PA

Bushong, Judy
Solanco HS
Quarryville, PA

Buszinski, Carrie
Bentworth SR HS
Bentleyville, PA

Butina, Barry
Bishop Mc Devitt
Harrisburg, PA

Butler, Beverly
Central HS
Roaring Sprg, PA

Butler, Nathanael
Cedar Grove
Christian Academy
Philadelphia, PA

Butler, Tracy Ann
Archbishop Ryan
HS For Girls
Philadelphia, PA

Butrie, Matthew
Marian HS
Lansford, PA

Butterworth,
Melanie
Neshaminy HS
Oakford, PA

Buttillo, Tony
Salisbury HS
Allentown, PA

Butts, Valerie
West Allegheny HS
Oakdale, PA

Butzler, Thomas M
Bethel Park HS
Bethel Park, PA

Buynak, Sonya
Philipsburg-Osceola
SR HS
Osceola Mills, PA

Buzzell, Dawn
Waynesboro Area
SR HS
Blue Ridge Smt, PA

Bybee, Patrick
Waynesboro Area
SR HS
Waynesboro, PA

Byers, Ann
Fairview HS
Erie, PA

Byers, Darlene
Purchase Line HS
Mahaffey, PA

Byers, Jon
Kiski Area HS
Vandergrift, PA

Byers, Robert
Trinity HS
Amity, PA

Byler, Lara
Northern Lebanon
JR SR HS
Fredericksburg, PA

Bynum, Dietra
Rittenhouse Acad
Philadelphia, PA

Byrne, John
Perry Traditional
Millvale, PA

Byrnes, Heather
Salisbury HS
Allentown, PA

Byrnes, Lisa
Cambria Heights HS
Hastings, PA

Cachules, Jim
Bethlehem Catholic
Bethlehem, PA

Cadwalader, Jason
Lake-Lehman HS
Dallas, PA

Caffrey, Phaedra
Creative &
Performing Arts HS
Philadelphia, PA

Cagni, Bertha Anne
Peters Twp HS
Mc Murray, PA

Caiazzo, Toni S
Bangor Area HS
E Bangor, PA

Cain, Martha
Kiski Area HS
Apollo, PA

Cain, Melissa
Kiski Area HS
Apollo, PA

Calabro, Joseph C
Scranton Prep
Clarks Summit, PA

Calafut, Maria
Sacred Heart HS
Carbondale, PA

Caldwell, Debbie
Upper Moreland SR
Hatboro, PA

Caldwell, Russell
Waynesburg Central
Waynesburg, PA

Caldwell, Susie
Upper Moreland HS
Hatboro, PA

Calizzi, Michael D
Kiski Area HS
Apollo, PA

Callahan, Bill
Our Lady Of
Lourdes Regiona
Shamokin, PA

Callander, Mary
Allegheny-Clarion
Valley HS
Parker, PA

Callas, Maria
Turtle Creek HS
E Pittsburgh, PA

Callipare, James
Mt Pleasant Area SR HS
Mount Pleasant, PA

Calviero, Laurie A
Bangor Area Joint
Roseto, PA

Camarda, Antoinette
Shaler Area SR HS
Pittsburgh, PA

Cambruzzi, Rita
Yough SR HS
Ruffsdale, PA

Cameron, A Christine
East Juniata HS
Millerstown, PA

Cameron, Carla
Milton SR HS
Milton, PA

Cameron, Christine
East Juniata HS
Millerstown, PA

Cameron, Robert
East Juniata HS
Millerstown, PA

Cammack, Stacey C
Bishop Mc Devitt
Harrisburg, PA

Cammerata, Jeffrey D
Manheim Township
Lancaster, PA

Campalong, Robert
Sto-Rox HS
Mc Kees Rocks, PA

Campbell, Bob
Albert Gallatin SR
Smithfield, PA

Campbell, Dawn
Juniata HS
Port Royal, PA

Campbell, Denny
Seneca Valley SR
Mars, PA

Campbell, Jim
Clarion Area HS
Clarion, PA

Campbell, Kelly
West Greene Middle SR HS
Graysville, PA

Campbell, Kristen
Altoona Area HS
Altoona, PA

Campbell, Mary Ellen
Bishop Kenrick HS
Norristown, PA

Campbell, Megan
West Middlesex HS
Pulaski, PA

Campbell, Stephen A
Ephrata SR HS
Ephrata, PA

Campbell, Timothy
Williamsburg HS
Williamsburg, PA

Cancel, Suejean
Delaware Valley HS
Milford, PA

Cannella, Joseph
Upper Darby HS
Upper Darby, PA

Cantolina, Paula
West Branch JR SR
Morrisdale, PA

Cantone, Audra
Allentown Central Catholic HS
Macungie, PA

Cantor, Selena A
Lower Moreland HS
Huntingdon Valley, PA

Capatosti, Jennifer
Brownsville Area SR
Brownsville, PA

Caperoon, Ray
Central Dauphin HS
Linglestown, PA

Caplinger, James
Tulpehocken HS
Bethel, PA

Capone, Nina Christine
Merion Mercy Acad
Drexel Hill, PA

Caputo, Diane
St Hubert HS
Philadelphia, PA

Capuzzi, Maryann
Saltsburg JR SR HS
Saltsburg, PA

Carabin, Lisa
Central Dauphin HS
Harrisburg, PA

Carathers, Christy
Bentworth HS
Bentleyville, PA

Caravella, Christy
New Castle SR HS
New Castle, PA

Carbaugh, Michelle
Waynesboro Area SR HS
S Mountain, PA

Carbonaro, Domenick
West Catholic H S For Boys
Philadelphia, PA

Card, Shawna
Norhtwestern SR
Albion, PA

Cardillo, Lisa
Wyoming Valley West HS
Forty Fort, PA

Carenzo, Michael T
Lower Dauphin HS
Hershey, PA

Carey, Kimberly
Nativity B V M HS
New Philadelphia, PA

Carl, Valerie
Tri-Valley HS
Valley View, PA

Carlisle, Anthony Todd
Ambridge HS
Ambridge, PA

Carlson, Camme
Blue Mountain Acad
Hatfield, PA

Carlson, Joely
North Allegheny SR
Wexford, PA

Carnack, Jr Daniel E
Connellsville Area SR HS
Dunbar, PA

Carnes, Dorenda A
Methacton SR HS
Audubon, PA

Caroselli, Joseph
Cardinal O Hara HS
Springfield, PA

Carpenter, Timothy
Blue Ridge HS
Hallstead, PA

Carpin, Espranza
St Marys Area HS
Weedville, PA

Carpin, Tracey
St Marys Area HS
Weedville, PA

Carr, Barbara
Ligonier Valley SR
Latrobe, PA

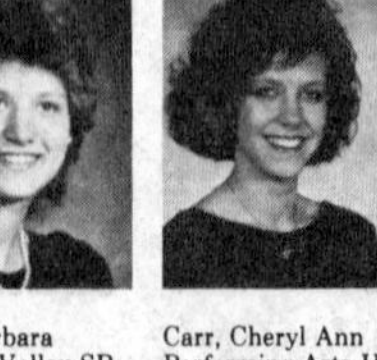
Carr, Cheryl Ann
Performing Arts HS Of Phila
Somerdale, NJ

Carr, Deborah
Middletown Area
Middletown, PA

Carrigan, Andrew Stuart
Church Farm Schl
Philadelphia, PA

Carroll, John
St John Neumann
Philadelphia, PA

Carroll, Lorie M
Archbishop Carroll
Haverford, PA

Carroll, Michael
Shikellamy SR HS
Northumberland, PA

Carson, Albert
Rocky Grove JR-SR
Franklin, PA

Carson, II Albert Patrick
Belle Vernon Area
Pricedale, PA

Carson, Tammy S
Central Dauphin HS
Harrisburg, PA

Carson, Wayne E
Indiana Wesleyan
Indiana, PA

Carter, David
Curwensville HS
Curwensville, PA

Carter, Gwenzetta
Bensalem HS
Trevose, PA

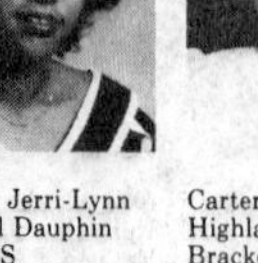
Carter, Jerri-Lynn
Central Dauphin East HS
Harrisburg, PA

Carter, Mary Jo
Highlands SR HS
Brackenridge, PA

Carter, Mike
Corry Area HS
Corry, PA

Carter, Phoebe
Bishop Mc Devitt
Glenside, PA

Carter, Stephanie Ann
Wissahickon HS
Ambler, PA

Carter, Tillary
Boyertown Area SR
Boyertown, PA

Cartin, Joseph W
Archbishop Wood
For Boys
Warminster, PA

Cartwright, Clifford
Westbranch Area JR
SR HS
Philipsburg, PA

Cartwright, Donna
Calvary Baptist
Norwood, PA

Carver, Laura
Lincoln HS
Ellwood City, PA

Casciani, Marc
Belle Vernon Area
Belle Vernon, PA

Case, Chris
Millville HS
Millville, PA

Case, Lynn
Northwestern SR
Albion, PA

Casey, Angela
Lake Lehman HS
Shavertown, PA

Caskie, Stephen
Tulpehocken HS
Myerstown, PA

Casper, Theresa
Creative And
Performing Arts
Philadelphia, PA

Cassel, Curtis
Northern Lebanon
Myerstown, PA

Cassidy, Jr Robert
D
St Josephs Prep
Philadelphia, PA

Castro, Bridget
Mifflinburg Area HS
Lewisburg, PA

Casuccio, Diana
Hopewell SR HS
Aliquippa, PA

Cates, Christine Ann
Kiski Area HS
New Kensington,
PA

Cates, Denise
Kiski Area HS
New Kensington,
PA

Catlin, Kimberly L
Union Area Middle
New Castle, PA

Cavada, Anthony
Jeannette SR HS
Jeannette, PA

Cawley, Cynthia
Baldwin HS
Pittsburgh, PA

Cays, John Michael
Pocono Mountain
Stroudsburg, PA

Cease, Jason
John S Fine HS
Nanticoke, PA

Cebula, Karen
Somerset Area SR
Friedens, PA

Ceccato, Angela
Plum SR HS
Pittsburgh, PA

Cecchett, Dawn
Rene
Yough SR HS
West Newton, PA

Cella, Jeffrey
Churchill HS
Pittsburgh, PA

Cellini, Lisa A
Bishop Hafey HS
Nuremberg, PA

Centini, Jacqueline
Northern York Co
Dillsburg, PA

Cernicky, Shawn
Belle Vernon Area
Belle Vernon, PA

Cervenak, Joseph C
Moshannon Valley
Morann, PA

Cervone, Marissa
Meadville Area SR
Meadville, PA

Cessna, Julie
Meyersdale Area HS
Wellersburg, PA

Chaapel, Kitrina
Canton JR SR HS
Grover, PA

Chalfant, Michele
Charleroi JR SR HS
Charleroi, PA

Chambers, Kelly
Blairsville SR HS
Black Lick, PA

Chambers, Shanee
Mc Keesport HS
Mckeesport, PA

Chan, Frances
St Huberts HS Girls
Philadelphia, PA

Chandler, Cassandra
L
Towanda HS
Towanda, PA

Chang, Eugene J
Shady Side Acad
Greensburg, PA

Chanitz, Jen
Sun Valley HS
Brookhaven, PA

Chapell, Allan
Coulersport Area JR
SR HS
Coudersport, PA

Chapin, Alan
Benton Area HS
Benton, PA

Chapman, Jessica
Oxford Area HS
Lincoln Universit,
PA

Chapman, Katharine
Canon-Mc Millan
Canonsburg, PA

Chapnell, David
Lincoln HS
Ellwood City, PA

Chappell, Cyndi
Richland HS
Gibsonia, PA

Chappell, Todd R
Lewisburg Area HS
Lewisburg, PA

Charles, James W
Lampeter Strasburg
Willow Street, PA

Charney, Susan
Pittston Area HS
Pittston, PA

Chaskin, Brenna
Hazleton SR HS
Hazleton, PA

Chastain, Curtis
Pocono Mountain
Swiftwater, PA

Chastain, Patty
South Fayette JRSR
Bridgeville, PA

Chatfield, Jeff
North Hills HS
Pittsburgh, PA

Check, Kellie
Carlynton HS
Pittsburgh, PA

Cheek, Lee
Waynesburg Central
Waynesburg, PA

Chen, Douglas
Council Rock HS
Washington Cros,
PA

Chenevey, Steve
Wilmington Area
New Wilmington,
PA

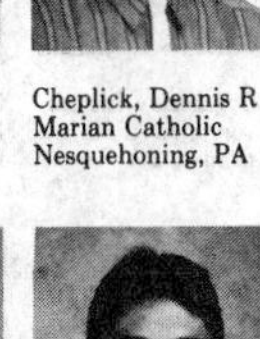

Cheplick, Dennis R
Marian Catholic
Nesquehoning, PA

Cherry, Ken
Bellwood-Antis HS
Tyrone, PA

Cherry, Steven
Lower Moreland HS
Huntingdon Valley,
PA

Cherwony, Beth
Neshaminy HS
Langhorne, PA

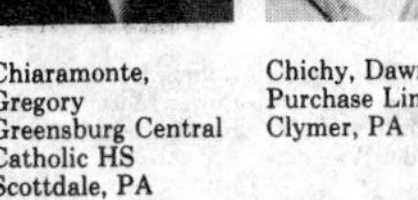

Chiaramonte,
Gregory
Greensburg Central
Catholic HS
Scottdale, PA

Chichy, Dawn
Purchase Line HS
Clymer, PA

Chickini, James J
Moon SR HS
Coraopolis, PA

Chickirda, Jennifer
Tamaqua Area HS
Tamaqua, PA

Chieffalo, Daniel
Bishop Hannan HS
Scranton, PA

Chiesa, Lisa
Highlands SR HS
Natrona Heights,
PA

Chilson, John
Millersburg Area HS
Millersburg, PA

Chin, Song-Ok
Susan
Plymouth
Whitemarsh HS
Conshohocken, PA

Chnupa, Keith
Clearfield Area HS
Clearfield, PA

Cho, Susan
Avon Grove HS
West Grove, PA

Choi, Un Jung
Plymouth
Whitemarsh HS
Conshohocken, PA

Chris, Michelle
Corry Area HS
Corry, PA

Christ, Cheryl
Peters TWP HS
Venetia, PA

Christensen, Peter
N
Central SR HS
York, PA

Christian, Thad
New Brighton HS
New Brighton, PA

Christie, Craig
Central Bucks West
Chalfont, PA

Chu, Siao Mei
Lock Haven HS
Lock Haven, PA

Chubin, Ellen
Pennsbury HS
Yardley, PA

Chudy, Frank
Springdale HS
Cheswick, PA

Chulvick, Mary Jo
James M Coughlin
Wilkes-Barre, PA

Chung, Elizabeth
Bethlehem Catholic
Bethlehem, PA

Chupak, Leslie
West Middlesex HS
W Middlesex, PA

Chupka, Paul
Ambridge Area HS
Ambridge, PA

Chvala, Keith
Kiso Arco HS
Vandergrift, PA

Ciabattoni, David
Exeter Township
Reading, PA

Cianelli, Lori
Canon-Mcmillan SR
Canonsburg, PA

Cianelli, Nick
Canon Mc Millan
SR HS
Canonsburg, PA

Cianflone, Ross
Old Forge HS
Old Forge, PA

Ciaramella, Terri
Geibel HS
Masontown, PA

Ciarrocchi, Carla
Abington SR HS
Willow Grove, PA

Ciccocioppo, Barry
Trinity HS
Marysville, PA

Cicero, Kathleen
Pleasanty Valley HS
Kunkletown, PA

Cichonski, Janeen
Saint Hubert HS
Philadelphia, PA

Cichonski, Jay M
North-East Catholic
Philadelphia, PA

Cifelli, Cynthia
Perry Traditional
Pittsburgh, PA

Cimino, Priscilla
Scr Central HS
Scranton, PA

Cimochowski,
Andrew
Neshamwy HS
Levittown, PA

Cindrich, Dave
Beth-Center HS
Marianna, PA

Cipolloni, Mark
West Catholic HS
Philadelphia, PA

Cisney, Amber
Dover Area HS
Dover, PA

Citrone, Greg
St John Neumann
Philadelphia, PA

Civiletti, Pia
Wyoming Area HS
Pittston, PA

Clark, Aaron D
State College Area
Bedford, PA

Clark, Beth
Manheim Central
Manheim, PA

Clark, Deurward W
Martin Luther King
Phila, PA

Clark, Diana
Everett Area HS
Clearville, PA

Clark, Douglas
Bentworth HS
Scenery Hill, PA

Clark, Douglas
Cornell SR HS
Coraopolis, PA

Clark, Lisa
Bishop Hannan HS
Scranton, PA

Clark, Melissa
Northern Bedford
County HS
Everett, PA

Clark, Rebecca L
Downingtown SR
West Chester, PA

Clark, Jr Robert
Blacklick Valley HS
Ebensburg, PA

Clark, Sheryl
Lake-Lehman HS
Dallas, PA

Clark, Susan
Meadville HS
Meadville, PA

Clausen, Ken
Strong Vincent HS
Erie, PA

Clausner, Carrie
Mary Fuller Frazier
Mem SR HS
Perryopolis, PA

Clawges, Tracy
Pennsbury HS
Yardley, PA

Clayton, Kimberly
Anne
Jeannette SR HS
Jeannette, PA

Clayton, Michelle
Shady Side Acad
Pittsburgh, PA

Clemens, Natalie
Danville Area SR
Danville, PA

Clifford, Tammy Jo
Bangor Area HS
Bangor, PA

Cline, Juli
Middletown Area
Middletown, PA

Cline, Nicole
Biglerville HS
Gardners, PA

Clingerman, Lisa A
Everett Area HS
Artemas, PA

Clink, Vicky
Northeast Bradford
Le Raysville, PA

Clinton, Autumn
Sullivan County HS
Dushore, PA

Clouser, Jeffrey
Boyertown Area SR
Bechtelsville, PA

Clowser, Richard
Pottsgrove SR HS
Pottstown, PA

Coakley, Kellie
Bald Eagle Area HS
Bellefonte, PA

Cobb, Christopher
Penn Hills SR HS
Pittsburgh, PA

Cobb, Eugene
Ambridge Area HS
Ambridge, PA

Coble, Scott
Elizabethtown Area
Elizabethtown, PA

Coble, Tracey
Purchase Line HS
Burnside, PA

Coburn, Corrine
State College Area
State College, PA

Coccagna, Carol
West Catholic Girls
Philadelphia, PA

Cochran, Dawn R
Du Bois Area HS
Sykesville, PA

Cockrum, Stephany
A
Lock Haven HS
Lock Haven, PA

Coe, Julie
Highlands SR HS
Natrona Hts, PA

Coffman, Samara
Robyn
Lower Moreland HS
Huntingdon Valley,
PA

Cohen, Beth
Lower Moreland HS
Huntingdon Valley,
PA

Cohen, Dan
Upper Dublin HS
Dresher, PA

Cohen, Jennifer
Lower Moreland HS
Huntingdon Valley, PA

Cohen, Judith D
Cheltenham HS
Elkins Park, PA

Cohen, Michael E
Harriton HS
Gladwyne, PA

Colangelo, Domenic
Hopewell HS
Aliquippa, PA

Cole, Christine
Meadville Area SR
Meadville, PA

Cole, Lisa
Bishop Guilfoyle HS
Altoona, PA

Cole, Patty
Mansfield HS
Mansfield, PA

Colello, Joseph
Altoona Area HS
Altoona, PA

Coleman, Dana
Joann Marie
Lutheran HS
Philadelphia, PA

Coleman, Joann
Central York SR HS
York, PA

Coleman, Joyce L
St Pauls Cathedral
Pittsburgh, PA

Coles, Dawna
Western Beaver JR SR HS
Midland, PA

Coleson, Brian
Ephrata HS
Ephrata, PA

Colia, Lisa Ann
Neshannock HS
New Castle, PA

Colinear, Jennifer
Norwin HS
N Huntingdon, PA

Collins, Jeannette
Moniteau HS
Chicora, PA

Collins, Jessica
Fox Chapel HS
Pittsbg, PA

Collins, Katherine A
Wilson SR HS
West Lawn, PA

Collins, Kevin
Curwensville Area
Curwensville, PA

Collins, Lenora
Belle Vernon Area
West Newton, PA

Collins, Sean
St Josephs Prep HS
Philadelphia, PA

Collins, Stephanie
Everett Area HS
Clearville, PA

Collison, James
Bishop Kenrick HS
Norristown, PA

Collura, Joseph
Palmyra SR HS
Palmyra, PA

Colombo, Mark
Cardinal O Hara HS
Media, PA

Colon, Jose
Souderton Area HS
Souderton, PA

Colon, Maria
Little Flower HS
Philadelphia, PA

Colwell, Carole
Red Land HS
York Haven, PA

Comella, Christine
Bethel Park HS
Bethel Park, PA

Comstock, Jeanette
Benton Area HS
Stillwater, PA

Condadina, Andrea
Cardinal O Hara HS
Broomall, PA

Confer, Julie
Lock Haven HS
Lock Haven, PA

Conforti, Kip
Anthony
Scranton Central
Moscow, PA

Conjelko, Brian J
Richland SR HS
Johnstown, PA

Conklin, Tim
Salisbury HS
Allentown, PA

Connell, Laura
Villa Maria Acad
Exton, PA

Connelly, Sharon
Penn-Trafford HS
Trafford, PA

Connelly, Stephanie
Bald Eagle Area HS
Howard, PA

Conner, Dawn
Bellwood-Antis HS
Tyrone, PA

Connor, Carol Ann
Susquehanna
Township HS
Harrisburg, PA

Connors, Lisa
Southmoreland SR
Scottdale, PA

Consiglio, Jackie
Bishop Guilfoyle HS
Altoona, PA

Consiglio, Kellie L
Hollidaysburg Area
Hollidaysburg, PA

Constantino, Todd
Shady Side Acad
Pittsburgh, PA

Cook, Ellen
Reynolds HS
Greenville, PA

Cook, Lori
Montgomery Area
Montgomery, PA

Cook, Rosalyn
Bellevernon Area
Belle Vernon, PA

Cooper, Amanda L
North Allegheny SR
Wexford, PA

Cooper, Cathryn
North Allegheny SR
Wexford, PA

Cooper, Dawn
Lewistown Area HS
Lewistown, PA

Cooper, Di Anna
Southmoreland HS
Scottdale, PA

Cooper, Hope
Upper Dauphin
Area HS
Elizabethville, PA

Cooper, Lisa
Ford City HS
Ford City, PA

Cooper, Marissa
Churchill HS
Pittsburgh, PA

Cooperman, Camie
Phila High For
Creative & Pref Arts
Philadelphia, PA

Coopie, Jennifer
Steel Valley HS
Munhall, PA

Cope, Carl
Louis E Dieruff HS
Allentown, PA

Copenhaver, Dawn
M
Conrad Weiser JS
Robesonia, PA

Coppens, Suzan
Harry S Truman HS
Croydon, PA

Coppola, Daniel
Northeast Catholic
Philadelphia, PA

Corace, Colleen
Gwynedd Mercy
Gwynedd Valley, PA

Corba, Maryann
St Maria Goretti HS
Philadelphia, PA

Corbett, Tyrus
Center HS
Monaca, PA

Corbin, Melissa
Huntingdon Area
Huntingdon, PA

Cordas, David
Pennsbury HS
Yardley, PA

Cordero, Brenda
Freedom HS
Bethlehem, PA

Corkran, Vicki L
Southmoreland HS
Scottdale, PA

Cornelison, Roberta
Greenwood HS
Millerstown, PA

Cornelius, Patricia
Ann
Kennett HS
Kennett Sq, PA

Cornell, Lewis
Forest Hills HS
Sidman, PA

Cornett, Cynthia L
Delone Catholic HS
Gettysburg, PA

Cornitcher, Monica
Phila HS For Girls
Philadelphia, PA

Corpuz, III Marcelo N
Shady Side Acad
Pittsburgh, PA

Corr, Warren V
Wilson Area HS
Easton, PA

Corso, Bonita
Burgettstown HS
Burgettstown, PA

Cortezzo, Conni
Pen Argyl Area HS
Pen Argyl, PA

Cosgrove, Kristie Lee
Steel Valley HS
Munhall, PA

Cosgrove, Stacey L
Commodore Perry
Hadley, PA

Costanzo, Valarie
Canon-Mc Millan
Canonsburg, PA

Costello, Colleen
Scranton Prep Schl
Dunmore, PA

Costello, Kelly
Northwestern Lehigh HS
Schnecksvile, PA

Costello, Michele
Connellsville SR HS
Connellsville, PA

Coughenour, Jr William E
Meyersdale Area HS
Salisbury, PA

Covert, Heather
Butler Area SR HS
Butler, PA

Cowell, Danelle
West Mifflin Area
W Mifflin, PA

Cowell, William
West Mifflin Area
West Mifflin, PA

Cox, Michelle
Hatboro Horsham SR HS
Horsham, PA

Coyle, Donna
Nazareth SR HS
Nazareth, PA

Coyne, Susan L
Steel Valley HS
Munhall, PA

Cozart, Selena Diane
Philadelphia HS For
Philadelphia, PA

Crable, Jennifer
Uniontown Area HS
Uniontown, PA

Craig, Deabra
Punxsutawney Area
Punxsutawney, PA

Craley, Matthew
Northeastern HS
Mt Wolf, PA

Cramer, Lori
United HS
Blairsville, PA

Cramton, Michael J
Wyoming Seminary
Shavertown, PA

Cranga, Michael
Carlisle SR HS
Carlisle, PA

Craven, Kimberly
Little Flower C H G
Philadelphia, PA

Crawford, Julie L
Redbank Valley HS
New Bethlehem, PA

Crawford, Kathleen
Sacred Heart HS
Pittsburgh, PA

Crawford, Kathleen
York County Vo-Tech HS
York, PA

Crawford, Stacy Alan
Dover HS
Dover, PA

Creamer, Michael
Souderton HS
Telford, PA

Creasy, Theresa M
Bloomsburg Area SR HS
Bloomsburg, PA

Crichton, Paige
Unionville HS
Kennett Square, PA

Crider, Matthew
Elizabethtown Area
Elizabethtown, PA

Crider, Roger
Seneca Valley HS
Evans City, PA

Crilley, Joseph Peter
Northwestern SR
E Springfield, PA

Criniti, Rosa
St Maria Goretti HS
Philadelphia, PA

Crist, Brian
Williams Valley HS
Reinerton, PA

Crist, Michelle
Halifax Area HS
Halifax, PA

Crist, Michelle Denise
Eastern York HS
York, PA

Croce, Christina
Lock Haven HS
Lock Haven, PA

Crockard, James
Carmichaels Area SR HS
Carmichaels, PA

Croll, Michelle L
West Hazleton HS
Zion Grove, PA

Cross, Brian G
Germantown Acad
Wyncote, PA

Crothers, Ray
Canon Mc Millan
Canonsburg, PA

Croushore, Deanna
Belle Vernon Area
Belle Vernon, PA

Croushore, Jr William
Southmoreland SR
Ruffsdale, PA

Crowley, Alisa
Alto-Eldred JR SR
Eldred, PA

Croy, Michele
Grove City HS
Grove City, PA

Cruz, Lynn
East SR HS
West Chester, PA

Cruz, Rose
Little Flower HS
Philadelphia, PA

Cucuzza, Robert J
Bradford Central Christian HS
Bradford, PA

Cuff, Tom
Cardinal Brennan
Frackville, PA

Culbertson, Deanne
Youngsville HS
Youngsville, PA

Culler, Brent
Mc Connellsburg HS
Mcconnellsburg, PA

Culp, Kimberly
Dallas SR HS
Dallas, PA

Cummings, Craig
Sun Valley HS
Brookhaven, PA

Cummings, Michael
Scranton Tech
Scranton, PA

Cumpston, Michele
Burgettstown Area
Langeloth, PA

Cunard, Rebecca
Christian Schl Of
York, PA

Cunkelman, Brian
Balirsville Sr HS
Blairsville, PA

Cunningham, Christine
Valley View JR SR
Blakely, PA

Cunningham, Janet
Homer-Center SR
Homer City, PA

Cunningham, Nicole
Warren Area HS
Warren, PA

Cupec, Jennifer
Our Lady Of The Sacred Heart HS
Aliquippa, PA

Cupples, Joycelyn
Ridley HS
Ridley Park, PA

Curran, Mary Kristen
Mc Keesport HS
White Oak, PA

Curran, Vincent
St Josephs Prep
Villanova, PA

Curry, Jennifer
Nazareth Acad
Philadelphia, PA

Curtis, Stephen
Western Wayne HS
Waymart, PA

Cussins, Donnie
North Clarion HS
Lucinda, PA

Custodio, Maribel
Bethlehem Catholic
Bethlehem, PA

Cutlip, Michele Kay
Central SR HS
York, PA

Cwiertnie, Victoria
Sun Valley HS
Aston, PA

Cycak, Wanda Kay
Lock Haven HS
Castanea, PA

Cyphert, Amy
Wilmington Area
New Wilmington,
PA

Cytrynowicz, Steven
Upper Moreland SR
Willow Grove, PA

Czajkowski, Dawn
Marie
St Huberts HS
Philadelphia, PA

Czarnecki, Barbara
Nazareth Academy
Philadelphia, PA

Czarnecki, John A
Bishop Mc Devitt
Harrisburg, PA

D Alessandris, Paula
Our Lady Of The
Sacred Heart
Aliquippa, PA

D Alessandro,
Noelle
Creative And
Performing Arts
Philadelphia, PA

D Amico, Melanie
Scranton Central
Scranton, PA

D Arcy, Jr William
F
Archbishop Wood
Holland, PA

Dahlin, Philip
Bishop Egan HS
Hulmeville, PA

Dainty, Daniel
Belle Vernon Area
Belle Vernon, PA

Daisley, Dawn
Reynolds HS
Greenville, PA

Dait, Marianne
Perkiomen Schl
Lehighton, PA

Dait, Pierre
Perkiomen HS
Lehighton, PA

Dale, III Clark
West Branch Area
Morrisdale, PA

Dalessandri, Susan
Aliquippa HS
Aliquippa, PA

Daley, Gena
Lackawanna Trl HS
Factoryvle, PA

Dalfo, Thomas J
Archbishop Wood H
S For Boys
Warminster, PA

Dallas, Michael
Wilson HS
West Lawn, PA

Dalton, Kate
North Allegheny SR
Pittsburgh, PA

Damiano, Gena
Marie
Panther Valley HS
Nesquehoning, PA

Damiano, Karen
Old Forge HS
Old Forge, PA

Damon, Mark
Northeaster SR HS
Manchester, PA

Damon, Jr Paul
Gateway HS
Mornoeville, PA

Dampf, Julie
Knoch HS
Butler, PA

Dandeneau, Nicole
Emmaus HS
Macungie, PA

Dando, Lisa
Mary Fuller Frazier
Me JR SR HS
Fayette City, PA

Daniels, Kathy
Forest Hills SR HS
St Michael, PA

Danielson, Nancy L
Mercer Area JR SR
Mercer, PA

Danko, Patricia A
Lansdale Catholic
Lansdale, PA

Danowski, Rebecca
Hatboro-Horsham
Hatboro, PA

Daresta, Annette
Unionville HS
West Chester, PA

Darnell, Beverly
Connellsville Area
Dunbar, PA

Darnell, Kelly
Bangor Area SR HS
Mt Bethel, PA

Dasovich, E Marty
Conneaut Valley HS
Conneautville, PA

Date, Lisa
Moshannon Valley
Smoke Run, PA

Daugherty, Colleen
Upper St Clair &
Canonmac HS
Canonsburg, PA

Daugherty, Lisa
Red Lion SR HS
Red Lion, PA

Daura, Keith
Penn-Trafford HS
Irwin, PA

Davidson, Daryl
Sharon HS
Sharon, PA

Davis, Brenda
Kiski Area HS
Vandergrift, PA

Davis, Chris
Elizabeth Area HS
Elizabethtown, PA

Davis, Chris
Williamsburg HS
Williamsburg, PA

Davis, Christina M
Ontario Street
Baptist Church Schl
Philadelphia, PA

Davis, Deanna
Faith Christian Schl
Stroudsburg, PA

Davis, Gary
Carmichaels Area
JR SR HS
Carmichaels, PA

Davis, Jonathan
Leigh
New Hope-Solebury
New Hope, PA

Davis, Kelley
Downingtown SR
Downingtown, PA

Davis, Linda
Creative &
Performings Arts
Philadelphia, PA

Davis, Lori
Brookville Area HS
Brookville, PA

Davis, Mary
Brookville Area JR
SR HS
Brookville, PA

Davis, Michael
Clarion-Limestone
Strattanville, PA

Davis, Mindy
Fairchance-Georges
Uniontownd, PA

Davis, Paris
Chester HS
Chester, PA

Davis, Paul
West Catholic HS
Philadelphia, PA

Davis, Scott
Council Rock HS
New Hope, PA

Davis, Stephani
Columbia-Montour
Area Vo Tech Schl
Catawissa, PA

Davison, Charles
Seneca Valley HS
Harmony, PA

Davison, Heather
Hanover Area HS
Lower Askam, PA

Davy, Tereasa
Lockhaven SR HS
Blanchard, PA

Dawson, Andrew S
Red Lion Area SR
Delta, PA

Dawson, Jeffrey
Bishop Mc Cort HS
Conemaugh, PA

Dawson, Kathleen
Bishop Shanahan
West Chester, PA

Dawson, Pam
Coudersport JR SR
Coudersport, PA

Day, Steve
Du Bois Area HS
Reynoldsville, PA

De Angelo, Leslie
North Pocono HS
Moscow, PA

De Arment, John M
Altoona Area HS
Altoona, PA

De Baker, Jodi
Canon Mc Millan
Canonsburg, PA

De Bellis, John Jay
Northampton Area
SR HS
Northampton, PA

De Berardinis, Andrea
Cardinal O Hara HS
Aston, PA

De Biase, Toni
East Pennsboro HS
Enola, PA

De Caria, James
Lincoln HS
Ellwood City, PA

De Carlucci, Henry Keith
Laurel Highlands
Uniontown, PA

De Caro, Donald
Greensbury Central
Catholic HS
Greensburg, PA

De Fusco, Jr Pasquale
West Catholic Boys
Philadelphia, PA

De Groat, Renee L
Sun Valley HS
Aston, PA

De Heck, Beth
Central Bucks East
Jamison, PA

De Lisio, Adrienne
Hopewell HS
Aliquippa, PA

De Long, Lisa
Du Bois Area HS
Du Bois, PA

De Luca, Deborah Lynn
Center Area HS
Aliquippa, PA

De Morrow, Denise
Mid-Valley HS
Dickson City, PA

De Pietro, Marisa
West Scranton HS
Scranton, PA

De Roos, Lisa
Mechanicsburg S
Mechanicsburg, PA

De Rosa, Ann
Central Bucks High
School East
Danboro, PA

De Rose, Laura
Ambridge Area HS
Baden, PA

De Ross, Daniel
Saegertown HS
Saegertown, PA

De Santis, Maureen
Cntry Day Schl Of
The Sacred Heart
Berwyn, PA

De Wire, Timothy
Mechanicsburg Area
SR HS
Mechanicsburg, PA

De Witt, Denise Marie
Schuylkill Haven
Area HS
Schuylkill Haven

De Woody, Elizabeth
Canon Mcmillan HS
Eighty Four, PA

Deaner, Stephanie
Cedar Crest HS
Lebanon, PA

Deangelis, Cara
Connellsville Area
Millrun, PA

Deangelis, Melissa
Muhlenberg HS
Laureldale, PA

Deaver, Wendy
Northern HS
Dillsburg, PA

Decarlo, Danielle
Canon-Mc Millan
Mcdonald, PA

Deckman, John
Northern Lebanon
Lebanon, PA

Deegan, Gregory
Pottstown SR HS
Pottstown, PA

Deemer, Kim
Seneca Valley HS
Evans City, PA

Deemer, Traci
Lincoln HS
Ellwood City, PA

Defilippi, Matthew
Leechburg Area HS
Leechburg, PA

Degler, Douglas
Muhlenberg HS
Reading, PA

Dehner, Sharon
North Clarion HS
Tylersburg, PA

Deibert, Julie
Tri-Valley HS
Sacramento, PA

Delconte, Lisa
Cardinal O Hara HS
Broomall, PA

Delgado, Abel
St Josephs Prep
Philadelphia, PA

Delgrosso, Patricia
Freedom HS
Bethlehem, PA

Delio, Jennifer
Bishop Shanahan
Downingtown, PA

Delisio, Robert F
New Brighton HS
New Brighton, PA

Demarchi, Jr Frank
William Allen HS
Allentown, PA

Demellier, Leah
E L Meyers HS
Wilkes Barre, PA

Demko, Timothy
Mahonoy Area HS
Mahanoy City, PA

Demmitt, Tom
Northeastern HS
York, PA

Demnyan, Sean
Canon Mcmillan SR
Canonsburg, PA

Demora, Sam
Lakeland HS
Jermyn, PA

Dempsey, Patricia
Archbishop
Kennedy HS
Philadelphia, PA

Demster, Deborah S
Lower Merion HS
Narberth, PA

Dennehy, Eileen
Abington Heights
Dalton, PA

Denney, Mindi
Connellsville SR HS
Connellsville, PA

Denniston, John J
Trinity HS
Mechanicsburg, PA

Dennler, Dena M
North Catholic HS
Pittsburgh, PA

Dentith, Amy Jo
Pen Argyl HS
Pen Argyl, PA

Denver, Karen
St Hubert For Girls
Philadelphia, PA

Depoe, Craig
Donegal HS
Mt Joy, PA

Derion, Kristin
Bethel Park SR HS
Bethel Park, PA

Derk, G Eric
Wilson HS
Wyomissing, PA

Derose, Joseph
Bentworth HS
Cokeburg, PA

Dest, Sandra
Nazareth Area SR
Nazareth, PA

Detter, Jennifer
York Suburban SR
York, PA

Detweiler, Lisa
Pen Argyl Area HS
Pen Argyl, PA

Dever, Mary Ann
Nazareth Acad
Philadelphia, PA

Devlin, Michael
Cardinal O Hara HS
Havertown, PA

Devorick, Dennis
Greater Johnstown
Area Vo-Tech
Johnstown, PA

Dewit, Christopher
Moon SR HS
Coraopolis, PA

Dherit, Gregory
Northeastern HS
Manchester, PA

Di Cesare, Jr
Patrick J
Greensburg Central
Catholic HS
Jeannette, PA

Di Cicco, Andrea
Nazareth Acad
Philadelphia, PA

Di Cio, Dan
Canon-Mc Millan
SR HS
Canonsburg, PA

Di Domenico,
Margaret
Archbishop
Kennedy HS
Ambler, PA

Di Gilarmo, Bob
Central Christian
Dubois, PA

Di Lucia, Mary
Mount St Joseph
Norristown, PA

Di Marcella,
Kathleen M
Bishop Kenrick HS
Norristown, PA

Di Martino, Lynn
Greensburg Central
Catholic HS
Irwin, PA

Di Matteo, Steven J
Monongahela Valley
Catholic HS
Monongahela, PA

Di Muro, John
The Hill Schl
E Brunswick, NJ

Di Palma, Giovanna
St Maria Goretti HS
Philadelphia, PA

Di Paolo, John P
Holy Ghost
Preparatory Schl
Philadelphia, PA

Di Paolo, Patrick
Cathedral
Preparatory Schl
Erie, PA

Di Piano, Jennifer
Perkiomen Valley
Collegeville, PA

Di Pietro, Maria
St Maria Goretta
Philadelphia, PA

Di Santo, Denise
Norristown Area HS
Norristown, PA

Diascro, Matthew
Perkiomen HS
Red Hill, PA

Dice, Tina
Waynesboro Area
SR HS
Chambersburg, PA

Dick, Catherine
Penn Trafford HS
Irwin, PA

Dickson, James
Red Lion Area SR
Red Lion, PA

Dickson, Sue
Conemaugh
Township Area HS
Johnstown, PA

Dicola, Robyn
Butler HS
Butler, PA

Diederich, Michelle
York Catholic HS
Jacobus, PA

Diefenderfer, Denise
West Hazleton HS
West Hazleton, PA

Dieffenbach, Todd
Carson Long
Military Inst
Bethel, PA

Diehl, Eric
Greater Latrobe SR
Latrobe, PA

Diehl, Eric
Kutztown Area HS
Kutztown, PA

Diehl, Kelly
Portage Area HS
Portage, PA

Diem, Vincent P
Pequea Valley HS
Kinzers, PA

Dieringer, Noelle
Du Bois Area HS
Rockton, PA

Dieterle, III Neal
Laurence
Northeastern SR HS
Mt Wolf, PA

Dietrich, II David
Norwin HS
N Huntingdon, PA

Dietrich, Doug
Pequea Valley HS
Paradise, PA

Dietrich, Wade
Lykens Christian
Williamstown, PA

Dietz, Robert
East HS
Erie, PA

Diffenderfer, Jennie
Manheim Central
Manheim, PA

Diggs, Reecella
Valley HS
New Kensington,
PA

Dill, Anthony
York Catholic HS
York, PA

Dillard, Grace
Cedar Grove
Christian Acad
Philadelphia, PA

Dillon, Kathy
Moshannon Valley
Houtzdale, PA

Dilts, Vivian
Philipsburg-Osceola
West Decatur, PA

Dimarcella, Daniel
Bishop Kenrick HS
Norristown, PA

Dimenno, Joseph
Anon Mc Millan HS
Canonsburg, PA

Dimmick, Jack
Mahanoy Area HS
Mahanoy City, PA

Dinant, Scott
Philipsburg-Osceola
Philipsburg, PA

Diomedo, Adam
Notre Dame HS
Easton, PA

Dion, Bill
Council Rock HS
Wash Crsng, PA

Dionne, Edward
Northampton HS
Walnutport, PA

Disabato, Lisa
Altoona Area HS
Altoona, PA

Dishauzi, David A
Center HS
Aliquippa, PA

Ditz, Beverly
North Clarion JRSR
Fryburg, PA

Ditzler, Marcie
Elizabeth
Lancaster Catholic
Conestoga, PA

Dneaster, Michael
Meyersdale Area HS
Garrett, PA

Doak, Eric
West Allegheny HS
Oakdale, PA

Dobbs, Marc
Ford City JR SR
Vandergrift, PA

Dodson, Chris
Girard College HS
Wilmington, DE

Dodson, Debbie
Clysburg-Kimmel
E Freedom, PA

Dodson, Dena
Everett HS
Clearville, PA

Dodson, Gayle
Claysburg-Kimmel
Claysburg, PA

Doebler, Antoinette
Meadowbrook
Christian Schl
Milton, PA

Doel, Peter
Plum SR HS
Pittsburgh, PA

Doering, Ryan
Pottsgrave HS
Pottstown, PA

Doherty, Francis
Crestwoodd HS
Mountaintop, PA

Dolezal, Kari
New Hope Salebury
New Hope, PA

Doluisio, Michael
Freedom HS
Bethlehem, PA

Domaracki,
Christine
Connellsville Area
SR HS
Connellsville, PA

Domen, David M
Laurel Highlands
SR HS
Uniontown, PA

Domer, Christina
Red Lion SR HS
York, PA

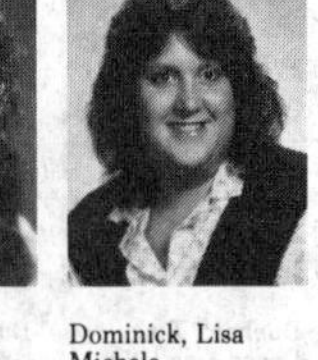
Dominick, Lisa
Michele
Pittston Area HS
Pittston, PA

Donaldson, Bob
Cambridge Springs
Cambridge Springs, PA

Doney, De Vonne Danelle
Waynesburg Central
Waynesburg, PA

Donkers, Lynn
Brownsville Area HS
Brownsville, PA

Donnelly, Noreen C
Cardinal Dougherty
Philadelphia, PA

Donnelly, Susan
Creative & Performing Arts
Philadelphia, PA

Donovan, Heather
Wilson Area HS
Riegelsville, PA

Donovan, Maureen
Archbishop Wood HS For Girls
Churchville, PA

Doral, Dina
Strath Haven HS
Wallingford, PA

Doraski, Lisa
Southern Columbia
Catawissa, PA

Dorich, Darlene Ann
Mercyhurst Prepatory Schl
Erie, PA

Dorman, Robert
Freedom SR HS
Bethlehem, PA

Dornenburg, William
Carlynton JR SR
Carnegie, PA

Dorozowski, Diane
Freedom HS
Bethlehem, PA

Dorwart, Stephen
Neshaminy HS
Trevose, PA

Doshi, Amol N
Shadyside Acad
Pittsburgh, PA

Doud, Tina
Mansfield JR & SR
Mansfield, PA

Douds, Mike
Bethel Park HS
Bethel Park, PA

Dougherty, Colleen
Bishop Shanahan
Exton, PA

Dougherty, Judith A
West Scranton HS
Scranton, PA

Dougherty, Laura Ann
West Perry HS
Loysville, PA

         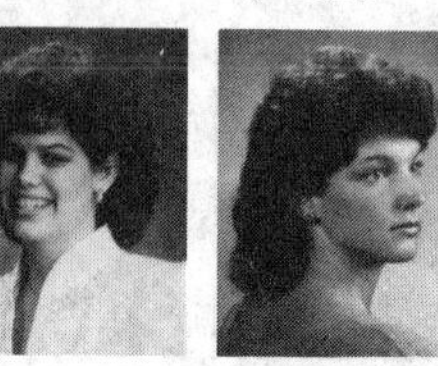

Doughty, Linda
Hopewell SR HS
Hookstown, PA

Dowler, Michael H
Greenville HS
Greenville, PA

Downey, John
West Branch HS
Morrisdale, PA

Doyle, Carole
Mt St Joseph Acad
Warminster, PA

Doyle, Erica
Abington Heights
Clarks Summit, PA

Doyle, Michael
Interboro HS
Lester, PA

Dragon, Amy
The Christian Acad
Wallingford, PA

Drake, Tracey
Chichester SR HS
Boothwyn, PA

Drakulic, Milana
Norwin SR HS
Ardara, PA

Draovitch, Kathleen M
St Clair Area HS
Pottsville, PA

Draper, Kelli Danielle
Chester HS
Chester, PA

Dressler, Theresa
Dallas SR HS
Dallas, PA

Drew, Phelicia
Villa Maria Acad
Erie, PA

Drewencki, Beth
Knoch JR SR HS
Cabot, PA

Driggs, Roberto L
Cardinal Dougherty
Phila, PA

Droz, Michelle L
Sylvania Hills Christian Acad
Rochester, PA

Drozda, Jennifer
Vincentian HS
Wexford, PA

Drozdo, Michael
Oil City SR HS
Seneca, PA

Dubbs, Scheri
Williams Valley SR SR HS
Reinerton, PA

Dubyak, Melissa
Cambria Heights HS
Patton, PA

Ducar, Mary Beth
West Mifflin Area
Whitaker, PA

Duffield, Amy
Frankford HS
Philadelphia, PA

Duffy, James
Upper Moreland SR
Willow Grove, PA

Dugan, Jacqueline
Cardinal O Hara HS
Drexel Hill, PA

Dugan, Kathleen
Bristol JR SR HS
Bristol, PA

Dugan, Sean
Bald Eagle Area HS
Howard, PA

Duggan, Colleen
West Scranton SR
Scranton, PA

Duggan, Jeanne
Pocono Mountain
Pocono Lake, PA

Duggins, Michele
Pleasant Valley HS
Saylorsburg, PA

Duke, John
Portage Area HS
Lilly, PA

    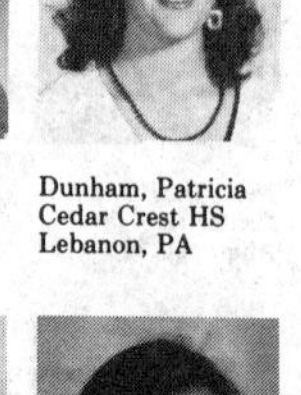

Dulaney, Kelly
Waynesburg Central
Waynesburg, PA

Dumbaugh, Erin
Butler SR HS
West Sunbury, PA

Dumblosky, Stephanie
Steel Valley HS
Munhall, PA

Dunaway, Debbie
Connellsville Area
Dunbar, PA

Dunbar, Chavock
Harrisburg Steelton High Spire Vo-Tech
Harrisburg, PA

Duncan, Debbie
Hopewell SR HS
Aliquippa, PA

Duncan, Eric
Springdale HS
Cheswick, PA

Dunegan, M Bernadette
Cambria Heights HS
Patton, PA

Dunham, Michael Ray
Albert Gallatin SR
Smithfield, PA

Dunham, Patricia
Cedar Crest HS
Lebanon, PA

Dunham, Tracy
Dover Area HS
Dover, PA

Dunkerley, Doug
Grove City Area HS
Grove City, PA

Dunkle, Jennifer
Northern York County HS
Dillsburg, PA

Dunkle, Kristi
Bedford HS
Everett, PA

Dunlap, Tracy
Marian HS
Delano, PA

Dunn, Jennifer
St Pius X HS
Phoenixville, PA

Dunn, Sherry
Canon Mc Millan
Canonsburg, PA

Dunning, Karyn
Bishop Shanahan
Wheaton, IL

Dunski, Jonathan F
Whitehall HS
Whitehall, PA

Durbeck, Lisa
Cumberland Valley
Mechanicsburg, PA

Durham, Kyle
Ringgold HS
Venetia, PA

Durkin, Lawrence
Scranton Prep
Dunmore, PA

Durner, Carol L
Parkland HS
Allentown, PA

Durning, Karen
Bethel Park HS
Bethel Park, PA

Dutchko, Donna
Mon-Valley Catholic
Elizabeth, PA

Dutkiewicz, Margie
St Hubert HS
Philadelphia, PA

Duvall, Sean
Charleroi Area JR SR HS
Charleroi, PA

Dy, Sylim
University City HS
Philadelphia, PA

Dydynski, Lori
Wyoming Valley West HS
Plymouth, PA

Dziak, Jason
Bentworth HS
Ellsworth, PA

Dziedzicki, Amy
Southmoreland SR
Everson, PA

Eakins, James S
Central Bucks HS
Chalfont, PA

Earle, Chrissa Janel
Pine Forge Acad
S Floral Park, NY

East, M Shane
Chambersburg Area SR HS
Fayetteville, PA

Easterday, Jennifer
Downington SR HS
Exton, PA

Eaves, Margaret
Cardinal Dougherty
Phila, PA

Ebbert, Dolores
Vincentian HS
Pittsburgh, PA

Eberly, Lisa
Ephrata SR HS
Ephrata, PA

Ebersole, Melissa
Salisbury HS
Allentown, PA

Ebling, Roseann
Schuylkill Haven Area HS
Schuylkill Haven, PA

Ecenrode, Risha
Governor Mifflin SR
Shillington, PA

Eck, Carol
West Forest HS
Tionesta, PA

Eckenrode, Tonya
Penn Cambria HS
Gallitzin, PA

Eddowes, Annette
Upper Dublin HS
Ft Washington, PA

Eddy, Allyson
Archbishop John Carroll Girls HS
Brewster, MA

Eddy, Robin
Bradford Central Christian HS
Bradford, PA

Edelstein, Michael E
Gateway SR HS
Monroeville, PA

Eder, Paul
Bethlehem Catholic
Bethlehem, PA

Edge, Dawn M
Geo Washgtn Carver H S Of Engr & Sci
Philadelphia, PA

Edgell, Lisa
New Brighton HS
New Brighton, PA

Edling, Yvonne
Ambridge Area HS
Freedom, PA

Edris, Gregory
Blue Mountain Acad
Leesport, PA

Edwards, Michael
William Penn HS
Philadelphia, PA

Edwards, Niki
William Penn HS
Philadelphia, PA

Edwards, Shelley
Garden Spot HS
Terre Hill, PA

Eells, Paul
Mosignor Bonner
Glenolden, PA

Egan, Elizabeth
Upper Dublin HS
Ft Washington, PA

Eggleston, Michele
Interboro HS
Glenolden, PA

Eggleston, Robert Bubba
Wyoming Seminary
Wilkes Barre, PA

Ehmann, Christopher
West Catholic Boys
Philadelphia, PA

Ehrhardt, Kathleen
Parkland HS
Allentown, PA

Eibs, Janet
Keystone Oaks HS
Pittsburgh, PA

Eicher, Tracy
Fairchance-Georges
Fairchance, PA

Eidemiller, Marsha
Cocalico SR HS
Ephrata, PA

Eikov, Lee
Notre Dame HS
Stroudsburg, PA

Eisaman, Carl Edward
Hempfield Area HS
Greensburg, PA

Eisenacher, Ronald C
Sun Valley HS
Aston, PA

Eisenbise, Christine Louise A
Cocalico HS
Reinholds, PA

Eisley, Patricia
Milton SR HS
New Columbia, PA

Eister, Mark
Shikellamy HS
Northumberland, PA

Elder, Terry
Hanover SR HS
Hanover, PA

Elder, Trudy
Wilmington Area
New Wilmington, PA

Elek, Kathleen
Fairchance Georges JR SR HS
Fairchance, PA

Elick, Raymond
Tunkhannock Area
Tunkhannock, PA

Elliott, Kelly
Fairview HS
Erie, PA

Ellis, Dina
Central Duphin HS
Harrisburgh, PA

Ellis, Jodi Lynn
Elk Lake HS
Montrose, PA

Ellison, James Philip
Hanover HS
Hanover, PA

Elmaleh, Francine J
Cheltenham HS
Elkins Park, PA

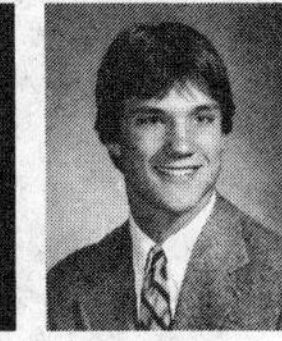
Elwell, Mike
Upper Dublin HS
Ft Washington, PA

Ely, Jill
SheffieldJR Sr HS
Clarendon, PA

Ely, Susan
Eastern York HS
Wrightsville, PA

Emel, Melissa Jean
Bald Eagle Area HS
Glendale, NY

Emerich, Shelly
Tulpehocken HS
Bethel, PA

Emil, Rodney
Dallas SR HS
Dallas, PA

Emmett, Rose
Forest City Regional
Forest City, PA

Enders, Kris
Council Rock HS
Richboro, PA

Endler, Edward F
Meyers HS
Wilkes Barre, PA

Engart, Timothy R
Upper Moreland HS
Hatboro, PA

Engel, Karen
Montoursville HS
Montoursville, PA

Engel, Tricia L
Greensburg Central
Catholic HS
Export, PA

Engelman, Jr Lowell
Monaca JR SR HS
Monaca, PA

Engle, Karyn
Pottstown SR HS
Pottstown, PA

Engle, Terry A
Upper Dauphin
Area HS
Elizabethville, PA

English, Brady
W Branch Area HS
Morrisdale, PA

English, Janine
St Huberts HS For
Philadelphia, PA

Enlow, James
Sayre HS
Sayre, PA

Epps, Dexter
University City HS
Phialdelphia, PA

Epstein, Amy
Harritown HS
Gladwyne, PA

Erb, Lester
Milton Area HS
Milton, PA

Erickson, Kirsten
Unionville HS
West Chester, PA

Erickson, Kristen
Downingtown SR
Chester Springs, PA

Ermocida, Vicky
Saint Maria Goretti
Philadelphia, PA

Ernst, Carl
Governor Mifflin HS
Shillington, PA

Eshbach, Debbie
Freedom HS
Bethlehem, PA

Eshenower, Kristin
Cnetral Dauphin HS
Harrisburg, PA

Esposito, Rosa
Quigley HS
Midland, PA

Esposto, Nunzio
Butler Area SR HS
Butler, PA

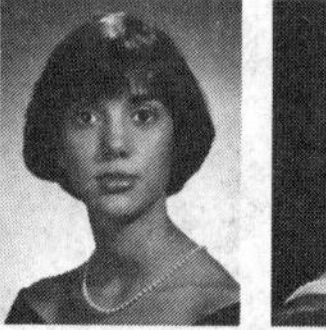
Estel, Sandra
Abington HS
Abington, PA

Etriss, Diane
Cardinal O Hara HS
Brookhaven, PA

Eury, Troy
Seneca Valley SR
Renfrew, PA

Evangelista, Angela
St Maria Goretti HS
Philadelphia, PA

Evans, Dana
Hickory HS
Hermitage, PA

Evans, II Daniel E
Mon Valley Catholic
Donora, PA

Evans, Dennis
Altoona Area HS
Altoona, PA

Evans, Eric
Liberty HS
Bethlehem, PA

Evans, Heather Ann
Elmer L Meyers HS
Wilkes-Barre, PA

Evans, Joseph
Bishop Mc Cort HS
Johnstown, PA

Evans, Katherine
Tunkhannock Area
Tunkhannock, PA

Evans, Kathleen
Our Lady Of The
Sacred Heart HS
Aliquippa, PA

Evans, Kelly
Neshaminy SR HS
Feasterville, PA

Evans, Melissa
Seneca Valley SR
Harmony, PA

Evans, Rhonda
Mary Fuller Frazier
Perryopolis, PA

Evans, Shelley
Albert Gallatin SR
Lake Lynn, PA

Evans, Jr Terrence J
Bishop Neumann
Williamsport, PA

Evens, Jamie
Port Allegany JR
SR HS
Port Allegany, PA

Everett, Donna
Lynn
Mechanicsburg Area
SR HS
Mechanicsburg, PA

Evers, James
Bradford Area HS
Bradford, PA

Evert, Tom
Bensalem HS
Bensalem, PA

Ewald, Frederic S
Council Rock HS
Ivyland, PA

Ewalt, Jacquelyn
Our Lady Of The
Sacred Heart
Coraopolis, PA

Ewaskey, Rae Ann
Chartiers Valley HS
Bridgeville, PA

Fabbri, Leslie
Penn Cambria SR
Gallitzin, PA

Fafalios, M Kristine
Belle Vernon Area
Belle Vernon, PA

Fair, Todd
Plum SR HS
Pittsburgh, PA

Fairlie, Steve
Hatboro Horsham
Prospectville, PA

Falbo, Nicole
Charleroi JR SR HS
Charleroi, PA

Falcone, Yvonne
Pen Argyl Area SR
Pen Argyl, PA

Falise, Marlene
Montour HS
Mc Kees Rocks, PA

Falvo, Rob
Trinity HS
Washington, PA

Fannin, Cathy
St Marys Area HS
Weedville, PA

Fant, Shelley
Elizabeth Forward
Elizabeth, PA

Fantiri, Mark
Norristown Annex
Norristown, PA

Faraone, Toni
New Castle HS
New Castle, PA

Farber, Mike
State College Area
State College, PA

Farleigh, Michael
Bishop Hafey HS
Hazleton, PA

Farmer, Andrea
Northern Lebanon
Fredericksburg, PA

Farpour, Laura
Salisbury HS
Allentown, PA

Farrar, Jeffrey
Ambridge Area HS
Ambridge, PA

Farrier, Monica
Carmichael Area JR
SR HS
Carmichaels, PA

Farrow, Christina
Elizabethtown Area
Elizabethtown, PA

Fassnacht, Matthew
Ephrata SR HS
Akron, PA

Fath, Jr David Kelly
Palmyra Area HS
Annville, PA

Fattori, Deanne
Gribel HS
Connellsville, PA

Fatula, Keith
Johnstown HS
Johnstown, PA

Fauser, Paul D
Manheim Central
Manheim, PA

Faust, Jennifer
Lampeter-Strasburg
Lancaster, PA

Faust, Lori
Salisbury HS
Allentown, PA

Fawcett, John
Gaughan
Ambridge Area SR
Baden, PA

Fay, Tracy
Corry Area HS
Corry, PA

Feagley, Dawn
Upper Dauphin Area HS
Elizabethville, PA

Fedyk, Nicholas
St Pius X HS
Pottstown, PA

Fee, William
Halifax Area HS
Halifax, PA

Feeman, Scot
Lebanon Catholic
Lebanon, PA

Feeney, Terry
Fox Chapel HS
Pittsburgh, PA

Feeser, Matthew
York Catholic HS
York, PA

Feggins, Joel
St John Neumann
Philadelphia, PA

Fegley, Matt
Greenwood HS
Millerstown, PA

Fehnel, Douglas
Nazareth Area SR
Nazareth, PA

Fehnel, Sharin
Wilson Area HS
Easton, PA

Feick, Joseph H
Brownsville Area HS
Chestnut Ridge, PA

Feilbach, Carol
Emmaus HS
East Texas, PA

Felesky, Caroline
North Star HS
Boswell, PA

Felix, Christina
Seneca Valley SR
Evans City, PA

Feller, Amy
Conrad Weiser HS
Reinholds, PA

Feltenberger, Michelle
Franklin JR SR HS
Polk, PA

Feltz, Thomas William
Hatboro-Horsham SR HS
Ambler, PA

Feng, Wu-Che
State College Area SR HS
State College, PA

Fenton, Christine
Corry Area HS
Corry, PA

Fenton, Tammy
Wyalusing Valley JR & SR HS
Sugar Run, PA

Fenwick, Jr Harry B
Tunkhannock Area
Mehoopany, PA

Ference, Shannon
Yough SR HS
Rillton, PA

Ferguson, Monica
Mt St Joseph Acad
Phila, PA

Ferguson, Paul
Philipsburg Oscela
Philipsburg, PA

Ferrand, Jeff
Ambridge Area HS
Ambridge, PA

Ferraro, Judith
West Scranton HS
Scranton, PA

Ferree, Lynn
Eastn York HS
Yorkana, PA

Ferri, Brenda
Council Rock HS
Holland, PA

Ferrigno, Denise
West Phila Catholic Girls HS
Philadelphia, PA

Feryo, Chris
Nativity B V M HS
St Clair, PA

Feryo, Christopher
Nativity BVM HS
St Clair, PA

Fetherman, Jodi
Conrad Weiser JS
Robesonia, PA

Fetherman, Melinda
Conrad Weiser HS
Robesonia, PA

Fetter, Kathleen
Hamburg Area HS
Hamburg, PA

Fetterolf, Jodi
Juniata HS
Mifflintown, PA

Fichtner, Michele
Solanco HS
Quarryville, PA

Fidalgo, Rui
Olney HS
Philadelphia, PA

Fielding, Preston
South Philadelphia
Philadelphia, PA

Fields, Rex
Central Fulton HS
Mcconnellsburg, PA

Figura, Rachelle
Dubois Area HS
Dubois, PA

Filippone, Eric
West Philadelphia Catholic HS
Philadelphia, PA

Finamore, Joan
Creative & Performing Arts
Philadelphia, PA

Finch, Carleen
Peters Township HS
Mcmurray, PA

Finger, Caroline
Northern SR HS
Dillsburg, PA

Fink, Bryan
East Brady JR SR
Cowansville, PA

Fink, Charles C
Allentown Central Catholic HS
Macungie, PA

Fink, Kelly
Tyrone Area HS
Tyrone, PA

Fink, Mitch
Fleetwood Area HS
Fleetwood, PA

Finnegan, Leslie
Chambersburg Area SR HS
Chambersburg, PA

Finnerty, John P
Scranton Central
Scranton, PA

Firestone, Blaney-Cay
Greensburg Central Catholic HS
Irwin, PA

Firmstone, Kenneth
Southmoreland HS
Mt Pleasant, PA

Firth, Roswitha M
Sewickley Acad
Thornburg, PA

Fischer, Danny
Franklin HS
Franklin, PA

Fischer, Jane
Middletown HS
Middletown, PA

Fischer, Steph
St Benedict Acad
Erie, PA

Fisher, Amy
Harry S Truman HS
Levittown, PA

Fisher, Donna
Blue Mountain Acad
Hamburg, PA

Fisher, Georgina
Lampeter-Straburg
Strasburg, PA

Fisher, Heath Jon
Conrad Weiser HS
Robesonia, PA

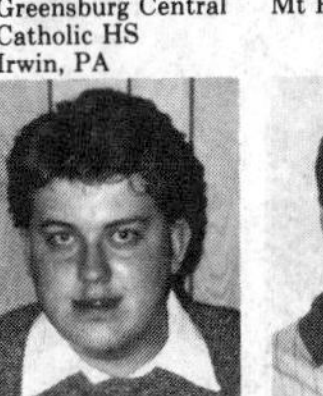
Fisher, Kevin
Carbondale Area HS
Simpson, PA

Fisher, Larry
Marion Center Area
Home, PA

Fisher, Lisa Anne
St Hubert HS
Philadelphia, PA

Fisher, Rodney
Bald Eagle Area HS
Fleming, PA

Fitzgerald, IV James J
William Penn Charter Schl
Philadelphia, PA

Fitzpatrick, Margaret M
Archbishop Wood
Warrington, PA

Fitzpatrick, Sheila Marie
Central Bucks West
Doylestown, PA

Fitzsimmons, Karen
Harriton HS
Gladwyne, PA

Fiumara, Theresa
Catasauqua HS
Allentown, PA

Flaherty, Susie
Mahanoy Area HS
Morea, PA

Flamini, Ellen
Central Daupin East SR HS
Steelton, PA

Flanagan, Kelly
West Mifflin Area
W Mifflin, PA

Flaxman, Michelle Lisa
Pocono Mountain
Mt Pocono, PA

Fleck, Jon
Altoona Area HS
Altoona, PA

Fleegle, Lee Ann
Ferndale Area HS
Johnstown, PA

Fleek, Melanie A
Phoenixville HS
Phoenixville, PA

Fleisher, Alysia
Lewistown Area HS
Granville, PA

Fleming, Kristin
Emmaus HS
Emmaus, PA

Fleming, Leisa
Bensalem SR HS
Bensalem, PA

Fleming, Lisa
Knoch JR SR HS
Butler, PA

Fleming, Patrick
Chestnut Ridge HS
Schellsburg, PA

Flemings, Martin S
Thomas A Edison
Philadelphia, PA

Fletcher, Angel
Ambridge Area HS
Baden, PA

Fletcher, Paula
Bishop Conwell HS
Morrisvl, PA

Fletcher, Rita
Southern Fulton HS
Warfordsburg, PA

Flores, Florence Elyssabeth I
St Marys Area HS
Saint Marys, PA

Flynn, Bill
Father Judge HS
Philadelphia, PA

Flynn, David
Lakeland JR SR HS
Jermyn, PA

Focht, Sherry
Altoona HS
Altoona, PA

Focht, Tamara
Tulpehocken HS
Bernville, PA

Fogel, Andrea
St Pius X HS
Schwenksville, PA

Fogel, Bonnie
Northampton SR
Bath, PA

Foley, Christina
St Hubert Catholic For Girls HS
Philadelphia, PA

Foley, Jacqueline J
Methacton HS
Trooper, PA

Fonarow, Nicole
Hastboro-Horsham SR HS
Horsham, PA

Fondren, Kelly
Downingtown HS
Downingtown, PA

Foor, Charlene
Chestnut Ridge SR
Manns Choice, PA

Foose, Cindy
Pennsburg HS
Yardley, PA

Ford, Alisa A
Bishop Mc Devitt
Philadelphia, PA

Ford, Bethany A
Downingtown SR
Downingtown, PA

Foreman, Tim
Philipsburg Osceola
Philipsburg, PA

Forish, Debra L
Ferndale Area HS
Johnstown, PA

Forker, Samuel
Donegal HS
Marietta, PA

Fornwalt, Danielle
Middletown Area
Middletown, PA

Forren, Anita
The Christian Acad
Claymont, DE

Forrest, Jennifer Lynn
Punxsutawney Area
Punxsutawney, PA

Forsburg, Brian
South Williamsport Area HS
Williamsport, PA

Forsythe, Dawn
Seneca Valley SR
Callery, PA

Forsythe, Kelly
Marion Center Area
Marion Ctr, PA

Forsythe, Rayna
Southmoreland SR
Scottdale, PA

Foster, Amy
Peters Township HS
Venetia, PA

Foster, Jason
Cornell HS
Coraopols, PA

Foster, Keith
Seneca Valley HS
Evans City, PA

Foster, Sean
Philipsburg-Osceola Area HS
West Decatur, PA

Fotia, Crista
Lincoln HS
Ellwood City, PA

Fotopoulos, Afroditi
Wm Allen HS
Allentown, PA

Fotopoulos, Jake
William Allen HS
Allentown, PA

Fought, Kevin
Millville HS
Millville, PA

Fowler, John
Waynesburg Central
Waynesburg, PA

Fowler, Regis R
Shaler Area HS
Glenshaw, PA

Fox, David
Northampton HS
Bath, PA

Fox, Holly
Gettysburg SR HS
Gettysburg, PA

Fox, Jennifer L
Western Wayne HS
Waymart, PA

Fox, Michele
Scranton Preparatory Schl
Scranton, PA

Fox, Trisha
Rocky Grove HS
Oil City, PA

Foy, Maureen
Archbishop Prendergast HS
Lansdowne, PA

Franceski, Amy
Susquehanna Community HS
Thompson, PA

Franchak, Michael
Richland HS
Wexford, PA

Franck, Lorie
Warwick HS
Lititz, PA

Franek, Ann Marie
Hazleton HS
Hazleton, PA

Frankenfield, Brenda
Pottsgrove HS
Pottstown, PA

Franklin, Anthony
Coatesville Area SR
Coatesville, PA

Franklin, Ben
Northern Cambria
Barnesboro, PA

Frantz, Michele
Donegal HS
Mount Joy, PA

Frantz, Sonia
Parkland HS
Slatington, PA

Franzis, Peter
Dover Greg SR HS
Dover, PA

Frattini, Nicole
Nazareth Acad
Philadelphia, PA

Frattone, Michael
St John Neumann
Philadelphia, PA

Frazer, Christin
Homer Center HS
Homer City, PA

Frazier, Lori
Trinity HS
Washington, PA

Frederick, Joseph B
Owen J Roberts HS
Spring City, PA

Frederick, Lisa
Central HS
Martinsburg, PA

Frederickson, Julie
Grace Christian Schl
Sinking Spring, PA

Freeberry, Jeannine
Interboro HS
Norwood, PA

Freeman, Dianne
Harbor Creek HS
Erie, PA

Freese, Jr John H
Pottstown HS
Pottstown, PA

French, Jennifer
Susan
Nazareth Acad HS
Philadelphia, PA

Frese, William G
Abraham Lincoln
Philadelphia, PA

Freudenberg,
Susanne
Greater Latrobe SR
Greensburg, PA

Frey, Kathryn L
Newport JR SR HS
Newport, PA

Friday, Edward
Blacklick Valley HS
Nanty Glo, PA

Friday, Erin
Downingtown SR
Exton, PA

Fridrick, Kathy
Western Beaver JR
SR HS
Midland, PA

Friend, Kelly
Mapletown HS
Bobtown, PA

Fritz, Dawn
Brandyvwine
Heights HS
Mertztown, PA

Fritz, Kelly E
North Hills HS
Pittsburgh, PA

Fritz, Ted P
Indiana Area HS
Indiana, PA

Frye, Randy
Central Dauphin HS
Harrisburg, PA

Fuerman, Richard
The Hill Schl
Pottstown, PA

Fuga, Michael
Phoenixville Area
Phoenixville, PA

Fuhrman, Richard
Newport JR SR HS
Newport, PA

Fuleno, Melissa
New Castle SR HS
New Castle, PA

Fuller, Deanne Lynn
Aliquippa HS
Aliquippa, PA

Fuller, Kim
Conneaut Lake HS
Cochranton, PA

Fulmer, David R
Yough SR HS
Herminie, PA

Fulmer, Kristin
Wissahickon HS
Norristown, PA

Fulmer, Shirley
Yough SR HS
West Newton, PA

Fulmer, Wendy
Spring-Ford SR HS
Collegeville, PA

Funk, April
Swissvale HS
Pittsbuirgh, PA

Funkhouser, Mark
Hopewell SR HS
Aliquippa, PA

Funyak, Jawn
Charles
Seneca Valley HS
Mars, PA

Furia, Claire
Archbishop Carroll
Haverford, PA

Fusco, Catherine
St Maria Goretti HS
Philadelphia, PA

Gabel, Martin
Bishop O Reilly HS
Swoyersville, PA

Gabig, Sarah
Trinity HS
Camp Hill, PA

Gadbois, Chris
Bethlehem Catholic
Bethlehem, PA

Gadonas, Michele
St Pius X HS
Phoenixville, PA

Gage, Karen
Strath Haven HS
Wallingford, PA

Gajewski, Joseph
Cardinal O Hara HS
Glenolden, PA

Galante, Elaine
Bensalem HS
Bensalem, PA

Galbraith, Mindy
Big Spring HS
Carlisle, PA

Gall, Daniele Lee
Seneca Valley SR
Harmony, PA

Gall, Walt
Butler HS
Butler, PA

Gallagher, Carolyn
Interboro HS
Essington, PA

Gallagher, John
Cardinal O Hara HS
Broomall, PA

Gallagher, Kathleen
Bethlehem Catholic
Bethlehem, PA

Gallagher, Margaret
Little Flower
Catholic HS
Philadelphia, PA

Gallaher, Careena
Homer-Center JR
SR HS
Lucernemines, PA

Galt, Danielle
Harbor Creek HS
Erie, PA

Gamble, Lisa
Avella JR SR HS
Washington, PA

Ganoe, Craig
Seneca HS
Union City, PA

Ganter, Bob
Bethel Park SR HS
Bethel Park, PA

Gantz, John
Shenandoah Valley
Shenandoah, PA

Garbacik, Edward J
West Hazleton SR
W Hazleton, PA

Garber, Alice
Hempfield Area SR
Greensburg, PA

Garbutt, Beth
Abington HS
Abington, PA

Gardiner, Laura
State College Area
SR HS
State College, PA

Gardner, Cindy
Chestnut Ridge HS
Bedford, PA

Gardner, Darylin
Penn Hills HS
Verona, PA

Gargasz, Joseph
New Wilmington
Area HS
Volant, PA

Garlesky, Jackie
Windber Area HS
Windber, PA

Garman, Dave
Hershey HS
Hershey, PA

Garmen, Bradley
Carlisle SR HS
Carlisle, PA

Garner, Barbara
North Penn HS
N Wales, PA

Garner, Deirdre Rae
St Marys Area HS
Saint Marys, PA

Garner, Pamela
Commodore Perry
Hadley, PA

Garr, Kathy
Nazareth Area SR
Nazareth, PA

Garrett, Jason
Peters Township HS
Venetia, PA

Garrison, Joseph
Crestwood JR Sr HS
Mountaintop, PA

Garrone, Carla
Trinity HS
Washington, PA

Gartner, Judy
Greater Works Acad
Verona, PA

Garver, Timothy
Altoona Area HS
Altoona, PA

Gaskin, Ramonah
Philadelphia HS For
Philadelphia, PA

Gatski, Lynn
Hazleton HS
Hazleton, PA

Gatta, Graziella
Saint Maria Goretti
Philadelphia, PA

Gaudio, Alyson C
Villa Maria HS
Youngstown, OH

Gausman, Nancy
St Marys Area HS
St Marys, PA

Gawel, Edward
Johnstown Voc Tech
Johnstown, PA

Gawlas, Carol
E L Meyers HS
Wilkes-Barre, PA

Gay, Yolanda
New Castle SR HS
New Castle, PA

Gayton, Karen
James M Coughlin
Wilkes-Barre, PA

Gazi, Leah Marie
California Area HS
Roscoe, PA

Gealy, Joe
Lakeview HS
Jackson Center, PA

Geary, Brian
Kisk Area HS
Apollo, PA

Geary, Michelle
Belle Vernon Area
Belle Vernon, PA

Geary, Staci
Somerset SR HS
Somerset, PA

Gebicki, Jennifer
Greater Latrobe SR
Latrobe, PA

Gedmark, Ann M
Red Land HS
New Cumberland, PA

Gegnas, Laura D
Central Bucks HS
Furlong, PA

Gehret, Carolan
Fleetwood Area HS
Fleetwood, PA

Geier, Anthony
Girard College HS
Philadelphia, PA

Geiger, Jennifer
Catasauqua Area HS
N Catasauqua, PA

Geiger, Scott
Hempfield HS
Irwin, PA

Geisler, Richard W
Bradford Area HS
Bradford, PA

Geisler, Ronald J
Washington HS
Washington, PA

Geist, Jayme
Calvary Baptist
Chrisitian Acad
Meadville, PA

Geletei, Kathy
Charleroi Area JR SR HS
Charleroi, PA

Gelli, Jennifer
James M Coughlin
Plains, PA

Genicola, Lance S
Whitehall HS
Whitehall, PA

Genteel, Corey
Bangor SR HS
Roseto, PA

Gentile, Cecilia
Highlands HS
Tarentum, PA

Gentile, Danielle
Merion Mercy Acad
Havertown, PA

Gentile, Deanna
Mt Alvernia HS
Pittsburgh, PA

George, Bethany
Purchase Line HS
Commodore, PA

George, Jeffrey
St Josephs Prep
Wallingford, PA

George, Pam
Canon-Mc Millan SR HS
Canonsburg, PA

George, Tammy
Greater Johnstown Area Vo-Tech Schl
Salix, PA

George, Tracey
James M Coughlin
Wilkes Barre, PA

Georgulis, Christopher
Belle Vernon Area
Belle Vernon, PA

Gerace, Julie
Bethel Park SR HS
Bethel Park, PA

Geramita, Kim
South Hills HS
Pittsburgh, PA

Gerber, Ronna
Penns Manor HS
Clymer, PA

Geregach, George
Montour HS
Coraopolis, PA

Gerenda, Michael
Bristol JR SR HS
Bristol, PA

Gerhards, Kimberly A
Northern Lebanon JR SR HS
Annville, PA

Gerhart, Lisa
Cocalico SR HS
Stevens, PA

Gernert, Amy
Waynesburg Central
Waynesburg, PA

Geroff, Adam
Lowe Moreland HS
Huntingdon Valley, PA

Gerster, Amy
North Hills HS
Pittsburgh, PA

Getz, Michael
Altoona Area HS
Altoona, PA

Giacomin, Melanie Ann
Penn-Trafford HS
Irwin, PA

Gianelle, Eric
Abington SR HS
Roslyn, PA

Gianferante, Lisa
Danville SR HS
Riverside, PA

Giardina, Lisa
Cardinal O Hara HS
Brookhaven, PA

Gibbons, Molly
Hopewell HS
Hookstown, PA

Gibbs, Michaela
Yough SR HS
Irwin, PA

Giberson, Scott
Wyoming Area HS
W Wyoming, PA

Gibson, James
Simon Gratz HS
Philadelphia, PA

Gibson, Wayne Lawrence
Spring Grove Area SR HS
Seven Valleys, PA

Gilbert, III Frank M
Lower Dauphin HS
Hummelstown, PA

Gilbertson, Bryan
Ford City HS
Manorville, PA

Gilbertson, Jeffrey E
East HS
West Chester, PA

Gilboy, Ann
Shenango HS
New Castle, PA

Gilbride, Thomas
Scranton Central
Scranton, PA

Gildroy, John
Southmoreland HS
Mt Pleasant, PA

Gileot, Angel
Moon SR HS
Coraopolis, PA

Giles, Eric J
Blackhawk HS
Beaver Falls, PA

Gill, Craig
Tyrone Area HS
Tyrone, PA

Gill, Tammy
Neshaminy HS
Langhorne, PA

Gillespie, Karen
Unionville HS
West Chester, PA

Gillespie, Rita
Cardinal O Hara HS
Aston, PA

Gillette, Margo
Dunmore HS
Dunmore, PA

Gilliland, George A
Portersville
Christian HS
Butler, PA

Gillow, Romaine
Pittston Area SR
Avoca, PA

Gilmer, Michelle
Canon-Mc Millan
SR HS
Canonsburg, PA

Gilmore, Annemarie
Nazareth Acad
Philadelphia, PA

Gilmore, Karen
Murrell Dobbins
Philadelphia, PA

Gilmore, Shane
Penn Wood HS
Yeadon, PA

Gilroy, Robert
Trinity HS
Mechanicsburg, PA

Gilson, III Charles A
Moshannon Ralley
JS HS
Smithmills, PA

Gimbel, Rita Mary
St Huberts HS
Philadelphia, PA

Gindlesperger, Kristine
Forest Hills SR HS
Windber, PA

Gingrich, Paul
Dover Area HS
Dover, PA

Giordano, Barbara
St Maria Goretti HS
Philadelphia, PA

Giovannelli, Perry
Valley HS
New Kensington, PA

Girardat, Denille Rae
Cochranton HS
Cochranton, PA

Girardi, Paul Thomas
Dubois Central
Christian HS
Curwensville, PA

Girone, Christine
Interboro HS
Prospect Park, PA

Giuntoli, Michael
St Joseph Prep Schl
Haddonfield, NJ

Giuntoli, II Robert L
St Josephs
Preparatory Schl
Haddonfield, NJ

Gjurich, Dana
Penn Cambria HS
Cresson, PA

Glackin, Christine
St Hubert Catholic
Philadelphia, PA

Glaser, Sally
Central Dauphin
East HS
Oberlin, PA

Glasl, Karen
Northwestern SR
Albion, PA

Glass, Nancy
Montour HS
Pittsburgh, PA

Glass, Sean
Greater Johnstown
Johnstown, PA

Glass, Tiffany
Muhlenberg HS
Temple, PA

Glenn, Terrance
South Vo-Tech HS
Pittsburgh, PA

Glinsky, III John
Mid-Valley HS
Throop, PA

Glisan, Carla
Uniontown HS
Markleysburg, PA

Glisan, Charlene
Northern SR HS
Dover, PA

Glover, Gordon
William Allen HS
Allentown, PA

Gnan, Maria
St Marys Area HS
St Marys, PA

Gobrecht, Renee
Northern Cambria
Barnesboro, PA

Gocella, Joe
Bradford Central
Christian HS
Bradford, PA

Gochtovtt, Annabel C
Bishop Shanahan
Exton, PA

Godish, Donna
Penn Cambria SR
Lilly, PA

Godwin, Kenton R
South Fayette HS
Bridgeville, PA

Goehring, Earl
Seneca Valley HS
Harmony, PA

Goehrs, Suzanne M
Harry S Touman
Fairless Hills, PA

Goida, Paul E
Panther Valley HS
Lansford, PA

Goldinger, Brian P
Ford City HS
Freeport, PA

Goldman, Suzanne
Harriton HS
Narberth, PA

Goldsborough, Jennifer L
Lower Merion HS
Bala Cynwyd, PA

Golembiesky, Jennifer
Freeport Area HS
Freeport, PA

Gomer, Shawn
Lower Moreland HS
Huntingdon Valley, PA

Gomez, Christopher
Hazleton HS
Drums, PA

Gonta, Darlene
Hempfield Area SR
Greensburg, PA

Gonzalez, Iris
South Philadelphia
Philadelphia, PA

Good, Denise
Bishop Mc Devitt
Harrisburg, PA

Good, Scott
Donegal HS
Mt Joy, PA

Goodfellow, Paul
Yough SR HS
West Newton, PA

Goodin, Culleen Irene
Quakertown Comm
Trumbauersville, PA

Goodman, Kellie
Wyalusing Valley
Wyalusing, PA

Goodwin, Larry
Troy SR HS
Troy, PA

Goodwin, Michael
Tunkhannock HS
Mehoopany, PA

Goon, Christopher
Altoona Area HS
Altoona, PA

Goos, Lara
Northampton Area
SR HS
Northampton, PA

Gordanier, Michael
Carson Long
Military HS
Linden, NJ

Gordon, Angela
Westinghouse HS
Pittsburgh, PA

Gordon, Jeffrey
Pennsbury HS
Morrisville, PA

Gordon, Matt
Dover Area HS
Dillsburg, PA

Gordon, Robert
Abington SR HS
Jenkintown, PA

Gori, Michael
Freedom HS
Bethlehem, PA

Gorman, Hillary
Cheltenham HS
Stockton, CA

Goshorn, Terry
Susquenita HS
Duncannon, PA

Gosin, Karen
Abraham Lincoln
Philadelphia, PA

Gossert, Dana A
CarlisleSR HS
Carlisle, PA

Gotlieb, Steve
Marple,newtown HS
Newtown Square, PA

Gould, Amy
Greenville HS
Greenville, PA

Gould, Todd E
Lower Dauphin SR
Middletown, PA

Gowatski, Kelly
Connellsville Area
Mt Pleasant, PA

Gowaty, Margaret
Serra Catholic HS
Mc Keesport, PA

Gowton, Stephanie
Connellsville SR HS
Mt Pleasant, PA

Graaf, Michele
Weatherly Area HS
Weatherly, PA

Grabarits, Richard
Northampton SR
Northampton, PA

Grabigel, Bryan
Highlands HS
Freeport, PA

Grable, Keith
Freedom HS
Rochester, PA

Grabowski, David A
Bethel Park HS
Bethel Park, PA

Grace, Lisa
Tussey Mountain
Hopewell, PA

Graczyk, Heather G
William Tennent
Warminster, PA

Grados, Robert
Fox Chapel Area HS
Monessen, PA

Grafton, Anissa
Leechburg Area HS
Schenley, PA

Graham, Antony
Pittston Area HS
Dupont, PA

Graham, Joanna
Frances
Vincentian HS
Pittsburgh, PA

Graham, Kristen
Crestwood HS
Wapwallopen, PA

Grainda, Lori
Central HS
Martinsburg, PA

Granato, Sherri
St Marra Goretti HS
Philadelphia, PA

Granbery, Anne
Marie
Seneca Valley HS
Zelienople, PA

Grandas, Frank Eric
North Star HS
Hooversville, PA

Grandinetti, Robert
Chartiers Valley HS
Pittsburgh, PA

Grannas, Chris
Bellwood-Antis HS
Bellwood, PA

Grant, David
Belle Vernon Area
Belle Vernon, PA

Grant, Mark W
Council Rock HS
Churchville, PA

Gray, David
Unionville HS
Kennett Sq, PA

Gray, Dionne Marie
Cedar Grove
Christian Acad
Abington, PA

Gray, Janet
Huntingdon Area
Huntingdon, PA

Gray, John
Quaker Valley HS
Sewickley, PA

Gray, Marla
Susquehanna
Township HS
Harrisburg, PA

Graybill, Lucinda
Middleburg HS
Richfield, PA

Graybill, Melinda
Middleburg HS
Richfield, PA

Grayson, Mary Beth
Open Door Christian
Greensburg, PA

Grazio, Paul
Emmaus HS
Macungie, PA

Grebe, Joann
Lower Moreland HS
Huntingdon Valley,
PA

Greck, Kristi
West Allegheny HS
Oakdale, PA

Greco, Cari
Mohawk Area HS
Edinburg, PA

Green, Jennifer
William Allen HS
Allentown, PA

Green, Stephanie
Harry S Truman HS
Bristol, PA

Green, Steven Kevin
Overbrook HS
Philadelphia, PA

Green, Tracey
Red Land HS
Etters, PA

Greener, Jill
Delaware County
Christian Schl
Havertown, PA

Greenwood, Mary
Ann
Wayneburg Centra
Waynesburg, PA

Greenwood,
Timothy
Yough HS
Ruffs Dale, PA

Grega, Brian
Dunmore HS
Dunmore, PA

Gregg, Carolyn
Avon Grove HS
Landenberg, PA

Gressly, Tammy L
Knoch HS
Butler, PA

Greybush, Mary
Freedom HS
Bethlehem, PA

Grieme, Amy
Pen Argyl Area HS
Pen Argyl, PA

Grier, Jennifer
Bald Eagle Area JR
SR HS
Karthaus, PA

Griffin, Deborah
Bethel Park SR HS
Bethel Park, PA

Griffin, Tiffany
Northern Lebanon
Jonestown, PA

Griffith, John
United HS
Indiana, PA

Griffith, Lisa L
Freeport Area SR
Sarver, PA

Griffiths, Jeff
Pine Grove Area HS
Tremont, PA

Grim, Susan
Boyertown HS
Barto, PA

Grimone, Billie Jo
Cameron County HS
Emporium, PA

Grinberg, Marni
Taylor Allderdice
Pittsburgh, PA

Gritzan, Robert W
Bethel Park HS
Bethel Park, PA

Groba, Steven R
Elizabeth-Forward
Greenock, PA

Grobinski, Anthony
John S Fine HS
Nanticoke, PA

Groff, Marcey
Grace Christian Schl
Ephrata, PA

Gromalski, Krista
Marian Catholic HS
Mahanoy City, PA

Groman, Michael J
Marion Center HS
Indiana, PA

Groover, Anita L
Canton Area HS
Canton, PA

Grosch, Lynn
MMI Prep School
Drums, PA

Grose, Wendy
Hanover Area HS
Wilkes Barre, PA

Groskopf, Nancy
North Hills HS
Pittsburgh, PA

Gross, Barbara
Exeter Twp SR HS
Douglassville, PA

Gross, Kirsten
Annville-Cleona HS
Lebanon, PA

Gross, Lori
Northeastern SR HS
Manchester, PA

Gross, Jr Steven H
York County
Manchester, PA

Gross, Jr Vincent R
West York Area HS
York, PA

Grosz, Elizabeth
Pennsbury HS
Morrisville, PA

Grove, Charles
Hopewell HS
Hookstown, PA

Grove, Peter
Uniontown Area HS
Uniontown, PA

Grow, Lisa
Shamokin Area HS
Shamokin, PA

Grubb, Chris
Springford HS
Royersford, PA

Grubbs, Gretchen
Albert Gallatin HS
Smithfield, PA

Grubbs, Kate
Avonworth HS
Pittsbg, PA

Gruber, Mark
East Pennsboro SR
Enola, PA

Gruber, Tim
Lower Dauphin HS
Hummelstown, PA

Grusky, Tori
Punxsutawney Area
SR HS
Anita, PA

Grzywinski, Patricia
Southmoreland SR
Scottdale, PA

Gsell, Debbi
Waynesboro Area
SR HS
Waynesboro, PA

Guerra, Cheryl
Phil-Mont Christian
Maple Glen, PA

Guiher, Kathy L
Saltsburg JR SR HS
Saltsburg, PA

Guilleux, Francois
Upper Dublin HS
Ambler, PA

Guilliams, Janet
Nazareth Acad
Philadelphia, PA

Guin, Mary
Bensalem HS
Rockaway
Township, NJ

Guindon, Kathryn
Lebanon SR HS
Lebanon, PA

Guinee, Patrick
Bishop Carroll HS
Cresson, PA

Guise, Lisa
Owen J Roberts HS
Pottstown, PA

Guistwhite, Jack B
Mechanicsburg HS
Mechanicsburg, PA

Gullo, Jr Jack
De Lone Catholic
New Windsor, MD

Gum, Sean
Governor Mifflin HS
Shillington, PA

Gussenhofen, Evelyn
Hopewell SR HS
Monaca, PA

Gustafson, Bryan
Curwensville HS
Clearfield, PA

Gustafson, Tina
Saegertown HS
Saegertown, PA

Gustas, Gerald
Wyoming Valley
West HS
Plymouth, PA

Gustetic, Adam
Saint Joseph HS
Brackenridge, PA

Guthrie, Melissa
Pen Argyl Area HS
Pen Argyl, PA

Gutowski, Karrie
Hopewell Area HS
Aliquippa, PA

Guyer, Suellen M
Northeastern SR HS
Mt Wolf, PA

Guziewicz, Richard
S
Archbishop
Kennedy HS
Philadelphia, PA

Haag, Daniel
Central York SR HS
York, PA

Haas, Farah
Owen J Roberts HS
Pottstown, PA

Haas, Karen
Blue Mountain Acad
Emmaus, PA

Haase, Justin
Conestoga Vly HS
Leola, PA

Habib, Thomas K
Bishop O Reilly HS
Kingston, PA

Hable, Kim
Garden Spot HS
New Holland, PA

Hack, Virginia A
Burrell HS
Lower Burrell, PA

Hackman, Joy
Lackawanna Trail
JR SR HS
Factoryville, PA

Haddick, Walter
Wyoming Valley
West HS
Swoyersville, PA

Haddock, Craig
Belle Vernon Area
W Newton, PA

Haehn, Lisa
Youngsville JR/SR
Grand Valley, PA

Hagemann, Amy
Liberty HS
Bethlehem, PA

Hahn, Pam
Warren Area HS
Warren, PA

Hahn, Peter Joon
The Haverford Schl
Broomall, PA

Haid, Lisa Rene
Altoona Area HS
Altoona, PA

Haig, Charles
Northeast Catholic
Philadelphia, PA

Haines, Barbara
Lewisburg Area HS
Lewisburg, PA

Haines, Victoria
Bethel Park HS
Bethel Park, PA

Hairston, Camille
Wilkingsburg HS
Pittsburgh, PA

Hakim, Tracey
James A Coughlin
Plains, PA

Hales, Tracey
Methacton HS
Audubon, PA

Hall, Andrew
Bensalem HS
Bensalem, PA

Hall, Andrew
Red Land SR HS
New Cumberland,
PA

Hall, Cynthia
Freedom HS
Bethlehem, PA

Hall, David
Lincoln HS
Ellwood City, PA

Hall, Heather
B Reed Henderson
West Chester, PA

Hall, Lynn
Altoona Area
Altoona, PA

Hall, Michael T
Forbes Road JR SR
Hustontown, PA

Hall, Risha Kaye
Central Columbia
Bloomsburg, PA

Hallam, Robert
Pocono Mountain
Cresco, PA

Hallam, Steve
Bethel Park SR HS
Bethel Park, PA

Halloran, Carrie
Coudersport JR SR
Coudersport, PA

Halverson, William
Interboro HS
Essington, PA

Hamerla, Diane
Upper Merion HS
King Of Prussia, PA

Hamilton, Anita
Yough SR HS
W Newton, PA

Hamilton, James
Dominick
Avella Area HS
Washington, PA

Hamilton, Jim
West Allegheny HS
Imperial, PA

Hamilton, Tracy
Ambridge Area HS
Baden, PA

Hammad, Soha
Penn Center Acad
Philadelphia, PA

Hammaker, Jr
Kenneth L
Cumberland Valley
Mechanicsburg, PA

Hammer, Lisa
St Marys Area HS
St Marys, PA

Hammerash, Jr
William J
Belle Vernon Area
Perryopolis, PA

Hammond, Pam
Saint Huberts HS
Philadelphia, PA

Hand, Kathy A
Tyrone Area HS
Tyrone, PA

Hanes, Victoria
Harbor Creek HS
Harbor Creek, PA

Haney, Barbra
Hopewell HS
Aliquippa, PA

Haney, Michele
Northern Lebanon
Jonestown, PA

Hanks, Pam
Harbor Creek HS
Harbor Creek, PA

Hanle, Barbara
Pennsburg HS
Yardley, PA

Hanlon, Jr Matthew
John S Fine HS
Lower Askam, PA

Hann, Jill Suzette
Connellsville Area
SR HS
Connellsville, PA

Hanna, James
Franklin HS
Harrisville, PA

Hanna, Mary
Conneaut Lake Area
Atlantic, PA

Hannan, Karen
North Allegheny HS
Pittsburgh, PA

Hannon, Kyle
Harbor Creek HS
Erie, PA

Hansen, Dawn
Northampton Area
SR HS
Bath, PA

Hansen, Jennifer
Churchill HS
East Pittsburgh, PA

Hanuska, Karl
Greater Johnstown
Johnstown, PA

Happ, Colleen
Henderson HS
West Chester, PA

Haraldson, Jennifer
Harborcreek HS
Erie, PA

Harbaugh, Wendy
Hempfield Area HS
Greensburg, PA

Hardel, Darcy
Upper Merion SR
Wayne, PA

Harden, Ruth
Blue Ridge HS
Great Bend, PA

Hardy, Damahn
West Catholic For
Philadelphia, PA

Harhart, James
Northampton SR
Walnutport, PA

Harkcom, Joni
Somerset Area SR
Somerset, PA

Harkins, John
Mechanicsburg Ares
SR HS
Mechanicsburg, PA

Harkins, Julianne
Baldwin HS
Pittsburgh, PA

Harkins, Keith
Cardinal Brennan
Shenandoah, PA

Harkins, Marigrace
Nazareth Acad
Philadelphia, PA

Harlacher, Selena
Christian School Of
East Berlin, PA

Harley, Brenda
Hollidaysburg Area
SR HS
Duncansville, PA

Harman, Dale
Richard
Fairview HS
Fairview, PA

Harman, Theresa
Biglerville HS
Biglerville, PA

Harmon, Michael
Shanksville Stony
Creek Vo Tech
Berlin, PA

Harney, Crissy
Norristown Area HS
Norristown, PA

Harnish, Eric
Dover Area HS
Dover, PA

Harp, Chadwick A
Norristown Area HS
Norristown, PA

Harpel, Cris A
Mars Area HS
Valencia, PA

Harper, Angela
Plymouth
Whitemarsh HS
Norristown, PA

Harper, Dorothy
Schenley Teachers
Center HS
Pittsburgh, PA

Harper, Rick
Conrad Weiser SR
Robesonia, PA

Harper, Troy
Ringgold HS
Donora, PA

Harris, Kira
Gateway SR HS
Monroeville, PA

Harris, Lisa
Portage Area HS
Portage, PA

Harris, Mark
Brookville Area HS
Brookville, PA

Harrison, Karen
Columbia Montour
Area Voc/Tech Schl
Stillwater, PA

Harrison, Kelli
The Swarthmore
Chester, PA

Harrison, Lisa
Trinity HS
Mechanicsburg, PA

Harrison, Lyndelle
Farrell HS
Farrell, PA

Harrison, Margaret
Saegertown HS
Saegertown, PA

Harrison, Stacey
Pocono Mountain
Mt Pocono, PA

Harrity, Daniel
Bishop Hannan HS
Scranton, PA

Hart, Brian
Rocky Grove HS
Franklin, PA

Hart, Deidre
Phil-Mont Christian
Philadelphia, PA

Hart, Jodie
Trinity Area HS
Washington, PA

Hart, Patrick
Newport JR SR HS
Newport, PA

Hart, Tracey
Burgettstown Area
JR-SR HS
Bulger, PA

Harter, Rebekah
Benton Area JR SR
Stillwater, PA

Hartill, Tom
Kiski Area SR HS
Vandergrift, PA

Hartlaub, Cindy
New Oxford SR HS
Mc Sherrystown, PA

Hartley, Melissa L
S Williamsport Area
S Williamsport, PA

Hartley, Robert
Quaker Valley HS
Sewickley, PA

Hartline, Heather L
Highlands HS
Tarentum, PA

Hartman, Joanne
Freedom HS
Bethlehem, PA

Hartman, Laurie
Blacklick Valley HS
Twin Rocks, PA

Hartman, Tommy
Charleroi JR SR HS
Stockdale, PA

Hartzell, Lorrie
Seneca Valley HS
Renfrew, PA

Harvey, Michael A
Pennsbury HS
Yardley, PA

Harvey, Wendy
Downington HS
Downingtown, PA

Harzinski, Debbie
Curwensville Area
Curwensville, PA

Haslam, Dawn
Hazleton HS
Mc Adoo, PA

Hassel, Eric
West Catholic Boys
Philadelphia, PA

Hasson, Cathy
Northern Cambria
Nicktown, PA

Hasson, Traci
Bristol JR SR HS
Bristol, PA

Hatch, Kelly
Altoona Area HS
Altoona, PA

Hatch, Mary Sue
Peters Township HS
Mc Murray, PA

Hatch, Melissa
Bradford Area HS
Rew, PA

Hatoff, Jacqueline
Lower Moreland HS
Huntingdon Valley, PA

Hauber, II William R
Manheim Township
Lancaster, PA

Hauck, Jessica L
Ephrata SR HS
Ephrata, PA

Haugland, Joseph
Interboro HS
Norwood, PA

Haus, Shannon
Milton Area HS
West Milton, PA

Hauser, Dean
Bald Eagle Area HS
Snow Shoe, PA

Hausman, Pamela
Northwestern Lehigh HS
New Tripoli, PA

Haussler, Jeanette
St Basil Acad
Philadelphia, PA

Havrilla, Jennifer
Little Flower Catholic HS Fo
Philadelphia, PA

Hawk, Lisa
E L Meyers HS
Wilkes Bare, PA

Hawk, Scott
Hanover HS
Hanover, PA

Hawley, Bryan
Altoona Area HS
Altoona, PA

Hawranko, Alyssa
M Fuller Franzier Mem JR SR HS
Perryopolis, PA

Hawthorne, Jeffery
Cornell Education
Coraopolis, PA

Hawthorne, Lori
Albert Gallatin HS
Lake Lynn, PA

Hay, Kelly
Northampton SR
Bath, PA

Hay, Kimberly
Berlin Brothers Valley HS
Berlin, PA

Hayden, Beth
Moniteau JR SR HS
W Sunbury, PA

Hayes, Amy
Kiski Area HS
Apollo, PA

Hayes, Ron
Fort Le Boeuf HS
Erie, PA

Hayes, Terry Lee
Corry HS
Corry, PA

Hayes, Wanda
Aliquippa SR HS
Aliquippa, PA

Hayney, Francis V
St Joseph Prep Schl
Camden, NJ

Hayward, Melinda
Clearfield HS
Clearfield, PA

Hayward, Melissa
Clearfield Area HS
Clearfield, PA

Haywood, Jenna
Pennsbury HS
Washington Crossi, PA

Heacock, Candice J
Perkiomen Valley
Perkiomenville, PA

Healy, Michelle
Pennsbury HS
Levittown, PA

Heard, Pamela
Wyoming Area HS
Wyoming, PA

Hearn, IV Chester G
Milton Area HS
Potts Grove, PA

Hearn, Kristina
Warwick HS
Lititz, PA

Heatwole, Jr Bill
Towanda Area HS
Towanda, PA

Hebert, John
Abraham Lincoln
Philadelphia, PA

Heck, Christopher J
Shady Side Acad
Glenshaw, PA

Heckman, April
Interboro HS
Norwood, PA

Heckman, Jeffrey
Lenape AVTS
Vandergrift, PA

Hedderick, Danny
Hamburg HS
Shoemakersville, PA

Heffelfinger, Ronald
Neshaminy HS
Penndel, PA

Hegarty, Maureen
Allentown Central Catholic HS
Whitehall, PA

Heidrich, Brenden
Cedar Crest HS
Lebanon, PA

Heil, Peter
Shadyside Acad
Pittsburgh, PA

Heim, Heather
Line Mountain HS
Dalmatia, PA

Heim, Lisa
Scranton Central
Scranton, PA

Heim, Mary Beth
Jersey Shore Area
Jersey Shore, PA

Heimbach, Mary Ann
Boyertown Area SR
Boyertown, PA

Hein, Dwight
Southern Lehigh HS
Coopersburg, PA

Heiney, Jeffrey
Lampeter Strasburg
Lancaster, PA

Heintzelman, Tammy
Central Dauphin HS
Harrisburg, PA

Heisen, Christopher
Pennsbury HS
Yardley, PA

Heisler, Shana
Plymouth-Whitemarsh HS
Lafayette Hill, PA

Heizmann, Noelle Beth
Central Bucks HS
Doylestown, PA

Helfrich, Gary A
Louis E Dieruff HS
Allentown, PA

Helfrich, Jenifer
William Penn SR
York, PA

Heller, Glenn J
Geibel HS
Scottdale, PA

Heller, Rachel
George Washington
Philadelphia, PA

Hellmann, Todd R
La Salle College HS
Buckingham, PA

Helm, Jodi L
Nazareth Area HS
Tatamy, PA

Helterbran, Tracey
Ambridge Area HS
Baden, PA

Hemperly, Laura
Middletown Area
Middletown, PA

Henderson, Bob
Warwick HS
Lititz, PA

Henderson, Cathy P
Hempfield Area SR
Greensburg, PA

Henderson, Erin
Meadville Area SR
Meadville, PA

Henderson, Kristi
Trinity HS
Washington, PA

Henderson, Stacey
William Penn SR
York, PA

Henes, Brian
Father Judge HS
Philadelphia, PA

Hengst, Tina
Greenwood HS
Millerstown, PA

Hengstenberg,
Nancy L
Penn-Trafford HS
Level Green, PA

Henneberry, Amy
Merion Mercy Acad
Phila, PA

Hennick, Amy
St Benedict Acad
Erie, PA

Henninger, Michelle
E
William Allen HS
Allentown, PA

Henry, Bobbi
Clarion-Limestone
Strattanville, PA

Henry, Mark
Geibel HS
Mount Pleasant, PA

Henry, Scott
Freedom HS
Easton, PA

Henry, Timothy
Sean
Kiski Area HS
Vandergrift, PA

Hensel, Tammy
Connellsville Area
SR HS
Mill Run, PA

Hensler, Patrick
Keystone Oaks HS
Pittsburgh, PA

Henson, Laurie
St Francis Acad
Eighty Four, PA

Heo, Su-Nam
Liberty HS
Bethlehem, PA

Hepburn, Alan
Montoursville HS
Mentoursville, PA

Hepler, Kathy
Blue Ridge HS
New Milford, PA

Hepner, Mark
Shikellamy HS
Sunbury, PA

Hepp, Barbara
Wyalusing Valley
JR/SR HS
Wyalusing, PA

Herb, Dawn
Williams Valley HS
Williamstown, PA

Herbert, Ken
Meadville Area SR
Provo, UT

Herbert, Sheryl
Little Flower Cath
HS For Girls
Philadelphia, PA

Herbert, Thomas
Lakeland JR SR HS
Olyphant, PA

Herforth, Robert C
Bishop Kenrick HS
Norristown, PA

Herman, Amy
Dover Area HS
Dover, PA

Herman, Brad
Northeastern HS
Manchester, PA

Herman, Danielle
Northeastern HS
York Haven, PA

Herman, Lisa
Plum SR HS
Pittsburgh, PA

Herman, Teresa
Canton Area HS
Roaring Branch, PA

Herrera, Andres J
Northeast Catholic
Philadelphia, PA

Hersh, Lisa
Spring Grove Area
Spg Grove, PA

Hershberger, Ross
Northern Bedford
County HS
Martinsburg, PA

Hershey, Tina M
William Penn SR
York, PA

Herstine, Carie
Canon-Mc Millan
Canonsburg, PA

Hertzog, Donna
Grace Christian HS
Newmanstown, PA

Herwig, Michelle
Lynn
Hatboro-Horsham
SR HS
Horsham, PA

Herzing, Nancy
Du Bois Area SR
Penfield, PA

Herzog, Kristy
Council Rock HS
Richboro, PA

Herzog, Richard
Hickory HS
Hermitage, PA

Hesidenz, Diana
Butler SR HS
Butler, PA

Hess, Barb
Garden Spot HS
New Holland, PA

Hess, Elisabeth
Harrisburg Acad
New Cumberland,
PA

Hess, Holly
Northeastern SR HS
Mt Wolf, PA

Hess, Howard
Spring-Ford HS
Spring City, PA

Hess, Lori
Glendale HS
Blandburg, PA

Hess, Stacey
Benton Area HS
Benton, PA

Hesson, Karen
Southmoreland HS
Scottdale, PA

Hester, Paul
Central York SR HS
York, PA

Hettler, Jessica
Penn Trafford HS
Irwin, PA

Heuscher, Derrick
Council Rock HS
Richboro, PA

Heyer, Jerre P
Seneca HS
Erie, PA

Hickman, Brett
Juniata HS
Port Royal, PA

Hicks, Kelli A
Lamberton HS
Philadelphia, PA

Higginbotham,
Sylvia Lynn
Burgettstown JR SR
Burgettstown, PA

Higgins, Leah
Dunmore HS
Dunmore, PA

Higgins, Tara
Westmont Hilltop
Johnstown, PA

Hile, Donald A
Reynolds HS
Fredonia, PA

Hiler, Matthew
Hershey HS
Hershey, PA

Hilk, Brian
Trinity HS
Washington, PA

Hill, Christina
Elkland Area HS
Nelson, PA

Hill, Curtis L
Southern Fulton HS
Needmore, PA

Hill, Jeffrey R
Valley Forge
Military Acad
Chatham Twp, NJ

Hill, Leonard
Penn Hills SR HS
Pittsburgh, PA

Hill, Steve
Linesville HS
Conneautville, PA

Hillard, Steve
Hollidaysburg Area
SR HS
Hollidaysburg, PA

Hillegass, Lonnie
Pottsgrove HS
Pottstown, PA

Hiller, Dawn
Quaker Valley HS
Leetsdale, PA

Hilliard, Gregory A
Olney HS
Philadelphia, PA

Hilliard, Patti
Butler SR HS
Renfrew, PA

Himes, Deborah
Blairsville SR HS
Blairsville, PA

Hinds, Barbie
Eastern York HS
Wrightsville, PA

Hines, Charles E
Bethlehem-Center
SR HS
Marianna, PA

Hinkle, Forrest
Marian HS
Weatherly, PA

Hinkle, Robert
Lehighton Area HS
Lehighton, PA

Hiriak, Kelly
Upper Perkiomen
Barto, PA

Hirsch, Joseph
United HS
Seward, PA

Hirsch, Scott
Upper Dauphin
Area HS
Lykens, PA

Hirsch, Tracy
Clearfield Area HS
Clearfield, PA

Hirschfield, Sue
David B Oliver HS
Pittsburgh, PA

Hirshman, Philip
Lower Moreland HS
Huntingdon Valley, PA

Hissong, Becky
Windber Area HS
Windber, PA

Hitt, Michele
Ambridge Area HS
South Hts, PA

Hittinger, Kyle
Saucon Valley SR
Bethlehem, PA

Hlatky, Greg
Northern HS
Dillsburg, PA

Hnot, Rebecca
Oil City SR HS
Oil City, PA

Ho, Willy W
Unionville HS
West Chester, PA

Hoagland, Kimberly
Shenandoah Valley
JR SR HS
Shenandoah, PA

Hobbs, Patrick
Cornell HS
Neville Isld, PA

Hobel, Daniel
Allentown Central
Catholic HS
Coplay, PA

Hoberney, Alan
Portage Area HS
Lilly, PA

Hockenberry, Denise
Pen Argyl Area HS
Nazareth, PA

Hockensmith, Lenny
Hanover HS
Hanover, PA

Hoden, Tim
Sheffield Area HS
Sheffield, PA

Hodil, Bryan
Shaler Area HS
Pittsburgh, PA

Hoefling, IV William A
Cedar Crest HS
Cornwall, PA

Hoeltzel, Steven R
Warwick HS
Lititz, PA

Hoff, Josh
Upper Moreland HS
Horsham, PA

Hoff, Wendy
Upper Dublin HS
Ft Washington, PA

Hoffer, Dawn
Eastern York HS
Wrightsville, PA

Hoffert, Sherry L
Liberty HS
Bethlehem, PA

Hoffman, Andrea
Bellwood-Antis HS
Altoona, PA

Hoffman, David M
Upper Perkiomen
Pennsburg, PA

Hoffman, Denise
Willias Valley JR
SR HS
Williamstown, PA

Hoffman, Francis
Northeast Catholic
Philadelphia, PA

Hoffman, Jill Ann
James M Coughlin
Wilkes-Barre, PA

Hoffman, Lee
William Allen HS
Allentown, PA

Hoffman, Yvonne
Boyertown Area SR
Boyertown, PA

Hofmann, Johanna
Linden Hall HS
Richland, PA

Hogan, Edward
Father Judge HS
Philadelphia, PA

Hogans, Pam
Altoona Area HS
Altoona, PA

Hogeland, Patricia
Danville HS
Danville, PA

Hogue, II Jack
New Brighton HS
New Brighton, PA

Hohl, Vicki L
Emmaus HS
Wescosville, PA

Hoke, Julia
Manheim Township
Lancaster, PA

Holby, Lisa
United HS
Homer City, PA

Holcombe, Bradford W
Susquehanna
Township HS
Harrisburg, PA

Holden, Scott
Philipsburg-Osceola
Area HS
Philipsburg, PA

Holderman, Kathy
Bellefonte Area HS
Bellefonte, PA

Holdredge, Jacqueline M
Dallas SR HS
Dallas, PA

Holecek, Lisa
Abraham Lincoln
Philadelphia, PA

Holland, Marc C
Penn-Trafford HS
Jeannette, PA

Hollenbaugh, David
New Hope-Solebury
Solebury, PA

Holler, Becky L
Springdale HS
Cheswick, PA

Hollinger, Chris
Northern Bedford
County HS
Roaring Spgs, PA

Hollis, Mark
Bentworth HS
Bentley Ville, PA

Holly, Karen
Cameron Counmty
Emporium, PA

Holm, Jennifer L
Methacton HS
Audubon, PA

Holmes, Lee
Hopewell SR HS
Aliquippa, PA

Holmes, Lee
Saucon Valley HS
Hellertown, PA

Holmes, Leslie
Moravian Acad
Bethelem, PA

Holoman, Tricia
West Mifflin Area
West Mifflin, PA

Holt, Melissa
York Catholic HS
York, PA

Holtz, Tara
Mt Lebanon HS
Pittsburgh, PA

Holtzman, Jr
Charles D
Bishop Mc Cort HS
Johnstown, PA

Holub, Timothy
Bentworth HS
Bentleyville, PA

Holzer, Stacey
Churchill HS
Pittsburgh, PA

Homer, Beth
Greenwood HS
Millerstown, PA

Homick, Jr Paul S
Highlands SR HS
Brackenridge, PA

Homola, Michelle
Cardinal Ohara HS
Chester, PA

Homulka, Gary J
Mt Pleasant Area
SR HS
Mt Pleasant, PA

Honey, Christine
Strong Vincent HS
Erie, PA

Hood, Dianna
Hempfield SR HS
Greensburg, PA

Hood, John
Cardinal Brennan
Ashland, PA

Hook, Michelle
Solanco SR HS
Peach Bottom, PA

Hooks, Tami
West Greene HS
New Freeport, PA

Hoover, Elizabeth
Bishop Guilfoyle HS
Altoona, PA

Hoover, Joel
Hershey SR HS
Hershey, PA

Hoover, Nancy
Big Spring HS
Newville, PA

Hoover, Verna
Bald Eagle Area HS
Karthaus, PA

Hoovler, Mark
General Mc Lane
Mckean, PA

Hopkins, Mary
Clare
Bishop Hannan HS
Scranton, PA

Hopkins, Sherry
State College Area
SR HS
State College, PA

Horak, Ellen
Springdale HS
Springdale, PA

Horan, Suzanne
Carbondale JR SR
Carbondale, PA

Horinko, Maria
Teresa
Hazleton HS
Hazleton, PA

Horn, Dedra Ann
Huntingdon Area
Mill Creek, PA

Hornak, Gena
Nicole
Boyertown Sr HS
Perkiomenville, PA

Hornak, Lorie
Pleasant Valley HS
Gilbert, PA

Hornberger, Jodie
Line Mountain HS
Shamokin, PA

Hornbuckle,
Timothy
Chamberrsburg Area
SR HS
Chambersburg, PA

Hornchek, Eric
Harry S Truman HS
Fairless Hills, PA

Horne, Gregory
Columbia-Montour
Berwick, PA

Hornik, Lisa
Strong Vincent HS
Erie, PA

Horst, Jared
Annville-Cleona HS
Cleona, PA

Horton, Clyde
Ringgold HS
Donora, PA

Horton, Vicki L
Hamburg Area HS
Hamburg, PA

Horvath, Theresa
Lakeland JR SR HS
Carbondale, PA

Horwatt, Christina
Lynn
Connellsville Area
SR HS
Dunbar, PA

Horwatt, De Ricci
Canon Mcmillan SR
Canonsburg, PA

Hosfeld, Matthew
Liberty HS
Bethlehem, PA

Hoshower, Victoria
Manheim Township
Lancaster, PA

Hosking, Christine
Benton Area JR SR
Benton, PA

Hostetler, Roy
Somerset Area HS
Somerset, PA

Hostetter, Roberta
Cedar Crest HS
Lebanon, PA

Hostler, Robert
Dover Area HS
Dover, PA

Houis, Curtis
Franklin HS
Emlenton, PA

House, Robert
Upper Dublin SR
Ft Washington, PA

Houser, Amy
West Branch Area
JR SR HS
Morrisdale, PA

Houser, Jr Donald E
Lock Haven HS
Lock Haven, PA

Houston, Sonja
Harrisburg Steelton
Highspire Vo Tech
Harrisburg, PA

Houston, Timothy J
North Hills HS
Pittsburgh, PA

Howard, Jeffrey M
Emmaus HS
Emmaus, PA

Howard, Wayne
West Catholic Boys
Philadelphia, PA

Howells, Kimberlee
A
Upper Moreland HS
Horsham, PA

Howles, Valerie
Cambridge Springs
Saegertown, PA

Howsare, Bobbi Ann
Chestnut Ridge HS
Bedford, PA

Howsare, Chris
Upper Moreland SR
Hatboro, PA

Howsare, Jacqueline
Hatboro Horsham
Hatboro, PA

Howsare, Janie Linn
Bedford HS
Bedford, PA

Hoy, Cheryl
Penns Manor HS
Clymer, PA

Hoysan, Bill
Liberty HS
Bethlehem, PA

Hreben, Matthew
Scranton Prep
Moosic, PA

Hribar, Monica
Center Area HS
Aliquippa, PA

Hrvoich, Steven J
Ambridge Area HS
Baden, PA

Hsu, Gwelleh
North Hills SR HS
Pittsburgh, PA

Huckestein, Angie
Seneca Valley SR
Evans City, PA

Hudler, Christine
Oxford Area HS
Lincoln Univ, PA

Hudock, Robert
Geibel HS
Uniontown, PA

Huey, Romayne
Yough SR HS
W Newton, PA

Huey, Vickie
Hamburg Area HS
Hamburg, PA

Huff, Donna
Slippery Rock HS
Prospect, PA

Huff, Karen
West Hazleton HS
Conyngham, PA

Hufford, Christine
Central HS
Martinsburg, PA

Hugh, Stephanie
Knoch HS
Butler, PA

Hughes, Aaron
Chief Logan HS
Burnham, PA

Hughes, Ginger
West Greene JR SR
Aleppo, PA

Hughes, Kelli
South Park HS
Library, PA

Hughes, Michael
Archbishop John
Carroll HS
Wayne, PA

Hughes, Polly Ann
West Side Area
Luzerne, PA

Hughes, Retonia
Kay
Philadelphia Schl Of
Performng Arts
Camden, NJ

Hughes, Stephen R
Hampton HS
Allison Pk, PA

Hughes, Susan
Lenape Vo-Tech
Spring Church, PA

Hughes, Suzanne
West Hazleton HS
Sugarloaf, PA

Hughes, Tiffany
Freedom HS
Bethlehem, PA

Hughes, Tracy
Central Cambria HS
Ebensburg, PA

Hull, Annmarie
Pen Argyl HS
Nazareth, PA

Hull, Shawn
Mt Pleasant Area
SR HS
Acme, PA

Hulsey, Amy
Canon Mc Millan
Canonsburg, PA

Humbert, Steven
Somerset Area SR
Friedens, PA

Humenick, Janice
Marie
Bishop Hafey HS
Hazleton, PA

Hummel, David
Upper Moreland HS
Hatboro, PA

Hummel, Harvey
Bensalem SR HS
Bensalem, PA

Hummel, Julie Ann
Bangor Area SR HS
Bangor, PA

Hummel, Virginia
Hopewell HS
Aliquippa, PA

Hummell, Amy
Washington HS
Washington, PA

Humphreys, David
South Park HS
Pittsburgh, PA

Humphreys, Debra
South Park HS
Pittsburgh, PA

Humphreys, John
Peters Township HS
Mc Murray, PA

Hundertmark, Jay
Bethlehem Center
Fredericktown, PA

Hunt, Elisa
Corry Area HS
Corry, PA

Hunt, Roberta
Seneca HS
Wattsburg, PA

Huntington, Gene
Troy Area HS
Columbia Cross Rd,
PA

Hurd, William
Clearfield Area HS
Clearfield, PA

Hurly, Stephen
Downingtown HS
Laurel, MD

Hurst, Carol
Archbishop
Prendergast HS
Collingdale, PA

Hurta, Todd
Ambridge HS
Freedom, PA

Hutchison, Jr
William R
Brownsville Area HS
Grindstone, PA

Hutton, Jennifer
Harmony HS
Mahaffey, PA

Hutzler, Kimberly
Fairview HS
Fairview, PA

Hyduk, Stephanie
Norwin SR HS
N Huntingdon, PA

Iannitti, Theresa
Chichester SR HS
Boothwyn, PA

Ianson, Bert
Cowanesque Valley
Middlebury Ctr, PA

Ickes, Carol
Altoona Area HS
Altoona, PA

Ickes, Kandi
Big Spring HS
Newville, PA

Igoe, Mark
Father Judge HS
Philadelphia, PA

Imber, Christopher
Lower Moreland HS
Huntingdon Valley,
PA

Ingel, Barbara
Bishop Conwell HS
Levittown, PA

Ingram, Dara
William Penn HS
Philadelphia, PA

Innamorato, Mary
Saint Huberts HS
Philadelphia, PA

Instone, John
Bishop Mc Cort HS
Johnstown, PA

Irons, Julie Anne
Center Area HS
Monaca, PA

Irwin, Flo
Delone Catholic HS
Hanover, PA

Irwin, III Frederick
H
Conrad Weiser HS
Womelsdorf, PA

Irwin, Jay
Clearfield SR HS
Woodland, PA

Irwin, Jr Jeffery
Warren Area HS
Warren, PA

Irwin, Joseph J
La Salle College HS
Philadelphia, PA

Irwin, Tracy Linn
Mc Guffey SR HS
Claysville, PA

Isabella, Gina Elyse
Penn-Trafford HS
Irwin, PA

Isler, Jamie
Brownsville Area HS
Brownsville, PA

Jack, Nick
Carmichaels Area
Carmichaels, PA

Jackson, Jr George
C B East HS
Doylestown, PA

Jackson, Heidi
Valley View JR SR
Blakely, PA

Jackson, Jane
Parkland HS
Allentown, PA

Jackson, Patricia
York Catholic HS
Hellam, PA

Jackson, Susan
Bensalem SR HS
Bensalem, PA

Jackson, Tammy
Philadelphia HS For
Philadelphia, PA

Jackson, Tammy
Pittston Area HS
Avoca, PA

Jackson, Tracey
Northgate HS
Pittsburgh, PA

Jackson, Tracy
Pennsbury HS
Levittown, PA

Jackson, Yolanda D
G W Carver HS Of
Engineering- Science
Philadelphia, PA

Jacob, Larry
Emmaus HS
Macungie, PA

Jacobs, John
Shady Side Acad
Glenshaw, PA

Jacobs, Kim
Bethel Park HS
Bethel Pk, PA

Jacoby, Monica
Northampton SR
Northampton, PA

Jacoway, La Vina
Delores
Farrell SR HS
Farrell, PA

Jakubec, Amy
Kennedy Christian
Fowler, OH

Janak, James
Richland Twp HS
Johnstown, PA

Janczak, Jay
Lower Moreland HS
Huntingdon Valley, PA

Janicki, Carl
Saint Pius X HS
Collegeville, PA

Janik, Diane
Cumberland Valley
Camp Hill, PA

Jannone, John
Wyalusing Valley JR SR HS
Camptown, PA

Janosik, Lesley
Laurel Highlands SR HS
Uniontown, PA

Jarrett, Aimee
State College Area
State College, PA

Jaskowiak, III
Walter A
Ridley HS
Ridley Park, PA

Jaskulski, Jodi
West Mifflin Area
West Mifflin, PA

Jayne, Kevin
Sullivan County HS
Dushore, PA

Jayne, Tamra
Wyalusing Valley
Laceyville, PA

Jeannerette, Mike
Otto-Eldred HS
Duke Center, PA

Jeanty, Marie Sheila
Bishop Mcdevitt HS
Elkins Park, PA

Jeddic, Denise
Wyoming Area SR
West Wyoming, PA

Jeffrey, Kimberly D
Dover Area HS
York, PA

Jeffreys, Pamela
Greater Johnstown SR HS
Johnstown, PA

Jegasothy, S
Manjula
Harriton HS
Rosemont, PA

Jeitner, David
Northeast HS
Philadelphia, PA

Jenkins, Deborah
Upper Darby HS
Drexel Hl, PA

Jenkins, Elizabeth Ann
West Scranton HS
Scranton, PA

Jenkins, Mary
Katherine
Cambria Heights HS
Patton, PA

Jenkins, Vicky Lynn
Lampeter-Strasburg
Willow St, PA

Jennings, Carrie
Plymouth-Whitemarsh HS
Ft Washington, PA

Jensen, Michael
Altoona Area HS
Altoona, PA

Jerich, Joe
Springdale HS
Springdale, PA

Jeschonek, Tonya
Greater Johnstown
Johnstown, PA

Jimmie, Dana
Dunmore HS
Dunmore, PA

Jindal, Binu
Central Dauphin East HS
Harrisburg, PA

Jobes, Shane W
Mc Guffey HS
Claysville, PA

John, IV Frank
Abington Heights
Dalton, PA

Johnson, Christy
Owen J Roberts HS
St Peters, PA

Johnson, Darlene
Andrea
Wallenpaupack Area
Hawley, PA

Johnson, Denise
Philadelphia HS For
Philadelphia, PA

Johnson, Edward
Cedar Cliff HS
New Cumberland, PA

Johnson, Erica
Berwick Area SR
Berwick, PA

Johnson, Jennifer
William Tennent SR
Southampton, PA

Johnson, Kimberly
Chartiers Valley HS
Carnegie, PA

Johnson, Lori
York Catholic HS
York, PA

Johnson, Mary
Youngsville JR SR
Youngsville, PA

Johnson, Melanie F
Shenango HS
New Castle, PA

Johnson, Pamela
W Phila Catholic HS For Girls
Philadelphia, PA

Johnson, Selina
Harry S Truman HS
Levittown, PA

Johnson, Sidney
Neshaminy HS
Langhorne, PA

Johnson, Tinna
Towanda Area HS
Towanda, PA

Johnston, Daren
Marion Center HS
Creekside, PA

Jokubetz, Jo Anne
Canon Mc Millan SR HS
Canonsburg, PA

Jones, Bill C
Freeport SR HS
Freeport, PA

Jones, Brian
Newport HS
Newport, PA

Jones, Darrin L
Hopewell SR HS
Aliquippa, PA

Jones, Denise
West Green JR-SR
Brave, PA

Jones, Hazel
Lynnette
Villa Maria HS
Wheatland, PA

Jones, Jennifer Ami
Schuylkill Valley HS
Leesport, PA

Jones, Karen
Downingtown SR
Downingtown, PA

Jones, Kathleen
Villa Joseph Marie
Huntingdon Valley, PA

Jones, Lauren
Strath Haven HS
Swarthmore, PA

Jones, Leonard
Chichester HS
Twin Oaks Farms, PA

Jones, Lisa
Brownsville Area HS
Brownsville, PA

Jones, Michael
West Allegheny SR
Oakdale, PA

Jones, Michael J
Monsignor Bonner
Clifton Heights, PA

Jones, Michele
Scranton Prep
Scranton, PA

Jones, Morrya
Purchase Line HS
Commodore, PA

Jones, Richard
Manhiem Township
Lancaster, PA

Jones, Robert
Quigley HS
Aliquippa, PA

Jones, Robyn
Unionville HS
Chadds Ford, PA

Jordan, Andrew
Bensalem SR HS
Bensalem, PA

Jordan, Joe
Mc Keesport SR HS
Mckeesport, PA

Jordan, Kelly
N Schuylkill HS
Frackville, PA

Jordan, Terry
Clearfield Area HS
Woodland, PA

Jorden, Heather
Kaye
Meadville SR HS
Meadville, PA

Joseph, Beth
Kiski Area HS
Export, PA

Joseph, Peter
East Stroudsburg
E Stroudsburg, PA

Joshi, Kalpesh
Cedar Crest HS
Lebanon, PA

Jover, Doreen
Valley View HS
Peckville, PA

Joyce, Stephen P
Brentwood JR SR
Pittsburgh, PA

Junkin, Julie
Fannett-Metal HS
Dry Run, PA

Jurasko, Diane
Hopewell HS
Aliquippa, PA

Jurista, Brent
Tunkhannock Area
Tunkhannock, PA

Justice, Kevin
Central Bucks East
Doylestown, PA

Kacik, Melissa
South Allegheny HS
Port Vue, PA

Kaczynski, Kris
North Hills HS
Pittsburgh, PA

Kagarise, Brian
Northern Bedford
County HS
Loysburg, PA

Kaguyutan, Janice
Victoria
The Mercersburg
Gettysburg, PA

Kahkonen, Gay L
Trinity HS
Washington, PA

Kahkonen, Sonja
Trinity HS
Washington, PA

Kahler, Allan
Upper Darby HS
Upr Darby, PA

Kahn, Jessica
Cheltenham HS
Wyncote, PA

Kalichuk, Lisa
Plum SR HS
Pittsburgh, PA

Kaliney, George
West Middlesex HS
W Middlesex, PA

Kalkbrenner,
Shawntelle
Claysburg-Kimmel
Claysburg, PA

Kalmanir, Heather
Windber Area HS
Windber, PA

Kalochie, Jennifer
Minersville Area HS
Minersville, PA

Kamdar, Melissa
St Basil Acad
Rydal, PA

Kaminski, Jeffri A
Norwin HS
N Huntingdon, PA

Kana-Collins,
Michelle
Unionville HS
Kennett Sq, PA

Kane, Apryl
Lock Haven SR HS
Lock Haven, PA

Kane, Mark
North Pocono HS
Lake Ariel, PA

Kane, II Ronald R
Immaculate
Conception HS
Amity, PA

Kang, Hae Eun
Cheltenham HS
Melrose Park, PA

Kang, Sue-Jin
Lower Moreland HS
Huntingdon Valley,
PA

Kara, Holly
Brownsville HS
Brownsville, PA

Karch, Mike
Kutztown HS
Kutztown, PA

Karchner, Bonnie
Berwick SR HS
Nescopeck, PA

Kardelis, Anthony C
Notre Dame HS
Easton, PA

Karenbauer, Marcy
Ellen
Butler SR HS
Butler, PA

Kargo, Ray
Portage Area HS
Portage, PA

Karlski, Valerie
Belle Vernon Area
Belle Vernon, PA

Karol, Bradford S
Moon SR HS
Coraopolis, PA

Karuzie, Lisa
Old Forge HS
Old Forge, PA

Kasanicky,
Stephanie
Ford City HS
Ford City, PA

Kasarda, Janene
Lake Lehman HS
Harveys Lake, PA

Kase, Terri
Shikellamy HS
Northumberland,
PA

Kassel, Kathy
Phoenixville Area
Phoenixville, PA

Kasun, Paige
Mc Caskey HS
Lancaster, PA

Katekovich,
Kathleen
Beaver Area HS
Beaver, PA

Katsuleris, Kelly
Ringgold HS
Monongahela, PA

Katzenbach, Nicole
Pottstown SR HS
Pottstown, PA

Kaucher, Joseph
Central Catholic HS
Reading, PA

Kauffman, Amanda
Lewiston Area HS
Lewistown, PA

Kavelines, Patricia
Scranton Technical
Scranton, PA

Kayafas, Kristen
Springdale HS
Harwick, PA

Kazmerski, Patricia
Our Lady Of
Lourdes Regiona
Shamokin, PA

Kearns, Christa
Chief Logan HS
Mcclure, PA

Kearns, Natalie
Louise
Riverview HS
Oakmont, PA

Keating, Christine A
Bishop Shanahan
West Chester, PA

Keating, James Alan
Penn-Trafford HS
Level Green, PA

Kebberly, Michele L
Uniontown Area SR
Chalk Hill, PA

Kecer, Tammy
Hutchinson
Corry Area HS
Columbus, PA

Keebler, Marty
St Marys Area HS
Kersey, PA

Keefer, Laureen L
North Allegheny HS
Allison Pk, PA

Keefer, Leona
Dover Area HS
Dover, PA

Keefer, Sandra
Palmyra Area HS
Palmyra, PA

Keefer, William
Connellsville Arew
SR HS
S Connellsville, PA

Keen, Denny
Central Dauphin HS
Harrisburg, PA

Keeney, Yvonne
Central York SR HS
York, PA

Keeton, Kimberly
Seneca Valley HS
Harmony, PA

Keffer, Kristy
Belle Vernon Area
Fayette City, PA

Kegerise, Kevin
Conrad Weiser HS
Womelsdorf, PA

Kehler, Michael T
Wilson Area HS
Easton, PA

Keifer, Jennifer
Bensalem SR HS
Bensalem, PA

Keil, Jennifer
Oil City SR HS
Oil City, PA

Keim, David M
Penn Hills SR HS
Pittsburgh, PA

Keim, Kathy
Phoenixville HS
Phoenixville, PA

Keiper, Joseph C
William Allen HS
Allentown, PA

Kell, David
West Perry HS
New Bloomfield, PA

Kellar, Peg
Cardinal O Hara HS
Havertown, PA

Keller, Lori
Middletown Area
Middletown, PA

Keller, Robert
Emmaus HS
Wescosville, PA

Kellerman, Shawn P
Seneca Valley SR
Evans City, PA

Kelley, Sharon
Connellsville Area
SR HS
Connellsville, PA

Kelley, Tammy
Altoona Area HS
Altoona, PA

Kelley, Tracy
Altoona Area HS
Altoona, PA

Kellner, Ralph E
West Allegheny SR
Oakdale, PA

Kelly, Christopher
Norwin SR HS
Ardara, PA

Kelly, Christopher J
Bethel Park SR HS
Bethel Park, PA

Kelly, Marie J
Bishop Shanahan
West Chester, PA

Kempf, III Edward
J
Northwestern HS
Cranesville, PA

Kempf, Gwendolyn
Towanda Area HS
Towanda, PA

Kempter, Joy
Archbishop Wood
HS For Girls
Holland, PA

Kendall, Lucia
Fox Chapel Area HS
Pittsburgh, PA

Kendig, Vicki
Norhteastern HS
Mt Wolf, PA

Kendrella, Nanci
Mt Pleasant HS
Mt Pleasant, PA

Kennedy, Barb
Knoch JR SR HS
Butler, PA

Kennedy, Edward J
West Mifflin Area
West Mifflin, PA

Kennedy, Patricia
St Pius X HS
Pennsburg, PA

Kennedy, Shannon
Yough HS
Herminie, PA

Kennell, Tammy
Hyndman HS
Hyndman, PA

Kenney, Kathy
Moshannon Valley
Houtzdale, PA

Kenney, Sean
Geibel HS
Scottdale, PA

Kenny, Erin
B Reed Henderson
Westchester, PA

Kephart, Brent
Philipsburg Osceola
Area HS
Osceola Mills, PA

Kephart, Michelle
Clearfield Area HS
Olanta, PA

Keppie, Ken
Franklin Regional
Delmont, PA

Kerner, Scott
Marion Center HS
Creekside, PA

Kerner, Troy
Hamburg HS
Bernville, PA

Kerr, Denise
St Hubert HS
Philadelphia, PA

Kerr, Erik
Trinity HS
Washington, PA

Kerr, Kara
Hopewell SR HS
Aliquippa, PA

Kerr, Laura Beth
Pennsbury HS
Yardley, PA

Kerris, Diane
Lourdes Regional
Mt Carmel, PA

Kertzel, Amy
Northeastern SR HS
Dover, PA

Keshishian, Arousiag
St Basil Acad
Phila, PA

Keslar, Tammy
Mt Pleasant Area
SR HS
Acme, PA

Kester, Mark C
Pennridge HS
Hilltown, PA

Kettering, Joelle C
Lancaster Christian
Thomson, IL

Keys, Richard D
Beth Center HS
Brownsville, PA

Kief, Randy
Canon-Mc Millian
Canonsburg, PA

Kieffer, Pam
Central Bucks East
Furlong, PA

Kikola, Dennis
Seneca HS
Wattsburg, PA

Kilbert, Jennifer
West Mifflin Area
W Mifflin, PA

Kilcoyne, Kelly
Mt Alvernia HS
Pittsburgh, PA

Killen, Dawn
Nazareth Acad
Philadelphia, PA

Killip, Eric W
Moon SR HS
Coraopolis, PA

Kim, John
Cheltenham HS
Elkins Pk, PA

Kimberland, Kelly
Ann
Canon Mc Millan
Eighty Four, PA

Kime, Andrew M
Ridley SR HS
Woodlyn, PA

Kimmel, Pamela
Tri Valley HS
Hegins, PA

Kimmen, Angela
Lyn
Bellwood-Antis HS
Bellwood, PA

Kinard, Brian
Central York HS
York, PA

Kindt, Stephanie
Wilson Area HS
Easton, PA

King, Aaron
Bradford Area HS
Bradford, PA

King, Deborah
Dover Area HS
Dover, PA

King, James
Saucon Valley HS
Bethlehem, PA

King, Kenneth S
Brookville Area HS
Brookville, PA

King, Pamela
Pocono Mountain
Long Pond, PA

Kingsley, Robyn
Butler Area SR HS
Butler, PA

Kiniry, Patricia J
Bishop Mc Cort HS
Johnstown, PA

Kinkella, Susan
Southmoreland HS
Ruffsdale, PA

Kinsey, Dawn
Ligonier Valley SR
Ligonier, PA

Kirch, Jeffrey
Bethel Park HS
Bethel Park, PA

Kirchner, Eric
Blacklick Valley HS
Vintondale, PA

Kirkland, Belinda
Blairsville SR HS
Blairsville, PA

Kirkland, John
Cardinal O Hara HS
Newtown Sq, PA

Kirkpatrick, Amy
Beth
Belle Vernon Area
Belle Vernon, PA

Kirkpatrick, Patricia
Bishop Guilfoyle HS
Altoona, PA

Kirschner, William
Cardinal O Hara HS
Broomall, PA

Kirtland, Kelly
York Catholic HS
York, PA

Kirwin, Brian
Father Judge HS
Philadelphia, PA

Kis Halas, Krisztina
Upper Merion Area
SR HS
King Of Prussia, PA

Kiscadden, Jennifer
Cedar Crest HS
Lebanon, PA

Kishbaugh, Wayne
Wyalusing Valley
Laceyville, PA

Kissinger, Kurt
Mechanisburg Area
SR HS
Mechanicsburg, PA

Kistler, Douglas G
Central York HS
York, PA

Kitchen, Jana
Danville SR HS
Danville, PA

Klahr, Amy
Conrad Weiser HS
Robesonia, PA

Kleckner, Jacque
Lock Haven SR HS
Lock Haven, PA

Kleckner, Zoe
Delaware County
Christian Schl
Haverton, PA

Klein, Letha
East Pennsboro HS
Enola, PA

Klein, Sharon
North Hills HS
Pittsburgh, PA

Kleinfelter, Scott
Palmyra Area HS
Campbelltown, PA

Kleist, Stacey
Meadville Area SR
Meadville, PA

Klems, Darlene E
Chicester SR HS
Boothwyn, PA

Klepper, Paula
Hatboro-Horsham
SR HS
Hatboro, PA

Klim, Pamela Jo
Chartiers Valley HS
Carnegie, PA

Kline, Beth
Eastern HS
Wrightsville, PA

Kline, Francesca
Lock Haven SR HS
Lock Haven, PA

Kline, John
Trinity HS
New Cumberland,
PA

Kline, Pamela
Everett Area HS
Everett, PA

Kline, Sandi
Hamburg Area HS
Hamburg, PA

Kline, Steve
Eastern York HS
Wrightsville, PA

Kline, Tina
Pann Cambria HS
Easton, PA

Klinefelter, Debbie
Shaler Area HS
Pittsburgh, PA

Kling, Craig
Altoona Area HS
Altoona, PA

Klingaman, Randy
Parkland SR HS
Trexlertown, PA

Klinger, Barbara
Southern Columbia
Area HS
Catawissa, PA

Klock, Jodi
Shikellamy HS
Sunbury, PA

Klos, Helena M
Plum SR HS
Pittsburgh, PA

Kluck, Carolyn
Carbondale Area HS
Simpson, PA

Kluck, John
Venango Christian
Rouseville, PA

Kmetz, Paul
Westmont Hilltop
Johnstown, PA

Knapp, Chris
Shenandoah Valley
Shenandoah, PA

Knapp, Dave
Beaver Area HS
Beaver, PA

Knapp, Leo R
Cardinal O Hara HS
Springfield, PA

Knauff, Damian
Bethel Park SR HS
Bethel Park, PA

Knebel, Steven W
Seneca Valley SR
Mars, PA

Knee, Celeste
Penn Cambria SR
Gallitzin, PA

Knee, Randy S
York Suburban SR
York, PA

Knefley, Cheryl M
Susquehannock HS
New Freedom, PA

Knight, Beth
New Brighton Area
New Brighton, PA

Knight, Philip
Aliquippa HS
West Aliquippa, PA

Knisel, Lynne
Forest Hills HS
Summerhill, PA

Knoll, Carolyn
Karns City HS
Chicora, PA

Knouse, III Theron
I
John S Fine HS
Wapwallopen, PA

Knupp, Traci
Rocky Grove HS
Franklin, PA

Kobilic, Lisa M
Monongahela Valley
Catholic HS
Lititz, PA

Kobuck, Lori
Tyrone Area HS
Warriors Mk, PA

Koch, Shannon
Oil City Area SR
Oil City, PA

Koch, Todd A
Blue Mountain HS
New Ringgold, PA

Kocher, Anne
Eastern Lebanon
County HS
Myerstown, PA

Kocis, Christine
Connellsville Area
SR HS
Cnlvle, PA

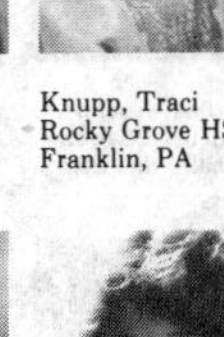

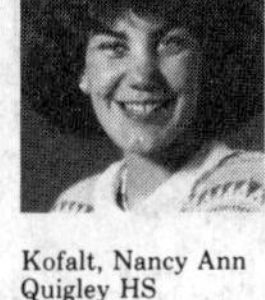

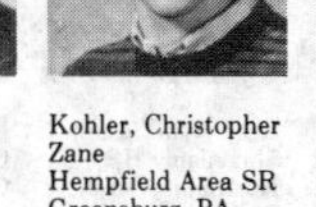

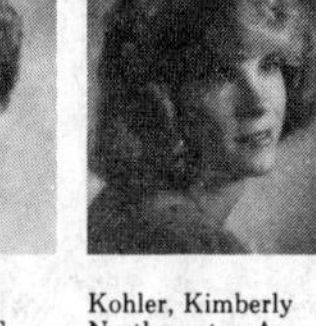

Koehler, Beth Ann
Abington Heights
Clarks Green, PA

Koehler, Jason
Trinity HS
Washington, PA

Koehn, David A
Bishop Hafey HS
Drums, PA

Koener, Chantelle
Greater Johnstown
Johnstown, PA

Kofalt, Nancy Ann
Quigley HS
Beaver, PA

Koffel, Christine
Rose
Pennridge SR HS
Perkasie, PA

Kofluk, Shawn
Schuylkill Haven
Auburn, PA

Kohler, Christopher
Zane
Hempfield Area SR
Greensburg, PA

Kohler, Debra
Easton Area HS
Easton, PA

Kohler, Kimberly
Northampton Area
SR HS
Walnutport, PA

Kohn, Kimberley
Lincoln HS
Philadelphia, PA

Kolakowski, Michael
Apollo-Ridge HS
Clarksburg, PA

Kolb, Cheri
Owen J Roberts HS
Spring City, PA

Kolick, Karen
Jefferson-Morgan
Clarksville, PA

Kolling, Scott R
Montour HS
Coraopolis, PA

Kolodychak, Michael
Charleroi Area JR SR HS
N Charleroi, PA

Koloshinsky, Karen R
Greater Latrobe HS
Latrobe, PA

Koman, Kristan G
Trinity HS
Washington, PA

Komishock, Jr Paul
Bishop Hafey HS
Hazleton, PA

Kompass, Lynn
Emmaus HS
Emmaus, PA

Kondras, Bryan
Elizabethtown Area
Mount Joy, PA

Konopke, Walt
Lake Lehman HS
Noxen, PA

Konzel, Stephen
Catherdral Preparatory HS
Erie, PA

Kool, Lisa
Harriton HS
Pen Vly, PA

Koons, Molly
Crestwood HS
Mountaintop, PA

Kopas, Julianne
Norwin SR HS
Westmoreland City, PA

Kopec, Michael
Bishop Kenrick HS
Norristown, PA

Kopelcheck, Kathleen
Danville Area HS
Danville, PA

Kopp, Michael J
Fox Chapel Area HS
Sharpsburg, PA

Koppenhaver, Kelly
Halifax Area HS
Halifax, PA

Korda, Susan
Villa Maria HS
Youngstown, OH

Kordes, Jeff
Meadville Area SR
Meadville, PA

Korzeniowski, Katria
St Basil Acad
Philadelphia, PA

Korzi, Michael
Windber Area HS
Windber, PA

Koski, Susan Marie
Canon Mc Millan SR HS
Eighty Four, PA

Kossar, Todd
Belle Vernon Area
Belle Vernon, PA

Kossmann, Bobbi
Hazleton HS
Hazleton, PA

Kost, Brian
Quigley HS
Freedon, PA

Kotarski, Anthony
James M Coughlin
Laflin, PA

Kotsko, John
John S Fine HS
Nanticoke, PA

Koukis, Kristine
Kennedy Christian
Farrell, PA

Koursaros, Hari
Reading SR HS
Reading, PA

Kovach, Sue
Pottstown SR HS
Pottstown, PA

Koval, Michelle R
Hazleton HS
Hazleton, PA

Kovaloski, James
Glendale JRSR HS
Irvona, PA

Kowalo, Jr Dan
Canon Mac Millian
Mc Donald, PA

Kowalski, II Stan J
Williamsport Area
Williamsport, PA

Kowasic, Jr William Charles
Belle Vernon Area
Belle Vernon, PA

Kowker, Michael
Mahanoy Area HS
Gilberton, PA

Koyack, Jim
Shamokin HS
Ranshaw, PA

Kozlansky, Gerald
Central HS
Scranton, PA

Kozloff, Samuel
Wyomissing Area
Wyomissing, PA

Kozlowski, Sharon
Freedom HS
Bethlehem, PA

Kozub, Lori
Gateway SR HS
Monroeville, PA

Kraft, Melissa
Freedom SR HS
Bethlehem, PA

Krajc, Elizabeth
Greensburg Central Catholic HS
Greensburg, PA

Kramer, Meredith
Upper Dublin HS
Ambler, PA

Kramer, Scott
Pine Grove HS
Pine Grove, PA

Kramer, Sherri
Penn-Trafford HS
Irwin, PA

Krasnitsky, Sandy
Minersville Area HS
Pottsville, PA

Kratofil, Kristen
Yough HS
Irwin, PA

Kratz, Michele
Crestwood HS
Nuangola, PA

Kraus, Kurt
Fox Chapel HS
Pittsbg, PA

Kraus, Jr Rich J
Center HS
Aliquippa, PA

Kravitz, Kyle
Cheltenham HS
Elkins Pk, PA

Kraynak, James S
Connellsville Area
Connellsville, PA

Kraynak, Joseph
Connellsville Area
Connellsville, PA

Krebs, Robert
Clearfield Area HS
Clearfield, PA

Kreider, Lori D
Garden Spot HS
E Earl, PA

Kreiser, Travis
Palmyra Area HS
Palmyra, PA

Kreitzer, Jr Eugene
Northern Lebanon
Fredericksburg, PA

Krejnus, Susan
Cambria Heights SR
Elmora, PA

Kremer, Jr Joseph L
Shikellamy HS
Northumberland, PA

Krenitsky, Victoria
Old Forge HS
Old Forge, PA

Kresovich, Joseph
Bellefonte HS
Bellefonte, PA

Kress, Karen
Fort Cherry HS
Mcdonald, PA

Kress, Melissa
Northeast HS
Philadelphia, PA

Kressler, Jill
Saucon Valley SR
Hellertown, PA

Kretschmer, Dawn
Cheltenham HS
Elkins Pk, PA

Krisch, Paul
Hanover Area HS
Wilkes Barre, PA

Krise, Tina Marie
Windber Area HS
Windber, PA

Kriser, Robyn
Punxsutawney Area
Delancey, PA

Krishna, Mohan
Emmaus HS
Macungie, PA

Kristen, Scot
Elizabeth Forward
Mckeesport, PA

Kroh, Mark
The Hill Schl
Aaronsburg, PA

Kropp, Richard
Vincentian HS
Wexford, PA

Krouse, Jennifer
Red Lion Area SR
Airville, PA

Krout, Paula M
Dallastown Area HS
Dallastown, PA

Kroznuskie, Millie
Staint Clair HS
New Philadelphia, PA

Krumm, Cheryl
Wallenpaupock HS
Hawley, PA

Krumrine, Richard H
Octorara Area HS
Parkesburg, PA

Krupski, Donna
North Pocono HS
Lake Ariel, PA

Kruth, Paul
Shaler Area HS
Pittsburgh, PA

Krutz, Mary
Lakeland HS
Mayfield, PA

Krysiak, Brendalyn
Cowanesque Valley
Westfield, PA

Kubel, John
Notre Dame HS
Easton, PA

Kubic, Tricia
Norwin SR HS
N Huntingdon, PA

Kubina, Kimberly
Bensalem HS
Warminster, PA

Kuck, Laura
Richland HS
Gibsonia, PA

Kudlik, Cheryl
Monessen JR SR
Monessen, PA

Kudrick, Rachel
Keystone HS
Knox, PA

Kuehner, Karen
Northampton HS
Cherryville, PA

Kugler, Michele
Saint Huberts HS
Philadelphia, PA

Kuhlman, Karen
Marple Newtown
Media, PA

Kuhns, Karla L
Liberty HS
Bethlehem, PA

Kujawa, Kimberly
Frazier HS
Dawson, PA

Kuklinski, Rebecca
St Benedict Acad
Erie, PA

Kulchinsky, Alisa
Northamption Area SR HS
Walnutport, PA

Kulich, Pam
Saint Benedict Acad
Erie, PA

Kulick, Lisa
Leechburg Area HS
Leechburg, PA

Kulish, Janice
Canon Mc Millan SR HS
Canonsburg, PA

Kulp, Walter P
Saint Josephs Prep
Philadelphia, PA

Kulyk, Jay
Northwestern SR
Albion, PA

Kuncheriah, Shyla
George Washington
Philadelphia, PA

Kuntz, Susan Ann
Waynesburg Central
Waynesburg, PA

Kupfer, Deborah A
Taylor Allderdice
Pittsburgh, PA

Kupfer, Jennifer E
Meadville Area SR
Meadville, PA

Kurash, Jody
Penn Cambria HS
Cresson, PA

Kurinko, Sherri Lynn
Saegertown HS
Saegertown, PA

Kurneck, Robert
Hampton HS
Allison Pk, PA

Kurpiel, Kathy
Southmoreland HS
Mt Pleasant, PA

Kurtz, Andrew N
Rochester JR-SR
Rochester, PA

Kurtz, Melissa
St Pius X HS
East Greenville, PA

Kurtz, Stacy
Plymouth Whitemarsh SR HS
Lafayette Hill, PA

Kurtz, Virginia
Shenandoah Valley
Shenandoah, PA

Kutzler, Jennifer
Liberty HS
Bethlehem, PA

Kuznicki, Noel
Lake-Lehman HS
Shavertown, PA

Kyle, Susan
Saucon Valley SR
Bethlehem, PA

Kyper, Aleisa
Mechanicsburg SR
Grantham, PA

Kyper, Sheila
Mechanicsburg Area
Grantham, PA

La Civita, Annmarie
St Maria Goretti HS
Philadelphia, PA

La Follette, Jean-Paul
The Mercersburg
Fairmont, WV

La Monaca, Stephanie
St Maria Goretti HS
Philadelphia, PA

La Plante, Treff
Central Dauphin East HS
Dauphin, PA

La Salle, Robert
Upper Perkiomen
East Greenville, PA

Labor, Kelly
Slippery Rock Area
Slippery Rock, PA

Lacko, Jennifer
Northampton Area SR HS
Walnutport, PA

Ladley, Stacy
Peters Twp HS
Bridgeville, PA

Lafferty, Richard
Interboro HS
Norwood, PA

Lagiovane, Sharon
Shaler Area SR HS
Allison Park, PA

Lahiri, Indra
Solebury Schl
Chalfont, PA

Lahr, Tina
Boyertown Area SR
Bally, PA

Lahr, William D
Upper Dauphin HS
Lykens, PA

Laird, Stephanie Jean
Indiana Area SR HS
Indiana, PA

Lako, Jamie
Monongahela Vly
Elizabeth, PA

Lally, III Edmund J
Interboro HS
Norwood, PA

Lambert, Aimee
Ringgold HS
Monongahela, PA

Lambert, Deborah
Cardinal O Hara HS
Chester, PA

Lambert, Juliet E
Parkland SR HS
Fogelsville, PA

Lambert, Renee
California Area HS
Coal Center, PA

Lamoreau, Amy
Moshannon Valley
JR SR HS
Ramey, PA

Lamoreux, Linda
Bishop Hoban HS
Swoyersville, PA

Lampron, Colleen
Downingtown HS
Downingtown, PA

Lanatto, Christine
Merion Mercy Acad
Phila, PA

Lancaster, Marlo
Roxborough HS
Philadelphia, PA

Landau, Helene
Northern HS
Dillsburg, PA

Landfried, Darryl
North Allegheny HS
Allison Park, PA

Landis, Chris
Canton HS
Troy, PA

Landis, Dawn
Kiski Area SR HS
Leechburg, PA

Landis, Kim
Canton Area JR SR
Troy, PA

Landis, Lisa
Octorara HS
Lancaster, PA

Landis, Marla
Bellefonte Area HS
Howard, PA

Landis, Matt
Bishop Shanahan
W Chester, PA

Landis, Raymond
Souderton Area HS
Harleysville, PA

Landis, Sharon
Souderton Area HS
Telford, PA

Landolina, Maria
Shaler Area SR HS
Glenshaw, PA

Lane, Denise
Lewistown Area HS
Lewistown, PA

Laney, Renee
Purchase Line HS
Cherry Tree, PA

Lang, Brett
Kennett HS
Kennett Sq, PA

Lang, Deborah Anne
Calvary Baptist
Christian Acad
Meadville, PA

Langdon, Debra
Cardinal O Hara HS
Essington, PA

Langer, Todd
Moon SR HS
Corapolis, PA

Langhorne, Wistar A
East HS
West Chester, PA

Langley, Robyn
Red Lion Area SR
Felton, PA

Langston, Senate
Perry Traditional
Pittsburgh, PA

Langton, Annette
Hopewell Area SR
Aliquippa, PA

Lanham, Traci
Yough HS
West Newton, PA

Lansberry, Cindy
Curwensville Area
Curwensville, PA

Lantelme, Amy
Leechburg Area HS
Leechburg, PA

Lanzendorfer, Lorie
Central HS
Duncanville, PA

Lapinas, Keith A
Central Dauphin HS
Harrisburg, PA

Lapp, Barbara Jean
Ringgold HS
Eighty Four, PA

Larimer, William J
Bethel Park SR HS
Bethel Park, PA

Larosse, Marle C
Greenwood HS
Newport, PA

Larson, Christine
Dunmore HS
Dunmore, PA

Lasch, Lori
Nazareth Acad
Philadelphia, PA

Lasco, Cori B
Towando Area HS
Towanda, PA

Lash, Dina
Curwensville Area
Grampian, PA

Lashay, Jacquelyn
Our Lady Of
Lourdes Regiona
Shamokin, PA

Lasher, Scott
Kittanning SR HS
Adrian, PA

Laskas, Karl M
East Allegheny HS
North Versailles, PA

Laskey, Carrie
Archbishop
Prendergast HS
Collingdale, PA

Laslo, Gregory
Annville Cleona HS
Annville, PA

Laspina, Lazae
Penn-Trafford HS
Irwin, PA

Lassiter, Tracey
Creative &
Performing Arts HS
Philadelphia, PA

Latimore, Karen
Moniteau HS
W Sunbury, PA

Latshaw, Shanon L
Shamokin Area HS
Shamokin, PA

Latshaw, Sherry
Pottstown SR HS
Pottstown, PA

Lauber, Kellyanne
St Basil Acad
Philadelphia, PA

Laughlin, James B
South Side HS
Hookstown, PA

Launtz, Michele
Westmont Hilltop
Johnstown, PA

Laurito, Kimberly
Aliquippa HS
Aliquippa, PA

Lavelle, David J
Bethel Park HS
Bethel Park, PA

Lavery, Mark
Notre Dame HS
Palmer, PA

Lavin, Meredith
Harriton HS
Narberth, PA

Lavrich, Joann
Shaler Area SR HS
Pittsburgh, PA

Lawrence, Brooks
Hampton HS
Allison Pk, PA

Lawrence, Carol
Villa Maria HS
Youngstown, OH

Lawrence, David
Hempfield HS
Lancaster, PA

Lawson, Beth
Middletown Area
Middletown, PA

Lawson, Eric
Hanover Area JR
SR HS
Ashley, PA

Lawson, Jeanne
Liverty JR SR HS
Liberty, PA

Lawson, Lisa
Charleroi Area HS
Charleroi, PA

Lawton, Micah
William Penn HS
Philadelphia, PA

Lawver, Wayne
Littlestown SR HS
Littlestown, PA

Layton, Joy
Garden Spot HS
New Holland, PA

Lazicki, Tammy
Our Lady Of
Lourdes HS
Ranshaw, PA

Lazzaretti, Judy
Our Lady Of The
Sacred Heart HS
Ambridge, PA

Le, Trang
Somerset Area SR
Somerset, PA

Le Febvre, Marie T
Hatboro-Horsham
SR HS
Horsham, PA

Leakey, Lestie
Garden Spot HS
Blue Ball, PA

Leardi, Kathleen
Cardinal O Hara HS
Springfield, PA

Leary, Maureen
Lampeter-Strasburg
Lancaster, PA

Leas, Noel
Lackawana Trail JR
SR HS
Dalton, PA

Leasgang, Lisa
St Marys Area HS
Kersey, PA

Leathers, Joy
High Point Baptist
Acad HS
Birdsboro, PA

Leckey, Ronald
Portage Area HS
Portage, PA

Ledbetter, William
Cambridge Springs
Saegertown, PA

Lee, Charles P
La Salle HS
Southampton, PA

Lee, Chi
Central HS
Philadelphia, PA

Lee, David
Exeter Township SR
Reading, PA

Lee, Dennis
Monaca JR SR HS
Monaca, PA

Lee, Gerald
Harbor Creek HS
Erie, PA

Lee, Jeffrey
Sayre Area HS
Sayre, PA

Lee, Kee
Hatboro-Horsham
SR HS
Horsham, PA

Lee, Leroy
Walter Biddle Saul
Philadelphia, PA

Lee, Lisa
Governor Mifflin HS
Reading Flying Hi,
PA

Lee, Michelle
Archbishop Rayn
HS For Girls
Philadelphia, PA

Lee, Susan Ann
South Fayette HS
Oakdale, PA

Lee, Jr Tyrone T
Taylor Allderice HS
Pittsburgh, PA

Legarht, Jr Dale L
Pine Grove Area HS
Pine Grove, PA

Lehett, Amy
West Middlesex HS
W Middlesex, PA

Lehman, Christine
Central York SR HS
Emigsville, PA

Lehman, David
Cheltenham HS
Cheltenham, PA

Lehman, Scott
Northern Potter HS
Ulysses, PA

Lehmann, Katrina
Pottstown SR HS
Pottstown, PA

Lehn, Kristen E
Cedar Crest HS
Lebanon, PA

Lehr, Kenneth W
La Salle HS
Southampton, PA

Leibman, Karen
James M Couglin
Wilkes Barre, PA

Leiby, Wendy
Tamaqua Area SR
Tamaqua, PA

Leichliter, Michael
G
William Penn SR
York, PA

Leighthardt, Joseph
Archbishop Ryan
For Boys
Philadelphia, PA

Leiker, Nicole
Philadelphia High
School For Girls
Philadelphia, PA

Leinheiser, Patrice
Harry S Truman HS
Edgely, PA

Lellock, David E
Punxsutawney Area
SR HS
Punxsutawney, PA

Lemon, Cindy Lynn
Rochester Area HS
Rochester, PA

Lencer, Jr Henry
North Clarion JR
SR HS
Leeper, PA

Lenetsky, Mara
Neshaminy HS
Langhorne, PA

Lenhart, Tamara
Clearfield Area HS
Clearfield, PA

Lent, Beth
Central Dauphin HS
Harrisburg, PA

Lentz, Edward T
Wyomissing Area
Wyomissing, PA

Leo, Jr Charles
Meyers HS
Wilkes Barre, PA

Leonard, Larissa
Connellsville HS
Dawson, PA

Leonard, Leann
Hempfield Area HS
Irwin, PA

Leone, Monica M
Archbishop Wood
For Girls
Feasterville, PA

Lepich, Jeanine
Fairview HS
Fairview, PA

Lepley, Michael
West Snyder HS
Beaver Spgs, PA

Lepore, Jeffrey
Wyoming Valley
West HS
Kingston, PA

Leppert, Tammy
Trinity HS
Washington, PA

Lerch, Jennifer
Pen Argyl HS
Nazareth, PA

Lerch, Suzanne
Middletown Area
Middletown, PA

Lerda, Elizabeth
Peters Township HS
Mc Murray, PA

Lerwick, Tanya
Wissahickon S HS
Ambler, PA

Leschek, Lisa
Gateway SR HS
Monroeville, PA

Lescott, Beth
Peters Twp HS
Bridgeville, PA

Lesh, Julie Kay
Bedford HS
Bedford, PA

Lesher, Jr James M
Upper Dauphin
Area HS
Gratz, PA

Leskusky, Vincent
St Pius X HS
Pottstown, PA

Leslie, Kristie
Bishop Shanahan
Coatesville, PA

Letchford, Ardean
Tyrone HS
Tyrone, PA

Levan, Pamela
Pine Grove Area HS
Pine Grove, PA

Leventhal, Mark
Upper Dublin HS
Dresher, PA

Levi, Daniel
Canon Mcmillan SR
Eighty Four, PA

Levin, Wendy
Clearfield Area HS
Clearfield, PA

Levitsky, Janet
Northwestern
Lehigh HS
Breinigsvile, PA

Lewis, Aaron
Danville Area HS
Danville, PA

Lewis, Andrea
Lincoln HS
Ellwood City, PA

Lewis, Arley
Punxsutawney Area
SR HS
Punxsutawney, PA

Lewis, David
Hanover Area JR
SR HS
Wilkes Barre, PA

Lewis, Greg
Council Rock HS
Newtown, PA

Lewis, Jannet
Meadville HS
Meadville, PA

Lewis, Mark K
Pocono Mountain
Cresco, PA

Lewis, Scott
Oil City SR HS
Oil City, PA

Lewis, Wally
West Scranton HS
Scranton, PA

Leysock, Sherri
Homer Center HS
Lucerne Mines, PA

Liberati, Nick
Springdale HS
Cheswick, PA

Libonati, Michael
Central HS
Philadelphia, PA

Lichty, Larry
Emmaus HS
Wescosville, PA

Licker, Lorane
Lebanon SR HS
Lebanon, PA

Lieb, Pamela M
Northampton SR
Bath, PA

Liebetrau, Emilie
Carlisle SR HS
Carlisle, PA

Liebling, William
Gateway SR HS
Monroeville, PA

Lied, Tracy
Ephrata HS
Ephrata, PA

Liedtka, Stephen
Bishop Egan HS
Morrisville, PA

Liesche, Darrin
Abington SR HS
Phila, PA

Lightner, Tina
Bishop Guilfoyle HS
Altoona, PA

Lilley, Chandra
Manheim Township
Lancaster, PA

Limbacher, John E
Knoch HS
Saxonburg, PA

Lin, Angela
Ephrata SR HS
Ephrata, PA

Lin, Charrissa Y
Freedom HS
Bethlehem, PA

Lindrose, Valarie
Blacklick Valley JR SR HS
Nanty Glo, PA

Lindsay, Roberta
Benton Area HS
Benton, PA

Lindsey, Brenda
Corry Area HS
Corry, PA

Lindsey, Carol
Downingtown SR
Downingtown, PA

Lindsey, II Kirby C
Sheffield Area JR SR HS
Sheffield, PA

Lindstrom, Lynn
Clearfield SR HS
Clearfield, PA

Linneman, Doug
Unionville HS
West Chester, PA

Lint, Tammy
Frazier HS
Dawson, PA

Linton, David
Donegal HS
Mount Joy, PA

Linton, Tammy
Shamokin Area HS
Shamokin, PA

Lippe, Craig
Shady Side Acad
Pittsburgh, PA

Lisella, Guy
Towanda Area HS
Towanda, PA

Lishinsky, David
Punxsutawney Area
Punxsutawney, PA

Lishman, Jennifer
Brandywine Heights Area HS
Topton, PA

Littell, Kirk
Richland HS
Gibsonia, PA

Little, Heather
Richland HS
Gibsonia, PA

Little, Jeff
South Western HS
Hanover, PA

Litz, Jennifer Lynn
Butler Area SR HS
Butler, PA

Litzenberger, Charlene
Cocalico HS
Stevens, PA

Livolsi, Joe
Canon Mc Millan
Canonsburg, PA

Lizzul, Kathleen
Shamokin Area HS
Shamokin, PA

Lladoc, Sarah M
Notre Dame HS
Stroudsburg, PA

Lloyd, Diane
Exeter SR HS
Reading, PA

Lloyd, Jeffrey
Greater Latrobe SR
Latrobe, PA

Lloyd, Kathy A
Belle Vernon Area
Perryopolis, PA

Lloyd, Mark W
Susquehanna Township HS
Harrisburg, PA

Lobel, Susan
New Hope-Solebury
Doylestown, PA

Lober, Walt
Mc Guffey SR HS
Washington, PA

Lobley, Jennifer
New Hope Solebury JR SR HS
New Hope, PA

Lobron, Neil
Saint Josephs Preparatory HS
Philadelphia, PA

Lockard, Jennifer
Immaculate Conception HS
Washington, PA

Lockard, Shelly
Chestnut Ridge SR
Imler, PA

Lockerman, Laurie
Vincentian HS
Pittsburgh, PA

Lockett, Monica
Valley HS
New Kensington, PA

Lockwood, Deborah A
Kutztown Area HS
Kutztown, PA

Loercher, Lauren
Warwick HS
Lititz, PA

Lohr, Christina
Bensalem HS
Bensalem, PA

Lombardo, Danielle
St Maria Goretti HS
Philadelphia, PA

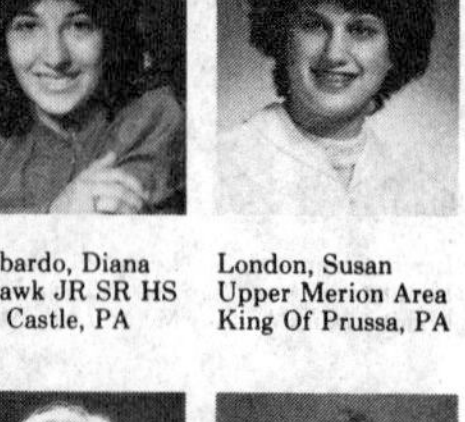
Lombardo, Diana
Mohawk JR SR HS
New Castle, PA

London, Susan
Upper Merion Area
King Of Prussa, PA

Long, Penny
Pine Grove Area HS
Tremont, PA

Long, Sandy
Downingtown HS
Downingtown, PA

Longenbach, Lynn
Allentown Central Catholic HS
Allentwn, PA

Longman, Abbe M
Radnor HS
Villanova, PA

Longnecker, Mark
Red Lion Area SR
Red Lion, PA

Longo, Carmela
St Maria Goretti HS
Philadelphia, PA

Longo, Peter
Girard Academic Music Program
Philadelphia, PA

Lopez, Donato
Pennsbury HS
Fairless Hills, PA

Lorah, Audra
W Hazleton HS
Ringtown, PA

Lorah, Heather
Moon SR HS
Corapolis, PA

Lord, Cathy
Mt Alvernia HS
Pittsburgh, PA

Lord, Lisa
Creative &
Performing Arts
Philadelphia, PA

Lordi, Toni
Lincoln HS
Ellwood City, PA

Loriso, Robert
South Park HS
Library, PA

Loucks, Thaddeus
James
Altoona Area HS
Altoona, PA

Louder, Dana
Clarion Area HS
Clarion, PA

Loughery, Rob
Central Bucks East
Warrington, PA

Loutzenhiser,
Timothy Paul
East Pennsporo HS
Enola, PA

Lovelace, Mauri
Hanover HS
Hanover, PA

Loving, Debbie
Bethlehem Catholic
Hellertown, PA

Lovrinic, Christine
Tunkhannock Area
Tunkhannock, PA

Lowden, Melissa
Shaler Area HS
Glenshaw, PA

Lowe, Eric
Manheim Central
SR HS
Manheim, PA

Lowe, James P
Muncy JR SR HS
Muncy, PA

Lowe, Rod
Great Valley SR HS
Malvern, PA

Lower, David A
Richland HS
Gibsonia, PA

Lowery, Enjay
Wilkinsburg JRSR
Pittsburgh, PA

Lowery, Leann
Northwestern HS
Albion, PA

Lowry, Mardi A
State College Area
State College, PA

Lowson, Alan
Waynesboro SR HS
Mont Alto, PA

Lubinski, Lynn
Tunkhannock Area
Tunkhannock, PA

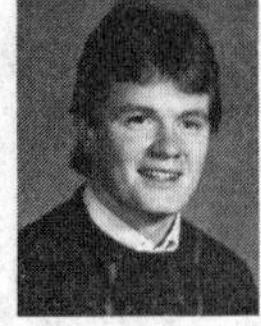
Luby, Dave
Bensalem SR HS
Bensalem, PA

Lucas, Kelly
North Allegheny HS
Pittsburgh, PA

Lucas, Pamela
Bald Eagle Area JR
SR HS
Howard, PA

Lucas, Tracy L
Freeport SR HS
Freeport, PA

Lucchetti, Louis
Central Catholic HS
Allentown, PA

Lucci, Joseph
Center HS
Aliquippa, PA

Lucci, Robert
Chartiers Valley HS
Pittsburgh, PA

Luchko, Robin
Dunmore HS
Dunmore, PA

Luckenbaugh,
Daniel
Central York SR HS
York, PA

Luckey, Judith
Elizabeth Forward
Elizabeth, PA

Luckock, David R
Conneaut Lake HS
Conneaut Lake, PA

Ludovici, Amy
Ambridge Area HS
Ambridge, PA

Luffey, William
Moon SR HS
Coraopolis, PA

Luffy, Elizabeth
Moon SR HS
Coraopolis, PA

Luft, Donna
Exeter SR HS
Reading, PA

Luisi, Kimberly P
Kiski Area HS
Apollo, PA

Luisi, Kristin
Canon Mc Millan
Canonsburg, PA

Lukos, Kimberlee
Moon Area HS
Coraopolis, PA

Luncher, Mark
Penn Hills SR HS
Pittsburgh, PA

Lupold, Linda
Solanco HS
New Providence, PA

Luptak, Sheryl
Wilmington Area
New Bedford, PA

Luque, Eric
Conestoga Valley
Leola, PA

Lusckay, Dori
West Mifflin Area
W Mifflin, PA

Lusk, Bill
Chapel Christian
Bentleyville, PA

Lutton, Alan
Sun Valley HS
Aston, PA

Lutz, George
Columbia Montour
Danville, PA

Lutz, Kenneth
West Side Vo Tech
Courtdale, PA

Lutz, Michael
Danville SR HS
Danville, PA

Lutz, Susan L
Conrad Weiser HS
Womelsdorf, PA

Lutz, Vikki L
Hempfield Area SR
Jeannette, PA

Lutzi, Dawn
Wilson Area HS
Easton, PA

Luzier, Cathy
Clearfield Area HS
Clearfield, PA

Luzier, Jeff
Clearfield Area HS
Clearfield, PA

Lydick, Terri L
Blairsville SR HS
Blairsville, PA

Lyman, Jennifer
Downingtown SR
Downingtown, PA

Lyman, Shannon
Coudersport JR SR
Coudersport, PA

Lyman, Steve
Greater Latrobe HS
Greensburg, PA

Lynch, Jeanine
Abington Heights
Clarks Summit, PA

Lynch, Kathleen V
Cardinal Dougherty
Cheltenham, PA

Lynch, Kris
Archbishop Wood
HS For Boys
Warminster, PA

Lynch, Sherry
Owen J Roberts HS
Spring City, PA

Lynn, Sandy
Ford City HS
Ford City, PA

Lyons, Linda
Butler Area SR HS
Connoquenessing,
PA

Lysaght, James
Cardinal O Hara HS
Warrenton, VA

Lysek, Spencer M
Saucon Valley HS
Bethlehem, PA

Maben, Paul
Wissahickon HS
Springhouse, PA

Mabius, Bryan J
East Pennsboro HS
Summerdale, PA

Mac Farland, Mike
Carlynton HS
Carnegie, PA

Mac Krell, Garry
Karns City Area HS
Chicora, PA

Machamer, Michele
Northwest Area HS
Hunlock Creek, PA

Macher, Scott
West Allegheny SR
Coraopolis, PA

Mack, Edward L
H S For Perform &
Creative Arts
Philadelphia, PA

Mackewicz, David
Pottstown HS
Pottstown, PA

Macomber, Mary
Claysburg-Kimmel
Portage, PA

Macwilliams, Laura
Lynn
Harborcreek JR/SR
Erie, PA

Madaya, Kevin
Northampton Area
Northampton, PA

Maddas, Mardi
Connellsville SR HS
Dunbar, PA

Madden, Pamela
Knoch JR SR HS
Butler, PA

Madden, Sandra A
Gwynedd-Mercy
Acad HS
Churchville, PA

Madison, Marc A
La Salle College HS
Philadelphia, PA

Madonna, Nan
Ambridge HS
Alquippa, PA

Madonna, Sandra A
Penn Cambria HS
Gallitzin, PA

Madore, Eric
Connellsville Area
Cnlvle, PA

Magaro, Stephanie
Northern HS
Wellsville, PA

Magda, Frank Alan
Bethlehem-Center
Millsboro, PA

Magdich, Mary
Anne
Canon Mc Millan
SR HS
Canonsburg, PA

Magera, George
Bentworth SR HS
Cokeburg, PA

Maggs, Michele
Henderson HS
West Chester, PA

Magill, Mike
Philipsburg Osceola
SR HS
Sandy Ridge, PA

Magiso, Peter
Marple Newtown
Newtown Square,
PA

Magnotta, Joe H
Center HS
Monaca, PA

Mahlon, Barbara J
Curwensville Area
Grampion, PA

Maholic, Julie
Council Rock HS
Richboro, PA

Maier, Christine
Greater Works Acad
Pittsburgh, PA

Main, George
Trinity HS
Washington, PA

Maiorano, Rosanne
St Maria Goretti HS
Philadelphia, PA

Maisano, Anita
St Maria Goretti HS
Philadelphia, PA

Maish, III George O
Saucon Valley HS
Bethlehem, PA

Majumdar, Joey
Quigley HS
Monaca, PA

Makaravage, Donna
G A R Memorial HS
Wilkes-Barre, PA

Malarney, Katie
Cumberland Valley
Mechanicsburg, PA

Malick, Jr Earl J
Shikellamy HS
Sunbury, PA

Malicki, Mark
Philipsburg Osceola
Area HS
Philipsburg, PA

Malingowski, Chris
Behtel Park HS
Bethel Pk, PA

Malinsky, Michael
Albert Gallatin SR
Masontown, PA

Malkowski, Robert
Northeast Catholic
Philadelphia, PA

Malloy, Bernadette
Christian School Of
York HS
York, PA

Malloy, Michelle
Freeport Area HS
Sarver, PA

Malloy, Tammy A
Bethel Park HS
Bethel Park, PA

Maloney, Kristen
Gettysburg SR HS
Gettysburg, PA

Manasseri, Michelle
Pen Argyl Area HS
Pen Argyl, PA

Mancuso, Greg
Sacred Heart HS
Carbondale, PA

Mandalakas, Anna
Norwin SR HS
N Huntingdon, PA

Maney, Douglas
Bald Eagle Area HS
Karthaus, PA

Manfredi, Michael
Bishop Hafey HS
Hazleton, PA

Mangini, Melissa
Greater Latrobe SR
Crabtree, PA

Manker, Gordon
David B Oliver HS
Pittsburgh, PA

Mankevich, Marilyn
Sharyl
Seneca Valley SR
Mars, PA

Manko, Gerard
Our Lady Of The
Sacred Heart HS
Ambridge, PA

Manley, Laura
Celeste
Country Day School
Of The Sacred
Haverford, PA

Mann, Kelly
South Park JR SR
Library, PA

Mann, Patricia
Altoona Area HS
Altoona, PA

Mann, Tabitha R
David B Oliver HS
Pittsburgh, PA

Manning, Jami
Trinity HS
Washington, PA

Manning, Jeffrey S
Hempfield HS
Lancaster, PA

Manno, James
Elk County
Christian HS
Ridgway, PA

Mansberger, James
Mount Union Area
Calvin, PA

Mansfield, Brian
West York Area HS
York, PA

Mansur, Andrew K
Downingtown HS
Downingtown, PA

Mantel, Brian K
Liberty HS
Bethlehem, PA

Mantz, Lee
Panther Valley
Jointure HS
Summit Hill, PA

Mao, Kelvin
Emmaus HS
Emmaus, PA

Marasco, Michael
Farrell SR HS
Farrell, PA

Marburger, Gregory
E
Seneca Valley HS
Harmony, PA

Marchesini,
Claudette
Bethlehem Center
Millsboro, PA

Marcheski, Jennifer
A
Danville HS
Danville, PA

Marchetti, Jr
Anthony
St Josephs Prep
Philadelphia, PA

Marchetti, Danielle
Bishop Hafey HS
Hazleton, PA

Mardis, Pamela A
United HS
Vintondale, PA

Maresco, Rita
St Maria Goretti HS
Philadelphia, PA

Marhanka, Curtis
Greensburg Salem
Delmont, PA

Marhefka, Susan
Upper Dublin HS
Maple Glen, PA

Mariano, Darren
Canevin HS
Pittsburgh, PA

Marine, Kathleen
St Puis X HS
Pottstown, PA

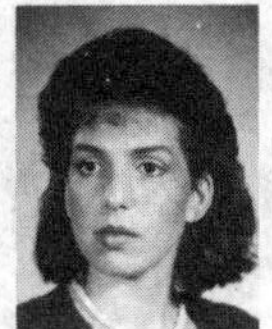
Marino, Angela
Pleasant Valley HS
Wind Gap, PA

Marino, Suzanna
Northern Cambria
Barnesboro, PA

Mark, Julie
Bellefonte Area HS
Howard, PA

Markee, Kathleen
West Philadelphia
Catholic Girls
Philadelphia, PA

Markey, Karen
Christian School Of
York HS
York, PA

Markiewich, Carla
Carmichaels Area
JR SR HS
Carmichaels, PA

Markowski, Annette
Conrad Wriser
Womelsdorf, PA

Marks, Sean
Downingtown SR
West Chester, PA

Marley, Todd A
Canon Mc Millan
Mc Murray, PA

Marmagin, Joelle
Ambridge Area HS
Baden, PA

Marnell, Mary
Greensburg Central
Catholic HS
Greensburg, PA

Maronic, Daryl
Central Dauphin HS
Harrisburg, PA

Marotta, Paul
Notre Dame HS
E Stroudsburg, PA

Marouchoc, Jim
Freedom HS
Allentown, PA

Marquardt, Mark
North Hills HS
Pittsburgh, PA

Marraccini, Mark
Elizabeth Forward
Elizabeth, PA

Marsh, James E
Greater Latrobe HS
Latrobe, PA

Marsh, Kelly A
Trinty HS
Washington, PA

Marsh, Lori
Ambridge Area HS
Baden, PA

Marshall, Richard
Chambersburg Area
SR HS
Chambersburg, PA

Marsteller, Gary
Lakeview HS
Sandy Lake, PA

Martin, Aliza
Greater Works Acad
Pittsburgh, PA

Martin, Bernard G
Lancaster Catholic
Columbia, PA

Martin, Curtis
Cocalico HS
Denver, PA

Martin, Deborah
North Allegheny HS
Pittsburgh, PA

Martin, Eldred
Chad
Charleroi Area HS
Stockdale, PA

Martin, Greg
Upper Dublin HS
Dresher, PA

Martin, Heather
United HS
Seward, PA

Martin, Karen
Carbondale Area JR
SR HS
Carbondale, PA

Martin, Lisa
West Perry HS
Shermans Dale, PA

Martin, Michelle R
Williamsburg HS
Williamsburg, PA

Martinak, Lori
Belle Vernon Area
Fayette, PA

Martinelli, Bernard
Waynesburg Central
Waynesburg, PA

Martinie, John
Devon Preparatory
Exton, PA

Martino, Paul
Upper Moreland SR
Hatboro, PA

Martinsen, Dana
Bensalem HS
Bensalem, PA

Martocci, Joseph
Pius X HS
Roseto, PA

Martz, Dana Lee
Line Mountain HS
Dalmatia, PA

Masci, Mary Beth
Sheffield Area JR
SR HS
Clarendon, PA

Masci, Valerie
St Maria Goretti HS
Philadelphia, PA

Mascilli, Scott
Valley HS
Arnold, PA

Masi, Sonia Rene
Punxsutawney Area
Punxsutawney, PA

Maskrey, Kris
Plum SR HS
Pittsburgh, PA

Maslowski, Scott
State College Area
State College, PA

Masney, Jr Richard
Mon Valley Catholic
Merrittstown, PA

Mason, David
Waynesburg Central
Morgantown, WV

Mason, Perry
Purchase Line HS
Commodore, PA

Mason, Richard T
Du Bois Area HS
Du Bois, PA

Massaro, Paul
New Castle SR HS
New Castle, PA

Massey, Audrey
Marie
Methacton SR HS
Collegeville, PA

Massey, Cynthia
Greater Latrobe HS
Greensburg, PA

Mastrangelo,
Christine
Canon-Mc Millan
SR HS
Muse, PA

Mastrangelo, Lisa
Interboro HS
Prospect Park, PA

Mastroianni, Angela
Bishop Hannan HS
Scranton, PA

Matarazzi, Jenny
Lebanon County
AVTS HS
Lebanon, PA

Mateer, IV John C
Upper Dauphin
Area HS
Elizabethville, PA

Mathias, Dénise
Spring Grove SR HS
Spring Grove, PA

Mathias, Patrick
Hershey HS
Hummelstown, PA

Mathna, Pam
Shippensburg Area
SR HS
Newburg, PA

Matia, Robert
Moshanon Valley
Houtzdale, PA

Matlock, Kellee
Pius X HS
Nazerath, PA

Matos, Stacey E
Freedom HS
Bethlehem, PA

Matsinger, Lisa
John Bartram HS
Philadelphia, PA

Mattei, Martin
Old Forge HS
Old Forge, PA

Matteo, Kristen
Kiski Area SR HS
Apollo, PA

Matter, Heather
Sacred Heart HS
Pittsburgh, PA

Mattson, John
Coatesville Area SR
Coatesville, PA

Matyjevich, Pete
West Scranton HS
Scranton, PA

Matz, Terrie
Governor Mifflin SR
Mohnton, PA

Mauger, Janet L
Methacton HS
Audubon, PA

Maurer, III Charles
V
Nativity B V M HS
Pottsville, PA

Mavrich, Angie
Hopewell HS
Aliquippa, PA

Mawby, Andrea
Britt
Villa Maria HS
New Castle, PA

Maximo, Lisa
Cardinal O Hara HS
Berwyn, PA

Maxwell, Scott L
Seneca Valley HS
Evans City, PA

May, Jr Ronald
John S Vine HS
Nanticoke, PA

May, Terry
Connellsville Area
SR HS
Mill Run, PA

May, Todd
Trinity HS
Camp Hill, PA

Maylish, David
Upper Darby HS
Secane, PA

Maynard, Inger
Marlo
Cheltenham HS
Elkins Pk, PA

Mazur, Michelle
Ambridge Area HS
Baden, PA

Mazzatesta, Jennifer
Susquehanna
Township HS
Harrisburg, PA

Mazzei, Damian
New Brighton Area
New Brighton, PA

Mazzoni, Carla M
Carbondale Area HS
Carbondale, PA

Mazzuca, David
Millville HS
Benton, PA

Mc Adoo, James
Punxsutawney SR
Glen Campbell, PA

Mc Afee, Heather
West Hazleton HS
Zion Grove, PA

Mc Aleer, Lori
Freedom HS
Bethlehem, PA

Mc Anlis, Colleen
Mohjawk Area JR
HS HS
Enon Valley, PA

Mc Bride, Karon
Seneca Valley SR
Evans City, PA

Mc Cabe, Tracey
John
Connellsville Area
SR HS
Mt Pleasant, PA

Mc Cafferty,
Malinda
Interboro HS
Essington, PA

Mc Cain, James
Meadville Area SR
Meadville, PA

Mc Callion, George
St John Neumann
Philadelphia, PA

Mc Candless, David
M
James Buchanan HS
Mercersburg, PA

Mc Cann, Michael
Canon Mcmillan HS
Canonsburg, PA

Mc Canney, Marsha
A
Central HS
Philadelphia, PA

Mc Cardle, Jennifer
Chief Logan HS
Yeagertown, PA

Mc Cartney, Erin
Marian HS
Mahanoy City, PA

Mc Cartney, Nancy
Bald Eagle Area HS
Howard, PA

Mc Carty, Trudy L
Charleroi Area JR
SR HS
Van Voorhis, PA

Mc Causland, Nancy
Jamestown Area JR
SR HS
Jamestown, PA

Mc Clain, Becky
Belle Vernon Area
Belle Vernon, PA

Mc Claine, Toni
Punxsutawney Area
Punxsutawney, PA

Mc Cleary, Heather
Grove City HS
Grove City, PA

Mc Clellan, Cindy
West Greene HS
Sycamore, PA

Mc Closkey, James
Bristol JR SR HS
Bristol, PA

Mc Closkey, Scott
Bellwood Antis HS
Bellwood, PA

Mc Clung, Sandra
Downingtown SR
Glenmoore, PA

Mc Clure, Brian D
Central HS
Martinsburg, PA

Mc Clymonds, Ann
Grove City Area SR
Grove City, PA

Mc Connell, Christie
Fairview HS
Erie, PA

Mc Conville, Melissa
Freeport SR HS
Sarver, PA

Mc Cormick, Diana
L
Mc Guffey HS
Washington, PA

Mc Cowan, Debbie
Warwick HS
Lititz, PA

Mc Coy, Amy Jo
Ambridge Area HS
Ambridge, PA

Mc Coy, Margo
Oil City HS
Franklin, PA

Mc Coy, Mary
Grove City Area SR
Slippery Rock, PA

Mc Cracken, Andrea
Commodore Perry
Hadley, PA

Mc Cray, Darren
Corry Area HS
Corry, PA

Mc Cray, Michael L
Central HS
Philadelphia, PA

Mc Crea, Michael
North Hills HS
Pittsburgh, PA

Mc Cuch, Thomas A
Devon Prep
Gulph Mills, PA

Mc Cullough, David
Mercer Area HS
Mercer, PA

Mc Cullough,
Douglas
Belle Vernon Area
Belle Vernon, PA

Mc Cullough, Kelly
Bishop Shanahan
W Chester, PA

Mc Cullough, Tom
Lanape AVTS
Worthington, PA

Mc Cutcheon, Amy
Cornell Education
Coraopolis, PA

Mc Cutcheon, Linda
Riverview HS
Oakmont, PA

Mc Dade, Craig
William
Elk County
Christian HS
Johnsonburg, PA

Mc Dade, Karen
Penn Hills SR HS
Verona, PA

Mc Dermott, Nicole
Marple Newtown
Newtown Square,
PA

Mc Dermott,
Stephanie
St Maria Goretti HS
Philadelphia, PA

Mc Donald, Colleen
Lancaster Catholic
Lancaster, PA

Mc Donald, Maria
Purchase Line HS
Cherry Tree, PA

Mc Donald, Tammy
Belle Vernon Area
Belle Vernon, PA

Mc Donald, Tisa
Danville SR HS
Danville, PA

Mc Donnell, Kelly
St Basil Acad
Philadelphia, PA

Mc Donnell, Patrick J
State College Area SR HS
State College, PA

Mc Donnell, Stephen
Eastern Montgomery C
Cheltenham, PA

Mc Donnell, William
St Josephs Prep
Drexel Hill, PA

Mc Donough, Linda
Cardinal O Hara HS
Broomall, PA

Mc Dyre, Cullen
Central Bucks High School East
Furlong, PA

Mc Elhaney, Cheryl
Connellsville Area SR HS
S Connellsville, PA

Mc Elhaney, Melanie
Connellsville SR HS
So Connellsville, PA

Mc Ewen, Heidi
Canon-Mc Millan
Eighty Four, PA

Mc Fadden, Kenneth J
Northeast Catholic
Philadelphia, PA

Mc Fadden, Michele
Bethel Park HS
Bethel Park, PA

Mc Farland, Sean
Bishop Hannan HS
Old Forge, PA

Mc Garry, Daniel
Hazleton SR HS
Hazleton, PA

Mc Gee, Kim
Mc Keesport SR HS
Mckeesport, PA

Mc Gee, III Tim F
Marian Catholic HS
Lehighton, PA

Mc Gettigan, David
Council Rock HS
Holland, PA

Mc Gill, Danielle
Acad Of Notre Dame De Namur
Springfield, PA

Mc Ginley, Joseph
Cardinal O Hara HS
Broomall, PA

Mc Ginley, Melissa
Butler HS
Renfrew, PA

Mc Ginnis, Marlo
Ligonier Valley SR
Ligonier, PA

Mc Givern, Pat
Hopewell SR HS
Aliquippa, PA

Mc Glynn, Michele
Blacklick Valley JR SR HS
Twin Rocks, PA

Mc Gonagle, Denise
Council Rock HS
Churchville, PA

Mc Govern, Shaun
Cardinal O Hara HS
Drexel Hill, PA

Mc Gowan, Brian
Fort Le Boeuf HS
Erie, PA

Mc Gowan, Cathy
Cardinal O Hara HS
Havertown, PA

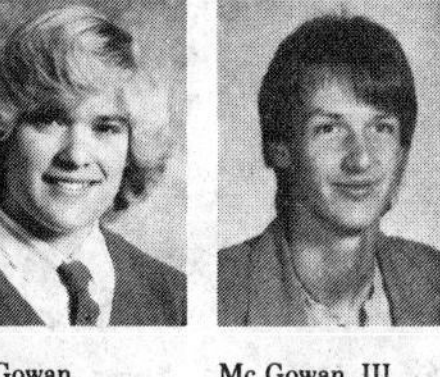
Mc Gowan, Kimberly L
The Christian Acad
Media, PA

Mc Gowan, III Nicholas
Saucon Valley SR
Bethlehem, PA

Mc Granahan, Devin
Warren Area HS
Warren, PA

Mc Grath, Dennis
Mars Area HS
Mars, PA

Mc Graw, Robert
West Scranton HS
Scranton, PA

Mc Grosky, Mark
Bethel Park HS
Bethel Pk, PA

Mc Grotty, Kyle
Upper Moreland HS
Huntingdon Vly, PA

Mc Guckin, Tracey
St Maria Goretti HS
Philadelphia, PA

Mc Guigan, Patrick J
Clarion Area JR SR
Clarion, PA

Mc Guire, Margaret
Monn SR HS
Coraopolis, PA

Mc Gurrin, Patrick
Technical HS
Scranton, PA

Mc Hale, Denise
Little Flower HS
Philadelphia, PA

Mc Hugh, Lisa
Cardinal O Hara HS
Broomall, PA

Mc Intire, Tammy
Waynesburg Central
Mt Morris, PA

Mc Kee, Alicia
Hollidaysburg SR
Hollidaysburg, PA

Mc Kee, Kelly
Milton SR HS
New Columbia, PA

Mc Kee, Veronica
Upper Darby SR HS
Primos, PA

Mc Keever, Joe
New Hope Solebury
Doylestown, PA

Mc Keever, Scott
Saltsburg JR SR HS
Clarksburg, PA

Mc Keown, Shannon
Manheim Township
Leola, PA

Mc Kimm, Jr Ralph
Cameron County HS
Emporium, PA

Mc Kinney, Colleen Renee
Ringgold HS
Finleyville, PA

Mc Kinney, Michael S
Bishop Shanahan
West Chester, PA

Mc Kinney, Rebecca
Seneca Valley SR
Evans City, PA

Mc Kissock, Matt
Youngsville HS
Youngsville, PA

Mc Kito, Joe
Ringgold HS
Donora, PA

Mc Kown, Michael T
Sheffield Area JR SR HS
Sheffield, PA

Mc Kruit, Christine
Valley SR HS
New Kensington, PA

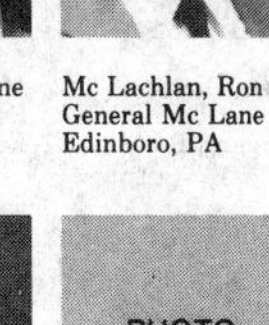
Mc Lachlan, Ron
General Mc Lane
Edinboro, PA

Mc Lain, Lori
North Pocono HS
Moscow, PA

Mc Lain, Phyllis Anaice
West Phila Catholic Girls HS
Richmond, VA

Mc Laughlin, II Charles W
Ringgold HS
Donora, PA

Mc Laughlin, Laura
Wilmington Area
New Wilmington, PA

Mc Laughlin, Michelle
New Hope-Solebury
New Hope, PA

Mc Leod, Karen
Du Bois Area SR
Reynoldsville, PA

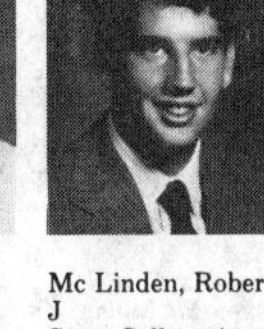
Mc Linden, Robert J
State College Area SR HS
Port Matilda, PA

Mc Mahon, Amy
Bradford Area HS
Bradford, PA

Mc Mahon, Kelli
Bensalem HS
Bensalem, PA

PHOTO NOT AVAILABLE

Mc Mahon, Mary
West Greene HS
Waynesburg, PA

Mc Mahon, Patricia
Boyertown SR HS
Green Lane, PA

Mc Mullen, Mark
Blacklick Valley HS
Nanty Glo, PA

Mc Navish, Lori
Chartiers-Houston
Houston, PA

Mc Neal, Caroline
Sayre Area HS
Sayre, PA

Mc Neal, Greg
Sheffield HS
Sheffield, PA

Mc Nicholas, Megan A
Archbishop Ryan HS For Girls
Philadelphia, PA

Mc Nulty, Kelly
Lower Dauphin SR
Middletown, PA

Mc Phelim, Barbara
Archbishop John Carroll HS
Audubon, PA

Mc Queen, Julie
Chambersburg Area SR HS
Fayetteville, PA

Mc Queen, Todd
Coatesville Area SR
Coatesville, PA

Mc Sparran, Vicki
Elizabethtown Area
Elizabethtown, PA

Mc Swain, William
West Chester Henderson HS
West Chester, PA

Mc Tavish, Lori
Clearfield HS
W Decatur, PA

Mc Tiernan, Kelly
Norwin SR HS
N Huntingdon, PA

Mc Williams, Sean
Norristown Area HS
Norristown, PA

Meadow, Shari
Central Bucks West
Chalfont, PA

Meadows, Cheryl
New Hope-Solebury JR SR HS
New Hope, PA

Means, Paul
Connellsville Area
Connellsville, PA

Mearkle, Sheri Dee
Shippensburg HS
Shippensburg, PA

Mech, Barbara Ann
Hanover Area JR-SR HS
Ashley, PA

Meckley, Ann Margaret
Chambersburg Area SR HS
Chambersburg, PA

Medina, Mabel
Central Catholic HS
Walnutport, PA

Medina, Patricia
Bentworth SR HS
Bentleyville, PA

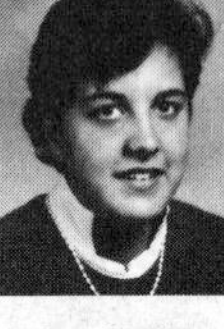

Medrick, Linda
Meadville Area HS
Meadville, PA

Meehan, Jennifer
Central Dauphin HS
Harrisburg, PA

Mehallo, Christopher
West Hazleton HS
Harwood, PA

Meisenbach, Michelle
Bishop Conwell HS
Melbourne, FL

Melego, Larry
Mt Pleasant Area
Mt Pleasant, PA

Mellinger, Heather
Eastern York HS
Wrightsville, PA

Mellor, Jennifer
Little Flower Catholic H S Fo
Philadelphia, PA

Melovich, Suzanne
Pennsburg HS
Levittown, PA

Melton, William C
Hollidaysburg Area
Hollidaysburg, PA

Mendola, Edward
Charleroi Area HS
Charleroi, PA

Mengel, Tim
Hamburg Area HS
Hamburg, PA

Menkel, Linda Sherri Arlene
John A Brashear HS
Pittsburgh, PA

Mensinger, Racquel
Hazleton HS
Hazleton, PA

Mercadante, Lisa Ann
Hopewell HS
Aliquippa, PA

Mercaldo, Vittoria Maria
Bishop Neumann
Williamsport, PA

Merlino, Joann
Creative And Performing Arts
Philadelphia, PA

Merlot, Tracy
Riverview HS
Oakmont, PA

Merschat, John
Turkeyfoot Valley Area HS
Markleysburg, PA

Mershon, II Charles
Blue Ride HS
New Milford, PA

Mershon, Jill
Blue Ridge HS
New Milford, PA

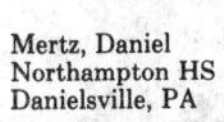

Mertz, Daniel
Northampton HS
Danielsville, PA

Mertz, Kim
Lehighton Area HS
Lehighton, PA

Mertz, Matt
Northampton HS
Walnutport, PA

Mesaros, Jody
William Allen HS
Allentown, PA

Meshyock, Lacrisha
Huntingdoin Area
Mill Creek, PA

Mesich, Beth Ann
Albert Gallatin SR
Masontown, PA

Mesnar, Ginger
Highlands SR HS
Tarentum, PA

Messenger, Michael
Fort Le Boeuf HS
Waterford, PA

Metcalfe, Sonya
Charleroi HS
Charleroi, PA

Metheny, Dana K
Trinity HS
Washington, PA

Metro, Michael
Marian Catholic HS
Lansford, PA

Metz, Bill
Bensalem HS
Bensalem, PA

Metz, Donna
Greater Latrobe SR
Latrobe, PA

Metz, Gail
Exeter Township SR
Reading, PA

Metz, Kathy
Bensalem HS
Bensalem, PA

Metz, Lisa
Hamburg Area HS
Hamburg, PA

Metzler, Ross
Manheim Central
Manheim, PA

Meyer, David
The Baptist HS
Clarks Summit, PA

Meyer, Kristen M
Canon Mc Millan
Canonsburg, PA

Meyer, Mark
Wyoming Seminary College Prep Schl
Kingston, PA

Meyer, Vicki
Burrell HS
Lower Burrell, PA

Meyers, George
Northeast Catholic
Philadelphia, PA

Meyers, Stephanie
James Buchanan HS
St Thomas, PA

Mezan, Kelly
Jefferson-Morgan
Rices Landing, PA

Michael, Tara
Northern Lebanon
Fredericksburg, PA

Michael, Vicki
Northern Lebanon
Jonestown, PA

Michalka, Denise
Canon-Mc Millan SR HS
Mc Donald, PA

Michel, Ricardo
West Catholic Boys
Phila, PA

Michell, Brian
Archbishop Jon Carroll HS
W Conshohocken, PA

Michuck, Ronna
Brockway Area HS
Brockway, PA

Mickel, Christine
William Allen HS
Allentown, PA

Mickey, Scott
Penn Trafford HS
Trafford, PA

Micsky, Russell
James
Reynolds HS
Greenville, PA

Middekauff, Ronda
Lackawanna Trail
Dalton, PA

Middleton, Brett
Pleasant Valley HS
Sciota, PA

Mihoci, Mike
Conneaut Lake HS
Conneault Lake, PA

Mika, Molly
James M Coughlin
Wilkes Barre, PA

Mika, Pamela
Burgettstown Area
JRSR HS
Burgettstown, PA

Mikhael, Juliet
Dinkha
Waynesboro SR HS
Odessa, TX

Mikita, Kelly
North Schuylkill HS
Ringtown, PA

Mikovch, Eric J
Northwestern HS
Cranesville, PA

Miksa, Lorri
Saint Hubert H S
For Girls
Philadelphia, PA

Mikula, Eric
Altoona Area HS
Altoona, PA

Miley, Arthur
Carbondale Area
JR-SR HS
Carbondale, PA

Milkent, Heather
Belle Vernon Area
Belle Vernon, PA

Milkovich, Amy
Westmon Hilltop
Johnstown, PA

Miller, Bart
Dover Area HS
Dover, PA

Miller, Brandy
Wilson Area HS
Easton, PA

Miller, Brett
Liberty HS
Bethlehem, PA

Miller, Camela
Central Dauphin
East HS
Dauphin, PA

Miller, Chad
Palmyra HS
Palmyra, PA

Miller, Christine
Altoona Area HS
Altoona, PA

Miller, Christopher
William Penn SR
York, PA

Miller, Christy
Peters Township HS
Mcmurray, PA

Miller, Corey D
Bellefonte SR HS
Bellefonte, PA

Miller, Dale
Aliquippa HS
Aliquippa, PA

Miller, Dane R
Mc Connellsburg HS
Big Cove Tannery,
PA

Miller, David
Lompeter Strasburg
Strasburg, PA

Miller, Debra
Lock Haren SR HS
Castanea, PA

Miller, Elizabeth
Benton Area HS
Orangeville, PA

Miller, Erik R
Emmaus HS
Allentown, PA

Miller, Heather
Central HS
Martinsburg, PA

Miller, Heather
Cocalico HS
Reamstown, PA

Miller, Heather
Scranton Technical
Scranton, PA

Miller, James
Pine Grove Area HS
Pine Grove, PA

Miller, James
Portersville
Christian Schl
Portersville, PA

Miller, Jeff
Harmony Area HS
Cherry Tree, PA

Miller, Jennifer
Cumberland Valley
Mechanicsburg, PA

Miller, John
Conrad Weiser HS
Robesonia, PA

Miller, Kara
Ringgold HS
Eighty Four, PA

Miller, Karen
Mechanicsburg SR
Mechanicsburg, PA

Miller, Kristine
Bellwood-Antis HS
Bellwood, PA

Miller, Lisa
Cambridge Springs
Cambridge Springs,
PA

Miller, Michael
Lewisburg Area HS
Lewisburg, PA

Miller, Michael
Marple Newtown SR
Newtown Square,
PA

Miller, Paul
J N Coughlin HS
Wilkes Barre, PA

Miller, Quentin
Lancaster
Mennonite HS
Mt Joy, PA

Miller, Roberta F
St Puis X HS
Pottstown, PA

Miller, Roxanne
Lock Haven SR HS
Castanea, PA

Miller, Scott A
Mechanicsburg HS
Mechanicsburg, PA

Miller, Shane
Greater Lafrobe SR
Youngstown, PA

Miller, Shannon
Hollidaysburg Area
SR HS
Hollidaysburg, PA

Miller, Sherry Lynn
Central Bucks HS
Doylestown, PA

Miller, Teri
Mt Pleasant Area
Mt Pleasant, PA

Miller, Tracy
Rocky Grove JR SR
Franklin, PA

Miller, William P
Berwick Area HS
Berwick, PA

Millette, Donna
Oxford Area HS
Lincoln Univ, PA

Millheim, Steven M
Pen Argyl Area HS
Nazareth, PA

Milliner, Karen
Wyoming Valley
West HS
Edwardsville, PA

Mills, Michele
Bishop Shanahan
W Chester, PA

Mills, Richard
Altoona Area HS
Altoona, PA

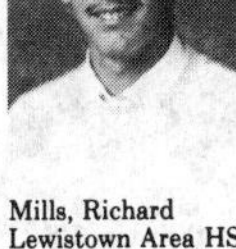
Mills, Richard
Lewistown Area HS
Lewistown, PA

Miloser, Michael
Lincoln HS
Wampum, PA

Minardi, Nicole
Conestoga Valley SR
Leola, PA

Mincer, Christy
Butler Area SR HS
Butler, PA

Minch, Jay
Mc Guffey HS
W Alexander, PA

Minech, Laura
Moon Area SR HS
Coraopolis, PA

Mineweaser, Patricia
J
Brookville Area HS
Brookville, PA

Mingle, Michelle
Bensalem HS
Bensalem, PA

Mink, Therese L
Greater Works Acad
Pittsburgh, PA

Minnich, Ann
Nazareth HS
Nazareth, PA

Mirabella, Mike
Bellwood-Antis HS
Tyrone, PA

Mirasola, Lisa
York Catholic HS
York, PA

Mish, Lori
Conemaugh Twp
Area HS
Davidsville, PA

Mistrano, Sam
Lower Moreland HS
Huntingdon Valley, PA

Mistysyn, Vince
Nativity B V M HS
Pottsville, PA

Mitchell, Andrea
Central Dauphin HS
Harrisburg, PA

Mitchell, Dean A
Smethport Area JR
SR HS
Smethport, PA

Mitchell, Diane
Clearfield Area HS
Clearfield, PA

Mitchell, Donald
Council Rock HS
Churchville, PA

Mitchell, Jill
Waynesboro Area
SR HS
Mont Alto, PA

Mitchell, Lance
Ephrata SR HS
Ephrata, PA

Mitchell, Laurie
Burrell SR HS
Lower Burrell, PA

Mitchell, Letha
Frazier HS
Grindstone, PA

Mitchell, Mellissa
Dianne
Exeter Township
Reiffton, PA

Mitman, Mark
Freedom HS
Bethlehem, PA

Modesitt, Keith
Center HS
Aliquippa, PA

Mody, Bhavana G
Frankford HS
Philadelphia, PA

Moebus, Jonathan
Ringgold HS
Monongahela, PA

Moffa, Anthony
Hatboro Horsham
Horsham, PA

Mohr, Rhonda
Bayertown Area HS
New Berlinvl, PA

Mohr, Thomas
Emmaus HS
Macungie, PA

Mollo, Benjamin
Blairsville SR HS
Blairsville, PA

Molnar, Jr George
M
Frazier HS
Perryopolis, PA

Monaco, Steven
Peters Township HS
Mc Murray, PA

Monahan, Teri
West Scranton HS
Scranton, PA

Moniot, Margot
North Hills SR HS
Glenshaw, PA

Monk, Susan S
Kennett HS
Mendenhall, PA

Monks, Robyn L
Jersey Shore Area
Jersey Shore, PA

Monroe, Andrea La
Shawn
Mt Pleasant SR HS
Mt Pleasant, PA

Montgomery, Donna
Clarion Area HS
Sligo, PA

Montgomery, Edwin
Penn Hills SR HS
Verona, PA

Montgomery, Pattie
Fairview HS
Erie, PA

Moody, John
Shamokin Area HS
Paxinos, PA

Moore, Christian S
Cedar Cliff HS
Camp Hill, PA

Moore, Christina
Northern Chester
County Tech Schl
Phoenixville, PA

Moore, Colleen
Archbishop
Kennedy HS
Conshohocken, PA

Moore, Kevin D
Henderson SR HS
West Chester, PA

Moore, Kristina L
High Schl Of
Engineering An
Philadelphia, PA

Moore, Michael T
Elderton JR-SR HS
Ford City, PA

Moore, Michele
Washington HS
Washington, PA

Moore, Pete
Mt Pleasant Area
Mt Pleasant, PA

Moore, Tim
Bald Eagle-Nittany
Mill Hall, PA

Moore, Wendy
Du Bois Area HS
Reynoldsville, PA

Moorhatch, Steve
Delaware County
Christian Schl
Paoli, PA

Moose, Travis
Emmaus HS
Emmaus, PA

Moran, Kim
Haverford SR HS
Havertown, PA

Morello, Gregory L
Carlisle HS
Carlisle, PA

Morgan, Amy
Union Area HS
New Castle, PA

Morgan, Chris
Newport HS
Newport, PA

Morgan, John
Wm Allen HS
Allentown, PA

Morgan, Michael
Bishop Hoban HS
Kingston, PA

Morgan, Pamela
Saint Huberts HS
Philadelphia, PA

Morgan, Rhonda
Rockwood Area HS
Rockwood, PA

Morgan, Tina
Line Mountain HS
Trevorton, PA

Morgano, Viola
Sacred Heart HS
Pittsburgh, PA

Morocco, Mary Ann
Penn-Trafford SR
Irwin, PA

Morreale, Dawn
Coughlin HS
Plains, PA

Morrell, Marc J
Pennridge HS
Sellersville, PA

Morris, Cheryl
Scranton Central
Scranton, PA

Morris, III Harris L
Penncrest HS
Media, PA

Morris, Sonja
Central Dauphin
East HS
Harrisburg, PA

Morrison, Colette
Warrne Area HS
Warren, PA

Morrison, Jerry
Clearfield Area HS
Clearfield, PA

Morrison, Lynne
South Western HS
Hanover, PA

Morrow, Julie
Upper Darby HS
Upper Darby, PA

Morrow, Megan
Freeport Area HS
Freeport, PA

Morrow, Susan
Plum SR HS
Pitts, PA

Morse, Karin
Northwestern HS
E Springfield, PA

Mort, Mark
United HS
Seward, PA

Mosier, Jr Frank A
Manheim Township
Lancaster, PA

Mosier, Joy Dawn
Belle Vernon Area
Belle Vernon, PA

Moskyok, Debra Jean
Gateway SR HS
Monroeville, PA

Mosley, Sue Juan
Susqushanna SR HS
Harrisburg, PA

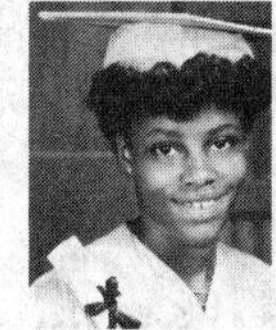
Moss, Lisa
William Penn HS
Philadelphia, PA

Moss, Richard
West Catholic Boys
Phila, PA

Mossel, Lisa
Unionville HS
Chadds Ford, PA

Mountain, Maryjane B
Baldwin SR HS
Pittsburgh, PA

Mowrey, Kelly
Yough SR HS
Herminie, PA

Mowry, Wally
Hyndman Middle SR HS
Hyndman, PA

Moye, Monique
St Benedict Acad
Erie, PA

Moyer, Beth
Berwick SR HS
Berwick, PA

Moyer, Bob
Lincoln HS
Ellwood City, PA

Moyer, Bruce
Liberty HS
Bethlehem, PA

Moyer, Jaclyn L
Ephrata HS
Ephrata, PA

Moyer, Melissa
Kutztown Area HS
Lenhartsville, PA

Mozes, Raymond P
Commodore Perry
Greenville, PA

Mozina, Samantha
Cambria Heights HS
Patton, PA

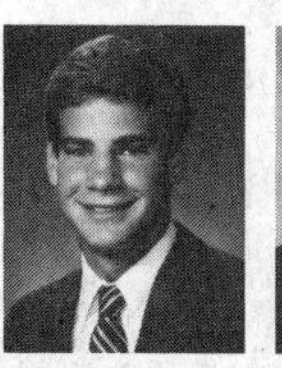
Mraz, Joseph M
Exeter Township SR
Reading, PA

Mueller, David
Penn Hills SR HS
Pittsburgh, PA

Mulholland, Joseph
Holy Ghost Prep
Philadelphia, PA

Mullen, Julie
Le Banon SR HS
Lebnaon, PA

Mullen, Kelly
Valley View HS
Eynon, PA

Mullican, Michael
Wyalusing Valley
Wyalusing, PA

Mullins, Shelly
Curwensville Area
Curwensville, PA

Mulraney, Deanna
Northern Cambria
Spangler, PA

Mulroney, Kelly
Mount St Joseph
Meadowbrook, PA

Mulroy, Jean
St Pius X HS
Collegeville, PA

Mumma, Joyce
Waynesboro Area
Waynesboro, PA

Mummert, Mark
Unionville HS
Chadds Ford, PA

Murcko, Cindy
Farrell SR HS
Farrell, PA

Murgas, Sandra
State College Area SR HS
State College, PA

Murnaghan, Jacqueline
Academy Of Notre
Yeadon, PA

Murphey, Melissa
North Star HS
Boswell, PA

Murphy, Donna
Johnstown Area Voc Tech Schl
South Fork, PA

Murphy, Francis
Archbishop Kennedy HS
Ambler, PA

Murphy, Kelly
Minersville Area HS
Pottsville, PA

Murphy, Lisa
Abington Sr HS
Roslyn, PA

Murphy, Michael
Northeastern HS
Mt Wolf, PA

Murray, Annemarie
St Maria Goretti HS
Philadelphia, PA

Murray, Debra
Greenwood HS
Liverpool, PA

Murray, Katie
Our Lady Of The Sacred Heart HS
Mckees Rocks, PA

Murry, Shane
Hempfield HS
Columbia, PA

Musial, Pamela
St Basil Acad
Philadelphia, PA

Musser, Donna J
Blue Mountain Acad
Elizabethtown, PA

Musser, John Evans
Mt Pleasant Area
Somerset, PA

Musser, Stephen J
Solanco SR HS
New Prvidence, PA

Musta, Laurie
Carlynton HS
Pittsburgh, PA

Musto, Pamela
Old Forge HS
Old Forge, PA

Myers, Amy Sue
Bald Eagle Area HS
Port Matilda, PA

Myers, Andrew
M M I Prep
Mountaintop, PA

Myers, Ann
Kennard-Dale HS
Stewartstown, PA

Myers, Christina L
Red Lion Area SR
Red Lion, PA

Myers, Denise
West York Area HS
York, PA

Myers, Doug
Newport HS
Newport, PA

Myers, Gregory
Northeastern HS
Mt Wolf, PA

Myers, Jeffrey L
Mt Zion Christian
Mt Pleasant, PA

Myers, Jennifer
Warriore Run HS
Allenwood, PA

Myers, Karen
Leechburg Area HS
Leechburg, PA

Myers, Kellie
Littlestown HS
Littlestown, PA

Myers, Michael T
Dover Area HS
Dover, PA

Myers, Russell A
The Christian Acad
Upper Darby, PA

Myers, Tamara
Ford City HS
Ford City, PA

Myers, Tracy
Greencastle-Antrim
Greencastle, PA

Myirski, Lynda
Freedom HS
Bethlehem, PA

Mysza, Frank
Mc Guffey Area HS
Washington, PA

Naessig, Cheryl
E L Meyers HS
Wilkes Barre, PA

Nagle, Deanna
William Allen HS
Allentown, PA

Nagy, Jr Michael S
Fort Cherry HS
Mc Donald, PA

Nagy, Robert G
Downingtown SR
Downingtown, PA

Nagy, Thomas C
Malvern Prepartory
Malvern, PA

Nair, Brendan
Redbank Valley HS
New Bethlehem, PA

Naleppa, Heidi
Chartiers Valley HS
Carnegie, PA

Nall, Jennifer
Brookville Area HS
Brookville, PA

Nance, Reggie
Monongahela Valley
Catholic HS
Brownsville, PA

Nardis, Stacey
West Greene HS
Wind Ridge, PA

Nardone, Dominque
Wyoming Area HS
West Pittston, PA

Nase, Pamela
Souderton Area HS
Souderton, PA

Nathan, David
Lower Moreland HS
Huntingdon Valley, PA

Naus, Kimberly
Berrwick Area SR
Berwick, PA

Naylor, Richard
Harry S Truman HS
Croydon, PA

Neal, Charles
Butler SR HS
Butler, PA

Neal, Dawn
Tussey Mountain
Saxton, PA

Neal, Eric J
Blairsville SR HS
Blairsville, PA

Neal, Robin
Franklin HS
Polk, PA

Neal, Tara
Punxsutawney Area
Punxsutawney, PA

Nearhoof, Sharon
Tyrone Area HS
Warriors Mark, PA

Nease, Matthew
Blairsville SR HS
Blairsville, PA

Necciai, William
Ringgold HS
Donora, PA

Neddoff, John
G A R Memorial HS
Wilkes Barre, PA

Nederostek, Beth
Parkland HS
Allentown, PA

Neff, Cynthia
Butler Area SR HS
Chicora, PA

Nehrer, Daniel B
North Allegheny SR
Sewickley, PA

Neidlinger, Jr Ronald
Tulpehocken HS
Myerstown, PA

Neimeyer, Sheila
Brandywine Heights
Mertztown, PA

Neisworth, Heather
Quighley HS
Ambridge, PA

Nejman, Paul
Technical Memorial
Erie, PA

Nelko, Matthew J
Ambridge Area HS
Baden, PA

Nelson, Aimee
Coudersport JR SR
Coudersport, PA

Nepomuceno, Randy Ray
St Josephs Preparatory Schl
Jenkintown, PA

Nero, Pam
New Castle HS
New Castle, PA

Nesbitt, Stephanie
Avon Grove HS
Lincoln Univ, PA

Nesfeder, Jr David G
William Allen HS
Allentown, PA

Nesmith, Emmilyn L
J R Masterman HS
Philadelphia, PA

Neulight, Joseph
Parkland SR HS
Allentown, PA

Neumyer, Todd M
Central Dauphin East HS
Harrisburg, PA

Nevel, Michael
Berwick Area SR
Berwick, PA

Nevison, Scott
Harry S Truman HS
Fairless Hills, PA

Newcaster, Jayanne
Butler Area SR HS
Butler, PA

Newcome, Jennifer
Brookville Area HS
Brookville, PA

Newlin, III Paul F
Spring-Ford SR HS
Schwenksville, PA

Newlin, Shelley K
North Allegheny HS
Sewickley, PA

Newman, Michael E
West Greene HS
Rogersville, PA

Newman, Myrna
Hopewell SR HS
Clinton, PA

Nguyen, Can
Central HS
Philadelphia, PA

Nichols, Dwayne
Millville HS
Bloomsburg, PA

Nichols, Sharon
Wmsport Area HS
Williamsport, PA

Nicholson, Dana
Turkeyfoot Valley Area HS
Confluence, PA

Nicholson, Shelly
Turkeyfoot Valley Area HS
Fort Hill, PA

Nickey, Constance
Chichester SR HS
Boothwyn, PA

Nickey, Ronda
Big Spring HS
Walnut Bottom, PA

Nicklas, Mary E
Little Flower HS
Philadelphia, PA

Nickleach, Traci Lempe
Vocational-Technica
Worthington, PA

Nicolette, Jr Lawrence J
Penn-Trafford HS
Harrison City, PA

Niedecker, Stacy
Shaler Area HS
Glenshaw, PA

Niehaus, William J
Wyomissing Area SR HS
Wyomissing, PA

Niemritz, Tracey
Johnstown HS
Johnstown, PA

Niklaus, Neal
Shaler Area HS
Glenshaw, PA

Niles, Laurence
East HS
Reston, VA

Nissly, Sharon L
Donegal HS
Mt Joy, PA

Nitchman, Tina
West York Area HS
York, PA

Noah, Dawn
Western Beaver HS
Industry, PA

Noble, Sean P
Methacton HS
Audubon, PA

Noble, William
Penn Trafford HS
Harrison Cty, PA

Noel, Kelley
Danville SR HS
Danville, PA

Noel, Michelle
Bellwood-Antis HS
Bellwood, PA

Noga, Mary
York Catholic HS
York, PA

Nogowski, Joanne
Little Flower Catholic HS
Philadelphia, PA

Nohaile, Michael
Altoona Area HS
Altoona, PA

Noll, Diane Louise
Muhlenberg HS
Laureldale, PA

Nolt, Timothy
Hempfield HS
Lancaster, PA

Nonemaker, Joan
Downingtown SR
Exton, PA

Noon, Melissa
Chestnut Ridge HS
Imler, PA

Noone, Kelley
New Hope-Solebury
New Hope, PA

Nordstrom, Eric
The Hill Schl
Leola, PA

North, Susan
Purchase Line HS
Mahaffey, PA

Notarianni, Lisa
West Scranton HS
Scranton, PA

Novack, Mark
Weatherly Area HS
Weatherly, PA

Novak, Frances
G A R Memorial HS
Wilkes Barre, PA

Novobilski, Theresa M
Carbondale Area HS
Simpson, PA

Novotny, Jessica
St Piux X HS
Pennsburg, PA

Nowacki, Maria
Nazareth Acad
Philadelphia, PA

Noyer, Carol
Iroquois HS
Erie, PA

Noyes, Jr David
Governor Mifflin HS
Shillington, PA

Nudo, Daniel R
E L Meyers HS
Wilkes Barre, PA

Null, Michael
Charleroi Area HS
Charleroi, PA

Nulty, Amy
Mazareth Academy
Philadelphia, PA

Nulty, Leslie
Nazareth Acad
Philadelphia, PA

Nuttall, Michelle A
Hampton HS
Allison Pk, PA

Nutter, Scott
Christian School Of York HS
Wrightsville, PA

Nye, Robyn
Dowingtown SR HS
Downingtown, PA

Nypaver, Patty
Springdale HS
Harwick, PA

O Barto, Wendy
South Allegheny HS
Glassport, PA

O Brien, Erin
William Allen HS
Allentown, PA

O Brien, Patrick
Tyrone Area HS
Tyrone, PA

O Connell, Jayne
Williamsport Area
Williamsport, PA

O Donnell, Christine
Lancaster Catholic
Lancaster, PA

O Donnell, Karren
Solanco HS
Nottingham, PA

O Hara, Kara Ann
Hollidaysburg Area
Jupiter, FL

O Hara, Nannette
Marple Newtown
Broomall, PA

O Leary, Anne
Villa Maria Acad
Erie, PA

O Neal, Bridget
Mercyhurst Prep HS
Erie, PA

O Neil, Michelle
Allegheny-Clarion Valley HS
Parker, PA

O Neill, Brian James
Strath Haven HS
Gwynedd, PA

O Neill, Dianne
Little Flower HS
Philadelphia, PA

O Neill, Mary M
Merion Mercy Acad
Ardmore, PA

O Neill, Patti
Norwin SR HS
North Huntingdon, PA

O Reilly, Amy
Saint Basil Acad
Philadelphia, PA

O Rorke, Barry J
Shaler Area HS
Glenshaw, PA

O Shell, Todd
Harmony HS
Cherry Tree, PA

O Toole, Margaret
Sacred Heart HS
Pittsburgh, PA

Oakley, Aneida Jean
Penn Hills SR HS
Pittsburgh, PA

Obenour, Caitie L
Fort Cherry HS
Hickory, PA

Obenreder, Christine
Harbor Creek HS
Erie, PA

Ober, Danette M
Elizabeth Area HS
Elizabethtown, PA

Oberkircher, Amy
Danville SR HS
Danville, PA

Obrzut, Annette
Mahonoy Area HS
Mahanoy City, PA

Ochotorena, Chris
Berwick SR HS
Berwick, PA

Ochwat, Karen
St Paul Cathedral
Cheswick, PA

Oddo, Tana Jean
Serra Catholic HS
Jefferson Boro, PA

Odell, Brian
Kennedy Christian
Brookfield, OH

Oesterling, Dianne
Butler SR HS
Butler, PA

Ogburn, Tricia
Trinity HS
Washingon, PA

Ogden, Valerie
West York HS
York, PA

Ogline, Timothy E
Montrose Area HS
Hallstead, PA

Ohlrich, Tina
Tech Memorial HS
Erie, PA

Okamoto, Neil
Council Rock HS
Holland, PA

Olczak, Ted
Council Rock HS
New Hope, PA

Oldrati, Brian E
St John Neumann
Philadelphia, PA

Olenchock, Michael
Greensburg Central Catholic HS
Latrobe, PA

Olexy, Laura
Riverside HS
Taylor, PA

Oliva, Cathy
Pius X HS
Pen Argyl, PA

Olszewski, Mary
E L Meyers HS
Wilkes-Barre, PA

Olweiler, Laura
Elizabethtown Area
Elizabethtown, PA

Omalley, Patrick
North Allegheney
Pittsburgh, PA

Omarzai, Najibullah
Roxborough HS
Philadelphia, PA

Onder, Sharon
Portage Area HS
Portage, PA

Ondo, Diana
Reynolds HS
Greenville, PA

Ongiri, Amy A
St Francis Acad
Bethlehem, PA

Opalisky, Kim
St Hubert HS
Philadelphia, PA

Opher, Dorit R
Akiba Hebrew Acad
Havertown, PA

Orange, Kellie
Penn Trafford HS
Jeannette, PA

Orazzi, Michael J
Lakeland HS
Carbondale, PA

Orlandi, Lisa
Sharon HS
Sharon, PA

Orlow, Marc Stewart
Northeast HS
Philadelphia, PA

Ormond, Valdamir
Father Judge HS
Philadelphia, PA

Orndorff, Karen
Littlestown SR HS
Gettysburg, PA

Orndorff, Robbie
Connellsville Area
SR HS
Mill Run, PA

Orner, Debra
Bishop Mc Cort HS
Johnstown, PA

Orr, Bill
Blairsville HS
Blairsville, PA

Orr, Deanne
Charleori JR SR HS
Charleroi, PA

Orr, Mark
Bishop Egan HS
Croydon, PA

Orr, Rhonda
Linesville HS
Linesville, PA

Orsborn, Jeffrey M
Butler SR HS
Renfrew, PA

Orsino, Tina M
Cranberry Area HS
Franklin, PA

Osgood, Barbara
Marion Center HS
Manassas, VA

Oslick, Lynn
Montour SR HS
Mc Kees Rocks, PA

Ostrosky, John J
Windber Area HS
Windber, PA

Ostrowski, Kimberly
Baldwin HS
Pittsburgh, PA

Ostrowski, Lori
Pittston Area HS
Pittston, PA

Otto, Roseanne
Scotland Schl For
Veterans Children
Aldan, PA

Overman, Carol
Unionville HS
W Chester, PA

Owens, Joseph A
South Side Catholic
Pittsburgh, PA

Owens, Melanie
Clearfield Area HS
Clearfield, PA

Owens, Sara
Clearfield Area HS
Frenchville, PA

Oyefeso, Olanike
Villa Maria HS
Berea, OH

Ozegovich, Dawn R
Yough SR HS
Smithtown, PA

Pabis, Dennis
Bishop O Hara HS
Blakely, PA

Pabst, Bill
Scranton Central
Scranton, PA

Pacek, Karen Lynn
St Joseph HS
Natrona Heights, PA

Packard, Richard
Canton Area JR SR
Canton, PA

Paczek, Stephen
Windber Area HS
Windber, PA

Padamonsky, George P
Northwestern
Lehigh HS
Schnecksville, PA

Pagac, Christy
Bethlehem Center
Brownsville, PA

Pagac, Edward
Bethlehem-Center
Richeyville, PA

Paglio, Kimberly
Mt Pleasant Area
SR HS
Mt Pleasant, PA

Paida, Douglas
Bishop Shanahan
W Chester, PA

Paine, Gail
Calvary Baptist
Christian HS
Wilkes-Barre, PA

Palach, Steve
Saegertown HS
Saegertown, PA

Paladino, Dawn
Milton Secondary
Lewisburg, PA

Palermini, Jr John J
Shade Central City
Hooversville, PA

Palichat, Patricia
Ambridge Area HS
Ambridge, PA

Pallone, Arthur K
Southmoreland HS
Scottdale, PA

Pallone, Nick
Westside Tech Schl
Courtdale, PA

Palmer, Kim
Waynesburg Central
Waynesburg, PA

Palmer, Mark
Deer Lakes JR/SR
Gibsonia, PA

Palombo, Michael
Canevin HS
Pittsburgh, PA

Palumbo, Kelly
Neshannock HS
New Castle, PA

Pambianco, Maria
Bishop Hoban HS
Plains, PA

Pampena, Marie Annette Jean
Sacred Heart HS
Pittsburgh, PA

Pan, Dorothy
Blue Mountain Acad
Limekiln, PA

Pancholi, Meeta
Bethel Park SR HS
Pittsburgh, PA

Pancu, Diana
Philadelphia HS For
Philadelphia, PA

Panebianco, Annette Marie
Canevin Catholic
Pittsburgh, PA

Pantaleo, Kim
Hopewell HS
Aliquippa, PA

Pantas, Lee J
Council Rock HS
Washington Crssng, PA

Paone, Anthony
St John Neumann
Philadelphia, PA

Papoutsis, John
Waynsboro Area SR
Waynesboro, PA

Papp, Suzanne
Cardinal O Hara HS
Morton, PA

Paquet, Karen
Interboro HS
Prospect Park, PA

Paquet, Laurie
Interboro SR HS
Prospect Park, PA

Parfitt, Anthony
Hempfield Area HS
Bovard, PA

Parise, Ralph
Washington HS
Washington, PA

Parisella, Jill
Bradford Area HS
Bradford, PA

Park, Judy
North Penn HS
North Wales, PA

Park, Sang
Harry S Truman HS
Fairless Hills, PA

Park, Steve
Northeast HS
Philadelphia, PA

Parke, Amy
Kiski Area HS
Apollo, PA

Parks, Eric
Kittanning SR HS
Worthington, PA

Parks, Jared
Kennedy Christian
Farrell, PA

Parks, Stacy
Lewistown Area HS
Lewistown, PA

Parks, Thomas
Kennard-Dale HS
Stewartstown, PA

Parry, Bryan
Canon-Mc Millan
SR HS
Mc Donald, PA

Parson, Lisa
West Greene HS
Graysville, PA

Partington, Statia
Portersville
Christian Schl
Ellwood City, PA

Pascoe, Pamela
Hanover Area JR
SR HS
Sugar Notch, PA

Pascoe, Vickie
New Castle SR HS
New Castle, PA

Pasquinelli, Paula
St Marys Area HS
Saint Marys, PA

Pass, Melissa
Moon SR HS
Corapolis, PA

Passio, Lori
St Maria Goretti HS
Philadelphia, PA

Passmore, Howard
Joseph
Neshaminy SR HS
Feasterville, PA

Pasterick, Gene
Belle Vernon Area
Belle Vernon, PA

Pastierik, Jennifer
Valley HS
New Kensington,
PA

Pastor, Jr Frank
Nroth Hills HS
Pittsburgh, PA

Pastore, Theresa
Lower Moreland HS
Huntingdon Valley,
PA

Patel, Jyotin
Upper Darby HS
Clifton Heights, PA

Patel, Kiren
Bishop O Hara HS
Dunmore, PA

Patel, Shailesh M
La Salle College HS
Huntingdon Vly, PA

Patrick, Kenneth G
Greensburg-Salem
Greensburg, PA

Patrick, Krishni
St Francis Acad
Bethlehem, PA

Patrick, Lynn
Chapel Christian
Belle Vernon, PA

Patterson, Eric
Wellsboro SR HS
Wellsboro, PA

Patterson, Gina
Elizabeth-Forward
Monongahela, PA

Patterson, Joan
Richland HS
Gibsonia, PA

Patterson, VI John J
West Perry SR HS
New Bloomfield, PA

Patterson, Kelly
Kiski Area SR HS
Leechburg, PA

Patterson, Valerie
Coatesville Area SR
Coatesville, PA

Patton, Bill
Tunkhannock Area
Noxen, PA

Patynski, Walter M
Milton Area SR HS
Milton, PA

Paul, Lisa
Berlin
Brothersvalley HS
Garrett, PA

Paul, Raymond
Shickshinny HS
Shickshinny, PA

Paules, Jonathan W
Central York SR HS
York, PA

Paulson, Denise
Cardinal O Hara HS
Glen Mills, PA

Paulson, Drew
Delaware County
Christian HS
Berwyn, PA

Pavelek, III Michael
Hershey HS
Hershey, PA

Pavlik, Andrea
Norwin SR HS
N Huntingdon, PA

Pavolic, Cassandra J
Coatesville Area SR
Coatesville, PA

Pavtis, Laurie
Belle Vernon Area
Belle Vernon, PA

Pawlik, Magdalena
Saucon Valley SR
Hellertown, PA

Pawlosky, Michael
Canon-Mc Millan
SR Schl
Canonsburg, PA

Payne, Celeste
Central Dauphin E
Harrisburg, PA

Payne, Christine
The Christan Acad
Chester, PA

Payne, Jr James L
Christian School Of
Dover, PA

Payne, John
Father Judge HS
Philadelphia, PA

Payne, Joseph R
Everett Area HS
Breezewood, PA

Payne, Sandra K
Hempfield Area SR
Greensburg, PA

Payne, Ursula
Union Area JR SR
New Castle, PA

Pcsolyar, Chad
Quigley HS
Baden, PA

Peacock, Robert
Tunkhannock HS
Tunkhannock, PA

Pearce, Glenn
Wm Allen HS
Allentown, PA

Pechatsko, Victoria
Fairchance-Georges
SR HS
Uniontown, PA

Peck, Jeannine
Nazareth Acad
Feasterville, PA

Pedano, Monica A
Merion Mercy Acad
Merion, PA

Peet, Debbie
The Baptist HS
Hop Bottom, PA

Peffley, Mike
Lebanon HS
Lebanon, PA

Pelka, Tamara
Tunkhannock Area
Tunkhannock, PA

Pellegrino, Valerie A
Exeter Twp SR HS
Birdsboro, PA

Pellicano, Rachel
Lincoln HS
Ellwood City, PA

Peloro, Letizia A
Bishop Kenrick HS
Norristown, PA

Pena, Marisol
Mt Pleasant Area
Mt Pleasant, PA

Pencek, Matthew
Tunkhannock HS
Tunkhannock, PA

Penecale, Gina
Upper Moreland HS
Hatboro, PA

Penland, Claude
Archbishop Carroll
Wayne, PA

Penner, Gary
Upper Moreland HS
Hatboro, PA

Pennington, James
V
Sharpvsville SR HS
Shaprsville, PA

Peno, Melissa
Cowanesque HS
Westfield, PA

Penrod, Wendy
Windber Area HS
Windber, PA

Penrose, Sean
St John Neumann
Philadelphia, PA

Pensenstadler,
Elaine
Ambridge HS
Ambridge, PA

Pensis, Bobbi
Charleroi Area JR
SR HS
Charleroi, PA

Percherke, James
North Star HS
Boswell, PA

Percosky, Kathy
Forest Hills HS
Windber, PA

Peretin, Joe
Baldwin HS
Pittsburgh, PA

Perez, Delton
Blue Mountain Acad
Waterbury, CT

Perez, Gemma
Geibel HS
Connellsville, PA

Perfecky, Marta
Abington HS
Glenside, PA

Perich, Michele
South Allegheny JR SR HS
Mc Keesport, PA

Perinis, Mary
Mt Lebanon HS
Pittsburgh, PA

Perkins, Martin
Glen Mills Schls
Concordville, PA

Pero, Jeff
Upper Moreland HS
Willow Grove, PA

Perrine, Melissa
Laural Highlands SR HS
Uniontown, PA

Perrins, Gerald
Pittston Area HS
Pittston, PA

Perry, Abby
Freedom HS
Bethlehem, PA

Perry, Brian
Towanda Area HS
Towanda, PA

Persun, Sherry
Highlands SR HS
Tarentum, PA

Pesta, Laura
York Catholic HS
Shrewsbury, PA

Pete, Debbie
Lock Haven SR HS
Lock Haven, PA

Pete, Matthew
Bishop Mccort HS
Johnstown, PA

Peter, Priscilla
Cedar Grove Christian Acad
Philadelphia, PA

Peterman, Tanya
Slippery Rock Area
Slippery Rock, PA

Peters, James
Northampton Area SR HS
Bethlehem, PA

Peters, Melinda M
Middletown Area
Middletown, PA

Peters, Michele
Valley View JR SR
Jessup, PA

Peters, Stephen
Parkland HS
Orefield, PA

Petersen, Stephanie
Garden Spot HS
Narvon, PA

Peterson, Candace
Glendale JR SR HS
Irvona, PA

Peterson, John
Greater Latrobe SR
Latrobe, PA

Peterson, Kristen
Dallastown Area HS
Dallastown, PA

Petey, Mark
Center HS
Monaca, PA

Petitjean, Beth
Governor Mifflin HS
Shillington, PA

Petlikowski, Lisa
East HS
West Chester, PA

Petlikowski, Renee
East HS
West Chester, PA

Petravich, Alan
Pine Grove Area HS
Pine Grove, PA

Petrelli, Gina
Plum SR HS
New Kensington, PA

Petrilak, John
Pen Argyl SR HS
Pen Argyl, PA

Petrilli, Denise
St Marys Area HS
Saint Marys, PA

Petrishen, Nick
Highland SR HS
Natrona Hts, PA

Petritsch, Kellie
Cardinal Brennan
Shenandoah, PA

Petro, Christine
Ringgold HS
Donora, PA

Petrole, Chris
Marian Catholic HS
Tresckow, PA

Petroske, Jennifer
Ringgold HS
Donora, PA

Petruzzelli, John Paul
Archbishop Ryan H S For Boys
Philadelphia, PA

Pettko, Lisa M
Mon Valley Catholic
Belle Vernon, PA

Peyton, Kelly
Shaler Area SR HS
Pittsburgh, PA

Pfeffer, David
Bishop Mc Devitt
Willow Grove, PA

Pfeufer, Kelly
Elk County Christian HS
St Marys, PA

Pfister, Brian D
A W Beattie-North Allegheny HS
Sewickley, PA

Pfisterer, Karin Beth
Palisades JR SR HS
Upper Black Eddy, PA

Pfrogner, Kimberly
Mt Pleasant Area
Mt Pleasant, PA

Phanco, Thomas Wayne
Chief Logan Joint
Mc Clure, PA

Phayre, Jenifer
Chichester HS
Boothwyn, PA

Phelan, Katie
Franklin Regional
Murrysville, PA

Phillips, A Benjamin M
Moravian Acad
Allentown, PA

Phillips, Calvin
Canton JR SR HS
Marsh Hill, PA

Phillips, Christopher J
Corry Area HS
Corry, PA

Phillips, Paul
Plum Boro SR HS
Pittsburgh, PA

Phillips, Ricky
Philipsburg-Osceola SR HS
West Decatur, PA

Phillips, Sharon
St Maria Goretti HS
Philadelphia, PA

Phillips, Tammy
Philipsburg-Osceola Area SR HS
Philipsburg, PA

Phillips, Jr William G
Windber Area HS
Windber, PA

Piatt, Howard Scott
Lock Haven SR HS
Lock Haven, PA

Pichler, Jennifer
St Marys Area HS
Kersey, PA

Pickett, Deborah
Wyalusing Valley JR SR HS
Laceyville, PA

Piechnick, Craig
Canon Mc Millan SR HS
Canonsburg, PA

Pierce, Stephanie Lyne
Solanco HS
Kirkwood, PA

Pierce, Vanessa
Troy SR HS
Col X Rds, PA

Pighetli, Gina
Bald Eagle Area HS
Howard, PA

Pikulsky, Richelle
Uniontown Area SR
Uniontown, PA

Pilewski, Julie
Venango Christian
Oil City, PA

Pilla, Mary Jo
St Maria Goretti HS
Philadelphia, PA

Pilston, Rebecca
Highlands SR HS
Tarentum, PA

Pincher, Beth
Altoona Area HS
Altoona, PA

Pinkett, Sean
Chester HS
Chester, PA

Pinti, Kim
Sharon SR HS
Sharon, PA

Piper, Edith
Meadow Brook
Christian Schl
Matteson, IL

Piper, Richard
Center HS
Monaca, PA

Pipkins, Chris
York Catholic HS
York, PA

Pireaux, Kellie
Charleroi Area JR
SR HS
N Charleroi, PA

Pirrotta, Elizabeth
A
Peters Township HS
Mcmurray, PA

Pirrotta, Kathryn
Peters Township HS
Mc Murray, PA

Pisano, Francene
Wyoming Area HS
Exeter, PA

Pisarchick, Tammy
Linesville HS
Linesville, PA

Pisarski, Cindy
Forest Hills HS
Summerhill, PA

Pistoria, Mike
Upper Perkiomen
Pennsburg, PA

Pitman, William
Wilmington Area
New Wilmington,
PA

Pittas,
Ann-Margaret
Brentwood HS
Pittsburgh, PA

Pitzer, Michele
Wilmington Area
New Wilmington,
PA

Place, Mary
Grove City Area SR
Grove City, PA

Placek, Tracy
Our Lady Of The
Sacred Heart Acad
Coraopolis, PA

Plasha, Wayne W
Lower Moreland HS
Huntingdon Valley,
PA

Plassio, Shelly
Yough SR HS
Irwin, PA

Pleban, Chris
Weatherly Area HS
Weatherly, PA

Pletcher, Allen
Rockwood Area HS
Rockwood, PA

Plocinik, Lynda
Rochester Area HS
Rochester, PA

Plowey, Jeffrey M
Hampton HS
Allison Pk, PA

Pluciennik, Betsy
Scranton
Preparatory Schl
Scranton, PA

Plumley, Mary
J R Masterman HS
Philadelphia, PA

Poall, Amy
George Washington
Philadelphia, PA

Pocratsky, Raymond
Mount Pleasant
Area SR HS
Mt Pleasant, PA

Podlesny, Christine
Manheim Central
Manheim, PA

Podolak, Greg
Crestwood HS
Mountaintop, PA

Poerio, Janine
Southmoreland HS
Scottdale, PA

Pohlot, Marylou
Bentworth SR HS
Bentleyville, PA

Polansky, G Michael
Bellefonte HS
Bellefonte, PA

Polin, Scott
Council Rock HS
Richboro, PA

Polka, Thomas
Apollo Ridge HS
Apollo, PA

Polkis, Eric M
Northgate HS
Pitsburgh, PA

Pollack, Amee
Lower Moreland HS
Huntingdon Valley,
PA

Pollack, Anne
Bishop Hafey HS
Freeland, PA

Pollard, Dennis B
Northeast HS
Philadelphia, PA

Pollins, Scott
Manheim Township
Lancaster, PA

Pollock, Janet S
Tamaqua Area HS
Tamaqua, PA

Pollock, Stephanie
Henderson HS
West Chester, PA

Pologrot, Mike
Mt Pleasant Area
Mount Pleasant, PA

Pologruto, Elizabeth
Mt Plesant Area HS
Mt Pleasant, PA

Polsenberg, Lisarose
Lebanon Catholic
Palmyra, PA

Polzer, Robert J
Allentown Central
Catholic HS
Coplay, PA

Pompeo, Alexis
Our Lady Of The
Sacred Heart
W Aliquippa, PA

Poniatowski,
Caroline
Fort Le Boeuf HS
Erie, PA

Pontani, Deanna
Penns Manor HS
Penn Run, PA

Pontious, Hope
Ridgway Area HS
Ridgway, PA

Pontzer, Heide
St Marys Area HS
Kersey, PA

Pontzer, Melissa
St Marys Area HS
Kersey, PA

Popielarz, Barbara
Merion Mercy Acad
Phila, PA

Port, Moses
Altoona Area HS
Altoona, PA

Porter, Andra
Chichester SR HS
Marcus Hook, PA

Porter, Bryan
Unionville HS
Kennett Sq, PA

Porter, Cheryl Diane
Nazareth Acad
Trevose, PA

Posey, Karen
Peters Twp HS
Mc Murray, PA

Posey, Vicki Renee
Harrisburg HS
Harrisburg, PA

Postreich, Leslie
Tyrone Area HS
Tyrone, PA

Potochnik, Christina
Churchill HS
Turtle Creek, PA

Potocki, Timothy J
North Allegheny HS
Wexford, PA

Potoka, Judi
Mt Pleasant SR HS
Mt Pleasant, PA

Potter, Jennifer
Villa Maria Acad
Erie, PA

Powell, Amy
New Brighton HS
New Brighton, PA

Powell, David D
Mt Lebanon HS
Pittsburgh, PA

Powell, Melanie
Penn Hills SR HS
Pgh, PA

Powers, Lori A
Bishop Shanahan
Exton, PA

Powers, Michele
Lock Haven HS
Lock Haven, PA

Praschak, Paula
Riverside JR SR HS
Taylor, PA

Prather, Diane
Susquehanna
Township HS
Harrisburg, PA

Prather, William
Hempfield HS
Lancaster, PA

Pratkanis, Joe
Kiski Area HS
Vandergrift, PA

Pratt, Barbara
Wissahickon HS
Norristown, PA

Pratt, Sheila Marie
Langley HS
Pittsburgh, PA

Pratt, William A
Conemaugh Twp
Area HS
Hollsopple, PA

Preaux, Cheryl
Elizabeth
Canon Mc Millan
Cecil, PA

Preisler, Victoria Jo
Freedom HS
Bethlehem, PA

Presant, Janet E
Council Rock HS
Churchville, PA

Presogna, Christine
Villa Maria Acad
Erie, PA

Preteroti, Pete
Canon Mc Millan
SR HS
Canonsburg, PA

Prevost, Jonet
Penn Center Acad
Philadelphia, PA

Pribicko, Jon
Homer Center JR
SR HS
Homer City, PA

Price, Becky
Slippery Rock Area
Portersville, PA

Price, Daryl
Canon-Mc Millan
Canonsburg, PA

Price, Jennifer
Wyalusing Valley
Dushore, PA

Price, Kristi
State College SR HS
State College, PA

Prichard, Jill
Harbor Creek HS
Erie, PA

Primrose, Scott
East Stroudsburg
E Stroudsburg, PA

Primus, Guy W
Penn Hills HS
Verona, PA

Prince, Tonya
Frankford HS
Philadelphia, PA

Pringle, Debra
Bald Eagle-Nittany
Salona, PA

Prisk, Kathryn
Curwensville Area
Curwensville, PA

Procovich, Michael
T
Rochester Area HS
Rochester, PA

Proctor, Leslie
Renee
Penn Trafford HS
Trafford, PA

Prosek, Marianne
Lynn
Mc Dowell SR HS
Erie, PA

Prosper, Marie
Jeanine
Our Lady Of The
Sacred Heart HS
Aliquippa, PA

Provance, Scott
Uniontown Area SR
Mill Run, PA

Provins, Cathleen A
Bethel Park SR HS
Bethel Park, PA

Prowell, Jodi
Northeast)rn HS
Mt Wolf, PA

Prue, Scott
Mt Pleasant Area
SR HS
Norvelt, PA

Prum, Piset Ang
Lebanon SR HS
Lebanon, PA

Pruss, Kim
Western Wayne HS
Sterling, PA

Prutzer, Carla
Perkiomen Valley
Perkiomenville, PA

Pryer, Darin
West Catholic HS
For Boys
Phila, PA

Pryle, Barbara A
Penn Hills SR HS
Pittsburgh, PA

Prynda, Michele
Carbondale Arca HS
Simpson, PA

Pryor, Maria
E L Meyers HS
Wilkes-Barre, PA

Przybylek, Andrew
North Allegheny HS
Allison Park, PA

Pudlak, Joseph P
Bethel Park SR HS
Bethel Park, PA

Pugh, Rebecca
Fannet-Metal HS
Dry Run, PA

Puglise, Andrew J
Quigley HS
Aliquippa, PA

Pulford, Erin
Carrick HS
Pittsburgh, PA

Pulkownik, Frank
West Greene HS
Wind Ridge, PA

Pullo, Tracy
St Maria Goretti HS
Philadelphia, PA

Purcell, Amy
Villa Maria Acad
Erie, PA

Purinton, Kimberly
Tunkhannock HS
Tunkhannock, PA

Purner, Amy
Cardinal O Hara HS
Media, PA

Purvis, Jennifer
Seneca Valley HS
Evans City, PA

Puscavage, Kimberly
Pittston Area SR
Pittston, PA

Pushwa, Valerie
Greensburg Central
Catholic HS
Greensburg, PA

Pyle, Christine
Northwestern HS
Cranesville, PA

Pyle, Randy
Heritage Christian
Erie, PA

Pysh, Sandra
Carlynton HS
Carnegie, PA

Quaglieri, Lisa
Gateway HS
Monroeville, PA

Quear, Paula
Freedom HS
Bethlehem, PA

Quinn, Mary G
Cardinal O Hara HS
Springfield, PA

Quinn, Matthew
St Josephs
Preparatory Schl
W Trenton, NJ

Quinn, Rachel
Reading Central
Oley, PA

Quinn, Thomas
Henderson HS
West Chester, PA

Quinney, Colleen
Chichester SR HS
Boothwyn, PA

Quli, Farhat
MMI Prep
Mountaintop, PA

Raab, Cheryl
Northampton SR
Walnutport, PA

Rabberman, Jr
Robert C
Hatboro-Horsham
Hatboro, PA

Rabits, Jennifer
Bishop Guilfoyle HS
Altoona, PA

Race, Patricia
Norwin SR HS
N Huntingdon, PA

Racicot, Arthur
Carson Long
Military Inst
Drayton Plains, MI

Racine, Brian
Hamburg Area HS
Hamburg, PA

Raciti, Linda
Bishop Kenrick HS
Norristown, PA

Raczkowski, John
Canton HS
Roaring Br, PA

Radinovsky, Lisa M
Penn Manor HS
Lancaster, PA

Radomski, David F
Lansdale Catholic
Chalfont, PA

Radwick, Thomas A
Downingtown SR
Exton, PA

Rady, Stephanie
St Clair Area HS
St Clair, PA

Rafferty, Emmett
Beth-Center SR HS
Vestaburg, PA

Ragnelli, Dina
Northwester Lehigh
Germansvile, PA

Ragni, Gregory
Bethlehem Catholic
Bethlehem, PA

Railey, Rebecca
Beaver Valley
Christian Acad
Beaver, PA

Raisley, Michael L
Seneca Valley HS
Harmony, PA

Rajan, Ravikanth
Rob
Central HS
Philadelphia, PA

Rambeau, David H
Portage Area HS
Cassandra, PA

Rambeau, Dawn
Renee
Portage Area HS
Cassandra, PA

Ramberger, Eric
Halifax Area HS
Halifax, PA

Ramirez, Luis
Harry S Truman HS
Bristol, PA

Ramsay, Karlyn
Albert Gallatin SR
Smithfield, PA

Randall, Jeffrey
Todd
Garden Spot HS
Narvon, PA

Randall, Kimberly
Mc Keesport Area
SR HS
Mckeesport, PA

Randolph, Curtis
Danville SR HS
Danville, PA

Ranieri, Pam
Freeport SR HS
Freeport, PA

Rao, Vani
Mechanicsburg Area
SR HS
Mechanicsburg, PA

Rapsey, Jeanna
Cedar Cliff HS
Camp Hill, PA

Rarick, Susan
Tamaqua Area HS
Tamaqua, PA

Ras, Joann
GAR Memorial HS
Wilkes Barre, PA

Rath, Debbie
Solanco SR HS
Quarryville, PA

Rathman, Clayton
Lincoln
Ephrata SR HS
Ephrata, PA

Ratica, Arlene
Greensburg Central
Catholix HS
Greensburg, PA

Rayer, Thomas J
Marple-Newtown
Broomall, PA

Rea, Kelly
Seneca HS
Union City, PA

Rea, Tim
Upper Perkiamen
Pennsburg, PA

Reagle, Douglas
Franklin JR SR HS
Franklin, PA

Reardon, Dave
Central Dauphin HS
Harrisburg, PA

Reber, Mike
Middletown Area
Middletown, PA

Rebert, Daniel
Quentin
York Vocational
York, PA

Rebich, E Todd
Rochester Area HS
Rochester, PA

Rebich, Kelly
Charleroi JR SR HS
Charleroi, PA

Rebich, Lynette M
Center HS
Aliquippa, PA

Rebuck, Craig
Line Mountain HS
Klingerstown, PA

Rech, Aaron
East SR HS
West Chester, PA

Rechel, Wendy
Lock Haven SR HS
Lock Haven, PA

Rechlicz, Nina
Abington Heights
Clarks Summit, PA

Reckus, Janet Alexis
Harry S Truman HS
Levittown, PA

Recupero, Frank
Northern HS
Dillsburg, PA

Reddin, Jr James J
Northeast Catholic
Philadelphia, PA

Redding, Mark
Hanover HS
Hanover, PA

Redlich, Beth
Hempfield Area SR
North Miami Bch,
FL

Redmond, Lisa
California Area HS
California, PA

Reduzzi, Tracy
Pen Argyle Area HS
Pen Argyl, PA

Reed, Eric S
Cedar Crest HS
Lebanon, PA

Reed, Mary
Hopewell SR HS
Aliquippa, PA

Reed, Michael
Williams Valley JR
SR HS
Wiconisco, PA

Reed, Michelle
Kishacoquillas HS
Milroy, PA

Reed, William L
Du Bois Area HS
Troutville, PA

Reeder, Mike
Lampeter-Strasburg
Strasburg, PA

Rees, Walter
Otto-Eldred JR SR
Eldred, PA

Reffitt, Darin M
Carson Long Inst
Colmar, PA

Regina, Ron
Canon-Mc Millan
Bridgeville, PA

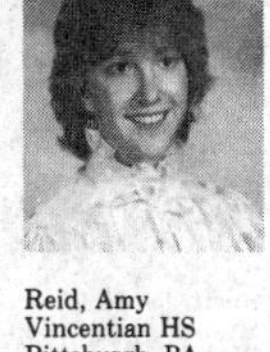
Reid, Amy
Vincentian HS
Pittsburgh, PA

Reifenstein, Rick
Deer Lakes JR SR
Tarentum, PA

Reiff, Melanie
Cedar Cliff HS
New Cumberland,
PA

Reighley,
Christopher Lee
Wilson SR HS
West Lawn, PA

Reigner, Barbara
Ann
Boyertown HS
Barto, PA

Reihart, Michelle
Juniata Valley HS
Huntingdon, PA

Reihart, Robert E
Juniata Valley HS
Alexandria, PA

Reilly, Kerri
Freedom HS
Bethlehem, PA

Reimer, Sheri
Bangor Area SR HS
Bangor, PA

Reinecke, Rachel A
Emmaus HS
Macungie, PA

Reiner, Denise
Line Mountain HS
Leck Kill, PA

Reinhard, Penny J
Whitehall HS
Whitehall, PA

Reininger, Vicki
Greater Johnstown
Johnstown, PA

Reinsel, Kristi
Hampton HS
Allison Pk, PA

Reisinger, Stacy
Seneca Valley HS
Harmony, PA

Reitano, Jill
St Maria Goretti HS
Philadelphia, PA

Reitler, Robert
Norwin HS
N Huntingdon, PA

Rendos, Karen M
Ambridge Area HS
Baden, PA

Rennie, David
Northampton Area
Northampton, PA

Renninger, Catherine
Ringgold SR HS
Monongahela, PA

Renzo, Zane
Lock Haven SR HS
Lock Haven, PA

Reppert, Angela
Allentown Central Catholic HS
Northampton, PA

Reppert, Melissa
Allen HS
Allentown, PA

Resek, Peter
Reynolds HS
Fredonia, PA

Resser, Kori
Northeastern HS
Manchester, PA

Restuccia, Nadine
Pittston Area HS
Pittston, PA

Reuss, Karla
Pen Argyl Area SR JR HS
Nazareth, PA

Reuther, Ken
North Pocono HS
Moscow, PA

Revilla, Juan A
Strath Haven HS
New York, NY

Rexroth, Lynnelle
York County Area
Mt Wolf, PA

Reynolds, Susan
Danville SR HS
Danville, PA

Rhiew, Betty
Scranton Preparatory Schl
Clarks Green, PA

Rhines, Amanda
Hopewell HS
Aliquippa, PA

Rhoades, Jr William
Homer Center HS
Homer City, PA

Rhodes, Mary Jane
Meadowview Christian Acad
Elysburg, PA

Rhodes, Michael
Central HS
Roaring Spring, PA

Rhodes, Tina
California Area HS
Elco, PA

Riccio, Richard
Hazleton SR HS
Hazleton, PA

Riccitelli, Dina
Quigley HS
Aliquippa, PA

Rice, Anita
Abington Senior HS
Abington, PA

Rice, Keith
Shenandoah Valley
Shenandoah, PA

Rice, Russell
Pennsbury HS
Yardley, PA

Rice, Susan
Susquenita HS
Duncannon, PA

Rich, Cheryl
Nazareth Acad
Philadelphia, PA

Richard, Christine
Shaler Area HS
Glenshaw, PA

Richard, Katie
Newport HS
Wila, PA

Richards, Kristy L
Mcconnellsburg HS
Mc Connellsburg, PA

Richards, Piper
Moshannon Valley
Brisbin, PA

Richards, Ralph
Marian HS
Mahanoy City, PA

Richardson, Jr John A
Harry S Truman HS
Croydon, PA

Richardson, Tina
Mc Keesport Area
White Oak, PA

Richter, Penny
Springdale HS
Springdale, PA

Rickard, Jennifer D
Curwensville HS
Curwensville, PA

Rickert, Jennifer
Bishop Kenrick HS
Norristown, PA

Ridenour, Kristin
Southmoreland SR
Scottdale, PA

Rider, Clint
Bellefonte HS
Pleasant Gap, PA

Riedel, Richard
W B Saul HS
Phialelphia, PA

Riedel, Ted
Red Land HS
New Cumberland, PA

Riehl, Gary
Hamburg Area HS
Strausstown, PA

Riehl, Rose
Dequea Valley HS
Kinzers, PA

Rieker, Michael
Annville-Cleona HS
Cleona, PA

Riendeau, Ralph
Father Judge HS
Philadelphia, PA

Riesmeyer, Teresa
Seneca Valley SR
Evans City, PA

Rigatti, Brian
Highlands SR HS
Natrona Hts, PA

Rigot, Gregg
Central Catholic HS
W Mifflin, PA

Rilatt, Joseph F
Henderson HS
West Chester, PA

Riley, Kevin
Pocono Central Catholic HS
Scotrun, PA

Riley, Kim
Waynesburg Central
Waynesburg, PA

Riley, Leslie
Penn Hills SR HS
Pittsburgh, PA

Rinaldi, Lisa
Marple Newtown SR
Newtown Square, PA

Rindgen, Pamela
Wyoming Area SR
Harding, PA

Rishel, Susan M
East Juniata HS
Thompsontown, PA

Rishel, Wendy S
Millville HS
Bloomsburg, PA

Rissinger, Ellen F
Conrad Weiser Area Schl District
Robesonia, PA

Rissinger, Michael S
Conrad Weiser Area
Robesonia, PA

Ritchey, Jim
Baldwin HS
Pittsburgh, PA

Ritenour, Carol
Laurel Valley HS
New Florence, PA

Ritter, Denise
West Perry HS
Loysville, PA

Ritterson, Christoph C
Gettysburg SR HS
Gettysburg, PA

Riverso, Joann
Ste Maria Goretti
Philadelphia, PA

Rivkin, Bill
Abington SR HS
Roslyn, PA

Rizor, Bill
West Allegheny SR
Imperial, PA

Rizzardi, Lisa
Warren Area HS
Warren, PA

Roba, Anthony C
Bishop Egan HS
Bensalem, PA

Robb, II William D
Lock Haven SR HS
Lock Haven, PA

Roberson, Helene
Harry S Truman HS
Levittown, PA

Roberts, Carol E
Central Dauphin
East HS
Swatara, PA

Roberts, Elizabeth
Wyoming Valley
West HS
Kingston, PA

Roberts, Tony
Unionville HS
Coatesville, PA

Robinson, Christine
State College Area
State College, PA

Robinson, Daniel D
Conneaut Lake HS
Conneaut Lake, PA

Robinson, Matt
Chief Logan HS
Lewistown, PA

Robinson, Jr
Thomas V
Central HS
Philadelphia, PA

Robledo, Vivian
Freedom HS
Bethlehem, PA

Roboski, Corienne
Mt Penn HS
Santa Clara, CA

Robsock, Mary Ann
Berwick Area SR
Berwick, PA

Robuck, Tania
Altoona Area HS
Altoona, PA

Rocco, Dominick
Mid-Valley HS
Throop, PA

Rocco, Francis
Central Christian
Reynoldsville, PA

Rock, Nerissa T
Bedford SR HS
Bedford, PA

Rock, Timothy
Ambridge Area HS
Baden, PA

Rockefeller, Jill
Pennsbury HS
Fairless Hills, PA

Rockmuller, Steve
Cash HS
Pittsburgh, PA

Rockwood, Chris
Trinity HS
Carlisle, PA

Rodavich, Rod
Waynesburg Central
Waynesburg, PA

Roddy, Kelly
East Pennsboro
Area HS
Enola, PA

Roddy, Rebecca
Bethel Christian HS
Erie, PA

Rodger, Heidi
Northeastern HS
York, PA

Rodgers, Keirsten
Parkland HS
Allentown, PA

Rodgers, Laura
Hempfield Area SR
Seekonk, MA

Rodgers, Rebecca
Chief Logan HS
Lewistown, PA

Rodgers, Susan
Grove City HS
Grove City, PA

Rodgers, Tammi K
Rocky Grove HS
Reno, PA

Rodrigues, Mark
Mt Lebanon HS
Mt Lebanon, PA

Roe, Rhonda
Penn-Trafford HS
Trafford, PA

Roebuck, Michael
Mapletown HS
Dilliner, PA

Roeske, Nicole
Cedar Crest HS
Lebanon, PA

Rogalewicz, Roger
West Scranton HS
Scranton, PA

Rogan, Kelli
Trinity HS
Carlisle, PA

Rogers, Antoinette
Philadelphia-Montg
omery Chrst
Philadelphia, PA

Rohland, Bryan
Middleburg HS
Middleburg, PA

Rohland, Jack
Freeport Area HS
Sarver, PA

Rohrer, Christopher
Donegal HS
Marietta, PA

Rohrer, Kerry
Solanco HS
Quarryville, PA

Roke, Lisa
John S Fine HS
Glen Lyon, PA

Roles, Elizabeth
Blacklick Valley HS
Nanty Glo, PA

Rolinski, Anthony
M
Penn Hills SR HS
Pittsburgh, PA

Rollin, Kristin
Donell
Elizabeth Forward
SR HS
Elizabeth, PA

Rollman, John
Shamokin Area HS
Shamokin, PA

Roman, James
West Mifflin Area
W Mifflin, PA

Romanic, Mary
Lynne
St Marys Area HS
Byrnedale, PA

Romano, Debbie
St Maria Goretti HS
Philadelphia, PA

Romano, Kenneth A
Father Judge HS
Philadelphia, PA

Romanosky, Michael
Norristown Area HS
Norristown, PA

Romanowski, Mary
Elaine
Scranton Tech
Scranton, PA

Romberger, Julie
Annville Cleona HS
Annville, PA

Romeo, Jr Dominic
P
Chambersburg Area
SR HS
Fayetteville, PA

Romig, Tom
Hamburg Area HS
Hamburg, PA

Romigh, Kelly
Sewickley Acad
Beaver, PA

Rondinelli, Lisa B
Bangor Area SR HS
Bangor, PA

Roney, Marcie
Punxsutawney Area
Punxsutawney, PA

Rooney, Elizabeth
Vincentian HS
Pi Tsburgh, PA

Roop, Gina
Cardinal O Hara HS
Aston, PA

Roos, Colette
E L Meyers HS
Wilkes Barre, PA

Roos, Rhonda
Manheim Central
Manheim, PA

Rorick, Donna
Technical HS
Scranton, PA

Rosati, Richard
Girard Academic
Music Program
Philadelphia, PA

Rosato, Anthony
B Redd Henderson
West Chester, PA

Rosato, Maria
Saint Maria Goretti
Philadelphia, PA

Rosborough, Vickie
Monessen HS
Monessen, PA

Rose, Brenda
Freedom Area HS
Rochester, PA

Rose, Peter
Bellefonte Area HS
Bellefonte, PA

Roseberry, Erin
Chambersburg Area
SR HS
Marion, PA

Rosenberger, Brian
Souderton HS
Telford, PA

Rosengrant, Lori
West Scranton HS
Scranton, PA

Rosenstiehl, Alicia
Cardinal O Hara HS
Upland, PA

Ross, Christopher
Downingtown SR
Downingtown, PA

Ross, Debby
Marple Newtown SR
Broomall, PA

Ross, Denise L
Greater Works Acad
Pittsburgh, PA

Ross, Ellen
Cumberland Valley
Mechanicsburg, PA

Ross, Michele Rae
Troy SR HS
Troy, PA

Ross, Scott
Abington Heights
Clarks Summit, PA

Ross, Susan
Corry Area HS
Corry, PA

Rossi, Lisa
Hopewell SR HS
Aliquippa, PA

Rosso, Anita
Uniontown Area SR
Uniontown, PA

Roth, Kurt
Sharpsville Area HS
Sharpsville, PA

Roth, Lisa
Garden Spot HS
New Holland, PA

Rotondo, Nadine
Upper Merion Area
Bridgeport, PA

Rouse, Brigitte
North Allegheny SR
Pittsburgh, PA

Rouse, Reginald
Abraham Lincoln
Philadelphia, PA

Roush, Judy Lee
Fort Le Boeuf HS
Waterford, PA

Route, Denny
Canton Area HS
Ralston, PA

Rovinsky, David
Bishop O Reilly HS
Swoyersville, PA

Rowe, Donald
Crawford
Chestnut Ridge SR
Schellsburg, PA

Rowe, Linda
Chestnut Ridge HS
Schellsburg, PA

Rowker, Kellie
Crestwood HS
Mountaintop, PA

Rowland, Amy
Big Spring HS
Carlisle, PA

Rowles, Dawn
East Juniata HS
Mcalistervl, PA

Rowles, Jane
Clearfield Area HS
Clearfield, PA

Royce, Danielle
Susquehanna Comm
Susquehanna, PA

Royer, Melynda
Ephrata SR HS
Ephrata, PA

Rozell, Michael
Connellsville Area
SR HS
Connellsville, PA

Rozman, John
West Allegheny HS
Oakdale, PA

Rubish, Barb
Frazier Mem JR SR
Perryopolis, PA

Ruby, Monica Lynn
Indiana Area SR HS
Indiana, PA

Ruda, Johnine
North Allegheny HS
Wexford, PA

Rudar, Stacey
Ringgold HS
Venetia, PA

Rudock, Chris
Solanco HS
Nottingham, PA

Rudolph, Scott
Richland HS
Wexford, PA

Rudolph, Theodore
Cardinal O Hara HS
Springfield, PA

Rudy, Tammi L
William Penn HS
Harrisburg, PA

Ruev, Cassandra
Ringgold HS
Donora, PA

Ruff, Jennifer
Lower Moreland HS
Huntingdon Valley, PA

Ruffin, Janene
Abp John Carroll
Wayne, PA

Ruffner, Kristine
Derry Area SR HS
Derry, PA

Ruggiero, Tricia
Bishop Hafey HS
Sugarloaf, PA

Ruggles, Lori
Central HS
E Freedom, PA

Rumbaugh, Richard
Laurel HS
Volant, PA

Runas, Richard
Deer Lakes HS
Gibsonia, PA

Runge, Rebecca
Octorara Area HS
Cochranville, PA

Rupert, Christopher
Tussey Mountain
Saxton, PA

Ruppert, Kimberly
Dover Area HS
Dover, PA

Ruppert, Tony
Eastern HS
York, PA

Rush, Amy
Washnington HS
Washington, PA

Rush, James
Mahonoy Area HS
New Boston, PA

Rush, Karen
Cumberland Valley
Camp Hill, PA

Rushton, Mark
Northeast Catholic
Philadelphia, PA

Rusnak, Susan E
General Mc Lane
Mckean, PA

Russ, Amy
Mc Keesport Area
Mc Keesport, PA

Russell, Brad
Clearfield Area HS
Clearfield, PA

Russell, Renee
Hanover Area HS
Wilkes Barre, PA

Russell, Sharon
Mechanicsburg Area
SR HS
Mechanicsburg, PA

Russo, Linda
Abp Prendergast HS
Havertown, PA

Russo, Maria
Bishop Kenrick HS
Norristown, PA

Russo, Shawn
Karns City JR SR
Parker, PA

Ruth, Michael
Christopher Dock
Souderton, PA

Ruth, Pegeron
Churchill HS
Rankin, PA

Rutkowski, Joseph
Upper Perkiomen
Red Hill, PA

Rutt, Daryl
Mount Calvary
Christian HS
Mt Joy, PA

Ruzzi, Vincent
Strath Haven HS
Wallingford, PA

Ryan, Frank
Meyersdale Area HS
Meyersdale, PA

Ryan, Kellie
Clearfield Area HS
Clearfield, PA

Ryan, Lisa Ann
York Suburban HS
York, PA

Ryan, Regina
Geibel HS
Connellsville, PA

Ryder, Elizabeth
North Allegheny
Senior HS
Sweickley, PA

Rydeski, P Thomas
Plum HS
Pittsburgh, PA

Ryley, Thomas R
Northeast Catholic
Philadelphia, PA

Rzeszotarski, Tracey
M
Sullivan County HS
Dushore, PA

Saab, Kara Lynn M
Salisbury HS
Allentown, PA

Sabatasse, Tina
Burgettstown Area
JR-SR HS
Burgettstown, PA

Sabol, Christy
Carmichaels Area
Carmichaels, PA

Sabol, Elizabeth
William Allen HS
Allentown, PA

Sabol, Jeff
Bethel Park SR HS
Bethel Park, PA

Sabol, Stephen
Uniontown Area HS
Uniontown, PA

Sabol, Tracy L
Fort Leboeuf HS
Erie, PA

Sach, Lois
Sun Valley HS
Brookhaven, PA

Sachon, Sean
Calvary Baptist Schl
Nesquehoning, PA

Sacik, Michael
Ford City JRSR HS
Ford City, PA

Sadecky, Beth
Highlands HS
Tarentum, PA

Sadecky, James
Highlands HS
Natrona Hts, PA

Sadler, Nannette A
Monongahela Valley
Catholic HS
Chareroi, PA

Sadlik, Lola Ann
Little Flower
Catholic HS
Philadelphia, PA

Saia, Frances
St Maria Goretti HS
Philadelphia, PA

Sakulich, Amy
Abington Heights
Clarks Summit, PA

Salak, Mike
Western Wayne HS
Waymart, PA

Saldukas, Janice
Shenandoah Valley
JR & SR HS
Shenandoah, PA

Salem, Ken
Bishop Mc Cort HS
Johnstown, PA

Salkeld, Brett
Cumberland Valley
Mechanicsburg, PA

Sallash, Robert
Freedom HS
Bethlehem, PA

Salvati, Louis
Lincoln HS
Ellwood City, PA

Sanchez, Michael
Salisbury HS
Allentown, PA

Sandelstein, Tammy
Academy HS
Erie, PA

Sanders, Michele
Mc Guffey HS
Prosperity, PA

Sanders, Sandra R
Kennedy Christian
Wheatland, PA

Sands, Kim
Shenandoah Valley
JR SR HS
Shenandoah, PA

Sands, IV William
Upper Perkiomen
Pennsburg, PA

Santiago, Daniel
Lutheran HS
Philadelphia, PA

Santini, David
California Area HS
California, PA

Santoli, Beth
Highlands SR HS
Natrona Hts, PA

Santos, Tyrone J
Dover Area HS
Dover, PA

Sapp, Debbie
Marion Center HS
Marion Center, PA

Sarachek, Liz
Parkland SR HS
Allentown, PA

Sarnecki, Kimberly
Coughlin HS
Plains, PA

Sarsfield, Shannon
West Allegheny HS
Coraopolis, PA

Sarver, Holly
Brockway Area HS
Brockway, PA

Sassaman, Shelley
Danville HS
Danville, PA

Satchell, Nicola
St Maria Goretti HS
Philadelphia, PA

Satterlee, Karen
Saegertown HS
Saegertown, PA

Saul, Lorie
Christopher Dock
Gilbertsville, PA

Sautter, Cheryl
Pocono Mountian
Long Pond, PA

Savage, Brenda
Plum SR HS
Pittsburgh, PA

Savage, Kimberly
Benton Area JR/SR
Benton, PA

Savaglio, Jr Italo R
Central Dauphin
East HS
Harrisburg, PA

Sawdey, Lori K
Great Valley SR HS
Malvern, PA

Sawin, Elizabeth A
Girard HS
Girard, PA

Sawka, Linda
Shenandoah Valley
Shenandoah, PA

Sawka, Raelin
Bethlehem SR HS
Denbo, PA

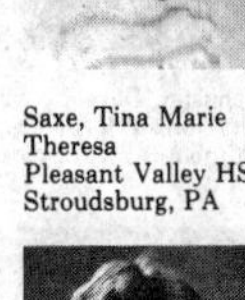
Saxe, Tina Marie
Theresa
Pleasant Valley HS
Stroudsburg, PA

Sayers, Constance S
Clarion-Limestone
Area HS
Summerville, PA

Scalercio, Nancy
Ambridge HS
Ambridge, PA

Scandle, Bethany L
Shamokin Area HS
Sunbury, PA

Scanlan, Patrick
Blue Mountain HS
Schuylkill Haven,
PA

Scanlon, Nicolle
Bethel Park HS
Bethel Pk, PA

Scarsellone, Richard
Aliquippa HS
Aliquippa, PA

Scekeres, Don
Mt Pleasant Area
SR HS
United, PA

Schach, Crystal
Pine Grove Area HS
Pine Grove, PA

Schade, Eric
The Christian Acad
Aston, PA

Schaefer, William E
Cardinal Dougherty
Philadelphia, PA

Schafer, Marisa
Penn Hills SR HS
Pittsburgh, PA

Schank, Rachel
Norwin SR HS
N Huntingdon, PA

Schantz, Justine
Perkiomen Valley
Spg Mt, PA

Schappell, Lisa
Hamburg Area HS
Hamburg, PA

Scharnberger,
Robert C
Penn Manor HS
Millersville, PA

Schell, Elizabeth
Clearfield Area HS
Clearfield, PA

Schell, Jenni
Cedar Cliff HS
Camp Hill, PA

Schell, Stephanie
Berwick Area HS
Nescopeck, PA

Scheller, Jason
Le Dieruff HS
Allentown, PA

Scheller, Michael J
Brentwood HS
Pittsburgh, PA

Schellhamer, Chris D
Northwestern Lehigh HS
Slatington, PA

Schellin, Karen M
Emmaus HS
Emmaus, PA

Scherfel, Jennifer
Harry S Truman HS
Levittown, PA

Schermerhorn, Gail
Phil Montgomery Christian Acad
Ardsley, PA

Schied, David M
Central Bucks West
Chalfont, PA

Schildt, Steve
Central Bucks East
Pipersville, PA

Schill, Lane
Johnsonburg Area
Johnsonburg, PA

Schittler, Linda
Brandywine Heights Area HS
Alburtis, PA

Schlack, Bobbi
Shenandoah Valley JR SR HS
Shenandoah, PA

Schlegel, Jon
Richland HS
Gibsonia, PA

Schlegel, Marc
Norwin SR HS
N Huntingdon, PA

Schlick, Denielle La Rue
Pottstown HS
Pottstown, PA

Schloss, Judeanne
Cardinal O Hara HS
Eddystone, PA

Schmader, Gretta
Clarion Area HS
Shippenville, PA

Schmid, Tracey
Knoch JR SR HS
Butler, PA

Schmidt, Eric William
Hempfield HS
Manheim, PA

Schmidt, Jeannine
Cambridge Springs
Conneautville, PA

Schmidt, Robert
Cambridge Springs
Saegertown, PA

Schmouder, Lon
Liberty HS
Liberty, PA

Schneck, Barbra J
Pine Grove Area HS
Pine Grove, PA

Schneck, Susan
Washington HS
Washington, PA

Schneider, Edward
North Catholic HS
Philadelphia, PA

Schneider, Joe
Council Rock HS
Holland, PA

Schneider, Melanie Dael
Central York SR HS
York, PA

Schnepp, Kimberly
Sto-Rox HS
Mc Kees Rocks, PA

Schnetzka, Teresa
York County Area Vo-Tech Schl
Brodbecks, PA

Schok, Tina Marie
Interboro HS
Essington, PA

Scholl, Eric
Freedom HS
Bethlehem, PA

Schott, Ryan
Galeton Area HS
Galeton, PA

Schrack, Susan
Northern York County HS
Dillsburg, PA

Schramm, Dorothy
Palisades HS
Coopersberg, PA

Schramm, Mary
Cardinal O Hara HS
Swarthmore, PA

Schramm, Robert
Notre Dame HS
E Stroudsburg, PA

Schrantz, Scott
Freedom HS
Bethlehem, PA

Schrecengast, Amber
Chief Logan HS
Lewistown, PA

Schremp, Doug
Radnor HS
Wayne, PA

Schroeder, Thomas
Springford HS
Royersford, PA

Schrope, Elizabeth
Williams Valley JR SR HS
Williamstown, PA

Schubert, Amy
Henderson HS
Westchester, PA

Schubert, Patricia
Villa Maria Acad
Downingtown, PA

Schultheis, Rebecca L
Gateway HS
Monroeville, PA

Schultz, Andrew
Salem Christian
Zionsville, PA

Schultz, Angela
Exeter HS
Reading, PA

Schultz, Karen L
Salisbury HS
Allentown, PA

Schultz, Laurie A
St Pius X HS
Red Hill, PA

Schultz, Lynaia
Pennsbury HS
Levittown, PA

Schulz, Linda
Cheltenham HS
Glenside, PA

Schumacher, Lauren
Salisbury SR HS
Allentown, PA

Schumann, Darci
Pennsbury HS
Levittown, PA

Schupbach, Stephanie
Peters Township HS
Mcmurray, PA

Schuster, Dave
Northwestern SR
Edinboro, PA

Schutz, Susanna
Nazareth Acad
Churchville, PA

Schwab, Gretchen
Council Rock HS
Newtown, PA

Schwandt, Christopher
Souderton Area SR
Harleysville, PA

Schwartz, Susan
Navitity B V M HS
New Philadelphia, PA

Schwartzer, Stacey
Saint Huberts HS
Philadelphia, PA

Schweidler, Glenn
Arch Bishop Wood For Boys
Warminster, PA

Schwenk, David A
Wyoming Valley West HS
Swoyersville, PA

Scialabba, John M
Penn Hills SR HS
Pittsburgh, PA

Sciortino, Christopher R
William Penn SR
York, PA

Scolnik, Chrissa J
Strath Haven HS
Wallingford, PA

Scopel, Darren
Ford City HS
Ford City, PA

Scopelliti, Debi
Scranton Central
Scranton, PA

Scorza, Lari
Charleroi SR HS
Charleroi, PA

Scott, Dionne
Carlisle SR HS
Harker Hts, TX

Scott, Du Juan
St John Neumann
Philadelphia, PA

Scott, William
Juniata HS
Mifflintohn, PA

Sculli, Monica L
Cardinal O Hara HS
Springfield, PA

Seaburn, Robin
Lincoln HS
Wampum, PA

Seaks, Tim
Dover Area HS
Dover, PA

Seaman, Daniel
East Juniata HS
Richfield, PA

Seaman, Daniel
Newport HS
Newport, PA

Seaman, David
Newport HS
Newport, PA

Searle, Nicola
Unionville HS
West Chester, PA

Searls, Coleen
Meadville SR HS
Meadville, PA

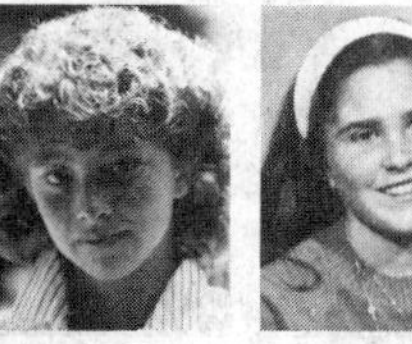

Seavey, Valerie
Archbishop
Prendergast HS
Collingdale, PA

Sebes, Pamela
Ringgold HS
Finleyville, PA

Sechler, Craig
Cheif Logan HS
Lewistown, PA

Sechler, Scott
Rockwood Area HS
Rockwood, PA

Secrest, Troy
Mount Union Area
Shirleysburg, PA

Sedowsky, Christine
Perkiomen Valley
Collegeville, PA

Sees, III Joseph
Danville Area HS
Danville, PA

Sees, Nedd Randall
Danville Area HS
Danville, PA

Segal, Stephanie
Pennsbury HS
Yardley, PA

Segin, Rosalie
Belle Vernon Area
Belle Vernon, PA

Seibert, Christie
Peters Township HS
Library, PA

Seibert, Daniel L
Mountain View
Christian Schl
Elizabethtown, PA

Seiders, Dana
Mc Connelsburg HS
Mc Connellsburg, PA

Seiler, Angele
Pennsbury HS
Morrisville, PA

Sejvar, Jim
Franklin Regional
Murrysville, PA

Sekelsky, Stephen
Norwin HS
Westmoreland City, PA

Selby, Julie
Freedom HS
Easton, PA

Sellers, Tina
East Juniata HS
Thompsontown, PA

Selway, Michael
Trinity HS
Washington, PA

Seman, Karen
Gateway SR HS
Mornoeville, PA

Sembower, Jr John
Penn Hills SR HS
Pittsburgh, PA

Semic, Beth
Central Dauphin
East HS
Harrisburg, PA

Semisch, Bruce
The Hill Schl
Newtown Sq, PA

Senss, Susan
St Maria Goretti HS
Philadelphia, PA

Serafin, Taso
Upper Darby HS
Upper Darby, PA

Serafini, Stefani
Chambersburg Area
SR HS
Chambersburg, PA

Serhienko, Amy
Phoenixville Area
Phoenixville, PA

Serrao, Martina
Penn Hills HS
Pittsburgh, PA

Sessa, Andrea
Quaker Valley HS
Sewickley, PA

Sesso, Andrew
W Scranton SR HS
Scranton, PA

Severo, Josephine
St Maria Goretti HS
Philadelphia, PA

Sevick, Denise
South Hills
Christian HS
Monongahela, PA

Sexton, Laura
Palmyra Area HS
Palmyra, PA

Seybert, Craig
Columbia-Montour
Berwick, PA

Seymour, Kimber
Waynesburg Central
Mt Morris, PA

Sferedes, Joanna
St Hubert HS
Philadelphia, PA

Shade, Diane
Cocalico HS
Denver, PA

Shaffer, Amy
Cardinal O Hara HS
Springfield, PA

Shaffer, Darrell
Shikellamy HS
Camp Hill, PA

Shaffer, Donna
Blacklick Valley HS
Twin Rocks, PA

Shaffer, Jr James M
Montgomery Area
Schl District
Montgomery, PA

Shaffer, Lori
Elderton JR SR HS
Spring Church, PA

Shah, Ameeta
Montour SR HS
Mckees Rocks, PA

Shah, Ashesh
Wissahickon HS
Norristown, PA

Shalikashvili, Amy
Carlisle SR HS
Carlisle, PA

Shaner, Sandra
Ford City JR/SR
Ford City, PA

Shank, Dean P
Bermudian Springs
East Berlin, PA

Shannon, Colleen
Brockway Area HS
Brockway, PA

Shappell, Tammy
Milton Area HS
Milton, PA

Shardy, Jennifer
Reynolds HS
Fredonia, PA

Sharp, Lisa
Central-York SR HS
York, PA

Sharpe, Kimberley
Clarion Area HS
Shippenville, PA

Shatto, John
Central Dauphin HS
Harrisburg, PA

Shatz, Ellyn
Upper Dublin HS
Willow Grove, PA

Shatzer, Melanie
Laurel Valley JR SR
New Florence, PA

Shaw, Brian
South Allegheny HS
Mc Keesport, PA

Shaw, Marcie
New Castle HS
New Castle, PA

Shaw, Mark Andrew
Keystone Oaks HS
Pittsburgh, PA

Shaw, Virginia
Carninal O Hara HS
Springfield, PA

Shea, Jennifer
Warren Area HS
Warren, PA

Shea, Sherry
Tunkhannock HS
Tunkhannock, PA

Sheaffer, Annmarie
Owen J Roberts HS
Elverson, PA

Sheaffer, Diane
Central Dauphu
East SR HS
Harrisburg, PA

Sheaffer, Keith
Greenwood HS
Millerstown, PA

Sheaffer, Matthew
South Western HS
Hanover, PA

Shearer, Mark J
Red Land HS
Etters, PA

Shearer, Peter W
Belle Vernon Area
Belle Vernon, PA

Shearer, Todd
Canon Mc Millan
Canonsburg, PA

Sheehan, Christa
Cardinal O Hara HS
Springfield, PA

Sheets, Pamela J
Waynesburg Central
Nantucket, MA

Sheets, Rebecca
Sullivan County HS
Muncy Valley, PA

Sheetz, Randy
Cumberland Valley
Mechanicsburg, PA

Sheffer, Travis
Dover Area HS
Dover, PA

Sheffield, Shelly
Marie
Moon Area SR HS
Moon Township, PA

Sheffield, Tanya
Montour HS
Mckees Rocks, PA

Shehy, Darla
Wilmington Area
Pulaski, PA

Shellenberger, Amy
J
Milton Area SR HS
Milton, PA

Shellenberger,
Parrish
Juniata HS
Port Royal, PA

Shellenberger,
Tammy
Juniata HS
Mifflintown, PA

Sheller, Melinda
Bishop Guilfoyle HS
Altoona, PA

Shellhamer, Debra C
Northwestern
Lehigh HS
Germansville, PA

Shelpman, Tracy
Bethel Park SR HS
Bethel Park, PA

Sheltman, William
Lewisburg Area HS
W Milton, PA

Shelton, Page
Unionville HS
Chadds Ford, PA

Shenck, Joni
Cedar Cliff HS
New Cumberland,
PA

Shenosky, Don
Punxsutawney HS
Punxsutawney, PA

Shephard, Gretchen
Farrell HS
Farrell, PA

Sheptock, Marybeth
Bethlehem Catholic
Bethlehem, PA

Sherfy, Beth
Elizabethtown Area
Elizabethtown, PA

Sheridan, John
Hershey HS
Hummelstown, PA

Sherif, Hassan H
Valley Forge
Military Acad
Malvern, PA

Sherman, James
Northern Potter JR
SR HS
Westfield, PA

Sherman, Mary
Anne
Central Christian
Du Bois, PA

Sherman, Michelle
Bald Eagle Nittany
Mill Hall, PA

Shertzer, Jere
Lancaster Christian
Lancaster, PA

Sherwin, Robert
Canevin HS
Pittsburgh, PA

Sherwood, Rhonda
Blacklick Valley HS
Belsano, PA

Shetromph, Carol
Hempfield HS
East Petersburg, PA

Shields, Lorianne
Pittston Area SR
Hughestown, PA

Shienbaum, Alan J
Lower Moreland SR
Huntingdon Valley,
PA

Shiffer, Angel
Minersville Area HS
Minersville, PA

Shimel, Tina
Curwensville Area
Curwensville, PA

Shimmel, Vanessa
Clearfield Area HS
Clearfield, PA

Shindler, Alana L
Garden Spot HS
New Holland, PA

Shinke, Stephen W
South Side Beaver
Hookstown, PA

Shinsky, David A
Geibel HS
Uniontown, PA

Shinsky, Rachel
Hempfield HS
Lancaster, PA

Shipley, Angela
Freedom HS
Bethlehem, PA

Shipp, Diane
Towanda Area SR
Towanda, PA

Shirey, Anita
United HS
Robinson, PA

Shirey, Brent
Union HS
Rimersburg, PA

Shiring, Steve
Western Beaver JR
SR HS
Beaver, PA

Shively, Sarah
Abigail
Phoenixville Area
Phoenixville, PA

Shives, Michael
Berwick Area SR
Berwick, PA

Shockey, Sally
Portage Area HS
Portage, PA

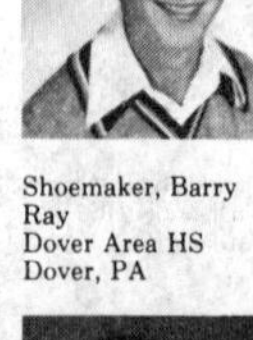
Shoemaker, Barry
Ray
Dover Area HS
Dover, PA

PHOTO
NOT
AVAILABLE

Shoemaker, Theresa
B Ishop Guilfoyle
Altoona, PA

Shoenfelt, Susan
Bishop Guilfoyle HS
Altoona, PA

Short, Brian
Marion Center Area
Home, PA

Shotwell, Diana
Elizabeth Forward
Elizabeth, PA

Shoup, Tammy
Saltsburg JR-SR HS
Saltsburg, PA

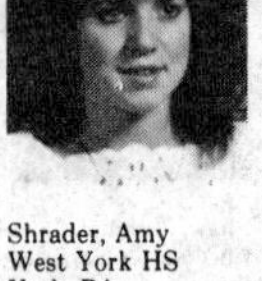
Shrader, Amy
West York HS
York, PA

Shreck, Mark
Milton Area HS
W Milton, PA

Shreffler, Shawn
West Perry HS
Blain, PA

Shriver, Michelle A
Trinity HS
Mechanicsburg, PA

Shriver, Wendy
Waynesburg Central
Waynesburg, PA

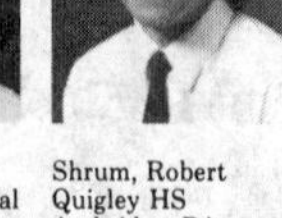
Shrum, Robert
Quigley HS
Ambridge, PA

Shuber, Michael
Norwin SR HS
N Huntingdon, PA

Shuey, Bill
Central Dauphin
East HS
Harrisburg, PA

Shultz, Mike
York County
Vo-Tech HS
York Haven, PA

Shumek, Jr George
Montour HS
Mckees Rocks, PA

Shutt, Kerri
Hempfield SR HS
Bovard, PA

Shuttleworth, Stacy
Conestoga Valley
Leola, PA

Shutty, Michael
Bishop Carroll HS
Hastings, PA

Shwallon, Chris
Brownsville Area HS
W Brownsville, PA

Siberski, Scott
Wyoming Valley
West HS
Plymouth, PA

Sibley, III William
Faith Christian Schl
Stroudsburg, PA

Sickles, Scott C
North Hills HS
Pittsburgh, PA

Sieber, Shelby
East Juniata HS
Mcalisterville, PA

Siecko, Lori Ann
Berwick Area SR
Berwick, PA

Siegel, Angie
North Clarion JR
SR HS
Tionesta, PA

Siegel, Cinnamon
North Clarion HS
Lucinda, PA

Siggers, Christine
New Castle SR HS
New Castle, PA

Sikorski, Cindy S
Chartiers Valley HS
Carnegie, PA

Silfies, Jeffrey
Dennis
Bethlehem Catholic
Bethlehem, PA

Silver, Lynda
Penn Wood HS
Darby, PA

Silverman, Isaac E
Lower Merion HS
Wynnewood, PA

Silvester, David
Richland HS
Gibsonia, PA

Silvestri, Jacqueline
Central Bucks HS
Doylestown, PA

Silvey, Lois Ann
Juniata Valley HS
Alexandria, PA

Simari, Geri Lynn
Mohawk HS
Hillsville, PA

Simcox, Cori J
Lock Haven SR HS
Farrandsville, PA

Simcox, Michael
Wayne
Clearfiel Area HS
Clearfield, PA

Simmons, Aishah
Philadelphia High
Schl For Grls
Philadelphia, PA

Simmons, Bryon
Susquenita HS
Duncannon, PA

Simms, Shelley Y
Philadelphia High
Schl For Girls
Philadelphia, PA

Simon, Kathleen
Villa Joseph Marie
Hatboro, PA

Simon, Michele
Canevin HS
Pittsburgh, PA

Simon, Vickie
Upper Ublin HS
Ft Washington, PA

Simons, Brian
HS For Creative &
Performing Arts
Philadelphia, PA

Simpson, Amy
Methacton SR HS
Norristown, PA

Simpson, Brian
Carlisle SR HS
Carlisle, PA

Simpson, Donella
Churchill HS
Pittsburgh, PA

Simpson, Fred
Blairsville SR HS
Blairsville, PA

Simpson, Heather
Monaca HS
Monaca, PA

Simpson, Lori
James M Coughlin
Wilkes Barre, PA

Simpson, Samuel
Pine Forge Acad
Brooklyn, NY

Singer, Douglas
Lebanon SR HS
Lebanon, PA

Singh, Reeta
Cedar Cliff HS
Camp Hill, PA

Singo, Christiann
Connellsville HS
Dunbar, PA

Sinko, John
Ringgold HS
Monongahela, PA

Sippy, Kinta
Saegertown HS
Saegertown, PA

Sirko, Marybeth
Forest Hills HS
Summerhill, PA

Sitler, Susan
Saint Hubert HS
Philadelphia, PA

Siuniak, Stephanie
Blacklick Valley JR
SR HS
Nanty Glo, PA

Sivilich, Kurt R
Berwick Area SR
Berwick, PA

Siwinski, David R
Archbishop Ryan
High Schl For Boys
Philadelphia, PA

Skaff, Tom
E L Meyers HS
Wilkes Barre, PA

Skelton, Brenda
Tyrone Area HS
Tyrone, PA

Skero, Tim
Sharon HS
Sharon, PA

Skidmore, Sherry
Greater Johnstown
Johnstown, PA

Skowronski, Gina
Archbishop
Kennedy HS
Philadelphia, PA

Skripkar, Lydia
Penn-Trafford HS
Jeannette, PA

Skul, Andrea
Lincoln HS
Ellwood City, PA

Slachta, Kathleen
Cardinal O Hara HS
Aston, PA

Slavek, Jennifer
Souderton Area HS
Telford, PA

Slaymaker, Michael
Lampeter-Strasburg
Strasburg, PA

Sleith, Shelly
Yough SR HS
West Newton, PA

Slenn, Brad
Abington SR HS
Huntington Valley,
PA

Slenn, Murray
Abington SR HS
Huntigton, PA

Slichter, Chanda
Hamburg Area HS
Shoemakersville, PA

Slimick, Jill
Highlands HS
Tarentum, PA

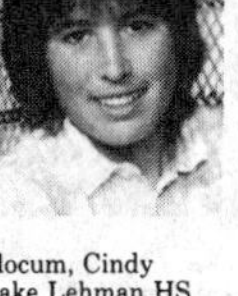
Slocum, Cindy
Lake Lehman HS
Dallas, PA

Slocum, Susie
Lake-Lehman HS
Dallas, PA

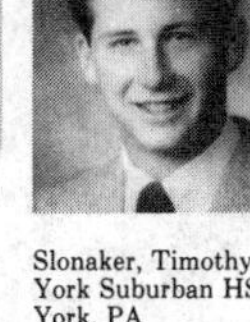
Slonaker, Timothy J
York Suburban HS
York, PA

Sloss, Douglas
Lower Moreland HS
Huntingdon Valley,
PA

Slovak, Tammy
New Brighton HS
New Brighton, PA

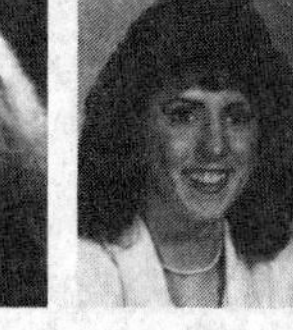
Slyhoff, Kim
Council Rock HS
Churchville, PA

Smale, Mary
Bangor Area SR HS
Bangor, PA

Smalley, Joseph
Northeast Catholic
Philadelphia, PA

Smalls, Lori
James M Coughlin
Wilkes-Barre, PA

Smay, Heather
Knoch JR SR HS
Saxonburg, PA

Smeal, Beth
West Branch HS
Hawk Run, PA

Smedley, Jana
Lock Haven SR HS
Lock Haven, PA

Smelko, Karen
Punxsutawney Area
Reynoldsville, PA

Smeltz, Dale E
Upper Dauphin
Area HS
Lykens, PA

Smerroskie, Dawn
Our Lady Of
Lourdes Regiona
Shamokin, PA

Smink, David M
Conestoga HS
Berwyn, PA

Smith, Betsy
E L Meyers HS
Wilkes Bare, PA

Smith, Colleen A
Bishop Hodan HS
Wilkes Barre, PA

Smith, Courtney
Hanover SR HS
Hanover, PA

Smith, Darleen
Mercyhurst Prep
North East, PA

Smith, David T
Phoenixville Area
Phoenixville, PA

Smith, Dawn
Cheltenham HS
Laverockk, PA

Smith, Debbie L
Yough SR HS
Rillton, PA

Smith, Debra
Greater Johnstown
Johnstown, PA

Smith, Debra
Our Lady Of The
Sacred Heart HS
Coraopolis, PA

Smith, Georgetta
Lyn
Mary Fuller Frazier
Memorial HS
Grindstone, PA

Smith, Gregory D
Ambridge Area HS
Baden, PA

Smith, Heather
Du Bois Area HS
Reynoldsville, PA

Smith, Heidi
Faith Baptist
Christian Acad
Levittown, PA

Smith, Jackie
Northern Cambria
Spangler, PA

Smith, Jamie
Lower Moreland HS
Huntingdon Valley,
PA

Smith, Jeff
Bishop Mc Corr HS
Johnstown, PA

Smith, Jennifer
Loyalsock HS
Montoursville, PA

Smith, Joanne
Catasauqua HS
Catasauqua, PA

Smith, Jodeen
Blair County
Christian HS
Duncansville, PA

Smith, John S
Thomas Jefferson
Pittsburgh, PA

Smith, Judy
Hempfield Area HS
Madison, PA

Smith, Julie
Brockway Area HS
Brockport, PA

Smith, Karol A
Octorara Area HS
Parkesburg, PA

Smith, Kelli
Penn Hills HS
Pittsburgh, PA

Smith, Kellyann
Bishop Kenrick HS
Norristown, PA

Smith, Kristin
Northeast Bradford
Rome, PA

Smith, Kristin Ann
Thomas Jefferson
Clairton, PA

Smith, Leslie
Chambersburg Area
SR HS
Fayetteville, PA

Smith, Jr Leslie
Brockway Area HS
Brockway, PA

Smith, Lori
Catasauqua HS
Catasauqua, PA

Smith, Maggie
Fox Chapel Area HS
Pittsburgh, PA

Smith, Megan
Harrisburg Acad
Carlisle, PA

Smith, Melissa
Du Bois Area SR
Penfield, PA

Smith, Michael A
Milton Hershey Schl
King Of Prussia, PA

Smith, Patricia
Avon Grove HS
W Grove, PA

Smith, Paula
Oxford Area HS
Nottingham, PA

Smith, Renee M
Penn Cambria HS
Gallitzin, PA

Smith, Rhonda
Westinghouse HS
Pittsburgh, PA

Smith, Robert
Southmoreland SR
Alverton, PA

Smith, Ronna Rae
Freeport Area Joint
Sarver, PA

Smith, Tracey
Punxsutawney Area
Punxsutawney, PA

Smith, Tracy
Boyertown HS
Bechtelsville, PA

Smith, Vicki
Lower Moreland HS
Huntingdon Valley,
PA

Smith, Wendy E
Crestwood HS
Wapwallopen, PA

Smith, William
Greater Johnstown
Johnstown, PA

Smithmyer, Ann
Bishop Carroll HS
Loretto, PA

Smoker, Ken
Northern Potter HS
Genesee, PA

Smyers, Bertrand
North Catholic HS
Glenshaw, PA

Snare, Eric
Lincoln HS
Ellwood City, PA

Snare, Robert
Tussey Mountain
Saxton, PA

Snee, Michelle
West Greene HS
Wind Ridge, PA

Snee, Thomas
Plum HS
Pittsburgh, PA

Sneeringer, Jo Ann
Delone Catholic HS
Hanover, PA

Snyder, Bryan
Salisbury HS
Bethlehem, PA

Snyder, Grace E
South Park HS
Library, PA

Snyder, Holly
Governor Mifflin HS
Shillington, PA

Snyder, Melissa
Muhlenberg HS
Reading, PA

Snyder, Michelle
Southern Columbia
Area HS
Elysburg, PA

Snyder, Patricia
Solanco HS
Quarryville, PA

Snyder, Wendy
Milton SR HS
Milton, PA

Snyder, William
William Allen HS
Allentown, PA

Soforic, Vanessa
Geibel HS
Scottdale, PA

Sohns, Lori J
Lakeland HS
Olyphant, PA

Solomon, Keith
Penn-Trafford HS
Level Green, PA

Solsman, Debra
Dunmore HS
Dunmore, PA

Soltis, Carole
W Branch Area HS
Hawk Run, PA

Somensky, Frani
St Hubert HS For
Philadelphia, PA

Somers, Rebecca
Bald Eagle Area HS
Milesburg, PA

Sommer, Gregory
Bethlehem Catholic
Bethlehem, PA

Sonnen, David
Conrad Weiser HS
Richland, PA

Soo Hoo, Lea
Northern Lebanon
Lebanon, PA

Soos, Angela
Owen J Roberts HS
Spring City, PA

Soranno, Thomas
Bishop Ohara HS
Peckville, PA

Sorrentino, Eric
George David
Manor HS
Ft Relvior, VA

Sortman, Trina
Shikellamy SR HS
Sunbury, PA

Sosko, Jeff
Mt Pleasant Area
Mount Pleasant, PA

Sotak, Amy L
Bethlehem Ctr
Brownsville, PA

Soto, Edwin
Bensalem HS
Trevose, PA

Sottile, Louise
Bishop Hannan HS
Scranton, PA

Souders, Martha
Archbishop Ryan
High Schl For Girls
Philadelphia, PA

Southerling, E
Andrew
Farther Judge HS
Jenkintown, PA

Sowers, Lisa
Grove City SR HS
Grove City, PA

Spadell, Susan
Crestwood HS
Wh Haven, PA

Spagnolo, Beth
Richland HS
Wexford, PA

Spahr, Damion
Hanover SR HS
Hanover, PA

Spahr, Lisa
Northern HS
Wellsville, PA

Spak, Ann
Punxsutawney Area
Reynoldsville, PA

Spangler, Dane
Governor Mifflin SR
Reading, PA

Spangler, Lorie
Northeastern SR HS
Dover, PA

Spargo, Todd A
Tussey Mt HS
Riddlesburg, PA

Sparvero, Louis J
Fox Chapel Area HS
Pittsburgh, PA

Spatola, Kevin
Hamburg Area HS
Hamburg, PA

Spayd, Carl
Muhlenberg SR HS
Laureldale, PA

Spector, Jill
Springfield
Township HS
Wyndmoor, PA

Spector, Larry
Abington HS
Huntingdon Valley, PA

Speelman, Veronica
Connellsville Area
Connellsville, PA

Speer, Sharon
Central Bucks West
Chalfont, PA

Spencer, Charles
Curwensville Area
Grampian, PA

Spencer, Shannon
Central Dauphin
East HS
Harrisburg, PA

Spencer, Susan
Bishop Mc Devitt
Wyncote, PA

Spennati, Amy
Aliquippa HS
Aliquippa, PA

Spickerman, Nancy
New Brighton Area
SR HS
New Brighton, PA

Spiewak, Joseph
Father Judge HS
Philadelphia, PA

Spina, Christina
Canon Mc Millan
Canonsburg, PA

Spirko, Jennifer
Mt Pleasant Area
SR HS
Mt Pleasant, PA

Splain, John M
Columbia Boro JR
SR HS
Columbia, PA

Spock, Shawn
Shamokin Area HS
Shamokin, PA

Spolar, Renee
Ambridge Area HS
Baden, PA

Spoonhour, Corey
Chambersburg Area
SR HS
Chambersburg, PA

Sporner, Diane
Elk County
Christian HS
St Marys, PA

Spotts, Beth
Penns Manor HS
Penn Run, PA

Spotts, Dale
Line Mountain HS
Dalmatia, PA

Spotts, Jeff
Southern Columbia
Area HS
Shamokin, PA

Spotts, Jr Richard D
Seneca Valley SR
Renfrew, PA

Spotts, Vincent J
Seneca Valley HS
Renfrew, PA

Spresser, Rebecca
Mc Keesport Area
Mckeesport, PA

Spring, Penny
Hughesville HS
Muncy Valley, PA

Srbinovich, Michael
Mapletown HS
Bobtown, PA

St Amant, Kelly
Rocky Grove HS
Franklin, PA

Staab, Rachel
Carlynton HS
Carnegie, PA

Stacey, Robert
Altoona Area HS
Altoona, PA

Stachacz, James
Bishop O Hara HS
Dickson City, PA

Stachel, Wendy
Scranton HS
Scranton, PA

Stade, William R
Strath Haven HS
Wallingford, PA

Stafford, Christie
Canon-Mc Millan
Clearwater, FL

Stafford, Darlene
Marie
Norristown Area HS
Norristown, PA

Stahle, Rachel
Dallastown Area HS
Dallastown, PA

Stahley, Deborah L
Perkiomen Valley
Schwenksville, PA

Stains, Brent
Greencastle-Antrim
Chambersburg, PA

Stairs, Ann
Hempfield HS
Monheim, PA

Stambaugh, Denise
Hatboro-Horsham
Hatboro, PA

Stambaugh, Paige
Homburg Area HS
Strausstown, PA

Stambaugh, Steve
Central SR HS
York, PA

Staph, Allison
Pocono Mountain
SR HS
Pocono Pines, PA

Stapleton, Mary
Ann
United HS
Indiana, PA

Stark, Sean
Saucon Valley SR
Hellertown, PA

Starner, Tamala
Southwestern HS
Hanover, PA

Starr, Jean
Saint Maria Goretti
Philadelphia, PA

Starr, Patrick
Freedom HS
Bethlehem, PA

Stas, Eric A
Emmaus HS
Macungie, PA

Stassi, Phil
Neshaminy HS
Langhorne, PA

Staub, D Deette
Delone Catholic HS
Hanover, PA

Staudt, Todd
Troy Area HS
Troy, PA

Stauffer, Kirk
Thomas
Manheim Township
Lancaster, PA

Stauffer, Robert
Northern Cambria
Barnesboro, PA

Stauffer, Tracy
Emmaus HS
Emmaus, PA

Stawarz, Margaret
Windber Area HS
Windber, PA

Stawitz, Eric
Cumberland Valley
Camp Hill, PA

Steadman, Heather
Conrad Weiser JS
Robesonia, PA

Steals, Tyrone T
Aliquippa SR HS
Aliquippa, PA

Stebbins, Sonja
Newport HS
Newport, PA

Stec, Dave
Scranton Central
Scranton, PA

Steele, Douglas
Henderson SR HS
West Chester, PA

Steele, Lu Ann
Central Dauphin HS
Harrisburg, PA

Steele, Teresa
Punxsutawney HS
Punxsutawney, PA

Steff, Paul A
Western Beaver JR
SR HS
Industry, PA

Steffens, Paul A
Germantown Acad
Ft Washington, PA

Steffy, Ann
Cedar Crest HS
Lebanon, PA

Steffy, Dana
Punxsutawney Area
Punxsutawney, PA

Steffy, Marijo
Exeter SR HS
Reading, PA

Stegenga, II David I
Chartiers-Houston
Houston, PA

Stein, Brian
Bensalem HS
Bensalem, PA

Stein, Jennifer
Akiba Hebrew Acad
Philadelphia, PA

Stein, Michelle
Ambridge Area HS
Ambridge, PA

Steinbring, Michele
Lea
Greater Johnstown
Johnstown, PA

Steinhauer, R
Douglas
Warwick HS
Lititz, PA

Stelacone, Lee
Wyoming Area HS
Wyoming, PA

Stellwagen, Robin
Neshaminy HS
Trevose, PA

Stepaniuk, Kimberly
Bishop Conwell HS
Morrisville, PA

Stephens, Amy
Rocky Grove HS
Franklin, PA

Sterling, Shannon
Saegertown Area HS
Saegertown, PA

Steup, Clayton
Robert
Quaker Valley SR
Edgeworth, PA

Stevenson, Dale
Solanco HS
New Providence, PA

Stevenson, Dean
Grace Christian Schl
Myerstown, PA

Stewart, Amy
Fannett-Metal HS
Doylesburg, PA

Stewart, Angela
Karns City HS
Bruin, PA

Stewart, Beth
Carlynton HS
Carnegie, PA

Stewart, Daphne A
Central Dauphin
East HS
Dauphin, PA

Stewart, Lisa
West Phila Catholic
Girls HS
Philadelphia, PA

Stewart, Nicole Dee
Ephrata HS
Akron, PA

Stewart, Rachel
York County Area
York, PA

Stewart, Robert
Greensburg-Salem
Greensburg, PA

Stewart, William
Trnity HS
Carlisle, PA

Sticklin, Danielle
Danville Area HS
Danville, PA

Stier, John
Penn Hills SR HS
Verona, PA

Stifel, Elizabeth
Winchester-Thursto
n HS
Pittsburgh, PA

Stiffey, Brian
Hempfield Area HS
Greensburg, PA

Stiffler, Kristine
Quigley HS
Aliquippa, PA

Still, Kirsten
Freedom HS
Bethlehem, PA

Stillions, Jerry
Kiski Area HS
E Vandergrift, PA

Stine, Sandra
Downingtown SR
Chester Springs, PA

Stinson, Renita
Trinity HS
Washington, PA

Stites, Shannon
Elizabethtown Area
Elizabethtown, PA

Stockman, Matt
Canon Mc Millan
SR HS
Wash, PA

Stoe, Christy
Lancaster Country
Day Schl
Lancaster, PA

Stohl, Hollylynne
Mt Pleasant Area
Mt Pleasant, PA

Stoianoff, Jennifer
Chief Logan HS
Mcclure, PA

Stolze, Brian
Avella Area HS
Burgettstown, PA

Stone, Daniel
Benjamin
Warren Area HS
Buffalo, NY

Stoner, Jodie
Blair County
Christian HS
Ebensburg, PA

Stoops, Kim
Slippery Rock Area
Harrisville, PA

Storey, Jennifer
Peters Township HS
Mc Murray, PA

Storms, Eric
Altoona Area HS
Altoona, PA

Stotka, Lisa
Hopewell HS
Aliquippa, PA

Stouffer, Lawrence
Greater Latrobe SR
Latrobe, PA

Stout, Taylorina
Yough SR HS
Herminie, PA

Stover, Melissa
Middleburg Joint
New Berlin, PA

Strachan, Bill
Norwin SR HS
Irwin, PA

Strait, Chris
Mc Connellsburg HS
Harrisonville, PA

Strait, Janet
Mc Connellsburg HS
Mcconnellsburg, PA

Straka, Joel W
Sewickley Acad
Sewickley, PA

Strank, Paula
Conemaugh Valley
JR SR HS
Johnstown, PA

Stratts, George
Archbishop Carroll
Newtown Sq, PA

Strauss, Leslie
Northern Lebanon
Jonestown, PA

Strauss, Mary Grace
Centger HS
Aliquippa, PA

Strausser, Beth
Phoenixville Area
Phoenixville, PA

Strayer, Shelley
Chestnut Ridge HS
Schellsburg, PA

Strelecky, Beth
Upper Perkiomen
Pennsburg, PA

Streletzky, Linda
Bethlehem Catholic
Bethlehem, PA

Stricker, Robert
Newport HS
Newport, PA

Strickland, Karen
Archbishop Wood
Girls HS
Doylestown, PA

Stringer, Penney
Governor Mifflin HS
Reading, PA

Strnisa, Chris
Canon-Mc Millan
Canonsburg, PA

Strojek, Leslie
Ambridge Area HS
Ambridge, PA

Strong, Ashley
Villa Maria Acad
Erie, PA

Stroud, Alisa R
South Hills HS
Pittsburgh, PA

Strozyk, Kathleen
Canton Area JR SR
Canton, PA

Stuart, Robert
Northeastern SR HS
Mt Wolf, PA

Stubanas, Diedre
Spring-Ford SR HS
Montclare, PA

Stuck, III William
Chief Logan HS
Yeagertown, PA

Stuckey, Tom
Newport HS
Newport, PA

Student, Joseph D
West Hazleton HS
W Hazelton, PA

Stull, Monica
Geibel HS
Scottdale, PA

Stump, Lori
Juaniata HS
Mifflintown, PA

Stumpo, Jeff
Westmont Hilltop
Johnstown, PA

Stumpo, Paulalee
St Huberts Catholic
Philadelphia, PA

Sturiale, Lisa
Kiski Area HS
Avonmore, PA

Stutzman, Andrew
K
Cedar Cliff HS
New Cumberland,
PA

Stutzman, Lee Ann
Rockwood Area HS
Somerset, PA

Styer, Yvonne
Philadelphia HS For
Philadelphia, PA

Stys, Deanna
Trinity HS
Washington, PA

Suchar, Mike
Bethel Park HS
Pittsburgh, PA

Suchy, Laura A
Bethel Park HS
Bethel Park, PA

Suhy, David A
Bethel Park HS
Bethel Park, PA

Sukay, Missy
Greensburg Salem
Greensburg, PA

Sulak, Mary
Fairchance Georges
Uniontown, PA

Sulikowski, Miranda
Pennsbury HS
Fairless Hills, PA

Sullivan, Kathleen
Nortre Dame Of
Green Pond HS
Easton, PA

Sullivan, Michelle
St Hubert HS
Philadelphia, PA

Sullivan, Neil
Bishop Mc Devitt
Harrisburg, PA

Sulouff, Christine
Shikellamy HS
Northumberland,
PA

Sultage, C Nicole
Tyrone Area HS
Tyrone, PA

Sultzer, Marcy
Mt Pleasant Area
SR HS
Mt Pleasant, PA

Summerly, Lynn C
Mc Keesport Area
White Oaks, PA

Summers, Kathy
Elizabethtown Area
Elizabethtown, PA

Summers, Melissa
Octorara Area HS
Kinzers, PA

Summerson, Valarie
Cameron County HS
Sinnamanoning, PA

Sunderman, Rebecca
Lynn
Center HS
Aliquippa, PA

Sundy, George
Chartiers Valley HS
Bridgeville, PA

Surkovich, Nancy
Moshannon Valley
Houtzdale, PA

Susko, Joanne
Salisbury Township
SR HS
Allentown, PA

Sutcavage, Beth A
Dallas SR HS
Trucksville, PA

Sutkowski, Beverly
Lincoln HS
Ellwood City, PA

Sutton, Jack C
Saegertown HS
Saegertown, PA

Sutts, Annarie
Monongahela Valley
Catholic HS
Monongahela, PA

Svitak, Lisa Marie
Little Flower
Catholic HS Fo
Philadelphia, PA

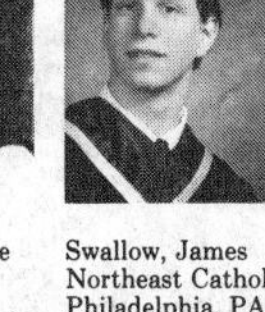

Swallow, James
Northeast Catholic
Philadelphia, PA

Swanson, Kelly
State College Area
State College, PA

Swartz, Kristin L
Northeastern SR HS
York, PA

Swartz, Matt
Pottstown HS
Pottstown, PA

Swartz, Michael
Todd
Hollidaysburg Area
Duncansville, PA

Sweatman, Patricia
A
B Reed Henderson
W Chester, PA

Sweeney, Kathe
Pius X HS
E Bangor, PA

Sweet, Anita
Fairchance George
JR SR HS
Smithfield, PA

Sweigert, Edward
Marian Catholic HS
Brockton, PA

Sweitzer, David
Connellsville Area
SR HS
Mt Pleasant, PA

Swift, Aaron
Clearfield Area HS
Clearfield, PA

Swigart, Karen
Lenape Area
Vocational Tech
Worthington, PA

Swineford, David
Brookville Area HS
Brookville, PA

Swinehart, Lisa
Nothern York HS
Dillsburg, PA

Swisher, Susan
Downingtown HS
Coatesville, PA

Switalski, Lori Ann
North Catholic HS
Glenshaw, PA

Swope, Allen
Altoona Area HS
Altoona, PA

Swope, Gary
Cumberlan Valley
Christian HS
Waynesboro, PA

Swope, Randall
Du Bois Area SR
Luthersburg, PA

Sword, Stacie
Harmony HS
Westover, PA

Sypolt, Cynthia
Kiski Area HS
Apollo, PA

Szanyi, Neil
Liberty HS
Bethlehem, PA

Szczublewski, Susan
Mount Alvernia HS
Pittsburgh, PA

Szekeresh, Lynn
Central Cambria HS
Johnstown, PA

Szepesi, Michelle
Connellsville Area
S Connellsville, PA

Szolis, Leigh A
Richland HS
Wexford, PA

Szuszczewicz,
Brenda
Nazareth Academy
Philadelphia, PA

Szymanski, Thomas
Peabody HS
Pittsburgh, PA

Szymecki, Julie
Harborcreek HS
Erie, PA

Tabarrini, Tara
Old Forge HS
Old Forge, PA

Tabatabai, Ali
Lower Merion HS
Narberth, PA

Tabron, Judith L
Chambersburg Area
SR HS
Scotland, PA

Taczak, Marcy L
Avella Area JR-SR
Burgettstown, PA

Tagliaboski, Larie
Bald Eagle Area HS
Bellefonte, PA

Tagliente, Don
Clearfield HS
Clearfield, PA

Taglieri, Vincent J
Father Judge HS
Philadelphia, PA

Tainton, Tracy L
Lakeview HS
Sandy Lake, PA

Tallaksen, Stephanie
Northampton HS
Northampton, PA

Talone, Stephanie
Connellsville SR HS
Connellsville, PA

Talotta, Angel
St Maria Goretti HS
Philadelphia, PA

Taluba, Denise
James M Coughlin
Wilkes Barre, PA

Tamarkin, Susan
York Suburban SR
York, PA

Tamburro, David
Springdale HS
Springdale, PA

Tanner, Angela
Wm Allen HS
Allentown, PA

Tarabrella, Christina
Elizabeth Forward
Elizabeth, PA

Tarcson, Tim
Central Christian
Du Bois, PA

Tarnosky, Jerry
Canevin HS
Carnegie, PA

Tarquinio, Suzanne
Canevin HS
Coraopolis, PA

Tasker, Heather
Delaware County
Christian Schl
Berwyn, PA

Tasker, Tim
Pennsburg HS
Yardley, PA

Tatman, II Lester
St Josephs Prep HS
Philadelphia, PA

Taylor, Jr B
Theodore
Pequea Valley HS
Gordonville, PA

Taylor, Brett
North Penn HS
North Wales, PA

Taylor, Cherie
Germantown HS
Philadelphia, PA

Taylor, Debbie
Lourdes Regional
Shamokin, PA

Taylor, Elizabeth H
Cardinal O Hara HS
Aston, PA

Taylor, John A
Mount Carmel Area
Mt Carmel, PA

Taylor, Keith
Chester HS
Chester, PA

Taylor, Kristin
Red Lion Area SR
Red Lion, PA

Taylor, Maureen
Shippensburg Area
SR HS
Shippensburg, PA

Taylor, Scott
Elk County
Christian HS
St Marys, PA

Teague, Carol
Chambersburg Area
SR HS
Chambersburg, PA

Teeter, Glenn
Peters Township HS
Venetia, PA

Ten Broeck, Leslie
A
Conestoga SR HS
Strafford, PA

Tereshko, Olga J
Hempfield Area SR
Greensburg, PA

Terotta, Tina
Scranton
Preparatory Schl
Old Forge, PA

Terranova, Jr
Leonard J
St Josephs
Preparatory Schl
Philadelphia, PA

Terrill, Robert
Cathedral Prep
Erie, PA

Terroni, Christopher
M
Council Rock HS
Holland, PA

Terry, Lisa-Ann
Marian Catholic HS
Lansford, PA

Tessitore, Dan
Central Bucks HS
Warrington, PA

Testa, IV Vincent
James
Burgettstown Area
JR SR HS
Burgettstown, PA

Theal, Barbara
Manheim Central
Manheim, PA

Theorgood, Jillian
Moon HS
Corapolis, PA

Therit, Tracey
Littlestown HS
Hanover, PA

Thi, Ut Vo
Mc Caskey HS
Lancaster, PA

Thieler, Dolly
Connellsville Area
SR HS
Mt Pleasant, PA

Thomas, Aimee
Old Forge HS
Old Forge, PA

Thomas, Catherine
Manheim Central
Manheim, PA

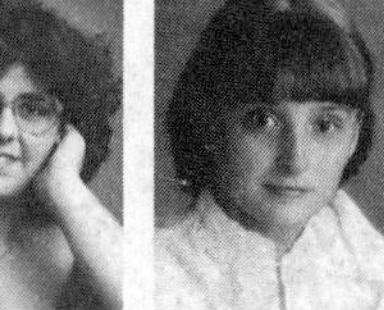
Thomas, Christina L
Harborcreek HS
Erie, PA

Thomas, Holly L
Mifflinburg Area HS
Mifflinburg, PA

Thomas, Jami
Millville Area HS
Bloomsburg, PA

Thomas, Pamela
Pine Grove Area HS
Tremont, PA

Thomas, Rebecca
Fairview HS
Erie, PA

Thomas, Robert J
West Allegheny HS
Oakdale, PA

Thomas, Sean
Barkley
Abraham Lincoln
Philadelphia, PA

Thomason, Jr Bruce
Saint James
Catholic HS
Brookhaven, PA

Thompson,
Alexander
Pottsgrove HS
Pottstown, PA

Thompson, Alice
Mount Calvary
Christian Schl
Mt Joy, PA

Thompson, Angela
M
Harrisburg HS
Harrisburg, PA

Thompson, Brian E
Leechburg Area HS
Leechburg, PA

Thompson, II David
C
Kennedy Christian
Transfer, PA

Thompson, David N
Red Lion Area SR
Airville, PA

Thompson, John
Henry
Penncrest HS
Media, PA

Thompson, Laurel
Hatboro-Horsham
SR HS
Horsham, PA

Thompson, Pauline
Berwick Area SR
Wapwallopen, PA

Thompson,
Stephanie
Kennard-Dale HS
Stewartstown, PA

Thompson, Tracey
Shaler Area HS
Pittsburgh, PA

Thompson, Trudi
Christina
Berwick Area SR
Wapwallopen, PA

Thoms, Richard
Chambersburg Area
SR HS
Chambersburg, PA

Thomson, Laura
Plum SR HS
Pittsburgh, PA

Thrower, Stephanie
Knoch JR SR HS
Saxonburg, PA

Tiberio, Joanna
Western Beaver HS
Industry, PA

Tilghman, Gregory S
Northeast HS
Philadelphia, PA

Timblin, Becky
Bald Eagle Area HS
Howard, PA

Timko, Lisa
Our Lady Of The
Sacred Heart HS
W Aliquippa, PA

Tincler, Rose Irene
Venango Christian
Kill Devil Hills, NC

Tinkey, Lori
Connellsville Area
Indian Head, PA

Tirdel, David
Valley HS
New Kensington,
PA

Tkacik, Kristin
Franklin Regional
Murrysville, PA

Tobin, Timothy
Mahanoy Area HS
Gilberton, PA

Toboz, Stephen
Lock Haven HS
Lock Haven, PA

Toliver, Walter
Saint Josephs Prep
Philadelphia, PA

Toltesi, Suzanne
Freedom HS
Bethlehem, PA

Tomanchek, Michael
Hazleton HS
Hazleton, PA

Tomaro, Mary Ann
Connellsville Area
Cnlvle, PA

Tomasello, Denise
South Allegheny HS
Liberty Boro, PA

Tomko, Kerrie
West Middlesex HS
Sharon, PA

Tomko, Stephen
Vincent
Mc Keesport Area
White Oak, PA

Tommasin, Lisa
Canon-Mc Millan
SR HS
Canonsburg, PA

Tonty, Pamela Jane
Mercyhurst Prep
Erie, PA

Toole, Padraic
Fox Chapel HS
Cheswick, PA

Topaz, Rhonda
Lawer Moreland HS
Huntingdon Valley,
PA

Torboli, Lisa
Trinity HS
Washington, PA

Toth, Gayle
Belle Vernon Area
Belle Vernon, PA

Toth, Michele
Liberty HS
Bethlehem, PA

Toubo, Michelle
Moshannon Valley
JR SR HS
Madera, PA

Touvell, Charlene
Brookville Area HS
Brookville, PA

Townsend, Resha
Kiski Area HS
Vandergrift, PA

Toy, Tim
Freedom HS
Bethlehem, PA

Trachtenberg, David
Upper Moreland HS
Huntingdon Valley,
PA

Traggiai, Regina
Knoch JR SR HS
Cabot, PA

Train, Timothy
Delawae County
Christian HS
Newtown Sq, PA

Tran, Cuong
Allentown Central
Catholic HS
Allentown, PA

Tran, Dung
Souderton Area HS
Philadelphia, PA

Tranguch, Katy
Bishop Hafey HS
Hazleton, PA

Trautman, Kimberly
A
Central HS
E Freedom, PA

Trautz, Thom
Northeast Catholic
Philadelphia, PA

Travers, Colleen
Merion Mercy Acad
Havertown, PA

Treece, Georgia
Mapletown JR SR
Greensboro, PA

Treffinger, Christine
A
Upper Perkiomen
East Greenville, PA

Trego, Pam
Downingtown SR
Downingtown, PA

Tremewen, Susan
Archbishop Wood H
S For Girls
Holland, PA

Trent, Richard
Glendale JR SR HS
Coalport, PA

Trexler, Melissa
Northampton HS
Northampton, PA

Triantafillou, Greg
Upper Darby HS
Upper Darby, PA

Trice, Scott
Mt Pleasant Area
Mt Pleasant, PA

Trimmer, Heather
Northern York
County HS
Lewisbury, PA

Trinidad, Tracie
Philipsburg-Osceola
Philipsburg, PA

Tritt, Julie
Big Spring SR HS
Plainfield, PA

Troiani, Annmarie
Quigley HS
Midland, PA

Trombley, Jr
Theodore
Hatboro-Horsham
SR HS
Hatboro, PA

Trost, Deborah
Ringgold HS
Monongahela, PA

Trotter, Bruce
Northwestern
Lehigh HS
Kempton, PA

Troup, Deanna
West Snyder HS
Beaver Springs, PA

Trout, Andrew
Northern Lebanon
Lebanon, PA

Trout, Teresa
Greater Latrobe SR
Greensburg, PA

Troutman, John
W Hazleton SR HS
Conyngham, PA

Troutman, Joy
Meyersdale Area HS
Hyndman, PA

Trozzolillo, Maria
Bishop Hannon HS
Scranton, PA

Truax, Holly
Cardinal Ohara HS
Chester, PA

True, Anne Michelle
Greencastle Antrim
Greencastle, PA

Trullender, Renee
Hollidaysburg Area
SR HS
Altoona, PA

Trump, Andrea
Eastern Lebanon
County HS
Myerstown, PA

Truong, Do
Elizabethtown HS
Elizabethtown, PA

Trussler, Shari
The Baptist HS
Clarks Summit, PA

Tubbs, Melissa
Curwensville Area
Curwensville, PA

Tucker, Belinda
Mc Connellsburg HS
Harrisonville, PA

Tukloff, Stacy
Henderson HS
West Chester, PA

Tullar, Courtney
Avonworth JR/SR
Pittsbg, PA

Tullock, Christen
Liberty HS
Bethlehem, PA

Tuman, John
Northeast Catholic
Philadelphia, PA

Tuohy, IV Edward
Robert
Council Rock HS
Newtown, PA

Turchi, Joseph
Plymouth-Whitemar
sh HS
Norristown, PA

Turchiarolo, Mario J
Archbishop John
Carroll For Boys
Philadelphia, PA

Turley, Laura
John S Fine SR HS
Nanticoke, PA

Turlip, Mary Ellen
Bishop O Hara HS
Archbald, PA

Turner, Joseph
Father Judge RC
Philadelphia, PA

Turner, Kimberly
Mercyhurst Prep
Erie, PA

Turner, Marquette
W
Central Catholic HS
Pittsburgh, PA

Turner, Scott
Coughlin HS
Wilkes Barre, PA

Turner, Tracie
Forest City Regional
Pleasant Mt, PA

Turner, Trent
Lock Haven SR HS
Lock Haven, PA

Tutera, David A
Duquesne HS
Duquesne, PA

Tutrone, Edward
Pocono Mt HS
Pocono Pines, PA

Tuttle, Wayne
Harbor Creek HS
Erie, PA

Twist, Todd
Milton SR HS
Milton, PA

Tyger, Tonya
Punxsutawney HS
Glen Campbell, PA

Typovsky, Kelly
CA Area HS
Daisytown, PA

Tytke, William
Steel Valley HS
Munhall, PA

Uber, Phil
Grove City HS
Grove City, PA

Uberti, Michelle
Du Bois Area HS
Penfield, PA

Udell, Harran
Upper Dublin HS
Ambler, PA

Ufberg, David
Parkland HS
Allentown, PA

Uhlman, Lori
Connecut Valley HS
Linesville, PA

Ukryn, Heather Joy
Hempfield SR HS
Irwin, PA

Umphrey, Patti L
Canon Mc Millan
SR HS
Strabane, PA

Unger, Heidi
Michele
Moon SR HS
Coraopolis, PA

Unger, Jr James G
Kenneth HS
Chadds Ford, PA

Urban, Ian
Conestoga SR HS
Wayne, PA

Urban, Rachel
Hershey HS
Hershey, PA

Urbany, Lisa M
Trinity HS
Washington, PA

Urich, Michael
West Perry SR HS
Elliottsburg, PA

Usaitis, Robert
Wyoming Valley
West HS
Kingston, PA

Vaccari, Natalie
Ringgold SR HS
Finleyville, PA

Vaccone, Michelle
Strath Haven HS
Wallingford, PA

Vaclavik, Steven
Upper Dauphin
Area HS
Millersburg, PA

Vahaly, Perry
Belle Vernon Area
Belle Vernon, PA

Valderrama, Wendy
Wyoming Seminary
Prep Schl
Shavertown, PA

Valenti, Mark
New Castle HS
New Castle, PA

Valentine, Hope
Pottstown SR HS
Pottstown, PA

Valentine, Laura
Pleasant Valley HS
Columbia, NJ

Valeriano, Deena R
Oley Valley HS
Oley, PA

Van, Cheryl
Delaware Valley SR
Milford, PA

Van Cleve, Jacqui
Bristol JR SR HS
Bristol, PA

Van Fleet, Brian
Lackawann Trail HS
Dalton, PA

Van Sickle, Scott
Uniontown HS
Uniontown, PA

Van Voorhis, Gregg
Franklin Regional
Murrysville, PA

Vandegrift, Cheryl
Neshaminy HS
Levittown, PA

Vanek, Dennis
Valley HS
New Kensington, PA

Vannucci, Dave
Frazier HS
Fayette City, PA

Varadhachary, Arun
Council Rock HS
Newtown, PA

Varady, Joseph
Owen J Roberts HS
Phoenixville, PA

Vargo, Robert
Nazareth Area SR
Nazareth, PA

Varner, Keith
Forest Hills HS
Johnstown, PA

Varner, Michelle Rayne
Seneca Valley SR
Harmony, PA

Vattieri, Teresa
Saint Huberts Catholic HS
Philadelphia, PA

Vaughn, Jeffrey
Philipsburg-Osceola SR HS
Sandy Ridge, PA

Vavrick, Michelle
Dunmore HS
Dunmore, PA

Vayansky, Tom
Mon Valley Catholic
Belle Vernon, PA

Vayda, Ron
Swissvale HS
Pittsburgh, PA

Veard, Christine
Cornell HS
Coraopolis, PA

Velisaris, Elaine
Canon Mc Millan SR HS
Canonsburg, PA

Venarchick, Kelly
Danville SR HS
Danville, PA

Veno, Arthur
Mid-Valley HS
Dickson City, PA

Verba, Michael
Saucon Valley SR
Hellertown, PA

Verduci, Carmela A
Bishop Shanahan
Westchester, PA

Vereb, Melissa
Villa Maria Acad
Erie, PA

Vergenes, Denise
Sto-Rox SR HS
Mc Kees Rocks, PA

Verna, Lori
Norwin SR HS
N Huntingdon, PA

Vernon, Sara E
Central Bucks H S
Doylestown, PA

Veronesi, David
Belle Vernon Area
Belle Vernon, PA

Victor, Tina
Bentworth HS
Bentleyville, PA

Vigna, Bill
Leechburg Area HS
Leechburg, PA

Vilchock, Tamara
Old Forge HS
Old Forge, PA

Vilcko, Kenneth
Hazleton HS
Drums, PA

Vincenti, Tracy
Burgettstown JR SR
Burgettstown, PA

Vinci, Donna
St Maria Goretti HS
Philadelphia, PA

Vinglas, Oriana
Penn Cambria HS
Portage, PA

Viola, Jason
Archbishop Kennedy HS
Philadelphia, PA

Viola, Michael
Father Judge HS
Philadelphia, PA

Virus, Lisa
Upper Perkiomen
Barto, PA

Vishneski, Kelly
Downingtown SR
West Chester, PA

Vitale, Anthony
Belle Vernon Area
Belle Vernon, PA

Vitelli, Mark
Pittston Area HS
Pittston, PA

Vituszynski, Laura
Cedar Crest HS
Lebanon, PA

Voci, Frank
St Josephs Prep
Cherry Hill, NJ

Voeghtly, Carla
Johnstown Vo-Tech
Johnstown, PA

Vogel, Valarie
Shady Side Acad
Monroeville, PA

Voit, Michael
Shaler HS
Glenshaw, PA

Volz, Kelly
Seneca Valley HS
Evans Cty, PA

Von Campbell, Timothy
Shenango HS
New Castle, PA

Vosefski, Theresa
Northampton Area SR HS
Bath, PA

Vrcek, Taris
Sto-Rox HS
Mc Kees Rocks, PA

Vresilovic, John
Homer Center HS
Coral, PA

Vucelich, Danice
Plum SR HS
Pittsburgh, PA

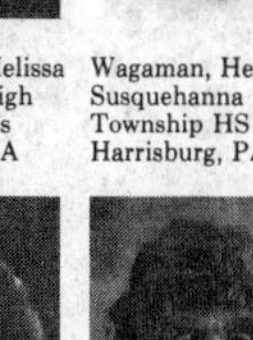

Vukmanic, Todd J
Bishop Mc Devitt
Bressler Steelto, PA

Vullo, Tamara Ann
Riverside JR SR HS
Taylor, PA

Wadhwani, Geeta
Bethleham Ctr
Brownsville, PA

Wadsworth, Bill
Shaler Area HS
Glenshaw, PA

Wadsworth, Jeff
Connellsville Area
Scottdale, PA

Wafford, Ivy Melissa
Philadelphia High School For Girls
Philadelphia, PA

Wagaman, Heidi N
Susquehanna Township HS
Harrisburg, PA

Wagman, Allan
Wissahickon SR HS
Ambler, PA

Wagner, Gregory
Sacred Heart HS
Jermyn, PA

Wagner, Liesl
Lock Haven SR HS
Woolrich, PA

Wagner, Matthew
Downington SR HS
Downingtown, PA

Wagner, Patricia
Plymouth-Whitemarsh HS
Conshohocken, PA

Wagner, Robert
Notre Dame HS
Easton, PA

Wagner, Sharon
Cedar Crest HS
Lebanon, PA

Waite, Sherry A
Clearfield Area HS
Clearfield, PA

Wajler, Bonita J
Neshannock HS
New Castle, PA

Wales, Sheri
Dallastown Area HS
Dallastown, PA

Walker, Gary
Weatherly Area HS
Weatherly, PA

Walker, Kristina
Blairsville SR HS
Blairsville, PA

Walker, Lee M
Cocalico HS
Denver, PA

Walker, Melissa
Bensalem HS
Bensalem, PA

Walkow, Marc
Seneca Valley SR
Harmony, PA

Walkup, Doug
Upper Darby HS
Drexel Hl, PA

Wall, Kevin
Yough SR HS
Ruffsdale, PA

Wallace, John
Penn Trafford HS
Irwin, PA

Wallace, Libby
Conneaut Lake HS
Atlantic, PA

Wallace, Michael
Altoona Area HS
Altoona, PA

Walls, Orville
William Penn
Charter Schl
Philadelphia, PA

Walsh, Brian
Emmaus HS
Macungie, PA

Walsh, Laurene
Center Area HS
Monaca, PA

Walsh, Thomas
Council Rock HS
Newtown, PA

Walter, Brian
Big Spring HS
Newville, PA

Walter, Mark
Nazareth Area SR
Nazareth, PA

Walter, Nolita
Westside Christian
Dover, PA

Walters, Dianne
Cocalico HS
Denver, PA

Walters, Judy
Northampton SR
Northampton, PA

Walters, Lowell
Northern Bedford
County HS
Bakers Summit, PA

Walther, Donald E
Conestoga SR HS
Wayne, PA

Walton, David J
North Penn HS
N Wales, PA

Wampler, Sherri
Cedar Crest HS
Lebanon, PA

Wampler, Suzanne
Central Dauphin HS
Harrisburg, PA

Wanamaker, Marie
Cheltenham HS
Elkins Pk, PA

Wandel, Kelly
Lake-Lehman HS
Dallas, PA

Ward, Constance L
Lower Moreland HS
Huntingdon Vly, PA

Ward, Lonie
Trinity HS
Washington, PA

Ward, Sabine
Belle Vernon Area
Belle Vernon, PA

Ward, Wanda
Otto-Eldred JR SR
Eldred, PA

Wareham, Gregory S
Gateway SR HS
Pitcairn, PA

Warf, Juliane M
Ambridge Area HS
Baden, PA

Warholak, Terri
Canon Mc Millan
SR HS
Canonsburg, PA

Warner, Donna
Norristown Area HS
Norristown, PA

Warrach, Andrea
Immaculate
Conception HS
Canonsburg, PA

Warren, Jeff
Linesville HS
Linesville, PA

Warrey, Lisa
York Catholic HS
Thomasville, PA

Waselko, David
Kiski Area HS
Leechburg, PA

Washington,
Leonard
Trinity HS
Washington, PA

Washmon, John
The Hill Schl
Brownsville, TX

Wasilewski, Lisa
Hanover Area JR
SR HS
Wilkes Barre, PA

Wasson, Paul
East HS
West Chester, PA

Waterman, Michael
Lock Haven SR HS
Lock Haven, PA

Waters, Kathy
Central Dauphin HS
Harrisburg, PA

Watkins, Brad
Towanda Area HS
Monroeton, PA

Watkins, Tim
Blairsville SR HS
Blairsville, PA

Watley, Leonard B
Harry S Truman HS
Bristol, PA

Watson, David N
New Brighton Area
New Brighton, PA

Watson, Heather
Trinity HS
Washington, PA

Watson, Marc
Oxford Area HS
Oxford, PA

Watt, Katherine
Altoona Area HS
Altoona, PA

Watt, Jr Ronald
Jamestown HS
Greenville, PA

Way, Charlie
Clearfield Area HS
Clearfield, PA

Way, Todd B
State Colege Area
SR HS
Lemont, PA

Wayne, Tina
Altoona Area HS
Altoona, PA

Waynebern, Scott
Upper Dublin HS
Dresher, PA

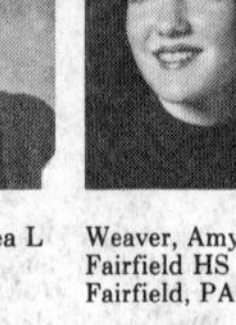
Wealand, Andrea L
Cocalico HS
Stevens, PA

Weaver, Amy
Fairfield HS
Fairfield, PA

Weaver, Amy
Hollidaysburg Area
Newry, PA

Weaver, Dianna
Blair County
Christian Schl
E Freedom, PA

Weaver, Kevin S
Bald Eagle Area HS
Howard, PA

Weaver, Michael
Conrad Weiser HS
Wernersville, PA

Weaver, Pamela
Bald Eagle Area HS
Howard, PA

Weaver, Renee
Manheim Central
Manheim, PA

Weaver, Shari
Chambersburgh
Area SR HS
Chambersburg, PA

Webber, Audrey
Mercersburg Acad
Hickory, NC

Weber, Barbara
Boyertown HS
Douglassville, PA

Weber, Melissa
Towanola Area HS
Towanda, PA

Weber, Timothy W
Du Bois Area HS
Grampian, PA

Webster,
Christopher Shawne
Mercy Vocational
Philadelphia, PA

Webster, Michael
Philipsburg-Osceola
SR HS
Philipsburg, PA

Wechsler, Francis
Allentown Central
Catholic HS
Allentown, PA

Weddigen, Raymond
Bethlehem Catholic
Hellertown, PA

Weddle, Katie
Lebanon SR HS
Lebanon, PA

Wedekind, Brenda
Fairview HS
Fairview, PA

Wehrung, Keith
Chestnut Ridge HS
Alum Bank, PA

Weidman, Jodi
Elizabethtown Area
Mt Joy, PA

Weidner, III
Richard L
Manheim Township
Lancaster, PA

Weinberg, Ellen
Altoona Area HS
Altoona, PA

Weinberger,
Roxanne
Western Wayne HS
Waymart, PA

Weingartner, Betsy
Shenango JR SR HS
New Castle, PA

Weirich, Debra
Northeastern HS
Manchester, PA

Weisbrod, Patricia
Steel Valley HS
W Homestead, PA

Weiss, Jr David P
Shaler Area SR HS
Glenshaw, PA

Weiss, Sandra M
Altoona Area HS
Altoona, PA

Weiss, Tammy
Bishop Hannan HS
Scranton, PA

Welch, Christopher
D
Upper St Clair HS
Upper St Clair, PA

Weller, Martin
Boyertown Area HS
Gilbertsvl, PA

Wells, Charles A
Elizabethtown Area
Elizabethtown, PA

Welty, James
Boiling Springs SR
Boiling Spgs, PA

Wenerowicz, Paula
St Benedict Acad
Erie, PA

Wengryn, Lou Ann
Chartiers Valley HS
Carnegie, PA

Wenrich, Scott
Northern Potter HS
Harrison Vly, PA

Wentz, Darlene
Bellefonte Area HS
Bellefonte, PA

Wenzel, Amy
Elizabeth
North Allegheny SR
Pittsburgh, PA

Werner, Amy
Richland HS
Gibsonia, PA

Werner, James Paul
Ambridge Area HS
Sewickley, PA

Werner, Melissa
Blue Mountain Acad
Tamaqua, PA

Werner, Shaun
Knoch JR SR HS
Cabot, PA

Werner, Tina
Mt Calvary
Christian Schl
Bainbridge, PA

Wert, Corey
Milton Area SR HS
Milton, PA

Wert, Kevin
Halifax HS
Halifax, PA

Wert, Shelley
Cedar Crest HS
Lebanon, PA

Wesley, Rosemary
Scranton Technical
Scranton, PA

Wesner, Michelle
Marian Catholic HS
Tamaqua, PA

Wessner, Debra
Kutztown Area HS
Lenhartsville, PA

West, Caroline
Fox Chapel Area HS
Pittsburgh, PA

West, Rick
Trinity HS
Washington, PA

Westcott, Steven
St Joseph Prep Schl
Wyndmoor, PA

Weston, Michele
Salisbury HS
Allentown, PA

Westover, Lynn
Central Columbia
Lightstreet, PA

Wetmore, Tamara
Riv Erview HS
Oakmont, PA

Wetzel, Maya
Christine
Beaver Area JRSR
Beaver, PA

Wetzel, William
Curwensville HS
Curwensville, PA

Whalen, Pamela
Pottstown SR HS
Pottstown, PA

Whalen, Terese
North Allegheny HS
Allison Park, PA

Wheeler, Roxanne
North Star HS
Jennerstown, PA

Wheeler, Stacy
Lynn
Williams Valley JR
SR HS
Williamstown, PA

Whieldon, Laura
Blue Mt HS
New Ringgold, PA

Whitaker, Wendy
Carlynton JR SR
Carnegie, PA

White, Edna
Lewistown Area HS
Granville, PA

White, Greg
Gov Mifflin SR HS
Shillington, PA

White, Jennifer
Council Rock HS
Newtown, PA

White, Leann
Clearfield Area HS
Olanta, PA

White, Marci
Punxsutawney Area
Punxsutawney, PA

White, Tricia
Northeastern HS
Dover, PA

Whitehead, Cori
Norwin SR HS
N Huntingdon, PA

Whiteman, Lisa
Elk County
Christian HS
St Marys, PA

Whiteman, Susan E
Central Bucks H S
Hartsville, PA

Whitfield, Melissa
Somerset Area HS
Somerset, PA

Whitmoyer, Alan
Millville Area HS
Millville, PA

Whittaker, Jim
Cedar Crest HS
Lebanon, PA

Whittington, Amy
Millville HS
Millville, PA

Whittle, III
Randolph G
Greater Johnstown
Johnstown, PA

Whorton, John
Dunmore HS
Dunmore, PA

Whytosek, Eugene
Archbishop Wood
Ivyland, PA

Wiand, Samuel
Middletown Area
Middletown, PA

Wible, Sharon L
Baldwin HS
Pittsburgh, PA

Wick, Richard
Upper Dublin HS
Ft Washington, PA

Wickel, Sandralee
North Pocono HS
Moscow, PA

Wickman, Deborah
L
North Hills HS
Alpharetta, GA

Widmer, Jeffrey
Canevin HS
Bridgeville, PA

Wieder, Darren
Lower Moreland HS
Huntington Valley,
PA

Wieland, Wendy S
Chartiers Valley HS
Pittsburgh, PA

Wieloch, Patricia
Perry Traditional
Pittsburgh, PA

Wiemann, Kimberly
Seneca Valley HS
Renfrew, PA

Wierman, Molly Jeanne
Hanover HS
Hanover, PA

Wiggins, Wendy
Meadville Area SR
Meadville, PA

Wigglesworth, Craig
Dover Area HS
Dover, PA

Wilbert, Georgia
Bensalem HS
Bensalem, PA

Wilcox, Susan
Western Beaver HS
Industry, PA

Wilenzik, Roslyn
Central Bucks East
Doylestown, PA

Wilke, Philip
Peters Township HS
Mcmurray, PA

Wilkinson, Dan
Gettysburg SR HS
Gettysburg, PA

Wilks, Danielle
Greater Johnstown
Johnstown, PA

Will, Philip
Somerset Area HS
Friedens, PA

Willert, Patricia
Cardinal O Hara HS
Woodlyn, PA

Williams, Adrienne
Pen Argyl Area HS
Wind Gap, PA

Williams, Aimee
New Hope Solebury
New Hope, PA

Williams, Amber E
Unionville HS
Daphne, AL

Williams, Anissa
Manheim Central
Manheim, PA

Williams, Chris
Upper Dublin HS
Oreland, PA

Williams, Curtis
Trinity Christian
Pittsburgh, PA

Williams, Heidi
Blair County Christian Schl
Duncansville, PA

Williams, Karen
Butler Area SR HS
Renfrew, PA

Williams, Keith
Trinity Christian
Pittsburgh, PA

Williams, Kristin
Bishop Shanlhan
W Chester, PA

Williams, Maria
Chambersburg Area SR HS
Chambersburg, PA

Williams, Maureen
Wallenpaupack Area
Greentown, PA

Williams, Michael
C A S HS
Chambersburg, PA

Williams, Michelle
Ambridge Area HS
Ambridge, PA

Williams, Nicole
William Allen HS
Allentown, PA

Williams, Peggy
Western Wayne HS
Lake Ariel, PA

Williams, Rasheed B
Martin Luther King
Philadelphia, PA

Williams, Shannon
Clearfield HS
Clearfield, PA

Williams, Terri
Tyrone Area HS
Altoona, PA

Williams, Todd
Clearfield HS
Woodland, PA

Williams, Wendy
G A R Memorial HS
Wilkes Barre, PA

Williams, Wendy
Harry S Truman HS
Levittown, PA

Williams, William F
Chambersburg Area SR HS
Chambersburg, PA

Williamson, Cristal
Chester HS
Brookhaven, PA

Williamson, Stephannie
Chambersburg Area
Chambersburg, PA

Willner, Tom
Mansfield HS
Mansfield, PA

Wills, Ted
Altoona Area HS
Altoona, PA

Wilson, Beth
Emmaus HS
Wescosville, PA

Wilson, Bill
N Pocono HS
Moscow, PA

Wilson, Carolyn Sue
Huntingdon Area
Huntingdon, PA

Wilson, Gary
Shaler Area SR HS
Glenshaw, PA

Wilson, Jodi
The Baptist HS
Clarks Summit, PA

Wilson, Melissa
Rochester Area HS
Rochester, PA

Wilson, Parrish
South Philadelphia
Philadelphia, PA

Wilson, Sarah Teri
Germantown HS
Philadelphia, PA

Wilt, Faith
Millersburg Area HS
Millersburg, PA

Winck, Jr Dwight
Everett Area HS
Breezewood, PA

Winebarger, Glenda
Northern Lebanon
Jonestown, PA

Winebarger, Julie
Northern Lebanon
Jonestown, PA

Winey, Denise
Garden Spot HS
New Holland, PA

Wingard, Kevin
West Middlesex HS
Sharon, PA

Wingard, Shelly
Connellsvilel HS
Dunbar, PA

Wingrove, Elisabeth
Mt Carmel Christian
Vanderbilt, PA

Winkler, Robert
Bangor Area SR HS
Bangor, PA

Winkowski, David
St Josephs Prep
Philadelphia, PA

Winne, Suzanne
Reading Central Catholic HS
Mt Penn, PA

Winterhalter, Erik
Mary Fuller Frazier
Dawson, PA

Wirdzek, Adam
Connellsville HS
Acme, PA

Wirth, Greg
Norwin HS
N Huntingdon, PA

Wisniewski, John
Hampton HS
Gibsonia, PA

Witcoski, John C
Neshaminy HS
Levittown, PA

Witcoski, Suzanna
Shenandoah Valley
Shenandoah, PA

Witt, Brent
Connellsville Area
Connellsville, PA

Witt, Catherine
Villa Maria Acad
Broomall, PA

Woeber, Teena K
North Allenghey SR
Wexford, PA

Woelfling, R John
Cedar Crest HS
Lebanon, PA

Woessner, Lori S
Conrad Weiser HS
Robesonia, PA

Wojnarowski, Darlene
West Greene HS
Wind Ridge, PA

Wolf, Darren
Turtle Creek HS
N Braddock, PA

Wolf, III Donald Henry
Palmyra Area HS
Palmyra, PA

Wolf, Joseph
Du Bois Area HS
Dubois, PA

Wolfe, Cathy
Hanover SR HS
Hanover, PA

Wolfe, Christina
Bellwood Antis HS
Altoona, PA

Wolfe, Jenny
Northern Lebanon
Jonestown, PA

Wolfe, Traci
Marion Center Area
Indiana, PA

Wolfgang, Debbie
Middletown Area
Middletown, PA

Wolfgang, Jr Raymond F
Central Dauphin HS
Harrisburg, PA

Wolko, Suzanne
St Hubert Catholic
Philadelphia, PA

Wolter, Eric Eno
Mon Valley Cath
Charleroi, PA

Womer, Kristie
Loyalsock Township
Montoursville, PA

Wong, Edwin
Perkomen Schl
Pennsburg, PA

Wong, Wilbur
Hampton HS
Gibsonia, PA

Wood, Braian
Towanda Area HS
Monroeton, PA

Wood, David
Penn Wood HS
Yeadon, PA

Wood, Jim
Waynesburg Central
Waynesburg, PA

Wood, Shawn
Corry Area HS
Corry, PA

Wood, Tammy S
Corry Area HS
Corry, PA

Wood, Tania
East Allegheny HS
N Versailles, PA

Woodlief, Gregory
Waynesboro Area SR HS
Waynesboro, PA

Woodman, Mary
Red Land HS
Etters, PA

Woodring, Steve
Harbor Creek HS
Erie, PA

Woodring, Tammy
Philipsburg-Osceola
Osceola Mills, PA

Woodson, Carmen
Canon-Mc Millan
Canonsburg, PA

Woodward, Lisa
Juniata HS
Honey Grove, PA

Woolever, Ernest J
North Pocono HS
Moscow, PA

Worcester, Carol
Annville-Cleona HS
Annville, PA

Workman, Leashell
Central York SR HS
York, PA

Wormley, Cecilia
Bishop Mc Devitt
Roslyn, PA

Worrall, Lisa
Pottsgrove HS
Pottstown, PA

Worthington, Chance J
Hatboro-Horsham
Horsham, PA

Woten, Jr David L
Ambridge Area SR
Baden, PA

Wozniak, Craig
Bishop Hafey HS
Conyngham, PA

Wozniak, Wendy
Plum SR HS
Pittsburgh, PA

Wright, Amy
Newport JR/SR HS
Newport, PA

Wright, April
Upper Merion HS
Bridgeport, PA

Wright, Brian J
North Allegheny HS
Allison Pk, PA

Wright, Lendina F
Winchester-Thursto n HS
Pittsburgh, PA

Wright, Linda C
Catasauqua HS
Catasauqua, PA

Wright, Mark
Punxsutawney Area SR HS
Summerville, PA

Wright, Teresa
West Greene HS
Aleppo, PA

Wu, Wendy L
Villa Maria HS
Edgerton, OH

Wuchter, Travis M
Northampton Area SR HS
Northampton, PA

Wyandt, Mary A
Greater Johnstown
Johnstown, PA

Wyatt, Jr Samuel J
Chester HS
Chester, PA

Wypa, Lynn
Lake Lehman HS
Shavertown, PA

Xiong, Ka Youa
Mercyhurst Prep HS
Erie, PA

Yacabucci, Jan
Clearfield HS
Clearfield, PA

Yacapsin, Gene
Marian HS
Nesquehoning, PA

Yakupkovic, Francine
Quigley HS
Aliquippa, PA

Yale, Dina
Bishop Hafey HS
Hazleton, PA

Yancich, Luann
Brownsville Area HS
Brownsville, PA

Yannacone, Teresa
Cardinal O Hara HS
Media, PA

Yanochko, Anne Marie
Bethlehem Catholic
Bethlehem, PA

Yantek, John
Bentworth HS
Bentleyville, PA

Yaple, Marylyn
Berwick Area SR
Berwick, PA

Yard, Cynthia
Rocky Grove HS
Franklin, PA

Yarnell, Stacy
Chestnut Ridge SR
Alum Bunk, PA

Yatcilla, Peter
St Josephs Prep
Philadephia, PA

Yauger, Melissa
Fairchance-Georges
Uniontownd, PA

Yeager, Tara
William Allen High
Allentown, PA

Yeager, Teresa
Lakeview HS
Clarks Mills, PA

Yeagley, Pam
Elizabethtown Area
Elizabethtown, PA

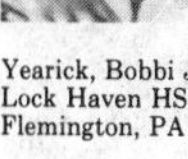
Yearick, Bobbi Jo
Lock Haven HS
Flemington, PA

Yearick, Johnni
Bellefonte Area SR
Bellefonte, PA

Yeigh, Tracy
Middleburg Joint
Kreamer, PA

Yen, David
William Allen HS
Allentown, PA

Yerace, Elizabeth
Norwin SR HS
N Huntingdon, PA

Yerger, Yvonne E
Schuylkill Valley HS
Leesport, PA

Yerkey, Jennifer
Monongahela Vly
Cath HS
Belle Vernon, PA

Yesville, Marylou
Pleasant Valley HS
Saylorsburg, PA

Yingling, Meghan P
Blairsville SR HS
Blairsville, PA

Yingst, Stacy
Blue Mountain Acad
Quarryville, PA

Yocum, Karen
Sun Valley HS
Aston, PA

Yoder, Keith
Conemaugh Twp
Area HS
Davidsville, PA

Yohe, Diane
Dubois Area HS
Du Bois, PA

Yokiel, Margaret
Brownsville Area SR
Grindstone, PA

Yokopenic, Pamela
Hempfield Area SR
Greensburg, PA

Yonkoski, Shirleen
Coughlin HS
Wilkes Barre, PA

Yorns, Eddie
New Brighton HS
New Brighton, PA

Yost, Heather
Greater Latrobe HS
Latrobe, PA

Yotko, Christine
Cardinal Brennen
Lavelle, PA

You, Song C
Upper Darby HS
Upper Darby, PA

Youd, Steven J
Bradford Area HS
Bradford, PA

Youells, Amy
Tunkhannock Area
Tunkhannock, PA

Young, Brenda
Belle Vernon Area
Fayette City, PA

Young, Douglas A
Everett Area HS
Breezewood, PA

Young, Greg
Cedar Crest HS
Lebanon, PA

Young, Kimberly
Penns Manor Joint
JR SR HS
Penn Run, PA

Young, Missy
Slippery Rock Area
Slippery Rock, PA

Young, Shawn A
Northern York
County HS
Dillsburg, PA

Young, Sherri
Kutztown Area HS
Kutztown, PA

Younker, Deidra A
West Hazleton HS
Tresckow, PA

Yourish, Bradley
Deer Lake S HS
Cheswick, PA

Yovetich, Barbara
Peters Township HS
Mc Murray, PA

Yuhas, Michelle
Greater Johnstown
Johnstown, PA

Yurchak, Kirk
Liberty HS
Bethlehem, PA

Yurcina, Angie
Hopewell HS
Aliquippa, PA

Yurich, Mike
South Allegheny HS
Port Vue, PA

Yutzler, Heidi
Upper Dublin SR
Maple Glen, PA

Zagorski, Dave
Lincoln HS
Ellwood City, PA

Zahniser, Kimberly
West Middlexex HS
W Middlesex, PA

Zalar, Amy
Mapletown HS
Waynesburg, PA

Zamulevic, Diane
Southside Catholic
Pittsburgh, PA

Zankel, James
Cornell HS
Coraopolis, PA

Zatratz, Denise
Holy Name HS
Mohnton, PA

Zawistoski,
Marybeth
Mercyhurst Prep
Erie, PA

Zdanavage, Corey
John S Fine SR HS
Nanticoke, PA

Zdrilich, Erica
Villa Maria HS
Poland, OH

Zedek, Kimberly
Kaye
Northern Cambria
Herndon, VA

Zeiset, G Elaine
Garden Spot HS
Denver, PA

Zelahy, Sandy M
Plum SR HS
Plum Boro, PA

Zelmore, Jason
Southmoreland SR
Mt Pleasant, PA

Zemble, Beth
Lower Moreland HS
Huntingdon Valley,
PA

Zemetro, John
Hanvoer Area JR
SR HS
Warrior Run, PA

Zeranick, Doreen
Ambridge HS
Freedom, PA

Zerla, Andrew
Mc Guffey HS
Washington, PA

Zeszutek, Dawn M
Canon Mc Millan
Cecil, PA

Zettelmayer, Erik J
North Catholic HS
Pittsburgh, PA

Zettlemoyer,
Michael
Brandywine HS
Mertztown, PA

Zibura, Maryann
Forest Hills HS
Beaverdale, PA

Ziccardi, Mary Jo
West Catholic Girls
Philadelphia, PA

Ziegler, Barbara
Nazareth Acad
Washington Crsg,
PA

Zimmerman, Brenda
Punxsutawney Area
Sykesville, PA

Zimmerman,
Constance M
Forest Hills SR HS
South Fork, PA

Zimmerman,
Daphne
Cocalico HS
Stevens, PA

Zimmerman, David
Northwest Area HS
Hunlock Creek, PA

Zimmerman, Eric
Ephrate SR HS
Akron, PA

Zimmerman, Ronald
Jason
Mt Pleasant Area
Norvelt, PA

Zinger, Victoria C
Boyertown Area SR
Boyertown, PA

Zinobile, Angela
Southern
Huntingdon Count
Mapleton Depot, PA

Zipp, Joy
Harborcreek JR SR
Harbor Creek, PA

Zola, Christine M
Shaler Area HS
Pittsburgh, PA

Zoranski, Kyra
Wyoming Valley
West HS
Kingston, PA

Zore, Cathy
St Marys Area HS
Saint Marys, PA

Zoretich, Maria
Chester HS
Chester, PA

Zuccarello, Michelle
W C East HS
West Chester, PA

Zucco, Lisa
Plum SR HS
Pittsburgh, PA

Zuczek, Matthew
Bishop O Hara HS
Dickson City, PA

Zukoski, Joseph
Hanover Area JR SR HS
Wilkes Barre, PA

Zulewski, Elizabeth
Nazareth Acad
Philadelphia, PA

Zupsic, Robert
Center Area HS
Monaca, PA

Zurkovski, Susan A
Baldwin HS
Pittsburgh, PA

Zweier, Scott
Lebanon HS
Lebanon, PA

Zweig, Kelly
Greater Nanticoke Area HS
Hunlock Creek, PA

Zygmunt, Susan
Nazareth Acad
Philadelphia, PA